April 2019

Dear Subscriber,

CSC®, in cooperation with legal publisher LexisNexis®, is pleased to provide you with the Spring 2019 Edition of *New York Laws Governing Business Entities Annotated*. This two-volume resource contains up-to-date annotated New York business entity legislation, as well as other valuable features that make your research faster and more efficient.

In this Edition you will find the latest legislative changes through Chapter 19 of the 2019 Session, including amendments to the Business Corporation Law, Limited Liability Company Law and Not-for-Profit Corporation Law. Blackline notes following each amended section illustrate exactly what text was added and deleted.

To ensure you don't miss any judicial decisions that could impact your clients, we have included over 65 new case notes from New York state and federal courts interpreting the law. You will also find five new full-text cases covering recent legal developments regarding LLC membership, presuit demand, memoranda of understanding and corporate taxation.

To assist in your practice, the companion CD-ROM in Volume 2 contains over 100 up-to-date fillable business entity forms including newly added county forms for general partnerships. A listing of the forms can be found in the book's appendix.

Our goal is to provide you with the resources you need to work faster and more efficiently. If there are new topics that you would like us to include in our books, please tell us. We want to hear from you!

Thank you for choosing this CSC publication.

Warm regards,

Eric Geringswald
Director
CSCPublishing
Eric.Geringswald@cscglobal.com

NEW YORK

LAWS GOVERNING BUSINESS ENTITIES
Annotated

———

Business Corporation Law
Limited Liability Company Law
Partnership Law
Not-for-Profit Corporation Law
Cooperative Corporations Law
Religious Corporation Law
Transportation Corporation Law
Uniform Commercial Code:

General Provisions
Investment Securities
Secured Transactions

2019 **SPRING**
VOLUME 1

CSC® and LexisNexis®

CSC and LexisNexis work in partnership to provide you with the highest quality publications and services you need.

For questions regarding content, billing, or subscriptions for this and other CSC publications, contact LexisNexis at 1.800.833.9844, or visit us on the web at **www.lexisnexis.com/PrintCDSC**.

To learn more about the products and services of CSC, call us at 1.800.927.9800, fax us at 302.636.5454, or visit our website at **www.cscglobal.com**.

ISBN: 978-1-5221-7273-4

© 2019 Matthew Bender & Company, Inc., a member of the LexisNexis Group®.

Pub No. 25570

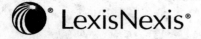

Table of Contents

————

VOLUME ONE

————

————

————

VOLUME TWO

———

Acknowledgments

———

Thank you to all of our team members at CSC and LexisNexis for their efforts and expertise in creating and producing this 2019 Spring Edition of *New York Laws Governing Business Entities Annotated*:

Pam Bruno, Meg Campbell, Sherry Dickerson, Scott Marinaro, Sonja Mundy, Jason Schuck, John van der Wal, and Monique Weaver.

We would also like to thank Robin Alperstein of Becker, Glynn, Muffly, Chassin & Hosinski LLP for her expert review of the material.

Eric Geringswald
Director
CSCPublishing
Eric.Geringswald@cscglobal.com

April 2019

About the Senior Legal Advisor
to CSCPublishing

———

Matthew J. O'Toole is a partner at Potter Anderson & Corroon LLP in Wilmington, Delaware (www.potteranderson.com). He is also the co-author of the treatise *Symonds & O'Toole on Delaware Limited Liability Companies*.

Mr. O'Toole is the current chair of the Delaware State Bar Association committee responsible for proposing amendments to the Delaware Limited Liability Company Act, and to Delaware's limited partnership and general partnership laws. He has testified numerous times before the Delaware General Assembly on proposed statutory amendments.

Mr. O'Toole is the immediate past chairman of the Council of the Corporation Law Section of the Delaware State Bar Association, which monitors and proposes amendments to the General Corporation Law of the State of Delaware.

Mr. O'Toole also served as a principal drafter of the Delaware Insurance Company Mutual-to-Stock Conversion Act and the Delaware Revised Captive Insurance Company Act.

Table of Sections Affected by 2018 Legislation

BUSINESS CORPORATION LAW [VOLUME 1]

Code Citation	Act Citation	Effects
§ 1503	Chapter 302	Amended

LIMITED LIABILITY COMPANY LAW [VOLUME 1]

Code Citation	Act Citation	Effects
§ 1105	Chapter 302	Amended

NOT-FOR-PROFIT CORPORATION LAW [VOLUME 1]

Code Citation	Act Citation	Effects
§ 202	Chapter 476	Amended
§ 301	Chapter 476	Amended
§ 601	Chapter 411	Amended
§ 712-a	Chapter 468	Amended
§ 1402	Chapter 476	Amended
§ 1402	Chapter 500	Amended
§ 1402	Chapter 513	Amended
§ 1506	Chapter 296	Amended
§ 1506-a	Chapter 296	Amended
§ 1603	Chapter 508	Amended
§ 1608	Chapter 483	Amended

RELIGIOUS CORPORATIONS LAW [VOLUME 1]

Code Citation	Act Citation	Effects
§ 7	Chapter 296	Amended

TAX LAW [VOLUME 2]

Code Citation	Act Citation	Effects
§ 209-L	Chapter 290	Added
§ 209-L	Chapter 294	Added
§ 209-L	Chapter 374	Added
§ 210-B	Chapter 518	Amended
§ 292	Chapter 369	Amended

TRANSPORTATION CORPORATION LAW [VOLUME 1]

Code Citation	Act Citation	Effects
§ 30	Chapter 476	Amended

UNIFORM COMMERCIAL CODE [VOLUME 1]

Code Citation	Act Citation	Effects
§ 9-102	Chapter 312	Amended

Table of New Annotations

BUSINESS CORPORATION LAW [VOLUME 1]

Code Citation	Case Citation	General Topic
§ 304	*Aybar v Aybar*, 2019 N.Y. App. Div. LEXIS 444 (N.Y. App. Div. 2d Dep't 2019)	Jurisdiction
§ 619	*Wynkoop v 622A President St. Owners Corp.*, 2019 N.Y. App. Div. LEXIS 1369 (N.Y. App. Div. 2d Dep't 2019)	Grounds for interventions
§ 626	*Mason-Mahon v Flint*, 2018 N.Y. App. Div. LEXIS 7689 (N.Y. App. Div. 2d Dep't 2018)	Derivative action—Demand excused
§ 706	*Wynkoop v 622A President St. Owners Corp.*, 2019 N.Y. App. Div. LEXIS 1369 (N.Y. App. Div. 2d Dep't 2019)	Board of directors—Elections
§ 1301	*Aybar v Aybar*, 2019 N.Y. App. Div. LEXIS 444 (N.Y. App. Div. 2d Dep't 2019)	Jurisdiction over foreign corporations
§ 1304	*Aybar v Aybar*, 2019 N.Y. App. Div. LEXIS 444 (N.Y. App. Div. 2d Dep't 2019)	Jurisdiction over foreign corporations
§ 1312	*Guangzhou Sanhua Plastic Co., Ltd. v Fine Line Prods. Corp.*, 2018 N.Y. App. Div. LEXIS 6870 (N.Y. App. Div. 2d Dep't 2018)	Pleadings & burden of proof

LIMITED LIABILITY COMPANIES CODE [VOLUME 1]

Code Citation	Case Citation	General Topic
§ 102	*Matter of Murphy v New York State Tax Appeals Trib.*, 2018 N.Y. App. Div. LEXIS 7354 (N.Y. App. Div. 3d Dep't 2018)	Distributions & allocations of profit
§ 602	*Kaminski v Sirera*, 2019 N.Y. App. Div. LEXIS 1057 (N.Y. App. Div. 2d Dep't 2019)	Standing
§ 603	*Matter of Murphy v New York State Tax Appeals Trib.*, 2018 N.Y. App. Div. LEXIS 7354 (N.Y. App. Div. 3d Dep't 2018)	Income tax

NOT FOR PROFIT CORPORATION LAW [VOLUME 1]

Code Citation	Case Citation	General Topic
§ 715	*Matter of The People of The State of New York v The Lutheran Care Network, Inc.*, 2018 N.Y. App. Div. LEXIS 8666 (N.Y. App. Div. 3d Dep't 2018)	Rescission of management fees

Code Citation	Case Citation	General Topic
§ 720	*Matter of The People of The State of New York v The Lutheran Care Network, Inc.*, 2018 N.Y. App. Div. LEXIS 8666 (N.Y. App. Div. 3d Dep't 2018)	Pleadings—Complaint
§ 1507	*Matter of White Plains Rural Cemetery Assn. v City of White Plains*, 2019 N.Y. App. Div. LEXIS 605 (N.Y. App. Div. 2d Dep't 2019)	Variance

UNIFORM COMMERCIAL CODE [VOLUME 1]

Code Citation	Case Citation	General Topic
§ 1-201	*McCormack v Maloney*, 160 A.D.3d 1098, 75 N.Y.S.3d 294, 2018 N.Y. App. Div. LEXIS 2384 (N.Y. App. Div. 3d Dep't 2018)	Holder
§ 1-201	*OneWest Bank, N.A. v FMCDH Realty, Inc.*, 165 A.D.3d 128, 83 N.Y.S.3d 612, 2018 N.Y. App. Div. LEXIS 6066 (N.Y. App. Div. 2d Dep't 2018)	Holder
§ 1-201	*Bayview Loan Servicing, LLC*, 166 A.D.3d 843, 2018 N.Y. App. Div. LEXIS 7992 (N.Y. App. Div. 2d Dep't 2018)	Holder
§ 1-201	*Bank of Am., N.A. v Tobin*, 2019 N.Y. App. Div. LEXIS 96 (N.Y. App. Div. 2d Dep't 2019)	Holder
§ 8-102	*Thaler v GJ & JF Realty Holdings, Inc. (In re Jaghab)*, 584 B.R. 472, 95 U.C.C. Rep. Serv. 2d (CBC) 826, 2018 Bankr. LEXIS 1151 (Bankr. E.D.N.Y. 2018)	Perfection of security interest
§ 9-102	*Matter of Abele Tractor & Equip. Co., Inc. v Schaeffer*, 2018 N.Y. App. Div. LEXIS 8694 (N.Y. App. Div. 3d Dep't 2018)	Good faith purchaser
§ 9-102	*Thaler v GJ & JF Realty Holdings, Inc. (In re Jaghab)*, 584 B.R. 472, 95 U.C.C. Rep. Serv. 2d (CBC) 826, 2018 Bankr. LEXIS 1151 (Bankr. E.D.N.Y. 2018)	Unperfected security interest
§ 9-106	*Thaler v GJ & JF Realty Holdings, Inc. (In re Jaghab)*, 584 B.R. 472, 95 U.C.C. Rep. Serv. 2d (CBC) 826, 2018 Bankr. LEXIS 1151 (Bankr. E.D.N.Y. 2018)	Adequate control of security entitlement
§ 9-203	*In re Tara Retail Grp., Inc.*, 2018 Bankr. LEXIS 655 (Bankr. N.D. W. Va. Feb. 14, 2018)	Attachment of security interest
§ 9-312	*Thaler v GJ & JF Realty Holdings, Inc. (In re Jaghab)*, 584 B.R. 472, 95 U.C.C. Rep. Serv. 2d (CBC) 826, 2018 Bankr. LEXIS 1151 (Bankr. E.D.N.Y. 2018)	Secured interest priority
§ 9-322	*TSA Stores, Inc. v M J Soffe, LLC (In re TSAWD Holdings, Inc.)*, 2018 Bankr. LEXIS 3681 (Bankr. D. Del. Nov. 26, 2018).	Perfected interest—Order of filing

Code Citation	Case Citation	General Topic
§ 9-609	*Matter of Abele Tractor & Equip. Co., Inc. v Schaeffer*, 2018 N.Y. App. Div. LEXIS 8694 (N.Y. App. Div. 3d Dep't 2018)	Right to repossess

CIVIL LAW AND PROCEDURE [VOLUME 2]

Code Citation	Case Citation	General Topic
§ 213	*County of Suffolk v Suburban Hous. Dev. & Research, Inc.*, 160 A.D.3d 607, 76 N.Y.S.3d 177, 2018 N.Y. App. Div. LEXIS 2294 (N.Y. App. Div. 2d Dep't 2018)	Performance of services
§ 213	*21st Mtge. Corp. v Osorio*, 167 A.D.3d 823, 90 N.Y.S.3d 274, 2018 N.Y. App. Div. LEXIS 8576 (N.Y. App. Div. 2d Dep't 2018)	Mortgages
§ 213	*US Bank Trust, N.A. v Williams*, 2019 N.Y. App. Div. LEXIS 618 (N.Y. App. Div. 2d Dep't 2019)	Mortgages
§ 213	*Epiphany Community Nursery Sch. v Levey*, 2019 N.Y. App. Div. LEXIS 835 (N.Y. App. Div. 1st Dep't 2019)	Tolling
§ 213	*McNeary v Charlebois*, 2019 N.Y. App. Div. LEXIS 1468 (N.Y. App. Div. 3d Dep't 2019)	Part payment
§ 213	*Lehman XS Trust, Series 2006-GP2 v GreenPoint Mortg. Funding, Inc.*, 2019 U.S. App. LEXIS 3727 (2d Cir. N.Y. Feb. 6, 2019)	Part payment
§ 213	*JP Morgan Chase Bank, N.A. v Mbanefo*, 166 A.D.3d 742, 88 N.Y.S.3d 420, 2018 N.Y. App. Div. LEXIS 7707 (N.Y. App. Div. 2d Dep't 2018)	Actions on contract
§ 213	*Krog Corp. v Vanner Group, Inc.*, 158 A.D.3d 914, 72 N.Y.S.3d 178, 2018 N.Y. App. Div. LEXIS 868 (N.Y. App. Div. 3d Dep't 2018)	Discovery of fraud
§ 213	*U.S. Bank N.A. v Joseph*, 159 A.D.3d 968, 73 N.Y.S.3d 238, 2018 N.Y. App. Div. LEXIS 2067 (N.Y. App. Div. 2d Dep't 2018)	Actions on mortgage
§ 213	*Freedom Mtge. Corp. v Engel*, 163 A.D.3d 631, 81 N.Y.S.3d 156, 2018 N.Y. App. Div. LEXIS 5138 (N.Y. App. Div. 2d Dep't 2018)	Actions on mortgage
§ 213	*Bank of N.Y. Mellon v Celestin*, 164 A.D.3d 733, 83 N.Y.S.3d 166, 2018 N.Y. App. Div. LEXIS 5832 (N.Y. App. Div. 2d Dep't 2018)	Actions on mortgage
§ 213	*Sejin Precision Indus. Co. v Citibank, N.A.*, 726 Fed. Appx. 27, 2018 U.S. App. LEXIS 5524 (2d Cir. N.Y. 2018)	Discovery of fraud

Code Citation	Case Citation	General Topic
§ 7511	*Matter of Wendt v BondFactor Co., LLC*, 2019 N.Y. App. Div. LEXIS 1050 (N.Y. App. Div. 2d Dep't 2019)	Statute of limitations

GENERAL BUSINESS LAW [VOLUME 2]

Code Citation	Case Citation	General Topic
§ 349-d	*Matter of National Energy Marketers Assn. v New York State Pub. Serv. Commn.*, 2018 N.Y. App. Div. LEXIS 7361 (N.Y. App. Div. 3d Dep't 2018)	Authority of New York State Public Service Commission
§ 5-1510C	*Bronstein v Clements*, 2019 N.Y. App. Div. LEXIS 1447 (N.Y. App. Div. 3d Dep't 2019)	Revocation

NEW YORK LAWS GOVERNING BUSINESS ENTITIES

Analysis of Legislative Changes to
New York Laws Governing Business Entities

(Compiled by the Publisher's Staff from New York legislative bill histories)

Business Corporations Law § 1503; Limited Liability Company Law § 1105 (Amended)

Subdivisions (b-6) and (b-7) of paragraph (1) of § 1503 of the Business Corporation Law allow business corporations to become professional service corporations and design professional service corporations by amending their certificates of incorporation, and subdivision (a) of 1105 of the Limited Liability Company Law allows limited liability companies to become professional limited liability companies by amending their certificates of organization. The purpose of these provisions is to allow these conversions to take place without dissolving and starting up businesses, which could result in adverse tax consequences, burdensome paperwork and possible cancellation of existing contracts. The sunset of these provisions has resulted in a situation wherein geologists who are still "in the pipeline" to satisfy the Education Department's licensing requirements would become unable to take advantage of the benefits conferred under Chapter 260 of the Laws of 2016. This bill provides some "breathing room" to these individuals by extending the provisions of this chapter to March 1, 2019. [Ch. 302, AB 10220]

Not-for-Profit Corporations § 601 (Amended)

Under the Not-For-Profit Corporation Law (NPCL), a single individual is authorized to be the only member of a charitable nonprofit corporation. Charitable nonprofits utilize a governance structure known as a "member model," whereby a membership comprising one or more individuals or entity members reserves the right to elect a board of directors. Current law does not prevent one sole member of a charitable nonprofit from electing a board of directors. This is a significant loophole. Amending the NPCL to preclude the possibility that a charitable nonprofit be controlled by any one member will prevent abuse by individuals who may try to use a charitable nonprofit for their own private interest. This bill amends paragraph a of section 601 of the NPCL to provide that as of July 1, 2019, no corporation except a corporation that has no members, shall have a membership comprising fewer than 3 persons. A corporation may have a corporation, joint-stock association, unincorporated association or partnership as a sole member, if such corporation, joint-stock association, unincorporated association, or partnership is owned or controlled by no fewer than 3 persons [Ch. 411, AB 10336]

Not-for-Profit Corporations § 712-a (Amended)

Many nonprofit corporations are made up of a nonprofit (generally referred to as a "parent") that controls one or more subsidiaries. This legislation will expressly permit voting directors from subsidiaries, who do not themselves serve on the parent nonprofit's board of directors, to serve as voting members of a parent's audit committee, for the purposes of overseeing audits of the parent or any subsidiary corporations. Currently, the NPCL provides that only the board of directors of a parent, or a designated "committee of the board" of such parent, may assume sole oversight of all financial audits, for both the parent and any subsidiaries. Amending the NPCL to include voting directors of subsidiaries in the audit process would allow for the service of informed and financially knowledgeable individuals. This bill amends paragraph d of section 712-a of the NPCL to provide that directors from one or more controlled corporations may serve on any designated audit committee of the board of the controlling corporation and perform the duties required by this section for each corporation and any controlled corporations. [Ch. 468, AB 10534]

Tax Law § 28 (Amended)

The Empire State Commercial Production tax credit is an essential component of maintaining a viable and expanding commercial advertising business in New York. Since the credit's enactment in 2006, commercial production activity in the State, after declining by more than 50 percent the previous 10 years, has increased 60 percent. This bill extends the sunset for the qualified commercial production companies, currently scheduled in section 28 of the Tax Law for taxable years beginning before the January 1, 2019, until taxable years beginning on or after January 1, 2024. [Ch. 518, AB 10768]

Tax Law § 292 (Amended)

Substantial amendments were made to the Internal Revenue Code which became effective on January 1, 2018. One of these changes was to provide for an unrelated business tax (UBIT) on any amount a non-profit employer has paid or incurred for commuter benefits such as transit or parking. New York law currently imposes a state tax of 9 percent of UBIT whenever federal law does. As a result, without this legislation, New York will automatically follow the new federal statute, imposing this additional 9 percent tax on not-for-profits. This unintended new tax could divert millions of dollars from the nonprofit sector each year. This bill excludes the payments for transportation costs such as mass transit, commuter and parking fees paid to employees from this tax imposition. The revenue that will be diverted to the state from nonprofits was unintentional, and these funds were not considered in the SFY 2018-19 Budget. The work performed by not-for-profit employees, and the compensation paid to them, including transportation benefits, certainly advances the purposes and mission of the not-for-profit. Should this new tax be enforced, it is certain that not-for profits will have fewer funds to perform their mission serving New Yorkers across the state, and some will undoubtedly be forced to close. This bill amends paragraph 4 of subdivision (a) of section 292 of the Tax Law to subtract from the federal unrelated business taxable income any amount which is included therein solely by reason of internal Revenue Code section 512(a)(7). [Ch. 369, AB 11051]

Summary of Featured New York Full-Text Cases

———

(Full text of these case opinions may be found in Appendix A)

Derivative Suits—Pre-Suit Demand

Case: *Deckter v Andreotti*, 2019 N.Y. App. Div. LEXIS 1699 (March 12, 2019)

Summary: The court properly dismissed a shareholder's complaint with prejudice because pre-suit demand was not excused where, while the issuance of false or misleading statements in public filings constituted a violation of the board's oversight duties and even though the complaint alleged that the corporation's audit committee and senior management knew about gaps in the company's internal controls, the directors were exculpated from liability except for claims based on fraudulent, illegal, or bad faith conduct, and the shareholder failed to establish bad faith or scienter where the document submitted by directors on their motion to dismiss showed that each internal audit report also included specific remedial actions.

LLC Membership

Case: *Kaminski v Sirera*, 2019 N.Y. App. Div. LEXIS 1057 (Feb. 13, 2019)

Summary: When plaintiff purchaser of an interest in an LLC sued defendant's managing member and the LLC's attorneys for breach of fiduciary duty, it was error not to dismiss the purchaser's claims because the purchaser lacked standing, as the purchaser did not obtain the consent of the LLC's nonselling members to be admitted as a member of the LLC, as required by the LLC's operating agreement and Limited Liability Company Law § 602.

Memorandum of Understanding

Case: *Doller v Prescott*, 167 A.D.3d 1298, 2018 N.Y. App. Div. LEXIS 8671 (3d Dept. 2018)

Summary: The parties' memorandum of understanding (MOU), memorializing, among other things, plaintiff's future right of first refusal to acquire "equity" in defendant corporation, was unenforceable because the parties left open for future negotiation both the type of equity and the "precise manner" in which that equity would be offered; in effect, the MOU was an unenforceable agreement to agree in the future on terms of a "definitive agreement" regarding the offer of equity; [2]-The trial court erred in determining that defendant foreign corporation was not properly served because there was no sworn evidence to rebut the process server's sworn affidavit that service was made upon a person expressly authorized to accept service.

Qualified Empire Zone Enterprise Tax Reduction

Case: *Matter of Purcell v New York State Tax Appeals Trib.*, 167 A.D.3d 1101, 89 N.Y.S.3d 41 (3d Dept. 2018)

Summary: A taxpayer, who was a resident shareholder of New York S corporation, was not eligible for qualified empire zone enterprise (QEZE) tax reduction credits for income earned by the corporation in Virginia because the phrase "allocated within the state" required that the income taxes attributable to a New York S corporation's out-of-state income be excluded when calculating the taxpayer's QEZE tax reduction credit.

Taxation—LLC Distributions & Allocations

Case: *Matter of Murphy v New York State Tax Appeals Trib.*, 166 A.D.3d 1096, 87 N.Y.S.3d 684 (3d Dept. 2018)

Summary: The determination sustaining a notice of deficiency of personal income tax was affirmed because as the assignee of a membership interest, petitioner was not automatically entitled to participate in the management or affairs of the limited liability company but was entitled to receive the distributions and allocations of profits and losses to which the assignor would be entitled, thus, the assessment was properly imposed.

PUBLICATION AND FEE TABLES

_____

Limited Liability, Limited Liability Partnership and Limited Partnership Publishing Requirements — New York State

	Requirements Prior to June 1, 2006	*Requirements Effective June 1, 2006*	*Requirements Prior to June 1, 2006*
Publication Timeframe Requirements	Within 120 days of Formation/Qualification of Entity.	Within 120 days of Formation/Qualification of Entity.	Entities formed prior to 1/1/1999 are exempt from publishing requirements.
Duration of Publishing	1x each week for 6 consecutive weeks in 2 newspapers.	1x each week for 6 consecutive weeks in 2 newspapers. One to be published weekly and one daily.	
Content of Notice	For domestic LLC: • Name of Entity. • Date of Filing. • County where office is located. • SOP Address. • Purpose. • Date of Dissolution (if any).	For domestic LLC: • Name of Entity. • Date of Filing and Formation (if different from filing date). • County where office is located. • SOP Address. • Purpose. • Street Address of Principal Business Location, if any (or state "none"). • Date of Dissolution (if any).	Varies by entity type — see below for statutory citations.
Where to Publish	County where office of business is located.	County where office of business is located as indicated in the initial formation filing.*	* Any changes can be outlined in the notice; however, the notice must reference information from the original filing.
Newspaper Determination	County clerk designates newspaper.	County clerk designates newspaper.	
Proof of Publishing Requirements	File 2 affidavits of publication as issued by the authorized person at the newspaper.	File Certificate of Publication with the Department of State attaching both Affidavits of Publication as issued by an authorized person from the newspaper within 120 days of formation.	Make sure text of publication is legible and can be microfilmed.
Certificate of Publication Execution Requirements: LLC	N/A.	LLC: Member, Manager, Authorized Person or Attorney-in-Fact (must state the name and capacity of the person that they are signing on behalf of).	LP: requires signature by General Partner or Attorney-in-Fact. LLP: requires signature of Partner.
Penalty for Failure to File within 120 days	Prohibition against maintaining any action or special proceeding.	Suspension of authority to conduct business.	

Statutes Governing Publication Requirements:

Domestic LLC: LLC § 206
Foreign LLC: LLC § 802
Conversion to LLC: LLC § 1006
Domestic Professional Service LLC: LLC § 1203
Foreign Professional Service LLC: LLC § 1306

Domestic Limited Partnership: PL § 91, PL § 121-201
Foreign Limited Partnership: PL § 121-902
Domestic Registered LLP: PL § 121-1500
Foreign Registered LLP: PL § 121-1502

---

*Disclaimer: The information contained in this document is intended merely to alert CSC customers. This information is subject to change without notice. Nothing in this document should be construed as legal advice or counsel. The reader assumes all risk and liability resulting from the use of this information.

Publication and Fee Tables

FEE TABLES

Fees under the Business Corporation Law
(All section references are to BCL sections unless otherwise stated)

Reservation of a corporate name (§ 303)	$ 20
Resignation of a registered agent for service of process (§ 305)	$ 60
Resignation for receipt for process (§ 306-A)	$ 60
Service of process on the secretary of state (§§ 306, 306-A(e), and 307)	$ 40*
*No fee shall be collected for process served on behalf of a county, city, town, village, or other political subdivision of the state.	
Filing a certificate of incorporation (§ 402)	$ 125
Filing a certificate of amendment (§ 805)	$ 60
Filing a certificate of change (§ 805-A(a))	$ 30
Filing a certificate of change (§ 805-A(b))	$ 5
Filing a restated certificate of incorporation (§ 807)	$ 60
Filing a certificate of merger or consolidation (§ 904)	$ 60
Filing a certificate of merger of a subsidiary corporation (§ 905)	$ 60
Filing a certificate of merger or consolidation (§§ 904-a and 904-b)	$ 60
Filing a certificate of merger or consolidation of domestic and foreign corporations (§ 907)	$ 60
Filing a certificate of dissolution (§ 1003)	$ 60
Filing an application by a foreign corporation for authority to do business in New York state (§ 1304)	$ 225
Filing a certificate of amendment of an application for authority by a foreign corporation (§ 1309)	$ 60
Filing a certificate of change of application for authority by a foreign corporation (§ 1309-A(b))	$ 30
Filing a certificate of change (§ 1309-A(c))	$ 5
Filing a certificate of surrender of authority (§ 1310)	$ 60
Filing a statement of the termination of existence of a foreign corporation (§ 1311)	$ 60
Filing by an authorized officer of the jurisdiction of incorporation of a foreign corporation of a certificate that the foreign corporation has been dissolved or its authority or existence has been otherwise terminated or cancelled in its jurisdiction of incorporation	No fee
Filing a certificate of incorporation by a professional service corporation (§ 1503)	$ 125

Filing a statement or amendment (§ 408)	$ 9
Filing any other certificate or instrument	$ 60

Fees under the Limited Liability Company Law
(All section references are to LLC sections)

Reservation of limited liability company name (§ 205)	$ 20
Change of address of a registered agent for service of process (§ 302)	$ 20
Resignation of a registered agent for service of process (§ 302)	$ 20
Filing articles of organization (§ 209)	$ 200
Filing a certificate of amendment (§ 211)	$ 60
Filing articles of dissolution (§ 705)	$ 60
Filing restated articles of organization (§ 214)	$ 60
Filling a judicial dissolution (§ 702)	$ 60
Filing an application for authority (§ 802)	$ 250
Filing an application for authority – Professional Service	$ 200
Filing an amendment to an application for authority (§ 804)	$ 60
Filing a certificate of surrender of authority (§ 806)	$ 60
Filing a certificate of termination of existence (§807)	$ 60
Filing a certificate of merger or consolidation (§ 1003)	$ 60
Filing a certificate of correction (§ 212)	$ 60
Filing a certificate of conversion (§ 1006)	$ 200
Filing a certificate of publication with affidavits of publication annexed thereto (§§ 206, 802, 1203, and 1306)	$ 50
Filing a certificate of resignation for receipt for process (§ 301-A)	$ 10
Service of process on the secretary of state (§§ 301-A(e) and 303)*	$ 40
*no fee shall be collected for process served on behalf of a county, city, town, village, or other political subdivision of the state.	
Filing a certificate of change (§§ 211-A(a) and 804-A(a))	$ 30
Filing a certificate of change (§§ 211-A(b) and 804-A(b))	$ 5

Fees under the Partnership Law
(All section references are to PL sections)

Reservation of a limited partnership name (§ 121-103)	$ 20
Resignation of a registered agent for service of process (§ 121-105(c))	$ 10
Filing a certificate of limited partnership (§ 121-201)	$ 200
Filing a certificate of publication with affidavits of publication annexed thereto (§§ 121-201 and 121-902)	$ 50
Filing a certificate of amendment (§ 121-202)	$ 60
Filing a certificate of cancellation (§ 121-203)	$ 60
Filing a restated certificate of limited partnership (§ 121-208)	$ 60
Filing a judicial dissolution (§ 121-802)	$ 60
Filing an application for authority (§ 121-902)	$ 200
Filing an amendment to an application for authority (§ 121-903)	$ 60
Filing a certificate of surrender of authority (§ 121-905)	$ 60
Filing a certificate of termination of existence (§ 121-906)	$ 60
Filing a certificate of merger or consolidation (§ 121-1103)	$ 60
Filing a certificate of adoption (§ 121-1202)	$ 200
Filing a certificate of resignation for receipt for process (§ 121-104-A)	$ 10
Service of process on the secretary of state (§§ 121-104-A and 121-109)	$ 40*
*no fee shall be collected for process served on behalf of a county, city, town, village, or other political subdivision of the state.	
Filing a certificate of change (§§ 121-202-A(a) and 121-903-A(a))	$ 30
Filing a certificate of change (§§ 121-202-A(b) and 121-903-A(b))	$ 5
Reservation of a limited partnership name (§ 121-103)	$ 20

Publication and Fee Tables

Fees under the Not-for-Profit Corporation Law
(All section references are to NPC sections)

Reservation of corporate name (§ 303)	$ 10
Resignation of a registered agent for service of process (§ 305)	$ 30
Service of process on the secretary of state (§§ 306 and 307)	$ 40
Service of process on the secretary of state if the service is in an action brought solely to recover a sum of money not in excess of $200 and the process is so endorsed	$ 10
Service of process on the secretary of state if the process is served on behalf of a county, city, town, village, or other subdivision of the state	$ 10
Filing a certificate of incorporation (§ 402)	$ 75
Filing a certificate of amendment (§ 803)	$ 30
Filing a certificate of change (§ 803-A)	$ 20
Filing a restated certificate of incorporation (§ 805)	$ 30
Filing a certificate of merger or consolidation (§ 904)	$ 30
Filing a certificate of merger or consolidation of domestic and foreign corporations (§ 906)	$ 30
Filing a certificate of dissolution (§ 1003)	$ 30
Filing a certificate of annulment of dissolution (§ 1012)	$ 30
Filing an application by a foreign corporation for authority to do business in New York state (§ 1304)	$ 135
Filing a certificate of amendment of an application for authority by a foreign corporation (§ 1309)	$ 30
Filing a certificate of change of application for authority by a foreign corporation (§ 1310)	$ 20
Filing a certificate of surrender of authority (§ 1311)	$ 30
Filing a statement of the termination of existence of a foreign corporation (§ 1312)	$ 30
Filing by an authorized officer of the jurisdiction of incorporation of a foreign corporation of a certificate that the foreign corporation has been dissolved or its authority or existence has been otherwise terminated or cancelled in its jurisdiction of incorporation	No fee
Filing any other certificate or instrument	$ 30

Publication and Fee Tables

BUSINESS CORPORATION LAW

ARTICLE 1
SHORT TITLE; DEFINITIONS; APPLICATION; CERTIFICATES, MISCELLANEOUS

History: Add, L 1961, ch 855, eff Sept 1, 1963.

Schedule of sections, amd, L 1962, ch 317, § 1, L 1963, ch 748, § 1, eff Sept 1, 1963, L 1963, ch 749, eff Sept 1, 1963.

Laws 1962, ch 317, § 30, provides as follows:

§ 30. This act shall take effect on the same day when a chapter of the laws of nineteen hundred sixty-two, entitled "An act in relation to civil practice and prescribing rules of civil procedure governing generally the civil procedure in the courts of the state of New York and before the judges thereof, constituting chapter eight of the consolidated laws," takes effect.

§ 101.   Short title

This chapter shall be known as the "Business Corporation Law".

History: Add, L 1961, ch 855, eff Sept 1, 1963.

§ 102.   Definitions

(a) As used in this chapter, unless the context otherwise requires, the term:

(1) "Authorized person" means a person, whether or not a shareholder, officer or director, who is authorized to act on behalf of a corporation or foreign corporation.

(2) "Bonds" includes secured and unsecured bonds, debentures, and notes.

(3) "Certificate of incorporation" includes (A) the original certificate of incorporation or any other instrument filed or issued under any statute to form a domestic or foreign corporation, as amended, supplemented or restated by certificates of amendment, merger or consolidation or other certificates or instruments filed or issued under any statute; or (B) a special act or charter creating a domestic or foreign corporation, as amended, supplemented or restated.

(4) "Corporation" or "domestic corporation" means a corporation for profit formed under this chapter, or existing on its effective date and theretofore formed under any other general statute or by any special act of this state for a purpose or purposes for which a corporation may be formed under this chapter, other than a corporation which may be formed under the cooperative corporations law.

(5) "Director" means any member of the governing board of a corporation, whether designated as director, trustee, manager, governor, or by any other title. The term "board" means "board of directors".

(6) [Repealed]

(7) "Foreign corporation" means a corporation for profit formed under laws other than the statutes of this state, which has as its purpose or among its purposes a purpose for which a corporation may be formed under this chapter, other than a corporation which, if it were to be formed currently under the laws of this state, could not be formed under this chapter. "Authorized", when used with respect to a foreign corporation, means having authority under article 13 (Foreign corporations) to do business in this state.

(7-a) "Infant" means a person who has not attained the age of eighteen years.

(8) "Insolvent" means being unable to pay debts as they become due in the usual course of the debtor's business.

(9) "Net assets" means the amount by which the total assets exceed the total liabilities. Stated capital and surplus are not liabilities.

(10) "Office of a corporation" means the office the location of which is stated in the certificate of incorporation of a domestic corporation, or in the application for authority of a foreign corporation or an amendment thereof. Such office need not be a place where business activities are conducted by such corporation.

(11) "Process" means judicial process and all orders, demands, notices or other papers required or permitted by law to be personally served on a domestic or foreign corporation, for the purpose of acquiring jurisdiction of such corporation in any action or proceeding, civil or criminal, whether judicial, administrative, arbitrative or otherwise, in this state or in the federal courts sitting in or for this state.

(12) "Stated capital" means the sum of (A) the par value of all shares with par value that have been issued, (B) the amount of the consideration received for all shares without par value that have been issued, except such part of the consideration therefor as may have been allocated to surplus in a manner permitted by law, and (C) such amounts not included in clauses (A) and (B) as have been transferred to stated capital, whether upon the distribution of shares or otherwise, minus all reductions from such sums as have been effected in a manner permitted by law.

(13) "Surplus" means the excess of net assets over stated capital.

(14) "Treasury shares" means shares which have been issued, have been subsequently acquired, and are retained uncancelled by the corporation. Treasury shares are issued shares, but not outstanding shares, and are not assets.

History: Add, L 1961, ch 855, eff Sept 1, 1963; amd, L 1962, ch 834, § 1, eff Sept 1, 1963; L 1964, ch 725, § 1; L 1966, ch 664, § 14, eff Sept 1, 1967; L 1974, ch 899, eff Sept 1, 1974; L 1997, ch 449, § 1, eff Feb 22, 1998; L 1998, ch 375, § 1, eff Aug 13, 1998.

CASE ANNOTATIONS

1. In general
2. Venue
3. Service of process
4. Under former law

1. In general

For purposes of stock repurchase agreement whereby price per share was to be determined by dividing total number of shares "issued and outstanding" into an amount equal to 3.75 times the gross annual fees for servicing mortgages for the company's last full fiscal year, treasury stock was, under statutory definition, issued but not outstanding, and thus the divisor in the contractual formula should be 5,833, after subtracting the 4,167 treasury shares from the total of 10,000 issued shares. Britton v Dorman & Wilson, Inc., 54 A.D.2d 953, 388 N.Y.S.2d 631, 1976 N.Y. App. Div. LEXIS 14857 (N.Y. App. Div. 2d Dep't 1976).

Parties who deal with entity holding itself out as corporation and receive performance from such entity are estopped from avoiding their obligations to it. Judarl L.L.C. v Cycletech Inc., 246 A.D.2d 736, 667 N.Y.S.2d 451, 1998 N.Y. App. Div. LEXIS 73 (N.Y. App. Div. 3d Dep't 1998).

Subd a (10) makes it quite clear that "office of a corporation" means location stated in its certificate or application and that such office need not be place where business activities are conducted. General Precision, Inc. v Ametek, Inc., 45 Misc. 2d 451, 257 N.Y.S.2d 120, 1965 N.Y. Misc. LEXIS 2280 (N.Y. Sup. Ct.), aff'd, 24 A.D.2d 757, 263 N.Y.S.2d 470, 1965 N.Y. App. Div. LEXIS 3338 (N.Y. App. Div. 2d Dep't 1965).

The language of Business Corporation Law §§ 1301 (a) and 1312 is limited strictly to foreign corporations organized for profit. Anti-Defamation League of B'Nai B'Rith v American Italian Anti-Defamation League, Inc., 54 Misc. 2d 830, 283 N.Y.S.2d 828, 1967 N.Y. Misc. LEXIS 1207 (N.Y. Sup. Ct. 1967).

Commercial entity of foreign sovereign cannot be deemed "foreign corporation" as defined under CLS Bus Corp § 102(a)(7). Lippus v Dahlgren Mfg. Co., 644 F. Supp. 1473, 1986 U.S. Dist. LEXIS 19865 (E.D.N.Y. 1986).

Where the corporate debtor was shown by a preponderance of the evidence to have been continuously insolvent since July 1, 2003 under N.Y. Bus. Corp. Law §§ 102(a)(8) and 513 (2003), it could avoid payments made after that date under a stock redemption agreement to a former shareholder's estate. Thaler v Estate of Arbore (In re Poseidon Pool & Spa Rec., Inc.), 2010 Bankr. LEXIS 3457 (Bankr. E.D.N.Y. Sept. 30, 2010), app. denied, 443 B.R. 271, 2010 U.S. Dist. LEXIS 130184 (E.D.N.Y. 2010).

In deciding whether the trust fund doctrine applied so as to find that debtor owed a fiduciary duty to preserve the assets of a corporation of which she was the sole shareholder and director for the benefit of creditors, although neither party offered evidence on whether, or at what point, the corporation was insolvent under either the Bankruptcy Code definition of insolvency or the New York Business Corporations Law definition, it appeared that the earliest point at which its liabilities exceeded its assets, or it became unable to pay its debts as they became due, was when its loan repayment checks began to bounce. Pappas v Gucciardo (In re Gucciardo), 577 B.R. 23, 64 Bankr. Ct. Dec. (LRP) 238, 2017 Bankr. LEXIS 4009 (Bankr. E.D.N.Y. 2017).

2. Venue

Where both parties to a commercial action were foreign corporations authorized to do business in New York, the proper venue of the suit was the county designated by the plaintiff in its statement as the county where its office was to be located, and the mere fact that the corporation has its office in a county other than that designated does not change its residence for the purpose of legal procedure. General Precision, Inc. v Ametek, Inc., 24 A.D.2d 757, 263 N.Y.S.2d 470, 1965 N.Y. App. Div. LEXIS 3338 (N.Y. App. Div. 2d Dep't 1965).

For purposes of venue, the residence of a corporation is in the county set forth in its certificate of incorporation as its principal place of business. Wegorzewski v Macrose Lumber & Trim Co., 28 A.D.2d 713, 280 N.Y.S.2d 994, 1967 N.Y. App. Div. LEXIS 3836 (N.Y. App. Div. 2d Dep't 1967).

Absent any indication that Congress intended section 94 of title 12 of the United States Code to be the exclusive venue provision governing transitory actions brought against national banks in courts of this State, State venue provisions are also applicable and where both parties to an action had their principal offices outside the county in which the action was brought, it was not a proper place for trial under New York law. (CPLR 503, subds [a], [c]; Business Corporation Law, § 102, subd [a], par [10].) Accordingly, the venue of the action was properly changed to the county in which the bank had its principal place of business. Walhalla Associates, Inc. v National Commercial Bank & Trust Co., 71 A.D.2d 154, 422 N.Y.S.2d 152, 1979 N.Y. App. Div. LEXIS 13242 (N.Y. App. Div. 3d Dep't 1979), aff'd, 54 N.Y.2d 857, 444 N.Y.S.2d 916, 429 N.E.2d 423, 1981 N.Y. LEXIS 3076 (N.Y. 1981).

Although plaintiff corporation relocated its entire office and manufacturing facility to another county, the residence of the corporation for purposes of venue was in the county set forth in its certificate of incorporation as its principal place of business. Reliable Displays Corp. v Maro Industries, Inc., 67 Misc. 2d 747, 325 N.Y.S.2d 616, 1971 N.Y. Misc. LEXIS 1305 (N.Y. Sup. Ct. 1971).

3. Service of process

Notice of appropriation is not a "process" as defined by the Business Corporation Law and, therefore, personal service is not perfected upon a corporation by serving a notice of appropriation upon the Secretary of State. Ebbets v State, 88 Misc. 2d 358, 387 N.Y.S.2d 969, 1976 N.Y. Misc. LEXIS 2614 (N.Y. Ct. Cl. 1976), aff'd, 64 A.D.2d 794,

408 N.Y.S.2d 556, 1978 N.Y. App. Div. LEXIS 12641 (N.Y. App. Div. 3d Dep't 1978).

Service upon Secretary of State was effective to subject defendants to jurisdiction of Civil Court of New York City, New York County, in action for earned insurance premiums even though defendants had moved their place of business from New York County to Westchester County prior to service since office designated in defendants' certificate of incorporation was care of attorneys in New York County and office need not be placed where business activities are conducted. Fireman's Fund Ins. Co. v Kashmir Krafts, Inc., 131 Misc. 2d 338, 500 N.Y.S.2d 604, 1986 N.Y. Misc. LEXIS 2394 (N.Y. Civ. Ct. 1986).

4. Under former law

For purposes of judicial procedure the residence or domicile of a corporation is the seat of government, and it makes no difference where the administrative departments and physical property of the corporation happen to be located. Gould v Texas & P. R. Co., 176 A.D. 818, 163 N.Y.S. 479, 1917 N.Y. App. Div. LEXIS 5154 (N.Y. App. Div. 1917).

The trustees of an educational corporation chartered by the Board of Regents had the same status, under former General Corporation Law, as directors. In re Lake Placid Co., 274 A.D. 205, 81 N.Y.S.2d 36, 1948 N.Y. App. Div. LEXIS 3040 (N.Y. App. Div. 1948).

Under the definition of "director" in § 3 of former General Corporation Law as a person duly chosen or designated to manage the affairs of a corporation, the so-called "Spiritual Leader" of an incorporated society who was only an ex-officio member of the Board of Directors, without right to vote or in any manner conduct business affairs of the organization, was not a director upon whom process could be served pursuant to § 228 subd. 8 of the Civil Practice Act. Plainview Plumbing & Heating Co. v Ethical Culture Soc., 24 Misc. 2d 1005, 205 N.Y.S.2d 419, 1960 N.Y. Misc. LEXIS 2428 (N.Y. Sup. Ct. 1960).

The terms "principal place of business" and "principal office" were not synonymous and were not used synonymously in § 3 of former General Corporation Law. Mason & Hanger Co. v Sharon, 231 F. 861, 1916 U.S. App. LEXIS 1721 (2d Cir. N.Y.), cert. denied, 241 U.S. 670, 36 S. Ct. 554, 60 L. Ed. 1230, 1916 U.S. LEXIS 1809 (U.S. 1916).

Corporations have been regarded as residents of the county where the office of the company is located and its general business is carried on. Wienbroer v United States Shipping Board Emergency Fleet Corp., 299 F. 972, 1924 U.S. Dist. LEXIS 1595 (D.N.Y. 1924).

UNDER FORMER LAW

For purposes of judicial procedure the residence or domicile of a corporation is the seat of government, and it makes no difference where the administrative departments and physical property of the corporation happen to be located. Gould v Texas & P. R. Co. (1917) 176 A.D. 818, 163 N.Y.S. 479

The trustees of an educational corporation chartered by the Board of Regents had the same status, under former General Corporation Law, as directors. Re Lake Placid Co. (1948) 274 A.D. 205, 81 N.Y.S.2d 36

Under the definition of "director" in § 3 of former General Corporation Law as a person duly chosen or designated to manage the affairs of a corporation, the so-called "Spiritual Leader" of an incorporated society who was only an ex-officio member of the Board of Directors, without right to vote or in any manner conduct business affairs of the organization, was not a director upon whom process could be served pursuant to § 228 subd. 8 of the Civil Practice Act. Plainview Plumbing & Heating Co. v Ethical Culture Soc. (1960) 24 Misc. 2d 1005, 205 N.Y.S.2d 419

Corporations have been regarded as residents of the county where the office of the company is located and its general business is carried on. Wienbroer v United States Shipping Board Emergency Fleet Corp. (1924, DC NY) 299 F 972

The terms "principal place of business" and "principal office" were not synonymous and were not used synonymously in § 3 of former General Corporation Law. Mason & Hanger Co. v Sharon (1916, CA2 NY) 231 F 861, cert den 241 US 670, 60 L Ed 1230, 36 S Ct 554

An educational corporation authorized to issue stock, in which holders share in surplus profits, was formerly considered a stock corporation. 1910 Ops Atty Gen 548

§ 103.   Application

(a) This chapter applies to every domestic corporation and to every foreign corporation which is authorized or does business in this state. This chapter also applies to any other domestic corporation or foreign corporation of any type or kind to the extent, if any, provided under this chapter or any law governing such corporation and, if no such provision for application is made, to the extent, if any, that the stock corporation law applied to such corporation immediately prior to the effective date of this chapter.

This chapter also applies to a corporation of any type or kind, formed for profit under any other chapter of the laws of this state except a chapter of the consolidated laws, to the extent that provisions of this chapter do not conflict with the provisions of such unconsolidated law. If an applicable provision of such unconsolidated law relates to a matter embraced in this chapter but is not in conflict therewith, both provisions shall apply. Any corporation to which this chapter is made applicable by this paragraph shall be treated as a "corporation" or "domestic corporation" as such terms are used in this chapter, except that the purposes of any such corporation formed or formable under such unconsolidated law shall not thereby be extended. For the purpose of this paragraph, the effective date of this chapter as to corporations to which this chapter is made applicable by this paragraph shall be June one, nineteen hundred seventy-three.

This chapter shall not apply to a domestic corporation of any type or kind heretofore or hereafter formed under the banking law, insurance law, railroad law, transportation corporations law or cooperative corporations law, or under any other statute or special act for a purpose or purposes for which a corporation may be formed under any of such laws except to the extent, if any, provided under such law. It shall not apply, except to the extent, if any, provided under the banking law, insurance law, railroad law, transportation corporations law or cooperative corporations law, to a foreign corporation of any type or kind heretofore or hereafter formed which (1) has as its purpose or among its purposes a purpose for which a corporation may be formed only under the insurance law, banking law, railroad law, transportation corporations law or cooperative corporations law, and (2) is either an authorized insurer as defined in the insurance law or does in this state only the kind of business which can be done lawfully by a corporation formed under the banking law, railroad law, transportation corporations law or cooperative corporations law, as the case may be. After the effective date of this chapter the stock corporation law shall not apply to any corporation of any type or kind. The general corporation law shall not apply to a corporation of any type or kind to which this chapter applies. A reference in any statute of this state, which makes a provision of the stock corporation law applicable to a corporation of any type or kind, shall be deemed and construed to refer to and make applicable the corresponding provision, if any, of this chapter.

(b) This chapter applies to commerce with foreign nations and among the several states, and to corporations formed by or under any act of congress, only to

Business Corporation Law

the extent permitted under the constitution and laws of the United States.

(c) The enactment of this chapter shall not affect the duration of a corporation which is existing on the effective date of this chapter. Any such existing corporation, its shareholders, directors and officers shall have the same rights and be subject to the same limitations, restrictions, liabilities and penalties as a corporation formed under this chapter, its shareholders, directors and officers.

(d) This chapter shall not affect any cause of action, liability, penalty or action or special proceeding, which on the effective date of this chapter, is accrued, existing, incurred or pending but the same may be asserted, enforced, prosecuted or defended as if this chapter had not been enacted.

(e) After the effective date of this chapter no corporation shall be formed under the stock corporation law.

History: Add, L 1961, ch 855, eff April 1, 1963; amd, L 1963, ch 692, eff Sept 1, 1963; L 1964, ch 725, § 2; L 1966, ch 664, § 15; L 1973, ch 388, eff June 1, 1973.

CASE ANNOTATIONS

Provision of subd d of above statute that provisions of Business Corporation Law should not affect any cause of action which was pending on its effective date, applied. Schlegel v Schlegel Mfg. Corp. (1965, 4th Dept) 23 A.D.2d 808, 258 N.Y.S.2d 587

Dismissal of an action by a subcontractor to foreclose a mechanic's lien on the theory that the plaintiff did not have legal capacity to sue was improper, where it did not appear from the papers submitted that the contract between the plaintiff and the general contractor had been made in this state. Kosson & Sons v Carleton (1966, 2d Dept) 26 A.D.2d 582, 272 N.Y.S.2d 81

Suffolk County Legislature had implicit power to impose reasonable fiscal conditions on approval of for-profit New York business corporation's application for rate increase for ferry service between Shelter Island and Greenport, on Long Island's mainland (Suffolk County Code § 287-3), but Legislature could not interfere with corporation's internal accounting procedures and corporate decision-making, nor could it usurp responsibilities, duties, and functions consigned by law exclusively to corporation's officers, directors, and shareholders; thus, conditions constituting such improper interference, imposed by Legislature on approval of resolution approving rate increase, were properly vacated. North Ferry Co. v Suffolk County Legislature (2000, 2d Dept) 272 A.D.2d 548, 708 N.Y.S.2d 144, app den 95 N.Y.2d 761, 714 N.Y.S.2d 711, 737 N.E.2d 953

The claim of a foreign trucking corporation for property damage caused by alleged negligence in maintaining state highways which accrued on March 20, 1963, was not barred by legislation that provided that an unauthorized foreign corporation could not maintain any action in the state of New York until it obtained authority to do business in this state, which became effective on April 1, 1963, notwithstanding that suit was instituted on June 14, 1963, since the Act had been amended and the effective date extended to September 1, 1963. Tetreault v State (1966) 50 Misc. 2d 170, 269 N.Y.S.2d 812

Leasing corporation was not precluded from bringing suit against a guarantor in New York because a letter from the state banking department indicated that a bank intended to establish a "representative office" in New York and that the representative office was registered with the banking department. Studebaker-Worthington Leasing v Cervera (2010, Sup) 28 Misc 3d 430, 243 NYLJ 84, 904 NYS2d 644.

This statutory provision states that this chapter of the Business Corporation Law shall not "affect" any such cause of action or liability, and a cause of action is not "affected" if substantive rights or obligations are not enlarged or impaired. Lumbermens Mut. Casualty Co. v Borden Co. (1967, SD NY) 268 F. Supp. 303

The intention of Business Corporation Law § 103(d) seems to be that a party may utilize the Business Corporation Law to pursue a cause of action that arose before its effective date, but that no provision in the Business Corporation Law can affect the substantive rights and obligations of the parties that arose out of such cause of action, and to this extent, Business Corporation Law § 307 neither enlarges nor impairs the rights of the parties and therefore may be retroactively applied. Lumbermens Mut. Casualty Co. v Borden Co. (1967, SD NY) 268 F. Supp. 303

New York's Business Corporation Law does not apply to a corporation formed under its own Banking Law, but it does apply to a corporation by or under any Act of Congress. Wolpert v First Nat. Bank (1974, ED NY) 381 F. Supp. 625

CLS Business Corporation Law § 103 provides that the law of the state of incorporation governs the internal affairs of a corporation. Cohen v Ayers (1978, ND Ill) 449 F. Supp. 298, CCH Fed Secur L Rep ¶ 96575, affd (CA7 Ill) 596 F.2d 733, CCH Fed Secur L Rep ¶ 96836

§ 104. Certificates; requirements, signing, filing, effectiveness

(a) Every certificate or other instrument relating to a domestic or foreign corporation which is delivered to the department of state for filing under this chapter, other than a certificate of existence under section 1304 (Application for authority; contents), shall be in the English language, except that the corporate name may be in another language if written in English letters or characters.

(b) [Repealed]

(c) Whenever such instrument is required to set forth the date when a certificate of incorporation was filed by the department of state, the original certificate of incorporation is meant. This requirement shall be satisfied, in the case of a corporation created by special act, by setting forth the chapter number and year of passage of such act.

(d) Every such certificate required under this chapter to be signed and delivered to the department of state shall, except as otherwise specified in the section providing for such certificate, be signed either by an officer, director, attorney-in-fact or duly authorized person and include the name and the capacity in which such person signs such certificate.

(e) If an instrument which is delivered to the department of state for filing complies as to form with the requirements of law and there has been attached to it the consent or approval of the state official, department, board, agency or other body, if any, whose consent to or approval of such instrument or the filing thereof is required by any statute of this state and the filing fee and tax, if any, required by any statute of this state in connection therewith have been paid, the instrument shall be filed and indexed by the department of state. No certificate of authentication or conformity or other proof shall be required with respect to any verification, oath or acknowledgment of any instrument delivered to the department of state under this chapter, if such verification, oath or acknowledgment purports to have been made before a notary public, or person performing the equivalent function, of one of the states, or any subdivision thereof, of the United States or the District of Columbia. Without limiting the effect of section four hundred three of this chapter, filing and indexing by the department of state shall not be deemed a finding that a certificate conforms to law, nor shall it be deemed to constitute an approval by the department of state of the name of the corporation or the contents of the certificate, nor shall it be deemed to prevent any person with appropriate standing from contesting the legality thereof in an appropriate forum.

(f) Except as otherwise provided in this chapter, such instrument shall become effective upon the filing thereof by the department of state.

(g) The department shall make, certify and transmit electronically a copy of each such instrument to the clerk of the county in which the office of the domestic or foreign corporation is or is to be located. The county clerk shall file and index such copy.

History: Add, L 1961, ch 855, eff Sept 1, 1963; amd, L 1962, ch 834, § 2, eff Sept 1, 1963, L 1965, ch 609, eff Sept 1, 1965, L 1982, ch 832, § 1, eff Oct 25, 1982 L 1997, ch 449, § 2, eff Feb 22, 1998, L 1998, ch 375, §§ 2, 3, eff Aug 13, 1998, L 1999, ch 172, § 1, eff July 6, 1999, L 2014, ch 57, § 1 (Part O), eff March 31, 2014.

CASE ANNOTATIONS

Plaintiff was not precluded from recovering on 3 promissory notes executed before its formation as corporation where defendant received proceeds of loan, and plaintiff filed its articles of organization and paid proper fees. Judarl L.L.C. v Cycletech Inc. (1998, 3d Dept) 246 A.D.2d 736, 667 N.Y.S.2d 451

A chairman of the board of directors is not one of the usual officers designated in Business Corporation L § 715, but §§ 104 and 508 of such Law do recognize the existence of such an office and accept it for certain purposes as an alternative to the presidency. American Express Co. v Lopez (1973) 72 Misc. 2d 648, 340 N.Y.S.2d 82

Chairman of board of directors of corporation had apparent authority to get himself a credit card and charge the corporation with responsibility for it. American Express Co. v Lopez (1973) 72 Misc. 2d 648, 340 N.Y.S.2d 82

Filing of an amendatory certificate of incorporation commences the effective date of the amendment; approval of a Supreme Court justice is a mere condition precedent to the right to file the amendment and is not conclusive on either the public or Secretary of State; however, such approval indicates that the purpose of the amendment is lawful and an acceptance by the Secretary enforces such view. Crohn v Firemen's Benev. Fund Asso. (1973) 79 Misc. 2d 536, 359 N.Y.S.2d 599

A tax deed issued by Rockland County to plaintiff corporation following a public auction must be set aside since plaintiff had not yet filed its certificate of incorporation at the time of the auction and was therefore incapable under the law of placing a bid at the auction (General Corporation Law, § 8); title shall revest in the county subject to any jurisdictional defects which can be proven by defendant, the alleged equitable owner of the property who has two years to rebut the presumption of regularity of the proceedings leading to the issuance of the tax deed to the county on March 30, 1979. R.M. Investors Corp. v Maggi (1980) 104 Misc. 2d 41, 427 N.Y.S.2d 919

Failure of a contractor to plead and establish itself as a corporation with regard to his breach of contract and quantum meruit suit against a homeowner did not provide a ground for the homeowner to have the unanimous verdict in favor of the contractor for unpaid services vacated or to obtain a new trial. However, because the contractor was unlicensed, as required by New York City, N.Y., Admin. Code §§ 20-386(2) and 20-385, he was precluded from recovering the unpaid balance of the services rendered, even on a quantum meruit basis, thus, the verdict was set aside and the complaint was dismissed. Nemard Constr. Corp. v Deafeamkpor (2008, Sup) 21 Misc 3d 320, 863 NYS2d 546.

UNDER FORMER GEN CORP § 8

Mere execution of a certificate of incorporation did not create a de facto corporation if the incorporators had not complied with § 8 of the General Corp. L. and, therefore, where the incorporators, prior to any attempt made in good faith to comply with that section, transferred all the stock of the proposed corporation in exchange for certain rights under alleged contracts owned by a third party, the transfer was without consideration and it was error to dismiss a complaint of a judgment creditor seeking to sequester the assets of the corporation and to recover on personal liability of the stockholders. Stevens v Episcopal Church History Co. (1910) 140 A.D. 570, 125 N.Y.S. 573

A corporation which had failed to comply with the requirements of § 8 of the General Corp. L. was not a corporation authorized to do business nor a de facto corporation and the Secretary of State was not justified in refusing to file the certificate of another corporation on the grounds of similarity of name. Brooks Clothing of California, Ltd. v Flynn (1931) 232 A.D. 346, 250 N.Y.S. 69

While § 8 of the General Corporation Law permitted the title of a corporation to be in foreign words, if composed of English letters, nevertheless the application, in such case, had to be accompanied by an affidavit explaining the meaning of the words, so that a justice could, if called upon to approve the application, determine whether the proposed name would engender discord or injure the feelings of the community. Re Daughters of Israel Orphan Aid Soc. (1925) 125 Misc 217, 210 N.Y.S. 541; disapproved Association for Preservation of Freedom of Choice, Inc. v Shapiro, (1961) 9 N.Y.2d 376, 214 N.Y.S.2d 388, 174 N.E.2d 487, reh den (1962) 11 N.Y.2d 662, 225 N.Y.S.2d 740, 180 N.E.2d 898), which provided that justice is not at liberty to grant or deny application for certificate of incorporation based on his personal notion of what is contrary to public policy or injurious to community

Where a company went out of existence as a result of merger and no new corporation was formed under § 85 of the Stk. Corp. Law, § 8 of the Gen. Corp. L. did not apply. O'Donnell v Milling & Lighting Co. (1937) 163 Misc 860, 298 N.Y.S. 9

Article 78 of the Civil Practice Act is not available to review an alleged erroneous filing of a certificate of incorporation, for the statutory authority "to review a determination" relates only to the determination of a body or an officer exercising quasi-judicial functions, and, in receiving a certificate for filing, the Department of State is acting in a ministerial capacity, except where there is some conflict of names. Where the certificate is in conformity with law there is a duty to receive and file it. New York State Soc. of Professional Engineers, Inc. v Department of State (1940) 174 Misc 173, 20 N.Y.S.2d 62

§ 104-A. Fees

Except as otherwise provided, the department of state shall collect the following fees pursuant to this chapter:

(a) For the reservation of a corporate name pursuant to section three hundred three of this chapter, twenty dollars.

(b) For the resignation of a registered agent for service of process pursuant to section three hundred five of this chapter, and for the resignation for receipt for process pursuant to section three hundred six-A of this chapter, sixty dollars.

(c) For service of process on the secretary of state pursuant to section three hundred six, paragraph (e) of section three hundred six-A, or three hundred seven of this chapter, forty dollars. No fee shall be collected for process served on behalf of a county, city, town or village or other political subdivision of the state.

(d) For filing a certificate of incorporation pursuant to section four hundred two of this chapter, one hundred twenty-five dollars.

(e) For filing a certificate of amendment pursuant to section eight hundred five of this chapter, sixty dollars.

(f) For filing a certificate of change pursuant to paragraph (a) of section eight hundred five-A of this chapter, thirty dollars, and for filing a certificate of change pursuant to paragraph (b) of section eight hundred five-A of this chapter, five dollars.

(g) For filing a restated certificate of incorporation pursuant to section eight hundred seven of this chapter, sixty dollars.

(h) For filing a certificate of merger or consolidation pursuant to section nine hundred four of this chapter, or a certificate of exchange pursuant to section nine hundred thirteen (other than paragraph (g) of section nine hundred thirteen) of this chapter, sixty dollars.

(i) For filing a certificate of merger of a subsidiary corporation pursuant to section nine hundred five of this chapter, or a certificate of exchange pursuant to paragraph (g) of section nine hundred thirteen of this chapter, sixty dollars.

(j) For filing a certificate of merger or consolidation pursuant to section nine hundred four-a of this chapter, a certificate of merger or consolidation pursuant to section nine hundred four-b of this chapter, or a certificate of merger or consolidation of domestic and foreign corporations pursuant to section nine hundred seven of this chapter, sixty dollars.

(k) For filing a certificate of dissolution pursuant to section one thousand three of this chapter, sixty dollars.

(l) For filing an application by a foreign corporation for authority to do business in New York state pursuant to section thirteen hundred four of this chapter, two hundred twenty-five dollars.

(m) For filing a certificate of amendment of an application for authority by a foreign corporation pursuant to section thirteen hundred nine of this chapter, sixty dollars.

(n) For filing a certificate of change of application for authority by a foreign corporation pursuant to paragraph (b) of section thirteen hundred nine-A of this chapter, thirty dollars, and for filing a certificate of change pursuant to paragraph (c) of section thirteen hundred nine-A of this chapter, five dollars.

(o) For filing a certificate of surrender of authority pursuant to section thirteen hundred ten of this chapter, sixty dollars.

(p) For filing a statement of the termination of existence of a foreign corporation pursuant to section thirteen hundred eleven of this chapter, sixty dollars. There shall be no fee for the filing by an authorized officer of the jurisdiction of incorporation of a foreign corporation of a certificate that the foreign corporation has been dissolved or its authority or existence has been otherwise terminated or cancelled in the jurisdiction of its incorporation.

(q) For filing a certificate of incorporation by a professional service corporation pursuant to section fifteen hundred three of this chapter, one hundred twenty-five dollars.

(r) For filing a statement or amendment pursuant to section four hundred eight of this chapter with the department of state, nine dollars. This fee shall not apply to statements submitted through the department of taxation and finance pursuant to paragraph eight of section four hundred eight of this chapter.

(s) For filing any other certificate or instrument, sixty dollars.

History: Add, L 1982, ch 591, § 1, eff Sept 20, 1982; amd, L 1984, ch 198, § 1, eff June 12, 1984; L 1986, ch 117, § 5, eff Sept 1, 1986; L 1987, ch 39, § 2, eff Oct 1, 1987; L 1991, ch 166, § 270, eff June 12, 1991; L 1992, ch 55, § 400, eff April 10, 1992; L 1994, ch 170, § 201, eff July 1, 1994; L 1997, ch 469, § 3, eff Nov 24, 1997; L 1998, ch 448, § 1, eff Oct 20, 1998; L 1999, ch 172, § 2, eff July 6, 1999; L 2000, ch 172, § 1, eff July 18, 2000; L 2008, ch 177, § 1, eff July 7, 2008; L 2014, ch 59, § 108 (Part A), eff Jan 1, 2015; L 2015, ch 59, § 1 (Part S), eff April 13, 2015.

CASE ANNOTATIONS

Plaintiff was not precluded from recovering on 3 promissory notes executed before its formation as corporation where defendant received proceeds of loan, and plaintiff filed its articles of organization and paid proper fees. Judarl L.L.C. v Cycletech Inc. (1998, 3d Dept) 246 A.D.2d 736, 667 N.Y.S.2d 451

§ 105.   Certificates; corrections

Any certificate or other instrument relating to a domestic or foreign corporation filed by the department of state under this chapter may be corrected with respect to any informality or error apparent on the face, incorrect statement or defect in the execution thereof including the deletion of any matter not permitted to be stated therein. A certificate, entitled "Certificate of correction of .... (correct title of certificate and name of corporation)" shall be signed and delivered to the department of state. It shall set forth the name of the corporation, the date the certificate to be corrected was filed by the department of state, a statement as to the nature of the informality, error, incorrect statement or defect, the provision in the certificate as corrected or eliminated and if the execution was defective, the proper execution. The filing of the certificate by the department of state shall not alter the effective time of the instrument being corrected, which shall remain as its original effective time, and shall not affect any right or liability accrued or incurred before such filing. A corporate name may not be changed or corrected under this section. The provisions of this section shall apply to all instruments and certificates heretofore and hereafter filed with the department of state.

History: Add, L 1961, ch 855; amd, L 1962, ch 834, § 3, eff Sept 1, 1963; L 1989, ch 495, § 1, eff July 16, 1989; L 1999, ch 172, § 3, eff July 6, 1999.

CASE ANNOTATIONS

UNDER FORMER GEN CORP § 10

Section 10 of the Gen. Corp. L. was designed to cover amendments due to errors in phraseology or language which failed accurately to express the true object of the corporation which the incorporators had in mind, and not to permit amendments which were the result of afterthought. Re Horace Keane Aeroplanes, Inc. (1920) 194 A.D. 873, 185 N.Y.S. 163

Amendment of a certificate of incorporation by elimination therefrom of a clause relating to preferred stock dividends could not be secured by a proceeding instituted under § 10 of the Gen. Corp. L. Re Horace Keane Aeroplanes, Inc. (1920) 194 A.D. 873, 185 N.Y.S. 163

Membership corporations could amend their charter under § 10 of the Gen. Corp. L. so as to truly set forth the object and purpose of the corporation. Re Creditors' Audit & Adjustment Ass'n (1911) 72 Misc 461, 131 N.Y.S. 263

Mistake in spelling in corporate title may be corrected by amended certificate. 1910 Ops Atty Gen 408

Under the Gen. Corp. L., certificate changing corporate name could not be filed except under § 40. 1910 Ops Atty Gen 410

Amended certificate proposing reduction of capital could not be made. 1911 Ops Atty Gen 23

Insertion of new word in the name is not a correction of an informality. 1921 Ops Atty Gen 237

Where the nature of a membership corporation was such as to require approval of its certificate by the state board of public welfare, the certificate could not be amended to delete a condition set forth in the original certificate without that board's approval. 1941 Ops Atty Gen Feb 18

A change of corporate name may not be effected by filing of a certificate of amendment of certificate of incorporation even though proposed change is merely of word "women's" to "woman's". 1946 Ops Atty Gen Sep 10

The failure of a membership corporation to obtain the necessary approval of the Board of Social Welfare to a certificate of extension of corporate existence was a defect which could not be corrected by an amendatory certificate or by the Board's nunc pro tunc approval. However, a remedy lay in the filing of a certificate of revival of corporate existence pursuant to General Corporation Law § 49. 1952 Ops Atty Gen Feb 15

§ 106. Certificates as evidence

(a) Any certificate or other instrument filed by the department of state relating to a domestic or foreign corporation and containing statements of fact required or permitted by law to be contained therein, shall be received in all courts, public offices and official bodies as prima facie evidence of such facts and of the execution of such instrument.

(b) Whenever by the laws of any jurisdiction other than this state, any certificate by any officer in such jurisdiction or a copy of any instruments certified or exemplified by any such officer, may be received as prima facie evidence of the incorporation, existence or capacity of any foreign corporation incorporated in such jurisdiction, or claiming so to be, such certificate when exemplified, or such copy of such instrument when exemplified shall be received in all courts, public offices and official bodies of this state, as prima facie evidence with the same force as in such jurisdiction. Such certificate or certified copy of such instrument shall be so received, without being exemplified, if it is certified by the secretary of state, or official performing the equivalent function as to corporate records, of such jurisdiction.

History: Add, L 1961, ch 855, eff Sept 1, 1963.

Par (b), amd, L 1962, ch 834, § 4, eff Sept 1, 1963.

§ 107. Corporate seal as evidence

The presence of the corporate seal on a written instrument purporting to be executed by authority of a domestic or foreign corporation shall be prima facie evidence that the instrument was so executed.

History: Add, L 1961, ch 855, eff Sept 1, 1963

CASE ANNOTATIONS

Presence of corporate seal on document giving mortgagee permission to enter upon mortgagor's property and take possession of its inventory was prima facie evidence that such document was duly authorized, and such document would be upheld, in absence of evidence to the contrary. Rakosi v General Electric Credit Corp. (1977, 2d Dept) 59 A.D.2d 553, 397 N.Y.S.2d 416, 22 UCCRS 204

If the agreement was signed by the sole stockholders in their individual capacity and there appears on the agreement the corporate seal, the court is justified in finding that the agreement is binding on the corporation and the two individual stockholders where it does not appear that corporate creditors' rights are violated. Re Klaum's Will (1968) 58 Misc. 2d 262, 294 N.Y.S.2d 877

§ 108. When notice or lapse of time unnecessary; notices dispensed with when delivery is prohibited

(a) Whenever, under this chapter or the certificate of incorporation or by-laws of any corporation or by the terms of any agreement or instrument, a corporation or the board or any committee thereof is authorized to take any action after notice to any person or persons or after the lapse of a prescribed period of time, such action may be taken without notice and without the lapse of such period of time, if at any time before or after such action is completed the person or persons entitled to such notice or entitled to participate in the action to be taken or, in the case of a shareholder, by his attorney-in-fact, submit a signed waiver of notice of such requirements.

(b) Whenever any notice or communication is required to be given to any person by this chapter, the certificate of incorporation or by-laws, or by the terms of any agreement or instrument, or as a condition precedent to taking any corporate action and communication with such person is then unlawful under any statute of this state or of the United States or any regulation, proclamation or order issued under said statutes, then the giving of such notice or communication to such person shall not be required and there shall be no duty to apply for license or other permission to do so. Any affidavit, certificate or other instrument which is required to be made or filed as proof of the giving of any notice or communication required under this chapter shall, if such notice or communication to any person is dispensed with under this paragraph, include a statement that such notice or communication was not given to any person with whom communication is unlawful. Such affidavit, certificate or other instrument shall be as effective for all purposes as though such notice or communication had been personally given to such person.

(c) Whenever any notice or communication is required or permitted by this chapter to be given by mail, it shall, except as otherwise expressly provided in this chapter, be mailed to the person to whom it is directed at the address designated by him for that purpose or, if none is designated, at his last known address. Such notice or communication is given when deposited, with postage thereon prepaid, in a post office or official depository under the exclusive care and custody of the United States post office department. Such mailing shall be by first class mail except where otherwise required by this chapter.

History: Add, L 1961, ch 855, eff Sept 1, 1963; amd, L 1963, ch 748, § 2, eff Sept 1, 1963; L 1963, ch 749, eff Sept 1, 1963; L 1964, ch 725, § 3, eff June 1, 1964; L 1965, ch 803, § 1, eff Sept 1, 1965.

§ 109.   Actions or special proceedings by attorney-general

(a) The attorney-general may maintain an action or special proceeding:

(1) To annul the corporate existence or dissolve a corporation that has acted beyond its capacity or power or to restrain it from the doing of unauthorized business;

(2) To annul the corporate existence or dissolve any corporation that has not been duly formed;

(3) To restrain any person or persons from acting as a domestic or foreign corporation within this state without being duly incorporated or from exercising in this state any corporate rights, privileges or franchises not granted to them by the law of the state;

(4) To procure a judgment removing a director of a corporation for cause under section 706 (Removal of directors);

(5) To dissolve a corporation under article 11 (Judicial dissolution);

(6) To restrain a foreign corporation or to annul its authority to do business in this state under section 1303 (Violations).

(7) Upon written application, ex parte, for an order to the supreme court at a special term held within the judicial district where the office of the corporation is located, and if the court so orders, to inspect the books and records of the corporation to the extent that such inspection is available to shareholders and directors under the law of this state. Such application shall contain a statement that the inspection is necessary to protect the interests of the people of this state. This paragraph applies to every corporation, no shares of which are listed on a national securities exchange or regularly quoted in an over-the-counter market by one or more members of a national or an affliated, [affiliated]* securities association. This paragraph does not apply to a corporation all shares of which are owned either directly or through a wholly owned subsidiary by a corporation or corporations to which this paragraph does not apply.

(8) To collect any fines payable to the department of state pursuant to section four hundred nine of this chapter.

* Bracketed language inserted by Publisher.

(b) In an action or special proceeding brought by the attorney-general under any of the provisions of this chapter:

(1) If an action, it is triable by jury as a matter of right.

(2) The court may confer immunity in accordance with the provisions of section 50.20 of the criminal procedure law.

(3) A temporary restraining order to restrain the commission or continuance of the unlawful acts which form the basis of the action or special proceeding may be granted upon proof, by affidavit, that the defendant or defendants have committed or are about to commit such acts. Application for such restraining order may be made ex parte or upon such notice as the court may direct.

(4) If the action or special proceeding is against a foreign corporation, the attorney-general may apply to the court at any stage thereof for the appointment of a temporary receiver of the assets in this state of such foreign corporation, whenever it has assets or property of any kind whatsoever, tangible or intangible, within this state.

(5) When final judgment in such action or special proceeding is rendered against the defendant or defendants, the court may direct the costs to be collected by execution against any or all of the defendants or by order of attachment or other process against the person of any director or officer of a corporate defendant.

(6) In connection with any such proposed action or special proceeding, the attorney-general may take proof and issue subpoenas in accordance with the civil practice law and rules.

(c) In any such action or special proceeding against a foreign corporation which has not designated the secretary of state as its agent for service of process under section 304 (Statutory designation of secretary of state as agent for service of process), any of the following acts in this state by such foreign corporation shall constitute the appointment by it of the secretary of state as its agent upon whom process against such foreign corporation may be served:

(1) As used in this paragraph the term "resident" shall include individuals, domestic corporations and foreign corporations authorized to do business in the state.

(2) Any act done, or representation made as part of a course of the solicitation of orders, or the issuance, or the delivery, of contracts for, or the sale of, property, or the performance of services to residents which involves or promotes a plan or scheme to defraud residents in violation of the laws or the public policy of the state.

(3) Any act done as part of a course of conduct of business in the solicitation of orders from residents for property, goods or services, to be delivered or rendered within this state to, or on their behalf, where the orders or contracts are executed by such

residents within this state and where such orders or contracts are accompanied or followed by an earnest money desposit [deposit]* or other down payment or any installment payment thereon or any other form of payment, which payment is either delivered in or transmitted from the state.

(4) Any act done as part of the conduct of a course of business with residents which defrauds such residents or otherwise involves or promotes an attempt by such foreign corporation to circumvent the laws of this state.

* Bracketed language inserted by Publisher.

(d) Paragraphs (b), (c), (d) and (e) of section 307 (Service of process on unauthorized foreign corporation) shall apply to process served under paragraph (c).

History: Add, L 1961, ch 855, eff Sept 1, 1963; amd, L 1962, ch 317, § 3, eff Sept 1, 1963; L 1967, ch 680; L 1971, ch 895, eff June 25, 1971; L 1971, ch 1097, § 4, eff Sept 1, 1971; L 1992, ch 55, § 401, eff April 10, 1992.

CASE ANNOTATIONS

UNDER FORMER LAW
1. In general
2. Particular actions
3. Injunctions
4. Jury trials

Authority of the Attorney General to issue subpoenaes to investigate alleged violations of the law is not impaired by his obligation to prosecute such violations. Sigety v Hynes (1975) 38 N.Y.2d 260, 379 N.Y.S.2d 724, 342 N.E.2d 518, cert den 425 US 974, 48 L Ed 2d 798, 96 S Ct 2174

Section 2302 of the CPLR, authorizing certain persons and officials to issue subpoenas without court order, does not make it necessary for the Attorney General to obtain a court order in order to issue a subpoena under this section. Security Advertising Co. v Lefkowitz (1964) 21 A.D.2d 860, 248 N.Y.S.2d 453, app dismd 14 N.Y.2d 840, 251 N.Y.S.2d 686, 200 N.E.2d 577

Immunity from civil suit in New York on the ground that the foreign corporation is not doing business here does not preclude the invocation of investigatory machinery by the Attorney General to determine whether it is violating any laws. Wm. G. Roe & Co. v State (1964) 43 Misc. 2d 417, 251 N.Y.S.2d 151

Where the Attorney General was conducting an investigation of private abortion referral agencies in order to determine whether the facts warranted the institution of judicial dissolution under Article II of the Business Corporations Law or action under Executive Law § 63, subd 12 where fraud and illegal business activities might exist causing harm to the public, he could issue a subpoena duces tecum to a physician who was involved in the setting up of the agencies and was a major stockholder in two of the corporations. Petition of Weitzner (1971) 66 Misc. 2d 721, 321 N.Y.S.2d 925

In action in nature of quo warranto to annul corporate charter for unlawful and unauthorized acts, defendant was not entitled to order extending its time to answer until after conclusion of criminal prosecution pending against it on theory that answer would compel disclosure of defenses usable in criminal prosecution and thus deny to indicted individuals their constitutional privilege against self-incrimination, where affirmation in support of motion denied that corporation or other defendants in the criminal proceeding had violated the law and restatement in an answer would disclose nothing additional. State v Brooklyn Trade Waste Asso. (1975) 81 Misc. 2d 174, 363 N.Y.S.2d 793

Evidence showed that individual and corporations engaged in fraudulent acts involving practice of hypnosis such as to warrant entry of permanent injunction, cancelling certificates of incorporation of corporations, and prohibiting respondents from engaging in further business in state of New York. People v Lefkowitz v Therapeutic Hypnosis, Inc. (1975) 83 Misc. 2d 1068, 374 N.Y.S.2d 576

UNDER FORMER LAW

1. In general
Quo warranto is the appropriate, if not the only action, to test the legality of a corporation formed under former General Village Act. People ex rel. Kingsland v Clark (1877) 70 N.Y. 518

The attorney general cannot maintain an action against a corporation under this provision (former CPA § 1217) to abate a public nuisance in the highways of the state when the matter can be dealt with effectually by the local officials, to whom the state has delegated a portion of its authority. People v Equity Gaslight Co. (1894) 141 N.Y. 232, 36 N.E. 194

The validity of a municipal corporation, created by proceedings legal and regular in form, cannot be questioned collaterally by a private individual, but can only be determined in proceedings in the nature of quo warranto instituted by the attorney general and in the name of the people. Prankard v Cooley (1911) 147 A.D. 145, 132 N.Y.S. 289

Former General Corporation Law, § 36, was applicable to a corporation created by Laws 1895, ch. 1033, and where organization did not take place within two years the attorney general could maintain suit for its dissolution. People v Stilwell (1912) 78 Misc 96, 138 N.Y.S. 693

Provision of former section, authorizing a warrant of attachment against a director, etc., to collect the costs, did not apply to an action brought under former General Corp. Law, § 131, but applied only to an action brought under former article 74 of the CPA. People v Cohocton Stone Road (1881, NY) 25 Hun 13

2. Particular actions
In an action brought by the people under this section (former CPA § 1217) against persons attempting to act as a corporation, the charter having expired, the corporation was not a proper party though relief may be granted against the other defendants. People ex rel. Haberman v James (1896) 5 A.D. 412, 39 N.Y.S. 313

Complaint by people to dissolve religious corporation for activities unauthorized by its certificate of incorporation was not insufficient because statutory regulations to effect dissolution are lacking. People v Volunteer Rescue Army, Inc. (1941) 262 A.D. 237, 28 N.Y.S.2d 994

Where the charter of a corporation prescribed that its powers should cease if it did not organize and commence business within three years an action may be brought under this section (former CPA § 1217) restraining certain persons from exercising corporate rights thereunder, where such corporation did not commence business until ten years after its incorporation. People v Equity Gas Works Const. Co. (1893) 3 Misc 333, 23 N.Y.S. 124, revd 141 N.Y. 232, 36 N.E. 194

The attorney general may maintain an action against underwriters carrying on a Lloyd's insurance; an action under this section (former CPA § 1217) will lie in every case where a franchise was unlawfully asserted and used. People v Loew (1896) 19 Misc 248, 44 N.Y.S. 42

An action to prevent the unlawful use or exercise of a railroad through public streets may be maintained by the attorney general upon his own information or upon the complaint of a private person. People v Bleecker S. & F. F. R. Co. (1910) 67 Misc 577, 124 N.Y.S. 782, affd 140 A.D. 611, 125 N.Y.S. 1045, affd 201 N.Y. 594, 95 N.E. 1136

If a mutual insurance association exercises franchises not conferred by its charter, or without complying with statutory conditions, it may be restrained by application to the court. People v Mutual Endow. & Acci. Asso. (1883) 17 Week Dig 174

3. Injunctions
A temporary injunction in quo warranto to prevent a deputy commissioner from assuming his principal's place on the city council upon the latter's resignation was sustained in view of the twofold nature of the principal's office, and the deputy was allowed only to succeed to the administrative side as commissioner. People ex rel. Finley v Gorman (1927) 219 A.D. 466, 219 N.Y.S. 275, affd 245 N.Y. 580, 157 N.E. 865

A temporary injunction may be granted upon satisfactory proof by affidavit that defendants are acting or threatening to act for and in behalf of a corporation not legally constituted. People v Smith (1923) 121 Misc 338, 200 N.Y.S. 863

Where complaint and affidavits of attorney general alleged that Colorado charitable corporation had obtained certificate to do business in New York but had continuously solicited funds without establishing hospital, temporary injunction was granted. People v

Business Corporation Law

Jewish Consumptives' Relief Soc. (1949) 196 Misc 579, 92 N.Y.S.2d 157

Attorney-general may invoke state police power to enjoin foreign hospital corporation from mailing letters, soliciting contributions or receiving money where fraudulent representations are made by it. People v National Cancer Hospital (1951) 200 Misc 363, 102 N.Y.S.2d 103; People v National Cancer Hospital (1954) 284 A.D. 935, 135 N.Y.S.2d 619, mod on other grounds 285 A.D. 871, 137 N.Y.S.2d 827 and affd 1 N.Y.2d 802, 153 N.Y.S.2d 63, 135 N.E.2d 596

4. Jury trials

Actions to try the title to public office are triable by a jury and are not of equitable cognizance. People v Albany & S. R. Co. 57 N.Y. 161 (1874), affg 5 Lans 25, revg 1 Lans 308, 7 Abb Pr NS 265, 55 Barb 344, 38 How Pr 228; and this right to jury trial is not affected by uniting with the equitable cause of action. People v Flanagan (1876) 66 N.Y. 237

In proceeding to revoke decree admitting will to probate, where executor interposed an answer raising issue as to relationship of petitioner to decedent, petitioner had no right to trial by jury on such issue. Re Reinhardt's Will (1915) 92 Misc 96, 156 N.Y.S. 171

A special jury will not be ordered to try the question of title to the office of a justice of a district court in the City of New York, there being nothing in the circumstances to make it such an extreme case as would warrant a special jury. People ex rel. Stemmler v McGuire (1872) 43 How Pr 67

§ 110. Reservation of power

The legislature reserves the right, at pleasure, to alter, amend, suspend or repeal in whole or in part this chapter, or any certificate of incorporation or any authority to do business in this state, of any domestic or foreign corporation, whether or not existing or authorized on the effective date of this chapter.

History: Add, L 1961, ch 855, eff Sept 1, 1963, deriving from N.Y. Const Art X § 1.

CASE ANNOTATIONS

UNDER FORMER LAW

The right to alter or repeal the charter of a corporation was reserved to the legislature by the N.Y. Const., former Art. VIII, § 1 (now Art. 10, § 1) and by § 5 of former Gen. Corp. L. Breslav v New York & Queens Electric Light & Power Co. (1936) 249 A.D. 181, 291 N.Y.S. 932, affd 273 N.Y. 593, 7 N.E.2d 708

Although the legislature has long possessed reserve power to alter and repeal all corporate charters, it is well settled that a statute authorizing a reduction in capital and the proceedings under it may not affect any vested right nor impair force of any corporate obligation. Jay Ronald Co. v Marshall Mortg. Corp. (1943) 265 A.D. 622, 40 N.Y.S.2d 391, revd on other grounds 291 N.Y. 227, 52 N.E.2d 108

The power to alter or amend a corporate charter is subject to the fundamental mandate that property shall not be taken without due process of law. The corporation cannot be deprived of its property nor can the rights of third parties be taken away. McNulty v W. & J. Sloane (1945) 184 Misc 835, 54 N.Y.S.2d 253

The reserved power extends not only to the contract between the corporation and the state but to the contract between the corporation and the stockholder or between the stockholders inter sese. McNulty v W. & J. Sloane (1945) 184 Misc 835, 54 N.Y.S.2d 253

Under its reserved powers the legislature may authorize a corporation to change a preferential right of the different classes of stock. McNulty v W. & J. Sloane (1945) 184 Misc 835, 54 N.Y.S.2d 253

§ 111. Effect of invalidity of part of chapter; severability

If any provision of this chapter or application thereof to any person or circumstances is held invalid, such invalidity shall not affect other provisions or applications of this chapter which can be given effect without the invalid provision or application, and to this end the provisions of this chapter are declared severable.

History: Add, L 1961, ch 855, eff Sept 1, 1963.

§ 112. References

Unless otherwise stated, all references in this chapter to articles or sections refer to the articles or sections of this chapter, and all references in any section of this chapter to a lettered or numbered paragraph or subparagraph refer to the paragraph or subparagraph so lettered or numbered in such section.

History: Add, L 1961, ch 855, eff Sept 1, 1963.

ARTICLE 2
CORPORATE PURPOSES AND POWERS

§ 201. Purposes
§ 202. General powers
§ 203. Defense of ultra vires

History: Add, L 1961, ch 855, eff Sept 1, 1963.

§ 201. Purposes

(a) A corporation may be formed under this chapter for any lawful business purpose or purposes except to do in this state any business for which formation is permitted under any other statute of this state unless such statute permits formation under this chapter. If, immediately prior to the effective date of this chapter, a statute of this state permitted the formation of a corporation under the stock corporation law for a purpose or purposes specified in such other statute, such statute shall be deemed and construed to permit formation of such corporation under this chapter, and any conditions, limitations or restrictions in such other statute upon the formation of such corporation under the stock corporation law shall apply to the formation thereof under this chapter.

(b) The approval of the industrial board of appeals is required for the filing with the department of state of any certificate of incorporation, certificate of merger or consolidation or application of a foreign corporation for authority to do business in this state which states as the purpose or one of the purposes of the corporation the formation of an organization of groups of working men or women or wage earners, or the performance, rendition or sale of services as labor consultant or as advisor on labor-management relations or as arbitrator or negotiator in labor-management disputes.

(c) In time of war or other national emergency, a corporation may do any lawful business in aid thereof, notwithstanding the purpose or purposes set forth in its certificate of incorporation, at the request or direction of any competent governmental authority.

(d) A corporation whose statement of purposes specifically includes the establishment or operation of a child day care center, as that term is defined in section three hundred ninety of the social services law, shall provide a certified copy of the certificate of incorporation, each amendment thereto, and any certificate of merger, consolidation or dissolution involving such corporation to the office of children and family services within thirty days after the filing of such certificate, amendment, merger, consolidation or dissolution with the department of state. This requirement shall also apply to any foreign corporation filing an application for authority under article thirteen of this chapter, any amendments thereto, and any surrender of authority or termination of authority in this state of such corporation.

(e) A corporation may not include as its purpose or among its purposes the establishment or maintenance of a hospital or facility providing health related services, as those terms are defined in article twenty-eight of the public health law unless its certificate of incorporation shall so state and such certificate shall have annexed thereto the approval of the public health and health planning council.

History: Add, L 1961, ch 855, eff Sept 1, 1963; amd, L 1963, ch 692, eff Sept 1, 1963; L 1965, ch 803, § 2, eff Sept 1, 1965; L 1977, ch 669, § 13, eff Oct 1, 1977; L 1981, ch 182, § 1, eff June 2, 1981; L 2006, ch 58, § 2 (Part D), eff April 12, 2006; L 2010, ch 58, § 71 (Part A), eff Dec 1, 2010.

Laws 1977, ch 669, §§ 1, 6 and 17-26, provides as follows:

Section 1. It is the purpose of this act to transfer certain direct administrative functions, powers and duties currently performed by the state board of social welfare, relating to operational and programmatic supervision of facilities, agencies and programs providing care or services to children and adults, and relating to the solicitation and collection of funds for charitable purposes, so that the board can more effectively perform its constitutional role of visitation and inspection of such facilities, agencies and programs and such new functions, powers and duties as may be conferred upon the board by this act, to help assure that state and local agencies having direct supervisory responsibilities for child and adult care or services appropriately utilize their resources to improve the quality of such programs. It is also the purpose of this act to more clearly delineate the respective responsibilities of the state departments of social services and mental hygiene, the division for youth, and other state and local government agencies having direct or indirect responsibilities for all or part of the resident population of such facilities, and to help assure by the provision of this act and by cooperative agreements entered into pursuant thereto that duplication of effort, overlapping of responsibilities, and the fragmentation of program planning and operational supervision are minimized.

§ 6. All of the functions and powers possessed by and all the obligations and duties of the board of social welfare relating to solicitation and collection of funds for charitable purposes and approval of certificates of incorporation which include the study and prevention of poverty; the relieving or reducing of unemployment among youth; the promoting or providing of employment of youth or the solicitation of contributions for any such purpose or purposes, are hereby transferred and assigned to, assumed and devolved upon the secretary of state. To effectuate such transfer there shall also be transferred such officers and employees as are necessary, all appropriations or reappropriations, to the extent of remaining unexpended or unencumbered balances thereof, whether allotted or unallotted or whether obligated or unobligated and all necessary books, papers, records and property. All rules, regulations, acts, determinations and decisions in force at the time of such transfer and proceedings or other business matters undertaken or commenced by or before the board of social welfare pertaining to the functions herein transferred and assigned, in force at the time of such transfer, assignment, assumption or devolution shall continue in force and effect until duly modified, obligated or completed by the secretary of state. References to the board of social welfare or office, bureau or other unit thereof contained in laws, rules, contracts and other documents relating to the functions herein transferred shall be deemed to be references to the secretary of state or the corresponding office, bureau or unit of the department of state as the case may be.

§ 17. Any provision of any special or general law heretofore or hereafter enacted relating to those functions, powers and duties of the state board of social welfare with respect to supervision of residential programs for children and adults which are by this act transferred to the state department of social services, shall be deemed to refer to such department rather than to such board.

§ 18. All the functions and powers possessed by, and all the obligations and duties of, the state board of social welfare in relation to direct supervision of residential programs for children and adults which are transferred to the state department of social services by this act are hereby transferred and assigned to, assumed and devolved upon the state department of social services.

§ 19. All functions and powers possessed by, and all the obligations and duties of the state board of social welfare related to functions which are transferred to the department of social services, health or mental hygiene are hereby transferred and assigned to, assumed by and devolved upon each such department.

§ 20. Upon the transfer of functions to the department of social services in accordance with this act, provision shall be made, subject to the approval of the director of the budget, for the transfer of such employees of the state board of social welfare as are engaged in carrying out functions transferred to the state department of social services by this act as may be determined necessary by the commissioner of social services for the exercise of such functions by the department. Upon the transfer of functions to the department of state in accordance with this act, provision shall be made, subject to the approval of the director of the budget, for the transfer of such employees of the state board of social welfare as are engaged in carrying out functions transferred to the department of state by this act and as may be determined necessary by the secretary of the state for the exercise of such functions by the department. Employees so transferred shall be transferred without further examination or classification and shall retain their respective civil service classification status. For the purpose of determination the employee holding permanent appointment in the competitive class position to be transferred, such employee shall be selected without such class or preference in the order of their original appointment, with due regard to the right of preference in retention of disabled and nondisabled veterans, any such employee, who at the time of such transfer, has a temporary or provisional appointment shall be transferred subject to the same right and removal or termination as though such transfer had not been made.

§ 21. The state board of social welfare shall deliver all books, papers, records and property of the board as the state commissioner of social services may deem necessary for the performance of functions transferred by this act, to the state department of social services.

§ 22. For the purpose of succession to all functions, powers, duties and obligations transferred, assigned to, devolved upon and assumed by it pursuant to this chapter, the state department of social services shall be deemed and held to constitute the state board of social welfare with respect to those functions transferred by this act.

§ 23. Any business or other matter undertaken or commended by the state board of social welfare pertaining to or connected with the functions, powers and duties hereby transferred to the state department of social services and pending on the effective date of this chapter may be conducted and completed by such department in the same manner and under the same terms and conditions and with the same effect as if conducted and completed by such board.

§ 24. All rules, regulations, determinations and decisions of the state board of social welfare pertaining to the functions herein transferred and assigned in force at the time of such transfer and assignment shall continue in force and effect as rules, regulations, determinations and decisions of the state department of social services. Whenever the terms "board" or "state board of social welfare" are referred to or indicated in any contract or document pertaining to the functions, powers and duties hereby transferred and assigned, such reference or designation shall be deemed to refer to the state department of social services.

§ 25. Existing rights and remedies preserved. No existing right or remedy of any character shall be lost, impaired or affected by reason of this act.

§ 26. By no later than the first day of March, nineteen hundred seventy-eight, the department of state shall prepare and submit to the governor and to the legislature a detailed report regarding the functions, powers and duties of the department of state with respect to the solicitation and collection of funds for charitable purposes as transferred by this act. The report shall include an analysis of the adequacy of the provisions of this act to satisfy the purposes of the state in regulating the solicitation of funds for charitable purposes, and shall include an analysis of the impact that any federal statutes or federal regulation may have on those provisions. Such report shall also set forth any recommendations for statutory changes that may be necessary to improve the operation and administration of the program regulating the solicitation and collection of funds for charitable purposes.

Laws 2010, ch 58, § 86 (f) (Part A), eff July 2, 2010, deemed eff on and after April 1, 2010, provides as follows:

§ 86. This act shall take effect immediately and shall be deemed to have been in full force and effect on and after April 1, 2010, provided however that:

(f) sections forty-three through eighty-five of this act shall take effect December 1, 2010, provided however, that the public health and health planning council shall be authorized to complete action on any application, regulation, complaint or other matter under consideration by the public health council or state hospital review and planning council on such effective date; and provided further that any final approval granted or regulation adopted by the public health council or state hospital review and planning council shall remain in effect according to its terms after the effective date of this act, unless otherwise lawfully annulled, revoked, modified, amended, limited or suspended.

CASE ANNOTATIONS

UNDER FORMER STK CORP § 5
1. In general
2. Allowed purposes
3. Prohibited purposes

A subsidiary of the Urban Development Corporation may incorporate under the Business Corporation Law without forfeiting its public status. The subsidiary may not pay profits to private investors, and upon dissolution of the corporation, the assets belong to the State. 1980 Op Atty Gen Oct. 20

UNDER FORMER STK CORP § 5

1. In general

Plaintiff lacked standing to bring a declaratory judgment suit alleging discrimination in unmet housing needs, municipal services, and lack of representation on the planning and zoning boards on behalf of its shareholders as plaintiff, which was formed to assert the objectives of the shareholders, could not do so as a for-profit corporation under N.Y. Bus. Corp. Law § 201(a); plaintiff's claims were maintainable under N.Y. Not-for-Profit Corp. Law § 201(b). United Fairness, Inc. v Town of Woodbury (2011, Sup) 932 NYS2d 895.

"Any lawful business" is not acceptable as a purpose of incorporation. 1911 Ops Atty Gen 69

2. Allowed purposes

A corporation organized under former § 5 of the Stk. Corp. L. might lawfully engage in the operation of freight terminal facilities. American Dock Co. v New York (1940) 174 Misc 813, 21 N.Y.S.2d 943, affd 261 A.D. 1063, 26 N.Y.S.2d 704, affd without op 286 N.Y. 658, 36 N.E.2d 696

Where a stock corporation was legally operating a licensed proprietary hospital when former § 35-b of the Social Welfare Law became effective, it was regarded as within the saving clause permitting continuance of operation, including use of the word "hospital" in the corporate name. Application of Hayes-Seventy-Third Corp. v De Sapio (1959) 16 Misc. 2d 371, 188 N.Y.S.2d 351, revd on ground license was to a physician (3d Dept) 9 A.D.2d 454, 195 N.Y.S.2d 566, affd 8 N.Y.2d 827, 203 N.Y.S.2d 89, 168 N.E.2d 531

Corporations could be organized under former Stock Corp. L. for the purpose of utilizing funds of the reconstruction finance corporation or other federal agencies. 1933 Ops Atty Gen 304

A corporation could be formed under former § 5 of the Stock Corp. Law for the following purpose: "to purchase, lease or to otherwise acquire, install and operate in any privately owned buildings either under contract of sale or of lease, plants and boilers for the furnishing of steam and/or hot water and to distribute and supply such products solely through private property to all parts of the building within which said products are produced, and also to supply same to adjoining buildings, likewise privately owned, and which will not be available to the general public, and which will not operate on public property." 1939 Ops Atty Gen 234

A corporation could be formed under former § 5 of the Stk. Corp. L. for the construction and operation of highways and bridges for which tolls are charged. 1946 Ops Atty Gen Feb 11

The Attorney General has ruled that a corporation could be formed under former Stock Corporation Law to engage in the business of stabling, breeding and training horses, but not for the purpose of conducting race meetings, as to which incorporation under special law is required. 1949 Ops Atty Gen Feb 21

The Secretary of State would not be justified in refusing to file a certificate of incorporation of a corporation whose purposes would be marriage counseling. There is no statute making such an enterprise unlawful and there is not involved such a situation as would justify the refusal to file on account of public policy, in the absence of statute. 1956 Ops Atty Gen Nov 1

3. Prohibited purposes

Cemetery corporations and those having a stated purpose of engaging in acquisition, management, or sale of cemetery lots, are, for the most part, subject to incorporation under special statutes only and cannot be organized under general laws. Grace v Repose Mausoleums, Inc. (1912) 78 Misc 213, 139 N.Y.S. 300; 1929 Ops Atty Gen 114, 118; 1937 Ops Atty Gen 222

An application for an order of mandamus directing the secretary of state to accept for filing a proposed certificate of incorporation enumerating among the proposed purposes of incorporation, "to do, render and perform optometrical and oculists' work and services and to engage in the practice of optometry, provided it (the corporation) employs only licensed optometrists to do the work," must be denied. Stern v Flynn (1935) 154 Misc 609, 278 N.Y.S. 598

Incorporation for the purpose of placing or collecting bets on horse races, in behalf of persons not in attendance, involves prohibited activities, and the Secretary of State properly refuses to file a certificate of incorporation revealing such a purpose. Application of Stewart (1940) 174 Misc 902, 22 N.Y.S.2d 164, affd 260 A.D. 979, 23 N.Y.S.2d 226; 1940 Ops Atty Gen 288; 1950 Ops Atty Gen Nov 27

A stock corporation for the purpose of conducting a private sanitarium or hospital, giving treatment, etc., could not be formed under the provisions of former Bus. Corp. Law § 2 or 2-a. 1909 Ops Atty Gen 517

A business corporation is prohibited from engaging in the business of issuing collateral trust income bonds secured by real property, the title of which is in a trustee under a trust agreement; such powers may be exercised only by a corporation formed under the provisions of the Banking Law. 1912 Ops Atty Gen 188

Corporations could not be organized under former Stock Corporation Law or the earlier Business Corporation Law to engage in any aspect of the banking business within the coverage of the Banking Law. 1918 Ops Atty Gen 86; 1929 Ops Atty Gen 242

A hospital may not be incorporated under this title. 1926 Ops Atty Gen 192

Corporations are prohibited by § 280 of the Penal Law from practicing medicine, and hence cannot be organized for the purpose of making physical examinations of persons. 1929 Ops Atty Gen 121

A corporation may not be formed for purpose of furnishing board, lodging and nursing services to private patients. 1934 Ops Atty Gen 220

A corporation could not be lawfully organized for the purpose of engaging in optometric practice. 1935 Ops Atty Gen 226

A business corporation may not be organized to contract with individuals to obtain medical service for them and to contract with physicians to treat and care for such individuals. 1935 Ops Atty Gen 240

The secretary of state is not required to file a certificate of incorporation, the stated purpose of which is to procure certain classes of persons to give professional work to certain optometrists, "at a substantial discount from prevailing rates of optometrists," thus violating or evading rules forbidding optometrists to advertise prices. 1946 Ops Atty Gen Nov 12

§ 202.   General powers

(a) Each corporation, subject to any limitations provided in this chapter or any other statute of this state or its certificate of incorporation, shall have power in furtherance of its corporate purposes:

(1) To have perpetual duration.

(2) To sue and be sued in all courts and to participate in actions and proceedings, whether judicial, administrative, arbitrative or otherwise, in like cases as natural persons.

(3) To have a corporate seal, and to alter such seal at pleasure, and to use it by causing it or a facsimile to be affixed or impressed or reproduced in any other manner.

(4) To purchase, receive, take by grant, gift, devise, bequest or otherwise, lease, or otherwise acquire, own, hold, improve, employ, use and otherwise deal in and with, real or personal property, or any interest therein, wherever situated.

(5) To sell, convey, lease, exchange, transfer or otherwise dispose of, or mortgage or pledge, or create a security interest in, all or any of its property, or any interest therein, wherever situated.

(6) To purchase, take, receive, subscribe for, or otherwise acquire, own, hold, vote, employ, sell, lend, lease, exchange, transfer, or otherwise dispose of, mortgage, pledge, use and otherwise deal in and with, bonds and other obligations, shares, or other securities or interests issued by others, whether engaged in similar or different business, governmental, or other activities.

(7) To make contracts, give guarantees and incur liabilities, borrow money at such rates of interest as the corporation may determine, issue its notes, bonds and other obligations, and secure any of its obligations by mortgage or pledge of all or any of its property or any interest therein, wherever situated.

(8) To lend money, invest and reinvest its funds, and take and hold real and personal property as security for the payment of funds so loaned or invested.

(9) To do business, carry on its operations, and have offices and exercise the powers granted by this chapter in any jurisdiction within or without the United States.

(10) To elect or appoint officers, employees and other agents of the corporation, define their duties, fix their compensation and the compensation of directors, and to indemnify corporate personnel.

(11) To adopt, amend or repeal by-laws, including emergency by-laws made pursuant to subdivision seventeen of section twelve of the state defense emergency act, relating to the business of the corporation, the conduct of its affairs, its rights or powers or the rights or powers of its shareholders, directors or officers.

(12) To make donations, irrespective of corporate benefit, for the public welfare or for community fund, hospital, charitable, educational, scientific, civic or similar purposes, and in time of war or other national emergency in aid thereof.

(13) To pay pensions, establish and carry out pension, profit-sharing, share bonus, share purchase, share option, savings, thrift and other retirement, incentive and benefit plans, trusts and provisions for any or all of its directors, officers and employees.

(14) To purchase, receive, take, or otherwise acquire, own, hold, sell, lend, exchange, transfer or otherwise dispose of, pledge, use and otherwise deal in and with its own shares.

(15) To be a promoter, partner, member, associate or manager of other business enterprises or ventures, or to the extent permitted in any other jurisdiction to be an incorporator of other corporations of any type or kind.

(16) To have and exercise all powers necessary or convenient to effect any or all of the purposes for which the corporation is formed.

(b) No corporation shall do business in New York state under any name, other than that appearing in its certificate of incorporation, without compliance with the filing provisions of section one hundred thirty of the general business law governing the conduct of business under an assumed name.

History: Add, L 1961, ch 855, eff Sept 1, 1963, deriving from NY Const Art X § 4; amd, L 1962, ch 834, § 5, eff Sept 1, 1963; L 1963, ch 748, § 3, eff Sept 1, 1963; L 1978, ch 693, eff Jan 1, 1979.

CASE ANNOTATIONS

UNDER FORMER LAW
1. **In general**
2. **"Sue and be sued"**
3. **Compensation and benefits**
4. **Contracts, guarantees and liabilities**
5. **Acquisition, holding and disposition of property**
6. **Dealings with related corporations**
7. **Banking activities**
8. **By-laws**
9. **Miscellaneous**

Respondent corporation was entitled to stay of arbitration of dispute arising from breach of plaintiffs' agreement with related corporation where it was not party to arbitration agreement between plaintiffs and related corporation (which was subsidiary of same parent corporation as respondent) because, even if respondent corporation dominated signatory corporation, plaintiffs failed to show that respondent's control resulted in some fraud or wrong mandating disregard of corporate form for purpose of imputing agreement to arbitrate to respondent; in fact, respondent had agreed to assume signatory's financial obligations if signatory failed to fulfill them. TNS Holdings v MKI Secs. Corp. (1998) 92 N.Y.2d 335

In computing unincorporated business taxable income, limited partnership was entitled to a deduction for personal services of a corporate partner actively engaged in the business of partnership. Mutual Mortg. Co. v State Tax Com. (1974, 3d Dept) 44 A.D.2d 273, 354 N.Y.S.2d 448

In terms of legal responsibility, parents, subsidiaries or affiliated corporations are treated separately and independently, and one will not be held liable for contractual obligations of other, unless it is shown that there was exercise of complete dominion and control; furthermore, one corporation will generally not have legal standing to exercise rights of other associated corporations. Alexander & Alexander, Inc. v Fritzen (1985, 1st Dept) 114 A.D.2d 814, 495 N.Y.S.2d 386

Corporate resolution properly granted owner's personal friend and business associate right to execute lease renewal of cooperative apartment of which corporation was tenant of record and friend was designated occupant on lease, even though friend was not corporate officer or shareholder; corporation has power to designate persons, who are not corporate officers or employees, to occupy apartments leased by corporation. North Star Graphics, Inc. v Spitzer (1987, 1st Dept) 135 A.D.2d 401, 521 N.Y.S.2d 699, app dismd without op 72 N.Y.2d 841, 530 N.Y.S.2d 556, 526 N.E.2d 47

State lacked compelling interest in permitting public utilities to charge their charitable contributions to ratepayers as legitimate operating expenses over ratepayers' free speech objections, despite charitable donation provision of CLS Bus Corp § 202, since giving of charitable contributions under statute is wholly discretionary, ratepayers lacked option of choosing other utilities due to their status as monopolies, and there was no necessary relationship between providing utility service and making charitable donations. Cahill v Public Service Com. (1989, 3d Dept) 147 A.D.2d 49, 542 N.Y.S.2d 394, affd 76 N.Y.2d 102, 556 N.Y.S.2d 840, 556 N.E.2d 133, cert den (US) 112 L Ed 2d 309, 111 S Ct 344

Attorney General's request for refunds to ratepayers for charitable contributions made by public utilities in derogation of ratepayers' free speech rights would not be granted where utilities relied on validity of Public Service Commission's policy allowing such contributions as operating expenses, computation of refunds would be monumental task, and refunds were not necessary to vindicate ratepayers' constitutional rights. Cahill v Public Service Com. (1989, 3d Dept) 147 A.D.2d 49, 542 N.Y.S.2d 394, affd 76 N.Y.2d 102, 556 N.Y.S.2d 840, 556 N.E.2d 133, cert den (US) 112 L Ed 2d 309, 111 S Ct 344

Corporate defendant's execution of agreement seeking to bring about disposition of lease held by its wholly-owned subsidiary was in furtherance of corporate defendant's own corporate purposes, and was thus authorized by CLS Bus Corp § 202. Garrick-Aug Assocs. Store Leasing, Inc. v Wein (2000, 1st Dept) 271 A.D.2d 344, 707 N.Y.S.2d 76

The service of process upon a corporation which held itself out to be a joint venturer or a partner of several other corporations was sufficient to constitute good and effective service so as to grant the court jurisdiction over the other several corporations. John's, Inc. v Island Garden Center of Nassau, Inc. (1966) 49 Misc. 2d 1086, 269 N.Y.S.2d 231, affd 53 Misc. 2d 1021, 280 N.Y.S.2d 34

Although the Internal Revenue Code exempts from income taxation "corporations organized for the exclusive purpose of holding title to property, collecting income therefrom, and turning over the entire amount thereof, less expenses, to an organization which itself is exempt under this section," the New York tax exemption statute is more restrictive; the owning corporation must be organized or conducted exclusively for one of the statutorily prescribed purposes and the property must be used for that purpose. Return Realty Corp. v Ranieri (1974) 78 Misc. 2d 825, 359 N.Y.S.2d 611

Telephone utility's use of its poles was not limited to a use for telephone purposes; utility had statutory right to enter into contractual arrangements with others for use of space on its poles. New York Tel. Co. v North Hempstead (1975) 86 Misc. 2d 487, 385 N.Y.S.2d 436, affd (2d Dept) 52 A.D.2d 934, 385 N.Y.S.2d 505, mod on other grounds 41 N.Y.2d 691, 395 N.Y.S.2d 143, 363 N.E.2d 694

A cause of action grounded on a claim that when the defendant corporation purchased some of its own common stock from a stockholder above the market price it was obliged to offer the same terms and conditions of purchase to all other stockholders on a prorated basis would be dismissed, as there is no such duty since a corporation has the right to purchase its own stock, with no limitations, in the absence of fraud or overreaching or the impairment of capital or harm to creditors. Karfunkel v USLIFE Corp. (1982) 116 Misc. 2d 841, 455 N.Y.S.2d 937

A stock transfer assessment imposed by the board of directors of a cooperative corporation on all tenant shareholders when they transfer their shares of stock to a third party is proper and would be upheld where it was consistent with the broad grant of powers to the board contained in the cooperative's by-laws, the provisions of the Cooperative Corporations Law, and the Business Corporation Law. Berglund v 411 East 57th Corp. (1984) 122 Misc. 2d 702, 471 N.Y.S.2d 803

No-fault health care provider who never filed assumed name certificate with Secretary of State as required by CLS Bus Corp § 202(b) and CLS Gen Bus § 130(1)(b) did not have legal authority, as matter of standing, to bill insurer for no-fault services rendered under assumed name. Park Health Ctr. v United Fin. Adjusting Co. (2001, Civ Ct) 186 Misc. 2d 667, 719 N.Y.S.2d 841 (criticized in State Farm Mut. Auto. Ins. Co. v Mallela (ED NY) 175 F. Supp. 2d 401)

Action by two shareholders in a closely-held corporation to refinance a loan so that the corporation became primarily liable for the loan and to authorize the issuance of promissory notes to themselves which would be satisfied by the issuance of additional shares of stock were not illegal and did not warrant dissolution of the corporation, and the appellate court dismissed an appeal which the Superintendent of Insurance of the State of New York took from a trial court's judgment denying dissolution of the corporation after the Superintendent acquired shares in the corporation that were owned by a bankrupt shareholder. Estate of Lawrence v Quail Aero Serv. (In re Dissolution of Quail Aero Serv.) (2002, A.D., 3d Dept) 755 N.Y.S.2d 103

To the extent that public utility's contribution to a non-partisan referendum was prompted by concern for the state of transportation and its multiplier effects on the economy as a whole it was protected by the specific words of Business Corporation Law § 202 and was not an ultra vires act. Schwartz v Romnes (1974, CA2 NY) 495 F.2d 844

Where security agreement is executed by corporation for purpose of attempting to avert bankruptcy of parent and principal customer, security agreement serves a valid corporate purpose and shareholder ratification of agreement is not necessary. Re Ollag Constr. Equipment Corp. (1978, CA2 NY) 578 F.2d 904, 4 BCD 549, 17 CBC 612, CCH Bankr L Rptr ¶ 66881, later app (CA2 NY) 665 F.2d 43, 8 BCD 619

The pledge of the assets of a wholly owned subsidiary to secure its previous guaranty of the indebtedness of its parent corporation in an attempt to prevent the bankruptcy of the parent corporation and principal customer was in furtherance of its corporate purposes so that shareholder approval of such transaction was not required. Re Ollag Constr. Equipment Corp. (1978, WD NY) 446 F. Supp. 586, affd in part and revd in part on other grounds (CA2 NY) 578 F.2d 904, 4 BCD 549, 17 CBC 612, CCH Bankr L Rptr ¶ 66881, later app (CA2 NY) 665 F.2d 43, 8 BCD 619

Allegation that corporation's sole shareholder agreed to guarantee corporation's obligations to plaintiff under employment contract with corporation did not warrant piercing corporate veil in order to hold shareholder liable for corporation's breach of employment contract, in absence of evidence that corporation either would not or could not itself have paid plaintiff. Mass v McClenahan (1995, SD NY) 893 F. Supp. 225, 67 BNA FEP Cas 1597, 66 CCH EPD ¶ 43564

Claim that a trademark owner fraudulently obtained a trademark registration when it was not in operation failed because, at all relevant times, the owner was an existing New York corporation and, thus, was capable of suing and being sued in a court of law. Total Control Apparel, Inc. v DMD Int'l Imports, LLC (2006, SD NY) 409 F Supp 2d 403

A county clerk may not accept for filing a certificate of a corporation doing business under an assumed name, but may accept for filing a certificate of a corporation and others doing business as partners under a partnership name. 1963 Ops Atty Gen Oct 29

It is permissible for a county clerk to accept for filing a certificate of limited partnership in which the general partner is a corporation. 1979 Op Atty Gen July 19 (informal)

A corporation cannot be a licensed funeral director. A corporation may serve as a partner in a partnership operating a funeral home. The partnership's registered manager has responsibility for management and control of the partnership's funeral home. 1987 Op Atty Gen No. 87-F3

Assuming that co-operative property/casualty insurance company was organized and licensed under requirements in Insurance Law Art 66, board of directors of company would be allowed to provide hearing aids to executive officer who worked for insurer if officer's health insurance failed to cover that cost. Insurance Department, Opinions of General Counsel, Opinion Number 02-01-31

UNDER FORMER LAW

1. In general

A corporation is an intangible entity which can act only through its officers, employees and agents. Powell v Shepard Niles Crane & Hoist Corp. (1960) 25 Misc. 2d 485, 201 N.Y.S.2d 683

2. "Sue and be sued"

The president of a corporation whose bylaws contained no reference to any authority on the part of the president or any other officer to institute litigation may not bring suit on his own initiative after the board of directors has voted down a proposal authorizing the institution of such litigation, in the absence of evidence to overcome the presumption of good faith of the directors or evidence indicating a special emergency. Sterling Industries, Inc. v Ball Bearing Pen Corp. (1949) 298 N.Y. 483, 84 N.E.2d 790, 10 ALR2d 694

There is no statutory prohibition which prevents a stock corporation from maintaining a summary dispossess proceeding as the agent of a landlord pursuant to § 1414 of former Civil Practice Act. Mutual Life Ins. Co. v Prever Lumber Co. (1938) 168 Misc 358, 6 N.Y.S.2d 28

A corporation cannot sue in all kinds of actions, but only in those which relate to their corporate rights, and therefore a corporate taxpayer may not maintain a taxpayer's action to nullify an alleged illegal appointment by the State Liquor Authority. J. D. L. Corp. v Bruckman (1939) 171 Misc 3, 11 N.Y.S.2d 741

3. Compensation and benefits

In view of the broad power conferred upon corporations by former subd. (13) of this section, to set up pension and profit-sharing plans for, and to grant stock options, etc., to officers, directors, and employees, and in the light of construction given similar provisions of the Gen. Corp. L., it is doubtful whether a regulatory commission, such as the Public Service Commission, is authorized to disapprove or interfere with such arrangements to the extent that such action would invade the field of corporate management. Brooklyn Union Gas Co. v Public Service Com. (1959, 3d Dept) 8 A.D.2d 210, 187 N.Y.S.2d 207, affd 8 N.Y.2d 815, 202 N.Y.S.2d 322, 168 N.E.2d 390

Corporations generally through their board of directors may pay or promise to pay to officers or other employees extra compensation in the way of a bonus and when properly authorized it is not in itself a fraud upon dissenting stockholders, nor is it illegal or against public policy unless the directors acted under an illegal bylaw, provided that the officers are not thereby receiving more in the way of a salary and bonus than the fair value of their service. Diamond v Davis (1942, Sup) 38 N.Y.S.2d 103, affd without op 265 A.D. 919, 39 N.Y.S.2d 412, affd 292 N.Y. 552, 54 N.E.2d 683

The fixation of compensation to executive officers and employees of a corporation is a question of internal management to be determined by the corporation itself in which neither the people of the state nor the public generally are interested; and the stockholders are entitled to determine what, if any, compensation should be paid to the officers. Diamond v Davis (1942, Sup) 38 N.Y.S.2d 103, affd without op 265 A.D. 919, 39 N.Y.S.2d 412, affd 292 N.Y. 552, 54 N.E.2d 683

4. Contracts, guarantees and liabilities

The general power of a corporation to "make contracts" is essential to being engaged in business and is as broad as its stated purposes, and activities incidental thereto, permit; whether or not persons acting for the corporation in making or executing a contract are likewise individually bound depends upon the terms of the contract and the apparent intention of the parties. See, for example, Mencher v Weiss (1953) 306 N.Y. 1, 114 N.E.2d 177, 32 BNA LRRM 2539, 24 CCH LC ¶ 67797

An individual has no right to make use of a corporation owned by himself to pay individual debts. Republican Art Printery v David (1916) 173 A.D. 726, 159 N.Y.S. 1010

The president of a business corporation has prima facie authority to enter into a contract in behalf of the corporation, where the contract is of such a nature that the directors of the corporation could authorize or ratify it legally. Greenpoint Coal Docks, Inc. v Newtown Creek Realty Corp. (1949) 5 Misc. 2d 812, 91 N.Y.S.2d 466

Mere existence of power to guarantee the obligation of another does not, however, mean that anyone can bind a corporation by casually stating that it guarantees another's obligation without due approval of the board of directors or stockholders. Rusch & Co. v Syndicate First Corp. (1956) 7 Misc. 2d 198, 155 N.Y.S.2d 369

Former Section 19 of the Stock Corporation Law likewise empowered corporations to guarantee obligations for payment of money,

Business Corporation Law

without specifically including such power or purpose in their certificates of incorporation, and it was held that, in view of the statutory grant of power, a corporation could not defend against liability on its guarantee of accounts of third persons on the ground, alone, that the guarantee was not incidental to or in furtherance of the business of the corporation. Fleet-Wing Corp. v Pease Oil Co. (1961) 29 Misc. 2d 437, 212 N.Y.S.2d 871, mod on other grounds (4th Dept) 14 A.D.2d 728, 218 N.Y.S.2d 533

Similarly, one corporation may legitimately guarantee the obligations of another corporation, where it has a real concern and interest in the latter's welfare and continued existence. Nurick v Baker (1939, Sup) 14 N.Y.S.2d 503

A corporation clearly has general power to enter into contracts of employment which continue to be binding, according to their terms, notwithstanding existence of general power in the management to fix compensation of officers and employees and to discharge or remove them. Re Paramount Publix Corp. (1937, CA2 NY) 90 F.2d 441

5. Acquisition, holding and disposition of property

General statutory power of a corporation to purchase, hold, and convey property is subject to such limitations and restrictions as may be imposed by other statutes or applicable law. Application of Kensico Cemetery (1949) 275 A.D. 681, 86 N.Y.S.2d 737, affd 299 N.Y. 752, 87 N.E.2d 670

Wherever property is devised to a corporation, partly for its own use and partly for the use of others, the corporation may take and hold the property for its own use and, as a necessary incident, it has power to execute that part of the trust which relates to others. Re Esmond's Will (1932) 144 Misc 609, 258 N.Y.S. 961

Authority of a corporation to acquire and hold an interest in property as cestui of a trust, under earlier corporation laws, was doubtful, having been denied in at least one instance. Re De Forest's Estate (1933) 147 Misc 82, 263 N.Y.S. 135

The words "take" and "hold," as used in § 15 of former Gen. Corp. L., taken in conjunction with § 14 of that law, were construed as broad enough to sanction acquisition of property by a corporation by gift, devise, or bequest. Re Hohn's Estate (1943) 180 Misc 384, 40 N.Y.S.2d 237; Re Clark's Estate (1938, Sur) 7 N.Y.S.2d 299, affd without op 257 A.D. 982, 14 N.Y.S.2d 157; Re Keene's Estate (1934) 152 Misc 424, 273 N.Y.S. 532; Re McQuirk's Estate (1927) 130 Misc 336, 224 N.Y.S. 431, affd without op 224 A.D. 724, 229 N.Y.S. 880

A newspaper corporation could receive a bequest of funds to be used in furtherance of a charitable project which it was sponsoring. Re Estate of Arnold (1956) 4 Misc. 2d 970, 157 N.Y.S.2d 448, affd (1st Dept) 3 A.D.2d 998, 165 N.Y.S.2d 433, app den (1st Dept) 4 A.D.2d 832, 166 N.Y.S.2d 298

Other decisions, however, took the view that there was nothing in the law to prevent a corporation from accepting and holding an interest as trust beneficiary. Alcoma Corp. v Ackerman (1960) 26 Misc. 2d 678, 207 N.Y.S.2d 137; Re Johnson's Estate (1933) 148 Misc 218, 265 N.Y.S. 395

Thus it was held that authority to take and hold "personal property" included choses in action, and that accordingly a New York corporation could be a beneficiary of a New York real property trust and acquire and hold certificates evidencing beneficial interest therein. Alcoma Corp. v Ackerman (1960) 26 Misc. 2d 678, 207 N.Y.S.2d 137

6. Dealings with related corporations

A corporation which has acquired and holds stock in another corporation has power to borrow money, or obtain it through issuance and sale of its own obligations, in order to provide funds for use of the second corporation and keep the latter in operation. Venner v New York C. & H. R. R. Co. (1914) 160 A.D. 127, 145 N.Y.S. 725, affd 217 N.Y. 615, 111 N.E. 487 and later app (Sup) 151 N.Y.S. 534, app dismd 167 A.D. 934, 152 N.Y.S. 1105 and later app 168 A.D. 345, 153 N.Y.S. 879, affd 217 N.Y. 119, 111 N.E. 484

Power to hold and vote shares in other corporations has been considered as sanctioning interlocking directorates. Chelrob, Inc. v Barrett (1943) 265 A.D. 455, 266 A.D. 669, 39 N.Y.S.2d 625, affd in part and revd in part 293 N.Y. 442, 57 N.E.2d 825, reh den 293 N.Y. 859, 59 N.E.2d 446

A corporation may legitimately borrow money and lend it to a subsidiary corporation. Such power is limited to situations where the benefit to the subsidiary is also a benefit to the parent, and it is at least doubtful whether an arrangement comes within this classification where the effect will be to increase the investment of the parent company in the subsidiary and at the same time reduce its stock ownership from a majority to a minority interest. Silverman v Lehrman (1960) 25 Misc. 2d 339, 203 N.Y.S.2d 171

A corporation's guarantee of payment of rent by another corporation for leased property is within the protection of former subd. (a) of this section where the lessee corporation was affiliated and related to the guarantor corporation as a subsidiary of the latter, which owned 51% of its stock, with close business ties and common officers, directors and employees. Chester Airport, Inc. v Aeroflex Corp. (1962) 37 Misc. 2d 145, 237 N.Y.S.2d 752, mod on other grounds (1st Dept) 18 A.D.2d 998, 238 N.Y.S.2d 715

Authority to acquire, hold, transfer, and deal in obligations, shares, bonds, and securities issued by others is a mere general grant of power, subject to implied restriction to doing so only in contemplated furtherance of the stated purposes of the acquiring corporation and not engaging in activities requiring incorporation under special statutes, such as the Banking Law. 1921 Ops Atty Gen 304; 1929 Ops Atty Gen 242

The chairman of the workmen's compensation board has a right to authorize the consolidation of security deposits of a parent corporation and one or more subsidiary corporations. 1947 Ops Atty Gen Feb 19

7. Banking activities

In the "discounting" field, the transaction was not prohibited if it was an isolated occurrence and did not amount to "carrying on the business" of discounting bills, notes, or the like. Meserole Secur. Co. v Cosman (1930) 253 N.Y. 130, 170 N.E. 519; Amherst Factors, Inc. v Kochenburger (1957, 2d Dept) 4 A.D.2d 745, 164 N.Y.S.2d 815, affd 4 N.Y.2d 203, 173 N.Y.S.2d 570, 149 N.E.2d 863; Pennsylvania Factors Corp. v S. Oldman, Inc. (1947) 272 A.D. 1049, 74 N.Y.S.2d 670; County Industrial Corp. v Francia (1957) 5 Misc. 2d 602, 164 N.Y.S.2d 415, affd (2d Dept) 4 A.D.2d 748, 165 N.Y.S.2d 699, affd 4 N.Y.2d 988, 177 N.Y.S.2d 507, 152 N.E.2d 530; New York Credit Men's Adjustment Bureau, Inc. v Samuel Breiter & Co. (1958, CA2 NY) 253 F.2d 675; Straf v Colonial Factors Corp. (1960, CA8 Mo) 273 F.2d 554

Some such business financing transactions, by virtue of the particular manner in which they were handled, were upheld as not violating these bank-protective statutes. James Talcott, Inc. v J. J. Ozdoba, Inc. (1954) 306 N.Y. 869, 119 N.E.2d 42; James Talcott, Inc. v Shindler (1954) 306 N.Y. 871, 119 N.E.2d 42; Re Worth Lighting & Fixture Co. (1923, DC NY) 292 F 769

A factoring and discounting corporation could not loan money to another corporation and deduct in advance a "discount charge" or "bonus." Miller v Discount Factors, Inc. (1956) 1 N.Y.2d 275, 152 N.Y.S.2d 273, 135 N.E.2d 33

Former Section 18 of the Gen. Corp. L. prohibited corporations, not formed under the banking laws, with certain exceptions, from carrying on the business of "discounting" bills, notes, and other evidences of indebtedness, "receiving deposits," "buying and selling bills of exchange," issuing instruments to circulate as money, or "engaging in any other form of banking"; and these restrictions were often literally and strictly imposed. Flatbush Auto Discount Corp. v McCarthy-Bernhardt Buick, Inc. (1961) 9 N.Y.2d 776, 215 N.Y.S.2d 78, 174 N.E.2d 749; Miller v Discount Factors, Inc. (1956) 1 N.Y.2d 275, 152 N.Y.S.2d 273, 135 N.E.2d 33; Feuchtwanger Corp. v South American Commodities, Inc. (1957) 9 Misc. 2d 624, 173 N.Y.S.2d 390; 1912 Ops Atty Gen 185; 1913 Ops Atty Gen 188

A corporation, organized under general corporation statutes, although it had express or implied power to lend money and take security for loans made, was prohibited from doing so except "in furtherance of its corporate purposes" and from invading the field of banking by former § 18 of the Gen. Corp. L. as construed in the light of § 131 of the Bank L. Flatbush Auto Discount Corp. v McCarthy-Bernhardt Buick, Inc. (1961) 9 N.Y.2d 776, 215 N.Y.S.2d 78, 174 N.E.2d 749

However, an ordinary business corporation was not considered as acting in violation of former § 18 of the Gen. Corp. L. merely because it sold goods, property, or services on an instalment payment plan after a "deposit" down. Gimbel Bros., Inc. v White (1939) 256 A.D. 439, 10 N.Y.S.2d 666; 1942 Ops Atty Gen Apr 22

Business financing arrangements, in connection with which accounts receivable, conditional sales contracts, or chattel mortgages were assigned over, "factorage" contracts, advancements against inventory pledged or mortgaged, and the like, presented the most difficult field in determining what was, or was not, engaging in the banking business. Not infrequently such dealings and transactions were held to be in violation of the statutes protecting the banking business against unauthorized competition. Ernst v Terminal Clearing House Ass'n (1914) 86 Misc 295, 149 N.Y.S. 181, affd without op 167 A.D. 902, 151 N.Y.S. 1114; Re Worth Lighting & Fixture Co. (1923, DC NY) 292 F 769

Section 18 of former Gen. Corp. L. was not violated by the discounting by defendant corporation of customer's notes transferred to it by plaintiff at one and one-half percent per month, such notes being non-interest bearing, where there was substantial proof to sustain findings that the transactions between plaintiff and defendant represented selling of some of its accounts receivable to defendant rather than merely placing them with defendant as security for loans. Sigman v Claar Bros., Inc. (1961, CA2 NY) 291 F.2d 820

The test of whether the corporation in question was engaged in transactions of the types prohibited to such extent as to be engaged in the banking business was similarly applied to exculpate other relatively isolated or unique dealings, which, if persisted in, might have been deemed in violation of these statutes. Wolf v Aero Factors Corp. (1954, DC NY) 126 F. Supp. 872, affd (CA2 NY) 221 F.2d 291

The 1958 amendments of § 131 of the Banking Law and § 18 of former General Corporation Law were designed to limit the implications of the decision of the Court of Appeals in Miller v Discount Factors, Inc. 1 N.Y.2d 275, wherein it was held that a company which loaned funds in exchange for a series of notes and deducted a flat "bonus charge" in advance was engaged in "making discounts" within the terms of these sections as they stood prior to such amendment, and it has since become well settled that the acquisition by a factorage corporation of notes representing the purchase price of goods sold by the transferor of the notes, though at a discount, is not a violation of these provisions. Sigman v Claar Bros., Inc. (1960, SD NY) 184 F. Supp. 193, affd (CA2 NY) 291 F.2d 820

A foreign transportation corporation was prohibited from issuing, buying and selling drafts or bills of exchange or issuing evidences of debt for circulation as money. 1911 Ops Atty Gen 544

Leasing out personalty and deducting interest or other charges in advance, was, for example, considered an invasion of the banking field. 1913 Ops Atty Gen 194

Issuing or giving out trading stamps or similar redeemable certificates was not usually considered within the coverage of these "banking business" prohibitions. 1916 Ops Atty Gen 344

8. By-laws

The test of illegality of bylaws is whether they are "inconsistent with the law." Benintendi v Kenton Hotel, Inc. (1943) 181 Misc 897, 45 N.Y.S.2d 705, affd without op 268 A.D. 857, 50 N.Y.S.2d 843, mod on other grounds 294 N.Y. 112, 60 N.E.2d 829 (superseded by statute on other grounds as stated in Application of Burkin, 1 N.Y.2d 570, 154 N.Y.S.2d 898, 136 N.E.2d 862, 64 ALR2d 638)

Under former § 14 of the Gen. Corp. L. it was held that a by-law, that no resolution shall be adopted except by unanimous vote of the stockholders, is inconsistent with law and invalid. Benintendi v Kenton Hotel, Inc. (1943) 181 Misc 897, 45 N.Y.S.2d 705, affd without op 268 A.D. 857, 50 N.Y.S.2d 843, mod on other grounds 294 N.Y. 112, 60 N.E.2d 829 (superseded by statute as stated in Application of Burkin, 1 N.Y.2d 570, 154 N.Y.S.2d 898, 136 N.E.2d 862, 64 ALR2d 638)

A by-law requiring a unanimous vote of the shareholders for an amendment of the by-laws is legal. Benintendi v Kenton Hotel, Inc. (1943) 181 Misc 897, 45 N.Y.S.2d 705, affd without op 268 A.D. 857, 50 N.Y.S.2d 843, mod on other grounds 294 N.Y. 112, 60 N.E.2d 829 (superseded by statute as stated in Application of Burkin, 1 N.Y.2d 570, 154 N.Y.S.2d 898, 136 N.E.2d 862, 64 ALR2d 638)

9. Miscellaneous

Officers of a corporation have no implied power to transact unusual business on behalf of a corporation, and where the business transacted is unusual, a person relying upon the authority of the officers must show that they had specific authority to act for the corporation. Trulock v Kings County Iron Foundry, Inc. (1926) 216 A.D. 439, 215 N.Y.S. 587

§ 203. Defense of ultra vires

(a) No act of a corporation and no transfer of real or personal property to or by a corporation, otherwise lawful, shall be invalid by reason of the fact that the corporation was without capacity or power to do such act or to make or receive such transfer, but such lack of capacity or power may be asserted:

(1) In a[...]
poration to enjo[...]
of real or personal [...]
the unauthorized act o[...]
is being, or is to be, per[...]
contract to which the corpora[...]
may, if all of the parties to the c[...]
the action and if it deems the sam[...]
set aside and enjoin the performance of [...]
and in so doing may allow to the corporatio[...]
other parties to the contract, as the case may b[...]
compensation as may be equitable for the loss[...]
damage sustained by any of them from the action o[...]
the court in setting aside and enjoining the performance of such contract; provided that anticipated profits to be derived from the performance of the contract shall not be awarded by the court as a loss or damage sustained.

(2) In an action by or in the right of the corporation to procure a judgment in its favor against an incumbent or former officer or director of the corporation for loss or damage due to his unauthorized act.

(3) In an action or special proceeding by the attorney-general to annul or dissolve the corporation or to enjoin it from the doing of unauthorized business.

History: Add, L 1961, ch 855, eff Sept 1, 1963.

CASE ANNOTATIONS

Section 203 of the Business Corporation Law does not shield a corporation from the consequences of noncompliance with § 908, but shareholder acquiescence and ratification may be sufficient in equity to bar challenge to the corporate action. Commercial Trading Co. v 120 Jane Corp. (1966, 1st Dept) 27 A.D.2d 533, 275 N.Y.S.2d 621

Corporation dissolved pursuant to CLS Tax § 203-a lacks capacity to bring suit on claim arising out of conduct of prohibited new business; furthermore, such corporation has neither de jure nor de facto existence for purposes of ultra vires defense under CLS Bus Corp § 203. Lorisa Capital Corp. v Gallo (1986, 2d Dept) 119 A.D.2d 99, 506 N.Y.S.2d 62

Corporate defendant's execution of agreement seeking to bring about disposition of lease held by its wholly-owned subsidiary was in furtherance of corporate defendant's own corporate purposes, and was thus authorized by CLS Bus Corp § 202. Garrick-Aug Assocs. Store Leasing, Inc. v Wein (2000, 1st Dept) 271 A.D.2d 344, 707 N.Y.S.2d 76

Where all stockholders participate in a transaction and approve it, and it does not appear that harm resulted to the public or to creditors, a defense of ultra vires is not available. Finke v Sil-Gold Corp. (1962) 33 Misc. 2d 1064, 227 N.Y.S.2d 582

This section is not limited to situation where ultra vires is raised as a defense, notwithstanding title of section. 711 Kings Highway Corp. v F. I. M.'s Marine Repair Service, Inc. (1966) 51 Misc. 2d 373, 273 N.Y.S.2d 299

This section applies even though contract which is claimed to be ultra vires is executory. 711 Kings Highway Corp. v F.I.M.'s Marine Repair Service, Inc. (1966) 51 Misc. 2d 373, 273 N.Y.S.2d 299

Lease restricting use of premises to motion picture theater, in other respects valid, was not invalid as to corporate lessee whose charter did not authorize it to operate motion picture theater. 711 Kings Highway Corp. v F.I.M.'s Marine Repair Service, Inc. (1966) 51 Misc. 2d 373, 273 N.Y.S.2d 299

Licensed plumbing contractors could not urge that gas company's installation of gas pipes beyond consumer's property line was ultra vires since such a claim is only available to a stockholder, the corporation itself, or the attorney general. Jaffe Plumbing & Heating Co. v Brooklyn Union Gas Co. (1966) 51 Misc. 2d 1083, 275 N.Y.S.2d 24, affd 29 A.D.2d 1051, 29 A.D.2d 1052, 290 N.Y.S.2d 1022, affd 26 N.Y.2d 851, 309 N.Y.S.2d 597, 258 N.E.2d 93 ship or from any name the right to which is reserved by or on behalf of any domestic or foreign limited liability company or limited partnership.

(3) Shall not contain any word or phrase, or any abbreviation or derivative thereof, the use of which is prohibited or restricted by any other statute of this state, unless in the latter case the restrictions have been complied with.

(4) Shall not contain any word or phrase, or any abbreviation or derivative thereof, in a context which indicates or implies that the corporation, if domestic, is formed or, if foreign, is authorized for any purpose or is possessed in this state of any power other than a purpose for which, or a power with which, the domestic corporation may be and is formed or the foreign corporation is authorized.

(5) (A) Shall not contain any of the following phrases, or any abbreviation or derivative thereof:

board of trade	state police	urban development
chamber of commerce	state trooper	urban relocation
community renewal	tenant relocation	

(B) Shall not contain any of the following words, or any abbreviation or derivative thereof:

acceptance	endowment loan
annuity	fidelity mortgage
assurance	finance savings
bank	guaranty surety
benefit	indemnity title
bond	insurance trust
casualty	investment underwriter
doctor	lawyer

unless the approval of the superintendent of financial services is attached to the certificate of incorporation, or application for authority or amendment thereof; or that the word "doctor" or "lawyer" or an abbreviation or derivation thereof is used in the name of a university faculty practice corporation formed pursuant to section fourteen hundred twelve of the not-for-profit corporation law or a professional service corporation formed pursuant to article fifteen of this chapter, or a foreign professional service corporation authorized to do business in this state pursuant to article fifteen-A of this chapter, the members or shareholders of which are composed exclusively of doctors or lawyers, respectively, or are used in a context which clearly denotes a purpose other than the practice of law or medicine.

(6) Shall not, unless the approval of the state board of standards and appeals is attached to the certificate of incorporation, or application for authority or amendment thereof, contain any of the following words or phrases, or any abbreviation or derivative thereof: union, labor, council, industrial organization, in a context which indicates or implies that the domestic corporation is formed or the foreign corporation authorized as an organization of working men or women or wage earners or for the performance, rendition or sale of services as labor or management consultant, adviser or specialist, or as negotiator or arbitrator in labor-management disputes.

1963.

...this chapter, the name o... ...ation:

(1) Shall contain ... ...ion", "incorporated" or "limited", or an a... ... of one of such words; or, in the case of a foreign c...oration, it shall, for use in this state, add at the end of its name one of such words or an abbreviation thereof.

(2) (i) Shall be such as to distinguish it from the names of corporations of any type or kind, or a fictitious name of an authorized foreign corporation filed pursuant to article thirteen of this chapter, as such names appear on the index of names of existing domestic and authorized foreign corporations of any type or kind, including fictitious names of authorized foreign corporations filed pursuant to article thirteen of this chapter, in the department of state, division of corporations, or a name the right to which is reserved.

(ii) Shall be such as to distinguish it from (A) the names of domestic limited liability companies, (B) the names of authorized foreign limited liability companies, (C) the fictitious names of authorized foreign limited liability companies, (D) the names of domestic limited partnerships, (E) the names of authorized foreign limited partnerships, or (F) the fictitious names of authorized foreign limited partnerships, in each case, as such names appear on the index of names of existing domestic and authorized foreign limited liability companies, including fictitious names of authorized foreign limited liability companies, in the department of state, or on the index of names of existing domestic or authorized foreign limited partnerships, including fictitious names of authorized foreign limited partnerships, in the department of state, or names the rights to which are reserved; provided, however, that no corporation that was formed prior to the effective date of this clause and no foreign corporation that was qualified to do business in this state prior to such effective date shall be required to change the name or fictitious name it had on such effective date solely by reason of such name or fictitious name being indistinguishable from the name or fictitious name of any domestic or authorized foreign limited liability company or limited partner-

(7) Shall not, unless the approval of the state department of social services is attached to the certificate of incorporation, or application for authority or amendment thereof, contain the word "blind" or "handicapped". Such approval shall be granted by the state department of social services, if in its opinion the word "blind" or "handicapped" as used in the corporate name proposed will not tend to mislead or confuse the public into believing that the corporation is organized for charitable or non-profit purposes related to the blind or the handicapped.

(8) Shall not contain any words or phrases, or any abbreviation or derivation thereof in a context which will tend to mislead the public into believing that the corporation is an agency or instrumentality of the United States or the state of New York or a subdivision thereof or is a public corporation.

(9) Shall not contain any word or phrase, or any abbreviation or derivation thereof, which, separately, or in context, shall be indecent or obscene, or shall ridicule or degrade any person, group, belief, business or agency of government, or indicate or imply any unlawful activity.

(10) Shall not, unless the approval of the attorney general is attached to the certificate of incorporation, or application for authority or amendment thereof, contain the word "exchange" or any abbreviation or derivative thereof. Such approval shall not be granted by the attorney general, if in his opinion the use of the word "exchange" in the proposed corporate name would falsely imply that the corporation conducts its business at a place where trade is carried on in securities or commodities by brokers, dealers, or merchants.

(11) Shall not, unless the consent of the commissioner of education is endorsed on or annexed to the certificate of incorporation, contain the words "school;" "education;" "elementary;" "secondary;" "kindergarten;" "prekindergarten;" "preschool;" "nursery school;" "museum;" "history;" "historical;" "historical society;" "arboretum;" "library;" "college;" "university" or other term restricted by section two hundred twenty-four of the education law; "conservatory," "academy," or "institute," or any abbreviation or derivative of such terms. Such consent shall not be granted by the commissioner of education, if in the commissioner's opinion, the use of such terms in the corporate name is likely to mislead or confuse the public into believing that the corporation is organized for non-profit educational purposes or for educational business purposes that are not specified in the corporate purposes and powers contained in its certificate of incorporation.

History: Add, L 1961, ch 855, eff Sept 1, 1963; amd, L 1963, ch 861, eff April 26, 1963, L 1965, ch 765, eff Sept 1, 1965, L 1971, ch 537, eff Sept 1, 1971, L 1973, ch 961, L 1974, ch 750, eff June 7, 1974, L 1978, ch 555, § 43, eff July 24, 1978, L 1981, ch 120, § 1, eff May 18, 1981, L 1982, ch 590, § 1, eff Oct 20, 1982, L 1982, ch 832, §§ 2, 3, eff Oct 25, 1982, L 1983,

ch 9, § 1, eff March 18, 1983, L 1983, ch 505, § 4, eff Oct 17, 1983, L 1993, ch 555, § 2, eff July 28, 1993, L 1999, ch 172, §§ 4, 5, eff July 6, 1999, L 2004, ch 344, § 2, eff Aug 10, 2004, L 2005, ch 316, § 5, eff Jan 1, 2006, L 2011, ch 62, § 104 (Part A), eff Oct 3, 2011, L 2012, ch 155, § 46, eff July 18, 2012.

CASE ANNOTATIONS

UNDER FORMER GEN CORP
1. In general
2. Indication of corporate status
3. Requirement of dissimilarity
4. Prohibited words or phrases
5. Miscellaneous

Corporation would not be allowed to change its name to "Financial World" in view of fact that "financial" was clearly a derivative of "finance" and therefore proscribed by ¶ 5 of subd (2) of § 301. Guenther Publishing Corp. v Lomenzo (1968, 3d Dept) 29 A.D.2d 708, 286 N.Y.S.2d 497

The prohibition set forth in ¶ 5 is absolute and there is not, as in ¶ 4 of subd (a), any requirement that the public be misled. Guenther Publishing Corp. v Lomenzo (1968, 3d Dept) 29 A.D.2d 708, 286 N.Y.S.2d 497

The Secretary of State is vested with discretion in the matter of permitting the amendment of a corporate name. Frank Boufford Co. v Lomenzo (1972, 3d Dept) 38 A.D.2d 986, 329 N.Y.S.2d 644

A corporation which had used the word "Vantage" in its name prior to its use by a second corporation was not entitled to have the second corporation enjoined from using the word as part of its corporate name or business, since there was little evidence of the likelihood of confusion in light of the businesses' different geographical locations and the dissimilar kinds of services in which they specialized; however, the second corporation would be required to use some qualifying word or phrase in conjunction with the word that would clearly distinguish its business from that of the other. Vantage Careers, Inc. v Vantage Agency, Inc. (1981, 1st Dept) 79 A.D.2d 912, 434 N.Y.S.2d 428

Subject to limitations imposed by the Constitution of the United States, a foreign corporation may be prevented from doing business in this state, and, if granted leave to do business here, conditions may accompany the privilege. Jervis Corp. v Secretary of State (1964) 43 Misc. 2d 185, 250 N.Y.S.2d 544

The general purpose of the statutes limiting use of corporate names is to protect the public and to prevent deception and confusion. Jervis Corp. v Secretary of State (1964) 43 Misc. 2d 185, 250 N.Y.S.2d 544

It is significant that former § 9 of the General Corporation Law, dealing with name similarities, uses the expression "calculated" to deceive, whereas in this provision of the Business Corporation Law the word used is "tend." Jervis Corp. v Secretary of State (1964) 43 Misc. 2d 185, 250 N.Y.S.2d 544

Store manager was personally liable on debt as agent of undisclosed corporate principal where there was no indication of corporate existence either in the name of the store or in business dealings between the parties, and where the only public indication of corporate existence was a small sales tax authorization certificate in front window of store. Judith Garden, Inc. v Mapel (1973) 73 Misc. 2d 810, 342 N.Y.S.2d 486

State racing commission regulation requiring that a thoroughbred horse's racing name be registered by its user with the Jockey Club annually and giving the Jockey Club, a private organization right, in its discretion the right to refuse such registration went beyond the scope of commission's power as granting to private organization the power to nullify effects of statutes regulating the use of trade names, business designations and assumed name and to substitute its judgment for that of state agencies and courts concerning who may or may not use a particular name. Halpern v Lomenzo (1975) 81 Misc. 2d 467, 367 N.Y.S.2d 653

The application of three licensed New York corporations, Shigoto International Corp., Shigoto Industries, Ltd., and Sekai Manufacturing Co., Inc., seeking to direct the Secretary of State to strike the names Shigoto Far East Importers, Ltd., and Sekai Far East Importers, Ltd., from the index of authorized foreign corporations is granted on the ground that the challenged corporate names are clearly so similar, either with or without "Importers" added thereto, and tending to confuse and deceive the public (Business Corporation Law, § 301, subd [a], par [2]) that the Secretary of State's approval of the proposed corporate names was an abuse of discretion, and it is irrelevant if the petitioner corporations are not yet doing business; although the Department of State has wide discretion in approving or denying proposed corporate names under the statute, if the choice of the name is so wanting in logical premise as to be violative of good sense and reason, the choice will be deemed an abuse of discretion. Shigoto International Corp. v Cuomo (1978) 101 Misc. 2d 646, 421 N.Y.S.2d 784

Any corporation using an assumed name prior to January 1, 1979, or seeking to now use an assumed name, is now required to file a certificate with the Secretary of State pursuant to Section 130 of the General Business Law. A corporation which is listed as a partner on a certificate filed with the county clerk prior to January 1, 1979, must register with the Secretary of State if it is doing business under any name other than its corporate name. 1979 Op Atty Gen Mar 14. (Informal)

The proscription against use in a corporate name of the words set forth in Business Corporation Law, § 301(a)(5) is applicable to corporations, domestic or foreign, unless the corporation had been authorized to do business by the incorporating State prior to September 1, 1963. 1980 Op Atty Gen Sept 10 (formal)

Name of limited partnership may not contain word "limited" or abbreviation thereof without any additional indication that entity is organized as limited partnership. Ops Atty Gen 88-61 (Informal)

UNDER FORMER GEN CORP

1. In general

This section has been referred to, in the light of legislative intent in adopting the new Business Corporation Law, as indicating how equivalent provisions of § 9 of the former General Corporation Law with respect to right to use the name of a corporation after taking over all of its assets should be construed. Industrial Psychology, Inc. v Simon (1962, 1st Dept) 16 A.D.2d 114, 226 N.Y.S.2d 148

Only the corporate name may be used by a corporation in the conduct of or in connection with its business. A corporation may not conduct its business under an assumed name. People ex rel. Bayer v Ferdinand (1939) 172 Misc 595, 15 N.Y.S.2d 506

The requirement under § 9 of the former Gen. Corp. L. that corporations shall take names that serve to distinguish them from individual proprietors and partnerships applied only to corporations formed after Jan. 1, 1912. Recamier Mfg. Co. v Harriet Hubbard Ayer, Inc. (1932, DC NY) 59 F.2d 802

Prohibited words may not be combined with others in the name of a business corporation. 1928 Ops Atty Gen 168

The rule of practical interpretation did not apply in case of inadvertent acceptance of a corporate name which violated the provisions of § 9 of the former Gen. Corp. L. through administrative error. 1961 Ops Atty Gen Nov 15

2. Indication of corporate status

Where the name of a foreign corporation does not clearly indicate that it is a corporation and it is not willing to use in this state such an affix or prefix as will indicate the necessary distinction the Secretary of State may deny its application for authority to do business in this state. People ex rel. United Verde Copper Co. v Hugo (1917) 181 A.D. 149, 168 N.Y.S. 80

Application of the "American Cigar Lighter Company" for leave to change its corporate name to "Electric Cigar Lighter Company" denied, on the ground that the proposed name has not, as a part thereof, some word, abbreviation, affix or prefix thereto, which clearly indicated that the applicant was a corporation, as required by § 9 of the former Gen. Corp. L, the word "company" does not indicate corporate nature. Re American Cigar Lighter Co. (1912) 77 Misc 643, 138 N.Y.S. 455

The word "limited" in a corporate name was in compliance with § 9 of the former Gen. Corp. L. 1912 Ops Atty Gen 65

Under § 9 of the former Gen. Corp. L., even a membership corporation having for its purposes giving of voluntary aid and furtherance of charity among its members was not relieved from the requirements necessitating words in its title indicating that it was a corporation. 1913 Ops Atty Gen 144

A change of name by a foreign corporation had to comply with the "corporate status" requirements of § 9 of the former Gen Corp L, notwithstanding it was authorized to do business in New York prior to existence of the requirement. 1963 Ops Atty Gen Mar 27

3. Requirement of dissimilarity

Sections 210 and 212 of the Former Gen. Corp. L. circumscribed the official action to be taken by the Secretary of State under former § 9. He was not bound to go beyond the documents on file or presented to him in accordance with the statute in order to determine whether to deny a certificate on the grounds of similarity of name. Historical data, good faith and other equities were beyond the inquest which the Secretary of State is required to make. Barber Co. v Department of State (1938) 277 N.Y. 55, 12 N.E.2d 790

Where the Material Men's Mercantile Association, Limited, sues to enjoin the New York Material Men's Mercantile Association, Inc., from using its corporate name, and there is no evidence that the plaintiff has lost any customers to the defendant because of similarity, but it is shown that some of plaintiff's customers have been led to believe that business solicited by the defendant was solicited by the plaintiff, the plaintiff is not entitled to exclusive use of words in its name, but the defendant cannot use its name without adding other words clearly distinguishing it from that of the plaintiff. Material Men's Mercantile Ass'n v New York Material Men's Mercantile Ass'n (1915) 169 A.D. 843, 155 N.Y.S. 706, affd without op 224 N.Y. 670, 121 N.E. 878

Notwithstanding § 40 of the former Gen. Corp. L., a court, having inherent power to modify or vacate its own orders and judgments in interest of justice, would grant a motion for "Public National Bank of New York" to vacate an order permitting "Bank of Europe" to assume name of "Republic Bank of New York," on ground that public was liable to be deceived by similarity of names. Re Bank of Europe (1919) 109 Misc 363, 179 N.Y.S. 664, affd without op 191 A.D. 905, 181 N.Y.S. 927

Action of the Secretary of State in denying a certificate to do business to a foreign corporation called Motor Club of America, was upheld where the resemblance of the name to that of the local Automobile Club of America, Inc. was so close "as to be calculated to deceive" within the restriction of this section, especially where the corporate powers were almost identical and the places of business were the same, the test applied in restraining unfair competition not necessarily being the same as under § 9 of the former Gen. Corp. L. Motor Club of America v Curran (1948) 193 Misc 157, 83 N.Y.S.2d 733, affd 274 A.D. 1083, 85 N.Y.S.2d 552, affd without op 299 N.Y. 776, 87 N.E.2d 678

The absence of any element of fraud in the use of the proposed new name bearing similarity to the name of another corporation is not controlling; if there are reasonable grounds to conclude that the granting of the change will result in injury to the complaining corporation it should be denied. Re United States Mortg. Co. (1895) 83 Hun 572, 32 N.Y.S. 11

The fact of incorporation in New York under a certain name is not alone sufficient reason for granting injunctive relief against the use of a similar name by a foreign corporation. The granting of a franchise by the state merely sanctions the use of a name if it is otherwise lawful. It is not an adjudication of the legality of the name nor a decision as to whether it may be used. Sterling Products Corp. v Sterling Products, Inc. (1942, DC NY) 43 F. Supp. 548, 52 USPQ 454

4. Prohibited words or phrases

Since the word "Lloyds" has by general usage become synonymous with "insurance", the secretary of state was justified in refusing to file a certificate incorporating a business corporation under the name "Lloyds, New York, Incorporated," which proposed to act as agent for unincorporated Lloyds association, on grounds that it was likely to deceive the public in that other companies were doing business under that name and because § 9 of the former Gen. Corp. L. forbade organization of any corporation with the name "insurance" except under Bank. Law or Insur. Law. Re Barker (1909) 135 A.D. 16, 119 N.Y.S. 777

Word "bank" used in combination with the word "electric," making word "Bankelectric" as part of the name of a proposed corporation, violated, in letter and spirit, the provisions of § 9 of the former Gen. Corp. L. People ex rel. Meyer Bank v Flynn (1930) 231 A.D. 763, 246 N.Y.S. 125

Use of the word "finance," "financing," or an equivalent, in the name of a corporation organized under general corporation laws was likewise prohibited by the former Gen. Corp. L., as construed in conjunction with the Banking Law. Retailers Collateral Secur. Trading Corp. v Department of State (1958, 3d Dept) 6 A.D.2d 975, 176 N.Y.S.2d 429, reh and app den (3d Dept) 6 A.D.2d 1018, 178 N.Y.S.2d 639; 1926 Ops Atty Gen 117

While § 9 of the former Gen. Corp. L. did not expressly provide that the word "aid" should not be used in a corporate name, it did prohibit the word "benefit", and the word "aid" would clearly indicate a benefit so that it would seem clear that the meaning and intent of the statute was to prohibit the use of such word. Re Antipoller Mut. Aid Soc. (1917) 100 Misc 589, 166 N.Y.S. 386

The purpose specified in a proposed certificate of incorporation for "Hotel Roosevelt Employees Welfare Association," that the corporation was designed to promote the well-being of employees, brought the proposed corporation within former § 9-a and Mem. Corp. Law, § 11, subd. 1-a. Breen v Picard (1938) 167 Misc 561, 4 N.Y.S.2d 301, 3 BNA LRRM 797

The word "union" as used in § 9-a of the former Gen. Corp. L. was intended to refer to its generally accepted meaning as a labor union or organization of workers, and a corporation which admittedly was not such an organization was properly denied the right to use such a name. Tool Owners Union v Roberts (1947) 190 Misc 577, 76 N.Y.S.2d 239

Use of the words "insurance," "assurance," and other terms commonly associated with being engaged in the insurance, casualty, or indemnity business by issuance of policies or contracts of insurance or indemnity, in the names of corporations organized under general laws, was likewise prohibited by § 9 of the former Gen. Corp. L. and other statutes. 1933 Ops Atty Gen 558

Use of name "Dealerbanc Corporation" for a business corporation not engaged in banking was prohibited. 1940 Ops Atty Gen Mar 18

"Bancredit" was prohibited as a corporate name. 1946 Ops Atty Gen Sept 10

A foreign corporation may not be authorized to do business in this State if the word "lawyer" is part of its name and it is not a non-profit membership corporation, the membership of which is composed exclusively of lawyers, notwithstanding that it was formed in the foreign state prior to the enactment of the prohibitory provision. 1948 Ops Atty Gen Dec 1

Mere use of the word "insurance" in corporate names was forbidden regardless of the purposes of the corporation or the character of the title as a whole. Hence, a certificate for the "Greater New York Insurance Co., Inc." was properly refused for filing although corporation's business was to publicize the insurance industry and make arrangement for demonstration and exhibitions on a day officially declared to be "Greater New York Insurance Day" by the mayor of New York City. 1953 Ops Atty Gen Oct 7

Even a corporation licensed pursuant to Banking Law Art 11-b to engage in the business of a sales finance company was not thereby authorized to use the word "finance" as part of its corporate title. 1957 Ops Atty Gen Oct 24

The word "banknote" may be used as part of a corporate name, notwithstanding the prohibition on use of the word "bank" in such names. 1961 Ops Atty Gen Oct 10

5. Miscellaneous

The state board of standards and appeals, under § 9-a of the former Gen. Corp. L. and Mem. Corp. Law, § 11, subd. 1-a (as both were amended by L 1937 c 820), could approve or disapprove a proposed certificate of incorporation of a corporation having for its purpose the formation of an organization of groups of working men and women, depending on whether or not the corporation was one consistent in all respects with provisions of Labor Law, §§ 700 to 716, as added by L 1937 c 443. Campbell v Picard (1937) 165 Misc 148, 300 N.Y.S. 515

A proposed certificate of incorporation for a corporation organized to conduct a registry or placement service for nurses or other medical or hospital employees as a paid employment agency for such persons, is unobjectionable and should be permitted to be filed. Such a corporation would not constitute the corporate practice of a profession where the nurses and others would not be employees of the corporation but would enter into direct contractual arrangement with those who need their services. 1953 Ops Atty Gen Oct 19

§ 302. Corporate name; exceptions

(a) Any reference to a corporation in this section except as otherwise provided herein shall include both domestic and foreign corporations.

(b) The provisions of section 301 (Corporate name; general):

(1) Shall not require any corporation, existing or authorized under any statute on the effective date of this chapter, to add to, modify or otherwise change its corporate name; provided, however, that any corporation organized or qualified to do business in this state under this chapter which contains in its name any of the following words or phrases or any abbreviation or derivation thereof, "community renewal", "tenant relocation", "urban development" or "urban relocation", shall plainly and legibly state immediately following its name in any writing issued or authorized to be issued by it upon which its name appears, including, but not limited to, advertising material letterheads, business cards and building directories and signs, the phrase "not a governmental agency".

(2) Shall not prevent a corporation with which another corporation is merged, or which is formed by the reorganization or consolidation of one or more other corporations or upon a sale, lease, exchange or other disposition to a domestic corporation of all or substantially all the assets of another domestic corporation, including its name, as provided in paragraph (b) of Section 909 (Sale, lease, exchange or other disposition of assets), from having the same name as any of such corporations if at the time such other corporation was authorized or existing under any statute of this state.

(3) Shall not prevent a foreign corporation from being authorized under a name which is similar to the name of a corporation of any type or kind existing or authorized under any statute, if the department of state finds, upon proof by affidavit or otherwise as it may determine, that a difference between such names exists in the terms or abbreviations indicating corporate character or otherwise, that the applicant has engaged in business as a corporation under its said name for not less than ten consecutive years immediately prior to the date of its application that the business to be conducted in this state is not the same as or similar to the business conducted by the corporation with whose name it may conflict and that the public is not likely to be confused or deceived, and if the applicant shall agree in its application for authority to use with its corporate name, in this state, to be placed immediately under or following such name, the words "a .... (name of jurisdiction of incorporation) corporation".

(4) Shall not prevent a "small business investment corporation" as defined in an act of congress entitled "Small Business Investment Act of 1958" from including the word "investment" as part of its name if such word is coupled with the words "small business".

(5) Shall not prevent an "investment company" as defined in an act of congress entitled "Investment Company Act of 1940" from including the word "finance" or "bond" as part of its name, if the approval of the superintendent of financial services is attached to the certificate of incorporation, application for authority, or amendment thereof.

Business Corporation Law

(6) Shall not prevent a broker or dealer in securities, as defined in an act of congress entitled "Securities Exchange Act of 1934", from including the word "investment" as part of its name if such word is coupled with the words "broker" or "brokers" and if such broker or dealer is registered with the securities and exchange commission under the provisions of section fifteen of the securities exchange act of nineteen hundred thirty-four and is also registered with the attorney general under the provisions of section three hundred fifty-nine-e of the general business law.

(7) Shall not prevent an association of banks or trust companies organized as a non-profit membership corporation for the promotion of the interests of member banks from including the word "bankers" as part of its corporate name.

(8) Shall not prevent a bank holding company, as long as it is required to be registered under article III-A of the banking law or under the federal Bank Holding Company Act, as each may be amended from time to time, from using the words "bank", "banker" or "trusts" or any abbreviation, derivative or combination thereof as part of its corporate name, if the approval of the superintendent of financial services is attached to the certificate of incorporation, application for authority, or amendment thereof.

History: Add, L 1961, ch 855, eff Sept 1, 1963; amd, L 1962, ch 834, § 6; L 1963, ch 748, § 4, eff Sept 1, 1963; L 1965, ch 904, eff July 17, 1965; L 1967, ch 339; L 1967, ch 700; L 1969, ch 200, eff May 24, 1969; L 1971, ch 537, eff Sept 1, 1971; L 1976, ch 619, eff July 21, 1976; L 1981, ch 892, § 1, eff July 31, 1981; L 2011, ch 62, § 104 (Part A), eff Oct 3, 2011.

CASE ANNOTATIONS

This § 302 of the Business Corp. L. has been referred to as drafted in the light of legislative intent that § 9 of the former Gen. Corp. L. should give a reorganized corporation or one succeeding to all the rights of a prior corporation the right to use the latter's corporate name, notwithstanding it contains some word the use of which, since adoption of the name by the predecessor and prior to the take-over, has been prohibited. Industrial Psychology, Inc. v Simon (1962, 1st Dept) 16 A.D.2d 114, 226 N.Y.S.2d 148

The requirements imposed by subd (b) (3) of this section permit a corporation to file its certificate to do business here, notwithstanding similarity of name, provided the State Department finds it has been engaged in business for ten years and that its business is not the same as, or similar to, that conducted by another corporation already licensed under a similar name and applicant agrees to place after its name a designation indicating the state of its incorporation. Jervis Corp. v Secretary of State (1964) 43 Misc. 2d 185, 250 N.Y.S.2d 544

The proscription against use in a corporate name of the words set forth in Business Corporation Law, § 301(a)(5) is applicable to corporations, domestic or foreign, unless the corporation had been authorized to do business by the incorporating State prior to September 1, 1963. 1980 Op Atty Gen Sept 10 (formal)

UNDER FORMER LAW

A corporation was not the reorganized successor of another foreign corporation of the same name, so as to entitle it to the benefit of the provisions of former § 9 of the Gen. Corp. L. where it had in no sense succeeded to the franchises of the other corporation and had not supplanted or taken the place of the old corporation. People ex rel. United Verde Copper Co. v Hugo (1917) 181 A.D. 149, 168 N.Y.S. 80

Use of a name similar to that of another corporation cannot be denied where a corporation desires to reincorporate under the same name which it has theretofore borne. People ex rel. United States

Grand Lodge of O. B. A. v Payn (1899) 28 Misc 275, 59 N.Y.S. 851, affd without op 43 A.D. 621, 60 N.Y.S. 1146, affd 161 N.Y. 229, 55 N.E. 849

Petitioner corporation was entitled to an order directing respondent Secretary of State to issue a certificate of authority to do business in New York under the name "Industrial Psychology, Inc." under which a prior Illinois corporation had been licensed to do business in New York, upon a showing that the Illinois corporation had adopted and consummated a plan of reorganization whereby all its assets were transferred to petitioner in return for petitioner's stock, whereupon the Illinois corporation ceased to do business, filed a certificate of dissolution in Illinois, and tendered its certificate of authority to the New York Secretary of State. Industrial Psychology, Inc. v Simon (1962, 1st Dept) 16 A.D.2d 114, 226 N.Y.S.2d 148

A foreign co-operative corporation may be authorized to do business in this State even though its name does not include the word "co-operative." 1948 Ops Atty Gen Sept 25

Upon the consolidation pursuant to former Stock Corporation Law § 91 of a Maryland corporation incorporated in May 1914 and authorized to do business in this State in 1928, having the term "Engineering", as part of its corporate name, and a Delaware corporation, the latter to be the surviving corporation, the consolidated corporation could adopt the name of the Maryland corporation and qualify in this State under such name. 1952 Ops Atty Gen July 2

A corporation could be formed under former Stock Corporation Law § 5 for the purpose of operating under the Small Business Investment Act of 1958. Such a corporation could not be incorporated pursuant to Banking Law Art. XII. Certificate of incorporation should contain a statement that the corporation shall not act as a depository and its incidental powers should be limited to those not otherwise prohibited by the laws of this State. 1958 Ops Atty Gen Dec 10

§ 303. Reservation of name

(a) A corporate name may be reserved by:

(1) Any person intending to form a domestic corporation.

(2) Any domestic corporation intending to change its name.

(3) Any foreign corporation intending to apply for authority to do business in this state.

(4) Any authorized foreign corporation intending to change its name.

(5) Any person intending to incorporate a foreign corporation and to have it apply for authority to do business in this state.

(b) A fictitious name for use pursuant to section 1301 of this chapter, may be reserved by:

(1) Any foreign corporation intending to apply for authority to do business in this state, pursuant to paragraph (d) of section 1301 of this chapter.

(2) Any authorized foreign corporation intending to change its fictitious name under which it does business in this state.

(3) Any authorized foreign corporation which has changed its corporate name in its jurisdiction, such new corporate name not being available in this state.

(c) Application to reserve a corporate name shall be delivered to the department of state. It shall set forth the name and address of the applicant, the name to be reserved and a statement of the basis under paragraph (a) or (b) for the application. The secretary of state may require that there be included in the application a statement as to the nature of the business to be conducted by the corporation. If the name is available for corporate use, the department of state shall reserve the name for the use of the applicant for a period of sixty days and issue a certificate of reservation. The restrictions and qualifications set forth in subparagraphs (a) (3), (4), (5), (6) and (7) of section 301 (Corporate name; general) are not waived by the issuance of a certificate of reservation. The certificate of reservation shall include the name of the applicant, the name reserved and the date of the reservation. The certificate of reservation (or in lieu thereof an affidavit by the applicant or by his agent or attorney that the certificate of reservation has been lost or destroyed) shall accompany the certificate of incorporation or the application for authority when either is delivered to the department of state.

(d) The secretary of state may extend the reservation for additional periods of not more than sixty days each, upon the written request of the applicant, his attorney or agent delivered to the department of state, to be filed before the expiration of the reservation period then in effect. Such request shall have attached to it the certificate of reservation of name. Not more than two such extensions shall be granted.

(e) Upon the request of the applicant, delivered to the department of state before the expiration of the reserved period, the department shall cancel the reservation.

(f) Any application or request under this section shall be signed by the applicant, his attorney or agent.

History: Add, L 1961, ch 855, eff Sept 1, 1963; amd, L 1964, ch 725, § 4; L 1965, ch 803, § 3; L 1969, ch 114, eff March 25, 1969; relettered par (c), L 1982, ch 590, § 2, eff Oct 20, 1982; L 1984, ch 241, § 1, eff June 19, 1984.

§ 304.   Statutory designation of secretary of state as agent for service of process

(a) The secretary of state shall be the agent of every domestic corporation and every authorized foreign corporation upon whom process against the corporation may be served.

(b) No domestic or foreign corporation may be formed or authorized to do business in this state under this chapter unless in its certificate of incorporation or application for authority it designates the secretary of state as such agent.

(c) Any designation by a domestic or a foreign corporation of the secretary of state as such agent, which designation is in effect on the effective date of this chapter, shall continue. Every domestic or foreign corporation, existing or authorized on the effective date of this chapter, which has not designated the secretary of state as such agent, shall be deemed to have done so. Any designation prior to the effective date of this chapter by a foreign corporation of an agent other than the secretary of state shall terminate on the effective date of this chapter.

(d) Any designated post-office address to which the secretary of state shall mail a copy of process served upon him as agent of a domestic corporation or a foreign corporation, shall continue until the filing of a certificate under this chapter directing the mailing to a different post-office address.

History: Add, L 1961, ch 855, eff Sept 1, 1963; amd, L 1962, ch 417, eff Sept 1, 1963.

CASE ANNOTATIONS

1. In general
2. Jurisdiction
3. Service of process
4. Under former law

1. In general
Where summons was mailed to defendant corporation by Secretary of State in care of its former counsel and, due to clerical error in the mail room of the law firm, the unopened letter was returned to the Secretary of State marked "Refused", default judgment would be opened for "mistake, inadvertence, surprise, or excusable neglect." Horn v Intelectron Corp., 294 F. Supp. 1153, 1968 U.S. Dist. LEXIS 8047 (S.D.N.Y. 1968).

2. Jurisdiction
In an action by plaintiff New York corporation alleging that it made two contracts for the sale and delivery of fuel oil with defendant Delaware Corporation and that defendant had failed to deliver the oil as agreed to plaintiff's barge at defendant's designated New York harbor terminal, defendant's authorization to do business in New York and concomitant designation of the secretary of state as its agent for surface of process pursuant to Bus Corp Law § 304(b) constitutes consent to in personam jurisdiction under CPLR § 301. Augsbury Corp. v Petrokey Corp., 97 A.D.2d 173, 470 N.Y.S.2d 787, 1983 N.Y. App. Div. LEXIS 20345 (N.Y. App. Div. 3d Dep't 1983).

Foreign car and tire makers did not consent to the personal general jurisdiction of New York courts in an action arising from an automobile accident occurring in Virginia by registering to do business in New York or appointing the Secretary of State as the makers' agent because, under evolving in personam jurisdiction jurisprudence, such acts did not consent to New York courts' general jurisdiction on claims unrelated to New York. Aybar v Aybar, 2019 N.Y. App. Div. LEXIS 444 (N.Y. App. Div. 2d Dep't 2019).

Provisions of the Business Corporation Law authorizing service of process on the Secretary of State do not extend the territorial jurisdiction of a city court outside the City of New York but merely provide an alternative method of service since, if the requirements are met, personal service could be made upon such defendant directly. O'Rourke v Ted's Ford, Inc., 89 Misc. 2d 986, 393 N.Y.S.2d 160, 1977 N.Y. Misc. LEXIS 2755 (N.Y. City Ct. 1977).

Territorial limitations upon service of summons contained the Uniform City Court Act and the Constitution with respect to city courts outside of the City of New York do not prohibit the domestic and foreign corporations from consenting to other means of acquiring jurisdiction, such as service upon the Secretary of State, even though such consent is required as a precondition for doing business in the state. O'Rourke v Ted's Ford, Inc., 89 Misc. 2d 986, 393 N.Y.S.2d 160, 1977 N.Y. Misc. LEXIS 2755 (N.Y. City Ct. 1977).

3. Service of process
In an action against a foreign corporation, defendant-corporation was subject to personal service by delivery of process to the Secretary of State where corporation's certificate of authority to do business in New York State was filed in 1917 and was still in effect although the corporation no longer was doing business in New York. Robfogel Mill-Andrews Corp. v Cupples Co., Mfrs., 67 Misc. 2d 623, 323 N.Y.S.2d 381, 1971 N.Y. Misc. LEXIS 1440 (N.Y. Sup. Ct. 1971).

Notice of appropriation is not a "process" as defined by the Business Corporation Law and, therefore, personal service is not perfected upon a corporation by serving a notice of appropriation upon the Secretary of State. Ebbets v State, 88 Misc. 2d 358, 387 N.Y.S.2d 969, 1976 N.Y. Misc. LEXIS 2614 (N.Y. Ct. Cl. 1976), aff'd, 64 A.D.2d 794, 408 N.Y.S.2d 556, 1978 N.Y. App. Div. LEXIS 12641 (N.Y. App. Div. 3d Dep't 1978).

Chapter 7 trustee failed to complete valid service of process on adversary defendants in a timely manner, or to offer a basis for excusable neglect of completing the service, and his motion to excuse tardy service was denied. Goldstein v Ill. Sec. Agency (In re Just for Feet, Inc.), 299 B.R. 343, 2003 Bankr. LEXIS 1102 (Bankr. D. Del. 2003).

Corporation's failure to comply with N.Y. Bus. Corp. Law § 304(a)-(b) and update its address in the Secretary of State's register explained why the corporation did not receive notice of the pension fund trustees' suit against it; the address was, however, the one on file with the New York Secretary of State, and the corporation's failure to comply with N.Y. Bus. Corp. Law § 304(a)-(b) did not change the fact that process—served on the Secretary of State as the corporation's agent—was proper and complete pursuant to N.Y. Bus. Corp. Law § 306(b)(1) and that it conferred the personal jurisdiction of the district court over the corporation. Trs. of the Local 531 Pension Fund v Am. Indus. Gases, Inc., 708 F. Supp. 2d 272, 2010 U.S. Dist. LEXIS 41204 (E.D.N.Y. 2010).

4. Under former law

Failure to make service in accordance with the provisions of § 24 of the former Stock Corp. L. could be waived where the corporation participated in the action on the merits, even though the corporation contended that it was appearing specially. In re East River Sa v Bank, 294 N.Y. 356, 62 N.E.2d 601, 294 N.Y. (N.Y.S.) 356, 1945 N.Y. LEXIS 760 (N.Y. 1945).

Where the designated agent for service of process upon a foreign corporation authorized to do business in this state died, and the corporation designated no other person in his place, service of summons upon the secretary of state in an action against said corporation upon a liability arising without this state was futile, where the defendant was not shown to have property in this state, and on motion would be set aside. Eastern Products Corp. v Tennessee C., I. & R. Co., 170 N.Y.S. 100, 102 Misc. 557, 1918 N.Y. Misc. LEXIS 852 (N.Y. Sup. Ct. 1918).

However, under § 213 of the former Gen. Corp. L. it was held that service of summons by the plaintiff, a resident of this state, upon the secretary of state as agent for the defendant, a Florida corporation, based upon a transitory cause of action arising in Florida, was invalid, since service, upon the agent designated solely by statute of the state wherein suit is brought, is valid only in respect to cause of action originating in that state. Powell v Home Seekers' Realty Co., 228 N.Y.S. 131, 131 Misc. 590, 1928 N.Y. Misc. LEXIS 785 (N.Y. App. Term 1928).

Under the provisions of the former Gen. Corp. L. and the former Stock Corp. L. from which this section was derived, either a domestic corporation, or a foreign corporation authorized to do business in New York, could be effectively served with process by serving the secretary of state. Application of Weiss, 5 Misc. 2d 501, 164 N.Y.S.2d 504, 1957 N.Y. Misc. LEXIS 3633 (N.Y. Sup. Ct. 1957); Durand v Lipman, 299 N.Y.S. 769, 165 Misc. 1, 1937 N.Y. Misc. LEXIS 1871 (N.Y. Mun. Ct. 1937).

The provisions of the former Gen. Corp. L. and of the former Stock Corp. L. making the secretary of state statutory agent for service of process on domestic and also on foreign corporations authorized to do business in New York superseded former Civil Practice Act provisions to the extent of conflict, but were to be read in conjunction with the latter to the extent that both could apply. Midvale Paper Board Co. v Cup Craft Paper Corp., 19 N.Y.S.2d 135, 173 Misc. 786, 1940 N.Y. Misc. LEXIS 1629 (N.Y. City Ct. 1940); Cohen v American Window Glass Co., 41 F. Supp. 48, 1941 U.S. Dist. LEXIS 2605 (D.N.Y. 1941), modified, 126 F.2d 111, 1942 U.S. App. LEXIS 4074 (2d Cir. N.Y. 1942).

Where service was not made upon the Secretary of State pursuant to statute until after limitations had run against the cause of action, the statute of limitations could be raised as a defense against the action notwithstanding a prior ineffective attempt to make personal service of the sums. Federspiel v R. J. & E. Corp., 34 Misc. 2d 44, 226 N.Y.S.2d 547, 1962 N.Y. Misc. LEXIS 3500 (N.Y. Sup. Ct. 1962).

Where a domestic corporation is served with process by serving the Secretary of State, default judgment taken against the corporation is subject to opening upon an adequate showing of meritorious defense and that the corporation never received copies of the process from the Secretary of State's office. Montulli v Sherlo Realty, Inc., 37 Misc. 2d 655, 234 N.Y.S.2d 754, 1962 N.Y. Misc. LEXIS 2145 (N.Y. Sup. Ct. 1962), aff'd, 18 A.D.2d 1139, 239 N.Y.S.2d 864, 1963 N.Y. App. Div. LEXIS 5482 (N.Y. App. Div. 4th Dep't 1963).

Service or process upon a domestic corporation by serving the Secretary of State is deemed personal service upon a designated agent under former § 228 of the Civil Practice Act and accordingly is not nullified by failure of the Secretary of State's office to mail the papers to the corporation. Montulli v Sherlo Realty, Inc., 37 Misc. 2d 655, 234 N.Y.S.2d 754, 1962 N.Y. Misc. LEXIS 2145 (N.Y. Sup. Ct.

1962), aff'd, 18 A.D.2d 1139, 239 N.Y.S.2d 864, 1963 N.Y. App. Div. LEXIS 5482 (N.Y. App. Div. 4th Dep't 1963).

Where the agent appointed to receive service of process died and no new agent had been appointed the federal district court in New York obtained jurisdiction where service was made on the secretary of state even though it was a foreign cause of action. Cohen v American Window Glass Co., 126 F.2d 111, 1942 U.S. App. LEXIS 4074 (2d Cir. N.Y. 1942).

§ 305. Registered agent for service of process

(a) In addition to such designation of the secretary of state, every domestic corporation or authorized foreign corporation may designate a registered agent in this state upon whom process against such corporation may be served. The agent shall be a natural person who is a resident of or has a business address in this state or a domestic corporation or foreign corporation of any type or kind formed, or authorized to do business in this state, under this chapter or under any other statute of this state.

(b) Any such designation of a registered agent may be made, revoked or changed as provided in this chapter.

(c) A registered agent may resign as such agent. A certificate, entitled "Certificate of resignation of registered agent of .... (name of designating corporation) under section 305 of the Business Corporation Law", shall be signed by him and delivered to the department of state. It shall set forth:

(1) That he resigns as registered agent for the designating corporation.

(2) The date the certificate of incorporation or the application for authority of the designating corporation was filed by the department of state.

(3) That he has sent a copy of the certificate of resignation by registered mail to the designating corporation at the post office address on file in the department of state specified for the mailing of process or if such address is the address of the registered agent, then to the office of the designating corporation in the jurisdiction of its formation or incorporation.

(d) The designation of a registered agent shall terminate thirty days after the filing by the department of state of a certificate of resignation or a certificate containing a revocation or change of the designation, whichever is filed earlier. A certificate designating a new registered agent may be delivered to the department of state by the corporation within the thirty days or thereafter.

History: Add, L 1961, ch 855, eff Sept 1, 1963; amd, L 1985, ch 131, § 1, eff May 28, 1985; L 1998, ch 375, § 4, eff Aug 13, 1998.

CASE ANNOTATIONS

Service upon attorney of respondent under rule of American Arbitration Association conferred jurisdiction upon court to vacate arbitrator's interim award and, complied with notice provisions of order to show cause to extent that it mandated "personal service" and such service also satisfied requirements of due process. Board of Education v Half Hollow Hills Teachers Asso. (1974) 79 Misc. 2d 223, 358 N.Y.S.2d 285, 87 BNA LRRM 2281

UNDER FORMER LAW

A New York corporation can maintain an action against a nonresident partnership where the partnership, under terms of a distributor franchise agreement, has appointed an agent for service of process in this state. Emerson Radio & Phonograph Corp. v Eskind (1957) 32 Misc. 2d 1038, 228 N.Y.S.2d 841

When a foreign corporation domesticated itself under § 24 of former Stock Corp. L. whereby it designated an agent for the service of process within this state, the Federal district court had jurisdiction of an action brought under the Federal Antitrust Laws though the defendant was served with process in another Federal district and even though the foreign corporation did no business in the district in which it was sued. Bertha Bldg. Corp. v National Theatres Corp. (1952, DC NY) 103 F. Supp. 712; Hintz v Austenal Laboratories, Inc. (1952, DC NY) 105 F. Supp. 187

§ 306. Service of process

(a) Service of process on a registered agent may be made in the manner provided by law for the service of a summons, as if the registered agent was a defendant.

(b) (1) Service of process on the secretary of state as agent of a domestic or authorized foreign corporation shall be made by personally delivering to and leaving with the secretary of state or a deputy, or with any person authorized by the secretary of state to receive such service, at the office of the department of state in the city of Albany, duplicate copies of such process together with the statutory fee, which fee shall be a taxable disbursement. Service of process on such corporation shall be complete when the secretary of state is so served. The secretary of state shall promptly send one of such copies by certified mail, return receipt requested, to such corporation, at the post office address, on file in the department of state, specified for the purpose. If a domestic or authorized foreign corporation has no such address on file in the department of state, the secretary of state shall so mail such copy, in the case of a domestic corporation, in care of any director named in its certificate of incorporation at the director's address stated therein or, in the case of an authorized foreign corporation, to such corporation at the address of its office within this state on file in the department.

(2) An additional service of the summons may be made pursuant to paragraph four of subdivision (f) of section thirty-two hundred fifteen of the civil practice law and rules.

(c) If an action or special proceeding is instituted in a court of limited jurisdiction, service of process may be made in the manner provided in this section if the office of the domestic or foreign corporation is within the territorial jurisdiction of the court.

(d) Nothing in this section shall affect the right to serve process in any other manner permitted by law.

History: Add, L 1961, ch 855, eff Sept 1, 1963; amd, L 1962, ch 834, § 7, eff Sept 1, 1963; L 1967, ch 17, eff Feb 28, 1967; L 1984, ch 93, § 1, eff Apr 24, 1984; L 1990, ch 419, § 1, eff Jan 1, 1991.

CASE ANNOTATIONS

1. In general
2. Jurisdictions
3. Foreign corporation
4. Meritorious defense
5. Service of process
6. Actual notice
7. Hearing
8. Proof of service
9. Avoidance of service
10. Failure to update filings
11. Under former law

1. In general

It was abuse of discretion and unduly harsh penalty for trial court, in contract action, to deny defendant's motion to vacate default judgment where defendants first notice of lawsuit occurred when it was served with levy on its property and where defendant had at all times had office and had been actively engaged in business in City of New York. Lang v French & Co., 48 A.D.2d 641, 368 N.Y.S.2d 25, 1975 N.Y. App. Div. LEXIS 9630 (N.Y. App. Div. 1st Dep't 1975).

In proceeding to enforce charging lien pursuant to CLS Jud § 475, court was not precluded from granting relief requested, even though corporate respondent (which was necessary party) had not been served with notice of petition and other papers, where service of process was made on Secretary of State under CLS Bus Corp § 306 as agent of corporate respondent, and, in any event, individual respondent, who was personally served with process, never moved to dismiss based on nonjoinder of necessary party. Rubin & Rothman v McNelis, 130 A.D.2d 643, 515 N.Y.S.2d 572, 1987 N.Y. App. Div. LEXIS 46658 (N.Y. App. Div. 2d Dep't 1987).

Failure to comply with CLS Bus Corp § 306 does not constitute "reasonable excuse" for corporation seeking to vacate its default under CLS CPLR § 5015(a)(1). Lawrence v Esplanade Gardens, 213 A.D.2d 216, 623 N.Y.S.2d 586, 1995 N.Y. App. Div. LEXIS 2761 (N.Y. App. Div. 1st Dep't 1995), reh'g denied, 1995 N.Y. App. Div. LEXIS 8578 (N.Y. App. Div. 1st Dep't Aug. 3, 1995).

Supreme court properly granted a corporation's motion to vacate its default in answering plaintiff's complaint provided that the answer did not include defenses predicated upon lack of personal jurisdiction and the statute of limitations, and denied the motion dismiss the complaint pursuant to N.Y. C.P.L.R. 3211(a)(8), because although the corporation maintained that it never received notice of the commencement of plaintiff's action to recover damages for assault, service was complete upon delivery of process to the State Secretary of State pursuant to N.Y. Bus. Corp. Law § 306(b)(1) and payment of the appropriate fee. Perkins v 686 Halsey Food Corp., 36 A.D.3d 881, 829 N.Y.S.2d 185, 2007 NY Slip Op 620, 2007 N.Y. App. Div. LEXIS 972 (N.Y. App. Div. 2d Dep't 2007).

Service of appearance ticket on Secretary of State under CLS Bus Corp § 306 satisfies requirements of CLS CPL § 600.10(1) for securing attendance of corporation for purposes of commencement of criminal action, and otherwise satisfies due process requirements. People v New York Paving, Inc.,, 155 Misc. 2d 934, 591 N.Y.S.2d 318, 1992 N.Y. Misc. LEXIS 526 (N.Y. City Crim. Ct. 1992).

Landlord was entitled to a default judgment against a tenant because it was uncontradicted that the landlord served the tenant pursuant to N.Y. Bus. Corp. Law § 306, and that service was complete when the landlord provided an authorized agent of the Secretary of the state of New York with a copy of the summons and complaint; under § 306 the tenant had 30 days to appear in the action and failed to do so.360 Motor Parkway, LLC v Mortgage Zone, Inc., 887 N.Y.S.2d 419, 2009 NY Slip Op 29378, 25 Misc. 3d 971, 2009 N.Y. Misc. LEXIS 2349 (N.Y. Sup. Ct. 2009).

Where a supplier did not substantiate its claim that the dissolved corporation operated as a de facto corporation under N.Y. Bus. Law §§ 1005(a)(2), 1006(a), (b), a judicial hearing officer properly set aside the N.Y. Bus. Corp. Law § 306 service on the Secretary of State; where the dissolved corporation only sought vacatur of a default judgment and leave to serve an answer pursuant to N.Y. C.P.L.R. 5015, the trial court properly granted the relief sought. Bruce Supply Corp. v New Wave Mech., Inc., 4 A.D.3d 444, 773 N.Y.S.2d 408, 2004 N.Y. App. Div. LEXIS 1725 (N.Y. App. Div. 2d Dep't 2004).

Under New York practice, service on a New York corporation can be made by simply serving the Secretary of State, and a domestic corporation is subject to such service in the state regardless of where in the state its principal place of business is located. Chilean Line, Inc. v United States, 344 F.2d 757, 1965 U.S. App. LEXIS 5778 (2d Cir. N.Y. 1965).

Assignee of leasehold may not recover under NY Real P Actions & Pr Law § 853, where assignee claimed that owner unconstitutionally obtained default judgment against assignor by serving assignor pursuant to NY Bus Corp Law § 306 while knowing that assignor's address listed with Secretary of State was incorrect and owner knew assignor's true address, because present action is untimely since it was filed more than three years after termination of prior action by owner to terminate lease, which occurred when U.S. Second Circuit affirmed refusal to overturn default judgment, and therefore NY CPLR § 205(a) would not act to toll statute of limitations. Baker v Latham Sparrowbush Assoc., 808 F. Supp. 981, 1992 U.S. Dist. LEXIS 3534 (S.D.N.Y. 1992).

Negligence action need not be remanded to New York State Supreme Court, even though plaintiff served Secretary of State with summons and complaint pursuant to CLS Bus Corp Law § 306(b) on June 20 and defendant did not file notice of removal until July 22, because defendant did not receive pleadings at its office until June 26, when 30-day removal period began to run. Medina v Wal-Mart Stores, 945 F. Supp. 519, 1996 U.S. Dist. LEXIS 16907 (W.D.N.Y. 1996).

Requirement of second mailing under CLS CPLR § 3215(g) is not jurisdictional in nature, but rather is protective measure specific to New York courts, designed to provide notice to corporations and to prevent unnecessary defaults. I.L.G.W.U. Nat'l Retirement Fund v Meredith Grey, Inc., 986 F. Supp. 816, 1997 U.S. Dist. LEXIS 19489 (S.D.N.Y. 1997).

2. Jurisdiction

Where plaintiff successfully established a cause of action under § 404 of the Uniform District Court Act, § 306(c) of the Business Corporation Law did not limit the jurisdiction of the District Court to effect personal jurisdiction on a corporate defendant by service upon the Secretary of State. 146-150 West Sunrise Highway Corp. v Lee's Hobby Speedway, Inc., 54 Misc. 2d 913, 283 N.Y.S.2d 790, 1967 N.Y. Misc. LEXIS 1260 (N.Y. Dist. Ct. 1967).

Provisions of the Business Corporation Law authorizing service of process on the Secretary of State do not extend the territorial jurisdiction of a city court outside the City of New York but merely provide an alternative method of service since, if the requirements are met, personal service could be made upon such defendant directly. O'Rourke v Ted's Ford, Inc., 89 Misc. 2d 986, 393 N.Y.S.2d 160, 1977 N.Y. Misc. LEXIS 2755 (N.Y. City Ct. 1977).

Territorial limitations upon service of summons contained the Uniform City Court Act and the Constitution with respect to city courts outside of the City of New York do not prohibit the domestic and foreign corporations from consenting to other means of acquiring jurisdiction, such as service upon the Secretary of State, even though such consent is required as a precondition for doing business in the state. O'Rourke v Ted's Ford, Inc., 89 Misc. 2d 986, 393 N.Y.S.2d 160, 1977 N.Y. Misc. LEXIS 2755 (N.Y. City Ct. 1977).

In order for city court outside the City of New York to obtain jurisdiction, the complaint must show that the corporate defendant has an office within the court's territorial jurisdiction and the summons must state that the action is within the court's jurisdiction. O'Rourke v Ted's Ford, Inc., 89 Misc. 2d 986, 393 N.Y.S.2d 160, 1977 N.Y. Misc. LEXIS 2755 (N.Y. City Ct. 1977).

Service of process on Secretary of State in Albany pursuant to CLS Bus Corp § 306(c) did not confer jurisdiction over nonappearing defendant corporation in Watertown City Court; CLS NY Const Art VI § 1(c), which excludes state-wide jurisdiction for City Courts outside New York City, limits process of Watertown City Court to Jefferson County or adjoining counties. United Communs. Corp. v 1st Tee, Inc., 179 Misc. 2d 896, 686 N.Y.S.2d 679, 1999 N.Y. Misc. LEXIS 71 (N.Y. City Ct. 1999).

3. Foreign corporation

In an action brought by a longshoreman against the foreign owner of a vessel on which he was working when injured, service on an officer of a New York corporation that was claimed to have been the agent for the foreign corporate owner would be ineffective where the New York corporation had not born any relationship to the foreign corporation and had not been under any obligation to transmit notice of service to it, despite the fact that the New York corporation had claimed that it had transmitted notice of service to the foreign corporation. De Candia v Hudson Waterways, Inc., 89 A.D.2d 506, 452 N.Y.S.2d 196, 1982 N.Y. App. Div. LEXIS 17542 (N.Y. App. Div. 1st Dep't 1982).

Personal jurisdiction was obtained over defendant foreign corporation, which was authorized to do business in state, even though service was effected under CLS Bus Corp § 307 which provides for method of service on foreign corporations not authorized to do business in state since (1) provisions of CLS CPLR § 311(1) regarding service on corporations are to be liberally construed, (2) process was delivered to proper person and at proper place for service on Secretary of State, (3) defendant received copy of process via registered mail with return receipt requested, and (4) only difference between method of service employed and mandated method of service was identity of person who actually placed defendant's copy of process in mail. Marine Midland Realty Credit Corp. v Welbilt Corp., 145 A.D.2d 84, 537 N.Y.S.2d 669, 1989 N.Y. App. Div. LEXIS 1249 (N.Y. App. Div. 3d Dep't 1989).

Order which denied defendant's motion to dismiss summons with notice affirmed–service on foreign corporation unauthorized to do business in New York in accordance with Business Corporation Law § 306, which is applicable to domestic corporations and foreign corporations authorized to do business in New York, is sufficient to invoke court's jurisdiction; summons with notice was personally served on Secretary of State at her office in Albany, which constituted literal compliance with jurisdictional requirements of CPLR 311 (1), which allows for personal service on corporation by delivering summons to agent authorized by law to receive service; process was delivered to proper person at proper place for service on Secretary of State, and defendant received copy of process via registered mail with return receipt requested albeit mailing was initiated by Secretary rather than by plaintiff or someone on his behalf, as required by Business Corporation Law § 307, which is applicable to unauthorized foreign corporations; since defendant received actual notice of action and suffered no prejudice by reason of plaintiff's method of service, omissions herein were mere irregularities that fail to deprive court of jurisdiction. Flick v Stewart-Warner Corp., 151 A.D.2d 823, 542 N.Y.S.2d 407, 1989 N.Y. App. Div. LEXIS 7144 (N.Y. App. Div. 3d Dep't 1989), rev'd, 76 N.Y.2d 50, 556 N.Y.S.2d 510, 555 N.E.2d 907, 1990 N.Y. LEXIS 1066 (N.Y. 1990).

4. Meritorious defense

Judgment and amended judgment which assessed damages in favor of plaintiffs affirmed–plaintiff fell when basement door located on defendant's construction site gave way beneath her, causing her to suffer serious personal injuries; service was effected pursuant to Business Corporation Law § 306 by delivering summons and complaint to Secretary of State; defendant never received notice of lawsuit and default judgment was entered, with damages to be assessed at future trial; shortly thereafter, defendant moved to vacate default judgment; finding meritorious defense lacking, Supreme Court denied motion, without prejudice to renewal; inquest was held and it was stipulated that plaintiff would make herself available to be examined by defendant regarding circumstances surrounding happening of accident; that examination was conducted, and Supreme Court determined that plaintiff's damages, reduced by one third for her contributory negligence, were $50,000–Supreme Court did not abuse its discretion in denying defendant's motion to vacate default judgment; meritorious defense has not been set forth. Wilcox v Parkland Dev. Corp., 157 A.D.2d 998, 550 N.Y.S.2d 478, 1990 N.Y. App. Div. LEXIS 552 (N.Y. App. Div. 3d Dep't 1990).

Order which granted defendant's motion to vacate default judgment entered against it affirmed–plaintiff was allegedly injured at restaurant when stereo speaker that was suspended overhead fell on him; plaintiff sued defendant restaurant owner and codefendants, parties that allegedly furnished, installed and maintained speaker; complaint alleges that defendant and codefendants were negligent in failing to adequately install, inspect and maintain speaker and in failing to warn customers of restaurant of dangerous condition; plaintiff effectuated service on defendant pursuant to Business Corporation Law § 306 by serving Secretary of State; Secretary of State mailed summons and complaint to defendant's designated corporate address, but letter was returned "unclaimed"; defendant never answered or appeared in action and plaintiff obtained default judgment in March 1989; defendant contends that it was unaware that plaintiff had commenced action until March 1989, when it was served with summons and cross claim by codefendants; in support of its motion to vacate default judgment, defendant's president averred that he had never received notice of original action and default was unintentional; defendant submitted affidavits stating that codefendants owned speaker that fell and were responsible for installing and maintaining it; it was averred that speaker had never come loose before and that defendant "did not install or maintain the speaker, did not control same, and had no prior knowledge that the speaker might pose a problem"–general rule is that owner who hires independent contractor to do work is not liable for contractor's negligence which causes injury to third parties; whether exception applies which imposed nondelegable duty upon defendant will depend on several factors, such as whether work at issue could be characterized as inherently dangerous in nature; facts do not support only conclusion that nondelegable duty existed in this case; nor is fact that there was no specific allegation that defendant's employees inspected speaker fatal since there is no evidence to indicate that such inspection would have disclosed that speaker's support was defective; thus, defendant's averments set forth potentially meritorious defense sufficient to entitle it to vacatur of default judgment. Hermance v Daddy-O's Restaurant Corp., 159 A.D.2d 924, 553 N.Y.S.2d 239, 1990 N.Y. App. Div. LEXIS 3576 (N.Y. App. Div. 3d Dep't 1990).

Where address of defendant, which had applied to commissioners of State Insurance Fund for workmen's compensation insurance, was inadvertently not updated and therefore defendant never received notice of lawsuit by commissioners to recover difference in premiums based on reclassification, defendant acted promptly to move to vacate default judgment, and controversy on its face articulated meritorious defense as to whether floating dry dock painted by defendant was a "dry-dock" or a "vessel" for workmen's compensation insurance purposes, adequate excuse and meritorious defense were presented and thus vacatur of default was providently granted. Commissioners of State Ins. Fund v Atlantic Sandblasting Service, Inc., 58 A.D.2d 751, 396 N.Y.S.2d 224, 1977 N.Y. App. Div. LEXIS 12893 (N.Y. App. Div. 1st Dep't 1977).

The trial court improperly denied defendant's motion to vacate a default judgment that had occurred as the result of defendant's agent's failure to notify the Secretary of State of a change of address, where service had been effected on the Secretary of State, in that, pursuant to CPLR § 317, a person so served is permitted to defend the action within one year after he obtains knowledge of entry of judgment, provided that the court finds that he did not personally receive notice of the summons in time to defend and has a meritorious defense; moreover, in light of a previous Civil Court proceeding, plaintiff's assertion that he did not know of any other address at which defendant could be served personally was unpersuasive, particularly in view of the lack of any attempt either to secure an appearance on behalf of defendant from its prior attorneys, or to obtain information from them as to where personal service could be effected. Seijas v Rawhide Ranch, Inc., 99 A.D.2d 739, 472 N.Y.S.2d 385, 1984 N.Y. App. Div. LEXIS 17103 (N.Y. App. Div. 1st Dep't 1984).

In a personal injury action arising from an incident in which plaintiff, an elderly man, allegedly slipped and fell on premises under defendant's control, defendant's motion, under CPLR § 317, to vacate a default entered by plaintiff and for leave to interpose an answer to the complaint was improperly denied where defendant showed that he did not personally receive notice of the pending lawsuit in time to defend it, in that process was served pursuant to Bus Corp Law § 306 at an incorrect address, and where defendant appeared to have a meritorious defense to the action. Winters v Albany Executive House Apartments, Inc., 102 A.D.2d 985, 477 N.Y.S.2d 794, 1984 N.Y. App. Div. LEXIS 19228 (N.Y. App. Div. 3d Dep't 1984).

Corporate defendant was entitled to vacatur of default judgment entered against it on ground that service was never received where notice sent by Secretary of State to defendant's designated corporate address was returned marked "unclaimed," defendant did not occupy premises to which notice was sent and in fact did not receive notice, plaintiff was aware of defendant's actual address, there was no showing that default was deliberate or intentional, and defendant raised prima facie meritorious defense; defendant's lack of reasonable excuse for not maintaining correct address with Secretary of State did not preclude relief under CLS CPLR § 317. Pabone v Jon-Bar Enterprises Corp., 140 A.D.2d 872, 528 N.Y.S.2d 912, 1988 N.Y. App. Div. LEXIS 5331 (N.Y. App. Div. 3d Dep't 1988).

Parties who failed to allege facts sufficient to demonstrate meritorious defense were not entitled to vacatur of judgment of foreclosure and sale although it was uncontroverted that they did not receive notice of summons and complaint in time to defend action following service on Secretary of State pursuant to CLS Bus Corp § 306. Halali v Gabbay, 223 A.D.2d 623, 636 N.Y.S.2d 838, 1996 N.Y. App. Div. LEXIS 420 (N.Y. App. Div. 2d Dep't 1996).

Trial court erred in granting an LLC's N.Y. C.P.L.R. 317 motion to vacate a default judgment because, although the LLC met its burden of showing that it did not receive actual notice of the summons, which was served on the Secretary of State, in time to defend, the LLC failed to submit competent evidence to demonstrate the existence of a potentially meritorious defense to plaintiff's N.Y. Lab. Law § 240(1) personal injury action. Thakurdyal v 341 Scholes St., LLC, 50 A.D.3d 889, 855 N.Y.S.2d 641, 2008 NY Slip Op 3447, 2008 N.Y. App. Div. LEXIS 3378 (N.Y. App. Div. 2d Dep't 2008).

5. Service of process

Under provisions of subd b of above statute, service upon corporation is complete when Secretary of State is served in accordance with such subdivision and such a corporation's failure to receive duplicate copy of summons and complaint mailed to it by such Secretary in and of itself and without excuse, does not furnish a ground for opening a default judgment against it; where it is clear that corporation's failure to receive notice was through its own fault or design since envelope containing it was mailed to address listed in certificate of incorporation there is no valid reason for opening the default in the absence of any meritorious defense. Cascione v Acme Equipment Corp., 23 A.D.2d 49, 258 N.Y.S.2d 234, 1965 N.Y. App. Div. LEXIS 4432 (N.Y. App. Div. 1st Dep't 1965).

Where the method of service of process, chosen by the plaintiff was not authorized, it was invalid. Rosman v Clark, 27 A.D.2d 839, 278 N.Y.S.2d 39, 1967 N.Y. App. Div. LEXIS 4729 (N.Y. App. Div. 2d Dep't 1967).

Where plaintiff in action to recover commissions served summons with notice upon Secretary of State, but due to staff error, summons was not mailed to corporate defendant, defendant's default was excusable, and trial court did not err in vacating default judgment. Micarelli v Regal Apparel, Ltd., 52 A.D.2d 524, 381 N.Y.S.2d 511, 1976 N.Y. App. Div. LEXIS 12053 (N.Y. App. Div. 1st Dep't 1976).

In action to recover commissions, service of process was complete when Secretary of State was served, and court acquired jurisdiction, even though summons was not forwarded to corporate defendant. Micarelli v Regal Apparel, Ltd., 52 A.D.2d 524, 381 N.Y.S.2d 511, 1976 N.Y. App. Div. LEXIS 12053 (N.Y. App. Div. 1st Dep't 1976).

Special Term erred in dismissing petition brought against corporation for failure of service, even though petitioner failed to serve corporation's principal officer, since petitioner achieved service within allotted time by serving Secretary of State pursuant to CLS CPLR § 311 and CLS Bus Corp § 306. Anthony v New York City Loft Bd., 122 A.D.2d 725, 511 N.Y.S.2d 600, 1986 N.Y. App. Div. LEXIS 59259 (N.Y. App. Div. 1st Dep't 1986).

Service on corporation by delivery of process to Secretary of State is not personal delivery to corporation or agent designated under CLS CPLR § 318; for purposes of statute, personal delivery is defined as "in-hand" delivery. Fleetwood Park Corp. v Jerrick Waterproofing Co., 203 A.D.2d 238, 615 N.Y.S.2d 695, 1994 N.Y. App. Div. LEXIS 3196 (N.Y. App. Div. 2d Dep't 1994).

Plaintiff did not obtain personal jurisdiction over "Olliver's Restaurant Corporation" by serving Secretary of State with summons and complaint on which defendant's name was misspelled and misstated as "Oliver's Restaurant, Inc." where defendant's attorney affirmed that separate corporation with misstated name was registered with Secretary of State. Pereira v Oliver's Restaurant, Inc., 260 A.D.2d 358, 687 N.Y.S.2d 704, 1999 N.Y. App. Div. LEXIS 3649 (N.Y. App. Div. 2d Dep't 1999).

Service was properly effectuated upon a corporation in an underlying action when a pedestrian delivered a copy of the summons and verified complaint to the New York Secretary of State under N.Y. Bus. Corp. Law § 306(b)(1) and N.Y. C.P.L.R. 3215(g)(4). Konig v Hermitage Ins. Co., 93 A.D.3d 643, 940 N.Y.S.2d 116, 2012 NY Slip Op 1659, 2012 N.Y. App. Div. LEXIS 1662 (N.Y. App. Div. 2d Dep't 2012).

After a youth club received 461 notices of violation (NOVs) issued by the New York City Environmental Control Board for posting handbills, the trial court erred in denying the club's petition with respect to 230 challenged NOVs because the affidavits of service with respect to the 230 challenged NOVs did not demonstrate that any of the NOVs was served by certified mail and no indication that delivery of the mailings was restricted to the club. Matter of New York Youth Club v New York City Envtl. Control Bd., 131 A.D.3d 615, 2015 NY Slip Op 06592, 2015 NY Slip Op 06592, 2015 NY Slip Op 6592, 2015 NY Slip Op 6592, 15 N.Y.S.3d 199, 2015 N.Y. App. Div. LEXIS 6464 (N.Y. App. Div. 2d Dep't 2015).

Plaintiff's motion for summary judgment in lieu of complaint seeking to enforce a Florida default judgment was properly denied, even though the trial court erred in requiring proof of personal jurisdiction in the Florida action, because defendants were served under N.Y. Bus. Corp. Law § 306 and an affidavit of the additional service required by N.Y. C.P.L.R. 3215 was not filed. TCA Global

Credit Master Fund, L.P. v Puresafe Water Sys., Inc., 151 A.D.3d 1098, 2017 NY Slip Op 05259, 2017 NY Slip Op 5259, 2017 N.Y. App. Div. LEXIS 5178 (N.Y. App. Div. 2d Dep't 2017).

Trial court properly granted the plaintiffs' motion to add the law firm as an additional defendant because the record included an affidavit of service from a process server indicating that service upon the law firm was effected by delivery of the original summons and complaint to the Secretary of State, which created a presumption of proper service on the law firm and the law firm did not submit any evidence to rebut this prima facie showing of proper service. Josephs v AACT Fast Collections Servs., Inc., 155 A.D.3d 1010, 66 N.Y.S.3d 17, 2017 N.Y. App. Div. LEXIS 8444 (N.Y. App. Div. 2d Dep't 2017).

Although there is no specific provision in the NYC Civil Ct Act authorizing the service of process beyond the territorial jurisdiction of that court, service of process upon the Secretary of State, pursuant to Bus Corp Law § 306 would be sufficient to confer jurisdiction over a domestic corporation sued in that court, since NYC Civil Ct Act § 403 has been interpreted as authorizing just such service. Boston Old Colony Ins. Co. v Tanya Casuals, Ltd., 121 Misc. 2d 734, 468 N.Y.S.2d 838, 1983 N.Y. Misc. LEXIS 3993 (N.Y. Civ. Ct. 1983).

Service upon Secretary of State was effective to subject defendants to jurisdiction of Civil Court of New York City, New York County, in action for earned insurance premiums even though defendants had moved their place of business from New York County to Westchester County prior to service since office designated in defendants' certificate of incorporation was care of attorneys in New York County and office need not be placed where business activities are conducted. Fireman's Fund Ins. Co. v Kashmir Krafts, Inc., 131 Misc. 2d 338, 500 N.Y.S.2d 604, 1986 N.Y. Misc. LEXIS 2394 (N.Y. Civ. Ct. 1986).

Defendant corporation was entitled to vacatur of default judgment pursuant to CLS CPLR § 317 where plaintiff served Secretary of State with process after defendant failed to return signed acknowledgment admitting service by mail pursuant to CLS CPLR § 312-a, and Secretary of State mailed summons and complaint to defendant's former address rather than its new address, since (1) service under § 312-a by certified mail rather than by required "first class mail" was defective, (2) fact that someone signed certified mail return receipt on behalf of defendant did not cure defective service, (3) service of process on Secretary of State did not constitute "personal delivery" on defendant for purposes of § 317, and (4) defendant did not receive process in time to oppose plaintiff's motion for default judgment. Miron Lumber Co. v Phylco Realty Dev. Co., 151 Misc. 2d 139, 572 N.Y.S.2d 992, 1991 N.Y. Misc. LEXIS 362 (N.Y. Civ. Ct. 1991).

CLS Bus Corp § 306(c), which in courts of limited jurisdiction permits substituted service on Secretary of State with respect to corporations within territorial jurisdiction of court, permitted substituted service to acquire jurisdiction in New York City Civil Court action over corporation not located within city for cause of action for conversion occurring within city where long-arm provisions of CLS NYC Civil Ct Act § 404 were satisfied, since CLS NYC Civil Ct Act § 404(b) provides that service may be made in same manner as that which would confer jurisdiction on Supreme Court in like case, and if instant action had been maintained in Supreme Court plaintiff could have served Secretary of State under CLS Bus Corp § 306(b). Woodbury Automotive Warehouse, Inc. v Island Speed Auto Supplies, Inc., 155 Misc. 2d 381, 588 N.Y.S.2d 536, 1992 N.Y. Misc. LEXIS 416 (N.Y. Civ. Ct. 1992).

Service by ordinary mail of administrative summons alleging that petitioner, licensed owner, allowed its for-hire vehicles to operate while overdue for inspection did not violate NYC Charter § 2303(c), which provides that notice of violation issued by New York City Taxi and Limousine Commission (TLC) must be served in same manner as summons in plenary action, since service under § 2303(c) requires such service only when agency seeks to enter decision or order imposing civil penalties as judgment in civil court, without court proceedings, for violations as to unlicensed vehicles or drivers for-hire, and since owner was licensed by TLC, such provision was inapplicable. Humming Bird Car Serv. v New York City Taxi & Limousine Comm'n, 184 Misc. 2d 146, 706 N.Y.S.2d 850, 2000 N.Y. Misc. LEXIS 90 (N.Y. Sup. Ct. 2000), aff'd, 286 A.D.2d 654, 731 N.Y.S.2d 356, 2001 N.Y. App. Div. LEXIS 8844 (N.Y. App. Div. 1st Dep't 2001).

Where an assignor was properly served under N.Y. Bus. Corp. Law § 306 with a summons and complaint, despite the misstatement of its name, a motion court was not deprived of jurisdiction; as a result, an assignee had no demonstrable defense to a foreclosure action by another lender. Household Fin. Realty Corp. v Emanuel, 2

A.D.3d 192, 769 N.Y.S.2d 511, 2003 N.Y. App. Div. LEXIS 12996 (N.Y. App. Div. 1st Dep't 2003).

6. Actual notice

Defendant's motion to vacate a default judgment was granted, where it was undisputed that defendant was served pursuant to Bus Corp Law § 306 and never received the summons and complaint, where the affidavit of defendant's president established the existence of a meritorious defense, and where plaintiff's contention that defendant failed to demonstrate a reasonable excuse for not filing a change of address with the Secretary of State was irrelevant, for while defendant's failure to demonstrate such excuse would preclude relief pursuant to CPLR § 5015, it would not preclude relief pursuant to CPLR § 317. Meyer v Chas. Fisher & Sons Dental Laboratory, Inc., 90 A.D.2d 889, 456 N.Y.S.2d 520, 1982 N.Y. App. Div. LEXIS 19158 (N.Y. App. Div. 3d Dep't 1982).

Defendant corporation failed to show that it did not receive actual notice of summons in time to defend action where plaintiffs effected service on defendant in 1992 by delivering 2 copies of summons and complaint to Secretary of State, defendant did not contend that address on file with Secretary of State was incorrect, and defendant did not rebut plaintiffs' evidence that copies of summons and complaint were delivered in 1992 to defendant at its business address in Brooklyn. Rivera v 999 Realty Mgmt., 246 A.D.2d 637, 666 N.Y.S.2d 962, 1998 N.Y. App. Div. LEXIS 606 (N.Y. App. Div. 2d Dep't 1998).

In a proceeding instituted against a domestic corporation pursuant to article 7 of the Real Property Actions and Proceedings Law, section 735 of which requires that service of the notice of petition and petition be made "by personally delivering them to the respondent", service of a summons with notice on the Secretary of State, as statutory agent of the domestic corporation (Business Corporation Law, § 306), is insufficient to obtain jurisdiction of the corporation. Puteoli Realty Corp. v Mr. D's Fontana di Trevi Restaurant, Inc., 95 Misc. 2d 108, 407 N.Y.S.2d 118, 1978 N.Y. Misc. LEXIS 2390 (N.Y. Dist. Ct. 1978).

Corporate defendant was entitled to have criminal default judgment vacated on ground that it did not receive actual notice of prosecution until after judgment was entered against it, even though failure to receive notice was due in part to its own negligent failure to keep current corporate address on file with Secretary of State, since (1) there was no evidence that corporation's failure to receive notice was result of deliberate attempt to avoid notice, and (2) method of service chosen by People was not most direct or reliable means of assuring actual notice to corporation. People v Sage Realty Corp., 155 Misc. 2d 832, 590 N.Y.S.2d 660, 1992 N.Y. Misc. LEXIS 508 (N.Y. City Crim. Ct. 1992).

Defendants' failure to receive summons served under CLS Bus Corp § 306(b)(1) was not sufficient excuse to vacate default judgment against them in action for breach of commercial lease, attorney's fees, brokerage commissions and re-rental expenses. 342 Madison Ave. Assocs. v Suzuki Assocs., 187 Misc. 2d 488, 722 N.Y.S.2d 729, 2001 N.Y. Misc. LEXIS 58 (N.Y. Sup. Ct. 2001).

7. Hearing

A corporate defendant was entitled to a hearing on its motion for relief from default where plaintiff had served the summons and complaint on the Secretary of State, the Secretary of State sent the papers to defendant's address but the papers had been returned unclaimed, defendant did business at that address but claimed it had not received the papers, and there was no showing as to whether defendant had received notice by certified mail of the papers. Rifenburg v Liffiton Homes, Inc., 107 A.D.2d 1015, 486 N.Y.S.2d 529, 1985 N.Y. App. Div. LEXIS 42827 (N.Y. App. Div. 4th Dep't 1985).

8. Proof of service

In an action alleging medical malpractice, personal jurisdiction was not obtained over a corporate defendant whose principal denied that he had been personally served by a sheriff in Louisiana and claimed that he had found the summons and complaint on the desk in his office, since the denial shifted the burden of proof to plaintiffs, who chose to rely on the sheriff's affidavits, which were devoid of factual detail, and were thus insufficient to rebut the denial, since delivery of process to one of the corporation's employees, together with a subsequent mailing, failed to satisfy the requirements of CPLR § 308(2), and since CPLR § 313 requires that service outside the state be effected in the same manner as service within the state, and plaintiffs failed to show compliance with either CPLR § 311(1), in that there was no evidence establishing that the summons and complaint had been served upon any individual authorized to receive service on the corporation's behalf, or Bus Corp Law § 306, in that there was no allegation that the summons and complaint had been served upon the Secretary of State or the corporation's registered agent, notwithstanding the fact that the corporation had clearly received actual notice of the suit. De Zego v Bruhn, 99 A.D.2d 823, 472 N.Y.S.2d 414, 1984 N.Y. App. Div. LEXIS 17226 (N.Y. App. Div. 2d Dep't 1984), app. dismissed, 63 N.Y.2d 770, 1984 N.Y. LEXIS 5979 (N.Y. 1984), aff'd, 67 N.Y.2d 875, 501 N.Y.S.2d 801, 492 N.E.2d 1217, 1986 N.Y. LEXIS 17664 (N.Y. 1986).

Affidavit evidencing service upon corporation by service on Secretary of State, which was not controverted by sworn denial or otherwise, was sufficient proof of service and thus corporation's affirmative defense alleging lack of personal jurisdiction should have been stricken on plaintiff's motion. Del Priore v Furnival Machinery Co., 124 A.D.2d 695, 508 N.Y.S.2d 206, 1986 N.Y. App. Div. LEXIS 62002 (N.Y. App. Div. 2d Dep't 1986).

Court would vacate and set aside default in action against corporation for goods sold and delivered where corporation, by affidavit of its officer, established that it was never served with copy of summons and complaint by office of Secretary of State pursuant to CLS Bus Corp § 306, no return receipt or other proof of service by Secretary of State was produced, and corporation set forth colorable defense as to certain amounts claimed to have been due and owing to plaintiff. Charmer Industries, Inc. v 71 Grand Liquor Corp., 128 A.D.2d 825, 513 N.Y.S.2d 747, 1987 N.Y. App. Div. LEXIS 44518 (N.Y. App. Div. 2d Dep't 1987).

Defendants in personal injury action were entitled to vacatur of their default in appearing, even though plaintiffs claimed to have effected service of process on corporate defendant under CLS Bus Corp § 306 and on individual defendant under CLS Veh & Tr § 254, where record contained no affidavits of service, defendants showed that neither received copy of summons or complaint in time to defend action, and accident report containing admission by plaintiffs proper affidavit of merit. Aloi v Firebird Freight Serv. Corp., 251 A.D.2d 608, 675 N.Y.S.2d 107, 1998 N.Y. App. Div. LEXIS 7976 (N.Y. App. Div. 2d Dep't 1998).

Service on domestic corporation under CLS Bus Corp § 306(b) was not shown where corporation established that it did not receive process, there was no indication in record that plaintiff served Secretary of State in conformance with § 306(b), and it was apparent that plaintiff's papers had been returned to him by Department of State because they were served by mail and were not accompanied by mandatory fee. Strong v Bi-Lo Wholesalers, 265 A.D.2d 745, 698 N.Y.S.2d 738, 1999 N.Y. App. Div. LEXIS 10938 (N.Y. App. Div. 3d Dep't 1999).

Order granting those branches of a corporation's cross-motion to vacate its default in appearing or answering the complaint and for leave to serve and file a late answer was improper because the denial of service by the corporation's president was insufficient to rebut the presumption of proper service on the Secretary of State raised by the affidavit of service; furthermore, the affirmation of the corporation's attorney that there was an incorrect address for service of process on file with the Secretary of State did not constitute a reasonable excuse for the corporation's delay in appearing or answering the complaint. Further, the corporation did not adequately rebut the presumption that it received notice of the summons approximately two weeks after service of the summons and the complaint in the regular course of the mail. Levine v Forgotson's Cent. Auto & Elec., Inc., 41 A.D.3d 552, 840 N.Y.S.2d 598, 2007 NY Slip Op 5232, 2007 N.Y. App. Div. LEXIS 7426 (N.Y. App. Div. 2d Dep't 2007).

In a breach of contract action, a corporation was not entitled to have a default judgment vacated pursuant to N.Y. C.P.L.R. § 317 because service was made on the Secretary of State pursuant to N.Y. Bus. Corp. Law § 306 and the corporation's uncorroborated denial of timely receipt of notice by mail at its current address did not overcome the presumption of timely delivery. Brightly v Florida N., Inc., 54 A.D.3d 1127, 863 N.Y.S.2d 842, 2008 NY Slip Op 6920, 2008 N.Y. App. Div. LEXIS 6755 (N.Y. App. Div. 3d Dep't 2008).

Trial court properly denied defendant's motion for relief from a default judgment because plaintiff submitted proof of service of the summons and complaint, proof of the facts constituting the claim, and proof of defendant's default, and defendant's unsubstantiated denial of receipt of the summons and complaint served through the Secretary of State did not amount to a reasonable excuse for its default. Jing Shan Chen v R & K 51 Realty, Inc., 148 A.D.3d 689, 2017 N.Y. Slip Op 01541, 2017 NY Slip Op 1541, 48 N.Y.S.3d 474, 2017 N.Y. App. Div. LEXIS 1523 (N.Y. App. Div. 2d Dep't 2017).

9. Avoidance of service

Court properly denied corporate defendant's motion to vacate default judgment under CLS CPLR §§ 317 and 5015 on ground that it did not receive copies of process served on Secretary of State pursuant to CLS Bus Corp § 306 since corporation had failed to apprise Secretary of State of its current address for more than 10 months although it was on notice that incorrect address was on file by virtue of its previous successful motion to vacate default judgment against it on same ground; under circumstances, it could be inferred that corporation was deliberately attempting to avoid receiving notice of summons. Paul Conte Cadillac, Inc. v C.A.R.S. Purchasing Service, Inc., 126 A.D.2d 621, 511 N.Y.S.2d 58, 1987 N.Y. App. Div. LEXIS 41754 (N.Y. App. Div. 2d Dep't 1987).

Although failure of corporation to comply with CLS Bus Corp § 306 does not preclude vacatur of default judgment under CLS CPLR § 317, relief was not warranted where corporation deliberately attempted to avoid notice of action for 2 ½ years after it received actual notice of plaintiff's accident and of identity of plaintiff's counsel. Lawrence v Esplanade Gardens, 213 A.D.2d 216, 623 N.Y.S.2d 586, 1995 N.Y. App. Div. LEXIS 2761 (N.Y. App. Div. 1st Dep't 1995), reh'g denied, 1995 N.Y. App. Div. LEXIS 8578 (N.Y. App. Div. 1st Dep't Aug. 3, 1995).

Defendant was not entitled to relief from default judgment under CLS CPLR § 317 where plaintiff showed that at least 5 months before commencement of action, defendant was placed on notice that address on file with Secretary of State was not correct, and defendant did not notify Secretary of State of its purported change of address. Santiago v Sansue Realty Corp., 243 A.D.2d 622, 663 N.Y.S.2d 235, 1997 N.Y. App. Div. LEXIS 10239 (N.Y. App. Div. 2d Dep't 1997).

10. Failure to update filings

Defendant was entitled to vacation of a default judgment in an action by the Secretary of State, where defendant's excuse for the default was its unintentional failure to provide the Secretary of State with its new office address, making it impossible for the Secretary to forward a copy of the summons and complaint, and where defendant's papers indicated that it may have had a meritorious defense to the action; however, as a condition for vacating the default, defendant would be required to pay $250.00 costs to the Secretary for the inconvenience caused by the delay. Reid v Ron Delsener Enterprises, Ltd., 84 A.D.2d 712, 444 N.Y.S.2d 9, 1981 N.Y. App. Div. LEXIS 15866 (N.Y. App. Div. 1st Dep't 1981).

In an action by plaintiff who was allegedly injured while entering an office against the owner and operator of the building, owner's motion to vacate its default would be granted where the original summons and complaint were never received by owner due to the fact that owner had changed its address without filing an amendment of its certificate of incorporation, and where it could not be said that owner acted intentionally in failing to file the address change with the secretary of state. Teichman v Gendelman, 87 A.D.2d 745, 448 N.Y.S.2d 678, 1982 N.Y. App. Div. LEXIS 16164 (N.Y. App. Div. 1st Dep't 1982).

Defendant corporation's motion to vacate a default judgment against it was properly denied where service of the summons and complaint was properly made on the Secretary of State, and where the corporation's failure to receive copies of process was the result of its own failure to keep a current address on file with the Secretary of State. Cristo Bros., Inc. v M. Cristo, Inc., 91 A.D.2d 807, 458 N.Y.S.2d 50, 1982 N.Y. App. Div. LEXIS 19704 (N.Y. App. Div. 3d Dep't 1982), app. dismissed, 59 N.Y.2d 760, 1983 N.Y. LEXIS 4990 (N.Y. 1983), app. dismissed, 60 N.Y.2d 701, 1983 N.Y. LEXIS 6252 (N.Y. 1983).

Corporation was itself responsible for alleged failure to receive notice of summons where, by its own admission, it failed to inform Secretary of State of its current address for some 5 years. Ameritek Constr. Corp. v Gas, Wash & Go, 247 A.D.2d 418, 668 N.Y.S.2d 663, 1998 N.Y. App. Div. LEXIS 1052 (N.Y. App. Div. 2d Dep't 1998).

Because a company was properly served by a private actor with notice of a foreclosure action in accordance with N.Y. Bus. Corp. Law § 306, and because the company failed to keep a current address on file with the Secretary of State, the company failed to provide a reasonable excuse to vacate the judgment. NYCTL 1999-1 Trust v 114 Tenth Ave. Assoc., Inc., 44 A.D.3d 576, 845 N.Y.S.2d 235, 2007 NY Slip Op 8115, 2007 N.Y. App. Div. LEXIS 10945 (N.Y. App. Div. 1st Dep't 2007), app. dismissed, 10 N.Y.3d 757, 853 N.Y.S.2d 540, 883 N.E.2d 366, 2008 N.Y. LEXIS 292 (N.Y. 2008), cert. denied, 555 U.S. 970, 129 S. Ct. 458, 172 L. Ed. 2d 327, 2008 U.S. LEXIS 7841 (U.S. 2008).

Corporate defendant could not attack service of process made on Secretary of State even though it did not receive actual notice, since it had failed to keep Secretary of State apprised of change in location of its office, and slight discrepancy in corporate name as it appeared in process papers was caused by corporations' principal. Citibank, N. A. v Press Realty Corp., 139 Misc. 2d 558, 528 N.Y.S.2d 307, 1988 N.Y. Misc. LEXIS 217 (N.Y. Sup. Ct. 1988).

Corporation's failure to comply with N.Y. Bus. Corp. Law § 304(a)-(b) and update its address in the Secretary of State's register explained why the corporation did not receive notice of the pension fund trustees' suit against it; the address was, however, the one on file with the New York Secretary of State, and the corporation's failure to comply with N.Y. Bus. Corp. Law § 304(a)-(b) did not change the fact that process—served on the Secretary of State as the corporation's agent—was proper and complete pursuant to N.Y. Bus. Corp. Law § 306(b)(1) and that it conferred the personal jurisdiction of the district court over the corporation. Trs. of the Local 531 Pension Fund v Am. Indus. Gases, Inc., 708 F. Supp. 2d 272, 2010 U.S. Dist. LEXIS 41204 (E.D.N.Y. 2010).

11. Under former law

Under earlier provisions, at least, it was held that where a foreign corporation had designated an agent for service of process on it, service on the designated agent was not limited to causes of action arising out of business transacted in New York and was effective as tantamount to personal service on the corporation itself, if the corporation was subject to suit in New York and the asserted cause of action was such that the New York court could take cognizance of it. Bagdon v Philadelphia & Reading Coal & Iron Co., 217 N.Y. 432, 111 N.E. 1075, 217 N.Y. (N.Y.S.) 432, 1916 N.Y. LEXIS 1327 (N.Y. 1916), superseded by statute as stated in , Rockefeller Univ. v Ligand Pharms. Inc., 581 F. Supp. 2d 461, 2008 U.S. Dist. LEXIS 40528 (S.D.N.Y. 2008); Smolik v Philadelphia & Reading Coal & Iron Co., 222 F. 148, 1915 U.S. Dist. LEXIS 1506 (D.N.Y. 1915).

But if the cause of action asserted arose within the court's area of limited jurisdiction, and the corporation had an office or was doing business within that area, personal jurisdiction over the corporation could be obtained by serving the Secretary of State; and if the corporation's "stated" or "principal" office or place of business was within the court's territorial jurisdiction, right to obtain personal jurisdiction over it by serving the Secretary of State was even clearer. Pohlers v Exeter Mfg. Co., 293 N.Y. 274, 56 N.E.2d 582, 293 N.Y. (N.Y.S.) 274, 1944 N.Y. LEXIS 1314 (N.Y. 1944); Less v 11 West 42nd Street, Inc., 274 A.D. 932, 83 N.Y.S.2d 607, 1948 N.Y. App. Div. LEXIS 4151 (N.Y. App. Div. 1948); Midvale Paper Board Co. v Cup Craft Paper Corp., 19 N.Y.S.2d 135, 173 Misc. 786, 1940 N.Y. Misc. LEXIS 1629 (N.Y. City Ct. 1940); Durand v Lipman, 299 N.Y. 769, 165 Misc. 1, 1937 N.Y. Misc. LEXIS 1871 (N.Y. Mun. Ct. 1937).

Jurisdiction over a defendant corporation could not be secured by service of process of the [former] Municipal Court of the Borough of Manhattan on the Secretary of State in Albany pursuant to § 25 of former Stock Corp. L., even though the defendant corporation was a resident of the City of New York. Glaser v Northwestern Provision Packers Corp., 265 A.D. 929, 38 N.Y.S.2d 450, 1942 N.Y. App. Div. LEXIS 6614 (N.Y. App. Div. 1942).

An action brought in justice court on a policy of insurance issued within the state, service having been effected on the superintendent of insurance pursuant to § 59 of the Insurance Law, was within the jurisdiction of such a court even though the defendant insurance company had no office within the jurisdiction and service was not made upon the Secretary of State under this section. Jackson v National Grange Mut. Liability Co., 274 A.D. 330, 83 N.Y.S.2d 602, 1948 N.Y. App. Div. LEXIS 3075 (N.Y. App. Div. 1948), app. dismissed, 299 N.Y. 333, 87 N.E.2d 283, 299 N.Y. (N.Y.S.) 333, 1949 N.Y. LEXIS 939 (N.Y. 1949).

Jurisdiction in rem was obtained by the city court of New York by attachment levy in an action against a foreign corporation served with summons and complaint within thirty days after the granting of the warrant by service on the secretary of state at Albany. Swedosh v Belding Hosiery Mills, Inc., 6 N.Y.S.2d 532, 168 Misc. 673, 1938 N.Y. Misc. LEXIS 1886 (N.Y. City Ct. 1938).

The provision in former subd. (c) of this section with respect to service of process on corporations in connection with proceedings in courts of limited jurisdiction seems to accord with decisions construing provisions of former Gen. Corp. L. and former Stock Corp. L. generally authorizing service on corporations by serving their designated agents or the Secretary of State. It was generally held that these special provisions as to mode of service could not aid or

augment basic territorial limits on the court's jurisdiction. McCulloch v American Carrier Corp., 15 N.Y.S.2d 566, 172 Misc. 450, 1939 N.Y. Misc. LEXIS 2432 (N.Y. Mun. Ct. 1939), app. denied, 260 A.D. 933, 24 N.Y.S.2d 129, 1940 N.Y. App. Div. LEXIS 5517 (N.Y. App. Div. 1940); De Cesare v American Cyanamid Co., 136 N.Y.S.2d 843, 1954 N.Y. Misc. LEXIS 3531 (N.Y. App. Term 1954).

A corporation, upon whom service had been made pursuant to § 25 of former Stock Corp. L., had thirty days after service of the summons in which to serve an answer upon the plaintiff's attorneys, in view of the provision of subdivision 9 of § 228 of former Civil Practice Act. Olson v Jordan, 43 N.Y.S.2d 348, 181 Misc. 942, 1943 N.Y. Misc. LEXIS 2205 (N.Y. Sup. Ct. 1943).

Service of process on a foreign corporation authorized to do business in New York, pursuant to § 217 of former Gen. Corp. L., had to be made as prescribed by that section, to subject it to liability in a personal injury action arising out of an automobile accident, and it was considered that there was no authority for serving the corporation pursuant to former § 52 of the Veh. & Traf. Law merely because the accident occurred in another state. Schlago v Seaboard Freight Lines, Inc., 65 N.Y.S.2d 369, 187 Misc. 732, 1946 N.Y. Misc. LEXIS 2827 (N.Y. Sup. Ct. 1946).

Dissolved corporation was not entitled to discretionary relief from default judgment even though it never received process which was served on Secretary of State, since it had failed to advise the Secretary of State of its change of address. Laurendi v Cascade Development Co., 5 Misc. 2d 688, 165 N.Y.S.2d 832, 1957 N.Y. Misc. LEXIS 3368 (N.Y. County Ct. 1957), aff'd, 4 A.D.2d 852, 167 N.Y.S.2d 240, 1957 N.Y. App. Div. LEXIS 4559 (N.Y. App. Div. 4th Dep't 1957).

Commencement of action to foreclose mechanic's lien was timely where plaintiff caused summons to be delivered to sheriff for service within one year after filing of lien, and when sheriff was unable to serve process, plaintiff, within 60 days of delivery to the sheriff, caused the summons to be served on the Secretary of State. Reliable Constr. Corp. v Relide Realty Corp., 6 Misc. 2d 857, 162 N.Y.S.2d 550, 1957 N.Y. Misc. LEXIS 3053 (N.Y. Sup. Ct. 1957).

Where a foreign corporation licensed to do business in this state filed an instrument with the Secretary of State designating him as agent for service of process and specifying the address of its office within New York State, and § 217 of former Gen. Corp. L. was complied with in serving the Secretary of State, a default judgment obtained against the corporation was not subject to being set aside on the ground that the corporation inadvertently failed to provide the Secretary of State with its full address and accordingly did not receive the notice of service forwarded to it by the Secretary of State. General Crane Service, Inc. v Whiting-Turner Contracting Co., 27 Misc. 2d 403, 208 N.Y.S.2d 244, 1960 N.Y. Misc. LEXIS 2110 (N.Y. Sup. Ct. 1960).

Under § 25 of former Stock Corp L service of process upon a domestic corporation by serving the Secretary of State was deemed service on a designated agent and not nullified by failure of the Secretary of State's office to mail the papers to the corporation, but a default judgment obtained against it could be opened upon adequate showing of meritorious defense and non-receipt of papers from the Secretary of State's office. Montulli v Sherlo Realty, Inc., 37 Misc. 2d 655, 234 N.Y.S.2d 754, 1962 N.Y. Misc. LEXIS 2145 (N.Y. Sup. Ct. 1962), aff'd, 18 A.D.2d 1139, 239 N.Y.S.2d 864, 1963 N.Y. App. Div. LEXIS 5482 (N.Y. App. Div. 4th Dep't 1963).

Service of summons and complaint upon a dissolved domestic corporation as provided by § 25 of former Stock Corp. L. was held to be valid in view of provisions of Tax Law that provisions of former General Corporation Law should apply to any corporation dissolved under the Tax Law and in view of provisions of former General Corporation Law that corporate existence of dissolved corporation continues for stated purposes. Public Fuel Service, Inc. v Hillgun Holding Corp., 133 N.Y.S.2d 850, 1954 N.Y. Misc. LEXIS 2459 (N.Y. Sup. Ct. 1954).

Where action was commenced in a court of limited territorial jurisdiction and service of process could not be made on the Secretary of State under this section plaintiff should not be required to commence a separate action in Supreme Court and consolidate the action pending in the lower court in order to comply with "due diligence" requirements of statute providing for order of substituted service of process. De Cesare v American Cyanamid Co., 136 N.Y.S.2d 843, 1954 N.Y. Misc. LEXIS 3531 (N.Y. App. Term 1954).

Where the agent appointed to receive service of process died and no new agent had been appointed the federal district court in New York obtained jurisdiction where service was made on the secretary of state even though it was a foreign cause of action. Cohen v American Window Glass Co., 126 F.2d 111, 1942 U.S. App. LEXIS 4074 (2d Cir. N.Y. 1942).

Where foreign corporation maintained regular and established place of business in New York within jurisdiction of N. Y. Fed. Dist. Ct. and had obtained license to do business in New York, and designated Secretary of State of New York as its agent to receive process in New York, such service was valid. American Blower Corp. v B. F. Sturtevant Co., 61 F. Supp. 756, 1945 U.S. Dist. LEXIS 2055 (D.N.Y. 1945).

UNDER FORMER LAW

Under earlier provisions, at least, it was held that where a foreign corporation had designated an agent for service of process on it, service on the designated agent was not limited to causes of action arising out of business transacted in New York and was effective as tantamount to personal service on the corporation itself, if the corporation was subject to suit in New York and the asserted cause of action was such that the New York court could take cognizance of it. Bagdon v Philadelphia & Reading Coal & Iron Co. (1916) 217 N.Y. 432, 111 N.E. 1075; Smolik v Philadelphia & Reading Coal & Iron Co. (1915, DC NY) 222 F 148

But if the cause of action asserted arose within the court's area of limited jurisdiction, and the corporation had an office or was doing business within that area, personal jurisdiction over the corporation could be obtained by serving the Secretary of State; and if the corporation's "stated" or "principal" office or place of business was within the court's territorial jurisdiction, right to obtain personal jurisdiction over it by serving the Secretary of State was even clearer. Pohlers v Exeter Mfg. Co. (1944) 293 N.Y. 274, 56 N.E.2d 582; Less v 11 West 42nd Street, Inc. (1948) 274 A.D. 932, 83 N.Y.S.2d 607; Midvale Paper Board Co. v Cup Craft Paper Corp. (1940) 173 Misc 786, 19 N.Y.S.2d 135; Durand v Lipman (1937) 165 Misc 1, 299 N.Y.S. 769

Service of summons and complaint upon a dissolved domestic corporation as provided by § 25 of former Stock Corp. L. was held to be valid in view of provisions of Tax Law that provisions of former General Corporation Law should apply to any corporation dissolved under the Tax Law and in view of provisions of former General Corporation Law that corporate existence of dissolved corporation continues for stated purposes. Public Fuel Service, Inc. v Hillgun Holding Corp. (1954, Sup) 133 N.Y.S.2d 850

Where action was commenced in a court of limited territorial jurisdiction and service of process could not be made on the Secretary of State under this section plaintiff should not be required to commence a separate action in Supreme Court and consolidate the action pending in the lower court in order to comply with "due diligence" requirements of statute providing for order of substituted service of process. De Cesare v American Cyanamid Co. (1954, Sup App T) 136 N.Y.S.2d 843

Jurisdiction over a defendant corporation could not be secured by service of process of the [former] Municipal Court of the Borough of Manhattan on the Secretary of State in Albany pursuant to § 25 of former Stock Corp. L., even though the defendant corporation was a resident of the City of New York. Glaser v Northwestern Provision Packers Corp. (1942) 265 A.D. 929, 38 N.Y.S.2d 450

An action brought in justice court on a policy of insurance issued within the state, service having been effected on the superintendent of insurance pursuant to § 59 of the Insurance Law, was within the jurisdiction of such a court even though the defendant insurance company had no office within the jurisdiction and service was not made upon the Secretary of State under this section. Jackson v National Grange Mut. Liability Co. (1948) 274 A.D. 330, 83 N.Y.S.2d 602, app gr 274 A.D. 1076, 85 N.Y.S.2d 330 and app dismd 299 N.Y. 333, 87 N.E.2d 283

Jurisdiction in rem was obtained by the city court of New York by attachment levy in an action against a foreign corporation served with summons and complaint within thirty days after the granting of the warrant by service on the secretary of state at Albany. Swedosh v Belding Hosiery Mills, Inc. (1938) 168 Misc 673, 6 N.Y.S.2d 532

The provision in former subd. (c) of this section with respect to service of process on corporations in connection with proceedings in courts of limited jurisdiction seems to accord with decisions construing provisions of former Gen. Corp. L. and former Stock Corp. L. generally authorizing service on corporations by serving their designated agents or the Secretary of State. It was generally held that these special provisions as to mode of service could not aid or

augment basic territorial limits on the court's jurisdiction. McCulloch v American Carrier Corp. (1939) 172 Misc 450, 15 N.Y.S.2d 566, app den 260 A.D. 933, 24 N.Y.S.2d 129; De Cesare v American Cyanamid Co. (1954, Sup App T) 136 N.Y.S.2d 843

A corporation, upon whom service had been made pursuant to § 25 of former Stock Corp. L., had thirty days after service of the summons in which to serve an answer upon the plaintiff's attorneys, in view of the provision of subdivision 9 of § 228 of former Civil Practice Act. Olson v Jordan (1943) 181 Misc 942, 43 N.Y.S.2d 348

Service of process on a foreign corporation authorized to do business in New York, pursuant to § 217 of former Gen. Corp. L., had to be made as prescribed by that section, to subject it to liability in a personal injury action arising out of an automobile accident, and it was considered that there was no authority for serving the corporation pursuant to former § 52 of the Veh. & Traf. Law merely because the accident occurred in another state. Schlago v Seaboard Freight Lines, Inc. (1946) 187 Misc 732, 65 N.Y.S.2d 369

Dissolved corporation was not entitled to discretionary relief from default judgment even though it never received process which was served on Secretary of State, since it had failed to advise the Secretary of State of its change of address. Laurendi v Cascade Development Co. (1957) 5 Misc. 2d 688, 165 N.Y.S.2d 832, affd (4th Dept) 4 A.D.2d 852, 167 N.Y.S.2d 240

Commencement of action to foreclose mechanic's lien was timely where plaintiff caused summons to be delivered to sheriff for service within one year after filing of lien, and when sheriff was unable to serve process, plaintiff, within 60 days of delivery to the sheriff, caused the summons to be served on the Secretary of State. Reliable Constr. Corp. v Relide Realty Corp. (1957) 6 Misc. 2d 857, 162 N.Y.S.2d 550

Where a foreign corporation licensed to do business in this state filed an instrument with the Secretary of State designating him as agent for service of process and specifying the address of its office within New York State, and § 217 of former Gen. Corp. L. was complied with in serving the Secretary of State, a default judgment obtained against the corporation was not subject to being set aside on the ground that the corporation inadvertently failed to provide the Secretary of State with its full address and accordingly did not receive the notice of service forwarded to it by the Secretary of State. General Crane Service, Inc. v Whiting-Turner Contracting Co. (1960) 27 Misc. 2d 403, 208 N.Y.S.2d 244

Under § 25 of former Stock Corp L service of process upon a domestic corporation by serving the Secretary of State was deemed service on a designated agent and not nullified by failure of the Secretary of State's office to mail the papers to the corporation, but a default judgment obtained against it could be opened upon adequate showing of meritorious defense and non-receipt of papers from the Secretary of State's office. Montulli v Sherlo Realty, Inc. (1962) 37 Misc. 2d 655, 234 N.Y.S.2d 754, affd 18 A.D.2d 1139, 239 N.Y.S.2d 864

Where the agent appointed to receive service of process died and no new agent had been appointed the federal district court in New York obtained jurisdiction where service was made on the secretary of state even though it was a foreign cause of action. Cohen v American Window Glass Co. (1942, CA2 NY) 126 F.2d 111

Where foreign corporation maintained regular and established place of business in New York within jurisdiction of N.Y. Fed. Dist. Ct. and had obtained license to do business in New York, and designated Secretary of State of New York as its agent to receive process in New York, such service was valid. American Blower Corp. v B. F. Sturtevant Co. (1945, DC NY) 61 F. Supp. 756, 66 USPQ 278

Under § 217 of former Gen. Corp. L., it was at one time ruled that service on the Secretary of State, as statutory agent for service on a corporation, must be made upon either the Secretary or a Deputy Secretary; but a later ruling indicated that the Secretary could authorize other persons in his office to receive such service and that subsequent reclassification of some of the office positions would not defeat such authorization. 1933 Ops Atty Gen 288; 1954 Ops Atty Gen Aug 20

Service was properly effectuated upon a corporation in an underlying action when a pedestrian delivered a copy of the summons and verified complaint to the New York Secretary of State under N.Y. Bus. Corp. Law § 306(b)(1) and N.Y. C.P.L.R. 3215(g)(4). Konig v Hermitage Ins. Co. (2012, 2d Dept) 93 App Div 3d 643, 940 NYS2d 116.

Business Corporation Law

§ 306-A.   Resignation for receipt of process

(a) The party (or his/her legal representative) whose post office address has been supplied by a domestic corporation or authorized foreign corporation as its address for process may resign. A certificate entitled "Certificate of Resignation for Receipt of Process under Section 306-A of the Business Corporation Law" shall be signed by such party and delivered to the department of state. It shall set forth:

(1) The name of the corporation and the date that its certificate of incorporation or application of authority was filed by the department of state.

(2) That the address of the party has been designated by the corporation as the post office address to which the secretary of state shall mail a copy of any process served on the secretary of state as agent for such corporation, and that such party wishes to resign.

(3) That sixty days prior to the filing of the certificate of resignation with the department of state the party has sent a copy of the certificate of resignation for receipt of process by registered or certified mail to the address of the registered agent of the designating corporation, if other than the party filing the certificate of resignation, for receipt of process, or if the resigning corporation has no registered agent, then to the last address of the designating corporation known to the party, specifying the address to which the copy was sent. If there is no registered agent and no known address of the designating corporation, the party shall attach an affidavit to the certificate stating that a diligent but unsuccessful search was made by the party to locate the corporation, specifying what efforts were made.

(4) That the designating corporation is required to deliver to the department of state a certificate of amendment or change providing for the designation by the corporation of a new address and that upon its failure to file such certificate, its authority to do business in this state shall be suspended, unless the corporation has previously filed a biennial statement under section four hundred eight of this chapter, in which case the address of the principal executive office stated in the last filed biennial statement shall constitute the new address for process of the corporation, and no such certificate of amendment or change need be filed.

(b) Upon the failure of the designating corporation to file a certificate of amendment or change providing for the designation by the corporation of the new address after the filing of a certificate of resignation for receipt of process with the secretary of state, its authority to do business in this state shall be suspended unless the corporation has previously filed a statement under section four hundred eight of this chapter, in which case the address of the principal executive office stated in the last filed statement, shall constitute the new address for process of the corporation provided such address is different from the previous address for process, and the corporation shall not be deemed suspended.

(c) The filing by the department of state of a certificate of amendment or change or statement under section four hundred eight of this chapter providing for a new address by a designating corporation shall annul the suspension and its authority to do business in this state shall be restored and continue as if no suspension had occurred.

(d) The resignation for receipt of process shall become effective upon the filing by the department of state of a certificate of resignation for receipt of process.

(e) (1) In any case in which a corporation suspended pursuant to this section would be subject to the personal or other jurisdiction of the courts of this state under article three of the civil practice law and rules, process against such corporation may be served upon the secretary of state as its agent pursuant to this section. Such process may issue in any court in this state having jurisdiction of the subject matter.

(2) Service of such process upon the secretary of state shall be made by personally delivering to and leaving with him or his deputy, or with any person authorized by the secretary of state to receive such service, at the office of the department of state in the city of Albany, a copy of such process together with the statutory fee, which fee shall be a taxable disbursement. Such service shall be sufficient if notice thereof and a copy of the process are:

(i) delivered personally within or without this state to such corporation by a person and in [the]* manner authorized to serve process by law of the jurisdiction in which service is made, or

(ii) sent by or on behalf of the plaintiff to such corporation by registered or certified mail with return receipt requested to the last address of such corporation known to the plaintiff.

(3) (i) Where service of a copy of process was effected by personal service, proof of service shall be by affidavit of compliance with this section filed, together with the process, within thirty days after such service, with the clerk of the court in which the action or special proceeding is pending. Service of process shall complete ten days after such papers are filed with the clerk of the court.

(ii) Where service of a copy of process was effected by mailing in accordance with this section, proof of service shall be by affidavit of compliance with this section filed, together with the process, within thirty days after receipt of the return receipt signed by the corporation, or other official proof of delivery or of the original envelope mailed. If a copy of the process is mailed in accordance with this section, there shall be filed with the affidavit of compliance either the return receipt signed by such corporation or other official proof of delivery, if acceptance was refused by it, the original envelope with a notation by the postal authorities that acceptance was refused. If acceptance was refused, a copy of the notice and process together with notice of the mailing by registered or certified mail and refusal to accept shall be promptly sent to such corporation at the same address by ordinary mail and the affidavit of compliance shall so state. Service of process shall be complete ten days after such papers are filed with the clerk of the court. The refusal to accept delivery of the registered or certified mail or to sign the return receipt shall not affect the validity of the service and such corporation refusing to accept such registered or certified mail shall be charged with knowledge of the contents thereof.

(4) Service made as provided in this section without the state shall have the same force as personal service made within this state.

(5) Nothing in this section shall affect the right to serve process in any other manner permitted by law.

* The bracketed word has been inserted by the Publisher.

History: Add, L 1997, ch 469, § 1, eff Nov 24, 1997; amd, L 1999, ch 172, § 6, eff July 6, 1999; L 2015, ch 59, § 2 (Part S), eff April 13, 2015.

§ 307.   Service of process on unauthorized foreign corporation

(a) In any case in which a non-domiciliary would be subject to the personal or other jurisdiction of the courts of this state under article three of the civil practice law and rules, a foreign corporation not authorized to do business in this state is subject to a like jurisdiction. In any such case, process against such foreign corporation may be served upon the secretary of state as its agent. Such process may issue in any court in this state having jurisdiction of the subject matter.

(b) Service of such process upon the secretary of state shall be made by personally delivering to and leaving with him or his deputy, or with any person authorized by the secretary of state to receive such service, at the office of the department of state in the city of Albany, a copy of such process together with the statutory fee, which fee shall be a taxable disbursement. Such service shall be sufficient if notice thereof and a copy of the process are:

(1) Delivered personally without this state to such foreign corporation by a person and in the manner authorized to serve process by law of the jurisdiction in which service is made, or

(2) Sent by or on behalf of the plaintiff to such foreign corporation by registered mail with return receipt requested, at the post office address specified for the purpose of mailing process, on file in the department of state, or with any official or body performing the equivalent function, in the jurisdiction of its incorporation, or if no such address is there specified, to its registered or other office there specified, or if no such office is there specified, to the last address of such foreign corporation known to the plaintiff.

(c) 1. Where service of a copy of process was effected by personal service, proof of service shall be by affidavit of compliance with this section filed, together with the process, within thirty days after such service, with the clerk of the court in which the action or special proceeding is pending. Service of process shall be complete ten days after such papers are filed with the clerk of the court.

2. Where service of a copy of process was effected by mailing in accordance with this section, proof of service shall be by affidavit of compliance with this section filed, together with the process, within thirty days after receipt of the return receipt signed by the foreign corporation, or other official proof of delivery or of the original envelope mailed. If a copy of the process is mailed in accordance with this section, there shall be filed with the affidavit of compliance either the return receipt signed by such foreign corporation or other official proof of delivery or, if acceptance was refused by it, the original envelope with a notation by the postal authorities that acceptance was refused. If acceptance was refused, a copy of the notice and process together with notice of the mailing by registered mail and refusal to accept shall be promptly sent to such foreign corporation at the same address by ordinary mail and the affidavit of compliance shall so state. Service of process shall be complete ten days after such papers are filed with the clerk of the court. The refusal to accept delivery of the registered mail or to sign the return receipt shall not affect the validity of the service and such foreign corporation refusing to accept such registered mail shall be charged with knowledge of the contents thereof.

(d) Service made as provided in this section shall have the same force as personal service made within this state.

(e) Nothing in this section shall affect the right to serve process in any other manner permitted by law.

History: Add, L 1961, ch 855, eff Sept 1, 1963; amd, L 1965, ch 803, § 4, eff Sept 1, 1965; L 1967, ch 725; L 1968, ch 60, eff March 19, 1968.

CASE ANNOTATIONS

1. In general
2. "Transacting business", generally
3. – Jurisdiction upheld
4. – Jurisdiction not upheld
5. Methods of service
6. Proof of service
7. Miscellaneous

1. In general

Special Term erred in denying defendant's motion to vacate default judgment; plaintiff effectuated service on defendant pursuant to Business Corporation Law § 307 by serving Secretary of State with summons and complaint, and by sending notice of this service and copy of pleadings by registered mail to defendant's last known address in Tokyo, Japan; when this letter was refused, plaintiff sent another copy of notice and pleadings by ordinary mail; defendant asserted as reasonable excuse for its default that it had moved its business offices prior to this service, and that it did not receive notice of action until plaintiff had executed on judgment; defendant further contends that it is improper party defendant in that it is neither successor corporation nor responsible for liabilities of company which allegedly breached its contract with plaintiff; plaintiff provided evidence that there is some relationship between two corporations; because defendant provided reasonable excuse for its default and potentially meritorious defense that raises substantial issues of fact, it was improvident exercise of discretion to deny defendant's motion to vacate its default. Mark III Assocs. v HEC Eng'g Co., 148 A.D.2d 990

CLS Bus Corp § 307 establishes mandatory sequence and progression of service completion options to acquire jurisdiction over foreign corporation not authorized to do business in New York, and such steps are requirements of jurisdictional nature which must be strictly satisfied; thus, court should have granted defendant's motion to dismiss for lack of personal jurisdiction where plaintiff did not file required affidavit of compliance under CLS Bus Corp § 307(c)(2). Flannery v General Motors Corp. (1995, 1st Dept) 214 A.D.2d 497, 625 N.Y.S.2d 556, affd, ctfd ques ans 86 N.Y.2d 771, 631 N.Y.S.2d 135, 655 N.E.2d 176

CLS Bus Corp § 307 does not provide sole method by which unauthorized foreign corporation may be served; rather, it is merely alternative to CLS CPLR § 311. Van Wert v Black & Decker (1998, 3d Dept) 246 A.D.2d 773, 667 N.Y.S.2d 770

The Supreme Court would not be deprived of jurisdiction over defendant Japanese corporation, where plaintiffs established that summons and complaint were served by registered mail on defendant and by personal service on the Secretary of State, although notice of service on the Secretary of State was not included when the summons and complaint were mailed to defendant; where there had been substantial compliance with the other major provisions of Bus Corp Law § 307 and where there was no allegation or proof of prejudice to defendant, such omission is a mere irregularity that does not deprive the court of jurisdiction. Ormandy v Lynn (1984) 122 Misc. 2d 954, 472 N.Y.S.2d 274

Section 307 of the Business Corporation Law does not permit service upon the secretary of state as agent for an unauthorized foreign corporation with respect to jurisdictional acts set forth in § 302(a) (1) of the CPLR since under the latter section service must be made upon a nondomiciliary defendant under §§ 311 and 313 of the CPLR which require delivery of the summons to an officer or agent of the corporation within or without the state. Railex Corp. v White Machine Co. (1965, EDNY) 243 F. Supp. 381, 145 USPQ 652

The intention of Business Corporation Law § 103(d) seems to be that a party may utilize the Business Corporation Law to pursue a cause of action that arose before its effective date, but that no provision in the Business Corporation Law can effect the substantive rights and obligations of the parties that arose out of such cause of action, and to this extent, Business Corporation Law § 307 neither enlarges nor impairs the rights of the parties and therefore may be retroactively applied. Lumbermens Mut. Casualty Co. v Borden Co. (1967, SDNY) 268 F. Supp. 303

Foreign Sovereign Immunities Act (28 USCS § 1608(b)) fully preempts state law, such that service of process upon commercial entity of foreign sovereign pursuant to state law in order to subject commercial entity to personal jurisdiction under state law is invalid and insufficient, and service must be made pursuant to Foreign Sovereign Immunities Act, as to allow service under state law would vitiate clear intent of congress to reserve to federal law exclusive method for service of process. Lippus v Dahlgren Mfg. Co. (1986, ED NY) 644 F. Supp. 1473

This section sets forth procedures for serving an unauthorized foreign corporation that are jurisdictional and require strict compliance. Issing v Madison Sq. Garden Ctr., (2009 App Div, 1st Dept) 878 NYS2d 723.

2. "Transacting business", generally

Where at the time alleged service was made upon a foreign corporation by serving the Secretary of State, the Secretary of State was not authorized to receive service for a foreign corporation not authorized to do business in this state which was not actually doing business here; the fact that Business Corporation Law § 307 was later amended authorizing service in cases covered by CPLR Art 3 would not serve to correct jurisdictionally defective service when made. Central School Dist. v C. R. Evans Corp. (1966) 49 Misc. 2d 924, 268 N.Y.S.2d 800

The essential criteria with which the doing business test is concerned is presence, and a corporation to be doing business in New York must be present here, not occasionally or casually, but with a fair measure of permanence and continuity. Central School Dist. v C. R. Evans Corp. (1966) 49 Misc. 2d 924, 268 N.Y.S.2d 800

This section permits the Secretary of State to receive process on behalf of an unauthorized foreign corporation when the defendant corporation transacts business in this state and the cause of action arises out of such transaction of business. Lumbermens Mut. Casualty Co. (1967, SDNY) v Borden Co. 268 F. Supp. 303

Business Corporation Law § 307(a) provides for a method of service on foreign corporations when jurisdiction is obtainable under the "transacting business" standards of the New York long-arm statute (CPLR 302), and since this section of the CPLR has been held to apply retroactively, Business Corporation Law § 307 which merely provides an additional method of service when long-arm jurisdiction is attainable, should also be held to apply retroactively. Lumbermens Mut. Casualty Co. v Borden Co. (1967, SD NY) 268 F. Supp. 303

Business Corporation Law § 307(a) embodies the "transacting business" test of CPLR 307. Lumbermens Mut. Casualty Co. v Borden Co. (1967, SD NY) 268 F. Supp. 303

3. – Jurisdiction upheld

German corporation not authorized to do business in New York was properly served with process under CLS Bus Corp § 307(b)(2) when plaintiffs personally served New York Secretary of State and mailed copy of summons and complaint by registered mail to corporation's wholly owned subsidiary located in New Jersey since prior decisional law had established that New Jersey subsidiary was mere department of corporation. Stewart v Volkswagen of America, Inc. (1992, 2d Dept) 181 A.D.2d 4, 584 N.Y.S.2d 886

Company contracting to supply granite for construction project in New York, under contract signed in New York, and company issuing surety bond to guarantee substantial performance of such contract, both being foreign corporations not licensed to do business in New York, were subject to service of process, and to jurisdiction of New York courts, in action for breach of contract, under CLS Bus Corp § 307 and CLS Ins § 1213. A. J. McNulty & Co. v Rocamat (1986) 132 Misc. 2d 1064, 506 N.Y.S.2d 393

In action for nonpayment of insurance claims, court had jurisdiction over foreign insurance company that had no office in New York since it transacted business in New York by issuing and delivering group insurance policies to corporations with offices in New York; company was chargeable with knowledge that its corporate insureds intended to provide coverage to their employees who were New York residents. Comprehensive Foot Care Group v Lincoln Nat. Life (1987) 135 Misc. 2d 862, 517 N.Y.S.2d 652

Foreign corporation which entered into a contract in New York, and executed said contract in New York, and whose representatives visited New York on 24 different negotiations in connection with the negotiations of said contract and whose representatives made nine visits to New York concerning settlement discussions was transacting business within the state of New York so as to subject it to in personam jurisdiction. Lumbermens Mut. Casualty Co. v Borden Co. (1967, SD NY) 268 F. Supp. 303

4. – Jurisdiction not upheld

Failure of defendant, a New Jersey corporation, to set aside service of summons and complaint upon its registered agent in New Jersey on the ground that it is a foreign corporation not doing business in New York and not subject to process therein within 30 days after the alleged service, was no bar to granting of the motion, although it advertised its New Jersey resort and hotel in New York publications, giving a New York telephone number which was also listed in New York telephone directories, where calls to that number for the making of reservations were directly connected to defendant in New Jersey. Greenberg v R. S. P. Realty Corp. (1964, 2d Dept) 22 A.D.2d 690, 253 N.Y.S.2d 344

Jurisdiction over defendant nonresident corporation was not obtained by service of summons of secretary of state pursuant to business corporation law § 307, where defendant's only contacts with New York State consisted of shipping caps into the state and the appearance of its name in listings and advertisements in regional and national trade directories. Simplicity Machine & Mfg. Co. v Stevens Co. (1968, 4th Dept) 30 A.D.2d 768, 292 N.Y.S.2d 259

In an action against a foreign corporation not qualified to do business in New York, arising out of an automobile accident in a foreign country while plaintiff was driving a car purchased in New York for delivery to him in the foreign country, the trial court erred in denying defendant's motion to dismiss the complaint where plaintiff did not effect valid service on the foreign corporation pursuant to Bus Corp Law § 307. Low v Bayerische Motoren Werke, AG. (1982, 1st Dept) 88 A.D.2d 504, 449 N.Y.S.2d 733

In an action against a Japanese corporation that was not authorized to transact business in New York, service of the amended summons and complaint by registered mail, return receipt requested, and delivery of a copy to the New York Secretary of State, though in compliance over defendant in that it failed to comply with the service requirements of the Convention on the Service Abroad of Judicial and Extrajudicial Documents in Civil or Commercial Matters (Hague Convention). Reynolds v Koh (1985, 3d Dept) 109 A.D.2d 97, 490 N.Y.S.2d 295

A foreign corporation who merchandized its products in New York through distributors who might have been special agents for certain limited purposes, but were not true agents, and who had no offices, warehouses, employees and telephone listing in New York was not doing business in this state. Central School Dist. v C. R. Evans Corp. (1966) 49 Misc. 2d 924, 268 N.Y.S.2d 800

Solicitation by telephone of employer in New York by personnel placement agency in Connecticut did not constitute such transaction of business in this state as would subject agency to New York long-arm jurisdiction. Electronic Devices, Inc. v Mark Rogers Associates (1970) 63 Misc. 2d 243, 311 N.Y.S.2d 413

New Jersey corporation which did not have a warehouse inventory or place of business within New York-the corporation having fourteen distributors and one salesman located within New York and paying nothing towards the maintenance of the salesman's home in New York-was not doing business in New York within the sections providing for service of process on foreign corporations. Railex Corp. v White Machine Co. (1965, ED NY) 243 F. Supp. 381, 145 USPQ 652

5. Methods of service

When plaintiff chooses to try to acquire personal jurisdiction under CLS Bus Corp § 307, which provides for service constructively on Secretary of State, provisions must be strictly complied with and second constructive service mechanism is not authorized. Stewart v Volkswagen of Am., Inc. (1993) 81 N.Y.2d 203, 597 N.Y.S.2d 612, 613 N.E.2d 518

CLS Bus Corp § 307 offers no alternatives for notification through agent, whether involuntary or not, when jurisdiction is invoked initially by service on Secretary of State. Stewart v Volkswagen of Am., Inc. (1993) 81 N.Y.2d 203, 597 N.Y.S.2d 612, 613 N.E.2d 518

New Jersey address of German corporation's American distributor did not constitute "last known address" of German corporation for purposes of CLS Bus Corp § 307, even if American distributor were mere department of German corporation, where plaintiff seeking jurisdiction was informed of corporation's address in Germany. Stewart v Volkswagen of Am., Inc. (1993) 81 N.Y.2d 203, 597 N.Y.S.2d 612, 613 N.E.2d 518

In personal injury action, order which granted motion of defendant to dismiss complaint and cross claim against it for lack of personal jurisdiction reversed-plaintiff was allegedly injured by commercial washing machine allegedly manufactured by defendant, Pennsylvania corporation not licensed to do business in New York; machine allegedly contained "washer-extractor" manufactured by codefendant; plaintiff timely served defendant pursuant to Business Corporation Law § 307 which governs service upon foreign corporation unauthorized to do business in New York by serving Secretary of State of New York, and by forwarding process to it by certified mail, return receipt requested, to its corporate offices in Pennsylvania; although Business Corporation Law § 307 (b) (2) prescribes service by "registered mail with return receipt requested", in absence of prejudice, this is not fatal defect; similarly, plaintiff's failure to timely file her proof of service with clerk of court in which action was pending did not divest court of jurisdiction; these defects and other service defects complained of were mere irregularities and did not deprive court of jurisdiction. Piekarz v Columbia Laundry Mach. Co., 150 A.D.2d 539

Where the method of service of process chosen by the plaintiff was not authorized, it was invalid. Rosman v Clark (1967, 2d Dept) 27 A.D.2d 839, 278 N.Y.S.2d 39

Where defendant was incorporated under laws of Delaware and only place where it actually had an office and did business was Puerto Rico, summons and complaint served pursuant to business corporation law by personally serving Secretary of State of New York and by mailing copy to another defendant in Illinois did not satisfy requirements of business corporation law and motion to dismiss for lack of personal jurisdiction should have been granted. Newman v G. D. Searle & Co. (1975, 2d Dept) 50 A.D.2d 574, 374 N.Y.S.2d 713

In actions to recover damages for personal injuries arising out of an explosion at a manufacturing plant, plaintiffs were properly permitted to cure the defect in their service of process on one foreign corporation where the only error was plaintiffs' failure to include a notice of service on the Secretary of State together with the copy of the summons and complaint that was served on the foreign corporation, where no prejudice to the corporation was shown, and where the

irregularity was properly cured nunc pro tunc by mailing the notice of service to the corporation. Orzechowski v Warner-Lambert Co. (1982, 2d Dept) 91 A.D.2d 681, 457 N.Y.S.2d 323

In a wrongful death action against a foreign automobile manufacturer, the complaint would be dismissed for lack of in personam jurisdiction where substituted service had been made on the Secretary of State in his New York City office, and where Bus Corp Law § 307(b) had required service in the city of Albany. Meyer v Volkswagen of America, Inc. (1983, 1st Dept) 92 A.D.2d 488, 459 N.Y.S.2d 82

Plaintiff's causes of action against Japanese corporation, which neither did business nor had agent to accept service in this country, should not have been dismissed on ground that service of summons and complaint pursuant to CLS Bus Corp § 307 was not authorized under article 10(a) of Hague Convention on the Service Abroad of Judicial and Extrajudicial Documents in Civil or Criminal Matters; reference in article 10(a) to "freedom to send judicial documents, by postal channels, directly to persons abroad" would be superfluous unless it was related to sending of such documents for purpose of service, and since Japan has not objected to use of "postal channels" under article 10(a), service by registered mail was appropriate. Rissew v Yamaha Motor Co. (1987, 4th Dept) 129 A.D.2d 94, 515 N.Y.S.2d 352

Plaintiff properly and timely served foreign corporation under CLS Bus Corp § 307 by serving Secretary of State, and by forwarding process to corporation by certified mail, return receipt requested, at its corporate offices in Pennsylvania, even though statute prescribes service by "regis tered mail with return receipt requested" and plaintiff failed to timely file her proof of service with clerk of court in which action was pending, where corporation was not prejudiced by such defects. Piekarz v Columbia Laundry Machine Co. (1989, 2d Dept) 150 A.D.2d 539, 541 N.Y.S.2d 439

Plaintiff did not acquire jurisdiction over German automobile manufacturer in action arising from accident involving automobile manufactured by United States subsidiary where summons and complaint were delivered to Secretary of State and mailed to German manufacturer, but mailing was rejected by German manufacturer, and attempt to serve did not comply with procedural requirements of Hague Service Convention. Derso v Volkswagen of America, Inc. (1990, 4th Dept) 159 A.D.2d 937, 552 N.Y.S.2d 1001

Mere service of summons and complaint on regional branch of California subsidiary of foreign parent company not authorized to do business in New York was wholly inadequate to confer personal jurisdiction over parent company. Vesligaj v PMT Forklift Corp. (1995, 2d Dept) 213 A.D.2d 541, 624 N.Y.S.2d 54

Court erred in dismissing action on ground of improper service where plaintiffs strictly complied with CLS Bus Corp § 307(b)(2) by mailing process to address in Colorado which was listed in documents on file with Colorado Secretary of State as address of each of defendant corporation's "place of business." Hernandez v Cottrell, Ltd. (1996, 2d Dept) 228 A.D.2d 648, 646 N.Y.S.2d 12

Japanese corporation was entitled to dismissal, for lack of personal jurisdiction, of complaint against it where it had no business address or designated agent in New York, and substituted service on Secretary of State was ineffective because Japan clearly indicated its preference for personal service by objecting to paragraphs of Hague Convention that would allow foreign substituted service. Sardanis v Sumitomo Corp. (2001, 1st Dept) 279 A.D.2d 225, 718 N.Y.S.2d 66, subsequent app (1st Dept) 282 A.D.2d 322, 723 N.Y.S.2d 466

Plaintiff properly served a manufacturer under N.Y. C.P.L.R. 311 because N.Y. C.P.L.R. 311(a)(1) determined the method of service upon any domestic or foreign corporation, and provided that a business corporation may also be served pursuant to N.Y. Bus. Corp. Law §§ 306 or N.Y. Bus. Corp. Law § 307; here, service was properly effected under N.Y. C.P.L.R. 311 because plaintiff personally served the manufacturer's authorized agent for service in accordance with N.Y. C.P.L.R. 311(a)(1) and thus, contrary to the manufacturer's contention, plaintiff was not required to comply with the provisions of § 307. Halas v Dick's Sporting Goods (2013, 4th Dept) 105 App Div 3d 1411, 964 NYS2d 808.

This section was not complied with where copies of summons and complaint were served upon Indiana corporation by service upon Secretary of State and copies were sent by registered mail to a manufacturer's representative in New York City who represented the defendant instead of mailing copies directly to the corporation in Indiana since the mailing did not follow the priority of addresses mandated by the statute, and defect was not cured either by fact that representative, upon receipt of the registered envelope, transmitted its contents by ordinary mail to defendant corporation in Indiana, or by letter from plaintiff's attorney likewise sent by ordinary mail to defendant's address in Indiana. Koepke v Bilnor Corp. (1968) 55 Misc. 2d 928, 286 N.Y.S.2d 719

In action for wrongful death allegedly resulting from defective and unsafe medical machinery, plaintiff's mistaken service on foreign division of domestic corporation was deemed service on domestic corporation where the 2 entities were considered to be one and the same. Nolan v Ohio Medical Products (1973) 75 Misc. 2d 620, 348 N.Y.S.2d 497

In a products liability action, the plaintiff effected valid service of process on a Japanese corporation by serving a summons with notice upon the defendant in Japan pursuant to the Hague Convention on the Service Abroad of Judicial and Extrajudicial Documents in Civil or Commercial Matters, where there was no requirement in the convention, or in New York law, that a plaintiff serve a complaint with the notice and summons, and where service in accordance with the provisions of the convention obviates the necessity of serving the Secretary of State with notice to the unauthorized foreign corporation. Re v Breezy Point Lumber Co. (1983) 118 Misc. 2d 206, 460 N.Y.S.2d 264

Service on foreign unauthorized corporation may be effected by service on secretary of state of foreign state only if laws of that jurisdiction appoint foreign secretary of state as agent for service of process. Breer v Sears, Roebuck & Co. (2000, Sup) 184 Misc. 2d 916, 709 N.Y.S.2d 798

Service of process upon Secretary of State within 2-year period prescribed by statute for commencing wrongful death actions does not constitute effective service of process sufficient to toll running of period set forth in applicable statute of limitations when defendant is foreign corporation unauthorized to conduct business in state and was not served with process by mail until after expiration of period. Singer v Black & Decker Mfg. Co. (1987, WD NY) 668 F. Supp. 160

Negligence/strict products liability plaintiff failed to effect service on unauthorized foreign corporation pursuant to CLS Bus Corp Law § 307, even though plaintiff took preliminary steps to serve and filed with court affidavit of compliance together with original and 2 copies of returned registered mail attempted service, because affidavit of compliance does not state that plaintiff complied with last step of § 307(b)(2) procedure-sending (1) copy of notice and process, together with notice of (2) mailing by registered mail and (3) [refusal to accept, to corporation] by ordinary mail. Anderson v John Royle & Sons (1992, ND NY) 784 F. Supp. 955

Service of process by registered mail on Swiss corporation not authorized to do business in New York did not confer jurisdiction on court since service violated requirement of Swiss law that service of process is governmental function. East Continental Gems, Inc. v Yakutiel (1992, Sup) 153 Misc. 2d 883, 582 N.Y.S.2d 594

Plaintiff properly served a manufacturer under N.Y. C.P.L.R. 311 because N.Y. C.P.L.R. 311(a)(1) determined the method of service upon any domestic or foreign corporation, and provided that a business corporation may also be served pursuant to N.Y. Bus. Corp. Law §§ 306 or N.Y. Bus. Corp. Law § 307; here, service was properly effected under N.Y. C.P.L.R. 311 because plaintiff personally served the manufacturer's authorized agent for service in accordance with N.Y. C.P.L.R. 311(a)(1) and thus, contrary to the manufacturer's contention, plaintiff was not required to comply with the provisions of § 307. Halas v Dick's Sporting Goods (2013, 4th Dept) 105 App Div 3d 1411, 964 NYS2d 808.

6. Proof of service

Once jurisdiction and service of process are questioned, plaintiffs have burden of proving satisfaction of statutory and due process prerequisites. Stewart v Volkswagen of Am., Inc. (1993) 81 N.Y.2d 203, 597 N.Y.S.2d 612, 613 N.E.2d 518

The trial court in a suit against a Saudi Arabian corporation erred in denying a motion to vacate a default judgment claimed by the corporation to have been entered without proper service of process, even though the corporation had on at least five occasions been served copies of the complaint and never denied receiving those copies, where plaintiff admitted that it never received from the postal authorities either a return receipt signed by the corporation or the original envelope with a notation that acceptance was refused, thus demonstrating that no proof of compliance as required by Bus Corp Law § 307 could have been made, where notice received by means other than those authorized by statute could not serve to bring the corporation within the jurisdiction of the court, and where it did not

appear that there was a willful default but rather that the corporation entertained a good-faith belief, based in part at least on the advice of counsel, that service was improper. Lansdowne Financial Services, Ltd. v Binladen Telecommunications Co. (1983, 1st Dept) 95 A.D.2d 711, 463 N.Y.S.2d 826

Plaintiff's failure to comply with CLS Bus Corp § 307(c)(2) by not filing affidavit of compliance with clerk of court within statute of limitations constituted jurisdictional defect, and such omission was not mere irregularity that could be remedied by resort to CLS CPLR §§ 2001 and 2004. Smolen v Cosco, Inc. (1994, 2d Dept) 207 A.D.2d 441, 616 N.Y.S.2d 228

Court has power under CPLR § 2004 to extend 30-day time limit for proof of service of this section. Sassand-Ilic v Calzaturificio San Giorgio (1966) 51 Misc. 2d 553, 273 N.Y.S.2d 502

Because a plaintiff's notice was not in strict compliance with N.Y. Bus. Corp. Law § 307(c)(2), a foreign corporation had a reasonable excuse for failure to properly and timely appear based on the plaintiff's rejection of the answer and the failure to be served with papers at its actual corporate offices. TAZ Prods., Inc. v Rentacom, Inc. (2008, Civ Ct) 19 Misc 3d 965, 239 NYLJ 92, 858 NYS2d 534.

Where individuals' attorney submitted an unrebutted affidavit which stated that his firm never received the return receipt from the registered mailing of process to a foreign corporation, and that it was not until he received the corporation's motion to dismiss that he was officially notified that the registered mailing was received by the corporation, the corporation's motion to dismiss was the "official proof of delivery" described in N.Y. Bus. Corp. Law § 307(c)(2), and thus the individuals filed their proof of service within the requisite 30 days in accordance with N.Y. Bus. Corp. Law § 307(c)(2); the corporation's motion to dismiss was properly denied. Reed v Gowanda Nursing Home (2004, A.D., 4th Dept) 773 N.Y.S.2d 311

In multi-district asbestos litigation, plaintiffs (who offered fully detailed account of their repeated and ultimately successful attempts to serve unauthorized foreign corporation) established full compliance with service of process requirements of CLS Bus Corp § 307(b) and (c) where copies of papers served on corporation included notice of service on Secretary of State, and plaintiffs provided copies of 2 separate affidavits of compliance filed with clerk of court after each attempt to serve corporation. Asbestos Litig. (1997, SD NY) 963 F. Supp. 247, motion den (SD NY) 986 F. Supp. 761

7. Miscellaneous

In action arising from lease of allegedly defective car from wholly-owned subsidiary of West German corporation, West German corporation was not entitled to dismissal of complaint on ground that service of process by delivering papers to Secretary of State and to subsidiary corporation was legally defective since (1) assumption of liability by subsidiary on behalf of foreign parent was sufficient to sustain service under CLS Bus Corp § 307 where subsidiary was express warrantor on behalf of parent and plaintiffs acquired car during term of express warranty, and (2) service was not invalid for failure to comply with Hague Service Convention since plaintiffs did not attempt to serve documents abroad. Luciano v Garvey Volkswagen, Inc. (1987, 3d Dept) 131 A.D.2d 253, 521 N.Y.S.2d 119

Personal jurisdiction was obtained over defendant foreign corporation, which was authorized to do business in state, even though service was effected under CLS Bus Corp § 307 which provides for method of service on foreign corporations not authorized to do business in state since (1) provisions of CLS CPLR § 311(1) regarding service on corporations are to be liberally construed, (2) process was delivered to proper person and at proper place for service on Secretary of State, (3) defendant received copy of process via registered mail with return receipt requested, and (4) only difference between method of service employed and mandated method of service was identity of person who actually placed defendant's copy of process in mail. Marine Midland Realty Credit Corp. v Welbilt Corp. (1989, 3d Dept) 145 A.D.2d 84, 537 N.Y.S.2d 669

Where service is properly made on local corporation that is so controlled by foreign corporation as to be deemed mere department thereof, local corporation is to be considered foreign corporation's involuntary agent for purposes of service. Stewart v Volkswagen of America, Inc. (1992, 2d Dept) 181 A.D.2d 4, 584 N.Y.S.2d 886

Without further development of record regarding defendant's corporate structure, Appellate Division would not disturb denial of defendant's motion to dismiss products liability complaint on ground that plaintiff had served process on wrong corporation by serving "Black & Decker Corporation," incorporated in Maryland, rather than "Black & Decker, Inc.," incorporated in Delaware; even if served corporation did not manufacture subject toaster, service of process on subsidiary corporation may effectuate service on parent under proper circumstances. Van Wert v Black & Decker (1998, 3d Dept) 246 A.D.2d 773, 667 N.Y.S.2d 770

Defendants were not entitled to dismissal of action as to defendant foreign corporation on ground of improper service where plaintiff was not required to serve it in manner set forth in CLS Bus Corp § 307 but also had option of serving it through agent authorized by appointment to receive service under CLS CPLR § 311, plaintiff served legal assistant at New York corporation that apparently was subsidiary of foreign corporation, and assistant allegedly stated that she was authorized to accept service for foreign corporation and endorsed summons acknowledging her acceptance of process for it, even though she later submitted affidavit stating that she was not so authorized. Hessel v Goldman, Sachs & Co. (2001, 1st Dept) 281 A.D.2d 247, 722 N.Y.S.2d 21, reargument den (NY A.D., 1st Dept) 2001 N.Y. A.D. LEXIS 6382 and app den 97 N.Y.2d 625, 735 N.Y.S.2d 485, 760 N.E.2d 1280

Defendant foreign corporation was not entitled to dismissal of complaint on ground of allegedly untimely service of process, despite defendant's claim that service was not "complete" until 10 days after plaintiff filed affidavit of compliance with court clerk under CLS Bus Corp § 307(c)(2), where (1) CLS Bus Corp § 306-b requires that service be "made," not that it be "complete," and (2) plaintiff complied with service requirements of CLS Bus Corp § 307 and filed requisite affidavit of compliance within 120-day period in § 306-b. Sorrento v Rice Barton Corp. (2001, 4th Dept) 286 A.D.2d 873, 730 N.Y.S.2d 604

In a mortgage foreclosure action service of a summons and complaint against a foreign corporation which did not do business in New York by service upon the Secretary of State pursuant to Business Corporation Law § 307(a) was proper, where no personal judgment was sought against the defendant and it was alleged that defendant had a lien subordinate to the lien of the mortgage on property upon which plaintiffs sought to foreclose. Petrossi v Ontario Properties, Inc. (1968) 55 Misc. 2d 601, 285 N.Y.S.2d 928

Delivery of summons and complaint to Secretary of State under CLS Bus Corp § 307 was not sufficient to confer jurisdiction over defendant religious corporation, and thus plaintiff's motion for default judgment was denied. Schoenthal v Beth Jacob Teachers Seminary of Am. (1998, Sup) 176 Misc. 2d 958, 675 N.Y.S.2d 756

§ 308.   Records and certificates of department of state

The department of state shall keep a record of each process served upon the secretary of state under this chapter, including the date of service. It shall, upon request made within ten years of such service, issue a certificate under its seal certifying as to the receipt of the process by an authorized person, the date and place of such service and the receipt of the statutory fee. Process served upon the secretary of state under this chapter shall be destroyed by him after a period of ten years from such service.

History: Add, L 1961, ch 855, eff Sept 1, 1963.

ARTICLE 4
FORMATION OF CORPORATIONS

History: Add, L 1961, ch 855, eff Sept 1, 1963.

Schedule of sections, amd, L 1962, ch 317, § 4, eff Sept 1, 1963.

§ 401.   Incorporators

One or more natural persons of the age of eighteen years or over may act as incorporators of a corporation to be formed under this chapter.

History: Add, L 1961, ch 855, eff Sept 1, 1963, amd, L 1974, ch 900, eff Sept 1, 1974.

CASE ANNOTATIONS

Pursuant to Business Corporation Law § 401 thousands of cabs are legally owned by individual drivers who conduct their business through corporations, each carrying only the minimum insurance required by § 370 of the Vehicle and Traffic Law. Walkovszky v Carlton (1966) 18 N.Y.2d 414, 276 N.Y.S.2d 585, 223 N.E.2d 6

Since the responsibility for imposing conditions on the privilege of incorporation has been committed by the constitution to the Legislature and it may not be implied that the Legislature intended, without discussion or debate, to require taxi corporations to carry automobile liability insurance over and above that mandated by the Vehicle and Traffic Law, a complaint was insufficient to hold an individual defendant liable merely by alleging that he was a stockholder in ten corporations, each of which had but two cabs registered in its name and covered by merely the minimum automobile liability insurance required. Walkovszky v Carlton (1966) 18 N.Y.2d 414, 276 N.Y.S.2d 585, 223 N.E.2d 6

§ 402.   Certificate of incorporation; contents

(a) A certificate, entitled "Certificate of incorporation of .... (name of corporation) under section 402 of the Business Corporation Law", shall be signed by each incorporator, with his name and address included in such certificate and delivered to the department of state. It shall set forth:

(1) The name of the corporation.

(2) The purpose or purposes for which it is formed, it being sufficient to state, either alone or with other purposes, that the purpose of the corporation is to engage in any lawful act or activity for which corporations may be organized under this chapter, provided that it also state that it is not formed to engage in any act or activity requiring the consent or approval of any state official, department, board, agency or other body without such consent or approval first being obtained. By such statement all lawful acts and activities shall be within the purposes of the corporation, except for express limitations therein or in this chapter, if any.

(3) The county within this state in which the office of the corporation is to be located.

(4) The aggregate number of shares which the corporation shall have the authority to issue; if such shares are to consist of one class only, the par value of the shares or a statement that the shares are without par value; or, if the shares are to be divided into classes, the number of shares of each class and the par value of the shares having par value and a statement as to which shares, if any, are without par value.

(5) If the shares are to be divided into classes, the designation of each class and a statement of the

relative rights, preferences and limitations of the shares of each class.

(6) If the shares of any preferred class are to be issued in series, the designation of each series and a statement of the variations in the relative rights, preferences and limitations as between series insofar as the same are to be fixed in the certificate of incorporation, a statement of any authority to be vested in the board to establish and designate series and to fix the variations in the relative rights, preferences and limitations as between series and a statement of any limit on the authority of the board of directors to change the number of shares of any series of preferred shares as provided in paragraph (e) of section 502 (Issue of any class of preferred shares in series).

(7) A designation of the secretary of state as agent of the corporation upon whom process against it may be served and the post office address within or without this state to which the secretary of state shall mail a copy of any process against it served upon him.

(8) If the corporation is to have a registered agent, his name and address within this state and a statement that the registered agent is to be the agent of the corporation upon whom process against it may be served.

(9) The duration of the corporation if other than perpetual.

(10) [Repealed]

(b) The certificate of incorporation may set forth a provision eliminating or limiting the personal liability of directors to the corporation or its shareholders for damages for any breach of duty in such capacity, provided that no such provision shall eliminate or limit:

(1) the liability of any director if a judgment or other final adjudication adverse to him establishes that his acts or omissions were in bad faith or involved intentional misconduct or a knowing violation of law or that he personally gained in fact a financial profit or other advantage to which he was not legally entitled or that his acts violated section 719, or

(2) the liability of any director for any act or omission prior to the adoption of a provision authorized by this paragraph.

(c) The certificate of incorporation may set forth any provision, not inconsistent with this chapter or any other statute of this state, relating to the business of the corporation, its affairs, its rights or powers, or the rights or powers of its shareholders, directors or officers including any provision relating to matters which under this chapter are required or permitted to be set forth in the by-laws. It is not necessary to set forth in the certificate of incorporation any of the powers enumerated in this chapter.

History: Add, L 1961, ch 855, eff Sept 1, 1963; amd, L 1962, ch 834, § 7, eff Sept 1, 1963; L 1975, ch 364; L 1979, ch 154, § 1, eff May 29, 1979; L 1982, ch 832, § 4, eff Oct 25, 1982; L 1985, ch 499, § 1, eff Oct 22, 1985; L 1987, ch 367, § 1, eff July 23, 1987; L

1997, ch 449, § 3, eff Feb 22, 1998; L 1998, ch 375, § 5, eff Aug 13, 1998.

CASE ANNOTATIONS

Court properly dismissed shareholders' derivative action for alleged breach of fiduciary duties under CLS Bus Corp § 720 where (1) pursuant to CLS Bus Corp § 402(b), corporation's certificate of incorporation shielded its board of directors from personal liability, subject to certain exceptions, for negligent acts or omissions that occurred in their capacity as directors, and (2) plaintiffs' conclusory allegations did not support contention that directors' conduct rose to level of intentional misconduct, bad faith, or knowing violation of law. Bildstein v Atwater (1995, 2d Dept) 222 A.D.2d 545, 635 N.Y.S.2d 88

In action against foreign corporation, plaintiffs properly relied on defendant's designation of New York County on its certificate of incorporation in selecting venue, and thus defendant's motion to change venue to Suffolk County (plaintiffs' county of residence) on ground that it had no principal office or place of business in New York when action was commenced, and that its principal office was located in Virginia, should have been denied. Cooper v Mobil Oil Corp. (1999, 1st Dept) 264 A.D.2d 578, 694 N.Y.S.2d 65

Although the Internal Revene Code exempts from income taxation "corporations organized for the exclusive purpose of holding title to property, collecting income therefrom, and turning over the entire amount thereof, less expenses, to an organization which itself is exempt under this section," the New York tax exemption statute is more restrictive; the owning corporation must be organized or conducted exclusively for one of the statutorily prescribed purposes and the property must be used for that purpose. Return Realty Corp. v Ranieri (1974) 78 Misc. 2d 825, 359 N.Y.S.2d 611

While the language of a corporation's amendment to its certificate of incorporation did not explicitly say that the corporation was waiving N.Y. Bus. Corp. Law § 912, it nonetheless clearly evinced an intention to supercede it; the two schemes often conflicted with one another, and contained numerous similar, but not identical, definitions, standards and requirements. Vassell v Reliance Sec. Group (2004, SD NY) 328 F. Supp. 2d 454

UNDER FORMER LAW

A certificate of incorporation may be deficient in stating the rights of preferred stock and stockholders where it merely states that they shall have a preference to payment at par in case of liquidation or dissolution, and shall be entitled to dividends, "if any," as provided by the by-laws. People ex rel. Siegel v Lyons (1922) 201 A.D. 530, 194 N.Y.S. 484

Under § 5 of former Stock Corp. L., restrictions on transfer and ownership of capital stock could be stated and imposed in and by provisions of the certificate of incorporation. Hassel v Pohle (1925) 214 A.D. 654, 212 N.Y.S. 561

Restrictions on rights otherwise conferred on stockholders, or a majority thereof, could formerly, at least, be imposed only by the certificate of incorporation, not by the by-laws. Christal v Petry (1949) 275 A.D. 550, 90 N.Y.S.2d 620, affd 301 N.Y. 562, 93 N.E.2d 450; Peets v Manhasset Civil Engineers, Inc. (1946) 4 Misc. 2d 683, 68 N.Y.S.2d 338

The secretary of state has the right to pass upon the form of the certificate and as to whether or not it is entitled to be filed under the statute, subject to review in a proper proceeding. People ex rel. Davenport v Rice (1893) 68 Hun 24, 22 N.Y.S. 631

Recitation of facts is not a statement of them, requirement of this section that certificate of incorporation shall state certain facts is not satisfied by recitation of them in certificate. Re Wendover Athletic Ass'n (1911) 70 Misc 273, 128 N.Y.S. 561

A provision in a proposed certificate of incorporation, restraining the stockholders' freedom to contract is improper. 1911 Ops Atty Gen 600

The secretary of state need not file a certificate of incorporation where execution is proved by subscribing witness and not by acknowledgment. 1911 Ops Atty Gen 651

§ 403. Certificate of incorporation; effect

Upon the filing of the certificate of incorporation by the department of state, the corporate existence shall begin, and such certificate shall be conclusive evidence that all conditions precedent have been fulfilled and that the corporation has been formed under this chapter, except in an action or special proceeding brought by the attorney-general. Notwithstanding the above, a certificate of incorporation may set forth a date subsequent to filing, not to exceed ninety days after filing, upon which date corporate existence shall begin.

History: Add, L 1961, ch 855; amd, L 1962 ch 317, § 6, eff Sept 1, 1963; L 1962, ch 317, eff Sept 1, 1963; L 1962, ch 834, § 8, eff Sept 1, 1963; L 1986, ch 590, § 1, eff Sept 1, 1986.

CASE ANNOTATIONS

Buyer was not entitled to specific performance of contract for sale of real property where buyer's certificate of incorporation was not filed until 18 months after contract was executed, and thus buyer lacked capacity to contract at time of execution. 183 Holding Corp. v 183 Lorraine St. Assocs. (1998, 2d Dept) 251 A.D.2d 386, 673 N.Y.S.2d 745, later proceeding (2d Dept) 251 A.D.2d 400, 675 N.Y.S.2d 543, motion den (2d Dept) 259 A.D.2d 694, 686 N.Y.S.2d 710 and later proceeding (App Div, 2d Dept) 700 N.Y.S.2d 756, later proceeding (App Div, 2d Dept) 700 N.Y.S.2d 757 and related proceeding (NY A.D., 2d Dept) 2000 N.Y. A.D. LEXIS 8379, later proceeding (NY A.D., 2d Dept) 2000 N.Y. A.D. LEXIS 8382

Individual defendants were individually liable for materials purchased from plaintiff lumber company on credit prior to formation of corporation by defendants. Tarolli Lumber Co. v Andreassi (1977, 4th Dept) 59 A.D.2d 1011, 399 N.Y.S.2d 739

In action to pierce corporate veil and hold owners of undercapitalized corporation personally liable for judgment debt in amount of $66,928.88, court misconstrued action as one for fraud and erred in holding plaintiffs to clear and convincing standard of proof; action to pierce corporate veil is equitable in nature and, although proof of fraud is relevant, plaintiff is not required to plead or prove actual fraud. Rotella v Derner (2001, 4th Dept) 283 A.D.2d 1026, 723 N.Y.S.2d 801, app den 96 N.Y.2d 720, 733 N.Y.S.2d 372, 759 N.E.2d 371 and reargument den (4th Dept) 286 A.D.2d 1003, 733 N.Y.S.2d 660

Town lacked standing to file N.Y. C.P.L.R. art. 78 proceeding since: (1) it was not an established corporation, since it had filed no incorporation papers with the New York Department of State under N.Y. Bus. Corp. Law §§ 403 and N.Y. Not-for-Profit Corp. Law §§ 403 and 904(a), (2) the state's highest court had not recognized it as a corporation, or as the governing body of the town, (3) the town failed to show that it was the successor corporation to the original incorporated proprietors of the town, (4) a municipal corporation was a political subdivision of the State having only the authority delegated to it by the State under N.Y. Const. art. IX, § 2, and (5) another town specifically included the town, and was a legitimate municipal corporation with the authority to govern the town under N.Y. Town Law § 2. Matter of Town of Montauk, Inc. v Pataki (2007, 2d Dept) 40 App Div 3d 772, 835 NYS2d 447, motion den (2007, 2d Dept) 40 App Div 3d 772, 834 NYS2d 661

It would seem that the failure to file a certificate of incorporation bars the application of the de facto doctrine. Mindlin v Gehrlein's Marina, Inc. (1968) 58 Misc. 2d 153, 295 N.Y.S.2d 172

If it is held that the defendant had not achieved the status of a de facto corporation at the time an order of attachment was granted, it being conceded that it was not a de jure corporation at such time, it follows that it had no legal existence at all and could not sue or be sued. Mindlin v Gehrlein's Marina, Inc. (1968) 58 Misc. 2d 153, 295 N.Y.S.2d 172

Where 2 corporations had been granted identical corporate name, first corporation was in business of managing property and had been dissolved by Secretary of State for failure to pay its corporate franchise taxes, and second corporation had later been formed to conduct business of dissemination and communication of sports information, first corporation remained de facto corporation by continuing to conduct new business after its dissolution, and court would grant each corporation's motion for preliminary injunction, with first corporation being enjoined from initiating any new court action or proceeding pending further order and from using corporate name in connection with any educational or sports publication, and second corporation being enjoined from interfering with business of

first corporation, including its pending lawsuits, and from exercising any control over property owned by first corporation, and each corporation would be ordered to file undertaking. H.E.G. Dev. & Mgmt. Corp. v Blumberg (1997, Sup) 171 Misc. 2d 740, 656 N.Y.S.2d 127

UNDER FORMER LAW

Although plaintiff corporation had not filed a certificate of incorporation and was not in existence under N.Y. Bus. Corp. Law § 403, the corporation existed under the doctrine of corporation estoppel because defendants, a partner in the corporation and his brother-in-law, had engaged in business dealings about the corporation, during which they recognized its corporate status; moreover, the partner was the person who signed a lease, a lease modification agreement, and a lease termination agreement, each time in his capacity as "president" of plaintiff corporation. Rubenstein v Mayor (2007, 2d Dept) 41 App Div 3d 826, 839 NYS2d 170

The existence of a corporation is not affected by the fact that no stock was ever actually issued, if its certificate of incorporation was duly filed and payment of the tax and filing fee was made. Gale-Hasslacher Corp. v Carmen Contracting Corp. (1961, Sup) 219 N.Y.S.2d 212

A Secretary of State's responsibility in passing upon certificates of authority is limited. Industrial Psychology, Inc. v Simon (1962, 1st Dept) 16 A.D.2d 114, 226 N.Y.S.2d 148

§ 404. Organization meeting

(a) After the corporate existence has begun, an organization meeting of the incorporator or incorporators shall be held within or without this state, for the purpose of adopting by-laws, electing directors to hold office until the first annual meeting of shareholders, except as authorized under section 704 (Classification of directors), and the transaction of such other business as may come before the meeting. If there are two or more incorporators, the meeting may be held at the call of any incorporator, who shall give at least five days' notice thereof by mail to each other incorporator, which notice shall set forth the time and place of the meeting. Notice need not be given to any incorporator who attends the meeting or submits a signed waiver of notice before or after the meeting. If there are more than two incorporators, a majority shall constitute a quorum and the act of the majority of the incorporators present at a meeting at which a quorum is present shall be the act of the incorporators. An incorporator may act in person or by proxy signed by the incorporator or his attorney-in-fact.

(b) Any action permitted to be taken at the organization meeting may be taken without a meeting if each incorporator or his attorney-in-fact signs an instrument setting forth the action so taken.

(c) If an incorporator dies or is for any reason unable to act, action may be taken as provided in such event in paragraph (c) of section 615 (Written consent of shareholders, subscribers or incorporators without a meeting).

History: Add, L 1961, ch 855, eff Sept 1, 1963; amd, L 1963, ch 748, § 5, eff Sept 1, 1963.

CASE ANNOTATIONS

In a proceeding upon a director and half owner's petition for a judicial dissolution of a corporation, petitioner was a proper party to seek dissolution of the corporation, pursuant to Bus Corp Law § 1104(a), where, even though the corporation had not had an organizational meeting as required by Bus Corp Law § 404(a), each incorporator had signed an instrument setting forth the action taken, and where petitioner had paid consideration for his shares in full, although no stock certificates had been issued. Re Rappaport (1985, 2d Dept) 110 A.D.2d 639, 487 N.Y.S.2d 376

§ 405. [Repealed]

History: Add, L 1974, ch 168; amd, L 1978, ch 405, § 44, eff July 24, 1978; repealed, L 2006, ch 58, § 3 (Part D), eff April 12, 2006.

§ 405-a. Institution for children; approval of certificate

Every certificate of incorporation which includes among its corporate purposes, the authority to care for children through the establishment or operation of an institution for destitute, delinquent, abandoned, neglected or dependent children shall have endorsed thereon or annexed thereto the approval of the office of children and family services. Provided, however, nothing herein shall authorize such corporation to place out or board out children, as those terms are defined in the social services law, or to care for children in a facility other than an institution possessing an operating certificate issued by the office of children and family services. No certificate of incorporation shall be approved pursuant to this section on or after June first, two thousand seven.

History: Add, L 1997, ch 436, § 50 (Part B), eff Aug 20, 1997; amd, L 2007, ch 107, § 2, eff July 3, 2007, deemed eff on and after June 1, 2007.

§ 406. Filing of a certificate of incorporation; facility for alcoholism or alcohol abuse, substance abuse, substance dependence, or chemical abuse or dependence

Every certificate of incorporation which includes among its corporate purposes the establishment or operation of a program of services for alcoholism or alcohol abuse, substance abuse, substance dependence, or chemical abuse or dependence shall have endorsed thereon or annexed thereto the approval of the commissioner of the state office of alcoholism and substance abuse services.

History: Add, L 1984, ch 211, § 1, eff June 12, 1984; amd, L 1999, ch 558, § 24, eff Oct 5, 1999.

§ 407. [Repealed]

History: Add, L 1985, ch 99, § 1, eff May 21, 1985; repealed, L 1999, ch 558, § 25, eff Oct 5, 1999.

§ 408. Statement; filing

1. Except as provided in paragraph eight of this section, each domestic corporation, and each foreign corporation authorized to do business in this state, shall, during the applicable filing period as determined by subdivision three of this section, file a statement setting forth:

(a) The name and business address of its chief executive officer.

(b) The street address of its principal executive office.

(c) The post office address within or without this state to which the secretary of state shall mail a copy of any process against it served upon him or her. Such address shall supersede any previous address on file with the department of state for this purpose.

2. Except as provided in paragraph eight of this section, such statement shall be made on forms prescribed by the secretary of state, and the information therein contained shall be given as of the date of the execution of the statement. Such statement shall only request reporting of information required under paragraph one of this section. It shall be signed and delivered to the department of state.

3. Except as provided in paragraph eight of this section, for the purpose of this section the applicable filing period for a corporation shall be the calendar month during which its original certificate of incorporation or application for authority were filed or the effective date thereof if stated. The applicable filing period shall only occur: (a) annually, during the period starting on April 1, 1992 and ending on March 31, 1994; and (b) biennially, during a period starting on April 1 and ending on March 31 thereafter. Those corporations that filed between April 1, 1992 and June 30, 1994 shall not be required to file such statements again until such time as they would have filed, had this subdivision not been amended.

4. The provisions of paragraph (g) of section one hundred four of this chapter shall not be applicable to filings pursuant to this section.

5. The provisions of this section and section 409 of this article shall not apply to a farm corporation. For the purposes of this subdivision, the term "farm corporation" shall mean any domestic corporation or foreign corporation authorized to do business in this state under this chapter engaged in the production of crops, livestock and livestock products on land used in agricultural production, as defined in section 301 of the agriculture and markets law. However, this exception shall not apply to farm corporations that have filed statements with the department of state which have been submitted through the department of taxation and finance pursuant to paragraph eight of this section.

6. No such statement shall be accepted for filing when a certificate of resignation for receipt of process has been filed under section three hundred six-A of this chapter unless the corporation has stated a different address for process which does not include the name of the party previously designated in the address for process in such certificate.

7. A domestic corporation or foreign corporation may amend its statement to change the information required by subparagraphs (a) and (b) of paragraph one of this section. Such amendment shall be made on forms prescribed by the secretary of state. It shall be signed and delivered to the department of state.

8. (a) The commissioner of taxation and finance and the secretary of state may agree to allow corporations to provide the statement specified in paragraph one of this section on tax reports filed with the department of taxation and finance in lieu of biennial

statements. This agreement may apply to tax reports due for tax years starting on or after January first, two thousand sixteen.

(b) If the agreement described in subparagraph (a) of this paragraph is made, each corporation required to file the statement specified in paragraph one of this section that is also subject to tax under article nine or nine-A of the tax law shall include such statement annually on its tax report filed with the department of taxation and finance in lieu of filing a statement under this section with the department of state and in a manner prescribed by the commissioner of taxation and finance. However, each corporation required to file a statement under this section must continue to file the biennial statement required by this section with the department of state until the corporation in fact has filed a tax report with the department of taxation and finance that includes all required information. After that time, the corporation shall continue to deliver annually the statement specified in paragraph one of this section on its tax report in lieu of the biennial statement required by this section.

(c) If the agreement described in subparagraph (a) of this paragraph is made, the department of taxation and finance shall deliver to the department of state for filing the statement specified in paragraph one of this section for each corporation that files a tax report containing such statement. The department of taxation and finance must, to the extent feasible, also include the current name of the corporation, department of state identification number for such corporation, the name, signature and capacity of the signer of the statement, name and street address of the filer of the statement, and the email address, if any, of the filer of the statement.

History: Add, L 1998, ch 375, § 6, eff Aug 13, 1998; amd, L 1992, ch 55, § 399, eff April 10, 1992; L 1994, ch 170, § 200, eff July 1, 1994; L 1997, ch 469, § 2, eff Nov 24, 1997; L 1998, ch 375, § 7, eff Aug 13, 1998; L 1999, ch 172, § 7, eff July 6, 1999,8, eff July 6, 1999; L 2000, ch 172, § 2, eff July 18, 2000; L 2015, ch 59, § 3 (Part S), eff April 13, 2015.

§ 409. Penalty for failure to file; cure

1. Each corporation which has failed to file its statement within the time required by this chapter after thirty days shall be shown to be past due on the records of the department of state.

2. Each corporation which has failed to file its statement for two years shall be shown to be delinquent on the records of the department of state sixty days after a notice of delinquency has been mailed to the last known address of such corporation. Such delinquency shall be removed from the records of the department of state upon the filing of the current statement required by section four hundred eight of this article, and the payment of a fine of two hundred fifty dollars.

3. The notice of delinquency shall state the cure and fine for such delinquency as determined by subdivision two of this section and the period during which such delinquency shall be foreborne without the imposition of such fine.

4. This section shall not apply to corporations that have submitted a statement pursuant to paragraph eight of section four hundred eight of this chapter.

History: Add, L 1992, ch 55, § 399, eff April 10, 1992; L 2015, ch 59, § 4 (Part S), eff April 13, 2015.

ARTICLE 5
CORPORATE FINANCE

History: Add, L 1961, ch 855, eff Sept 1, 1963.

Schedule of sections, amd, L 1962, ch 834, § 9, L 1963, ch 738, eff Sept 1, 1963.

§ 501. Authorized shares

(a) Every corporation shall have power to create and issue the number of shares stated in its certificate of incorporation. Such shares may be all of one class or may be divided into two or more classes. Each class shall consist of either shares with par value or shares without par value, having such designation and such relative voting, dividend, liquidation and other rights, preferences and limitations, consistent with this chapter, as shall be stated in the certificate of incorporation. The certificate of incorporation may deny, limit or otherwise define the voting rights and may limit or otherwise define the dividend or liquidation rights of shares of any class, but no such denial, limitation or definition of voting rights shall be effective unless at the time one or more classes of outstanding shares or bonds, singly or in the aggregate, are entitled to full voting rights, and no such limitation or definition of dividend or liquidation rights shall be effective unless at the time one or more classes of outstanding shares, singly or in the aggregate, are entitled to unlimited dividend and liquidation rights.

Business Corporation Law

(b) If the shares are divided into two or more classes, the shares of each class shall be designated to distinguish them from the shares of all other classes. Shares which are entitled to preference in the distribution of dividends or assets shall not be designated as common shares. Shares which are not entitled to preference in the distribution of dividends or assets shall be common shares, even if identified by a class or other designation, and shall not be designated as preferred shares.

(c) Subject to the designations, relative rights, preferences and limitations applicable to separate series and except as otherwise permitted by subparagraph two of paragraph (a) of section five hundred five of this article, each share shall be equal to every other share of the same class. With respect to corporations owning or leasing residential premises and operating the same on a cooperative basis, however, provided that (1) liquidation or other distribution rights are substantially equal per share, (2) changes in maintenance charges and general assessments pursuant to a proprietary lease have been and are hereafter fixed and determined on an equal per-share basis or on an equal per-room basis or as an equal percentage of the maintenance charges, and (3) voting rights are substantially equal per share or the certificate of incorporation provides that the shareholders holding the shares allocated to each apartment or dwelling unit owned by the corporation shall be entitled to one vote in the aggregate regardless of the number of shares allocated to the apartment or dwelling unit or the number of shareholders holding such shares, shares of the same class shall not be considered unequal because of variations in fees or charges payable to the corporation upon sale or transfer of shares and appurtenant proprietary leases that are provided for in proprietary leases, occupancy agreements or offering plans or properly approved amendments to the foregoing instruments.

History: Add, L 1961, ch 855, eff Sept 1, 1963; amd, L 1962, ch 834, § 10, eff Sept 1, 1963; L 1965, ch 803, § 5, eff Sept 1, 1965; L 1986, ch 598, § 1; L 1988, ch 743, §§ 2, 4; L 1989, ch 81, § 3 (which amendment was repealed, L 1992, ch 510, § 1, eff July 24, 1992, deemed eff May 3, 1989); L 1989, ch 81, § 1, eff May 3, 1989, deemed eff July 24, 1986; L 1996, ch 59, § 1, eff April 15, 1996.

CASE ANNOTATIONS

1. Generally
2. Retroactive application
3. Cooperative apartment transfer fees; generally
4. – Fees held enforceable
5. – Fees not held enforceable
6. Other fees and surcharges
7. –10. [Reserved for future use.]
11. Under former law

1. Generally

Cause of action for breach of fiduciary duty was not barred by res judicata, although plaintiffs had raised claim in federal court action that corporate merger violated CLS Bus Corp § 501(c), where federal court had refused to retain pendent jurisdiction as to any cause of action based on nonfederal claim, thus state claim was not within federal court's stated jurisdiction, and federal court did not consider claim on merits. Beaumont v American Can Co. (1990, 1st Dept) 160 A.D.2d 174, 553 N.Y.S.2d 145

Arrangement asserted by shareholder-tenant of cooperative apartment, by which he was relieved of financial obligations which other shareholders of same class had to pay, was prohibited by CLS Bus Corp § 501(c), and thus shareholder-tenant would be declared bound by written terms of proprietary lease. Jones v Fordham Hill Owners Corp. (1996, 1st Dept) 225 A.D.2d 465, 639 N.Y.S.2d 384

Defendant shareholders' voluntary waiver of their right to dividends on their stock in plaintiff corporation was enforceable where (1) they received, in exchange, valuable contract to service corporation's real property, (2) nothing in CLS Bus Corp § 501(c) prohibits such waiver, and (3) no public policy was otherwise implicated; so long as there is no violation of public policy, statutory right may be waived if made with knowledge of right and intention to waive it. Cherry Green Prop. Corp. v Wolf (2001, 1st Dept) 281 A.D.2d 367, 722 N.Y.S.2d 537

Partnership minority discount did not contravene the distinctly corporate statutory proscription against treating holders of the same class of stock differently, or undermine the remedial goal of the appraisal statutes to protect shareholders from being forced to sell at unfair values, or inevitably encourage oppressive majority conduct; nor did a decreased marketability discount implicate policy concerns, as it applied equally to all partnership interests, not those of the deceased partner only. Vick v Albert (2008, 1st Dept) 47 App Div 3d 482, 849 NYS2d 250.

Because a bankruptcy trustee failed to disburse the family members the $2,000 per share for their stock, the family members, who were express third-party beneficiaries under a merger agreement, had the right to enforce its terms by way of an action for breach of contract under N.Y. Bus. Corp. Law § 501(c). Kassover v Prism Venture Partners, LLC (2008, 1st Dept) 53 App Div 3d 444, 862 NYS2d 493.

Four of the minority shareholders' causes of action were properly dismissed because, while two of the minority shareholders had standing to assert a cause of action against the corporation for failure to pay equal profit distributions with other shareholders in their class, the minority shareholders failed to allege specific facts supporting their contention that the directors were interested, such that a futility demand was not required. JAS Family Trust v Oceana Holding Corp. (2013, 2d Dept) 109 App Div 3d 639, 970 NYS2d 813.

Trial court properly granted a cooperative corporation's summary judgment motion pursuant to N.Y. C.P.L.R. 3212 and ruled in favor of a cooperative corporation in a tenant's declaratory judgment action alleging that the cooperative's managing agent improperly withheld consent to sublet an apartment; provisions of a lease and cooperative by-laws violated N.Y. Bus. Corp. Law § 501(c) by giving original purchasers more favorable subletting rights than non-original purchasers, and the cooperative did not waive its right to assert the illegality pursuant to N.Y. C.P.L.R. 3018(b). Spiegel v 1065 Park Ave. Corp. (2003, A.D., 1st Dept) 759 N.Y.S.2d 461

Business Corporation Law § 501(c) did not prohibit an offering plan or proprietary lease from exempting a holder of unsold shares from sublet fees or board-approval requirements applicable to other shareholders. Yatter v Continental Owners Corp. (2005, A.D., 2d Dept) 802 N.Y.S.2d 239

Owner was entitled to summary judgment in shareholder's suit challenging enactment of resolution barring certain subleasing without board approval because, among other things, N.Y. Bus. Corp. Law § 501(c) precluded any such special subletting rights. Bregman v 111 Tenants Corp. (2012, App Div, 1st Dept) 943 NYS2d 100

2. Retroactive application

Legislature expressly intended that CLS Bus Corp § 501(c), as amended by L 1986, ch 598 § 1, be applied retroactively, so as to validate transfer fee provisions in bylaws and certificates of incorporation already in existence at date of enactment. Vaughn v Manor Towers Owners Corp. (1987, 1st Dept) 135 A.D.2d 380, 521 N.Y.S.2d 680

Amendment to CLS Bus Corp § 501(c) (L 1986, ch 598) applies to shareholders of cooperative apartment corporations from and after date of execution of proprietary leases and occupancy agreements executed before effective date of act. Thomas v 81-87 Owners Corp. (1989) 142 Misc. 2d 237, 536 N.Y.S.2d 946

3. Cooperative apartment transfer fees; generally

Under CLS Bus Corp Law § 501(c), fee on transfer of shares in cooperative apartment corporation ("flip tax") may not be imposed by corporation's board of directors, when bylaws of corporation authorize board to impose on such transfer and assignment only "reasonable fee to cover actual expenses and attorneys' fees of Corporation, service fee of Corporation and such other conditions as it may determine"; nor may flip tax which is not in proportion to shares held by assignor be imposed under either "cash requirements" or "assignment" provisions of proprietary lease, or, in view of mandate of § 501(c), by amendment of bylaws. Fe Bland v Two Trees Management Co. (1985) 66 N.Y.2d 556, 498 N.Y.S.2d 336, 489 N.E.2d 223

Under proper circumstances, fee on transfer of shares in cooperative apartment corporation ("flip tax") may be adopted, as long as such tax conforms to requirements of CLS Bus Corp L § 501(c). Fe Bland v Two Trees Management Co. (1985) 66 N.Y.2d 556, 498 N.Y.S.2d 336, 489 N.E.2d 223

Co-operative may lawfully require shareholders to tender transfer fee ("flip tax") before co-operative agrees to waive its option to purchase shareholders' shares. Lowy v Bay Terrace Cooperative, Section VIII, Inc. (1988, ED NY) 698 F. Supp. 1058, affd (CA2 NY) 869 F.2d 174

4. – Fees held enforceable

Fee imposed on transfer of shares in cooperative apartment corporation did not violate equality-of-shares mandate of CLS Bus Corp § 501(c) merely because charges assessed were not equal per share and certain preferences and exemptions had been created for holders of unsold shares, since fee was validly adopted under terms of offering plan, proprietary lease and bylaws, and every shareholder of record was entitled to one vote for each share owned. Mogulescu v 255 West 98th Street Owners Corp. (1988, 1st Dept) 135 A.D.2d 32, 523 N.Y.S.2d 801, app dismd 71 N.Y.2d 964, 529 N.Y.S.2d 74, 524 N.E.2d 428 and app dismd, app den 73 N.Y.2d 868, 537 N.Y.S.2d 487, 534 N.E.2d 325

Imposition of "waiver of option" fee on outgoing shareholders in housing cooperative who wished to sell their shares on open market rather than resell them to cooperative corporation at book value, as their agreement provided, was valid exercise of cooperative board's power where fee was applied in evenly proportioned fashion, and thus did not violate mandate of CLS Bus Corp § 501(c) that each share of stock be equal to every other share in same class. Meichsner v Valentine Gardens Cooperative, Inc. (1988, 2d Dept) 137 A.D.2d 797, 525 N.Y.S.2d 345

In action for reimbursement of waiver of option fee imposed by cooperative association, defendant was entitled to summary judgment since imposition of 40 percent waiver of option fee upon sale of plaintiff's shares in cooperative, as authorized by amendment to bylaws of association, did not contravene CLS Bus Corp § 501(c) even though fee schedule contained in bylaw provision sanctioned assessment of unequal fees in respect to holders of same class of stock. Amer v Bay Terrace Cooperative Section II, Inc. (1988, 2d Dept) 142 A.D.2d 704, 531 N.Y.S.2d 33

Cooperative corporation was entitled to summary judgment dismissing action to recover transfer fee (flip tax) exacted at closing of sale and assignment of plaintiff's cooperative apartment in 1984 since 1986 amendment to CLS Bus Corp § 501 authorized such fees retroactive to date of execution of any existing proprietary lease when fee is "provided for in proprietary lease, occupancy agreements or offering plans or properly approved amendments to the foregoing instruments," and fee in instant case was included in amendment to offering plan prior to plaintiff's purchase and was also included in bylaws. De Mello v 79th Street Tenants Corp. (1987) 136 Misc. 2d 73, 517 N.Y.S.2d 892

Although cooperative apartment corporation was entitled to partial summary judgment upholding its authority to impose transfer tax under CLS Bus Corp § 501(c), there was triable fact issue as to amount of tax shareholder was obligated to pay at time of sale. Thomas v 81-87 Owners Corp. (1989) 142 Misc. 2d 237, 536 N.Y.S.2d 946

Action of cooperative corporation's board of directors in assessing transfer fee or "flip tax" on transferors of shares in corporation was within its authority under CLS Bus Corp § 501(c) where fee was covered in governing bylaw set forth in second amended offering plan, notwithstanding fact that amended bylaw also specified that fee provision was not to apply to sponsor or holders of unsold shares, since § 501(c) permits variations among shareholders in calculating such fee. 1326 Apartments Corp. v Barbosa (1990) 147 Misc. 2d 264, 555 N.Y.S.2d 560

Action of cooperative corporation's board of directors in assessing transfer fee or "flip tax" on transferors of shares in corporation was within its authority under CLS Bus Corp § 501(c) where (1) terms of governing bylaw set forth in second amended offering plan described

manner of calculating fee and provided that, for first 36 months after closing of cooperative conversion, calculations could not be changed but that thereafter board could "modify or extend" fee, and (2) board continued fee without modification through time of defendants' sale of their shares to third party. 1326 Apartments Corp. v Barbosa (1990) 147 Misc. 2d 264, 555 N.Y.S.2d 560

Action of cooperative corporation's board of directors in assessing transfer fee or "flip tax" on transferors of shares in corporation was within its authority under CLS Bus Corp § 501(c) where fee was covered in governing bylaws set forth in second amended offering plan, notwithstanding absence of provision for fee in form proprietary lease. 1326 Apartments Corp. v Barbosa (1990) 147 Misc. 2d 264, 555 N.Y.S.2d 560

5. – Fees not held enforceable

Cooperative corporation was not entitled to vacatur of default judgment pursuant to CLS CPLR § 317 in action by shareholder to recover transfer fees imposed in violation of CLS Bus Corp § 501 where shareholder sought to move from current apartment to smaller one in same building, she sold her shares of stock and purchased fewer shares from another, and corporation charged member $6 per share waiver of option fee on her own shares and $12 per share transfer fee for acquisition of new shares; since unequal charge was provided for only in resolution of board of directors, rather than by terms of offering plan, proprietary lease, bylaws or amendments, as required by § 501, corporation failed to set forth meritorious defense warranting vacatur. Reisch v Greenwood Arms Coop. Corp. (1989, 2d Dept) 153 A.D.2d 844, 545 N.Y.S.2d 364

A resolution passed by defendant board of directors of a cooperative apartment building without shareholder approval, which raised the fee on the resale or transfer of shares and imposed a higher fee for owners of less than five years and original purchasers than for longer-term owners and outside purchasers who resold, would be voided, since the resolution violated the cooperative's certificate of incorporation and Bus Corp Law § 501(c), by imposing significantly different charges on owners of shares of the same class. Fe Bland v Two Trees Management Co. (1984) 125 Misc. 2d 111, 479 N.Y.S.2d 123

To require that a purchaser from an original subscriber to a cooperative corporation pay a transfer fee when he sells his shares, but not require the purchaser from a holder of unsold shares to pay the same under similar circumstances, results in shareholders, all of whom own the same class of shares, possessing different rights, and such unequal treatment of shareholders would be found to contravene Bus Corp Law § 501(c); the statute does not authorize the board of directors to enact bylaws creating preferences among shareholders, all of whom own the same class and series of shares. Mullins v 510 East 86th Street Owners, Inc. (1984) 126 Misc. 2d 758, 483 N.Y.S.2d 631

System of transfer fees ("flip taxes") instituted by co-operative, whereby shareholders who happened to purchase their shares between 1974 and 1976 pay to co-operative amounts much greater than waiver of option fees exacted from all other selling shareholders, is illegal under CLS Bus Corp L § 501(c), where nothing in proprietary lease, occupancy agreement, or offering plan of co-operative authorizes enactment of rules governing sale of apartments that differed depending on when shareholder bought apartment; resale policy which exacts different percentages of sale profits from shareholders, depending on number of shares shareholder has held stock, violates § 501(c). Lowy v Bay Terrace Cooperative, Section VIII, Inc. (1988, ED NY) 698 F. Supp. 1058, affd (CA2 NY) 869 F.2d 174

6. Other fees and surcharges

Subleasing fee imposed by cooperative corporation did not violate CLS § 501(c) since (1) surcharge was same for all shareholders (5 percent of rent collected in those instances where rent exceeded maintenance cost), (2) inside purchasers were not assessed differently than outsiders, and (3) fee was not affected by length of ownership, bore no relationship to number or class of shares owned, and was strictly dependent on rent received by sublessor. McCabe v Hoffman (1988, 1st Dept) 138 A.D.2d 287, 526 N.Y.S.2d 93

Contract rider whereby cooperative corporation imposed maintenance surcharge on dentist in event he brought in associate, although not included in contract or proprietary lease for another dentist occupying office in building, did not violate requirement of CLS Bus Corp § 501(c) that "each share shall be equal to every other share of the same class," since other dentist's agreement with board might well have been reached under different market conditions, and was in form of consent to subletthat required credit and other references from proposed subtenants. Cohen v 120 Owners Corp. (1994, 1st Dept) 205 A.D.2d 394, 613 N.Y.S.2d 615

Although 1986 amendment to CLS Bus Corp § 501(c) carved out exception for flip tax on sale of shares, it did not change statute's general mandate that shares of same class be treated equally. Wapnick v Seven Park Ave. Corp. (1997, 1st Dept) 240 A.D.2d 245, 658 N.Y.S.2d 604

Prohibition of variation in fees in CLS Bus Corp § 501(c) applies to subletting and assignment of shares as well as sale of shares. Wapnick v Seven Park Ave. Corp. (1997, 1st Dept) 240 A.D.2d 245, 658 N.Y.S.2d 604

Lessees' claim that assessments imposed by a residential cooperative corporation for repairs which the corporation made to terraces and greenhouses appurtenant to the lessees' apartments violated N.Y. Bus. Corp. Law § 501(c) was without merit. Mariaux v Turtle Bay Towers Corp. (2003, A.D., 1st Dept) 753 N.Y.S.2d 505

Corporation established its entitlement to judgment as a matter of law by demonstrating that it properly exercised its authority to impose the waiver of option fee, as such fee was validly adopted pursuant to the amended by-laws and the proprietary lease/occupancy agreement, when considered in conjunction with each other. Zilberfein v Palmer Terrace Coop., Inc. (2005, A.D., 2d Dept) 796 N.Y.S.2d 115

7. –10. [Reserved for future use.]

11. Under former law

The words "preference as to principal" have been used to distinguish certain kinds of preferred stock from stock preferred as to dividends only, and § 11 of the former Stock Corp. L. did not purport to limit the preference, but merely required that it be made definite and certain. People ex rel. Recess Exporting & Importing Corp. v Hugo (1920) 191 A.D. 628, 182 N.Y.S. 9

Section 11 of former Stock Corp. L. was construed as authorizing, unless violative of public policy, provisions in a corporate certificate requiring a class vote for particular kinds of corporate action, or a greater percentage of class approval than the statute itself would require. 1948 Ops Atty Gen Dec 14

A certificate of incorporation may provide for fractional voting rights in certain classes of stock. 1949 Ops Atty Gen March 28

§ 502.   Issue of any class of preferred shares in series

(a) If the certificate of incorporation so provides, a corporation may issue any class of preferred shares in series. Shares of each such series when issued, shall be designated to distinguish them from shares of all other series.

(b) The number of shares included in any or all series of any classes of preferred shares and any or all of the designations, relative rights, preferences and limitations of any or all such series may be fixed in the certificate of incorporation, subject to the limitation that, unless the certificate of incorporation provides otherwise, if the stated dividends and amounts payable on liquidation are not paid in full, the shares of all series of the same class shall share ratably in the payment of dividends including accumulations, if any, in accordance with the sums which would be payable on such shares if all dividends were declared and paid in full, and in any distribution of assets other than by way of dividends in accordance with the sums which would be payable on such distribution if all sums payable were discharged in full.

(c) If any such number of shares or any such designation, relative right, preference or limitation of the shares of any series is not fixed in the certificate of incorporation, it may be fixed by the board, to the extent authorized by the certificate of incorporation.

Unless otherwise provided in the certificate of incorporation, the number of preferred shares of any series so fixed by the board may be increased (but not above the total number of authorized shares of the class) or decreased (but not below the number of shares thereof then outstanding) by the board. In case the number of such shares shall be decreased, the number of shares by which the series is decreased shall, unless eliminated pursuant to paragraph (e) of this section, resume the status which they had prior to being designated as part of a series of preferred shares.

(d) Before the issue of any shares of a series established by the board, a certificate of amendment under section 805 (Certificate of amendment; contents) shall be delivered to the department of state. Such certificate shall set forth:

(1) The name of the corporation, and, if it has been changed, the name under which it was formed.

(2) The date the certificate of incorporation was filed by the department of state.

(3) That the certificate of incorporation is thereby amended by the addition of a provision stating the number, designation, relative rights, preferences, and limitations of the shares of the series as fixed by the board, setting forth in full the text of such provision.

(e) Action by the board to increase or decrease the number of preferred shares of any series pursuant to paragraph (c) of this section shall become effective by delivering to the department of state a certificate of amendment under section 805 (Certificate of amendment; contents) which shall set forth:

(1) The name of the corporation, and, if it has been changed, the name under which it was formed.

(2) The date its certificate of incorporation was filed with the department of state.

(3) That the certificate of incorporation is thereby amended to increase or decrease, as the case may be, the number of preferred shares of any series so fixed by the board, setting forth the specific terms of the amendment and the number of shares so authorized following the effectiveness of the amendment.

When no shares of any such series are outstanding, either because none were issued or because no issued shares of any such series remain outstanding, the certificate of amendment under section 805 may also set forth a statement that none of the authorized shares of such series are outstanding and that none will be issued subject to the certificate of incorporation, and, when such certificate becomes accepted for filing, it shall have the effect of eliminating from the certificate of incorporation all matters set forth therein with respect to such series of preferred shares.

History: Add, L 1961, ch 855, eff Sept 1, 1963; amd, L 1962, ch 834, § 11, eff Sept 1, 1963; L 1963, ch 738, eff Sept 1, 1963; L 1965, ch 803, § 6, eff Sept 1, 1965; L 1997, ch 449, §§ 5, 6, eff Feb 22, 1998; L 1997, ch 494, § 1, eff Feb 22, 1998.

§ 503. Subscription for shares; time of payment, forfeiture for default

(a) Unless otherwise provided by the terms of the subscription, a subscription for shares of a corporation to be formed shall be irrevocable, except with the consent of all other subscribers or the corporation, for a period of three months from its date.

(b) A subscription, whether made before or after the formation of a corporation, shall not be enforceable unless in writing and signed by the subscriber.

(c) Unless otherwise provided by the terms of the subscription, subscriptions for shares, whether made before or after the formation of a corporation, shall be paid in full at such time, or in such installments and at such times, as shall be determined by the board. Any call made by the board for payment on subscriptions shall be uniform as to all shares of the same class or of the same series. If a receiver of the corporation has been appointed, all unpaid subscriptions shall be paid at such times and in such installments as such receiver or the court may direct.

(d) In the event of default in the payment of any installment or call when due, the corporation may proceed to collect the amount due in the same manner as any debt due the corporation or the board may declare a forfeiture of the subscriptions. The subscription agreement may prescribe other penalties, not amounting to forfeiture, for failure to pay installments or calls that may become due. No forfeiture of the subscription shall be declared as against any subscriber unless the amount due thereon shall remain unpaid for a period of thirty days after written demand has been made therefor. If mailed, such written demand shall be deemed to be made when deposited in the United States mail in a sealed envelope addressed to the subscriber at his last post office address known to the corporation, with postage thereon prepaid. Upon forfeiture of the subscription, if at least fifty percent of the subscription price has been paid, the shares subscribed for shall be offered for sale for cash or a binding obligation to pay cash at a price at least sufficient to pay the full balance owed by the delinquent subscriber plus the expenses incidental to such sale, and any excess of net proceeds realized over the amount owed on such shares shall be paid to the delinquent subscriber or to his legal representative. If no prospective purchaser offers a cash price or a binding obligation to pay cash sufficient to pay the full balance owed by the delinquent subscriber plus the expenses incidental to such sale, or if less than fifty percent of the subscription price has been paid, the shares subscribed for shall be cancelled and restored to the status of authorized but unissued shares and all previous payments thereon shall be forfeited to the corporation and transferred to surplus.

(e) Notwithstanding the provisions of paragraph (d) of this section, in the event of default in payment or other performance under the instrument evidencing a subscriber's binding obligation to pay a portion of the subscription price or perform services, the corporation may pursue such remedies as are provided in such instrument or a related agreement or under law.

History: Add, L 1961, ch 855, eff Sept 1, 1963; amd, L 1962, ch 834, § 12; L 1963, ch 738, eff Sept 1, 1963; amd, L 1997, ch 449, §§ 7, 8, eff Feb 22, 1998; L 1997, ch 494, § 2, eff Feb 22, 1998.

CASE ANNOTATIONS

UNDER FORMER LAW
1. In general
2. Liability of subscriber
3. Fraudulently obtained
4. Default and forfeiture
5. Miscellaneous

Action to enforce alleged oral subscription agreements, and to compel issuance of shares of stock in 2 corporations, was not barred by statute of frauds where plaintiffs argued that they had fully paid for their shares, and triable issues of fact existed as to whether sums paid by them unequivocally referred to purchase of shares; mere fact that plaintiffs were never formally issued stock certificates did not preclude finding that they had rights of shareholders. Serdaroglu v Serdaroglu (1994, 2d Dept) 209 A.D.2d 600, 621 N.Y.S.2d 806

CLS Bus Corp § 503(b) was inapplicable to action for accounting with regard to purported oral agreement between plaintiffs (as preparers of bid proposal for newsstands at railroad stations) and individual defendants (owner-operators of such newsstands), in which plaintiffs sought 50 percent of shares of stock in corporate defendant. Himani v Mojawalla (1996, 2d Dept) 232 A.D.2d 455, 649 N.Y.S.2d 157, 33 UCCRS2d 889

Plaintiff alleging to be equitable owner of 44 percent of stock of acquisition corporation cannot succeed, where subscription agreement must be in writing to be enforceable under NYCLS Bus Corp Law § 503(b), as must agreement to transfer stock under NYCLS UCC § 8-319(a), because 3 writings signed by alleged joint venturer with plaintiff are insufficient to memorialize unwritten agreement. Zahr v Wingate Creek Acquisition Corp. (1993, SD NY) 827 F. Supp. 1061, 21 UCCRS2d 1140

UNDER FORMER LAW

1. In general
The object of a subscription is to carry out the legitimate purposes of the corporation. United States Vinegar Co. v Foehrenbach (1895) 148 N.Y. 58, 42 N.E. 403

A subscriber who enters into a valid subscription agreement becomes a stockholder subject to all of the stockholder's liabilities, even though a certificate of stock has never issued to him. Allen v Ryan (1927) 219 A.D. 634, 221 N.Y.S. 77, affd without op 246 N.Y. 609, 159 N.E. 671

A subscription contract may be on separate papers. Sodus B. & C. R. Co. v Hamlin (1881, NY) 24 Hun 390; Buffalo & J. R. Co. v Gifford (1882) 87 N.Y. 294

2. Liability of subscriber
Although this section of former Bus. Corp. L. contains no such provision, it was, at least formerly, the law that a subscriber to stock in a corporation was not bound to pay assessments on his subscription until all the stated capital had been subscribed for, although he waived this implied condition by paying prior assessments without objection on that score. Myers v Sturges (1908) 123 A.D. 470, 108 N.Y.S. 528, affd without op 197 N.Y. 526, 90 N.E. 1162

Although a subscriber for the stock of a corporation not yet in existence is not bound by his subscription, he becomes bound when after due organization he accepts the script and gives a check in payment therefor. Avon Springs Sanitarium Co. v Kellogg (1908) 125 A.D. 51, 109 N.Y.S. 153, affd without op 194 N.Y. 567, 88 N.E. 1129

A subscriber is liable for the unpaid balance due on a subscription even though the corporation is a bankrupt and a stock certificate cannot be issued. Allen v Ryan (1927) 219 A.D. 634, 221 N.Y.S. 77, affd without op 246 N.Y. 609, 159 N.E. 671

Where the theory of the complaint relating to corporate stock, fairly interpreted, is that the defendant is liable, not as a purchaser but as a subscriber, an allegation of tender of the stock is unnecessary. Mills v Friedman (1920) 111 Misc 253, 181 N.Y.S. 285, affd without op 194 A.D. 942, 184 N.Y.S. 937 and affd without op 194 A.D. 932, 184 N.Y.S. 613, affd 233 N.Y. 517, 135 N.E. 899

3. Fraudulently obtained

An action in equity will lie to rescind subscriptions for corporate stock which were obtained by fraud; in such an action the corporation and its officers may be restrained from asserting the validity of the subscription and from bringing or maintaining an action based upon such subscription. Mack v Latta (1904) 178 N.Y. 525, 71 N.E. 97

Subscriptions induced by fraud may be set aside. Talmage v Sanitary Secur. Co. (1898) 31 A.D. 498, 52 N.Y.S. 139; Bosley v National Machine Co. (1890) 123 N.Y. 550, 25 N.E. 990; McDermott v Harrison (1890, Sup) 9 N.Y.S. 184

4. Default and forfeiture

Forfeitures are not favored by law, and parties seeking to enforce them must pursue exactly all necessary requirements. Re Election of Directors (1911) 145 A.D. 623, 130 N.Y.S. 414

Where a corporation declared a forfeiture of stock under § 68 of former Stock Corp. L., it was necessary for the board of directors itself to determine whether notice should be given, and when, in order to make the forfeiture valid. Re Election of Directors (1911) 145 A.D. 623, 130 N.Y.S. 414

Where a resolution providing for a warning notice was passed at a meeting of the board of directors at which there was not a quorum present any attempted forfeiture thereunder was void. Re Election of Directors (1911) 145 A.D. 623, 130 N.Y.S. 414

Where, in all the proceedings and minutes of a corporation meeting at which a warning notice was directed to be sent, it was characterized as a meeting of the board of directors. the corporation was estopped from asserting, for the purpose of validating the notice which would otherwise be invalid for lack of a quorum of directors, that it was a meeting of the executive committee of the board. Re Election of Directors (1911) 145 A.D. 623, 130 N.Y.S. 414

Forfeiture of corporate stock for failure to pay the installments of the subscription price is a corporate act involving the exercise of judgment and discretion. Re Election of Directors (1911) 145 A.D. 623, 130 N.Y.S. 414

A letter stating that, unless his subscription was paid within ten days, a certificate of stock would be issued covering the amount already paid and his right to further stock would be waived, would not accomplish a forfeiture under § 68 of former Stock Corp. L. but, both parties having apparently acquiesced in the cancellation or waiver for nearly two years, it would be question of fact whether plaintiff corporation was not estopped from asserting any obligation on part of defendant subscriber. Armleder Motor Truck Co. v Barnes (1923) 207 A.D. 764, 202 N.Y.S. 472

The trustee in bankruptcy of a bankrupt corporation has authority to sue for the unpaid balance on share subscriptions. Allen v Ryan (1927) 219 A.D. 634, 221 N.Y.S. 77, affd without op 246 N.Y. 609, 159 N.E. 671

One who neither paid his subscription nor received a certificate though not a stockholder of record may be entitled to enjoy all the privileges of a stockholder until his rights are forfeited under this section. Re Automotive Mfrs. Ass'n (1923) 120 Misc 405, 199 N.Y.S. 313

5. Miscellaneous

A contract to pay for the construction of a railroad in bonds and stocks of the company is not a stock subscription. Bostwick v Young (1907) 118 A.D. 490, 103 N.Y.S. 607, affd without op 194 N.Y. 516, 87 N.E. 1115

§ 504. Consideration and payment for shares

(a) Consideration for the issue of shares shall consist of money or other property, tangible or intangible; labor or services actually received by or performed for the corporation or for its benefit or in its formation or reorganization; a binding obligation to pay the purchase price or the subscription price in cash or other property; a binding obligation to perform services having an agreed value; or a combination thereof. In the absence of fraud in the transaction, the judgment of the board or shareholders, as the case may be, as to the value of the consideration received for shares shall be conclusive.

(b) [Repealed]

(c) Shares with par value may be issued for such consideration, not less than the par value thereof, as is fixed from time to time by the board.

(d) Shares without par value may be issued for such consideration as is fixed from time to time by the board unless the certificate of incorporation reserves to the shareholders the right to fix the consideration. If such right is reserved as to any shares, a vote of the shareholders shall either fix the consideration to be received for the shares or authorize the board to fix such consideration.

(e) Treasury shares may be disposed of by a corporation on such terms and conditions as are fixed from time to time by the board.

(f) Upon distribution of authorized but unissued shares to shareholders, that part of the surplus of a corporation which is concurrently transferred to stated capital shall be the consideration for the issue of such shares.

(g) In the event of a conversion of bonds or shares into shares, or in the event of an exchange of bonds or shares for shares, with or without par value, the consideration for the shares so issued in exchange or conversion shall be the sum of (1) either the principal sum of, and accrued interest on, the bonds so exchanged or converted, or the stated capital then represented by the shares so exchanged or converted, plus (2) any additional consideration paid to the corporation for the new shares, plus (3) any stated capital not theretofore allocated to any designated class or series which is thereupon allocated to the new shares, plus (4) any surplus thereupon transferred to stated capital and allocated to the new shares.

(h) Certificates for shares may not be issued until the amount of the consideration therefor determined to be stated capital pursuant to section 506 (Determination of stated capital) has been paid in the form of cash, services rendered, personal or real property or a combination thereof and consideration for the balance (if any) complying with paragraph (a) of this section has been provided, except as provided in paragraphs (e) and (f) of section 505 (Rights and options to purchase shares; issue of rights and options to directors, officers and employees).

(i) When the consideration for shares has been provided in compliance with paragraph (h) of this section, the subscriber shall be entitled to all the rights and privileges of a holder of such shares and to a certificate representing his shares, and such shares shall be fully paid and nonassessable.

(j) Notwithstanding that such shares may be fully paid and nonassessable, the corporation may place in escrow shares issued for a binding obligation to pay cash or other property or to perform future services, or make other arrangements to restrict the transfer of the shares, and may credit distributions in respect of the shares against the obligation, until the obligation is performed. If the obligation is not performed in whole or in part, the corporation may pursue such remedies as are provided in the instrument evidencing the obligation or a related agreement or under law.

History: Add, L 1961, ch 855, eff Sept 1, 1963; amd, L 1962, ch 834, § 13, eff Sept 1, 1963; L 1963, ch 738, eff Sept 1, 1963; L 1997, ch 449, § 9, eff Feb 22, 1998; L 1998, ch 17, § 1, eff Feb 19, 1998, deemed eff Feb 22, 1998.

CASE ANNOTATIONS

UNDER FORMER LAW
1. **In general**
2. **Consideration, generally**
3. **– Particular cases**
4. **Remedies and defenses**
5. **Miscellaneous**

In proceeding under CLS Bus Corp § 619 for judicial enforcement of petitioners' shareholder status in law firm, estoppel theory did not apply absent exceptional circumstances, where corporate bylaws stated that "no certificate representing shares shall be issued until the full amount of consideration therefor has been paid, except as otherwise permitted by law"; equitable considerations might generate indefiniteness, and detrimentally diminish stability and stake of already inherently vulnerable minority shareholders in professional corporations and other types of small business corporations. Heisler v Gingras (1997) 90 N.Y.2d 682, 665 N.Y.S.2d 59, 687 N.E.2d 1342, reargument den (NY) 1997 N.Y. LEXIS 4279

In proceeding under CLS Bus Corp § 619, petitioner established that he acquired shareholder status in law firm where (1) he provided consideration for shares as prescribed by corporate bylaws and CLS Bus Corp § 504 by bringing 15 years of experience and professional relationship to firm, which had encouraged him to join so that he might open its new office, (2) he did open and manage firm's new office, (3) firm publicly proclaimed that he was joining as managing shareholder, and (4) he regularly participated in shareholder meetings and voted as shareholder. Heisler v Gingras (1997) 90 N.Y.2d 682, 665 N.Y.S.2d 59, 687 N.E.2d 1342, reargument den (NY) 1997 N.Y. LEXIS 4279

In proceeding under CLS Bus Corp § 619, petitioner failed to establish that he acquired shareholder status in law firm where he was informed that he would not become shareholder or be issued any shares of stock until specific amount of consideration for shares was determined and paid, he expressly declined to pay any consideration for shares offered to him, and record did not demonstrate that he ever voted as shareholder. Heisler v Gingras (1997) 90 N.Y.2d 682, 665 N.Y.S.2d 59, 687 N.E.2d 1342, reargument den (NY) 1997 N.Y. LEXIS 4279

In action to recover damages for wrongful expulsion from corporation as shareholder, defendants' motion for summary judgment should have been denied-plaintiff and individual defendants executed stockholders' agreement whereby they formed defendant corporation, racquetball club; while plaintiff was performing his regular services at club, pursuant to consultation and employment agreements, he was called into meeting during which his contracts were terminated; meeting was held without prior notice being given to plaintiff-plaintiff had paid large percentage of his capital contribution and individual defendants had considered him as stockholder and principal of corporation since its inception; since they never moved to declare his shares void by reason of fact that they had been issued in violation of Business Corporation Law § 504 they are now estopped from arguing that plaintiff was not shareholder or that shares are void-further, stockholders' agreement provided that 100 shares to be distributed to plaintiff and one of individual defendants were to be distributed proportionately to their capital contributions; since plaintiff had fully paid for approximately 71 shares of corporate stock, representing 35.5% of outstanding stock, his affirmative vote was necessary for corporation to obtain 75% affirmative vote required for it to conduct business-Business Corporation Law § 606, which states that notice of meeting is waived if shareholder attends meeting without protesting lack of notice of such meeting, is inapplicable; plaintiff attended subject meeting but argues that he protested lack of notice and voted "no"; while defendants contest plaintiff's claim, conspicuous absence of plaintiff's signature from minutes of that meeting supports his claim-finally, defendants concede that club opened for business;

under terms of consultation agreement, plaintiff's employment was only to be terminated on date corporation ceases operation; various contentions as to whether or not corporation had net positive cash flow out of which plaintiff was to be paid raise question of fact which triers of fact must decide. Block v Magee, 146 A.D.2d 730

Cash purchase of par value stock cannot be made for less than par value. Frankowski v Palermo (1975, 4th Dept) 47 A.D.2d 579, 363 N.Y.S.2d 159

In determining whether full par value has been paid for issuance of par value stock, cancellation of corporation debt is considered equivalent to cash payment in amount of debt. Frankowski v Palermo (1975, 4th Dept) 47 A.D.2d 579, 363 N.Y.S.2d 159

Where 44 shares of stock of corporation of par value of $100 per share were issued to corporation president in exchange for cancellation of corporate debt in amount of $2,726, and president therefore paid $1,674 less than par value of shares issued, transaction was voidable at option of other shareholders. Frankowski v Palermo (1975, 4th Dept) 47 A.D.2d 579, 363 N.Y.S.2d 159

In action to recover damages for wrongful expulsion from corporation as shareholder, court would reject argument of defendants that plaintiff was not shareholder because he had not paid his full subscription since, although CLS Bus Corp § 504 made clear that obligations for future payments do not constitute payments or part payments for shares, statute rendered shares held by plaintiff merely voidable, rather than void, and defendants never moved to declare plaintiff's shares void for violation of statute; defendants were thus estopped from arguing that plaintiff was not shareholder or that shares were void. Block v Magee (1989, 2d Dept) 146 A.D.2d 730, 537 N.Y.S.2d 215

Trustees were not entitled to order directing defendant to issue them certificate for common shares based on their prior delivery of preferred shares in exchange offer where (1) common stock had already been issued to cotrustees, and cotrustees had voted common shares and received dividends, and (2) trustees never notified defendant of any claim of loss or wrongful taking of stock certificates. Roth v Gulf & Western Industries, Inc. (1990, 1st Dept) 160 A.D.2d 525, 554 N.Y.S.2d 176

Petitioners who purchased 50 percent of corporation's stock had standing to maintain proceeding for dissolution under CLS Bus Corp § 1104(a)(3) even though they had not been issued certificates reflecting ownership and purchase agreement provided that stock would be held in escrow by corporation's accountant until full purchase price was paid, where escrow provision was mere security arrangement, and agreement (and simultaneously executed Irrevocable Stock Power) unambiguously provided for present immediate sale of stock; furthermore, court should have granted petitioners' motion to compel issuance of stock certificates to them where seller, in sworn affidavit, forgave any balance due on purchase price. In re Dissolution of M. Kraus, Inc. (1996, 1st Dept) 229 A.D.2d 347, 645 N.Y.S.2d 304, reh den (NY A.D., 1st Dept) 1996 N.Y. A.D. LEXIS 9608 and app dismd without op 89 N.Y.2d 916, 653 N.Y.S.2d 919, 676 N.E.2d 501

Respondents, professional corporation and several of its officers and shareholders, were estopped from arguing that petitioners were not shareholders where respondents invited petitioners to become shareholders and held them out to public, courts, and clients as shareholders, without requiring payment of any monetary consideration. Heisler v Gingras (1997, 3d Dept) 235 A.D.2d 900, 652 N.Y.S.2d 841, motion gr 89 N.Y.2d 1007, 657 N.Y.S.2d 401, 679 N.E.2d 640 and app dismd (3d Dept) 238 A.D.2d 702, 656 N.Y.S.2d 70 and mod, affd 90 N.Y.2d 682, 665 N.Y.S.2d 59, 687 N.E.2d 1342, reargument den 91 N.Y.2d 867, 668 N.Y.S.2d 563, 691 N.E.2d 635

Plaintiff was not entitled to partial summary judgment on his claim that sale of his minority interest in defendant corporation to individual defendant was invalid under CLS Bus Corp § 504, on ground that price of stock was less than its par value and such defect could not be cured by individual defendant's promises of future consideration, as § 504 has no bearing on resale of issued shares among shareholders. Torres v Speiser (2000, 1st Dept) 268 A.D.2d 253, 701 N.Y.S.2d 360

In action for specific performance and damages for breach of stock buy-back agreement and for accounting, there was no merit in counterclaim alleging that particular plaintiff was not entitled to shares of stock because those shares originally had been issued in exchange for future services that were not provided, in violation of CLS Bus Corp former § 504, where issuance of stock under parties preincorporation agreement was not conditioned on performance of future services but, rather, on payment of money. Smith v Long

(2001, 4th Dept) 281 A.D.2d 897, 723 N.Y.S.2d 584, related proceeding (4th Dept) 281 A.D.2d 998, 721 N.Y.S.2d 856

Judgment for former clients in an attorney's suit for specific performance of a retainer agreement was error because the president of the former clients, both corporations, had at least apparent authority to enter into the agreement; N.Y. Bus. Corp. Law §§ 504, 505 did not stand as an impediment to the former clients' performance of the agreement, under which the attorney was to be paid two percent of the stock of one of the former clients because the agreement was binding on the former clients whether or not the president had actual authority to engage in the transaction or sought any necessary corporate approval. Goldston v Bandwidth Tech. Corp. (2008, 1st Dept) 52 App Div 3d 360, 859 NYS2d 651.

The judgment of the corporation directors as to the value of labor taken in payment for stock is conclusive in the absence of fraud, and, therefore, the president of a corporation has no power to enter into an employment contract which provides that part of the employee's compensation is to be paid in corporation stock. Goldenberg v Bartell Broadcasting Corp. (1965) 47 Misc. 2d 105, 262 N.Y.S.2d 274

Action by two shareholders in a closely-held corporation to re-finance a loan so that the corporation became primarily liable for the loan and to authorize the issuance of promissory notes to themselves which would be satisfied by the issuance of additional shares of stock were not illegal and did not warrant dissolution of the corporation, and the appellate court dismissed an appeal which the Superintendent of Insurance of the State of New York took from a trial court's judgment denying dissolution of the corporation after the Superintendent acquired shares in the corporation that were owned by a bankrupt shareholder. Estate of Lawrence v Quail Aero Serv. (In re Dissolution of Quail Aero Serv.) (2002, A.D., 3d Dept) 755 N.Y.S.2d 103

Executive officer's stock purchase arose from his employment with the corporation, not as result of a tender offer; since the corporation's directors authorized the purchase at a price set by the directors, pursuant to N.Y. Bus. Law §§ 504, 505, compliance with the Securities Takeover Disclosure Act, N.Y. Bus. Corp. Law art. 16, was unneeded. In re Application of Presher (2003, Sup) 765 N.Y.S.2d 210

Judgment declaring that a subtenant was not a corporate shareholder was proper because there was no evidence showing an understanding or a meeting of the minds between the subtenant and the stockholder sufficient to invoke N.Y. Bus. Corp. Law § 504; among other things, the stockholder testified that she never agreed to share the corporation with subtenant and that the subtenant never mentioned to her that she wanted to be a fifty percent shareholder, and the subtenant never asked for or received any forms to report a shareholder's distributed share of income from the corporation, corporate tax forms, or any other indicia of shareholder status. Further, the subtenant continued in the relationship without demanding any rights of a shareholder for two years after learning that she was not a shareholder. Kun v Fulop (2010, 2d Dept) 71 App Div 3d 832, 896 NYS2d 462.

Where the defendant, both president and chairman of the board of the defendant corporation, received 50,000 shares of stock in consideration of his obligation to make future payments, the transaction was voidable under CLS Bus Corp L § 504, subd b. S. & S. Realty Corp. v Kleer-Vu Industries, Inc. (1978, CA2 NY) 575 F.2d 1040, CCH Fed Secur L Rep ¶ 96409

The prohibition of Business Corporation Law § 504 is not limited in its application only to newly formed corporations, and on the contrary, the broad reach of the statute suggests that creditors, public and other stockholders are to be protected at all times during life of corporation. Lewis v Dansker (1973, SD NY) 357 F. Supp. 636, CCH Fed Secur L Rep ¶ 93916

Proposal of outright sale of shares of corporation to principal officers and stockholders evidenced by series of non-interest bearing promissory notes was violative of Business Corporation Law § 504, subd b. Lewis v Dansker (1973, SD NY) 357 F. Supp. 636, CCH Fed Secur L Rep ¶ 93916

Business Corporation Law § 504(e) authorizes corporate directors to fix consideration to be received for treasury shares being sold and under Business Corporation Law § 504(h) directors' judgment as to adequacy of consideration received for grant of option to purchase treasury shares of stock is conclusive in absence of fraud. Buffalo Forge Co. v Ogden Corp. (1983, WD NY) 555 F. Supp. 892, CCH Fed Secur L Rep ¶ 99079

UNDER FORMER LAW

1. In general

It is the policy of the state to require all corporations to be organized honestly, with a bona fide capital stock to be issued only for cash, labor or property, and thus provide the necessary means for carrying out purposes of their creation, and thereby prevent frauds upon creditors and the public. Winston v Saugerties Farms, Inc. (1940, Sup) 21 N.Y.S.2d 841, revd on other grounds 262 A.D. 435, 29 N.Y.S.2d 292, affd without op 287 N.Y. 718, 39 N.E.2d 934

2. Consideration, generally

A business corporation has no authority to issue shares without any consideration, and shares issued without any such consideration as the statutes require are void, or voidable, at least in the hands of the person to whom originally issued. Barnes v Brown (1880) 80 N.Y. 527; Winston v Saugerties Farms, Inc. (1940, Sup) 21 N.Y.S.2d 841, revd on other grounds 262 A.D. 435, 29 N.Y.S.2d 292, affd without op 287 N.Y. 718, 39 N.E.2d 934; Sarasohn v Andrew Jergens Co. (1943, Sup) 45 N.Y.S.2d 888; Eisenberg v Grossman (1948, Sup) 84 N.Y.S.2d 118, app dismd (AD) 87 N.Y.S.2d 227 and revd on other grounds 275 A.D. 946, 89 N.Y.S.2d 787; Kittinger v Churchill (1936) 161 Misc 3, 292 N.Y.S. 35, affd 249 A.D. 703, 292 N.Y.S. 51

The word "property" as used in § 69 of former Stock Corp. L. was broadly construed as including almost anything of apparent present value in doing business, such as a leasehold, the good will and other assets of a going business, or a license to use trademarks, patents, or the like, regardless of what success, or lack of success, the corporation might ultimately have in profiting from such acquisitions. Close v Noye (1895) 147 N.Y. 597, 41 N.E. 570; Sarasohn v Andrew Jergens Co. (1943, Sup) 45 N.Y.S.2d 888; Estate Planning Corp. v Commissioner (1939, CA2) 101 F.2d 15, 39-1 USTC ¶ 9235; Williams v McClave (1915) 168 A.D. 192, 154 N.Y.S. 38; Alpha Portland Cement Co. v Schratwieser (1914, DC NY) 215 F 982, affd (CA2 NY) 221 F 258; Washburn v National Wall-Paper Co. (1897, CA2 NY) 81 F 17

The liability of persons receiving capital stock without consideration in kind and amount as required by statute is limited to the amount which should have been paid for such stock. Shaw v Ansaldi Co. (1917) 178 A.D. 589, 165 N.Y.S. 872

Under former Stock Corp. L., a corporation could distribute a new issue of stock, such as of preferred shares, among its existing stockholders, without any new or additional consideration paid in by them. Frank Gilbert Paper Co. v Prankard (1923) 204 A.D. 83, 198 N.Y.S. 25

Under former Stock Corp. L., it was held that stock having a fixed par value could not be issued for cash less than par, although there was no specific provision to that effect in the statute itself. Stone v Young (1924) 210 A.D. 303, 206 N.Y.S. 95

Under § 69 of former Stock Corp. L., as under subd. (a) of this section, judgment of the board of directors of the corporation as to value of consideration, other than money, received for shares, was conclusive in the absence of fraud or bad faith. Winter v Anderson (1934) 242 A.D. 430, 275 N.Y.S. 373; Van Vleet v Jones (1894) 75 Hun 340, 26 N.Y.S. 1082

Former Stock Corp. L. did not require that stock be paid for with money, property, or labor of the person to whom the stock was issued, but merely that the corporation receive whatever the consideration might be. Winston v Saugerties Farms, Inc. (1941) 262 A.D. 435, 29 N.Y.S.2d 292, affd without op 287 N.Y. 718, 39 N.E.2d 934

Where no rights of creditors or of the public are involved, however, there is some authority to the effect that the remaining shareholders may ratify issuance of shares to one or more holders who have not paid or contributed consideration as contemplated by statute. Kimmel Sales Corp. v Lauster (1938) 167 Misc 514, 4 N.Y.S.2d 88

An issue of stock for less than par was not void under § 69 of former Stock Corp L, and the stock was to be regarded as actually "issued" until the transaction was duly attacked for insufficiency of consideration. Bonsall v Commissioner (1963, CA2) 317 F.2d 61, 63-1 USTC ¶ 9462

A corporation may not provide in its certificate of incorporation for the issuance of stock without par value which shall be subject to assessment by the board of directors. 1929 Ops Atty Gen 258

3. – Particular cases

A contract providing for the rendition of services by an employee and for the payment therefor by stock in the employer corporation after such services had been rendered to the company's satisfaction was not subject to the prohibition of § 69 of the former Stock Corp. L. where there was no claim by the employee until after his services had been completed. Morgan v Bon Bon Co. (1917) 222 N.Y. 22, 118 N.E. 205

The exclusive right to sell the product of another corporation is not "property." Powell v Murray (1896) 3 A.D. 273, 38 N.Y.S. 233, affd without op 157 N.Y. 717, 53 N.E. 1130

An agreement of a person to co-operate with a publisher to extent of becoming editor of history and to suggest competent persons to write same, does not constitute property for which stock may be issued, within the requirements of this section. Stevens v Episcopal Church History Co. (1910) 140 A.D. 570, 125 N.Y.S. 573

Under § 69 of former Stock Corp. L., stock could be issued for property received, or labor or services already performed, but not on the basis of services to be rendered in the future. B. & C. Electrical Const. Co. v Owen (1917) 176 A.D. 399, 163 N.Y.S. 31, affd without op 227 N.Y. 569, 126 N.E. 927; Shaw v Ansaldi Co. (1917) 178 A.D. 589, 165 N.Y.S. 872; Stevens v Episcopal Church History Co. (1910) 140 A.D. 570, 125 N.Y.S. 573

If the defendant contemplated the purchase of stock of a merged corporation, or the issuance of stock to him not in violation of this section, the contract on his part to assign to the plaintiff part of it for services in bringing about the merger would be valid. Dancey v Brieger Press, Inc. (1932) 235 A.D. 861, 257 N.Y.S. 547

Contrary to the provisions of subd. (a) of this section, under § 69 of former Stock Corp. L. stock could not validly be issued in payment for services rendered in promoting or forming the corporation. Lamphear v Lang (1913) 157 A.D. 306, 141 N.Y.S. 967, revd on other grounds 213 N.Y. 585, 108 N.E. 82; Ludlam v Riverhead Bond & Mortg. Corp. (1935) 244 A.D. 113, 278 N.Y.S. 487; Winston v Saugerties Farms, Inc. (1940, Sup) 21 N.Y.S.2d 841, revd on other grounds 262 A.D. 435, 29 N.Y.S.2d 292, affd without op 287 N.Y. 718, 39 N.E.2d 934

Where a farmer voluntarily contracted to join in the formation of a corporation, to convey his farm and business to it in return for all of its capital stock, and to give one-half of this stock to defendant and defendant on his part agreed that he would assume entire management of the farm and business without salary or compensation except such as he might derive from profits or dividends after the payment of all expenses which included payment of twenty-five dollars a week to the farmer, and defendant performed the agreement faithfully on his part for at least ten months and the farmer accepted the benefits, requirement of full value for stock was fully met by the conveyance to the corporation by the farmer of property whose value was far in excess of the amount of the capital stock. Winston v Saugerties Farms, Inc. (1941) 262 A.D. 435, 29 N.Y.S.2d 292, affd without op 287 N.Y. 718, 39 N.E.2d 934

A director of a corporation who authorized the issuance of corporate stock in consideration of recipients' entering corporation's employ was held to have violated § 69 of former Stock Corp. L. even though recipients might have had special knowledge, experience or contacts of value to the corporation. Brown v Watson (1955) 285 A.D. 587, 139 N.Y.S.2d 628

Since § 69 of former Stock Corp. L. prohibited issuance of stock except for a valuable consideration, where the members of a partnership agreed to transfer all its assets to a corporation in exchange for all stock of the latter and then set up a second corporation to hold title to the realty formerly belonging to the partnership, one of the partners had no basis for demanding stock in the second corporation on the basis of transferring the realty to it, as equitable title was already in the first corporation by virtue of the agreement for transfer of all assets to it. Hochadel v G. & H. Enterprises, Inc. (1962, 4th Dept) 16 A.D.2d 874, 228 N.Y.S.2d 479

It was held, however, under § 69 of former Stock Corp. L., that a mere contract for purchase of property, held by a contractor who had not invested one cent in it, would not entitle him to issuance of stock in a corporation. Macklem v Marine Park Homes, Inc. (1955) 17 Misc. 2d 439, 191 N.Y.S.2d 374, affd (2d Dept) 8 A.D.2d 824, 191 N.Y.S.2d 545, affd 8 N.Y.2d 1076, 207 N.Y.S.2d 451, 170 N.E.2d 455

Obligations or promises of the purchaser, or of another, were not ordinarily considered "property" for which a corporation organized under former Stock Corp. L. could issue stock certificates. Re Waterloo Organ Co. (1904, CA2 NY) 134 F 341. See however Bowers v Max Kaufmann & Co. (1927, CA2 NY) 18 F.2d 69, 5 USTC ¶ 1458

A binding and adequately secured obligation to pay, entered into in good faith, may be considered as "property" given in payment for stock, at least where the transaction is entered into good faith. See American Radiator & Standard Sanitary Corp. v United States (1961) 155 Ct Cl 515, 295 F.2d 939, 61-2 USTC ¶ 9731, dealing with the problem in connection with federal excess profits credit

4. Remedies and defenses

The receiver of a corporation may sue directors or officers, either in tort or upon implied contract, to recover the amount which they should have paid in, but did not, for stock issued to themselves. Lamphear v Lang (1913) 157 A.D. 306, 141 N.Y.S. 967, revd on other grounds 213 N.Y. 585, 108 N.E. 82

Section 69 of former Stock Corp. L. did not prevent recovery on a note given by a subscriber in part payment for stock where the subscription was not for the original issue of stock but for stock which had been issued and reacquired by the corporation. Furlong v Johnston (1924) 209 A.D. 198, 204 N.Y.S. 710, affd 239 N.Y. 141, 145 N.E. 910

And notwithstanding statutory prohibitions, express or implied, against issuance or sale of shares without consideration in kind and amount as specified, violation of such provisions has not ordinarily been deemed a defense available to a person who has obtained the shares under a contract or promise to pay or perform, unless the corporation, its creditors, or someone acting in its behalf or in behalf of its creditors, with authority to bind it, has seen fit to rescind the transaction. Backus v Hutson (1930) 136 Misc 290, 240 N.Y.S. 610

But a defense of estoppel could not be interposed in an action based on violation of § 69 of former Stock Corp. L. for the cancelation of illegally issued stock. Winston v Saugerties Farms, Inc. (1940, Sup) 21 N.Y.S.2d 841, revd on other grounds 262 A.D. 435, 29 N.Y.S.2d 292, affd without op 287 N.Y. 718, 39 N.E.2d 934

The statute of limitations was available as a defense in an action based upon § 69 of former Stock Corp. L. inasmuch as stock issued under that section was voidable rather than void. Eisenberg v Grossman (1948, Sup) 84 N.Y.S.2d 118, app dismd (AD) 87 N.Y.S.2d 227 and revd on other grounds 275 A.D. 946, 89 N.Y.S.2d 787

Where it is alleged stock has been improperly issued for insufficient property or services, the questions of overvaluation and fraud are for the jury. Powers v Knapp (1895) 85 Hun 38, 32 N.Y.S. 622, affd without op 159 N.Y. 534, 53 N.E. 1132; Brown v Smith (1880) 80 N.Y. 650; Lake Superior Iron Co. v Drexel (1882) 90 N.Y. 87; National Tube-Works Co. v Gilfillan (1891) 124 N.Y. 302, 26 N.E. 538; Douglass v Ireland (1878) 73 N.Y. 100

Section 58 of former Stock Corp. L., in prohibition withdrawal of a certain portion of their initial investment in a corporation by stockholders, was designed to require a corporation to retain its stated capital unimpaired for satisfaction of all creditors, and accordingly gave rise to a cause of action if capital was impaired regardless of whether the particular distribution caused insolvency. Field v Bankers Trust Co. (1961, CA2 NY) 296 F.2d 109, cert den 369 US 859, 8 L Ed 2d 17, 82 S Ct 948

5. Miscellaneous

An issue to purchase stock and bonds of a rival company to prevent ruinous competition is for a "lawful purpose." Rafferty v Buffalo City Gas Co. (1899) 37 A.D. 618, 56 N.Y.S. 288

A corporation has no authority to agree to throw in a bonus of one share of its common stock with each purchase of two shares of its preferred stock where its only assets will be funds received from stock subscriptions and it presently has no common stock in its treasury or available for distribution. Stone v Young (1924) 210 A.D. 303, 206 N.Y.S. 95

§ 505. Rights and options to purchase shares; issue of rights and options to directors, officers and employees

(a) (1) Except as otherwise provided in this section or in the certificate of incorporation, a corporation may create and issue, whether or not in connection with the issue and sale of any of its shares or bonds, rights or options entitling the holders thereof to purchase from the corporation, upon such consideration, terms and conditions as may be fixed by the board, shares of any class or series, whether authorized but unissued shares, treasury shares or shares to be purchased or acquired or assets of the corporation.

(2) (i) In the case of a domestic corporation that has a class of voting stock registered with the Securities and Exchange Commission pursuant to section

Business Corporation Law

twelve of the Exchange Act, the terms and conditions of such rights or options may include, without limitation, restrictions or conditions that preclude or limit the exercise, transfer or receipt of such rights or options by an interested shareholder or any transferee of any such interested shareholder or that invalidate or void such rights or options held by any such interested shareholder or any such transferee. For the purpose of this subparagraph, the terms "voting stock", "Exchange Act" and "interested shareholder" shall have the same meanings as set forth in section nine hundred twelve of this chapter;

(ii) Determinations of the board of directors whether to impose, enforce or waive or otherwise render ineffective such limitations or conditions as are permitted by clause (i) of this subparagraph shall be subject to judicial review in an appropriate proceeding in which the courts formulate or apply appropriate standards in order to insure that such limitations or conditions are imposed, enforced or waived in the best long-term interests and short-term interests of the corporation and its shareholders considering, without limitation, the prospects for potential growth, development, productivity and profitability of the corporation.

(b) The consideration for shares to be purchased under any such right or option shall comply with the requirements of section 504 (Consideration and payment for shares).

(c) The terms and conditions of such rights or options, including the time or times at or within which and the price or prices at which they may be exercised and any limitations upon transferability, shall be set forth or incorporated by reference in the instrument or instruments evidencing such rights or options.

(d) The issue of such rights or options to one or more directors, officers or employees of the corporation or a subsidiary or affiliate thereof, as an incentive to service or continued service with the corporation, a subsidiary or affiliate thereof, or to a trustee on behalf of such directors, officers or employees, shall be authorized as required by the policies of all stock exchanges or automated quotation systems on which the corporation's shares are listed or authorized for trading, or if the corporation's shares are not so listed or authorized, by a majority of the votes cast at a meeting of shareholders by the holders of shares entitled to vote thereon, or authorized by and consistent with a plan adopted by such vote of shareholders. If, under the certificate of incorporation, there are preemptive rights to any of the shares to be thus subject to rights or options to purchase, either such issue or such plan, if any shall also be approved by the vote or written consent of the holders of a majority of the shares entitled to exercise preemptive rights with respect to such shares and such vote or written consent shall operate to release the preemptive rights with respect thereto of the holders of all

the shares that were entitled to exercise such preemptive rights.

In the absence of preemptive rights, nothing in this paragraph shall require shareholder approval for the issuance of rights or options to purchase shares of the corporation in substitution for, or upon the assumption of, rights or options issued by another corporation, if such substitution or assumption is in connection with such other corporation's merger or consolidation with, or the acquisition of its shares or all or part of its assets by, the corporation or its subsidiary.

(e) A plan adopted by the shareholders for the issue of rights or options to directors, officers or employees shall include the material terms and conditions upon which such rights or options are to be issued, such as, but without limitation thereof, any restrictions on the number of shares that eligible individuals may have the right or option to purchase, the method of administering the plan, the terms and conditions of payment for shares in full or in installments, the issue of certificates for shares to be paid for in installments, any limitations upon the transferability of such shares and the voting and dividend rights to which the holders of such shares may be entitled, though the full amount of the consideration therefor has not been paid; provided that under this section no certificate for shares shall be delivered to a shareholder, prior to full payment therefor, unless the fact that the shares are partly paid is noted conspicuously on the face or back of such certificate.

(f) If there is shareholder approval for the issue of rights or options to individual directors, officers or employees, but not under an approved plan under paragraph (e), the terms and conditions of issue set forth in paragraph (e) shall be permissible except that the grantees of such rights or options shall not be granted voting or dividend rights until the consideration for the shares to which they are entitled under such rights or options has been fully paid.

(g) If there is shareholder approval for the issue of rights and options, such approval may provide that the board is authorized by certificate of amendment under section 805 (Certificate of amendment; contents) to increase the authorized shares of any class or series to such number as will be sufficient, when added to the previously authorized but unissued shares of such class or series, to satisfy any such rights or options entitling the holders thereof to purchase from the corporation authorized but unissued shares of such class or series.

(h) In the absence of fraud in the transaction, the judgment of the board shall be conclusive as to the adequacy of the consideration, tangible or intangible, received or to be received by the corporation for the issue of rights or options for the purchase from the corporation of its shares.

(i) The provisions of this section are inapplicable to the rights of the holders of convertible shares or bonds to acquire shares upon the exercise of conversion privileges under section 519 (Convertible shares and bonds).

History: Add, L 1961, ch 855; amd, L 1962, ch 834, § 14, eff Sept 1, 1963,15, eff Sept 1, 1963; amd, L 1963, ch 738, eff Sept 1, 1963; relettered par (h), L 1963, ch 738, eff Sept 1, 1963; L 1963, ch 749, eff Sept 1, 1963; amd, L 1965, ch 803, § 7, eff Sept 1, 1965; L 1981, ch 288, § 1, eff June 22, 1981; L 1988, ch 743, §§ 3, 5; L 1989, ch 81, § 2, eff May 3, 1989, deemed eff July 24, 1986, 4 (which amendment was repealed); L 1992, ch 510, § 1, eff July 24, 1992, deemed eff May 3, 1989; L 1996, ch 404, § 1, eff Jan 26, 1997; L 1997, ch 449, § 10, eff Feb 22, 1998; L 2000, ch 543, § 1, eff Oct 11, 2000.

CASE ANNOTATIONS

Court properly dismissed, as barred by collateral estoppel, derivative claims alleging that defendants breached their fiduciary duty and committed corporate waste by issuing warrants giving individual defendants options to purchase stock in defendant corporation, where plaintiff's prior RICO action against same defendants, alleging that warrants were unauthorized and unsupported by valid consideration, was dismissed by federal court which concluded that warrants were properly issued and were economically justified as compensation for individual defendants' service to corporation. Pinnacle Consultants, Ltd. v Leucadia Nat'l Corp. (2000) 94 N.Y.2d 426, 706 N.Y.S.2d 46, 727 N.E.2d 543

Corporation that issued warrants to purchase specified number of shares of stock for 10 cents per share was not entitled to judgment declaring that warrants should be adjusted to reflect one-for-5 reverse stock split later authorized by shareholders, as warrants did not incorporate provision requiring adjustment in event of reverse stock split, and fact that warrant agreements did not address contingency of reverse stock split did not, of itself, create ambiguity permitting court to imply allegedly missing term. Reiss v Fin. Performance Corp. (2001) 97 N.Y.2d 195, 738 N.Y.S.2d 658, 764 N.E.2d 958

In action to enforce warrants to purchase shares of stock of defendant corporation in accordance with their stated terms, and to reform expiration date of warrants to date in late 2000, where Supreme Court and Appellate Division dismissed both causes of action and Court of Appeals, in 2001, reinstated enforcement cause of action but plaintiffs had not advocated reinstating reformation cause of action (which, if granted in 2001, would leave them with nothing but expired warrants), case was remitted to Supreme Court for further proceedings, and if court determined that plaintiffs were entitled to declaration in their favor on reinstated cause of action, then it should resolve remaining remedial issues concerning reformation of warrants and whether plaintiffs' attempt to exercise warrants, together with their cause of action seeking extension of warrants' expiration date, preserved their right to exercise warrants upon successful conclusion of litigation. Reiss v Fin. Performance Corp. (2001) 97 N.Y.2d 195, 738 N.Y.S.2d 658, 764 N.E.2d 958

Corporation's 2-year delay in issuing stock warrants did not require 2-year extension of warrants' expiration date, where warrant holders were at all times aware of warrants' existence and never sought to compel their physical delivery, nor was there any indication that they desired to exercise their right to purchase stock before warrants were physically delivered. Reiss v Financial Performance Corp. (2000, 1st Dept) 279 A.D.2d 13, 715 N.Y.S.2d 29, reargument den, app gr (1st Dept) 280 A.D.2d 1012, 721 N.Y.S.2d 765 and affd in part and mod in part, remitted, ctfd ques ans (NY) 2001 N.Y. LEXIS 3815

Following corporation's one-for-5 reverse stock split, plaintiff stock warrant holders were limited to purchasing shares proportionally adjusted as to both number and price to reflect the split, where warrants were silent as to effect of reverse stock split on warrant holder's right to purchase shares of stock and there was no evidence that parties to warrants contemplated otherwise; just as plaintiffs should not suffer from possibility of dilution of their warrants resulting from stock split, corporation should not suffer from consolidation of its shares resulting from declaration of reverse stock split. Reiss v Financial Performance Corp. (2000, 1st Dept) 279

A.D.2d 13, 715 N.Y.S.2d 29, reargument den, app gr (1st Dept) 280 A.D.2d 1012, 721 N.Y.S.2d 765 and affd in part and mod in part, remitted, ctfd ques ans (NY) 2001 N.Y. LEXIS 3815

Judgment for former clients in an attorney's suit for specific performance of a retainer agreement was error because the president of the former clients, both corporations, had at least apparent authority to enter into the agreement; N.Y. Bus. Corp. Law §§ 504, 505 did not stand as an impediment to the former clients' performance of the agreement, under which the attorney was to be paid two percent of the stock of one of the former clients because the agreement was binding on the former clients whether or not the president had actual authority to engage in the transaction or sought any necessary corporate approval. Goldston v Bandwidth Tech. Corp. (2008, 1st Dept) 52 App Div 3d 360, 859 NYS2d 651.

Options to purchase shares of corporate capital stock must be approved by board of directors to be valid. Scarpinato v National Patent Development Corp. (1973) 75 Misc. 2d 94, 347 N.Y.S.2d 623

Alleged oral agreement for option to purchase stock was unenforceable against alleged offeror not only because such agreement failed to comply with requirements that contract for sale of securities be in writing and be signed by person against whom it is sought to be enforced (UCC § 8-319), that also because plaintiff failed to meet burden of proving that defendant's board of directors had ever considered the option, as required by Business Corporation Law § 505(a). Scarpinato v National Patent Development Corp. (1973) 75 Misc. 2d 94, 347 N.Y.S.2d 623

Where stock subscription agreement, which provided that corporate employer would repurchase shares of voting stock issued to employee, was integral part of employee's original two year employment contract as a form of deferred compensation, and employee's employment was extended by implication on year to year basis after expiration of original two years of employment, right to stock and right to sell stock back arose each year until employee terminated employment with company. Schlaifer v Kaiser (1975) 84 Misc. 2d 817, 377 N.Y.S.2d 356, affd (1st Dept) 50 A.D.2d 749, 378 N.Y.S.2d 639

Stock subscription agreement, which provided that corporation would issue employee 15 shares, out of total of 100, of voting stock at one dollar per share to be repurchased out of surplus by company at end of two-year employment contract or, in event there was no surplus, by majority stockholder for cash, and which was entered into contemporaneously with employment contract, was in effect deferred compensation plan and was enforceable even though employee did not pay one dollar per share purchase price and did not receive certificates of stock. Schlaifer v Kaiser (1975) 84 Misc. 2d 817, 377 N.Y.S.2d 356, affd (1st Dept) 50 A.D.2d 749, 378 N.Y.S.2d 639

Where employee's right to stock and right to sell stock back to corporation under stock subscription agreement arose each year after expiration of employee's original two-year employment contract until employee terminated his employment with company, employee was entitled to assert his claim at end of each year, and thus six year contract statute of limitations, which began to run at end of each year as cause of action to be paid book value for stock for that year accrued, barred only claims sought to be asserted by employee in arbitration for fiscal years ending more than six years prior to service of demand for arbitration. Schlaifer v Kaiser (1975) 84 Misc. 2d 817, 377 N.Y.S.2d 356, affd (1st Dept) 50 A.D.2d 749, 378 N.Y.S.2d 639

The motion of plaintiff corporation, which seeks to acquire defendant corporation, for a preliminary injunction enjoining defendant from enforcing the "flip-in" provision of a rights agreement shall be granted since plaintiff has demonstrated a likelihood of success on the merits, and irreparable injury without the requested relief is likely in that without such relief the tender offer, economically, could not be completed within the time limits imposed by regulatory agencies. The "flip-in" provision, which grants those shareholders who have not acquired control of 20% or more of the shares of defendant the right to purchase $400 worth of common stock in defendant for $200, greatly dilutes the acquirer's 20% equity and voting rights and, thus, makes acquisition of all or a majority of the shares extremely expensive for that acquirer; accordingly, the "flip-in" provision works an impermissible discrimination among shareholders of the same class by favoring certain shareholders over others in violation of Business Corporation Law § 501 (c). The resulting discrimination is not a permissible distribution of rights (see, Business Corporation Law § 505) and is not authorized by the preemptive rights provisions of Business Corporation Law § 622, which should not be read to contradict the express mandate of section 501 (c). Moreover, the court will not, on the instant record, direct

Business Corporation Law

defendant to give approval or waive rights under Business Corporation Law § 912, which provides a comprehensive defensive mechanism, since such direction could only be made after a complete factual hearing on the issue of defendant's board's exercise of its business judgment. Bank of N.Y. Co. v Irving Bank Corp., 142 Misc. 2d 145

Executive officer's stock purchase arose from his employment with the corporation, not as result of a tender offer; since the corporation's directors authorized the purchase at a price set by the directors, pursuant to N.Y. Bus. Law §§ 504, 505, compliance with the Securities Takeover Disclosure Act, N.Y. Bus. Corp. Law art. 16, was unneeded. In re Application of Presher (2003, Sup) 765 N.Y.S.2d 210

A proxy statement given to shareholders which accompanied a resolution to ratify the actions of the board of directors in canceling and regranting, at lower prices, stock option plans for employees did not have to include statements which the directors did not believe to be true. Cohen v Ayers (1978, ND Ill) 449 F. Supp. 298, CCH Fed Secur L Rep ¶ 96575, affd (CA7 Ill) 596 F.2d 733, CCH Fed Secur L Rep ¶ 96836

Since CLS Business Corporation Law § 505, subd d does not indicate how many details must be disclosed before shareholder authorization of a stock option plan for employees is valid, it was not necessary to include details such as the composition of the Executive Committee and the name of plaintiff's attorney where the proxy statement filed with the resolution to ratify the action of the board of directors which permitted the cancellation and regranting, at lower prices, of previously granted options was more detailed than proxy statements which accompanied the original authorization for the plans, and the shareholders had before them the plaintiff's complaint, copies of the previous plans, and other relevant detailed information. Cohen v Ayers (1978, ND Ill) 449 F. Supp. 298, CCH Fed Secur L Rep ¶ 96575, affd (CA7 Ill) 596 F.2d 733, CCH Fed Secur L Rep ¶ 96836

Shareholders' authorization of a stock option plan, put forth under CLS Business Corporation Law § 505, subd d by resolution of the board of directors which permitted the cancellation and regrant, at substantially lower prices, of stock options to employees, was not invalid even though a proxy statement which accompanied the resolution did not spell out the information concerning the prior stock option plans, since all that was necessary was shareholder approval of the particular grant of the option. Cohen v Ayers (1978, ND Ill) 449 F. Supp. 298, CCH Fed Secur L Rep ¶ 96575, affd (CA7 Ill) 596 F.2d 733, CCH Fed Secur L Rep ¶ 96836

The actions of the directors of a New York corporation permitting employees who held stock options to cancel previously granted options and then regranting such options at substantially lower prices, even if inconsistent with previous plans, were valid where the shareholders authorized such action under CLS Business Corporation Law § 505, subd d. Cohen v Ayers (1978, ND Ill) 449 F. Supp. 298, CCH Fed Secur L Rep ¶ 96575, affd (CA7 Ill) 596 F.2d 733, CCH Fed Secur L Rep ¶ 96836

Sending proxy statement to corporate officers, urging approval of stock warrants, did not constitute predicate act of wire fraud for purpose of shareholder's civil RICO claim in derivative action against corporate officers and directors, as stock warrants were properly issued as compensation in compliance with CLS Bus Corp § 505 in that consideration received by corporation was services rendered by officers; § 505 did not require guarantee of continued service. Pinnacle Consultants ex rel. Shareholders of Leucadia Nat'l Corp. v Leucadia Nat'l Corp. (1995, SD NY) 923 F. Supp. 439

Corporate directors could not be held liable for conversion or fraud in shareholders' derivative action challenging issuance of stock warrants to them, where stock warrants were legally valid, and proxy statements urging approval of issuance of stock warrants disclosed all relevant facts. Pinnacle Consultants ex rel. Shareholders of Leucadia Nat'l Corp. v Leucadia Nat'l Corp. (1995, SD NY) 923 F. Supp. 439

UNDER FORMER LAW

A determination of the Public Service Commission disapproving a restricted stock option plan for key personnel of a gas corporation was beyond the administrative function of the Commission because it invaded the field of management. But the Public Service Commission's order was nonetheless confirmed where the proposed stock issue for the plan was not one within the purposes specified by § 69 of the Public Service Law. Brooklyn Union Gas Co. v Public Service Com. (1959, 3d Dept) 8 A.D.2d 210, 187 N.Y.S.2d 207, affd 8 N.Y.2d 815, 202 N.Y.S.2d 322, 168 N.E.2d 390

Where stock option rights were given to certain officers and employees of a corporation, with stockholder approval, containing certain provisions for adjustment in case of recapitalization but without mentioning subsequent stock dividends, directors could not be found guilty of fraud or misconduct in subsequently adjusting the terms of the options to conform with the results of later stock dividends and the effect of such dividends on share values. Amdur v Meyer (1962, 1st Dept) 15 A.D.2d 425, 224 N.Y.S.2d 440, motion to dismiss app den 11 N.Y.2d 1051, 230 N.Y.S.2d 206, 184 N.E.2d 179

Resolutions of the board of directors violated preemptive rights of shareholders where the attempt was to authorize issuance of several thousands of shares at one cent per share to employees and management in consideration of past services rendered. Hyman v Behar (1963) 39 Misc. 2d 617, 241 N.Y.S.2d 625

Stockholders had no pre-emptive rights with respect to shares issued to employees pursuant to an incentive plan under § 14 of former Stock Corp L, and the only remedy of stockholders disapproving such a plan was to seek appraisal of the value of their shares. Hyman v Behar (1963) 39 Misc. 2d 617, 241 N.Y.S.2d 625

Where there is nothing to show that the by-laws of a company provide for the transfer of stock other than on the books of the company, it is a transfer on the books, not a transfer of the certificate which transfers title. Gideon v Representative Secur. Corp. (1916, DC NY) 232 F 184

§ 506. Determination of stated capital

(a) Upon issue by a corporation of shares with a par value, the consideration received therefor shall constitute stated capital to the extent of the par value of such shares.

(b) Upon issue by a corporation of shares without par value, the entire consideration received therefor shall constitute stated capital unless the board within a period of sixty days after issue allocates to surplus a portion, but not all, of the consideration received for such shares. No such allocation shall be made of any portion of the consideration received for shares without par value having a preference in the assets of the corporation upon involuntary liquidation except all or part of the amount, if any, of such consideration in excess of such preference, nor shall such allocation be made of any portion of the consideration for the issue of shares without par value which is fixed by the shareholders pursuant to a right reserved in the certificate of incorporation, unless such allocation is authorized by vote of the shareholders.

(c) The stated capital of a corporation may be increased from time to time by resolution of the board transferring all or part of the surplus of the corporation to stated capital. The board may direct that the amount so transferred shall be stated capital in respect of any designated class or series of shares.

History: Add, L 1961, ch 855, eff Sept 1, 1963; amd, L 1962, ch 738, ch 834, § 16, eff Sept 1, 1963.

§ 507. Compensation for formation, reorganization and financing

The reasonable charges and expenses of formation or reorganization of a corporation, and the reasonable expenses of and compensation for the sale or underwriting of its shares may be paid or allowed by the corporation out of the consideration received by it in payment for its shares without thereby impairing the fully paid and nonassessable status of such shares.

History: Add, L 1961, ch 855, eff Sept 1, 1963.

CASE ANNOTATIONS

UNDER FORMER STK CORP § 69

Under § 69 of former Stock Corp. L., where the sole incorporators of a corporation agreed that stock should be issued to them as compensation for the performance of their usual and ordinary duties as officers of the corporation, and themselves approved of the issue as "fully paid and non-assessable," in the absence of statute, charter or by-law authorizing them to be paid for serving as directors or officers, the agreement was invalid under this section and said incorporators may be held liable for the amount unpaid upon their subscriptions. Palmer v Scheftel (1918) 183 A.D. 77, 170 SNYS 588

The fact that plaintiff was to receive, for his promotional services, a percentage of shares of corporation to be organized did not render agreement for floating of a Canadian corporation illegal. Nastasi v Moore (1956) 7 Misc. 2d 226, 156 N.Y.S.2d 521

§ 508. Certificates representing shares

(a) The shares of a corporation shall be represented by certificates or shall be uncertificated shares. Certificates shall be signed by the chairman or a vice-chairman of the board or the president or a vice-president and the secretary or an assistant secretary or the treasurer or an assistant treasurer of the corporation, and may be sealed with the seal of the corporation or a facsimile thereof. The signatures of the officers upon a certificate may be facsimiles if: (1) the certificate is countersigned by a transfer agent or registered by a registrar other than the corporation itself or its employee, or (2) the shares are listed on a registered national sercurity exchange. In case any officer who has signed or whose facsimile signature has been placed upon a certificate shall have ceased to be such officer before such certificate is issued, it may be issued by the corporation with the same effect as if he were such officer at the date of issue.

(b) Each certificate representing shares issued by a corporation which is authorized to issue shares of more than one class shall set forth upon the face or back of the certificate, or shall state that the corporation will furnish to any shareholder upon request and without charge, a full statement of the designation, relative rights, preferences and limitations of the shares of each class authorized to be issued and, if the corporation is authorized to issue any class of preferred shares in series, the designation, relative rights, preferences and limitations of each such series so far as the same have been fixed and the authority of the board to designate and fix the relative rights, preferences and limitations of other series.

(c) Each certificate representing shares shall state upon the face thereof:

(1) That the corporation is formed under the laws of this state.

(2) The name of the person or persons to whom issued.

(3) The number and class of shares, and the designation of the series, if any, which such certificate represents.

(d) Shares shall be transferable in the manner provided by law and in the by-laws.

(e) The corporation may issue a new certificate for shares in place of any certificate theretofore issued by it, alleged to have been lost or destroyed, and the board may require the owner of the lost or destroyed certificate, or his legal representative, to give the corporation a bond sufficient to indemnify the corporation against any claim that may be made against it on account of the alleged loss or destruction of any such certificate or the issuance of any such new certificate.

(f) Unless otherwise provided by the articles of incorporation or bylaws, the board of directors of a corporation may provide by resolution that some or all of any or all classes and series of its shares shall be uncertificated shares, provided that such resolution shall not apply to shares represented by a certificate until such certificate is surrendered to the corporation. Within a reasonable time after the issuance or transfer of uncertificated shares, the corporation shall send to the registered owner thereof a written notice containing the information required to be set forth or stated on certificates pursuant to paragraphs (b) and (c) of this section. Except as otherwise expressly provided by law, the rights and obligations of the holders of uncertificated shares and the rights and obligations of the holders of certificates representing shares of the same class and series shall be identical.

History: Add, L 1961, ch 855; amd, L 1962, ch 834, § 17, eff Sept 1, 1963; L 1963, ch 738, eff Sept 1, 1963; L 1965, ch 803, § 8, eff Sept 1, 1965; L 1982, ch 928, §§ 35, 36, eff Dec 21, 1982; L 1985, ch 578, § 1, eff Aug 25, 1985.

CASE ANNOTATIONS

In an action by representatives of a deceased shareholder of a corporation formed as a private club brought against the corporation and its sole surviving shareholder to declare a provision of the corporation's by-laws restricting the transferability of stock and requiring the deceased member's stock to be returned to the corporation void as against public policy, the restriction on the transferability of shares was void as an absolute restraint on the power of alienation violative of state public policy and, therefore, the corporation would be required to transfer the stock to plaintiffs; however, the remaining provisions of the article prohibiting transfers survived, with the result that current stockholders, as well as any new stockholders, would be able to carry out the purposes of corporation by purchasing, leasing or acquiring land and by protecting and promoting the interest of legitimate sport with rod and gun. Quinn v Stuart Lakes Club, Inc. (1982) 57 N.Y.2d 1003, 457 N.Y.S.2d 471, 443 N.E.2d 945

CLS CPLR §§ 213 and 214 barred action for breach of contract and breach of fiduciary duty commenced in 1993 arising from defendants' alleged delay in transferring proceeds from redemption of 30,000 stock shares of defendant corporation to plaintiff, and thus court properly granted defendants' motion for summary judgment and denied plaintiff's cross motion for leave to serve amended complaint and to compel further discovery, where plaintiff's problems arose from its alleged failure to receive stock certificate in 1985, and defendants promptly redeemed shares on plaintiff's submission of satisfactory proof that stock certificate was lost and submission of indemnity bond pursuant to CLS Bus Corp § 508(e). Local 381 Pension Fund v Chemical Bank (1995, 2d Dept) 222 A.D.2d 415, 635 N.Y.S.2d 242, app dismd, in part, app den, in part 88 N.Y.2d 830, 644 N.Y.S.2d 491, 666 N.E.2d 1364

Plaintiff, who was vice-president of corporation for which no stock certificates had been issued, failed to prove that he was 50 percent owner of corporation where, inter alia, defendant (who was president of corporation and plaintiff's older brother) conducted virtually all of corporation's business, plaintiff did not contribute any money to corporation, and plaintiff admitted on several occasions that he had no ownership in corporation. Hunt v Hunt (1995, 3d Dept) 222 A.D.2d 759, 634 N.Y.S.2d 804

In action to invalidate cooperative corporation's exercise of option contained in by-laws which allowed it to repurchase plaintiff's shares at book value (as opposed to market value) on termination of her tenancy for cause, court erred in denying summary judgment to cooperative on ground that, as movant, it had burden to show non-existence of bad faith or breach of fiduciary duty; instead, after cooperative submitted proof that plaintiff executed acknowledgment and occupancy agreements while represented by counsel and thus was on notice that transfer of her shares was subject to restrictions in by-laws, plaintiff bore burden of showing that cooperative's exercise of repurchase option was "unjust and unconscionable" and thus beyond scope of protection afforded by business judgment rule. Jones v Surrey Coop. Apts., Inc. (1999, 1st Dept) 263 A.D.2d 33, 700 N.Y.S.2d 118

In action seeking partition of undivided interest in certain shares of stock allegedly held by plaintiff's former law firm as convenience to investors, who were members of law firm, investment entity was not necessary party under CLS CPLR § 1001 because, in event plaintiff's partition claim was granted, only effect would that plaintiff's proportionate share of revenue from his investment would be remitted directly to him and not remitted to him through his former law firm. Taub v Brockman (2000, 1st Dept) 270 A.D.2d 180, 706 N.Y.S.2d 21

Defendant shareholders' voluntary waiver of their right to dividends on their stock in plaintiff corporation was binding on their transferees where (1) general rule is that in absence of contrary provisions in statute under which corporation is organized or in its bylaws, transferee of corporation's shares takes with no greater rights, and subject to same liabilities, as those of transferor, and (2) there was no merit in shareholders' claim that general rule does not apply if all shares are of same class. Cherry Green Prop. Corp. v Wolf (2001, 1st Dept) 281 A.D.2d 367, 722 N.Y.S.2d 537

A chairman of the board of directors is not one of the usual officers designated in Business Corporation L § 715, but §§ 104 and 508 of such Law do recognize the existence of such an office and accept it for certain purposes as an alternative to the presidency. American Express Co. v Lopez (1973) 72 Misc. 2d 648, 340 N.Y.S.2d 82

Before shareholder tenant of co-operative apartment corporation may dispose of his stock, board of directors of corporation may require payment of $2,000 fee for waiver of its right to first option to purchase stock. Jamil v Southridge Cooperative, Section 4, Inc. (1979) 102 Misc. 2d 404, 425 N.Y.S.2d 905, affd 77 A.D.2d 822, 429 N.Y.S.2d 340, cert den 450 US 919, 67 L Ed 2d 346, 101 S Ct 1366, reh den 450 US 1050, 68 L Ed 2d 247, 101 S Ct 1771

Plaintiff's purported class action seeking $1,000,000 in compensatory damages, $1,000,000 in punitive damages, specific performance, removal of all corporate officers and an award of 1,000 shares of defendant's stock for himself arising from defendant's refusal to replace two shares of its stock allegedly lost by plaintiff unless plaintiff provided a surety bond is baseless and is dismissed in view of the explicit statutory authority permitting a corporation to require an owner of lost or destroyed shares to post a bond sufficient to indemnify it against any future claim that might be made against the lost shares (Business Corporation Law § 508 [e]). Furthermore, in view of plaintiff's willful action in pursuing a claim he knew was wholly lacking in merit (plaintiff having graduated from law school but having been denied admission to the Illinois Bar) and in view of plaintiff's long history of bringing baseless claims in a variety of forums that resulted in his having been permanently enjoined from prosecuting claims in the Federal courts, the court, sua sponte, imposes a sanction against plaintiff in the amount of $5,000 (22 NYCRR 130-1.1 [d]) and enjoins him from pursuing any further actions in State courts on a pro se basis. Martin-Trigona v Capital Cities/ABC, Inc., 145 Misc. 2d 405

UNDER FORMER LAW

Stock certificates do not possess the full character of negotiable paper. Weaver v Barden (1872) 49 N.Y. 286; Jarvis v Manhattan Beach Co. (1896) 148 N.Y. 652, 43 N.E. 68; Knox v Eden Musee American Co. (1896) 148 N.Y. 441, 42 N.E. 988

Stock certificates regular on their face are presumed to be valid. Sarasohn v Andrew Jergens Co. (1943, Sup) 45 N.Y.S.2d 888

Innocent transferees of shares of stock are not legally bound by an agreement between the original owners thereof providing in effect for the election of directors by cumulative voting, and such transferees

cannot be compelled to give up their right to insist that directors be elected by a plurality of votes cast by the holders of voting stock, each share being entitled to one vote. Binon v Boel (1946, Sup) 64 N.Y.S.2d 518

The bylaws of a corporation cannot limit the unconditional right to transfer its shares of stock. Kinnan v Sullivan County Club (1898) 26 A.D. 213, 50 N.Y.S. 95

Issuance of a stock certificate is not essential to stockholder status, or to liability, if any, as a stockholder, or to liability for the balance due on a stock subscription contract. Allen v Ryan (1927) 219 A.D. 634, 221 N.Y.S. 77, affd without op 246 N.Y. 609, 159 N.E. 671; Beals v Buffalo Expanded Metal Const. Co. (1900) 49 A.D. 589, 63 N.Y.S. 635

Capital surplus created by reduction in capital of corporation may be retained by corporation as corporate surplus and need not be distributed to stock holders. Jay Ronald Co. v Marshall Mortg. Corp. (1943) 291 N.Y. 227, 52 N.E.2d 108

Reasonable restrictions upon the transfer of stock of a corporation which are imposed by the charter, articles of association or certificate of incorporation, and notice of which is stamped on the certificates, are legal. Bloomingdale v Bloomingdale (1919) 107 Misc 646, 177 N.Y.S. 873

While an absolute prohibition of transfer of stock unlimited as to time would be against public policy, an agreement expressly permitting the free sale of stock after its purchase has been refused by the other stockholders is valid. Bloomingdale v Bloomingdale (1919) 107 Misc 646, 177 N.Y.S. 873

One who has assigned to a corporation certain contracts to purchase lands upon an agreement that the assignor should become a subscriber for its capital stock but that certificates should not be delivered until the payment of the purchase price of the lots should be completed, is entitled to vote in the election of directors since the existence or nonexistence of a certificate does not affect his relation to the corporation. Re Timen (1923) 120 Misc 815, 200 N.Y.S. 488

An amendment to the bylaws of a corporation to make all subsequent transfers of stock subject to certain restrictions is of no force and effect since it would be necessary to replace the outstanding certificates with new certificates stating on the face thereof the restrictions of the agreement. Peets v Manhasset Civil Engineers, Inc. (1946) 4 Misc. 2d 683, 68 N.Y.S.2d 338

In what purported to be a stockholder's derivative suit, the evidence was insufficient to show that plaintiff was either a stockholder, or had an equitable and beneficial interest in stock of the defendant corporation, as nominee of her husband, where it was established that no stock was duly authorized to be issued by any properly elected officer of the corporation or actually issued, either to plaintiff or her husband, but merely that a stock certificate had been made out in the husband's name. Cavanagh v L & R Trucking & Warehouse Co. (1961) 29 Misc. 2d 576, 215 N.Y.S.2d 902

A clause in a certificate providing that shares of stock cannot be transferred without the consent in writing of the board of directors is invalid as against public policy. 1910 Ops Atty Gen 404

§ 509.   Fractions of a share or scrip authorized

(a) A corporation may, but shall not be obliged to, issue fractions of a share either represented by a certificate or uncertificated, which shall entitle the holder, in proportion to his fractional holdings, to exercise voting rights, receive dividends and participate in liquidating distributions.

(b) As an alternative, a corporation may pay in cash the fair value of fractions of a share as of the time when those entitled to receive such fractions are determined.

(c) As an alternative, a corporation may issue scrip in registered or bearer form over the manual or facsimile signature of an officer of the corporation or of its agent, exchangeable as therein provided for full shares, but such scrip shall not entitle the holder to any rights of a shareholder except as therein provided. Such scrip may be issued subject to the condition

that it shall become void if not exchanged for certificates representing full shares or uncertificated full
shares before a specified date, or subject to the
condition that the shares for which such scrip is
exchangeable may be sold by the corporation and the
proceeds thereof distributed to the holders of such
scrip, or subject to any other conditions which the
board may determine.

(d) A corporation may provide reasonable opportunity for persons entitled to fractions of a share or
scrip to sell such fractions of a share or scrip or to
purchase such additional fractions of a share or scrip
as may be needed to acquire a full share.

History: Add, L 1961, ch 855, eff Sept 1, 1963;
amd, L 1962, ch 834, § 18, eff Sept 1, 1963,19, eff Sept
1, 1963; L 1982, ch 928, § 37, eff Dec 21, 1982; L 1997,
ch 449, § 11, eff Feb 22, 1998.

CASE ANNOTATIONS

UNDER FORMER LAW

Under earlier statutes, it was ruled that a stock corporation could
not provide for the issuance of fractional shares of stock. 1934 Ops
Atty Gen 237

§ 510. Dividends or other distributions in cash or property

(a) A corporation may declare and pay dividends
or make other distributions in cash or its bonds or its
property, including the shares or bonds of other
corporations, on its outstanding shares, except when
currently the corporation is insolvent or would
thereby be made insolvent, or when the declaration,
payment or distribution would be contrary to any
restrictions contained in the certificate of incorporation.

(b) Dividends may be declared or paid and other
distributions may be made either (1) out of surplus,
so that the net assets of the corporation remaining
after such declaration, payment or distribution shall
at least equal the amount of its stated capital, or (2)
in case there shall be no such surplus, out of its net
profits for the fiscal year in which the dividend is
declared and/or the preceding fiscal year. If the
capital of the corporation shall have been diminished
by depreciation in the value of its property or by
losses or otherwise to an amount less than the aggregate amount of the stated capital represented by the
issued and outstanding shares of all classes having a
preference upon the distribution of assets, the directors of such corporation shall not declare and pay out
of such net profits any dividends upon any shares
until the deficiency in the amount of stated capital
represented by the issued and outstanding shares of
all classes having a preference upon the distribution
of assets shall have been repaired. A corporation
engaged in the exploitation of natural resources or
other wasting assets, including patents, or formed
primarily for the liquidation of specific assets, may
declare and pay dividends or make other distributions in excess of its surplus, computed after taking
due account of depletion and amortization, to the
extent that the cost of the wasting or specific assets
has been recovered by depletion reserves, amortization or sale, if the net assets remaining after such
dividends or distributions are sufficient to cover the
liquidation preferences of shares having such preferences in involuntary liquidation.

(c) [Repealed]

History: Add, L 1961, ch 855, eff Sept 1, 1963;
amd, L 1962, ch 834, § 20, eff Sept 1, 1963; L 1963, ch
738, eff Sept 1, 1963; L 1997, ch 449, § 12, eff Feb 22,
1998; L 2008, ch 313, § 1, eff July 21, 2008.

CASE ANNOTATIONS

UNDER FORMER LAW
1. In general
2. What constitutes dividend
3. Determining surplus
4. Role of directors
5. Insolvency as factor
6. Wrongful declaration
7. Miscellaneous

In proceeding to decide a beneficial interest in stock dividends
wherein critical issue was whether financial transaction on which
complaint was based was or was intended to be a transaction in
praesenti or in futuro, discussions between parties and clear
language of agreement stating that "upon receipt of the check to be
delivered on August 1, 1967, Seller will deliver to Buyers certificate
for the shares to be sold by it" established that seller's intention was
to defer passage of title until a time certain in the future. Deering
Milliken, Inc. v Clark Estates, Inc. (1977, 1st Dept) 57 A.D.2d 773,
394 N.Y.S.2d 436, affd 43 N.Y.2d 545, 402 N.Y.S.2d 987, 373 N.E.2d
1212

Judgment creditor was not proper party to bring action under CLS
Bus Corp §§ 510 and 719 for enforcement of director's liability to
corporate debtor for unlawful distribution of corporate assets into
employee benefit plan in which he claimed 80 percent of funds since
remedies of § 719 are given exclusively to corporation, not to its
creditors; furthermore, even if judgment creditor were proper party,
action would not lie under § 719 since statute does not authorize
action to set aside unlawful conveyances or transfers of corporate
assets. Planned Consumer Marketing, Inc. v Coats & Clark, Inc.
(1987, 1st Dept) 127 A.D.2d 355, 513 N.Y.S.2d 417, affd, ctfd ques ans
71 N.Y.2d 442, 527 N.Y.S.2d 185, 522 N.E.2d 30, 9 EBC 1796

Cause of action alleging payment of dividends and distributions in
violation of CLS Bus Corp §§ 510 and 719(a)(1) was not subject to
dismissal for failure to comply with pleading requirements of CLS
CPLR § 3016 since allegations were not based on fraud. Menaker v
Alstaedter (1987, 2d Dept) 134 A.D.2d 412, 521 N.Y.S.2d 35

Corporate directors were entitled to summary judgment on shareholders' claims based on directors' failure to pay dividends in
particular year where uncontradicted evidence revealed that directors
were prohibited from declaring dividends because there was stockholder equity deficit. Jones v Jones (1996, 1st Dept) 223 A.D.2d 483,
637 N.Y.S.2d 83

In action for judicial determination of value of 3 deceased physicians' interests in partnership and corporation that owned and
operated hospital, trial court properly held that redemption ratios
established at 1982 and 1983 annual meetings of partnership and
corporation were valid and controlling. Livack v Central Gen. Hosp.
(1997, 2d Dept) 242 A.D.2d 684, 664 N.Y.S.2d 935

In action for judicial determination of value of 3 deceased physicians' interests in partnership and corporation that owned and
operated hospital, trial court properly concluded that one physician's
interests in hospital were ineligible for inclusion in any computation
for quorum and voting purposes, by reason of that physician's felony
conviction and stipulation of withdrawal. Livack v Central Gen.
Hosp. (1997, 2d Dept) 242 A.D.2d 684, 664 N.Y.S.2d 935

In action for judicial determination of value of 3 deceased physicians' interests in partnership and corporation that owned and
operated hospital, trial court employed proper methodology to
determine redemption ratios applicable to plaintiffs' interests, where
partnership and stockholder agreements, read together, expressly

provided for alternative valuation methods. Livack v Central Gen. Hosp. (1997, 2d Dept) 242 A.D.2d 684, 664 N.Y.S.2d 935

Question of whether or not dividend is to be declared or distribution of some kind should be made is exclusively a matter of business judgment for corporation's board of directors. Kamin v American Express Co. (1976) 86 Misc. 2d 809, 383 N.Y.S.2d 807, affd (1st Dept) 54 A.D.2d 654, 387 N.Y.S.2d 993

New York's debtor and creditor law does not authorize actions against those who aid and abet violations of CLS Bus Corp §§ 510, 719, or 720. Atlanta Shipping Corp. v Chemical Bank (1987, CA2 NY) 818 F.2d 240, 3 UCCRS2d 1618

Surplus out of which declaration or payment of dividends may be made under CLS Bus Corp L § 510(b) need not be based on valuation assets reflected on books of corporation. British Printing & Communication Corp. plc v Harcourt Brace Jovanovich, Inc. (1987, SD NY) 664 F. Supp. 1519, CCH Fed Secur L Rep ¶ 93318

A subsidiary of the Urban Development Corporation may incorporate under the Business Corporation Law without forfeiting its public status. The subsidiary may not pay profits to private investors, and upon dissolution of the corporation, the assets belong to the State. 1980 Op Atty Gen Oct. 20

UNDER FORMER LAW

1. In general

The earnings of a corporation remain its property until a division is made or a dividend declared; until that time whatever interest a stockholder has therein passes with the transfer of his stock as incident thereto. Robertson v Brulatour (1907) 188 N.Y. 301, 80 N.E. 938, affg 111 A.D. 882, 98 N.Y.S. 15

It was the law under § 58 of former Stock Corp. L., as it is, generally, under the phrasing of subd. (a) (1) of this section, that dividends could be declared and paid, or other distributions to shareholders made, only out of surplus of "stated" (usually depletion of "stated" (usually referred to in older decisions as "chartered" or "authorized") capital. Randall v Bailey (1940, Sup) 23 N.Y.S.2d 173, affd without op 262 A.D. 844, 29 N.Y.S.2d 512, affd 288 N.Y. 280, 43 N.E.2d 43

It is fundamental that dividends can only legally be paid from profits or net assets in excess of capital. Case v New York C. R. Co. (1962, Sup) 232 N.Y.S.2d 702, revd on other grounds (1st Dept) 19 A.D.2d 383, 243 N.Y.S.2d 620, revd on other grounds 15 N.Y.2d 150, 256 N.Y.S.2d 607, 204 N.E.2d 643

Section 58 of former Stock Corp. L., in its general prohibition against paying dividends which would deplete authorized or stated capital, was applicable to foreign corporations authorized to do business in New York without regard to whether there was such a restriction in the laws of the jurisdiction under which the foreign corporation was organized. International Ticket Scale Corp. v United States (1948, CA2 NY) 165 F.2d 358, 48-1 USTC ¶ 9124; Hayman v Morris (1942, Sup) 36 N.Y.S.2d 756; Re Burnet-Clark, Ltd. (1932, CA2 NY) 56 F.2d 744

2. What constitutes dividend

Where a stock corporation, formed for sole purpose of trading in real estate, disposed of all its real estate, receiving payment therefor partly in cash and partly in purchase-money mortgages, and distributed cash among stockholders, mere collection of principal and interest of mortgage and distribution thereof among stockholders did not constitute distribution of dividends from business of corporation, within meaning of Tax Law, § 182. People ex rel. Ridgewood Land & Improv. Co. v Saxe (1916) 174 A.D. 344, 160 N.Y.S. 752, affd without op 219 N.Y. 637, 114 N.E. 1080

An agreement to provide a shareholder, or some group of shareholders, with benefits, special rights, or privileges at the corporation's expense or in deprivation of commercial use of property or assets," in lieu of" dividends, has been considered, in some instances, as tantamount to a dividend or distribution of assets. 791 Corp. v Engel (1934) 152 Misc 107, 273 N.Y.S. 322; Stevens v Olus Mfg. Co. (1911) 72 Misc 508, 130 N.Y.S. 22, affd without op 146 A.D. 951, 131 N.Y.S. 1145

A cancelation of indebtedness due to a corporation did not constitute a dividend violating § 58 of former Stock Corp. L., even though such cancelation would result in an impairment of the capital of the company, where there were sufficient liquid assets to pay all creditors in full and all stockholders consented to the cancelation along with an amendment to the certificate of incorporation reclassifying the shares of stock to avoid any impairment of capital resulting from the said cancelation. Re Maijgren's Will (1949) 194 Misc 389, 86 N.Y.S.2d 760

Execution of a chattel mortgage by which stockholders impose a lien upon corporate assets for their own benefit and to secure payments on sales of their stock, was, in effect, the payment of a secret dividend to stockholders in derogation of rights of present and future creditors and a distribution of assets such as § 58 of the former Stock Corp. L. forbids. Re Bay Ridge Inn, Inc. (1938, CA2 NY) 98 F.2d 85

But withdrawals of corporate funds without any dividend declaration, and apparently by way of loans or salary payments, were not considered "distributions" of assets within the meaning of § 58 of former Stock Corp. L. Newfield v Oosterhuis (1943, CA2 NY) 137 F.2d 437

What constitutes a "dividend" or "other distribution" under statutes using such terms is not too clear, but it would appear from decisions under § 664 of the Penal Law and § 58 of former Stock Corp. L. that any kind of benefit conferred at corporate expense on shareholders generally, or a particular class of shareholders, such as payment of insurance premiums for their benefit, falls within the coverage. Carson, Pirie Scott & Co. v Duffy-Powers, Inc. (1934, DC NY) 9 F. Supp. 199

3. Determining surplus

Property or other assets accumulated by a corporation in excess of chartered or authorized capital was considered "surplus" available for distribution to shareholders. Equitable Life Assur. Soc. v Union P. R. Co. (1914) 162 A.D. 81, 147 N.Y.S. 382, affd 212 N.Y. 360, 106 N.E. 92

Gains and profits made by fortunate investment, and in converting bonds into common stock are distributable as dividends in discretion of board of directors of a solvent corporation in precisely the same manner as gains and profits made in operation. Equitable Life Assur. Soc. v Union P. R. Co. (1914) 162 A.D. 81, 147 N.Y.S. 382, affd 212 N.Y. 360, 106 N.E. 92

In valuing assets to determine whether or not a surplus exists from which dividends may be paid, unrealized appreciation or depreciation may be taken into consideration; in other words value rather than cost may be used in determining whether or not there exists a surplus out of which dividends can be paid. Randall v Bailey (1940, Sup) 23 N.Y.S.2d 173, affd without op 262 A.D. 844, 29 N.Y.S.2d 512, affd 288 N.Y. 280, 43 N.E.2d 43

Assessed value of property for tax purposes is at least competent evidence as to its value in determining existence and extent of a surplus, and it may be practically conclusive where the assessment is at a fair market value as arrived at in connection with negotiations and proceedings between the corporation and the taxing authorities to determine that value. Randall v Bailey (1940, Sup) 23 N.Y.S.2d 173, affd without op 262 A.D. 844, 29 N.Y.S.2d 512, affd 288 N.Y. 280, 43 N.E.2d 43

Good will of the corporation as a going concern could be assigned a reasonable value in determining existence and amount of surplus. Randall v Bailey (1940, Sup) 23 N.Y.S.2d 173, affd without op 262 A.D. 844, 29 N.Y.S.2d 512, affd 288 N.Y. 280, 43 N.E.2d 43

Net income of a corporation for dividend purposes cannot be determined until all taxes, depreciation, maintenance and upkeep expenses have been deducted. Case v New York C. R. Co. (1962, Sup) 232 N.Y.S.2d 702, revd on other grounds (1st Dept) 19 A.D.2d 383, 243 N.Y.S.2d 620, revd on other grounds 15 N.Y.2d 150, 256 N.Y.S.2d 607, 204 N.E.2d 643

4. Role of directors

Whether or not to declare a dividend, and the amount of the dividend, if declared, rests in the discretion and sound business judgment of the corporate management, usually the board of directors, and the management will not be judicially compelled to make a dividend declaration, or to distribute any particular amount, notwithstanding funds are available for the purpose, unless bad faith in failing to do so is clearly demonstrated. Strout v Cross, Austin & Ireland Lumber Co. (1940) 283 N.Y. 406, 28 N.E.2d 890; City Bank Farmers' Trust Co. v Hewitt Realty Co. (1931) 257 N.Y. 62, 177 N.E. 309; Strassburger v Singer Mfg. Co. (1942) 263 A.D. 518, 33 N.Y.S.2d 424; Lockley v Robie (1950) 276 A.D. 291, 94 N.Y.S.2d 335, mod on other grounds 301 N.Y. 371, 93 N.E.2d 895, reh den 301 N.Y. 731, 95 N.E.2d 409

In the light of statutory limitations on dividend sources, such as § 58 of former Stock Corp. L., it has been considered that any contract whereby a corporation or its board of directors is unrestrictedly required to pay dividends is contrary to public policy. Kennedy v Kennedy (1949) 22 Misc. 2d 924, 91 N.Y.S.2d 294; 791 Corp. v Engel (1934) 152 Misc 107, 273 N.Y.S. 322

Where directors have declared dividends, the presumption is that they exercised their discretion in good faith, that there were net profits available for this purpose, and that their action in declaring or paying dividends was legal and proper, and courts will not interfere unless the powers have been illegally or unconscientiously executed; or unless it be made to appear that the acts were fraudulent or collusive, and destructive of the rights of the stockholders. Gallagher v New York Dock Co. (1940, Sup App T) 19 N.Y.S.2d 789, affd 263 A.D. 878, 32 N.Y.S.2d 348

It is recognized that value of corporate assets is not static, and it is considered to be the duty of the board of directors to ascertain in connection with each dividend declaration, if in doubt, whether there is sufficient surplus available to cover the dividend. For this purpose it is usually enough for the board to consider what the assets then are and their existing values, without calling in independent and professional appraisers or altering book values item by item. Randall v Bailey (1940, Sup) 23 N.Y.S.2d 173, affd without op 262 A.D. 844, 29 N.Y.S.2d 512, affd 288 N.Y. 280, 43 N.E.2d 43

Where, in valuing the assets of a corporation to determine whether or not a surplus exists from which dividends may be paid, the directors have in fact exercised an informed judgment with respect thereto, the courts will be exceedingly slow to override that judgment, and clear and convincing evidence will be required to justify a finding that such judgment was not in accordance with the facts. Randall v Bailey (1940, Sup) 23 N.Y.S.2d 173, affd without op 262 A.D. 844, 29 N.Y.S.2d 512, affd 288 N.Y. 280, 43 N.E.2d 43

5. Insolvency as factor

On dissolution of a domestic corporation, whose assets remaining after payment of its debts were not sufficient to pay both preferred and common stock at par, preferred stockholders were not entitled, in addition to payment for their stock at par, to receive dividends on said stock, to exclusion of common stockholders, where no dividends were declared and none could have been legally declared thereon under § 58 of the former Stock Corp. L. Michael v Cayey-Caguas Tobacco Co. (1920) 190 A.D. 618, 180 N.Y.S. 532

A certificate of incorporation providing that the preferred stock should be entitled to cumulative dividend "as and when declared" and that upon dissolution, after the payment of debts, the corporate assets were to be applied to the payment of the par value of the preferred stock with any arrearages of dividends to which the stockholders "may be entitled" was construed to mean that the arrearages of preferred dividends on dissolution referred only to declared dividends which were not paid. Wouk v Merin (1954) 283 A.D. 522, 128 N.Y.S.2d 727

Where a parent corporation held the bonds of its subsidiary in the amount of $4,000,000 and the subsidiary was indebted to the parent corporation for an additional sum, and the parent corporation owned 98 percent of the preferred stock of the subsidiary, dividends declared on the stock out of surplus at a time when the subsidiary corporation was making money rather than applying the surplus to a reduction of the subsidiary's indebtedness to the parent corporation was not improper in the absence of bad faith on the part of the directors. Schwartz v Kahn (1944) 183 Misc 252, 50 N.Y.S.2d 931

Section 58 of former Stock Corp. L. was designed to prevent the depreciation of the fund upon which creditors rely in extending credit to the corporation and which they resort to for payment; if there were no creditors, that section had no application and the prohibition was without effect. Hayman v Morris (1942, Sup) 36 N.Y.S.2d 756

It is not impossible that this section of former Bus. Corp. L., though phrased quite differently from § 58 of former Stock Corp. L., might be regarded, as was the latter in some decisions, as sort of a general prohibition against invasion of the captial of a corporation, or sanctioning its use, for the benefit of officers or shareholders, particularly if the corporation was then insolvent or might thereby be rendered insolvent. Re Yukon Ice Cream Co. (1941, DC NY) 41 F. Supp. 466

6. Wrongful declaration

The illegal act of directors declaring dividends where no surplus in fact existed may not be ratified. Cowin v Jonas (1943, Sup) 43 N.Y.S.2d 468, affd without op 267 A.D. 947, 48 N.Y.S.2d 460, affd 293 N.Y. 838, 59 N.E.2d 436

Where corporation agreed to return plaintiff's paid-in capital by a certain date, it could not avoid its obligation on the ground of ultra vires in the absence of proof that at such date it lacked surplus out of which to make the payment. Moro v Soldo (1955, Sup) 143 N.Y.S.2d 863

A bank to which the president and sole stockholder of a corporation is individually indebted, is not chargeable with notice from the mere fact the debtor makes a payment on his indebtedness by check drawn on the account of the corporation in another bank that the payment will impair stated capital of the corporation in violation of § 58 of former Stock Corp. L. or to make inquiry concerning the possibility of such impairment. Field v Bankers Trust Co. (1961, CA2 NY) 296 F.2d 109, cert den 369 US 859, 8 L Ed 2d 17, 82 S Ct 948

Section 58 of the former Stock Corp. L. was sometimes referred to in connection with asserted bank liability for paying, honoring, or accepting checks drawn on a corporate bank account and used to pay personal debts or obligations of the officer signing the check or making the withdrawal, thereby impairing corporate capital. It has been said that the New York decisions are not too clear in this field, but held, by a Federal Court of Appeals decision, that a bank should not be held liable for the capital impairment where it acted pursuant to corporate authorization in honoring checks so drawn and had no actual knowledge that corporate capital was being impaired. This decision dealt with a situation where the sole stockholder of the corporation was using its checking account to pay his personal debts. Field v Bankers Trust Co. (1961, CA2 NY) 296 F.2d 109, cert den 369 US 859, 8 L Ed 2d 17, 82 S Ct 948

The wrongful declaration of a dividend out of capital in violation of § 58 of former Stock Corp. L. was a wrong of those committing it, innocent participants were not accomplices to its commission; and in order to hold a stockholder who received such a dividend liable, it was necessary to positively allege and prove the stockholder's complicity in and knowledge of the wrong. Fried v Cano (1958, DC NY) 167 F. Supp. 625

7. Miscellaneous

Where, according to the terms to the recital on the stock certificates the owners of preferred shares were entitled "to a 7 per cent cumulative annual dividend", a preferred stockholder cannot be compelled without her consent to accept a property dividend rather than a cash dividend in payment of the accrued amount owed her. Strout v Cross, Austin & Ireland Lumber Co. (1940) 283 N.Y. 406, 28 N.E.2d 890

In the construction and application of will and trust provisions, questions have frequently arisen as to whether a particular dividend is to be considered a "cash" or ordinary dividend, a stock dividend, or a distribution out of capital, as bearing on right to the dividend as between a life beneficiary or remainderman. The problem is primarily to determine intent of the testator or creator of the trust, but the corporation laws are sometimes referred to in trying to arrive at what his probable intent was. See, for example, Re Benary's Will (1949) 194 Misc 271, 86 N.Y.S.2d 679; Re Lissberger's Estate (1947) 189 Misc 277, 71 N.Y.S.2d 585, affd without op 273 A.D. 881, 78 N.Y.S.2d 199

Under § 58 of former Stock Corp. L. and § 664 of the Penal L., a corporation could not buy up its own shares except out of surplus. Grasselli Chemical Co. v Aetna Explosives Co. (1918, DC NY) 258 F 66

§ 511.   Share distributions and changes

(a) A corporation may make pro rata distributions of its authorized but unissued shares to holders of any class or series of its outstanding shares, subject to the following conditions:

(1) If a distribution of shares having a par value is made, such shares shall be issued at not less than the par value thereof and there shall be transferred to stated capital at the time of such distribution an amount of surplus equal to the aggregate par value of such shares.

(2) If a distribution of shares without par value is made, the amount of stated capital to be represented by each such share shall be fixed by the board, unless the certificate of incorporation reserves to the shareholders the right to fix the consideration for the issue of such shares, and there shall be transferred to stated capital at the time of such distribution an amount of surplus equal to the aggregate stated capital represented by such shares.

(3) A distribution of shares of any class or series may be made to holders of the same or any other class or series of shares unless the certificate of incorporation provides otherwise, provided, however, that in the case of a corporation incorporated prior to the effective date of subparagraph (4) of this paragraph, then so long as any shares of such class remain outstanding a distribution of shares of any class or series of shares of such corporation may be made only to holders of the same class or series of shares unless the certificate of incorporation permits distribution to holders of another class or series, or unless such distribution is approved by the affirmative vote or the written consent of the holders of a majority of the outstanding shares of the class or series to be distributed.

(4) A distribution of any class or series of shares shall be subject to the preemptive rights, if any, applicable to such shares pursuant to this chapter.

(b) A corporation making a pro rata distribution of authorized but unissued shares to the holders of any class or series of outstanding shares may at its option make an equivalent distribution upon treasury shares of the same class or series, and any shares so distributed shall be treasury shares.

(c) A change of issued shares of any class which increases the stated capital represented by those shares may be made if the surplus of the corporation is sufficient to permit the transfer, and a transfer is concurrently made, from surplus to stated capital, of an amount equal to such increase.

(d) No transfer from surplus to stated capital need be made by a corporation making a distribution of its treasury shares to holders of any class of outstanding shares; nor upon a split up or division of issued shares of any class into a greater number of shares of the same class, or a combination of issued shares of any class into a lesser number of shares of the same class, if there is no increase in the aggregate stated capital represented by them.

(e) Nothing in this section shall prevent a corporation from making other transfers from surplus to stated capital in connection with share distributions or otherwise.

(f) Every distribution to shareholders of certificates representing a share distribution or a change of shares which affects stated capital or surplus shall be accompanied by a written notice (1) disclosing the amounts by which such distribution or change affects stated capital and surplus, or (2) if such amounts are not determinable at the time of such notice, disclosing the approximate effect of such distribution or change upon stated capital and surplus and stating that such amounts are not yet determinable.

(g) When issued shares are changed in any manner which affects stated capital or surplus, and no distribution to shareholders of certificates representing any shares resulting from such change is made, disclosure of the effect of such change upon the stated capital and surplus shall be made in the next finan-cial statement covering the period in which such change is made that is furnished by the corporation to holders of shares of the class or series so changed or, if practicable, in the first notice of dividend or share distribution or change that is furnished to such shareholders between the date of the change of shares and the next such financial statement, and in any event within six months of the date of such change.

History: Add, L 1961, ch 855; amd, L 1962, ch 834, § 21, eff Sept 1, 1963; amd, L 1963, ch 738, eff Sept 1, 1963; L 1965, ch 803, § 9, eff Sept 1, 1965; L 1997, ch 449, § 13, eff Feb 22, 1998.

CASE ANNOTATIONS
UNDER FORMER LAW

A stipulation settling an action brought by preferred stockholders to enjoin corporation from carrying out proposal that preferred stock be reduced from $100 to $1.00 per share, solely by vote of the common stock, was improper where the settlement plan included a plan of recapitalization and an adjustment of claims between the corporation and others. Brill v Blakely (1955) 308 N.Y. 951, 127 N.E.2d 96

Under § 21 of former Stock Corp. L. a corporation, instead of utilizing its surplus to pay back dividends on preferred stock, could adopt a plan of reclassification. Liebschutz v Schaffer Stores Co. (1951) 279 A.D. 96, 108 N.Y.S.2d 476

A cause of action for alleged breach of contract on the part of defendants to purchase certain shares of stock fails, where plaintiff is unable to tender the original stock which has been reclassified into new stock, and has impliedly consented to the reclassification. Goebbel v Gross (1934) 153 Misc 637, 275 N.Y.S. 308

Reclassification of stock does not result in the "purchase" of stock by the stockholders within the meaning of the Securities Act of 1934. Roberts v Eaton (1953, DC NY) 119 F. Supp. 362, affd (CA2 NY) 212 F.2d 82, cert den 348 US 827, 99 L Ed 652, 75 S Ct 44

§ 512. Redeemable shares

(a) Subject to the restrictions contained in section 513 (Purchase, redemption and certain other transactions by a corporation with respect to its own shares) and paragraph (b) of this section, a corporation may provide in its certificate of incorporation for one or more classes or series of shares which are redeemable, in whole or in part, at the option of the corporation, the holder or another person or upon the happening of a specified event.

(b) No redeemable common shares, other than shares of an open-end investment company, as defined in an act of congress entitled "Investment Company Act of 1940", as amended, or of a member corporation of a national securities exchange registered under a statute of the United States such as the Securities Exchange Act of 1934, as amended, or of a corporation described in this paragraph, shall be issued or redeemed unless the corporation at the time has outstanding a class of common shares that is not subject to redemption. Any common shares of a corporation which directly or through a subsidiary has a license or franchise to conduct its business, which license or franchise is conditioned upon some or all of the holders of such corporation's common shares possessing prescribed qualifications, may be made subject to redemption by the corporation to the extent necessary to prevent the loss of, or to reinstate, such license or franchise.

(c) Shares of any class or series which may be made redeemable under this section may be redeemed for cash, other property, indebtedness or other securities of the same or another corporation, at such time or times, price or prices, or rate or rates, and with such adjustments, as shall be stated in the certificate of incorporation.

(d) Nothing in this section shall prevent a corporation from creating sinking funds for the redemption or purchase of its shares to the extent permitted by section 513 (Purchase, redemption and certain other transactions by a corporation with respect to its own shares).

History: Add, L 1961, ch 855, eff Sept 1, 1963; amd, L 1963, ch 738, eff Sept 1, 1963; L 1970, ch 927, eff June 17, 1970; L 1984, ch 603, § 1, eff July 27, 1984; L 1987, ch 125, § 1, eff June 15, 1987; L 1997, ch 449, § 14, eff Feb 22, 1998.

CASE ANNOTATIONS

Where statute (Business Corporation Law § 512) prohibiting the issuance of redeemable common shares in the absence of an outstanding of a class of common shares that is not subject to redemption, was adopted subsequent to certificate of incorporation, reacquisition of shares by a trade association where a shareholder ceased membership therein or transferred his shares to a nonmember, was not a "redemption" barred by the statute. Glens Falls Ins. Co. v National Board of Fire Underwriters Bldg. Corp. (1970) 63 Misc. 2d 989, 314 N.Y.S.2d 80, affd 36 A.D.2d 793, 318 N.Y.S.2d 915

The right of a business or trade association to reacquire or repurchase the shares of stock on a limited option was a reasonable restriction on the shareholders' right of transfer. Glens Falls Ins. Co. v National Board of Fire Underwriters Bldg. Corp. (1970) 63 Misc. 2d 989, 314 N.Y.S.2d 80, affd 36 A.D.2d 793, 318 N.Y.S.2d 915

§ 513. Purchase, redemption and certain other transactions by a corporation with respect to its own shares

(a) Notwithstanding any authority contained in the certificate of incorporation, the shares of a corporation may not be purchased by the corporation, or, if redeemable, convertible or exchangeable shares, may not be redeemed, converted or exchanged, in each case for or into cash, other property, indebtedness or other securities of the corporation (other than shares of the corporation and rights to acquire such shares) if the corporation is then insolvent or would thereby be made insolvent. Shares may be purchased or redeemed only out of surplus.

(b) When its redeemable, convertible or exchangeable shares are purchased by the corporation within the period during which such shares may be redeemed, converted or exchanged at the option of the corporation, the purchase price thereof shall not exceed the applicable redemption, conversion or exchange price stated in the certificate of incorporation. Upon a redemption, conversion or exchange, the amount payable by the corporation for shares having a cumulative preference on dividends may include the stated redemption, conversion or exchange price plus accrued dividends to the next dividend date following the date of redemption, conversion or exchange of such shares.

(c) No domestic corporation which is subject to the provisions of section <u>nine hundred twelve of</u> this chapter shall purchase or agree to purchase more than ten percent of the stock of the corporation from a shareholder for more than the market value thereof unless such purchase or agreement to purchase is approved by the affirmative vote of the board of directors and a majority of the votes of all outstanding shares entitled to vote thereon at a meeting of shareholders unless the certificate of incorporation requires a greater percentage of the votes of the outstanding shares to approve.

The provisions of this paragraph shall not apply when the corporation offers to purchase shares from all holders of stock or for stock which the holder has been the beneficial owner of for more than two years.

The terms "stock", "beneficial owner", and "market value" shall be as defined in section nine hundred twelve of this chapter.

History: Add, L 1961, ch 855, deriving from Penal Law § 664; amd, L 1962, ch 834, § 22, eff Sept 1, 1963; L 1963, ch 738, eff Sept 1, 1963; L 1985, ch 915, § 1, eff Feb 14, 1986; L 1996, ch 404, § 2, eff Jan 27, 1997,2, eff Jan 26, 1997; L 1997, ch 449, § 15, eff Feb 22, 1998; L 1998, ch 17, § 2, eff Feb 19, 1998, deemed eff Feb 19, 1998,2, eff Feb 19, 1998, deemed eff Feb 22, 1998.

CASE ANNOTATIONS

In an action in which a shareholder in three close corporations sought to enforce each corporation's agreement to redeem his stock and each corporation's guaranty of the other two corporations' redemption agreements, the trial court erred in rendering judgment for the shareholder, although the court determined that each corporation possessed a surplus sufficient to enable it to perform its agreement, where the court failed to determine whether each corporation's performance of its redemption agreement or its guaranty contract would render it equitably insolvent. Vowteras v Argo Compressor Service Corp. (1981, 2d Dept) 81 A.D.2d 582, 437 N.Y.S.2d 689, later app (2d Dept) 83 A.D.2d 834, 441 N.Y.S.2d 562

In an action to enforce an agreement to redeem stock in three close corporations, a corporation failed to establish that compliance with any of its obligations would have rendered it equitably insolvent where the corporation stated that its monthly income exceeded its expenses but there was a substantial likelihood that it could have obtained financing to satisfy its obligations, and the other corporations involved established that they lacked sufficient surplus at the time of the alleged default to satisfy their obligations on the guarantee pursuant to the stock purchase agreement, but failed to establish that they lacked sufficient surplus to satisfy their accelerated obligations, as principal obligors, nor did they establish that compliance with the acceleration clause would have rendered them equitably insolvent. Vowteras v Argo Compressor Service Corp. (1981, 2d Dept) 83 A.D.2d 834, 441 N.Y.S.2d 562

Proper formula for calculating stock redemption price was "formula" contained in unequivocal language of parties' agreements. Resnick v Maxim Group (1995, 4th Dept) 221 A.D.2d 957, 633 N.Y.S.2d 910, app dismd without op 87 N.Y.2d 1055, 644 N.Y.S.2d 147, 666 N.E.2d 1061 and app den 89 N.Y.2d 803, 653 N.Y.S.2d 280, 675 N.E.2d 1233

While a corporation may have no funds to purchase stock, this is not an impediment to the maintenance of an action for specific performance as the corporation has a right to demand performance, the offer to be accepted by it if it can perform, or by a remaining stockholder if it cannot even when the transfer to a third party may have been completed. Cicero Industrial Development Corp. v Roberts (1970) 63 Misc. 2d 565, 312 N.Y.S.2d 893

Corporate directors may be held jointly and severally liable to corporation for benefit of creditors or shareholders for improper purchases of its stock in violation of statute. Nakano v Nakano

McGlone Nightingale Advertising, Inc. (1975) 84 Misc. 2d 905, 377 N.Y.S.2d 996, reh gr, in part 84 Misc. 2d 905, 377 N.Y.S.2d 1001

Redemption of stock where there is an undisputed deficit in corporate surplus account would violate both criminal and civil law. Nakano v Nakano McGlone Nightingale Advertising, Inc. (1975) 84 Misc. 2d 905, 377 N.Y.S.2d 996, reh gr, in part 84 Misc. 2d 905, 377 N.Y.S.2d 1001

Where creditors become such with notice of corporate purchase of its own stock, and redemption is in good faith, the purchase does not infringe upon or prejudice creditor's rights. Nakano v Nakano McGlone Nightingale Advertising, Inc. (1975) 84 Misc. 2d 905, 377 N.Y.S.2d 996, reh gr, in part 84 Misc. 2d 905, 377 N.Y.S.2d 1001

As corporate defendant, against which suit was brought on note executed to redeem stock, failed to establish, on motion for reargument and/or renewal of special term's decision and order thereon granting plaintiff's motion for summary judgment in lieu of complaint to recover $44,000 with interest, that special term overlooked or misapprehended any relevant fact or misapplied controlling principles of law, there was no basis for reargument; but in view of newly submitted financial records establishing the non-availability of a corporate surplus from which payment for the stock could be made, defendant's alternative motion would be granted, with payments to be made when a surplus was available for that purpose. Nakano v Nakano McGlone Nightingale Advertising, Inc. (1975) 84 Misc. 2d 905, 377 N.Y.S.2d 1001

In action upon promissory note issued by corporation to redeem and purchase plaintiff's corporate stock following alleged discharge of plaintiff from employment, plaintiff was entitled to summary judgment, where defendant asserted only that a deficit existed at time that payment under note was to be made but the existence of a deficit was premised upon the barest and most general obligations, totally conclusory in form and substance, and failed to lay bare proof by evidentiary facts sufficient to raise genuine issue for submission to trier of facts. Nakano v Nakano McGlone Nightingale Advertising, Inc. (1975) 84 Misc. 2d 905, 377 N.Y.S.2d 996, reh gr, in part 84 Misc. 2d 905, 377 N.Y.S.2d 1001

Actions of a majority shareholder group in eliminating a petitioner and his son from participation in the active operation of a corporation in which they had previously participated, and in which they had every reasonable expectation of being able to continue to participate, constituted "oppressive" conduct within the meaning of Business Corporation Law (BCL) § 1104-a concerning judicial dissolution of a corporation. Since the corporation was permitted to purchase the shares of the petitioner, pursuant to BCL § 1118, it was entitled to appear and obtain a stay of a dissolution proceeding authorized by that section, but merely establishing that the corporation was legally and financially able to pay the fair value of the shares under the limitations prescribed by BCL § 513 was not a condition precedent to the grant of the stay mandated by § 1118. Although a letter from a corporation offering to purchase the petitioner's shares for a specified price could not constitute an election to purchase required to trigger a stay, the corporation's answer to the petition, together with an affidavit by a majority shareholder on the corporation's behalf, did constitute an election to purchase at fair value. Furthermore, a motion for summary judgment pursuant to CPLR § 3213 brought by the petitioner for repayment of loans of $215,000 allegedly made by him to the corporation would be consolidated, pursuant to the court's discretion provided in CPLR § 602, with proceedings on the shareholder's petition for dissolution, contingent on a denial of the motion for summary judgment. Gene Barry One Hour Photo Process, Inc. (1981) 111 Misc. 2d 559, 444 N.Y.S.2d 540

Insurance proceeds paid to a decedent's widow as the beneficiary of a group employee benefit life insurance policy should not have been applied against the purchase price of the decedent's shares of stock in a corporation, which had exercised its right to purchase the decedent's shares under the buy-sell provisions of the shareholders' agreement, where the provisions of the agreement permitting the corporation to fund such a buy-back with insurance on a shareholder's life related to insurance policies owned by the corporation itself and in which the corporation was named as the beneficiary, and where the fact that employees other than the signatories on the agreement were covered by the group plan and that the corporation took a tax deduction for the group insurance premiums supported the conclusion that the group coverage was not intended to fund the redemption of a deceased shareholder's stock by the corporation. Re Estate of Sirotta (1983) 117 Misc. 2d 1088, 460 N.Y.S.2d 242

A restriction in the certificate of incorporation of a close corporation, which provided that no stock "shall be transferred... until it has first been offered for sale" to the corporation, although otherwise valid and enforceable as a reasonable and valid business purpose of the corporation, would not be enforceable against the estate of a deceased shareholder in the absence of any provision in the certificate clearly expressing the intention of the incorporators to so bind the estate, since a restriction concerning a "transfer" of stock does not generally include the passing of title by operation of law; accordingly, the administratrix would not be required to offer the stock back to the corporation, and she would be allowed to distribute it in kind to the distributees of the deceased stockholder. Re Estate of Spaziani (1984) 125 Misc. 2d 901, 480 N.Y.S.2d 854

In action arising from highly-leveraged buyout of corporation, former owners of corporation, as guarantors on note, were entitled to summary judgment in lieu of complaint indemnifying them for money paid to corporation's creditors after corporation defaulted; purchasers of corporation were not members of class intended to be protected by CLS Bus Corp § 513, and thus were not protected from liability on basis that financing scheme created for sale of corporation violated § 513, where they were not creditors of corporation and were intimately involved in financial gimmickry that eventually led corporation to fail. Sarkin v Nates Auto Parts (1995, Sup) 166 Misc. 2d 913, 636 N.Y.S.2d 985

UNDER FORMER LAW

A stockholder has no constitutionally protected right to continue as a stockholder so long as the value of his interest is compensable. Blumenthal v Roosevelt Hotel (1952) 202 Misc 988, 115 N.Y.S.2d 52

§ 514. Agreements for purchase by a corporation of its own shares

(a) An agreement for the purchase by a corporation of its own shares shall be enforceable by the shareholder and the corporation to the extent such purchase is permitted at the time of purchase by section 513 (Purchase or redemption by a corporation of its own shares).

(b) The possibility that a corporation may not be able to purchase its shares under section 513 shall not be a ground for denying to either party specific performance of an agreement for the purchase by a corporation of its own shares, if at the time for performance the corporation can purchase all or part of such shares under section 513.

History: Add, L 1961, ch 855, amd, L 1962, ch 834, § 23, eff Sept 1, 1963.

CASE ANNOTATIONS

Either the corporation itself or any of its officers may maintain an action for specific performance of the terms of an agreement or contract to preserve and protect the corporate interests. Cicero Industrial Development Corp. v Roberts (1970) 63 Misc. 2d 565, 312 N.Y.S.2d 893

While a corporation may have no funds to purchase stock, this is not an impediment to the maintenance of an action for specific performance as the corporation has a right to demand performance, the offer to be accepted by it if it can perform, or by a remaining stockholder if it cannot even when the transfer to a third party may have been completed. Cicero Industrial Development Corp. v Roberts (1970) 63 Misc. 2d 565, 312 N.Y.S.2d 893

Specific performance of an agreement executed by a real estate development corporation and all its shareholders providing that no shareholder may sell shares of stock owned by him unless he first offers to sell his stock to the corporation at book value, as defined in the agreement, was authorized and the Secretary-Treasurer was entitled to enjoin the other shareholders from selling any of the corporate assets or dissolving the corporation pending transfer of the stock and the shareholders must sell all of their stock to either the corporation or, in the alternative, to the Secretary-Treasurer. Cicero Industrial Development Corp. v Roberts (1970) 63 Misc. 2d 565, 312 N.Y.S.2d 893

The Secretary-Treasurer's actions could not result in a waiver or estoppel of the corporation's rights nor of his own rights; there was no waiver because his actions and desire to continue in the corporation were frequently expressed; nor was there estoppel since there was no fraud or misrepresentation upon his part and the other stockholders knew his wishes and were completely aware of what was taking place. Cicero Industrial Development Corp. v Roberts (1970) 63 Misc. 2d 565, 312 N.Y.S.2d 893

An agreement by a corporation to purchase or redeem its stock is both valid and legal, subject to certain limitations on its enforceability, requiring the existence of a corporate surplus from which the purchase must be made. Nakano v Nakano McGlone Nightingale Advertising, Inc. (1975) 84 Misc. 2d 905, 377 N.Y.S.2d 996, reh gr, in part 84 Misc. 2d 909, 377 N.Y.S.2d 1001

In an action against corporation to enforce a contract of redemption of its stock, burden of proof rests upon corporation to establish that it would be illegal to proceed with the purchase of redemption. Nakano v Nakano McGlone Nightingale Advertising, Inc. (1975) 84 Misc. 2d 905, 377 N.Y.S.2d 996, reh gr, in part 84 Misc. 2d 909, 377 N.Y.S.2d 1001

On issue of right to enforce purchase or redemption of its stock by corporation, there is no presumption one way or another as to the existence of requisite surplus. Nakano v Nakano McGlone Nightingale Advertising, Inc. (1975) 84 Misc. 2d 905, 377 N.Y.S.2d 996, reh gr, in part 84 Misc. 2d 909, 377 N.Y.S.2d 1001

If a surplus which existed at time of agreement of corporation to purchase or redeem its stock disappears, or shrinks to a deficit, the agreement is rendered unenforceable. Nakano v Nakano McGlone Nightingale Advertising, Inc. (1975) 84 Misc. 2d 905, 377 N.Y.S.2d 996, reh gr, in part 84 Misc. 2d 909, 377 N.Y.S.2d 1001

Burden is on corporation to establish that, at time payments were made for purchase or redemption of its stock, it lacked necessary surplus to make payments called for by contract and, where such proof is lacking, it is incumbent upon trial judge to award judgment to plaintiff, even where corporation, at the time of trial, is without sufficient surplus and is, in fact, insolvent. Nakano v Nakano McGlone Nightingale Advertising, Inc. (1975) 84 Misc. 2d 905, 377 N.Y.S.2d 996, reh gr, in part 84 Misc. 2d 905, 377 N.Y.S.2d 1001

§ 515. Reacquired shares

(a) Shares that have been issued and have been purchased, redeemed or otherwise reacquired by a corporation shall be cancelled if they are reacquired out of stated capital, or if they are converted shares, or if the certificate of incorporation requires that such shares be cancelled upon reacquisition.

(b) Any shares reacquired by the corporation and not required to be cancelled may be either retained as treasury shares or cancelled by the board at the time of reacquisition or at any time thereafter.

(c) Neither the retention of reacquired shares as treasury shares, nor their subsequent distribution to shareholders or disposition for a consideration shall change the stated capital. When treasury shares are disposed of for a consideration, the surplus shall be increased by the full amount of the consideration received.

(d) Shares cancelled under this section are restored to the status of authorized but unissued shares. However, if the certificate of incorporation prohibits the reissue of any shares required or permitted to be cancelled under this section, the board by certificate of amendment under section 805 (Certificate of amendment; contents) shall reduce the number of authorized shares accordingly.

History: Add, L 1961, ch 855, eff Sept 1, 1963; amd, L 1962, ch 834, § 24; L 1963, ch 738, eff Sept 1, 1963; L 1965, ch 803, § 10, eff Sept 1, 1965; L 1997, ch 449, § 16, eff Feb 22, 1998.

CASE ANNOTATIONS

UNDER FORMER STK CORP § 36

Where the owner of all the outstanding shares of a corporation except for those held by another, wishing to own all of the outstanding stock, purchases the shares held by the other stockholder, paying therefor with funds of the corporation, the gain is taxable as a gain resulting from the sale or exchange of a capital asset rather than as a gain resulting from a distribution in partial liquidation of the corporation, where the parties did not intend to permanently retire the stock and, since § 36 of former Stock Corp. L. was not complied with, the power to reissue the shares continued to exist. Alpers v Commissioner (1942, CA2) 126 F.2d 58, 42-1 USTC ¶ 9297

§ 516. Reduction of stated capital in certain cases

(a) Except as otherwise provided in the certificate of incorporation, the board may at any time reduce the stated capital of a corporation in any of the following ways:

(1) by eliminating from stated capital any portion of amounts previously transferred by the board from surplus to stated capital and not allocated to any designated class or series of shares;

(2) by reducing or eliminating any amount of stated capital represented by issued shares having a par value which exceeds the aggregate par value of such shares;

(3) by reducing the amount of stated capital represented by issued shares without par value; or

(4) by applying to an otherwise authorized purchase, redemption, conversion or exchange of outstanding shares some or all of the stated capital represented by the shares being purchased, redeemed, converted or exchanged, or some or all of any stated capital that has not been allocated to any particular shares, or both. Notwithstanding the foregoing, if the consideration for the issue of shares without par value was fixed by the shareholders under section 504 (Consideration and payment for shares), the board shall not reduce the stated capital represented by such shares except to the extent, if any, that the board was authorized by the shareholders to allocate any portion of such consideration to surplus.

(b) No reduction of stated capital shall be made under this section unless after such reduction the stated capital exceeds the aggregate preferential amounts payable upon involuntary liquidation upon all issued shares having preferential rights in the assets plus the par value of all other issued shares with par value.

(c) When a reduction of stated capital has been effected under this section, the amount of such reduction shall be disclosed in the next financial statement covering the period in which such reduction is made that is furnished by the corporation to all its shareholders or, if practicable, in the first notice of

Business Corporation Law

dividend or share distribution that is furnished to the holders of each class or series of its shares between the date of such reduction and the next such financial statement, and in any event to all its shareholders within six months of the date of such reduction.

History: Add, L 1961, ch 855; amd, L 1963, ch 738, eff Sept 1, 1963; L 1997, ch 449, § 17, eff Feb 22, 1998.

CASE ANNOTATIONS

UNDER FORMER LAW

"Reduced capital" implies decreased capital stock, not corporate assets. 1910 Ops Atty Gen 403

A statement that the whole amount of debts and liabilities is less than the amount to which it is sought to reduce the capital, was substantial compliance with the requirement of § 36 of former Stock Corp. L. that the whole amount of ascertained debts and liabilities should be stated. 1915 Ops Atty Gen 308

A corporation's right to the benefit of tax deductions upon the filing of a certificate changing its capital (Tax Law § 180(1)), was not affected by the earlier filing of a certificate of reduction of capital pursuant to § 28 of former Stock Corp. L. The latter certificate was not tantamount to a certificate of amendment authorized to be filed under Section 36 of that law, the filing of which within five years from the time of change of capital, would affect such tax deductions. 1950 Ops Atty Gen Dec 7

§ 517.   [Repealed]

History: Add, L 1961, ch 855, eff Sept 1, 1963; amd, L 1963, ch 738, eff Sept 1, 1963; repealed, L 1997, ch 449, § 18, eff Feb 22, 1998.

§ 518.   Corporate bonds

(a) No corporation shall issue bonds except for money or other property, tangible or intangible; labor or services actually received by or performed for the corporation or for its benefit or in its formation or reorganization; a binding obligation to pay the purchase price thereof in cash or other property; a binding obligation to perform services having an agreed value; or a combination thereof. In the absence of fraud in the transaction, the judgment of the board as to the value of the consideration received shall be conclusive.

(b) If a distribution of its own bonds is made by a corporation to holders of any class or series of its outstanding shares, there shall be concurrently transferred to the liabilities of the corporation in respect of such bonds an amount of surplus equal to the principal amount of, and any accrued interest on, such bonds. The amount of the surplus so transferred shall be the consideration for the issue of such bonds.

(c) A corporation may, in its certificate of incorporation, confer upon the holders of any bonds issued or to be issued by the corporation, rights to inspect the corporate books and records and to vote in the election of directors and on any other matters on which shareholders of the corporation may vote.

History: Add, L 1961, ch 855; amd, L 1962, ch 834, § 25; L 1963, ch 738, eff Sept 1 1963; L 1963, ch 738, eff Sept 1, 1963; L 1997, ch 449, § 19, eff Feb 22, 1998.

CASE ANNOTATIONS

UNDER FORMER LAW

Bonds taken as a bonus to stock were not valid. Duncomb v New York, H. & N. R. Co. (1881) 84 N.Y. 190, later app 88 N.Y. 1; but see Christensen v Eno (1887) 106 N.Y. 97, 12 N.E. 648

Bonds could be issued to a bank by a company already in debt to the bank under an agreement that they be issued at their fair market value or at par for property in the nature of advances, loans, discounts, etc., received for the use and lawful purposes of the corporation. Re Waterloo Organ Co. (1904, CA2 NY) 134 F 345, cert den 197 US 621, 49 L Ed 910, 25 S Ct 798

Section 69 of former Stock Corp. L. permitted issuance of bonds for less than their fair market value. Westinghouse Electric & Mfg. Co. v Brooklyn Rapid Transit Co. (1923, DC NY) 288 F 221

But bonds given solely to evidence liability for pre-existing indebtedness were, under § 69 of former Stock Corp. L., invalid, even though the objective was to extend time for payment. Joseph W. Woods & Sons Co. v Southern Trust Co. (1926, CA3 NJ) 13 F.2d 367; Re Progressive Wall Paper Corp. (1916, CA2 NY) 229 F 489; David v Seneca Falls Mfg. Co. (1925, DC NY) 8 F.2d 546, mod in other respects (CA2 NY) 17 F.2d 546; Re Paul Delaney Co. (1927, DC NY) 23 F.2d 737, affd in part and revd in part on other grounds (CA2 NY) 26 F.2d 961

Where loans were made to a corporation by banking institutions prior to the issue of certain bonds by the corporation and prior to their pledge as collateral, on the understanding that, when issued, the bonds should be pledged, the bonds were validly pledged and not given for an antecedent debt. Joseph W. Woods & Sons Co. v Southern Trust Co. (1926, CA3 NJ) 13 F.2d 367

Section 69 of former Stock Corporation L. did not require that corporation bonds be issued for their exact par value. Re Paul Delaney Co. (1927, DC NY) 23 F.2d 737, affd in part and revd in part on other grounds (CA2 NY) 26 F.2d 961; Re Paul Delaney Co. (1928, DC NY) 26 F.2d 937, affd (CA2 NY) 30 F.2d 1018; MacQuoid v Queens Estates (1911) 143 A.D. 134, 127 N.Y.S. 867

Bonds issued pursuant to an agreement providing for the cancellation of a mortgage for which the bonds secured by a trust mortgage were to be substituted, were validly issued. Re Paul De Laney Co. (1928, CA2 NY) 26 F.2d 961

Property of any value could serve as consideration for bonds, under § 69 of former Stock Corp. L., if really intended as such and not merely as a cover for means of evidencing a pre-existing debt. Re Paul De Laney Co. (1928, CA2 NY) 26 F.2d 961

The legislature of the state has the authority to give to the directors of a corporation, the power to determine the value of bonds issued. Estate Planning Corp. v Commissioner (1939, CA2) 101 F.2d 15, 39-1 USTC ¶ 9235

§ 519.   Convertible or exchangeable shares and bonds

(a) Unless otherwise provided in the certificate of incorporation, and subject to the restrictions in section 513 (Purchase, redemption and certain other transactions by a corporation with respect to its own shares) and paragraphs (c) and (d) of this section, a corporation may issue shares or bonds convertible into or exchangeable for, at the option of the holder, the corporation or another person, or upon the happening of a specified event, shares of any class or shares of any series of any class or cash, other property, indebtedness or other securities of the same or another corporation.

(b) If there is shareholder approval for the issue of bonds or shares convertible into, or exchangeable for, shares of the corporation, such approval may provide that the board is authorized by certificate of amendment under section 805 (Certificate of amendment; contents) to increase the authorized shares of any class or series to such number as will be sufficient, when added to the previously authorized but unissued shares of such class or series, to satisfy the conversion or exchange privileges of any such bonds or shares convertible into, or exchangeable for, shares of such class or series.

(c) No issue of bonds or shares convertible into, or exchangeable for, shares of the corporation shall be made unless:

(1) A sufficient number of authorized but unissued shares, or treasury shares, of the appropriate class or series are reserved by the board to be issued only in satisfaction of the conversion or exchange privileges of such convertible or exchangeable bonds or shares when issued;

(2) The aggregate conversion or exchange privileges of such convertible or exchangeable bonds or shares when issued do not exceed the aggregate of any shares reserved under subparagraph (1) and any additional shares which may be authorized by the board under paragraph (b); or

(3) In the case of the conversion or exchange of shares of common stock other than into other shares of common stock, there remains outstanding a class or series of common stock not subject to conversion or exchange other than into other shares of common stock, except in the case of corporations of the type described in the exceptions to the provisions of paragraph (b) of section 512 (Redeemable shares).

(d) No privilege of conversion may be conferred upon, or altered in respect to, any shares or bonds that would result in the receipt by the corporation of less than the minimum consideration required to be received upon the issue of new shares. The consideration for shares issued upon the exercise of a conversion or exchange privilege shall be that provided in paragraph (g) of section 504 (Consideration and payment for shares).

(e) When shares have been converted or exchanged, they shall be cancelled. When bonds have been converted or exchanged, they shall be cancelled and not reissued except upon compliance with the provisions governing the issue of convertible or exchangeable bonds.

History: Add, L 1961, ch 855; amd, L 1962, ch 834, § 26, eff Sept 1, 1963,26, incorporated in par (a); amd, L 1963, ch 738, eff Sept 1, 1963; relettered par (b), L 1963, ch 738, eff Sept 1, 1963; amd, L 1963, ch 749, eff Sept 1, 1963; L 1965, ch 803, § 11, eff Sept 1, 1965; L 1970, ch 927, eff June 17, 1970; L 1997, ch 449, § 20, eff Feb 22, 1998.

§ 520. Liability for failure to disclose required information

Failure of the corporation to comply in good faith with the notice or disclosure provisions of paragraphs (f) and (g) of section 511 (Share distributions and changes), or paragraph (c) of section 516 (Reduction of stated capital in certain cases), shall make the corporation liable for any damage sustained by any shareholder in consequence thereof.

History: Add, L 1961, ch 855; amd, L 1962, ch 834, § 27; L 1963, ch 738, eff Sept 1, 1963; L 1997, ch 449, § 21, eff Feb 22, 1998; L 1998, ch 17, § 3, eff Feb 19, 1998, deemed eff Feb 22, 1998.

ARTICLE 6
SHAREHOLDERS

History: Add L 1961, ch 855, eff Sept 1, 1963.

Schedule of sections, amd, L 1962, ch 417, L 1963, ch 746, eff Sept 1, 1963.

§ 601. By-laws

(a) The initial by-laws of a corporation shall be adopted by its incorporator or incorporators at the organization meeting. Thereafter, subject to section 613 (Limitations on right to vote), by-laws may be adopted, amended or repealed by a majority of the votes cast by the shares at the time entitled to vote in the election of any directors. When so provided in the certificate of incorporation or a by-law adopted by the shareholders, by-laws may also be adopted, amended or repealed by the board by such vote as may be therein specified, which may be greater than the vote otherwise prescribed by this chapter, but any by-law adopted by the board may be amended or repealed by the shareholders entitled to vote thereon as herein provided. Any reference in this chapter to a "by-law adopted by the shareholders" shall include a by-law adopted by the incorporator or incorporators.

(b) The by-laws may contain any provision relating to the business of the corporation, the conduct of its affairs, its rights or powers or the rights or powers of its shareholders, directors or officers, not inconsistent with this chapter or any other statute of this state or the certificate of incorporation.

History: Add, L 1961, ch 855, eff Sept 1, 1963; amd, L 1962, ch 834, § 28; L 1963, ch 746, eff Sept 1, 1963; L 1965, ch 803, § 12, eff Sept 1, 1965; L 1997, ch 449, § 22, eff Feb 22, 1998; L 1998, ch 17, § 4, eff Feb 19, 1998, deemed eff Feb 22, 1998.

CASE ANNOTATIONS

Where a corporation president calls a special stockholder meeting for a purpose requiring stockholder action under a bylaw giving him the power to do so without limitations, that call may not be cancelled by the Board of Directors, either directly or indirectly, or by a succeeding president to the one who made the call. Republic Corp. v Carter (1964, 1st Dept) 22 A.D.2d 29, 253 N.Y.S.2d 280, affd 15 N.Y.2d 661, 255 N.Y.S.2d 875, 204 N.E.2d 206

Court properly denied petitioner's motion to confirm election of board of directors of corporation where election was conducted in violation of offering plan and by-laws, inasmuch as sponsor used its votes to elect all 7 board members after having nominated 3 sponsor-related members. Flagg Court Realty Co. v Flagg Court Owners Corp. (1996, 2d Dept) 230 A.D.2d 740, 646 N.Y.S.2d 298

Court incorrectly gave effect to shareholder unanimity provision contained in corporation's original bylaws where corporation's certificate of incorporation did not contain shareholder unanimity provision. Stile v Antico (2000, 2d Dept) 272 A.D.2d 403, 707 N.Y.S.2d 227

Certain amendments to corporate bylaws which were adopted at purported meeting of board of directors were null and void where bylaws required quorum of 2 directors to transact corporate business, and there was only one director present at meeting in question. Stile v Antico (2000, 2d Dept) 272 A.D.2d 403, 707 N.Y.S.2d 227

Original corporate bylaws could not be amended at shareholders meeting to provide for restructuring of board of directors from 2 to 4 directors, nor could bylaws be amended to eliminate requirement that directors be chosen from among shareholders, where bylaws required quorum of 2 directors to transact corporate business, and only one director was present at meeting. Stile v Antico (2000, 2d Dept) 272 A.D.2d 403, 707 N.Y.S.2d 227

UNDER FORMER GEN CORP §§ 14, 27

Section 27 of former Gen. Corp. L. was construed as prohibiting the adoption of a bylaw which would require unanimous approval by the stockholders of any corporate act which must, by statute or under the terms of the corporation's certificate of incorporation, have stockholder approval or be submitted to the stockholders for approval. Benintendi v Kenton Hotel, Inc. (1945) 294 N.Y. 112, 60 N.E.2d 829 (superseded by statute as stated in Application of Burkin, 1 N.Y.2d 570, 154 N.Y.S.2d 898, 136 N.E.2d 862, 64 ALR2d 638)

Removal of the chairman of the board of a corporation was illegal where effected without cause in violation of a by-law requiring cause for removal which was adopted by the stockholders and never validly amended. Petition of Buckley (1944) 183 Misc 189, 50 N.Y.S.2d 54

By-laws providing that no contract for more than one year shall be valid unless approved by a majority of the stockholders, that no director shall be eligible to vote for ratification of any contract from which he derives a financial benefit, and that no resolution which provides for the payment of a bonus to any officer in excess of 5% of the corporation's net annual income shall be valid unless approved by a majority of the stockholders, did not violate § 27 of former Gen. Corp. L. and were not otherwise illegal. Ripley v Storer (1955) 1 Misc. 2d 281, 139 N.Y.S.2d 786, affd 286 A.D. 844, 142 N.Y.S.2d 269, mod 309 N.Y. 506, 132 N.E.2d 87, motion to vacate den 309 N.Y. 976, 132 N.E.2d 335

Where the Board of Directors of a corporation, at a special meeting, amended by-laws of the corporation so as to prohibit nominations for director from the floor at the annual meeting, but the notice of annual meetings sent to the stockholders merely stated that, pursuant to § 27 of former Gen. Corp. L., the by-laws had been amended, and the chairman of the annual meeting refused to give the

stockholders any opportunity to pass upon validity of the amendment, his ruling was not in consonance with that section, which implied that such an amendment must be submitted to the stockholders for their approval or rejection. Re Scharf (1961) 28 Misc. 2d 869, 216 N.Y.S.2d 775, mod and remitted for trial on all issues (2d Dept) 15 A.D.2d 563, 223 N.Y.S.2d 307

§ 602.   Meetings of shareholders

(a) Meetings of shareholders may be held at such place, within or without this state, as may be fixed by or under the by-laws, or if not so fixed, at the office of the corporation in this state.

(b) A meeting of shareholders shall be held annually for the election of directors and the transaction of other business on a date fixed by or under the by-laws. A failure to hold the annual meeting on the date so fixed or to elect a sufficient number of directors to conduct the business of the corporation shall not work a forfeiture or give cause for dissolution of the corporation, except as provided in paragraph (c) of section 1104 (Petition in case of deadlock among directors or shareholders).

(c) Special meetings of the shareholders may be called by the board and by such person or persons as may be so authorized by the certificate of incorporation or the by-laws. At any such special meeting only such business may be transacted which is related to the purpose or purposes set forth in the notice required by section 605 (Notice of meetings of shareholders).

(d) Except as otherwise required by this chapter, the by-laws may designate reasonable procedures for the calling and conduct of a meeting of shareholders, including but not limited to specifying: (i) who may call and who may conduct the meeting, (ii) the means by which the order of business to be conducted shall be established, (iii) the procedures and requirements for the nomination of directors, (iv) the procedures with respect to the making of shareholder proposals, and (v) the procedures to be established for the adjournment of any meeting of shareholders. No amendment of the by-laws pertaining to the election of directors or the procedures for the calling and conduct of a meeting of shareholders shall affect the election of directors or the procedures for the calling or conduct in respect of any meeting of shareholders unless adequate notice thereof is given to the shareholders in a manner reasonably calculated to provide shareholders with sufficient time to respond thereto prior to such meeting.

History: Add, L 1961, ch 855, eff Sept 1, 1963; amd, L 1965, ch 803, § 13, eff Sept 1, 1965; L 1997, ch 449, § 23, eff Feb 22, 1998.

CASE ANNOTATIONS

This section expressly authorizes the inclusion in the corporate bylaws of provisions for fixing the annual meeting date in the discretion of the board of directors. Re Unexcelled, Inc. (1967, 1st Dept) 28 A.D.2d 44, 281 N.Y.S.2d 173

An order setting aside the election of directors on March 21, 1967, and directing that a new election be held on July 12, was reversed, where the corporate bylaws provided that the directors could in their discretion hold an annual meeting no later than the fourth Wednesday of July, notwithstanding that the directors had been elected on

July 12, 1966 and had voluntarily chosen to shorten their own terms of office. Re Unexcelled, Inc. (1967, 1st Dept) 28 A.D.2d 44, 281 N.Y.S.2d 173

In an action brought by shareholders alleging that they were entitled, pursuant to a shareholders' agreement, to designate a successor director in the place of their prior designee, who resigned both as a director and the holder of an irrevocable proxy, the agreement having entitled plaintiffs to designate a successive proxy holder but having made no provision for the procedure to be employed in the filling of a vacancy on the board of directors, the plaintiff shareholders were not entitled to designate a successor director in the place of their prior designee since the question of whether an ambiguity exists must be ascertained from the face of the agreement without regard to extrinsic evidence, and when the board of directors selected their own successor to fill the vacancy, the action was not interdicted by any language in the shareholders' agreement but was consisted with the authority vested in their remaining directors by Bus Corp Law §§ 602(b), 705.Schmidt v Magnetic Head Corp. (1983, 2d Dept) 97 A.D.2d 151, 468 N.Y.S.2d 649

Original corporate bylaws could not be amended at shareholders meeting to provide for restructuring of board of directors from 2 to 4 directors, nor could bylaws be amended to eliminate requirement that directors be chosen from among shareholders, where bylaws required quorum of 2 directors to transact corporate business, and only one director was present at meeting. Stile v Antico (2000, 2d Dept) 272 A.D.2d 403, 707 N.Y.S.2d 227

Because a corporate president had authority to act on behalf of a corporation, and because the shareholders lacked authority to call a special meeting under N.Y. Bus. Corp. Law § 602(c), the trial court erred in granting the shareholders' N.Y. C.P.L.R. § 6312(c) motion for a preliminary injunction. Eklund v Pinkey (2006, 3d Dept) 31 App Div 3d 908, 819 NYS2d 586.

Corporation, its shareholders, and its director were entitled to summary judgment dismissing causes of action relating to events that occurred at special meeting at which plaintiff was replaced as corporate director, even though meeting was not called at written request of majority of shareholders as required by corporate bylaws, since special meeting could also be called by president, which occurred here, and it was undisputed that plaintiff received timely notice thereof. Hakim v Mahdavian (1992, 3d Dept) 185 A.D.2d 428, 585 N.Y.S.2d 828

UNDER FORMER LAW

Where the by-laws of a corporation required the president to call a special meeting whenever requested in writing to do so by stockholders owning a majority of capital stock entitled to vote at such a meeting, the president could be required to hold such a meeting at the request of 55% of the holders of one class of the voting stock for the purpose of endorsing the administration of a former president, to amend the charter and by-laws to provide that vacancies caused by the removal or resignation of directors shall be filled only by the stockholders theretofore represented by the removed or resigned directors and to hear charges against four of the directors representing that class of stock and to remove them if the charges be proven. Auer v Dressel (1954) 306 N.Y. 427, 118 N.E.2d 590, 48 ALR2d 604

Section 5 of former Stock Corp. L., insofar as it provided that if meetings were to be held only within the state, the certificate of incorporation or by-laws must so provide, was declaratory of the general rule in the absence of express provision. Russian Reinsurance Co. v Stoddard (1925) 211 A.D. 132, 207 N.Y.S. 574, revd on other grounds 240 N.Y. 149, 147 N.E. 703, reh den 240 N.Y. 682, 148 N.E. 757

Sections 45 and 55 of former Stock Corp. L. had reference to only those meetings which were called by officers or directors in the proper performance of their duties. Petition of Bloch (1947) 272 A.D. 218, 70 N.Y.S.2d 530

In an action to compel directors of a corporation to call a special meeting of stockholders for the purposes set forth in a proposed notice of special meeting which the officers have refused to send to the stockholders, the court will not modify the proposed notice to eliminate defects therefrom because it is a necessary prerequisite of granting an application of this character that the officers shall have refused to comply with a proper demand upon them. Fierman v Rose (1940) 175 Misc 102, 22 N.Y.S.2d 215

Where an annual meeting for the election of directors was adjourned because it became so turbulent that it could not be conducted peacefully, directors can be validly elected at the adjourned meeting.

Re Election of Directors of Bushwick Sav. & Loan Ass'n (1947) 189 Misc 316, 70 N.Y.S.2d 478

§ 603. Special meeting for election of directors

(a) If, for a period of one month after the date fixed by or under the by-laws for the annual meeting of shareholders, or if no date has been so fixed, for a period of thirteen months after the formation of the corporation or the last annual meeting, there is a failure to elect a sufficient number of directors to conduct the business of the corporation, the board shall call a special meeting for the election of directors. If such special meeting is not called by the board within two weeks after the expiration of such period or if it is so called but there is a failure to elect such directors for a period of two months after the expiration of such period, holders of ten percent of the votes of the shares entitled to vote in an election of directors may, in writing, demand the call of a special meeting for the election of directors specifying the date and month thereof, which shall not be less than sixty nor more than ninety days from the date of such written demand. The secretary of the corporation upon receiving the written demand shall promptly give notice of such meeting, or if he fails to do so within five business days thereafter, any shareholder signing such demand may give such notice. The meeting shall be held at the place fixed in the by-laws or, if not so fixed, at the office of the corporation.

(b) At any such special meeting called on demand of shareholders, notwithstanding section 608 (Quorum of shareholders), the shareholders attending, in person or by proxy, and entitled to vote in an election of directors shall constitute a quorum for the purpose of electing directors, but not for the transaction of any other business.

History: Add, L 1961, ch 855, eff Sept 1, 1963; amd, L 1962, ch 834, § 29, eff Sept 1, 1963; L 1963, ch 746, eff Sept 1, 1963; amd, L 1971, ch 768, eff Sept 1, 1971; L 1997, ch 449, § 24, eff Feb 22, 1998.

CASE ANNOTATIONS

Business Corporation Law does not permit number of directors constituting corporate board to be determined by custom, usage and acquiescence absent governing provision in corporate bylaws; pursuant to CLS Business Corporation Law § 702(a), where corporate bylaws make no provision whatsoever for size of board of directors, number thereof shall be 3; where corporation has no governing bylaw whatsoever, deviation from number of directors explicitly fixed by statute could only be effectuated by proper enactment by shareholders of statutorily requisite bylaw. Re Rye Psychiatric Hospital Center, Inc. (1985) 66 N.Y.2d 333, 497 N.Y.S.2d 317, 488 N.E.2d 63

Where 6 shareholders of respondent corporation conducted business as though 6 of them constituted board of directors, but bylaws remained silent on number of directors, CLS Business Corporation Law § 702 governs and board thereby, comprised 3 members; consequently, 3 individual respondent shareholders, acting as lawful § 603(b) quorum of shareholders, filled all directorships at special meeting when they elected themselves to corporate board and, because number of directors was already fixed by operation of statutory law at 3, no § 608 quorum consisting of holders of majority of shares was necessary to "reduce" size of board to that number. Re Rye Psychiatric Hospital Center, Inc. (1985) 66 N.Y.2d 333, 497 N.Y.S.2d 317, 488 N.E.2d 63

Since the legislature wanted to protect shareholders and the corporation from an undue extension by the directors of their terms of office, § 603 of the Business Corporation Law provides that a special meeting of the shareholders may be called for an election of directors if a regular meeting for such purpose has not been called within 30 days after the date fixed by the by-laws for the annual meeting or since the last annual meeting. Re Unexcelled, Inc. (1967, 1st Dept) 28 A.D.2d 44, 281 N.Y.S.2d 173

A special meeting of the shareholders of a corporation called by the corporate secretary "for the purpose of electing directors" would not be declared void on the ground that the notice of such meeting was insufficient on the basis that it failed to specify the name of the person who demanded the meeting and that the meeting was called pursuant to Bus Corp Law § 603 since, when the corporate secretary calls a special meeting, neither Bus Corp Law § 603 nor § 605 requires inclusion in the notice of the nameof the person demanding that the meeting be called nor requires inclusion of a reference in the notice that the meeting is being held pursuant to a specific statutory provision or by-law. Rye Psychiatric Hospital Center, Inc. v Schoenholtz (1984, 2d Dept) 101 A.D.2d 309, 476 N.Y.S.2d 339

Where three of six shareholder-directors entitled to vote attended a special shareholders' meeting, there existed a sufficient quorum to elect themselves to new terms as three of the six directors, and the election of only three directors did not render such election void, but there was an insufficient quorum to effect a change in the number of directors constituting the entire board from six to three; however, since the newly elected directors were not sufficient in number to constitute a quorum of the board under the corporate by-laws or Bus Corp Law § 707 for the purpose of electing themselves corporate officers, said elections would be set aside. Rye Psychiatric Hospital Center, Inc. v Schoenholtz (1984, 2d Dept) 101 A.D.2d 309, 476 N.Y.S.2d 339

Judicial relief in the form of mandamus may be used to compel action by the officers of a corporation and, accordingly, a petition brought by minority shareholders of a corporation to compel the officers and members of the board of directors to hold an annual meeting of shareholders, pursuant to the by-laws, would be granted; the fact that another remedy existed under Bus Corp Law § 603(a) would not require denial of mandamus since the Bus Corp Law remedy was not equally speedy, convenient, complete and beneficial.Silver v Farrell (1982) 113 Misc. 2d 443, 450 N.Y.S.2d 938

Under CLS Bus Corp L § 603, annual meetings are contemplated to occur no later than 13 months after last such meeting; special meeting must be called by directors no later than 15 months after last annual meeting. Ocilla Industries, Inc. v Katz (1987, ED NY) 677 F. Supp. 1291

UNDER FORMER LAW

Where the by-laws of a corporation required the president to call a special meeting whenever requested in writing to do so by stockholders owning a majority of capital stock entitled to vote at such a meeting, the president could be required to hold such a meeting at the request of 55% of the holders of one class of the voting stock for the purpose of endorsing the administration of a former president, to amend the charter and by-laws to provide that vacancies caused by the removal or resignation of directors shall be filled only by the stockholders theretofore represented by the removed or resigned directors and to hear charges against four of the directors representing that class of stock and to remove them if the charges be proven. Auer v Dressel (1954) 306 N.Y. 427, 118 N.E.2d 590, 48 ALR2d 604

Under § 22 of former Gen. Corp. L., stockholders were likewise authorized to call a special meeting for election of directors where the management failed to call one as required by statute or bylaws, without necessity for instituting a judicial proceeding to compel management to issue such a call. Petition of Bloch (1947) 272 A.D. 218, 70 N.Y.S.2d 530

Corporate vice-president had the right to sign a notice of meeting for the election of directors and officers, where he had caused a letter to be addressed to the attorneys for the corporation demanding that a meeting of the stockholders be called. Re Petition of Shulman (1956) 2 Misc. 2d 896, 151 N.Y.S.2d 819

A special meeting of a corporation for the purpose of electing a new Board of Directors was valid, where notice thereof conformed to the by-laws provision that special meetings were callable at any time by a majority of the directors. Application of Miller (1956) 4 Misc. 2d 555, 150 N.Y.S.2d 520

Where a president of a corporation would apparently not sign any notice of special meeting which the stockholders might request and where there had been no annual meeting for several years, the stockholders were entitled to proceed in accordance with the provi-

sions of § 22 of former Gen. Corp. L. and were not required to comply with the provisions of former Stock Corporation Law § 45. Salerno v J S Painting Corp. (1958) 12 Misc. 2d 856, 171 N.Y.S.2d 323

Five-day notice of meeting for election of directors, which was mailed by holders of 50% of the stock, was not governed by § 45 of former Stock Corp. Law, since that section was limited to notices mailed by corporation officers, but was governed by § 22 of former General Corporation Law which required two weeks' notice. Re M. & O. Realty Corp. (1958) 16 Misc. 2d 562, 182 N.Y.S.2d 186

If no annual meeting of a corporation had been held for several years, and the officers and directors refused to sign a notice of meeting at the request of the stockholders, the stockholders were entitled to proceed in accordance with § 22 of former Gen. Corp. L. Goldberg v Creative Country Day School, Inc. (1960) 24 Misc. 2d 889, 201 N.Y.S.2d 243

It was held that the provisions of former Gen. Corp. L. for calling a meeting of stockholders to elect directors were not designed to meet the case of a two-man corporation, which had been conducted substantially as a partnership without formal election of directors, or to permit one of the two stockholders to call a meeting and then proceed, by himself, to elect directors. Re Election of Directors (1961) 28 Misc. 2d 987, 212 N.Y.S.2d 807

Notice of a meeting of stockholders for election of directors met the requirements of § 22 of former Gen. Corp. L. where, although the notice was not published in two newspapers, the corporate by-laws authorized giving notice by personal service or by mailing not less than ten days nor more than 40 days to each stockholder, and service in this manner was established. M & E Luncheonette, Inc. v Freilich (1961) 30 Misc. 2d 637, 218 N.Y.S.2d 125

The provision in § 23 of former Gen. Corp. L. that, at a special meeting of stockholders for election of directors, "the members attending shall constitute a quorum," were not deemed to supersede the requirement of § 55 of that law as to what would constitute a quorum of stockholders at stockholders' meetings. M & E Luncheonette, Inc. v Freilich (1961) 30 Misc. 2d 637, 218 N.Y.S.2d 125

§ 604.   Fixing record date

(a) For the purpose of determining the shareholders entitled to notice of or to vote at any meeting of shareholders or any adjournment thereof, or to express consent to or dissent from any proposal without a meeting, or for the purpose of determining shareholders entitled to receive payment of any dividend or the allotment of any rights, or for the purpose of any other action, the by-laws may provide for fixing or, in the absence of such provision, the board may fix, in advance, a date as the record date for any such determination of shareholders. Such date shall not be more than sixty nor less than ten days before the date of such meeting, nor more than sixty days prior to any other action.

(b) If no record date is fixed:

(1) The record date for the determination of shareholders entitled to notice of or to vote at a meeting of shareholders shall be at the close of business on the day next preceding the day on which notice is given, or, if no notice is given, the day on which the meeting is held.

(2) The record date for determining shareholders for any purpose other than that specified in subparagraph (1) shall be at the close of business on the day on which the resolution of the board relating thereto is adopted.

(c) When a determination of shareholders of record entitled to notice of or to vote at any meeting of shareholders has been made as provided in this section, such determination shall apply to any adjournment thereof, unless the board fixes a new record date under this section for the adjourned meeting.

History: Add, L 1961, ch 855, eff Sept 1, 1963; amd, L 1997, ch 449, § 25, eff Feb 22, 1998.

CASE ANNOTATIONS

In an action to set aside the election of directors of co-operative apartments on the ground that one of the elected directors, who became a co-operative member five days prior to the election, was ineligible to serve on the board by virtue of his failure to comply with a co-operative by-law prohibiting the transfer of membership within 10 days preceding the annual stockholders' meeting, petitioner has waived his right to contest the election by his participation as a director in numerous board meetings during which respondent was sitting as a voting and active member of the board, and more particularly, by petitioner's accepting respondent's seconding motions made by petitioner; in addition, petitioner's request that the board be discharged would necessitate vacating all actions on which the board has given its approval subsequent to the election and would be highly disruptive and prejudicial to the election and to the interests of the co-operators; furthermore, neither section 604 of the Business Corporation Law, which provides for the fixing of a record date to establish shareholder ownership for the purpose of determining shareholder eligibility to notice or to vote, nor section 60 of the Cooperative Corporations Law, which requires directors of a co-operative corporation to be elected from among its members, prohibits a person who is a member of a co-operative as of the date of board elections from being an eligible candidate for a directorship; moreover, the by-law in question, which forbids membership transfer within 10 days preceding the annual meeting, imposes only a technical restriction and furthermore is not concerned with board membership. Re Willoughby Walk Cooperative Apartments, Inc. (1980) 104 Misc. 2d 477, 428 N.Y.S.2d 574

UNDER FORMER LAW

Under § 47 of former Stock Corp. L. providing that "unless otherwise provided in the certificate of incorporation or other certificate filed pursuant to law or in the by-laws," the board of directors of a stock corporation may prescribe a period, prior to meetings of stockholders, during which no transfer of stock on the books of the corporation may be made, or may fix a day and hour as of which stockholders entitled to vote at such meetings shall be determined, refusals to transfer stock on the books of a corporation on the ground that the demand was made less than fifteen days before the annual stockholders' meeting was not justified, where the directors had adopted the latter of the two alternatives. Re Fleetwood Bank (1940) 283 N.Y. 157, 27 N.E.2d 974, reh den 284 N.Y. 574, 29 N.E.2d 394

Where cash dividends on stock, were declared prior to testator's death but made payable to stockholders of record as of date subsequent to death, such dividends should be allocated to income in absence of expression of intention in will as to whether date of declaration of dividends or record date should control. Re Goldman (1945) 295 N.Y. 609, 64 N.E.2d 352

Section 62 of former Stock Corp. L. gave no authority to corporation to fix date for determination of record owner prior to date of resolution declaring dividend. Lunt v Genesee Valley Trust Co. (1937) 162 Misc 859, 297 N.Y.S. 27

Section 62 of former Stock Corp. L. determined person in whose favor right was created as against corporation. Re Bashford's Estate (1942) 178 Misc 951, 36 N.Y.S.2d 651

However, it has been pointed out that corporations were protected from liability in distributing dividends according to share ownership on a set record date by § 164 of the Pers. Prop. L. even prior to the enactment of § 62 of former Stock Corp. L. Re Bashford's Estate (1942) 178 Misc 951, 36 N.Y.S.2d 651

Statutes according power to corporate management to fix a record date as determining who shall be entitled to rights and benefits as holder or owner of shares are designed to permit the corporation to act safely on the basis of its own stock records in recognizing voting rights, distributing dividends, and the like, do not purport to determine rights as between the record owner and others, and do not preclude others from demanding an accounting from the record owner for benefits received or from asserting adverse claims to the shares in question. Re Alling's Estate (1945) 186 Misc 192, 63 N.Y.S.2d 427; Re Depew's Estate (1943) 179 Misc 1074, 41 N.Y.S.2d 19

Where corporate directors fixed record date for determining what stockholders could vote at annual meeting in May, and May meeting was adjourned until June, the directors could thereafter change the record date for the adjourned meeting. McDonough v Foundation Co. (1956) 7 Misc. 2d 571, 155 N.Y.S.2d 67

A corporation could not hide behind § 62 of former Stock Corp. L. in refusing to replace burned certificate of stock with new certificate, where for a period of 10 years it had recognized both deceased and plaintiff as the owner of the certificate of stock and paid dividends thereon. Komar v General Electric Co. (1959) 17 Misc. 2d 24, 183 N.Y.S.2d 762

Section 62 of former Stock Corp. L. did not affect the pre-existing common-law rule to the effect that the owner of stock at the date of the declaration of a dividend secured a vested property right; and that the provision for payment to stockholders of record of a certain future date was a mere convenience for the sole benefit of the corporation. Helvering v McGlue's Estate (1941, CA4) 119 F.2d 167, 41-1 USTC ¶ 9403

Section 62 of former Stock Corp. L. was passed merely for the purpose of protecting a corporation from liability where, without any notice of a stock transfer, the corporation pays dividends to the person who appears on its books as the owner of particular stock. Helvering v McGlue's Estate (1941, CA4) 119 F.2d 167, 41-1 USTC ¶ 9403

A dividend which has been declared prior to the date of the stockholder's death but according to the terms of the declaration is payable to stockholders of a record date that is subsequent to the date of the stockholder's death creates a corporate debt as of the declaration of the dividend and accordingly the stockholder's right to the dividend has "accrued" as of the time of the stockholder's death and such dividend, therefore, is subject to taxation under § 42 of the Internal Revenue Code (Revenue Act 1934, § 42, 26 USCA). Helvering v McGlue's Estate (1941, CA4) 119 F.2d 167, 41-1 USTC ¶ 9403

§ 605. Notice of meetings of shareholders

(a) Whenever under the provisions of this chapter shareholders are required or permitted to take any action at a meeting, notice shall be given stating the place, date and hour of the meeting and, unless it is the annual meeting, indicating that it is being issued by or at the direction of the person or persons calling the meeting. Notice of a special meeting shall also state the purpose or purposes for which the meeting is called. Notice of any meeting of shareholders may be written or electronic. If, at any meeting, action is proposed to be taken which would, if taken, entitle shareholders fulfilling the requirements of section 623 (Procedure to enforce shareholder's right to receive payment for shares) to receive payment for their shares, the notice of such meeting shall include a statement of that purpose and to that effect and shall be accompanied by a copy of section 623 or an outline of its material terms. Notice of any meeting shall be given not fewer than ten nor more than sixty days before the date of the meeting, provided, however, that such notice may be given by third class mail not fewer than twenty-four nor more than sixty days before the date of the meeting, to each shareholder entitled to vote at such meeting. If mailed, such notice is given when deposited in the United States mail, with postage thereon prepaid, directed to the shareholder at the shareholder's address as it appears on the record of shareholders, or, if the shareholder shall have filed with the secretary of the corporation a request that notices to the shareholder be mailed to some other address, then directed to him at such other address. If transmitted electronically, such notice is given when directed to the shareholder's electronic mail address as supplied by the shareholder to the secretary of the corporation or as otherwise directed pursuant to the shareholder's authorization or instructions. An affidavit of the secretary or other person giving the notice or of a transfer agent of the corporation that the notice required by this section has been given shall, in the absence of fraud, be prima facie evidence of the facts therein stated.

(b) When a meeting is adjourned to another time or place, it shall not be necessary, unless the by-laws require otherwise, to give any notice of the adjourned meeting if the time and place to which the meeting is adjourned are announced at the meeting at which the adjournment is taken, and at the adjourned meeting any business may be transacted that might have been transacted on the original date of the meeting. However, if after the adjournment the board fixes a new record date for the adjourned meeting, a notice of the adjourned meeting shall be given to each shareholder of record on the new record date entitled to notice under paragraph (a).

History: Add, L 1961, ch 855; amd, L 1962, ch 417, eff Sept 1, 1963; amd, L 1963, ch 746, eff Sept 1, 1963; L 1965, ch 803, § 14, eff Sept 1, 1965; L 1982, ch 202, § 2, eff Sept 1, 1982; L 1986, ch 735, § 1, eff Sept 1, 1986; L 1997, ch 449, § 26, eff Feb 22, 1998; L 1998, ch 498, § 1, eff July 29, 1998.

CASE ANNOTATIONS

A special meeting of the shareholders of a corporation called by the corporate secretary "for the purpose of electing directors" would not be declared void on the ground that the notice of such meeting was insufficient on the basis that it failed to specify the name of the person who demanded the meeting and that the meeting was called pursuant to Bus Corp Law § 603 since, when the corporate secretary calls a special meeting, neither Bus Corp Law § 603 nor § 605 requires inclusion in the notice of the name of the person demanding that the meeting be called nor requires inclusion of a reference in the notice that the meeting is being held pursuant to a specific statutory provision or by-law. Rye Psychiatric Hospital Center, Inc. v Schoenholtz (1984, 2d Dept) 101 A.D.2d 309, 476 N.Y.S.2d 339

Since notice of an October 13, 2005 meeting, at which a director was elected, was given at the September 8, 2005 meeting, attended by an attorney on behalf of an owner, the election of the director was valid; the owner received notice of the September meeting as evidenced by the presence of her agent, and she therefore clearly waived any defect in notice. Matter of McDaniel v 162 Columbia Hgts. Hous. Corp. (2009, Sup) 873 NYS2d 468.

UNDER FORMER LAW

The terms and conditions under which certain shares or securities have been issued, and provisions in other contracts, may require issuance of additional or special notice of a meeting of shareholders to take action on a measure affecting rights of holders, and failure to give notice as prescribed in such agreements may give rise to liability either for breach of contract or for fraud. Davison v Parke, Austin & Lipscomb (1941) 285 N.Y. 500, 35 N.E.2d 618, remittitur den 286 N.Y. 673, 36 N.E.2d 910; Danzig v Lacks (1932) 235 A.D. 189, 256 N.Y.S. 769

However, a notice which states that the purpose of the meeting is to elect directors and "take up such other business as may arise" is not inadequate as warning that a change in management and policies may come about when the new directors take office. Re William Faehndrich, Inc. (1957) 2 N.Y.2d 468, 161 N.Y.S.2d 99, 141 N.E.2d 597

Where a special stockholders' meeting originally scheduled to be held on Nov. 24th was not held because of a temporary injunction and the motion upon which the temporary injunction was based was decided adversely to the moving party, whereupon at 10:45 A.M. on Nov. 28th the attorney for the moving party, who was also a minority stockholder, was informed of the decision and at 12:15 notified him that the stockholders would reconvene between 2 P.M. and 2:30 P.M. of that same day, but the order upon the motion was not served upon the moving party's attorney until 6 P.M. of that day, there was insufficient notice under § 45 of former Stock Corp. L. of the meeting to the moving party shareholder and the action taken at the meeting removing him and his wife as directors was invalid. Re J. A. Maurer, Inc. (1947, Sup) 77 N.Y.S.2d 159

Statutory provisions as to form and manner of giving notice to shareholders are mandatory and must be at least substantially complied with in order to bind stockholders who do not expressly waive notice and who fail to attend in person or by proxy. Re J. A. Maurer, Inc. (1947, Sup) 77 N.Y.S.2d 159; Alexander v Quality Leather Goods Corp. (1934) 150 Misc 577, 269 N.Y.S. 499

In stating the purpose or purposes of a special meeting, general references to "any and all other business which may come before the meeting," or the like, are insufficient to broaden the scope of matters which may properly be passed upon. Fierman v Rose (1940) 175 Misc 102, 22 N.Y.S.2d 215

Where an annual meeting for the election of directors has been adjourned, no additional notice is necessary because the notice given respecting the original meeting extends to all adjourned meetings and the corporation may transact any business at the adjourned meeting which it could have done at the original meeting. Re Election of Directors of Bushwick Sav. & Loan Ass'n (1947) 189 Misc 316, 70 N.Y.S.2d 478

Stockholders who refuse to vote and participate in an adjourned meeting for the election of directors will be deemed to have virtually consented that the election should be made by those who choose to exercise their privilege and they cannot afterward object that directors have been selected of whom they have not approved. Re Election of Directors of Bushwick Sav. & Loan Ass'n (1947) 189 Misc 316, 70 N.Y.S.2d 478

A by-law requiring the directors to call a special meeting of the stockholders whenever so requested in writing by stockholders representing not less than 51 per cent of the capital stock of the company does not violate any provision of law and is a legal and enforceable by-law which is binding upon the directors. Weisblum v Li Falco Mfg. Co. (1947) 193 Misc 473, 84 N.Y.S.2d 162

A corporate vice-president had the right to sign a notice of meeting for the election of directors and officers, where he had caused a letter to be addressed to the attorneys for the corporation demanding that a meeting of the stockholders be called. Re Petition of Shulman (1956) 2 Misc. 2d 896, 151 N.Y.S.2d 819

A special meeting of a corporation for the purpose of electing a new Board of Directors was valid, where notice thereof conformed to the by-laws provision that special meetings were callable at any time by a majority of the directors. Application of Miller (1956) 4 Misc. 2d 555, 150 N.Y.S.2d 520

Notice of stockholders' meeting was valid where it was sent to all stockholders on August 13, 1956 calling for a meeting to be held on August 28, 1956. Teperman v Atcos Baths, Inc. (1957) 6 Misc. 2d 162, 163 N.Y.S.2d 221, affd (2d Dept) 7 A.D.2d 854, 182 N.Y.S.2d 765

While this section of former Bus. Corp. L. does not require that notice of an annual meeting state the purposes of the meeting, under earlier statutes election of directors at a meeting the notice for which failed to state that election of directors was one of the purposes for which it was called could be set aside at the instance of shareholders who did not expressly waive notice or attend. Re 74 & 76 West Tremont Ave. Corp. (1958) 10 Misc. 2d 662, 173 N.Y.S.2d 154

The statutory time limitations on the period prior to date set for the meeting within which notice must be given are material, and the notice is insufficient if not given within the specified time bracket. Re M. & O. Realty Corp. (1958) 16 Misc. 2d 562, 182 N.Y.S.2d 186; Davison v Parke, Austin & Lipscomb, Inc. (1937) 165 Misc 32, 299 N.Y.S. 960, mod 256 A.D. 1071, 12 N.Y.S.2d 358

A notice of special stockholders' meeting to pass on a consolidation proposal was not an entire nullity, under § 45 of the Stock Corp L, because it was not in fact signed by the officer whose signature it purported to bear, where it properly stated the time, place, and purposes of the meeting, and those who attended and participated in the meeting must, in any event, be considered as waving defects in the notice. Andrews v Precision Apparatus, Inc. (1963, SD NY) 217 F. Supp. 679

§ 606. Waivers of notice

Notice of meeting need not be given to any shareholder who submits a waiver of notice whether before or after the meeting. Waiver of notice may be written or electronic. If written, the waiver must be executed by the shareholder or the shareholder's authorized officer, director, employee or agent by signing such waiver or causing his or her signature to be affixed to such waiver by any reasonable means, including, but not limited to, facsimile signature. If electronic, the transmission of the waiver must either set forth or be submitted with information from which it can reasonably be determined that the transmission was authorized by the shareholder. The attendance of any shareholder at a meeting, in person or by proxy, without protesting prior to the conclusion of the meeting the lack of notice of such meeting, shall constitute a waiver of notice by such shareholder.

History: Add, L 1961, ch 855, amd, L 1962, ch 834, § 30, eff Sept 1, 1963.

Amd, L 1998, ch 498, § 2, eff July 29, 1998.

CASE ANNOTATIONS

Generally failure to give notice in accord with Business Corporation Law § 606 and the corporate by-laws would render an election void, and, if void, a new election would be required even without a showing that the result of the elections would, or might have been, different. Goldfield Corp. v General Host Corp. (1971) 29 N.Y.2d 264, 327 N.Y.S.2d 330, 277 N.E.2d 387

Where the plaintiff-shareholder was not the owner of record on the record date, it was not, without more, entitled to notice of the election, and thus, at least on that ground, the election was invulnerable. Goldfield Corp. v General Host Corp. (1971) 29 N.Y.2d 264, 327 N.Y.S.2d 330, 277 N.E.2d 387

If the plaintiff, challenging the validity of an election, had been the record owner at the time of the election, it would have been entitled to receive notice of the meeting, and although persons connected with the plaintiff attended the meeting and presented its views, there was no waiver since those persons were not allowed to participate by voice or vote as the plaintiff's representative. Goldfield Corp. v General Host Corp. (1971) 29 N.Y.2d 264, 327 N.Y.S.2d 330, 277 N.E.2d 387

In action to recover damages for wrongful expulsion from corporation as shareholder, defendants' motion for summary judgment should have been denied-plaintiff and individual defendants executed stockholders' agreement whereby they formed defendant corporation, racquetball club; while plaintiff was performing his regular services at club, pursuant to consultation and employment agreements, he was called into meeting during which his contracts were terminated; meeting was held without prior notice being given to plaintiff-plaintiff had paid large percentage of his capital contribution and individual defendants had considered him as stockholder and principal of corporation since its inception; since they never moved to declare his shares void by reason of fact that they had been issued in violation of Business Corporation Law § 504 they are now estopped from arguing that plaintiff was not shareholder or that shares are void-further, stockholders' agreement provided that 100 shares to be issued to plaintiff and one of individual defendants were to be distributed proportionately to their capital contributions; since plaintiff had fully paid for approximately 71 shares of corporate stock, representing 35.5% of outstanding stock, his affirmative vote was necessary for corporation to obtain 75% affirmative vote required for it to conduct business-Business Corporation Law § 606, which states that notice of meeting is waived if shareholder attends meeting without protesting lack of notice of such meeting, is inapplicable; plaintiff attended subject meeting but argues that he protested lack of notice and voted "no"; while defendants contest plaintiff's claim, conspicuous absence of plaintiff's signature from minutes of that meeting supports his claim-finally, defendants concede that club opened for business; under terms of consultation agreement, plaintiff's employment was only to be terminated on date corporation ceases operation; various contentions as to whether or not corporation had net positive cash flow out of which plaintiff was to be paid raise question of fact which triers of fact must decide. Block v Magee, 146 A.D.2d 730

In action to recover damages for wrongful expulsion from corporation as shareholder, CLS Bus Corp § 606 was inapplicable to effect waiver of notice of meeting in which defendants expelled plaintiff where plaintiff conceded that he attended meeting but argued that he protested lack of notice and voted "no" on motion to terminate his consultation and employment contracts; although defendants contested plaintiff's claim, conspicuous absence of plaintiff's signature from minutes of meeting supported his claim since it was inconceivable that one whose vote could block proposal, and who in fact believed at time that his vote could block proposal, would decide not to vote on proposal with which he disagreed. Block v Magee (1989, 2d Dept) 146 A.D.2d 730, 537 N.Y.S.2d 215

Since notice of an October 13, 2005 meeting, at which a director was elected, was given at the September 8, 2005 meeting, attended by an attorney on behalf of an owner, the election of the director was valid; the owner received notice of the September meeting as evidenced by the presence of her agent, and she therefore clearly waived any defect in notice. Matter of McDaniel v 162 Columbia Hgts. Hous. Corp. (2009, Sup) 873 NYS2d 468.

UNDER FORMER LAW

A stockholder of a corporation was deemed to have participated in the regular annual meeting of stockholders and to have waived any right he might otherwise have had to question the validity of the meeting for lack of sufficient notice, where it appeared that at the meeting he participated in the discussion of the financial statement; that he made suggestions in regard thereto; and that he moved through his attorney that the financial statement be spread on the minutes. Frankel v 447 Cent. Park West Corp. (1941) 176 Misc 701, 28 N.Y.S.2d 505, affd without op 263 A.D. 950, 34 N.Y.S.2d 136

Attendance at a shareholder's meeting and participation in the business transacted without objection to lack of notice or on the ground that such notice as was given was inadequate or defective have likewise been deemed to waive the deficiencies or give rise to an estoppel to object at a later date. Re Roosevelt Leather Hand Bag Co. (1947, Sup) 68 N.Y.S.2d 735

Written waivers of notice of meetings of shareholders were held effective to preclude objections based on absence of notice or defects in giving notice under earlier statutes.1910 Ops Atty Gen 823

§ 607. List of shareholders at meetings

A list of shareholders as of the record date, certified by the corporate officer responsible for its preparation or by a transfer agent, shall be produced at any meeting of shareholders upon the request thereat or prior thereto of any shareholder. If the right to vote at any meeting is challenged, the inspectors of election, or person presiding thereat, shall require such list of shareholders to be produced as evidence of the right of the persons challenged to vote at such meeting, and all persons who appear from such list to be shareholders entitled to vote thereat may vote at such meeting.

History: Add, L 1961, ch 855, amd, L 1963, ch 746, eff Sept 1, 1963.

CASE ANNOTATIONS

The beneficial or true owners or any other person entitled to possession of shares have no right to vote if they are not record holders.Stewart Becker, Ltd. v Horowitz (1978) 94 Misc. 2d 766, 405 N.Y.S.2d 571

Under the Business Corporation Law, possession is not the criterion by which the right to vote is determined; the record of shareholders is conclusive upon the election inspectors, and they may not look behind the list to determine whether or not the record owners are the true owners entitled to vote the stock, nor may shareholders of record be required to produce their share certificates as evidence of their continuing ownership before being permitted to vote.Stewart Becker, Ltd. v Horowitz (1978) 94 Misc. 2d 766, 405 N.Y.S.2d 571

§ 608.   Quorum of shareholders

(a) The holders of a majority of the votes of shares entitled to vote thereat shall constitute a quorum at a meeting of shareholders for the transaction of any business, provided that when a specified item of business is required to be voted on by a particular class or series of shares, voting as a class, the holders of a majority of the votes of shares of such class or series shall constitute a quorum for the transaction of such specified item of business.

(b) The certificate of incorporation or by-laws may provide for any lesser quorum not less than one-third of the votes of shares entitled to vote, and the certificate of incorporation may, under section 616 (Greater requirement as to quorum and vote of shareholders), provide for a greater quorum.

(c) When a quorum is once present to organize a meeting, it is not broken by the subsequent withdrawal of any shareholders.

(d) The shareholders present may adjourn the meeting despite the absence of a quorum.

History: Add, L 1961, ch 855, eff Sept 1, 1963; amd, L 1962, ch 834, § 31; L 1963, ch 746, eff Sept 1, 1963; L 1997, ch 449, § 27, eff Feb 22, 1998; L 1998, ch 17, § 5, eff Feb 19, 1998, deemed eff Feb 22, 1998.

CASE ANNOTATIONS

Business Corporation Law does not permit number of directors constituting corporate board to be determined by custom, usage and acquiescence absent governing provision in corporate bylaws; pursuant to CLS Business Corporation Law § 702(a), where corporate bylaws make no provision whatsoever for size of board of directors, number thereof shall be 3; where corporation has no governing bylaw whatsoever, deviation from number of directors explicitly fixed by statute could only be effectuated by proper enactment by shareholders of statutorily requisite bylaw. Re Rye Psychiatric Hospital Center, Inc. (1985) 66 N.Y.2d 333, 497 N.Y.S.2d 317, 488 N.E.2d 63

Where 6 shareholders of respondent corporation conducted business as though 6 of them constituted board of directors, but bylaws remained silent on number of directors, CLS Business Corporation Law § 702 governs and board thereby, comprised 3 members; consequently, 3 individual respondent shareholders, acting as lawful § 603(b) quorum of shareholders, filled all directorships at special meeting when they elected themselves to corporate board and, because number of directors was already fixed by operation of statutory law at 3, no § 608 quorum consisting of holders of majority of shares was necessary to "reduce" size of board to that number. Re Rye Psychiatric Hospital Center, Inc. (1985) 66 N.Y.2d 333, 497 N.Y.S.2d 317, 488 N.E.2d 63

In proceeding under CLS Bus Corp § 619 to set aside election of corporate directors, Special Term correctly concluded that election was properly conducted, even though petitioning shareholder alleged that he had attended shareholders' meeting only to protest fact that meeting was held at improper location and contended that his shares should not have been counted in determining whether there was quorum present, where shareholder had attended meeting without complaining as to its location, and thus waived any objection which he might have had in that respect. Chiulli v Cross Westchester Dev. Corp. (1987, 2d Dept) 130 A.D.2d 616, 515 N.Y.S.2d 546, later proceeding (2d Dept) 130 A.D.2d 617, 515 N.Y.S.2d 547, later proceeding (2d Dept) 130 A.D.2d 618, 515 N.Y.S.2d 717

In proceeding under § 619 of the Business Corporation Law to declare invalid the election of directors and officers of a corporation, the petitioner, the president of the corporation, who, according to the bylaws, was to preside at all meetings, could not unilaterally adjourn a duly constituted meeting of the shareholders, at which a quorum was present, and thereby prevent the termination of his term of office and thwart any elective or other action the corporate body might wish

to take, and the election of directors and officers at such meeting would be confirmed. Re Petition of Dollinger Corp. (1966) 51 Misc. 2d 802, 274 N.Y.S.2d 285

UNDER FORMER LAW

A by-law provision requiring a quorum of two-thirds of the corporate shares at special meetings of stockholders is invalid where not authorized by the certificate of incorporation. Re William Faehndrich, Inc. (1957) 2 N.Y.2d 468, 161 N.Y.S.2d 99, 141 N.E.2d 597

The minimum number constituted as a quorum by bylaws or statute has no significance when more than that number are present and vote. Re Lake Placid Co. (1948) 274 A.D. 205, 81 N.Y.S.2d 36

The annual meeting for the election of directors may be adjourned if it becomes necessary or advisable and if the meeting becomes so turbulent that it cannot be conducted peacefully and without the aid of police officers an adjournment is proper. Re Election of Directors of Bushwick Sav. & Loan Ass'n (1947) 189 Misc 316, 70 N.Y.S.2d 478

No quorum was present at a special meeting called by a stockholder for election of directors, and the action taken at such meeting was accordingly a nullity, where the stockholder calling the meeting was the only one in attendance and did not own a majority of the shares. M & E Luncheonette, Inc. v Freilich (1961) 30 Misc. 2d 637, 218 N.Y.S.2d 125

But § 9 of former Stock Corp. L. was deemed to authorize a provision in a certificate of incorporation requiring presence of a quorum of shareholders and unanimous voting by them for the transaction of any business at a shareholders' meeting. Re Application of Venice Amusement Corp. (1961) 32 Misc. 2d 122, 222 N.Y.S.2d 889

§ 609.   Proxies

(a) Every shareholder entitled to vote at a meeting of shareholders or to express consent or dissent without a meeting may authorize another person or persons to act for him by proxy.

(b) No proxy shall be valid after the expiration of eleven months from the date thereof unless otherwise provided in the proxy. Every proxy shall be revocable at the pleasure of the shareholder executing it, except as otherwise provided in this section.

(c) The authority of the holder of a proxy to act shall not be revoked by the incompetence or death of the shareholder who executed the proxy unless, before the authority is exercised, written notice of an adjudication of such incompetence or of such death is received by the corporate officer responsible for maintaining the list of shareholders.

(d) Except when other provision shall have been made by written agreement between the parties, the record holder of shares which he holds as pledgee or otherwise as security or which belong to another, shall issue to the pledgor or to such owner of such shares, upon demand therefor and payment of necessary expenses thereof, a proxy to vote or take other action thereon.

(e) A shareholder shall not sell his vote or issue a proxy to vote to any person for any sum of money or anything of value, except as authorized in this section and section 620 (Agreements as to voting; provision in certificate of incorporation as to control of directors); provided, however, that this paragraph shall not apply to votes, proxies or consents given by holders of preferred shares in connection with a proxy or consent solicitation made available on identical terms to all holders of shares of the same class or series and remaining open for acceptance for at least twenty business days.

(f) A proxy which is entitled "irrevocable proxy" and which states that it is irrevocable, is irrevocable when it is held by any of the following or a nominee of any of the following:

(1) A pledgee;

(2) A person who has purchased or agreed to purchase the shares;

(3) A creditor or creditors of the corporation who extend or continue credit to the corporation in consideration of the proxy if the proxy states that it was given in consideration of such extension or continuation of credit, the amount thereof, and the name of the person extending or continuing credit;

(4) A person who has contracted to perform services as an officer of the corporation, if a proxy is required by the contract of employment, if the proxy states that it was given in consideration of such contract of employment, the name of the employee and the period of employment contracted for;

(5) A person designated by or under an agreement under paragraph (a) of section 620.

(g) Notwithstanding a provision in a proxy, stating that it is irrevocable, the proxy becomes revocable after the pledge is redeemed, or the debt of the corporation is paid, or the period of employment provided for in the contract of employment has terminated, or the agreement under paragraph (a) of section 620 has terminated; and, in a case provided for in subparagraphs (f) (3) or (4), becomes revocable three years after the date of the proxy or at the end of the period, if any, specified therein, whichever period is less, unless the period of irrevocability is renewed from time to time by the execution of a new irrevocable proxy as provided in this section. This paragraph does not affect the duration of a proxy under paragraph (b).

(h) A proxy may be revoked, notwithstanding a provision making it irrevocable, by a purchaser of shares without knowledge of the existence of the provision unless the existence of the proxy and its irrevocability is noted conspicuously on the face or back of the certificate representing such shares.

(i) Without limiting the manner in which a shareholder may authorize another person or persons to act for him as proxy pursuant to paragraph (a) of this section, the following shall constitute a valid means by which a shareholder may grant such authority.

(1) A shareholder may execute a writing authorizing another person or persons to act from him as proxy. Execution may be accomplished by the shareholder or the shareholder's authorized officer, director, employee or agent signing such writing or causing his or her signature to be affixed to such writing by any reasonable means including, but not limited to, by facsimile signature.

(2) A shareholder may authorize another person or persons to act for the shareholder as proxy by transmitting or authorizing the transmission of a telegram, cablegram or other means of electronic transmission to the person who will be the holder of the proxy or to a proxy solicitation firm, proxy support service organization or like agent duly authorized by the person who will be the holder of the proxy to receive such transmission, provided that any such telegram, cablegram or other means of electronic transmission must either set forth or be submitted with information from which it can be reasonably determined that the telegram, cablegram or other electronic transmission was authorized by the shareholder. If it is determined that such telegrams, cablegrams or other electronic transmissions are valid, the inspectors or, if there are no inspectors, such other persons making that determination shall specify the nature of the information upon which they relied.

(j) Any copy, facsimile telecommunication or other reliable reproduction of the writing or transmission created pursuant to paragraph (i) of this section may be substituted or used in lieu of the original writing or transmission for any and all purposes for which the original writing or transmission could be used, provided that such copy, facsimile telecommunication or other reproduction shall be a complete reproduction of the entire original writing or transmission.

History: Add, L 1961, ch 855, eff Sept 1, 1963; amd, L 1962, ch 834, § 32, eff Sept 1, 1963; L 1963, ch 746, eff Sept 1, 1963; L 1965, ch 803, § 15, eff Sept 1, 1965 (see 1965 note under § 108); L 1997, ch 449, §§ 28, 29, eff Feb 22, 1998; L 1998, ch 17, § 6, eff Feb 19, 1998, deemed eff Feb 22, 1998.

CASE ANNOTATIONS

The dismissal of a petition brought pursuant to Bus Corp Law § 619 to set aside the election of the board of directors at an annual shareholders' meeting and to vacate passage of amendments to articles of incorporation authorizing issuance of new shares would be reversed, since in order to overturn an election of the board of directors it must be shown by a preponderance of the evidence that the irrevocable proxies signed as a result of a shareholders' agreement are invalid, since the preponderance of evidence criterion was inappropriately utilized upon the motion to dismiss, in that every reasonable inference must be drawn from the record in plaintiff's favor, since Bus Corp Law § 609 allows for the creation of irrevocable general proxies within the rubric of a shareholders' agreement, since if the agreement is subject to attack the proxies will be vulnerable, and since a trial was necessary to determine if the shareholders' agreement should be reformed or rescinded. Re Schmidt (1983, 2d Dept) 97 A.D.2d 244, 468 N.Y.S.2d 663

Proxies voted by the management of respondent Federal Savings and Loan Association in the election for directors, some of which were valid for the period of 40 years, others which called for no time limit other than "from year to year" until canceled, and other proxies bearing the overstamp "Revocable Proxy", which were altered by the management after the date of execution, are invalid as being contrary to State law limiting the life of a revocable proxy to 11 months (Business Corporation Law, § 609) and the applicable regulations of the Federal Home Loan Bank Board (12 CFR 569.2) pertaining to proxies, which regulations have the force and effect of a statute. Although an election should not be lightly set aside, a new election is required since the use of the invalid proxies precluded a free and unfettered election, resulting in the perpetuation in office of the board of directors. Re McVann (1978) 96 Misc. 2d 879, 409 N.Y.S.2d 923

Section 611 of the Business Corporation Law, which delineates the authority of an inspector of elections, is a codification of prior law and provides that the inspector's function is purely ministerial and does not extend to the quasi-judicial role of resolving disputes; accordingly, the inspector's function is to ascertain that the holders of shares are record owners as appears on the list of stockholders produced at the shareholders' meeting; the inspector has no authority to investigate that list, examine allegations of forged or fraudulently obtained proxies, adjudicate disputes involving the ownership of shares, or question the right or mental competency of the record holder of shares to execute a proxy (see Business Corporation Law, § 609, subd [c]); while the inspector's discretionary powers permit him to examine irregularities which appear on a proxy, once its facial validity is established he must accept it and the proxy may vote the shares he holds. Gunzburg v Gunzburg (1979) 101 Misc. 2d 896, 422 N.Y.S.2d 577, affd (2d Dept) 74 A.D.2d 636, 425 N.Y.S.2d 151

Section 609 (subd [f], par [3]) of the Business Corporation Law, which was intended to make credit more readily available to satisfy the needs of corporations whose stockholders were prepared to yield voting rights during the period of the extension of credit, provides that a proxy that is entitled "irrevocable proxy" and states that it is irrevocable, is irrevocable when it is held by a creditor or creditors of the corporation who extend or continue to extend credit to the corporation in consideration of the proxy, if the proxy states such consideration, the amount of credit extended or continued and the name of the creditor. Accordingly, where it is clear that a lease agreement, referred to as the consideration in and for an "irrevocable proxy", is an extension of credit and the proxy makes reference to a written lease in which the total amount of the rent to be paid and the term thereof is clear and precise, the "amount" of the credit is thereby stated and defendants, the shareholders who granted the proxies, should not be permitted to avoid their undertaking by means of a narrow, semantic interpretation of the statement of "amount" requirement contrary to the intention of the statute, while defendant creditor corporation has lived up to its undertaking; defendants' motion for summary judgment which sought a judgment declaring that the proxies were revocable and were, in fact, revoked, was denied and plaintiff's motion to compel depositions was granted.Schulman v Spera (1979) 102 Misc. 2d 179, 423 N.Y.S.2d 115

UNDER FORMER LAW

A statutory provision that a shareholder shall not sell his vote to anyone for money or anything of value is violated where a shareholder requests another to buy certain stock and vote for reelection of directors, agreeing to pay a portion of whatever loss the purchaser might sustain on subsequent resale of the stock, and illegality of the transaction can be raised by way of defense to an action on the agreement for recovery of loss sustained on the resale. Morgenstern v Cohon (1957) 2 N.Y.2d 302, 160 N.Y.S.2d 633, 141 N.E.2d 314

Under § 47 of former Stock Corp. L., it was held that a vendor of stock could be compelled to give a proxy to his vendee. Re Atlantic City Ambassador Hotel Corp. (1946, Sup) 62 N.Y.S.2d 62

Section 609 of former Bus. Corp. L. now deals with "irrevocable" proxies in a clear and specific manner, and some of its provisions trace back to § 47-a of former Stock Corp. L. It may be noted that an "irrevocable" proxy given prior to the effective date of § 47-a, not for any of the purposes specified in that section, was considered invalid as contrary to public policy. Re Norton & Schneider, Inc. (1954, Sup) 137 N.Y.S.2d 269

There is no common-law right on the part of a member of a stock corporation to vote by proxy. Dal-Tran Service Co. v Fifth Ave. Coach Lines, Inc. (1961, 1st Dept) 14 A.D.2d 349, 14 A.D.2d 764, 220 N.Y.S.2d 549, application gr 11 N.Y.2d 659, 225 N.Y.S.2d 738, 180 N.E.2d 897

The burden is upon those who seek to have proxies declared invalid to establish their right to relief by a preponderance of evidence. Dal-Tran Service Co. v Fifth Ave. Coach Lines, Inc. (1961, 1st Dept) 14 A.D.2d 349, 14 A.D.2d 764, 220 N.Y.S.2d 549, application gr 11 N.Y.2d 659, 225 N.Y.S.2d 738, 180 N.E.2d 897

For fraud and concealment in solicitation of proxies the courts have power to set aside an election of directors, and proxies wrongfully obtained may be challenged by the persons who gave them. Dal-Tran Service Co. v Fifth Ave. Coach Lines, Inc. (1961, 1st Dept) 14 A.D.2d 349, 14 A.D.2d 764, 220 N.Y.S.2d 549, application gr 11 N.Y.2d 659, 225 N.Y.S.2d 738, 180 N.E.2d 897

Shareholders soliciting proxies from fellow shareholders assume a fiduciary relation and proxies wrongfully obtained may be challenged either by those who gave them or by those affected, but only if the

proxy statement failed to inform stockholders of all material facts. Dal-Tran Service Co. v Fifth Ave. Coach Lines, Inc. (1961, 1st Dept) 14 A.D.2d 349, 14 A.D.2d 764, 220 N.Y.S.2d 549, application gr 11 N.Y.2d 659, 225 N.Y.S.2d 738, 180 N.E.2d 897

Under § 47 of former Stock Corp. L., beneficial owners of shares could, under stated circumstances, require the owners of record to issue proxies entitling them to vote the shares. Fierman v Rose (1940) 175 Misc 102, 22 N.Y.S.2d 215

A proxy is subject to the directions of the owner of the stock as to how it shall be voted, and can be compelled to vote as directed. Wilson v Rensselaer & S. R. Co. (1945) 184 Misc 218, 52 N.Y.S.2d 847, affd 268 A.D. 1076, 53 N.Y.S.2d 306

If a proxy is so phrased as to limit the authority conferred to voting at some particular meeting, or at "general" meetings of shareholders, it is restricted to the meeting or type of meetings specified and does not confer authority to vote the shares on other occasions or at "special" meetings.Societe Anonyme D'Innovations Chimiques v American Alcolac Corp. (1957) 8 Misc. 2d 166, 171 N.Y.S.2d 149

Where a proxy runs to two named individuals, but fails to state that either of them may exercise the voting power conferred, presence of one of them only at the meeting cannot be counted either for voting or for quorum purposes. Petition of Melloh (1959) 17 Misc. 2d 902, 187 N.Y.S.2d 203

But where a statute confers the right to vote by proxy, without specifying formal details beyond basic requirements, it can validly run to any one of a number of persons, in the alternative, such as any member of the existing board of directors, and use of such a proxy form as solicited by one of the factions seeking control is not subject to injunction as "misleading."Prince v Albin (1960) 23 Misc. 2d 194, 200 N.Y.S.2d 843

A married woman, stockholder in a corporation, did not lose her status as a principal, and thus her rights as a stockholder, merely because she gave her husband a proxy and appointed him her agent in corporate affairs. Ohlstein v Hillcrest Paper Co. (1959) 24 Misc. 2d 212, 195 N.Y.S.2d 920

§ 610. Selection of inspectors at shareholders' meetings

(a) The board of directors shall appoint one or more inspectors to act at the meeting or any adjournment there of and make a written report thereof. The board of directors may designate one or more persons as alternate inspectors to replace any inspector who fails to act. If no inspector or alternate has been appointed, or if such persons are unable to act at a meeting of shareholders, the person presiding at the meeting shall appoint one or more inspectors to act at the meeting. Each inspector, before entering upon the discharge of his duties, shall take and sign an oath faithfully to execute the duties of inspector at such meeting with strict impartiality and according to the best of his ability.

(b) Unless otherwise provided in the certificate of incorporation or by-laws, paragraph (a) of this section shall not apply to a corporation that does not have a class of voting stock that is listed on a national securities exchange or authorized for quotation on an interdealer quotation system of a registered national securities association. Notwithstanding the foregoing, any corporation may take the actions set forth in paragraph (a) of this section.

History: Add, L 1961, ch 855; amd, L 1963, ch 746, eff Sept 1, 1963; L 1964, ch 725, § 5; L 1965, ch 803, § 16, eff Sept 1, 1965; L 1997, ch 449, § 30, eff Feb 22, 1998.

Under earlier statutes it was held that appointment of inspectors of election could be covered by the bylaws without any provision for their selection or approval by the stockholders. Re Remington Typewriter Co. (1922) 234 N.Y. 296, 137 N.E. 335

They could be designated as "tellers" rather than inspectors, the duties and functions being the same. Data-Guide, Inc. v Marcus (1958) 16 Misc. 2d 541, 181 N.Y.S.2d 945

§ 611. Duties of inspectors at shareholders' meetings

(a) The inspectors shall determine the number of shares outstanding and the voting power of each, the shares represented at the meeting, the existence of a quorum, the validity and effect of proxies, and shall receive votes, ballots or consents, hear and determine all challenges and questions arising in connection with the right to vote, count and tabulate all votes, ballots or consents, determine the result, and do such acts as are proper to conduct the election or vote with fairness to all shareholders. On request of the person presiding at the meeting or any shareholder entitled to vote thereat, the inspectors shall make a report in writing of any challenge, question or matter determined by them and execute a certificate of any fact found by them. Any report or certificate made by them shall be prima facie evidence of the facts stated and of the vote as certified by them.

(b) In determining the validity and counting of proxies, ballots and consents, the inspectors shall be limited to an examination of the proxies, any envelopes submitted with those proxies and consents, any information provided in accordance with section 609 (Proxies), ballots and the regular books and records of the corporation, except that the inspectors may consider other reliable information for the limited purpose of reconciling proxies, ballots and consents submitted by or on behalf of banks, brokers, their nominees or similar persons which represent more votes than the holder of a proxy is authorized by the record owner to cast or more votes than the stockholder holds of record. If the inspectors consider other reliable information for the limited purpose permitted herein, the inspectors at the time they make their certification pursuant to paragraph (a) of this section shall specify the precise information considered by them including the person or persons from whom they obtained the information, when the information was obtained, the means by which the information was obtained and the basis for the inspectors' belief that such information is reliable.

(c) The date and time (which need not be a particular time of day) of the opening and the closing of the polls for each matter upon which the shareholders will vote at a meeting shall be announced by the person presiding at the meeting at the beginning of the meeting and, if no date and time is so announced, the polls shall close at the end of the meeting, including any adjournment thereof. No ballot, proxies or consents, nor any revocation thereof or changes thereto, shall be accepted by the inspectors after the closing of polls in accordance with section 605 (Notice of meetings of shareholders) unless the supreme court at a special term held within the judicial district where the office of the corporation is located upon application by a shareholder shall determine otherwise.

(d) Unless otherwise provided in the certificate of incorporation or by-laws, paragraphs (a) and (c) of this section shall not apply to a corporation that does not have a class of voting stock that is listed on a national securities exchange or authorized for quotation on an interdealer quotation system of a registered national securities association. Notwithstanding the foregoing, any corporation may take the actions set forth in paragraphs (a) and (c) of this section.

History: Add, L 1961, ch 855, eff Sept 1, 1963; amd, L 1997, ch 449, § 31, eff Feb 22, 1998.

CASE ANNOTATIONS

An action brought under Bus Corp Law § 611 to annul the tabulation of votes at an annual corporate shareholders' meeting on the ground that the election inspectors were not disinterested, breached their duties, and were negligent and unfair was properly dismissed, since § 611 only prescribes the duties of an inspector at the shareholders' meeting and does not provide the mechanism for challenging the results of such a meeting, and since the exclusive methods for testing the validity of an election are either an action in the nature of quo warranto brought by the attorney general or a proceeding instituted under Bus Corp Law § 619. A proceeding brought pursuant to § 619 several days earlier, however, alleging that the vote was invalid because of certain irregularities, was sufficiently broad to cover the matters raised in the purported § 611 action. Re Schmidt (1983, 2d Dept) 97 A.D.2d 244, 468 N.Y.S.2d 663

Proxies voted for directors elected to respondent Federal Savings and Loan Association, not verified or inspected by the inspectors of the election prior to the election, in violation of the inspectors' duties at shareholders' meetings (Business Corporation Law, § 611) are invalid. The rights of members in Federal Savings and Loan Associations are analogous to those of a corporate shareholder, and since applicable Federal law does not provide for the verification of proxies or prohibit the inspectors of the election from undertaking such activity (US Code, tit 12, § 1464; 12 CFR Part 544), State law prevails entitling petitioner, as a minority shareholder, to enjoy all the rights enumerated in section 611 of the Business Corporation Law. Re McVann (1978) 96 Misc. 2d 879, 409 N.Y.S.2d 923

Section 611 of the Business Corporation Law, which delineates the authority of an inspector of elections, is a codification of prior law and provides that the inspector's function is purely ministerial and does not extend to the quasi-judicial role of resolving disputes; accordingly, the inspector's function is to ascertain that the holders of shares are record owners as appears on the list of stockholders produced at the shareholders' meeting; the inspector has no authority to investigate that list, examine allegations of forged or fraudulently obtained proxies, adjudicate disputes involving the ownership of shares, or question the right or mental competency of the record holder of shares to execute a proxy (see Business Corporation Law, § 609, subd [c]); while the inspector's discretionary powers permit him to examine irregularities which appear on a proxy, once its facial validity is established he must accept it and the proxy may vote the shares he holds. Gunzburg v Gunzburg (1979) 101 Misc. 2d 896, 422 N.Y.S.2d 577, affd (2d Dept) 74 A.D.2d 636, 425 N.Y.S.2d 151

UNDER FORMER LAW

If a vote is challenged, an inspector cannot determine the question, but must call for the production of corporate books as evidence of the right to vote. Data-Guide, Inc. v Marcus (1958) 16 Misc. 2d 541, 181 N.Y.S.2d 945

Business Corporation Law

§ 612.   Qualification voters

(a) Every shareholder of record shall be entitled at every meeting of shareholders to one vote for every share standing in his name on the record of shareholders, unless otherwise provided in the certificate of incorporation.

(b) Treasury shares and shares held by another domestic or foreign corporation of any type or kind, if a majority of the shares entitled to vote in the election of directors of such other corporation is held by the corporation, shall not be shares entitled to vote or to be counted in determining the total number of outstanding shares.

(c) Shares held by an administrator, executor, guardian, conservator, committee, or other fiduciary, except a trustee, may be voted by him, either in person or by proxy, without transfer of such shares into his name. Shares held by a trustee may be voted by him, either in person or by proxy, only after the shares have been transferred into his name as trustee or into the name of his nominee.

(d) Shares held by or under the control of a receiver may be voted by him without the transfer thereof into his name if authority so to do is contained in an order of the court by which such receiver was appointed.

(e) A shareholder whose shares are pledged shall be entitled to vote such shares until the shares have been transferred into the name of the pledgee, or a nominee of the pledgee.

(f) Redeemable shares which have been called for redemption shall not be deemed to be outstanding shares for the purpose of voting or determining the total number of shares entitled to vote on any matter on and after the date on which written notice of redemption has been sent to holders thereof and a sum sufficient to redeem such shares has been deposited with a bank or trust company with irrevocable instruction and authority to pay the redemption price to the holders of the shares upon surrender of certificates therefor.

(g) Shares standing in the name of another domestic or foreign corporation of any type or kind may be voted by such officer, agent or proxy as the by-laws of such corporation may provide, or, in the absence of such provision, as the board of such corporation may determine.

(h) If shares are registered on the record of shareholders of a corporation in the name of two or more persons, whether fiduciaries, members of a partnership, joint tenants, tenants in common, tenants by the entirety or otherwise, or if two or more persons have the same fiduciary relationship respecting the same shares, unless the secretary of the corporation is given written notice to the contrary and is furnished with a copy of the instrument or order appointing them or creating the relationship wherein it is so provided, their acts with respect to voting shall have the following effect:

(1) If only one votes, the vote shall be accepted by the corporation as the vote of all;

(2) If more than one vote, the act of the majority so voting shall be accepted by the corporation as the vote of all;

(3) If more than one vote, but the vote is equally divided on any particular matter, the vote shall be accepted by the corporation as a proportionate vote of the shares; unless the corporation has evidence, on the record of shareholders or otherwise, that the shares are held in a fiduciary capacity. Nothing in this paragraph shall alter any requirement that the exercise of fiduciary powers be by act of a majority, contained in any law applicable to such exercise of powers (including section 10-10.7 of the estates, powers and trusts law);

(4) When shares as to which the vote is equally divided are registered on the record of shareholders of a corporation in the name of, or have passed by operation of law or by virtue of any deed of trust or other instrument to two or more fiduciaries, any court having jurisdiction of their accounts, upon petition by any of such fiduciaries or by any party in interest, may direct the voting of such shares for the best interest of the beneficiaries. This subparagraph shall not apply in any case where the instrument or order of the court appointing fiduciaries shall otherwise direct how such shares shall be voted; and

(5) If the instrument or order furnished to the secretary of a corporation shows that a tenancy is held in unequal interests, a majority or equal division for the purposes of this paragraph shall be a majority or equal division in interest.

(i) Notwithstanding the foregoing paragraphs, a corporation shall be protected in treating the persons in whose names shares stand on the record of shareholders as the owners thereof for all purposes.

History: Add, L 1961, ch 855, eff Sept 1, 1963; amd, L 1962, ch 834, § 33, eff Sept 1, 1963; L 1963, ch 746, eff Sept 1, 1963; L 1964, ch 681, § 4, eff June 1, 1965; repealed, L 1981, ch 62, § 1, eff Apr 8, 1981.

CASE ANNOTATIONS

UNDER FORMER LAW

1. **In general**
2. **"Shareholder of record", generally**
3. **– Right to vote**
4. **Fiduciaries**
5. **Pledged shares**
6. **Non-voting shares**
7. **Miscellaneous**

Partnership which owned approximately 58 percent interest in publicly held corporation was not barred by cross-voting restrictions of CLS Bus Corp § 612(b) from voting its shares in favor of merger with another corporation, regardless of whether it was effectively controlled by other corporation, as § 612(b) explicitly applies only to corporations, not to partnerships. Pinnacle Consultants, Ltd. v Leucadia Nat'l Corp. (2000) 94 N.Y.2d 426, 706 N.Y.S.2d 46, 727 N.E.2d 543

Stockholders of corporation may validly agree to bylaws which provide that one person's stock is entitled to three votes per share while another's is entitled to only one vote per share; thus, in declaratory judgment action, defendant was entitled to summary judgment declaring that he was entitled to three votes per share of stock, despite technicality that special voting provisions were not authorized in certificate of incorporation or amendment thereto, pursuant to Bus Corp Law § 612(a). Garson v Garson (1984, 2d Dept) 105 A.D.2d 726, 481 N.Y.S.2d 162, affd 66 N.Y.2d 928, 498 N.Y.S.2d 796, 489 N.E.2d 765

Plaintiff sponsor of condominium apartment complex was entitled to summary judgment declaring that it was entitled to vote its unsold shares in election of new directors, notwithstanding contention of defendant (cooperative corporation that owned and operated buildings) that offering plan barred sponsor from exercising voting control over board of directors after sponsor owned less than 50 percent of outstanding shares, since mere fact that new directors may be elected with sponsor's votes cannot, without more, be equated with exercising voting control as matter of law; defendant must show that directors so elected were on sponsor's slate of directors, or were on sponsor's payroll or received other remuneration from sponsor. Rego Park Gardens Assoc. v Rego Park Gardens Owners, Inc. (1991, 1st Dept) 174 A.D.2d 337, 570 N.Y.S.2d 550, app den 78 N.Y.2d 859, 575 N.Y.S.2d 456, 580 N.E.2d 1059

Provision of offering plan whereby "Sponsor will vote its shares so that its votes and those of other holders of Unsold Shares will not elect a majority of the Board of Directors" did not prohibit sponsor from combining her votes with those of other resident shareholders, who were not holders of unsold shares, to elect 3 or more members of 5-member board of directors. Madison v Striggles (1996, 1st Dept) 228 A.D.2d 170, 644 N.Y.S.2d 6, later proceeding (NY A.D., 1st Dept) 1996 N.Y. A.D. LEXIS 9603

Plaintiff as executrix of estate of her husband-shareholder had right to institute stockholders' derivative action even though coexecutrix, who was a defendant and whose husband was a codefendant, did not consent to the suit, and plaintiff was not required to apply to the Surrogate's Court for permission to prosecute suit on behalf of the estate. Greenberg v Acme Folding Box Co. (1975) 84 Misc. 2d 181, 374 N.Y.S.2d 997

Under the Business Corporation Law, possession is not the criterion by which the right to vote is determined; the record of shareholders is conclusive upon the election inspectors, and they may not look behind the list to determine whether or not the record owners are the true owners entitled to vote the stock, nor may shareholders of record be required to produce their share certificates as evidence of their continuing ownership before being permitted to vote.Stewart Becker, Ltd. v Horowitz (1978) 94 Misc. 2d 766, 405 N.Y.S.2d 571

The beneficial or true owners or any other person entitled to possession of shares have no right to vote if they are not record holders.Stewart Becker, Ltd. v Horowitz (1978) 94 Misc. 2d 766, 405 N.Y.S.2d 571

Under the terms of a proprietary lease stipulating that a tenant could make an assignment without the approval of defendant cooperative's board of directors, provided that a written consent to such assignment was given by the lessees owning of record at least the majority of the capital stock of the lessor accompanying proprietary leases then in force, plaintiff tenants, who obtained the majority of consents needed, were entitled to assign their shares and proprietary lease, even though six of the signatories, whose failure to be counted would deprive plaintiffs of their majority, were joint shareholders whose vote was accepted as the vote of their joint shareholder, since Bus Corp Law § 612(h) provides that if shares are registered on the record of the shareholders of a corporation in the name of two or more persons, the act of one shareholder in giving consent is the act of all tenants in common in the absence of a disclaimer or other action provided for in § 612(h); the absence of protest from the silent joint shareholders was valid for the consent of the commonly owned shares.Ebner v 91st Street Tenants Corp. (1984) 126 Misc. 2d 108, 481 N.Y.S.2d 198

CLS Bus Corp § 612 was not violated by corporate merger on ground that partnership controlled by defendant corporation was permitted to vote on merger, as § 612 is inapplicable to partnerships. Pinnacle Consultants, Ltd. v Leucadia Nat'l Corp. (1999, 1st Dept) 261 A.D.2d 164, 689 N.Y.S.2d 497, app gr 93 N.Y.2d 815, 697 N.Y.S.2d 562, 719 N.E.2d 923 and affd 94 N.Y.2d 426, 706 N.Y.S.2d 46, 727 N.E.2d 543

There was no indication that shares were required by a corporation to be cancelled upon reacquisition, and their subsequent sale, upon authorization by the board, would contraindicate such cancellation; the evidence supported the corporation's contention that the shares were retained as treasury shares and were subsequently disposed for fair consideration. An owner's argument in reliance on

N.Y. Bus. Corp. Law §§ 515, 612(b) was ineffective to overcome the legitimate acts of the board in transferring the shares. Matter of McDaniel v 162 Columbia Hgts. Hous. Corp. (2009, Sup) 873 NYS2d 468.

CLS Bus Corp § 612(b) did not prohibit partnership from voting its majority block of corporate shares in favor of corporate merger, despite contention that partnership effectively constituted subsidiary corporation because it was indirectly owned by putative parent corporation due to complex ownership structure whereby 3 entities essentially held majority interest in each other; § 612(b) does not apply to partnerships and, even if it did, complaint did not establish that putative parent corporation owned controlling interest in putative subsidiary. Pinnacle Consultants ex rel. Shareholders of Leucadia Nat'l Corp. v Leucadia Nat'l Corp. (1995, SD NY) 923 F. Supp. 439

UNDER FORMER LAW

1. In general

One objective of statutes dealing with qualifications or eligibility to vote corporate shares at shareholders' meetings is to facilitate and lend certainty in the conduct of corporate affairs, and hence, where a corporation keeps stock books and records, these records are ordinarily regarded as conclusive as to stock ownership for voting purposes. Re Bruder's Estate (1950) 302 N.Y. 52, 96 N.E.2d 84; Application of Morrison (1958, 1st Dept) 7 A.D.2d 42, 180 N.Y.S.2d 760; Flagg-Utica Corp. v Baselice (1958) 14 Misc. 2d 476, 178 N.Y.S.2d 860

2. "Shareholder of record", generally

In the case of a family corporation which has no stock book, however, and other small corporations which are managed and operated by agreement among stockholders, some decisions indicate that record ownership of shares is of less importance in determining the outcome of proceedings at a stockholders' meeting than what the individuals in interest have agreed upon. See, for example,Re Bruder's Estate (1950) 302 N.Y. 52, 96 N.E.2d 84, revg 277 A.D. 871, 98 N.Y.S.2d 459

The corporation is not required to conduct investigations into the ownership of its individual shares, as matter of law and equity, before proceeding with the business at hand, nor is a dispute over ownership of shares a matter for summary judicial determination merely because right to vote them is in controversy. Re William Faehndrich, Inc. (1957) 2 N.Y.2d 468, 161 N.Y.S.2d 99, 141 N.E.2d 597; Flagg-Utica Corp. v Baselice (1958) 14 Misc. 2d 476, 178 N.Y.S.2d 860

Persons who are the owners of stock and entitled to be recorded in the books of the corporation as the owners must procure certificates of the shares in their own names if they desire to vote; their failure to do so, particularly in the absence of any explanation or excuse for their inaction, affords a presumption that they intended to permit the present record holders of the stock to vote. Re D. J. Salvator, Inc. (1944) 268 A.D. 919, 51 N.Y.S.2d 342

The outcome of voting by shareholders of record, and their proxies, ordinarily binds other owners of shares in the corporation who have failed to make their ownership of record at the time when the records become closed for purposes of the particular meeting, notwithstanding some of the shares have been assigned or transferred to others between record date and date of the meeting. Re Henry Harrison Co. (1941, DC NY) 40 F. Supp. 733

3. – Right to vote

Under § 47 of former Stock Corp L, the record holder of all stock in a corporation has the right to vote it, even if he holds it merely as security or as "trustee" under an instrument giving him the voting power.Sire Plan, Inc. v Mintzer (1963) 38 Misc. 2d 920, 237 N.Y.S.2d 123

Although all stock of certain corporations stood of record in the name of a particular individual as "trustee," he nevertheless had the right to vote such stock where the terms of the trust instrument gave him such right as pledgee in the event of default.Sire Plan, Inc. v Mintzer (1963) 38 Misc. 2d 920, 237 N.Y.S.2d 123

The record holder of all stock in a certain corporation has the right, under this section, to vote such stock, even if he held the stock only as security for a default which had not occurred.Sire Plan, Inc. v Mintzer (1963) 38 Misc. 2d 920, 237 N.Y.S.2d 123

Where the record owner of all stock in a corporation is the sole stockholder, and under the by-laws of the corporation directors may be removed at any time by affirmative vote of the holders of a majority of shares at a special meeting called for that purpose, such stockholder could remove all directors by simply voting for their removal, without a special meeting, as the calling of a special meeting would be only for the benefit of other stockholders, and there were none.Sire Plan, Inc. v Mintzer (1963) 38 Misc. 2d 920, 237 N.Y.S.2d 123

Continued possession of the stock certificate issued to a holder of record is not the test of his right to vote the stock, and his right continues as long as he remains holder of record, notwithstanding the holder of the remaining 50% of the stock has come into possession of his certificate. Application for Dissolution of Homer Fabrics, Inc. (1955, Sup) 137 N.Y.S.2d 701

Generally speaking, one who is not a shareholder of record as of the record date fixed for the meeting, is not entitled to vote, unless he holds a proxy from the record owner, notwithstanding he may be the owner of some interest in outstanding shares or even the actual legal owner of the shares which he seeks to vote. Re Henry Harrison Co. (1941, DC NY) 40 F. Supp. 733

Where a stock transfer was actually made of record, the stock could only be voted by the record owner as of record date, and accordingly it was immaterial whether it was voted under a proxy given to the purchaser by the record owner or by the record owner as of record date, as long as it would have been voted the same way in either event. Andrews v Precision Apparatus, Inc. (1963, SD NY) 217 F. Supp. 679

The voting rights of stockholders cannot be based upon the amount of fees paid to or business done with the corporation during the preceding fiscal year.1957 Ops Atty Gen Oct 16

4. Fiduciaries

Where the executors of an estate of a decedent are unable to agree on how stock of certain corporations shall be voted with respect to their proposed dissolution, after several years of controversy, although the Surrogate cannot direct them how to vote, he can direct sale of the stock at public auction unless those in interest consent to its distribution in kind, thereby terminating the dispute for the benefit of all concerned. Re Bourne's Will (1960, 1st Dept) 11 A.D.2d 128, 202 N.Y.S.2d 452, affd 8 N.Y.2d 1041, 207 N.Y.S.2d 65, 170 N.E.2d 388

Trustees of a trust part of the corpus of which consists of corporate stock, in voting the stock, are under a fiduciary obligation to do so in furtherance of the purposes of the trust and for the benefit of the cestuis, and accordingly cannot properly join in a voting agreement the carrying out of which would or could conflict with this fiduciary obligation. Re Palmer's Will (1954, Sur) 132 N.Y.S.2d 311

5. Pledged shares

The owner of pledged stock was entitled to all the rights of a stockholder subject to the lien of the pledgee, and until the pledge was enforced and title made absolute in the pledge, the pledgor was entitled to vote. Monitor Co. v Confianza Furniture & Appliance Corp. (1955, Sup) 142 N.Y.S.2d 140

6. Non-voting shares

Insofar as this section of the Business Corporation Law prohibits voting of treasury shares, or shares held by one corporation in such amount as to constitute a majority of the shares entitled to vote in an election of directors at a shareholders' meeting of another corporation, the concept is not entirely new in New York law, as there were already New York decisions precluding exercise of control over one corporation by another through acquisition and voting of a majority of the latter's stock if it would involve fraud or defeat public interests. Dal-Tran Service Co. v Fifth Ave. Coach Lines, Inc. (1961) 30 Misc. 2d 236, 217 N.Y.S.2d 193, revd on other grounds (1st Dept) 14 A.D.2d 349, 14 A.D.2d 764, 220 N.Y.S.2d 549, application gr 11 N.Y.2d 659, 225 N.Y.S.2d 738, 180 N.E.2d 897

7. Miscellaneous

Statutory provisions that each shareholder shall be entitled to "one vote for every share standing in his name" on the record of shareholders, "unless otherwise provided in the certificate of incorporation," or the like, have been construed as precluding bylaws which would require shareholders to vote all the shares individually held by them for but one candidate for director. Re Crown Heights Hospital, Inc. (1944) 183 Misc 563, 49 N.Y.S.2d 658

§ 613. Limitations on right to vote

The certificate of incorporation may provide, except as limited by section 501 (Authorized shares), either absolutely or conditionally, that the holders of any designated class or series of shares shall not be entitled to vote, or it may otherwise limit or define the respective voting powers of the several classes or series of shares, and, except as otherwise provided in this chapter, such provisions of such certificate shall prevail, according to their tenor, in all elections and in all proceedings, over the provisions of this chapter which authorizes any action by the shareholders.

History: Add, L 1961, ch 855, amd, L 1962, ch 834, § 34, eff Sept 1, 1963.

CASE ANNOTATIONS

UNDER FORMER STK CORP §§ 47, 51

Doubt existed under § 51 of former Stock Corp. L. as to whether stockholders in an established corporation could be compelled to share exclusive voting rights conferred upon them by the terms of the certificate of incorporation and under which they acquired their stock with other stockholders. Re Riggi Bros. Co. (1930, CA2 Vt) 42 F.2d 174, cert den 282 US 881, 75 L Ed 777, 51 S Ct 85

Where a stock transfer was duly recorded, under § 47 of former Stock Corp L the stock in question could only be voted by its owner as of record date, but it was immaterial whether it was voted by proxy given to the purchaser or by the owner of record date as long as it would have been voted the same way in either event. Andrews v Precision Apparatus, Inc. (1963, SD NY) 217 F. Supp. 679

The voting rights of stockholders could not, under § 51 of former Stock Corp. L., be based upon the amount of fees paid to or business done with the corporation during the preceding fiscal year.1957 Ops Atty Gen Oct 16

§ 614. Vote of shareholders

(a) Directors shall, except as otherwise required by this chapter or by the by-laws or certificate of incorporation as permitted by this chapter, be elected by a plurality of the votes cast at a meeting of shareholders by the holders of shares entitled to vote in the election.

(b) Whenever any corporate action, other than the election of directors, is to be taken under this chapter by vote of the shareholders, it shall, except as otherwise required by this chapter or by the certificate of incorporation as permitted by this chapter or by the specific provisions of a by-law adopted by the shareholders, be authorized by a majority of the votes cast in favor of or against such action at a meeting of shareholders by the holders of shares entitled to vote thereon. Except as otherwise provided in the certificate of incorporation or the specific provision of a by-law adopted by the shareholders, an abstention shall not constitute a vote cast.

History: Add, L 1961, ch 855, eff Sept 1, 1963; amd, L 1997, ch 449, § 32, eff Feb 22, 1998; L 2008, ch 314, § 1, eff July 21, 2008.

CASE ANNOTATIONS

Only if the by-laws and the certificate of incorporation make no provision for the removal of a director without cause or, so providing, do not stipulate the plurality of shares to accomplish the result, does subdivision (b) of Business Corporation Law § 614 come into play. Re Laser Tech, Inc. (1970, 2d Dept) 35 A.D.2d 994, 317 N.Y.S.2d 853

The effect of Business Corporation Law § 614, subdivision (b) is to provide a rule of procedure of voting if no different procedure is otherwise permitted by the Business Corporation Law or the certificate of incorporation and since Business Corporation Law § 706, in the case of the removal of a director without cause, permits the provisions of the by-laws to control, Business Corporation Law § 614, subdivision (b) does not apply. Re Laser Tech, Inc. (1970, 2d Dept) 35 A.D.2d 994, 317 N.Y.S.2d 853

In an action brought by two of three equal shareholders in a closely held corporation against the third shareholder, the trial court erred in holding that a paragraph in the parties' shareholders' agreement which required changes in the corporate structure to receive unanimous shareholder approval was void as requiring, in the absence of an amendment to the corporation's certificate of incorporation to reflect such a provision, a voting majority greater than that specified by law, where the parties, in unanimously approving the shareholders' agreement, had intended that the ministerial act of amending the corporation's certificate of incorporation would be accomplished so as to effectuate the agreement's provisions; as requested by the third stockholder's counterclaim, judgment would be entered amending the certificate of incorporation to include the unanimity provision of the shareholders' agreement. Adler v Svingos (1981, 1st Dept) 80 A.D.2d 764, 436 N.Y.S.2d 719

Court properly denied petitioner's motion to confirm election of board of directors of corporation where election was conducted in violation of offering plan and by-laws, inasmuch as sponsor used its votes to elect all 7 board members after having nominated 3 sponsor-related members. Flagg Court Realty Co. v Flagg Court Owners Corp. (1996, 2d Dept) 230 A.D.2d 740, 646 N.Y.S.2d 298

When all shareholders of corporation agree that it is necessary or desirable to require unanimous consent of board of directors for corporate action for which consent of board of directors is required, and further consent to amendment of certificate to reflect this understanding, and where no rights of third parties are implicated, it is proper to reform certificate of incorporation. Ench v Breslin (1997, 2d Dept) 241 A.D.2d 475, 659 N.Y.S.2d 893

Court incorrectly gave effect to shareholder unanimity provision contained in corporation's original bylaws where corporation's certificate of incorporation did not contain shareholder unanimity provision. Stile v Antico (2000, 2d Dept) 272 A.D.2d 403, 707 N.Y.S.2d 227

Proposed amendment to corporate bylaws was validly approved at shareholders' meeting by "majority" of votes cast for purposes of CLS Bus Corp § 614(b) where 7,698,692 shares were cast in favor, 7,243,554 against, and 476,985 abstained; proxy cards marked "abstained" could not be counted in order to determine number of shares required to constitute majority given that "abstain" box was specifically provided in proxy to enable shareholders to not vote on issue or issues. Bank of New York Co. v Irving Bank Corp. (1988) 140 Misc. 2d 508, 531 N.Y.S.2d 730

Corporate election procedure was neither illegal nor improper where plaintiff was removed as director for cause at adjourned annual shareholder's meeting by affirmative vote of at least 80 percent of outstanding shares of company entitled to vote, as required by corporate bylaws, after election polls had been closed on 2 resolutions but left open on proposal to remove plaintiff when preliminary results at initial meeting indicated that 80 percent vote had not yet been achieved; in absence of controlling statute or bylaws, decisions as to whether polls are kept open is matter within discretion of election inspectors, who may keep polls open beyond specified hour. Smith v Orange & Rockland Utils. (1994, Sup) 162 Misc. 2d 606, 617 N.Y.S.2d 278

UNDER FORMER LAW

Section 55 of former Stock Corp. L. was regarded as mandatory in providing for election of directors by "plurality vote" of the shareholders, and neither a certificate of incorporation, nor bylaw provisions, could require their election by unanimous vote. Benintendi v Kenton Hotel, Inc. (1945) 294 N.Y. 112, 60 N.E.2d 829 (superseded by statute as stated in Application of Burkin, 1 N.Y.2d 570, 154 N.Y.S.2d 898, 136 N.E.2d 862, 64 ALR2d 638); Re Boulevard Theatre & Realty Co. (1921) 195 A.D. 518, 186 N.Y.S. 430, affd without op 231 N.Y. 615, 132 N.E. 910

Although a provision in a stockholders' agreement that all the stockholders would continue to vote for themselves as directors was legal, a provision for the continuance of specified persons as officers and employees was valid only if such persons remained faithful and efficient and were not guilty of acts or omissions which would constitute good cause for their removal or discharge. Re Roosevelt Leather Hand Bag Co. (1947, Sup) 68 N.Y.S.2d 735

An agreement by a stockholder to vote for a certain person as a director was not prohibited by § 55 of former Stock Corp. L. Slonim v Brodie (1951, Sup) 109 N.Y.S.2d 440, affd 281 A.D. 861, 119 N.Y.S.2d 916

A contract whereby directors were to be elected by other than a plurality vote was void. Reiss v Levy (1916) 175 A.D. 938, 161 N.Y.S. 1048

Bylaws could not, moreover, under earlier statutes, preclude the holder of a block of shares from spreading his votes among candidates for the board of directors by requiring that he vote all of his shares for not more than one director. Re Crown Heights Hospital, Inc. (1944) 183 Misc 563, 49 N.Y.S.2d 658

Where a certificate of incorporation provided for unanimous vote or consent of all stockholders for transaction of corporate business, election of a board of directors by a plurality vote, pursuant to a by-law of the corporation, was invalid, since the provision in the certificate took priority over the by-law. Re Election of Directors of Radiant Knitting Mills, Inc. (1959) 20 Misc. 2d 915, 194 N.Y.S.2d 232

§ 615. Written consent of shareholders, subscribers or incorporators without a meeting

(a) Whenever under this chapter shareholders are required or permitted to take any action by vote, such action may be taken without a meeting on written consent, setting forth the action so taken, signed by the holders of all outstanding shares entitled to vote thereon or, if the certificate of incorporation so permits, signed by the holders of outstanding shares having not less than the minimum number of votes that would be necessary to authorize or take such action at a meeting at which all shares entitled to vote thereon were present and voted. In addition, this paragraph shall not be construed to alter or modify the provisions of any section or any provision in a certificate of incorporation not inconsistent with this chapter under which the written consent of the holders of less than all outstanding shares is sufficient for corporate action.

(b) No written consent shall be effective to take the corporate action referred to therein unless, within sixty days of the earliest dated consent delivered in the manner required by this paragraph to the corporation, written consents signed by a sufficient number of holders to take action are delivered to the corporation by delivery to its registered office in this state, its principal place of business, or an officer or agent of the corporation having custody of the book in which proceedings of meetings of shareholders are recorded. Delivery made to a corporation's registered office shall be by hand or by certified or registered mail, return receipt requested.

(c) Prompt notice of the taking of the corporate action without a meeting by less than unanimous written consent shall be given to those shareholders who have not consented in writing.

(d) Written consent thus given by the holders of such number of shares as is required under paragraph (a) of this section shall have the same effect as a valid vote of holders of such number of shares, and any certificate with respect to the authorization or taking of any such action which is to be delivered to the department of state shall recite that written consent has been given in accordance with this section and that written notice has been given as and to the extent required by this section.

Business Corporation Law

Business
Corporation Law

(e) When there are no shareholders of record, such action may be taken on the written consent signed by a majority in interest of the subscribers for shares whose subscriptions have been accepted or their successors in interest or, if no subscription has been accepted, on the written consent signed by the incorporator or a majority of the incorporators. When there are two or more incorporators, if any dies or is for any reason unable to act, the other or others may act. If there is no incorporator able to act, any person for whom an incorporator was acting as agent may act in his stead, or if such other person also dies or is for any reason unable to act, his legal representative may act.

History: Add, L 1961, ch 855, eff Sept 1, 1963; amd, L 1963, ch 746, eff Sept 1, 1963; L 1997, ch 449, § 33, eff Feb 22, 1998.

CASE ANNOTATIONS

In action arising under business reorganization agreements providing, inter alia, that if plaintiff ceased to be full-time employee before maturity of promissory note given by defendants to acquire share of plaintiffs' company, then defendants' purchase price would be zero, neither side was entitled to summary judgment on cause of action alleging that defendants' ouster of plaintiff 9 months after reorganization was unlawful, where issue existed as to unanimity of defendants' written consent (CLS Gen Bus § 615) to remove plaintiff as officer and director. Shea v Hambros PLC (1998, 1st Dept) 244 A.D.2d 39, 673 N.Y.S.2d 369

UNDER FORMER LAW

Earlier provisions were not as broad as the provisions of this section, but it was recognized that actual consent of a majority, or of some specifically required percentage, of shareholders, to particular corporate action, before or after such action was taken by the board of directors or managing officers, if consent could be established, would preclude the corporation from backing out of the transaction. Gottfried v Gottfried Baking Co. (1956, 1st Dept) 1 A.D.2d 994, 151 N.Y.S.2d 583, app den (1st Dept) 2 A.D.2d 664, 153 N.Y.S.2d 544; Gottfried v Gottfried Baking Co. (1956, Sup) 155 N.Y.S.2d 215, app dismd (1st Dept) 3 A.D.2d 648, 161 N.Y.S.2d 557

Even though the statute specified consent "in writing," actual consent of the requisite number of shareholders was sufficient, if it could be established, and "signed" consents were enough notwithstanding failure to comply in full as to the manner in which the consent was stated or filed. Re Paul Delaney Co. (1928, DC NY) 26 F.2d 937, affd (CA2 NY) 30 F.2d 1018. See also Re Paul Delaney Co. (1927, DC NY) 23 F.2d 737, affd in part and revd in part on other grounds (CA2 NY) 26 F.2d 961; Re Paul De Laney Co. (1928, CA2 NY) 26 F.2d 961; Re Constantine Tobacco Co. (1923, CA2 NY) 290 F 128

§ 616. Greater requirement as to quorum and vote of shareholders

(a) The certificate of incorporation may contain provisions specifying either or both of the following:

(1) That the proportion of votes of shares, or the proportion of votes of shares of any class or series thereof, the holders of which shall be present in person or by proxy at any meeting of shareholders, including a special meeting for election of directors under section 603 (Special meeting for election of directors), in order to constitute a quorum for the transaction of any business or of any specified item of business, including amendments to the certificate of incorporation, shall be greater than the proportion prescribed by this chapter in the absence of such provision.

(2) That the proportion of votes of shares, or votes of shares of a particular class or series of shares, that shall be necessary at any meeting of shareholders for the transaction of any business or of any specified item of business, including amendments to the certificate of incorporation, shall be greater than the proportion prescribed by this chapter in the absence of such provision.

(b) An amendment of the certificate of incorporation which changes or strikes out a provision permitted by this section, shall be authorized at a meeting of shareholders by two-thirds of the votes of the shares entitled to vote thereon, or of such greater proportion of votes of shares, or votes of shares of a particular class or series of shares, as may be provided specifically in the certificate of incorporation for changing or striking out a provision permitted by this section.

(c) If the certificate of incorporation of any corporation contains a provision authorized by this section, the existence of such provision shall be noted conspicuously on the face or back of every certificate for shares issued by such corporation, except that this requirement shall not apply to any corporation having any class of any equity security registered pursuant to Section twelve of the Securities Exchange Act of 1934, as amended.

History: Add, L 1961, ch 855, eff Sept 1, 1963; amd, L 1962, ch 834, § 35, eff Sept 1, 1963; L 1963, ch 746, eff Sept 1, 1963; L 1965, ch 803, § 17, eff Sept 1, 1965; L 1984, ch 603, § 2, eff July 27, 1984; L 1997, ch 449, § 34, eff Feb 22, 1998; L 1998, ch 17, § 7, eff Feb 19, 1998, deemed eff Feb 22, 1998.

CASE ANNOTATIONS

In an action brought by two of three equal shareholders in a closely held corporation against the third shareholder, the trial court erred in holding that a paragraph in the parties' shareholders' agreement which required changes in the corporate structure to receive unanimous shareholder approval was void as requiring, in the absence of an amendment to the corporation's certificate of incorporation to reflect such a provision, a voting majority greater than that specified by law, where the parties, in unanimously approving the shareholders' agreement, had intended that the ministerial act of amending the corporation's certificate of incorporation would be accomplished so as to effectuate the agreement's provisions; as requested by the third stockholder's counterclaim, judgment would be entered amending the certificate of incorporation to include the unanimity provision of the shareholders' agreement. Adler v Svingos (1981, 1st Dept) 80 A.D.2d 764, 436 N.Y.S.2d 719

Supermajority provision in shareholder's agreement, even if otherwise valid, cannot be applied to decision regarding dissolution of corporation where shareholder has statutory right to seek judicial dissolution under CLS Bus Corp § 1104. In re Dissolution of Validation Review Assocs. (1997, 2d Dept) 236 A.D.2d 477, 653 N.Y.S.2d 373, subsequent app (2d Dept) 237 A.D.2d 614, 655 N.Y.S.2d 1005 and app gr 89 N.Y.2d 817, 659 N.Y.S.2d 858, 681 N.E.2d 1305

When all shareholders of corporation agree that it is necessary or desirable to require unanimous consent of board of directors for corporate action for which consent of board of directors is required, and further consent to amendment of certificate to reflect this understanding, and where no rights of third parties are implicated, it is proper to reform certificate of incorporation. Ench v Breslin (1997, 2d Dept) 241 A.D.2d 475, 659 N.Y.S.2d 893

Court incorrectly gave effect to shareholder unanimity provision contained in corporation's original bylaws where corporation's certificate of incorporation did not contain shareholder unanimity provision. Stile v Antico (2000, 2d Dept) 272 A.D.2d 403, 707 N.Y.S.2d 227

Original corporate bylaws could not be amended at shareholders meeting to provide for restructuring of board of directors from 2 to 4 directors, nor could bylaws be amended to eliminate requirement that directors be chosen from among shareholders, where bylaws required quorum of 2 directors to transact corporate business, and only one director was present at meeting. Stile v Antico (2000, 2d Dept) 272 A.D.2d 403, 707 N.Y.S.2d 227

Requirement of attaining 80 percent shareholders' vote for removal of director for cause, in case of public utility, violated public policy and was unenforceable; it was unconscionable that public utility could skirt rule that shareholders may not be deprived of their right to discharge director for cause by requiring millions of shares to be voted. Smith v Orange & Rockland Utils. (1994, Sup) 162 Misc. 2d 606, 617 N.Y.S.2d 278

UNDER FORMER LAW

Where the certificate of incorporation required unanimity of stockholders to transact any business, the ouster of a minority stockholder as a director for alleged misconduct could not be made the subject of an action and hence, could not be made the subject of an arbitration proceeding. Application of Burkin (1956) 1 N.Y.2d 570, 154 N.Y.S.2d 898, 136 N.E.2d 862, 64 ALR2d 638

A complaint to compel the attorney for the organizers of a corporation to amend the certificate of incorporation to provide for the unanimous consent of its stockholders and directors to certain acts, as provided for in an agreement, was insufficient where the corporation was not made a party and it was not alleged that such attorney was a stockholder and that all other stockholders had consented, or been made parties defendant. Lapidos v Harkavy (1954, Sup) 137 N.Y.S.2d 419

Unanimous consent or approval of shareholders to proposed corporate action is not normally required, and such a requirement, if relied upon, must ordinarily appear in the certificate of incorporation. Teperman v Atcos Baths, Inc. (1957) 6 Misc. 2d 162, 163 N.Y.S.2d 221, affd (2d Dept) 7 A.D.2d 854, 182 N.Y.S.2d 765

The 1954 amendment of § 9 of former Stock Corp. L., authorizing certificates of incorporation to increase the percentage of stockholder consent beyond that which existing statutes would require, was not retroactive, and hence it gave no vitality to a requirement in a 1924 certificate for 75% approval of sale of a corporation's real estate as against the two-thirds approval sufficient under § 20 of that law. Wells v Beekman Terrace, Inc. (1960) 23 Misc. 2d 22, 197 N.Y.S.2d 79

Agreements among stockholders that certain action shall not be taken, such as sale of real property by the corporation, without their unanimous consent, are not necessarily invalid or unenforceable inter sese; but, unless included in the certificate of incorporation, and agreement that all corporate acts must be unanimously approved by stockholders is so broad that it cannot be binding, and, where the primary business of the corporation is dealing in real estate, an agreement requiring unanimous consent for disposition of any such property amounts to the same thing. Fromkin v Merrall Realty, Inc. (1961) 30 Misc. 2d 288, 215 N.Y.S.2d 525, affd (2d Dept) 15 A.D.2d 919, 225 N.Y.S.2d 632

Under § 9 of former Stock Corp L as amended in 1949, a by-law inconsistent with the certificate of incorporation or with a 1953 agreement executed by all stockholders, providing for appointment of all servants and employees by the president of the corporation, subject to approval of the Board of Directors, had to yield to the law as amended. Lasker v Moreida (1963) 38 Misc. 2d 348, 238 N.Y.S.2d 16

The executrix of an estate charged with setting up a corporation to take over assets of the decedent's business and form a corporation to distribute stock in such corporation to herself and other designated persons with full power to determine particulars of incorporation and other matters had no power or authority to insist upon inclusion of restrictions in the certificate of incorporation requiring greater than majority or plurality vote of directors and stockholders. Re Burns' Will (1963) 40 Misc. 2d 377, 243 N.Y.S.2d 96

Consent by the required percentage of shareholders to a particular transaction carries with it consent to normal incidents in connection with it, such as extension of an option on corporate property after giving of the option has initially been approved, without necessity for calling another meeting to obtain consent to the extension. Texas Co. v Z. & M. Independent Oil Co. (1946, CA2 NY) 156 F.2d 862

The provisions of this section for amending certificates of incorporation by increasing requirements as to a quorum of shareholders for voting purposes could not be based on shareholder resolutions

adopted 33 years earlier and then contrary to public policy and which continued to be contrary to public policy until 1948 amendment of § 9 of former Stock Corporation Law. Globe Slicing Machine Co. v Hasner (1963, SD NY) 223 F. Supp. 589, affd (CA2 NY) 333 F.2d 413, cert den 379 US 969, 13 L Ed 2d 562, 85 S Ct 666

§ 617.   Voting by class or classes of shares

(a) The certificate of incorporation may contain provisions specifying that any class or classes of shares or of any series thereof shall vote as a class in connection with the transaction of any business or of any specified item of business at a meeting of shareholders, including amendments to the certificate of incorporation.

(b) Where voting as a class is provided in the certificate of incorporation, it shall be by the proportionate vote so provided or, if no proportionate vote is provided, in the election of directors, by a plurality of the votes cast at such meeting by the holders of shares of such class entitled to vote in the election, or for any other corporate action, by a majority of the votes cast at such meeting by the holders of shares of such class entitled to vote thereon.

(c) Such voting by class shall be in addition to any other vote, including vote by class, required by this chapter and by the certificate of incorporation as permitted by this chapter.

History: Add, L 1961, ch 855, eff Sept 1, 1963.

Par (b), amd, L 1962, ch 834, § 36, eff Sept 1, 1963.

§ 618.   Cumulative voting

The certificate of incorporation of any corporation may provide that in all elections of directors of such corporation each shareholder shall be entitled to as many votes as shall equal the number of votes which, except for such provisions as to cumulative voting, he would be entitled to cast for the election of directors with respect to his shares multiplied by the number of directors to be elected, and that he may cast all of such votes for a single director or may distribute them among the number to be voted for, or any two or more of them, as he may see fit, which right, when exercised, shall be termed cumulative voting.

History: Add, L 1961, ch 855, eff Sept 1, 1963.

CASE ANNOTATIONS

UNDER FORMER LAW

Sections 47 and 49 of former Stock Corp. L. likewise sanctioned cumulative voting for directors, but only if it was provided for in the certificate of incorporation. Re American Fibre Chair Seat Corp. (1934) 265 N.Y. 416, 193 N.E. 253, reh den 266 N.Y. 500, 195 N.E. 171; Re Crown Heights Hospital, Inc. (1944) 183 Misc 563, 49 N.Y.S.2d 658

A bylaw provision for cumulative voting, unanimously adopted and expressly subject to amendment only by 85% of the shares, was, however, considered a contract binding among the shareholders, not against public policy, and enforcible. Re American Fibre Chair Seat Corp. (1934) 241 A.D. 532, 272 N.Y.S. 206, affd 265 N.Y. 416, 193 N.E. 253, reh den 266 N.Y. 500, 195 N.E. 171

Prior to authorization of cumulative voting by § 49 of former Stock Corp. L., if provided for in the certificate of incorporation, statutory provisions for election of directors by plurality vote of stockholders were deemed mandatory and as conferring a right to have directors elected on such a basis, as an ordinary incident to stock ownership, notwithstanding an agreement among some of the stockholders for cumulative voting, which right could be asserted by one not a party to the agreement. Binon v Boel (1946, Sup) 64 N.Y.S.2d 518

§ 619. Powers of supreme court respecting elections

Upon the petition of any shareholder aggrieved by an election, and upon notice to the persons declared elected thereat, the corporation and such other persons as the court may direct, the supreme court at a special term held within the judicial district where the office of the corporation is located shall forthwith hear the proofs and allegations of the parties, and confirm the election, order a new election, or take such other action as justice may require.

History: Add, L 1961, ch 855, eff Sept 1, 1963.

CASE ANNOTATIONS

1. In general
2. Notice and time limitations
3. Parties
4. Reviewable issues
5. Grounds for interventions
6. Power of directors
7. Miscellaneous

UNDER FORMER GEN CORP § 25

1. In general
2. Applicability
3. Notice and time limitations
4. Parties
5. Reviewable issues
6. Grounds for intervention
7. Remedial action
8. Power of directors
9. Miscellaneous

1. In general

Unlike § 25 of former General Corporation Law, from which this section was derived, the Supreme Court is no longer limited to merely confirming a challenged corporate election or ordering a new one but may likewise "take such other action as justice may require," and therefor, with respect to a disputed election which took place after effective date of this section, the court may proceed to make arrangements for decision of all necessary issues, including the question of stock ownership. Unbekant v Bohl Tours Travel Agency, Inc. (1964, 3d Dept) 21 A.D.2d 317, 250 N.Y.S.2d 397, app dismd 14 N.Y.2d 959, 253 N.Y.S.2d 996, 202 N.E.2d 377

This section endows the court with broad equitable powers to direct a new election of directors where the election under review is so clouded with doubt or tainted with questionable circumstances that standards of fair dealing require such an order. Carter v Muscat (1964, 1st Dept) 21 A.D.2d 543, 251 N.Y.S.2d 378

The "judicial review" of corporate elections has been broadened by this section to empower the court to hear proof and allegations of the parties as to all issues relevant to the validity of such elections. Crass v Budd Publications, Inc. (1967, 1st Dept) 28 A.D.2d 1100, 284 N.Y.S.2d 156

The dismissal of a petition brought pursuant to Bus Corp Law § 619 to set aside the election of the board of directors at an annual shareholders' meeting and to vacate passage of amendments to articles of incorporation authorizing issuance of new shares would be reversed, since in order to overturn an election of the board of directors it must be shown by a preponderance of the evidence that the irrevocable proxies signed as a result of a shareholders' agreement are invalid, since the preponderance of evidence criterion was inappropriately utilized upon the motion to dismiss, in that every reasonable inference must be drawn from the record in plaintiff's favor, since Bus Corp Law § 609 allows for the creation of irrevocable general proxies within the rubric of a shareholders' agreement, since if the agreement is subject to attack the proxies will be vulnerable, and since a trial was necessary to determine if the shareholders' agreement should be reformed or rescinded. Re Schmidt (1983, 2d Dept) 97 A.D.2d 244, 468 N.Y.S.2d 663

2. Notice and time limitations

In connection with a proceeding under this section to invalidate election of certain named directors on the ground that their election on July 11, 1963 was illegal failure of petitioners to act within a reasonable period of time after the election of directors was confirmed, with full disclosure of circumstances, at the annual meeting held April 8, 1964, supported dismissal of the petition. Carter v Muscat (1964, 1st Dept) 21 A.D.2d 543, 251 N.Y.S.2d 378

CPLR 217 and § 619 of the Business Corporation Law must be construed together, and a minority stockholder who waited eight months after the stockholder's meeting to institute an action against the corporation, was guilty of laches and the long delay constituted a waiver of his objections. Scheeler v Buffalo Wire Works Co. (1966) 50 Misc. 2d 158, 269 N.Y.S.2d 897

The four month period of limitation of CPLR 217 applies to this section. Christ v Lake Erie Distributors, Inc. (1966) 51 Misc. 2d 811, 273 N.Y.S.2d 878, mod on other grounds (4th Dept) 28 A.D.2d 817, 282 N.Y.S.2d 728 and and order affd 28 A.D.2d 825, 282 N.Y.S.2d 728

Petition instituted on Sept. 30 to set aside election of corporate directors and to order a new election under this section was barred by four month limitation of CPLR § 217, where election of said directors and their acceptance occurred on March 12. Christ v Lake Erie Distributors, Inc. (1966) 51 Misc. 2d 811, 273 N.Y.S.2d 878, mod on other grounds (4th Dept) 28 A.D.2d 817, 282 N.Y.S.2d 728 and and order affd 28 A.D.2d 825, 282 N.Y.S.2d 728

3. Parties

A proceeding to contest election of directors may only be brought by a stockholder "aggrieved" by the election, and the stockholder cannot complain of irregularities in an election wherein he had no right to vote. Petition of Caplan (1964, 1st Dept) 20 A.D.2d 301, 246 N.Y.S.2d 913, affd 14 N.Y.2d 679, 249 N.Y.S.2d 877, 198 N.E.2d 908

Where plaintiff was vice president of corporation and one defendant was president and other was secretary and treasurer thereof, if plaintiff felt aggrieved at action of defendants in calling a special meeting of stockholders at which new officers and directors were elected, his remedy was provided by the above statute. Boyer v Legal Estates, Inc. (1964) 44 Misc. 2d 1065, 255 N.Y.S.2d 955

4. Reviewable issues

In a proceeding to set aside the issuance of previously unissued stock and the subsequent election of directors based on the votes of the new shareholdings, it is inappropriate to determine the scope or application of the equitable doctrine that, in issuing authorized but heretofore unissued shares of stock, corporate directors have a fiduciary responsibility to treat all their shareholders fairly and evenly, without first determining the equitable ownership of the outstanding shares of stock on which to predicate a decision. A determination of the underlying beneficial interests of the parties is necessary to an enforcement of their rights with respect to the corporation and, accordingly, the case is remitted to the Supreme Court for a determination of such ownership. Re Buckley (1978) 44 N.Y.2d 560, 406 N.Y.S.2d 739, 378 N.E.2d 103

This section provides for hearing proofs and allegations of the parties, which would permit determination of issues as to whether ownership of stock represented by respondents constituted "working control" of the corporation, had the proceeding been timely instituted. Carter v Muscat (1964, 1st Dept) 21 A.D.2d 543, 251 N.Y.S.2d 378

In challenge to election of corporate officers, hearing was appropriate to determine relationship of parties and their status or lack thereof as corporate directors or officers. Abelow v Diamond (1976, 1st Dept) 54 A.D.2d 656, 388 N.Y.S.2d 10

Validity of removal of petitioner as director and question of application of provisions of shareholders' agreement concerning rights of shareholder to be retained as director by other shareholders were not legal issues reviewable under Business Corporation Law section providing for summary review of validity of elections of directors. Springut v Don & Bob Restaurants, Inc. (1977, 4th Dept) 57 A.D.2d 302, 394 N.Y.S.2d 971

Whether a director can be removed before end of term of office is question governed by certificate of incorporation, bylaws, applicable shareholder agreements and the Business Corporation Law, and removal is not cognizable under section providing for summary review of validity of elections of directors. Springut v Don & Bob Restaurants, Inc. (1977, 4th Dept) 57 A.D.2d 302, 394 N.Y.S.2d 971

An action brought under Bus Corp Law § 611 to annul the tabulation of votes at an annual corporate shareholders' meeting on the ground that the election inspectors were not disinterested, breached their duties, and were negligent and unfair was properly dismissed, since § 611 only prescribes the duties of an inspector at the shareholders' meeting and does not provide the mechanism for challenging the results of such a meeting, and since the exclusive methods for testing the validity of an election are either an action in the nature of quo warranto brought by the attorney general or a proceeding instituted under Bus Corp Law § 619. A proceeding brought pursuant to § 619 several days earlier, however, alleging that the vote was invalid because of certain irregularities, was sufficiently broad to cover the matters raised in the purported § 611 action. Re Schmidt (1983, 2d Dept) 97 A.D.2d 244, 468 N.Y.S.2d 663

In proceeding under CLS Bus Corp § 619 to determine propriety of election of corporate directors, it was unnecessary to determine whether 30 shares of stock held by certain corporate entity were validly issued, since election result would have been same even if those shares had not been voted. Chiulli v Cross Westchester Dev. Corp. (1987, 2d Dept) 130 A.D.2d 616, 515 N.Y.S.2d 546, later proceeding (2d Dept) 130 A.D.2d 617, 515 N.Y.S.2d 547, later proceeding (2d Dept) 130 A.D.2d 618, 515 N.Y.S.2d 717

In action for fraud and to enjoin defendant from acting as corporate president, shareholder's cause of action alleging invalidity of election of corporate directors was properly dismissed with prejudice where issue had already been litigated in prior proceeding pursuant to CLS Bus Corp § 619; statutory proceeding is exclusive method available to shareholder to test validity of election of director. Chiulli v Reiter (1987, 2d Dept) 130 A.D.2d 617, 515 N.Y.S.2d 547, later proceeding (2d Dept) 130 A.D.2d 618, 515 N.Y.S.2d 717

Court erred in allowing each shareholder to vote "on each of the agenda items considered at the Special Meeting of March 6, 1996" at new special meeting; under CLS Bus Corp § 619, only validity of election may be challenged, and validity of other action taken at meeting is not subject to review. Heisler v Gingras (1997, 3d Dept) 235 A.D.2d 900, 652 N.Y.S.2d 841, motion gr 89 N.Y.2d 1007, 657 N.Y.S.2d 401, 679 N.E.2d 640 and app dismd (3d Dept) 238 A.D.2d 702, 656 N.Y.S.2d 70 and mod, affd 90 N.Y.2d 682, 665 N.Y.S.2d 59, 687 N.E.2d 1342, reargument den 91 N.Y.2d 867, 668 N.Y.S.2d 563, 691 N.E.2d 635

5. Grounds for interventions

Order requiring that new election be held for board of directors of closely held corporation was within Supreme Court's discretionary equity powers under CLS Bus Corp § 619 where shareholder who held voting rights of majority of corporation's stock had voted to adjourn shareholders' meeting and walked out, and remaining shareholders had then elected slate of directors in his absence. Ronnen v Ajax Elec. Motor Corp. (1996) 88 N.Y.2d 582, 648 N.Y.S.2d 422, 671 N.E.2d 534

In proceeding under CLS Bus Corp § 619 to set aside election of corporate directors, Special Term correctly concluded that election was properly conducted, even though petitioning shareholder alleged that he had attended shareholders' meeting only to protest fact that meeting was held at improper location and contended that his shares should not have been counted in determining whether there was quorum present, where shareholder had attended meeting without complaining as to its location, and thus waived any objection which he might have had in that respect. Chiulli v Cross Westchester Dev. Corp. (1987, 2d Dept) 130 A.D.2d 616, 515 N.Y.S.2d 546, later proceeding (2d Dept) 130 A.D.2d 617, 515 N.Y.S.2d 547, later proceeding (2d Dept) 130 A.D.2d 618, 515 N.Y.S.2d 717

Trial court properly determined that purported elections to elect a board of directors were not valid and directed a new special shareholders' meeting be held and supervised by a referee, where the meeting was held after the parties entered into an on-the-record stipulation in an earlier action in which they agreed that all four shareholders were to serve as directors. Further, the bylaws provided that a board member could be removed only upon a vote of a majority of the directors or shareholders, and it was undisputed that a majority of the directors or shareholders did not vote for the removal. Wynkoop v 622A President St. Owners Corp., 2019 N.Y. App. Div. LEXIS 1369 (N.Y. App. Div. 2d Dep't 2019).

In proceeding under this section to declare invalid the election of directors and officers of a corporation, the petitioner, the president of the corporation, who, according to the bylaws, was to preside at all meetings, could not unilaterally adjourn a duly constituted meeting of the shareholders, at which a quorum was present, and thereby prevent the termination of his term of office and thwart any elective or other action the corporate body might wish to take, and the election of directors and officers at such meeting would be confirmed.

Re Petition of Dollinger Corp. (1966) 51 Misc. 2d 802, 274 N.Y.S.2d 285

In a derivative action by shareholders of a bank, the recent re-election of the defendant board of directors was set aside where the plaintiffs' proposed nominees for the election had been arbitrarily rejected at the election meeting, and where at least three of the rejected nominees could have been elected by cumulative voting of the plaintiffs and their allies. Wolpert v First Nat. Bank (1974, ED NY) 381 F. Supp. 625

6. Power of directors

Where corporate by-laws provided that vacancies in the board of directors could be filled by the directors in office, a vote of two of the three directors in office was sufficient to fill a vacancy on the board despite a charter and by-law provision that a quorum should consist of 75 percent of the directors and the votes of 75 percent of the directors were necessary for the transaction of business. Jacobson v Moskowitz (1970) 27 N.Y.2d 67, 313 N.Y.S.2d 684, 261 N.E.2d 613

Where corporate bylaws provide that the Board of Directors may remove any officer, with or without cause, the Board of Directors has power to discharge a dissenting and uncooperative president without limitation or restriction. Republic Corp. v Carter (1964, 1st Dept) 22 A.D.2d 29, 253 N.Y.S.2d 280, affd 15 N.Y.2d 661, 255 N.Y.S.2d 875, 204 N.E.2d 206

Certain amendments to corporate bylaws which were adopted at purported meeting of board of directors were null and void where bylaws required quorum of 2 directors to transact corporate business, and there was only one director present at meeting in question. Stile v Antico (2000, 2d Dept) 272 A.D.2d 403, 707 N.Y.S.2d 227

Original corporate bylaws could not be amended at shareholders meeting to provide for restructuring of board of directors from 2 to 4 directors, nor could bylaws be amended to eliminate requirement that directors be chosen from among shareholders, where bylaws required quorum of 2 directors to transact corporate business, and only one director was present at meeting. Stile v Antico (2000, 2d Dept) 272 A.D.2d 403, 707 N.Y.S.2d 227

Petitioner's election to board of directors of her cooperative was not invalid on ground that she was delinquent on her carrying charges for August and September 1988 and thus ineligible under cooperative's by-laws to have her name placed in nomination on September 13, 1988 since (1) by allowing petitioner to make late payments of 3 to 4 weeks each month over past year without notifying her that future rent had to be paid on first of month, cooperative waived its right to enforce provision of by-laws that tenant nominated to run for directorship not be delinquent in payment of carrying charges at time of nomination, and (2) uncontroverted evidence established that petitioner's August carrying charge check was, through no fault of petitioner, incorrectly refused payment by her bank.Smith v Ellerbe (1988, Sup) 141 Misc. 2d 699, 534 N.Y.S.2d 100

7. Miscellaneous

Since only the validity of elections may be challenged by summary proceeding under Business Corporation Law § 619, the validity of other action taken at the meeting may not be considered. Goldfield Corp. v General Host Corp. (1971) 29 N.Y.2d 264, 327 N.Y.S.2d 330, 277 N.E.2d 387

In proceeding under CLS Bus Corp § 619 for judicial enforcement of petitioners' shareholder status in law firm, estoppel theory did not apply absent exceptional circumstances, where corporate bylaws stated that "no certificate representing shares shall be issued until the full amount of consideration therefor has been paid, except as otherwise permitted by law"; equitable considerations might generate indefiniteness, and detrimentally diminish stability and stake of already inherently vulnerable minority shareholders in professional corporations and other types of small business corporations. Heisler v Gingras (1997) 90 N.Y.2d 682, 665 N.Y.S.2d 59, 687 N.E.2d 1342, reargument den (NY) 1997 N.Y. LEXIS 4279

In proceeding under CLS Bus Corp § 619, petitioner established that he acquired shareholder status in law firm where (1) he provided consideration for shares as prescribed by corporate bylaws and CLS Bus Corp § 504 by bringing 15 years of experience and professional relationship to firm, which had encouraged him to join so that he might open its new office, (2) he did open and manage firm's new office, (3) firm publicly proclaimed that he was joining as managing shareholder, and (4) he regularly participated in shareholder meetings and voted as shareholder. Heisler v Gingras (1997) 90 N.Y.2d 682, 665 N.Y.S.2d 59, 687 N.E.2d 1342, reargument den (NY) 1997 N.Y. LEXIS 4279

Business Corporation Law

In proceeding under CLS Bus Corp § 619, petitioner failed to establish that he acquired shareholder status in law firm where he was informed that he would not become shareholder or be issued any shares of stock until specific amount of consideration for shares was determined and paid, he expressly declined to pay any consideration for shares offered to him, and record did not demonstrate that he ever voted as shareholder. Heisler v Gingras (1997) 90 N.Y.2d 682, 665 N.Y.S.2d 59, 687 N.E.2d 1342, reargument den (NY) 1997 N.Y. LEXIS 4279

In proceeding under CLS Bus Corp § 619 seeking either to confirm corporate election held at special shareholders' meeting, or to order new election, professional corporation's annual statement filed under CLS Bus Corp § 1514, which listed petitioners as shareholders, was not determinative of issue of petitioners' status and entitlement to be treated as shareholders in law firm. Heisler v Gingras (1997) 90 N.Y.2d 682, 665 N.Y.S.2d 59, 687 N.E.2d 1342, reargument den (NY) 1997 N.Y. LEXIS 4279

Proceedings under this section for the removal of a corporate officer are not limited to a stockholder's action or a proceeding by way of quo warranto unless usurpation of the office is claimed. Republic Corp. v Carter (1964, 1st Dept) 22 A.D.2d 29, 253 N.Y.S.2d 280, affd 15 N.Y.2d 661, 255 N.Y.S.2d 875, 204 N.E.2d 206

Although Bus Corp Law § 619 does not authorize judicial inquiry into the validilty of amendments to articles of incorporation adopted at an annual shreholders' meeting, since the adoption of the amendments was not relevant to the election, dismissal of the proceeding challenging the amendments was not warranted, for the proceeding, pursuant to CPLR § 103, could be deemed converted into an action to determine the validilty of the amendments and for other appropriate relief. Re Schmidt (1983, 2d Dept) 97 A.D.2d 244, 468 N.Y.S.2d 663

Court properly denied petition to set aside election of directors of cooperative corporation where result would have been same even if petitioner had been allowed to vote all shares he allegedly was entitled to vote. In re Laufer (1995, 2d Dept) 221 A.D.2d 342, 633 N.Y.S.2d 512

Court properly denied petitioner's motion to confirm election of board of directors of corporation where election was conducted in violation of offering plan and by-laws, inasmuch as sponsor used its votes to elect all 7 board members after having nominated 3 sponsor-related members. Flagg Court Realty Co. v Flagg Court Owners Corp. (1996, 2d Dept) 230 A.D.2d 740, 646 N.Y.S.2d 298

Court incorrectly gave effect to shareholder unanimity provision contained in corporation's original bylaws where corporation's certificate of incorporation did not contain shareholder unanimity provision. Stile v Antico (2000, 2d Dept) 272 A.D.2d 403, 707 N.Y.S.2d 227

Application for judgment declaring that petitioner and 2 others were duly elected directors of subject corporation, and to enjoin respondents from acting or holding themselves out as officers, directors, employees or representatives of corporation, was properly denied where (1) corporate bylaws stated that petitioner could not act both personally and by proxy at meeting at which he was elected, and thus proxy used by him as device for his nomination to board was invalid and ensuing election was nullity, and (2) court was not required to order new election under CLS Bus Corp § 619. Cinotti v Davidsohn (2001, 1st Dept) 283 A.D.2d 280, 724 N.Y.S.2d 312

Trial court properly denied a resident's motion pursuant to N.Y. Bus. Corp. Law § 619 to set aside the election of the board of directors of a residential cooperative corporation, because the resident did not come to court with clean hands and therefore could not obtain equitable relief. Lago v 87-10 51st Ave. Owners Corp. (2003, A.D., 2d Dept) 753 N.Y.S.2d 733

UNDER FORMER GEN CORP § 25

1. In general

According to most decisions, § 25 of former Gen. Corp. L. was so phrased as to constrain the court to one of two alternative determinations, either confirming the election in question, or setting it aside, in which latter case it could likewise order a new election. Application of Kaminsky (1937) 251 A.D. 132, 295 N.Y.S. 989, reh den 251 A.D. 795, 298 N.Y.S. 171 and affd without op 277 N.Y. 524, 13 N.E.2d 456; Re Machinery Builders, Inc. (1943, Sup) 44 N.Y.S.2d 198; Burke v Wiswall (1948) 193 Misc 14, 85 N.Y.S.2d 187

Section 25 of former Gen. Corp. L. was enacted to give the court power to test title to corporate offices in a summary manner and without resort to the cumbersome proceedings incident to quo warranto. Re William Faehndrich, Inc. (1957) 2 N.Y.2d 468, 161

N.Y.S.2d 99, 141 N.E.2d 597;Re Lake Placid Co. (1948) 274 A.D. 205, 81 N.Y.S.2d 36; Re George Ringler & Co. (1912) 204 N.Y. 30, 97 N.E. 593

The power of a court under former § 25 was to confirm an election or order a new election, as justice might require, and it had no authority to go far beyond this by setting aside an election already held and ordering a new election where there was a deadlock in control and no possibility of a change in result. Jacobs v Ostow & Jacobs, Inc. (1960, 1st Dept) 12 A.D.2d 613, 209 N.Y.S.2d 37

Some decisions, however, did not so narrowly circumscribe the court's authority and discretion under § 25 of former Gen. Corp. L., sanctioning a broad exercise of equitable powers if the election was clouded with doubt or tainted with questionable circumstances. Wyatt v Armstrong (1945) 186 Misc 216, 59 N.Y.S.2d 502

Section 25 of former Gen. Corp. L. was not regarded as providing an exclusive remedy, and the remedy under § 1208 of former Civil Practice Act, to test right to office, remained available, with right of recourse to either. Tabulating Card Co. v Leidesdorf (1961) 32 Misc. 2d 720, 223 N.Y.S.2d 652; Application of Porea (1961) 29 Misc. 2d 48, 215 N.Y.S.2d 881; Merchants' Loan & Invest. Corp. v Abramson (1925) 214 A.D. 252, 212 N.Y.S. 193, affd without op 242 N.Y. 587, 152 N.E. 438

2. Applicability

Remedies other than under § 25 of former Gen. Corp. L. or by quo warranto were not ordinarily considered available where § 25 covered the situation. Re Moscowitz (1923) 206 A.D. 289, 200 N.Y.S. 630; People ex rel. Putzel v Simonson (1891) 61 Hun 338, 16 N.Y.S. 118

Elections held by boards of directors, such as those to fill vacancies, as well as elections by shareholders, were within the coverage of § 25 of former Gen. Corp. L. Re National Pleasure Tours, Inc. (1927) 131 Misc 84, 225 N.Y.S. 307; Re George Ringler & Co. (1912) 204 N.Y. 30, 97 N.E. 593; Gearing v Kelly (1962) 11 N.Y.2d 201, 227 N.Y.S.2d 897, 182 N.E.2d 391

Section 25 of former Gen Corp L was considered applicable to election of directors for a savings and loan association, as well as other corporations, providing a more appropriate remedy than a declaratory judgment suit for challenging validity of by-laws of the association involved in the dispute.Stuberfield v Long Island City Sav. & Loan Asso. (1962) 37 Misc. 2d 811, 235 N.Y.S.2d 908

Action taken to oust or remove directors, however, was not deemed an "election" within the coverage of § 25 of former Gen. Corp. L. Re Tama (1954, Sup) 137 N.Y.S.2d 248; Roossin v Louis Roossin Soda Fountain Co. (1943) 181 Misc 938, 43 N.Y.S.2d 389

3. Notice and time limitations

Under varying circumstances, petitioners seeking to have elections set aside were held to be estopped or to have waived their rights to invoke § 25 of former Gen. Corp. L. One such circumstance was deliberately refraining from attending the meeting after receipt of due notice. Re P. F. Keogh, Inc. (1920) 192 A.D. 624, 183 N.Y.S. 408

But if institution of the proceedings is so long delayed, or they become so involved and protracted, as to remain undetermined on approach of the next annual meeting, at which the same problems are likely to arise, the court is justified in staying the next meeting until a determination can be reached. Ohrbach v Kirkeby (1957, 1st Dept) 3 A.D.2d 269, 161 N.Y.S.2d 371

No time limitation was placed on institution of proceedings to challenge election of directors under § 25 of former Gen. Corp. L.; the four-month general limitation statute was held to be inapplicable to such proceedings, and delay in instituting them would not preclude their maintenance, at least in the absence of showing injury sustained by respondents because of the delay. Wyatt v Armstrong (1945) 186 Misc 216, 59 N.Y.S.2d 502

Where plaintiff, seeking vacation of an election of directors, not only received registered notice of the meeting, but, in addition, executed a waiver of notice of such meeting, and there is nothing to indicate that the election was improper, the petition must be denied. Saull v Seplowe (1961, Sup) 218 N.Y.S.2d 777

A petition can be sustained, moreover, where it is based on failure of the notice to shareholders to state the purpose of the meeting, regardless of petitioner's knowledge of its purpose, particularly if a litigious situation existed between factions of shareholders. Re 74 & 76 West Tremont Ave. Corp. (1958) 10 Misc. 2d 662, 173 N.Y.S.2d 154

4. Parties

The stock record and stock transfer books of the corporation did not necessarily furnish the irrefutable evidence, or the only evidence, which the court could consider in passing upon rights involved,

interests affected, or who was "aggrieved" by the election in question.
Re George Ringler & Co. (1912) 204 N.Y. 30, 97 N.E. 593

A holder of 50% of the stock of a corporation would not be granted
relief in an action to set aside election of directors because it took
place in her absence and without presence of a quorum where she
deliberately and intentionally stayed away from the meeting for the
sole purpose of preventing a quorum from assembling. Gearing v
Kelly (1962) 11 N.Y.2d 201, 227 N.Y.S.2d 897, 182 N.E.2d 391

A stockholder was not entitled to intervene in a proceeding to
annul an election of directors where she merely alleged that she was
a stockholder at the time of the motion, and did not show that she
was a stockholder at the date of election or that the former holder of
her stock did not vote for the directors whose election was sought to
be set aside. Re Scheel (1909) 134 A.D. 442, 119 N.Y.S. 295

Failure to take advantage of an opportunity to be duly represented
at the meeting and to participate in the voting may give rise to an
estoppel. Re Triennial Election of Catholic R. & B. Ass'n (1911) 142
A.D. 307, 127 N.Y.S. 143

Individual ownership of shares by petitioner was not a requisite to
proceeding under § 25 of former Gen. Corp. L.; the statute could be
invoked by the legal representative of a shareholder, such as the
executor of a shareholder's estate. Re P. F. Keogh, Inc. (1920) 192
A.D. 624, 183 N.Y.S. 408

The corporation was a necessary party defendant to proceedings
under § 25 of former Gen. Corp. L. Re P. F. Keogh, Inc. (1920) 192
A.D. 624, 183 N.Y.S. 408

Section 619 of the Bus. Corp. L. uses the words "shareholder
aggrieved" in reference to who may institute the proceeding, but
under § 25 of former Gen. Corp. L. the proceedings could be instituted
by "members" or others actually aggrieved, such as defeated candidates for election, without necessity of showing share ownership, and
even the corporation itself could maintain the proceeding. Re
Workmen's Ben. Fund (1942) 265 A.D. 176, 38 N.Y.S.2d 429, app den
265 A.D. 991, 39 N.Y.S.2d 990; Re Election of Directors of Hammond
Light & Power Co. (1928) 131 Misc 747, 228 N.Y.S. 70, affd 224 A.D.
684, 229 N.Y.S. 865

Voting in a previous election and in the election complained of,
knowing that no provision had been made for classification of
directors as required by the charter, did not constitute such ratification of an illegal act that the petitioner was not an aggrieved person,
particularly where he objected at the election and was assured that
the directors would be classified after the election. Re Election of
Directors of Baldwinsville Federal Sav. & Loan Ass'n (1944) 268 A.D.
414, 51 N.Y.S.2d 816

A petitioner seeking to have an election set aside under § 25 of
former Gen. Corp. L. had to show that he was "aggrieved" by the
result, but it was usually enough to show, in this connection, that he
was a shareholder and that the election was irregularly conducted or
that the meeting at which it was held was not duly called and
noticed. Re Lake Placid Co. (1948) 274 A.D. 205, 81 N.Y.S.2d 36;
Gearing v Kelly (1961) 29 Misc. 2d 674, 215 N.Y.S.2d 609, revd on
other grounds (1st Dept) 15 A.D.2d 219, 222 N.Y.S.2d 474, affd 11
N.Y.2d 201, 227 N.Y.S.2d 897, 182 N.E.2d 391; Petition of Melloh
(1959) 17 Misc. 2d 902, 187 N.Y.S.2d 203; Re Workmen's Ben. Fund
(1942, Sup) 36 N.Y.S.2d 662, app dismd 265 A.D. 176, 38 N.Y.S.2d
429, app den 265 A.D. 991, 39 N.Y.S.2d 990; Re Green Bus Lines, Inc.
(1937) 166 Misc 800, 2 N.Y.S.2d 556

Shareholders who attended the meeting as originally called, or a
proper adjournment thereof, at which directors could be validly
elected, but did not vote, were not entitled to complain of election of
directors not of their choice. Re Election of Directors of Bushwick Sav.
& Loan Ass'n (1947) 189 Misc 316, 70 N.Y.S.2d 478

If the petition is based on fraud in the solicitation of proxies by a
group seeking control of management, petitioner need not show that
he, himself, was deceived by the misstatements. Re R. Hoe & Co.
(1954) 14 Misc. 2d 500, 137 N.Y.S.2d 142, affd 285 A.D. 927, 139
N.Y.S.2d 883, affd 309 N.Y. 719, 128 N.E.2d 420, reh den 309 N.Y.
802, 130 N.E.2d 603

There is at least one decision to the effect that petitioner's unwarranted personal domination of the affairs of the corporation, and use
of it for his personal ends, prior to the meeting in question, may
preclude him from challenging election of others at such meeting on
the basis of mere informalities in connection with the election.
Hungarian Freedom Fighters Federation, Inc. v Samson (1961) 30
Misc. 2d 354, 219 N.Y.S.2d 348

The corporation itself was not considered a person aggrieved who
could, under § 25 of former Gen Corp L, challenge an election of

officers by its shareholders or members. Veverka v Suffolk County
Patrolemen's Benev. Asso. (1963, Sup) 236 N.Y.S.2d 917

5. Reviewable issues

The courts recognized that § 25 of former Gen. Corp. L., predecessor of this section of the Bus. Corp. L., was designed to provide an
early determination of doubts concerning validity of corporate
elections, and hence that proceedings thereunder must be conducted
in a fairly summary manner. Some decisions accordingly held that
the court could not ordinarily go into questions of actual ownership or
title to shares, such issues being properly determinable only in a
plenary action. Re William Faehndrich, Inc. (1957) 2 N.Y.2d 468, 161
N.Y.S.2d 99, 141 N.E.2d 597; Re Bruder's Estate (1950) 302 N.Y. 52,
96 N.E.2d 84; Application of Morrison (1958, 1st Dept) 7 A.D.2d 42,
180 N.Y.S.2d 760; Re Robert Clarke, Inc. (1919) 186 A.D. 216, 174
N.Y.S. 314; Farmer v A. D. Farmer & Son Type Founding Co. (1903)
83 A.D. 218, 82 N.Y.S. 228; Re Utica Fire Alarm Tel. Co. (1906) 115
A.D. 821, 101 N.Y.S. 109

Where material, the court could investigate assertions that the
election was invalid because shares issued at less than par or without
such consideration as the law requires were voted, or because shares
voted or allegedly owned by the petitioner were invalid for other
reasons. Re Prophet (1932) 236 A.D. 524, 260 N.Y.S. 239, reh den 238
A.D. 765, 261 N.Y.S. 1037; Application of Sugarman (1954) 14 Misc.
2d 507, 133 N.Y.S.2d 754, affd 285 A.D. 947, 139 N.Y.S.2d 904

Some decisions held that the court had ample authority to take
evidence concerning anything incidental to the controversy and
necessarily involved in its disposition, but not to decide equitable
claims or extraneous matters. Application of Kaminsky (1937) 251
A.D. 132, 295 N.Y.S. 989, reh den 251 A.D. 795, 298 N.Y.S. 171 and
affd without op 277 N.Y. 524, 13 N.E.2d 456

When it appeared that the adverse claims of the parties to the
proceeding were in sharp conflict with respect to matters which were
originally for determination by the inspectors of election, the court
might simply refuse to substitute itself in exercise of judgment.
Juster v Morrison (1956) 15 Misc. 2d 998, 182 N.Y.S.2d 940

6. Grounds for intervention

Section 25 of former Gen. Corp. L. was regarded as not directed to
challenging elections on the basis of technical irregularities, unless
they were of such nature and substance as to effect the result; it did
not warrant the setting aside of an election that there had been some
minor deviation from procedural requirements in calling the meeting
or holding the election, if the defect was non-prejudicial to persons in
interest and outcome of the election would obviously have been the
same in any event. George v Holstein-Friesian Ass'n of America
(1924) 238 N.Y. 513, 144 N.E. 776; Application of Siebenmann (1961)
32 Misc. 2d 92, 222 N.Y.S.2d 707; Hungarian Freedom Fighters
Federation, Inc. v Samson (1961) 30 Misc. 2d 354, 219 N.Y.S.2d 348;
Re Workmen's Ben. Fund (1942, Sup) 36 N.Y.S.2d 662, app dismd
265 A.D. 176, 38 N.Y.S.2d 429, app den 265 A.D. 991, 39 N.Y.S.2d
990; Re Crown Heights Hospital, Inc. (1944) 183 Misc 563, 49
N.Y.S.2d 658

Where amendments adopted at the annual meeting were void, an
election which followed thereunder must be set aside. Re Flushing
Hospital & Dispensary (1942) 288 N.Y. 125, 41 N.E.2d 917, remittitur
amd 288 N.Y. 735, 43 N.E.2d 356 and remittitur den 289 N.Y. 654, 44
N.E.2d 626

However, a purported election of directors at a rump session of
part of those attending an annual meeting, at a different place,
cannot be sustained. Re Bogart (1925) 215 A.D. 45, 213 N.Y.S. 137

In a proceeding under § 25 of former General Corporation Law
directors elected by less than a quorum present, and less than a
plurality of votes, under Stock Corporation Law § 55, were properly
unseated when the illegality of two proxies by the majority stockholder necessitated disregard of those votes. Re Lake Placid Co. (1948)
274 A.D. 205, 81 N.Y.S.2d 36

Fraud or intentional concealment of facts in connection with solicitation of proxies by persons seeking control over management, or
continuance of existing management, could constitute ground for
setting aside the election, if demonstrated to be a material factor in
the result. Re Petition of Ideal Mut. Ins. Co. (1959, 1st Dept) 9 A.D.2d
60, 190 N.Y.S.2d 895

Election of directors, and other business transacted at an annual
meeting of stockholders, were not subject to invalidation because
proxy solicitation statements failed to state specifically the amount of
annual retirement benefits of certain officers under a proposal to be
submitted at the meeting, or to advise stockholders of an extraordi-
narily large first quarter deficit sustained by the corporation, where it

was not the practice of the corporation to include financial statements and there was nothing in the proxy statements which was misleading. Dal-Tran Service Co. v Fifth Ave. Coach Lines, Inc. (1961, 1st Dept) 14 A.D.2d 349, 14 A.D.2d 764, 220 N.Y.S.2d 549, application gr 11 N.Y.2d 659, 225 N.Y.S.2d 738, 180 N.E.2d 897

A certain amount of misstatement or failure to make full and frank disclosure in soliciting proxies will not require overturning the results of an election, on the other hand, where it is not shown that the election was tainted with fraud, that an inequitable result was accomplished, or that the result would have been different in the absence of fraud. Dal-Tran Service Co. v Fifth Ave. Coach Lines, Inc. (1961, 1st Dept) 14 A.D.2d 349, 14 A.D.2d 764, 220 N.Y.S.2d 549, application gr 11 N.Y.2d 659, 225 N.Y.S.2d 738, 180 N.E.2d 897; Stone v Auslander (1961) 28 Misc. 2d 384, 212 N.Y.S.2d 777; Re R. Hoe & Co. (1954) 14 Misc. 2d 500, 137 N.Y.S.2d 142, affd 285 A.D. 927, 139 N.Y.S.2d 883, affd 309 N.Y. 719, 128 N.E.2d 420, reh den 309 N.Y. 802, 130 N.E.2d 603

Existence of general confusion at an annual meeting of stockholders for election of directors will not suffice to invalidate the election where no one was deprived of an opportunity to nominate candidates or to vote and it does not appear that the outcome of the election would have been different under other circumstances. Dal-Tran Service Co. v. Fifth Ave. Coach Lines, Inc. (1961, 1st Dept) 14 A.D.2d 349, 14 A.D.2d 764, 220 N.Y.S.2d 549, application gr 11 N.Y.2d 659, 225 N.Y.S.2d 738, 180 N.E.2d 897

An election of directors of a corporation must be set aside as illegal where it appears that prior to said election several stockholders transferred their stock, aggregating ninety-five shares, to the petitioner and others to whom were issued new certificates; that said transfers were later held invalid and void; that thirty-five of the ninety-five shares of stock, though represented at the annual meeting, which petitioner attended, as lawful owner of thirty shares, by proxies executed to certain stockholders, among whom were said transferees of stock, were deprived of a vote for directors, notwithstanding the fact that the transferees did not attempt to vote the stock as owners thereof but only as duly authorized representatives of the lawful owners. Re Mt. Vernon Dye Casting Corp. (1926) 127 Misc 169, 216 N.Y.S. 317

An election of five directors of corporation is voidable where the certificate of incorporation fixes the number of directors at three and this number has not been increased as provided by statute. Such an election may be set aside in a proceeding by stockholders where said stockholders did not personally or through their assignors participate in the election. Re Election of Directors of Hammond Light & Power Co. (1928) 131 Misc 747, 228 N.Y.S. 70, affd 224 A.D. 684, 229 N.Y.S. 865

Where proxies were solicited without informing the electors that the persons on whose behalf they were solicited had previously submitted undated resignations and, at least in some cases, the proxies were used to give control of the corporation to others than those named as nominees for the directorships involved, the court was justified in setting aside the election. Wyatt v Armstrong (1945) 186 Misc 216, 59 N.Y.S.2d 502

Mere existence of dispute over eligibility to vote certain shares or the validity and effectiveness of certain proxies would not justify court intervention, if these matters were duly and impartially considered at the time of the meeting and not disposed of in an arbitrary manner. Burke v Wiswall (1948) 193 Misc 14, 85 N.Y.S.2d 187

An adjournment of the meeting at which the election was held, or the fact that the meeting was held in some slightly different place, pursuant to notice of adjournment or change of place, was not ordinarily considered sufficient ground for setting the election aside, where the change was in good faith and the notice, under the circumstances, was reasonable, though not fully in accord with notice of meeting requirements. Petition of Weinstein (1953) 203 Misc 975, 119 N.Y.S.2d 457; Application of Havender (1943) 181 Misc 989, 44 N.Y.S.2d 213, affd without op 267 A.D. 860, 47 N.Y.S.2d 114, reh and app den 267 A.D. 901, 48 N.Y.S.2d 325

An election of certain directors was not invalidated under § 25 of former Gen. Corp. L. merely because campaign material given by a group of stockholders to workers soliciting proxies had not been cleared by the Securities and Exchange Commission. Re R. Hoe & Co. (1954) 14 Misc. 2d 500, 137 N.Y.S.2d 142, affd 285 A.D. 927, 139 N.Y.S.2d 883, affd 309 N.Y. 719, 128 N.E.2d 420, reh den 309 N.Y. 802, 130 N.E.2d 603

Misrepresentation as to how proxies solicited will be used and voted may likewise be sufficient to warrant the setting aside of an election, at the instance of interested persons who were misled by the misrepresentations and aggrieved by the result. Re Petition of Ideal Mut. Ins. Co. (1959) 18 Misc. 2d 127, 190 N.Y.S.2d 887, affd (1st Dept) 9 A.D.2d 60, 190 N.Y.S.2d 895; Re R. Hoe & Co. (1954) 14 Misc. 2d 500, 137 N.Y.S.2d 142, affd 285 A.D. 927, 139 N.Y.S.2d 883, affd 309 N.Y. 719, 128 N.E.2d 420, reh den 309 N.Y. 802, 130 N.E.2d 603

In a proceeding pursuant to § 25 of former Gen. Corp. L. for an order setting aside election of directors at a stockholders' annual meeting, the application was granted and a new election ordered in the interest of justice because the Board of Directors, shortly before the annual meeting, had amended the by-laws so as to preclude nomination of directors from the floor, but the chairman of the meeting refused to submit validity of this by-law change to a vote of the stockholders. Re Scharf (1961) 28 Misc. 2d 869, 28 M2d 869, 216 N.Y.S.2d 775, mod and remitted for trial on all issues (1st Dept) 15 A.D.2d 563, 223 N.Y.S.2d 307

A petition seeking to set aside an election because petitioner was uninformed concerning bylaws providing for a three-man board of directors, and thought that eleven would be elected because the certificate of incorporation authorized a board of from three to eleven directors, is insufficient to invoke judicial consideration. Application of Siebenmann (1961) 32 Misc. 2d 92, 222 N.Y.S.2d 707

The court directed a new election where great majority of stockholders at election had no warning that an attempt was to be made to alter the customary course of corporate elections. Application of Garrett (1954, Sup) 132 N.Y.S.2d 373

7. Remedial action

Under § 25 of former Gen. Corp. L. it was held that the court had no power to supervise an election which it had ordered. Re Flushing Hospital & Dispensary (1942) 289 N.Y. 654, 44 N.E.2d 626

In one former § 25 decision by the Court of Appeals it was flatly stated that the Supreme Court, in a proceeding under that section of the Gen. Corp. L., could not vacate a corporate election without ordering a new one. Re William Faehndrich, Inc. (1957) 2 N.Y.2d 468, 161 N.Y.S.2d 99, 141 N.E.2d 597

The court sat as a court of equity in proceedings under § 25 of former Gen. Corp. L., and, while it could order a new election if justice so required, would not do so merely to permit a holder of 50% of the stock to attack action taken by the board of directors by reason of conduct of one of them which she had actively encouraged. Gearing v Kelly (1962) 11 N.Y.2d 201, 227 N.Y.S.2d 897, 182 N.E.2d 391

The court could, however, properly provide in its order that all persons who are stockholders when a new election is held shall be allowed to vote thereat and to restrain issuance of new stock or bonds pending election. Re Election of Directors (1911) 145 A.D. 623, 130 N.Y.S. 414

Ordinarily, where the grounds advanced by petitioner in a former § 25 proceeding were determined in his favor, such as that his right to vote was defeated by an invalid forfeiture of his stock, the court should set aside the election and order a new election. Re Election of Directors (1911) 145 A.D. 623, 130 N.Y.S. 414

That section of former Gen. Corp. L., moreover, could be invoked only after a purported election had been held and furnished no basis for court intervention in advance to determine voting rights and other potential disputes which might arise, except in connection with ordering a new election after exercising its power to set aside one already held. Re Trustees of Washington Ave. Baptist Church (1926) 215 A.D. 529, 214 N.Y.S. 259; Salerno v J S Painting Corp. (1958) 12 Misc. 2d 856, 171 N.Y.S.2d 323; Re Green Bus Lines, Inc. (1937) 166 Misc 800, 2 N.Y.S.2d 556

Under former § 25 the court had no authority to dismiss the proceedings without prejudice to a new proceeding if the directors had not been classified as to terms of office at the next annual election, lack of such classification being the basis for the existing proceeding. Re Election of Directors of Baldwinsville Federal Sav. & Loan Ass'n (1944) 268 A.D. 414, 51 N.Y.S.2d 816

But it is not to be implied from existence of a statutory remedy for challenging an election after it has taken place that a court necessarily lacks power to enjoin holding of an election in advance of the event, upon an adequate showing of fraud in solicitation of proxies, or the like, the objective being to stay the election pending investigation of the charges. Segal v Bresnick (1952) 30 Misc. 2d 569, 222 N.Y.S.2d 768

A motion to disaffirm the election of directors and officers of two corporations was granted but a new election was not ordered where the stockholders had previously agreed that all corporate action must be by unanimous vote and that for ten years the officers and directors could not be removed except by voluntary resignation. Application of Katz (1955) 2 Misc. 2d 325, 143 N.Y.S.2d 282, affd (1st Dept) 1 A.D.2d 657, 147 N.Y.S.2d 10, see Re Application of Katz (1955) 308 N.Y. 789, 125 N.E.2d 433

It was likewise held that the summary nature of former § 25 proceedings made it improper to pray or petition for summary determination of validity of a corporate election in a plenary action in equity in the nature of a stockholders' derivative suit, seeking damages and other relief. Saull v Seplowe (1961, Sup) 218 N.Y.S.2d 777

8. Power of directors

If an election of directors is not duly challenged, those who are declared elected ordinarily attain the status of directors and officers at least de facto, as such, eligible to call subsequent meetings of directors and shareholders. Petition of Weinstein (1953) 203 Misc 975, 119 N.Y.S.2d 457

9. Miscellaneous

Section 25 of former Gen. Corp. L., because of the broad scope of that law in application to all manner of corporations, was not confined to stock, profit, or business corporations and was often availed of to test right to elected office in a membership or other type of non-profit corporation and various corporations organized under special laws. See, for example,Re Election of Directors of Baldwinsville Federal Sav. & Loan Ass'n (1944) 268 A.D. 414, 51 N.Y.S.2d 816; Re Lawrence-Cedarhurst Bank (1936) 247 A.D. 528, 288 N.Y.S. 301, affd 272 N.Y. 646, 5 N.E.2d 374; Re Empire State Supreme Lodge D. of H. (1907) 118 A.D. 616, 103 N.Y.S. 1124; Stone v Auslander (1961) 28 Misc. 2d 384, 212 N.Y.S.2d 777

The proceedings envisioned by § 25 of former Gen. Corp. L. were considered, in one decision, too summary in nature to lend themselves to the delays entailed in taking depositions. Re Scharf (1961) 28 Misc. 2d 869, 216 N.Y.S.2d 775, mod (2d Dept) 15 A.D.2d 563, 223 N.Y.S.2d 307

Nothing in § 25 of former Gen. Corp. L. required the court to take testimony, and it could accordingly determine the controversy on the basis of a written stipulation of facts, no provision being made for trial of issues by a jury. Petition of Serenbetz (1943, Sup) 46 N.Y.S.2d 475, affd 267 A.D. 836, 46 N.Y.S.2d 127

§ 620. Agreements as to voting; provision in certificate of incorporation as to control of directors

(a) An agreement between two or more shareholders, if in writing and signed by the parties thereto, may provide that in exercising any voting rights, the shares held by them shall be voted as therein provided, or as they may agree, or as determined in accordance with a procedure agreed upon by them.

(b) A provision in the certificate of incorporation otherwise prohibited by law because it improperly restricts the board in its management of the business of the corporation, or improperly transfers to one or more shareholders or to one or more persons or corporations to be selected by him or them, all or any part of such management otherwise within the authority of the board under this chapter, shall nevertheless be valid:

(1) If all the incorporators or holders of record of all outstanding shares, whether or not having voting power, have authorized such provision in the certificate of incorporation or an amendment thereof; and

(2) If, subsequent to the adoption of such provision, shares are transferred or issued only to persons who had knowledge or notice thereof or consented in writing to such provision.

(c) A provision authorized by paragraph (b) shall be valid only so long as no shares of the corporation are listed on a national securities exchange or regularly quoted in an over-the-counter market by one or more members of a national or affiliated securities association.

(d) (1) Except as provided in paragraph (e), an amendment to strike out a provision authorized by paragraph (b) shall be authorized at a meeting of shareholders by (A) (i) for any corporation in existence on the effective date of subparagraph (2) of this paragraph, two-thirds of the votes of the shares entitled to vote thereon and (ii) for any corporation in existence on the effective date of this clause the certificate of incorporation of which expressly provides such and for any corporation incorporated after the effective date of subparagraph (2) of this paragraph, a majority of the votes of the shares entitled to vote thereon or (B) in either case, by such greater proportion of votes of shares as may be required by the certificate of incorporation for that purpose.

(2) Any corporation may adopt an amendment of the certificate of incorporation in accordance with the applicable clause or subclause of subparagraph (1) of this paragraph to provide that any further amendment of the certificate of incorporation that strikes out a provision authorized by paragraph (b) of this section shall be authorized at a meeting of the shareholders by a specified proportion of votes of the shares, or votes of a particular class or series of shares, entitled to vote thereon, provided that such proportion may not be less than a majority.

(e) Alternatively, if a provision authorized by paragraph (b) shall have ceased to be valid under this section, the board may authorize a certificate of amendment under section 805 (Certificate of amendment; contents) striking out such provision. Such certificate shall set forth the event by reason of which the provision ceased to be valid.

(f) The effect of any such provision authorized by paragraph (b) shall be to relieve the directors and impose upon the shareholders authorizing the same or consenting thereto the liability for managerial acts or omissions that is imposed on directors by this chapter to the extent that and so long as the discretion or powers of the board in its management of corporate affairs is controlled by any such provision.

(g) If the certificate of incorporation of any corporation contains a provision authorized by paragraph (b), the existence of such provision shall be noted conspicuously on the face or back of every certificate for shares issued by such corporation.

History: Add, L 1961, ch 855, eff Sept 1, 1963; amd, L 1962, ch 834, § 37, eff Sept 1, 1963; L 1963, ch 746, eff Sept 1, 1963; L 1964, ch 725, § 6, eff June 1, 1964; L 1965, ch 803, §§ 18, 19, eff Sept 1, 1965; L 1997, ch 449, § 35, eff Feb 22, 1998; L 1998, ch 17, § 8, eff Feb 19, 1998, deemed eff Feb 22, 1998.

CASE ANNOTATIONS

An agreement between corporate shareholders, which includes illegal provisions regarding the election of corporate officers and the fixation of their compensation, does not preclude enforcement of a provision for a stock purchase option contained in the same agreement, where, during the seven-year life of the agreement, there was no intrusion on the unfettered management of corporate affairs by the board of directors, as the parties ignored and made no attempt to enforce the illegal portions of their agreement, and the parties did not consider enforcement of the stock purchase option to be contingent on observance of the illegal portions of the agreement. Triggs v Triggs (1978) 46 N.Y.2d 305, 413 N.Y.S.2d 325, 385 N.E.2d 1254

When all of the stockholders of a Delaware corporation enter into a written agreement which provides that, except as specified in their agreement, no "business or activities" of the corporation shall be conducted without the consent of a minority stockholder, the agreement is, as between the original parties to it, enforceable, even though all formal steps required by Delaware statute to effectuate such an agreement, including amendment of the corporate charter, have not been taken, since such a provision, although it takes all management functions away from the directors, is not against the public policy of Delaware (Delaware General Corporation Law, §§ 350, 351, 354), whose law governs said "internal matters" under the terms of the agreement and the accepted choice-of-law rule, since no New York policy stands in the way of the application of Delaware statutory and decisional law (Business Corporation Law, § 620, subd [b]) and since there are no intervening rights of third parties affected; moreover, the certificate of incorporation may be ordered reformed to reflect the stockholders' agreement by requiring the majority stockholder to file the appropriate amendments, or, more directly, he may be held estopped to rely on the absence of those amendments from the corporate charter to validate action taken over the minority stockholder's objection. Accordingly, such an agreement was violated when the corporation entered into two agreements without the minority stockholder's consent, but was not violated by the formation of two subsidiary corporations with the minority stockholder's consent, and the consent provision continues in existence as provided in the agreement, there being no mutual mistake warranting reformation of the contract to alter the minority stockholder's veto power; the intention of the parties being determinable from the words of their written agreements, interpretation of those agreements is for the court and summary judgment based on that interpretation is proper. Zion v Kurtz (1980) 50 N.Y.2d 92, 428 N.Y.S.2d 199, 405 N.E.2d 681,15 ALR4th 1061

Agreement between sister and brother, as major shareholders of closely held corporation, providing that brother would exercise voting rights over shares owned by both parties "with respect to any and all matters relating to...day-to-day operations and corporate management" conferred on brother right to vote sister's shares in election of board of directors, since management of corporation's business was, under authority of CLS Bus Corp § 701, exclusively under direction of its board of directors; different result was not required by other provisions of agreement reciting that parties agreed to vote their shares to ensure sister seat on board of directors, to ensure sister access to corporate reports, and to place cap on brother's executive compensation. Ronnen v Ajax Elec. Motor Corp. (1996) 88 N.Y.2d 582, 648 N.Y.S.2d 422, 671 N.E.2d 534

Complaint stated cause of action for breach of agreement between two sole stockholders of "incorporated partnership" that each would vote at stockholders' and directors' meetings so that the board of directors would consist of these two sole stockholders both of whom would be necessary to constitute a quorum for the transaction of business.Shubin v Surchin (1967, 1st Dept) 27 A.D.2d 452, 280 N.Y.S.2d 55

Where certificate of incorporation and bylaws were not included in record on appeal, evaluation of their applicability to petitioner's removal as director could not be made and case would therefore be remitted for further proceedings by way of motion or trial concerning validity of petitioner's removal in light of application of Business Corporation Law sections relating to removal of directors by shareholders and to agreement among shareholders as to voting rights.Springut v Don & Bob Restaurants, Inc. (1977, 4th Dept) 57 A.D.2d 302, 394 N.Y.S.2d 971

In an action brought by two of three equal shareholders in a closely held corporation against the third shareholder, the trial court erred in holding that a paragraph in the parties' shareholders' agreement which required changes in the corporate structure to receive unanimous shareholder approval was void as requiring, in the absence of an amendment to the corporation's certificate of incorporation to reflect such a provision, a voting majority greater than that specified by law, where the parties, in unanimously approving the sharehold-

ers' agreement, had intended that the ministerial act of amending the corporation's certificate of incorporation would be accomplished so as to effectuate the agreement's provisions; as requested by the third stockholder's counterclaim, judgment would be entered amending the certificate of incorporation to include the unanimity provision of the shareholders' agreement. Adler v Svingos (1981, 1st Dept) 80 A.D.2d 764, 436 N.Y.S.2d 719

In a shareholder's action to reform the shareholders' agreement in order to provide that no corporate action could be taken without the unanimous consent of all three shareholders of a corporation that operated a fast-food restaurant chain, the two other shareholders would not be enjoined from accepting management fees where the shareholders' agreement had been void and unenforceable insofar as it provided that there could be no increase of salaries without unanimous shareholders' approval, in view of the fact that the certificate of incorporation did not provide for the legality of this provision of the agreement. Gazda v Kolinski (1982, 4th Dept) 91 A.D.2d 860, 458 N.Y.S.2d 387

When all shareholders of corporation agree that it is necessary or desirable to require unanimous consent of board of directors for corporate action for which consent of board of directors is required, and further consent to amendment of certificate to reflect this understanding, and where no rights of third parties are implicated, it is proper to reform certificate of incorporation. Ench v Breslin (1997, 2d Dept) 241 A.D.2d 475, 659 N.Y.S.2d 893

Requirement in stockholders' agreement that named person be elected officer and director of corporation would not be specifically enforced where such named person was guilty of conduct such that his employment by corporation might be disruptive or otherwise against corporation's best interests. Puro v Puro (1976) 89 Misc. 2d 856, 393 N.Y.S.2d 633

Where stockholders' agreement expressly provided that it could be amended by signatories thereto, signatories' ability to modify agreement was not terminated when beneficiary under trust of corporation's shares, whom agreement required to be elected as officer and director, brought suit seeking to enforce rights thereunder. Puro v Puro (1976) 89 Misc. 2d 856, 393 N.Y.S.2d 633

Beneficiary under trust of shares of corporate stock had no vested right under provision of stockholders' agreement requiring that he be elected director and officer of corporation where such agreement expressly reserved parties' right to amend it; thus, if there ever were duty on part of signatories to elect beneficiary, that duty ended when agreement was amended so as to eliminate provision for beneficiary's election. Puro v Puro (1976) 89 Misc. 2d 856, 393 N.Y.S.2d 633

Lack of mutuality of relief barred nonparty to stockholders' agreement from obtaining specific performance of provisions of agreement requiring that he be made director and officer of corporation. Puro v Puro (1976) 89 Misc. 2d 856, 393 N.Y.S.2d 633

Amendment to "rights" plan, adopted by board of directors of banking corporation in response to second corporation's tender offer for all outstanding shares, which restricted power of duly elected directors by creating different classes of directors and permitting members of present board if reelected to act on tender offer by majority vote while prohibiting board other than current board or those approved by it from so acting unless by supermajority 2/3 vote, was invalid since certificate of incorporation contained no provision restricting action of future board nor provision requiring supermajority vote; thus, in view of probability that presence of amendment would taint yearly election of board of directors, court would enjoin enforcement thereof. Bank of New York Co. v Irving Bank Corp. (1988) 139 Misc. 2d 665, 528 N.Y.S.2d 482

Where agreement between controlling shareholders provided that parties would vote their shares "only in a mannerin which they both agree," and at later meeting of board of directors, parties to agreement and other board members chose management slate for re-election to board, sending to shareholders proxy solicitation seeking support for slate, only reasonable inference was that board members would vote personal shares in support of management slate, and shareholders' agreement was violated when party sent out counter proxy solicitation seeking votes to elect two of his designees to board. Neuman v Pike (1978, SD NY) 456 F. Supp. 1192, affd in part and revd in part on other grounds, (CA2 NY) 591 F.2d 191

UNDER FORMER LAW

There is nothing which prohibits an agreement among all stockholders as to the manner in which shares may be voted, provided such agreement does not limit the right to cast one vote for each share. Re American Fibre Chair Seat Corp. (1934) 241 A.D. 532, 272 N.Y.S. 206, affd 265 N.Y. 416, 193 N.E. 253, reh den 266 N.Y. 500, 195 N.E. 171

The commencement of a proceeding under § 25 of former Gen. Corp. L. to set aside an election of directors constituted an irrevocable election and a waiver of whatever rights the stockholders may have had under an agreement whereby stockholders would vote their stock as a unit. The arbitration called for in the stockholders' agreement could therefore not be compelled. Application of Gerakares (1956, 2d Dept) 2 A.D.2d 850, 155 N.Y.S.2d 771, reh and app den (2d Dept) 2 A.D.2d 894, 157 N.Y.S.2d 907

An agreement whereby six shareholders of a theatrical producing corporation turned back their common stock to the corporation, and which provided that three of the shareholders should each retain one share of common stock, and that two of them should have the active management of the corporation, the number of directors being reduced from six to three, and that the other directors should receive shares of new nonvoting preferred stock, was not illegal under § 27 of former Gen. Corp. L. since the management of the corporation was still in the hands of the common stockholders.Simonson v Helburn (1950) 198 Misc 430, 97 N.Y.S.2d 406

Pendency of an action by a stockholder to set aside election of existing directors, on the ground that directors must be stockholders under the certificate of incorporation and bylaws, was not ground for motion to dismiss an action by plaintiff for specific performance of a stockholders' agreement calling for her election as a director, the causes of action being different. Ohlstein v Hillcrest Paper Co. (1959) 24 Misc. 2d 212, 195 N.Y.S.2d 920

While not all agreements providing for unanimity among shareholders had to be authorized by the certificate of incorporation under earlier law, it was held, referring to § 9 of former Stock Corp. L., that an agreement which would require unanimous approval of shareholders for any corporate action would not be binding unless so authorized, and, accordingly, that disposition of property by a corporation organized to deal in real estate could not be subjected to a unanimous approval agreement not embodied in the corporation's certificate of incorporation. Fromkin v Merrall Realty, Inc. (1961) 30 Misc. 2d 288, 215 N.Y.S.2d 525, affd (2d Dept) 15 A.D.2d 919, 225 N.Y.S.2d 632

This section recognizes the right of shareholders to have their shares voted in accordance with an agreement entered into as part of the terms of a sale of certain shares as to how the shares acquired by the purchaser shall be voted.721 Corp. v Morgan Guaranty Trust Co. (1963) 40 Misc. 2d 395, 243 N.Y.S.2d 198

An agreement between shareholders to elect designated persons as directors is valid and binding, and it is enforceable as between the contracting parties as long as it does not contravene any express charter or statutory provision or contemplate fraud or wrongdoing.721 Corp. v Morgan Guaranty Trust Co. (1963) 40 Misc. 2d 395, 243 N.Y.S.2d 198

§ 621. Voting trust agreements

(a) Any shareholder or shareholders, under an agreement in writing, may transfer his or their shares to a voting trustee or trustees for the purpose of conferring the right to vote thereon for a period not exceeding ten years upon the terms and conditions therein stated. The certificates for shares so transferred shall be surrendered and cancelled and new certificates therefor issued to such trustee or trustees stating that they are issued under such agreement, and in the entry of such ownership in the record of the corporation that fact shall also be noted, and such trustee or trustees may vote the shares so transferred during the term of such agreement.

(b) The trustee or trustees shall keep available for inspection by holders of voting trust certificates at his or their office or at a place designated in such agreement or of which the holders of voting trust certificates have been notified in writing, correct and complete books and records of account relating to the trust, and a record containing the names and addresses of all persons who are holders of voting trust certificates and the number and class of shares represented by the certificates held by them and the dates when they became the owners thereof. The record may be in written form or any other form capable of being converted into written form within a reasonable time.

(c) A duplicate of every such agreement shall be filed in the office of the corporation and it and the record of voting trust certificate holders shall be subject to the same right of inspection by a shareholder of record or a holder of a voting trust certificate, in person or by agent or attorney, as are the records of the corporation under section 624 (Books and records; right of inspection, prima facie evidence). The shareholder or holder of a voting trust certificate shall be entitled to the remedies provided in that section.

(d) At any time within six months before the expiration of such voting trust agreement as originally fixed or as extended one or more times under this paragraph, one or more holders of voting trust certificates may, by agreement in writing, extend the duration of such voting trust agreement, nominating the same or substitute trustee or trustees, for an additional period not exceeding ten years. Such extension agreement shall not affect the rights or obligations of persons not parties thereto and shall in every respect comply with and be subject to all the provisions of this section applicable to the original voting trust agreement.

History: Add, L 1961, ch 855, eff Sept 1, 1963; amd, L 1962, ch 834, § 38; L 1963, ch 746, eff Sept 1, 1963.

CASE ANNOTATIONS
UNDER FORMER LAW
1. In general
2. Validity
3. Creation and terms
4. Rights, duties and liabilities
5. Extension and termination
6. Non-depositing shareholders

UNDER FORMER LAW

1. In general

A voting trust agreement under § 50 of former Stock Corp. L. need not be confined to a specifically designated purpose as required by older case law, and the voting trustees could be given discretion in formulating corporate policy to be pursued. Mannheimer v Keehn (1943) 30 Misc. 2d 584, 41 N.Y.S.2d 542, mod on other grounds 268 A.D. 813, 49 N.Y.S.2d 304, amd 268 A.D. 845, 51 N.Y.S.2d 750

2. Validity

The essence of a voting trust is that all shareholders be privileged to subscribe to the trust if they choose to do so, and a plan establishing a compulsory voting trust for all stockholders, which will deprive minority stockholders of a voice in the management of the corporation is invalid and will be enjoined.Eisenberg v Central Zone Property Corp. (1953) 306 N.Y. 58, 115 N.E.2d 652

A voting trust agreement established pursuant to § 50 of former Stock Corp. L. was prima facie valid if it did not or contemplate fraud, oppression, or wrong against other stockholders or creditors. Dal-Tran Service Co. v Fifth Ave. Coach Lines, Inc. (1961, 1st Dept) 14 A.D.2d 349, 14 A.D.2d 764, 220 N.Y.S.2d 549, application gr 11 N.Y.2d 659, 225 N.Y.S.2d 738, 180 N.E.2d 897; De Marco v Paramount Ice Corp. (1950) 30 Misc. 2d 158, 102 N.Y.S.2d 692; Mannhei-

Business Corporation Law

mer v Keehn (1943) 30 Misc. 2d 584, 41 N.Y.S.2d 542, mod on other grounds 268 A.D. 813, 49 N.Y.S.2d 304, amd 268 A.D. 845, 51 N.Y.S.2d 750

A voting trust agreement is not invalid because it may deprive minority stockholders of any right to participate directly in the election of directors of a distinct corporation in which their corporation holds a controlling interest. Dal-Tran Service Co. v Fifth Ave. Coach Lines, Inc. (1961, 1st Dept) 14 A.D.2d 349, 14 A.D.2d 764, 220 N.Y.S.2d 549, application gr 11 N.Y.2d 659, 225 N.Y.S.2d 738, 180 N.E.2d 897

Circular voting, or placing the voting power in the directors of one corporation to vote for directors of another corporation in which the first corporation holds stock, is of doubtful validity in New York, and a voting trust agreement which is designed to obviate such voting by voting as empowered by a majority of the voting shareholders, with certain discretionary and independent powers, is not invalid. Dal-Tran Service Co. v Fifth Ave. Coach Lines, Inc. (1961, 1st Dept) 14 A.D.2d 349, 14 A.D.2d 764, 220 N.Y.S.2d 549, application gr 11 N.Y.2d 659, 225 N.Y.S.2d 738, 180 N.E.2d 897

A voting trust agreement which complied structurally with the requirements of § 50 of former Stock Corp. L. and violated no provision of the by-laws of the corporation or the corporate charter, but aimed to assure stability and continuity of management for the benefit of stockholders, or likewise to consolidate and control management of another corporation in which the particular corporation had control, was not invalid, and there was no presumption that it would operate oppressively in favor of the dominant shareholders against the minority. Dal-Tran Service Co. v Fifth Ave. Coach Lines, Inc. (1961, 1st Dept) 14 A.D.2d 349, 14 A.D.2d 764, 220 N.Y.S.2d 549, application gr 11 N.Y.2d 659, 225 N.Y.S.2d 738, 180 N.E.2d 897

A voting trust agreement capable of a construction which will make it valid will not be adjudged illegal; only powers prohibited would be deemed to be withheld, if the agreement contained powers forbidden by law. Mannheimer v Keehn (1943) 30 Misc. 2d 584, 41 N.Y.S.2d 542, mod on other grounds 268 A.D. 813, 49 N.Y.S.2d 304, amd 268 A.D. 845, 51 N.Y.S.2d 750

Failure to file trust agreement does not make it invalid, but merely renders it inoperative to permit trustees to exercise the voting rights granted thereby until it is so filed, and where agreement is filed prior to trial, plaintiff's objections based on noncompliance at commencement of action will be disregarded.De Marco v Paramount Ice Corp. (1950) 30 Misc. 2d 158, 102 N.Y.S.2d 692

A provision that voting trustees be directors was valid as was a stockholders' agreement that they would continue to vote for themselves as directors.De Marco v Paramount Ice Corp. (1950) 30 Misc. 2d 158, 102 N.Y.S.2d 692

3. Creation and terms

Even though it be assumed that a voting trust agreement could contain provisions authorizing the voting trustees to consent to the destruction of the corporation and of the right of the stockholders, the power to destroy the value of such stock would not be implied merely from a power to vote the stock; only by the use of clear language can such an extraordinary power be conferred. Application of Bacon (1941) 287 N.Y. 1, 38 N.E.2d 105

Where a voting trust agreement grants power to the trustees to possess and exercise all rights of the stockholders "of every name and nature, including the right to vote or give any consent in respect of any and all shares of the capital stock of the company as may be deposited with them" but further provides for the calling by the trustees of a meeting of the holders of certificates at which they are to be entitled to vote on whether or not the business of the company shall be liquidated, the trustees have no authority to consent on behalf of the certificate holders to a sale of substantially all the assets of the corporation, except as to those who at a meeting called pursuant to the trust agreement advised the trustees to sell. Application of Bacon (1941) 287 N.Y. 1, 38 N.E.2d 105

It has been held that a statutory requirement that a voting trust agreement be "in writing" is satisfied by a court order in reorganization proceedings under the Bankruptcy Act directing, in connection with approval of a plan of reorganization, transfer of certain shares to a voting trustee to be held and voted by the trustee in accordance with the plan.277 Park Ave. Corp. v New York C. R. Co. (1949) 194 Misc 417, 90 N.Y.S.2d 214, affd without op 275 A.D. 1028, 91 N.Y.S.2d 838

A voting trust agreement is not effective until the voting trustees accept the trust. Mannheimer v Keehn (1943) 30 Misc. 2d 584, 41 N.Y.S.2d 542, mod on other grounds 268 A.D. 813, 49 N.Y.S.2d 304, amd 268 A.D. 845, 51 N.Y.S.2d 750

A voting trust agreement providing that the voting trustees shall possess and be entitled to exercise all rights, of every name and nature, including the right to vote, in respect of any and all shares of stock of the company deposited pursuant to the agreement, at any and all meetings of the stockholders of the company, upon any and all propositions which may come up at any such meeting or meetings, is not so broad as to render the instrument void in its entirety. Mannheimer v Keehn (1943) 30 Misc. 2d 584, 41 N.Y.S.2d 542, mod on other grounds 268 A.D. 813, 49 N.Y.S.2d 304, amd 268 A.D. 845, 51 N.Y.S.2d 750

Circular letters soliciting signatures of stockholders including former voting trust certificate holders for a new trust agreement in which unsigned printed copies of the new agreement were included which the stockholders were requested to sign and return do not constitute an acceptance by the voting trustees of the trust and the deposit of securities in exchange for voting trust certificates prior to the date of their official acceptance does not change the result. Mannheimer v Keehn (1943) 30 Misc. 2d 584, 41 N.Y.S.2d 542, mod on other grounds 268 A.D. 813, 49 N.Y.S.2d 304, amd 268 A.D. 845, 51 N.Y.S.2d 750

A provision concerning all questions arising among voting trustees with respect to voting, giving stockholders' consent to corporate actions, or any other matter or thing, relates exclusively to action which trustees could take as representatives of stockholders.De Marco v Paramount Ice Corp. (1950) 30 Misc. 2d 158, 102 N.Y.S.2d 692

A requirement in a trust agreement of ownership of a certain number of shares limited eligibility as voting trustees but was not a qualification for participation as a stockholder.De Marco v Paramount Ice Corp. (1950) 30 Misc. 2d 158, 102 N.Y.S.2d 692

It was held, under § 50 of former Stock Corp. L., that a "voting trust" was not created by a shareholder's testamentary bequest of stock to two trustees, only one of whom was given power to vote the stock, and that such section did not have any bearing upon a testator's right to bequeath stock subject to specific conditions. Feldsine v Feldsine (1953, Sup) 119 N.Y.S.2d 220; Re Estate of Tourneau (1956) 4 Misc. 2d 941, 156 N.Y.S.2d 793

4. Rights, duties and liabilities

A stockholder who deposits his stock under a voting trust agreement parts with the right to vote but he retains the beneficial ownership of the stock. Application of Bacon (1941) 287 N.Y. 1, 38 N.E.2d 105

Voting trust certificate holders who have objected to the sale of substantially all the assets of the corporation in process of reorganization under the Bankruptcy Act are entitled to the appointment of appraisers to determine the value of their stock or the certificates representing such stock, even though the voting trustees voted in favor of the sale. Application of Bacon (1941) 287 N.Y. 1, 38 N.E.2d 105

The nature and extent of the rights of a beneficial holder of a voting trust certificate, who has assigned his right to vote to certain voting trustees, can only be ascertained by reference to the voting trust agreement itself. Brentmore Estates v Hotel Barbizon (1942) 263 A.D. 389, 33 N.Y.S.2d 331

However, § 50 of former Stock Corp. L. was construed, in one decision, as not entitling a voting trust certificate holder to issuance of an additional certificate on the basis of a stock dividend declaration by the corporation, since the certificate holder was not a "stockholder" with respect to the additional shares constituting the dividend merely by virtue of the dividend declaration. Gertenbach v Rodnon (1939) 171 Misc 302, 12 N.Y.S.2d 518

Stockholder has no vested right to become a voting trustee or director.De Marco v Paramount Ice Corp. (1950) 30 Misc. 2d 158, 102 N.Y.S.2d 692

The provision in § 50 of former Stock Corporation Law that a stockholder, by agreement in writing, "may" transfer his stock to a voting trustee was permissive only and did not sanction compulsion of a shareholder to surrender his shares to voting trustees with surrender of his voting rights and right freely to alienate his interests. Re Kanewsky's Will (1963) 40 Misc. 2d 840, 244 N.Y.S.2d 180

While trustees of a corporation organized pursuant to a Burchill Act plan of reorganization would not be directed to permit the holder of a substantial block of voting trust certificates to inspect the voting trust certificate books and to make a list of the names, addresses and holdings of the holders of voting trust certificates in the absence of any facts from which the necessity or motivation of the application might be discerned, the trustees would be directed to mail, at the applicant's expense, any communication or communications which he might desire to send to voting trust certificate holders, provided said communications represented the facts fairly and commented fairly and no matter how unpalatable the contents might be to the trustees. Bresnick v Saypol (1945, Sup) 57 N.Y.S.2d 904, mod 270 A.D. 837, 61 N.Y.S.2d 376

Subdivision (c) of this section of the Bus. Corp. L. deals to some extent with the right to inspect records concerning voting trust certificate holders and grants holders of such certificates the remedies provided to shareholders under § 624 with respect to inspection of corporate books and records. Section 50 of former Stock Corp. L. imposed essentially the same requirements on right to inspect voting trust records as § 624 of the Bus. Corp. L. now imposes on right to inspect other corporate records. These requirements, fundamentally involving an affidavit of "good faith" in seeking the inspection, were construed in like manner as similar provisions elsewhere in the Corporation Laws. Application of Spanierman (1945, Sup) 58 N.Y.S.2d 10, adhered to (Sup) 58 N.Y.S.2d 322, affd 269 A.D. 1023, 59 N.Y.S.2d 400 and affd without op 270 A.D. 885, 61 N.Y.S.2d 923

5. Extension and termination

An oral agreement for continuing management and control of a corporation by means of a voting trust, which, by its terms, would continue for more than ten years, was unenforceable. Wygod v Makewell Hats (1942) 265 A.D. 286, 38 N.Y.S.2d 587, app den 265 A.D. 992, 39 N.Y.S.2d 988 and app dismd 290 N.Y. 656, 49 N.E.2d 619

Section 50 of former Stock Corp. L. was construed as making void any provision in a voting trust agreement which would preclude its termination and continue it in effect after ten years. Kittinger v Churchill Evangelistic Ass'n (1934) 151 Misc 350, 271 N.Y.S. 510, affd 244 A.D. 876, 281 N.Y.S. 680, reh den 245 A.D. 805, 281 N.Y.S. 409 and affd 244 A.D. 877, 281 N.Y.S. 681

But, directing attention to the permissible extension provisions of subd. (d) thereof, there was nothing in § 50 of former Stock Corp. L. to preclude a series of 10-year voting trusts if those who had deposited their stock with the trustee were permitted to withdraw at the end of the initial 10-year period. Mannheimer v Keehn (1943) 30 Misc. 2d 584, 41 N.Y.S.2d 542, mod on other grounds 268 A.D. 813, 49 N.Y.S.2d 304, amd 268 A.D. 845, 51 N.Y.S.2d 750

When a voting trust expires the trustees become trustees of a "dry trust" and such a trustee may be compelled by the beneficiary to give him a proxy. Re Atlantic City Ambassador Hotel Corp. (1946, Sup) 62 N.Y.S.2d 62

Objections of a stockholder to an option given to the corporation in connection with his acquisition of stock under an employee purchase plan and through stock dividends that a voting trust agreement, in support of which the option was given to the corporation to repurchase stock so acquired, was invalid under § 50 of former Stock Corp. L. because the term of the trust was more than ten years, and for other reasons, were all rejected on the basis of his acquiescence and consent to what was done and the absence of any prohibition in that section against a series of ten-year voting trust agreements. Martin v Graybar Electric Co. (1961, CA7 Ill) 285 F.2d 619, 41 CCH LC ¶ 50122

6. Non-depositing shareholders

The depositing stockholders under a voting trust agreement are not necessary parties in an action by a nondepositing stockholder to have the trust agreement set aside. Mannheimer v Keehn (1943) 30 Misc. 2d 584, 41 N.Y.S.2d 542, mod on other grounds 268 A.D. 813, 49 N.Y.S.2d 304, amd 268 A.D. 845, 51 N.Y.S.2d 750

A stockholder who is not a party to a voting trust agreement will be assumed to have standing in court to set the agreement aside where management of the corporation and the non-depositing stockholders are necessarily affected by existence of the trust. Mannheimer v Keehn (1943) 30 Misc. 2d 584, 41 N.Y.S.2d 542, mod on other grounds 268 A.D. 813, 49 N.Y.S.2d 304, amd 268 A.D. 845, 51 N.Y.S.2d 750

§ 622. Preemptive rights

(a) As used in this section, the term:

(1) "Unlimited dividend rights" means the right without limitation as to amount either to all or to a share of the balance of current or liquidating dividends after the payment of dividends on any shares entitled to a preference.

(2) "Equity shares" means shares of any class, whether or not preferred as to dividends or assets, which have unlimited dividend rights.

(3) "Voting rights" means the right to vote for the election of one or more directors, excluding a right so to vote which is dependent on the happening of an event specified in the certificate of incorporation which would change the voting rights of any class of shares.

(4) "Voting shares" means shares of any class which have voting rights, but does not include bonds on which voting rights are conferred under section 518 (Corporate bonds).

(5) "Preemptive right" means the right to purchase shares or other securities to be issued or subjected to rights or options to purchase, as such right is defined in this section.

(b) (1) With respect to any corporation incorporated prior to the effective date of subparagraph (2) of this paragraph, except as otherwise provided in the certificate of incorporation, and except as provided in this section, the holders of equity shares of any class, in case of the proposed issuance by the corporation of, or the proposed granting by the corporation of rights or options to purchase, its equity shares of any class or any shares or other securities convertible into or carrying rights or options to purchase its equity shares of any class, shall, if the issuance of the equity shares proposed to be issued or issuable upon exercise of such rights or options or upon conversion of such other securities would adversely affect the unlimited dividend rights of such holders, have the right during a reasonable time and on reasonable conditions, both to be fixed by the board, to purchase such shares or other securities in such proportions as shall be determined as provided in this section.

(2) With respect to any corporation incorporated on or after the effective date of this subparagraph, the holders of such shares shall not have any preemptive right, except as otherwise expressly provided in the certificate of incorporation.

(c) Except as otherwise provided in the certificate of incorporation, and except as provided in this section, the holders of voting shares of any class having any preemptive right under this paragraph on the date immediately prior to the effective date of subparagraph (2) of paragraph (b) of this section, in case of the proposed issuance by the corporation of, or the proposed granting by the corporation of rights or options to purchase, its voting shares of any class or any shares or other securities convertible into or carrying rights or options to purchase its voting shares of any class, shall, if the issuance of the voting shares proposed to be issued or issuable upon exercise of such rights or options or upon conversion of such other securities would adversely affect the voting rights of such holders, have the right during a reasonable time and on reasonable conditions, both to be fixed by the board, to purchase such shares or other securities in such proportions as shall be determined as provided in this section.

(d) The preemptive right provided for in paragraphs (b) and (c) shall entitle shareholders having such rights to purchase the shares or other securities to be offered or optioned for sale as nearly as practicable in such proportions as would, if such preemptive right were exercised, preserve the relative unlimited dividend rights and voting rights of such holders and at a price or prices not less favorable than the price or prices at which such shares or other securities are proposed to be offered for sale to others, without deduction of such reasonable expenses of and compensation for the sale, underwriting or purchase of such shares or other securities by underwriters or dealers as may lawfully be paid by the corporation. In case each of the shares entitling the holders thereof to preemptive rights does not confer the same unlimited dividend right or voting right, the board shall apportion the shares or other securities to be offered or optioned for sale among the shareholders having preemptive rights to purchase them in such proportions as in the opinion of the board shall preserve as far as practicable the relative unlimited dividend rights and voting rights of the holders at the time of such offering. The apportionment made by the board shall, in the absence of fraud or bad faith, be binding upon all shareholders.

(e) Unless otherwise provided in the certificate of incorporation, shares or other securities offered for sale or subjected to rights or options to purchase shall not be subject to preemptive rights under paragraph (b) or (c) of this section if they:

(1) Are to be issued by the board to effect a merger or consolidation or offered or subjected to rights or options for consideration other than cash;

(2) Are to be issued or subjected to rights or options under paragraph (d) of section 505 (Rights and options to purchase shares; issue of rights and options to directors, officers and employees);

(3) Are to be issued to satisfy conversion or option rights theretofore granted by the corporation;

(4) Are treasury shares;

(5) Are part of the shares or other securities of the corporation authorized in its original certificate of incorporation and are issued, sold or optioned within two years from the date of filing such certificate; or

(6) Are to be issued under a plan of reorganization approved in a proceeding under any applicable act of congress relating to reorganization of corporations.

(f) Shareholders of record entitled to preemptive rights on the record date fixed by the board under section 604 (Fixing record date), or, if no record date is fixed, then on the record date determined under section 604, and no others shall be entitled to the right defined in this section.

(g) The board shall cause to be given to each shareholder entitled to purchase shares or other securities in accordance with this section, a notice directed to him in the manner provided in section 605 (Notice of meetings of shareholders) setting forth the time within which and the terms and conditions upon which the shareholder may purchase such shares or other securities and also the apportionment made of the right to purchase among the shareholders entitled to preemptive rights. Such notice shall be given personally or by mail at least fifteen days prior to the expiration of the period during which the shareholder shall have the right to purchase. All shareholders entitled to preemptive rights to whom notice shall have been given as aforesaid shall be deemed conclusively to have had a reasonable time in which to exercise their preemptive rights.

(h) Shares or other securities which have been offered to shareholders having preemptive rights to purchase and which have not been purchased by them within the time fixed by the board may thereafter, for a period of not exceeding one year following the expiration of the time during which shareholders might have exercised such preemptive rights, be issued, sold or subjected to rights or options to any other person or persons at a price, without deduction of such reasonable expenses of and compensation for the sale, underwriting or purchase of such shares by underwriters or dealers as may lawfully be paid by the corporation, not less than that at which they were offered to such shareholders. Any such shares or other securities not so issued, sold or subjected to rights or options to others during such one year period shall thereafter again be subject to the preemptive rights of shareholders.

(i) Except as otherwise provided in the certificate of incorporation and except as provided in this section, no holder of any shares of any class shall as such holder have any preemptive right to purchase any other shares or securities of any class which at any time may be sold or offered for sale by the corporation. Unless otherwise provided in the certificate of incorporation, holders of bonds on which voting rights are conferred under section 518 shall have no preemptive rights.

History: Add, L 1961, ch 855, eff Sept 1, 1963; amd, L 1962, ch 834, § 39, eff Sept 1, 1963; L 1963, ch 746, eff Sept 1, 1963; L 1997, ch 449, § 36, eff Feb 22, 1998.

CASE ANNOTATIONS

Although preemptive rights, as such, do not attach to treasury stock in the absence of specific provision in the certificate of incorporation, members of a corporate board of directors nevertheless owe a fiduciary responsibility to the shareholders in general and to individual shareholders in particular to treat all shareholders fairly and evenly.Schwartz v Marien (1975) 37 N.Y.2d 487, 373 N.Y.S.2d 122, 335 N.E.2d 334

Where a stockholder in a corporation sells a right to subscribe to bonds thereof to a non-stockholder, the rights of such buyer are as a general rule no more and no less than that of his seller. Sass v New Yorker Towers, Ltd. (1965, 1st Dept) 23 A.D.2d 105, 258 N.Y.S.2d 765

Although under Bus Corp L § 622, subdivision (e)(4) treasury stock is not subject to preemptive rights absent a specific provision in certificate of incorporation, directors' refusal to sell such shares to stockholder, while selling such shares to employees and directors of corporation, must accord with established legal standards of honesty and fair dealing in the management of the corporation; fact issue of whether corporate directors had so acted precluded summary judgment for corporation.Schwartz v Marien (1974, 4th Dept) 43 A.D.2d 307, 351 N.Y.S.2d 216, affd 37 N.Y.2d 487, 373 N.Y.S.2d 122, 335 N.E.2d 334

Judicial hearing officer in divorce action properly valued husband's minority interest in closely-held corporation by fixing value at price stated in shareholder's agreement, despite greatly enhanced value that could be obtained if shares were sold outside agreement, where (1) agreement was bona fide buy-sell agreement predating period of marital discord, (2) shares were subject to agreement for another 14 years beyond date of trial, (3) no evidence existed of any pending sale of corporate assets or its outstanding shares or of any other action which might vitiate husband's obligation under agreement, and (4) any appraisal of value of shares based upon potential sale outside agreement would be purely speculative. Amodio v Amodio (1986, 2d Dept) 122 A.D.2d 757, 505 N.Y.S.2d 645, app gr 68 N.Y.2d 883, 508 N.Y.S.2d 943, 501 N.E.2d 592 and affd 70 N.Y.2d 5

UNDER FORMER LAW

Under earlier provisions, the holder of preferred stock was not entitled to subscribe prorata to a new issue of common stock, issued by the corporation in good faith. Russell v American Gas & Electric Co. (1912) 152 A.D. 136, 136 N.Y.S. 602

Where capital stock of corporation had been increased to pay debts, minority stockholder who was financially unable to purchase his pro rata share had no cause for complaint. The corporation had the right to allow stockholders to purchase shares not purchased by other stockholders and bad faith was not shown by the fact that some of the creditors are stockholders.Schramme v Cowin (1923) 205 A.D. 20, 199 N.Y.S. 98

A certificate of incorporation may be amended so as to deprive consenting stockholders of their pre-emptive rights to purchase stock, but such an amendment cannot bind a stockholder who opposes its adoption. Albrecht, Maguire & Co. v General Plastics, Inc. (1939) 256 A.D. 134, 9 N.Y.S.2d 415, affd without op 280 N.Y. 840, 21 N.E.2d 887

Earlier statutes did not grant or preserve any preemptive right in shareholders to purchase bonds merely because the bonds could, under stated conditions, be converted into stock. Venner v American Tel. & Tel. Co. (1920) 110 Misc 118, 181 N.Y.S. 45, affd without op (Sup App T) 189 N.Y.S. 1

With respect to 5000 shares of stock which had not been validly issued when preemptive rights of all stockholders to share in unissued stock became effective, April 16, 1958, under subd. (4)(d) of § 39 of former Stock Corp. L. the directors' meeting at which they were purportedly issued being void, subsequent purported ratification of the action taken at that meeting at a stockholders' meeting held December 26, 1958 could not deprive nonconsenting stockholders of their preemptive rights. Tabulating Card Co. v Leidesdorf (1961) 32 Misc. 2d 720, 223 N.Y.S.2d 652

Resolutions of the board of directors violated preemptive rights of shareholders where the attempt was to authorize issuance of several thousand shares at one cent per share to employees and management in consideration of services already rendered. Hyman v Behar (1963) 39 Misc. 2d 617, 241 N.Y.S.2d 625

§ 623. Procedure to enforce shareholder's right to receive payment for shares

(a) A shareholder intending to enforce his right under a section of this chapter to receive payment for his shares if the proposed corporate action referred to therein is taken shall file with the corporation, before the meeting of shareholders at which the action is submitted to a vote, or at such meeting but before the vote, written objection to the action. The objection shall include a notice of his election to dissent, his name and residence address, the number and classes of shares as to which he dissents and a demand for payment of the fair value of his shares if the action is taken. Such objection is not required from any shareholder to whom the corporation did not give notice of such meeting in accordance with this chapter or where the proposed action is authorized by written consent of shareholders without a meeting.

(b) Within ten days after the shareholders' authorization date, which term as used in this section means the date on which the shareholders' vote authorizing such action was taken, or the date on which such consent without a meeting was obtained from the requisite shareholders, the corporation shall give written notice of such authorization or consent by registered mail to each shareholder who filed written objection or from whom written objection was not required, excepting any shareholder who voted for or consented in writing to the proposed action and who thereby is deemed to have elected not to enforce his right to receive payment for his shares.

(c) Within twenty days after the giving of notice to him, any shareholder from whom written objection was not required and who elects to dissent shall file with the corporation a written notice of such election, stating his name and residence address, the number and classes of shares as to which he dissents and a demand for payment of the fair value of his shares. Any shareholder who elects to dissent from a merger under section 905 (Merger of subsidiary corporation) or paragraph (c) of section 907 (Merger or consolidation of domestic and foreign corporations) or from a share exchange under paragraph (g) of section 913 (Share exchanges) shall file a written notice of such election to dissent within twenty days after the giving to him of a copy of the plan of merger or exchange or an outline of the material features thereof under section 905 or 913.

(d) A shareholder may not dissent as to less than all of the shares, as to which he has a right to dissent, held by him of record, that he owns beneficially. A nominee or fiduciary may not dissent on behalf of any beneficial owner as to less than all of the shares of such owner, as to which such nominee or fiduciary has a right to dissent, held of record by such nominee or fiduciary.

(e) Upon consummation of the corporate action, the shareholder shall cease to have any of the rights of a shareholder except the right to be paid the fair value of his shares and any other rights under this section. A notice of election may be withdrawn by the shareholder at any time prior to his acceptance in writing of an offer made by the corporation, as provided in paragraph (g), but in no case later than sixty days from the date of consummation of the corporate action except that if the corporation fails to make a timely offer, as provided in paragraph (g), the time for withdrawing a notice of election shall be extended until sixty days from the date an offer is made. Upon expiration of such time, withdrawal of a notice of election shall require the written consent of the corporation. In order to be effective, withdrawal of a notice of election must be accompanied by the return to the corporation of any advance payment made to the shareholder as provided in paragraph (g). If a notice of election is withdrawn, or the corporate action is rescinded, or a court shall determine that the shareholder is not entitled to receive payment for his shares, or the shareholder shall otherwise lose his dissenters' rights, he shall not have the right to receive payment for his shares and he shall be reinstated to all his rights as a shareholder as of the consummation of the corporate action, including any intervening preemptive rights and the right to payment of any intervening dividend or other distribution or, if any such rights have expired or any such dividend or distribution other than in cash has been completed, in lieu thereof, at the election of the corporation, the fair value thereof in cash as determined by the board as of the time of such expiration or completion, but without prejudice otherwise to any corporate proceedings that may have been taken in the interim.

(f) At the time of filing the notice of election to dissent or within one month thereafter the shareholder of shares represented by certificates shall submit the certificates representing his shares to the corporation, or to its transfer agent, which shall forthwith note conspicuously thereon that a notice of election has been filed and shall return the certificates to the shareholder or other person who submitted them on his behalf. Any shareholder of shares represented by certificates who fails to submit his certificates for such notation as herein specified shall, at the option of the corporation exercised by written notice to him within forty-five days from the date of filing of such notice of election to dissent, lose his dissenter's rights unless a court, for good cause shown, shall otherwise direct. Upon transfer of a certificate bearing such notation, each new certificate issued therefor shall bear a similar notation together with the name of the original dissenting holder of the shares and a transferee shall acquire no rights in the corporation except those which the original dissenting shareholder had at the time of transfer.

(g) Within fifteen days after the expiration of the period within which shareholders may file their notices of election to dissent, or within fifteen days after the proposed corporate action is consummated, whichever is later (but in no case later than ninety days from the shareholders' authorization date), the corporation or, in the case of a merger or consolidation, the surviving or new corporation, shall make a written offer by registered mail to each shareholder who has filed such notice of election to pay for his shares at a specified price which the corporation considers to be their fair value. Such offer shall be accompanied by a statement setting forth the aggregate number of shares with respect to which notices of election to dissent have been received and the

aggregate number of holders of such shares. If the corporate action has been consummated, such offer shall also be accompanied by (1) advance payment to each such shareholder who has submitted the certificates representing his shares to the corporation, as provided in paragraph (f), of an amount equal to eighty percent of the amount of such offer, or (2) as to each shareholder who has not yet submitted his certificates a statement that advance payment to him of an amount equal to eighty percent of the amount of such offer will be made by the corporation promptly upon submission of his certificates. If the corporate action has not been consummated at the time of the making of the offer, such advance payment or statement as to advance payment shall be sent to each shareholder entitled thereto forthwith upon consummation of the corporate action. Every advance payment or statement as to advance payment shall include advice to the shareholder to the effect that acceptance of such payment does not constitute a waiver of any dissenters' rights. If the corporate action has not been consummated upon the expiration of the ninety day period after the shareholders' authorization date, the offer may be conditioned upon the consummation of such action. Such offer shall be made at the same price per share to all dissenting shareholders of the same class, or if divided into series, of the same series and shall be accompanied by a balance sheet of the corporation whose shares the dissenting shareholder holds as of the latest available date, which shall not be earlier than twelve months before the making of such offer, and a profit and loss statement or statements for not less than a twelve month period ended on the date of such balance sheet or, if the corporation was not in existence throughout such twelve month period, for the portion thereof during which it was in existence. Notwithstanding the foregoing, the corporation shall not be required to furnish a balance sheet or profit and loss statement or statements to any shareholder to whom such balance sheet or profit and loss statement or statements were previously furnished, nor if in connection with obtaining the shareholders' authorization for or consent to the proposed corporate action the shareholders were furnished with a proxy or information statement, which included financial statements, pursuant to Regulation 14A or Regulation 14C of the United States Securities and Exchange Commission. If within thirty days after the making of such offer, the corporation making the offer and any shareholder agree upon the price to be paid for his shares, payment therefor shall be made within sixty days after the making of such offer or the consummation of the proposed corporate action, whichever is later, upon the surrender of the certificates for any such shares represented by certificates.

(h) The following procedure shall apply if the corporation fails to make such offer within such period of fifteen days, or if it makes the offer and any dissenting shareholder or shareholders fail to agree with it within the period of thirty days thereafter upon the price to be paid for their shares:

(1) The corporation shall, within twenty days after the expiration of whichever is applicable of the two periods last mentioned, institute a special proceeding in the supreme court in the judicial district in which the office of the corporation is located to determine the rights of dissenting shareholders and to fix the fair value of their shares. If, in the case of merger or consolidation, the surviving or new corporation is a foreign corporation without an office in this state, such proceeding shall be brought in the county where the office of the domestic corporation, whose shares are to be valued, was located.

(2) If the corporation fails to institute such proceeding within such period of twenty days, any dissenting shareholder may institute such proceeding for the same purpose not later than thirty days after the expiration of such twenty day period. If such proceeding is not instituted within such thirty day period, all dissenter's rights shall be lost unless the supreme court, for good cause shown, shall otherwise direct.

(3) All dissenting shareholders, excepting those who, as provided in paragraph (g), have agreed with the corporation upon the price to be paid for their shares, shall be made parties to such proceeding, which shall have the effect of an action quasi in rem against their shares. The corporation shall serve a copy of the petition in such proceeding upon each dissenting shareholder who is a resident of this state in the manner provided by law for the service of a summons, and upon each nonresident dissenting shareholder either by registered mail and publication, or in such other manner as is permitted by law. The jurisdiction of the court shall be plenary and exclusive.

(4) The court shall determine whether each dissenting shareholder, as to whom the corporation requests the court to make such determination, is entitled to receive payment for his shares. If the corporation does not request any such determination or if the court finds that any dissenting shareholder is so entitled, it shall proceed to fix the value of the shares, which, for the purposes of this section, shall be the fair value as of the close of business on the day prior to the shareholders' authorization date. In fixing the fair value of the shares, the court shall consider the nature of the transaction giving rise to the shareholder's right to receive payment for shares and its effects on the corporation and its shareholders, the concepts and methods then customary in the relevant securities and financial markets for determining fair value of shares of a corporation engaging in a similar transaction under comparable circumstances and all other relevant factors. The court shall determine the fair value of the shares without a jury and without referral to an appraiser or referee. Upon application by the corporation or by any shareholder who is a party to the proceeding, the court may, in its

discretion, permit pretrial disclosure, including, but not limited to, disclosure of any expert's reports relating to the fair value of the shares whether or not intended for use at the trial in the proceeding and notwithstanding subdivision (d) of section 3101 of the civil practice law and rules.

(5) The final order in the proceeding shall be entered against the corporation in favor of each dissenting shareholder who is a party to the proceeding and is entitled thereto for the value of his shares so determined.

(6) The final order shall include an allowance for interest at such rate as the court finds to be equitable, from the date the corporate action was consummated to the date of payment. In determining the rate of interest, the court shall consider all relevant factors, including the rate of interest which the corporation would have had to pay to borrow money during the pendency of the proceeding. If the court finds that the refusal of any shareholder to accept the corporate offer of payment for his shares was arbitrary, vexatious or otherwise not in good faith, no interest shall be allowed to him.

(7) Each party to such proceeding shall bear its own costs and expenses, including the fees and expenses of its counsel and of any experts employed by it. Notwithstanding the foregoing, the court may, in its discretion, apportion and assess all or any part of the costs, expenses and fees incurred by the corporation against any or all of the dissenting shareholders who are parties to the proceeding, including any who have withdrawn their notices of election as provided in paragraph (e), if the court finds that their refusal to accept the corporate offer was arbitrary, vexatious or otherwise not in good faith. The court may, in its discretion, apportion and assess all or any part of the costs, expenses and fees incurred by any or all of the dissenting shareholders who are parties to the proceeding against the corporation if the court finds any of the following: (A) that the fair value of the shares as determined materially exceeds the amount which the corporation offered to pay; (B) that no offer or required advance payment was made by the corporation; (C) that the corporation failed to institute the special proceeding within the period specified therefor; or (D) that the action of the corporation in complying with its obligations as provided in this section was arbitrary, vexatious or otherwise not in good faith. In making any determination as provided in clause (A), the court may consider the dollar amount or the percentage, or both, by which the fair value of the shares as determined exceeds the corporate offer.

(8) Within sixty days after final determination of the proceeding, the corporation shall pay to each dissenting shareholder the amount found to be due him, upon surrender of the certificates for any such shares represented by certificates.

(i) Shares acquired by the corporation upon the payment of the agreed value therefor or of the

Business
Corporation Law

amount due under the final order, as provided in this section, shall become treasury shares or be cancelled as provided in section 515 (Reacquired shares), except that, in the case of a merger or consolidation, they may be held and disposed of as the plan of merger or consolidation may otherwise provide.

(j) No payment shall be made to a dissenting shareholder under this section at a time when the corporation is insolvent or when such payment would make it insolvent. In such event, the dissenting shareholder shall, at his option:

(1) Withdraw his notice of election, which shall in such event be deemed withdrawn with the written consent of the corporation; or

(2) Retain his status as a claimant against the corporation and, if it is liquidated, be subordinated to the rights of creditors of the corporation, but have rights superior to the non-dissenting shareholders, and if it is not liquidated, retain his right to be paid for his shares, which right the corporation shall be obliged to satisfy when the restrictions of this paragraph do not apply.

(3) The dissenting shareholder shall exercise such option under subparagraph (1) or (2) by written notice filed with the corporation within thirty days after the corporation has given him written notice that payment for his shares cannot be made because of the restrictions of this paragraph. If the dissenting shareholder fails to exercise such option as provided, the corporation shall exercise the option by written notice given to him within twenty days after the expiration of such period of thirty days.

(k) The enforcement by a shareholder of his right to receive payment for his shares in the manner provided herein shall exclude the enforcement by such shareholder of any other right to which he might otherwise be entitled by virtue of share ownership, except as provided in paragraph (e), and except that this section shall not exclude the right of such shareholder to bring or maintain an appropriate action to obtain relief on the ground that such corporate action will be or is unlawful or fraudulent as to him.

(l) Except as otherwise expressly provided in this section, any notice to be given by a corporation to a shareholder under this section shall be given in the manner provided in section 605 (Notice of meetings of shareholders).

(m) This section shall not apply to foreign corporations except as provided in subparagraph (e)(2) of section 907 (Merger or consolidation of domestic and foreign corporations).

History: Add, L 1961, ch 855, eff Sept 1, 1963; amd, L 1962, ch 834, § 40; L 1963, ch 746, eff Sept 1, 1963; L 1965, ch 803, §§ 20- 22, eff Sept 1, 1965; L 1982, ch 202, §§ 3-9, eff Sept 1, 1982 (see 1982 note below); L 1982, ch 928, §§ 38-40, eff Dec 21, 1982; L 1986, ch 117, § 3, eff Sept 1, 1986.

CASE ANNOTATIONS

1. In general

1. In general

Protection afforded to minority shareholders under statute authorizing stockholders to petition for appraisal of value of stock held by them should not be wielded as an offensive weapon nor employed to cause unwarranted expense or embarrassment to corporation. Dimmock v Reichhold Chemicals, Inc. (1977) 41 N.Y.2d 273, 392 N.Y.S.2d 396, 360 N.E.2d 1079, later app (2d Dept) 75 A.D.2d 870, 428 N.Y.S.2d 38

In proceeding pursuant to Business Corporation Law § 623 (h) (2) to enforce shareholder's right to receive payment for fair value of her shares, summary judgment is granted dismissing proceeding, since formation of two subsidiaries, both wholly owned by respondent corporation, and transfer of camping operations and its buses to subsidiaries do not fall within purview of Business Corporation Law §§ 909 and 910-these transactions did not result in liquidation, in whole or in part, of camp business operated by respondent, which retained ownership of corporate land and buildings-consequently, subject transactions did not give rise to right under New York law of dissenting stockholder to have her shares redeemed. Matter of Resnick v Karmax Camp Corp., 149 A.D.2d 709

Petitioner stated cause of action under CLS Bus Corp § 623 to determine fair value of his shares in corporation where it was undisputed that corporation had abolished petitioner's preemptive right to purchase new shares to preserve his percentage interest in corporation, and petitioner had filed notice of objection at special shareholders' meeting prior to vote being taken. Carroll v Seacroft Plaza, Ltd. (1988, 2d Dept) 141 A.D.2d 724, 529 N.Y.S.2d 588

Petitioner did not waive his right to appraisal by failing to file notice of objection before shareholders voted on proposal that effectively abolished his preemptive rights to purchase stock since (1) corporation had failed to send petitioner notice of meeting or copy of CLS Bus Corp § 623 or summary of its material terms, (2) petitioner's tardiness in serving notice of objection was insignificant (15 minutes after vote), and (3) corporation was not unduly prejudiced thereby. Carroll v Seacroft, Ltd. (1988, 2d Dept) 141 A.D.2d 726, 529 N.Y.S.2d 829

Under New York law, stockholder who exercises his appraisal rights may not later maintain action for breach of fiduciary duty. Mullen v Academy Life Ins. Co. (1983, CA8 Mo) 705 F.2d 971

2. Purpose

Purpose of subsection (h)(1) of statute is to place upon corporation the obligation of initiating the appraisal procedure and to prevent multiplicity of actions that might otherwise ensue, which procedure would have the salutary effect of avoiding divergent decisions on similar facts that might result from a multiplicity of actions in different courts. Petition of Gruntal & Co. (1972) 69 Misc. 2d 121, 328 N.Y.S.2d 141

3. Applicability

In a proceeding under Bus Corp Law § 1104-a to dissolve certain corporations, Bus Corp Law § 623(g), (h) were not applicable to the determination of fair value of stock in those corporations, since there was no legislative design that those provisions were intended to govern a court's determination of fair value under Bus Corp Law § 1118, in which corporations exercise their option to purchase the shares of the person petitioning to dissolve. Re Fleischer (1980, 2d Dept) 79 A.D.2d 636, 433 N.Y.S.2d 614

In action by minority shareholders challenging majority shareholders' approval of extension of sublease agreement and provision granting option to subtenant to purchase leased premises, defendants were entitled to summary judgment dismissing claims for breach of fiduciary duty and fraud, as plaintiffs' sole remedy was to seek appraisal under CLS Bus Corp § 623, where complaint alleged that challenged transactions were within purview of CLS Bus Corp § 910, triggering plaintiffs' appraisal rights, and that defendants improperly failed to advise them of their appraisal rights. Norte & Co. v New York & H. R.R. (1995, 1st Dept) 222 A.D.2d 357, 635 N.Y.S.2d 629, app den (NY A.D., 1st Dept) 1996 N.Y. A.D. LEXIS 5947 and app den 88 N.Y.2d 811, 649 N.Y.S.2d 378, 672 N.E.2d 604

Although the corporation in question was not actively conducting a profit-making business or commercial enterprise, its principal activity being that of landlord leasing its property to a golf club, where it had been organized under former Stock Corporation Law its dissolution was subject to the provisions of this section. Sands Point Land Co. v Rossmoore (1964) 43 Misc. 2d 368, 251 N.Y.S.2d 197

4. Acts subject to dissent

In an action for fraud and breach of a fiduciary relationship brought against a corporation by a shareholder who dissented from the terms of a corporate merger and sought rescission of the merger, an accounting, and damages, the corporation's motion to dismiss would be granted where the shareholder, in an amended complaint, had dropped the claim for rescission and accounting, since, in the absence of any primary request for equitable relief, the shareholder's sole remedy is a statutory proceeding for appraisal of the value of its shares pursuant to Bus Corp Law § 623(k). Walter J. Schloss Associates v Arkwin Industries, Inc. (1984) 61 N.Y.2d 700, 472 N.Y.S.2d 605, 460 N.E.2d 1090

On finding that corporate merger was not yet consummated and might well be abandoned, and that corporation was not proceeding untimely, special term properly concluded that proceeding by minority stockholders for valuation was premature and denied application without prejudice to renewal either upon merger's consummation or passage of unreasonable period of time without either consummation or abandonment. Goldberg v Arrow Electronics, Inc. (1973, 1st Dept) 42 A.D.2d 890, 347 N.Y.S.2d 597, app dismd 33 N.Y.2d 1004, 353 N.Y.S.2d 966, 309 N.E.2d 428

A shareholder failed to state a cause of action in a proceeding to determine his right to payment and to have the fair value of his shares fixed, based on his dissent to a merger plan, where the plan or merger effected no change in his rights as a shareholder in the surviving corporation. In addition, the shareholder failed to file a timely notice of election to dissent as provided in Bus Corp Law § 623 where his notice of dissent was filed more than 20 days after he had received notice from the corporation. McGowan v Grand Island Transit Corp. (1981, 4th Dept) 80 A.D.2d 731, 437 N.Y.S.2d 158

Majority shareholder of a corporation improperly acted alone in conveying real property that constituted substantially all the corporate assets to a limited liability company without first obtaining the approval of the minority shareholders under N.Y. Bus. Law § 909 as despite the fact that all the shareholders were family members, the requirements of § 909 were mandatory based on the use of the language "shall"; strict construction of the provisions was necessary to preserve the rights of any minority shareholder who might wish to object and have their shares appraised and bought by the corporation pursuant to N.Y. Bus. Corp. Law §§ 623, 910(a)(1)(B). Bear Pond Trail v Am. Tree Co. (2009, 3d Dept) 61 App Div 3d 1195, 876 NYS2d 571.

Where corporate action objected to prior to shareholder's meeting pursuant to Business Corporation Law § 623(a) was not taken and only action taken at meeting related to replacement of petitioner as an officer, director and employee of the corporation, such action did not entitle shareholder to payment of fair value of her shares under statute. Valando v Data Boutique, Ltd. (1971) 67 Misc. 2d 515, 323 N.Y.S.2d 608

Shareholders' suit against the corporation under N.Y. Bus. Corp. Law §§ 623 and 806, seeking payment of fair value for their shares, was dismissed; as an amendment to the certificate of incorporation did not constitute an adverse alteration for purposes of § 806(b)(6), the shareholders did not have a right to appraisal under § 623. Matter of Celauro v 4C Foods Corp., 956 N.Y.S.2d 821, 38 Misc. 3d 636, 2012 N.Y. Misc. LEXIS 5425 (N.Y. Sup. Ct. 2012), reh'g denied, in part, 972 N.Y.S.2d 142, 39 Misc. 3d 1234(A), 2013 N.Y. Misc. LEXIS 2269 (N.Y. Sup. Ct. 2013), in part, 2013 NY Slip Op 31768(U), 2013 N.Y. Misc. LEXIS 3414 (N.Y. Sup. Ct. Aug. 2, 2013), in part, 2016 NY Slip Op 31917(U), 2016 N.Y. Misc. LEXIS 3711 (N.Y. Sup. Ct. Oct. 12, 2016).

5. – Procedural compliance

Petitioners, minority shareholders in appellant corporation, dissented to merger of corporation but failed to submit their stock certificates for notation pursuant to Business Corporation Law § 623 (f), and were precluded from exercising their dissenters' rights where appellant failed, within 45 days of date petitioners filed their notice of dissent, to exercise its option pursuant to statute to terminate dissenters' rights-court properly held that appellant, by failing to exercise its option to terminate petitioners' dissenters' rights, is precluded from arguing petitioners are not entitled to have their shares appraised; appellant is incorrect in its assertion that petitioners, by failing to demonstrate good cause for their delay in submitting their certificates for notation, were precluded from obtaining dissenters' rights; Business Corporation Law § 623 (f) indicates shareholder need only demonstrate "good cause" to reinstate his or her dissenter's rights after they have been vitiated by corporation's exercise of option provided for in statute. Matter of Rosenblum (Arkwin Indus.), 166 A.D.2d 597

A procedure to enforce a shareholder's right to receive payment for her shares is conditioned upon the shareholder's adherence to the time requirements of the statute. However equity requires that the court have some discretion to waive absolute compliance where special circumstances justify such a determination. Davis v Adirondack Industries, Inc. (1970, 4th Dept) 33 A.D.2d 1100, 308 N.Y.S.2d 107

In order for a shareholder to avail himself of his right of appraisal, he must follow the procedure established by the legislature, and the courts may not alter that procedure as the time requirements of the statute are mandatory. Endicott Johnson Corp. v Bade (1973, 3d Dept) 42 A.D.2d 236, 346 N.Y.S.2d 33

Corporation was precluded from refusing shareholders their dissenters' rights, even though shareholders failed to submit their stock certificates for notation under CLS Bus Corp § 623(f), where corporation failed to exercise its option under statute to terminate dissenters' rights within 45 days of date that shareholders filed their notice of dissent. Re Rosenblum (1990, 2d Dept) 166 A.D.2d 597, 560 N.Y.S.2d 884

Defendant lost his right to appraisal of his shares in corporation when he failed to serve his notice of election to dissent until after merger vote; CLS Bus Corp § 623(a) contains no provision for judicial excuse of noncompliance for good cause. Albany-Plattsburgh United Corp. v Bell (1994, 3d Dept) 202 A.D.2d 800, 609 N.Y.S.2d 113, app gr 84 N.Y.2d 807

Defendant did not lose his right to appraisal of his shares in corporation where he served notice of election to dissent before merger vote, but thereafter failed to tender his shares in timely manner, since defendant established good cause for his failure to tender shares where he had lost, and did not have possession of, certificates. Albany-Plattsburgh United Corp. v Bell (1994, 3d Dept) 202 A.D.2d 800, 609 N.Y.S.2d 113, app gr 84 N.Y.2d 807

Defendant corporation was entitled to dismissal of complaint seeking money damages to compensate plaintiffs for alleged undervaluation of stock formerly held by them in corporation whose merger with defendant occasioned purchase of their shares, as appraisal is exclusive remedy for stockholders dissenting to terms on which corporation has offered its shares for sale in context of corporate merger, except that action in equity is permissible to challenge fraudulent or illegal corporate activity, and plaintiffs, having failed to comply with procedural requirements of CLS Bus Corp § 623, forfeited their appraisal rights and were relegated to seeking relief in equity. Theodore Trust v Smadbeck (2000, 1st Dept) 277 A.D.2d 67, 717 N.Y.S.2d 7, app den 96 N.Y.2d 703, 723 N.Y.S.2d 130, 746 N.E.2d 185

A dissenting shareholder who fails to comply with the provisions of this section and § 910 as to acts to be done and time schedule for doing them, or to make any reasonable attempt to do so, is not entitled to have his stock appraised. Application of Wiedersum (1964) 41 Misc. 2d 936, 246 N.Y.S.2d 638

A dissenting shareholder sufficiently complied with the requirements of this section when, upon receipt of notice of special meeting to take up a plan for complete liquidation with sale of all assets, he notified the corporation by letter that he objected to the plan and intended to demand payment for his shares, and, after the plan was adopted, notified the corporation of his dissent and demanded payment of fair value for his shares. Sands Point Land Co. v Rossmoore (1964) 43 Misc. 2d 368, 251 N.Y.S.2d 197

The beneficial owner of shares who notified the corporation of his objection to a merger and intent to demand appraisal before the special meeting on the proposed merger was held is entitled to written notice of the corporation's action as he has put the corporation on notice of his ownership; since the corporation failed to give him notice of the merger, the shareholder's demand for appraisal is timely, although it would have come too late had he been given notice, and since the corporation failed to bring a proceeding to fix the value of the shares of dissenting shareholders, the dissenting beneficial shareholder is entitled to do so. Re Bowwan (1978) 98 Misc. 2d 1043

Trial court erred in granting a shareholder additional time to commence an action under N.Y. Bus. Corp. Law § 623 to determine the fair value of shares in a corporation, as the shareholder failed to file a notice of election to dissent in the statutory time frame, so the shareholder had no right to bring the proceeding. Matter of Sikorski (2006, App Div, 2d Dept) 815 NYS2d 753

6. Judicial intervention under § 623(h), generally

Reading paragraphs 1, 2, and 4 of subd (h) of statute together, it appears that the statutory scheme is that the corporation in its action under subsection (h)(1) may ask the court to determine a questioned dissenter's right to payment and, if it fails to do so, then the aggrieved shareholder can have his right to payment determined in a special proceeding brought by him under subsection (h)(2) within 30 days after the 20 day period given exclusively to the corporation elapses, and that "dissenting shareholder" includes those whose right to appraisal is questioned or denied by the corporation. Petition of Gruntal & Co. (1972) 69 Misc. 2d 121, 328 N.Y.S.2d 141

7. – Justification for intervention

Where an offer to purchase the shares of a dissenting stockholder was made in good faith and was treated as such by the stockholder, the fact that the offer was not complete in that it was not accompanied by a balance sheet of the corporation whose shares the dissenting shareholder held as of the latest available date, did not invalidate the offer to the extent that the stockholder would be required to proceed under Business Corporation Law § 623(h). Application of Davis (1969) 59 Misc. 2d 1098, 301 N.Y.S.2d 340, affd (4th Dept) 33 A.D.2d 1100, 308 N.Y.S.2d 107

8. – Determination of value

Although net asset value, investment value and market value are relevant to determination of "fair value" of shares owned by those stockholders dissenting to proposed corporate merger, all three elements do not have to influence the result in every valuation proceeding; it suffices if they are all considered; compelling consideration of all of them, including those which may turn out unreliable in a particular case, has the salutary effect of assuring more complete justification by the appraiser of the conclusion he reaches and also provides a more concrete basis for court review. Endicott Johnson Corp. v Bade (1975) 37 N.Y.2d 585, 376 N.Y.S.2d 103, 338 N.E.2d 614

Where corporation was not being liquidated but was to continue to operate as part of the surviving parent, it made good business and legal sense not to attempt any estimation of net asset value in determining the value of shares held by those stockholders dissenting to proposed merger. Endicott Johnson Corp. v Bade (1975) 37 N.Y.2d 585, 376 N.Y.S.2d 103, 338 N.E.2d 614

Assigning limited weight to market value in determining fair value of shares held by those stockholders dissenting to proposed corporate merger was proper where the stock had been delisted from the New York Stock Exchange and had come to be 70% owned by the parent corporation and there was a radical change in management resulting in a turnaround of the financial picture. Endicott Johnson Corp. v Bade (1975) 37 N.Y.2d 585, 376 N.Y.S.2d 103, 338 N.E.2d 614

Right of stockholders dissenting to a proposed merger to obtain fair value, rather than market value, for their stock protects them from being forced to sell at unfair values arbitrarily and unilaterally fixed by those who may dominate a corporation; however, market value is an ingredient that must enter into the calculation of fair value. Endicott Johnson Corp. v Bade (1975) 37 N.Y.2d 585, 376 N.Y.S.2d 103, 338 N.E.2d 614

Where in computing fair value of those shares held by stockholders dissenting to proposed merger detailed consideration was given to matters like investment credit, tax-loss carry forward and, especially depreciation, it could not be said that Appellate Division was not within its province in deciding that negative good will, which represented excess of book value of acquired corporation's assets over price paid by acquiring corporation, was not a separate aliquot element of special value that was to be added to preponderating investment considerations. Endicott Johnson Corp. v Bade (1975) 37 N.Y.2d 585, 376 N.Y.S.2d 103, 338 N.E.2d 614

Stockholders dissenting to a proposed merger are entitled to be paid the "fair value" of their stock excluding any appreciation or depreciation due to the merger or its proposal. Endicott Johnson Corp. v Bade (1975) 37 N.Y.2d 585, 376 N.Y.S.2d 103, 338 N.E.2d 614

Net asset value, investment value and market value are factors relevant to determination of fair value of shares owned by those stockholders dissenting to a corporate merger; while in order to provide the elasticity deemed necessary to reach a just result, all three factors are to be considered, the weight to be accorded to each varies with the facts and circumstances of the particular case. Endicott Johnson Corp. v Bade (1975) 37 N.Y.2d 585, 376 N.Y.S.2d 103, 338 N.E.2d 614

To extent that ultimate valuation of shares held by those stockholders dissenting to a proposed corporate merger is confined to the issues of fact, it rests largely within the discretion of the lower courts, to whose review the appraiser's findings are subject. Endicott Johnson Corp. v Bade (1975) 37 N.Y.2d 585, 376 N.Y.S.2d 103, 338 N.E.2d 614

In assessing fair value of shares in CLS Bus Corp § 623 stock appraisal proceeding, court abused its discretion by disregarding tax deduction that corporation became entitled to on consummation of its merger with second corporation; dissenting shareholders are entitled to receive fair value for their securities as determined by consideration of all relevant factors, including prospective, nonspeculative tax benefits accruing to acquired corporation from merger. Cawley v SCM Corp. (1988) 72 N.Y.2d 465, 534 N.Y.S.2d 344, 530 N.E.2d 1264

Dissenting shareholder was entitled to his aliquot share of tax benefit which accrued to corporation on its merger with second corporation since each share of stock within given class must be treated equally; tax advantages attendant to corporate actions must be distributed proportionately among all shareholders in calculating fair value. Cawley v SCM Corp. (1988) 72 N.Y.2d 465, 534 N.Y.S.2d 344, 530 N.E.2d 1264

Personal income tax liability of dissenting shareholder is not element of future value to corporation arising from merger, and so should not be considered in valuing shares pursuant to CLS Bus Corp § 623 proceeding. Cawley v SCM Corp. (1988) 72 N.Y.2d 465, 534 N.Y.S.2d 344, 530 N.E.2d 1264

Principles governing appraisal rights of dissenting shareholders under CLS Bus Corp § 623 include: (1) fair value of dissenter's shares is to be determined on their worth in going concern, not in liquidation, and fair value is not necessarily tied to market value as reflected in actual stock trading, (2) 3 major elements of fair value are net asset value, investment value, and market value, with particular facts and circumstances dictating which element predominates, and not all 3 elements necessarily influencing result, (3) fair value requires that dissenting stockholder be paid for his or her proportionate interest in going concern (i.e., intrinsic value of shareholder's economic interest in corporate enterprise), (4) by virtue of 1982 amendments to CLS Bus Corp § 623(h)(4) (L 1982 ch 202, § 9), fair value determinations should take into account subsequent economic impact on value of very transaction giving rise to appraisal rights, as supplemental to 3 basic value factors, and (5) such fair value determinations are governed by provisions of Business Corporation Law that require equal treatment of all shares of same class of stock. Friedman v Beway Realty Corp. (1995) 87 N.Y.2d 161, 638 N.Y.S.2d 399, 661 N.E.2d 972

There is no difference in analysis between stock fair value determinations under CLS Bus Corp § 623 and fair value determinations under CLS Bus Corp § 1118; in fixing fair value, courts should determine minority shareholder's proportionate interest in going concern value of corporation as whole (i.e., what willing purchaser, in arm's length transaction, would offer for corporation as operating business). Friedman v Beway Realty Corp. (1995) 87 N.Y.2d 161, 638 N.Y.S.2d 399, 661 N.E.2d 972

Imposing minority discount on compensation payable to dissenting stockholders for their shares in proceeding under CLS Bus Corp § 623 or § 1118 would necessarily deprive minority shareholders of their proportionate interest in going concern, and would result in minority shares being valued below that of majority shares, thus violating mandate of equal treatment of all shares of same class in minority stockholder buyouts. Friedman v Beway Realty Corp. (1995) 87 N.Y.2d 161, 638 N.Y.S.2d 399, 661 N.E.2d 972

In proceeding under CLS Bus Corp § 623 for judicial determination of fair value of minority stockholders' shares in close corporations, there was nothing improper in court's failure to assign any additional diminution in value of shares because they were subject to contractual restrictions on voluntary transfer; statutory acquisition of minority shares by corporation under Business Corporation Law is not voluntary sale of corporate shares as contemplated by restrictive stockholder agreement, and thus express covenant was literally inapplicable. Friedman v Beway Realty Corp. (1995) 87 N.Y.2d 161, 638 N.Y.S.2d 399, 661 N.E.2d 972

In determining applicable unmarketability discount, court erred in removing nonexistent minority discount element from reduction in value of minority shareholders' shares that corporations' expert attributed to shares' lack of marketability where (1) court's determination was based on its erroneous finding that expert arrived at 30.4 percent discount by analyzing privately transacted sales of stock with restrictive sales provisions and found that they exhibited median discount of 30.4 percent relative to net asset value, and further that expert's unmarketability discount must also have contained element of reduced value because sales analyzed were of minority shares, (2) in actuality, expert calculated unmarketability factor by comparing purchase prices of registered, publicly traded minority shares in comparative corporations to purchase prices of same class of minority shares in same corporations that were unregistered and thus not publicly traded but purchased under trading restrictions in private placements, and (3) because expert always compared prices of marketable set of minority shares to prices of set of minority shares when same stock was unmarketable, difference in prices of shares did not contain any additional minority discount element, and discount was solely attributable to difference in marketability of shares in same stock. Friedman v Beway Realty Corp. (1995) 87 N.Y.2d 161, 638 N.Y.S.2d 399, 661 N.E.2d 972

While market price of actively traded and listed stock is factor in determining value of stock of dissenting shareholders, it is not controlling factor and other circumstances having direct bearing on market price, such as investment value and asset value, are also to be considered. Marvin Josephson Associates, Inc. v Randeria (1976, 1st Dept) 52 A.D.2d 523, 381 N.Y.S.2d 675

Sale of all corporation's assets pursuant to contract entered into within month of valuation date was best indication of corporation's value. Quill v Cathedral Corp. (1995, 3d Dept) 215 A.D.2d 960, 627 N.Y.S.2d 157, app dismd without op 86 N.Y.2d 838, 634 N.Y.S.2d 446, 658 N.E.2d 224

Court properly relied on risk factor incorporated in report of dissenting shareholder's expert, who placed risk factor at 0.75 as opposed to 3.75 as offered by corporation's expert, where such determination was based on corporation's stable client base, stable revenues, abundant cash assets, and low debt level. Quill v Cathedral Corp. (1995, 3d Dept) 215 A.D.2d 960, 627 N.Y.S.2d 157, app dismd without op 86 N.Y.2d 838, 634 N.Y.S.2d 446, 658 N.E.2d 224

Court properly refused to apply marketability discount to subsidiary corporation, even though shares therein were not publicly traded, where parent corporation received inquiries for its subsidiary from 4 or 5 buyers, it obtained 2 firm offers, and it finally sold subsidiary for asking price. Quill v Cathedral Corp. (1995, 3d Dept) 215 A.D.2d 960, 627 N.Y.S.2d 157, app dismd without op 86 N.Y.2d 838, 634 N.Y.S.2d 446, 658 N.E.2d 224

Court properly did not include pension plans as excess asset for valuation purposes where all 4 alternatives to valuing pension plans were not workable. Quill v Cathedral Corp. (1995, 3d Dept) 215

A.D.2d 960, 627 N.Y.S.2d 157, app dismd without op 86 N.Y.2d 838, 634 N.Y.S.2d 446, 658 N.E.2d 224

In proceeding under CLS Bus Corp § 623 to determine fair value of shares in corporation, there was no basis for disturbing court's unmarketability discount of 10 percent, given essential distinction between permissible discount for lack of marketability and impermissible discount applied to minority shares for minority shareholder's lack of control of close corporation. Carolina Gardens, Inc. v Menowitz (1997, 1st Dept) 238 A.D.2d 189, 655 N.Y.S.2d 536

Valuation of corporation's stock based, to some extent, on appreciation in value resulting from merger that gave rise to appraisal proceeding was inappropriate with respect to merger that occurred prior to 1982 amendment to CLS Bus Corp § 623(h)(4). Greek Peak Inc. v Armstrong (1999, 3d Dept) 265 A.D.2d 760, 697 N.Y.S.2d 375

Valuation of corporation's stock was improper where record did not support finding that court applied discount to reflect stock's lack of marketability, even though court indicated that it considered marketability. Greek Peak Inc. v Armstrong (1999, 3d Dept) 265 A.D.2d 760, 697 N.Y.S.2d 375

Investment value as of valuation date could not be computed retrospectively based on corporation's reported actual earnings for fiscal year ending 11 months after valuation date since fair value may include elements of future value only if known or susceptible of proof as of date of merger and not product of speculation. Miller Bros. Indus. v Lazy River Inv. Co. (2000, 1st Dept) 272 A.D.2d 166, 709 N.Y.S.2d 162, app den 95 N.Y.2d 761, 714 N.Y.S.2d 711, 737 N.E.2d 953

There was no need to give net asset value any weight in appraising fair value of dissenting shareholders' shares of corporation's stock where tender offer price reliably reflected corporation's market value as going concern as of valuation date, and liquidation was not contemplated at time of merger. Miller Bros. Indus. v Lazy River Inv. Co. (2000, 1st Dept) 272 A.D.2d 166, 709 N.Y.S.2d 162, app den 95 N.Y.2d 761, 714 N.Y.S.2d 711, 737 N.E.2d 953

Price offered for the shares of an acquired company was properly found fair in a N.Y. Bus. Corp. Law § 623 proceeding because neither the grant of an option to purchase property nor an agreement to sell certain assets to take effect immediately after the merger breached a ground lease were the subject of the valuation proceeding; moreover, even if arguendo these were breaches, they did not warrant termination of the lease so as to trigger the underwriter's obligation to pay the acquired entity the proceeds for assets sold over the years and to include such payment in the valuation. The trial court's acceptance of the opinions of the underwriter's experts and rejection of the opinions of other experts was proper. Matter of American Premier Underwriters, Inc. v Abelow (2008, 1st Dept) 54 App Div 3d 638, 864 NYS2d 19.

In an action to determine the value of stock held by shareholders dissenting from a corporate recapitalization, there are at least three constant formulae which may be used, market value, investment value, or net asset value. Lipe-Rollway Corp. v Seligson (1969) 59 Misc. 2d 805, 300 N.Y.S.2d 478

Date used to determine minority shareholder's value of her shares was April 28, not April 30 as sought in petition, where April 29 was shareholders' authorization date in instant proceeding. Direct Media/DMI v Rubin (1997, Sup) 171 Misc. 2d 505, 654 N.Y.S.2d 986

Trial court's findings in a N.Y. Bus. Corp. Law § 623 proceeding as to the valuation of a dissenting shareholder's stock were supported by the evidence, including the trial court's acceptance of the valuation by the shareholder's expert utilizing the market multiple, comparable transaction, and discounted cash flow methods of valuation and the rejection of the valuation by the corporation's expert utilizing financial projections based on his own judgment. Jersey Partners, Inc. v McCully (2007, App Div, 1st Dept) 847 NYS2d 170

9. – Procedural matters

Dissenting shareholder's stock appraisal proceeding under CLS Bus Corp § 623 was not class action or functional equivalent where shareholder was only one to perfect his right to fair valuation determination as provided by statute, and thus he would be only shareholder entitled to value greater than tender offer price if court found shares to have greater value after considering tax benefit to corporation. Cawley v SCM Corp. (1988) 72 N.Y.2d 465, 534 N.Y.S.2d 344, 530 N.E.2d 1264

Formation of 2 subsidiaries, both wholly owned by respondent corporation, and transfer of its camping operations and buses to subdivisions, did not fall within purview of CLS Bus Corp §§ 909 and 910 since such transactions did not result in liquidation, in whole or in part, of camp business operated by respondent, which retained ownership of corporate land and buildings; thus, respondent was entitled to summary judgment dismissing proceeding brought under CLS Bus Corp § 623(h)(2) to enforce shareholder's right to receive payment for fair value of her shares. Resnick v Karmax Camp Corp. (1989, 2d Dept) 149 A.D.2d 709, 540 N.Y.S.2d 503

In an action on behalf of minority public shareholders of a principal corporation to enjoin the merger with a corporation which had been newly formed by the controlling stockholders for the sole purpose of the merger, a stockholder who owned a small number of shares which he had purchased at a low price fairly represented the interests of other minority stockholders in a class action, since he advanced the same legal claims as were asserted by other stockholders. A dissenting stockholder, by seeking an appraisal of his stock, did not waive his rights to challenge a settlement, since an appraisal is not the exclusive remedy of a stockholder where fraud or illegality is claimed. A proposed merger which would work to freeze out public stockholders was subject to the strict scrutiny test as to the discharge of the fiduciary duty owed by the controlling stockholders and the principal inquiry was whether the conditions of the merger as a whole compelling a liquidation of the minority interests was fair to all concerned. A settlement agreement would be set aside as unfair where the offer per share had been arrived at by an over-weighting of market value as opposed to book value. On remand the lower court would be required to make a determination of the fair offer for the stock according to the same process ordinarily in effect under a statutory appraisal (Bus Corp Law § 623), and the court would have authority to appoint an expert to assist by examining books and other pertinent records of the corporation, and to report his findings on the fair value of the shares, with fees and other costs charged to the corporation. Klurfeld v Equity Enterprises, Inc. (1981, 2d Dept) 79 A.D.2d 124, 436 N.Y.S.2d 303

In a special proceeding brought under Bus Corp Law § 623 to determine the rights of dissenting shareholders who did not accept the corporation's offer respecting the fair value of their shares as part of a merger of the corporation with another company, the statute required that all dissenting shareholders must be made parties except those who had agreed with the corporation upon price; therefore, the trial court should have granted plaintiff's request for an order directing the merging corporations to join all other dissenting shareholders as parties to the proceeding. Weiss v Summit Organization, Inc. (1981, 1st Dept) 80 A.D.2d 526, 436 N.Y.S.2d 6

Court properly declined to give retroactive application to 1982 amendment to CLS Bus Corp § 623(h) (which forbids courts in special proceedings brought under statute from ordering "referral to an appraiser or referee") since there is no clear expression of legislative purpose to justify retroactive application, and such application would affect proceedings already taken in such actions. Alpert v 79 Realty Corp. (1995, 1st Dept) 214 A.D.2d 478, 625 N.Y.S.2d 521

Where a dissenting stockholder did not have sufficient information before her in order to make a decision on an offer of purchase, motion to dismiss a petition to determine the fair value of the stock as being untimely brought was dismissed and a delay of 25 days in serving the petition granted where it appeared that the corporation would not be prejudiced in any way by the delay. Application of Davis (1969) 59 Misc. 2d 1098, 301 N.Y.S.2d 340, affd (4th Dept) 33 A.D.2d 1100, 308 N.Y.S.2d 107

Three accountants who are being paid a contingent fee by petitioners to testify as expert witnesses in a consolidated appraisal proceeding (Business Corporation Law, § 623) brought by two groups of dissenting shareholders, are not incompetent to testify in the appraisal proceeding by reason of the contingent fee since the nature of an expert's fee arrangement is relevant only to his credibility not his competency to testify. DR 7-109 (C) of the Code of Professional Responsibility which prohibits a lawyer from offering to pay or acquiescing in the "payment of compensation to a witness contingent upon the content of his testimony or the outcome of the case" only represents an indirect "legislative judgment" with respect to contingent fees and in no way limits the applicability of CPLR 4512 which does not preclude a witness from testifying "by reason of his interest in the event". The disciplinary rule only gives the Appellate Division, through its disciplinary powers over attorneys, the power to indirectly limit the provisions of CPLR 4512 and does not provide an exception thereto. Re Shore (1978) 93 Misc. 2d 933, 403 N.Y.S.2d 990, affd (2d Dept) 67 A.D.2d 526, 415 N.Y.S.2d 878, app dismd 48 N.Y.2d 634, 421 N.Y.S.2d 196, 396 N.E.2d 479

Respondent, formerly a "public" corporation which went "private" to enable the major shareholder to repay his personal indebtedness,

waived its right to a stay of a nonjury appraisal proceeding (Business Corporation Law, § 623) pending the determination of the Federal court class action suit brought against respondent and its officers for damages arising out of misrepresentations made in a prospectus, by successfully opposing petitioner's prior application for a stay pending the outcome of the Federal action. Respondent should have been aware at the time of petitioner's application for a stay that its right to a jury trial on the issue of damages in the Federal action could be lost by the application of collateral estoppel based on a finding of fair market value in the appraisal proceeding. Re Shore (1978) 93 Misc. 2d 933, 403 N.Y.S.2d 990, affd (2d Dept) 67 A.D.2d 526, 415 N.Y.S.2d 878, app dismd 48 N.Y.2d 634, 421 N.Y.S.2d 196, 396 N.E.2d 479

A class action is not necessary in a special proceeding for appraisal of shares since all dissenting shareholders must be joined and the question of fair value of their shares must be considered jointly. Re Bowman (1978) 98 Misc. 2d 1028, 414 N.Y.S.2d 951

10. – Costs and interest

Increasing from $15,000 to $30,000 counsel fee awarded several shareholders dissenting from proposed corporate merger was not abuse of discretion in light of result achieved, time spent on the case and fact that, as representatives of the largest number of shares in the proceeding, the attorneys appeared to have had the laboring oar of acting as lead counsel. Endicott Johnson Corp. v Bade (1975) 37 N.Y.2d 585, 376 N.Y.S.2d 103, 338 N.E.2d 614

For certain proof to be admissible or entitled to consideration on issue whether a shareholder's refusal to accept corporate offer of payment for his shares incident to merger was not in good faith so as to preclude an allowance of interest to shareholder in a proceeding commenced by him to determine fair value of his shares, there must be a relevance between such proof and the good faith in issue.Dimmock v Reichhold Chemicals, Inc. (1977) 41 N.Y.2d 273, 392 N.Y.S.2d 396, 360 N.E.2d 1079, later app (2d Dept) 75 A.D.2d 870, 428 N.Y.S.2d 38

In proceeding in which shareholder sought to have fair value of his shares of corporation's stock determined incident to its merger into another corporation, consideration of events occurring after shareholder refused to accept corporate offer of payment for his shares as at least a partial basis for denial of an interest allowance to shareholder from shareholder's authorization date to date of payment and for an assessment of half of costs and expenses of appraiser against shareholder was error.Dimmock v Reichhold Chemicals, Inc. (1977) 41 N.Y.2d 273, 392 N.Y.S.2d 396, 360 N.E.2d 1079, later app (2d Dept) 75 A.D.2d 870, 428 N.Y.S.2d 38

In proceeding in which shareholder sought to have fair value of his shares of corporation's stock determined incident to its merger into another corporation and in which stock was found to have value of $4.75 per share, refusal to award counsel fees and expenses of experts to shareholder, who had rejected corporate offer of $3.82 per share and who had a prior proceeding to determine fair value dismissed because it was commenced one day late, was not error if refusal was not influenced by trial court's determination that shareholder had not acted in good faith in respect to his application for interest and expenses of proceeding.Dimmock v Reichhold Chemicals, Inc. (1977) 41 N.Y.2d 273, 392 N.Y.S.2d 396, 360 N.E.2d 1079, later app (2d Dept) 75 A.D.2d 870, 428 N.Y.S.2d 38

Where the fair value of the shares as fixed by appraisers materially exceeded the amount which the corporation offered to pay, the fees and the cost of experts and counsel should be assessed against the corporation. Lipe-Rollway Corp. v Abrams (1970, 4th Dept) 33 A.D.2d 1094, 308 N.Y.S.2d 130

Dissenting shareholders who failed to establish bad faith were not entitled to interest on value of their stock from date merger was authorized to date of abandonment thereof, nor were said shareholders entitled to attorneys' fees. Goldberg v Arrow Electronics, Inc. (1973, 1st Dept) 42 A.D.2d 890, 347 N.Y.S.2d 597, app dismd 33 N.Y.2d 1004, 353 N.Y.S.2d 966, 309 N.E.2d 428

Interest at rate of six percent on fair value of shares owned by dissenters to proposed corporate merger was equitable. Endicott Johnson Corp. v Bade (1974) 45 A.D.2d 407, 357 N.Y.S.2d 738, affd 37 N.Y.2d 585, 376 N.Y.S.2d 103, 338 N.E.2d 614

Petitioners' request for interim allowances to be paid to their expert witnesses and attorneys in a consolidated appraisal proceeding (Business Corporation Law, § 623) was properly denied; absent a final determination of the fair value of the shares to be exchanged for cash, there is no basis upon which a court can exercise its discretion in awarding fees. Re Shore (1979, 2d Dept) 67 A.D.2d 526, 415

N.Y.S.2d 878, app dismd 48 N.Y.2d 634, 421 N.Y.S.2d 196, 396 NW2d 479

The testimony of three expert witnesses for petitioners in a consolidated appraisal proceeding (Business Corporation Law, § 623) need not be stricken on the ground that their fee arrangements, which included an understanding that they would receive no fee unless petitioners were successful, are violative of public policy, since the fee arrangements are not unethical and actually reflect the public policy of the State in affording minority shareholders true access to the appraisal remedy which was enacted for their protection in that the costs of the proceeding are generally assessed against the corporation and only where the dissenting shareholders acted arbitrarily, vexatiously or otherwise not in good faith, does the statute provide that such costs and expenses may be apportioned and assessed against the dissenting shareholders (Business Corporation Law, § 623, subd [h], par [7]), the compensation to be paid to the experts was not fixed between them and the experts in any sum or percentage dependent upon success, and there was no indication that the experts were asked to do anything other than to give their honest opinions; although an agreement to pay a certain percentage of petitioners' recovery would run afoul of both the Code of Professional Responsibility (DR 7-109 [C]) and the Professional Standards of the American Institute of Certified Public Accountants (rule 302), the latter rule provides that fees are not regarded as contingent if fixed by courts, and the former is inapplicable where an attorney acquiesces in an arrangement whereby the witness agrees to look to the court for his fee. Re Shore (1979, 2d Dept) 67 A.D.2d 526, 415 N.Y.S.2d 878, app dismd 48 N.Y.2d 634, 421 N.Y.S.2d 196, 396 N.E.2d 479

In evidentiary hearing on issue of reasonable value of services necessarily rendered on behalf of petitioners for appraisal under CLS Business Corporation § 623, court properly denies leave to conduct pre-hearing discovery under CLS CPLR § 408 since discovery would significantly delay resolution of fee issue and would entail monumental inquiry on issue wholly ancillary to substance of law suit; pre-hearing discovery may be denied where petitioners fail to demonstrate that information they seek is necessary to resolution of fee issue. Re Shore (1985, 2d Dept) 109 A.D.2d 842, 486 N.Y.S.2d 368

In proceeding under CLS Bus Corp § 623 to determine fair value shares in corporation, court properly required each side to bear its own costs and fees under CLS Bus Corp § 623(h)(7), absent finding of material disparity between corporation's offer and eventual determination of fair value. Carolina Gardens, Inc. v Menowitz (1997, 1st Dept) 238 A.D.2d 189, 655 N.Y.S.2d 536

In proceeding under CLS Bus Corp § 623 to determine fair value shares in corporation, award of interest was required where trial court found only that award of interest was not warranted under circumstances but did not make finding, required for denial of interest under CLS Bus Corp § 623(h)(6), that conduct was arbitrary, vexatious, or otherwise not in good faith; shareholders' purportedly vexatious conduct in connection with litigation was not relevant to issue of their good faith in rejecting corporation's offer. Carolina Gardens, Inc. v Menowitz (1997, 1st Dept) 238 A.D.2d 189, 655 N.Y.S.2d 536

Court properly awarded attorney fees to shareholders in proceeding under CLS Bus Corp § 623(h) to determine fair value of their stock where case involved complicated valuation proceeding in which shareholders were largely successful, as court determined that fair value of each share was $900.25, materially exceeding $600 per share offer made to shareholders; comparison of hourly rates of shareholders' counsel ($110 to $185) to those charged by respondent's counsel ($90 to $120) did not require conclusion that former were unreasonable. Quill v Cathedral Corp. (1997, 3d Dept) 241 A.D.2d 593, 659 N.Y.S.2d 919, app den 90 N.Y.2d 812, 666 N.Y.S.2d 100, 688 N.E.2d 1383

In shareholders' proceeding under CLS Bus Corp § 623(h) to determine fair value of their stock, Supreme Court did not err in refusing to apportion costs between parties, since costs of bringing such proceeding might have "chilling effect" on dissenting shareholders, making case less appropriate for apportionment than dissolution cases. Quill v Cathedral Corp. (1997, 3d Dept) 241 A.D.2d 593, 659 N.Y.S.2d 919, app den 90 N.Y.2d 812, 666 N.Y.S.2d 100, 688 N.E.2d 1383

In assessing costs in shareholders' proceeding under CLS Bus Corp § 623(h) to determine fair value of their stock, Supreme Court properly exercised its discretion to include costs incurred prosecuting appeals. Quill v Cathedral Corp. (1997, 3d Dept) 241 A.D.2d 593, 659

N.Y.S.2d 919, app den 90 N.Y.2d 812, 666 N.Y.S.2d 100, 688 N.E.2d 1383

In awarding attorney fees to shareholders in their proceeding under CLS Bus Corp § 623(h) to determine fair value of their stock, Supreme Court properly assessed interest on such fees where court's decision had stated shareholder's entitlement to costs, including counsel fees, and established respondent's liability for those costs within meaning of CLS CPLR § 5002, and judgment later entered on issue of costs was money judgment on which interest runs from time of docketing under CLS CPLR § 5003. Quill v Cathedral Corp. (1997, 3d Dept) 241 A.D.2d 593, 659 N.Y.S.2d 919, app den 90 N.Y.2d 812, 666 N.Y.S.2d 100, 688 N.E.2d 1383

In awarding attorney fees to shareholders in their proceeding under CLS Bus Corp § 623(h) to determine fair value of their stock, court properly refused to include fees for shareholders' Massachusetts counsel where he essentially acted as liaison between shareholders and other professionals involved in proceedings, there was no explanation of purpose for his occasional meetings with persons involved, record indicated that his services were duplicative, and to extent that he provided legal services in Massachusetts, nothing in record supported need for such services. Quill v Cathedral Corp. (1997, 3d Dept) 241 A.D.2d 593, 659 N.Y.S.2d 919, app den 90 N.Y.2d 812, 666 N.Y.S.2d 100, 688 N.E.2d 1383

Stockholders who petitioned for the appointment of three persons to appraise the value of the shares of stock held by them pursuant to Insurance Law § 503, were not required to pay the expenses of such appraisal under the Business Corporation Law, since Insurance Law § 503 is determinative of the liability for such charges in view of the provision in § 7 of the Insurance Law that if any provision of the Business Corporation Law conflicts with any provision of the Insurance Law the Insurance Law shall prevail and the conflicting provision of the Business Corporation Law shall not apply in such case. Kuflik v New Amsterdam Casualty Co. (1966) 53 Misc. 2d 436, 278 N.Y.S.2d 725

Simplistic method of appraisal based solely upon over-the-counter stock prices is not sufficient; appraisals must be based on three factors: net asset value, investment (or earnings) value, and market value.DiRose v PK Management Corp (1982, CA2 NY) 691 F.2d 628, (US) 77 L Ed 285, 103 S Ct 1896

11. Other relief under § 623(k)

This section is a codification of the judicial principle that equity will act, despite the existence of a stock appraisal remedy under Insurance Law § 503, where there is fraud or illegality in a given merger. Willcox v Stern (1966) 18 N.Y.2d 195, 273 N.Y.S.2d 38, 219 N.E.2d 401

Under Bus Corp Law §§ 623(k) and 910, which give corporate shareholders dissenting from a corporate merger the right to have their shares appraised in a judicial proceeding, shareholders who exercised that right were barred from maintaining any derivative action on behalf of the merged corporation. Under Bus Corp Law § 623(k), the shareholders were not allowed to pursue an action for damages for fraud in connection with the merger absent a primary request for equitable relief. Breed v Barton (1981) 54 N.Y.2d 82, 444 N.Y.S.2d 609, 429 N.E.2d 128

Technical compliance with the Business Corporation Law's requirements will not necessarily exempt a merger from further judicial review, even though generally the remedy of a shareholder dissenting from a merger and the offered "cash-out" price is to obtain the fair value of his or her stock through an appraisal proceeding, since, when the merger is unlawful or fraudulent as to that shareholder, an action for equitable relief is authorized by Bus Corp Law § 623(k). Alpert v 28 Williams St. Corp. (1984) 63 N.Y.2d 557, 483 N.Y.S.2d 667, 473 N.E.2d 19

Appraisal proceeding pursuant to CLS Bus Corp § 623 is dissenting shareholders' exclusive remedy following merger or other corporate action where equitable relief based on unlawful or fraudulent action by corporation is not pursued. Cawley v SCM Corp. (1988) 72 N.Y.2d 465, 534 N.Y.S.2d 344, 530 N.E.2d 1264

Although plaintiff had previously initiated appraisal proceedings as a minority stockholder, dissenting from the transfer by majority stockholders of all the assets of the subject corporations, plaintiff was not barred from asserting causes of action for equitable relief upon a proper showing that the transfer was fraudulent or unlawful as to him.Yoss v Sacks (1966, 2d Dept) 26 A.D.2d 671, 272 N.Y.S.2d 387

In action by minority shareholders who challenged approval by majority shareholders of extension of sublease agreement for balance of lease term and agreement allowing subtenant to purchase certain leased properties, plaintiffs were precluded from invoking exception to exclusivity rule under CLS Bus Corp § 623(k) because their causes of action for breach of fiduciary duty and fraud, although labeled as individual and class actions, asserted claims primarily on behalf of corporation, and thus were derivative. Norte & Co. v New York & H. R.R. (1995, 1st Dept) 222 A.D.2d 357, 635 N.Y.S.2d 629, app den (NY A.D., 1st Dept) 1996 N.Y. A.D. LEXIS 5947 and app den 88 N.Y.2d 811, 649 N.Y.S.2d 378, 672 N.E.2d 604

Action alleging fraud, overreaching, and breach of fiduciary duties by individual defendants, who were directors of defendant corporation, in their adoption of and participation in stock option plan was not barred by exclusivity provisions of CLS Bus Corp § 623(k) where complaint sought as one of its primary requests rescission of stock option plan, imposition of constructive trust on stock issued under stock option plan, and accounting; moreover, plaintiffs showed that breach of fiduciary duty occurred, then defendants' actions were unlawful and plaintiffs might be entitled to equitable relief. Lazar v Robinson Knife Mfg. Co. (1999, 4th Dept) 262 A.D.2d 968, 692 N.Y.S.2d 539

While a shareholder claimed an exception to the exclusivity provision in N.Y. Bus. Corp. Law § 623(k) based on a claim that he was fraudulently induced to sign a consent to a sale of the assets of first and second corporations under N.Y. Bus. Corp. Law § 909(a), the exclusivity provision did not apply to the derivative causes of action asserted by the shareholder. Kingston v Breslin (2008, 2d Dept) 56 App Div 3d 430, 866 NYS2d 778.

Principle of subd (k) of above statute permitting shareholder to maintain appropriate action on ground that corporate action will be fraudulent as to him, applied to merger of insurance corporations. Willcox v Stern (1964) 44 Misc. 2d 827, 255 N.Y.S.2d 38, mod on other grounds 24 A.D.2d 845, 263 N.Y.S.2d 1005, affd 18 N.Y.2d 195, 273 N.Y.S.2d 38, 219 N.E.2d 401

Minority shareholder did not waive her right to assert cross claims of breach of fiduciary duty by majority shareholders when she sought appraisal rights under CLS Bus Corp § 623, even though shareholder may not seek appraisal and also commence separate action to recover money damages for improper corporate action (CLS Bus Corp § 623(k)); discharge of majority's fiduciary duty to minority can be weighed in determining fair value of dissenting shareholder's shares, in appraisal proceeding, and minority shareholder's only means to challenge alleged improper prior corporate actions was in appraisal proceeding, disallowance of which would violate public policy. Direct Media/DMI v Rubin (1997, Sup) 171 Misc. 2d 505, 654 N.Y.S.2d 986

Trial court's order was reversed, defendants' motion to dismiss was granted, and complaint was dismissed as under N.Y. P'ship Law § 121-1102(d), since no limited partner (LP) exercised rights under § 121-1102(b) and (c), subsequent action by LPs in law or equity to attack validity of merger, or to have merger set aside or rescinded, was barred; the LPs' invitation to rewrite the statute and graft the fraud exception of N.Y. Bus. Corp. Law § 623(k) onto an otherwise clear legislative pronouncement was rejected.. Appleton Acquisition, LLC v National Hous. Partnership (2006, 1st Dept) 34 App Div 3d 339, 826 NYS2d 7

Employee-shareholder of employee-owned company was limited to her statutory appraisal right or equitable relief, and thus was not entitled to compensatory and punitive damages for alleged breach of fiduciary duty by company's controlling officer, based on his acceptance of payment for hisshares in merger of company, since (1) under CLS Bus Corp § 623(k), money damages are not available to dissenting shareholder except as "ancillary to a grant of traditionally equitable relief," (2) employee-shareholder made no attempt to obtain traditional equitable relief such as rescission of merger, and (3) her request for "accounting" was not for equitable relief from controlling officer as to funds belonging to company but rather sought funds which he had received in his individual capacity, which was merely request for damages in another form. Burke v Jacoby (1992, CA2 NY) 981 F.2d 1372, CCH Fed Secur L Rep ¶ 97649, cert den (US) 124 L Ed 2d 249, 113 S Ct 2338

Class relief is unavailable in appraisal proceeding. Pellman v Cinerama, Inc. (1980, SD NY) 503 F. Supp. 107, CCH Fed Secur L Rep ¶ 97707, later proceeding (SD NY) 89 FRD 386, CCH Fed Secur L Rep ¶ 97868, 32 FR Serv 2d 1182

Dissenter's action pursuant to CLS Bus Corp Law § 623(k) exception clause must fail, even though complaint originally requested equitable remedy of rescission, where case in its present state seeks only damages, because action suffers from "fatal absence of any

primary request for equitable relief." Grace v Rosenstock (1998, ED NY) 23 F. Supp. 2d 326

12. Miscellaneous

A shareholder derivative action may be maintained even though commenced after the subject corporation has effected a dissolution and distributed its assets inasmuch as a shareholder has the necessary standing where he meets the dual requirement as to the ownership of stock contained in subdivision (b) of section 626 of the Business Corporation Law, which requires plaintiff to be a shareholder at the time of bringing the action and at the time of the transaction of which he complains; a shareholder of a dissolved corporation has a sufficient interest in a derivative action to satisfy the spirit of the rule requiring ownership at the commencement of the action and, furthermore, pursuant to section 1006 of the Business Corporation Law, the rights and remedies of the shareholders existing prior to dissolution are viewed as if the dissolution never occurred. Accordingly, since the dissolution of a corporation, without more, does not deprive the shareholders of their derivative remedy, it was error to dismiss such a derivative action except as to those shareholders who availed themselves of their appraisal rights under subdivision (e) of section 623 of the Business Corporation Law. IndependentInvestor Protective League v Time, Inc. (1980) 50 N.Y.2d 259, 428 N.Y.S.2d 671, 406 N.E.2d 486

In action arising out of purported merger of plaintiff corporation and another closely held corporation of which defendant was minority shareholder, it was error to grant plaintiff's motion for summary judgment declaring that defendant lost his appraisal rights because he failed to dissent prior to vote as required by CLS Bus Corp § 623, since defendant had raised defense of lack of compliance with preincorporation agreement as well as invalidity of merger itself, and it was necessary to resolve issue as to validity of preincorporation agreement prior to addressing legal efficacy of plaintiff's actions leading up to and culminating in merger vote. Albany-Plattsburgh United Corp. v Bell (1995) 85 N.Y.2d 948, 626 N.Y.S.2d 1004, 650 N.E.2d 851

In an equitable action brought by dissenting shareholders to rescind a corporate merger on the ground that it was illegal, fraudulent, and a violation of the corporate management's fiduciary duty, the trial court erred in failing to balance the competing interests involved prior to ruling that certain communications between the corporation and its attorneys were nondiscoverable by virtue of the attorney-client privilege conferred by CPLR § 4503(a), since the corporate management had the burden to show the existence of circumstances that justified recognition of the privilege, and such recognition should only be accorded if the injury that would result from disclosure is greater than the benefit thereby gained; furthermore, plaintiffs' initiation of a related proceeding pursuant to Bus Corp Law § 623 to obtain a judicial determination of the value of plaintiffs' stock would not preclude access to the requested information, since the statute specifically protects the rights of shareholders to bring such equitable actions. Beard v Ames (1983, 4th Dept) 96 A.D.2d 119, 468 N.Y.S.2d 253

In dispute over value of shares of realty corporation held by petitioner minority shareholders, in which respondents refused to disclose various appraisal, income and expense reports on basis of attorney-client privilege, minority shareholders were entitled to order requiring respondents to identify all attorneys and others who had seen assertedly privileged documents; respondents should be required to furnish sufficient information to assure that confidentiality was maintained with respect to assertedly privileged documents. In re Alpert (1995, 1st Dept) 214 A.D.2d 316, 624 N.Y.S.2d 588

Denial of any interest was erroneous under CLS Bus Corp § 623(h)(6) where court expressly found that dissenting shareholders' initial refusal to accept offer was not arbitrary, vexatious, or in bad faith; thus, judgment would be modified to award interest on 20 percent portion of corporation's offer for dissenting shareholders' stock that was withheld under CLS Bus Corp § 623(g). Miller Bros. Indus. v Lazy River Inv. Co. (2000, 1st Dept) 272 A.D.2d 166, 709 N.Y.S.2d 162, app den 95 N.Y.2d 761, 714 N.Y.S.2d 711, 737 N.E.2d 953

Supreme Court's determination that plaintiff was shareholder in defendant corporation, and that she therefore had standing to maintain shareholders' derivative action, constituted finding of fact which was not independently appealable. Aragona v CIN-MAR Developers, Inc. (2000, 2d Dept) 277 A.D.2d 266, 715 N.Y.S.2d 659

Minority shareholder who did not bring proceeding to value his shares under CLS Bus Corp § 623 could sue for money damages where corporation sold all or substantially all of its assets, sale was not made in usual or regular course of business, and corporation had failed to give shareholder proper notice under CLS Bus Corp § 909(a). Collins v Telcoa Int'l Corp. (2001, 2d Dept) 283 A.D.2d 128, 726 N.Y.S.2d 679

Stockholder should have been accorded rights as a dissenting minority shareholder in a post-merger proceeding; the record did not show that the underwriter requested proof of beneficial ownership of his shares despite ample opportunity to do so, and the only ground asserted in its letter to the stockholder and in the petition was that he was not an owner of record. Matter of American Premier Underwriters, Inc. v Abelow (2008, 1st Dept) 54 App Div 3d 638, 864 NYS2d 19.

Restrictions on sale or transfer of corporate stock, although valid, are strictly construed, and ordinarily they apply only to voluntary sales. Sands Point Land Co. v Rossmoore (1964) 43 Misc. 2d 368, 251 N.Y.S.2d 197

The fact that the certificate of incorporation of the corporation in which a minority shareholder was seeking payment of the fair value of his shares on the basis of dissent to a liquidation proposition contained a restriction on sale or assignment of shares without first offering them to the corporation could not affect rights of the shareholder to fair value though the proposition objected to was one for sale of all assets and liquidation of the corporation. Sands Point Land Co. v Rossmoore (1964) 43 Misc. 2d 368, 251 N.Y.S.2d 197

UNDER FORMER STK CORP

I. In General

1. In general

Such rights as minority stockholders have under legislation of this kind to insist upon being bought out if they disagree with proposed corporate action are of very real importance, and corporate acts which would result in impairing them, without consent of minority shareholders, may, for that reason, be invalid. Murrin v Archbald Consol. Coal Co. (1921) 196 A.D. 107, 187 N.Y.S. 606, affd 232 N.Y. 541, 134 N.E. 563

2. Purpose

The purpose of § 21 of former Stock Corp L was to save a dissenting shareholder from loss by reason of a change in the nature of the business. Petition of McKay (1962, 1st Dept) 17 A.D.2d 299, 234 N.Y.S.2d 531

Section 21 of former Stock Corp. L., from which this section of the Bus. Corp. L. was derived, was designed to protect the interests of non-consenting minority stockholders and is to be construed in the light of that objective. Ribakove v Rich (1958) 13 Misc. 2d 98, 173 N.Y.S.2d 306; Re Rowe (1919) 107 Misc 549, 176 N.Y.S. 753

3. Applicability

Section 21 of former Stock Corp. L. did not state that it was applicable to foreign corporations, and it was doubted whether dissenting shareholders of a foreign corporation had any remedy thereunder. November v National Exhibition Co. (1958) 10 Misc. 2d 537, 173 N.Y.S.2d 490. But see, in this connection, § 1319 of this Bus. Corp. L

4. Exclusive remedy

In the absence of some basis for a cause of action, such as fraudulent conspiracy or individual fraud, the remedy of a minority shareholder merely disagreeing with action taken by the majority was solely and exclusively under § 21 of former Stock Corp. L. Liebschutz v Schaffer Stores Co. (1949) 276 A.D. 1, 93 N.Y.S.2d 125, reh and app den 276 A.D. 944, 94 N.Y.S.2d 808

Section 21 of former Stock Corp. L., where available to dissenting shareholders, was deemed to provide an adequate remedy, but not necessarily their exclusive remedy. Katz v R. Hoe & Co. (1950) 199 Misc 459, 103 N.Y.S.2d 106, app dismd 277 A.D. 1035, 100 N.Y.S.2d 1022 and affd 278 A.D. 766, 104 N.Y.S.2d 14, cert den 342 US 886, 96 L Ed 665, 72 S Ct 176; Re Fensterer's Estate (1948, Sur) 79 N.Y.S.2d 427

Where a corporation transfers its assets to another corporation for shares of the latter, then proposes to distribute such shares among its own shareholders, not by way of dividend but as a liquidation, on a basis of ten shares of the stock acquired for each common share of its own stock, but only three shares of the stock received for each share of its preferred, a holder of the preferred stock is entitled to apply for an injunction against such a distribution on the ground of its inequality. Newman v Arabol Mfg. Co. (1963) 41 Misc. 2d 184, 245 N.Y.S.2d 442

Where a complaint alleged that the plaintiffs were the holders of 50% of the stock of a corporation and that the requirements of notification and consent in respect of the sale of corporate assets had not been met, the provisions of § 21 of former Stock Corp. L. were not applicable and not the sole remedy and, hence, plaintiffs were entitled to bring an action of rescission on behalf of the corporation. Cachules v 116 East 57th Street, Inc. (1953, Sup) 125 N.Y.S.2d 97

II. Objections and Dissents

5. In general

Section 21 of former Stock Corp. L. was construed as requiring that the dissenting shareholder at least have taken a definite position against the measure and made an unequivocal demand for payment, in order to be entitled to insist upon appraisal of and payment for his shares. Re O'Brien (1943) 182 Misc 577, 45 N.Y.S.2d 208

Section 21 of former Stock Corp. L. merely required that the dissenting shareholder have objected to the proposed action and demanded payment for his shares. His motives in objecting and demanding payment were immaterial, if he was legally entitled to object. Re Nulle's Estate (1949) 194 Misc 622, 87 N.Y.S.2d 565

6. Standing to object

Under some circumstances, holders of voting trust certificates were entitled to seek appraisal and require purchase of their shares, under § 21 of former Stock Corp. L., at least if voting of shares in the trust was subject to their direction under the terms of the voting trust agreement and they objected to the proposal for which the shares were voted. Application of Bacon (1941) 287 N.Y. 1, 38 N.E.2d 105; Blumenthal v Roosevelt Hotel (1952) 202 Misc 988, 115 N.Y.S.2d 52

Holders of stock which had no voting power with respect to the action objected to had no standing to seek payment for their shares under § 21 of former Stock Corp. L., which was deemed applicable only to voting stock. Application of Harwitz (1948) 192 Misc 91, 80 N.Y.S.2d 570

One who was not a holder of shares according to the corporation's stock records by the record date fixed for the particular meeting, as determining eligibility to vote thereat, had no basis for demanding an appraisal of his stock under § 21 of former Stock Corp. L. because of his personal disagreement with action taken by majority vote at the meeting. Flagg-Utica Corp. v Baselice (1958) 14 Misc. 2d 476, 178 N.Y.S.2d 860

A petitioner who acquired one share of stock some three weeks following adoption of a resolution calling a special meeting of stockholders to vote approval of a proposed sale, and who was found by the court to have purchased the stock with knowledge of the impending transaction, was likewise precluded from exercising the statutory remedy provided by §§ 20 and 21 of former Stock Corp. L. Corwin v Shelter Island Light & Power Co. (1960, Sup) 199 N.Y.S.2d 866

7. Acts subject to dissent

A minority stockholder of some particular class of shares had no basis for demanding appraisal and purchase of his shares on the basis of a recapitalization plan or proposed change in preferential rights as between different classes and issues, where the proposal would not materially change his existing rights. Re Kinney (1939) 279 N.Y. 423, 18 N.E.2d 645, reh den 280 N.Y. 569, 20 N.E.2d 18; Standard Brewing Co. v Peachey (1951) 202 Misc 279, 108 N.Y.S.2d 583

But if it was not clear that rights of holders of the particular kind of shares would not be adversely affected by the act challenged, and there was some ground for contending that they would be, a dissenting holder of such stock was entitled to demand that appraisal proceedings go forward. Marcus v R. H. Macy & Co. (1947) 297 N.Y. 38, 74 N.E.2d 228; Re International Superpower Corp. (1933) 261 N.Y. 538, 185 N.E. 729; Re Gohn (1940) 174 Misc 188, 20 N.Y.S.2d 254

Where preferred stockholders could vote only in specified contingencies and the corporation proposed to grant them equal voting rights with common stock, the effect on the common stock "limits their voting rights" pro rata, and a nonconsenting common stockholder who gave written notice of objection and demand for payment and voted against the amendment was entitled to an appraisal of her stock. Marcus v R. H. Macy & Co. (1947) 297 N.Y. 38, 74 N.E.2d 228

This section of the Bus. Corp. L. does not specify what acts and proposals a minority shareholder is entitled to dissent to and demand purchase of his shares. Section 21 of former Stock Corp. L., from which it was derived, was construed as directed only to action requiring affirmative vote of an appropriate number of shareholders. As to any corporate action within its coverage a stockholder, entitled to vote on the measure, was likewise entitled to dissent and demand payment for his shares, notwithstanding further action by management would be required to effectuate the act. Re McKinney (1954) 306 N.Y. 207, 117 N.E.2d 256

It was generally held, under § 21 of former Stock Corp. L., that there was no practical objective to be served by going into appraisal proceedings, or going forward with them, where the proposition objected to was still in the formative stage, might fail of adoption, would still be subject to exercise of discretion by management, or had already been dropped or rescinded. Re McKinney (1954) 306 N.Y. 207, 117 N.E.2d 256; Application of Eaton (1949) 276 A.D. 7, 92 N.Y.S.2d 867

Where the action taken by the corporation was, under the circumstances, mandated by law, a minority stockholder had no right to have his stock appraised and be bought out. Re Bronson (1917) 177 A.D. 374, 164 N.Y.S. 179, affd without op 221 N.Y. 661, 117 N.E. 1062

An application by dissenting shareholders for appointment of appraisers should not be granted where, before the order of appointment is entered, the project to which they object has been definitely abandoned by the board of directors with stockholder approval. Re Millard (1927) 221 A.D. 113, 222 N.Y.S. 633, affd without op 246 N.Y. 546, 159 N.E. 645

If there was doubt as to whether the dissenting shareholder's rights would be materially and adversely affected by the measure to which he was objecting, he was however, entitled to a determination of whether he could be forced into a position of abiding by the majority decision and accepting whatever came his way as a result, or could insist on being bought out. Liebschutz v Schaffer Stores Co. (1949) 276 A.D. 1, 93 N.Y.S.2d 125, reh and app den 276 A.D. 944, 94 N.Y.S.2d 808

An appraisal was not proper where, although stockholders adopted a resolution authorizing officers to sell all corporate property, the officers had taken no action on the resolution except to lease real property and to sell unneeded personal property. Application for appraisal was directed to be held in abeyance to permit corporation to rescind resolution within a reasonable time. Petition of Hake (1955) 285 A.D. 316, 136 N.Y.S.2d 817, app dismd 308 N.Y. 940, 127 N.E.2d 90

The superimposition of a new class of stock on existing classes does not, standing alone, give a right of appraisal to a holder of stock in an existing class. Re Gohn (1940) 174 Misc 188, 20 N.Y.S.2d 254

Where, however, majority stockholder approval of proposed action, such as a sale of assets, was all that was necessary to authorize management to proceed, the authorization, in and of itself, was sufficient to sustain a demand for appraisal of his stock by a dissenting minority shareholder and for immediate appointment of appraisers, notwithstanding management had, as yet, taken no steps to exercise its authority. Geiler v Brooklyn-Manhattan Transit Corp. (1939, Sup) 18 N.Y.S.2d 788; Application of Harwitz (1948) 192 Misc 91, 80 N.Y.S.2d 570

8. Procedural compliance

Failure to commence the proceedings within the time limit was ground for dismissal and not ordinarily excusable. Re McKinney (1954) 306 N.Y. 207, 117 N.E.2d 256

Section 21 of former Stock Corp. L. contained a precise timetable for preliminary objections by nonconsenting stockholders, for demands by them for payment, and for bringing a proceeding for appraisal if those demands for payment were not met. Where such stockholders failed to comply with the mandatory time requirements of the statute, their proceeding for an appraisal of their stock should be dismissed. Re McKinney (1954) 306 N.Y. 207, 117 N.E.2d 256

The time limitation for commencement of appraisal proceedings under former Stock Corp. L. provisions commenced to run when the measure objected to was approved by the majority stockholders, notwithstanding further action would be required by management before it could be effectuated. Re McKinney (1954) 306 N.Y. 207, 117 N.E.2d 256; Application of Isaac (1950) 198 Misc 85, 97 N.Y.S.2d 634

Dissenting stockholders should be relieved of their default in presenting their stock for notation where they opposed a sale of corporation assets from the start and gave formal and timely notice of their opposition and appeared by counsel in opposition at the stockholders' meeting and were prevented from obtaining access to the stock by reason of illness. Re Kunin (1953) 281 A.D. 635, 121 N.Y.S.2d 220, affd 306 N.Y. 967, 120 N.E.2d 228, reh den 307 N.Y. 686, 120 N.E.2d 856

The purpose of § 21 of former Stock Corp. L. in requiring that a petition by a minority stockholder for appraisal of his shares be made returnable "on the 50th day after the last day on which" he could demand payment for his shares was to fix a maximum, rather than a minimum, time for effectuating the rights of a dissenting stockholder, and such an application was not subject to dismissal because it fixed an earlier return date. Petition of McKay (1962, 1st Dept) 17 A.D.2d 299, 234 N.Y.S.2d 531

No inquiry was permitted under § 20 of former Stock Corp. L. into the motive of nonconsenting shareholders seeking an appraisal of their stock after having given timely notice of their objection upon the decision of the corporation to sell its assets and practically cease operations. Re Nulle's Estate (1949) 194 Misc 622, 87 N.Y.S.2d 565

Subdivision 8 of § 21 of former Stock Corp. L., requiring the dissenting shareholder, seeking an appraisal of his shares, to submit his stock certificate to the corporation within a limited time for notation of demand for payment, was deemed to have been introduced for protection of the corporation, therefore subject to waiver by it, and as being waived where the corporation refused to accept a certificate timely presented for the purpose of noting the demand thereon. Application of Wood (1951, Sup) 103 N.Y.S.2d 110

Stockholders instituting such proceedings were not entitled to withdraw without the corporation's consent. Application of Deutschmann (1952, Sup) 113 N.Y.S.2d 823, mod on other grounds 281 A.D. 14, 116 N.Y.S.2d 578

III. Valuation

9. "Fair value"

The objective is to reach a fair value; such as to give the nonconsenting shareholder the equivalent of his aliquot part in the assets of the corporation. Murrin v Archbald Consol. Coal Co. (1921) 196 A.D. 107, 187 N.Y.S. 606, affd 232 N.Y. 541, 134 N.E. 563

Particularly where the amount of stock held by dissenters is very small in relation to the total shares outstanding, the appraisal proceeding should not go beyond what is necessary to award petitioners fair value. Application of Marcus (1948) 273 A.D. 725, 79 N.Y.S.2d 76, reh and app den 274 A.D. 822, 81 N.Y.S.2d 199

On appraisal, dissenting stockholders are not entitled to a premium or a bonus but there is a clear obligation to pay them the true value of their stock in accordance with the mandate of the statute. Application of Silverman (1953) 282 A.D. 252, 122 N.Y.S.2d 312

Valuation of stock held by dissenting shareholders necessarily involves determination, either by the appraiser or by the court, of what portion of validity outstanding shares is represented by those held by the dissenters, if validity of some of the outstanding stock is seriously questioned. Tabulating Card Co. v Leidesdorf (1961) 32 Misc. 2d 720, 223 N.Y.S.2d 652

10. Factors in determining value, generally

While there is no fixed legal formula for valuing the shares of dissenting shareholders in appraisement proceedings, and proper valuation remains a matter of judgment to be arrived at on the basis of the particular facts, accepted principles require the taking into account of market value, investment value, and net asset value, and none of these factors should be excluded from consideration, where all are present, in favor of placing complete reliancy upon any other. Re Tudor City Fifth Unit, Inc. (1962, 1st Dept) 17 A.D.2d 794, 232 N.Y.S.2d 758, app dismd 12 N.Y.2d 993, 239 N.Y.S.2d 121, 189 N.E.2d 618 and affd 13 N.Y.2d 812, 242 N.Y.S.2d 345, 192 N.E.2d 222; Application of Behrens (1946, Sup) 61 N.Y.S.2d 179, affd without op 271 A.D. 1007, 69 N.Y.S.2d 910

11. – Market value

Market value has frequently been considered as the dominant factor where there was a free and open market for the stock at and before the date as of which value is to be determined. Application of Marcus (1948) 273 A.D. 725, 79 N.Y.S.2d 76, reh and app den 274 A.D. 822, 81 N.Y.S.2d 199 (and revg 191 Misc 808, 77 N.Y.S.2d 529 which also recognized controlling effect of market value; Re Karlin (1951) 202 Misc 792, 111 N.Y.S.2d 96

The value of shares as reflected in sales on a recognized securities exchange is always material, but is not conclusive and its existence does not preclude the necessity for a hearing or the introduction of other evidence bearing upon actual or potential value. Re Kaufmann, Alsberg & Co. (1961, 1st Dept) 15 A.D.2d 468, 222 N.Y.S.2d 305; Application of Wood (1951, Sup) 103 N.Y.S.2d 110; Amella v Consolidated Edison Co. (1947, Sup) 73 N.Y.S.2d 263, affd 273 A.D. 755, 75 N.Y.S.2d 513

In appraising the stock of a dissenting stockholder, market value is of very little significance where the trading is so limited that it can hardly be said to reflect judgment of informed buyers and sellers. Re Tudor City Fifth Unit, Inc. (1962, 1st Dept) 17 A.D.2d 794, 232 N.Y.S.2d 758, app dismd 12 N.Y.2d 993, 239 N.Y.S.2d 121, 189 N.E.2d 618 and affd 13 N.Y.2d 812, 242 N.Y.S.2d 345, 192 N.E.2d 222

Some decisions, however, place the emphasis on fair value, regardless of market value, and require that every item of value that can be established be given due consideration. Blumenthal v Roosevelt Hotel (1952) 202 Misc 988, 115 N.Y.S.2d 52; Amella v Consolidated Edison Co. (1947, Sup) 73 N.Y.S.2d 263, affd 273 A.D. 755, 75 N.Y.S.2d 513

There is some conflict in the decisions dealing with propriety of taking into consideration antecedent influences on market value of the shares. One decision takes the position that an anticipatory increase in market price looking to a proposed consolidation, with respect to which the dissenting shareholder has objected, is not to be excluded in valuing his shares.Dynamics Corp. of America v Abraham & Co. (1956) 5 Misc. 2d 652, 166 N.Y.S.2d 128, mod on other grounds (1st Dept) 6 A.D.2d 683, 174 N.Y.S.2d 952

In appraisal proceedings a wide market on an established exchange under normal conditions is entitled to great and probably controlling weight; a narrow or spasmodic market over the counter, or a market which is subjected to abnormal influences one way or another is not entitled to much weight. Application of Behrens (1946, Sup) 61 N.Y.S.2d 179, affd without op 271 A.D. 1007, 69 N.Y.S.2d 910

12. – Net asset value

Net asset value should not be the basis of determining the value as a going concern of stock of a great industrial corporation. Application of Silverman (1953) 282 A.D. 252, 122 N.Y.S.2d 312

In appraising the value of stock held by a dissenting stockholder in a real estate corporation, the net asset value is entitled to maximum weight. Re Tudor City Fifth Unit, Inc. (1962, 1st Dept) 17 A.D.2d 794, 232 N.Y.S.2d 758, app dismd 12 N.Y.2d 993, 239 N.Y.S.2d 121, 189 N.E.2d 618 and affd 13 N.Y.2d 812, 242 N.Y.S.2d 345, 192 N.E.2d 222

Net asset, or liquidation, value is not a fair basis for appraising stock in a growing and profitable business. Tabulating Card Co. v Leidesdorf (1961) 32 Misc. 2d 720, 223 N.Y.S.2d 652

In appraisal proceedings, net asset value is entitled to weight, but it must be remembered that the stock must be appraised on a going concern basis with a posibility in different cases that the value of the stock may be substantially above or below net asset or breakup value; the nature of the business, the nature of the assets, their liquidity and profitable use, are factors bearing upon the weight to be given to net asset value. Application of Behrens (1946, Sup) 61 N.Y.S.2d 179, affd without op 271 A.D. 1007, 69 N.Y.S.2d 910

13. – Investment value

Investment value of stock held by a dissenting stockholder, reflecting such factors as capitalization, earnings and dividend record, position in the industry and prospects of the business and industry with over-all value of securities in relation to general market conditions should be given some weight, but in the case of a real estate corporation not nearly as much as in the case of an industrial or commercial concern, and giving this factor a weight of 55% was considered too high. Re Tudor City Fifth Unit, Inc. (1962, 1st Dept) 17 A.D.2d 794, 232 N.Y.S.2d 758, app dismd 12 N.Y.2d 993, 239 N.Y.S.2d 121, 189 N.E.2d 618 and affd 13 N.Y.2d 812, 242 N.Y.S.2d 345, 192 N.E.2d 222

Investment value takes account of such factors as the capitalization of the company, earnings and dividend record, position in the industry, prospects of the business and the industry, and the over-all value of its securities in relation to general market conditions and the market values of comparable securities. Application of Behrens (1946, Sup) 61 N.Y.S.2d 179, affd without op 271 A.D. 1007, 69 N.Y.S.2d 910

14. – Date of valuation

The date as of which value of stock held by dissenting shareholders is to be determined is that on which the action objected to was taken by majority shareholders, without taking into consideration how such action may have, or will in future, affect share values. Re Clark's Will (1931) 257 N.Y. 487, 178 N.E. 766; Re Kinney (1939) 257 A.D. 343, 13 N.Y.S.2d 446; Application of Behrens (1946, Sup) 61 N.Y.S.2d 179, affd without op 271 A.D. 1007, 69 N.Y.S.2d 910

More precisely, under later versions of these valuation and appraisal statutes, value should be fixed as of the close of business on the day preceding date of the meeting at which the action objected to was taken, without reference to appreciation or depreciation of value as a result of such action, and the court, in passing upon propriety of the valuation determined by the appraisers, should view the evidence in this light. Application of Silverman (1953) 282 A.D. 252, 122 N.Y.S.2d 312

15. – Other factors

Where the good will of a corporation which has been in existence only a few years is a factor in valuing its stock, it has been considered proper to arrive at it by dividing total net earnings by the number of

months it has been in existence and doing business, multiply the result by the approximate number of years it has been in business to arrive at a per annum average, and then deduct interest on invested capital. Seaich v Mason Seaman Transp. Co. (1915) 170 A.D. 686, 156 N.Y.S. 579, affd without op 219 N.Y. 634, 114 N.E. 1083

An arithmetical average of "bid" quotations of the common stock on the over-the-counter market for a period of two years prior to the time of the vote should not be the determining factor in the evaluating of stock under this section. Market value has been the controlling consideration where there is a free and open market on a recognized stock exchange and the volume of transactions and conditions make it a fair reflection of the judgment of the buying and selling public. But in respect of stock not listed on any exchange, there is a marked difference between the reliability of market price as a guide to value. Application of Silverman (1953) 282 A.D. 252, 122 N.Y.S.2d 312

In appraising the preferred stock of a non-consenting stockholder, the appraisers have the right to take into consideration accumulated surplus. Re Clark's Will (1928) 131 Misc 151, 226 N.Y.S. 141

Another holds that depressive influence on market price of an antitrust decree and the existence of certain outstanding stock options do not warrant requiring the production of records relating to the company's assets, in an effort to establish their actual value. Re Karlin (1951) 202 Misc 792, 111 N.Y.S.2d 96

With respect to high valuations placed upon the holdings of dissenting stockholders in a relatively young corporation, it was unreasonable to overlook unlikelihood of dividends in the foreseeable future, pending expiration of certain contracts with the Government, relative probability of competition in the field, internal discord between stockholders, and absence of any established market for the company's stock. Tabulating Card Co. v Leidesdorf (1961) 32 Misc. 2d 720, 223 N.Y.S.2d 652

16. Particular cases

In the absence of any challenge suggesting that the market was insufficient to represent the opinion of the buying and selling public or that it was subject to any abnormal conditions or influences, one holding only fifty shares in a corporation having outstanding in excess of 1,650,000 shares cannot turn an appraisal of his stock into an appraisal of the underlying assets of the corporation merely upon the claim that the corporation may have undervalued its assets in the light of inflationary conditions, in carrying fixed assets at cost and inventories at cost or market value whichever was lower. Application of Marcus (1948) 273 A.D. 725, 79 N.Y.S.2d 76, reh and app den 274 A.D. 822, 81 N.Y.S.2d 199, and revg 191 Misc 808, 77 N.Y.S.2d 529

A preferred stock which was callable at $25.00 a share, not counting accrued and unpaid dividends, and which therefore had a ceiling value of that amount and which was paying a dividend rate of only four percent when similar preferred stocks were yielding upward of five percent cannot be appraised at an amount in excess of $25.00 if due weight is given to market and investment value. Application of Behrens (1946, Sup) 61 N.Y.S.2d 179, affd 271 A.D. 1007, 69 N.Y.S.2d 910

In a proceeding, under this section to obtain an appraisal of preferred stock of a going corporation which had outstanding common stock and an accumulated surplus from undivided profits, where all of the stockholders except petitioner had voted to sell all of the corporate assets including good will, it was error for appraisers to determine the value of the preferred stock by dividing sum of surplus and capital stock account by total number of shares issued, common and preferred, thereby allotting to preferred stock proportionate share of surplus. Holders of preferred stock had no interest in surplus except preference given by terms of certificate of incorporation as to dividends. Continental Ins. Co. v United States (1922) 259 US 156, 66 L Ed 871, 42 S Ct 540; Cole v Wells (1916) 224 Mass 504, 113 N.E. 189 (disapproved on other grounds Martignette v Sagamore Mfg. Co., 340 Mass 136, 163 N.E.2d 9); Re Clark's Will (1931) 257 N.Y. 487, 178 N.E. 766

17. Miscellaneous

An objection to the application of stockholders dissenting from a merger for appraisal and value of their stock, that petitioners' holdings were "negligible", was without foundation where it appeared that petitioners held 5,000 shares of stock in one of the corporations, of approximately $145,000 value. Re Kaufmann, Alsberg & Co. (1961) 30 Misc. 2d 1025, 220 N.Y.S.2d 151, affd (1st Dept) 15 A.D.2d 468, 222 N.Y.S.2d 305

Stipulation of settlement of representative dissenting stockholders action to enjoin sale of corporate assets, which provided stockholders with an option of liquidating their stock at a price in keeping with appraisals submitted by the corporation or exchanging them for stocks in purchasing corporation with an option to sell within a certain period for a price greater than the appraised value was fair, reasonable and adequate. Blumenthal v Roosevelt Hotel, Inc. (1952, Sup) 116 N.Y.S.2d 94

IV. Appraisal Proceedings

18. Role of appraisers

An order giving to the appraisers the right to select certified public accountants "to prepare and audit report or reports" merely authorizes the appraisers to hire certified public accountants who will assemble the data and evidence adduced before the appraisers for their benefit; it does not authorize the employment of certified public accountants to make an independent audit of the books of the corporation generally. Re Kinney (1939) 257 A.D. 343, 13 N.Y.S.2d 446

The appraisers are entitled to take into consideration their own observations based on general knowledge and testimony without going into details with respect to fixed assets and inventory values, and may consider, among other things, market value of comparable securities issued by other companies in the same field. Application of Marcus (1948) 273 A.D. 725, 79 N.Y.S.2d 76, reh and app den 274 A.D. 822, 81 N.Y.S.2d 199

Function of the appraiser or appraisers is solely to determine value of the stock in question, and they are not properly concerned with allegations of the petition and answer on the basis of which they were appointed. Tabulating Card Co. v Leidesdorf (1959) 17 Misc. 2d 573, 188 N.Y.S.2d 23

Generally, value of the shares of dissenting shareholders as determined by the appraisers, rather than the amount per share offered by the corporation, should be confirmed and upheld where it appears that the appraisers have duly taken into account the recognized elements of market value, investment value, and net asset value in making their determination. Application of Dorsey (1961) 31 Misc. 2d 747, 221 N.Y.S.2d 927

The method of appraisal to be employed, the factors to be considered, and the weight to be given them, in proceedings for determining value of dissenting stockholders' stock, depends upon the circumstances of each individual case, and an appraiser must use his own judgment and give such consideration to the various factors involved as he may deem proper. Tabulating Card Co. v Leidesdorf (1961) 32 Misc. 2d 720, 223 N.Y.S.2d 652

Low valuations placed by experts on stock of dissenting stockholders were not binding upon the appraiser where they failed to take into consideration the corporation's favorable position in the industry, its phenomenal growth in a short period, gross sales and net revenues after taxes, substantial development possibilities, skillful management, popularity of stocks in growth industries, etc. Tabulating Card Co. v Leidesdorf (1961) 32 Misc. 2d 720, 223 N.Y.S.2d 652

19. Power of court

Under earlier provisions, there was some doubt as to whether the court could even entertain exceptions to the report of the appraisers. Re Bickerton (1921) 196 A.D. 231, 187 N.Y.S. 267, app dismd 232 N.Y. 1, 133 N.E. 41 and app dismd 232 N.Y. 495, 134 N.E. 544; Re Arnold (1921) 232 N.Y. 495, 134 N.E. 544; Re Erlanger (1921) 232 N.Y. 496, 134 N.E. 544

The court, in proceedings under § 21 of former Stock Corp. L., had no authority to act except such as was conferred by that section, and accordingly could not order a corporation to make part payment to the shareholder prior to completion and confirmation or modification of the appraisal. Re Nulle's Estate (1949) 194 Misc 622, 87 N.Y.S.2d 565

Later decisions, however, hold that the court is not bound to accept the appraisers' valuation, but can test their report in the light of accepted legal standards and modify their valuation as application of these standards dictates, or completely review the record. Amella v Consolidated Edison Co. (1947, Sup) 73 N.Y.S.2d 263, affd 273 A.D. 755, 75 N.Y.S.2d 513; Application of Behrens (1946, Sup) 61 N.Y.S.2d 179, affd 271 A.D. 1007, 69 N.Y.S.2d 910

20. Procedural matters

The order appointing appraisers is not a final order, or subject to review, except as incident to a final order confirming or rejecting their report. Re Seaich (1916) 219 N.Y. 634, 114 N.E. 1083; Re Bickerton (1921) 232 N.Y. 1, 133 N.E. 41

Dissenting stockholders who had turned in their stock and received payment therefor after Special Term had fixed its value in an appraisal proceeding could nevertheless appeal where they contested

the appraisers' valuation. Re Silverman (1953) 305 N.Y. 13, 110 N.E.2d 402, remittitur den 305 N.Y. 626, 111 N.E.2d 737

The petition for an appraisal could not be filed by a person acting merely as purported agent for the dissenting shareholder, without any averment as to his authority to act. Application of Baker (1939) 257 A.D. 1024, 13 N.Y.S.2d 408, mod on other grounds 284 N.Y. 1, 29 N.E.2d 241

Proceedings for appraisal of value of stock of dissenting stockholders, under § 21 of former Stock Corp. L., were designed to be somewhat summary, or at least not long protracted and unduly expensive for any of the parties concerned, or so conducted as to impair ordinary functioning of the corporation. Hence it has been held that dissenting shareholders are not entitled to subpoena or tie up all books, records, and working papers of the corporation for minute investigation, or to require a detailed accounting with respect to all transactions. Re Kaufmann, Alsberg & Co. (1961, 1st Dept) 15 A.D.2d 468, 222 N.Y.S.2d 305; Application of Marcus (1948) 273 A.D. 725, 79 N.Y.S.2d 76, reh and app den 274 A.D. 822, 81 N.Y.S.2d 199 and revg 191 Misc 808, 77 N.Y.S.2d 529; Tanenbaum v Consolidated Edison Co. (1947, Sup) 72 N.Y.S.2d 493

The appraiser in charge of proceedings for valuing stock of dissenting stockholders is charged with keeping the proceedings within reasonable bounds, and the corporation has its remedies against any subpoena, too broad in its terms, which may be served in the proceeding. Re Kaufmann, Alsberg & Co. (1961, 1st Dept) 15 A.D.2d 468, 222 N.Y.S.2d 305, affg 30 Misc. 2d 1025, 220 N.Y.S.2d 151

Under § 21 of former Stock Corp L, the court had discretion to consolidate appraisal proceedings, and it was accordingly considered improper to dismiss one such proceeding because of the pendency of another; object of the 1950 amendment of that section, requiring five days' notice of the petition and making it returnable on the 50th day, was to facilitate consolidation of such actions as might be then pending. Petition of McKay (1962, 1st Dept) 17 A.D.2d 299, 234 N.Y.S.2d 531

Under § 21 of former Stock Corp. L., the application for appraisal of a dissenting stockholder's stock could be made in any county within the judicial district in which the office of the corporation was situated. Application of Harwitz (1948) 192 Misc 91, 80 N.Y.S.2d 570

A subpoena duces tecum addressed to a subsidiary corporation and calling for the production of the records of the subsidiary in an attempt to establish the value of assets consisting of plant and equipment on a present replacement basis would be set aside where such present replacement value had slight if any material bearing upon the value of the stock. Application of Deutschmann (1951, Sup) 111 N.Y.S.2d 140, affd (AD) 107 N.Y.S.2d 1008

21. Costs and interest

Under § 21 of former Stock Corp. L., if a number of appraisal proceedings were initiated with respect to different dissenting shareholders or groups of shareholders, and these proceedings were consolidated, the court, on confirmation of the appraisers' report, could reserve the question of costs for further consideration and could, thereafter, award individual motion costs to each of the petitioners, but any award of trial fees and disbursements to them had to be in favor of all, as a group. Applications of Baker (1940) 284 N.Y. 1, 29 N.E.2d 241

Dissenting shareholders were likewise entitled to payment of their expense in procuring and introducing expert testimony as to value of their holdings, where the corporation failed to make any cash offer for their stock. Application of Silverman (1953) 305 N.Y. 628, 111 N.E.2d 889

Dissenting shareholders, as initiators or parties to appraisal proceedings under § 21 of former Stock Corp. L., were acting under, and with rights subject to, the special provisions of that section, to which some of the cost provisions of the Civil Practice Act were deemed inapplicable. Application of Cheney (1939) 257 A.D. 401, 13 N.Y.S.2d 403, mod 284 N.Y. 1, 29 N.E.2d 241

Dissenting stockholders were each entitled to motion costs against the corporation and their expense in obtaining a stenographic transcript of the testimony in the appraisal proceeding was properly charged against the corporation where the corporation made no offer to the dissenters whereby they could surrender stock to the corporation for a fair value and they were forced to apply for an appraisal. Application of Silverman (1953) 282 A.D. 252, 122 N.Y.S.2d 312

If dissenting stockholders seeking valuation of their stock were not shown to be acting in bad faith, they could be denied interest on the appraised value and likewise charged with costs and expenses of the appraisal proceeding. Re Kaufmann, Alsberg & Co. (1961, 1st Dept) 15 A.D.2d 468, 222 N.Y.S.2d 305, affg 30 Misc. 2d 1025, 220 N.Y.S.2d 151

Under a 1934 amendment of § 21 of former Stock Corp. L., a stockholder objecting to consolidation of his corporation with another could be awarded interest from date of the consolidation.Skipwith v Federal Water & Gas Corp. (1945) 185 Misc 248, 56 N.Y.S.2d 804

An application to the court to find that the shareholders' refusal to accept the corporation's offer of payment for their stock was arbitrary and capricious, made with a view to imposing appraisal costs and expenses on them, is premature where made before the appraisal is complete and the court has had an opportunity to review the record and report of the appraisers. Tabulating Card Co. v Leidesdorf (1959) 17 Misc. 2d 467, 188 N.Y.S.2d 26

Although the valuation of stock of dissenting stockholders in appraisal proceedings was only $3.50 per share above the $24 offer made by the corporation, the court, in its discretion, found that the appraisal materially exceeded the corporation's offer, in view of the number of shares held, entitling petitioner to reasonable expenses involved in prosecution of the appraisal proceeding, including expense of expert witnesses. Application of Dorsey (1961) 31 Misc. 2d 747, 221 N.Y.S.2d 927

Appraiser's valuation of stock held by dissenting stockholders at $1,100,000, being greatly in excess of the corporation's offer of $8,000 for such stock, the dissenting stockholders were entitled to reimbursement for fees paid to expert witnesses upon the basis of whose testimony the appraiser's estimate was reached. Tabulating Card Co. v Leidesdorf (1961) 32 Misc. 2d 720, 223 N.Y.S.2d 652

Under § 21 of former Stock Corp. L., as amended, as under this section of the Bus. Corp. L., the court had discretion to assess costs and expenses of the appraisal proceeding either against the corporation or the dissenting shareholders, or to apportion them. The costs and expenses would not be assessed against the shareholders, however, in the absence of clear and convincing proof of lack of good faith on their part in demanding the appraisal. Application of Deutschmann (1952, Sup) 113 N.Y.S.2d 823, mod on other grounds 281 A.D. 14, 116 N.Y.S.2d 578

§ 624. Books and records; right of inspection, prima facie evidence

(a) Each corporation shall keep correct and complete books and records of account and shall keep minutes of the proceedings of its shareholders, board and executive committee, if any, and shall keep at the office of the corporation in this state or at the office of its transfer agent or registrar in this state, a record containing the names and addresses of all shareholders, the number and class of shares held by each and the dates when they respectively became the owners of record thereof. Any of the foregoing books, minutes or records may be in written form or in any other form capable of being converted into written form within a reasonable time.

(b) Any person who shall have been a shareholder of record of a corporation upon at least five days' written demand shall have the right to examine in person or by agent or attorney, during usual business hours, its minutes of the proceedings of its shareholders and record of shareholders and to make extracts therefrom for any purpose reasonably related to such person's interest as a shareholder. Holders of voting trust certificates representing shares of the corporation shall be regarded as shareholders for the purpose of this section. Any such agent or attorney shall be authorized in a writing that satisfies the requirements of a writing under paragraph (b) of section 609 (Proxies). A corporation requested to provide information pursuant to this paragraph shall make available such information in written form and in any other format in which such information is maintained by the corporation and shall not be required to provide such information in any other format. If a request made pursuant to this paragraph includes a request to furnish information regarding beneficial owners, the corporation shall make available such information in its possession regarding beneficial owners as is provided to the corporation by a registered broker or dealer or a bank, association or other entity that exercises fiduciary powers in connection with the forwarding of information to such owners. The corporation shall not be required to obtain information about beneficial owners not in its possession.

(c) An inspection authorized by paragraph (b) may be denied to such shareholder or other person upon his refusal to furnish to the corporation, its transfer agent or registrar an affidavit that such inspection is not desired for a purpose which is in the interest of a business or object other than the business of the corporation and that he has not within five years sold or offered for sale any list of shareholders of any corporation of any type or kind, whether or not formed under the laws of this state, or aided or abetted any person in procuring any such record of shareholders for any such purpose.(d) Upon refusal by the corporation or by an officer or agent of the corporation to permit an inspection of the minutes of the proceedings of its shareholders or of the record of shareholders as herein provided, the person making the demand for inspection may apply to the supreme court in the judicial district where the office of the corporation is located, upon such notice as the court may direct, for an order directing the corporation, its officer or agent to show cause why an order should not be granted permitting such inspection by the applicant. Upon the return day of the order to show cause, the court shall hear the parties summarily, by affidavit or otherwise, and if it appears that the applicant is qualified and entitled to such inspection, the court shall grant an order compelling such inspection and awarding such further relief as to the court may seem just and proper.

(e) Upon the written request of any shareholder, the corporation shall give or mail to such shareholder an annual balance sheet and profit and loss statement for the preceding fiscal year, and, if any interim balance sheet or profit and loss statement has been distributed to its shareholders or otherwise made available to the public, the most recent such interim balance sheet or profit and loss statement. The corporation shall be allowed a reasonable time to prepare such annual balance sheet and profit and loss statement.

(f) Nothing herein contained shall impair the power of courts to compel the production for examination of the books and records of a corporation.

(g) The books and records specified in paragraph (a) shall be prima facie evidence of the facts therein stated in favor of the plaintiff in any action or special proceeding against such corporation or any of its officers, directors or shareholders.

History: Add, L 1961, ch 855, eff Sept 1, 1963; amd, L 1962, ch 834, § 41, eff Sept 1, 1963; L 1963, ch 746, eff Sept 1, 1963; L 1964, ch 725, § 7, eff June 1, 1964; L 1997, ch 449, § 37, eff Feb 22, 1998.

CASE ANNOTATIONS

1. In general
2. Applicability
3. Location of records
4. Sufficiency of records
5. Balance sheet; profit and loss statement
7. Prima facie evidence; particular matters
8. Right to inspect, generally
9. Who may inspect
10. Material subject to inspection
11. Effect of corporate dissolution
12. Relation to common-law right
13. Demand
14. Refusal by corporation, generally
15. Grounds for refusal
16. Judicial proceedings, generally
17. Who may institute proceedings
18. Good faith requirement, generally
19. – Particular cases
20. Other grounds and factors
21. Procedural matters

1. In general

Statute providing for shareholder inspection of corporate books and records should be liberally construed in favor of the shareholder whose welfare as a stockholder or the corporation's welfare may be affected. Crane Co. v Anaconda Co. (1976) 39 N.Y.2d 14, 382 N.Y.S.2d 707, 346 N.E.2d 507

Suffolk County Legislature had implicit power to impose reasonable fiscal conditions on approval of for-profit New York business corporation's application for rate increase for ferry service between Shelter Island and Greenport, on Long Island's mainland (Suffolk County Code § 287-3), but Legislature could not interfere with corporation's internal accounting procedures and corporate decision-making, nor could it usurp responsibilities, duties, and functions consigned by law exclusively to corporation's officers, directors, and shareholders; thus, conditions constituting such improper interference, imposed by Legislature on approval of resolution approving rate increase, were properly vacated. North Ferry Co. v Suffolk County Legislature (2000, 2d Dept) 272 A.D.2d 548, 708 N.Y.S.2d 144, app den 95 N.Y.2d 761, 714 N.Y.S.2d 711, 737 N.E.2d 953

2. Applicability

Section 10 of former Stock Corp. L. was considered inapplicable as a basis for seeking inspection of corporate records by a proceeding in the nature of mandamus where the objective was to obtain evidence for use by the petitioner in an action against individual directors personally. Re Taylor (1907) 117 A.D. 348, 101 N.Y.S. 1039

Section 10 of former Stock Corp. L., from which this section was principally derived, was construed as applicable only to domestic corporations and not to banks or corporations formed under special laws containing their own provisions as to records to be kept and right to inspect such records, to the extent of conflict with such special statutes. Lauer v Bayside Nat. Bank (1935) 244 A.D. 601, 280 N.Y.S. 139; Re Rappleye (1899) 43 A.D. 84, 59 N.Y.S. 338, app dismd 161 N.Y. 615, 55 N.E. 1100; Broderick v Adamson (1936) 159 Misc 634, 288 N.Y.S. 688

3. Location of records

The requirement of § 10 of former Stock Corp. L. that a corporation's business account books be kept "at its office" was regarded as controlling over bylaw or other provisions, and as extending to the corporation's minute book as well as other business records, and hence a bylaw requiring that the minute book be kept in custody of the secretary was construed as requiring it to be kept in his custody at the office of the corporation. Jamosa Holding Corp. v Bleendes (1939) 173 Misc 492, 18 N.Y.S.2d 190

If a corporation formed under former Stock Corp. L. kept its books and records at an office outside the state, the court, in connection with a shareholder's application for an inspection order, could require the corporation to bring them into the State for examination by the applicant. Wyman v Sombrerete Mining Co. (1959) 32 Misc. 2d 276, 222 N.Y.S.2d 996

However, the place where the books and records were actually kept was not apparently regarded as of vital importance, if no one's inspection rights were frustrated. Thus, in one case wherein a shareholder demanded inspection of business records kept outside the State, the court balanced the equities and relative inconvenience of requiring the corporation to bring them into the state against the shareholder's need for information and provided a choice of options as to how and where inspection might take place, for substituting photostatic copies for the originals, etc. Wyman v Sombrerete Mining Co. (1959) 32 Misc. 2d 276, 222 N.Y.S.2d 996

Where a corporation had only two shareholders and its affairs were managed by one of them from his home, where he kept the books and records, upon his death a court order was issued at the instance of the survivor requiring decedent's widow to turn over the records to petitioner as the person upon whom management of the corporation naturally devolved, since he could not be expected to manage the business fom decedent's home. Fisher v Meyerowitz (1961) 31 Misc. 2d 624, 220 N.Y.S.2d 920

That books and records were in custody of one of the corporation's officers or directors did not satisfy the statutory requirement. Orr v Bedford (1954, Sup) 137 N.Y.S.2d 216

4. Sufficiency of records

A stock certificate book containing the necessary information to answer all requirements of the statute, showing who the stockholders were, the number of shares held by them, and when they became owners thereof was sufficient. Re Utica Fire Alarm Tel. Co. (1906) 115 A.D. 821, 101 N.Y.S. 109

Under § 10 of former Stock Corp. L., a stock corporation was required to "keep at its office correct books of account of all its business and transactions," and likewise a "stock book" showing names and residences of all stockholders and the number of shares held by each. These provisions clearly required the keeping of reasonably detailed and accurate records. A partnership which controlled a number of corporations was liable to a judgment creditor of one of the corporations upon its insolvency where correct books of account were not kept separately for each of the subsidiary corporations and it appeared that transfers of assets of the insolvent corporation were systematically made to another of the controlled corporations. Salner Realty Corp. v Nancy Lee Millinery, Inc. (1941) 262 A.D. 491, 30 N.Y.S.2d 596

5. Balance sheet; profit and loss statement

In a proceeding to compel a corporation to deliver certain of its financial statements, the petition was insufficient as to any interim balance sheets or profit and loss statements where it made no showing as required by Business Corporation Law § 624(e) that such a document had been distributed to the corporate respondent's stockholders or otherwise been made available to the public. Levine v Pat-Plaza Amusements, Inc. (1971) 67 Misc. 2d 485, 324 N.Y.S.2d 145

Limitations imposed by statute on the right of inspection of corporate books does not apply to right of shareholder to receive copy of annual balance sheet and profit and loss statement. Apple v Careerco, Inc. (1974) 82 Misc. 2d 468, 370 N.Y.S.2d 289

Statute which provides that any shareholder for a period of at least six months may request, and a corporation must give, an annual balance sheet and profit and loss statement is mandatory; there are no restrictions or limitations on that right and no requirement of good faith. Apple v Careerco, Inc. (1974) 82 Misc. 2d 468, 370 N.Y.S.2d 289

If, at some future time, minority shareholder attempted to use corporate profit and loss statement as a basis for harassment of her former husband, who was president of the corporation, she would have no standing, but she was nonetheless entitled to receive annual balance sheet and profit and loss statement even though the motive for wishing the financial information might have been with reference to the marital dispute. Apple v Careerco, Inc. (1974) 82 Misc. 2d 468, 370 N.Y.S.2d 289

Section 77 of former Stock Corp. L. was pointed at the obtaining by stockholders of record of not less than 3% of outstanding shares of a stock corporation, upon demand, of a verified statement concerning the corporation's financial status and condition. The demandant could exact a penalty for failure to comply with his demand. Section 77 has not been carried forward into the new law, except to the extent of right conferred upon any shareholder to demand the most recent balance sheet and profit and loss statement which has been distributed to shareholders or made public. Under the former Stock Corp. L., the rights and remedies of shareholders under §§ 10 and 77 were regarded as distinct, and ownership of 3% or more of outstanding stock was not a necessary qualification for proceeding to demand an inspection of records under § 10. Re Lay (1943, Sup) 44 N.Y.S.2d 430

7. Prima facie evidence; particular matters

Some decisions have referred to the stock book as "conclusive" as to such matters as right to vote stock. Re Bruder's Estate (1950) 302 N.Y. 52, 96 N.E.2d 84

Minutes of proceedings of board of directors of corporation are prima facie evidence of action taken by corporation.DFI Communications, Inc. v Greenberg (1977) 41 N.Y.2d 602, 394 N.Y.S.2d 586, 363 N.E.2d 312

The stock book and stock records of a corporation are at least presumptive evidence as to who are holders of its shares, entitled to assert rights as such. Breck v Brewster (1912) 150 A.D. 202, 134 N.Y.S. 697, later app 153 A.D. 800, 138 N.Y.S. 821. See also subd. (i) of § 612 of the Bus. Corp. L

A corporation is ordinarily entitled to rely on its stock records, and to deny recognition as a shareholder to one who does not appear on those records as a shareholder of record, notwithstanding his assertion of claim to legal ownership of shares or some interest therein. Re D. J. Salvator, Inc. (1944) 268 A.D. 919, 51 N.Y.S.2d 342; Davis v Fraser (1953, Sup) 121 N.Y.S.2d 643, affd 283 A.D. 657, 127 N.Y.S.2d 838, affd 307 N.Y. 433, 121 N.E.2d 406, reh den 308 N.Y. 736, 124 N.E.2d 716

Although the stock book and books of account of a corporation are prima facie evidence of the fact therein stated in favor of a plaintiff in any action or special proceeding against it or any of its officers, directors or stockholders, they are not conclusive as to who is a stockholder nor as to the ownership of stock. Porco v Catherwood (1969, 3d Dept) 32 A.D.2d 983, 302 N.Y.S.2d 219

Where 44 shares of stock of corporation of par value of $100 per share were issued to corporation president in exchange for cancellation of corporate debt in amount of $2,726, and president therefore paid $1,674 less than par value of shares issued, transaction was voidable at option or other shareholders. Frankowski v Palermo (1975, 4th Dept) 47 A.D.2d 579, 363 N.Y.S.2d 159

Corporation's books are to be treated as prima facie evidence but are not conclusive of matters stated therein, and where reports of FCC on ownership of stock in radio station corporation conflict with corporate records on issue of stock ownership, question of fact is created. Kyle v Kyle (1985, 3d Dept) 111 A.D.2d 537, 489 N.Y.S.2d 409

Court properly granted application to inspect respondent corporation's books and records where special referee's finding that petitioner owned 40 of 200 shares of respondent's stock was supported by, inter alia, stock purchase agreement evidencing purchase of 160 shares by respondent's principals, subsequently issued stock certificate certifying petitioner's ownership of 40 shares, and testimony of banking department examiner on significance of certain documents that respondent was required to file, which mentioned petitioner as stockholder. In re Greenberg (1995, 1st Dept) 220 A.D.2d 205, 632 N.Y.S.2d 7

In the absence of evidence to the contrary, § 10 of former Stock Corp L was regarded as making a corporation's stock ledger presumptive evidence of facts therein stated concerning date of issuance of certain stock. Bonsall v Commissioner (1963, CA2) 317 F.2d 61, 63-1 USTC ¶ 9462

8. Right to inspect, generally

Because personal gain and benefit to the corporation are not mutually exclusive objectives, stockholder has right to inspect the corporation's list of stockholders for the sole purpose of soliciting sales of stock in the corporation to such stockholder. Crane Co. v Anaconda Co., (1976) 39 N.Y.2d 14, 382 N.Y.S.2d 707, 346 N.E.2d 507

To the extent that a right to inspect the records of a corporation exists, it includes the right to make extracts from such records. People ex rel. Lorge v Consolidated Nat. Bank (1905) 105 A.D. 409, 94 N.Y.S. 173

A shareholder's right to inspect the corporation's stock records exists irrespective of his motive or objective, if he furnishes the required affidavit and has himself been a shareholder of record for six months or more. People ex rel. Britton v American Press Ass'n (1911) 148 A.D. 651, 133 N.Y.S. 216

Proper purposes for which shareholder has common-law right to inspect corporate books and records include efforts to ascertain financial condition of corporation, to learn propriety of dividend distributions, to calculate value of stock, to investigate management's conduct, and to obtain information in aid of legitimate litigation; improper purposes are those which are inimical to corporation, such as to discover business secrets to aid competitor of corporation, to secure prospects for future business, to find technical defects in corporate transactions for purpose of instituting "strike suits," and to locate information to pursue one's own social or political goals. Tatko v Tatko Bros. Slate Co. (1991, 3d Dept) 173 A.D.2d 917, 569 N.Y.S.2d 783

Defendants were ordered to provide the owner of a condominium unit with contact information for the condominium's other unit owners because, while the owner was not entitled under Business Corporation Law to examine the books and records of the condominium, right of a stockholder to examine the books and records of a corporation existed at common law, and did not depend on a statute; the unit owners collectively owned the common elements of the condominium and were responsible for the common expenses under N.Y. Real Prop. Law §§ 339-i, 339-m, so the rationale that existed for a shareholder to examine a corporation's books and records at common law applied equally to a unit owner vis-a-vis a condominium. The owner had rights similar to those of a shareholder under N.Y. Bus. Corp. Law § 624, at least where elections for a condominium board were concerned. Pomerance v McGrath (2013, 1st Dept) 104 App Div 3d 440, 961 NYS2d 83.

Defendants were ordered to provide the owner of a condominium unit with contact information for the condominium's other unit owners because, while the owner was not entitled under Business Corporation Law to examine the books and records of the condominium, right of a stockholder to examine the books and records of a corporation existed at common law, and did not depend on a statute; the unit owners collectively owned the common elements of the condominium and were responsible for the common expenses under N.Y. Real Prop. Law §§ 339-i, 339-m, so the rationale that existed for a shareholder to examine a corporation's books and records at common law applied equally to a unit owner vis--vis a condominium. The owner had rights similar to those of a shareholder under N.Y. Bus. Corp. Law § 624, at least where elections for a condominium board were concerned. Pomerance v McGrath (2013, 1st Dept) 104 App Div 3d 440, 961 NYS2d 83.

9. Who may inspect

Directors as well as stockholders have generally been conceded to have the right to inspect corporate books and records, but this is by virtue of necessity to enable them to perform the duties of office, rather than any statutory authorization. Overland v Le Roy Foods, Inc. (1952) 304 N.Y. 573, 107 N.E.2d 74; People ex rel. Leach v Central Fish Co. (1907) 117 A.D. 77, 101 N.Y.S. 1108

Shareholder agreement was specific enough to be more than a profit sharing agreement and unambiguously demonstrated that a former employee was a minority shareholder; as such, the former employee was entitled to inspect the company's books and records upon demand. World Ambulette Transp., Inc. v Lee, 161 A.D.3d 1028, 78 N.Y.S.3d 137, 2018 N.Y. App. Div. LEXIS 3509 (N.Y. App. Div. 2d Dep't 2018).

The fact that shares standing of record in the name of a demandant had been pledged to another as security for indebtedness did not, however, defeat the pledgor's right to demand inspection. Pray v Todd (1902) 71 A.D. 391, 75 N.Y.S. 947; Booth v Consolidated Fruit Jar Co. (1909) 62 Misc 252, 114 N.Y.S. 1000

A successor in interest by operation of law to shares registered in the name of another has been regarded as entitled to assert his predecessor's right to inspect the corporate records, in some instances, upon establishing his acquisition of title, as in the case of a purchaser at execution sale or the personal representative, or a distributee, of the estate of a deceased shareholder. Re Hastings (1908) 128 A.D. 516, 112 N.Y.S. 800, affd 194 N.Y. 546, 87 N.E. 1120; Monitor Co. v Confianza Furniture & Appliance Corp. (1955, Sup) 142 N.Y.S.2d 140; Application of Schnepf (1948, Sup) 84 N.Y.S.2d 416

If a director or other officer is a stockholder of record as well as engaged in management of the corporation, he can rest his right of inspection upon either his status as shareholder or on his duties and responsibilities in his official capacity, or upon both. Townsend v Davis (1912) 153 A.D. 599, 138 N.Y.S. 758; Re Bush Terminal Co. (1935, CA2 NY) 78 F.2d 662; see also Re Bush Terminal Co. (1935, DC NY) 10 F. Supp. 315

While this section of the Bus. Corp. L. clearly brings holders of voting trust certificates within the ambit of "shareholders" entitled to demand an inspection, lack of any such language in earlier provisions precluded them from being regarded as stockholders of record and hence, ordinarily, from having rights as such under § 10 of former

Business Corporation Law

Stock Corp. L. Brentmore Estates v Hotel Barbizon (1942) 263 A.D. 389, 33 N.Y.S.2d 331

An officer's right of inspection is not subject to denial, if he still holds office, merely because he has acquired adverse interests or is, in fact, hostile to those in control of its affairs. Davis v Keilsohn Offset Co. (1948) 273 A.D. 695, 79 N.Y.S.2d 540. See also Javits v Investors League, Inc. (1949, Sup) 92 N.Y.S.2d 267; People ex rel. Leach v Central Fish Co. (1907) 117 A.D. 77, 101 N.Y.S. 1108

It is not sufficient that the shareholder, in requesting an examination of corporate records, appear to the court to be "qualified;" he must also appear to the court to be "entitled" to the inspection. Gottdenker v Philadelphia & Reading Corp. (1968, 1st Dept) 31 A.D.2d 152, 295 N.Y.S.2d 682 (petition for right of inspection denied without prejudice to renewal upon a showing of the purpose for which the inspection was desired)

Plaintiff who alleged an agreement to enter into business with individual defendant in a corporation to be formed in which plaintiff was to be president and director and to be issued shares of stock could not examine the corporate books until he established that he was a stockholder or director or had a vested contract right thereto and was not entitled to an accounting until he established an agreement that he share in the profits, nor was he entitled to examine individual defendant's income tax returns, but for limited purpose of establishing his rights to share in corporate profits, and thus his right to accounting as opposed to an accounting itself, plaintiff was entitled to examine defendants and their business records. Lo Verde v Interex Design & Equipment Corp. (1976, 4th Dept) 54 A.D.2d 1090, 388 N.Y.S.2d 770

In action arising from failed merger of petitioner corporation into defendant corporation, petitioners were entitled to order under CLS Bus Corp § 624 directing defendant corporation to produce its books and records for inspection, even though parties' contract was ambiguous as to whether petitioners were actually shareholders of defendant corporation, since examination of books was necessary to establish that petitioners were shareholders, and statute does not impair power of courts to compel examination of books and records of corporations. Koch v Specto Optical, Inc. (1992, 2d Dept) 184 A.D.2d 701, 585 N.Y.S.2d 448

Even after removal of minority shareholder from his positions as officer and director of 8 related corporations and partnerships, he retained right to inspect books of those entities in order to determine true value of his shares in response to buy-out offer where he was still partner in partnerships and shareholder in corporations. Berkowitz v Astro Moving & Storage Co. (1997, 2d Dept) 240 A.D.2d 450, 658 N.Y.S.2d 425

A shareholder, to be entitled as such to demand an inspection or financial statement under §§ 10 and 77 of former Stock Corp. L., had to be a stockholder of record at the time of making the demand. Tighe v Lavery (1917) 98 Misc 245, 162 N.Y.S. 1005

Both at common law and by statute a stockholder has a qualified right to inspect the corporate books and records, such right being qualified only by a requirement of good faith and proper purpose.Smilkstein v J. Smilkstein & Sons, Inc. (1961) 32 Misc. 2d 882, 223 N.Y.S.2d 561

Stockholder who was in competitive business was entitled to examine books of defendant corporation where there appeared to be evidence of irregularities in the conduct of the respondent corporation's affairs; however, respondent corporations were entitled to protection from disclosure of any business secrets which should be withheld from petitioner. Malone v Dimco Corp. (1969) 68 Misc. 2d 610, 328 N.Y.S.2d 65

An officer and director of a corporation has an absolute right to inspection of the records of such corporation. Leisner v Kent Investors, Inc. (1970) 62 Misc. 2d 132, 307 N.Y.S.2d 293

It was generally held, moreover, that one who had the right to inspect corporate records need not make the inspection alone and in person, but could invoke the assistance of his attorney or accountant. Re Hassuk (1945, Sup) 57 N.Y.S.2d 798. See also Davis v Keilsohn Offset Co. (1948) 273 A.D. 695, 79 N.Y.S.2d 540

Existence of any right to demand inspection of corporate books and records, under § 10 of former Stock Corp. L., without a court order, required, as to alleged stockholders, record ownership of stock in the demandant, or those authorizing him in writing to make the demand, at the time it was made. There was some doubt as to whether one who had already entered into a binding contract to sell and transfer his shares could enforce such a demand.Diamond v Jarold Shops, Inc.

(1949, Sup) 91 N.Y.S.2d 585, revd on other grounds 275 A.D. 919, 90 N.Y.S.2d 683

10. Material subject to inspection

Section 10 of former Stock Corp. L. dealt with a shareholder's right to inspect the "stock book," but this was construed, in the light of a reference in § 47 of former Stock Corp. L. to "books and papers containing the list of stockholders," as extending to any records containing information equivalent to that which § 10 required to be set forth in the "stock book," if the corporation did not keep a "stock book" within the statutory concept, such as a stock certificate book, and other documents. Re Bruder's Estate (1950) 302 N.Y. 52, 96 N.E.2d 84

A distinction has consistently been recognized between right to inspect a corporation's records concerning ownership of its outstanding shares and right to inspect its business and other records and documents. Shareholders were considered to have a common-law right to inspect records as to share ownership, in the absence of bad faith, of which right they could not be denied; but neither shareholders nor anyone else except managing personnel had any absolute right of access to other records. This distinction was inherent in the phrasing of § 10 of former Stock Corp. L., and has been carefully retained in § 624 of the Bus. Corp. L. People ex rel. Callanan v Keeseville, A. C. & L. C. R. Co. (1905) 106 A.D. 349, 94 N.Y.S. 555; Schulman v Louis Dejonge & Co. (1945) 270 A.D. 147, 59 N.Y.S.2d 119; Feinberg v Enselberg (1946, Sup) 63 N.Y.S.2d 891; Green v Baltic Shipping Co. (1947, Sup) 76 N.Y.S.2d 608, revd on other grounds 275 A.D. 700, 87 N.Y.S.2d 354. See also Application of Schnepf (1948, Sup) 84 N.Y.S.2d 416; Seff v Williamsburgh Maternity, Inc. (1948, Sup) 81 N.Y.S.2d 584

Petitioner, owner of 178,000 shares in respondent corporation, seeks to compel respondent to disclose certain shareholder records for use in soliciting proxies in connection with election of respondent's board of directors; order granting petition inappropriately limits petitioner's access to records sought; Business Corporation Law § 624, pursuant to which petitioner seeks to examine respondent's "record of shareholders", is to be liberally construed so as to facilitate communication among shareholders on issues respecting corporate affairs; statute seeks, to extent possible, to place shareholders on equal footing with management in obtaining access to shareholders; affirmance of order under review would leave respondent's management with exclusive access to materials necessary to expeditiously locate and communicate with respondent's shareholders in upcoming proxy battle; such advantage is not required by statute's language and does not comport with its purpose; orders modified accordingly. Matter of Bohrer v International Banknote Co., 150 A.D.2d 196

Petitioner, who sought certain shareholder records for use in soliciting proxies in connection with election of corporate board of directors, was entitled to (1) immediate access to any "NOBO" list in possession of corporation, (2) access to "CEDE" breakdown of holders of shares by nominees for beneficial owners thereof, (3) magnetic computer tapes listing common shareholders and preference shareholders with name, address and number of shares held by them, and (4) access to daily transfer sheets; CLS Bus Corp § 624 is to be construed liberally so as to place shareholders on equal footing with management in obtaining access to shareholders. Bohrer v International Banknote Co. (1989, 1st Dept) 150 A.D.2d 196, 540 N.Y.S.2d 445

Stockholders were not entitled under § 10 of former Stock Corp. L. to "copies of income statements" of the corporation, where they had been duly furnished with "a statement of its affairs, under oath, embracing a particular account of all its assets and liabilities," less than one year perviously. Feinberg v Enselberg (1946, Sup) 63 N.Y.S.2d 891

It could be said, under §§ 10 and 77 of former Stock Corp. L., and earlier decisions, that a shareholder, as one having a legal interest in the business conducted and the welfare of the corporation, had, in a sense, a "right" to inspect records other than the stock book; but it was a right unenforceable without a court order and whether to grant the application for such an order rested in the court's sound discretion. Seff v Williamsburgh Maternity, Inc. (1948, Sup) 81 N.Y.S.2d 584; Re Lay (1943, Sup) 44 N.Y.S.2d 430

Trial court judgment awarding a stockholder the right to inspect corporate financial records was modified because the scope of the inspection granted by the court under N.Y. Bus. Corp. Law § 624 was overly broad; therefore, the matter was remitted to the trial court for a hearing to determine the proper scope of inspection. Because the stockholder sought to verify the corporation's book value to determine the correct value of his shares, the stockholder's right of inspection should have been limited to those books and records relevant and necessary to establish the book value of the stockholder's stock. Matter of Dwyer v Di Nardo & Metschl, P.C. (2007, 4th Dept) 41 App Div 3d 1177, 838 NYS2d 745

11. Effect of corporate dissolution

After a corporation has been dissolved, however, inspection rights as they existed by statute or otherwise prior to dissolution cease to exist, or at least can no longer be asserted as absolute on the basis of prior official position and interest in its affairs. Bellman v Standard Match Co. (1924) 208 A.D. 4, 202 N.Y.S. 840

After sale of all corporate assets in connection with a voluntary liquidation, acceptance of payment of the liquidating dividend, and execution of mutual releases, a stockholder's rights of inspection under § 10 of former Stock Corp. L. and likewise under common-law principles terminated as completely and effectively as if his stock had been sold outright.Schor v Barshor Realty Co. (1961, Sup) 218 N.Y.S.2d 11

12. Relation to common-law right

Right of examination of corporate records granted by subd b of this section is not exclusive of common-law right to inspect stock books of corporation if such inspection is sought in good faith and for valid purpose as is shown by the provision in subd f, and therefore stockholder has such common-law right although he has not been shareholder of record of corporation for at least 6 months as required by subd b, and is in fact not stockholder of record at all.Sivin v Schwartz (1964, 2d Dept) 22 A.D.2d 821, 254 N.Y.S.2d 914

A stockholder has the common law right to inspection and examination of the corporate books at a proper time and place and for a proper purpose. Malone v Dimco Corp. (1969) 68 Misc. 2d 610, 328 N.Y.S.2d 65

The common law recognized no right to a financial statement as distinct from inspection of the corporation's books and the making of extracts thereof. Levine v Pat-Plaza Amusements, Inc. (1971) 67 Misc. 2d 485, 324 N.Y.S.2d 145

Business Corporation Law § 624 is in addition to and not in substitution for the rights accorded stockholders by the common law and the common law did not insist, as does the statute, that the petitioner be either a holder of record or own or speak for any given percentage of outstanding stock. Levine v Pat-Plaza Amusements, Inc. (1971) 67 Misc. 2d 485, 324 N.Y.S.2d 145

Plaintiff, the beneficial owner of 100 shares of a corporation, is entitled to examine and copy the current record list of shareholders of the corporation for the purpose of ascertaining the identity of the shareholders in order to inform them of a tender offer, despite the fact that plaintiff has not been a shareholder of record for at least six months and does not own at least 5% of the corporation's outstanding shares as required by subdivision (b) of section 624 of the Business Corporation Law, since there is a common-law right of inspection independent of section 624, which does not require that a shareholder own his stock for six months or have 5% of the outstanding shares, as long as the inspection is sought for a valid purpose. Johncamp Realty, Inc. v Sanders (1979) 98 Misc. 2d 949, 415 N.Y.S.2d 192

Common-law right of inspection survived enactment of § 624 of New York Business Corporation Law. Rockwell v SCM Corp. (1980, SD NY) 496 F. Supp. 1123

Business Corporation Law § 624, subd b's 6-month requirement is not exclusive, and any shareholder, including one not of record, has common law right to inspect the shareholders list if the inspection is sought in good faith and for a valid purpose, which purpose includes inducing a sufficient number of shareholders to join as co-plaintiffs in derivative suit to obviate need for posting security. Weisfeld v Spartans Industries, Inc. (1972, SD NY) 58 FRD 570, 17 FR Serv 2d 331

13. Demand

Where the demand to inspect stock records has a clearly legitimate objective, such as a desire to locate and contact other shareholders with a view to purchasing their shares, the demand cannot be refused and the demandant has a right to copy the list of shareholders, or such part of it as he may wish. People ex rel. Lorge v Consolidated Nat. Bank (1905) 105 A.D. 409, 94 N.Y.S. 173

A preliminary demand for leave to inspect corporate records, or for disclosure of information to be found in the records, or alleged to appear therein, has always been necessary in order to place the corporation in the wrong in refusing to permit the inspection or provide the information and to provide a foundation for Art. 78 proceedings to compel the disclosure. Re Hitchcock (1912) 149 A.D.

824, 134 N.Y.S. 174, later app 157 A.D. 328, 142 N.Y.S. 247; People ex rel. Clason v Nassau Ferry Co. (1895) 86 Hun 128, 33 N.Y.S. 244

If the demand was by a stockholder of record, he did not have to produce his share certificate to sustain it. Re McCafferty's Estate (1933) 147 Misc 179, 264 N.Y.S. 38

It was sufficient compliance with a demand for a financial statement, under § 77 of former Stock Corp. L., to send the statement to him by registered mail or deliver the statement to his duly authorized agent. Daddazio v Ontario Sand & Gravel Co. (1940) 175 Misc 518, 24 N.Y.S.2d 179, affd 264 A.D. 821, 35 N.Y.S.2d 464

Under both Business Corporation Law § 624(b) and at common law, a demand is a prerequisite to the inspection of the books of a corporation. Levine v Pat-Plaza Amusements, Inc. (1971) 67 Misc. 2d 485, 324 N.Y.S.2d 145

A demand for inspection of records under § 10 of former Stock Corp. L. had to be made at, or addressed to, the office where the record was required to be kept, but it could be made by registered mail and did not have to be delivered in person. Green v Baltic Shipping Co. (1947, Sup) 76 N.Y.S.2d 608, revd on other grounds 275 A.D. 700, 87 N.Y.S.2d 354; Buker v Steele (1896, Co Ct) 43 N.Y.S. 346

In a suit between brothers, who were also former business partners, based on defendants' alleged unlawful transfer of jointly held assets, plaintiff's claim for an accounting failed because he did not allege that he made any inspection demand upon the corporate defendants prior to fling suit, as required by N.Y. Corp. Bus. Law 624(b). Kermanshah v Kermanshah (2008, SD NY) 580 F Supp 2d 247, injunction den (2008, SD NY) 2008 US Dist LEXIS 87581.

14. Refusal by corporation, generally

Under the statute the corporation may not constitute itself the judge of the propriety of a shareholder's purpose in requesting an inspection of records; its right in this regard is limited to a demand for an affidavit as prescribed by statute. Gottdenker v Philadelphia & Reading Corp. (1968, 1st Dept) 31 A.D.2d 152, 295 N.Y.S.2d 682

In an action by a stockholder to obtain an audit of the corporation's books and records the trial court properly held the corporation in contempt and directed it to produce certain corporate books and records where the corporation failed to demonstrate any lack of good faith by plaintiff or any other reason why the documents requested should not be produced as required by Bus Cor Law § 624. Traktman v Atlantic & Pacific Oil Co. (1983, 2d Dept) 98 A.D.2d 719, 469 N.Y.S.2d 124

The corporation's right to refuse a demand for inspection of its stock records was substantially the same under § 10 of former Stock Corp. L. as it now is under § 624 of the Bus. Corp. L. It could deny the request if the shareholder making it failed to furnish an affidavit, or otherwise establish, that inspection was not sought in the interest of a business or object other than that of the corporation and that demandant had not within five years sold or offered to sell any list of corporate shareholders or aided and abetted such a project. These implied conditions on the right to inspect stock records must both be met, upon request, before the right became absolute. Petition of Holzer (1960) 26 Misc. 2d 934, 209 N.Y.S.2d 846; Bresnick v Saypol (1945, Sup) 57 N.Y.S.2d 904, mod in other respects 270 A.D. 837, 61 N.Y.S.2d 376

15. Grounds for refusal

A request to examine the stock book was not deemed to have been denied where it was made at the office of the corporation and the demandant was told that the stock book was not there, but at the office of the president only a short distance away, where he would be at liberty to inspect it. Lozier v Saratoga Gas, Electric Light & Power Co. (1901) 59 A.D. 390, 69 N.Y.S. 247

Financial condition of a corporation cannot be considered confidential when a stockholder is concerned; it is only when the stockholder attempts to misuse the financial information to the detriment of the corporation that his actions will be limited. Apple v Careerco, Inc. (1974) 82 Misc. 2d 468, 370 N.Y.S.2d 289

The fact that a stockholder is highly temperamental or disputatious does not deprive him of the right of inspection. Re Chanel (1947, Sup) 74 N.Y.S.2d 203

If it appears that the demand for inspection was made by an eligible shareholder and in good faith, for some legitimate purpose in furtherance of his interest as a shareholder, it is not a sufficient reason for denying it that the applicant was offered, instead, a prepared financial statement. Re Chanel (1947, Sup) 74 N.Y.S.2d 211

Presence of the demandant's attorney to take part in the proposed inspection is likewise not a sound reason for denying it. People ex rel. Clason v Nassau Ferry Co. (1895) 86 Hun 128, 33 N.Y.S. 244

16. Judicial proceedings, generally

Where the demand is for inspection of records other than, or in addition to, stock records, the corporation can legally refuse to grant it for any reason whatsoever and thereby place the demandant under necessity of resorting to Art. 78 judicial proceedings. But if its refusal is not for good cause and sound reasons, but merely because it denies any mismanagement or wastage of assets, or the like, in an Art. 78 proceeding it is likely to be overruled with costs of the proceeding to obtain an order for inspection assessed against it.Durr v Paragon Trading Corp. (1936) 270 N.Y. 464, 1 N.E.2d 967; Seff v Williamsburgh Maternity, Inc. (1948, Sup) 81 N.Y.S.2d 584; Lewis v Nat Lewis Retail Corp. (1949) 194 Misc 427, 86 N.Y.S.2d 823; Re Hassuk (1945, Sup) 57 N.Y.S.2d 798; Re Lay (1943, Sup) 44 N.Y.S.2d 430

Common-law requirement of a bona fide intention on part of him who seeks access to corporation's books and records is equally applicable when statutory relief is sought. Crane Co. v Anaconda Co. (1976) 39 N.Y.2d 14, 382 N.Y.S.2d 707, 346 N.E.2d 507

If a request or demand for leave to inspect corporate books and records is denied by the corporation, whether the request relates to share records, other records, or both, the remedy of the person seeking the inspection is usually by a proceeding in the nature of mandamus under Art.78 of the Civil Practice Act. Spector v Rosman Metal Body Co. (1944) 268 A.D. 929, 51 N.Y.S.2d 468

A stockholder is not entitled to inspect the complete books and records of the corporation in which he holds stock as matter of right, but can seek a court order for their inspection in an art. 78 proceeding, in which, if an objection is made in point of law by motion to dismiss the petition, the court, upon denying the motion, should permit respondent to answer. Application of Black (1964, 1st Dept) 21 A.D.2d 645, 249 N.Y.S.2d 389

A special proceeding in the nature of mandamus is a procedure whereby the right to inspect corporate books for a proper purpose is enforced. Leisner v Kent Investors, Inc. (1970) 62 Misc. 2d 132, 307 N.Y.S.2d 293

17. Who may institute proceedings

Under § 10 of former Stock. Corp. L., it was held that an attorney in fact could not institute inspection proceedings in his own name individually, not being the real party in interest. Application of Gill (1948) 192 Misc 283, 80 N.Y.S.2d 400

Such a proceeding could be instituted by an attorney thereunto duly authorized in behalf of his client, at least in emergency circumstances where the client was out of the state; and it was likewise held that one petitioning as a shareholder could be presumed to be a shareholder of record on the basis of the corporation's stock records and continued recognition of his shareholder status. Seff v Williamsburgh Maternity, Inc. (1948, Sup) 81 N.Y.S.2d 584; Schacher v G. Taus & Sons, Inc. (1946) 188 Misc 259, 67 N.Y.S.2d 337

18. Good faith requirement, generally

When stockholder seeking to enforce right to inspect corporate books and records alleges compliance with statute, the bona fides of the stockholder will be assumed and it becomes incumbent on the corporation to justify its refusal by showing an improper purpose or bad faith. Crane Co. v Anaconda Co. (1976) 39 N.Y.2d 14, 382 N.Y.S.2d 707, 346 N.E.2d 507

Dispositive inquiry in determining whether to require corporation to produce record of shareholders for inspection by stockholder is whether the corporation can prove that inspection is sought for a purpose which is contrary to the best interests of the corporation or its stockholders. Crane Co. v Anaconda Co. (1976) 39 N.Y.2d 14, 382 N.Y.S.2d 707, 346 N.E.2d 507

Although an application by a shareholder of record to inspect the stock book and stock records has often been referred to as based on absolute right, decisions construing and applying § 10 of former Stock Corp. L. indicate that the court, in an Art. 78 proceeding to compel the corporation to submit its stock records to stockholder inspection, has discretion to deny the application if satisfied that the application was not made in good faith and that its objective does not accord with the business of the corporation, this area of discretion being quite broad. Baker v Macfadden Publications, Inc. (1946) 270 A.D. 440, 59 N.Y.S.2d 841, revd on other grounds 300 N.Y. 325, 90 N.E.2d 876; Tate v Sonotone Corp. (1947) 272 A.D. 103, 69 N.Y.S.2d 535; People ex rel. Britton v American Press Ass'n (1911) 148 A.D. 651, 133 N.Y.S. 216; Application of Huber (1960) 26 Misc. 2d 563, 210 N.Y.S.2d 211; Hecht v Select Theatres Corp. (1949, Sup) 91 N.Y.S.2d 464; Javits v Investors League, Inc. (1949, Sup) 92 N.Y.S.2d 267

As to good or bad faith in making the application for an inspection, several decisions state that a shareholder applicant is not under the burden of proving his own good faith, either stating or implying that the burden of establishing his bad faith is on those opposing the application, but frequently adding that the petition should be denied unless the papers before the court establish that purpose of inspection is related to petitioner's welfare as a stockholder and for protection of his stockholder interest. Tate v Sonotone Corp. (1947) 272 A.D. 103, 69 N.Y.S.2d 535; Re Combined Industries, Inc. (1961) 28 Misc. 2d 649, 212 N.Y.S.2d 129; Hecht v Select Theatres Corp. (1949, Sup) 91 N.Y.S.2d 464; Re Chanel (1947, Sup) 74 N.Y.S.2d 203

A hearing on issue of lack of good faith on part of shareholder who sought inspection of corporation's records was not necessary; a proper disposition could be made on the assumption of the truth of the allegations of shareholder's affidavits.S. & S. Realty Corp. v Kleer-Vu Industries, Inc. (1976, 1st Dept) 53 A.D.2d 552, 384 N.Y.S.2d 796

Shareholder's authority to inspect corporation's books and records pursuant to CLS Bus Corp § 624 is qualified and can be asserted only where shareholder is acting in good faith and has established that inspection is for proper purpose. Niggli v Richlin Mach., Inc. (1999, 2d Dept) 257 A.D.2d 623, 684 N.Y.S.2d 254

The former § 10 requirement that a stockholder seeking inspection of the stock book must establish that the inspection sought was not for the purpose of "communicating with stockholders in the interest of a business or object other than the business of the corporation" was viewed as similar to the common-law requirement of good faith in connection with stockholder applications to inspect books and records of the corporation other than its stock books.Young v Columbia Broadcasting System, Inc. (1959) 28 Misc. 2d 512, 215 N.Y.S.2d 950

An inspection will not be ordered, where an issue has been duly raised as to whether the application is made in good faith or for some ulterior purpose, until such issue has been determined, and this may involve questions of fact for submission to a jury. Re Chanel (1947, Sup) 74 N.Y.S.2d 203; Schulman v Louis Dejonge & Co. (1945) 270 A.D. 147, 59 N.Y.S.2d 119

Where the corporation raised a question as to whether the former president's request for information pursuant to N.Y. Bus. Corp. Law § 624 was motivated by bad faith and/or improper motives, and the court scheduled a hearing on that issue. In re Application of Presher (2003, Sup) 765 N.Y.S.2d 210

19. – Particular cases

Shareholder's interest in pursuing a selective and direct approach to stockholders with respect to shareholder's pending tender offer involving over one-fifth of the corporation's common stock, and shareholder's refusal of corporation's offer to have corporation's transfer agent transmit the tender offer prospectus to all stockholders, was not improper and did not render shareholder's request for inspection contrary to the best interests of the corporation or its stockholders. Crane Co. v Anaconda Co. (1976) 39 N.Y.2d 14, 382 N.Y.S.2d 707, 346 N.E.2d 507

Stockholder's request to inspect corporation's record of shareholders in order to present stockholders with information pertinent to stockholder's pending tender offer involving over one-fifth of the corporation's common stock did not involve a purpose other than the business of the corporation. Crane Co. v Anaconda Co. (1976) 39 N.Y.2d 14, 382 N.Y.S.2d 707, 346 N.E.2d 507

A shareholder desiring to discuss relevant aspects of a tender offer should be granted access to the shareholder list unless it is sought for a purpose inimical to the corporation or its stockholders. Crane Co. v Anaconda Co. (1976) 39 N.Y.2d 14, 382 N.Y.S.2d 707, 346 N.E.2d 507

Any application to a court for an order to require a corporation to submit books and records to stockholder inspection is addressed to the court's discretion and may be denied if it is not directed to something which the applicant has a right to know or it appears to have been made merely for the purpose of annoying and impeding the corporation. People ex rel. McElwee v Produce Exch. Trust Co. (1900) 53 A.D. 93, 65 N.Y.S. 926; Martin v Columbia Pictures Co. (1953, Sup) 133 N.Y.S.2d 469, affd 283 A.D. 926, 130 N.Y.S.2d 300, affd 307 N.Y. 922, 123 N.E.2d 572, reh den 308 N.Y. 745, 125 N.E.2d 103; Cravatts v Klozo Fastener Corp. (1954) 205 Misc 781, 133 N.Y.S.2d 235

The application is not in good faith if it is made for an ulterior purpose and to aid undisclosed persons in some undisclosed scheme against the corporation. People ex rel. Hunter v National Park Bank (1907) 122 A.D. 635, 107 N.Y.S. 369

Where the applicant has a considerable stake or interest in the corporation and shows reason for suspecting mismanagement or wastage of assets, his good faith is usually evident and his application should ordinarily be granted. People ex rel. Ludwig v Ludwig & Co.

(1908) 126 A.D. 696, 111 N.Y.S. 94; Lewis v Nat Lewis Retail Corp. (1949) 194 Misc 427, 86 N.Y.S.2d 823

Where it is asserted in connection with a stockholder's petition for leave to inspect the corporate books and records that the petitioner has been consorting with competitors and is not acting in good faith, the judge is not free to exercise his discretion and to conclude, without a hearing, that petitioner has shown good faith and is entitled to an order for inspection. Santomauro v Pollio Products Corp. (1962, 2d Dept) 15 A.D.2d 944, 225 N.Y.S.2d 994

Although a wife who was 25 percent owner of stock in close corporation would be afforded the opportunity of ascertaining the true condition of affairs of the corporation of which she was a substantial part owner where it appeared that she had been denied all information as to the affairs of said corporation, she would not be permitted to use an inspection and examination as a means of securing data to be utilized in a matrimonial action or for the purpose of harassing her husband who owned the remaining stock in the corporation along with two other persons. Botwin v Central Structural Steel Co. (1967, 1st Dept) 28 A.D.2d 522, 279 N.Y.S.2d 741

Where owner of 5,000 corporate shares sought to examine corporate minutes, accounts and records from 1968 in order to ascertain reasons for corporation's financial difficulties, and particularly where corporate directors offered to buy such owner's shares at greatly reduced price, special term abused its discretion in denying any part of application, and inspection would be allowed subject only to provision that corporation be not unduly disturbed in conduct of its affairs. Bondi v Business Education Forum, Inc. (1976, 4th Dept) 52 A.D.2d 1046, 384 N.Y.S.2d 291

Petitioner shareholder's specified purpose in seeking inspection of list of shareholders to solicit shareholders not to reelect the incumbent members of board of directors for the reason that they had engaged in a questionable financial transaction with the corporation was not a purpose proscribed by statute even though the transaction occurred before petitioner became a shareholder.S. & S. Realty Corp. v Kleer-Vu Industries, Inc. (1976, 1st Dept) 53 A.D.2d 552, 384 N.Y.S.2d 796

Plaintiff's request to inspect shareholder lists and books and records of corporation in order to value stock of corporation was made in bad faith in light of shareholder's agreement, which contained names of all shareholders and agreed on method for valuing stock. Vasinkevich v Elm Drugs (1994, 2d Dept) 208 A.D.2d 522, 616 N.Y.S.2d 808

Shareholder demonstrated good faith and facially valid purpose for his petition to compel corporation to produce its books and records for inspection and copying, where he averred that he required information in question to evaluate worth of his shares and pursue his concerns regarding corporation's failure to declare any dividends for more than 20 years; matter was remitted for hearing to determine what information, and for what time period, was relevant and necessary for shareholder's purposes. Troccoli v L & B Contract Indus., Inc. (1999, 2d Dept) 259 A.D.2d 754, 687 N.Y.S.2d 400

See alsoPeople ex rel. Colby v Imbrie & Co. (1926) 126 Misc 457, 214 N.Y.S. 53, affd 216 A.D. 713, 214 N.Y.S. 819

Where it sufficiently appears from the showing made in opposition to a stockholder's application for leave to inspect the stock books that his purpose and motive are to harass the corporation in the interest of another company of which he is president and a substantial stockholder, rather than, as alleged in the application, to inform other stockholders of a conflict of interest on the part of a nominee for election to the board of directors, the application should be denied.Young v Columbia Broadcasting System, Inc. (1959) 28 Misc. 2d 512, 215 N.Y.S.2d 950

It cannot be said that an attempt by a group of stockholders to induce their fellow stockholders to reject a merger plan suggested by management and to encourage a merger with some other group is in itself an improper motive or bad faith such as to disentitle them to their right of inspection of the stock book of the corporation, notwithstanding the fact that the particular merger they seek to promote would be beneficial to them individually as holders of stock in both corporations. Application of Huber (1960) 26 Misc. 2d 563, 210 N.Y.S.2d 211

A stockholder's application to examine the books and records of the corporation, for the alleged purpose of determining value of his holdings, was for a legitimate purpose and must be granted as against contentions that the corporation was a family affair operated by brothers of the petitioner, and petitioner was making the application merely by way of a bludgeon to attain a better price for his stock

out of the operating brothers.Smilkstein v J. Smilkstein & Sons, Inc. (1961) 32 Misc. 2d 882, 223 N.Y.S.2d 561

A close corporation would be directed to allow a minority shareholder full access to all records, notwithstanding the fact that the minority shareholder had previously stolen from the corporation, since in the absence of bad faith a shareholder has a statutory right to inspect shareholder records pursuant to Bus Corp Law § 624, and a common law right to examine the corporate books of account. Gimpel v Bolstein (1984) 125 Misc. 2d 45, 477 N.Y.S.2d 1014

Hearing was required to determine whether a majority shareholder was, in fact, acting in good faith and with a proper purpose under N.Y. Bus. Corp. Law § 624 and the common law because an issue of fact was raised as to whether the majority shareholder was acting for the improper purpose of obtaining personal business or a competitive advantage. Matter of Liaros v Ted's Jumbo Red Hots, Inc. (2012, App Div, 4th Dept) 946 NYS2d 387

20. Other grounds and factors

Although agreement between parties provided that certified determination by corporation's accountant, made in accordance with sound accounting practice, should be binding as to book value, stockholder who offered to sell stock was entitled to inspect books and records where accountant's statement was not certified and standards and sound accounting practices were not followed. Glassman v Louis Shiffman, Inc. (1977, 1st Dept) 56 A.D.2d 824, 393 N.Y.S.2d 33

Ordinarily, sale to corporation by shareholder is valid ground for inspection of corporation's books and records but where parties agree that accountant's report would be final as to what books show, party is entitled solely to accountant's unchallenged report and audit of books and records is not permitted. Glassman v Louis Shiffman, Inc. (1977, 1st Dept) 56 A.D.2d 824, 393 N.Y.S.2d 33

Issuance of order compelling corporation to produce books and records was not abuse of discretion where allegation that petitioner owned five percent of the corporate stock was substantiated by letters from one respondent and affidavit of another shareholder, officer and director. Blank v Premium Gas Service, Inc. (1977, 3d Dept) 59 A.D.2d 970, 399 N.Y.S.2d 282

Whether the fact that the demandant has already been permitted an inspection of the records will suffice as a reason for denying a later request depends upon circumstances, including lapse of time since the prior inspection and whether or not the stated purposes of the inspection are within the same field. Palley v Chase Nat. Bank (1942) 178 Misc 536, 35 N.Y.S.2d 958, affd 264 A.D. 764, 35 N.Y.S.2d 717

Mismanagement is not the only ground upon which an inspection order can issue, and an averment of mismanagement is accordingly not essential to consideration of such an application. Re Chanel (1947, Sup) 74 N.Y.S.2d 203

The relatively slight amount of stock interest held by petitioner can be taken into consideration against granting his application where the objective in seeking an inspection is to back up minor grievances and differences of opinion with management policy and majority control. Adler v Oppenheim Collins & Co. (1948, Sup) 81 N.Y.S.2d 293

However, the mere fact that a surplus of some size has been allowed to accumulate without declaration of a dividend, and that the petitioning shareholder lacks detailed knowledge of the affairs of the corporation will not require issuance of an inspection order, in the absence of any claim of waste or mismanagement. Hecht v Select Theatres Corp. (1949, Sup) 91 N.Y.S.2d 464

Because a shareholder's conclusory claims of corporate waste were insufficient to justify a limited review of a corporation's books and records under N.Y. C.P.L.R. art. 78 and N.Y. Bus. Corp. Law § 624, and because the shareholder's remaining contentions were without merit, the shareholder's stock in a corporation was declared to be determined by book value. Lapsley v Sorfin Intl., Ltd. (2007, 2d Dept) 43 App Div 3d 1113, 843 NYS2d 141

21. Procedural matters

In proceeding to enforce right to inspect corporate books and records, the stockholder must allege compliance with statute. Crane Co. v Anaconda Co. (1976) 39 N.Y.2d 14, 382 N.Y.S.2d 707, 346 N.E.2d 507

When asserting a common-law right of access to corporate books and records the shareholder must plead and prove that inspection is desired for a proper purpose. Crane Co. v Anaconda Co. (1976) 39 N.Y.2d 14, 382 N.Y.S.2d 707, 346 N.E.2d 507

Even where an inspection of books and records of the corporation is sanctioned by court order, the court has power and discretion to impose terms and conditions as to time, place, manner, and extent of the inspection, and, if the shareholder is engaged in a competing business, may deny him access to business secrets, such as the names and addresses of customers. Newmark v C & C Super Corp. (1957, 1st Dept) 3 A.D.2d 823, 160 N.Y.S.2d 936, affd 3 N.Y.2d 790, 164 N.Y.S.2d 42, 143 N.E.2d 796; Re Chanel (1947, Sup) 74 N.Y.S.2d 203; Hansen v Marblette Corp. (1940, Sup) 24 N.Y.S.2d 200, affd 260 A.D. 866, 23 N.Y.S.2d 842

In Article 78 proceeding to compel disclosure of corporation records under CLS Bus Corp § 624, court erred in dismissing proceeding on ground that petitioner failed to satisfy condition of stock purchase agreement requiring franchisor approval, and was therefore never actually issued stock as required by statute, since fact issues existed as to when parties intended stock transfer to occur and whether corporate president interfered with petitioner's attempts to obtain franchisor approval; further, corporation and its president could be equitably estopped from claiming petitioner's lack of stock ownership if it were shown that petitioner refrained from attempting to get approval in reliance on president's representation that he would obtain approval. Benincasa v Garrubbo (1988, 2d Dept) 141 A.D.2d 636, 529 N.Y.S.2d 797

Court erred in declaring defendant to be sole stockholder of corporations in question where, in prior CLS Art 78 proceedings to permit inspection of corporate books and records in accordance with CLS Bus Corp § 624, plaintiff's decedent had been found to be shareholder of at least 5 percent of corporations; since defendant was afforded full and fair opportunity to contest decedent's claims in prior litigation, court was collaterally estopped from finding that defendant was sole shareholder. Blank v Blank (1998, 3d Dept) 256 A.D.2d 688, 681 N.Y.S.2d 377

Hearing was required in Article 78 proceeding to compel production of corporation's books and records pursuant to CLS Bus Corp § 624 where corporation raised substantial question of fact concerning petitioner's good faith and motive. Niggli v Richlin Mach., Inc. (1999, 2d Dept) 257 A.D.2d 623, 684 N.Y.S.2d 254

Seeking an inspection of corporate books and papers under § 10 of former Stock Corp. L., and seeking to subpoena such books and records in connection with discovery proceedings in course of ordinary litigation, under general provisions of the Civil Practice Act, were regarded as distinct matters. Existence of § 10 did not impair right of recourse to ordinary discovery proceedings in proper case, and it is obvious from subd. (f) of § 624 of the Bus. Corp. L. that this section, likewise, does not impair power of courts to compel "the production for examination of the books and records of a corporation."Diamond v 87 Nassau Street Corp. (1956) 4 Misc. 2d 408, 152 N.Y.S.2d 244

In order to defeat the issuance of an order to inspect the stock book of a corporation, the corporation must make a direct and positive denial of the essential facts relied upon to support the application. Green v Baltic Shipping Co. (1947, Sup) 76 N.Y.S.2d 608, revd on other grounds 275 A.D. 700, 87 N.Y.S.2d 354

In proceeding to inspect corporate records, the court may order trial of an issue with respect to petitioner's ownership of stock prior to ordering such inspection. Rudolfer v Hudson Shipping Co. (1956, Sup) 158 N.Y.S.2d 948, app dismd (1st Dept) 2 A.D.2d 959, 159 N.Y.S.2d 469

§ 625. Infant shareholders and bondholders

(a) A corporation may treat an infant who holds shares or bonds of such corporation as having capacity to receive and to empower others to receive dividends, interest, principal and other payments and distributions, to vote or express consent or dissent, in person or by proxy, and to make elections and exercise rights relating to such shares or bonds, unless, in the case of shares, the corporate officer responsible for maintaining the list of shareholders or the transfer agent of the corporation or, in the case of bonds, the treasurer or paying officer or agent has received written notice that such holder is an infant.

(b) An infant holder of shares or bonds of a corporation who has received or empowered others to receive payments or distributions, voted or expressed consent or dissent, or made an election or exercised a right relating thereto, shall have no right thereafter to disaffirm or avoid, as against the corporation, any such act on his part, unless prior to such receipt, vote, consent, dissent, election or exercise, as to shares, the corporate officer responsible for maintaining the list of shareholders or its transfer agent or, in the case of bonds, the treasurer or paying officer had received written notice that such holder was an infant.

(c) This section does not limit any other statute which authorizes any corporation to deal with an infant or limits the right of an infant to disaffirm his acts.

History: Add, L 1961, ch 855, eff Sept 1, 1963.

§ 626. Shareholders' derivative action brought in the right of the corporation to procure a judgment in its favor

(a) An action may be brought in the right of a domestic or foreign corporation to procure a judgment in its favor, by a holder of shares or of voting trust certificates of the corporation or of a beneficial interest in such shares or certificates.

(b) In any such action, it shall be made to appear that the plaintiff is such a holder at the time of bringing the action and that he was such a holder at the time of the transaction of which he complains, or that his shares or his interest therein devolved upon him by operation of law.

(c) In any such action, the complaint shall set forth with particularity the efforts of the plaintiff to secure the initiation of such action by the board or the reasons for not making such effort.

(d) Such action shall not be discontinued, compromised or settled, without the approval of the court having jurisdiction of the action. If the court shall determine that the interests of the shareholders or any class or classes thereof will be substantially affected by such discontinuance, compromise, or settlement, the court, in its discretion, may direct that notice, by publication or otherwise, shall be given to the shareholders or class or classes thereof whose interests it determines will be so affected; if notice is so directed to be given, the court may determine which one or more of the parties to the action shall bear the expense of giving the same, in such amount as the court shall determine and find to be reasonable in the circumstances, and the amount of such expense shall be awarded as special costs of the action and recoverable in the same manner as statutory taxable costs.

(e) If the action on behalf of the corporation was successful, in whole or in part, or if anything was received by the plaintiff or plaintiffs or a claimant or claimants as the result of a judgment, compromise or settlement of an action or claim, the court may award the plaintiff or plaintiffs, claimant or claimants, reasonable expenses, including reasonable attorney's fees, and shall direct him or them to account to the corporation for the remainder of the proceeds so received by him or them. This paragraph shall not apply to any judgment rendered for the benefit of injured shareholders only and limited to a recovery of the loss or damage sustained by them.

History: Add, L 1961, ch 855, eff Sept 1, 1963; amd, L 1962, ch 834, § 42; L 1963, ch 746, eff Sept 1, 1963.

CASE ANNOTATIONS

1. In general

Subd a of above statute was enacted to overruleGordon v Elliman (1954) 306 N.Y. 456, 119 N.E.2d 331, but has no applicability to causes of action pending on effective date of the Business Corporation Law in view of the provision of § 103, subd d, against such application. Schlegel v Schlegel Mfg. Corp. (1965, 4th Dept) 23 A.D.2d 808, 258 N.Y.S.2d 587

Generally, any recovery obtained in shareholders' derivative suit is for benefit of injured corporation; where, however, shareholder sues in individual capacity to recover damages resulting in harm, not to corporation, but to individual shareholders, suit is personal, not derivative, and it is appropriate for damages to be awarded directly to those shareholders. Glenn v Hoteltron Systems, Inc. (1989) 74 N.Y.2d 386, 547 N.Y.S.2d 816, 547 N.E.2d 71

Court of Appeals has historically been reluctant to permit shareholder derivative suits, since power of courts to direct management of corporation's affairs should be exercised with restraint. Marx v Akers (1996) 88 N.Y.2d 189, 644 N.Y.S.2d 121, 666 N.E.2d 1034

In addition to dealing with shareholders' derivative actions in behalf of the corporation, § 61 of former Gen. Corp. L. likewise sanctioned actions by individual officers or directors to require other officers or directors to account for their conduct or misconduct in managing the corporation's affairs. Wangrow v Wangrow (1924) 211 A.D. 552, 207 N.Y.S. 132; Manix v Fantl (1924) 209 A.D. 756, 205 N.Y.S. 174; Higgins v Applebaum (1918) 183 A.D. 527, 170 N.Y.S. 228; Scott v Funaroff (1948, Sup) 84 N.Y.S.2d 144; Wyckoff v Sagall (1945) 16 Misc. 2d 630, 56 N.Y.S.2d 392; Kehaya v Axton (1940, DC NY) 32 F. Supp. 266

An individual may not bring a direct action solely on his own behalf for a wrong committed against the corporation of which he is a shareholder; a derivative suit is the proper remedy.Empleton v D'Elia Gemstones Corp. (1974, 1st Dept) 46 A.D.2d 751, 360 N.Y.S.2d 683

Surrogate's Court did not have subject matter jurisdiction over stockholder derivative action instituted by executor and testamentary trustee (petitioner) on behalf of estate of deceased stockholder where relief sought did not relate to affairs of decedent and would not affect administration of estate; fact that estate owns stock in corporation does not confer jurisdiction on Surrogate's Court to resolve all matters involving that corporation. Lincoln First Bank, N.A. v Sanford (1991, 4th Dept) 173 A.D.2d 65, 579 N.Y.S.2d 781

A "representative" action must be distinguished from a "derivative" suit, the former being by plaintiff as representative of a class for the benefit of the class or such members thereof as care to join in the action, whereas the latter, while it may redound to the benefit of all shareholders, is strictly and technically in behalf of the corporation. Handler v Belmare Lighting Co. (1957) 8 Misc. 2d 687, 168 N.Y.S.2d 288; Lazar v Knolls Cooperative Section No. 2, Inc. (1954) 205 Misc 748, 130 N.Y.S.2d 407

The entire purpose of this section and § 720 of the Business Corp Law is to allow a derivative action in the name of the corporation and for its benefit when the board of directors has refused, under certain circumstances to bring an action, and a stockholder's derivative action cannot be obviated by a majority vote of the board of directors not to bring the action in the first place, especially where the corporation is controlled by the alleged wrongdoers.Syracuse Television, Inc. v Channel 9 Syracuse, Inc. (1966) 52 Misc. 2d 246, 275 N.Y.S.2d 190

In determining whether a cause of action is derivative in nature pursuant to the Business Corporation Law, if the primary injury is to the corporation, the direct cause of action belongs to the corporation, even though all shareholders may be injured by a diminution in the value of their shares, and a shareholder cannot proceed individually to assert the corporate claim but must proceed by derivative suit and the same criteria must be used in determining whether a limited partner's claim is derivative or personal. Alpert v Haimes (1970) 64 Misc. 2d 608, 315 N.Y.S.2d 332

Action by majority shareholders and directors of defunct corporation against minority shareholder who managed business should have been instituted under CLS Bus Corp § 720(a)(1) rather than CLS Bus Corp § 626, where complaint sought accounting and related relief as to defendant shareholder's conversion, fraud, misappropriation of corporate funds, and breach of fiduciary duty. Bouhayer v Georgalis (1996, Sup) 169 Misc. 2d 779, 645 N.Y.S.2d 1008

1963 addition of words "in its favor" to definition of derivative suits was intended to limit the definition of such suits and to further distinguish between derivative and representative suits.Eisenberg v Flying Tiger Line, Inc. (1971, CA2 NY) 451 F.2d 267

Section 626(d) reflects clear legislative policy that once suit has been initiated, it may not be terminated in any fashion without approval of court. Mokhiber on behalf of Ford Motor Co. v Cohn (1986, CA2 NY) 783 F.2d 26

Derivative action may not be settled without approval of court having jurisdiction; approval of court is required for settlement even though prior to settlement action was dismissed on grounds of forum non conveniens. Mokhiber on behalf of Ford Motor Co. v Cohn (1985, SD NY) 608 F. Supp. 616

2. Grounds for suit

In shareholders' derivative action against various parties, shareholders stated cause of action against certain attorneys by alleging that, in connection with prior litigation, corporation paid fees and other charges of attorneys for legal services rendered in personal defense of certain individuals and other corporate defendants, and that attorneys received such payment with knowledge that it was not for services rendered to corporation. Blank v Schafrann (1987) 70 N.Y.2d 887, 524 N.Y.S.2d 377, 519 N.E.2d 288, motion den 71 N.Y.2d 835, 527 N.Y.S.2d 756, 522 N.E.2d 1054

Minority shareholders' request, in derivative action, for recision of merger that was contemplated by corporation's majority shareholders was equitable remedy that remained viable-and only became tenable-after merger was completed. Re Colt Industries Shareholder Litigation (1991) 77 N.Y.2d 185, 565 N.Y.S.2d 755, 566 N.E.2d 1160

Stockholder, who had stored collection of gems with the corporation and who charged that corporation refused to return the balance of the gems or the proceeds of the gems sold, could not bring a direct action against the corporation and others to recover for alleged conspiracy between the corporate and individual defendants to willfully defraud plaintiff of his property by manipulation of corporate books; such a cause of action was to be initiated as a derivative suit.Empleton v D'Elia Gemstones Corp. (1974, 1st Dept) 46 A.D.2d 751, 360 N.Y.S.2d 683

Derivative action was appropriate vehicle by which stockholder could claim some right to corporate assets allegedly converted after dissolution, and appropriate vehicle for protection of rights of corporation's creditors. Maki v Estate of Ziehm (1977, 3d Dept) 55 A.D.2d 454, 391 N.Y.S.2d 705

In shareholder's derivative action, court properly voided disproportionate salary increase to majority shareholder/sole director/president/secretary, as well as personal loan by corporation to same person and corporate loan to another corporation, where there were 2 shareholders in corporation but there was never more than one director (in violation of CLS Bus Corp § 702), corporation was not authorized to take challenged actions, and other shareholder had no knowledge of actions. Rodgers v Bell (1994, 4th Dept) 202 A.D.2d 1040, 610 N.Y.S.2d 111

In shareholder derivative action, court did not err in denying defendants' request to sanction plaintiff for bringing corporate dissolution proceeding, as it would not have been unreasonable for her to have believed that improprieties had occurred in light of acrimonious atmosphere that existed when she was fired from her position and removed as director, and informal and lax recordkeeping procedures being practiced at that time. Di Pace v Figueroa (1996, 3d Dept) 223 A.D.2d 949, 637 N.Y.S.2d 222

A stockholder cannot succeed in a true "derivative action" unless he demonstrates a cause of action in favor of the corporation, and he fails to do this where his complaint merely sets forth the grievance of certain minority shareholders against management in exercising discretion and business judgment to withhold a distribution of profits from sale of assets for the time being and invest such profits in securities of other corporations pending solution of certain tax problems, particularly where it appears that this action was taken in good faith and those objecting could sell their stock on the market at a considerable profit. Lippman v New York Water Service Corp. (1960) 25 Misc. 2d 267, 205 N.Y.S.2d 541, app dismd 12 A.D.2d 611, 214 N.Y.S.2d 715

Upon proper allegations, a stockholder may not be estopped from questioning, through judicial proceedings, the legality of salaries paid to officers and directors. Abramson v Blakeley (1960) 25 Misc. 2d 967, 202 N.Y.S.2d 586

An action brought under § 720 to require officers and directors to account for their official duties in the management of a corporation, is, according to this section, derivative in nature, since the cause of action belongs to the corporation. Syracuse Television, Inc. v Channel 9, Syracuse, Inc. (1966) 51 Misc. 2d 188, 273 N.Y.S.2d 16

It has long been recognized that waste, mismanagement, and interference with a corporation's business are wrongs to the corporation which do not ordinarily give rise to a cause of action in favor of any individual shareholder and can be redressed only by action or proceeding taken by the corporation as an entity or by someone in interest acting in its behalf. Weinstein v Behn (1946, Sup) 65 N.Y.S.2d 536, affd 272 A.D. 1045, 75 N.Y.S.2d 284, app den 273 A.D. 877, 77 N.Y.S.2d 391 and app dismd 298 N.Y. 506, 80 N.E.2d 656; Jeantet v Allbrand Appliance & Tel. Inc. (1959) 20 Misc. 2d 94, 189 N.Y.S.2d 722; Hyde v Everett Van Kleeck & Co. (1959) 17 Misc. 2d 375, 190 N.Y.S.2d 914; Re Tama (1954, Sup) 137 N.Y.S.2d 248; Deitch v Atlas (1954, Sup) 132 N.Y.S.2d 803

Shareholders' action challenging severance package of member of corporation's board of directors was properly dismissed, because sole person having direct financial interest in that package was that director. In re Woolworth Corp. Shareholder Derivative Litig. (1997, 1st Dept) 240 A.D.2d 189, 658 N.Y.S.2d 869

Shareholder was entitled to summary judgment as to his claims against a corporation's founder in a shareholder's derivative suit under N.Y. Bus. Corp. Law § 626 arising out of the corporation's indemnification of the founder for his legal expenses as: (1) the founder's conduct resulted in a five-count felony indictment against him and the corporation, (2) the founder admitted knowingly and willfully violating the Federal Election Campaign Act and the tax laws, (3) the conduct, punished with a sentence of fines and imprisonment, was not little more than a technical violation of an obscure malum prohibitum statute, (4) the founder's sworn admissions left no room for finding that he was entitled to indemnification by the corporation because he acted in good faith, for a purpose he reasonably believed to be in the best interest of the corporation, and had no reasonable cause to believe that his conduct was unlawful, for which indemnification was permitted under N.Y. Bus. Corp. Law § 722(a), and (5) indemnification in this circumstance was prohibited under N.Y. Bus. Corp. Law §§ 721 and 722(b). Bansbach v Zinn (2003) 1 NY3d 1, 769 N.Y.S.2d 175, 801 N.E.2d 395, reargument den (2004, NY) 2004 N.Y. LEXIS 50

Plaintiff's claim of corporate waste is properly asserted by way of derivative action under CLS, Business Corporation Law § 626(a). Lewis v S. L. & E., Inc. (1980, CA2 NY) 629 F.2d 764

3. Shareholders as parties

Trial court committed no error in refusing to give minority shareholder opportunity to exclude itself from class of minority shareholders when class was first certified in derivative action which sought injunction to prevent (and, failing that, recision of) corporate merger since there is no due process right to opt out of class that seeks predominantly equitable relief that will necessarily benefit class as whole if granted; moreover, unlike Fed Rules Civ Pro rule 23, CLS CPLR Art 9 does not specifically mandate opt-out for cases of certain type, although court may choose to exercise discretion to permit class member to opt out of class. Re Colt Industries Shareholder Litigation (1991) 77 N.Y.2d 185, 565 N.Y.S.2d 755, 566 N.E.2d 1160

Analysis set forth in Phillips Petroleum Co. v Shutts, 472 US 797 was relevant in determining whether out-of-state minority shareholder had right to opt out of class in shareholder derivative action which merged 15 separate shareholder suits in New York court. Re Colt Industries Shareholder Litigation (1991) 77 N.Y.2d 185, 565 N.Y.S.2d 755, 566 N.E.2d 1160

Approval of merger by corporation's shareholders did not moot all equitable claims of minority shareholders in their class action, and thus particular minority shareholder would not necessarily have due process right (under Phillips Petroleum Co. v Shutts, 472 US 797) to receive notification of class action, and to seek exclusion from class on ground that action had been converted into one for damages, where the only element of complaint that became moot on consummation of merger was request for injunction preventing merger from going forward, and class' request for equitable remedy of rescission obviously became tenable only after merger had been completed. Re Colt Industries Shareholder Litigation (1991) 77 N.Y.2d 185, 565 N.Y.S.2d 755, 566 N.E.2d 1160

Minority shareholders' request for fees and expenses contained in their consolidated class complaint in derivative action was improperly characterized by Appellate Division as claim for damages, and thus particular minority shareholder would not necessarily have due process right (under Phillips Petroleum Co. v Shutts, 472 US 797) to receive notification of class action and to seek exclusion from class on ground that action had been converted into one for damages, where complaint sought equitable relief in form of injunction (to prevent merger from going forward) and recision (should merger be consummated). Re Colt Industries Shareholder Litigation (1991) 77 N.Y.2d 185, 565 N.Y.S.2d 755, 566 N.E.2d 1160

Shareholder in publicly held corporation who abstained from voting for or against corporate merger was not thereby estopped from subsequently challenging merger, especially where predetermined number of affirmative votes were required to approve merger, which made abstention equivalent of negative vote. Pinnacle Consultants, Ltd. v Leucadia Nat'l Corp. (2000) 94 N.Y.2d 426, 706 N.Y.S.2d 46, 727 N.E.2d 543

The stockholder of a corporation which controls another corporation which, in turn controls a third corporation may maintain a derivative action against the third corporation for waste of assets of such subsidiary corporation. Kaufman v Wolfson (1956, 1st Dept) 1 A.D.2d 555, 151 N.Y.S.2d 530

Rule requiring that stockholder bring derivative action to assert right to corporate assets upon their final distribution is applicable even where complaining stockholder owns all or substantially all of the corporate stock. Maki v Estate of Ziehm (1977, 3d Dept) 55 A.D.2d 454, 391 N.Y.S.2d 705

An action for an accounting brought by the sole shareholder in a corporation that had entered into a joint venture agreement with a tire manufacturer, which held the controlling interest in the joint venture as against plaintiff's corporation's minority interest, was properly dismissed by the trial court, since plaintiff had chosen to conduct business with the tire manufacturer through the corporate form, so that his appropriate remedy was a stockholder's derivative action in the right of the corporation in which he held a controlling interest. Beck v General Tire & Rubber Co. (1983, 2d Dept) 98 A.D.2d 756, 469 N.Y.S.2d 785

Action against defendant commenced by plaintiff on behalf of corporation should have been dismissed where (although no stock had been issued and no formal corporate activities had taken place) it was undisputed that plaintiff and defendant were intended to have equal interest in and control over corporation, since where there are only 2 stockholders, each with 50 percent share, action cannot be maintained in name of corporation by one against other; proper remedy is stockholder's derivative action. Executive Leasing Co. v Leder (1993, 1st Dept) 191 A.D.2d 199, 594 N.Y.S.2d 217

Surviving member of family partnership, who was also surviving owner of plaintiff corporation following his brother's death, had authority to authorize action by corporation's action to recover $71,000 allegedly lent to deceased partner (who was also half-owner of corporation); court would not apply rule that one 50 percent shareholder cannot maintain action against other 50 percent shareholder in name of corporation, where action did not name shareholders or indicate their respective interests. Blank v Blank (1995, 3d Dept) 222 A.D.2d 851, 634 N.Y.S.2d 886

Court erred in dismissing shareholder's derivative action for lack of standing where plaintiff was 50 percent shareholder and officer and director of plaintiff corporation; plaintiff's deposition testimony, which reflected his confusion as non-lawyer as to nature of shareholder's derivative action, was not fairly probative of his standing to sue on corporation's behalf. Rafield v Brotman (1999, 1st Dept) 261 A.D.2d 257, 690 N.Y.S.2d 263

Stockholder of bank acquired by another bank lacked standing to challenge merger where (1) her allegations-that bank was acquired at unfairly depressed price at stockholders' expense as result of excessive compensation and bonus arrangements provided by acquired bank's board of directors to certain directors and executives-set forth wrong to corporation only, for which shareholder may sue derivatively but not individually, and (2) she neither made demand on bank's board of directors to initiate action on bank's behalf nor pleaded why such demand would have been futile, and thus she did not satisfy requisites for maintenance of shareholder's derivative action. Fischbein v Beitzel (2001, 1st Dept) 281 A.D.2d 167, 721 N.Y.S.2d 515, app den 96 N.Y.2d 715, 729 N.Y.S.2d 442, 754 N.E.2d 202

A person holding stock in a representative capacity, such as an administrator or executor of an estate, has the right to institute a stockholders' derivative action. Greenberg v Acme Folding Box Co. (1975) 84 Misc. 2d 181, 374 N.Y.S.2d 997

When stockholders are estopped, because of their own knowledge, ratification or participation in the wrongdoing, from questioning wrongs done their corporation, they cannot redress those wrongs through a derivative suit brought on behalf of the corporation. Greenberg v Acme Folding Box Co. (1975) 84 Misc. 2d 181, 374 N.Y.S.2d 997

A shareholder who brought a derivative action alleging that defendant corporation president breached a fiduciary duty to the corporation failed to establish that she would fairly and adequately represent the interest of shareholders and the corporation free from adverse personal interest and animus where she was involved in a divorce action with defendant, had offered to discontinue suit if she was paid a premium of approximately $1,000,000 over the market value of her shares, and where the total circumstances indicated that the action was instituted to obtain leverage in the matrimonial preceeding. In addition, the shareholder was estopped by equitable principles from challenging alleged improper expenditures by defendant since his wife she had shared in his assertedly extravagant life style. Steinberg v Steinberg (1980) 106 Misc. 2d 720, 434 N.Y.S.2d 877

Derivative action cannot be maintained by former shareholder after cash-out merger of corporation whereby shareholder is divested of all rights other than to collect sum agreed on for purchase of stock. Bronzaft v Caporali (1994, Sup) 162 Misc. 2d 281, 616 N.Y.S.2d 863

In a "demand refused" case, a shareholder lacked standing to pursue a derivative action regarding losses associated with the corporation's collateralized debt obligation and subprime mortgage-related assets because the shareholder failed to plead any particularized facts to raise a reasonable doubt as to the good faith or reasonableness of the investigation by the board of directors of the shareholder's demand, and the business judgment rule shielded the board from further inquiry. Lerner v Prince (2012, Sup) 36 Misc 3d 297, 945 NYS2d 520

Stockholders initiating a derivative action are nominal parties only deriving their authority to bring the action from the statute. They are qualified to initiate the action by reason of their status as stockholders but, having initiated it, the action survives and continues without abatement regardless of any change in that status.Smith v Bradlee (1942, Sup) 37 N.Y.S.2d 512, mod on other grounds 265 A.D. 931, 38 N.Y.S.2d 379

It can be said, generally, that a stockholder, as such, regardless of the number of shares held, has capacity to assert a derivative cause of action in behalf of the corporation upon a proper showing that the board of directors has refused to take such action or is so dominated by persons in adverse interest that it cannot be induced to take such action.Sussman v Goldberg (1961, Sup) 215 N.Y.S.2d 650

Plaintiff's standing in shareholder derivative action was governed by Delaware law where Delaware was state of subject corporation's

incorporation. CPF Acquisition Co. by Kagan v CPF Acquisition Co. (1998, 1st Dept) 255 A.D.2d 200, 682 N.Y.S.2d 3

Where a co-shareholder sued on behalf of a corporation and had standing to sue as a co-shareholder, the trial court properly directed an accounting and the imposition of a constructive trust on real property owned by the corporation. Frederick v Fried (2003, A.D., 2d Dept) 765 N.Y.S.2d 371

Because the corporation, on whose behalf a shareholder was presumably suing, ceded to the shareholder's demand and authorized the commencement of an action against the officer and directors, the shareholder failed to assert a proper shareholders' derivative suit under Business Corporation Law § 626. Rafiy v Javaheri (2011) 32 Misc. 3d 734, 927 N.Y.S.2d 554.

Appellate court held that in order for shareholders to have had standing to pursue a derivative action under Fed. R. Civ. P. 23.1 or N.Y. Bus. Corp. Law § 626(b), the shareholders were required to have owned stock in the corporation, a bank, before the core of the allegedly wrongful conduct transpired, which in the instant case, involved alleged unlawful conduct committed by certain corporate officers during the bank's expansion into the Russian banking industry, which occurred primarily between 1992 and 1996, and because the shareholders did not acquire their stock until July 21, 1998, they lacked standing; in reaching its decision, the appellate court declined to adopt the expansive definition of the term "transaction" that was inherent in the continuing wrong doctrine and focused instead on when the "core" of the alleged wrongdoing took place. Kaliski v Bacot (In re Bank of N.Y. Derivative Litig.) (2003, CA2 NY) 320 F.3d 291

Person holding stock in representative capacity, such as administrator or executor of estate, has right to institute stockholders' derivative action; further, where minority stockholder asserts cause of action for wrong done to corporation, it is immaterial whether minority stockholder has large or small interest. Jacobs v Adams (1979, CA5 Fla) 601 F.2d 176, 28 FR Serv 2d 47

Derivative action could be maintained by a shareholder on behalf of the corporation because the economic benefit of the summary proceeding belonged to the corporation, not the shareholder; since the corporation was the owner of the premises and would receive the benefit of the summary proceeding, an action could be brought under N.Y. Real Prop. Acts. Law § 721 because the corporation was the owner of the property. Gorbrook Assoc. Inc. v Silverstein (2013, Dist Ct) 40 Misc 3d 425, 965 NYS2d 851.

Shareholder lacked the authority to authorize litigation in the name of the corporation because he was at complete odds with the vice president and one of the directors, who objected to the proceeding. Gorbrook Assoc. Inc. v Silverstein (2013, Dist Ct) 40 Misc 3d 425, 965 NYS2d 851.

Shareholder met obligations imposed on him by New York Law to derivatively defend instant lawsuit because shareholder both took efforts to get limited liability to defend action, and once company elected not to defend action, he adequately explained why he should be allowed to derivatively defend it, i.e., company's good faith and well-reasoned consent. Horowitz v 148 South Emerson Assocs. LLC, 888 F.3d 13, 2018 U.S. App. LEXIS 9971 (2d Cir. N.Y. 2018).

4. Corporation as party

In an action by plaintiff, who was the sole stockholder of a parent corporation with numerous subsidiaries and associated companies, in which it was alleged that defendant had been hired to manage cash flow problems with those various companies and had committed various acts of fraud and mismanagement, the complaint was properly dismissed where the plaintiff's companies and not plaintiff himself were the real parties in interest so that the claims should have been asserted in a derivative action on behalf of said companies. Overmyer v Todd (1981) 55 N.Y.2d 766, 447 N.Y.S.2d 246, 431 N.E.2d 971

In a stockholder's derivative action, the corporation is an indispensable party. The corporation cannot be made a party simply by act of the defendant in inserting the name of the corporation in his answer as an additional defendant. Thus, a motion to dismiss a counterclaim seeking an accounting by the plaintiff was granted with leave to file an amended answer after compelling the plaintiff to join the corporation as a party defendant. Meier v Holmes (1953) 282 A.D. 1030, 126 N.Y.S.2d 655

In stockholders' derivative action under this statute corporation itself was substituted as plaintiff where circumstances demonstrated strong probability that it would prosecute action in good faith, court saying that it need not now decide whether such substitution would destroy derivative nature of action so that corporation could enter a voluntary dismissal thereof without approval of the court as required by subd d. Lazar v Merchants' Nat. Properties, Inc. (1964, 1st Dept) 22 A.D.2d 253, 254 N.Y.S.2d 712

Where an officer and director sued another officer and director for waste and mismanagement of corporate assets, while the cause of action and right of recovery actually belongs to the corporation and the director is suing as a representative, the corporation is only a proper party, neither necessary nor indispensable. Conant v Schnall (1970, 3d Dept) 33 A.D.2d 326, 307 N.Y.S.2d 902

Although in derivative action, corporation is usually passive litigant, in particular cases relief sought may require appearance and answer by corporate defendant and such appearance must be by independent counsel whose interests will not conflict with those of individual defendants. Russo v Zaharko (1976, 2d Dept) 53 A.D.2d 663, 385 N.Y.S.2d 105

Since the derivative action was permitted, the corporation had to be named as a respondent since it was an indispensable party. Gorbrook Assoc. Inc. v Silverstein (2013, Dist Ct) 40 Misc 3d 425, 965 NYS2d 851.

5. Officers and directors as parties

An officer or director of a corporation may bring an action against another officer or director under § 720 of the Business Corporation Law and such director may sue in his own name and need not allege his representative capacity. Conant v Schnall (1970, 3d Dept) 33 A.D.2d 326, 307 N.Y.S.2d 902

Where plaintiff brought action for various equitable remedies against director of corporation as shareholder and former director and officer of corporation, on behalf of himself and all other shareholders of corporation similarly situated, and in right of said corporation, plaintiff was required to comply with Business Corporation Law provisions concerning such derivative suits. Galasso v Pioneer Home Improv. Corp. (1976, 2d Dept) 52 A.D.2d 901, 383 N.Y.S.2d 376

President/treasurer of 2-man corporation lacked authority to bring action on behalf of corporation against vice-president/secretary to terminate latter's employment contract and recover amount of compensation and fringe benefits provided to him after his receipt of disability benefits where each man owned 50 percent of stock, and thus, by implication from CLS Bus Corp §§ 701 and 702(a), deadlock could not be remedied by exercise of presidential power, and proper remedy was shareholder's derivative action. Stone v Frederick (1997, 3d Dept) 245 A.D.2d 742, 666 N.Y.S.2d 294

Although individual claim by president/treasurer of 2-man corporation against vice-president/secretary stated cause of action for specific performance of shareholder agreement, action would be enjoined where further use of corporate funds to prosecute it would be obvious abuse of plaintiff's fiduciary relationship with corporation. Stone v Frederick (1997, 3d Dept) 245 A.D.2d 742, 666 N.Y.S.2d 294

Resignation of one of the defendants in a stockholder's derivative suit, eight days after conclusion of an allegedly fraudulent settlement of a claim of the corporation against a third person, in which settlement defendant is alleged to have participated, will not entitled him to dismissal of the charges against him. Gluck v Unger (1960) 25 Misc. 2d 554, 202 N.Y.S.2d 832, app den (1st Dept) 10 A.D.2d 911, 203 N.Y.S.2d 1005

Plaintiff could not sue derivatively under Business Corporation Law § 626 charging a corporate president with the wasting of assets, misconduct and breach of fiduciary duty, where he was an officer when the alleged misconduct, waste and breach of duty occurred but was not a stockholder. Alan v Landau-Alan Gallery, Inc. (1971) 66 Misc. 2d 350, 320 N.Y.S.2d 853

In absence of claim by defendant officers and directors of corporation that plaintiff who brought derivative suit was a participant in defendants' alleged wrongdoing, plaintiff was not estopped from maintaining action simply because defendants, as stockholders, would benefit from any recovery by the corporation. Greenberg v Acme Folding Box Co. (1975) 84 Misc. 2d 181, 374 N.Y.S.2d 997

Shareholder was not entitled to summary judgment in his shareholder's derivative suit under N.Y. Bus. Corp. Law § 626 against corporate officers and directors for their actions in approving the indemnification of the corporation's founder for legal expenses he incurred defending himself from criminal charges as factual issues remained as to the motivation for the actions of the officers and directors, particularly in light of their failure to do more than note the existence of a report of independent legal counsel, upon which they placed heavy reliance under N.Y. Bus. Corp. Law § 723(b)(2)(A).

Bansbach v Zinn (2003) 1 NY3d 1, 769 N.Y.S.2d 175, 801 N.E.2d 395, reargument den (2004, NY) 2004 N.Y. LEXIS 50

6. Others as parties

Shareholders' derivative action for waste and diversion of corporate assets is proper vehicle for relief against not only corporate officials, but also third parties who were beneficiaries of their misconduct. Blank v Schafrann (1987) 70 N.Y.2d 887, 524 N.Y.S.2d 377, 519 N.E.2d 288, motion den 71 N.Y.2d 835, 527 N.Y.S.2d 756, 522 N.E.2d 1054

Association of tenants, in contract dispute with sponsors of conversion of apartment building to cooperative ownership, was entitled to dismissal of sponsor's counterclaim alleging waste and mismanagement of association's assets where sponsor made no showing as to how association would be prejudiced if association prevailed in dispute, where sponsor was apparently not proper party shareholder necessary to bring derivative claim based on corporate mismanagement and waste, and where association's action was properly authorized by executive committee duly appointed by association's board of directors. 305 East 24th Owners Corp. v Parman Co. (1986, 1st Dept) 122 A.D.2d 684, 505 N.Y.S.2d 999, app gr, motion den (1st Dept) 124 A.D.2d 503, 507 N.Y.S.2d 1002

Where plaintiff was beneficiary of trust holding stock in defendant corporation, he was entitled to institute shareholder derivative action. Cassata on behalf of A. J. Hughes Screw Products Co. v Cassata (1989, 4th Dept) 148 A.D.2d 944, 538 N.Y.S.2d 960, app dismd without op 74 N.Y.2d 892, 547 N.Y.S.2d 849, 547 N.E.2d 104

Due to conflict of interest, sponsor who owned 78 percent of shares in cooperative corporation and held wraparound mortgage was improper party to commence shareholder's derivative action, and thus complaint was properly dismissed with leave to replead. Sigfeld Realty ex rel. 200 E. 16th St. Hous. Corp. v Landsman (1996, 1st Dept) 234 A.D.2d 148, 651 N.Y.S.2d 35

Plaintiff's oral transfer of 50 percent interest in family-owned corporation to his estranged wife, who already owned other 50 percent, constituted valid inter vivos gift that left him without standing to assert derivative claim on behalf of corporation for misappropriation of corporate assets. Chien v Chien (2000, 1st Dept) 276 A.D.2d 426, 714 N.Y.S.2d 292

A stockholder's derivative suit is an equitable action and is, in effect, a combination of two suits, one against the corporation for refusing to comply with the stockholder's request and the other against the third party which contests the matter in controversy with the corporation, such third party being a necessary party to any such action. Halpern v Pennsylvania R. Co. (1960, ED NY) 189 F. Supp. 494, 40 CCH LC ¶ 66749, 3 FR Serv 2d 360

Under Bus Corp § 626(b) and federal law, stranger to corporation who buys stock with knowledge of alleged wrongs may not maintain derivative action even if wrongs complained of are continuing wrongs. In re Bank of N.Y. Derivative Litig. (2001, SD NY) 173 F. Supp. 2d 193

Creditor of debtor corporation is not entitled to sue derivatively on behalf of such corporation. Brooks v Weiser (1972, DC NY) 57 FRD 491

7. Intervention and substitution

Ownership of stock of a corporation which in turn owns the stock of the corporation involved in a stockholder's derivative action does not permit intervention. A double derivative suit may be maintained only where the relationship between the two corporations is that of holding and operating companies or where a parent owns and controls a subsidiary. Breswick & Co. v Harrison-Rye Realty Corp. (1952) 280 A.D. 820, 114 N.Y.S.2d 25, app dismd 304 N.Y. 840, 109 N.E.2d 712

Generally, motion for substitution of corporation as plaintiff should not be granted without notice to all stockholders for whose benefit action was brought similar in purpose and effect to notice contemplated by subd d of this statute. Lazar v Merchants' Nat. Properties, Inc. (1964, 1st Dept) 22 A.D.2d 253, 254 N.Y.S.2d 712

Substitution of parties in a stockholder's derivative action will be permitted where the assignee of the corporation is the substituted party, and at the time of the assignment the plaintiff was a stockholder. In such a case, the plaintiffs, if successful, are entitled to be reimbursed for their costs and expenses even though the assignee is a foreign corporation. Marco v Sachs (1951) 201 Misc 928, 106 N.Y.S.2d 522, affd 304 N.Y. 912, 110 N.E.2d 737

Where district court determined that shareholders did not have standing to pursue a derivative action under Fed. R. Civ. P. 23.1 or N.Y. Bus. Corp. Law § 626(b) because the shareholders did not own stock in the corporation, a bank, before the core of the allegedly wrongful conduct transpired, the appellate court held that the district court did not abuse its discretion in denying the motion to intervene pursuant to Fed. R. Civ. P. 24 by a plaintiff who owned stock during the relevant time period because the case had been pending for two years with considerable media attention, and the potential plaintiff had notice of the action but failed to intervene earlier, and further, the potential plaintiff's interests would have been adequately protected in parallel state court proceedings stemming from the same conduct. Kaliski v Bacot (In re Bank of N.Y. Derivative Litig.) (2003, CA2 NY) 320 F.3d 291

In a stockholder's derivative action seeking damages, an accounting, injunctive and other relief, a motion for leave to intervene was denied where the putative intervenors merely alleged that they have been stockholders of the corporation during the time of a major portion of the transactons complained of, such conclusory allegations failing to meet the requirements of § 61 of former Gen. Corp. L. Bauer v Servel, Inc. (1958, SD NY) 168 F. Supp. 478, 1 FR Serv 2d 410

8. Burden of proof

Plaintiffs who allege excessive corporate compensation must prove wrongdoing or waste as to compensation arrangements regarding disinterested directors or shareholders, but directors who approve their own compensation bear burden of proving that transaction was fair to corporation. Marx v Akers (1996) 88 N.Y.2d 189, 644 N.Y.S.2d 121, 666 N.E.2d 1034

One who seeks to maintain a derivative action in behalf of a corporation has the burden of proving that he was a bona fide stockholder at the time of the transaction of which he complains. Cavanagh v L & R Trucking & Warehouse Co. (1961) 29 Misc. 2d 576, 215 N.Y.S.2d 902

Dismissal of a shareholder's derivative action was appropriate because the shareholder had not established futility of making a demand as required by N.Y. Bus. Corp. Law § 626(c). Stein v Immelt (2012, CA2 NY) 2012 US App LEXIS 13888 (UNPUBLISHED)

9. Complaint

In shareholders' derivative action asserting that board of directors wasted corporate assets by awarding excessive compensation to executives and outside directors, plaintiff failed to allege with particularity that demand on board of directors to initiate lawsuit would have been futile where (1) only 3 directors were alleged to have received benefit of executive compensation scheme, (2) allegations that board used faulty accounting procedures were mere conclusory allegations of wrongdoing, and (3) no particular facts were alleged to demonstrate that board failed to deliberate or exercise its business judgment. Marx v Akers (1996) 88 N.Y.2d 189, 644 N.Y.S.2d 121, 666 N.E.2d 1034

Allegation that corporate board of directors voted themselves compensation does not give rise to cause of action, since directors are statutorily entitled to set those levels; nor is cause of action stated by conclusory allegation that compensation directors have set for themselves is excessive. Marx v Akers (1996) 88 N.Y.2d 189, 644 N.Y.S.2d 121, 666 N.E.2d 1034

To survive dismissal motion, complaint challenging excessiveness of director compensation must allege compensation rates excessive on their face or other facts which call into question whether compensation was fair to corporation when approved, good faith of directors setting those rates, or that decision to set compensation could not have been product of valid business judgment. Marx v Akers (1996) 88 N.Y.2d 189, 644 N.Y.S.2d 121, 666 N.E.2d 1034

Bare allegations in shareholders' derivative action that executive compensation set by board of directors lacked relationship to duties performed or to cost of living were insufficient as matter of law to state cause of action for excessive compensation constituting corporate waste. Marx v Akers (1996) 88 N.Y.2d 189, 644 N.Y.S.2d 121, 666 N.E.2d 1034

In shareholders' derivative action, order which denied defendants' cross motion for summary judgment dismissing complaint affirmed-minority shareholders seek reimbursement of corporate funds used by majority shareholders to pay for defense of dissolution proceeding-complaint failed to comply with Business Corporation Law § 626 (c), which provides that in shareholders' derivative action complaint shall set forth with particularity efforts of plaintiff to secure initiation of such action by board or reasons for not making such effort; majority shareholders argued to Supreme Court only that minority failed to request receiver to bring action or to explain futility of such request; consequently, majority shareholders' claim as it concerns requests made of board is not properly before Appellate Division; claim as it

pertains to receiver, while properly before Appellate Division, is meritless because receiver had not yet been appointed at time complaint was filed-action does not constitute second suit involving same two parties for purposes of res judicata; in dissolution proceeding, actual interaction between parties was one involving minority shareholders against majority shareholders; corporation had only passive presence in that proceeding; in this action, actual interaction between parties concerns corporation and majority shareholders; minority shareholders are only nominal parties. Gunzburg v Gunzburg, 152 A.D.2d 537

In a derivative action by a shareholder who alleged corporate waste, the allegations of the shareholder were insufficient to establish charges of improper conduct where the complaint failed to set forth any specific allegations showing that an award of a contingent bonus to the president of the corporation was in bad faith or otherwise improper, and where it was obvious that the issuance of the bonus was an added incentive to the president to continue to increase the profits of the corporation. Lewis v Riklis (1981, 1st Dept) 82 A.D.2d 789, 440 N.Y.S.2d 658

In an action brought by the plaintiff against the corporation which owned the cooperative apartment in which both the plaintiff and the individual defendant, who was the president of the corporation, lived, the causes of action alleging that the defendant president "misled" the board of directors as to her intentions regarding a possible sublet of a portion of her apartment and then prepared minutes of the board's meeting so as to recite incorrectly the proposal which she made and the action by the board, were derivative in nature. Condren v Slater (1981, 1st Dept) 85 A.D.2d 507, 444 N.Y.S.2d 454

In a shareholder's derivative action against a corporation, Special Term properly denied defendant's motion to dismiss the complaint where the shareholder complied with Bus Corp Law § 626(c) by alleging with sufficient particularity that it would have been futile to attempt to secure initiation of the action by the corporate board of directors in that defendant majority stockholder had power under the by-laws to remove plaintiff and his wife, who were the other directors, without cause. Miller v Kastner (1984, 4th Dept) 100 A.D.2d 728, 473 N.Y.S.2d 656

Complaint by minority shareholder against majority shareholders of family close corporation which merely contained general charges of mismanagement, waste, and taking of corporate assets failed to state cause of action since no specific factual averments were provided as to when and what wrongful acts were attributed to each defendant, and affidavits submitted in support of claim by plaintiff and her attorney were unexecuted; however, court would grant leave to serve amended complaint within 20 days.Di Pace v Figueroa (1987, 3d Dept) 128 A.D.2d 942, 512 N.Y.S.2d 593

Court properly declined to dismiss cause of action purported to be stockholders' derivative action, although plaintiffs were not entitled to maintain such action, where action was pleaded in plaintiffs' individual capacity and sufficient facts were stated to make out cause of action for breach of contract; it did not matter that plaintiffs had mislabeled their cause of action. Pullin v Feinsod (1988, 2d Dept) 142 A.D.2d 561, 530 N.Y.S.2d 226

Complaint in shareholder's derivative action was properly dismissed for failure to state cause of action where plaintiff failed to plead any particularized facts creating reasonable doubt that defendants were disinterested or that challenged transaction was other than valid exercise of business judgment. Strougo v Hoyt (1997, 1st Dept) 245 A.D.2d 210, 665 N.Y.S.2d 902

Brief references to unsuccessful attempts to obtain consent of other shareholders of corporation to commence instant actions in right of that corporation did not comply with CLS Bus Corp § 626(c). Charos v Charos (1999, 2d Dept) 264 A.D.2d 495, 694 N.Y.S.2d 702

Even if stockholder of bank acquired by another bank had standing to challenge merger, her allegations-that bank was acquired at unfairly depressed price at stockholders' expense as result of excessive compensation and bonus arrangements provided by acquired bank's board of directors to certain directors and executives-did not state viable cause of action, and thus her complaint was properly dismissed, and her motion to replead was properly denied, where her allegations, which were mainly conclusory, did not allege compensation rates excessive on their face or other facts that called into question whether (1) compensation was fair to corporation when approved, (2) directors acted in good faith in setting those rates, or (3) decision to set compensation was product of valid business judgment. Fischbein v Beitzel (2001, 1st Dept) 281 A.D.2d 167, 721 N.Y.S.2d 515, app den 96 N.Y.2d 715, 729 N.Y.S.2d 442, 754 N.E.2d 202

Business Corporation Law

It was error to dismiss for failure to state a claim a derivative action in which a shareholder claimed that a law firm had improperly advised a corporation that its chairman's son could be involved in a project despite his securities violations. Evidence that other factors contributed to the loss did not mean that the shareholder could not prove causation as a matter of law; the law firm had not established that it had not departed from the requisite standard of care; because the shareholder alleged that the malpractice continued after it acquired its shares, it had standing to bring the action; and the shareholder had showed that demand would have been futile because the chairman dominated two of the other four members of the board. Voluto Ventures, LLC v Jenkens & Gilchrist Parker Chapin LLP (2007, 1st Dept) 46 App Div 3d 354, 847 NYS2d 559.

The complaint in a stockholder's derivative action charging misconduct on the part of officers and directors in voting excessive salaries and improper stock options, is sufficient, in alleging facts rather than mere conclusions of the pleader, where it gives full details of the employment agreements and other transactions, with dates, figures, and the naming of individuals. Abramson v Blakeley (1960) 25 Misc. 2d 967, 202 N.Y.S.2d 586

Because of the fact that the basic cause of action is in the corporate entity, not in any individual shareholder, the complaint in a stockholder's derivative suit should make clear that the action is brought in behalf of the corporation, but an averment that it is brought "derivatively and in the right and for the benefit" of the corporation, or to like effect, is sufficient to apprise all parties of plaintiff's position. Abramson v Blakeley (1960) 25 Misc. 2d 967, 202 N.Y.S.2d 586

Complaint in shareholder's derivative action against corporate directors, which did not clearly indicate whether plaintiff was proceeding on theory that individual directors breached their fiduciary duty trust in failing to act in good faith or that they were negligent or inattentive to affairs of corporation, was deficient for failure to make clear theory on which plaintiff was proceeding. Kutik v Taylor (1975) 80 Misc. 2d 839, 364 N.Y.S.2d 387

To comply properly with § 61 of former Gen. Corp. L., it was incumbent upon a plaintiff to set forth in the complaint the date when it was claimed he became a stockholder. Myers v Jeffe (1952, Sup) 111 N.Y.S.2d 384

Defendants were entitled to dismissal of shareholder derivative action alleging waste of corporate assets and breach of fiduciary duty, where proxy statement discussing facts regarding challenged corporate merger informed shareholders that failure to respond would be counted as vote in favor of transaction, and plaintiff did not allege that it voted in opposition to merger; by its silence, plaintiff acquiesced in merger and was estopped from maintaining suit. Pinnacle Consultants, Ltd. v Leucadia Nat'l Corp. (1999, 1st Dept) 261 A.D.2d 164, 689 N.Y.S.2d 497, app gr 93 N.Y.2d 815, 697 N.Y.S.2d 562, 719 N.E.2d 923 and affd 94 N.Y.2d 426, 706 N.Y.S.2d 46, 727 N.E.2d 543

Because the shareholder's complaint did not allege with particularity that the challenged transaction was so egregious on its face that it could not have been the product of sound business judgment of the directors, it did not comply with N.Y. Bus. Corp. Law § 626(c); therefore, the trial court erred in failing to dismiss the complaint. Matter of Omnicom Group Inc. (2007, 1st Dept) 43 App Div 3d 766, 842 NYS2d 408

Corporate directors could not be held liable for conversion or fraud in shareholders' derivative action challenging issuance of stock warrants to them, where stock warrants were legally valid, and proxy statements urging approval of issuance of stock warrants disclosed all relevant facts. Pinnacle Consultants ex rel. Shareholders of Leucadia Nat'l Corp. v Leucadia Nat'l Corp. (1995, SD NY) 923 F. Supp. 439

In shareholders' derivative action, complaint stated claims for breach of fiduciary duty and corporate waste based on allegations that defendant directors dominated and controlled their fellow directors financially, that board approved issuance and repurchase of stock warrants solely to funnel cash and corporate control into defendants' pockets, that defendants were substantially overpaid, and that board was aware that challenged transactions were not in company's best interests. Pinnacle Consultants ex rel. Shareholders of Leucadia Nat'l Corp. v Leucadia Nat'l Corp. (1995, SD NY) 923 F. Supp. 439

10. Miscellaneous procedural issues and remedies

Trial court erred, as matter of law, in seeking to bind absent minority shareholder, with no ties to New York, to shareholder derivative class action settlement that purported to extinguish shareholder's due process rights to bring action for damages in another jurisdiction, even though (1) shareholder had notice of action,

(2) court was not required to give it opportunity to opt out of class at time class was certified, and (3) shareholder could have chosen to appear to contest settlement. Re Colt Industries Shareholder Litigation (1991) 77 N.Y.2d 185, 565 N.Y.S.2d 755, 566 N.E.2d 1160

Court properly dismissed, as barred by collateral estoppel, derivative claims alleging that defendants breached their fiduciary duty and committed corporate waste by issuing warrants giving individual defendants options to purchase stock in defendant corporation, where plaintiff's prior RICO action against same defendants, alleging that warrants were unauthorized and unsupported by valid consideration, was dismissed by federal court which concluded that warrants were properly issued and were economically justified as compensation for individual defendants' service to corporation. Pinnacle Consultants, Ltd. v Leucadia Nat'l Corp. (2000) 94 N.Y.2d 426, 706 N.Y.S.2d 46, 727 N.E.2d 543

Neither vacating of corporate resolutions, which amended corporate bylaw and permitted purchase of stock from deceased shareholder's estate as treasury stock, nor setting aside of election of directors was warranted, absent any showing of fraud. Maybrown v Malverne Distributors, Inc. (1977, 2d Dept) 57 A.D.2d 548, 393 N.Y.S.2d 67

Although, ordinarily, the provisions of CPLR § 3101 as to scope of disclosure are liberally construed and applied, the rule in shareholder derivative actions is that an individual defendant should not be examined before trial, absent an evidentiary showing of special circumstances. Condren v Slater (1981, 1st Dept) 85 A.D.2d 507, 444 N.Y.S.2d 454

In shareholder's derivative action whereby board of directors of incorporated hospital were deadlocked due to struggle for control over closely held corporation in which there were two sets of bylaws thus creating on two separate papers, distinct boards with different spheres of authority, which in actuality functioned as one entity, court, pursuant to parties' stipulation and in response to plaintiff's motion to enjoin proposed executive committee meeting pending resolution of derivative action, properly restricted agenda of proposed executive committee meeting to day-to-day administration of hospital so as to maintain status quo with respect to corporate matters. Lauer v Schoenholtz (1984, 2d Dept) 106 A.D.2d 552, 482 N.Y.S.2d 849, later proceeding (2d Dept) 106 A.D.2d 551, 483 N.Y.S.2d 70

In hybrid proceedings and actions seeking judicial dissolution of corporations pursuant to CLS Bus Corp Art 11 and seeking to preserve assets of corporations pursuant to CLS Bus Corp §§ 626 and 1202(a)(3), Supreme Court erred in appointing permanent receiver and ordering defendant to make accounting to each corporation since litigation was at early stage; papers submitted by plaintiff-petitioner were sufficient only to support appointment of temporary receiver to preserve assets and carry out business of each corporation. Imbriale v Imbriale (1988, 2d Dept) 144 A.D.2d 557, 534 N.Y.S.2d 418

Prior dissolution proceeding was not res judicata to shareholders' derivative action seeking, inter alia, reimbursement and accounting since dissolution proceeding involved minority shareholders against majority shareholders, with corporation having only passive presence therein, whereas present action concerned corporation and majority shareholders, with minority shareholders only nominal parties. Gunzburg v Gunzburg (1989, 2d Dept) 152 A.D.2d 537, 543 N.Y.S.2d 474

In shareholder derivative action defendants were entitled to summary judgment where documentary evidence and affidavits from persons with firsthand knowledge demonstrated that plaintiff's allegations of wrongdoing were meritless, and only material proffered by plaintiff to substantiate her claims was her deposition testimony which consisted merely of hearsay and conclusory allegations, which was insufficient to withstand summary judgment. Di Pace v Figueroa (1996, 3d Dept) 223 A.D.2d 949, 637 N.Y.S.2d 222

In shareholder derivative action, plaintiff presented no compelling reason to permit further discovery prior to granting defendants' summary judgment motion where she had conducted discovery permitted by previous court order and failed to perfect appeal from that order, she was permitted to depose 2 individual defendants and was given access to many corporate documents, and affidavits submitted by persons who would be expected to have personal knowledge of events at issue did not suggest that other evidence supporting her position might be uncovered. Di Pace v Figueroa (1996, 3d Dept) 223 A.D.2d 949, 637 N.Y.S.2d 222

Court properly denied stay in stockholder derivative action against bank, which sought stay pending action by Special Litigation Committee (SLC) it had appointed, given bank's delay in appointing

SLC, and inclusion on SLC of members whose impartiality was suspect. Katz v Renyi (2001, 1st Dept) 282 A.D.2d 262, 722 N.Y.S.2d 860

With respect to a charge, in a stockholder's derivative suit, that defendant officers and directors gave illegal stock options to certain officers, market value of the stock at the time of the grant is immaterial and the question is whether or not the corporation receives full value of the stock, either in cash or services, at the time the option is exercised. Abramson v Blakeley (1960) 25 Misc. 2d 967, 202 N.Y.S.2d 586

In shareholders' derivative action, court granted plaintiffs' motion to compel production of outlines, notes and summaries of witness interviews conducted by defendant corporation's special litigation committee, which formed basis of committee's pending motion to dismiss plaintiffs' action as not in corporation's best interests, where witness interviews were not transcribed and material requested by plaintiffs was only means by which to assess reasonableness and good faith of committee's investigation; court's in camera review would ensure that no privileges were violated. Weiser v Grace (1998, Sup) 179 Misc. 2d 116, 683 N.Y.S.2d 781

Minority shareholders' motion for reargument and renewal seeking injunction in derivative action was not made moot by majority shareholder's agreement to personally pay his criminal defense costs (for which use of corporate funds was objected to by minority shareholders) where minority shareholders were attacking validity of any expenditures by corporation on majority shareholder's behalf, including considerable sums that corporation had already spent on his criminal defense, as well as any future proceedings and civil actions. Pilipiak v Keyes (2000, Sup) 185 Misc. 2d 636, 712 N.Y.S.2d 757

Real estate investor had no standing to assert derivative claims on behalf of a real estate venture formed by others with whom he had participated in other real estate ventures in the past, as he had no actual, equitable or beneficial interest in any shares of the new venture, under N.Y. Bus. Corp. Law § 626(a) and (b). Tal v Malekan (2003, A.D., 1st Dept) 760 N.Y.S.2d 36

11. Demand, generally

In respect to a shareholder's derivative action, the requirement of a demand on the board of directors, or of sufficient explanation for failure to make one, derives from one of the basic principles of corporate law, namely, that the management of a corporation is entrusted to its board of directors who have primary responsibility for acting in the name of corporation and who are often in a position to correct alleged abuses without resort to the courts. Barr v Wackman (1975) 36 N.Y.2d 371, 368 N.Y.S.2d 497, 329 N.E.2d 180, 99 ALR3d 1023

In respect to a shareholder's derivative action, the demand requirement is generally designed to weed out unnecessary or illegitimate shareholder derivative suits, but that prophylactic device should not be allowed to frustrate the true derivative suit, the very thing it was designed to protect. Barr v Wackman (1975) 36 N.Y.2d 371, 368 N.Y.S.2d 497, 329 N.E.2d 180, 99 ALR3d 1023

In a shareholder's derivative action, the better approach, in respect to the necessity for a demand on the board of directors, is to rest the determination of that issue in the sound discretion of the court to which the issue is first presented, to be determined from the sufficiency of the complaint, liberally construed. Barr v Wackman (1975) 36 N.Y.2d 371, 368 N.Y.S.2d 497, 329 N.E.2d 180, 99 ALR3d 1023

In shareholders' derivative action, purposes of requiring plaintiff to first demand that board of directors initiate lawsuit are (1) to relieve courts from deciding matters of internal corporate governance by providing corporate directors with opportunities to correct alleged abuses, (2) to provide corporate boards with reasonable protection from harassment by litigation on matters clearly within discretion of directors, and (3) to discourage "strike suits" commenced by shareholders for personal gain rather than benefit of corporation; demand is generally designed to weed out unnecessary or illegitimate shareholder derivative suits. Marx v Akers (1996) 88 N.Y.2d 189, 644 N.Y.S.2d 121, 666 N.E.2d 1034

Majority shareholders of close corporation were not entitled to dismissal of derivative action on ground that complaint failed to comply with CLS Bus Corp § 626(c) in that minority shareholders failed to request receiver to bring action or explain futility of such request since receiver had not yet been appointed at time complaint was filed. Gunzburg v Gunzburg (1989, 2d Dept) 152 A.D.2d 537, 543 N.Y.S.2d 474

Individual cotrustee of testamentary trusts involving stock of 2 closely held corporations had standing to object to accountings of those trusts filed by corporate cotrustee, despite corporate cotrustee's claims that objection could be asserted only through shareholder's derivative action and that individual cotrustee was precluded from maintaining derivative action by her failure to comply with CLS Bus Corp § 626(c), where individual cotrustee was shareholder of both corporations and director of one, and she did not allege breach of duty owed to corporations but rather alleged corporate cotrustee's breach of fiduciary duty as trustee and sought relief that would directly benefit trusts. In re Estate of Mooney (1999, 3d Dept) 263 A.D.2d 727, 694 N.Y.S.2d 784

A shareholder does not sue in his own right but in the right of the corporation, and is authorized to act when the corporation fails to act. However, it is therefore incumbent on him to allege with particularity his efforts to secure initiation of the action by the board of directors or the reason for not making such effort. Syracuse Television, Inc. v Channel 9, Syracuse, Inc. (1966) 51 Misc. 2d 188, 273 N.Y.S.2d 16

This section, as originally introduced in the legislature, contained in subdivision c the requirement that a demand be made on shareholders, but that requirement was removed because it was considered too onerous. A litigating shareholder need therefore not comply with any such condition. Syracuse Television, Inc. v Channel 9, Syracuse, Inc. (1966) 51 Misc. 2d 188, 273 N.Y.S.2d 16

Requirement of Business Corporation Law that shareholder make demand on corporate directors before initiating derivative suit would apply to derivative action brought by a shareholder in a Massachusetts business trust. Rottenberg v Pfeiffer (1976) 86 Misc. 2d 556, 383 N.Y.S.2d 189, affd (2d Dept) 59 A.D.2d 756, 398 N.Y.S.2d 703

In a shareholders' derivative action, the trial court erred in denying summary judgment to an abstract company and its president dismissing a third-party complaint, because defendant third-party plaintiff merely asserted conclusory allegations of wrongdoing and control insufficient to circumvent the requirement of a demand on the board of directors under N.Y. Bus. Corp. Law § 626(c). Danzy v NIA Abstract Corp. (2007, 2d Dept) 40 App Div 3d 804, 835 NYS2d 738

There is no reason to excuse demand requirement where plaintiff shareholder is sole shareholder of corporation and presumably could secure compliance with demand if one were made. Texwood, Ltd. v Gerber (1985, SD NY) 621 F. Supp. 585, CCH Fed Secur L Rep ¶ 92374

Board of directors were entitled to dismiss a shareholder's claims that certain current and former outside directors wasted corporate assets in engaging in the investigation of the shareholder's demand to sue regarding losses associated with the corporation's collateralized debt obligation and subprime mortgage-related assets because the shareholder failed to make a pre-suit demand, or to plead facts establishing futility of such a demand. Lerner v Prince (2012, Sup) 36 Misc 3d 297, 945 NYS2d 520

12. Sufficiency of demand

Corporation directors were not entitled to dismissal of shareholder's derivative action for failure to comply with requirement under CLS Bus Corp § 626(c) that efforts to secure initiation of action by board of directors, or reasons for not making such effort, be set forth with particularity where pleadings alleged that directors were in exclusive control of corporation and were involved in series of specific transactions which were detrimental to corporation, thus setting forth sufficient details from which it could be inferred that making of demand would have been futile. Curreri v Verni (1989, 2d Dept) 156 A.D.2d 420, 548 N.Y.S.2d 540

Pleading in shareholder's derivative action does not comply with CLS Bus Corp § 626(c) requirement that efforts to secure initiation of action by board of directors, or reasons for not making such effort, be set forth with particularity where it merely names majority of board of directors as parties defendant and contains conclusory allegations of wrongdoing. Curreri v Verni (1989, 2d Dept) 156 A.D.2d 420, 548 N.Y.S.2d 540

Plaintiff shareholders satisfied demand requirement of CLS Bus Corp § 626(c) by forwarding draft copy of complaint with demand letter to defendant directors 2 1/2 months prior to instituting action. Jones v Jones (1996, 1st Dept) 223 A.D.2d 483, 637 N.Y.S.2d 83

A demand under this section need not assume any particular form or recite any specific language since no such requirement is set forth in subdivision c, and a memo which itemized the grounds for the demand with particularity and advised that in the absence of corporate action plaintiff would proceed to protect its rights, was sufficient.Syracuse Television, Inc. v Channel 9, Syracuse, Inc. (1966) 51 Misc. 2d 188, 273 N.Y.S.2d 16

There was no substance to the allegation by the directors of a defendant corporation that stockholder suing them to account for their official duties in the management of the corporation had made no demand specifically requesting action against the program director, where the demand by the stockholder referred to appropriate action against any and all persons appearing to be responsible for loss or waste or diversion of the corporation's assets for non-corporate purposes, and there was a specific allegation that the program director had used over $1,000 worth of airline tickets belonging to the corporation for his personal benefit.Syracuse Television, Inc. v Channel 9, Syracuse, Inc. (1966) 51 Misc. 2d 188, 273 N.Y.S.2d 16

Shareholders' allegations were insufficient to prove with particularity that corporation's board of directors would not have been responsive to demand under CLS Bus Corp § 626(c) to take action with respect to challenged accounting irregularities where most of those allegations tracked publicly disseminated report issued by special committee set up by board of directors to investigate those irregularities, in response to which board took remedial action. In re Woolworth Corp. Shareholder Derivative Litig. (1997, 1st Dept) 240 A.D.2d 189, 658 N.Y.S.2d 869

Dismissal of a shareholder's derivative suit was proper because the complaint failed to adequately plead a demand or demand futility pursuant to N.Y. Bus. Corp. Law § 626(c); among other things, while the shareholder's claims that three directors received backdated options sufficiently alleged that they were interested, the allegations as to other directors were insufficient to establish that any of them were interested. The amended complaint failed to plead with the requisite particularity that the directors had specific information or reason to inform themselves about the details of the issuance of stock options, and failed to do so, and allegations, based on a report acknowledging backdating but indicating that the misdating was generally by a matter of days, did not rise to the level required. Wandel v Eisenberg (2009, App Div, 1st Dept) 871 NYS2d 102.

Defendants' motion to dismiss plaintiff's derivative action alleging breach of fiduciary duty and other causes of action had to be granted, because plaintiff failed to make a demand for action on the corporation's board of directors, and futility was not pled with particularity in accord with N.Y. Bus. Corp. Law § 626(c). Wandel v Eisenberg (2007, Sup) 237 NYLJ 101, affd (2009, 1st Dept) 60 App Div 3d 77, 871 NYS2d 102.

While demand to sue need not assume a particular form or be made in any special language, it must inform the board with particularity of the complained of acts and the potential defendants. A demand, therefore, must fairly and adequately apprise the directors of the potential cause of action so that they, in the first instance, can discharge their duty of authorizing actions that in their considered opinion are in the best interests of the corporation. Kalin v Xanboo, Inc., 2009 US Dist LEXIS 34954 (SD NY March 30, 2009).

13. Demand excused

A futile demand on the board of directors need not be made before a shareholder's derivative action is instituted. Barr v Wackman (1975) 36 N.Y.2d 371, 368 N.Y.S.2d 497, 329 N.E.2d 180, 99 ALR3d 1023

Allegations of directorial fraud or self-interest are not in every case a prerequisite to excusing a derivative shareholder from making a demand upon the board of directors. Barr v Wackman (1975) 36 N.Y.2d 371, 368 N.Y.S.2d 497, 329 N.E.2d 180, 99 ALR3d 1023

A demand on the board of directors will be excused, as a condition precedent to the institution of a shareholder's derivative action, where the alleged wrongdoers control or comprise a majority of the directors. Barr v Wackman (1975) 36 N.Y.2d 371, 368 N.Y.S.2d 497, 329 N.E.2d 180, 99 ALR3d 1023

Where the shareholder's derivative complaint, liberally construed, alleged acts for which a majority of the board of directors might be liable, plaintiff reasonably concluded that the board would not be responsive to a demand to secure initation of an action in favor of the corporation or to otherwise remedy the acts of which complaint was made. Barr v Wackman (1975) 36 N.Y.2d 371, 368 N.Y.S.2d 497, 329 N.E.2d 180, 99 ALR3d 1023

In respect to a shareholder's derivative action, a demand on the subject corporation's board of directors to secure initiation of an action in favor of the corporation or to otherwise remedy the acts of which plaintiff complains is excused where the board itself is accused of patent breach of its fiduciary duties and its members are named as parties defendant. Barr v Wackman (1975) 36 N.Y.2d 371, 368 N.Y.S.2d 497, 329 N.E.2d 180, 99 ALR3d 1023

In shareholder's derivative action, plaintiff's allegations of board participation in and approval of acts involving bias and self-dealing by minority "affiliated" directors and breach of fiduciary duties of the due care and diligence by the remaining majority "unaffiliated" directors through their participation and approval, though there was no claim of self-dealing as to them, were sufficient to withstand a motion to dismiss for failure to make a demand on the board of directors to initiate an action in favor of the corporation or to otherwise remedy the acts of which plaintiff complained. Barr v Wackman (1975) 36 N.Y.2d 371, 368 N.Y.S.2d 497, 329 N.E.2d 180, 99 ALR3d 1023

A derivative shareholder's complaint may, in a particular case, withstand a motion to dismiss for failure to make a demand upon the board of directors, even though a majority of the board are not individually charged with fraud or self-dealing; particular allegations of formal board participation in and approval of active wrongdoing may suffice to defeat a dismissal motion. Barr v Wackman (1975) 36 N.Y.2d 371, 368 N.Y.S.2d 497, 329 N.E.2d 180, 99 ALR3d 1023

While justification for failure to give directors notice prior to the institution of a derivative action is not automatically to be found in bare allegations which merely set forth prima facie personal liability of directors without spelling out some detail, such justification may be found when the claim of liability is based on formal board action in which the individual directors were participants; however, it is not sufficient merely to name a majority of the directors as parties defendant with conclusory allegations of wrongdoing or control by wrongdoers. Barr v Wackman (1975) 36 N.Y.2d 371, 368 N.Y.S.2d 497, 329 N.E.2d 180, 99 ALR3d 1023

Under rule that plaintiff may commence shareholders' derivative action only after demanding that board of directors initiate lawsuit, demand would be considered futile if complaint alleges with particularity (1) that majority of directors are interested in transaction, (2) that directors failed to inform themselves to degree reasonably necessary about transaction, or (3) that directors failed to exercise their business judgment in approving transaction. Marx v Akers (1996) 88 N.Y.2d 189, 644 N.Y.S.2d 121, 666 N.E.2d 1034

Conclusory allegations of wrongdoing against each member of board of directors are not sufficient to excuse requirement that plaintiff in shareholders' derivative suit first demand that board initiate lawsuit. Marx v Akers (1996) 88 N.Y.2d 189, 644 N.Y.S.2d 121, 666 N.E.2d 1034

In shareholders' derivative suit, requirement that plaintiff first demand that board of directors initiate lawsuit is not excused by fact that majority of board members who approved transaction are named as defendants. Marx v Akers (1996) 88 N.Y.2d 189, 644 N.Y.S.2d 121, 666 N.E.2d 1034

Demand that board of directors initiate lawsuit, as prerequisite to shareholders' derivative action, is excused on ground of futility when complaint alleges with particularity that majority of board is interested in challenged transaction; director interest may either be self-interest in transaction, or loss of independence because director with no direct interest in transaction is "controlled" by self-interested director. Marx v Akers (1996) 88 N.Y.2d 189, 644 N.Y.S.2d 121, 666 N.E.2d 1034

Demand that board of directors initiate lawsuit, as prerequisite to shareholders' derivative action, is excused on grounds of futility when complaint alleges with particularity that board of directors did not fully inform themselves about challenged transaction to extent reasonably appropriate under circumstances; director does not exempt himself from liability by failing to do more than passively rubber-stamp decisions of active managers. Marx v Akers (1996) 88 N.Y.2d 189, 644 N.Y.S.2d 121, 666 N.E.2d 1034

Demand that board of directors initiate lawsuit, as prerequisite to shareholders' derivative action, is excused on ground of futility when complaint alleges with particularity that challenged transaction was so egregious on its face that it could not have been product of sound business judgment of directors. Marx v Akers (1996) 88 N.Y.2d 189, 644 N.Y.S.2d 121, 666 N.E.2d 1034

Requirement that plaintiff demand that board of directors initiate lawsuit, as prerequisite to commencement of shareholders' derivative action, should have been excused as to that part of complaint that challenged fixing of directors' compensation; directors are self-interested in challenged transaction where they will receive direct financial benefit from transaction which is different from benefit to shareholders generally. Marx v Akers (1996) 88 N.Y.2d 189, 644 N.Y.S.2d 121, 666 N.E.2d 1034

In shareholder's derivative action, requirement of demand upon board of directors pursuant to Business Corporation Law § 626 (c) will be excused where such demand would be futile or where alleged wrongdoers control or comprise majority of directors; although pleading is deemed insufficient if it merely names majority of directors as parties defendants and contains conclusory allegations of wrongdoing, here amended pleadings allege that appellants were in exclusive control of corporation and that they were involved in series of specific transactions which were detrimental to corporation; amended pleadings therefore set forth sufficient details from which it may be inferred that making of demand would indeed be futile; additionally, there are triable issues of fact as to composition of board of directors which can only be resolved at trial. Curreri v Verni, 156 A.D.2d 420

For purposes of withstanding motion to dismiss complaint in shareholder's derivative action, plaintiff shareholder's unrefuted allegation that individual defendants controlled board of directors constituted sufficient compliance with statute requiring that a complaint in a shareholder's derivative action set forth the reasons for not making an effort to secure the initiation of such an action by board of directors. Joseph v Amrep Corp. (1977, 1st Dept) 59 A.D.2d 841, 399 N.Y.S.2d 3

In a shareholder's derivative action, the trial court improperly dismissed plaintiffs' cause of action against two defendants where the three plaintiffs and the three defendants each owned one-sixth of the voting shares of the corporation and constituted its board of directors, which had been deadlocked for a lengthy period, even though the allegations failed to state a cause of action against the two defendants for breach of their fiduciary duties as corporate directors, since the allegations were sufficient to show such bias and antagonism on their part such as would render futile any demand by plaintiffs on the board to take corrective action regarding the third defendant's alleged misconduct and thus the allegation satisfied the requirements of Bus Corp Law § 626. Lauer v Schoenholtz (1984, 2d Dept) 106 A.D.2d 551, 483 N.Y.S.2d 70

Plaintiff sufficiently set forth reasons why he did not make demand on defendant corporation before commencing action where he asserted that (1) he and his business associate were sole officers and directors of corporation, (2) business associate raided corporate bank account by unilaterally altering corporate banking resolution, and (3) demand on business associate, who was director in control of corporation, would have been futile. Tong v Hang Seng Bank (1994, 1st Dept) 210 A.D.2d 99, 620 N.Y.S.2d 42

In shareholder derivative action alleging breach of fiduciary duties and waste of corporate assets, it was error to dismiss complaint for failure to comply with condition precedent set forth in CLS Bus Corp § 626(c) where plaintiff alleged that demand on board of directors would have been futile because defendant had "hand-picked" members of board, who were his personal friends and had business relationships with him as well. Bansbach v Zinn (1999, 3d Dept) 258 A.D.2d 710, 685 N.Y.S.2d 332

Dismissal of a shareholder derivative action was erroneous under N.Y. Bus. Corp. Law § 626(c) because the appointment by the board of directors of a special committee to investigate and rectify the alleged backdating of stock option grants to officers and directors, and the steps which the committee had undertaken, did not establish the board's willingness to take appropriate action to protect the interests of the corporation. Matter of Comverse Tech., Inc. (2008, 1st Dept) 56 App Div 3d 49, 866 NYS2d 10.

If the shareholder derivative action against individual defendants and the bank, plaintiff was not required to make a demand on the board prior to bringing suit because demand was excused as futile where, inter alia, the amended complaint alleged with particularity that the board of directors did not fully inform itself about the challenged transactions to the extent reasonably appropriate under the circumstances. Mason-Mahon v Flint, 2018 N.Y. App. Div. LEXIS 7689 (N.Y. App. Div. 2d Dep't 2018).

With regard to prior demand on the directors before instituting a stockholder's derivative suit, while an allegation that demand would be futile because the entire board is constituted of appointees of one individual and subservient to him is, standing alone, insufficient, additional allegations that the remainder of the defendant officers participated in the wrongs alleged sufficiently satisfies the demand requirements. Abramson v Blakeley (1960) 25 Misc. 2d 967, 202 N.Y.S.2d 586

In shareholders' derivative action against minority shareholder who managed business, where majority shareholders sought to recover for corporate waste, fraud, conversion and diversion and appropriation of corporate opportunity, failure to strictly comply with pleading prerequisites contained in CLS Bus Corp § 626(c) would be excused, and defendant's motion to dismiss complaint on that basis would be denied. Bouhayer v Georgalis (1996, Sup) 169 Misc. 2d 779, 645 N.Y.S.2d 1008

Shareholder was not collaterally estopped by a prior lawsuit against corporate management from claiming that demand upon the management prior to instituting a shareholder's derivative suit, as required by N.Y. Bus. Corp. Law § 626(c), would have been futile as there was no identity of issues; that the intermediate court had concluded that the officers and directors were not subject to the founder's control with respect to stock options and warrants did not insulate their conduct from similar claims forever. Bansbach v Zinn (2003) 1 NY3d 1, 769 N.Y.S.2d 175, 801 N.E.2d 395, reargument den (2004, NY) 2004 N.Y. LEXIS 50

Shareholder established that a demand on a corporation's officers and directors prior to instituting a shareholder's derivative suit under N.Y. Bus. Corp. Law § 626 would have been futile as: (1) the officers and directors immediately covered the founder's legal expenses incurred in connection with a criminal investigation concerning his actions, yet delayed reimbursement, and continued to advance defense costs after the founder admitted in open court having implicated the corporation in his criminal conduct, (2) they sought only partial reimbursement, and (3) they voted to indemnify the founder for all his legal costs and expenses, including the fine assessed against him, after the shareholder's suit was dismissed, but before it was reinstated. Bansbach v Zinn (2003) 1 NY3d 1, 769 N.Y.S.2d 175, 801 N.E.2d 395, reargument den (2004, NY) 2004 N.Y. LEXIS 50

Shareholder's derivative action against officers and directors of corporation is not dismissed, where shareholder did not make demand on corporation but specified its reasons for not doing so, including fact that defendants were directors of company and approved alleged wrongdoing, because, in light of this, plaintiff is excused from making demand on corporation. Pinnacle Consultants ex rel. Shareholders of Leucadia Nat'l Corp. v Leucadia Nat'l Corp. (1995, SD NY) 923 F. Supp. 439

Shareholder's derivative action against officers and directors of corporation is not dismissed, where shareholder did not make demand on corporation but specified its reasons for not doing so, including fact that defendants were directors of company and approved alleged wrongdoing, because, in light of this, plaintiff is excused from making demand on corporation. Pinnacle Consultants ex rel. Shareholders of Leucadia Nat'l Corp. v Leucadia Nat'l Corp. (1995, SD NY) 923 F. Supp. 439

In a derivative action concerning backdated stock options where the shareholder argued that demand on the board was futile, the complaint failed to support the assertion that a majority of the directors should have been treated as interested in the transaction. Three inside directors were alleged to have received backdated options, but the allegations as to the other seven directors were insufficient to establish that any of them were interested. Also, the complaint failed to plead with the requisite particularity that the directors had specific information or reason to inform themselves about the details of the issuance of stock options, and failed to do so. Finally, the allegations, based on a report acknowledging backdating but indicating that the misdating was generally by a matter of days, did not rise to the level required. Wandel v Eisenberg, (2009, App Div, 1st Dept) 871 NYS2d 102.

Pursuant to N.Y. Bus. Corp. Law § 626(c), a shareholder adequately pleaded grounds establishing that demand upon the board of directors would be futile, and the shareholder alleged specific facts that the other directors would not be impartial. Gorbrook Assoc. Inc. v Silverstein (2013, Dist Ct) 40 Misc 3d 425, 965 NYS2d 851.

Limited liability company's (LLC's) non-managing members (NMMs) had standing to pursue professional negligence claim against an independent auditor because the NMMs sufficiently pleaded the LLC's managing member (MM) had a direct financial interest in the auditor's issuance of clean audit opinions in the form of higher fees for the MM as well as inflated fees based on a percentage of the LLC's fictitious profits, and, as such, demand upon the MM to assert the claim was futile. Sacher v Beacon Assoc. Mgt. Corp. (2014, App Div, 2d Dept) 980 NYS2d 121.

14. Refusal to act

Not only must plaintiff make a demand on the corporation prior to commencing a derivative action (unless such demand is futile), but the demand must be met by a wrongful refusal not justified by the exercise of reasonable discretion by the directors, and the failure to sue must be the result of a breach of duty on the part of the board of directors, and not merely an error in judgment. Consequently, where plaintiff had formally presented to the board in the form of a motion information of alleged mismanagement and waste, and the motion failed for want of a second, the board taking none of the many actions which might be anticipated in view of the gravity of the charges, the refusal of the stockholder's demand was not a mere error of judgment and did not prevent the stockholder from bringing a derivative action on behalf of the corporation to compel directors and officers thereof to take appropriate action to recover the losses resulting from waste and mismanagement in their failure and refusal to act.Syracuse Television, Inc. v Channel 9, Syracuse, Inc. (1966) 51 Misc. 2d 188, 273 N.Y.S.2d 16

Simply naming a board member as a defendant and alleging claims of breach of fiduciary duty and negligence based on the director's inaction are insufficient to establish interest. M+J Savitt, Inc. v Savitt, 2009 US Dist LEXIS 21321 (SD NY March 17, 2009).

15. Holder of interest, generally

The requirement presently appearing in subd. (b) of this section, that it must appear that plaintiff, initiating a derivative suit, is holder of a share interest at the time of bringing the action and was likewise such at the time of the transaction of which he complains, or that his shares or interest devolved upon him by operation of law, was originally introduced into § 61 of the Gen. Corp. L. by amendment of 1944, prior to which time there was no such specific requirement, and which amendment was not retroactive. Coane v American Distilling Co. (1948) 298 N.Y. 197, 81 N.E.2d 87; Gottfried v Gottfried (1952, Sup) 112 N.Y.S.2d 431

Since 1944, failure of plaintiff to allege and prove that he has a share interest at time of initiating the action and likewise that he had such an interest at the time of the transactions complained of has usually been regarded as fatal to any attempt on his part to enforce a cause of action in behalf of the corporation.Eisenberg v Grossman (1949) 275 A.D. 946, 89 N.Y.S.2d 787; Myer v Myer (1946) 271 A.D. 465, 66 N.Y.S.2d 83, app dismd 271 A.D. 823, 66 N.Y.S.2d 618 and affd 296 N.Y. 979, 73 N.E.2d 562; Manowitz v Colorado Mining Corp. (1954, Sup) 135 N.Y.S.2d 714; Breswick & Co. v Harrison-Rye Realty Corp. (1952) 280 A.D. 820, 114 N.Y.S.2d 25, app dismd 304 N.Y. 840, 109 N.E.2d 712; Weinstein v Behn (1946, Sup) 65 N.Y.S.2d 536, affd 272 A.D. 1045, 75 N.Y.S.2d 284, app den 273 A.D. 877, 77 N.Y.S.2d 391 and app dismd 298 N.Y. 506, 80 N.E.2d 656; Wyckoff v Sagall (1945) 16 Misc. 2d 630, 56 N.Y.S.2d 392; White v Phillips (1945) 185 Misc 960, 58 N.Y.S.2d 52

Purported stockholders' derivative action could not be maintained where stock warrants on which plaintiffs based their right to bring action were not operative because they were never signed; plaintiffs were therefore not holders of warrants, and were not beneficial owners of shares of stock in corporation within meaning of CLS Bus Corp § 626. Pullin v Feinsod (1988, 2d Dept) 142 A.D.2d 561, 530 N.Y.S.2d 226

In stockholder's derivative action on behalf of 2 corporations, alleging waste and mismanagement, defendants were not entitled to summary judgment dismissing complaint for lack of standing since record showed that plaintiff owned stock in both corporations at time alleged wrongs occurred where corporate defendants admitted that he appeared to own stock in both corporations and conceded that he was present at stockholders' meeting at which vote relating to acts of alleged mismanagement was held; moreover, concession by individual defendant that one corporation had made advances to plaintiff's grandmother against her "interest" in corporate shares established that plaintiff held "interest" sufficient to grant him standing, since plaintiff and his grandmother held equal interests, each having acquired stock by devise contained in plaintiff's grandfather's will.Schoettmer v F.G.S. Realty Corp. (1988, 2d Dept) 143 A.D.2d 128, 531 N.Y.S.2d 587

Motion to dismiss the complaint to the extent that it asserted claims by respondent in a shareholder derivative capacity against them under N.Y. Bus. Corp. Law § 626(b) based on documentary evidence should have been granted; the parties' former corporation was dissolved in 1996, some seven years before the alleged wrongdoing upon which respondent sued. Pursnani v Stylish Move Sportswear, Inc. (2012, 2d Dept) 92 App Div 3d 663, 938 NYS2d 333.

In a stockholder's derivative action only those stockholders who held stock at the time of the alleged wrong may be included among those instituting the action. Ripley v International Railways of Cent. America (1949) 196 Misc 798, 95 N.Y.S.2d 202, mod on other grounds 276 A.D. 1006, 95 N.Y.S.2d 871

The object of the requirement is to protect business corporations from those who had no interest in such corporations when certain transactions occurred or had no interest when wholly-owned corporations had transactions unobjectionable because such corporations may, with the consent of their stockholders, dispose of their assets almost as they please free from vexatious lawsuits. Northridge Cooperative Section No. 1, Inc. v 32nd Ave. Constr. Corp. (1955) 207 Misc 164, 136 N.Y.S.2d 737, mod 286 A.D. 422, 142 N.Y.S.2d 534, affd 2 N.Y.2d 514, 161 N.Y.S.2d 404, 141 N.E.2d 802

The requirement that plaintiff have a share interest at the time of initiating a derivative suit is just as mandatory, and as much insisted upon, as that of having a share interest at time of the transaction complained of, and some decisions carry it further, requiring that plaintiff's share interest continue to exist through trial of the action and at time of entry of final judgment.Sorin v Shahmoon Industries, Inc. (1961) 30 Misc. 2d 408, 429, 220 N.Y.S.2d 760; Harris v Averick (1960) 24 Misc. 2d 1039, 204 N.Y.S.2d 372

Claims against a former property manager, arising from his conduct with respect to the sale of a limited liability company's real property and the distribution of proceeds, survived challenge by the manager's motion to dismiss with respect to a holder of a beneficial interest in the company, as the holder was a beneficiary of the estate of a deceased interest holder, such that he had standing. Neary v Burns (2014, Sup) 44 Misc 3d 280, 982 NYS2d 868

The language of § 61 of former Gen. Corp. L. did not require that plaintiff have been a stockholder "of record" at the time of the transaction complained of, and it was sufficient if he could show that he then had a share interest, legal or equitable, or that his predecessor in interest then had such an interest to which he succeeded by operation of law. Lewin v New York Ambassador, Inc. (1946, Sup) 61 N.Y.S.2d 492, affd 271 A.D. 927, 67 N.Y.S.2d 706; Law v Alexander Smith & Sons Carpet Co. (1947) 271 A.D. 705, 68 N.Y.S.2d 143; Oltarsh v National Velvet Corp. (1949) 195 Misc 634, 90 N.Y.S.2d 630; Salter v Columbia Concerts, Inc. (1948) 191 Misc 479, 77 N.Y.S.2d 703; Singer v State Laundry, Inc. (1947) 188 Misc 583, 68 N.Y.S.2d 808

Constitutionality of this 1944 amendment was upheld generally and likewise as against contentions that it violated due process and equal protection clauses of the constitution. Weinstein v Behn (1946, Sup) 65 N.Y.S.2d 536, affd 272 A.D. 1045, 75 N.Y.S.2d 284, app den 273 A.D. 877, 77 N.Y.S.2d 391 and app dismd 298 N.Y. 506, 80 N.E.2d 656; Myer v Myer (1946) 271 A.D. 465, 66 N.Y.S.2d 83, app dismd 271 A.D. 823, 66 N.Y.S.2d 618 and affd 296 N.Y. 979, 73 N.E.2d 562

Since § 61 of former Gen Corp L unequivocally required that plaintiff in a stockholder's derivative action have been a stockholder at time of the transaction complained of, the corporate defendant was entitled to pre-trial examination of plaintiffs concerning whether they met this requirement. Tel-A-Sign, Inc. v Weesner (1963, Sup) 237 N.Y.S.2d 420

The purpose of introducing the requirement that plaintiff be owner of a share interest at time of bringing the action and likewise at time of the transaction complained of was said to be to limit champerty and maintenance. Bauer v Servel, Inc. (1958, SD NY) 168 F. Supp. 478, 1 FR Serv 2d 410

16. Sufficiency of interest

A shareholder derivative action may be maintained even though commenced after the subject corporation has effected a dissolution and distributed its assets inasmuch as a shareholder has the necessary standing where he meets the dual requirement as to the ownership of stock contained in subdivision (b) of section 626 of the Business Corporation Law, which requires plaintiff to be a shareholder at the time of bringing the action and at the time of the transaction of which he complains; a shareholder of a dissolved corporation has a sufficient interest in a derivative action to satisfy the spirit of the rule requiring ownership at the commencement of the action and, furthermore, pursuant to section 1006 of the Business Corporation Law, the rights and remedies of the shareholders existing prior to dissolution are viewed as if the dissolution never occurred. Accordingly, since the dissolution of a corporation, without more, does not deprive the shareholders of their derivative remedy, it was error to dismiss such a derivative action except as to those shareholders who availed themselves of their appraisal rights under subdivision (e) of section 623 of the Business Corporation Law. Independent Investor Protective League v Time, Inc. (1980) 50 N.Y.2d 259, 428 N.Y.S.2d 671, 406 N.E.2d 486

Should plaintiff, who alleged that corporation and its president perpetrated fraud on him in connection with stock purchase agreement, succeed in obtaining reformation or rescission of agreement, plaintiff would possess equitable interest in stock of corporation and have right to institute stockholder's derivative suit, and thus plaintiff's derivative action should be severved pending disposition of his cause of action seeking reformation or rescission of stock purchase agreement. Bernstein v Polo Fashions, Inc. (1976, 1st Dept) 55 A.D.2d 530, 389 N.Y.S.2d 368

A stockholder is not deprived of his right to bring a stockholder's derivative suit because his stock has been placed in escrow pursuant to an option for purchase of the same by another, as long as the option has not been exercised. Malkan v General Transistor Corp. (1960) 27 Misc. 2d 275, 210 N.Y.S.2d 289, motion den 13 A.D.2d 691, 215 N.Y.S.2d 714, app dismd (2d Dept) 14 A.D.2d 693, 219 N.Y.S.2d 936

An allegation in the complaint in a stockholders' derivative action that "at all times mentioned herein" plaintiff owned 25% of the capital stock of the corporations in question is sufficient to satisfy the requirement that plaintiff was a stockholder at the time of the transaction of which he complains. Tomasello v Trump (1961) 30 Misc. 2d 643, 217 N.Y.S.2d 304

Right of plaintiff to sue derivatively did not depend upon the smallness of her holdings or upon the fact that she was the sole complaining stockholder. Greenberg v Acme Folding Box Co. (1975) 84 Misc. 2d 181, 374 N.Y.S.2d 997

Complaint brought by a former limited liability company (LLC) member asserting self-dealing and other claims against the remaining members was dismissed since the former member lacked standing to bring suit due to no longer being a member. Further, the complaint asserted harm to the detriment of the LLC, not individual harm and was, therefore, derivative in nature. Billings v Bridgepoint Partners, LLC (2008, Sup) 21 Misc 3d 535, 240 NYLJ 66, 863 NYS2d 591.

A stockholder's derivative action will not be dismissed as to small stockholders under the doctrine de minimis non curat lex for neither the proportion nor the value of the plaintiff's holdings of stock is relevant to the right to bring the action.Smith v Bradlee (1942, Sup) 37 N.Y.S.2d 512, mod on other grounds 265 A.D. 931, 38 N.Y.S.2d 379

A stockholder, who had placed shares of a foreign corporation doing business in New York in a revocable trust and who was the sole income beneficiary of the trust, held, within the meaning of the statute, a beneficial interest in the shares and was entitled to maintain a derivative action under Business Corporation Law § 1319(a)(2).Stephenson v Landegger (1971, SD NY) 337 F. Supp. 591, affd (CA2 NY) 464 F.2d 133, cert den 409 US 1039, 34 L Ed 2d 488, 93 S Ct 520

17. Time of ownership

The complaint in an attempted stockholders' action under § 61 of former Gen Corp L was insufficient to state a cause of action where it was primarily directed at a contractual transaction entered into when all stock of the corporation was held by one person, who was not a party plaintiff. Chaft v Kass, 19 A.D.2d 610, 241 N.Y.S.2d 284 (1963)

Motion to dismiss shareholder derivative action was properly granted where plaintiffs, who were shareholders of corporate minority shareholder of injured corporation, were shareholders of injured corporation when action was commenced but not at time alleged wrongs were committed, as required by CLS Bus Corp § 626(b); double derivative action may not be maintained by shareholder of corporation which merely owns stock in wronged corporation where first corporation does not control second. Pessin v Chris-Craft Industries, Inc. (1992, 1st Dept) 181 A.D.2d 66, 586 N.Y.S.2d 584

Motion to dismiss shareholder derivative action was properly granted where plaintiffs, who were shareholders of corporate minority shareholder of injured corporation, were shareholders of injured corporation when action was commenced but not at time alleged wrongs were committed; CLS Bus Corp § 626(b) mandates that shareholders instituting derivative action demonstrate that they owned stock both when lawsuit was brought and at time of transactions complained of, unless their interest devolves upon them by operation of law. Pessin v Chris-Craft Industries, Inc. (1992, 1st Dept) 181 A.D.2d 66, 586 N.Y.S.2d 584

In shareholder derivative action, issue of contemporaneous ownership was governed not by law of state of incorporation (Delaware) but by CLS Bus Corp § 626(b); controlling effect had to be given to law of jurisdiction which, because of its relationship or contact with occurrence or parties, had greatest concern with issue raised in litigation. Pessin v Chris-Craft Industries, Inc. (1992, 1st Dept) 181 A.D.2d 66, 586 N.Y.S.2d 584

Recipient of stock certificates (plaintiff) satisfied "contemporaneous ownership" requirement of CLS Bus Corp § 626(b) and therefore had standing as shareholder to bring shareholder suit where disputed but credible evidence showed that, contemporaneously with or prior to issuance of stock certificates, plaintiff provided services in organizing corporation's predecessor, provided corporation and its predecessor with business opportunities, and paid debts of corporation and its predecessor in amount exceeding par value of issued shares. Rocha Toussier y Asociados, S.C. v Rivero (1992, 1st Dept) 184 A.D.2d 397, 585 N.Y.S.2d 384

Mere existence or nonexistence of certificates of stock is not determinative of shareholder status under CLS Bus Corp § 626. Rocha Toussier y Asociados, S.C. v Rivero (1992, 1st Dept) 184 A.D.2d 397, 585 N.Y.S.2d 384

Plaintiffs were entitled to bring a stockholders' derivative action seeking to restrain the performance of an option agreement made by the corporation, where they became owners of stock in defendant corporation after the corporation granted the option but before it was exercised.Sorin v Shahmoon (1956) 3 Misc. 2d 953, 152 N.Y.S.2d 521, affd (1st Dept) 2 A.D.2d 678, 153 N.Y.S.2d 562

One or more stockholders instituting a stockholder's derivative suit, or intervening therein, have the right to continue the action for the purpose of obtaining an accounting with respect to funds allegedly fraudulently obtained or misappropriated by any of the individual defendants, if they held stock at the time of the misconduct complained of and thereafter up to rendition of final judgment, whether or not other plaintiffs or intervenors have standing to prosecute other causes of action asserted.Sorin v Shahmoon Industries, Inc. (1961) 30 Misc. 2d 408, 429, 220 N.Y.S.2d 760

A stockholder lost capacity to maintain a derivative action where, although he held a considerable block of stock at time of the transaction complained of and later acquired more, he sold it all after institution of suit. Gresov v Shattuck Denn Mining Corp. (1963) 40 Misc. 2d 569, 243 N.Y.S.2d 760

If the plaintiff in a stockholder's derivative action disposes of all his stockholdings after institution of suit, he loses capacity to proceed with the action, notwithstanding, just prior to trial, he reacquires a certain number of shares. Gresov v Shattuck Denn Mining Corp. (1963) 40 Misc. 2d 569, 243 N.Y.S.2d 760

Defendant's motion to dismiss a shareholders' derivative action on the ground that plaintiff did not have legal capacity to sue, in that she was not a shareholder according to the records of the defendant corporation at the time of the transaction complained of and continually thereafter, would be denied where the plaintiff raised an inference of continuous ownership from the time of the transaction through her submission of a comfirmation slip and brokerage account statements showing her ownership or recent purchase of a substantial number of shares, which inference was not rebutted, in that the fact that the shares were held for the plaintiff by a nominee did not detract from the plaintiff's ownership. Karfunkel v USLIFE Corp. (1982) 116 Misc. 2d 841, 455 N.Y.S.2d 937

Where a complaint alleges acts of the defendant both prior and subsequent to the acquisition by the plaintiff of his stock interest, and the allegations are not readily separable, the entire complaint must be dismissed. Milton v Krivit (1948, Sup) 82 N.Y.S.2d 38

As otherwise stated, the fact that a transaction took place before the plaintiff or any intervenor became a stockholder ordinarily constitutes a complete defense to a derivative stockholders' action.Semensohn v Weisblum (1952, Sup) 118 N.Y.S.2d 57

If several causes of action are combined, some of which are necessarily derivative in nature, the complaint fails as to these derivative causes unless it avers the required share interest in plaintiff at the time of the transaction complained of; and if the plaintiff is complaining of a number of different transactions, it fails as to such of them as took place prior to acquisition of stock interest.Scutt v Kinney's Bakery, Inc. (1955, Sup) 141 N.Y.S.2d 174; Schwartz v Kahn (1944) 183 Misc 252, 50 N.Y.S.2d 931

Minority stockholder in railroad which leased property to another railroad was not entitled to contest validity of lease agreement which was entered into before shareholder obtained its stock. Re Penn Cent. Transp. Co. (1972, ED Pa) 354 F. Supp. 759

18. Exceptions to ownership requirement

Minority stockholders of a railroad company need not have held stock therein at the time a preferential rate agreement was given to a corporation holding practical control of the railroad, in order to maintain a stockholder's suit to require the controlling corporation to pay fair value for services rendered. Ripley v International Railways of Cent. America (1960) 8 N.Y.2d 430, 209 N.Y.S.2d 289, 171 N.E.2d 443, affg (1st Dept) 8 A.D.2d 310, 188 N.Y.S.2d 62

There is one recognized modification of the requirement of share interest in plaintiff at the time of the transaction complained of. This is with reference to instances where his complaint goes to a "continuing wrong," something which started or was initiated prior to his acquisition of share interest but had not yet been completed or executed or was still going on.York Properties, Inc. v Neidoff (1957) 10 Misc. 2d 439, 170 N.Y.S.2d 683; Austin v Gardiner (1947) 188 Misc 538, 68 N.Y.S.2d 664

A stockholder's derivative action can be based on wrongful conduct of officers and directors, after plaintiff became a stockholder, in taking no action with respect to wrongful conduct on the part of other directors and officers, which prior conduct occurred before plaintiff became a stockholder, as the "cover-up" of the original wrong is a new and independent wrong. Gluck v Unger (1960) 25 Misc. 2d 554, 202 N.Y.S.2d 832; app den (1st Dept) 10 A.D.2d 911, 203 N.Y.S.2d 1005

Where it is charged in a stockholder's derivative action that rights of action in favor of the corporation arising out of a merger transaction with another corporation, occurring before plaintiff became a stockholder, were settled, after plaintiff became a stockholder, by a fraudulent, unfair, and invalid settlement agreement, the loss resultant from the fraudulent settlement is proper subject of complaint. Gluck v Unger (1960) 25 Misc. 2d 554, 202 N.Y.S.2d 832, app den (1st Dept) 10 A.D.2d 911, 203 N.Y.S.2d 1005

A director's action in behalf of the corporation against fellow directors, unlike a stockholder's derivative action, does not require ownership of stock by plaintiff, or that plaintiff still be a director at time of instituting the action. Gresov v Shattuck Denn Mining Corp. (1963) 40 Misc. 2d 569, 243 N.Y.S.2d 760

Notwithstanding the plaintiff in a stockholder's derivative action disposes of all his stockholdings and thereby deprives himself of capacity to sue as a stockholder, the action can go forward as a director's action in behalf of the corporation if he was likewise a director of the corporation and if the action is against other directors, the complaint being broad enough to sustain the action as a director's suit in behalf of the corporation. Gresov v Shattuck Denn Mining Corp. (1963) 40 Misc. 2d 569, 243 N.Y.S.2d 760

A complaint could allege acts which occurred prior to plaintiff's acquisition of the stock in order to set forth relevant facts by way of inducement or background tending to show existence of continuing wrongs. Such allegations, however, must be limited in scope to material appropriate to their purpose. Milton v Krivit (1948, Sup) 82 N.Y.S.2d 38

19. Devolution by operation of law

Acquisition of stock as trustees under a trust agreement was not a transfer by operation of law within the meaning of § 61 of former Gen. Corp. L. Myer v Myer (1946) 271 A.D. 465, 66 N.Y.S.2d 83, app dismd 271 A.D. 823, 66 N.Y.S.2d 618 and affd 296 N.Y. 979, 73 N.E.2d 562

20. Discontinuance, generally

In a shareholder's derivative action, a motion by defendant corporation to dismiss the complaint for failure to state a cause of action, based upon the decision of a special litigation committee appointed by the corporation's board of directors that it would not be in the best interests of the corporation for the action to proceed, was properly denied by the trial court where it appeared that two of the three members of the special litigation committee may not have been truly independent, and that the methods of investigation of the committee were somewhat suspect, and where the business judgment doctrine did not shield the members of the special litigation committee from inquiry into their disinterested independence or the adequacy and appropriateness of the committee's investigative procedures and methodologies. Rosen v Bernard (1985, 2d Dept) 108 A.D.2d 906, 485 N.Y.S.2d 791

Since stockholders of the corporation, in a stockholder's derivative action, might be substantially affected by the granting of the motion of the substitute plaintiff, the corporation, to discontinue the action with prejudice, the interests of all litigants would best be served by

referring the issue presented in the motion to a referee for his inquiry and recommendations.Elgin Nat. Industries, Inc. v Zale Corp. (1972) 71 Misc. 2d 468, 336 N.Y.S.2d 275

In shareholders' derivative action, judicial approval of proposed settlement was warranted where all parties favored proposed settlement, plaintiffs had not shown likelihood of prevailing, and litigation had been ongoing for over 5 years. Seinfeld ex rel. American Express Co. v Robinson (1997, Sup) 172 Misc. 2d 159, 656 N.Y.S.2d 707, remanded, revd (1st Dept) 246 A.D.2d 291, 676 N.Y.S.2d 579

Section 626(d) reflects clear legislative policy that once suit has been initiated, it may not be terminated in any fashion without approval of court. Mokhiber on behalf of Ford Motor Co. v Cohn (1986, CA2 NY) 783 F.2d 26

21. Notice

Since this section requires court approval of a stipulation for discontinuance of a shareholder's derivative action, the court may order that notice of such an application be given to those whose interest may be affected, and the motion should not be granted except upon fairly decisive showing that there was no cause of action, which requirement is not satisfied by a mere statement from the corporation that the action will "likely" be defeated. Borden v Guthrie (1964) 42 Misc. 2d 879, 248 N.Y.S.2d 913

22. Ratification

Stockholders of a defendant corporation demonstrated factual issues with respect to alleged void acts constituting gift and waste of corporate assets by directors of the corporation sufficient to defeat a motion for summary judgment, notwithstanding the subsequent ratification of said actions by a majority vote of the stockholders, where the complaint alleged that rent reductions and other transactions including the purchase of certain equipment with corporate funds were unaccompanied by lease modifications and resulted in a loss of profits to the corporation; voidable transactions may be ratified by a majority vote of the stockholders but void acts, such as waste or a gift of corporate assets, cannot be so ratified. Aronoff v Albanese (1982, 2d Dept) 85 A.D.2d 3, 446 N.Y.S.2d 368

Where the activities of defendants in a stockholder's derivative suit were voidable rather than void, the acts could be ratified by the majority of the stockholders as long as the conduct of the alleged wrongdoers was not fraudulent or collusive.Syracuse Television, Inc. v Channel 9 Syracuse, Inc. (1966) 52 Misc. 2d 246, 275 N.Y.S.2d 190

Where circumstances would require a unanimous vote in order to ratify the illegal acts of corporate directors or officers, the majority of the stockholders would not be allowed to ratify the directors' decision not to bring a suit in the name of the corporation and thus defeat the derivative cause of action.Syracuse Television, Inc. v Channel 9 Syracuse, Inc. (1966) 52 Misc. 2d 246, 275 N.Y.S.2d 190

Where the question remained whether the stockholders of a corporation acted reasonably and in good faith in ratifying the action by the board of directors in discontinuing a derivative suit against directors and officers for alleged wrongdoings, so as to make the decision of the board binding on the corporation, the question must be resolved upon a full trial in order to determine whether the ratification of the acts challenged was done honestly and in good faith, and motion for summary judgment under CPLR 3212 was denied.Syracuse Television, Inc. v Channel 9 Syracuse, Inc. (1966) 52 Misc. 2d 246, 275 N.Y.S.2d 190

Ratification of wrongdoing by the officers or directors of a corporation cannot be accomplished indirectly under the guise of the refusal of the directors to bring an action, but the ratification by a majority of the stockholders to discontinue a derivative suit would be binding upon the corporation if the ratification was done reasonably and in good faith and would not constitute a ratification of a fraudulent or illegal act.Syracuse Television, Inc. v Channel 9 Syracuse, Inc. (1966) 52 Misc. 2d 246, 275 N.Y.S.2d 190

23. Fees and expenses

CLS Bus Corp § 626(e) does not authorize imposition of legal expenses and attorney's fees on losing party in shareholders' derivative action, although statute does provide that successful plaintiff in action may recoup such expenses from proceeds of judgment. Glenn v Hoteltron Systems, Inc. (1989) 74 N.Y.2d 386, 547 N.Y.S.2d 816, 547 N.E.2d 71

Application for any such special expense allowance in behalf of the plaintiff in a shareholder's derivative suit should be made to the court in the same action, not by special and independent proceeding, and if there is doubt as to collectibility of the judgment obtained in favor of the corporation determination of the application should be deferred until benefit, if any, to the corporation can be ascertained. Masholie v

Salvator (1945) 269 A.D. 846, 55 N.Y.S.2d 395; Smith v Bradlee (1942, Sup) 37 N.Y.S.2d 512, mod on other grounds 265 A.D. 931, 38 N.Y.S.2d 379

But, to sustain a special expense allowance in favor of a participating shareholder, it is not necessary that he have been the initiating or sole plaintiff, or that the benefit to the corporation be in the form of a money judgment in its favor for some specific amount. New York C. R. Co. v New York & H. R. Co. (1949) 275 A.D. 604, 90 N.Y.S.2d 309, affd 301 N.Y. 567, 93 N.E.2d 451

Allowances to attorneys for successful plaintiffs depend upon the benefits to the corporation attributable to their joint or several services, and where probable future benefits can be foreseen, but their extent can only be estimated, the future benefits are an indefinite factor which can only be taken into consideration in a general way. No weight should be given to interest on the judgment, or to amounts collected as the result of merely threatening suit and before any action was actually instituted. Ripley v International R. of Central America (1962, 1st Dept) 16 A.D.2d 260, 227 N.Y.S.2d 64, affd 12 N.Y.2d 814, 236 N.Y.S.2d 64, 187 N.E.2d 131

"Cost" allowances in shareholders' derivative actions are made pursuant to court rules and general statutes relating to costs, but a right to special expense allowances in favor of plaintiff is often asserted on the basis of success in recovering benefits for the corporation and the making of such special allowances was at one time the subject of a former § 61-a of former Gen. Corp. L., since repealed. It has been held that an attorney-shareholder who brings such an action is not entitled to compensation for his own professional services in the proceedings, or that his right to compensation out of the recovery is at least doubtful. Ripley v International R. of Central America (1962, 1st Dept) 16 A.D.2d 260, 227 N.Y.S.2d 64, affd 12 N.Y.2d 814, 236 N.Y.S.2d 64, 187 N.E.2d 131; Eisenberg v Central Zone Property Corp. (1956, 1st Dept) 1 A.D.2d 353, 149 N.Y.S.2d 840, affd 3 N.Y.2d 729, 163 N.Y.S.2d 968, 143 N.E.2d 516, cert den 355 US 884, 2 L Ed 2d 113, 78 S Ct 151; Masholie v Salvator (1944) 182 Misc 523, 46 N.Y.S.2d 596, mod on other grounds 269 A.D. 846, 55 N.Y.S.2d 395; Drivas v Lekas (1944) 182 Misc 567, 48 N.Y.S.2d 785

Attorneys who did not appear as attorneys of record for parties to the action, but merely assisted counsel of record under a fee-splitting agreement, have no standing to seek a direct fee allowance out of the recovery or against the corporation, and those who come in at a late stage after certain benefits have already resulted to the corporation are not entitled to participate in the portion or benefits already obtained or accrued. Ripley v International R. of Central America (1962, 1st Dept) 16 A.D.2d 260, 227 N.Y.S.2d 64, affd 12 N.Y.2d 814, 236 N.Y.S.2d 64, 187 N.E.2d 131

Claim for counsel fees and expenses by policyholder of mutual insurance company bringing derivative action against company was not established on basis that action originally brought to prevent investment by company in urban renewal development resulted in increased investment therein which proved successful. Garfield v Equitable Life Assur. Soc. (1965, 1st Dept) 24 A.D.2d 74, 263 N.Y.S.2d 922, affd 17 N.Y.2d 841, 271 N.Y.S.2d 281, 218 N.E.2d 322

Doctrine of "substantial benefit" does not require creation of cash fund as prerequisite to award of counsel fees, nor need benefit accruing to corporation have readily ascertainable monetary value; overriding concern involves equitable considerations. Seinfeld v Robinson (1998, 1st Dept) 246 A.D.2d 291, 676 N.Y.S.2d 579

Award of attorneys' fees under CLS Bus Corp § 626(e) was appropriate in shareholders' derivative action challenging alleged misconduct by corporate officers and directors as to corporation's response to activities of private detective with criminal record hired by corporation's public relations department, which culminated in settlement requiring corporation's general counsel to approve any contract to hire outside investigators costing over $150,000 and further requiring corporation to preserve records of all contracts with and payments to outside investigators, including all related expense vouchers. Seinfeld v Robinson (1998, 1st Dept) 246 A.D.2d 291, 676 N.Y.S.2d 579

In a putative shareholder derivative action, the shareholders were precluded from recovering attorneys' fees or other litigation costs, despite the shareholders' claim that the action resulted in a substantial benefit to the corporation, because the shareholders failed to make a pre-suit demand or particularized allegations establishing the futility of such demand; the shareholders sought an award of attorneys fees of $5 million. Central Laborers' Pension Fund v Blankfein (2013, 1st Dept) 111 App Div 3d 40, 971 NYS2d 282.

Plaintiffs who create fund for benefit of corporation are entitled to their expenses and reasonable attorneys' and accountants' fees out of

fund; former § 61-a was declaratory in this respect. Neuberger v Barrett (1942) 180 Misc 222, 39 N.Y.S.2d 575

A successful party was entitled to allowance of expenses under former § 61-a of former Gen. Corp. L. regardless of specific demand therefor in complaint on the principle that those sharing benefits should share expenses of producing benefit. Gildener v Lynch (1945) 184 Misc 427, 54 N.Y.S.2d 827

Where a stockholder's derivative action had been in litigation in state and federal courts for approximately ten years and resulted in the acquisition of control of the corporation, an award of $1,876,000 for counsel fees, consulting fees, and disbursements was justified. Zenn v Anzalone (1965) 46 Misc. 2d 378, 259 N.Y.S.2d 747

Court would deny plaintiffs' counsels' request for award of attorney's fees and reimbursement of expenses where plaintiffs had not prevailed in action, action had not produced tangible benefit for corporation or its shareholders, and such award would have detrimental effect of penalizing corporation for negotiating reasonable settlement of prior dispute, which gave rise to instant derivative action, and which had beneficial effect of avoiding litigation, with its attendant unfavorable publicity. Seinfeld ex rel. American Express Co. v Robinson (1997, Sup) 172 Misc. 2d 159, 656 N.Y.S.2d 707, remanded, revd (1st Dept) 246 A.D.2d 291, 676 N.Y.S.2d 579

If a shareholder's derivative action is discontinued as to some plaintiffs and severed but continued as to others, an expense award in favor of plaintiffs cannot be made until its final termination.Smith v Bradlee (1942, Sup) 37 N.Y.S.2d 512, mod on other grounds 265 A.D. 931, 38 N.Y.S.2d 379

Production of a fund was not necessarily a prerequisite foundation for allowance of fees and expenses under § 67 of former Gen. Corp. L., under which the basic test was success in prosecution or defense of the action. Bysheim v Miranda (1943, Sup) 45 N.Y.S.2d 473

A shareholder is not entitled to an allowance for expenses and attorney's fees merely because he attains some measure of success in an action against the corporation or some of its officers unless the action was "derivative" and brought for the benefit and in the right of the corporation and results in some actual benefit to it. Fontheim v Walker (1955, Sup) 141 N.Y.S.2d 62; Masholie v Salvator (1944) 182 Misc 523, 46 N.Y.S.2d 596, mod on other grounds 269 A.D. 846, 55 N.Y.S.2d 395

Where the recovery inured to the benefit of the corporation, the District Court erroneously ordered the president and holder of 50 percent of the corporate stock to personally pay plaintiff's attorney's fees in a derivative action brought by the holder of the other 50 percent of the corporation's stock for diversion of corporate assets. Jones v Uris Sales Corp. (1967, CA2 NY) 373 F.2d 644

CLS, Business Corporation Law § 626(e) permits the award of attorneys' fees for the attorney for a successful derivative plaintiff, out of the corporation's recovery from the defendants. Lewis v S. L. & E., Inc. (1980, CA2 NY) 629 F.2d 764

Under CLS Bus Corp L § 626(e), court approval is required before payment by corporation of counsel fees in derivative action; further, in derivative action that is discontinued by stipulation "without costs," counsel fees cannot be awarded thereafter. Parker Chapin Flattau & Klimpl v Blackman (1983, SD NY) 566 F. Supp. 1112

New York law provides no basis for law firm's recovery of attorney's fees for assisting toy company shareholder in convincing company to stop unnecessary payment of royalties under expired patents, where firm on behalf of shareholder sent 2 demand letters to company but never actually sued, because making demand upon corporation without actually instituting litigation does not constitute "action" warranting attorney's fees award under CLS Bus Corp Law § 626(e). Kaufman Malchman & Kirby, P.C. v Hasbro, Inc. (1995, SD NY) 897 F. Supp. 719

24. Damages

In shareholders' derivative suit arising from diversion of corporate asset, damages should be awarded to injured corporation, not directly to innocent shareholder, even though innocent and guilty shareholders each held 50 percent of shares and guilty shareholder thus would ultimately share in proceeds of award, since such prospect exists in any successful derivative action in which wrongdoer is shareholder; moreover, awarding corporate asset directly to shareholder could impair rights of creditors whose claims may be superior to that of innocent shareholder. Glenn v Hoteltron Systems, Inc. (1989) 74 N.Y.2d 386, 547 N.Y.S.2d 816, 547 N.E.2d 71

In shareholders' derivative action, Supreme Court acted reasonably in examining wrongdoing shareholder's withdrawals from his solely-owned corporation (into which he had diverted jointly-owned

Business Corporation Law

corporation's assets and opportunities) in order to calculate net profits diverted from jointly-owned corporation. Glenn v Hoteltron Systems, Inc. (1989) 74 N.Y.2d 386, 547 N.Y.S.2d 816, 547 N.E.2d 71

In shareholder derivative actions, it was improper for court to award damages to plaintiff shareholder rather than to corporation on behalf of which action was commenced. Glenn v Hoteltron Systems, Inc. (1988, 2d Dept) 138 A.D.2d 568, 526 N.Y.S.2d 149, app gr 73 N.Y.2d 706, 539 N.Y.S.2d 299, 536 N.E.2d 628 and app gr 73 N.Y.2d 706, 539 N.Y.S.2d 299, 536 N.E.2d 628 and app gr 73 N.Y.2d 706, 539 N.Y.S.2d 299, 536 N.E.2d 628 and affd 74 N.Y.2d 386, 547 N.Y.S.2d 816, 547 N.E.2d 71

Award of damages to individual defendant, at trial on complaint alleging conversion of funds from account of closely held corporation, was error where injury to plaintiff's decedent was real but only derivative; thus, funds should have been awarded to corporation, even if it would permit defendant wrongdoer to share in proceeds and such result might be insufficient deterrence to wrongdoing. Paradiso & DiMenna, Inc. v DiMenna (1996, 1st Dept) 232 A.D.2d 257, 649 N.Y.S.2d 126

In action by plaintiff who owned 20 percent of closely-held family corporation operated by defendants, wherein it was determined after non-jury trial that defendants concealed certain corporate profits and converted them to their own use for which they were liable to plaintiff, appellate court would vacate award of damages to plaintiff individually and modified judgment to award damages to corporation because, although plaintiff sued individually as well as derivatively, action actually sought vindication of her rights as shareholder and recovery of corporate assets and profits diverted from her in that status. Wolf v Rand (1999, 1st Dept) 258 A.D.2d 401, 685 N.Y.S.2d 708

§ 627. Security for expenses in shareholders' derivative action brought in the right of the corporation to procure a judgment in its favor

In any action specified in section 626 (Shareholders' derivative action brought in the right of the corporation to procure a judgment in its favor), unless the plaintiff or plaintiffs hold five percent or more of any class of the outstanding shares or hold voting trust certificates or a beneficial interest in shares representing five percent or more of any class of such shares, or the shares, voting trust certificates and beneficial interest of such plaintiff or plaintiffs have a fair value in excess of fifty thousand dollars, the corporation in whose right such action is brought shall be entitled at any stage of the proceedings before final judgment to require the plaintiff or plaintiffs to give security for the reasonable expenses, including attorney's fees, which may be incurred by it in connection with such action and by the other parties defendant in connection therewith for which the corporation may become liable under this chapter, under any contract or otherwise under law, to which the corporation shall have recourse in such amount as the court having jurisdiction of such action shall determine upon the termination of such action. The amount of such security may thereafter from time to time be increased or decreased in the discretion of the court having jurisdiction of such action upon showing that the security provided has or may become inadequate or excessive.

History: Add, L 1961, ch 855, amd, L 1962, ch 834, § 43, eff Sept 1, 1963, L 1965, ch 803, § 23 eff Sept 1, 1965.

CASE ANNOTATIONS

1. In general

2. Purpose
3. Applicable to derivative actions
4. Applicable in federal courts
5. Minimum holding requirement
6. – Joinder of parties
7. – Consolidation of actions
8. Value of holdings
9. Time of demand; delay
10. Failure to obtain security
11. Discretion of court
12. Miscellaneous

1. In general

This section was derived from, and is substantially the same as, § 61-b of former Gen. Corp. L., the constitutionality of which was upheld against all attacks. Baker v MacFadden Publications, Inc. (1949) 300 N.Y. 325, 90 N.E.2d 876; Shielcrawt v Moffett (1944, Sup) 49 N.Y.S.2d 64, affd 268 A.D. 352, 51 N.Y.S.2d 188, revd on other grounds 294 N.Y. 180, 61 N.E.2d 435, reh den 294 N.Y. 840, 62 N.E.2d 392; Wolf v Atkinson (1944) 182 Misc 675, 49 N.Y.S.2d 703

They are based on a corporation's obligation to defend and take part in an action initiated by shareholders as a derivative suit, and to indemnify its officers who are made defendants for expense incurred if the outcome of the litigation is such as to indicate that they were unjustly accused of wrongdoing. Gilbert v Case (1957, 2d Dept) 3 A.D.2d 930, 163 N.Y.S.2d 179, reh and app den (2d Dept) 4 A.D.2d 688, 164 N.Y.S.2d 995, motion dismd 3 N.Y.2d 876, 166 N.Y.S.2d 498, 145 N.E.2d 176

A foreign corporation could invoke the right to require security under § 61-b of former Gen. Corp. L., if subjected to jurisdiction of a New York court in connection with a shareholder's derivative action. Gilbert v Case (1957, 2d Dept) 3 A.D.2d 930, 163 N.Y.S.2d 179, reh and app den (2d Dept) 4 A.D.2d 688, 164 N.Y.S.2d 995, motion dismd 3 N.Y.2d 876, 166 N.Y.S.2d 498, 145 N.E.2d 176

From the viewpoint of conflict of laws, § 61-b, of former Gen. Corp. L. was regarded as procedural rather than substantive in nature. Shielcrawt v Moffett (1945) 184 Misc 1074, 56 N.Y.S.2d 134

The right to demand security from plaintiff stockholders in connection with a stockholder's derivative suit can be asserted only by the corporation itself, not by an individual defendant. Sorin v Shahmoon Industries, Inc. (1961) 30 Misc. 2d 408, 429, 220 N.Y.S.2d 760

On the other hand, it has been asserted that the security requirement provisions of former § 61-b are to be strictly construed as not permitting the corporation to recover all its expenses in a derivative action, though successful in defending it, out of the plaintiffs, but only out of such security as it may require them to put up and to the extent of the security which the court orders them to give. Tyler v Gas Consumers Asso. (1962) 35 Misc. 2d 801, 231 N.Y.S.2d 15

Such provisions are not arbitrary or unduly discriminatory, and similar statutes have been upheld as not violating due process or equal protection clauses of the federal constitution. Cohen v Beneficial Industrial Loan Corp. (1949) 337 US 541, 93 L Ed 1528, 69 S Ct 1221; Lapchak v Baker (1948) 298 N.Y. 89, 80 N.E.2d 751; Isensee v Long Island Motion Picture Co. (1945) 184 Misc 625, 54 N.Y.S.2d 556

Court has power under General Corporation Law § 627 to require filing of bond in shareholders' derivative action when plaintiff's stockholdings consist of less than 5 percent of any class of standing voting stock or have fair value of less than $50,000. Haberman v Tobin (1979, SD NY) 466 F. Supp. 447

2. Purpose

The obvious purpose of § 61-b of former Gen. Corp. L. was to require a plaintiff holding less than 5% "of the outstanding shares of any class" of the stock, on whose behalf he claims to sue, to post security for expenses unless his stockholdings had a market value in excess of $50,000. And so, in computing percentage of stock owned, shares of a wrongdoing defendant had to be counted as "outstanding" even though he might own 98% thereby making it impossible for any plaintiff to muster 5% of the shares. Tropper v Bysshe (1958) 4 N.Y.2d 397, 175 N.Y.S.2d 811, 151 N.E.2d 610

It has been said of § 61-b of former Gen. Corp. L. that it should be construed reasonably to effectuate its primary purpose, which was to frustrate "nuisance" actions by holders of small stock interests lacking actual or substantial interest in the outcome. Richman v Felmus (1958) 16 Misc. 2d 377, 182 N.Y.S.2d 210, mod on other grounds (2d Dept) 8 A.D.2d 985, 190 N.Y.S.2d 920

The purpose was to prevent or curtail abuses which through the years had developed in stockholders' derivative actions where persons owning insignificant amounts of stock, frequently bought for litigious reasons, and more intent upon self-interest than protecting the rights of corporations and the stockholders, foisted heavy expense upon them. Fuller v American Machine & Foundry Co. (1951, DC NY) 97 F. Supp. 742

The purpose of security statutes is the deterrence of "strike suits." Mintz v Allen (1966, SD NY) 254 F. Supp. 1012

3. Applicable to derivative actions

There is no merit in a contention that minority shareholders have no right to institute an equitable proceeding to compel dissolution of the corporation upon a showing that the directors and those in control are looting its assets and keeping it alive only for selfish purposes because such a course will permit them to escape the statutory requirements of this section under which, if they brought derivative actions, they could be required to furnish security under this section. Leibert v Clapp (1963) 13 N.Y.2d 313, 247 N.Y.S.2d 102, 196 N.E.2d 540

Section 61-b of former Gen. Corp. L. was construed as applicable only to stockholders' derivative suits, being those based on a right of action in the corporation rather than an individual cause of action running to plaintiff or to plaintiff and others as shareholders, and accordingly it did not apply to "representative" actions brought, not in behalf of the corporation, but in behalf of plaintiff individually "and other shareholders similarly situated."Sherman v P & Q Shops, Inc. (1949) 275 A.D. 788, 87 N.Y.S.2d 759; Fontheim v Walker (1955, Sup) 141 N.Y.S.2d 62; Davidson v Rabinowitz (1951, Sup) 140 N.Y.S.2d 875; Lehrman v Godchaux Sugars, Inc. (1955) 207 Misc 314, 138 N.Y.S.2d 163; Imberman v Alexander (1952) 203 Misc 576, 116 N.Y.S.2d 609, affd 281 A.D. 656, 117 N.Y.S.2d 682, affd 305 N.Y. 820, 113 N.E.2d 560; Lennan v Blakeley (1948, Sup) 80 N.Y.S.2d 288

An action to compel payment of dividends was not within § 61-b of former Gen. Corp. L.Swinton v W. J. Bush & Co. (1951) 199 Misc 321, 102 N.Y.S.2d 994, affd 278 A.D. 754, 103 N.Y.S.2d 1019, app den 278 A.D. 823, 105 N.Y.S.2d 408

An action by a stockholder to compel a corporation to declare a dividend is derivative, and accordingly plaintiff must post security unless a sufficient number of stockholders join in the action. Gordon v Elliman (1952) 202 Misc 612, 115 N.Y.S.2d 567, affd 280 A.D. 655, 116 N.Y.S.2d 671, affd 306 N.Y. 456, 119 N.E.2d 331

Where a complaint in an action instituted by shareholders states a number of causes of action, one or more of which are derivative in nature, though the others are not, the corporate defendant is entitled to seek security if plaintiffs do not have sufficient stock interest to be exempt from such a demand, notwithstanding the relief sought is an injunction against holding a special meeting of shareholders to take action on a proposed merger. Williams v Bartell (1962) 34 Misc. 2d 552, 226 N.Y.S.2d 187, mod on other grounds (1st Dept) 16 A.D.2d 21, 225 N.Y.S.2d 351

Nature of the cause of action asserted was determinative as to whether the action was derivative or merely representative, rather than the manner in which the complaint was phrased or in whose behalf it was stated to be brought, in passing upon an application by the corporation to require plaintiffs to give security. White v National Bondholders Corp. (1947, Sup) 117 N.Y.S.2d 450; Ritter v Hilo Varnish Corp. (1960, SD NY) 185 F. Supp. 43; Dalva v Bailey (1957, DC NY) 153 F. Supp. 548

An action by stockholder to enjoin corporation and two directors from exercising certain stock options allegedly given without consideration is in fact an action to prevent "waste and mismanagement of corporate assets" and as such is maintained in the right of the corporation, and, under the terms of § 61-b of the former Gen. Corp. L., security could be demanded, in situations within that section, of the person instituting or maintaining the action. Selman v Allen (1953, Sup) 121 N.Y.S.2d 142

Mismanagement or waste of corporate assets, if challenged, is plainly challenged in the right of the corporation although the final injury is usually that the equity interest of the stockholder is jeopardized. Similarly, imposition upon the corporation of an unserviceable debt structure (as part of a plan of reorganization) threatening insolvency and foreclosure of the mortgaged property comprising the life blood of the corporation is a disservice to the corporation and all its owners and not merely to one class of stock. Hence, in an action to set aside a proposed voluntary plan of reorganization, the corporation was entitled to security under § 61-b of

former Gen. Corp. L. Christie v Fifth Madison Corp. (1953, Sup) 124 N.Y.S.2d 492

Class action by shareholder to contest reorganization and merger whereby the corporation in which he owned stock became a wholly owned subsidiary of a holding company whose stockholders were the former stockholders of the defendant corporation was a personal class action rather than a derivative action and thus the statutory provision as to posting of security for costs in derivative actions did not apply.Eisenberg v Flying Tiger Line, Inc. (1971, CA2 NY) 451 F.2d 267

4. Applicable in federal courts

In federal court proceedings, § 61-b of former Gen. Corp. L. was considered as expressing policy of the state of New York with respect to shareholders' derivative suits, and usually given application in like manner and to like extent as it would have been had the action been in a court of the State of New York, but whether and how to apply it rested to some extent in the federal court's discretion. Cohen v Beneficial Industrial Loan Corp. (1949) 337 US 541, 93 L Ed 1528, 69 S Ct 1221; Aspinook Corp. v Bright (1947, CA2 NY) 165 F.2d 294, cert den 333 US 846, 92 L Ed 1129, 68 S Ct 664; Neuwirth v Namm-Loeser's, Inc. (1958, DC NY) 161 F. Supp. 828; Elkins v Bricker (1956, DC NY) 147 F. Supp. 609; Schreiber v Butte Copper & Zinc Co. (1951, DC NY) 98 F. Supp. 106; Montro Corp. v Prindle (1952, DC NY) 105 F. Supp. 460; Donovan v Queensboro Corp. (1947, DC NY) 75 F. Supp. 131; Boyd v Bell (1945, DC NY) 64 F. Supp. 22; Craftsman Finance & Mortg. Co. v Brown (1945, DC NY) 64 F. Supp. 168

However, that section was applicable in federal court proceedings only where jurisdiction of the court was based on diversity of citizenship and not where a violation of the Securities and Exchange Act was the basis of suit and jurisdiction. McClure v Borne Chemical Co. (1961, CA3 Pa) 292 F.2d 824, 4 FR Serv 2d 418, cert den 368 US 939, 7 L Ed 2d 339, 82 S Ct 382; Stella v Kaiser (1948, DC NY) 81 F. Supp. 807

In the federal courts, § 61-b of former Gen. Corp. L. was not regarded as such a strict declaration of New York public policy as to preclude application of a different rule under the law of a foreign corporation's domicile. Hausman v Buckley (1962, CA2 NY) 299 F.2d 696, 93 ALR2d 1340, cert den 369 US 885, 8 L Ed 2d 286, 82 S Ct 1157

Statutory requirement providing for posting of security for costs in derivative action may be invoked by foreign corporation where plaintiff is New York resident and corporation is doing business in the state, even though New York substantive law does not apply to the action.Eisenberg v Flying Tiger Line, Inc. (1971, CA2 NY) 451 F.2d 267

Where the issue to be tried in a stockholder's derivative action in Federal Court was whether the plaintiff had any interest at all in two corporations, he was not required to give security under this section, since, if he had no interest, the action would fall immediately.Drews v Eastern Sausage & Provision Co. (1954, DC NY) 125 F. Supp. 289

Where the basis of federal court jurisdiction was diversity of citizenship, and the corporation in question was a New York corporation or the situation was otherwise such that a New York state court would have had to recognize the corporation's right to seek security from plaintiffs, some federal decisions took the position that recognition of this right was likewise mandatory on the federal court. Goldstein v Weisman (1960, SD NY) 185 F. Supp. 242

Requirements of this section are applicable to federal claims. Kane v Central American Mining & Oil, Inc. (1964, SD NY) 235 F. Supp. 559

Where plaintiffs alleged a separate cause of action under state law for breach of fiduciary duty and corporate waste against the directors and officers of the defendant corporation, the corporation was entitled to security for reasonable expenses whether federal jurisdiction was based on diversity of citizenship or on pendent jurisdiction and it is immaterial that the same expense may be involved in the defense of both federal and state claims. Entel v Allen (1967, SD NY) 270 F. Supp. 60

Under Business Corporation Law § 627, plaintiff's purchase of additional $50,000 worth of stock after shareholders' derivative action was begun did not constitute compliance with order requiring him to post $100,000 security for costs; however, federal court may not dismiss plaintiff's federal claims for failure to meet bond requirement since federal court may enforce state security requirements for shareholders' derivative actions only as to state causes of action. Haberman v Tobin (1979, SD NY) 480 F. Supp. 425, affd (CA2 NY) 626 F.2d 1101

Business Corporation Law

5. Minimum holding requirement

Where plaintiff in a stockholder's derivative suit owned more than 5 percent of the Class A stock at the inception of the action, the corporation's demand for security was properly denied, notwithstanding that the corporation had issued new stock after the action had been commenced. Roach v Franchises International, Inc. (1969, 2d Dept) 32 A.D.2d 247, 300 N.Y.S.2d 630

The share interests required of plaintiffs, to be exempt from a security demand by the corporation, were recognized as being in the alternative, and if their holdings or interests, in the aggregate, or the interests of any one of them, amounted to 5% or more of outstanding shares of some class of stock or $50,000 or more in value, and the plaintiff or plaintiffs in question were qualified to bring a derivative action, the corporation had no right to demand security. Perry v Shahmoon Industries, Inc. (1958) 11 Misc. 2d 137, 172 N.Y.S.2d 245, affd (1st Dept) 6 A.D.2d 1010, 178 N.Y.S.2d 612, app den (1st Dept) 7 A.D.2d 634, 179 N.Y.S.2d 846

Section 61-b of former Gen. Corp. L. could not be invoked by the corporation if the plaintiff or plaintiffs held 5% or more of some class of stock issued by the corporation or the market value of their share interests exceeded $50,000. There has been some conflict in the decisions as to the date as of which these share percentages and values are to be determined. Most decisions appear to relate determination of value, with respect to initial plaintiffs, to date of commencement of the action, and, as to intervening plaintiffs, to date of their intervention. Weinstein v Behn (1947, Sup) 68 N.Y.S.2d 199, affd 272 A.D. 1045, 75 N.Y.S.2d 284, app den 273 A.D. 877, 77 N.Y.S.2d 391 and app dismd 298 N.Y. 506, 80 N.E.2d 656; Sorin v Shahmoon Industries, Inc. (1961) 30 Misc. 2d 408, 429, 220 N.Y.S.2d 760

In view of a 1962 amendment of this section of the Bus. Corp. L., it more closely conforms to the language of § 61-b of former Gen. Corp. L. in stating the percentage of stock interest which will exempt plaintiffs from a security demand. Section 61-b did not require plaintiffs to hold 5% of total outstanding stock where there were different classes of stock outstanding, or 5% of each class of stock, but merely 5% of a class of outstanding stock. Auerbach v Feder (1952, Sup) 115 N.Y.S.2d 67

Where one count in a shareholders' suit seeking to enjoin the holding of a shareholders' meeting to pass on a merger proposal charged false and misleading statements by officers of the corporation in regard to the proposed merger, under this section the court could impose security requirements on plaintiffs unless they established that they held more than the minimum number or amount of shares to escape the statutory requirements. Phelps v Burnham (1964, CA2 NY) 327 F.2d 812

In a stockholders' derivative action, plaintiffs who owned more than five percent of the outstanding preferred stock were not required to give security under the section. Lowell Wiper Supply Co. v Helen Shop, Inc. (1964, SD NY) 235 F. Supp. 640

6. – Joinder of parties

Later decisions, however, took the position that joinder of additional stockholders as plaintiffs, bringing the aggregate of share holdings by plaintiffs above the 5% of outstanding shares or the $50,000 in value, would defeat a motion by the corporation to require security, if it had not previously been made, or permit the court to vacate a security order, if one had already issued, and that the court could delay or condition issuance of a security order in such manner as to permit other qualified holders of share interests to join as plaintiffs and obviate the security demand. Baker v MacFadden Publications, Inc. (1949) 300 N.Y. 325, 90 N.E.2d 876; Perry v Shahmoon Industries, Inc. (1958) 11 Misc. 2d 137, 172 N.Y.S.2d 245, affd (1st Dept) 6 A.D.2d 1010, 178 N.Y.S.2d 612, app den (1st Dept) 7 A.D.2d 634, 179 N.Y.S.2d 846; Davidson v Rabinowitz (1951, Sup) 140 N.Y.S.2d 875

An early decision held that ownership of stock by the original plaintiff or plaintiffs was controlling as to right of the corporation to seek security against costs and expenses, and that such right could not be defeated by later acquisition of more shares by plaintiff or by joinder of other shareholders as plaintiffs. Noel Associates, Inc. v Merrill (1944) 184 Misc 646, 53 N.Y.S.2d 143

A stockholder joining in a stockholder's derivative action is not immune from a security demand because he was assured by plaintiff's general counsel that success was certain and no liability for costs or otherwise would be involved.Sorin v Shahmoon Industries, Inc. (1961) 30 Misc. 2d 408, 429, 220 N.Y.S.2d 760

It has gradually become customary to condition an order requiring the plaintiff or plaintiffs in a derivative suit to put up security upon failure to procure joinder of additional plaintiffs holding enough qualifying additional stock to avoid the security requirements within a specified period of time, with leave to seek vacation of the security order if such joinder can be attained. If plaintiff has sought leave to inspect the corporation's stock records as an aid in recruiting assistance, the time limit can be tied to when he is given access to these records. Auerbach v Shafstor, Inc. (1962) 34 Misc. 2d 658, 229 N.Y.S.2d 927, affd (2d Dept) 19 A.D.2d 531, 240 N.Y.S.2d 146, app dismd 13 N.Y.2d 891, 243 N.Y.S.2d 673, 193 N.E.2d 501; Ratzkin v Harris (1961, Sup) 219 N.Y.S.2d 665; Himmelblau v Haist (1961, SD NY) 195 F. Supp. 356, 5 FR Serv 2d 409

Such a conditional security order is not complied with by merely going out and acquiring some more stock by the initial plaintiff or plaintiffs, and the complaint is subject to dismissal if joinder of additional different shareholders in sufficient amount is not obtained within the specified time limit. Tyler v Gas Consumers Asso. (1962) 34 Misc. 2d 947, 229 N.Y.S.2d 169

Where the plaintiff in a derivative action is seeking to avoid a security demand or comply with a conditional security order, by inducing enough additional shareholders to join as plaintiffs to meet the security-exemption requirements, the decisions indicate that results are the measure of success, though attained in disregard of bylaw provisions or through reckless promises of success or that he will personally assume the expense liabilities.Solomon v Hirsch (1962) 35 Misc. 2d 716, 230 N.Y.S.2d 625; Hoover v Allen (1960, SD NY) 180 F. Supp. 263, 3 FR Serv 2d 442

See alsoNeuwirth v Wyman (1953, Sup) 119 N.Y.S.2d 266, affd 282 A.D. 1044, 126 N.Y.S.2d 895

Effectiveness of joinder of other shareholders as plaintiffs in a stockholder's derivative suit, as sufficiently bolstering the litigation, was not defeated by the fact that some of them sold their shares from three to five months after joining the action or that some of them did not hold stock at the time that the original transactions began which were the subject of litigation, particularly where the wrongs charged were of a continuing nature. Hoover v Allen (1960, SD NY) 180 F. Supp. 263, 3 FR Serv 2d 442

Under Business Corporation Law § 627 defendant motion picture studio is entitled to security where plaintiff did not own shares representing 5 percent or more of class of voting shares or value exceeding $50,000; however, in lieu of posting security, court will grant plaintiff's application to be furnished list of company's shareholders so that she may seek to join as plaintiff sufficient number of shareholders to avoid security requirement. Nemo v Allen (1979, SD NY) 466 F. Supp. 192, CCH Fed Secur L Rep ¶ 96765

7. – Consolidation of actions

Plaintiff and intervening stockholders, who held stock having a market value in excess of $50,000 in respect to second cause of action, were not required to put up security on the ground that stock holdings were less than $50,000 on first cause of action. Richman v Felmus (1958) 16 Misc. 2d 377, 182 N.Y.S.2d 210, mod on other grounds (2d Dept) 8 A.D.2d 985, 190 N.Y.S.2d 920

Consolidation of plaintiff's action with a similar action filed by another person, was denied, where the consolidation would prejudicially affect the plaintiff, if it was determined on appeal that security for costs was required. Richman v Felmus (1959) 20 Misc. 2d 46, 188 N.Y.S.2d 608, app dismd (2d Dept) 8 A.D.2d 985, 190 N.Y.S.2d 922

Where stockholders' derivative suits have been commenced by various different stockholders, stating various causes of action, and consolidated, and some of the complaints have been dismissed for failure to state or to establish the causes of action asserted, the stock holdings of the plaintiffs in the dismissed actions are not to be included in determining whether or not shares of sufficient market value are owned by the remaining plaintiffs, to escape a demand for security, with respect to the remaining causes of action.Sorin v Shahmoon Industries, Inc. (1961) 30 Misc. 2d 408, 429, 220 N.Y.S.2d 760

But it was considered to be clear that the provisions of § 61-b of former Gen. Corp. L. did not require the original plaintiff, alone, or in association with others, to have the required share interest, in number or value, with respect to each wrongful act alleged or each cause of action pleaded.Sorin v Shahmoon Industries, Inc. (1961) 30 Misc. 2d 408, 429, 220 N.Y.S.2d 760

8. Value of holdings

While a corporation defendant in a stockholders' derivative action may be able to ascertain at all times the status of the plaintiffs' stock holdings held in their names, such ascertainment is well-nigh impossible where stock is held in a "street name."Amdur v Meyer (1964, 1st Dept) 22 A.D.2d 655, 253 N.Y.S.2d 65

Section 627 of Bus. Corp. L., in dealing with the aggregate value of shares held by plaintiffs which will preclude the corporation from moving for security, uses the adjective "fair" in connection with "value," whereas § 61-b of former Gen. Corp. L. referred to "market value." Under the latter section it was held that intervening shareholders did not have to show outright and clear ownership of their share interests, on the ground that equity value rather than full market value could be a controlling factor. Richman v Felmus (1958) 16 Misc. 2d 377, 182 N.Y.S.2d 210, mod on other grounds (2d Dept) 8 A.D.2d 985, 190 N.Y.S.2d 920

Some defer the date for determination of value or percentage of outstanding shares to the date of the corporation's application to require security, or even to the return date of a motion resisting the corporation's application.Sorin v Shahmoon Industries, Inc. (1961) 30 Misc. 2d 408, 429, 220 N.Y.S.2d 760; Dalva v Bailey (1957, DC NY) 158 F. Supp. 204

As pointed out in one decision, the legislature, in authorizing the court to increase or decrease security which plaintiffs may be required to give, did not intend to have the right to demand security fluctuate with market value of the shares after the action was commenced, and therefore assessment of value of share interests of plaintiffs should not be made as of a date later than return day of a motion to permit additional shareholders to intervene.Sorin v Shahmoon Industries, Inc. (1961) 30 Misc. 2d 408, 429, 220 N.Y.S.2d 760

Since § 61 of former Gen. Corp. L., like § 626 of the Bus. Corp. L., required that a shareholder, to qualify as plaintiff in a derivative action, must have been such at the time of the transaction complained of, it was held that only the share holdings of plaintiffs having that qualification were to be considered in determining the percentage and value of shares held by plaintiffs.Elkins v Bricker (1956, DC NY) 147 F. Supp. 609

9. Time of demand; delay

Section 61-b of former Gen Corp L required defendant corporation to seek posting of security by plaintiffs "before final judgment," but it also authorized the making of such a demand at any stage prior thereto. It was held that the demand could be made at any time prior to a mandate determining rights of the parties. Where, prior to any such mandate, plaintiffs were ordered to post security but later obtained a cancellation of that order then proceeded to dispose of their share holdings to such extent as once again to be subject to the security requirement, the corporation was entitled to move for reinstatement of the security order, notwithstanding dismissal of the complaint, there having been no "final judgment."Amdur v Meyer (1963, 1st Dept) 17 A.D.2d 571, 237 N.Y.S.2d 352, affd 13 N.Y.2d 1089, 246 N.Y.S.2d 408, 196 N.E.2d 63

On the other hand, it was held that the corporate defendant could not avoid assessment of costs of the proceeding against it by making its security demand only after most of plaintiffs' expenses had already been incurred. Tichner v Andrews (1949) 193 Misc 1050, 85 N.Y.S.2d 760, app dismd 275 A.D. 749, 90 N.Y.S.2d 920

The usually appropriate time for a defendant corporation to apply for security is after service of answers by the several defendants.Sorin v Shahmoon Industries, Inc. (1962) 34 Misc. 2d 1008, 231 N.Y.S.2d 6

At whatever stage of the proceedings security was demanded, if the situation was found to be within § 61-b of former Gen. Corp. L. and plaintiffs were ordered to give security the security then posted related back to commencement of the action and was applicable to expenses of the corporation already paid or incurred as well as subsequent expenses.Sorin v Shahmoon Industries, Inc. (1962) 34 Misc. 2d 1008, 231 N.Y.S.2d 6

Where there was delay in seeking security on the part of the corporation, however, questions could arise as to whether, plaintiffs having been already partially successful in obtaining accounting orders against some of the individual defendants, the security demand, in the light of § 67 of former Gen. Corp. L., was justified. It was held in at least one case that a security demand already granted should not be overturned by vacating the order in this situation, if the corporation might still be subject to an order to reimburse the individual defendants in question for their expenses in further defending.Sorin v Shahmoon Industries, Inc. (1962) 34 Misc. 2d 1008, 231 N.Y.S.2d 6

Section 61-b of former Gen. Corp. L. permitted the corporation to seek security for costs at any stage of the proceedings, and plaintiff

accordingly could not ordinarily avoid the demand or find ground for objecting to it because of delay in making it, or stall it by some specious counter-motion such as an objection to propriety of representation of the corporation by its attorney of record.Solomon v Hirsch (1962) 35 Misc. 2d 716, 230 N.Y.S.2d 625; Abramson v Blakeley (1960) 25 Misc. 2d 967, 202 N.Y.S.2d 586

10. Failure to obtain security

Under this section, a corporation involved in a stockholders' derivative action cannot recover costs in that action from the plaintiffs where no security for costs has been given. Amdur v Meyer (1964, 1st Dept) 22 A.D.2d 655, 253 N.Y.S.2d 65

Where a corporation involved in a stockholders' derivative action wherein the decision goes against plaintiffs is unable to recover costs because plaintiffs gave no security, if plaintiffs' stock holdings in defendant corporation were disposed of to a point where their value fell below the statutory minimum of $50,000 it should be able to recover under some other provision or theory for the unnecessary trouble and expense to which it has been put, and legislation to this effect has been recommended. Amdur v Meyer (1964, 1st Dept) 22 A.D.2d 655, 253 N.Y.S.2d 65

The importance of moving to require security for costs in a stockholder's derivative action, where the situation was such as to permit such a motion by the corporation under § 61-b of former Gen. Corp. L., lay not alone in the possibility of stopping the action then and there if required security was not put up, but in the fact that that section was construed as limiting the corporation's recovery, though successful, to ordinary court costs, without any right to demand and recover its general expenses in defending except out of special security demanded and supplied. Auerbach v Shafstor, Inc. (1962) 34 Misc. 2d 658, 229 N.Y.S.2d 927, affd (2d Dept) 19 A.D.2d 531, 240 N.Y.S.2d 146, app dismd 13 N.Y.2d 891, 243 N.Y.S.2d 673, 193 N.E.2d 501; Tyler v Gas Consumers Asso. (1962) 35 Misc. 2d 801, 231 N.Y.S.2d 15

Although a corporation may move to require the shareholders to post security at any stage during the pendency of the action under N.Y. Bus. Corp. § 627, the statutory language indicated that the corporation's entitlement to security for the reasonable expenses incurred in the action terminated with the entry of a final judgment. Shapiro v Rockville Country Club, Inc. (2005, A.D., 2d Dept) 802 N.Y.S.2d 717

11. Discretion of court

An appeal does not lie from an order denying a motion made by the respondent to require plaintiff to furnish security.Sherman v P & Q Shops, Inc. (1950) 277 A.D. 782, 97 N.Y.S.2d 342

On motion of the corporate defendant in a stockholder's derivative action to require plaintiff stockholder, holding only a small number of shares of slight value, to give security under this section in the amount of $75,000, an order was entered requiring plaintiff to give security in the amount of $35,000. Auerbach v Shafstor, Inc. (1962) 34 Misc. 2d 658, 229 N.Y.S.2d 927, affd (2d Dept) 19 A.D.2d 531, 240 N.Y.S.2d 146, app dismd 13 N.Y.2d 891, 243 N.Y.S.2d 673, 193 N.E.2d 501

The last sentence of § 61-b of former Gen. Corp. L. was considered broad enough to permit court review at any time of the amount of security to be required of. plaintiffs. Although an earlier order requiring posting of $35,000 security was vacated upon intervention of additional plaintiffs bringing total share holdings above $50,000, it was held in one case that the security requirement could be reimposed pending appeal from final judgment where, by then, plaintiffs had disposed of enough of their holdings to reduce market value below $50,000. Amdur v Meyer (1962) 36 Misc. 2d 433, 233 N.Y.S.2d 15, affd (1st Dept) 17 A.D.2d 571, 237 N.Y.S.2d 352, affd 13 N.Y.2d 1089, 246 N.Y.S.2d 408, 196 N.E.2d 63

Where a corporation was a nominal defendant in a stockholder's derivative action, it was held that a bond of $1000 was ample security to be given by the plaintiff, but that the corporation could apply to have it increased when it demonstrated to the court that its position in the action is not neutral and that the amount of security has become inadequate. Neuwirth v Namm-Loeser's, Inc. (1958, DC NY) 161 F. Supp. 828

On motion of the corporation and individual defendants served with process in a stockholder's derivative action to require plaintiffs, as holders of less than the required minimum in quantity and value of stock, to put up security in the amount of $70,000 as a condition to proceeding with the action, upon consideration of all the allegations of the complaint and various affidavits, the fact that judgment was sought only against part of the defendants, and that none of such defendants were presently officers of the corporation, plaintiffs were ordered to furnish security in the sum of $5,000, without prejudice to right of any party to move for increase or decrease of the security. Goldstein v Weisman (1960, SD NY) 185 F. Supp. 242

The amount of the security required by this section may from time to time be increased or decreased in the discretion of the court upon a showing that the security provided has or may become inadequate or excessive. Neuwirth v Merin (1967, SD NY) 267 F. Supp. 333, 11 FR Serv 2d 913

12. Miscellaneous

The fact that directors of the corporate defendant in whose right a stockholder's derivative action is brought are not named as parties to the action and that no relief is sought against them does not dispense with right of the corporation to seek security for costs and expenses. Auerbach v Shafstor, Inc. (1962) 34 Misc. 2d 658, 229 N.Y.S.2d 927, affd (2d Dept) 19 A.D.2d 531, 240 N.Y.S.2d 146, app dismd 13 N.Y.2d 891, 243 N.Y.S.2d 673, 193 N.E.2d 501

When defendants move to have the plaintiff post security under this section in a stockholder's derivative action in New York State courts, the plaintiff can generally obtain, upon his cross motion, an order for the production of the stockholders' list but federal court lacks power to grant such relief. Neuwirth v Merin (1967, SD NY) 267 F. Supp. 333, 11 FR Serv 2d 913

§ 628. Liability of subscribers and shareholders

(a) A holder of or subscriber for shares of a corporation shall be under no obligation to the corporation for payment for such shares other than the obligation to pay the unpaid portion of his subscription which in no event shall be less than the amount of the consideration for which such shares could be issued lawfully.

(b) Any person becoming an assignee or transferee of shares or of a subscription for shares in good faith and without knowledge or notice that the full consideration therefor has not been paid shall not be personally liable for any unpaid portion of such consideration, but the transferor shall remain liable therefor.

(c) No person holding shares in any corporation as collateral security shall be personally liable as a shareholder but the person pledging such shares shall be considered the holder thereof and shall be so liable. No executor, administrator, guardian, trustee or other fiduciary shall be personally liable as a shareholder, but the estate and funds in the hands of such executor, administrator, guardian, trustee or other fiduciary shall be liable.

History: Add, L 1961, ch 855, eff Sept 1, 1963; amd, L 1963, ch 746, eff Sept 1, 1963.

CASE ANNOTATIONS

1. Nature and basis of liability
2. Holder or subscriber status
3. Enforcement of obligation
4. Restrictions and defenses
5. Procedural matters
6. Miscellaneous

1. Nature and basis of liability

However, the personal liability imposed by § 70 of former Stock Corp. L. on shareholders and subscribers in favor of creditors of the corporation was several rather than joint, and a creditor could sue any or all of the delinquents, leaving those sued to work out contribution rights from such as were not made defendants. Aspinwall v Sacchi (1874) 57 N.Y. 331; John A. Roebling's Sons Co. v Federal Storage Battery Car Co. (1918) 185 A.D. 430, 173 N.Y.S. 297

Limited partner who "takes part in the control of" limited partnership's business should not automatically be insulated from individual liability merely by benefit of status as officer and sole owner of corporate general partner; limited partner in such dual capacity bears heavy burden when seeking to elude personal liability and must, at least, prove that any relevant actions taken were performed solely in capacity as officer of general partner. Gonzalez v Chalpin (1990) 77 N.Y.2d 74, 564 N.Y.S.2d 702, 565 N.E.2d 1253

Limited partner was properly denied limited liability protection of CLS Partn § 96, despite his contention that he acted at all times solely in his capacity as officer of corporate general partner when he took part in control of limited partnership's business, where (1) the only evidence he produced consisted of certificate of limited partnership, signed by him on behalf of general partnership, which stated that he was limited partner, and (2) evidence in refutation consisted of limited partnership checks signed by limited partner in his own name which failed to name general partnership or to indicate that he was signing in any representative capacity. Gonzalez v Chalpin (1990) 77 N.Y.2d 74, 564 N.Y.S.2d 702, 565 N.E.2d 1253

A creditor, suing in his own behalf and for the benefit of other creditors, could be required to join as defendants all subscribers and shareholders from whom any balance was due on subscriptions or shares, as well as the personal representatives of any of them who had died, so that they could be compelled to contribute pro rata to a fund to be shared by the various creditors. Warth v Moore Blind Stitcher & Overseamer Co. (1911) 146 A.D. 28, 130 N.Y.S. 748, affd 207 N.Y. 673, 100 N.E. 1135

The creditor's basis of claim, however, under § 70 of former Stock Corp. L., was the original debt of the corporation to him rather than the judgment obtained against the corporation on that debt. Graeber v Ehrgott (1918) 182 A.D. 377, 169 N.Y.S. 32

Sole shareholder of corporation that owned taxicab was not entitled to dismissal of personal injury action as against him personally on basis that taxicab was owned by corporate entity in that complaint set forth cognizable cause of action for piercing corporate veil where it alleged that he owned 16 other taxi corporations, that all 17 corporations were operated centrally and maintained as one entity, and that corporations were mere shams whose only purpose was to enable him to defraud public, including injured plaintiff. Goldberg v Lee Express Cab Corp. (1995, Sup) 166 Misc. 2d 668, 634 N.Y.S.2d 337

Sole shareholder of corporation was properly held personally liable under lease for damage to residential premises, even though original lease was signed by corporation, where shareholder used corporation to rent premises for his own use as weekend residence, and shareholder personally negotiated extensions of lease with owner's agent. Walling v Holman (1988, CA2 NY) 858 F.2d 79, cert den (US) 103 L Ed 2d 842

Showing of fraud or disregard of corporate form such as intermingling of corporate and personal funds is necessary to warrant piercing corporate veil under New York law. Bank Saderat Iran v Amin Beydoun, Inc. (1983, SD NY) 555 F. Supp. 770

2. Holder or subscriber status

Under § 70 and certain other provisions of former Stock Corp. L., it had to appear that the subscriber or shareholder sued by a creditor was such at the time the corporation's indebtedness to such creditor was contracted, and some decisions interpreted this requirement, in view of the provisions of § 73, as extending likewise to necessity of showing that defendant still owed something on his shares or subscription when judgment was obtained against the corporation. Tucker v Gilman (1890) 121 N.Y. 189, 24 N.E. 302; Dyer v Drucker (1905) 108 A.D. 238, 95 N.Y.S. 749

Pre-incorporation subscribers were under the same liability to creditors, whether or not they signed the certificate of incorporation or received any stock certificate, even though the certificate of incorporation varied to some extent from the powers and purposes of the corporation as originally contemplated. Lyell Ave. Lumber Co. v Lighthouse (1910) 137 A.D. 422, 121 N.Y.S. 802, later app 151 A.D. 902, 135 N.Y.S. 1124

However, the fact that the defendant signed a proxy, a consent to an increase of capital, and a waiver of notice of a special meeting in which he described himself as stockholder of record was not conclusive evidence that he was a "holder of capital stock" within the meaning of § 70 of former Stock Corp. L. Breck v Brewster (1912) 150 A.D. 202, 134 N.Y.S. 697, later app 153 A.D. 800, 138 N.Y.S. 821

Section 70 of former Stk Corp. L. imposed shareholder liability to creditors on the basis of having entered into a valid stock subscription agreement, regardless of whether any stock certificate had issued. Allen v Ryan (1927) 219 A.D. 634, 221 N.Y.S. 77, affd 246 N.Y. 609, 159 N.E. 671; Granger & Co. v Allen (1925) 214 A.D. 367, 212 N.Y.S.

356, affd 244 N.Y. 587, 155 N.E. 907; George Irish Paper Corp. v White (1915) 91 Misc 261, 154 N.Y.S. 778

The signers of a paper who agreed to "subscribe" for a certain number of shares in a corporation in the process of formation and to pay for their stock when called upon by the directors were liable for the amount subscribed, although, in the certificate subsequently filed, their names were not included as subscribers, and they never took any part in the formation or in the affairs of the corporation and never demanded or were tendered the stock. Woods Motor Vehicle Co. v Brady (1902) 39 Misc 79, 78 N.Y.S. 203, affd 90 A.D. 610, 85 N.Y.S. 1151, revd 181 N.Y. 145, 73 N.E. 674

3. Enforcement of obligation

A trustee in bankruptcy of the corporation, receiver, or assignee for the benefit of creditors, foreign or domestic, could enforce shareholder and subscriber liability for unpaid amounts or share commitments, as representing, and for the benefit of, creditors who would themselves have been entitled to enforce it.Stoddard v Lum (1899) 159 N.Y. 265, 53 N.E. 1108; Wigton v Kenney (1900) 51 A.D. 215, 64 N.Y.S. 924; Mills v Friedman (1920) 111 Misc 253, 181 N.Y.S. 285, affd 194 A.D. 942, 184 N.Y.S. 937 and affd 194 A.D. 932, 184 N.Y.S. 613, affd 233 N.Y. 517, 135 N.E. 899; Allen v Ryan (1927) 219 A.D. 634, 221 N.Y.S. 77, affd 246 N.Y. 609, 159 N.E. 671

Under § 70 of former Stock Corp. L., the decisions dealt mostly with shareholders' liability as enforceable by or for the benefit of creditors. The liability for unpaid amounts due on original issuance of shares is now directly to the corporation, but with a view to right of judgment creditors, trustees in bankruptcy, etc., to enforce such liability. The § 70 decisions are accordingly not entirely obsolete. It was held, for instance, that stockholders' liability for the balance due on shares was not limited to commercial creditors of the corporation and could be enforced with respect to obligations generally undertaken by the corporation. Bottlers' Seal Co. v Rainey (1926) 243 N.Y. 333, 153 N.E. 437; Hallett v Metropolitan Messenger Co. (1902) 69 A.D. 258, 74 N.Y.S. 639

Under § 70 of former Stock Corp. L., liability of stockholders to creditors was not considered an asset of the corporation, the corporation itself could not invoke that section to enforce subscription liabilities or unpaid balances legally due it for shares issued, and neither, according to some decisions, could its assignee for the benefit of creditors, or its trustee in bankruptcy, enforce such liability merely as its representative or assignee of its assets. Breck v Brewster (1912) 153 A.D. 800, 138 N.Y.S. 821; Thompson v Knight (1902) 74 A.D. 316, 77 N.Y.S. 599; Rathbone v Ayer (1903) 84 A.D. 186, 82 N.Y.S. 235

4. Restrictions and defenses

Where a creditor brought an action against a single stockholder, the defendant could set off a debt due from the company. Weeks v Love (1872) 50 N.Y. 568; Christensen v Colby (1887, NY) 43 Hun 362, affd 110 N.Y. 660, 18 N.E. 480

Section 70 of former Stock Corp. L. gave a creditor of the corporation no standing to sue a shareholder until the debt to him had become absolute and due, and, in suing a shareholder, a creditor was not acting in behalf of the corporation, but in his own behalf, or in behalf of himself and other creditors of the corporation. Bottlers' Seal Co. v Rainey (1919) 225 N.Y. 369, 122 N.E. 200; Stull v Terry & Tench, Inc. (1948, City Ct) 81 N.Y.S.2d 43

An action by a creditor of a corporation against a holder of stock not fully paid was not barred by the dissolution of the corporation and the appointment of a receiver of its assets. Lyell Ave. Lumber Co. v Lighthouse (1910) 137 A.D. 422, 121 N.Y.S. 802, later app 151 A.D. 902, 135 N.Y.S. 1124

Defects in incorporation were defense to stockholder liability to creditors under § 70 of former Stock Corp. L., if, notwithstanding the defects, de facto corporate existence came into being and defendant thereafter acted or held himself out as a stockholder in an existing corporation. Lyell Ave. Lumber Co. v Lighthouse (1910) 137 A.D. 422, 121 N.Y.S. 802, later app 151 A.D. 902, 135 N.Y.S. 1124

Various defenses were not available to a stock subscriber in a creditor's action under § 70 of former Stock Corp. L., which might have been available to him in a direct action by the corporation to enforce his subscription agreement, such as that his subscription was conditional or contingent and had not become absolute, or was induced by fraud. Lyell Ave. Lumber Co. v Lighthouse (1910) 137 A.D. 422, 121 N.Y.S. 802, later app 151 A.D. 902, 135 N.Y.S. 1124; George Irish Paper Corp. v White (1915) 91 Misc 261, 154 N.Y.S. 778; Moosbrugger v Walsh (1895) 89 Hun 564, 35 N.Y.S. 550

The provisions of § 73 of former Stock Corp. L. imposing certain restrictions and limitations on shareholder and subscriber liability to creditors (which were not carried forward in the Bus. Corp. L.) were taken into consideration, where applicable, in decisions dealing with § 70. One of these was that judgment must first have been obtained against the corporation with execution returned unsatisfied in favor of the particular creditor before such creditor had a right to enforce liability under § 70 and other sections imposing individual liability for corporate debts. Granger & Co. v Allen (1925) 214 A.D. 367, 212 N.Y.S. 356, affd 244 N.Y. 587, 155 N.E. 907; Graeber v Ehrgott (1918) 182 A.D. 377, 169 N.Y.S. 32

Plaintiff would be required to pursue its remedy for breach of contract against subsidiary corporations to judgment before it could resort to suing either the parent corporation or the stockholders or directors of said parent corporation.Eskimo Pie Corp. v Whitelawn Dairies, Inc. (1967, SD NY) 266 F. Supp. 79

Creditors of a corporation may not recover from a parent corporation, or its stockholders or directors until they have exhausted their legal remedies against the corporation by recovery of a judgment against it, and return of an execution wholly or partially unsatisfied, unless such creditor shows that it was impossible or would have been useless to proceed against the corporation.Eskimo Pie Corp. v Whitelawn Dairies, Inc. (1967, SD NY) 266 F. Supp. 79

5. Procedural matters

A complaint by a trustee in bankruptcy or other creditor representative, seeking to enforce shareholder or subscriber liability, had to disclose necessity of recourse to such liability for the benefit of creditors whose claims were not barred, but subject to payment in the bankruptcy or other pending proceedings, and who could have enforced the liability under §§ 70, 73, and other provisions of former Stock Corp. L. Business Advisory Bureau, Inc. v Stallforth (1941) 262 A.D. 162, 28 N.Y.S.2d 437, affd 289 N.Y. 792, 47 N.E.2d 48; John A. Roebling's Sons Co. v Federal Storage Battery Car Co. (1918) 185 A.D. 430, 173 N.Y.S. 297

A subscriber could intervene in an action by a creditor against the corporation, where a judgment had been taken against the corporation by default.Stull v Terry & Tench, Inc. (1948, City Ct) 81 N.Y.S.2d 43

6. Miscellaneous

The liability of a subscriber for unpaid subscriptions in a New Jersey corporation is to be determined by New Jersey law.Southworth v Morgan (1912) 205 N.Y. 293, 98 N.E. 490; Manufacturers' Commercial Co. v Heckscher (1911) 144 A.D. 601, 129 N.Y.S. 556, affd 203 N.Y. 560, 96 N.E. 1121

Individual defendant was entitled to summary judgment dismissing fraud complaint against him, even though he was sole shareholder, director, and officer of corporate defendant, where allegedly fraudulent letter, which represented that certain premises "will be delivered vacant at closing," was signed by individual defendant in his corporate capacity, and thus plaintiff failed to meet its burden of piercing corporate veil so as to impose general liability on individual defendant. Madison Home Equities, Inc. v Echeverria (1999, 2d Dept) 266 A.D.2d 435, 698 N.Y.S.2d 703

Out-of-possession landlord and its shareholders were entitled to summary judgment dismissing action for personal injuries sustained in tenant's car repair shop where mechanic accidentally started car that hit plaintiff, landlord was in no way responsible for accident, and shareholders could not be held liable for acts of corporation. Abdurakhmanov v Ruinsky (2000, 2d Dept) 273 A.D.2d 420, 710 N.Y.S.2d 606

§ 629. Certain transfers or assignments by shareholders or subscribers; effect

Any transfer or assignment by a shareholder of his shares, or by a subscriber for shares of his interest in the corporation, shall not relieve him of any liability as a shareholder or subscriber if at the time of such transfer or assignment the aggregate of the corporation's property, exclusive of any property which it may have conveyed, transferred, concealed, removed, or permitted to be concealed or removed, with intent to defraud, hinder or delay its creditors, is not at a fair valuation sufficient in amount to pay its debts, or if such condition is imminent.

History: Add, L 1961, ch 855, eff Sept 1, 1963.

CASE ANNOTATIONS

This section, although said to have its source in some of the provisions of § 15 of former Stock Corp. L., actually bears so little relationship to § 15, which dealt with preferential transfers of corporate assets when the corporation was "insolvent," leaving such transfers subject to invalidation at suit of creditors, etc., that the decisions construing and applying § 15 are of no assistance in construing or applying the much more limited terms here used, directed to an entirely distinct objective. See for example Bartle v Warren-Jefferson Properties, Inc. (1960) 27 Misc. 2d 328, 210 N.Y.S.2d 736

An essential element of a recovery under former New York Stock Corporation Law § 15 was an intent by the debtor to give a preference. Ackman v Walter E. Heller & Co. (1968, SD NY) 307 F. Supp. 971, affd (CA2 NY) 420 F.2d 1380

§ 630. Liability of shareholders for wages due to laborers, servants or employees

(a) The ten largest shareholders, as determined by the fair value of their beneficial interest as of the beginning of the period during which the unpaid services referred to in this section are performed, of every domestic corporation or of any foreign corporation, when the unpaid services were performed in the state, no shares of which are listed on a national securities exchange or regularly quoted in an over-the-counter market by one or more members of a national or an affiliated securities association, shall jointly and severally be personally liable for all debts, wages or salaries due and owing to any of its laborers, servants or employees other than contractors, for services performed by them for such corporation. Before such laborer, servant or employee shall charge such shareholder for such services, he shall give notice in writing to such shareholder that he intends to hold him liable under this section. Such notice shall be given within one hundred and eighty days after termination of such services, except that if, within such period, the laborer, servant or employee demands an examination of the record of shareholders under paragraph (b) of section 624 (Books and records; right of inspection, prima facie evidence) of this article, such notice may be given within sixty days after he has been given the opportunity to examine the record of shareholders. An action to enforce such liability shall be commenced within ninety days after the return of an execution unsatisfied against the corporation upon a judgment recovered against it for such services. The provisions of this paragraph shall not apply to an investment company registered as such under an act of congress entitled "Investment Company Act of 1940."

(b) For the purposes of this section, wages or salaries shall mean all compensation and benefits payable by an employer to or for the account of the employee for personal services rendered by such employee. These shall specifically include but not be limited to salaries, overtime, vacation, holiday and severance pay; employer contributions to or payments of insurance or welfare benefits; employer contributions to pension or annuity funds; and any other moneys properly due or payable for services rendered by such employee.

(c) A shareholder who has paid more than his pro rata share under this section shall be entitled to contribution pro rata from the other shareholders liable under this section with respect to the excess so paid, over and above his pro rata share, and may sue them jointly or severally or any number of them to recover the amount due from them. Such recovery may be had in a separate action. As used in this paragraph, "pro rata" means in proportion to beneficial share interest. Before a shareholder may claim contribution from other shareholders under this paragraph, he shall, unless they have been given notice by a laborer, servant or employee under paragraph (a), give them notice in writing that he intends to hold them so liable to him. Such notice shall be given by him within twenty days after the date that notice was given to him by a laborer, servant or employee under paragraph (a).

History: Add, L 1961, ch 855, eff Sept 1, 1963; amd, L 1962, ch 834, § 44; L 1963, ch 746, eff Sept 1, 1963; L 1964, ch 725, § 8; L 1965, ch 803, § 24, eff Sept 1, 1965; L 1984, ch 212, § 1, eff June 12, 1984; L 2015, ch 421, § 1, eff Jan 20, 2016; L 2016, ch 5, § 1, eff Jan 19, 2016.

CASE ANNOTATIONS

1. In general
2. Purpose
3. Applicability
4. "Employee"
5. "Wages" and other terms
6. Notice, generally
7. – Particular cases
8. Execution unsatisfied
9. Parties; subrogation
10. Timeliness of action
11. Jurisdiction
12. Miscellaneous

1. In general

Section 71 of former Stock Corp. L., from which this section of the Bus. Corp. L. is said to have been "derived," was dissimilar in a number of respects, most notably in its application to all stockholders and regardless of whether the corporation's shares were listed on a recognized securities exchange. Section 71 was inapplicable to foreign corporations, and their shareholders were not personally liable for amounts due employees thereunder, even though the corporation did business in New York and the contract was entered into and the services rendered in New York. Armstrong v Dyer (1935) 268 N.Y. 671, 198 N.E. 551; Spector v Brandriss (1933) 184 Misc 40, 54 N.Y.S.2d 527; Gonzales v Tuttman (1945, DC NY) 59 F. Supp. 858, 9 CCH LC ¶ 62524; Bogardus v Fitzpatrick (1931) 139 Misc 533, 247 N.Y.S. 692

Business Corporation § 630 is not pre-empted by Employee Retirement Income Security Act (29 USCS § 1144) on grounds that it impermissibly regulates terms and conditions of employee benefit plans; trustees of welfare and pension plan may seek recovery of payments which corporation failed to contribute to welfare and pension plan from shareholders of corporation pursuant to Business Corporation § 630. Sasso v Vachris (1985) 66 N.Y.2d 28, 494 N.Y.S.2d 856, 484 N.E.2d 1359, 6 EBC 2393

A proceeding against a principal stockholder of a corporation to require him to pay a judgment obtained against the corporation pursuant to § 71 of the Stock Corporation Law could only, after effective date of this law (September 1, 1963) be commenced and carried forward under this section of the Business Corporation Law and within the 90-day period prescribed herein. Tessler v Suskind (1964) 42 Misc. 2d 27, 247 N.Y.S.2d 537, 49 CCH LC ¶ 51116

Statute permitting employees to bring action for wages or salaries due and owing for services performed for corporation in which defendants hold stock does not require termination of employment relationship as condition precedent to bringing action thereunder. Grossman v Sendor (1977) 89 Misc. 2d 952, 392 N.Y.S.2d 997, mod on other grounds (1st Dept) 64 A.D.2d 561, 407 N.Y.S.2d 22

Action brought under CLS Bus Corp § 630 is not renewed determination on merits but constitutes enforcement mechanism to protect employees of closely held corporation, so that large shareholder may not collaterally attack judgment for which there was full opportunity to litigate. Matarazzo v Segall (1992, Civ Ct) 153 Misc. 2d 176, 580 N.Y.S.2d 644

But former Stk Corp § 71 was considered penal in nature and to be strictly construed. Kabaker v Gelb (1941, City Ct) 52 N.Y.S.2d 678; Harris v Lederfine (1949) 196 Misc 410, 92 N.Y.S.2d 645; Burns v Stento (1939, Co Ct) 9 N.Y.S.2d 736

CLS Bus Corp § 630, providing that in certain cases obligation to make contributions to employee benefit funds could be enforced against 10 largest corporate shareholders, made explicit reference to ERISA plans and significantly affected ERISA plans, and thus related to ERISA plans and was preempted by ERISA; although statute did not specifically reference ERISA plans, references to insurance or welfare benefits and pension or annuity funds that were supported by employer contributions described with sufficient specificity welfare benefit plans regulated under ERISA and, by changing remedies, statute would alter incentives for employers to create and maintain ERISA plans. Romney v Lin (1996, CA2 NY) 94 F.3d 74, 20 EBC 1816

CLS Bus Corp § 630, providing that in certain cases obligation to make contributions to employee benefit funds could be enforced against 10 largest corporate shareholders, did not serve basic purpose of ERISA preemption (namely, to avoid multiplicity of regulation in order to permit nationally uniform administration of employee benefits) and thus was preempted by ERISA, as it provided alternative enforcement mechanism to ERISA. Romney v Lin (1996, CA2 NY) 94 F.3d 74, 20 EBC 1816

Union's claim under CLS Bus Corp § 630 for recovery of arbitration award was not preempted by federal Labor Management Relations Act § 301, and thus majority shareholders who were held liable for award in state court action were not entitled to judgment declaring such preemption, since § 630 requires that action may be commenced only after there has been adjudication of amount due and owing, judgment and rights created by collective-bargaining agreements (CBAs) were determined by arbitrators prior to action under § 630, and court in § 630 action would therefore not be required to interpret CBAs. Albradco, Inc. v Bevona (1992, CA2 NY) 982 F.2d 82, 16 EBC 1279, 142 BNA LRRM 2282, 124 CCH LC ¶ 10498

CLS Bus Corp § 630 (which provides that 10 largest shareholders of corporation are jointly and severally liable for debts owing to employees, including amounts owed to employee benefit funds) is not preempted by Labor Management Relations Act. Romney v Lin (1995, SD NY) 894 F. Supp. 163

Employee Retirement Income Security Act (ERISA) preempts CLS Bus Corp § 630 (which provides that 10 largest shareholders of corporation are jointly and severally liable for debts owing to employees, including amounts owed to employee benefit funds), since question of whether shareholders of corporate employer are to be held liable for unpaid contributions to benefit fund has "connection" to benefit fund, and § 630 contradicts ERISA (which does not authorize any action against officers and stockholders of corporate employer to recover contributions owed to ERISA fund). Romney v Lin (1995, SD NY) 894 F. Supp. 163

2. Purpose

The phrasing and purpose of § 71 of former Stock Corp. L. were regarded as excluding stockholder liability for amounts due to a major stockholder, principal contributor, director, or principal executive, even though the claim was asserted as one for services rendered. Askowith v Carlton (1928) 249 N.Y. 579, 164 N.E. 590; Kabaker v Gelb (1941, City Ct) 52 N.Y.S.2d 678; Harris v Lederfine (1949) 196 Misc 410, 92 N.Y.S.2d 645

Defendants, the income beneficiaries and remaindermen of a trust which was comprised of the preferred stock in a corporation, would be deemed shareholders for the purposes of Bus Corp Law § 630 and therefore would be jointly and severably liable for the payment of wages due the corporation's employees in the form of fringe benefit contributions, since by specifying in the statute that the ten largest shareholders are to be determined by valuing their "beneficial interests" in the corporation, the legislature made clear its intention not to make a fiduciary holding legal title personally liable therein, but to make the equitable owners of the stock responsible for the payment of employee wage claims. Sasso v Gallucci (1982) 112 Misc. 2d 865, 447 N.Y.S.2d 618

Section 71 of former Stock Corp. L. had for its purpose the protection of all classes of labor beneath the grade of a vice-principal or a direct representative of the employer. Kabaker v Gelb (1941, City Ct) 52 N.Y.S.2d 678

Purpose of Business Corporation Law § 630 is to safeguard those protected by it from being left without recourse for payment of wages and salaries due in case of insolvency of corporation within meaning of statute; this purpose would be significantly undermined by requiring member of protected class to pursue those responsible for payment of wages and salaries in remote jurisdiction and, thus, defendants' ownership of shares in New York corporation allegedly subject to terms and conditions of § 630 is purposeful activity from which instant cause of action arises which satisfies requirements of transaction of business in New York for actions brought against nondomiciliary under CPLR § 302(a)(1). Kane v Benson (1980, ED NY) 86 FRD 460

3. Applicability

An action relating to the recovery of a deposit made by the plaintiff with the corporation as a guaranty of the faithful performance of his duties, was not one brought to recover a debt for services performed. Bradigan v Bayliss (1938) 255 A.D. 934, 8 N.Y.S.2d 756

Claim, that two individual majority stockholders, who owned more than majority of shares of corporate majority stockholder, conspired to depress profits of bankrupt corporation and to increase profits of corporate majority stockholder and that the two individual majority stockholders wasted assets of bankrupt corporation to benefit of corporate majority stockholder, belonged to the bankrupt corporation rather than to stockholders and should have been brought as a derivative suit. Carpenter v Sisti (1974, 1st Dept) 45 A.D.2d 529, 360 N.Y.S.2d 13

CLS Bus Corp § 630(a) applied, and thus defendants' motion to dismiss complaint was properly denied, where plaintiffs sought compensation for labor and services performed before subject New York corporation merged with foreign corporation, and merger did not extinguish defendants' liability for that compensation. La Vigne v Feinbloom (1998, 4th Dept) 255 A.D.2d 896, 680 N.Y.S.2d 348, related proceeding (4th Dept) 255 A.D.2d 897, 680 N.Y.S.2d 882

An action by trustees of a union welfare fund under Bus Corp Law § 630 to hold officers and shareholders of a bankrupt corporation liable for the corporation's failure to pay contributions to the welfare fund on behalf of union employees as required by the terms of a collective bargaining agreement would be dismissed, since the subject employee benefit plan falls within the purview of federal law (ERISA) which nearly totally preempts regulation of employee benefit plans and which grants federal courts exclusive jurisdiction of such an action. Sasso v Vachris (1982) 116 Misc. 2d 797, 456 N.Y.S.2d 629

Because the use of the term "corporation" in N.Y. Bus. Corp. Law § 630 was plainly limited to domestic corporations, and because the corporation in question was a defunct Delaware corporation, the shareholders' motion to dismiss an employee's claims brought pursuant to that statute had to be granted. Stuto v Kerber (2009, Sup) 888 NYS2d 872.

District Court will not exercise ancillary jurisdiction over law firm's attorney's fees claims against individual shareholders of corporate employer which firm represented in underlying wage and hour cause of action, where judgment has not been entered in underlying wage and hour action against corporate employer, because, under CLS Bus Corp Law § 630, personal liability of 10 largest shareholders is not only contingent upon judgment against corporation for employee compensation but is subject of separate action commenced within 90 days of judgment against corporation. Wong v East River Chinese Restaurant (1995, ED NY) 884 F. Supp. 663

Action to collect money owed to union benefit funds is dismissed, where employer failed to pay funds, judgment was obtained, and amount owed is now sought from principal shareholder of employer, because statute authorizing such collection action against "ten largest shareholders of every corporation," CLS Bus Corp Law § 630, is preempted by ERISA (29 USCS §§ 1001 et seq.) as state law relating to employee benefit plan. Romney v Lin (1995, SD NY) 894 F. Supp. 163

4. "Employee"

An attorney at law was not deemed to be in the "employee" class, notwithstanding he was regularly employed. Bristor v Smith (1899) 158 N.Y. 157, 53 N.E. 42

The plaintiffs, whose principal duties were to travel around the country instructing the purchasers of annealing furnaces in the method of their operation, necessitating the actual operation of furnaces, making research tests and doing stenographic and typing work, for which they received meagre salaries in keeping with such positions, were "employees" within the meaning of § 71 of former Stock Corp. L. Evans v Lawrence Stern & Co. (1936) 270 N.Y. 177, 200 N.E. 777

The word "employee" included a bookkeeper employed at a weekly salary who, in addition to the usual duties of such position, attended to the banking business of the corporation and answered inquiries in the absence of officers. It seems, that such an employee is within the terms of the statute although he receives an annual salary. Farnum v Harrison (1915) 167 A.D. 704, 152 N.Y.S. 835, affd 218 N.Y. 672, 113 N.E. 1055

A salesman employed by corporation and at all times subject to the direction and control of his employer, which is entitled to command his entire time and attention, was an "employee" and within the protection of § 71 of former Stock Corp. L., though he was paid commission on accepted sales. Hitchcock v Pagenstecher (1921) 198 A.D. 511, 190 N.Y.S. 706

Despite what plaintiff described as his "fancy title" of "Sr. Vice-President-Sales," he stated cause of action for recovery of unpaid wages as "employee" under CLS Bus Corp § 630 where he alleged that he had no supervisory responsibilities over other employees, no authority to make spending decisions, no check writing privileges, and no financial interest in corporation, that his sole responsibility was to sell finished products, and that all of his contracts were subject to approval of corporation's president. Moses v Polk (1998, 1st Dept) 251 A.D.2d 75, 673 N.Y.S.2d 678

Court erred in granting defendants' summary judgment motion in action under CLS Bus Corp § 630 on ground that plaintiff lacked standing inasmuch as he was attorney and not "employee" within meaning of statute since plaintiff was full-time salaried employee of corporation, who throughout his employment was under direction and control of corporation's managers and officers. Klepner v Dorfman (1998, 1st Dept) 256 A.D.2d 163, 681 N.Y.S.2d 532

Plaintiff whose claim against largest stockholders of insolvent corporation was for sums due him from corporation was an integral part of buy-out agreement under which plaintiff sold his shares to corporation and received cash plus a noncancelable ten-year contract for a guaranteed salary of $1,000 per month was not an "employee" within meaning of statute making ten largest stockholders of certain corporations which become insolvent liable for debts, wages and salaries of laborers, servants and employees of corporation. Herman v Levanne (1974) 77 Misc. 2d 653, 354 N.Y.S.2d 361

The word "laborer" was considered to have the same connotation as the word "workman" as used in § 17 of the Bankruptcy Act, giving certain claims priority status in bankruptcy proceedings. Re Fabbri (1934, DC NY) 8 F. Supp. 35

5. "Wages" and other terms

Employer contributions for welfare benefits and two pension funds are expressly included as wages and salaries, and action may be taken against shareholders for unpaid contributions to pension trust funds. Sasso v Vachris (1985) 66 N.Y.2d 28, 494 N.Y.S.2d 856, 484 N.E.2d 1359, 6 EBC 2393

Although § 71 of former Stock Corp. L. was less specific than this section of the Bus. Corp. L. with respect to what constituted "wages" and "salaries" as including special pay and "fringe benefits," it was construed as permitting trustees of a Union Health and Welfare Fund to impose personal liability on stockholders where the corporation failed to pay contributions to the fund as required by a collective bargaining agreement. Greenberg v Corwin (1961) 31 Misc. 2d 736, 222 N.Y.S.2d 80

See also Corenti v Kulik (1962) 36 Misc. 2d 996, 234 N.Y.S.2d 28, 47 CCH LC ¶ 50809

While contributions to welfare and pension plans may not qualify as "wages" for purpose of determining priority of claims in bankruptcy, they do qualify as "wages" for purpose of statute permitting employees to bring action for wages or salaries due and owing for services performed for corporation in which defendants hold stock, and union has standing to bring action under that statute. Grossman v Sendor (1977) 89 Misc. 2d 952, 392 N.Y.S.2d 997, mod on other grounds (1st Dept) 64 A.D.2d 561, 407 N.Y.S.2d 22

Use of word "such" in statute permitting employees to bring action for wages or salaries due and owing for services performed for corporation in which defendants hold stock and requiring that notice be given stockholders within 90 days after termination of "such services" indicates that "services" referred to are those which have already been "performed" and for which wages are "due and owing"; thus prospective relationship of employer and employee is not material, since statute makes stockholders liable only for services which have already been completed and not for those which will be completed at some point in future; "termination" therefore refers to services, not to employment relationship. Grossman v Sendor (1977) 89 Misc. 2d 952, 392 N.Y.S.2d 997, mod on other grounds (1st Dept) 64 A.D.2d 561, 407 N.Y.S.2d 22

Section 71 of former Stock Corp. L. required the notice of intention to enforce stockholder liability to be given within a specified time after "termination of employment," and these words were given their usual and ordinary meaning, "termination" being broad enough to include either voluntary quitting or involuntary discharge. Burns v Stento (1939, Co Ct) 9 N.Y.S.2d 736

6. Notice, generally

Section 71 of former Stock Corp. L. likewise contained time limitations within which notice of intention to enforce stockholder liability must be given, and within which an action to enforce such liability must be brought. Failure to meet these limitations was ground for dismissal of the action. Denise v Welch (1934) 242 A.D. 34, 273 N.Y.S. 921

If the notice was actually received within the prescribed time by the stockholder to whom it was directed, the service was good and valid, even though the service was by mail; the manner of service was of no great importance. Horowitz v Winter (1927) 129 Misc 814, 222 N.Y.S. 233

Section 71 of former Stock Corp. L., like this section of the Bus. Corp. L., contained a preliminary notice requirement which was a condition precedent to right to enforce stockholder liability. The purpose of the requirement was to give the stockholder notified a chance to take measures to compel payment of the wage demand by the corporation, or others in interest, before being sued and actually subjected to personal liability. Horowitz v Winter (1927) 129 Misc 814, 222 N.Y.S. 233

Section 71 of former Stock Corp. L. required the notice of intention to enforce stockholder liability to be given within a specified time after "termination of employment," and these words were given their usual and ordinary meaning, "termination" being broad enough to include either voluntary quitting or involuntary discharge. Burns v Stento (1939, Co Ct) 9 N.Y.S.2d 736

7. – Particular cases

Corporation allegedly terminated services of one of its employees, plaintiff, at time when it was allegedly indebted to plaintiff for past-due wages and salary in amount in excess of $50,000; plaintiff's negotiations with corporation culminated in settlement and following one payment, corporation apparently failed to continue payments to plaintiff; corporation thereafter filed for reorganization and plaintiff gave notice to defendant, one of 10 largest shareholders of corporation, of his intent to hold defendant liable pursuant to Business Corporation Law § 630 for amount corporation owed him for services rendered-while Business Corporation Law § 630 provides that 10 largest shareholders shall jointly and severally be personally liable for debts owing to its employees for services rendered, such liability is conditioned on explicit statutory directive that notice of intent to hold shareholder liable shall be given within 180 days after termination of services; plaintiff's notice of intent is dated May 21, 1986 and states that plaintiff's services were terminated on April 5, 1985; notice thus failed to satisfy 180-day limitation period; accordingly, complaint was properly dismissed-plaintiff's equitable estoppel argument is rejected; there is no proof that defendant, by resort to settlement negotiations, intended to lull plaintiff into refraining from giving timely notice of intent within 180 days of termination; in any event, settlement negotiations did not involve defendant, which therefore cannot be bound by any equitable estoppel assertable against corporation. Beam v Key Venture Capital Corp., 152 A.D.2d 825

Where payments corporation was required to make to union's welfare, pension and special displacement benefit trust funds, calculated as percentage of gross earnings of employees, were "due and owing" only at end of each month, in order to hold stockholders of corporation, which filed petition in bankruptcy, liable for payment due May 31, June 30, and July 31, only one notice need be served within 90 days after termination of such services. Grossman v Sendor (1978) (1st Dept) 64 A.D.2d 561, 407 N.Y.S.2d 22

Terminated employee was not entitled to hold large shareholder of employer company liable for amount owed him for services rendered to company, pursuant to CLS Bus Corp § 630, where employee was terminated in April 1985 but did not send notice of intent to hold shareholder liable until May 1986, and thus failed to satisfy 180-day limitation set forth in § 630(a); employee's argument that settlement with employer made in November 1985 led him to believe suit would not be necessary was without merit where there was no evidence that employer intended to lull employee into failing to give timely notice of intent. Beam v Key Venture Capital Corp. (1989, 3d Dept) 152 A.D.2d 825, 544 N.Y.S.2d 35

Labor union, in order to comply with 180-day notice requirement of CLS Bus Corp § 630(a), had to serve notice of intent on shareholder by February 1, 1991 for first period and by September 21, 1991 for second period, since unpaid services in question (contributions to union welfare fund) were performed between November 1, 1989 and August 1, 1990, and between October 1, 1990 and March 21, 1991; plaintiff's failure to serve notice until May 16, 1992 required dismissal of action. Gannone v Wittman (1996, 1st Dept) 232 A.D.2d 298, 649 N.Y.S.2d 14

Because an employee who sought to recover unpaid wages from a former employer's sole shareholder did not retain counsel until after this section's notice period had expired, at which time an action against the shareholder was precluded, a legal malpractice complaint failed to state a claim. The notice period began to run upon cessation of services, regardless of when the employment relationship was deemed to have ended under federal law for visa status purposes, and tolling was unavailable. Ingvarsdottir v Gaines, Gruner, Ponzini & Novick, LLP, 144 A.D.3d 1099, 43 N.Y.S.3d 68, 2016 N.Y. App. Div. LEXIS 7898 (2d Dep't 2016).

Notice of intention to hold corporation stockholders liable given by registered mail was sufficient notice within meaning of § 71 of former Stock Corp. L., where the proof showed receipt of the notice within thirty days after termination of plaintiff's services and within thirty days after return unsatisfied of execution in an action in which judgment was recovered against corporation for said services. Horowitz v Winter (1927) 129 Misc 814, 222 N.Y.S. 233

The requirement that notice of intention to hold a stockholder liable for unpaid wages be given within 30 days after termination of services was not met by the trustees of a union insurance fund where the corporation had gone into bankruptcy and all services by employees had ceased long before notice of intention to enforce stockholder liability was given. Corenti v Kulik (1962) 36 Misc. 2d 996, 234 N.Y.S.2d 28, 47 CCH LC ¶ 50809

The fact that employees in a petition and verified proof of claim in a bankruptcy proceeding fixed the date of termination of their services as a date more than 30 days prior to service of notice on the stockholders did not estop such employees from proving a different date in an action against the stockholders for wages. Burns v Stento (1939, Co Ct) 9 N.Y.S.2d 736

8. Execution unsatisfied

The judgment obtained against the corporation did not have to be a judgment of a court of record, and neither did the execution issued and returned unsatisfied have to issue out of a court of record. Padros v Swarzenbach (1909) 134 A.D. 811, 119 N.Y.S. 589

Claim that there was no execution returned unsatisfied against bankrupt corporation prior to payment by majority stockholders of employees' wage claims, and claim, that two individual majority stockholders, who owned more than majority of shares of corporate majority stockholder, conspired to depress profits of bankrupt corporation and to increase profits of corporate stockholder and that the individual majority stockholders wasted assets of bankrupt corporation to benefit of corporate majority stockholder, was valid affirmative defense to allegation that majority shareholders paid more than their pro rata share of wages owned to employees of bankrupt corporation and that they were entitled to contribution from minority shareholders. Carpenter v Sisti (1974, 1st Dept) 45 A.D.2d 529, 360 N.Y.S.2d 13

In an action by a union against a corporation for payment of specified funds in which defendant corporate president served a crossclaim on defendant corporate vice-president alleging that liability of the individual defendants flowed from Bus Corp Law § 630 and Labor Law § 198-c and that the president was entitled to recoup from the vice-president as vice-president and largest shareholder his pro rata share of the amount paid by the president in satisfaction of the union's claim, summary judgment dismissing the crosscomplaint was proper since Bus Corp Law § 630 requires as a condition precedent to an action against shareholders that judgment be recovered against the corporation and that execution on such judgment be returned unsatisfied, and the proof showed that the president settled the claim by payment of $55,000, that the corporation was still operating, that

the president was still its president, and that the vice-president, employed as plant superintendent without executive authority, did not fall within the categories of corporate officer as specified in Labor Law § 198-c. Powers v Adcraft Typographers, Inc. (1982, 1st Dept) 86 A.D.2d 566, 446 N.Y.S.2d 292

Before suing stockholders to enforce their individual liability, under § 71 of former Stock Corp. L., as construed with § 73 of that Law, the claimant must first have brought an action against the corporation, obtained judgment against it, and had execution issued thereon returned unsatisfied. Arenwald v Douglas Machinery Co. (1944) 183 Misc 627, 50 N.Y.S.2d 39

In reference to statute providing that action by employees against stockholders of corporate employer shall be commenced within 90 days after return of execution unsatisfied against corporation upon judgment recovered against it for services rendered, fact that plaintiff union was stayed from commencing any action against corporation, which employed members of union, to recover unpaid balance owed union's welfare, pension and special displacement benefit trust funds once corporation filed petition in bankruptcy did not make it impossible to collect full amount in bankruptcy proceedings, although that was unlikely, and as long as it was theoretically possible to collect debt from corporation, stockholders were not liable, for purpose of statute was to create exception to rule of limited liability only where employees could not collect their wages because of insolvency of corporation. Grossman v Sendor (1977) 89 Misc. 2d 952, 392 N.Y.S.2d 997, mod on other grounds (1st Dept) 64 A.D.2d 561, 407 N.Y.S.2d 22

In an action brought by trustees of union welfare and pension trust funds against sole stockholder and alleged corporate officers for fringe benefits due from corporate employer, summary judgment in favor of union trustees would be granted since plaintiffs were not required to wait for the return of an unsatisfied execution of judgment against the corporation when plaintiffs were prevented from proceeding against the corporate employer by an automatic stay of the bankruptcy law and where plaintiffs' established a prima facie case pursuant to Bus Corp Law § 630 for fringe benefits due and a prima facie case under Labor Law § 198-c for failure to remit the requisite payments to the welfare and pension trust funds. Sasso v Millbrook Enterprises, Inc. (1981) 108 Misc. 2d 562, 438 N.Y.S.2d 59

9. Parties; subrogation

A wage claimant or other creditor within the coverage of § 71 of former Stock Corp. L. could proceed individually or in behalf of himself and other such claimants, and could maintain an action to enforce stockholder liability against all, part, or any one of the stockholders with respect to whom he had met the preliminary requirements. Pfohl v Simpson (1878) 74 N.Y. 137; Citizens' Bank of Buffalo v Weinberg (1899) 26 Misc 518, 57 N.Y.S. 495; Horowitz v Winter (1927) 129 Misc 814, 222 N.Y.S. 233

Plaintiff, as head of union which had negotiated collective bargaining agreements with defendant, which operated through 2 alter ego corporations, had standing to bring action under CLS Bus Corp § 630 for recovery of wage differentials and unpaid union pension and health funds contributions, even in absence of former employees. Bevona v Albradco, Inc. (1991, 1st Dept) 173 A.D.2d 419, 570 N.Y.S.2d 47

Court erred in granting defendants' summary judgment motion in action under CLS Bus Corp § 630 on ground that plaintiff lacked standing inasmuch as he was attorney and not "employee" within meaning of statute since plaintiff was full-time salaried employee of corporation, who throughout his employment was under direction and control of corporation's managers and officers. Klepner v Dorfman (1998, 1st Dept) 256 A.D.2d 163, 681 N.Y.S.2d 532

An action pursuant to § 71 of former Stock Corp. L. could not succeed against an individual defendant if he had ceased to be a stockholder long prior to its commencement. Murphy v Meyer (1935) 155 Misc 753, 280 N.Y.S. 550

Although debtor-in-possession is new legal entity distinct from debtor and is therefore a "new" employer for bankruptcy purposes, the actual employment of the debtor's workers may be continued and such continuation does not preclude an action against the debtor's shareholders to recover wages, salaries or pension benefits due the debtor's employees. Grossman v Sendor (1977) 89 Misc. 2d 952, 392 N.Y.S.2d 997, mod on other grounds (1st Dept) 64 A2d 561, 407 N.Y.S.2d 22

A stockholder was not subrogated to employee's wage claims where she advanced money to a bankrupt corporation to pay wage claims of the corporation's employees before her liability under § 71 of former Stock Corp. L. had arisen. Lacks v Frummer (1957, CA2 NY) 242 F.2d 216

10. Timeliness of action

Plaintiffs' CLS Bus Corp § 630 claims were properly dismissed since they were not interposed within 90 days of return of unsatisfied execution as required by CLS Bus Corp § 630(a), and claims could not be saved through application of CLS CPLR §§ 205(a) or former 306-b. Wing Wong v King Sun Yee (1999, 1st Dept) 262 A.D.2d 254, 693 N.Y.S.2d 536, 5 BNA WH Cas 2d 1087

Action, brought against stockholders of corporation which employed members of plaintiff union after corporation filed petition in bankruptcy, to recover unpaid balance owed plaintiff's welfare, pension and special displacement benefit trust funds, payments to which were calculated as percentage of gross earnings of employees, was timely where commenced within 90 days of bankruptcy confirmation order, as opposed to date of filing of bankruptcy petition. Grossman v Sendor (1977) 89 Misc. 2d 952, 392 N.Y.S.2d 997, mod on other grounds (1st Dept) 64 A.D.2d 561, 407 N.Y.S.2d 22

Service of summons upon one stockholder within the time limited for institution of the action was considered sufficient to meet that limitation with respect to all stockholders. Ryan v Dash (1952, Sup) 114 N.Y.S.2d 36

11. Jurisdiction

Although the State Supreme Court had jurisdiction over a cause of action based on Bus Corp Law § 630, in which plaintiffs, trustees of an employees' welfare and pension fund, sought to hold defendant shareholders liable for contributions which should have been made to the fund, such cause of action would not be maintainable in State Court, since the broad plain language of the Federal Employee Retirement Income Security Act (ERISA) applies to supersede § 630 insofar as the latter relates to employee benefit plans covered by the Federal statute, notwithstanding the fact that the State statute neither conflicts with nor frustrates the general objectives of ERISA; insofar as § 630 "relates to" employee benefit plans by providing a potential enforcement mechanism not encountered in ERISA for plans governed by ERISA, it falls within the Federal preemption statute. Sasso v Vachris (1984, 2d Dept) 106 A.D.2d 132, 482 N.Y.S.2d 875, revd 66 N.Y.2d 28, 494 N.Y.S.2d 856, 484 N.E.2d 1359, 6 EBC 2393

Since the liability of stockholders to employees was quasi-contractual in nature, the municipal court of New York City had jurisdiction of an action by an employee under § 71 of former Stock Corp. L. Halkin v Hume (1924) 123 Misc 815, 206 N.Y.S. 702; Horowitz v Winter (1927) 129 Misc 814, 222 N.Y.S. 233

Purchase of 10,000 shares of a New York corporation by New York residents, coupled with knowledge of and participation in the operation of the corporation, was "purposeful activity" within long-arm statute, especially when the stock purchase constituted the purchasers, as joint tenants, the largest shareholders in the corporation, and third-party cause of action against the purchasers for pro rata payment of liability imposed on the ten largest shareholders for unpaid wages earned by employee of the corporation arose from business transacted within the state, so that there was personal jurisdiction over the purchasers, who had moved to Indiana, in the third-party action. Havlicek v Bach (1976) 86 Misc. 2d 1084, 385 N.Y.S.2d 750

Labor union's state law cause of action against employer's principal shareholder to collect delinquent contributions to ERISA plans (which was preempted by ERISA) fell within scope of ERISA's civil enforcement provisions, and thus was properly removed to federal court; ERISA provides means for collecting delinquent ERISA contributions without imposing direct liability on shareholders such that permitting suits against shareholders pursuant to CLS Bus Corp § 630 would reallocate burden and benefits for class of New York corporations establishing ERISA plans and would afford those plans special and stringent means of civil enforcement. Romney v Lin (1996, CA2 NY) 94 F.3d 74, 20 EBC 1816

12. Miscellaneous

A stockholder could not be charged with costs incurred in the defense of an action prosecuted against the corporation for damages upon causes of action other than that embraced in the statute making him liable. Card v Groesbeck (1912) 204 N.Y. 301, 97 N.E. 728

Action to recover damages for unpaid wages, brought under CLS Bus Corp § 630 against respondents in their alleged capacity as 2 of 10 largest shareholders of corporate defendants, was properly dismissed where plaintiff's did not allege that judgment had been entered against any of defendant corporations and returned unsatis-

fied. Garcia v Tamir (2000, 2d Dept) 269 A.D.2d 423, 702 N.Y.S.2d 904

Plaintiff, who in a prior action against the corporate defendant was awarded a judgment for breach of an employment contract, could not maintain a suit pursuant to Business Corporation Law § 630 against the corporation and the largest stockholder thereof as an individual, where there was no allegation that plaintiff had not been paid for work, labor, or services performed by her and in fact the plaintiff's statement that she was paid in full for all work rendered for the corporation appeared in the papers. Lindsey v Winkler (1967) 52 Misc. 2d 1037, 277 N.Y.S.2d 768

While CLS Bus Corp § 630 is essentially enforcement mechanism permitting employees of closely held corporations to bring suit against shareholder for wages due, shareholder was nevertheless entitled to day in court to litigate issues involved, and summary judgment was thus inappropriate notwithstanding prior federal court action which determined amount of liability. Matarazzo v Segall (1993, Sup App T) 156 Misc. 2d 1, 600 N.Y.S.2d 890

Labor union's CLS Bus Corp § 630 action to collect delinquent pension fund contributions directly from principal shareholder of corporate employer fell within civil enforcement provision of Employee Retirement Income Security Act (ERISA) and was preempted by 29 USCS § 1132(a) even though shareholder would not be liable for ERISA violations. Romney v Lin (1997, CA2) 105 F.3d 806, 20 EBC 2446

ARTICLE 7
DIRECTORS AND OFFICERS

History: Add, L 1961, ch 855, eff Sept 1, 1963.

Schedule of sections, amd, L 1962, ch 819, eff Sept 1, 1963.

§ 701.   Board of directors

Subject to any provision in the certificate of incorporation authorized by paragraph (b) of section 620 (Agreements as to voting; provision in certificate of incorporation as to control of directors) or by paragraph (b) of section 715 (Officers), the business of a corporation shall be managed under the direction of its board of directors, each of whom shall be at least eighteen years of age. The certificate of incorporation or the by-laws may prescribe other qualifications for directors.

History: Add, L 1961, ch 855, eff Sept 1, 1963, amd, L 1965, ch 803, § 25, L 1974, ch 899, L 1977, ch 432, § 1, eff Sept 1, 1977.

CASE ANNOTATIONS

1. Eligibility
2. Powers, generally
3. Litigation
4. Other powers
5. Interference with control
6. Judicial review
7. Liability for unauthorized acts

1. Eligibility

Under § 55 of former Stock Corp. L., a person could be a director, though not a stockholder, if the charter or bylaws so provided, and eligibility for election as a director was not limited to holders of common stock but could be extended by the bylaws to a holder of any kind of the capital stock. Re Haecker (1925) 212 A.D. 167, 207 N.Y.S. 561; Buffalo Electro-Plating Co. v Day (1912) 151 A.D. 237, 135 N.Y.S. 1054

2. Powers, generally

Directors have general power to do any act which falls within what properly may be regarded as management of ordinary business of the corporation. Amdur v Meyer (1962, 1st Dept) 15 A.D.2d 425, 224 N.Y.S.2d 440, motion to dismiss app den 11 N.Y.2d 1051, 230 N.Y.S.2d 206, 184 N.E.2d 179

Matters of discretion and the exercise of business judgment in the management of corporate affairs may not be settled by arbitration. Application of Vogel (1966, 1st Dept) 25 A.D.2d 212, 268 N.Y.S.2d 237, affd 19 N.Y.2d 589, 278 N.Y.S.2d 236, 224 N.E.2d 738

Actions taken in regard to leasing of vehicles for closely-held corporation were not matters of corporate policy that required formal action by board of directors. Bahar v Schwartzreich (1994, 2d Dept) 204 A.D.2d 441, 611 N.Y.S.2d 619

A stock transfer assessment imposed by the board of directors of a cooperative corporation on all tenant shareholders when they transfer their shares of stock to a third party is proper and would be upheld where it was consistent with the broad grant of powers to the board contained in the cooperative's by-laws, the provisions of the Cooperative Corporations Law, and the Business Corporation Law. Berglund v 411 East 57th Corp. (1984) 122 Misc. 2d 702, 471 N.Y.S.2d 803

3. Litigation

Under § 27 of former Gen. Corp. L., control over institution of litigation in behalf of the corporation was regarded as a function of management to such extent that the president of a corporation lacked authority to institute it as against refusal of the board of directors, to sanction the action, notwithstanding the position taken by the directors was the result of a deadlock on the board. Sterling Industries, Inc. v Ball Bearing Pen Corp. (1949) 298 N.Y. 483, 84 N.E.2d 790, 10 ALR2d 694

The business of a corporation is managed by its board of directors. Hence, a president, a 50% stockholder, of a corporation could not bring an action against its vice-president, also a 50% stockholder, without the approval of its board of directors. The presumption that a president may sue without approval of the board of directors has no force when he attempts to sue one who has equal control of the corporation. Tidy-House Paper Corp. v Adlman (1957, 1st Dept) 4 A.D.2d 619, 168 N.Y.S.2d 448

President/treasurer of 2-man corporation lacked authority to bring action on behalf of corporation against vice-president/secretary to terminate latter's employment contract and recover amount of compensation and fringe benefits provided to him after his receipt of disability benefits where each man owned 50 percent of stock, and thus, by implication from CLS Bus Corp §§ 701 and 702(a), deadlock could not be remedied by exercise of presidential power, and proper remedy was shareholder's derivative action. Stone v Frederick (1997, 3d Dept) 245 A.D.2d 742, 666 N.Y.S.2d 294

Where plaintiff was a closed corporation having two equal stockholders who were its two directors, a suit initiated by president in name of plaintiff corporation for monies had and received against his co-equal director could not be maintained where board refused its

sanction. Schillinger & Albert Inc. v Myral Hats Inc. (1967) 55 Misc. 2d 178, 284 N.Y.S.2d 780

Shareholder lacked the authority to authorize litigation in the name of the corporation because he was at complete odds with the vice president and one of the directors, who objected to the proceeding. Gorbrook Assoc. Inc. v Silverstein (2013, Dist Ct) 40 Misc 3d 425, 965 NYS2d 851.

Filing of a petition seeking voluntary adjudication of a corporation in bankruptcy has been considered such an act of management as to require approval of the board of directors. Re Jefferson Casket Co. (1910, DC NY) 182 F 689

In absence of lawful authorization by corporation, third-party complaint brought in corporation's name may not lawfully proceed. Wilson v Westmoreland Farm (1998, ED NY) 989 F. Supp. 451

4. Other powers

Any understanding between shareholders of a corporation as to how profits of the business were to be shared as between them was subject to the statutory directive that the business of the corporation shall be managed by its Board of Directors. Weber v Sidney (1963, 1st Dept) 19 A.D.2d 494, 244 N.Y.S.2d 228, affd 14 N.Y.2d 929, 252 N.Y.S.2d 327, 200 N.E.2d 867

Bylaw provisions of a corporation whereby salaries of all officers are to be fixed by the Board of Directors and dividends were to be paid from earnings upon proper action taken by the Board are to be given the force and effect of a contract as between shareholders. Weber v Sidney (1963, 1st Dept) 19 A.D.2d 494, 244 N.Y.S.2d 228, affd 14 N.Y.2d 929, 252 N.Y.S.2d 327, 200 N.E.2d 867

The matter of disposal of a corporation's non-franchise assets and the nonexercise of the option to repurchase the same, were matters for the business judgment of the corporation's directors. Greenbaum v American Metal Climax, Inc. (1967, 1st Dept) 27 A.D.2d 225, 278 N.Y.S.2d 123

Imposition of "waiver of option" fee on outgoing shareholders in housing cooperative who wished to sell their shares on open market rather than resell them to cooperative corporation at book value, as their agreement provided, was valid exercise of cooperative board's power where fee was applied in evenly proportioned fashion, and thus did not violate mandate of CLS Bus Corp § 501(c) that each share of stock be equal to every other share in same class. Meichsner v Valentine Gardens Cooperative, Inc. (1988, 2d Dept) 137 A.D.2d 797, 525 N.Y.S.2d 345

Cooperative corporation was entitled to summary judgment in action, brought by executrix of deceased shareholder, for return of "waiver of option" fee imposed by corporation in connection with transfer of shares of cooperative housing stock where executrix, on informing corporation of her intent to sell premises, signed document in which she agreed to pay such fee; imposition of fee on outgoing shareholders who wish to sell their shares on open market, rather than to resell them to corporation at book value, is valid exercise of cooperative board's power as granted by statute and corporate bylaws. Badowski v Roosevelt Terrace Cooperative, Inc. (1989, 2d Dept) 148 A.D.2d 406, 538 N.Y.S.2d 562

The power to lease property of one corporation to another is primarily in the board of directors. Green v People's Gaslight & Coke Co. (1922) 118 Misc 1, 192 N.Y.S. 232, affd 206 A.D. 647, 198 N.Y.S. 917

It was within the powers of directors of a corporation to provide for a drawing account or salary for one of the officers thereof, and, where the contract is supported by sufficient consideration, it is valid. Harris v Harris (1930) 137 Misc 73, 241 N.Y.S. 474

A contract between a theater producing corporation and two of its three directors covering compensation for their duties as administrative directors of the corporation was not invalid under § 27 of former Gen. Corp. L. as an improper delegation of management power, since under it the Board retained power to withdraw the duties assigned whenever it saw fit. Simonson v Helburn (1950) 198 Misc 430, 97 N.Y.S.2d 406

Since plaintiff tenant never informed defendant co-operative apartment corporation, in writing, of his intention to leave the co-operative as required by the co-operative's by-laws, he could not assign his lease and dispose of his stock in the co-operative without affording defendant the first option to purchase his shares and he is, therefore, not entitled to the return of a $2,000 "waiver of option" fee paid to defendant in return for defendant's waiver of its right to purchase plaintiff's shares; moreover, the "waiver of option" fee is a valid exercise of the power of defendant's board of directors (Cooperative Corporations Law, § 5; Business Corporation Law, § 701) and the complaint must, therefore, be dismissed. Jamil v Southridge Cooperative, Section No. 4, Inc. (1979)

Business Corporation Law

102 Misc. 2d 404, 425 N.Y.S.2d 905, affd 77 A.D.2d 822, 429 N.Y.S.2d 340, cert den 450 US 919, 67 L Ed 2d 346, 101 S Ct 1366, reh den 450 US 1050, 68 L Ed 2d 247, 101 S Ct 1771

A transfer fee imposed by a cooperative board of directors on shares of stock in the cooperative corporation was valid when the authority to impose such a fee is conferred by the corporations's by-laws, the Cooperative Corporations Law, and the Business Corporation Law, and a court will not upset an act of a cooperative board of directors when it is undertaken in good faith, for legitimate corporate purposes, and not in violation of the board's fiduciary duty to stockholders. Mayerson v 3701 Tenants Corp. (1984) 123 Misc. 2d 235, 473 N.Y.S.2d 123

The owner of a cooperative apartment was entitled to recover the money she paid the cooperative corporation as a "flip tax" of 15 percent of her profits on the sale of her apartment where, after she entered into the sales agreement, the tax was authorized by the board in violation of provisions of the proprietary lease forbidding retroactive changes in rent and charges, where neither the corporate bylaws nor the proprietary lease authorized imposition of the tax, and where the tax was not within the board's power to collect expenses incidental to the transfer of an apartment. McIntyre v Royal Summit Owners, Inc. (1984) 126 Misc. 2d 930, 487 N.Y.S.2d 474

5. Interference with control

The provision of § 27 of former Gen. Corp. L. that the business of the corporation should be managed by its board of directors did not, however, invalidate a contract in which the controlling stockholder agreed to keep the only other stockholder as a director and general manager. Clark v Dodge (1936) 269 N.Y. 410, 199 N.E. 641

Section 27 of former Gen. Corp. L., in vesting management of corporate business in the directors, was regarded as rendering invalid, or at least unenforceable, private agreements which would impede or interfere with control over matters of normal business management, such as control by the directors over salaries and personnel, or place management in another corporation or some particular group or class of shareholders. Long Park, Inc. v Trenton-New Brunswick Theatres Co. (1948) 297 N.Y. 174, 77 N.E.2d 633 (superseded by statute as stated in Zion v Kurtz, 50 N.Y.2d 92, 428 N.Y.S.2d 199, 405 N.E.2d 681, 15 ALR4th 1061); McQuade v Stoneham (1934) 263 N.Y. 323, 189 N.E. 234, reh den 264 N.Y. 460, 191 N.E. 514 and (superseded by statute as stated in Zion v Kurtz, 50 N.Y.2d 92, 428 N.Y.S.2d 199, 405 N.E.2d 681, 15 ALR4th 1061); Abby v Meyerson (1949) 299 N.Y. 557, 85 N.E.2d 789

Under agreement for purchase and sale of stock which provided that both parties would vote their shares together for a majority of the directors nominated by purchaser and for a minority nominated by seller and that if the directors designated by the purchaser were elected and if so requested by seller, purchaser would use his best efforts to cause the company to register under appropriate laws for the sale or distribution of other shares owned by seller, the agreement could not possibly be deemed illegal because purchaser later became a director and thereupon came to regard his agreement as an interference with his independent duty as a director, since the purchaser was not required to interfere with the directors, to elect officers or to do any act of interference with the corporate management. Glekel v Gluck (1972) 30 N.Y.2d 93, 330 N.Y.S.2d 371, 281 N.E.2d 171

Agreement between sister and brother, as major shareholders of closely held corporation, providing that brother would exercise voting rights over shares owned by both parties "with respect to any and all matters relating to...day-to-day operations and corporate management" conferred on brother right to vote sister's shares in election of board of directors, since management of corporation's business was, under authority of CLS Bus Corp § 701, exclusively under direction of its board of directors; different result was not required by other provisions of agreement reciting that parties agreed to vote their shares to ensure sister seat on board of directors, to ensure sister access to corporate reports, and to place cap on brother's executive compensation. Ronnen v Ajax Elec. Motor Corp. (1996) 88 N.Y.2d 582, 648 N.Y.S.2d 422, 671 N.E.2d 534

Agreements precluding directors from exercising discretion and judgment in the discharge of their duties are void and against public policy. Glekel v Gluck (1971, 1st Dept) 37 A.D.2d 1, 321 N.Y.S.2d 956, revd on other grounds 30 N.Y.2d 93, 330 N.Y.S.2d 371, 281 N.E.2d 171

No contract can bind directors to predestined corporate action or policy, irrespective of their own judgment and discretion. Glekel v Gluck (1971, 1st Dept) 37 A.D.2d 1, 321 N.Y.S.2d 956, revd on other grounds 30 N.Y.2d 93, 330 N.Y.S.2d 371, 281 N.E.2d 171

Provisions of an agreement restricting the management from risking the last $15,000 of the working capital and preventing the board from reappointing administrative directors after they had resigned without first obtaining the consent of certain persons, if in violation of § 27 of former Gen. Corp. L., constituted so slight an infringement as to be innocuous. Simonson v Helburn (1950) 198 Misc 430, 97 N.Y.S.2d 406

Where a contract provided that, at the end of a corporate fiscal year, before the declaration of any dividends there should be paid to each of the parties thereto a salary and equal share of the net earnings and also that the individual plaintiff would personally guarantee payment by corporation to defendant of 50 per cent of net earnings of the corporation and that salaries of the parties should be in such amount as might from time to time be authorized by a resolution of the board of directors, did not violate § 27 of former Gen. Corp. L. because it did not deprive the board of directors of their powers of management. Slonim v Brodie (1951, Sup) 109 N.Y.S.2d 440, affd 281 A.D. 861, 119 N.Y.S.2d 916

Limited liability companies were improperly granted partial summary judgment as to the validity of letter agreements with a corporation because provisions of the contract requiring directors of the corporation to select and maintain certain individuals as corporate officers were void as they violated N.Y. Bus. Corp. Law § 701 and factual issues remained as to whether the illegal provisions actually restricted the board of directors and whether other provisions of the agreements could survive the illegal provisions. Torvec, Inc. v CXO on Go of Del., LLC (2007, 4th Dept) 38 App Div 3d 1175, 831 NYS2d 800, subsequent app (2007, 4th Dept) 38 App Div 3d 1177 and subsequent app (2007, 4th Dept) 38 App Div 3d 1177

6. Judicial review

Authorization of a particular corporate act by the board of directors, if made in their considered opinion that it is in the best interests of the corporation, and fair to the corporation, will not be interfered with by the courts. Barr v Wackman (1975) 36 N.Y.2d 371, 368 N.Y.S.2d 497, 329 N.E.2d 180, 99 ALR3d 1023

Business judgment rule prohibits judicial inquiry into actions of corporate directors taken in good faith and in exercise of honest judgment in lawful and legitimate furtherance of corporate purposes; so long as directors have not breached their fiduciary obligation to corporation, exercise of their powers for common and general interests of corporation may not be questioned, even if results show that what they did was unwise or inexpedient. Levandusky v One Fifth Ave. Apartment Corp. (1990) 75 N.Y.2d 530, 554 N.Y.S.2d 807, 553 N.E.2d 1317

Action by board of directors of corporation that comes within business judgment rule cannot be characterized as arbitrary and capricious, or abuse of discretion, for purpose of Article 78 proceeding. Levandusky v One Fifth Ave. Apartment Corp. (1990) 75 N.Y.2d 530, 554 N.Y.S.2d 807, 553 N.E.2d 1317

Decision of publicly-traded corporation and its future purchaser to wait until close of markets when negotiations were complete and agreement was final before publicly announcing that major new deal had been struck fell within business judgment rule, absent allegations or showing of some countervailing misconduct or manipulation, and thus shareholders' complaint against corporation alleging breach of fiduciary duty in not revealing agreement would fail. Lindner Fund v Waldbaum, Inc. (1993) 82 N.Y.2d 219, 604 N.Y.S.2d 32, 624 N.E.2d 160

The soundness or wisdom of judgment of the board of directors of a private corporation will not be judicially reviewed where there is neither bad faith nor fraud. Accordingly, a court of equity will not restrain paying of property dividend by defendant through distribution of stock of another corporation held by defendant, where the only evidence of bad faith on the part of the directors is that a result of the distribution of stock will be to deprive minority stockholders of defendant of power to elect two directors of the corporation whose stock it holds. Liebman v Auto Strop Co. (1925) 212 A.D. 306, 208 N.Y.S. 589, affd 241 N.Y. 427, 150 N.E. 505

Evidence failed to show that the sale of a corporation's nonfranchise assets were at a grossly inadequate price or that the directors acted in the transaction otherwise than conscientiously and in the best interests of the corporation, and further failed to establish that any director acted in self-interest or in a dual capacity in the transaction. Greenbaum v American Metal Climax, Inc. (1967, 1st Dept) 27 A.D.2d 225, 278 N.Y.S.2d 123

In action seeking declaration that corporate resolution which provided for discontinuance of eviction proceeding commenced in Justice Court was validly adopted by board of directors and binding on defendant, it was error for Supreme Court to dismiss complaint on ground that eviction proceeding was in nature of shareholder's derivative claim immune from board action, and to direct parties to litigate issues raised by defendant's counterclaim in Justice Court, as such ruling essentially determined that resolution was properly adopted procedurally, while referring defendant's substantive challenges to Justice Court, which was beyond Justice Court's subject matter jurisdiction. TJI Realty, Inc. v Harris (1998, 2d Dept) 250 A.D.2d 596, 672 N.Y.S.2d 386

Residential cooperative corporation's alleged wrongful withdrawal of approval for alterations to plaintiffs' apartment was not valid exercise of discretion protected by business judgment rule, as plaintiffs sought to enforce specific rights granted to them by approved alteration agreement and, while it may be good business judgment to walk away from contract, this is no defense to breach of contract claim. Whalen v 50 Sutton Place S. Owners, Inc. (2000, 1st Dept) 276 A.D.2d 356, 714 N.Y.S.2d 269

7. Liability for unauthorized acts

Decision of State Division of Housing and Community Renewal (DHCR) would not be annulled, in Article 78 proceeding, where there was substantial evidence that petitioner, in her capacity as president of corporation's board of directors, violated CLS Bus Corp § 701, CLS Priv Hous Fin § 32(1), and 9 NYCRR § 1738-1.3, hearing was fair in both its conduct and outcome, and DHCR did not violate rules that it promulgated to ensure fair adjudication in agency possessing both prosecutorial and adjudicative power. Hazell v New York State Div. of Hous. & Community Renewal (1998, 1st Dept) 251 A.D.2d 132, 673 N.Y.S.2d 311, app den 92 N.Y.2d 812, 680 N.Y.S.2d 905, 703 N.E.2d 763

Corporation was not liable on its guaranty where it was not made in connection with its exercise of corporate powers, or in connection with the negotiation of an obligation owned by it, and the guarantor corporation did not directly or indirectly own at least a majority of the voting shares of the principal corporation, and the guaranty was not approved by a resolution of the Board of Directors of the defendant corporation or by its stockholders. Rusch & Co. v Syndicate First Corp. (1956) 7 Misc. 2d 198, 155 N.Y.S.2d 369

§ 702.   Number of directors

(a) The board of directors shall consist of one or more members. The number of directors constituting the board may be fixed by the by-laws, or by action of the shareholders or of the board under the specific provisions of a by-law adopted by the shareholders. If not otherwise fixed under this paragraph, the number shall be one. As used in this article, "entire board" means the total number of directors which the corporation would have if there were no vacancies.

(b) The number of directors may be increased or decreased by amendment of the by-laws, or by action of the shareholders or of the board under the specific provisions of a by-law adopted by the shareholders, subject to the following limitations:

(1) If the board is authorized by the by-laws to change the number of directors, whether by amending the by-laws or by taking action under the specific provisions of a by-law adopted by the shareholders, such amendment or action shall require the vote of a majority of the entire board.

(2) No decrease shall shorten the term of any incumbent director.

History: Add, L 1961, ch 855; amd, L 1962, ch 834, § 45, eff Sept 1, 1963; L 1965, ch 803, § 26, eff Sept 1, 1965; L 1997, ch 449, § 38, eff Feb 22, 1998.

CASE ANNOTATIONS

A provision in the certificate of incorporation of a corporation organized under the earlier "Business Corporation Law," fixing number of directors at four, with number not subject to change except by unanimous stockholder consent, was upheld as authorized by § 13 of former Gen. Corp. L. and not in conflict with § 26 of former Stock Corp. L. Ripin v Atlantic Mercantile Co. (1912) 205 N.Y. 442, 98 N.E. 855

Where 6 shareholders of respondent corporation conducted business as though 6 of them constituted board of directors, but bylaws remained silent on number of directors, CLS Business Corporation Law § 702 governs and board thereby, comprised 3 members; consequently, 3 individual respondent shareholders, acting as lawful § 603(b) quorum of shareholders, filled all directorships at special meeting when they elected themselves to corporate board and, because number of directors was already fixed by operation of statutory law at 3, no § 608 quorum consisting of holders of majority of shares was necessary to "reduce" size of board to that number. Re Rye Psychiatric Hospital Center, Inc. (1985) 66 N.Y.2d 333, 497 N.Y.S.2d 317, 488 N.E.2d 63

Business Corporation Law does not permit number of directors constituting corporate board to be determined by custom, usage and acquiescence absent governing provision in corporate bylaws; pursuant to CLS Business Corporation Law § 702(a), where corporate bylaws make no provision whatsoever for size of board of directors, number thereof shall be 3; where corporation has no governing bylaw whatsoever, deviation from number of directors explicitly fixed by statute could only be effectuated by proper enactment by shareholders of statutorily requisite bylaw. Re Rye Psychiatric Hospital Center, Inc. (1985) 66 N.Y.2d 333, 497 N.Y.S.2d 317, 488 N.E.2d 63

Under § 14 of former Gen. Corp. L., a by-law attempting to restrict right of majority shareholders to increase the number of directors by amending the certificate of incorporation was considered invalid. Christal v Petry (1949) 275 A.D. 550, 90 N.Y.S.2d 620, affd 301 N.Y. 562, 93 N.E.2d 450

Where a resolution adopted by stockholders at an annual meeting increases the number of directors from four to five, but such action on the part of stockholders contravenes a bylaw providing that directors shall have the power to increase their own number when stockholders are not assembled in a meeting, the action taken by the stockholders is invalid as against the bylaw. Model, Roland & Co. v Industrial Acoustics Co. (1964, 1st Dept) 21 A.D.2d 70, 248 N.Y.S.2d 387, affd 16 N.Y.2d 703, 261 N.Y.S.2d 896, 209 N.E.2d 533

Complaint stated cause of action for breach of agreement between two sole stockholders of "incorporated partnership" that each would vote at stockholders' and directors' meetings so that the board of directors would consist of these two sole stockholders both of whom would be necessary to constitute a quorum for the transaction of business. Shubin v Surchin (1967, 1st Dept) 27 A.D.2d 452, 280 N.Y.S.2d 55

Since the legislature wanted to protect directors from an undue involuntary shortening of the term for which they were elected, § 702(b)(2) provides for the prevention of the precipitous removal of a director by the ruse of reducing the number of directors, although a director may still be removed for cause before the end of his term. Re Unexcelled, Inc. (1967, 1st Dist) 28 A.D.2d 44, 281 N.Y.S.2d 173

President/treasurer of 2-man corporation lacked authority to bring action on behalf of corporation against vice-president/secretary to terminate latter's employment contract and recover amount of compensation and fringe benefits provided to him after his receipt of disability benefits where each man owned 50 percent of stock, and thus, by implication from CLS Bus Corp §§ 701 and 702(a), deadlock could not be remedied by exercise of presidential power, and proper remedy was shareholder's derivative action. Stone v Frederick (1997, 3d Dept) 245 A.D.2d 742, 666 N.Y.S.2d 294

The stockholders could elect the additional directors where an increase in the number of directors was authorized, whether the authorization was contained in the by-laws, an amendment thereto, or by amendment of the charter. Fierman v Rose (1940) 175 Misc 102, 22 N.Y.S.2d 215

In the absence of a provision in the certificate of incorporation requiring unanimous consent of all stockholders to an increase in number of directors, a majority could amend the certificate to increase the number notwithstanding this would impair effectiveness of an oral agreement between existing directors, the validity of which as between the parties had been judicially upheld. Ripley v Storer

(1955) 1 Misc. 2d 281, 139 N.Y.S.2d 786, affd 286 A.D. 844, 142 N.Y.S.2d 269, mod on other grounds 309 N.Y. 506, 132 N.E.2d 87, motion to vacate den 309 N.Y. 976, 132 N.E.2d 335

This section's sanctioning of establishment of one-man corporations is in accord with decisions already recognizing the propriety of incorporation of closely held corporations as a shelter from personal liability and for the doing of an act permitted for a corporation but forbidden to an individual. Alfred P. Sloan Foundation, Inc. v Atlas (1964) 42 Misc. 2d 603, 248 N.Y.S.2d 524, affd 23 A.D.2d 820, 258 N.Y.S.2d 807

Retailing company did not violate N.Y. Bus Corp Law § 702(b)(2), where company reduced number of directors from 15 to 10 effective at its annual stockholders meeting, because § 702(b)(2) prohibits involuntary shortening of director's term and each of the five directors to be eliminated had resigned voluntarily prior to meeting. Re Sears, Roebuck & Co. Secur. Litigation (1992, ED Pa) 792 F. Supp. 977, CCH Fed Secur L Rep ¶ 96959

Section 5 of former Stock Corp. L. required a minimum of three directors, without exception. 1955 Ops Atty Gen Aug 4 (informal)

§ 703. Election and term of directors

(a) At each annual meeting of shareholders, directors shall be elected to hold office until the next annual meeting except as authorized by section 704 (Classification of directors). The certificate of incorporation may provide for the election of one or more directors by the holders of the shares of any class or series, or by the holders of bonds entitled to vote in the election of directors pursuant to section 518 (Corporate bonds), voting as a class.

(b) Each director shall hold office until the expiration of the term for which he is elected, and until his successor has been elected and qualified.

History: Add, L 1961, ch 855, eff Sept 1, 1963; amd, L 1962, ch 834, § 46, eff Sept 1, 1963.

CASE ANNOTATIONS

Election of directors could be directly challanged under § 25 of former Gen. Corp. L., and either confirmed or set aside as justice required, in like manner as authorized by § 619 of this law. Re Lake Placid Co. (1948) 274 A.D. 205, 81 N.Y.S.2d 36

An order setting aside the election of directors on March 21, 1967, and directing that a new election be held on July 12, was reversed, where the corporate bylaws provided that the directors could in their discretion hold an annual meeting no later than the fourth Wednesday of July, notwithstanding that the directors had been elected on July 12, 1966 and had voluntarily chosen to shorten their own terms of office. Re Unexcelled, Inc. (1967, 1st Dept) 28 A.D.2d 44, 281 N.Y.S.2d 173

In the absence of a showing that a successor to the director had been elected, the director of a corporation continued as director and had an absolute right to inspect the books and records of the corporation barring a claim of circumstance that his action was inimical to the interests of the corporation; furthermore, the director was entitled to inspect the books and records where it was a close corporation and he owned one-third of the shares. Griffin v Varflex Corp. (1980, 4th Dept) 79 A.D.2d 857, 434 N.Y.S.2d 488

Pursuant to corporate by-laws providing that special meetings of board of directors could be held only on prior notice given in accordance with by-laws, board meeting held immediately after special meeting of shareholders which was initiated by written notice to shareholders was improperly convened, and election of officers and board chairman conducted at meeting was void, since no prior notice of board meeting itself had been given to directors. Shevlin v National Conservation Corp. (1993, 4th Dept) 199 A.D.2d 995, 605 N.Y.S.2d 593

An agreement between the holders of all the stock in a corporation to vote their stock so as to retain themselves as directors, officers and employees for life, conditioned upon faithful performance of duties, is valid. Martocci v Martocci (1943) 2 Misc. 2d 330, 42 N.Y.S.2d 222, affd 266 A.D. 840, 43 N.Y.S.2d 516, app den 266 A.D. 917, 43 N.Y.S.2d 517

Although this section provides for election of directors "at each annual meeting" of shareholders, similar earlier provisions were not construed as precluding election of directors at a special meeting called for that purpose in accordance with the by-laws, if not annual meeting was held or no directors were elected at such meeting. Petition of Stylemaster Dept. Store, Inc. (1956) 7 Misc. 2d 207, 154 N.Y.S.2d 58

If the notice of meeting of shareholders at which directors are purportedly elected fails to meet statutory or by-law requirements, authority of the newly-elected directors is, of course, subject to challenge and their participation in action taken by the board as reconstituted may invalidate that action. Janaug, Inc. v Szlapka (1957) 6 Misc. 2d 84, 162 N.Y.S.2d 668

The provision in this section for holding office after expiration of the term for which a director is elected, and until a successor has been elected and qualified, is not new, a similar provision having appeared in § 21 of former Gen. Corp. L. Martoccia v Cardinal Agency, Inc. (1960) 24 Misc. 2d 1095, 204 N.Y.S.2d 426

Section 27 of former Gen. Corp. L. provided that if any by-law regulating an impending election of directors was adopted, amended, or repealed by the board of directors, notice of the next meeting of stockholders must so state. Its purpose was said to be to enable stockholders to ratify or disaffirm the by-law change and thus prevent directors in control from perpetuating themselves in office contrary to wishes of the majority of stockholders. Re Scharf (1961) 28 Misc. 2d 869, 216 N.Y.S.2d 775, mod and remitted for trial of all issues (2d Dept) 15 A.D.2d 563, 223 N.Y.S.2d 307

Election of corporate directors at annual shareholders meeting, conducted by insurgent shareholders at corporation's office after chairman designated to preside at scheduled meeting adjourned it to later date due to inadequacy of space at office to accommodate number of shareholders who showed up, would not be confirmed due to numerous irregularities, including failure to ascertain identity and eligibility of voters and failure to elect directors by ballot as required by corporation's bylaws. Jordan v Allegany Co-Op Ins. Co. (1990) 147 Misc. 2d 768, 558 N.Y.S.2d 806

Shareholder, who participated in and voted as director at board meeting at which chairman to preside at annual meeting of shareholders was designated, waived right to object to action taken at meeting and hence to designated chairman's approval. Jordan v Allegany Co-Op Ins. Co. (1990) 147 Misc. 2d 768, 558 N.Y.S.2d 806

An election at which less than one fourth of the directors were elected, as required by § 55 of former Stock Corp. L. would not be set aside some two or more years after the illegal election took place, since such relief was barred by laches. Re Empire Title & Guarantee Co. (1947, Sup) 73 N.Y.S.2d 84

A hold-over director retains the same right to inspect corporate records as he had during the term for which he was elected. Application of Goldman (1960, Sup) 207 N.Y.S.2d 309, app dismd (1st Dept) 10 A.D.2d 915, 203 N.Y.S.2d 1002

1930 resolutions of shareholders permitting directors to be elected by a plurality vote were contrary to law as it then existed and against state public policy as in violation of this section at the time of their adoption. Globe Slicing Machine Co. v Hasner (1963, SD NY) 223 F. Supp. 589, affd (CA2 NY) 333 F.2d 413, cert den 379 US 969, 13 L Ed 2d 562, 85 S Ct 666

§ 704. Classification of directors

(a) The certificate of incorporation or the specific provisions of a by-law adopted by the shareholders may provide that the directors be divided into either two, three or four classes. All classes shall be as nearly equal in number as possible. The terms of office of the directors initially classified shall be as follows: that of the first class shall expire at the next annual meeting of shareholders, the second class at the second succeeding annual meeting, the third class, if any, at the third succeeding annual meeting, and the fourth class, if any, at the fourth succeeding annual meeting.

(b) At each annual meeting after such initial classification, directors to replace those whose terms expire at such annual meeting shall be elected to hold office until the second succeeding annual meeting if there are two classes, the third succeeding annual meeting if there are three classes, or the fourth succeeding annual meeting if there are four classes.

(c) If directors are classified and the number of directors is thereafter changed:

(1) Any newly created directorships or any decrease in directorships shall be so apportioned among the classes as to make all classes as nearly equal in number as possible.

(2) When the number of directors is increased by the board and any newly created directorships are filled by the board, there shall be no classification of the additional directors until the next annual meeting of shareholders.

History: Add, L 1961, ch 855, eff Sept 1, 1963; amd, L 1962, ch 834, § 47, eff Sept 1, 1963; L 1997, ch 449, § 39, eff Feb 22, 1998.

CASE ANNOTATIONS

Section 55 of former Stock Corp. L. contained a provision that "at least one fourth" in numbers of the directors must be elected annually, which was designed to prevent any director from holding office for more than four years without renewed stockholder approval and to "stagger" terms of directors. Re Empire Title & Guarantee Co. (1947, Sup) 73 N.Y.S.2d 84; Wyatt v Armstrong (1945) 186 Misc 216, 59 N.Y.S.2d 502

§ 705. Newly created directorships and vacancies

(a) Newly created directorships resulting from an increase in the number of directors and vacancies occurring in the board for any reason except the removal of directors without cause may be filled by vote of the board. If the number of the directors then in office is less than a quorum, such newly created directorships and vacancies may be filled by vote of a majority of the directors then in office. Nothing in this paragraph shall affect any provision of the certificate of incorporation or the by-laws which provides that such newly created directorships or vacancies shall be filled by vote of the shareholders, or any provision of the certificate of incorporation specifying greater requirements as permitted under section 709 (Greater requirements as to quorum and vote of directors).

(b) Unless the certificate of incorporation or the specific provisions of a by-law adopted by the shareholders provide that the board may fill vacancies occurring in the board by reason of the removal of directors without cause, such vacancies may be filled only by vote of the shareholders.

(c) A director elected to fill a vacancy, unless elected by the shareholders, shall hold office until the next meeting of shareholders at which the election of directors is in the regular order of business, and until his successor has been elected and qualified.

(d) Unless otherwise provided in the certificate of incorporation or by-laws, notwithstanding the provisions of paragraphs (a) and (b) of this section, whenever the holders of any class or classes of shares or series thereof are entitled to elect one or more directors by the certificate of incorporation, any vacancy that may be filled by the board or a majority of the directors then in office, as the case may be, shall be filled by a majority of the directors elected by such class or classes or series thereof then in office, or, if no such director is in office, then as provided in paragraph (a) or (b) of this section, as the case may be.

History: Add, L 1961, ch 855, eff Sept 1, 1963; amd, L 1962, ch 834, § 48, eff Sept 1, 1963; L 1965, ch 803, § 27, eff Sept 1, 1965; L 1971, ch 768, eff Sept 1, 1971; L 1972, ch 462, eff Sept 1, 1972; L 1997, ch 449, § 40, eff Feb 22, 1998.

CASE ANNOTATIONS

Because only two directors constituted the entire board, the board member remaining after the resignation of the other was authorized to appoint a second director to fill the vacancy; under the circumstances, the single director constituted a "majority." Matter of McDaniel v 162 Columbia Hgts. Housing Corp., 2009 NY Slip Op 29047 (Kings Cty Sup Ct February 3, 2009).

Where corporate by-laws provided that vacancies in the board of directors could be filled by the directors in office, a vote of two of the three directors in office was sufficient to fill a vacancy on the board despite a charter and by-law provision that a quorum should consist of 75 percent of the directors and the votes of 75 percent of the directors were necessary for the transaction of business. Jacobson v Moskowitz (1970) 27 N.Y.2d 67, 313 N.Y.S.2d 684, 261 N.E.2d 613

Under § 27 of former General Corp. L., vacancies on the board of directors were to be filled as the by-laws might provide, subject to statutory limitations. Gearing v Kelly (1961, 1st Dept) 15 A.D.2d 219, 222 N.Y.S.2d 474, affd 11 N.Y.2d 201, 227 N.Y.S.2d 897, 182 N.E.2d 391

Subdivision (a) of this section provides that vacancies on the Board of Directors may be filled by vote of a majority of those remaining in office unless the bylaws provide that vacancies shall be filled by stockholders, and bylaws cannot be said to require filling of vacancies by stockholders where they do not so specifically require and merely relate to what constitutes a quorum of directors and what quorum is necessary for doing business. Petition of Caplan (1964, 1st Dept) 20 A.D.2d 301, 246 N.Y.S.2d 913, affd 14 N.Y.2d 679, 249 N.Y.S.2d 877, 198 N.E.2d 908

Where a court orders removal of directors in a proceeding under § 619, it should not order their continuance in office until new directors may be elected by the stockholders in the absence of a corporate bylaw requiring filling of vacancies on the Board of Directors by stockholders, notwithstanding removal of the directors will result in less than a quorum remaining on the Board, as subd. (a) of this section does not require a quorum of directors to make vacancy appointments in such case. Petition of Caplan (1964, 1st Dept) 20 A.D.2d 301, 246 N.Y.S.2d 913, affd 14 N.Y.2d 679, 249 N.Y.S.2d 877, 198 N.E.2d 908

In an action brought by shareholders alleging that they were entitled, pursuant to a shareholders' agreement, to designate a successor director in the place of their prior designee, who resigned both as a director and the holder of an irrevocable proxy, the agreement having entitled plaintiffs to designate a successive proxy holder but having made no provision for the procedure to be employed in the filling of a vacancy on the board of directors, the plaintiff shareholders were not entitled to designate a successor director in the place of their prior designee since the question of whether an ambiguity exists must be ascertained from the face of the agreement without regard to extrinsic evidence, and when the board of directors selected their own successor to fill the vacancy, the action was not interdicted by any language in the shareholders' agreement but was consisted with the authority vested in their remaining directors by Bus Corp Law §§ 602(b), 705. Schmidt v Magnetic Head Corp. (1983, 2d Dept) 97 A.D.2d 151, 468 N.Y.S.2d 649

Section 55 of former Stock Corp. L. looked to filling vacancies on the board by the remaining directors only where a vacancy resulted from death, resignation, removal, or the like, and reduced the required membership. Fierman v Rose (1940) 175 Misc 102, 22 N.Y.S.2d 215

Where a member of a corporate board died, and the two remaining directors constituted a quorum, they could elect a temporary director to fill the vacancy by their joint action without preliminary notice or the other usual formalities. Jacobs v Ostow & Jacobs, Inc. (1959) 20 Misc. 2d 655, 194 N.Y.S.2d 164

Vacancies occurring in a corporation board of directors by reason of resignations may be filled by a majority of the directors then in office, notwithstanding the absence of a quorum. Avien, Inc. v Weiss (1966) 50 Misc. 2d 127, 269 N.Y.S.2d 836

Where owners of a class of stock were entitled under the terms of its issuance to elect two out of six directors, one who owned all such stock outstanding was entitled to fill a vacancy brought about by her own resignation as director by simply filing a certificate designating her successor, without the formality of a meeting, and the corporation was bound to recognize the successor upon his consent to acceptance of the post. Wohl v Avon Electrical Supplies, Inc. (1945, Sup) 55 N.Y.S.2d 252

§ 706.   Removal of directors

(a) Any or all of the directors may be removed for cause by vote of the shareholders. The certificate of incorporation or the specific provisions of a by-law adopted by the shareholders may provide for such removal by action of the board, except in the case of any director elected by cumulative voting, or by the holders of the shares of any class or series, or holders of bonds, voting as a class, when so entitled by the provisions of the certificate of incorporation.

(b) If the certificate of incorporation or the by-laws so provide, any or all of the directors may be removed without cause by vote of the shareholders.

(c) The removal of directors, with or without cause, as provided in paragraphs (a) and (b) is subject to the following:

(1) In the case of a corporation having cumulative voting, no director may be removed when the votes cast against his removal would be sufficient to elect him if voted cumulatively at an election at which the same total number of votes were cast and the entire board, or the entire class of directors of which he is a member, were then being elected; and

(2) When by the provisions of the certificate of incorporation the holders of the shares of any class or series, or holders of bonds, voting as a class, are entitled to elect one or more directors, any director so elected may be removed only by the applicable vote of the holders of the shares of that class or series, or the holders of such bonds, voting as a class.

(d) An action to procure a judgment removing a director for cause may be brought by the attorney-general or by the holders of ten percent of the outstanding shares, whether or not entitled to vote. The court may bar from re-election any director so removed for a period fixed by the court.

History: Add, L 1961, ch 855, eff Sept 1, 1963; amd, L 1962, ch 834, §§ 49, 50; L 1963, ch 689, § 1, eff Sept 1, 1963.

CASE ANNOTATIONS

1. In general
2. For cause
3. Without cause
4. Special meeting

1. In general

Since the legislature wanted to protect directors from an undue involuntary shortening of the term for which they were elected, § 702(b)(2) provides for the prevention of the precipitous removal of a director by the ruse of reducing the number of directors, although a director may still be removed for cause before the end of his term. In re Unexcelled, Inc., 28 A.D.2d 44, 281 N.Y.S.2d 173, 1967 N.Y. App. Div. LEXIS 3659 (N.Y. App. Div. 1st Dep't 1967).

The procedure laid down in the certificate of incorporation or the by-laws must be followed before the removal of a director without cause may be affected. In re Laser Tech, Inc., 35 A.D.2d 994, 317 N.Y.S.2d 853, 1970 N.Y. App. Div. LEXIS 3053 (N.Y. App. Div. 2d Dep't 1970).

Where certificate of incorporation and bylaws were not included in record on appeal, evaluation of their applicability to petitioner's removal as director could not be made and case would therefore be remitted for further proceedings by way of motion or trial concerning validity of petitioner's removal in light of application of Business Corporation Law sections relating to removal of directors by shareholders and to agreement among shareholders as to voting rights. Springut v Don & Bob Restaurants, Inc., 57 A.D.2d 302, 394 N.Y.S.2d 971, 1977 N.Y. App. Div. LEXIS 10960 (N.Y. App. Div. 4th Dep't 1977).

Trial court properly determined that purported elections to elect a board of directors were not valid and directed a new special shareholders' meeting be held and supervised by a referee, where the meeting was held after the parties entered into an on-the-record stipulation in an earlier action in which they agreed that all four shareholders were to serve as directors. Further, the bylaws provided that a board member could be removed only upon a vote of a majority of the directors or shareholders, and it was undisputed that a majority of the directors or shareholders did not vote for the removal. Wynkoop v 622A President St. Owners Corp., 2019 N.Y. App. Div. LEXIS 1369 (N.Y. App. Div. 2d Dep't 2019).

A corporation was not entitled to a declaratory judgment in respect of a clear and unambiguous agreement between officers, directors and stockholders providing for the unanimous consent for the removal of any officer or director. Jos. H. Carter, Inc. v Carter, 127 N.Y.S.2d 518, 205 Misc. 192, 1953 N.Y. Misc. LEXIS 2572 (N.Y. Sup. Ct. 1953), aff'd, 283 A.D. 858, 129 N.Y.S.2d 898, 1954 N.Y. App. Div. LEXIS 5532 (N.Y. App. Div. 1954).

A proceeding to annual action of stockholders in removing a director was not the proper method of seeking to enforce an agreement that he was to be retained in office as long as he or his designee was a stockholder. However, a petition for such relief may be sufficient as matter of pleading and as against a motion to dismiss. Teperman v Atcos Baths, Inc., 6 Misc. 2d 162, 163 N.Y.S.2d 221, 1957 N.Y. Misc. LEXIS 3078 (N.Y. Sup. Ct. 1957), aff'd, 7 A.D.2d 854, 182 N.Y.S.2d 765, 1959 N.Y. App. Div. LEXIS 10347 (N.Y. App. Div. 2d Dep't 1959).

2. For cause

Notwithstanding that a shareholders' agreement requires maintenance in office of a particular director designated by a stockholder, director may be removed for cause since implicit in any agreement to maintain a particular director in office is director's duty to fulfill faithfully the requirements of his office. Springut v Don & Bob Restaurants, Inc., 57 A.D.2d 302, 394 N.Y.S.2d 971, 1977 N.Y. App. Div. LEXIS 10960 (N.Y. App. Div. 4th Dep't 1977).

Dismissal of a former director's claim that he was improperly removed from a corporation's board of directors upon the issuance of a security slip violation was error because N.Y. Bus. Corp. Law §§ 706, 708, and the corporation's by-laws provided for a board member's removal only upon a vote of a majority of the corporation's shareholders. Chaudhry v Vital Holding Co. of NY, Inc., 51 A.D.3d 844, 858 N.Y.S.2d 740, 2008 N.Y. App. Div. LEXIS 4400 (N.Y. App. Div. 2d Dep't 2008).

3. Without cause

The effect of Business Corporation Law § 614, subdivision (b) is to provide a rule of procedure of voting if no different procedure is otherwise permitted by the Business Corporation Law or the certificate of incorporation and since Business Corporation Law § 706, in the case of the removal of a director without cause, permits the provisions of the by-laws to control, Business Corporation Law § 614, subdivision (b) does not apply. In re Laser Tech, Inc., 35 A.D.2d 994, 317 N.Y.S.2d 853, 1970 N.Y. App. Div. LEXIS 3053 (N.Y. App. Div. 2d Dep't 1970).

It was held under earlier provisions that an amendment of the certificate of incorporation by vote of stockholders to provide for cumulative voting for directors invalidated a by-law whereby a director could be removed without cause by majority vote of the stockholders. In re Rogers Imports, Inc., 116 N.Y.S.2d 106, 202 Misc. 761, 1952 N.Y. Misc. LEXIS 1820 (N.Y. Sup. Ct. 1952).

4. Special meeting

Where the by-laws of a corporation required the president to call a special meeting whenever requested in writing to do so by stockholders owning a majority of capital stock entitled to vote at such a meeting, the president could be required to hold such a meeting at the request of 55% of the holders of one class of the voting stock for the purpose of endorsing the administration of a former president, to amend the charter and by-laws to provide that vacancies caused by the removal or resignation of directors shall be filled only by the stockholders theretofore represented by the removed or resigned directors and to hear charges against four of the directors representing that class of stock and to remove them if the charges be proven. Auer v Dressel, 306 N.Y. 427, 118 N.E.2d 590, 306 N.Y. (N.Y.S.) 427, 1954 N.Y. LEXIS 1024 (N.Y. 1954).

§ 707. Quorum of directors

Unless a greater proportion is required by the certificate of incorporation, a majority of the entire board shall constitute a quorum for the transaction of business or of any specified item of business, except that the certificate of incorporation or the by-laws may fix the quorum at less than a majority of the entire board but not less than one-third thereof.

History: Add, L 1961, ch 855, eff Sept 1, 1963.

CASE ANNOTATIONS

Reading together § 27 and § 28 of former Gen. Corp. L. and examining their legislative history, the court concluded that there never was legislative intent so to change the common-law rule as to quorums as to authorize a by-law requiring unanimous vote of directors. Benintendi v Kenton Hotel, Inc. (1945) 294 N.Y. 112, 60 N.E.2d 829 (superseded by statute as stated in Application of Burkin, 1 N.Y.2d 570, 154 N.Y.S.2d 898, 136 N.E.2d 862, 64 ALR2d 638)

Sections 27 and 28 of former Gen. Corp. L. did not forbid a by-law requiring a two-thirds' vote of a quorum of directors. Re Lake Placid Co. (1948) 274 A.D. 205, 81 N.Y.S.2d 36

A by-law provision that a "majority of the directors shall constitute a quorum" is ambiguous as to whether the reference is to a majority of the remaining directors in case of a vacancy or to a majority of the authorized number of members, but where other by-law provisions indicate a distinction between action which can only be taken by a majority of the "whole" board, or by a certain fraction of the whole board, it can be implied that in instances where the whole board is not called for the "board" consists of the directors actually in office. Gearing v Kelly (1961, 1st Dept) 15 A.D.2d 219, 222 N.Y.S.2d 474, affd 11 N.Y.2d 201, 227 N.Y.S.2d 897, 182 N.E.2d 391

Where three of six shareholder-directors entitled to vote attended a special shareholders' meeting, there existed a sufficient quorum to elect themselves to new terms as three of the six directors, and the election of only three directors did not render such election void, but there was an insufficient quorum to effect a change in the number of directors constituting the entire board from six to three; however, since the newly elected directors were not sufficient in number to constitute a quorum of the board under the corporate by-laws or Bus Corp Law § 707 for the purpose of electing themselves corporate officers, said elections would be set aside. Rye Psychiatric Center, Inc. v Schoenholtz (1984, 2d Dept) 101 A.D.2d 309, 476 N.Y.S.2d 339

Section 9 of former Stock Corp. L. was deemed to authorize such provisions in a certificate of incorporation as a requirement that all directors must be present to constitute a quorum for doing business at a directors' meeting and must vote unanimously in favor of any action to be taken, and similar provisions as to presence and unanimous voting by all shareholders at shareholders' meetings. Re Application of Venice Amusement Corp. (1961) 32 Misc. 2d 122, 222 N.Y.S.2d 889

Vacancies occurring in a corporation board of directors by reason of resignations may be filled by a majority of the directors then in office, notwithstanding the absence of a quorum. Avien, Inc. v Weiss (1966) 50 Misc. 2d 127, 269 N.Y.S.2d 836

A corporate charter provision for election of two directors by each of three classes of stock, and a provision that five of the six directors constituted a quorum, was not illegal or inequitable. Wohl v Avon Electrical Supplies, Inc. (1945, Sup) 55 N.Y.S.2d 252

It appears to be the legislative intent that a board of directors can act by a majority of a quorum, irrespective of the number of other directors who may merely be present at the meeting. Crowley v Commodity Exchange, Inc. (1944, CA2 NY) 141 F.2d 182

§ 708.   Action by the board

(a) Except as otherwise provided in this chapter, any reference in this chapter to corporate action to be taken by the board shall mean such action at a meeting of the board.

(b) Unless otherwise restricted by the certificate of incorporation or the by-laws, any action required or permitted to be taken by the board or any committee thereof may be taken without a meeting if all members of the board or the committee consent in writing to the adoption of a resolution authorizing the action. The resolution and the written consents thereto by the members of the board or committee shall be filed with the minutes of the proceedings of the board or committee.

(c) Unless otherwise restricted by the certificate of incorporation or the by-laws, any one or more members of the board or any committee thereof may participate in a meeting of such board or committee by means of a conference telephone or similar communications equipment allowing all persons participating in the meeting to hear each other at the same time. Participation by such means shall constitute presence in person at a meeting.

(d) Except as otherwise provided in this chapter, the vote of a majority of the directors present at the time of the vote, if a quorum is present at such time, shall be the act of the board.

History: Add, L 1961, ch 855, eff Sept 1, 1963; amd, L 1974, ch 517, eff Sept 1, 1974; L 1975, ch 227, eff Sept 1, 1975; L 1977, ch 296, eff June 21, 1977; L 1997, ch 449, § 41, eff Feb 22, 1998.

CASE ANNOTATIONS

Reading together § 27 and § 28 of former Gen. Corp. L. and examining their legislative history, the court concluded that there never was legislative intent so to change the common-law rule as to quorums as to authorize a by-law requiring unanimous vote of directors. Benintendi v Kenton Hotel, Inc. (1945) 294 N.Y. 112, 60 N.E.2d 829 (superseded by statute as stated in Application of Burkin, 1 N.Y.2d 570, 154 N.Y.S.2d 898, 136 N.E.2d 862, 64 ALR2d 638)

Directors have power to manage the corporation only when acting as a board. Acting singly the directors cannot bind the corporation. Knapp v Rochester Dog Protective Ass'n (1932) 235 A.D. 436, 257 N.Y.S. 356

Sections 27 and 28 of former Gen. Corp. L. were regarded as not forbidding a bylaw requirement that two-thirds of a quorum of directors must concur in action taken. Re Lake Placid Co. (1948) 274 A.D. 205, 81 N.Y.S.2d 36

The provision in § 27 of former Gen. Corp. L. requiring presence of a majority of directors at a meeting "duly assembled" in order to have a quorum in attendance was considered as implying that each director must have had, or waived, proper notice of the meeting. Cirrincione v Polizzi (1961, 4th Dept) 14 A.D.2d 281, 220 N.Y.S.2d 741

In an action to enforce a restrictive covenant contained in an employment agreement enjoining a former member of a medical corporation from practicing medicine and/or performing surgery within a ten-mile radius of the office of the corporate plaintiff, plaintiffs were not entitled to enforce the restrictive covenants contained in defendant's employment contract where the defendant had been unilaterally expelled from the corporation by proceedings which were illegal and invalid since the removal of defendant as a director left the corporation with only one director and therefore without a validly constituted board of directors. Lehman v Piontkowski (1983, 2d Dept) 93 A.D.2d 809, 460 N.Y.S.2d 817

Dismissal of a former director's claim that he was improperly removed from a corporation's board of directors upon the issuance of a security slip violation was error because N.Y. Bus. Corp. Law §§ 706, 708, and the corporation's by-laws provided for a board member's removal only upon a vote of a majority of the corporation's shareholders. Chaudhry v Vital Holding Co. of NY, Inc. (2008, 2d Dept) 51 App Div 3d 844, 858 NYS2d 740.

Section 28 of former Gen. Corp. L. was said to evidence legislative intent that a board of directors could act by majority of a quorum, irrespective of the number present at the meeting. Crowley v Commodity Exchange, Inc. (1944, CA2 NY) 141 F.2d 182

Under N.Y. Bus. Corp. Law § 708(b), the members of a subsidiary's board of directors properly approved a debt offering by written consent. The members' failure to hold a meeting before approving the debt offering did not constitute a breach of the members' fiduciary duties. RSL Communs. PLC v Bildirici (2009, SD NY) 649 F Supp 2d 184.

§ 709. Greater requirement as to quorum and vote of directors

(a) The certificate of incorporation may contain provisions specifying either or both of the following:

(1) That the proportion of directors that shall constitute a quorum for the transaction of business or of any specified item of business shall be greater than the proportion prescribed by this chapter in the absence of such provision.

(2) That the proportion of votes of directors that shall be necessary for the transaction of business or of any specified item of business shall be greater than the proportion prescribed by this chapter in the absence of such provision.

(b) (1) An amendment of the certificate of incorporation which changes or strikes out a provision permitted by this section shall be authorized at a meeting of shareholders by (A) (i) for any corporation in existence on the effective date of subparagraph (2) of this paragraph, two-thirds of the votes of all outstanding shares entitled to vote thereon, and (ii) for any corporation in existence on the effective date of this clause the certificate of incorporation of which expressly provides such and for any corporation incorporated after the effective date of subparagraph (2) of this paragraph, a majority of the votes of all outstanding shares entitled to vote thereon or (B) in either case, such greater proportion of votes of shares, or votes of a class or series of shares, as may be provided specifically in the certificate of incorporation for changing or striking out a provision permitted by this section.

(2) Any corporation may adopt an amendment of the certificate of incorporation in accordance with any applicable clause or subclause of subparagraph (1) of this paragraph to provide that any further amendment of the certificate of incorporation that changes or strikes out a provision permitted by this section shall be authorized at a meeting of the shareholders by a specified proportion of the votes of the shares, or particular class or series of shares, entitled to vote thereon, provided that such proportion may not be less than a majority.

(c) [Repealed]

History: Add, L 1961, ch 855, eff Sept 1, 1963; amd, L 1962, ch 834, § 51, eff Sept 1, 1963; L 1963, ch 689, § 2, eff Sept 1, 1963; L 1986, ch 852, § 1, eff Aug 2, 1986; L 1997, ch 449, § 42, eff Feb 22, 1998; L 1998, ch 17, § 9, eff Feb 19, 1998, deemed eff Feb 22, 1998.

CASE ANNOTATIONS

Where corporate by-laws provided that vacancies in the board of directors could be filled by the directors in office, a vote of two of the three directors in office was sufficient to fill a vacancy on the board despite a charter and by-law provision that a quorum should consist of 75 percent of the directors and the votes of 75 percent of the directors were necessary for the transaction of business. Jacobson v Moskowitz (1970) 27 N.Y.2d 67, 313 N.Y.S.2d 684, 261 N.E.2d 613

A bylaw requiring unanimous vote of directors to sale of the entire business or any bulk portion of its assets other than in usual course of business was not in violation of § 27 of former Gen. Corp. L. Levin v Mayer (1914) 86 Misc 116, 149 N.Y.S. 112

The executrix of an estate charged with setting up a corporation to take over assets of the decedent's business and form a corporation to distribute stock in such corporation to herself and other designated persons with full power to determine particulars of incorporation and other matters had no power or authority to insist upon inclusion of restrictions in the certificate of incorporation requiring greater than majority or plurality vote of directors and stockholders. Re Burns' Will (1963) 40 Misc. 2d 377, 243 N.Y.S.2d 96

One decision held, however, that no valid provision could be made by stockholders' agreement or otherwise requiring the concurrence of more than a majority of a quorum of the board of directors of a domestic corporation. Goldfarb v Dorset Products, Inc. (1948, Sup) 82 N.Y.S.2d 42

Section 9 of former Stock Corp. L. was considered as sanctioning provisions in a certificate of incorporation requiring a class vote of more than a majority for the taking of particular corporate action. 1948 Ops Atty Gen Dec 14

Section 9 of former Stock Corp. L. likewise required shareholder approval of amendments of the certificate of incorporation which would change the required number of votes by the board for taking action, and the attorney general ruled that a certificate of amendment should not be accepted for filing if its approval by the shareholders in accordance with law was not shown. 1957 Ops Atty Gen July 2

§ 710. Place and time of meetings of the board

Meetings of the board, regular or special, may be held at any place within or without this state, unless otherwise provided by the certificate of incorporation or the by-laws. The time and place for holding meetings of the board may be fixed by or under the by-laws, or, if not so fixed, by the board.

History: Add, L 1961, ch 855, eff Sept 1, 1963.

CASE ANNOTATIONS

Suffolk County Legislature had implicit power to impose reasonable fiscal conditions on approval of for-profit New York business corporation's application for rate increase for ferry service between Shelter Island and Greenport, on Long Island's mainland (Suffolk County Code § 287-3), but Legislature could not interfere with corporation's internal accounting procedures and corporate decision-making, nor could it usurp responsibilities, duties, and functions consigned by law exclusively to corporation's officers, directors, and shareholders; thus, conditions constituting such improper interference, imposed by Legislature on approval of resolution approving rate increase, were properly vacated. North Ferry Co. v Suffolk County Legislature (2000, 2d Dept) 272 A.D.2d 548, 708 N.Y.S.2d 144, app den 95 N.Y.2d 761, 714 N.Y.S.2d 711, 737 N.E.2d 953

§ 711. Notice of meetings of the board

(a) Unless otherwise provided by the by-laws, regular meetings of the board may be held without notice if the time and place of such meetings are fixed by the by-laws or the board. Special meetings of the board shall be held upon notice to the directors.

(b) The by-laws may prescribe what shall constitute notice of meeting of the board. A notice, or waiver of notice, need not specify the purpose of any regular or special meeting of the board, unless required by the by-laws.

(c) Notice of a meeting need not be given to any director who submits a signed waiver of notice whether before or after the meeting, or who attends the meeting without protesting, prior thereto or at its commencement, the lack of notice to him.

(d) A majority of the directors present, whether or not a quorum is present, may adjourn any meeting to another time and place. If the by-laws so provide, notice of any adjournment of a meeting of the board to another time or place shall be given to the directors who were not present at the time of the adjournment and, unless such time and place are announced at the meeting, to the other directors.

History: Add, L 1961, ch 855, eff Sept 1, 1963.

Par (c), amd, L 1963, ch 689, § 3, eff Sept 1, 1963.

CASE ANNOTATIONS

Where a directors' meeting was a special meeting, notice to the directors was required, and, in the absence of ratification, failure to notify directors of the special meeting rendered actions taken at the meeting invalid. Rapoport v Schneider (1972) 29 N.Y.2d 396, 328 N.Y.S.2d 431, 278 N.E.2d 642

The provision in § 27 of former Gen. Corp. L. that a majority of the directors at a meeting "duly assembled" should constitute a quorum was construed as requiring that each director be given proper notice of a meeting of the board, unless he waived notice. Cirrincione v Polizzi (1961, 4th Dept) 14 A.D.2d 281, 220 N.Y.S.2d 741

Under earlier provisions it was held that where a majority of stockholders, under the by-laws, had the right to request a special meeting for the purpose of electing directors and to proceed to elect directors at such meeting, a directors' meeting following the election was legally constituted. Petition of Stylemaster Dept. Store, Inc. (1956) 7 Misc. 2d 207, 154 N.Y.S.2d 58

Want of notice or material defects in such notice as was given of either a directors' or stockholders' meeting, resulting in lack of attendance of all members or shareholders, may result in ground for invalidating whatever action was taken at the meeting at the instance of those who did not attend, or on the score that a different result would have been attained had proper notice been given. Janaug, Inc. v Szlapka (1957) 6 Misc. 2d 84, 162 N.Y.S.2d 668

Absence of notice or defective notice of a directors' meeting has usually been regarded as immaterial with respect to those actually in attendance. Kahn v Blinn (1946, Sup) 60 N.Y.S.2d 413

§ 712. Executive committee and other committees

(a) If the certificate of incorporation or the by-laws so provide, the board, by resolution adopted by a majority of the entire board, may designate from among its members an executive committee and other committees, each consisting of one or more directors, and each of which, to the extent provided in the resolution or in the certificate of incorporation or by-laws, shall have all the authority of the board, except

that no such committee shall have authority as to the following matters:

(1) The submission to shareholders of any action that needs shareholders' approval under this chapter.

(2) The filling of vacancies in the board of directors or in any committee.

(3) The fixing of compensation of the directors for serving on the board or on any committee.

(4) The amendment or repeal of the by-laws, or the adoption of new by-laws.

(5) The amendment or repeal of any resolution of the board which by its terms shall not be so amendable or repealable.

(b) The board may designate one or more directors as alternate members of any such committee, who may replace any absent or disqualified member or members at any meeting of such committee.

(c) Each such committee shall serve at the pleasure of the board. The designation of any such committee, the delegation thereto of authority, or action by any such committee pursuant to such authority shall not alone constitute performance by any member of the board who is not a member of the committee in question, of his duty to the corporation under section 717 (Duty of directors).

History: Add, L 1961, ch 855, eff Sept 1, 1963; amd, L 1965, ch 803, § 28, eff Sept 1, 1965; L 1977, ch 432, § 2, eff Sept 1, 1977; L 1997, ch 449, § 43, eff Feb 22, 1998.

CASE ANNOTATIONS

It has long been common practice in the New York to set up an executive committee to advise and deal with ordinary business problems arising between meetings of the board of directors. Olcott v Tioga R. Co. (1863) 27 N.Y. 546; First Nat. Bank v Commercial Travelers' Home Asso. (1905) 108 A.D. 78, 95 N.Y.S. 454, affd 185 N.Y. 575, 78 N.E. 1103

The allegations of the complaint alleging breach of duties imposed on officers and directors and executive committees merit a full and plenary trial and the issues should not be limited to whether the stockholders and directors ratified the actions of the defendants and voted to discontinue suits in good faith and with full knowledge of the facts. Syracuse Television, Inc. v Channel 9, Syracuse, Inc. (1967, 4th Dept) 28 A.D.2d 638, 280 N.Y.S.2d 287

Corporate boards may delegate policymaking powers to committees. Ostrove v New York State Teachers Retirement System Board (1969, 3d Dept) 32 A.D.2d 163, 300 N.Y.S.2d 663, affd 27 N.Y.2d 623, 313 N.Y.S.2d 757, 261 N.E.2d 664

Even though not provided for in the bylaws of the corporation, the board of directors had the power to adopt a resolution creating an executive committee for the purpose of acting as a sounding board to assist and advise the president between regular meetings of the board and to receive periodic lists of corporate checks to be signed for their information and approval, to check travel expenses and expense accounts of employees, to investigate "trade deals", to work with management between board meetings, to investigate and adjust problems not readily understandable by the full board, and to make recommendations. Syracuse Television, Inc. v Channel 9, Syracuse, Inc. (1966) 51 Misc. 2d 188, 273 N.Y.S.2d 16

Member of corporate board of directors could not be denied access to salary information regarding corporate employees on ground that salaries were fixed by committee of directors and "were not to be disclosed to the other directors," since board member could be held liable for payment of excessive compensation to corporate employees, and such committees are not exempt from oversight and supervision of entire board; however, board member would be required to keep salary information strictly confidential in accordance with his fiduciary capacity and duty of loyalty to corporation. Baker v Henry Glass & Co. (1988) 140 Misc. 2d 836, 531 N.Y.S.2d 746

By-laws of membership corporation may provide for an executive committee of the board of directors. Requirement that at least five members of executive committee be chosen from directors of another corporation was not proper. 1955 Ops Atty Gen Mar 21

§ 713. Interested directors

(a) No contract or other transaction between a corporation and one or more of its directors, or between a corporation and any other corporation, firm, association or other entity in which one or more of its directors are directors or officers, or have a substantial financial interest, shall be either void or voidable for this reason alone or by reason alone that such director or directors are present at the meeting of the board, or of a committee thereof, which approves such contract or transaction, or that his or their votes are counted for such purpose:

(1) If the material facts as to such director's interest in such contract or transaction and as to any such common directorship, officership or financial interest are disclosed in good faith or known to the board or committee, and the board or committee approves such contract or transaction by a vote sufficient for such purpose without counting the vote of such interested director or, if the votes of the disinterested directors are insufficient to constitute an act of the board as defined in section 708 (Action by the board), by unanimous vote of the disinterested directors; or

(2) If the material facts as to such director's interest in such contract or transaction and as to any such common directorship, officership or financial interest are disclosed in good faith or known to the shareholders entitled to vote thereon, and such contract or transaction is approved by vote of such shareholders.

(b) If a contract or other transaction between a corporation and one or more of its directors, or between a corporation and any other corporation, firm, association or other entity in which one or more of its directors are directors or officers, or have a substantial financial interest, is not approved in accordance with paragraph (a), the corporation may avoid the contract or transaction unless the party or parties thereto shall establish affirmatively that the contract or transaction was fair and reasonable as to the corporation at the time it was approved by the board, a committee or the shareholders.

(c) Common or interested directors may be counted in determining the presence of a quorum at a meeting of the board or of a committee which approves such contract or transaction.

(d) The certificate of incorporation may contain additional restrictions on contracts or transactions between a corporation and its directors and may provide that contracts or transactions in violation of such restrictions shall be void or voidable by the corporation.

(e) Unless otherwise provided in the certificate of incorporation or the by-laws, the board shall have authority to fix the compensation of directors for services in any capacity.

History: Add, L 1971, ch 768, eff Sept 1, 1971; amd, L 1997, ch 449, § 44, eff Feb 22, 1998.

CASE ANNOTATIONS

A director is "interested" if he is an officer or director of another corporation apparently involved in the questioned transaction. Rapoport v Schneider (1972) 29 N.Y.2d 396, 328 N.Y.S.2d 431, 278 N.E.2d 642

Interested director within the meaning of Business Corporation Law § 713(a)(1) could not have voted in his capacity as such for acceptance of his offer of sale of stock at the challenged joint meeting of shareholders and directors even if he had been present, and where fourth director was absent and did not vote, the attempt by the remaining 2 directors to effectuate the contract was void and invalid as violative of the corporation's charter and bylaws calling for a 75 percent vote of the directors for corporate action. Lewis v Steinhart (1972, 1st Dept) 40 A.D.2d 817, 338 N.Y.S.2d 552

Defendants (corporation, its shareholders, and its director) were not entitled to summary judgment dismissing cause of action challenging payments made by corporation to 2 shareholders for services rendered since 2 shareholders were also members of corporation's board of directors which authorized payments, and defendants failed to offer evidentiary proof to support their claim that transactions were fair and reasonable. Hakim v Mahdavian (1992, 3d Dept) 185 A.D.2d 428, 585 N.Y.S.2d 828

In shareholder's derivative action involving retirement agreement, Supreme Court properly granted summary judgment in favor of defendant corporate director, despite fact that he had interest in agreement, where he demonstrated that he did not vote on agreement, that he disclosed his interest in agreement to boards of directors, their committees, and shareholders, and that agreement was fair and reasonable. Freer v Mayer (1996, 2d Dept) 223 A.D.2d 667, 637 N.Y.S.2d 425

Corporate director was entitled to summary judgment in his action to vacate agreement of reciprocal easements between corporation and certain partnership where agreement had been authorized by second director who had failed to disclose to plaintiff his interest in partnership, benefit received by corporation from transaction was far outweighed by value of easements corporation had relinquished, and defendants had failed to raise triable questions of fact relevant to establishing that agreement was fair and reasonable. Ench v Breslin (1997, 2d Dept) 241 A.D.2d 475, 659 N.Y.S.2d 893

In action by residential cooperative corporation (plaintiff) to enjoin law firm (defendant) from prosecuting earlier action purportedly brought on plaintiff's behalf against its sponsors seeking rescission of cooperative conversion, court properly granted defendant's summary judgment motion, despite plaintiff's contention that it never validly retained defendant, or, if it did, that it validly discharged defendant in subsequent resolution adopted by its 5-person board of directors, where there was no evidence rebutting plaintiff's then-president's presumptive authority to have instituted action on plaintiff's behalf and engage counsel therefor without formal authorization from plaintiff's board, and evidence showed that resolution to terminate retainer was not supported by majority of plaintiff's disinterested directors (CLS Bus Corp § 713(a)(1)). Park River Owners Corp. v Bangser Klein Rocca & Blum, LLP (2000, 1st Dept) 269 A.D.2d 313, 703 N.Y.S.2d 465

Assignment by corporation of legal claims constituting all or substantially all of its assets, to entity in which its chairman and his son had substantial financial interest, was void where it was made without approval of 3 members of 5-person board of directors, and was transaction outside scope of corporation's usual or regular course of business. Sardanis v Sumitomo Corp. (2001, 1st Dept) 282 A.D.2d 322, 723 N.Y.S.2d 466

Corporate officer who surreptitiously arranged assignment to himself of legal claims constituting all or substantially all of corporation's assets, in violation of CLS Bus Corp §§ 713 and 909(a), had unclean hands and was precluded from relying on equitable defenses such as estoppel. Sardanis v Sumitomo Corp. (2001, 1st Dept) 282 A.D.2d 322, 723 N.Y.S.2d 466

Even assuming that the directors of a corporation failed to comply with N.Y. Bus. Corp. Law § 713(a)(1) with respect to a stock option plan, they established that the plan was fair and reasonable as to the corporation when it was approved; therefore, they were entitled to summary judgment in a shareholder's derivative action. Anderson v Blabey (2008, 4th Dept) 52 App Div 3d 1234, 860 NYS2d 341.

Dealings between corporations having one or more directors in common did not necessarily involve diversion of loyalty and breach of trust. Kutik v Taylor (1975) 80 Misc. 2d 839, 364 N.Y.S.2d 387

Because the disinterested directors knew, before a majority shareholder purchased a competitor's periodical, that their corporation was in serious financial trouble, their consent to the transaction was binding on the corporation under N.Y. Bus. Corp. Law § 713(a)(1); the business judgment rule barred judicial inquiry into the transaction. Owen v Hamilton (2007, App Div, 1st Dept) 843 NYS2d 298, subsequent app, motion gr (2007, App Div, 1st Dept) 843 NYS2d 827

The appellate court will reverse the District Court's finding that plaintiff shareholder failed to carry his burden of proving waste since the transaction involved in the derivative action involved interested directors, and under Bus Corp § 713 interested directors had the burden of proving a transaction to be fair and reasonable to the corporation. Lewis v S. L. & E., Inc. (1980, CA2 NY) 629 F.2d 764

In a derivative suit claiming that the directors' action in cancelling and regranting stock options was invalid because of the directors' personal interest, summary judgment was granted to the directors since the corporation was not harmed by the transactions insofar as the replacement options were never exercised the material facts as to the directors' interests in the stock option plans was disclosed in the shareholder ratification proxy statement, and the shareholders approved the interested directors' transactions in accordance with Bus Corp § 713(a)(2). Cohen v Ayers (1978, ND Ill) 449 F. Supp. 298, CCH Fed Secur L Rep ¶ 96575, affd (CA7 Ill) 596 F.2d 733, CCH Fed Secur L Rep ¶ 96836

If shareholders or directors approve the canceling and regranting of stock option plans to directors, it is unnecessary for the interested directors to affirmatively esatblish that the transaction was fair and reasonable when made. Cohen v Ayers (1978, ND Ill) 449 F. Supp. 298, CCH Fed Secur L Rep ¶ 96575, affd (CA7 Ill) 596 F.2d 733, CCH Fed Secur L Rep ¶ 96836

Even though Bus Corp § 713 provides that interested director transactions are not void if certain substantive or procedural requirements are met, if the board of directors is interested in the disbursement of corporate assets, the court will review the terms to decide independently whether the consideration is adequate, despite deference to the business judgment of directors; even if the transaction is valid under CLS Business Corporation Law § 713, the interested directors may be liable for waste. Cohen v Ayers (1978, ND Ill) 449 F. Supp. 298, CCH Fed Secur L Rep ¶ 96575, affd (CA7 Ill) 596 F.2d 733, CCH Fed Secur L Rep ¶ 96836

§ 714.   Loans to directors

(a) A corporation may not lend money to or guarantee the obligation of a director of the corporation unless:

(1) the particular loan or guarantee is approved by the shareholders, with the holders of a majority of the votes of the shares entitled to vote thereon constituting a quorum, but shares held of record or beneficially by directors who are benefitted by such loan or guarantee shall not be entitled to vote or to be included in the determination of a quorum; or

(2) with respect to any corporation in existence on the effective date of this subparagraph (2) the certificate of incorporation of which expressly provides such and with respect to any corporation incorporated after the effective date of this subparagraph (2), the board determines that the loan or guarantee benefits the corporation and either approves the specific loan or guarantee or a general plan authorizing loans and guarantees.

(b) The fact that a loan or guarantee is made in violation of this section does not affect the borrower's liability on the loan.

History: Add, L 1997, ch 449, § 45, eff Feb 22, 1998; amd, L 1998, ch 17, § 10, eff Feb 19, 1998, deemed eff Feb 22, 1998.

CASE ANNOTATIONS

UNDER FORMER STK CORP § 59

Section 59 of former Stock Corp. L. did not make it improper for a corporation to reimburse a shareholder for money advanced in its behalf or take over an obligation entered into by the shareholder to acquire property necessary in its business, with the consent, express or implied, of all directors and stockholders. New York Credit Men's Ass'n v Dingfelder (1942) 287 N.Y. 531, 41 N.E.2d 86

Section 59 of former Stock Corp. L. was considered primarily for the benefit of creditors of the corporation, and there was some authority to the effect that only creditors could enforce the liability imposed thereby for making prohibited loans, and that not even a receiver or bankruptcy trustee could do so. Flexner v B. T. Babbitt, Inc. (1943) 290 N.Y. 604, 48 N.E.2d 707; Hauben v Morris (1938) 255 A.D. 35, 5 N.Y.S.2d 721, affd 281 N.Y. 652, 22 N.E.2d 482; Waters v Spalt (1948) 22 Misc. 2d 937, 80 N.Y.S.2d 681; Gottfried v Gottfried (1944, Sup) 50 N.Y.S.2d 951; Klages v Cohen (1945, CA2 NY) 146 F.2d 641; United States v E. Regensburg & Sons (1954, DC NY) 124 F. Supp. 687, 54-2 USTC ¶ 9620, affd (CA2 NY) 221 F.2d 336, 55-1 USTC ¶ 9358, cert den 350 US 842, 100 L Ed 751, 76 S Ct 83

Section 59 of former Stock Corp. L., which dealt with making loans to anyone who happened to own stock in the corporation, was regarded as penal in nature, and it was deemed to be violated by approval, by the directors, of a loan to any stockholder with knowledge that he was a shareholder in the corporation. American Broadcasting-Paramount Theatres, Inc. v Frye (1960) 8 N.Y.2d 232, 203 N.Y.S.2d 850, 168 N.E.2d 669, affg (1st Dept) 9 A.D.2d 735, 193 N.Y.S.2d 441; Wyle v Gould (1951) 22 Misc. 2d 935, 110 N.Y.S.2d 113; Waters v Spalt (1948) 22 Misc. 2d 937, 80 N.Y.S.2d 681; Lincoln Nat. Bank v John Peirce Co. (1917) 98 Misc 325, 164 N.Y.S. 421, affd 185 A.D. 932, 172 N.Y.S. 904, affd 228 N.Y. 359, 127 N.E. 253, reh den 229 N.Y. 537, 129 N.E. 906

A creditor could enforce the liability imposed by § 59 of former Stock Corp. L. for making prohibited loans though he had not reduced his claim against the corporation to judgment and did not become a creditor until after the loan was made; he could sue as an individual creditor and need not purport to represent all other creditors similarly situated unless he chose to do so. American Broadcasting-Paramount Theatres, Inc. v Frye (1960) 8 N.Y.2d 232, 203 N.Y.S.2d 850, 168 N.E.2d 669, affg (1st Dept) 9 A.D.2d 735, 193 N.Y.S.2d 441; Union Dime Sav. Bank v Restaurants & Patisseries Longchamps, Inc. (1947) 272 A.D. 761, 70 N.Y.S.2d 142; David McDonough, Inc. v Berger (1959) 22 Misc. 2d 646, 192 N.Y.S.2d 702; Bil-Jax, Inc. v Pine (1958) 15 Misc. 2d 434, 181 N.Y.S.2d 566

Section 59 of former Stock Corp. L. was likewise construed as precluding use of corporate funds for payment of a shareholder's individual debts or obligations, even though he owned all, or practically all, of its stock. Republican Art Printery v David (1916) 173 A.D. 726, 159 N.Y.S. 1010

A contract to make a loan to a shareholder was within the prohibition of § 59 of former Stock Corp. L., and accordingly a nullity. Kennedy v Kennedy (1949) 22 Misc. 2d 924, 91 N.Y.S.2d 294

However, it was held that limitations did not commence to run against a creditor's cause of action until he had obtained judgment and an execution had been returned unsatisfied against the corporation. Storer v Ripley (1958) 12 Misc. 2d 466, 171 N.Y.S.2d 14

That section of former Stock Corp. L. likewise did not make a bank liable for permitting withdrawals or honoring checks against a corporate bank account actually used to pay personal obligations of a shareholder, where it was authorized by resolution of the directors to permit withdrawals or honor checks of the kind in question and had no knowledge that corporate funds were being misappropriated. Willcox v Goess (1937, CA2 NY) 92 F.2d 8, cert den 303 US 647, 82 L Ed 1108, 58 S Ct 646

To extent that moneys advanced by corporation to shareholder to enable shareholder to pay personal income taxes may be viewed as loans to shareholder, apt characterization since corporation carried

Business Corporation Law

advances on its books as accounts receivable, circumstances surrounding loan placed them in violation of predecessor to Business Corporation Law § 714 since corporation had no legitimate corporate purpose behind advances. Fidelity & Deposit Co. v USAFORM Hail Pool, Inc. (1979, MD Fla) 465 F. Supp. 478

§ 715.　Officers

(a) The board may elect or appoint a president, one or more vice-presidents, a secretary and a treasurer, and such other officers as it may determine, or as may be provided in the by-laws.

(b) The certificate of incorporation may provide that all officers or that specified officers shall be elected by the shareholders instead of by the board.

(c) Unless otherwise provided in the certificate of incorporation or the by-laws, all officers shall be elected or appointed to hold office until the meeting of the board following the next annual meeting of shareholders or, in the case of officers elected by the shareholders, until the next annual meeting of shareholders.

(d) Each officer shall hold office for the term for which he is elected or appointed, and until his successor has been elected or appointed and qualified.

(e) Any two or more offices may be held by the same person. When all of the issued and outstanding stock of the corporation is owned by one person, such person may hold all or any combination of offices.

(f) The board may require any officer to give security for the faithful performance of his duties.

(g) All officers as between themselves and the corporation shall have such authority and perform such duties in the management of the corporation as may be provided in the by-laws or, to the extent not so provided, by the board.

(h) An officer shall perform his duties as an officer in good faith and with that degree of care which an ordinarily prudent person in a like position would use under similar circumstances. In performing his duties, an officer shall be entitled to rely on information, opinions, reports or statements including financial statements and other financial data, in each case prepared or presented by:

(1) one or more other officers or employees of the corporation or of any other corporation of which at least fifty percentum of the outstanding shares of stock entitling the holders thereof to vote for the election of directors is owned directly or indirectly by the corporation, whom the officer believes to be reliable and competent in the matters presented, or

(2) counsel, public accountants or other persons as to matters which the officer believes to be within such person's professional or expert competence, so long as in so relying he shall be acting in good faith and with such degree of care, but he shall not be considered to be acting in good faith if he has knowledge concerning the matter in question that would cause such reliance to be unwarranted. A person who so performs his duties shall have no liability by reason of being or having been an officer of the corporation.

History: Add, L 1961, ch 855, eff Sept 1, 1963; amd, L 1963, ch 689, § 4, eff Sept 1, 1963; L 1970, ch 780; L 1971, ch 810, eff June 25, 1971; L 1977, ch 432, § 3, eff Sept 1, 1977; L 1997, ch 449, § 46, eff Feb 22, 1998.

CASE ANNOTATIONS

1. **In general**
2. **Officers**
3. **Authority for action**
4. **Individual liability**
5. **Piercing the corporate veil**
6. **Business judgment rule**
7. **De facto corporation**
8. **Under former Stk Corp § 60**

1. In general

Defendants' motion to dismiss complaint was properly granted; plaintiff seeks declaration he is shareholder of corporation and direction that corporation distributes certain funds in accordance with percentage of stock owned by each shareholder; corporation was incorporated on April 24, 1981 by defendant attorney, to acquire and develope real property; plaintiff does not deny that, on May 29, 1981, he entered attorney's office without permission, removed corporate kit and issued to himself two stock certificates purportedly representing 500 shares in corporation; plaintiff issued certificates to himself as president and secretary, contrary to prohibition of Business Corporation Law § 715 (e), and he offers not explanation of circumstances under which certificates were supposedly issued; on June 11, 1981, attorney wrote to plaintiff, objecting to removal of corporate kit and demanding its return; plaintiff never replied, but rather brought underlying action on March 17, 1988, seeking declaration he is shareholder and distribution of corporation's property–plaintiff's claim is barred by six-year Statute of Limitations for "action for which no limitation is specifically prescribed by law" (CPLR 213 [1]); plaintiff's claim is most closely analogous to contract cause of action which would have expired no later than June 11, 1987. Stern v BSL Dev. Corp., 163 A.D.2d 35, 557 N.Y.S.2d 89, 1990 N.Y. App. Div. LEXIS 8084 (N.Y. App. Div. 1st Dep't 1990).

In action to foreclose mortgage, plaintiff's motion for summary judgment was properly denied where there were triable issues of fact as to whether (1) individual defendant had actual authority, under corporation's bylaws, to mortgage corporate defendant's sole asset, (2) individual defendant had apparent authority to execute mortgage on behalf of corporate defendant, (3) plaintiff fulfilled its duty to conduct reasonable inquiry into scope of individual defendant's authority, and (4) corporate defendant ratified mortgage or should be estopped from denying individual defendant's authority to execute it. U.O.M. Trading Corp. v 85 South Ocean Realty Corp., 251 A.D.2d 652, 676 N.Y.S.2d 481, 1998 N.Y. App. Div. LEXIS 7897 (N.Y. App. Div. 2d Dep't 1998).

Suffolk County Legislature had implicit power to impose reasonable fiscal conditions on approval of for-profit New York business corporation's application for rate increase for ferry service between Shelter Island and Greenport, on Long Island's mainland (Suffolk County Code § 287-3), but Legislature could not interfere with corporation's internal accounting procedures and corporate decision-making, nor could it usurp responsibilities, duties, and functions consigned by law exclusively to corporation's officers, directors, and shareholders; thus, conditions constituting such improper interference, imposed by Legislature on approval of resolution approving rate increase, were properly vacated. North Ferry Co. v Suffolk County Legislature, 272 A.D.2d 548, 708 N.Y.S.2d 144, 2000 N.Y. App. Div. LEXIS 5806 (N.Y. App. Div. 2d Dep't), app. denied, 95 N.Y.2d 761, 714 N.Y.S.2d 711, 737 N.E.2d 953, 2000 N.Y. LEXIS 3286 (N.Y. 2000).

Judgment for a town against a corporation's officers arising from the officers' refusal to seek insurance coverage from the New York State Insurance Fund was error because, inter alia, an action against an officer for misconduct was circumscribed by N.Y. Bus. Corp. Law § 720, which limited the relief available in such an action, and § 720 may not have been used to obtain a money judgment in an action at law. Town of Amherst v Hilger, 106 A.D.3d 120, 962 N.Y.S.2d 837, 2013 N.Y. App. Div. LEXIS 1901 (N.Y. App. Div. 4th Dep't 2013).

In an adversary proceeding, a trustee's claim against a bank based on the theory of deepening insolvency was dismissed for failure to state a claim because there was no absolute duty to shut down and liquidate an insolvent corporation; however, the trustee could have stated a claim against insiders of the debtor by making additional allegations. Kittay v Atl. Bank (In re Global Serv. Group LLC), 316 B.R. 451, 2004 Bankr. LEXIS 1702 (Bankr. S.D.N.Y. 2004).

2. Officers

The business manager and program director of a defendant corporation were not officers thereof, nor were they directors, and no cause of action could be stated against them for mismanagement of the corporate affairs under Bus Corp § 720. Syracuse Television, Inc. v Channel 9, Syracuse, Inc., 51 Misc. 2d 188, 273 N.Y.S.2d 16, 1966 N.Y. Misc. LEXIS 1646 (N.Y. Sup. Ct. 1966).

A chairman of the board of directors is not one of the usual officers designated in Bus Corp § 715, but §§ 104 and 508 of such Law do not recognize the existence of such an office and accept it for certain purposes as an alternative to the presidency. American Express Co. v Lopez, 72 Misc. 2d 648, 340 N.Y.S.2d 82, 1973 N.Y. Misc. LEXIS 2317 (N.Y. Civ. Ct. 1973).

Chairman of board of directors of corporation had apparent authority to get himself a credit card and charge the corporation with responsibility for it. American Express Co. v Lopez, 72 Misc. 2d 648, 340 N.Y.S.2d 82, 1973 N.Y. Misc. LEXIS 2317 (N.Y. Civ. Ct. 1973).

Person who, by reason of provisions of shareholders' agreement, is entitled to be elected treasurer and secretary of close corporation, does not impliedly possess certain powers and is not required to be assigned specific duties, other than those prescribed by statute, absent any provision to such effect in certificate of incorporation, shareholders' agreement or bylaws, and only duties required of treasurer and secretary are mere ministerial functions. Landorf v Glottstein, 131 Misc. 2d 432, 500 N.Y.S.2d 494, 1986 N.Y. Misc. LEXIS 2514 (N.Y. Sup. Ct. 1986), aff'd, 127 A.D.2d 1016, 511 N.Y.S.2d 776, 1987 N.Y. App. Div. LEXIS 42820 (N.Y. App. Div. 1st Dep't 1987).

Claim that defendant breached her fiduciary duties in her capacity as debtor's vice president failed as a matter of law because although corporate officers owed fiduciary duties of due care, good faith, and loyalty under New York law, a vice president had no specific duties. Geltzer v Bedke (In re Mundo Latino Mkt.), 2018 Bankr. LEXIS 2435 (Bankr. S.D.N.Y. Aug. 16, 2018).

3. Authority for action

Defendant was not entitled to dismissal of complaint where he alleged that plaintiff's president resigned in December 1988 as part of arrangement with creditor, and thus did not have authority to commence action in January 1989, but plaintiff presented (1) affidavit of ex-president stating that at time action was commenced he was secretary of plaintiff, and (2) affidavit of creditor confirming ex-president's statement and adding that action was authorized by board of directors. Happy Banana, Ltd. v Tishman Constr. Corp., 179 A.D.2d 562, 578 N.Y.S.2d 574, 1992 N.Y. App. Div. LEXIS 728 (N.Y. App. Div. 1st Dep't 1992).

Condominium company was authorized to commence action for breach of contract where its president executed resolution authorizing commencement of action, and majority of its board of managers approved commencement of action. Board of Managers of Stewart Place Condo. v Stewart Place Acquisition Corp., 255 A.D.2d 351, 679 N.Y.S.2d 842, 1998 N.Y. App. Div. LEXIS 11781 (N.Y. App. Div. 2d Dep't 1998).

Purported assignment of patent rights from corporation to 50-percent shareholder was unauthorized and is invalid, even though assignment was later filed in U.S. Patent and Trademark Office, where alleged assignment amounted to disposition of substantially all assets of corporation, because such unilateral act was not authorized absent unanimous vote by board under bylaws and CLS Bus Corp Law § 715, or two-thirds vote of shareholders under CLS Bus Corp Law § 909(a). COR Mktg. & Sales v Greyhawk Corp., 994 F. Supp. 437, 1998 U.S. Dist. LEXIS 1544 (W.D.N.Y. 1998).

4. Individual liability

In action for negligent misrepresentation, defendant (chief financial officer and chairman of corporation) could not escape liability on basis of provisions of CLS Bus Corp §§ 715 and 717—that corporate officer or director may rely on information and opinions provided by corporate employees when officer or director believes those employees to be reliable and competent in matters presented—where employees on whom defendant relied were "woefully negligent and abysmally uninformed," and defendant had little or no personal dealings with them, had no basis for assessing their competence, and failed to make any inquiry into basis or methodology of their projections; defendant's

failure to make any inquiry as to those matters constituted negligence. Kimmell v Schaefer, 89 N.Y.2d 257, 652 N.Y.S.2d 715, 675 N.E.2d 450, 1996 N.Y. LEXIS 3574 (N.Y. 1996).

In a complaint by an employee, who entered into a two-year employment contract with defendant consulting corporation, which contract was signed by the president and majority shareholder on behalf of the corporation, and who made a loan of $25,000 to the corporation, which loan was secured by a six-month note at 15 percent interest that was also signed by the president and majority shareholder of the corporation, in return for which the employee apparently received shares of the corporation and acted as its chief financial officer, causes of action for repayment of the loan and recovery of unpaid salary had vitality only against the corporation, since the president and majority shareholder signed the note in his representative capacity and incurred no individual liability, and since the corporation, as employer, was the only one obligated to make salary payments. Rossi v Kelly, 96 A.D.2d 451, 465 N.Y.S.2d 1, 1983 N.Y. App. Div. LEXIS 18962 (N.Y. App. Div. 1st Dep't 1983).

Defendant, who allegedly had falsely represented himself as architect, was not entitled to dismissal of apartment owner's action for defective design work, despite architect's contention that written agreement was between owner and "DGR Design, Inc.," not architect, where agreement contained "DGR" logo but word "Inc." did not appear, there was no indication that "DGR" was corporation, and architect signed his own name without any indication that he was acting as agent or representative of any other entity, thus apparently binding himself personally to contract obligations. Gardner v Rivas, 162 A.D.2d 354, 556 N.Y.S.2d 912, 1990 N.Y. App. Div. LEXIS 7740 (N.Y. App. Div. 1st Dep't 1990).

Supreme Court did not err in dismissing contract action as against individual defendant where contract in question was entered into between plaintiff and corporate defendant, individual defendant signed contract as president on behalf of corporation, and there were no allegations that individual defendant exceeded scope of his authority in acting on behalf of corporation or that he committed separate tort from that of corporation. Ruti v Knapp, 193 A.D.2d 662, 598 N.Y.S.2d 50, 1993 N.Y. App. Div. LEXIS 4712 (N.Y. App. Div. 2d Dep't 1993).

Defendant, who owned 50 percent of plaintiff corporation and served as its president and treasurer, breached his duty of good faith under CLS Bus Corp §§ 715 and 717 by converting corporation's business assets and opportunities, where he virtually put corporation out of business by taking all of its employees and customers and converting its assets, and he incorporated his own firm with almost identical name to that which corporation operated under to avoid sharing profits and proceeds with plaintiffs. Howard v Carr, 222 A.D.2d 843, 635 N.Y.S.2d 326, 1995 N.Y. App. Div. LEXIS 13006 (N.Y. App. Div. 3d Dep't 1995).

Court should have granted motion to dismiss cause of action asserted against defendant personally where individual defendant was not in privity of contract with plaintiffs because relevant contract was made with his professional corporation. Shiel v Termini, 242 A.D.2d 528, 662 N.Y.S.2d 269, 1997 N.Y. App. Div. LEXIS 8580 (N.Y. App. Div. 2d Dep't 1997).

Summary judgment dismissing cause of action that sought to hold corporation's president personally liable on unsecured promissory note was properly granted where president signed note in his representative capacity. Martorano v Herman Miller, Inc., 255 A.D.2d 367, 680 N.Y.S.2d 20, 1998 N.Y. App. Div. LEXIS 11832 (N.Y. App. Div. 2d Dep't 1998), app. denied, 93 N.Y.2d 802, 687 N.Y.S.2d 626, 710 N.E.2d 273, 1999 N.Y. LEXIS 145 (N.Y. 1999).

5. Piercing the corporate veil

Court properly pierced corporate veil to impose corporate obligation on individual defendant where misrepresentation was intentionally made by corporate seller's sole officer, director, and stockholder. Classic Office Supplies v Classic Commer. Office Prods., 238 A.D.2d 221, 657 N.Y.S.2d 7, 1997 N.Y. App. Div. LEXIS 4073 (N.Y. App. Div. 1st Dep't 1997).

Plaintiff was entitled to pierce corporate veil in order to compel defendants to satisfy default judgment against closely held corporation where defendants held offices of president, vice-president, secretary, and treasurer of corporation, constituted majority of its shareholders and directors, were in privity with corporation, had control over litigation that resulted in default judgment, had opportunity to participate in that case instead of permitting default judgment, and should reasonably have expected that they might be held personally accountable for corporation's obligations. Sterling Doubleday Enters., L.P. v Marro, 238 A.D.2d 502, 656 N.Y.S.2d 676, 1997 N.Y. App. Div. LEXIS 4002 (N.Y. App. Div. 2d Dep't 1997).

Individual defendant was entitled to summary judgment dismissing fraud complaint against him, even though he was sole shareholder, director, and officer of corporate defendant, where allegedly fraudulent letter, which represented that certain premises "will be delivered vacant at closing," was signed by individual defendant in his corporate capacity, and thus plaintiff failed to meet its burden of piercing corporate veil so as to impose general liability on individual defendant. Madison Home Equities, Inc. v Echeverria, 266 A.D.2d 435, 698 N.Y.S.2d 703, 1999 N.Y. App. Div. LEXIS 12064 (N.Y. App. Div. 2d Dep't 1999).

6. Business judgment rule

Decision of publicly-traded corporation and its future purchaser to wait until close of markets when negotiations were complete and agreement was final before publicly announcing that major new deal had been struck fell within business judgment rule, absent allegations or showing of some countervailing misconduct or manipulation, and thus shareholders' complaint against corporation alleging breach of fiduciary duty in not revealing agreement would fail. Lindner Fund v Waldbaum, Inc., 82 N.Y.2d 219, 604 N.Y.S.2d 32, 624 N.E.2d 160, 1993 N.Y. LEXIS 3895 (N.Y. 1993).

Business judgment rule did not warrant dismissal of a breach of fiduciary duty claim because the pleadings suggested a lack of good faith. Neogenix Oncology, Inc. v Gordon, 133 F. Supp. 3d 539, 2015 U.S. Dist. LEXIS 135663 (E.D.N.Y. 2015).

7. De facto corporation

Person who deals with a de facto corporation cannot later deny its existence and proceed against its officers personally. L-TEC Elecs. Corp. v Cougar Elec. Org., Inc., 198 F.3d 85, 1999 U.S. App. LEXIS 30719 (2d Cir. N.Y. 1999).

Where de facto corporation later pays its taxes and is reinstated, its corporate status is restored nunc pro tunc, and any contracts into which it may have entered are retroactively validated. L-TEC Elecs. Corp. v Cougar Elec. Org., Inc., 198 F.3d 85, 1999 U.S. App. LEXIS 30719 (2d Cir. N.Y. 1999).

8. Under former Stk Corp § 60

An agreement between the two major stockholders of a corporation who held most but not all the corporation stock to the effect that the ownership of a stated number of shares of stock in the corporation would entitle the holder thereof to one of the three offices of the corporation was invalid as a violation of § 60 of former Stock Corp. L. since such a provision unduly restricted the discretion of the board of directors and was therefore unenforceable. Lockley v Robie, 276 A.D. 291, 94 N.Y.S.2d 335, 1950 N.Y. App. Div. LEXIS 4849 (N.Y. App. Div.), modified, 301 N.Y. 371, 93 N.E.2d 895, 301 N.Y. (N.Y.S.) 371, 1950 N.Y. LEXIS 815 (N.Y. 1950).

Under § 60 of former Stock Corp. L., the function of appointing or electing officers rested with the board of directors, and the board could ignore or summarily remove an "officer" selected or purportedly elected by the shareholders, notwithstanding by-law provisions for election of certain officers by the shareholders. Bechtold v Stillwagon, 195 N.Y.S. 66, 119 Misc. 177, 1922 N.Y. Misc. LEXIS 1349 (N.Y. Sup. Ct. 1922).

Agreements looking to perpetuation in office are not inherently invalid, and are binding upon the parties to them if possessing the requisites of an enforceable contract. Martocci v Martocci, 2 Misc. 2d 330, 42 N.Y.S.2d 222, 1943 N.Y. Misc. LEXIS 1478 (N.Y. Sup. Ct.), aff'd, 266 A.D. 840, 43 N.Y.S.2d 516, 1943 N.Y. App. Div. LEXIS 4780 (N.Y. App. Div. 1943).

One who has resigned as president of a corporation may not restore himself to the office of president by any voluntary act subsequent to his resignation without his election thereto pursuant to the by-laws of the corporation. Harry Levi & Co. v Feldman, 61 N.Y.S.2d 639, 1946 N.Y. Misc. LEXIS 2111 (N.Y. App. Term 1946).

Agreements among shareholders for perpetuation in office, while not contrary to public policy, cannot override statutes authorizing removal of officers for cause and must be construed as binding only so long as duties of the office are faithfully and efficiently performed. Goldfarb v Dorset Products, Inc., 82 N.Y.S.2d 42, 1948 N.Y. Misc. LEXIS 3016 (N.Y. Sup. Ct. 1948); In re Roosevelt Leather Hand Bag Co., 68 N.Y.S.2d 735, 1947 N.Y. Misc. LEXIS 2137 (N.Y. Sup. Ct. 1947); In re Block's Will, 60 N.Y.S.2d 639, 186 Misc. 945, 1946 N.Y. Misc. LEXIS 1913 (N.Y. Sur. Ct. 1946).

Notes to Unpublished Decisions

1.In general
1. In general

Unpublished decision: Debtor, a father who had founded a corporation in which his son, a plaintiff in a nondischargeability complaint per 11 U.S.C.S. § 523(a)(4), ultimately owned 95% of the stock, could not discharge his obligation for the $362,760 that the debtor removed from the corporation's investment account and deposited into an entity that debtor himself controlled because debtor, given his various offices and roles with the corporation over the years, owed a fiduciary duty to the company and to his son under various rules including N.Y. Bus. Corp. Law § 717 and N.Y. Bus. Corp. Law § 715(h). Because all of the criteria for nondischargeability under § 523(a)(4) were satisfied, judgment for plaintiffs was proper. Am. Legal Commer. Printers, Inc. v Russo (In re Russo), 2012 Bankr. LEXIS 1236 (Bankr. W.D.N.Y. Mar. 20, 2012).

§ 716.   Removal of officers

(a) Any officer elected or appointed by the board may be removed by the board with or without cause. An officer elected by the shareholders may be removed, with or without cause, only by vote of the shareholders, but his authority to act as an officer may be suspended by the board for cause.

(b) The removal of an officer without cause shall be without prejudice to his contract rights, if any. The election or appointment of an officer shall not of itself create contract rights.

(c) An action to procure a judgment removing an officer for cause may be brought by the attorney-general or by ten percent of the votes of the outstanding shares, whether or not entitled to vote. The court may bar from re-election or reappointment any officer so removed for a period fixed by the court.

History: Add, L 1961, ch 855, eff Sept 1, 1963; amd, L 1962, ch 834, § 53, eff Sept 1, 1963; L 1963, ch 689, § 5, eff Sept 1, 1963; L 1997, ch 449, § 47, eff Feb 22, 1998.

CASE ANNOTATIONS

Fact that three days after his handwritten election for early retirement vice president of corporation also executed one on corporation's printed form did not in any wise vitiate effect of earlier document which resulted in termination of his employment and automatic commencement of retirement, making him no longer subject to discharge. Hadden v Consolidated Edison Co. (1977, 1st Dept) 58 A.D.2d 154, 396 N.Y.S.2d 210, mod on other grounds 45 N.Y.2d 466, 410 N.Y.S.2d 274, 382 N.E.2d 1136

Issues of corporate governance are determined by state in which corporation is chartered. Kikis v McRoberts Corp. (1996, 1st Dept) 225 A.D.2d 455, 639 N.Y.S.2d 346

Where the defendant had been removed as president of the plaintiff corporation by a vote of the board of directors, a quorum being present, the corporation was entitled to enjoin the defendant from acting as president, since under the circumstances, the board had the power to remove the defendant with or without cause. Avien, Inc. v Weiss (1966) 50 Misc. 2d 127, 269 N.Y.S.2d 836

UNDER FORMER LAW

Board of directors could remove an unfaithful officer or employee, under § 27 of former Gen. Corp. L., notwithstanding he was in office pursuant to stockholders' agreement, as the agreement would be illegal and contrary to public policy if it required his retention under such circumstances. Fells v Katz (1931) 256 N.Y. 67, 175 N.E. 516; Re Allied Fruit & Extract Co. (1934) 243 A.D. 52, 276 N.Y.S. 153

The resignation of an individual as president and director of a corporation which states that it is to take effect at once becomes effective when tendered. Harry Levi & Co. v Feldman (1946, Sup App T) 61 N.Y.S.2d 639

A director and secretary of a life insurance company could be removed from the office of secretary by order of the Board of Directors where he had poor working habits, inferior ability, and had openly defied the Board although a life insurance company was prohibited under Insurance Law § 198 from coercing any officer to support certain candidates. Petition of Holmes (1955) 286 A.D. 500, 145 N.Y.S.2d 26, affd in part and app dismd in part 2 N.Y.2d 1001, 163 N.Y.S.2d 614, 143 N.E.2d 348

Under § 61 of former Gen. Corp. L., an action for removal of officers and directors of a corporation could be brought only by the attorney general. Cirrincione v Polizzi (1961, 4th Dept) 14 A.D.2d 281, 220 N.Y.S.2d 741; Purdy v Humphrey (1947) 192 Misc 309, 82 N.Y.S.2d 92, affd 274 A.D. 841, 82 N.Y.S.2d 388

It was held that a by-law could restrict removal power of the directors to removals for cause, notwithstanding the provisions of § 60 of former Stock Corp. L. Petition of Buckley (1944) 183 Misc 189, 50 N.Y.S.2d 54

The court would not entertain a petition for an order setting aside a special meeting of the board of directors of a corporation, and vacating the removal of a corporate officer. Heller v Clark Merchandisers, Inc. (1955) 9 Misc. 2d 106, 154 N.Y.S.2d 150

Section 60 of former Stock Corp. L. permitted the board of directors to remove any officer of the corporation with or without cause, in the absence of a binding contract protecting tenure in office against removal except for cause. Some decisions likewise referred to the general management powers vested in the board by § 27 of the former Gen. Corp. L. in support of such action. Heller v Clark Merchandisers, Inc. (1955) 9 Misc. 2d 106, 154 N.Y.S.2d 150; Re Roosevelt Leather Hand Bag Co. (1947, Sup) 68 N.Y.S.2d 735

It was likewise held that § 60 of former Stock Corp. L. could not protect a corporation from liability for breach of an employment contract running for a fixed period, in the event of its breach of the contract without cause. Heller v Clark Merchandisers, Inc. (1955) 9 Misc. 2d 106, 154 N.Y.S.2d 150; Re Paramount Publix Corp. (1937, CA2 NY) 90 F.2d 441

The sole stockholder of a corporation may remove all directors without calling a special meeting for the purpose, notwithstanding its by-laws call for holding a special meeting of shareholders to accomplish such a purpose and for procedure by majority vote of shareholders. Sire Plan, Inc. v Mintzer (1963) 38 Misc. 2d 920, 237 N.Y.S.2d 123

§ 717. Duty of directors

(a) A director shall perform his duties as a director, including his duties as a member of any committee of the board upon which he may serve, in good faith and with that degree of care which an ordinarily prudent person in a like position would use under similar circumstances. In performing his duties, a director shall be entitled to rely on information, opinions, reports or statements including financial statements and other financial data, in each case prepared or presented by:

(1) one or more officers or employees of the corporation or of any other corporation of which at least fifty percentum of the outstanding shares of stock entitling the holders thereof to vote for the election of directors is owned directly or indirectly by the corporation, whom the director believes to be reliable and competent in the matters presented,

(2) counsel, public accountants or other persons as to matters which the director believes to be within such person's professional or expert competence, or

(3) a committee of the board upon which he does not serve, duly designated in accordance with a provision of the certificate of incorporation or the bylaws, as to matters within its designated authority, which committee the director believes to merit confidence, so long as in so relying he shall be acting in good faith and with such degree of care, but he shall not be considered to be acting in good faith if he

has knowledge concerning the matter in question that would cause such reliance to be unwarranted. A person who so performs his duties shall have no liability by reason of being or having been a director of the corporation.

(b) In taking action, including, without limitation, action which may involve or relate to a change or potential change in the control of the corporation, a director shall be entitled to consider, without limitation, (1) both the long-term and the short-term interests of the corporation and its shareholders and (2) the effects that the corporation's actions may have in the short-term or in the long-term upon any of the following:

(i) the prospects for potential growth, development, productivity and profitability of the corporation;

(ii) the corporation's current employees;

(iii) the corporation's retired employees and other beneficiaries receiving or entitled to receive retirement, welfare or similar benefits from or pursuant to any plan sponsored, or agreement entered into, by the corporation;

(iv) the corporation's customers and creditors; and

(v) the ability of the corporation to provide, as a going concern, goods, services, employment opportunities and employment benefits and otherwise to contribute to the communities in which it does business.

Nothing in this paragraph shall create any duties owed by any director to any person or entity to consider or afford any particular weight to any of the foregoing or abrogate any duty of the directors, either statutory or recognized by common law or court decisions.

For purposes of this paragraph, "control" shall mean the possession, directly or indirectly, of the power to direct or cause the direction of the management and policies of the corporation, whether through the ownership of voting stock, by contract, or otherwise.

History: Add, L 1961, ch 855, eff Sept 1, 1963; amd, L 1977, ch 432, § 4, eff Sept 1, 1977; L 1987, ch 367, § 2, eff July 23, 1987; L 1989, ch 228, § 1, eff June 30, 1989.

CASE ANNOTATIONS

1. **In general**
2. **Duty of loyalty**
3. **Duty of care**
4. **Majority stockholders**
5. **Procedural matters**

1. In general

Business judgment rule prohibits judicial inquiry into actions of corporate directors taken in good faith and in exercise of honest judgment in lawful and legitimate furtherance of corporate purposes; so long as directors have not breached their fiduciary obligation to corporation, exercise of their powers for common and general interests of corporation may not be questioned, even if results show that what they did was unwise or inexpedient. Levandusky v One Fifth Ave. Apartment Corp. (1990) 75 N.Y.2d 530, 554 N.Y.S.2d 807, 553 N.E.2d 1317

Action by board of directors of corporation that comes within business judgment rule cannot be characterized as arbitrary and capricious, or abuse of discretion, for purpose of Article 78 proceeding. Levandusky v One Fifth Ave. Apartment Corp. (1990) 75 N.Y.2d 530, 554 N.Y.S.2d 807, 553 N.E.2d 1317

In action for negligent misrepresentation, defendant (chief financial officer and chairman of corporation) could not escape liability on basis of provisions of CLS Bus Corp §§ 715 and 717-that corporate officer or director may rely on information and opinions provided by corporate employees when officer or director believes those employees to be reliable and competent in matters presented-where employees on whom defendant relied were "woefully negligent and abysmally uninformed," and defendant had little or no personal dealings with them, had no basis for assessing their competence, and failed to make any inquiry into basis or methodology of their projections; defendant's failure to make any inquiry as to those matters constituted negligence. Kimmell v Schaefer (1996) 89 N.Y.2d 257, 652 N.Y.S.2d 715, 675 N.E.2d 450

Corporate directors in their dealings with third persons are considered somewhat as agents for the corporation, but their relation to the property of the corporation is that of a fiduciary, and are bound to exercise standards of honesty, morality, and to care for the corporate interests in good faith. Application of Vogel (1966, 1st Dept) 25 A.D.2d 212, 268 N.Y.S.2d 237, affd 19 N.Y.2d 589, 278 N.Y.S.2d 236, 224 N.E.2d 738

In shareholder's derivative action, business judgment rule was applicable to decision of corporate directors regarding retirement agreement in absence of evidence that directors had interest in agreement or that they lacked good faith or committed fraud when considering whether to enter into agreement. Freer v Mayer (1996, 2d Dept) 223 A.D.2d 667, 637 N.Y.S.2d 425

The director of a corporation has a duty to act in what he believes to be the best interests of the corporation and its stockholders. Dankoff v Bowling Proprietors Assn. (1972) 69 Misc. 2d 658, 331 N.Y.S.2d 109

In an adversary proceeding, a trustee's claim against a bank based on the theory of deepening insolvency was dismissed for failure to state a claim because there was no absolute duty to shut down and liquidate an insolvent corporation; however, the trustee could have stated a claim against insiders of the debtor by making additional allegations. Kittay v Atl. Bank (In re Global Serv. Group LLC) (2004, BC SD NY) 316 BR 451

Due to nature and terms of joint venture agreement between Health Research, Incorporated (not-for-profit corporation closely affiliated with Department of Health) and private for-profit corporation, and due to Department of Health's vast authority over matters concerning public health, there was appearance of conflict of interest in violation of CLS Pub O § 74 for Commissioner of Health to serve as chair or member of board of directors of for-profit corporation. State Ethics Comm Adv Op No. 93-3

Due to broad responsibilities of Public Health Council, there was appearance of conflict of interest under CLS Pub O § 74 for chair of Public Health Council to sit on board of directors of private for-profit corporation involved in joint venture with Health Research, Incorporated (not-for-profit corporation closely affiliated with Department of Health). State Ethics Comm Adv Op No. 93-3

It violated CLS Pub O § 74 for executive director of Health Research, Incorporated (not-for-profit corporation closely affiliated with Department of Health), in his position as executive director or as member of Department of Health's Institutional Review Board for Human Research Review, to serve as member of board of directors and secretary/treasurer of private for-profit corporation involved in joint venture with Health Research, Incorporated. State Ethics Comm Adv Op No. 93-3

2. Duty of loyalty

Decision of publicly-traded corporation and its future purchaser to wait until close of markets when negotiations were complete and agreement was final before publicly announcing that major new deal had been struck fell within business judgment rule, absent allegations or showing of some countervailing misconduct or manipulation, and thus shareholders' complaint against corporation alleging breach of fiduciary duty in not revealing agreement would fail. Lindner Fund v Waldbaum, Inc. (1993) 82 N.Y.2d 219, 604 N.Y.S.2d 32, 624 N.E.2d 160

The requirement that directors and officers discharge the duties of their respective positions in good faith means that they shall not assume and engage in promotion of personal interests incompatible with the superior interests of the corporation, to whom they owe their undivided and unqualified loyalty. Foley v D'Agostino, (1964, 1st Dept) 21 A.D.2d 60, 248 N.Y.S.2d 121

An officer or director who actually engages in a rival or competing business to the detriment of his corporation is answerable to it for injury thereby sustained. Foley v D'Agostino (1964, 1st Dept) 21 A.D.2d 60, 248 N.Y.S.2d 121

Rejection by a corporation of the opportunity of taking over a rival and competing business does not release officers and directors of the corporation, remaining in office and in its employ, from their continuing and overriding obligation of loyalty and good faith to the corporation or authorize them to take over and operate the competing business. Foley v D'Agostino (1964, 1st Dept) 21 A.D.2d 60, 248 N.Y.S.2d 121

Directors and officers are bound by their duty of undivided and unqualified loyalty to their corporations, a duty which encompasses good faith efforts to insure that their personal profit is not at the expense of their corporations; in cases of self-dealing, defendants have the burden of demonstrating the fairness of the transactions. Limmer v Medallion Group, Inc. (1980, 1st Dept) 75 A.D.2d 299, 428 N.Y.S.2d 961

Judgment would be granted to one of two shareholders in an electronics corporation in a shareholder derivative action against a corporation, where the other shareholder-officer, in complete disregard of his fiduciary duty to the corporation, had seized all of the corporate assets of the corporation, had entered into a unilateral royalty agreement with another corporation that he had created himself to manufacture and sell the products to which the first corporation had patent and trademark rights, and then proceeded to carry on under the name of the second corporation the business for which the first corporation had been formed. Schachter v Kulik (1983, 2d Dept) 96 A.D.2d 1038, 466 N.Y.S.2d 444

Complaint of tenant-shareholders of cooperative apartment stated cause of action where it alleged breach of fiduciary duty on part of board of directors and its individual members in failing to act in good faith toward tenants in violation of CLS Bus Corp § 717 by board's rejection of transfer of shares and assignment of proprietary lease in next-door cooperative apartment to tenants, and that one or more board members attempted to purchase next-door apartment in question below market so as to sell it to third party. Bernheim v 136 East 64th Street Corp. (1987, 1st Dept) 128 A.D.2d 434, 512 N.Y.S.2d 825

Remaining owner of closely-held family corporation did not breach his fiduciary duty as officer and director owed to former owner when he extinguished debt owed to corporation as part of consideration given by him to debtor in exchange for parcel of property which remaining owner acquired in his own name where former owner had known of debt when he left corporation, he had made no effort to recover it for corporation, and debt had been recovered on remaining owner's initiative; however, remaining owner was properly directed by referee to account to corporation for amount of debt. Gargano v V.C.&J. Constr. Corp. (1989, 2d Dept) 148 A.D.2d 417, 538 N.Y.S.2d 955, later proceeding (2d Dept) 148 A.D.2d 492, 538 N.Y.S.2d 953

In action for corporate waste and mismanagement brought under CLS Bus Corp § 720, directors were not protected by business judgment rule where plaintiff alleged that corporate decisions lacked legitimate business purpose and were tainted by fraud. Amfesco Industries, Inc. v Greenblatt (1991, 1st Dept) 172 A.D.2d 261, 568 N.Y.S.2d 593

Former shareholder was entitled to summary judgment in derivative action alleging that former officer of corporation breached his fiduciary duty to corporation where (1) it was undisputed that officer unilaterally discontinued corporation's business after incorporating second business, he appropriated corporation's fixtures and tools for use by second business, second business occupied same space that corporation had occupied, and second business used same employees, identical telephone number, and like stationery as that used by corporation, and (2) it was established that major customer of corporation was thereby induced to believe that 2 entities were "synonymous" and that there had been mere change in name of corporation; officer's actions constituted misappropriation of corporation's tangible assets and good will. Plotnik v Greenberg (In re Greenberg) (1994, 4th Dept) 206 A.D.2d 963, 614 N.Y.S.2d 825

Defendant, who owned 50 percent of plaintiff corporation and served as its president and treasurer, breached his duty of good faith under CLS Bus Corp §§ 715 and 717 by converting corporation's business assets and opportunities, where he virtually put corporation out of business by taking all of its employees and customers and converting its assets, and he incorporated his own firm with almost identical name to that which corporation operated under to avoid sharing profits and proceeds with plaintiffs. Howard v Carr (1995, 3d Dept) 222 A.D.2d 843, 635 N.Y.S.2d 326

In action for diversion of corporate assets, there was no judicial or statutory authority for defendant's theory that, essentially, his fiduciary duties as 50 percent shareholder, director, and officer of corporation were on sliding scale so that plaintiff committed bad acts, defendant's duties were reduced or limited proportionately. Ross v Moyer (2001, 1st Dept) 286 A.D.2d 610, 730 N.Y.S.2d 318, related proceeding (1st Dept) 286 A.D.2d 611, 730 N.Y.S.2d 225

Doctrine of unclean hands barred recovery in action against 50 percent shareholder, director, and officer of corporation for diversion of corporate assets where, inter alia, plaintiff, who held similar position, secretly wired to himself $670,000 in corporate funds. Ross v Moyer (2001, 1st Dept) 286 A.D.2d 610, 730 N.Y.S.2d 318, related proceeding (1st Dept) 286 A.D.2d 611, 730 N.Y.S.2d 225

Dealings between corporations having one or more directors in common did not necessarily involve diversion of loyalty and breach of trust. Kutik v Taylor (1975) 80 Misc. 2d 839, 364 N.Y.S.2d 387

Director of corporation will be held liable for conduct or acts which involve fraud, bad faith, or intent to promote self-interest or interest of others at expense of corporation. Kutik v Taylor (1975) 80 Misc. 2d 839, 364 N.Y.S.2d 387

Director's duty to creditors does not arise only when liquidation is imminent and foreseeable, but upon insolvency. Clarkson Co. v Shaheen (1981, CA2 NY) 660 F.2d 506, cert den (US) 71 L Ed 2d 850, 102 S Ct 1614

Shareholder's claims that two of the directors breached their fiduciary duties of loyalty and care by offering to purchase additional shares of the corporation were dismissed because mere attempts by a director to increase his stake in the company as a shareholder are not actionable as a breach of fiduciary duty. Patrick v Allen (2005, SD NY) 355 F. Supp. 2d 704

Complaint in action by trustee in bankruptcy alleging self-serving mismanagement on part of directors, officers, and employees of corporation stated a cause of action. Bush v Masiello (1972, SD NY) 55 FRD 72

Debtor, a father who had founded a corporation in which his son, a plaintiff in a nondischargeability complaint per 11 U.S.C.S. § 523(a)(4), ultimately owned 95% of the stock, could not discharge his obligation for the $ 362,760 that the debtor removed from the corporation's investment account and deposited into an entity that debtor himself controlled because debtor, given his various offices and roles with the corporation over the years, owed a fiduciary duty to the company and to his son under various rules including N.Y. Bus. Corp. Law § 717 and N.Y. Bus. Corp. Law § 715(h). Because all of the criteria for nondischargeability under § 523(a)(4) were satisfied, judgment for plaintiffs was proper. Am. Legal Commer. Printers, Inc. v Russo (In re Russo) (2012, BC WD NY) 2012 Bankr LEXIS 1236 (UNPUBLISHED)

3. Duty of care

The officers and directors of a corporation were properly held liable to the former sole shareholder of the corporation, to whom the stock of the corporation had been pledged in connection with plaintiff's sale of the business, for their wrongful dissipation of the corporation's assets, since plaintiff, pursuant to the pledge agreement, possessed a beneficial interest in the corporation's stock, so that defendants had a fiduciary duty to protect plaintiff's stock interest and were required to discharge such duty "in good faith and with that degree of care which an ordinary prudent person in a like position would use under similar circumstances" pursuant to Bus Corp Law § 717, and since the evidence showed that defendants had breached such duty in that their wrongful diversion and squandering of the corporation's assets in speculative enterprises, their granting of excessive credit, and their payments of salary to themselves beyond the point at which they had defaulted in their installment payments to plaintiff amounted, at least, to willful or wanton negligence with respect to the corporation's assets. Giblin v Murphy (1983, 3d Dept) 97 A.D.2d 668, 469 N.Y.S.2d 211

The care and skill of directors in management are relative concepts depending not only on the type of corporation, the circumstances involved, but also the corporate role of the directors whose duty is measured by all the circumstances. The fact that a board delegated certain responsibilities to some of the directors as an executive or advisory committee, in which capacity such directors acted, is a fact

to be considered along with all others present to determine the knowledge they had of the corporation's affairs and possible mismanagement thereof. A director is charged with knowledge he actually possesses or which he might have possessed had he diligently pursued his duties, and this is so whether the executive or advisory committee is de jure, de facto, or a nullity. Their duty is to be measured by what prudent men would do in similar circumstances. Having injected themselves into the more detailed management of the corporation and thereby acquired additional knowledge, they are charged with that knowledge when their conduct is judged. In this case their responsibility encompassed matters passed upon by the Committee, and because of their participation in these decisions the diligence required of them was greater and the liability stricter than that of the other board members. Syracuse Television, Inc. v Channel 9, Syracuse, Inc. (1966) 51 Misc. 2d 188, 273 N.Y.S.2d 16

Duty of care of directors and officers of corporations is measured by circumstances. Kutik v Taylor (1975) 80 Misc. 2d 839, 364 N.Y.S.2d 387

Complaint, which asserted that corporate directors breached their fiduciary duties to corporation by failing to collect from subsidiaries full amount due under contract for services rendered to subsidiaries, but which neither alleged circumstances constituting director's alleged misconduct, nor alleged facts from which inference of negligence or lack of due care could be drawn, was insufficient. Kutik v Taylor (1975) 80 Misc. 2d 839, 364 N.Y.S.2d 387

Where a corporate committee composed of disinterested directors always accepted the recommendation of management as to the stock option grants to employees who were not officers and directors but had full personal knowledge of the performance and responsibilities of the optionee-directors and acted independently as to stock option grants to such directors, the committee did not subject its action to independent court review by abdicating its function to the management of the corporation and its decisions are conclusive under the business judgment rule, especially where the first replacement options to the directors were not exercised and the second regrant was for only 75 percent of shares previously held while other employees received the full number of options. Cohen v Ayers (1978, ND Ill) 449 F. Supp. 298, CCH Fed Secur L Rep ¶ 96575, affd (CA7 Ill) 596 F.2d 733, CCH Fed Secur L Rep ¶ 96836

Breach of fiduciary duty by corporate director is not found where director, in performing his corporate functions, relies on advice of corporate attorney, even where advice is unsound. Buffalo Forge Co. v Ogden Corp. (1983, WD NY) 555 F. Supp. 892, CCH Fed Secur L Rep ¶ 99079

Directors' motion to dismiss was granted to the extent the shareholder claimed that the directors breached their fiduciary duties of loyalty and care by failing to negotiate for a sale of the property because the directors were not elected to the corporation's board of directors until after the offer was made, and the complaint did not allege any facts that would have supported the conclusory allegation that they failed to negotiate a sale of the property. Patrick v Allen (2005, SD NY) 355 F. Supp. 2d 704

Under N.Y. Bus. Corp. Law § 717(a), members of a subsidiary's board of directors did not owe a fiduciary duty of care to the subsidiary's creditors while the subsidiary allegedly operated in the zone of insolvency for a period of between thirty and sixty days during which the subsidiary and its parent company were having difficulty raising financing to address their liquidity needs. RSL Communs. PLC v Bildirici (2009, SD NY) 649 F Supp 2d 184.

4. Majority stockholders

Defendant's motion, in a representative stockholders' action seeking dissolution of the corporation and other relief, for judgment on the pleadings or summary judgment, should not be granted where there is discoverable in the language of the complaint assertion, supported by allegations as to particular transactions, that the corporation has been and is being exploited exclusively for private benefit of its managing and controlling stockholders. Gaines v Adler (1962, 1st Dept) 15 A.D.2d 743, 223 N.Y.S.2d 1011

Majority shareholders' exclusion of one minority shareholder from some "special" meetings during her tenure on board of close corporation, and denial of access to corporate books and records, did not rise to level of "oppressive conduct" entitling plaintiff minority shareholders to compensatory and injunctive relief for breach of fiduciary duty, where special meetings involved only ministerial matters and minutes were distributed at annual board meetings, plaintiffs had no reasonable expectation of assuming management positions in company, and plaintiffs failed to show that defendants violated any corporate resolution or bylaw. Orloff v Weinstein Enters. (1998, 1st Dept) 247 A.D.2d 63, 677 N.Y.S.2d 544

Majority stockholders owe the minority the utmost good faith, and may not, in defiance of this fiduciary duty, use their power to disregard or defeat rights of minority shareholders wishing to dissent from action taken by the majority of a right to be paid the fair value of their shares. Rank Organization Ltd. v Pathe Laboratories, Inc. (1962) 33 Misc. 2d 748, 227 N.Y.S.2d 562

Where president of corporation and his wife were trustees of trust holding majority of outstanding voting shares of corporation, court upheld finding that amendment of certificate of incorporation to replace voting preferred shares with voting common, to authorize additional voting shares, to remove restriction requiring two-thirds approval for issuance or disposition of new voting stock, and to abolish shareholders' pre-emptive rights and cumulative voting for directors, was made in good faith in furtherance of corporate objectives. Renz v Beeman (1978, CA2 NY) 589 F.2d 735, cert den 444 US 834, 62 L Ed 2d 43, 100 S Ct 65

5. Procedural matters

The allegations of the complaint alleging breach of duties imposed on officers and directors and executive committees merit a full and plenary trial and the issues should not be limited to whether the stockholders and directors ratified the actions of the defendants and voted to discontinue suits in good faith and with full knowledge of the facts. Syracuse Television, Inc. v Channel 9, Syracuse, Inc. (1967, 4th Dept) 28 A.D.2d 638, 280 N.Y.S.2d 287

In shareholder's derivative action involving retirement agreement, Supreme Court properly granted summary judgment in favor of defendant corporate director, despite fact that he had interest in agreement, where he demonstrated that he did not vote on agreement, that he disclosed his interest in agreement to boards of directors, their committees, and shareholders, and that agreement was fair and reasonable. Freer v Mayer (1996, 2d Dept) 223 A.D.2d 667, 637 N.Y.S.2d 425

In action seeking declaration that corporate resolution which provided for discontinuance of eviction proceeding commenced in Justice Court was validly adopted by board of directors and binding on defendant, it was error for Supreme Court to dismiss complaint on ground that eviction proceeding was in nature of shareholder's derivative claim immune from board action, and to direct parties to litigate issues raised by defendant's counterclaim in Justice Court, as such ruling essentially determined that resolution was properly adopted procedurally, while referring defendant's substantive challenges to Justice Court, which was beyond Justice Court's subject matter jurisdiction. TJI Realty, Inc. v Harris (1998, 2d Dept) 250 A.D.2d 596, 672 N.Y.S.2d 386

The complaint of a bankruptcy trustee alleging violations of fiduciary obligations adequately set forth facts which were intertwined with a preceding federal cause of action which, if provable, could support a claim upon which relief could be granted pursuant to Business Corporation Law §§ 717, 720 and the trustee had standing to sue under Business Corporation Law § 720. Bush v Masiello (1972, SD NY) 55 FRD 72

Bankruptcy court found that corporate officers violated their fiduciary duties because they extended direct loans (approximately $ 8.5 million) and trade credit (approximately $ 18 million) to a corporation, with only modest analysis and even less in the way of traditional corporate formalities. Additionally, the officers made direct loans totaling $ 8.5 million in the aggregate, on an unsecured basis, without requiring any promissory notes. Fox v Koplik (In re Perry H. Koplik & Sons, Inc.) (2012, BC SD NY) 476 BR 746, adversary proceeding, request gr (2012, BC SD NY) 2012 Bankr LEXIS 3139 and objection overruled, accepted, in part, rejected, in part (2013, SD NY) 2013 US Dist LEXIS 123254.

Claim that defendant breached her fiduciary duties as debtor's director under New York law survived a motion to dismiss, as the trustee plead around the business judgment rule because the thrust of his complaint was that defendant closed her eyes to debtor's affairs and failed to take reasonable steps to inform herself about a dishonest employee's activities and debtor's operations. Geltzer v Bedke (In re Mundo Latino Mkt.), 2018 Bankr. LEXIS 2435 (Bankr. S.D.N.Y. Aug. 16, 2018).

§ 718.   List of directors and officers

(a) If a shareholder of a corporation, in person or by his attorney or agent, or a representative of the district attorney or of the secretary of state, the attorney general, or other state official, makes a written demand on a corporation to inspect a current list of its directors and officers, the corporation shall, within two business days after receipt of the demand and for a period of one week thereafter, make the list available for such inspection at its office during usual business hours.

(b) Upon refusal by the corporation to make a current list of its directors and officers available, as provided in paragraph (a), the person making a demand for such list may apply, ex parte, to the supreme court at a special term held within the judicial district where the office of the corporation is located for an order directing the corporation to make such list available. The court may grant such order or take such other action as it may deem just and proper.

History: Add, L 1961, ch 855, eff Sept 1, 1963; amd, L 1971, ch 895, eff June 25, 1971; L 1997, ch 449, § 48, eff Feb 22, 1998; L 1997, ch 494, § 3, eff Feb 22, 1998.

§ 719.   Liability of directors in certain cases

(a) Directors of a corporation who vote for or concur in any of the following corporate actions shall be jointly and severally liable to the corporation for the benefit of its creditors or shareholders, to the extent of any injury suffered by such persons, respectively, as a result of such action:

(1) The declaration of any dividend or other distribution to the extent that it is contrary to the provisions of paragraphs (a) and (b) of section 510 (Dividends or other distributions in cash or property).

(2) The purchase of the shares of the corporation to the extent that it is contrary to the provisions of section 513 (Purchase or redemption by a corporation of its own shares).

(3) The distribution of assets to shareholders after dissolution of the corporation without paying or adequately providing for all known liabilities of the corporation, excluding any claims not filed by creditors within the time limit set in a notice given to creditors under articles 10 (Non-judicial dissolution) or 11 (Judicial dissolution).

(4) The making of any loan contrary to section 714 (Loans to directors).

(b) A director who is present at a meeting of the board, or any committee thereof, when action specified in paragraph (a) is taken shall be presumed to have concurred in the action unless his dissent thereto shall be entered in the minutes of the meeting, or unless he shall submit his written dissent to the person acting as the secretary of the meeting before the adjournment thereof, or shall deliver or send by registered mail such dissent to the secretary of the corporation promptly after the adjournment of the meeting. Such right to dissent shall not apply to a director who voted in favor of such action. A director who is absent from a meeting of the board, or any committee thereof, when such action is taken shall be presumed to have concurred in the action unless he shall deliver or send by registered mail his dissent thereto to the secretary of the corporation or shall cause such dissent to be filed with the minutes of the proceedings of the board or committee within a reasonable time after learning of such action.

(c) Any director against whom a claim is successfully asserted under this section shall be entitled to contribution from the other directors who voted for or concurred in the action upon which the claim is asserted.

(d) Directors against whom a claim is successfully asserted under this section shall be entitled, to the extent of the amounts paid by them to the corporation as a result of such claims:

(1) Upon payment to the corporation of any amount of an improper dividend or distribution, to be subrogated to the rights of the corporation against shareholders who received such dividend or distribution with knowledge of facts indicating that it was not authorized by section 510, in proportion to the amounts received by them respectively.

(2) Upon payment to the corporation of any amount of the purchase price of an improper purchase of shares, to have the corporation rescind such purchase of shares and recover for their benefit, but at their expense, the amount of such purchase price from any seller who sold such shares with knowledge of facts indicating that such purchase of shares by the corporation was not authorized by section 513.

(3) Upon payment to the corporation of the claim of any creditor by reason of a violation of subparagraph (a) (3), to be subrogated to the rights of the corporation against shareholders who received an improper distribution of assets.

(4) Upon payment to the corporation of the amount of any loan made contrary to section 714, to be subrogated to the rights of the corporation against a director who received the improper loan.

(e) A director shall not be liable under this section if, in the circumstances, he performed his duty to the corporation under paragraph (a) of section 717.

(f) This section shall not affect any liability otherwise imposed by law upon any director.

History: Add, L 1961, ch 855, eff Sept 1, 1963, amd, L 1962, ch 834, § 54, eff Sept 1, 1963, L 1963, ch 689, § 6, eff Sept 1, 1963, L 1977, ch 432, § 5, eff Sept 1, 1977.

Par (e), amd, L 1987, ch 367, § 3, eff July 23, 1987.

CASE ANNOTATIONS

1. In general
2. Impairment of capital
3. Other actions warranting liability
4. Enforcement of liability; limitations
5. Participation by directors; dissent

1. In general

With respect to liability of directors of foreign corporations for acts of the nature of those set forth in this section, the law of the corpora-

tion's domicile has been regarded as the touchstone. De Raismes v United States Lithograph Co. (1914) 161 A.D. 781, 146 N.Y.S. 813

Section 58 of former Stock Corp. L. has been regarded as not penal in nature but merely as requiring directors to compensate for damage sustained by reason of their wrongful acts. Stratton v Bertles (1933) 238 A.D. 87, 263 N.Y.S. 466; Waters v Spalt (1948) 22 Misc. 2d 937, 80 N.Y.S.2d 681; Greene v Boardman (1932) 143 Misc 201, 256 N.Y.S. 340

Judgment creditor's cause of action against director of corporate judgment debtor would be dismissed, without prejudice and with leave to replead, where it was alleged only that director was personally liable under Business Corporation Law to corporate debtor for unlawful distributions of corporate assets and that creditor was entitled to satisfy its judgment from director's interest in assets of employee benefit plan, and it appeared from wording that cause of action was grounded on CLS Bus Corp §§ 510 and 719; while § 719 would not apply to such cause, and CLS Bus Corp § 720 does permit action against director by judgment creditor to set aside unlawful conveyance where transferee knew of its unlawfulness, essential elements of § 720 action could not be deemed to have been pleaded even under liberal rules regarding construction of pleadings. Planned Consumer Marketing, Inc. v Coats & Clark, Inc. (1987, 1st Dept) 127 A.D.2d 355, 513 N.Y.S.2d 417, affd, ctfd ques ans 71 N.Y.2d 442, 527 N.Y.S.2d 185, 522 N.E.2d 30, 9 EBC 1796

Individual defendant was entitled to summary judgment dismissing fraud complaint against him, even though he was sole shareholder, director, and officer of corporate defendant, where allegedly fraudulent letter, which represented that certain premises "will be delivered vacant at closing," was signed by individual defendant in his corporate capacity, and thus plaintiff failed to meet its burden of piercing corporate veil so as to impose general liability on individual defendant. Madison Home Equities, Inc. v Echeverria (1999, 2d Dept) 266 A.D.2d 435, 698 N.Y.S.2d 703

The statutes provide for actions against defaulting directors and officers under certain circumstances, but such actions are by or for the benefit of the corporation and are clearly equitable in nature. Krauss v Dinerstein (1970) 62 Misc. 2d 682, 309 N.Y.S.2d 962

Bank which functioned as primary creditor of judgment debtor, which was neither director of debtor nor recipient of dividend or distribution made by debtor, could not be held liable under BCL § 719 merely as aider and abettor of prohibited transaction under statute. Atlanta Shipping Corp. v Chemical Bank (1986, SD NY) 631 F. Supp. 335

2. Impairment of capital

Ignorance concerning the financial condition of the corporation would not excuse a director from liability for voting a dividend impairing capital, and there was usually very little by way of defense which could be raised where personal liability was asserted on a charge of voting for or acquiescing in an illegal distribution of assets. Irving Trust Co. v Gunder (1932) 234 A.D. 252, 254 N.Y.S. 630; Wesp v Muckle (1910) 136 A.D. 241, 120 N.Y.S. 976, reh den 136 A.D. 945, 121 N.Y.S. 1151 and affd 201 N.Y. 527, 94 N.E. 1100

When the damage consisted in an impairment of capital, as by the payment of an unlawful dividend or making an improper and unwarranted distribution of assets, liability of directors was limited to the loss sustained by the corporation or its creditors by reason of the capital impairment. Friedman v Video Television, Inc. (1953) 281 A.D. 815, 118 N.Y.S.2d 844; Shaw v Ansaldi Co. (1917) 178 A.D. 589, 165 N.Y.S. 872

Under § 58 of former Stock Corp. L., a director present at a meeting of the board when action was taken impairing capital would incur personal liability though he did not vote on the proposal, if he failed to register dissent. Furthermore, one who was not even a member of the board when the action was taken, but subsequently became a director, could be held liable on the basis of acquiescence or ratification. Union Discount Co. v Macrobert (1929) 134 Misc 107, 234 N.Y.S. 529; Walker v Man (1931) 142 Misc 277, 253 N.Y.S. 458

See also Walker v Man (1931) 142 Misc 288, 253 N.Y.S. 472

Section 58 of former Stock Corp. L., in imposing express liability for impairment of capital on directors, did not preclude assertion of liability against a transferee of corporate assets to the extent of what he received, if he was chargeable with knowledge when he accepted the property that it would illegally impair assets. Field v Bankers Trust Co. (1961, CA2 NY) 296 F.2d 109, cert den 369 US 859, 8 L Ed 2d 17, 82 S Ct 948

3. Other actions warranting liability

Directors distributing assets of a corporation in process of dissolution in disregard of the rights of a creditor entitled to participate in the distribution, became jointly and severally liable to take care of the debt remaining due him. J. F. Tapley Co. v Keller (1909) 133 A.D. 54, 117 N.Y.S. 817

Administrative penalties for violating regulations of Department of Environmental Conservation were properly levied, jointly and severally, against directors of corporation which had run refuse operation where directors had voluntarily dissolved corporation without covering abandoned landfill and without making adequate arrangements for possible damage and penalty claims, and where directors had been put on notice of applicable regulations 3 years prior to corporate dissolution. Fiorillo v New York State Dept. of Environmental Conservation (1987, 3d Dept) 123 A.D.2d 151, 510 N.Y.S.2d 775, app dismd 70 N.Y.2d 641, 512 N.E.2d 557

In shareholders' derivative action against directors of corporation for breach of fiduciary duty and corporate waste in sale of 41 percent of corporation's stock for allegedly grossly inadequate consideration, plaintiffs raised reasonable doubt as to adequacy of investigation into that sale by special committee appointed by directors where committee was advised by attorney who had represented corporation in connection with sale, and committee's 2-page report on sale failed to document committee's procedures, reasoning, and conclusions, thus effectively insulating its investigation from scrutiny by courts. Brinckerhoff v JAC Holding Corp. (1999, 1st Dept) 263 A.D.2d 352, 692 N.Y.S.2d 381

In action for diversion of corporate assets, there was no judicial or statutory authority for defendant's theory that, essentially, his fiduciary duties as 50 percent shareholder, director, and officer of corporation were on sliding scale so that as plaintiff committed bad acts, defendant's duties were reduced or limited proportionately. Ross v Moyer (2001, 1st Dept) 286 A.D.2d 610, 730 N.Y.S.2d 318, related proceeding (1st Dept) 286 A.D.2d 611, 730 N.Y.S.2d 225

Doctrine of unclean hands barred recovery in action against 50 percent shareholder, director, and officer of corporation for diversion of corporate assets where, inter alia, plaintiff, who held similar position, secretly wired to himself $670,000 in corporate funds. Ross v Moyer (2001, 1st Dept) 286 A.D.2d 610, 730 N.Y.S.2d 318, related proceeding (1st Dept) 286 A.D.2d 611, 730 N.Y.S.2d 225

An officer or director of a corporation is personally liable for his acts which constitute a conversion of the property of a third person and it is no answer to such liability that the act was done while the officer or director was acting for the corporation. Admiral Corp. v Cohen (1971) 68 Misc. 2d 687, 327 N.Y.S.2d 422

A complaint filed against officers, directors and sole stockholders of a corporation alleging a cause of action in contract, in that the named defendants personally and knowingly sold trust items and failed to remit to plaintiff the invoiced amounts, and a cause of action in conversion, alleged two viable causes of action, one in conversion and the other in breach of contract. Admiral Corp. v Cohen (1971) 68 Misc. 2d 687, 327 N.Y.S.2d 422

Neither Business Corporation Law § 719 nor 720 permits an action against officers and directors and sole stockholders of a corporation for the selling of items of merchandise "out of trust" and failing to remit to the plaintiffs the proceeds received from such sales, which items had been delivered in accordance with a floor agreement, but the statutes preserve liability of officers and directors in those instances where they actually participated in frauds, misfeasance or other kinds of tortious conduct injurious to third parties. Admiral Corp. v Cohen (1971) 68 Misc. 2d 687, 327 N.Y.S.2d 422

New York's debtor and creditor law does not authorize actions against those who aid and abet violations of CLS Bus Corp §§ 510, 719, or 720. Atlanta Shipping Corp. v Chemical Bank (1987, CA2 NY) 818 F.2d 240, 3 UCCRS2d 1618

4. Enforcement of liability; limitations

As against judgment creditors, or their representatives, limitations did not run against enforcement of director liability until six years after return of execution against the corporation unsatisfied. Rosenkranz v Doran (1942) 264 A.D. 335, 35 N.Y.S.2d 413; Klages v Cohen (1947, DC NY) 7 FRD 218

In an action to recover a real estate brokerage commission and for punitive damages based upon the defendants' failure to pay plaintiff a commission after the plaintiff produced a signed lease for commercial space in a building owned by the defendant corporation, the trial court properly dismissed the complaint against the individual defendants, where the evidence established that the individual defendants, who represented the corporation in the course of the parties' negotiations, never obligated themselves in their personal capacities; however, the trial court erred in dismissing the complaint as against the corporate defendant, inasmuch as the parties had expressly provided that the plaintiff's commission would not be earned until an agreement had been reached and the tenant had bound itself to a lease, and the evidence demonstrated the existence of issues of fact as to whether the signed lease with certain changes mirrored the agreement reached by the parties or whether it contained unauthorized departures from their oral agreement as to material terms. Williamson, Picket, Gross, Inc. v Hirschfeld (1983, 1st Dept) 92 A.D.2d 289, 460 N.Y.S.2d 36

Cause of action alleging payment of dividends and distributions in violation of CLS Bus Corp §§ 510 and 719(a)(1) was not subject to dismissal for failure to comply with pleading requirements of CLS CPLR § 3016 since allegations were not based on fraud. Menaker v Alstaedter (1987, 2d Dept) 134 A.D.2d 412, 521 N.Y.S.2d 35

If a creditor's action to enforce directors' liability was predicated on §§ 90 and 91 of former Gen. Corp. L., he must have first obtained judgment against the corporation and had execution thereon returned unsatisfied. Waters v Spalt (1948) 22 Misc. 2d 937, 80 N.Y.S.2d 681; Island Paper Co. v Carthage Timber Corp. (1926) 128 Misc 246, 218 N.Y.S. 346

A director's liability under this section of the Bus. Corp. L. is specifically "to the corporation" for the benefit of its creditors or shareholders, whereas, under § 58 of former Stock Corp. L., in the case of injured creditors, it was directly to any creditor damaged, who could proceed individually to enforce it, if he saw fit, without first exhausting other remedies or making his action representative in character in behalf of himself and all other creditors. Quintal v Greenstein (1932) 142 Misc 854, 256 N.Y.S. 462, affd 236 A.D. 719, 257 N.Y.S. 1034; Huron Milling Co. v Hedges (1958, CA2 NY) 257 F.2d 258

Limitations do not commence to run against such a cause of action accruing to a trustee in bankruptcy until after his appointment as trustee. Callaghan v Bailey (1942) 179 Misc 673, 38 N.Y.S.2d 203, affd 266 A.D. 915, 43 N.Y.S.2d 516, affd 293 N.Y. 396, 57 N.E.2d 729

The creditor, pursuing his individual remedy under § 58 of former Stock Corp. L., did not have to aver or prove that he was a creditor at the time of the wrongful act complained of, or that there were other creditors at that time, or when the action was commenced, as every creditor of a corporation is entitled to rely on the unimpaired condition of its capital as against depletion by illegal conduct of its directors. David McDonough, Inc. v Berger (1959) 22 Misc. 2d 646, 192 N.Y.S.2d 702; New York Credit Men's Ass'n v Harris (1939) 170 Misc 988, 11 N.Y.S.2d 435, affd 262 A.D. 826, 29 N.Y.S.2d 505; Aktieselskabet Christianssand v Federal S.S. Corp. (1923) 121 Misc 627, 201 N.Y.S. 504

Creditors of a corporation may not recover from a parent corporation, or its stockholders or directors until they have exhausted their legal remedies against the corporation by recovery of a judgment against it, and return of an execution wholly or partially unsatisfied, unless such creditor shows that it was impossible or would have been useless to proceed against the corporation. Eskimo Pie Corp. v Whitelawn Dairies, Inc. (1967, SD NY) 266 F. Supp. 79

Plaintiff would be required to pursue its remedy for breach of contract against subsidiary corporations to judgment before it could resort to suing either the parent corporation or the stockholders or directors of said parent corporation. Eskimo Pie Corp. v Whitelawn Dairies, Inc. (1967, SD NY) 266 F. Supp. 79

5. Participation by directors; dissent

However, some linkage between the defendant director and the action taken by the board had to be established, expressly or by implication, in order to show his participation or acquiescence in the action of the board, and some decisions stated that evidence of bad faith or negligence was necessary. Murray v Smith (1918) 224 N.Y. 40, 120 N.E. 60; Diamond v Davis (1942, Sup) 38 N.Y.S.2d 103, affd 265 A.D. 919, 39 N.Y.S.2d 412, affd 292 N.Y. 552, 54 N.E.2d 683

While this section of the Bus. Corp. L. excuses a director from liability if he has duly recorded his dissent from the illegal action taken by the board, or if he has "discharged his duty to the corporation under § 717," defenses of good faith and due care were not generally recognized in proceedings to enforce liability under § 58 of former Stock Corp. L. Cowin v Jonas (1944) 293 N.Y. 838, 59 N.E.2d 436; Cowin v Jonas (1943, Sup) 43 N.Y.S.2d 468, affd 267 A.D. 947, 48 N.Y.S.2d 460, affd 293 N.Y. 838, 59 N.E.2d 436

Directors of corporation who did not take any actions leading to pecuniary gain realized by one director who sold his shares to another and received a premium in exchange for his promise to aid buyer in obtaining control and acquiring certain corporate offices and who did not realize any personal profit themselves as a result of the transaction could not be held liable jointly or severally with the selling shareholder for the illegal profit realized by the selling stockholder, even though the directors did give certain votes which aided the buyer's goals. Brecher v Gregg (1975) 89 Misc. 2d 457, 392 N.Y.S.2d 776, affd (1st Dept) 56 A.D.2d 525, 391 N.Y.S.2d 829

§ 720. Action against directors and officers for misconduct

(a) An action may be brought against one or more directors or officers of a corporation to procure a judgment for the following relief:

(1) Subject to any provision of the certificate of incorporation authorized pursuant to paragraph (b) of section 402, to compel the defendant to account for his official conduct in the following cases:

(A) The neglect of, or failure to perform, or other violation of his duties in the management and disposition of corporate assets committed to his charge.

(B) The acquisition by himself, transfer to others, loss or waste of corporate assets due to any neglect of, or failure to perform, or other violation of his duties.

(C) In the case of directors or officers of a benefit corporation organized under article seventeen of this chapter: (i) the failure to pursue the general public benefit purpose of a benefit corporation or any specific public benefit set forth in its certificate of incorporation; (ii) the failure by a benefit corporation to deliver or post an annual report as required by section seventeen hundred eight of article seventeen of this chapter; or (iii) the neglect of, or failure to perform, or other violation of his or her duties or standard of conduct under article seventeen of this chapter.

(2) To set aside an unlawful conveyance, assignment or transfer of corporate assets, where the transferee knew of its unlawfulness.

(3) To enjoin a proposed unlawful conveyance, assignment or transfer of corporate assets, where there is sufficient evidence that it will be made.

(b) An action may be brought for the relief provided in this section, and in paragraph (a) of section 719 (Liability of directors in certain cases) by a corporation, or a receiver, trustee in bankruptcy, officer, director or judgment creditor thereof, or, under section 626 (Shareholders' derivative action brought in the right of the corporation to procure a judgment in its favor), by a shareholder, voting trust certificate holder, or the owner of a beneficial interest in shares thereof.

(c) This section shall not affect any liability otherwise imposed by law upon any director or officer.

History: Add, L 1961, ch 855, eff Sept 1, 1963; amd. L 1965, ch 803, § 30, eff Sept 1, 1965, L 1987, ch 367, § 4, eff July 23, 1987, L 2011, ch 599, § 4, eff Feb 10, 2012.

CASE ANNOTATIONS
1. In general

1.5. Relationship to federal law
2. Accounting actions, generally
3. Waste or mismanagement, generally
4. Excessive compensation
5. – Other waste or mismanagement
6. Unlawful transfers
7. – Particular cases
8. Conversion
9. Other grounds for action
10. Parties, generally
11. Shareholders
12. Directors and officers
13. Creditors
14. Receivers to bring action
15. Corporation
16. Defenses; good faith
17. Participation or ratification
18. Other defenses
19. Jurisdiction
20. Joinder of parties and claims
21. Time limitations
22. Pre-trial examinations; discovery
23. Other procedural matters

1. In general

Purpose of CLS Bus Corp § 720 is to furnish means of redressing wrongful disposition of corporate assets by corporation's officers and directors. Planned Consumer Marketing, Inc. v Coats & Clark, Inc. (1988) 71 N.Y.2d 442, 527 N.Y.S.2d 185, 522 N.E.2d 30, 9 EBC 1796

Provisions in prior corporation laws according rights of action against officers and directors for official misconduct or dereliction of duty have been regarded as remedial rather than penal, and accordingly not subject to strict construction, but nevertheless, to the extent that they were in derogation of the common law, not to be extended beyond situations fairly within their terms. Caesar v Bernard (1913) 156 A.D. 724, 141 N.Y.S. 659, affd 209 N.Y. 570, 103 N.E. 1122; Newfield v Ettlinger (1959) 22 Misc. 2d 769, 194 N.Y.S.2d 670, app dismd (1st Dept) 10 A.D.2d 947, 205 N.Y.S.2d 908; Palmer v Intermediate Factors Co. (1949, Sup) 88 N.Y.S.2d 559; Matters v Manufacturers' Trust Co. (1932, CA2 NY) 54 F.2d 1010

The remedies afforded by prior similar provisions were not necessarily exclusive and did not supersede or abolish relief by creditors' bill. Rubenstein v Berch (1941) 261 A.D. 265, 25 N.Y.S.2d 202; Bailey v Colleen Products Corp. (1923) 120 Misc 297, 198 N.Y.S. 418

Where plaintiff brought action for various equitable remedies against director of corporation as shareholder and former director and officer of corporation, on behalf of himself and all other shareholders of corporation similarly situated, and in right of said corporation, plaintiff was required to comply with Business Corporation Law provisions concerning such derivative suits. Galasso v Pioneer Home Improv. Corp. (1976, 2d Dept) 52 A.D.2d 901, 383 N.Y.S.2d 376

Corporate officer who participates in commission of tort by corporation is personally liable therefor; he is not held liable for negligence of corporation simply because of his official relationship, and he must be shown to have participated in wrongful conduct; officer of construction corporation is personally liable for failure to construct home in workmanlike manner where he supervises construction and personally does some of work. Clark v Pine Hill Holmes, Inc. (1985, 4th Dept) 112 A.D.2d 755, 492 N.Y.S.2d 253

The entire purpose of this section and § 626 of the Business Corp Law is to allow a derivative action in the name of the corporation and for its benefit when the board of directors has refused, under certain circumstances to bring an action, and a stockholder's derivative action cannot be obviated by a majority vote of the board of directors not to bring the action in the first place, especially where the corporation is controlled by the alleged wrongdoers. Syracuse Television, Inc. v Channel 9 Syracuse, Inc. (1966) 52 Misc. 2d 246, 275 N.Y.S.2d 190

The statutes provide for actions against defaulting directors and officers under certain circumstances, but such actions are by or for the benefit of the corporation and are clearly equitable in nature. Krauss v Dinerstein (1970) 62 Misc. 2d 682, 309 N.Y.S.2d 962

Judgment for a town against a corporation's officers arising from the officers' refusal to seek insurance coverage from the New York State Insurance Fund was error because, inter alia, an action against an officer for misconduct was circumscribed by N.Y. Bus. Corp. Law

§ 720, which limited the relief available in such an action, and § 720 may not have been used to obtain a money judgment in an action at law. Town of Amherst v Hilger (2013, App Div, 4th Dept) 962 NYS2d 837, subsequent app (2013, 4th Dept) 104 App Div 3d 1268, 960 NYS2d 922.

Section 720 of New York Business Corporation Law is to be broadly construed and is to cover every form of waste of assets and violation of corporate duty. Re Princeton Industries, Inc. (1984, BC SD NY) 39 BR 140

Where appraisal remedy is not available to minority dissenting shareholders, courts in New York have displayed no hesitancy in granting injunctive relief. Goldberg v Meridor (1977, CA2 NY) 567 F.2d 209, cert den 434 US 1069, 55 L Ed 2d 771, 98 S Ct 1249 and on remand (SD NY) 81 FRD 105, CCH Fed Secur L Rep ¶ 96754, 27 FR Serv 2d 1360

New York's debtor and creditor law does not authorize actions against those who aid and abet violations of CLS Bus Corp §§ 510, 719, or 720. Atlanta Shipping Corp. v Chemical Bank (1987, CA2 NY) 818 F.2d 240, 3 UCCRS2d 1618

Common law principle that corporate director has fiduciary duty to manage corporate assets in a reasonable way and that he is liable for any waste or misappropriation of corporate property is embodied in CLS Business Corporation Law § 720, which is explicitly an extension of the common law and not a limit on it. Superintendent of Ins. v Freedman (1977, SD NY) 443 F. Supp. 628, affd without op (CA2 NY) 594 F.2d 852 and affd without op (CA2 NY) 594 F.2d 852

Action under New York Business Corporation Law § 720 is not stockholder's derivative suit. Re Application of Blakeman (1981, ED NY) 512 F. Supp. 325

Pennsylvania carpet maker is entitled to dismissal of "directorial negligence" claim under CLS Bus Corp Law § 720, even if customer had evidence that maker's negligence caused customer's alleged loss of carpet, because there is no evidence sufficient to warrant inference that maker is or was doing business in New York. Air India v Pennsylvania Woven Carpet Mills (1997, SD NY) 978 F. Supp. 500

1.5. Relationship to federal law

It is not basis for stay of arbitration under Federal Arbitration Act (9 USCS §§ 1 et seq.) that arbitrator may be called upon to consider issues of waste and overreaching on part of corporate officer that are also involved in state court action under state law (CLS Business Corporation Law § 720) brought by corporation against officer, or that party to court proceeding may later argue that arbitrator's determination should be given preclusive effect. GAF Corp. v Werner (1985) 66 N.Y.2d 97, 495 N.Y.S.2d 312, 485 N.E.2d 977, cert den (US) 89 L Ed 2d 720, 106 S Ct 1463

Supersedure clause of Employee Retirement Income Security Act (ERISA), 29 USCS § 1144, did not preclude enforcement proceeding under CLS CPLR Art 52 where judgment creditor alleged that director and officer of corporate debtor (who was also ERISA plan trustee) violated CLS Bus Corp § 720 by wrongfully distributing corporate assets to plan, and where proceeding did not purport to relate to management of ERISA trust or to trustee's fiduciary obligations. Planned Consumer Marketing, Inc. v Coats & Clark, Inc. (1988) 71 N.Y.2d 442, 527 N.Y.S.2d 185, 522 N.E.2d 30, 9 EBC 1796

In action for corporate waste and mismanagement brought under CLS Bus Corp § 720, court would reject contention that recovery by corporation could subject directors to duplicate liability, even though class of shareholders had commenced action against directors for same frauds alleged in instant action, and individual creditors had brought and settled their own claims for credit fraud, since stockholder action had been brought under anti-fraud provisions of SEC for damages caused to shareholders rather than corporation, and claims asserted by creditors were not identical to those asserted by corporation. Amfesco Industries, Inc. v Greenblatt (1991, 1st Dept) 172 A.D.2d 261, 568 N.Y.S.2d 593

Supreme Court would not make equitable exception to antialienation provisions of ERISA, even if proceeds of sale of judgment debtor's property were unlawfully transferred to pension fund trustees in violation of CLS Dr & Cr §§ 273, 273-a, 276, and 276-a and CLS Bus Corp § 720; in judgment creditor's turnover action, parties' motions for summary judgment would be denied where there were triable issues of fact as to how sale proceeds were disbursed and whether transfers were wrongful. Majteles v AVL Corp. (1999, Sup) 182 Misc. 2d 140, 696 N.Y.S.2d 748

Bankruptcy trustee had standing to bring an action on behalf of the debtor against a controlling shareholder and others alleging, among other claims, fraud because (1) the Wagoner rule was not

invoked where the complaint alleged that the controlling shareholder, while purportedly acting as the manager of the debtor, in reality was an agent of the debtor's franchisor and the franchisor's credit company and was put in control of the debtor by those parties specifically to control the debtor for their benefit; (2) even if the Wagoner rule applied, the allegations of the complaint were sufficient to invoke the adverse interest exception because it was alleged that throughout his tenure as a manager of the debtor, the controlling shareholder was acting either to benefit third parties or for his own benefit; and (3) the sole actor rule did not apply because the complaint adequately alleged that an innocent shareholder, i.e., the debtor, existed who could have stopped the fraudulent scheme had she known it was being committed where the debtor, as a 48 percent shareholder had standing to commence a derivative action or an action to enforce her rights pursuant to N.Y. Bus. Corp. Law § 720. Nisselson v Ford Motor Co. (In re Monahan Ford Corp.) (2006, BC ED NY) 340 BR 1, 46 BCD 93

Under New York law, claims for waste, mismanagement, and breach of fiduciary duty belonged to corporation and once bankruptcy ensued, became property of estate that Chapter 7 trustee alone had standing to assert, and movants made prima facie showing that creditor violated stay by demanding payment from movants (debtor's former officers, directors, and shareholder) on account of these estate claims. However, movants failed to identify any damages proximately caused by stay violation other than their attorneys' fees and legal expenses incurred in responding to letter and prosecuting motion, and in absence of any actual damages, award was not merited. In re Ampal-Am. Isr. Corp. (2013, BC SD NY) 502 BR 361, 58 BCD 246.

2. Accounting actions, generally

Any action brought to require an accounting for official conduct of corporate officers under § 60 of former Gen. Corp. L. was deemed one to require an accounting to the corporation for the benefit of all persons in interest, not merely the plaintiff. Wangrow v Wangrow (1924) 211 A.D. 552, 207 N.Y.S. 132

Former shareholder of defendant corporation could maintain action for accounting against officers and directors of corporation in their individual capacities, although CLS Bus Corp § 720 did not create cause of action personal to him by which he might proceed against them, where he alleged that they caused corporation to offer him inadequate price for his stock and redistributed his shares among themselves without compensating him when he declined to sell, in order to deprive him of his share of corporation's profits; redress of wrong personal to plaintiff was available to plaintiff personally despite right of present shareholder to redress wrong in derivative action so far as it related to corporation, and thus defense motion for summary judgment was properly denied. Tornick v Dinex Furniture Industries, Inc. (1989, 2d Dept) 148 A.D.2d 602, 539 N.Y.S.2d 68

An action brought under this section to require directors and officers to account for their official duties in the management of the corporation is, according to § 626, derivative in nature since the cause of action belongs to the corporation. Syracuse Television, Inc. v Channel 9, Syracuse, Inc. (1966) 51 Misc. 2d 188, 273 N.Y.S.2d 16

Statute permitting action against corporate director for "the neglect of, or failure to perform, or other violations of his duties in the management and disposition of corporate assets committed to his charge" does not mean that director is chargeable with ordinary negligence for having made improper decision, or having acted imprudently; "neglect" referred to in statute is neglect of duties, i.e., malfeasance or nonfeasance, and not misjudgment. Kamin v American Express Co. (1976) 86 Misc. 2d 809, 383 N.Y.S.2d 807, affd (1st Dept) 54 A.D.2d 654, 387 N.Y.S.2d 993

Action by majority shareholders and directors of defunct corporation against minority shareholder who managed business should have been instituted under CLS Bus Corp § 720(a)(1) rather than CLS Bus Corp § 626, where complaint sought accounting and related relief as to defendant shareholder's conversion, fraud, misappropriation of corporate funds, and breach of fiduciary duty. Bouhayer v Georgalis (1996, Sup) 169 Misc. 2d 779, 645 N.Y.S.2d 1008

Computer game creator's accounting, breach of contract, trade secret misappropriation, and tortious interference claims were unique to it, rather than derivative claims belonging to a buyer under N.Y. Bus. Corp. Law § 720, and were not barred by a bankruptcy settlement in the buyer's bankruptcy proceeding since the causes of action alleged a direct injury to property rights unique to the creator, rather than the corporation or all of the creditors, because: (1) recovery of damages by the corporation would not rectify the creator's injury, (2) allegations that defendants breached their assigned contract obligations to the creator did not implicate the buyer such that it could assert a claim on its own behalf, and (3) because the creator asserted that the buyer participated in the alleged misconduct, the buyer could not assert the tortious interference or misappropriation of trade secrets causes of action on its own. Andrew Greenberg, Inc. v Svane, Inc. (2007, 3d Dept) 36 App Div 3d 1094, 830 NYS2d 358

An action pursuant to § 60 of former Gen Corp L has always been considered one in equity for an accounting, rather than one at law for damages, but the officers charged with misconduct were not regarded as trustees of the corporate assets in the strict legal sense, even though it was in process of liquidation. Chambers v Blickle Ford Sales, Inc. (1963, CA2 Conn) 313 F.2d 252

Because an action under § 60 of former Gen Corp L to require corporate officers to account for misconduct was regarded as equitable, time to commence it was governed by limitations applicable to accounting suits rather than the shorter limitation period for tort actions. Chambers v Blickle Ford Sales, Inc. (1963, CA2 Conn) 313 F.2d 252

Shareholder's demand for an accounting from several orange juice manufacturers and their corporate officers was dismissed as such an action could only be brought in a shareholder derivative action brought on behalf of the corporation. Fisher v Big Squeeze (NY), Inc. (2004, ED NY) 349 F. Supp. 2d 483

3. Waste or mismanagement, generally

Director of corporation who is entitled to bring suit under CLS Business Corporation § 720 on behalf of corporation for waste committed by another director or officer does not violate CLS Civil Rights § 70 by commencing such suit. Di Dominici v Parmet (1986, 2d Dept) 118 A.D.2d 618, 499 N.Y.S.2d 768

Court properly dismissed third-party complaint by tenant that had performed repairs on landlord's building, alleging that landlord's officers and directors sold building for less than fair value in violation of CLS Dr & Cr § 273, improperly retained proceeds of sale, wasted landlord's assets, and intended to defraud landlord's creditors, including repairing tenant, where (1) debt no longer existed for purposes of § 273, because landlord had filed bond in excess of amount of tenant's mechanic's lien claim, (2) tenant's allegations of insolvency, fraud, and lack of fair consideration were unsubstantiated and conclusory, and (3) there was insufficient evidence to pierce landlord's corporate veil, and thus landlord's officers and directors were not liable for landlord's alleged corporate debts. Washington 1993 Inc. v Reles (1998, 3d Dept) 255 A.D.2d 745, 680 N.Y.S.2d 715

It is well settled that in a stockholders' derivative action it must be shown, among other things, (1) that the corporation has a cause of action, and (2) that the directors have unreasonably refused to prosecute such cause of action. Markewich v Newberg (1960) 27 Misc. 2d 1040, 210 N.Y.S.2d 299

Shareholder was entitled to be reimbursed for money advanced on behalf of a corporation for legal fees and settlement money in a prior litigation because other officers had ratified the shareholder's actions, and the shareholder's erroneous opinion concerning payment by an insurer did not show bad faith for N.Y. Bus. Corp. Law § 722(a) purposes; the facts did not establish the requisite bad faith, self-dealing, or fraud required to overcome the presumption under the business judgment rule. The termination of the litigation by settlement did not create a presumption of bad faith or a purpose which did not serve the best interest of the corporation. McDaniel v 162 Columbia Hgts. Hous. Corp. (2009, Sup) 25 Misc 3d 1024, 886 NYS2d 562.

CLS Business Corporation Law § 720, subd a(3), which grants injunctive relief against misconduct by corporate directors, is broad and covers every form of waste of assets and violation of duty whether as result of intention, negligence, or predatory acquisition and is applicable to foreign corporations pursuant to CLS Business Corporation Law § 1317, subd a(2). Goldberg v Meridor (1977, CA2 NY) 567 F.2d 209, cert den 434 US 1069, 55 L Ed 2d 771, 98 S Ct 1249 and on remand (SD NY) 81 FRD 105, CCH Fed Secur L Rep ¶ 96754, 27 FR Serv 2d 1360

In an action, for misconduct of corporate directors and officers, charging waste, the particular acts constituting the waste, from which the court may conclude neglect, must appear, and conclusory allegations that such corporate directors and officers were neglectful because their neglect caused waste and a dissipation of assets, are not sufficient. Mooney v Vitolo (1969, SD NY) 301 F. Supp. 198, affd (CA2 NY) 435 F.2d 838, 14 FR Serv 2d 683

An action for waste or mismanagement of corporate assets must be brought on behalf of the corporation and not for the personal benefit of a shareholder or creditor. Zeiler v Work Wear Corp. (1978, SD NY) 450 F. Supp. 891

In New York, suits challenging alleged corporate mismanagement must be brought as derivative actions. Downey v Vernitron Corp. (1983, DC Mass) 559 F. Supp. 1081

Directors' motion to dismiss the shareholder's claim that their actions in failing to negotiate a sale of the property and leasing it to the golf club at below-market rent constituted corporation waste of the corporation's lone asset was denied because neither the complaint nor the documents incorporated therein dictated that the present use of the property was consistent with the corporate purpose of the corporation and thus, the shareholder had pled corporate waste sufficiently to survive the motion to dismiss. Patrick v Allen (2005, SD NY) 355 F. Supp. 2d 704

4. Excessive compensation

A cause of action brought under section 720 of the Business Corporation Law, alleging that the individual defendants, acting as corporate officials, wasted the assets of plaintiff corporation by causing excessive payments to be made into the pension plan over which they had exclusive control, is not so related to the pension plan as to require pre-emption under the provisions of ERISA (US Code, tit 29, § 1001 *et seq.*); the pension plan was no more than the instrumentality by which the defendants accomplished the alleged misappropriation of plaintiff's funds; ERISA was not meant to shield such misconduct from State law especially where, as here, no interest protected by the act is involved. ERISA, however, does pre-empt a separate cause of action alleging an improper lump-sum payment, and, accordingly, such cause of action must be stricken from the complaint. Cornell Mfg. Co. v Mushlin (1979, 2d Dept) 70 A.D.2d 123, 420 N.Y.S.2d 231

Any claim that plaintiff's decedent withdrew more than his share of compensation from corporation of which he and defendant were sole shareholders could be brought as derivative action on corporation's behalf and was not defense to personal obligation imposed by promissory note. Furia v Cerone (1995, 2d Dept) 218 A.D.2d 682, 630 N.Y.S.2d 551

Corporate directors were entitled to summary judgment in shareholder derivative action alleging their receipt of stock options and warrants that wasted corporate assets where 3 outside directors were brought in and served on special litigation committee(SLC), which determined that continuation of derivative action was not in corporation's best interest, SLC members were shown to have "disinterested independence" in making their investigation, and SLC's investigative procedures were appropriate and sufficient. Lichtenberg v Zinn (1999, 3d Dept) 260 A.D.2d 741, 687 N.Y.S.2d 817, app den 94 N.Y.2d 754, 701 N.Y.S.2d 340, 723 N.E.2d 89

A complaint in a stockholder's derivative suit is insufficient to state facts showing misconduct on the part of defendant officers where it points only to payment of salary in the amount of $3,000 to the president of the corporation and the remaining allegations are merely conclusory. Sucher v Radiant Briar Pipe Co. (1960) 27 Misc. 2d 428, 211 N.Y.S.2d 317

Where plaintiffs, in a stockholder's derivative suit, seek to charge directors with waste and mismanagement in paying excessive salary and bonuses to the president, who is likewise the principal stockholder, the burden is upon defendants to justify such payments, but the individual defendants cannot be held liable where the salary paid was justified by results and not out of line with prior salary paid to previous officers, likewise being fully disclosed to the stockholders, who continued to reelect the officer allegedly overpaid. Sorin v Shahmoon Industries, Inc. (1961) 30 Misc. 2d 408, 429, 220 N.Y.S.2d 760

Although the business manager and program director of the defendant corporation were neither officers nor directors thereof under § 715 of the Business Corporation Law, an action might lie against them to recover excessive salaries or enjoin future excessive salary payments, or for knowingly receiving corporate assets for their personal use, and such action might be joined with an action against the directors and other officers of the corporation to account for their official duties in the management thereof. Syracuse Television, Inc. v Channel 9, Syracuse, Inc. (1966) 51 Misc. 2d 188, 273 N.Y.S.2d 16

Excessiveness of salaries or compensation authorized by or paid to directors or officers can serve as the basis for waste charges against management, and personal liability can be imposed on the directors or managing officers to the extent that any such payment is clearly excessive and unwarranted. Baker v Cohn (1942, Sup) 42 N.Y.S.2d 159, mod on other grounds 266 A.D. 715, 40 N.Y.S.2d 623, affd 292 N.Y. 570, 54 N.E.2d 689

In shareholders' derivative action, complaint stated claims for breach of fiduciary duty and corporate waste based on allegations that defendant directors dominated and controlled their fellow directors financially, that board approved issuance and repurchase of stock warrants solely to funnel cash and corporate control into defendants' pockets, that defendants were substantially overpaid, and that board was aware that challenged transactions were not in company's best interests. Pinnacle Consultants ex rel. Shareholders of Leucadia Nat'l Corp. v Leucadia Nat'l Corp. (1995, SD NY) 923 F. Supp. 439

5. – Other waste or mismanagement

Officers and directors of a solvent corporation who, confronted with unfavorable business conditions, sold all the corporate property at public auction without notice to creditors, are prima facie liable to creditors for waste of the corporate assets if the proceeds of the property at the auction were less than its full value. New York Credit Men's Adjustment Bureau, Inc. v Weiss (1953) 305 N.Y. 1, 110 N.E.2d 397

A corporation having been organized to engage in and carry on the business of importing, buying and selling laces and, generally, to carry on any other business, whether manufacturing or otherwise, which might seem to the company capable of being carried on in connection therewith, had no right to purchase stocks and cotton on margin, and directors and stockholders of the corporation could not lawfully, as against creditors, authorize themselves, acting for the corporation, to use its funds in such speculations, without subjecting themselves to risk of accountability to judgment creditors, for losing or wasting the property of the corporation. Hemsley & Co. v C. C. Duncan Co. (1917) 98 Misc 338, 164 N.Y.S. 282, mod on other grounds 178 A.D. 882, 164 N.Y.S. 670

Complaint in an action by the trustee in bankruptcy of a corporation to recover from the defendants, as former directors thereof, for dereliction of duty and mismanagement in the conduct of the affairs of the corporation, stated a good cause of action where the defendants were not only charged with misfeasance but with nonfeasance and not only with doing wrongful acts and committing waste but with acquiescing in and confirming wrongdoing of others and doing nothing to retrieve waste. Walker v Man (1931) 142 Misc 277, 253 N.Y.S. 458

See also Walker v Man (1931) 142 Misc 288, 253 N.Y.S. 472; Walker v Man (1931) 142 Misc 293, 253 N.Y.S. 478

A complaint in a stockholders' derivative suit which, far from showing that the directors have refused to press a claim against an officer of the corporation for alleged misconduct, shows that they have required him to settle for a large sum of money, is insufficient to charge that they refused to pursue the corporation's right of action in the absence of a statement of facts showing that the settlement was, in fact, inadequate. Markewich v Newberg (1960) 27 Misc. 2d 1040, 210 N.Y.S.2d 299

Allegation in stockholder's derivative action that director "negligently permitted the declaration and payment" of dividend, without alleging fraud, dishonesty or malfeasance, was to state merely that decision was taken with which one disagreed, and thus did not state cause of action under statute permitting action against corporate director for neglect of, or failure to perform, or other violations of his duties in management and disposition of corporate assets committed to his charge. Kamin v American Express Co. (1976) 86 Misc. 2d 809, 383 N.Y.S.2d 807, affd (1st Dept) 54 A.D.2d 654, 387 N.Y.S.2d 993

Allegation that four corporate directors, who were also officers and employees of corporation, engaged in self-dealing when they voted to approve dividend in kind, unanimously approved by 20-member board of directors, board action which allegedly resulted in overstatement of corporate earnings and affected officers' compensation, was highly speculative and standing alone was insufficient to support inference of self-dealing, where there was no claim or showing that four company directors dominated and controlled 16 outside members of board. Kamin v American Express Co. (1976) 86 Misc. 2d 809, 383 N.Y.S.2d 807, affd (1st Dept) 54 A.D.2d 654, 387 N.Y.S.2d 993

Where the corporation received consideration in the form of the continued services of the optionee employees, the board of directors' actions allowing the cancellation and regranting, at lower prices, of stock options to key employees were not gifts to the optionees or a waste of corporate assets. Cohen v Ayers (1978, ND Ill) 449 F. Supp.

298, CCH Fed Secur L Rep ¶ 96575, affd (CA7 Ill) 596 F.2d 733, CCH Fed Secur L Rep ¶ 96836

Since a board of directors does not have the power to give away the assets of a corporation and is liable to the corporation for waste if it does so, whether or not the directors benefit personally, the board may not grant stock options for no consideration, and minority shareholders may bring a derivative action under CLS Business Corporation Law § 720, subd a(1)(B) to recover for waste if the grant of stock options is a gift. Cohen v Ayers (1978, ND Ill) 449 F. Supp. 298, CCH Fed Secur L Rep ¶ 96575, affd (CA7 Ill) 596 F.2d 733, CCH Fed Secur L Rep ¶ 96836

Complaint in action by trustee in bankruptcy alleging self-serving mismanagement on part of directors, officers, and employees of corporation stated a cause of action. Bush v Masiello (1972, SD NY) 55 FRD 72

6. Unlawful transfers

Fraudulent and illegal transfers of corporate assets were dealt with in distinct categories and much greater detail in earlier corporation laws, as becomes readily apparent from a comparison of §§ 60 and 61 of former Gen. Corp. L., and § 15 of former Stock Corp. L., with the broad terms of this § 720 of the Bus. Corp. L. Decisions construing and applying the earlier provisions accordingly have little value in determining the scope and meaning of this section, but they do tend to emphasize the concepts of corporate assets as trust funds for creditors and the fiduciary obligation of management to both creditors and shareholders in handling and disposing of the assets. See, for example, John S. Lane & Son, Inc. v Westchester County (1928) 248 N.Y. 298, 162 N.E. 86; Salner Realty Corp. v Nancy Lee Millinery, Inc. (1941) 262 A.D. 491, 30 N.Y.S.2d 596; Anton Larsen & Son, Inc. v Newmark & Davis, Inc. (1918) 182 A.D. 724, 170 N.Y.S. 268; Cullen v Friedland (1912) 152 A.D. 124, 136 N.Y.S. 659

Under §§ 60 and 61 of former Gen. Corp. L. and § 15 of former Stock Corp. L., a creditor of a corporation could bring an action to set aside a transfer of its assets in violation of any of the provisions of these sections, and could likewise seek and obtain a money judgment against officers or directors who approved or sanctioned the transfer, whether or not they individually profited or benefited by the transfer. Thorne Neale & Co. v New York Southern Coal Terminal Corp. (1946) 270 A.D. 816, 59 N.Y.S.2d 833, affd 295 N.Y. 977, 68 N.E.2d 56; Caesar v Bernard (1913) 156 A.D. 737, 141 N.Y.S. 669, affd 209 N.Y. 570, 103 N.E. 1122; Feldman v Capitol Piece Dye Works, Inc. (1960, SD NY) 185 F. Supp. 426, revd on other grounds (CA2 NY) 293 F.2d 889, cert den 368 US 948, 7 L Ed 2d 344, 82 S Ct 389; New York Credit Men's Asso. v Hasenberg (1938, DC NY) 26 F. Supp. 877, affd (CA2 NY) 107 F.2d 1020, cert den 309 US 666, 84 L Ed 1013, 60 S Ct 592; Irving Trust Co. v Manufacturers' Trust Co. (1934, DC NY) 6 F. Supp. 185; Pennsylvania R. Co. v Pedrick (1915, DC NY) 222 F 75,

In the minority shareholders' action for rescission of a merger transaction that would involve the cancellation of their minority shares, the trial court's judgment that the directors and majority shareholders would be liable with respect to the merger would be reversed, and the matter remanded for determination of whether the merger had been tainted with fraud, conflict of interest, or self-dealing, since courts will not interfere with the proper business judgment of directors in the absence of a showing of fraud, illegality, or self-dealing, as long as there is some proper corporate purpose for the merger other than the forced buy-out of the minority shares. Alpert v 28 Williams St. Corp. (1982, 1st Dept) 91 A.D.2d 530, 457 N.Y.S.2d 4

A stockholder's derivative action could be based on § 60 of former Gen. Corp. L. for the recovery of assets illegally conveyed or disposed of by management. Deitch v Atlas (1954, Sup) 132 N.Y.S.2d 803

An injunction could be obtained, in proper case, against a transfer which, if made, would violate these older statutes. Margolin v Greenberg (1954, Sup) 135 N.Y.S.2d 94

Where a New York corporation, in New York, disposed of assets in violation of § 15 of former Stock Corp. L. to a foreign corporation or nonresident of the state, that section was nonetheless applicable in determining validity of the transaction and rights of persons in interest allegedly damaged by the transaction. McGill v Commercial Credit Co. (1917, DC Md) 243 F 637, error dismd (CA4 Md) 255 F 989

7. – Particular cases

But one creditor was not entitled to priority as against others in the same category merely by virtue of being the one to institute proceedings to set aside a fraudulent or illegal transfer of assets of the corporate debtor, as the result of setting aside the transfer was to restore the asset to the corporation, not to make it property of the plaintiff. Lodi Chemical Co. v National Lead Co. (1899) 41 A.D. 535, 58 N.Y.S. 717

The element of insolvency on the part of the debtor corporation, or inability to pay debts as they matured, was a specified factor under some of these earlier provisions giving a creditor the right to pursue and recover assets of the corporation or seek damages from officers making or approving the transfer, and, in these respects, there was duplication and confusion of concepts as between the corporation laws and the more general provisions of the Debtor and Creditor Law. See, for example, Whalen v Strong (1930) 230 A.D. 617, 246 N.Y.S. 40; Hazzan v Herman (1961) 30 Misc. 2d 832, 219 N.Y.S.2d 405; Beol, Inc. v Dorf (1959) 22 Misc. 2d 798, 193 N.Y.S.2d 394, affd (1st Dept) 12 A.D.2d 459, 209 N.Y.S.2d 267, reh and app den (1st Dept) 12 A.D.2d 616, 210 N.Y.S.2d 753, app dismd 9 N.Y.2d 963, 218 N.Y.S.2d 43, 176 N.E.2d 499; Lazar v Towne House Restaurant Corp. (1955, Sup) 142 N.Y.S.2d 315, affd (2d Dept) 5 A.D.2d 794, 171 N.Y.S.2d 334, affd 6 N.Y.2d 923, 190 N.Y.S.2d 997, 161 N.E.2d 211; Yankiver Realty Corp. v Yankiver (1945, Sup) 55 N.Y.S.2d 427

Evidence held insufficient to sustain alleged misconduct on the part of corporate officers in making payments to another corporation with identical share interests and officers. Bartle v Finkelstein (1963, 4th Dept) 19 A.D.2d 256, 241 N.Y.S.2d 655

Where corporation continued to be actively engaged in business throughout 1973, employing eight employees and paying president his regular weekly salary without increases from prior years, president testified that he devoted all of his time to corporation, and there was no evidence that his salary was either excessive or unreasonable or that corporation did not receive full value in return, salary paid president was not unlawful transfer of corporate assets in violation of Business Corporation Law nor a fraudulent conveyance of assets within meaning of Debtor and Creditor Law. Cilco Cement Corp. v White (1976, 2d Dept) 55 A.D.2d 668, 390 N.Y.S.2d 178

Complaint alleging that defendant officers and directors caused corporation to acquire from defendants stock in corporation which had almost no net worth, granted defendants second mortgage on acquired corporation's only asset after dissolving it, and then transferred asset to outside corporation owned by defendants, stated a cause of action. Duffy v Cross Country Industries, Inc. (1977, 4th Dept) 57 A.D.2d 1063, 395 N.Y.S.2d 852

In action by shareholder/lender arising from defendant board of directors' issuance of new stock in defendant corporation, in alleged contravention of anti-dilution clause of plaintiff's shareholders' agreement, defendants were not entitled to partial summary judgment dismissing cause of action for breach of fiduciary duty on ground that settlement agreement whereby loan agreement was terminated required plaintiff to transfer back its shares immediately, since factual questions existed as to terms of settlement agreement, which was executed in Japanese (although certified translation of settlement agreement was in record), where plaintiff contended that its stock was not to be transferred back until loan amount had actually been repaid. First Transcable Corp. v Avalon Pictures, Inc. (1992, 1st Dept) 184 A.D.2d 254, 585 N.Y.S.2d 195

In action for breach of fiduciary duty arising from defendant board of directors' issuance of new stock in defendant corporation, in alleged contravention of anti-dilution clause of shareholders' agreement, it was error to grant partial summary judgment to individual directors on theory that they were acting pursuant to "corporate purposes" since (1) such standard vastly understated fiduciary duties of directors to afford shareholders fair, uniform, and equal treatment, and (2) record showed that plaintiff shareholder had demonstrated prima facie case of unequal treatment in connection with directors' attempt extinguish anti-dilution rights on short notice and without adequate disclosure, thus shifting burden to directors to justify stock offering. First Transcable Corp. v Avalon Pictures, Inc. (1992, 1st Dept) 184 A.D.2d 254, 585 N.Y.S.2d 195

Complaint in restitution action was properly dismissed for failure to show that defendant law firm was not holder in due course of checks given to it by plaintiff corporation as payment for services rendered where complaint failed to show that firm had actual knowledge of corporation's defense to checks-namely, that its chief executive officer lacked authority to use its funds to bring shareholder's derivative action and that funds so used had been secretly diverted from corporation's regular account. Transglobal Mktg. Corp. v Derfner & Mahler, LLP (1998, 1st Dept) 246 A.D.2d 482, 667 N.Y.S.2d 751

Section 15 of former Stock Corp. L. did not prevent a corporation from paying or securing its debts, or make such action on its part illegal, notwithstanding it was in financial difficulties, if it still expected to continue in business. Male v National Pure Water Co. (1940) 176 Misc 743, 27 N.Y.S.2d 984, affd 261 A.D. 1050, 27 N.Y.S.2d 1023

Officer's transfer of fewer than a majority of his corporation's shares, at a price in excess of that prevailing in the market, accompanied by his promise to effect the transfer of offices and control in the corporation to the buyer breaches the fiduciary duty owed to the corporation; officer must forfeit that portion of his profit ascribable to the unlawful promise as he has been unjustly enriched. Brecher v Gregg (1975) 89 Misc. 2d 457, 392 N.Y.S.2d 776, affd (1st Dept) 56 A.D.2d 525, 391 N.Y.S.2d 829

A creditor, if the assets or their proceeds were traceable and had not reached asylum in the hands of an innocent purchaser for value, could follow them and subject them to the lien of his judgment. Lazar v Towne House Restaurant Corp. (1955, Sup) 142 N.Y.S.2d 315, affd (2d Dept) 5 A.D.2d 794, 171 N.Y.S.2d 334, affd 6 N.Y.2d 923, 190 N.Y.S.2d 997, 161 N.E.2d 211

See also Re Fred Stern & Co. (1931, CA2 NY) 54 F.2d 478

There are clear indications that New York courts would consider payment out of corporate funds in furtherance of conspiracy to violate federal conflict of interest statute (18 USCS § 203) to be diversion of property to other than proper corporate purposes, and under New York law, creditor or trustee in bankruptcy may recover corporate payments from one who received such payments in violation of statute. Re Leasing Consultants, Inc. (1979, CA2 NY) 592 F.2d 103, 5 BCD 34, CCH Bankr L Rptr ¶ 67040

Since Business Corporation Law § 720 is broad enough to cover every form of waste of assets in violation of fiduciary duty, question of whether pursuit of relief in action against corporate president to set aside certain fraudulent transfers and transfers involving voidable preferences is labeled as action for accounting or suit for damages is of little consequence; amending ad damnum clause in plaintiff's second cause of action to make it demand that corporate president account for company's damages will cause no change of substance, nor will it prejudice corporate president in any manner. Klein v Tabatchnick (1979, CA2 NY) 610 F.2d 1043, 5 BCD 1159, 21 CBC 911

BCL § 720 authorizes claim alleging that creditor of judgment debtor violated statute by aiding and abetting debtor's directors in transferring corporate assets in breach of creditor's fiduciary duties to debtor. Atlanta Shipping Corp. v Chemical Bank (1986, SD NY) 631 F. Supp. 335

Former shareholders of defunct corporation are not entitled to relief in action against former executive vice-president and director for misappropriation of 39 checks, each in amount of $3,000, drawn on corporate checking account for "expenses," because (1) defendant testified that payments were authorized by corporation for his lodging in New York City while his family lived in Florida, and (2) CPA testified that corporation's financial statements would not be certified if checks like ones at issue here were not found to be authorized. Establissement Kadaq Vaduz v Piha (1995, SD NY) 901 F. Supp. 139

8. Conversion

In an action by a foreign corporation against two individual defendants engaged in the business of brokering promissory notes and a corporation in which one of the individual defendants was the principal shareholder and the other was both a director and one of two minority shareholders, to recover for the conversion of the proceeds of promissory notes, the director could not be held liable for the principal shareholder's action in converting the proceeds where the director had no knowledge that the proceeds had been deposited in the corporation's bank account and there was no proof linking him to the receipt or disposition of the notes, and where, even if the director could be considered culpable of nonfeasance in regard to his corporate duties in approving a loan by the corporation (funded by the converted proceeds) without first obtaining or reviewing the corporation's bank statements, his liability did not extend to the foreign corporation. Ecuador Importadora-Exportadora Cia. Ltda. v ITF (Overseas) Corp. (1983, 1st Dept) 94 A.D.2d 113, 463 N.Y.S.2d 208

At the other extreme are clear-cut conversions of corporate funds or assets by individual officers or directors, or their wanton diversion of assets to third persons or other corporate entities. In such instances, misconduct and liability are obvious. Newfield v Ettlinger (1959) 22 Misc. 2d 769, 194 N.Y.S.2d 670, app dismd conditionally (1st Dept) 10 A.D.2d 947, 205 N.Y.S.2d 908; De Rosa v Bloch (1934) 150 Misc 160, 270 N.Y.S. 255

An officer or director of a corporation is personally liable for his acts which constitute a conversion of the property of a third person and it is no answer to such liability that the act was done while the officer or director was acting for the corporation. Admiral Corp. v Cohen (1971) 68 Misc. 2d 687, 327 N.Y.S.2d 422

Corporate directors could not be held liable for conversion or fraud in shareholders' derivative action challenging issuance of stock warrants to them, where stock warrants were legally valid, and proxy statements urging approval of issuance of stock warrants disclosed all relevant facts. Pinnacle Consultants ex rel. Shareholders of Leucadia Nat'l Corp. v Leucadia Nat'l Corp. (1995, SD NY) 923 F. Supp. 439

9. Other grounds for action

In an action by directors and stockholders against other directors to prevent the allegedly improper payment of a duplicate claim, a cause of action was stated where it was alleged that a resolution, adopted at a director's meeting was invalid, which resolution authorized payment of the claim, where there was lack of proper notice and a conflict of interest of some directors who voted for it, and further that the defendant directors knowingly authorized payment of an improper claim. Rapoport v Schneider (1972) 29 N.Y.2d 396, 328 N.Y.S.2d 431, 278 N.E.2d 642

Majority shareholders of closely held corporation were not entitled to summary judgment dismissing action for breach of fiduciary duty for issuing stock options to themselves without granting minority shareholder opportunity to make similar purchase in proportion to his shares, since fact issues existed as to whether such actions were undertaken in good faith for legitimate corporate purpose and whether other means to accomplish their stated goals were available. Goldberg v Goldberg (1988, 2d Dept) 139 A.D.2d 695, 527 N.Y.S.2d 451

Officer and majority shareholder breached her fiduciary duty to minority shareholders of small corporation, whose sole asset was apartment building, since she improperly placed her own interest over that of corporation when she obtained corporate note and mortgage in repayment of prior loans made to corporation, where prior loans were unenforceable because of statute of limitations. Szelega v O'Hara (1990, 3d Dept) 159 A.D.2d 890, 553 N.Y.S.2d 526

Plaintiff stated cause of action for corporate waste and mismanagement under CLS Bus Corp § 720 where plaintiff alleged that (1) corporation was controlled by family until it went public, (2) 1/3 of stock was sold to public, while 2 brothers retained remainder of stock, (3) one brother bought out other brother, (4) remaining brother then operated corporation purely for his own pecuniary advantage, he extracted kickbacks from salesmen, incurred loans for capital expenditures that he knew could never be repaid, and he hid losses and declared nonexistent profits, and (5) corporation finally went bankrupt due to debt that was unnecessarily imposed on it. Amfesco Industries, Inc. v Greenblatt (1991, 1st Dept) 172 A.D.2d 261, 568 N.Y.S.2d 593

Directors of corporation are not liable to stockholder for having caused corporation to break its contract with another corporation; such an extension of doctrine of interfering with contract right would tend to leave directors open to tort claims whenever corporation had failed to perform a contract. Lukach v Blair (1919) 108 Misc 20, 178 N.Y.S. 8, affd 191 A.D. 957, 182 N.Y.S. 935

Complaint in an action, under § 60 of former Gen. Corp. L., to compel directors of a corporation to account for profits acquired in violation of duties of their office, stated a good cause of action where it not only alleged that the directors were motivated by the aim of placing a competitive concern in a position to dominate the corporation, but also that directors had made use of relations of trust and confidence in order to promote some selfish interest. Stanton v Schenck (1931) 142 Misc 406, 252 N.Y.S. 172

In a stockholder's derivative action, a charge that there was any fraud in connection with the making of an agreement or the price at which treasury stock of the corporation was sold to the principal stockholders by action of an executive committee was unsubstantiated where it appeared that the corporation, at the time, was desperately in need of funds, unable to obtain bank loans, others were not interested in making the purchase, the principal stockholder agreed to the deal at a price above then market price of the stock, and the stockholders were fully apprised of the situation and the terms of the arrangement and approved it. Sorin v Shahmoon Industries, Inc. (1961) 30 Misc. 2d 408, 429, 220 N.Y.S.2d 760

Neither Business Corporation Law § 719 nor 720 permits an action against officers and directors and sole stockholders of a corporation for the selling of items of merchandise "out of trust" and failing to remit to the plaintiffs the proceeds received from such sales, which items had been delivered in accordance with a floor agreement,

but the statutes preserve liability of officers and directors in those instances where they actually participated in frauds, misfeasance or other kinds of tortious conduct injurious to third parties. Admiral Corp. v Cohen (1971) 68 Misc. 2d 687, 327 N.Y.S.2d 422

A complaint filed against officers, directors and sole stockholders of a corporation alleging a cause of action in contract, in that the named defendants personally and knowingly sold trust items and failed to remit to plaintiff the invoiced amounts, and a cause of action in conversion, alleged two viable causes of action, one in conversion and the other in breach of contract. Admiral Corp. v Cohen (1971) 68 Misc. 2d 687, 327 N.Y.S.2d 422

Evidence did not show that transaction between one shareholder and buyer of shareholder's stock was the proximate cause of failure of FCC to approve corporation's purchase of a radio station so that, even though the sale of stock was illegal, the selling director was not required to forfeit to the corporation the value of the bargain which the corporation lost when FCC approval for the purchase of the radio station was not given before the owners of the radio station exercised their right under the contract to cancel the sale because of the delay in FCC approval. Brecher v Gregg (1975) 89 Misc. 2d 457, 392 N.Y.S.2d 776, affd (1st Dept) 56 A.D.2d 525, 391 N.Y.S.2d 829

Shareholders in recycling company adequately pleaded elements of constructive fraud where complaint alleged that (1) directors, who owed them fiduciary duty, falsely promised them in prospectus (and after dissemination of prospectus) that new recycling plant would be built, and that escrowed shares would be released quickly, and (2) they agreed to escrow their shares in reliance thereon. Barsam v Pure Tech Int'l (1994, SD NY) 864 F. Supp. 1440

Minority shareholders adequately pleaded breach of fiduciary duty where complaint alleged that directors fraudulently induced them to waive their preemptive rights, that additional shares were subsequently issued by corporation, and that they could have claimed additional shares but for alleged fraudulent inducement. Barsam v Pure Tech Int'l (1994, SD NY) 864 F. Supp. 1440

10. Parties, generally

Creditors' committee had standing to maintain action against directors of bankrupt corporation for failure to keep themselves properly informed of corporation's financial condition where federal bankruptcy court had authorized committee to commence such action, and it was not necessary that trustee or receiver be appointed to maintain action. Official Secured Creditors' Committee of Amfesco Industries, Inc. v Greenblatt (1989, 1st Dept) 156 A.D.2d 215, 548 N.Y.S.2d 476

Plaintiff, as officer and 50 percent owner of plaintiff corporation, was not estopped from maintaining shareholder's derivative action to redress wrong to corporation committed by other 50 percent owner on basis that he failed to prevent defendant's alleged improprieties, withdrew money from corporate account causing corporate checks to be returned for insufficient funds, and caused client to withhold payment of commissions earned by plaintiff corporation, where record demonstrated that plaintiff's actions were undertaken to protect corporation from defendant, that bank account funds were placed in new account requiring 2 signatures for withdrawal, and that plaintiff never benefited from new account or from withdrawal of funds. Howard v Carr (1995, 3d Dept) 222 A.D.2d 843, 635 N.Y.S.2d 326

Trial court properly denied the shareholders' motion for a preliminary injunction, and granted cooperative's cross-motion to dismiss because, inter alia, the shareholders' first cause of action—to reduce an individual shareholder's votes from two to one—was barred by the four-month statute of limitations, a director of the cooperative had standing to bring the causes of action pursuant to the Business Corporation Law without a pre-suit demand, and they were not entitled to additional discovery where they did not specify the discovery they sought. Valyrakis v 346 W. 48th St. Hous. Dev. Fund Corp., 161 A.D.3d 404, 76 N.Y.S.3d 523, 2018 N.Y. App. Div. LEXIS 3061 (N.Y. App. Div. 1st Dep't 2018).

Where a complaint purportedly based on § 61 of former Gen. Corp. L. failed to allege that plaintiff came within any of the classes specified in that section as authorized to enforce it, as a creditor, director, officer, or stockholder, it failed to state a cause of action. Geller v Acwa Sportswear Mfg. Co. (1951, Sup) 110 N.Y.S.2d 20

11. Shareholders

Under this section of the Bus. Corp. L., however, it is very clear that a shareholder can, in like manner and instances as he could under §§ 60 and 61 of former Gen. Corp. L., maintain a derivative action in the corporation's behalf, based upon misconduct of its officers or directors, if he has such share interest at time of starting suit and likewise had it when the misconduct occurred as to meet the requirements of § 626 of the Bus. Corp. L. Malkan v General Transistor Corp. (1960) 27 Misc. 2d 275, 210 N.Y.S.2d 289, motion den 13 A.D.2d 691, 215 N.Y.S.2d 714, app dismd (2d Dept) 14 A.D.2d 693, 219 N.Y.S.2d 936; Sorin v Shahmoon Industries, Inc. (1961) 30 Misc. 2d 408, 429, 220 N.Y.S.2d 760

A stockholder is not precluded from maintaining a stockholder's derivative suit against individual defendants merely because he voted for their election as directors or granted proxies for that purpose. Sorin v Shahmoon Industries, Inc. (1961) 30 Misc. 2d 408, 429, 220 N.Y.S.2d 760

Only a stockholder who was such at the time of the transaction complained of is entitled to maintain a derivative action. Jaret v 2210 Church Ave. Realty Corp. (1962) 36 Misc. 2d 1003, 234 N.Y.S.2d 528

Minority shareholders, who have been divested of their shares in both old and new corporations and who had been made creditors by majority shareholders to be paid out at appraised value of their former shares, could not sue as stockholders for alleged conspiracy on part of majority shareholders to loot corporation, until and unless their stockholdings were reinstated by judicial decree or otherwise. Levine v Chavkin (1974) 82 Misc. 2d 441, 369 N.Y.S.2d 588

A single stockholder, suing as an individual, could not maintain an individual action against officers and directors under § 60 of former Gen. Corp. L. Re Tama (1954, Sup) 137 N.Y.S.2d 248

Shareholder's breach of fiduciary duty claim against several orange juice manufacturers and corporate officers was dismissed where the alleged breach was incurred by the corporation, the shareholder's alleged emotional harm did not provide a basis for recovery, his financial interest in the corporation's products and trademarks was no different than that of the other shareholders, and as a result, the shareholder should have brought the claim derivatively. Fisher v Big Squeeze (NY), Inc. (2004, ED NY) 349 F. Supp. 2d 483

12. Directors and officers

Action, brought by one of the directors as such, has been held not to abate if and when he ceases to be a director, by ouster or otherwise, notwithstanding he remains a shareholder. Manix v Fantl (1924) 209 A.D. 756, 205 N.Y.S. 174

There is likewise later authority to the effect that a director's suit to compel individual defendants to account to the corporation, which is likewise made a defendant, does not abate merely by his ceasing to hold office. Tenney v Rosenthal (1958, 1st Dept) 6 A.D.2d 510, 179 N.Y.S.2d 728, affd 6 N.Y.2d 204, 189 N.Y.S.2d 158, 160 N.E.2d 463

An officer or director of a corporation may bring an action against another officer or director under § 720 of the Business Corporation Law and such director may sue in his own name and need not allege his representative capacity. Conant v Schnall (1970, 3d Dept) 33 A.D.2d 326, 307 N.Y.S.2d 902

Judgment would be granted to one of two shareholders in an electronics corporation in a shareholder derivative action against a corporation, where the other shareholder-officer, in complete disregard of his fiduciary duty to the corporation, had entered into a unilateral royalty agreement with another corporation that he had created himself to manufacture and sell the products to which the first corporation had patent and trademark rights, and then proceeded to carry on under the name of the second corporation the business for which the first corporation had been formed. Schachter v Kulik (1983, 2d Dept) 96 A.D.2d 1038, 466 N.Y.S.2d 444

In corporate president's action for judgment declaring percentages of ownership of shares of stock in corporation, defendant, as vice-president of corporation, was proper party to interpose counterclaim against president to compel him to return $6,000 to corporate treasury, and to return files belonging to corporation to corporate offices. Siegel v Protiva (1987, 2d Dept) 130 A.D.2d 569, 515 N.Y.S.2d 511

Corporate vice-president had standing to recover damages, on behalf of corporation, for alleged mismanagement by corporate president since vice-president and president were only 2 persons who held interest in family-owned business, and although right of recovery belonged to corporation, claim could be brought in vice-president's name without necessity of joining corporation as party. Brown v Brown (1988, 2d Dept) 143 A.D.2d 248, 532 N.Y.S.2d 157, app den, in part, app dismd, in part 75 N.Y.2d 797, 552 N.Y.S.2d 100, 551 N.E.2d 593

President/treasurer of 2-man corporation lacked authority to bring action on behalf of corporation against vice-president/secretary to terminate latter's employment contract and recover amount of

compensation and fringe benefits provided to him after his receipt of disability benefits where each man owned 50 percent of stock, and thus, by implication from CLS Bus Corp §§ 701 and 702(a), deadlock could not be remedied by exercise of presidential power, and proper remedy was shareholder's derivative action. Stone v Frederick (1997, 3d Dept) 245 A.D.2d 742, 666 N.Y.S.2d 294

Although individual claim by president/treasurer of 2-man corporation against vice-president/secretary stated cause of action for specific performance of shareholder agreement, action would be enjoined where further use of corporate funds to prosecute it would be obvious abuse of plaintiff's fiduciary relationship with corporation. Stone v Frederick (1997, 3d Dept) 245 A.D.2d 742, 666 N.Y.S.2d 294

An illegal ouster from office does not, however, have this effect. Wyckoff v Sagall (1945) 16 Misc. 2d 630, 56 N.Y.S.2d 392; Wangrow v Wangrow (1924) 211 A.D. 552, 207 N.Y.S. 132

The president of a corporation has the authority to institute an action in its name, and to retain attorneys for that purpose to protect its economic self-preservation even against a majority of directors, when their conduct allegedly constitutes a breach of trust. Lasker v Moreida (1963) 38 Misc. 2d 348, 238 N.Y.S.2d 16

Though plaintiff, who had been divested of his shares in both old and new corporations, could not sue as a stockholder for alleged conspiracy on part of majority stockholders to loot corporation, where plaintiff was also a director of corporation, plaintiff could continue suit as a director. Levine v Chavkin (1974) 82 Misc. 2d 441, 369 N.Y.S.2d 588

Fact that defendants, by their corporate maneuvers as majority stockholders, were able to divest plaintiff of his shares as a minority stockholder, thus making plaintiff a creditor of corporation, did not mean that defendant also had a right to divest plaintiff as a director of his right to maintain suit for alleged conspiracy to loot corporation, even though plaintiff was no longer a director, where plaintiff was a director at time action was commenced and, as a stockholder or creditor, had an interest in value of corporation or an interest in value of shares to be appraised. Levine v Chavkin (1974) 82 Misc. 2d 441, 369 N.Y.S.2d 588

A director or officer of the corporation, currently in office and not for some reason estopped from doing so, could bring an action for the benefit of the corporation against other directors or officers charging violation of § 60 or § 61 of former Gen. Corp. L. Peets v Manhasset Civil Engineers, Inc. (1946, Sup) 68 N.Y.S.2d 335; Rothbart v Star Wet Wash Laundry Co. (1919) 185 A.D. 807, 174 N.Y.S. 76

Purchaser could not recover damages against principal of insolvent supplier under provisions of CLS Bus Corp §§ 720 and 1317 that allow action against directors and officers of corporation for negligence in management and disposition of corporate assets, where supplier was not New York corporation, and evidence did not warrant inference that it was doing business in New York. Air India v Pennsylvania Woven Carpet Mills (1997, SD NY) 978 F. Supp. 500

Directors' motion to dismiss was granted to the extent the shareholder claimed that the directors breached their fiduciary duties by failing to negotiate for a sale of the property because the directors were not elected to the corporation's board of directors until after the offer was made, and the complaint did not allege any facts that would have supported the conclusory allegation that they failed to negotiate a sale of the property. Patrick v Allen (2005, SD NY) 355 F. Supp. 2d 704

Shareholder's claims that two of the directors breached their fiduciary duties by offering to purchase additional shares of the corporation were dismissed because mere attempts by a director to increase his stake in the company as a shareholder are not actionable as a breach of fiduciary duty. Patrick v Allen (2005, SD NY) 355 F. Supp. 2d 704

13. Creditors

Violations of § 15 of former Stock Corp. L., dealing with fraudulent and preferential transfers by corporations, could be attacked by any judgment creditor in his own right and for his individual benefit. Buttles v Smith (1939) 281 N.Y. 226, 22 N.E.2d 350; Feuer, Inc. v Peoples Bank of Johnstown (1941) 261 A.D. 1118, 27 N.Y.S.2d 63, affd 294 N.Y. 748, 61 N.E.2d 746; Pennsylvania R. Co. v Pedrick (1915, DC NY) 222 F 75

Some decisions regarded a proceeding against officers and directors for misconduct brought under § 60 or § 61 of former Gen. Corp. L. as a strictly equitable action, which could not take the form of an action at law and which must, if instituted by a creditor, be a representative suit in behalf of plaintiff and all other creditors similarly situated. Davis v Wilson (1912) 150 A.D. 704, 135 N.Y.S. 825; Schwartzreich v Bauman (1920) 112 Misc 464, 183 N.Y.S. 440

There was no doubt as to the right of a single judgment creditor to sue officers and directors for misconduct without purporting to represent other creditors if the rights of no other creditors were involved. Buckley v United Cloak & Suit Co. (1913) 155 A.D. 735, 140 N.Y.S. 953, affd 214 N.Y. 679, 108 N.E. 1090

Only judgment creditors of the corporation were given a right of action against officers and directors for misconduct by §§ 60 and 61 of former Gen. Corp. L. Steele v Isman (1914) 164 A.D. 146, 149 N.Y.S. 488; Beol, Inc. v Dorf (1959) 22 Misc. 2d 798, 193 N.Y.S.2d 394, affd (1st Dept) 12 A.D.2d 459, 209 N.Y.S.2d 267, reh and app den (1st Dept) 12 A.D.2d 616, 210 N.Y.S.2d 753, app dismd 9 N.Y.2d 963, 218 N.Y.S.2d 43, 176 N.E.2d 499; Kendall v Oakland Golf Club (1953, Sup) 123 N.Y.S.2d 907, affd 282 A.D. 1057, 126 N.Y.S.2d 379, affd 307 N.Y. 753, 121 N.E.2d 554; Island Paper Co. v Carthage Timber Corp. (1926) 128 Misc 246, 218 N.Y.S. 346; Bristol Mfg. Corp. v Elk Textile Co. (1923) 121 Misc 138, 200 N.Y.S. 860, affd 209 A.D. 95, 204 N.Y.S. 427; Levy v Paramount Publix Corp. (1933) 149 Misc 129, 266 N.Y.S. 271, affd 241 A.D. 711, 269 N.Y.S. 997, affd 265 N.Y. 629, 193 N.E. 418

In proceedings instituted in Bankruptcy Court, plaintiff was authorized to commence action against directors of corporate debtor in possession for waste, mismanagement and negligence; while complaint is insufficient to state cause of action and was properly dismissed, plaintiff, creditors' committee, has standing; corporation, as debtor in possession in bankruptcy proceeding, is specifically authorized to maintain action under Business Corporation Law § 720; moreover, qualified right of creditors' committee to initiate adversary proceedings in name of debtor in possession has been recognized when that entity unjustifiably or in abuse of its discretion fails to bring suit. Official Secured Creditors' Comm. v Greenblatt, 156 A.D.2d 215

Business Corp § 720 did not authorize action by creditors to obtain money judgment against corporation officers and directors who allegedly transferred assets from one corporation to another in derogation of creditors' rights. Ali Baba Creations, Inc. v Congress Textile Printers, Inc. (1973, 1st Dept) 41 A.D.2d 924, 343 N.Y.S.2d 712

In short, a creditor could maintain an action based on either § 60 or § 61 of former Gen. Corp. L. by reason of waste of corporate assets without pinpointing the expenditures as coming from capital or surplus, and it would not be assumed they were out of surplus rather than capital merely because the corporation had at one time accumulated surplus earnings. New York Credit Men's Ass'n v Harris (1939) 170 Misc 988, 11 N.Y.S.2d 435, affd 262 A.D. 826, 29 N.Y.S.2d 505

Generally speaking, for any creditor to have a right of action against officers or directors for misconduct under § 60 of former Gen. Corp. L., there must have been creditors of the corporation in existence at the time of the misconduct or unlawful transaction complained of. New York Credit Men's Ass'n v Harris (1939) 170 Misc 988, 11 N.Y.S.2d 435, affd 262 A.D. 826, 29 N.Y.S.2d 505

But where the acts complained of resulted in an impairment of stated capital of the corporation, some decisions took the view that creditors were entitled to rely upon stated capital being kept intact and not depleted by misconduct of management, and hence that it was immaterial that plaintiff creditor did not become a creditor until after the depletion took place or whether there were any creditors when that occurred. New York Credit Men's Ass'n v Harris (1939) 170 Misc 988, 11 N.Y.S.2d 435, affd 262 A.D. 826, 29 N.Y.S.2d 505

Other decisions, however, referring to §§ 60 and 133 of former Gen. Corp. L., and § 278 of former Debtor and Creditor L., have permitted a single judgment creditor to maintain an action against officers and directors, while denying him the right to sue as representative of other creditors in the same action. Lazar v Towne House Restaurant Corp. (1955, Sup) 142 N.Y.S.2d 315, affd (2d Dept) 5 A.D.2d 794, 171 N.Y.S.2d 334, affd 6 N.Y.2d 923, 190 N.Y.S.2d 997, 161 N.E.2d 211

A creditor who does not have the status of a judgment creditor does not have standing to bring suit under Business Corporation L § 720, subd b. Coleman v Golkin, Bomback & Co. (1977, CA2 NY) 562 F.2d 166

Creditors are not able to sue derivatively on behalf of the debtor corporation. Brooks v Weiser (1972, DC NY) 57 FRD 491

14. Receivers to bring action

See also Allaire v Silberberg (1924) 210 A.D. 109, 205 N.Y.S. 634; Re Paul Delaney Co. (1928, DC NY) 26 F.2d 937, affd (CA2 NY) 30 F.2d 1018; Re Paul Delaney Co. (1927, DC NY) 23 F.2d 737, affd in part and revd in part on other grounds (CA2 NY) 26 F.2d 961

A receiver appointed for the corporation, or in supplementary proceedings, could enforce earlier provisions relating to liability of directors and officers for misconduct. Potter v Emerson-Steuben Corp. (1936) 248 A.D. 630, 288 N.Y.S. 170; Hitz v Garfinkel (1935) 246 A.D. 728, 283 N.Y.S. 872; Klages v Cohen (1945, CA2 NY) 146 F.2d 641

Bankruptcy trustee has standing to bring action under § 720 of New York Business Corporation Law. Re Princeton Industries, Inc. (1984, BC SD NY) 39 BR 140

Trustee of debtor corporation need not establish that it has no adequate remedy at law to bring action under § 720 of New York Business Corporation Law. Re Princeton Industries, Inc. (1984, BC SD NY) 39 BR 140

A trustee in bankruptcy of the corporation could enforce at least the provisions of § 15 of former Stock Corp. L. relating to preferment of creditors and fraudulent conveyances. Cardozo v Brooklyn Trust Co. (1915, CA2 NY) 228 F 333

The complaint of a bankruptcy trustee alleging violations of fiduciary obligations adequately set forth facts which were intertwined with a preceding federal cause of action which, if provable, could support a claim upon which relief could be granted pursuant to Business Corporation Law §§ 717, 720 and the trustee had standing to sue under Business Corporation Law § 720. Bush v Masiello (1972, SD NY) 55 FRD 72

15. Corporation

Where an action is brought against defendant officers, and the complaint states no cause of action against the corporation itself, it states but a single cause of action, although the corporation is properly made party defendant to whom the individual defendants will be directed to account and pay over. Higgins v Applebaum (1918) 183 A.D. 527, 170 N.Y.S. 228

If the proceeding was in the form of a stockholder's derivative action, the corporation was an indispensable party defendant. Meier v Holmes (1953) 282 A.D. 1030, 126 N.Y.S.2d 655

This section expressly authorizes a corporation to maintain an action against its officers, directors and agents to recover for misconduct, mismanagement and waste in its affairs. Platt Corp. v Platt (1964, 1st Dept) 21 A.D.2d 116, 249 N.Y.S.2d 75, affd 15 N.Y.2d 705, 256 N.Y.S.2d 335, 204 N.E.2d 495

Independently of this section the corporation is the proper party to sue for injury and damages sustained by reason of mismanagement or misconduct of directors, officers, or employees, and statutory remedies for such wrongs are an extension, not an exclusion, of existing remedies, statutory, equitable, or at common law. Platt Corp. v Platt (1964, 1st Dept) 21 A.D.2d 116, 249 N.Y.S.2d 75, affd 15 N.Y.2d 705, 256 N.Y.S.2d 335, 204 N.E.2d 495

Where an officer and director sued another officer and director for waste and mismanagement of corporate assets, while the cause of action and right of recovery actually belongs to the corporation and the director is suing as a representative, the corporation is only a proper party, neither necessary nor indispensable. Conant v Schnall (1970, 3d Dept) 33 A.D.2d 326, 307 N.Y.S.2d 902

While a shareholder lacked standing to bring an action against the corporate president for actions that took place before the shareholder became a shareholder, the corporation could and did state a cause of action alleging waste of corporate assets pursuant to N.Y. Bus. Corp. Law § 720. Gabel v Gabel (2013, 2d Dept) 104 App Div 3d 910, 961 NYS2d 569.

While this section of the Bus. Corp. L., sanctions an action by "a corporation" to require directors and officers to account for their misconduct, or to recover assets illegally transferred by them, one decision referring to § 61 of former Gen. Corp. L. took the position that if no stockholder of the corporation in question could maintain a stockholders' derivative suit, all the stock having been bought up by a single individual subsequent to the transaction in question, the "corporation" could not sue, either. Ford Tank Maintenance Co. v Ford (1960) 24 Misc. 2d 261, 203 N.Y.S.2d 542

16. Defenses; good faith

As against a charge of misconduct levelled by a creditor, it is a defense that he has been fully paid, or that the action taken was in good faith and in exercise of what could be considered sound business judgment and did not violate any statute. Curran v Oppenheimer (1914) 164 A.D. 746, 150 N.Y.S. 369, affd 222 N.Y. 615, 118 N.E. 1055; Lazar v Libby (1960) 28 Misc. 2d 131, 219 N.Y.S.2d 362

In action for corporate waste and mismanagement brought under CLS Bus Corp § 720, directors were not protected by business judgment rule where plaintiff alleged that corporate decisions lacked legitimate business purpose and were tainted by fraud. Amfesco Industries, Inc. v Greenblatt (1991, 1st Dept) 172 A.D.2d 261, 568 N.Y.S.2d 593

Complaint in shareholder's derivative action was properly dismissed for failure to state cause of action where plaintiff failed to plead any particularized facts creating reasonable doubt that defendants were disinterested or that challenged transaction was other than valid exercise of business judgment. Strougo v Hoyt (1997, 1st Dept) 245 A.D.2d 210, 665 N.Y.S.2d 902

In shareholder derivative action, court erred in denying plaintiffs' motion to prohibit defendants' use of corporate funds in defense of action where corporation had made no provisions for indemnification of shareholders or directors (CLS Bus Corp § 721), there was no receipt of undertaking by or on behalf of director or officer in question, and with shareholder or board approval (CLS Bus Corp § 723(c)), litigation had barely commenced, and defendants' "good faith" and motives were plainly at issue (CLS Bus Corp § 722(a) and (b)). Donovan v Rothman (1998, 1st Dept) 253 A.D.2d 627, 677 N.Y.S.2d 327

Bad faith in bringing a stockholders' derivative suit is not necessarily to be implied from the fact that plaintiff stockholder has violated an agreement made with the corporation defendant not to enter into a competing business by almost immediately setting up a competing corporation, notwithstanding it is contended that the objective of his action is to benefit his competing corporation at the expense of defendant corporation. Malkan v General Transistor Corp. (1960) 27 Misc. 2d 275, 210 N.Y.S.2d 289, motion den 13 A.D.2d 691, 215 N.Y.S.2d 714, app dismd (2d Dept) 14 A.D.2d 693, 219 N.Y.S.2d 936

Directors and officers of a corporation cannot be called to account for good faith acts in exercise of their best judgment under emergency conditions, where there is no attempt to conceal the situation or their proposed solution of it from the shareholders and others in interest and no one objects or suggests otherwise. Sorin v Shahmoon Industries, Inc. (1961) 30 Misc. 2d 408, 429, 220 N.Y.S.2d 760

Complaint which alleges merely that some course of action other than that pursued by corporation's board of directors would have been more advantageous gives rise to no cognizable cause of action; directors' room rather than courtroom is appropriate forum for thrashing out purely business questions which will have impact on profits, market prices, competitive situations, or tax advantages, and substitution of someone else's business judgment for that of directors is no business for any court to follow. Kamin v American Express Co. (1976) 86 Misc. 2d 809, 383 N.Y.S.2d 807, affd (1st Dept) 54 A.D.2d 654, 387 N.Y.S.2d 993

Corporate directors are entitled to exercise their honest business judgment on information before them, and to act within their corporate powers; that they may be mistaken, that other courses of action might have differing consequences, or that their action might benefit some shareholders more than others presents no basis for superimposition of judicial judgment, so long as it appears that directors have been acting in good faith. Kamin v American Express Co. (1976) 86 Misc. 2d 809, 383 N.Y.S.2d 807, affd (1st Dept) 54 A.D.2d 654, 387 N.Y.S.2d 993

Good faith on the part of particular individual defendants is not a defense if the conduct complained of was in violation of law, such as the declaration and payment of an illegal dividend. Cowin v Jonas (1943, Sup) 43 N.Y.S.2d 468, affd 267 A.D. 947, 48 N.Y.S.2d 460, affd 293 N.Y. 838, 59 N.E.2d 436

Good faith in taking the particular action or making the particular disposition of assets can be a defense, or at least aid in escaping personal liability, if the point at issue is whether sound business judgment was exercised in the field of general corporate management wherein much is necessarily left to discretion of directors and managing officers. Doyle v Gordon (1954, Sup) 158 N.Y.S.2d 248

17. Participation or ratification

Plaintiff's own concurrence or acquiescence in the action taken may, of itself, give rise to a defense by way of estoppel. Darcy v Brooklyn & N.Y. Ferry Co. (1909) 196 N.Y. 99, 89 N.E. 461; John H. Giles Dyeing Mach. Co. v Klauder-Weldon Dyeing Mach. Co. (1922) 233 N.Y. 470, 135 N.E. 854, reh den 234 N.Y. 531, 138 N.E. 435; Male v National Pure Water Co. (1940) 176 Misc 743, 27 N.Y.S.2d 984, affd 261 A.D. 1050, 27 N.Y.S.2d 1023

On the other hand, if all statutory requirements were fully met in connection with the transaction complained of, as in connection with a bulk sale of corporate assets to another solvent corporation, unanimously approved by shareholders, in conjunction with which the acquiring corporation assumed indebtedness of the vendor, a creditor of the vendor has no standing to complain. John H. Giles Dyeing Mach. Co. v Klauder-Weldon Dyeing Machine Co. (1925) 212 A.D. 771, 209 N.Y.S. 616, affd 243 N.Y. 547, 154 N.E. 599

In action arising from defendant board of directors' issuance of new stock in defendant corporation, it was error to grant partial summary judgment dismissing cause of action for breach of fiduciary duty on ground that plaintiff shareholder waived its right to purchase additional shares pro rata in accordance with terms of anti-dilution provisions of shareholders' agreement by not responding within 11-day period set for exercise of right in notice sent by directors, since notice was deficient, inter alia, in failing to provide specific details of proposed new issuance, failing to disclose terms of proposed loan agreement with related company to which additional shares were to be issued, and failing to disclose that new issuance would exceed maximum number of shares authorized by certificate of incorporation. First Transcable Corp. v Avalon Pictures, Inc. (1992, 1st Dept) 184 A.D.2d 254, 585 N.Y.S.2d 195

In an action by directors of a corporation to compel defendant directors to restore to said defendant corporation moneys and assets which were allegedly wasted or fraudulently transferred at grossly inadequate prices, it was not a defense that the plaintiffs were estopped because they might have participated in or ratified said wrongs. Williams v Robinson (1957) 9 Misc. 2d 774, 169 N.Y.S.2d 811, affd (1st Dept) 5 A.D.2d 823, 170 N.Y.S.2d 991

A director or officer of a corporation was liable under § 60 of former Gen. Corp. L. where he participated in an illegal transaction or transfer or permitted it to take place with active knowledge of its occurrence, but not merely by virtue of holding office. Each case is sui generis as to negligence, and the degree of care required necessarily depends upon the facts of the particular case. Newfield v Ettlinger (1959) 22 Misc. 2d 769, 194 N.Y.S.2d 670, app dismd conditionally (1st Dept) 10 A.D.2d 947, 205 N.Y.S.2d 908

Closely-held family corporations are not required to be directed with the same degree of care and responsibility as larger corporations whose stock is more widely distributed, and one who is an officer in name only of a family corporation, having little to do with its operation by her son, is not liable for illegal transfers made by her son without her knowledge. Newfield v Ettlinger (1959) 22 Misc. 2d 769, 194 N.Y.S.2d 670, app dismd conditionally (1st Dept) 10 A.D.2d 947, 205 N.Y.S.2d 908

Where the activities of defendants in a stockholders' derivative suit were voidable rather than void, the acts could be ratified by the majority of the stockholders as long as the conduct of the alleged wrongdoers was not fraudulent or collusive. Syracuse Television, Inc. v Channel 9 Syracuse, Inc. (1966) 52 Misc. 2d 246, 275 N.Y.S.2d 190

Ratification of wrongdoing by the officers or directors of a corporation cannot be accomplished indirectly under the guise of the refusal of the directors to bring an action, but the ratification by a majority of the stockholders to discontinue a derivative suit would be binding upon the corporation if the ratification was done reasonably and in good faith and would not constitute a ratification of a fraudulent or illegal act. Syracuse Television, Inc. v Channel 9 Syracuse, Inc. (1966) 52 Misc. 2d 246, 275 N.Y.S.2d 190

A violation of statute cannot be disregarded on the ground that the action taken was ratified by stockholders or others. Cowin v Jonas (1943, Sup) 43 N.Y.S.2d 468, affd 267 A.D. 947, 48 N.Y.S.2d 460, affd 293 N.Y. 838, 59 N.E.2d 436

It is not a defense that the misconduct in question was that of other officers or directors, if it can be shown that the particular defendant ratified or acquiesced in what was done. Kehaya v Axton (1940, DC NY) 30 F. Supp. 838

18. Other defenses

Directors of a corporation who sold and transferred its assets without complying with § 60 of former Gen. Corp. L. and with requirements of the former Stock Corp. L. could not relieve themselves from personal liability in a suit by a judgment creditor of the corporation merely by alleging that, at time of the transfer, a fund was placed in trust for payment of all debts and that plaintiff lost his rights by failing to present his claim. Shalek v Jetter (1915) 171 A.D. 364, 155 N.Y.S. 975

The most obvious defense to a charge of misconduct against an officer or director of a corporation is that he was not guilty of the misconduct alleged or that no misconduct was involved in the challenged transactions. Lonas v Layman Pressed Rod Co. (1934) 242 A.D. 444, 275 N.Y.S. 27, affd 269 N.Y. 529, 199 N.E. 520

Court properly dismissed shareholders' derivative action for alleged breach of fiduciary duties under CLS Bus Corp § 720 where (1) pursuant to CLS Bus Corp § 402(b), corporation's certificate of incorporation shielded its board of directors from personal liability, subject to certain exceptions, for negligent acts or omissions that occurred in their capacity as directors, and (2) plaintiffs' conclusory allegations did not support contention that directors' conduct rose to level of intentional misconduct, bad faith, or knowing violation of law. Bildstein v Atwater (1995, 2d Dept) 222 A.D.2d 545, 635 N.Y.S.2d 88

Widow of the founder of a corporation's business, who was an officer and director of the corporation, was not liable as a transferee of assets of the corporation with knowledge of its insolvency where, during the period in question, she loaned more to the corporation than was paid out to her in the form of repayment of the loan, salary, or alleged business expenses. Newfield v Ettlinger (1959) 22 Misc. 2d 769, 194 N.Y.S.2d 670, app dismd (1st Dept) 10 A.D.2d 947, 205 N.Y.S.2d 908

A stockholders' derivative suit cannot be based upon failure of the directors to compel officers of the corporation to account for small gifts received from persons dealing with the corporation in the absence of anything to indicate that the best interests of the corporation would be furthered or that fraud was involved. Markewich v Newberg (1960) 27 Misc. 2d 1040, 210 N.Y.S.2d 299

In a stockholders' derivative action alleging that officers and directors of the defendant corporation caused the corporation to purchase some of its own stock from one of its shareholders at a price higher than market value for the sole purpose of enabling the officers and directors to maintain their positions and to remove a threat or potential threat to the continuance of their control of the corporation, summary judgment for the defendant would be granted, where there was no showing that any of the directors personally profitted by the transaction, the transaction complained of actually improved the condition of the other stockholders of the defendant corporation by increasing the book value of the remaining shares, there were sound business reasons for the transactions, and there was no tangible threat to the control of the corporation; the summary judgment remedy should be fully utilized and given due effect to challenge stockholders' derivative suits which appear to be in the nature of a strike suit or otherwise lack apparent merit. Karfunkel v USLIFE Corp. (1982) 116 Misc. 2d 841, 455 N.Y.S.2d 937

Plaintiff's derivative action against members of cooperative board, alleging that specially appointed committee of directors improperly permitted several tenant-shareholders to combine separate apartments into single unit without updating building's certificate of occupancy, was barred by business judgment rule where (1) cooperative board submitted unrebutted proof of committee members' disinterested independence, as well as proof of appropriateness and sufficiency of investigative procedure chosen and pursued by them, and (2) plaintiff failed to raise issue of fact as to whether committee's investigation was so restricted in scope, so shallow in execution, or otherwise so pro forma as to constitute pretext or sham. Ungerleider v One Fifth Ave. Apartment Corp. (1995, Sup) 164 Misc. 2d 118, 623 N.Y.S.2d 711

Shareholder sufficiently alleged that, because of the directors' status as members of the golf club to which the corporation leased its property, they were not disinterested directors with respect to the transactions involving the golf club. Thus, the court could not conclude that the business judgment rule protected the directors' decisions concerning the golf club and the property. Patrick v Allen (2005, SD NY) 355 F. Supp. 2d 704

19. Jurisdiction

Issues of corporate governance are determined by state in which corporation is chartered. Kikis v McRoberts Corp. (1996, 1st Dept) 225 A.D.2d 455, 639 N.Y.S.2d 346

While derivative actions may be brought in New York in connection with the affairs of a foreign corporation, such actions are not authorized for the benefit of the stockholder plaintiff but only for the benefit of the corporation and are not to be regarded with favor where equivalent proceedings are already brought and pending in the state of the corporation's domicile. Markewich v Newberg (1960) 27 Misc. 2d 1040, 210 N.Y.S.2d 299

In proper case, an action charging misconduct on the part of officers or directors of a corporation could be brought in federal court, or a New York court could assume jurisdiction notwithstanding the affairs

of a foreign corporation were involved, if the foreign corporation had been doing business in New York. Schwarz v Artcraft Silk Hosiery Mills, Inc. (1940, CA2 NY) 110 F.2d 465; Jacobs v Manufacturers Trust Co. (1948, DC NY) 81 F. Supp. 394; Kehaya v Axton (1940, DC NY) 30 F. Supp. 838

20. Joinder of parties and claims

In proceedings to charge directors or officers with liability for misconduct under § 60 of former Gen. Corp. L., liability of the individual defendants was several and plaintiff could proceed against one or more without joining all. Buckley v United Cloak & Suit Co. (1913) 155 A.D. 735, 140 N.Y.S. 953, affd 214 N.Y. 679, 108 N.E. 1090

Any number and variety of alleged acts of misconduct could be asserted in the same complaint, and considerable liberality was allowed in stating violations of different sections of the earlier corporation laws, such as §§ 60 and 61 of former Gen. Corp. L. and § 15 of former Stock Corp. L. as a single cause of action, notwithstanding different or alternative types of relief were sought. Whalen v Strong (1930) 230 A.D. 617, 246 N.Y.S. 40; Scott v Funaroff (1948, Sup) 84 N.Y.S.2d 144

A preliminary injunction staying an action was improperly granted, where the plaintiffs in a second action failed to demonstrate a clear likelihood of success on the merits and showed only that minority shareholders and perhaps a single officer of a corporation objected to the litigation, and where the plaintiff in the first action established that all three directors of the corporation had ratified the institution of the action. In addition, a plaintiff's attempt to stay the first action as an officer of the corporation was defective where she failed to join any officer or director of the corporation as a defendant in the second action. NYF Properties Corp. v SB Investors, Ltd. (1983, 1st Dept) 96 A.D.2d 481, 465 N.Y.S.2d 37

However, according to one decision, legal and equitable claims may not properly be joined in the same count. Gans v Hearst (1940) 173 Misc 662, 17 N.Y.S.2d 834, affd 259 A.D. 861, 20 N.Y.S.2d 400

It was not necessary, in an action by an officer or director charging violation of § 61 of former Gen. Corp. L. by other officers or directors, to allege prior demand upon the corporation to bring the action, and recipients of assets transferred in violation of that section could be joined as parties defendant. Katz v Braz (1946) 188 Misc 581, 66 N.Y.S.2d 722, affd 271 A.D. 970, 69 N.Y.S.2d 324

Complaint against debtor's director for breach of fiduciary duties was not dismissed for failure to join required parties, as the liability of a director for breach of fiduciary duty was joint and several under New York law, and the trustee could proceed against one or more directors without joining all of them. Geltzer v Bedke (In re Mundo Latino Mkt.), 2018 Bankr. LEXIS 2435 (Bankr. S.D.N.Y. Aug. 16, 2018).

21. Time limitations

Limitations did not commence to run against a creditor's cause of action under § 58 of former Stock Corp. L. or § 60 of former Gen. Corp. L. charging misconduct on the part of officers or directors until he had first obtained judgment against the corporation with execution returned unsatisfied. Buttles v Smith (1939) 281 N.Y. 226, 22 N.E.2d 350; Rosenkranz v Doran (1942) 264 A.D. 335, 35 N.Y.S.2d 413; Hastings v H. M. Byllesby & Co. (1942, Sup) 38 N.Y.S.2d 201

Once a cause of action came into being in favor of a creditor under § 60 of former Gen. Corp. L., the limitation period applicable depended upon the nature of the misconduct charged, or what was sometimes referred to as "the gravemen of the cause of action," and the problem was often regarded in the light of what kind or type of action the corporation itself would have had against the wrongdoer, had it been plaintiff. Coane v American Distilling Co. (1948) 298 N.Y. 197, 81 N.E.2d 87; Hastings v H. M. Byllesby & Co. (1944) 293 N.Y. 404, 57 N.E.2d 733, cert den 324 US 860, 89 L Ed 1417, 65 S Ct 864; Luke v Polstein (1944) 268 A.D. 921, 51 N.Y.S.2d 427, affd 294 N.Y. 896, 63 N.E.2d 27; Corash v Texas Co. (1942) 264 A.D. 292, 35 N.Y.S.2d 334; Purdy v Humphrey (1947) 192 Misc 309, 82 N.Y.S.2d 92, affd 274 A.D. 841, 82 N.Y.S.2d 388; Baker v Cohn (1942, Sup) 42 N.Y.S.2d 159, mod on other grounds 266 A.D. 715, 40 N.Y.S.2d 623, affd 292 N.Y. 570, 54 N.E.2d 689

Action alleging waste and dissipation of corporate assets by corporate officers and directors was "action... on behalf of a corporation" governed by 6-year limitations period of CLS CPLR § 213(7) where plaintiff judgment creditor sought accounting, recovery of funds allegedly wrongfully diverted by corporate officers and directors, and damages allegedly incurred by corporation and its creditors; thus, director added as defendant more than 3 years after action was commenced was not entitled to dismissal of complaint against her as time barred by CLS CPLR § 214(2). Rupert v Tigue (1999, 4th Dept) 259 A.D.2d 946, 687 N.Y.S.2d 502, related proceeding (4th Dept) 259 A.D.2d 947, 688 N.Y.S.2d 454

Judgment creditor's claims under N.Y. B.C.L. § 720 were not timely and were dismissed pursuant to Fed. R. Civ. P. 12(b)(6) where it waited substantially more than three years after becoming a judgment creditor to attempt to bring direct claims against a judgment debtor corporation such that the claims were time-barred under N.Y. C.P.L.R. § 214(2). JSC Foreign Econ. Ass'n Technostroyexport v Int'l Dev. & Trade Servs. (2003, SD NY) 295 F. Supp. 2d 366

22. Pre-trial examinations; discovery

Plaintiff, in an action under § 60 of former Gen. Corp. L., had the usual right to demand pre-trial examination of the individual defendants. Eckman v Lindbeck (1917) 178 A.D. 720, 165 N.Y.S. 145

However, examinations before trial are not favored, in the first department, in the stockholders' derivative suits, will be allowed only in special circumstances, and cannot ordinarily be availed of to fish for facts which might give rise to a cause of action. Markewich v Newberg (1960) 27 Misc. 2d 1040, 210 N.Y.S.2d 299

23. Other procedural matters

When corporation commences state court action against corporate officer, among others, charging mismanagement, waste, unfairness and self-dealing, after officer, whose employment has been terminated, has demanded arbitration pursuant to employment agreement and has began state court action against corporation for compensatory and punitive damages for breach of stock option agreements, corporation's motion to stay arbitration will be denied, officer's cross-motion to compel arbitration will be granted, and corporation's motion for consolidation of officer's stock option action with corporation's action will be granted but trial will be stayed of so much of consolidated action as relates to officer's compensation rights under employment agreement until completion of arbitration. GAF Corp. v Werner (1985) 66 N.Y.2d 97, 495 N.Y.S.2d 312, 485 N.E.2d 977, cert den (US) 89 L Ed 2d 720, 106 S Ct 1463

It is doubtful whether an officer or director of a corporation, called upon to account for waste and mismanagement, can counterclaim for moneys loaned or advanced to the corporation, or assert a cross-claim against others in interest. Ritter v Mountain Camp Holding Corp. (1937) 252 A.D. 602, 299 N.Y.S. 876; Orto Theatres Corp. v Newins (1955) 207 Misc 414, 138 N.Y.S.2d 550; Burgess v Stevens (1933) 148 Misc 450, 266 N.Y.S. 79

Individual defendants have a right to demand a jury trial with respect to causes of action at law asserted against them, notwithstanding the complaint is for an accounting to the corporation. Duane Jones Co. v Burke (1952) 280 A.D. 889, 115 N.Y.S.2d 529

A cause of action by an officer and director against another officer and director stating that the corporation had suffered a loss because of waste and mismanagement was sufficient without an allegation that the cause of action was a class action on behalf of all similarly situated stockholders, that a demand was made on the directors of the corporation, or the reasons why the corporation failed to bring the action. Conant v Schnall (1970, 3d Dept) 33 A.D.2d 326, 307 N.Y.S.2d 902

Corporation was properly ordered to make certain records available to its director, even though corporation contended that director was the principal of a competing corporation, was hostile to corporation, and would use the information to the detriment of corporation. Dusel v Castellani (1973, 4th Dept) 43 A.D.2d 799, 350 N.Y.S.2d 258

Judgment creditor's cause of action against director of corporate judgment debtor would be dismissed, without prejudice and with leave to replead, where it was alleged only that director was personally liable under Business Corporation Law to corporate debtor for unlawful distributions of corporate assets and that creditor was entitled to satisfy its judgment from director's interest in assets of employee benefit plan, and it appeared from wording that cause of action was grounded on CLS Bus Corp §§ 510 and 719; while § 719 would not apply to such cause, and CLS Bus Corp § 720 does permit action against director by judgment creditor to set aside unlawful conveyance where transferee knew of its unlawfulness, essential elements of § 720 action could not be deemed to have been pleaded even under liberal rules regarding construction of pleadings. Planned Consumer Marketing, Inc. v Coats & Clark, Inc. (1987, 1st Dept) 127 A.D.2d 355, 513 N.Y.S.2d 417, affd, ctfd ques ans 71 N.Y.2d 442, 527 N.Y.S.2d 185, 522 N.E.2d 30, 9 EBC 1796

Cause of action alleging violations of CLS Bus Corp § 720(a)(1) was not subject to dismissal for failure to comply with pleading requirements of CLS CPLR § 3016 since prohibitions of § 720 are not based on fraud. Menaker v Alstaedter (1987, 2d Dept) 134 A.D.2d 412, 521 N.Y.S.2d 35

In action for accounting and damages for corporate mismanagement, breach of fiduciary duty, and conversion, plaintiff's affidavit was insufficient to defeat defendants' summary judgment motion where plaintiff merely claimed that unsworn third parties gave him reason to believe that defendants committed complained of acts and he admitted that his suspicions were "sheer speculation." Lipshie v Peck (1988, 2d Dept) 139 A.D.2d 702, 527 N.Y.S.2d 981

In action seeking declaration that corporate resolution which provided for discontinuance of eviction proceeding commenced in Justice Court was validly adopted by board of directors and binding on defendant, it was error for Supreme Court to dismiss complaint on ground that eviction proceeding was in nature of shareholder's derivative claim immune from board action, and to direct parties to litigate issues raised by defendant's counterclaim in Justice Court, as such ruling essentially determined that resolution was properly adopted procedurally, while referring defendant's substantive challenges to Justice Court, which was beyond Justice Court's subject matter jurisdiction. TJI Realty, Inc. v Harris (1998, 2d Dept) 250 A.D.2d 596, 672 N.Y.S.2d 386

A complaint, on the other hand, which is vague, general, and wholly conclusory, or one which merely alleges some discrepancy in records or accounts over a short period of time, is insufficient. Arvonio v Arvonio (1961) 31 Misc. 2d 5, 219 N.Y.S.2d 635; Cirrincione v Polizzi (1961, 4th Dept) 14 A.D.2d 281, 220 N.Y.S.2d 741

A counsel fee to a successful plaintiff who happens to be a creditor is appropriate where a substantial benefit to the corporation has resulted from the action. Gutman v Branden (1971) 65 Misc. 2d 232, 317 N.Y.S.2d 221

Since stockholders of the corporation, in a stockholder's derivative action, might be substantially affected by the granting of the motion of the substitute plaintiff, the corporation, to discontinue the action with prejudice, the interests of all litigants would best be served by referring the issue presented in the motion to a referee for his inquiry and recommendations. Elgin Nat. Industries, Inc. v Zale Corp. (1972) 71 Misc. 2d 468, 336 N.Y.S.2d 275

Whether pursuit of relief under § 720 of New York Business Corporation Law is labeled accounting or suit for damages is inconsequential. Re Princeton Industries, Inc. (1984, BC SD NY) 39 BR 140

§ 721. Nonexclusivity of statutory provisions for indemnification of directors and officers

The indemnification and advancement of expenses granted pursuant to, or provided by, this article shall not be deemed exclusive of any other rights to which a director or officer seeking indemnification or advancement of expenses may be entitled, whether contained in the certificate of incorporation or the by-laws or, when authorized by such certificate of incorporation or by-laws, (i) a resolution of shareholders, (ii) a resolution of directors, or (iii) an agreement providing for such indemnification, provided that no indemnification may be made to or on behalf of any director or officer if a judgment or other final adjudication adverse to the director or officer establishes that his acts were committed in bad faith or were the result of active and deliberate dishonesty and were material to the cause of action so adjudicated, or that he personally gained in fact a financial profit or other advantage to which he was not legally entitled. Nothing contained in this article shall affect any rights to indemnification to which corporate personnel other than directors and officers may be entitled by contract or otherwise under law.

History: Add, L 1961, ch 855, eff Sept 1, 1963.

Amd, L 1986, ch 513, § 1, eff July 24, 1986.

Business Corporation Law

Section heading, amd, L 1986, ch 513, § 1, eff July 24, 1986.

CASE ANNOTATIONS

Director of cooperative apartment corporation who denied proposed tenants' sublease application based on their race and retaliated against shareholder for opposing his actions, failed to state indemnification cause of action against corporation where corporate by-laws provided for indemnification of director or officer who "acted in good faith, for a purpose which he reasonably believed to be in the best interests of the Corporation"; underlying judgment, finding that director violated various civil rights law, established that he acted in bad faith. Biondi v Beekman Hill House Apt. Corp. (2000) 94 N.Y.2d 659, 709 N.Y.S.2d 861, 731 N.E.2d 577

Reading CLS Bus Corp §§ 721 and 722 together, key to indemnification is director's good faith toward corporation, and judgment against director, standing alone, is not dispositive of whether he or she acted in good faith; however, willful racial discrimination against proposed tenants cannot be considered to be in corporation's best interest. Biondi v Beekman Hill House Apt. Corp. (2000) 94 N.Y.2d 659, 709 N.Y.S.2d 861, 731 N.E.2d 577

The allegations of the complaint alleging breach of duties imposed on officers and directors and executive committees merit a full and plenary trial and the issues should not be limited to whether the stockholders and directors ratified the actions of the defendants and voted to discontinue suits in good faith and with full knowledge of the facts. Syracuse Television, Inc. v Channel 9, Syracuse, Inc. (1967, 4th Dept) 28 A.D.2d 638, 280 N.Y.S.2d 287

In shareholder derivative action, court erred in denying plaintiffs' motion to prohibit defendants' use of corporate funds in defense of action where corporation had made no provisions for indemnification of shareholders or directors (CLS Bus Corp § 721), there was no receipt of undertaking by or on behalf of director or officer in question, and with shareholder or board approval (CLS Bus Corp § 723(c)), litigation had barely commenced, and defendants' "good faith" and motives were plainly at issue (CLS Bus Corp § 722(a) and (b)). Donovan v Rothman (1998, 1st Dept) 253 A.D.2d 627, 677 N.Y.S.2d 327

Corporation was entitled to dismissal of corporate director's claim for indemnification, under corporate by-laws, of sum he owed as punitive damages pursuant to his settlement of lawsuit in which he had been held liable after trial. Biondi v Beekman Hill House Apt., Corp. (1999, 1st Dept) 257 A.D.2d 76, 692 N.Y.S.2d 304, app gr 93 N.Y.2d 819, 697 N.Y.S.2d 566, 719 N.E.2d 927

It was abuse of discretion to deny plaintiffs' motion to preliminarily enjoin defendants from expending corporate funds in defense of proceeding before New York State Department of Insurance where individual defendant had been convicted of grand larceny and scheme to defraud in first degree: it was unlawful for corporation to indemnify individual defendant for expenses he incurred in defending criminal action inasmuch as element of intent under CLS Penal §§ 155.05 and 190.65 required finding of deliberate dishonesty. Pilipiak v Keyes (2001, 1st Dept) 286 A.D.2d 231, 729 N.Y.S.2d 99, app den 97 N.Y.2d 653, 737 N.Y.S.2d 54, 762 N.E.2d 932

Shareholder was entitled to be reimbursed for money advanced on behalf of a corporation for legal fees and settlement money in a prior litigation because other officers had ratified the shareholder's actions, and the shareholder's erroneous opinion concerning payment by an insurer did not show bad faith for N.Y. Bus. Corp. Law § 722(a) purposes; the facts did not establish the requisite bad faith, self-dealing, or fraud required to overcome the presumption under the business judgment rule. The termination of the litigation by settlement did not create a presumption of bad faith or a purpose which did not serve the best interest of the corporation. McDaniel v 162 Columbia Hgts. Hous. Corp. (2009, Sup) 25 Misc 3d 1024, 886 NYS2d 562.

Directors have no common law right to reimbursement for expenses. Bailey v Bush Terminal Co. (1943, Sup) 46 N.Y.S.2d 877, affd 267 A.D. 899, 48 N.Y.S.2d 324, affd 293 N.Y. 735, 56 N.E.2d 739

Although a corporation could grant expanded indemnification rights by contract if it was authorized to do so in its certificate of incorporation or bylaws, the corporation's adoption of expanded indemnification through its amended bylaws, and the corporate executives' subsequent indemnity agreements, violated a preliminary injunction that the federal trial court had entered against the corporation in litigation against it and, thus, the trial court erred in awarding counsel fees to the corporate executives based on their indemnification claim pursuant to the indemnification agreements. Marincovich v Dunes Hotels & Casinos, Inc. (2007, 3d Dept) 41 App Div 3d 1006, 839 NYS2d 553

Shareholder was entitled to summary judgment as to his claims against a corporation's founder in a shareholder's derivative suit under N.Y. Bus. Corp. Law § 626 arising out of the corporation's indemnification of the founder for his legal expenses as: (1) the founder's conduct resulted in a five-count felony indictment against him and the corporation, (2) the founder admitted knowingly and willfully violating the Federal Election Campaign Act and the tax laws, (3) the conduct, punished with a sentence of fines and imprisonment, was not little more than a technical violation of an obscure malum prohibitum statute, (4) the founder's sworn admissions left no room for finding that he was entitled to indemnification by the corporation because he acted in good faith, for a purpose he reasonably believed to be in the best interest of the corporation, and had no reasonable cause to believe that his conduct was unlawful, for which indemnification was permitted under N.Y. Bus. Corp. Law § 722(a), and (5) indemnification in this circumstance was prohibited under N.Y. Bus. Corp. Law §§ 721 and 722(b). Bansbach v Zinn (2003) 1 NY3d 1, 769 N.Y.S.2d 175, 801 N.E.2d 395, reargument den (2004, NY) 2004 N.Y. LEXIS 50

§ 722. Authorization for indemnification of directors and officers

(a) A corporation may indemnify any person made, or threatened to be made, a party to an action or proceeding (other than one by or in the right of the corporation to procure a judgment in its favor), whether civil or criminal, including an action by or in the right of any other corporation of any type or kind, domestic or foreign, or any partnership, joint venture, trust, employee benefit plan or other enterprise, which any director or officer of the corporation served in any capacity at the request of the corporation, by reason of the fact that he, his testator or intestate, was a director or officer of the corporation, or served such other corporation, partnership, joint venture, trust, employee benefit plan or other enterprise in any capacity, against judgments, fines, amounts paid in settlement and reasonable expenses, including attorneys' fees actually and necessarily incurred as a result of such action or proceeding, or any appeal therein, if such director or officer acted, in good faith, for a purpose which he reasonably believed to be in, or, in the case of service for any other corporation or any partnership, joint venture, trust, employee benefit plan or other enterprise, not opposed to, the best interests of the corporation and, in criminal actions or proceedings, in addition, had no reasonable cause to believe that his conduct was unlawful.

(b) The termination of any such civil or criminal action or proceeding by judgment, settlement, conviction or upon a plea of nolo contendere, or its equivalent, shall not in itself create a presumption that any such director or officer did not act, in good faith, for a purpose which he reasonably believed to be in, or, in the case of service for any other corporation or any partnership, joint venture, trust, employee benefit plan or other enterprise, not opposed to, the best interests of the corporation or that he had reasonable cause to believe that his conduct was unlawful.

(c) A corporation may indemnify any person made, or threatened to be made, a party to an action by or in the right of the corporation to procure a judgment in its favor by reason of the fact that he, his testator or intestate, is or was a director or officer of the corporation, or is or was serving at the request of the corporation as a director or officer of any other corporation of any type or kind, domestic or foreign, of any partnership, joint venture, trust, employee benefit plan or other enterprise, against amounts paid in settlement and reasonable expenses, including attorneys' fees, actually and necessarily incurred by him in connection with the defense or settlement of such action, or in connection with an appeal therein, if such director or officer acted, in good faith, for a purpose which he reasonably believed to be in, or, in the case of service for any other corporation or any partnership, joint venture, trust, employee benefit plan or other enterprise, not opposed to, the best interests of the corporation, except that no indemnification under this paragraph shall be made in respect of (1) a threatened action, or a pending action which is settled or otherwise disposed of, or (2) any claim, issue or matter as to which such person shall have been adjudged to be liable to the corporation, unless and only to the extent that the court in which the action was brought, or, if no action was brought, any court of competent jurisdiction, determines upon application that, in view of all the circumstances of the case, the person is fairly and reasonably entitled to indemnity for such portion of the settlement amount and expenses as the court deems proper.

(d) For the purpose of this section, a corporation shall be deemed to have requested a person to serve an employee benefit plan where the performance by such person of his duties to the corporation also imposes duties on, or otherwise involves services by, such person to the plan or participants or beneficiaries of the plan; excise taxes assessed on a person with respect to an employee benefit plan pursuant to applicable law shall be considered fines; and action taken or omitted by a person with respect to an employee benefit plan in the performance of such person's duties for a purpose reasonably believed by such person to be in the interest of the participants and beneficiaries of the plan shall be deemed to be for a purpose which is not opposed to the best interests of the corporation.

History: Formerly § 723, renumbered § 722 and amd, L 1986, ch 513, § 1, eff July 24, 1986.

CASE ANNOTATIONS

1. In general
2. Good faith
3. Criminal prosecution
4. Indemnification for reasonable fees
5. Foreign corporations
6. "Undertaking"
7. "Otherwise disposed of"
8. Under former law

1. In general
Where a corporate officer is successful in the defense of an underlying action, within the meaning of N.Y. Bus. Corp. Law § 723(a), where the corporation unsuccessfully contests the duty to indemnify and contests with partial success the amount of indemnification, and where there is no bad faith on the part of the corporation, the phrase 'attorneys' fees actually and necessarily incurred as a result of such action or proceeding,' as used in N.Y. Bus. Corp. Law § 722(a), does not provide for recovery of reasonable fees incurred by a corporate officer in making an application for fees before a court as authorized N.Y. Bus. Corp. Law § 724(a). Baker v Health Mgmt. Sys., 98 N.Y.2d 80, 745 N.Y.S.2d 741, 772 N.E.2d 1099, 2002 N.Y. LEXIS 899 (N.Y. 2002).

"Good faith" of the corporate officer charged with misconduct likewise had to be established in order to entitle him to reimbursement for expenses of litigation from the corporation under § 64 of former Gen. Corp. L. If his initial misconduct was not in good faith, belated efforts on his part to protect remaining assets and prevent further wastage of funds would not entitle him to reimbursement out of remaining assets at stockholder expense. People v Uran Mining Corp., 13 A.D.2d 419, 216 N.Y.S.2d 985, 1961 N.Y. App. Div. LEXIS 9856 (N.Y. App. Div. 4th Dep't 1961).

Business Corporation L § 723 is applicable to "derivative suits". Professional Ins. Co. v Barry, 60 Misc. 2d 424, 303 N.Y.S.2d 556, 1969 N.Y. Misc. LEXIS 1837 (N.Y. Sup. Ct. 1969), aff'd, 32 A.D.2d 898, 302 N.Y.S.2d 722, 1969 N.Y. App. Div. LEXIS 3451 (N.Y. App. Div. 1st Dep't 1969), overruled in part, Baker v Health Mgmt. Sys., 98 N.Y.2d 80, 745 N.Y.S.2d 741, 772 N.E.2d 1099, 2002 N.Y. LEXIS 899 (N.Y. 2002).

Although a corporation could grant expanded indemnification rights by contract if it was authorized to do so in its certificate of incorporation or bylaws, the corporation's adoption of expanded indemnification through its amended bylaws, and the corporate executives' subsequent indemnity agreements, violated a preliminary injunction that the federal trial court had entered against the corporation in litigation against it and, thus, the trial court erred in awarding counsel fees to the corporate executives based on their indemnification claim pursuant to the indemnification agreements. Marincovich v Dunes Hotels & Casinos, Inc., 41 A.D.3d 1006, 839 N.Y.S.2d 553, 2007 NY Slip Op 5193, 2007 N.Y. App. Div. LEXIS 7326 (N.Y. App. Div. 3d Dep't 2007).

If an action is not of the kind covered under N.Y. Bus. Corp. Law § 722, then neither N.Y. Bus. Corp. Law § 723 nor N.Y. Bus. Corp. Law § 724 is applicable, and the court has no statutory basis to order such indemnification. Mercado v Coes FX, Inc., 815 N.Y.S.2d 806, 2006 NY Slip Op 26172, 12 Misc. 3d 766, 235 N.Y.L.J. 100, 2006 N.Y. Misc. LEXIS 1018 (N.Y. Sup. Ct. 2006).

Federal District Court has jurisdiction over motion for attorney fees under CLS Business Corporation § 725 where claimed fees were incurred in course of representation before same court; lack of pendency of lawsuit does not destroy rights to indemnification since corporate director who has been wholly successful on merits and defense of civil action is entitled to indemnification and statute does not require pendency of action as basis for attorney fees motion. Buffalo Forge Co. v Ogden Corp., 595 F. Supp. 593, 1984 U.S. Dist. LEXIS 23336 (W.D.N.Y. 1984).

2. Good faith
Director of cooperative apartment corporation who denied proposed tenants' sublease application based on their race and retaliated against shareholder for opposing his actions, failed to state indemnification cause of action against corporation where corporate by-laws provided for indemnification of director or officer who "acted in good faith, for a purpose which he reasonably believed to be in the best interests of the Corporation"; underlying judgment, finding that director violated various civil rights law, established that he acted in bad faith. Biondi v Beekman Hill House Apt. Corp., 94 N.Y.2d 659, 709 N.Y.S.2d 861, 731 N.E.2d 577, 2000 N.Y. LEXIS 520 (N.Y. 2000).

A person could not claim right to reimbursement for litigation expense from the corporation under § 64 of former Gen. Corp. L. on the ground that he was actually merely one of its employees, without knowledge of what was going on, where he was also in fact one of its designated officers and directors, as such, chargeable with knowledge and with want of good faith. People v Uran Mining Corp., 13 A.D.2d 419, 216 N.Y.S.2d 985, 1961 N.Y. App. Div. LEXIS 9856 (N.Y. App. Div. 4th Dep't 1961).

In shareholder derivative action, court erred in denying plaintiffs' motion to prohibit defendants' use of corporate funds in defense of action where corporation had made no provisions for indemnification of shareholders or directors (CLS Bus Corp § 721), there was no receipt of undertaking by or on behalf of director or officer in question, and with shareholder or board approval (CLS Bus Corp § 723(c)), litigation had barely commenced, and defendants' "good faith" and motives were plainly at issue (CLS Bus Corp § 722(a) and (b)). Donovan v Rothman, 253 A.D.2d 627, 677 N.Y.S.2d 327, 1998 N.Y. App. Div. LEXIS 9335 (N.Y. App. Div. 1st Dep't 1998).

Shareholder was entitled to be reimbursed for money advanced on behalf of a corporation for legal fees and settlement money in a prior litigation because other officers had ratified the shareholder's actions, and the shareholder's erroneous opinion concerning payment by an insurer did not show bad faith for N.Y. Bus. Corp. Law § 722(a) purposes; the facts did not establish the requisite bad faith, self-dealing, or fraud required to overcome the presumption under the business judgment rule. The termination of the litigation by settlement did not create a presumption of bad faith or a purpose which did not serve the best interest of the corporation. McDaniel v 162 Columbia Hgts. Hous. Corp., 886 N.Y.S.2d 562, 2009 NY Slip Op 29390, 25 Misc. 3d 1024, 2009 N.Y. Misc. LEXIS 2677 (N.Y. Sup. Ct. 2009).

3. Criminal prosecution

Shareholder was entitled to summary judgment as to his claims against a corporation's founder in a shareholder's derivative suit under N.Y. Bus. Corp. Law § 626 arising out of the corporation's indemnification of the founder for his legal expenses as: (1) the founder's conduct resulted in a five-count felony indictment against him and the corporation, (2) the founder admitted knowingly and willfully violating the Federal Election Campaign Act and the tax laws, (3) the conduct, punished with a sentence of fines and imprisonment, was not little more than a technical violation of an obscure malum prohibitum statute, (4) the founder's sworn admissions left no room for finding that he was entitled to indemnification by the corporation because he acted in good faith, for a purpose he reasonably believed to be in the best interest of the corporation, and had no reasonable cause to believe that his conduct was unlawful, for which indemnification was permitted under N.Y. Bus. Corp. Law § 722(a), and (5) indemnification in this circumstance was prohibited under N.Y. Bus. Corp. Law §§ 721 and 722(b). Bansbach v Zinn, 1 N.Y.3d 1, 769 N.Y.S.2d 175, 801 N.E.2d 395, 2003 N.Y. LEXIS 3408 (N.Y. 2003).

Court erred in granting summary judgment to plaintiff, corporate officer, in action for indemnification for expenses incurred in connection with criminal prosecution against him since certificate of incorporation provided for indemnification to fullest extent permitted by CLS Bus Corp §§ 721- 725, and whether he acted in good faith, and whether he had reasonable cause to know that his actions were unlawful were matters exclusively within his knowledge. Titley v Amerford Int'l Corp., 249 A.D.2d 380, 671 N.Y.S.2d 497, 1998 N.Y. App. Div. LEXIS 3981 (N.Y. App. Div. 2d Dep't 1998).

It was abuse of discretion to deny plaintiffs' motion to preliminarily enjoin defendants from expending corporate funds in defense of proceeding before New York State Department of Insurance where individual defendant had been convicted of grand larceny and scheme to defraud in first degree: it was unlawful for corporation to indemnify individual defendant for expenses he incurred in defending criminal action inasmuch as element of intent under CLS Penal §§ 155.05 and 190.65 required finding of deliberate dishonesty. Pilipiak v Keyes, 286 A.D.2d 231, 729 N.Y.S.2d 99, 2001 N.Y. App. Div. LEXIS 7925 (N.Y. App. Div. 1st Dep't 2001), app. denied, 97 N.Y.2d 653, 737 N.Y.S.2d 54, 762 N.E.2d 932, 2001 N.Y. LEXIS 3458 (N.Y. 2001).

4. Indemnification for reasonable fees

Defendant did not qualify for discretionary allowance by court, under CLS Bus Corp § 722, for his reasonable expenses in defending declaratory judgment action where his submissions were insufficient to raise genuine issue of fact regarding his assertion that he held office of president or chief executive officer in plaintiff corporation, plaintiff's documentary evidence proved that defendant never was corporate officer, and even if he were, action against him was not brought "by reason of" such status or for any action allegedly taken by him as officer. Brittania 54 Hotel Corp. v Freid, 251 A.D.2d 49, 673 N.Y.S.2d 668, 1998 N.Y. App. Div. LEXIS 6417 (N.Y. App. Div. 1st Dep't 1998).

Although a president of a corporation might be entitled to indemnification for legal fees incurred in defending an action under N.Y. Bus. Corp. Law § 720 brought by the corporation's director, the president was responsible for the legal services incurred on her behalf as the president made partial payments on invoices and acknowledged an obligation for payment. Mintz & Gold, LLP v Hart, 48 A.D.3d 526, 852 N.Y.S.2d 248, 2008 NY Slip Op 1312, 2008 N.Y. App. Div. LEXIS 1256 (N.Y. App. Div. 2d Dep't 2008).

Corporate president was properly denied indemnification for attorney's fees because (1) the discontinuance, without prejudice, of claims against the president seeking to compel the issuance of a stock certificate and for breach of fiduciary duty did not show the president prevailed on the merits, and (2) indemnification was barred where a matter was settled. Tulino v Tulino, 148 A.D.3d 755, 2017 NY Slip Op 01589, 48 N.Y.S.3d 258, 2017 N.Y. App. Div. LEXIS 1572 (N.Y. App. Div. 2d Dep't 2017).

Denying minority shareholder's cross-motion for reimbursement of expenses related to defending against corporations and individual defendants; counterclaims was error as all shareholder was required by the statute to do was raise a genuine issue of fact or law, which he did, and denying his cross motion to restrain use of corporate funds to pay for defense expenses related to a dissolution claim was also error. Feldmeier v Feldmeier Equip., Inc., 2018 N.Y. App. Div. LEXIS 5843 (N.Y. App. Div. 4th Dep't 2018).

In an action instituted by a corporation against a former director in which the director counterclaimed for indemnity and filed a third party complaint seeking indemnification from a second corporation by whom he was allegedly employed and served as director of the plaintiff corporation at the request of and for the benefit of the second corporation, it was held that Business Corporation Law § 722 and § 723 are not exclusive so that asserting rights to indemnification under one section did not preclude assertion of rights to indemnification under the other. Rejecting the contention the director failed to establish a "reasonable probability of success", the court noted that no such requirement was set forth in applicable sections of the Business Corporation Law. Professional Ins. Co. v Barry, 60 Misc. 2d 424, 303 N.Y.S.2d 556, 1969 N.Y. Misc. LEXIS 1837 (N.Y. Sup. Ct. 1969), aff'd, 32 A.D.2d 898, 302 N.Y.S.2d 722, 1969 N.Y. App. Div. LEXIS 3451 (N.Y. App. Div. 1st Dep't 1969), overruled in part, Baker v Health Mgmt. Sys., 98 N.Y.2d 80, 745 N.Y.S.2d 741, 772 N.E.2d 1099, 2002 N.Y. LEXIS 899 (N.Y. 2002).

Shareholders made requisite finding under CLS Bus Corp § 723(b)(2)(B) that majority shareholder met standard of conduct required by CLS Bus Corp § 722 (i.e., good faith and concern for best interests of company) in approving corporate indemnification to majority shareholder for his personal legal expenses where majority shareholder owned 59 percent of shares, and thus his vote alone was sufficient to approve indemnification; his personal interest in indemnification did not preclude him from voting on issue, or from making requisite finding of good faith. Pilipiak v Keyes, 185 Misc. 2d 636, 712 N.Y.S.2d 757, 2000 N.Y. Misc. LEXIS 319 (N.Y. Sup. Ct. 2000), rev'd, 286 A.D.2d 231, 729 N.Y.S.2d 99, 2001 N.Y. App. Div. LEXIS 7925 (N.Y. App. Div. 1st Dep't 2001), abrogated as stated in Spitzer v Soundview Health Ctr., 233 N.Y.L.J. 18, 2005 N.Y. Misc. LEXIS 3249 (N.Y. Sup. Ct. 2005).

Where a first company did not establish that an employee was not an officer of a second company, the second company was entitled to indemnification for the employee's legal fees under N.Y. Bus. Corp. Law § 722(a); pursuant to N.Y. C.P.L.R. 6312(b), all damages and costs that were sustained by reason of an improperly imposed injunction should have been considered. Marietta Corp. v Pac. Direct, Inc., 9 A.D.3d 815, 781 N.Y.S.2d 387, 2004 N.Y. App. Div. LEXIS 10035 (N.Y. App. Div. 3d Dep't 2004).

5. Foreign corporations

Under Business Corporation Law § 723, made applicable to foreign corporations doing business in New York by Business Corporation Law § 1319, and providing that in order for a director of a corporation to obtain the benefits of indemnification and to be reimbursed for the expense of contesting an action against him it must be by reason of his being or having been a director, the director of a membership corporation, sued on the ground that he had conspired to injure an equipment supplier's business by criticizing the supplier's competition with the membership corporation, was not precluded from recovering the full amount of costs, expenses and fees incurred in defending the suit by reason of his having been paid half of such amount by an insurer. Dankoff v Bowling Proprietors Ass'n, 69 Misc. 2d 658, 331 N.Y.S.2d 109, 1972 N.Y. Misc. LEXIS 2072 (N.Y. Sup. Ct. 1972).

6. "Undertaking"

"Undertaking" made under Business Corporation Law is distinct from "undertaking" made under CLS CPLR Art 25 in that former, unlike latter, is repayment commitment by director or officer to its corporation which is enforceable against its principal on delivery, it may apply to director's or officer's ongoing expenses for defending both civil or criminal actions or proceedings, it does not need to be filed, served on other parties or acknowledged, and it can be made "by or on behalf of" indemnified director or officer (meaning that principal making undertaking can act as his or her own surety). Pilipiak v Keyes, 185 Misc. 2d 636, 712 N.Y.S.2d 757, 2000 N.Y. Misc. LEXIS 319 (N.Y. Sup. Ct. 2000), rev'd, 286 A.D.2d 231, 729 N.Y.S.2d 99, 2001 N.Y. App. Div. LEXIS 7925 (N.Y. App. Div. 1st Dep't 2001), abrogated as stated in Spitzer v Soundview Health Ctr., 233 N.Y.L.J. 18, 2005 N.Y. Misc. LEXIS 3249 (N.Y. Sup. Ct. 2005).

7. "Otherwise disposed of"

When an officer and a corporation stipulated that counterclaims brought against the officer by the corporation were to be dismissed without prejudice, they had been "otherwise disposed of" under N.Y. Bus. Corp. Law § 722, and the officer could not be indemnified for counsel fees incurred in their defense. The statute ruled out indemnification in cases where an action against an officer or a director had been disposed of in some manner other than on the merits. Mercado v Coes FX, Inc., 815 N.Y.S.2d 806, 2006 NY Slip Op 26172, 12 Misc. 3d 766, 235 N.Y.L.J. 100, 2006 N.Y. Misc. LEXIS 1018 (N.Y. Sup. Ct. 2006).

8. Under former law

Earlier provisions for reimbursement of corporate officers by the corporation for litigation expense did not extend to their expense in defending against criminal charges. Schwarz v General Aniline & Film Corp., 305 N.Y. 395, 113 N.E.2d 533, 305 N.Y. (N.Y.S.) 395, 1953 N.Y. LEXIS 808 (N.Y. 1953); Petition of Schwarz, 94 F. Supp. 129, 1950 U.S. Dist. LEXIS 2074 (D.N.Y. 1950).

Under § 64 of former Gen. Corp. L., a conviction of a corporate officer upon a plea of nolo contendere amounted to an adjudication of misconduct, precluding any right to reimbursement. Schwarz v General Aniline & Film Corp., 102 N.Y.S.2d 325, 198 Misc. 1046, 1951 N.Y. Misc. LEXIS 1504 (N.Y. Sup. Ct. 1951), aff'd, 279 A.D. 996, 112 N.Y.S.2d 146, 1952 N.Y. App. Div. LEXIS 5588 (N.Y. App. Div. 1952).

Under earlier statutes, an individual defendant in a stockholder's derivative action was not entitled to expense reimbursement merely because the complaint was dismissed, but only if it was dismissed against him on the merits. Thus, he was not entitled to reimbursement where the complaint was dismissed because plaintiff had participated in the acts complained of. Diamond v Diamond, 307 N.Y. 263, 120 N.E.2d 819, 307 N.Y. (N.Y.S.) 263, 1954 N.Y. LEXIS 988 (N.Y. 1954).

Section 64 of former Gen. Corp. L. was regarded, by some authority, as sanctioning reimbursement of an officer or director for expense in defending charges against him, only where the charge was made and defended in a stockholder's derivative action. People v Uran Mining Corp., 13 A.D.2d 419, 216 N.Y.S.2d 985, 1961 N.Y. App. Div. LEXIS 9856 (N.Y. App. Div. 4th Dep't 1961).

Under § 64 of former Gen. Corp. L., read in conjunction with § 61-b, an individual defendant in a stockholder's derivative action was entitled to reimbursement from the corporation for expense incurred in defending the suit if there was no adjudication rendering him liable for negligence or misconduct, and accordingly dismissal of such an action because of plaintiff's failure to give security as required by court order under § 61-b would ipso facto entitle an individual defendant who was joined as such by reason of officer status to expense reimbursement. Tyler v Gas Consumers Asso., 35 Misc. 2d 801, 231 N.Y.S.2d 15, 1962 N.Y. Misc. LEXIS 3110 (N.Y. Sup. Ct. 1962).

UNDER FORMER § 722

Under earlier statutes, an individual defendant in a stockholder's derivative action was not entitled to expense reimbursement merely because the complaint was dismissed, but only if it was dismissed against him on the merits. Thus, he was not entitled to reimbursement where the complaint was dismissed because plaintiff had participated in the acts complained of. Diamond v Diamond (1954) 307 N.Y. 263, 120 N.E.2d 819

Section 64 of former Gen. Corp. L. was regarded, by some authority, as sanctioning reimbursement of an officer or director for expense in defending charges against him, only where the charge was made and defended in a stockholder's derivative action. People v Uran Mining Corp. (1961, 4th Dept) 13 A.D.2d 419, 216 N.Y.S.2d 985

Under § 64 of former Gen. Corp. L., read in conjunction with § 61-b, an individual defendant in a stockholder's derivative action was entitled to reimbursement from the corporation for expense incurred in defending the suit if there was no adjudication rendering him liable for negligence or misconduct, and accordingly dismissal of such an action because of plaintiff's failure to give security as required by court order under § 61-b would ipso facto entitle an individual defendant who was joined as such by reason of officer status to expense reimbursement. Tyler v Gas Consumers Asso. (1962) 35 Misc. 2d 801, 231 N.Y.S.2d 15

In an action instituted by a corporation against a former director in which the director counterclaimed for indemnity and filed a third party complaint seeking indemnification from a second corporation by whom he was allegedly employed and served as director of the plaintiff corporation at the request of and for the benefit of the second corporation, it was held that Business Corporation Law § 722 and § 723 are not exclusive so that asserting rights to indemnification under one section did not preclude assertion of rights to indemnification under the other. Rejecting the contention the director failed to establish a "reasonable probability of success", the court noted that no such requirement was set forth in applicable sections of the Business Corporation Law. Professional Ins. Co. v Barry (1969) 60 Misc. 2d 424, 303 N.Y.S.2d 556, affd (1st Dept) 32 A.D.2d 898, 302 N.Y.S.2d 722

Earlier provisions were construed as permitting a certificate of incorporation to provide for indemnification of a director, officer or employee in an action brought against him as such, and likewise for expenses in settlement of an alleged or asserted cause of action if the settlement was court-approved, but not in the absence of court approval. 1953 Ops Atty Gen Dec 31

§ 723. Payment of indemnification other than by court award

(a) A person who has been successful, on the merits or otherwise, in the defense of a civil or criminal action or proceeding of the character described in section 722 shall be entitled to indemnification as authorized in such section.

(b) Except as provided in paragraph (a), any indemnification under section 722 or otherwise permitted by section 721, unless ordered by a court under section 724 (Indemnification of directors and officers by a court), shall be made by the corporation, only if authorized in the specific case:

(1) By the board acting by a quorum consisting of directors who are not parties to such action or proceeding upon a finding that the director or officer has met the standard of conduct set forth in section 722 or established pursuant to section 721, as the case may be, or,

(2) If a quorum under subparagraph (1) is not obtainable or, even if obtainable, a quorum of disinterested directors so directs;

(A) By the board upon the opinion in writing of independent legal counsel that indemnification is proper in the circumstances because the applicable standard of conduct set forth in such sections has been met by such director or officer, or

(B) By the shareholders upon a finding that the director or officer has met the applicable standard of conduct set forth in such sections.

(c) Expenses incurred in defending a civil or criminal action or proceeding may be paid by the corporation in advance of the final disposition of such action or proceeding upon receipt of an undertaking by or on behalf of such director or officer to repay such amount as, and to the extent, required by paragraph (a) of section 725.

History: Formerly § 724, renumbered § 723 and amd, L 1986, ch 513, § 1, eff July 24, 1986.

CASE ANNOTATIONS

1. In general
2. Good faith
3. Independent legal counsel
4. "Undertaking"

1. In general

Corporate president was properly denied indemnification for attorney's fees because (1) the discontinuance, without prejudice, of claims against the president seeking to compel the issuance of a stock certificate and for breach of fiduciary duty did not show the president prevailed on the merits, and (2) indemnification was barred where a matter was settled. Tulino v Tulino, 148 A.D.3d 755, 2017 NY Slip Op 01589, 48 N.Y.S.3d 258, 2017 N.Y. App. Div. LEXIS 1572 (N.Y. App. Div. 2d Dep't 2017).

According to some decisions dealing with §§ 63 and 64 of former Gen. Corp. L., an officer or director of a corporation was not entitled as matter of right to reimbursement by the corporation for expense of defending charges against him, merely on the basis of plaintiffs' lack of success in establishing his liability and dismissal of the action. Diamond v Diamond, 307 N.Y. 263, 120 N.E.2d 819, 307 N.Y. (N.Y.S.) 263, 1954 N.Y. LEXIS 988 (N.Y. 1954); People v Uran Mining Corp., 13 A.D.2d 419, 216 N.Y.S.2d 985, 1961 N.Y. App. Div. LEXIS 9856 (N.Y. App. Div. 4th Dep't 1961); Spring v Moncrieff, 10 Misc. 2d 731, 173 N.Y.S.2d 86, 1958 N.Y. Misc. LEXIS 3756 (N.Y. Sup. Ct. 1958).

Where a corporate officer is successful in the defense of an underlying action, within the meaning of N.Y. Bus. Corp. Law § 723(a), where the corporation unsuccessfully contests the duty to indemnify and contests with partial success the amount of indemnification, and where there is no bad faith on the part of the corporation, the phrase "attorneys' fees actually and necessarily incurred as a result of such action or proceeding," as used in N.Y. Bus. Corp. Law § 722(a), does not provide for recovery of reasonable fees incurred by a corporate officer in making an application for fees before a court as authorized N.Y. Bus. Corp. Law § 724(a). Baker v Health Mgmt. Sys., 98 N.Y.2d 80, 745 N.Y.S.2d 741, 772 N.E.2d 1099, 2002 N.Y. LEXIS 899 (N.Y. 2002).

No allowance could be made for services rendered by the attorneys for the executor of a deceased director, who was made an individual party defendant in a stockholders' derivative action, where they were successful only in defeating a second cause of action which was directed against the corporation and not against its directors. Christie v Fifth Madison Corp., 35 Misc. 2d 570, 231 N.Y.S.2d 541, 1962 N.Y. Misc. LEXIS 2950 (N.Y. Sup. Ct. 1962).

Final dismissal of action by reason of plaintiffs' failure to comply with a security order made pursuant to § 61-b of former Gen. Corp. L., without any finding of liability on the part of an individual defendant who, as an officer, was charged with liability to the corporation, entitled him to seek expense reimbursement from the corporation. Tyler v Gas Consumers Asso., 35 Misc. 2d 801, 231 N.Y.S.2d 15, 1962 N.Y. Misc. LEXIS 3110 (N.Y. Sup. Ct. 1962).

Corporation's indemnification of majority shareholder for his personal legal expenses was duly authorized by shareholders, regardless of when or whether corporate board of directors validly approved indemnification, since, under CLS Bus Corp § 723(b)(2)(B), shareholders' vote alone validated indemnification. Pilipiak v Keyes, 185 Misc. 2d 636, 712 N.Y.S.2d 757, 2000 N.Y. Misc. LEXIS 319 (N.Y. Sup. Ct. 2000), rev'd, 286 A.D.2d 231, 729 N.Y.S.2d 99, 2001 N.Y. App. Div. LEXIS 7925 (N.Y. App. Div. 1st Dep't 2001), abrogated as stated in Spitzer v Soundview Health Ctr., 233 N.Y.L.J. 18, 2005 N.Y. Misc. LEXIS 3249 (N.Y. Sup. Ct. 2005).

Shareholders made requisite finding under CLS Bus Corp § 723(b)(2)(B) that majority shareholder met standard of conduct required by CLS Bus Corp § 722 (i.e., good faith and concern for best interests of company) in approving corporate indemnification to majority shareholder for his personal legal expenses where majority shareholder owned 59 percent of shares, and thus his vote alone was sufficient to approve indemnification; his personal interest in indemnification did not preclude him from voting on issue, or from making requisite finding of good faith. Pilipiak v Keyes, 185 Misc. 2d 636, 712 N.Y.S.2d 757, 2000 N.Y. Misc. LEXIS 319 (N.Y. Sup. Ct. 2000), rev'd, 286 A.D.2d 231, 729 N.Y.S.2d 99, 2001 N.Y. App. Div. LEXIS 7925 (N.Y. App. Div. 1st Dep't 2001), abrogated as stated in Spitzer v Soundview Health Ctr., 233 N.Y.L.J. 18, 2005 N.Y. Misc. LEXIS 3249 (N.Y. Sup. Ct. 2005).

If an action is not of the kind covered under N.Y. Bus. Corp. Law § 722, then neither N.Y. Bus. Corp. Law § 723 nor N.Y. Bus. Corp. Law § 724 is applicable, and the court has no statutory basis to order such indemnification. Mercado v Coes FX, Inc., 815 N.Y.S.2d 806, 2006 NY Slip Op 26172, 12 Misc. 3d 766, 235 N.Y.L.J. 100, 2006 N.Y. Misc. LEXIS 1018 (N.Y. Sup. Ct. 2006).

Federal District Court has jurisdiction over motion for attorney fees under CLS Business Corporation § 725 where claimed fees were incurred in course of representation before same court; lack of pendency of lawsuit does not destroy rights to indemnification since corporate director who has been wholly successful on merits and defense of civil action is entitled to indemnification and statute does not require pendency of action as basis for attorney fees motion. Buffalo Forge Co. v Ogden Corp., 595 F. Supp. 593, 1984 U.S. Dist. LEXIS 23336 (W.D.N.Y. 1984).

2. Good faith

In shareholder derivative action, court erred in denying plaintiffs' motion to prohibit defendants' use of corporate funds in defense of action where corporation had made no provisions for indemnification of shareholders or directors (CLS Bus Corp § 721), there was no receipt of undertaking by or on behalf of director or officer in question, and with shareholder or board approval (CLS Bus Corp § 723(c)), litigation had barely commenced, and defendants' "good faith" and motives were plainly at issue (CLS Bus Corp § 722(a) and (b)). Donovan v Rothman, 253 A.D.2d 627, 677 N.Y.S.2d 327, 1998 N.Y. App. Div. LEXIS 9335 (N.Y. App. Div. 1st Dep't 1998).

3. Independent legal counsel

Shareholder was not entitled to summary judgment in his shareholder's derivative suit under N.Y. Bus. Corp. Law § 626 against corporate officers and directors for their actions in approving the indemnification of the corporation's founder for legal expenses he incurred defending himself from criminal charges as factual issues remained as to the motivation for the actions of the officers and directors, particularly in light of their failure to do more than note the existence of a report of independent legal counsel, upon which they placed heavy reliance under N.Y. Bus. Corp. Law § 723(b)(2)(A). Bansbach v Zinn, 1 N.Y.3d 1, 769 N.Y.S.2d 175, 801 N.E.2d 395, 2003 N.Y. LEXIS 3408 (N.Y. 2003).

In an action brought by shareholders alleging that they were entitled pursuant to a shareholders' agreement, to designate a successor director in the place of their prior designee who resigned, plaintiffs' motion to preliminarily enjoin the defendant corporation from paying the legal fees or expenses of the individual defendant directors was properly denied since Bus Corp Law § 724(b)(2)(A) provides that such expenses may be paid by the corporation and authorized by the board upon the opinion of independent legal counsel that indemnification is proper, and "independent legal counsel" means an attorney who is free from past connections with the corporation or the persons to be indemnified and the attorney retained constituted "independent legal counsel" notwithstanding that the attorney had been retained by a partner in the firm which represented the corporation and the defendant directors, the attorney owned no stock in the corporation, had not previously represented the corporation, and had no past relationship with any of the company's officers or directors. Schmidt v Magnetic Head Corp., 97 A.D.2d 151, 468 N.Y.S.2d 649, 1983 N.Y. App. Div. LEXIS 20344 (N.Y. App. Div. 2d Dep't 1983).

4. "Undertaking"

"Undertaking" made under Business Corporation Law is distinct from "undertaking" made under CLS CPLR Art 25 in that former, unlike latter, is repayment commitment by director or officer to its corporation which is enforceable against its principal on delivery, it may apply to director's or officer's ongoing expenses for defending both civil or criminal actions or proceedings, it does not need to be filed, served on other parties or acknowledged, and it can be made "by or on behalf of" indemnified director or officer (meaning that principal making undertaking can act as his or her own surety). Pilipiak v Keyes, 185 Misc. 2d 636, 712 N.Y.S.2d 757, 2000 N.Y. Misc. LEXIS 319 (N.Y. Sup. Ct. 2000), rev'd, 286 A.D.2d 231, 729 N.Y.S.2d 99, 2001 N.Y. App. Div. LEXIS 7925 (N.Y. App. Div. 1st Dep't 2001), abrogated as stated in Spitzer v Soundview Health Ctr., 233 N.Y.L.J. 18, 2005 N.Y. Misc. LEXIS 3249 (N.Y. Sup. Ct. 2005).

§ 724. Indemnification of directors and officers by a court

(a) Notwithstanding the failure of a corporation to provide indemnification, and despite any contrary resolution of the board or of the shareholders in the specific case under section 723 (Payment of indemnification other than by court award), indemnification shall be awarded by a court to the extent authorized under section 722 (Authorization for indemnification of directors and officers), and paragraph (a) of section 723. Application therefor may be made, in every case, either:

(1) In the civil action or proceeding in which the expenses were incurred or other amounts were paid, or

(2) To the supreme court in a separate proceeding, in which case the application shall set forth the disposition of any previous application made to any court for the same or similar relief and also reasonable cause for the failure to make application for such relief in the action or proceeding in which the expenses were incurred or other amounts were paid.

(b) The application shall be made in such manner and form as may be required by the applicable rules of court or, in the absence thereof, by direction of a court to which it is made. Such application shall be upon notice to the corporation. The court may also direct that notice be given at the expense of the corporation to the shareholders and such other persons as it may designate in such manner as it may require.

(c) Where indemnification is sought by judicial action, the court may allow a person such reasonable expenses, including attorneys' fees, during the pendency of the litigation as are necessary in connection with his defense therein, if the court shall find that the defendant has by his pleadings or during the course of the litigation raised genuine issues of fact or law.

History: Formerly § 725, renumbered § 724 and amd, L 1986, ch 513, § 1, eff July 24, 1986; amd, L 1962, ch 819, eff Sept 1, 1963; L 1963, ch 689, § 8, eff Sept 1, 1963.

CASE ANNOTATIONS

1. In general
2. Applicability
3. Jurisdiction
4. Construction
5. Statute of limitations
6. Arbitration agreements
7. Under former law

1. In general

Where indemnification for legal expenses incurred in defense of action is sought in special proceeding, petitioner must show reasonable cause for failure to seek relief in original action. Klimczak v Connrex Corp., 49 A.D.2d 1031, 374 N.Y.S.2d 497, 1975 N.Y. App. Div. LEXIS 11394 (N.Y. App. Div. 4th Dep't 1975).

Court erred in denying defendants' motion for pendente lite indemnification of their reasonable attorneys' fees and expenses under CLS Bus Corp § 724(c) where questions of fact and law were raised warranting such relief, defendants having previously succeeded in obtaining dismissal of fraud and certain breach of lease claims, and

having presently succeeded in opposing plaintiff's attempt to add RICO claim. 136 East 56th St. Owners v Darnet Realty Assocs., 248 A.D.2d 327, 670 N.Y.S.2d 97, 1998 N.Y. App. Div. LEXIS 3382 (N.Y. App. Div. 1st Dep't 1998).

Defendant did not qualify for discretionary allowance by court, under CLS Bus Corp § 722, for his reasonable expenses in defending declaratory judgment action where his submissions were insufficient to raise genuine issue of fact regarding his assertion that he held office of president or chief executive officer in plaintiff corporation, plaintiff's documentary evidence proved that defendant never was corporate officer, and even if he were, action against him was not brought "by reason of" such status or for any action allegedly taken by him as officer. Brittania 54 Hotel Corp. v Freid, 251 A.D.2d 49, 673 N.Y.S.2d 668, 1998 N.Y. App. Div. LEXIS 6417 (N.Y. App. Div. 1st Dep't 1998).

In an action instituted by a corporation against a former director in which the director counterclaimed for indemnity and filed a third party complaint seeking indemnification from a second corporation by whom he was allegedly employed and served as director of the plaintiff corporation at the request of and for the benefit of the second corporation, it was held that Business Corporation Law § 722 and § 723 are not exclusive so that asserting rights to indemnification under one section did not preclude assertion of rights to indemnification under the other. Rejecting the contention the director failed to establish a "reasonable probability of success", the court noted that no such requirement was set forth in applicable sections of the Business Corporation Law. Professional Ins. Co. v Barry, 60 Misc. 2d 424, 303 N.Y.S.2d 556, 1969 N.Y. Misc. LEXIS 1837 (N.Y. Sup. Ct. 1969), aff'd, 32 A.D.2d 898, 302 N.Y.S.2d 722, 1969 N.Y. App. Div. LEXIS 3451 (N.Y. App. Div. 1st Dep't 1969), overruled in part, Baker v Health Mgmt. Sys., 98 N.Y.2d 80, 745 N.Y.S.2d 741, 772 N.E.2d 1099, 2002 N.Y. LEXIS 899 (N.Y. 2002).

Former corporate executive against whom corporation brought RICO action is entitled to interim payments of expenses and fees, where executive protested his innocence, notwithstanding fact that corporation brought RICO claim alleging that executive acted in bad faith, because executive raised genuine issues of fact. Sequa Corp. v Gelmin, 828 F. Supp. 203, 1993 U.S. Dist. LEXIS 10005 (S.D.N.Y. 1993).

2. Applicability

Where a corporate officer is successful in the defense of an underlying action, within the meaning of N.Y. Bus. Corp. Law § 723(a), where the corporation unsuccessfully contests the duty to indemnify and contests with partial success the amount of indemnification, and where there is no bad faith on the part of the corporation, the phrase "attorneys' fees actually and necessarily incurred as a result of such action or proceeding," as used in N.Y. Bus. Corp. Law § 722(a), does not provide for recovery of reasonable fees incurred by a corporate officer in making an application for fees before a court as authorized N.Y. Bus. Corp. Law § 724(a). Baker v Health Mgmt. Sys., 98 N.Y.2d 80, 745 N.Y.S.2d 741, 772 N.E.2d 1099, 2002 N.Y. LEXIS 899 (N.Y. 2002).

Court erred in granting interim indemnification under CLS Bus Corp § 724(c) to ex-employee of Delaware corporation, who was alleged to have improperly obtained information as to plaintiff's customers during term of his employment, since Delaware's General Corporation Law provided for interim indemnification at corporation's discretion on posting of undertaking by person indemnified to repay such amount if it was ultimately determined that that person was not entitled to indemnification (Del Code Annot., title 8, § 145(e)), but contained no provision for court-ordered interim indemnification analogous to CLS Bus Corp § 724(c). Bear, Stearns & Co. v D.F. King & Co., 243 A.D.2d 252, 663 N.Y.S.2d 12, 1997 N.Y. App. Div. LEXIS 9286 (N.Y. App. Div. 1st Dep't 1997).

Because a shareholder's siblings raised sufficient genuine issues of fact or law in the shareholder's action for breach of fiduciary duty, conversion, fraud, an accounting, common-law dissolution, appointment of a temporary receiver, and injunctive relief, the siblings were entitled to advancement of their expenses under N.Y. Bus. Corp. Law § 724(c). Lemle v Lemle, 92 A.D.3d 494, 939 N.Y.S.2d 15, 2012 NY Slip Op 1106, 2012 N.Y. App. Div. LEXIS 1124 (N.Y. App. Div. 1st Dep't 2012).

If an action is not of the kind covered under N.Y. Bus. Corp. Law § 722, then neither N.Y. Bus. Corp. Law § 723 nor N.Y. Bus. Corp. Law § 724 is applicable, and the court has no statutory basis to order such indemnification. Mercado v Coes FX, Inc., 815 N.Y.S.2d 806,

2006 NY Slip Op 26172, 12 Misc. 3d 766, 235 N.Y.L.J. 100, 2006 N.Y. Misc. LEXIS 1018 (N.Y. Sup. Ct. 2006).

In a federal criminal action in which defendants sought advancement of defense costs from a former employer, an accounting firm, the procedures established in 8 Del. C. § 145(k) and N.Y. Bus. Corp. Law §§ 724(a) and 1319(a)(4) for litigating advancement disputes in state courts did not apply; however, the scope of the issues properly considered in an advancement proceeding was governed by state law. United States v Stein, 452 F. Supp. 2d 230, 2006 U.S. Dist. LEXIS 63445 (S.D.N.Y. 2006).

3. Jurisdiction

Civil Court of City of New York could not grant corporation's motion for summary judgment in action brought by former officer seeking indemnification under CLS Bus Corp § 724, despite complaint's apparent lack of merit, since statute provides that such proceedings may only be brought as part of original action or in Supreme Court; thus, case would be transferred to Supreme Court. Kaufman v CBS, Inc., 135 Misc. 2d 64, 514 N.Y.S.2d 620, 1987 N.Y. Misc. LEXIS 2178 (N.Y. Civ. Ct. 1987).

Federal District Court has jurisdiction over motion for attorney fees under CLS Business Corporation § 725 where claimed fees were incurred in course of representation before same court; lack of pendency of lawsuit does not destroy rights to indemnification since corporate director who has been wholly successful on merits and defense of civil action is entitled to indemnification and statute does not require pendency of action as basis for attorney fees motion. Buffalo Forge Co. v Ogden Corp., 595 F. Supp. 593, 1984 U.S. Dist. LEXIS 23336 (W.D.N.Y. 1984).

4. Construction

Corporate president was properly denied indemnification for attorney's fees because (1) the discontinuance, without prejudice, of claims against the president seeking to compel the issuance of a stock certificate and for breach of fiduciary duty did not show the president prevailed on the merits, and (2) indemnification was barred where a matter was settled. Tulino v Tulino, 148 A.D.3d 755, 2017 NY Slip Op 01589, 48 N.Y.S.3d 258, 2017 N.Y. App. Div. LEXIS 1572 (N.Y. App. Div. 2d Dep't 2017).

Fees on fees recovery was denied because state law required a substantial nexus between the expense on which indemnification was sought and the underlying securities fraud litigation against which the corporate officer was forced to defend. Baker v Health Mgmt. Sys., 298 F.3d 146, 2002 U.S. App. LEXIS 15111 (2d Cir. N.Y. 2002).

Plaintiff's malicious prosecution action against his former corporate employers would be dismissed for failure to allege that corporations' lawsuit was terminated in plaintiff's favor, or under circumstances indicating his innocence, where corporations voluntarily discontinued their lawsuit against him "without prejudice" after trial judge ruled that his denials of wrongdoing and "protestations of innocence" raised "genuine issues of fact" sufficient to require corporations to indemnify him for legal expenses under CLS Bus Corp § 724(c); corporate officer seeking indemnification under § 724(c) need not even show probability of success. O'Brien v Alexander, 898 F. Supp. 162, 33 Fed. R. Serv. 3d (Callaghan) 608, 1995 U.S. Dist. LEXIS 12587 (S.D.N.Y. 1995), aff'd in part and rev'd in part, 101 F.3d 1479, 36 Fed. R. Serv. 3d (Callaghan) 558, 1996 U.S. App. LEXIS 32632 (2d Cir. N.Y. 1996).

5. Statute of limitations

An action for attorneys fees under former General Corporation Law § 64 would not be governed by the 20 year statute of limitations of CPLR § 211 concerning money judgments since the judgment for defendant in the underlying suit "together with the cost and disbursements of the action" did not include the specific findings which must be made before attorneys' fees can be awarded; until such findings are made, no "money judgment" for attorneys' fees has been awarded. Phillips v Investors Diversified Services, Inc., 426 F. Supp. 208, 1976 U.S. Dist. LEXIS 11832 (S.D.N.Y. 1976).

In an action by an attorney to recover the "reasonable value" of his services rendered as a successful attorney pro se defending an earlier shareholders' derivative action against him and others as directors of a corporation, plaintiff would not be entitled to recover under former General Corporation Law §§ 64 and 68 since his claim was barred by the six year statute of limitations formerly provided by CPA § 48(2), and because his own services as attorney pro se did not qualify as "reasonable expenses, including attorneys' fees" for which the statute permitted reimbursement. Phillips v Investors Diversified Services, Inc., 426 F. Supp. 208, 1976 U.S. Dist. LEXIS 11832 (S.D.N.Y. 1976).

6. Arbitration agreements

In a criminal case in which the court had ancillary jurisdiction over defendants' claims against a former employer, an accounting firm, for advancement of defense costs, the advancement dispute was not arbitrable under 9 U.S.C.S. § 2 of the Federal Arbitration Act, 9 U.S.C.S. § 1 et seq., because there was no evidence that all defendants were parties to an arbitration agreement, partnership agreements demonstrated that the obligation of former partners to arbitrate ended when their status as partners terminated, and enforcement of any applicable arbitration clauses would have violated public policy. Requiring arbitration (1) would have limited the court's ability to ensure that proceedings against defendants were fair, (2) would have undermined the court's responsibility under the Constitution and Criminal Justice Act, 18 U.S.C.S. § 3006A(f), to ensure that property available to defendants was used for their defense, (3) would have undermined the public interest in a speedy trial in accordance with the Sixth Amendment and the Speedy Trial Act, 18 U.S.C.S. § 3161 et seq., and (4) would have implicated the public interest, as found in 8 Del. C. § 145(k) and N.Y. Bus. Corp. Law §§ 724(a) and 1319(a)(4), in the timely resolution of disputes concerning advancement of defense costs. United States v Stein, 452 F. Supp. 2d 230, 2006 U.S. Dist. LEXIS 63445 (S.D.N.Y. 2006).

7. Under former law

Section 63 of former Gen. Corp. L. was regarded as in derogation of the common law and accordingly as subject to strict construction. Diamond v Diamond, 307 N.Y. 263, 120 N.E.2d 819, 307 N.Y. (N.Y.S.) 263, 1954 N.Y. LEXIS 988 (N.Y. 1954).

There was no right to an expense reimbursement allowance against the corporation, under § 64 of former Gen. Corp. L., where the charge against the corporate officer was strictly criminal, or based upon his individual misconduct as contrasted with his conduct as an officer or representative of the corporation. Diamond v Diamond, 307 N.Y. 263, 120 N.E.2d 819, 307 N.Y. (N.Y.S.) 263, 1954 N.Y. LEXIS 988 (N.Y. 1954); Schwarz v General Aniline & Film Corp., 305 N.Y. 395, 113 N.E.2d 533, 305 N.Y. (N.Y.S.) 395, 1953 N.Y. LEXIS 808 (N.Y. 1953); Hennessey v Fein, 176 F. Supp. 228, 1959 U.S. Dist. LEXIS 2779 (D.N.Y. 1959); Petition of Schwarz, 94 F. Supp. 129, 1950 U.S. Dist. LEXIS 2074 (D.N.Y. 1950).

It was usually the practice, under sections of former Gen. Corp. L. dealing with reimbursement allowances against corporations, to apply for such allowances by motion directed to the court and in the action in connection with which the expenses were incurred, if the corporation was a party to that action. In re Bailey, 265 A.D. 758, 40 N.Y.S.2d 746, 1943 N.Y. App. Div. LEXIS 6411 (N.Y. App. Div. 1943), aff'd, 291 N.Y. 534, 50 N.E.2d 653, 291 N.Y. (N.Y.S.) 534, 1943 N.Y. LEXIS 1692 (N.Y. 1943).

There was no right to a reimbursement allowance against the corporation under § 64 of former Gen. Corp. L. in behalf of an officer who was merely a nominal party to the action and not called upon, or required, to defend. Warnecke v Forty Wall Street Bldg., Inc., 16 Misc. 2d 467, 183 N.Y.S.2d 925, 1959 N.Y. Misc. LEXIS 4406 (N.Y. Sup. Ct. 1959), aff'd, 13 A.D.2d 630, 215 N.Y.S.2d 720, 1961 N.Y. App. Div. LEXIS 11440 (N.Y. App. Div. 1st Dep't 1961), superseded by statute as stated in Schmidt v Magnetic Head Corp., 97 A.D.2d 151, 468 N.Y.S.2d 649, 1983 N.Y. App. Div. LEXIS 20344 (N.Y. App. Div. 2d Dep't 1983).

Some decisions held that the reimbursement application, under earlier statutes, could be made only by the corporate officer involved in the litigation, or in his name, not by his attorney acting in his own right. Buchman & Buchman v Lanston Industries, Inc., 25 Misc. 2d 818, 200 N.Y.S.2d 445, 1960 N.Y. Misc. LEXIS 3367 (N.Y. Sup. Ct. 1960).

If, for some reason, an application for expense reimbursement could not be made by motion in a pending action, it was recognized that a special proceeding would lie to determine propriety and amount of the claim. But where the application could be, and was, made by motion in the action in which the expense was incurred, it was held that the judge, in the absence of exceptional circumstances, should make the determination personally without referring the matter to an official referee. Tharaud v James Bros. Realty Co., 28 Misc. 2d 921, 216 N.Y.S.2d 1012, 1961 N.Y. Misc. LEXIS 2753 (N.Y. Sup. Ct. 1961).

While an expense allowance against the corporation and in favor of one of its officers who was made a party defendant to a shareholder's derivative action could not successfully be applied for and obtained if the officer was found guilty of the misconduct charged, his complete vindication on the merits was not a condition to making such an allowance under § 64 of former Gen. Corp. L., and he was entitled to apply for it when and if the action was dismissed by reason of plaintiff's failure to give security for costs. Tyler v Gas Consumers Asso., 35 Misc. 2d 801, 231 N.Y.S.2d 15, 1962 N.Y. Misc. LEXIS 3110 (N.Y. Sup. Ct. 1962); Tichner v Andrews, 85 N.Y.S.2d 760, 193 Misc. 1050, 1949 N.Y. Misc. LEXIS 1695 (N.Y. Sup. Ct. 1949), app. dismissed, 275 A.D. 749, 90 N.Y.S.2d 920, 1949 N.Y. App. Div. LEXIS 4321 (N.Y. App. Div. 1949).

The provisions of former Gen. Corp. L. from which this section was derived were upheld as valid and constitutional. Hayman v Morris, 37 N.Y.S.2d 884, 1942 N.Y. Misc. LEXIS 2111 (N.Y. Sup. Ct. 1942).

Under § 64 of former Gen. Corp. L., it was held that successful individual defendants in a stockholder's derivative action could be granted an expense reimbursement allowance against the corporation, notwithstanding the plaintiff shareholders were also deemed entitled to an award out of the recovery by reason of their success in the action in other respects. Cohn v Columbia Pictures Corp., 117 N.Y.S.2d 809, 1952 N.Y. Misc. LEXIS 2079 (N.Y. Sup. Ct. 1952).

Matter of making any allowances out of the assets of a corporation involved in proceedings under the Bankruptcy Act was strictly for the bankruptcy court. Le Boeuf v Austrian, 240 F.2d 546, 1957 U.S. App. LEXIS 4372 (4th Cir. Va. 1957), cert. denied, 353 U.S. 965, 77 S. Ct. 1049, 1 L. Ed. 2d 914, 1957 U.S. LEXIS 908 (U.S. 1957); Austrian v Williams, 216 F.2d 278, 1954 U.S. App. LEXIS 3925 (2d Cir. N.Y. 1954), cert. denied, 348 U.S. 953, 75 S. Ct. 441, 99 L. Ed. 745 (U.S. 1955).

UNDER FORMER LAW

In a federal criminal action in which defendants sought advancement of defense costs from a former employer, an accounting firm, the procedures established in 8 Del. C. § 145(k) and N.Y. Bus. Corp. Law §§ 724(a) and 1319(a)(4) for litigating advancement disputes in state courts did not apply; however, the scope of the issues properly considered in an advancement proceeding was governed by state law. United States v Stein (2006, SD NY) 452 F Supp 2d 230, 98 AFTR 2d 6520, motion to strike gr (2006, SD NY) 452 F Supp 2d 276, stay den (2006, SD NY) 452 F Supp 2d 281, 98 AFTR 2d 7160, motion den (2006, SD NY) 2006 US Dist LEXIS 80572, costs/fees proceeding, motion den (2006, SD NY) 461 F Supp 2d 201, motion den (2006, SD NY) 98 AFTR 2d 8016, later proceeding (2007, SD NY) 2007 US Dist LEXIS 1825

In a criminal case in which the court had ancillary jurisdiction over defendants' claims against a former employer, an accounting firm, for advancement of defense costs, the advancement dispute was not arbitrable under 9 U.S.C.S. § 2 of the Federal Arbitration Act, 9 U.S.C.S. § 1 et seq., because there was no evidence that all defendants were parties to an arbitration agreement, partnership agreements demonstrated that the obligation of former partners to arbitrate ended when their status as partners terminated, and enforcement of any applicable arbitration clauses would have violated public policy. Requiring arbitration (1) would have limited the court's ability to ensure that proceedings against defendants were fair, (2) would have undermined the court's responsibility under the Constitution and Criminal Justice Act, 18 U.S.C.S. § 3006A(f), to ensure that property available to defendants was used for their defense, (3) would have undermined the public interest in a speedy trial in accordance with the Sixth Amendment and the Speedy Trial Act, 18 U.S.C.S. § 3161 et seq., and (4) would have implicated the public interest, as found in 8 Del. C. § 145(k) and N.Y. Bus. Corp. Law §§ 724(a) and 1319(a)(4), in the timely resolution of disputes concerning advancement of defense costs. United States v Stein (2006, SD NY) 452 F Supp 2d 230, 98 AFTR 2d 6520, motion to strike gr (2006, SD NY) 452 F Supp 2d 276, stay den (2006, SD NY) 452 F Supp 2d 281, 98 AFTR 2d 7160, motion den (2006, SD NY) 2006 US Dist LEXIS 80572, costs/fees proceeding, motion den (2006, SD NY) 461 F Supp 2d 201, motion den (2006, SD NY) 98 AFTR 2d 8016, later proceeding (2007, SD NY) 2007 US Dist LEXIS 1825

Section 63 of former Gen. Corp. L. was regarded as in derogation of the common law and accordingly as subject to strict construction. Diamond v Diamond (1954) 307 N.Y. 263, 120 N.E.2d 819

There was no right to an expense reimbursement allowance against the corporation, under § 64 of former Gen. Corp. L., where the charge against the corporate officer was strictly criminal, or based upon his individual misconduct as contrasted with his conduct as an officer or representative of the corporation. Diamond v Diamond (1954) 307 N.Y. 263, 120 N.E.2d 819; Schwarz v General Aniline & Film Corp. (1953) 305 N.Y. 395, 113 N.E.2d 533; Hennessey v Fein

(1959, DC NY) 176 F. Supp. 228; Petition of Schwarz (1950, DC NY) 94 F. Supp. 129

It was usually the practice, under sections of former Gen. Corp. L. dealing with reimbursement allowances against corporations, to apply for such allowances by motion directed to the court and in the action in connection with which the expenses were incurred, if the corporation was a party to that action. Re Bailey (1943) 265 A.D. 758, 40 N.Y.S.2d 746, affd 291 N.Y. 534, 50 N.E.2d 653

There was no right to a reimbursement allowance against the corporation under § 64 of former Gen. Corp. L. in behalf of an officer who was merely a nominal party to the action and not called upon, or required, to defend. Warnecke v Forty Wall Street Bldg., Inc. (1959) 16 Misc. 2d 467, 183 N.Y.S.2d 925, affd (1st Dept) 13 A.D.2d 630, 215 N.Y.S.2d 720, reh den (1st Dept) 13 A.D.2d 760, 216 N.Y.S.2d 674, affd 11 N.Y.2d 679, 225 N.Y.S.2d 755, 180 N.E.2d 909

Some decisions held that the reimbursement application, under earlier statutes, could be made only by the corporate officer involved in the litigation, or in his name, not by his attorney acting in his own right. Buchman & Buchman v Lanston Industries, Inc. (1960) 25 Misc. 2d 818, 200 N.Y.S.2d 445

If, for some reason, an application for expense reimbursement could not be made by motion in a pending action, it was recognized that a special proceeding would lie to determine propriety and amount of the claim. But where the application could be, and was, made by motion in the action in which the expense was incurred, it was held that the judge, in the absence of exceptional circumstances, should make the determination personally without referring the matter to an official referee. Tharaud v James Bros. Realty Co. (1961) 28 Misc. 2d 921, 216 N.Y.S.2d 1012

While an expense allowance against the corporation and in favor of one of its officers who was made a party defendant to a shareholder's derivative action could not successfully be applied for and obtained if the officer was found guilty of the misconduct charged, his complete vindication on the merits was not a condition to making such an allowance under § 64 of former Gen. Corp. L., and he was entitled to apply for it when and if the action was dismissed by reason of plaintiff's failure to give security for costs. Tyler v Gas Consumers Asso. (1962) 35 Misc. 2d 801, 231 N.Y.S.2d 15; Tichner v Andrews (1949) 193 Misc 1050, 85 N.Y.S.2d 760, app dismd 275 A.D. 749, 90 N.Y.S.2d 920

The provisions of former Gen. Corp. L. from which this section was derived were upheld as valid and constitutional. Hayman v Morris (1942, Sup) 37 N.Y.S.2d 884, settled 179 Misc 265, 38 N.Y.S.2d 782

Under § 64 of former Gen. Corp. L., it was held that successful individual defendants in a stockholder's derivative action could be granted an expense reimbursement allowance against the corporation, notwithstanding the plaintiff shareholders were also deemed entitled to an award out of the recovery by reason of their success in the action in other respects. Cohn v Columbia Pictures Corp. (1952, Sup) 117 N.Y.S.2d 809

Matter of making any allowances out of the assets of a corporation involved in proceedings under the Bankruptcy Act was strictly for the bankruptcy court. Le Boeuf v Austrian (1957, CA4 Va) 240 F.2d 546, cert den 353 US 965, 1 L Ed 2d 914, 77 S Ct 1049; Austrian v Williams (1954, CA2 NY) 216 F.2d 278, cert den 348 US 953, 99 L Ed 745, 75 S Ct 441

Because a shareholder's siblings raised sufficient genuine issues of fact or law in the shareholder's action for breach of fiduciary duty, conversion, fraud, an accounting, common-law dissolution, appointment of a temporary receiver, and injunctive relief, the siblings were entitled to advancement of their expenses under N.Y. Bus. Corp. Law § 724(c). Lemle v Lemle (2012, 1st Dept) 92 App Div 3d 494, 939 NYS2d 15.

§ 725. Other provisions affecting indemnification of directors and officers

(a) All expenses incurred in defending a civil or criminal action or proceeding which are advanced by the corporation under paragraph (c) of section 723 (Payment of indemnification other than by court award) or allowed by a court under paragraph (c) of section 724 (Indemnification of directors and officers by a court) shall be repaid in case the person receiving such advancement or allowance is ultimately found, under the procedure set forth in this article, not to be entitled to indemnification or, where indemnification is granted, to the extent the expenses so advanced by the corporation or allowed by the court exceed the indemnification to which he is entitled.

(b) No indemnification, advancement or allowance shall be made under this article in any circumstance where it appears:

(1) That the indemnification would be inconsistent with the law of the jurisdiction of incorporation of a foreign corporation which prohibits or otherwise limits such indemnification;

(2) That the indemnification would be inconsistent with a provision of the certificate of incorporation, a by-law, a resolution of the board or of the shareholders, an agreement or other proper corporate action, in effect at the time of the accrual of the alleged cause of action asserted in the threatened or pending action or proceeding in which the expenses were incurred or other amounts were paid, which prohibits or otherwise limits indemnification; or

(3) If there has been a settlement approved by the court, that the indemnification would be inconsistent with any condition with respect to indemnification expressly imposed by the court in approving the settlement.

(c) If any expenses or other amounts are paid by way of indemnification, otherwise than by court order or action by the shareholders, the corporation shall, not later than the next annual meeting of shareholders unless such meeting is held within three months from the date of such payment, and, in any event, within fifteen months from the date of such payment, mail to its shareholders of record at the time entitled to vote for the election of directors a statement specifying the persons paid, the amounts paid, and the nature and status at the time of such payment of the litigation or threatened litigation.

(d) If any action with respect to indemnification of directors and officers is taken by way of amendment of the by-laws, resolution of directors, or by agreement, then the corporation shall, not later than the next annual meeting of shareholders, unless such meeting is held within three months from the date of such action, and, in any event, within fifteen months from the date of such action, mail to its shareholders of record at the time entitled to vote for the election of directors a statement specifying the action taken.

(e) Any notification required to be made pursuant to the foregoing paragraph (c) or (d) of this section by any domestic mutual insurer shall be satisfied by compliance with the corresponding provisions of section one thousand two hundred sixteen of the insurance law.

(f) The provisions of this article relating to indemnification of directors and officers and insurance therefor shall apply to domestic corporations and foreign corporations doing business in this state, except as provided in section 1320 (Exemption from certain provisions).

History: Formerly § 726, renumbered § 725 and amd, L 1986, ch 513, § 1, eff July 24, 1986; amd, L 1988, ch 774, § 2, eff Dec 29, 1988.

CASE ANNOTATIONS

Defendant, a Delaware corporation authorized to do business in New York State, is exempt from the indemnification provisions of sections 721 through 726 of the Business Corporation Law since its shares are traded on the New York Stock Exchange (Business Corporation Law, § 726, subd [d]; § 1319, subd [a], par [4]; § 1320, subd [a], par [1]); accordingly, a claim against defendant by a former officer for indemnification for legal expenses incurred in connection with his appearance before a Federal Grand Jury must be decided under Delaware law. Stewart v Continental Copper & Steel Industries, Inc. (1979, 1st Dept) 67 A.D.2d 293, 414 N.Y.S.2d 910

Court erred in granting interim indemnification under CLS Bus Corp § 724(c) to ex-employee of Delaware corporation, who was alleged to have improperly obtained information as to plaintiff's customers during term of his employment, since Delaware's General Corporation Law provided for interim indemnification at corporation's discretion on posting of undertaking by person indemnified to repay such amount if it was ultimately determined that that person was not entitled to indemnification (Del Code Annot, title 8, § 145(e)), but contained no provision for court-ordered interim indemnification analogous to CLS Bus Corp § 724(c). Bear, Stearns & Co. v D.F. King & Co. (1997, 1st Dept) 243 A.D.2d 252, 663 N.Y.S.2d 12

§ 726. Insurance for indemnification of directors and officers

(a) Subject to paragraph (b), a corporation shall have power to purchase and maintain insurance:

(1) To indemnify the corporation for any obligation which it incurs as a result of the indemnification of directors and officers under the provisions of this article, and

(2) To indemnify directors and officers in instances in which they may be indemnified by the corporation under the provisions of this article, and

(3) To indemnify directors and officers in instances in which they may not otherwise be indemnified by the corporation under the provisions of this article provided the contract of insurance covering such directors and officers provides, in a manner acceptable to the superintendent of financial services, for a retention amount and for co-insurance.

(b) No insurance under paragraph (a) may provide for any payment, other than cost of defense, to or on behalf of any director or officer:

(1) if a judgment or other final adjudication adverse to the insured director or officer establishes that his acts of active and deliberate dishonesty were material to the cause of action so adjudicated, or that he personally gained in fact a financial profit or other advantage to which he was not legally entitled, or

(2) in relation to any risk the insurance of which is prohibited under the insurance law of this state.

(c) Insurance under any or all subparagraphs of paragraph (a) may be included in a single contract or supplement thereto. Retrospective rated contracts are prohibited.

(d) The corporation shall, within the time and to the persons provided in paragraph (c) of section 725 (Other provisions affecting indemnification of directors or officers), mail a statement in respect of any insurance it has purchased or renewed under this section, specifying the insurance carrier, date of the contract, cost of the insurance, corporate positions insured, and a statement explaining all sums, not previously reported in a statement to shareholders, paid under any indemnification insurance contract.

(e) This section is the public policy of this state to spread the risk of corporate management, notwithstanding any other general or special law of this state or of any other jurisdiction including the federal government.

History: Formerly § 727, amd, L 1962, ch 819, eff Sept 1, 1963; renumbered § 726 and amd, L 1986, ch 513, § 1, eff July 24, 1986; L 1969, ch 1007, eff Sept 1, 1969; L 2011, ch 62, § 104 (Part A), eff Oct 3, 2011.

CASE ANNOTATIONS

Insurer under directors and officers liability policy was entitled to allocation of expenses incurred by insured corporation in defending against stockholders' class actions, in which both corporation and its officers and directors were sued for same violations of federal securities laws, since insurer was only liable under policy to reimburse corporation for expenses of defending officers and directors and not for expenses incurred by corporation in defending itself. Health-Chem Corp. v National Union Fire Ins. Co. (1990) 148 Misc. 2d 187, 559 N.Y.S.2d 435

In action by corporation, as insured under directors and officers liability policy, brought against its insurer for reimbursement of expenses incurred in defending against stockholders' class actions in which both corporation and its officers and directors had been sued for same violations of federal securities laws, neither party would be granted summary judgment on claim for reimbursement for services rendered by corporation's general counsel since issues of fact existed as to what services were rendered for defense of corporation rather than officers and directors covered by policy, and whether insurer was properly notified that general counsel would take part in defense of actions. Health-Chem Corp. v National Union Fire Ins. Co. (1990) 148 Misc. 2d 187, 559 N.Y.S.2d 435

Although other states statutes authorizing corporations to purchase indemnity insurance may draw distinction between insurance purchased to cover liability of persons serving as directors of indemnifying corporation than that of persons serving as directors of second corporation at request of first, Business Corporations Law § 727 draws no such distinction. Continental Copper & Steel Industries, Inc. v Johnson (1980, SD NY) 491 F. Supp. 360, affd (CA2 NY) 641 F.2d 59 and affd without op (CA2 NY) 647 F.2d 161

Neither section 17 nor section 18 of the Public Officers Law covers officers and directors of Safe Affordable Housing, Inc., a not-for-profit community development corporation organized by the Division of Housing and Community Renewal, even though the officers and directors are also officers and employees of the division. The corporation is authorized to indemnify its officers and directors. 1982 Op Atty Gen July 13 (formal)

§ 727. [Renumbered]

History: Add, L 1969, ch 1007, eff Sept 1, 1969; renumbered § 726, L 1986, ch 513, § 1, eff July 24, 1986.

§ 727. Annual reports for certain transactions required

(a) A condominium created pursuant to the real property law or a cooperative housing corporation created pursuant to this chapter, shall, at least once each year:

(1) require that each director, as defined in paragraph five of subdivision (a) of section one hundred two of this chapter, receive a copy of section seven hundred thirteen of this chapter; and

(2) submit an annual report to the shareholders, which shall be signed by each such director, containing information on any contracts made, entered into, or otherwise voted on by the board of directors where one or more of the directors was an interested director, pursuant to section seven hundred thirteen of this chapter.

(b) The annual report required by subdivision (a) of this section shall include, but not be limited to, the following:

(1) a list of all contracts voted on by the board of directors, including information on the contract recipient, contract amount, and the purpose of entering into the contract;

(2) the record of each meeting including director attendance, voting records for contracts, and how each director voted on such contracts; and

(3) the date of each vote on each contract, and the date the contract would be and remain valid.

(c) If the annual report required by subdivision (a) of this section would, notwithstanding the requirements of this section, contain no information because of the absence of any actions taken by the board that would otherwise qualify for inclusion in such annual report, then the board shall instead submit to the shareholders a document, signed by each director, indicating: "No actions taken by the board were subject to the annual report required pursuant to section 727 of the Business Corporation Law".

History: Add, L 2017, ch 305, § 2, eff Jan 1, 2018; amd, L 2018, ch 9, § 2, eff Jan 1, 2018.

Laws 2017, ch 305, § 3, eff Jan 1, 2018, provides:

§ 3. This act shall take effect on the first of January next succeeding the date on which it shall have become a law.

Laws 2018, ch 9, § 3, eff January 1, 2018, provides:

§ 3. This act shall take effect on the same date and in the same manner as a chapter of the laws of 2017, amending the not-for-profit corporation law and the business corporation law, relating to conflicts of interests for condominium and cooperative housing, as proposed in legislative bills numbers S.6652-A and A.8261-A, takes effect.

ARTICLE 8
AMENDMENTS AND CHANGES

History: Add, L 1961, ch 855, eff Sept 1, 1963

§ 801. Right to amend certificate of incorporation

(a) A corporation may amend its certificate of incorporation, from time to time, in any and as many respects as may be desired, if such amendment contains only such provisions as might be lawfully contained in an original certificate of incorporation filed at the time of making such amendment.

(b) In particular, and without limitation upon such general power of amendment, a corporation may amend its certificate of incorporation, from time to time, so as:

(1) To change its corporate name.

(2) To enlarge, limit or otherwise change its corporate purposes.

(3) To specify or change the location of the office of the corporation.

(4) To specify or change the post office address to which the secretary of state shall mail a copy of any process against the corporation served upon him.

(5) To make, revoke or change the designation of a registered agent, or to specify or change the address of its registered agent.

(6) To extend the duration of the corporation or, if the corporation ceased to exist because of the expiration of the duration specified in its certificate of incorporation, to revive its existence.

(7) To increase or decrease the aggregate number of shares, or shares of any class or series, with or without par value, which the corporation shall have authority to issue.

(8) To remove from authorized shares any class of shares, or any shares of any class, whether issued or unissued.

(9) To increase the par value of any authorized shares of any class with par value, whether issued or unissued.

(10) To reduce the par value of any authorized shares of any class with par value, whether issued or unissued.

(11) To change any authorized shares, with or without par value, whether issued or unissued, into a different number of shares of the same class or into the same or a different number of shares of any one or more classes or any series thereof, either with or without par value.

(12) To fix, change or abolish the designation of any authorized class or any series thereof or any of the relative rights, preferences and limitations of any shares of any authorized class or any series thereof, whether issued or unissued, including any provisions in respect of any undeclared dividends, whether or not cumulative or accrued, or the redemption of any shares, or any sinking fund for the redemption or purchase of any shares, or any preemptive right to acquire shares or other securities.

(13) As to the shares of any preferred class, then or theretofore authorized, which may be issued in series, to grant authority to the board or to change or revoke the authority of the board to establish and designate series and to fix the number of shares and the relative rights, preferences and limitation as between series.

(14) To strike out, change or add any provision, not inconsistent with this chapter or any other statute, relating to the business of the corporation, its affairs, its rights or powers, or the rights or powers of its shareholders, directors or officers, including any provision which under this chapter is required or permitted to be set forth in the by-laws, except that a certificate of amendment may not be filed wherein the duration of the corporation shall be reduced.

(c) A corporation created by special act may accomplish any or all amendments permitted in this article, in the manner and subject to the conditions provided in this article.

History: Add, L 1961, ch 855, eff Sept 1, 1963; amd, L 1962, ch 834, § 55, eff Sept 1, 1963, L 1963, § 6, ch 748, § 6, eff Sept 1, 1963; L 1965, ch 803, §§ 31, 51, eff Sept 1, 1965; L 1966, ch 502, eff June 7, 1966.

CASE ANNOTATIONS

All that is required to effectuate a corporate name change is a simple amendment of the entity's certificate of incorporation pursuant to N.Y. Bus. Corp. Law § 801(b)(1). Because a certificate of incorporation is a public record, a company that had entered into a guaranty contract with a corporation could and should have easily ascertained that the corporation's purported "name change" was not a change in name only, but that a separate entity had been formed which was not the legal equivalent of the original bond obligor. 95 Lorimer, LLC v Insurance Co. of State of Pa. (2004, Sup) 6 Misc 3d 500, 789 N.Y.S.2d 833

Where corporation changes its name but takes no other action to amend its certificate of incorporation in any other respect, organization before and after name change constitutes single continuous corporate entity and there is no need for formal assignment of trademark rights from corporation under old name to corporation under new name. Department of Justice, Federal Bureau of Investigation v Calspan Corp. (1978, Cust & Pat App) 578 F.2d 295, 198 USPQ 147

Where president of corporation and his wife were trustees of trust holding majority of outstanding voting shares of corporation, court upheld finding that amendment of certificate of incorporation to replace voting preferred shares with voting common, to authorize additional voting shares, to remove restriction requiring two-thirds approval for issuance or disposition of new voting stock, and to abolish shareholders' pre-emptive rights and cumulative voting for directors, was made in good faith in furtherance of corporate objectives. Renz v Beeman (1978, CA2 NY) 589 F.2d 735, cert den 444 US 834, 62 L Ed 2d 43, 100 S Ct 65

UNDER FORMER LAW

Earlier provisions with regard to amendment of corporate certificates were less broad and comprehensive than this section of the Bus. Corp. L. Under § 35 of former Stock Corp. L. a change in purposes of the corporation was restricted to business "of the same general character," and thus a corporation organized to engage in private business could not, by amendment of its certificate, become a public service corporation. People ex rel. Cayuga Power Corp. v Public Service Com. (1919) 226 N.Y. 527, 124 N.E. 105

Under earlier statutes it was held that a corporation organized to engage in the business of supplying merchants with financial reports on customers could amend its certificate so as to assume responsibility for accuracy of such reports but limit damages recoverable in case of inaccuracy. People ex rel. Daily Credit Service Corp. v May (1914) 162 A.D. 215, 147 N.Y.S. 487, affd 212 N.Y. 561, 106 N.E. 1039

Where there was an adequate statute providing means by which a corporation could extend the objects of its business by altering its certificate of incorporation, corporations seeking to extend their businesses were remitted to that method of obtaining such authority and could not seek like authority by some other method or under a different statute. Re Horace Keane Aeroplanes, Inc. (1920) 194 A.D. 873, 185 N.Y.S. 163

Section 35 of former Stock Corp. L. authorized the making of various changes with respect to "shares, capital stock or capital" of a corporation, including the "classification or reclassification" of its shares. A reclassification of stock by amending the certificate of incorporation was held to constitute an issuance of stock. Public Service Com. v New York & Richmond Gas Co. (1935) 244 A.D. 398, 279 N.Y.S. 824

The right to "reclassify" or "classify" shares did not extend to making a non-callable issue callable by simply amending a certificate of incorporation, as such a change would be in violation of rights of holders of outstanding shares. Breslav v New York & Queens Electric Light & Power Co. (1936) 249 A.D. 181, 291 N.Y.S. 932, affd 273 N.Y. 593, 7 N.E.2d 708

Revival of the existence of a corporation whose period of existence has expired, by amendment of its certificate of incorporation, was authorized by § 49 of former Gen. Corp. L., and the validity of this provision was upheld as against objections that it violated the rights of minority stockholders to obtain their share of the assets on dissolution and liquidation. Garzo v Maid of Mist S.B. Co. (1951) 278 A.D. 508, 106 N.Y.S.2d 4, affd 303 N.Y. 516, 104 N.E.2d 882

The State constitutional provision as to reserved control of the legislature over corporations and power to amend and repeal laws relating to corporations is broad enough to sanction legislation in regard to amendment of their charters. Hollender v Rochester Food Products Corp. (1923) 124 Misc 130, 207 N.Y.S. 319, affd 215 A.D. 751, 212 N.Y.S. 833, affd 242 N.Y. 490, 152 N.E. 271

A corporation did not die or "cease to exist" merely by changing its name by amendment of its certificate of incorporation. Williams Grain Co. v Leval & Co. (1960, CA8 Ark) 277 F.2d 213, 3 FR Serv 2d 474

Reclassification of stock did not, however, result in "purchase" of any stock by the shareholders within the meaning of the Securities Act of 1934. Roberts v Eaton (1953, DC NY) 119 F. Supp. 362, affd (CA2 NY) 212 F.2d 82, cert den 348 US 827, 99 L Ed 652, 75 S Ct 44

The fact that a corporation was created by special legislation was not considered as precluding it from filing an amended certificate of incorporation extending its objects and purposes. 1921 Ops Atty Gen 232

A name change did not effect liability of a surety on an undertaking in behalf of the corporation under its earlier name, or the corporation's right to collect on obligations running to it under the old name. 1941 Ops Atty Gen May 20; 1911 Ops Atty Gen 588

An opinion has also been expressed that a membership corporation could revive its existence by amending its certificate of incorporation pursuant to § 49 of former Gen. Corp. L., although it would otherwise have to obtain approval of an administrative agency in order to carry on activities. 1952 Ops Atty Gen Feb 15

§ 802. Reduction of stated capital by amendment

(a) A corporation may reduce its stated capital by an amendment of its certificate of incorporation under section 801 (Right to amend certificate of incorporation) which:

(1) Reduces the par value of any issued shares with par value.

(2) Changes issued shares under subparagraph (b)(11) of section 801 that results in a reduction of stated capital.

(3) Removes from authorized shares, shares that have been issued, reacquired and cancelled by the corporation.

(b) This section shall not prevent a corporation from reducing its stated capital in any other manner permitted by this chapter.

History: Add, L 1961, ch 855, eff Sept 1, 1963.

Par (a), subpar (3), amd, L 1965, ch 803, § 32, eff Sept 1, 1965.

CASE ANNOTATIONS

UNDER FORMER LAW

Under prior provisions, notably §§ 35 and 37 of former Stock Corp. L., a corporation, by amendment of its charter, could change and reduce its stated capital and the stated par value of its shares, and change its shares from having a stated par value to no-par, and vice versa. Jay Ronald Co. v Marshall Mortg. Corp, (1943) 291 N.Y. 227, 52 N.E.2d 108; People v Liberty Light & Power Co. (1923) 121 Misc 424, 201 N.Y.S. 302

Section 35 of former Stock Corp. L. permitted the corporation to retain a surplus resulting from reduction of capital, even though its capital was represented by non-par shares and no immediate distribution to shareholders was contemplated. Jay Ronald Co. v Marshall Mortg. Corp. (1943) 291 N.Y. 227, 52 N.E.2d 108

Corporations subject to the Public Service Law, however, had to obtain consent and approval of the public service commission in order to effectuate a reduction of capital, including amounts which had been transferred to capital by action of their directors. Rochester Gas & Electric Corp. v Maltbie (1940) 258 A.D. 682, 18 N.Y.S.2d 630, affd 284 N.Y. 626, 29 N.E.2d 936

Reduction of par value of shares was deemed a "classification or reclassification" of shares within the meaning of § 35 of former Stock Corp. L. Sterling v 16 Park Ave., Inc. (1954, Sup) 132 N.Y.S.2d 921, mod on other grounds 284 A.D. 1033, 136 N.Y.S.2d 363

Subdivision 3 of § 35 of former Stock Corporation Law, relating to amendment of a certificate of incorporation to eliminate cumulative dividends, whether or not accrued, "which shall not have been declared," recognizes a difference between "accrued" and "declared" dividends, and hence holders of cumulative preferred stock may well be entitled on distribution of corporate assets in course of dissolution to preferential payment for cumulative dividends, whether or not declared. Re Chandler & Co. (1962, Sup) 230 N.Y.S.2d 1012

§ 803. Authorization of amendment or change

(a) Amendment or change of the certificate of incorporation may be authorized by vote of the board, followed by vote of a majority of all outstanding shares entitled to vote thereon at a meeting of shareholders; provided, however, that, whenever the certificate of incorporation requires action by the board of directors, by the holders of any class or series of shares, or by the holders of any other securities having voting power by the vote of a greater number or proportion than is required by any section of this article, the provision of the certificate of incorporation requiring such greater vote shall not be altered, amended, or repealed except by such greater vote; and provided further that an amendment to the certificate of incorporation for the purpose of reducing the requisite vote by the holders of any class or series of shares or by the holders of any other securities having voting power that is otherwise provided for in any section of this chapter that would otherwise require more than a majority of the votes of all outstanding shares entitled to vote thereon shall not be adopted except by the vote of such holders of class or series of shares or by such holders of such other securities having voting power that is at least equal to that which would be required to take the action provided in such other section of this chapter.

(b) Alternatively, any one or more of the following changes may be authorized by or pursuant to authorization of the board:

(1) To specify or change the location of the corporation's office.

(2) To specify or change the post office address to which the secretary of state shall mail a copy of any process against the corporation served upon him.

(3) To make, revoke or change the designation of a registered agent, or to specify or change the address of its registered agent.

(c) This section shall not alter the vote required under any other section for the authorization of an amendment referred to therein, nor alter the authority of the board to authorize amendments under any other section.

(d) Amendment or change of the certificate of incorporation of a corporation which has no shareholders of record, no subscribers for shares whose subscriptions have been accepted and no directors may be authorized by the sole incorporator or a majority of the incorporators.

History: Add, L 1961, ch 855, eff Sept 1, 1963; amd, L 1962, ch 834, § 56; L 1963, ch 748, § 7, eff Sept 1, 1963; L 1965, ch 803, § 33, eff Sept 1, 1965; L 1984, ch 603, § 3, eff July 27, 1984; L 1987, ch 49, § 1, eff April 21, 1987; L 1997, ch 449, § 49, eff Feb 22, 1998; L 2004, ch 93, § 1, eff Nov 21, 2004.

CASE ANNOTATIONS

A dissenting minority shareholder's usual remedy is to file written objections to the action of the majority and demand payment of the value of his shares, and, where this remedy is considered adequate, and exists, he may have no other. Re McKinney (1954) 306 N.Y. 207, 117 N.E.2d 256; Application of Isaac (1950) 198 Misc 85, 97 N.Y.S.2d 634

A subsisting and valid agreement binding more than a majority of the shareholders may, however, be invoked against their approval of an amendment in violation of it. Ripley v Storer (1956) 309 N.Y. 506, 132 N.E.2d 87, motion to vacate den 309 N.Y. 976, 132 N.E.2d 335

An agreement by stockholders not to increase or decrease the number of directors of a corporation was not binding on subsequent owners of stock purchased in good faith and without notice. Bond v Atlantic Terra Cotta Co. (1910) 137 A.D. 671, 122 N.Y.S. 425

An amendment decreasing the number of directors has been deemed not to impair any vested right of shareholders, notwithstanding it will have the practical effect of requiring more of them to combine votes in order to obtain representation on the board. Bond v Atlantic Terra Cotta Co. (1910) 137 AD-671, 122 N.Y.S. 425

Neither contracts entered into by the corporation nor agreements among some of its stockholders can impair the statutory right of a majority of shareholders not bound thereby to put through an amendment which is permissible by law. Bond v Atlantic Terra Cotta Co. (1910) 137 A.D. 671, 122 N.Y.S. 425

Where a corporation's certificate of incorporation can be amended only with the consent or upon authorization by shareholders, it is doubtful whether a dissenting minority shareholder can be effectively deprived of fundamental rights, such as his pre-emptive rights to purchase new stock to be issued, or his contractual rights under stock already held, by an amendment, notwithstanding its approval by the required majority. Albrecht, Maguire & Co. v General Plastics, Inc. (1939) 256 A.D. 134, 9 N.Y.S.2d 415, affd 280 N.Y. 840, 21 N.E.2d 887; 1911 Ops Atty Gen 24

The Public Service Commission may not make its approval of an amendment to the certificate of incorporation of a utility corporation, permitting increase of capital stock, contingent upon the corporation's compliance with requirements made by the commission in other unrelated matters. Rochester Gas & Electric Corp. v Maltbie (1948) 273 A.D. 114, 76 N.Y.S.2d 671, resettled 274 A.D. 856, 82 N.Y.S.2d 390 and affd 298 N.Y. 867, 84 N.E.2d 635

Section 35 of former Stock Corp. L. required more than a majority vote of shareholders for the adoption of specified types of amendments, but an amendment increasing the number of directors was not one of these, and accordingly a bylaw requiring 75% approval of such an amendment was deemed invalid. Christal v Petry (1949) 275 A.D. 550, 90 N.Y.S.2d 620, affd 301 N.Y. 562, 93 N.E.2d 450

In the absence of a unanimous written agreement of the stockholders to the contrary, the holder of a majority of the voting stock has the right to amend the certificate of incorporation so as to increase the number of directors. Christal v Petry (1949) 275 A.D. 550, 90 N.Y.S.2d 620, affd 301 N.Y. 562, 93 N.E.2d 450

An amendment extending the sphere of permissible business activities of the corporation to include operations incidental to those already authorized, did not require unanimous stockholder approval under § 35 of former Stock Corp. L. Clarke v American Press Ass'n (1932) 145 Misc 370, 259 N.Y.S. 478

The constitutionality of prior provisions of similar nature has been upheld. McNulty v W & J Sloane (1945) 184 Misc 835, 54 N.Y.S.2d 253

A subsidiary of the Urban Development Corporation may incorporate under the Business Corporation Law without forfeiting its public status. The subsidiary may not pay profits to private investors, and upon dissolution of the corporation, the assets belong to the State. 1980 Op Atty Gen Oct. 20

§ 804.   Class voting on amendment

(a) Notwithstanding any provision in the certificate of incorporation, the holders of shares of a class shall be entitled to vote and to vote as a class upon the authorization of an amendment and, in addition to the authorization of the amendment by a majority of the votes of all outstanding shares entitled to vote thereon, the amendment shall be authorized by a majority of the votes of all outstanding shares of the class when a proposed amendment would:

(1) Exclude or limit their right to vote on any matter, except as such right may be limited by voting rights given to new shares then being authorized of any existing or new class or series.

(2) Change their shares under subparagraphs (b) (10), (11) or (12) of section 801 (Right to amend certificate of incorporation) or provide that their shares may be converted into shares of any other class or into shares of any other series of the same class, or alter the terms or conditions upon which their shares are convertible or change the shares issuable upon conversion of their shares, if such action would adversely affect such holders, or

(3) Subordinate their rights, by authorizing shares having preferences which would be in any respect superior to their rights.

(b) If any proposed amendment referred to in paragraph (a) would adversely affect the rights of the holders of shares of only one or more series of any class, but not the entire class, then only the holders of those series whose rights would be affected shall be considered a separate class for the purposes of this section.

Business
Corporation Law

History: Add, L 1961, ch 855, eff Sept 1, 1963; amd, L 1963, ch 748, § 8, eff Sept 1, 1963; L 1997, ch 449, § 50, eff Feb 22, 1998.

CASE ANNOTATIONS

Under some earlier provisions, such as § 35 and former § 36 of former Stock Corp. L., holders of preferred stock were regarded as having vested contractual rights to performance of the terms and conditions of the shares held by them, such as cumulation of dividends to the extent deferred and unpaid, of which they could not be deprived without their consent. Davison v Parke, Austin & Lipscomb (1941) 285 N.Y. 500, 35 N.E.2d 618, remittitur den 286 N.Y. 673, 36 N.E.2d 910; Wiedersum v Atlantic Cement Products, Inc. (1941) 261 A.D. 305, 25 N.Y.S.2d 496

Section 38 of former Stock Corp. L. permitted a corporation, having outstanding common stock and also outstanding cumulative non-callable preferred stock is authorized, by consent of two-thirds of the holders of each kind of stock, to amend its charter so as to reclassify such preferred stock into common stock. W. N. Clark Co. v Anderson (1942) 288 N.Y. 570, 42 N.E.2d 23

Section 38 of former Stock Corp. L. was held applicable only where a proposed charter amendment would alter preferential rights of outstanding shares, and there was doubt as to whether even the consent or approval of two-thirds of the holders of stock having special contractual rights could deprive non-consenting holders of such stock of their right to unpaid dividends accrued through lapse of time. Wiedersum v Atlantic Cement Products, Inc. (1941) 261 A.D. 305, 25 N.Y.S.2d 496; Breslav v New York & Queens Electric Light & Power Co. (1936) 249 A.D. 181, 291 N.Y.S. 932, affd 273 N.Y. 593, 7 N.E.2d 708

Where the owner of preferred stock of a corporation undertaking a reclassification program was left with the alternative of taking new stock or proceeding with an appraisal, he was entitled to a trial of the facts to determine whether the forcing of the alternatives was a coercive act forbidden in view of the fiduciary duty owed by a corporation to its stockholders. Liebschutz v Schaffer Stores Co. (1949) 276 A.D. 1, 93 N.Y.S.2d 125, reh and app den 276 A.D. 944, 94 N.Y.S.2d 808

The amendment of 1943 to former §§ 36, 37 was not limited to dividends accruing after its effective date but applied also to cumulative dividends which accrued, through lapse of time, prior to the effective date of the amendment. McNulty v W & J Sloane (1945) 184 Misc 835, 54 N.Y.S.2d 253

In the absence of a contractual obligation to pay dividends on preferred stock, however, or existence of a debtor-creditor relationship by the declaration of a particular dividend on such stock, potential dividend rights could be eliminated by a stock reclassification pursuant to § 35 of former Stock Corp. L. Arstein v Robert Reis & Co. (1948, Sup) 77 N.Y.S.2d 303, affd 273 A.D. 963, 79 N.Y.S.2d 314, cert den 335 US 860, 93 L Ed 407, 69 S Ct 135

Under § 51 of former Stock Corp. L., preferred shareholders had right to vote on amendment reducing par value of preferred shares of stock where such reduction would adversely affect their interests. Sterling v 16 Park Ave., Inc. (1954, Sup) 132 N.Y.S.2d 921, mod on other grounds 284 A.D. 1033, 136 N.Y.S.2d 363

§ 805. Certificate of amendment; contents

(a) To accomplish any amendment, a certificate of amendment, entitled "Certificate of amendment of the certificate of incorporation of .... (name of corporation) under section 805 of the Business Corporation Law", shall be signed and delivered to the department of state. It shall set forth:

(1) The name of the corporation and, if it has been changed, the name under which it was formed.

(2) The date its certificate of incorporation was filed by the department of state.

(3) Each amendment effected thereby, setting forth the subject matter of each provision of the certificate of incorporation which is to be amended or eliminated and the full text of the provision or provisions, if any, which are to be substituted or added.

(4) If an amendment provides for a change of shares, the number, par value and class of issued shares changed, the number, par value and class of issued shares resulting from such change, the number, par value and class of unissued shares changed, the number, par value and class of unissued shares resulting from such change and the terms of each such change. If an amendment makes two or more such changes, a like statement shall be included in respect to each change.

(5) If any amendment reduces stated capital, then a statement of the manner in which the same is effected and the amounts from which and to which stated capital is reduced.

(6) The manner in which the amendment of the certificate of incorporation was authorized. If the amendment was authorized under paragraph (d) of section eight hundred three of this chapter, then a statement that the corporation does not have any shareholders of record or any subscribers for shares whose subscriptions have been accepted and no directors.

(b) Any number of amendments or changes may be included in one certificate under this section. Such certificate may also include any amendments or changes permitted by other sections and in that case the certificate shall set forth any additional statement required by any other section specifying the contents of a certificate to effect such amendment or change.

(c) In the case of a change of shares, the shares resulting from such change, shall upon the filing of the certificate of amendment, be deemed substituted for the shares changed, in accordance with the stated terms of change.

History: Add, L 1961, ch 855, eff Sept 1, 1963; amd, L 1962, ch 834, § 57, eff Sept 1, 1963; L 1963, ch 748, § 9, eff Sept 1, 1963; L 1964, ch 725, §§ 9-11, eff June 1, 1964; L 1965, ch 803, § 34; L 1966, ch 316, eff May 10, 1966; L 1984, ch 242, § 1, eff July 8, 1984; L 1985, ch 101, § 1, eff May 21, 1985; L 1987, ch 49, § 2, eff April 21, 1987; L 1998, ch 375, § 8, eff Aug 13, 1998.

CASE ANNOTATIONS

The requirements of § 37 of former Stock Corp. L. as to form, signing, verification, and various statements and affidavits which must accompany a certificate of amendment, in order to make it eligible for acceptance and filing by the department of state, were considerably more elaborate than those of § 805 of the Bus. Corp. L., and strict compliance therewith was usually demanded. Boornazian v Sarkisian (1952, Sup) 110 N.Y.S.2d 350

If the formal requirements were met, however, and the nature of the amendment was not on its face outside the scope of permissive amendments, purposes, and powers of the particular corporation or kind of corporation, it was not considered within the functions of the Secretary of State to quibble about its legality. 1949 Ops Atty Gen May 5

A certificate of amendment of the charter of an interstate railroad corporation could be accepted and filed by the Secretary of State without approval of the State Public Service Commission, where accompanied by a certificate establishing approval by the Interstate

Commerce Commission and the changes effected related solely to matters within the exclusive control of the ICC. 1953 Ops Atty Gen July 7

§ 805-A. Certificate of change; contents

(a) Any one or more of the changes authorized by paragraph (b) of section 803 (Authorization of amendment or change) may be accomplished by filing a certificate of change which shall be entitled "Certificate of change of .... (name of corporation) under section 805-A of the Business Corporation Law" and shall be signed and delivered to the department of state. It shall set forth:

(1) The name of the corporation, and if it has been changed, the name under which it was formed.

(2) The date its certificate of incorporation was filed by the department of state.

(3) Each change effected thereby.

(4) The manner in which the change was authorized.

(b) A certificate of change which changes only the post office address to which the secretary of state shall mail a copy of any process against a corporation served upon him or the address of the registered agent, provided such address being changed is the address of a person, partnership or other corporation whose address, as agent, is the address to be changed or who has been designated as registered agent for such corporation, may be signed, verified and delivered to the department of state by such agent. The certificate of change shall set forth the statements required under subparagraphs (a) (1), (2) and (3) of this section; that a notice of the proposed change was mailed to the corporation by the party signing the certificate not less than thirty days prior to the date of delivery to the department and that such corporation has not objected thereto; and that the party signing the certificate is the agent of such corporation to whose address the secretary of state is required to mail copies of process or the registered agent, if such be the case. A certificate signed, verified and delivered under this paragraph shall not be deemed to effect a change of location of the office of the corporation in whose behalf such certificate is filed.

History: Add, L 1964, ch 725, § 12, eff June 1, 1964.

Par (a), opening par, amd, L 1998, ch 375, § 9, eff Aug 13, 1998.

§ 806. Provisions as to certain proceedings

(a) The department of state shall not file a certificate of amendment reviving the existence of a corporation unless the consent of the state tax commission to the revival is delivered to the department. If the name of the corporation being revived is not available under section 301 (Corporate name; general) for use by a corporation then being formed under this chapter, the certificate of amendment shall change the name to one which is available for such use.

(b) The following provisions shall apply to amendments and changes under this article, except under section 808 (Reorganization under act of congress):

(1) The stated capital in respect of any shares without par value resulting from a change of issued shares shall be the amount of stated capital in respect of the shares changed or, if such stated capital is reduced by the amendment, the reduced amount stated in the certificate of amendment. No corporation shall change issued shares into both shares with par value and shares without par value unless the stated capital in respect of the shares so changed or, if such stated capital is reduced by the amendment, the reduced amount of stated capital stated in the certificate of amendment, exceeds the par value of the shares with par value resulting from such change; and the amount of such excess shall be the stated capital in respect of the shares without par value resulting from such change.

(2) No corporation shall increase the aggregate par value of its issued shares with par value, unless, after giving effect to such increase, the stated capital is at least equal to the amount required by subparagraph (a) (12) of section 102 (Definitions).

(3) No reduction of stated capital shall be made by amendment unless after such reduction the stated capital exceeds the aggregate preferential amount payable upon involuntary liquidation upon all issued shares having preferential rights in assets plus the par value of all other issued shares with par value.

(4) Any changes that may be made in the relative rights, preferences and limitations of the authorized shares of any class by any certificate of amendment which does not eliminate such shares from authorized shares or change them into shares of another class, shall not for the purpose of any statute or rule of law effect an issue of a new class of shares.

(5) No amendment or change shall affect any existing cause of action in favor of or against the corporation, or any pending suit to which it shall be a party, or the existing rights of persons other than shareholders; and in the event the corporate name shall be changed, no suit brought by or against the corporation under its former name shall abate for that reason.

(6) A holder of any adversely affected shares who does not vote for or consent in writing to the taking of such action shall, subject to and by complying with the provisions of section 623 (Procedure to enforce shareholder's right to receive payment for shares), have the right to dissent and to receive payment for such shares, if the certificate of amendment (A) alters or abolishes any preferential right of such shares having preferences; or (B) creates, alters or abolishes any provision or right in respect of the redemption of such shares or any sinking fund for the redemption or purchase of such shares; or (C) alters or abolishes any preemptive right of such holder to acquire shares or other securities; or (D) excludes or limits the right of

such holder to vote on any matter, except as such right may be limited by the voting rights given to new shares then being authorized of any existing or new class.

History: Add, L 1961, ch 855, eff Sept 1, 1963; amd, L 1962, ch 834, § 58, eff Sept 1, 1963; L 1963, ch 748, § 10, eff Sept 1, 1963; L 1965, ch 803, § 35; L 1966, ch 869, eff July 29, 1966.

CASE ANNOTATIONS

1. **Corporate domicile or residence**
2. **Rights of dissenting holders, generally**
3. **– Particular cases**
4. **Reacquisition of shares**

1. Corporate domicile or residence

And if an actual change of location had taken place, service of process on the corporation at the new location was valid and venue of an action involving the corporation could be based on its true location, without right in the corporation to a change of venue because its certificate of incorporation designated a different place of business or "residence." Carvel Court Realty Co. v Jonas (1921) 195 A.D. 662, 186 N.Y.S. 802; Kern Horse Remedy Co. v Selner (1916) 172 A.D. 152, 158 N.Y.S. 192; Gorman v A. B. Leach & Co. (1926, DC NY) 11 F.2d 454

Third persons were entitled to rely on the statement in the certificate of incorporation, as long as such statement remained unchanged, in determining residence or domicile of the corporation for purposes of fixing the proper locus for filing chattel mortgages, and the like. Re General Assignment of Norma Footwear Corp. (1956, 1st Dept) 2 A.D.2d 24, 153 N.Y.S.2d 80, affd 2 N.Y.2d 887, 161 N.Y.S.2d 143, 141 N.E.2d 628

There was, however, some authority to the effect that books and records should be kept at the principal office or place of business of the corporation, wherever that might be, regardless of a change in location from that stated in the certificate of incorporation. Jamosa Holding Corp. v Bleendes (1939) 173 Misc 492, 18 N.Y.S.2d 190

A corporation was not entitled to have a default judgment taken against it set aside on the ground of failure to receive notice of the action through service of process on the Secretary of State, where the failure was due to its fault in not legally changing its office location or in not notifying the Secretary of State of a change of address. Laurendi v Cascade Development Co. (1957) 5 Misc. 2d 688, 165 N.Y.S.2d 832, affd (4th Dept) 4 A.D.2d 852, 167 N.Y.S.2d 240

It has been the general view under prior corporation laws that the place designated in a corporation's certificate of incorporation as that where its principal office or place of business is located is where its books and records should be kept and determinative as to its domicile or residence for purposes of venue or taxation. Acme Kalamein Door & Sash Co. v Bronxville-Devon Corp. (1954, Sup) 135 N.Y.S.2d 184; Re Hillmark Associates, Inc. (1942, DC NY) 47 F. Supp. 605

2. Rights of dissenting holders, generally

Right to demand payment for shares held, as the result of adverse effect of an amendment of the certificate of incorporation on their value, was dependent upon compliance with the procedural and other requirements of § 21 of former Stock Corp. L., dealing generally with right of a dissenting stockholder to demand payment, and, if necessary, an appraisal of the value of his shares. Re McKinney (1954) 306 N.Y. 207, 117 N.E.2d 256; Goebbel v Gross (1934) 151 Misc 512, 271 N.Y.S. 727

If there was doubt as to whether the amendment would in fact adversely affect rights of the objecting shareholder and value of his stock, he was entitled to have that doubt judicially determined in a proceeding under § 21 of former Stock Corp. L., the appraisal proceeding to go forward if probable damage to his interests was found to exist. Re Seiler (1933) 239 A.D. 400, 267 N.Y.S. 567

With respect to amendments of certificates of incorporation decreasing or impairing the rights of shareholders, or their rights under the terms of particular share issues, §§ 37 and 38 of former Stock Corp. L. expressly gave stockholders adversely affected a right to object or dissent and to demand payment for their shares. Brill v Blakeley (1953) 281 A.D. 532, 120 N.Y.S.2d 713, affd 308 N.Y. 951, 127 N.E.2d 96; Application of New York Hanseatic Corp. (1951) 200 Misc 530, 103 N.Y.S.2d 698

Petitioner did not waive his right to appraisal by failing to file notice of objection before shareholders voted on proposal that effectively abolished his preemptive rights to purchase stock since (1) corporation had failed to send petitioner notice of meeting or copy of CLS Bus Corp § 623 or summary of its material terms, (2) petitioner's tardiness in serving notice of objection was insignificant (15 minutes after vote), and (3) corporation was not unduly prejudiced thereby. Carroll v Seacroft, Ltd. (1988, 2d Dept) 141 A.D.2d 726, 529 N.Y.S.2d 829

Section 38 of former Stock Corp. L. did not confer a right on any stockholder objecting to an amendment of the certificate of incorporation to be bought out, merely because he disagreed with the majority of his fellows, but only where his individual rights and the value of shares held by him would be clearly and necessarily adversely affected by the amendment objected to. Re Eaton (1947) 189 Misc 303, 69 N.Y.S.2d 846, affd 276 A.D. 7, 92 N.Y.S.2d 867; Re Gohn (1940) 174 Misc 188, 20 N.Y.S.2d 254

3. – Particular cases

Similarly, a holder of preferred stock could object and demand to be bought out if the amendment would impair or endanger his existing rights to preferential payment in the event of dissolution of the corporation. Max Fine & Sons, Inc. v Lindarose, Inc. (1928) 247 N.Y. 553, 161 N.E. 179; Application of Silberkraus (1929) 250 N.Y. 242, 165 N.E. 279

Section 38 of former Stock Corp. L. was considered inapplicable, however, as basis for a demand to be bought out, where the amendment did not disturb preferential rights as between presently outstanding shares but merely subjected such shares to a new issue of stock and the rights to be accorded purchasers of the new issue. Re Kinney (1939) 279 N.Y. 423, 18 N.E.2d 645, reh den 280 N.Y. 569, 20 N.E.2d 18; Application of Woodruff (1941) 175 Misc 819, 26 N.Y.S.2d 679, affd 262 A.D. 814, 28 N.Y.S.2d 756; Re Gohn (1940) 174 Misc 188, 20 N.Y.S.2d 254

A holder of common stock has a legitimate objection to a proposal to give equal voting rights to preferred stock which was issued with only limited voting privileges, and to demand payment for his shares if a resolution to amend the certificate of incorporation is adopted over his objection. Marcus v R. H. Macy & Co. (1947) 297 N.Y. 38, 74 N.E.2d 228

In view of the provisions of § 38 of former Stock Corp. L., a shareholder dissenting from or disapproving a reorganization or recapitalization proposal involving an exchange of new stock for old had a choice of acceding to the exchange or demanding the value of his shares; there was no other alternative; but the corporation would not be permitted to penalize him for voicing his disapproval by calling his shares, alone, for redemption. Liebschutz v Schaffer Stores Co. (1949) 276 A.D. 1, 93 N.Y.S.2d 125, reh and app den 276 A.D. 944, 94 N.Y.S.2d 808

But if impairment of rights of the objector or of the value of his stock was purely ephemeral, or any resolution or action taken which might have impaired his rights had already been rescinded prior to determination of value of his stock in the appraisal proceedings, those proceedings would be dismissed. Application of Eaton (1949) 276 A.D. 7, 92 N.Y.S.2d 867; Standard Brewing Co. v Peachey (1951) 202 Misc 279, 108 N.Y.S.2d 583

Thus a holder of preferred shares could dissent and demand to be bought out where the amendment would involve deferment in payment of cumulative dividends and use of surplus to retire outstanding preferred stock, or abolish restrictions on payment of dividends on common stock which had been imposed for the protection of preferred dividends. Brill v Blakeley (1953) 281 A.D. 532, 120 N.Y.S.2d 713, affd 308 N.Y. 951, 127 N.E.2d 96; Application of New York Hanseatic Corp. (1951) 200 Misc 530, 103 N.Y.S.2d 698

Where plan of merger adopted by corporation did not effect change in petitioner's rights as shareholder in surviving corporation, petitioner has no right to payment and has failed to state cause of action under Bus. Corp. Law § 806(b)(6). McGowan v Grand Island Transit Corp. (1981, 4th Dept) 80 A.D.2d 731, 437 N.Y.S.2d 158

Petitioner stated cause of action under CLS Bus Corp § 623 to determine fair value of his shares in corporation where it was undisputed that corporation had abolished petitioner's preemptive right to purchase new shares to preserve his percentage interest in corporation, and petitioner had filed notice of objection at special shareholders' meeting prior to vote being taken. Carroll v Seacroft Plaza, Ltd. (1988, 2d Dept) 141 A.D.2d 724, 529 N.Y.S.2d 588

Shareholders' suit against the corporation under N.Y. Bus. Corp. Law §§ 623 and 806, seeking payment of fair value for their shares, was dismissed; as an amendment to the certificate of incorporation did not constitute an adverse alteration for purposes of § 806(b)(6), the shareholders did not have a right to appraisal under § 623.

Business Corporation Law

Matter of Celauro v 4C Foods Corp., 956 N.Y.S.2d 821, 38 Misc. 3d 636, 2012 N.Y. Misc. LEXIS 5425 (N.Y. Sup. Ct. 2012), reh'g denied, in part, 972 N.Y.S.2d 142, 39 Misc. 3d 1234(A), 2013 N.Y. Misc. LEXIS 2269 (N.Y. Sup. Ct. 2013), in part, 2013 NY Slip Op 31768(U), 2013 N.Y. Misc. LEXIS 3414 (N.Y. Sup. Ct. Aug. 2, 2013), in part, 2016 NY Slip Op 31917(U), 2016 N.Y. Misc. LEXIS 3711 (N.Y. Sup. Ct. Oct. 12, 2016).

An amendment might have the effect of impairing a preferred shareholder's rights on dissolution if it would defeat his right to payment of cumulative but undeclared dividends which have accrued before any distribution is made to holders of subordinate issues. Re Chandler & Co. (1962, Sup) 230 N.Y.S.2d 1012

4. Reacquisition of shares

The right of a business or trade association to reacquire or repurchase the shares of stock on a limited option was a reasonable restriction on the shareholders' right of transfer. Glens Falls Ins. Co. v National Board of Fire Underwriters Bldg. Corp. (1970) 63 Misc. 2d 989, 314 N.Y.S.2d 80, affd 36 A.D.2d 793, 318 N.Y.S.2d 915

Where statute (Business Corporation Law § 512) prohibiting the issuance of redeemable common shares in the absence of an outstanding of a class of common shares that is not subject to redemption, was adopted subsequent to certificate of incorporation, reacquisition of shares by a trade association where a shareholder ceased membership therein or transferred his shares to a nonmember, was not a "redemption" barred by the statute. Glens Falls Ins. Co. v National Board of Fire Underwriters Bldg. Corp. (1970) 63 Misc. 2d 989, 314 N.Y.S.2d 80, affd 36 A.D.2d 793, 318 N.Y.S.2d 915

§ 807.   Restated certificate of incorporation

(a) A corporation, when authorized by the board, may restate in a single certificate the text of its certificate of incorporation without making any amendment or change thereby, except that it may include any one or more of the amendments or changes which may be authorized by the board without a vote of shareholders under this chapter. Alternatively, a corporation may restate in a single certificate the text of its certificate of incorporation as amended thereby to effect any one or more of the amendments or changes authorized by this chapter, when authorized by the required vote of the holders of shares entitled to vote thereon.

(b) A restated certificate of incorporation, entitled "Restated certificate of incorporation .... (name of corporation) under section 807 of the Business Corporation Law", shall be signed and delivered to the department of state. It shall set forth:

(1) The name of the corporation and, if it has been changed, the name under which it was formed.

(2) The date its certificate of incorporation was filed by the department of state.

(3) If the restated certificate restates the text of the certificate of incorporation without making any amendment or change, then a statement that the text of the certificate of incorporation is thereby restated without amendment or change to read as therein set forth in full.

(4) If the restated certificate restates the text of the certificate of incorporation as amended or changed thereby, then a statement that the certificate of incorporation is amended or changed to effect one or more of the amendments or changes authorized by this chapter, specifying each such amendment or change and that the text of the certificate of incorporation is thereby restated as amended or changed to read as therein set forth in full.

(5) If an amendment, effected by the restated certificate, provides for a change of issued shares, the number and kind of shares changed, the number and kind of shares resulting from such change and the terms of change. If any amendment makes two or more such changes, a like statement shall be included in respect to each such change.

(6) If the restated certificate contains an amendment which effects a reduction of stated capital, then a statement of the manner in which the same is effected and the amounts from which and to which stated capital is reduced.

(7) The manner in which the restatement of the certificate of incorporation was authorized.

(c) A restated certificate need not include statements as to the incorporator or incorporators, the original subscribers for shares or the first directors.

(d) Any amendment or change under this section shall be subject to any other section, not inconsistent with this section, which would be applicable if a separate certificate were filed to effect such amendment or change.

(e) Notwithstanding that the corporation would be required by any statute to secure from any state official, department, board, agency or other body, any consent or approval to the filing of its certificate of incorporation or a certificate of amendment, such consent or approval shall not be required with respect to the restated certificate if such certificate makes no amendment and if any previously required consent or approval had been secured.

(f) Upon filing by the department, the original certificate of incorporation shall be superseded and the restated certificate of incorporation, including any amendments and changes made thereby, shall be the certificate of incorporation of the corporation.

History: Add, L 1961, ch 855, eff Sept 1, 1963; amd, L 1962, ch 834, § 59; L 1963, ch 748, § 11, eff Sept 1, 1963; L 1965, ch 803, § 36; L 1966, ch 316, eff May 10, 1966; L 1981, ch 210, §§ 1-3, eff June 9, 1981; L 1998, ch 375, § 10, eff Aug 13, 1998.

§ 808.   Reorganization under act of congress

(a) Whenever a plan of reorganization of a corporation has been confirmed by a decree or order of a court in proceedings under any applicable act of congress relating to reorganization of corporations, the corporation shall have authority, without action of its shareholders or board, to put into effect and carry out the plan and decree and orders of the court relative thereto, and take any proceeding and any action for which provision is made in any statute governing the corporation or for which provision is or might be made in its certificate of incorporation or by-laws and which is provided for in such plan or directed by any such decree or order.

(b) Such authority may be exercised, and such proceedings and actions may be taken, as may be directed by any such decree or order, by the trustee or trustees of such corporation appointed in the reorganization proceedings, or if none is acting, by any person or persons designated or appointed for the purpose by any such decree or order, with like effect as if exercised and taken by unanimous action of the board and shareholders of the corporation.

(c) Any certificate, required or permitted by law to be filed or recorded to accomplish any corporate purpose, shall be signed, and verified or acknowledged, under any such decree or order, by such trustee or trustees or the person or persons referred to in paragraph (b), and shall certify that provision for such certificate is contained in the plan of reorganization or in a decree or order of the court relative thereto, and that the plan has been confirmed, as provided in an applicable act of congress, specified in the certificate, with the title and venue of the proceeding and the date when the decree or order confirming the plan was made, and such certificate shall be delivered to the department of state.

(d) A shareholder of any such corporation shall have no right to receive payment for his shares and only such rights, if any, as are provided in the plan of reorganization.

(e) Notwithstanding section 504 (Consideration and payment for shares), such corporation may, after the confirmation of such plan, issue its shares, bonds and other securities for the consideration specified in the plan of reorganization and may issue warrants or other optional rights for the purchase of shares upon such terms and conditions as may be set forth in such plan.

(f) If after the filing of any such certificate by the department of state, the decree or order of confirmation of the plan of reorganization is reversed or vacated or such plan is modified, such other or further certificates shall be executed and delivered to the department of state as may be required to conform to the plan of reorganization as finally confirmed or to the decree or order as finally made.

(g) Except as otherwise provided in this section, no certificate filed by the department of state hereunder shall confer on any corporation any powers other than those permitted to be conferred on a corporation formed under this chapter.

(h) If, in any proceeding under any applicable act of congress relating to reorganization of corporations, a decree or order provides for the formation of a new domestic corporation or for the authorization of a new foreign corporation to do business in this state under a name the same as or similar to that of the corporation being reorganized, the certificate of incorporation of the new domestic corporation or the application of the new foreign corporation shall set forth that it is being delivered pursuant to such decree or order and be endorsed with the consent of the court having jurisdiction of the proceeding. After such certificate of incorporation or application has been filed, the corporation being reorganized shall not continue the use of its name except in connection with the reorganization proceeding and as may be necessary to adjust

and wind up its affairs, and thirty days after such filing, the reorganized domestic corporation shall be automatically dissolved or the authority of the reorganized foreign corporation to transact business in this state shall cease. To the extent that the adjustment and winding up of the affairs of such dissolved corporation is not accomplished as a part of the proceeding or prescribed by the decree or order of such court, it shall proceed in accordance with the provisions of article 10 (Non-judicial dissolution).

(i) This section shall not relieve any corporation from securing from any state official, department, board, agency or other body, any consent or approval required by any statute.

History: Add, L 1961, ch 855, eff Sept 1, 1963; amd, L 1962, ch 834, § 60; L 1963, ch 748, § 12, eff Sept 1, 1963.

CASE ANNOTATIONS

The creditor of a corporation that was involved in a Chapter 11 bankruptcy proceeding would not be permitted to recover the diminution of his share in the bankruptcy estate from the president of the corporation, who allegedly wrongfully dissipated the assets of the bankruptcy estate in breach of his fiduciary duties, since, though the corporate president could be held personally liable for his wrongful or unauthorized use of corporate funds, such liability would properly be redressed through the president's compensation of the bankruptcy estate for such loss in that the ultimate recovery of all creditors had been diminished by any dissipation of corporate funds, and plaintiff had not suffered any injury not suffered by the other creditors of the corporation, and since the creditor's action for his individual loss would not be maintainable under a federal statute that permitted actions to redress torts committed in furtherance of a debtor's business in that such statute had no apparent application to a loss caused by a breach of fiduciary duties in the administration of a bankruptcy estate. Maguire v Puente (1983) 120 Misc. 2d 871, 466 N.Y.S.2d 934

Unless the Bankruptcy Court orders the appointment of a trustee, the debtor in a Chapter 11 bankruptcy proceeding will remain in possession of the property in the bankruptcy estate as a debtor in possession, and will have, with limited exceptions, all of the rights, powers, and duties of a trustee; accordingly, the president of a corporation that was involved in a Chapter 11 bankruptcy proceeding would not be free of fiduciary responsibilities in connection with the affairs of the corporation, since, though the corporation itself was technically the debtor in possession, the onus in such a situation is upon the officers and managing employees of the corporation to conduct the debtor's affairs in accordance with the normal fiduciary duties of the trustee. Maguire v Puente (1983) 120 Misc. 2d 871, 466 N.Y.S.2d 934

ARTICLE 9
MERGER OR CONSOLIDATION; GUARANTEE; DISPOSITION OF ASSETS; SHARE EXCHANGES

History: Add, L 1961, ch 855, eff Sept 1, 1963.

Schedule of sections, amd, L 1963, ch 689, § 11, eff Sept 1, 1963.

Art heading, amd, L 1986, ch 117, § 2, eff Sept 1, 1986.

§ 901.   Power of merger or consolidation

(a) Two or more domestic corporations may, as provided in this chapter:

(1) Merge into a single corporation which shall be one of the constituent corporations; or

(2) Consolidate into a single corporation which shall be a new corporation to be formed pursuant to the consolidation.

(b) Whenever used in this article:

(1) "Merger" means a procedure of the character described in subparagraph (a)(1).

(2) "Consolidation" means a procedure of the character described in subparagraph (a)(2).

(3) "Constituent corporation" means an existing corporation that is participating in the merger or consolidation with one or more other corporations.

(4) "Surviving corporation" means the constituent corporation into which one or more other constituent corporations are merged.

(5) "Consolidated corporation" means the new corporation into which two or more constituent corporations are consolidated.

(6) "Constituent entity" means a domestic or foreign corporation or other business entity, that is participating in the merger or consolidation with one or more domestic or foreign corporations.

(7) "Other business entity" means any person other than a natural person, general partnership (including any registered limited liability partnership or registered foreign limited liability partnership) or a domestic or foreign business corporation.

(8) "Person" means any association, corporation, joint stock company, estate, general partnership (including any registered limited liability partnership or foreign limited liability partnership), limited association, limited liability company (including a professional service limited liability company), foreign limited liability company (including a foreign professional service limited liability company), joint venture, limited partnership, natural person, real estate investment trust, business trust or other trust, custodian, nominee or any other individual or entity in its own or any representative capacity.

(c) One or more domestic corporations and one or more other business entities, or one or more foreign corporations and one or more other business entities may as provided by any other applicable statute and this chapter:

(1) Merge into a single domestic or foreign corporation or other business entity, which shall be one of the constituent entities; or

(2) Consolidate into a single domestic or foreign corporation or other business entity, which shall be a new domestic or foreign corporation or other business entity to be formed pursuant to the consolidation.

History: Add, L 1961, ch 855, eff Sept 1, 1963; amd, L 1997, ch 449, § 51, eff Feb 22, 1998; L 1997, ch 470, §§ 17, 18, eff Aug 26, 1997; L 1997, ch 494, § 6, eff Feb 22, 1998; L 1998, ch 374, §§ 1, 3, eff Sept 12, 1998; L 1999, ch 172, § 9, eff July 6, 1999.

CASE ANNOTATIONS

To be effective, a merger or consolidation involving a corporation subject to the provisions of former Stock Corp. L. had to be arranged, agreed upon, and carried out in accordance with the procedure and requirements set forth in § 86 and other sections of that law. People v North River Sugar Refining Co. (1890) 121 N.Y. 582, 24 N.E. 834; Unckles v Colgate (1896) 148 N.Y. 529, 43 N.E. 59

Some decisions failed to draw clear lines of distinction between "mergers" and "consolidations," and it was held, for instance, that a merger might be accomplished, at least in some instances, by simply amending the certificate of incorporation of one of the corporations involved and taking over the assets and liabilities of the other, with shareholder consent and approval. People ex rel. Municipal Gas Co. v Rice (1893) 138 N.Y. 151, 33 N.E. 846

Compliance with statutory requirements in effecting a merger or consolidation, moreover, did not preclude a court from looking into the cause, reason, or effect of the consolidation. Small v Sullivan (1927) 245 N.Y. 343, 157 N.E. 261, reh den 245 N.Y. 621, 157 N.E. 883

Former Stock Corp. L. merger and consolidation provisions were originally complex and involved, but were later amended in what was referred to as an effort to meet a "nation-wide demand for simplification," particularly in favor of utility mergers. Beloff v Consolidated Edison Co. (1949) 300 N.Y. 11, 87 N.E.2d 561

Statutory provisions authorizing consolidations and mergers were not regarded as invalid or unconstitutional because they permitted such combinations involving one or more corporations formed under less comprehensive provisions or not sanctioning consolidations. Beloff v Consolidated Edison Co. (1949) 300 N.Y. 11, 87 N.E.2d 561

Earlier corporation laws were likewise liberal in sanctioning mergers and consolidations, and the terms of any agreement among shareholders, or between them and the corporation in which they held stock, were deemed drawn in the light of this fact and not to bar entry of the corporation into arrangements for merger or consolidation with another corporation unless clearly and explicitly so providing. Zobel v American Locomotive Co. (1943) 182 Misc 323, 44 N.Y.S.2d 33

In cases of corporate merger, there is no violation of fiduciary duty owed by dominant stockholders to public stockholders if there is proper corporate purpose for merger and there has been neither fraud, self-dealing nor price manipulation, and alternatives afforded to public shareholders are a fair price fairly determined or statutory right to appraisal. Schulwolf v Cerro Corp. (1976) 86 Misc. 2d 292, 380 N.Y.S.2d 957

Where there was valid corporate purpose of combining management and resources and providing for intercompany transactions which warranted proposed corporate merger, and terms of merger were worked out and negotiations leading to it were conducted by an apparently independent committee, and stockholders of merged corporation would receive stock interest in surviving corporation, stockholders of merged corporation were not entitled to preliminary injunction restraining such proposed merger. Schulwolf v Cerro Corp. (1976) 86 Misc. 2d 292, 380 N.Y.S.2d 957

Only where merger is for sole benefit of insiders is use of corporate funds to purchase the stock improper. Schulwolf v Cerro Corp. (1976) 86 Misc. 2d 292, 380 N.Y.S.2d 957

Term "constituent corporation" under N.Y. Bus. Corp. Law § 901(b)(3) plainly excluded an entity such as a non-profit subsidiary of the New York Stock Exchange (NYSE) that was created at the time of or after the merger of the NYSE from a non-profit corporation into a for-profit entity; thus, the state attorney general did not have the authority to pursue claims against the former CEO of the NYSE under N.Y. Not-for-Profit Corp. Law § 720(b). People v Grasso (2008, App Div, 1st Dept) 861 NYS2d 627.

Some decisions rather clearly recognized a distinction between mergers and consolidations, as by declaring that no merger resulted where a new corporation, of different name and stated period of existence, was to take the place of two constituent corporations. Swedish Iron & Steel Corp. v Edwards (1932, DC NY) 1 F. Supp. 335, affd (CA2 NY) 69 F.2d 1018

The merger and consolidation provisions of former Stock Corp. L. were regarded as confined in application to corporations organized under or subject to that law and not broad enough to include those formed under special laws, such as the Transportation Law. 1911 Ops Atty Gen 140; 1912 Ops Atty Gen 33; 1960 Ops Atty Gen May 19

A cooperative corporation could not consolidate with an ordinary business corporation because of fundamentally different purposes and powers. 1961 Ops Atty Gen Dec 7

De facto merger doctrine did not render an attorney liable to an assignee as a successor by merger to the professional service limited liability company (PSLLC) inasmuch as the PSLLC was created pursuant to N.Y. Ltd. Liab. Co. Law art. 12, any merger or consolidation between the attorney and the PSLLC would be governed by that article and the attorney was a "natural person," despite the fact that he practiced law under an assumed name and the fact that his law practice was characterized as a sole proprietorship; thus, even if the attorney and the PSLLC desired to be merged, rather than having such merger imposed upon them by a judicially created doctrine, such a merger could not be accomplished under the Limited Liability Company Law. Hamilton Equity Group, LLC v Juan E. Irene, PLLC (2012, 4th Dept) 101 App Div 3d 1703, 957 NYS2d 527, subsequent app (2012, 4th Dept) 101 App Div 3d 1702, 955 NYS2d 903.

§ 902.   Plan of merger or consolidation

(a) The board of each corporation proposing to participate in a merger or consolidation under section 901 (Power of merger or consolidation) shall adopt a plan of merger or consolidation, setting forth:

(1) The name of each constituent entity and, if the name of any of them has been changed, the name under which it was formed; and the name of the surviving corporation, or the name, or the method of determining it, of the consolidated corporation.

(2) As to each constituent corporation, the designation and number of outstanding shares of each class and series, specifying the classes and series entitled to vote and further specifying each class and series, if any, entitled to vote as a class; and, if the number of any such shares is subject to change prior to the effective date of the merger or consolidation, the manner in which such change may occur.

(3) The terms and conditions of the proposed merger or consolidation, including the manner and basis of converting the shares of each constituent corporation into shares, bonds or other securities of the surviving or consolidated corporation, or the cash or other consideration to be paid or delivered in exchange for shares of each constituent corporation, or a combination thereof.

(4) In case of merger, a statement of any amendments or changes in the certificate of incorporation of

the surviving corporation to be effected by such merger; in case of consolidation, all statements required to be included in a certificate of incorporation for a corporation formed under this chapter, except statements as to facts not available at the time the plan of consolidation is adopted by the board.

(5) Such other provisions with respect to the proposed merger or consolidation as the board considers necessary or desirable.

History: Add, L 1961, ch 855, eff Sept 1, 1963; amd, L 1962, ch 834, § 61, eff Apr 1, 1963; L 1963, ch 689, § 12, eff Sept 1, 1963; L 1965, ch 803, § 37, eff Sept 1, 1965; L 1998, ch 374, § 4, eff Sept 12, 1998.

CASE ANNOTATIONS

Under § 86 of former Stock Corp. L., working out of the initial agreement and plans for a merger or consolidation was likewise left to the boards of directors of the corporations contemplating such a move, subject to stockholder approval, and a court would not substitute its judgment as to economic wisdom of the plan for that of the directors and stockholders in the absence of a very plain showing of fraud or improvidence. Katz v R. Hoe & Co. (1950) 199 Misc 459, 103 N.Y.S.2d 106, app dismd 277 A.D. 1035, 100 N.Y.S.2d 1022 and affd 278 A.D. 766, 104 N.Y.S.2d 14, cert den 342 US 886, 96 L Ed 665, 72 S Ct 176

§ 903.   Authorization by shareholders

(a) The board of each constituent corporation, upon adopting such plan of merger or consolidation, shall submit such plan to a vote of shareholders in accordance with the following:

(1) Notice of meeting shall be given to each shareholder of record, as of the record date fixed pursuant to section 604 (Fixing record date), whether or not entitled to vote. A copy of the plan of merger or consolidation or an outline of the material features of the plan shall accompany such notice.

(2) The plan of merger or consolidation shall be adopted at a meeting of shareholders by (i) for corporations in existence on the effective date of this clause the certificate of incorporation of which expressly provides such or corporations incorporated after the effective date of subclause (A) of clause (ii) of this subparagraph, a majority of the votes of the shares entitled to vote thereon or (ii) for other corporations in existence on the effective date of this clause, two-thirds of the votes of all outstanding shares entitled to vote thereon. Notwithstanding any provision in the certificate of incorporation, the holders of shares of a class or series of a class shall be entitled to vote together and to vote as a separate class if both of the following conditions are satisfied:

(A) such shares will remain outstanding after the merger or consolidation or will be converted into the right to receive shares of stock of the surviving or consolidated corporation or another corporation, and

(B) the certificate or articles of incorporation of the surviving or consolidated corporation or of such other corporation immediately after the effectiveness of the merger or consolidation would contain any provision which, is not contained in the certificate of incorporation of the corporation and which, if contained in an amendment to the certificate of incorporation, would entitle the holders of shares of such class or such one or more series to vote and to vote as a separate class thereon pursuant to section 804 (Class voting on amendment).

In such case, in addition to the authorization of the merger or consolidation by the requisite number of votes of all outstanding shares entitled to vote thereon pursuant to the first sentence of this subparagraph (2), the merger or consolidation shall be authorized by a majority of the votes of all outstanding shares of the class entitled to vote as a separate class. If any provision referred to in subclause (B) of clause (ii) of this subparagraph would affect the rights of the holders of shares of only one or more series of any class but not the entire class, then only the holders of those series whose rights would be affected shall together be considered a separate class for purposes of this section.

(b) Notwithstanding shareholder authorization and at any time prior to the filing of the certificate of merger or consolidation, the plan of merger or consolidation may be abandoned pursuant to a provision for such abandonment, if any, contained in the plan of merger or consolidation.

History: Add, L 1961, ch 855, eff Sept 1, 1963; amd, L 1962, ch 834, § 62; L 1963, ch 689, § 13, eff Sept 1, 1963; L 1965, ch 803, § 38, eff Sept 1, 1965; L 1997, ch 449, § 53, eff Feb 22, 1998; L 1997, ch 494, § 4, eff Feb 22, 1998, 1998; L 1998, ch 17, § 11, eff Feb 19, 1998, deemed eff Feb 22, 1998.

CASE ANNOTATIONS

In the absence of statute authorizing merger or consolidation of corporations with the approval of holders of two-thirds, or some other fixed percentage, of their outstanding stock, unanimous shareholder consent would be required; and the statutes sanctioning merger or consolidation on the basis of percentage approval have substituted a percentage majority control in this field with right in dissenting shareholders to retire or be retired from the enterprise, upon payment of the value of their shares, if they do not wish to go along with the majority. Anderson v International Minerals & Chemical Corp. (1946) 295 N.Y. 343, 67 N.E.2d 573

Section 86 of former Stock Corp. L. required that the shareholders of both corporations involved in a proposed consolidation approve the proposal. People ex rel. Consolidated Kansas City Smelting & Refining Co. v Secretary of State (1897) 13 A.D. 50, 43 N.Y.S. 51

Temporary injunction enjoining defendant corporation from counting 125,000 shares in determining whether proposed merger had been authorized by vote of holders of two-thirds of outstanding shares of common stock, vacated as moot, upon showing that more than two-thirds of such shares, exclusive of contested shares, had voted in favor of merger. David Brown Corp. v Hewitt-Robins, Inc. (1965, 1st Dept) 23 A.D.2d 490, 255 N.Y.S.2d 893

Where the law requires shareholder approval of a proposal or of action to be taken by the corporation or its board of directors on the part of holders of a specific percentage of outstanding stock, as in the case of a proposal to merge or consolidate, it has been held that a by-law provision requiring unanimous approval of corporate acts is void for inconsistency with the statute. Benintendi v Kenton Hotel, Inc. (1943) 181 Misc 897, 45 N.Y.S.2d 705, affd 268 A.D. 857, 50 N.Y.S.2d 843, mod on other grounds 294 N.Y. 112, 60 N.E.2d 829 (superseded by statute as stated in Application of Burkin, 1 N.Y.2d 570, 154 N.Y.S.2d 898, 136 N.E.2d 862, 64 ALR2d 638)

Where proposal for corporate merger and its terms were announced publicly November 19, 1975, and proxy statement was mailed January 27, 1976, but order to show cause commencing action to enjoin merger was not obtained by stockholders of merged corporation and served until February 18, 1976, returnable February 20, four days before scheduled stockholders' meeting, such stockholders were chargeable with gross laches. Schulwolf v Cerro Corp. (1976) 86 Misc. 2d 292, 380 N.Y.S.2d 957

In action by shareholder of defendant banking corporation for judgment declaring that defendant's plan to acquire another banking corporation constituted de facto merger and thus required approval by 2/3 of defendant's shareholders pursuant to CLS Bus Corp § 903, plaintiff was not entitled to summary judgment or preliminary injunction preventing defendant from implementing plan based on CLS Bus Corp § 912, which would prevent merger for 5 years after date of acquisition without approval of other corporation's board of directors, since defendant planned to purchase other corporation's stock, not its assets, and did not intend to immediately dissolve business of other corporation or assume its debts and obligations; while merger might occur in future, instant transaction was not merger but acquisition of subsidiary. Irving Bank Corp. v Bank of New York Co. (1988) 140 Misc. 2d 363, 530 N.Y.S.2d 757

Section 86 of former Stock Corp. L., unlike this section of the Business Corp. L., did not require approval of the proposal by shareholders who, under the terms of the stock held by them, had no voting rights or who were entitled to vote only on other distinctly specified measures or conditions, no matter how the proposed terms for consolidation or merger might affect their rights or the value of their stock. Jewel Tea Co. v United States (1937, CA2 NY) 90 F.2d 451, 37-2 USTC ¶ 9331, affg (SD NY) 217 F. Supp. 679

Under § 91 of former Stock Corp L, a consolidation of corporations did not require affirmative approval of their boards of directors but only authorization by the necessary two-thirds of shareholders, and was not subject to stay by injunction at the instance of an objecting shareholder who failed to file his objections in time. Andrews v Precision Apparatus, Inc. (1963, SD NY) 217 F. Supp. 679

§ 904.   Certificate of merger or consolidation; contents

(a) After adoption of the plan of merger or consolidation by the board and shareholders of each constituent corporation, unless the merger or consolidation is abandoned in accordance with paragraph (b) of section 903 (Authorization by shareholders), a certificate of merger or consolidation, entitled "Certificate of merger (or consolidation) of .... and .... into .... (names of corporations) under section 904 of the Business Corporation Law", shall be signed on behalf of each constituent corporation and delivered to the department of state. It shall set forth:

(1) The statements required by subparagraphs (a) (1), (2) and (4) of section 902 (Plan of merger or consolidation).

(2) The effective date of the merger or consolidation if other than the date of filing of the certificate of merger or consolidation by the department of state.

(3) In the case of consolidation, any statement required to be included in a certificate of incorporation for a corporation formed under this chapter but which was omitted under subparagraph (a) (4) of section 902.

(4) The date when the certificate of incorporation of each constituent corporation was filed by the department of state.

(5) The manner in which the merger or consolidation was authorized with respect to each constituent corporation.

(b) The surviving or consolidated corporation shall thereafter cause a copy of such certificate, certified by the department of state, to be filed in the office of the clerk of each county in which the office of a constituent corporation, other than the surviving corporation, is located, and in the office of the official who is the recording officer of each county in this state in which real property of a constituent corporation, other than the surviving corporation, is situated.

History: Add, L 1961, ch 855, eff Sept 1, 1963; renumbered subpar (5), L 1965, ch 803, § 39; renumbered subpar (3), L 1969, ch 401, eff June 8, 1969; renumbered subpar (4), L 1969, ch 401, eff June 8, 1969; renumbered subpar (5), L 1969, ch 401, eff June 8, 1969; L 1962, ch 834, § 63; deleted, L 1963, ch 689, § 14, eff Sept 1, 1963; deleted, L 1965, ch 803, § 39, eff Sept 1, 1965; deleted, L 1969, ch 401, eff June 8, 1969; L 1998, ch 375, § 11, eff Aug 13, 1998.

CASE ANNOTATIONS

Subsidiary, which owned a factory, was not immune from a negligence suit on the ground that it no longer existed as a corporate entity as the subsidiary failed to comply with the requirements for domestic corporations to convey property by way of merger, and for the court to conclude that the subsidiary and its successor in interest, the employer, were immune from suit in spite of those failings would render illusory the Business Corporation Law's requirements for conveyance of real property by merger. Preston v. APCH, Inc., (2011, 4th Dept) 89 App Div 3d 65, 930 N.Y.S.2d 722.

Under § 89 of former Stock Corp. L., filing of a certificate of consolidation automatically vested property of the constituent corporations in the consolidated corporation, but the transfer was nevertheless considered voluntary rather than by operation of law and accordingly not exempt from federal stamp tax. Niagara Hudson Power Corp. v Hoey (1940, DC NY) 34 F. Supp. 302, 40-2 USTC ¶ 9588, affd (CA2 NY) 117 F.2d 414, 41-1 USTC ¶ 9234, cert den 313 US 571, 85 L Ed 1529, 61 S Ct 958

Date of filing of the certificate of consolidation was to be considered the date of transfer of assets. United States v Niagara Hudson Power Corp. (1944, DC NY) 53 F. Supp. 796, 44-1 USTC ¶ 9148

§ 904-a. Merger or consolidation of corporations with other business entities; certificate of merger or consolidation

(a) After adoption of the agreement of merger or consolidation by the board and shareholders of each corporation participating in the merger or consolidation, unless the merger or consolidation is abandoned in accordance with paragraph (b) of section nine hundred three of this article, subdivision (d) of section one thousand two of the limited liability company law or other applicable statute, and the surviving or resulting entity is a corporation, foreign corporation, or other business entity for which the laws of this state do not provide for the filing of a certificate of merger or consolidation with the department of state, a certificate of merger or consolidation, entitled "Certificate of merger (or consolidation) .... and .... into .... (names of constituent entities) under section nine hundred four-a of the business corporation law," shall be signed on behalf of each constituent entity and delivered to the department of state. It shall set forth:

(1) The name of each constituent entity and, if the name of any of them has been changed, the name under which it was formed;

(2) The date when the certificate of incorporation or articles of organization of each domestic constituent entity was filed by the department of state;

(3) If a constituent entity is a foreign business corporation or foreign other business entity, the jurisdiction and date of filing of its initial certificate of incorporation or formation document, if any and the date when its application for authority was filed by the department of state or if no such application has been filed, a statement to such effect and (if the constituent foreign corporation is the surviving entity) that it is not to do business in this state until an application for such authority shall have been filed with the department of state;

(4) A statement that an agreement of merger or consolidation has been approved and executed by each constituent entity;

(5) The name of the surviving or consolidated corporation;

(6) If the surviving or resulting entity is a domestic corporation, in case of a merger, a statement of any amendments or changes in the certificate of incorporation of the surviving corporation to be effected by such merger; in case of consolidation, all statements required to be included in a certificate of incorporation for a corporation formed under this chapter;

(7) If the surviving or resulting entity is a foreign corporation or other business entity, an agreement that the surviving or consolidated foreign corporation or other business entity may be served with process in this state in any action or special proceeding for the enforcement of any liability or obligation of any domestic or foreign entity, previously amenable to suit in this state, which is a constituent entity in such merger or consolidation, and for the enforcement, as provided in this chapter, of the right of shareholders or members of any constituent domestic entity to receive payment for their interests against the surviving or consolidated corporation;

(8) If the surviving or resulting entity is a foreign corporation or other business entity, a designation of the secretary of state as its agent upon whom process against it may be served in the manner set forth in paragraph (b) of section three hundred six of this chapter, in any action or special proceeding, and a post office address, within or without this state, to which the secretary of state shall mail a copy of any process against it served upon him. Such post office address shall supersede any prior address designated as the address to which process shall be mailed;

(9) If the surviving or resulting entity is a foreign corporation, an agreement that, subject to the provisions of section six hundred twenty-three of this chapter, section one thousand five of the limited liability company law and any applicable statute, the surviving or consolidated foreign corporation will promptly pay to the shareholders of each constituent domestic corporation and owners of any constituent other business entity the amount, if any, to which

they shall be entitled under the provisions of this chapter and the limited liability company law or any applicable statute relating to the right of shareholders, owners and members to receive payment for their interests;

(10) The effective date of the merger or consolidation if other than the date of filing of the certificate of merger or consolidation by the department of state;

(11) For each foreign corporation, foreign limited liability company or other business entity, a statement that such merger or consolidation is permitted by its jurisdiction of incorporation or organization and is in compliance therewith;

(12) That the agreement of merger or consolidation is on file at a place of business of the surviving or resulting domestic or foreign corporation and shall state the address thereof.

(b) The surviving or consolidated domestic or foreign corporation shall thereafter cause a copy of such certificate, certified by the department of state, to be filed in the office of the clerk of each county in which each office of a participating domestic or foreign corporation, other than the surviving corporation, is located, and in the office of the official who is the recording officer of each county in this state in which real property of a participating domestic or foreign corporation, other than the surviving corporation, is situated.

History: Add, L 1997, ch 470, § 19, eff Aug 26, 1997 (see 1997 note below); amd, L 1998, ch 374, § 5, eff Sept 12, 1998; L 2008, ch 177, § 2, eff July 7, 2008.

§ 904-b. Merger or consolidation of business corporations into non-profit corporations

(a) A domestic business corporation may be merged or consolidated into a domestic corporation formed under section two hundred one (Purposes) of the not-for-profit corporation law and authorized to do business under article forty-three of the insurance law.

(b) With respect to procedure, including approval by members or authorization by shareholders, the domestic not-for-profit corporation shall comply with the not-for-profit corporation law and the domestic business corporation shall comply with the provisions of this chapter.

(c) The plan of merger or consolidation, pursuant to this section, shall set forth all matters required by section nine hundred two of the not-for-profit corporation law or section 902 (Plan of merger or consolidation) and the terms and conditions of the proposed merger or consolidation, including the manner and basis of converting shares, bonds or other securities in each constituent corporation into membership or other interest of the surviving or consolidated corporation, or the cash or other consideration to be paid or delivered in exchange for shares, bonds or other securities in each constituent corporation, or a combination thereof.

(d) After adoption of the plan of merger or consolidation by the board and shareholders or members of each constituent corporation, unless the merger or consolidation is abandoned in accordance with paragraph (b) of section 903 (Authorization by shareholders) and paragraph (b) of section nine hundred three of the not-for-profit corporation law, a certificate of merger or consolidation, entitled "Certificate of merger (or consolidation) of .... and .... into .... (names of corporations) under section 904-b of the Business Corporation Law", shall be signed on behalf of each constituent corporation and delivered to the department of state.

(e) The certificate required to be filed pursuant to this section shall set forth the statements required by paragraph (a) of section nine hundred four of the not-for-profit corporation law or paragraph (a) of section nine hundred four (Adoption of the plan of merger or consolidation).

(f) No certificate shall be filed pursuant to this section until an order approving the plan of merger or consolidation and authorizing the filing of the certificate has been made by the supreme court, as provided in section nine hundred seven of the not-for-profit corporation law.

(g) Upon the filing of the certificate of merger or consolidation by the department of state or on such date subsequent thereto, not to exceed thirty days, as shall be set forth in such certificate, the merger or consolidation shall be effected.

(h) The surviving or consolidated domestic corporation shall thereafter cause a copy of such certificate, certified by the department of state, to be filed in the office of the clerk of each county in which the office of a constituent corporation, other than the surviving corporation, is located, and in the office of the official who is the recording officer of each county in this state in which real property of a constituent corporation, other than the surviving corporation, is situated.

(i) When such merger or consolidation has been effected, it shall be subject to the not-for-profit corporation law and the effect of such merger or consolidation shall be the same as in the case of the merger or consolidation of domestic corporations under section nine hundred five of the not-for-profit corporation law, except that in subparagraph three of paragraph (b) of such section the word "member" shall be read to include the word "shareholder" as the latter is defined in this chapter.

History: Add, L 1999, ch 485, § 1, eff Sept 7, 1999.

§ 905. Merger of parent and subsidiary corporations

(a) Any domestic corporation owning at least ninety percent of the outstanding shares of each class of another domestic corporation or corporations may either merge such other corporation or corporations into itself without the authorization of the shareholders of any such corporation or merge itself and one or more of such other corporations into one of such other corporations with the authorization of the parent corporation's shareholders in accordance with paragraph (a) of section 903 (Authorization by shareholders). In either case, the board of such parent corporation shall adopt a plan of merger, setting forth:

(1) The name of each corporation to be merged and the name of the surviving corporation, and if the name of any of them has been changed, the name under which it was formed.

(2) The designation and number of outstanding shares of each class of each corporation to be merged and the number of such shares of each class, if any, owned by the surviving corporation; and if the number of any such shares is subject to change prior to the effective date of the merger, the manner in which such change may occur.

(3) The terms and conditions of the proposed merger, including the manner and basis of converting the shares of each subsidiary corporation to be merged not owned by the parent corporation into shares, bonds or other securities of the surviving corporation, or the cash or other consideration to be paid or delivered in exchange for shares of each such subsidiary corporation, or a combination thereof.

(4) If the parent corporation is not the surviving corporation, provision for the pro rata issuance of shares of the surviving corporation to the shareholders of the parent corporation on surrender of any certificates therefor.

(5) If the parent corporation is not the surviving corporation, a statement of any amendments or changes in the certificate of incorporation of the surviving corporation to be effected by the merger.

(6) Such other provisions with respect to the proposed merger as the board considers necessary or desirable.

(b) If the surviving corporation is the parent corporation, a copy of such plan of merger or an outline of the material features thereof shall be given, personally or by mail, to all holders of shares of each subsidiary corporation to be merged not owned by the parent corporation, unless the giving of such copy or outline has been waived by such holders.

(c) A certificate of merger, entitled "Certificate of merger of .... into .... (names of corporations) under section 905 of the Business Corporation Law", shall be signed and delivered to the department of state by the surviving corporation. If the surviving corporation is the parent corporation and such corporation does not own all shares of each subsidiary corporation to be merged, such certificate shall be delivered not less than thirty days after the giving of a copy or outline of the material features of the plan of merger to shareholders of each such subsidiary corporation, or at any time after the waiving thereof by the holders of all of the outstanding shares of each such subsidiary corporation not owned by the surviving corporation. The certificate shall set forth:

(1) The statements required by subparagraphs (a) (1), (2), (4) and (5) of this section.

(2) The effective date of the merger if other than the date of filing of the certificate of merger by the department of state.

(3) The date when the certificate of incorporation of each constituent corporation was filed by the department of state.

(4) A statement that the plan of merger was adopted by the board of directors of the parent corporation.

(5) If the surviving corporation is the parent corporation and such corporation does not own all the shares of each subsidiary corporation to be merged, either the date of the giving to holders of shares of each such subsidiary corporation not owned by the surviving corporation of a copy of the plan of merger or an outline of the material features thereof, or a statement that the giving of such copy or outline has been waived, if such is the case.

(6) If the parent corporation is not the surviving corporation, a statement that the proposed merger has been approved by the shareholders of the parent corporation in accordance with paragraph (a) of section 903 (Authorization by shareholders).

(d) The surviving corporation shall thereafter cause a copy of such certificate, certified by the department of state, to be filed in the office of the clerk of each county in which the office of a constituent corporation, other than the surviving corporation, is located, and in the office of the official who is the recording officer of each county in this state in which real property of a constituent corporation, other than the surviving corporation, is situated.

(e) Paragraph (b) of section 903 (Authorization by shareholders) shall apply to a merger under this section.

(f) The right of merger granted by this section to certain corporations shall not preclude the exercise by such corporations of any other right of merger or consolidation under this article.

History: Add, L 1961, ch 855, eff Sept 1, 1963; amd, L 1962, ch 834, § 64, eff Sept 1, 1963; L 1963, ch 689, § 15, eff Sept 1, 1963; L 1965, ch 803, §§ 40-42, eff Sept 1, 1965; L 1966, ch 626; L 1969, ch 401, eff June 8, 1969; L 1982, ch 202, § 10, eff Sept 1, 1982; L 1991, ch 390, § 1, eff July 15, 1991; L 1998, ch 375, § 12, eff Aug 13, 1998.

CASE ANNOTATIONS

The "cash payout" by which minority stockholders may be frozen out of continued participation in a corporation merged under § 85 of former Stock Corporation Law, closely analogous to this section, does not deprive such stockholders of due process or of contract rights, and, so long as the value of the stockholders' interest is compensable, there is no constitutionally protected right to continue as a stockholder. Willcox v Stern (1966) 18 N.Y.2d 195, 273 N.Y.S.2d 38, 219 N.E.2d 401

Where corporate owner of leased premises merged into another corporation, there was no separation or divestment of corporate assets from corporate landlord owner of leased premises and corporation into which owner of leased premises merged became the successor to all rights and obligations of corporate landlord as if corporate landlord continued in independent existence. Torrey Delivery, Inc. v Chautauqua Truck Sales & Service, Inc. (1975, 4th Dept) 47 A.D.2d 279, 366 N.Y.S.2d 506

The provisions of § 85 of former Stock Corp. L. for summary merger of a subsidiary into a parent corporation owning 95% or more of the subsidiary's outstanding stock, by action of the parent corporation's board of directors and without shareholder authorization, closely paralleled those of this § 905 of the Bus. Corp. L., and the earlier provisions were upheld against attacks on their constitutionality. Alpren v Consolidated Edison Co. (1938) 168 Misc 381, 5 N.Y.S.2d 254

The fact that one of two corporations involved in a merger is a wholly owned subsidiary of the other has never been regarded as precluding merger, under general statutes authorizing such corporate joinders. Zobel v American Locomotive Co. (1943) 182 Misc 323, 44 N.Y.S.2d 33

Earlier versions of § 85 of former Stock Corp. L. required that the parent corporation own all outstanding shares of the subsidiary before it could simply take over and absorb the subsidiary by action of the board of directors. Application of Gerstle-Rhein S. A. (1949) 194 Misc 795, 87 N.Y.S.2d 778

Where there is some outstanding stock of the subsidiary, though it is small in amount and not more than 5% with the balance all held by the parent corporation, giving the latter the required 95% control for effectuation of a summary merger, the board of directors of the parent corporation owes the minority shareholder a duty to proceed in good faith and in such manner as to assure that he receives timely notice of its action and has opportunity to object and demand payment for his shares within the statutory period for taking such steps. Rank Organization Ltd. v Pathe Laboratories, Inc. (1962) 33 Misc. 2d 748, 227 N.Y.S.2d 562

In a case where the board of directors of a corporation owning 95% of the outstanding stock of a subsidiary adopted a merger resolution without the knowledge of a British holder of the remaining 5% stock interest, and merely sent notice of the action taken to such minority shareholder by ordinary, instead of by air, mail, filing the certificate of merger to be effective so quickly that the British shareholder failed to receive notice in time to dissent, the parent corporation was held to be estopped to raise the time limitation under § 21 of former Stock Corp. L. for interposition of objections and demanding payment for stock as a bar to such a demand. Rank Organization Ltd. v Pathe Laboratories, Inc. (1962) 33 Misc. 2d 748, 227 N.Y.S.2d 562

In proceeding to annul the action of the Superintendent of Insurance in approving merger of insurance corporations, standard of 95% ownership set by Bus Corp § 905(a) did not violate but rather carried out the requirement of fairness and equity set by Ins § 486. Willcox v Stern (1964) 44 Misc. 2d 827, 255 N.Y.S.2d 38, mod on other grounds 24 A.D.2d 845, 263 N.Y.S.2d 1005, affd 18 N.Y.2d 195, 273 N.Y.S.2d 38, 219 N.E.2d 401

Acquiring corporation's offer for shares of corporation to be acquired through short form merger was not a palpable or gross undervaluation and did not warrant injunctive relief to complaining minority stockholder, despite fact that offer of 8.125 dollars per share was less than book value per share of $15.77 and was less than minority stockholder's estimate of fair market value of $12.27 per share, in view of fact that possible price adjustments would be made in appraisal proceedings. Tanzer Economic Associates, Inc. Profit Sharing Plan v Universal Food Specialties, Inc. (1976) 87 Misc. 2d 167, 383 N.Y.S.2d 472

Pursuant to section 906 (subd [b], par [2]) of the Business Corporation Law, when a merger or consolidation has been effected between corporations, all of the property, real and personal, including subscription to shares, causes of action and every other asset of each of the corporations vests in the surviving or consolidated corporation without further act or deed. Accordingly, plaintiff's cause of action against defendant, the corporate owner of the building in which plaintiff's employer is located and in which plaintiff was injured in the course of employment, was dismissed for failure to state a cause of action, where the defendant corporation and the employer corporation had merged, with the employer corporation surviving, and had filed a certificate of merger with the Department of State before the injury occurred, since plaintiff's only remedy is under the Workers' Compensation Law; although the surviving corporation did not file a copy of such certificate with the County Clerk as it is required to do by subdivision (d) of section 905 of the Business Corporation Law, so that the record owner of the building appeared to be a separate corporate entity from plaintiff's employer when plaintiff searched the record, this requirement is procedural in nature and must give way to the substantive law of section 906. Fioranelli v News Bldg. Corp. (1980) 102 Misc. 2d 825, 424 N.Y.S.2d 677

A short form merger of a closely held public corporation into a private corporation would be proper, since there was significant financial saving in becoming private, the merger eliminated a conflict of interest between the majority stockholder as guarantor of corporate loans and minority shareholder interests, it eliminated the conflict between the profit and dividend interests of minority shareholders and the growth and expansion objections of the majority interest, and it removed plaintiff competitor as a minority shareholder, which combined to establish a valid business purpose for the merger untainted by fraud, nondisclosure, or breach of fiduciary reponsibility. Cross v Communication Channels, Inc. (1982) 116 Misc. 2d 1019, 456 N.Y.S.2d 971

Plaintiff shareholder failed to state claim for fraud arising from merger of defendant corporation and corporation which it controlled, where all relevant facts regarding merger were disclosed in proxy statement sent to shareholders. Pinnacle Consultants, Ltd. v Leucadia Nat'l Corp. (1999, 1st Dept) 261 A.D.2d 164, 689 N.Y.S.2d 497, app gr 93 N.Y.2d 815, 697 N.Y.S.2d 562, 719 N.E.2d 923 and affd 94 N.Y.2d 426, 706 N.Y.S.2d 46, 727 N.E.2d 543

The "short form" merger statute (former Stock Corporation Law § 85) requires that the parent corporation own at least 95 percent of the merged subsidiary's stock. NLRB v Mastro Plastics Corp. (1965, CA2) 354 F.2d 170, 60 BNA LRRM 2578, 52 CCH LC ¶ 16787, cert den 384 US 972, 16 L Ed 2d 682, 86 S Ct 1862, 62 BNA LRRM 2292, 53 CCH LC ¶ 11270

New York law authorizes a corporation owning at least 95 percent of the outstanding shares of each class of another corporation to merge the latter corporation with the former without the authorization of the shareholders of the latter corporation, on approval of the board of the former corporation; and the consent of the remaining 5 percent stockholders is not required to effectuate the merger, although those stockholders are given an opportunity to obtain the fair value of their shares either by agreement or by appraisal. Vine v Beneficial Finance Co. (1967, CA2 NY) 374 F.2d 627, cert den 389 US 970, 19 L Ed 2d 460, 88 S Ct 463

§ 906.   Effect of merger or consolidation

(a) Upon the filing of the certificate of merger or consolidation by the department of state or on such date subsequent thereto, not to exceed thirty days, as shall be set forth in such certificate, the merger or consolidation shall be effected.

(b) When such merger or consolidation has been effected:

(1) Such surviving or consolidated corporation shall thereafter, consistently with its certificate of incorporation as altered or established by the merger or consolidation, possess all the rights, privileges, immunities, powers and purposes of each of the constituent corporations.

(2) All the property, real and personal, including subscriptions to shares, causes of action and every other asset of each of the constituent entities, shall vest in such surviving or consolidated corporation without further act or deed.

(3) The surviving or consolidated corporation shall assume and be liable for all the liabilities, obligations and penalties of each of the constituent entities. No liability or obligation due or to become due, claim or demand for any cause existing against any such constituent entity, or any shareholder, member, officer or director thereof, shall be released or impaired by such merger or consolidation. No action or proceeding, whether civil or criminal, then

pending by or against any such constituent entity, or any shareholder, member, officer or director thereof, shall abate or be discontinued by such merger or consolidation, but may be enforced, prosecuted, settled or compromised as if such merger or consolidation had not occurred, or such surviving or consolidated corporation may be substituted in such action or special proceeding in place of any constituent entity.

(4) In the case of a merger, the certificate of incorporation of the surviving corporation shall be automatically amended to the extent, if any, that changes in its certificate of incorporation are set forth in the plan of merger; and, in the case of a consolidation, the statements set forth in the certificate of consolidation and which are required or permitted to be set forth in a certificate of incorporation of a corporation formed under this chapter shall be its certificate of incorporation.

History: Add, L 1961, ch 855, eff Sept 1, 1963; amd, L 1962, ch 834, § 65, eff Sept 1, 1963; L 1997, ch 470, § 20, eff Aug 26, 1997.

CASE ANNOTATIONS

1. In general
2. Effects of merger, generally
3. Rights, privileges and powers
4. Property and other assets
5. Liabilities, obligations and penalties
6. Miscellaneous

1. In general

There was no occasion to decide whether liability for insider trading could be imposed against nonparticipating but acquiescing directors of a foreign corporation, since plaintiff in a shareholders' derivative action against the foreign corporation had no standing to continue the action, in that Bus Corp Law § 906, which permits continuation of a shareholders' action on behalf of a merged corporation in certain circumstances was not one of the enumerated laws specifically applicable to foreign corporations. Rubinstein v Catacosinos (1983) 60 N.Y.2d 890, 470 N.Y.S.2d 570, 458 N.E.2d 1247

Filing of certificate of merger may not be regarded as inconsequential technicality, in view of significant legal import assigned by CLS Bus Corp §§ 906 and 907 to filing of certificate. Holmberg v Attractions Land (1997, 3d Dept) 230 A.D.2d 362, 657 N.Y.S.2d 816

A merger becomes effective under New York Law upon filing the Certificate of Consolidation with the Secretary of State. Hilton Hotels Corp. v United States (1969, CA7 Ill) 410 F.2d 194, 69-1 USTC ¶ 9336, revd on other grounds 397 US 580, 25 L Ed 2d 585, 90 S Ct 1307, 70-1 USTC ¶ 9349

2. Effects of merger, generally

When corporations were consolidated pursuant to the provisions of former Stock Corp. L., the constituent corporations were deemed dissolved. People v New York, C. & S. L. R. Co. (1892) 129 N.Y. 474, 29 N.E. 959

Constituent corporations involved in a merger did not, cease to exist for all purposes. Re Kaufmann, Alsberg & Co. (1961) 30 Misc. 2d 1025, 220 N.Y.S.2d 151, affd (1st Dept) 15 A.D.2d 468, 222 N.Y.S.2d 305

3. Rights, privileges and powers

A merged corporation is entitled to enforce a guaranty of an obligation running to one of its constituent corporations. W. H. McElwain Co. v Primavera (1917) 180 A.D. 288, 167 N.Y.S. 815

Generally speaking, nothing is lost by merger of corporations and any right lawfully belonging to either can be asserted by the surviving or new corporation. Platt Corp. v Platt (1964, 1st Dept) 21 A.D.2d 116, 249 N.Y.S.2d 75, affd 15 N.Y.2d 705, 256 N.Y.S.2d 335, 204 N.E.2d 495

If an action has already been brought to recover upon a cause of action in favor of one corporation at time of its merger with another, and it is still then pending, the action does not abate and may be continued in the name of the original owner thereof until a substitution of parties is effected. Platt Corp. v Platt (1964, 1st Dept) 21 A.D.2d 116, 249 N.Y.S.2d 75, affd 15 N.Y.2d 705, 256 N.Y.S.2d 335, 204 N.E.2d 495

Right to take over and assume the name of one of the constituents was recognized even though, by some change in the governing statutes, such a name or manner of designation could no longer be used or availed of by a corporation newly incorporating under the Stock Corporation Law. Sizer Lumber Corp. v Knapp (1925) 124 Misc 669, 209 N.Y.S. 197

Under § 85 of former Stock Corp. L., all the rights, privileges, powers, and purposes of a constituent corporation passed, on merger or consolidation, to the surviving or consolidated corporation. By virtue of this provision, the surviving or consolidated corporation could expand its business and exercise powers theretofore lacking, such as power to acquire and hold securities of other corporations. Lippman v New York Water Service Corp. (1960) 25 Misc. 2d 267, 205 N.Y.S.2d 541, app dismd 12 A.D.2d 611, 214 N.Y.S.2d 715

An insurer's issuance of a product liability insurance policy to an insured cast upon the insurer contingent contractual obligations which constituted an indebtedness owing to the insured, and this asset of the insured, upon its merger with another corporation, automatically vested in the surviving corporation by virtue of the statute; nothing is lost by a merger of corporations and any right lawfully belonging to any of the constituent corporations merged together can be asserted by the surviving corporation. Chatham Corp. v Argonaut Ins. Co. (1972) 70 Misc. 2d 1028, 334 N.Y.S.2d 959

Franchises to engage in a particular type of business and to use streets, highways, etc., also passed to the surviving or consolidated corporation. Re New York Water Service Corp. (1946, Sup) 67 N.Y.S.2d 850, affd 271 A.D. 1019, 69 N.Y.S.2d 508, affd 296 N.Y. 1016, 73 N.E.2d 724

A right to special billing at reduced cost for electricity consumed at the plant of one of the constituent corporations involved in a consolidation, which was limited in availability to customers being served by the utility at a specified date prior to the consolidation, did not pass to the consolidated corporation because such right depended on identity of the user rather than legal succession. First Sterling Corp. v Lundy (1961, Sup) 232 N.Y.S.2d 645, affd (3d Dept) 14 A.D.2d 193, 217 N.Y.S.2d 646, affd 11 N.Y.2d 836, 227 N.Y.S.2d 447, 182 N.E.2d 118

While pending statutory claims against, inter alia, the former CEO of the New York Stock Exchange (NYSE) were not completely extinguished by virtue of N.Y. Bus. Corp. Law § 906(b)(3) following the NYSE's merger into a for-profit entity from a non-profit corporation as the NYSE could bring the claims itself, the public policy concerns supporting the state attorney general's authority under N.Y. Not-for-Profit Corp. § 720(b) to bring the claims no longer existed as the public interest was not involved in the NYSE as a private corporation. People v Grasso (2008, App Div, 1st Dept) 861 NYS2d 627.

Under §§ 85 and 86 of former Stock Corp. L., a merger or consolidation of corporations passed to the consolidated or surviving corporation all rights, property, and assets of the constituent corporations, including such equitable rights as licenses under patents. Hartford-Empire Co. v Demuth Glass Works, Inc. (1937, DC NY) 19 F. Supp. 626

Right to use the name of either constituent likewise passed to the surviving or consolidated corporation, but this right could only be made effective by formally adopting such name in the certificate of consolidation or merger or by filing a new or amended certificate of incorporation, if variant from the existing name of the surviving corporation. 1921 Ops Atty Gen 366

4. Property and other assets

Shares of stock of other corporations owned by the constituents of consolidation are not subject to stock transfer tax, under Tax Law, § 270, on the consolidation of two corporations as the transfer of such shares to the new corporation results by operation of law. Electric Bond & Share Co. v State (1937) 249 A.D. 371, 293 N.Y.S. 175, affd 274 N.Y. 625, 10 N.E.2d 583

A different view was taken as to shares of stock in a third corporation held and owned by a constituent corporation and passing to the surviving or consolidated corporation under the statute. The New York state tax on stock transfers was held inapplicable as only directed at ordinary sales and transfers. Electric Bond & Share Co. v State (1937) 249 A.D. 371, 293 N.Y.S. 175, affd 274 N.Y. 625, 10 N.E.2d 583

Conveyance of leased premises from corporate landlord to corporation into which corporate landlord merged did not constitute a proposed sale of premises within the meaning of lease provision granting tenant right of first refusal in the event of proposed sale of premises. Torrey Delivery, Inc. v Chautauqua Truck Sales & Service, Inc. (1975, 4th Dept) 47 A.D.2d 279, 366 N.Y.S.2d 506

Merger of corporate owner of leased premises with another corporation did not constitute a sale of the leased premises within meaning of lease agreement granting tenant first refusal in the event of proposed sale of demised premises. Torrey Delivery, Inc. v Chautauqua Truck Sales & Service, Inc. (1975, 4th Dept) 47 A.D.2d 279, 366 N.Y.S.2d 506

Where corporate owner of leased premises merged into another corporation, there was no separation or divestment of corporate assets from corporate landlord owner of leased premises and corporation into which owner of leased premises merged became the successor to all rights and obligations of corporate landlord as if corporate landlord continued in independent existence. Torrey Delivery, Inc. v Chautauqua Truck Sales & Service, Inc. (1975, 4th Dept) 47 A.D.2d 279, 366 N.Y.S.2d 506

Filing date of certificate of merger covering liquidation of seller into its parent buyer was not effective date of transfer of ownership of land where valid and binding assignment of seller's interest in land to parent existed, establishing operative conveyance date. Cayea v Lake Placid Granite Co. (1997, 3d Dept) 245 A.D.2d 659, 665 N.Y.S.2d 127

In the absence of a lawful merger complying with statutory requirements, directors selected by a parent corporation for a subsidiary have no legal right to divert revenues of the subsidiary to the parent except by declaration of dividends which will be paid on subsidiary stock held by the parent. Green v People's Gaslight & Coke Co. (1922) 118 Misc 1, 192 N.Y.S. 232, affd 206 A.D. 647, 198 N.Y.S. 917

Compliance with § 15 of the Lien Law is unnecessary where a corporation acquires the lien as a part of the assets of another corporation which it acquired by merger. American Cement Corp. v Dunetz Bros., Inc. (1965) 47 Misc. 2d 747, 263 N.Y.S.2d 119

Pursuant to section 906 (subd [b], par [2]) of the Business Corporation Law, when a merger or consolidation has been effected between corporations, all of the property, real and personal, including subscription to shares, causes of action and every other asset of each of the corporations vests in the surviving or consolidated corporation without further act or deed. Accordingly, plaintiff's cause of action against defendant, the corporate owner of the building in which plaintiff's employer is located and in which plaintiff was injured in the course of employment, was dismissed for failure to state a cause of action, where the defendant corporation and the employer corporation had merged, with the employer corporation surviving, and had filed a certificate of merger with the Department of State before the injury occurred, since plaintiff's only remedy is under the Workers' Compensation Law; although the surviving corporation did not file a copy of such certificate with the County Clerk as it is required to do by subdivision (d) of section 905 of the Business Corporation Law, so that the record owner of the building appeared to be a separate corporate entity from plaintiff's employer when plaintiff searched the record, this requirement is procedural in nature and must give way to the substantive law of section 906. Fioranelli v News Bldg. Corp. (1980) 102 Misc. 2d 825, 424 N.Y.S.2d 677

Merger of wholly-owned subsidiary corporation into its parent corporation did not constitute assignment within meaning of nonassignment covenant in real property lease where merger did not change beneficial ownership, possession, or control of subsidiary's property or leasehold estate, and merely affected corporate form. Brentsun Realty Corp. v D'Urso Supermarkets, Inc. (1992, 2d Dept) 182 A.D.2d 604, 582 N.Y.S.2d 216

There was some question as to whether the transfer of property and assets to the surviving or consolidated corporation was by "operation of law" so as to be exempt from documentary stamp taxes and similar property transfer imposts. Some decisions and administrative opinions took the position that the transfer, though pursuant to statute, was not wholly by operation of law, but voluntary, and hence not exempt from such taxes. Niagara Hudson Power Corp. v Hoey (1941, CA2 NY) 117 F.2d 414, 41-1 USTC ¶ 9234, cert den 313 US 571, 85 L Ed 1529, 61 S Ct 958, and affg (DC NY) 34 F. Supp. 302, 40-2 USTC ¶ 9588; United States v Niagara Hudson Power Corp. (1944, DC NY) 53 F. Supp. 796, 44-1 USTC ¶ 9148. See also 1930 Ops Atty Gen 166

Upon similar reasoning, it was ruled that a merger of corporations did not cause expiration of registration of motor vehicles registered in the name of one of the constituents by reason of the statutory transfer of title to the other as the surviving corporation. 1934 Ops Atty Gen 205

5. Liabilities, obligations and penalties

In the field of liabilities undertaken or assumed by a consolidated or surviving corporation, as the result of a merger or consolidation, former Stock Corp. L. was explicit in providing protection for creditors of the constituents. The burden of liability was cast on the new or surviving corporation, and this burden could not be impaired by agreement. Re Utica Nat. Brewing Co. (1897) 154 N.Y. 268, 48 N.E. 521; United States v Oswego Falls Corp. (1939, DC NY) 28 F. Supp. 872, 39-2 USTC ¶ 9633, affd (CA2 NY) 113 F.2d 322, 40-2 USTC ¶ 9590

Under the trust-fund theory treating assets of a debtor corporation as held in trust for the benefit of its creditors, a creditor of a corporation involved in a merger or consolidation, notwithstanding absence of any express assumption of that corporation's debts and liabilities by the successor corporation, is entitled, after exhausting his legal remedies, to proceed in equity against assets of the debtor coming into possession of the successor, if he can adequately trace and identify them. Irvine v New York Edison Co. (1913) 207 N.Y. 425, 101 N.E. 358

Where a railroad company by a covenant in a deed of land agreed to pay for all damage caused by sparks, ashes, cinders or coal dust to ice in a lake beyond fifty feet on each side of its right of way, an action to recover such damages could be maintained against its successor in interest under merger agreement whereby it became vested with all property and railroad rights and bound by all of obligations of its predecessor. Morgan Lake Co. v New York, N. H. & H. R. Co. (1933) 262 N.Y. 234, 186 N.E. 685

Where, although claimant was working for different corporate employer at the time that he filed formal claim for total disability benefits than he was working for at the time of his injury, the corporate employer was a successor corporation which had absorbed as a subsidiary the employer for whom the workman was working at the time of his injury, advance payments of compensation which had been made by the initial corporate employer and an intermediary corporate employer within three years of time that claim was filed were binding on the corporate entity which was employing the workman at the time of his claim so that liability could not be shifted to the Special Fund, for reopened cases. Riley v Aircraft Products, Mfg. Corp. (1976) 40 N.Y.2d 366, 386 N.Y.S.2d 838, 353 N.E.2d 801

Under Business Corporations L § 906, subdivision (b)(3), merger of corporation did not preclude derivative action against it or representative action against its directors personally for alleged improper conduct resulting in depressed price of merged corporation's stock. Albert v Salzman (1973, 1st Dept) 41 A.D.2d 501, 344 N.Y.S.2d 457

Cause of action for setting aside merger due to alleged improper conduct with respect to merged corporation's stock belonged solely to merged corporation and could not be maintained by individual shareholders thereof against merging corporation under Business Corporations L § 906, subd b(3). Albert v Salzman (1973, 1st Dept) 41 A.D.2d 501, 344 N.Y.S.2d 457

Although a purchase of corporate assets may ordinarily be arranged so as to insulate the purchaser from the seller's liabilities, the purchase must be for fair consideration and undertaken in good faith as a bona fide transaction. Gardner v Fyr-Fyter Co. (1975, 4th Dept) 47 A.D.2d 591, 363 N.Y.S.2d 693

A stockholder who instituted a derivate action on behalf of a corporation did not, under Delaware law, continue to have the right to prosecute the action after there had been a merger which resulted in the conversion of his stock into the right to receive a fixed sum of cash from the surviving corporation, in that he ceased to be a stockholder and became more like a creditor, notwithstanding Bus Corp Law § 906(b)(3), which preserves the continuation of the claim on behalf of the corporation, but does not preserve the standing of a nonstockholder to enforce that claim on behalf of the corporation against the corporation's. will. Rubinstein v Catacosinos (1983, 1st Dept) 91 A.D.2d 445, 459 N.Y.S.2d 286

Individual's personal injury action against corporation was properly dismissed even though deed on file with county clerk indicated property where individual was hurt was owned by corporation; corporation ceased to be owner of subject property when it was merged into another company prior to individual's accident, and thus corporation could not be held liable for injuries since it ceased to exist on merger date. La Porta v Enten Corp. (1986, 2d Dept) 125 A.D.2d 367, 509 N.Y.S.2d 91

In action under CLS Labor § 240, Minnesota corporation which was plaintiff's employer when accident occurred, and thus was immune from liability under CLS Work Comp § 11, was nevertheless answerable as third-party tortfeasor for any liability owed by New York corporate owner of premises where accident occurred, where merger between corporate employer and corporate owner did not become effective until after date of accident. Holmberg v Attractions Land (1997, 3d Dept) 230 A.D.2d 362, 657 N.Y.S.2d 816

Successors to corporation after de facto merger were not liable on corporation's unpaid promissory note; successor corporate liability after de facto merger is relevant to products liability tort law but not to action to collect on promissory note. Martorano v Herman Miller, Inc. (1998, 2d Dept) 255 A.D.2d 367, 680 N.Y.S.2d 20, app den 93 N.Y.2d 802, 687 N.Y.S.2d 626, 710 N.E.2d 273

CLS Bus Corp § 906(b)(3) applied, and thus defendants' motion to dismiss complaint was properly denied, where defendants did not become stockholders of foreign corporation until after plaintiffs' claim for wages already had accrued. La Vigne v Feinbloom (1998, 4th Dept) 255 A.D.2d 896, 680 N.Y.S.2d 348, related proceeding (4th Dept) 255 A.D.2d 897, 680 N.Y.S.2d 882

De facto merger doctrine creates exception to general rule that acquiring corporation does not become responsible thereby for preexisting liabilities of acquired corporation; doctrine is applied when acquiring corporation has not purchased another corporation merely for purpose of holding it as subsidiary but, rather, has effectively merged with acquired corporation. Fitzgerald v Fahnestock & Co. (2001, 1st Dept) 286 A.D.2d 573, 730 N.Y.S.2d 70

Although stock purchase agreement alone is insufficient to prove de facto merger as exception to general rule that acquiring corporation does not become responsible thereby for preexisting liabilities of acquired corporation, there may be such merger even though acquired subsidiary is not legally dissolved, so long as acquired corporation is shorn of its assets and has become, in essence, shell. Fitzgerald v Fahnestock & Co. (2001, 1st Dept) 286 A.D.2d 573, 730 N.Y.S.2d 70

De facto merger doctrine, which creates exception to general rule that acquiring corporation does not become responsible thereby for preexisting liabilities of acquired corporation, is not limited to tort actions and applies to breach of contract actions. Fitzgerald v Fahnestock & Co. (2001, 1st Dept) 286 A.D.2d 573, 730 N.Y.S.2d 70

Complaint sufficiently alleged cause of action for defendant's liability for acquired corporation's breach of contract by application of de facto merger doctrine, which creates exception to general rule that acquiring corporation does not become responsible thereby for preexisting liabilities of acquired corporation, where plaintiff alleged that (1) shortly after defendant's acquisition of all of subsidiary's stock, subsidiary ceased issuance of it own annual audited financial report, (2) instead, defendant later included such information in its own annual report, (3) subsidiary's trading, compliance, legal, and management departments were subsumed into those of defendant, (4) registration of subsidiary's employees with National Association of Securities Dealers was transferred in bulk to defendant, and (5) subsidiary withdrew its membership from New York Stock Exchange, surrendered its broker/dealer number, and thereafter conducted trades under defendant's number. Fitzgerald v Fahnestock & Co. (2001, 1st Dept) 286 A.D.2d 573, 730 N.Y.S.2d 70

Past statutes have not dealt with the effect of a merger on the rights and liabilities of a surety for one of the constituent corporations, and this problem has accordingly been considered as left for determination under general principles of law. Worth Corp. v Metropolitan Casualty Ins. Co. (1932) 142 Misc 734, 255 N.Y.S. 470, affd 235 A.D. 782, 256 N.Y.S. 1007

The obligation to abide by a fair trade agreement with respect to retail prices of goods sold, such agreement being binding upon a constituent corporation, became one of the obligations assumed and undertaken by the new or surviving corporation. Emerson Radio & Phonograph Corp. v Standard Appliances, Inc. (1952) 201 Misc 821, 112 N.Y.S.2d 615

Where, under a corporate "reorganization," defendant acquired all the assets and current liabilities of corporate plaintiff in exchange for defendant's stock and continued to operate plaintiffs' business as a division of defendant acquiring corporation, staffed by corporate plaintiff's former employees, plaintiffs were entitled to summary judgment declaring defendant liable to indemnify and defend products liability actions involving products sold by plaintiff corpora-

tion, notwithstanding that the injuries occurred after the acquisition. Grant-Howard Associates v General Housewares Corp. (1982) 115 Misc. 2d 704, 454 N.Y.S.2d 521

Pursuant to N.Y. Bus. Corp. Law § 906(b)(3), the obligation of the licensee to pay royalties to the licensor was not terminated by the licensee's mere acquisition of the licensor; it was terminated by the agreement under which the licensor granted the licensee a royalty-free license. Joan Hansen & Co. v Everlast World's Boxing Headquarters Corp. (2003, A.D., 1st Dept) 768 N.Y.S.2d 329

Subsidiary, which owned a factory, was not immune from a negligence suit on the ground that it no longer existed as a corporate entity as the subsidiary failed to comply with the requirements for domestic corporations to convey property by way of merger, and for the court to conclude that the subsidiary and its successor in interest, the employer, were immune from suit in spite of those failings would render illusory the Business Corporation Law's requirements for conveyance of real property by merger. Preston v. APCH, Inc., (2011, 4th Dept) 89 App Div 3d 65, 930 N.Y.S.2d 722.

Rights of action already accrued against the constituent corporations did not cease to exist, and actions pending against either of them did not abate and could go forward and proceed as if no consolidation or merger had occurred. Creditors could not be prejudiced by the technical change in title to assets. Employers' Liability Assur. Corp. v Astoria Mahogany Co. (1924, CA2 NY) 299 F 579; Evans v Lawton (1888, CC Mo) 34 F 233

A tax liability of a constituent, such as for federal documentary stamp tax in connection with stock in another corporation which was transferred by the terms of § 86 of former Stock Corp. L. to the new or surviving corporation, became the latter's obligation if not paid by the constituent. Niagara Hudson Power Corp. v Hoey (1941, CA2 NY) 117 F.2d 414, 41-1 USTC ¶ 9234, cert den 313 US 571, 85 L Ed 1529, 61 S Ct 958, and affg (DC NY) 34 F. Supp. 302, 40-2 USTC ¶ 9588

Section 90 of former Stock Corp L was taken into consideration by a federal court in holding that a consolidated corporation must submit to a union demand for arbitration of points covered by a collective bargaining agreement between the union and a constituent of the consolidation. Livingston v John Wiley & Sons, Inc. (1963, CA2 NY) 313 F.2d 52, 52 BNA LRRM 2223, 46 CCH LC ¶ 18037, affd 376 US 543, 11 L Ed 2d 898, 84 S Ct 909, 55 BNA LRRM 2769, 49 CCH LC ¶ 18846

Service on an officer of a corporation subsequent to merger by such corporation with another corporation is invalid to bind such corporation as if unmerged where the plaintiff declines to hold the successor corporation which is willing to enter appearance by substitution. O'Brien v New York Edison Co. (1937, DC NY) 19 F. Supp. 968

The statutory liability of the successor corporation was, at least for most purposes, as if it had originally entered into the obligation or so acted as to create the liability. Kopitko v J. T. Flagg Knitting Co. (1953, DC NY) 111 F. Supp. 549

The surviving corporation is liable for acts of merged corporation committed before merger where merger occurs prior to commencement of action. Service is made personally upon surviving corporation or upon Secretary of State or registered agent of corporation. 1971 Ops Atty Gen Sept 27

6. Miscellaneous

In action alleging that individual defendants had fraudulently induced plaintiff to part with his partnership interest in mortgage lending venture, bank that acquired individual defendants' interests in certain closely held corporation was properly granted summary judgment dismissing complaint against it as (1) individual defendants, when they committed alleged tortious acts and when they sold their corporate interests to bank, were acting for their own benefit and not for corporation, (2) plaintiff did not possess any shares or certificates evidencing his alleged ownership interest in subject corporation, and (3) bank did not assume any corporate obligation to plaintiff under CLS Bus Corp § 906(b)(3) when it acquired corporation in arms-length good-faith transaction. Held v Kaufman (1999, 2d Dept) 261 A.D.2d 509, 690 N.Y.S.2d 612

A shareholder whose stock is held in the name of his stockbroker is entitled to demand appraisal from a corporation that proposes a merger, although he is not the shareholder of record, since section 910 (subd [a], par [1]) of the Business Corporation Law does not specifically exclude shareholders who are the beneficial owners from the right of appraisal, the statutory phrase "entitled to vote thereon" restricting the right of appraisal to owners of voting rather than nonvoting shares, and since provisions in the Business Corporation Law allowing nominees and fiduciaries to demand appraisal do not prevent beneficial owners from demanding appraisal. Re Bowman (1978) 98 Misc. 2d 1028, 414 N.Y.S.2d 951

It was held, under the earlier "Business Corporation Law," that after effectuation of a consolidation stockholders of either participating corporation have the right to demand that the terms of the plan of consolidation be carried out by exchanging old stock for that of the new corporation, and in other respects affecting their individual interests. Re Interborough Consol. Corp. (1920, DC NY) 267 F 914

§ 907. Merger or consolidation of domestic and foreign corporations

(a) One or more foreign corporations and one or more domestic corporations may be merged or consolidated into a corporation of this state or of another jurisdiction, if such merger or consolidation is permitted by the laws of the jurisdiction under which each such foreign corporation is incorporated. With respect to such merger or consolidation, any reference in paragraph (b) of section 901 (Power of merger or consolidation) to a corporation shall, unless the context otherwise requires, include both domestic and foreign corporations.

(b) With respect to procedure, including the requirement of shareholder authorization, each domestic corporation shall comply with the provisions of this chapter relating to merger or consolidation of domestic corporations, and each foreign corporation shall comply with the applicable provisions of the law of the jurisdiction under which it is incorporated.

(c) The procedure for the merger of a subsidiary corporation or corporations under section 905 (Merger of parent and subsidiary corporations) shall be available where either a subsidiary corporation or the corporation owning at least ninety percent of the outstanding shares of each class of a subsidiary is a foreign corporation, and such merger is permitted by the laws of the jurisdiction under which such foreign corporation is incorporated.

(d) If the surviving or consolidated corporation is, or is to be, a domestic corporation, a certificate of merger or consolidation shall be signed and delivered to the department of state as provided in section 904 (Certificate of merger or consolidation; contents) or 905 (Merger of parent and subsidiary corporations), as the case may be. In addition to the matters specified in such sections, the certificate shall set forth as to each constituent foreign corporation the jurisdiction and date of its incorporation and the date when its application for authority to do business in this state was filed by the department of state, and its fictitious name used in this state pursuant to article thirteen of this chapter, if applicable, or, if no such application has been filed, a statement to such effect.

(e) If the surviving or consolidated corporation is, or is to be, formed under the law of any jurisdiction other than this state:

(1) It shall comply with the provisions of this chapter relating to foreign corporations if it is to do business in this state.

(2) It shall deliver to the department of state a certificate, entitled "Certificate of merger (or consolidation) of .... and .... into ....

(names of corporations) under section 907 of the Business Corporation Law", which shall be signed on behalf of each constituent domestic and foreign corporation. It shall set forth:

(A) If the procedure for the merger or consolidation of a constituent domestic corporation was effected in compliance with sections 902 (Plan of merger or consolidation) and 903 (Authorization by shareholders), the following:

(i) The statements required by subparagraphs (a) (1) and (2) of section 902.

(ii) The effective date of the merger or consolidation if other than the date of filing of the certificate of merger or consolidation by the department of state.

(iii) The manner in which the merger or consolidation was authorized with respect to each constituent domestic corporation and that the merger or consolidation is permitted by the laws of the jurisdiction of each constituent foreign corporation and is in compliance therewith.

(B) If the procedure for the merger of a subsidiary corporation was effected in compliance with section 905, the following:

(i) The statements required by subparagraphs (a) (1), (2), (4) and (5) of section 905.

(ii) The effective date of the merger if other than the date of filing of the certificate of merger by the department of state.

(iii) If the surviving foreign corporation is the parent corporation and such corporation does not own all the shares of a subsidiary domestic corporation being merged, either the date of the giving to holders of shares of each subsidiary domestic corporation not owned by the surviving foreign corporation of a copy of the plan of merger or an outline of the material features thereof, or a statement that the giving of such copy or outline has been waived, if such is the case.

(iv) That the merger is permitted by the laws of the jurisdiction of each constituent foreign corporation and is in compliance therewith.

(v) If the parent domestic corporation is not the surviving corporation, a statement that the proposed merger has been approved by the shareholders of the parent domestic corporation in accordance with paragraph (a) of section 903 (Authorization by shareholders).

(C) The jurisdiction and date of incorporation of the surviving or consolidated foreign corporation, the date when its application for authority to do business in this state was filed by the department of state, and its fictitious name used in this state pursuant to article thirteen of this chapter, if applicable, or, if no such application has been filed, a statement to such effect and that it is not to do business in this state until an application for such authority shall have been filed by such department.

(D) The date when the certificate of incorporation of each constituent domestic corporation was filed by the department of state and the jurisdiction and date of incorporation of each constituent foreign corporation, other than the surviving or consolidated foreign corporation, and, in the case of each such corporation authorized to do business in this state, the date when its application for authority was filed by the department of state.

(E) An agreement that the surviving or consolidated foreign corporation may be served with process in this state in any action or special proceeding for the enforcement of any liability or obligation of any domestic corporation or of any foreign corporation, previously amenable to suit in this state, which is a constituent corporation in such merger or consolidation, and for the enforcement, as provided in this chapter, of the right of shareholders of any constituent domestic corporation to receive payment for their shares against the surviving or consolidated corporation.

(F) An agreement that, subject to the provisions of section 623 (Procedure to enforce shareholder's right to receive payment for shares), the surviving or consolidated foreign corporation will promptly pay to the shareholders of each constituent domestic corporation the amount, if any, to which they shall be entitled under the provisions of this chapter relating to the right of shareholders to receive payment for their shares.

(G) A designation of the secretary of state as its agent upon whom process against it may be served in the manner set forth in paragraph (b) of section 306 (Service of process), in any action or special proceeding, and a post office address, within or without this state, to which the secretary of state shall mail a copy of any process against it served upon him. Such post office address shall supersede any prior address designated as the address to which process shall be mailed.

(H) (i) A certification that all fees and taxes (including penalties and interest) administered by the department of taxation and finance which are then due and payable by each constituent domestic corporation have been paid and that a cessation franchise tax report (estimated or final) through the anticipated date of the merger or consolidation (which return, if estimated, shall be subject to amendment) has been filed by each constituent domestic corporation and (ii) an agreement that the surviving or consolidated foreign corporation will within thirty days after the filing of the certificate of merger or consolidation file the cessation franchise tax report, if an estimated report was previously filed, and promptly pay to the department of taxation and finance all fees and taxes (including penalties and interest), if any, due to the department of taxation and finance by each constituent domestic corporation.

(f) Upon the filing of the certificate of merger or consolidation by the department of state or on such date subsequent thereto, not to exceed ninety days, as shall be set forth in such certificate, the merger or consolidation shall be effected.

(g) The surviving or consolidated domestic corporation or foreign corporation shall thereafter cause a copy of such certificate, certified by the department of state, to be filed in the office of the clerk of each county in which the office of a constituent corporation other than the surviving corporation is located, and in the office of the official who is the recording officer of each county in this state in which real property of a constituent corporation, other than the surviving corporation, is situated.

(h) If the surviving or consolidated corporation is, or is to be, formed under the law of this state, the effect of such merger or consolidation shall be the same as in the case of the merger or consolidation of domestic corporations under section 906 (Effect of merger or consolidation). If the surviving or consolidated corporation is, or is to be, incorporated under the law of any jurisdiction other than this state, the effect of such merger or consolidation shall be the same as in the case of the merger or consolidation of domestic corporations, except in so far as the law of such other jurisdiction provides otherwise.

History: Add, L 1961, ch 855; L 1962, ch 834, § 66; L 1963, ch 689, § 16, eff Sept 1, 1963; L 1965, ch 803, §§ 43, 44, eff Sept 1, 1965; L 1967, ch 179, eff Apr 10, 1967; L 1969, ch 401, eff June 8, 1969; amd, L 1970, ch 225, eff Apr 24, 1970; L 1970, ch 230, eff Apr 24, 1970; L 1982, ch 202, § 11, eff Sept 1, 1982; L 1982, ch 590, §§ 4, 5, eff Oct 20, 1982; L 1986, ch 590, § 2, eff Sept 1, 1986; L 1991, ch 390, § 2, eff July 15, 1991; L 1997, ch 449, § 56, eff Feb 22, 1998; L 1998, ch 375, § 13, eff Aug 13, 1998; L 1999, ch 172, §§ 10, 11, eff July 6, 1999.

CASE ANNOTATIONS

Although, when a subsidiary consolidates with its parent corporation under this section, the consolidated corporation succeeds to all rights, privileges, franchises and interests of the subsidiary, this does not include the subsidiary's right to conjunctional billing for a group of buildings owned by the subsidiary under an electric utility rate schedule making such billing privilege available only to customers who were taking service under such tariff on a certain date, which date antedates consolidation, as the right to such billing is not a matter of general legal succession but rather a problem of identity. First Sterling Corp. v Lundy (1961, 3d Dept) 14 A.D.2d 193, 217 N.Y.S.2d 646, affd without op 11 N.Y.2d 836, 227 N.Y.S.2d 447, 182 N.E.2d 118

In an action to recover for money had and received, jurisdiction existed over defendant pursuant to Bus Corp Law § 907(e)(2) by virtue of defendant's assuming under a mortgage agreement the obligations of a domestic corporation, notwithstanding that defendant failed to file the certificate of merger setting forth its consent to jurisdiction as required by that section, where defendant did carry on business in New York through that corporation, in that having effectively derived the benefit of the merger statute, defendant could not advance its blatant disregard of the statute to contest jurisdiction and would be estopped from doing so. Armour Handcrafts, Inc. v Miami Decorating & Design Center, Inc. (1984, 2d Dept) 99 A.D.2d 521, 471 N.Y.S.2d 607

Filing of certificate of merger may not be regarded as inconsequential technicality, in view of significant legal import assigned by CLS Bus Corp §§ 906 and 907 to filing of certificate. Holmberg v Attractions Land (1997, 3d Dept) 230 A.D.2d 362, 657 N.Y.S.2d 816

In action under CLS Labor § 240, Minnesota corporation which was plaintiff's employer when accident occurred, and thus was immune from liability under CLS Work Comp § 11, was nevertheless answerable as third-party tortfeasor for any liability owed by New York corporate owner of premises where accident occurred, where merger between corporate employer and corporate owner did not become effective until after date of accident. Holmberg v Attractions Land (1997, 3d Dept) 230 A.D.2d 362, 657 N.Y.S.2d 816

The provisions of § 90 of former Stock Corporation Law, made applicable to consolidation with foreign corporations by subd. 6 thereof, do not mean merely that for all purposes the consolidation shall be ignored and have no legal effect or that no rights of parties can be affected thereby, and the prohibition against impairment of rights of creditors should not be interpreted so as to preserve the "right" to impose on New York courts litigation which should not be in those courts after the plaintiff has first, with full knowledge of the facts, brought suit in an appropriate forum and then discontinued it. Michels v McCrory Corp. (1964) 44 Misc. 2d 212, 253 N.Y.S.2d 485

Subsidiary, which owned a factory, was not immune from a negligence suit on the ground that it no longer existed as a corporate entity as the subsidiary failed to comply with the requirements for domestic corporations to convey property by way of merger, and for the court to conclude that the subsidiary and its successor in interest, the employer, were immune from suit in spite of those failings would render illusory the Business Corporation Law's requirements for conveyance of real property by merger. Preston v. APCH, Inc., (2011, 4th Dept) 89 App Div 3d 65, 930 N.Y.S.2d 722.

Unless a taxing statute clearly requires it, formal differences in state laws relating to consolidations and mergers should not be made the basis of discrimination in the assessment of federal taxes. Niagara Hudson Power Corp. v Hoey (1941, CA2 NY) 117 F.2d 414, 41-1 USTC ¶ 9234, cert den 313 US 571, 85 L Ed 1529, 61 S Ct 958, and affg (DC NY) 34 F. Supp. 302, 40-2 USTC ¶ 9588

New York law authorizes a corporation owning at least 95 percent of the outstanding shares of each class of another corporation to merge the latter corporation with the former without the authorization of the shareholders of the latter corporation, on approval of the board of the former corporation; and the consent of the remaining 5 percent stockholers is not required to effectuate the merger, although those stockholders are given an opportunity to obtain the fair value of their shares either by agreement or by appraisal. Vine v Beneficial Finance Co. (1967, CA2 NY) 374 F.2d 627, cert den 389 US 970, 19 L Ed 2d 460, 88 S Ct 463

No vote of directors on consolidation of corporations is required by New York law, authority from the necessary two-thirds of the shares being sufficient in itself. Andrews v Precision Apparatus, Inc. (1963, SD NY) 217 F. Supp. 679

Where a stockholder dissenting from a proposed consolidation had ample time to file his objections between receipt of the notice of stockholders' meeting and filing of the consolidation documents, his only alternatives were to go along with the consolidation or receive the appraised value of his shares and it was too late for him to seek an injunction against the consolidation. Andrews v Precision Apparatus, Inc. (1963, SD NY) 217 F. Supp. 679

Rights of company pursuant to guaranty agreement survives merger of such company with another even where originally guananteed company is not survivor corporation of merger. CBS Inc v Film Corp of America (1982 ED Pa) 545 F. Supp. 1382

The Attorney General has ruled that where a domestic corporation consolidates with a foreign corporation which is authorized to do business in this state and the name of which includes a word proscribed for stock corporations formed under New York law, and likewise with a Delaware corporation which is to be the surviving corporation, the consolidated corporation can adopt the name of the other foreign corporation and still qualify to do business in this state under that name. 1952 Ops Atty Gen July 2

The excess of capital stock resulting from a merger of a domestic insurance corporation with a foreign insurance corporation where the domestic corporation survives is taxable under Tax Law § 180 regardless of the classification ascribed for other purposes. 1953 Ops Atty Gen July 15

§ 908. Guarantee authorized by shareholders

A guarantee may be given by a corporation, although not in furtherance of its corporate purposes, when authorized at a meeting of shareholders by two-thirds of the votes of all outstanding shares entitled to vote thereon. If authorized by a like vote, such guarantee may be secured by a mortgage or pledge of, or the creation of a security interest in, all or any part of the corporate property, or any interest therein, wherever situated.

History: Add, L 1961, ch 855, amd, L 1963, ch 689, § 17, eff Sept 1, 1963.

Amd, L 1997, ch 449, § 57, eff Feb 22, 1998.

CASE ANNOTATIONS

Section 203 of the Business Corporation Law does not shield a corporation from the consequences of noncompliance with § 908, but shareholder acquiescence and ratification may be sufficient in equity to bar challenge to the corporate action. Commercial Trading Co. v 120 Jane Corp. (1966, 1st Dept) 27 A.D.2d 533, 275 N.Y.S.2d 621

Mortgagor, in purchasing from bank-mortgagee notes issued by another corporation controlled by the same principals who controlled the mortgagor, did not give a guaranty but, instead, simply undertook an indebtedness as principal debtor and purchase the obligations of another corporation, thereby becoming the creditor of that other corporation. Chester Nat. Bank v Rondout Marine, Inc. (1974, 3d Dept) 46 A.D.2d 985, 362 N.Y.S.2d 268

In an action to recover money on a guarantee given by a realty corporation as collateral security for a line of credit extended to another corporation, the realty corporation was properly held liable on its guarantee where shareholder approval of the guarantee was not required inasmuch as the interrelationship of the two corporations with respect to ownership, common officers, employees, organization, and tenancy justified the conclusion that the realty corporation's guarantee was given in furtherance of its corporate purposes. Westinghouse Credit Corp. v N. D. P. Auto Supplies, Inc. (1982, 2d Dept) 88 A.D.2d 933, 450 N.Y.S.2d 876

Even in the absence of statute, a corporation, under the common law, could guarantee payment of rent and performance of the terms of a lease for one of its customers, and the propriety of such a guarantee was even clearer where the lessee was likewise an affiliated subsidiary. Chester Airport, Inc. v Aeroflex Corp. (1962) 37 Misc. 2d 145, 237 N.Y.S.2d 752, mod on other grounds (1st Dept) 18 A.D.2d 998, 238 N.Y.S.2d 715

Section 19 of former Stock Corp. L. similarly required approval by two-thirds of outstanding stock entitled to vote to make a guaranty by a corporation of some obligation not incidental to its stated purposes effective and enforceable. It was held, however, that this requirement was met where the guaranty was indorsed on the back of a promissory note signed by a different corporation, and the indorsement of guaranty was signed by the president of the corporate guarantor, who owned 100% of its stock. Art Craft Paper Box Co. v Interdisca, Inc. (1962, City Ct) 228 N.Y.S.2d 192

Where the execution of a note and mortgage represented a gratuitous guarantee by a company of its former president's personal debt, a transaction that was not part of the company's ordinary course of business, the transaction required the consent of two-thirds of the company's shareholders; because the consent was not given or implied, the trial court properly discharged the note and mortgage because the former president lacked apparent authority to execute the note and mortgage. Lindenbaum v Albany Post Prop. Assocs. (2002, A.D., 2d Dept) 747 N.Y.S.2d 118

Where security agreement is executed by corporation for purpose of attempting to avert bankruptcy of parent and principal customer, security agreement serves a valid corporate purpose and shareholder ratification of agreement is not necessary. Re Ollag Constr. Equipment Corp. (1978, CA2 NY) 578 F.2d 904, 4 BCD 549, 17 CBC 612, CCH Bankr L Rptr ¶ 66881, later app (CA2 NY) 665 F.2d 43, 8 BCD 619

The pledge of the assets of a wholly owned subsidiary to secure its previous guaranty of the indebtedness of its parent corporation in an attempt to prevent the bankruptcy of the parent corporation and principal customer was in furtherance of its corporate purposes so that shareholder approval of such transaction was not required. Ollag Constr. Equipment Corp. (1978, DC NY) 446 F. Supp. 586, revd on Re Ollag Constr. Equipment Corp. (1978, WD NY) 446 F. Supp. 586, affd in part and revd in part on other grounds (CA2 NY) 578 F.2d 904, 4 BCD 549, 17 CBC 612, CCH Bankr L Rptr ¶ 66881, later app (CA2 NY) 665 F.2d 43, 8 BCD 619

§ 909. Sale, lease, exchange or other disposition of assets

(a) A sale, lease, exchange or other disposition of all or substantially all the assets of a corporation, if not made in the usual or regular course of the business actually conducted by such corporation, shall be authorized only in accordance with the following procedure:

(1) The board shall authorize the proposed sale, lease, exchange or other disposition and direct its submission to a vote of shareholders.

(2) Notice of meeting shall be given to each shareholder of record, whether or not entitled to vote.

(3) The shareholders shall approve such sale, lease, exchange or other disposition and may fix, or may authorize the board to fix, any of the terms and conditions thereof and the consideration to be received by the corporation therefor, which may consist in whole or in part of cash or other property, real or personal, including shares, bonds or other securities of any other domestic or foreign corporation or corporations, by vote at a meeting of shareholders of (A) for corporations in existence on the effective date of this clause the certificate of incorporation of which expressly provides such or corporations incorporated after the effective date of this clause, a majority of the votes of all outstanding shares entitled to vote thereon or (B) for other corporations in existence on the effective date of this clause, two-thirds of the votes of all outstanding shares entitled to vote thereon.

(b) A recital in a deed, lease or other instrument of conveyance executed by a corporation to the effect that the property described therein does not constitute all or substantially all of the assets of the corporation, or that the disposition of the property affected by said instrument was made in the usual or regular course of business of the corporation, or that the shareholders have duly authorized such disposition, shall be presumptive evidence of the fact so recited.

(c) An action to set aside a deed, lease or other instrument of conveyance executed by a corporation affecting real property or real and personal property may not be maintained for failure to comply with the requirements of paragraph (a) unless the action is commenced and a notice of pendency of action is filed within one year after such conveyance, lease or other instrument [instrument]* is recorded or within six months after this subdivision takes effect, whichever date occurs later.

* Bracketed language inserted by Publisher.

(d) Whenever a transaction of the character described in paragraph (a) involves a sale, lease, exchange or other disposition of all or substantially all the assets of the corporation, including its name, to a new corporation formed under the same name as the existing corporation, upon the expiration of thirty days from the filing of the certificate of incorporation of the new corporation, with the consent of the state tax commission attached, the existing corporation shall be automatically dissolved, unless, before the end of such thirty-day period, such corporation has changed its name. The adjustment and winding up of the affairs of such dissolved corporation shall proceed in accordance with the provisions of article 10 (Nonjudicial dissolution).

(e) The certificate of incorporation of a corporation formed under the authority of paragraph (d) shall set forth the name of the existing corporation, the date when its certificate of incorporation was filed by the department of state, and that the shareholders of such corporation have authorized the sale, lease, exchange or other disposition of all or substantially all the assets of such corporation, including its name, to the new corporation to be formed under the same name as the existing corporation.

(f) Notwithstanding shareholder approval, the board may abandon the proposed sale, lease, exchange or other disposition without further action by the shareholders, subject to the rights, if any, of third parties under any contract relating thereto.

History: Add, L 1961, ch 855, eff Sept 1, 1963; amd, L 1962, ch 834, § 68, eff Sept 1, 1963; L 1965, ch 803, §§ 45, 46, eff Sept 1, 1965; L 1966, ch 533, eff June 7, 1966; L 1976, ch 13, eff March 2, 1976; amd, L 1997, ch 449, § 58, eff Feb 22, 1998.

CASE ANNOTATIONS

1. In general
2. Applicability
3. Disposition of assets
4. Regular course of business
5. "All or substantially all"
6. Notice
7. Shareholder approval, generally
8. Who can approve
9. When approval required; particular cases
10. Effect of approval
11. Liability and remedies
12. Defenses
13. Miscellaneous

1. In general

At common law neither the majority stockholders nor the directors could bring about a sale or cause a transfer of any portion of the property, essential for the transaction of its customary business, of a solvent, prosperous corporation, which was justifying the reason for its corporate existence, against the will of a minority, however small. Eisenberg v Central Zone Property Corp. (1953) 306 N.Y. 58, 115 N.E.2d 652

Section 20 of former Stock Corp L was to be construed with § 21, both being designed to enable a two-third majority of stockholders to authorize sale of corporate assets but to protect rights of minority stockholders if they regarded the sale as opposed to their interest. Petition of McKay (1962, 1st Dept) 17 A.D.2d 299, 234 N.Y.S.2d 531

Sections 20 and 21 of former Stock Corp. L. were enacted to overcome prior inequities in the common law and to enable a majority of two-thirds of the stockholders to sell if they deem it advisable, and at the same time to protect minority stockholders if the latter regarded the sale as opposed to their interest. Ribakove v Rich (1958) 13 Misc. 2d 98, 173 N.Y.S.2d 306

Section 20 of former Stock Corp. L. was regarded as enacted for the dual purpose of ameliorating the common-law requirement of unanimous agreement with respect to any sale or disposition of a major portion of the corporation's assets, but leaving sales and dispositions not in the regular course of business subject to approval of two-thirds of the outstanding stock entitled to vote and thus requiring more than mere majority approval of any disposition of assets which would result in inability of the corporation to carry on the business which it was organized to conduct. Frankel v Tremont Norman Motors Corp. (1959) 21 Misc. 2d 20, 193 N.Y.S.2d 722, affd

(1st Dept) 10 A.D.2d 680, 197 N.Y.S.2d 576, affd 8 N.Y.2d 901, 204 N.Y.S.2d 146, 168 N.E.2d 823; 277 Park Ave. Corp. v New York C. R. Co. (1949) 194 Misc 417, 90 N.Y.S.2d 214, affd 275 A.D. 1028, 91 N.Y.S.2d 838; Strauss v Midtown Enterprises, Inc. (1945) 5 Misc. 2d 823, 60 N.Y.S.2d 601, affd 270 A.D. 837, 61 N.Y.S.2d 378

2. Applicability

A sale or disposition of assets in liquidation proceedings directed to dissolution of the corporation, or an involuntary sale under legal process, or pursuant to judicial directive, was not within the coverage of §§ 20 and 21 of former Stock Corp. L. Application of Kokol (1950) 300 N.Y. 685, 91 N.E.2d 333; Re Miglietta (1942) 287 N.Y. 246, 39 N.E.2d 224, reh den 288 N.Y. 661, 42 N.E.2d 749; Application of Kokol (1949) 275 A.D. 1021, 92 N.Y.S.2d 103, affd 300 N.Y. 685, 91 N.E.2d 333

After a corporation had ceased to do business, a sale of its entire property, ratified by a majority of stockholders, was considered outside the scope of § 20 of former Stock Corp. L., and for this reason a dissenting shareholder had no right, under § 21 of that law, to demand payment for his stock. Re MacDonald (1923) 205 A.D. 579, 199 N.Y.S. 873

Former Stock Corp. L. was applicable to stock corporations generally, except as to matters for which provision was made in some "other corporate law," and since provisions appeared in some of the laws under which corporations were organized for specific purposes with respect to sale or disposition of assets in bulk, § 20 of the former Stock Corp. L. was deemed inapplicable to some such corporations, for instance, "salvage" corporations. Continental Bank & Trust Co. v W. A. R. Realty Corp. (1946) 270 A.D. 577, 61 N.Y.S.2d 273, affd 295 N.Y. 877, 67 N.E.2d 517 and app dismd 295 N.Y. 884, 67 N.E.2d 519

This section, when it became effective September 1, 1963, adopted an earlier minority view, but it was inapplicable to a proposed sale of practically all corporate assets submitted to shareholders prior to the effective date. Petition of McKay (1963, 1st Dept) 19 A.D.2d 815, 243 N.Y.S.2d 591, app dismd 13 N.Y.2d 1058, 246 N.Y.S.2d 34, 195 N.E.2d 762

Business Corporation Law § 1005, not § 909, governs corporate procedure following dissolution. Helfand v Cohen (1985, 2d Dept) 110 A.D.2d 751, 487 N.Y.S.2d 836

Defendant, incorporated "to do everything suitable, proper and conducive to the successful conduct of a real estate business," was entitled to summary judgment dismissing action for specific performance of real estate sales contract executed by corporation's president since sale involved property which was corporation's sole asset, thereby requiring approval of 2/3 of corporation's shareholders under CLS Bus Corp § 909(a), which applies to sales not made in usual or regular course of business "actually conducted" by such corporation; although corporation was authorized to sell real property, its regular business was managing its one piece of property, and plaintiffs failed to establish that corporation's president possessed implied or apparent authority so as to estop corporation from asserting § 909(a) as defense. Vig v Deka Realty Corp. (1988, 2d Dept) 143 A.D.2d 185, 531 N.Y.S.2d 633, app den 73 N.Y.2d 708, 540 N.Y.S.2d 1003, 538 N.E.2d 355

Certain federal legislation, such as the Federal Public Utility Holding Company Act, was deemed to supersede the requirements of § 20 of former Stock Corp. L. where the sale or other disposition of assets was incidental to reorganization proceedings governed by the federal statute. Application of Okin (1946) 187 Misc 697, 65 N.Y.S.2d 23

A sale or lease of assets by a trustee in bankruptcy or in connection with reorganization proceedings under the Bankruptcy Act seems to have been considered in the same category, as not within the intended coverage of § 20 of former Stock Corp. L., although sometimes consent and approval of two-thirds of the voting stock was sought for and obtained as a precautionary measure. 277 Park Ave. Corp. v New York C. R. Co. (1949) 194 Misc 417, 90 N.Y.S.2d 214, affd 275 A.D. 1028, 91 N.Y.S.2d 838

Mortgage is not conveyance within boundaries of CLS Bus Corp § 909, and legislative intent was that statute would not apply to mortgages. Rols Capital Co. v Panvaspan Realties, Inc. (1993, Sup) 157 Misc. 2d 449, 597 N.Y.S.2d 266

However, a sale and transfer of property by one corporation to another corporation of the same name could fall within § 20 of former Stock Corp. L. where there was no merger or consolidation of the corporations because of failure to comply with the statutory merger and consolidation sections. 1938 Ops Atty Gen 191 (dealing with necessity of reregistering motor vehicles so sold)

3. Disposition of assets

Section 20 of former Stock Corp. L. was less comprehensive, at least prior to 1954 amendment, than present § 909 of the Bus. Corp. L. in listing the kinds of asset dispositions requiring shareholder approval. As long as it referred only to "sales" of property, transactions by way of lease or exchange were not deemed within the coverage of § 20. "Assignments" were likewise not considered as "sales." La Vin v La Vin (1954) 283 A.D. 809, 128 N.Y.S.2d 518, affd 307 N.Y. 790, 121 N.E.2d 620; Re Knaisch (1922) 203 A.D. 725, 197 N.Y.S. 116; Dieselcraft Corp. v Joca Realty Corp. (1957, Sup) 161 N.Y.S.2d 761

Lease held not to be affected by provisions of above statute. Janoff v Sheepshead Towers, Inc. (1964, 2d Dept) 22 A.D.2d 950, 256 N.Y.S.2d 45, affd 16 N.Y.2d 949, 265 N.Y.S.2d 100, 212 N.E.2d 535

Sale of corporate stock does not constitute sale of corporate property. Torrey Delivery, Inc. v Chautauqua Truck Sales & Service, Inc. (1975, 4th Dept) 47 A.D.2d 279, 366 N.Y.S.2d 506

Right of corporation with respect to corporate property is entirely distinct from right of stockholders who are the ultimate or equitable owners of its assets, and even complete ownership of capital stock does not operate to transfer a title to corporate property. Torrey Delivery, Inc. v Chautauqua Truck Sales & Service, Inc. (1975, 4th Dept) 47 A.D.2d 279, 366 N.Y.S.2d 506

Tenant, given right of first refusal in event of sale of leased property owned by corporation, contracted with the corporate owner rather than its sole stockholder so that passage of control of corporation from sole stockholder to his estate and eventually to another individual did not change ownership of the leased property and sale of corporate landlord's stock did not constitute a sale of the leased premises within meaning of lease option. Torrey Delivery, Inc. v Chautauqua Truck Sales & Service, Inc. (1975, 4th Dept) 47 A.D.2d 279, 366 N.Y.S.2d 506

Material questions of fact were presented as to whether contract for sale of corporation's assets was void because of noncompliance with business corporation law and because corporation was not able to deliver title, precluding summary judgment in action by escrow agents. Oppenheim v Simon (1977, 3d Dept) 57 A.D.2d 1006, 394 N.Y.S.2d 500

In an action for specific performance of an agreement between a purchaser and a sole shareholder of the selling corporation for the sale of corporate assets, the trial court properly denied the selling corporation's motion for summary judgment where the allegations of the purchasing corporation raised material issues of fact concerning the sole shareholder's operation of the selling corporation, her participation in the underlying contract of sale, and whether such operation and participation were such as to overcome the necessity for the usual formal technicalities of corporate action so as to estop the sole shareholder from taking advantage of those technicalities. Leslie, Semple & Garrison, Inc. v Gavit & Co. (1981, 3d Dept) 81 A.D.2d 950, 439 N.Y.S.2d 707

The 1954 amendment of § 20 of former Stock Corp. L. extended its specific coverage to "exchanges" and leases, and thereafter the section was held applicable to an exchange of property for trust certificates, though they were to be issued to stockholders of the transferring corporation as part of a contemplated dissolution, thereby making § 21 applicable to permit a dissenting shareholder to demand payment for his shares. Alcoma Corp. v Ackerman (1960) 26 Misc. 2d 678, 207 N.Y.S.2d 137

President of joint venture was without power to sell all of debtor's assets, and was also without power to bind debtor to pay commission to broker for procuring willing purchaser; debtor's president failed to obtain requisite consent prescribed under § 909 of the New York Business Corporation Law, and president's conduct violated express language of joint venture agreement requiring unanimous vote by debtor's board of directors to sell unimproved land to third party. Re Eadie Properties, Inc. (1983, BC SD NY) 31 BR 812

4. Regular course of business

Ultra vires activities of a corporation cannot be considered part of its regular business for purposes of determining what transactions are in course thereof, within the meaning of statutes such as these. Eisen v Post (1957) 3 N.Y.2d 518, 169 N.Y.S.2d 15, 146 N.E.2d 779

Sale of corporate assets was not in regular course of business and was such as to render the corporation unable in whole or part to accomplish its purposes, entitling appellants to appraisal of their stock under § 21 of the Stock Corporation Law. Petition of McKay (1963) 13 N.Y.2d 1058, 246 N.Y.S.2d 34, 195 N.E.2d 762, dismissing app (1st Dept) 19 A.D.2d 815, 243 N.Y.S.2d 591

A transfer of properties of a petroleum products corporation to a newly-organized corporation, in exchange for stock in the latter, was not deemed to require compliance with § 20 of former Stock Corp. L. where it was beneficial to the transferring corporation, designed to complement its marketing and supply requirements, and essential to market maintenance. Re Leventall (1934) 241 A.D. 277, 271 N.Y.S. 493

It was held that the business of a corporation formed to effectuate a reorganization under the Burchill Act was to liquidate assets for the benefit of bondholders who were likewise its stockholders, and hence that its disposition of the last and chief asset under its control was not a transaction within the contemplation of § 20 of former Stock Corp. L. requiring stockholder approval. Continental Bank & Trust Co. v W. A. R. Realty Corp. (1946) 270 A.D. 577, 61 N.Y.S.2d 273, affd 295 N.Y. 877, 67 N.E.2d 517 and app dismd 295 N.Y. 884, 67 N.E.2d 519

As to what constituted a sale or disposition of assets in the usual or regular course of the corporation's business, for that reason not requiring stockholder approval under § 20 of former Stock Corp. L., much depended upon the nature of the property regarded in the light of what the corporation's business actually was or was authorized to be. If it was a corporation formed and organized to deal in real estate, its sales, exchanges, or leases of real property were usually considered as in ordinary course of business, notwithstanding the high percentage of assets involved. Re Roehner (1958, 1st Dept) 6 A.D.2d 580, 180 N.Y.S.2d 586, affd 6 N.Y.2d 280, 189 N.Y.S.2d 644, 160 N.E.2d 519; Epstein v Gosseen (1932) 235 A.D. 33, 256 N.Y.S. 49; Greenpoint Coal Docks, Inc. v Newtown Creek Realty Corp. (1949) 5 Misc. 2d 812, 91 N.Y.S.2d 466; Strauss v Midtown Enterprises, Inc. (1945) 5 Misc. 2d 823, 60 N.Y.S.2d 601, affd 270 A.D. 837, 61 N.Y.S.2d 378

A sale of real estate by a real estate corporation in ordinary course of its business did not fall within the shareholder-approval requirements of § 20 of former Stock Corp. L., so as to entitle a dissenting minority shareholder to payment for his stock under § 21, notwithstanding amendment of its certificate of incorporation pursuant to stockholder agreement to require consent of holders of 70% of its stock to the transaction or any business of any kind. Re Rosenshein (1962, 1st Dept) 16 A.D.2d 537, 229 N.Y.S.2d 14

Where a corporation had power under its charter to do all things necessary for its business and it was operating at a loss in New York, it could sell its property in New York and shift its operation to its low-cost plant in South Carolina, without the consent of two-thirds of its stockholders. Petition of Avard (1955) 5 Misc. 2d 817, 144 N.Y.S.2d 204, app dismd (4th Dept) 2 A.D.2d 647, 156 N.Y.S.2d 970

Where corporation in its whole corporate life has been entirely devoted to owning managing and operating single piece of property, vice-president of corporation has no authority to execute on behalf of corporation, contract for sale of such property without consent of directors and stockholders of such corporation, even though it would appear from its certificate of incorporation that it was corporation formed for purpose of doing real estate business generally. Boyer v Legal Estates, Inc. (1964) 44 Misc. 2d 1065, 255 N.Y.S.2d 955

5. "All or substantially all"

Sale of the business, assets and property, including good will, of an independent and important department or branch of the business, although for lack of capital to carry it on, required approval of two-thirds of the outstanding stock entitled to vote. Re Timmis (1910) 200 N.Y. 177, 93 N.E. 522

Where principals of defendant had been directors of plaintiff and transferred trademark from plaintiff to defendant and trademark was principal asset of plaintiff, disposal of principal asset of plaintiff without approval of board of directors and two-thirds of the outstanding shares of plaintiff may violate Business Corporation Law § 909 and temporary injunction should have been issued. Shorell Laboratories, Inc. v H. Allen Lightman, Inc. (1965, 1st Dept) 24 A.D.2d 856, 264 N.Y.S.2d 829, app dismd 17 N.Y.2d 870, 271 N.Y.S.2d 300, 218 N.E.2d 336

Section 20 of former Stock Corp. L. required consent or approval of two-thirds of outstanding stock entitled to vote only where the transaction involved sale or other disposition of all or substantially all assets of the corporation. If the disposition of assets reached these proportions, stockholder approval was essential to its validity. Kaszubowski v Buffalo Tel. Corp. (1928) 131 Misc 563, 227 N.Y.S. 435

Subsidiary, which corporation was about to sell, did not constitute "all or substantially all" of corporation's assets, so as to require shareholder approval, where corporation's remaining assets would be of value approximately equal to those sold, although, for past two years, subsidiary's assets constituted corporation's sole income-producing assets. Story v Kennecott Copper Corp. (1977) 90 Misc. 2d 333, 394 N.Y.S.2d 353

If management of a stock corporation desired to sell all of its assets, it was essential to comply with all the requirements of both § 20 and § 45 of former Stock Corp. L. in order to leave dissenting or disgruntled shareholders in a position where their only remedy was to seek payment for their stock pursuant to § 21. Starrett Corp. v Fifth Ave. & Twenty-Ninth St. Corp. (1932, DC NY) 1 F. Supp. 868

A sale was regarded as involving enough property or assets to require shareholder approval only if it imperiled operation of some department of the business important to carrying it on. Insufficient assets were involved to bring the transaction within the intendment of § 20 of former Stock Corp. L. if their loss would not put an end to the business or some important part of it and practically result in dissolution. Re United Gas Corp. (1944, DC Del) 58 F. Supp. 501, affd (CA3 Del) 162 F.2d 409

6. Notice

Where, prior to effective date of this section, a corporation sent out notices to shareholders of a special meeting at which a proposed sale of practically all corporate assets would be submitted to them which stated that any stockholder entitled to vote and not voting in favor of the proposition could object and demand his rights under § 21 of the Stock Corporation Law, the corporation was estopped from attempting to deny dissenting shareholders' rights demanded in accordance with the terms of the notice. Petition of McKay (1963, 1st Dept) 19 A.D.2d 815, 243 N.Y.S.2d 591, app dismd 13 N.Y.2d 1058, 246 N.Y.S.2d 34, 195 N.E.2d 762

7. Shareholder approval, generally

It has been consistently held that a sale of property by a corporation in regular course of its business does not require shareholder approval under statutes like § 20 of former Stock Corp. L., at least in the absence of a provision in its certificate of incorporation requiring such approval. Re Rosenshein (1962, 1st Dept) 16 A.D.2d 537, 229 N.Y.S.2d 14

Under § 909 of the Business Corporation Law, "shareholders" refers to shareholders of record. Cross Properties, Inc. v Brook Realty Co. (1971, 2d Dept) 37 A.D.2d 193, 322 N.Y.S.2d 773, affd 31 N.Y.2d 938, 340 N.Y.S.2d 928, 293 N.E.2d 95

Although plaintiff purchaser had believed that defendant was sole shareholder of corporation, court properly refused to grant specific performance of contract for sale of automotive repair business entered into by defendant in his capacity as corporate treasurer where holders of 46 percent of company's stock refused to authorize sale, since CLS Bus Corp § 909 requires proposed sale to be approved by 2/3 vote and precludes claim of apparent authority. Bouton v Thomas Bros. Sales Corp. (1992, 2d Dept) 179 A.D.2d 612, 578 N.Y.S.2d 232

Trial court properly granted the defendants' motions to dismiss a 1% shareholder's action for damages and to set aside a conveyance of real property based upon, inter alia, alleged breaches of fiduciary duty by his now deceased grandfather (an officer and director), whose actions were allegedly aided and abetted by the other defendants because the shareholder's breach of fiduciary duty claim was time-barred, the shareholder was collaterally estopped from asserting a proposed cause of action regarding the sale since the issue of his standing was decided in a prior proceeding, the written consent of 99% of the shareholders to the conveyance satisfied the "consents in writing," and the shareholder's remaining arguments were unavailing. Romanoff v Romanoff, 148 A.D.3d 614, 51 N.Y.S.3d 36 (N.Y. App. Div. 1st Dep't 2017).

Shareholder approval was, of course, not essential to the validity of a disposition of assets not covered by § 20 of former Stock Corporation Law, some other statute, or a specific requirement in the certificate of incorporation of the transferring corporation. Behrens v Clark (1928) 131 Misc 712, 227 N.Y.S. 717

1954 amendment of § 20 of former Stock Corp. L. was construed as superseding a requirement placed in the certificate of incorporation of a corporation formed prior to its enactment which would have required more than two-thirds stock approval for a sale of assets. Wells v Beekman Terrace, Inc. (1960) 23 Misc. 2d 22, 197 N.Y.S.2d 79

8. Who can approve

It has been declared that an agreement among shareholders of a corporation formed to deal in real estate requiring their unanimous consent to disposition of any property would be invalid and unenforceable as in contravention of state policy, unless the restriction was further specifically imposed by a provision to such effect set forth in the certificate of incorporation. Fromkin v Merrall Realty, Inc. (1962, 2d Dept) 15 A.D.2d 919, 225 N.Y.S.2d 632

Under N.Y. Bus. Corp. Law § 1511, a nonprofessional shareholder is only permitted to vote on corporate action pursuant to either N.Y. Bus. Corp. Law §§ 909 or 1001. Matter of Bernfeld and Kurilenko (2011, 2d Dept) 86 App Div 3d 244, 925 NYS2d 122.

The administrator of the estate of the sole and only stockholder was held to have plenary power to sell all assets of the corporation. Karp v Twenty-Three Thirty Ryer Corp. (1945, Sup) 55 N.Y.S.2d 856, affd 270 A.D. 758, 59 N.Y.S.2d 919

It was also held that the president of a corporation who owned two-thirds of its stock had a right to sell all or substantially all of its property. Re Fensterer's Estate (1948, Sur) 79 N.Y.S.2d 427

The requirement of § 20 of former Stock Corporation Law of stock-holder approval for voluntary sale, lease or exchange of corporate property otherwise than in regular course of business is not satisfied by showing that the conveyance was made by the president of the corporation who is assertedly its sole stockholder where his status as sole stockholder is contested, and the burden of proving lack of compliance with the statute is on the party who asserts it. Re 716 Third Ave. Holding Corp. (1964, SD NY) 225 F. Supp. 268, revd on other grounds (CA2 NY) 340 F.2d 42, cert den 381 US 913, 14 L Ed 2d 434, 85 S Ct 1535

9. When approval required; particular cases

A sale of remaining assets pursuant to court order by a corporation set up to take over the property of an existing corporation in reorganization proceedings under the Burchill Act could be made without notice to or consent of stockholders. Continental Bank & Trust Co. v W. A. R. Realty Corp. (1946) 295 N.Y. 877, 67 N.E.2d 517

Formation of 2 subsidiaries, both wholly owned by respondent corporation, and transfer of its camping operations and buses to subdivisions, did not fall within purview of CLS Bus Corp §§ 909 and 910 since such transactions did not result in liquidation, in whole or in part, of camp business operated by respondent, which retained ownership of corporate land and buildings; thus, respondent was entitled to summary judgment dismissing proceeding brought under CLS Bus Corp § 623(h)(2) to enforce shareholder's right to receive payment for fair value of her shares. Resnick v Karmax Camp Corp. (1989, 2d Dept) 149 A.D.2d 709, 540 N.Y.S.2d 503

A sale of substantially all the assets of "Dollar US" and "County Dollar," two New York corporations, "Dollar US" being owned by "County Dollar," which in turn was wholly-owned by "Dollar Canada," a Canadian corporation, 90 percent of which was owned by "Dollar England," a publicly-held English corporation, need not be approved, under § 909 of the Business Corporation Law, by the ultimate beneficial owners, i. e., two-thirds of the shareholders of "Dollar England," where the boards of directors of "County Dollar" and "Dollar Canada", being the shareholders of record of "Dollar US" and "County Dollar" respectively, had consented to the sale as required by law. Cross Properties, Inc. v Brook Realty Co. (1971, 2d Dept) 37 A.D.2d 193, 322 N.Y.S.2d 773, affd 31 N.Y.2d 938, 340 N.Y.S.2d 928, 293 N.E.2d 95

Mere transfer of company's operations from one building to another did not require shareholder approval under CLS Bus Corp § 909 since company continued to be in same business as it had before move and transaction did not result in liquidation, in whole or in part, of any of company's business; accordingly, company was entitled to summary judgment dismissing action to set aside conveyance. Dukas v Davis Aircraft Products Co. (1987, 2d Dept) 131 A.D.2d 720, 516 N.Y.S.2d 781

President of corporate buyer of land did not have authority, at closing, to assign contract to another corporation of which he was president, since in absence of shareholder approval he did not have actual authority under CLS Bus Corp § 909 to assign corporation's only asset. Highland Views Corp. v Gerdts (1993, 3d Dept) 190 A.D.2d 954, 593 N.Y.S.2d 902

Sale of building did not require shareholder authorization under CLS Bus Corp § 909 where corporation retained other valuable property, certificate of incorporation provided that corporation was formed for purpose of purchasing, owning and selling real property, and sale would not change nature of company's business. Soho Gold, Inc. v 33 Rector St. (1996, 1st Dept) 227 A.D.2d 314, 642 N.Y.S.2d 684, app den (NY A.D., 1st Dept) 1996 N.Y. A.D. LEXIS 8643 and app den 89 N.Y.2d 806, 654 N.Y.S.2d 716, 677 N.E.2d 288

Court properly granted defendants' summary judgment motion in action to set aside conveyance of real property under CLS Bus Corp § 909 since conveyance in question was made in usual or regular course of business actually conducted by corporation, and corporation retained valuable leasehold interest in second parcel of land of comparable size and location following conveyance in question. Posner v Post Rd. Dev. Equity, L.L.C. (1998, 2d Dept) 253 A.D.2d 866, 678 N.Y.S.2d 350

Assignment by corporation of legal claims constituting all or substantially all of its assets, to entity in which its chairman and his son had substantial financial interest, was void where it was made without approval of 3 members of 5-person board of directors, and was transaction outside scope of corporation's usual or regular course of business. Sardanis v Sumitomo Corp. (2001, 1st Dept) 282 A.D.2d 322, 723 N.Y.S.2d 466

Majority shareholder of a corporation improperly acted alone in conveying real property that constituted substantially all the corporate assets to a limited liability company without first obtaining the approval of the minority shareholders under N.Y. Bus. Corp. Law § 909 as despite the fact that all the shareholders were family members, the requirements of § 909 were mandatory based on the use of the language "shall"; strict construction of the provisions was necessary to preserve the rights of any minority shareholder who might wish to object and have their shares appraised and bought by the corporation pursuant to N.Y. Bus. Corp. Law §§ 623, 910(a)(1)(B). Bear Pond Trail v Am. Tree Co. (2009, 3d Dept) 61 App Div 3d 1195, 876 NYS2d 571.

A transfer or disposition of assets by a corporation pursuant to a plan of merger or consolidation usually required approval by two-thirds of the outstanding stock of each corporation, under the merger and consolidation provisions of the corporation laws, and a dissenting shareholder was entitled to demand payment for his stock; but this was by virtue of provisions other than § 20 of former Stock Corp. L. Re Jevons (1932) 146 Misc 434, 262 N.Y.S. 205

Sale of real estate by real estate corporation, even if such property constituted its sole asset, would not require shareholder approval since this was company's ordinary function. Tarbert Realty Co. v Manny Realty Corp. (1987) 134 Misc. 2d 607, 512 N.Y.S.2d 634

Trial court erred by denying an investor's motion for an order enjoining his cousin from selling a corporation after it found that the investor owned 60 percent of the corporation because the cousin owned less than two-thirds of the corporation's shares and he could not approve a sale. LaConti v Urban (2003, A.D., 2d Dept) 765 N.Y.S.2d 634

10. Effect of approval

An attempt to sell or transfer all or substantially all of the assets of a stock corporation, not in ordinary course of its business and without stockholder consent as required by § 20 of former Stock Corp. L., was void, not only under that section and § 15 of the former Stock Corp. L., but also as to creditors under the Debtor and Creditor Law. Re Rosenshein (1962, 1st Dept) 16 A.D.2d 537, 229 N.Y.S.2d 14; Re Valhalla Cemetery (1940, DC NY) 32 F. Supp. 616

Formal approval of the sale at a stockholders' meeting called for that purpose did not consummate the transaction, but merely authorized the proper officers of the corporation to consummate it. Delay in concluding the agreement or making the transfer following shareholder approval was usually considered as of no consequence and not affecting validity of the transaction, in the absence of evidence prejudice. Geiler v Brooklyn-Manhattan Transit Corp. (1939, Sup) 18 N.Y.S.2d 788; Re Algonquin Electric Co. (1932, CA2 NY) 61 F.2d 779

Under § 20 of former Stock Corp. L., particularly since 1954 amendment and even according to some earlier decisions, consent of two-thirds of outstanding stock to disposition of assets would validate and sustain the action of management in making the agreement for sale, or the like, or making the transfer, if it was evidenced by writing, whether or not all terms and conditions had then been fully agreed upon, and whether or not it was in the form of a resolution adopted at a stockholders' meeting. Gottfried v Gottfried Baking Co. (1956, Sup) 155 N.Y.S.2d 215, app dismd (1st Dept) 3 A.D.2d 648, 161 N.Y.S.2d 557; Gottfried v Gottfried Baking Co. (1956, 1st Dept) 1 A.D.2d 994, 151 N.Y.S.2d 583, app den (1st Dept) 2 A.D.2d 664, 153 N.Y.S.2d 544; Neponsit Holding Corp. v Ansorge (1926) 215 A.D. 371, 214 N.Y.S. 91; Mattiello v Flagg (1958) 14 Misc. 2d 597, 178 N.Y.S.2d 179; Texas Co. v Z. & M. Independent Oil Co. (1945, DC NY) 66 F. Supp. 957, affd (CA2 NY) 156 F.2d 862

It was reasoned that, if two-thirds of the outstanding stock could authorize a sale, they could likewise authorize the giving of an irrevocable option to purchase, and, in such case, their consent would not have to be obtained anew for an extension of the option. Texas Co. v Z. & M. Independent Oil Co. (1946, CA2 NY) 156 F.2d 862

11. Liability and remedies

If the statutory procedure was not followed to seek and obtain stockholder approval of a sale or similar transaction requiring it, any stockholder could institute an action to enjoin or nullify the transaction. Eisenberg v Central Zone Property Corp. (1953) 306 N.Y. 58, 115 N.E.2d 652; Cachules v 116 East 57th Street, Inc. (1953, Sup) 127 N.Y.S.2d 795; Goldfarb v Dorset Products, Inc. (1948, Sup) 82 N.Y.S.2d 42

Escrow agents pursuant to agreement for sale of corporation's assets were trustees and had duty to act for any party with beneficial interest in the trust corpus and were real parties in interest and could bring action to require purchasers to pay the unpaid balance of contract price. Oppenheim v Simon (1977, 3d Dept) 57 A.D.2d 1006, 394 N.Y.S.2d 500

Escrow agent who was not party to alleged agreement between corporation's purported president and purchasers of corporation's assets by which purchasers in return for cash payment were to be relieved of personal liability could not be liable to purchasers who claimed breach of oral agreement and sought return of the money paid. Oppenheim v Simon (1977, 3d Dept) 57 A.D.2d 1006, 394 N.Y.S.2d 500

Where the individual defendant held himself out as having the authority to make the sale, the corporate undisclosed principal would be estopped to deny his authority. Kursh v Verderame (1982, 1st Dept) 87 A.D.2d 803, 449 N.Y.S.2d 500

In mortgage foreclosure action, mortgagee was entitled to partial summary judgment dismissing counterclaim in which individual defendant sought to set aside mortgage for lack of requisite approval of board of directors and shareholders of defendant corporation, as required by CLS Bus Corp § 909, since counterclaim was asserted more than one year after mortgage was recorded and thus failed to comply with § 909(c). Chemical Bank v Colonna (1994, 2d Dept) 208 A.D.2d 583, 618 N.Y.S.2d 243

Minority shareholder who did not bring proceeding to value his shares under CLS Bus Corp § 623 could sue for money damages where corporation sold all or substantially all of its assets, sale was not made in usual or regular course of business, and corporation had failed to give shareholder proper notice under CLS Bus Corp § 909(a). Collins v Telcoa Int'l Corp. (2001, 2d Dept) 283 A.D.2d 128, 726 N.Y.S.2d 679

While a shareholder claimed an exception to the exclusivity provision in N.Y. Bus. Corp. Law § 623(k) based on a claim that he was fraudulently induced to sign a consent to a sale of the assets of first and second corporations under N.Y. Bus. Corp. Law § 909(a), the exclusivity provision did not apply to the derivative causes of action asserted by the shareholder. Kingston v Breslin (2008, 2d Dept) 56 App Div 3d 430, 866 NYS2d 778.

Another remedy available to a stockholder if the procedural requirements to obtain his approval had not been met was to seek an accounting by managing officers for the value of the property transferred. Alexander v Quality Leather Goods Corp. (1934) 150 Misc 577, 269 N.Y.S. 499

Most decisions, however, required that a stockholder's suit to nullify the transaction be a derivative action in the right of the corporation, involving reimbursement of the transferee for anything of value paid for the property. Burg v Burg Trucking Corp. (1960) 26 Misc. 2d 619, 203 N.Y.S.2d 699; November v National Exhibition Co. (1958) 10 Misc. 2d 537, 173 N.Y.S.2d 490; 5912 Corp v Fuller-Searles Corp. (1946, Sup) 65 N.Y.S.2d 563; Losie v Ken-Vic, Inc. (1943, Sup) 43 N.Y.S.2d 914, affd 266 A.D. 1045, 44 N.Y.S.2d 473

Creditors could attack the transfer if it was preferential in nature under § 15 of former Stock Corp. L. or fraudulent as to them under the provisions of the Debtor and Creditor Law or any other statute, but their attacks have usually been based on some alleged damage to their rights or status as creditors, rather than on lack of stockholder approval. See, for example, Biscayne-Gallowhur Corp. v Smith (1961) 32 Misc. 2d 304, 223 N.Y.S.2d 301, mod (1st Dept) 17 A.D.2d 930, 233 N.Y.S.2d 723, affd 14 N.Y.2d 629, 249 N.Y.S.2d 177, 198 N.E.2d 369; Hewlett Park Co. v 1193-1205 East Broadway of Hewlett, Inc. (1961) 32 Misc. 2d 691, 223 N.Y.S.2d 756, affd (1st Dept) 17 A.D.2d 736, 232 N.Y.S.2d 391

Corporate officers and directors are answerable for any damages resulting to the corporation by the sale of substantially all the corporate assets without proper authorization. Mageloff v Sarkin (1966) 52 Misc. 2d 737, 276 N.Y.S.2d 708

The purchaser, moreover, could not demand specific performance of the agreement for sale without a showing of the required stockholder approval or if it appeared that more than one-third of the vendor's shareholders had not consented or acquiesced. Rednib Realty Corp. v Greeley Square Bldg. Corp. (1952, Sup) 115 N.Y.S.2d 158

The directors of a New Jersey corporation had no duty to continue the corporation in operation or existence when in their opinion to do so would not be expedient, and the decision to sell the corporation would not be disturbed in the absence of proof of fraud or that less than the requisite two thirds majority of stockholders had voted in favor of the sale or dissolution. Richland v Crandall (1967, SD NY) 262 F. Supp. 538

In a proceeding to dissolve a corporation, when the corporation's majority shareholder sought to join the purchaser of the corporation's sole asset from a minority shareholder, the purchaser could not claim the minority shareholder had apparent authority to sell the asset because (1) an extraordinary transaction to sell substantially all the assets of a corporation required the approval of two-thirds of shareholders, and (2) such provision precluded any claim of apparent authority since those who dealt with corporations were bound by the statutory limitations on the authority of corporate officers. Matter of Shau Chung Hu v Lowbet Realty Corp. (2012, Sup) 956 NYS2d 400.

12. Defenses

A stockholder who participates in a meeting at which the sale is approved, and likewise in closing the deal, is estopped even from bringing a derivative action to set aside the conveyance on the ground of lack of required shareholder consent, her conduct being such as to amount to approval of the sale. Bradley v East Williston Shopping Center, Inc. (1961, 2d Dept) 15 A.D.2d 560, 222 N.Y.S.2d 943

In action for specific performance of real estate sales contract executed by corporate defendant's president, defendant was not estopped from asserting defense under CLS Bus Corp § 909(a), requiring that sale of all or substantially all of corporation's assets be approved by 2/3 of shareholders, since buyers were aware that property owner was corporation, sale of sole significant asset of corporation was unusual and extraordinary, and those who deal with corporations are bound by statutory limitations on authority of corporate officers. Vig v Deka Realty Corp. (1988, 2d Dept) 143 A.D.2d 185, 531 N.Y.S.2d 633, app den 73 N.Y.2d 708, 540 N.Y.S.2d 1003, 538 N.E.2d 355

Corporate officer who surreptitiously arranged assignment to himself of legal claims constituting all or substantially all of corporation's assets, in violation of CLS Bus Corp §§ 713 and 909(a), had unclean hands and was precluded from relying on equitable defenses such as estoppel. Sardanis v Sumitomo Corp. (2001, 1st Dept) 282 A.D.2d 322, 723 N.Y.S.2d 466

A sole stockholder who signs a contract for sale of corporate property is at least estopped from asserting that the sale was not approved by holders of two-thirds of its outstanding shares. Frankel v Tremont Norman Motors Corp. (1959) 21 Misc. 2d 20, 193 N.Y.S.2d 722, affd (1st Dept) 10 A.D.2d 680, 197 N.Y.S.2d 576, affd 8 N.Y.2d 901, 204 N.Y.S.2d 146, 168 N.E.2d 823

Where all stockholders participate in a transaction and approve it, and it does not appear that harm resulted to the public or to creditors, a defense of ultra vires is not available. Finke v Sil-Gold Corp. (1962) 33 Misc. 2d 1064, 227 N.Y.S.2d 582

Confession of judgment (COJ) and lease assignment were entitled to full force and effect because all of the corporate entities were closely held by two equal shareholders who agreed to and/or acquiesced in and ratified the COJ and assignment, and to permit them to utilize N.Y. Bus. Corp. Law § 909 as a sword would effect an injustice. MP Assoc. Suffolk, Inc. v Americana Petroleum Corp. (2013, Sup) 39 Misc 3d 341, 957 NYS2d 849.

Trial court properly determined that the statute of limitations contained in N.Y. Bus. Corp. Law § 909(c) did not apply to the claimant's third cause of action to cancel certain mortgages in a case where the claimant filed a shareholder's derivative action; that statute applied to actions to set aside a deed, lease, or other instrument of conveyance and a mortgage was not such a conveyance. Fischer v Sadov Realty Corp. (2006, 2d Dept) 34 App Div 3d 630, 824 NYS2d 434, subsequent app (2006, 2d Dept) 34 App Div 3d 632, 823 NYS2d 899

Minority shareholders were not estopped from relying upon the formal requirements of this section even where the dominant shareholder operated the corporation in disregard of corporate formalities for many years with the acquiescence of the minority shareholders. Bear Pond Trail v Am. Tree Co., (2009 App Div, 3d Dept) 876 NYS2d 571.

Confession of judgment (COJ) and lease assignment were entitled to full force and effect because all of the corporate entities were closely held by two equal shareholders who agreed to and/or acquiesced in and ratified the COJ and assignment, and to permit them to utilize N.Y. Bus. Corp. Law § 909 as a sword would effect an injustice. MP Assoc. Suffolk, Inc. v Americana Petroleum Corp. (2013, Sup) 39 Misc 3d 341, 957 NYS2d 849.

13. Miscellaneous

The terms of a voting trust agreement set up in connection with a corporate reorganization proceeding could be such as to give a dissenting shareholder a right to demand payment for his shares, regardless of whether he would be entitled to make such a demand under the statute. Application of Bacon (1941) 287 N.Y. 1, 38 N.E.2d 105

Court properly dismissed action seeking rescission of agreement modifying lease, which was based on alleged violations of CLS Bus Corp § 909, were documentary evidence established that party who signed lease modification was in fact sole shareholder of plaintiff corporation. Kalivia Food Corp. v Hunts Point Coop. Mkt. (1997, 2d Dept) 244 A.D.2d 460, 664 N.Y.S.2d 347

Tenant was entitled to summary judgment declaring that lease entered into 25 years earlier was valid, and that it properly exercised its option to renew thereunder, as (1) corporate owner of premises was time-barred and equitably estopped from attempting to invalidate lease, and (2) in any case, lease was validly entered into and its terms were not unconscionable at time of its making. Knutson v Tillotson (2000, 2d Dept) 270 A.D.2d 268, 704 N.Y.S.2d 118, related proceeding (App Div, 2d Dept) 722 N.Y.S.2d 763

Administrator of the estate of three professional corporations' (PCs) sole shareholder, officer, and director (SH) could not be substituted under N.Y. C.P.L.R. 1017 for the PCs in suits seeking assigned first-party benefits because: (1) the SH's administrator had not been appointed a receiver for the PCs and they had not been dissolved; (2) no one was authorized to act on behalf of the PCs; (3) the administrator could not act under N.Y. Bus. Corp. Law §§ 1507, 1508, and 1511 because the PCs were authorized to practice medicine, and the administrator was not licensed to practice medicine; and (4) the administrator could only vote the shares in the PCs for the N.Y. Bus. Corp. Law §§ 909, 1001, and 1511 purposes. Painless Med., P.C. v GEICO (2011, Civ Ct) 32 Misc 3d 715, 929 NYS2d 357.

§ 910. Right of shareholder to receive payment for shares upon merger or consolidation, or sale, lease, exchange or other disposition of assets, or share exchange

(a) A shareholder of a domestic corporation shall, subject to and by complying with section 623 (Procedure to enforce shareholder's right to receive payment for shares), have the right to receive payment of the fair value of his shares and the other rights and benefits provided by such section, in the following cases:

(1) Any shareholder entitled to vote who does not assent to the taking of an action specified in clauses (A), (B) and (C).

(A) Any plan of merger or consolidation to which the corporation is a party; except that the right to receive payment of the fair value of his shares shall not be available:

(i) To a shareholder of the parent corporation in a merger authorized by section 905 (Merger of parent and subsidiary corporations), or paragraph (c) of section 907 (Merger or consolidation of domestic and foreign corporations); or

(ii) To a shareholder of the surviving corporation in a merger authorized by this article, other than a merger specified in subclause (i), unless such merger effects one or more of the changes specified in subparagraph (b) (6) of section 806 (Provisions as to certain proceedings) in the rights of the shares held by such shareholder; or

(iii) Notwithstanding subclause (ii) of this clause, to a shareholder for the shares of any class or series of stock, which shares or depository receipts in respect thereof, at the record date fixed to determine the shareholders entitled to receive notice of the meeting of shareholders to vote upon the plan of merger or consolidation, were listed on a national securities exchange or designated as a national market system security on an interdealer quotation system by the National Association of Securities Dealers, Inc.

(B) Any sale, lease, exchange or other disposition of all or substantially all of the assets of a corporation which requires shareholder approval under section 909 (Sale, lease, exchange or other disposition of assets) other than a transaction wholly for cash where the shareholders' approval thereof is conditioned upon the dissolution of the corporation and the distribution of substantially all of its net assets to the shareholders in accordance with their respective interests within one year after the date of such transaction.

(C) Any share exchange authorized by section 913 in which the corporation is participating as a subject corporation; except that the right to receive payment of the fair value of his shares shall not be available to a shareholder whose shares have not been acquired in the exchange or to a shareholder for the shares of any class or series of stock, which shares or depository receipt in respect thereof, at the record date fixed to determine the shareholders entitled to receive notice of the meeting of shareholders to vote upon the plan of exchange, were listed on a national securities exchange or designated as a national market system security on an interdealer quotation system by the National Association of Securities Dealers, Inc.

(2) Any shareholder of the subsidiary corporation in a merger authorized by section 905 or paragraph (c) of section 907, or in a share exchange authorized by paragraph (g) of section 913, who files with the corporation a written notice of election to dissent as provided in paragraph (c) of section 623.

(3) Any shareholder, not entitled to vote with respect to a plan of merger or consolidation to which the corporation is a party, whose shares will be cancelled or exchanged in the merger or consolidation for cash or other consideration other than shares of the surviving or consolidated corporation or another corporation.

History: Add, L 1961, ch 855, eff Sept 1, 1963; amd, L 1962, ch 834, § 69, eff Sept 1, 1963; amd, L 1963, ch 689, § 18, eff Sept 1, 1963; L 1965, ch 803, § 47, eff Sept 1, 1965; L 1986, ch 117, § 4, eff Sept 1,

1986; L 1991, ch 390, § 3, eff July 15, 1991; L 1997, ch 449, § 59, eff Feb 22, 1998; L 1998, ch 17, § 12, eff Feb 19, 1998, deemed eff Feb 22, 1998.

CASE ANNOTATIONS

1. In general
2. Who may demand
3. Availability of right
4. Good faith
5. Statutory requirements
6. Remedies of dissenting holders
7. Valuation
8. Effects of approval

1. In general

The provisions of §§ 20, 21, 85, 87, and 91 of former Stock Corp. L., by amendment and sort of a process of evolution, came around to conferring approximately the same rights on dissenting minority stockholders with respect to mergers, consolidations, and bulk dispositions of assets, as does this § 910 of the Business Corp. L. All such provisions are directed to providing fair treatment for minority shareholders and preventing arbitrary "freeze-outs" of minority interests through exercise of majority control. Anderson v International Minerals & Chemical Corp. (1946) 295 N.Y. 343, 67 N.E.2d 573; Amella v Consolidated Edison Co. (1947, Sup) 73 N.Y.S.2d 263, affd 273 A.D. 755, 75 N.Y.S.2d 513; Beloff v Consolidated Edison Co. (1948, Sup) 81 N.Y.S.2d 440, affd 274 A.D. 980, 85 N.Y.S.2d 303, affd 300 N.Y. 11, 87 N.E.2d 561

Right of a disapproving minority shareholder to demand payment for his shares by reason of a disposition of corporate assets has usually been limited to instances clearly within the coverage of statutes granting such right. Borea v Locust Court Apartments, Inc. (1932) 234 A.D. 450, 255 N.Y.S. 215; Re Knaisch (1922) 203 A.D. 725, 197 N.Y.S. 116; Re Cohen (1954, Sup) 134 N.Y.S.2d 294; Petition of Avard (1955) 5 Misc. 2d 817, 144 N.Y.S.2d 204, app dismd (4th Dept) 2 A.D.2d 647, 156 N.Y.S.2d 970; Application of Harwitz (1948) 192 Misc 91, 80 N.Y.S.2d 570; Application of Woodruff (1941) 175 Misc 819, 26 N.Y.S.2d 679, affd 262 A.D. 814, 28 N.Y.S.2d 756

2. Who may demand

Ownership of stock or some interest therein as of date of seeking and obtaining shareholder approval is obviously essential to having any right to demand payment for the shares. Dynamics Corp. of America v Abraham & Co. (1956) 4 Misc. 2d 50, 152 N.Y.S.2d 807, mod as to date of public notice (1st Dept) 1 A.D.2d 1005, 153 N.Y.S.2d 533, app den (1st Dept) 2 A.D.2d 673, 153 N.Y.S.2d 554

A shareholder had no right to demand payment for his shares by instituting appraisal proceedings where failure to receive notice of a meeting called to approve a measure requiring stockholder approval was due to his lack of record ownership of the stock as of date of closing of the stock books for the meeting, without fraud or fault on the part of management. Rubel v Rubel Corp. (1960) 25 Misc. 2d 388, 206 N.Y.S.2d 396; Flagg-Utica Corp. v Baselice (1958) 14 Misc. 2d 476, 178 N.Y.S.2d 860; Dynamics Corp. of America v Abraham & Co. (1956) 4 Misc. 2d 50, 152 N.Y.S.2d 807, mod as to date of public notice (1st Dept) 1 A.D.2d 1005, 153 N.Y.S.2d 533, app den (1st Dept) 2 A.D.2d 673, 153 N.Y.S.2d 554

But record ownership of shares at the time of majority approval of a proposal for disposition of assets is not, of itself, essential to right of a beneficial owner or actual owner to demand payment for shares if proper objection was made and dissent noted by someone representing the shares in question. Re Kaufmann, Alsberg & Co. (1961) 30 Misc. 2d 1025, 220 N.Y.S.2d 151, affd (1st Dept) 15 A.D.2d 468, 222 N.Y.S.2d 305; Re Rowe (1919) 107 Misc 549, 176 N.Y.S. 753

3. Availability of right

Some decisions treat the right to demand payment for shares as dependent on consummation of the transaction, or sanction holding proceedings for appraisal of value of a dissenter's shares in abeyance for a reasonable time to permit the corporation to rescind the action to which he objects. Petition of Hake (1955) 285 A.D. 316, 136 N.Y.S.2d 817, app dismd 308 N.Y. 940, 127 N.E.2d 90; Re O'Hara (1928) 133 Misc 184, 231 N.Y.S. 60

Formation of 2 subsidiaries, both wholly owned by respondent corporation, and transfer of its camping operations and buses to subdivisions, did not fall within purview of CLS Bus Corp §§ 909 and 910 since such transactions did not result in liquidation, in whole or in part, of camp business operated by respondent, which retained ownership of corporate land and buildings; thus, respondent was entitled to summary judgment dismissing proceeding brought under CLS Bus Corp § 623(h)(2) to enforce shareholder's right to receive payment for fair value of her shares. Resnick v Karmax Camp Corp. (1989, 2d Dept) 149 A.D.2d 709, 540 N.Y.S.2d 503

Majority shareholder of a corporation improperly acted alone in conveying real property that constituted substantially all the corporate assets to a limited liability company without first obtaining the approval of the minority shareholders under N.Y. Bus. Corp. Law § 909 as despite the fact that all the shareholders were family members, the requirements of § 909 were mandatory based on the use of the language "shall"; strict construction of the provisions was necessary to preserve the rights of any minority shareholder who might wish to object and have their shares appraised and bought by the corporation pursuant to N.Y. Bus. Corp. Law §§ 623, 910(a)(1)(B). Bear Pond Trail v Am. Tree Co. (2009, 3d Dept) 61 App Div 3d 1195, 876 NYS2d 571.

The weight of authority is to the effect that a dissenting minority shareholder's right to demand payment for his shares accrues when proposal of a transaction involving disposition of assets and requiring shareholder consent is approved by the required percentage of shares, whether or not the proposed transaction is effectuated or consummated. Application of Harwitz (1948) 192 Misc 91, 80 N.Y.S.2d 570; Geiler v Brooklyn-Manhattan Transit Corp. (1939, Sup) 18 N.Y.S.2d 788

Where a summary merger of a subsidiary into the parent corporation took place under § 85 of former Stock Corp. L., by virtue of the parent corporation's ownership of 95% of the outstanding shares of the subsidiary, not requiring shareholder approval, subd. 7 of that section nevertheless gave holders of the remaining outstanding minority shares the right to demand payment for their shares and to proceed under § 21 of that law to obtain it. Re Lewis (1962) 34 Misc. 2d 180, 227 N.Y.S.2d 823, affd (1st Dept) 16 A.D.2d 772, 228 N.Y.S.2d 462

The right of appraisal under this section is not available to a holder of non-voting preferred stock with respect to a proposal to distribute shares of stock in another corporation, received in exchange for assets in a transaction not objected to by its preferred and common stockholders, on a basis more favorable to the owners of common than the holders of preferred shares. Newman v Arabol Mfg. Co. (1963) 41 Misc. 2d 184, 245 N.Y.S.2d 442

But if management takes all the required statutory steps to obtain shareholder approval, but fails to obtain approval by the required percentage of outstanding stock, there is some authority to the effect that a minority shareholder's only right is to treat the disposition of assets as invalid; that, in this situation, he is not entitled to demand payment for his shares. Cachules v 116 East 57th Street, Inc. (1953, Sup) 125 N.Y.S.2d 97

4. Good faith

Although the courts have sometimes looked into the good faith of a minority shareholder in seeking payment for his shares, it has been pointed out that sections of former Stock Corp. L. giving the right to dissent and demand to be bought out did not in any way qualify or limit such right or sanction an inquiry into the motives of a shareholder invoking the right. Re Kaufmann, Alsberg & Co. (1961) 30 Misc. 2d 1025, 220 N.Y.S.2d 151, affd (1st Dept) 15 A.D.2d 468, 222 N.Y.S.2d 305

Good faith in opposing a merger and seeking appraisal and payment for stock after the plan has been approved by the requisite amount of outstanding stock notwithstanding objections is not, at least, open to question with respect to shares purchased a considerable length of time in advance of the time for objecting. Re Kaufmann, Alsberg & Co. (1961) 30 Misc. 2d 1025, 220 N.Y.S.2d 151, affd (1st Dept) 15 A.D.2d 468, 222 N.Y.S.2d 305

5. Statutory requirements

On the other hand, it is enough to protect a statutory right to demand payment for minority shares that the holder has taken timely steps to make clear his dissent in such manner as the statute prescribes or permits. Re Timmis (1910) 200 N.Y. 177, 93 N.E. 522; Re Kaufmann, Alsberg & Co. (1961) 30 Misc. 2d 1025, 220 N.Y.S.2d 151, affd (1st Dept) 15 A.D.2d 468, 222 N.Y.S.2d 305; Flagg-Utica Corp. v Baselice (1958) 14 Misc. 2d 476, 178 N.Y.S.2d 860

Shareholders and holders of voting trust certificates who assent or advise their representatives to assent to the proposed transaction, or who fail to file written objections or dissents under statutes imposing such conditions on right to demand payment for shares, in time and manner as specified in the statute, ordinarily lose any right which they might otherwise have to demand payment or to institute proceedings for appraisal of value of their shares. Application of Bacon (1941) 287 N.Y. 1, 38 N.E.2d 105

Some decisions have indicated that delay in meeting all statutory requirements for noting dissent to a merger, consolidation, or disposition of corporate assets, as a basis for demanding payment for shares, is to some extent excusable upon a showing of practical inability to take all required steps within the statutory time limit notwithstanding due diligence, or of lack of prompt notice of the contemplated transaction under circumstances indicative of intentional deception. Re Kunin (1953) 281 A.D. 635, 121 N.Y.S.2d 220, affd 306 N.Y. 967, 120 N.E.2d 228, reh den 307 N.Y. 686, 120 N.E.2d 856; Rank Organization Ltd. v Pathe Laboratories, Inc. (1962) 33 Misc. 2d 748, 227 N.Y.S.2d 562

In a proceeding by minority stockholders to have their stock appraised and to be paid its value, petitioners' failure to make timely submission of their stock certificates to the corporation for notation of their demand as required by subd 8 of this section could be excused if the corporation was not prejudiced by the delay and at no time during the five-day period did the corporation have reason to believe that they would relinquish their right to appraisal and payment and denying them this right would deprive them of their right to payment and relegate them to status of minority stockholders in a close corporation the stock of which had no market. Sasseen v Danco Industries, Inc. (1964, 2d Dept) 20 A.D.2d 657, 246 N.Y.S.2d 440, motion to dismiss app withdrawn 14 N.Y.2d 754, 250 N.Y.S.2d 436, 199 N.E.2d 514

A shareholder failed to state a cause of action in a proceeding to determine his right to payment and to have the fair value of his shares fixed, based on his dissent to a merger plan, where the plan or merger effected no change in his rights as a shareholder in the surviving corporation. In addition, the shareholder failed to file a timely notice of election to dissent as provided in Bus Corp Law § 623 where his notice of dissent was filed more than 20 days after he had received notice from the corporation. McGowan v Grand Island Transit Corp. (1981, 4th Dept) 80 A.D.2d 731, 437 N.Y.S.2d 158

Failure to meet the statutory requirements as to time and manner of filing notice of dissent is not excusable, however, and precludes enforcement of the payment demand in the absence of unusual circumstances the impact of which could not have been avoided by due diligence. Application of Gerstle-Rhein S. A. (1949) 194 Misc 795, 87 N.Y.S.2d 778

A minority shareholder of the remaining 5% or less of outstanding stock of the subsidiary was entitled to fair treatment by management of the merging parent corporation in connection with a summary § 85 merger, so that he would have time to meet the requirements of § 21 of former Stock Corp. L. in demanding payment for his shares, if he saw fit to do so. Rank Organization Ltd. v Pathe Laboratories, Inc. (1962) 33 Misc. 2d 748, 227 N.Y.S.2d 562

Sections 623 and 910 of this law set forth a time schedule for acts to be done by a dissenting minority stockholder who wants to have the value of his stock appraised and be paid the fair value thereof, and where he fails to take such steps within at least even a reasonable time after that fixed by these sections the shareholder is not entitled to demand appraisal and payment. Application of Wiedersum (1964) 41 Misc. 2d 936, 246 N.Y.S.2d 638

6. Remedies of dissenting holders

If the procedure to obtain shareholder approval of the transfer of assets is substantially complied with, and there is no indication of fraud or deceit, a disapproving shareholder, after approval by the required majority of outstanding shares, has a right to such benefits as the terms of the deal may offer, or he can file dissent and demand payment for his shares, but he cannot do both. Anderson v International Minerals & Chemical Corp. (1946) 295 N.Y. 343, 67 N.E.2d 573

If the statutory procedure is duly followed by giving notice of a shareholders' meeting to consider and approve a merger, consolidation, or other disposition of assets not in usual course of business, a shareholder not in favor of the proposal is put to his remedy of filing objection or dissent and demanding payment for his shares, and that is his only remedy in case the proposal is approved by the required percentage of outstanding shares entitled to vote. Beloff v Consolidated Edison Co. (1949) 300 N.Y. 11, 87 N.E.2d 561; Burg v Burg Trucking Corp. (1960) 26 Misc. 2d 619, 203 N.Y.S.2d 699; Blumenthal v Roosevelt Hotel (1952) 202 Misc 988, 115 N.Y.S.2d 52; Re O'Brien (1943) 182 Misc 577, 45 N.Y.S.2d 208

If he can show fraud, deceit, or some material defect in the proceedings to obtain shareholder approval, he is, however, in a position to attack their validity and seek an injunction or nullification of the

transaction supposedly approved. Eisenberg v Central Zone Property Corp. (1953) 306 N.Y. 58, 115 N.E.2d 652; Williams v Bartell (1962) 34 Misc. 2d 552, 226 N.Y.S.2d 187, mod on other grounds (1st Dept) 16 A.D.2d 21, 225 N.Y.S.2d 351; Burg v Burg Trucking Corp. (1960) 26 Misc. 2d 619, 203 N.Y.S.2d 699

Under Bus Corp Law §§ 623(k) and 910, which give corporate shareholders dissenting from a corporate merger the right to have their shares appraised in a judicial proceeding, shareholders who exercised that right were barred from maintaining any derivative action on behalf of the merged corporation. Under Bus Corp Law § 623(k), the shareholders were not allowed to pursue an action for damages for fraud in connection with the merger absent a primary request for equitable relief. Breed v Barton (1981) 54 N.Y.2d 82, 444 N.Y.S.2d 609, 429 N.E.2d 128

In instances where a statute requires the giving of notice of a meeting and shareholder approval of a disposition of assets, failure of management to meet these requirements leaves a non-consenting and dissatisfied shareholder in a position to institute proceedings for payment of the value of his shares, or to seek an injunction against or nullification of the transaction, without any short time limitation on taking such steps. Hodes v 1299 Realty Corp. (1951) 278 A.D. 803, 104 N.Y.S.2d 206; Re Drosnes (1919) 187 A.D. 425, 175 N.Y.S. 628; Rank Organization Ltd. v Pathe Laboratories, Inc. (1962) 33 Misc. 2d 748, 227 N.Y.S.2d 562

In action by minority shareholders challenging majority shareholders' approval of extension of sublease agreement and provision granting option to subtenant to purchase leased premises, defendants were entitled to summary judgment dismissing claims for breach of fiduciary duty and fraud, as plaintiffs' sole remedy was to seek appraisal under CLS Bus Corp § 623, where complaint alleged that challenged transactions were within purview of CLS Bus Corp § 910, triggering plaintiffs' appraisal rights, and that defendants improperly failed to advise them of their appraisal rights. Norte & Co. v New York & H. R.R. (1995, 1st Dept) 222 A.D.2d 357, 635 N.Y.S.2d 629, app den (NY A.D., 1st Dept) 1996 N.Y. A.D. LEXIS 5947 and app den 88 N.Y.2d 811, 649 N.Y.S.2d 378, 672 N.E.2d 604

If he seeks a temporary injunction against holding of a stockholders' meeting to pass upon the proposal, the fact that he will be entitled to demand payment for his shares, if approval is obtained, may be weighed against his application for the injunction. Williams v Bartell (1962) 34 Misc. 2d 552, 226 N.Y.S.2d 187, mod on other grounds (1st Dept) 16 A.D.2d 21, 225 N.Y.S.2d 351

Upon the filing of a Certificate of Consolidation with the Secretary of State, objecting stockholders have no interest other than to receive payment of the fair value of their stock. Hilton Hotels Corp. v United States (1969, CA7 Ill) 410 F.2d 194, 69-1 USTC ¶ 9336, revd on other grounds 397 US 580, 25 L Ed 2d 585, 90 S Ct 1307, 70-1 USTC ¶ 9349

7. Valuation

In appraising the stock of a dissenting stockholder, market value is of very little significance where the trading is so limited that it can hardly be said to reflect judgment of informed buyers and sellers. Re Tudor City Fifth Unit, Inc. (1962, 1st Dept) 17 A.D.2d 794, 232 N.Y.S.2d 758, app dismd 12 N.Y.2d 993, 239 N.Y.S.2d 121, 189 N.E.2d 618, affd 13 N.Y.S.2d 812, 242 N.Y.S.2d 345, 192 N.E.2d 222

In appraising the value of stock held by a dissenting stockholder in a real estate corporation, the net asset value is entitled to maximum weight. Re Tudor City Fifth Unit, Inc. (1962, 1st Dept) 17 A.D.2d 794, 232 N.Y.S.2d 758, app dismd 12 N.Y.2d 993, 239 N.Y.S.2d 121, 189 N.E.2d 618, affd 13 N.Y.2d 812, 242 N.Y.S.2d 345, 192 N.E.2d 222

Investment value of stock held by a dissenting stockholder, reflecting such factors as capitalization, earnings and dividend record, position in the industry and prospects of the business and industry with over-all value of securities in relation to general market conditions should be given some weight, but in the case of a real estate corporation, not nearly as much as in the case of an industrial or commercial concern, and giving this factor a weight of 55% was considered too high. Re Tudor City Fifth Unit, Inc. (1962, 1st Dept) 17 A.D.2d 794, 232 N.Y.S.2d 758, app dismd 12 N.Y.2d 993, 239 N.Y.S.2d 121, 189 N.E.2d 618, affd 13 N.Y.2d 812, 242 N.Y.S.2d 345, 192 N.E.2d 222

The weight to be accorded market value, investment value, and net asset value in proceedings for appraisal of dissenting stockholders' stock varies in accordance with the facts, but all factors relevant on actual value should be taken into consideration. Re Tudor City Fifth Unit, Inc. (1962, 1st Dept) 17 A.D.2d 794, 232 N.Y.S.2d 758, app dismd 12 N.Y.2d 993, 239 N.Y.S.2d 121, 189 N.E.2d 618, affd without op 13 N.Y.2d 812, 242 N.Y.S.2d 345, 192 N.E.2d 222

Provisions requiring appraisal and payment of the value of stock held by non-consenting stockholders, however, should be construed to the end of not depriving them of contemplated benefits. Re Kaufmann, Alsberg & Co. (1961) 30 Misc. 2d 1025, 220 N.Y.S.2d 151, affd (1st Dept) 15 A.D.2d 468, 222 N.Y.S.2d 305

Stipulation of settlement of representative dissenting stockholders action to enjoin sale of corporate assets, which provided stockholders an option of liquidating their stock at a price in keeping with appraisals submitted by the corporation or exchanging them for stocks in purchasing corporation with an option to sell within a certain period for a price greater than the appraised value was fair, reasonable and adequate. Blumenthal v Roosevelt Hotel, Inc. (1952, Sup) 116 N.Y.S.2d 94

8. Effects of approval

A shareholder who exchanges his shares for new ones as authorized by a plan of merger or consolidation accedes to all terms and conditions of the plan and cannot demand additional rights, such as payment of dividends which had accrued on his former shares. Anderson v International Minerals & Chemical Corp. (1946) 295 N.Y. 343, 67 N.E.2d 573

Failure to carry out the agreement as approved or to fully perform it gives an approving shareholder no standing to reverse his position and seek payment for his shares. Roehner v Gracie Manor, Inc. (1959) 6 N.Y.2d 280, 189 N.Y.S.2d 644, 160 N.E.2d 519

See also Amella v Consolidated Edison Co. (1947, Sup) 73 N.Y.S.2d 263, affd 273 A.D. 755, 75 N.Y.S.2d 513; Tanenbaum v Consolidated Edison Co. (1947, Sup) 72 N.Y.S.2d 493

A shareholder who accedes to or who expressly or impliedly approves or consents to the plan or transaction has no standing to complain of it, in the absence of fraud, cannot attack it for lack of approval by other shareholders, or maintain a derivative action on the ground of waste or mismanagement, and even dissenting shareholders are in the same predicament once they have been paid the value of their shares. Beloff v Consolidated Edison Co. (1948, Sup) 81 N.Y.S.2d 440, affd 274 A.D. 980, 85 N.Y.S.2d 303, affd 300 N.Y. 11, 87 N.E.2d 561

§ 911.   Mortgage or pledge of, or security interest in, corporate property

The board may authorize any mortgage or pledge of, or the creation of a security interest in, all or any part of the corporate property, or any interest therein, wherever situated. Unless the certificate of incorporation provides otherwise, no vote or consent of shareholders shall be required to approve such action by the board.

History: Add, L 1961, ch 855, amd, L 1962, ch 552, L 1963, ch 689, § 19, eff Sept 1, 1963, ch 749, eff Sept 1, 1963, L 1965, ch 803, § 48, eff Sept 1, 1965.

Section heading, amd, L 1963, ch 689, § 19, eff Sept 1, 1963.

CASE ANNOTATIONS

Corporate board of directors had power to authorize mortgage since certificate of incorporation did not restrict such power, notwithstanding that there was clause in bylaws which restricted corporate action without majority vote of shareholders. Chiulli v Reiter (1991, 2d Dept) 173 A.D.2d 672, 570 N.Y.S.2d 820

Court erred in granting defendant corporations' motions for summary judgment dismissing action seeking enforcement of security interest, on ground that corporations' boards of directors failed to approve security agreements, since fact issues existed as to propriety of execution of security agreements on corporations' behalf; permissive language of CLS Bus Corp § 911 does not pose absolute bar to creation of security interests without board approval. Saleh v Saleh (1997, 1st Dept) 239 A.D.2d 165, 657 N.Y.S.2d 52

Even under § 16 of former Stock Corp. L., which required two-thirds stockholder approval of corporate mortgages, where two-thirds of the shareholders either took an active part in authorizing the mortgage or clearly acquiesced in the transaction, they were estopped

to attack its validity. Re Endicott Laundry Co. (1926) 128 Misc 413, 219 N.Y.S. 632

Mortgage is not conveyance within boundaries of CLS Bus Corp § 909, and legislative intent was that statute would not apply to mortgages. Rols Capital Co. v Panvaspan Realties, Inc. (1993, Sup) 157 Misc. 2d 449, 597 N.Y.S.2d 266

It has been held that stockholders who join in voting approval of a chattel mortgage to be given by the corporation on property held by it under conditional sale contract are not liable personally to the conditional vendor for its conversion, as their act does not constitute the conversion, but rather the resolution of the directors directing execution of the mortgage. Aeroglide Corp. v Zeh (1962, CA2 NY) 301 F.2d 420, cert den 371 US 822, 9 L Ed 2d 61, 83 S Ct 38

§ 912.   Requirements relating to certain business combinations

(a) For the purposes of this section:

(1) "Affiliate" means a person that directly, or indirectly through one or more intermediaries, controls, or is controlled by, or is under common control with, a specified person.

(2) "Announcement date", when used in reference to any business combination, means the date of the first public announcement of the final, definitive proposal for such business combination.

(3) "Associate", when used to indicate a relationship with any person, means (A) any corporation or organization of which such person is an officer or partner or is, directly or indirectly, the beneficial owner of ten percent or more of any class of voting stock, (B) any trust or other estate in which such person has a substantial beneficial interest or as to which such person serves as trustee or in a similar fiduciary capacity, and (C) any relative or spouse of such person, or any relative of such spouse, who has the same home as such person.

(4) "Beneficial owner", when used with respect to any stock, means a person:

(A) that, individually or with or through any of its affiliates or associates, beneficially owns such stock, directly or indirectly; or

(B) that, individually or with or through any of its affiliates or associates, has (i) the right to acquire such stock (whether such right is exercisable immediately or only after the passage of time), pursuant to any agreement, arrangement or understanding (whether or not in writing), or upon the exercise of conversion rights, exchange rights, warrants or options, or otherwise; provided, however, that a person shall not be deemed the beneficial owner of stock tendered pursuant to a tender or exchange offer made by such person or any of such person's affiliates or associates until such tendered stock is accepted for purchase or exchange; or (ii) the right to vote such stock pursuant to any agreement, arrangement or understanding (whether or not in writing); provided, however, that a person shall not be deemed the beneficial owner of any stock under this item if the agreement, arrangement or understanding to vote such stock (X) arises solely from a revocable proxy or consent given in response to a proxy or consent solicitation made in accordance with the applicable rules and regulations under the Exchange Act and (Y)

Business Corporation Law

is not then reportable on a Schedule 13D under the Exchange Act (or any comparable or successor report); or

(C) that has any agreement, arrangement or understanding (whether or not in writing), for the purpose of acquiring, holding, voting (except voting pursuant to a revocable proxy or consent as described in item (ii) of clause (B) of this subparagraph), or disposing of such stock with any other person that beneficially owns, or whose affiliates or associates beneficially own, directly or indirectly, such stock.

(5) "Business combination", when used in reference to any domestic corporation and any interested shareholder of such corporation, means:

(A) any merger or consolidation of such corporation or any subsidiary of such corporation with (i) such interested shareholder or (ii) any other corporation (whether or not itself an interested shareholder of such corporation) which is, or after such merger or consolidation would be, an affiliate or associate of such interested shareholder;

(B) any sale, lease, exchange, mortgage, pledge, transfer or other disposition (in one transaction or a series of transactions) to or with such interested shareholder or any affiliate or associate of such interested shareholder of assets of such corporation or any subsidiary of such corporation (i) having an aggregate market value equal to ten percent or more of the aggregate market value of all the assets, determined on a consolidated basis, of such corporation, (ii) having an aggregate market value equal to ten percent or more of the aggregate market value of all the outstanding stock of such corporation, or (iii) representing ten percent or more of the earning power or net income determined on a consolidated basis, of such corporation;

(C) the issuance or transfer by such corporation or any subsidiary of such corporation (in one transaction or a series of transactions) of any stock of such corporation or any subsidiary of such corporation which has an aggregate market value equal to five percent or more of the aggregate market value of all the outstanding stock of such corporation to such interested shareholder or any affiliate or associate of such interested shareholder except pursuant to the exercise of warrants or rights to purchase stock offered, or a dividend or distribution paid or made, pro rata to all shareholders of such corporation;

(D) the adoption of any plan or proposal for the liquidation or dissolution of such corporation proposed by, or pursuant to any agreement, arrangement or understanding (whether or not in writing) with, such interested shareholder or any affiliate or associate of such interested shareholder;

(E) any reclassification of securities (including, without limitation, any stock split, stock dividend, or other distribution of stock in respect of stock, or any reverse stock split), or recapitalization of such corporation, or any merger or consolidation of such corporation with any subsidiary of such corporation, or any

other transaction (whether or not with or into or otherwise involving such interested shareholder), proposed by, or pursuant to any agreement, arrangement or understanding (whether or not in writing) with, such interested shareholder or any affiliate or associate of such interested shareholder, which has the effect, directly or indirectly, of increasing the proportionate share of the outstanding shares of any class or series of voting stock or securities convertible into voting stock of such corporation or any subsidiary of such corporation which is directly or indirectly owned by such interested shareholder or any affiliate or associate of such interested shareholder, except as a result of immaterial changes due to fractional share adjustments; or

(F) any receipt by such interested shareholder or any affiliate or associate of such interested shareholder of the benefit, directly or indirectly (except proportionately as a shareholder of such corporation) of any loans, advances, guarantees, pledges or other financial assistance or any tax credits or other tax advantages provided by or through such corporation.

(6) "Common stock" means any stock other than preferred stock.

(7) "Consummation date", with respect to any business combination, means the date of consummation of such business combination, or, in the case of a business combination as to which a shareholder vote is taken, the later of the business day prior to the vote or twenty days prior to the date of consummation of such business combination.

(8) "Control", including the terms "controlling", "controlled by" and "under common control with", means the possession, directly or indirectly, of the power to direct or cause the direction of the management and policies of a person, whether through the ownership of voting stock, by contract, or otherwise. A person's beneficial ownership of ten percent or more of a corporation's outstanding voting stock shall create a presumption that such person has control of such corporation. Notwithstanding the foregoing, a person shall not be deemed to have control of a corporation if such person holds voting stock, in good faith and not for the the the purpose of circumventing this section, as an agent, bank, broker, nominee, custodian or trustee for one or more beneficial owners who do not individually or as a group have control of such corporation.

(9) "Exchange Act" means the Act of Congress known as the Securities Exchange Act of 1934, as the same has been or hereafter may be amended from time to time.

(10) "Interested shareholder", when used in reference to any domestic corporation, means any person (other than such corporation or any subsidiary of such corporation) that

(A) (i) is the beneficial owner, directly or indirectly, of twenty percent or more of the outstanding voting stock of such corporation; or

(ii) is an affiliate or associate of such corporation and at any time within the five-year period immediately prior to the date in question was the beneficial owner, directly or indirectly, of twenty percent or more of the then outstanding voting stock of such corporation; provided that

(B) for the purpose of determining whether a person is an interested shareholder, the number of shares of voting stock of such corporation deemed to be outstanding shall include shares deemed to be beneficially owned by the person through application of subparagraph four of this paragraph but shall not include any other unissued shares of voting stock of such corporation which may be issuable pursuant to any agreement, arrangement or understanding, or upon exercise of conversion rights, warrants or options, or otherwise.

(11) "Market value", when used in reference to stock or property of any domestic corporation, means:

(A) in the case of stock, the highest closing sale price during the thirty-day period immediately preceding the date in question of a share of such stock on the composite tape for New York stock exchange-listed stocks, or, if such stock is not quoted on such composite tape or if such stock is not listed on such exchange, on the principal United States securities exchange registered under the Exchange Act on which such stock is listed, or, if such stock is not listed on any such exchange, the highest closing bid quotation with respect to a share of such stock during the thirty-day period preceding the date in question on the National Association of Securities Dealers, Inc. Automated Quotations System or any system then in use, or if no such quotations are available, the fair market value on the date in question of a share of such stock as determined by the board of directors of such corporation in good faith; and

(B) in the case of property other than cash or stock, the fair market value of such property on the date in question as determined by the board of directors of such corporation in good faith.

(12) "Preferred stock" means any class or series of stock of a domestic corporation which under the by-laws or certificate of incorporation of such corporation is entitled to receive payment of dividends prior to any payment of dividends on some other class or series of stock, or is entitled in the event of any voluntary liquidation, dissolution or winding up of the corporation to receive payment or distribution of a preferential amount before any payments or distributions are received by some other class or series of stock.

(13) [Repealed]

(14) "Stock" means:

(A) any stock or similar security, any certificate of interest, any participation in any profit sharing agreement, any voting trust certificate, or any certificate of deposit for stock; and

(B) any security convertible, with or without consideration, into stock, or any warrant, call or other option or privilege of buying stock without being bound to do so, or any other security carrying any right to acquire, subscribe to or purchase stock.

(15) "Stock acquisition date", with respect to any person and any domestic corporation, means the date that such person first becomes an interested shareholder of such corporation.

(16) "Subsidiary" of any person means any other corporation of which a majority of the voting stock is owned, directly or indirectly, by such person.

(17) "Voting stock" means shares of capital stock of a corporation entitled to vote generally in the election of directors.

(b) Notwithstanding anything to the contrary contained in this chapter (except the provisions of paragraph (d) of this section), no domestic corporation shall engage in any business combination with any interested shareholder of such corporation for a period of five years following such interested shareholder's stock acquisition date unless such business combination or the purchase of stock made by such interested shareholder on such interested shareholder's stock acquisition date is approved by the board of directors of such corporation prior to such interested shareholder's stock acquisition date. If a good faith proposal is made in writing to the board of directors of such corporation regarding a business combination, the board of directors shall respond, in writing, within thirty days or such shorter period, if any, as may be required by the Exchange Act, setting forth its reasons for its decision regarding such proposal. If a good faith proposal to purchase stock is made in writing to the board of directors of such corporation, the board of directors, unless it responds affirmatively in writing within thirty days or such shorter period, if any, as may be required by the Exchange Act, shall be deemed to have disapproved such stock purchase.

(c) Notwithstanding anything to the contrary contained in this chapter (except the provisions of paragraphs (b) and (d) of this section), no domestic corporation shall engage at any time in any business combination with any interested shareholder of such corporation other than a business combination specified in any one of subparagraph (1), (2) or (3):

(1) A business combination approved by the board of directors of such corporation prior to such interested shareholder's stock acquisition date, or where the purchase of stock made by such interested shareholder on such interested shareholder's stock acquisition date had been approved by the board of directors of such corporation prior to such interested shareholder's stock acquisition date.

(2) A business combination approved by the affirmative vote of the holders of a majority of the outstanding voting stock not beneficially owned by such interested shareholder or any affiliate or associate of such interested shareholder at a meeting called

for such purpose no earlier than five years after such interested shareholder's stock acquisition date.

(3) A business combination that meets all of the following conditions:

(A) The aggregate amount of the cash and the market value as of the consummation date of consideration other than cash to be received per share by holders of outstanding shares of common stock of such corporation in such business combination is at least equal to the higher of the following:

(i) the highest per share price paid by such interested shareholder at a time when he was the beneficial owner, directly or indirectly, of five percent or more of the outstanding voting stock of such corporation, for any shares of common stock of the same class or series acquired by it (X) within the five-year period immediately prior to the announcement date with respect to such business combination, or (Y) within the five-year period immediately prior to, or in, the transaction in which such interested shareholder became an interested shareholder, whichever is higher; plus, in either case, interest compounded annually from the earliest date on which such highest per share acquisition price was paid through the consummation date at the rate for one-year United States treasury obligations from time to time in effect; less the aggregate amount of any cash dividends paid, and the market value of any dividends paid other than in cash, per share of common stock since such earliest date, up to the amount of such interest; and

(ii) the market value per share of common stock on the announcement date with respect to such business combination or on such interested shareholder's stock acquisition date, whichever is higher; plus interest compounded annually from such date through the consummation date at the rate for one-year United States treasury obligations from time to time in effect; less the aggregate amount of any cash dividends paid, and the market value of any dividends paid other than in cash, per share of common stock since such date, up to the amount of such interest.

(B) The aggregate amount of the cash and the market value as of the consummation date of consideration other than cash to be received per share by holders of outstanding shares of any class or series of stock, other than common stock, of such corporation is at least equal to the highest of the following (whether or not such interested shareholder has previously acquired any shares of such class or series of stock):

(i) the highest per share price paid by such interested shareholder at a time when he was the beneficial owner, directly or indirectly, of five percent or more of the outstanding voting stock of such corporation, for any shares of such class or series of stock acquired by it (X) within the five-year period immediately prior to the announcement date with respect to such business combination, or (Y) within the five-year period immediately prior to, or in, the transaction in which such interested shareholder became an interested shareholder, whichever is higher; plus, in either case, interest compounded annually from the earliest date on which such highest per share acquisition price was paid through the consummation date at the rate for one-year United States treasury obligations from time to time in effect; less the aggregate amount of any cash dividends paid, and the market value of any dividends paid other than in cash, per share of such class or series of stock since such earliest date, up to the amount of such interest;

(ii) the highest preferential amount per share to which the holders of shares of such class or series of stock are entitled in the event of any voluntary liquidation, dissolution or winding up of such corporation, plus the aggregate amount of any dividends declared or due as to which such holders are entitled prior to payment of dividends on some other class or series of stock (unless the aggregate amount of such dividends is included in such preferential amount); and

(iii) the market value per share of such class or series of stock on the announcement date with respect to such business combination or on such interested shareholder's stock acquisition date, whichever is higher; plus interest compounded annually from such date through the consummation date at the rate for one-year United States treasury obligations from time to time in effect; less the aggregate amount of any cash dividends paid, and the market value of any dividends paid other than in cash, per share of such class or series of stock since such date, up to the amount of such interest.

(C) The consideration to be received by holders of a particular class or series of outstanding stock (including common stock) of such corporation in such business combination is in cash or in the same form as the interested shareholder has used to acquire the largest number of shares of such class or series of stock previously acquired by it, and such consideration shall be distributed promptly.

(D) The holders of all outstanding shares of stock of such corporation not beneficially owned by such interested shareholder immediately prior to the consummation of such business combination are entitled to receive in such business combination cash or other consideration for such shares in compliance with clauses (A), (B) and (C) of this subparagraph.

(E) After such interested shareholder's stock acquisition date and prior to the consummation date with respect to such business combination, such interested shareholder has not become the beneficial owner of any additional shares of voting stock of such corporation except:

(i) as part of the transaction which resulted in such interested shareholder becoming an interested shareholder;

(ii) by virtue of proportionate stock splits, stock dividends or other distributions of stock in respect of stock not constituting a business combination under clause (E) of subparagraph five of paragraph (a) of this section;

(iii) through a business combination meeting all of the conditions of paragraph (b) of this section and this paragraph; or

(iv) through purchase by such interested shareholder at any price which, if such price had been paid in an otherwise permissible business combination the announcement date and consummation date of which were the date of such purchase, would have satisfied the requirements of clauses (A), (B) and (C) of this subparagraph.

(d) The provisions of this section shall not apply:

(1) to any business combination of a domestic corporation that does not have a class of voting stock registered with the Securities and Exchange Commission pursuant to section twelve of the Exchange Act, unless the certificate of incorporation provides otherwise; or

(2) to any business combination of a domestic corporation whose certificate of incorporation has been amended to provide that such corporation shall be subject to the provisions of this section, which did not have a class of voting stock registered with the Securities and Exchange Commission pursuant to section twelve of the Exchange Act on the effective date of such amendment, and which is a business combination with an interested shareholder whose stock acquisition date is prior to the effective date of such amendment; or

(3) to any business combination of a domestic corporation (i) the original certificate of incorporation of which contains a provision expressly electing not to be governed by this section, or (ii) which adopts an amendment to such corporation's by-laws prior to March thirty-first, nineteen hundred eighty-six, expressly electing not to be governed by this section, or (iii) which adopts an amendment to such corporation's by-laws, approved by the affirmative vote of a majority of votes of the outstanding voting stock of such corporation, excluding the voting stock of interested shareholders and their affiliates and associates, expressly electing not to be governed by this section, provided that such amendment to the by-laws shall not be effective until eighteen months after such vote of such corporation's shareholders and shall not apply to any business combination of such corporation with an interested shareholder whose stock acquisition date is on or prior to the effective date of such amendment; or

(4) to any business combination of a domestic corporation with an interested shareholder of such corporation which became an interested shareholder inadvertently, if such interested shareholder (i) as soon as practicable, divests itself of a sufficient amount of the voting stock of such corporation so that it no longer is the beneficial owner, directly or indirectly, of twenty percent or more of the outstanding voting stock of such corporation, and (ii) would not at any time within the five-year period preceding the announcement date with respect to such business combination have been an interested shareholder but for such inadvertent acquisition; or

(5) to any business combination with an interested shareholder who was the beneficial owner, directly or indirectly, of five percent or more of the outstanding voting stock of such corporation on October thirtieth, nineteen hundred eighty-five, and remained so to such interested shareholder's stock acquisition date.

History: Add, L 1985, ch 915, § 2, eff Dec 16, 1985; amd, L 1988, ch 704, § 1, eff Sept 2, 1988; L 1996, ch 404, § 3-9, eff Jan 26, 1997; L 1997, ch 449, § 60, eff Feb 22, 1998.

CASE ANNOTATIONS

In action by shareholder of defendant banking corporation for judgment declaring that defendant's plan to acquire another banking corporation constituted de facto merger and thus required approval by 2/3 of defendant's shareholders pursuant to CLS Bus Corp § 903, plaintiff was not entitled to summary judgment or preliminary injunction preventing defendant from implementing plan based on CLS Bus Corp § 912, which would prevent merger for 5 years after date of acquisition without approval of other corporation's board of directors, since defendant planned to purchase other corporation's stock, not its assets, and did not intend to immediately dissolve business of other corporation or assume its debts and obligations; while merger might occur in future, instant transaction was not merger but acquisition of subsidiary. Irving Bank Corp. v Bank of New York Co. (1988) 140 Misc. 2d 363, 530 N.Y.S.2d 757

Plaintiff, corporation attempting hostile takeover of another corporation, did not demonstrate eminent threat of harm sufficient to warrant preliminary injunctive relief against application of New York Anti-Takeover Law (CLS Bus Corp § 912) where plaintiff controlled only 8.3 percent of stock and no provisions of statute apply until plaintiffs acquire 20 percent of target's shares. Salant Acquisition Corp. v Manhattan Industries, Inc. (1988, SD NY) 682 F. Supp. 199, CCH Fed Secur L Rep ¶ 93673

Express election by a corporation to waive the New York Business Corporation Law's (BCL) statutory scheme will be found where an amendment to a corporation's by-laws or articles of incorporation unambiguously demonstrates the corporation's intention to waive its protections under BCL, not just where the resolution adopting the amendment states that it expressly elects not to be governed by N.Y. Bus. Corp. Law § 912. Vassell v Reliance Sec. Group (2004, SD NY) 328 F. Supp. 2d 454

Corporation "opted out" of N.Y. Bus. Corp. Law § 912 by amending its certificate of incorporation to create a comprehensive anti-takeover regime; even though the language of the amendment did not explicitly say that the corporation was waiving N.Y. Bus. Corp. Law § 912, it nonetheless clearly evinced an intention to supercede it. Vassell v Reliance Sec. Group (2004, SD NY) 328 F. Supp. 2d 454

§ 913. Share exchanges

(a) (1) Two domestic corporations may, as provided in this section, participate in the consummation of a plan for binding share exchanges.

(2) Whenever used in this article:

(A) "Acquiring corporation" means a corporation that is participating in a procedure pursuant to which such corporation is acquiring all of the outstanding shares of one or more classes of a subject corporation.

(B) "Subject corporation" means a corporation that is participating in a procedure pursuant to which all of the outstanding shares of one or more classes of such corporation are being acquired by an acquiring corporation.

(b) The board of the acquiring corporation and the board of the subject corporation shall adopt a plan of exchange, setting forth:

(1) The name of the acquiring corporation and the name of the subject corporation, and, if the name of either of them has been changed, the name under which it was formed;

(2) As to the acquiring corporation and the subject corporation, the designation and number of outstanding shares of each class and series, specifying the classes and series entitled to vote and further specifying each class and series, if any, entitled to vote as a class; and, if the number of any such shares is subject to change prior to the effective date of the exchange, the manner in which such change may occur;

(3) The terms and conditions of the proposed exchange, including the manner and basis of exchanging the shares to be acquired for shares, bonds or other securities of the acquiring corporation, or the cash or other consideration to be paid or delivered in exchange for such shares to be acquired, or a combination thereof; and

(4) Such other provisions with respect to the proposed exchange as the board considers necessary or desirable.

(c) The board of the subject corporation, upon adopting the plan of exchange, shall submit such plan, except as provided in paragraph (g) of this section, to a vote of shareholders in accordance with the following:

(1) Notice of meeting shall be given to each shareholder of record, as of the record date fixed pursuant to section 604 (Fixing record date), whether or not entitled to vote. A copy of the plan of exchange or an outline of the material features of the plan shall accompany such notice.

(2) (A) The plan of exchange shall be adopted at a meeting of shareholders by (i) for any corporation in existence on the effective date of subclause (ii) of this clause, two-thirds of the votes of all outstanding shares entitled to vote thereon and (ii) for any corporation in existence on the effective date of this subclause the certificate of incorporation of which expressly provides such and for any corporation incorporated after the effective date of this subclause, a majority of the votes of all outstanding shares entitled to vote thereon. Notwithstanding any provision in the certificate of incorporation, the holders of shares of a class or series of a class shall be entitled to vote together and to vote as a separate class if both of the following conditions are satisfied:

1. Such shares will be converted into shares of the acquiring corporation, and

2. The certificate or articles of incorporation of the acquiring corporation immediately after the share exchange would contain any provision which is not contained in the certificate of incorporation of the subject corporation and which, if contained in an amendment to the certificate of incorporation of the subject corporation, would entitle the holders of shares of such class or such one or more series to vote and to vote as a separate class thereon pursuant to section 804 (Class voting on amendment).

In such case, in addition to the authorization of the exchange by the proportion of votes indicated above of all outstanding shares entitled to vote thereon, the exchange shall be authorized by a majority of the votes of all outstanding shares of the class entitled to vote as a separate class. If any provision referred to in subclause 2 of this clause (A) would affect the rights of the holders of shares of only one or more series of any class but not the entire class, then only the holders of those series whose rights would be affected shall together be considered a separate class for purposes of this section.

Notwithstanding shareholder authorization and at any time prior to the filing of the certificate of exchange, the plan of exchange may be abandoned pursuant to a provision for such abandonment, if any, contained in the plan of exchange.

(B) Any corporation may adopt an amendment of the certificate of incorporation which provides that such plan of exchange shall be adopted at a meeting of the shareholders by vote of a specified proportion of the holders of outstanding shares, or class or series of shares, entitled to vote thereon, provided that such proportion may not be less than a majority and subject to the second sentence of clause (A) of this subparagraph (2).

(d) After adoption of the plan of exchange by the board of the acquiring corporation and the board of the subject corporation and by the shareholders of the subject corporation entitled to vote thereon, unless the exchange is abandoned in accordance with paragraph (c), a certificate of exchange, entitled "Certificate of exchange of shares of ...., subject corporation, for shares of ...., acquiring corporation, or other consideration, under section 913 of the Business Corporation Law", shall be signed on behalf of each corporation and delivered to the department of state. It shall set forth:

(1) the statements required by subparagraphs (1) and (2) of paragraph (b) of this section;

(2) the effective date of the exchange if other than the date of filing of the certificate of exchange by the department of state;

(3) the date when the certificate of incorporation of each corporation was filed by the department of state;

(4) the designation of the shares to be acquired by the acquiring corporation and a statement of the consideration for such shares; and

(5) the manner in which the exchange was authorized with respect to each corporation.

(e) Upon the filing of the certificate of exchange by the department of state or on such date subsequent thereto, not to exceed thirty days, as shall be set forth in such certificate, the exchange shall be effected. When such exchange has been effected, ownership of the shares to be acquired pursuant to the plan of exchange shall vest in the acquiring corporation, whether or not the certificates for such shares have been surrendered for exchange, and the acquiring corporation shall be entitled to have new certificates registered in its name or at its direction. Shareholders whose shares have been so acquired shall become entitled to the shares, bonds or other securities of the acquiring corporation, or the cash or other consideration, required to be paid or delivered in exchange for such shares pursuant to the plan. Subject to any terms of the plan regarding surrender of certificates theretofore evidencing the shares so acquired and regarding whether such certificates shall thereafter evidence securities of the acquiring corporation, such certificates shall thereafter evidence only the right to receive the consideration required to be paid or delivered in exchange for such shares pursuant to the plan or, in the case of dissenting shareholders, their rights under section 910 (Right of shareholder to receive payment for shares upon merger or consolidation, or sale, lease, exchange or other disposition of assets, or share exchange) and section 623 (Procedure to enforce shareholder's right to receive payment for shares).

(f) (1) A foreign corporation and a domestic corporation may participate in a share exchange, but, if the subject corporation is a foreign corporation, only if such exchange is permitted by the laws of the jurisdiction under which such foreign corporation is incorporated. With respect to such exchange, any reference in subparagraph (2) of paragraph (a) of this section to a corporation shall, unless the context otherwise requires, include both domestic and foreign corporations, and the provisions of paragraphs (b), (c), (d) and (e) of this section shall apply, except to the extent otherwise provided in this paragraph.

(2) With respect to procedure, including the requirement of shareholder authorization, a domestic corporation shall comply with the provisions of this chapter relating to share exchanges in which domestic corporations are participating, and a foreign corporation shall comply with the applicable provisions of the law of the jurisdiction under which it is incorporated.

(3) If the subject corporation is a foreign corporation, the certificate of exchange shall set forth, in addition to the matters specified in paragraph (d), the jurisdiction and date of incorporation of such corporation and a statement that the exchange is permitted by the laws of the jurisdiction of such corporation and is in compliance therewith.

(g) (1) Any corporation owning at least ninety percent of the outstanding common shares, having full voting rights, of another corporation may acquire by exchange the remainder of such outstanding common shares, without the authorization of the shareholders of any such corporation and with the

effect provided for in paragraph (e) of this section. The board of the acquiring corporation shall adopt a plan of exchange, setting forth the matters specified in paragraph (b) of this section. A copy of such plan of exchange or an outline of the material features thereof shall be given, personally or by mail, to all holders of shares of the subject corporation that are not owned by the acquiring corporation, unless the giving of such copy or outline has been waived by such holders.

(2) A certificate of exchange, entitled "Certificate of exchange of shares of....., subject corporation, for shares of....., acquiring corporation, or other consideration, under paragraph (g) of section 913 of the Business Corporation Law" and complying with the provisions of paragraph (d) and, if applicable, subparagraph (3) of paragraph (f) shall be signed, verified and delivered to the department of state by the acquiring corporation, but not less than thirty days after the giving of a copy or outline of the material features of the plan of exchange to shareholders of the subject corporation, or at any time after the waiving thereof by the holders of all the outstanding shares of the subject corporation not owned by the acquiring corporation.

(3) The right of exchange of shares granted by this paragraph to certain corporations shall not preclude the exercise by such corporations of any other right of exchange under this article.

(4) The procedure for the exchange of shares of a subject corporation under this paragraph (g) of this section shall be available where either the subject corporation or the acquiring corporation is a foreign corporation, and, in case the subject corporation is a foreign corporation, where such exchange is permitted by the laws of the jurisdiction under which such foreign corporation is incorporated.

(h) This section does not limit the power of a domestic or foreign corporation to acquire all or part of the shares of one or more classes of another domestic or foreign corporation by means of a voluntary exchange or otherwise.

(i) (1) A binding share exchange pursuant to this section shall constitute a "business combination" pursuant to section nine hundred twelve of this chapter (Requirements relating to certain business combinations) if the subject corporation is a domestic corporation and the acquiring corporation is an "interested shareholder" of the subject corporation, as such term is defined in section nine hundred twelve of this chapter.

(2) With respect to convertible securities and other securities evidencing a right to acquire shares of a subject corporation, a binding share exchange pursuant to this section shall have the same effect on the rights of the holders of such securities as a merger of the subject corporation.

(3) A binding share exchange pursuant to this section which is effectuated on or after September first, nineteen hundred ninety-one is intended to have

the same effect as a "merger" in which the subject corporation is a surviving corporation, within the meaning of any provision of the certificate of incorporation, bylaws or other contract or instrument by which the subject corporation was bound on September first, nineteen hundred eighty-six, unless it is apparent on the face of such instrument that the term "merger" was not intended to include a binding share exchange.

History: Add, L 1986, ch 117, § 1, eff Sept 1, 1986; amd, L 1996, ch 404, § 10, eff Jan 27, 1997; L 1997, ch 449, § 61, eff Feb 22, 1998; L 1998, ch 375, § 14, eff Aug 13, 1998.

CASE ANNOTATIONS

Share exchange between petitioner (investor-owned, regulated public utility) and wholly-owned subsidiary holding company, whereby holding company would acquire 100 percent of common stock of petitioner, would result in taxable conveyance of real property in accordance with CLS Tax §§ 1402, 1401(b), and 1401(e); however, since former common stock shareholders of petitioner would receive proportionately equal amount of holding company common stock as result of share exchange, conveyance would be exempt from real estate transfer tax as provided in CLS Tax § 1405(b)(6). N.Y. Adv Op Comm T & F TSB-A-97-(9)R

Share exchange between petitioner (investor-owned, regulated public utility) and wholly-owned subsidiary holding company, whereby holding company would acquire 100 percent of common stock of petitioner, would not be subject to stock transfer tax where, at effective time, shares of petitioner would no longer represent legally valid stock of petitioner, but instead would represent ownership interest in holding company and would be, in effect, originally issued shares of holding company. N.Y. Adv Op Comm T & F TSB-A-97-(9)R

Share exchange, whereby holding company would acquire 100 percent of common stock of gas and electric utility company (petitioner) as part of proposed restructuring in response to Competitive Opportunities Proceeding instituted by New York State Public Service Commission, resulted in taxable conveyance of real property under CLS Tax §§ 1402, 1401(b), and 1401(e); however, since former common stock shareholders of petitioner would receive proportionately equal amount of holding company common stock as result of share exchange, share exchange would be exempt from real estate transfer tax under CLS Tax § 1405(b)(6). N.Y. Adv Op Comm T & F TSB-A-98-(2)R

§ 914.   [Repealed]

History: Add, L 1997, ch 449, § 62, eff Feb 22, 1998; repealed, L 1997, ch 494, § 6, eff Feb 22, 1998.

§ 915.   [Repealed]

History: Add, L 1997, ch 449, § 62, eff Feb 22, 1998; repealed, L 1997, ch 494, § 6, eff Feb 22, 1998.

ARTICLE 10
NON-JUDICIAL DISSOLUTION

History: Add, L 1961, ch 855, eff Sept 1, 1963.

Schedule of sections, amd, L 1962, ch 834, § 70, L 1963, ch 748, § 13, eff Sept 1, 1963.

§ 1001.   Authorization of dissolution

(a) A corporation may be dissolved under this article. Such dissolution shall be authorized at a meeting of shareholders by (i) for corporations the certificate of incorporation of which expressly provides such or corporations incorporated after the effective date of paragraph (b) of this section, a majority of the votes of all outstanding shares entitled to vote thereon or (ii) for other corporations, two-thirds of the votes of all outstanding shares entitled to vote thereon, except, in either case, as otherwise provided under section 1002 (Dissolution under provision in certificate of incorporation).

(b) Any corporation may adopt an amendment of the certificate of incorporation providing that such dissolution shall be authorized at a meeting of shareholders by a specified proportion of votes of all outstanding shares entitled to vote thereon, provided that such proportion may not be less than a majority.

History: Add, L 1961, ch 855; amd, L 1963, ch 748, § 14, eff Sept 1, 1963; L 1997, ch 449, § 63, eff Feb 22, 1998.

CASE ANNOTATIONS

An agreement entered into by two-thirds of the stockholders to sell all corporate assets to another corporation and use the proceeds to establish a voting trust in the latter corporation would not give rise to a permissible dissolution under § 105 of former Stock Corp. L., and could be enjoined at the instance of a disagreeing minority shareholder. Eisenberg v Central Zone Property Corp. (1953) 306 N.Y. 58, 115 N.E.2d 652

A judgment directing the two directors of a corporation to take all steps necessary under Article 10 to cause the corporation to be dissolved was not justified on ground that the amount of bonuses received by one director so reduced the net profit of the corporation as to leave an insufficient amount to provide a fair return to minority stockholders on their stock. Kruger v Gerth (1965) 16 N.Y.2d 802, 263 N.Y.S.2d 1, 210 N.E.2d 355

In action by minority stockholders to compel dissolution of corporation where court ordered individual defendants who were majority of corporation's directors to take all steps and procedures provided by the above article (§§ 1001-1009) to cause such dissolution, court held that dissolution would not be compelled unless it was found that dominant stockholders or directors had been looting corporation's assets and impairing its capital or maintaining it for their own special benefit thereby enriching themselves at expense of minority stockholders, and that fact that corporation was operating profitably or that complaining stockholders had a right to relief by way of derivative suits or otherwise was not in itself bar to compelling dissolution. Plaintiffs complained that stockholder holding 53 per cent of corporate stock dominated and controlled affairs of the corporation, that he had taken salaries and bonuses in such amounts as to leave little net profit annually, that no dividends had ever been paid on common stock, that dividend payments on preferred stock which had begun only recently gave plaintiffs a meager return on their interest in corporation, that corporation could not be operated so as to increase its profits, and that such majority stockholder had a personal interest in continuing the corporate business, namely, to provide himself with employment at substantial salaries and bonuses, and that he had thereby been exploiting corporation to the detriment of other stockholders. Appellate Division, however, reversed the decision granting requested relief on grounds that it had not been shown that such stockholder did not deserve salaries and bonuses he received, and that it was not a sufficient showing to base dissolution that minority stockholders were not receiving fair return on their stock in corporation. Kruger v Gerth (1964, 2d Dist) 22

A.D.2d 916, 255 N.Y.S.2d 498 affd 16 N.Y.2d 802, 263 N.Y.S.2d 1, 210 N.E.2d 355

A provision of the by-laws of an incorporated hunting and fishing club which constituted a survivorship lottery would not be given effect, and since with this provision eliminated and the membership rolls closed, it became impossible to fulfill the corporate purposes, there was no justification for its continued existence and a proceeding to terminate its existence could be brought by any party claiming an interest in the corporation. Quinn v Stuart Lakes Club, Inc. (1981, 1st Dept) 80 A.D.2d 350, 439 N.Y.S.2d 30

Provision in shareholder's agreement, waiving statutory and common-law right to petition for judicial dissolution of closely-held corporation deadlocked in its operation, was unenforceable as against public policy for protection of shareholders, especially where parties had relationship akin to partners and owed each other high degree of fidelity and good faith; under supermajority provision of agreement, both shareholders were relegated to status of minority shareholder, thereby vitiating parties' statutory rights under CLS Bus Corp §§ 1104 and 1104-a. In re Validation Review Assocs. (1996, 2d Dept) 223 A.D.2d 134, 646 N.Y.S.2d 149

Supermajority provision in shareholder's agreement, even if otherwise valid, cannot be applied to decision regarding dissolution of corporation where shareholder has statutory right to seek judicial dissolution under CLS Bus Corp § 1104. In re Dissolution of Validation Review Assocs. (1997, 2d Dept) 236 A.D.2d 477, 653 N.Y.S.2d 373, subsequent app (2d Dept) 237 A.D.2d 614, 655 N.Y.S.2d 1005 and app gr 89 N.Y.2d 817, 659 N.Y.S.2d 858, 681 N.E.2d 1305

Plaintiff, minority shareholder who alleged that remaining shareholders voted for dissolution in furtherance of conspiracy to "take the accounts, good will and assets" of corporation and otherwise "freeze (him) out" of value of his stock, was properly denied preliminary injunction to enjoin dissolution pending arbitration he was contemplating since plaintiff was not so much challenging defendants' right to dissolve corporation as manner they intended to go about winding up its affairs and distributing its assets, plaintiff did not even describe award to which he might be entitled or otherwise identify particular, ripe controversies, shareholders agreement provided that on dissolution, corporate debts were to be paid and each shareholder given his pro rata share of value of remaining assets, as valued by independent appraiser, and plaintiff offered no evidence for suspecting that such would not occur or why award of money would not make him whole were defendants to divert physical assets. Karnavat v Jesse Bands, Inc. (2001, 1st Dept) 284 A.D.2d 266, 726 N.Y.S.2d 848

Under N.Y. Bus. Corp. Law § 1511, a nonprofessional shareholder is only permitted to vote on corporate action pursuant to either N.Y. Bus. Corp. Law §§ 909 or 1001. Matter of Bernfeld and Kurilenko (2011, 2d Dept) 86 App Div 3d 244, 925 NYS2d 122.

Section 105 of former Stock Corp. L. applied to insolvent as well as to solvent corporations. It contemplated a ratable distribution of assets. Re Flexlite Corp. (1943) 180 Misc 718, 43 N.Y.S.2d 948

As against a statute authorizing certain action by two-thirds or some other fixed percentage of outstanding stock entitled to vote, a bylaw requiring unanimous consent of such stock was deemed invalid. Benintendi v Kenton Hotel, Inc. (1943) 181 Misc 897, 45 N.Y.S.2d 705, affd 268 A.D. 857, 50 N.Y.S.2d 843, mod on other grounds 294 N.Y. 112, 60 N.E.2d 829 (superseded by statute as stated in Application of Burkin, 1 N.Y.2d 570, 154 N.Y.S.2d 898, 136 N.E.2d 862, 64 ALR2d 638)

Attempted voluntary dissolution of a corporation by action of its officers and directors without equitable distribution of assets to creditors constitutes fraud as matter of law, and if there is likewise fraud in fact any transfer, even to apply on antecedent indebtedness, is invalid and must be set aside. Beol, Inc. v Dorf (1959) 22 Misc. 2d 798, 193 N.Y.S.2d 394, affd (1st Dept) 12 A.D.2d 459, 209 N.Y.S.2d 267, reh and app den (1st Dept) 12 A.D.2d 616, 210 N.Y.S.2d 753, app dismd 9 N.Y.2d 963, 218 N.Y.S.2d 43, 176 N.E.2d 499

One of three persons owning all stock of a corporation was entitled to a temporary injunction against dissolution proceedings under subd. 4 of § 105 of former Stock Corp. L. upon the basis of an agreement among them that each would offer his stock to the others before selling to an outsider on a formula for assessing its value, violation of which would oust plaintiff as owner and operator of a printing establishment transferred to the corporation and leave the other two stockholders in control of its accounts. Levine v Styleart Press, Inc. (1961) 31 Misc. 2d 106, 217 N.Y.S.2d 688

In view of likelihood that delivery of shares of stock of professional corporation to sheriff for sale would not result in satisfaction of alimony arrears, and since delivery of property to sheriff must be made for sole purpose of sale to satisfy judgment, delivery of stock was ordered to be made to receiver, who could then do any act designed to satisfy judgment including dissolution of corporation. Udel v Udel (1975) 82 Misc. 2d 882, 370 N.Y.S.2d 426

Administrator of the estate of three professional corporations' (PCs) sole shareholder, officer, and director (SH) could not be substituted under N.Y. C.P.L.R. 1017 for the PCs in suits seeking assigned first-party benefits because: (1) the SH's administrator had not been appointed a receiver for the PCs and they had not been dissolved; (2) no one was authorized to act on behalf of the PCs; (3) the administrator could not act under N.Y. Bus. Corp. Law §§ 1507, 1508, and 1511 because the PCs were authorized to practice medicine, and the administrator was not licensed to practice medicine; and (4) the administrator could only vote the shares in the PCs for the N.Y. Bus. Corp. Law §§ 909, 1001, and 1511 purposes. Painless Med., P.C. v GEICO (2011, Civ Ct) 32 Misc 3d 715, 929 NYS2d 357.

Where a decedent bequeathed the decedent's shares of stock equally to petitioner and respondent, petitioner and respondent were the owners of the corporation and, as such, and absent their mutual agreement not present in the proceeding, their options for the relief requested in the petition, which sought an order directing the sale by the corporation of real property and the liquidation of the corporation for the payment and distribution of its shares to the parties, could have been found in either N.Y. Bus. Corp. Law art. 10 or N.Y. Bus. Corp. Law art. 11. Matter of Kagan (2005, Sur) 790 N.Y.S.2d 366

Voluntary liquidation and dissolution of a corporation are not equivalent to a merger, notwithstanding some of the same results may be sought or attained. Patten Fine Papers, Inc. v Commissioner (1957, CA7) 249 F.2d 776, 57-2 USTC ¶ 10050

The directors of a New Jersey corporation had no duty to continue the corporation in operation or existence when in their opinion to do so would not be expedient, and the decision to sell the corporation would not be disturbed in the absence of proof of fraud or that less than the requisite two thirds majority of stockholders had voted in favor of the sale or dissolution. Richland v Crandall (1967, SD NY) 262 F. Supp. 538

§ 1002. Dissolution under provision in certificate of incorporation

(a) The certificate of incorporation may contain a provision that any shareholder, or the holders of any specified number or proportion of shares or votes of shares, or of any specified number or proportion of shares or votes of shares of any class or series thereof, may require the dissolution of the corporation at will or upon the occurrence of a specified event. If the certificate of incorporation contains such a provision, a certificate of dissolution under section 1003 (Certificate of dissolution; contents) may be signed, verified and delivered to the department of state as provided in section 104 (Certificate; requirements, signing, filing, effectiveness) when authorized by a holder or holders of the number or proportion of shares or votes of shares specified in such provision, given in such manner as may be specified therein, or if no manner is specified therein, when authorized on written consent signed by such holder or holders; or such certificate may be signed, verified and delivered to the department by such holder or holders or by such of them as are designated by them.

(b) An amendment of the certificate of incorporation which adds a provision permitted by this section, or which changes or strikes out such a provision, shall be authorized at a meeting of shareholders by vote of all outstanding shares, whether or not otherwise entitled to vote on any amendment, or of such lesser proportion of shares and of such class or series of shares, but not less than a majority of all outstanding shares entitled to vote on any amendment, as may be provided specifically in the certificate of incorporation for adding, changing or striking out a provision permitted by this section.

(c) If the certificate of incorporation of any corporation contains a provision authorized by this section, the existence of such provision shall be noted conspicuously on the face or back of every certificate for shares issued by such corporation.

History: Add, L 1962, ch 834, § 71, with substance transferred from former § 1105; amd, L 1963, ch 748, § 15, eff Sept 1, 1963; L 1997, ch 449, § 64, eff Feb 22, 1998.

CASE ANNOTATIONS

Provision in shareholder's agreement, waiving statutory and common-law right to petition for judicial dissolution of closely-held corporation deadlocked in its operation, was unenforceable as against public policy for protection of shareholders, especially where parties had relationship akin to partners and owed each other high degree of fidelity and good faith; under supermajority provision of agreement, both shareholders were relegated to status of minority shareholder, thereby vitiating parties' statutory rights under CLS Bus Corp §§ 1104 and 1104-a. In re Validation Review Assocs. (1996, 2d Dept) 223 A.D.2d 134, 646 N.Y.S.2d 149

§ 1003. Certificate of dissolution; contents

(a) A certificate of dissolution, entitled "Certificate of dissolution of .... (name of corporation) under section 1003 of the Business Corporation Law", shall be signed and delivered to the department of state. It shall set forth:

(1) The name of the corporation and, if its name has been changed, the name under which it was formed.

(2) The date its certificate of incorporation was filed by the department of state.

(3) The name and address of each of its officers and directors.

(4) That the corporation elects to dissolve.

(5) The manner in which the dissolution was authorized.

History: Formerly § 1002, renumbered, L 1962, ch 834, § 72, eff Sept 1, 1963; amd, L 1998, ch 375, § 15, eff Aug 13, 1998.

CASE ANNOTATIONS

The existence of a corporation does not terminate until it is legally dissolved in accordance with the law of its creation. Eastern Grain Elevator Corp. v McGowan (1950, DC NY) 95 F. Supp. 40, 51-1 USTC ¶ 66003

§ 1004. Certificate of dissolution; filing

(a) The department shall not file such certificate unless the consent of the state department of taxation and finance to the dissolution is attached thereto. Upon such filing, the corporation is dissolved.

(b) Notwithstanding paragraph (a) of this section, with respect to any corporation that has done business in the city of New York and incurred liability for any tax or charge under chapter six, seven, eight, ten, eleven, twelve, thirteen, fourteen, fifteen, twenty-one,

twenty-four, twenty-five or twenty-seven of title eleven of the administrative code of the city of New York, the department shall not file such certificate unless the consent of the commissioner of finance of the city of New York to the dissolution is also attached thereto.

History: Formerly § 1003, renumbered, L 1962, ch 834, § 73, eff Sept 1, 1963; amd, L 2009, ch 201, § 73, eff Oct 1, 2009.

CASE ANNOTATIONS

In action by charitable foundation, seeking to set aside conveyance of certain real property to defendant corporation for noncompliance with CLS N-PCL §§ 510 and 511, substitution of corporation's president and sole shareholder as defendant was permissible under CLS CPLR § 1017, where he had deeded property in question to himself personally prior to commencement of action, and corporation's certificate of dissolution was not filed with Department of State until after action against corporation was commenced. Rose Ocko Found., Inc. v Lebovits (1999, 2d Dept) 259 A.D.2d 685, later proceeding 93 N.Y.2d 997, 696 N.Y.S.2d 107, 718 N.E.2d 412

Summary judgment granted in favor of the landlord in an action against the corporate officer was reversed because the landlord did not have an actionable claim against the officer personally, pursuant to N.Y. Bus. Corp. Law §§ 1004 and 1005, when the corporation's dissolution was annulled retroactively after the corporation's back franchise taxes were paid, pursuant to N.Y. Tax Law § 203-a. Flushing Plaza Assoc. #2 v Albert (2006, 2d Dept) 31 App Div 3d 494, 818 NYS2d 252

The filing of a certificate of dissolution of a corporation, when the corporation is insolvent, constitutes an act of bankruptcy under § 3, subpar a(5) of the Bankruptcy Act. Re Bonnie Classics, Inc. (1953, DC NY) 116 F. Supp. 646

§ 1005. Procedure after dissolution

(a) After dissolution:

(1) The corporation shall carry on no business except for the purpose of winding up its affairs.

(2) The corporation shall proceed to wind up its affairs, with power to fulfill or discharge its contracts, collect its assets, sell its assets for cash at public or private sale, discharge or pay its liabilities, and do all other acts appropriate to liquidate its business.

(3) After paying or adequately providing for the payment of its liabilities:

(A) The corporation, if authorized at a meeting of shareholders by a majority of the votes of all outstanding shares entitled to vote thereon may sell its remaining assets, or any part thereof, for shares, bonds or other securities or partly for cash and partly for shares, bonds or other securities, and distribute the same among the shareholders according to their respective rights. In the case of a sale under this subparagraph where the consideration is in whole or in part other than cash, any shareholder, entitled to vote thereon, who does not vote for or consent in writing to such sale, shall, subject to and by complying with the provisions of section 623 (Procedure to enforce shareholder's right to receive payment for shares), have the right to receive payment for his shares. Section 909 (Sale, lease, exchange or other disposition of assets) is not applicable to a sale of assets under this paragraph.

(B) The corporation, whether or not it has made a sale under subparagraph (A), may distribute any remaining assets, in cash or in kind or partly each, among its shareholders according to their respective rights.

(b) When there are no shareholders, upon dissolution all subscriptions for shares shall be cancelled and all obligations of the corporation to issue shares or of the subscribers to pay their subscriptions shall terminate, except for such payments as may be required to enable the corporation to pay its liabilities.

(c) Upon the winding up of the affairs of the corporation, any assets distributable to a creditor or shareholder who is unknown or cannot be found, or who is under disability and for whom there is no legal representative, shall be paid to the state comptroller as abandoned property within six months from the date fixed for the payment of the final liquidating distribution, and be subject to the provisions of the abandoned property law.

History: Formerly § 1004, renumbered, L 1962, ch 834, § 74, eff Sept 1, 1963; amd, L 1963, ch 748, § 16, eff Sept 1, 1963; amd, L 1997, ch 449, § 65, eff Feb 22, 1998.

CASE ANNOTATIONS

1. In general
2. Winding up
3. —Legal actions
4. —Obligations
5. Distribution of assets

1. In general

New York City Corporation Counsel's interpretation of "eligibility" of dissolved corporation to seek release of its tax-foreclosed property under New York City Administrative Code § 11-424(f), and his approval of application for release, were neither arbitrary nor irrational merely because application was not checked against provisions of Business Corporation Law pertaining to dissolved corporations that might render otherwise eligible corporation ineligible to apply for release. 172 East 122 172 E. 122 St. Tenants Ass'n v Schwarz, 73 N.Y.2d 340, 540 N.Y.S.2d 420, 537 N.E.2d 1281, 1989 N.Y. LEXIS 395 (N.Y. 1989).

On designation of receiver for corporation, it was necessary that corporate liability be extinguished before any corporate assets be distributed to stockholders. Business Corporation Law §§ 1005, 1111. Maki v Estate of Ziehm, 55 A.D.2d 454, 391 N.Y.S.2d 705, 1977 N.Y. App. Div. LEXIS 9999 (N.Y. App. Div. 3d Dep't 1977).

Business Corporation Law § 1005, not § 909, governs corporate procedure following dissolution. Helfand v Cohen, 110 A.D.2d 751, 487 N.Y.S.2d 836, 1985 N.Y. App. Div. LEXIS 48653 (N.Y. App. Div. 2d Dep't 1985).

Allowance of counsel fees to permanent receiver appointed under Business Corporation Law was not barred as matter of law, even though receiver conceded that employee of dissolved corporation had performed work in contravention of CLS Bus Corp § 1005, and that receiver had made personal telephone calls on corporate telephone, since such acts did not rise to level of gross mismanagement. Corcoran v Joseph M. Corcoran, Inc., 135 A.D.2d 531, 521 N.Y.S.2d 757, 1987 N.Y. App. Div. LEXIS 52483 (N.Y. App. Div. 2d Dep't 1987).

Trial court improperly sua sponte appointed a referee to hear and report as to the value of the corporation's properties and leasehold interest and the appropriate procedures following dissolution in the judicial dissolution of the corporation; post-dissolution procedures in a judicial proceeding, provided for in N.Y. Bus. Corp. Law §§ 1005-1008, as provided under N.Y. Bus. Corp. Law § 1117, did not include the appointment of a referee. In re Oak St. Mgmt., 307 A.D.2d 320, 762 N.Y.S.2d 522, 2003 N.Y. App. Div. LEXIS 8264 (N.Y. App. Div. 2d Dep't 2003), app. dismissed, 100 N.Y.2d 640, 769 N.Y.S.2d 204, 801 N.E.2d 425, 2003 N.Y. LEXIS 3422 (N.Y. 2003).

Summary judgment granted in favor of the landlord in an action against the corporate officer was reversed because the landlord did not have an actionable claim against the officer personally, pursuant to N.Y. Bus. Corp. Law §§ 1004 and 1005, when the corporation's dissolution was annulled retroactively after the corporation's back franchise taxes were paid, pursuant to N.Y. Tax Law § 203-a. Flushing Plaza Assoc. #2 v Albert, 31 A.D.3d 494, 818 N.Y.S.2d 252, 2006 NY Slip Op 5586, 2006 N.Y. App. Div. LEXIS 9144 (N.Y. App. Div. 2d Dep't 2006).

Plaintiff had standing as a dissolved corporation could transfer its shares and sell the tanning beds to plaintiff as part of winding up its affairs and defendants did not show that the transactions constituted impermissible new business. Lots 4 Less Stores, Inc. v Integrated Props., Inc., 152 A.D.3d 1181, 2017 NY Slip Op 05529, 2017 NY Slip Op 5529, 2017 N.Y. App. Div. LEXIS 5371 (N.Y. App. Div. 4th Dep't 2017).

Trial court erred in searching the record and awarding summary judgment to a dissolved corporate seller in a buyer's breach of contract action and in cancelling the buyer's notice of pendency because no shareholder authorization was required where the subject transaction was entirely for cash, and there was insufficient evidence to determine whether the seller's secretary had actual or apparent authority to represent it. Heights Props. 1388, LLC v Make Realty Corp., 151 A.D.3d 825, 2017 NY Slip Op 04822, 2017 NY Slip Op 4822, 58 N.Y.S.3d 78, 2017 N.Y. App. Div. LEXIS 4738 (N.Y. App. Div. 2d Dep't 2017).

Motion for summary judgment could have been considered as a motion to dismiss under N.Y. C.P.L.R. 3211(a)(1) where the defense was founded on documentary evidence of plaintiff corporation's dissolution proclamation; it could have been considered under N.Y. C.P.L.R. 3211(a)(2) for lack of subject matter jurisdiction, as the plaintiff dissolved corporation did not exist, and thus there was no case or controversy; and it could have been considered under N.Y. C.P.L.R. 1017, 1021 and/or N.Y. Bus. Corp. Law §§ 1005, 1006 dealing with the substitution of parties for a dissolved corporation. Lance Int'l, Inc. v First Nat'l City Bank, 878 N.Y.S.2d 572, 2009 NY Slip Op 29210, 24 Misc. 3d 1109, 241 N.Y.L.J. 72, 2009 N.Y. Misc. LEXIS 1165 (N.Y. Civ. Ct. 2009), aff'd in part and rev'd in part, 898 N.Y.S.2d 752, 2010 NY Slip Op 20050, 27 Misc. 3d 13, 2010 N.Y. Misc. LEXIS 293 (N.Y. App. Term 2010).

In short, under § 105 of former Stock Corp. L., a dissolved corporation survived for the purpose of liquidating its assets and satisfying its existing liabilities and obligations, and, generally speaking, for that purpose only. Colburn v Geneva Nursery Co., 29 N.Y.S.2d 892, 1941 N.Y. Misc. LEXIS 2172 (N.Y. Sup. Ct. 1941).

Statutory procedure for dissolution of corporations was set up primarily to avoid the injustices of the common-law rule that, upon dissolution, corporate assets escheated to the sovereign. Northern Properties, Inc. v Kuf Realty Corp., 30 Misc. 2d 1, 217 N.Y.S.2d 355, 1961 N.Y. Misc. LEXIS 2923 (N.Y. Sup. Ct. 1961).

President's summary judgment motion alleging that he could not be held personally liable on a contract he executed as a corporate officer was denied as there were triable issues as to the president's knowledge of the corporation's status and his own bad faith where 11 years passed between a corporation's dissolution for the nonpayment of taxes and its reinstatement; the corporation was only reinstated after a suit was filed. Lodato v Greyhawk N. Am., L.L.C., 807 N.Y.S.2d 818, 2005 NY Slip Op 25428, 10 Misc. 3d 418, 234 N.Y.L.J. 82, 2005 N.Y. Misc. LEXIS 2218 (N.Y. Sup. Ct. 2005), aff'd, 39 A.D.3d 496, 834 N.Y.S.2d 237, 2007 NY Slip Op 2902, 2007 N.Y. App. Div. LEXIS 4308 (N.Y. App. Div. 2d Dep't 2007).

President and chief operating officer of corporation which is dissolved by state for failure to file reports or pay taxes is not personally liable for debts incurred by corporation in absence of fraud since, as general rule, no one but state may question de facto corporation's existence. Prentice Corp. v Martin, 624 F. Supp. 1114, 1986 U.S. Dist. LEXIS 30913 (E.D.N.Y. 1986).

2. Winding up

On dissolution of corporation under CLS Tax § 203-a, corporation is authorized to conduct business only to extent necessary to wind up its affairs. Brandes Meat Corp. v Cromer, 146 A.D.2d 666, 537 N.Y.S.2d 177, 1989 N.Y. App. Div. LEXIS 734 (N.Y. App. Div. 2d Dep't 1989).

In action for account stated against individual owner of meat market for value of meats and other goods, plaintiff was entitled to summary judgment where defendant acknowledged that plaintiff was owed stated sum but asserted that, at time of transactions in question, he was acting as agent for corporation, since corporation had been dissolved 3 years earlier pursuant to CLS Tax § 203-a and plaintiff's sale of products to defendant was clearly not transaction relating to winding up of corporation; therefore, defendant was personally liable for obligations which he incurred. Brandes Meat Corp. v Cromer, 146 A.D.2d 666, 537 N.Y.S.2d 177, 1989 N.Y. App. Div. LEXIS 734 (N.Y. App. Div. 2d Dep't 1989).

Absent agreement, parties to dissolution are entitled to recover their share of fees that corporation earns from pending contingency fee cases. DelCasino v Koeppel, 207 A.D.2d 374, 615 N.Y.S.2d 454, 1994 N.Y. App. Div. LEXIS 8217 (N.Y. App. Div. 2d Dep't 1994).

Where trustees or successors of dissolved corporation do not choose to maintain preexisting lease in effect, landlord may seek to enforce its rights under lease against estate or assets of dissolved corporation. Goldberg v Harwood, 216 A.D.2d 152, 628 N.Y.S.2d 105, 1995 N.Y. App. Div. LEXIS 6612 (N.Y. App. Div. 1st Dep't 1995), aff'd, 88 N.Y.2d 911, 646 N.Y.S.2d 663, 669 N.E.2d 821, 1996 N.Y. LEXIS 1179 (N.Y. 1996), reh'g denied, 1995 N.Y. App. Div. LEXIS 9763 (N.Y. App. Div. 1st Dep't).

Absent express assumption of rights and obligations of preexisting lease by purchaser of assets of dissolved corporation, and landlord's consent to assignment, as required by lease, landlord continued to be dissolved corporation's creditor with claim against proceeds of sale of its assets. Goldberg v Harwood, 216 A.D.2d 152, 628 N.Y.S.2d 105, 1995 N.Y. App. Div. LEXIS 6612 (N.Y. App. Div. 1st Dep't 1995), aff'd, 88 N.Y.2d 911, 646 N.Y.S.2d 663, 669 N.E.2d 821, 1996 N.Y. LEXIS 1179 (N.Y. 1996), reh'g denied, 1995 N.Y. App. Div. LEXIS 9763 (N.Y. App. Div. 1st Dep't).

Partnership had capacity to commence tax certiorari proceedings as part of its obligation to wind up its affairs under CLS Bus Corp § 1005(a) and (b) and CLS Partn §§ 60 et seq. Fox Meadow Partners, Ltd. v Board of Assessment Review, 273 A.D.2d 472, 710 N.Y.S.2d 610, 2000 N.Y. App. Div. LEXIS 7358 (N.Y. App. Div. 2d Dep't 2000).

When a record production company, which had been dissolved, acted as trustee for two recording artists by receiving royalties to which the artists were entitled, it was improper to grant this dissolved company the indefinite right to receive and administer the royalties belonging, largely, to the artists, as this was unrelated to the winding up of the company's business, under N.Y. Bus. Corp. Law § 1005(a)(2). Noise in the Attic Prods., Inc. v London Records, 10 A.D.3d 303, 782 N.Y.S.2d 1, 2004 N.Y. App. Div. LEXIS 10333 (N.Y. App. Div. 1st Dep't 2004).

New York Public Service Commission had a rational basis upon which to deny the corporation's request for restoration of service as part of the relief that the corporation sought from the telephone company because the corporation was dissolved and was not supposed to be carrying on any business except for that required to wind up its affairs. Matter of Community Network Serv., Inc. v New York State Dept. of Pub. Serv., 32 A.D.3d 640, 820 N.Y.S.2d 184, 2006 NY Slip Op 6186, 2006 N.Y. App. Div. LEXIS 9951 (N.Y. App. Div. 3d Dep't 2006).

The assets, or their proceeds, were primarily and first of all held in trust for creditors, and they could be subjected to claims of unpaid creditors even in the hands of a transferee unless the transfer was in good faith and for adequate consideration, or adequate provision was made for payment of debts and demands. Colburn v Geneva Nursery Co., 29 N.Y.S.2d 892, 1941 N.Y. Misc. LEXIS 2172 (N.Y. Sup. Ct. 1941); Willey v Diepress Co., 281 N.Y.S. 907, 156 Misc. 762, 1935 N.Y. Misc. LEXIS 1379 (N.Y. Sup. Ct. 1935); United States v Oscar Frommel & Bro., 50 F.2d 73, 1931 U.S. App. LEXIS 4412 (2d Cir. N.Y. 1931), cert. denied, 284 U.S. 647, 52 S. Ct. 25, 76 L. Ed. 549, 1931 U.S. LEXIS 697 (U.S. 1931).

Assets of a solvent corporation, or their proceeds, could be distributed to shareholders, free from liability for debts, but only if proper and adequate provision was made for payment and satisfaction of outstanding obligations. Shanik v Empire Power Corp., 58 N.Y.S.2d 176, 1945 N.Y. Misc. LEXIS 2410 (N.Y. Sup. Ct. 1945), aff'd, 270 A.D. 925, 62 N.Y.S.2d 760, 1946 N.Y. App. Div. LEXIS 4681 (N.Y. App. Div. 1946).

It could still accept a use variance with respect to zoning requirements though the variance was not granted until after distribution of the property in question to its stockholders, acting, to that extent, as agent for the distributees, and a deed to the corporation executed in accordance with subd. 8 of § 105 of former Stock Corp. L. was valid. Feneck v Murdock, 16 Misc. 2d 789, 181 N.Y.S.2d 441, 1958 N.Y. Misc. LEXIS 2405 (N.Y. Sup. Ct. 1958); Bank of New York v Kenne-

dy, 54 N.Y.S.2d 122, 183 Misc. 819, 1944 N.Y. Misc. LEXIS 1473 (N.Y. Sup. Ct. 1944), aff'd, 269 A.D. 747, 55 N.Y.S.2d 115, 1945 N.Y. App. Div. LEXIS 3606 (N.Y. App. Div. 1945).

When it came to a distribution of surplus assets among shareholders, and there was more than one issue of series of stock outstanding, rights as between holders of different issues depend upon terms of issuance and specific priorities granted and agreed to and which should ordinarily appear in the certificate of incorporation. Thus there may be a right in certain shareholders to payment of specified or cumulative dividends, notwithstanding failure to declare the dividend in question. In re Chandler & Co., 230 N.Y.S.2d 1012 (N.Y. Sup. Ct. 1962); Shanik v Empire Power Corp., 58 N.Y.S.2d 176, 1945 N.Y. Misc. LEXIS 2410 (N.Y. Sup. Ct. 1945), aff'd, 270 A.D. 925, 62 N.Y.S.2d 760, 1946 N.Y. App. Div. LEXIS 4681 (N.Y. App. Div. 1946).

Corporations undergoing dissolution may continue to function for the purpose of winding up the affairs of the corporation in the same manner as if the dissolution had not taken place and the dissolution does not affect either the right of the corporation to collect and distribute its assets or to sue in its corporate name; therefore, a corporation which was dissolved pursuant to Tax Law § 203-a for nonpayment of taxes was permitted to exercise an option to purchase real estate since the option constituted a valuable asset and the exercise of that option was a significant part of winding up the affairs of the corporation. Bowditch v 57 Laight Street Corp., 111 Misc. 2d 255, 443 N.Y.S.2d 785, 1981 N.Y. Misc. LEXIS 3257 (N.Y. Sup. Ct. 1981).

3. —Legal actions

New York City Corporation Counsel properly determined that corporation dissolved under CLS Tax § 203-a could obtain release of its tax-foreclosed property under New York City Administrative Code § 11-424(f), without violating statutory prohibition against such corporations carrying on new business, since CLS Bus Corp § 1006 permits dissolved corporation to pursue any remedy available to it in respect to reacquisition of property it owned prior to its dissolution, such remedy does not depend on whether that property could be characterized as corporate asset after dissolution, and code permits recapture of property right possessed by corporation prior to its dissolution. 172 East 122 172 E. 122 St. Tenants Ass'n v Schwarz, 73 N.Y.2d 340, 540 N.Y.S.2d 420, 537 N.E.2d 1281, 1989 N.Y. LEXIS 395 (N.Y. 1989).

Distributor of asbestos which was dissolved in 1999 was permitted to bring a contribution or indemnification claim against the employer of an employee who had been diagnosed with asbestos-related illnesses in 2000 because bringing such a claim was a normal part of winding up the distributor's affairs, N.Y. Bus. Corp. Law §§ 1005(a)(1) and 1006(a); the distributor had to either settle or defend asbestos claims to wind up its affairs, and a third-party claim for contribution or indemnification was a normal part of defending such a claim. Tedesco v A.P. Green Indus., Inc., 8 N.Y.3d 243, 832 N.Y.S.2d 141, 2007 NY Slip Op 1423, 864 N.E.2d 65, 2007 N.Y. LEXIS 190 (N.Y. 2007).

The trial court improperly dismissed a complaint brought by a dissolved corporation to recover on a fire insurance policy obtained by the corporation one year after dissolution, where the power to keep corporation property insured against fire and other hazards was inherent in the power possessed by a corporation winding up its affairs following dissolution. Igbara Realty Corp. v New York Property Ins. Underwriting Asso., 94 A.D.2d 79, 463 N.Y.S.2d 211, 1983 N.Y. App. Div. LEXIS 17952 (N.Y. App. Div. 1st Dep't 1983), modified, 63 N.Y.2d 201, 481 N.Y.S.2d 60, 470 N.E.2d 858, 1984 N.Y. LEXIS 4613 (N.Y. 1984).

Corporation dissolved pursuant to CLS Tax § 203-a lacks capacity to bring suit on claim arising out of conduct of prohibited new business; furthermore, such corporation has neither de jure nor de facto existence for purposes of ultra vires defense under CLS Bus Corp § 203. Lorisa Capital Corp. v Gallo, 119 A.D.2d 99, 506 N.Y.S.2d 62, 1986 N.Y. App. Div. LEXIS 56313 (N.Y. App. Div. 2d Dep't 1986).

Corporation dissolved by secretary of state may defend foreclosure action relating to its corporate assets. Harris v Stony Clove Lake Acres, 221 A.D.2d 833, 633 N.Y.S.2d 691, 1995 N.Y. App. Div. LEXIS 12131 (N.Y. App. Div. 3d Dep't 1995).

Dissolved corporation was entitled to file notice of mechanic's lien to enforce claim that existed before dissolution where corporation was winding up its affairs rather than engaging in prohibited new business. Schenectady Mun. Hous. Auth. v Keystone Metals Corp., 245 A.D.2d 725, 665 N.Y.S.2d 744, 1997 N.Y. App. Div. LEXIS 12949

(N.Y. App. Div. 3d Dep't 1997), app. denied, 92 N.Y.2d 804, 677 N.Y.S.2d 779, 700 N.E.2d 318, 1998 N.Y. LEXIS 1848 (N.Y. 1998).

Where a supplier did not substantiate its claim that the dissolved corporation operated as a de facto corporation under N.Y. Bus. Law §§ 1005(a)(2), 1006(a), (b), a judicial hearing officer properly set aside the N.Y. Bus. Corp. Law § 306 service on the Secretary of State; where the dissolved corporation only sought vacatur of a default judgment and leave to serve an answer pursuant to N.Y. C.P.L.R. 5015, the trial court properly granted the relief sought. Bruce Supply Corp. v New Wave Mech., Inc., 4 A.D.3d 444, 773 N.Y.S.2d 408, 2004 N.Y. App. Div. LEXIS 1725 (N.Y. App. Div. 2d Dep't 2004).

Although a mortgagor was a dissolved corporation, exercising its right to redeem three mortgages on two parcels was not engaging in new business prohibited by N.Y. Bus. Corp. Law § 1005(a)(1) but pursuing a remedy to reacquire property it owned prior to its dissolution; thus, the assignee of the mortgagees was required to provide the mortgagor with payoff letters. Luna Light., Inc. v Just Indus., Inc., 45 A.D.3d 814, 847 N.Y.S.2d 126, 2007 NY Slip Op 9369, 2007 N.Y. App. Div. LEXIS 12115 (N.Y. App. Div. 2d Dep't 2007), app. denied, 10 N.Y.3d 712, 861 N.Y.S.2d 272, 891 N.E.2d 307, 2008 N.Y. LEXIS 1587 (N.Y. 2008).

Trial court erred in denying a request for leave to allow a corporation to assert direct claims because both the complaint and first amended complaint provided a former employee with notice that the corporation allegedly sustained damages as a result of the former employee's conduct, no new facts or theories were injected by the requests that the corporation be permitted to assert direct claims, and, thus, the former employee would not have sustained any prejudice as a result of the amendment; it was demonstrated that the corporation's proposed direct claims were potentially meritorious. The corporation, while dissolved, was permitted to prosecute the action, which sought to recover damages sustained prior to its dissolution, as part of the course of winding up its affairs. Schorr v Steiner, 46 A.D.3d 435, 849 N.Y.S.2d 39, 2007 NY Slip Op 10074, 2007 N.Y. App. Div. LEXIS 12788 (N.Y. App. Div. 1st Dep't 2007).

Law firm's motion to dismiss legal malpractice suit on the alternate ground that the corporate client lacked the capacity to commence the action against the law firm should have been granted because the client had been dissolved for failure to pay franchise taxes; a lawyer had represented the client prior to its dissolution, and thus, under N.Y. Bus. Corp. Law § 1006(b), the client retained the capacity to sue her relating to such representation. However, the law firm was not retained until after the client was dissolved and this action did not relate to the winding up of the client's affairs, so the client thus lacked the capacity to use the courts to enforce obligations arising out of the law firm's representation of the corporation until it secured retroactive de jure status by payment of delinquent franchise taxes. Moran Enters., Inc. v Hurst, 66 A.D.3d 972, 888 N.Y.S.2d 109, 2009 NY Slip Op 7807, 2009 N.Y. App. Div. LEXIS 7681 (N.Y. App. Div. 2d Dep't 2009).

Order vacating a tax deed, subsequent conveyances, and a mortgage was affirmed because the trial court found that the notice to redeem sent to the owner failed to comply with due process; contrary to the assignee's contention, the owner, a corporation, had the capacity to commence this action despite its dissolution.89 Pine Hollow Rd. Realty Corp. v American Tax Fund, 96 A.D.3d 995, 948 N.Y.S.2d 617, 2012 NY Slip Op 5136, 2012 N.Y. App. Div. LEXIS 5046 (N.Y. App. Div. 2d Dep't 2012).

Plaintiff's breach of contract action, which allegedly arose from the purchase and sale of many properties, was properly brought in his capacity as corporate assignee, as although the corporations had been dissolved before the action was commenced, there was no prima facie showing that the action did not relate to the winding up of the corporate affairs. Singer v Riskin, 137 A.D.3d 999, 2016 NY Slip Op 01825, 2016 NY Slip Op 01825, 2016 NY Slip Op 1825, 2016 NY Slip Op 1825, 27 N.Y.S.3d 209, 2016 N.Y. App. Div. LEXIS 1812 (N.Y. App. Div. 2d Dep't 2016).

Although a corporation had fitfully pursued a problematic lawsuit for four and a half decades after the events in issue transpired and after the business declared bankruptcy, three and a half decades after the corporation was dissolved did not sound like a limited winding up of affairs during which time the dissolved corporation had limited existence pursuant to N.Y. Bus. Corp. Law §§ 1005(a)(1) and 1006. Lance Int'l, Inc. v First Nat'l City Bank, 878 N.Y.S.2d 572, 2009 NY Slip Op 29210, 24 Misc. 3d 1109, 241 N.Y.L.J. 72, 2009 N.Y. Misc. LEXIS 1165 (N.Y. Civ. Ct. 2009), aff'd in part and rev'd in part, 898

N.Y.S.2d 752, 2010 NY Slip Op 20050, 27 Misc. 3d 13, 2010 N.Y. Misc. LEXIS 293 (N.Y. App. Term 2010).

4. —Obligations

But it was not dead for all purposes and thus remained bound by the terms of a contract with a labor union to employ only members of the particular union, to the extent that it continued to have employees. Hudak v Hornell Industries, Inc., 304 N.Y. 207, 106 N.E.2d 609, 304 N.Y. (N.Y.S.) 207, 1952 N.Y. LEXIS 761 (N.Y. 1952).

Under § 105 of former Stock Corp. L., a corporation was considered as out of business, or precluded from engaging in any further new business, when it took adequate steps to effectuate a dissolution. Thus its employees became entitled to severance pay under a collective bargaining agreement calling for severance pay in case of discharge. In re Brooklyn Citizen, 1 Misc. 2d 162, 90 N.Y.S.2d 99, 1949 N.Y. Misc. LEXIS 1657 (N.Y. Sup. Ct. 1949).

If a corporation distributes property held by it in trust for the benefit of an employee, the property remains burdened with the trust in the hands of the shareholders, whether or not the shareholders have actual knowledge of the trust. Coleman v Golkin, Bomback & Co., 562 F.2d 166, 1977 U.S. App. LEXIS 11636 (2d Cir. N.Y. 1977).

As case law regarding preemption distinguishes between state laws which "relate to" employee benefit plans and those that have only "tenuous, remote, or peripheral" impact, § 1005 is not preempted by ERISA (Employee Retirement Income Security Act of 1974). Retirement Fund of Fur Mfg. Industry v Getto & Getto, Inc., 714 F. Supp. 651, 1989 U.S. Dist. LEXIS 6121 (S.D.N.Y. 1989).

For purposes of determining whether a Chapter 7 debtor transferred hardware store assets with the actual intent to hinder, delay, or defraud creditors, a court determined that those assets were an interest of debtor in property. Debtor, who was the hardware store's sole shareholder and an officer, continued to operate the business for 20 months after it was dissolved and not for purposes of winding up its affairs and thus, under New York law, he became personally responsible for its debts, and property acquired as a result of carrying on business after dissolution belonged to debtor, not the corporation. Carver Fed. Sav. Bank v Cedillo (In re Cedillo), 2017 Bankr. LEXIS 2568 (Bankr. E.D.N.Y. Sept. 11, 2017).

5. Distribution of assets

A transfer of assets to a successor corporation under subd. 9 of § 105 of former Stock Corp. L. was regarded as in the nature of a reorganization, and a stockholder of the dissolving corporation who failed to deposit his stock in accordance with the plan of reorganization lost any preference rights which he might otherwise have had against new stockholders under the plan. In re Duer, 270 N.Y. 343, 1 N.E.2d 457, 270 N.Y. (N.Y.S.) 343, 1936 N.Y. LEXIS 1551 (N.Y. 1936).

There may likewise be a right to interest on dividends declared, but not paid or received, and hence left on deposit bearing interest. Griffin v Dyett, 262 A.D. 368, 29 N.Y.S.2d 486, 1941 N.Y. App. Div. LEXIS 5367 (N.Y. App. Div. 1941).

Personal representatives of deceased stockholders and directors of dissolved corporation were not entitled to stay arbitration of claim against corporation for alleged breach of contract, since dissolution of corporation more than 30 years prior to present proceedings made it futile for contracting party to even attempt to sue corporation directly and he was therefore entitled to directly sue trustees of corporate assets under predecessor statutes to current CLS Bus Corp §§ 1005 and 1006, particularly where contracting party sought to pierce corporate veil on theory that corporation did not have existence separate from its stockholders; under valid and broad arbitration agreement contained in contract, it was properly within arbitrator's jurisdiction to decide issue relating to subsequent acts (dissolution of corporation and death of stockholders) which might effect cancellation or termination of contract. Rodgers v Logan, 121 A.D.2d 250, 503 N.Y.S.2d 36, 1986 N.Y. App. Div. LEXIS 58237 (N.Y. App. Div. 1st Dep't 1986).

Tenant's complaint against landlord alleging violation of first refusal clause in lease was properly dismissed for failure to state cause of action where clause read "landlord agrees to give" first refusal "on sale of building," and ownership of building was transferred from corporate landlord to corporation's sole shareholder on voluntary dissolution, since distribution of corporate assets to shareholders upon voluntary dissolution is not "sale" of those assets. Kings Antiques Corp. v Varsity Properties, Inc., 121 A.D.2d 885, 503 N.Y.S.2d 575, 1986 N.Y. App. Div. LEXIS 59017 (N.Y. App. Div. 1st

Dep't 1986), app. dismissed, 70 N.Y.2d 641, 518 N.Y.S.2d 1031, 512 N.E.2d 557, 1987 N.Y. LEXIS 17460 (N.Y. 1987).

Court improperly granted summary judgment of plaintiff in action seeking to assess personal liability against individual defendant for corporate debt on "successor in interest" theory allegedly arising because corporation was voluntarily dissolved and individual defendant, as sole shareholder and recipient of corporate assets, became personally responsible for debts of corporation, where details of corporate dissolution more minimal, and there was suggestion that title to sole asset of corporation remained in corporation, thus raising fact issues as to personal liability of individual defendant. Wells v Ronning, 269 A.D.2d 690, 702 N.Y.S.2d 718, 2000 N.Y. App. Div. LEXIS 1580 (N.Y. App. Div. 3d Dep't 2000).

The liquidation process included sale or other disposition of all assets for such price or consideration as could be obtained, including such intangibles as trade names or trade marks and good will, if any. Speed Products Co. v Tinnerman Products, Inc., 179 F.2d 778, 1949 U.S. App. LEXIS 4622 (2d Cir. N.Y. 1949).

Since a distribution of assets by a corporation is not a sale, stockholders receiving the assets are not bona fide purchasers. Coleman v Golkin, Bomback & Co., 562 F.2d 166, 1977 U.S. App. LEXIS 11636 (2d Cir. N.Y. 1977).

Subdivision 9 of § 105 of former Stock Corp. L. contained provisions analogous to those appearing in § 1005 of the Business Corp. L., permitting a dissolving corporation to sell its assets to a corporation to take its place, taking securities of the latter in whole or in part by way of consideration, for distribution among shareholders of the vendor according to their respective rights. These were regarded as broad enough to sanction acceptance and distribution of trust certificates. Alcoma Corp. v Ackerman, 26 Misc. 2d 678, 207 N.Y.S.2d 137, 1960 N.Y. Misc. LEXIS 2372 (N.Y. Sup. Ct. 1960).

Shareholders to whom remaining assets of dissolved corporation are distributed hold such assets in trust for benefit of corporation's creditors, and may be liable to retirement fund to extent of corporate property they have received. Retirement Fund of Fur Mfg. Industry v Getto & Getto, Inc., 714 F. Supp. 651, 1989 U.S. Dist. LEXIS 6121 (S.D.N.Y. 1989).

Section 1005 would seem to permit recovery of corporate assets from stockholders regardless of motive or distribution; nothing in language of section or case law suggests that, in order to recover, plaintiffs must show that defendants defrauded corporation's creditors. Retirement Fund of Fur Mfg. Industry v Getto & Getto, Inc., 714 F. Supp. 651, 1989 U.S. Dist. LEXIS 6121 (S.D.N.Y. 1989).

Fact that corporate employer was not obliged to make ERISA withdrawal liability payments until after corporation was dissolved, when amount of its debt liability was calculated, did not preclude collection of corporate assets distributed to sole shareholders within previous 2 years; even if debt could be characterized as "contingent", term "liability" in § 1005 has been held to include contingent claims. Retirement Fund of Fur Mfg. Industry v Getto & Getto, Inc., 714 F. Supp. 651, 1989 U.S. Dist. LEXIS 6121 (S.D.N.Y. 1989).

Notes to Unpublished Decisions

1. In general

1. In general

Unpublished decision: Partial summary judgment in favor of defendants was proper because defendants were not liable as de facto owners under the Comprehensive Environmental Remediation, Compensation and Liability Act of 1980, nothing suggested that defendants directed or controlled the sublessee's daily operations in such a way as to cause contamination, and the sublessee's operations were "wound up" and its affairs fully-adjusted long before plaintiffs commenced the action. Next Millennium Realty v Adchem Corp., 2017 U.S. App. LEXIS 8476 (2d Cir. N.Y. May 11, 2017).

§ 1006. Corporate action and survival of remedies after dissolution

(a) A dissolved corporation, its directors, officers and shareholders may continue to function for the purpose of winding up the affairs of the corporation in the same manner as if the dissolution had not taken place, except as otherwise provided in this chapter or by court order. In particular, and without limiting the generality of the foregoing:

(1) The directors of a dissolved corporation shall not be deemed to be trustees of its assets; title to such assets shall not vest in them, but shall remain in the corporation until transferred by it in its corporate name.

(2) Dissolution shall not change quorum or voting requirements for the board or shareholders, or provisions regarding election, appointment, resignation or removal of, or filling vacancies among, directors or officers, or provisions regarding amendment or repeal of by-laws or adoption of new by-laws.

(3) Shares may be transferred and determinations of shareholders for any purpose may be made without closing the record of shareholders until such time, if any, as such record may be closed, and either the board or the shareholders may close it.

(4) The corporation may sue or be sued in all courts and participate in actions and proceedings, whether judicial, administrative, arbitrative or otherwise, in its corporate name, and process may be served by or upon it.

(b) The dissolution of a corporation shall not affect any remedy available to or against such corporation, its directors, officers or shareholders for any right or claim existing or any liability incurred before such dissolution, except as provided in sections 1007 (Notice to creditors; filing or barring claims) or 1008 (Jurisdiction of supreme court to supervise dissolution and liquidation).

History: Formerly § 1005, renumbered, L 1962, ch 834, § 75, eff Sept 1, 1963; amd, L 1963, ch 748, § 17, eff Sept 1, 1963.

CASE ANNOTATIONS

1. In general
2. Actions and liabilities preserved
3. Other activities preserved
4. Directors; liability
5. Procedural matters

1. In general

The differences, however, were more superficial than fundamental, as all of these provisions have sedulously preserved rights, remedies, liabilities, and the status of pending litigation and proceedings notwithstanding steps duly taken for dissolution. Country Tweeds, Inc. v Clyde Fashions, Ltd. (1955) 286 A.D. 491, 145 N.Y.S.2d 267, reh and app den 286 A.D. 1089, 147 N.Y.S.2d 674; Petition of Lynch (1945, Sup) 54 N.Y.S.2d 111; I. Kalfus Co. v Ad Press, Ltd. (1945) 184 Misc 285, 53 N.Y.S.2d 496, revd on other grounds 185 Misc 214, 56 N.Y.S.2d 373; Treemond Co. v Schering Corp. (1941, CA3 NJ) 122 F.2d 702, 50 USPQ 593; Stentor Electric Mfg. Co. v Klaxon Co. (1940, CA3 Del) 115 F.2d 268, 47 USPQ 193, revd on other grounds 313 US 487, 85 L Ed 1477, 61 S Ct 1020, 49 USPQ 515, on remand (CA3 Del) 125 F.2d 820, 52 USPQ 404, cert den 316 US 685, 86 L Ed 1757, 62 S Ct 1284, 53 USPQ 685; O'Neil v American Radiator Co. (1942, DC NY) 43 F. Supp. 543; Bloedorn v Washington Times Co. (1937) 67 App DC 91, 89 F.2d 835

Earlier provisions, notably § 29 of former Gen. Corp. L. and § 105 of former Stock Corp. L., differed from this § 1006 of the Business Corp. L in continuing corporate existence after the filing of a certificate of dissolution for the purpose of liquidating and winding up its affairs, and designated the board of directors "trustees" of the assets for this purpose. Re Baldwin Trading Corp. (1959, 2d Dept) 8 A.D.2d 968, 190 N.Y.S.2d 949, affd 8 N.Y.2d 144, 202 N.Y.S.2d 312, 168 N.E.2d 383; Central Union Trust Co. v American R. T. Co. (1921) 198 A.D. 303, 190 N.Y.S. 674, affd 233 N.Y. 531, 135 N.E. 905; Bank of New York v Kennedy (1944) 183 Misc 819, 54 N.Y.S.2d 122, affd 269 A.D. 747, 55 N.Y.S.2d 115; Steinhardt Import Corp. v Levy (1940)

174 Misc 184, 20 N.Y.S.2d 360; Marine Trust Co. v Tralles (1933) 147 Misc 426, 263 N.Y.S. 750; Wilson v Brown (1919) 107 Misc 167, 175 N.Y.S. 688, affd 190 A.D. 926, 179 N.Y.S. 958

Court improperly granted summary judgment of plaintiff in action seeking to assess personal liability against individual defendant for corporate debt on "successor in interest" theory allegedly arising because corporation was voluntarily dissolved and individual defendant, as sole shareholder and recipient of corporate assets, became personally responsible for debts of corporation, where details of corporate dissolution more minimal, and there was suggestion that title to sole asset of corporation remained in corporation, thus raising fact issues as to personal liability of individual defendant. Wells v Ronning (2000, 3d Dept) 269 A.D.2d 690, 702 N.Y.S.2d 718

Respondent corporations, which entered into new business relationship with petitioner corporation at time when its corporate status had lapsed due to non-compliance with unspecified provisions of Nevada corporations law, could not rely on "winding up" provision of CLS Bus Corp § 1005(a), since respondent was not exercising right or remedy existing as of its dissolution; fact that respondent was dissolved in another state was of no moment, since it continued as de facto corporation. Intelligent Bank Management v East Coast Fin. Corp. (1994, 1st Dept) 207 A.D.2d 760, 616 N.Y.S.2d 618

Corporation that was dissolved could continue to function for the purpose of winding up its affairs but did not have a claim against the telephone company for restoration of its phone service as part of the relief requested in a protracted dispute, and the Public Service Commission had a rational basis for denying the corporation's request to have service restored. Matter of Community Network Serv., Inc. v New York State Dept. of Pub. Serv. (2006, App Div, 3d Dept) 820 NYS2d 184

Law firm's motion to dismiss legal malpractice suit on the alternate ground that the corporate client lacked the capacity to commence the action against the law firm should have been granted because the client had been dissolved for failure to pay franchise taxes; a lawyer had represented the client prior to its dissolution, and thus, under N.Y. Bus. Corp. Law § 1006(b), the client retained the capacity to sue her relating to such representation. However, the law firm was not retained until after the client was dissolved and this action did not relate to the winding up of the client's affairs, so the client thus lacked the capacity to use the courts to enforce obligations arising out of the law firm's representation of the corporation until it secured retroactive de jure status by payment of delinquent franchise taxes. Moran Enters., Inc. v Hurst (2009, App Div, 2d Dept) 888 NYS2d 109.

Judgment for a town against a corporation's officers arising from the officers' refusal to seek insurance coverage from the New York State Insurance Fund was error because, inter alia, the town's claim against the corporation was the subject of litigation at the time of the corporation's dissolution and thus could not have been barred by the Business Corporation Law even if notice of the dissolution had been provided to the town; thus, the town's claim with respect to the harm flowing from the officers' alleged violation of the Business Corporation Law was of no moment. Town of Amherst v Hilger (2013, App Div, 4th Dept) 962 NYS2d 837, subsequent app (2013, 4th Dept) 104 App Div 3d 1268, 960 NYS2d 922.

2. Actions and liabilities preserved

Compromise and settlement of both rights and liabilities were permissible, including tax claims, and arbitration could be agreed to or demanded under the terms of antecedent agreements. Milton L. Ehrlich, Inc. v Unit Frame & Floor Corp. (1959) 5 N.Y.2d 275, 184 N.Y.S.2d 334, 157 N.E.2d 495, 71 ALR2d 1115; Parish & Bingham Corp. v United States (1930) 71 Ct Cl 90, 44 F.2d 993, 2 USTC ¶ 600

A shareholder derivative action may be maintained even though commenced after the subject corporation has effected a dissolution and distributed its assets inasmuch as a shareholder has the necessary standing where he meets the dual requirement as to the ownership of stock contained in subdivision (b) of section 626 of the Business Corporation Law, which requires plaintiff to be a shareholder at the time of bringing the action and at the time of the transaction of which he complains; a shareholder of a dissolved corporation has a sufficient interest in a derivative action to satisfy the spirit of the rule requiring ownership at the commencement of the action and, furthermore, pursuant to section 1006 of the Business Corporation Law, the rights and remedies of the shareholders existing prior to dissolution are viewed as if the dissolution never occurred. Accordingly, since the dissolution of a corporation, without more, does not deprive the shareholders of their derivative remedy, it

was error to dismiss such a derivative action except as to those shareholders who availed themselves of their appraisal rights under subdivision (e) of section 623 of the Business Corporation Law. Independent Investor Protective League v Time, Inc. (1980) 50 N.Y.2d 259, 428 N.Y.S.2d 671, 406 N.E.2d 486

Order which denied cross motion of defendants for summary judgment dismissing complaint and cross claims against them affirmed-plaintiff, carpenter for subcontractor, fell from roof and sustained serious injuries; individual defendant is builder who has incorporated several business entities which perform general contracting duties; on date of plaintiff's accident, corporate defendant was acting as general contractor on subject subdivision, although it subsequently changed its name and second corporation with same name as defendant corporation was incorporated; successor corporation later filed certificate of dissolution, following which action was commenced with service on individual defendant personally and as president of defendant corporation-defendant corporation was acting as general contractor on date of plaintiff's accident and corporate name change cannot affect its liability (Business Corporation Law § 806 [b] [5]); its subsequent dissolution cannot prevent suit against it because Business Corporation Law § 1006 (a) (4) and (b) permit suit against dissolved corporation as part of winding up its affairs; thus, Supreme Court properly granted summary judgment against defendant corporation-agent of general contractor can be liable under Labor Law § 240 (1) if agent exercises sufficient supervision and control over activity; individual defendant's testimony and affidavit reveal he was personally involved on almost daily basis at building site; he described building project in personal terms, referring to work as his own; whether this involvement provides sufficient supervision and control is question for jury to resolve. Briere v Barbera, 163 A.D.2d 659

The trial court improperly dismissed a complaint brought by a dissolved corporation to recover on a fire insurance policy obtained by the corporation one year after dissolution, where the power to keep corporation property insured against fire and other hazards was inherent in the power possessed by a corporation winding up its affairs following dissolution. Igbara Realty Corp. v New York Property Ins. Underwriting Asso. (1983, 1st Dept) 94 A.D.2d 79, 463 N.Y.S.2d 211

Personal representatives of deceased stockholders and directors of dissolved corporation were not entitled to stay arbitration of claim against corporation for alleged breach of contract, since dissolution of corporation more than 30 years prior to present proceedings made it futile for contracting party to even attempt to sue corporation directly and he was therefore entitled to directly sue trustees of corporate assets under predecessor statutes to current CLS Bus Corp §§ 1005 and 1006, particularly where contracting party sought to pierce corporate veil on theory that corporation did not have existence separate from its stockholders; under valid and broad arbitration agreement contained in contract, it was properly within arbitrator's jurisdiction to decide issue relating to subsequent acts (dissolution of corporation and death of stockholders) which might effect cancellation or termination of contract. Rodgers v Logan (1986, 1st Dept) 121 A.D.2d 250, 503 N.Y.S.2d 36

In action by carpenter under CLS Labor § 240(1) for injuries sustained in fall from roof, carpenter was properly awarded summary judgment against general contractor, and president of general contractor was properly denied summary judgment where (1) president was builder who incorporated several business entities to perform general contracting duties, and (2) after accident, general contractor changed its name and then was dissolved, and new corporation with same name as general contractor was then incorporated; general contractor was properly sued since CLS Bus Corp § 1006 permits dissolved corporation to be sued as part of winding up of its affairs, and question existed as to whether president was sufficiently personally involved with general contractor as to be held personally liable. Briere v Barbera (1990, 3d Dept) 163 A.D.2d 659, 558 N.Y.S.2d 278

Criminal prosecution of corporation did not abate on corporation's dissolution in view of state's strong public policy in favor of maintaining corporate liability beyond dissolution. People v Pymm Thermometer Corp. (1992, 2d Dept) 188 A.D.2d 560, 591 N.Y.S.2d 459, app den 81 N.Y.2d 1018, 600 N.Y.S.2d 206, 616 N.E.2d 863

Corporation dissolved by secretary of state may defend foreclosure action relating to its corporate assets. Harris v Stony Clove Lake Acres (1995, 3d Dept) 221 A.D.2d 833, 633 N.Y.S.2d 691

A defendant corporation was estopped to set up a defense that it has been dissolved and was no longer in existence where it had continued to do business for a period of several years following the alleged dissolution. Wilkins v Sirael Realty Corp. (1940) 174 Misc 1002, 21 N.Y.S.2d 1017

Corporations undergoing dissolution may continue to function for the purpose of winding up the affairs of the corporation in the same manner as if the dissolution had not taken place and the dissolution does not affect either the right of the corporation to collect and distribute its assets or to sue in its corporate name; therefore, a corporation which was dissolved pursuant to Tax Law § 203-a for nonpayment of taxes was permitted to exercise an option to purchase real estate since the option constituted a valuable asset and the exercise of that option was a significant part of winding up the affairs of the corporation. Bowditch v 57 Laight Street Corp. (1981) 111 Misc. 2d 255, 443 N.Y.S.2d 785

In action wherein employer, which was found 25 percent liable, settled for more than its equitable share, and corporate manufacturer, which was found 40 percent liable, was dissolved before trial, distributor's liability for noneconomic loss was limited by CLS CPLR § 1601 to 35 percent as found by jury and could not be increased by manufacturer's liability of 40 percent to 75 percent, notwithstanding plaintiffs' claim that they did not have jurisdiction to enforce judgment against manufacturer. Dominguez v Fixrammer Corp. (1997, Sup) 172 Misc. 2d 868, 656 N.Y.S.2d 111

In action wherein employer was found 25 percent liable but settled for more than its equitable share, corporate manufacturer was found 40 percent liable but was dissolved before trial, and distributor was found 35 percent liable, each nonsettling tortfeasor's share of noneconomic damages would be limited under CLS CPLR §.1601 to 40 percent and 35 percent, respectively, regardless of amount of liability remaining after applying set-off provisions of CLS Gen Oblig § 15-108 pertaining to releases by other joint tortfeasors. Dominguez v Fixrammer Corp. (1997, Sup) 172 Misc. 2d 868, 656 N.Y.S.2d 111

Contingent as well as fixed liabilities continued and could be asserted against the corporation during the winding up period, and the corporation could still accept gifts, take action to collect debts due to it, and receive, accept, and hold anything to which it might be entitled under the terms of an antecedent transaction. School of Music of Brooklyn Free Musical Society, Inc. v Moritt (1955, Sup) 145 N.Y.S.2d 645; Commissioners of State Ins. Fund v H. L. & F. McBride, Inc. (1949) 195 Misc 362, 90 N.Y.S.2d 416; Re Mohr's Estate (1941) 175 Misc 706, 24 N.Y.S.2d 977; Display Stage Lighting Co. v Century Lighting, Inc. (1941, DC NY) 41 F. Supp. 937, 52 USPQ 163

Upon completion of dissolution, under the earlier statutes, the corporation lacked capacity to sue. Dieselcraft Corp. v Joca Realty Corp. (1957, Sup) 161 N.Y.S.2d 761

Distributor of asbestos which was dissolved in 1999 was permitted to bring a contribution or indemnification claim against the employer of an employee who had been diagnosed with asbestos-related illnesses in 2000 because bringing such a claim was a normal part of winding up the distributor's affairs, N.Y. Bus. Corp. Law §§ 1005(a)(1) and 1006(a); the distributor had to either settle or defend asbestos claims to wind up its affairs, and a third-party claim for contribution or indemnification was a normal part of defending such a claim. Tedesco v A.P. Green Indus., Inc. (2007) 8 NY3d 243, 832 NYS2d 141, 864 NE2d 65, reported at (2007, NY) 2007 NY LEXIS 207

Although a corporation had fitfully pursued a problematic lawsuit for four and a half decades after the events in issue transpired and after the business declared bankruptcy, three and a half decades after the corporation was dissolved did not sound like a limited winding up of affairs during which time the dissolved corporation had limited existence pursuant to N.Y. Bus. Corp. Law §§ 1005(a)(1) and 1006. Lance Int'l v First Nat'l City Bank (2009, Civ Ct) 241 NYLJ 72, 878 NYS2d 572.

New York law establishes corporation's continuing obligation to respond to subpoenas relating to pre-dissolution conduct as well as its amenability to sanctions should it fail to do so. Re Grand Jury Subpoenas Issued to Thirteen Corps. (1985, CA2 NY) 775 F.2d 43, 85-2 USTC ¶ 9768

New York corporation which was dissolved for nonpayment of corporate franchise taxes could file petition for reorganization under Chapter 11 of Bankruptcy Code since CLS Bus Corp § 1006 permits dissolved corporation to wind up its affairs and participate in actions and proceedings as if dissolution had not taken place, and CLS Tax § 203-a permits dissolved corporation to be reinstated nunc pro tunc

on filing of certificate that all taxes, penalties and interest charges have been paid. Re Cedar Tide Corp. (1988, CA2 NY) 859 F.2d 1127, 18 BCD 843, CCH Bankr L Rptr ¶ 72480, cert den (US) 104 L Ed 2d 405, 109 S Ct 1933

Among liabilities deemed preserved by the earlier statutes was that incurred for violation of a federal criminal or penal provision. United States v Brakes, Inc. (1958, DC NY) 157 F. Supp. 916

Corporation no longer in existence remains responsible for its liabilities until its affairs are fully adjusted, and included as corporate liabilities are contractual obligations. Flute, Inc. v Rubel (1988, SD NY) 682 F. Supp. 184

Dissolved company was subject to suit in state's action under federal law to recover costs incurred in cleanup of site formerly owned by company, where dissolved company continued to exist under Bus Corp § 1006 to wind up its affairs. New York v Longboat, Inc. (2001, ND NY) 140 F. Supp. 2d 174

Where a dissolved race systems company brought an action for patent infringement against a competitor, the court held that N.Y. Bus. Corp. Law § 1006(a) did not prevent the race systems company, as a dissolved corporation, from bringing the lawsuit. Race Safe Sys. v Indy Racing League (2003, ND NY) 251 F. Supp. 2d 1106

Plaintiff venturers could bring a second suit to address post-judgment wrongdoing by defendants with respect to their appropriation of a film project; case was remanded to state court where removal based on fraudulent joinder argument failed. Briarpatch Ltd., L.P. v Thomas (2003, SD NY) 265 F. Supp. 2d 219

Order vacating a tax deed, subsequent conveyances, and a mortgage was affirmed because the trial court found that the notice to redeem sent to the owner failed to comply with due process; contrary to the assignee's contention, the owner, a corporation, had the capacity to commence this action despite its dissolution. 89 Pine Hollow Rd. Realty Corp. v American Tax Fund (2012, 2d Dept) 96 App Div 3d 995, 948 NYS2d 617, related proceeding (2012, 2d Dept) 96 App Div 3d 981, 946 NYS2d 878

Cross-plaintiff (CP) had the capacity to maintain its cross claims, even though it had been dissolved by proclamation, as the checks at issue were allegedly transferred and the cross claims were asserted before the dissolution, and the claims could be pursued in the course of winding up CP's affairs. Greater Bright Light Home Care Servs., Inc. v Jeffries-El, 151 A.D.3d 818, 2017 NY Slip Op 04821, 2017 NY Slip Op 4821, 58 N.Y.S.3d 68, 2017 N.Y. App. Div. LEXIS 4740 (N.Y. App. Div. 2d Dep't 2017).

3. Other activities preserved

Plaintiff had standing as a dissolved corporation could transfer its shares and sell the tanning beds to plaintiff as part of winding up its affairs and defendants did not show that the transactions constituted impermissible new business. Lots 4 Less Stores, Inc. v Integrated Props., Inc., 2017 NY Slip Op 05529, 2017 N.Y. App. Div. LEXIS 5371 (N.Y. App. Div. 4th Dep't 2017).

Executives of the corporation were not precluded from acting in the corporation's behalf in such matters as executing conveyances or other instruments in its name or retaining counsel to represent it, because of the statutory designation of the board of directors as "trustees" in liquidation, particularly if they did so at the direction or with the acquiescence of the directors. Gaillard Realty Co. v Manhattan Brass Co. (1933) 238 A.D. 84, 263 N.Y.S. 397; O. G. Orr & Co. v Fireman's Fund Ins. Co. (1932) 235 A.D. 1, 256 N.Y.S. 79; Northern Properties, Inc. v Kuf Realty Corp. (1961) 30 Misc. 2d 1, 217 N.Y.S.2d 355

The filing of a certificate of dissolution did not preclude a corporation from entering into a fixed-fee agreement retaining counsel to prosecute damage claims in its behalf. Application of Peters (1946) 271 A.D. 518, 67 N.Y.S.2d 305, mod on other grounds 296 N.Y. 974, 73 N.E.2d 560

Where trustees or successors of dissolved corporation do not choose to maintain preexisting lease in effect, landlord may seek to enforce its rights under lease against estate or assets of dissolved corporation. Goldberg v Harwood (1995, 1st Dept) 216 A.D.2d 152, 628 N.Y.S.2d 105, reh den (NY A.D., 1st Dept) 1995 N.Y. A.D. LEXIS 9763 and app gr 87 N.Y.2d 806, 641 N.Y.S.2d 597, 664 N.E.2d 508 and affd (NY) 1996 N.Y. LEXIS 1179

Absent express assumption of rights and obligations of preexisting lease by purchaser of assets of dissolved corporation, and landlord's consent to assignment, as required by lease, landlord continued to be dissolved corporation's creditor with claim against proceeds of sale of its assets. Goldberg v Harwood (1995, 1st Dept) 216 A.D.2d 152, 628 N.Y.S.2d 105, reh den (NY A.D., 1st Dept) 1995 N.Y. A.D. LEXIS

9763 and app gr 87 N.Y.2d 806, 641 N.Y.S.2d 597, 664 N.E.2d 508 and affd (NY) 1996 N.Y. LEXIS 1179

New York City Corporation Counsel properly determined that corporation dissolved under CLS Tax § 203-a could obtain release of its tax-foreclosed property under New York City Administrative Code § 11-424(f), without violating statutory prohibition against such corporations carrying on new business, since CLS Bus Corp § 1006 permits dissolved corporation to pursue any remedy available to it in respect to reacquisition of property it owned prior to its dissolution, such remedy does not depend on whether that property could be characterized as corporate asset after dissolution, and code permits recapture of property right possessed by corporation prior to its dissolution. 172 East 122 Street Tenants Asso. v Schwarz (1989) 73 N.Y.2d 340, 540 N.Y.S.2d 420, 537 N.E.2d 1281

4. Directors; liability

The board of directors, notwithstanding their general designation as "trustees" of the corporate assets by § 29 of former Gen. Corp. L., were not considered trustees of an express trust as that term is used in certain provisions of the Real and Personal Property Laws, and were not subject to suit as such. Actions by creditors to recover judgment or enforce rights had to be against the corporation as such, not against its board of directors. Similarly the directors could not sue, as such, on an obligation running to the corporation; the action had to be in the name of the corporation. Cunningham v Glauber (1909) 133 A.D. 10, 117 N.Y.S. 866; Parish-Watson v Chalom Art Gallery, Inc. (1943) 181 Misc 299, 43 N.Y.S.2d 179; Hassett v Kimball (1932) 144 Misc 50, 258 N.Y.S. 17; Giovannangeli v Levich & Pollach, Inc. (1929) 134 Misc 245, 235 N.Y.S. 28

Although § 29 of former Gen. Corp. L. left liquidation and winding up of the affairs of a corporation generally in the hands of its board of directors as trustees, someone else could be appointed trustee or liquidator by court sanction upon a showing of good cause, as where, for example, the directors were equally divided and unable to agree on action to be taken. De Martini v McCaldin (1918) 184 A.D. 222, 171 N.Y.S. 528; Gutwirth & Errante Homes, Inc. v Jacobowitz (1948, Sup) 81 N.Y.S.2d 607

While judgment creditors had certain rights of action against the directors as liquidating trustees in the event of failure to make adequate provision for payment of obligations due them, or wasting assets deemed to be held in trust for their benefit, under §§ 90 and 91 of former Gen. Corp. L., an ordinary creditor had no right to proceed against the directors as such under § 105 of former Stock Corp. L. and must first proceed against the corporation. Bristol Mfg. Corp. v Elk Textile Co. (1924) 209 A.D. 95, 204 N.Y.S. 427

Right to charge individual directors acting as trustees in liquidation with fraud or waste in the handling and disposition of assets remained primarily in the corporation, notwithstanding it was in process of dissolution, and the proper method for demanding an accounting to protect rights of shareholders was apparently to bring a derivative action. Brennan v Barnes (1928) 133 Misc 340, 232 N.Y.S. 112

Compare however, Alexander v Quality Leather Goods Corp. (1934) 150 Misc 577, 269 N.Y.S. 499

Company dissolved for failure to pay franchise taxes can be considered de facto corporation. L-TEC Elecs. Corp. v Cougar Elec. Org., Inc. (1999, CA2 NY) 198 F.3d 85

Where de facto corporation later pays its taxes and is reinstated, its corporate status is restored nunc pro tunc, and any contracts into which it may have entered are retroactively validated. L-TEC Elecs. Corp. v Cougar Elec. Org., Inc. (1999, CA2 NY) 198 F.3d 85

Creditor may maintain action directly against directors or shareholders, where it is impossible or futile to obtain judgment against defunct corporation. Flute, Inc. v Rubel (1988, SD NY) 682 F. Supp. 184

Debtors who dissolved a catering business they owned before they declared bankruptcy, but who did not inform a creditor or a state court that the business was dissolved, were jointly and severally liable under New York law for a debt their catering business owed the creditor, and the debt was nondischargeable under 11 U.S.C.S. § 523(a)(2)(A) and (a)(3). The debt was nondischargeable under § 523(a)(2)(A) because the debtors concealed a material fact when they did not tell the creditor they were dissolving their business, and it was nondischargeable under § 523(a)(3) because the debtors did not list the creditor or a lawsuit involving the creditor in their bankruptcy petition. In re Hartley (2011, BC SD NY) 458 BR 145.

5. Procedural matters

The corporation itself was likewise a necessary party to a stockholders' suit to set aside a transfer of corporate property. Security Trust Co. v Pritchard (1922) 201 A.D. 142, 194 N.Y.S. 486

Plaintiff corporation which was defunct but not judicially dissolved could be examined before trial through its former officers, agents, or employees. Rugby Excavators, Inc. v Juliano (1972, 2d Dept) 40 A.D.2d 1024, 338 N.Y.S.2d 983

Where all stockholders, officers and presumably directors of corporation were before court and represented, proceeding, on claim against decedent's estate which should have been brought as derivative action, for alleged misappropriation of corporate assets by decedent would not be dismissed for nonjoinder of parties, though receiver, who failed to qualify, was not joined, and corporation was not joined. Business Corporation Law §§ 1006, 1111, 1206(a). Maki v Estate of Ziehm (1977, 3d Dept) 55 A.D.2d 454, 391 N.Y.S.2d 705

Adverse inference could properly be drawn against dissolved corporation (defendant) for its failure to produce its president at trial of action for breach of sublease since dissolution does not affect liability occurring prior to dissolution, and thus defendant remained obligated to respond to subpoenas. Simplicity Pattern Co. v Miami Tru-Color Off-Set Serv. (1994, 1st Dept) 210 A.D.2d 24, 619 N.Y.S.2d 29

Error in defendant's notice of dissolution under CLS Bus Corp § 1007, by which another undissolved corporation was named instead of defendant, rendered notice ineffective to limit defendant's liability to claims brought within prescribed period (CLS Bus Corp § 1006), and thus, although defendant was dissolved and its assets distributed, it could be sued in connection with claims that arose prior to its dissolution. Fernandez v Kinsey (1994, 1st Dept) 205 A.D.2d 448, 613 N.Y.S.2d 894

Court erred in dismissing action against corporation for lack of personal jurisdiction where action arose before purported dissolution of corporation, and corporation did not deny that it received service of process from Secretary of State. Gutman v Club Mediterranee Int'l (1995, 2d Dept) 218 A.D.2d 640, 630 N.Y.S.2d 343

Service of process could be made upon the corporation in like manner as prior to institution of the dissolution proceedings. Laurendi v Cascade Development Co. (1957) 5 Misc. 2d 688, 165 N.Y.S.2d 832, affd (4th Dept) 4 A.D.2d 852, 167 N.Y.S.2d 240; Public Fuel Service, Inc. v Hillgun Holding Corp. (1954, Sup) 133 N.Y.S.2d 850; Garibaldi v Yonkers (1949) 198 Misc 1100, 102 N.Y.S.2d 200, affd 278 A.D. 571, 102 N.Y.S.2d 426

Trial court improperly sua sponte appointed a referee to hear and report as to the value of the corporation's properties and leasehold interest and the appropriate procedures following dissolution in the judicial dissolution of the corporation; post-dissolution procedures in a judicial proceeding, provided for in N.Y. Bus. Corp. Law §§ 1005-1008, as provided under N.Y. Bus. Corp. Law § 1117, did not include the appointment of a referee. In re Oak St. Mgmt. (2003, A.D., 2d Dept) 762 N.Y.S.2d 522

New York City Corporation Counsel's interpretation of "eligibility" of dissolved corporation to seek release of its tax-foreclosed property under New York City Administrative Code § 11-424(f), and his approval of application for release, were neither arbitrary nor irrational merely because application was not checked against provisions of Business Corporation Law pertaining to dissolved corporations that might render otherwise eligible corporation ineligible to apply for release. 172 East 122 Street Tenants Asso. v Schwarz (1989) 73 N.Y.2d 340, 540 N.Y.S.2d 420, 537 N.E.2d 1281

Motion for summary judgment could have been considered as a motion to dismiss under N.Y. C.P.L.R. 3211(a)(1) where the defense was founded on documentary evidence of plaintiff corporation's dissolution proclamation; it could have been considered under N.Y. C.P.L.R. 3211(a)(2) for lack of subject matter jurisdiction, as the plaintiff dissolved corporation did not exist, and thus there was no case or controversy; and it could have been considered under N.Y. C.P.L.R. 1017, 1021 and/or N.Y. Bus. Corp. Law §§ 1005, 1006 dealing with the substitution of parties for a dissolved corporation. Lance Int'l v First Nat'l City Bank (2009, Civ Ct) 241 NYLJ 72, 878 NYS2d 572.

N.Y. Bus. Corp. Law §§ 1006 and 1117 stand for the proposition that N.Y. C.P.L.R. 1017 can be disregarded and substitution avoided in a case of corporate dissolution. The specific provisions of the Business Corporation Law override the more general provisions of the CPLR. Lance Int'l v First Nat'l City Bank (2009, Civ Ct) 241 NYLJ 72, 878 NYS2d 572.

Although a corporation filed suit before its dissolution, based on pre-dissolution transactions, the reasoning of Lorisa, that courts had to foster compliance with N.Y. Tax Law § 203-a(10), and that a dissolved corporation may only "wind up" its affairs, under N.Y. Bus. Corp. Law §§ 1009 and 1006, had to be brought to bear in determining a dissolved corporation's capacity to sue. Lance Int'l v First Nat'l City Bank (2009, Civ Ct) 241 NYLJ 72, 878 NYS2d 572.

Court did not have long-arm jurisdiction over corporation that was dissolved prior to alleged wrongful acts. Linzer v EMI Blackwood Music (1995, SD NY) 904 F. Supp. 207

Where a supplier did not substantiate its claim that the dissolved corporation operated as a de facto corporation under N.Y. Bus. Law §§ 1005(a)(2), 1006(a), (b), a judicial hearing officer properly set aside the N.Y. Bus. Corp. Law § 306 service on the Secretary of State; where the dissolved corporation only sought vacatur of a default judgment and leave to serve an answer pursuant to N.Y. C.P.L.R. 5015, the trial court properly granted the relief sought. Bruce Supply Corp. v New Wave Mech., Inc. (2004, A.D., 2d Dept) 773 N.Y.S.2d 408

§ 1007. Notice to creditors; filing or barring claims

(a) At any time after dissolution, the corporation may give a notice requiring all creditors and claimants, including any with unliquidated or contingent claims and any with whom the corporation has unfulfilled contracts, to present their claims in writing and in detail at a specified place and by a specified day, which shall not be less than six months after the first publication of such notice. Such notice shall be published at least once a week for two successive weeks in a newspaper of general circulation in the county in which the office of the corporation was located at the date of dissolution. On or before the date of the first publication of such notice, the corporation shall mail a copy thereof, postage prepaid and addressed to his last known address, to each person believed to be a creditor of or claimant against the corporation whose name and address are known to or can with due diligence be ascertained by the corporation. The giving of such notice shall not constitute a recognition that any person is a proper creditor or claimant, and shall not revive or make valid, or operate as a recognition of the validity of, or a waiver of any defense or counterclaim in respect of any claim against the corporation, its assets, directors, officers or shareholders, which has been barred by any statute of limitations or become invalid by any cause, or in respect of which the corporation, its directors, officers or shareholders, has any defense or counterclaim.

(b) Any claims which shall have been filed as provided in such notice and which shall be disputed by the corporation may be submitted for determination to the supreme court under section 1008 (Jurisdiction of supreme court to supervise dissolution and liquidation). A claim filed by the trustee or paying agent for the holders of bonds or coupons shall have the same effect as if filed by the holder of any such bond or coupon. Any person whose claim is, at the date of the first publication of such notice, barred by any statute of limitations is not a creditor or claimant entitled to any notice under this section or section 1008. The claim of any such person and all other claims which are not timely filed as provided in such notice except claims which are the subject of litigation on the date

of the first publication of such notice, and all claims which are so filed but are disallowed by the court under section 1008, shall be forever barred as against the corporation, its assets, directors, officers and shareholders, except to such extent, if any, as the court may allow them against any remaining assets of the corporation in the case of a creditor who shows satisfactory reason for his failure to file his claim as so provided. If the court requires a further notice under section 1008, any reference to a notice in this section shall, to the extent that the court so orders, mean such further notice, except that a claim which has been filed in accordance with a notice under this section need not be refiled under such further notice.

(c) Notwithstanding this section and section 1008, tax claims and other claims of this state, of the United States and of the department of finance of the city of New York shall not be required to be filed under those sections, and such claims shall not be barred because not so filed, and distribution of the assets of the corporation, or any part thereof, may be deferred until determination of any such claims.

(d) Laborer's wages shall be preferred claims and entitled to payment before any other creditors out of the assets of the corporation in excess of valid prior liens or encumbrances.

History: Formerly § 1006, renumbered, L 1962, ch 834, § 76, eff Sept 1, 1963; amd, L 1963, ch 748, § 18, eff Sept 1, 1963; L 2009, ch 201, § 74, eff Oct 1, 2009.

CASE ANNOTATIONS

In proceeding arising out of dissolution of closely held corporation, landlord of corporate tenant was entitled to enforce its claim as creditor against assets of dissolved corporation, and referee properly ordered satisfaction of that claim from proceeds of sale of corporation's assets where (1) terms of public auction sale identified lease of premises where corporation conducted business as corporate asset, (2) at time of sale, corporate tenant had defaulted in payment of rent due under lease, (3) landlord advised referee prior to sale that it was corporation's creditor for balance due under lease, and (4) highest bidder at auction sale purchased all of corporation's assets. Goldberg v Harwood (1996) 88 N.Y.2d 911, 646 N.Y.S.2d 663, 669 N.E.2d 821

Under provision of Business Corporation Law governing nonjudicial dissolution of the corporation that the bar of an order confirming dissolution does not extend to claims which were subject to litigation on the date of first publication of notice of dissolution, the dissolved corporation must be a party to any litigation relied on as preserving claims against it. Gardner v Fyr-Fyter Co. (1975, 4th Dept) 47 A.D.2d 591, 363 N.Y.S.2d 690

Error in defendant's notice of dissolution under CLS Bus Corp § 1007, by which another undissolved corporation was named instead of defendant, rendered notice ineffective to limit defendant's liability to claims brought within prescribed period (CLS Bus Corp § 1006), and thus, although defendant was dissolved and its assets distributed, it could be sued in connection with claims that arose prior to its dissolution. Fernandez v Kinsey (1994, 1st Dept) 205 A.D.2d 448, 613 N.Y.S.2d 894

Trial court improperly sua sponte appointed a referee to hear and report as to the value of the corporation's properties and leasehold interest and the appropriate procedures following dissolution in the judicial dissolution of the corporation; post-dissolution procedures in a judicial proceeding, provided for in N.Y. Bus. Corp. Law §§ 1005-1008, as provided under N.Y. Bus. Corp. Law § 1117, did not include the appointment of a referee. In re Oak St. Mgmt. (2003, A.D., 2d Dept) 762 N.Y.S.2d 522

After obtaining a judgment against a lessor, the lessee was permitted to amend the complaint to include the defunct lessor's director pursuant to N.Y. Uniform Dist. Ct. Act §§ 1813(a) and 1814(a) because while N.Y. Bus. Corp. Law § 1007 allowed informal dissolution of corporations without notice to creditors, the director could not be shielded against corporate creditor liability. Parent v Amity Autoworld, Ltd. (2007, Dist Ct) 15 Misc 3d 633, 832 NYS2d 775

Judgment for a town against a corporation's officers arising from the officers' refusal to seek insurance coverage from the New York State Insurance Fund was error because, inter alia, the town's claim against the corporation was the subject of litigation at the time of the corporation's dissolution and thus could not have been barred by the Business Corporation Law even if notice of the dissolution had been provided to the town; thus, the town's claim with respect to the harm flowing from the officers' alleged violation of the Business Corporation Law was of no moment. Town of Amherst v Hilger (2013, App Div, 4th Dept) 962 NYS2d 837, subsequent app (2013, 4th Dept) 104 App Div 3d 1268, 960 NYS2d 922.

Debtors who dissolved a catering business they owned before they declared bankruptcy, but who did not inform a creditor or a state court that the business was dissolved, were jointly and severally liable under New York law for a debt their catering business owed the creditor, and the debt was nondischargeable under 11 U.S.C.S. § 523(a)(2)(A) and (a)(3). The debt was nondischargeable under § 523(a)(2)(A) because the debtors concealed a material fact when they did not tell the creditor they were dissolving their business, and it was nondischargeable under § 523(a)(3) because the debtors did not list the creditor or a lawsuit involving the creditor in their bankruptcy petition. In re Hartley (2011, BC SD NY) 458 BR 145.

§ 1008. Jurisdiction of supreme court to supervise dissolution and liquidation

(a) At any time after the filing of a certificate of dissolution under this article the supreme court in the judicial district where the office of the corporation was located at the date of its dissolution, in a special proceeding instituted under this section, upon the petition of the corporation, or, in a situation approved by the court, upon the petition of a creditor, claimant, director, officer, shareholder, subscriber for shares, incorporator or the attorney-general, may suspend or annul the dissolution or continue the liquidation of the corporation under the supervision of the court and may make all such orders as it may deem proper in all matters in connection with the dissolution or the winding up of the affairs of the corporation, and in particular, and without limitation of the generality thereof, in respect of the following:

(1) The determination of the validity of the authorization of the dissolution of the corporation and of the execution and delivery of the certificate of dissolution under this article.

(2) The adequacy of the notice given to creditors and claimants and if it is determined to have been inadequate, the requirement of such further notice as the court may deem proper.

(3) The determination of the validity and amount or invalidity of any claims which have been presented to the corporation.

(4) The barring of all creditors and claimants who have not timely filed claims as provided in any such notice, or whose claims have been disallowed by the court, as against the corporation, its assets, directors, officers and shareholders.

(5) The determination and enforcement of the liability of any director, officer, shareholder or subscriber for shares, to the corporation or for the liabilities of the corporation.

(6) The payment, satisfaction or compromise of claims against the corporation, the retention of assets for such purpose, and the determination of the adequacy of provisions made for payment of the liabilities of the corporation.

(7) The disposition or destruction of records, documents and papers of the corporation.

(8) The appointment and removal of a receiver under article 12 (Receivership) who may be a director, officer or shareholder of the corporation.

(9) The issuance of injunctions for one or more of the purposes and as provided in section 1115 (Injunction).

(10) The return of subscription payments to subscribers for shares, and the making of distributions, in cash or in kind or partly each, to the shareholders.

(11) The payment to the state comptroller, as abandoned property, of assets under paragraph (c) of section 1005 (Procedure after dissolution).

(b) Orders under this section may be entered ex parte, except that if such special proceeding was not instituted upon petition of the corporation, notice shall be given to the corporation in such manner as the court may direct. Notice shall be given to such other persons interested, and in such manner, as the court may deem proper, of any hearings and of the entry of any orders on such matters as the court shall deem proper. All orders made by the court under this section shall be binding upon the attorney-general, the corporation, its officers, directors, shareholders, subscribers for shares, incorporators, creditors and claimants.

(c) (1) Simultaneously with the institution of such special proceeding for annulment of the dissolution, the petitioner shall apply to the department of state to reserve the corporation name to the corporation. If such name shall not be available for use, the petitioner forthwith upon being notified thereof shall apply to such department for the reservation of another and available name and any judgment or order of annulment made in such proceeding shall order and direct the petitioner to execute a certificate of change of the corporate name to such other name.

(2) The clerk of the court, or such other person as the court may direct, shall transmit a certified copy of the judgment or order of annulment of the dissolution, together with the certificate of change of corporate name in the appropriate case, to the department of state, and a certified copy of such judgment or order to the clerk of the county in which the office of the corporation was located on the date of the dissolution. Upon filing by the department of state, the annulment of dissolution shall be effected.

History: Formerly § 1007, renumbered, L 1962, ch 834, § 77, eff Sept 1, 1963; amd, L 1963, ch 748, §§ 19, 20 eff Sept 1, 1963; L 1970, ch 226, eff April 24, 1970.

CASE ANNOTATIONS

This section was derived from § 106 of former Stock Corp. L., the purpose of which was to provide for speedy termination of corporate affairs under judicial supervision with proper notice to all parties concerned, with the objectives, among others, of supplying judicial approval of steps taken in liquidation and distribution of assets and permitting presentation of claims without necessity of instituting individual actions. Re Baldwin Trading Corp. (1960) 8 N.Y.2d 144, 202 N.Y.S.2d 312, 168 N.E.2d 383, affg (2d Dept) 8 A.D.2d 968, 190 N.Y.S.2d 949

The Supreme Court, under former § 106, could require liquidating directors to account for all financial transactions in proposed liquidation, but it was doubtful whether it could, under this section, require a director to account for alleged misconduct in management of the corporation as a going concern. Application of Bittner (1943) 265 A.D. 490, 39 N.Y.S.2d 658

It has been stated that the provisions of § 106 of former Stock Corp. L. should be invoked to determine the time and manner of distribution of assets where stockholders have opposing views. Stephens v Maust (1960, 1st Dept) 11 A.D.2d 1004, 205 N.Y.S.2d 913

Since third-party claim asserted by assembler and/or distributor of fire extinguisher against the designer was not cognizable until judicial decision permitting an actively negligent party to seek apportionment of damages by way of impleader action, the trial court had discretionary power to allow third-party claim against remaining assets of dissolved corporation, which allegedly negligently designed fire extinguisher and allegedly failed to conduct recall of the defective products; change in law was a satisfactory reason for failure to file claim against the corporation prior to order confirming dissolution. Gardner v Fyr-Fyter Co. (1975, 4th Dept) 47 A.D.2d 591, 363 N.Y.S.2d 690

Since corporate designer of allegedly defective fire extinguisher had its main office in Rockland County, fire extinguisher distributor should have proceeded in that judicial district, which was supervising dissolution of the designer, for leave to file its third-party claim rather than in Allegany County, where the main action was pending; however, proceedings could continue in Allegany County where to require the distributors to proceed in a proper manner would only add to the substantial delay which the plaintiff had already experienced as result of the problems created by the multiple and complex transactions involving all other parties. Gardner v Fyr-Fyter Co. (1975, 4th Dept) 47 A.D.2d 591, 363 N.Y.S.2d 690

It having already been decided that summary expulsion of petitioner as officer and director of corporation was act of oppression entitling petitioner to relief, IAS Court acted within broad supervisory and injunctive powers conferred under CLS Bus Corp §§ 1008(a)(3), 1113, and 1115(a)(1) when it directed corporation to pay petitioner same compensation and benefits as those paid to other shareholders, retroactive to date of his summary firing and exclusion from corporate premises. In re Dissolution of HGK Asset Mgmt. (1997, 1st Dept) 238 A.D.2d 291, 656 N.Y.S.2d 264

Granting of retroactive compensation and benefits to corporate officer and director who was victim of oppressive summary expulsion from corporation did not require showing of irreparable injury. In re Dissolution of HGK Asset Mgmt. (1997, 1st Dept) 238 A.D.2d 291, 656 N.Y.S.2d 264

Court should not have summarily dismissed, albeit with leave to renew, creditor's petition under CLS Bus Corp § 1008 to annul allegedly fraudulent voluntary dissolution of corporation where there were disputed issued regarding new corporation formed by principals of former corporation, its ownership, and transfers of assets. Sunwest Enters. v Tilani Enters. (2001, 1st Dept) 282 A.D.2d 236, 723 N.Y.S.2d 448

The Supreme Court had no authority to make a summary determination of the validity and amount of a claim made by a 50% stockholder against a dissolved corporation, where the other 50% stockholder had instituted an action in Municipal Court. Re Bishop & Sinclair, Inc. (1956) 4 Misc. 2d 155, 152 N.Y.S.2d 527

Court had authority to order respondents, dissolved corporation and its sole shareholder, to provide accounting of distribution of corporate assets, despite their claim that since corporation had been divested of its assets there was nothing left for court to supervise, since corporation's assets had been distributed to sole shareholder, and there was allegation that, 7 months before petition for voluntary dissolution was filed, respondents were aware that petitioners had brought claims in federal court seeking damages for corporation's

alleged contamination of local air, soil and water; under circumstances, public interest required court to exercise its equitable powers to supervise dissolution. State v Abalene Pest Control Service, Inc. (1989) 142 Misc. 2d 396

The fundamental requirement that capital cannot be impaired by declaration of dividends out of capital assets does not apply to a corporation in course of liquidation, and holders of cumulative preferred stock with whom the corporation has contracted to pay dividends out of assets on distribution are entitled to payment of cumulative dividends in addition to par value, whether or not such dividends have been declared, if such was the agreement. Re Chandler & Co. (1962, Sup) 230 N.Y.S.2d 1012

With respect to distribution of assets of a dissolved corporation under § 106 of former Stock Corporation Law, it was held that holders of First Preferred Stock, originally issued as $100 par value stock and later changed by amendment of certificate to no par stock, in the light of the terms of issuance were entitled to be paid $100 per share plus accrued dividends, whether or not such dividends had been declared, before other stockholders were paid anything. Re Chandler & Co. (1962, Sup) 230 N.Y.S.2d 1012

Trial court improperly sua sponte appointed a referee to hear and report as to the value of the corporation's properties and leasehold interest and the appropriate procedures following dissolution in the judicial dissolution of the corporation; post-dissolution procedures in a judicial proceeding, provided for in N.Y. Bus. Corp. Law §§ 1005-1008, as provided under N.Y. Bus. Corp. Law § 1117, did not include the appointment of a referee. In re Oak St. Mgmt. (2003, A.D., 2d Dept) 762 N.Y.S.2d 522

Although a town's theories for its claim against a corporation's officers arising from the officers' refusal to seek insurance coverage from the New York State Insurance Fund (SIF) had no merit, the case was remitted for the trial court to join the corporation as a necessary party, convert the action to a special proceeding pursuant to N.Y. Bus. Corp. Law § 1008, and exercise its authority under that statute, which included the power to force the corporation to seek coverage from SIF with respect to the town judgment. Town of Amherst v Hilger (2013, App Div, 4th Dept) 962 NYS2d 837, subsequent app (2013, 4th Dept) 104 App Div 3d 1268, 960 NYS2d 922.

A petition for judicial supervision under § 106 of former Stock Corp. L. could properly be denied where it was presented by a stockholder, but there was no chance that he, not being a creditor, would be entitled to participate in the assets. Garifled v Lowy (1957, CA2 NY) 245 F.2d 132

Although § 106 of former Stock Corp. L. permitted the supreme court to enter an order permitting destruction of the corporate records, in the absence of entry of such an order mere pendency of dissolution proceedings would not excuse failure or refusal of an officer of a corporation having custody to comply with a subpoena duces tecum for their production. United States v Johnson (1957, CA2 NY) 247 F.2d 5, cert den 355 US 867, 2 L Ed 2d 74, 78 S Ct 116

§ 1009. Applicability to dissolution under other provisions

The provisions of sections 1005 (Procedure after dissolution), 1006 (Corporate action and survival of remedies after dissolution), 1007 (Notice to creditors; filing or barring claims) and 1008 (Jurisdiction of supreme court to supervise dissolution and liquidation) shall apply to a corporation dissolved by expiration of its period of duration or under section two hundred three-a of the tax law.

History: Formerly § 1008, renumbered, amd, L 1962, ch 834, § 78, amd, L 1963, ch 748, § 21, eff Sept 1, 1963.

CASE ANNOTATIONS

Sections 105 and 106 of former Stock Corp. L. had no application to corporate dissolutions under Art. 9 of former Gen. Corp. L. Re Greenwald (1936) 248 A.D. 590, 287 N.Y.S. 362

This section would seem to clear up doubts previously existing as to rights, powers, liabilities, and procedure to be followed in connection with liquidation and winding up of the affairs of a corporation whose existence has been terminated under § 203-a of the Tax Law for delinquency in paying franchise tax, notwithstanding a 1940 amendment of that section referring dissolution procedure to § 29 of former Gen. Corp. L. For decisions dealing with various aspects of this problem, see Application of S. M. & J. Eisenstadt, Inc. (1939) 256 A.D. 488, 10 N.Y.S.2d 868, app dismd 282 N.Y. 611, 25 N.E.2d 391 and affd 283 N.Y. 578, 27 N.E.2d 439; Vestal Products v Manufacturers Trust Co. (1935, Sup) 60 N.Y.S.2d 183; Carton Plumbing & Heating Co. v Fuscaldo (1943) 179 Misc 946, 40 N.Y.S.2d 423; 1480 Popham Corp. v Fordham Bus Corp. (1941) 176 Misc 508, 26 N.Y.S.2d 571; Wilner Friends Credit Ass'n v Scheffres (1941) 175 Misc 909, 25 N.Y.S.2d 664; Hub Commercial Co. v Rosenblum (1940, City Ct) 21 N.Y.S.2d 426; Seventy-Three First Ave. Corp. v Braunstein Bros. Carbonic Sales Corp. (1938) 168 Misc 842, 6 N.Y.S.2d 664, affd 170 Misc 657, 10 N.Y.S.2d 868; N.Y. Rayon Importing Co. v United States (1946) 105 Ct Cl 606, 64 F. Supp. 684, mod on other grounds 329 US 654, 91 L Ed 577, 67 S Ct 601

Corporations undergoing dissolution may continue to function for the purpose of winding up the affairs of the corporation in the same manner as if the dissolution had not taken place and the dissolution does not affect either the right of the corporation to collect and distribute its assets or to sue in its corporate name; therefore, a corporation which was dissolved pursuant to Tax Law § 203-a for nonpayment of taxes was permitted to exercise an option to purchase real estate since the option constituted a valuable asset and the exercise of that option was a significant part of winding up the affairs of the corporation. Bowditch v 57 Laight Street Corp. (1981) 111 Misc. 2d 255, 443 N.Y.S.2d 785

Although a corporation filed suit before its dissolution, based on pre-dissolution transactions, the reasoning of Lorisa, that courts had to foster compliance with N.Y. Tax Law § 203-a(10), and that a dissolved corporation may only "wind up" its affairs, under N.Y. Bus. Corp. Law §§ 1009 and 1006, had to be brought to bear in determining a dissolved corporation's capacity to sue. Lance Int'l v First Nat'l City Bank (2009, Civ Ct) 241 NYLJ 72, 878 NYS2d 572.

ARTICLE 11
JUDICIAL DISSOLUTION

History: Add, L 1961 ch 855, eff Sept 1, 1963.

Schedule of sections, amd, L 1962, ch 834, § 79, L 1963, ch 748, § 22, eff Sept 1, 1963.

§ 1101. Attorney-general's action for judicial dissolution

(a) The attorney-general may bring an action for the dissolution of a corporation upon one or more of the following grounds:

(1) That the corporation procured its formation through fraudulent misrepresentation or concealment of a material fact.

(2) That the corporation has exceeded the authority conferred upon it by law, or has violated any provision of law whereby it has forfeited its charter, or carried on, conducted or transacted its business in a persistently fraudulent or illegal manner, or by the abuse of its powers contrary to the public policy of the state has become liable to be dissolved.

(b) An action under this section is triable by jury as a matter of right.

(c) The enumeration in paragraph (a) of grounds for dissolution shall not exclude actions or special proceedings by the attorney-general or other state officials for the annulment or dissolution of a corporation for other causes as provided in this chapter or in any other statute of this state.

History: Add L 1961, ch 855, eff Sept 1, 1963.

Par (b), amd, L 1962, ch 834, § 80, eff Sept 1, 1963.

CASE ANNOTATIONS

1. In general
2. Leave of court
3. Grounds
4. Discretion and authority of Attorney General
5. Procedural matters
6. Miscellaneous

1. In general

Section 91 of former Gen. Corp. L. neither extended corporate liability nor provided for determination of its existence. It merely enumerated instances in which the attorney general could seek leave of court to proceed for annulment or vacation of a charter and stated the procedure to be followed. People v Atlantic A. R. Co. (1891) 125 N.Y. 513, 26 N.E. 622

No private individual had a right to institute charter annulment or forfeiture proceedings under § 91 of former Gen. Corp. L., which sanctioned the institution of such proceedings only by the Attorney General. People ex rel. Lehmaier v Interurban S. R. Co. (1904) 177 N.Y. 296, 69 N.E. 596; Re Brooklyn E. R. Co. (1891) 125 N.Y. 434, 26 N.E. 474; Re Trustees of Congregational Church & Soc. (1892) 131 N.Y. 1, 30 N.E. 43; Re Petition of New York E. R. Co. (1877) 70 N.Y. 327; Fredonia v Fredonia Natural Gas Light Co. (1914) 87 Misc 592, 149 N.Y.S. 964, affd 169 A.D. 690, 155 N.Y.S. 212

Former General Corp. L. sections from which this section was derived were applicable only to domestic corporations, and they were considered inapplicable to certain kinds of domestic corporations, such as insolvent banks, as to which dissolution or going out of business was controlled by district statutes. Hagmayer v Alten (1901) 36 Misc 59, 72 N.Y.S. 623; Wilkinson v North River Constr. Co. (1884) 66 How Pr 423

2. Leave of court

Whether to grant the application of the attorney general for leave to proceed with an action for annulment or vacation of the corporation's charter rested in the discretion of the court, and the prime consideration in the exercise of that discretion was whether the alleged excesses or abuses of power by the corporation were such as to threaten or harm public welfare. People v North River Sugar Refining Co. (1890) 121 N.Y. 582, 24 N.E. 834; People v Abbott Maintenance Corp. (1960, 1st Dept) 11 A.D.2d 136, 201 N.Y.S.2d 895, affd 9 N.Y.2d 810, 215 N.Y.S.2d 761, 175 N.E.2d 341; People v Bleecker S. & F. F. R. Co. (1910) 140 A.D. 611, 125 N.Y.S. 1045, affd 201 N.Y. 594, 95 N.E. 1136; People v B. C. Associates, Inc. (1959) 22 Misc. 2d 43, 194 N.Y.S.2d 353

If the attorney general was satisfied that ground existed for forfeiture or annulment of a corporate charter pursuant to § 91 of former Gen. Corp. L., he could proceed upon a petition in the name of the people without a "relator," but his initial move had to be an application for leave of court, in connection with which the court, under § 92, could require giving of notice to the corporation with leave to contest the application. People v Buffalo Stone & Cement Co. (1892) 131 N.Y. 140, 29 N.E. 947; People v Ulster & D. R. Co. (1891) 128 N.Y. 240, 28 N.E. 635; People ex rel. Hearst v Ramapo Water Co. (1900) 51 A.D. 145, 64 N.Y.S. 532; Herring v New York, L. E. & W. R. Co. (1887) 105 N.Y. 340, 12 N.E. 763; People v Bleecker S. & F. F. R. Co. (1910) 140 A.D. 611, 125 N.Y.S. 1045, affd 201 N.Y. 594, 95 N.E. 1136; Goodyear Aluminum Products, Inc. v State (1960) 21 Misc. 2d 725, 203 N.Y.S.2d 256, revd on other grounds (3d Dept) 12 A.D.2d 692, 207 N.Y.S.2d 904; People v Boston, H. T. & W. R. Co. (1882, NY) 27 Hun 528

An order granting leave to the attorney general to bring a charter annulment action, being discretionary, would not be reviewed by an appellate tribunal except in extreme instances. People v Boston, H. T. & W. R. Co. (1882, NY) 27 Hun 528

Court which granted leave could likewise reconsider and revoke it. People v Boston, H. T. & W. R. Co. (1882, NY) 27 Hun 528

3. Grounds

Failure to exercise corporate powers by starting business within two years after incorporation was likewise ground for annulment of charter under § 30 of former Gen. Corp. L., and would sustain an application by the attorney general under § 91 to institute an annulment action; but these provisions have not been carried forward herein. Re Brooklyn E. R. Co. (1891) 125 N.Y. 434, 26 N.E. 474; Day v Ogdensburg & L. C. R. Co. (1887) 107 N.Y. 129, 13 N.E. 765; People v Kingston & M. Turnpike Road Co. (1840) 23 Wend 193

A temporary shutdown or failure to exercise corporate powers, particularly if brief or excusable, has not ordinarily been considered ground for annulment of charter. People v Atlantic A. R. Co. (1891) 125 N.Y. 513, 26 N.E. 622

The application for leave of court could be based on any violation of statutory requirements by the corporation for which its charter was subect to forfeiture, such as failure to make and file reports, regardless of existence of alternative penalties or remedies. People v Buffalo Stone & Cement Co. (1892) 131 N.Y. 140, 29 N.E. 947

Failure of a business corporation to collect in and attain the amount of its stated capital constituted a defect in its formation or a fraud for which it could be subjected to charter annulment proceedings. People v Buffalo Stone & Cement Co. (1892) 131 N.Y. 140, 29 N.E. 947

The provision in § 91 of former Gen. Corp. L. authorizing institution of proceedings for forfeiture of charter for "violation of any provision" of law was broad enough to extend to violation of laws not particularly directed to corporate activities or found among the various "corporation laws," and thus as extending not only to prohibited or illegal mergers and consolidations but likewise to combinations in restraint of trade or designed to fix and control prices. People v Milk Exchange, Ltd. (1895) 145 N.Y. 267, 39 N.E. 1062; People v North River Sugar Refining Co. (1890) 121 N.Y. 582, 24 N.E. 834; People v Abbott Maintenance Corp. (1960, 1st Dept) 11 A.D.2d 136, 201 N.Y.S.2d 895, affd 9 N.Y.2d 810, 215 N.Y.S.2d 761, 175 N.E.2d 341

Engaging in unauthorized business or enterprises was ground for seeking leave to bring charter annulment proceedings under § 91 of former Gen. Corp. L. People v Standard Plate Glass & Salvage Co. (1916) 174 A.D. 501, 156 N.Y.S. 1012

Persistent fraudulent advertising and business practices were considered within the coverage of § 91 of former Gen. Corp. L. People v Abbott Maintenance Corp. (1960, 1st Dept) 11 A.D.2d 136, 201 N.Y.S.2d 895, affd 9 N.Y.2d 810, 215 N.Y.S.2d 761, 175 N.E.2d 341

Dissolution of defendant corporation was warranted under CLS Bus Corp § 1101(a)(2) where (1) defendant corporation, which operated 4 business schools in New York and participated in Guaranteed Student Loan (GSL) program, used refund money rightfully belonging to its former students to solve its own cash flow problems, in violation of federal and state regulations governing GSL program, and (2) problem kept escalating for 2 years after defendant promised GSL administrators that it would stop. People by Abrams v Oliver Sch. (1994, 4th Dept) 206 A.D.2d 143, 619 N.Y.S.2d 911

Evidence showed that individual and corporations engaged in fraudulent acts involving practice of hypnosis such as to warrant entry of permanent injunction, cancelling certificates of incorporation of corporations, and prohibiting respondents from engaging in further business in state of New York. People by Lefkowitz v Therapeutic Hypnosis, Inc. (1975) 83 Misc. 2d 1068, 374 N.Y.S.2d 576

A corporation which engaged in a trade, business, or profession prohibited to corporations was subject to charter revocation. 1916 Ops Atty Gen 455

4. Discretion and authority of Attorney General

The attorney general was not required to take such action even where advised of possible grounds for proceeding, and grounds for forfeiture of charter were subject to waiver. Re Petition of New York E. R. Co. (1877) 70 N.Y. 327; People v Ulster & D. R. Co. (1891) 128 N.Y. 240, 28 N.E. 635; People v Tobacco Mfg. Co. (1871) 42 How Pr 162

In order to make sure of the facts on the basis of which a charter annulment could be sought, the attorney general had authority to instigate an investigation and issue subpoenas. Lawrence Aluminum Industries, Inc. v Lefkowitz (1960) 20 Misc. 2d 739, 196 N.Y.S.2d 844

Pendency of voluntary dissolution proceedings with respect to the corporation did not preclude the attorney general from proceeding under § 91 of former Gen. Corp. L. to seek annulment of its charter. People v Seneca Lake Grape & Wine Co. (1889) 52 Hun 174, 5 N.Y.S. 136, affd 126 N.Y. 631, 27 N.E. 410; People v Murray Hill Bank (1896) 10 A.D. 328, 41 N.Y.S. 804

5. Procedural matters

Parties in interest other than the corporation should be joined as parties to a charter annulment suit where they have important rights and interests dependent upon continued corporation existence and ability to do business. People v Albany & V. R. Co. (1879) 77 N.Y. 232

Attorney General's suit on behalf of State to enjoin certain allegedly fraudulent practices, obtain redress for defrauded persons and dissolve corporations engaged in fraudulent practices, was not "action to recover upon a liability, penalty, or forfeiture created or imposed by statute" and therefore was not controlled by three-year statute of limitations applicable to such actions. State v Cortelle Corp. (1975) 38 N.Y.2d 83, 378 N.Y.S.2d 654, 341 N.E.2d 223

Defendant corporation, which participated in Guaranteed Student Loan (GSL) program in connection with its operation of 4 business schools in New York, was not entitled to jury trial in dissolution proceeding under CLS Bus Corp § 1101(b) arising from charge that it used refund money belonging to its former students to solve its own cash flow problems, thus violating federal and state regulations governing GSL program, where it did not contest figures as to number of students involved, amount of refunds owed, or obvious fact that amount increased during 2 years that it said it was trying to resolve problem; Attorney General was entitled to summary judgment since no contested material fact issues were presented. People by Abrams v Oliver Sch. (1994, 4th Dept) 206 A.D.2d 143, 619 N.Y.S.2d 911

No due process violation arose from grant of summary judgment in proceeding to dissolve defendant corporation pursuant to CLS Bus Corp § 1101 on basis that it conducted its business in persistently illegal manner, since lengthy negotiations between state and defendant prior to litigation, and lengthy interval between commencement of litigation and grant of summary judgment, provided defendant with sufficient opportunity to be heard at meaningful time and in meaningful manner. People by Abrams v Oliver Sch. (1994, 4th Dept) 206 A.D.2d 143, 619 N.Y.S.2d 911

The two-year statute of limitations was considered applicable in asserting grounds for annulment of charter. People v Society of St. Joseph Palo Del Colle, Inc. (1941) 177 Misc 419, 30 N.Y.S.2d 551

6. Miscellaneous

Temporary injunction entered in Attorney General's action on behalf of State to enjoin certain allegedly fraudulent practices, obtain redress from defrauded persons and dissolve corporations engaged in fraudulent practices, which restrained defendants from disposing of any property having a source related to transactions described in complaint or "similar transactions," was not unduly vague. State v Cortelle Corp. (1975) 38 N.Y.2d 83, 378 N.Y.S.2d 654, 341 N.E.2d 223

Institution of proceedings for annulment of a corporate charter under § 91 of former Gen. Corp. L. did not deprive the corporation of existing property rights or rights of action, or clear it of liabilities, and a receivership or dissolution proceedings were usually required to work out these matters and to liquidate and equitably distribute such assets as it might have. Mutual Brewing Co. v New York & C. P. Ferry Co. (1897) 16 A.D. 149, 45 N.Y.S. 101

§ 1102. Directors' petition for judicial dissolution

If a majority of the board adopts a resolution that finds that the assets of a corporation are not sufficient to discharge its liabilities or that a dissolution will be beneficial to the shareholders, it may present a petition for its dissolution.

History: Add, L 1961, ch 855, eff Sept 1, 1963.

CASE ANNOTATIONS

Section 101 of former Gen. Corp. L., from which this section was derived, and subsequent sections of the same Article, constituted the sole and exclusive guide to court authority to act in proceedings originally instituted in behalf of the corporation at the instance of directors or shareholders seeking judicial dissolution, and the court had no authority to exercise ordinary equity powers. Re Importers' & Grocers' Exchange (1892) 132 N.Y. 212, 30 N.E. 401; Re Malcom Brewing Co. (1903) 78 A.D. 592, 79 N.Y.S. 1057; Re Application of Boynton Saw & File Co. (1884, NY) 34 Hun 369; Re George Ringler & Co. (1911) 70 Misc 576, 127 N.Y.S. 934; Gutwirth & Errante Homes, Inc. v Jacobowitz (1948, Sup) 81 N.Y.S.2d 607; Re Directors of Binghamton General Electric Co. (1894) 143 N.Y. 261, 38 N.E. 297

Such proceedings were classified as "special proceedings" rather than actions. Re Hulbert (1899) 160 N.Y. 9, 54 N.E. 571; Re Stoll-Meyer Woodcrafters, Inc. (1948, Sup) 84 N.Y.S.2d 757

Where the application was made by the directors, the petition had to be verified by a majority of them. Re Dolgeville Electric Light & Power Co. (1899) 160 N.Y. 500, 55 N.E. 287; Re Christian Jensen Co. (1891) 128 N.Y. 550, 28 N.E. 665; Application of Ades (1958) 12 Misc. 2d 915, 177 N.Y.S.2d 574

Section 101 of former Gen. Corp. L. was not construed as requiring a formal meeting of the board of directors as a prerequisite to filing of a petition by a majority of them, as the petition contemplated was an act of the majority, individually, rather than of the corporation. Zeltner v Henry Zeltner Brewing Co. (1903) 174 N.Y. 247, 66 N.E. 810; Application of Gail Kiddie Clothes, Inc. (1945, Sup) 56 N.Y.S.2d 117

It is necessary that service be made upon the attorney-general of the state of notice of application for an order to show cause under this section to give the supreme court jurisdiction of a special proceeding instituted to dissolve a membership benevolent corporation. Re Society of Justice (1922) 233 N.Y. 691, 135 N.E. 972

Under other provisions, notice of the application ordinarily had to be given to the attorney general. Re Board of Directors of Broadway Ins. Co. (1897) 23 A.D. 282, 48 N.Y.S. 299

De facto directors could join in such a petition, notwithstanding their de jure status as directors might be open to question. Re Manoca Temple Ass'n (1908) 128 A.D. 796, 113 N.Y.S. 172

The right of directors to petition for judicial dissolution was recognized under § 101 of former Gen. Corp. L., where a majority could agree on that course, notwithstanding the special provisions of § 103 for seeking dissolution because of a deadlock in control of the corporation. Re McLoughlin (1917) 176 A.D. 653, 163 N.Y.S. 547

The petition did not have to be granted merely because a majority of the directors, likewise owning more than a majority of the outstanding stock, signed and presented it, if those not joining in it showed good cause for dissenting or disagreeing. Re Cowles Realty Co. (1920) 193 A.D. 874, 184 N.Y.S. 778

Relief via dissolution is available on petition of a minority shareholder as a matter of judicial sponsorship where it is alleged that the directors and others in control are looting and thereby enriching themselves at expense of minority shareholders or are continuing corporation's existence for sole purpose of benefiting those in control at expense of minority. Horne v Radiological Health Services, P.C. (1975) 83 Misc. 2d 446, 371 N.Y.S.2d 948, affd (2d Dept) 51 A.D.2d 544, 379 N.Y.S.2d 374

A heavier burden is required to sustain an action by minority shareholder for dissolution than is required to sustain a derivative action for waste since purpose of dissolution action is not to strengthen corporation but to end its life. Horne v Radiological Health Services, P.C. (1975) 83 Misc. 2d 446, 371 N.Y.S.2d 948, affd (2d Dept) 51 A.D.2d 544, 379 N.Y.S.2d 374

It is not sufficient in a dissolution proceeding by a minority shareholder to show merely that corporation has continued for purpose of providing a salary and bonus to majority even where that precludes possibility of dividends. Horne v Radiological Health Services, P.C. (1975) 83 Misc. 2d 446, 371 N.Y.S.2d 948, affd (2d Dept) 51 A.D.2d 544, 379 N.Y.S.2d 374

§ 1103. Shareholders' petition for judicial dissolution

(a) If the shareholders of a corporation adopt a resolution stating that they find that its assets are not sufficient to discharge its liabilities, or that they deem a dissolution to be beneficial to the shareholders, the shareholders or such of them as are designated for that purpose in such resolution may present a petition for its dissolution.

(b) A shareholders' meeting to consider such a resolution may be called, notwithstanding any provision in the certificate of incorporation, by the holders of shares representing ten percent of the votes of all outstanding shares entitled to vote thereon, or if the certificate of incorporation authorizes a lesser proportion of votes of shares to call the meeting, by such lesser proportion. A meeting under this paragraph may not be called more often than once in any period of twelve consecutive months.

(c) Such a resolution may be adopted at a meeting of shareholders by vote of a majority of the votes of all outstanding shares entitled to vote thereon or if the certificate of incorporation requires a greater proportion of votes to adopt such a resolution, by such greater proportion.

History: Add, L 1961, ch 855, eff Sept 1, 1963; amd, L 1997, ch 449, § 66, eff Feb 22, 1998; L 1998, ch 17, § 13, eff Feb 19, 1998, deemed eff Feb 22, 1998.

CASE ANNOTATIONS

Although it is ordinarily for the directors to determine whether the best interests of shareholders require its dissolution and to make application therefor in accordance with statute, minority shareholders are entitled to institute equitable proceedings to require its dissolution where the directors and others in control are keeping it alive for purposes of looting its assets in disregard of the rights of the minority. Leibert v Clapp (1963) 13 N.Y.2d 313, 247 N.Y.S.2d 102, 196 N.E.2d 540

As between contesting stockholders, good faith of petitioner in a proceeding for dissolution by reason of deadlock in control is an issue, but, under § 103 of former Gen Corp L, the corporation in question could not itself initiate such a proceeding or challenge it on the basis of an asserted privilege to remain undissolved. Re Application of Clemente Bros., Inc. (1963, 3d Dept) 19 A.D.2d 568, 239 N.Y.S.2d 703, affd 13 N.Y.2d 963, 244 N.Y.S.2d 641, 194 N.E.2d 602

Derivative action by stockholder alleging that defendant unlawfully diverted corporation's assets for their own use could properly be consolidated with proceedings for judicial dissolution of the corporation. Grammas v Charla (1974, 2d Dept) 45 A.D.2d 756, 357 N.Y.S.2d 23

At trial of stockholder's derivative action alleging that defendants unlawfully diverted corporation's assets for their own use, or of the derivative action consolidated with proceeding for dissolution of the corporation, trial court could consider the facts and equities as they might exist at the time of trial and mold the relief which it might be fit to grant to any of the parties according to the exigencies of the case as they might then exist. Grammas v Charla (1974, 2d Dept) 45 A.D.2d 756, 357 N.Y.S.2d 23

Plaintiff was not entitled to judicial dissolution of corporation where (1) plaintiff formed corporation to own and manage building, (2) in year of formation, plaintiff sold 50 percent interest, (3) one year later, plaintiff agreed to sell remainder of his interest to other shareholders, with sales price to be paid in monthly installments, and (4) other shareholders never made any installment payments, but plaintiff waited 12 years before asserting claim and commencing action; plaintiff was barred by 6-year statute of limitations (CLS CPLR § 213) and by laches since (1) he had endorsed stock certificate and written "void" across its face, and (2) other shareholders had relied on plaintiff's acquiescence, and had dedicated their time and finances to preservation of property. Paris v Anthony Ave. Realty Corp. (1990, 1st Dept) 160 A.D.2d 541, 554 N.Y.S.2d 192

Court properly denied motion to intervene in special proceeding to dissolve corporation where proposed intervenors owned stock in "satellite corporations" in which corporation also owned stock, but they did not own stock in corporation itself. Osman v Sternberg (1990, 2d Dept) 168 A.D.2d 490, 562 N.Y.S.2d 731

Estate executor, a nonprofessional who was the transferee of a majority of shares in a professional services corporation, lacked standing to obtain judicial dissolution of the corporation pursuant to N.Y. Bus. Corp. Law § 1103. N.Y. Bus. Corp. Law § 1511 did not authorize the action. Matter of Bernfeld and Kurilenko (2011, 2d Dept) 86 App Div 3d 244, 925 NYS2d 122.

A bylaw requiring unanimous vote of all shareholders for adoption of any resolution was deemed invalid as in conflict with § 102 of former Gen. Corp. L. and other provisions in the corporation laws authorizing taking of specific action on the basis of a favoring majority or percentage vote. Benintendi v Kenton Hotel, Inc. (1943) 181 Misc 897, 45 N.Y.S.2d 705, affd 268 A.D. 857, 50 N.Y.S.2d 843, mod on other grounds 294 N.Y. 112, 60 N.E.2d 829 (superseded by statute as stated in Application of Burkin, 1 N.Y.2d 570, 154 N.Y.S.2d 898, 136 N.E.2d 862, 64 ALR2d 638)

Section 102 of former Stock Corp. L., from which this section of the Business Corp. L. is derived, was unlike this section in requiring even a majority of shareholders agreeing on dissolution to act through the board of directors, by passing a resolution directing the board to file a petition for dissolution. Application of Ades (1958) 12 Misc. 2d 915, 177 N.Y.S.2d 574; Re Friedlieb (1920, Sup) 184 N.Y.S. 753; Hayman v Brown (1941) 176 Misc 176, 26 N.Y.S.2d 898

The statutory procedures for dissolution of corporations were set up primarily to avoid injustice of the common-law rule escheating the assets of a corporation, upon termination of its existence, to the sovereign. Northern Properties, Inc. v Kuf Realty Corp. (1961) 30 Misc. 2d 1, 217 N.Y.S.2d 355

It is not sufficient in a dissolution proceeding by a minority shareholder to show merely that corporation has continued for purpose of providing a salary and bonus to majority even where that precludes possibility of dividends. Horne v Radiological Health Services, P.C. (1975) 83 Misc. 2d 446, 371 N.Y.S.2d 948, affd (2d Dept) 51 A.D.2d 544, 379 N.Y.S.2d 374

Relief via dissolution is available on petition of a minority shareholder as a matter of judicial sponsorship where it is alleged that the directors and others in control are looting and thereby enriching themselves at expense of minority shareholders or are continuing corporation's existence for sole purpose of benefiting those in control at expense of minority. Horne v Radiological Health Services, P.C. (1975) 83 Misc. 2d 446, 371 N.Y.S.2d 948, affd (2d Dept) 51 A.D.2d 544, 379 N.Y.S.2d 374

Where a decedent bequeathed the decedent's shares of stock equally to petitioner and respondent, petitioner and respondent were the owners of the corporation and, as such, and absent their mutual agreement not present in the proceeding, their options for the relief requested in the petition, which sought an order directing the sale by the corporation of real property and the liquidation of the corporation for the payment and distribution of its shares to the parties, could have been found in either N.Y. Bus. Corp. Law art. 10 or N.Y. Bus. Corp. Law art. 11. Matter of Kagan (2005, Sur) 790 N.Y.S.2d 366

§ 1104. Petition in case of deadlock among directors or shareholders

(a) Except as otherwise provided in the certificate of incorporation under section 613 (Limitations on right to vote), the holders of shares representing one-half of the votes of all outstanding shares of a corporation entitled to vote in an election of directors may present a petition for dissolution on one or more of the following grounds:

(1) That the directors are so divided respecting the management of the corporation's affairs that the votes required for action by the board cannot be obtained.

(2) That the shareholders are so divided that the votes required for the election of directors cannot be obtained.

(3) That there is internal dissension and two or more factions of shareholders are so divided that dissolution would be beneficial to the shareholders.

(b) If the certificate of incorporation provides that the proportion of votes required for action by the board, or the proportion of votes of shareholders required for election of directors, shall be greater than that otherwise required by this chapter, such a petition may be presented by the holders of shares representing more than one-third of the votes of all outstanding shares entitled to vote on non-judicial dissolution under section 1001 (Authorization of dissolution).

(c) Notwithstanding any provision in the certificate of incorporation, any holder of shares entitled to vote at an election of directors of a corporation, may present a petition for its dissolution on the ground that the shareholders are so divided that they have failed, for a period which includes at least two consecutive annual meeting dates, to elect successors to directors whose terms have expired or would have expired upon the election and qualification of their successors.

History: Add, L 1961, ch 855, eff Sept 1, 1963; amd, L 1963, ch 748, § 23, eff Sept 1, 1963; L 1997, ch 449, § 67, eff Feb 22, 1998; L 1998, ch 17, § 14, eff Feb 19, 1998, deemed eff Feb 22, 1998.

CASE ANNOTATIONS

1. In general
2. Shareholder status
3. Deadlock among directors
4. Deadlock among shareholders, generally
5. Deadlock precluding election of directors
6. Miscellaneous instances of shareholder deadlock
7. Arbitration
8. Proceedings by minority holders
9. Discretion and authority of court
10. Procedural matters
11. Miscellaneous

1. In general

Sections 101 and 103 of former Gen. Corp. L. were treated as independent provisions, so that the filing of a petition under either section did not preclude the filing of a petition under the other. Re McLoughlin (1917) 176 A.D. 653, 163 N.Y.S. 547

Generally speaking, § 103 of former Gen. Corp. L., as amended, authorized the filing of a petition for judicial dissolution only upon petition of at least a majority of holders of outstanding voting stock and a showing that dissension or disagreement among directors or controlling shareholders was preventing or seriously hampering the effective development and carrying on of business which the corporation was formed to conduct. It could not be availed of by minority shareholders merely because of disagreement with majority policies. Fontheim v Walker (1953) 282 A.D. 373, 122 N.Y.S.2d 642, affd 306 N.Y. 926, 119 N.E.2d 605

In a proceeding upon a director and half owner's petition for a judicial dissolution of a corporation, petitioner was a proper party to seek dissolution of the corporation, pursuant to Bus Corp Law § 1104(a), where, even though the corporation had not had an organizational meeting as required by Bus Corp Law § 404(a), each incorporator had signed an instrument setting forth the action taken, and where petitioner had paid consideration for his shares in full, although no stock certificates had been issued. Re Rappaport (1985, 2d Dept) 110 A.D.2d 639, 487 N.Y.S.2d 376

In determining whether judicial dissolution of corporation is in order, issue is not who is at fault for deadlock precluding successful and profitable conduct of corporation's affairs, but whether deadlock exists. In re Kaufmann v Kaufmann (1996, 2d Dept) 225 A.D.2d 775, 640 N.Y.S.2d 569

Petitioner failed to show that dissention between him and his brother with regard to corporation they acquired from their late father had resulted in deadlock precluding successful and profitable conduct of corporation's affairs where petitioner did not show that disagreements between him and his brother posed irreconcilable barrier to continued functioning and prosperity of corporation. In re Kaufmann v Kaufmann (1996, 2d Dept) 225 A.D.2d 775, 640 N.Y.S.2d 569

Application for judicial dissolution of corporation pursuant to CLS Bus Corp § 1104(a) should have been denied, and petition dismissed without prejudice to commencement of new proceeding under CLS Bus Corp § 1104-a, where complaint merely alleged that there had been only one shareholders' meeting since inception of venture, that financial information was not regularly disseminated, and that one 50 percent shareholder exercised sole control over daily management of corporation. In re Parveen (1999, 1st Dept) 259 A.D.2d 389, 687 N.Y.S.2d 90

In order to bring a petition to dissolve a corporation, the petitioner must have represented at least one-half of the votes in case of deadlock or 20 percent of the votes in case of oppression; petitions to dissolve corporations were properly dismissed as the petitioner was not a shareholder or had sold his interests in the corporations. Artigas v Renewal Arts Realty Corp. (2005, A.D., 1st Dept) 803 N.Y.S.2d 12

2. Shareholder status

In proceeding pursuant to Business Corporation Law § 1104 for judicial dissolution of closely held corporation, question of fact exists as to whether petitioner holds one half of outstanding shares giving him standing to maintain proceeding for judicial dissolution; circumstances warrant evidentiary inquiry into whether grounds exist for judicial dissolution; therefore, matter is remitted for evidentiary hearing on these issues-court incorrectly directed appointment of appraiser to assess value of corporation; buy-out remedy set forth in Business Corporation Law § 1118 does not apply where dissolution proceeding is brought pursuant to Business Corporation Law § 1104. Matter of Lake Mahopac Tailor, 146 A.D.2d 774

Under former § 103 of the General Corporation Law (now included in this section of the Business Corporation Law) dissolution of a corporation could only be sought by holders of one-half of the stock entitled to vote at an election of directors, and whether a petitioner seeking dissolution has the required stockholder status requires determination prior to ordering dissolution and appointing a receiver, particularly where his stockholder status is already under attack in an independent action. Re Application of Three Hundred Fifty West Forty-Sixth Street, Inc. (1964, 1st Dept) 20 A.D.2d 685, 246 N.Y.S.2d 501

Corporation was entitled to dismissal of action seeking its dissolution pursuant to CLS Bus Corp § 1104 on ground that petitioner was not real party in interest where (1) petitioner and former business employee incorporated corporation, but petitioner requested that no stock be issued to him at time because of potential liability from former employment, (2) thereafter, petitioner filed for bankruptcy and failed to disclose alleged ownership interest in corporation, and (3) after being discharged in bankruptcy, petitioner requested issuance of stock representing 50 percent of corporation, but corporation denied request; asserted stock interest and any claims of injury inuring to that interest vested in trustee in bankruptcy since petitioner failed to disclose alleged ownership interest. Re C & M Plastics, Inc. (1991, 3d Dept) 168 A.D.2d 160, 571 N.Y.S.2d 343

Fifty percent shareholder in main corporation was not disqualified from petitioning for relief under CLS Bus Corp § 1104, based on theory that 5 satellite corporations and main corporation were single, unified franchise, and thus his interest in 6-corporation enterprise was less than 50 percent, even though corporations shared interlocking officers and directors to varying degrees, where (1) each corporation pertained to store which had its own manager and conducted day-to-day operations independently, (2) main corporation's involvement was largely service oriented, and (3) on dissolution of main corporation, each of 5 satellites would be capable of either recreating

centralized administrative office or independently performing its own administration. Sternberg v Osman (1992, 2d Dept) 181 A.D.2d 897, 582 N.Y.S.2d 206, app dismd 80 N.Y.2d 892, 587 N.Y.S.2d 902, 600 N.E.2d 629

Petitioners who purchased 50 percent of corporation's stock had standing to maintain proceeding for dissolution under CLS Bus Corp § 1104(a)(3) even though they had not been issued certificates reflecting ownership and purchase agreement provided that stock would be held in escrow by corporation's accountant until full purchase price was paid, where escrow provision was mere security arrangement, and agreement (and simultaneously executed Irrevocable Stock Power) unambiguously provided for present immediate sale of stock; furthermore, court should have granted petitioners' motion to compel issuance of stock certificates to them where seller, in sworn affidavit, forgave any balance due on purchase price. In re Dissolution of M. Kraus, Inc. (1996, 1st Dept) 229 A.D.2d 347, 645 N.Y.S.2d 304, reh den (NY A.D., 1st Dept) 1996 N.Y. A.D. LEXIS 9608 and app dismd without op 89 N.Y.2d 916, 653 N.Y.S.2d 919, 676 N.E.2d 501

Section 1104 of the Business Corporation Law, which sets forth the grounds upon which the holders of one half of all outstanding shares of a corporation entitled to vote in an election of directors may present a petition for dissolution of the corporation has a limited base which does not allow for the determination of complex factual questions raised by the petition for dissolution, including questions of ownership of shares in the corporation; therefore, respondents' motion to dismiss on the grounds that the court has no jurisdiction and that petitioners fail to state a cause of action should be granted, since petitioners' status with respect to the ownership of stock must be determined before issues concerning dissolution can be considered under section 1104 of the Business Corporation Law. Re Cassaro (1978) 93 Misc. 2d 1096, 403 N.Y.S.2d 887

The purchaser of a sharehold interest in a corporation pursuant to an agreement which provides for installment payments of a portion of the purchase price and for the shares purchased to be held in escrow until payment of the full price, and which further provides that he is to enjoy all voting rights and the right to receive "dividends accruing from the ownership of such stock", is a "holder" within the meaning of subdivision (a) of section 1104 of the Business Corporation Law, which provides that "the holders of one-half of all outstanding shares of a corporation entitled to vote in an election of directors may present a petition for dissolution" on one or more of specified grounds. Stewart Becker, Ltd. v Horowitz (1978) 94 Misc. 2d 766, 405 N.Y.S.2d 571

Fact that petitioner was not real party in interest in action seeking dissolution of corporation pursuant to CLS Bus Corp § 1104 could not be cured by substitution of real party in interest, and therefore corporation was entitled to dismissal of proceeding. Re C & M Plastics, Inc. (1991, 3d Dept) 168 A.D.2d 160, 571 N.Y.S.2d 343

Trial court properly dismissed petitioner stockholder's N.Y. Bus. Corp. Law § 1104 action seeking dissolution of a corporation where the stockholder did not own 50 percent of the stock, as was required to demonstrate standing. In re Sakow (2002, A.D., 1st Dept) 746 N.Y.S.2d 159

Because a trial court did not elaborate on the basis for its finding that a shareholder lacked standing to direct the judicial dissolution of a closely-held corporation under N.Y. Bus. Corp. Law § 1104, intelligent appellate review was foreclosed. Matter of Sunburst Assoc., Inc. (2012, 3d Dept) 93 App Div 3d 1045, 941 NYS2d 289.

3. Deadlock among directors

The ground for seeking dissolution under § 103 of former Gen. Corp. L. was present where there was such discord among those in control as to prevent effective management. Re Importers' & Grocers' Exchange (1892) 132 N.Y. 212, 30 N.E. 401; Application of Casale-Chadwick, Inc. (1961) 31 Misc. 2d 699, 221 N.Y.S.2d 608

The mere failure to hold stockholders' meetings in and of itself does not constitute sufficient grounds to bring about a dissolution under the statute. Nelkin v H. J. R. Realty Corp. (1969) 25 N.Y.2d 543, 307 N.Y.S.2d 454, 255 N.E.2d 713

A petition disclosing that the corporation had an even number of directors so divided in opinion as to management that no efficient progress could be made sufficiently brought the situation within § 103 of former Gen. Corp. L. Cachules v Finkelstein (1951) 279 A.D. 173, 109 N.Y.S.2d 272, reh and app den 279 A.D. 778, 109 N.Y.S.2d 360 and motion den 279 A.D. 778, 109 N.Y.S.2d 360; Re Gotham Tissue Corp. (1945) 269 A.D. 922, 57 N.Y.S.2d 550; Application of Stutman (1954, Sup) 132 N.Y.S.2d 538

Above statute applied to dissolve five corporations where stock of each was owned equally by each of two persons whose discord had become so great that efficient management became impossible and in each of which an even number of directors were equally divided in respect to management of corporate affairs. Application of Sheridan Constr. Corp. (1965, 4th Dept) 22 A.D.2d 390, 256 N.Y.S.2d 210, affd 16 N.Y.2d 680, 261 N.Y.S.2d 300, 209 N.E.2d 290

A proceeding for involuntary judicial dissolution of a corporation, pursuant to Bus Corp Law §§ 1104, 1104-a, on the basis of a deadlock in the management of the corporation, was properly referred for determination of the fair value of petitioner's shares as of the day prior to the filing of the petition, where respondent timely elected to purchase petitioner's stock under Bus Corp Law § 1118, and where, although the statutory buy-out remedy does not apply to actions pursuant to Bus Corp Law § 1104, petitioner was entitled to petition for dissolution under both Bus Corp Law § 1104 and Bus Corp Law § 1104-a, and was properly prohibited from amending the petition to delete any reference to Bus Corp Law § 1104-a. Re Dissolution of Public Relations Aids, Inc. (1985, 1st Dept) 109 A.D.2d 502, 492 N.Y.S.2d 736

Court would affirm dismissal of petition for judicial dissolution of corporations where (1) corporations continued to operate during periods in which 2 principals did not speak directly to each other (discussions were held via their sons and companies' comptroller), and (2) operation of businesses continued after negotiations on division of assets came to stalemate only because one side unilaterally ended negotiations and commenced proceeding in hope of avoiding more expensive buy-out of other side. Hayes v Festa (1994, 1st Dept) 202 A.D.2d 277, 612 N.Y.S.2d 561, related proceeding (1st Dept) 202 A.D.2d 278, 612 N.Y.S.2d 824

An allegation that one of the directors, capable of swinging a majority vote on the board, was a mere "dummy", would not sustain the petition, where no deadlock actually existed or could exist as long as there was an odd number of directors. Petition of Binder (1939) 172 Misc 634, 15 N.Y.S.2d 4, revd 258 A.D. 1041, 17 N.Y.S.2d 1020

In a situation where the affairs of interlocking corporations are so deadlocked by disagreement among those in their common control that neither can effectively do business, both can, if considered advisable by the court, be dissolved in simultaneous proceedings. Application of Fulton-Washington Corp. (1956) 3 Misc. 2d 277, 151 N.Y.S.2d 417, affd (2d Dept) 2 A.D.2d 981, 157 N.Y.S.2d 894; Application of Ansol Holding Corp. (1954, Sup) 137 N.Y.S.2d 184

A temporary stalemate, because one of three directors is in military service and the remaining directors disagree on policy, has been considered insufficient foundation for a § 103 dissolution petition. Application of Ades (1958) 12 Misc. 2d 915, 177 N.Y.S.2d 574

Claim that not more than one board meeting had actually been held and therefore it could not be said that the board would not act would be rejected where evidence established that both parties in closed corporation would not agree and that therefore calling of board meeting would have been a vain act. Application of Surchin (1967) 55 Misc. 2d 888, 286 N.Y.S.2d 580

A petition for the dissolution of a corporation would be granted where the differences and animosity between the two principals in a service company were such as to present an irreconcilable barrier to the continued functioning of the corporation under efficient management; moreover, the act of one of the parties in seeking to discontinue the business would not constitute bad faith, notwithstanding allegations that he wished to dissolve the corporation so as to set up another company, in the case of a deadlock and consequent loss of profit by the parties, who were not working together to provide services to their clients. Re Probe Personnel Consultants, Inc. (1982) 117 Misc. 2d 21, 457 N.Y.S.2d 170

Plaintiff's claim that plaintiff had no power under the by-laws to call a board meeting before or after the lease was signed was of no moment as plaintiff made no effort to convene the board, or to dissolve the corporation under N.Y. Bus. Corp. Law §§ 1104 or 1104-a; that the president knew that two of the four directors opposed the signing of the lease and deliberately failed to call a meeting to pass upon the question did not preclude him from instituting the suit. Hellman v Hellman (2010) 31 Misc 3d 265, 919 NYS2d 764, affd (2010, 4th Dept) 79 App Div 3d 1813, 913 NYS2d 600, lv to app den (2011) 16 NY3d 711, 923 NYS2d 415, 947 NE2d 1194.

But mere failure of management to take such action as the petitioners advocated was not enough, nor was it ordinarily sufficient to show a stalemate in management unless there was likewise such discord among shareholders that the situation could not be remedied

by election of new or different directors. Petition of Williamson (1948, Sup) 85 N.Y.S.2d 93; Application of Gail Kiddie Clothes, Inc. (1945, Sup) 56 N.Y.S.2d 117

A petition seeking dissolution by reason of deadlock was insufficient to meet the statutory requirements where it appeared that the corporation was set up to have an odd number of directors, there was nothing to explain how a deadlock could exist, and the petitioner seemed to be merely claiming that he had been defrauded out of an alleged right to 40% of the stock under a joint venture agreement. Dissolution of Roanoke Homes, Inc. (1962, Sup) 234 N.Y.S.2d 109

4. Deadlock among shareholders, generally

A deadlock among shareholders was not sufficient ground for a petition under § 103 of former Gen. Corp. L. if the corporation was financially sound and the management was functioning normally and efficiently, notwithstanding it had an even number of directors who could have disagreed. Application of Cantelmo (1949) 275 A.D. 231, 88 N.Y.S.2d 604

Where a point is reached when the stockholders who are actively conducting the business of the corporation cannot agree, it becomes in the best interest of those shareholders to order a dissolution. Application of Weiss (1969, 1st Dept) 32 A.D.2d 279, 301 N.Y.S.2d 839

In a proceeding pursuant to Bus Corp Law §§ 1104 and 1104-a, seeking judicial dissolution of a corporation whose stock was equally divided between two shareholders, the court improperly dismissed one shareholder's cross petition under Bus Corp Law § 118 to purchase the other shareholder's stock, since the second shareholder owned more than 20 percent of the shares of the corporation and thus fell within the class entitled to bring a petition under § 1104-a, and since § 1118 unambiguously provides for an election to purchase such a shareholder's shares in all cases that include allegations under § 1104-a. Re Cristo Bros., Inc. (1983, 3d Dept) 97 A.D.2d 274, 470 N.Y.S.2d 781

A petition for the judicial dissolution of a closely held corporation failed to state a cause of action where it did not allege any facts that would justify dissolution on any grounds set forth in Bus Corp Law §§ 1104, 1104-a, or at common law; plaintiffs, as 50 percent shareholders, failed to allege that the control of the corporation's daily management by the party resisting dissolution had led to a single instance of internal dissension which resulted in a deadlock over management decision or a performance of a duty by management that was either oppressive, illegal, fraudulent, or breached a fiduciary responsibility; moreover, allegations that the corporation had substantial liquid assets and that plaintiffs had personal financial problems totally unrelated to the corporation did not state grounds for judicial dissolution. Re Dubonnet Scarfs, Inc. (1985, 1st Dept) 105 A.D.2d 339, 484 N.Y.S.2d 541

Provision in shareholder's agreement, waiving statutory and common-law right to petition for judicial dissolution of closely-held corporation deadlocked in its operation, was unenforceable as against public policy for protection of shareholders, especially where parties had relationship akin to partners and owed each other high degree of fidelity and good faith; under supermajority provision of agreement, both shareholders were relegated to status of minority shareholder, thereby vitiating parties' statutory rights under CLS Bus Corp §§ 1104 and 1104-a. In re Validation Review Assocs. (1996, 2d Dept) 223 A.D.2d 134, 646 N.Y.S.2d 149

Dissolution of law firm was appropriate where firm could not continue to function effectively due to dissension between 2 50 percent shareholders, notwithstanding that dissension had not yet had appreciable impact on firm's profitability, and there were no fact issues as to possibility of reconciliation. Molod v Berkowitz (1996, 1st Dept) 233 A.D.2d 149, 649 N.Y.S.2d 438, app dismd without op 89 N.Y.2d 1029, 658 N.Y.S.2d 244, 680 N.E.2d 618

Dispute between the only two shareholders of corporation, owning equal numbers of shares, does not necessarily mandate dissolution. Siegel v 141 Bowery Corp. (1974) 80 Misc. 2d 255, 362 N.Y.S.2d 897, affd (1st Dept) 51 A.D.2d 209, 380 N.Y.S.2d 232

Dissolution under N.Y. Bus. Corp. Law § 1104 was unwarranted because the shareholder failed to set forth a prima facie case that the parties were deadlocked; the shareholder and the administrator each controlled half of the company's stock, and the shareholder did not assert that an election was held or show that a deadlock was harming the parties, but, rather, the parties had agreed on an interim operating arrangement which was never implemented due to the shareholder's unilateral decision to petition for dissolution. The only factual issue in dispute was whether, despite the absence of an official appointment, the shareholder had become an officer of the company, and as this fact was not material to the issue of whether the shareholder, a 50 percent stockholder, engaged in oppressive conduct, and given that he apparently never requested a hearing, the trial court was not required to hold one. Matter of Clever Innovations, Inc. (Dooley) (2012, App Div, 3d Dept) 941 NYS2d 777.

5. Deadlock precluding election of directors

Dissolution of a corporation pursuant to the statute is not warranted where it is not alleged that the shareholders are so divided that they have failed to elect directors but merely that the corporation failed to call a meeting for such purpose for several years. Nelkin v H. J. R. Realty Corp. (1969) 25 N.Y.2d 543, 307 N.Y.S.2d 454, 255 N.E.2d 713

Business Corporation L § 1104 applied to action for dissolution of corporation in which two families each owned equal stock shares but because of a deadlock between the two groups, there was a failure to fill a vacancy on the board of directors resulting from the death of a member of one of the families. Application of Goldstone (1972, 1st Dept) 40 A.D.2d 971, 338 N.Y.S.2d 756

Second cause of action in a shareholder's 2007 petition for dissolution of a corporation was improperly dismissed as it sufficiently stated a claim for dissolution under N.Y. Bus. Corp. Law § 1104(c) based on the failure to hold annual meetings for more than two years, thereby preventing the election of directors and impeding the corporation's ability to conduct business. Matter of El-Roh Realty Corp. (2008, 4th Dept) 55 App Div 3d 1431, 865 NYS2d 475.

Such dissension among stockholders as to preclude the election of a board of directors, or of new directors, was ground for a shareholder petition under the express language of § 103 of former Gen. Corp. L., regardless of the fact that existing directors were still holding over in office. Re Application of Venice Amusement Corp. (1961) 32 Misc. 2d 122, 222 N.Y.S.2d 889; Application of Pivot Punch & Die Corp. (1959) 15 Misc. 2d 713, 182 N.Y.S.2d 459, mod on other grounds (4th Dept) 9 A.D.2d 861, 193 N.Y.S.2d 34; Petition of Acker (1953, Sup) 124 N.Y.S.2d 298, affd 282 A.D. 641, 126 N.Y.S.2d 194; Petition of Williamson (1948, Sup) 85 N.Y.S.2d 93

Inability of two 50 percent shareholders to agree on the election of a third director was not grounds for a corporate dissolution, absent factual proof that the competing interests prevented the efficient management and corporate success; the stockholders also failed to demonstrate that the dissension between them and the shareholder resulted in a deadlock precluding the successful and profitable conduct of the corporation's affairs, and the shareholder's alleged refusal to grant the stockholders access to the corporate books and records was not a ground for dissolution under the circumstances. Fazio Realty Corp. v Neiss (2004, A.D., 2d Dept) 781 N.Y.S.2d 118

6. Miscellaneous instances of shareholder deadlock

The situation was otherwise, however, where the corporation could not take action necessary to its continuation of business without shareholder support or approval, and there was such discord among shareholders as to prevent the taking of such action, or where, for other reasons, irreconcilable discord among stockholders had stymied management and progress. Application of Numode Realty Co. (1951) 278 A.D. 979, 105 N.Y.S.2d 588; Re Application of Venice Amusement Corp. (1961) 32 Misc. 2d 122, 222 N.Y.S.2d 889; Re Clemente Bros. Inc. (1960, 3d Dept) 12 A.D.2d 694, 207 N.Y.S.2d 821; Re Kaufman Circle Express Co. (1941) 177 Misc 106, 29 N.Y.S.2d 264; Application of Bown Bros., Inc. (1920) 111 Misc 294, 181 N.Y.S. 460

Business Corporation L § 1104 with respect to dissolution in the event of deadlock applied to suit for dissolution based on waste of corporate assets. Application of Goldstone (1972, 1st Dept) 40 A.D.2d 971, 338 N.Y.S.2d 756

Court properly granted dissolution of corporations owned in equal shares by 2 brothers, based on (1) undisputed evidence of intense strife which effectively crippled brothers' ability to agree on any corporate decisions including hiring and firing of employees, election of officers and allocation of corporate spending, and (2) allegations by each brother that other misappropriated corporate money for personal use. Greer v Greer (1986, 2d Dept) 124 A.D.2d 707, 508 N.Y.S.2d 217

Petitioner was entitled to summary judgment dissolving corporation on ground of dissension and deadlock between shareholders, where it was undisputed that shareholders had fundamental differences in opinion regarding, inter alia, expansion nd direction of corporation's business profit distribution, salary and bonus treatment of employees, and their respective roles in operation of corporation's business. In re Dissolution of Validation Review Assocs. (1997, 2d

Dept) 236 A.D.2d 477, 653 N.Y.S.2d 373, subsequent app (2d Dept) 237 A.D.2d 614, 655 N.Y.S.2d 1005 and app gr 89 N.Y.2d 817, 659 N.Y.S.2d 858, 681 N.E.2d 1305

A petition was sufficient to sustain an application for dissolution of a corporation where it stated that petitioner and her sister each owned one-half of the stock in the corporation and had jointly exercised control over it up to a certain time, when irreconcilable disputes and differences arose with respect to its affairs, resulting in an impasse, following which respondent asserted and assumed sole management, diverting the assets to her own use and excluding petitioner from the corporate premises and access to the books and records, etc. Re Victorian Sales Corp. (1961) 32 Misc. 2d 275, 223 N.Y.S.2d 119

Since the word "beneficial" is applicable both in respect of the mental and physical well being of the shareholder as well as in respect to financial gain to him, dissolution of a closed corporation would be ordered when evidence established that one of the two active shareholders, who was an active director and active officer of the corporation, issued threats of personal violence, listened in surreptitiously on his associate's telephone calls, seized and cut telephone wires, acted in presence of employees so as to demean his associate as employer in the corporation, took trips at corporate expense without advance mutual consent, left the shop inadequately manned, and engaged in other activities as if he were the sole owner of the business. Application of Surchin (1967) 55 Misc. 2d 888, 286 N.Y.S.2d 580

A corporation could be dissolved under this section where majority and minority stockholders had numerous disputes and corporate certificate provided for unanimity of action, even though majority stockholders by ignoring veto rights of minority interests kept the corporation mobile and prosperous. Application of Bankhalter (1953, Sup) 128 N.Y.S.2d 81

Summary judgment granting petition to dissolve a corporation under N.Y. Bus. Corp. Law § 1104(a)(3) was appropriate because petitioner shareholders had not acted in bad faith to create dissension solely to compel dissolution as respondent shareholders had sole control and petitioners had been excluded from the corporation's management. Matter of Eklund Farm Mach., Inc. (2007, 3d Dept) 40 App Div 3d 1325, 836 NYS2d 732

7. Arbitration

In proceeding to dissolve corporation, motion to compel arbitration should have been granted where stockholders' agreement provided that "any controversy or claim arising out of or relating to this contract or the breach thereof" was made arbitrable, such provision rendered subject to arbitration the issues on which it was claimed there was a deadlock of the five signing stockholders, four of whom were members of the board of directors, even though such issues might otherwise be the predicate of the claim for dissolution under Business Corporation Law § 1104. Moskowitz v Surrey Sleep Products, Inc. (1968, 2d Dept) 30 A.D.2d 820, 292 N.Y.S.2d 748

Half-owners of clothing manufacturer did not waive their right to arbitrate issues raised by co-owners' undertaking to dissolve manufacturer, despite half-owners having commenced action for damages and injunctive relief prior to co-owners' dissolution petition, where management agreements between parties specifically authorized each side to seek injunctive relief in event of specified material breaches by other side, without waiving any other remedies to which moving party might be entitled, and half-owners alleged only violations that fell within scope of those parts of agreement which authorized injunctive relief. Assael v Assael (1987, 1st Dept) 132 A.D.2d 4, 521 N.Y.S.2d 226

Supreme Court should have stayed proceeding for judicial dissolution of profession corporation and granted director-shareholder's motion to compel arbitration where shareholders' agreement provided that "any disputes or controversies of whatever kind or nature which may arise in connection with, for breach or on account of the performance or nonperformance of this agreement, shall be decided by arbitration," and dispute as to whether, and on what terms, shareholders should sever their corporate ties, was more than reasonably related to general subject matter of agreement establishing those ties. Ehrlich v Stein (1988, 2d Dept) 143 A.D.2d 908, 533 N.Y.S.2d 517

Agreements among stockholders for settlement or arbitration of disputes did not preclude a stockholder petition for dissolution based on § 103 of former Gen. Corp. L. if a situation within the coverage of that section was shown to exist notwithstanding the agreement.

Business Corporation Law

Application of Cohen (1944) 183 Misc 1034, 52 N.Y.S.2d 671, affd 269 A.D. 663, 53 N.Y.S.2d 467, app den 269 A.D. 690, 54 N.Y.S.2d 389

Where, inter alia, stock purchase agreement between employer and employee gave employer option to repurchase stock in close corporation from employee with increase in stock value to be determined by arbitration, and subsequent shareholders' agreement included as subject to arbitration all disputes arising out of "the conduct of the business of the company or the relationship between the parties hereto," issues relating to dissolution of subsequently formed corporation, which corporation was not a party to arbitration agreement and which was not in existence at time of arbitration agreement but which was owned in equal shares by employer and employee and rented its only asset, a building, to initial corporation, were subject to arbitration. Siegel v 141 Bowery Corp. (1974) 80 Misc. 2d 255, 362 N.Y.S.2d 897, affd (1st Dept) 51 A.D.2d 209, 380 N.Y.S.2d 232

Where the stockholders of a corporation have entered into a broad arbitration agreement which subjects to arbitration issues which might be the predicate of a claim for dissolution, it is appropriate to stay the dissolution and direct arbitration. Stewart Becker, Ltd. v Horowitz (1978) 94 Misc. 2d 766, 405 N.Y.S.2d 571

8. Proceedings by minority holders

Where a corporation was formed by tenants of a building in order to manage the same, no cause for dissolution in an action brought by minority stockholders was stated by the mere allegation that the shareholders' agreement was invalid and that the rents paid by the majority stockholders pursuant thereto were unreasonably low. Nelkin v H. J. R. Realty Corp. (1969) 25 N.Y.2d 543, 307 N.Y.S.2d 454, 255 N.E.2d 713

Court properly dismissed CLS Bus Corp § 1104 petition where, under properly confirmed finding of special referee, it was determined that petitioner was only 30 percent shareholder in tax law professional corporation in which respondent was 70 percent owner, and thus petitioner did not meet 50 percent ownership requirement for bringing petition for judicial dissolution due to internal distention under CLS Bus Corp § 1104(a)(3). In re Luttati (2000, 1st Dept) 271 A.D.2d 362, 707 N.Y.S.2d 86, subsequent app 95 N.Y.2d 861, 714 N.Y.S.2d 705, 737 N.E.2d 947

Relief via dissolution is available on petition of a minority shareholder as a matter of judicial sponsorship where it is alleged that the directors and others in control are looting and thereby enriching themselves at expense of minority shareholders or are continuing corporation's existence for sole purpose of benefiting those in control at expense of minority. Horne v Radiological Health Services, P.C. (1975) 83 Misc. 2d 446, 371 N.Y.S.2d 948, affd (2d Dept) 51 A.D.2d 544, 379 N.Y.S.2d 374

It is not sufficient in a dissolution proceeding by a minority shareholder to show merely that corporation has continued for purpose of providing a salary and bonus to majority even where that precludes possibility of dividends. Horne v Radiological Health Services, P.C. (1975) 83 Misc. 2d 446, 371 N.Y.S.2d 948, affd (2d Dept) 51 A.D.2d 544, 379 N.Y.S.2d 374

Actions by a majority shareholder group in eliminating a petitioner and his son from participation in the active operation of a corporation in which they had previously participated, and in which they had every reasonable expectation of being able to continue to participate, constituted "oppressive" conduct within the meaning of Business Corporation Law (BCL) § 1104-a concerning judicial dissolution of a corporation. Since the corporation was permitted to purchase the shares of the petitioner, pursuant to BCL § 1118, it was entitled to appear and obtain a stay of a dissolution proceeding authorized by that section, but merely establishing that the corporation was legally and financially able to pay the fair value of the shares under the limitations prescribed by BCL § 513 was not a condition precedent to the grant of the stay mandated by § 1118. Although a letter from a corporation offering to purchase the petitioner's shares for a specified price could not constitute an election to purchase required to trigger a stay, the corporation's answer to the petition, together with an affidavit by a majority shareholder on the corporation's behalf, did constitute an election to purchase at fair value. Furthermore, a motion for summary judgment pursuant to CPLR § 3213 brought by the petitioner for repayment of loans of $215,000 allegedly made by him to the corporation would be consolidated, pursuant to the court's discretion provided in CPLR § 602, with proceedings on the shareholder's petition for dissolution, contingent on a denial of the motion for summary judgment. Gene Barry One Hour Photo Process, Inc. (1981) 111 Misc. 2d 559, 444 N.Y.S.2d 540

A petition could be filed under § 103 of former Gen. Corp. L. by a widow who was likewise administratrix of the estate of her deceased husband, either in her individual or representative capacity, where several affiliated corporations were deadlocked and she personally owned stock in some of them and stock in the others was part of the assets of the husband's estate. Application of Guaranteed Pictures Co. (1953, Sup) 124 N.Y.S.2d 176, later app 282 A.D. 1028, 126 N.Y.S.2d 526

9. Discretion and authority of court

Although the cause of action for dissolution should have been asserted in an action and not in a special proceeding, where the Supreme Court had obtained jurisdiction over the necessary parties, the court did not abuse its discretion by entertaining the nonstatutory cause of action. Nelkin v H. J. R. Realty Corp. (1969) 25 N.Y.2d 543, 307 N.Y.S.2d 454, 255 N.E.2d 713

An application for dissolution of a corporation pursuant to § 103 of former Gen. Corp. L. was classified as a "special proceeding," and the court was without power to make an allowance of attorney's fees. Application of Cantelmo (1951) 278 A.D. 800, 104 N.Y.S.2d 282; Re Stoll-Meyer Woodcrafters, Inc. (1948, Sup) 84 N.Y.S.2d 757

An order directing immediate dissolution by public sale of a corporation unless the parties in the corporation reached an agreement as to terms of private sale was the only viable remedy to fully protect the business and financial interest of the parties and to advance the ends of justice, where more than three years had elapsed since the commencement of the proceeding seeking judicial dissolution, where the principals had failed to reach any accord under the guidance of a temporary receiver, and where the continuation of the proceeding in its present posture would serve no purpose except to undermine the financial stability of the coporation and the security of the shareholders. Re T. J. Ronan Paint Corp. (1983, 1st Dept) 97 A.D.2d 283, 469 N.Y.S.2d 931, recalled, vacated, op replaced (1st Dept) 98 A.D.2d 413

But the petition had to disclose a situation within the statutory coverage, where the application was based on former § 103, or the court was without authority to grant it. It could not grant such a petition on the basis of ordinary equity powers or jurisdiction. Coucounas v Coucounas (1962) 33 Misc. 2d 559, 225 N.Y.S.2d 410; Gutwirth & Errante Homes, Inc. v Jacobowitz (1948, Sup) 81 N.Y.S.2d 607; Application of Landau (1944) 183 Misc 876, 51 N.Y.S.2d 651

The court to which a petition for dissolution was presented under § 103 of former Gen. Corp. L. had discretion to deny it, notwithstanding the petition and proof disclosed a situation within the coverage of that section, if the court considered dissolution not in the best interest of those concerned or of the public. Re Norton & Schneider, Inc. (1954, Sup) 137 N.Y.S.2d 269.

10. Procedural matters

Although the statute provides for a hearing in connection with the dissolution of a corporation, the provision is not jurisdictional. It cannot be maintained that a dissolution otherwise properly granted was a nullity because there was no hearing. A hearing is only required where there is some contested issue determinative of the validity of the application, and in the absence of such an issue there is nothing in the nature of the proceeding that distinguishes it from any other litigated proceeding in this respect. Application of Weiss (1969, 1st Dept) 32 A.D.2d 279, 301 N.Y.S.2d 839

Even though petitioner for the dissolution of a corporation had attempted to squeeze out the respondent for an inadequate consideration, the institution of a proceeding for the dissolution of the corporation precludes such a contention. Application Weiss (1969, 1st Dept) 32 A.D.2d 279, 301 N.Y.S.2d 839

Where it is determined that a corporation should be dissolved an order charging the receiver with the duty of formulating a plan of dissolution and distribution of assets which plan shall be subject to the final approval of the court, is a proper application of Business Corporation Law § 1111(c). While the statute does not specifically so provide, the application for approval should be on notice to all parties with a suitable opportunity to be heard. Application of Weiss (1969, 1st Dept) 32 A.D.2d 279, 301 N.Y.S.2d 839

Where the essential issue common to stockholders derivative action and action for dissolution of corporation was the corporate assets subject to waste, the dissolution proceedings should not have been stayed pending determination of the derivative stockholders suit, even though all the parties were the same, as the derivative action covered past activities only, but the demand for dissolution contemplated the future. Application of Goldstone (1972, 1st Dept) 40 A.D.2d 971, 338 N.Y.S.2d 756

Where it did not appear that corporation was insolvent, or that its assets were being diverted or wasted, appointment of temporary receiver pending determination on merits of proceeding to dissolve corporation was unwarranted. Di Bona v General Rayfin, Ltd. (1974, 1st Dept) 45 A.D.2d 696, 357 N.Y.S.2d 71

Issue of right to commence dissolution proceeding under CLS Bus Corp § 1104 may be determined as part of dissolution proceeding itself. Re Three Hours Plants & Flowers, Ltd. (1987, 1st Dept) 135 A.D.2d 396, 521 N.Y.S.2d 690

In proceeding pursuant to CLS Bus Corp § 1104 for judicial dissolution of closely held corporation in business of dry cleaning, court would remit matter for evidentiary hearing since question of fact existed as to whether petitioner held 1/2 of outstanding shares, which would give him standing to maintain proceeding for judicial dissolution, where (1) corporation was founded by petitioner and 2 other individuals and stock of corporation was divided equally by them, (2) petitioner alleged that shares of one other stockholder had been purchased by corporation and retired, so that he owned 1/2 of outstanding shares, and (3) respondent alleged that she and 2 other individuals had purchased shares which petitioner alleged had been retired. Re Lake Mahopac Tailor, Inc. (1989, 2d Dept) 146 A.D.2d 774, 537 N.Y.S.2d 256, appeal after remand (2d Dept) 172 A.D.2d 525, 568 N.Y.S.2d 336

In proceeding for dissolution of corporation brought under CLS Bus Corp § 1104, those paragraphs of petition specifically addressing claims relating to corporate deadlock should not have been stricken since they were clearly relevant to such proceeding. Del Bueno v Barrionuevo (1989, 1st Dept) 147 A.D.2d 392, 537 N.Y.S.2d 813

Evidentiary hearing with regard to petition to dissolve corporation in case of deadlock is not mandated by law; hearing is required only if there is some contested issue determinative of validity of petition. In re Kaufmann v Kaufmann (1996, 2d Dept) 225 A.D.2d 775, 640 N.Y.S.2d 569

It was error for court to convert proceeding under CLS Bus Corp § 1104 to one under CLS Bus Corp § 1104-a over petitioner's objection, and to permit respondent to elect to purchase petitioner's interest in corporation pursuant to CLS Bus Corp § 1118, as it is petitioner who chooses statutory basis for dissolution (CLS Bus Corp § 1105), and buyout option under § 1118 is not available in proceeding brought exclusively under § 1104. Giordano v Stark (1996, 2d Dept) 229 A.D.2d 493, 645 N.Y.S.2d 517

Court properly denied respondent's application to have petition for dissolution under CLS Bus Corp § 1104(a)(3) deemed one brought under CLS Bus Corp § 1104-a and to stay proceeding for valuation hearing under CLS Bus Corp § 118; it is petitioner who chooses statutory authority under which relief is sought. Toscano v Southampton Brick & Tile (1996, 2d Dept) 233 A.D.2d 515, 650 N.Y.S.2d 297

In shareholder's action alleging, inter alia, breach of fiduciary duty and conversion of corporate assets, court erred in ruling that plaintiff's dissolution allegations pleaded CLS Bus Corp § 1104-a cause of action, in directing plaintiff to amend his complaint to comply with CLS Bus Corp §§ 1105 and 1106, and in permitting forced buy of out his shares pursuant to CLS Bus Corp § 1118, where his pleadings never cited § 1104-a as basis for dissolution and he made it clear that he was requesting common-law dissolution only as alternative to primary relief requested in his first 6 causes of action. Fedele v Seybert (1998, 1st Dept) 250 A.D.2d 519, 673 N.Y.S.2d 421

Supreme Court erred in granting relief under CLS CPLR § 5015(a)(5) reinstating plaintiff's cause of action for breach of anti-judicial dissolution provision of parties' shareholder agreement on ground that Court of Appeals, by reversing Appellate Division's order determining that anti-judicial dissolution provision violated public policy, in effect determined that such provision was enforceable; rather, in reversing Appellate Division's orders in dissolution proceeding and directing Supreme Court to dismiss dissolution proceeding as academic (because corporation was already in dissolution and receiver had been appointed), Court of Appeals did not reach merits of substantive issues and, while Appellate Division's orders predicated on rationale that anti-judicial dissolution provision violated public policy were not binding authority, its rationale remained persuasive authority. Schimel v Berkun (1999, 2d Dept) 264 A.D.2d 725, 696 N.Y.S.2d 49, app dismd 94 N.Y.2d 797, 700 N.Y.S.2d 429, 722 N.E.2d 509 and reargument den 94 N.Y.2d 876, 705 N.Y.S.2d 7, 726 N.E.2d 484

Court did not err in denying motion by one petitioner to discontinue CLS Bus Corp § 1104 dissolution proceeding to extent it sought relief on his behalf where (1) if one petitioner was permitted to withdraw, other petitioner would have insufficient shares to maintain proceeding, and (2) derivative claims interposed by respondent on corporation's behalf would be extirpated, requiring respondent to commence another action more than one year after interposing such claims and 2 years after alleged conduct giving rise thereto. In re Bronsky-Graff Orthodontics P.C. (2000, 3d Dept) 270 A.D.2d 792, 705 N.Y.S.2d 711

Court erred in dismissing petition seeking declaratory judgment that petitioner was 50 percent shareholder in corporation, and for dissolution of corporation, where (1) petitioner alleged that, after forming corporation, he accepted respondents' offer to fund cost of renovating premises in exchange for 50 percent ownership, and that respondents thereafter changed locks on doors, prohibiting his access, and (2) documentary evidence submitted by respondents did not definitively dispose of petitioner's claims. In re Loukoumi, Inc. (2001, 2d Dept) 285 A.D.2d 595, 728 N.Y.S.2d 383

In judicial dissolution proceeding arising from alleged shareholder deadlock, wherein respondents' answer and cross motion pleaded grounds typically falling under CLS Bus Corp § 1104-a and they requested injunction and bond based on petitioner's alleged corporate looting and misconduct, court ordered petitioner to post undertaking to preserve corporation's assets pending dissolution. In re Judicial Dissolution of 212 E. 52nd St. Corp. (2000, Sup) 185 Misc. 2d 95, 712 N.Y.S.2d 777

A heavier burden is required to sustain an action by minority shareholder for dissolution than is required to sustain a derivative action for waste since purpose of dissolution action is not to strengthen corporation but to end its life. Horne v Radiological Health Services, P.C. (1975) 83 Misc. 2d 446, 371 N.Y.S.2d 948, affd (2d Dept) 51 A.D.2d 544, 379 N.Y.S.2d 374

Supreme Court lacked jurisdiction to grant preliminary injunction under CLS Bus Corp § 1115 in conjunction with CLS Bus Corp § 1104 dissolution proceeding of Delaware corporation with principal place of business in New York, as New York court may not dissolve corporation domiciled elsewhere even with parties' consent and, if court may not adjudicate dissolution proceeding, logically it may not grant § 1115 relief. In re Dissolution of Chris Kole Enters. (2001, Sup) 188 Misc. 2d 207, 725 N.Y.S.2d 838

Once the trial court properly dismissed petitioner stockholder's N.Y. Bus. Corp. Law § 1104 action for dissolution because the stockholder owned insufficient stock to have standing, the trial court erred in sua sponte converting the action into a proceeding under N.Y. Bus. Corp. Law § 1104-a and ordering an appraisal hearing to value the stockholder's shares for a forced buy-out under N.Y. Bus. Corp. Law § 1118, as (1) the stockholder opposed the conversion and never sought such relief; (2) the right of appraisal provided by § 1118 applied only where dissolution was sought under N.Y. Bus. Corp. Law § 1104-a; and (3) the stockholder sought statutory dissolution under a section which did not afford respondents, a corporation and others, a buy-out remedy. In re Sakow (2002, A.D., 1st Dept) 746 N.Y.S.2d 159

In a proceeding for judicial dissolution of a corporation pursuant to N.Y. Bus. Corp. Law § 1104 the appointment of a receiver to liquidate the corporation's property at a public sale was proper; the prior resolution of this issue by the appeals court constituted the law of the case and the shareholders failed to show any basis for changing the prior determination. In re Oak St. Mgmt. (2005, A.D., 2d Dept) 799 N.Y.S.2d 556

A statement by the vice-president, director, and 50 percent shareholder and his wife, as a director, to the effect that a corporation was unable to pay any of its creditors and should be adjudged a bankrupt was binding upon the corporation. Re Henry's Systems Northeast, Inc. (1968, SD NY) 284 F. Supp. 841

11. Miscellaneous

Business Corporation Law § 1104 did not provide an adequate alternate legal remedy to temporary injunction against corporate president's writing checks on corporate account resulting in dissipation thereof after he had relinquished management control. R & J Bottling Co. v Rosenthal (1972, 3d Dept) 40 A.D.2d 911, 337 N.Y.S.2d 783

In a proceeding for a judicial dissolution of two close corporations in which respondent had pending a notice to purchase the petitioner's shares at their fair market value, the trial court erred in granting the dissolution following respondent's failure to post security for petitioner's shares, since her failure to do so would not serve as a predicate for frustrating her right under § 1118 to purchase petitioner's shares nor would it serve, as a basis for vacating the stay since petitioner's stock remained in her possession and control and respondent's failure to post the undertaking is not a basis for dissolution under the Business Corporation Law. Re Delinko (1981, 1st Dept) 85 A.D.2d 561, 445 N.Y.S.2d 706

In a corporate dissolution proceeding, an order directing the valuation of stock would be reversed, where a stock valuation can be directed when the proceeding is instituted under Bus Corp Law § 1104-a, when an election has been made under Bus Corp Law § 1118 by a shareholder to buy out the other shareholders, or an application has been made to stay the dissolution proceedings, and where the dissolution proceeding was instituted under Bus Corp Law § 1104, not under § 1104-a, where neither of the two principal shareholders had made an election to buy out the other, and where no one had moved to stay the dissolution. Re Application of Duffy (1983, 1st Dept) 97 A.D.2d 694, 468 N.Y.S.2d 116

Petition for judicial dissolution of hospital corporation under CLS Bus Corp § 1104 constituted proposed "passage or disposition of shares" within meaning of shareholders' agreement, thus triggering buy-out provision of agreement and entitling nonpetitioning shareholders to specific performance of their right to buy shares of petitioners, where agreement provided that shares must be offered for sale following "any proposed passage or disposition of shares whatsoever, including but not limited to passage or disposition by sale, delivery, assignment, gift, exchange, transfer (or) distribution," since language was unambiguous and required conclusion that proceeding for judicial dissolution was one means by which buy-out provisions of agreement would be triggered; even if language were considered ambiguous, nonpetitioning shareholders would be entitled to specific performance on basis of evidence that parties entered into agreement in ignorance of concept of corporate dissolution and could not have had any intention to exclude dissolution from all-inclusive language of agreement, and that purpose of agreement was for parties to be able to continue operation of hospital under ownership of all shareholders, or those shareholders who desired to do so. Doniger v Rye Psychiatric Hospital Center, Inc. (1986, 2d Dept) 122 A.D.2d 873, 505 N.Y.S.2d 920

In action pursuant to CLS Bus Corp § 1104 seeking dissolution of corporations owned in equal shares by 2 brothers, court did not err in rejecting one brother's offer, made after hearing was concluded, to buy out his brother's interest since buy-out provision contained in CLS Bus Corp § 1118 applies only to petitions pursuant to CLS Bus Corp § 1104-a. Greer v Greer (1986, 2d Dept) 124 A.D.2d 707, 508 N.Y.S.2d 217

In proceeding pursuant to CLS Bus Corp § 1104 for judicial dissolution of closely held corporation in business of dry cleaning, court erred in appointing appraiser to assess value of corporation for purpose of buy-out of petitioner's shares since buy-out remedy of CLS Bus Corp § 1118 does not apply where dissolution proceeding is brought under CLS Bus Corp § 1104. Re Lake Mahopac Tailor, Inc. (1989, 2d Dept) 146 A.D.2d 774, 537 N.Y.S.2d 256, appeal after remand (2d Dept) 172 A.D.2d 525, 568 N.Y.S.2d 336

Proceeding for judicial dissolution of corporation pursuant to CLS Bus Corp § 1104 would not be converted into proceeding for common-law dissolution where petitioners were each 50 percent shareholders and constituted all officers and directors of corporation; remedy of common law dissolution is available only to minority shareholders who accuse majority shareholders, officers, or directors of looting corporation and violating their fiduciary duty. Sternberg v Osman (1992, 2d Dept) 181 A.D.2d 897, 582 N.Y.S.2d 206, app dismd 80 N.Y.2d 892, 587 N.Y.S.2d 902, 600 N.E.2d 629

Supermajority provision in shareholder's agreement, even if otherwise valid, cannot be applied to decision regarding dissolution of corporation where shareholder has statutory right to seek judicial dissolution under CLS Bus Corp § 1104. In re Dissolution of Validation Review Assocs. (1997, 2d Dept) 236 A.D.2d 477, 653 N.Y.S.2d 373, subsequent app (2d Dept) 237 A.D.2d 614, 655 N.Y.S.2d 1005 and app gr 89 N.Y.2d 817, 659 N.Y.S.2d 858, 681 N.E.2d 1305

In a proceeding brought by a shareholder pursuant to Business Corporation Law § 1104(a)(1), (3), seeking dissolution of a corporation, the trial court properly held that the commencement of the proceeding triggered a provision in the parties' agreement that required the shareholder to offer to sell her shares to the corporation; the trial court also properly granted the motion for partial summary judgment on a stockholder's counterclaim seeking specific performance of that part of the agreement requiring the shareholder to offer to sell her shares to the corporation. Dismissal of the sharehold-

er's petition, however, was improper, because, in the event that the corporation or the remaining shareholders did not purchase the shareholder's shares, the shareholder will have been deprived of the ability to dispose of her shares and will have had no remedy. Matter of El-Roh Realty Corp. (2008, 4th Dept) 48 App Div 3d 1190, 851 NYS2d 777, subsequent app (2008, App Div, 4th Dept) 849 NYS2d 865.

Equitable standards applicable in a case of partnership dissolution are not applicable to question of dissolving a closed corporation on behalf of minority. Horne v Radiological Health Services, P.C. (1975) 83 Misc. 2d 446, 371 N.Y.S.2d 948, affd (2d Dept) 51 A.D.2d 544, 379 N.Y.S.2d 374

In a special proceeding for corporate dissolution there would be no basis for provisional relief by way of a declaratory judgment pendente lite, i.e., a "reverse injunction" declaring that petitioners' proposed competitive conduct was permissible, since CPLR § 3001 permits only final declaratory judgment and not an interim declaratory judgment in a pending proceeding, and since a grant of interim relief would result in a de facto dissolution of the corporation before the issues could be heard. Tigler v Peskin (1981) 113 Misc. 2d 1077, 450 N.Y.S.2d 358

A judicial dissolution of corporation would not be warranted by the inability to get along of the three shareholders, petitioner and two brothers, of closely held corporations which sold detergents to the maritime industry and cleaned ships in port by blasting their surfaces with detergents, after a 15 year relationship, due to petitioner's removal as manager of the blasting operation, the firing of petitioner's son because of his establishment of a competing business, and a dispute over the bookkeeper's handling of an invoice, since judicial dissolution of a close corporation is only authorized in the case of minority stockholders who are being treated unfairly by the majority or are being "squeezed out" because of "oppressive" conduct of the majority which fair-minded people would find objectionable, and petitioner has failed to show the required "oppressive" behavior in view of his endorsement of his son's actions and his "unfair" demand for a speedy buy out. Mardikos v Arger (1982) 116 Misc. 2d 1028, 457 N.Y.S.2d 371

In action for dissolution pursuant to CLS Bus Corp § 1104, shareholder did not have buy-out option under CLS Bus Corp § 1118; buy-out option is available in dissolution actions under CLS Bus Corp § 1104-a, but not in those under § 1104(a). Re Field, Rich & Associates, Inc. (1986) 134 Misc. 2d 216, 510 N.Y.S.2d 47

N.Y. Bus. Corp. Law § 1104(a) gives certain rights to holders of shares representing one-half of the votes of all outstanding shares of a corporation entitled to vote in an election of directors; even if respondent were determined to be a joint tenant of all of the shares of the corporation, his interest would be an undivided interest in all of the shares, and he could not be deemed a holder of one-half of the shares as required by § 1104(a). Rust v Turgeon (2002, A.D., 4th Dept) 746 N.Y.S.2d 223

Petition for dissolution under N.Y. Bus. Corp. Law § 1104 filed by a shareholder's conservator was equivalent to a voluntary offer to sell that triggered a provision in a stockholders agreement providing for the forced sale of the ward's shares, because the agreement used the expansive language, "in any manner whatsover," in defining the circumstances that would trigger a forced sale of shares. Matter of Johnsen v ACP Distrib., Inc. (2006, App Div, 1st Dept) 814 NYS2d 142

Order granting a petition for dissolution of a limited liability company (LLC) under N.Y. Ltd. Liab. Co. Law § 702 was error because, inter alia, the petitioning member failed to establish, in the context of the terms of the operating agreement, that (1) the management of the LLC was unable or unwilling to reasonably permit or promote the stated purpose of the LLC to be realized or achieved, or (2) continuing the LLC was financially unfeasible; "deadlock" was a basis, in and of itself, for judicial dissolution under N.Y. Bus. Corp. Law § 1104, but no such independent ground for dissolution was available under § 702. It was improper to apply partnership dissolution standards to a cause for dissolution of a limited liability company. Matter of 1545 Ocean Ave., LLC v Crown Royal Ventures, LLC (2010, App Div, 2d Dept) 893 NYS2d 590.

§ 1104-a.   Petition for judicial dissolution under special circumstances

(a) The holders of shares representing twenty percent or more of the votes of all outstanding shares of a corporation, other than a corporation registered as an investment company under an act of congress entitled "Investment Company Act of 1940", no shares of which are listed on a national securities exchange or regularly quoted in an over-the-counter market by one or more members of a national or an affiliated securities association, entitled to vote in an election of directors may present a petition of dissolution on one or more of the following grounds:

(1) The directors or those in control of the corporation have been guilty of illegal, fraudulent or oppressive actions toward the complaining shareholders;

(2) The property or assets of the corporation are being looted, wasted, or diverted for non-corporate purposes by its directors, officers or those in control of the corporation.

(b) The court, in determining whether to proceed with involuntary dissolution pursuant to this section, shall take into account:

(1) Whether liquidation of the corporation is the only feasible means whereby the petitioners may reasonably expect to obtain a fair return on their investment; and

(2) Whether liquidation of the corporation is reasonably necessary for the protection of the rights and interests of any substantial number of shareholders or of the petitioners.

(c) In addition to all other disclosure requirements, the directors or those in control of the corporation, no later than thirty days after the filing of a petition hereunder, shall make available for inspection and copying to the petitioners under reasonable working conditions the corporate financial books and records for the three preceding years.

(d) The court may order stock valuations be adjusted and may provide for a surcharge upon the directors or those in control of the corporation upon a finding of wilful or reckless dissipation or transfer of assets or corporate property without just or adequate compensation therefor.

History: Add, L 1979, ch 217, § 1, eff June 11, 1979; amd, L 1989, ch 141, § 1, eff June 9, 1989; L 1990, ch 822, § 1, eff July 25, 1990; L 1997, ch 449, § 68, eff Feb 22, 1998; L 1998, ch 17, § 15, eff Feb 19, 1998, deemed eff Feb 22, 1998.

CASE ANNOTATIONS

1. Generally

Minority shareholder who had invested his entire life's work in family-owned business established "oppression" within meaning of CLS Bus Corp § 1104-a where (1) he was not reelected as officer or director of corporation although he had held both positions in preceding years, (2) he was denied access to corporate records, (3) his employment with corporation was terminated, and (4) he received no salary or dividends after he was terminated except for one dividend declared on eve of trial. Re Burack (1988, 2d Dept) 137 A.D.2d 523, 524 N.Y.S.2d 457, app dismd without op 73 N.Y.2d 851, 537 N.Y.S.2d 495, 534 N.E.2d 333

CLS Bus Corp § 1104-a was enacted to provide protection to minority shareholders of closely held corporations who are subject, inter alia, to "oppressive" conduct of majority. Re Rambusch (1988, 1st Dept) 143 A.D.2d 605, 533 N.Y.S.2d 423

Proceeding for judicial dissolution of corporation pursuant to CLS Bus Corp § 1104 would not be converted into proceeding for dissolution pursuant to CLS Bus Corp § 1104-a where neither party pleaded "special circumstances" enunciated in § 1104-a, and evidence adduced did not support any theory thereunder. Sternberg v Osman (1992, 2d Dept) 181 A.D.2d 897, 582 N.Y.S.2d 206, app dismd 80 N.Y.2d 892, 587 N.Y.S.2d 902, 600 N.E.2d 629

Provision in shareholder's agreement, waiving statutory and common-law right to petition for judicial dissolution of closely-held corporation deadlocked in its operation, was unenforceable as against public policy for protection of shareholders, especially where parties had relationship akin to partners and owed each other high degree of fidelity and good faith; under supermajority provision of agreement, both shareholders were relegated to status of minority shareholder, thereby vitiating parties' statutory rights under CLS Bus Corp §§ 1104 and 1104-a. In re Validation Review Assocs. (1996, 2d Dept) 223 A.D.2d 134, 646 N.Y.S.2d 149

Court erred in concluding that offer to purchase petitioner's shares in corporation constituted election under CLS Bus Corp § 1118 that relieved petitioner of burden as to proving allegations of oppressive conduct where, prior to filing of petition under CLS Bus Corp § 1104-a, offeror exercised option to purchase actioner's shares under terms of shareholders' agreement, and thus his offer could not be deemed clear and unequivocal election to purchase petitioner's shares at fair market value. In re Apple (1996, 4th Dept) 224 A.D.2d 1016, 637 N.Y.S.2d 534, reh den (NY A.D., 4th Dept) 1996 N.Y. A.D. LEXIS 5750 and app den 88 N.Y.2d 811, 649 N.Y.S.2d 378, 672 N.E.2d 604

Petitioner could proceed with his application for dissolution under CLS Bus Corp § 1104-a despite fact that court lacked personal jurisdiction over individual who claimed to be shareholder of corporation. In re Finando (1996, 2d Dept) 226 A.D.2d 634, 641 N.Y.S.2d 384

It was error for court to convert proceeding under CLS Bus Corp § 1104 to one under CLS Bus Corp § 1104-a over petitioner's objection, and to permit respondent to elect to purchase petitioner's interest in corporation pursuant to CLS Bus Corp § 1118, as it is petitioner who chooses statutory basis for dissolution (CLS Bus Corp § 1105), and buyout option under § 1118 is not available in proceeding brought exclusively under § 1104. Giordano v Stark (1996, 2d Dept) 229 A.D.2d 493, 645 N.Y.S.2d 517

Court erred in denying respondents' motion to consolidate proceeding to dissolve corporation under CLS Bus Corp § 1104-a with respondents' action alleging, inter alia, that petitioner had misappropriated corporation's assets and destroyed its business in favor of competing business that he opened. In re Dissolution of Tosca Brick Oven Bread (1997, 1st Dept) 243 A.D.2d 416, 665 N.Y.S.2d 252

In proceeding under CLS Bus Corp § 1104-a for dissolution of corporation, it was proper exercise of discretion for referee to order petitioner to pay 1-half copying costs spent by respondents in for failing petitioner's voluminous document request. In re Krissler Bus. Inst. (1997, 2d Dept) 244 A.D.2d 486, 664 N.Y.S.2d 112

In action arising from removal of plaintiff as officer and director of closely held corporation, defendants were not entitled to summary judgment dismissing cause of action for judicial dissolution or fair market value, as moot, on ground that companies had already been dissolved by act of their board of directors, where validity of boards' actions in removing plaintiff as officer and director hinged on plaintiff's status as shareholder, as to which triable issue was raised. Shea v Hambros PLC (1998, 1st Dept) 244 A.D.2d 39, 673 N.Y.S.2d 369

In proceeding for dissolution of corporation under CLS Bus Corp § 1104-a for fraudulent or oppressive acts of shareholders, court properly found that respondent shareholders' testimony was not credible in light of contrary documentary evidence and testimony of their former employee, who was responsible for drafting minutes of all corporate meetings, coupled with shareholders' admission to perpetrating fraud on public for almost 10 years in representing petitioner to be 1/3 owner in all corporate entities. In re Dissolution of Pickwick Realty (1998, 3d Dept) 246 A.D.2d 863, 668 N.Y.S.2d 84

In an action for judicial dissolution of a closely held corporation, as the gravamen of the petition was that respondent majority shareholders breached their fiduciary duties to petitioner minority shareholders, and judicial dissolution was an equitable remedy, N.Y. C.P.L.R. 213(1)'s six-year limitations period applied; and as the suit was filed within six years of respondents' force-out attempt—"an open repudiation by the fiduciary"—it was not time-barred. Matter of Twin Bay Vil., Inc. v Kasian, 153 A.D.3d 998, 60 N.Y.S.3d 560, 2017 N.Y. App. Div. LEXIS 5970 (N.Y. App. Div. 3d Dep't 2017), app. denied, 31 N.Y.3d 902, 77 N.Y.S.3d 657, 2018 N.Y. LEXIS 482 (N.Y. 2018), app. dismissed, in part, 162 A.D.3d 1265, 79 N.Y.S.3d 702, 2018 N.Y. App. Div. LEXIS 4339 (N.Y. App. Div. 3d Dep't 2018).

In judicial dissolution proceeding arising from alleged shareholder deadlock, wherein respondents' answer and cross motion pleaded grounds typically falling under CLS Bus Corp § 1104-a and they requested injunction and bond based on petitioner's alleged corporate looting and misconduct, court ordered petitioner to post substantial bond to preserve corporation's assets pending dissolution. In re Judicial Dissolution of 212 E. 52nd St. Corp. (2000, Sup) 185 Misc. 2d 95, 712 N.Y.S.2d 777

Once the trial court properly dismissed petitioner stockholder's N.Y. Bus. Corp. Law § 1104 action for dissolution because the stockholder owned insufficient stock to have standing, the trial court erred in sua sponte converting the action into a proceeding under N.Y. Bus. Corp. Law § 1104-a and ordering an appraisal hearing to value the stockholder's shares for a forced buy-out under N.Y. Bus. Corp. Law § 1118, as (1) the stockholder opposed the conversion and never sought such relief; (2) the right of appraisal provided by § 1118 applied only where dissolution was sought under N.Y. Bus. Corp. Law § 1104-a; and (3) the stockholder sought statutory dissolution under a section which did not afford respondents, a corporation and others, a buy-out remedy. In re Sakow (2002, A.D., 1st Dept) 746 N.Y.S.2d 159

Minority shareholder's claim for order dissolving corporation and limited partnership and appointing receiver to administer dissolution, pursuant to Bus Corp §§ 1104-a, 1113, and 1201 et seq., is dismissed without prejudice, where shareholder can obtain full relief in New York Supreme Court, because adjudicating his discretionary claims has potential to interfere with New York's regulatory scheme governing its corporations. Feiwus v Genpar, Inc. (1999, ED NY) 43 F. Supp. 2d 289

2. Application to foreign corporations

Court properly dismissed, on its own motion, dissolution proceeding brought pursuant to CLS Bus Corp § 1104-a regarding foreign corporation; foreign corporation is controlled, as to its dissolution, by laws of its domicile, and is not affected by laws which are intended to govern dissolution of corporations created under local laws. Warde-McCann v Commex, Ltd. (1987, 2d Dept) 135 A.D.2d 541, 522 N.Y.S.2d 19

Corporate dissolution proceeding by 28 percent shareholder of Florida corporation was properly dismissed because foreign corporation is controlled, as to its dissolution, by laws of its domicile. Porciello v Sound Moves, Inc. (1998, 2d Dept) 253 A.D.2d 467, 675 N.Y.S.2d 903

Corporate dissolution proceeding by 28 percent shareholder of Florida corporation was properly dismissed because foreign corporation is controlled, as to its dissolution, by laws of its domicile. Porciello v Sound Moves, Inc. (1998, 2d Dept) 253 A.D.2d 467, 675 N.Y.S.2d 903

New York court had subject matter jurisdiction over petition brought by minority shareholder under CLS Bus Corp § 1104-a for dissolution of Delaware corporation since corporation's sole contact with Delaware was its certificate of incorporation, and all or most of corporation's assets, employees, officers, and 2 of its 5 directors were located in New York. Re Dohring (1989) 142 Misc. 2d 429, 537 N.Y.S.2d 767

3. Standing to petition

The sole minority shareholder of a corporation had no standing to commence a statutory action for dissolution under the provision of Bus Corp Law § 1104-a, since he held less than 20 percent of the shares; however, the minority shareholder could commence a common-law suit to dissolve the corporation for alleged director violation of fiduciary duty to shareholders (fraud, misappropriation, and use of corporate assets for personal gain), since the common-law action has no minimum-share ownership requirement. Lewis v Jones (1985, 3d Dept) 107 A.D.2d 931, 483 N.Y.S.2d 868

In a proceeding for the dissolution of several closely held corporations, the petition was properly dismissed as against all the corporations other than the corporation in which petitioner owned one third of the voting shares. Petitioner did not own 20 percent of the voting stock, as required by Bus Corp Law § 1104-a, in any of the other corporations. Furthermore, even if the corporations constituted a single entity, petitioner owned far less than the necessary 20 percent of the aggregate voting stock in the corporations. Re Wiedy's Furniture Clearance Center Co. (1985, 3d Dept) 108 A.D.2d 81, 487 N.Y.S.2d 901

Although shares are in name of children of stockholders, stockholders are entitled to petition for dissolution where children assign shares to respective fathers. Gunzberg v Art-Lloyd Metal Products Corp. (1985, 2d Dept) 112 A.D.2d 423, 492 N.Y.S.2d 83

Petitioner, who was divested of her interest in closely held corporation under option agreement for repurchase of stock, had no standing to bring proceeding to dissolve corporation under CLS Bus Corp § 1104-a. Martin Enterprises, Inc. v Janover (1988, 2d Dept) 140 A.D.2d 587, 528 N.Y.S.2d 855

Plaintiff did not have standing to petition for judicial dissolution of corporation pursuant to CLS Bus Corp § 1104-a where (1) employment contract specifically stated that, on termination for any cause, employee was required to surrender his or her shares in corporation, and (2) employment of plaintiff by corporation was terminated, and court had vacated preliminary injunction obtained by him pending appeal. Weiner v Anesthesia Assocs., P. C. (1994, 2d Dept) 203 A.D.2d 455, 610 N.Y.S.2d 608

In denying application for dissolution of corporation, court correctly held that shares in hands of trustees of Pemberton pension and profit sharing plan could not be used to satisfy 20 percent standing requirement of CLS Bus Corp § 1104-a where plan had been amended before start of present proceeding to eliminate "pass through" voting rights of equitable owners of its shares; it was irrelevant that elimination of pass through might have been motivated by desire of majority shareholders to deprive applicant of ownership interest needed to maintain dissolution proceeding where they otherwise had right to amend plan. In re Dissolution of TDA Indus. (1997, 1st Dept) 240 A.D.2d 262, 659 N.Y.S.2d 12, app den 91 N.Y.2d 805, 668 N.Y.S.2d 561, 691 N.E.2d 633

Hearing was required on issue of whether plaintiff owned requisite number of shares (20 percent or more) in professional service corporation to have standing to bring dissolution action under CLS Bus Corp § 1104-a(a)(1) and (2) where plaintiff alleged that he was made 50 percent shareholder, and certificate of incorporation reflected that he was "to be [one of] the original stockholders, directors and officers of the corporation." LaBarbera v D'Amico (1997, 2d Dept) 240 A.D.2d 640, 659 N.Y.S.2d 96

In action arising out of removal of plaintiff as officer and director of closely held corporation, defendants were not entitled to summary judgment dismissing plaintiff's claim for judicial dissolution or fair market value on ground that he lacked standing under CLS Bus Corp § 1104-a because he owned only 12.5 percent interest, as material question of fact existed as to threshold question of plaintiff's status as shareholder where defendants had failed to record 37.5 percent interest in corporation purportedly issued to other parties. Shea v Hambros PLC (1998, 1st Dept) 244 A.D.2d 39, 673 N.Y.S.2d 369

In proceeding for dissolution of corporation under CLS Bus Corp § 1104-a for fraudulent or oppressive acts of shareholders, petitioner's shares were voidable, not void, despite his outstanding debt, where he bought his shares for $100,000 with $10,000 down payment and promissory note for remaining $90,000, and thus he had protectable interest. In re Dissolution of Pickwick Realty (1998, 3d Dept) 246 A.D.2d 863, 668 N.Y.S.2d 84

Terminated members of worker cooperative corporation were not holders of 20 percent or more of outstanding membership shares of defendant company, and thus lacked standing to commence judicial dissolution proceeding under CLS Bus Corp § 1104-a, where their membership shares were automatically deemed transferred to corporation on termination of their work in corporation. In re Judicial Dissolution of Good Co. Gen. Store Coop. (1998, Sup) 178 Misc. 2d 210, 679 N.Y.S.2d 230

Plaintiff's claim that plaintiff had no power under the by-laws to call a board meeting before or after the lease was signed was of no moment as plaintiff made no effort to convene the board, or to dissolve the corporation under N.Y. Bus. Corp. Law §§ 1104 or 1104-a; that the president knew that two of the four directors opposed the signing of the lease and deliberately failed to call a meeting to pass upon the question did not preclude him from instituting the suit. Hellman v Hellman (2010) 31 Misc 3d 265, 919 NYS2d 764, affd (2010, 4th Dept) 79 App Div 3d 1813, 913 NYS2d 600, lv to app den (2011) 16 NY3d 711, 923 NYS2d 415, 947 NE2d 1194.

Court erroneously ordered dissolution of medical professional corporations on theory that corporations were in fact alter egos of certain other corporations in which petitioner owned 20 percent of shares since petitioner was not authorized to practice medicine, and thus she could own shares in those corporations, if that all, only as "transferee of shares by operation of law or court decree" (CLS Bus Corp §§ 1511, 1503, and 1507); even if petitioner were entitled, by "operation of law," to transfer 20 percent of shares in medical professional corporations, she would still be forbidden from voting those shares "for any purpose whatsoever except with respect to corporate action under (Business Corporation Law) section nine hundred nine and section one thousand one." Fromcheck v Brentwood Pain & Med. Servs., P.C. (1998, 2d Dept) 254 A.D.2d 485, 679 N.Y.S.2d 632

Where petitioners sought judicial dissolution of a closely held corporation, as petitioners one and two were beneficial owners of shares in the corporation with no right to vote, they lacked standing, but petitioner three had standing because he had the power to vote shares held by him as custodian and trustee that represented over 20 percent of all outstanding shares. Matter of Twin Bay Vil., Inc. v Kasian, 153 A.D.3d 998, 60 N.Y.S.3d 560, 2017 N.Y. App. Div. LEXIS 5970 (N.Y. App. Div. 3d Dep't 2017), app. denied, 31 N.Y.3d 902, 77 N.Y.S.3d 657, 2018 N.Y. LEXIS 482 (N.Y. 2018), app. dismissed, in part, 162 A.D.3d 1265, 79 N.Y.S.3d 702, 2018 N.Y. App. Div. LEXIS 4339 (N.Y. App. Div. 3d Dep't 2018).

In an N.Y. Bus. Corp. Law § 1104-a proceeding, where the lower court granted appellee's pre-answer summary motion to dismiss the petition and complaint after a nonjury trial on the ground that appellant lacked standing, the appellate court's standard of review was not limited to whether the trial court's verdict was against the weight of the evidence; its scope of review was as broad as that of the trial court. Capizola v Vantage Int'l, Ltd. (2003, A.D., 2d Dept) 770 N.Y.S.2d 395

In a judicial dissolution pursuant to N.Y. Bus. Corp. Law § 1104-a, the lower court erred in granting appellees' summary judgment motion to dismiss the petition and complaint on the ground that appellant lacked standing, the lower court ignored or relegated to insignificance the overwhelming proof that the owner petitioner was a 20 percent shareholder of one of the companies. Capizola v Vantage Int'l, Ltd. (2003, A.D., 2d Dept) 770 N.Y.S.2d 395

4. Pleadings

A petition for the judicial dissolution of a closely held corporation failed to state a cause of action where it did not allege any facts that would justify dissolution on any grounds set forth in Bus Corp Law §§ 1104, 1104-a, or at common law; plaintiffs, as 50 percent shareholders, failed to allege that the control of the corporation's daily management by the party resisting dissolution had led to a single instance of internal dissension which resulted in a deadlock over management decision or a performance of a duty by management that was either oppressive, illegal, fraudulent, or breached a fiduciary responsibility; moreover, allegations that the corporation had substantial liquid assets and that plaintiffs had personal financial problems totally unrelated to the corporation did not state grounds for judicial dissolution. Re Dubonnet Scarfs, Inc. (1985, 1st Dept) 105 A.D.2d 339, 484 N.Y.S.2d 541

Court erred in dismissing petition for judicial dissolution of closely held corporation for failure to state cause of action where petitioner alleged and supported allegations of oppressive behavior of majority stockholders by affidavit showing facts that majority stockholders froze petitioner out from corporation started by his grandfather, where he had been employed for 36 years, and in which he had served in executive positions and owned over 30 percent of stock. Re Rambusch (1988, 1st Dept) 143 A.D.2d 605, 533 N.Y.S.2d 423

In proceeding under CLS Bus Corp § 1104-a for judicial dissolution of close corporation, court should not have dismissed petition, without hearing, where parties' affidavits and affirmations created fact issues, inter alia, as to whether petitioner was shareholder in corporation,

and whether other shareholder forced petitioner out of business. Singer v Evergreen Decorators (1994, 2d Dept) 205 A.D.2d 694, 613 N.Y.S.2d 667

Court properly denied respondent's application to have petition for dissolution under CLS Bus Corp § 1104(a)(3) deemed one brought under CLS Bus Corp § 1104-a and to stay proceeding for valuation hearing under CLS Bus Corp § 118; it is petitioner who chooses statutory authority under which relief is sought. Toscano v Southampton Brick & Tile (1996, 2d Dept) 233 A.D.2d 515, 650 N.Y.S.2d 297

Court erred in granting minority shareholder's motion for summary judgment for judicial dissolution under CLS Bus Corp § 1104-a, even though he showed oppressive conduct by majority shareholders, since fact issue existed as to whether minority shareholder's actions were undertaken with view toward forcing dissolution in order to aid competing insurance agency in which he had financial interest. Cassata v Brewster-Allen-Wichert, Inc. (1998, 2d Dept) 248 A.D.2d 710, 670 N.Y.S.2d 552

In shareholder's action alleging, inter alia, breach of fiduciary duty and conversion of corporate assets, court erred in ruling that plaintiff's dissolution allegations pleaded CLS Bus Corp § 1104-a cause of action, in directing plaintiff to amend his complaint to comply with CLS Bus Corp §§ 1105 and 1106, and in permitting forced buy of out his shares pursuant to CLS Bus Corp § 1118, where his pleadings never cited § 1104-a as basis for dissolution and he made it clear that he was requesting common-law dissolution only as alternative to primary relief requested in his first 6 causes of action. Fedele v Seybert (1998, 1st Dept) 250 A.D.2d 519, 673 N.Y.S.2d 421

Petition for dissolution of closely held cooperative apartment corporation was improperly denied without hearing to determine validity of allegations that corporation engaged in oppressive conduct when it failed to credit petitioners' maintenance payments, thereby manufacturing default for purposes of obtaining their eviction, and that corporation engaged in waste when it used corporate funds to perform repairs that were obligation of individual apartment shareholders. Cunningham v 344 6th Ave. Owners Corp. (1998, 2d Dept) 256 A.D.2d 406, 681 N.Y.S.2d 593

In an action which a minority shareholder and former officer of a closely held corporation filed, pursuant to N.Y. Bus. Corp. Law § 1104-a, seeking dissolution of the corporation on the grounds that other shareholders engaged in illegal and fraudulent actions and were guilty of oppressive conduct, the evidence raised issues of fact about whether the former officer breached his fiduciary duty to the corporation when he leased property to the corporation, and the trial court properly denied the former officer's motion for partial summary judgment on the corporation's counterclaims seeking an order imposing a constructive trust on the property and alleging that he converted assets belonging to the corporation. In re Dissolution of Watson Landscaping, Inc. (2004, A.D., 4th Dept) 778 N.Y.S.2d 658

5. What constitutes "oppressive" conduct; generally

Given the nature of closed corporations and the remedial purpose of the statute, utilizing a complaining shareholder's "reasonable expectations" as a means of identifying and measuring conduct alleged to be oppressive is appropriate, and a court must investigate what the majority shareholders knew, or should have known, to be the petitioner's expectations in entering the particular enterprise. Oppression should be deemed to arise only when the majority conduct substantially defeats expectations that, objectively viewed, were both reasonable under the circumstances, and were central to the petitioner's decision to join the venture. Re Kemp & Beatley, Inc. (1984) 64 N.Y.2d 63, 484 N.Y.S.2d 799, 473 N.E.2d 1173

In a proceeding by a corporate shareholder pursuant to Bus Corp Law § 1104-a for judicial dissolution of two close corporations, an order denying the corporation's motion to dismiss the petition and granting the petition was erroneous where the issue of oppressive conduct by defendants, as alleged by the petitioner, was determined by Special Term solely on the papers presented by the parties without a hearing on the issue of whether defendants were guilty of such conduct toward the petitioner. Re Rosen (1984, 2d Dept) 102 A.D.2d 855, 476 N.Y.S.2d 625

Fact that corporation paid dividends does not mean that corporate policy is not oppressive as to closely held corporation in which shareholder has reasonable expectation of continued employment. Gunzberg v Art-Lloyd Metal Products Corp. (1985, 2d Dept) 112 A.D.2d 423, 492 N.Y.S.2d 83

"Oppression" within meaning of statute arises only when majority conduct substantially defeats expectations that, objectively viewed, were both reasonable under circumstances and were central to petitioner's decision to join venture. Re Mintz (1985, 2d Dept) 113 A.D.2d 803, 493 N.Y.S.2d 488

Where petitioner, although largest single corporation stockholder, and her family, had received no return on investment for over 12 years, and good faith and judgment of directors was called into question by their freezing all cash surpluses of company for several years; issues existed as to whether corporation had been engaged in oppressive conduct to freeze out petitioner by stock piling surplus or by attempting to force her to sell below value or whether other shareholders had been receiving dividends in form of excessive salaries or other benefits to exclusion of petitioner. Re Mintz (1985, 2d Dept) 113 A.D.2d 803, 493 N.Y.S.2d 488

Supreme Court erred in striking company's affirmative defenses to shareholder's petition seeking judicial dissolution under CLS Bus Corp § 1104-a where company alleged facts which, if true, would constitute partial defenses to shareholder's claim of oppressive conduct in that they (1) contradicted shareholder's claims that no dividends had been declared and that he had no access to business records, and (2) asserted that buy-out offer had been made to shareholder and that business had flourished since shareholder left company board. Petraglia v Whirlwind Music Distributors, Inc. (1987, 4th Dept) 126 A.D.2d 948, 511 N.Y.S.2d 718

In proceeding pursuant to CLS Bus Corp § 1104-a(a)(1) for involuntary dissolution of corporation on ground that majority shareholders were guilty of oppressive conduct, test to determine whether conduct was oppressive by examination of minority shareholder's "reasonable expectations" applies in situation where minority shareholder's stock interest was gift. Re Schlachter (1989, 2d Dept) 154 A.D.2d 685, 546 N.Y.S.2d 891, app den 76 N.Y.2d 705, 560 N.Y.S.2d 128, 559 N.E.2d 1287

In a proceeding by a minority shareholder seeking judicial dissolution, pursuant to Bus Corp Law § 1104a, of two close corporations after controlling corporate shareholders allegedly engaged in oppressive actions in discharging the minority shareholder as employee and officer, the minority shareholder is entitled to petition for dissolution where the controlling shareholders' actions severely damaged the minority shareholder's reasonable expectation and constituted a freeze-out of the minority shareholder's interest; in such a situation, however, the court may permit purchase for fair value of the minority shareholder's interest by the other shareholders where the other shareholders have made such an election. Topper v Park Sheraton Pharmacy, Inc. (1980) 107 Misc. 2d 25, 433 N.Y.S.2d 359

The "reasonable expectations" test, which sets a standard for describing oppressive conduct by majority shareholders pursuant to which dissolution of the corporation may be ordered pursuant to Bus Corp Law § 1104-a, is an inappropriate means to determine the rights of the parties in a dissolution proceeding when the close corporation in questions is in its fifty-third year of existence and all present holders of voting shares are two generations removed from the adoption of the corporate form, since the test is an examination into the spoken and unspoken understanding upon which the founders relied when entering into the venture and, inasmuch as all present shareholders acquired their interest by bequest or gift, they in no sense chose each other as business associates. Gimpel v Bolstein (1984) 125 Misc. 2d 45, 477 N.Y.S.2d 1014

The trial court properly ordered two closely-held corporations dissolved, because the majority shareholders' actions, including alleged usurpation of corporate opportunities by selling four undeveloped plots to two other corporations, one of which was entirely owned by a majority shareholder, and alleged failure distribute dividends and compensate a minority shareholder for his services, constituted oppression of the minority shareholders. In re Charleston Square, Inc. (2002, A.D., 2d Dept) 743 N.Y.S.2d 170

6. – Oppressive conduct found

A policy whereby the majority shareholders of a closed corporation award de facto dividends to all shareholders except a class of minority shareholders may constitute "oppressive actions" and serve as a basis for an order of judicial dissolution under Bus Corp Law § 1104-a. Accordingly, an order for dissolution, subject to an opportunity for a buy-out of petitioners' shares, was properly based on a finding that the recharacterization of distributions of corporate income as extra compensation for services rendered to the corporation, rather than as a distribution on stockholdings, amounted to nothing less than an attempt to exclude petitioners from gaining any return on their investment. Re Kemp & Beatley, Inc. (1984) 64 N.Y.2d 63, 484 N.Y.S.2d 799, 473 N.E.2d 1173

A change of policy for distributions of corporate income, designed to offer petitioners no return on their investment in an attempted "squeeze-out," constituted "oppressive actions" as a basis for an order of judicial dissolution. Re Kemp & Beatley, Inc. (1984) 64 N.Y.2d 63, 484 N.Y.S.2d 799, 473 N.E.2d 1173

Petitioner, the holder of one third of the voting stock in one of several closely held corporations established by members of his family, was subjected to oppressive conduct within the context of Bus Corp Law § 1104-a(a)(1) where, in 1974, petitioner returned to the family business with a reasonable expectation of being actively involved in the management and operation of the new corporation in which he held the one-third interest, utilized his own funds in getting the new venture under way, not simply as an investment, but to provide employment and a future for himself, and, until his discharge, had turned the new corporation into a highly profitable venture, and where, under such circumstances, petitioner's reasonable expectations as a minority shareholder were clearly frustrated by his discharge. Furthermore, a hearing into the factual allegations of oppression was not required, since respondents conceded that petitioner was squeezed out of the corporation for no legitimate reason other than family animosity. Re Wiedy's Furniture Clearance Center Co. (1985, 3d Dept) 108 A.D.2d 81, 487 N.Y.S.2d 901

Shareholder who owned 20 percent of close corporation which operated transmission shop was subjected to "oppressive actions" under CLS Bus Corp § 1104-a, and was entitled to dissolve corporation, where he had invested in corporation on basis of understanding that it would employ him as mechanic at particular salary, but other shareholders later decided to discontinue paying salary, forcing him to resign. Re Imperatore (1987, 2d Dept) 128 A.D.2d 707, 512 N.Y.S.2d 904

Minority shareholder who had invested his entire life's work in family-owned business established "oppression" within meaning of CLS Bus Corp § 1104-a where (1) he was not reelected as officer or director of corporation although he had held both positions in preceding years, (2) he was denied access to corporate records, (3) his employment with corporation was terminated, and (4) he received no salary or dividends after he was terminated except for one dividend declared on eve of trial. Re Burack (1988, 2d Dept) 137 A.D.2d 523, 524 N.Y.S.2d 457, app dismd without op 73 N.Y.2d 851, 537 N.Y.S.2d 495, 534 N.E.2d 333

Cause of action for involuntary dissolution on ground of oppressive conduct under CLS Bus Corp § 1104-a was stated by allegations that respondents cut off petitioner's weekly salary, bonuses, and other perquisites, denied him unrestricted access to corporate records and facilities, prevented his active participation in business, and terminated employment of his family members. DiMino v DeVeaux Servs. (1997, 4th Dept) 238 A.D.2d 943, 661 N.Y.S.2d 550

In proceeding for dissolution of corporation under CLS Bus Corp § 1104-a for fraudulent or oppressive acts of shareholders, dissolution was proper and fully necessary to protect petitioner's interest where respondent shareholders attempted to nullify petitioner's shares, falsified corporate documents, and denied petitioner access to records and documents. In re Dissolution of Pickwick Realty (1998, 3d Dept) 246 A.D.2d 863, 668 N.Y.S.2d 84

Evidence supported the trial court's findings that petitioner physician was an oppressed shareholder under N.Y. Bus. Corp. Law § 1104-a(a)(1) where respondents, two associates, excluded the physician from the daily operations of respondent group practice, made personnel decisions without consulting the physician, and generally undertook a course of conduct that frustrated the physician's reasonable expectations that the physician would have an active role in the group practice, that respondents would not interfere with the physician's practice or its growth, and that respondents would not deprive the physician of a reasonable opportunity to earn a living by impermissibly terminating the physician's employment. In re Dissolution of Upstate Med. Assocs. P.C. (2002, 3d Dept) 292 A.D.2d 732, 739 N.Y.S.2d 766

Trial court did not err in granting petitioner minority shareholders' application for judicial dissolution of a closely held corporation because the record supported its findings that the majority shareholders looted corporate assets by removing large amounts of cash from the corporation and oppressed petitioners by diluting and seeking to extinguish their ownership interest in the corporation. Matter of Twin Bay Vil., Inc. v Kasian, 153 A.D.3d 998, 60 N.Y.S.3d 560, 2017 N.Y. App. Div. LEXIS 5970 (N.Y. App. Div. 3d Dep't 2017), app. denied, 31 N.Y.3d 902, 77 N.Y.S.3d 657, 2018 N.Y. LEXIS 482

(N.Y. 2018), app. dismissed, in part, 162 A.D.3d 1265, 79 N.Y.S.3d 702, 2018 N.Y. App. Div. LEXIS 4339 (N.Y. App. Div. 3d Dep't 2018).

Discharged corporate officer and minority shareholder is entitled to order dissolving 2 closely held corporations pursuant to Business Corporation Law § 1104-a where controlling shareholders' actions severely damage minority shareholder's reasonable expectation and constitute freeze-out of minority shareholder's interest; however, in view of election made by majority shareholders, they are permitted to purchase for fair value, minority shareholder's interest in corporation. Topper v Park Sheraton Pharmacy, Inc. (1980) 107 Misc. 2d 25, 433 N.Y.S.2d 359

"Oppressive conduct" within meaning of Business Corporation Law § 1104-a is found where majority father-and-son shareholder groups eliminates minority father and son from active operation of corporation in which minority father and son shareholders participated and in which they had every reasonable expectation of being able to continue to participate after son having been "creator and moving force behind corporation" and relocating to New York to become full time employee of corporation, establishing residence in New York for purposes of overseeing operation of corporation, and where majority shareholders allege no facts stating circumstances leading to removal other than certain conclusory allegations in their affidavit. Re Gene Barry One Hour Photo Process, Inc. (1981) 111 Misc. 2d 559, 444 N.Y.S.2d 540

Frustration of interest of minority shareholder, including systematic expulsion of shareholder from day-to-day operations of company, culminating in his termination as officer and director constitutes oppressive actions and are basis for grant of order in minority shareholder's favor dissolving corporation pursuant to Business Corporation Law § 1104-a. O'Donnel v Marine Repair Services, Inc. (1982, SD NY) 530 F. Supp. 1199

7. – Oppressive conduct not found

Minority shareholder failed to establish "oppressive action" under CLS Bus Corp § 1104-a based on majority shareholder's laxity in maintaining certain records, failure to regularly consult with him, erroneous belief that she was sole owner of corporation, and failure to cooperate in allowing him access to corporate records where (1) minority shareholder was passive investor who did not seek role in day-to-day management or expect corporation to provide him with occupation, (2) there was insufficient evidence of disparity between financial returns paid to him and those paid to majority shareholder to support claim of oppression, and (3) his initial investment of $20,000 had resulted in one-third ownership of corporation with assets valued at $500,000; thus, application for judicial dissolution of corporation was properly denied. Re Farega Realty Corp. (1987, 3d Dept) 132 A.D.2d 797, 517 N.Y.S.2d 610

Action to dissolve corporation under CLS Bus Corp § 1104-a should have been dismissed where petitioner alleged that corporation was mismanaged by virtue of inadequate bookkeeping and that shareholders' agreement failed to set forth buy-out procedure originally contemplated, or to provide, in event of stock transfer, for payment of mortgage note secured solely by petitioner's property, since (1) petition merely set forth dissatisfaction with corporate management, which would not support finding of oppressive action by majority of shareholders, (2) there was no showing of corporate waste or looting, or continuation of corporate existence solely for other shareholders' benefit at petitioner's expense, and (3) no appeal had been taken from prior order dismissing petitioner's action for reformation of buy-out agreement based on court's holding that buy-out procedure provided petitioner with fair return on his investment. Re Brach (1987, 2d Dept) 135 A.D.2d 711, 522 N.Y.S.2d 612, app den 73 N.Y.2d 701, 535 N.Y.S.2d 595, 532 N.E.2d 101

In action for judicial dissolution of 3 affiliated, family-owned corporations, where petitioner established "oppression" under CLS Bus Corp § 1104-a with respect to primary corporation based on majority shareholders' decision to terminate his employment and not re-elect him as officer and director of primary corporation, trial court properly determined that petitioner did not establish "oppression" as to 2 remaining corporations which were run separately from primary corporation, inasmuch as he was still officer and director of those corporations. Re Burack (1988, 2d Dept) 137 A.D.2d 523, 524 N.Y.S.2d 457, app dismd without op 73 N.Y.2d 851, 537 N.Y.S.2d 495, 534 N.E.2d 333

Stockholder who owned 1/3 of closely held corporations was not entitled to dissolution of corporations pursuant to CLS Bus Corp § 1104-a on ground that majority shareholders had subjected him to oppressive actions where (1) stockholder, who was California

resident, had essentially been passive shareholder from time he inherited interest in 1981 and sought neither responsibilities in day-to-day management of corporations nor employment with corporations, (2) despite his acknowledged receipt of notices of annual shareholders' meetings, stockholder's first sign of interest in corporations was in 1986 when he attended his first annual meeting, (3) prior to 1986, he had never inquired as to affairs of corporations and had never requested that dividends be declared, and (4) at 1986 annual meeting, stockholder's motion to become member of board of directors was defeated. Re Smith (1989, 2d Dept) 154 A.D.2d 537, 546 N.Y.S.2d 382

Failure to declare dividends did not constitute oppression under CLS Bus Corp § 1104-a since (1) as was common with closely held corporations, no policy of declaring dividends appeared to exist, and (2) shareholder made no demand for such declaration, and thus there was no refusal by board of directors. Re Smith (1989, 2d Dept) 154 A.D.2d 537, 546 N.Y.S.2d 382

In proceeding pursuant to CLS Bus Corp § 1104-a for judicial dissolution of closely held corporation on basis that corporation's major shareholder had engaged in oppressive conduct, including misappropriation of over $50,000 in corporate assets, petitioner was not entitled to summary judgment where (1) majority shareholder averred that corporate assets were expended for valid business reasons and were not converted to her personal use, and (2) while assertion was largely unsupported by documentary proof, it was inferable that any inability to produce documentary corroboration was attributable to careless record keeping, rather than to any intent to defraud. Re Schwen (1989, 2d Dept) 154 A.D.2d 601, 546 N.Y.S.2d 429

Respondents were entitled to summary judgment dismissing minority shareholder's petition for dissolution of closely held corporations pursuant to CLS Bus Corp § 1104-a(a)(1) after termination of employment of her husband by one of corporations, notwithstanding allegation that corporations were guilty of oppressive conduct, since (1) petitioner's husband was employed prior to her acquisition of stock and was employee at will, and therefore petitioner could have had no reasonable expectation that he would continue to be employed or that she would continue to receive ancillary benefits that flowed to her husband as employee, and (2) petitioner never sought role in day-to-day operations of corporations or their management. Re Schlachter (1989, 2d Dept) 154 A.D.2d 685, 546 N.Y.S.2d 891, app den 76 N.Y.2d 705, 560 N.Y.S.2d 128, 559 N.E.2d 1287

Petition for dissolution of corporation pursuant to CLS Bus Corp § 1104-a was properly denied since (1) petitioners' claim regarding their removal as directors was subject to arbitration under shareholders' agreement, and (2) proposed merger, which was objected to by petitioners, did not receive necessary approval of Public Health Council, and therefore did not occur. Alleman v Sunrest Health Facilities, Inc. (1991, 2d Dept) 176 A.D.2d 287, 574 N.Y.S.2d 216

Court erred in granting petition to dissolve closely held corporation where petitioners' proof, including majority shareholders' failure to regularly account to them as to corporate operations, laxness in maintaining certain records, and failure to allow them access to corporate records, was insufficient to show requisite "oppressive action" since petitioners had been passive shareholders from time they purchased their shares, they did not seek responsibilities in date-to-day management of corporation, and they did not express interest in shareholders' meetings or in electing corporate officers. Brickman v Brickman Estate at the Point, Inc. (1998, 2d Dept) 253 A.D.2d 812, 677 N.Y.S.2d 600, app den 92 N.Y.2d 488, 92 N.Y.2d 817, 684 N.Y.S.2d 488, 707 N.E.2d 443

Minority stockholder seeking dissolution of closely held corporation failed to prove oppressive conduct by majority stockholder under CLS Bus Corp § 1104-a where, inter alia, (1) as to alleged impropriety in repayment of personal funds lent to corporation, petitioner signed corporate promissory notes at issue, thus negating at least any intent by majority stockholder to conceal those transactions, (2) apparent purchase of personal item for majority stockholder with corporate funds was explained as inadvertent "accounting error" that was corrected when brought to his attention, and (3) petitioner's affidavit in response to motion to dismiss did not address alleged oppressive conduct but focused on parties' failed buy-out negotiations and suspension of his salary after he had "agreed" to resign and after parties had begun to discuss tender of his shares. In re Dissolution of Rencor Controls, Inc. (1999, 3d Dept) 263 A.D.2d 845, 693 N.Y.S.2d 717

Trial court properly granted respondent summary judgment dismissing the N.Y. Bus. Corp. Law § 1104-a cause of action because there was no dispute with the evidence that established that respondent's alleged conduct did not defeat petitioner's reasonable expectations or otherwise amount to oppressive conduct within the meaning of the statute. Matter of Tehan, 144 A.D.3d 1530, 40 N.Y.S.3d 858, 2016 N.Y. App. Div. LEXIS 7458 (4th Dep't 2016).

8. Other grounds for dissolution

Mere fact that closely held corporation may have substantial liquid assets which minority shareholder wishes to reach in order to obtain better return on money elsewhere is insufficient basis for judicial dissolution. Re Murphy (1986, 2d Dept) 120 A.D.2d 733, 502 N.Y.S.2d 518

Company was not entitled to dismissal of plaintiff shareholder's petition seeking judicial dissolution pursuant to CLS Bus Corp § 1104-a where plaintiff alleged (1) diversion of company's opportunities to second company formed by other shareholders, (2) failure of other shareholders to pay dividends or make distributions from either company, and (3) refusal of other shareholders to grant plaintiff access to business records of either company; however, second company was entitled to dismissal of dissolution petition as against it since plaintiff held no shares in second company, and § 1104-a requires that dissolution petition be brought by holder of at least 20 percent of shares of corporation sought to be dissolved. Petraglia v Whirlwind Music Distributors, Inc. (1987, 4th Dept) 126 A.D.2d 948, 511 N.Y.S.2d 718

In proceeding brought by shareholder for dissolution of closely held corporations under CLS Bus Corp § 1104-a, evidence did not support findings that salaries paid to majority shareholders were in lieu of dividends or that work they performed was duplicative where (1) court sustained objection by petitioner shareholder to direct examination of majority shareholders' expert witness as to whether salaries were excessive relative to work performed on basis that salary levels were not relevant, and (2) no evidence was adduced as to appropriateness of salary levels relative to work performed or corporations' manpower requirements. Re Smith (1989, 2d Dept) 154 A.D.2d 537, 546 N.Y.S.2d 382

In dissolution proceeding, plaintiff failed to establish that sale of building and land which housed corporation's business, to one shareholder individually, constituted improper usurpation of corporate opportunity, where sellers unequivocally averred that they would not have sold to corporation, or to plaintiff, but only to particular shareholder individually. Di Pace v Figueroa (1996, 3d Dept) 223 A.D.2d 949, 637 N.Y.S.2d 222

Summary judgment as to liability under N.Y. Bus. Corp. Law § 1104-a(a)(2) in favor of an administrator and against a shareholder was proper in a turnover proceeding pursuant to N.Y. Surr. Ct. Proc. Act §§ 2103, 2104, because the administrator showed that the shareholder and other stockholders of corporation had looted, wasted, or diverted corporate assets; as corporate officers, the surviving stockholders stood in a fiduciary relationship to the corporation, and their establishment of a new corporation with two of the same principals, which used the same office, equipment, and furniture, and which served many of the same clients, violated that duty. In opposition, the shareholder failed to raise a fact issue sufficient to defeat summary judgment on the issue of his liability, and, specifically, he failed to adduce any evidence in support of his contention that the administrator had steered the decedent's clients away from the corporation in an attempt to force a judicial dissolution. Matter of Verdeschi (2009, 2d Dept) 63 App Div 3d 1084, 882 NYS2d 440.

9. Dissolution as proper remedy; generally

The appropriateness of an order of judicial dissolution of a closed corporation pursuant to Bus Corp Law § 1104-a is in every case vested in the sound discretion of the court considering the application. Once oppressive conduct is found, consideration must be given to the totality of circumstances to determine whether some remedy short of, or other than, dissolution constitutes a feasible means of satisfying both the petitioners' expectations and the rights and interests of any other substantial group of shareholders. It was not an abuse of discretion to order dissolution subject to an opportunity for a buy-out of petitioners' shares, where the court found that the controlling faction of the company was, in effect, attempting to "squeeze-out" petitioner minority shareholders, and where it was not unreasonable for the court to have determined that a forced buy-out of petitioners' shares or liquidation of the corporation's assets was the only means by which petitioners could be guaranteed a fair return on

their investments. Re Kemp & Beatley, Inc. (1984) 64 N.Y.2d 63, 484 N.Y.S.2d 799, 473 N.E.2d 1173

After a petitioner seeking judicial dissolution of a closed corporation pursuant to Bus Corp Law § 1104-a has set forth a prima facie case of oppressive conduct, it is incumbent upon the parties seeking to forestall dissolution to demonstrate to the court the existence of an adequate, alternative remedy. A court should not hesitate to order dissolution when fulfillment of the oppressed petitioner's expectations by alternate means is doubtful, but every such order of dissolution must be conditioned upon permitting any shareholder of the corporation to elect to purchase the complaining shareholder's stock at fair value. Re Kemp & Beatley, Inc. (1984) 64 N.Y.2d 63, 484 N.Y.S.2d 799, 473 N.E.2d 1173

Where petitioner has set forth prima facie case of oppressive conduct, it is incumbent upon party seeking to forestall dissolution to demonstrate to court existence of adequate alternative remedy. Gunzberg v Art-Lloyd Metal Products Corp. (1985, 2d Dept) 112 A.D.2d 423, 492 N.Y.S.2d 83

Fact that petitioner seeking judicial dissolution of closely held corporation has demonstrated grounds for dissolution does not require court to enter order of involuntary dissolution where petitioner may obtain fair return on investment pursuant to buy-out provisions of shareholder's agreement. Re Harris (1986, 2d Dept) 118 A.D.2d 646, 500 N.Y.S.2d 5

"Reasonable expectation" standard under CLS Bus Corp § 1104-a(b)(1) can be applied to case in which stock interest is inherited; however, petitioner shareholder's conduct did not evidence reasonable expectation of being active participant in management of closely held corporation given his prior acquiescence in majority shareholders' exercise of control over day-to-day management of corporation. Re Smith (1989, 2d Dept) 154 A.D.2d 537, 546 N.Y.S.2d 382

Court erred in ordering dissolution of closely-held corporation, without hearing, in view of parties' conflicting assertions. In re Fancy Windows & Doors Mfg. Corp. (1997, 2d Dept) 244 A.D.2d 484, 664 N.Y.S.2d 113

Dissolution of a corporation pursuant to Bus Corp Law § 1104-a is discretionary and a drastic remedy which should be ordered when it is the only means by which complainant shareholders can reasonably expect to receive a fair return on their investment, and when it is reasonably necessary to protect their rights and interests. Gimpel v Bolstein (1984) 125 Misc. 2d 45, 477 N.Y.S.2d 1014

A proceeding for dissolution of a closed corporation pursuant to Bus Corp Law § 1104-a would be stayed pending the court's attempt to fashion a more feasible means whereby petitioner might obtain relief by determining the fair market value of petitioner's shares so that respondent majority shareholder could buy petitioner's shares pursuant to Bus Corp Law, § 1118, where petitioner's action seemed motivated primarily by frustration over the alleged uncooperative attitude of respondent in facilitating an inspection of the corporate records, petitioner had not been involved in the day-to-day operations of the corporation for some time pursuant to his separation and divorce from respondent, and the corporation was a going concern. Re Chariot Taxi, Inc. (1984) 126 Misc. 2d 394

Trial court properly found that an estate established the "special circumstances" required to invoke N.Y. Bus. Corp. Law § 1104-a, and properly ordered that a shareholder buy the estate's shares, because of the shareholder's unwillingness to either negotiate sale of the estate's shares or to include the administrator in company's operation of the company; the shareholder's conduct in operating the company to the exclusion of the administrator substantially defeated the estate's reasonable expectations for cooperation and disclosure of relevant business information. The only factual issue in dispute was whether, despite the absence of an official appointment, the shareholder had become an officer of the company, and as this fact was not material to the issue of whether the shareholder, a 50 percent stockholder, engaged in oppressive conduct, and given that he apparently never requested a hearing, the trial court was not required to hold one. Matter of Clever Innovations, Inc. (Dooley) (2012, App Div, 3d Dept) 941 NYS2d 777.

10. – Dissolution granted

An order of dissolution, subject to an opportunity for a buy-out of petitioners' shares, was proper where a complete deterioriation of relations between the parties, and the absence of any suggestion of a feasible alternative remedy by respondents, rendered doubtful the possibility that petitioners' expectations could be fulfilled by alternative means. Re Kemp & Beatley, Inc. (1984) 64 N.Y.2d 63, 484 N.Y.S.2d 799, 473 N.E.2d 1173

Petitioner's allegation that he was involuntarily ousted from any involvement or ownership in respondent corporation, of which he was founding 1/3 shareholder, by other 2 1/3 shareholders, not only stated cause of action for involuntary dissolution based on oppressive action, but also warranted granting of petition, where papers submitted on respondents' dismissal motion (which effectively constituted answer) failed to raise any genuine issues of fact on question of oppression. Williamson v Williamson, Picket, Gross, Inc. (In re Williamson) (1999, 1st Dept) 259 A.D.2d 362, 687 N.Y.S.2d 53

Trial court properly found that an estate established the "special circumstances" required to invoke N.Y. Bus. Corp. Law § 1104-a, and properly ordered that a shareholder buy the estate's shares, because of the shareholder's unwillingness to either negotiate sale of the estate's shares or to include the administrator in company's operation of the company; the shareholder's conduct in operating the company to the exclusion of the administrator substantially defeated the estate's reasonable expectations for cooperation and disclosure of relevant business information. The only factual issue in dispute was whether, despite the absence of an official appointment, the shareholder had become an officer of the company, and as this fact was not material to the issue of whether the shareholder, a 50 percent stockholder, engaged in oppressive conduct, and given that he apparently never requested a hearing, the trial court was not required to hold one. Matter of Clever Innovations, Inc. (Dooley) (2012, App Div, 3d Dept) 941 NYS2d 777.

Petitioner's reasonable expectations at the time of his acquisition of stock in both corporations was long-term employment, a role in corporate management and compensation in the form of profit-sharing, and respondent's actions defeated those expectations; petitioner had established grounds for dissolution of both corporations. Matter of Gould Erectors & Rigging, Inc. (Digeser—Flach), 146 A.D.3d 1128, 45 N.Y.S.3d 270, 2017 N.Y. App. Div. LEXIS 224 (3d Dep't 2017).

Petitioner's reasonable expectations at the time of his acquisition of stock in both corporations was long-term employment, a role in corporate management and compensation in the form of profit-sharing, and respondent's actions defeated those expectations; petitioner had established grounds for dissolution of both corporations. Matter of Gould Erectors & Rigging, Inc. (Digeser—Flach), 146 A.D.3d 1128, 45 N.Y.S.3d 270 (N.Y. App. Div. 3d Dep't 2017).

11. – Dissolution denied

In an action by two shareholders of a corporation, seeking a declaration of a reasonable dividend, the removal of the officers and directors, and compensatory and punitive damages, the trial court should not have directed the dissolution of the corporation where one substantial shareholder had not been a party to the action, where defendant directors had not been given an opportunity to contest the dissolution, where the plaintiff shareholders had not sought dissolution, and where the trial court had not considered whether dissolution was the only feasible means by which the shareholders could expect to receive a fair return on their investment. Muller v Silverstein (1983, 1st Dept) 92 A.D.2d 455, 458 N.Y.S.2d 597

In action for judicial dissolution of parties' closely held corporation, where petitioner established that he was "oppressed" within meaning of CLS Bus Corp § 1104-a, court properly ordered buyout of stock owned by petitioner rather than dissolution where corporation was multimillion dollar enterprise employing many people and acting as major competitor in its field. Re Burack (1988, 2d Dept) 137 A.D.2d 523, 524 N.Y.S.2d 457, app dismd without op 73 N.Y.2d 851, 537 N.Y.S.2d 495, 534 N.E.2d 333

In dissolution proceeding, plaintiff failed to establish that adoption of plan for infusion of equity into corporation was not improper attempt to dilute her holdings, where she was offered opportunity to purchase additional shares on same terms as other shareholders; determination of whether additional capital was needed, as well as price which shares were offered, was plainly in realm of business judgment which court would not disturb absent evidence of bad faith or fraud. Di Pace v Figueroa (1996, 3d Dept) 223 A.D.2d 949, 637 N.Y.S.2d 222

Parol evidence rule precluded plaintiff from presenting extrinsic evidence that written agreement by which he pledged his shares of stock in corporation was sham, and plaintiff was equitably estopped from denying that he had pledged his shares as security for his debts to corporation, where (1) he admitted his complicity in scheme to defeat legitimate claims of creditors by assigning personal assets, including his stock in corporation, to corporation to secure antecedent debt, (2) he fraudulently backdated that document in order to give

corporation priority in those assets over claims of creditors, and (3) he deceived court into granting corporation such priority; thus, he was no longer shareholder of corporation and lacked standing to bring shareholder's suit to dissolve corporation on grounds of waste, mismanagement, looting, and oppression or to bring proceeding to compel production of corporation's books and records under Business Corporation Law and CLS CPLR Art 78. Davis v Davis (1999, 4th Dept) 266 A.D.2d 867, 697 N.Y.S.2d 888, related proceeding (4th Dept) 266 A.D.2d 869, 698 N.Y.S.2d 193, related proceeding (4th Dept) 266 A.D.2d 869, 698 N.Y.S.2d 195, app den 94 N.Y.2d 761 and app den 94 N.Y.2d 761 and app den 94 N.Y.2d 761, 706 N.Y.S.2d 81

Petitioner, who was 25 percent shareholder of subject corporation, was not entitled to judicial dissolution based on his objections to terms of "definitive" agreement adopted by other 2 shareholders, because he failed to show that his expectations of either job security or right to participate in corporation's management were reasonable, or that conduct of other 2 shareholders defeated any of his reasonable expectations, where he had been employed by corporation for less than 2 years in nonmanagerial at-will position, and preliminary shareholders' agreement noted that all matters of corporate governance were subject to affirmative vote of other 2 shareholders and gave other 2 shareholders right to repurchase his shares at their initial purchase price if he did not agree to terms to be set forth in "definitive" agreement. In re Bitter (2000, 1st Dept) 270 A.D.2d 101, 704 N.Y.S.2d 250, app den 95 N.Y.2d 764, 716 N.Y.S.2d 39, 739 N.E.2d 295

Action by two shareholders in a closely-held corporation to refinance a loan so that the corporation became primarily liable for the loan and to authorize the issuance of promissory notes to themselves which would be satisfied by the issuance of additional shares of stock were not illegal and did not warrant dissolution of the corporation, and the appellate court dismissed an appeal which the Superintendent of Insurance of the State of New York took from a trial court's judgment denying dissolution of the corporation after the Superintendent acquired shares in the corporation that were owned by a bankrupt shareholder. Estate of Lawrence v Quail Aero Serv. (In re Dissolution of Quail Aero Serv.) (2002, A.D., 3d Dept) 755 N.Y.S.2d 103

12. Buyout of petitioner's shares

In proceedings brought by the holder of 50 percent of a closed corporation's stock for judicial dissolution under both Bus Corp Law §§ 1104, 1104-a, the holder of the remaining 50 percent stock was entitled to buy out petitioner's shares under Bus Corp Law § 1118, which allows buyout under § 1104-a, but is silent regarding the right to buy out under § 1104. Re Cristo Bros., Inc. (1985) 64 N.Y.2d 975, 489 N.Y.S.2d 35, 478 N.E.2d 176

Close corporation's election to buy minority shareholder's shares under shareholders' agreement, or alternatively under CLS Bus Corp § 1118, relieved shareholder of need to prove allegations of fraud, mismanagement, et al. underlying his petition to dissolve corporation, so no hearing on allegations was required; while fixing blame is material under dissolution proceeding of CLS Bus Corp § 1104-a, it is immaterial under § 1118. Re Pace Photographers, Ltd. (1988) 71 N.Y.2d 737, 530 N.Y.S.2d 67, 525 N.E.2d 713

Close corporation's election to buy minority shareholder's shares under shareholders' agreement, or alternatively under CLS Bus Corp § 1118, made it unnecessary for Court of Appeals to decide whether shareholders' agreement fixing value in and of itself precluded relief for shareholder in his dissolution proceeding under CLS Bus Corp § 1104-a, despite his allegations of fraud, mismanagement, et al., since § 1104-a provides that court must take into account whether "liquidation of the corporation is the only feasible means whereby the petitioners may reasonably expect to obtain a fair return on their investment"; on election, central question became one of valuation under § 1118, not liquidation under § 1104-a. Re Pace Photographers, Ltd. (1988) 71 N.Y.2d 737, 530 N.Y.S.2d 67, 525 N.E.2d 713

Closely-held corporation clearly and unequivocally elected to purchase minority shareholder's shares under shareholders' agreement, or alternatively under CLS Bus Corp § 1118, on shareholder's instigation of dissolution proceeding for fraud, mismanagement, et al. under CLS Bus Corp § 1104-a where corporation did not contend that its offer was hedged or conditional, and it maintained consistent position in litigation before both Supreme Court and Appellate Division. Re Pace Photographers, Ltd. (1988) 71 N.Y.2d 737, 530 N.Y.S.2d 67, 525 N.E.2d 713

Where one shareholder in close corporation petitioned for dissolution under CLS Bus Corp § 1104-a and another shareholder elected to purchase his shares at fair value, petitioning shareholder's vested right to recover fair value for his corporate stock survived his death. In re Penepent Corp. (2001) 96 N.Y.2d 186, 726 N.Y.S.2d 345, 750 N.E.2d 47

In a proceeding pursuant to Bus Corp Law §§ 1104 and 1104-a, seeking judicial dissolution of a corporation whose stock was equally divided between two shareholders, the court improperly dismissed one shareholder's cross petition under Bus Corp Law § 118 to purchase the other shareholder's stock, since the second shareholder owned more than 20 percent of the shares of the corporation and thus fell within the class entitled to bring a petition under § 1104-a, and since § 1118 unambiguously provides for an election to purchase such a shareholder's shares in all cases that include allegations under § 1104-a. Re Cristo Bros., Inc. (1983, 3d Dept) 97 A.D.2d 274, 470 N.Y.S.2d 781

A proceeding for involuntary judicial dissolution of a corporation, pursuant to Bus Corp Law §§ 1104, 1104-a, on the basis of a deadlock in the management of the corporation, was properly referred for determination of the fair value of petitioner's shares as of the day prior to the filing of the petition, where respondent timely elected to purchase petitioner's stock under Bus Corp Law § 1118, and where, although the statutory buy-out remedy does not apply to actions pursuant to Bus Corp Law § 1104, petitioner was entitled to petition for dissolution under both Bus Corp Law § 1104 and Bus Corp Law § 1104-a, and was properly prohibited from amending the petition to delete any reference to Bus Corp Law § 1104-a. Re Dissolution of Public Relations Aids, Inc. (1985, 1st Dept) 109 A.D.2d 502, 492 N.Y.S.2d 736

Appellate Division would dismiss appeal by majority shareholders from injunction order granted to minority shareholders in their action for dissolution under CLS Bus Corp § 1104-a where it was conceded at oral argument that majority shareholders had subsequently elected to purchase minority's shares pursuant to CLS Bus Corp § 1118, and mandatory stay provisions of § 1118 had been triggered; parties should proceed with remedy provided by § 1118 as substitute for § 1104-a proceeding. Re Seagroatt Floral Co. (1988, 3d Dept) 140 A.D.2d 841, 528 N.Y.S.2d 225

In proceeding under CLS Bus Corp § 1104-a, nonpetitioning shareholder was properly permitted to revoke his election to purchase shares owned by party seeking dissolution where fire destroyed corporation's business after election was made since election was made prior to effective date of amendment to CLS Bus Corp § 1118 limiting right to revoke, and thus nonpetitioning shareholder may have assumed that he would not be bound by his election, which may have influenced his decision to elect; moreover, even if amendment applied retroactively, revocation was properly allowed as matter of discretion, since it would be inequitable to force nonpetitioning shareholder to purchase essentially worthless stock owing to unforeseeable fire, absent evidence that election was made as delaying tactic or that nonpetitioning shareholder failed to act in good faith. Rey v Pan American Cash & Carry Corp. (1989, 2d Dept) 152 A.D.2d 246, 548 N.Y.S.2d 524

Defendants were entitled to summary judgment in dissolution proceeding where plaintiff could obtain fair return on her investment by selling her shares to defendants, who had signalled their willingness to update price set by parties' buy-out agreement and to purchase plaintiff's shares in accordance therewith. Di Pace v Figueroa (1996, 3d Dept) 223 A.D.2d 949, 637 N.Y.S.2d 222

Court abused its discretion in allowing majority shareholders to revoke their election to purchase minority shareholders' shares on ground of "impossibility of performance" due to financial difficulties experienced by one of majority shareholders since all majority shareholders had assured court that remaining majority shareholders would be able to effectuate buy out even if majority shareholder in question proved unable to participate, and they waited more than 3 years until after minority shareholders' initial proceeding to compel dissolution, and their own election to purchase shares, to move for revocation. Smith v Russo (1996, 2d Dept) 230 A.D.2d 863, 646 N.Y.S.2d 711

In proceeding under CLS Bus Corp Art 11 by minority stockholder for dissolution of closely held corporation, majority stockholder could not be forced to buy out petitioner at price to be determined by court if parties could not agree on value of petitioner's shares where petitioner failed to prove that dissolution was appropriate. In re Dissolution of Rencor Controls, Inc. (1999, 3d Dept) 263 A.D.2d 845, 693 N.Y.S.2d 717

13. – Effect of parties' agreement

In an action brought by a shareholder of a corporation who alleged that he had been "frozen-out" of his interest and who sought an award based on his interest in the corporation at the time of the alleged "freeze-out", the plaintiff was not entitled to recover the value of his interest on the basis of an alleged "buyout" agreement where the agreement had not been concluded, no decision on valuation having been reached by the parties. Robbins v Panitz (1984) 61 N.Y.2d 967, 475 N.Y.S.2d 274, 463 N.E.2d 615

Where one shareholder in close corporation petitioned for dissolution under CLS Bus Corp § 1104-a and another shareholder elected to purchase his shares at fair value, but petitioning shareholder died before determination of fair value, other shareholder was not entitled to revoke his election and acquire petitioning shareholder's stock pursuant to shareholder agreement which provided that deceased shareholder's estate must surrender deceased's stock to corporation in exchange for specified price, which was less than fair value; divestiture event under shareholder agreement (shareholder's death) did not occur until one1/2 years after CLS Bus Corp § 1118 election was made. In re Penepent Corp. (2001) 96 N.Y.2d 186, 726 N.Y.S.2d 345, 750 N.E.2d 47

Stock sale and repurchase provisions of shareholder's agreement, which were triggered by petitioner's termination from employment, did not, as matter of law, bar petitioner's proceeding to dissolve corporation pursuant to CLS Bus Corp § 1104-a where agreement did not explicitly provide that provisions were exclusive remedy available to minority shareholder; thus, question of fact existed as to whether fair return on investment requirement of CLS Bus Corp § 1104-a(b)(1) had been met. Mariello v Sovran Group, Inc. (1989, 4th Dept) 152 A.D.2d 1007, 544 N.Y.S.2d 749

Court would deny application for judicial dissolution of corporation under CLS Bus Corp § 1104-a, and would grant cross motion to dismiss, without prejudice to petitioner's right to commence arbitration, since arbitration clause in shareholders' agreement was broad enough to reach dispute between shareholders over control of corporation where dispute involved attempt by group of shareholders to buy out individual shareholder under shareholders' agreement. Re Herrero (1990, 1st Dept) 168 A.D.2d 343, 562 N.Y.S.2d 665

Plaintiff shareholders were not entitled to summary judgment granting specific performance of corporate agreement to purchase defendant's shares of their family corporation at specified price, on ground that defendant attempted to "dispose of" his stock within meaning of agreement by commencing dissolution proceeding under CLS Bus Corp § 1104-a, since (1) commencement of dissolution proceeding does not automatically result in sale and purchase of shares, and thus defendant did not attempt to "dispose of" his stock, (2) forced sale provisions of CLS Bus Corp § 1118 would require that any purchase thereunder be at fair value determined by court, and (3) shareholders' agreement clearly contemplated that forced sale at predetermined value would be triggered only in event of disposal of stock to outsiders. James Mirabito & Sons, Inc. v Mirabito (1986) 137 Misc. 2d 972, 523 N.Y.S.2d 711

Corporation could, without the consent of the petitioning shareholder, invoke its N.Y. Bus. Corp. Law § 1118 right of election because the shareholders did not explicitly limit its ability to exercise the right following the filing of a voluntary dissolution under N.Y. Bus. Corp. Law § 1104-a. Ferolito v Vultaggio (2012, App Div, 1st Dept) 949 NYS2d 356, injunction den, partial summary judgment den (2012, NY Sup) 2012 NY Slip Op 32047U, 2012 NY Misc LEXIS 3740, injunction den, partial summary judgment den (2012, NY Sup) 2012 NY Slip Op 51523U, 2012 NY Misc LEXIS 3869

14. Valuation of parties' interests

Where one shareholder in close corporation petitioned for dissolution under CLS Bus Corp § 1104-a and another shareholder invoked CLS Bus Corp § 1118, fair value of petitioner's shares was not affected by fact that third shareholder's dissolution proceeding was currently pending against corporation and other shareholders' § 1118 election in that proceeding would result in petitioner being "minority shareholder." In re Penepent Corp. (2001) 96 N.Y.2d 186, 726 N.Y.S.2d 345, 750 N.E.2d 47

In a proceeding under Bus Corp Law § 1104-a to dissolve certain corporations, Bus Corp Law § 623(g), (h) were not applicable to the determination of fair value of stock in those corporations, since there was no legislative design that those provisions were intended to govern a court's determination of fair value under Bus Corp Law § 1118, in which corporations exercise their option to purchase the shares of the person petitioning to dissolve. Re Fleischer (1980, 2d Dept) 79 A.D.2d 636, 433 N.Y.S.2d 614

In a corporate dissolution proceeding, an order directing the valuation of stock would be reversed, where a stock valuation can be directed when the proceeding is instituted under Bus Corp Law § 1104-a, when an election has been made under Bus Corp Law § 1118 by a shareholder to buy out the other shareholders, or an application has been made to stay the dissolution proceedings, and where the dissolution proceeding was instituted under Bus Corp Law § 1104, not under § 1104-a, where neither of the two principal shareholders had made an election to buy out the other, and where no one had moved to stay the dissolution. Re Application of Duffy (1983, 1st Dept) 97 A.D.2d 694, 468 N.Y.S.2d 116

Following a corporation's election under Bus Corp Law § 1118 to buy out a minority shareholder who had commenced a special proceeding under Bus Corp Law § 1104-a to dissolve the corporation, the referee, in valuing the shareholder's interest in the corporation: properly applied a multiplier of only one to gross commission revenue in determining the corporation's goodwill, since the insurance industry was "soft" due to direct billing of premiums; erred in valuing the shareholder's interest at 25 percent rather than 40 percent, since, while the shares of a closely held corporation cannot be readily sold on a public market, a minority interest in closely held corporate stock should not be discounted solely because it is a minority interest; erred in failing to award interest on the fair value of the shareholder's shares in the corporation, as justice demanded; and properly refused to discount the shareholder's share of net tangible assets, despite the argument that such an approach failed to account for the working capital needs of the corporation, where the corporation had never paid any dividends, and where the corporation's balance sheet, prior to the filing of the dissolution petition showed that it had sufficient capital even after paying the shareholder. Blake v Blake Agency, Inc. (1985, 2d Dept) 107 A.D.2d 139, 486 N.Y.S.2d 341

In action by minority shareholder of close corporation for dissolution pursuant to CLS Bus Corp § 1104-a(a) on grounds of oppressive conduct and looting by corporate directors and majority shareholders, court erred in ordering, without hearing, appraisal of defendants' shares and buy out of those shares by majority shareholders since hearing on allegations was required before remedy could be fashioned. Re MacDougall (1989, 1st Dept) 150 A.D.2d 160, 540 N.Y.S.2d 245

Petitioners were entitled to disclosure of relevant information in proceeding under CLS Bus Corp § 1104-a to dissolve 2 closely-held corporations in which majority shareholder elected to buy out petitioners subject to CLS Bus Corp § 1118, although election of majority shareholder to buy out petitioners made allegations of misconduct contained in petition superfluous with respect to dissolution under CLS Bus Corp § 1104-a, where allegations were still relevant with regard to impact of alleged misconduct on fair value of corporation. Gerzof v Coons (1990, 2d Dept) 168 A.D.2d 619, 563 N.Y.S.2d 458, later proceeding (2d Dept) 177 A.D.2d 487, 576 N.Y.S.2d 29

In proceeding under CLS Bus Corp § 1104-a for judicial dissolution, it was not error for court to direct referee to complete his valuation of petitioner's stock as soon as possible, rather than by specified date, where petitioner's motion papers requested only that referee be directed to submit his appraisal forthwith. Whalen v Whalen's Moving & Storage Co. (1994, 2d Dept) 204 A.D.2d 468, 612 N.Y.S.2d 165

In proceeding under CLS Bus Corp § 1104-a for judicial dissolution of closely held corporation, it was not improper for court to instruct referee to express value of petitioner's shares in terms of their fair market value and to further instruct referee to discount value of shares in recognition of their lack of marketability. Whalen v Whalen's Moving & Storage Co. (1994, 2d Dept) 204 A.D.2d 468, 612 N.Y.S.2d 165

In proceeding under CLS Bus Corp § 1104-a to dissolve closely-held corporation, whose only assets were cash and real property, judicial hearing officer improperly used fair market rental value of real property to determine fair market value pursuant to income capitalization method of valuing real property without consideration that property was subject to below-market-value lease. Cinque v Largo Enters. (1995, 1st Dept) 212 A.D.2d 608, 622 N.Y.S.2d 735

Respondents, who answered petition for judicial dissolution by filing election to purchase petitioners' shares for fair value under CLS Bus Corp § 1118, were improperly granted summary judgment as to issue that petitioners' shares must be valued solely by methodology set forth in parties' agreement (which gave respondents unilateral option to purchase petitioners' shares at price to be established in accordance with contractual formula), since (1) option was to be exercisable only after business had been in operation for 2 years, with active participation by petitioners during that time, and (2) petitioners' assertion that they were effectively barred by respondents participating in business in any meaningful way, if true, would have denied petitioners' receipt of consideration promised in exchange for option, thus precluding respondents' enforcement of option; in sum, before actual effect of option clause on fair value of petitioners' shares could be determined, factual questions had to be resolved as to respondents allegedly oppressive conduct and fraud, insofar as they were relevant to issue of whether respondents breached agreement. In re Dissolution of Funplex Inc. (1995, 3d Dept) 214 A.D.2d 858, 624 N.Y.S.2d 681

Court erred in granting petitioner's motion of dissolve corporation under CLS Bus Corp § 1104-a without holding hearing to determine fair value of petitioner's shares as provided by CLS Bus Corp § 1104-a where respondents were unable to agree with petitioner on fair value of his shares, they timely elected to purchase his shares, and they requested hearing to determine fair value of shares. In re Dissolution of Tosca Brick Oven Bread (1997, 1st Dept) 243 A.D.2d 416, 665 N.Y.S.2d 252

In proceeding to dissolve corporation, court properly determined valuation date of corporation and its shares as day prior to filing of petition. Wolk v Kornberg (In re Vetco, Inc.) (1999, 2d Dept) 260 A.D.2d 642, 687 N.Y.S.2d 270

In a proceeding to determine the fair value of petitioner's shares in a corporation organized by three equal shareholders and capitalized by loans of equal amounts from each shareholder, the court, pursuant to Bus Corp Law § 1118(b) would evaluate said shares by the investment value method, since the net asset method relies heavily on accounting methods which do not provide an accurate measure of a going business and is therefore inappropriate since the corporation had elected to continue as a going business and since the market value method of valuation was also inappropriate, in that petitioner's stock would have no value at all if measured by that method; using the investment value method, the court found that a prudent informed investor would have been willing to pay double the adjusted annual cash flow for the business and, after allocating a portion of that sum to repayment of the outstanding shareholders' loans to the corporation, petitioner would be entitled to one third of the balance; however, the court declined to impose terms and conditions permitting a deferred payment for said shares due to the nature of the oppressive conduct engaged in by the two remaining shareholders in ousting petitioner from the corporation. Taines v Gene Barry One Hour Photo Process, Inc. (1983) 123 Misc. 2d 529, 474 N.Y.S.2d 362

When a petition to judicially dissolve a corporation was filed, a provision in a shareholders' agreement which gave certain shareholders the exclusive right to use a certain trade name upon dissolution did not give those shareholders ownership of the trade name or the exclusive right to the value of the corporation's goodwill associated with that trade name, and the value of that goodwill was a distributable corporate asset. Greenberg v Siskin (In re Leslie & Penny for Penny Preville, Inc.) (2003, A.D., 2d Dept) 757 N.Y.S.2d 302

Co-operative corporation's transfer of 400 shares appurtenant to a garden unit in a building owned by the corporation and a proprietary lease for that apartment were valid, and an owner's interest in the corporation was thus 20 percent for purposes of the corporation's N.Y. Bus. Corp. Law § 1118 election to purchase her interest, because a single director was a "majority" and was therefore able to validly fill a board vacancy pursuant to N.Y. Bus. Corp. Law § 705(a). Matter of McDaniel v 162 Columbia Hgts. Hous. Corp. (2009, Sup) 873 NYS2d 468.

With respect to a closely held corporation owner's application for dissolution pursuant to N.Y. Bus. Corp. Law § 1104-a, the trial court's valuation of the corporation and of the owner's shares therein was supported by the record evidence. Matter of McKeown (2012, 4th Dept) 94 App Div 3d 1445, 942 NYS2d 715.

With respect to a closely held corporation owner's application for dissolution pursuant to N.Y. Bus. Corp. Law § 1104-a, the trial court's award of interest should have accrued from the date of the filing of the petition. Matter of McKeown (2012, 4th Dept) 94 App Div 3d 1445, 942 NYS2d 715.

Business Corporation Law

After a trial court appointed a receiver to segregate the assets of five corporations in accordance with the parties' ownership interests, in lieu of dissolution, the court erred in crediting the majority shareholder's assertion that $ 750,000 in settlement proceeds were used to pay corporate debts and not diverted for personal use because the majority shareholder did not offer any documentation of any corporate debt or attorney's fees paid with the proceeds. Matter of Wenger v L.A. Wenger Contr. Co., Inc. (2014, App Div, 2d Dept) 979 NYS2d 692.

§ 1105. Contents of petition for judicial dissolution

A petition for dissolution shall specify the section or sections of this article under which it is authorized and state the reasons why the corporations should be dissolved. It shall be verified by the petitioner or by one of the petitioners.

History: Formerly § 1106, renumbered L 1962, ch 834, § 82, amd, L 1963, ch 748, § 24, eff Sept 1, 1963.

Former § 1105, add, L 1961, ch 855, repealed, L 1962, ch 834, § 81, eff Sept 1, 1963.

CASE ANNOTATIONS

Under § 104 of former Gen. Corp. L., a "schedule" had to be annexed to the petition listing all creditors and giving a complete inventory of property, and this was considered mandatory, although defects or omissions in the "schedule" were subject to amendment or to cure by evidence introduced at the hearing. Re Majority of Trustees of Santa Eulalia Silver Min. Co. (1889) 115 N.Y. 657, 21 N.E. 1119; Re Greenwald (1936) 248 A.D. 590, 287 N.Y.S. 362; Re Dubois (1857) 15 How Pr 7

Section 104 of former Gen. Corp. L. laid down the general requirements for a petition "and schedules" seeking judicial dissolution of a corporation under Art. 9 of that law. It was construed as applicable whether the dissolution was sought under § 101 or § 103, but not requiring allegations which would warrant dissolution under both such sections. Re McLoughlin (1917) 176 A.D. 653, 163 N.Y.S. 547

Court erred in dismissing petition for judicial dissolution of closely held corporation for failure to state cause of action where petitioner alleged and supported allegations of oppressive behavior of majority stockholders by affidavit showing facts that majority stockholders froze petitioner out from corporation started by his grandfather, where he had been employed for 36 years, and in which he had served in executive positions and owned over 30 percent of stock. Re Rambusch (1988, 1st Dept) 143 A.D.2d 605, 533 N.Y.S.2d 423

It was error for court to convert proceeding under CLS Bus Corp § 1104 to one under CLS Bus Corp § 1104-a over petitioner's objection, and to permit respondent to elect to purchase petitioner's interest in corporation pursuant to CLS Bus Corp § 1118, as it is petitioner who chooses statutory basis for dissolution (CLS Bus Corp § 1105), and buyout option under § 1118 is not available in proceeding brought exclusively under § 1104. Giordano v Stark (1996, 2d Dept) 229 A.D.2d 493, 645 N.Y.S.2d 517

Court properly denied respondent's application to have petition for dissolution under CLS Bus Corp § 1104(a)(3) deemed one brought under CLS Bus Corp § 1104-a and to stay proceeding for valuation hearing under CLS Bus Corp § 118; it is petitioner who chooses statutory authority under which relief is sought. Toscano v Southampton Brick & Tile (1996, 2d Dept) 233 A.D.2d 515, 650 N.Y.S.2d 297

In shareholder's action alleging, inter alia, breach of fiduciary duty and conversion of corporate assets, court erred in ruling that plaintiff's dissolution allegations pleaded CLS Bus Corp § 1104-a cause of action, in directing plaintiff to amend his complaint to comply with CLS Bus Corp §§ 1105 and 1106, and in permitting forced buy of out his shares pursuant to CLS Bus Corp § 1118, where his pleadings never cited § 1104-a as basis for dissolution and he made it clear that he was requesting common-law dissolution only as alternative to primary relief requested in his first 6 causes of action. Fedele v Seybert (1998, 1st Dept) 250 A.D.2d 519, 673 N.Y.S.2d 421

§ 1106. Order to show cause; issuance; publication, service, filing

(a) Upon the presentation of such a petition, the court shall make an order requiring the corporation and all persons interested in the corporation to show cause before it, or before a referee designated in the order, at a time and place therein specified, not less than four weeks after the granting of the order, why the corporation should not be dissolved. In connection therewith, the court may order the corporation, its officers and directors, to furnish the court with a schedule of all information, known or ascertainable with due diligence by them, deemed pertinent by the court, including a statement of the corporate assets and liabilities, and the name and address of each shareholder and of each creditor and claimant, including any with unliquidated or contingent claims and any with whom the corporation has unfulfilled contracts.

(b) A copy of the order to show cause shall be published as prescribed therein, at least once in each of the three weeks before the time appointed for the hearing thereon, in one or more newspapers, specified in the order, of general circulation in the county in which the office of the corporation is located at the date of the order.

(c) A copy of the order to show cause shall be served upon the state tax commission and the corporation and upon each person named in the petition, or in any schedule provided for in paragraph (a), as a shareholder, creditor or claimant, except upon a person whose address is stated to be unknown, and cannot with due diligence be ascertained by the corporation. The service shall be made personally, at least ten days before the time appointed for the hearing, or by mailing a copy of the order, postage prepaid, at least twenty days before the time so appointed, addressed to the person to be served at his last known address.

(d) A copy of the order to show cause and the petition shall be filed, within ten days after the order is entered, with the clerk of the county where the office of the corporation is located at the date of the order. A copy of each schedule furnished to the court under this section shall, within ten days thereafter, be filed with such clerk.

(e) Publication, service and filing provided for in this section shall be effected by the corporation or such other persons as the court may order.

History: Formerly § 1107, renumbered, L 1962, ch 834, § 82, eff Sept 1, 1963; amd, L 1963, ch 748, § 25, eff Sept 1, 1963.

CASE ANNOTATIONS

Section 106 of former Gen. Corp. L. did not require that a copy of the petition and schedule, as well as a copy of the order to show cause, be served on stockholders, creditors, and others in interest; it was sufficient to serve a copy of the show cause order on such persons. Re Christian Jensen Co. (1891) 128 N.Y. 550, 28 N.E. 665

Service of the initial show cause order on creditors, etc., did not require them to take notice of all subsequent steps in the dissolution proceedings, and they should likewise be given notice of such later proceedings as an application for approval of a receiver's accounts. Re Simonds Mfg. Co. (1899) 39 A.D. 576, 57 N.Y.S. 776

Proceedings under Art. 9 of former Gen. Corp. L. for judicial dissolution of a corporation were purely statutory, the various provisions must be complied with in order to give the court authority to proceed, and the court, even then, had only such authority as the statute gave it. Re Seneca Oil Co. (1912) 153 A.D. 594, 138 N.Y.S. 78, affd 208 N.Y. 545, 101 N.E. 1121

A show cause order could properly issue upon a petition by the owner of 50% of outstanding stock showing existence of a condition of hopeless deadlock in management of the corporation's affairs, pursuant to § 103 of former Gen. Corp. L., as, in such case, the show cause order was primarily directed to investigation of the alleged situation. Re Clemente Bros. Inc. (1960, 3d Dept) 12 A.D.2d 694, 207 N.Y.S.2d 821

In a proceeding by one stockholder to dissolve a corporation because of a deadlock in control, the primary issue is whether dissolution will be beneficial to the stockholders and not injurious to the public, and, as between the contesting stockholders, good faith of petitioner is an issue. Re Application of Clemente Bros., Inc. (1963, 3d Dept) 19 A.D.2d 568, 239 N.Y.S.2d 703, affd 13 N.Y.2d 963, 244 N.Y.S.2d 641, 194 N.E.2d 602

The corporation sought to be dissolved is itself a proper party to a proceeding by one of two equal owners of its shares of stock for its dissolution by reason of a stalemate in control, for the limited and passive purpose of rendering it amenable to orders of the court. Re Application of Clemente Bros. (1963, 3d Dept) 19 A.D.2d 568, 239 N.Y.S.2d 703, affd 13 N.Y.2d 963, 244 N.Y.S.2d 641, 194 N.E.2d 602

Although this section authorizes the court upon presentation of a dissolution petition, to issue an order requiring the corporation and all persons interested to show cause before it, or before a referee, why the corporation should not be dissolved, such a show cause order may be made returnable at Special Term, and a reference should not be directed where the issue as to whether the corporation is to be dissolved is not complex. Re Willmark Service System, Inc. (1964, 1st Dept) 21 A.D.2d 478, 251 N.Y.S.2d 267

An action seeking judicial dissolution of defendant corporation was improperly instituted by plaintiffs by service of a summons and complaint, rather than by commencing a proceeding pursuant to Bus Corp Law § 1106 upon presentation of verified petition to the court. Since the trial court failed to direct amendment of the plaintiffs' papers or issue nunc pro tunc the appropriate orders with regard to publication, service, and filing of an order to show cause and verified petition, consideration of the dissolution cause of action was improper. La Sorsa v Algen Press Corp. (1984, 2d Dept) 105 A.D.2d 771, 481 N.Y.S.2d 716

Petitioner could proceed with his application for dissolution under CLS Bus Corp § 1104-a despite fact that court lacked personal jurisdiction over individual who claimed to be shareholder of corporation. In re Finando (1996, 2d Dept) 226 A.D.2d 634, 641 N.Y.S.2d 384

In shareholder's action alleging, inter alia, breach of fiduciary duty and conversion of corporate assets, court erred in ruling that plaintiff's dissolution allegations pleaded CLS Bus Corp § 1104-a cause of action, in directing plaintiff to amend his complaint to comply with CLS Bus Corp §§ 1105 and 1106, and in permitting forced buy of out his shares pursuant to CLS Bus Corp § 1118, where his pleadings never cited § 1104-a as basis for dissolution and he made it clear that he was requesting common-law dissolution only as alternative to primary relief requested in his first 6 causes of action. Fedele v Seybert (1998, 1st Dept) 250 A.D.2d 519, 673 N.Y.S.2d 421

The trial court erred in granting a petition to dissolve a closely-held corporation, because N.Y. Bus. Corp. Law § 1106(b) required, among other things, that a copy of an order to show cause seeking dissolution be published at least once in each of the three weeks before the time appointed for the hearing thereon as prescribed in the order, and that a copy of the order be served upon the New York State Tax Commission, and the petitioner's order to show cause did not provide for publication, was not published, and was not served on the tax commission. In re WTB Props. (2002, 2d Dept) 291 A.D.2d 566, 737 N.Y.S.2d 654

Former § 137 of Gen Corp specifically required service of all motion papers and applications to the court in connection with dissolution proceedings on the attorney general, and this section was deemed applicable to dissolution proceedings under Art. 9, notwithstanding it appeared in a different article of that law. Re Petition of Clemente Bros., Inc. (1959) 32 Misc. 2d 665, 228 N.Y.S.2d 320

The required order to show cause was in the nature of process for bringing interested persons before the court, and it accordingly had to be entered in manner and form and served in strict compliance with the statute. Re Petition of Clemente Bros., Inc. (1959) 32 Misc. 2d 665, 228 N.Y.S.2d 320; Re Pyrolusite Manganese Co. (1883, NY) 29 Hun 429; People v Seneca Lake Grape & Wine Co. (1889) 52 Hun 174, 5 N.Y.S. 136, affd 126 N.Y. 631, 27 N.E. 410

But if a petition for dissolution failed to state required facts and was not approved by the court and brought on for hearing pursuant to order to show cause, it could not be granted. Coucounas v Coucounas (1961, Sup) 222 N.Y.S.2d 592

Where parties to a proceeding seeking dissolution of a corporation under the Gen Corp L entered into a stipulation waiving notice of hearing and setting up a plan for liquidation under management of specified directors, but the plan could not be carried out as agreed, petitioner should be allowed to withdraw consent and permitted to seek a dissolution decree and appointment of a receiver. Re Venice Amusement Corp. (1962, Sup) 235 N.Y.S.2d 54

§ 1107. Amending papers

At any stage, before final order, the court may grant an order amending the petition or any other paper filed in the action or special proceeding, with like effect as though originally filed as amended, or otherwise as the court may direct.

History: Formerly § 1108, renumbered, L 1962, ch 834, § 82, eff Sept 1, 1963.

Former § 1107, add, L 1961, ch 855, renumbered § 1106, L 1962, ch 834, § 82, eff Sept 1, 1963.

CASE ANNOTATIONS

In proceeding for judicial dissolution of a corporation under Art. 9 of former Gen. Corp. L., § 115 of that law authorized amendment of the petition by leave of court up to entry of final order, and it was held that purely formal defects in the order to show cause could be cured by entry of an order nunc pro tunc. Re Christian Jensen Co. (1891) 128 N.Y. 550, 28 N.E. 665; Re Greenwald (1936) 248 A.D. 590, 287 N.Y.S. 362; Re Lenox Corp. (1901) 57 A.D. 515, 68 N.Y.S. 103, affd 167 N.Y. 623, 60 N.E. 1115

In a proceeding to dissolve a corporation, the corporation's majority shareholder was allowed to join the purchaser of the corporation's sole asset because (1) the majority shareholder alleged that the sale was fraudulent, (2) the sale violated a court order, and (3) the majority shareholder's claims against the purchaser arose from the same series of transactions as, and shared a common nucleus of operative fact with, the dissolution proceeding. Matter of Shau Chung Hu v Lowbet Realty Corp. (2012, Sup) 956 NYS2d 400.

§ 1108. Referee

If a referee was not designated in the order to show cause, the court, in its discretion, may appoint a referee when or after the order is returnable. The court may at any time appoint a successor referee.

History: Formerly § 1109, renumbered, L 1962, ch 834, § 82, eff Sept 1, 1963.

Former § 1108, add, L 1961, ch 855, renumbered § 1107, L 1962, ch 834, § 82, eff Sept 1, 1963.

CASE ANNOTATIONS

Making of a compulsory reference, ex parte and without giving interested persons an opportunity to object, may constitute an abuse of discretion. Application of Audio-Scriptions, Inc. (1947) 272 A.D. 50, 69 N.Y.S.2d 27

A referee's determination of facts in this type of proceeding is binding upon the court, and therefore that the court should make the determination itself in the first instance unless the facts are so intricate and complex as to require undue consumption of judicial time. Application of 3260 Perry Ave. Realty Corp. (1954) 285 A.D. 71, 135 N.Y.S.2d 551, resettlement den 285 A.D. 882, 140 N.Y.S.2d 506

Under Art. 9 of former Gen. Corp. L., the court similarly had discretion as to appointing a referee or making a reference to an official referee where it appeared that questions of fact or matters of detail would require protracted investigation and attention. Re Sahara Beach Club, Inc. (1957, 2d Dept) 3 A.D.2d 933, 163 N.Y.S.2d 315

In corporate dissolution matters determination of facts made by referee becomes binding upon Special Term. Therefore in absence of complex issues or necessity for extended hearings better practice is for the court to try issue. Dalminter, Inc. v Siderexport (1965, 1st Dept) 23 A.D.2d 749, 258 N.Y.S.2d 954

§ 1109.　Hearing and decision

At the time and place specified in the order to show cause, or at any other time and place to which the hearing is adjourned, the court or the referee shall hear the allegations and proofs of the parties and determine the facts. The decision of the court or the report of the referee shall be made and filed with the clerk of the court with all convenient speed.

History: Formerly § 1110, renumbered, L 1962, ch 834, § 82, amd, L 1963, ch 748, § 26, eff Sept 1, 1963.

CASE ANNOTATIONS

If the petition fails to show or indicate that dissolution will be beneficial to the shareholders and not injurious to the public, it can be summarily dismissed without any hearing, reference, or the taking of any proof. Re Radom & Neidorff, Inc. (1954) 307 N.Y. 1, 119 N.E.2d 563, motion den 307 N.Y. 701, 120 N.E.2d 865

If the referee appointed or designated to hold the hearing on the petition resigns the court can appoint another in his place and stead, upon notice, and direct the hearing to proceed before the new referee or adjourn it to such time and place as the new referee may designate, if no-one's rights will be impaired thereby. Application of Baumann (1922) 201 A.D. 136, 194 N.Y.S. 243, affd 234 N.Y. 555, 138 N.E. 444

It was considered unnecessary to publish and serve notice of hearing again merely because the court, after hearing and considering objections to referring fact issues involved, overruled the objections and made the reference. Application of Audio-Scriptions, Inc. (1947) 272 A.D. 50, 69 N.Y.S.2d 27

Since the proceeding is deemed a "special proceeding" within the coverage of § 308 of [former] Civil Practice Act, special term has discretion to permit a pre-trial examination in connection with the dissolution petition. Re Sahara Beach Club, Inc. (1957, 2d Dept) 3 A.D.2d 933, 163 N.Y.S.2d 315

In a proceeding for judicial dissolution of a corporation, the defendants have the right to introduce evidence at the hearing in opposition to the proposed corporate dissolution. Re Allchester Development Co. (1970, 2d Dept) 34 A.D.2d 660, 310 N.Y.S.2d 110

In a proceeding by a corporate shareholder pursuant to Bus Corp Law § 1104-a for judicial dissolution of two close corporations, an order denying the corporation's motion to dismiss the petition and granting the petition was erroneous where the issue of oppressive conduct by defendants, as alleged by the petitioner, was determined by Special Term solely on the papers presented by the parties without a hearing on the issue of whether defendants were guilty of such conduct toward the petitioner. Re Rosen (1984, 2d Dept) 102 A.D.2d 855, 476 N.Y.S.2d 625

Its abuse of discretion to fail to order hearing under CLS Business Corporation § 1109 to resolve disputed issues of fact where record conclusively shows disagreement between 50 percent shareholder in corporation and 2 shareholders holding remaining 50 percent. Ricci v First Time Around, Inc. (1985, 4th Dept) 112 A.D.2d 794, 492 N.Y.S.2d 295

Court improperly dissolved judgment debtor corporation and appointed receiver on basis of alleged improper payment to shareholders where only issue framed by parties was whether funds sought to be turned over were in fact corporate property; underlying turnover proceeding did not seek appointment of receiver or corporate dissolution, and no party to proceeding requested such relief. Breiterman v Chemical Bank (1992, 2d Dept) 181 A.D.2d 675, 580 N.Y.S.2d 463

Court erroneously determined that principals of judgment debtor had wrongfully dissipated corporate assets where single incident of alleged impropriety was failure to properly apportion closing expenses of sale of 2 parcels of real property, one owned by judgment debtor and other by its 2 shareholders, and no testimony tended to show that principals had embarked on campaign to systematically loot corporation's assets; court's remedy should have been to direct each of 2 individual shareholders to return principal sum to corporation. Breiterman v Chemical Bank (1992, 2d Dept) 181 A.D.2d 675, 580 N.Y.S.2d 463

In proceeding under CLS Bus Corp § 1104-a for judicial dissolution, it was not error for court to direct referee to complete his valuation of petitioner's stock as soon as possible, rather than by specified date, where petitioner's motion papers requested only that referee be directed to submit his appraisal forthwith. Whalen v Whalen's Moving & Storage Co. (1994, 2d Dept) 204 A.D.2d 468, 612 N.Y.S.2d 165

In proceeding under CLS Bus Corp § 1104-a for judicial dissolution of closely held corporation, it was not improper for court to instruct referee to express value of petitioner's shares in terms of their fair market value and to further instruct referee to discount value of shares in recognition of their lack of marketability. Whalen v Whalen's Moving & Storage Co. (1994, 2d Dept) 204 A.D.2d 468, 612 N.Y.S.2d 165

In proceeding under CLS Bus Corp § 1104-a for judicial dissolution of close corporation, court should not have dismissed petition, without hearing, where parties' affidavits and affirmations created fact issues, inter alia, as to whether petitioner was shareholder in corporation, and whether other shareholder forced petitioner out of business. Singer v Evergreen Decorators (1994, 2d Dept) 205 A.D.2d 694, 613 N.Y.S.2d 667

Court does not have to have personal jurisdiction over all putative stockholders in order to conduct hearing under CLS Bus Corp § 1109. In re Finando (1996, 2d Dept) 226 A.D.2d 634, 641 N.Y.S.2d 384

In proceeding for dissolution of professional corporation engaged in practice of law, where petitioner alleged that majority shareholder had acted against interests of corporation by (among other things) charging gasoline and photocopying expenses of his wife to corporation and providing her with rent-free suite in corporate offices, majority shareholder's wife was properly disqualified from acting as co-counsel because it was likely that petitioner would call her as witness, and her testimony likely would be detrimental to her client. Stober v Gaba & Stober, P.C. (1999, 2d Dept) 259 A.D.2d 554, 686 N.Y.S.2d 440

One who objects to the petition or opposes the application on a particular ground may be estopped to shift to a conflicting ground of opposition at a later stage of the proceedings. Re Wolsky (1955) 11 Misc. 2d 766, 151 N.Y.S.2d 239

On the other hand, where the petition shows disagreement and distrust between holders of equal amounts of outstanding stock, a stalemate in electing directors, and lack of profits, absence of benefit to shareholders or the public from continued corporate functioning is to be implied provided the allegations are true, and a hearing should be set to determine their truth. Re Application of Milton Point Realty Co. (1958) 13 Misc. 2d 277, 178 N.Y.S.2d 151, mod on other grounds (1st Dept) 6 A.D.2d 1033, 178 N.Y.S.2d 1018

The issue involved where the dissolution petition alleged insufficiency of assets to meet liabilities was whether or not the corporation was able to pay its debts in ordinary course of business. Application of Gail Kiddie Clothes, Inc. (1945, Sup) 56 N.Y.S.2d 117

Hearing and determination on a petition for judicial dissolution of a corporation should be prompt and not unduly protracted or delayed. No stay should be granted merely because of the pendency of other litigation which has no bearing upon sufficiency of the dissolution petition. Petition of Acker (1953, Sup) 124 N.Y.S.2d 298, affd 282 A.D. 641, 126 N.Y.S.2d 194

Dissolution under N.Y. Bus. Corp. Law § 1104 was unwarranted because the shareholder failed to set forth a prima facie case that the parties were deadlocked; the shareholder and the administrator each controlled half of the company's stock, and the shareholder did not assert that an election was held or show that a deadlock was harming the parties, but, rather, the parties had agreed on an interim operating arrangement which was never implemented due to the shareholder's unilateral decision to petition for dissolution. The only factual issue in dispute was whether, despite the absence of an official appointment, the shareholder had become an officer of the company, and as this fact was not material to the issue of whether the shareholder, a 50 percent stockholder, engaged in oppressive conduct, and given that he apparently never requested a hearing, the trial court was not required to hold one. Matter of Clever Innovations, Inc. (Dooley) (2012, App Div, 3d Dept) 941 NYS2d 777.

Trial court properly found that an estate established the "special circumstances" required to invoke N.Y. Bus. Corp. Law § 1104-a, and properly ordered that a shareholder buy the estate's shares, because of the shareholder's unwillingness to either negotiate sale of the estate's shares or to include the administrator in company's operation of the company; the shareholder's conduct in operating the company to the exclusion of the administrator substantially defeated the estate's reasonable expectations for cooperation and disclosure of relevant business information. The only factual issue in dispute was whether, despite the absence of an official appointment, the shareholder had become an officer of the company, and as this fact was not material to the issue of whether the shareholder, a 50 percent stockholder, engaged in oppressive conduct, and given that he apparently never requested a hearing, the trial court was not required to hold one. Matter of Clever Innovations, Inc. (Dooley) (2012, App Div, 3d Dept) 941 NYS2d 777.

§ 1110. Application for final order

When the hearing is before a referee, a motion for a final order must be made to the court upon notice to each party to the action or special proceeding who has appeared therein. The notice of motion may be served as prescribed for the service of papers upon an attorney in an action in such court. When the hearing is before the court, a motion for a final order may be made at the hearing or at such time and upon such notice as the court prescribes.

History: Formerly § 1111, renumbered, L 1962, ch 834, § 82, eff Sept 1, 1963.

§ 1111. Judgment or final order of dissolution

(a) In an action or special proceeding under this article if, in the court's discretion, it shall appear that the corporation should be dissolved, it shall make a judgment or final order dissolving the corporation.

(b) In making its decision, the court shall take into consideration the following criteria:

(1) In an action brought by the attorney-general, the interest of the public is of paramount importance.

(2) In a special proceeding brought by directors or shareholders, the benefit to the shareholders of a dissolution is of paramount importance.

(3) In a special proceeding brought under section 1104 (Petition in case of deadlock among directors or shareholders) or section 1104-a (Petition for judicial dissolution under special circumstances) dissolution is not to be denied merely because it is found that the corporate business has been or could be conducted at a profit.

(c) If the judgment or final order shall provide for a dissolution of the corporation, the court may, in its discretion, provide therein for the distribution of the property of the corporation to those entitled thereto according to their respective rights.

(d) The clerk of the court or such other person as the court may direct shall transmit certified copies of the judgment or final order of dissolution to the department of state and to the clerk of the county in which the office of the corporation was located at the

date of the judgment or order. Upon filing by the department of state, the corporation shall be dissolved.

(e) The corporation shall promptly thereafter transmit a certified copy of the judgment or final order to the clerk of each other county in which its certificate of incorporation was filed.

History: Formerly § 1112, renumbered, L 1962, ch 834, § 83, eff Sept 1, 1963; amd, L 1979, ch 217, § 2, eff June 11, 1979.

CASE ANNOTATIONS

1. In general
2. Discretion of court, generally
3. Public interest
4. – Deadlock; interest of holders
5. – Effect of corporate solvency
6. Receivership; asset distribution
7. Procedural matters
8. Miscellaneous

1. In general
Substance of provisions of former General Corporation Law § 117 has been incorporated in above statute. Application of Sheridan Constr. Corp. (1965, 4th Dept) 22 A.D.2d 390, 256 N.Y.S.2d 210, affd 16 N.Y.2d 680, 261 N.Y.S.2d 300, 209 N.E.2d 290

2. Discretion of court, generally
Decree ruling that a shareholder was individually liable for a proportionate share of an estate's interest in a closely-held corporation in the sum of $189,112 was proper because, as the surrogate's order properly granted summary judgment on the issue of liability upon the establishment of grounds for the dissolution of the corporation pursuant to N.Y. Bus. Corp. Law § 1104-a(a)(2), the trial court was authorized, in its discretion, to provide for the distribution of the decedent's interest in the corporation to the estate pursuant to N.Y. Bus. Corp. Law § 1111(c); the trial court providently exercised its discretion in fashioning a remedy, and there was no reason to disturb it. Matter of Verdeschi (2009, 2d Dept) 63 App Div 3d 1084, 882 NYS2d 440.

Decisions dealing with judicial dissolutions under Art. 9 of former Gen. Corp. L. usually stated that whether or not a petition for such dissolution should be granted rested in the discretion of the court to whom the petition was addressed, at least where the petition was not based upon and supported by a showing of insolvency, such discretion to be exercised in the light of whether or not shareholders would benefit by dissolution and whether or not it would be in the public interest or detrimental to public interest and welfare. Re Application of Admiral Rubber Corp. (1958) 12 Misc. 2d 355, 172 N.Y.S.2d 952

3. Public interest
Dissolution could not be considered injurious to the public where the number of persons employed by the corporation was steadily decreasing due to disagreements over policy and management. Application of Pivot Punch & Die Corp. (1959) 15 Misc. 2d 713, 182 N.Y.S.2d 459, mod on other grounds (4th Dept) 9 A.D.2d 861, 193 N.Y.S.2d 34

4. – Deadlock; interest of holders
The rights and interests of all shareholders, minority as well as majority, were to be weighed in determining whether dissolution would be beneficial or harmful to shareholders. Re Rateau Sales Co. (1911) 201 N.Y. 420, 94 N.E. 869

Mere existence of disputes between shareholders was not sufficient to warrant a dissolution decree, if the corporate objectives, assets, functions, and creditors were not in jeopardy. Application of Cantelmo (1949) 275 A.D. 231, 88 N.Y.S.2d 604; Re Application of Admiral Rubber Corp. (1958) 12 Misc. 2d 355, 172 N.Y.S.2d 952

But a petition for dissolution based on deadlock was held to have been improperly dismissed on the merits where it was presented by the owner of one-half of the total stock, disclosed disagreement with respondents over management, their failure to attend stockholders' meetings, and their refusal to permit inspection of the corporate books or to account for its income, as it could not be determined, from the pleadings alone, that dissolution would not be for the best interests of the shareholders. Application of Numode Realty Co. (1951) 278 A.D. 979, 105 N.Y.S.2d 588

Where a clear-cut deadlock appeared between shareholders owning or controlling equal blocks of stock, according to the allegations of the petition, the court should investigate the situation and take evidence to ascertain the truth of the allegations and whether the positions of the parties in interest were irreconcilable and the deadlock unbreakable and likely to continue. If the court so found, it was usually considered in the best interest of the shareholders to decree dissolution. Application of A. B. C. Wholesale Florists, Inc. (1952) 280 A.D. 785, 113 N.Y.S.2d 397; Re Bob's Fashion Furriers, Inc. (1944, Sup) 52 N.Y.S.2d 279

The fact alone that those in control of the corporation were allegedly operating it for their own benefit would not require granting of a dissolution order at the instance of a minority shareholder, at least in the absence of substantiating evidence. Gross v Price (1954) 284 A.D. 964, 134 N.Y.S.2d 649

Where a point is reached when the stockholders who are actively conducting the business of the corporation cannot agree, it becomes in the best interest of those shareholders to order a dissolution. Application of Weiss (1969, 1st Dept) 32 A.D.2d 279, 301 N.Y.S.2d 839

Corporation ordered dissolved under evidence that it completed its last house in 1966 and conveyed it to the purchaser also in 1966; that the directors and majority stockholders had been wasting the assets of the corporation for their own benefit and at the expense of the minority stockholders; and that there were few remaining assets. Marcone v Mott (1970, 2d Dept) 33 A.D.2d 919, 307 N.Y.S.2d 518, app dismd 26 N.Y.2d 1016, 311 N.Y.S.2d 914, 260 N.E.2d 545

Good faith of a petitioner for dissolution by reason of an alleged deadlock is a point in issue, as a court of equity will not permit use of the statute merely for petitioner's personal gain; but if it appears that the petition is obviously presented in good faith, motives of those in interest neither require nor proscribe judgment of dissolution. Mares v Foster (1962) 35 Misc. 2d 852, 231 N.Y.S.2d 707, affd 19 A.D.2d 695, 242 N.Y.S.2d 606

In special proceeding for judicial dissolution of corporation pursuant to CLS Bus Corp § 1104, order directing dissolution of corporation by private sale of one 50 percent shareholder's interest in corporate assets to other 50 percent shareholder without prior calculation of corporation's tax liability was improper, even though court's purpose was to preserve structure, functioning, and profitability of corporation, since "benefit to the shareholders" as contemplated by CLS Bus Corp § 1111 would not be maximized by judicial fiat forcing one shareholder to buy out other's interest encumbered by unascertained tax debt. Sternberg v Osman (1992, 2d Dept) 181 A.D.2d 899, 582 N.Y.S.2d 208, app den 80 N.Y.2d 891, 587 N.Y.S.2d 902, 600 N.E.2d 629

5. – Effect of corporate solvency

Where profits and the ratio of assets to liabilities had been steadily going downward for a considerable period of time, nearing a point where there would soon be nothing left for distribution to shareholders, a dissolution decree was usually warranted. Jameson v Hartford Fire Ins. Co. (1897) 14 A.D. 380, 44 N.Y.S. 15

In some instances it was deemed not in the best interests of shareholders to decree dissolution because, notwithstanding grave disagreement among them, management of the corporation was still operating efficiently and at a profit, or its operations did not appear to be paralyzed. Application of Radom (1953) 282 A.D. 854, 124 N.Y.S.2d 424, affd 307 N.Y. 1, 119 N.E.2d 563, motion den 307 N.Y. 701, 120 N.E.2d 865; Application of George W. Anderson, Inc. (1951, Sup) 104 N.Y.S.2d 184, affd 279 A.D. 594, 107 N.Y.S.2d 556

A petition for voluntary dissolution by a corporation was denied in the exercise of discretion where the business was solvent, was being conducted in the interest of consenting creditors and the stockholders and the corporation failed to comply with the provisions of § 104 of former Gen. Corp. L. Application of Hickory House, Inc. (1958) 13 Misc. 2d 761, 177 N.Y.S.2d 356

The fact that a corporation is operating profitably is no bar to a minority shareholder's action in equity to require its dissolution upon allegations that the directors and controllng interests are keeping it alive merely for purposes of looting its assets and selfish gain at expense of the minority. Leibert v Clapp (1963) 13 N.Y.S.2d 313, 247 N.Y.S.2d 102, 196 N.E.2d 540

6. Receivership; asset distribution

Where it is determined that a corporation should be dissolved an order charging the receiver with the duty of formulating a plan of dissolution and distribution of assets which plan shall be subject to the final approval of the court is a proper application of Business Corporation Law § 1111(c). While the statute does not specifically so provide, the application for approval should be on notice to all parties with a suitable opportunity to be heard. Application of Weiss (1969, 1st Dept) 32 A.D.2d 279, 301 N.Y.S.2d 839

Finality of dissolution of corporation was not contingent upon appointed receiver's qualifying to carry out his duties, and failure of designated receiver to file required bond was not determinative of corporate status; corporation was effectively dissolved by order. Maki v Estate of Ziehm (1977, 3d Dept) 55 A.D.2d 454, 391 N.Y.S.2d 705

7. Procedural matters

Procedure for judicial dissolution of a corporation under Art 9 of former Gen. Corp. L., in case a reference was made for hearing on the petition, left the referee's findings of fact binding upon the court, including his finding as to whether or not dissolution would benefit the shareholders. If the referee found that the shareholders would not benefit, his finding could be reviewed and reversed only upon appeal to the Appellate Division. Re Seamerlin Operating Co. (1954) 307 N.Y. 407, 121 N.E.2d 392

Upon appeal in proceedings for dissolution of a corporation under § 103 of former Gen. Corp. L., based on deadlock in control and management, the decision could be remanded to Special Term for reconsideration where it appeared from statements of counsel that the parties in interest had agreed on sale of the corporation as a going business, to be operated under judicial supervision. Application for Dissolution of Venice Amusement Corp. (1961, 1st Dept) 14 A.D.2d 742, 220 N.Y.S.2d 47

Where a stockholder sought dissolution of the corporation under § 103 of former Gen Corp L, because of a deadlock in control, the corporation was a proper party to the proceedings but without standing to raise an issue or be heard on whether dissolution would be beneficial to its shareholders or injurious to the public. Re Application of Clemente Bros., Inc. (1963, 3d Dept) 19 A.D.2d 568, 239 N.Y.S.2d 703, affd 13 N.Y.2d 963, 244 N.Y.S.2d 641, 194 N.E.2d 602

The burden was deemed to be upon the petitioner or petitioners for dissolution to establish that dissolution would not be injurious, but beneficial, to the shareholders and not injurious to the public. Application for Topper's Hamburger of Distinction, Inc. (1961) 28 Misc. 2d 626, 213 N.Y.S.2d 117; Application for Dissolution of Homer Fabrics, Inc. (1955, Sup) 137 N.Y.S.2d 701; Re Norton & Schneider, Inc. (1954, Sup) 137 N.Y.S.2d 269

8. Miscellaneous

If there was an agreement among shareholders under which one opposing dissolution was entitled to buy out those seeking dissolution at book value of their shares, as determined by their own accountant, and the oppositor was ready to buy on those terms, a judgment of dissolution could be denied in favor of leaving the dispute to settlement under the agreement. Application for Topper's Hamburger of Distinction, Inc. (1961) 28 Misc. 2d 626, 213 N.Y.S.2d 117

Trial court properly found that an estate established the "special circumstances" required to invoke N.Y. Bus. Corp. Law § 1104-a, and properly ordered that a shareholder buy the estate's shares, because of the shareholder's unwillingness to either negotiate sale of the estate's shares or to include the administrator in company's operation; the shareholder's conduct in operating the company to the exclusion of the administrator substantially defeated the estate's reasonable expectations for cooperation and disclosure of relevant business information. The only factual issue in dispute was whether, despite the absence of an official appointment, the shareholder had become an officer of the company, and as this fact was not material to the issue of whether the shareholder, a 50 percent stockholder, engaged in oppressive conduct, and given that he apparently never requested a hearing, the trial court was not required to hold one. Matter of Clever Innovations, Inc. (Dooley) (2012, App Div, 3d Dept) 941 NYS2d 777.

§ 1112. Venue

An action or special proceeding under this article shall be brought in the supreme court in the judicial district in which the office of the corporation is located at the time of the service on the corporation of a summons in such action or of the presentation to the court of the petition in such special proceeding.

History: Formerly § 1113, renumbered, L 1962, ch 834, § 84, eff Sept 1, 1963.

CASE ANNOTATIONS

While this section provides that an action or a special proceeding for dissolution of a corporation shall be brought in the Supreme Court and judicial district in which the office of the corporation is located, failure to comply with this requirement is not a jurisdictional defect and involves only a question of venue which is waived if objection thereto is not timely raised by the parties. Application of Elishewitz Hat Co. (1964) 42 Misc. 2d 51, 247 N.Y.S.2d 806

§ 1113. Preservation of assets; appointment of receiver

At any stage of an action or special proceeding under this article, the court may, in its discretion, make all such orders as it may deem proper in connection with preserving the property and carrying on the business of the corporation, including the appointment and removal of a receiver under article 12 (Receivership), who may be a director, officer or shareholder of the corporation.

History: Formerly 1114, renumbered, L 1962, ch 834, § 84, eff Sept 1, 1963.

CASE ANNOTATIONS

A temporary receiver, where appointed, may be authorized to finish and complete outstanding contracts of the corporation; but such a receiver should not be authorized to sell property except for cogent reasons. Re Malcom Brewing Co. (1903) 78 A.D. 592, 79 N.Y.S. 1057; Nason Mfg. Co. v Garden (1900) 52 A.D. 363, 65 N.Y.S. 147

It was flatly stated in some decisions, in fact, that a temporary receiver could not, or would not, be appointed for a corporation unless it was insolvent. Re Greenwald (1936) 248 A.D. 590, 287 N.Y.S. 362; Garibaldi v Yonkers (1949) 198 Misc 1100, 102 N.Y.S.2d 200, affd 278 A.D. 571, 102 N.Y.S.2d 426; Re Kaufman Circle Express Co. (1941) 177 Misc 106, 29 N.Y.S.2d 264

Under the provisions of former Gen. Corp. L. dealing with judicial dissolution of corporations, it was held that there was no necessity for the appointment of a receiver where there was no showing of insolvency and rights of outside creditors were not involved. Application for Dissolution of Whitehall Art Co. (1958, 1st Dept) 6 A.D.2d 399, 178 N.Y.S.2d 338; Re Hy-Lite Plastics, Inc. (1957) 8 Misc. 2d 101, 165 N.Y.S.2d 888

Petitioner, owner of 50% of stock of corporation, did not establish absolute right to dissolution where hostility had developed between him and owner of other 50%. However, parties are entitled to a hearing. Issue should be decided by a court and not by a referee. And there was no necessity for the appointment of a temporary receiver where there was no showing of insolvency and no outside creditors were involved. Application for Dissolution of Whitehall Art Co. (1958, 1st Dept) 6 A.D.2d 399, 178 N.Y.S.2d 338

Substance of former General Corporation Law § 118 has been incorporated in provisions of above statute. Application of Sheridan Constr. Corp. (1965, 4th Dept) 22 A.D.2d 390, 256 N.Y.S.2d 210, affd 16 N.Y.2d 680, 261 N.Y.S.2d 300, 209 N.E.2d 290

On petition to appoint receiver under CLS Bus Corp § 1113 in connection with dissolution of close corporation, shareholder should be permitted to have corporation's books and records examined by accountant. Re Imperatore (1987, 2d Dept) 128 A.D.2d 707, 512 N.Y.S.2d 904

Supreme Court was authorized, under CLS N.Y. Const Art VI § 7 and CLS Jud § 140-b, to order parties to execute credit facility documents in furtherance of preservation of assets pending proceedings for judicial dissolution of their partnership and closely held corporations. Re Schwartzreich (1988, 2d Dept) 136 A.D.2d 642, 523 N.Y.S.2d 880

In proceedings for judicial dissolution of parties' 3 closely held corporations and one partnership, in which petitioners had obtained preliminary injunction requiring those in control of businesses to take "all steps reasonably necessary to protect and preserve" assets of businesses, Supreme Court should have granted respondents' motion for order under CLS Bus Corp § 1113 compelling petitioners to execute documents necessary to secure line of credit where (1) prior line of credit had been revoked after one petitioner informed bank of pendency of dissolution proceedings, and (2) court-appointed referee stated that profitability of primary corporation was negatively affected by absence of line of credit and that establishment of line of credit was reasonably necessary to preserve corporate assets. Re Schwartzreich (1988, 2d Dept) 136 A.D.2d 642, 523 N.Y.S.2d 880

In corporate dissolution proceeding, order granting petitioners' motion for appointment of receiver would be modified to extent of deleting receiver's appointment on condition that respondent post undertaking in amount of $250,000, given that respondent had made election to purchase petitioners' shares. Re Androtsakis (1988, 1st Dept) 139 A.D.2d 471, 527 N.Y.S.2d 407, app dismd without op 72 N.Y.2d 914, 532 N.Y.S.2d 848, 529 N.E.2d 178, later app (1st Dept) 159 A.D.2d 442, 553 N.Y.S.2d 125

In hybrid proceedings and actions seeking judicial dissolution of corporations pursuant to CLS Bus Corp Art 11 and seeking to preserve assets of corporations pursuant to CLS Bus Corp §§ 626 and 1202(a)(3), Supreme Court erred in appointing permanent receiver and ordering defendant to make accounting to each corporation since litigation was at early stage; papers submitted by plaintiff-petitioner were sufficient only to support appointment of temporary receiver to preserve assets and carry out business of each corporation. Imbriale v Imbriale (1988, 2d Dept) 144 A.D.2d 557, 534 N.Y.S.2d 418

In dissolution proceeding, court properly determined amount by which court-appointed receiver was overpaid, but judgment reflecting that amount should have been entered in favor of corporation only, rather than jointly in favor of corporation and its sole shareholder. Re Kane (1989, 2d Dept) 151 A.D.2d 672, 543 N.Y.S.2d 934, app gr 74 N.Y.2d 613, 547 N.Y.S.2d 847, 547 N.E.2d 102 and affd 75 N.Y.2d 511, 554 N.Y.S.2d 457, 553 N.E.2d 1005

Supreme Court had authority to direct receiver of corporation in dissolution to suspend payment of 2 principles' $4,100 per week salaries after court-appointed accountant alerted court that corporation was being assessed for up to $1,900,000 in unpaid taxes, since order was in furtherance of preservation of corporation's assets, and court had jurisdiction over principals and corporation. Osman v Sternberg (1992, 2d Dept) 181 A.D.2d 868, 582 N.Y.S.2d 444

Court abused its discretion when it sua sponte appointed temporary receiver of corporation's property where there was no evidence that such appointment was necessary to preserve corporation's assets, operate business, or protect parties' interests. Hessert v Brooklyn Home Dialysis Training Ctr. (1996, 2d Dept) 231 A.D.2d 719, 647 N.Y.S.2d 1000

It having already been decided that summary expulsion of petitioner as officer and director of corporation was act of oppression entitling petitioner to relief, IAS Court acted within broad supervisory and injunctive powers conferred under CLS Bus Corp §§ 1008(a)(3), 1113, and 1115(a)(1) when it directed corporation to pay petitioner same compensation and benefits as those paid to other shareholders, retroactive to date of his summary firing and exclusion from corporate premises. In re Dissolution of HGK Asset Mgmt. (1997, 1st Dept) 238 A.D.2d 291, 656 N.Y.S.2d 264

Granting of retroactive compensation and benefits to corporate officer and director who was victim of oppressive summary expulsion from corporation did not require showing of irreparable injury. In re Dissolution of HGK Asset Mgmt. (1997, 1st Dept) 238 A.D.2d 291, 656 N.Y.S.2d 264

Fifty percent shareholder was properly denied appointment as receiver of corporation in proceeding for judicial dissolution where he had been convicted in federal court of altering certified check, and his father, who had also participated in corporation's management, had negotiated invalid $100,000 check. In re Broder (1999, 1st Dept) 265 A.D.2d 218, 696 N.Y.S.2d 459

Extreme hostility between 50 percent owners of corporation militated against nomination of one owner as receiver in proceeding for judicial dissolution, and such appointment would be remanded for appointment of neutral receiver. In re Broder (1999, 1st Dept) 265 A.D.2d 218, 696 N.Y.S.2d 459

The mere filing of a petition for judicial dissolution under Art. 9 of former Gen. Corp. L., and appointment of a temporary receiver for the corporation, did not strip its officers and managing agents of all powers, and they could still be served with process as representatives of the corporation. Garibaldi v Yonkers (1949) 198 Misc 1100, 102 N.Y.S.2d 200, affd 278 A.D. 571, 102 N.Y.S.2d 426

In judicial dissolution proceeding arising from alleged shareholder deadlock, wherein respondents' answer and cross motion pleaded

Business Corporation Law

grounds typically falling under CLS Bus Corp § 1104-a and they requested injunction and bond based on petitioner's alleged corporate looting and misconduct, court ordered petitioner to post undertaking to preserve corporation's assets pending dissolution. In re Judicial Dissolution of 212 E. 52nd St. Corp. (2000, Sup) 185 Misc. 2d 95, 712 N.Y.S.2d 777

Impropriety of appointing a temporary receiver, in the absence of insolvency, was asserted in some instances notwithstanding the dissolution petition was based on a deadlock in control or management of the corporation. Re Hy-Lite Plastics, Inc. (1957) 8 Misc. 2d 101, 165 N.Y.S.2d 888

Upon ordering dissolution of a closed corporation pursuant to § 1104(2)(3) attorneys for respective parties would be appointed receivers and the question of the amount of their bond, the question as to how long the business was to continue, the question as to what employees were to be engaged, including employees who were officers of the corporation, and other questions having to do with the preservation of the property in carrying on of the business of the corporation, would be matters for the determination of the receivers who would act under the aegis of the court and on their responsibility as specially appointed representatives of the court, and they would also be charged with the responsibility of presenting to the court, in due course, a plan for orderly dissolution and for the disposition of the property of the corporation including its name and goodwill. Application of Surchin (1967) 55 Misc. 2d 888, 286 N.Y.S.2d 580

Where state brought action to dissolve corporation which accepted fees under false pretenses that it could use its influence to help an applicant gain admission to a professional school, had refused to make promised refunds, and its checks had been returned as insufficient funds, a temporary receiver was appointed to preserve the assets of the corporation pendente lite. State v Remedial Education, Inc. (1972) 70 Misc. 2d 1068, 335 N.Y.S.2d 353

In action to dissolve corporations, state held not entitled to the appointment of a receiver, where court held that granting of a preliminary injunction restraining transfer of property was sufficient. State v Cortelle Corp. (1972) 73 Misc. 2d 352, 341 N.Y.S.2d 640, affd 43 A.D.2d 668, 349 N.Y.S.2d 653, mod on other grounds 38 N.Y.2d 83, 378 N.Y.S.2d 654, 341 N.E.2d 223

After appointing a receiver, the court may insist upon his continuance in possession as long as problems remain as to who is entitled to distribution of assets. Re Application of St. Luke Stockholders, Inc. (1954, Sup) 133 N.Y.S.2d 457

A temporary receiver has been appointed in some instances where dissolution was sought on the ground of deadlock, however, where it appeared that the situation was such that no one, under the circumstances, could act with authority as representative of the corporation in handling funds, preserving assets, paying obligations, and the like, without reference to whether the corporation was actually insolvent. Application of Ansol Holding Corp. (1954, Sup) 137 N.Y.S.2d 184

Where petitioner attorney, in a proceeding pursuant to N.Y. Bus. Corp. Law art. 11 to dissolve a professional corporation that was formed by the attorney and respondent partner, alleged that the partner, who was also a lawyer, had failed to adequately safeguard a corporate asset, i.e., an attorney's charging lien on certain settlement proceeds, and moved for an order directing the partner to post to an undertaking in the amount of $17,500, which was to be paid to the attorney if the partner either failed to perfect an appeal from the dismissal of the corporation's action to collect on the lien or perfected an appeal but lost, the trial court properly denied the motion to direct the attorney to post the undertaking, as an appeal from the order dismissing the action to recover on the charging lien was rendered academic by the partner's settlement of the lien claim with the relevant insurance company for $7,500, and the attorney failed to provide sufficient evidence from which the trial court could have concluded that the settlement did not represent fair compensation to the dissolved firm. Juron v Minzner (In re Juron & Minzner, P.C.) (2003, A.D., 2d Dept) 756 N.Y.S.2d 439

§ 1114. Certain sales, transfers, security interests and judgments void

A sale, mortgage, conveyance or other transfer of, or the creation of a security interest in, any property of a corporation made, without prior approval of the court, after service upon the corporation of a summons in an action, or of an order to show cause in a special proceeding, under this article in payment of or as security for an existing or prior debt or for any other or for no consideration, or a judgment thereafter rendered against the corporation by confession or upon the acceptance of any offer, shall be void as against such persons and to such extent, if any, as the court shall determine.

History: Formerly § 1115, renumbered, L 1962, ch 834, § 84, amd, L 1962, ch 552, L 1963, ch 748, § 27, eff Sept 1, 1963.

CASE ANNOTATIONS

1. Applicability
2. Particular determinations

1. Applicability

In a proceeding for the judicial dissolution of a close corporation brought by one of the two 50 percent shareholders, the court supervising the dissolution proceedings could hear a motion under Bus Corp Law § 1114 for an order setting aside a consent judgment of eviction rendered against the corporation where such judgment had been entered after the dissolution proceeding was already pending, where an earlier civil court denial of the motion did not bar the relief sought in that the motion was denied with express leave to move in the court supervising the dissolution for the same relief, and where, although the corporation's leased premises had been demolished, the parties' rights could still be quantified and compensated as the leasehold had some value. Re Schramm (1980) 107 Misc. 2d 393, 434 N.Y.S.2d 333

Record supported the referee's conclusion that defendant violated the statute by conveying parcels to himself after service of the petition that commenced the proceeding to dissolve the corporation; although he claimed that a 1997 dissolution agreement authorized his actions, the court had previously determined that his claim for specific performance of that agreement was time-barred. Sutton v Burdick, 135 A.D.3d 1016, 22 N.Y.S.3d 633 (3d Dep't 2016).

Prohibition imposed by CLS Bus Corp § 1114 on transfers of corporate property would not preclude payment of sales tax. N.Y. Tax Appeals Tribunal TSB-D-93(45)S

In a proceeding to dissolve a corporation, the corporation's majority shareholder was allowed to join the purchaser of the corporation's sole asset because (1) the majority shareholder alleged that the sale was fraudulent, (2) the sale violated a court order, and (3) the majority shareholder"s claims against the purchaser arose from the same series of transactions as, and shared a common nucleus of operative fact with, the dissolution proceeding. Matter of Shau Chung Hu v Lowbet Realty Corp. (2012, Sup) 956 NYS2d 400.

2. Particular determinations

In an action seeking rescission of a sale of real property predicated on fraud and pursuant to this section, allegations that the signature and authority to convey were acquired by fraudulent means, but not that the signature was forged, would not make the deed void ab initio, but only voidable. The buyer reasonably relied on the apparent authority of the signer, whose control over the seller's business indicated authority to enter into a real estate transaction on its behalf. Matter of Shau Chung Hu v Lowbet Realty Corp., 2018 N.Y. App. Div. LEXIS 3489 (N.Y. App. Div. 2d Dep't 2018).

§ 1115. Injunction

(a) At any stage of an action or special proceeding under this article, the court may, in its discretion, grant an injunction, effective during the pendency of the action or special proceeding or such shorter period as it may specify in the injunction, for one or more of the following purposes:

(1) Restraining the corporation and its directors and officers from transacting any unauthorized business and from exercising any corporate powers, except by permission of the court.

(2) Restraining the corporation and its directors and officers from collecting or receiving any debt or

other property of the corporation, and from paying out or otherwise transferring or delivering any property of the corporation, except by permission of the court.

(3) Restraining the creditors of the corporation from beginning any action against the corporation, or from taking any proceedings in an action theretofore commenced, except by permission of the court. Such injunction shall have the same effect and be subject to the same provisions of law as if each creditor upon whom it is served was named therein.

(b) [Repealed]

History: Formerly § 1116, renumbered, L 1962, ch 834, § 84, eff Sept 1, 1963; amd, L 1962, ch 317, § 7, eff Sept 1, 1963.

CASE ANNOTATIONS

Minority shareholder's petition for an injunction and a bond or other suitable security were denied because the majority shareholders elected to purchase his shares for their fair value and the bond request was made for the first time in reply and was unsupported by proof persuasively demonstrating a need for such relief. O'Connor v Coccadotts, Inc., 3 N.Y.S.3d 567, 2015 N.Y. Misc. LEXIS 87 (N.Y. Sup. Ct. 2015).

Issuance of an injunction pursuant to § 73 of former Gen. Corp. L. did not work a dissolution of the corporation. Kincaid v Dwinelle (1875) 59 N.Y. 548

Section 135 of former Gen. Corp. L., dealing with injunctions suspending general and ordinary business of a corporation or suspending the powers of an officer or director, conditioned the issuance of such injunctions upon giving notice of the application to management or to the officers whose powers would be affected. Goss v Warp Twisting-in Mach. Co. (1909) 133 A.D. 122, 117 N.Y.S. 228; Ciancimino v Man (1892) 1 Misc 121, 20 N.Y.S. 702; Wilkie v Rochester & S. L. R. Co. (1877, NY) 12 Hun 242; Ft. Edward v Hudson V. R. Co. (1908) 127 A.D. 438, 111 N.Y.S. 753

Section 111 of former Gen. Corp. L. authorized enjoining of actions by creditors only where a receiver was legally appointed, and since it sanctioned only injunctions against actions for the recovery of "a sum of money," it was not considered as authorizing injunctions against lien foreclosures or enforcement of rights against pledged property. Re Greenwald (1936) 248 A.D. 590, 287 N.Y.S. 362; Re French (1918) 181 A.D. 719, 168 N.Y.S. 988, affd 224 N.Y. 555, 120 N.E. 863

It having already been decided that summary expulsion of petitioner as officer and director of corporation was act of oppression entitling petitioner to relief, IAS Court acted within broad supervisory and injunctive powers conferred under CLS Bus Corp §§ 1008(a)(3), 1113, and 1115(a)(1) when it directed corporation to pay petitioner same compensation and benefits as those paid to other shareholders, retroactive to date of his summary firing and exclusion from corporate premises. In re Dissolution of HGK Asset Mgmt. (1997, 1st Dept) 238 A.D.2d 291, 656 N.Y.S.2d 264

Granting of retroactive compensation and benefits to corporate officer and director who was victim of oppressive summary expulsion from corporation did not require showing of irreparable injury. In re Dissolution of HGK Asset Mgmt. (1997, 1st Dept) 238 A.D.2d 291, 656 N.Y.S.2d 264

Court properly enjoined two-thirds majority shareholder in closely-held corporation from using corporate funds to pay counsel fees incurred in defending dissolution proceeding. In re Park Inn Ford, Inc. (1998, 2d Dept) 249 A.D.2d 307, 671 N.Y.S.2d 288

In judicial dissolution proceeding arising from alleged shareholder deadlock, wherein respondents' answer and cross motion pleaded grounds typically falling under CLS Bus Corp § 1104-a and they requested injunction and bond based on petitioner's alleged corporate looting and misconduct, court ordered petitioner to post undertaking to preserve corporation's assets pending dissolution. In re Judicial Dissolution of 212 E. 52nd St. Corp. (2000, Sup) 185 Misc. 2d 95, 712 N.Y.S.2d 777

However, § 135 of former Gen. Corp. L. was so phrased that it was construed as not requiring preliminary notice and as permitting an ex parte injunction restraining exercise of certain powers by a director, if such restraint would not result in suspending general and ordinary business of the corporation. Furthermore, a court could restrain, ex parte or otherwise, specific corporate acts in order to preserve status quo, if general and ordinary business capacity would not thereby be suspended. United Democratic Regular Organization of Sixteenth Assembly Dist., Inc. v Lewis (1959) 21 Misc. 2d 822, 194 N.Y.S.2d 225; People v Borg-Johnson (1958) 11 Misc. 2d 928, 176 N.Y.S.2d 167

State was entitled to preliminary injunction restraining defendant corporations from transferring property upon allegations that such corporations had conspired to loan money to individuals whose homes were being foreclosed provided that such individuals signed over the deed to their property as collateral for loans, representing that such individuals would be able to repurchase their homes at a subsequent date, which representations were known to be false. State v Cortelle Corp. (1972) 73 Misc. 2d 352, 341 N.Y.S.2d 640, affd 43 A.D.2d 668, 349 N.Y.S.2d 653, mod on other grounds 38 N.Y.2d 83, 378 N.Y.S.2d 654, 341 N.E.2d 223

Supreme Court lacked jurisdiction to grant preliminary injunction under CLS Bus Corp § 1115 in conjunction with CLS Bus Corp § 1104 dissolution proceeding of Delaware corporation with principal place of business in New York, as New York court may not dissolve corporation domiciled elsewhere even with parties' consent and, if court may not adjudicate dissolution proceeding, logically it may not grant § 1115 relief. In re Dissolution of Chris Kole Enters. (2001, Sup) 188 Misc. 2d 207, 725 N.Y.S.2d 838

Notice was nonetheless required by § 135 of former Gen. Corp. L. because the business sought to be enjoined was unlawful. New York v Starin (1888) 56 N.Y. Super Ct 153, 2 N.Y.S. 346

N.Y. Bus. Corp. Law § 1115 authorizes an injunction at any stage of an action or proceeding pursuant to N.Y. Bus. Corp. Law art. 11 effective during the pendency of the action or special proceeding or such shorter period as it may specify in the injunction, but N.Y. Bus. Corp. § 1115 does not refer to either an undertaking or N.Y. C.P.L.R. art. 63. Rust v Turgeon (2002, A.D., 4th Dept) 746 N.Y.S.2d 223

§ 1116. Discontinuance of action or special proceeding

An action or special proceeding for the dissolution of a corporation may be discontinued at any stage when it is established that the cause for dissolution did not exist or no longer exists. In such event, the court shall dismiss the action or special proceeding and direct any receiver to redeliver to the corporation all its remaining property.

History: Formerly § 1117, renumbered, L 1962, ch 834, § 84, eff Sept 1, 1963.

CASE ANNOTATIONS

Nor could such a petition be dismissed summarily and without passing on its merits, where the petition made out a sufficient showing of deadlock and inability of those in control to agree on policies and management, without a showing that dissolution would be for the best interest of shareholders. Application of Numode Realty Co. (1951) 278 A.D. 979, 105 N.Y.S.2d 588

It was abuse of discretion to allow shareholder to discontinue dissolution proceedings against corporations, thereby depriving them of statutory buy-out remedy of CLS Bus Corp § 1118, for despite shareholder's assertion that he had become convinced that grounds for dissolution alleged in his petition-that other corporate directors had attempted to wrongfully freeze him out as director and shareholder-no longer existed, it was reasonably clear that his desire to discontinue was response to corporations' exercise of buy-out remedy, given that shareholder had commenced dissolution proceeding only after he had failed to obtain negotiated buy-out and sought leave to discontinue when corporations elected to purchase his shares; moreover, in light of shareholder's veto power, it was not inconceivable that he would seek to deadlock corporations, which could be avoided by allowing corporations to purchase his stock. Re Musilli (1987, 2d Dept) 134 A.D.2d 15, 523 N.Y.S.2d 120, later op (NY A.D. 2nd Dept) LEXIS slip op

"Discontinuance" of proceedings for judicial dissolution under this section of the Bus. Corp. L. seems to be a matter of voluntary termination of the proceedings or discontinuance by agreement as distinguished from a dismissal on the merits or in the court's discretion under § 1111. Under the judicial dissolution provisions of former Gen. Corp. L., a petition for such a dissolution was not subject to dismissal merely because of the pendency of other litigation between the petitioner and the corporation. Application of Pivot Punch & Die Corp. (1959) 15 Misc. 2d 713, 182 N.Y.S.2d 459, mod on other grounds (4th Dept) 9 A.D.2d 861, 193 N.Y.S.2d 34

Order requiring a temporary receiver in a judicial dissolution matter to disburse funds he held to a former shareholder of the corporation was improper; the dissolution no longer existed because the parties had reached an agreement whereby the former shareholder sold his interest in the corporation to the remaining shareholder and in that situation, the funds should have been returned to the corporation. Lipton v Carmel Prof'l Office Park, Inc. (2003, A.D., 2d Dept) 764 N.Y.S.2d 124

§ 1117. Applicability of other provisions

(a) Subject to the provisions of this article, the provisions of sections 1005 (Procedure after dissolution), 1006 (Corporate action and survival of remedies after dissolution), 1007 (Notice to creditors; filing or barring claims) and 1008 (Jurisdiction of supreme court to supervise dissolution and liquidation) shall apply to a corporation dissolved under this article.

(b) Any orders provided for in section 1008, may be made at any stage of an action or special proceeding for dissolution of a corporation under this article, and if the corporation is dissolved under this article, the court may retain jurisdiction for the purpose of making such orders, after the dissolution, in such action or special proceeding. The court may also make such orders in separate special proceedings, as provided in section 1008.

(c) Notice to creditors and claimants, provided for in section 1007, may also be given, by order of the court, at any stage of an action or special proceeding for dissolution of a corporation under this article.

History: Formerly § 1118, renumbered and amd, L 1962, ch 834, § 85, eff Sept 1, 1963; amd, L 1963, ch 748, § 28, eff Sept 1, 1963.

CASE ANNOTATIONS

Trial court improperly sua sponte appointed a referee to hear and report as to the value of the corporation's properties and leasehold interest and the appropriate procedures following dissolution in the judicial dissolution of the corporation; post-dissolution procedures in a judicial proceeding, provided for in N.Y. Bus. Corp. Law §§ 1005-1008, as provided under N.Y. Bus. Corp. Law § 1117, did not include the appointment of a referee. In re Oak St. Mgmt. (2003, A.D., 2d Dept) 762 N.Y.S.2d 522

N.Y. Bus. Corp. Law §§ 1006 and 1117 stand for the proposition that N.Y. C.P.L.R. 1017 can be disregarded and substitution avoided in a case of corporate dissolution. The specific provisions of the Business Corporation Law override the more general provisions of the CPLR. Lance Int'l v First Nat'l City Bank (2009, Civ Ct) 241 NYLJ 72, 878 NYS2d 572.

§ 1118. Purchase of petitioner's shares; valuation

(a) In any proceeding brought pursuant to section eleven hundred four-a of this chapter, any other shareholder or shareholders or the corporation may, at any time within ninety days after the filing of such petition or at such later time as the court in its discretion may allow, elect to purchase the shares owned by the petitioners at their fair value and upon such terms and conditions as may be approved by the court, including the conditions of paragraph (c)

herein. An election pursuant to this section shall be irrevocable unless the court, in its discretion, for just and equitable considerations, determines that such election be revocable.

(b) If one or more shareholders or the corporation elect to purchase the shares owned by the petitioner but are unable to agree with the petitioner upon the fair value of such shares, the court, upon the application of such prospective purchaser or purchasers or the petitioner, may stay the proceedings brought pursuant to section 1104-a of this chapter and determine the fair value of the petitioner's shares as of the day prior to the date on which such petition was filed, exclusive of any element of value arising from such filing but giving effect to any adjustment or surcharge found to be appropriate in the proceeding under section 1104-a of this chapter. In determining the fair value of the petitioner's shares, the court, in its discretion, may award interest from the date the petition is filed to the date of payment for the petitioner's share at an equitable rate upon judicially determined fair value of his shares.

(c) In connection with any election to purchase pursuant to this section:

(1) If such election is made beyond ninety days after the filing of the petition, and the court allows such petition, the court, in its discretion, may award the petitioner his reasonable expenses incurred in the proceeding prior to such election, including reasonable attorneys' fees;

(2) The court, in its discretion, may require, at any time prior to the actual purchase of petitioner's shares, the posting of a bond or other acceptable security in an amount sufficient to secure petitioner for the fair value of his shares.

History: Add, L 1979, ch 217, § 3, eff June 11, 1979; amd, L 1986, ch 861, § 1, eff Sept 1, 1986; L 1990, ch 822, § 2, eff July 25, 1990.

CASE ANNOTATIONS

1. Generally
2. Application to proceeding under § 1104
3. Application to interlinked corporations
4. Election to purchase; generally
5. – As obviating proof of grounds for dissolution
6. – Revocation of election
7. Imposition of restrictive covenant on petitioner
8. Stay of proceedings
9. Discontinuance of proceedings
10. Valuation of parties' interests; generally
11. – Effect of parties' agreement
12. – Marketability of stock as factor
13. – "Minority discount"
14. – Costs, fees, expenses and interest
15. Posting of bond

1. Generally

In proceeding for dissolution of closely-held corporation under CLS Bus Corp § 1104-a, majority shareholder could not be forced to buy out minority shareholder where minority shareholder failed to establish that dissolution was in order, since compulsory buy out under CLS Bus Corp § 1118 is alternative to dissolution. Re Farega Realty Corp. (1987, 3d Dept) 132 A.D.2d 797, 517 N.Y.S.2d 610

It was error to deny defendants' motion for immediate valuation under CLS Bus Corp § 1118(a); just as it would be unfair to preclude plaintiff shareholder from pursuing derivative action, alleging corporate waste and diversion of corporate assets for non-corporate purposes, by staying such action while permitting alleged wrongdoers in control of corporation to use election under CLS Bus Corp § 1118 to purchase all of shareholder's shares at fair value, thereby divesting shareholder of standing, such derivative or non-dissolution claims should likewise be no impediment to defendants exercising their statutory buy-out option. Edmonds v Amnews Corp. (1996, 1st Dept) 224 A.D.2d 358, 638 N.Y.S.2d 85

In action arising from removal of plaintiff as officer and director of closely held corporation, defendants were not entitled to summary judgment dismissing cause of action for judicial dissolution or fair market value, as moot, on ground that companies had already been dissolved by act of their board of directors, where validity of boards' actions in removing plaintiff as officer and director hinged on plaintiff's status as shareholder, as to which triable issue was raised. Shea v Hambros PLC (1998, 1st Dept) 244 A.D.2d 39, 673 N.Y.S.2d 369 Covenant restricting transferability of shares in a closely held corporation was properly held to apply only to voluntary transfers. Because it did not explicitly deem a forced sale or buyout to be a transfer, it did not apply to an election of a right under N.Y. Bus. Corp. Law §§ 623 or 1118, and in case of dissolution, the covenant would not apply because corporate property, not shares, would be sold under N.Y. Bus. Corp. Law § 1111. Eklund v Pinkey (2006, App Div, 3d Dept) 816 NYS2d 912, related proceeding (2006, NY App Div, 3d Dept) 2006 NY Slip Op 5692, 2006 NY App Div LEXIS 9246

2. Application to proceeding under § 1104

In proceedings brought by the holder of 50 percent of a closed corporation's stock for judicial dissolution under both Bus Corp Law §§ 1104, 1104-a, the holder of the remaining 50 percent stock was entitled to buy out petitioner's shares under Bus Corp Law § 1118, which allows buyout under § 1104-a, but is silent regarding the right to buy out under § 1104. Re Cristo Bros., Inc. (1985) 64 N.Y.2d 975, 489 N.Y.S.2d 35, 478 N.E.2d 176

In a corporate dissolution proceeding, an order directing the valuation of stock would be reversed, where a stock valuation can be directed when the proceeding is instituted under Bus Corp Law § 1104-a, when an election has been made under Bus Corp Law § 1118 by a shareholder to buy out the other shareholders, or an application has been made to stay the dissolution proceedings, and where the dissolution proceeding was instituted under Bus Corp Law § 1104, not under § 1104-a, where neither of the two principal shareholders had made an election to buy out the other, and where no one had moved to stay the dissolution. Re Application of Duffy (1983, 1st Dept) 97 A.D.2d 694, 468 N.Y.S.2d 116

A proceeding for involuntary judicial dissolution of a corporation, pursuant to Bus Corp Law §§ 1104, 1104-a, on the basis of a deadlock in the management of the corporation, was properly referred for determination of the fair value of petitioner's shares as of the day prior to the filing of the petition, where respondent timely elected to purchase petitioner's stock under Bus Corp Law § 1118, and where, although the statutory buy-out remedy does not apply to actions pursuant to Bus Corp Law § 1104, petitioner was entitled to petition for dissolution under both Bus Corp Law § 1104 and Bus Corp Law § 1104-a, and was properly prohibited from amending the petition to delete any reference to Bus Corp Law § 1104-a. Re Dissolution of Public Relations Aids, Inc. (1985, 1st Dept) 109 A.D.2d 502, 492 N.Y.S.2d 736

In action pursuant to CLS Bus Corp § 1104 seeking dissolution of corporations owned in equal shares by 2 brothers, court did not err in rejecting one brother's offer, made after hearing was concluded, to buy out his interest since buy-out provision contained in CLS Bus Corp § 1118 applies only to petitions pursuant to CLS Bus Corp § 1104-a. Greer v Greer (1986, 2d Dept) 124 A.D.2d 707, 508 N.Y.S.2d 217

In proceeding pursuant to CLS Bus Corp § 1104 for judicial dissolution of closely held corporation in business of dry cleaning, court erred in appointing appraiser to assess value of corporation for purpose of buy-out of petitioner's shares since buy-out remedy of CLS Bus Corp § 1118 does not apply where dissolution proceeding is brought under CLS Bus Corp § 1104. Re Lake Mahopac Tailor, Inc. (1989, 2d Dept) 146 A.D.2d 774, 537 N.Y.S.2d 256, appeal after remand (2d Dept) 172 A.D.2d 525, 568 N.Y.S.2d 336

It was error for court to convert proceeding under CLS Bus Corp § 1104 to one under CLS Bus Corp § 1104-a over petitioner's objection, and to permit respondent to elect to purchase petitioner's interest in corporation pursuant to CLS Bus Corp § 1118, as it is petitioner who chooses statutory basis for dissolution (CLS Bus Corp § 1105), and buyout option under § 1118 is not available in proceeding brought exclusively under § 1104. Giordano v Stark (1996, 2d Dept) 229 A.D.2d 493, 645 N.Y.S.2d 517

Court properly denied respondent's application to have petition for dissolution under CLS Bus Corp § 1104(a)(3) deemed one brought under CLS Bus Corp § 1104-a and to stay proceeding for valuation hearing under CLS Bus Corp § 118; it is petitioner who chooses statutory authority under which relief is sought. Toscano v Southampton Brick & Tile (1996, 2d Dept) 233 A.D.2d 515, 650 N.Y.S.2d 297

In shareholder's action alleging, inter alia, breach of fiduciary duty and conversion of corporate assets, court erred in ruling that plaintiff's dissolution allegations pleaded CLS Bus Corp § 1104-a cause of action, in directing plaintiff to amend his complaint to comply with CLS Bus Corp §§ 1105 and 1106, and in permitting forced buy of out his shares pursuant to CLS Bus Corp § 1118, where his pleadings never cited § 1104-a as basis for dissolution and he made it clear that he was requesting common-law dissolution only as alternative to primary relief requested in his first 6 causes of action. Fedele v Seybert (1998, 1st Dept) 250 A.D.2d 519, 673 N.Y.S.2d 421

In action for dissolution pursuant to CLS Bus Corp § 1104, shareholder did not have buy-out option under CLS Bus Corp § 1118; buy-out option is available in dissolution actions under CLS Bus Corp § 1104-a, but not in those under § 1104(a). Re Field, Rich & Associates, Inc. (1986) 134 Misc. 2d 216, 510 N.Y.S.2d 47

Once the trial court properly dismissed petitioner stockholder's N.Y. Bus. Corp. Law § 1104 action for dissolution because the stockholder owned insufficient stock to have standing, the trial court erred in sua sponte converting the action into a proceeding under N.Y. Bus. Corp. Law § 1104-a and ordering an appraisal hearing to value the stockholder's shares for a forced buy-out under N.Y. Bus. Corp. Law § 1118, as (1) the stockholder opposed the conversion and never sought such relief; (2) the right of appraisal provided by § 1118 applied only where dissolution was sought under N.Y. Bus. Corp. Law § 1104-a; and (3) the stockholder sought statutory dissolution under a section which did not afford respondents, a corporation and others, a buy-out remedy. In re Sakow (2002, A.D., 1st Dept) 746 N.Y.S.2d 159

Trial court did not err in ordering the extraordinary remedy of a forced buyout in a N.Y. Bus. Corp. Law § 1104 proceeding where the parties no longer desired to continue in business together, and it was clear from the record that, had they reached agreement on a price, the shareholder would have purchased the estate's shares; with the decedent's passing, the shareholder maintained the primary relationship with the company's customers and, considering his actions designed to move the operation of the company beyond the administrator's reach, the trial court was justified in finding that, through dissolution, the shareholder sought to avoid paying the estate the fair value of its shares while personally continuing to profit by operating the company's business either individually or through a new corporation. Matter of Clever Innovations, Inc. (Dooley) (2012, App Div, 3d Dept) 941 NYS2d 777.

3. Application to interlinked corporations

Court erred in imposing joint and several liability on 2 interlinked, closely-held corporations under CLS Bus Corp § 1118, even though financial statements of the 2 entities were consolidated in order to determine true value of minority shareholders' shares, since (1) joint and several liability is generally inconsistent with language and goals of statute, (2) allowing third party-by satisfying entire "joint and several" judgment-to purchase shares of petitioning shareholders would inject element of uncertainty and new ownership interest into continued operation of enterprises, and (3) imposition of such liability might jeopardize payments to preferred shareholders and corporations' status as "S" corporations for federal tax purposes. Re Seagroatt Floral Co. (1991) 78 N.Y.2d 439, 576 N.Y.S.2d 831, 583 N.E.2d 287

Supreme Court properly issued single order and single judgment in proceeding brought under CLS Bus Corp § 1118 to determine value of 2 closely-held, interlinked corporations, even though separate proceedings had been commenced by minority shareholders and no party moved for consolidation, where proceedings were prosecuted together in single hearing before referee, single report was issued by referee without objection, and the 2 sets of records and briefs submitted on appeal were virtually identical except for name of corporations. Re Seagroatt Floral Co. (1990, 3d Dept) 167 A.D.2d 586, 563 N.Y.S.2d 539, app gr 77 N.Y.2d 805, 568 N.Y.S.2d 913, 571 N.E.2d 83 and mod on other grounds, remanded 78 N.Y.2d 439, 576 N.Y.S.2d 831, 583 N.E.2d 287

Business Corporation Law

4. Election to purchase; generally

Closely-held corporation clearly and unequivocally elected to purchase minority shareholder's shares under shareholders' agreement, or alternatively under CLS Bus Corp § 1118, on shareholder's instigation of dissolution proceeding for fraud, mismanagement, et al. under CLS Bus Corp § 1104-a where corporation did not contend that its offer was hedged or conditional, and it maintained consistent position in litigation before both Supreme Court and Appellate Division. Re Pace Photographers, Ltd. (1988) 71 N.Y.2d 737, 530 N.Y.S.2d 67, 525 N.E.2d 713

Where one shareholder in close corporation petitioned for dissolution under CLS Bus Corp § 1104-a and another shareholder elected to purchase his shares at fair value, petitioning shareholder's vested right to recover fair value for his corporate stock survived his death. In re Penepent Corp. (2001) 96 N.Y.2d 186, 726 N.Y.S.2d 345, 750 N.E.2d 47

In a proceeding pursuant to Bus Corp Law §§ 1104 and 1104-a, seeking judicial dissolution of a corporation whose stock was equally divided between two shareholders, the court improperly dismissed one shareholder's cross petition under Bus Corp Law § 118 to purchase the other shareholder's stock, since the second shareholder owned more than 20 percent of the shares of the corporation and thus fell within the class entitled to bring a petition under § 1104-a, and since § 1118 unambiguously provides for an election to purchase such a shareholder's shares in all cases that include allegations under § 1104-a. Re Cristo Bros., Inc. (1983, 3d Dept) 97 A.D.2d 274, 470 N.Y.S.2d 781

Actions of a majority shareholder group in eliminating a petitioner and his son from participation in the active operation of a corporation in which they had previously participated, and in which they had every reasonable expectation of being able to continue to participate, constituted "oppressive" conduct within the meaning of Business Corporation Law (BCL) § 1104-a concerning judicial dissolution of a corporation. Since the corporation was permitted to purchase the shares of the petitioner, pursuant to BCL § 1118, it was entitled to appear and obtain a stay of a dissolution proceeding authorized by that section, but merely establishing that the corporation was legally and financially able to pay the fair value of the shares under the limitations prescribed by BCL § 513 was not a condition precedent to the grant of the stay mandated by § 1118. Although a letter from a corporation offering to purchase the petitioner's shares for a specified price could not constitute an election to purchase required to trigger a stay, the corporation's answer to the petition, together with an affidavit by a majority shareholder on the corporation's behalf, did constitute an election to purchase at fair value. Furthermore, a motion for summary judgment pursuant to CPLR § 3213 brought by the petitioner for repayment of loans of $215,000 allegedly made by him to the corporation would be consolidated, pursuant to the court's discretion provided in CPLR § 602, with proceedings on the shareholder's petition for dissolution, contingent on a denial of the motion for summary judgment. Gene Barry One Hour Photo Process, Inc. (1981) 111 Misc. 2d 559, 444 N.Y.S.2d 540

Holder of shares of family corporation who commenced dissolution proceeding under CLS Bus Corp § 1104-a was not entitled to declaration that other shareholders' commencement of action for specific performance of parties' stock purchase agreement, which was dismissed by court, constituted election to purchase his shares at fair value under CLS Bus Corp § 1118, since other shareholders, by seeking to enforce stock purchase agreement, apparently sought to purchase shares at value ascribed to them in such agreement, and it was ambiguous whether they would elect to purchase his shares at their fair value. James Mirabito & Sons, Inc. v Mirabito (1986) 137 Misc. 2d 972, 523 N.Y.S.2d 711

Corporation could, without the consent of the petitioning shareholder, invoke its N.Y. Bus. Corp. Law § 1118 right of election because the shareholders did not explicitly limit its ability to exercise the right following the filing of a voluntary dissolution under N.Y. Bus. Corp. Law § 1104-a. Ferolito v Vultaggio (2012, App Div, 1st Dept) 949 NYS2d 356, injunction den, partial summary judgment den (2012, NY Sup) 2012 NY Slip Op 32047U, 2012 NY Misc LEXIS 3740, injunction den, partial summary judgment den (2012, NY Sup) 2012 NY Slip Op 51523U, 2012 NY Misc LEXIS 3869

5. – As obviating proof of grounds for dissolution

Close corporation's election to buy minority shareholder's shares under shareholders' agreement, or alternatively under CLS Bus Corp § 1118, relieved shareholder of need to prove allegations of fraud, mismanagement, et al. underlying his petition to dissolve corpora-

tion, so no hearing on allegations was required; while fixing blame is material under dissolution proceeding of CLS Bus Corp § 1104-a, it is immaterial under § 1118. Re Pace Photographers, Ltd. (1988) 71 N.Y.2d 737, 530 N.Y.S.2d 67, 525 N.E.2d 713

Concept of wrongdoing is alien to proceeding under CLS Bus Corp § 1118 since such proceeding seeks to determine fair value of petitioning shareholders' interests and not their initial allegations of misconduct. Re Seagroatt Floral Co. (1991) 78 N.Y.2d 439, 576 N.Y.S.2d 831, 583 N.E.2d 287

Where shareholders make election to purchase petitioner's shares, petitioner does not have to prove any allegations upon which to base petition for dissolution of corporation on grounds that other shareholders had been taking assets out for personal use without properly accounting for them. Re Gargano (1985, 2d Dept) 112 A.D.2d 225, 491 N.Y.S.2d 440, later proceeding Re Gargano (1985, 2d Dept) 112 A.D.2d 224, 491 N.Y.S.2d 441

Court erred in concluding that offer to purchase petitioner's shares in corporation constituted election under CLS Bus Corp § 1118 that relieved petitioner of burden as to proving allegations of oppressive conduct where, prior to filing of petition under CLS Bus Corp § 1104-a, offeror exercised option to purchase actioner's shares under terms of shareholders' agreement, and thus his offer could not be deemed clear and unequivocal election to purchase petitioner's shares at fair market value. In re Apple (1996, 4th Dept) 224 A.D.2d 1016, 637 N.Y.S.2d 534, reh den (NY A.D., 4th Dept) 1996 N.Y. A.D. LEXIS 5750 and app den 88 N.Y.2d 811, 649 N.Y.S.2d 378, 672 N.E.2d 604

Court properly granted petition to stay arbitration with regard to dissolution of parties' corporation, as dissolution would not be appropriate because appellant had buy-out procedure available to him which would provide him with fair return on his investment. Gold v Gold (1996, 2d Dept) 229 A.D.2d 495, 645 N.Y.S.2d 328

Minority shareholder's petition for an injunction and a bond or other suitable security were denied because the majority shareholders elected to purchase his shares for their fair value and the bond request was made for the first time in reply and was unsupported by proof persuasively demonstrating a need for such relief. O'Connor v Coccadotts, Inc., 3 N.Y.S.3d 567, 2015 N.Y. Misc. LEXIS 87 (N.Y. Sup. Ct. 2015).

6. – Revocation of election

Where one shareholder in close corporation petitioned for dissolution under CLS Bus Corp § 1104-a and another shareholder elected to purchase his shares at fair value, but petitioning shareholder died before determination of fair value, other shareholder was not entitled to revoke his election and acquire petitioning shareholder's stock pursuant to shareholder agreement which provided that deceased shareholder's estate must surrender deceased's stock to corporation in exchange for specified price, which was less than fair value; divestiture event under shareholder agreement (shareholder's death) did not occur until one1/2 years after CLS Bus Corp § 1118 election was made. In re Penepent Corp. (2001) 96 N.Y.2d 186, 726 N.Y.S.2d 345, 750 N.E.2d 47

In proceeding under CLS Bus Corp § 1104-a, nonpetitioning shareholder was properly permitted to revoke his election to purchase shares owned by party seeking dissolution where fire destroyed corporation's business after election was made since election was made prior to effective date of amendment to CLS Bus Corp § 1118 limiting right to revoke, and thus nonpetitioning shareholder may have assumed that he would not be bound by his election, which may have influenced his decision to elect; moreover, even if amendment applied retroactively, revocation was properly allowed as matter of discretion, since it would be inequitable to force nonpetitioning shareholder to purchase essentially worthless stock owing to unforeseeable fire, absent evidence that election was made as delaying tactic or that nonpetitioning shareholder failed to act in good faith. Rey v Pan American Cash & Carry Corp. (1989, 2d Dept) 152 A.D.2d 246, 548 N.Y.S.2d 524

Corporation would not be permitted to revoke its election to purchase shares under CLS Bus Corp § 1118 after Court of Appeals rendered decision finding suggested price did not constitute fair value, especially as there were no just and equitable considerations to allow revocation. Re Pace Photographers, Ltd. (1990, 2d Dept) 163 A.D.2d 316, 557 N.Y.S.2d 443

Amendment to CLS Bus Corp § 1118(a), which precluded revocation of election to purchase petitioner's share in corporation unless election was deemed by court to be revocable, applied where dissolution action was commenced prior to amendment of statute, but election was made after amendment of statute. In re Chu (1993, 1st Dept) 192 A.D.2d 315, 595 N.Y.S.2d 465

Court abused its discretion in allowing majority shareholders to revoke their election to purchase minority shareholders' shares on ground of "impossibility of performance" due to financial difficulties experienced by one of majority shareholders since all majority shareholders had assured court that remaining majority shareholders would be able to effectuate buy out even if majority shareholder in question proved unable to participate, and they waited more than 3 years until after minority shareholders' initial proceeding to compel dissolution, and their own election to purchase shares, to move for revocation. Smith v Russo (1996, 2d Dept) 230 A.D.2d 863, 646 N.Y.S.2d 711

It was improper to allow defendants to withdraw their CLS Bus Corp § 1118 election after judicial hearing officer adopted plaintiff's appraisal of property. F.P.D. Realty Corp. v Tru-Way Private Taxi Corp. (1999, 1st Dept) 267 A.D.2d 111, 700 N.Y.S.2d 146

7. Imposition of restrictive covenant on petitioner

Restrictive covenant in shareholders' agreement regarding extent to which minority shareholder could conduct business in competition with corporation would be inapplicable to sale of shareholder's shares where agreement was, by its terms, limited to "sale of shares of stock as herein provided," and sale was to proceed not by agreement but by court order under CLS Bus Corp § 1118; whether or not reasonable restriction could be imposed by way of implied covenant in connection with sale of goodwill would be open question that would require resolution by trial court on remittal. Re Pace Photographers, Ltd. (1988) 71 N.Y.2d 737, 530 N.Y.S.2d 67, 525 N.E.2d 713

Where respondent corporations avoided dissolution by electing, pursuant to Bus Corp Law § 1118, to buy out a minority shareholder, it was not error to decline to impose restrictive covenants on the shareholder, enjoining him from competing with respondents or soliciting their customers. Inasmuch as there was no express or implied computation of the value of corporate goodwill or of the shareholder's share of said goodwill in arriving at the fair value of his interest, there was no reason to impose a restrictive covenant on him; moreover, there is no specific statutory authority to impose such a restrictive covenant, nor was there a prior written agreement amongst the parties with regard to a noncompetition pact. Re Fleischer (1985, 2d Dept) 107 A.D.2d 97, 486 N.Y.S.2d 272

Referee correctly refused to prohibit the minority shareholder from competing against the corporation and soliciting the corporation's customers, since an acquisition premium was appropriate only when the entire corporation was being sold to an outside third party willing to pay an acquisition premium in exchange for capturing the assets of the corporation, and since the minority shareholder was not getting the value of a sale to an outside third party that might entitle him to an acquisition premium or the nonapplication of an illiquidity discount. Re Gift Pax, Inc. (1984) 123 Misc. 2d 830, 475 N.Y.S.2d 324

8. Stay of proceedings

Appellate Division would dismiss appeal by majority shareholders from injunction order granted to minority shareholders in their action for dissolution under CLS Bus Corp § 1104-a where it was conceded at oral argument that majority shareholders had subsequently elected to purchase minority's shares pursuant to CLS Bus Corp § 1118, and mandatory stay provisions of § 1118 had been triggered; parties should proceed with remedy provided by § 1118 as substitute for § 1104-a proceeding. Re Seagroatt Floral Co. (1988, 3d Dept) 140 A.D.2d 841, 528 N.Y.S.2d 225

A proceeding for dissolution of a closed corporation pursuant to Bus Corp Law § 1104-a would be stayed pending the court's attempt to fashion a more feasible means whereby petitioner might obtain relief by determining the fair market value of petitioner's shares so that respondent majority shareholder could buy petitioner's shares pursuant to Bus Corp Law, § 1118, where petitioner's action seemed motivated primarily by frustration over the alleged uncooperative attitude of respondent in facilitating an inspection of the corporate records, petitioner had not been involved in the day-to-day operations of the corporation for some time pursuant to his separation and divorce from respondent, and the corporation was a going concern. Re Chariot Taxi, Inc. (1984) 126 Misc. 2d 394

9. Discontinuance of proceedings

It was abuse of discretion to allow shareholder to discontinue dissolution proceedings against corporations, thereby depriving them of statutory buy-out remedy of CLS Bus Corp § 1118, for despite shareholder's assertion that he had become convinced that grounds for dissolution alleged in his petition-that other corporate directors

had attempted to wrongfully freeze him out as director and share-holder-no longer existed, it was reasonably clear that his desire to discontinue was response to corporations' exercise of buy-out remedy, given that shareholder had commenced dissolution proceeding only after he had failed to obtain negotiated buy-out and sought leave to discontinue when corporations elected to purchase his shares; moreover, in light of shareholder's veto power, it was not inconceivable that he would seek to deadlock corporations, which could be avoided by allowing corporations to purchase his stock. Re Musilli (1987, 2d Dept) 134 A.D.2d 15, 523 N.Y.S.2d 120, later op (NY A.D. 2nd Dept) LEXIS slip op

10. Valuation of parties' interests; generally

There is no difference in analysis between stock fair value determinations under CLS Bus Corp § 623 and fair value determinations under CLS Bus Corp § 1118; in fixing fair value, courts should determine minority shareholder's proportionate interest in going concern value of corporation as whole (i.e., what willing purchaser, in arm's length transaction, would offer for corporation as operating business). Friedman v Beway Realty Corp. (1995) 87 N.Y.2d 161, 638 N.Y.S.2d 399, 661 N.E.2d 972

In a proceeding under Bus Corp Law § 1104-a to dissolve certain corporations, Bus Corp Law § 623(g), (h) were not applicable to the determination of fair value of stock in those corporations, since there was no legislative design that those provisions were intended to govern a court's determination of fair value under Bus Corp Law § 1118 in which corporations exercise their option to purchase the shares of the person petitioning to dissolve. Re Fleischer (1980, 2d Dept) 79 A.D.2d 636, 433 N.Y.S.2d 614

In evaluating a minority shareholder's one-third interest in certain closely held corporations for the purpose of the purchase of his shares by the corporations pursuant to Bus Corp Law § 1118, the trial court used acceptable valuation methods in multiplying each corporation's income by a multiplier based on the price-earnings ratio of comparable publicly traded corporations, and adding to that sum the adjusted net assets and securities of the corporation. Re Fleischer (1985, 2d Dept) 107 A.D.2d 97, 486 N.Y.S.2d 272

Following a corporation's election under Bus Corp Law § 1118 to buy out a minority shareholder who had commenced a special proceeding under Bus Corp Law § 1104-a to dissolve the corporation, the referee, in valuing the shareholder's interest in the corporation: properly applied a multiplier of only one to gross commission revenue in determining the corporation's goodwill, since the insurance industry was "soft" due to direct billing of premiums. Blake v Blake Agency, Inc. (1985, 2d Dept) 107 A.D.2d 139, 486 N.Y.S.2d 341

Referee properly refused to discount the shareholder's share of net tangible assets, despite the argument that such an approach failed to account for the working capital needs of the corporation, where the corporation had never paid any dividends, and where the corporation's balance sheet, prior to the filing of the dissolution petition showed that it had sufficient capital even after paying the shareholder. Blake v Blake Agency, Inc. (1985, 2d Dept) 107 A.D.2d 139, 486 N.Y.S.2d 341

In dissolution proceeding wherein closely held corporations elected to buy out petitioner under CLS Bus Corp § 1118, court properly valued petitioner's shares based on salary figures proposed by corporations' expert witness, although he relied primarily on 2 studies which were outside record, since his figures were supported by evidence in record, including study showing median salaries, and salaries of top 10 percent of executives for various corporations, as well as testimony concerning subject corporations' growth records; nor was it abuse of discretion to multiply corporations' earnings by 10 to arrive at realistic price that impartial buyer would pay, but court erred by refusing to discount petitioner's shares to reflect fact that they could not be freely traded. Raskin v Walter Karl, Inc. (1987, 2d Dept) 129 A.D.2d 642, 514 N.Y.S.2d 120

In dissolution proceeding, it was error to appoint referee to hear and report on value of petitioner's stock where matter did not involve complex issues or necessity for extended hearing; under circumstances, it would be to shareholders' advantage and in best interests of small close corporation for court to try issue or refer it to judicial hearing officer rather than burdening litigants with expense of private referee. Mitchell v A.J. Medical Supply, Inc. (1988, 2d Dept) 141 A.D.2d 732, 529 N.Y.S.2d 589

Referee in valuation proceeding brought under CLS Bus Corp § 1118 properly deducted $18,000 for value of outstanding shares of preferred stock where valuation method used by minority shareholders' expert took into account value of dividend produced by preferred stock, but no adjustment was made for value of stock itself. Re Seagroatt Floral Co. (1990, 3d Dept) 167 A.D.2d 586, 563 N.Y.S.2d 539, app gr 77 N.Y.2d 805, 568 N.Y.S.2d 913, 571 N.E.2d 83 and mod on other grounds, remanded 78 N.Y.2d 439, 576 N.Y.S.2d 831, 583 N.E.2d 287

Petitioners were entitled to disclosure of relevant information in proceeding under CLS Bus Corp § 1104-a to dissolve 2 closely-held corporations in which majority shareholder elected to buy out petitioners subject to CLS Bus Corp § 1118, although election of majority shareholder to buy out petitioners made allegations of misconduct contained in petition superfluous with respect to dissolution under CLS Bus Corp § 1104-a, where allegations were still relevant with regard to impact of alleged misconduct on fair value of corporation. Gerzof v Coons (1990, 2d Dept) 168 A.D.2d 619, 563 N.Y.S.2d 458, later proceeding (2d Dept) 177 A.D.2d 487, 576 N.Y.S.2d 29

In corporate dissolution proceeding under CLS Bus Corp § 1104-a, Supreme Court properly rejected valuation submitted by respondent's expert on ground that it failed to account for excessive executive compensation. In re Walt's Submarine Sandwiches, Inc. (1991, 3d Dept) 173 A.D.2d 980, 569 N.Y.S.2d 492, app den 78 N.Y.2d 860, 576 N.Y.S.2d 218, 582 N.E.2d 601

In proceeding under CLS Bus Corp § 1104-a to dissolve closely-held corporation, whose only assets were cash and real property, judicial hearing officer improperly used fair market rental value of real property to determine fair market value pursuant to income capitalization method of valuing real property without consideration that property was subject to below-market-value lease. Cinque v Largo Enters. (1995, 1st Dept) 212 A.D.2d 608, 622 N.Y.S.2d 735

Court erred in granting petitioner's motion of dissolve corporation under CLS Bus Corp § 1104-a without holding hearing to determine fair value of petitioner's shares as provided by CLS Bus Corp § 1104-a where respondents were unable to agree with petitioner on fair value of his shares, they timely elected to purchase his shares, and they requested hearing to determine fair value of shares. In re Dissolution of Tosca Brick Oven Bread (1997, 1st Dept) 243 A.D.2d 416, 665 N.Y.S.2d 252

Court's failure to recognize and correct error in respondent's expert's use of "capital deficiency" adjustment produced valuation that was against weight of evidence, even though it was not improper to consider amount of capital that purchaser would have to immediately contribute to business in arriving at price he or she would likely pay for it, since, having done so, expert neglected to consider effect which such presumed contribution would have on corporation's cash flow in first year, without providing any convincing explanation for such omission. In re Dissolution of Funplex, Inc. (1998, 3d Dept) 252 A.D.2d 923, 676 N.Y.S.2d 321

In proceeding to dissolve corporation, court properly determined valuation date of corporation and its shares as day prior to filing of petition. Wolk v Kornberg (In re Vetco, Inc.) (1999, 2d Dept) 260 A.D.2d 642, 687 N.Y.S.2d 270

Trial court could rely on the "investment value" approach in valuing a corporation that provided a service and could thereafter apply discounts for lack of marketability and general economic factors. Hessert v Berlyne (In re Brooklyn Home Dialysis Training Ctr., Inc.) (2002, 2d Dept) 293 A.D.2d 747, 741 N.Y.S.2d 280

In a proceeding to determine the fair value of petitioner's shares in a corporation organized by three equal shareholders and capitalized by loans of equal amounts from each shareholder, the court, pursuant to Bus Corp Law § 1118(b) would evaluate said shares by the investment value method, since the net asset method relies heavily on accounting methods which do not provide an accurate measure of a going business and is therefore inappropriate since the corporation had elected to continue as a going business and since the market value method of valuation was also inappropriate, in that petitioner's stock would have no value at all if measured by that method; using the investment value method, the court found that a prudent informed investor would have been willing to pay double the adjusted annual cash flow for the business and, after allocating a portion of that sum to repayment of the outstanding shareholders' loans to the corporation, petitioner would be entitled to one third of the balance; however, the court declined to impose terms and conditions permitting a deferred payment for said shares due to the nature of the oppressive conduct engaged in by the two remaining shareholders in ousting petitioner from the corporation. Taines v Gene Barry One Hour Photo Process, Inc. (1983) 123 Misc. 2d 529, 474 N.Y.S.2d 362

In determining fair value of petitioner's shares pursuant to CLS Bus Corp § 1118(b) in dissolution proceeding under CLS Bus Corp § 1104-a, neither party had burden of proof; rather, all parties were entitled to be heard on question of fair value, to enable court to make findings based on all relevant evidence. In re Cohen (1995, Sup) 168 Misc. 2d 91, 636 N.Y.S.2d 994

In determining fair value of petitioner's shares as of May 23, 1992, pursuant to CLS Bus Corp § 1118(b), special referee erred in rejecting respondent's zero valuation of shares as "incredible" and in crediting petitioner's valuation of shares at $1.5 million "as a starting point" as (1) mere fact that controlling shareholder was paid for his services did not mean that corporation was making profit, (2) fact that 1988 contract listed corporation for sale or soliciting investment for $1.25 million was not worthy reason to reject zero valuation as it merely constituted unconsummated offer for sale or investment, and (3) petitioner's "expert" was experienced in corporation's film business, but lacked experience in evaluating close corporations. In re Cohen (1995, Sup) 168 Misc. 2d 91, 636 N.Y.S.2d 994

In corporate dissolution proceeding, fair value of petitioner's shares would be fixed at $19,800, rather than zero valuation claimed by respondent or $1.25 million claimed by petitioner, where court-appointed expert arrived at value of $19,800 by analyzing net asset value and investment value of respondent film corporation, and properly accounted for difference between films that physically existed in libraries that he had evaluated previously and distribution rights sans physical properties in "libraries" of respondent and its subsidiaries, in addition to royalties required to generate income for respondent from prosecuting rights to distribute films in its "cornucopia"; furthermore, expert set forth his methodology in detailed reports, and his realistic treatment recognized that respondent, like any business, incurred expenses to generate revenues. In re Cohen (1995, Sup) 168 Misc. 2d 91, 636 N.Y.S.2d 994

Only realistic approach by which to determine fair value of shares of close corporation, whose only product was cigarette rolling papers, was "investment method" which involved determining what prudent informed investor would be willing to pay for entire business as going concern, considering all factors indicated by nature of company's business, risks involved, and expected projected return. In re Dissolution of Bambu Sales (1997, Sup) 177 Misc. 2d 459, 672 N.Y.S.2d 613

For evaluating shares of close corporation by investment method, 4 percent small stock premium set forth in "Ibbotson" evaluation manual (which was based on fund of publicly traded companies with capitalization of between $10 million and $150 million) was unrealistically low, and court assigned 20 percent risk factor, where corporation's only product was cigarette rolling papers, it had only one supplier and limited geographic sales market, its product was subject to extensive government regulation and thus ability to advertise was limited, and it had incurred more than $200,000 per year in 3-year period in legal and professional fees to protect its trademark which was continuing cost of doing business. In re Dissolution of Bambu Sales (1997, Sup) 177 Misc. 2d 459, 672 N.Y.S.2d 613

In determining fair value of shares of close corporation pursuant to investment value method, court (1) determined income stream by adjusting historical earnings, certain nonrecurring or unusual expenses, interest expenses and add-back of owner's compensation and benefits papers, (2) applied weighting factor to results of operations for years under review, with heavier weighting generally assigned to later years on assumption that recent years are more indicative of future results, (3) adopted 25 percent discount for lack of marketability, and (4) considered fair value to be value of all stock of company for sale. In re Dissolution of Bambu Sales (1997, Sup) 177 Misc. 2d 459, 672 N.Y.S.2d 613

In determining fair value of plaintiff's 45 percent share of stock in closely held corporation, for purchase by defendant in lieu of dissolution, referee did not err by relying on testimony of expert witness who used net asset approach despite anticipated continuation of corporation's business, where expert calculated value of corporation's goodwill and added that sum to his calculation of corporation's value under traditional net asset approach. Hall v King (1998, Sup) 177 Misc. 2d 126, 675 N.Y.S.2d 810

N.Y. Bus. Corp. Law §§ 1006 and 1117 stand for the proposition that N.Y. C.P.L.R. 1017 can be disregarded and substitution avoided in a case of corporate dissolution. The specific provisions of the Business Corporation Law override the more general provisions of the CPLR. Lance Int'l v First Nat'l City Bank (2009, Civ Ct) 241 NYLJ 72, 878 NYS2d 572.

Co-operative corporation's transfer of 400 shares appurtenant to a garden unit in a building owned by the corporation and a proprietary lease for that apartment were valid, and an owner's interest in the corporation was thus 20 percent for purposes of the corporation's N.Y. Bus. Corp. Law § 1118 election to purchase her interest, because a single director was a "majority" and was therefore able to validly fill a board vacancy pursuant to N.Y. Bus. Corp. Law § 705(a). Matter of McDaniel v 162 Columbia Hgts. Hous. Corp. (2009, Sup) 873 NYS2d 468.

In a case involving valuation of shares in a cooperative housing corporation under N.Y. Bus. Corp. Law § 1104-a and § 1118, equity was accomplished by a "closing adjustment" that did not award the shareholder any interest on a $825,000 payment but also did not award the corporation use and occupancy over and above the shareholder's maintenance of $973 a month. Matter of Balk v 125 W. 92nd St. Corp. (2005, A.D., 1st Dept) 805 N.Y.S.2d 352

Because the record was insufficient to determine the value of the corporation's shares and because the judicial hearing officer did not did not explain how the value of a minority shareholder's shares was determined, the matter was remitted for a new hearing pursuant to N.Y. Bus. Corp. Law § 1118. Matter of DeAngelis v AVC Servs., Inc. (2008, 2d Dept) 57 App Div 3d 989, 871 NYS2d 290.

Although the trial court properly valued a corporation's shares pursuant to N.Y. Bus. Corp. Law § 1118(b), it erred in granting each officer an additional pension, in determining the expected future rate of return, and in limiting the shareholders' postjudgment interest to 5%. Matter of Murphy v United States Dredging Corp. (2010, 2d Dept) 74 App Div 3d 815, 903 NYS2d 434.

11. – Effect of parties' agreement

In an action brought by a shareholder of a corporation who alleged that he had been "frozen-out" of his interest and who sought an award based on his interest in the corporation at the time of the alleged "freeze-out", the plaintiff was not entitled to recover the value of his interest on the basis of an alleged "buyout" agreement where the agreement had not been concluded, no decision on valuation having been reached by the parties. Robbins v Panitz (1984) 61 N.Y.S.2d 967, 475 N.Y.S.2d 274, 463 N.E.2d 615

Terms of shareholders' agreement governing voluntary sale of shares by shareholder to corporation should not dictate "fair value" of minority interest under CLS Bus Corp § 1118; on remand, court should determine "fair value" by taking into account not only agreement's provisions regarding value but also shareholder's own offer to buy, corporation's earlier efforts to sell business, and any other pertinent evidence. Re Pace Photographers, Ltd. (1988) 71 N.Y.2d 737, 530 N.Y.S.2d 67, 525 N.E.2d 713

Close corporation's election to buy minority shareholder's shares under shareholders' agreement, or alternatively under CLS Bus Corp § 1118, made it unnecessary for Court of Appeals to decide whether shareholders' agreement fixing value in and of itself precluded relief for shareholder in his dissolution proceeding under CLS Bus Corp § 1104-a, despite his allegations of fraud, mismanagement, et al., since § 1104-a provides that court must take into account whether "liquidation of the corporation is the only feasible means whereby the petitioners may reasonably expect to obtain a fair return on their investment"; on election, central question became one of valuation under § 1118, not liquidation under § 1104-a. Re Pace Photographers, Ltd. (1988) 71 N.Y.2d 737, 530 N.Y.S.2d 67, 525 N.E.2d 713

Court properly refused to hold hearing to determine fair value of stock under CLS Bus Corp § 1118(a) in light of uncontested submissions of corporation that its stock had no fair market value; court appropriately applied stock redemption agreement to determine value of petitioner's stock, despite his contention that redemption agreement did not cover forced redemptions. In re Kline (1995, 4th Dept) 212 A.D.2d 1002, 619 N.Y.S.2d 40, related proceeding (4th Dept) 212 A.D.2d 1070, 623 N.Y.S.2d 62, app den 85 N.Y.2d 808, 628 N.Y.S.2d 51, 651 N.E.2d 919

Respondents, who answered petition for judicial dissolution by filing election to purchase petitioners' shares for fair value under CLS Bus Corp § 1118, were improperly granted summary judgment as to issue that petitioners' shares must be valued solely by methodology set forth in parties' agreement (which gave respondents unilateral option to purchase petitioners' shares at price to be established in accordance with contractual formula), since (1) option was to be exercisable only after business had been in operation for 2 years, with active participation by petitioners during that time, and (2) petitioners' assertion that they were effectively barred by respondents participating in business in any meaningful way, if true, would have

denied petitioners' receipt of consideration promised in exchange for option, thus precluding respondents' enforcement of option; in sum, before actual effect of option clause on fair value of petitioners' shares could be determined, factual questions had to be resolved as to respondents allegedly oppressive conduct and fraud, insofar as they were relevant to issue of whether respondents breached agreement. In re Dissolution of Funplex Inc. (1995, 3d Dept) 214 A.D.2d 858, 624 N.Y.S.2d 681

In proceeding to determine fair value of plaintiff's 45 percent share of stock in closely held corporation, distribution of $180,000 by plaintiff to himself after valuation date (whether or not it was made by his wrongdoing) would be deducted from value of his shares inasmuch as it was not approved or ratified by defendant and necessarily impacted on value of corporation measured by net asset method; however, another distribution by plaintiff to himself made after valuation date, which was approved by defendant, would not be deducted from value of his shares. Hall v King (1998, Sup) 177 Misc. 2d 126, 675 N.Y.S.2d 810

12. – Marketability of stock as factor

While lack of public market for shares of closely-held corporation should be considered in determining what willing purchaser would pay for such shares under CLS Bus Corp § 1118, there is no single method for calculating that factor and Court of Appeals has never mandated one; thus, as matter of law, illiquidity may not be taken into account only byapplication of percentage discount against value. Re Seagroatt Floral Co. (1991) 78 N.Y.2d 439, 576 N.Y.S.2d 831, 583 N.E.2d 287

Appellate Division properly found that minority shareholders' expert had factored risk associated with lack of marketability of 2 closely-held corporations' shares into his formula to determine overall value, despite referee's rejection of expert's testimony as incredible, where expert had used capitalization rate which he believed was reasonable for pretax earnings of closely-held corporation, and he repeatedly explained that lack of marketability had been factor in his choice of capitalization rate. Re Seagroatt Floral Co. (1991) 78 N.Y.2d 439, 576 N.Y.S.2d 831, 583 N.E.2d 287

It was also appropriate for the trial court to discount the value of the minority shareholder's interest by 25 percent due to its lack of marketability. Re Fleischer (1985, 2d Dept) 107 A.D.2d 97, 486 N.Y.S.2d 272

In proceeding to determine fair value of stockholder's shares in closely held corporation upon election of corporation to purchase shares, judicial hearing officer erred in failing to apply discount to reflect lack of marketability of shares in closely held corporation, and under particular circumstances of case, appropriate discount would be 10 percent. Re Joy Wholesale Sundries, Inc. (1986, 2d Dept) 125 A.D.2d 310, 508 N.Y.S.2d 594

Referee in valuation proceeding under CLS Bus Corp § 1118 erred in applying 25 percent discount for lack of marketability, even though such discount is appropriate in valuing shares of closely-held corporation because those shares cannot readily be sold on public market, where valuation method used by minority shareholders' expert included marketability factor and referee had accepted remainder of expert's testimony concerning valuation. Re Seagroatt Floral Co. (1990, 3d Dept) 167 A.D.2d 586, 563 N.Y.S.2d 539, app gr 77 N.Y.2d 805, 568 N.Y.S.2d 913, 571 N.E.2d 83 and mod on other grounds, remanded 78 N.Y.2d 439, 576 N.Y.S.2d 831, 583 N.E.2d 287

In proceeding under CLS Bus Corp § 1104-a to dissolve closely-held corporation, whose only assets were cash and real property, judicial hearing officer properly refused to discount value of petitioner's shares of corporation due to their lack of marketability, since such discount is only applicable to portion of value of corporation that is attributable to good will. Cinque v Largo Enters. (1995, 1st Dept) 212 A.D.2d 608, 622 N.Y.S.2d 735

The referee who determined the fair value of a minority shareholder's stock which a corporation in dissolution had elected to purchase, erred in holding no discount for illiquidity because the corporation had become a willing and available buyer by electing to purchase the minority shareholder's stock, since that determinatin was contrary to the clear statutory requirement in Bus Corp Law § 1118 and that the fair value of the minority shareholder's stock be determined as of the day prior to the date on which the corporate dissolution petition was filed regardless of any element of value arising from the filing of that petition. Re Gift Pax, Inc. (1984) 123 Misc. 2d 830, 475 N.Y.S.2d 324

In proceeding to determine fair value of plaintiff's 45 percent share of stock in closely held corporation, for purchase by defendant in lieu of dissolution, 25 percent lack of marketability discount applied by referee was not excessive and was properly applied to entire valuation of plaintiff's shares, rather than just to valuation of corporation's intangible assets (i.e., goodwill). Hall v King (1998, Sup) 177 Misc. 2d 126, 675 N.Y.S.2d 810

Where respondent elected under N.Y. Bus. Corp. Law § 1118(b) to buy petitioner's shares in a corporate dissolution proceeding, the trial court erred in assessing that marketability of the corporations' real property assets was same as marketability of their shares; the costs and risks associated with corporate ownership of real estate should have been accounted for by a discount. The reduction of built-in capital gains to present value properly adjusted for embedded capital gains taxes that would not have been paid until a future time. Giaimo v Vitale (2012, 1st Dept) 101 App Div 3d 523, 956 NYS2d 41.

13. – "Minority discount"

Imposing minority discount on compensation payable to dissenting stockholders for their shares in proceeding under CLS Bus Corp § 623 or § 1118 would necessarily deprive minority shareholders of their proportionate interest in going concern, and would result in minority shares being valued below that of majority shares, thus violating mandate of equal treatment of all shares of same class in minority stockholder buyouts. Friedman v Beway Realty Corp. (1995) 87 N.Y.2d 161, 638 N.Y.S.2d 399, 661 N.E.2d 972

Where one shareholder in close corporation petitioned for dissolution under CLS Bus Corp § 1104-a and another shareholder invoked CLS Bus Corp § 1118, fair value of petitioner's shares was not affected by fact that third shareholder's dissolution proceeding was currently pending against corporation and other shareholders' § 1118 election in that proceeding would result in petitioner being "minority shareholder." In re Penepent Corp. (2001) 96 N.Y.2d 186, 726 N.Y.S.2d 345, 750 N.E.2d 47

While the shares of a closely held corporation cannot be readily sold on a public market, a minority interest in closely held corporate stock should not be discounted solely because it is a minority interest. Blake v Blake Agency, Inc. (1985, 2d Dept) 107 A.D.2d 139, 486 N.Y.S.2d 341

14. – Costs, fees, expenses and interest

In a proceeding to evaluate a minority shareholder's interest in certain closely held corporations for purposes of their purchase by the corporations under Bus Corp Law § 1118, the trial court properly exercised its discretion in dividing costs and fees amongst the parties according to their interests in the corporations, and in awarding the minority shareholder interest at the rate of 12 percent per annum on the fair value of his shares. Re Fleischer (1985, 2d Dept) 107 A.D.2d 97, 486 N.Y.S.2d 272

In proceeding to determine fair value of stockholder's shares upon election of corporation to purchase shares, stockholder was entitled to interest on fair value determined from day prior to filing of petition to date of payment since there was no evidence of bad faith on part of stockholder, and therefore statutory rate of 9 percent per annum would be awarded. Re Joy Wholesale Sundries, Inc. (1986, 2d Dept) 125 A.D.2d 310, 508 N.Y.S.2d 594

Referee in proceeding to determine value of 2 closely-held corporations under CLS Bus Corp § 1118 properly set interest rates and extended terms of corporations' payment to minority shareholders over 8-year period where his determinations were approved by Supreme Court; rate of interest and terms and conditions of purchase of minority shareholder's shares are discretionary matters for court to determine. Re Seagroatt Floral Co. (1990, 3d Dept) 167 A.D.2d 586, 563 N.Y.S.2d 539, app gr 77 N.Y.2d 805, 568 N.Y.S.2d 913, 571 N.E.2d 83 and mod on other grounds, remanded 78 N.Y.2d 439, 576 N.Y.S.2d 831, 583 N.E.2d 287

Under CLS Bus Corp § 1118, award of interest, and its rate, are discretionary with court, and such award should be refused if petitioner has acted in bad faith. Schneiderman v Luv-A-Cup Coffee Serv. (1994, 1st Dept) 204 A.D.2d 173, 614 N.Y.S.2d 112

Interest should have been awarded from approximate date used by parties for purpose of evaluating property. F.P.D. Realty Corp. v Tru-Way Private Taxi Corp. (1999, 1st Dept) 267 A.D.2d 111, 700 N.Y.S.2d 146

In proceeding to determine fair value of plaintiff's share of stock in closely held corporation for purchase by defendant in lieu of dissolution, inconclusive evidence that plaintiff acted in bad faith by allegedly engaging in competition with corporation while he was still

employed by it, and by causing inordinate delays in proceedings, did not warrant denying him 9 percent interest from date his petition for dissolution was filed. Hall v King (1998, Sup) 177 Misc. 2d 126, 675 N.Y.S.2d 810

15. Posting of bond

In a proceeding for a judicial dissolution of two close corporations in which respondent had pending a notice to purchase the petitioner's shares at their fair market value, the trial court erred in granting the dissolution following respondent's failure to post security for petitioner's shares, since her failure to do so would not serve as a predicate for frustrating her right under § 1118 to purchase petitioner's shares nor would it serve, as a basis for vacating the stay since petitioner's stock remained in her possession and control and respondent's failure to post the undertaking is not a basis for dissolution under the Business Corporation Law. Delinko v Sunshine Temporary Office Personnel (1981, 1st Dept) 85 A.D.2d 561, 445 N.Y.S.2d 706

In action for judicial dissolution of 2 close corporations, respondent's failure to obtain effective control of corporations by posting security to gain such control under court order may not serve as basis for frustrating respondent's rights under Business Corporation Law § 1118 to purchase petitioner's shares. Delinko v Sunshine Temporary Office Personnel (1981) 85 A.D.2d 561, 445 N.Y.S.2d 706

Where court dismissed proceeding to dissolve corporation commenced by petitioner who was 1/3-owner of corporation, based on 20 1/2 percent shareholder's election to purchase petitioner's shares, it was error for court to deny petitioner's application for undertaking to secure value of his interest in corporation pending outcome of valuation hearing. In re Dissolution of Elliot Kastle, Inc. (1996, 1st Dept) 234 A.D.2d 181, 651 N.Y.S.2d 485

ARTICLE 12
RECEIVERSHIP

History: Add, L 1961, ch 855, eff Sept 1, 1963.

Schedule of sections, amd, L 1962, ch 317, § 8, eff Sept 1, 1963.

§ 1201. Action by judgment creditor for sequestration

Where final judgment for a sum of money has been rendered against a corporation, and an execution issued thereupon to the sheriff of the county where the corporation does its general business, or where its office is located, has been returned wholly or partly unsatisfied, the judgment creditor may maintain an action to procure a judgment sequestrating the property of the corporation and providing for a distribution thereof.

History: Add, L 1961, ch 855, eff Sept 1, 1963.

CASE ANNOTATIONS

Shareholders, officers, and trustees were proper parties to a judgment creditor's sequestration action, if personal liability was asserted against them. Re Murray Hill Bank (1897) 153 N.Y. 199, 47 N.E. 298; Bagley & Sewall Co. v Lennig (1901) 61 A.D. 26, 70 N.Y.S. 242; Beals v Buffalo Expanded Metal Const. Co. (1900) 49 A.D. 589, 63 N.Y.S. 635

An assignee of a judgment against the corporation could maintain a sequestration action under § 70 of former Gen. Corp. L. if the assignment was full and complete and execution had been issued and returned unsatisfied before he commenced suit, but he was not entitled to proceed under the statutes unless his right to do so had fully accrued at time of instituting the action. Wappler v Woodbury Co. (1927) 246 N.Y. 152, 158 N.E. 56

Proof of insolvency was not essential to the maintenance of a sequestration action under § 70 of former Gen. Corp. L.; return of execution nulla bona brought the situation within the statute. But the remedy by issuance and return of execution unsatisfied must have been availed of in order to lay the necessary foundation. Buttles v Smith (1939) 281 N.Y. 226, 22 N.E.2d 350; Rodbourn v Utica, I. & E. R. Co. (1882, NY) 28 Hun 369; National Broadway Bank v Wessell Metal Co. (1891) 59 Hun 470, 13 N.Y.S. 744

This [former] section is practically identical with § 70 of former Gen. Corp. L., from which it was derived. A judgment creditor's action under § 70 was purely statutory, but equitable in nature. Proctor v Sidney Sash, Blind & Furniture Co. (1896) 8 A.D. 42, 40 N.Y.S. 454; Easton Nat. Bank v Buffalo Chemical Works (1888) 48 Hun 557, 1 N.Y.S. 250

The sequestration action would lie not only against the corporation, but likewise against those in possession of its assets, and parties necessary to determine controversies could be brought into the proceedings after their commencement. Proctor v Sidney Sash, Blind & Furniture Co. (1896) 8 A.D. 42, 40 N.Y.S. 454; Taylor v Ellsworth Bldg. Corp. (1920, Sup) 183 N.Y.S. 394, affd 198 A.D. 1022, 190 N.Y.S. 954; Woodard v Holland Medicine Co. (1891, Super Ct) 15 N.Y.S. 128

The complaint could likewise seek to set aside illegally preferential transfers to other creditors or to officers or shareholders, if the proper showing of knowledge and intent to prefer could be made. Abrams v Manhattan Consumers' Brewing Co. (1911) 142 A.D. 392, 126 N.Y.S. 844

Section 70 of former Gen. Corp. L. was inapplicable to foreign corporations, but a court of equity, as such, had power to sequester and protect the property of a foreign corporation for equitable distribution among its creditors. Horton v Thomas McNally Co. (1913) 155 A.D. 322, 140 N.Y.S. 357; Dreyfus v Charles Seale & Co. (1899) 37 A.D. 351, 55 N.Y.S. 1111; Wilkinson v North River Constr. Co. (1884) 66 How Pr 423

In the absence of objection by the corporation on the score that it was not subject to the statutory type of sequestration and receivership, such objection could be deemed waived by consent of the parties, and a third party who consented could not thereafter raise the objection. Horton v Thomas McNally Co. (1913) 155 A.D. 322, 140 N.Y.S. 357

Fraudulent transfers and conveyances by the corporation could be set aside in a sequestration action, if the transferees were made defendants, in order to reach the property sought to be sequestered, provided the complaint contained the necessary allegations to establish that the conveyance was made in fraud of creditors, but other creditors were entitled to share in the distribution of assets so recovered. Dagood Holding Corp. v Rosenbluth (1931) 231 A.D. 470, 247 N.Y.S. 489; Home Bank v J. B. Brewster & Co. (1897) 15 A.D. 338, 44 N.Y.S. 54, later app 33 A.D. 330, 53 N.Y.S. 867, app dismd 159 N.Y. 526, 53 N.E. 1126

A sequestration action by a judgment creditor was regarded as on to recover upon a liability created by statute and hence within subd. 2 of § 48 of former Civil Practice Act for purposes of limitations upon time to sue. Luke v Polstein (1944) 268 A.D. 921, 51 N.Y.S.2d 427, affd 294 N.Y. 896, 63 N.E.2d 27

Such an action was not one to dissolve the corporation and did not have that result or effect. People v Troy Steel & Iron Co. (1894) 82 Hun 303, 31 N.Y.S. 337

§ 1202. Appointment of receiver of property of a domestic or foreign corporation

(a) A receiver of the property of a corporation can be appointed only by the court, and in one of the following cases:

(1) An action or special proceeding brought under article 10 (Non-judicial dissolution) or 11 (Judicial dissolution).

(2) An action under section 1201 (Action by judgment creditor for sequestration).

(3) An action brought by the attorney-general or by a shareholder to preserve the assets of a corporation, which has no officer within this state qualified to administer them.

(4) An action to preserve the assets in this state, of any kind, tangible or intangible, of a foreign corporation which has been dissolved, nationalized or its authority or existence otherwise terminated or cancelled in the jurisdiction of its incorporation or which has ceased to do business, brought by any creditor or shareholder of such corporation or by one on whose behalf an order of attachment against the property of such corporation has been issued.

(b) A receiver shall be subject to the control of the court at all times and may be removed by the court at any time.

(c) All actions or special proceedings brought by or against a receiver shall have a preference upon the calendars of all courts next in order to actions or special proceedings brought by the people of the state of New York.

History: Add, L 1961, ch 855, eff Sept 1, 1963; amd, L 1962, ch 317, §§ 9, 10; L 1962, ch 834, § 86, eff Sept 1, 1963.

CASE ANNOTATIONS

1. **In general**
2. **Dissolution proceedings**
3. **Action by judgment creditor**
4. **Other proceedings**
5. **Action against foreign corporation, generally**
6. **Availability of remedy against foreign corporation**
7. **Nationalization**
8. **Authority of receiver as to foreign corporation**
9. **Jurisdiction and parties**
10. **Miscellaneous procedural matters**

1. In general

Receivership is creature of court, subject to control of court at all times, and functions in place of and as instrumentality of court itself; as special officer of court, with fiduciary responsibilities, receiver acts solely on court's behalf and is otherwise stranger to parties and their dispute. Re Kane (1990) 75 N.Y.2d 511, 554 N.Y.S.2d 457, 553 N.E.2d 1005

Provisional remedy of receivership may be invoked only if moving party has made clear evidentiary showing of necessity of conserving property and protecting that party's interests. Kristensen v Charleston Square, Inc. (2000, 2d Dept) 273 A.D.2d 312, 709 N.Y.S.2d 853

Attachment and receivership are not independent but auxiliary in character, and are designed to adjudge not finally substantive rights but to secure such judgment as may be rendered. Zittman v McGrath (1951) 341 US 446, 95 L Ed 1096, 71 S Ct 832 (not followed American

Business Corporation Law

International Group, Inc. v Islamic Republic of Iran, 211 App DC 468, 657 F.2d 430)

Receiver who is party to suit represents all stockholders who might be entitled to participate in fund, and so their absence is immaterial. United States v Belmont (1941, DC NY) 41 F. Supp. 943

Purpose of § 977-b of former New York Civil Practice Act (now § 1202(a)(4)) was to administer the New York assets of foreign corporation and to prescribe method of distribution irrespective of scheme of distribution in any other state, inclusive of domicile of foreign corporation. Markham v Taylor (1947, DC NY) 70 F. Supp. 202, app dismd (CA2 NY) 163 F.2d 940 and affd (CA2 NY) 169 F.2d 324, affd 337 US 472, 93 L Ed 1480, 69 S Ct 1333, reh den 338 US 841, 94 L Ed 514, 70 S Ct 33 and reh den 342 US 907, 96 L Ed 679, 72 S Ct 289

2. Dissolution proceedings

In dissolution proceedings, as distinguished from a judgment creditor's sequestration action, appointment of a receiver may or may not be appropriate, depending upon the fact situation, as liquidation and winding up of the affairs of the corporation to effectuate dissolution are usually left in the hands of its officers and directors in the absence of evident insolvency or some other cogent reason for placing an officer of the court in control.Ehret v George Ringler & Co. (1911) 144 A.D. 480, 129 N.Y.S. 551, app dismd 204 N.Y. 638, 98 N.E. 1102

Upon dissolution of corporate auto dealership owned in equal shares by 2 brothers, court properly exercised its discretion in appointing, as general manager and temporary receiver, brother who had run dealership almost exclusively for past several years and who had managerial control pursuant to dealership agreement with auto supplier, where such brother was ordered to post $500,000 bond, was restrained from selling corporate property, and would be accountable to referee for any money taken from corporation for personal use, thus sufficiently protecting other brother's interest in corporation. Greer v Greer (1986, 2d Dept) 124 A.D.2d 707, 508 N.Y.S.2d 217

In hybrid proceedings and actions seeking judicial dissolution of corporations pursuant to CLS Bus Corp Art 11 and seeking to preserve assets of corporations pursuant to CLS Bus Corp §§ 626 and 1202(a)(3), Supreme Court erred in appointing permanent receiver and ordering defendant to make accounting to each corporation since litigation was at early stage; papers submitted by plaintiff-petitioner were sufficient only to support appointment of temporary receiver to preserve assets and carry out business of each corporation. Imbriale v Imbriale (1988, 2d Dept) 144 A.D.2d 557, 534 N.Y.S.2d 418

Petitioners were not entitled to appointment of receiver to operate 2 corporations during pendency of proceedings to dissolve those corporations where value of real estate owned by corporations provided sufficient security to protect petitioners' interests; if future accounting revealed that majority shareholders had improperly taken fees and interest for loans made by them to corporations or had filed fraudulent tax records on behalf of corporations, setoff could be made against their remaining interest in corporate assets. Kristensen v Charleston Square, Inc. (2000, 2d Dept) 273 A.D.2d 312, 709 N.Y.S.2d 853

Where state brought action to dissolve corporation which accepted fees under false pretenses that it could use its influence to help an applicant gain admission to a professional school, had refused to make promised refunds, and its checks had been returned as insufficient funds, a temporary receiver was appointed to preserve the assets of the corporation pendente lite.State v Remedial Education, Inc. (1972) 70 Misc. 2d 1068, 335 N.Y.S.2d 353

3. Action by judgment creditor

Authorization by statute for the appointment of a receiver in connection with a sequestration action by a judgment creditor of a corporation under § 70 of former Gen. Corp. L. was necessary, as such a creditor had no right to demand appointment of a receiver for a domestic corporation in ordinary proceedings in aid of execution. Boucker Contracting Co. v W. H. Callahan Contracting Co. (1916) 218 N.Y. 321, 113 N.E. 257

If the judgment creditor was a foreign corporation not doing business in the state, a receiver could be appointed in ordinary supplementary proceedings in aid of execution for such of its property or assets as could be found within the state. Davis v Pneumatic Cushion Mfg. Corp. (1933) 146 Misc 578, 261 N.Y.S. 684

4. Other proceedings

In other types of litigation involving corporations and corporate affairs, the court ordinarily lacks power to appoint a receiver, either pendente lite or by final judgment.Schindler v George Ringler & Co. (1923) 206 A.D. 217, 200 N.Y.S. 692; Soloway v Junius Coal & Wood

Co. (1919) 186 A.D. 879, 175 N.Y.S. 1; Garifled v Lowy (1957, CA2 NY) 245 F.2d 132

In stockholder's derivative action, finding by referee that president of corporation had misappropriated approximately $19,000 belonging to corporation warranted the exercise of Supreme Court power to appoint a receiver during pendency of litigation. Sandfield v Goldstein (1968, 3d Dept) 29 A.D.2d 999, 289 N.Y.S.2d 733

Trial court erroneously dismissed shareholders' derivative action alleging misappropriation of corporate assets and seeking appointment of receiver since (1) even if plaintiffs erroneously joined their individual claims with those of corporation, dismissal was not required because they did not confuse individual and derivative claims within causes of action, (2) plaintiffs had clear legal right to bring derivative action, and thus it was immaterial that they may have sought to benefit themselves by bringing action, and (3) prayer for relief is not part of cause of action, and thus fact that plaintiffs mistakenly demanded appointment of receiver did not warrant dismissal. Baliotti v Walkes (1987, 2d Dept) 134 A.D.2d 554, 521 N.Y.S.2d 453

Appointment of temporary receiver of realty corporation was warranted where Attorney General had brought special proceeding under CLS Exec § 63 alleging that corporation's sole shareholder had repeatedly violated rent stabilization laws, Attorney General was then forced to bring second proceeding to enforce court order and to punish shareholder for contempt of court, court-appointed referee recommended appointment of guardian ad litem for shareholder on grounds that she was incapable of representing herself, and tenants in corporation's buildings brought third proceeding under CLS RPAPL Art 7-A in which they alleged serious lack of services; however, because hearing before referee and hearing on Art 7-A proceeding had not been completed, receiver should not be made permanent and should not be authorized to sell or mortgage properties in question. Abrams v Chatsworth Realty Corp. (1988, 1st Dept) 143 A.D.2d 596, 533 N.Y.S.2d 279, app dismd without op 73 N.Y.2d 995, 540 N.Y.S.2d 1006, 538 N.E.2d 358

Court did not abuse its discretion in appointing receiver and granting preliminary injunction enjoining defendant corporation from transferring assets where plaintiff showed likelihood of waste and fraudulent transfer of assets by defendant. Nesis v Paris Int'l Lighting, Inc. (1992, 1st Dept) 184 A.D.2d 485, 587 N.Y.S.2d 152

Receiver would be appointed for corporation in action which was essentially fight between 2 factions for control of corporation where (1) there were issues that could not yet be resolved as to whether stockholders' agreement remained in effect, whether any party had breached fiduciary duty to corporation, and whether one party usurped corporate opportunity, and (2) actions of various antagonists threatened wellbeing and continued viability of corporation. Modern Telecommunications, Inc. v Dalessandro (1992, 1st Dept) 185 A.D.2d 218, 587 N.Y.S.2d 315, reh den, in part, reh gr, in part, stay den (App Div, 1st Dept) 588 N.Y.S.2d 765

Appointment of temporary receiver for corporation was provident exercise of court's discretion in light of compelling evidence of struggle within corporation, threatening its continued viability. Rosan v Vassell (1999, 1st Dept) 257 A.D.2d 436, 683 N.Y.S.2d 516

In action for accounting, return of allegedly stolen documents, injunction prohibiting defendants from using stolen records in furtherance of their business, and punitive damages for alleged breach of fiduciary duty, plaintiff was not entitled to extraordinary remedy of appointment of receiver to collect proceeds of defendants' business where complaint did not seek appointment of receiver, and no party ever requested such relief. Rotary Watches (USA), Inc. v Greene (1999, 2d Dept) 266 A.D.2d 527, 699 N.Y.S.2d 106

While one claimant, seeking to recover the amount of a security deposit on lease, alleged that a trust should be imposed and rents collected by receiver in foreclosure action to the extent of its claim, such argument overlooked the fact that claimant did not establish that the receiver stood in the position of a trustee with respect to the claimant and the further fact that no evidence was offered nor did the account indicate that the receiver took possession of anything other than rent payments. Allison v Roslyn Plaza, Ltd. (1976) 86 Misc. 2d 849, 385 N.Y.S.2d 454

In an action which a corporation's director filed against the corporation, alleging breach of contract, breach of fiduciary duty, and breach of a shareholders' agreement, the trial court erred by granting the director's application to appoint a temporary receiver to oversee the corporation's business while litigation was pending, because none of the circumstances permitting appointment of a temporary receiver, pursuant to N.Y. Bus. Corp. Law § 1202(a), were present in the case. Hoffman v Eagle Box Co. (2003, A.D., 2d Dept) 759 N.Y.S.2d 387

In case of suit by appropriate government official against two rival claimants to same fund, there can be final judgment only when there is decision as to existence and ownership of property in dispute. Clark v Taylor (1947, CA2 NY) 163 F.2d 940

5. Action against foreign corporation, generally

This section (former CPA § 977-b) is not in contravention with the provisions of the United States Constitution. Oliner v American-Oriental Banking Corp. (1939) 258 A.D. 752, 15 N.Y.S.2d 428, affd 282 N.Y. 748, 27 N.E.2d 40. See United States v New York Trust Co. (1466, DC NY) 75 F. Supp. 583

It is policy of New York State to surrender assets of liquidated foreign corporation to statutory receiver appointed in State in which it was created, where there is reasonable assurance that rotable distribution of net assets will be made to all creditors.State Bank of Pearl River v Hudson Engineering & Tool Co. (1952) 280 A.D. 805, 113 N.Y.S.2d 345

This section (former CPA § 977-b) does not apply to corporations presently in liquidation by the Superintendent of Insurance under the provisions of the Insurance Law. Mejulis v First Russian Ins. Co. (1936) 161 Misc 715, 292 N.Y.S. 753, affd 249 A.D. 811, 293 N.Y.S. 621

The constitutionality of this section (former CPA § 977-b) is beyond dispute.Stephen v Zivnostenska Banka (1960) 23 Misc. 2d 855, 199 N.Y.S.2d 797, affd (1st Dept) 15 A.D.2d 111, 222 N.Y.S.2d 128, affd 12 N.Y.2d 781, 235 N.Y.S.2d 1, 186 N.E.2d 676

6. Availability of remedy against foreign corporation

The acceptance and retention by claimants of dividends paid to them by the liquidator of a banking corporation without filing any claim with him or solicitation on their part, does not constitute a waiver of their right to pursue their remedy under this section. Oliner v American-Oriental Banking Corp. (1939) 258 A.D. 752, 15 N.Y.S.2d 428, affd 282 N.Y. 748, 27 N.E.2d 40

Where no application for domestic receiver has been made pursuant to (former) CPA § 977-b and such statute is not invoked, such statute will not be considered.State Bank of River v Hudson Engineering & Tool Co. (1952) 280 A.D. 805, 113 N.Y.S.2d 345

The court "must appoint" a temporary receiver of local assets of a foreign corporation on an affidavit of the necessary facts in an action under (former) CPA § 977-b to protect local creditors and such ex parte order will not be vacated merely on the corporation's offer to post a bond. Patton v Compania Aerea Viajes Expresos De Venezuela (1958) 9 Misc. 2d 333, 169 N.Y.S.2d 981

Where Czechoslovakia corporation ostensibly owns property in this State, purchased with funds on deposit in New York bank, stockholder, seeking to pursue diversion of its funds which he alleges made his stock worthless, has right to avail himself of all remedies open to stockholders of corporations under (former) CPA § 977-b. Augstein v Banska A Hutni Akciova Spolecnost (1953, Sup) 124 N.Y.S.2d 446, mod 282 A.D. 929, 125 N.Y.S.2d 647

Though assets of Czechoslovakia corporations have been "nationalized," courts of New York deny any validity to effect such nationalization as to assets within state of New York, and court has jurisdiction of action by stockholder, seeking to pursue diversion of its funds which made his stock ownership worthless. Augstein v Banska A Hutni Akciova Spolecnost (1953, Sup) 124 N.Y.S.2d 446, mod on other grounds 282 A.D. 929, 125 N.Y.S.2d 647

7. Nationalization

A proceeding, instituted pursuant to this section (former CPA § 977-b), is in rem for the purpose of distribution of assets of a foreign corporation which has been nationalized and may not be vitiated because of the status of the United States as a claimant to the assets. A motion by the United States to vacate the appointment of a permanent receiver is denied. Meyer v Petrograd Metal Works (1939) 256 A.D. 1077, 11 N.Y.S.2d 125

Stockholder and creditor of foreign corporation must show that defendant corporation has been nationalized or has ceased to do business or has been liquidated or that its charter has been suspended, repealed, annulled or revoked, to prevail under (former) CPA § 977-b. Rothschild v Naamlooze Vennootschap Gebroeders Pappenhiem's Tabakshandel (1949) 194 Misc 889, 88 N.Y.S.2d 157

In proceeding by creditors of Czechoslovakian bank to throw its assets into permanent receivership upon premise that bank has been nationalized, where it was asserted that bank had been ordered to end its activities and cease to exist and where it was claimed that bank might pay its creditors, trial was ordered under subd 9 of

(former) CPA § 977-b, to determine whether bank could meet its obligations.Stephen v Zivnostenska Banka, Nat. Corp. (1955) 31 Misc. 2d 45, 140 N.Y.S.2d 323, affd 286 A.D. 999, 145 N.Y.S.2d 310

Nationalization decrees of foreign government are repugnant to the public policy of New York and are not given extra-territorial effect over assets which have their situs in New York.Stephen v Zivnostenska Banka (1960) 23 Misc. 2d 855, 199 N.Y.S.2d 797, affd (1st Dept) 15 A.D.2d 111, 222 N.Y.S.2d 128, affd 12 N.Y.2d 781, 235 N.Y.S.2d 1, 186 N.E.2d 676

Ex parte order appointing temporary receiver was vacated where plaintiff failed to establish that defendant corporation had been nationalized or had gone out of business. Compania Anonima Inversiones Venam v Punta Alegre Sugar Corp. (1960) 26 Misc. 2d 520, 208 N.Y.S.2d 361

Foreign nationalization decree will not be recognized as sufficient to defeat receiver's right to turnover order.Schwartz v Compania Azucarera Vertientes-Camaguey De Cuba (1960) 28 Misc. 2d 355, 208 N.Y.S.2d 833

It is contrary to the public policy of this state to enforce confiscatory decrees of Russia with respect to property located here at the date of the decree. United States v Belmont (1936, CA2 NY) 85 F.2d 542, revd on other grounds 301 US 324, 81 L Ed 1134, 57 S Ct 758

8. Authority of receiver as to foreign corporation

Where a Delaware statutory receiver, appointed in proceeding to dissolve corporation by Delaware court, under Delaware statutes vesting him with title to chose in action formerly belonging to corporation, permanent receiver of New York assets of such corporation, appointed in action brought for that purpose in New York under this section, has no legal capacity to sue for accounting against majority stockholder, alleging waste of corporate assets. Hirson v United Stores Corp. (1942) 263 A.D. 646, 34 N.Y.S.2d 122, affd 289 N.Y. 564, 43 N.E.2d 712

Suspension of right of nonresident alien enemy to prosecute actions in New York courts by existing war held not to apply to action brought by resident New York receiver of New York assets of Austrian corporation, since such receiver is accountable to court and can make no distribution of any recovery except upon order of court. Propper v Buck (1942) 178 Misc 76, 33 N.Y.S.2d 11, affd 263 A.D. 948, 34 N.Y.S.2d 134

Court has duty of recognizing any suggestion of immunity made by executive branch of government but where contravening ownership is shown the suggested immunity will be confined to property which, in fact, belongs to the foreign nation; motion to modify restraining provisions denied with leave to foreign government to present proofs of ownership as to contested assets to referee.Stephen v Zivnostenska Banka (1960) 23 Misc. 2d 855, 199 N.Y.S.2d 797, affd (1st Dept) 15 A.D.2d 111, 222 N.Y.S.2d 128, affd 12 N.Y.2d 781, 235 N.Y.S.2d 1, 186 N.E.2d 676

Temporary receiver under (former) CPA § 977-b is not vested with title by virtue of his appointment. Propper v Clark (1949) 337 US 472, 93 L Ed 1480, 69 S Ct 1333, reh den 338 US 841, 94 L Ed 514, 70 S Ct 33 and reh den 342 US 907, 96 L Ed 679, 72 S Ct 289

State law determines effect of appointment of receiver on title to property administered, but federal law determines whether event of appointment can free property from prior control of United States under freezing order issued under authority of Trading with Enemy Act. Propper v Clark (1949) 337 US 472, 93 L Ed 1480, 69 S Ct 1333, reh den 338 US 841, 94 L Ed 514, 70 S Ct 33 and reh den 342 US 907, 96 L Ed 679, 72 S Ct 289

Temporary receiver of New York assets of foreign society did not have such title as to defeat later freezing order of Executive prohibiting transfer of enemy funds and still later seizure by Alien Property Custodian. Clark v Propper (1948, CA2 NY) 169 F.2d 324, affd 337 US 472, 93 L Ed 1480, 69 S Ct 1333, reh den 338 US 841, 94 L Ed 514, 70 S Ct 33 and reh den 342 US 907, 96 L Ed 679, 72 S Ct 289

Existence of receiver or liquidator in foreign country does not preclude suit in this country by New York receiver. Bernstein v N. V. Nederlandsche-Amerikaansche Stoomvaart-Maatschappij (1949, CA2 NY) 173 F.2d 71, mandate amd (CA2) 210 F.2d 375 (disapproved on other grounds First Nat. City Bank v Banco Nacional de Cuba, 406 US 759, 32 L Ed 2d 466, 92 S Ct 1808, reh den 409 US 897, 34 L Ed 2d 155, 93 S Ct 92 and on remand (CA2 NY) 478 F.2d 191) as stated in Banco Nacional de Cuba v Chase Manhattan Bank (CA2 NY) 658 F.2d 875, 32 FR Serv 2d 79

Alien enemy's transfer of title to assets, without federal license, was void, and temporary receiver appointed pursuant to (former) CPA § 977-b can obtain no title to such assets. Bernstein v N. V.

Nederlandsche-Amerikaansche Stoomvaart-Maatschappij (1948, DC NY) 76 F. Supp. 335, reh den (DC NY) 79 F. Supp. 38, affd in part and mod in part (CA2 NY) 173 F.2d 71, amd (CA2) 210 F.2d 375 (disapproved on other grounds First Nat. City Bank v Banco Nacional de Cuba, 406 US 759, 32 L Ed 2d 466, 92 S Ct 1808, reh den 409 US 897, 34 L Ed 2d 155, 93 S Ct 92 and on remand (CA2 NY) 478 F.2d 191) as stated in Banco Nacional de Cuba v Chase Manhattan Bank (CA2 NY) 658 F.2d 875, 32 FR Serv 2d 79

Where Soviet government assigned its claims against New York bank, in which nationalized Russian bank had account, to United States, latter had claim superior to those of receiver of Russian bank appointed under (former) CPA § 977-b. United States v National City Bank (1950, DC NY) 90 F. Supp. 448

It is not essential to validity of appointment of temporary receiver that receiver ultimately appointed have requisite federal authority to distribute property. Bernstein v N. V. Nederlansche-Amerikaansche Stoomvaart-Maatschappij (1953, DC NY) 117 F. Supp. 898

9. Jurisdiction and parties

Dissolved foreign corporation is not indispensable party to judgment in stockholders' derivative action against directors for breach of fiduciary duties, where receiver was appointed to distribute payments on judgment. Weinert v Kinkel (1947) 296 N.Y. 151, 71 N.E.2d 445

Subdivision 19 of (former) CPA § 977-b, limiting extraterritorial effect of dissolution of foreign corporation as to property or choses in action within New York was not intended to include those acts of a foreign state to which the constitutional requirement of full faith and credit is applicable. Hirson v United Stores Corp. (1942) 263 A.D. 646, 34 N.Y.S.2d 122, affd 289 N.Y. 564, 43 N.E.2d 712

Persons who appeared specially in action to appoint permanent receiver of New York assets of foreign corporation were not parties to such action, and so not entitled to object to such appointment. Cohen v Tobacco Products Corp. (1942) 264 A.D. 703, 34 N.Y.S.2d 130

The plaintiff, an assignee of a judgment creditor's claim and judgment obtained in a court in France against the defendant, a dissolved Russian corporation, is, prima facie, a creditor of the defendant by virtue of the assignment to plaintiff of the debt owed to the assignor by the defendant, under the allegations of the complaint in this action under this section (former CPA § 977-b) for the appointment of a receiver of assets in this State of the defendant.Smith v Russo Asiatic Bank (1936) 160 Misc 417, 290 N.Y.S. 471

In action by plaintiff as stockholder and creditor of foreign corporation for appointment of receiver of its assets, court may enjoin such corporation from prosecuting subsequent proceeding before foreign tribunal to determine if plaintiff is such stockholder or creditor. Rothschild v Naamlooze Vennootschap Gebroeders Pappenheim's Tabakshandel (1949) 194 Misc 479, 87 N.Y.S.2d 189

Where verified complaint alleges that defendants are foreign corporations and have or may have assets within state of New York and have been nationalized by decree of Roumanian government, New York court has jurisdiction to appoint temporary receiver and court's order is not void for lack of jurisdiction. Talmon v Societatea Romana Pentru Industria De Bumbac (1954) 206 Misc 449, 132 N.Y.S.2d 776

New York court has jurisdiction to appoint temporary receiver of foreign corporation having assets within state of New York, upon showing by summons and verified complaint that action authorized by (former) CPA § 977-b is brought by one prima facie having status of creditor or stockholder. Talmon v Societatea Romana Pentru Industria De Bumbac (1954) 206 Misc 449, 132 N.Y.S.2d 776

Where the requisite jurisdictional facts for appointment of a receiver have been set forth by plaintiff, all issues as to such facts must be determined at trial, and not by affidavits. Manalich v Compania Cubana De Aviacion (1960) 28 Misc. 2d 136, 209 N.Y.S.2d 225

Stockholders of Russian corporation nationalized by decree of Soviet government are not indispensable parties to action by United States as assignee to recover funds of said corporation against receiver who represents stockholders. United States v Pink (1942) 315 US 203, 86 L Ed 796, 62 S Ct 552

10. Miscellaneous procedural matters

Where there are conflicting claims to personalty held by temporary receiver in action pursuant to (former) CPA § 977-b, title should be determined only after plenary trial and not upon petition. Manalich v Compania Cubana De Aviacion, S. A. (1960, 2d Dept) 12 A.D.2d 486, 206 N.Y.S.2d 746

In an action by stockholder pursuant to this section even though the word "must" is used therein, the court is not deprived of all discretion to examine the papers submitted, or to require proof of the

facts upon which the stated conclusions are based.Schwartz v Compania Azucarera Vertientes-Camaguey De Cuba (1960, 2d Dept) 12 A.D.2d 506, 207 N.Y.S.2d 288

Where action is brought to recover money by New York receiver of New York assets of Austrian corporation and defendant's examination before trial was in progress and bill of particulars had not been complied with when United States became belligerent, there was no satisfactory showing that present stay was necessary to protect defendant's rights. Propper v Buck (1942) 178 Misc 76, 33 N.Y.S.2d 11, affd 263 A.D. 948, 34 N.Y.S.2d 134

If the corporation is still doing business, it may serve an answer and obtain a preference for trial and corporation's assertion that it is still doing business merely presents an issue for trial. Patton v Compania Aerea Viajes Expresos De Venezuela (1958) 9 Misc. 2d 333, 169 N.Y.S.2d 981

In an action under (former) CPA § 977-b, the names and amounts of all creditors must be ascertained, since the action being in the nature of a class action, the rights of all creditors as well as those of the plaintiff should be protected. Patton v Compania Aerea Viajes Expresos De Venezuela (1958) 9 Misc. 2d 333, 169 N.Y.S.2d 981

A defendant, in action to appoint receiver to liquidate local assets of foreign corporation, by filing an answer promptly may obtain an early trial of the issues, and is entitled to a preference for a day certain. Manalich v Compania Cubana De Aviacion (1960) 28 Misc. 2d 136, 209 N.Y.S.2d 225

Publication of the summons in the English language in a foreign language newspaper was held to satisfy the statutory requirement. Hershbaum v Compania Petrolera Trans-Cuba, S. A. (1961, Sup) 215 N.Y.S.2d 898

Stockholder's action for appointment of receiver for foreign corporation pursuant to this section (former CPA § 977-b) was barred where a receiver had already been appointed in an earlier action brought by another stockholder and continued to functon. Hershbaum v Compania Petrolera Trans-Cuba S. A. (1961, Sup) 215 N.Y.S.2d 898

Despite the valuable services rendered by a receiver, because the receiver was appointed pursuant to N.Y. Bus. Corp. Law § 1202(a)(1), the receiver's commission was governed by the provisions of Business Corporation Law § 1217, which did not include a commission for based upon the value of the services rendered. Jakubowicz v A.C. Green Elec. Contrs., Inc. (2005, A.D., 1st Dept) 803 N.Y.S.2d 71

Right of New York receiver of German corporation to intervene in action by stockholder of such corporation, wherein complaint alleged its dissolution in 1939, was not outlawed, since governing statute was tolled by (former) CPA §§ 13 and 977-b subd. 18. Bernstein v N. V. Nederlandsche-Amerikaansche Stoomvaart-Maatschappij (1949, CA2 NY) 173 F.2d 71, mandate amd (CA2) 210 F.2d 375 (disapproved on other grounds First Nat. City Bank v Banco Nacional de Cuba, 406 US 759, 32 L Ed 2d 466, 92 S Ct 1808, reh den 409 US 897, 34 L Ed 2d 155, 93 S Ct 92 and on remand (CA2 NY) 478 F.2d 191) as stated in Banco Nacional de Cuba v Chase Manhattan Bank (CA2 NY) 658 F.2d 875, 32 FR Serv 2d 79

§ 1203. Temporary and permanent receiver

(a) At any stage before final judgment or final order in an action or special proceeding brought under this article, the court may appoint one or more receivers of the property of the corporation or of the property in this state of a foreign corporation against which an action has been brought under subparagraph (a) (4) of section 1202 (Appointment of receiver of property of a domestic or foreign corporation). Notice of an application for the appointment of a receiver shall be given to the attorney-general and to such other persons and in such manner as the court directs. The determination by the court of the necessity or advisability of appointing a receiver or an attorney for a receiver, and the allowance of expenses, commissions or compensation to the receiver or his attorney, shall be subject to review on appeal. This provision shall not affect any other right to review on appeal.

(b) A receiver appointed by or under a final judgment or order in an action or special proceeding, or a temporary receiver who is continued by the final judgment or order, is a permanent receiver. The court may confer upon a temporary receiver the powers, and subject him to the duties of a permanent receiver, or so much thereof as it deems proper.

History: Add, L 1961, ch 855, eff Sept 1, 1963.

Sub (a), amd, L 1962, ch 317, § 11, eff Sept 1, 1962.

CASE ANNOTATIONS

Under § 162 of former Gen. Corp. L., a temporary receiver was merely a custodian and agent of the court with respect to such property as was confided to him, title to which remained in the corporation, and he had no general authority to bring suits for the recovery of assets or the collection of claims or enforcement of corporate rights of action. Cohen v Sherman (1952) 279 A.D. 939, 111 N.Y.S.2d 439; Garibaldi v Yonkers (1949) 198 Misc 1100, 102 N.Y.S.2d 200, affd 278 A.D. 571, 102 N.Y.S.2d 426

After appointment of temporary receiver, corporation retains title to causes of action on its behalf and may institute an action in its own name. Daro Industries, Inc. v RAS Enterprises, Inc. (1977, 1st Dept) 56 A.D.2d 776, 392 N.Y.S.2d 446, affd 44 N.Y.2d 969, 408 N.Y.S.2d 329, 380 N.E.2d 160

Temporary receiver acquires no title to property of corporation but only the right of possession as a court officer. Daro Industries, Inc. v RAS Enterprises, Inc. (1977, 1st Dept) 56 A.D.2d 776, 392 N.Y.S.2d 446, affd 44 N.Y.2d 969, 408 N.Y.S.2d 329, 380 N.E.2d 160

In hybrid proceedings and actions seeking judicial dissolution of corporations pursuant to CLS Bus Corp Art 11 and seeking to preserve assets of corporations pursuant to CLS Bus Corp §§ 626 and 1202(a)(3), Supreme Court erred in appointing permanent receiver and ordering defendant to make accounting to each corporation since litigation was at early stage; papers submitted by plaintiff-petitioner were sufficient only to support appointment of temporary receiver to preserve assets and carry out business of each corporation. Imbriale v Imbriale (1988, 2d Dept) 144 A.D.2d 557, 534 N.Y.S.2d 418

Officers and managing agents are not stripped of their power by the mere filing of a petition or the appointment of a temporary receiver, and service of process on a managing agent after such appointment is valid. Garibaldi v Yonkers (1949) 198 Misc 1100, 102 N.Y.S.2d 200, affd 278 A.D. 571, 102 N.Y.S.2d 426

Section 162 of former Gen. Corp. L. likewise authorized the appointment of one or more receivers, and under this provision it was deemed proper to appoint a distinct receiver for each of several retail stores jointly operated by a group of entities the management of which was charged with waste, mismanagement, and misappropriation of assets. Nadrich v Nagelberg (1957) 8 Misc. 2d 339, 165 N.Y.S.2d 166

Section 162 of former Gen. Corp. L. also required giving of notice to the attorney general of an application for appointment of a receiver for a corporation, and this requirement was mandatory. Leonard v Soufoul (1957) 13 Misc. 2d 659, 172 N.Y.S.2d 11

A jurisdictional objection to the appointment of a receiver could not be based upon §§ 151 and 162 of former Gen. Corp. L. where the appointment was not based on Art. 11 of that law, but to protect against a transfer of stock by the executor of the estate of a deceased shareholder who was alleged to have acquired it fraudulently. Rolnick v Rolnick (1962) 35 Misc. 2d 456, 230 N.Y.S.2d 789

For failure to give proper notice to the Attorney General pursuant to subd. (a) of this section of an action by one of three promoters of a corporation against the other two and the corporation seeking to place the corporation in receivership and to enjoin certain acts on the part of defendants, plaintiff's request for a temporary receiver must be denied. P. B. G. Realty, Inc. v Putter (1963) 41 Misc. 2d 129, 245 N.Y.S.2d 45

§ 1204. Oath and security

(a) A receiver, before entering upon his duties, shall:

(1) Take and subscribe an oath that he will faithfully, honestly and impartially discharge the trust committed to him, and the oath shall be filed with the clerk of the court in which the action or special proceeding is pending.

(2) File with the clerk of such court a bond to the people, with at least two sufficient sureties or a bond executed by any fidelity or surety company authorized by the laws of this state to transact business, in a penalty fixed by the court appointing him, conditioned for the faithful discharge of his duties as receiver. The court may at any time direct a receiver to give a new bond with new sureties and with like conditions.

History: Add, L 1961, ch 855, eff Sept 1, 1963.

Par (a), opening clause, amd, L 1963, ch 748, § 29, eff Sept 1, 1963.

CASE ANNOTATIONS

Where permanent receiver for corporation failed to file bond and did not qualify to assume his duties as receiver, he did not become vested with title to assets of the corporation. Maki v Estate of Ziehm (1977, 3d Dept) 55 A.D.2d 454, 391 N.Y.S.2d 705

Finality of dissolution of corporation was not contingent upon appointed receiver's qualifying to carry out his duties, and failure of designated receiver to file required bond was not determinative of corporate status; corporation was effectively dissolved by order. Maki v Estate of Ziehm (1977, 3d Dept) 55 A.D.2d 454, 391 N.Y.S.2d 705

§ 1205. Designation of depositories by court

All orders appointing a receiver of a corporation shall designate therein one or more places of deposit, wherein all funds of the corporation not needed for immediate disbursement shall be deposited and no other deposits and no investment of such funds shall be made, except upon the order of the court.

History: Add, L 1961, ch 855, eff Sept 1, 1963.

§ 1206. Powers of permanent receiver

(a) A permanent receiver, upon qualifying under section 1204 (Oath and security), shall be vested with title to all the property of the corporation wherever situated or of the property in this state of a foreign corporation against which an action or special proceeding has been brought under subparagraph (a)(4) of section 1202 (Appointment of receiver of property of a domestic or foreign corporation), for the benefit of the creditors and shareholders of the corporation.

(b) A permanent receiver shall have the power:

(1) To sue in his own name or otherwise for the recovery of the property, debts and causes of action of the corporation. No set-off or counterclaim shall be allowed in any such action for any demand unless it was owing by the corporation to the defendant before the commencement of the action or special proceeding in which the receiver was appointed or unless it shall have been incurred by the receiver subsequent to his appointment.

(2) To sell at public or private sale all the property vested in him, in such manner and on such terms and conditions as the court shall direct, and to make necessary transfers and conveyances thereof.

(3) To examine on oath, to be administered by him, any person concerning any matter pertaining to or affecting the receivership.

(4) To settle or compound any demands by or against the receivership.

(c) When more than one receiver is appointed, all provisions in this article in reference to one receiver shall apply to them.

(d) When more than one receiver is appointed, the debts and property of the corporation may be collected and received by any of them; when more than two receivers are appointed, the powers and rights conferred on them may be exercised by any two.

(e) When more than one receiver is appointed, the survivor or survivors of such receivers shall have all the powers and right of the receivers.

History: Add, L 1961, ch 855, eff Sept 1, 1963.

Sub (a), amd, L 1962, ch 317, § 12, eff Sept 1, 1963.

CASE ANNOTATIONS

1. In general
2. Title to property
3. Power to sue
4. Power to sell property
5. Power to examine under oath

1. In general

A receiver, as an officer of the court, was not subject to suit without court permission. Re Commercial Bank (1898) 35 A.D. 224, 54 N.Y.S. 722

Where permanent receiver failed to qualify and thus did not become vested with title to assets of corporation, he was not indispensable party to proceeding which should have been brought as derivative action. Maki v Estate of Ziehm (1977, 3d Dept) 55 A.D.2d 454, 391 N.Y.S.2d 705

2. Title to property

The receiver's title was subject to any valid conditions or legal restraints on alienation existing at time of his appointment, but not subject to judgment liens or process under judgments thereafter obtained. Atty. Gen. v Atlantic Mut. Ins. Co. (1885) 100 N.Y. 279, 3 N.E. 193; Clark v Propper (1948, CA2 NY) 169 F.2d 324, affd 337 US 472, 93 L Ed 1480, 69 S Ct 1333, reh den 338 US 841, 94 L Ed 514, 70 S Ct 33 and reh den 342 US 907, 96 L Ed 679, 72 S Ct 289

Under § 168 of former Gen. Corp. L., a receiver's title to assets, upon qualifying for office by filing oath and giving security, related back to the date of his appointment. Re Lenox Corp. (1901) 57 A.D. 515, 68 N.Y.S. 103, affd 167 N.Y. 623, 60 N.E. 1115; Re Christian Jensen Co. (1891) 128 N.Y. 550, 28 N.E. 665

The receiver's title was no better than that of the corporation as of date of his appointment and was subject to any valid prior liens or transfers. National Park Bank v Clark (1904) 92 A.D. 262, 87 N.Y.S. 185; People v United States Law-Blank & Stationary Co. (1898) 24 Misc 535, 53 N.Y.S. 852; Herring v New York, L. E. & W. R. Co. (1887) 105 N.Y. 340, 12 N.E. 763

Where permanent receiver for corporation failed to file bond and did not qualify to assume his duties as receiver, he did not become vested with title to assets of the corporation. Maki v Estate of Ziehm (1977, 3d Dept) 55 A.D.2d 454, 391 N.Y.S.2d 705

A temporary receiver, appointed as such and whose appointment is not made permanent, in the absence of special authorization by the court, does not acquire title to its assets or supplant its existing management. Garibaldi v Yonkers (1949) 198 Misc 1100, 102 N.Y.S.2d 200, affd 278 A.D. 571, 102 N.Y.S.2d 426

3. Power to sue

Receiver could move to vacate judgments obtained against the corporation or affecting its property if they were obtained collusively or other good cause existed for taking such action. Whittlesey v Delaney (1878) 73 N.Y. 571; Yorkville Bank v Henry Zeltner Brewing

Co. (1903) 80 A.D. 578, 80 N.Y.S. 839, app dismd 178 N.Y. 572, 70 N.E. 1111

Receiver could sue to set aside transfers and conveyances, or incumbrances, invalid for want of shareholder approval, or which were fraudulent as to creditors. Vail v Hamilton (1881) 85 N.Y. 453; Atty. Gen. v Guardian Mut. Life Ins. Co. (1879) 77 N.Y. 272; Hubbell v Syracuse Iron Works (1886, NY) 42 Hun 182

Receiver could enforce individual liability of officers and directors to the corporation for negligence, waste, or mismanagement, sue to collect on unpaid stock subscriptions, or proceed against shareholders for the recovery of illegal dividends paid and received. Mason v Henry (1897) 152 N.Y. 529, 46 N.E. 837; Phoenix Warehousing Co. v Badger (1876) 67 N.Y. 294; Osgood v Layten (1867) 3 Keyes 521; Kelly v Dolan (1916, CA3 Pa) 233 F 635

Receiver could sue an officer of the corporation to recover money paid to and received by him to influence election of certain directors. McClure v Law (1899) 161 N.Y. 78, 55 N.E. 388

By virtue of § 169 and other sections of former Gen. Corp. L. from this section of the Business Corp. L. was derived, the permanent receiver of a corporation could sue for the recovery of property of the corporation, to collect debts due it, or to enforce almost any cause of action running in its favor. Mills v Ross (1899) 39 A.D. 563, 57 N.Y.S. 680, affd 168 N.Y. 673, 61 N.E. 1131; Higgins v Herrmann (1897) 23 A.D. 420, 48 N.Y.S. 244

Where corporation is in receivership or insolvent, receiver of corporation can bring "alter ego" action for benefit of company's creditors which seeks to pierce corporate veil of corporation. Corcoran v Frank B. Hall & Co. (1989, 1st Dept) 149 A.D.2d 165, 545 N.Y.S.2d 278

A contract purportedly entered into by a corporation after its corporate existence had been terminated for non-payment of franchise tax could not, however, be enforced. Re Solomon (1939, Sup) 16 N.Y.S.2d 472

It was doubtful whether a receiver for the corporation had any title to a cause of action against its officers for making a preferential transfer, as such, but under some circumstances he might assert a cause of action charging conversion of the asset transferred. Hubsch v Insler (1954, Sup) 129 N.Y.S.2d 619

The authority of such a receiver to institute actions was not confined to commencement of them in New York courts. Cohen v La Vin (1954, CA2 Conn) 210 F.2d 550

4. Power to sell property

A sale by a receiver of a leasehold subject to a claim for rent does not prevent the landlord who purchased at the receiver's sale from asserting his claim for rent accruing while the receiver was in possession.Schwartz v Cahill (1917) 220 N.Y. 174, 115 N.E. 451

Section 169 of former Gen. Corp. L. conferred on receivers power to sell any and all assets to which they acquired title by virtue of their appointment, but they could give no better title than they had and hence all sales were subject to existing liens. Mayer v Burr (1909) 133 A.D. 604, 118 N.Y.S. 203; Re Coleman (1903) 174 N.Y. 373, 66 N.E. 983

Trial court erred in granting a receiver's motion to, among other things, permit a sale of mortgaged property and mandating the lender's discharge of the mortgage because the receiver's deposit of the money into the escrow account of the lender's attorney—contingent upon the occurrence of the trial court's determination of the long-pending summary judgment motions—was not tantamount to possession of the collateral by the lender, the Uniform Commercial Code did not authorize the trial court to substitute the lender's collateral, and the receiver did not have the same power as a bankruptcy trustee to dispose of real property free and clear of all liens and mortgages. Krupnick v Windy Ridge Corp., 147 A.D.3d 1247, 48 N.Y.S.3d 536 (N.Y. App. Div. 3d Dep't 2017).

5. Power to examine under oath

While § 169 of former Gen. Corp. L. authorized a receiver to examine any person under oath with respect to matters pertaining to or affecting the receivership, it did not authorize him to issue subpoenas to compel attendance of witnesses for examination. Re Klein (1930) 138 Misc 282, 245 N.Y.S. 486

§ 1207. Duties of receiver upon appointment

(a) Upon appointment and qualification, a receiver shall have the following duties:

(1) To give immediate notice of his appointment by publication once a week for two successive weeks in two newspapers of general circulation in the county where the office of the corporation is located or, in the case of a foreign corporation against which an action has been brought under subparagraph (a)(4) of section 1202 (Appointment of receiver of property of a domestic or foreign corporation), in a newspaper of general circulation as directed by the court, requiring:

(A) All persons indebted to the corporation to render an account of all debts owing by them to the corporation and to pay the same to the receiver at a specified place and by a specified day.

(B) All persons having in their possession any property of the corporation to deliver the same to the receiver at the specified place and by the specified day.

(C) All creditors and claimants, including any with unliquidated or contingent claims and any with whom the corporation has unfulfilled contracts, to present their claims to the receiver in writing and in detail at a specified place and by a specified day, which shall not be less than six months after the first publication of such notice. Whenever a receiver is appointed in dissolution proceedings under article 10 (Non-judicial dissolution) or article 11 (Judicial dissolution), section 1007 (Notice to creditors; filing or barring claims) shall apply and shall control the giving of notice to creditors and claimants and the filing and barring of claims.

(2) To call a general meeting of the creditors of the corporation within four months from the date of his appointment by a notice to be published as directed in subparagraph (a) (1), setting forth the time and place of such meeting, which time shall be not more than two months, nor less than one month after the first publication of such notice. At such meeting, or at an adjournment thereof, the receiver shall present a statement of all accounts and demands for and against the corporation, its subsisting contracts, and the money and other assets in his hands.

(3) To keep true books of account of all moneys received and expended by him as receiver, which books shall be open for inspection at reasonable times by creditors or other persons interested therein. On or before the first day of February in each year, for the preceding calendar year, and at such other times as the court shall direct, the receiver shall file with the clerk of the court by which he was appointed a verified statement showing the assets received, the disposition thereof, the money on hand, all payments made, specifying the persons to whom paid and the purpose of the payments, the amount necessary to be retained to meet necessary expenses and claims against the receiver, and the distributive share in the remainder of each person interested therein. A copy of such statement shall be served by the receiver upon the attorney-general within five days after the filing thereof.

History: Add, L 1961, ch 855, eff Sept 1, 1963; amd, L 1962, ch 317, § 13; L 1962, ch 834, § 87, eff Sept 1, 1963; L 1963, ch 748, § 30, eff Sept 1, 1963.

CASE ANNOTATIONS

The receivership provisions of former Gen Corp L included receiverships in connection with foreclosure of mortgages on corporate property as well as receiverships in connection with dissolutions and judgment creditors' sequestration suits, and it was held, under § 174 of that law, that where the mortgage covered all property and income of the corporation the foreclosure receiver could proceed to give notice to all creditors and should proceed to perform the duties of a general receiver without necessity for appointing any other receiver.State Bank of Williamson v Lamoka Power Corp. (1935) 269 N.Y. 1, 198 N.E. 609

Court erroneously found that receiver's failure to keep certain written records required under CLS CPLR § 6404 (which governs duties of temporary receivers) constituted gross mismanagement so as to justify disallowance of receiver's necessary expenses, where receiver was appointed as permanent receiver under Business Corporation Law, and receiver complied with duty under CLS Bus Corp § 1207 by keeping detailed schedule setting forth all income received, date of receipt, and source as either account receivable or sale of material on hand. Corcoran v Joseph M. Corcoran, Inc. (1987, 2d Dept) 135 A.D.2d 531, 521 N.Y.S.2d 757, later proceeding (App Div, 2d Dept) 546 N.Y.S.2d 671

Attorney's affidavit of services rendered to receiver was deficient for not detailing time expended on each of legal services rendered; receiver would be granted leave to resubmit proper and sufficient affidavit of services rendered from his counsel. Corcoran v Joseph M. Corcoran, Inc. (1987, 2d Dept) 135 A.D.2d 531, 521 N.Y.S.2d 757, later proceeding (App Div, 2d Dept) 546 N.Y.S.2d 671

Fees for accounting services rendered subsequent to receiver's removal were not barred as matter of law where accountants were appointed pursuant to court order (which was controlling regarding scope of accountants' authority), and it was not clear that accountants were acting without authority during period subsequent to removal and prior to submission of final account; thus, receiver would be granted leave to renew his application for accountants' fees on submission of proper affidavit indicating nature of services performed on each date, and services which exceeded scope of order of appointment or did not directly benefit corporation would be obligation of receiver. Corcoran v Joseph M. Corcoran, Inc. (1987, 2d Dept) 135 A.D.2d 531, 521 N.Y.S.2d 757, later proceeding (App Div, 2d Dept) 546 N.Y.S.2d 671

Under § 174 of former Gen. Corp. L., claims not filed with the receiver within the time limited by his notice to creditors, and not barred by other limitations, could still be presented and passed upon if final payment of dividends and distribution of assets had not already been made. People v S. W. Straus & Co. (1936) 158 Misc 186,222, 285 N.Y.S. 648, mod on other grounds 248 A.D. 785, 289 N.Y.S. 209 and affd 248 A.D. 785, 290 N.Y.S. 423

§ 1208. Penalty for concealing property from receiver

Any persons having possession of property belonging to the corporation, who shall wrongfully withhold such property from the receiver after the day specified in the notice given under section 1207 (Duties of receiver upon appointment), shall forfeit to the receiver double the value of such property, and the same may be recovered in an action by the receiver.

History: Add, L 1961, ch 855, eff Sept 1, 1963.

§ 1209. Recovery of assets

(a) Whenever a receiver, by verified petition to the supreme court at a special term held in the judicial district in which he was appointed shall show that he has good reason to believe that any person has in his possession or under his control, or has wrongfully concealed, withheld or disposed of, any property of the corporation, or that any person can testify concerning such facts, the court, with or without notice, shall make an order requiring such person to appear before the court or a referee, at a time and place designated, and submit to an examination concerning such facts. In such order, or at any time thereafter, in its discretion, the court may enjoin and restrain such person from disposing of any property of the corporation in his possession or under his control.

(b) In any examination under such order, the court may confer immunity in accordance with the provisions of section 50.20 of the criminal procedure law; provided that no immunity shall be conferred except upon twenty-four hours prior written notice to the appropriate district attorney having an official interest therein.

(c) A person so ordered to appear shall be entitled to the same fees and mileage, to be paid at the time of serving the order, as are allowed by law to witnesses subpoenaed to attend and testify in an action in the supreme court, and shall be subject to the same penalties upon failure to appear and testify in obedience to such order as are provided by law in the case of witnesses who fail to obey a subpoena to appear and testify in an action.

(d) A person appearing for examination in obedience to such order shall be sworn, and shall be entitled to be represented on such examination by counsel, and may be cross-examined, or may make a voluntary statement in his own behalf concerning the subject of his examination.

(e) The testimony taken under such order shall be signed and sworn to by the person examined, and be filed in the office of the clerk of the county where the action or proceeding is pending. If it shall appear that any person is wrongfully concealing or withholding, or has in his possession or under his control, any property of the corporation, on notice to him, the court may make an order requiring him forthwith to deliver it to the receiver, subject to the further order of the court.

History: Add, L 1961, ch 855, eff Sept 1, 1963.

Par (b), amd, L 1967, ch 680, § 12, L 1971, ch 1097, § 5, eff Sept 1, 1971.

CASE ANNOTATIONS

A summary turnover order could not properly issue without giving the holder of the property an opportunity to be heard, or unless it was established that right of the receiver to possession was clear and that the alleged possessor still had possession. Re Delaney (1931) 256 N.Y. 315, 176 N.E. 407; Petition of Horowitz (1940) 260 A.D. 879, 22 N.Y.S.2d 946

Section 170 of former Gen. Corp. L. was only available in statutory receivership cases conducted under Art. 9 of former Gen. Corp. L. and to receivers appointed by a New York court. Re Myerberg (1936) 249 A.D. 149, 291 N.Y.S. 519; Howell v German Theater, Inc. (1909) 64 Misc 110, 117 N.Y.S. 1124

Golf range revenue that was subject to competing claims and was deposited into court by range operator when it brought interpleader

action should be retained by court until it could determine rightful owner where revenue was claimed under terms of lease by owner of golf range land and was claimed by range operator's receiver under terms of federal court order, which was conditioned on receiver's obtaining lawful possession of premises by specified date, and such lawful possession depended on whether owner's eviction of range operator was valid. Myung Suk Koh v Tappan Prop., Inc. (1998, 2d Dept) 255 A.D.2d 300, 679 N.Y.S.2d 416

In action for specific performance of shareholders' agreement, court properly granted receiver's motion to confirm real estate contract of sale and asset purchase agreement without first conducting hearing. Lubliner v A.E.B. Car Wash Ltd. (1999, 2d Dept) 263 A.D.2d 498, 691 N.Y.S.2d 921, app dismd 94 N.Y.2d 835, 703 N.Y.S.2d 66, 724 N.E.2d 761

Section 170 of former Gen. Corp. L., from which this section of the Business Corp. L. was derived, was considered as remedial in nature and to be given a broad and liberal construction. Although that section did not so state, witnesses called for examination could be required to produce documentary evidence pertinent to the inquiry.Smith v Russo-Asiatic Bank (1939) 170 Misc 408, 10 N.Y.S.2d 10

A statutory receiver was entitled to conduct an examination of persons whom he believed had knowledge or possession of assets, notwithstanding they had denied knowledge or possession and even filed affidavits to that effect. Talmon v Societatea Romana Pentru Industria De Bumbac (1954) 206 Misc 449, 132 N.Y.S.2d 776

§ 1210. Order of payment by receiver

(a) Laborers' wages shall be preferred claims and entitled to payment before any other creditors out of the assets of the corporation in excess of valid prior liens or encumbrances.

(b) The receiver shall subject to any prior liens or encumbrances distribute the residue of the moneys in his hands, among the creditors whose claims have been proved and allowed, as follows:

(1) All debts due by such corporation to the United States, and all debts entitled to a preference under the laws of the United States.

(2) All debts that may be owing by the corporation as trustee.

(3) Judgments against the corporation, to the extent of the value of the real property on which they are liens.

(4) All other creditors, in proportion to their respective demands, without preference to specialty debts.

History: Add, L 1961, ch 855, eff Sept 1, 1963.

CASE ANNOTATIONS

Court does not err in requiring corporation, as creditor, to prove its claim before allowing it. M & R Rubbish Removal, Inc. v Spaterella (1985, 2d Dept) 112 A.D.2d 202, 491 N.Y.S.2d 423

In proceeding to determine priorities of claims on settlement of account of receiver of nursing home, CLS Bus Corp § 1210 did not support contention of union, which represented employees of nursing home, that its claim for moneys due for fringe benefits took priority over claim by landlord for rent due.D'Guardia v Piffath (1992, 2d Dept) 180 A.D.2d 630, 579 N.Y.S.2d 447

When it comes to distribution of assets among creditors in the same priority class, or lacking any priority, it has been suggested that it should ordinarily be ratable without regard to the order in which they have filed or proved their claims. Application of Lyding (1962) 33 Misc. 2d 561, 226 N.Y.S.2d 12

While one claimant, seeking to recover the amount of a security deposit on lease, alleged that a trust should be imposed and rents collected by receiver in foreclosure action to the extent of its claim, such argument overlooked the fact that claimant did not establish that the receiver stood in the position of a trustee with respect to the claimant and the further fact that no evidence was offered nor did the account indicate that the receiver took possession of anything other than rent payments. Allison v Roslyn Plaza, Ltd. (1976) 86 Misc. 2d 849, 385 N.Y.S.2d 454

There was some question as to what constituted "laborers' wages," or the like, entitled to priority under § 180 of former Gen. Corp. L. The term used in that section was "employees' wages," and even that was somewhat strictly construed as not including amounts due to a department head part of whose compensation was on a sales-percentage basis, or covering amounts due a sales agent. MacGregor v Johnson-Cowdin-Emmerich, Inc. (1928, CA2 NY) 26 F.2d 311; De Vries v Alsen Cement Co. (1923, CA2 NY) 290 F 746

§ 1211. Final distribution by receiver

(a) If there remains property of the corporation after the first distribution, the receiver shall, within one year thereafter, make a final distribution among the creditors entitled thereto. Notice that such distribution will be the final distribution to creditors shall be published once a week for two consecutive weeks in a newspaper of general circulation in the county where the office of the corporation is located.

(b) A creditor or claimant who failed to prove his claim before the first distribution and who proves it before the final one shall receive the sum he would have been entitled to on the first distribution before any further distribution shall be made to other creditors or claimants.

(c) Unless the court shall otherwise direct, no other distribution shall be made thereafter to creditors, except to those having pending actions against the corporation or the receiver.

(d) After the final distribution to creditors, the receiver shall not be answerable to any creditor or claimant, unless his claim shall have been proved before or at the time specified in the notice of the final distribution.

History: Add, L 1961, ch 855, eff Sept 1, 1963.

§ 1212. Disposition of moneys retained; surplus; unclaimed distributions

(a) When any action pending at the time of the final distribution shall be terminated, the receiver shall apply the moneys retained by him to the payment of the amount recovered, and his necessary charges and expenses incurred therein.

(b) After the final distribution to creditors and after deducting his charges and expenses, the receiver shall distribute any surplus among the shareholders of the corporation, in accordance with their respective rights.

(c) Any portion of the assets distributable to a creditor or shareholder who is unknown or cannot be found, or who is under disability and for whom there is no legal representative, shall be paid by the receiver to the state comptroller as abandoned property within six months from the date fixed for the payment of the final liquidating distribution, and be subject to the provisions of the abandoned property law.

History: Add, L 1961, ch 855, eff Sept 1, 1963.

§ 1213. Omission or default of receiver

Upon notice to the attorney-general and upon such notice to creditors or others interested as the court shall direct, the court may, in the furtherance of justice, relieve a receiver from any omission or default, on such conditions as may be imposed, and, on compliance therewith, confirm his action.

History: Add, L 1961, ch 855, eff Sept 1, 1963.

§ 1214. Application by attorney-general for removal of receiver and to close receivership

(a) Whenever he deems it to be to the advantage of the shareholders, creditors or other persons interested in the assets of any corporation for which a receiver has been appointed, the attorney-general may move:

(1) For an order removing the receiver and appointing another in his stead;

(2) To compel the receiver to account;

(3) For such other and additional orders as may facilitate the closing of the receivership.

History: Add, L 1961, ch 855, eff Sept 1, 1963.

§ 1215. Resignation by receiver; filling any vacancy

(a) A receiver may petition the court appointing him for an order to show cause why he should not be permitted to resign.

(b) The petition shall be accompanied by a verified account of all the assets of the corporation received by him, of all payments or other disposition thereof made by him, of the remaining assets of the corporation in respect to which he was appointed receiver and the situation of the same, and of all his transactions as receiver. Thereupon, the court shall grant an order directing notice to be given to the sureties on his official bond and to all persons interested in the property of the corporation to show cause, at a time and place specified, why the receiver should not be permitted to resign. Such notice shall be published once in each week for six successive weeks in one or more newspapers as the court shall direct. If it shall appear that the proceedings of the receiver in the discharge of his trust have been fair and honest and that there is no good cause to the contrary, the court shall make an order permitting such receiver to resign. Thereupon he shall be discharged and his powers as receiver shall cease, but he shall remain subject to any liability incurred prior to the making of such order. The court, in its discretion, may require the expense of such proceeding to be paid by the receiver presenting the petition.

(c) Any vacancy created by resignation, removal, death or otherwise, may be filled by the court, and the property of the receivership shall be delivered to the remaining receivers or, if there are none, to the successor appointed by the court. The court may summarily enforce delivery by order in the action or special proceeding in which the receiver was appointed.

History: Add, L 1961, ch 855, eff Sept 1, 1963.

§ 1216. Final accounting; notice; duty of attorney-general

(a) Within one year after qualifying, the receiver shall apply to the court for a final settlement of his accounts and for an order for distribution, or, upon notice to the attorney-general, for an extension of time, setting forth the reasons therefor. If the receiver has not so applied for a settlement of his accounts or for such extension of time, the attorney-general or any creditor or shareholder may apply for an order that the receiver show cause why an accounting and distribution should not be had, and after the expiration of eighteen months from the time the receiver qualified, it shall be the duty of the attorney-general to apply for such an order on notice to the receiver.

(b) Before presenting a final account, the receiver shall give notice of his intention to file it by publication, under subparagraph (a) (1) of section 1207 (Duties of receiver upon appointment), setting forth the time and place of filing and presentation to the court. The receiver shall also give not less than eight days' written notice to the sureties on his official bond.

(c) Upon presentation of such account, the court shall hear the allegations, objections and proofs of all parties interested and allow or disallow such account, in whole or in part, and make a final order. The court may refer the account and the hearing, in whole or in part, to a referee who shall report thereon to the court.

History: Add, L 1961, ch 855, eff Sept 1, 1963.

CASE ANNOTATIONS

Where a temporary receiver is continued as permanent receiver the creditors may require him to account for everything received by him as temporary receiver. Re Simonds Mfg. Co. (1899) 39 A.D. 576, 57 N.Y.S. 776

Court erred in directing distribution of funds in account of temporary receiver without first conducting hearing in light of objections to proposed distribution. Lipton v Carmel Prof'l Office Park, Inc. (2001, 2d Dept) 286 A.D.2d 332, 728 N.Y.S.2d 679

§ 1217. Commissions

(a) A receiver shall be entitled, in addition to his necessary expenses, to such commissions upon the sums received and disbursed as may be allowed by the court, as follows:

(1) On the first twenty thousand dollars, not exceeding five percent;

(2) On the next eighty thousand dollars, not exceeding two and one-half percent; and

(3) On the remainder, not exceeding one percent.

(b) If the commissions of the receiver so computed do not amount to one hundred dollars, the court in its discretion may allow such sum not exceeding one hundred dollars as shall be reasonable.

(c) When more than one receiver shall be appointed, the compensation herein provided shall be divided between them, as the court directs.

History: Add, L 1961, ch 855, eff Sept 1, 1963.

CASE ANNOTATIONS

Court-appointed receiver was barred from privately negotiating fee without court approval in amount exceeding scheduled maximums set by CLS Bus Corp § 1217 as part of over-all settlement between 2 litigating shareholders of close corporation, despite absence of fraud, duress or unconscionability, since receiver is court's agent, not parties', and to allow receiver to receive commission higher than allowed by statute is contrary to its plain meaning. Re Kane (1990) 75 N.Y.2d 511, 554 N.Y.S.2d 457, 553 N.E.2d 1005

Where applicable, the provisions of § 192 of former Gen. Corp. L. were controlling as against any pre-existing arrangement for higher compensation. Salmon v Schenectady Mason Supply Corp. (1951) 278 A.D. 609, 102 N.Y.S.2d 91

Section 192 of former Gen. Corp. L. was regarded as the proper basis for allowing commissions to a temporary receiver appointed under § 162 of that law, as against § 1547 of former Civil Practice Act. La Vin v La Vin (1953) 281 A.D. 888, 119 N.Y.S.2d 573

Receiver waived his right to commission on amount received which was refund of sum placed in escrow account during sale of corporation's real property-it is premature for petitioner to complain about amount of total gross receipts with which receiver should be credited, because Supreme Court has not yet determined amount of his commission-Supreme Court properly held that receiver was appointed pursuant to Business Corporation Law rather than CPLR; thus, his commission should be calculated in accordance with Business Corporation Law § 1217; claim for compensation in excess of commission calculated under provisions of that section is rejected. Matter of Corcoran v Joseph M. Corcoran, Inc., 154 A.D.2d 671

Upon appeal from an order fixing the receiver's commissions and the fees of attorneys for the receivers by one of two equal stockholders of a dissolved corporation, the order was modified on the theory that the receiver's commissions should have been computed pursuant to § 191 of former General Corporation Law (now Business Corporation Law § 1217) and that the fees of the receiver's attorneys should be measured by the fair and reasonable value of the services rendered, and not by suggested fee recommendations by bar associations or Commercial Law Leagues, or by attorneys specializing in collection matters. Re F. G. A. Concrete Constr. Corp. (1966, 2d Dept) 26 A.D.2d 639, 272 N.Y.S.2d 458

Temporary receiver of corporation was not entitled to commissions on receipts and disbursements subsequent to the date upon which judgment entered in shareholders derivative action was paid. Re Kraemer (1972, 3d Dept) 40 A.D.2d 1053, 338 N.Y.S.2d 913

Temporary receiver was not entitled to commissions on the amount which was on deposit in the corporate bank account when he assumed his duties nor on the interest generated thereon, since such sums were not received and disbursed by him. Re Kraemer (1972, 3d Dept) 40 A.D.2d 1053, 338 N.Y.S.2d 913

In a proceeding seeking the involuntary judicial dissolution of a corporation, a receiver appointed by the court would not be entitled to fees and commissions determined in accordance with CPLR § 8004, but rather would be limited to the amount determined under Bus Corp Law § 1217, and the receiver's fee would be determined in accordance with that section regardless of whether the corporation was solvent or insolvent. Re T. J. Ronan Paint Corp. (1983, 1st Dept) 97 A.D.2d 283, 469 N.Y.S.2d 931, recalled, vacated, op replaced (1st Dept) 98 A.D.2d 413

Court was without authority to allow receiver compensation in excess of maximum receivership commission provided for by CLS Bus Corp § 1217; despite stipulation of parties, matter would be remitted for accounting. Re Kane (1987, 2d Dept) 132 A.D.2d 610, 517 N.Y.S.2d 771

Receiver who grossly mismanages his trust is not entitled to his "necessary expenses" under CLS Bus Corp § 1217, such as counsel fees and accountants' fees. Corcoran v Joseph M. Corcoran, Inc. (1987, 2d Dept) 135 A.D.2d 531, 521 N.Y.S.2d 757, later proceeding (App Div, 2d Dept) 546 N.Y.S.2d 671

Court erroneously found that receiver's failure to keep certain written records required under CLS CPLR § 6404 (which governs duties of temporary receivers) constituted gross mismanagement so as to justify disallowance of receiver's necessary expenses, where receiver was appointed as permanent receiver under Business Corporation Law, and receiver complied with duty under CLS Bus Corp § 1207 by keeping detailed schedule setting forth all income received, date of receipt, and source as either account receivable or sale of material on hand. Corcoran v Joseph M. Corcoran, Inc. (1987, 2d Dept) 135 A.D.2d 531, 521 N.Y.S.2d 757, later proceeding (App Div, 2d Dept) 546 N.Y.S.2d 671

Fact that permanent receiver appointed under Business Corporation Law hired his wife as secretary to assist in winding down corporation did not constitute gross mismanagement so as to justify disallowance of receiver's necessary expenses; to extent that wife's services were found to be unnecessary, appropriate remedy would be to disallow compensation for wife out of funds on hand. Corcoran v Joseph M. Corcoran, Inc. (1987, 2d Dept) 135 A.D.2d 531, 521 N.Y.S.2d 757, later proceeding (App Div, 2d Dept) 546 N.Y.S.2d 671

No evidence existed to support court's finding that permanent receiver appointed under Business Corporation Law unnecessarily delayed winding down of corporation by neglecting to perform major contract, so as to justify disallowance of his necessary expenses, where receiver learned that building materials necessary to complete contract according to specification were available only overseas, contractor directed receiver to order substitute materials domestically in order to expedite performance, and receiver properly refused to perform unless release were issued indemnifying dissolved corporation for claims based on its failure to complete contract according to specification. Corcoran v Joseph M. Corcoran, Inc. (1987, 2d Dept) 135 A.D.2d 531, 521 N.Y.S.2d 757, later proceeding (App Div, 2d Dept) 546 N.Y.S.2d 671

Allowance of counsel fees to permanent receiver appointed under Business Corporation Law was not barred as matter of law, even though receiver conceded that employee of dissolved corporation had performed work in contravention of CLS Bus Corp § 1005, and that receiver had made personal telephone calls on corporate telephone, since such acts did not rise to level of gross mismanagement. Corcoran v Joseph M. Corcoran, Inc. (1987, 2d Dept) 135 A.D.2d 531, 521 N.Y.S.2d 757, later proceeding (App Div, 2d Dept) 546 N.Y.S.2d 671

Receiver was not entitled to compensation for his services as attorney since CLS Bus Corp § 1217(a) sets commission for receiver based on "sums received and disbursed," and receiver was paid accordingly; however, receiver was also entitled to reimbursement of his "necessary expenses" since he presented adequate documentation thereof. Re Japan Diamond Polishing Works, Ltd. (1993, 1st Dept) 188 A.D.2d 359

Although receiver would be entitled to reimbursement for necessary expenses and, if necessary, could have hired managing agent, he was not entitled to receive salary or commission for providing management services in addition to commissions permitted under CLS Bus Corp § 1217, which provides maximum compensation to be paid to receiver. Goldman v Bernardini (1998, 2d Dept) 246 A.D.2d 510, 667 N.Y.S.2d 390, app dismd 92 N.Y.2d 919, 680 N.Y.S.2d 459, 703 N.E.2d 271

Compensation of a receiver appointed in connection with a mortgage foreclosure suit involving corporate property, and not under any of the provisions of Art. 9 of former Gen. Corp. L., was not subject to the provisions of § 192 of that law but to be based upon § 1547 of former Civil Practice Act. Murphy v Pfeiffer Glass, Inc. (1958) 15 Misc. 2d 214, 180 N.Y.S.2d 639, mod on other grounds (4th Dept) 11 A.D.2d 902, 202 N.Y.S.2d 937

A receiver's right to payment of fees and expenses has usually been recognized as entitled to priority in payment out of the assets, before all other claims, including his fees and expenses in connection with a reference for hearing in relation to the receivership in voluntary dissolution proceedings by reason of insolvency of the corporation. Application of Lyding (1962) 33 Misc. 2d 561, 226 N.Y.S.2d 12

Receiver who was appointed pursuant to N.Y. Bus. Corp. Law § 1217 as part of a corporate dissolution procedure could not recover a fee for a real estate transaction that transferred corporate property to the receiver because the transfer did not generate money for the corporation and the property was transferred back to the corporation as soon as the court had allowed the transfer. Jakubowicz v 709 9th Ave., LLC (2004, Sup) 777 N.Y.S.2d 609

Despite the valuable services rendered by a receiver, because the receiver was appointed pursuant to N.Y. Bus. Corp. Law § 1202(a)(1), the receiver's commission was governed by the provisions of Business Corporation Law § 1217, which did not include a commission for based upon the value of the services rendered. Jakubowicz v A.C. Green Elec. Contrs., Inc. (2005, A.D., 1st Dept) 803 N.Y.S.2d 71

§ 1218. Special provisions relating to actions or special proceedings against foreign corporations

(a) In any action or special proceeding brought against a foreign corporation under this article, the following provisions shall apply:

(1) Service of the summons in such action may be made personally within the state of New York, by delivery of the same to any officer or director of the corporation, or by publication pursuant to an order obtained as hereinafter provided.

(2) An order directing service by publication of the summons shall be made upon application of a plaintiff in any such action and shall be founded upon a verified complaint, alleging that the defendant is a foreign corporation and has or may have or may be entitled to assets, credits, choses in action or other property, tangible or intangible within the state and that such corporation has been dissolved, nationalized or that its authority or existence has been terminated or cancelled in the jurisdiction of its incorporation, or that it has ceased to do business, and upon an affidavit reciting that personal service of the summons cannot be effected within the state with due diligence and that a temporary receiver of its property within the state of New York has been appointed pursuant to this article in such action and that a copy of the order appointing the receiver has been served personally by or on behalf of such receiver upon a person, firm or corporation holding property, tangible or intangible, of the said foreign corporation, or against whom a claim or demand in favor of such foreign corporation exists and that demand therefor has been made upon such person, firm or corporation by or on behalf of such receiver.

(3) The order directing service of the summons shall require the publication thereof in a newspaper published in the state of New York in the English language at least once a week for four successive weeks, and shall also require the mailing on or before the date of the first publication of a copy of the summons, complaint and order to the corporation at its last known principal or head office in the state or country of its incorporation.

(4) In any such action, the summons shall be served personally or an order directing service thereof by publication shall be obtained and the first publication thereof made within sixty days after the appointment of the temporary receiver, and if served by publication, the service shall be made complete by the continuance thereof.

(5) If served by publication, service of the summons shall be deemed complete on the date of the last publication. The action shall be deemed commenced upon the issuance of the summons. The order appointing the receiver and the papers upon which the same is granted shall be filed in the office of the clerk

Business Corporation Law

of the court where the action is triable within ten days after the order is made.

(6) In the event that the defendant defaults in answering, or if after a trial the court is satisfied that the defendant has ceased to do business by reason of any thing or matter whatsoever, or that it has been dissolved, nationalized, or its authority or existence has been otherwise terminated or cancelled, the court shall thereupon direct judgment, appointing a permanent receiver and directing the receiver to liquidate the assets, credits, choses in action and property, tangible and intangible, in the state of New York of the said defendant, in the manner provided in this article.

(7) The time between the cessation of business by the corporation or its dissolution or nationalization or the termination or cancellation of its authority or existence and the appointment of a receiver in this state pursuant to this article, whichever time is longer, plus three years after such appointment, shall not be a part of the time limited by domestic or foreign law for the commencement of an action or for the assertion of a claim therein by or on behalf of or against said corporation or by or against said receiver, whether or not said action or claim has heretofore been barred by any statute of limitations of this state or of any other state or country.

(8) The existence of and causes of action of or against such corporation existing at the time of its dissolution, nationalization, or the termination or cancellation of its authority or existence, or arising thereafter, shall not be deemed ended, abated or affected thereby, nor shall actions brought by or against such corporation or a receiver appointed hereunder or any remedy therein be deemed to have ended or abated or to have been affected by reason of such dissolution, nationalization, or termination or cancellation of its authority or existence. This provision shall apply to all property, tangible and intangible, debts, demands, and choses in action of such corporation within the state of New York, and to all litigation heretofore or hereafter brought in the courts of the state or of the United States to which the corporation or the receiver of said corporation appointed pursuant to the provisions of this article is a party. Any receiver appointed pursuant to the provisions of this article may be substituted for such corporation in any action or proceeding pending in the courts of the state or of the United States to which such corporation is a party and may intervene in any action or proceeding which relates to or affects any of the assets or claims of the corporation and revive any action which shall have heretofore or which may hereafter have abated, and such dissolution, nationalization, or termination or cancellation of its authority or existence in the jurisdiction of its incorporation, or any confiscatory law or decree thereof, shall not be deemed to have any extraterritorial effect or validity as to the property, tangible or intangible, debts, demands or choses in action of such corporation within the state or any debts or

obligations owing to such corporation from persons, firms or corporations residing, sojourning or doing business in the state. Nothing contained in this subdivision shall be deemed to validate claims for or causes of action or actions to recover property located in or moneys payable in the jurisdiction of incorporation which are unenforcible under the laws of such jurisdiction.

(9) If any receiver or trustee has heretofore been appointed in this state for such corporation or its property in any action or proceeding, either before or supplementary to judgment, otherwise than in a action brought pursuant to this article, such receiver or trustee may be appointed or continued as the receiver in any action brought pursuant to the provisions of this article.

(10) The appointment of a receiver or the pendency of an action for the appointment of such receiver, shall until such receiver shall be discharged or until such action shall have terminated, be a bar to any subsequent application or action for the appointment of a receiver of the assets of the same corporation.

(11) An action shall be commenced within three years from the discovery by the plaintiff or his predecessor in interest, of any asset of said corporation in the state of New York.

History: Add, L 1962, ch 317, § 14, eff Sept 1, 1963; amd, L 1963, ch 747, eff Sept 1, 1963.

CASE ANNOTATIONS

Provision of Bus Corp § 1218(a)(8) in regard to dissolution of a foreign corporation is applicable only to receivership actions and not to an ordinary action for breach of contract.Dean Constr. Co. v Agricultural Ins. Co. (1964, 2d Dept) 22 A.D.2d 82, 254 N.Y.S.2d 196

Stockholders' request to have a receiver appointed to administer the assets of a corporation incorporated in Delaware and registered to do business in New York as a foreign corporation was time-barred where the shareholders knew that the assets of the corporation were located in New York, and thus, their action would have accrued in December 2001 when they were distinctly aware that the corporation was going to cease to do business, but had not commenced their action until the filing of the petition nearly four years later. Under 8 Del. C. § 278 and N.Y. Bus. Corp. Law § 1218(a)(11), the application for a receiver had to have been within three years, but pursuant to an exception under the Delaware statute, the shareholders could apply to the Court of Chancery of Delaware for the appointment of a receiver regardless of the aforementioned limitation, and a receiver could then be appointed at any time when good cause was shown. Potter v Arrington (2006, Sup) 810 NYS2d 312

ARTICLE 13
FOREIGN CORPORATIONS

History: Add, L 1961, ch 855, eff Sept 1, 1963.

Schedule of sections, amd, L 1962, ch 834, § 88, eff Sept 1, 1963.

§ 1301. Authorization of foreign corporations

(a) A foreign corporation shall not do business in this state until it has been authorized to do so as provided in this article. A foreign corporation may be authorized to do in this state any business which may be done lawfully in this state by a domestic corporation, to the extent that it is authorized to do such business in the jurisdiction of its incorporation, but no other business.

(b) Without excluding other activities which may not constitute doing business in this state, a foreign corporation shall not be considered to be doing business in this state, for the purposes of this chapter, by reason of carrying on in this state any one or more of the following activities:

(1) Maintaining or defending any action or proceeding, whether judicial, administrative, arbitrative or otherwise, or effecting settlement thereof or the settlement of claims or disputes.

(2) Holding meetings of its directors or its shareholders.

(3) Maintaining bank accounts.

(4) Maintaining offices or agencies only for the transfer, exchange and registration of its securities, or appointing and maintaining trustees or depositaries with relation to its securities.

(c) The specification in paragraph (b) does not establish a standard for activities which may subject a foreign corporation to service of process under this chapter or any other statute of this state.

(d) A foreign corporation whose corporate name is not acceptable for authorization pursuant to sections 301 and 302 of this chapter, may submit in its application for authority pursuant to section 1304 of this chapter, a fictitious name under which it shall do business in this state. A fictitious name submitted pursuant to this section shall be subject to the provisions of subparagraphs (2) through (9) of paragraph (a) of section 301 and 302 of this chapter. A foreign corporation authorized to do business in this state under a fictitious name pursuant to this section, shall use such fictitious name in all of its dealings with the secretary of state and in the conduct of its business in this state. The provisions of section one hundred thirty of the general business law shall not apply to any fictitious name filed by a foreign corporation pursuant to this section, and a filing under section one hundred thirty of the general business law shall not constitute the adoption of a fictitious name.

History: Add, L 1961, ch 855, eff Sept 1, 1963.

Par (a), amd, L 1962, ch 834, § 89, eff Sept 1, 1963, L 1964, ch 725, § 13, eff June 1, 1964.

Par (d), add, L 1982, ch 590, § 6, eff Oct 20, 1982.

CASE ANNOTATIONS

1. In general
2. Business authorized within state
3. Doing business, generally
4. Actions constituting "doing business"
5. Actions not constituting "doing business"
6. Failure to comply
7. Jurisdiction over foreign corporations

1. In general

The language of Business Corporation Law §§ 1301(a) and 1312 is limited strictly to foreign corporations organized for profit. Anti-Defamation League of B'Nai B'Rith v American Italian Anti-Defamation League, Inc. (1967) 54 Misc. 2d 830, 283 N.Y.S.2d 828, 156 USPQ 280

2. Business authorized within state

The business conducted in New York, moreover, must be in the field of, or incidental to, the business which the corporation was organized to conduct.Singer Mfg. Co. v Granite Spring Water Co. (1910) 66 Misc 595, 123 N.Y.S. 1088

Former Gen. Corp. L. provisions relating to foreign corporations permitted such corporations to engage only in such businesses as a similar New York corporation could be permitted to engage in.1921 Ops Atty Gen 307

3. Doing business, generally

Decisions as to what constitutes such "doing of business" in New York by a foreign corporation as to require authorization to protect rights of action which may accrue in its favor and against unfavorable measures which may otherwise be taken against it usually turn on the extent and nature of its activities in this state. Isolated transactions having no continuity, and those having no profit motive or commercial significance do not amount to "doing business," and whether or not the corporation maintains an office or place of business in New York is likewise a factor to be considered. McDowell v Starobin Electrical Supply Co. (1918) 104 Misc 596, 172 N.Y.S. 221. See also McDowell v Starobin Electrical Supply Co. (1920) 190 A.D. 676, 180 N.Y.S. 528; Berkshire Engineering Corp. v Scott-Paine (1961) 29 Misc. 2d 1010, 217 N.Y.S.2d 919; Whitney v Dudley (1943, Sup) 40 N.Y.S.2d 838, affd 266 A.D. 1056, 45 N.Y.S.2d 725

Such a corporation did not have to possess property in New York as a condition to being authorized to do business here. Colgate Palmolive Peet Co. v Planet Service Corp. (1939) 173 Misc 494, 15 N.Y.S.2d 558

No sound basis exists for interpreting N.Y. Bus. Corp. Law art. 13 as an integrated statutory scheme with the same standard for "doing business" applicable to each section in the article. Airtran N. Y., LLC v Midwest Air Group, Inc. (2007, App Div, 1st Dept) 844 NYS2d 233.

Since N.Y. Bus. Corp. Law § 1312 constitutes a statutory barrier to a foreign corporation's right to bring suit, a party seeking to impose the barrier, in order to rebut the presumption that the corporation does business in its state of incorporation rather than New York, has the burden of proving that the foreign corporation's activity in New York is systematic and regular, and the burden of showing "doing business" is therefore a heavy one since a lesser showing might infringe on Congress's constitutional power to regulate interstate commerce, and the same concern applies to the N.Y. Bus. Corp. Law § 1301 requirement that a foreign corporation be authorized to "do business" in New York, but those concerns do not apply to N.Y. Bus. Corp. Law § 1315(a), which implicates neither the restriction of a right nor the fear of constitutional infringement. Airtran N. Y., LLC v Midwest Air Group, Inc. (2007, App Div, 1st Dept) 844 NYS2d 233

4. Actions constituting "doing business"

Subletting to different tenants, of a building in city of New York leased to a foreign corporation under a lease delivered in this state, constitutes "doing business in this state."Cassidy's, Ltd. v Rowan (1917) 99 Misc 274, 163 N.Y.S. 1079

Regular and long-continued buying of goods in New York can constitute doing business here, however, in like manner as selling them or performing services for pay. Merchandise Reporting Co. v L. Oransky & Sons (1929) 133 Misc 890, 234 N.Y.S. 83

A Massachusetts corporation was clearly engaged in doing business in New York where, over a two and onehalf year period, it had been engaged in erecting houses and general building construction work in New York, where its employees resided for varying periods of time while working on such contracts, and where its machinery and equipment was stationed in New York for weeks and sometimes months. Berkshire Engineering Corp. v Scott-Paine (1961) 29 Misc. 2d 1010, 217 N.Y.S.2d 919

5. Actions not constituting "doing business"

Mere presence on occasions of an agent of the corporation in New York does not establish that the corporation is doing business here, unless it appears that his visitations have some permanency or regularity and are for "business" reasons. It has been well said that there is no precise test other than whether the corporate activities will enable the court to say that the corporation "is here" for business purposes. Tauza v Susquehanna Coal Co. (1917) 220 N.Y. 259, 115 N.E. 915

Transactions falling within the range of interstate commerce have ordinarily not been regarded as "doing business in New York" because of federal constitutional control in that field which precludes state interference, and thus the taking and solicitation of orders for goods in New York, subject to acceptance and not binding until accepted outside the state, or to be filled or performed elsewhere, has not been considered doing business in New York, even though a New York office with telephone service is maintained for the sales representative. Munoz v American Stevedores, Inc. (1960, 2d Dept) 10 A.D.2d 963, 201 N.Y.S.2d 640; National Folding Box Co. v Bisceglia Bros. Wines Corp. (1950, Sup) 147 N.Y.S.2d 361, app dismd 278 A.D. 711, 103 N.Y.S.2d 836; National Tool Salvage Co. v National Tool Salvage Industries, Inc. (1946) 186 Misc 833, 60 N.Y.S.2d 308, 68 USPQ 118; Re Dennin's Will (1942, Sur) 37 N.Y.S.2d 725

Mere maintenance of action by foreign corporation does not constitute "doing business" within state, and therefore statutory proscription against actions by unauthorized foreign corporations which are doing business in state is inapplicable.De Ran Landscaping Service, Inc. v De Ran Industries, Inc. (1985, 3d Dept) 109 A.D.2d 1040, 487 N.Y.S.2d 160

Foreign corporation had capacity to sue for breach of contract where commencement of that action was not "doing business" within state in violation of CLS Bus Corp §§ 1301(b)(1) and 1312 or CLS Gen Bus § 130. Federal Fin. Co. v Levine (2001, 2d Dept) 281 A.D.2d 454, 721 N.Y.S.2d 558

Trial court did not have personal jurisdiction over a Turkish telecommunications company in a shareholder's action for contribution and indemnification because the company's defense of an action in a federal district court in New York did not constitute "doing business" under N.Y. Bus. Corp. Law § 1301(b)(1); roaming agreements, which the company was not alleged to have entered, did not constitute doing business for the purpose of conferring general jurisdiction. Uzan v Telsim Mobil Telekomunikasyon Hizmetleri A.S. (2008, 1st Dept) 51 App Div 3d 476, 856 NYS2d 625.

A foreign corporation is not doing business in New York where such corporation sells 7 per cent of its total product in New York City through a commission salesman, who also represents eight other firms, and where such salesman is not an employee or managing agent of the corporation. New York Automatic Canteen Corp. v Keppel & Ruof, Inc. (1949) 195 Misc 526, 90 N.Y.S.2d 454

A credit corporation, set up as a subsidiary of a manufacturing corporation, the latter doing no business with dealers and the former having its principal office in Chicago and being organized under the laws of Delaware, was not doing business in New York where it merely, through the home office in Chicago, arranged to finance a dealer in New York through trust receipt financing, but had no personal contacts with the dealer. Samuels v Mott (1960) 29 Misc. 2d 705, 211 N.Y.S.2d 242

The maintenance of an office for transaction of business in New York is not essential to "doing business" in New York by a foreign corporation which has engaged in a series of extensive and persistent transactions in this state over varying periods of time signifying intention to establish a permanent business situs here. Berkshire Engineering Corp. v Scott-Paine (1961) 29 Misc. 2d 1010, 217 N.Y.S.2d 919

Foreign corporation which enters into single transaction in New York, maintains bank account in New York, and retains New York law firm to represent it, with partner of law firm being director of foreign corporation, is not "doing business" in New York, so as to be precluded from maintaining action in New York. Azuma N.V. v Sinks (1986, SD NY) 646 F. Supp. 122

Texas corporation was not "doing business" in New York and was thus not precluded, by virtue of being unlicensed under § 301, from maintaining action in New York, despite its solicitation of business in New York, where work performed need not by its nature have been performed in New York and plaintiff claimed to have performed all its work in Texas.Expense Reduction Services, Inc. v Jonathan Woodner Co. (1989, SD NY) 720 F. Supp. 262

Foreign corporations maintaining exhibits at New York World's Fair are not doing business in this state so as to be subject to taxation or require qualification.1938 Ops Atty Gen 331

Unauthorized alien insurer may maintain New York office that would not engage in doing insurance business, provided office did not use unauthorized insurer's name. Insurance Department, Opinions of General Counsel, Opinion Number 02-11-09

6. Failure to comply

Substantial business transactions consummated within this state through a foreign corporation unlicensed to do business in New York is a violation of this section, and no action pursuant to § 1312 of the Business Corporation Law may be maintained to enforce contracts entered into during the course of such business transactions.State by Lefkowitz v ITM, Inc. (1966) 52 Misc. 2d 39, 275 N.Y.S.2d 303, 3 UCCRS 775

Respondents acted as issuers, dealers and salesmen when they sold units of stock in unauthorized foreign corporation from their office in New York, and they violated CLS Bus Corp § 1301 and CLS Gen Bus §§ 352(1), 359-e(14)(l) and 359-f by failing to register under Martin Act, and by misrepresenting and failing to disclose facts regarding use of proceeds raised in offering. People v World Interactive Gaming Corp. (1999, Sup) 185 Misc. 2d 852, 714 N.Y.S.2d 844, reported at (NY Sup) 1999 N.Y. Misc LEXIS 662

Because the consumer debt settlement companies repeatedly engaged in deceptive business practices, false advertising, statutory fraud, and conducted business in New York without authorization, they violated N.Y. Exec. Law § 63(12), N.Y. Gen. Bus. Law §§ 349, 350, and N.Y. Bus. Corp. Law § 1301; accordingly, pursuant to N.Y. Bus. Corp. Law § 1303, N.Y. Gen. Bus. Law § 350-d, N.Y. C.P.L.R. 8303(a)(6), they were permanently enjoined from continuing such actions and required to pay a civil penalty, special court costs, and make restitution to certain consumers. People v Nationwide Asset Servs., Inc. (2009, Sup) 888 NYS2d 850.

Failure of a foreign corporation to seek and obtain authority to do business in New York will likewise not invalidate a mortgage executed by it in New York or covering property in New York. Re Heffron Co. (1914, DC NY) 216 F 642

7. Jurisdiction over foreign corporations

Foreign car and tire makers did not consent to the personal general jurisdiction of New York courts in an action arising from an automobile accident occurring in Virginia by registering to do business in New York or appointing the Secretary of State as the makers' agent because, under evolving in personam jurisdiction jurisprudence, such acts did not consent to New York courts' general jurisdiction on claims unrelated to New York. Aybar v Aybar, 2019 N.Y. App. Div. LEXIS 444 (N.Y. App. Div. 2d Dep't 2019).

Foreign unauthorized corporations and their principals had minimum contacts sufficient to establish personal jurisdiction in New York, even without physical presence in New York, where they operated offshore casino offering gambling to Internet users in New York, they engaged in advertising campaign to induce people to visit their web site and gamble, they made no attempt to exclude identifiable New Yorkers from their ads, and phone logs from their toll-free number (available to casino visitors on their web site) indicated that they had received phone calls from New Yorkers. People v World Interactive Gaming Corp. (1999, Sup) 185 Misc. 2d 852, 714 N.Y.S.2d 844, reported at (NY Sup) 1999 N.Y. Misc LEXIS 662

There was no jurisdiction over a corporation in a products liability case based on the "corporate presence" doctrine where the corporation was a nondomiciliary that was not doing business in New York, did not come into existence until after the injury at issue, and could not have engaged in tortious conduct that caused the injuries; while the corporation had purchased all of the manufacturer's assets, even if the corporation had a duty to warn, that duty did not arise until after it acquired the assets of the manufacturer, after the injury, and the trial court's ruling that under the "product line" exception, since the manufacturer was subject to long-arm jurisdiction, the corporation was likewise was subject to such jurisdiction as the successor, was error. Semenetz v Sherling & Walden, Inc. (2005, 3d Dept) 21 A.D. 3d 1138, 801 N.Y.S.2d 78, app gr (2005, NY) 2005 N.Y. LEXIS 3419

A foreign corporation is not necessarily to be considered as a resident of New York or domiciled here for purposes of federal court jurisdiction on the basis of diversity of citizenship, or venue, because it has actually been doing business here to such extent that it should have sought authorization. Moss v Atlantic C. L. R. Co. (1945, CA2 NY) 149 F.2d 701; Donahue v M. A. Henry Co. (1948, DC NY) 78 F. Supp. 91

In light of the plain language of the exclusionary clause contained in Business Corporation Law § 1301, subd c, defendant foreign corporation's contention that Business Corporation Law § 1301 precluded personal jurisdiction over it was without merit, and the question of whether it was "doing business" in New York was not the decisive consideration under CPLR 302. Gasarch v Ormand Industries, Inc. (1972, SD NY) 346 F. Supp. 550, CCH Fed Secur L Rep ¶ 93609

In an action for damages for wrongful refusal of a New York agent of a foreign corporation to exchange certain stock certificates, a tort, Business Corporation Law § 1301(c) did not preclude employment of the long-arm statute, CPLR § 302, to obtain jurisdiction over the foreign corporation since the commission of such a tortious act in New York could be imputed to the foreign corporation so as to render it amenable to suit in New York. Gasarch v Ormand Industries, Inc. (1972, SD NY) 346 F. Supp. 550, CCH Fed Secur L Rep ¶ 93609

Where Florida corporation could have subjected defendant Michigan corporation to jurisdiction of court in Florida or Michigan or in any state where defendant carried on its warehousing and wholesaling of plaintiff's products in action based on defendant's sale of such product below costs, and where witnesses would be more accessible and discovery imposed less of a burden on defendant in some states other than New York, New York was an inconvenient forum for the action. Medow Industries, Inc. v Kirsch Co. (1973, SD NY) 356 F. Supp. 52

Defendant's compliance with New York statutes governing powers and rights of foreign banking and other corporations doing business in New York did not make it citizen of New York for federal diversity purposes. Arab International Bank & Trust Co. v National Westminister Bank, Ltd. (1979, SD NY) 463 F. Supp. 1145

Since foreign corporation was authorized to do business in New York, it was "present" in state for purposes of personal jurisdiction.DCA Food Industries, Inc. v Hawthorn Mellody, Inc. (1979, SD NY) 470 F. Supp. 574, 202 USPQ 739

Although a German shipping company was authorized to do business in New York, this filing was a mere consent to be sued and did not establish its presence in the state for purposes of its being "found" within the jurisdiction under Supp. R. Certain Adm. & Mar. Cl. B(1)(a) where the company also did not have "continuous and systematic" contacts with New York as (1) it was incorporated in Germany, where all of its employees were based, (2) although it had several contracts with New York entities, only one of these contracts, which was for a weather service, was ongoing, and the New York contracts accounted for only two percent of its overall business, and (3) the company did not have a New York office or telephone line, and did no advertising within the state. Erne Shipping Inc. v HBC Hamburg Bulk Carriers GMBH & Co. KG (2006, SD NY) 409 F Supp 2d 427

In car owners' action against car manufacturer alleging concealment of known safety defect, the court lacked general jurisdiction over the car manufacturer because registration with the state did not amount to a consent to general jurisdiction. Spratley v FCA US LLC, 2017 U.S. Dist. LEXIS 147492 (N.D.N.Y. Sept. 12, 2017).

§ 1302. Application to existing authorized foreign corporations

Every foreign corporation which on the effective date of this chapter is authorized to do business in this state under a certificate of authority heretofore issued to it by the secretary of state shall continue to have such authority. Such foreign corporation, its shareholders, directors and officers shall have the same rights, franchises and privileges and shall be subject to the same limitations, restrictions, liabilities and penalties as a foreign corporation authorized under this chapter, its shareholders, directors and officers respectively. Reference in this chapter to an application for authority shall, unless the context otherwise requires, include the statement and designation and any amendment thereof required to be filed by the secretary of state under prior statutes to obtain a certificate of authority.

History: Add, L 1961, ch 855, eff Sept 1, 1963.

§ 1303. Violations

The attorney-general may bring an action to restrain a foreign corporation from doing in this state without authority any business for the doing of which it is required to be authorized in this state, or from doing in this state any business not set forth in its application for authority or certificate of amendment filed by the department of state. The attorney-general may bring an action or special proceeding to annul the authority of a foreign corporation doing in this state any business not set forth in its application for authority or certificate of amendment or the authority of which was obtained through fraudulent misrepresentation or concealment of a material fact or to enjoin or annul the authority of any foreign corporation which within this state contrary to law has done or omitted any act which if done by a domestic corporation would be a cause for its dissolution under section 1101 (Attorney-general's action for judicial dissolution) or to annul the authority of a foreign corporation that has been dissolved or had its authority or existence otherwise terminated or cancelled in the jurisdiction of its incorporation. The attorney-general shall deliver a certified copy of the order of annulment to the department of state. Upon the filing thereof by the department of state the authority of the foreign corporation to do business in this state shall be annulled. The secretary of state shall continue as agent of the foreign corporation upon whom process against it may be served in any action or special proceeding based upon any liability or obligation incurred by the foreign corporation within the state prior to the filing of the certified copy of the order of annulment by the department of state.

History: Add, L 1961, ch 855, eff Sept 1, 1963.

Amd, L 1984, ch 198, § 2, eff June 12, 1984.

CASE ANNOTATIONS

Because the consumer debt settlement companies repeatedly engaged in deceptive business practices, false advertising, statutory fraud, and conducted business in New York without authorization, they violated N.Y. Exec. Law § 63(12), N.Y. Gen. Bus. Law §§ 349, 350, and N.Y. Bus. Corp. Law § 1301; accordingly, pursuant to N.Y. Bus. Corp. Law § 1303, N.Y. Gen. Bus. Law § 350-d, N.Y. C.P.L.R. 8303(a)(6), they were permanently enjoined from continuing such actions and required to pay a civil penalty, special court costs, and make restitution to certain consumers. People v Nationwide Asset Servs., Inc. (2009, Sup) 888 NYS2d 850.

§ 1304. Application for authority; contents

(a) A foreign corporation may apply for authority to do business in this state. An application, entitled "Application for authority of............ (name of corporation) under section 1304 of the Business Corporation Law", shall be signed and delivered to the department of state. It shall set forth:

(1) The name of the foreign corporation.

(2) The fictitious name the corporation agrees to use in this state pursuant to section 1301 of this chapter, if applicable.

(3) The jurisdiction and date of its incorporation.

(4) The purpose or purposes for which it is formed, it being sufficient to state, either alone or with other purposes, that the purpose of the corporation is to engage in any lawful act or activity for which corporations may be organized under this chapter, provided that it also state that it is not formed to engage in any act or activity requiring the consent or approval of any state official, department, board, agency or other body without such consent or approval first being obtained. By such statement all lawful acts and activities shall be within the purposes of the corporation, except for express limitations therein or in this chapter, if any.

(5) The county within this state in which its office is to be located.

(6) A designation of the secretary of state as its agent upon whom process against it may be served and the post office address within or without this state to which the secretary of state shall mail a copy of any process against it served upon him.

(7) If it is to have a registered agent, his name and address within this state and a statement that the registered agent is to be its agent upon whom process against it may be served.

(8) A statement that the foreign corporation has not since its incorporation or since the date its authority to do business in this state was last surrendered, engaged in any activity in this state, except as set forth in paragraph (b) of section 1301 (Authorization of foreign corporations), or in lieu thereof the consent of the state tax commission to the filing of the application, which consent shall be attached thereto.

(b) Attached to the application for authority shall be a certificate by an authorized officer of the jurisdiction of its incorporation that the foreign corporation is an existing corporation. If such certificate is in a foreign language, a translation thereof under oath of the translator shall be attached thereto.

History: Add, L 1961, ch 855, eff Sept 1, 1963; amd, L 1962, ch 834, § 90, eff Sept 1, 1963; L 1963, ch 684, § 1, eff Sept 1, 1963; L 1975, ch 364, eff Sept 1, 1975; repealed, L 1980, ch 357, § 1, eff June 23, 1980; L 1982, ch 590, § 7, eff Oct 20, 1982; L 1983, ch 186, § 1, eff June 30, 1983; L 1985, ch 499, § 2, eff Oct 22, 1985; L 1998, ch 375, § 16, eff Aug 13, 1998.

CASE ANNOTATIONS

1. In general
2. Designated agent
3. Corporate name
4. Jurisdiction over foreign corporations.

1. In general

Under former Gen. Corp. L. it was held that if the name of a foreign corporation did not "clearly indicate" that it was a corporation, and it was unwilling to make such changes or additions as would result in meeting this general New York requirement with respect to corporate names, the secretary of state could deny its application for authority to do business in New York. People ex rel. United Verde Copper Co. v Hugo, 181 A.D. 149, 168 N.Y.S. 80, 1917 N.Y. App. Div. LEXIS 9054 (N.Y. App. Div. 1917).

A Secretary of State's responsibility in passing upon certificates of authority is, however, limited. Industrial Psychology, Inc. v Simon, 16 A.D.2d 114, 226 N.Y.S.2d 148, 1962 N.Y. App. Div. LEXIS 10836 (N.Y. App. Div. 1st Dep't 1962).

An incorporated alien insurer is not required to designate a residence office in its application for authority to do business filed with the secretary of state. General Accident Fire & Life Assurance Corp. v Allcity Ins. Co., 53 Misc. 2d 596, 279 N.Y.S.2d 422, 1967 N.Y. Misc. LEXIS 1630 (N.Y. Sup. Ct. 1967).

The "office" or "principal place of business" of a foreign corporation is at whatever location it designates in its application for authority to do business, but if it fails to seek such authority or designate such a location, the question, where material, becomes one of fact. Kibler v Transcontinental & Western Air, Inc., 63 F. Supp. 724, 1945 U.S. Dist. LEXIS 1770 (D.N.Y. 1945).

2. Designated agent

A state may constitutionally require a foreign corporation, as a condition of doing local business, to designate an agent upon whom service of process may be made. Neirbo Co. v Bethlehem Shipbuilding Corp., 308 U.S. 165, 60 S. Ct. 153, 84 L. Ed. 167, 1939 U.S. LEXIS 77 (U.S. 1939).

Designation of the secretary of state, or some other local agent for service of process in New York, amounts to consent to be sued there for purposes of federal jurisdiction and venue, and service on the designated agent of federal court process is thereby authorized. Roger v A. H. Bull & Co., 170 F.2d 664, 1948 U.S. App. LEXIS 4176 (2d Cir. N.Y. 1948); Trounstine v Bauer, Pogue & Co., 44 F. Supp. 767, 1942 U.S. Dist. LEXIS 2910 (D.N.Y. 1942), aff'd, 144 F.2d 379, 1944 U.S. App. LEXIS 2844 (2d Cir. N.Y. 1944); American Blower Corp. v B. F. Sturtevant Co., 61 F. Supp. 756, 1945 U.S. Dist. LEXIS 2055 (D.N.Y. 1945); Detachable Bit Co. v Timken Roller Bearing Co., 31 F. Supp. 632, 1940 U.S. Dist. LEXIS 3440 (D.N.Y. 1940).

Although plaintiff argued that defendants' registration pursuant to N.Y. Bus. Corp. Law § 1304 alone was insufficient to avoid attachment in the Southern District of New York, registration with the New York Department of State, pursuant to § 1304, to conduct business in New York and designation of an agent within the district upon whom process could be served constituted being found within the district for purposes of Supp. R. Adm. or Mar. Cl. & Asset Forfeiture Actions B (Rule B). Because plaintiff was not entitled to maintain its attachment by virtue of defendants' being found within the district, it could not demonstrate a likelihood of success on the merits for purposes of its motion, and, necessarily, it also lost the underlying appeal. STX Panocean (UK) Co. v Glory Wealth Shipping Pte Ltd., 560 F.3d 127, 2009 U.S. App. LEXIS 5751 (2d Cir. N.Y. 2009).

Service on the designated agent is nonetheless binding and effective because the corporation has actually not done business in New York, the designation not having been withdrawn. Aaron v Agwilines, Inc., 75 F. Supp. 604, 1948 U.S. Dist. LEXIS 3368 (D.N.Y. 1948).

Fact that defendant shipping company is authorized to do business in New York pursuant to certificate of authority under Business Corporation Law § 1304, which authorizes service of process on Secretary of State of New York does not defeat maritime attachment, since there was express provision in subject lease contract calling for service of process on company's agent and plaintiffs made unsuccessful attempt to mail notice to such agent. Integrated Container Service, Inc. v Starlines Container Shipping, Ltd., 476 F. Supp. 119, 1979 U.S. Dist. LEXIS 10599 (S.D.N.Y. 1979).

By registering to do business in New York, an alleged patent infringer consented to personal jurisdiction under the statute; even if registration alone was insufficient, when the alleged infringer's minimal contacts with New York were considered in connection with its registration to do business in the state, the requirements of due process were satisfied. Steuben Foods, Inc. v Oystar Group, 2013 U.S. Dist. LEXIS 187536 (W.D.N.Y. May 14, 2013).

3. Corporate name

Under former Gen Corp L, a foreign corporation's designation of the secretary of state as its agent for service of process was not limited to process in actions asserted against it as the principal defendant but broad enough to make service on the secretary of state valid and effective with respect to a subpoena issued in connection with supplementary proceedings. Nesbitt v Nesbitt, 39 Misc. 2d 855, 241 N.Y.S.2d 611, 1963 N.Y. Misc. LEXIS 1754 (N.Y. Sup. Ct. 1963).

An application by a corporation organized under the laws of the Territory of Virgin Islands to do business in New York was properly denied by the Secretary of State where the applicant's corporate name included the word "psychology," in view of art. 153 of the Education Law. Industrial Psychology, Inc. v Simon, 27 Misc. 2d 879, 211 N.Y.S.2d 256, 1960 N.Y. Misc. LEXIS 1968 (N.Y. Sup. Ct. 1960), dismissed, 15 A.D.2d 905, 1962 N.Y. App. Div. LEXIS 10838 (N.Y. App. Div. 1st Dep't 1962).

4. Jurisdiction over foreign corporations.

Foreign car and tire makers did not consent to the personal general jurisdiction of New York courts in an action arising from an automobile accident occurring in Virginia by registering to do business in New York or appointing the Secretary of State as the makers' agent because, under evolving in personam jurisdiction jurisprudence, such acts did not consent to New York courts' general jurisdiction on claims unrelated to New York. Aybar v Aybar, 2019 N.Y. App. Div. LEXIS 444 (N.Y. App. Div. 2d Dep't 2019).

Nonresident corporation could not be deemed to have consented to general jurisdiction by registering to transact business within the state. New York cases that had relied on a consent-by-registration theory of general jurisdiction are no longer persuasive in light of more recent Supreme Court case law holding that due process does not permit the exercise of general jurisdiction over corporations unless their activities in the state render them essentially at home. Wilderness USA, Inc. v Deangelo Bros. LLC, 265 F. Supp. 3d 301, 2017 U.S. Dist. LEXIS 135555 (W.D.N.Y. 2017).

§ 1305. Application for authority; effect

Upon filing by the department of state of the application for authority the foreign corporation shall be authorized to do in this state any business set forth in the application. Such authority shall continue so long as it retains its authority to do such business in the jurisdiction of its incorporation and its authority to do business in this state has not been surrendered, suspended or annulled in accordance with law.

History: Add, L 1961, ch 855, eff Sept 1, 1963.

§ 1306. Powers of authorized foreign corporations

An authorized foreign corporation shall have such powers as are permitted by the laws of the jurisdiction of its incorporation but no greater powers than those of a domestic corporation formed for the business set forth in the application for authority.

History: Add, L 1961, ch 855, eff Sept 1, 1963.

§ 1307. Tenure of real property

A foreign corporation may acquire and hold real property in this state in furtherance of its corporate purposes and may convey the same by deed or otherwise in the same manner as a domestic corporation.

History: Add, L 1961, ch 855, eff Sept 1, 1963.

CASE ANNOTATIONS

The power to "convey" property, granted by § 221 of former Gen. Corp. L., included power to mortgage. Re Heffron Co. (1914, DC NY) 216 F 642

If acquisition of similar property for similar purposes would require a domestic corporation to obtain approval of some state board or agency, a foreign corporation would likewise have to obtain such approval.1955 Ops Atty Gen Apr 20 (informal)

§ 1308. Amendments or changes

(a) An authorized foreign corporation may amend or change its application for authority from time to time in any and as many of the following respects as may be desired if the amendments contain only such provisions as might be lawfully contained in an application for authority at the time of making such amendment:

(1) To change its corporate name if such change has been effected under the laws of the jurisdiction of its incorporation.

(2) To change its fictitious name filed pursuant to paragraph (d) of section 1301 of this chapter, to another fictitious name, if its true corporate name is not available for use in this state.

(3) To delete its fictitious name filed pursuant to paragraph (d) of section 1301 of this chapter, if its true corporate name is now available for use in this state.

(4) To adopt a fictitious name when the corporate name is changed and is not available in this state.

(5) To enlarge, limit or otherwise change the business which it proposes to do in this state.

(6) To change the location of its office in this state.

(7) To specify or change the post office address to which the secretary of state shall mail a copy of any process against it served upon him.

(8) To make, revoke or change the designation of a registered agent or to specify or change his address.

(9) To change the jurisdiction of its incorporation if such change has been effected under laws permitting such a change to occur.

History: Add, L 1961, ch 855, eff Sept 1, 1963; amd, L 1962, ch 834, § 91, eff Sept 1, 1963; amd, L 1964, ch 725, § 14, eff June 1, 1964; L 1982, ch 590, § 8, eff Oct 20, 1982; L 1983, ch 186, § 2, eff June 30, 1983; L 1991, ch 20, § 1, eff March 15, 1991.

§ 1309. Certificate of amendment; contents, effect

(a) To accomplish such amendment a certificate, entitled "Certificate of amendment of application for authority of .... (name of corporation) under section 1309 of the Business Corporation Law", shall be signed and delivered to the department of state. It shall set forth:

(1) The name of the foreign corporation as it appears on the index of names of existing domestic and authorized foreign corporations of any type or kind in the department of state, division of corporations and the fictitious name the corporation has agreed to use in this state pursuant to paragraph (d) of section 1301 of this chapter.

(2) The jurisdiction of its incorporation. If the jurisdiction of its incorporation has been changed, a

Business Corporation Law

statement that the change of jurisdiction has been effected under laws permitting such a change to occur, citing such laws, and including the date the change in jurisdiction was so effected; and a statement that annexed to this certificate of amendment of application for authority is the certificate required by paragraph (b) of this section.

(3) The date it was authorized to do business in this state.

(4) Each amendment effected thereby.

(5) If the true corporate name of the foreign corporation is to be changed, a statement that the change of name has been effected under the laws of the jurisdiction of its incorporation and the date the change was so effected.

(6) If the business it proposes to do in this state is to be enlarged, limited or otherwise changed, a statement that it is authorized to do in the jurisdiction of its incorporation the business which it proposes to do in this state.

(b) If the jurisdiction of its incorporation has been changed, annexed to the certificate of amendment of application for authority shall be a certificate by an authorized officer of the new jurisdiction of its incorporation that such foreign corporation is an existing corporation domiciled in that jurisdiction. If the annexed certificate by an authorized officer is not in the English language, there shall be attached thereto a translation thereof in the English language under oath of the translator.

(c) If an authorized foreign corporation has changed its name in the jurisdiction of its incorporation, or has changed its jurisdiction of incorporation, it shall deliver to the department of state within twenty days after the change became effective in that jurisdiction a certificate of amendment under paragraph (a) of this section. Upon its failure to deliver such certificate, its authority to do business in this state shall upon the expiration of said twenty days be suspended. The filing by the department of state of a certificate of amendment changing the corporate name or jurisdiction of incorporation within one hundred twenty days after the effective date of the change of name in the jurisdiction of its incorporation or of the change of jurisdiction of its incorporation effected under laws permitting such a change to occur shall annul the suspension,and its authority to do business in this state shall be restored and continue as if no suspension had occurred. The secretary of state shall continue as agent of the foreign corporation upon whom process against the foreign corporation may be served in the manner set forth in paragraph (b) of section 306 (Service of process), in any action or special proceeding based upon any liability or obligation incurred by it within this state before the filing of the certificate of amendment changing the corporate name or changing the jurisdiction of incorporation.

History: Add, L 1961, ch 855, eff Sept 1, 1963; amd, L 1962, ch 834, § 92, eff Sept 1, 1963; L 1964, ch 71, eff Mar 2, 1964; L 1982, ch 590, § 9, eff Oct 20, 1982; L 1983, ch 186, § 3, eff June 30, 1983; L 1991, ch 20, § 2-4, eff March 15, 1991; L 1998, ch 375, § 17, eff Aug 13, 1998.

CASE ANNOTATIONS

Foreign corporation that failed to file amended certificate to do business in New York as required by CLS Bus Corp § 1309 lacked capacity to bring Article 78 proceeding to compel Department of Health to grant its request for hearing prior to revoking provisional approval for it to operate asbestos training facility under 10 NYCRR § 73.8(a). United Envtl. Techniques v State Dep't of Health (1996) 88 N.Y.2d 824, 643 N.Y.S.2d 959, 666 N.E.2d 552

Distributor failed to state cause of action against supplier and its parent for breach of exclusive distribution agreement where complaint was devoid of even conclusory allegations tending to show parent's liability, documents submitted in opposition to plaintiff's motion did not mention parent, plaintiff's affidavit contained no evidence of self-dealing, commingling of funds, lack of corporate formalities, or other veil-piercing indicia, there was no allegation that subsidiary was used for purpose of committing wrong, and there was no merit to claim that subsidiary failed to comply with CLS Bus Corp § 1309. Hartej Corp. v Pepsico World Trading Co. (1998, 1st Dept) 255 A.D.2d 233, 680 N.Y.S.2d 237

§ 1309-A. Certificate of change; contents

(a) In lieu of a certificate of amendment, an authorized foreign corporation, upon compliance with this section, may make any or all of the following changes in its application for authority:

(1) To change the location of its office in this state.

(2) To specify or change the post office address to which the secretary of state shall mail a copy of any process against it served upon him.

(3) To make, revoke or change the designation of a registered agent or specify or change his address.

(b) To accomplish such change, a certificate entitled "Certificate of change of application for authority of .... (name of corporation) under section 1309-A of the Business Corporation Law" shall be signed and delivered to the department of state.

It shall set forth:

(1) The name of the foreign corporation as it appears on the index of names of existing domestic and authorized foreign corporations of any type or kind in the department of state, division of corporations and the fictitious name the corporation has agreed to use in this state pursuant to paragraph (d) of section 1301 of this chapter.

(2) The jurisdiction of its incorporation.

(3) The date it was authorized to do business in this state.

(4) Each change effected thereby.

(c) A certificate of change of application for authority which changes only the post office address to which the secretary of state shall mail a copy of any process against an authorized foreign corporation served upon him or which changes the address of its registered agent, provided such address is the address of a person, partnership or other corporation whose address, as agent, is the address to be changed or who has been designated as registered agent for such authorized foreign corporation, may be signed and delivered to the department of state by such agent. The certificate of change of application for authority shall set forth the statements required under subparagraphs (1), (2), (3) and (4) of paragraph (b) of this section; that a notice of the proposed change was mailed by the party signing the certificate to the authorized foreign corporation not less than thirty days prior to the date of delivery to the department and that such corporation has not objected thereto; and that the party signing the certificate is the agent of such foreign corporation to whose address the secretary of state is required to mail copies of process or the registered agent, if such be the case. A certificate signed and delivered under this paragraph shall not be deemed to effect a change of location of the office of the corporation in whose behalf such certificate is filed.

History: Add, L 1964, ch 725, § 15, eff June 1, 1964; amd, L 1982, ch 590, § 10, eff Oct 20, 1982; L 1983, ch 186, § 4, eff June 30, 1983; L 1998, ch 375, § 18, eff Aug 13, 1998; L 1999, ch 172, § 12, eff July 6, 1999.

CASE ANNOTATIONS

In personal injury action against New Jersey corporation arising from accident that occurred in Nassau County, plaintiff properly placed venue in New York County on ground that New York County was defendant's principal place of business in New York on date of accident, and court erred in removing venue to Nassau County based on affidavit of defendant's vice-president and corporate counsel asserting that corporation's principal place of business was in Fort Lee, New Jersey, as defendant's initial designation of New York County, in its 1965 Application for Certificate of Authority, was not altered by Certificate of Change of Application for Authority filed in 1992 changing its address for service of process to Fort Lee, New Jersey. Nadle v L.O. Realty Corp. (2001, 1st Dept) 286 A.D.2d 130, 735 N.Y.S.2d 1

§ 1310. Surrender of authority

(a) An authorized foreign corporation may surrender its authority. A certificate, entitled "Certificate of surrender of authority of .... (name of corporation) under section 1310 of the Business Corporation Law", shall be signed and delivered to the department of state. It shall set forth:

(1) The name of the foreign corporation as it appears on the index of names of existing domestic and authorized foreign corporations of any type or kind in the department of state, division of corporations or, the fictitious name the corporation has agreed to use in this state pursuant to paragraph (d) of section 1301 of this chapter.

(2) The jurisdiction of its incorporation.

(3) The date it was authorized to do business in this state.

(4) That it surrenders its authority to do business in this state.

(5) That it revokes the authority of its registered agent, if any, previously designated and consents that process against it in any action or special proceeding based upon any liability or obligation incurred by it

within this state before the filing of the certificate of surrender may be served on the secretary of state after the filing thereof in the manner set forth in paragraph (b) of section 306 (Service of process).

(6) A post office address within or without this state to which the secretary of state shall mail a copy of any process against it served upon him.

(b) The department shall not file such certificate unless the consent of the state tax commission to the surrender of authority is attached thereto.

(c) The authority of the foreign corporation to do business in this state shall terminate on the filing by the department of state of the certificate of surrender of authority.

(d) The post office address specified under subparagraph (6) of paragraph (a) of this section may be changed. A certificate, entitled "Certificate of amendment of certificate of surrender of authority of .... (name of corporation) under section 1310 of the Business Corporation Law", shall be signed as provided in paragraph (a) of this section and delivered to the department of state. It shall set forth:

(1) The name of the foreign corporation.

(2) The jurisdiction of its incorporation.

(3) The date its certificate of surrender of authority was filed by the department of state.

(4) The changed post office address, within or without this state, to which the secretary of state shall mail a copy of any process against it served upon him.

History: Add, L 1961, ch 855, eff Sept 1, 1963; amd, L 1962, ch 834, § 93, eff Sept 1, 1963; L 1982, ch 590, § 11, eff Oct 20, 1982; L 1998, ch 375, § 19, eff Aug 13, 1998; L 1999, ch 172, § 13, eff July 6, 1999.

CASE ANNOTATIONS

Among "liabilities and obligations" of a corporation existing at time of filing of a certificate of surrender of authority was its duty or obligation to require officers and directors guilty of misconduct prior to such filing to account for wastage of assets, and the like; and it was accordingly held that summons could and should be served on the corporate defendant by serving the secretary of state, in a stockholder's derivative action charging such misconduct and failure or refusal of the corporate management to sue. Thorne v Brand (1938) 277 N.Y. 212, 14 N.E.2d 42; Herold v Wills (1952) 201 Misc 114, 110 N.Y.S.2d 321; Lissauer v Brown (1941, Sup) 86 N.Y.S.2d 35, affd 262 A.D. 723, 28 N.Y.S.2d 722; Druckerman v Harbord (1940) 174 Misc 1077, 22 N.Y.S.2d 595; Spielberger v Textron Inc. (1949, CA2 NY) 172 F.2d 85

Where foreign corporation has surrendered its authority to do business in New York and has consented to service on Secretary of State in accordance with subd a (5) of above statute, an instrument executed by it in New York while authorized to do business here guaranteeing an obligation of third party under sublease of business property in Massachusetts which later resulted in declaratory judgment there that specified sum of money was due upon such guarantee and action on Massachusetts judgment was brought in New York for such sum, such action was on liability or obligation incurred within this state within meaning of such subdivision. Jay's Stores, Inc. v Ann Lewis Shops, Inc. (1965) 15 N.Y.2d 141, 256 N.Y.S.2d 600, 204 N.E.2d 638

Under § 216 of former Gen. Corp. L., a foreign corporation's surrender of its authority to do business in New York had the effect of withdrawing its authorization for service of process against it on the secretary of state or other authorized agent with respect to future litigation generally, but not with respect to liabilities existing at time of filing the surrender certificate. Saxe v Sugarland Mfg. Co. (1919) 189 A.D. 204, 178 N.Y.S. 454; Mid-Continent Petroleum Corp. v Universal Oil Products Co. (1950) 198 Misc 1073, 102 N.Y.S.2d 74, affd 278 A.D. 564, 102 N.Y.S.2d 451; Green v Clark (1959, DC NY) 173 F. Supp. 233; General Motors Overseas Operations Div. v The Lichtenstein (1954, DC NY) 126 F. Supp. 395

Where a foreign corporation had filed a certificate of surrender of authority to do business in this state, in order to sustain service of process on the secretary of state the complaint must show that the liability was incurred within this state and prior to the surrender of authority to do business. Hexter v Day-Elder Motors Corp. (1920) 192 A.D. 394, 182 N.Y.S. 717

A transfer of corporate assets in fraud of creditors was considered as giving rise to corporate liability, and so was an alleged violation of the Sherman Anti-Trust Law, or some other federal penal statute, if occurring prior to surrender of authority, and either would warrant service on the secretary of state. Irving Trust Co. v Miss L. Brogan, Inc. (1936) 247 A.D. 275, 287 N.Y.S. 423; United States v Brakes, Inc. (1958, DC NY) 157 F. Supp. 916; Re Grand Jury Subpoenas Duces Tecum, etc. (1947, DC NY) 72 F. Supp. 1013

Section 216 of former Gen. Corp. L. authorized service of process against the corporation on the secretary of state with respect to liabilities existing at time of filing the certificate of surrender of authority, notwithstanding the surrender, and it was construed as requiring recourse to this method of service and rendering service on an officer or agent of the corporation, in a case involving such liabilities, improper and inadequate. Cappello v Union Carbide & Carbon Corp. (1950) 276 A.D. 277, 95 N.Y.S.2d 36

A reorganization proceeding under the Martin Act involved existing liabilities and obligations and could likewise be commenced by serving the secretary of state. People v Bankers' Capital Corp. (1930) 137 Misc 293, 241 N.Y.S. 693

The liability or obligation, to warrant service on the secretary of state after filing of a certificate of surrender of authority, under § 216 of former Gen. Corp. L., further must have been incurred within the State of New York; but it was deemed sufficient to satisfy this aspect that individual defendants in a stockholder's derivative suit were residents of New York and subject to the jurisdiction of its courts.Devlin v Webster (1946) 188 Misc 891, 66 N.Y.S.2d 464, affd 272 A.D. 793, 71 N.Y.S.2d 706; Druckerman v Harbord (1940) 174 Misc 1077, 22 N.Y.S.2d 595

A corporate liability or obligation could be regarded as "incurred within this state" if it ran to a resident of New York, notwithstanding the acts giving rise to it took place elsewhere. Carlton Properties, Inc. v 328 Properties, Inc. (1955) 208 Misc 776, 143 N.Y.S.2d 140

In an action for personal injuries against a foreign corporation which filed a certificate of surrender of authority with the Secretary of State and contended that, therefore, the Secretary lacked the power to accept service of process on the corporation's behalf after the date of filing the certificate, the corporation's motion to dismiss is denied since service was properly effectuated upon the corporation by service on the Secretary of State; the certificate, executed in accordance with the statutory requirements of Business Corporation Law § 1310, provided that the corporation consented to be served with process through the Secretary of State based upon any liability incurred within the State before the filing of the certificate, and although plaintiff's accident did not occur until after the date of filing, the allegedly defective product which the corporation manufactured was put into the stream of commerce prior to the filing date. The Hague Convention (20 UST 361), which the corporation contends provides the requirements of service, is not applicable since "there is [no] occasion to transmit a judicial or extrajudicial document for service abroad." However, insofar as any liability of the corporation may exist for acts subsequent to the filing of the certificate, plaintiff is bound by the provisions of the Convention and must effect service pursuant thereto. Karaszewski v Honda Motor Co.,142 Misc. 2d 653

Though a Delaware corporation, against which an action for accounting was brought, ceased to exist under Delaware laws, it might be still existent in New York so that the winding up of its business and administration of the assets could be carried on in New York where it did its business and where the controversy in suit arose. Trounstine v Bauer, Pogue & Co. (1942, DC NY) 44 F. Supp. 767, affd (CA2 NY) 144 F.2d 379, cert den 323 US 777, 89 L Ed 621, 65 S Ct 190

§ 1311. Termination of existence

When an authorized foreign corporation is dissolved or its authority or existence is otherwise terminated or cancelled in the jurisdiction of its incorporation or when such foreign corporation is merged into or consolidated with another foreign corporation, a certificate of the secretary of state, or official performing the equivalent function as to corporate records, of the jurisdiction of incorporation of such foreign corporation attesting to the occurrence of any such event or a certified copy of an order or decree of a court of such jurisdiction directing the dissolution of such foreign corporation, the termination of its existence or the cancellation of its authority shall be delivered to the department of state. The filing of the certificate, order or decree shall have the same effect as the filing of a certificate of surrender of authority under section 1310 (Surrender of authority). The secretary of state shall continue as agent of the foreign corporation upon whom process against it may be served in the manner set forth in paragraph (b) of section 306 (Service of process), in any action or special proceeding based upon any liability or obligation incurred by the foreign corporation within this state prior to the filing of such certificate, order or decree and he shall promptly cause a copy of any such process to be mailed by registered mail, return receipt requested, to such foreign corporation at the post office address on file in his office specified for such purpose. The post office address may be changed by signing and delivering to the department of state a certificate of change setting forth the statements required under section 1309-A (Certificate of change; contents) to effect a change in the post office address under subparagraph (a) (4) of section 1308 (Amendments or changes).

History: Add, L 1961, ch 855, amd, L 1962, ch 834, § 94, L 1963, ch 684, § 2, eff Sept 1, 1963, L 1964, ch 725, § 16, eff June 1, 1964.

Amd, L 1998, ch 375, § 20, eff Aug 13, 1998.

CASE ANNOTATIONS

Although New York permits service of process upon the Secretary of State to commence a suit against an authorized foreign corporation even after dissolution and provides for the appointment of receiver to liquidate assets in New York of any dissolved foreign corporation, there is no authority for holding a dissolved foreign corporation's former officers or directors personally liable for claims against the corporation.Schenin v Micro Copper Corp. (1967, SD NY) 272 F. Supp. 523

§ 1312. Actions or special proceedings by unauthorized foreign corporations

(a) A foreign corporation doing business in this state without authority shall not maintain any action or special proceeding in this state unless and until such corporation has been authorized to do business in this state and it has paid to the state all fees and taxes imposed under the tax law or any related statute, as defined in section eighteen hundred of such law, as well as penalties and interest charges related thereto, accrued against the corporation. This prohibition shall apply to any successor in interest of such foreign corporation.

(b) The failure of a foreign corporation to obtain authority to do business in this state shall not impair the validity of any contract or act of the foreign corporation or the right of any other party to the contract to maintain any action or special proceeding thereon, and shall not prevent the foreign corporation from defending any action or special proceeding in this state.

History: Add, L 1961, ch 855, eff Sept 1, 1963.

Par (b), amd, L 1963, ch 684, § 3, eff Sept 1, 1963.

Par (a), amd, L 1990, ch 190, § 1, eff May 25, 1990.

CASE ANNOTATIONS

1. In general
2. Prohibiting actions or special proceedings, generally
3. – Particular cases
4. Pleadings and burden of proof
5. Other procedural matters
6. Doing business within state, generally
7. – Not doing business
8. Interstate commerce
9. Relation to jurisdictional statute
10. Miscellaneous

UNDER FORMER GEN CORP § 218

1. In general
2. Actions in contract, generally
3. – Particular cases
4. Contract "made in New York"
5. Pleadings and burden of proof
6. Federal courts
7. Other procedural matters
8. Doing business within state, generally
9. – Not doing business
10. Interstate commerce
11. Validity of contracts or acts, generally
12. – Defenses and counterclaims

1. In general

In an action to foreclose on mortgages, the provisions of Bus Corp Law § 1312 had no application to plaintiff foreign corporation formed for banking purposes and carrying on banking business in New York, and did not preclude the maintenance of the action which was specifically authorized by Banking Law § 200. Commonwealth Bank & Trust Co. v Tioga Mills, Inc. (1980, 3d Dept) 78 A.D.2d 953, 433 N.Y.S.2d 519

Although a foreign corporation subrogee stands in the shoes of its subrogor and thus need not qualify under Business Corporation Law § 1312(a) in order to bring an action, a foreign corporation that was both a subrogee and an assignee was a real party in interest and thus was required to qualify. Safeco Ins. Co. v Gabbayan Ahdout Corp. (1984, 1st Dept) 99 A.D.2d 443, 470 N.Y.S.2d 620

CLS Business Corporation Law § 1312(a) is not designed to deny access to New York courts by foreign corporation; rather it is intended to require that those who do business in this state be authorized to do so. Tinterorias Ibericas de Peleteria, S.A. v GAFCO, Inc. (1985, 1st Dept) 114 A.D.2d 329, 494 N.Y.S.2d 318

CLS Bus Corp § 1312, which provides that foreign corporation doing business in state without authority may not maintain New York action unless authorized to do business in state, does not limit right of such foreign corporation to defend action by serving third-party complaint seeking contribution or indemnification. Reese v Harper Surface Finishing Systems (1987, 2d Dept) 129 A.D.2d 159, 517 N.Y.S.2d 522

CLS Bus Corp § 1312(a) was meant to regulate foreign corporations doing business in New York and to protect against avoidance of contractual obligations; however, absent proof that plaintiff foreign corporation is doing business in New York, it is presumed that it is doing business in state of its incorporation and not in New York.

Airline Exch., Inc. v Bag (1999, 2d Dept) 266 A.D.2d 414, 698 N.Y.S.2d 694

This section is not applicable where foreign corporation not authorized to do business in the state merges with a domestic corporation which furnished the materials which gave rise to the lien presently asserted by the foreign corporation. American Cement Corp. v Dunetz Bros., Inc. (1965) 47 Misc. 2d 747, 263 N.Y.S.2d 119

The language of Business Corporation Law §§ 1301 (a) and 1312 is limited strictly to foreign corporations organized for profit. Anti-Defamation League of B'Nai B'Rith v American Italian Anti-Defamation League, Inc. (1967) 54 Misc. 2d 830, 283 N.Y.S.2d 828, 156 USPQ 280

The purpose of requiring foreign corporations doing business in the state to comply with Business Corporation Law § 1312, subd (a) as a prerequisite to maintaining a suit in the state is to protect domestic corporations from unfair competition and to place them on an equal footing with corporations who are using the facilities provided by the state of New York in the conduct of their business.Dixie Dinettes, Inc. v Schaller's Furniture, Inc. (1972) 71 Misc. 2d 102, 335 N.Y.S.2d 632

Acting as third party plaintiff is not barred by defendant's noncompliance with CLS Bus Corp § 1312, as it is not defendant's choice to use New York as forum, judicial economy would not be served by forcing defendant to institute separate action to assert third party claims, and question of whether defendant can obtain jurisdiction over third party defendant outside of New York may arise. Williams Erectors of Suffolk County v Mulach Steel Corp. (1988, ED NY) 684 F. Supp. 357

2. Prohibiting actions or special proceedings, generally

No useful purpose would be served in annotating this § 1312 of the Business Corporation Law by going into detail as to what were or were not deemed contracts made by a foreign corporation in New York while lacking authority to do business here. The prohibition against enforcement of rights in a New York court is no longer thus limited. It may be noted, however, that if the contract was made in New York, it was immaterial that it was made with a nonresident or another foreign corporation, or that the particular transaction was in the field of interstate commerce.East Coast Oil Co. v Hollins (1918) 183 A.D. 67, 170 N.Y.S. 576; Talbot Mills, Inc. v Benezra (1962) 35 Misc. 2d 924, 231 N.Y.S.2d 229

Order which granted plaintiff's motion for summary judgment and judgment entered thereon affirmed-plaintiff commenced action to recover last of three installment payments due from defendant on contract entered into between parties-defendant argued that plaintiff, foreign corporation, was precluded from maintaining action under Business Corporation Law § 1312 (a), which provides that foreign corporation "doing business" in this State without authorization cannot maintain action in New York; only evidence defendant presented was that contract was executed and performed in New York and that plaintiff has New York address and New York bank account; this evidence was insufficient to support defendant's allegation that plaintiff was doing business in this State-defendant should not have been permitted to conduct further discovery on this issue; any unknown information was due to defendant's voluntary inaction, and in any event, failure to obtain authorization to do business is defect that is curable during pendency of action-defendant also claimed that he was fraudulently induced into contract by plaintiff's agent; defendant's assertions were too uncertain and conclusory to defeat summary judgment in plaintiff's favor; defendant in no way explains how or when alleged representations by agent were found to be false. Fine Arts Enters. v Levy, 149 A.D.2d 795

This section cannot constitute defense to causes of action which either accrued or existed prior to the effective date of the statute.St. Regis Paper Co. v Bellin, (1966, 1st Dept) 25 A.D.2d 523, 267 N.Y.S.2d 311

Failure of a foreign corporation doing business in New York to comply with the requirements of subd (a) of § 1312 of the Business Corporation Law affects that corporation's legal capacity to maintain an action; it does not affect jurisdiction. Hot Roll Mfg. Co. v Cerone Equipment Co. (1972, 3d Dept) 38 A.D.2d 339, 329 N.Y.S.2d 466

Plaintiff, Nevada corporation with its principal office in California, had standing as assignee on promissory note to bring action to recover on note where, other than taking steps necessary to carry out assignment of note in question, it did no business in New York. Platus Corp. Pension Plan v Nazareth (2000, 2d Dept) 271 A.D.2d 422, 705 N.Y.S.2d 649

This section prohibits maintenance of "any" action or proceeding by an unqualified foreign corporation unless and until it qualifies and makes restitution of all fees, etc., for the years in which it did business without authority, and, unlike § 218 of the General Corporation Law the prohibition is not limited to actions on contracts made in this state. Wm. G. Roe & Co. v State (1964) 43 Misc. 2d 417, 251 N.Y.S.2d 151

This section now prohibits the maintenance of an action or special proceeding by an unauthorized foreign corporation until it has obtained authority to do business in this state, but this new law does not affect any cause of action which had accrued or was pending as of September 1, 1963, its effective date. Garden State Brickface & Stone Co. v Oradell Constr. Corp. (1964) 44 Misc. 2d 22, 252 N.Y.S.2d 790

Above statute does not provide that foreign corporation doing business in this state without authority may not "commence" action here or that such action if instituted shall be forthwith dismissed. Rather it provides that such plaintiff may not "maintain" action here "unless and until such corporation has been authorized to do business in this state and it has paid to the state all fees, penalties and franchise taxes for the years or parts thereof during which it did business in this state without authority." Thus, upon receipt of such authority and payment of such sums, action previously commenced may be maintained. Oxford Paper Co. v S. M. Liquidation Co. (1965) 45 Misc. 2d 612, 257 N.Y.S.2d 395

Corporation doing business in New York without license may not bring suit in New York courts, but may itself be sued in New York. Traub v Robertson-American Corp. (1975) 82 Misc. 2d 222, 368 N.Y.S.2d 958

Foreign bank not licensed in New York could maintain action to enforce mortgage obligation on real property located in New York since general rule of CLS Bus Corp § 1312 precluding foreign corporation from bringing suit in state was rendered inapplicable by CLS Bank § 200, which expressly authorizes foreign banks without New York branches to make loans in state without qualification or license where loan is secured by mortgage on real property.Skylake State Bank v Solar Heat & Insulation, Inc. (1990) 148 Misc. 2d 32, 559 N.Y.S.2d 930

Corporation, though not qualified to do business in New York and unable to file action, may still raise counterclaims arising out of cause of action upon which corporation is sued. Printers II, Inc. v Professionals Pub., Inc. (1985, SD NY) 615 F. Supp. 767

Filing counterclaim in third party action is within meaning of "defending" action under CLS Bus Corp L § 1312(b), and therefore foreign corporation's failure to comply with § 1312 does not require dismissal. Williams Erectors of Suffolk County v Mulach Steel Corp. (1988, ED NY) 684 F. Supp. 357

3. – Particular cases

Foreign corporation that failed to file amended certificate to do business in New York as required by CLS Bus Corp § 1309 lacked capacity to bring Article 78 proceeding to compel Department of Health to grant its request for hearing prior to revoking provisional approval for it to operate asbestos training facility under 10 NYCRR § 73.8(a). United Envtl. Techniques v State Dep't of Health (1996) 88 N.Y.2d 824, 643 N.Y.S.2d 959, 666 N.E.2d 552

Where foreign corporation and all of its predecessors had paid the required fees and filed the appropriate applications for authority to do business in New York during all times it furnished merchandise to the defendant, foreign corporation was entitled to maintain action to recover for merchandise sold to defendant. Kerr-McGee Chemical Corp. v Bullard Orchards, Inc. (1974, 3d Dept) 45 A.D.2d 786, 356 N.Y.S.2d 734

Mere maintenance of action by foreign corporation does not constitute "doing business" within state, and therefore statutory proscription against actions by unauthorized foreign corporations which are doing business in state is inapplicable.De Ran Landscaping Service, Inc. v De Ran Industries, Inc. (1985, 3d Dept) 109 A.D.2d 1040, 487 N.Y.S.2d 160

Supreme Court did not err in permitting defendant (foreign corporation doing business in New York without authority) to move to compel contractual arbitration, since (1) CLS Bus Corp § 1312 provides that failure to obtain authority to do business in state does not impair validity of contract, and (2) by moving to compel arbitration, defendant was exercising its right to defend against action, and statute also states that unauthorized foreign corporation is not precluded from defending any action or special proceeding in New York. Ruti v Knapp (1993, 2d Dept) 193 A.D.2d 662, 598 N.Y.S.2d 50

CLS Bus Corp § 1312(a) did not require dismissal of action commenced by New York corporation which succeeded to interests of an

unauthorized foreign corporation. Meritor Credit Corp. v Eisenberg (1994, 2d Dept) 204 A.D.2d 284, 614 N.Y.S.2d 156

Court erred in granting defendant's motion to dismiss action on ground that plaintiff's assignor, Pennsylvania corporation, lacked capacity to sue under CLS Bus Corp § 1312(a), even though corporation shipped large amount of its product into New York, since it neither maintained office, telephone, or sales representative in New York, nor did it do any advertising in New York.S & T Bank v Spectrum Cabinet Sales (1998, 2d Dept) 247 A.D.2d 373, 668 N.Y.S.2d 641

Court should have dismissed fraud cause of action where only plaintiffs that loaned money to defendant, and thus only plaintiffs defrauded, were foreign corporations not authorized to do business in New York. Northway Exch., Inc. v Dufrane (1999, 3d Dept) 258 A.D.2d 766, 685 N.Y.S.2d 848

Plaintiff foreign corporation's failure to obtain certificate under CLS Bus Corp § 1312 could be cured before resolution of action and thus was insufficient basis on which to grant summary judgment for defendant. Uribe v Merchants Bank (1999, 1st Dept) 266 A.D.2d 21, 697 N.Y.S.2d 279

Order granting defendant's motion to dismiss would be modified to direct that complaint be dismissed unless within 60 days plaintiff complied with requirements of CLS Bus Corp § 1312(a).Showcase Limousine, Inc. v Carey (2000, 1st Dept) 269 A.D.2d 133, 703 N.Y.S.2d 22, motion gr, in part, mod (1st Dept) 273 A.D.2d 20, 716 N.Y.S.2d 551, subsequent app (App Div, 1st Dept) 716 N.Y.S.2d 552 and app dismd 95 N.Y.2d 902, 716 N.Y.S.2d 642, 739 N.E.2d 1147

The claim of a foreign trucking corporation for property damage caused by alleged negligence in maintaining state highways which accrued on March 20, 1963, was not barred by legislation that provided that an unauthorized foreign corporation could not maintain any action in the state of New York until it obtained authority to do business in this state, which became effective on April 1, 1963, notwithstanding that suit was instituted on June 14, 1963, since the Act had been amended and the effective date extended to September 1, 1963. Tetreault v State (1966) 50 Misc. 2d 170, 269 N.Y.S.2d 812

Foreign corporation which held license to sell bedding in New York state was not thereby rendered the right to access to New York courts to enforce a contract for the sale of dinette equipment.Dixie Dinettes, Inc. v Schaller's Furniture, Inc. (1972) 71 Misc. 2d 102, 335 N.Y.S.2d 632

A "foreign" bank, not licensed in New York, may maintain an action to enforce a mortgage obligation on real property located in the State since the general rule precluding a foreign corporation from bringing suit in the New York courts (Business Corporation Law § 1312) must give way to the specific statutory provision expressly authorizing foreign banks without New York branches to lend in this State without qualification or license where the loan is secured by a mortgage on real property (Banking Law § 200). It would be outrageous from any point of view to permit banks to lend money and obtain security in New York real property by the use of mortgages and then preclude them from enforcing their rights by closing the courts to them. If foreign banks were precluded from enforcement of the collateral in the New York courts, the secondary market for New York mortgage paper would be seriously impaired.Skylake State Bank v Solar Heat & Insulation,148 Misc. 2d 32

Appeals court had previously ruled that the lessor's suit, in part to enforce a payment bond against an insurer after it was not timely paid rent by a public improvement project subcontractor lessee, was timely commenced under N.Y. C.P.L.R. 205(a) and, with respect to whether the lessor was a proper plaintiff, that the lessor had complied with N.Y. Bus. Corp. Law § 1312(a), since the lessor had undoubtedly furnished materials and labor to the subcontractor and thus was covered by the bond by force of N.Y. State Fin. Law § 137(1); these rulings were the law of the case, but the lessor also proved at trial that it was a proper plaintiff.Scaffold-Russ Dilworth Ltd. v Shared Mgmt. Group, Ltd. (2003, A.D., 4th Dept) 768 N.Y.S.2d 65

Business Corporation Law § 1312(a) may not be raised as a defense in an action to compel arbitration brought pursuant to the United States Arbitration Act with diversity as the jurisdictional basis. Grand Bahama Petroleum Co. v Asiatic Petroleum Corp. (1977, CA2 NY) 550 F.2d 1320

Business Corporation Law § 1312 is bar to action by nonregistered Bermuda corporation engaged in business of lending against guarantors to recover under guarantee agreement unless and until Bermuda corporation pays state of New York all fees, penalties and franchise taxes, even though paragraph of guarantee agreement provide that any legal action or proceeding with respect to guarantee could be brought by lender in any jurisdiction where guarantor or its assets can be found or located since overriding policy contained in "door closing" statute may not be negated by private contract. Netherlands Shipmortgage Corp. v Madias (1983, SD NY) 554 F. Supp. 375

Although a producer's motion to remand a breach of contract and other claims against an actor and production company was denied under 28 U.S.C.S. § 1446(b), the motion was subject to renewal upon the granting of the producer's company's N.Y. Bus. Corp. Law 1312(a) application to conduct business in the state and the filing of a properly noticed motion for joinder of that company. Nasso v Seagal .(2003, ED NY) 263 F. Supp. 2d 596

Subcontractor, a foreign corporation doing business in New York without authorization, was nonetheless entitled to defend itself in court, including the right to assert counterclaims and third-party claims. MacQuesten Gen. Contr., Inc. v HCE, Inc. (2003, SD NY) 296 F. Supp. 2d 437

4. Pleadings and burden of proof

Court erred in dismissing, under CLS CPLR § 3211(a)(3), action by North Carolina corporation to recover on contract, concluding that plaintiff was doing business in New York without authority and was thus barred from maintaining action by CLS Bus Corp § 1312(a), where defendant's motion papers did not establish that contract between plaintiff and defendant was other than solitary transaction and that plaintiff's activities in New York were so systematic and regular as to manifest continuity of activity; nevertheless, defendant would not be precluded from setting forth appropriate allegations in its answer as defense. Interline Furniture, Inc. v Hodor Industries, Corp. (1988, 2d Dept) 140 A.D.2d 307, 527 N.Y.S.2d 544

Defense that corporate plaintiff lacked capacity to sue because it failed to comply with requirements of CLS Bus Corp § 1312 was waived where defendant merely stated, in his affidavit in support of motion to dismiss for failure to state cause of action, that plaintiff may not have complied with § 1312, since such defense must be raised by motion to dismiss or in responsive pleading. RCA Records, Div. of RCA Corp. v Wiener (1990, 1st Dept) 166 A.D.2d 221, 564 N.Y.S.2d 89

Determination by Department of Taxation and Finance, allowing foreign company to function in New York, was prima facie evidence of compliance with CLS Bus Corp § 1312(a), but was not entirely dispositive of corporate plaintiff's capacity to sue. McIntosh Builders, Inc. v Ball (1998, 3d Dept) 247 A.D.2d 103, 678 N.Y.S.2d 810

Defense that corporate plaintiff has failed to comply with require-ments of Business Corporation Law § 1312 is based on premise that plaintiff is without legal capacity to sue, and this defense is waived unless raised by motion to dismiss or in responsive pleading; in his affidavit in support of motion to dismiss for failure to state cause of action, defendant's mere statement that plaintiff may not have complied with Business Corporation Law § 1312, without seeking relief on this ground, was insufficient to raise it as defense and it was therefore waived. RCA Records v Wiener, 166 A.D.2d 221

Buyer failed to show its entitlement to dismissal of the seller's breach of contract and unjust enrichment claims on the basis that the seller, a Chinese corporation, lacked capacity to sue because the buyer did not show that the seller's business activities in New York were so systematic and regular as to manifest continuity of activity in New York, such that the seller would be required to have a certificate of authority from the New York Secretary of State to commence an action in New York. Guangzhou Sanhua Plastic Co., Ltd. v Fine Line Prods. Corp., 2018 N.Y. App. Div. LEXIS 6870 (N.Y. App. Div. 2d Dep't 2018).

In an action brought to recover for goods sold and delivered, the defendant had the burden of proving that the plaintiff, which had concededly not filed a certificate authorizing it to do business in this state, had been or was doing business in this state, or that the contract was made in New York. John's, Inc. v Island Garden Center of Nassau, Inc. (1966) 49 Misc. 2d 1086, 269 N.Y.S.2d 231, affd 53 Misc. 2d 1021, 280 N.Y.S.2d 34

Defendant's motion to dismiss plaintiff's complaint for lack of capacity to sue was denied, where it did not appear from the complaint or proofs that the foreign corporation was doing business in New York, and it was held that defendants must raise that issue in their answer and sustain it by proof. Dari-Delite, Inc. v Priest & Baker, Inc. (1966) 50 Misc. 2d 654, 271 N.Y.S.2d 355

Despite statutory provision that objection or defense based on legal incapacity to sue is waived unless raised either before service of responsive pleading or in responsive pleading, where New York defendant's motion to dismiss action by Pennsylvania corporate plaintiff was based on provision of Business Corporation Law precluding foreign corporation which does business in New York without certificate of authority from access to New York courts until it obtains such certificate, defendant did not waive objection by waiting until eve of trial to raise issue by motion to dismiss. Paper Mfrs. Co. v Ris Paper Co. (1976) 86 Misc. 2d 95, 381 N.Y.S.2d 959

Prior to the passage of section 1312 of the Business Corporation Law, which provides that a foreign corporation doing business in this State without authority shall not maintain any action or special proceeding in this State unless and until such corporation has been authorized to do business in this State and it has paid to the State all fees, penalties and franchise taxes for the years or parts thereof during which it did business in this State without authority, a complaint which did not allege that a subject contract was made in New York by a plaintiff foreign corporation was not demurrable; it was presumed that the complaint was sufficient and the court was precluded from speculating as to what the proof upon trial might or might not establish, which presumption is carried over under CPLR 3211 (subd [a]). Accordingly, where it does not appear, either from the complaint or the motion papers, that plaintiff foreign corporation is doing business in this State, defendants' motion for dismissal under CPLR 3211 (subd [a], pars 2, 7) must be denied, leaving the issue to be pleaded as a defense and sustained by trial proof, and the defect, if any, under section 1312 of the Business Corporation Law to be cured anytime prior to judgment; to hold otherwise would deny plaintiff foreign corporation access to the courts of New York, a violation of the commerce clause of the United States Constitution. Atlantic-Corey Crane Service, Inc. v Dory Leasing Corp. (1979) 100 Misc. 2d 995, 420 N.Y.S.2d 465

In a landlord-tenant case involving a dispute over a vault space, the tenant's affirmative defense of the landlord's lack of standing was stricken because the landlord had established that it was a Delaware limited liability company that was authorized to do business in New York; moreover, a party asserting a defense based on N.Y. Bus. Corp. Law § 1312 bore the burden of proof on the issue, and the tenant had submitted no evidence that the tenant lacked authority to do business in New York. Blenheim LLC v Il Posto LLC (2006, Civ Ct) 236 NYLJ 107, 827 NYS2d 620

It is apparent that the burden of proving a corporation must quali-fy before it can sue in the state courts of New York is upon the party attacking the corporate status. Textile Banking Co. v Colonial Chemical Corp. (1967, ND Ga) 285 F. Supp. 824

Defendant seeking to invoke Business Corporation Law § 1312(a) to terminate suit by adversary bears burden of establishing that plaintiff has not met requirements of section, and defendant must show that plaintiff has maintained and carried on regular and continuous course of business conduct in New York. Oliver Promo-tions, Ltd. v Tams-Witmark Music Library, Inc. (1982, SD NY) 535 F. Supp. 1224

5. Other procedural matters

The trial court erred in denying a Canadian corporation's motion to vacate an ex parte order of attachment which a second party had secured on certain funds, in the possession of a third party, to which the corporation claimed title, where the court had jurisdiction over the corporation's motion in that there was neither allegation nor proof that the corporation was transacting or had transacted business within the State of New York so as to bring into play Bus Corp Law § 1312(a), which prohibited the maintenance of an action or special proceeding in New York by a foreign corporation which was doing business in New York without authority, where CPLR § 6223(a) permitted any person having an interest in attached funds to move for the vacation of the order of attachment, and where the second party had failed to timely confirm the attachment. Great White Whale Advertising, Inc. v First Festival Productions (1981, 3d Dept) 81 A.D.2d 704, 438 N.Y.S.2d 655

Dismissal of action due to plaintiff corporation's lack of authority to do business in New York as required by CLS Bus Corp § 1312(a) did not prohibit plaintiff from commencing new action without having obtained authority to do business, and thus dismissal of second action brought by plaintiff within applicable limitations period, also due to lack of authority, did not preclude application of 6-month extension under CLS CPLR § 205(a) when plaintiff obtained authority and commenced third action 3 months after second action was dis-missed.E & L, Inc. v Liberty Mut. Fire Ins. Co. (1996, 1st Dept) 227 A.D.2d 303, 642 N.Y.S.2d 886

Business
Corporation Law

A New York court need not decline to exercise jurisdiction under the doctrine of forum non conveniens of an action by a foreign corporation, most of whose shareholders reside in New York, against a Canadian bank concerning a contract made and to be performed in Canada, where there is nothing to indicate that harm will result to any of those involved by retention of jurisdiction in New York. Plasticos Industriales Extrusos, A. A. v Bank of Nova Scotia (1963) 38 Misc. 2d 9, 237 N.Y.S.2d 802, affd 19 A.D.2d 592, 240 N.Y.S.2d 934

Pennsylvania corporation, which in agreement with plaintiff represented that it had complied with the provisions of Art 13 of the Business Corporation Law, had submitted itself to the jurisdiction of the state and should be estopped from denying it, especially in view of the policies expressed in such statutes as General Corporation Law § 218 and Penal Law § 964. Farmingdale Steer-Inn, Inc. v Steer Inn Realty Corp. (1966) 51 Misc. 2d 986, 274 N.Y.S.2d 379

Proof by foreign corporation that it was licensed during period in question to sell bedding in New York state was not relevant to issue of whether it was licensed to sell a dinette set, and compliance with the provisions of Business Corporation Law § 1312 was a prerequisite to bringing a suit on the contract for sale of such dinette set.Dixie Dinettes, Inc. v Schaller's Furniture, Inc. (1972) 71 Misc. 2d 102, 335 N.Y.S.2d 632

Forum would be convenient for suit against foreign corporation if it was doing business in New York or there were transactions in New York within long-arm statute. Traub v Robertson-American Corp. (1975) 82 Misc. 2d 222, 368 N.Y.S.2d 958

"Inconvenient forum" does not provide ticket out of town for every foreign corporation but only provides that court should not accept jurisdiction of cause having no substantial nexus with New York. Traub v Robertson-American Corp. (1975) 82 Misc. 2d 222, 368 N.Y.S.2d 958

An unincorporated association, operating under an informal status, formed under the laws of the United Kingdom would be permitted to file a new complaint in order to comply with the requirement of Gen Assn Law § 12 that its action be instituted in the name of its president, in the absence of any prejudice to defendant. Further, the plaintiff association, not being a joint stock association, a business trust, or a foreign corporation, was not required to file a certificate pursuant to Gen Assn Law § 18 designating the Secretary of State as agent for service of process, nor to qualify under Bus Corp Law § 1312 in order to do business in the State. Plaintiff would, however, be required to post security for costs pursuant to CPLR § 8503. Formula One Constructors Asso. v Watkins Glen Grand Prix Corp. (1981) 110 Misc. 2d 247, 441 N.Y.S.2d 864

Third party defendant's motion to amend answer to third party complaint to include affirmative defense that third party plaintiff was corporation which was not authorized to do business in State is granted on condition that third party defendant not raise any possible defense based on Statute of Limitations in subsequent action by plaintiff against third-party defendant based upon same facts as gave rise to third party action. Tynon v D. R. McClain & Son (1986) 131 Misc. 2d 203, 499 N.Y.S.2d 354

Where jurisdiction rests on diversity, CLS Bus Corp L § 1312 precludes maintaining of action by unauthorized foreign corporation not only in state courts but also in federal courts located in that state. Netherlands Shipmortgage Corp. v Madias (1983, CA2 NY) 717 F.2d 731

Court would not grant costs to successful plaintiff in diversity of citizenship action where there was some question as to the existence of a certificate to do business for the foreign corporation plaintiff in the state of New York, and said certificate had been in fact obtained during the course of the trial. Tolchester Lines, Inc. v Dowd (1966, SD NY) 253 F. Supp. 643

Acting as third party plaintiff is not barred by defendant's noncompliance with CLS Bus Corp § 1312, as it is not defendant's choice to use New York as forum, judicial economy would not be served by forcing defendant to institute separate action to assert third party claims, and question of whether defendant can obtain jurisdiction over third party defendant outside of New York may arise. Williams Erectors of Suffolk County v Mulach Steel Corp. (1988, ED NY) 684 F. Supp. 357

When jurisdiction in federal court rests on diversity, § 1312 precludes maintaining of an action not only in state courts of New York but also in federal courts located in New York.Expense Reduction Services, Inc. v Jonathan Woodner Co. (1989, SD NY) 720 F. Supp. 262

6. Doing business within state, generally

In order for foreign corporation to be "doing business" in New York under CLS Bus Corp § 1312(a), so as to require authorization before maintaining action, corporation must be engaged in regular and continuous course of conduct in state. Commodity Ocean Transp. Corp. v Royce (1995, 2d Dept) 221 A.D.2d 406, 633 N.Y.S.2d 541

Plaintiff, Canadian corporation that rented and sold scaffolding, could not maintain action because it was "doing business in this state without authority" (CLS Bus Corp § 1312(a)) where it had rented scaffolding to contractors at 8public and private construction projects in New York, and had leased facility in New York for storage of scaffolding and accessories for use on construction projects.Scaffold-Russ Dilworth, Ltd. v Shared Mgmt. Group, Ltd. (1998, 4th Dept) 256 A.D.2d 1087, 682 N.Y.S.2d 765

Appeals court affirmed order that denied officers' motion to dismiss breach of fiduciary duty claims brought by Mississippi entities, in which they had interests, in New York; they did not rebut presumption that entities did business primarily in Mississippi so as to be deprived of the right to sue in New York without being granted authority to do business in New York as a foreign corporation. Nick v Greenfield (2002, 1st Dept) 299 A.D.2d 172, 753 N.Y.S.2d 45

Under § 210 of former Gen Corp L it was held that a foreign insurance company which issued an insurance policy through a New York broker pursuant to § 122 of the Insurance Law, though not authorized to do business in New York, was entitled to maintain an action in a New York court to obtain a declaration of nonliability on such a policy, because it was legally doing business here to the extent permitted by that section of the Insurance Law.Empire Mut. Ins. Co. v International Tram-Po-Line Mfrs., Inc. (1963) 39 Misc. 2d 810, 242 N.Y.S.2d 28

Substantial business transactions consummated within this state through a foreign corporation unlicensed to do business in New York is a violation of Business Corporation Law § 1301 subsection a, and no action pursuant to this section may be maintained to enforce contracts entered into during the course of such business transactions.State by Lefkowitz v ITM, Inc. (1966) 52 Misc. 2d 39, 275 N.Y.S.2d 303, 3 UCCRS 775

Not every instance of business transactions in the state requires the procurement of a certificate of authority in accord with Business Corporation Law § 1312(a); the corporate activities must be more than casual or occasional and must be so systematic and regular as to manifest continuity of activities in this jurisdiction in order to require compliance therewith.Dixie Dinettes, Inc. v Schaller's Furniture, Inc. (1972) 71 Misc. 2d 102, 335 N.Y.S.2d 632

Where Pennsylvania paper manufacturer was regularly promoting its products to ultimate New York users with purpose of inducing users to specify its products when they placed orders with distributors, corporation's activities in New York constituted "doing business in New York" within meaning of Business Corporation Law provision which precludes foreign corporation doing business in New York without certificate of authority from access to New York courts until it obtains such certificate and pays all necessary fees. Paper Mfrs. Co. v Ris Paper Co. (1976) 86 Misc. 2d 95, 381 N.Y.S.2d 959

In the absence of evidence to the contrary, it was to be presumed that plaintiff trust company organized under Puerto Rican law maintained its apartment in New York for use by its officers and employees while they were there to transact the corporation's business and that the corporation would not maintain a permanent apartment in New York unless such business consisted of more than a casual, isolated, or occasional transaction. Maintenance of the apartment therefore constituted "doing business" in New York so as to require qualification under Bus Corp Law § 1312 as a condition precedent to the maintenance of an action for specific performance in New York. Girod Trust Co. v Kingsdown Corp. (1981) 108 Misc. 2d 759, 438 N.Y.S.2d 894

Foreign banking corporation, not licensed in New York but doing business through loan production office properly registered in New York, could maintain mortgage foreclosure action in New York, since (1) corporation had complied with New York law and regulations and was authorized to maintain loan production office, (2) it had been given authority to do limited business of loan production, and (3) it already had right to make mortgage loans at time it created that office in New York and had right to foreclose mortgages in default. Integra Bank N. v Gordon (1995, Sup) 164 Misc. 2d 691, 624 N.Y.S.2d 344

When determining whether a domestic corporation had a right, through a foreign corporation's shareholder, to require the foreign corporation to produce a list of the foreign corporation's shareholders, under N.Y. Bus. Corp. Law § 1315, the applicable standard to apply when determining if the foreign corporation was "doing business" in New York was the standard set forth in N.Y. C.P.L.R. 302, rather than the stricter standard applicable under N.Y. Bus. Corp. Law § 1312, because N.Y. Bus. Corp. Law § 1315 did not raise the Commerce Clause concerns involved when applying N.Y. Bus. Corp. Law § 1312. Airtran N. Y., LLC v Midwest Air Group, Inc. (2007, App Div, 1st Dept) 844 NYS2d 233

N.Y. Bus. Corp. Law § 1312(a), which denies an unauthorized foreign corporation "doing business" in New York capacity to sue there, employs a heightened "doing business" standard, fashioned specifically to avoid unconstitutional interference with interstate commerce under the Commerce Clause. Airtran N. Y., LLC v Midwest Air Group, Inc. (2007, App Div, 1st Dept) 844 NYS2d 233

Since N.Y. Bus. Corp. Law § 1312 constitutes a statutory barrier to a foreign corporation's right to bring suit, a party seeking to impose the barrier, in order to rebut the presumption that the corporation does business in its state of incorporation rather than New York, has the burden of proving that the foreign corporation's activity in New York is systematic and regular, and the burden of showing "doing business" is therefore a heavy one since a lesser showing might infringe on Congress's constitutional power to regulate interstate commerce, and the same concern applies to the N.Y. Bus. Corp. Law § 1301 requirement that a foreign corporation be authorized to "do business" in New York, but those concerns do not apply to N.Y. Bus. Corp. Law § 1315(a), which implicates neither the restriction of a right nor the fear of constitutional infringement. Airtran N. Y., LLC v Midwest Air Group, Inc. (2007, App Div, 1st Dept) 844 NYS2d 233

Dismissal of a Louisiana corporation's lawsuit pursuant to N.Y. Bus. Corp. Law § 1312(a) was proper because defendants submitted undisputed evidence that the Louisiana corporation's business activities in New York were not "casual or occasional," but rather were "systematic and regular," intrastate in character, and essential to its business; among other things, the Louisiana corporation's regional vice president regularly and continuously solicited potential companies in New York in an effort to persuade the companies to retain the Louisiana corporation to conduct and manage "special sales" in New York. The Louisiana corporation undertook an extensive advertising campaign with respect to the "special sales" aimed at New York consumers. Highfill, Inc. v Bruce & Iris, Inc. (2008, App Div, 2d Dept) 855 NYS2d 635.

Distributor's business activities in New York were not "casual or occasional" for N.Y. Bus. Corp. Law § 1312(a) purposes because, inter alia, the distributor had activities with New York based companies, and the essence of parties' contractual relationship described the distributor's network to, inter alia, substantial New York business contacts; the nature of the distributor's business-the supply of material to retail stores-necessarily did not include such case law indicia as advertising, and the distributor's practice did not require an office, telephone, or a sales representative in New York. Instead, the relationship arose out of an Internet auction, used by the distributor to provide services to, inter alia, New York businesses. Schwarz Supply Source v Redi Bag USA LLC (2008, Sup) 241 NYLJ 5, affd in part and mod in part (2009, 2d Dept) 64 App Div 3d 696, 881 NYS2d 900.

As a company had submitted evidence that it paid all applicable taxes and was otherwise fully authorized to do business in New York, the property owner's motion to dismiss the company's action, which sought a prescriptive easement or easement by necessity, was denied. Lew Beach Co. v Carlson (2010, 3d Dept) 77 App Div 3d 1127, 910 NYS2d 565.

Non-registered Bermuda corporation engaged in business of lending is doing business in New York within meaning of Business Corporation Law § 1312 where it engages in 19 consummated loan transactions which are partially closed in New York, and where corporation's chief operating officer travels to New York on regular and recurring basis to execute documents necessary to consummate transactions and to solicits business. Netherlands Shipmortgage Corp. v Madias (1983, SD NY) 554 F. Supp. 375

7. – Not doing business

Swiss corporation was not engaged in "doing business" in New York where it merely ships goods into that state for further shipment by New York corporation,and Swiss corporation could therefore institute suit in New York courts without qualifying as foreign corporation; in any case, Swiss corporation's activity in state was, under United States Constitution, beyond state interference. Von

Arx, AG v Breitenstein (1977) 41 N.Y.2d 958, 394 N.Y.S.2d 876, 363 N.E.2d 582

Activities of plaintiff corporation, which maintained no office, warehouse, telephone listing or bank account in New York, and which solicited orders through an independent sales agent that were then confirmed and accepted in Massachusetts, did not constitute "doing business in this state," within contemplation of statute providing, inter alia, that foreign corporation doing business in New York may not maintain any actions or special proceeding unless and until it has been authorized to do business in the state and has paid to the state all fees, penalties and franchise taxes for the years during which it did business in the state without authority.Sirois Leather, Inc. v Lea-Suede Corp. (1974, 1st Dept) 44 A.D.2d 815, 355 N.Y.S.2d 428

Foreign corporation which (1) kept all its officers and manufacturing facilities in Connecticut, (2) had no employees stationed in New York, (3) had no local New York telephone number, bank accounts or property, and (4) participated in activities in New York (solicitation of business from existing customers and assembly and installation of machines) which were clearly incidental to interstate sales of its surface finishing machines, was not "doing business" in New York under CLS Bus Corp § 1312. Reese v Harper Surface Finishing Systems (1987, 2d Dept) 129 A.D.2d 159, 517 N.Y.S.2d 522

New York activities of Argentina corporation were merely incidental to its business in interstate and international commerce, and thus it was not barred from suing on promissory note signed in New York by New York resident on ground that it was unauthorized foreign corporation doing business in New York within meaning of CLS Bus Corp § 1312; during 7 years that corporation maintained office in New York, it negotiated only 4 transactions, 3 with companies outside New York, and all pertaining to purchase of machinery to be shipped to Argentina. Alicanto, S. A. v Woolverton (1987, 2d Dept) 129 A.D.2d 601, 514 N.Y.S.2d 96

Evidence was insufficient to establish that defendant foreign corporation was doing business within state within meaning of CLS Bus Corp § 1312(a) where only evidence presented was that contract for sale of syndicated partnership interest in thoroughbred horse was executed and performed in state and that corporation had address within state and bank account within state. Fine Arts Enterprises, N. V. v Levy (1989, 3d Dept) 149 A.D.2d 795, 539 N.Y.S.2d 827

Plaintiff foreign corporation was not "doing business" in New York, and thus was not subject to conditions placed by CLS Bus Corp § 1312 on corporate capacity to sue, where plaintiff maintained no office or telephone listing, owned no real property, and had no employees in New York, and its in-state activities were limited to soliciting business and facilitating sale and delivery of merchandise incidental to its business in interstate and foreign commerce. Uribe v Merchants Bank (1999, 1st Dept) 266 A.D.2d 21, 697 N.Y.S.2d 279

Florida corporation's business activities in New York were not so systematic and regular as to manifest continuity, and thus CLS Bus Corp § 1312(a) did not bar it from maintaining action to foreclose mortgage, where it transacted almost all of its business in Florida, it maintained office in Florida and received its mail there, it had one New York bank account, it occasionally used New York office that its president maintained for his other business interests, and it entered into only 3 or 4 transactions in New York during at least 8-year period. Airline Exch., Inc. v Bag (1999, 2d Dept) 266 A.D.2d 414, 698 N.Y.S.2d 694

Foreign corporation had capacity to sue for breach of contract where commencement of that action was not "doing business" within state in violation of CLS Bus Corp §§ 1301(b)(1) and 1312 or CLS Gen Bus § 130. Federal Fin. Co. v Levine (2001, 2d Dept) 281 A.D.2d 454, 721 N.Y.S.2d 558

Trial court properly entered a judgment in favor of a Canadian judgment creditor in its action to enforce a Canadian money judgment against a judgment debtor because the debtor did not rebut the presumption that the creditor did not do business in New York, the Canadian judicial system provided impartial tribunals and procedures compatible with due process of law, and although the creditor failed to establish that the debtor was properly served with process in the Canadian action, the debtor purposefully transacted business in Canada, voluntarily appeared in the Canadian action, and did more than it had to do to preserve a jurisdictional objection. Gemstar Can., Inc. v George A. Fuller Co., Inc., 127 A.D.3d 689, 6 N.Y.S.3d 552 (2d Dep't 2015).

New Jersey corporation was not barred from commencing action in New York on basis that it did not comply with CLS Bus Corp § 1312(a) since evidence did not establish that corporation conducted systematic and regular business activities in New York that were essential to its corporate business; mere solicitation of sales in New York and placement of orders did not constitute "doing business" in state within meaning of statute. Maro Leather Co. v Aerolineas Argentinas (1994, Sup App T) 161 Misc. 2d 920, 617 N.Y.S.2d 617

Company whose connection to New York was limited to taking orders from and delivering goods to New York buyers, with no claim that it had office, advertised, regularly induced purchase of its products by New York users from its New York distributors, or otherwise transacted business in state, was not "doing business" in New York within meaning of CLS Bus Corp § 1312, and thus its unlicensed status did not bar it from maintaining action in New York courts for breach of contract. Bayonne Block Co. v Porco (1996, Civ Ct) 171 Misc. 2d 684, 654 N.Y.S.2d 961

Placement of orders within New York, maintenance of an office within the state, even if coupled with the employment of solicitors to transmit orders obtained here to the home office for acceptance, and even if the corporation's name appears on the door and is listed in telephone and business directories, does not constitute "doing business" with the resulting invocation that a foreign corporation could not bring diversity action in New York against New York corporation without qualifying to do business therein. Stafford-Higgins Industries, Inc. v Gaytone Fabrics, Inc. (1969, SD NY) 300 F. Supp. 65

Ohio corporation did not conduct any business in New York for purposes of application of Business Corporation Law § 1312(a) where it maintained no facilities or local telephone numbers in New York, did not maintain New York bank account, and its salesmen in New York were required to forward all orders to Ohio for processing. Invacare Corp. v John Nageldinger & Son, Inc. (1984, ED NY) 576 F. Supp. 1542

Foreign corporate lessee is not precluded from suing lessor in New York federal district court by CLS Bus Corp Law § 1312, where lessee entered into single contract for leasing of showroom and office space that was ultimately used by its subsidiary, New York corporation, because lessee's contacts with New York were incidental and not so systematic and regular as to make it unauthorized foreign corporation "doing business in state" under § 1312.Storwal Int'l, Inc. v Thom Rock Realty Co., L.P. (1992, SD NY) 784 F. Supp. 1141

Plaintiff's contention that an unauthorized foreign corporation doing business in this state was not entitled to compel arbitration was properly rejected, because such a corporation may seek to compel arbitration defensively. Mergent Servs. v. ITEX Corp., 130 A.D.3d 408, 13 N.Y.S.3d 367 (1 Dept. 2015).

8. Interstate commerce

Denial to foreign corporation engaged solely in interstate commerce of access to New York courts constitutes unlawful interference with foreign corporation's right to engage in interstate commerce. Von Arx, A. G. v Breitenstein (1976, 4th Dept) 52 A.D.2d 1049, 384 N.Y.S.2d 895, affd 41 N.Y.2d 958, 394 N.Y.S.2d 876, 363 N.E.2d 582

Law requiring foreign corporations doing business in state to qualify as such before bringing suit in state may not, under protections afforded by commerce clause of United States Constitution, deny foreign corporation access to New York courts where foreign corporation is engaged solely in interstate commerce. Colonial Mortg. Co. v First Federal Sav. & Loan Asso. (1977, 4th Dept) 57 A.D.2d 1046, 395 N.Y.S.2d 798

Where a foreign corporation's primary contact in New York is to solicit business or to merely facilitate the sale and delivery of its merchandise, such a corporation should be exempt from any burdens which New York laws place upon foreign corporations doing business in New York. Librairie Hachette v Paris Book Center, Inc. (1970) 62 Misc. 2d 873, 309 N.Y.S.2d 701

Where a foreign corporation transacting business within state without authorization prevails in federal court after full and fair trial of issues, District Court properly imposed stay of judgment pending foreign corporation's compliance with CLS Bus Corp § 1312, thus appropriately balancing state interest in enforcing its business licensing requirements with federal interest and efficient disposition of federal diversity cases involving interstate commerce.S & K Sales Co. v Nike, Inc. (1987, CA2 NY) 816 F.2d 843

9. Relation to jurisdictional statute

Judicial Hearing Officer did not err in denying defendant's motion to dismiss complaint for lack of jurisdiction; individual to whom summons was delivered was authorized by corporate officer to accept it on behalf of defendant; denial of motion to dismiss, based on alleged failure to allege and prove compliance with Business Corporation

Law § 1312 (a), was proper because compliance after commencement of action is permissible; furthermore, corporation of which plaintiffs claim to be assignees has been authorized to do business in New York since 1979; court did not err in finding that validity of plaintiffs' alleged assignment could only be determined at trial. Beer v Myers & Co., 159 A.D.2d 943

While some activities of foreign corporation might constitute "doing business" so as to subject foreign corporation to jurisdiction of New York courts, such finding does not necessarily render such corporation liable to qualification requirements of Business Corporation Law governing special proceedings by unauthorized foreign corporations "doing business" in state. Von Arx, A. G. v Breitenstein (1976, 4th Dept) 52 A.D.2d 1049, 384 N.Y.S.2d 895, affd 41 N.Y.2d 958, 394 N.Y.S.2d 876, 363 N.E.2d 582

Incidents of business transacted in New York by foreign corporation may be sufficient to subject it to service of New York process and yet insufficient to require it to take out certificate authorizing it to do business in New York. Colonial Mortg. Co. v First Federal Sav. & Loan Asso. (1977, 4th Dept) 57 A.D.2d 1046, 395 N.Y.S.2d 798

Standard of doing business for purpose of statute forbidding foreign corporation doing business in state without authority to maintain action in state until it is authorized to do business is different from standard required for jurisdictional purposes; foreign corporations, without aid of any license may engage in activities incidental to commerce between the states. Beltone Electronics Corp. v Selbst (1977, 1st Dept) 58 A.D.2d 560, 396 N.Y.S.2d 21

While a foreign corporation may be considered as present within the state for the purpose of ordinary jurisdiction over it, such a determination does not necessarily carry the conclusion that the corporation is "doing business" within the state to the extent of requiring compliance with Business Corporation Law § 1312. Librairie Hachette v Paris Book Center, Inc. (1970) 62 Misc. 2d 873, 309 N.Y.S.2d 701

Although CPLR 8501 permits a foreign corporation which is not conducting a systematic transaction of business herein to bring an action in the state on posting of costs, this statute may not be construed to permit a corporation which is engaged in a systematic transaction of business in the state to bring an action on posting of costs without otherwise complying with Business Corporation Law § 1312(a) as to payment of taxes, fees, etc.Dixie Dinettes, Inc. v Schaller's Furniture, Inc. (1972) 71 Misc. 2d 102, 335 N.Y.S.2d 632

Foreign corporation is not precluded from bringing action in New York court despite fact that corporation is not duly licensed in New York, since corporation is not "doing business" in New York, pursuant to CLS Bus Corp L § 1312, in that (1) corporation has never transacted business in New York with defendants, (2) defendants transmitted all orders for goods as well as payments to corporation's offices in Mexico, (3) corporation did not ship goods directly to defendant in New York, but rather to Texas in care of brokers designated by defendant and (4) corporation has never transacted business in New York unrelated to instant action. Virgilio Flores, S.A. v Jerome Radelman, Inc. (1982, ED NY) 567 F. Supp. 577

10. Miscellaneous

Delaware corporation lacked capacity to commence action in New York, notwithstanding correspondence from Department of Taxation and Finance stating that it was "cleared to operate in good standing" in New York state, given undisputed proof that it owed New York more than $38,000 in taxes, interest and penalties. McIntosh Builders, Inc. v Ball (1998, 3d Dept) 247 A.D.2d 103, 678 N.Y.S.2d 810

Proceeding commenced on Aug. 7, 1997, seeking to annul determination reauthorizing foreign corporation to do business in New York, was properly dismissed as time barred, despite petitioners' argument that November 25, 1996 reinstatement of corporation did not adversely impact on them until June 30, 1997 when court ruled that in view of reinstatement, whether properly granted or otherwise, corporation would be permitted to prosecute its underlying action against petitioners, since decision to reinstate corporation was discrete determination, unambiguous and with certain effect, of which petitioners were aware in January 1997, at latest. Ayres v New York State Comm'r of Taxation & Fin. (1998, 3d Dept) 252 A.D.2d 808, 675 N.Y.S.2d 678

Unlike compliance with CLS Bus Corp § 1312(a), licensing by New York City Taxi and Limousine Commission is not condition precedent to ability to sue.Showcase Limousine, Inc. v Carey (2000, 1st Dept) 269 A.D.2d 133, 703 N.Y.S.2d 22, motion gr, in part, mod (1st Dept) 273 A.D.2d 20, 716 N.Y.S.2d 551, subsequent app (App Div, 1st Dept)

716 N.Y.S.2d 552 and app dismd 95 N.Y.2d 902, 716 N.Y.S.2d 642, 739 N.E.2d 1147

In action by New Jersey leather importer against airline to recover for loss of goods shipped from Argentina, court did not abuse its discretion in rejecting airline's efforts to conduct discovery on eve of trial as to whether importer conducted business in New York within meaning of CLS Bus Corp § 1312(a) where (1) action had been pending for several months following its reinstatement and importer's response to notice to admit that it did business in New Jersey, (2) airline's own investigation into matter failed to ascertain volume of business in New York, both in number and dollar amounts, and (3) soon after importer filed notice of trial and certificate of readiness, defendant indicated that it had no desire for further discovery. Maro Leather Co. v Aerolineas Argentinas (1994, Sup App T) 161 Misc. 2d 920, 617 N.Y.S.2d 617

Fact that corporation offering plan of cooperative association was not authorized to do business in New York did not impair the validity of the prospectus of such plan. Tuvim v 10 E. 30 Corp. (1971) 75 Misc. 2d 612, 345 N.Y.S.2d 258, mod (1st Dept) 38 A.D.2d 895, 329 N.Y.S.2d 275, affd 32 N.Y.2d 541, 347 N.Y.S.2d 13, 300 N.E.2d 397

Acting as third party plaintiff is not barred by defendant's non-compliance with CLS Bus Corp § 1312, as it is not defendant's choice to use New York as forum, judicial economy would not be served by forcing defendant to institute separate action to assert third party claims, and question of whether defendant can obtain jurisdiction over third party defendant outside of New York may arise. Williams Erectors of Suffolk County v Mulach Steel Corp. (1988, ED NY) 684 F. Supp. 357

UNDER FORMER GEN CORP § 218

1. In general

A "business trust" formed elsewhere was not considered a "foreign corporation" subject to the provisions of § 218 of former Gen. Corp. L. Burgoyne v James (1935) 156 Misc 859, 282 N.Y.S. 18, affd 246 A.D. 605, 284 N.Y.S. 977

2. Actions in contract, generally

Under § 218 of former Gen. Corp. L., an unauthorized foreign corporation was simply prohibited from maintaining an action in New York upon a contract made in New York while it was doing business without authority in the state. This prohibition was not retroactive so as to preclude actions on contracts made before its effective date, and it did not cover actions to enforce contracts made and entered into before it commenced "doing business" to such extent and in such manner as to require authorization. Re Scheftel's Estate (1937) 275 N.Y. 135, 9 N.E.2d 809; Vilter Mfg. Co. v Dairymen's League Co-op. Ass'n (1948, Sup) 84 N.Y.S.2d 445, affd 275 A.D. 706, 88 N.Y.S.2d 248, resettled 275 A.D. 769, 88 N.Y.S.2d 902 and motion den 275 A.D. 769, 88 N.Y.S.2d 903 and reh and app den 275 A.D. 769, 88 N.Y.S.2d 903; Hanley v Bradley (1927) 145 Misc 285, 259 N.Y.S. 278

Section 218 of former Gen. Corp. L., unlike this § 1312 of the Business Corporation Law, prohibited only actions or special proceedings by an unauthorized foreign corporation which had been doing business in New York upon contracts made by the corporation in New York prior to becoming authorized, and the prohibition was quite strictly construed as limited in application to the enforcement of such contracts. American Middle East Corp. v Barouk (1961, 1st Dept) 13 A.D.2d 919, 215 N.Y.S.2d 843; Bertolf Bros., Inc. v Leuthardt (1941) 261 A.D. 981, 26 N.Y.S.2d 114; Stephenson v Wiltsee (1928) 223 A.D. 41, 227 N.Y.S. 230; Bradford Co. v Dunn (1919) 188 A.D. 454, 176 N.Y.S. 834; Bremer v Ringe (1911) 146 A.D. 724, 131 N.Y.S. 487; Eclipse Silk Mfg. Co. v Hiller (1911) 145 A.D. 568, 129 N.Y.S. 879; American Case & Register Co. v Griswold (1911) 143 A.D. 807, 128 N.Y.S. 206; James Talcott, Inc. v J. J. Delaney Carpet Co. (1961) 28 Misc. 2d 600, 213 N.Y.S.2d 354, affd (1st Dept) 14 A.D.2d 866, 222 N.Y.S.2d 312; National Merchandising Corp. v Powers (1957) 8 Misc. 2d 881, 168 N.Y.S.2d 507; John Dirkmaat Co. v Pruyser (1947, Sup) 72 N.Y.S.2d 797; Hedges & Bro. v Busch (1931) 141 Misc 493, 252 N.Y.S. 693; McDowell v Starobin Electrical Supply Co. (1918) 104 Misc 596, 172 N.Y.S. 221; Sterling Mfg. Co. v National Surety Co. (1916) 94 Misc 604, 159 N.Y.S. 979; Max Factor & Co. v Janel Sales Corp. (1962, CA2 NY) 298 F.2d 511

The prohibition of § 218 of former Gen. Corp. L. could not be avoided by basing the action on fraud, or some other non-contractual theory, if the underlying obligation was inescapably contractual and would not exist in the absence of contractual relationship between the parties. Knight Products, Inc. v Donnen-Fuel Co. (1940, Sup) 20

N.Y.S.2d 135. Compare however American Middle East Corp. v Barouk (1961) 31 Misc. 2d 823, 226 N.Y.S.2d 874

It was likewise held that an assignee of rights under a New York contract could maintain an action to enforce it if his assignor would not have been prohibited from doing so under the terms of § 218 of former Gen. Corp. L. because the assignor could not be considered as "doing business" in New York without authority. Nicolich v E. Muniz Ferreira & Cia (1956, Sup) 149 N.Y.S.2d 662

3. – Particular cases

Various rights and causes of action were enforceable under § 218 and other provisions of former Gen. Corp. L., by unauthorized foreign corporations and in New York courts, notwithstanding the rights asserted arose out of or were incidental to business done in New York without authority, if the cause of action was not founded upon contract or the contract involved was not one made in New York. These included, among others, actions sounding in tort and injunction suits charging unfair competition or violation of "fair trade" agreements. Hoevel Sand-Blast Mach. Co. v Hoevel (1915) 167 A.D. 548, 153 N.Y.S. 35; Dunkin' Donuts of America, Inc. v Dunkin Donuts, Inc. (1958) 12 Misc. 2d 380, 176 N.Y.S.2d 915, affd (3d Dept) 8 A.D.2d 228, 188 N.Y.S.2d 132, 122 USPQ 220; Meisel Tire Co. v Mar-Bel Trading Co. (1935) 155 Misc 664, 280 N.Y.S. 335; Max Factor & Co. v Janel Sales Corp. (1962, CA2 NY) 298 F.2d 511; United States Light & Heating Co. v United States Light & Heating Co. (1910, CC NY) 181 F 182; Max Factor & Co. v Park Row Cut Rate (1961, SD NY) 193 F. Supp. 462, affd (CA2 NY) 298 F.2d 511; Mutual Export & Import Corp. v Mutual Export & Import Corp. (1917, DC NY) 241 F 137

The word "action" as used in § 218 of former Gen. Corp. L. was deemed to include a proceeding in the Court of Claims to assert a claim based upon contract against the State. Amos D. Bridge's Sons, Inc. v State (1919) 188 A.D. 500, 177 N.Y.S. 3, affd 231 N.Y. 532, 132 N.E. 876; Pittsburgh & Shawmut Coal Co. v State (1922) 118 Misc 50, 192 N.Y.S. 310

Some decisions dealing with the application of § 218 of former Gen. Corp. L. held that its prohibition did not extend to rights inuring to an unauthorized foreign corporation by implication of law, or quasi-contractual rights of recovery by reason of defendant's unjust enrichment. Fairmount Film Corp. v New Amsterdam Casualty Co. (1919) 189 A.D. 246, 178 N.Y.S. 525; Evyan Perfumes, Inc. v Hamilton (1959) 20 Misc. 2d 950, 195 N.Y.S.2d 869

Holder in due course of a negotiable instrument could enforce it notwithstanding instrument was incidental to New York transaction with prior holder or payee which was foreign corporation doing business in New York without authority. Alliston Hill Trust Co. v Sarandrea (1932) 236 A.D. 189, 258 N.Y.S. 299

Decisions purporting to deal with former § 218 prohibition against actions or special proceedings by unauthorized foreign corporations to enforce contracts were not in complete agreement as to enforceability of arbitration provisions. Some of them seem to have regarded an application for compulsory arbitration as an assertion of statutory right rather than, in and of itself, an "action."T. J. Stevenson & Co. v International Coal Corp. (1953) 15 Misc. 2d 904, 185 N.Y.S.2d 599; Terminal Auxiliar Maritima v Cocotos S.S. Co. (1957) 11 Misc. 2d 697, 178 N.Y.S.2d 298. See also General Knitting Mills, Inc. v Rudd Plastic Fabrics Corp. (1961, Sup) 212 N.Y.S.2d 783

A mechanic's lien right based upon New York contract rights was within the prohibition of § 218 of formerGen. Corp. L. Berkshire Engineering Corp. v Scott-Paine (1961) 29 Misc. 2d 1010, 217 N.Y.S.2d 919; Italian Mosaic & Marble Co. v Niagara Falls (1928) 131 Misc 281, 227 N.Y.S. 64

According to some decisions, a judicial proceeding to enforce contract rights under an arbitration agreement could be considered an action or special proceeding within the prohibition of § 218 of former Gen. Corp. L. Application of Levys (1947, Sup) 73 N.Y.S.2d 801, affd 276 A.D. 953, 94 N.Y.S.2d 924; Re Vanguard Films, Inc. (1947) 188 Misc 796, 67 N.Y.S.2d 893

4. Contract "made in New York"

A contract was not deemed to have been made in New York where the acceptance which made it effective took place elsewhere; but the mere fact that it was dated outside the state or contained a statement as to place of making was not conclusive as to where it was, in fact and in law, made for purposes of falling within the provisions of § 218 of former Gen. Corp. L. Allen Industries, Inc. v Exquisite Form Brassiere, Inc. (1961) 31 Misc. 2d 673, 221 N.Y.S.2d 619, affd (1st Dept) 15 A.D.2d 760, 224 N.Y.S.2d 579; Samuels v Mott (1960) 29 Misc. 2d 705, 211 N.Y.S.2d 242

Business Corporation Law

Some decisions construed § 218 of former Gen. Corp. L. so strictly that a contract was not deemed "made by" the plaintiff foreign corporation in New York, and suit to enforce it was not prohibited as far as plaintiff was concerned, though plaintiff had been doing business in New York without authority, where plaintiff's rights were acquired by assignment from another. Landerton Co. v Sy-Jo Luncheonette, Inc. (1953, Sup) 118 N.Y.S.2d 478

5. Pleadings and burden of proof

A complaint by a foreign corporation was not open to motion to dismiss based on § 218 of former Gen. Corp. L. unless it was obvious therefrom that the corporation had been doing business in this state without authority and that the contract sued upon was made in this state, or treated the prohibition contained in that section as matter of substantive defense rather than requiring affirmative avoidance in the complaint. Alpha Portland Cement Co. v Schratwieser Fireproof Const. Co. (1911) 146 A.D. 571, 131 N.Y.S. 142; Nicolich v E. Muniz Ferreira & Cia (1956, Sup) 149 N.Y.S.2d 662; Frick Co. v Pultz (1914) 162 A.D. 209, 147 N.Y.S. 732

A complaint by a foreign corporation founded upon contract need not specifically negative all three factors in the statutory prohibition under § 218 of former Gen. Corp. L. by affirmatively alleging that the corporation was not "doing business" in New York, or that, if it was, it had authority to do so, or that the contract was not made in New York. Allegations short of this, as long as they did not indicate a situation within § 218, would throw the burden of defending under that section upon the defendant. Angldile Computing Scale Co. v Gladstone (1914) 164 A.D. 370, 149 N.Y.S. 807; Eclipse Silk Mfg. Co. v Hiller (1911) 145 A.D. 568, 129 N.Y.S. 879; William L. Bonnell Co. v Katz (1960) 23 Misc. 2d 1028, 196 N.Y.S.2d 763; Barney & Smith Car Co. v E. W. Bliss Co. (1917) 100 Misc 21, 164 N.Y.S. 800, affd 178 A.D. 919, 165 N.Y.S. 1076; E. H. Stafford Mfg. Co. v Newman (1912) 75 Misc 636, 133 N.Y.S. 1073

Where it appeared on the face of a complaint filed by a foreign corporation that the action was based on a contract made in New York while doing business here without authority, the complaint, by reason of § 218 of former Gen. Corp. L., was subject to dismissal; and some decisions stated that a complaint by a foreign corporation failing to show or allege that it had been authorized to do business in New York prior to making the contract was demurrable or subject to motion to dismiss.East Coast Oil Co. v Hollins (1918) 183 A.D. 67, 170 N.Y.S. 576; American Secur. Credit Co. v Empire Properties Corp. (1935) 154 Misc 191, 276 N.Y.S. 970; Dan Talmage's Sons Co. v American Dock Co. (1916) 93 Misc 535, 157 N.Y.S. 445; Meyers v Spangenberg & McLean Co. (1909) 65 Misc 475, 120 N.Y.S. 174

Allegations in a foreign corporation's complaint upon contract were sufficient to show a prima facie right of action in New York, notwithstanding § 218 of former Gen. Corp. L., if they clearly negatived the prohibitory elements therein which, in combination, could preclude the action. It was not necessary to go into details in order to achieve that result. Western Felt Works v Modern Carpet Cleaning & Storage Corp. (1931) 141 Misc 495, 252 N.Y.S. 696; United Bldg. Material Co. v Odell (1910) 67 Misc 584, 123 N.Y.S. 313, affd 141 A.D. 921, 125 N.Y.S. 1148

The defendant in an action by a foreign corporation always had the right to controvert plaintiff's allegations indicating right to sue notwithstanding § 218 of former Gen. Corp. L., or to set up an affirmative defense based on that section, and to prevail unless plaintiff established that it was inapplicable. In such case, issues of fact were raised and the complaint, ordinarily at least, was not subject to dismissal upon motion. J. H. Balmer Co. v Mallamo (1931) 142 Misc 100, 253 N.Y.S. 37; E. A. Strout Farm Agency v Hunter (1914) 85 Misc 476, 148 N.Y.S. 924

Some decisions regarded the burden of proving such an affirmative defense as resting on the defendant. La Mar Hosiery Mills, Inc. v Credit & Commodity Corp. (1961) 28 Misc. 2d 764, 216 N.Y.S.2d 186

A defensive pleading based on § 218 of former Gen. Corp. L. had to set forth sufficient facts to bring the case affirmatively within the prohibition of that section; otherwise, it was insufficient to raise the issue. Fleet-Wing Corp. v Pease Oil Co. (1961) 29 Misc. 2d 437, 212 N.Y.S.2d 871, mod on other grounds (4th Dept) 14 A.D.2d 728, 218 N.Y.S.2d 533; Gindy Mfg. Corp. v Fishman (1959, Sup) 189 N.Y.S.2d 56

6. Federal courts

Supreme Court of the United States, on the basis of its decision in Erie R. Co. v Tompkins (1938) 304 US 64, 82 L ed 1188, 58 S Ct 817, 11 Ohio Ops 246,, overruled earlier decisions as obsolete and held that § 218 of former Gen. Corp. L. must be construed as prohibiting an action by a corporation in a New York federal district court to enforce a New York contract in like manner and to like extent as it prohibited such actions "in this state."Woods v Interstate Realty Co. (1949) 337 US 535, 93 L Ed 1524, 69 S Ct 1235

For a long time, § 218 of former Gen. Corp. L. was not regarded, by its prohibition against the maintenance of actions "in this state" by an unauthorized foreign corporation to enforce New York contracts, as affording a defense against such actions in federal courts, even the federal district courts in New York districts. Johnson v New York Breweries Co. (1910, CA2 NY) 178 F 513; Richmond Cedar Works v Buckner (1910, CC NY) 181 F 424; Wing v McCallum (1926, DC Mass) 16 F.2d 645, affd (CA1 Mass) 30 F.2d 505, reh den (CA1 Mass) 31 F.2d 940; Bamberger Broadcasting Service, Inc. v William Irving Hamilton, Inc. (1940, DC NY) 33 F. Supp. 273

7. Other procedural matters

Defendant in an action by or in the right of a foreign corporation to enforce a contract, upon proper application and showing, was entitled to pre-trial examination of plaintiff to investigate whether or not plaintiff, or his assignor, lacked right to sue because of § 218 of former Gen. Corp. L.Stevens v Silverman (1935) 157 Misc 381, 283 N.Y.S. 744

8. Doing business within state, generally

Where it is shown that a foreign corporation sold and delivered goods in New York and that it maintained personal representatives in New York with an office for the transaction of business, such proof was sufficient to establish that it was doing business within the state thus necessitating compliance with former General Corporation Law § 15 as a prerequisite to bringing an action in the state. Warner Instrument Co. v Sweet (1909) 65 Misc 57, 119 N.Y.S. 166

A foreign corporation operating as a correspondence school is "doing business" in the state within former General Corporation Law § 15 where it has agencies in various parts of the state to solicit persons to contract with it for instruction, each district office being headed by a district superintendent of the corporation having under him a corps of the corporation's representatives, where the rent and other expenses of each of the officers are paid by the corporation, including the salaries of the superintendent and his corps of assistants, and the payments made by students are collected by the division superintendent, deposited in a special account in his own name in a bank in the city where his office is situated and sent by him from time to time to the corporation, and each of the division superintendents and representatives in the state is required to be qualified to give instruction in mathematics to his students, and assistance in mathematics is given by such superintendents at their division offices to such students as desire it. International Text-Book Co. v Connelly (1910) 67 Misc 49, 124 N.Y.S. 603, affd 140 A.D. 939, 125 N.Y.S. 1125, affd 206 N.Y. 188, 99 N.E. 722

On the other hand, it is not necessary that a foreign corporation maintain an office, or a permanent representative, in New York, in order to fall within the ambit of doing business here. Woodridge Heights Const. Co. v Gippert (1915) 92 Misc 204, 155 N.Y.S. 363

The phrase "doing business in this state" implies such continuity of corporate activity as is evidenced by investment of capital within the state, with maintenance of an office for transaction of business and such other incidental circumstances which attest corporate intent to avail itself of privilege to conduct business.Eatonton Cotton Mills, Inc. v Goodyear Tire & Rubber Co. (1924) 124 Misc 211, 208 N.Y.S. 218, affd 212 A.D. 885, 208 N.Y.S. 857

It is clear from the facts presented in some of the decisions dealing with application and construction of § 218 of former Gen. Corp. L. that the corporation in question was beyond doubt doing business in New York without authority, as where it had its principal office and a factory there, or employed in New York a district manager to take charge of its ordinary and usual business of selling portraits without limitation as to territory. Foreman & Clark Mfg. Co. v Bartle (1925) 125 Misc 759, 211 N.Y.S. 602; Chicago Crayon Co. v Slattery (1910) 68 Misc 148, 123 N.Y.S. 987. See also F. C. Russell Co. v Kaye (1954, Sup) 129 N.Y.S.2d 585, app dismd 284 A.D. 1037, 137 N.Y.S.2d 819

Recital in lease that plaintiff, a foreign corporation, had "principal office" in state, raises presumption, in absence of evidence to contrary, that it was "doing business" in the state at such time; "principal office" being synonymous with "principal place of business," and being the place where its principal affairs were transacted. Foreman & Clark Mfg. Co. v Bartle (1925) 125 Misc 759, 211 N.Y.S. 602

"Doing business" in state implies corporate continuity of conduct in that respect, such as might be evidenced by investment of capital in state, with maintenance of office, for transaction of business and incidental circumstances attesting intent to avail itself of privilege to carry on a business. Ideal Werke A. G. Fur Drahtlose Telephonie v Roos (1931) 140 Misc 298, 250 N.Y.S. 481

A foreign corporation is doing business in this state when its local activity transcends the ambit of transient, occasional, noncontinuous sphere, and becomes attended with an appreciable measure of volume, continuity and regularity. Lebanon Mill Co. v Kuhn (1932) 145 Misc 918, 261 N.Y.S. 172

Activities in New York State of foreign corporation, which was engaged in manufacture of toys outside New York, but which maintained Manhattan office for purposes of displaying its toys and taking orders therefor, and which was listed in phone directory, had name on door in Manhattan office, and had stationery listing Rhode Island and New York City addresses, were carried on with sufficient permanence, continuity, and regularity to constitute doing business within New York State, even though corporation may not have filed a qualifying certificate under the General Corporation Law. Neu v Teen Time, Inc. (1959) 18 Misc. 2d 234, 188 N.Y.S.2d 1018

The fact that a foreign corporation can be considered as present in New York for purposes of serving one of its officers or agents with process against it is not a true test of whether it is "doing business" in the state within the intendment of statutory prohibitions against maintaining an action in its own behalf. William L. Bonnell Co. v Katz (1960) 23 Misc. 2d 1028, 196 N.Y.S.2d 763; M. M. Mades Co. v Gassman (1948, City Ct) 77 N.Y.S.2d 236

Whether single transaction constitutes doing business within state depends upon whether it constitutes part of general attempt to transact business in violation of statute, and, if it does, first transaction is as illegal as second, third, or twentieth. Franklin Enterprises Corp. v Moore (1962) 34 Misc. 2d 594, 226 N.Y.S.2d 527

A cumulation of acts, transactions, circumstances, and occurrences, no one or distinct part of which would require the conclusion that the corporation was doing business in New York without authority, may well, when weighed together, call for such a conclusion. Such was the situation where the corporation not only maintained an office and bank account and telephone listing in New York, but its stationery indicated that such office was its main office and it repeatedly sold and accepted payment for goods through that office. Talbot Mills, Inc. v Benezra (1962) 35 Misc. 2d 924, 231 N.Y.S.2d 229

A corporation is "doing business within the state", within the meaning of the General Corporation Law, when it is exercising corporate franchises by maintaining an office in the state, having invested capital and carrying along a regular business of some kind as domestic corporations do. Re Dennin's Will (1942, Sur) 37 N.Y.S.2d 725

9. – Not doing business

A foreign corporation was not regarded as doing business in New York within the meaning of § 218 of former Gen. Corp. L. unless its activities there were along the lines of the business which it was organized to conduct under its charter and not merely such as any citizen might transact, like opening a bank account or taking out property insurance. Kline Bros. & Co. v German Union Fire Ins. Co. (1911) 147 A.D. 790, 132 N.Y.S. 181, affd 210 N.Y. 534, 103 N.E. 1125; Lebanon Mill Co. v Kuhn (1932) 145 Misc 918, 261 N.Y.S. 172

It is generally conceded that a single sale or other business transaction within the state, or even a series of isolated and independent transactions, without some degree of continuity indicative of more or less settled intention, will not constitute "doing business" within the state without authority to such extent as to call for application of a prohibition against enforcement of rights arising therefrom in New York courts. Kline Bros. & Co. v German Union Fire Ins. Co. (1911) 147 A.D. 790, 132 N.Y.S. 181, affd 210 N.Y. 534, 103 N.E. 1125; Lebanon Mill Co. v Kuhn (1932) 145 Misc 918, 261 N.Y.S. 172; Spiegel May Stern Co. v Mitchell (1925) 125 Misc 604, 211 N.Y.S. 495; Richmond Cedar Works v Buckner (1910, CC NY) 181 F 424

Local business in New York may be considered as "done" by a resident, rather than by the foreign corporation, where it is handled on a commission basis, or by the same person acting as representative for sale of several lines of merchandise and collecting and remitting to the various manufacturers or producers, less discount, only as sales are made.Eagle Mfg. Co. v Arkell & Douglas, Inc. (1921) 197 A.D. 788, 189 N.Y.S. 140, affd 234 N.Y. 573, 138 N.E. 451; Brookford Mills, Inc. v Baldwin (1913) 154 A.D. 553, 139 N.Y.S. 195; William L. Bonnell Co. v Katz (1960) 23 Misc. 2d 1028, 196 N.Y.S.2d 763; Lederwerke v Capitelli (1915) 92 Misc 260, 155 N.Y.S. 651

Procuring subscriptions to capital stock of a foreign corporation and issuing stock to subscribers was not doing business within the meaning of § 218 of former Gen. Corp. L.Southworth v Morgan (1910) 71 Misc 214, 128 N.Y.S. 598, affd 143 A.D. 648, 128 N.Y.S. 196, revd on other grounds 205 N.Y. 293, 98 N.E. 490

Taking or solicitation of orders for goods manufactured or to be shipped from points outside the state, through a representative not having a fixed or fairly steady base of operation here, has usually been considered not to amount to "doing business" here, particularly if the orders are subject to acceptance or approval at the home office in another state or elsewhere outside New York. McDowell v Starobin Electrical Supply Co. (1918) 104 Misc 596, 172 N.Y.S. 221. See also McDowell v Starobin Electrical Supply Co. (1920) 190 A.D. 676, 180 N.Y.S. 528; L. C. Page & Co. v Sherwood (1911) 146 A.D. 618, 131 N.Y.S. 322; Suss v Durable Knit Corp. (1955) 4 Misc. 2d 666, 147 N.Y.S.2d 363; National Folding Box Co. v Bisceglia Bros. Wines Corp. (1950, Sup) 147 N.Y.S.2d 361, app dismd 278 A.D. 711, 103 N.Y.S.2d 836; M. M. Mades Co. v Gassman (1948, City Ct) 77 N.Y.S.2d 236; National Tool Salvage Co. v National Tool Salvage Industries, Inc. (1946) 186 Misc 833, 60 N.Y.S.2d 308, 68 USPQ 118; L. C. Page Co. v Sherwood (1910) 65 Misc 543, 120 N.Y.S. 837

Maintenance of some sort of office facilities in New York State for the convenience of officers or representatives or in conjunction with others, even though it is used for display of samples or goods and listed in a telephone directory, does not, in and of itself, constitute doing business in New York, if nothing is actually sold or delivered there, the corporation does not pay the upkeep, or the amount of business done there is infrequent and insignificant. James Talcott, Inc. v J. J. Delaney Carpet Co. (1961) 28 Misc. 2d 600, 213 N.Y.S.2d 354, affd (1st Dept) 14 A.D.2d 866, 222 N.Y.S.2d 312; National Tool Salvage Co. v National Tool Salvage Industries, Inc. (1946) 186 Misc 833, 60 N.Y.S.2d 308, 68 USPQ 118; Ideal Werke A. G. Fur Drahtlose Telephonie v Roos (1931) 140 Misc 298, 250 N.Y.S. 481; Pittsburgh & Shawmut Coal Co. v State (1922) 118 Misc 50, 192 N.Y.S. 310

A foreign corporation, publishing a magazine, which keeps a local office in the state to enable agents to solicit business, which is accepted in its home office, where its magazine is published and from which it is distributed, is not "doing business in the state," within former General Corporation Law § 15, requiring a foreign corporation to secure a certificate of authority.System Co. v Advertisers' Cyclopedia Co. (1910, Supp App T) 121 N.Y.S. 611

A foreign manufacturing corporation, whose manufacturing plant and staff were outside of the state, was not doing business within the state, so as to be required to obtain a certificate by former General Corporation Law § 15 though it had a selling agent within the state who maintained an office, the expenses of which he personally paid, though he had the corporation's name on the door and in the telephone directory, where all contracts for sale made by him were made subject to approval by the home office.Schwarz v Sargent (1922, Sup App T) 197 N.Y.S. 216

Foreign corporation's maintenance of office in New York and having customers in New York was insufficient to show that corporation was "doing business" in New York within statute prohibiting foreign corporation doing business in New York without certificate of authority from maintaining action on contract made in New York. M. M. Mades Co. v Gassman (1948, City Ct) 77 N.Y.S.2d 236

10. Interstate commerce

A correspondence school business, for example, has been considered purely interstate and hence not within the application of § 218 of former Gen. Corp. L. notwithstanding representatives and solicitors of the foreign corporation conducting it are regularly engaged in soliciting membership or enrollment contracts in New York, where all such contracts require acceptance at and by the home office in another state and all instruction material and instructional assistance comes from the home office. International Text Book Co. v Tone (1917) 220 N.Y. 313, 115 N.E. 914

Numerous decisions dealing with construction and application of § 218 of former Gen. Corp. L. have pointed out that such a statute cannot apply to a corporation exclusively engaged in interstate or foreign commerce because of lack of state control or regulatory power in that field. Where the only business originated in New York is based on orders accepted or approved outside the state and carried out through interstate shipments and commerce, and practically no local New York business is done, the interstate and foreign business will not subject the corporation to the prohibition found in § 218. International Fuel & Iron Corp. v Donner Steel Co. (1926) 242 N.Y. 224, 151 N.E. 214; Munoz v American Stevedores, Inc. (1960, 2d Dept) 10 A.D.2d 963, 201 N.Y.S.2d 640; Ruby S.S. Corp. v American Merchant Marine Ins. Co. (1928) 224 A.D. 531, 231 N.Y.S. 503, affd 250 N.Y. 573, 166 N.E. 329; Stephenson v

Business Corporation Law

Wiltsee (1928) 223 A.D. 41, 227 N.Y.S. 230; Eatonton Cotton Mills, Inc. v Goodyear Tire & Rubber Co. (1924) 124 Misc 211, 208 N.Y.S. 218, affd 212 A.D. 885, 208 N.Y.S. 857; Pittsburgh & Shawmut Coal Co. v State (1922) 118 Misc 50, 192 N.Y.S. 310; Publicker Commercial Alcohol Co. v Roberts (1921) 114 Misc 551, 187 N.Y.S. 178; United Drug Co. v Parodney (1928, DC NY) 24 F.2d 577

If the business done in New York is purely interstate, the fact that the corporation maintains a permanent office in this state as an aid or incident to conducting it will not preclude the corporation from maintaining an action in New York courts to enforce rights arising out of it. Erie Beach Amusements, Ltd. v Spirella Co. (1918) 105 Misc 170, 173 N.Y.S. 626

11. Validity of contracts or acts, generally

Although § 218 of former Gen. Corp. L., unlike this § 1312 of the Business Corporation Law, did not expressly protect the general validity of contracts to which an unauthorized foreign corporation doing business within the state was a party and permit their enforcement by other parties to the contract, § 218 was construed in like manner as not intended to impair validity of the contract as such. Mahar v Harrington Park Villa Sites (1912) 204 N.Y. 231, 97 N.E. 587

12. – Defenses and counterclaims

Section 218 of former Gen. Corp. L. did not preclude or affect the right of a foreign corporation, as a defendant, from asserting any and all defenses which it might be able to establish against the asserted cause of action. Although there was doubt, as hereinabove indicated, as to whether a foreign corporation could institute or compel arbitration under a New York contract made while it was doing business without authority, it clearly had the right to be heard and participate in such a proceeding after it got under way. Tugee Laces v Mary Muffet, Inc. (1948) 297 N.Y. 914, 79 N.E.2d 744; Jones v Wells Fargo Express Co. (1914) 83 Misc 508, 145 N.Y.S. 601

A foreign corporation defendant could likewise counterclaim on the basis of a New York contract entered into while it was doing business without authority, at least if the counterclaim arose out of the same transaction with respect to which it was being sued, and some decisions indicate a right to counterclaim without regard to relationship of the counterclaim to plaintiff's asserted cause of action. Rolle v Rolle (1922) 201 A.D. 698, 194 N.Y.S. 661; James Howden & Co. v American Condenser & Engineering Corp. (1920) 194 A.D. 164, 185 N.Y.S. 159, affd 231 N.Y. 627, 132 N.E. 915; Bellak v Bon Specialty Co. (1948, Sup App T) 80 N.Y.S.2d 248; Conoley v Distileria Serralles, Inc. (1944, City Ct) 48 N.Y.S.2d 11; Carrier Engineering Corp. v International Mfg. Co. (1918) 104 Misc 191, 171 N.Y.S. 641

Right to assert counterclaims based on New York contracts was denied in one relatively early decision, however, because the defendant foreign corporation had failed to pay license tax for doing business in the state. This decision likewise indicated a distinction between counterclaims arising out of the transaction on which plaintiff is suing and independent or non-related counterclaims, the latter as being precluded by § 218 of former Gen. Corp. L. American Ink Co. v Riegel Sack Co. (1913) 79 Misc 421, 140 N.Y.S. 107

§ 1313. Actions or special proceedings by foreign corporations

An action or special proceeding may be maintained by a foreign corporation, in like manner and subject to the same limitations, as an action or special proceeding brought by a domestic corporation, except as otherwise prescribed by statute.

History: Add, L 1961, ch 855, eff Sept 1, 1963.

CASE ANNOTATIONS

It has long been the recognized law in New York that a foreign corporation which is not, and has not been, "doing business" in New York without authority has the same right of access to New York courts as a domestic corporation would have and is not excluded from enforcing rights and maintaining actions and special proceedings therein merely because it is organized under the laws of some other jurisdiction. Russian Reinsurance Co. v Stoddard (1925) 240 N.Y. 149, 147 N.E. 703, reh den 240 N.Y. 682, 148 N.E. 757; Maple Motor Co. v Beales (1951, Co Ct) 110 N.Y.S.2d 623

If the contract sued upon was valid under the laws of the state where executed, it has been held that it is likewise not a defense available against the foreign corporation plaintiff that a New York

domestic corporation would have been prohibited by law from entering into such a contract. City Nat. Bank v Lake Const. Co. (1929) 227 A.D. 85, 237 N.Y.S. 58

Since a foreign corporation is authorized to sue in New York on the same basis as a domestic corporation, except as otherwise provided where it has been doing business in New York without authority (§ 1312) or the like, it has been held that a foreign corporation's action to recover for services rendered is not subject to a defense of ultra vires. New York Factors, Inc. v Yam K. Seid (1961) 28 Misc. 2d 753, 213 N.Y.S.2d 294

A foreign corporation not regularly engaged in business in New York may file a notice of mechanic's lien with respect to work and materials furnished in an isolated New York transaction, and such notice of lien substantially meets the requirements of § 9 of the Lien Law where it states the actual principal place of business of the corporation rather than a purported place of business in New York. Garden State Brickface Co. v Artcourt Realty Corp. (1963) 40 Misc. 2d 712, 243 N.Y.S.2d 733

One foreign corporation is entitled to sue another foreign corporation in a New York court if a domestic corporation could maintain such an action and the defendant corporation is subject to suit here under the provisions governing actions against foreign corporations (see § 1314, infra). John Dirkmaat Co. v Pruyser (1947, Sup) 72 N.Y.S.2d 797

§ 1314. Actions or special proceedings against foreign corporations

(a) An action or special proceeding against a foreign corporation may be maintained by a resident of this state or by a domestic corporation of any type or kind for any cause of action.

(b) Except as otherwise provided in this article, an action or special proceeding against a foreign corporation may be maintained by another foreign corporation of any type or kind or by a non-resident in the following cases only:

(1) Where it is brought to recover damages for the breach of a contract made or to be performed within this state, or relating to property situated within this state at the time of the making of the contract.

(2) Where the subject matter of the litigation is situated within this state.

(3) Where the cause of action arose within this state, except where the object of the action or special proceeding is to affect the title of real property situated outside this state.

(4) Where, in any case not included in the preceding subparagraphs, a non-domiciliary would be subject to the personal jurisdiction of the courts of this state under section 302 of the civil practice law and rules.

(5) Where the defendant is a foreign corporation doing business or authorized to do business in this state.

(c) Paragraph (b) does not apply to a corporation which was formed under the laws of the United States and which maintains an office in this state.

History: Add, L 1961, ch 855, eff Sept 1, 1963; amd, L 1963, ch 684, § 4, eff Sept 1, 1963; L 1965, ch 803, § 49, eff Sept 1, 1965; L 1975, ch 117, eff May 27, 1975.

CASE ANNOTATIONS

1. Jurisdiction, generally
2. Action by resident or domestic corporation
3. Action by nonresident or foreign corporation

1. Jurisdiction, generally

The fact that §§ 224 and 225 of former Gen. Corp. L. authorized the maintenance of actions, or certain types of actions, in New York courts against foreign corporations was never deemed to sanction the maintenance of such an action in a court lacking jurisdiction of the subject matter, or one wherein the foreign corporation, or some of its assets, had not been subjected to the court's jurisdiction by due process of law.Simonson v International Bank (1962, 1st Dept) 16 A.D.2d 55, 225 N.Y.S.2d 392, affd 14 N.Y.2d 281, 251 N.Y.S.2d 433, 200 N.E.2d 427

Where jurisdiction over individual is obtained independent of statute concerning personal jurisdiction based upon acts of nondomiciliaries because individual was "doing business" in the state, jurisdiction will also attach with the respect to causes of action which did not arise in New York. ABKCO Industries, Inc. v Lennon (1976, 1st Dept) 52 A.D.2d 435, 384 N.Y.S.2d 781 (disagreed with on other grounds B. v H. (2d Dept) 84 A.D.2d 295, 445 N.Y.S.2d 579)

Defendant insurance company's motion to dismiss indemnification suit for lack of personal jurisdiction was premature, and plaintiff insurance company was entitled to discovery on limited issue of whether defendant was conducting business in New York sufficient to establish basis for personal jurisdiction, where plaintiff demonstrated that facts "may exist" to show that defendant, as wholly-owned subsidiary of parent company doing noninsurance business in New York, had directly done business within state. National Union Fire Ins. Co. v Ideal Mut. Ins. Co. (1986, 1st Dept) 122 A.D.2d 630, 505 N.Y.S.2d 416

If the corporation failed to challenge the court's jurisdiction over it by timely objection, defects in service, and likewise any question as to whether the corporation was in fact doing business in New York, or doing sufficient business in nature and amount to make it "present" there, were deemed waived and the court had jurisdiction over the person of the corporation by acquiescence or consent. Baltimore Pub. Co. v Swedish-American Mexico Line, Ltd. (1932) 143 Misc 229, 256 N.Y.S. 284

The limitation contained in the statute reflects the state policy against lending its courts to the resolution of disputes between nonresident parties, limits the subject-matter jurisdiction of the courts and cannot be waived by the defendant. Farrell v Piedmont Aviation, Inc. (1969, CA2 NY) 411 F.2d 812, cert den 396 US 840, 24 L Ed 2d 91, 90 S Ct 103

2. Action by resident or domestic corporation

Section 224 of former Gen. Corp. L., merely by authorizing a resident or domestic corporation to maintain an action on any manner of cause of action against a foreign corporation, did not, however, make it any easier to obtain personal jurisdiction over the foreign corporation by service of process upon it, and, if it had no designated agent for service of process upon it in New York, it still had to be doing a certain amount of business there before service on one of its agents or representatives who could be found in New York would bind it as personal service.Simonson v International Bank (1962, 1st Dept) 16 A.D.2d 55, 225 N.Y.S.2d 392, affd 14 N.Y.2d 281, 251 N.Y.S.2d 433, 200 N.E.2d 427; Emerson Radio & Phonograph Corp. v Eskind (1957) 32 Misc. 2d 1038, 228 N.Y.S.2d 841; Trautman v Taylor-Adams Co. (1931) 141 Misc 500, 252 N.Y.S. 701

New York courts of general jurisdiction have long had discretion to take jurisdiction over transitory causes of action sounding in tort and asserted in behalf of residents of the state, and § 224 of former Gen. Corp. L. permitted a resident or domestic corporation to invoke this jurisdiction against a foreign corporation. Rojzenblitt v Polish Trans-Atlantic Shipping Co. (1936) 162 Misc 251, 293 N.Y.S. 79

A Colorado corporation owning a department store in Denver, though it sold nothing in New York but only bought merchandise there, was held to have such contacts and presence in New York as to require it to defend an action brought against it in New York by a New York manufacturer for the price of goods sold to it by him, where, with other out-of-town stores, it had joined in organizing and sharing the expenses of a New York corporation which maintained a buying office in New York City managed by an office manager and used by store buyers when they came to New York, and the Colorado corporation's name was listed on the office door, in the building lobby, and in the Manhattan telephone directory. Kimberly Knitwear, Inc. v Mid-West Pool Car Asso. (1959) 21 Misc. 2d 730, 191 N.Y.S.2d 347

The fact alone that a cause of action against a foreign carrier in favor of a New York resident arose outside New York or even in a foreign country did not defeat right of the injured resident to sue the foreign corporation in New York under § 224 of former Gen. Corp. L., and, upon a showing that the plaintiff was physically and financially unable to maintain his action in the country where he was injured and where the corporation was domiciled and that the corporation had been doing a substantial amount of soliciting and arranging for business in New York, the New York court decided to retain jurisdiction as against objections that it would be unfair to the foreign corporation, and unconstitutional, to do so. Fuss v French Nat. Railroads (1962) 35 Misc. 2d 680, 231 N.Y.S. 2d 57, affd (1st Dept) 17 A.D.2d 941, 233 N.Y.S.2d 1013

3. Action by nonresident or foreign corporation

In instances where the action was by a nonresident against a foreign corporation, or by one foreign corporation against another, jurisdiction could not even be conferred by consent, acquiescence, or failure of the corporate defendant to object unless the cause of action fell within one of the first three subparagraphs of § 225 of former Gen. Corp. L. or the defendant was shown to have been "doing business in this state."Davis v Julius Kessler & Co. (1922) 118 Misc 292, 194 N.Y.S. 9, affd 202 A.D. 798, 194 N.Y.S. 927

When a foreign corporation sued another foreign corporation in a New York state court, under their contract choosing New York as their forum, the action had to be dismissed for lack of subject matter jurisdiction because it did not fit any of the categories under N.Y. Bus. Corp. Law § 1314(b) of actions which could be filed by one foreign corporation against another foreign corporation in New York courts, and, although they selected New York as their forum, they did not choose to apply the law of New York, so, under N.Y. Gen. Oblig. Law §§ 5-1401 and 5-1402, their forum selection clause could not be enforced. DDR Real Estate Servs. v Burnham Pac. Props., Inc. (2003, Sup) 769 N.Y.S.2d 832

N.Y. Bus. Corp. Law § 1314(b) is not a bar to maintenance of an action between foreign parties based on a foreign country's judgment. Byblos Bank Europe, S.A. v Sekerbank Turk Anonym Syrketi (2006, Sup) 12 Misc 3d 792, 819 NYS2d 412, later proceeding (2006, NY App Div, 1st Dept) 2006 NY App Div LEXIS 7880

Because N.Y. Bus. Corp. Law § 1314(b) was not a bar to the maintenance of an action between foreign parties based on a foreign country's judgment, a Belgian bank had a right to seek enforcement in New York of a Belgian judgment. However, because the Belgian bank did not show a probability that its motion under N.Y. C.P.L.R. 3213 for recognition of the Belgium judgment would be granted, a Turkish bank's motion to vacate an order of attachment that was based on the Belgium judgment had to be granted. Byblos Bank Europe, S.A. v Sekerbank Turk Anonym Syrketi (2006, Sup) 12 Misc 3d 792, 819 NYS2d 412, later proceeding (2006, NY App Div, 1st Dept) 2006 NY App Div LEXIS 7880

N.Y. Bus. Corp. Law § 1314(b)(2) allowed an action by a foreign corporation to be brought against another foreign corporation when the litigation's subject matter was located in New York, so that a Belgian bank had a right to seek an order of attachment in New York against a Turkish bank, based on a Belgian judgment. The locality of a judgment was the situs of the court where it was entered, and upon recognition and conversion of the Belgian judgment to a New York judgment, the subject matter of the litigation was thus located in the State of New York. Byblos Bank Europe, S.A. v Sekerbank Turk Anonym Syrketi (2006, Sup) 12 Misc 3d 792, 819 NYS2d 412, later proceeding (2006, NY App Div, 1st Dept) 2006 NY App Div LEXIS 7880

Delaware corporation which was consignee of fuel oil lost when a vessel disappeared at sea could maintain an action in New York courts against the owner of the vessel, a Panamanian corporation.

Coastal States Trading, Inc. v Zenith Navigation S. A. (1977, SD NY) 446 F. Supp. 330

4. Service of process

A foreign corporation must be doing some substantial part of its main business in this state to justify service of process upon its representative. Holzer v Dodge Bros. (1922) 233 N.Y. 216, 135 N.E. 268; Emerson Radio & Phonograph Corp. v Eskind (1957) 32 Misc. 2d 1038, 228 N.Y.S.2d 841; Simonson v International Bank (1962, 1st Dept) 16 A.D.2d 55, 225 N.Y.S.2d 392, affd 14 N.Y.2d 281, 251 N.Y.S.2d 433, 200 N.E.2d 427

A foreign corporation could, however, be subjected to the court's jurisdiction by personal service of process in New York on one of its officers or managing agents, if it was then doing business in New York.Elish v St, Louis S. R. Co. (1953) 305 N.Y. 267, 112 N.E.2d 842, reh den 305 N.Y. 824, 113 N.E.2d 560; Donner v Weinberger's Hair Shops, Inc. (1952) 280 A.D. 67, 111 N.Y.S.2d 310; Stark v Howe Sound Co. (1931) 141 Misc 148, 252 N.Y.S. 233, affd 234 A.D. 904, 254 N.Y.S. 959

Where the corporation had been authorized to do business in New York and had designated the secretary of state or some other agent for service of process upon it, service on such agent in accordance with law was sufficient to subject the corporation to the court's jurisdiction regardless of the nature of the action and whether the corporation was, in fact, doing any business in New York. Zacharakis v Bunker Hill Mut. Ins. Co. (1953) 281 A.D. 487, 120 N.Y.S.2d 418, app gr 281 A.D. 1019, 121 N.Y.S.2d 271; Karius v All States Freight, Inc. (1941) 176 Misc 155, 26 N.Y.S.2d 738; Bisbee Linseed Co. v Fireman's Fund Ins. Co. (1927) 128 Misc 851, 220 N.Y.S. 309; Trounstine v Bauer, Pogue & Co. (1942, DC NY) 44 F. Supp. 767, affd (CA2 NY) 144 F.2d 379, cert den 323 US 777, 89 L Ed 621, 65 S Ct 190

The fact that the officer or agent of the corporation served with process against it was a resident of New York would not, in and of itself, suffice, over timely objection, to subject the corporation to the court's jurisdiction. Western Hair Goods Co. v B. R. Haberkorn Co. (1928) 131 Misc 930, 229 N.Y.S. 273

In all actions against a foreign corporation, the corporate defendant has a right to question the validity of service of process upon it as subjecting it to the court's jurisdiction and thereby seek dismissal of the action. Kohn v Wilkes-Barre Dry Goods Co. (1930) 139 Misc 116, 246 N.Y.S. 425

5. Effect on interstate commerce

Subd. 4 of § 225 of former Gen. Corp. L. was declared to be unconstitutional when construed to subject an interstate carrier to necessity of defending suits, other than tort actions, in courts of this State, as imposing an unreasonable burden upon carrier, in violation of U. S. Const., Art. I, § 8, subd. 3. N. V. Brood en Beschuitfabriek V/H John Simons v Aluminum Co. of America (1931) 231 A.D. 693, 248 N.Y.S. 460

Other decisions, however, have rejected contentions of unconstitutionality of § 225 of former Gen. Corp. L. as sanctioning invasion of the foreign and interstate commerce field, or avoided such contentions by simply declining to exercise jurisdiction where the cause of action arose outside of the state as an incident of such commerce. Williamson v Palmer (1943) 181 Misc 610, 43 N.Y.S.2d 532

If the defendant corporation was doing business in New York, as well as being engaged in interstate commerce, and the cause of action arose here, a New York court can entertain the action without unduly invading the field of interstate commerce notwithstanding the loss or damage was incidental to a transaction or occurrence in course of such commerce. Cincis v Seaboard A. L. Ry. (1952) 201 Misc 887, 113 N.Y.S.2d 29; Jacobson v Baltimore & O. R. Co. (1936) 161 Misc 268, 291 N.Y.S. 628

Some decisions have taken the view that impairment of foreign or interstate commerce is not an invalidating factor merely because the cause of action asserted by the resident against the foreign corporation arose out of or in course of such commerce and the damage was sustained elsewhere than in New York. These recognize discretion in the New York court to decline to proceed with the case if trial in New York would place an undue burden on foreign or interstate commerce, but see no constitutional objection to proceeding under other circumstances. Fuss v French Nat. Railroads (1962) 35 Misc. 2d 680, 231 N.Y.S.2d 57, affd (1st Dept) 17 A.D.2d 941, 233 N.Y.S.2d 1013; Johnston v Atlantic C. L. R. Co. (1926) 128 Misc 82, 217 N.Y.S. 758

Under subdivision (b) (5) hereof an action is ordinarily maintainable against a foreign corporation doing business in New York and if such action is to be disallowed there must be an adequate showing that it would be an unreasonable burden on interstate commerce; action was improperly dismissed where the foreign corporation sued did business in New York under a certificate from the Secretary of State, kept records in New York, advertised its office in New York, its general agents and traffic manager had offices in New York, it employed 75 people in New York and its ships regularly plied the waters of New York Harbor, notwithstanding that the shipment in suit did not pass through New York. Ceravit Corp. Ag v Black Diamond S.S. Corp. (1965) 46 Misc. 2d 979, 260 N.Y.S.2d 848

The question involved where the action relates to interstate commerce can be regarded as primarily jurisdictional or one of comity between courts. Panstwowe Zaklady Graviozne v Automobile Ins. Co. (1928, DC NY) 36 F.2d 504

6. Discretion of court to entertain action

Although subd. (4) of § 225 of former Gen. Corp. L. upon its face seemed to accord a nonresident an absolute right to maintain an action against a foreign corporation, with like right in one foreign corporation to sue another foreign corporation, in a New York court, if jurisdiction over the foreign corporation could be obtained in New York State and the corporation had been "doing business" there, numerous decisions held that the court in which the action was brought had discretion, particularly where the cause of action asserted rested in tort and arose outside the state, to decline to entertain the action. Murnan v Wabash R. Co. (1927) 246 N.Y. 244, 158 N.E. 508; Seeley v Waterman S.S. Corp. (1947, Sup) 73 N.Y.S.2d 80, revd on other grounds 274 A.D. 934, 83 N.Y.S.2d 502; Yesuvida v Pennsylvania R. Co. (1951) 200 Misc 815, 111 N.Y.S.2d 417; Heydemann v Westinghouse Electric Mfg. Co. (1936, CA2 NY) 80 F.2d 837; Gilbert v Gulf Oil Corp. (1945, DC NY) 62 F. Supp. 291, revd on other grounds (CA2 NY) 153 F.2d 883, revd on other grounds 330 US 501, 91 L Ed 1055, 67 S Ct 839;

Shareholders' derivative action for breach of fiduciary duty and waste should have been dismissed on ground of forum non conveniens since Delaware, not New York, had paramount interest in deciding whether Delaware corporation properly purchased securities from group of its shareholders, especially where 9 additional actions involving same claims on behalf of same corporation were pending in Delaware, and dismissal would not impose undue hardship on plaintiff, who was man of substantial means. Hart v General Motors Corp. (1987, 1st Dept) 129 A.D.2d 179, 517 N.Y.S.2d 490, app den 70 N.Y.2d 608, 521 N.Y.S.2d 225, 515 N.E.2d 910

But if the defendant was not shown to be "doing business within the state" and the cause of action did not fall within any of the other subdivisions of § 225 of former Gen. Corp. L., the court could not entertain an action by a nonresident or foreign corporation against a foreign corporation, even with the defendant's consent. Davis v Julius Kessler & Co. (1922) 118 Misc 292, 194 N.Y.S. 9, affd 202 A.D. 798, 194 N.Y.S. 927

Expense and inconvenience in bringing witnesses into this state and trying the case here were not, in and of themselves, ground for refusing to entertain the action. Crane, Hayes & Co. v New York, N. H. & H. R. Co. (1927) 131 Misc 71, 225 N.Y.S. 775

It was sometimes broadly stated that the court had discretion to entertain the action, or not to entertain it, and some decisions indicated existence of such discretion in the court whether the action sounded in tort or upon contract.Emerson Quiet Kool Corp. v Eskind (1957) 32 Misc. 2d 1037, 1039, 228 N.Y.S.2d 839; Yesuvida v Pennsylvania R. Co. (1951) 200 Misc 815, 111 N.Y.S.2d 417; McCaskell Filters, Inc. v Goslin-Birmingham Mfg. Co. (1948, Sup) 81 N.Y.S.2d 309, affd 274 A.D. 761, 79 N.Y.S.2d 925; Rederiet Ocean Aktieselskab v W. A. Kirk & Co. (1944, Sup) 51 N.Y.S.2d 565; Williamson v Palmer (1943) 181 Misc 610, 43 N.Y.S.2d 532; Richter v Chicago R. I. & P. R. Co. (1924) 123 Misc 234, 205 N.Y.S. 128

Where New Jersey resident brought action against New Jersey corporation on contract made, performed, and broken in New Jersey and only reason plaintiff brought action in New York was to take advantage of New York's pre-judgment attachment statutes, court would refuse to hear case on doctrine of forum non conveniens. Wachsman v Craftool Co. (1973) 77 Misc. 2d 360, 353 N.Y.S.2d 78

7. Federal courts

Obtaining authority by a foreign corporation to do business in New York and designating the secretary of state or some other agent for service of process against it is deemed to authorize service of federal process in connection with actions commenced in a New York federal district court upon the designated agent, and to make such service binding and effective. It amounts to consent to be sued in a federal court sitting in New York. Neirbo Co. v Bethlehem Shipbuilding

Corp. (1939) 308 US 165, 84 L Ed 167, 60 S Ct 153; Bertha Bldg. Corp. v National Theatres Corp. (1952, DC NY) 103 F. Supp. 712; Hintz v Austenal Laboratories, Inc. (1952, DC NY) 105 F. Supp. 187; Aaron v Agwilines, Inc. (1948, DC NY) 75 F. Supp. 604, 14 CCH LC ¶ 64339

It has been held that mere doing of business by a foreign corporation, without authority, does not make it a New York resident for purposes of conferring jurisdiction on a federal court by reason of diversity of citizenship or affect the proper venue of actions in the federal courts. Moss v Atlantic C. L. R. Co. (1945, CA2 NY) 149 F.2d 701

The provisions of §§ 224 and 225 of former Gen. Corp. L., and likewise those of this § 1314 of the Business Corp. L., seem to be directed solely to authority to maintain actions against foreign corporations in courts of the State of New York, although they do not so state. At least some intimation is to be found that federal district courts in New York districts do not consider themselves bound to entertain a damage claim by a nonresident of New York against a foreign corporation merely because that company was doing business in New York.Summerall v United Fruit Co. (1935, DC NY) 11 F. Supp. 963, affd (CA2 NY) 80 F.2d 1020, cert den 298 US 658, 80 L Ed 1384, 56 S Ct 680

Where statute prohibited foreign corporation from maintaining suit in New York against another foreign corporation (with certain immaterial exceptions) federal court sitting in New York would not entertain diversity suit involving such parties. Aerotrade, Inc. v Banque Nationale de la Republique D'Haiti (1974, SD NY) 376 F. Supp. 1286

8. Miscellaneous

Property of a foreign corporation found within the State of New York, such as a deposit of funds in a New York bank, was subject to attachment under § 224 of former Gen. Corp. L., whether or not the corporation could be considered as "doing business" in New York. Madsen v Baltimore Mail S.S. Co. (1935) 244 A.D. 809, 279 N.Y.S. 766, cert den 298 US 675, 80 L Ed 1396, 56 S Ct 939

What constitutes subd. (c) of this § 1314 of the Business Corp. L. likewise appeared as the last unnumbered paragraph of § 225 of former Gen. Corp. L., and, under it, a federal corporation which maintained an office in New York could be sued by a nonresident in a New York court for damages for injuries sustained by plaintiff in Manila. Jacobsen v United States Shipping Board Emergency Fleet Corp. (1926) 128 Misc 138, 217 N.Y.S. 856

Attachment of debt owed by New York corporation to foreign corporation was improper where foreign corporation was not subject to the jurisdiction of New York courts under Business Corporation Law § 1314. Calzaturificio Giuseppe Garbuio S. A. S. v Dartmouth Outdoor Sports, Inc. (1977, SD NY) 435 F. Supp. 1209

9. Actions by residents or domestic corporations, generally

Section 224 of former Gen. Corp. L., like subd. (a) of this § 1314 of the Business Corp. L., broadly authorized the maintenance against a foreign corporation of an action, by a New York resident or domestic corporation, based upon any kind or manner of cause of action whatsoever. This statutory authorization was not conditioned upon where the cause of action arose, whether it sounded in tort or contract, or whether the corporation had been or was doing or authorized to do business in New York. Accordingly it was held that the court in which the action was brought had no power to dismiss it except for lack of jurisdiction or overriding policy or comity considerations. Gregonis v Philadelphia & Reading Coal & Iron Co. (1923) 235 N.Y. 152, 139 N.E. 223 (ovrld on other grounds Silver v Great American Ins. Co., 29 N.Y.2d 356, 328 N.Y.S.2d 398, 278 N.E.2d 619, on remand (1st Dept) 38 A.D.2d 932, 330 N.Y.S.2d 156); Fuss v French Nat. Railroads (1962) 35 Misc. 2d 680, 231 N.Y.S.2d 57, affd (1st Dept) 17 A.D.2d 941, 233 N.Y.S.2d 1013; Newtown Jackson Co. v Barclays Bank (1954, Sup) 133 N.Y.S.2d 726; Re Hamburg-American Line (1930) 135 Misc 715, 238 N.Y.S. 331, affd 228 A.D. 802, 239 N.Y.S. 914

10. "Resident" status

The person damaged or injured need not have been a resident of New York at the time he sustained the damage, but he must have attained and had resident status when he commenced the action.Silberfeld v Swiss Bank Corp. (1944) 268 A.D. 884, 50 N.Y.S.2d 841

"Resident" status for purposes of § 224 of former Gen. Corp. L. was acquired by taking up actual residence in New York with intention to remain indefinitely, and such status did not disappear until there was a change of residence to some place outside the state. Randolph v

American Packing Corp. (1947) 273 A.D. 105, 75 N.Y.S.2d 187, reh den 273 A.D. 807, 76 N.Y.S.2d 266

Even an alien residing in New York under a temporary visa was eligible to sue a foreign corporation in that state upon any cause of action he might have under § 224 of former Gen. Corp. L., provided he was an actual and bona fide resident when he instituted the action. Greiner v Bank of Adelaide (1941) 176 Misc 315, 26 N.Y.S.2d 515

A plaintiff, in order to qualify as a resident, within the meaning of § 224 of former Gen. Corp. L., must establish (1) his intent to make this state his permanent home, or (2) that he had no present intent to establish or have a permanent home elsewhere; to the extent thatGreiner v Bank of Adelaide (1941) 176 Misc 315, 26 N.Y.S.2d 515, and Von Petersdorff v Insurance Co. of North America (1944) 181 Misc 907, 46 N.Y.S.2d 651, are to the contrary, they will not be followed

A foreign corporation could not be deemed a "resident" of New York, for purposes of suing another foreign corporation, merely because it had been licensed and authorized to do business in New York.Schwartz v Zim Israel Navigation Co. (1958) 15 Misc. 2d 576, 181 N.Y.S.2d 283

Failure of a plaintiff to state in his original papers that he was then a resident of the state was not a fatal defect which could not be cured. Cantor v Mutual Trimming & Binding Co. (1940, City Ct) 23 N.Y.S.2d 429

11. Assignment of claims

Because of the broad phrasing of § 224 of former Gen. Corp. L., a New York resident or domestic corporation to whom a cause of action against a foreign corporation was assigned could maintain action as owner of the cause of action, regardless of its nature, notwithstanding inability of the assignor to sue the foreign corporation in New York because of the restrictions placed on actions by nonresidents against such corporations in that state by § 225 of former Gen. Corp. L., the essence of which likewise appears in this § 1314 of the Business Corp. L. Banque De France v Supreme Court of New York (1942) 287 N.Y. 483, 41 N.E.2d 65, cert den 316 US 646, 86 L Ed 1730, 62 S Ct 1279; Commission for Polish Relief, Ltd. v Banca Nationala A Romaniei (1941) 176 Misc 1064, 27 N.Y.S.2d 377, affd 288 N.Y. 332, 43 N.E.2d 345; Hewitt v Canadian P. R. Co. (1924) 124 Misc 186, 207 N.Y.S. 797, affd 212 A.D. 815, 207 N.Y.S. 851; Ball v Nippon Yusen (Kabushki Kaisha) (1931) 142 Misc 201, 253 N.Y.S. 260, affd 143 Misc 243, 256 N.Y.S. 298

One decision, promulgated in 1934, held that § 224 of former Gen. Corp. L. would be unconstitutional if construed as authorizing a resident assignee of a cause of action which accrued to a nonresident against a foreign corporation for damage to goods shipped in interstate commerce to sue such corporation in New York. The basis of decision was impairment of or interference with interstate commerce. Miele v Chicago, M., S. P. & P. R. Co. (1934) 151 Misc 137, 270 N.Y.S. 788

Assignment of causes of action to residents was a recognized and effectual method of circumventing the restrictions of § 225 of former Gen. Corp. L. on what actions a nonresident could maintain against a foreign corporation, and it was frankly stated that the fact that the assignment was made solely to enable the resident assignee to sue in New York was not to be considered against his right to sue. Segal Lock & Hardware Co. v Markey (1953, Sup) 124 N.Y.S.2d 181; Severnoe Secur. Corp. v Westminster Bank, Ltd. (1925) 214 A.D. 14, 210 N.Y.S. 629; McCauley v Georgia Railroad Bank (1924) 122 Misc 632, 203 N.Y.S. 550, affd 209 A.D. 886, 205 N.Y.S. 935, affd 239 N.Y. 514, 147 N.E. 175

A resident to whom a claim has been assigned for the sole purpose of enabling him to bring suit may maintain an action in the state court although the assignor could not. Farrell v Piedmont Aviation, Inc. (1969, CA2 NY) 411 F.2d 812, cert den 396 US 840, 24 L Ed 2d 91, 90 S Ct 103

12. Actions by nonresidents or foreign corporations, generally

Section 225 of former Gen. Corp. L., from which subd. (b) of this § 1314 of the Business Corp. L. was derived, was somewhat differently phrased and arranged, but fundamentally similar. It permitted a nonresident or foreign corporation to maintain an action in a New York court against a foreign corporation only on certain specified causes of action, such as those arising in the state or out of New York contracts, or to determine rights in and to New York property, unless the corporation was "doing business" in New York. If the situation was not within one of these categories the action simply would not lie, even by consent.Swift & Co. v Karline (1927) 245 N.Y. 570, 157 N.E. 861; Cala v Luis De Ridder Ltda., S. A. (1962, 1st Dept) 17 A.D.2d 729, 232 N.Y.S.2d 284; Gano-Moore Coal Mining Co. v W. E. Deegans Coal Co. (1925) 214 A.D. 634, 213 N.Y.S. 54; Fidan v Austral American Trading Corp. (1957) 8 Misc. 2d 598, 168 N.Y.S.2d 27; Rzeszotarski v Co-operative Ass'n Kasa Polska (1931) 139 Misc 400, 247 N.Y.S. 471; Electric Race Patrol, Inc. v National Trailer Convoy, Inc. (1961, SD NY) 191 F. Supp. 364;

If the nature of the cause of action asserted by the nonresident or foreign corporation was such as to fall strictly within the authorizing paragraphs of § 225 of former Gen. Corp. L., or the defendant was "doing business" in New York, the action "could be" maintained here. Gonzalez v Industrial Bank (of Cuba) (1961) 9 N.Y.2d 623, 210 N.Y.S.2d 227, 172 N.E.2d 80

This section, in delineating the classes of cases, including actions brought to recover damages for breach of contracts made within the state, in which New York courts may entertain an action by a nonresident against a foreign corporation, was designed solely to block out an area of subject-matter in which New York courts are available for suits against a foreign corporation, and it presupposes that the particular foreign corporation is otherwise subject to jurisdiction of New York courts.Simonson v International Bank (1964) 14 N.Y.2d 281, 251 N.Y.S.2d 433, 200 N.E.2d 427

13. Breach of contract

Section 225 of former Gen. Corp. L. specifically authorized a non-resident or foreign corporation to maintain an action in New York seeking damages for breach of a contract made in New York or relating to property in New York when the contract was made. This right was regarded as absolute, without any discretion in the court to refuse to entertain the action. N. V. Tonerde Maatschappij Voor Montaan-Chemie v Great Lakes Coal & Coke Co. (1935) 243 A.D. 640, 276 N.Y.S. 895; National Equipment Rental, Ltd. v Graphic Art Designers, Inc. (1962) 36 Misc. 2d 442, 234 N.Y.S.2d 61; Distillers Factors Corp. v Country Distillers Products, Inc. (1947) 189 Misc 497, 71 N.Y.S.2d 654; Panstwowe Zaklady Graviozne v Automobile Ins. Co. (1928, DC NY) 36 F.2d 504. See however, MacKenzie v Climax Industries, Inc. (1947, Sup) 73 N.Y.S.2d 504

The contract, to serve as absolute basis for a New York action by a nonresident against a foreign corporation or by one foreign corporation against another, must have been "made in" New York, and it was not enough that under its terms, or applicable principles in the field of conflict of laws, its construction, applicability, and validity would be determinable under New York law. Fremay, Inc. v Modern Plastic Machinery Corp. (1961, 1st Dept) 15 A.D.2d 235, 222 N.Y.S.2d 694

To be "made within" the State of New York, the last act necessary to formulation of the contract must have taken place in New York, and if that last act was its signing by defendant corporation, and that took place outside of New York, § 225, of former Gen. Corp. L. did not provide a basis for suit. Fremay, Inc. v Modern Plastic Machinery Corp. (1961, 1st Dept) 15 A.D.2d 235, 222 N.Y.S.2d 694

On the other hand, the fact that the contract indicated on its face that it was made elsewhere, or was to be considered as made elsewhere, or stated that it was to be construed in the light of the law of some other jurisdiction, did not defeat the statutory right to sue the foreign corporation in New York, if such contract was, in fact and in law, "made within" the State of New York. Allen Industries, Inc. v Exquisite Form Brassiere, Inc. (1962, 1st Dept) 15 A.D.2d 760, 224 N.Y.S.2d 579; Stagg v British Controlled Oilfields, Ltd. (1921) 117 Misc 474, 192 N.Y.S. 596

Where rights under a contract, such as one for transportation on a foreign shipping line, were the crux of the litigation, and the contract specified that all disputes must be litigated in the courts of the shipping corporation's domicile, and this was considered a reasonable condition, a New York court might defer to the contractual fixation of forum notwithstanding right to sue the corporation in New York might otherwise exist.Schwartz v Zim Israel Navigation Co. (1958) 15 Misc. 2d 576, 181 N.Y.S.2d 283

Provision in contract that it be construed under New York law does not make the contract one made in New York for purposes of Business Corporation Law § 1314, subdivision b(1). Calzaturificio Giuseppe Garbuio S. A. S. v Dartmouth Outdoor Sports, Inc. (1977, SD NY) 435 F. Supp. 1209

Clause in contract actually made outside of New York which provided that "this agreement shall be deemed to have been made in New York" did not confer jurisdiction in New York under Business Corporation Law § 1314, subdivision b(1). Calzaturificio Giuseppe

Garbuio S. A. S. v Dartmouth Outdoor Sports, Inc. (1977, SD NY) 435 F. Supp. 1209

14. Cause of action

A Cuban refugee's cause of action against a Cuban bank for directing a New York bank not to pay a draft drawn on it by the Cuban bank, for cash received, in favor of the refugee, was based on a cause of action arising in New York within the meaning of § 225 of the Gen Corp L, and his action was accordingly maintainable in a New York court. Gonzalez v Industrial Bank (of Cuba) (1962) 12 N.Y.2d 33, 234 N.Y.S.2d 210, 186 N.E.2d 410, reh den 12 N.Y.2d 835, 236 N.Y.S.2d 611, 187 N.E.2d 465, and revg (1st Dept) 16 A.D.2d 347, 228 N.Y.S.2d 81

Cause of action against a foreign bank arises in New York where the action is based upon nonpayment by a New York bank of a draft purchased from the foreign bank in a foreign country. Gonzalez v Industrial Bank (1962) 12 N.Y.2d 33, 234 N.Y.S.2d 210, 186 N.E.2d 410, reh den 12 N.Y.2d 835, 236 N.Y.S.2d 611, 187 N.E.2d 465, apparently ovrlg Gonzalez v Industrial Bank (1959) 22 Misc. 2d 874, 195 N.Y.S.2d 346, affd (1st Dept) 10 A.D.2d 624, 196 N.Y.S.2d 926, affd 9 N.Y.2d 623, 210 N.Y.S.2d 227, 172 N.E.2d 80

New York had jurisdiction over action by Israeli partnership, as the beneficiary of an irrevocable letter of credit established by defendant Ugandan bank, arising out of defendant's instructions to its New York agent bank to refrain from effecting reimbursement of checks drawn under the letter, since the Banking Law allows the maintenance of an action by a nonresident against a foreign banking corporation where the cause of action arose within New York, since defendant's order countermanding payment took effect in New York, and since reimbursement in New York was an essential provision in the arrangement. J. Zeevi & Sons, Ltd. v Grindlays Bank (Uganda), Ltd. (1975) 37 N.Y.2d 220, 371 N.Y.S.2d 892, 333 N.E.2d 168, cert den 423 US 866, 46 L Ed 2d 95, 96 S Ct 126

Section 225 of former Gen. Corp. L. likewise sanctioned an action by a nonresident against a foreign corporation or by one foreign corporation against another on a cause of action which arose in New York, except where the object of the action was to affect title to real property located elsewhere. Under this provision a suit could be maintained against a foreign banking corporation, in proper case, for conversion of funds belonging to plaintiff by wrongfully sending them out of the country, if the conversion technically took place in New York. Plesch v Banque Nationale De La Republique D'Haiti (1948) 273 A.D. 224, 77 N.Y.S.2d 43, affd 298 N.Y. 573, 81 N.E.2d 106

Section 225 was inapplicable to an action brought pursuant to a supervisory order of the alien property custodian.Yokohama Specie Bank, Ltd. v National City Bank (1944) 183 Misc 610, 52 N.Y.S.2d 97

15. Long-arm jurisdiction

Up to the time of effective date of § 302 of the CPLR (September 1, 1963) a foreign corporation, not authorized to do business in this state, was amenable to local suit only if it was engaged in such a continuous and systematic course of "doing business" here as to warrant a finding of its "presence" in this jurisdiction, and § 302 of the CPLR should not be construed retroactively to bring such a corporation within personal jurisdiction of the New York courts by virtue of service made on the corporation prior to its effective date. Simonson v International Bank (1964) 14 N.Y.2d 281, 251 N.Y.S.2d 433, 200 N.E.2d 427

A foreign corporation could not be subjected to personal jurisdiction by a New York court by service upon its president in New York in an action for negligence and breach of warranty in the manufacture of the steel tank on a gasoline tank truck which exploded on a New York highway, where such corporation did no business in New York and the alleged tortious act causing the injury, that of improperly designing and assembling the steel tank, occurred out of the state. Longines-Wittnauer Watch Co. v Barnes & Reinecke, Inc. (1965) 15 N.Y.2d 443, 261 N.Y.S.2d 8, 209 N.E.2d 68 24 ALR3d 508, cert den 382 US 905, 15 L Ed 2d 158, 86 S Ct 241

Section 302 of the CPLR authorizes judicial jurisdiction over an absent nonresident defendant where a cause of action arises from commission of a tortious act in New York State. Feathers v McLucas (1964, 3d Dept) 21 A.D.2d 558, 251 N.Y.S.2d 548, revd on other grounds Longines-Wittnauer Watch Co. v Barnes & Reinecke, Inc. 15 N.Y.2d 443, 261 N.Y.S.2d 8, 209 N.E.2d 68, 24 ALR3d 508, cert den 382 US 905, 15 L Ed 2d 158, 86 S Ct 241

Jurisdiction of a state may be extended over a foreign corporation where even a single or occasional act, because of its nature and quality, and the circumstances of its commission, may be deemed sufficient to render the corporation liable to suit on causes of action arising therefrom, pursuant to § 302 of the CPLR, incorporating the due process views of late decisions of the United States Supreme Court. Feathers v McLucas (1964, 3d Dept) 21 A.D.2d 558, 251 N.Y.S.2d 548, revd on other grounds Longines-Wittnauer Watch Co. v Barnes-Reinecke, Inc. 15 N.Y.2d 443, 261 N.Y.S.2d 8, 209 N.E.2d 68, cert den 382 US 905, 15 L Ed 2d 158, 86 S Ct 241, and revg 41 Misc. 2d 498, 245 N.Y.S.2d 282

Trial court had personal and subject matter jurisdiction over defendant, a Spanish company, because 1) defendant purposefully availed itself of the privilege of conducting activities within New York; 2) plaintiff's claim under this section arose from defendant's transaction of business in New York within the meaning of N.Y. C.P.L.R. 302(a)(1); and 3) the exercise of long-arm jurisdiction over defendant comported with federal due process as it established minimum contacts with New York by visiting the state on multiple occasions to promote its wine and selling wine to a New York-based distributor. D&R Global Selections, S.L. v Bodega Olegario Falcon Pineiro, 29 N.Y.3d 292, 2017 NY Slip Op 04494, 2017 NY Slip Op 4494, 2017 N.Y. LEXIS 1453 (N.Y. 2017).

Musical composer by his composing activities, which he exploited in the United States through attorneys and accountants whom he retained in New York on continuing basis, did business in New York, within purview of long-arm statute. ABKCO Industries, Inc. v Lennon (1976, 1st Dept) 52 A.D.2d 435, 384 N.Y.S.2d 781 (disagreed with on other grounds B. v H. (2d Dept) 84 A.D.2d 295, 445 N.Y.S.2d 579)

There was no jurisdiction over a corporation in a products liability case based on the "corporate presence" doctrine where the corporation was a nondomiciliary that was not doing business in New York, did not come into existence until after the injury at issue, and could not have engaged in tortious conduct that caused the injuries; while the corporation had purchased all of the manufacturer's assets, even if the corporation had a duty to warn, that duty did not arise until after it acquired the assets of the manufacturer, after the injury, and the trial court's ruling that under the "product line" exception, since the manufacturer was subject to long-arm jurisdiction, the corporation was likewise was subject to such jurisdiction as the successor, was error. Semenetz v Sherling & Walden, Inc. (2005, 3d Dept) 21 A.D. 3d 1138, 801 N.Y.S.2d 78, app gr (2005, NY) 2005 N.Y. LEXIS 3419

16. Doing business

Foreign corporation was not doing business in New York State within meaning of section 47 of former Gen. Corp. Law where corporation's only contact with state was its selling agent who maintained office in state and listed corporation's name in local telephone directory. Hamlin v G. E. Barrett & Co. (1927) 246 N.Y. 554, 159 N.E. 648

Defendant's motion to dismiss was properly denied at Special Term where plaintiff sued for tort in Paris committed by foreign airline which did not fly into New York but which maintained leased office here, employed several people and had bank account, did public relations and publicity work here and transmitted requests for space to European headquarters; test for "doing business" should be a simple, pragmatic one and was met on this showing. Bryant v Finnish Nat. Airline (1965) 15 N.Y.2d 426, 260 N.Y.S.2d 625, 208 N.E.2d 439

Once plaintiff established that the defendant corporation had been doing business in New York, plaintiff, though a nonresident or likewise a foreign corporation, was in a position to assert any kind of a cause of action against it, provided it could be considered as still doing business in New York when the action was commenced.Sukosky v Philadelphia & Reading Coal & Iron Co. (1919) 189 A.D. 689, 179 N.Y.S. 23; Smith v Compania Litografica De La Habana (1923) 121 Misc 368, 201 N.Y.S. 65

Apparent intention of the revisors was to carry forward and retain former recognized tests of what constitutes "doing business" by a foreign corporation in New York; a foreign corporation cannot be considered as "doing business" in New York within subd. (4) of § 225 of former Gen. Corp. L. unless it has done sufficient New York business in nature and amount as to satisfy the classic "presence" test set forth in leading cases. Fremay, Inc. v Modern Plastic Machinery Corp. (1961, 1st Dept) 15 A.D.2d 235, 222 N.Y.S.2d 694

Where both parties were foreign corporations, test for "doing business" in New York under statute providing for maintenance of action against foreign corporation by another or by nonresident where defendant is foreign corporation doing business in the state is same as under statute authorizing court to exercise such jurisdiction over persons, property or status as might have been exercised heretofore. ABKCO Industries, Inc. v Lennon (1976, 1st Dept) 52 A.D.2d 435,

384 N.Y.S.2d 781 (disagreed with on other grounds B. v H. (2d Dept) 84 A.D.2d 295, 445 N.Y.S.2d 579)

Purchase of merchandise within New York by foreign corporation does not constitute doing business within New York for purposes of § 47 of former Gen. Corp. Law.Scheinman v Bonwit Teller & Co. (1928) 132 Misc 311, 229 N.Y.S. 783

In order for nonresident to be able to sue foreign corporation in New York pursuant to § 47 of former Gen. Corp. Law, business done in this state by foreign corporation must be related to its main business and be substantial part of it; therefore, where foreign corporation was banking business which performed none of its banking functions in New York, but merely maintained office in New York to solicit business, corporation was not "doing business" within meaning of former § 47. Raiola v Los Angeles First Nat. Trust & Sav. Bank (1929) 133 Misc 630, 233 N.Y.S. 301

Where a considerable amount of local, non-interstate business had been done in New York through a local office or place of business or through agents and representatives more or less regularly attempting to promote the corporation's business in New York, the situation was within the "doing business" clause in § 225 of former Gen. Corp. L., notwithstanding the corporation had failed to seek or obtain authority to do business in New York. Murray v J. P. Ward Co. (1959) 15 Misc. 2d 944, 181 N.Y.S.2d 216; Madison Distributing Co. v Phoenix Piece Dye Works (1930) 135 Misc 543, 239 N.Y.S. 176

"Doing business" in New York implies corporate continuity of conduct such as might be evidenced by investment of capital here, with maintenance of office for transaction of business along with those incidental circumstances which attest to corporate intent to avail itself of privilege to carry on business. William L. Bonnell Co. v Katz (1960) 23 Misc. 2d 1028, 196 N.Y.S.2d 763

While foreign corporation may be considered as present in this state for purpose of obtaining jurisdiction over it, such determination does not carry with it conclusion that corporation is doing business here to extent that State may demand compliance with § 218 of former Gen. Corp. Law. M. M. Mades Co. v Gassman (1948, City Ct) 77 N.Y.S.2d 236

17. – Effect of authorization

If the action was not commenced until after defendant foreign corporation had entirely ceased doing business in the state and formally withdrawn its certificate of authority and designation of an agent for service of process, it was too late to qualify the action as one maintainable under subd. (4) of § 225 of former Gen. Corp. L.Simons v Inecto, Inc. (1934) 242 A.D. 275, 275 N.Y.S. 501

If the foreign corporation had applied for and obtained authority to do business in New York before the action against it was instituted, it could be presumed that it was doing business in New York. Hamilton v Berwind-White Coal Mining Co. (1945, Sup) 60 N.Y.S.2d 561; Bloom v Wrought Iron Novelty Corp. (1926) 128 Misc 460, 219 N.Y.S. 92; L. B. Foster Co. v Koppel Industrial Car & Equipment Co. (1926) 127 Misc 51, 215 N.Y.S. 214

But if the foreign corporation had never applied for or obtained authority to do business in New York, there was no presumption that it was doing business there, and another foreign corporation or nonresident seeking to maintain an action in a New York court against it solely on the ground that it had been, or was, doing business in New York, had the burden of so establishing.Electric Race Patrol, Inc. v National Trailer Convoy, Inc. (1961, SD NY) 191 F. Supp. 364

§ 1315. Record of shareholders

(a) Any resident of this state who shall have been a shareholder of record of a foreign corporation doing business in this state upon at least five days' written demand may require such foreign corporation to produce a record of its shareholders setting forth the names and addresses of all shareholders, the number and class of shares held by each and the dates when they respectively became the owners of record thereof and shall have the right to examine in person or by agent or attorney at the office of the foreign corporation in this state or at the office of its transfer agent or registrar in this state or at such other place in the county in this state in which the foreign corporation is doing business as may be designated by the foreign corporation, during the usual business hours, the record of shareholders or an exact copy thereof certified as correct by the corporate officer or agent responsible for keeping or producing such record and to make extracts therefrom. Resident holders of voting trust certificates representing shares of the foreign corporation shall for the purpose of this section be regarded as shareholders. Any such agent or authority shall be authorized in a writing that satisfies the requirements of a writing under paragraph (b) of section 609 (proxies). A corporation requested to provide information pursuant to this paragraph shall make available such information in the format in which such information is maintained by the corporation and shall not be required to provide such information in any other format. If a request made pursuant to this paragragh includes a request to furnish information regarding beneficial owners, the corporation shall make available such information in its possession regarding beneficial owners as is provided to the corporation by a registered broker or dealer or a bank, association or other entity that exercises fiduciary powers in connection with the forwarding of information to such owners. The corporation shall not be required to obtain information about beneficial owners not in its possession.

(b) An examination authorized by paragraph (a) may be denied to such shareholder or other person upon his refusal to furnish to the foreign corporation or its transfer agent or registrar an affidavit that such inspection is not desired for a purpose which is in the interest of a business or object other than the business of the foreign corporation and that such shareholder or other person has not within five years sold or offered for sale any list of shareholders of any corporation of any type or kind, whether or not formed under the laws of this state, or aided or abetted any person in procuring any such record of shareholders for any such purpose.

(c) Upon refusal by the foreign corporation or by an officer or agent of the foreign corporation to produce for examination or to permit an examination of the record of shareholders as herein provided, the person making the demand for production and examination may apply to the supreme court in the judicial district where the office of the foreign corporation within this state is located, upon such notice as the court may direct, for an order directing the foreign corporation, its officer or agent, to show cause why an order should not be granted directing such production and permitting such examination by the applicant. Upon the return day of the order to show cause, the court shall hear the parties summarily, by affidavit or otherwise, and if it appears that the applicant is qualified and entitled to such examination, the court shall grant an order compelling such production for examination and awarding such further relief as to the court may seem just and proper.

(d) Nothing herein contained shall impair the power of courts to compel the production for examination of the books of a foreign corporation. The record of shareholders specified in paragraph (a) shall be prima facie evidence of the facts therein stated in favor of the plaintiff in any action or special proceeding against such foreign corporation or any of its officers, directors or shareholders.

History: Add, L 1961, ch 855; amd, L 1963, ch 684, § 5, eff Sept 1, 1963; L 1964, ch 725, § 17, eff June 1, 1964; L 1997, ch 449, § 69, eff Feb 22, 1998.

CASE ANNOTATIONS

1. **In general**
2. **Right to inspect, generally**
3. **Prerequisites of right**
4. **Enforcement of right**
5. **Location and sufficiency of records**
6. **Purpose of inspection, generally**
7. **– Particular cases**
8. **Miscellaneous**

1. In general

Statute providing for shareholder inspection of corporate books and records should be liberally construed in favor of the shareholder whose welfare as a stockholder or the corporation's welfare may be affected. Crane Co. v Anaconda Co. (1976) 39 N.Y.S.2d 14, 382 N.Y.S.2d 707, 346 N.E.2d 507

This section does not abolish or qualify the common law right of a stockholder to the production of a list of all the shareholders of a foreign corporation licensed to do business in New York. Gittlin v Studebaker Corp. (1966) 49 Misc. 2d 964, 268 N.Y.S.2d 897, revd on other grounds (1st Dept) 25 A.D.2d 822, 269 N.Y.S.2d 143

Dissenting shareholders were entitled to compilation of list of non-objecting beneficial owners of corporation ("NOBO" list) under CLS Gen Bus § 1315, even though corporation, at time of demand, did not have NOBO list in its possession, where shareholders were qualified to demand shareholder records under statute, compilation was relatively simple mechanical task, and failure to provide list would, under corporate bylaws, result in management receiving automatic support of those beneficial owners not contacted. Sadler v NCR Corp. (1991, CA2 NY) 928 F.2d 48

Production, under CLS Bus Corp § 1315, of shareholder records of Maryland corporation doing business in New York did not subject corporation to inconsistent regulation in violation of "dormant" Commerce Clause, even though Maryland, as part of its own scheme of regulation, would not permit such production, since states are not prohibited from enacting regulations simply because they require more of entity that is already subject to some less demanding regulation elsewhere. Sadler v NCR Corp. (1991, CA2 NY) 928 F.2d 48

Shareholder record production requirement of CLS Bus Corp § 1315 creates no discrimination against interstate commerce since it applies equally to foreign and domestic corporations. Sadler v NCR Corp. (1991, CA2 NY) 928 F.2d 48

CLS Bus Corp Law § 1315(a) does not violate the Commerce Clause, where shareholders of Maryland corporation could compel production of shareholders list under New York law but not under Maryland law, and corporation contended that these different rules in different states would render unmanageable its business transactions, because availability of the list does not involve corporation in different controls or accountability. NCR Corp. v Wahl (1991, SD NY) 755 F. Supp. 91, later proceeding (SD NY) 1991 US Dist LEXIS 876 and affd (CA2 NY) 928 F.2d 48

2. Right to inspect, generally

The right to inspect stock records included the right to copy or make notes of what the records showed, and the inspection and copying could be done through or with the assistance of an authorized representative. Henry v Babcock & Wilcox Co. (1909) 196 N.Y. 302, 89 N.E. 942; Application of Joslyn (1948) 191 Misc 512, 78 N.Y.S.2d 183, affd 273 A.D. 945, 78 N.Y.S.2d 923; Althause v Giroux (1907) 56 Misc 508, 107 N.Y.S. 191

It was held that a director of a foreign corporation had no right, merely as such, under § 113 of former Stock Corp. L., to demand inspection of its records and that his application for a court order could be denied for such reasons as communist affiliations and failure to have security clearance. Posen v United Aircraft Products, Inc. (1952) 201 Misc 260, 111 N.Y.S.2d 261

3. Prerequisites of right

Section 113 of former Stock Corp. L. contained provisions similar to those now appearing in subd. (b) of this § 1315 of the Business Corp. L., giving the foreign corporation a right to require of the demanding shareholder a formal statement that he was not seeking the inspection for a purpose alien to the corporation's business or objectives and had not been a party to procuring and selling lists of shareholders. It was held that if a shareholder did not advise why he wanted to inspect the stock records, his demand could properly be denied.Shorten v Remington Rand, Inc. (1954) 206 Misc 834, 135 N.Y.S.2d 85

In a stockholder's derivative action, failure of plaintiff, following a security demand by the corporation pursuant to § 61-b of former General Corporation Law, to comply with a bylaw of the corporation in seeking leave to inspect its stock records, did not require denial of his motion in view of the broad powers encompassed in this section.Solomon v Hirsch (1962) 35 Misc. 2d 716, 230 N.Y.S.2d 625

The plaintiff who sought an order directing a corporation to furnish him with the names and addresses of all shareholders and the number of shares held by each pursuant to § 1315 of the Business Corporation Law possessed no absolute right under the statute to demand the list of shareholders where he had been a stockholder less than the six months' period required by the statute, and where he had been enjoined from using authorizations allegedly supplied to him by holders of more than five percent of the outstanding common stock until he had complied with the appropriate S. E. C. regulations. Gittlin v Studebaker Corp. (1966) 49 Misc. 2d 964, 268 N.Y.S.2d 897, revd on other grounds (1st Dept) 25 A.D.2d 822, 269 N.Y.S.2d 143

N.Y. Bus. Corp. Law § 1315(c), which requires a shareholder requesting a foreign corporation's shareholder records to apply for an order in a court in the judicial district where the foreign corporation's New York office is located, suggests that the foreign corporation, at a minimum, must have an office in New York before an order may be issued against it. Airtran NY, LLC v Midwest Air Group, Inc. (2007, Sup) 15 Misc 3d 467, 831 NYS2d 307, later proceeding (2007, NY App Div, 1st Dept) 2007 NY App Div LEXIS 5062

Foreign corporation was not obliged to turn over records of its shareholders to a New York limited liability company because it was not "doing business" in New York for purposes of N.Y. Bus. Corp. Law § 1315(a), as it had no office there, and the actions of its wholly-owned subsidiary in New York could not be imputed to it. Airtran NY, LLC v Midwest Air Group, Inc. (2007, Sup) 15 Misc 3d 467, 831 NYS2d 307, later proceeding (2007, NY App Div, 1st Dept) 2007 NY App Div LEXIS 5062

That a foreign corporation's New York contacts are sufficient to obtain long arm jurisdiction over it does not mean that they rise to the level of "doing business" in New York for purposes of N.Y. Bus. Corp. Law § 1315(a). Airtran NY, LLC v Midwest Air Group, Inc. (2007, Sup) 15 Misc 3d 467, 831 NYS2d 307, later proceeding (2007, NY App Div, 1st Dept) 2007 NY App Div LEXIS 5062

When determining whether a domestic corporation had a right, through a foreign corporation's shareholder, to require the foreign corporation to produce a list of the foreign corporation's shareholders, under N.Y. Bus. Corp. Law § 1315, the applicable standard to apply when determining if the foreign corporation was "doing business" in New York was the standard set forth in N.Y. C.P.L.R. 302, rather than the stricter standard applicable under N.Y. Bus. Corp. Law § 1312, because N.Y. Bus. Corp. Law § 1315 did not raise the Commerce Clause concerns involved when applying N.Y. Bus. Corp. Law § 1312. Airtran N. Y., LLC v Midwest Air Group, Inc. (2007, App Div, 1st Dept) 844 NYS2d 233.

Domestic corporation, through a foreign corporation's shareholder, was entitled to the foreign corporation's shareholder list, under N.Y. Bus. Corp. Law § 1315, because the foreign corporation did business in New York through the foreign corporation's subsidiary. Airtran N. Y., LLC v Midwest Air Group, Inc. (2007, App Div, 1st Dept) 844 NYS2d 233

Since N.Y. Bus. Corp. Law § 1312 constitutes a statutory barrier to a foreign corporation's right to bring suit, a party seeking to impose the barrier, in order to rebut the presumption that the corporation does business in its state of incorporation rather than New York, has the burden of proving that the foreign corporation's activity in New York is systematic and regular, and the burden of showing "doing

business" is therefore a heavy one since a lesser showing might infringe on Congress's constitutional power to regulate interstate commerce, and the same concern applies to the N.Y. Bus. Corp. Law § 1301 requirement that a foreign corporation be authorized to "do business" in New York, but those concerns do not apply to N.Y. Bus. Corp. Law § 1315(a), which implicates neither the restriction of a right nor the fear of constitutional infringement. Airtran N. Y., LLC v Midwest Air Group, Inc. (2007, App Div, 1st Dept) 844 NYS2d 233

Proper application of the rules of statutory construction and due respect for the admonition that N.Y. Bus. Corp. Law § 1315 be broadly construed lead to the conclusion that "doing business," as used in the statute, should be interpreted consistently with the precedents applying the usual standard for doing business. Airtran N. Y., LLC v Midwest Air Group, Inc. (2007, App Div, 1st Dept) 844 NYS2d 233

Plaintiff shareholders qualified under CLS Bus Corp § 1315 as persons entitled to obtain "record" of corporation's shareholders where corporation did business in state, plaintiffs were residents of state, and they had owned corporation's stock for 6 months prior to their demand. Sadler v NCR Corp. (1991, CA2 NY) 928 F.2d 48

Qualified shareholders should not be denied right to invoke CLS Gen Bus § 1315 in order to obtain "record" of all other shareholders, even though qualified shareholders had entered into agreement with corporate shareholder (which could not qualify on its own as entity entitled to obtain "record") by which corporate shareholder would reimburse and indemnify qualified shareholders for expenses incurred in their demand for record, where there was nothing in agreement which created risk of using statute for improper purpose or in bad faith. Sadler v NCR Corp. (1991, CA2 NY) 928 F.2d 48

4. Enforcement of right

A shareholder who established that he was qualified under § 113 of former Stock Corp. L. to demand inspection of the foreign corporation's stock records, and that the corporation was doing business in New York and otherwise under a duty to comply with his demand, had an absolute right to make the inspection, enforceable by a proceeding in the nature of mandamus. Henry v Babcock & Wilcox Co. (1909) 196 N.Y. 302, 89 N.E. 942; Application of King-Sze Publications, Inc. (1960, Sup) 203 N.Y.S.2d 637; Application of Joslyn (1948) 191 Misc 512, 78 N.Y.S.2d 183, affd 273 A.D. 945, 78 N.Y.S.2d 923; People ex rel. Miles v Montreal & B. Copper Co. (1903) 40 Misc 282, 81 N.Y.S. 974

In proceeding to enforce right to inspect corporate books and records, the stockholder must allege compliance with statute. Crane Co. v Anaconda Co. (1976) 39 N.Y.2d 14, 382 N.Y.S.2d 707, 346 N.E.2d 507

Where a shareholder of a foreign corporation applied for a court order to compel the corporation to accede to his demand for inspection of records, he was deemed, under § 113 of former Stock Corp. L., to be seeking exercise of the court's discretion and the court could, if good cause appeared, deny the application or condition its production order in such manner as to avoid unreasonable inconvenience to the corporation or tying up of its records. Newmark v C & C Super Corp. (1957, 1st Dept) 3 A.D.2d 823, 160 N.Y.S.2d 936, affd 3 N.Y.2d 790, 164 N.Y.S.2d 42, 143 N.E.2d 796; People ex rel. Althause v Giroux Consol. Mines Co. (1907) 122 A.D. 617, 107 N.Y.S. 188

Evasiveness on the part of corporate representatives in acceding to a shareholder's demand to inspect records was sufficient to sustain the latter's application for a court order. People ex rel. Miles v Montreal & B. Copper Co. (1903) 40 Misc 282, 81 N.Y.S. 974

A shareholder seeking enforcement of record inspection rights under § 113 of former Stock Corp. L. had the burden of making a showing as to all factors and circumstances necessary to qualify him to make the demand and to demonstrate the corporation's obligation to comply with it. Hollister v De Forest Wireless Tel. Co. (1905) 47 Misc 674, 94 N.Y.S. 504; Seydel v Corporation Liquidating Co. (1905) 46 Misc 576, 92 N.Y.S. 225

5. Location and sufficiency of records

Section 113 of former Stock Corp. L., dealing with records to be kept and made available to New York stockholders of a foreign corporation, was considered inapplicable if the corporation had no office for the transaction of business in this state, or if it was doubtful whether the corporation was doing business here. Hovey v De Long Hook & Eye Co. (1914) 211 N.Y. 420, 105 N.E. 667; People ex rel. Sarles v Kendall Products Corp. (1922) 119 Misc 611, 197 N.Y.S. 752; Althause v Guaranty Trust Co. (1912) 78 Misc 181, 137 N.Y.S. 945

Failure of the corporation to keep any stock records at its New York office was not, however, an acceptable reason for not meeting a legitimate demand by a qualified shareholder. Hovey v Procter & Gamble Co. (1910) 139 A.D. 521, 124 N.Y.S. 128

Having a transfer agent in New York State was not of itself, having an office for the "transaction of business" within § 113 of former Stock Corp. L. Wadsworth v Equitable Trust Co. (1912) 153 A.D. 737, 138 N.Y.S. 842

The place for inspection was the office of the company and the stockholder could not be compelled to go elsewhere. Recknagel v Empire Self Lighting Oil Lamp Co. (1898) 24 Misc 193, 52 N.Y.S. 635

If the stock records kept in the corporation's New York office were not complete, the shareholder was at least entitled to inspect such records as were kept there. Singer v Knickerbocker Trust Co. (1902) 38 Misc 446, 77 N.Y.S. 1000

A foreign corporation was subject to a shareholder demand for inspection of stock records under § 113 of former Stock Corp. L., however, if it was renting office space for a representative in permanent charge, from which money was deposited for payment of dividends, or could otherwise be considered as doing business here. People ex rel. Singer v Knickerbocker Trust Co. (1902) 38 Misc 446, 77 N.Y.S. 1000

When a stockholder goes to the office of a foreign corporation where its stock book is required to be kept and makes a demand, during office hours upon the person apparently in charge of the office that an inspection be permitted, a prima facie case is made out; he is not required to prove, in the first instance, that the person apparently in charge bore any particular relation to the company. Pelletreau v Greene Consol. Gold Min. Co. (1906) 49 Misc 233, 97 N.Y.S. 391

6. Purpose of inspection, generally

Dispositive inquiry in determining whether to require corporation to produce record of shareholders for inspection by stockholder is whether the corporation can prove that inspection is sought for a purpose which is contrary to the best interests of the corporation or its stockholders. Crane Co. v Anaconda Co. (1976) 39 N.Y.2d 14, 382 N.Y.S.2d 707, 346 N.E.2d 507

When asserting a common-law right of access to corporate books and records the shareholder must plead and prove that inspection is desired for a proper purpose. Crane Co. v Anaconda Co. (1976) 39 N.Y.2d 14, 382 N.Y.S.2d 707, 346 N.E.2d 507

Common-law requirement of a bona fide intention on part of him who seeks access to corporation's books and records is equally applicable when statutory relief is sought. Crane Co. v Anaconda Co. (1976) 39 N.Y.2d 14, 382 N.Y.S.2d 707, 346 N.E.2d 507

When stockholder seeking to enforce right to inspect corporate books and records alleges compliance with statute, the bona fides of the stockholder will be assumed and it becomes incumbent on the corporation to justify its refusal by showing an improper purpose or bad faith. Crane Co. v Anaconda Co. (1976) 39 N.Y.2d 14, 382 N.Y.S.2d 707, 346 N.E.2d 507

Where purpose of obtaining stockholder's list is one of general interest to stockholders in corporation, in connection with their common interest in corporation as stockholders, rationale for requesting such list is not "purpose which is in interest of business or object other than business of foreign corporation" within meaning of Business Corporation Law provision excluding inspection of stock records for such purposes. Crane Co. v Anaconda Co. (1976, 1st Dept) 51 A.D.2d 46, 378 N.Y.S.2d 713, mod on other grounds 39 N.Y.2d 14, 382 N.Y.S.2d 707, 346 N.E.2d 507

Upon application by the shareholder to a court for an order to compel inspection, affidavits bearing on good faith of the application could be received and considered. But if there was no showing of bad faith on the part of petitioner, and no formal statement as to why he made the request had been demanded, his petition was not subject to dismissal merely because it failed to aver that it was made in furtherance of the corporation's business or interests. Application of King-Sze Publications, Inc. (1960, Sup) 203 N.Y.S.2d 637; Application of Joslyn (1948) 191 Misc 512, 78 N.Y.S.2d 183, affd 273 A.D. 945, 78 N.Y.S.2d 923

7. – Particular cases

Shareholder's interest in pursuing a selective and direct approach to stockholders with respect to shareholder's pending tender offer involving over one-fifth of the corporation's common stock, and shareholder's refusal of corporation's offer to have corporation's transfer agent transmit the tender offer prospectus to all stockholders, was not improper and did not render shareholder's request for inspection contrary to the best interests of the corporation or its stockholders. Crane Co. v Anaconda Co. (1976) 39 N.Y.2d 14, 382 N.Y.S.2d 707, 346 N.E.2d 507

Stockholder's request to inspect corporation's record of shareholders in order to present stockholders with information pertinent to stockholder's pending tender offer involving over one-fifth of the corporation's common stock did not involve a purpose other than the business of the corporation. Crane Co. v Anaconda Co. (1976) 39 N.Y.2d 14, 382 N.Y.S.2d 707, 346 N.E.2d 507

A shareholder desiring to discuss relevant aspects of a tender offer should be granted access to the shareholder list unless it is sought for a purpose inimical to the corporation or its stockholders. Crane Co. v Anaconda Co. (1976) 39 N.Y.2d 14, 382 N.Y.S.2d 707, 346 N.E.2d 507

Qualified stockholder may inspect corporation's stock register to ascertain the identity of fellow stockholders for the avowed purpose of informing them directly of its exchange offer and soliciting tenders of stock. Crane Co. v Anaconda Co. (1976) 39 N.Y.2d 14, 382 N.Y.S.2d 707, 346 N.E.2d 507

If the enforcement order was sought for purely personal reasons, such as to obtain a list of prospective purchasers of other securities, having no relationship to the business or welfare of the respondent corporation, the court could deny the application. People ex rel. Althause v Giroux Consol. Mines Co. (1907) 122 A.D. 617, 107 N.Y.S. 188

Under evidence that largest stockholder of foreign corporation had filed affidavit stating that its request to gain access to stock records of corporation was for business purposes of corporation, that stockholder was itself corporation which had made offer to exchange its stock for that of foreign corporation, and that directors of foreign corporation had sent four letters to its stockholders registering opposition to largest stockholder's offer, Special Term improperly found that stockholder was not entitled to access to stock records because its purpose was "other than business of foreign corporation" within meaning of Business Corporation Law provision prohibiting inspection of stock records for such purposes. Crane Co. v Anaconda Co. (1976, 1st Dept) 51 A.D.2d 46, 378 N.Y.S.2d 713, mod on other grounds 39 N.Y.2d 14, 382 N.Y.S.2d 707, 346 N.E.2d 507

It is well settled that a stockholder is entitled to inspect the corporation's stock book in order to be able to communicate with other stockholders and seek to persuade them, by solicitation of proxies and otherwise, to oust existing directors and management and substitute a slate nominated or approved by the stockholder seeking the inspection, and the fact that the existing management may be innocent of charges of mismanagement made by the petitioning stockholder is no reason for denying inspection of the stock list. Murchison v Alleghany Corp. (1960) 27 Misc. 2d 290, 210 N.Y.S.2d 153, affd 12 A.D.2d 753, 210 N.Y.S.2d 975, app den (1st Dept) 12 A.D.2d 903, 212 N.Y.S.2d 997

The possibility that a stockholder petitioning for an order entitling him to inspect the stock book of a corporation intends to use the information obtained to negotiate purchases of large blocks of the company's stock through private sales or negotiations, is not, in itself, sufficient to deprive him of his statutory right of inspection. Murchison v Alleghany Corp. (1960) 27 Misc. 2d 290, 210 N.Y.S.2d 153, affd 12 A.D.2d 753, 210 N.Y.S.2d 975, app den (1st Dept) 12 A.D.2d 903, 212 N.Y.S.2d 997

Granting of a stockholder's application for leave to inspect the stock records of his corporation should not be held up to permit an investigation of charges that petitioner, and his associates, have been guilty of misconduct in attempting to further their personal interests in the handling of certain affairs of the corporation, particularly where the investigation would have to be very extensive, the charges have already been investigated and considered without merit by an investigating committee, and the charges, even if substantiated, would fail to establish that his application to inspect the stock records was not in good faith. Murchison v Alleghany Corp. (1960) 27 Misc. 2d 290, 210 N.Y.S.2d 153, affd 12 A.D.2d 753, 210 N.Y.S.2d 975, app den (1st Dept) 12 A.D.2d 903, 212 N.Y.S.2d 997

Since the right of inspection of stockholder books, absent proof of an improper purpose, is unconditional when based upon Business Corporation Law § 1315, the petitioner's application for an order directing respondent to allow petitioner to inspect the stockholder list was granted where the purpose advanced, that of enlisting shareholder opposition to a proposed merger, was entirely proper. Since the basis urged in support of this application was different than the facts of previous applications, those previous denials of a right of inspection could not preclude the ordered inspection under the application of res judicata. Crane Co. v Westinghouse Air Brake Co. (1968) 56 Misc. 2d 538, 288 N.Y.S.2d 984

A motion by the plaintiff in a stockholders' derivative suit for an order requiring the defendant corporation to supply plaintiff with a copy of its stock list at plaintiff's expense should be granted where the plaintiff's request is not for the purpose of seeking examination of all books of the corporation but merely to aid him in seeking joinder of other stockholders. Ratzkin v Harris (1961, Sup) 219 N.Y.S.2d 665

8. Miscellaneous

Section 113 of former Stock Corp. L. further contained a penal provision, which has not been carried forward into this § 1315 of the Business Corp. L. As against a claim for the penalty, it was enough to show that the records were not available in the New York office when the demand was made, or that the corporation was not doing business in New York but merely maintaining a stock transfer agent there. Other decisions dealing with the penal aspects of § 113 are likewise hereto appended, though they apparently lack significance under this § 1315 of the Business Corp. L. Cox v Paul (1903) 175 N.Y. 328, 67 N.E. 586; Kellner v Shelley (1917) 178 A.D. 657, 165 N.Y.S. 833; Wadsworth v Equitable Trust Co. (1912) 153 A.D. 737, 138 N.Y.S. 842; Althause v Giroux Consol. Mines Co. (1912) 150 A.D. 580, 135 N.Y.S. 500; Hovey v Eiswald (1910) 139 A.D. 433, 124 N.Y.S. 130; Tyng v Corporation Trust Co. (1905) 104 A.D. 486, 93 N.Y.S. 928

The manner of communication selected by stockholder desiring to discuss aspects of tender offer with fellow stockholders should be within the judgment of the shareholder. Crane Co. v Anaconda Co. (1976) 39 N.Y.2d 14, 382 N.Y.S.2d 707, 346 N.E.2d 507

In a proceeding filed pursuant to § 113 of former Stock Corp. L. for inspection of corporate books, the petitioner, a stockholder, was entitled to have the registration agent furnish a list of stockholders, despite protests of the corporation, where the list could be furnished with a minimum of expense and inconvenience by the registration agent and the stockholder was willing to pay for the expense involved. Mencher v Seminole Oil & Gas Corp. (1959) 20 Misc. 2d 56, 194 N.Y.S.2d 162

§ 1316. Voting trust records

(a) A voting trustee, appointed under a voting trust agreement to vote the shares of a foreign corporation doing business in this state, who either has an office in this state or has designated a transfer agent within this state, shall produce for examination and permit to be examined in this state, at the office of the foreign corporation or at his office or at the office of such transfer agent, a record of voting trust certificate holders setting forth their names, alphabetically arranged, and addresses, the number and class of shares represented by the certificates held by them respectively and the dates when they respectively became the owners thereof, upon the written demand of any resident of this state who shall have been a voting trust certificate holder or a shareholder of the foreign corporation for at least six months immediately preceding his demand, or of any resident of this state holding, or thereunto authorized in writing by the holders of, at least five percent of any class of the outstanding shares of such foreign corporation, either directly or as holders of voting trust certificates for such shares, subject to the same terms and conditions set forth with respect to the right of examination of the record of shareholders of the foreign corporation in section 1315 (Record of shareholders).

(b) The voting trustee shall deposit an exact copy of the voting trust agreement with the foreign corporation at its office in this state or at the office of the transfer agent in this state.

(c) The copy of the voting trust agreement shall be subject to the same right of examination by voting trust certificate holders and by shareholders of the

foreign corporation as is the record of shareholders of a corporation under section 624 (Books and records; right of inspection, prima facie evidence).

(d) Upon refusal by a voting trustee or his transfer agent to produce for examination or to permit an examination of the record of voting trust certificate holders or of such copy of the voting trust agreement as herein provided, the person making the demand may apply to the supreme court, upon such notice as the court may direct, for an order directing the voting trustee or his transfer agent to show cause why an order should not be granted directing such production and permitting such examination. Upon the return day of the order to show cause, the court shall hear the parties summarily, by affidavit or otherwise, and if it appears that the applicant is entitled to such examination, the court shall grant an order compelling such production for examination and awarding such further relief as to the court may seem just and proper.

(e) Where the voting trust agreement shall vest in the voting trustee the right to vote the shares of a foreign corporation which has an office in this state for the doing of business and either the principal business operation of which is conducted within this state or the greater part of its property is located within this state, the voting trust agreement is an express trust created under the laws of this state and the supreme court upon the petition of a voting trust certificate holder may exercise such power over the trustee named therein as is granted to the court by section one hundred twelve of the real property law.

History: Add, L 1961, ch 855, eff Sept 1, 1963; amd, L 1962, ch 834, § 95; L 1963, ch 684, § 6, eff Sept 1, 1963.

CASE ANNOTATIONS

As § 115 of former Stock Corp. L, from which this § 1316 of the Business Corp. L. was partially derived, was remedial in nature, it was held applicable to voting trusts existing at date of its enactment. Palley v Chase Nat. Bank (1942) 178 Misc 536, 35 N.Y.S.2d 958, affd 264 A.D. 764, 35 N.Y.S.2d 717

The right to an inspection is a continuing one and each application must be considered in the light of circumstances then existing. Palley v Chase Nat. Bank (1942) 178 Misc 536, 35 N.Y.S.2d 958, affd 264 A.D. 764, 35 N.Y.S.2d 717

See alsoPetition of Allen (1942) 178 Misc 541, 35 N.Y.S.2d 120, affd 264 A.D. 764, 35 N.Y.S.2d 717, reh and app den 264 A.D. 838, 35 N.Y.S.2d 764

Power of a court to remove the trustee of a voting trust was recognized prior to enactment of § 115 of former Stock Corp. L. on common-law principles. Petition of Allen (1942) 178 Misc 541, 35 N.Y.S.2d 120, affd 264 A.D. 764, 35 N.Y.S.2d 717, reh and app den 264 A.D. 838, 35 N.Y.S.2d 764

§ 1317. Liabilities of directors and officers of foreign corporations

(a) Except as otherwise provided in this chapter, the directors and officers of a foreign corporation doing business in this state are subject, to the same extent as directors and officers of a domestic corporation, to the provisions of:

(1) Section 719 (Liability of directors in certain cases) except subparagraph (a)(3) thereof, and

(2) Section 720 (Action against directors and officers for misconduct.)

(b) Any liability imposed by paragraph (a) may be enforced in, and such relief granted by, the courts in this state, in the same manner as in the case of a domestic corporation.

History: Formerly § 1318, renumbered and amd, L 1962, ch 834, §§ 97, 98, eff Sept 1, 1963.

CASE ANNOTATIONS

Section 114 of former Stock Corp. L., from which this § 1317 of the Business Corp. L. was in part derived, imposed, generally speaking, like liabilities upon officers, directors, and stockholders of foreign corporations doing business in New York as were imposed in connection with domestic corporations for such acts as making unauthorized dividends, illegal loans to stockholders, false certificates, reports, etc., and illegal transfer while insolvent or in danger of insolvency. It had the effect of making provisions in these fields applicable to foreign as well as domestic corporations. German-American Coffee Co. v Diehl (1915) 216 N.Y. 57, 109 N.E. 875; Upright v Brown (1938, CA2 NY) 98 F.2d 802; Feldman v Capitol Piece Dye Works, Inc. (1960, SD NY) 185 F. Supp. 426, revd on other grounds (CA2 NY) 293 F.2d 889, cert den 368 US 948, 7 L Ed 2d 344, 82 S Ct 389

The dividend had to be one which was "unauthorized" under the laws of the jurisdiction pursuant to which the corporation was organized, as well as under New York law, to sustain an action for its recovery or to sustain an action against directors for reimbursement; but if it was unauthorized under both laws, the action could be maintained in New York. Hutchinson v Stadler (1903) 85 A.D. 424, 83 N.Y.S. 509

Misconduct of an officer of a foreign corporation would not subject him to liability under § 114 of former Stock Corp. L. unless it fell within one of the categories of misconduct covered by that section. Greyhound Corp. v Commercial Casualty Ins. Co. (1940) 259 A.D. 317, 19 N.Y.S.2d 239; Braden v Perkins (1940) 174 Misc 885, 22 N.Y.S.2d 144

With respect to "unauthorized" dividends, § 114 of former Stock Corp. L. was regarded as aimed only at such dividends as would impair capital to the detriment of creditors, and thus was inapplicable in the absence of creditors or to the payment of a dividend on preferred stock which was merely excessive under the terms of its issuance. Diamond v Davis (1942, Sup) 38 N.Y.S.2d 103, affd 265 A.D. 919, 39 N.Y.S.2d 412, affd 292 N.Y. 552, 54 N.E.2d 683; Hayman v Morris (1942, Sup) 36 N.Y.S.2d 756. See however, Irving Trust Co. v Gunder (1932) 234 A.D. 252, 254 N.Y.S. 630

Although § 114 of former Stock Corp. L. did not explicity provide a remedy against a transferee of corporate property by sanctioning recovery of the property or setting aside of the transfer for fraud or illegality, it was assumed that such a remedy could be found. Irving Trust Co. v Maryland Casualty Co. (1936, CA2 NY) 83 F.2d 168, cert den 299 US 571, 81 L Ed 421, 57 S Ct 34

It was recognized, however, that a transfer of property situated outside the State of New York could not be declared void by virtue of such a statute unless it was likewise void or subject to avoidance under the lex rei sitae. Irving Trust Co. v Maryland Casualty Co. (1936, CA2 NY) 83 F.2d 168, cert den 299 US 571, 81 L Ed 421, 57 S Ct 34

If it appeared that the corporation was doing business in New York, liability on the part of its officers, etc., followed from the fact that the act, transaction, or occurrence was within the scope of § 114 of former Stock Corp. L. and equivalent provisions referring to liability of officers, etc., of domestic corporations. Upright v Brown (1938, CA2 NY) 98 F.2d 802

An officer of a foreign corporation did not have to account for illegal dividends received or credited to his account where they had already been applied against indebtedness of the corporation to him. Upright v Brown (1938, CA2 NY) 98 F.2d 802

CLS Business Corporation Law § 720, subd a(3), which grants injunctive relief against misconduct by corporate directors, is broad and covers every form of waste of assets and violation of duty whether as result of intention, negligence, or predatory acquisition and is applicable to foreign corporations pursuant to CLS Business Corporation Law § 1317, subd a(2). Goldberg v Meridor (1977, CA2

NY) 567 F.2d 209, cert den 434 US 1069, 55 L Ed 2d 771, 98 S Ct 1249 and on remand (SD NY) 81 FRD 105, CCH Fed Secur L Rep ¶ 96754, 27 FR Serv 2d 1360

For § 114 of former Stock Corp. L. to impose liability upon the officers, etc., of a foreign corporation, it must be averred and established that the corporation was "transacting business in this state."Jacobs v Manufacturers Trust Co. (1948, DC NY) 81 F. Supp. 394

Purchaser could not recover damages against principal of insolvent supplier under provisions of CLS Bus Corp §§ 720 and 1317 that allow action against directors and officers of corporation for negligence in management and disposition of corporate assets, where supplier was not New York corporation, and evidence did not warrant inference that it was doing business in New York. Air India v Pennsylvania Woven Carpet Mills (1997, SD NY) 978 F. Supp. 500

§ 1318. Liability of foreign corporations for failure to disclose required information

A foreign corporation doing business in this state shall, in the same manner as a domestic corporation, disclose to its shareholders of record who are residents of this state the information required under paragraph (c) of section 510 (Dividends or other distributions in cash or property), paragraphs (f) and (g) of section 511 (Share distributions and changes), paragraph (d) of section 515 (Reacquired shares), paragraph (c) of section 516 (Reduction of stated capital in certain cases), and shall be liable as provided in section 520 (Liability for failure to disclose required information) for failure to comply in good faith with these requirements.

History: Formerly § 1319, renumbered and amd, L 1962, ch 834, §§ 99, 100, eff Sept 1, 1963; amd, L 1962, ch 834, § 99, eff Sept 1, 1963,100, eff Sept 1, 1963; amd, L 1963, ch 684, § 7, eff Sept 1, 1963; L 1997, ch 449, § 70, eff Feb 22, 1998.

§ 1319. Applicability of other provisions

(a) In addition to articles 1 (Short title; definitions; application; certificates; miscellaneous) and 3 (Corporate name and service of process) and the other sections of article 13 (foreign corporations), the following provisions, to the extent provided therein, shall apply to a foreign corporation doing business in this state, its directors, officers and shareholders:

(1) Section 623 (Procedure to enforce shareholder's right to receive payment for shares).

(2) Section 626 (Shareholders' derivative action brought in the right of the corporation to procure a judgment in its favor).

(3) Section 627 (Security for expenses in shareholders' derivative action brought in the right of the corporation to procure a judgment in its favor).

(4) Section 630 (Liability of shareholders for wages due to laborers, servants or employees).

(5) Sections 721 (Nonexclusivity of statutory provisions for indemnification of directors and officers) through 726 (Insurance for indemnification of directors and officers), inclusive.

(6) Section 808 (Reorganization under act of congress).

(7) Section 907 (Merger or consolidation of domestic and foreign corporations).

History: Formerly § 1320, renumbered and amd, L 1962, ch 819; amd, L 1961, ch 834, § 101; L 1962, ch 317, § 15, eff Sept 1, 1963; L 1963, ch 684, § 8, eff Sept 1, 1963; L 1969, ch 1007, eff Sept 1, 1969; L 2016, ch 5, § 2, eff Jan 19, 2016.

CASE ANNOTATIONS

Defendant, a Delaware corporation authorized to do business in New York State, is exempt from the indemnification provisions of sections 721 through 726 of the Business Corporation Law since its shares are traded on the New York Stock Exchange (Business Corporation Law, § 726, subd [d]; § 1319, subd [a], par [4]; § 1320, subd [a], par [1]); accordingly, a claim against defendant by a former officer for indemnification for legal expenses incurred in connection with his appearance before a Federal Grand Jury must be decided under Delaware law.Stewart v Continental Copper & Steel Industries, Inc. (1979, 1st Dept) 67 A.D.2d 293, 414 N.Y.S.2d 910

Under Business Corporation Law § 723, made applicable to foreign corporations doing business in New York by Business Corporation Law § 1319, and providing that in order for a director of a corporation to obtain the benefits of indemnification and to be reimbursed for the expense of contesting an action against him it must be by reason of his being or having been a director, the director of a membership corporation, sued on the ground that he had conspired to injure an equipment supplier's business by criticizing the supplier's competition with the membership corporation, was not precluded from recovering the full amount of costs, expenses and fees incurred in defending the suit by reason of his having been paid half of such amount by an insurer. Dankoff v Bowling Proprietors Assn. (1972) 69 Misc. 2d 658, 331 N.Y.S.2d 109

In a stockholder's derivative action commenced in New York seeking to nullify the action of the board of directors of a Pennsylvania corporation in awarding bonuses to two executives, the law of Pennsylvania would be applied, pursuant to Bus Corp Law § 1319, to determine whether the requirement that the stockholders make a demand upon the board of directors as a prerequisite to suit was fulfilled since Pennsylvania has the most significant contacts with the corporation and, although Pennsylvania places the demand requirement within its procedural rules, it is a matter of substantive law governed by substantive conflict of laws rules among which is the rule that the State of Incorporation is a most significant contact. Lewis v Dicker (1982) 118 Misc. 2d 28, 459 N.Y.S.2d 215

In a stockholder's derivative action commenced in New York seeking to nullify the action of the board of directors of a Pennsylvania corporation in awarding bonuses to two executives, defendant's motion to dismiss would be granted where plaintiff's failure to make a demand on the board of directors to institute such action would bar plaintiff's action in that pursuant to the Pennsylvania law, a stockholder must demonstrate, as a prerequisite to suit against the board that all avenues were pursued in an effort to induce the board to bring such action, and plaintiff's allegation that he failed to make such demand because it would have been futile, inasmuch as the members of board as currently comprised either participated or acquiesced in the alleged wrongdoing, was insufficient to fulfill the required showing of futility. Lewis v Dicker (1982) 118 Misc. 2d 28, 459 N.Y.S.2d 215

A stockholder, who had placed shares of a foreign corporation doing business in New York in a revocable trust and who was the sole income beneficiary of the trust, held, within the meaning of Business Corporation Law § 626(a), a beneficial interest in the shares and was entitled to maintain a derivative action under the statute.Stephenson v Landegger (1971, SD NY) 337 F. Supp. 591, affd (CA2 NY) 464 F.2d 133, cert den 409 US 1039, 34 L Ed 2d 488, 93 S Ct 520

In a federal criminal action in which defendants sought advancement of defense costs from a former employer, an accounting firm, the procedures established in 8 Del. C. § 145(k) and N.Y. Bus. Corp. Law §§ 724(a) and 1319(a)(4) for litigating advancement disputes in state courts did not apply; however, the scope of the issues properly considered in an advancement proceeding was governed by state law. United States v Stein (2006, SD NY) 452 F Supp 2d 230, 98 AFTR 2d 6520, motion to strike gr (2006, SD NY) 452 F Supp 2d 276, stay den

(2006, SD NY) 452 F Supp 2d 281, 98 AFTR 2d 7160, motion den (2006, SD NY) 2006 US Dist LEXIS 80572, costs/fees proceeding, motion den (2006, SD NY) 461 F Supp 2d 201, motion den (2006, SD NY) 98 AFTR 2d 8016, later proceeding (2007, SD NY) 2007 US Dist LEXIS 1825

In a criminal case in which the court had ancillary jurisdiction over defendants' claims against a former employer, an accounting firm, for advancement of defense costs, the advancement dispute was not arbitrable under 9 U.S.C.S. § 2 of the Federal Arbitration Act, 9 U.S.C.S. § 1 et seq., because there was no evidence that all defendants were parties to an arbitration agreement, partnership agreements demonstrated that the obligation of former partners to arbitrate ended when their status as partners terminated, and enforcement of any applicable arbitration clauses would have violated public policy. Requiring arbitration (1) would have limited the court's ability to ensure that proceedings against defendants were fair, (2) would have undermined the court's responsibility under the Constitution and Criminal Justice Act, 18 U.S.C.S. § 3006A(f), to ensure that property available to defendants was used for their defense, (3) would have undermined the public interest in a speedy trial in accordance with the Sixth Amendment and the Speedy Trial Act, 18 U.S.C.S. § 3161 et seq., and (4) would have implicated the public interest, as found in 8 Del. C. § 145(k) and N.Y. Bus. Corp. Law §§ 724(a) and 1319(a)(4), in the timely resolution of disputes concerning advancement of defense costs. United States v Stein (2006, SD NY) 452 F Supp 2d 230, 98 AFTR 2d 6520, motion to strike gr (2006, SD NY) 452 F Supp 2d 276, stay den (2006, SD NY) 452 F Supp 2d 281, 98 AFTR 2d 7160, motion den (2006, SD NY) 2006 US Dist LEXIS 80572, costs/fees proceeding, motion den (2006, SD NY) 461 F Supp 2d 201, motion den (2006, SD NY) 98 AFTR 2d 8016, later proceeding (2007, SD NY) 2007 US Dist LEXIS 1825

§ 1320. Exemption from certain provisions

(a) Notwithstanding any other provision of this chapter, a foreign corporation doing business in this state which is authorized under this article, its directors, officers and shareholders, shall be exempt from the provisions of paragraph (e) of section 1316 (Voting trust records), subparagraph (a)(1) of section 1317 (Liabilities of directors and officers of foreign corporations), section 1318 (Liability of foreign corporations for failure to disclose required information) and subparagraph (a)(4) of section 1319 (Applicability of other provisions) if when such provision would otherwise apply:

(1) Shares of such corporation were listed on a national securities exchange, or

(2) Less than one-half of the total of its business income for the preceding three fiscal years, or such portion thereof as the foreign corporation was in existence, was allocable to this state for franchise tax purposes under the tax law.

History: Add, L 1962, ch 834, § 102, eff Sept 1, 1963; amd, L 1962, ch 819; L 1963, ch 684, § 9, eff Sept 1, 1963.

CASE ANNOTATIONS

Defendant, a Delaware corporation authorized to do business in New York State, is exempt from the indemnification provisions of sections 721 through 726 of the Business Corporation Law since its shares are traded on the New York Stock Exchange (Business Corporation Law, § 726, subd [d]; § 1319, subd [a], par [4]; § 1320, subd [a], par [1]); accordingly, a claim against defendant by a former officer for indemnification for legal expenses incurred in connection with his appearance before a Federal Grand Jury must be decided under Delaware law.Stewart v Continental Copper & Steel Industries, Inc. (1979, 1st Dept) 67 A.D.2d 293, 414 N.Y.S.2d 910

ARTICLE 14
[RENUMBERED]

History: Article 14 (consisting of § 1401), add, L 1961, ch 855, amd, L 1962, ch 837, renumbered Article 20 and § 2001, L 1976, ch 893, eff Nov 1, 1976. (Laws 1976, ch 894, § 6, changed the effective date from Sept 25, 1976 to Nov 1, 1976.).

§ 1401. [Repealed]

History: Add, L 1961, ch 855, and L 1962, ch 837, eff Apr 1, 1963, renumbered § 2001, L 1976, ch 893, eff Nov 1, 1976. (Laws 1976, ch 894, § 6, changed the effective date from Sept 25, 1976 to Nov 1, 1976.).

ARTICLE 15
PROFESSIONAL SERVICE
CORPORATION

History: Add, L 1970, ch 974, eff May 19, 1970.

§ 1501. Definitions

As used in this article, unless the context otherwise requires, the term:

(a) "licensing authority" means the regents of the university of the state of New York or the state education department, as the case may be, in the case of all professions licensed under title eight of the education law, and the appropriate appellate division of the supreme court in the case of the profession of law.

(b) "Profession" includes any practice as an attorney and counselor-at-law, or as a licensed physician, and those occupations designated in title eight of the education law.

(c) "Professional service" means any type of service to the public which may be lawfully rendered by a member of a profession within the purview of his or her profession.

(d) "Professional service corporation" means a corporation organized under this article.

(e) "Officer" does not include the secretary or an assistant secretary of a corporation having only one shareholder.

(f) "Other business entity" means any person other than a natural person, general partnership or a domestic or foreign business corporation, and includes a professional service limited liability company formed pursuant to the provisions of the New York limited liability company law.

(g) "Design professional service corporation" means a corporation organized under this article practicing professional engineering, architecture, landscape architecture, geology, or land surveying, or practicing any combination of such professions. The provisions of this article applicable to professional service corporations shall apply to design professional service corporations except to the extent that any provision is either inconsistent with a provision expressly applying to design professional service corporations or not relevant thereto.

(h) "Design professional" means an individual licensed and registered pursuant to title eight of the education law to practice professional engineering, architecture, landscape architecture, geology or land surveying.

(i) "Employee stock ownership plan" (ESOP) means a defined contribution plan established pursuant to Section 4975(e)(7) of the Internal Revenue Code.

History: Add, L 1970, ch 974, eff May 19, 1970, L 2011, ch 550, § 1, eff Jan 1, 2012, L 2011, ch 564, § 1, eff Sept 23, 2011; L 2013, ch 9, §§ 1, 2, eff March 15, 2013, deemed eff on and after Oct 3, 2012; L 2014, ch 475, § 13, eff Nov 21, 2016.

CASE ANNOTATIONS

Architecture firm's proposed use of initials "HOK" in its corporate name, representing last initials of three licensed firm members, was prohibited by Bus Corp L § 1512 as an assumed or fictitious name; thus Education Commissioner did not act arbitrarily, capriciously, or unreasonably in denying use of such initials in corporate name of firm. Kahn & Jacobs v Nyquist (1973) 76 Misc. 2d 355, 350 N.Y.S.2d 840

§ 1502. Corporations organized under other provisions of law

The provisions of this article shall not apply to corporations heretofore or hereafter duly organized under any other provision of law.

History: Add, L 1970, ch 974, eff May 19, 1970.

§ 1503. Organization

(a) Notwithstanding any other provision of law, one or more individuals duly authorized by law to render the same professional service within the state may organize, or cause to be organized, a professional service corporation for pecuniary profit under this article for the purpose of rendering the same professional service, except that one or more individuals duly authorized by law to practice professional engineering, architecture, landscape architecture, land surveying or geology within the state may organize, or cause to be organized, a professional service corporation or a design professional service corporation for pecuniary profit under this article for the purpose of rendering such professional services as such individuals are authorized to practice.

(b) The certificate of incorporation of a professional service corporation shall meet the requirements of this chapter and (i) shall state the profession or professions to be practiced by such corporation and the names and residence addresses of all individuals who are to be the original shareholders, directors and officers of such corporation, and (ii) shall have attached thereto a certificate or certificates issued by the licensing authority certifying that each of the proposed shareholders, directors and officers is authorized by law to practice a profession which the corporation is being organized to practice and, if applicable, that one or more of such individuals is authorized to practice each profession which the corporation will be authorized to practice.

(b-1) The certificate of incorporation of a design professional service corporation shall meet the requirements of this chapter, provided that shareholders may include employee stock ownership plans (ESOPs) and employees of the corporation not licensed as design professionals, and provided further however that:

(i) greater than seventy-five percent of the outstanding shares of stock of the corporation are owned by design professionals,

(ii) an ESOP, either in part or in its entirety, shall not constitute part of the greater than seventy-five percent owned by design professionals,

(iii) greater than seventy-five percent of the directors are design professionals,

(iv) greater than seventy-five percent of the officers are design professionals,

(v) the president, the chairperson of the board of directors and the chief executive officer or officers are design professionals, and

(vi) the single largest shareholder is either a design professional or an ESOP with greater than seventy-five percent of the plan's voting trustees being design professionals and greater than seventy-five percent of the plan's committee members being design professionals.

(b-2) The certificate of incorporation of a design professional service corporation shall:

(i) state the profession or professions to be practiced by such corporation,

(ii) state the names and residence addresses of all individuals or ESOPs who are to be the original shareholders, directors and officers of such corporation,

(iii) indicate the profession or professions of each original shareholder, director and officer who is a design professional,

(iv) state the ownership interest of each original shareholder, and

(v) indicate the names of the original officers and directors who are the president, the chairperson of the board of directors and the chief executive officer or officers.

(b-3) The certificate of incorporation of a design professional service corporation shall have attached thereto a certificate or certificates issued by the licensing authority certifying that each of the proposed shareholders, directors and officers who is listed as a design professional is authorized by law to practice a profession which the corporation is being organized to practice and, if applicable, that one or more of such individuals is authorized to practice each profession which the corporation will be authorized to practice. The attached certificate or certificates shall also certify that the president, the chairperson of the board of directors and the chief executive officer or officers are authorized by law to practice a profession which the corporation is being organized to practice.

(b-4) The certificate of incorporation of a design professional service corporation shall also have attached thereto a certificate or certificates issued by the licensing authority certifying that each of the shareholders, officers, directors and owners have been deemed to have been of good moral character as may be established by the regulations of the commissioner of education.

(b-5) On or after January first, two thousand twelve, the state education department and the department of state shall allow an existing professional service corporation organized under this article and practicing professional engineering, architecture, landscape architecture, geology or land surveying, or practicing any combination of such professions to become a design professional service corporation as defined in this article, provided the professional service corporation meets all of the requirements to become a design professional service corporation, including that its name shall end with the words "design professional corporation" or the abbreviation "D.P.C.", by amending its certificate of incorporation so that it contains the following statements:

(1) the names and residence addresses of all individuals or ESOPs who will be the shareholders, directors and officers of the original design professional service corporation; and

(2) the profession or professions of each shareholder, director and officer who is a design professional of the original design professional service corporation; and

(3) the ownership interest of each shareholder of the original design professional service corporation; and

(4) the names of the officers and directors who will be the president, the chairperson of the board of directors and the chief executive officer or officers of the original design professional service corporation.

(i) The certificate of amendment shall have attached thereto a certificate or certificates issued by the licensing authority certifying that each of the proposed shareholders, directors and officers who is listed as a design professional is authorized by law to practice a profession which the corporation is organized to practice and, if applicable, that one or more of such individuals is authorized to practice each profession which the corporation will be authorized to practice. The attached certificate or certificates shall also certify that the proposed president, the chairperson of the board of directors and the chief executive officer or officers are authorized by law to practice a profession which the corporation is organized to practice.

(ii) The certificate of amendment shall also have attached thereto a certificate or certificates issued by the licensing authority certifying that each of the proposed shareholders, officers, directors and owners listed have been deemed to have been of good moral character as may be established by the regulations of the commissioner of education.

(iii) The certificate of amendment shall also have attached thereto: (A) a tax clearance issued by the department of taxation and finance certifying that the existing professional service corporation is current with respect to payment of its state tax liabilities and (B) a certificate of good standing from the state education department certifying that the existing professional service corporation is authorized to provide professional services without restriction.

(b-6) (1) Prior to the first day of March, two thousand nineteen, the state education department and the department of state shall allow an existing business corporation organized under article four of this chapter to become a professional service corporation as defined in this article for the purpose of practicing professional geology, provided that the surviving corporation meet all of the requirements to become a professional service corporation, including that the name of a professional service corporation shall end with the words "professional corporation" or the abbreviation "P.C." by amending its certificate of incorporation so that it contains the following:

(i) the names and residence addresses of all individuals who will be the original shareholders, directors and officers of the professional service corporation;

(ii) a statement that the professional service corporation is formed pursuant to this section; and

(iii) a statement that the amendment shall not effect a dissolution of the corporation, but shall be deemed a continuation of its corporate existence, without affecting its then existing property rights or liabilities or the liabilities of its members or officers as such, but thereafter it shall have only such rights, powers and privileges, and be subject only to such other duties and liabilities, as a corporation created for the same purposes under this article.

(2) The certificate of amendment shall have attached thereto a certificate or certificates issued by the licensing authority certifying that each of the proposed shareholders, directors and officers listed:

(i) is authorized by law to practice a profession which the corporation is organized to practice and, if applicable, that one or more of such individuals is authorized to practice each profession which the corporation will be authorized to practice; and

(ii) has been deemed to be of good moral character as may be established by the regulations of the commissioner of education.

(3) The certificate of amendment shall also have attached thereto a tax clearance issued by the department of taxation and finance certifying that the existing business corporation is current with respect to payment of its state tax liabilities.

(4) Notwithstanding any provision of law to the contrary, any corporation formed under this section shall be required to comply with all applicable laws, rules, or regulations relating to the practice of a profession under title eight of the education law.

(b-7) (1) Prior to the first day of March, two thousand nineteen, the state education department and the department of state shall allow an existing business corporation organized under article four of this chapter to become a design professional service corporation as defined in this article for the purpose of practicing professional geology, provided that the surviving corporation meet all of the requirements to become a design professional service corporation, including that the name shall end with the words "design professional service corporation" or the abbreviation "D.P.C." by amending its certificate of incorporation so that it contains the following:

(i) the names and residence addresses of all individuals or ESOPs who will be the original shareholders, directors and officers of the professional service corporation;

(ii) a statement that the design professional service corporation is formed pursuant to this section;

(iii) the profession or profession of each shareholder, director and officer who is a design professional of the original design professional service corporation;

(iv) the names of the officers and directors who will be the president, the chairperson of the board of directors and the chief executive officer or officers of the original design professional service corporation;

(v) the ownership interest of each shareholder of the original design professional service corporation; and

(vi) a statement that the amendment shall not effect a dissolution of the corporation, but shall be deemed a continuation of its corporate existence, without affecting its then existing property rights or liabilities or the liabilities of its members or officers as such, but thereafter it shall have only such rights, powers and privileges, and be subject only to such other duties and liabilities, as a corporation created for the same purposes under this article.

(2) The certificate of amendment shall have attached thereto a certificate or certificates issued by the licensing authority certifying that each of the proposed shareholders, directors and officers listed:

(i) is authorized by law to practice a profession which the corporation is organized to practice and, if applicable, that one or more of such individuals is authorized to practice each profession which the corporation will be authorized to practice; and

(ii) has been deemed to be of good moral character as may be established by the regulations of the commissioner of education.

(3) The certificate of amendment shall also have attached thereto a tax clearance issued by the department of taxation and finance certifying that the existing business corporation is current with respect to payment of its state tax liabilities.

(4) Notwithstanding any provision of law to the contrary, any corporation formed under this section shall be required to comply with all applicable laws, rules, or regulations relating to the practice of a profession under title eight of the education law.

(c) A certified copy of the certificate of incorporation and of each amendment thereto shall be filed by the corporation with the licensing authority within thirty days after the filing of such certificate or amendment with the department of state.

(d) A professional service corporation, including a design professional service corporation, other than a corporation authorized to practice law, shall be under the supervision of the regents of the university of the state of New York and be subject to disciplinary proceedings and penalties, and its certificate of incorporation shall be subject to suspension, revocation or annulment for cause, in the same manner and to the same extent as is provided with respect to individuals and their licenses, certificates, and registrations in title eight of the education law relating to the applicable profession. Notwithstanding the provisions of this paragraph, a professional service corporation authorized to practice medicine shall be subject to the prehearing procedures and hearing procedures as is provided with respect to individual physicians and their licenses in title II-A of article two of the public health law.

(e) A corporation authorized to practice law shall be subject to the regulation and control of, and its certificate of incorporation shall be subject to suspension, revocation or annulment for cause by, the appellate division of the supreme court and the court of appeals in the same manner and to the same extent provided in the judiciary law with respect to individual attorneys and counselors-at-law. Such corporation need not qualify for any certification under section four hundred sixty-four of the judiciary law, take an oath of office under section four hundred sixty-six of such law or register under section four hundred sixty-seven of such law.

(f) The order of suspension, revocation or annulment of the certificate of incorporation of a profes-

sional service corporation pursuant to paragraphs (d) and (e) of this section shall be effective upon the filing of such order with the department of state.

(g) The practices of creative arts therapy, marriage and family therapy, mental health counseling, and psychoanalysis shall not be deemed the same professional service for the purpose of paragraph (a) of this section, notwithstanding that such practices are all licensed under article one hundred sixty-three of the education law.

History: Add, L 1970, ch 974, eff May 19, 1970; amd, L 1975, ch 109, § 35, eff Sept 1, 1975; L 2002, ch 676, § 12, eff Jan 1, 2005; L 2011, ch 550, § 2, eff Jan 1, 2012; L 2012, ch 467, § 1, eff Oct 3, 2012; L 2013, ch 9, § 3, eff March 15, 2013, deemed eff on and after Oct 3, 2012; L 2014, ch 475, §§ 14, 15, eff Nov 21, 2016; L 2016, ch 260, § 1, eff Nov 21, 2016; L 2018, ch 302, §§ 1, 2, eff Oct 1, 2018.

Blackline Showing Effect of 2018 Amendments. — (a) Notwithstanding any other provision of law, one or more individuals duly authorized by law to render the same professional service within the state may organize, or cause to be organized, a professional service corporation for pecuniary profit under this article for the purpose of rendering the same professional service, except that one or more individuals duly authorized by law to practice professional engineering, architecture, landscape architecture, land surveying or geology within the state may organize, or cause to be organized, a professional service corporation or a design professional service corporation for pecuniary profit under this article for the purpose of rendering such professional services as such individuals are authorized to practice.

(b) The certificate of incorporation of a professional service corporation shall meet the requirements of this chapter and (i) shall state the profession or professions to be practiced by such corporation and the names and resident addresses of all individuals who are to be the original shareholders, directors and officers of such corporation, and (ii) shall have attached thereto a certificate or certificates issued by the licensing authority certifying that each of the proposed shareholders, directors and officers is authorized by law to practice a profession which the corporation is being organized to practice and, if applicable, that one or more of such individuals is authorized to practice each profession which the corporation will be authorized to practice.

(b-1) The certificate of incorporation of a design professional service corporation shall meet the requirements of this chapter, provided that shareholders may include employee stock ownership plans (ESOPs) and employees of the corporation not licensed as design professionals, and provided further however that:

(i) greater than seventy-five percent of the outstanding shares of stock of the corporation are owned by design professionals,

(ii) an ESOP, either in part or in its entirety, shall not constitute part of the greater than seventy-five percent owned by design professionals,

(iii) greater than seventy-five percent of the directors are design professionals,

(iv) greater than seventy-five percent of the officers are design professionals,

(v) the president, the chairperson of the board of directors and the chief executive officer or officers are design professionals, and

(vi) the single largest shareholder is either a design professional or an ESOP with greater than seventy-five percent of the plan's voting trustees being design professionals and greater than seventy-five percent of the plan's committee members being design professionals.

(b-2) The certificate of incorporation of a design professional service corporation shall:

(i) state the profession or professions to be practiced by such corporation,

(ii) state the names and residence addresses of all individuals or ESOPs who are to be the original shareholders, directors and officers of such corporation,

(iii) indicate the profession or professions of each original shareholder, director and officer who is a design professional,

(iv) state the ownership interest of each original shareholder, and

(v) indicate the names of the original officers and directors who are the president, the chairperson of the board of directors and the chief executive officer or officers.

(b-3) The certificate of incorporation of a design professional service corporation shall have attached thereto a certificate or certificates issued by the licensing authority certifying that each of the proposed shareholders, directors and officers who is listed as a design professional is authorized by law to practice a profession which the corporation is being organized to practice and, if applicable, that one or more of such individuals is authorized to practice each profession which the corporation will be authorized to practice. The attached certificate or certificates shall also certify that the president, the chairperson of the board of directors and the chief executive officer or officers are authorized by law to practice a profession which the corporation is being organized to practice.

(b-4) The certificate of incorporation of a design professional service corporation shall also have attached thereto a certificate or certificates issued by the licensing authority certifying that each of the shareholders, officers, directors and owners have been deemed to have been of good moral character as may be established by the regulations of the commissioner of education.

(b-5) On or after January first, two thousand twelve, the state education department and the department of state shall allow an existing professional service corporation organized under this article and practicing professional engineering, architecture, landscape architecture, geology or land surveying, or practicing any combination of such professions to become a design professional service corporation as defined in this article, provided the professional service corporation meets all of the requirements to become a design professional service corporation, including that its name shall end with the words "design professional corporation" or the abbreviation "D.P.C.", by amending its certificate of incorporation so that it contains the following statements:

(1) the names and residence addresses of all individuals or ESOPs who will be the shareholders, directors and officers of the original design professional service corporation; and

(2) the profession or professions of each shareholder, director and officer who is a design professional of the original design professional service corporation; and

(3) the ownership interest of each shareholder of the original design professional service corporation; and

(4) the names of the officers and directors who will be the president, the chairperson of the board of directors and the chief executive officer or officers of the original design professional service corporation.

(i) The certificate of amendment shall have attached thereto a certificate or certificates issued by the licensing authority certifying that each of the proposed shareholders, directors and officers who is listed as a design professional is authorized by law to practice a profession which the corporation is organized to practice and, if applicable, that one or more of such individuals is authorized to practice each profession which the corporation will be authorized to practice. The attached certificate or certificates shall also certify that the proposed president, the chairperson of the board of directors and the chief executive officer or officers are authorized by law to practice a profession which the corporation is organized to practice.

(ii) The certificate of amendment shall also have attached thereto a certificate or certificates issued by the licensing authority certifying that each of the proposed shareholders, officers, directors and owners listed have been deemed to have been of good moral character as may be established by the regulations of the commissioner of education.

(iii) The certificate of amendment shall also have attached thereto: (A) a tax clearance issued by the department of taxation and finance certifying that the existing professional service corporation is current with respect to payment of its state tax liabilities and (B) a certificate of good standing from the state education department certifying that the existing professional service corporation is authorized to provide professional services without restriction.

(b-6) (1) Prior to the first day of March, two thousand ~~eighteen~~ nineteen, the state education department and the department of state shall allow an existing business corporation organized under article four of this chapter to become a professional <u>service</u> corporation as defined in this article for the purpose of practicing professional geology, provided that the surviving corporation meet all of the requirements to become a professional <u>service</u> corporation, including that the name of a professional <u>service</u> corporation shall end with the

words "professional corporation" or the abbreviation "P.C." by amending its certificate of incorporation so that it contains the following:

(i) the names and residence addresses of all individuals who will be the original shareholders, directors and officers of the professional service corporation;

(ii) a statement that the professional service corporation is formed pursuant to this section; and

(iii) a statement that the amendment shall not effect a dissolution of the corporation, but shall be deemed a continuation of its corporate existence, without affecting its then existing property rights or liabilities or the liabilities of its members or officers as such, but thereafter it shall have only such rights, powers and privileges, and be subject only to such other duties and liabilities, as a corporation created for the same purposes under this article.

(2) The certificate of amendment shall have attached thereto a certificate or certificates issued by the licensing authority certifying that each of the proposed shareholders, directors and officers listed:

(i) is authorized by law to practice a profession which the corporation is organized to practice and, if applicable, that one or more of such individuals is authorized to practice each profession which the corporation will be authorized to practice; and

(ii) has been deemed to be of good moral character as may be established by the regulations of the commissioner of education.

(3) The certificate of amendment shall also have attached thereto a tax clearance issued by the department of taxation and finance certifying that the existing business corporation is current with respect to payment of its state tax liabilities.

(4) Notwithstanding any provision of law to the contrary, any corporation formed under this section shall be required to comply with all applicable laws, rules, or regulations relating to the practice of a profession under title eight of the education law.

(b-7) (1) Prior to the first day of March, two thousand ~~eighteen~~ nineteen, the state education department and the department of state shall allow an existing business corporation organized under article four of this chapter to become a design professional service corporation as defined in this article for the purpose of practicing professional geology, provided that the surviving corporation meet all of the requirements to become a design professional service corporation, including that the name shall end with the words "design professional service corporation" or the abbreviation "D.P.C." by amending its certificate of incorporation so that it contains the following:

(i) the names and residence addresses of all individuals or ESOPs who will be the original shareholders, directors and officers of the professional service corporation;

(ii) a statement that the design professional service corporation is formed pursuant to this section;

(iii) the profession or profession of each shareholder, director and officer who is a design professional of the original design professional service corporation;

(iv) the names of the officers and directors who will be the president, the chairperson of the board of directors and the chief executive officer or officers of the original design professional service corporation;

(v) the ownership interest of each shareholder of the original design professional service corporation; and

(vi) a statement that the amendment shall not effect a dissolution of the corporation, but shall be deemed a continuation of its corporate existence, without affecting its then existing property rights or liabilities or the liabilities of its members or officers as such, but thereafter it shall have only such rights, powers and privileges, and be subject only to such other duties and liabilities, as a corporation created for the same purposes under this article.

(2) The certificate of amendment shall have attached thereto a certificate or certificates issued by the licensing authority certifying that each of the proposed shareholders, directors and officers listed:

(i) is authorized by law to practice a profession which the corporation is organized to practice and, if applicable, that one or more of such individuals is authorized to practice each profession which the corporation will be authorized to practice; and

(ii) has been deemed to be of good moral character as may be established by the regulations of the commissioner of education.

(3) The certificate of amendment shall also have attached thereto a tax clearance issued by the department of taxation and finance certifying that the existing business corporation is current with respect to payment of its state tax liabilities.

(4) Notwithstanding any provision of law to the contrary, any corporation formed under this section shall be required to comply with all applicable laws, rules, or regulations relating to the practice of a profession under title eight of the education law.

(c) A certified copy of the certificate of incorporation and of each amendment thereto shall be filed by the corporation with the licensing authority within thirty days after the filing of such certificate or amendment with the department of state.

(d) A professional service corporation, including a design professional service corporation, other than a corporation authorized to practice law, shall be under the supervision of the regents of the university of the state of New York and be subject to disciplinary proceedings and penalties, and its certificate of incorporation shall be subject to suspension, revocation or annulment for cause, in the same manner and to the same extent as is provided with respect to individuals and their licenses, certificates, and registrations in title eight of the education law relating to the applicable profession. Notwithstanding the provisions of this paragraph, a professional service corporation authorized to practice medicine shall be subject to the prehearing procedures and hearing procedures as is provided with respect to individual physicians and their licenses in title II-A of article two of the public health law.

(e) A corporation authorized to practice law shall be subject to the regulation and control of, and its certificate of incorporation shall be subject to suspension, revocation or annulment for cause by, the appellate division of the supreme court and the court of appeals in the same manner and to the same extent provided in the judiciary law with respect to individual attorneys and counselors-at-law. Such corporation need not qualify for any certification under section four hundred sixty-four of the judiciary law, take an oath of office under section four hundred sixty-six of such law or register under section four hundred sixty-seven of such law.

(f) The order of suspension, revocation or annulment of the certificate of incorporation of a professional service corporation pursuant to paragraphs (d) and (e) of this section shall be effective upon the filing of such order with the department of state.

(g) The practices of creative arts therapy, marriage and family therapy, mental health counseling, and psychoanalysis shall not be deemed the same professional service for the purpose of paragraph (a) of this section, notwithstanding that such practices are all licensed under article one hundred sixty-three of the education law.

CASE ANNOTATIONS

While it is established public policy of New York that medical providers may not engage in voluntary prospective fee-splitting arrangements, this blanket proscription against fee-splitting does not extend to licensed professional associated with or employed by professional corporation formed to provide medical services. Sheldon Rabin, P.C. v Hirshfield, 223 A.D.2d 535, 636 N.Y.S.2d 117, 1996 N.Y. App. Div. LEXIS 160 (N.Y. App. Div. 2d Dep't 1996).

Written consent in which plaintiff, provider of "architectural and interior design services," agreed to perform construction and design services to defendant for construction of restaurant was valid and enforceable, even though plaintiff, as regular business corporation, was not licensed professional corporation authorized to perform architectural services, since plaintiff did not perform any architectural services, and contract expressly called for plaintiff to obtain services of "qualified architect" and did not expressly or impliedly require it to perform services itself. SKR Design Group v Yonehama, Inc., 230 A.D.2d 533, 660 N.Y.S.2d 119, 1997 N.Y. App. Div. LEXIS 6745 (N.Y. App. Div. 1st Dep't 1997).

Court erroneously ordered dissolution of medical professional corporations on theory that corporations were in fact alter egos of certain other corporations in which petitioner owned 20 percent of shares since petitioner was not authorized to practice medicine, and thus she could own shares in those corporations, if that all, only as "transferee of shares by operation of law or court decree" (CLS Bus Corp §§ 1511, 1503, and 1507); even if petitioner were entitled, by "operation of law," to transfer 20 percent of shares in medical professional corporations, she would still be forbidden from voting those shares "for any purpose whatsoever except with respect to corporate action under (Business Corporation Law) section nine hundred nine and section one thousand one." Fromcheck v Brentwood Pain & Med. Servs., P.C., 254 A.D.2d 485, 679 N.Y.S.2d 632, 1998 N.Y. App. Div. LEXIS 11285 (N.Y. App. Div. 2d Dep't 1998).

Denial of a summary judgment motion filed by a professional corporation (PC) and its owner was proper in an insurer's suit

seeking, inter alia, a declaration that it was not obligated to pay no-fault claims pursuant to N.Y. Comp. Codes R. & Regs. tit. 11, § 65-3.16(a)(12) because the insurer submitted sufficient evidentiary proof to raise an issue of fact as to whether the PC was actually controlled by a management company owned by unlicensed individuals in violation of the Business Corporation Law. One Beacon Ins. Group, LLC v Midland Med. Care, P.C., 54 A.D.3d 738, 863 N.Y.S.2d 728, 2008 NY Slip Op 6813, 2008 N.Y. App. Div. LEXIS 6696 (N.Y. App. Div. 2d Dep't 2008).

An application for a certificate of incorporation pursuant to the Not For Profit Corporation Law § 402 for an organization which by virtue of its name and its state purposes indicated that it would provide legal services to students, parents, and the general public for improvement of the schools was withheld on the ground that it could not in fact provide professional legal services. Re Application of Queens Lay Advocate Service, Inc., 71 Misc. 2d 33, 335 N.Y.S.2d 583 (1972).

Architecture firm's proposed use of initials "HOK" in its corporate name, representing last initials of three licensed firm members, was prohibited by Bus Corp L § 1512 as an assumed or fictitious name; thus Education Commissioner did not act arbitrarily, capriciously, or unreasonably in denying use of such initials in corporate name of firm. Kahn & Jacobs v Nyquist, 76 Misc. 2d 355, 350 N.Y.S.2d 840, 1973 N.Y. Misc. LEXIS 1485 (N.Y. Sup. Ct. 1973).

Improperly licensed medical service provider was precluded under N.Y. Comp. Codes R. & Regs. tit. 11, § 65-3.16(a)(12) from recovering claims submitted prior to the amendment thereof, as the amendment was the clarification of the existing regulation; such a provider was ineligible for reimbursement, as any other interpretation of the regulation would have nullified existing statutory provisions which prohibited the medical corporation from being owned and operated by one other than a licensed medical doctor and from physicians sharing fees with non-physicians, pursuant to N.Y. Bus. Corp. Law § 1503(b), N.Y. Comp. Codes R. & Regs. tit. 8, § 29.1(b)(4) and N.Y. Educ. Law §§ 6511 and 6530(19). A.T. Med., P.C. v State Farm Mut. Ins. Co., 809 N.Y.S.2d 392, 2005 NY Slip Op 25461, 10 Misc. 3d 568, 2005 N.Y. Misc. LEXIS 2398 (N.Y. Civ. Ct. 2005).

Because an insurer's N.Y. C.P.L.R. § 3101 discovery requests to determine whether the owners of an acupuncturist were properly licensed in accordance with N.Y. Educ. Law § 8212, N.Y. Bus. Corp. Law §§ 1503(b), 1507, N.Y. Comp. Codes R. & Regs. tit. 11, § 65-3.16(a)(12) were germane to the question of whether the acupuncturist was eligible for reimbursement, pursuant to N.Y. C.P.L.R. § 3212(f), the acupuncturist's motion for summary judgment was premature. Lexington Acupuncture, P.C. v State Farm Ins Co., 820 N.Y.S.2d 385, 2006 NY Slip Op 26251, 12 Misc. 3d 90, 2006 N.Y. Misc. LEXIS 1605 (N.Y. App. Term 2006).

Because an insurer's discovery requests seeking information to determine whether the owners of an acupuncturist were properly licensed under N.Y. Educ. Law § 8212 and N.Y. Bus. Corp. Law §§ 1503(b), 1507 were germane to the question of whether the acupuncturist was eligible for reimbursement under N.Y. Comp. Codes R. & Regs. tit. 11, § 65-3.16(a)(12), the trial court erred in denying the requests and granting summary judgment to the acupuncturist. Midborough Acupuncture P.C. v State Farm Ins. Co., 823 N.Y.S.2d 822, 2006 NY Slip Op 26360, 13 Misc. 3d 58, 2006 N.Y. Misc. LEXIS 2411 (N.Y. App. Term 2006).

Insurance company was not required to pay monies to an improperly licensed professional corporation and could recoup any such monies paid through a claim for unjust enrichment. State Farm Mut. Auto. Ins. Co. v Grafman, 655 F. Supp. 2d 212, 2009 U.S. Dist. LEXIS 86451 (E.D.N.Y. 2009).

Insurer adequately stated a claim for relief under the Racketeer Influenced and Corrupt Organizations Act (RICO), 18 U.S.C.S. § 1962(c), by alleging that the providers were improperly licensed under Public Health Law § 2801-a, rendering them ineligible to collect under New York's no-fault law for the services provided to the insureds, even though state authorities had approved the providers, because insurers could test the validity of a provider's license pursuant to 11 NYCRR § 65.3.5(c). Allstate Ins. Co. v Elzanaty, 916 F. Supp. 2d 273, 2013 U.S. Dist. LEXIS 3696 (E.D.N.Y.), dismissed, in part, 929 F. Supp. 2d 199, 85 Fed. R. Serv. 3d (Callaghan) 1, 2013 U.S. Dist. LEXIS 33309 (E.D.N.Y. 2013).

Where defendants were charged with conspiracy to commit health care fraud and mail fraud in connection with an allegedly fraudulent no-fault insurance scheme, the indictment's fraudulent incorporation theory was not legally insufficient, because the question of whether defendants misrepresented the identity of the owners was properly viewed as one for the jury, the insurer's entitlement to withhold reimbursement was an interest in money or property, and the indictment rested on the alleged deprivation of their monetary interest in nonpayment of claims. United States v Zemlyansky, 945 F. Supp. 2d 438, 2013 U.S. Dist. LEXIS 71818 (S.D.N.Y. 2013).

§ 1504. Rendering of professional service

(a) No professional service corporation, including a design professional service corporation, may render professional services except through individuals authorized by law to render such professional services as individuals.

(b) Each final plan and report made or issued by a corporation practicing one or more of the professions of professional engineering, architecture, landscape architecture, land surveying or geology shall bear the name and seal of one or more professional engineers, architects, landscape architects, land surveyors or professional geologists, respectively, who are in responsible charge of such plan or report.

(c) Each report, diagnosis, prognosis, and prescription made or issued by a corporation practicing medicine, dentistry, podiatry, optometry, ophthalmic dispensing, veterinary medicine, pharmacy, nursing, physiotherapy or chiropractic shall bear the signature of one or more physicians, dentists, podiatrists, optometrists, ophthalmic dispensers, veterinarians, pharmacists, nurses, physiotherapists, or chiropractors, respectively, who are in responsible charge of such report, diagnosis, prognosis, or prescription.

(d) Each record, transcript, report and hearing report prepared by a corporation practicing certified shorthand reporting shall bear the signature of one or more certified shorthand reporters who are in responsible charge of such record, transcript, report, or hearing report.

(e) Each corporation practicing public accounting or certified public accounting shall maintain records indicating the identity of each public accountant or certified public accountant, respectively, who was responsible for each report or statement which is issued prepared or examined by such corporation.

(f) Each opinion prepared by a corporation practicing law shall bear the signature of one or more attorneys and counsellors-at-law who are in responsible charge of such opinion.

(g) In addition to the requirements in subdivisions (b) through (f), inclusive, each document prepared by a corporation which under the rules, regulations, laws or customs of the applicable profession is required to bear the signature of an individual in responsible charge of such document, shall be signed by one or more such individuals.

History: Add, L 1970, ch 974, eff May 19, 1970; amd, L 1983, ch 265, § 1, eff June 10, 1983, L 2011, ch 550, § 3, eff Jan 1, 2012; L 2014, ch 475, § 16 eff Nov 21, 2016.

CASE ANNOTATIONS

Continued existence and operation of professional service corporation is not restricted following shareholder's death and appointment of executor; corporation may properly carry out its practice through employment of authorized professionals during 6-month period allowed to executor for sale, transfer or redemption of deceased's shares. Re Olsson (1992, 2d Dept) 180 A.D.2d 739, 580 N.Y.S.2d 376

Requirement that corporation appear by attorney was inapplicable to professional corporation of attorneys in suit upon promissory note against maker and guarantor, in view of statute making each shareholder, employee, and agent of professional corporation of attorneys personally liable and in view of fact that each member of corporation was qualified to appear before the court and argue its case. Austrian, Lance & Stewart, P. C. v Hastings Properties, Inc. (1976) 87 Misc. 2d 25, 385 N.Y.S.2d 466, 19 UCCRS 1177

Petitioner physician, a former employee of respondent professional service corporation, would not be entitled to possession of the patient records of those patients for whom he was the primary treating physician while so employed, since it was the professional service corporation which practiced medicine and had patients (Bus Corp Law § 1504(a)), and thus had the property right in the patient records, rather than the individual physician who treated the patient and made the record as an agent of the corporation. Parsley v Associates in Internal Medicine, P. C. (1985) 126 Misc. 2d 996, 484 N.Y.S.2d 485

Attorney had resigned from the practice of law, and thus, he was not a member or shareholder of a legal professional corporation since he could no longer have rendered legal services; thus, the attorney's action seeking a declaratory judgment that he was a member of a professional corporation failed. Lubov v Welikson (2008, Sup) 21 Misc 3d 896, 240 NYLJ 80, 865 NYS2d 510.

A corporate acknowledgment of a professional service corporation practicing law is not required on a document satisfying a judgment when the attorney of record or the attorney named on a judgment docket is a professional service corporation.1974 Ops Atty Gen Aug 19 (informal)

Where owner(s) of professional services corporation (PC) is licensed to perform health services, and such services are performed by PC owner or employee under supervision of PC owner, services may be billed for under No-Fault Law (CLS Insurance Law Art 51) by PC as licensed provider of services. Insurance Department, Opinions of General Counsel, Opinion Number 01-02-13

Where health services are performed by provider who is independent contractor with professional services corporation (PC) and is not employee under direct supervision of PC owner, PC is not authorized to bill under No-Fault Law (CLS Insurance Law Art 51) as licensed provider of those services. Insurance Department, Opinions of General Counsel, Opinion Number 01-02-13

While in accordance with CLS Bus Corp Art 15 professional corporation (PC) may practice medicine through licensed physicians, there is no provision for professional employer organization (PEO) to so practice. Insurance Department, Opinions of General Counsel, Opinion Number 05-03-21

Under N.Y. Comp. Codes R. & Regs. tit. 11, § 65-3.16(a)(12), proper licensing and incorporation of a medical provider was a condition precedent to payment. An insurer did not have to pay a provider who did not comply with that rule even if the provider submitted a timely claim and the insurer did not timely deny the claim. Multiquest, PLLC v Allstate Ins. Co. (2005, Civ Ct) 9 Misc 3d 1031, 805 N.Y.S.2d 255 (criticized in Multiquest, P.L.L.C. v Allstate Ins. Co. (2005, Civ Ct) 10 Misc 3d 1061A)

§ 1505. Professional relationships and liabilities

(a) Each shareholder, employee or agent of a professional service corporation and a design professional service corporation shall be personally and fully liable and accountable for any negligent or wrongful act or misconduct committed by him or by any person under his direct supervision and control while rendering professional services on behalf of such corporation.

(b) The relationship of an individual to a professional service corporation or a design professional service corporation with which such individual is associated, whether as shareholder, director, officer, employee or agent, shall not modify or diminish the jurisdiction over him of the licensing authority and in the case of an attorney and counsellor-at-law, the other courts of this state.

History: Add, L 1970, ch 974, eff May 19, 1970; amd, L 2011, ch 550, § 4, eff Jan 1, 2012.

CASE ANNOTATIONS

Absent any showing of abuse of a corporate form of doing business, the shareholders of a professional service corporation cannot be held personally liable for an ordinary business debt of the corporation; Bus Corp Law § 1505(a) precludes the imposition of personal liability on shareholders of professional service corporations in instances not involving the direct rendition of professional services on behalf of the corporation, and the statute's plain words cannot be construed to include ordinary business debts within the definition of professional services. Accordingly, in an action by plaintiff landlord, the individual defendants, shareholders of a professional service corporation, could not be held liable in their individual capacities for rents due under a lease naming only the corporation as tenant. We're Associates Co. v Cohen, Stracher & Bloom, P.C. (1985) 65 N.Y.2d 148, 490 N.Y.S.2d 743, 480 N.E.2d 357, ALR4th 1527

The shareholders of a professional service corporation, organized pursuant to Bus Corp Law Article 15 for the purpose of engaging in the practice of law, could not be sued in their individual capacities for rents allegedly due under lease executed solely in the name of the corporation by one of its members as an officer, since the individual shareholders have no personal liability for the corporate obligations under the lease in that the personal liability of the individual shareholders is limited to liability arising out of conduct by the shareholder is someone acting under his direct supervision while rendering professional services on behalf of the corporation. We're Associates Co. v Cohen, Stracher & Bloom, P.C. (1984, 2d Dept) 103 A.D.2d 130, 478 N.Y.S.2d 670

In action for breach of fiduciary duty arising from attorney's representation of client, attorney's partners in professional corporation were entitled to dismissal of action against them where client failed to present anything beyond his allegation of "information and belief" that other partners might have participated in wrongful conduct. Krouner v Koplovitz (1991, 3d Dept) 175 A.D.2d 531, 572 N.Y.S.2d 959

Court properly dismissed, as untimely, medical malpractice claim against physician member of professional corporation to extent that his treatment of plaintiff ended more than 2 1/2 years before commencement of action, even though another member of corporation continued to treat plaintiff within limitations period, since fact that physician is shareholder, officer or employee of professional service corporation does not make him vicariously liable for malpractice of another doctor who is officer, director or employee of corporation in absence of showing that 2 doctors were agents of each other or that there was continuing relevant relationship between them regarding patient. Polokoff v Palmer (1993, 3d Dept) 190 A.D.2d 897, 593 N.Y.S.2d 129

Defendant, president and sole shareholder of professional dental corporation, was not entitled to summary judgment in action for injuries plaintiff suffered following tooth extraction that was performed by dentist whom defendant had hired to manage and provide dental services at separate office where fact issue existed as to degree of control and supervision that defendant exerted, or could have exerted, over dentist. Wise v Greenwald (1994, 3d Dept) 208 A.D.2d 1141, 617 N.Y.S.2d 591

Defendant, president and sole shareholder of professional dental corporation, was not entitled to summary judgment in action alleging that he acted negligently in hiring and failing to discharge dentist, despite contention that dentist was hired by corporation, that act of hiring another dentist does not constitute "rendering [of] professional services" (CLS Bus Corp § 1505(a)), and thus liability could not be imposed on him on basis of that act, since statute does not otherwise supplant ordinary principles of corporate responsibility and liability,

and it was undisputed that defendant himself actually hired dentist. Wise v Greenwald (1994, 3d Dept) 208 A.D.2d 1141, 617 N.Y.S.2d 591

In action to set aside alleged fraudulent conveyances made by defendant attorneys, who were sole shareholders in professional corporation that previously had been held liable to plaintiffs for malpractice and was thereafter dissolved, court should have granted summary judgment to defendants on ground that personal liability could not be established against either attorney for malpractice of professional corporation because attorneys were never individually named as defendants in malpractice action or served with legal malpractice complaint; CLS Bus Corp § 1505(a), which renders attorneys potentially liable for malpractice of professional corporation to extent of their own personal negligence or to extent of negligent acts committed at their direction, does not obviate need to acquire personal jurisdiction over potentially liable parties. Somer & Wand, P.C. v Rotondi (1996, 2d Dept) 219 A.D.2d 340, 642 N.Y.S.2d 937

Court properly refused to dismiss legal malpractice cause of action against member of law firm who alleged that he neither participated nor supervised or controlled other members of firm in any questioned actions, where he was officer of law firm/professional corporation and one of 2 members whose names made up corporate name, and he was also involved in underlying project from which legal representation arose. Beltrone v General Schuyler & Co. (1996, 3d Dept) 223 A.D.2d 938, 636 N.Y.S.2d 917, subsequent app (3d Dept) 229 A.D.2d 857, 645 N.Y.S.2d 914

In malpractice action against professional accounting corporation and its 2 principals for failure to timely file client's tax returns for years 1981 to 1987, one principal (Bernstein) was entitled to summary judgment where (1) client testified, before his death, that, to his knowledge, accounting services were provided exclusively by other principal (Zwaik) until Zwaik became ill in 1989, (2) there was no evidence that Bernstein handled client's account during relevant period or that he supervised anyone who did, and (3) Bernstein's 1990 cover letters to federal and state taxing authorities, which accompanied submission of client's late tax returns, showed only that Bernstein became involved in client's affairs after tax problem was discovered. Ecker v Zwaik & Bernstein, P.C. (1997, 2d Dept) 240 A.D.2d 360, 658 N.Y.S.2d 113

In action for nonpayment of legal fees, in which defendants counterclaimed for legal malpractice against plaintiff professional corporation, late amended counterclaim seeking to add individual shareholders as counterclaim defendants did not relate back to original counterclaim, and thus was time-barred, where counterclaimants were aware of identities of individual shareholders when they commenced action against corporation, and although counterclaimants contended that they intentionally did not name and serve shareholders because they believed that shareholders would be personally liable under CLS Bus Corp § 1505(a), they made mistake of law, which is not type of mistake contemplated by relation-back doctrine. Somer & Wand, P.C. v Rotondi (1998, 2d Dept) 251 A.D.2d 567, 674 N.Y.S.2d 770

In general, employee of professional corporation will not be held vicariously liable for acts of coemployee. Moller v Taliuaga (1998, 2d Dept) 255 A.D.2d 563, 681 N.Y.S.2d 90

Legal malpractice plaintiffs, who sought to amend complaint to add, as defendant, principal of professional corporation of which original defendant attorney was member, failed to prove applicability of relation-back doctrine under CLS CPLR § 203(b) in order to save proposed amendment from being time barred where unsubstantiated allegations of plaintiffs' present attorney were insufficient to prove that principal committed any negligent or wrongful acts in prosecution of underlying action or supervised wrongful conduct of original defendant attorney. Moller v Taliuaga (1998, 2d Dept) 255 A.D.2d 563, 681 N.Y.S.2d 90

Discharged attorney's action against law firm and its partner for breach of his employment contract was properly dismissed as to partner, notwithstanding attorney's contention that partner failed to perform his obligations as shareholder and officer of professional corporation under CLS Bus Corp § 1505(a), where partner's alleged misconduct was not committed in course of rendering professional services on behalf of firm. Lichtman v Estrin (2001, 1st Dept) 282 A.D.2d 326, 723 N.Y.S.2d 185

Trial court erred in granting the architects' motion to dismiss, should not have severed the action as to the architect, or amended the caption to eliminate the supervisor as a named defendant because N.Y. Bus. Corp. Law § 1505(a) rendered the supervisor potentially liable for the malpractice of the architect to the extent of the supervisor's own personal negligence or to the extent of negligent acts committed at the supervisor's direction. Crystal Clear Dev., LLC v Devon Architects of N.Y., P.C. (2012, 2d Dept) 97 App Div 3d 716, 949 NYS2d 398

Requirement that corporation appear by attorney was inapplicable to professional corporation of attorneys in suit upon promissory note against maker and guarantor, in view of statute making each shareholder, employee, and agent of professional corporation of attorneys personally liable and in view of fact that each member of corporation was qualified to appear before the court and argue its case. Austrian, Lance & Stewart, P. C. v Hastings Properties, Inc. (1976) 87 Misc. 2d 25, 385 N.Y.S.2d 466, 19 UCCRS 1177

Buyers of all of stock of professional corporation which bore name of podiatrist who formed professional corporation and who sold all stock in corporation and buyers' successors could not utilize founding podiatrist's name in connection with professional corporation. Weiner v Weiner (1976) 88 Misc. 2d 920, 390 N.Y.S.2d 359

Lawyer-shareholders of a professional corporation are individually liable for the business debts of the individual corporation since the purpose of permitting professional incorporation is to confer certain tax advantages and not to shield lawyers from just debts whether they arise out of commercial obligations or out of the lawyer-client relationship; moreover, the statutory qualification of Bus Corp Law § 1505(a) limiting the liability of professional corporation shareholders to acts committed "while rendering professional services on behalf of such corporation" applies to the private, as distinguished from corporate acts of the de facto partners of the corporation. Infosearch, Inc. v Horowitz (1982) 117 Misc. 2d 774, 459 N.Y.S.2d 348

A general release executed by a medical doctor individually, as releasor in settlement of a claim for property damage to a medical office arising out of the collision of two automobiles, would not preclude a subrogated claim brought on behalf of the doctor's professional service corporation, pursuant to Bus Corp Law § 1505, since the relationship of an individual to a professional service corporation, in which the individual is associated as a shareholder, director, officer, employee or agent, is not of such a representative or derivative nature as would make an individual release binding upon the professional service corporation. Allstate Ins. Co. v Horowitz (1983) 118 Misc. 2d 787, 461 N.Y.S.2d 218

Corporate veil would be pierced, and shareholder immunity for ordinary debts of corporation denied under CLS Bus Corp § 1505, in action for breach of lease and fraud against attorney who assigned long-term personal lease for office space to his professional corporation and vacated premises 2 weeks later to join another law firm, after which assignee corporation transacted no business. Glockhurst Corp. v Schechter (1988) 144 Misc. 2d 204, 544 N.Y.S.2d 266

Defendant, an attorney who entered into a 10-year lease for the rental of office space in 1983 and then, three years into the lease, assigned the lease to his professional corporation as he was permitted to do by the lease agreement, may not evade his personal liability for the rent owing by the assignment since the corporate veil of a professional corporation and a shareholder's immunity from personal liability for ordinary business debts of the corporation (Business Corporation Law § 1505) may be pierced "to prevent fraud" and defendant's conduct in vacating the premises to join another law firm two weeks after executing the assignment and the fact that there is no proof that thecorporation engaged in any transactions from the time of its formation in 1983 to the time of the lease assignment, give rise to an inference that the assignment was merely a fraudulent attempt to avoid personal liability. Glockhurst Corp. v Schechter,144 Misc. 2d 204

Where owner(s) of professional services corporation (PC) is licensed to perform health services, and such services are performed by PC owner or employee under supervision of PC owner, services may be billed for under No-Fault Law (CLS Insurance Law Art 51) by PC as licensed provider of services. Insurance Department, Opinions of General Counsel, Opinion Number 01-02-13

Where health services are performed by provider who is independent contractor with professional services corporation (PC) and is not employee under direct supervision of PC owner, PC is not authorized to bill under No-Fault Law (CLS Insurance Law Art 51) as licensed provider of those services. Insurance Department, Opinions of General Counsel, Opinion Number 01-02-13

N.Y. Bus. Corp. Law § 1505(a) did not shield a president of a professional corporation (PC) from personal liability for an employee's medical malpractice as fact issues remained as to the relationship of the employee, the president, and the PC, including questions as to the president's control in the employee's practice of anesthesiology and the nature of their relationship. Von Stackelberg v Goldweber (2011, Sup) 33 Misc 3d 1229A.

§ 1506. Purposes of incorporation

No professional service corporation or design professional service corporation shall engage in any business other than the rendering of the professional services for which it was incorporated; provided that such corporation may invest its funds in real estate, mortgages, stocks, bonds or any other type of investments.

History: Add, L 1970, ch 974, eff May 19, 1970, L 2011, ch 550, § 4, eff Jan 1, 2012.

CASE ANNOTATIONS

A professional service corporation consisting solely of attorneys duly licensed to practice law in New York State is exempt from licensure as a real estate broker and may earn real estate brokerage commissions.1980 Op Atty Gen June 9 (Formal)

§ 1507. Issuance of shares

(a) A professional service corporation may issue shares only to individuals who are authorized by law to practice in this state a profession which such corporation is authorized to practice and who are or have been engaged in the practice of such profession in such corporation or a predecessor entity, or who will engage in the practice of such profession in such corporation within thirty days of the date such shares are issued. No shareholder of a professional service corporation shall enter into a voting trust agreement, proxy, or any other type agreement vesting in another person, other than another shareholder of the same corporation or a person who would be eligible to become a shareholder if employed by the corporation, the authority to exercise voting power of any or all of his shares. All shares issued, agreements made, or proxies granted in violation of this section shall be void.

(b) A design professional service corporation may issue shares to individuals who are authorized by law to practice in this state a profession which such corporation is authorized to practice and who are or have been engaged in the practice of such profession in such corporation or a predecessor entity, or who will engage in the practice of such profession in such corporation within thirty days of the date such shares are issued. A design professional service corporation may also issue shares to employee stock ownership plans (ESOPs) and employees of the corporation not licensed as design professionals, provided that:

(i) greater than seventy-five percent of the outstanding shares of stock of the corporation are owned by design professionals,

(ii) an ESOP, either in part or in its entirety, shall not constitute part of the greater than seventy-five percent owned by design professionals,

(iii) greater than seventy-five percent of the directors are design professionals,

(iv) greater than seventy-five percent of the officers are design professionals,

(v) the president, the chairperson of the board of directors and the chief executive officer or officers are design professionals, and

(vi) the single largest shareholder is either a design professional or an ESOP with greater than seventy-five percent of the plan's voting trustees being design professionals and greater than seventy-five percent of the plan's committee members being design professionals.

No shareholder of a design professional service corporation shall enter into a voting trust agreement, proxy or any other type of agreement vesting in another person, other than another shareholder of the same corporation, the authority to exercise voting power of any or all of his or her shares. All shares issued, agreements made or proxies granted in violation of this section shall be void.

History: Add, L 1970, ch 974, amd, L 1971, ch 1022, eff July 2, 1971, L 2011, ch 550, § 5, eff Jan 1, 2012.

CASE ANNOTATIONS

1.In general
2.Unlicensed shareholders

1. In general

Denial of a summary judgment motion filed by a professional corporation (PC) and its owner was proper in an insurer's suit seeking, inter alia, a declaration that it was not obligated to pay no-fault claims pursuant to N.Y. Comp. Codes R. & Regs. tit. 11, § 65-3.16(a)(12) because the insurer submitted sufficient evidentiary proof to raise an issue of fact as to whether the PC was actually controlled by a management company owned by unlicensed individuals in violation of the Business Corporation Law. One Beacon Ins. Group, LLC v Midland Med. Care, P.C., 54 A.D.3d 738, 863 N.Y.S.2d 728, 2008 NY Slip Op 6813, 2008 N.Y. App. Div. LEXIS 6696 (N.Y. App. Div. 2d Dep't 2008).

Where an insurer alleged a professional corporation (PC) was not entitled to recover benefits for medical services rendered because it was controlled by non-physicians, the jury instruction on the elements of fraudulent incorporation was proper because it instructed the jury to look to the totality of the circumstances to determine whether non-physicians were de facto owners or exercised substantial control over the PC. Andrew Carothers, M.D., P.C. v Progressive Ins. Co., 150 A.D.3d 192, 2017 NY Slip Op 02614, 2017 NY Slip Op 02614, 2017 NY Slip Op 2614, 2017 NY Slip Op 2614, 51 N.Y.S.3d 551, 2017 N.Y. App. Div. LEXIS 2556 (N.Y. App. Div. 2d Dep't 2017).

Where an insurer alleged a professional corporation (PC) was not entitled to recover benefits for medical services rendered because it was controlled by non-physicians, the trial court did not err in declining to instruct the jury on fraudulent intent at the time of incorporation, because even if the PC did not intend to yield control to unlicensed parties at the time of incorporation, it nonetheless would be ineligible for no-fault reimbursement if the nominal physician owner yielded control of the PC at some later date. Andrew Carothers, M.D., P.C. v Progressive Ins. Co., 150 A.D.3d 192, 2017 NY Slip Op 02614, 2017 NY Slip Op 02614, 2017 NY Slip Op 2614, 2017 NY Slip Op 2614, 51 N.Y.S.3d 551, 2017 N.Y. App. Div. LEXIS 2556 (N.Y. App. Div. 2d Dep't 2017).

Court consolidated 61 actions involving no fault insurance for the purposes of amending the answer and setting a hearing as to whether the professional corporations were fraudulently incorporated under N.Y. Bus. Corp. Law §§ 1507, 1508 and N.Y. Educ. Law § 6507(4)(c) since the insurer articulated a founded belief that the health providers violated those laws. Metroscan Imaging P.C. v GEICO Ins. Co., 797 N.Y.S.2d 737, 2005 NY Slip Op 25228, 8 Misc. 3d 829, 233 N.Y.L.J. 115, 2005 N.Y. Misc. LEXIS 1165 (N.Y. Civ. Ct. 2005), aff'd, 823 N.Y.S.2d 818, 2006 NY Slip Op 26319, 13 Misc. 3d 35, 2006 N.Y. Misc. LEXIS 2150 (N.Y. App. Term 2006).

Summary judgment in favor of plaintiffs was reversed where an insurance company had served discovery on plaintiffs to determine if plaintiffs were properly licensed pursuant to N.Y. Bus. Corp. Law § 1507 because the issue was relevant to whether the insurance company was obligated to reimburse plaintiffs for medical services provided A.B. Med. Servs. PLLC v Utica Mut. Ins. Co., 813 N.Y.S.2d 845, 2006 NY Slip Op 26068, 11 Misc. 3d 71, 2006 N.Y. Misc. LEXIS 341 (N.Y. App. Term 2006).

Because an insurer's N.Y. C.P.L.R. § 3101 discovery requests to determine whether the owners of an acupuncturist were properly licensed in accordance with N.Y. Educ. Law § 8212, N.Y. Bus. Corp. Law §§ 1503(b), 1507, N.Y. Comp. Codes R. & Regs. tit. 11, § 65-3.16(a)(12) were germane to the question of whether the acupuncturist was eligible for reimbursement, pursuant to N.Y. C.P.L.R. § 3212(f), the acupuncturist's motion for summary judgment was premature. Lexington Acupuncture, P.C. v State Farm Ins Co., 820 N.Y.S.2d 385, 2006 NY Slip Op 26251, 12 Misc. 3d 90, 2006 N.Y. Misc. LEXIS 1605 (N.Y. App. Term 2006).

Because the promulgation of N.Y. Comp. Codes R. & Regs. tit. 11, § 65-3.16(a)(12) altered the common law prospectively, an insurer could amend its answer to assert an affirmative defense that an assignee was fraudulently incorporated under N.Y. Business Corporation Law §§ 1507, 1508 and N.Y. Education Law § 6507(4)(c). Metroscan Imaging, P.C. v GEICO Ins. Co., 823 N.Y.S.2d 818, 2006 NY Slip Op 26319, 13 Misc. 3d 35, 2006 N.Y. Misc. LEXIS 2150 (N.Y. App. Term 2006).

Because an insurer's discovery requests seeking information to determine whether the owners of an acupuncturist were properly licensed under N.Y. Educ. Law § 8212 and N.Y. Bus. Corp. Law §§ 1503(b), 1507 were germane to the question of whether the acupuncturist was eligible for reimbursement under N.Y. Comp. Codes R. & Regs. tit. 11, § 65-3.16(a)(12), the trial court erred in denying the requests and granting summary judgment to the acupuncturist. Midborough Acupuncture P.C. v State Farm Ins. Co., 823 N.Y.S.2d 822, 2006 NY Slip Op 26360, 13 Misc. 3d 58, 2006 N.Y. Misc. LEXIS 2411 (N.Y. App. Term 2006).

Jury verdict denying a corporation's no-fault first-party benefit claim was proper, and the corporation's motion to set the verdict aside was denied, because the jury was properly instructed, and found that the corporation was owned and controlled by two non-physician individuals, which established that the corporation was fraudulently incorporated and that it was not entitled to reimbursement pursuant to N.Y. Comp. Codes R. & Regs. tit. 11, § 65-3.16(a)(12); a medical corporation that was owned or controlled by non-physicians, in violation of N.Y. Bus. Corp. Law §§ 1507, 1508, at the time no-fault services were provided, was ineligible for reimbursement of first-party benefits, and the jury was properly instructed that in determining if corporation was fraudulently incorporated, they could consider the totality of the circumstances and all relevant factors. There was no reason why a violation of the latter part of N.Y. Bus. Corp. Law § 1507 should have been treated differently than a violation of that portion of § 1507 which prohibited non-physician ownership of medical corporations. Carothers, P.C. v Ins. Cos., 888 N.Y.S.2d 372, 2009 NY Slip Op 29413, 26 Misc. 3d 448, 2009 N.Y. Misc. LEXIS 2838 (N.Y. Civ. Ct. 2009).

Insurer, who was not a party to a previous declaratory judgment (DJ) action, was not permitted to proactively invoke collateral estoppel to bar a medical provider, who was a party to the DJ action, from recovering no-fault benefits due to the finding of fraudulent incorporation because the insurer did not amend its answer to raise Mallela as a defense and hence create an apparent identity of issues between the DJ action and the instant matter. Downtown Acupuncture PC v State Wide Ins. Co., 2015 NY Slip Op 25371, 50 Misc. 3d 461, 21 N.Y.S.3d 548, 2015 N.Y. Misc. LEXIS 4042 (N.Y. Civ. Ct. 2015).

Following question was certified to the New York Court of Appeals pursuant to N.Y. Comp. Codes R. & Regs. tit. 22, § 500.17 and 2nd Cir. R. § 0.27: Is a medical corporation that was fraudulently incorporated under N.Y. Bus. Corp. Law §§ 1507, 1508, and N.Y. Educ. Law § 6507(4)(c) entitled to be reimbursed by insurers, under N.Y. Ins. Law § 5101 et seq., and its implementing regulations, for medical services rendered by licensed medical practitioners? State Farm Mut. Auto. Ins. Co. v Mallela, 372 F.3d 500, 2004 U.S. App. LEXIS 12034 (2d Cir. N.Y. 2004).

In insurers' action for a declaratory judgment that a radiologist and a group of professional service corporations were ineligible for no fault reimbursement on the ground that they failed to comply with State licensing requirements, the corporations' motion for partial summary judgment on the ground that a professional service corporation was ineligible for no fault reimbursement only if it was fraudulently incorporated was denied because if the corporations were under the control of an unlicensed individual, the insurers would be entitled to a declaration that they could deny the corporations no fault reimbursement, regardless of whether they were fraudulently incorporated; a medical service corporation will be ineligible for no fault reimbursement if it is in violation of licensing requirements, regardless of whether the doctor intended to yield control to unlicensed parties at the time he formed the corporation. AIU Ins. Co. v Deajess Med. Imaging, P.C., 882 N.Y.S.2d 812, 2009 NY Slip Op 29079, 24 Misc. 3d 161, 241 N.Y.L.J. 42, 2009 N.Y. Misc. LEXIS 367 (N.Y. Sup. Ct. 2009).

Insurer adequately stated a claim for relief under the Racketeer Influenced and Corrupt Organizations Act (RICO), 18 U.S.C.S. § 1962(c), by alleging that the providers were improperly licensed under Public Health Law § 2801-a, rendering them ineligible to collect under New York's no-fault law for the services provided to the insureds, even though state authorities had approved the providers, because insurers could test the validity of a provider's license pursuant to 11 NYCRR § 65.3.5(c). Allstate Ins. Co. v Elzanaty, 916 F. Supp. 2d 273, 2013 U.S. Dist. LEXIS 3696 (E.D.N.Y. 2013), dismissed, in part, 929 F. Supp. 2d 199, 2013 U.S. Dist. LEXIS 33309 (E.D.N.Y. 2013).

Where defendants were charged with conspiracy to commit health care fraud and mail fraud in connection with an allegedly fraudulent no-fault insurance scheme, the indictment's fraudulent incorporation theory was not legally insufficient, because the question of whether defendants misrepresented the identity of the owners was properly viewed as one for the jury, the insurer's entitlement to withhold reimbursement was an interest in money or property, and the indictment rested on the alleged deprivation of their monetary interest in nonpayment of claims. United States v Zemlyansky, 945 F. Supp. 2d 438, 2013 U.S. Dist. LEXIS 71818 (S.D.N.Y. 2013).

2. Unlicensed shareholders

In determining value of veterinarian practice for purposes of equitable distribution, agreement wherein wife's father gave husband (veterinarian) money for use in practice and wife (veterinary technician) was granted 51 percent of partnership was void as against public policy since veterinarians are prohibited from being partners or joint shareholders in professional corporations established for practice of veterinary medicine. Sangiorgio v Sangiorgio, 173 Misc. 2d 625, 662 N.Y.S.2d 220, 1997 N.Y. Misc. LEXIS 361 (N.Y. Sup. Ct. 1997).

Administrator of the estate of three professional corporations' (PCs) sole shareholder, officer, and director (SH) could not be substituted under N.Y. C.P.L.R. 1017 for the PCs in suits seeking assigned first-party benefits because: (1) the SH's administrator had not been appointed a receiver for the PCs and they had not been dissolved; (2) no one was authorized to act on behalf of the PCs; (3) the administrator could not act under N.Y. Bus. Corp. Law §§ 1507, 1508, and 1511 because the PCs were authorized to practice medicine, and the administrator was not licensed to practice medicine; and (4) the administrator could only vote the shares in the PCs for the N.Y. Bus. Corp. Law §§ 909, 1001, and 1511 purposes. Painless Med., P.C. v GEICO, 929 N.Y.S.2d 357, 2011 NY Slip Op 21228, 32 Misc. 3d 715, 2011 N.Y. Misc. LEXIS 3233 (N.Y. Civ. Ct. 2011).

Court erroneously ordered dissolution of medical professional corporations on theory that corporations were in fact alter egos of certain other corporations in which petitioner owned 20 percent of shares since petitioner was not authorized to practice medicine and thus she could own shares in those corporations, if that all, only as "transferee of shares by operation of law or court decree" (CLS Bus Corp §§ 1511, 1503, and 1507); even if petitioner were entitled, by "operation of law," to transfer 20 percent of shares in medical professional corporations, she would still be forbidden from voting those shares "for any purpose whatsoever except with respect to corporate action under (Business Corporation Law) section nine hundred nine and section one thousand one." Fromcheck v Brentwood Pain & Med. Servs., P.C., 254 A.D.2d 485, 679 N.Y.S.2d 632, 1998 N.Y. App. Div. LEXIS 11285 (N.Y. App. Div. 2d Dep't 1998).

§ 1508. Directors and officers

(a) No individual may be a director or officer of a professional service corporation unless he is authorized by law to practice in this state a profession which such corporation is authorized to practice and is either a shareholder of such corporation or engaged in the practice of his profession in such corporation.

(b) The directors and officers of a design professional service corporation may include individuals who are not design professionals, provided however that greater than seventy-five percent of the directors, greater than seventy-five percent of the officers and the president, the chairperson of the board of directors and the chief executive officer or officers are authorized by law to practice in this state a profession which such corporation is authorized to practice, and are either shareholders of such corporation or engaged in the practice of their professions in such corporation.

History: Add, L 1970, ch 974, eff May 19, 1970; amd, L 2011, ch 550, § 6, eff Jan 1, 2012.

CASE ANNOTATIONS

1.In general
2.Unlicensed directors or officers

1. In general

Denial of a summary judgment motion filed by a professional corporation (PC) and its owner was proper in an insurer's suit seeking, inter alia, a declaration that it was not obligated to pay no-fault claims pursuant to N.Y. Comp. Codes R. & Regs. tit. 11, § 65-3.16(a)(12) because the insurer submitted sufficient evidentiary proof to raise an issue of fact as to whether the PC was actually controlled by a management company owned by unlicensed individuals in violation of the Business Corporation Law. One Beacon Ins. Group, LLC v Midland Med. Care, P.C., 54 A.D.3d 738, 863 N.Y.S.2d 728, 2008 NY Slip Op 6813, 2008 N.Y. App. Div. LEXIS 6696 (N.Y. App. Div. 2d Dep't 2008).

Where an insurer alleged a professional corporation (PC) was not entitled to recover benefits for medical services rendered because it was controlled by non-physicians, the jury instruction on the elements of fraudulent incorporation was proper because it instructed the jury to look to the totality of the circumstances to determine whether non-physicians were de facto owners or exercised substantial control over the PC. Andrew Carothers, M.D., P.C. v Progressive Ins. Co., 150 A.D.3d 192, 2017 NY Slip Op 02614, 2017 NY Slip Op 02614, 2017 NY Slip Op 2614, 2017 NY Slip Op 2614, 51 N.Y.S.3d 551, 2017 N.Y. App. Div. LEXIS 2556 (N.Y. App. Div. 2d Dep't 2017).

Where an insurer alleged a professional corporation (PC) was not entitled to recover no-fault benefits for medical services because it was controlled by non-physicians, the trial court did not err in declining to instruct the jury on fraudulent intent at the time of incorporation, because even if the PC did not intend to yield control to unlicensed parties at the time of incorporation, it nonetheless would be ineligible for no-fault reimbursement if the nominal physician owner yielded control of the PC at some later date. Andrew Carothers, M.D., P.C. v Progressive Ins. Co., 150 A.D.3d 192, 2017 NY Slip Op 02614, 2017 NY Slip Op 02614, 2017 NY Slip Op 2614, 2017 NY Slip Op 2614, 51 N.Y.S.3d 551, 2017 N.Y. App. Div. LEXIS 2556 (N.Y. App. Div. 2d Dep't 2017).

Court consolidated 61 actions involving no fault insurance for the purposes of amending the answer and setting a hearing as to whether the professional corporations were fraudulently incorporated under N.Y. Bus. Corp. Law §§ 1507, 1508 and N.Y. Educ. Law § 6507(4)(c) since the insurer articulated a founded belief that the health providers violated those laws. Metroscan Imaging P.C. v GEICO Ins. Co., 797 N.Y.S.2d 737, 2005 NY Slip Op 25228, 8 Misc. 3d 829, 233 N.Y.L.J. 115, 2005 N.Y. Misc. LEXIS 1165 (N.Y. Civ. Ct. 2005), aff'd, 823 N.Y.S.2d 818, 2006 NY Slip Op 26319, 13 Misc. 3d 35, 2006 N.Y. Misc. LEXIS 2150 (N.Y. App. Term 2006).

Jury verdict denying a corporation's no-fault first-party benefit claim was proper, and the corporation's motion to set the verdict aside was denied, because the jury was properly instructed, and found that the corporation was owned and controlled by two non-physician individuals, which established that the corporation was fraudulently incorporated and that it was not entitled to reimbursement pursuant to N.Y. Comp. Codes R. & Regs. tit. 11, § 65-3.16(a)(12); a medical corporation that was owned or controlled by non-physicians, in violation of N.Y. Bus. Corp. Law §§ 1507, 1508, at the time no-fault services were provided, was ineligible for reimbursement of first-party benefits, and the jury was properly instructed that in determining if corporation was fraudulently incorporated, they could consider the totality of the circumstances and all relevant factors. There was no reason why a violation of the latter part of N.Y. Bus. Corp. Law § 1507 should have been treated differently than a violation of that portion of § 1507 which prohibited non-physician ownership of medical corporations. Carothers, P.C. v Ins. Cos., 888 N.Y.S.2d 372, 2009 NY Slip Op 29413, 26 Misc. 3d 448, 2009 N.Y. Misc. LEXIS 2838 (N.Y. Civ. Ct. 2009).

Insurer, who was not a party to a previous declaratory judgment (DJ) action, was not permitted to proactively invoke collateral estoppel to bar a medical provider, who was a party to the DJ action, from recovering no-fault benefits due to the finding of fraudulent incorporation because the insurer did not amend its answer to raise *Mallela* as a defense and hence create an apparent identity of issues between the DJ action and the instant matter. Downtown Acupuncture PC v State Wide Ins. Co., 2015 NY Slip Op 25371, 50 Misc. 3d 461, 21 N.Y.S.3d 548, 2015 N.Y. Misc. LEXIS 4042 (N.Y. Civ. Ct. 2015).

Following question was certified to the New York Court of Appeals pursuant to N.Y. Comp. Codes R. & Regs. tit. 22, § 500.17 and 2nd Cir. R. § 0.27: Is a medical corporation that was fraudulently incorporated under N.Y. Bus. Corp. Law §§ 1507, 1508, and N.Y. Educ. Law § 6507(4)(c) entitled to be reimbursed by insurers, under N.Y. Ins. Law § 5101 et seq., and its implementing regulations, for medical services rendered by licensed medical practitioners? State Farm Mut. Auto. Ins. Co. v Mallela, 372 F.3d 500, 2004 U.S. App. LEXIS 12034 (2d Cir. N.Y. 2004).

In insurers' action for a declaratory judgment that a radiologist and a group of professional service corporations were ineligible for no fault reimbursement on the ground that they failed to comply with State licensing requirements, the corporations' motion for partial summary judgment on the ground that a professional service corporation was ineligible for no fault reimbursement only if it was fraudulently incorporated was denied because if the corporations were under the control of an unlicensed individual, the insurers would be entitled to a declaration that they could deny the corporations no fault reimbursement, regardless of whether they were fraudulently incorporated; a medical service corporation will be ineligible for no fault reimbursement if it is in violation of licensing requirements, regardless of whether the doctor intended to yield control to unlicensed parties at the time he formed the corporation. AIU Ins. Co. v Deajess Med. Imaging, P.C., 882 N.Y.S.2d 812, 2009 NY Slip Op 29079, 24 Misc. 3d 161, 241 N.Y.L.J. 42, 2009 N.Y. Misc. LEXIS 367 (N.Y. Sup. Ct. 2009).

Insurer adequately stated a claim for relief under the Racketeer Influenced and Corrupt Organizations Act (RICO), 18 U.S.C.S. § 1962(c), by alleging that the providers were improperly licensed under Public Health Law § 2801-a, rendering them ineligible to collect under New York's no-fault law for the services provided to the insureds, even though state authorities had approved the providers, because insurers could test the validity of a provider's license pursuant to 11 NYCRR § 65.3.5(c). Allstate Ins. Co. v Elzanaty, 916 F. Supp. 2d 273, 2013 U.S. Dist. LEXIS 3696 (E.D.N.Y. 2013), dismissed, in part, 929 F. Supp. 2d 199, 2013 U.S. Dist. LEXIS 33309 (E.D.N.Y. 2013).

Where defendants were charged with conspiracy to commit health care fraud and mail fraud in connection with an allegedly fraudulent no-fault insurance scheme, the indictment's fraudulent incorporation theory was not legally insufficient, because the question of whether defendants misrepresented the identity of the owners was properly viewed as one for the jury, the insurer's entitlement to withhold reimbursement was an interest in money or property, and the indictment rested on the alleged deprivation of their monetary interest in nonpayment of claims. United States v Zemlyansky, 945 F. Supp. 2d 438, 2013 U.S. Dist. LEXIS 71818 (S.D.N.Y. 2013).

2. Unlicensed directors or officers

In a Small Claims Court action the trial court properly refused to let a corporate secretary appearing on behalf of defendant medical service corporation cross-examine or present evidence when it was discovered that she was not an attorney, since no individual may be a director of a professional service corporation unless that person is authorized by law to practice in this state the profession that such corporation is authorized to practice and, though corporations may

appear in Small Claims Court by an officer, the corporate secretary did not allege that she was a medical doctor and therefore she could not legally be an officer of defendant corporation. Bradley v Weber, 122 Misc. 2d 428, 473 N.Y.S.2d 89, 1983 N.Y. Misc. LEXIS 4127 (N.Y. App. Term 1983).

Administrator of the estate of three professional corporations' (PCs) sole shareholder, officer, and director (SH) could not be substituted under N.Y. C.P.L.R. 1017 for the PCs in suits seeking assigned first-party benefits because: (1) the SH's administrator had not been appointed a receiver for the PCs and they had not been dissolved; (2) no one was authorized to act on behalf of the PCs; (3) the administrator could not act under N.Y. Bus. Corp. Law §§ 1507, 1508, and 1511 because the PCs were authorized to practice medicine, and the administrator was not licensed to practice medicine; and (4) the administrator could only vote the shares in the PCs for the N.Y. Bus. Corp. Law §§ 909, 1001, and 1511 purposes. Painless Med., P.C. v GEICO, 929 N.Y.S.2d 357, 2011 NY Slip Op 21228, 32 Misc. 3d 715, 2011 N.Y. Misc. LEXIS 3233 (N.Y. Civ. Ct. 2011).

Because the promulgation of N.Y. Comp. Codes R. & Regs. tit. 11, § 65-3.16(a)(12) altered the common law prospectively, an insurer could amend its answer to assert an affirmative defense that an assignee was fraudulently incorporated under N.Y. Business Corporation Law §§ 1507, 1508 and N.Y. Education Law § 6507(4)(c). Metroscan Imaging, P.C. v GEICO Ins. Co., 823 N.Y.S.2d 818, 2006 NY Slip Op 26319, 13 Misc. 3d 35, 2006 N.Y. Misc. LEXIS 2150 (N.Y. App. Term 2006).

§ 1509. Disqualification of shareholders, directors, officers and employees

If any shareholder, director, officer or employee of a professional service corporation, including a design professional service corporation, who has been rendering professional service to the public becomes legally disqualified to practice his profession within this state, he shall sever all employment with, and financial interests (other than interests as a creditor) in, such corporation forthwith or as otherwise provided in section 1510 of this article. All provisions of law regulating the rendering of professional services by a person elected or appointed to a public office shall be applicable to a shareholder, director, officer and employee of such corporation in the same manner and to the same extent as if fully set forth herein. Such legal disqualification to practice his profession within this state shall be deemed to constitute an irrevocable offer by the disqualified shareholder to sell his shares to the corporation, pursuant to the provisions of section 1510 of this article or of the certificate of incorporation, by-laws or agreement among the corporation and all shareholders, whichever is applicable. Compliance with the terms of such offer shall be specifically enforceable in the courts of this state. A professional service corporation's failure to enforce compliance with this provision shall constitute a ground for forfeiture of its certificate of incorporation and its dissolution.

History: Add, L 1970, ch 974, eff May 19, 1970; amd, L 2011, ch 550, § 6, eff Jan 1, 2012.

CASE ANNOTATIONS

Where a stockholders' agreement clearly specified that the purchase price of a withdrawing stockholder's shares would be book value as determined from the balance sheet prepared for that purpose, and that no value would be attached to any accounts receivable, the trial court erred in granting petitioner, an attorney required by Bus Corp Law §§ 1509 and 1510 to withdraw from a professional corporation upon her elevation to the bench, an order permitting discovery, apparently in aid of determining the value of her shares on a quantum meruit basis, in that petitioner should have been precluded from seeking a valuation method at variance with that expressly provided for by the agreement. Re Application of Danzig (1983, 1st Dept) 96 A.D.2d 803, 466 N.Y.S.2d 343

Attorney's claims seeking compensation for his interest in a professional corporation was dismissed because, inter alia, although, under N.Y. Bus. Corp. Law § 1510, an obligation existed to purchase or redeem the shares of a deceased or disqualified shareholder, there was no remedy in the statute for a discharged owner; further, "retirement from the practice of law" did not equal "disqualification from the practice of law" for the purposes of § 1510. Lubov v Welikson (2008, Sup) 21 Misc 3d 896, 240 NYLJ 80, 865 NYS2d 510.

Court dismissed a corporation's appeal from an order denying the corporation's motion for summary judgment because, upon the death of the corporation's sole officer, director, and shareholder during the pendency of the corporation's motion, the corporation became powerless to proceed with the action. Upon the officer's death, the officer's shares in the corporation became an asset of his estate, and the record did not establish that any of the corporation's subsequent actions in filing a notice of appeal and prosecuting the appeal were authorized by someone with the authority to do so in compliance with N.Y. Bus. Corp. Law §§ 1507 and 1511. Ocean Diagnostic Imaging, P.C. v Merchants Mut. Ins. Co. (2007, Sup App T) 15 Misc 3d 9, 832 NYS2d 383

§ 1510. Death or disqualification of shareholders

(a) A professional service corporation, including a design professional service corporation, shall purchase or redeem the shares of a shareholder in case of his death or disqualification pursuant to the provisions of section 1509 of this article, within six months after the appointment of the executor or administrator or other legal representative of the estate of such deceased shareholder, or within six months after such disqualification, at the book value of such shares as of the end of the month immediately preceding the death or disqualification of the shareholder as determined from the books and records of the corporation in accordance with its regular method of accounting. The certificate of incorporation, the by-laws of the corporation or an agreement among the corporation and all shareholders may modify this section by providing for a shorter period of purchase or redemption, or an alternate method of determining the price to be paid for the shares, or both. If the corporation shall fail to purchase or redeem such shares within the required period, a successful plaintiff in an action to recover the purchase price of such shares shall also be awarded reasonable attorneys' fees and costs. Limitations on the purchase or redemption of shares set forth in section 513 of this chapter shall not apply to the purchase or redemption of shares pursuant to this section. Nothing herein contained shall prevent a corporation from paying pension benefits or other deferred compensation to or on behalf of a former or deceased officer, director or employee thereof as otherwise permitted by law. The provisions of this section shall not be deemed to require the purchase of the shares of a disqualified shareholder where the period of disqualification is for less than six months, and the shareholder again becomes eligible to practice his profession within six months from the date of disqualification.

(b) Notwithstanding the provisions of paragraph (a) of this section, the corporation shall not be required to purchase or redeem the shares of a deceased

or disqualified shareholder if such shares, within the time limit prescribed by paragraph (a) of this section, are sold or transferred to another professional pursuant to the provisions of section 1511 of this article.

History: Add, L 1970, ch 974, eff May 19, 1970; amd, L 1971, ch 1022, eff July 2, 1971, L 2011, ch 550, § 7, eff Jan 1, 2012.

CASE ANNOTATIONS

Where a stockholders' agreement clearly specified that the purchase price of a withdrawing stockholder's shares would be book value as determined from the balance sheet prepared for that purpose, and that no value would be attached to any accounts receivable, the trial court erred in granting petitioner, an attorney required by Bus Corp Law §§ 1509 and 1510 to withdraw from a professional corporation upon her elevation to the bench, an order permitting discovery, apparently in aid of determining the value of her shares on a quantum meruit basis, in that petitioner should have been precluded from seeking a valuation method at variance with that expressly provided for by the agreement. Re Application of Danzig (1983, 1st Dept) 96 A.D.2d 803, 466 N.Y.S.2d 343

Executrix of deceased chiropractor, who had been sole shareholder of professional corporation, stated cause of action against decedent's former employee for injunction prohibiting former employee's solicitation of professional corporation's patients, since estate had valid interest in professional corporation's practice of chiropractic, and unauthorized solicitation of patients could impair value of that practice and value of professional corporation. Re Olsson (1992, 2d Dept) 180 A.D.2d 739, 580 N.Y.S.2d 376

Business Corporation Law requires executor of deceased shareholder in professional service corporation to sell, transfer, or have redeemed deceased's shares within 6 months of executor's appointment. Re Olsson (1992, 2d Dept) 180 A.D.2d 739, 580 N.Y.S.2d 376

Continued existence and operation of professional service corporation is not restricted following shareholder's death and appointment of executor; corporation may properly carry out its practice through employment of authorized professionals during 6-month period allowed to executor for sale, transfer or redemption of deceased's shares. Re Olsson (1992, 2d Dept) 180 A.D.2d 739, 580 N.Y.S.2d 376

Court erred in denying law firm's motion for summary judgment dismissing action by widow of partner to compel firm to formally redeem her late husband's shares in compliance with CLS Bus Corp § 1510, notwithstanding widow's claim that determination of book value of her husband's shares in accordance with firm's regular cash method of accounting excluded consideration of work in progress and accounts receivable which existed at time of husband's death, where firm conceded that its regular method of accounting required that widow be compensated for pro rata share of such work in progress and accounts receivable on "if, as and when collected" basis, placing her in same position vis-a-vis future earnings as other shareholders of firm. Licitra v Shaw, Licitra, Eisenberg, Esernio & Schwartz, P. C. (1992, 2d Dept) 187 A.D.2d 640, 590 N.Y.S.2d 269

Court exceeded requirements of CLS Bus Corp § 1510 in granting summary judgment directing surviving law firm shareholder to redeem deceased shareholder's 50 percent interest in professional corporation by paying book value calculated on accrual basis and including all accounts and other receivables and work-in-progress, since statute requires only redemption of book value as determined from books and records of corporation "in accordance with its regular method of accounting," and law firm's regular method of accounting was cash method omitting accounts receivable and work-in-progress from valuation; further discovery would be ordered to determine whether cash method of valuation would produce windfall to surviving shareholder or unjust hardship to estate of deceased shareholder.Diamond & Golomb, P. C. v Diamond (1993, 1st Dept) 189 A.D.2d 722, 592 N.Y.S.2d 743

Book value of decedent shareholder's shares in profession law corporation did not include pending cases where law firm's regular accounting procedure was cash method which did not recognize accounts receivable or work in progress as assets. In re Estate of Reichenbaum (1995, 2d Dept) 214 A.D.2d 48, 631 N.Y.S.2d 178

Attorney's claims seeking compensation for his interest in a professional corporation was dismissed because, inter alia, although, under N.Y. Bus. Corp. Law § 1510, an obligation existed to purchase or redeem the shares of a deceased or disqualified shareholder, there was no remedy in the statute for a discharged owner; further, "retirement from the practice of law" did not equal "disqualification from the practice of law" for the purposes of § 1510. Lubov v Welikson (2008, Sup) 21 Misc 3d 896, 240 NYLJ 80, 865 NYS2d 510.

Attorney basically claimed during trial, as reflected by the testimony, that after he was terminated by a professional corporation (PC), his shares were redistributed amongst the remaining shareholders, and, thus, the attorney's real claim appeared to be one of conversion; this cause of action came into being as part of the attorney's third amended complaint, filed four years after the attorney left the PC, and thus, on its facts, it was time barred under N.Y. C.P.L.R. 214 as a claim under N.Y. Bus. Corp. Law § 1510. Lubov v Welikson (2008, Sup) 21 Misc 3d 896, 240 NYLJ 80, 865 NYS2d 510.

§ 1511. Transfer of shares

(a) No shareholder of a professional service corporation or a design professional service corporation may sell or transfer his shares in such corporation except to another individual who is eligible to have shares issued to him by such corporation or except in trust to another individual who would be eligible to receive shares if he were employed by the corporation. Nothing herein contained shall be construed to prohibit the transfer of shares by operation of law or by court decree. No transferee of shares by operation of law or court decree may vote the shares for any purpose whatsoever except with respect to corporate action under sections 909 and 1001 of this chapter. The restriction in the preceding sentence shall not apply, however, where such transferee would be eligible to have shares issued to him if he were an employee of the corporation and, if there are other shareholders, a majority of such other shareholders shall fail to redeem the shares so transferred, pursuant to section 1510 of this article, within sixty days of receiving written notice of such transfer. Any sale or transfer, except by operation of law or court decree or except for a corporation having only one shareholder, may be made only after the same shall have been approved by the board of directors, or at a shareholders' meeting specially called for such purpose by such proportion, not less than a majority, of the outstanding shares as may be provided in the certificate of incorporation or in the by-laws of such professional service corporation. At such shareholders' meeting the shares held by the shareholder proposing to sell or transfer his shares may not be voted or counted for any purpose, unless all shareholders consent that such shares be voted or counted. The certificate of incorporation or the by-laws of the professional service corporation, or the professional service corporation and the shareholders by private agreement, may provide, in lieu of or in addition to the foregoing provisions, for the alienation of shares and may require the redemption or purchase of such shares by such corporation at prices and in a manner specifically set forth therein. The existence of the restrictions on the sale or transfer of shares, as contained in this article and, if applicable, in the certificate of incorporation, by-laws, stock purchase or stock redemption agreement, shall be noted conspicuously on the face or back of every certificate for shares issued by a professional service corporation. Any sale or transfer in violation of such restrictions shall be void.

(b) A design professional service corporation shall purchase or redeem the shares of a non-design professional shareholder in the case of his or her termination of employment within thirty days after such termination. A design professional service corporation shall not be required to purchase or redeem the shares of a terminated non-design professional shareholder if such shares, within thirty days after such termination, are sold or transferred to another employee of the corporation pursuant to this article.

History: Add, L 1970, ch 974, amd, L 1971, ch 1022, eff July 2, 1971, L 2011, ch 550, § 8, eff Jan 1, 2012.

CASE ANNOTATIONS

Estate executor, a nonprofessional who was the transferee of a majority of shares in a professional services corporation, lacked standing to obtain judicial dissolution of the corporation pursuant to N.Y. Bus. Corp. Law § 1103. N.Y. Bus. Corp. Law § 1511 did not authorize the action. Matter of Bernfeld and Kurilenko (2011, 2d Dept) 86 App Div 3d 244, 925 NYS2d 122.

Under N.Y. Bus. Corp. Law § 1511, a nonprofessional shareholder is only permitted to vote on corporate action pursuant to either N.Y. Bus. Corp. Law §§ 909 or 1001. Matter of Bernfeld and Kurilenko (2011, 2d Dept) 86 App Div 3d 244, 925 NYS2d 122.

In view of likelihood that delivery of shares of stock of professional corporation to sheriff for sale would not result in satisfaction of alimony arrears, and since delivery of property to sheriff must be made for sole purpose of sale to satisfy judgment, delivery of stock was ordered to be made to receiver, who could then do any act designed to satisfy judgment including dissolution of corporation. Udel v Udel (1975) 82 Misc. 2d 882, 370 N.Y.S.2d 426

Administrator of the estate of three professional corporations' (PCs) sole shareholder, officer, and director (SH) could not be substituted under N.Y. C.P.L.R. 1017 for the PCs in suits seeking assigned first-party benefits because: (1) the SH's administrator had not been appointed a receiver for the PCs and they had not been dissolved; (2) no one was authorized to act on behalf of the PCs; (3) the administrator could not act under N.Y. Bus. Corp. Law §§ 1507, 1508, and 1511 because the PCs were authorized to practice medicine, and the administrator was not licensed to practice medicine; and (4) the administrator could only vote the shares in the PCs for the N.Y. Bus. Corp. Law §§ 909, 1001, and 1511 purposes. Painless Med., P.C. v GEICO (2011, Civ Ct) 32 Misc 3d 715, 929 NYS2d 357.

Court erroneously ordered dissolution of medical professional corporations on theory that corporations were in fact alter egos of certain other corporations in which petitioner owned 20 percent of shares since petitioner was not authorized to practice medicine, and thus she could own shares in those corporations, if that all, only as "transferee of shares by operation of law or court decree" (CLS Bus Corp §§ 1511, 1503, and 1507); even if petitioner were entitled, by "operation of law," to transfer 20 percent of shares in medical professional corporations, she would still be forbidden from voting those shares "for any purpose whatsoever except with respect to corporate action under (Business Corporation Law) section nine hundred nine and section one thousand one." Fromcheck v Brentwood Pain & Med. Servs., P.C. (1998, 2d Dept) 254 A.D.2d 485, 679 N.Y.S.2d 632

Court dismissed a corporation's appeal from an order denying the corporation's motion for summary judgment because, upon the death of the corporation's sole officer, director, and shareholder during the pendency of the corporation's motion, the corporation became powerless to proceed with the action. Upon the officer's death, the officer's shares in the corporation became an asset of his estate, and the record did not establish that any of the corporation's subsequent actions in filing a notice of appeal and prosecuting the appeal were authorized by someone with the authority to do so in compliance with N.Y. Bus. Corp. Law §§ 1507 and 1511. Ocean Diagnostic Imaging,

P.C. v Merchants Mut. Ins. Co. (2007, Sup App T) 15 Misc 3d 9, 832 NYS2d 383

§ 1512. Corporate name

(a) Notwithstanding any other provision of law, the name of a professional service corporation, including a design professional service corporation, may contain any word which, at the time of incorporation, could be used in the name of a partnership practicing a profession which the corporation is authorized to practice, and may not contain any word which could not be used by such a partnership. Provided, however, the name of a professional service corporation may not contain the name of a deceased person unless

(1) such person's name was part of the corporate name at the time of such person's death; or

(2) such person's name was part of the name of an existing partnership and at least two-thirds of such partnership's partners become shareholders of the corporation.

(b) The name of a professional service corporation shall end with the words "Professional Corporation" or the abbreviation "P.C." The name of a design professional service corporation shall end with the words "design professional corporation" or the abbreviation "D.P.C." The provisions of subparagraph one of paragraph (a) of section 301 of this chapter shall not apply to a professional service corporation.

History: Add, L 1970, ch 974, eff May 19, 1970; amd, L 2011, ch 550, § 9, eff Jan 1, 2012.

CASE ANNOTATIONS

Architecture firm's proposed use of initials "HOK" in its corporate name, representing last initials of three licensed firm members, was prohibited by Bus Corp L § 1512 as an assumed or fictitious name; thus Education Commissioner did not act arbitrarily, capriciously, or unreasonably in denying use of such initials in corporate name of firm. Kahn & Jacobs v Nyquist (1973) 76 Misc. 2d 355, 350 N.Y.S.2d 840

Buyers of all of stock of professional corporation which bore name of podiatrist who formed professional corporation and who sold all stock in corporation and buyers' successors could not utilize founding podiatrist's name in connection with professional corporation. Weiner v Weiner (1976) 88 Misc. 2d 920, 390 N.Y.S.2d 359

§ 1513. Business corporation law applicable

This chapter, except article 13 and article 15-A, shall be applicable to a professional service corporation, including a design professional service corporation, except to the extent that the provisions thereof conflict with this article. A professional service corporation, including a design professional service corporation, may consolidate or merge only with another corporation organized under this article or authorized to do business in this state under article 15-A of this chapter or authorized and registered to practice the same profession, or in the case of a design professional service corporation one or more professions as provided in paragraph (e) of section 1501 of this article, pursuant to the applicable provisions of subdivision six of section seventy-two hundred nine of the education law, subdivision four of section seventy-three hundred seven of the education law or subdivision four of section seventy-three

hundred twenty-seven of the education law, or may be a member of a professional service limited liability company, a foreign professional service limited liability company, a registered limited liability partnership or foreign limited liability partnership, and only if all of the professions practiced by such corporations, limited liability companies or limited liability partnerships could be practiced by a single corporation organized under this article.

History: Add, L 1970, ch 974, eff May 19, 1970; amd, L 1983, ch 505, § 1, eff Oct 17, 1983, L 1992, ch 851, § 1, eff Dec 2, 1992, L 1994, ch 576, § 16, eff Oct 24, 1994, L 2011, ch 550, § 10, eff Jan 1, 2012.

CASE ANNOTATIONS

In breach of contract action involving legal fees and disbursements, defendant professional services corporation could appear pro se by its member lawyers, whether or not members could be held liable to plaintiff. Toren v Anderson, Kill & Olick, P.C. (2000, Sup) 185 Misc. 2d 23, 710 N.Y.S.2d 799

§ 1514. Triennial statement

(a) Each professional service corporation shall, at least once every three years on or before the date prescribed by the licensing authority, furnish a statement to the licensing authority listing the name and residence address of each shareholder, director and officer of such corporation and certifying that all such individuals are authorized by law in this state to practice a profession which such corporation is authorized to practice. The statement shall be signed by the president or any vice-president of the corporation and attested to by the secretary or any assistant secretary of the corporation.

(b) Each design professional service corporation shall, at least once every three years on or before the date prescribed by the licensing authority, furnish a statement to the licensing authority listing the names and residence addresses of each shareholder, director and officer of such corporation and certify as the date of certification and at all times over the entire three year period that:

(i) greater than seventy-five percent of the outstanding shares of stock of the corporation are and were owned by design professionals,

(ii) greater than seventy-five percent of the directors are and were design professionals,

(iii) greater than seventy-five percent of the officers are and were design professionals,

(iv) the president, the chairperson of the board of directors and the chief executive officer or officers are and were design professionals, and

(v) the single largest shareholder is and was either a design professional or an ESOP with greater than seventy-five percent of the plan's voting trustees being design professionals and greater than seventy-five percent of the plan's committee members being design professionals.

The statement shall be signed by the president or any design professional vice-president and attested to by the secretary or any assistant secretary of the corporation.

History: Add, L 1970, ch 974, eff May 19, 1970; amd, L 1987, ch 43, § 60, eff May 1, 1987 (see 1987 note below), L 2001, ch 538, § 9, eff Jan 11, 2002, L 2011, ch 550, § 11, eff Jan 1, 2012.

CASE ANNOTATIONS

In proceeding under CLS Bus Corp § 619 seeking either to confirm corporate election held at special shareholders' meeting, or to order new election, professional corporation's annual statement filed under CLS Bus Corp § 1514, which listed petitioners as shareholders, was not determinative of issue of petitioners' status and entitlement to be treated as shareholders in law firm. Heisler v Gingras (1997) 90 N.Y.2d 682, 665 N.Y.S.2d 59, 687 N.E.2d 1342, reargument den (NY) 1997 N.Y. LEXIS 4279

There is no requirement that upon the transfer of shares of professional corporation approval must be obtained from state authorities with regard to continued use of existing professional corporate name. Weiner v Weiner (1976) 88 Misc. 2d 920, 390 N.Y.S.2d 359

In proceeding to confirm election of directors by shareholders of professional corporation that did business as law firm, respondent attorneys were estopped from denying legitimacy of shareholders they had previously certified to Appellate Division pursuant to CLS Bus Corp § 1514. Heisler v Gingras (1996, Sup) 169 Misc. 2d 403, 646 N.Y.S.2d 264, mod on other grounds, affd (App Div, 3d Dept) 652 N.Y.S.2d 841, motion gr (NY) 1997 N.Y. LEXIS 439 and app dismd (NY A.D., 3d Dept) 1997 N.Y. A.D. LEXIS 3746, 1997 N.Y. Slip Op 3366

§ 1515. Regulation of professions

This article shall not repeal, modify or restrict any provision of the education law or the judiciary law regulating the professions referred to therein except to the extent in conflict herewith.

History: Add, L 1970, ch 974, eff May 19, 1970.

§ 1516. Corporate mergers, consolidations and other reorganizations

(a) Notwithstanding any inconsistent provision of this article, and subject to the limitations in paragraph (d) of this section, a professional service corporation, including a design professional service corporation, pursuant to the provisions of article nine of this chapter, may be merged or consolidated with another corporation formed pursuant to the provisions of this chapter, with a corporation authorized and registered to practice the same profession pursuant to the applicable provisions of subdivision six of section seventy-two hundred nine of the education law (engineer or land surveyor), subdivision four of section seventy-three hundred seven of the education law (architect) or subdivision four of section seventy-three hundred twenty-seven of the education law (landscape architect) of articles one hundred forty-five, one hundred forty-seven and one hundred forty-eight of the education law, or with a foreign corporation, or other business entity practicing the same profession or professions in this state or the state of its formation, or may be otherwise reorganized, provided that the corporation which survives or which is formed pursuant thereto is a professional service corporation, a design professional service corporation, a professional service limited liability company or a foreign professional service corporation practicing the same profession or professions in this

state or the state of incorporation or, if one of the original corporations is authorized to practice pursuant to the provisions of either subdivision six of section seventy-two hundred nine, subdivision four of section seventy-three hundred seven or subdivision four of section seventy-three hundred twenty-four of the education law, a corporation authorized and registered to practice the same profession pursuant to the applicable provisions of subdivision six of section seventy-two hundred nine of the education law (engineer or land surveyor), subdivision four of section seventy-three hundred seven of the education law (architect) of articles one hundred forty-five, one hundred forty-seven and one hundred forty-eight or subdivision four of section seventy-three hundred twenty-seven of the education law.

(b) If the surviving business entity is a professional corporation, the restrictions on the issuance, transfer or sale of shares of a professional service corporation or a design professional service corporation shall be suspended for a period not exceeding thirty days with respect to any issuance, transfer or sale of shares made pursuant to such merger, consolidation or reorganization, provided that: (i) no person who would not be eligible to be a shareholder in the absence of this section shall vote the shares of or receive any distribution from such corporation; (ii) after such merger, consolidation or reorganization, any professional service corporation or a design professional service corporation which survives or which is created thereby shall be subject to all of the provisions of this article; and (iii) shares thereafter only may be held by persons who are eligible to receive shares of such professional service corporation, design professional service corporation or such other corporation authorized and registered to practice the same profession pursuant to the applicable provisions of subdivision six of section seventy-two hundred nine of the education law (engineer or land surveyor), subdivision four of section seventy-three hundred seven of the education law (architect) or subdivision four of section seventy-three hundred twenty-seven of the education law (landscape architect) of articles one hundred forty-five, one hundred forty-seven and one hundred forty-eight of the education law, which survives. Nothing herein contained shall be construed as permitting the practice of a profession in this state by a corporation which is not incorporated pursuant to the provisions of this article or authorized to do business in this state pursuant to the provisions of article fifteen-A of this chapter, authorized pursuant to subdivision six of section seventy-two hundred nine of the education law, authorized pursuant to subdivision four of section seventy-three hundred seven of the education law, authorized pursuant to subdivision four of section seventy-three hundred twenty-seven of the education law or authorized and registered to practice a profession pursuant to the applicable provisions of article one hundred forty-five, one hundred forty-seven or one hundred forty-eight of the education law. For the purposes of this section, other reorganizations shall be limited to those reorganizations defined in paragraph one of subsection (a) of section three hundred sixty-eight of the internal revenue code.

(c) If the surviving business entity is a professional service limited liability company, the restrictions on the issuance, transfer or sale of membership interests of a professional service limited liability company other than the requirements of the first two sentences of subdivision (c) of section twelve hundred eleven of the limited liability company law, shall be suspended for a period not exceeding thirty days with respect to any issuance, transfer or sale of membership interests made pursuant to such merger or consolidation, provided that: (i) no person or business entity who would not be eligible to be a member in the absence of this section shall vote or receive any distribution from such limited liability company; (ii) after such merger or consolidation, any professional service limited liability company that survives or that is created thereby shall be subject to all the provisions of the limited liability company law; and (iii) membership interests thereafter may be held only by persons or business entities who are eligible to be a member of such professional service limited liability company. Nothing herein contained shall be construed as permitting the practice of a profession in this state by a limited liability company that is not formed pursuant to the provisions of the limited liability company law or authorized to do business in the state pursuant to the provisions of article thirteen of the limited liability company law.

(d) Notwithstanding the provisions contained in paragraphs (a), (b) and (c) of this section, no design professional service corporation shall be merged or consolidated with any entity unless such entity is a professional business organization lawfully organized to provide professional services pursuant to articles one hundred forty-five, one hundred forty-seven and one hundred forty-eight of the education law.

History: Add, L 1971, ch 1022, eff July 2, 1971; amd, L 1982, ch 567, § 1, eff July 22, 1982, L 1982, ch 567, § 1, eff July 22, 1982, L 1983, ch 505, § 2, eff Oct 17, 1983, L 1992, ch 851, § 2, eff Dec 2, 1992, L 2011, ch 564, § 2, eff Sept 23, 2011; L 2014, ch 475, § 18 eff Nov 21, 2016.

ARTICLE 15-A
FOREIGN PROFESSIONAL SERVICE CORPORATIONS

History: Add, L 1983, ch 505, § 3, eff Oct 17, 1983.

§ 1525. Definitions

As used in this article, unless the context otherwise requires, the term:

(a) "Licensing authority" means the regents of the university of the state of New York or the state education department, as the case may be, in the case of all professions licensed under title eight of the education law, and the appropriate appellate division of the supreme court in the case of the profession of law.

(b) "Profession" includes any practice as an attorney and counsellor-at-law, or as a licensed physician, and those professions designated in title eight of the education law.

(c) "Professional service" means any type of service to the public which may be lawfully rendered by a member of a profession within the purview of his profession.

(d) "Foreign professional service corporation" means a professional service corporation, whether or not denominated as such, organized under the laws of a jurisdiction other than this state, all of the shareholders, directors and officers of which are authorized and licensed to practice the profession for which such corporation is licensed to do business; except that all shareholders, directors and officers of a foreign professional service corporation which provides health services in this state shall be licensed in this state.

(e) "Officer" does not include the secretary or an assistant secretary of a corporation having only one shareholder.

History: Add, L 1983, ch 505, § 3, eff Oct 17, 1983.

§ 1526. Rendering of professional service

(a) No foreign professional service corporation may render professional services in this state except through individuals authorized by law to render such professional services as individuals in this state.

(b) Each final plan, drawing and report made or issued by a foreign professional service corporation practicing professional engineering, architecture, landscape architecture, geology or land surveying shall bear the name and seal of one or more professional engineers, architects, landscape architects, professional geologists or land surveyors, respectively, who are in responsible charge of such plan or report.

(c) Each report, diagnosis, prognosis, and prescription made or issued by a foreign professional service corporation practicing medicine, dentistry, podiatry, optometry, ophthalmic dispensing, veterinary medicine, pharmacy, nursing, physiotherapy or chiropractic shall bear the signature of one or more physicians, dentists, podiatrists, optometrists, ophthalmic dispensers, veterinarians, pharmacists, nurses, physiotherapists, or chiropractors, respectively, who are in responsible charge of such report, diagnosis, prognosis, or prescription.

(d) Each record, transcript, report and hearing report prepared by a foreign professional service corporation practicing certified shorthand reporting shall bear the signature of one or more certified shorthand reporters who are in responsible charge of such record, transcript, report, or hearing report.

(e) Each report and statement prepared by a foreign professional service corporation practicing public accounting or certified public accounting shall bear the signature of one or more public accountants or certified public accountants, respectively, who are in responsible charge of such report or statement.

(f) Each opinion prepared by a foreign professional service corporation practicing law shall bear the signature of one or more attorneys and counsellors-at-law who are in responsible charge of such opinion.

(g) In addition to the requirements in paragraphs (b) through (f) inclusive herein, each document prepared by a foreign professional service corporation which under the rules, regulations, laws or customs of the applicable profession is required to bear the signature of an individual in responsible charge of such document, shall be signed by one or more such individuals licensed to practice in this state.

History: Add, L 1983, ch 505, § 3, eff Oct 17, 1983; L 2014, ch 475, § 19 eff Nov 21, 2016.

§ 1527. Professional relationships and liabilities

(a) Each shareholder, employee or agent of a foreign professional service corporation who performs professional services in this state on behalf of the corporation shall be personally and fully liable and accountable for any negligent or wrongful act or misconduct committed by him or by any person under his direct supervision and control while rendering such professional services, and shall bear professional responsibility for compliance by such corporation with all laws, rules and regulations governing the practice of the profession in this state.

(b) The relationship of an individual to a foreign professional service corporation with which such individual is associated, whether as shareholder, director, officer, employee or agent, shall not modify or diminish the jurisdiction over him of the licensing authority and in the case of an attorney and counsellor-at-law, the other courts of this state.

History: Add, L 1983, ch 505, § 3, eff Oct 17, 1983.

CASE ANNOTATIONS

Shareholder of firm was not personally liable, under CLS Bus Corp § 1527, for breach of contract entered into by firm, as statute applies only to tort claims, not to breach of contract claims. Joseph v David M. Schwarz/Architectural Servs., P.C. (1997, SD NY) 957 F. Supp. 1334

§ 1528. Foreign professional service corporation

No foreign professional service corporation shall engage in any business in this state other than the rendering of the professional services for which it is incorporated and is authorized to do business in this state; provided that such corporation may invest its funds in real estate, mortgages, stocks, bonds or any other type of investments.

History: Add, L 1983, ch 505, § 3, eff Oct 17, 1983.

§ 1529. Business corporation law applicable

Except for the provisions of sections thirteen hundred three, thirteen hundred four, thirteen hundred sixteen, thirteen hundred seventeen and thirteen hundred twenty, this chapter shall be applicable to a foreign professional service corporation to the extent that the provisions thereof are not in conflict with the provisions of this article. A foreign professional service corporation may practice in this state, or may consolidate or merge with another corporation, or may be a member of a professional service limited liability company, a foreign professional service limited liability company, a registered limited liability partnership or foreign limited liability partnership, only if all of the professions practiced by such corporations, limited liability companies or limited liability partnerships could be practiced by a single professional service corporation organized in this state; and, further, only if such foreign professional service corporation is domiciled in a state or territory of the United States the laws of which, at the time of application by such corporation under section fifteen hundred thirty of this article, contain a reciprocal provision under which professional service corporations domiciled in this state may similarly apply for the privilege of doing business in any such state or territory; provided further however, that nothing herein shall authorize a foreign professional service corporation practicing professional engineering, land surveying, geology, architecture and/or landscape architecture to be a member or partner of a professional service limited liability company, a foreign professional service limited liability company, a registered limited liability partnership or a foreign limited liability partnership unless all of the shareholders, directors and officers of such foreign professional service corporation are licensed to practice one or more of such professions in this state.

History: Add, L 1983, ch 505, § 3, eff Oct 17, 1983; amd, L 1994, ch 576, § 17, eff Oct 24, 1994; L 2014, ch 475, § 20 eff Nov 21, 2016.

§ 1530. Filing requirements

(a) A foreign professional service corporation may apply for authority to do business in this state. An application entitled "Application for Authority of .... (name of corporation) under Section fifteen hundred thirty of the Business Corporation Law," shall be signed and delivered to the department of state. It shall set forth:

(1) The name of the foreign professional service corporation. If the name does not end with the words "Professional Corporation" or the abbreviation "P.C.", it shall in addition to the foregoing set forth the name to be used in this state, ending with the words "Professional Corporation" or the abbreviation "P.C."

(2) The jurisdiction and date of its incorporation.

(3) A statement of the profession or professions to be practiced in this state and a statement that the foreign professional service corporation is authorized to practice such profession or professions in the jurisdiction of its incorporation.

(4) The name, address and license number of each person within the foreign professional service corporation who is licensed to practice the profession or professions in this state.

(5) The city, incorporated village or town and the county within this state in which its office is to be located.

(6) A designation of the secretary of state as its agent upon whom process against it may be served and the post office address within or without this state to which the secretary of state shall mail a copy of any process against it served upon him.

(7) If it is to have a registered agent, his name and address within this state and a statement that the registered agent is to be its agent upon whom process against it may be served.

(8) A statement that the foreign professional service corporation has not since its incorporation or since the date its authority to do business in this state was last surrendered, engaged in any activity in this state, or in lieu thereof, the consent of the state tax commission to the filing of the application, which consent shall be attached thereto.

(b) Attached to the application for authority shall be:

(1) A certificate by an authorized officer of the jurisdiction of its incorporation that the foreign professional service corporation is an existing corporation.

(2) A certificate or certificates issued by the licensing authority that each individual within the corporation intending to practice the profession or professions in this state is licensed to practice said profession or professions in this state. In order to obtain said certificate or certificates, a copy of the certificate of incorporation shall be furnished to the licensing authority.

(3) A certificate or certificates issued by the licensing authority in the case of a foreign professional service corporation providing health services that each shareholder, officer and director of the foreign professional service corporation is licensed to practice said profession in this state.

(c) The fee for filing the application for authority shall be two hundred dollars, payable to the department of state, and the fee for a certificate of authority issued by the state education department shall be fifty dollars.

History: Add, L 1983, ch 505, § 3, eff Oct 17, 1983.

Par (a), opening par, amd, L 1998, ch 375, § 21, eff Aug 13, 1998.

§ 1531. Annual statement

Each foreign professional service corporation shall, at least once [of]* each year on or before the date prescribed by the licensing authority, furnish a statement to the licensing authority listing the name and residence address of each shareholder, director, officer and corporate employee licensed by such licensing authority and certifying that such individuals intending to practice a profession which such foreign professional service corporation is authorized to practice in this state are licensed to practice said profession in this state. In the case of a foreign professional service corporation providing health services, such statement shall also certify that each shareholder, officer and director of the corporation is licensed to practice said profession in this state. The statement shall be signed by the president or any vice-president of the corporation and attested to by the secretary or any assistant secretary of the corporation.

* Brackets have been inserted by the Publisher around this word as it is superfluous.

History: Add, L 1983, ch 505, § 3, eff Oct 17, 1983; amd, L 2001, ch 538, § 10, eff Jan 11, 2002.

§ 1532. Regulation of professions

(a) This article shall not repeal, modify or restrict any provision of the education law or the judiciary law or any rules or regulations adopted thereunder regulating the professions referred to therein except to the extent in conflict herewith.

(b) A foreign professional service corporation, other than a foreign professional service corporation authorized to practice law, shall be under the supervision of the regents of the university of the state of New York and be subject to disciplinary proceedings and penalties, and its authority to do business shall be subject to suspension, revocation or annulment for cause, in the same manner and to the same extent as is provided with respect to individuals and their licenses, certificates, and registrations in title eight of the education law relating to the applicable profession. Notwithstanding the provisions of this subdivision, a foreign professional service corporation authorized to practice medicine shall be subject to the prehearing procedures and hearing procedures as is provided with respect to individual physicians and their licenses in Title II-A of article two of the public health law.

(c) A foreign professional service corporation authorized to practice law shall be subject to the regulation and control of, and its authority to do business shall be subject to suspension, revocation or annulment for cause by, the appellate division of the supreme court and the court of appeals in the same manner and to the same extent provided in the judiciary law with respect to individual attorneys and counselors-at-law. Such corporation need not qualify for any certification under section four hundred sixty-four of the judiciary law, take an oath of office under section four hundred sixty-six of such law or register under section four hundred sixty-seven of such law.

History: Add, L 1983, ch 505, § 3, eff Oct 17, 1983.

§ 1533. Licensing of individuals

No officer, director, shareholder or employee of a foreign professional service corporation shall practice his or her profession in this state unless such individual is duly licensed to practice such profession in this state.

History: Add, L 1983, ch 505, § 3, eff Oct 17, 1983.

ARTICLE 16
SECURITY TAKEOVER DISCLOSURE ACT

History: Add, L 1976, ch 893, eff Nov 1, 1976; amd, L 1985, ch 915, § 4, eff Feb 14, 1986.

§ 1600. Short title

This article shall be known as the security takeover disclosure act.

History: Add, L 1976, ch 893, eff Nov 1, 1976; amd, L 1985, ch 915, § 4, eff Feb 14, 1986.

CASE ANNOTATIONS

Executive officer's stock purchase arose from his employment with the corporation, not as result of a tender offer; since the corporation's directors authorized the purchase at a price set by the directors, pursuant to N.Y. Bus. Law §§ 504, 505, compliance with the Securities Takeover Disclosure Act, N.Y. Bus. Corp. Law art. 16, was unneeded. In re Application of Presher (2003, Sup) 765 N.Y.S.2d 210

State business takeover law requiring registration with state prior to takeover bid constitutes burden on interstate commerce in violation of U.S. Constitution's commerce clause (Art I § 3 cl 8), and is invalid.Edgar v Mite Corp (1982) 457 US 624, 73 L Ed 2d 269, 102 S Ct 2629

§ 1601. Definitions

As used in this article, the following terms shall have the following meanings:

(a) "Takeover bid" means the acquisition of or offer to acquire by an offeror from an offeree, pursuant to a tender offer or request or invitation for tenders, any equity security of a target company, if after acquisition thereof the offeror would, directly or indirectly, be a beneficial owner of more than five percent of any class of the issued and outstanding equity securities of such target company.

Such term does not include:

(1) Bids made by a dealer for his own account in the ordinary course of his business of buying and selling such security;

(2) An offer to acquire such equity security solely in exchange for other securities, or the acquisition of such equity security pursuant to such offer, for the sole account of the offeror, in good faith and not for the purpose of avoiding this section, and not involving any public offering of such other securities within the meaning of section four of title one of the "Securities Act of 1933", (48 Stat.77, 15 U.S.C.77 d (2)); as amended;

(3) Any other offer to acquire an equity security, or the acquisition of such equity security pursuant to such offer, for the sole account of the offeror, from not more than fifty offerees, in good faith and not for the purpose of avoidingthe provisions of this article;

(4) Any offer or class of offer where, prior to making the offer, the offeror beneficially owns, directly or indirectly, a majority of the voting equity securities of the target company;

(b) "Offeror" means a person who makes, or in any way participates or aids in making, a takeover bid, and includes persons acting jointly or in concert, or who intend to exercise jointly or in concert any voting rights attached to the securities for which such takeover bid is made. An "offeror" includes an issuer of securities whose securities are or are to be the subject of a takeover bid whether or not the issuer, upon acquisition, will become the beneficial owner of such securities. "An offeror" does not include any bank or broker-dealer in securities loaning funds to the offeror in the ordinary course of the business of the bank or broker-dealer in securities and not otherwise participating in the takeover bid, or any bank, broker-dealer in securities, attorney, accountant or consultant furnishing information or advice to an offeror and not otherwise participating in the takeover bid.

(c) "Offeree" means the beneficial owner, residing in this state, of securities which an offeror acquires or offers to acquire in connection with a takeover bid.

(d) "Target company" means a corporation, organized under the laws of this state and having its principal executive offices or significant business operations located within this state.

(e) "Equity security" means any stock, bond, or other obligation of a target company, the holder of which has the right to vote for the election of members of the board of directors, or those exercising a similar function if the target company is not a corporation, of such target company. Equity security includes any security convertible into an equity security, and also includes any right, option or warrant to purchase an equity security.

History: Add, L 1976, ch 893, eff Nov 1, 1976; amd, L 1976, ch 894, eff Nov 1, 1976; L 1979, ch 588, §§ 1-4, eff July 10, 1979; L 1980, ch 733, § 1, eff June 30, 1980; L 1985, ch 915, § 4, eff Feb 16, 1986.

CASE ANNOTATIONS

Executive officer's stock purchase arose from his employment with the corporation, not as result of a tender offer; since the corporation's directors authorized the purchase at a price set by the directors, pursuant to N.Y. Bus. Law §§ 504, 505, compliance with the Securities Takeover Disclosure Act, N.Y. Bus. Corp. Law art. 16, was unneeded. In re Application of Presher (2003, Sup) 765 N.Y.S.2d 210

There is no "tender offer" signaling commencement of "takeover bid" under "Business Corporation Law 1601 (a) based merely on purchase of 8.7 percent of corporation's publicly traded stock. Condec Corp. v Farley (1983, SD NY) 578 F. Supp. 85

There is no "offer" under Business Corporation Law 1601 based on directions to broker to purchase shares in open market at particular price. Condec Corp. v Farley (1983, SD NY) 578 F. Supp. 85

Preliminary injunction ordering filing of registration statement under Business Corporation Law § 1601 is denied where, even if statement is required by New York Law, statement required under 15 USCS § 78m(d) has been filed and its adequacy will be determined in related action. Condec Corp. v Farley (1983, SD NY) 578 F. Supp. 85

§ 1602. Disclosure requirement

(a) No offeror shall make a takeover bid unless as soon as practicable on the date of commencement of the takeover bid he files with the attorney general at his New York city office and delivers to the target company at its principal executive offices a registration statement containing the information required by section sixteen hundred three of this article.

(b) An offeror shall make full and fair disclosure to offerees of the material information set forth in the registration statement filed pursuant to subdivision (a) of this section.

(c) No solicitation or recommendation to the offerees of a target company to accept or reject a takeover bid shall be made by or on behalf of an offeror or a target company unless at the time copies of such solicitation or recommendation are first published, sent or given to such offerees, the person making such solicitation or recommendation has filed copies of the solicitation or recommendation with the attorney general at his New York city office.

History: Add, L 1976, ch 893, eff Nov 1, 1976; amd, L 1976, ch 894, eff Nov 1, 1976; L 1980, ch 733, § 2, eff June 30, 1980; L 1985, ch 915, § 4, eff Feb 14, 1986.

CASE ANNOTATIONS

The action of the Attorney General in waiving the requirements of Bus Corp Law §§ 1602-1603 that require the filing of financial statements by the offeror in making a takeover bid respecting a New York corporation was unreasonable and without rational basis; moreover, it was not authorized by the Legislature when it conferred authority on the Attorney General to promulgate rules and regulations to carry out the purposes of the Disclosure Act (Bus Corp Law §§ 1601 et seq.). Injunctive relief, therefore, was available in petitioner's action challenging the validity of the waiver to direct the Attorney General to require the offeror to make the statutory disclosures. Buffalo Forge Co. v Abrams (1981, 1st Dept) 79 A.D.2d 140, 436 N.Y.S.2d 19

State business takeover law requiring registration with state prior to takeover bid constitutes burden on interstate commerce in violation of U.S. Constitution's commerce clause (Art I § 3 cl 8), and is invalid. Edgar v Mite Corp (1982) 457 US 624, 73 L Ed 2d 269, 102 S Ct 2629

§ 1603. Contents of registration statement

(a) The registration statement required to be filed pursuant to subdivision (a) of section sixteen hundred two of this article shall include:

1. Copies of all prospectuses, brochures, advertisements, circulars, letters, or other matter by means of which the offeror proposes to disclose to offerees all information material to a decision to accept or reject the offer;

2. The identity and background of all persons on whose behalf the acquisition of any equity security of the target company has been or is to be effected;

3. The exact title and number of shares outstanding of the class of equity securities being sought, the number of such securities being sought and the consideration being offered therefor;

4. The source and amount of funds or other consideration used or to be used in acquiring any equity security, including a statement describing any securities, other than the existing capital stock or long term debt of the offeror, which are being offered in exchange for the equity securities of the target company and also including copies of all loan or credit agreements and letters of commitment used or to be used to secure financing for the acquisition of any equity security of the target company;

5. A statement of any plans or proposals which the offeror, upon gaining control, may have to liquidate the target company, sell its assets, effect a merger or consolidation of it, or make any other major change in its business, corporate structure, management personnel, or policies of employment;

6. The number of shares of any equity security of the target company of which each offeror is beneficial or record owner or has a right to acquire, directly or indirectly, together with the name and address of each person defined in this section as an offeror;

7. Particulars as to any contracts, arrangements, or understandings to which an offeror is party with respect to any equity security of the target company, including without limitation transfers of any equity security, joint ventures, loans or option arrangements, puts and calls, guarantees of loan, guarantees against loss, guarantees of profits, division of losses or profits, or the giving or withholding of proxies, naming the persons with whom such contracts, arrangements, or understandings have been entered into;

8. Complete information on the organization and operations of the offeror, including without limitation the year of organization, form of organization, jurisdiction in which it is organized, a description of each class of the offeror's capital stock and of its long term debt, financial statements for the current period and for the three most recent annual accounting periods, a description of pending legal proceedings other than routine litigation to which the offeror or any of its

subsidiaries is a party or of which any of their property is the subject, a brief description of the business done and projected by the offeror and its subsidiaries and the general development of such business over the past five years, the names of all directors and executive officers together with biographical summaries of each for the preceding three years to date;

9. A statement as to the potential impact, if any, of the offeror's plans or proposals on the residents of New York state, including any material change in the location of the target company's offices or business activities within this state; any plant or facility relocation; any plant or facility closings; any significant reduction in the workforce at an individual plant or facility; any other material change in the number, job classification, compensation, or other terms and conditions of employment of persons employed by the target company in this state; any material change in the relationships of the target company with suppliers or customers within this state, or any other material changes in the target company's business, corporate structure, management, personnel or activities which would have a substantial impact on residents of this state;

10. Particulars as to any pension plans; profit sharing plans; savings plans; educational opportunities; relocation adjustments; labor relations records, including violations of the federal national labor relations act, occupational safety and health act of 1970, fair labor standards act, or employee retirement and income security act, as amended, finally adjudicated or settled within five years of the commencement of the takeover [takeover]* bid; earnings and dividend growth; community activities; and charitable, cultural, educational and civic contributions of the offeror;

11. If the offeror is a natural person, information concerning his identity and background, including without limitation financial statements for the current and three preceding years, a description of his business activities and affiliations during that time period, and a description of any pending legal or administrative proceedings, other than routine and immaterial litigation, to which the offeror is a party or of which any of his property is the subject; and

12. If debt securities or preferred stock are either offered in the takeover bid or used as a source of funds in making the takeover bid, the investment rating, if any, by a generally recognized rating service of such debt security or preferred stock.

* Bracketed language inserted by the Publisher.

(b) If any material change occurs in the facts set forth in the registration statement required by subdivision (a) of section sixteen hundred two of this article, the offeror who filed such statement shall promptly notify the attorney general and the target company of such change in writing or by telephone confirmed in writing and shall amend the registration statement to reflect such change promptly but not later than the date such change is first published, sent or given to offerees.

(c) The attorney general may permit the omission of any information required by subdivision (a) of this section to be included in the registration statement if he determines that such information is immaterial or otherwise unnecessary for the protection of offerees.

History: Add, L 1976, ch 893, eff Nov 1, 1976; amd, L 1976, ch 894, eff Nov 1, 1976; L 1985, ch 915, § 4, eff Feb 14, 1986.

§ 1604. Enforcement

(a) The attorney general may conduct such investigation as he deems necessary concerning any takeover bid for the purpose of determining compliance with the requirements of this article. As part of such investigation the attorney general may require persons to file statements in writing and under oath with his office, subpoena witnesses, compel their attendance, examine them under oath and require the production of books, records, documents and papers.

(b) In the event the attorney general determines that any person is violating or about to violate any provision of this article, or any order, rule or regulation issued pursuant thereto, he may seek, in a court of competent jurisdiction, an injunction temporarily or permanently barring that person from making or taking part in or continuing a takeover bid or from taking up or paying for shares tendered by offerees pursuant to a takeover bid, and the court may grant the relief applied for or so much thereof as it may deem proper.

History: Add, as § 1606, L 1976, ch 893, eff Nov 1, 1976; amd, L 1976, ch 894, eff Nov 1, 1976; L 1980, ch 733, § 2, eff June 30, 1980; renumbered and amd L 1985, ch 915, § 4, eff Feb 14, 1986.

CASE ANNOTATIONS

State business takeover law requiring registration with state prior to takeover bid constitutes burden on interstate commerce in violation of U.S. Constitution's commerce clause (Art I § 3 cl 8), and is invalid.Edgar v Mite Corp (1982) 457 US 624, 73 L Ed 2d 269, 102 S Ct 2629

Statement by members of Attorney General's staff that they were investigating a tender offer and might take jurisdiction over it conveyed a sufficient threat of bringing an injunctive or criminal action against the offeror so as to give the offeror standing to bring an action challenging the Security Takeover Disclosure Act, but when the Attorney General finally issued a "no action" letter, the challenge became moot. Great Western United Corp. v Kidwell (1977, ND Tex) 439 F. Supp. 420, CCH Fed Secur L Rep ¶ 96187, affd (CA5 Tex) 577 F.2d 1256, CCH Fed Secur L Rep ¶ 96529, revd on other grounds 443 US 173, 61 L Ed 2d 464, 99 S Ct 2710, CCH Fed Secur L Rep ¶ 96900, on remand (CA5 Tex) 602 F.2d 1246

§ 1605. Violations; penalties

(a) Every person who willfully violates any provision of this article shall be guilty of a class E felony; every person who willfully violates any order, rule or regulation issued pursuant thereto, shall be guilty of a class A misdemeanor.

(b) A violation of any provision of this article shall constitute a fraudulent practice within the meaning of article twenty-three-A of the general business law.

(c) Every person who violates any provision of this article shall be subject to a civil penalty of one thousand dollars per violation if a natural person or ten thousand dollars per violation if a corporation. When the violation is the failure to file a registration statement as required by subdivision (a) of section sixteen hundred two of this article, the failure to file a solicitation or recommendation as required by subdivision (c) of section sixteen hundred two of this article, or the failure to amend such registration statement as required by subdivision (b) of section sixteen hundred three of this article, each business day of non-registration or failure to file a recommendation or solicitation or failure to amend constitutes a separate violation. The penalty imposed by this section shall be cumulative and more than one penalty shall be recoverable in the same action in any court of competent jurisdiction.

History: Add as §1607, , L 1976, ch 893, eff Nov 1, 1976; amd, L 1976, ch 894, eff Nov 1, 1976; L 1980, ch 733, § 2, eff June 30, 1980; renumbered and amd, L 1985, ch 915, § 4, eff Feb 14, 1986.

CASE ANNOTATIONS

State business takeover law requiring registration with state prior to takeover bid constitutes burden on interstate commerce in violation of U.S. Constitution's commerce clause (Art § 3 cl 8), is invalid.Edgar v Mite Corp. (1982) 457 US 624, 73 L Ed 2d 269, 102 S Ct 2629

Statement by members of Attorney General's staff that they were investigating a tender offer and might take jurisdiction over it conveyed a sufficient threat of bringing an injunctive or criminal action against the offeror so as to give the offeror standing to bring an action challenging the Security Takeover Disclosure Act, but when the Attorney General finally issued a "no action" letter, the challenge became moot. Great Western United Corp. v Kidwell (1977, ND Tex) 439 F. Supp. 420, CCH Fed Secur L Rep ¶ 96187, affd (CA5 Tex) 577 F.2d 1256, CCH Fed Secur L Rep ¶ 96529, revd on other grounds 443 US 173, 61 L Ed 2d 464, 99 S Ct 2710, CCH Fed Secur L Rep ¶ 96900, on remand (CA5 Tex) 602 F.2d 1246

§ 1606. Administration

(a) This article shall be administered by the attorney general and employees designated by him within the department of law. The attorney general is hereby empowered to promulgate, alter, amend or revoke rules and regulations necessary to carry out the purposes of this article.

(b) The attorney general may establish fees for the filing of any registration statement, not to exceed two thousand five hundred dollars, to recover the costs of administering this article. Such fees may vary according to the maximum consideration payable by the offeror for the securities which are the subject of the takeover bid.

History: Add as §1608, L 1976, ch 893, eff Nov 1, 1976; amd, L 1976, ch 894, eff Nov 1, 1976; renumbered, L 1985, ch 915, § 4, eff Feb 14, 1986.

§ 1607. Prosecutions and immunity

(a) The attorney general may prosecute every person charged with the commission of a criminal offense arising from the violation of any provision of this article. In all such proceedings, the attorney general may appear in person or by his deputy before any court of record or any grand jury and exercise all the powers and perform all the duties in respect of such actions or proceedings which the district attorney would otherwise be authorized or required to exercise or perform; or the attorney general may in his discretion transmit evidence, proof and information as to such offense to the district attorney of the county or counties in which the alleged violation has occurred, and every district attorney to whom such evidence, proof and information is so transmitted shall forthwith proceed to prosecute any corporation, company, association, or officer, manager or agent thereof, or any firm or person charged with such violation. In any such proceeding, wherein the attorney general has appeared either in person or by deputy, the district attorney shall only exercise such powers and perform such duties as are required of him by the attorney general or the deputy attorney general so appearing.

(b) Upon any investigation before the attorney general or his deputy or other officer designated by him, or in any criminal proceeding before any court, magistrate or grand jury, pursuant to or for a violation of any of the provisions of this article, the attorney general, his deputy or other officer designated by him, or the court, magistrate or grand jury, may confer immunity in accordance with the provisions of section 50.20 of the criminal procedure law.

History: Add as §1609, L 1976, ch 893, eff Nov 1, 1976; amd, L 1976, ch 894, eff Nov 1, 1976; renumbered, L 1985, ch 915, § 4, eff Feb 14, 1986.

§ 1608. Designation of secretary of state for service

(a) Every nonresident offeror, whether or not such offeror has filed a registration statement, except a foreign corporation which has appointed and keeps a resident agent in this state, shall be deemed to have appointed the secretary of state as his agent upon whom may be served any lawful process, authorized by this article, with the same effect as though served upon the offeror personally.

(b) Service of process pursuant to this section shall be accomplished by leaving a copy of the process in the office of the secretary of state, but it shall not be effective unless notice of the service and a copy of the process is sent by certified or registered mail to the nonresident offeror served, at his last known address.

History: Add as §1610, L 1976, ch 893, eff Nov 1, 1976; amd, L 1976, ch 894, eff Nov 1, 1976; renumbered, L 1985, ch 915, § 4, eff Feb 14, 1986.

§ 1609. Fraudulent, deceptive or manipulative practices

(a) No person shall make any untrue statement of a material fact or omit to state any material fact necessary in order to make the statements made, in the light of the circumstances under which they are made, not misleading, or engage in any fraudulent, deceptive, or manipulative acts or practices, in connection with any takeover bid or any solicitation of offerees in opposition to or in favor of any such takeover bid.

(b) It shall constitute a violation of this article for any person who is in possession of material information relating to any takeover bid, which information he knows or has reason to know is nonpublic, which he acquired either before or after the commencement of the takeover bid, and which he knows or has reason to know has been acquired directly or indirectly from an offeror, a target company, or any officer, director, partner or employee or any other person acting on behalf of the offeror or target company, to purchase or sell or cause to be purchased or sold, within or from this state, any securities sought or to be sought by such takeover bid or any securities convertible into or exchangeable for any such securities or any option or right to obtain or to dispose of any such securities.

(c) Fraudulent, deceptive or manipulative acts or practices include without limitation those acts and practices proscribed by rules and regulations which the attorney general is hereby empowered to adopt, promulgate, amend and rescind as is necessary to carry out the provisions of this section.

History: Add as §1611, L 1976, ch 893, eff Nov 1, 1976; amd, L 1976, ch 894, eff Nov 1, 1976; renumbered, L 1985, ch 915, § 4, eff Feb 14, 1986.

§ 1610. Exclusions

This article shall not apply when:

(a) The offeror or the target company is a public utility or a public utility holding company as defined in section two of the "Public Utility Holding Company Act of 1935," (49 Stat. 803, 15 U.S.C. 79), as amended, and the takeover bid is subject to approval by the appropriate federal agency as provided in such act;

(b) The offeror or the target company is a bank or a bank holding company as subject to the "Bank Holding Company Act of 1956," (70 Stat. 133, 12 U.S.C. 1841), and subsequent amendments thereto, and the takeover bid is subject to approval by the appropriate federal agency as provided in such act;

(c) The offeror or the target company is a savings and loan holding company as defined in section two of the "Savings and Loan Holding Company Amendments of 1967," (82 Stat. 5, 12 U.S.C. 1730A), as amended, and the takeover bid is subject to approval by the appropriate federal agency as provided in such act;

(d) The offeror and the target company are banks and the offer is part of a merger transaction subject to approval by appropriate federal or state supervisory authorities.

History: Add as §1612, L 1976, ch 893, eff Nov 1, 1976; amd, L 1976, ch 894, eff Nov 1, 1976; renumbered, L 1985, ch 915, § 4, eff Feb 14, 1986.

§ 1611. Validity; saving clause

In the event any provision or application of this article shall be held illegal or invalid for any reason, such holding shall not affect the legality or validity of any other provision or application thereof.

History: Add as §1613, L 1976, ch 893, eff Nov 1, 1976; amd, L 1976, ch 894, eff Nov 1, 1976; renumbered, L 1985, ch 915, § 4, eff Feb 14, 1986.

§ 1612. Requirements for certain takeover bids

If the takeover bid is not subject to the requirements of section 14(d) of the Securities Exchange Act of 1934, 15 U.S.C. § 78n(d), the following additional requirements shall apply to the takeover bid:

(a) The takeover bid shall be made on the same terms to all offerees holding the same class or series of securities.

(b) The period of time within which equity securities may be deposited pursuant to a takeover bid shall not be less than thirty business days.

(c) Equity securities deposited pursuant to a takeover bid may be withdrawn at any time until the expiration of thirty business days after the commencement of the takeover bid and at any time after the expiration of sixty-five days from the commencement of the takeover bid, if the shares have not been purchased, and until the expiration of ten business days following the date of commencement of another offeror's takeover bid for the same equity securities if the shares have not been purchased and if the bidder has received notice or otherwise has knowledge of the commencement of such takeover bid.

(d) Where a takeover bid is made for less than all the outstanding equity securities of a class and where a greater number of such securities is deposited pursuant thereto than the offeror is bound or willing to take up and pay for, the securities taken up and paid for by the offeror shall be taken up and paid for as nearly as possible on a pro rata basis, disregarding fractions, according to the number of securities deposited by each shareholder.

(e) Where an offeror increases the consideration offered in a takeover bid, the offeror shall pay the increased consideration for all equity securities accepted, whether such securities have been accepted by the offeror before or after the increase in consideration.

(f) (1) Within ten days of the filing of a registration statement as required by section sixteen hundred two of this article the attorney general may schedule a public hearing or hearings or conduct such investigation as he deems necessary concerning any takeover bid for the purpose of determining compliance with the requirements of this article;

(2) Any such hearing or investigation shall be declared by order of the attorney general;

(3) Any initial hearing shall commence within twenty days of the filing of a registration statement.

(g) In the event the attorney general shall schedule a public hearing or otherwise conduct an investigation pursuant to subdivision (f) of this section, the attorney general may also, in his discretion, issue an order staying the offeror from purchasing or paying for any shares tendered in response to its takeover bid at any time prior to such purchasing or paying for shares tendered. Every person shall comply with every such order.

(h) In the event the attorney general shall issue a stay payment order pursuant to subdivision (g) of this section, the attorney general shall, no later than thirty days from the issuance of such stay payment order, issue an order containing his findings of fact and conclusions of law.

(i) Any stay payment order issued by the attorney general pursuant to subdivision (g) of this section shall automatically expire within sixty days from its issuance except where the attorney general has in his order containing findings of fact and conclusions of law conditioned the purchase and payment for shares tendered upon changes or modifications in the registration statement, in which event any stay payment order shall be vacated by the attorney general after he is satisfied that such changes or modifications have been publicly disseminated to offerees.

(j) The attorney general may apply, on notice to the offeror and the target company, to a court of competent jurisdiction, and such court may grant an application, for good cause, to extend any of the time periods set forth in this section if an extension is necessary for the protection of offerees.

History: Add, L 1985, ch 915, § 4, eff Feb 14, 1986.

§ 1613. Private right of action

Any offeree whose equity securities are the subject of a takeover bid and who has been injured by any violation of this article may bring an action in his or her own name to enjoin such unlawful act or practice and to recover actual damages together with reasonable attorney fees in the event the offeree is successful.

History: Add, L 1985, ch 915, § 4, eff Feb 14, 1986.

§ 1614. [Deleted]

History: Add, L 1980, ch 733, § 3, eff June 30, 1980; deleted, L 1985, ch 915, § 4, eff Feb 14, 1986.

ARTICLE 17
BENEFIT CORPORATIONS

§ 1701. Application and effect of article

(a) This article shall be applicable to all benefit corporations.

(b) The existence of a provision of this article shall not of itself create any implication that a contrary or different rule of law is or would be applicable to a business corporation that is not a benefit corporation. This article shall not affect any statute or rule of law that is or would be applicable to a business corporation that is not a benefit corporation.

(c) Except as otherwise provided in this article, this chapter shall be applicable to all benefit corporations. The specific provisions of this article shall control over the general provisions of this chapter.

(d) A provision of the certificate of incorporation or bylaws of a benefit corporation may not relax, be inconsistent with or supersede any provision of this article.

History: Add, L 2011, ch 599, § 3, eff Feb 10, 2012.

§ 1702. Definitions

As used in this article, unless the context otherwise requires, the term:

(a) "Benefit corporation" means a business corporation incorporated under this article and whose status as a benefit corporation has not been terminated as provided in this article.

(b) "General public benefit" means a material positive impact on society and the environment, taken as a whole, assessed against a third-party standard, from the business and operations of a benefit corporation.

(c) "Independent" means that a person has no material relationship with a benefit corporation or any of its subsidiaries. A material relationship between a person and a benefit corporation or any of its subsidiaries will be conclusively presumed to exist if:

(1) the person is, or has been within the last three years, an employee of the benefit corporation or any of its subsidiaries;

(2) an immediate family member of the person is, or has been within the last three years, an executive officer of the benefit corporation or any of its subsidiaries; or

(3) the person, or an entity of which the person is a director, officer or other manager or in which the person owns beneficially or of record five percent or more of the equity interests, owns beneficially or of record five percent or more of the shares of the benefit corporation. A percentage of ownership in an entity shall be calculated as if all outstanding rights to

acquire equity interests in the entity had been exercised.

(d) "Minimum status vote" means that, in addition to any other approval or vote required by this chapter, the certificate of incorporation or a bylaw adopted by the shareholders:

(1) The holders of shares of every class or series that are entitled to vote on the corporate action shall be entitled to vote as a class on the corporate action; and

(2) The corporate action must be approved by vote of the shareholders of each class or series entitled to cast at least three-quarters of the votes that all shareholders of the class or series are entitled to cast thereon.

(e) "Specific public benefit," includes:

(1) providing low-income or underserved individuals or communities with beneficial products or services;

(2) promoting economic opportunity for individuals or communities beyond the creation of jobs in the normal course of business;

(3) preserving the environment;

(4) improving human health;

(5) promoting the arts, sciences or advancement of knowledge;

(6) increasing the flow of capital to entities with a public benefit purpose; and

(7) the accomplishment of any other particular benefit for society or the environment.

(f) "Subsidiary" means an entity in which a person owns beneficially or of record fifty percent or more of the equity interests. A percentage of ownership in an entity shall be calculated as if all outstanding rights to acquire equity interests in the entity had been exercised.

(g) "Third-party standard" means a recognized standard for defining, reporting and assessing general public benefit that is:

(1) developed by a person that is independent of the benefit corporation; and

(2) transparent because the following information about the standard is publicly available:

(A) the factors considered when measuring the performance of a business;

(B) the relative weightings of those factors; and

(C) the identity of the persons who developed and control changes to the standard and the process by which those changes are made.

History: Add, L 2011, ch 599, § 3, eff Feb 10, 2012.

§ 1703. Formation of benefit corporations

A benefit corporation shall be formed in accordance with this chapter except that its certificate of incorporation shall also state that it is a benefit corporation.

History: Add, L 2011, ch 599, § 3, eff Feb 10, 2012.

§ 1704. Election of an existing business corporation to become a benefit corporation

(a) A business corporation may become a benefit corporation under this article by amending its certificate of incorporation so that it contains a statement that the corporation is a benefit corporation. The amendment shall not be effective unless it is adopted by at least the minimum status vote.

(b) Any corporation that is not a benefit corporation that is a party to a merger or consolidation in which the surviving or consolidated corporation will be a benefit corporation must approve the plan of merger or consolidation by at least the minimum status vote in addition to any other vote required by this chapter, the certificate of incorporation or the bylaws.

(c) Any corporation that is not a benefit corporation that is party to a merger or consolidation in which shares of stock of such corporation will be converted into a right to receive shares of stock of a benefit corporation must approve the plan of merger or consolidation by at least the minimum status vote in addition to any other vote required by this chapter, the certificate of incorporation or the bylaws.

History: Add, L 2011, ch 599, § 3, eff Feb 10, 2012.

§ 1705. Termination of benefit corporation status

(a) A benefit corporation may terminate its status as such and cease to be subject to this article by amending its certificate of incorporation to delete the statement that the corporation is a benefit corporation. The amendment shall not be effective unless it is adopted by at least the minimum status vote.

(b) If a benefit corporation is a party to a merger or consolidation in which the surviving or new corporation will not be a benefit corporation, the plan of merger or consolidation shall not be effective unless it is adopted by at least the minimum status vote in addition to any other vote required by this chapter, the certificate of incorporation or the bylaws.

(c) Any benefit corporation that is party to a merger or consolidation in which shares of stock of such benefit corporation will be converted into a right to receive shares of stock of a corporation that is not a benefit corporation must approve the plan of merger or consolidation by at least the minimum status vote in addition to any other vote required by this chapter, the certificate of incorporation or the bylaws.

(d) A sale, lease, conveyance, exchange, transfer, or other disposition of all or substantially all of the assets of a benefit corporation, unless the transaction is in the usual and regular course of business of the benefit corporation, shall not be effective unless the transaction is approved by at least the minimum status vote in addition to any other vote required by

Business Corporation Law

this chapter, the certificate of incorporation or the bylaws.

History: Add, L 2011, ch 599, § 3, eff Feb 10, 2012.

§ 1706. Corporate purposes

(a) Every benefit corporation shall have a purpose of creating general public benefit. This purpose is in addition to its purposes under section two hundred one of this chapter and any specific purpose set forth in its certificate of incorporation under paragraph (b) of this section. The purpose to create general public benefit shall be a limitation on the other purposes of the benefit corporation, and shall control over any inconsistent purpose of the benefit corporation.

(b) The certificate of incorporation of a benefit corporation may identify one or more specific public benefits that it is the purpose of the benefit corporation to create in addition to its purposes under section two hundred one of this chapter and paragraph (a) of this section. The identification of a specific public benefit under this paragraph does not limit the obligation of a benefit corporation to create general public benefit.

(c) The creation of general and specific public benefits as provided in paragraphs (a) and (b) of this section is in the best interests of the benefit corporation.

(d) A benefit corporation may amend its certificate of incorporation to add, amend or delete the identification of a specific public benefit that it is the purpose of the benefit corporation to create. The amendment shall not be effective unless it is adopted by at least the minimum status vote.

History: Add, L 2011, ch 599, § 3, eff Feb 10, 2012.

§ 1707. Standard of conduct for directors and officers

(a) In discharging the duties of their respective positions, the board of directors, committees of the board and individual directors and officers of a benefit corporation:

(1) shall consider the effects of any action upon:

(A) the ability for the benefit corporation to accomplish its general and any specific public benefit purpose;

(B) the shareholders of the benefit corporation;

(C) the employees and workforce of the benefit corporation and its subsidiaries and suppliers;

(D) the interests of customers as beneficiaries of the general or specific public benefit purposes of the benefit corporation;

(E) community and societal considerations, including those of any community in which offices or facilities of the benefit corporation or its subsidiaries or suppliers are located;

(F) the local and global environment; and

(G) the short-term and long-term interests of the benefit corporation, including benefits that may accrue to the benefit corporation from its long-term plans and the possibility that these interests may be best served by the continued independence of the benefit corporation;

(2) may consider:

(A) the resources, intent and conduct (past, stated and potential) of any person seeking to acquire control of the corporation; and

(B) any other pertinent factors or the interests of any other group that they deem appropriate; and

(3) shall not be required to give priority to the interests of any particular person or group referred to in subparagraphs one and two of this paragraph over the interests of any other person or group unless the benefit corporation has stated its intention to give priority to interests related to a specific public benefit purpose identified in its certificate of incorporation.

(b) The consideration of interests and factors in the manner required by paragraph (a) of this section:

(1) shall not constitute a violation of the provisions of sections seven hundred fifteen or seven hundred seventeen of this chapter; and

(2) is in addition to the ability of directors to consider interests and factors as provided in section seven hundred seventeen of this chapter.

(c) A director does not have a fiduciary duty to a person that is a beneficiary of the general or specific public benefit purposes of a benefit corporation arising from the status of the person as a beneficiary, unless otherwise stated in the certificate of incorporation or the bylaws of the benefit corporation.

History: Add, L 2011, ch 599, § 3, eff Feb 10, 2012.

§ 1708. Annual benefit report

(a) A benefit corporation must deliver to each shareholder an annual benefit report including:

(1) a narrative description of:

(A) the process and rationale for selecting the third party standard used to prepare the benefit report;

(B) the ways in which the benefit corporation pursued general public benefit during the year and the extent to which general public benefit was created;

(C) the ways in which the benefit corporation pursued any specific public benefit that the certificate of incorporation states it is the purpose of the benefit corporation to create and the extent to which that specific public benefit was created; and

(D) any circumstances that have hindered the creation by the benefit corporation of general or specific public benefit;

(2) an assessment of the performance of the benefit corporation, relative to its general public benefit purpose assessed against a third-party standard

applied consistently with any application of that standard in prior benefit reports or accompanied by an explanation of the reasons for any inconsistent application and, if applicable, assessment of the performance of the benefit corporation, relative to its specific public benefit purpose or purposes;

(3) the compensation paid by the benefit corporation during the year to each director in that capacity; and

(4) the name of each person that owns beneficially or of record five percent or more of the outstanding shares of the benefit corporation.

(b) The benefit report must be sent annually to each shareholder within one hundred twenty days following the end of the fiscal year of the benefit corporation. Delivery of a benefit report to shareholders is in addition to any other requirement to deliver an annual report to shareholders.

(c) A benefit corporation must post its most recent benefit report on the public portion of its website, if any, except that the compensation paid to directors and any financial or proprietary information included in the benefit report may be omitted from the benefit report as posted.

(d) Concurrently with the delivery of the benefit report to shareholders pursuant to paragraph (b) of this section, the benefit corporation must deliver a copy of the benefit report to the department for filing, except that the compensation paid to directors and any financial or proprietary information included in the benefit report may be omitted from the benefit report as filed under this section.

(e) The annual benefit report shall be in addition to all other reporting requirements under this chapter.

History: Add, L 2011, ch 599, § 3, eff Feb 10, 2012.

§ 1709. Conspicuous language on the face of certificates

All certificates representing shares of a benefit corporation shall contain, in addition to any other statements required by the business corporation law, the following conspicuous language on the face of the certificate:

"This entity is a benefit corporation organized under article seventeen of the New York business corporation law."

History: Add, L 2011, ch 599, § 3, eff Feb 10, 2012.

———

ARTICLE 20
EFFECTIVE DATE

History: Formerly Article 14, add, L 1961, ch 855, eff Sept 1, 1963, renumbered Article 20, L 1976, ch 893, eff Nov 1, 1976. (Laws 1976, ch 894, § 6, changed the effective date from Sept 25, 1976 to Nov 1, 1976.)

§ 2001. Effective date

This act shall take effect September first, nineteen hundred sixty-three.

History: Formerly § 1401, add, L 1961, ch 855, and L 1962, ch 837, eff Apr 1, 1963, renumbered § 2001, L 1976, ch 893, eff Nov 1, 1976. (Laws 1976, ch 894, § 6, changed the effective date from Sept 25, 1976 to Nov 1, 1976.)

LIMITED LIABILITY COMPANY LAW

History: Add, L 1994, ch 576, § 1, eff Oct 24, 1994.

ARTICLE I
SHORT TITLE AND DEFINITIONS

§ 101. Short title
§ 102. Definitions

History: Add, L 1994, ch 576, § 1, eff Oct 24, 1994.

§ 101. Short title

This chapter shall be known as the "New York Limited Liability Company Law."

History: Add, L 1994, ch 576, § 1, eff Oct 24, 1994.

CASE ANNOTATIONS

While express language was omitted from N.Y. Ltd. Liab. Co. Law § 101 et seq. permitting a limited liability company (LLC) member to bring a derivative action on behalf of the LLC, members were found to have standing to bring a derivative action alleging that a sale of a hotel owned by the LLC and the execution of a second (secret) lease was unauthorized and void because historically the judiciary had recognized a similar common-law right to bring a derivative action on behalf of a corporation or a limited partnership and most states provided a statutory right to an LLC member to bring a derivative claim. Tzolis v Wolff (2007, App Div, 1st Dept) 829 NYS2d 488

Although a member of a limited liability company (LLC) lacked standing to assert claims under 18 U.S.C.S. §§ 1962(b) and (d) and 1964(c) of the Racketeer Influenced and Corrupt Organizations Act, 18 U.S.C.S. § 1961 et seq., where the member's alleged loss of its share of the LLC's revenue was a derivative injury, the member was permitted to amend its complaint pursuant to Fed. R. Civ. P. 15(a) to assert a derivative action on behalf of the LLC because the question of whether Although a member of a limited liability company (LLC) lacked standing to assert claims under 18 U.S.C.S. §§ 1962(b) and (d) and 1964(c) of the Racketeer Influenced and Corrupt Organizations Act, 18 U.S.C.S. § 1961 et seq., where the member's alleged loss of its share of the LLC's revenue was a derivative injury, the member was permitted to amend its complaint pursuant to Fed. R. Civ. P. 15(a) to assert a derivative action on behalf of the LLC because the question of whether New York law, which did not expressly authorize derivative suits by members of limited liability companies, allowed the member to file a derivative action on behalf of the LLC was unsettled. At the Airport v ISATA, LLC (2006, ED NY) 438 F Supp 2d 55

§ 102. Definitions

(a) "Articles of organization" means the articles of organization filed with the department of state for the purpose of forming a limited liability company pursu-

ant to section two hundred three of this chapter, as amended or restated pursuant to section two hundred eleven or section two hundred fourteen of this chapter.

(a-1) "Affidavit of publication" means the affidavit of the printer or publisher of a newspaper in which a publication pursuant to sections two hundred six, eight hundred two, one thousand two hundred three, and one thousand three hundred six of this chapter has been made. The affidavit of publication shall be in a form substantially as follows:

"Affidavit of Publication Under Section _____ (specify applicable section) of the Limited Liability Company Law

State of New York,

County of _____, ss.:

The undersigned is the printer (or publisher) of _____ (name of newspaper), a _____ (daily or weekly) newspaper published in _____, New York. A notice regarding _____ (name of limited liability company) was published in said newspaper once in each week for six successive weeks, commencing on _____ and ending on _____.

The text of the notice as published in said newspaper is as set forth below, or in the annexed exhibit. This newspaper has been designated by the Clerk of _____ County for this purpose.

_____ (signature)
_____ (printed name),
_____ (jurat)"

The text of the notice set forth in or annexed to each affidavit of publication shall: (i) include only the text of the published notice, (ii) be free of extraneous marks, and (iii) if submitted in paper form, be printed on paper of such size, weight and color, and in ink of such color, and in such font, and be in such other qualities and form not inconsistent with any other provision of law as, in the judgment of the secretary of state, will not impair the ability of the department of state to include a legible and permanent copy thereof in its official records. Nothing in this subdivision shall be construed as requiring the department of state to accept for filing a document submitted in electronic form.

(b) "Authorized foreign limited liability company" means a foreign limited liability company authorized to do business in this state pursuant to article eight of this chapter.

(c) "Authorized person" means a person, whether or not a member, who is authorized by the operating agreement, or otherwise, to act on behalf of a limited liability company or foreign limited liability company.

(d) "Bankruptcy"means bankruptcy under the United States Bankruptcy Code, as amended, or insolvency under any state insolvency act.

(e) "Business" means every trade, occupation, profession or commercial activity.

(e-1) "Certificate of publication" means a certificate presented on behalf of the applicable limited liability company to the department of state together with the affidavits of publication pursuant to section two hundred six, eight hundred two, one thousand two hundred three, or one thousand three hundred six of this chapter. The certificate of publication shall be in a form substantially as follows:

"Certificate of Publication of _____ (name of limited liability company) Under Section _____ (specify applicable section) of the Limited Liability Company Law

The undersigned is the _____ (title) of _____ (name of limited liability company). The published notices described in the annexed affidavits of publication contain all of the information required by the above-mentioned section of the Limited Liability Company Law. The newspapers described in such affidavits of publication satisfy the requirements set forth in the Limited Liability Company Law and the designation made by the county clerk. I certify the foregoing statements to be true under penalties of perjury.

_____ Date
_____ Signature
_____ Printed Name"

(f) "Contribution" means any cash, property, services rendered, or a promissory note or other binding obligation to contribute cash or property or to render services that a member contributes to a limited liability company in his or her capacity as a member.

(g) "Corporation" means a corporation formed under the laws of this state or a foreign corporation as defined in subdivision (j) of this section.

(h) "Court" means every court and judge of competent jurisdiction with respect to a particular matter, action or case.

(i) "Distribution" means the transfer of property by a limited liability company to one or more of its members in his or her capacity as a member.

(j) "Foreign corporation" means a corporation formed under the laws of any jurisdiction, including any foreign country, other than the laws of this state.

(k) "Foreign limited liability company" means an unincorporated organization formed under the laws of any jurisdiction, including any foreign country, other than the laws of this state (i) that is not authorized to do business in this state under any other law of this state and (ii) of which some or all of the persons who are entitled (A) to receive a distribution of the assets thereof upon the dissolution of the organization or otherwise or (B) to exercise voting rights with respect to an interest in the organization have, or are entitled or authorized to have, under the laws of such other jurisdiction, limited liability for the contractual obligations or other liabilities of the organization.

(l) "Foreign limited partnership" means a partnership that is formed under the laws of any jurisdiction, including any foreign country, other than the laws of this state and that has as partners one or more general partners and one or more limited partners.

(m) "Limited liability company" and "domestic limited liability company" mean, unless the context otherwise requires, an unincorporated organization of one or more persons having limited liability for the contractual obligations and other liabilities of the business (except as authorized or provided in section six hundred nine or twelve hundred five of this chapter), other than a partnership or trust, formed and existing under this chapter and the laws of this state.

(n) "Limited partnership" means a limited partnership formed under the laws of this state or a foreign limited partnership as defined in subdivision (l) of this section.

(o) "Majority in interest of the members" means, unless otherwise provided in the operating agreement, the members whose aggregate share of the current profits of the limited liability company constitutes more than one-half of the aggregate of such shares of all members.

(p) "Manager" means, subject to section four hundred one of this chapter, a person designated by the members to manage the limited liability company as provided in the operating agreement.

(q) "Member" means a person who has been admitted as a member of a limited liability company in accordance with the terms and provisions of this chapter and the operating agreement and has a membership interest in a limited liability company with the rights, obligations, preferences and limitations specified under this chapter and the operating agreement.

(r) "Membership interest" means a member's aggregate rights in a limited liability company, including, without limitation: (i) the member's right to a share of the profits and losses of the limited liability company; (ii) the member's right to receive distributions from the limited liability company; and (iii) the member's right to vote and participate in the management of the limited liability company.

(s) "Office of the limited liability company" means the office of the limited liability company, the location of which is stated in the articles of organization of a domestic limited liability company, or in the application for authority of a foreign limited liability company. Such office need not be a place where business activities are conducted by such limited liability company.

(t) "One-third in interest of the members" means, unless otherwise provided in the operating agreement, the members whose aggregate share of the current profits of the limited liability company constitutes one-third of the aggregate of such shares of all members.

(u) "Operating agreement" means any written agreement of the members concerning the business of a limited liability company and the conduct of its affairs and complying with section four hundred seventeen of this chapter.

(v) "Other business entity" means any person other than a natural person or domestic limited liability company.

(w) "Person" means any association, corporation, joint stock company, estate, general partnership (including any registered limited liability partnership or foreign limited liability partnership), limited association, limited liability company (including a professional service limited liability company), foreign limited liability company (including a foreign professional service limited liability company), joint venture, limited partnership, natural person, real estate investment trust, business trust or other trust, custodian, nominee or any other individual or entity in its own or any representative capacity.

(x) "Process" means judicial process and all orders, demands, notices or other papers required or permitted by law to be personally served on a limited liability company or foreign limited liability company, for the purpose of acquiring jurisdiction of such limited liability company in any action or proceeding, civil or criminal, whether judicial, administrative, arbitrative or otherwise, in this state or in the federal courts sitting in or for this state.

(y) "State" means a state, territory or possession of the United States, the District of Columbia or the Commonwealth of Puerto Rico.

(z) "Two-thirds in interest of the members" means, unless otherwise provided in the operating agreement, the members whose aggregate share of the current profits of the limited liability company constitutes two-thirds of the aggregate of such shares of all members.

(aa) "Foreign related limited liability partnership" has the meaning given to it in section two of the partnership law.

(bb) "Profession" has the meaning given to it in subdivision (b) of section twelve hundred one of this chapter.

(cc) "Registered limited liability partnership" has the meaning given to it in section two of the partnership law.

(dd) "Foreign limited liability partnership" has the meaning given to it in section two of the partnership law.

(ee) "Professional service limited liability company" has the meaning given to it in subdivision (f) of section twelve hundred one of this chapter.

(ff) "Foreign professional service limited liability company" has the meaning given to it in subdivision (a) of section thirteen hundred one of this chapter.

(gg) "Professional service corporation" has the meaning given to it in subdivision (e) of section twelve hundred one of this chapter.

(hh) "Foreign professional service corporation" has the meaning given to it in subdivision (d) of section fifteen hundred twenty-five of the business corporation law.

History: Add, L 1994, ch 576, § 1, eff Oct 24, 1994; amd, L 1995, ch 643, § 1, eff Aug 8, 1995; L 2005, ch 767, §§ 1, 2, eff June 1, 2006; L 2006, ch 44, § 1, eff June 1, 2006.

CASE ANNOTATIONS

Plaintiff had standing pursuant to N.Y. Ltd. Liab. Co. Law § 702 to seek dissolution of a limited liability company (LLC), despite his submission of a resignation letter to company counsel; even if the company counsel was properly appointed, he was neither retained to address general business matters on behalf of the LLC nor authorized by the operating agreement to act on behalf of the LLC, and thus was not authorized to represent the LLC and thus could not have accepted plaintiff's purported resignation letter. Caplash v Rochester Oral & Maxillofacial Surgery Assoc. (2009, 4th Dept) 63 App Div 3d 1683, 881 NYS2d 270, subsequent app (2009, 4th Dept) 63 App Div 3d 1686, 880 NYS2d 594.

The determination sustaining a notice of deficiency of personal income tax was affirmed because as the assignee of a membership interest, petitioner was not automatically entitled to participate in the management or affairs of the limited liability company but was entitled to receive the distributions and allocations of profits and losses to which the assignor would be entitled, thus, the assessment was properly imposed. Matter of Murphy v New York State Tax Appeals Trib., 2018 N.Y. App. Div. LEXIS 7354 (N.Y. App. Div. 3d Dep't 2018).

Where there was no basis for a judicial dissolution under the provisions of the articles of organization of a limited liability company, which business relationship the members sought to end, the business operation of the limited liability company was bound by the statutory default provisions of the New York Limited Liability Company Law. Spires v Casterline (2004, Sup) 778 N.Y.S.2d 259

Although an insured's limited liability company was the named insured in an insurance policy, that did not preclude him, as the sole member thereof, from being entitled to coverage under N.Y. Ltd. Liab. Co. Law § 102(w) in order to avoid the policy provisions being illusory. Morette v Kemper, Unitrin Auto & Home Ins. Co., Inc. (2012, Sup) 35 Misc 3d 200, 941 NYS2d 440

Limited liability company's convictions of willful violation of health laws, N.Y. Pub. Health Law § 12-b(2), and second degree falsifying business records, N.Y. Penal Law § 175.05(1), were proper because, inter alia, a limited liability company was a "person" within the meaning of the N.Y. Penal Law § 10.00(7), which defined the term as including an unincorporated association, and may have been convicted of a crime; given the important public interest at issue and the regulatory nature of the crimes committed by defendant's employees, there was no rational basis to exempt defendant from criminal liability under these circumstances, when a corporate nursing home operator would have been held accountable pursuant to N.Y. Penal Law § 20.20. People v Highgate Ltc Mgt., LLC (2009, App Div, 3d Dept) 887 NYS2d 298.

Investor's suit against the CEO of a limited liability company (LLC) based on the CEO's withdrawal of $300,000 of his capital investment from the LLC was time barred because the withdraw was a distribution and subject to the three-year limitation period of N.Y. Ltd. Liab. Co. Law § 508(c) and 18 Del. C. § 18-607(c); the distribution occurred more than three years before the case was filed. The three-year time limitation imposed by § 508(c) overrides the limitation period applicable to any claim brought under the Debtor and Creditor Law with regard to distributions made by a limited liability company to a member. Mostel v Petrycki (2009, Sup) 242 NYLJ 50, 885 NYS2d 397.

Pursuant to N.Y. Ltd. Liab. Co. Law § 102(d), "bankruptcy" is defined as bankruptcy under the U.S. Bankruptcy Code, or applicable state insolvency statute. Liquidation was not synonymous with bankruptcy and the court would not equate the two for the purposes of including bankruptcy as an event requiring the consent of the member; if anything, the act of filing for bankruptcy is more equivalent to an act to "bring or defend, settle, pay, collect, compromise, arbitrate, resort to legal action, or otherwise adjust claims or demands of or against the (debtor)" which the Managing Member was expressly permitted to do. In re E. End Dev. (2013, BC ED NY) 491 BR 633, 57 BCD 250.

Annual filing fee per member imposed on limited liability company under CLS Tax § 658(c)(3) does not apply to investors who own contractual non-voting economic interest in portion of member's interest. N.Y. Adv Op Comm T & F TSB-A-02-(3)I

Limited liability company (LLC) seeking to be issued insurance agent's license may include as member natural person who is not licensed as insurance agent provided that LLC has named natural person (who meets same requirements that person seeking to be licensed as individual for same kind of license is required to meet) as its sub-licensee, to act individually as its agent. Insurance Department, Opinions of General Counsel, Opinion Number 03-10-15

Term "institution"as applied in CLS Ins Art 14 includes limited liability companies. Insurance Department, Opinions of General Counsel, Opinion Number 05-04-15

Ownership interests in limited liability company (LLC) are similar to "partnership interests"as defined by CLS Ins § 1401(a)(3), and thus where Insurance Law permits or prohibits particular partnership interest, ownership interest in LLC is permitted or prohibited, respectively. Insurance Department, Opinions of General Counsel, Opinion Number 05-04-15

Since limited liability corporations (LLCs) are similar to corporations, where CLS Ins Art 14 permits or prohibits certain investments in shares, investments in LLCs are permitted or prohibited, respectively, except where Insurance Law refers to specific type of shares, such as preferred shares, or interest in LLC, which fails to satisfy any other requirements for particular type of investment or context requires otherwise. Insurance Department, Opinions of General Counsel, Opinion Number 05-04-15

Order granting a petition for dissolution of a limited liability company (LLC) under N.Y. Ltd. Liab. Co. Law § 702 was error because, inter alia, the petitioning member failed to establish, in the context of the terms of the operating agreement, that (1) the management of the LLC was unable or unwilling to reasonably permit or promote the stated purpose of the LLC to be realized or achieved, or (2) continuing the LLC was financially unfeasible; "deadlock" was a basis, in and of itself, for judicial dissolution under N.Y. Bus. Corp. Law § 1104, but no such independent ground for dissolution was available under § 702. It was improper to apply partnership dissolution standards to a cause for dissolution of a limited liability company. Matter of 1545 Ocean Ave., LLC v Crown Royal Ventures, LLC (2010, App Div, 2d Dept) 893 NYS2d 590.

Pursuant to N.Y. Ltd. Liab. Co. Law § 102(d), "bankruptcy" is defined as bankruptcy under the U.S. Bankruptcy Code, or applicable state insolvency statute. Liquidation was not synonymous with bankruptcy and the court would not equate the two for the purposes of including bankruptcy as an event requiring the consent of the member; if anything, the act of filing for bankruptcy is more equivalent to an act to "bring or defend, settle, pay, collect, compromise, arbitrate, resort to legal action, or otherwise adjust claims or demands of or against the (debtor)" which the Managing Member was expressly permitted to do. In re E. End Dev. (2013, BC ED NY) 491 BR 633, 57 BCD 250.

ARTICLE II
FORMATION

History: Add, L 1994, ch 576, § 1, eff Oct 24, 1994.

§ 201.   Purpose

A limited liability company may be formed under this chapter for any lawful business purpose or purposes except to do in this state any business for which another statute specifically requires some other business entity or natural person to be formed or used for such business.

History: Add, L 1994, ch 576, § 1, eff Oct 24, 1994.

CASE ANNOTATIONS

Sewage-works corporation organized under Transportation Corporation Law may not reorganize as limited liability company. 1998 Ops Atty Gen I 98-47

Law firm and an affiliate lacked standing to seek a declaration that N.Y. R. Prof. Conduct 5.4 (N.Y. Comp. Codes R. & Regs. tit. 22, § 1200.0) was unconstitutional because it prohibited non-lawyer equity investment in law practices, as invalidating the rule would not have redressed the claimed injury. The affiliate was a limited liability company that was precluded from practicing law by N.Y. Jud. Law § 495; the practice of law was not a "lawful business purpose" under N.Y. Ltd. Liab. Co. Law § 201. Jacoby & Meyers, LLP v Presiding Justices of the Appellate Div. (2012, SD NY) 847 F Supp 2d 590.

Limited liability companies generally, as opposed to professional services limited liability companies, may not lawfully practice law in New York. Jacoby & Meyers, LLP v Presiding Justices of the Appellate Div. (2012, SD NY) 847 F Supp 2d 590

§ 202.   Powers

Unless the articles of organization provide otherwise and subject to any limitations provided in this chapter or any other law of this state, a limited liability company may:

(a) sue or be sued, or institute, participate in or defend any action or proceeding, whether judicial, arbitrative, administrative or otherwise, in its name;

(b) purchase, take, receive, lease or otherwise acquire, own, hold, improve, use or otherwise deal in or with real or personal property or an interest in real or personal property, wherever situated;

(c) sell, convey, assign, encumber, mortgage, pledge, lease, exchange, transfer, create a security interest in or otherwise dispose of all or part of its property or assets;

(d) purchase, take, receive, subscribe for or otherwise acquire, own, hold, vote, employ, sell, mortgage, lend, pledge or otherwise dispose of and otherwise use and deal in and with shares or other interests in, securities issued by and direct or indirect obligations of:

(1) other persons; or

(2) any government, state, territory, governmental district or municipality or of any instrumentality or subdivision of any of them;

(e) make contracts, including, but not limited to, contracts of guaranty and suretyship, incur liabilities, borrow money at such rates of interest as the limited liability company may determine, issue its notes, bonds or other obligations, secure any of its obligations by mortgage, pledge or other encumbrance of all or any part of its property, franchises and income, make contracts of guaranty and suretyship that are necessary or convenient to the conduct, promotion or attainment of the business of (i) a limited liability company or other person at least a majority of the outstanding membership or other ownership interests of which are owned, directly or indirectly, by the contracting limited liability company, (ii) a limited liability company or other person that owns, directly or indirectly, at least a majority of the outstanding membership interests of the contracting limited liability company or (iii) a limited liability company or other person at least a majority of the outstanding membership or other ownership interests of which are owned, directly or indirectly, by a limited liability company or other person that owns, directly or indirectly, at least a majority of the outstanding membership interests of the contracting limited liability company, which contracts of guaranty and suretyship shall be deemed to be necessary or convenient to the conduct, promotion or attainment of the business of the contracting limited liability company and make other contracts of guaranty and suretyship that are necessary or convenient to the conduct, promotion or attainment of the business of the contracting limited liability company. A limited liability company may make any contracts of guaranty and suretyship that are not necessary or convenient to the conduct, promotion or attainment of the business of the contracting limited liability company upon the vote of the percentage in interest of the members or class or classes of members provided in the operating agreement, or if no such percentage is so stated, upon the vote of a majority in interest of the members entitled to vote thereon; provided, however, that the operating agreement may provide that no such vote is required;

(f) lend money for any lawful purpose, invest or reinvest its funds, or take and hold real or personal property as security for the payment of funds so loaned or invested;

(g) conduct its business, carry on its operations, maintain offices and exercise the powers granted by this chapter in any state, foreign country or other jurisdiction;

(h) elect or appoint managers, employees and agents of the limited liability company, define their duties and fix their compensation;

(i) assist, lend money to and transact other business with a member, manager, agent or employee of such limited liability company;

(j) make and alter its operating agreement, not inconsistent with its articles of organization or with the laws of this state, concerning the business of the limited liability company and the conduct of its affairs;

(k) indemnify a member or manager or any other person;

(l) pay pensions and establish pension plans, pension trusts, profit-sharing plans, profit-sharing trusts, equity bonus plans, equity option plans and other incentive plans for any of its members, managers, employees, agents or consultants or any of the directors, officers, managers, employees, agents or consultants of its affiliates;

(m) make donations for the public welfare or for charitable, scientific, religious, civic, educational or similar purposes;

(n) transact any lawful business in aid of governmental policy;

(o) be a promoter, shareholder, general partner, limited partner, member, associate or manager of any association, corporation, partnership, limited partnership, limited liability company, joint venture, trust or other entity or enterprise;

(p) cease its activities, cancel its articles of organization or dissolve; and

(q) have and exercise all powers, in addition to those set forth in subdivisions (a) through (p) of this section, not inconsistent with law, necessary or convenient to effect any or all of the purposes for which the limited liability company is formed. In order for a limited liability company to exercise the powers enumerated in this chapter, it is not necessary to set forth such powers in the articles of organization.

History: Add, L 1994, ch 576, § 1, eff Oct 24, 1994.

Sub q, add, L 1997, ch 470, § 1, eff Aug 26, 1997.

§ 203. Formation

(a) One or more persons may act as an organizer or organizers to form a limited liability company by (i) preparing the articles of organization of such limited liability company in accordance with subdivision (e) of this section, (ii) executing such articles of organization in accordance with section two hundred seven of this article and (iii) filing such articles, entitled "Articles of organization of .... (name of limited liability company) under section two hundred three of the Limited Liability Company Law," in accordance with section two hundred nine of this article.

(b) An organizer may, but need not be, a member of the limited liability company that he or she forms.

(c) At the time of its formation, a limited liability company must have at least one member.

(d) A limited liability company is formed at the time of the filing of the initial articles of organization with the department of state or at any later time specified in the articles of organization, not to exceed sixty days from the date of such filing. The filing of the articles of organization shall, in the absence of actual fraud, be conclusive evidence of the formation of the limited liability company as of the time of filing or effective date if later, except in an action or special proceeding brought by the attorney general. A limited liability company formed under this chapter shall be a separate legal entity, the existence of which as a separate legal entity shall continue until the cancellation of the limited liability company's articles of organization.

(e) The articles of organization of a limited liability company shall set forth:

(1) the name of the limited liability company;

(2) the county within this state in which the office of the limited liability company is to be located or if the limited liability company shall maintain more than one office in this state, the county in which the principal office of the limited liability company is to be located;

(3) if the limited liability company is to have a specific date of dissolution in addition to the events of dissolution set forth in section seven hundred one of this chapter, the latest date on which the limited liability company is to dissolve;

(4) a designation of the secretary of state as agent of the limited liability company upon whom process against it may be served and the post office address within or without this state to which the secretary of state shall mail a copy of any process against the limited liability company served upon him or her;

(5) if the limited liability company is to have a registered agent, its name and address within this state and a statement that the registered agent is to be the agent of the limited liability company upon whom process against it may be served;

(6) if all or specified members are to be liable in their capacity as members for all or specified debts, obligations or liabilities of the limited liability company as authorized pursuant to section six hundred nine of this chapter, a statement that all or specified members are so liable for such debts, obligations or liabilities in their capacity as members of the limited liability company as authorized pursuant to section six hundred nine of this chapter; and

(7) any other provisions, not inconsistent with law, that the members elect to include in the articles or organization for the regulation of the internal affairs of the limited liability company, including, but not limited to, (A) the business purpose for which the limited liability company is formed, (B) a statement of whether there are limitations on the authority of members or managers or a class or classes thereof to bind the limited liability company and (C) any provisions that are required or permitted to be included in the operating agreement of the limited liability company pursuant to section four hundred seventeen of this chapter.

History: Add, L 1994, ch 576, § 1, eff Oct 24, 1994.

Sub a, amd, L 1997, ch 470, § 2, eff Aug 26, 1997.

Sub e, add, L 1997, ch 470, § 2, eff Aug 26, 1997.

CASE ANNOTATIONS

Sewage-works corporation organized under Transportation Corporation Law may not reorganize as limited liability company. 1998 Ops Atty Gen I 98-47

Purported transfer of real estate to a limited liability company was void because the deed was executed two weeks before the articles of organization were filed with the state as required by N.Y. Ltd. Liab. Co. Law § 203, and, as there had been no bona fide attempt to comply with the filing requirement, the limited liability company did not operate as a de facto company. Matter of Hausman (2009) 13 NY3d 408.

Where the purchaser, a limited liability company, entered into the real estate contract a month before the purchaser became a limited liability company by filing its articles of organization pursuant to N.Y. Ltd. Liab. Co. Law § 203, the purchaser lacked the capacity to enter into the contract. 442 Decatur St., LLC v Spheres Realty, Inc. (2005, A.D., 2d Dept) 787 N.Y.S.2d 669

Limited liability company's convictions of willful violation of health laws, N.Y. Pub. Health Law § 12-b(2), and second degree falsifying business records, N.Y. Penal Law § 175.05(1), were proper because, inter alia, a limited liability company was a "person" within the meaning of the N.Y. Penal Law § 10.00(7), which defined the term as including an unincorporated association, and may have been convicted of a crime; given the important public interest at issue and the regulatory nature of the crimes committed by defendant's employees, there was no rational basis to exempt defendant from criminal liability under these circumstances, when a corporate nursing home operator would have been held accountable pursuant to N.Y. Penal Law § 20.20. People v Highgate Ltc Mgt., LLC (2009, App Div, 3d Dept) 887 NYS2d 298.

Because the promoters planned a business venture, organized limited liability companies, and solicited the investors to invest in them, they violated their N.Y. Ltd. Liab. Co. Law § 203(a)(iii) fiduciary relationship by failing to reveal that they would receive commissions from others in addition to their disclosed profit from the venture. Roni LLC v Arfa (2010, 1st Dept) 74 App Div 3d 442, 903 NYS2d 352.

Where an insured, which sought coverage for a personal injury claim filed by one of the insured's tenants, claimed (1) that, due to the insured's failure to update its address with the Secretary of State, the insured's agent for service pursuant to N.Y. Limited Liability Company Law § 203(e)(4), the insured did not receive actual notice of the tenant's action when the tenant's complaint was served on the Secretary and (2) that the insured's obligation to notify the insurer was not triggered until the insured received actual, rather than constructive notice, of the tenant's action, the question of whether the insurer's disclaimer of coverage based on the insured's failure to provide earlier notice should be sustained was certified to the New York Court of Appeals pursuant to 2nd Cir. R. § 0.27 and N.Y. Comp. Codes R. & Regs. tit. 22, § 500.27(a) because the issue of when the notification requirement was triggered implicated broader questions of insurance law and public policy and the recurring question of state law had led to divergent opinions in the federal district courts. Briggs Ave., L.L.C. v Ins. Corp. (2008, CA2) 516 F3d 42.

While the limited liability company (LLC) was clearly a necessary party to plaintiff's derivative suit (the LLC was a separate legal entity with rights and obligations distinct from those of its members, and the court could not presume its interests were not also distinct from those of its members), it could not be made a party to the action without destroying jurisdiction (as the LLC shared citizenship with both plaintiff and defendant, the court would have lacked diversity jurisdiction under 28 U.S.C.S. § 1332 were it to be a party). Bartfield v Murphy (2008, SD NY) 578 F Supp 2d 638.

§ 204. Limited liability company name

The name of each limited liability company as set forth in its articles of organization:

(a) shall contain without abbreviation the words "Limited Liability Company" or the abbreviation "L.L.C." or "LLC";

(b) (1) shall be such as to distinguish it from the name of (i) any domestic limited liability company, (ii) any authorized foreign limited liability company or (iii) a fictitious name of an authorized foreign limited liability company filed pursuant to section eight hundred two of this chapter, in each case, as such names appear on the index of names of existing domestic and authorized foreign limited liability companies of any type or kind, including fictitious names of authorized foreign limited liability companies filed pursuant to section eight hundred two of this chapter, in the department of state, or names the right to which are reserved;

(2) shall be such as to distinguish it from (i) the names of domestic business corporations, domestic not-for-profit corporations and other domestic corporations of any type or kind that are formed by a filing in the department of state, (ii) the names of authorized foreign business corporations, authorized foreign not-for-profit corporations and other authorized foreign corporations of any type or kind that are authorized to do business or conduct activities in this state by reason of a filing in the department of state, (iii) the fictitious names of authorized foreign business corporations, authorized foreign not-for-profit corporations and other authorized foreign corporations of any type or kind that are authorized to do business or conduct activities in this state by reason of a filing in the department of state, (iv) the names of domestic limited partnerships, (v) the names of authorized foreign limited partnerships, or (vi) the fictitious names of authorized foreign limited partnerships, in each case, as such names appear on the index of names of existing domestic and authorized foreign corporations of any type or kind, including fictitious names of authorized foreign corporations of any type or kind, in the department of state, or on the index of names of existing domestic or authorized foreign limited partnerships, including fictitious names of authorized foreign limited partnerships, in the department of state, or names the rights to which are reserved; provided, however, that no limited liability company that was formed prior to the effective date of this paragraph and no foreign limited liability company that was qualified to do business in this state prior to such effective date shall be required to change the name or fictitious name it had on such effective date solely by reason of such name or fictitious name being indistinguishable from the name or fictitious name of any domestic or authorized foreign corporation or limited partnership or from any name the right to which is reserved by or on behalf of any domestic or foreign corporation or limited partnership;

(c) shall, unless the limited liability company or foreign limited liability company shall have complied with the provisions of section one hundred thirty of the general business law, be the name used by the limited liability company in its conduct of business;

(d) shall not contain any word or phrase, or any abbreviation or derivative thereof, the use of which is prohibited or restricted by any other statute of this state, unless in the latter case the restrictions have been complied with;

(e) shall not contain the following phrases or any abbreviation or derivative thereof:

board of trade	state police
chamber of commerce	state trooper
community renewal	tenant relocation
corporation	urban development
incorporated	urban relocation
partnership	

(f) shall not contain the following words, or any abbreviation or derivative thereof:

acceptance	guaranty
annuity	indemnity
assurance	insurance
attorney	investment
bank	lawyer
benefit	loan
bond	mortgage
casualty	savings
doctor	surety
endowment	title
fidelity	trust
finance	underwriter

unless the approval of the superintendent of financial services is attached to the articles of organization or unless the word "doctor" or "lawyer" or an abbreviation or derivative thereof is used in a context that clearly denotes a purpose other than the practice of law or medicine;

(g) shall not, unless the approval of the state department of social services is attached to the articles of organization or application for authority, contain the word "blind"or "handicapped."Such approval shall be granted by the state department of social services if in its opinion the word "blind"or "handicapped"as used in the limited liability company's proposed name will not tend to mislead or confuse the public into believing that the limited liability company is organized for charitable or nonprofit purposes related to the blind or the handicapped; and

(h) shall not, unless the approval of the attorney general is attached to the articles of organization or application for authority, contain the word "exchange"or any abbreviation or derivative thereof. Such approval shall not be granted by the attorney general if in his or her opinion the use of the word "exchange"in the limited liability company's proposed name would falsely imply that the limited liability company conducts its business at a place where trade is carried on in securities or commodities by brokers, dealers or merchants.

(i) shall not contain the following terms: "school," "education," "elementary," "secondary," "kindergarten," "prekindergarten," "preschool," "nursery school," "museum," "history," "historical," "historical society," "arboretum," "library," "college," "university"or other term restricted by section two hundred twenty-four of the education law; "conservatory," "academy," or "institute" or any abbreviation or derivative of such terms, shall have endorsed thereon or annexed thereto the consent of the commissioner of education.

History: Add, L 1994, ch 576, § 1, eff Oct 24, 1994; amd, , L 1995, ch 643, § 2; so designated sub (b), par (1), L 2004, ch 344, § 1, eff Aug 10, 2004, L 2005, ch 316, § 8, eff Jan 1, 2006, L 2011, ch 62, § 104 (Part A), eff Oct 3, 2011, L 2012, ch 155, § 63, eff July 18, 2012.

CASE ANNOTATIONS

With respect to timber home purchasers' breach of contract claims, first authorized representative of corporations was not entitled to summary judgment as to his personal liability as there was no reference in the construction contract to the status of the representative's company as a limited liability company under N.Y. Limited Liability Company Law § 204(a) or to the representative's status as an officer or representative of that company. DeAngelis v Timberpeg East, Inc. (2008, 3d Dept) 51 App Div 3d 1175, 858 NYS2d 410.

Limited liability companies generally, as opposed to professional services limited liability companies, may not lawfully practice law in New York. Jacoby & Meyers, LLP v Presiding Justices of the Appellate Div. (2012, SD NY) 847 F Supp 2d 590

§ 205.   Reservation of name

(a) Subject to section two hundred four of this article, the exclusive right to the use of a name may be reserved by:

(1) any person intending to form or cause the formation of a domestic limited liability company under this chapter;

(2) any domestic limited liability company or any authorized foreign limited liability company intending to change its name;

(3) any foreign limited liability company intending to apply for authority to do business in this state and to adopt that name; and

(4) any person intending to form a foreign limited liability company and intending to have it apply for authority to do business in this state.

(b) A fictitious name for use pursuant to section eight hundred two of this chapter may be reserved by:

(1) any foreign limited liability company intending to apply for authority to do business in this state pursuant to section eight hundred two of this chapter;

(2) any authorized foreign limited liability company intending to change the fictitious name under which it does business in this state; and

(3) any authorized foreign limited liability company that has changed its name in its jurisdiction, such new name not being available in this state.

(c) Application to reserve a limited liability company name shall be delivered to the department of state. It shall set forth the name and address of the applicant, the name to be reserved and a statement of the basis for the application under subdivision (a) or (b) of this section. The secretary of state may require that there be included in the application a statement as to the nature of the business to be conducted by the limited liability company it being sufficient to state, either alone, or with other purposes, that the limited liability company intends to conduct any lawful act or activity for which limited liability companies may be formed under this chapter, provided that it also state that it is not intended to be formed to engage in any act or activity requiring the consent or approval of any state official, department, board or agency or other body without such consent or approval first being obtained. If the name is available for use by the applicant for a limited liability company, the department of state shall reserve the name for the use of the applicant for a period of sixty days and issue a certificate of reservation. The restrictions and qualifications set forth in section two hundred four of this article are not waived by the issuance of a certificate of reservation. The certificate of reservation shall include the name of the applicant, the name reserved and the date of reservation. The certificate of reservation (or in lieu thereof an affidavit by the applicant or by his or her agent or attorney that the certificate of reservation has been lost or destroyed) shall accompany the articles of organization or the application for authority when either is delivered to the department of state. The secretary of state may extend the reservation for additional periods of not more than sixty days each, upon the written request of the applicant or his or her attorney in fact or agent delivered to the department of state and filed before expiration of the reservation period then in effect. Such request shall have attached to it the certificate of reservation. No more than two such extensions shall be granted.

(d) Upon request of the applicant, delivered to the department of state before the expiration of the reserved period, the department shall cancel the reservation.

History: Add, L 1994, ch 576, § 1, eff Oct 24, 1994. Sub (d), add, L 1997, ch 470, § 3, eff Aug 26, 1997.

§ 206.   Affidavits of publication

(a) Within one hundred twenty days after the effectiveness of the initial articles of organization as determined pursuant to subdivision (d) of section two hundred three of this article, a copy of the same or a notice containing the substance thereof shall be published once in each week for six successive weeks, in two newspapers of the county in which the office of the limited liability company is located, one newspaper to be printed weekly and one newspaper to be printed daily, to be designated by the county clerk. When such county is located within a city with a population of one million or more, such designation shall be as though the copy or notice were a notice or advertisement of judicial proceedings. Proof of the publication required by this subdivision , consisting of the certificate of publication of the limited liability company with the affidavits of publication of such newspapers annexed thereto, must be filed with the department of state. Notwithstanding any other provision of law, if the office of the limited liability company is located in a county wherein a weekly or daily newspaper of the county, or both, has not been so designated by the county clerk, then the publication herein required shall be made in a weekly or daily newspaper of any county, or both, as the case may be, which is contiguous to, such county, provided that any such newspaper meets all the other requirements of this subdivision. A copy or notice published in a newspaper other than the newspaper or newspapers designated by the county clerk shall not be deemed to be one of the publications required by this subdivision. The notice shall include: (1) the name of the limited liability company; (2) the date of filing of the articles of organization with the department of state and, if the date of formation is not the date of filing of the articles of organization, the date of the formation of the limited liability company; (3) the county within this state, in which the office of the limited liability company is located; (3-a) the street address of the principal business location, if any; (4) a statement that the secretary of state has been designated as agent of the limited liability company upon whom process against it may be served and the post office address within or without this state to which the secretary of state shall mail a copy of any process against it served upon him or her; (5) if the limited liability company is to have a registered agent, his or her name and address within this state and a statement that the registered agent is to be the agent of the limited liability company upon whom process against it may be served; (6) if the limited liability company is to have a specific date of dissolution in addition to the events of dissolution set forth in section seven hundred one of this chapter, the latest date upon which the limited liability company is to dissolve; and (7) the character or purpose of the business of such limited liability company. Where, at any time after completion of the first of the six weekly publications required by this subdivision and prior to the completion of the sixth such weekly publication, there is a change in any of the information contained in the copy or notice as published, the limited liability company may complete the remaining publications of the original copy or notice, and the limited liability company shall not be required to publish any further or amended copy or notice. Where, at any time after completion of the six weekly publications required by this subdivision, there is a change to any of the information contained in the copy or notice as published, no further or amended publication or republication shall be required to be made. If within one hundred twenty days after its formation, proof of such publication, consisting of the certificate of publication of the limited liability company with the affidavits of publication of the newspapers annexed thereto has not been filed with the department of state, the authority of such limited liability company to carry on, conduct or transact any business in this state shall be suspended, effective as of the expiration of such one hundred twenty day period. The failure of a limited liability company to cause such copy or notice to be published and such certificate of publication and affidavits of publication to be filed with the department of state within such one hundred twenty day period or the suspension of such limited liability company's authority to carry on, conduct or transact business in this state pursuant to this subdivision shall not limit or impair the validity of any contract or act of such limited liability company, or any right or remedy of

any other party under or by virtue of any contract, act or omission of such limited liability company, or the right of any other party to maintain any action or special proceeding on any such contract, act or omission, or right of such limited liability company to defend any action or special proceeding in this state, or result in any member, manager or agent of such limited liability company becoming liable for the contractual obligations or other liabilities of the limited liability company. If, at any time following the suspension of a limited liability company's authority to carry on, conduct or transact business in this state pursuant to this subdivision, such limited liability company shall cause proof of publication in substantial compliance with the provisions (other than the one hundred twenty day period) of this subdivision, consisting of the certificate of publication of the limited liability company with the affidavits of publication of the newspapers annexed thereto, to be filed with the department of state, such suspension of such limited liability company's authority to carry on, conduct or transact business shall be annulled.

(b)(1) A limited liability company which was formed prior to the effective date of this subdivision and which complied with the publication and filing requirements of this section as in effect prior to such effective date shall not be required to make any publication or republication or any filing under subdivision (a) of this section, and shall not be subject to suspension pursuant to this section.

(2) Within twelve months after the effective date of this subdivision, a limited liability company, which was formed prior to such effective date, and which did not comply with the publication and filing requirements of this section as in effect prior to such effective date, shall publish a copy of its articles of organization or a notice containing the substance thereof in the manner required (other than the one hundred twenty day period) by this section as in effect prior to such effective date and file proof of such publication, consisting of the certificate of publication of the limited liability company with the affidavits of publication of the newspapers annexed thereto, with the department of state.

(3) If a limited liability company that is subject to the provisions of paragraph two of this subdivision fails to file the required proof of publication with the department of state within twelve months after the effective date of this subdivision, its authority to carry on, conduct or transact any business in this state shall be suspended, effective as of the expiration of such twelve month period.

(4) The failure of a limited liability company that is subject to the provisions of paragraph two of this subdivision to fully comply with the provisions of said paragraph two or the suspension of such limited liability company's authority to carry on, conduct or transact any business in this state pursuant to paragraph three of this subdivision shall not impair or limit the validity of any contract or act of such

limited liability company, or any right or remedy of any other party under or by virtue of any contract, act or omission of such limited liability company, or the right of any other party to maintain any action or special proceeding on any such contract, act or omission, or right of such limited liability company to defend any action or special proceeding in this state, or result in any member, manager or agent of such limited liability company becoming liable for the contractual obligations or other liabilities of the limited liability company.

(5) If, at any time following the suspension of a limited liability company's authority to carry on, conduct or transact business in this state, pursuant to paragraph three of this subdivision, such limited liability company shall cause proof of publication in substantial compliance with the provisions (other than the one hundred twenty day period) of subdivision (a) of this section, consisting of the certificate of publication of the limited liability company with the affidavits of publication of the newspapers annexed thereto, to be filed with the department of state, such suspension of such limited liability company's authority to carry on, conduct or transact business shall be annulled.

(6) For the purposes of this subdivision, a limited liability company which was formed prior to the effective date of this subdivision shall be deemed to have complied with the publication and filing requirements of this section as in effect prior to such effective date if (i) the limited liability company was formed on or after January first, nineteen hundred ninety-nine and prior to such effective date and the limited liability company filed at least one affidavit of the printer or publisher of a newspaper with the department of state at any time prior to such effective date, or (ii) the limited liability company was formed prior to January first, nineteen hundred ninety-nine, without regard to whether the limited liability company did or did not file any affidavit of the printer or publisher of a newspaper with the secretary of state.

(c) The information in a notice published pursuant to this section shall be presumed to be in compliance with and satisfaction of the requirements of this section.

History: Add, L 1994, ch 576, § 1; amd, L 1997, ch 470, § 4, eff Aug 26, 1997 (see 1997 note below); L 1999, ch 420, § 1; L 2005, ch 767, § 3; L 2006, ch 44, § 3, eff June 1, 2006.

CASE ANNOTATIONS

N.Y. Ltd. Liab. Co. Law § 206, requiring a limited liability company to publish its articles of organization or comparable specified information for six successive weeks in two local newspapers within 120 days of its formation to be able to maintain an action in any New York court, did not violate the right of access to the civil courts, under N.Y. Const. art. 10, § 4, as limited liability companies had no such general right, or substantive due process, as the companies' right of access to the state's civil courts under state law was not arbitrarily altered or restricted, or equal protection, as the statute was rationally related to a legitimate governmental interest. Barklee Realty Co. LLC v Pataki (2003, A.D., 1st Dept) 765 N.Y.S.2d 599

Barring the maintenance of court proceedings by limited liability companies that had not complied with the publication requirement of N.Y. Ltd. Liab. Co. § 206 was rationally related to the goal of ensuring that those companies actually published the designated information. Barklee Realty Co. LLC v Pataki (2003, A.D., 1st Dept) 765 N.Y.S.2d 599

Motion to dismiss a breach of contract case alleging that a newspaper charged higher rates to publish legal notices relating to the formation of partnerships, limited liability companies, and other business entities based on geographical location was proper because such was not unlawful; while the various county clerks situated within the city of New York designated the publisher's newspaper as one of two for the publication of the legal notices at issue, the use of the publisher's newspaper as an officially-designated newspaper did not make the resulting absence of choice unconscionable because such designation was pursuant to legislative authority. NCJ Cleaners, LLC v ALM Media, Inc. (2008, 2d Dept) 48 App Div 3d 766, 852 NYS2d 384.

§ 207.   Execution of articles or certificates

(a) Each article or certificate required by this chapter to be filed with the department of state shall be executed in the following manner:

(1) the initial articles of organization must be signed by an organizer or organizers of the limited liability company;

(2) a certificate of amendment must be signed by at least one member, manager or authorized person of the limited liability company;

(3) restated articles of organization or amended and restated articles of organization must be signed by at least one member, manager or authorized person of the limited liability company;

(4) a certificate of correction must be signed by at least one member, manager or authorized person of the limited liability company;

(5) a certificate of cancellation must be signed by at least one member, manager or authorized person of the limited liability company; and

(6) all other certificates must be signed by at least one member, manager or authorized person of the limited liability company.

(b) Any person may sign any articles or certificate by an attorney in fact. Powers of attorney relating to the signing of articles or a certificate by an attorney in fact need not be filed with the department of state or provided as evidence of authority by the person filing but must be retained in the records of the limited liability company.

(c) Each article or certificate must be signed.

(d) Each article or certificate must include the name and capacity of each signer.

History: Add, L 1994, ch 576, § 1, eff Oct 24, 1994.

Sub (c), amd, L 1997, ch 470, § 5, eff Aug 26, 1997, L 1998, ch 375, § 23, eff Aug 13, 1998.

Sub (d), amd, L 1998, ch 375, § 23, eff Aug 13, 1998.

§ 208.   Execution, amendment or cancellation by judicial act

If a person required by section two hundred seven of this article to execute articles or a certificate fails or refuses to do so, any member or any permitted assignee of a membership interest who is adversely affected by such failure or refusal may petition the supreme court in the judicial district in which the office of the limited liability company is or is to be located to direct the execution of such articles or certificate. If the court finds that such articles or certificate should be executed and that such person has failed or refused to execute such articles or certificate, it shall order such person to file the appropriate articles or certificate.

History: Add, L 1994, ch 576, § 1, eff Oct 24, 1994.

§ 209. Filing with the department of state

A signed articles of organization and any signed certificate of amendment or other certificates filed pursuant to this chapter or of any judicial decree of amendment or cancellation shall be delivered to the department of state. If the instrument that is delivered to the department of state for filing complies as to form with the requirements of law and the filing fee required by any statute of this state in connection therewith has been paid, the instrument shall be filed and indexed by the department of state. The department of state shall not review such articles or certificates for legal sufficiency; its review shall be limited to determining that the form has been completed.

History: Add, L 1994, ch 576, § 1, eff Oct 24, 1994.

CASE ANNOTATIONS

Purported transfer of real estate to a limited liability company was void because the deed was executed two weeks before the articles of organization were filed with the state as required by N.Y. Ltd. Liab. Co. Law § 203, and, as there had been no bona fide attempt to comply with the filing requirement, the limited liability company did not operate as a de facto company. Matter of Hausman (2009) 13 NY3d 408.

Limited liability company's members' motion to dismiss action against them for the company's obligations was denied because the members did not provide a certified copy of the articles of organization they were required to file on the company's behalf nor any information pertaining to their consent to personal liability either by filing a consent or voting for the adoption of such a provision. Stuyvesant Fuel Serv. Corp. v 99-105 3rd Ave. Realty LLC (2002, Civ Ct) 745 N.Y.S.2d 680

§ 210. Liability for false statement in articles or certificates

(a) If any articles of organization, certificate of amendment or other certificate filed pursuant to this chapter contains a materially false statement, one who suffers loss by reasonable reliance on the statement may recover damages for the loss from:

(1) any person who executes the articles of organization or certificate, or caused another to execute it on his or her behalf, and knew, and any manager who knew of the filing of such articles or certificate and who knew or should have known with the exercise of reasonable care and diligence, the statement to be false in any material respect at the time the articles or certificate was executed; and

(2) any manager who thereafter knows of the filing of such articles or certificate and who knows or should have known with the exercise of reasonable care and diligence that any arrangement or other fact described in such articles or certificate has changed, making the statement false in any material respect.

(b) Notwithstanding paragraph two of subdivision (a) of this section, no person shall have any liability for failing to cause the amendment or cancellation of the articles of organization or a certificate to be filed or failing to file a petition for its amendment or cancellation, if the articles of organization, certificate or petition is filed within ninety days of the time when that person knew or should have known that the statement in the articles of organization or certificate was false in any material respect.

History: Add, L 1994, ch 576, § 1, eff Oct 24, 1994.

§ 211. Amendment of articles of organization

(a) A limited liability company may amend its articles of organization, from time to time, in any and as many respects as may be desired by (i) preparing a certificate of amendment, entitled "Certificate of amendment of the articles of organization of.... (name of limited liability company) under section two hundred eleven of the Limited Liability Company Law,"in accordance with this section, (ii) executing such certificate of amendment in accordance with section two hundred seven of this article and (iii) filing such certificate of amendment in accordance with section two hundred nine of this article.

(b) The certificate of amendment may set forth only such provisions as might be lawfully contained in the initial articles of organization filed at the time of making such amendment.

(c) The certificate of amendment shall set forth:

(1) the name of the limited liability company and, if it has been changed, the name under which it was formed;

(2) the date of filing its initial articles of organization; and

(3) each amendment effected thereby, setting forth the subject matter of each provision of the articles of organization that is to be amended or eliminated and the full text of the provision or provisions, if any, which are to be substituted or added.

(d) In particular, but without limiting the general power of amendment as stated in subdivision (b) of this section, a limited liability company shall amend its articles of organization no later than ninety days after the happening of any of the following events:

(1) a change in the name of the limited liability company;

(2) a change in the county within this state in which the office of the limited liability company is to be located;

(3) a change in the latest date, if any, on which the limited liability company is to dissolve;

(4) the continuation of the limited liability company under section seven hundred one of this chapter after an event of dissolution;

(5) a change in the name or street address of its registered agent in the state if such change is made

other than pursuant to section three hundred two of this chapter;

(6) a change in the post office address to which the secretary of state shall mail a copy of any process against the limited liability company served upon him or her if such change is made other than pursuant to section three hundred one of this chapter;

(7) a change in whether the limited liability company is to be managed by one or more members of a class or classes of members or by one or more managers or a class or classes of managers;

(8) the discovery of a materially false or inaccurate statement in the articles of organization; and

(9) the decision to change any other statement in the articles of organization.

(e) Unless otherwise provided in this chapter, a certificate of amendment shall be effective at the time of its filing with the department of state.

History: Add, L 1994, ch 576, § 1, eff Oct 24, 1994.

§ 211-A. Certificate of change

(a) A limited liability company may amend its articles of organization from time to time to (i) specify or change the location of the limited liability company's office; (ii) specify or change the post office address to which the secretary of state shall mail a copy of any process against the limited liability company served upon him; and (iii) make, revoke or change the designation of a registered agent, or specify or change the address of the registered agent. Any one or more such changes may be accomplished by filing a certificate of change which shall be entitled "Certificate of Change of.... (name of limited liability company) under section 211-A of the Limited Liability Company Law"and shall be signed and delivered to the department of state. It shall set forth:

(1) the name of the limited liability company, and if it has been changed, the name under which it was formed;

(2) the date the articles of organization were filed by the department of state; and

(3) each change effected thereby.

(b) A certificate of change which changes only the post office address to which the secretary of state shall mail a copy of any process against a limited liability company served upon him or the address of the registered agent, provided such address being changed is the address of a person, partnership or corporation whose address, as agent, is the address to be changed or who has been designated as registered agent for such limited liability company may be signed and delivered to the department of state by such agent. The certificate of change shall set forth the statements required under subdivision (a) of this section; that a notice of the proposed change was mailed to the domestic limited liability company by the party signing the certificate not less than thirty days prior to the date of delivery to the department of state and that such domestic limited liability company has not

objected thereto; and that the party signing the certificate is the agent of such limited liability company to whose address the secretary of state is required to mail copies of process or the registered agent, if such be the case. A certificate signed and delivered under this subdivision shall not be deemed to effect a change of location of the office of the limited liability company in whose behalf such certificate is filed.

History: Add, L 1998, ch 448, § 2, eff Oct 20, 1998.

§ 212. Certificate of correction

The articles of organization, any certificate or any other instrument relating to a domestic or foreign limited liability company filed with the department of state under this chapter may be corrected with respect to any informality or error apparent on the face, incorrect statement or defect in the execution thereof, including the deletion of any matter not permitted to be stated therein. A certificate, entitled "Certificate of correction of .... (title of articles or certificate and name of limited liability company) under section two hundred twelve of the Limited Liability Company Law,"shall be signed and delivered to the department of state. It shall set forth the name of the limited liability company, the date the articles or certificate to be corrected was filed by the department of state, a statement as to the nature of the informality, error, incorrect statement or defect, the provision in the articles or certificate as corrected or eliminated and, if the execution was defective, the proper execution. The filing of the certificate of correction with the department of state shall not alter the effective date of the instrument being corrected and shall not affect any right or liability accrued or incurred before such filing. A name of a limited liability company may not be changed or corrected pursuant to this section.

History: Add, L 1994, ch 576, § 1, eff Oct 24, 1994; amd, L 1998, ch 375, § 24, eff Aug 13, 1998.

§ 213. Authorization of amendment of articles of organization

(a) Except as provided in the operating agreement, an amendment of the articles of organization shall be authorized by at least a majority in interest of the members entitled to vote thereon.

(b) Notwithstanding subdivision (a) of this section, unless the operating agreement provides otherwise (including, but not limited to, by restricting or enlarging the management powers or responsibilities of one or more managers or classes of managers), if the limited liability company is managed by one or more managers then any of the following amendments may be authorized by a majority of such managers:

(1) to change the name or street address of the registered agent, if any, of the limited liability company in the state;

(2) to change the post office address to which the secretary of state shall mail a copy of any process

against the limited liability company served upon him or her; and

(3) to correct any error in the articles of organization pursuant to section two hundred twelve of this article.

History: Add, L 1994, ch 576, § 1, eff Oct 24, 1994.

Sub (b), opening par, amd, L 1995, ch 643, § 3, eff Aug 8, 1995.

§ 214. Restated articles of organization

(a) A limited liability company may at any time, and from time to time, restate in a single instrument entitled "Restated Articles of Organization of .... (name of limited liability company) under section two hundred fourteen of the Limited Liability Company Law", the text of its articles of organization, without making any amendment thereby. Alternatively, a limited liability company may restate in a single instrument the text of its articles of organization and as amended thereby to effect any one or more of the amendments authorized by this article.

(b) The restated or amended and restated articles of organization, as the case may be, shall be executed in accordance with section two hundred seven of this article.

(c) The restated articles of organization shall be filed with the department of state in accordance with section two hundred nine of this article and shall set forth:

(1) the name of the limited liability company and, if it has been changed, the name under which it was formed;

(2) the date of filing of its articles of organization; and

(3) if the restated articles of organization restate the text of the articles of organization without making any amendments, then a statement that the text of the articles of organization is thereby restated without amendment to read as therein set forth in full; or

(4) if the restated articles restate the text of the articles of organization, and is amended thereby, then a statement that the articles of organization is amended to effect one or more of the amendments authorized by this chapter, specifying each such amendment and that the text of the articles of organization is thereby restated as amended to read as therein set forth in full.

(d) Any amendments effected in connection with the restatement of the articles of organization shall be subject to any other provisions of this chapter, including, but not limited to, section two hundred thirteen of this article, that would apply if a separate certificate of amendment were filed to effect such amendment.

(e) Unless otherwise provided in this chapter, the restated or amended and restated articles of organization, as the case may be, shall be effective at the time of its filing with the department of state.

History: Add, L 1994, ch 576, § 1, eff Oct 24, 1994.

Sub (a), amd, L 1997, ch 470, § 6, eff Aug 26, 1997.

ARTICLE III
SERVICE OF PROCESS

History: Add, L 1994, ch 576, § 1, eff Oct 24, 1994.

§ 301. Statutory designation of secretary of state as agent for service of process

(a) The secretary of state shall be the agent of every domestic limited liability company that has filed with the department of state articles of organization making such designation and every foreign limited liability company upon which process may be served pursuant to this chapter.

(b) No domestic or foreign limited liability company may be formed or authorized to do business in this state under this chapter unless its articles of organization or application for authority designates the secretary of state as such agent.

(c) Any designated post office address to which the secretary of state shall mail a copy of process served upon him or her as agent of a domestic limited liability company or a foreign limited liability company shall continue until the filing of a certificate under this chapter directing the mailing to a different post office address.

(d) [Repealed]

(e) (1) Except as otherwise provided in this subdivision, every limited liability company to which this chapter applies, shall biennially in the calendar month during which its articles of organization or application for authority were filed, or effective date thereof if stated, file on forms prescribed by the secretary of state, a statement setting forth the post office address within or without this state to which the secretary of state shall mail a copy of any process accepted against it served upon him or her. Such address shall supersede any previous address on file with the department of state for this purpose.

(2) The commissioner of taxation and finance and the secretary of state may agree to allow limited liability companies to include the statement specified in paragraph one of this subdivision on tax reports filed with the department of taxation and finance in lieu of biennial statements and in a manner prescribed by the commissioner of taxation and finance. If this agreement is made, starting with taxable years beginning on or after January first, two thousand sixteen, each limited liability company required to file the statement specified in paragraph one of this

subdivision that is subject to the filing fee imposed by paragraph three of subsection (c) of section six hundred fifty-eight of the tax law shall provide such statement annually on its filing fee payment form filed with the department of taxation and finance in lieu of filing a statement under this section with the department of state. However, each limited liability company required to file a statement under this section must continue to file the biennial statement required by this section with the department of state until the limited liability company in fact has filed a filing fee payment form with the department of taxation and finance that includes all required information. After that time, the limited liability company shall continue to provide annually the statement specified in paragraph one of this subdivision on its filing fee payment form in lieu of the biennial statement required by this subdivision.

(3) If the agreement described in paragraph two of this subdivision is made, the department of taxation and finance shall deliver to the department of state the statement specified in paragraph one of this subdivision contained on filing fee payment forms. The department of taxation and finance must, to the extent feasible, also include the current name of the limited liability company, department of state identification number for such limited liability company, the name, signature and capacity of the signer of the statement, name and street address of the filer of the statement, and the email address, if any, of the filer of the statement.

History: Add, L 1994, ch 576, § 1, eff Oct 24, 1994; amd, L 1995, ch 643, § 4, eff Aug 8, 1995; L 1998, ch 448, § 3, eff Oct 20, 1998; amd, L 2015, ch 59, § 5 (Part S), eff April 13, 2015.

CASE ANNOTATIONS

In an action on an account stated, a limited liability company (LLC) failed to show a reasonable excuse for its default under N.Y. C.P.L.R. § 5015(a)(1) as it failed to change its address with the Secretary of State as required by N.Y. Limited Liability Company Law §§ 301(e) and 303 for a period of 15 months; the LLC never properly pleaded a defense that the debt was paid, either partially or fully. On Assignment v Medasorb Tech., LLC (2008, App Div, 1st Dept) 855 NYS2d 98.

§ 301-A.   Resignation for receipt of process

(a) The party (or his/her legal representative) whose post office address has been supplied by a domestic limited liability company or foreign limited liability company as its address for process may resign. A certificate entitled "Certificate of Resignation for Receipt of Process under section 301-A of the Limited Liability Company Law"shall be signed by such party and delivered to the department of state. It shall set forth:

(1) the name of the limited liability company and the date that its articles of organization or application for authority was filed by the department of state.

(2) that the address of the party has been designated by the limited liability company as the post office address to which the secretary of state shall mail a copy of any process served on the secretary of state as agent for such limited liability company, and that such party wishes to resign.

(3) that sixty days prior to the filing of the certificate of resignation with the department of state the party has sent a copy of the certificate of resignation for receipt of process by registered or certified mail to the address of the registered agent of the designated limited liability company, if other than the party filing the certificate of resignation, for receipt of process, or if the resigning limited liability company has no registered agent, then to the last address of the designated limited liability company known to the party, specifying the address to which the copy was sent. If there is no registered agent and no known address of the designating limited liability company, the party shall attach an affidavit to the certificate stating that a diligent but unsuccessful search was made by the party to locate the limited liability company, specifying what efforts were made.

(4) that the designated limited liability company is required to deliver to the department of state a certificate of amendment or change providing for the designation by the limited liability company of a new address, and that upon its failure to file such certificate its authority to do business in this state shall be suspended.

(b) Upon the failure of the designating limited liability company to file a certificate of amendment or certificate of change providing for the designation by the limited liability company of the new address after the filing of a certificate of resignation for receipt of process with the secretary of state, its authority to do business in this state shall be suspended.

(c) The filing by the department of state of a certificate of amendment or certificate of change or the filing of a statement under section three hundred one of this article providing for a new address by a designating limited liability company shall annul the suspension and its authority to do business in this state shall be restored and continued as if no suspension had occurred.

(d) The resignation for receipt of process shall become effective upon the filing by the department of state of a certificate of resignation for receipt of process.

(e) (1) In any case in which a limited liability company suspended pursuant to this section would be subject to the personal or other jurisdiction of the courts of this state under article three of the civil practice law and rules, process against such limited liability company may be served upon the secretary of state as its agent pursuant to this section. Such process may be issued in any court in this state having jurisdiction of the subject matter.

(2) Service of such process upon the secretary of state shall be made by personally delivering to and

leaving with him or his deputy, or with any person authorized by the secretary of state to receive such service, at the office of the department of state in the city of Albany, a copy of such process together with the statutory fee, which fee shall be a taxable disbursement. Such service shall be sufficient if notice thereof and a copy of the process are:

(i) delivered personally within or without that state to such limited liability company by a person and in the manner authorized to serve process by law of the jurisdiction in which service is made, or

(ii) sent by or on behalf of the plaintiff to such limited company [limited liability company]* by registered or certified mail with return receipt requested to the last address of such limited liability company known to the plaintiff.

(3) (i) Where service of a copy of process was effected by personal service, proof of service shall be by affidavit of compliance with the section filed, together with the process, within thirty days after such service, with the clerk of the court in which the action or special proceeding is pending. Service of process shall be complete ten days after such papers are filed with the clerk of the court.

(ii) Where service of a copy of process was effected by mailing in accordance with this section, proof of service shall be by affidavit of compliance with this section filed, together with the process, within thirty days after receipt of the return receipt signed by the limited liability company or other official proof of delivery or of the original envelope mailed. If a copy of the process is mailed in accordance with this section, there shall be filed with the affidavit of compliance either the return receipt signed by such limited company [limited liability company] * or other official proof of delivery, if acceptance was refused by it, the original envelope with a notation by the postal authorities that acceptance was refused. If acceptance was refused a copy of the notice and process together with notice of the mailing by registered or certified mail and refusal to accept shall be promptly sent to such limited liability company at the same address by ordinary mail and the affidavit of compliance shall so state. Service of process shall be complete ten days after such papers are filed with the clerk of the court. The refusal to accept delivery of the registered or certified mail or to sign the return receipt shall not affect the validity of the service and such limited liability company refusing to accept such registered or certified mail shall be charged with knowledge of the contents thereof.

(4) Service made as provided in this section without the state shall have the same force as personal service made within this state.

(5) Nothing in this section shall affect the right to serve process in any other manner permitted by law.

* The bracketed words have been inserted by the Publisher.

History: Add, L 1998, ch 448, § 4, eff Oct 20, 1998; amd, L 1999, ch 172, § 18, eff July 6, 1999; amd, L 2015, ch 59, §6 (Part S), eff April 13, 2015.

§ 302. Registered agent for service of process

(a) In addition to the designation of the secretary of state, each domestic limited liability company or authorized foreign limited liability company may designate a registered agent upon whom process against the limited liability company may be served.

(b) The agent must be either:

(1) a natural person who is a resident of this state or has a business address in this state;

(2) a domestic limited liability company or an authorized foreign limited liability company; or

(3) a domestic corporation or a foreign corporation authorized to do business in this state.

(c) [Repealed]

(d) The registered agent of a limited liability company may resign as such agent. The registered agent shall file a certificate with the department of state entitled "Certificate of resignation of registered agent of .... (name of limited liability company) under subdivision (d) of section three hundred two of the Limited Liability Company Law" and executed by such registered agent. Such certificate shall set forth:

(1) the name of the limited liability company, and if it has been changed, the name under which it was formed. With respect to a foreign limited liability company, there shall be set forth its name and, if applicable, the fictitious name the foreign limited liability company has agreed to use in this state pursuant to section eight hundred two of this chapter;

(2) the date the articles of organization or application for authority was filed by the department of state;

(3) that he or she resigns as registered agent of the limited liability company; and

(4) that he or she has sent a copy of the certificate of resignation by registered mail to the limited liability company at the post office address on file with the department of state specified for the mailing of process or, if such address is the address of the registered agent, to the office of the limited liability company in the jurisdiction of its formation.

(e) The designation of a registered agent shall terminate thirty days after the filing with the department of state of the certificate of resignation. A certificate designating a new registered agent may be delivered to the department of state by the limited liability company within the thirty days or thereafter.

History: Add, L 1994, ch 576, § 1, eff Oct 24, 1994.

Sub (c), repealed, L 1999, ch 172, § 19, eff July 6, 1999.

§ 303. Service of process on limited liability companies

(a) Service of process on the secretary of state as agent of a domestic limited liability company or authorized foreign limited liability company shall be made by personally delivering to and leaving with the secretary of state or his or her deputy, or with any person authorized by the secretary of state to receive such service, at the office of the department of state in the city of Albany, duplicate copies of such process together with the statutory fee, which fee shall be a taxable disbursement. Service of process on such limited liability company shall be complete when the secretary of state is so served. The secretary of state shall promptly send one of such copies by certified mail, return receipt requested, to such limited liability company at the post office address on file in the department of state specified for that purpose.

(b) Nothing in this section shall limit or affect the right to serve any process required or permitted by law to be served upon a limited liability company in any other manner now or hereafter permitted by law or applicable rules of procedure.

History: Add, L 1994, ch 576, § 1, eff Oct 24, 1994; amd, L 1999, ch 341, § 4, eff July 27, 1999.

CASE ANNOTATIONS

Court properly denied that branch of defendant's motion to dismiss for lack of personal jurisdiction because defendant submitted an affidavit from its managing member denying service, and the mere denial of receipt, without more, was insufficient to rebut the presumption of proper service created by the service upon the Secretary of State. Bank of N.Y. Mellon v Marolda, 2016 NY Slip Op 03692, 2016 NY Slip Op 3692, 2016 N.Y. App. Div. LEXIS 3549 (N.Y. App. Div. 2d Dep't May 11, 2016).

Trial court erred in denying the plaintiffs' motion for leave to enter a default judgment against the defendants and in granting the defendants' cross-motion to compel the plaintiffs to accept a late answer because the plaintiffs submitted proof of service of the summons and complaint via the Secretary of State, proof of the facts constituting the causes of action, and proof of the defendants' default, and the defendants failed to demonstrate a reasonable excuse for their delay in appearing or answering the complaint inasmuch as the individual defendants unsuccessfully attempted to appear on behalf of the defendant limited liability companies and the arbitration agreement they cited did not involve them. Seidler v Knopf, 2017 NY Slip Op 06310, 2017 NY Slip Op 6310, 2017 N.Y. App. Div. LEXIS 6279 (N.Y. App. Div. 2d Dep't 2017).

In plaintiff's slip and fall case, the supreme court properly denied defendant LLCs' motion to vacate the default judgment because service was made upon the defendants pursuant to N.Y. Ltd. Liab. Co. Law § 303 by delivery of the summons and complaint to the Secretary of State; the LCCs' owners' mere denial of receipt of the summons and complaint was insufficient to rebut the presumption of proper service. An LLC's failure to keep a current address on file with the Secretary of State did not constitute a reasonable excuse for its failure to appear or answer the complaint. Jian Hua Tan v AB Capstone Dev., LLC, 163 A.D.3d 937, 2018 N.Y. App. Div. LEXIS 5360 (N.Y. App. Div. 2d Dep't 2018).

In a summary proceeding against a limited liability company for nonpayment of rent, the tenant was properly served with process under N.Y. Real Prop. Acts. Law § 735 because N.Y. Limited Liability Company Law §§ 301-A(5) and 303(b) allowed service of process on a limited liability company by means existing under statutes other than the New York Limited Liability Law, and the tenant admitted receipt of service, so the protection afforded by the statute was achieved. 2505 Victory Blvd., LLC v Victory Holding, LLC (2007, Civ Ct) 18 Misc 3d 279, 238 NYLJ 113, 848 NYS2d 514.

Legislature gave limited liability companies the power to purchase, take, receive, lease, or otherwise acquire, own, hold, improve, use or otherwise deal in or with real or personal property or an interest in real or personal property, wherever situated, under N.Y. Limited Liability Company Law § 202(b), as well as to sue or be sued, or institute, participate in or defend any action or proceeding, under N.Y. Limited Liability Company Law § 202(a), and, when these clauses were read in concert with N.Y. Limited Liability Company Law §§ 301-A(5) and 303(b), the only conclusion to be drawn was that limited liability companies were subject to service under the N.Y. Real Prop. Acts. Law. 2505 Victory Blvd., LLC v Victory Holding, LLC (2007, Civ Ct) 18 Misc 3d 279, 238 NYLJ 113, 848 NYS2d 514.

In an action on an account stated, a limited liability company (LLC) failed to show a reasonable excuse for its default under N.Y. C.P.L.R. § 5015(a)(1) as it failed to change its address with the Secretary of State as required by N.Y. Limited Liability Company Law §§ 301(e) and 303 for a period of 15 months; the LLC never properly pleaded a defense that the debt was paid, either partially or fully. On Assignment v Medasorb Tech., LLC (2008, App Div, 1st Dept) 855 NYS2d 98.

§ 304. Service of process on unauthorized foreign limited liability companies

(a) In any case in which a non-domiciliary would be subject to the personal or other jurisdiction of the courts of this state under article three of the civil practice law and rules, a foreign limited liability company not authorized to do business in this state is subject to a like jurisdiction. In any such case, process against such foreign limited liability company may be served upon the secretary of state as its agent. Such process may issue in any court in this state having jurisdiction of the subject matter.

(b) Service of such process upon the secretary of state shall be made by personally delivering to and leaving with the secretary of state or his or her deputy, or with any person authorized by the secretary of state to receive such service, at the office of the department of state in the city of Albany, a copy of such process together with the statutory fee, which fee shall be a taxable disbursement.

(c) Such service shall be sufficient if notice thereof and a copy of the process are:

(1) delivered personally outside this state to such foreign limited liability company by a person and in the manner authorized to serve process by law of the jurisdiction in which service is made; or

(2) sent by or on behalf of the plaintiff to such foreign limited liability company by registered mail, return receipt requested, at the post office address specified for the purpose of mailing process, on file in the department of state, or with any official or body performing the equivalent function, in the jurisdiction of its formation, or if no such address is specified, to its registered or other office specified, or if no such office is specified, to the last address of such foreign limited liability company known to the plaintiff.

(d) Where service of a copy of process was effected by personal service, proof of service shall be by affidavit of compliance with this section filed, together with the process, within thirty days after such service, with the clerk of the court in which the action or special proceeding is pending. Service of process shall be complete ten days after such papers are filed with the clerk of the court.

(e) Where service of a copy of process was effected by mailing in accordance with this section, proof of service shall be by affidavit of compliance with this section filed, together with the process, within thirty days after receipt of the return receipt signed by the foreign limited liability company or other official proof of delivery or of the original envelope mailed. If a copy of the process is mailed in accordance with this section, there shall be filed with the affidavit of compliance either the return receipt signed by such foreign limited liability company or other official proof of delivery or, if acceptance was refused by it, the original envelope with a notation by the postal authorities that acceptance was refused. If acceptance was refused, a copy of the notice and process together with notice of the mailing by registered mail and refusal to accept shall be promptly sent to such foreign limited liability company at the same address by ordinary mail and the affidavit of compliance shall so state. Service of process shall be complete ten days after such papers are filed with the clerk of the court. The refusal to accept delivery of the registered mail or to sign the return receipt shall not affect the validity of the service and such foreign limited liability company refusing to accept such registered mail shall be charged with knowledge of the contents thereof.

(f) Service made as provided in this section shall have the same force as personal service made within this state.

(g) Nothing in this section shall limit or affect the right to serve any process required or permitted by law to be served upon a foreign limited liability company in any other manner now or hereafter permitted by law or applicable rules of procedure.

History: Add, L 1994, ch 576, § 1, eff Oct 24, 1994.

CASE ANNOTATIONS

Although a credit card servicing company had actual notice of a store owner's breach of contract action against it, because the owner did not file an affidavit of compliance with the court clerk in accordance with N.Y. Ltd. Liab. Co. Law § 304(c)(2), the court lacked personal jurisdiction over the company. Elzofri v American Express Co. (2010, Sup) 29 Misc 3d 898, 907 NYS2d 644.

Denial of an insurer's motion for leave to enter a default judgment against a medical service provider, arising from the insurer's coverage action for services rendered to the occupants from a vehicle accident, was warranted because strict compliance with the filing requirements was not shown. Interboro Ins. Co. v Tahir, 129 A.D.3d 1687, 12 N.Y.S.3d 688 (4th Dep't 2015).

Limited Liability Company Law § 304 is substantively identical to Business Corporation Law § 307, and both statutes apply to foreign business entities not authorized to do business in New York. Just as strict compliance with the procedures set forth in § 307 is required, strict compliance is likewise required for the procedures set forth in § 304. Interboro Ins. Co. v Tahir, 129 A.D.3d 1687, 12 N.Y.S.3d 688 (4 Dept. 2015).

Trial court erred in denying the motion to vacate the default judgment of the successor in interest to defendant because the court did not have jurisdiction over defendant because, although plaintiff filed an affidavit of service showing personal service upon the Secretary of State and a notation that service was made upon defendant by registered mail, return receipt requested, she did not file an affidavit of compliance; and, because plaintiff did not file an affidavit of compliance, she was unable to file a return receipt signed

by defendant or other official proof of delivery; furthermore, a copy of the envelope mailed to defendant by registered mail and returned to plaintiff as undeliverable, did not show proof of delivery. Chan v Onyx Capital, LLC, 156 A.D.3d 1361, 67 N.Y.S.3d 748, 2017 N.Y. App. Div. LEXIS 9035 (N.Y. App. Div. 4th Dep't 2017), app. denied, 102 N.E.3d 431, 77 N.Y.S.3d 655, 2018 N.Y. LEXIS 768 (N.Y. 2018).

§ 305. Records of process served on the secretary of state

The secretary of state shall keep a record of each process served upon the secretary of state under this chapter, including the date of such service and the action of the secretary of state with reference thereto.

History: Add, L 1994, ch 576, § 1, eff Oct 24, 1994.

ARTICLE IV
MANAGEMENT BY MEMBERS OR MANAGERS

History: Add, L 1994, ch 576, § 1, eff Oct 24, 1994.

§ 401. Management of the limited liability company by members

(a) Unless the articles of organization provides for management of the limited liability company by a manager or managers or a class or classes of managers, management of the limited liability company shall be vested in its members who shall manage the limited liability company in accordance with this chapter, subject to any provisions in the articles of organization or the operating agreement and section four hundred eighteen of this article granting or withholding the management powers or responsibilities of one or more members or classes of members.

(b) If management of a limited liability company is vested in its members, then (i) any such member exercising such management powers or responsibilities shall be deemed to be a manager for purposes of applying the provisions of this chapter, unless the context otherwise requires, and (ii) any such member shall have and be subject to all of the duties and liabilities of a manager provided in this chapter.

History: Add, L 1994, ch 576, § 1, eff Oct 24, 1994.

CASE ANNOTATIONS

Although provisions of the LLC's articles vested management in the members, under N.Y. Ltd. Liab. Co. Law § 401(a) the provisions of the articles were subject to the operating agreement's provisions, which granted management authority to the manager, who also was a member. Since the grant of management authority did not violate § 401(a), they were legal, were not to be voided. Nathanson v Nathanson (2005, 2d Dept) 20 App Div 3d 403, 799 NYS2d 83.

Order granting the limited liability company's (LLC's) motion to stay the action pending the conclusion of the investigation of the Special Litigation Committee (SLC) was reversed because the operating agreements at issue did not explicitly provide for such an appointment, and otherwise do not evince an intent to delegate core governance functions to nonmembers, thus, the outside attorney could not serve as the sole member of an SLC. LNYC Loft, LLC v Hudson Opportunity Fund I, LLC, 154 A.D.3d 109, 57 N.Y.S.3d 479, 2017 N.Y. App. Div. LEXIS 6108 (N.Y. App. Div. 1st Dep't 2017).

Evidence showing that individuals acting on behalf of defendant business entity, which was a member of comedy club that was organized as a limited liability company (LLC), did the comedy club's bookkeeping and obtained the comedy club's liquor license created a genuine issue as to whether defendant business entity was a managing member of the comedy club and whether defendant business entity thus owed a fiduciary duty to plaintiff, the other member of the LLC. However, defendant businessman could not be held liable in his personal capacity for breach of fiduciary duty because he was not a member on the LLC. Laugh Factory, Inc. v Basciano (2009, SD NY) 608 F Supp 2d 549.

§ 402.   Voting rights of members

(a) Except as provided in the operating agreement, in managing the affairs of the limited liability company, electing managers or voting on any other matter that requires the vote at a meeting of the members pursuant to this chapter, the articles of organization or the operating agreement, each member of a limited liability company shall vote in proportion to such member's share of the current profits of the limited liability company in accordance with section five hundred three of this chapter.

(b) Except as provided in the operating agreement, any member may vote in person or by proxy.

(c) Except as provided in the operating agreement, whether or not a limited liability company is managed by the members or by one or more managers, the vote of a majority in interest of the members entitled to vote thereon shall be required to:

(1) admit a person as a member and issue such person a membership interest in the limited liability company;

(2) approve the incurrence of indebtedness by the limited liability company other than in the ordinary course of its business; or

(3) adopt, amend, restate or revoke the articles of organization or operating agreement, subject to the provisions in subdivision (e) of this section, subdivision (b) of section six hundred nine of this chapter and subdivision (b) of section four hundred seventeen of this article.

(d) Except as provided in the operating agreement, whether or not a limited liability company is managed by the members or by one or more managers, the vote of at least a majority in interest of the members entitled to vote thereon shall be required to:

(1) approve the dissolution of the limited liability company in accordance with section seven hundred one of this chapter;

(2) approve the sale, exchange, lease, mortgage, pledge or other transfer of all or substantially all of the assets of the limited liability company; or

(3) approve a merger or consolidation of the limited liability company with or into another limited liability company or foreign limited liability company.

(e) Notwithstanding anything to the contrary in this section or section four hundred seventeen of this article, no applicable provision in either this chapter, the articles of organization or operating agreement, as the case may be, that provides for the vote or consent of a percentage in interest of the members or class of members shall be amended without the vote or consent of at least such percentage in interest of the members or such class of members.

(f) Whenever any action is to be taken under this chapter by the members or a class of members, it shall, except as otherwise required or specified by this chapter or the articles of organization or the operating agreement as permitted by this chapter, be authorized by a majority in interest of the members' votes cast at a meeting of members by members or such class of members entitled to vote thereon.

(g) A limited liability company whose original articles of organization were filed with the secretary of state and effective prior to the effective date of this subdivision shall continue to be governed by this section as in effect on such date and shall not be governed by this section, unless otherwise provided in the operating agreement.

History: Add, L 1994, ch 576, § 1, eff Oct 24, 1994.

Sub (d), opening par, amd, L 1999, ch 420, § 2, eff Aug 31, 1999.

Sub (g), add, L 1999, ch 420, § 2, eff Aug 31, 1999.

CASE ANNOTATIONS

Appellants limited liability companies and the other member, even as nonparties in a divorce action, could be bound by an injunction if they had knowledge of it, provided they were servants or agents of a party in the divorce action, or acted in collusion or combination with a party. There was sufficient financing and operation evidence to prove the husband, a 50 percent member, involved in financing and operations, acted in combination with appellants. Ricatto v Ricatto (2004, A.D., 2d Dept) 772 N.Y.S.2d 705

Trial court properly denied a motion by a limited liability company and its members for summary judgment and directed specific performance of a contract for sale because they failed to make a prima facie showing that the transfer of the subject property by the managing member was not authorized under the operating agreement or N.Y. Ltd. Liab. Co. Law § 402(d)(2). Ahmed v Fulton St. Bros. Realty, LLC (2013, 2d Dept) 107 App Div 3d 832, 968 NYS2d 523.

Manager's attempted sale of all the assets of the entity, investment in which was the only purpose for the existence of the limited liability company, without obtaining the statutorily required approvals was null and void; it was not authorized under the powers given to him in the operating agreement, because it was not in the ordinary course of business. TIC Holdings, LLC v HR Software Acquisition Group, Inc. (2002, Sup) 750 N.Y.S.2d 425

§ 403. Meetings of members

Except as provided in the operating agreement, a limited liability company shall hold meetings of members annually. Meetings of members may be held at a place, either within or outside this state, as may be fixed by or in accordance with the operating agreement, or if not so fixed, at the office of the limited liability company. Except as provided in the operating agreement, members of a limited liability company may participate in a meeting by means of conference telephone or similar communications equipment by means of which all persons participating in the meeting can hear each other. Such participation shall constitute presence in person at the meeting.

History: Add, L 1994, ch 576, § 1, eff Oct 24, 1994.

§ 404. Quorum of members

(a) Except as provided in the operating agreement, a majority in interest of the members entitled to vote shall constitute a quorum at a meeting of members for the transaction of any business, provided that when a specified item of business is required to be voted on by a class of members voting as a class, a majority in interest of the members of such class shall constitute a quorum for the transaction of such specified item of business.

(b) The operating agreement may provide for a greater quorum or a lesser quorum, provided that such lesser quorum shall not be less than one-third in interest of the members entitled to vote.

(c) When a quorum is once present to organize a meeting, it is not broken by the subsequent withdrawal of any members.

(d) The members present may adjourn the meeting despite the absence of a quorum.

History: Add, L 1994, ch 576, § 1, eff Oct 24, 1994.

§ 405. Notice of meetings of members

(a) Except as provided in the operating agreement, whenever under the provisions of this chapter members are required or permitted to take any action by vote at a meeting, written notice shall be given stating the place, date and hour of the meeting, indicating that it is being issued by or at the direction of the person or persons calling the meeting and, in the case of a special meeting, stating the purpose or purposes for which the meeting is called.

(b) Except as provided in the operating agreement, a copy of the notice of any meeting shall be given, personally or by first class mail, not less than ten or more than sixty days before the date of the meeting, provided, however, that a copy of such notice may be given by third class mail not less than twenty-four nor more than sixty days before the date of the meeting, to each member entitled to vote at such meeting. If mailed, such notice is given when deposited in the United States mail, with postage thereon prepaid, directed to the member at his or her address as it appears in the records of the limited liability company. An affidavit of a manager, if any, or other person giving the notice that the notice required by this section has been given shall, in the absence of fraud, be prima facie evidence of the facts therein stated.

(c) Except as provided in the operating agreement, when a meeting is adjourned to another time or place, it shall not be necessary to give any notice of the adjourned meeting if the time and place to which the meeting is adjourned are announced at the meeting at which the adjournment is taken, and at the adjourned meeting any business may be transacted that might have been transacted at the original date of the meeting.

History: Add, L 1994, ch 576, § 1, eff Oct 24, 1994.

§ 406. Waiver of notice

Except as provided in the operating agreement, notice of meeting need not be given to any member who submits a signed waiver of notice, in person or by proxy, whether before or after the meeting. The attendance of any member at a meeting, in person or by proxy, without protesting prior to the conclusion of the meeting the lack of notice of such meeting, shall constitute a waiver of notice by him or her.

History: Add, L 1994, ch 576, § 1, eff Oct 24, 1994.

§ 407. Action by members without a meeting

(a) Whenever under this chapter members of a limited liability company are required or permitted to take any action by vote, except as provided in the operating agreement, such action may be taken without a meeting, without prior notice and without a vote, if a consent or consents in writing, setting forth the action so taken shall be signed by the members who hold the voting interests having not less than the minimum number of votes that would be necessary to authorize or take such action at a meeting at which all of the members entitled to vote therein were present and voted and shall be delivered to the office of the limited liability company, its principal place of business or a manager, employee or agent of the limited liability company having custody of the records of the limited liability company. Delivery made to the office of the limited liability company shall be by hand or by certified or registered mail, return receipt requested.

(b) Every written consent shall bear the date of signature of each member who signs the consent, and, except as provided in the operating agreement, no written consent shall be effective to take the action referred to therein unless, within sixty days of the earliest dated consent delivered in the manner required by this section to the limited liability company, written consents signed by a sufficient number of members to take the action are delivered to the office of the limited liability company, its principal place of business or a manager, employee or agent of the limited liability company having custody of the records of the limited liability company. Delivery

Limited Liability Company Law

made to such office, principal place of business or manager, employee or agent shall be by hand or by certified or registered mail, return receipt requested.

(c) Prompt notice of the taking of the action without a meeting by less than unanimous written consent shall be given to those members who have not consented in writing but who would have been entitled to vote thereon had such action been taken at a meeting. In the event that the action that is consented to is such as would have required the filing of articles or a certificate under any other section of this chapter, if such action had been voted on by members at a meeting thereof, such articles or certificate filed under such other section shall state, in lieu of any statement required by such section concerning any vote of members, that written consent has been given in accordance with this section and that written notice has been given as provided in this section.

History: Add, L 1994, ch 576, § 1, eff Oct 24, 1994.

§ 408. Management by managers

(a) If the articles of organization provides that the management of the limited liability company shall be vested in a manager or managers or class or classes of managers, then the management of the limited liability company shall be vested in one or more managers or classes of managers in accordance with this chapter, subject to any provisions in the articles of organization or the operating agreement and section four hundred nineteen of this article granting or withholding the management powers or responsibilities of one or more managers or class or classes of managers. A manager shall hold such offices and have such responsibilities accorded to him or her by the members as provided in the operating agreement.

(b) Except as provided in the operating agreement and in accordance with section four hundred nineteen of this article, the managers shall manage the limited liability company by the affirmative vote of a majority of the managers.

(c) Except as provided in the operating agreement, any action required or permitted to be taken by a vote of the managers or a class of managers may be taken without a vote if all of the managers or all of the managers in such class, as the case may be, consent thereto in writing, and the writing is filed with the records of the limited liability company.

(d) Except as otherwise provided in the operating agreement, managers of a limited liability company may participate in a meeting by means of conference telephone or similar communications equipment by means of which all persons participating in the meeting can hear each other. Such participation shall constitute presence in person at the meeting.

History: Add, L 1994, ch 576, § 1, eff Oct 24, 1994.

§ 409. Duties of managers

(a) A manager shall perform his or her duties as a manager, including his or her duties as a member of any class of managers, in good faith and with that degree of care that an ordinarily prudent person in a like position would use under similar circumstances.

(b) In performing his or her duties, a manager shall be entitled to rely on information, opinions, reports or statements, including financial statements and other financial data, in each case prepared or presented by:

(1) one or more agents or employees of the limited liability company;

(2) counsel, public accountants or other persons as to matters that the manager believes to be within such person's professional or expert competence; or

(3) a class of managers of which he or she is not a member, duly designated in accordance with the operating agreement of the limited liability company, as to matters within its designated authority, which class the manager believes to merit confidence, so long as in so relying he or she shall be acting in good faith and with such degree of care, but he or she shall not be considered to be acting in good faith if he or she has knowledge concerning the matter in question that would cause such reliance to be unwarranted.

(c) A person who so performs his or her duties in accordance with this section shall have no liability by reason of being or having been a manager of the limited liability company.

History: Add, L 1994, ch 576, § 1, eff Oct 24, 1994.

CASE ANNOTATIONS

Since a limited liability company (LLC) member pleaded that the LLC's manager breached his N.Y. Ltd. Liab. Co. Law § 409(a) fiduciary duty by engaged in self-dealing by deferring payments of priority distributions so that the interest on those unpaid distributions could accrue at a 12 percent interest rate, those claims that were not barred by the three-year statute of limitations were not dismissed; however, a claim to impose a constructive trust over the LLC's only asset was dismissed since the member did not plead how the manager was unjustly enriched. Nathanson v Nathanson (2005, 2d Dept) 20 App Div 3d 403, 799 NYS2d 83.

Causes of action alleging derivative claims on behalf of defendant limited liability company (LLC) against defendant managing member should have been dismissed as defendant managing member's conduct was established as a matter of law to be consistent with his obligations under the operating agreement, which did not state that a membership interest would be given to an entity, such as plaintiff LLC, that did not contribute any capital, and N.Y. Limited Liability Company Law § 409; defendant managing member allegedly failed to share profits from the sale of defendant LLC's property with plaintiff LLC. East Quogue Jet, LLC v East Quogue Members, LLC (2008, 2d Dept) 50 App Div 3d 1089, 857 NYS2d 627.

Although a manager failed to conclusively establish that a shareholder lacked standing to sue, a complaint filed by the shareholder and the company properly alleged causes of action for wrongful interference with prospective contractual relations, unfair competition, and violation of the duty of fidelity under N.Y. Limited Liability Company Law § 409(a), and N.Y. Gen. Bus. Law §§ 360-k, 360-l. Out of the Box Promotions, LLC v Koschitzki (2008, 2d Dept) 55 App Div 3d 575, 866 NYS2d 677.

Since a fund did not unequivocally evince an intent to forego its obligation to make a payment requested by the partnership, and the partnership brought the action about 35 days before the date on which the fund was required to satisfy the redemption request, the partnership suffered no damages from any breach of fiduciary duty by a manager. Palmetto Partners, L.P. v AJW Qualified Partners, LLC (2011, 2d Dept) 83 App Div 3d 804, 921 NYS2d 260.

Claims by limited liability company interest owners against a former property manager, arising from his conduct with respect to the sale of the company's real property and the distribution of proceeds, survived challenge by a motion to dismiss because the owners sufficiently alleged that the manager engaged in bad faith or intentional misconduct. Neary v Burns (2014, Sup) 44 Misc 3d 280, 982 NYS2d 868

In an action in which a member of a limited liability company (LLC) alleged that a co-member and the co-member's managers fraudulently diverted the LLC's assets, the member lacked standing to assert claims pursuant to 18 U.S.C.S. §§ 1962(b) and (d) and 1964(c) of the Racketeer Influenced and Corrupt Organizations Act, 18 U.S.C.S. § 1961 et seq., because the member's alleged loss of its share of the LLC's revenue was a derivative injury; furthermore, the special duty exception was inapplicable because the duty the managers owed to the member under N.Y. Ltd. Liab. Co. Law § 409(a) was not distinguishable from the duty that the mangers owed to the LLC. At the Airport v ISATA, LLC (2006, ED NY) 438 F Supp 2d 55

Evidence showing that individuals acting on behalf of defendant business entity, which was a member of comedy club that was organized as a limited liability company (LLC), did the comedy club's bookkeeping and obtained the comedy club's liquor license created a genuine issue as to whether defendant business entity was a managing member of the comedy club and whether defendant business entity thus owed a fiduciary duty to plaintiff, the other member of the LLC. However, defendant businessman could not be held liable in his personal capacity for breach of fiduciary duty because he was not a member on the LLC. Laugh Factory, Inc. v Basciano (2009, SD NY) 608 F Supp 2d 549.

§ 410. Qualification of managers

(a) Unless otherwise provided in the operating agreement, a manager may, but need not, be a member of the limited liability company.

(b) The operating agreement may prescribe qualifications for managers.

History: Add, L 1994, ch 576, § 1, eff Oct 24, 1994.

§ 411. Interested managers

(a) No contract or other transaction between a limited liability company and one or more of its managers, or between a limited liability company and any other limited liability company or other business entity in which one or more of its managers are managers, directors or officers, or have a substantial financial interest, shall be either void or voidable for this reason alone or by reason alone that such manager or managers are present at the meeting of the managers, or of a class thereof, which approves such contract or transaction, or that his or her or their votes are counted for such purpose:

(1) if the material facts as to such manager's interest in such contract or transaction and as to any such common managership, directorship, officership or financial interest are disclosed in good faith or known to the other managers or class of managers, and the managers or such class approve such contract or transaction by a vote sufficient for such purpose without counting the vote of such interested manager or, if the votes of the disinterested managers are insufficient to constitute an act of the managers pursuant to section four hundred eight of this article, by unanimous vote of the disinterested managers; or

(2) if the material facts as to such manager's interest in such contract or transaction and as to any such common managership, directorship, officership or financial interest are disclosed in good faith or known to the members entitled to vote thereon, and

such contract or transaction is approved by vote of such members.

(b) If such good faith disclosure of the material facts as to the manager's interest in the contract or transaction and as to any such common managership, directorship, officership or financial interest is made to the managers or members, or known to the managers or class of managers or members approving such contract or transaction, as provided in subdivision (a) of this section, the contract or transaction may not be avoided by the limited liability company for the reasons set forth in subdivision (a) of this section. If there was no such disclosure or knowledge, or if the vote of such interested manager was necessary for the approval of such contract or transaction at a meeting of the managers or class of managers at which it was approved, the limited liability company may avoid the contract or transaction unless the party or parties thereto shall establish affirmatively that the contract or transaction was fair and reasonable as to the limited liability company at the time it was approved by the managers, a class of managers or the members.

(c) Common or interested managers may be counted in determining the presence of a quorum at a meeting of the managers or of a class of managers that approves such contract or transaction.

(d) The operating agreement may contain additional restrictions on contracts or transactions between a limited liability company and its managers and may provide that contracts or transactions in violation of such restrictions shall be void or voidable by the limited liability company.

(e) Unless otherwise provided in the operating agreement, the managers shall have authority to fix the compensation of managers for services in any capacity.

History: Add, L 1994, ch 576, § 1, eff Oct 24, 1994.

CASE ANNOTATIONS

While the appraisals for a property at the center of litigation had been obtained by a limited liability company's managers, who voted in favor of the sale, the appraisals were based on independently verified information and record evidence showed the sale was fair and reasonable when approved as required by N.Y. Ltd. Liab. Co. Law § 411(b). Wilcke v Seaport Lofts, LLC (2007, App Div, 1st Dept) 846 NYS2d 133

Application to dissolve a limited liability company does not flow from a claim under N.Y. Ltd. Liab. Co. Law § 411. Matter of 1545 Ocean Ave., LLC v Crown Royal Ventures, LLC (2010, App Div, 2d Dept) 893 NYS2d 590.

§ 412. Agency of members or managers

(a) Unless the articles of organization of a limited liability company provide that management shall be vested in a manager or managers, every member is an agent of the limited liability company for the purpose of its business, and the act of every member, including the execution in the name of the limited liability company of any instrument, for apparently carrying on in the usual way the business of the limited liability company, binds the limited liability company, unless (i) the member so acting has in fact no authority to act for the limited liability company in the particular matter and (ii) the person with whom he or she is dealing has knowledge of the fact that the member has no such authority.

(b) If the articles of organization of a limited liability company provide that management shall be vested in one or more managers:

(1) no member, solely by reason of being a member, is an agent of the limited liability company for the purpose of its business except to the extent that authority has been delegated to such member by the manager or managers or by the provisions of the operating agreement; and

(2) every manager is an agent of the limited liability company for the purpose of its business, and the act of every manager, including the execution in the name of the limited liability company of any instrument, for apparently carrying on in the usual way the business of the limited liability company binds the limited liability company, unless (A) the manager acting has in fact no authority to act for the limited liability company in the particular matter and (B) the person with whom he or she is dealing has knowledge of the fact that the manager has no such authority.

(c) An act of a member or manager that is not apparently for the carrying on of the business of the limited liability company in the usual way does not bind the limited liability company unless authorized in fact by the limited liability company in the particular matter.

(d) No act of a member, manager or other agent of a limited liability company in contravention of a restriction on authority shall bind the limited liability company to persons having knowledge of the restriction.

History: Add, L 1994, ch 576, § 1, eff Oct 24, 1994.

CASE ANNOTATIONS

Because the first member clothed a second member with apparent authority to act on behalf of an insurance agency, and the lenders reasonably relied upon such authority, pursuant to N.Y. Ltd. Liab. Co. Law §§ 402, 412, the successor was liable for the negligence of the agency. Merrell-Benco Agency, LLC v HSBC Bank USA (2005, 3d Dept) 20 App Div 3d 605, 799 NYS2d 590, app dismd, app den (2005, NY) 2005 NY LEXIS 3423.

Although there was no dispute that broker clearly earned its commission, the purported brokerage agreement was not signed by a managing member of the company, in accordance with the operating agreement and N.Y. Limited Liability Company Law § 412(b)(1); the matter was remitted to determine the amount of the commission to which the broker was entitled. Halstead Brooklyn, LLC v 96-98 Baltic, LLC (2008, 2d Dept) 49 App Div 3d 602, 854 NYS2d 437.

Plaintiff had standing pursuant to N.Y. Ltd. Liab. Co. Law § 702 to seek dissolution of a limited liability company (LLC), despite his submission of a resignation letter; the LLC was member-managed rather than manager-managed, and since the appointment of company counsel by a member was neither for carrying on the LLC's usual business, nor, as required by the operating agreement, sanctioned by majority vote of the LLC's members, the company counsel was not authorized to represent the company and thus could not have accepted plaintiff's purported resignation letter. Caplash v Rochester Oral & Maxillofacial Surgery Assoc. (2009, 4th Dept) 63 App Div 3d 1683, 881 NYS2d 270, subsequent app (2009, 4th Dept) 63 App Div 3d 1686, 880 NYS2d 594.

§ 413.   Election and term of managers

(a) Except as provided in the operating agreement, if the articles of organization provides that management shall be vested in one or more managers, the members shall vote in accordance with section four hundred two of this article to designate or elect annually the manager or managers of the limited liability company.

(b) Each manager shall hold the office and have the terms (which may be unlimited) and responsibilities accorded to him or her by the members and set out in the operating agreement until his or her successor has been elected and qualified or until his or her earlier resignation or removal.

(c) Except as provided in the operating agreement, the initial managers shall hold office until the first annual meeting of members and until their successors have been elected and qualified.

(d) The number of managers may be increased or decreased by amendment to and in the manner provided in the operating agreement.

History: Add, L 1994, ch 576, § 1, eff Oct 24, 1994.

§ 414.   Removal or replacement of managers

Except as provided in the operating agreement, any or all managers of a limited liability company may be removed or replaced with or without cause by a vote of a majority in interest of the members entitled to vote thereon.

History: Add, L 1994, ch 576, § 1, eff Oct 24, 1994.

CASE ANNOTATIONS

While the parties' operating agreement lacked a specific provision for the removal of a member-manager, the agreement was, by its terms, guided by the Limited Liability Company Law; thus, an individual and limited liability companies properly relied on N.Y. Limited Liability Company Law § 414 to remove a manager. Ross v Nelson (2008, 1st Dept) 54 App Div 3d 258, 861 NYS2d 670.

§ 415.   Resignation of managers

Except as provided in the operating agreement, a manager may resign at any time by giving written notice to the limited liability company; provided, however, that if the resignation violates any provision contained in the operating agreement or the provision of any contractual agreement between the manager and the limited liability company, the limited liability company may recover from such manager damages for such breach as provided by such operating agreement or contract or by law. The election of a manager shall not of itself create contract rights.

History: Add, L 1994, ch 576, § 1, eff Oct 24, 1994.

§ 416.   Vacancies

(a) Except as provided in the operating agreement, if management of the limited liability company is vested in a group of managers, any vacancies occurring in such group may be filled by the vote of a majority in interest of the members entitled to vote thereon.

(b) Except as provided in the operating agreement, a manager chosen to fill a vacancy shall serve the unexpired term of his or her predecessor.

(c) Except as provided in the operating agreement, any manager's position filled by reason of an increase in the number of managers shall be filled by the vote of a majority in interest of the members entitled to vote thereon.

(d) Except as provided in the operating agreement, a manager chosen to fill a position resulting from an increase in the number of managers shall hold office until the next annual meeting of members or until a successor has been elected and qualified.

History: Add, L 1994, ch 576, § 1, eff Oct 24, 1994.

§ 417. Operating agreement

(a) Subject to the provisions of this chapter, the members of a limited liability company shall adopt a written operating agreement that contains any provisions not inconsistent with law or its articles of organization relating to (i) the business of the limited liability company, (ii) the conduct of its affairs and (iii) the rights, powers, preferences, limitations or responsibilities of its members, managers, employees or agents, as the case may be.

The operating agreement may set forth a provision eliminating or limiting the personal liability of managers to the limited liability company or its members for damages for any breach of duty in such capacity, provided that no such provision shall eliminate or limit:

(1) the liability of any manager if a judgment or other final adjudication adverse to him or her establishes that his or her acts or omissions were in bad faith or involved intentional misconduct or a knowing violation of law or that he or she personally gained in fact a financial profit or other advantage to which he or she was not legally entitled or that with respect to a distribution the subject of subdivision (a) of section five hundred eight of this chapter his or her acts were not performed in accordance with section four hundred nine of this article; or

(2) the liability of any manager for any act or omission prior to the adoption of a provision authorized by this subdivision.

(b) The operating agreement of a limited liability company may be amended from time to time as provided therein; provided, however, that, except as otherwise provided in the operating agreement or the articles of organization, without the written consent of each member adversely affected thereby, (i) no amendment of the operating agreement or (ii) to the extent any provision concerning (A) the obligations of any member to make contributions, (B) the allocation for tax purposes of any items of income, gain, loss, deduction or credit, (C) the manner of computing the distributions of any member or (D) the compromise of an obligation of a member to make a contribution is contained in the articles of organization, no amendment of such provision in the articles of organization, shall be made that (i) increases the obligations of any member to make contributions, (ii) alters the allocation for tax purposes of any items of income, gain, loss, deduction or credit, (iii) alters the manner of computing the distributions of any member or (iv) allows the obligation of a member to make a contribution to be compromised by consent of less than all the members.

(c) An operating agreement may be entered into before, at the time of or within ninety days after the filing of the articles of organization. Regardless of whether such agreement was entered into before, at the time of or after such filing, such agreement, may be effective upon the formation of the limited liability company or at such later time or date as provided in the operating agreement; provided, however, under no circumstances shall an operating agreement become effective prior to the formation of such company.

History: Add, L 1994, ch 576, § 1, eff Oct 24, 1994.

Sub (a), first undesignated par, amd, L 1995, ch 643, § 5, eff Aug 8, 1995.

Sub (c), add, L 1996, ch 170, § 1, eff June 18, 1996.

CASE ANNOTATIONS

Where there was no basis for a judicial dissolution under the provisions of the articles of organization of a limited liability company, which business relationship the members sought to end, the business operation of the limited liability company was bound by the statutory default provisions of the New York Limited Liability Company Law. Spires v Casterline (2004, Sup) 778 N.Y.S.2d 259

Trial court erred in refusing to admit an operating agreement, purportedly entered into before the organization of a limited liability company (LLC) under N.Y. Ltd. Liab. Co. Law § 417(c), between defendant and plaintiff's son, which granted defendant the right to acquire up to 25 percent of the ownership interest in the LLC and the son the right to acquire the remaining 75 percent interest; the agreement was included as part of a closing statement prepared by the LLC's counsel that had previously been admitted into evidence on consent of the parties. Chiu v Chiu (2007, 2d Dept) 38 App Div 3d 619, 832 NYS2d 89

Manager's argument that a release from liability contained in the limited liability company's operating agreement was invalid to the extent that the complaint against him was based on allegations of willful and intentional wrongful conduct, because an exculpatory clause covering such conduct was unlawful. TIC Holdings, LLC v HR Software Acquisition Group, Inc. (2002, Sup) 750 N.Y.S.2d 425

Order granting a petition for dissolution of a limited liability company (LLC) under N.Y. Ltd. Liab. Co. Law § 702 was error because, inter alia, there was no allegation of fraud or frustration of the LCC's purpose, the operating agreement contained no specific provisions relating to dissolution and did not require regular meetings or quorums, the record showed that the managers communicated with each other on a regular basis without the formality of a noticed meeting and there was no showing that the LLC was unable to function as intended or that it was failing financially; the operating agreement was silent as to the issue of manager conflicts and the dispute between the two managers was not shown to be inimical to achieving the LLC's purpose. Where an operating agreement did not address certain topics, a limited liability company was bound by the default requirements set forth in the Limited Liability Company Law. Matter of 1545 Ocean Ave., LLC v Crown Royal Ventures, LLC (2010, App Div, 2d Dept) 893 NYS2d 590.

§ 418. Classes and voting of members

(a) The articles of organization of a limited liability company may provide for classes or groups of members having such relative rights, powers, prefer-

Limited Liability Company Law

ences and limitations as the operating agreement of such limited liability company may provide. The articles of organization may make provision for the future creation, in the manner provided in the operating agreement, of additional classes of members having such relative rights, powers, preferences and limitations as may from time to time be established pursuant to the operating agreement, including rights, powers, preferences, limitations and duties senior to existing classes of members. The operating agreement may grant to or withhold from all or one or more classes of members the right to vote upon any matter on the basis of capital contributions, capital commitments or capital accounts or on a per capita, class or other basis.

(b) The operating agreement may set forth provisions relating to notice of the time, place or purpose of any meeting at which any matter is to be voted on by any members, waiver of any such notice, action by consent without a meeting, the establishment of a record date, quorum requirements, voting in person or by proxy or any other matter with respect to the exercise of any such right to vote.

History: Add, L 1994, ch 576, § 1, eff Oct 24, 1994.

§ 419. Classes and voting of managers

(a) The articles of organization of a limited liability company may provide for classes or groups of managers having such relative rights, powers, preferences and limitations as the operating agreement may provide. The articles of organization may make provision for the future creation, in the manner provided in the operating agreement, of additional classes of managers having such relative rights, powers, preferences and limitations as may from time to time be established pursuant to the operating agreement, including rights, powers, preferences, limitations and duties senior to existing classes of managers. The operating agreement may provide for the classification of managers within classes of managers for the purpose of determining the terms of office of such managers and may grant to all or to one or more classes of managers the right to vote upon any matter on a per capita, class or other basis.

(b) The operating agreement may set forth provisions relating to notice of the time, place or purpose of any meeting at which any matter is to be voted on by any managers, waiver of any such notice, action by consent without a meeting, the establishment of a record date, quorum requirements, voting in person or by proxy or any other matter with respect to the exercise of any such right to vote.

History: Add, L 1994, ch 576, § 1, eff Oct 24, 1994.

§ 420. Indemnification

Subject to the standards and restrictions, if any, set forth in its operating agreement, a limited liability company may, and shall have the power to, indemnify and hold harmless, and advance expenses to, any member, manager or other person, or any

testator or intestate of such member, manager or other person, from and against any and all claims and demands whatsoever; provided, however, that no indemnification may be made to or on behalf of any member, manager or other person if a judgment or other final adjudication adverse to such member, manager or other person establishes (a) that his or her acts were committed in bad faith or were the result of active and deliberate dishonesty and were material to the cause of action so adjudicated or (b) that he or she personally gained in fact a financial profit or other advantage to which he or she was not legally entitled.

History: Add, L 1994, ch 576, § 1, eff Oct 24, 1994.

CASE ANNOTATIONS

Trial court properly denied the limited liability company members' motions for attorneys' fees incurred in obtaining indemnification under the operating agreements because the operating agreements, N.Y. Ltd. Liab. Co. Law § 420, and public policy of the State of New York did not support an award of attorneys' fees on fees. 546-552 W. 146th St. LLC v Arfa (2012, 1st Dept) 99 App Div 3d 117, 950 NYS2d 24

As there was no final adjudication on whether a former property manager breached his duties under the operating agreement of the parties' limited liability company, his claim for indemnification was premature. Neary v Burns (2014, Sup) 44 Misc 3d 280, 982 NYS2d 868

ARTICLE V
CONTRIBUTIONS AND DISTRIBUTIONS

History: Add, L 1994, ch 576, § 1, eff Oct 24, 1994.

§ 501. Form of capital contributions

The contribution of a member to the capital of a limited liability company may be in cash, property or services rendered or a promissory note or other obligation to contribute cash or property or to render services, or any combination of the foregoing.

History: Add, L 1994, ch 576, § 1, eff Oct 24, 1994; amd, L 1995, ch 643, § 6, eff Aug 8, 1995.

§ 502. Liability for contributions

(a) Except as provided in the operating agreement, a member is obligated to the limited liability company to perform any promise to contribute cash or property or to perform services that is otherwise enforceable in accordance with applicable law, even if he or she is unable to perform because of death, disability or any other reason. Except as provided in the operating agreement, if a member does not make any required contribution of property or services, he or she is obligated at the option of the limited liability company to contribute cash equal to that portion of the value, as stated in the records of the limited liability company, if so stated, of the contribution that he or she has not made. The foregoing option shall be in addition to, and not in lieu of, any other rights, including the right to specific performance, that the limited liability company may have against such member under the operating agreement or applicable law.

(b) Unless otherwise provided in the operating agreement and except as provided in section six hundred five of this chapter, the obligation of a member to make a contribution or to return money or other property paid or distributed in violation of this chapter may be compromised only by consent of all the members. Notwithstanding the compromise, a creditor of a limited liability company who extends credit in reliance on the obligation of any member may enforce the original obligation to the extent he or she reasonably relied on such obligation after the member signed a writing which reflects the obligation and the creditor extended credit before the compromise. A conditional obligation of a member to make a contribution or return money or other property to a limited liability company may not be enforced unless the conditions to the obligation have been satisfied or waived as to or by such member. Conditional obligations include contributions payable upon a discretionary call of a limited liability company or a member prior to the time the call occurs.

(c) The operating agreement may provide that the membership interest of any member who fails to make any required contribution shall be subject to specified consequences of such failure. Such consequences may include, but are not limited to, reduction or elimination of the defaulting member's interest, subordination of the defaulting member's interest to that of nondefaulting members, a forced sale of the defaulting member's interest, forfeiture of the defaulting member's interest, the lending by the other members of the amount necessary to meet the defaulting member's commitment, a fixing of the value of the defaulting member's interest by appraisal or by formula and redemption or sale of such member's interest at such value, or other consequences.

History: Add, L 1994, ch 576, § 1, eff Oct 24, 1994.

Sub (a), amd, L 1995, ch 643, § 7, eff Aug 8, 1995.

§ 503. Sharing of profits and losses

The profits and losses of a limited liability company shall be allocated among the members, and among the classes of members, if any, in the manner provided in the operating agreement. If the operating agreement does not so provide, profits and losses shall be allocated on the basis of the value, as stated in the records of the limited liability company if so stated, of the contributions of each member, but not including defaulted obligations to make contributions, to the extent they have been received by or promised to the limited liability company and have not been returned to any such member.

History: Add, L 1994, ch 576, § 1, eff Oct 24, 1994.

§ 504. Sharing of distributions

Distributions of cash or other assets of a limited liability company shall be allocated among the members, and among classes of members, if any, in the manner provided in the operating agreement, which may, among other things, establish record dates for distributions. If the operating agreement does not so provide, distributions shall be allocated on the basis of the value, as stated in the records of the limited liability company, if so stated, of the contributions of each member, but not including defaulted obligations to make contributions, to the extent they have been received by or promised to the limited liability company and have not been returned to any such member.

History: Add, L 1994, ch 576, § 1, eff Oct 24, 1994.

§ 505. Distributions in kind

(a) Except as provided in the operating agreement, a member, regardless of the nature of his or her contribution, has no right to demand and receive any distribution from the limited liability company in any form other than cash.

(b) Except as provided in the operating agreement, a member may not be compelled to accept a distribution of any asset in kind from a limited liability company to the extent that the percentage of the asset distributed to him or her exceeds a percentage of that asset that is equal to the percentage in which he or she shares in distributions from the limited liability company.

History: Add, L 1994, ch 576, § 1, eff Oct 24, 1994.

§ 506. Right to distribution

Subject to sections five hundred eight and seven hundred four of this chapter, at the time a member becomes entitled to receive a distribution, such member has the status of, and is entitled to all remedies available to, a creditor of the limited liability company with respect to the distribution.

History: Add, L 1994, ch 576, § 1, eff Oct 24, 1994.

§ 507. Interim distributions

Except as provided in this chapter, to the extent and at the times or upon the happening of events specified in the operating agreement, a member is entitled to receive distributions from a limited liability company before his or her withdrawal from the limited liability company and before the dissolution and winding up of the limited liability company.

History: Add, L 1994, ch 576, § 1, eff Oct 24, 1994.

§ 508. Limitations on distributions

(a) A limited liability company shall not make a distribution to a member to the extent that, at the time of the distribution, after giving effect to the distribution, all liabilities of the limited liability company, other than liabilities to members on ac-

Limited Liability Company Law

count of their membership interests and liabilities for which recourse of creditors is limited to specified property of the limited liability company, exceed the fair market value of the assets of the limited liability company, except that the fair market value of property that is subject to a liability for which the recourse of creditors is limited shall be included in the assets of the limited liability company only to the extent that the fair value of such property exceeds such liability.

(b) A member who receives a distribution in violation of subdivision (a) of this section, and who knew at the time of distribution that the distribution violated subdivision (a) of this section, shall be liable to the limited liability company for the amount of the distribution. A member who receives a distribution in violation of subdivision (a) of this section, and who did not know at the time of the distribution that the distribution violated subdivision (a) of this section, shall not be liable for the amount of the distribution. Subject to subdivision (c) of this section, this subdivision shall not affect any obligation or liability of a member under the operating agreement or other applicable law for the amount of a distribution.

(c) Unless otherwise agreed, a member who receives a wrongful distribution from a limited liability company shall have no liability under this article or other applicable law for the amount of the distribution after the expiration of three years from the date of the distribution.

History: Add, L 1994, ch 576, § 1, eff Oct 24, 1994.

CASE ANNOTATIONS

Claims by limited liability company interest owners against a former property manager, arising from his conduct with respect to the sale of the company's real property and the distribution of proceeds, survived challenge by a motion to dismiss because the owners sufficiently alleged that the manager engaged in bad faith or intentional misconduct. Neary v Burns (2014, Sup) 44 Misc 3d 280, 982 NYS2d 868

Bankruptcy court denied a Chapter 11 debtor's motion for an order expunging a creditor's unsecured nonpriority claim on promissory notes the debtor, a limited liability company (LLC), issued because, inter alia, there was no merit to the debtor's argument that payments on the notes could not be made without violating N.Y. Limited Liability Company Law § 508. The debtor's obligation to make payments on the notes did not violate § 508 because § 508 prohibited distributions to members of an LLC when the LLC was insolvent or distributions rendered the LLC insolvent, and neither the creditor nor another person who sold his interests to the LLC were members of the LLC after they sold their interests. In re 37-02 Plaza LLC (2008, BC ED NY) 387 BR 413, 50 BCD 14.

Investor's suit against the CEO of a limited liability company (LLC) based on the CEO's withdrawal of $300,000 of his capital investment from the LLC was time barred because the withdraw was a distribution and subject to the three-year limitation period of N.Y. Ltd. Liab. Co. Law § 508(c) and 18 Del. C. § 18-607(c); the distribution occurred more than three years before the case was filed. The three-year time limitation imposed by § 508(c) overrides the limitation period applicable to any claim brought under the Debtor and Creditor Law with regard to distributions made by a limited liability company to a member. Mostel v Petrycki (2009, Sup) 242 NYLJ 50, 885 NYS2d 397.

Whether challenged transfers were in fact "distributions" made to debtor's LLC "members" via an intermediary recipient, in order to invoke the three-year statute of repose, was a disputed issue of fact that could not be resolved on a motion to dismiss. Official Comm. of Unsecured Creditors of Vivaro Corp. v Leucadia Nat'l Corp. (In re Vivaro Corp.), 524 B.R. 536, 2015 Bankr. LEXIS 378 (Bankr. S.D.N.Y. 2015).

§ 509. Distribution upon withdrawal

Except as provided in this chapter, upon withdrawal as a member of the limited liability company, any withdrawing member is entitled to receive any distribution to which he or she is entitled under the operating agreement and, if not otherwise provided in the operating agreement, he or she is entitled to receive, within a reasonable time after withdrawal, the fair value of his or her membership interest in the limited liability company as of the date of withdrawal based upon his or her right to share in distributions from the limited liability company.

History: Add, L 1994, ch 576, § 1, eff Oct 24, 1994.

CASE ANNOTATIONS
1. Generally
2. Evidence

1. Generally

Order was modified dismissing a declaratory judgment action because instead of dismissing the action on the ground that the withdrawing limited liability member was not entitled to the relief he sought, the proper procedure was for the court to deny the motion and then declare the rights of the parties, including declaring the withdrawal and ordering the value of his membership interest and to follow the procedures pursuant to the operating agreement. Matter of Jacobs v Cartalemi, 156 A.D.3d 635, 66 N.Y.S.3d 503, 2017 N.Y. App. Div. LEXIS 8596 (N.Y. App. Div. 2d Dep't 2017).

2. Evidence

Two members of a limited liability company (LLC) were not entitled to summary judgment on a claim under this statute by the estate of a third member of the LLC, seeking a distribution upon withdrawal, because the only evidence supporting the members' claim that they offered the estate the fair value of the decedent's interest in the LLC as of the date of withdrawal was their attorney's affirmation, which had no probative or evidentiary value. Deerin v Ocean Rich Foods, LLC, 158 A.D.3d 603, 71 N.Y.S.3d 123, 2018 N.Y. App. Div. LEXIS 820 (N.Y. App. Div. 2d Dep't 2018).

ARTICLE VI
MEMBERS AND MEMBERSHIP

History: Add, L 1994, ch 576, § 1, eff Oct 24, 1994.

§ 601. Nature of membership interest

A membership interest in the limited liability company is personal property. A member has no interest in specific property of the limited liability company.

History: Add, L 1994, ch 576, § 1, eff Oct 24, 1994.

CASE ANNOTATIONS

Notices of pendency were properly cancelled under N.Y. C.P.L.R. 6514 because plaintiff's action did not directly affect title to or possession of real property under N.Y. C.P.L.R. 6501; plaintiff's true action was to enforce a promise to give plaintiff a 20% interest in a limited liability company (LLC) that acquired a building (which would not give plaintiff an interest in the LLC's property under N.Y. Ltd. Liab. Co. Law § 601), not to gain an ownership interest in the building itself. Yonaty v Glauber (2007, 3d Dept) 40 App Div 3d 1193, 834 NYS2d 744

Cause of action to wind up the affairs of a limited liability company, N.Y. Ltd. Liab. Co. Law § 703(a), did not support a notice of pendency, as a membership interest in the limited liability company was personal property, and, under N.Y. Ltd. Liab. Co. Law § 601, a member had no interest in specific property of the limited liability company. Sealy v Clifton, LLC (2009, App Div, 2d Dept) 890 NYS2d 598.

Claims that the assets of a limited liability company (LLC) were misappropriated alleged an injury to the LLC, and an injury to plaintiff, a member of the LLC, was entirely derivative of defendant's failure to preserve an asset owned by the LLC. Bartfield v Murphy (2008, SD NY) 578 F Supp 2d 638.

§ 602. Admission of members

(a) A person becomes a member of a limited liability company on the later of:

(1) the effective date of the initial articles of organization; or

(2) the date as of which the person becomes a member pursuant to this section or the operating agreement; provided, however, that if such date is not ascertainable, the date stated in the records of the limited liability company.

(b) After the effective date of a limited liability company's initial articles of organization, a person may be admitted as a member:

(1) in the case of a person acquiring a membership interest directly from the limited liability company, upon compliance with the operating agreement or, if the operating agreement does not so provide, upon the vote or written consent of a majority in interest of the members;

(2) in the case of an assignee of a membership interest of a member who has the power, as provided in the operating agreement, to grant the assignee the right to become a member, upon the exercise of that power and compliance with any conditions limiting the grant or exercise of the power; or

(3) unless otherwise provided in an agreement of merger or consolidation or the operating agreement, in the case of a person acquiring a membership interest in a surviving or resulting limited liability company pursuant to a merger or consolidation approved in accordance with subdivision (b) of section one thousand one of this chapter, at the time provided in and upon compliance with the operating agreement of the surviving or resulting limited liability company.

History: Add, L 1994, ch 576, § 1, eff Oct 24, 1994; amd, L 1995, ch 643, § 8, eff Aug 8, 1995; L 1996, ch 170, § 2, eff June 18, 1996.

CASE ANNOTATIONS

1. Applicability

When the purchaser of an interest in a limited liability company (LLC) sued a managing member and the LLC's attorneys for breach of fiduciary duty, it was error not to dismiss the purchaser's claims because the purchaser lacked standing, as the purchaser did not obtain the consent of the LLC's nonselling members to be admitted as a member of the LLC, as required by the LLC's operating agreement and statutorily. Kaminski v Sirera, 2019 N.Y. App. Div. LEXIS 1057 (N.Y. App. Div. 2d Dep't 2019).

§ 603. Assignment of membership interest

(a) Except as provided in the operating agreement,

(1) a membership interest is assignable in whole or in part;

(2) an assignment of a membership interest does not dissolve a limited liability company or entitle the assignee to participate in the management and affairs of the limited liability company or to become or to exercise any rights or powers of a member;

(3) the only effect of an assignment of a membership interest is to entitle the assignee to receive, to the extent assigned, the distributions and allocations of profits and losses to which the assignor would be entitled; and

(4) a member ceases to be a member and to have the power to exercise any rights or powers of a member upon assignment of all of his or her membership interest. Unless otherwise provided in the operating agreement, the pledge of, or the granting of a security interest, lien or other encumbrance in or against, any or all of the membership interest of a member shall not cause the member to cease to be a member or to cease to have the power to exercise any rights or powers of a member.

(b) The operating agreement may provide that a member's interest may be evidenced by a certificate issued by the limited liability company and may also provide for the assignment or transfer of any of the interest represented by such a certificate. A member's interest may be a certificated security or an uncertificated security within the meaning of section 8-102 of the uniform commercial code if the requirements of section 8-103(c) are met, and if the requirements are not met such interest shall, for purposes of the uniform commercial code, be deemed to be a general intangible asset. The existence of the restrictions on the sale or transfer of a membership interest, as contained in this chapter and, if applicable, in the operating agreement, shall be noted conspicuously on the face or back of every certificate representing a membership interest issued by a limited liability company. Any sale or transfer in violation of such restrictions shall be void.

(c) Unless otherwise provided in an operating agreement and except to the extent assumed by agreement, until the time, if any, that an assignee of a membership interest becomes a member, the assignee shall have no liability as a member solely as a result of the assignment.

History: Add, L 1994, ch 576, § 1, eff Oct 24, 1994.

Sub (a), par (3), amd, L 1995, ch 643, § 9, eff Aug 8, 1995.

Sub (b), amd, L 1997, ch 566, § 23, eff Oct 10, 1997.

Limited Liability Company Law

The determination sustaining a notice of deficiency of personal income tax was affirmed because as the assignee of a membership interest, petitioner was not automatically entitled to participate in the management or affairs of the limited liability company but was entitled to receive the distributions and allocations of profits and losses to which the assignor would be entitled, thus, the assessment was properly imposed. Matter of Murphy v New York State Tax Appeals Trib., 2018 N.Y. App. Div. LEXIS 7354 (N.Y. App. Div. 3d Dep't 2018).

Partnership includes a limited liability company which is deemed a partnership for federal income tax purposes. Matter of Murphy v New York State Tax Appeals Trib., 2018 N.Y. App. Div. LEXIS 7354 (N.Y. App. Div. 3d Dep't 2018).

Annual filing fee per member imposed on limited liability company under CLS Tax § 658(c)(3) does not apply to investors who own contractual non-voting economic interest in portion of member's interest. N.Y. Adv Op Comm T & F TSB-A-02-(3)I

§ 604. Rights of assignee to become a member

(a) Except as provided in the operating agreement, an assignee of a membership interest may not become a member without the vote or written consent of at least a majority in interest of the members, other than the member who assigned or proposes to assign such membership interest.

(b) An assignee who has become a member has, to the extent assigned, the rights, powers, preferences and limitations and is subject to the restrictions and liabilities, of a member under the articles of organization, the operating agreement and this chapter. Notwithstanding the foregoing, unless otherwise provided in the operating agreement, an assignee who becomes a member is liable for the obligations of his or her assignor to make contributions as provided in section five hundred two of this chapter, but shall not be liable for the obligations of his or her assignor under sections six hundred six and five hundred eight of this chapter. However, the assignee is not obligated for (i) liabilities, including the obligations of his or her assignor to make contributions as provided in section five hundred two of this chapter, unknown to the assignee at the time he or she becomes a member and that could not be ascertained from the operating agreement or (ii) any accrued liabilities of the assignor at the time of assignment unless the assignee specifically assumes such liabilities.

History: Add, L 1994, ch 576, § 1, eff Oct 24, 1994.

Annual filing fee per member imposed on limited liability company under CLS Tax § 658(c)(3) does not apply to investors who own contractual non-voting economic interest in portion of member's interest. N.Y. Adv Op Comm T & F TSB-A-02-(3)I

§ 605. Liability upon assignment

Whether or not an assignee of a membership interest becomes a member, the assignor of a membership interest is not released from any liability under this chapter or the operating agreement, except liabilities that arise after the effectiveness of the assignment and are pursuant to section two hundred ten of this chapter, section five hundred eight of this chapter or, in the event the assignee becomes a member, unless otherwise provided in the operating agreement, section five hundred two of this chapter.

History: Add, L 1994, ch 576, § 1, eff Oct 24, 1994.

§ 606. Withdrawal of a member

(a) A member may withdraw as a member of a limited liability company only at the time or upon the happening of events specified in the operating agreement and in accordance with the operating agreement. Notwithstanding anything to the contrary under applicable law, unless an operating agreement provides otherwise, a member may not withdraw from a limited liability company prior to the dissolution and winding up of the limited liability company. Notwithstanding anything to the contrary under applicable law, an operating agreement may provide that a membership interest may not be assigned prior to the dissolution and winding up of the limited liability company.

(b) A limited liability company whose original article [articles] * of organization were filed with the secretary of state and effective prior to the effective date of this subdivision shall continue to be governed by this section as in effect on such date and shall not be governed by this section, unless otherwise provided in the operating agreement.

* The bracketed word has been inserted by the Publisher.

History: Sub (a), formerly entire section, add, L 1994, ch 576, § 1, eff Oct 24, 1994; amd, L 1995, ch 643, § 10, eff Aug 8, 1995; so designated sub (a) and amd, L 1999, ch 420, § 3, eff Aug 31, 1999

Sub (b), add, L 1999, ch 420, § 3, eff Aug 31, 1999

2. Evidence

Court exercised its discretion and decreed judicial dissolution of a limited liability company as it was not reasonably practicable for the company to carry on its business in conformity with a statutory operating agreement that explicitly required the dissolution and winding up of the company prior to the withdrawal of one of its members. Spires v Casterline (2004, Sup) 778 N.Y.S.2d 259

Order was modified dismissing a declaratory judgment action because instead of dismissing the action on the ground that the withdrawing limited liability member was not entitled to the relief he sought, the proper procedure was for the court to deny the motion and then declare the rights of the parties, including declaring the withdrawal and ordering the value of his membership interest and to follow the procedures pursuant to the operating agreement. Matter of Jacobs v Cartalemi, 156 A.D.3d 635, 66 N.Y.S.3d 503, 2017 N.Y. App. Div. LEXIS 8596 (N.Y. App. Div. 2d Dep't 2017).

§ 607. Rights of creditors of members

(a) On application to a court of competent jurisdiction by any judgment creditor of a member, the court may charge the membership interest of the member with payment of the unsatisfied amount of the judgment with interest. To the extent so charged, the judgment creditor has only the rights of an assignee of the membership interest. This chapter does not deprive any member of the benefit of any exemption laws applicable to his or her membership interest.

(b) No creditor of a member shall have any right to obtain possession of, or otherwise exercise legal or equitable remedies with respect to, the property of the limited liability company.

History: Add, L 1994, ch 576, § 1, eff Oct 24, 1994.

CASE ANNOTATIONS

1. Generally

Trial court granted plaintiff's motion to appoint a receiver over defendant's interests in two limited liability companies (LLCs) in order to collect on the judgment plaintiff had obtained; though this section barred creditors from obtaining an interest in the property of an LLC, it did not bar them from executing on the debtor's membership interest itself. Coscia v Eljamal, 2015 NY Slip Op 25109, 8 N.Y.S.3d 882, 2015 N.Y. Misc. LEXIS 1100 (N.Y. Sup. Ct. 2015).

§ 608. Powers of estate of a deceased or incompetent member

If a member who is a natural person dies or a court of competent jurisdiction adjudges him or her to be incompetent to manage his or her person or his or her property, the member's executor, administrator, guardian, conservator or other legal representative may exercise all of the member's rights for the purpose of settling his or her estate or administering his or her property, including any power under the operating agreement of an assignee to become a member. If a member is a corporation, trust or other entity and is dissolved or terminated, the powers of that member may be exercised by its legal representative or successor.

History: Add, L 1994, ch 576, § 1, eff Oct 24, 1994.

CASE ANNOTATIONS

Cross-motion for the executor of the sole member's estate to intervene and be joined as a plaintiff in an action the limited liability company commenced prior to the sole member's passing should have been granted because pursuant to N.Y. Ltd. Liab. Co. Law § 608 and the terms of the limited liability company's operating agreement, the executor of the deceased sole member's estate was authorized to wind up the affairs of the limited liability company. Yew Prospect, LLC v Szulman (2003, A.D., 2d Dept) 759 N.Y.S.2d 357

§ 609. Liability of members, managers and agents

(a) Neither a member of a limited liability company, a manager of a limited liability company managed by a manager or managers nor an agent of a limited liability company (including a person having more than one such capacity) is liable for any debts, obligations or liabilities of the limited liability company or each other, whether arising in tort, contract or otherwise, solely by reason of being such member, manager or agent or acting (or omitting to act) in such capacities or participating (as an employee, consultant, contractor or otherwise) in the conduct of the business of the limited liability company.

(b) Notwithstanding the provisions of subdivision (a) of this section, all or specified members of a limited liability company may be liable in their capacity as members for all or specified debts, obligations or liabilities of a limited liability company if (l) a statement to such effect is specifically contained in the articles of organization of the limited liability company and (2) any such member so liable shall have (i) specifically consented in writing (A) to the adoption of such provisions or (B) to be bound by such provision or (ii) specifically voted for the adoption of such provision. The absence of either such statement in the articles of organization or such consent or vote of any such member shall in no way affect or impair the ability of a member to act as a guarantor or a surety for, provide collateral for or otherwise be liable for, the debts, obligations or liabilities of a limited liability company as authorized pursuant to section six hundred eleven of this article.

(c) Notwithstanding the provisions of subdivisions (a) and (b) of this section, the ten members with the largest percentage ownership interest, as determined as of the beginning of the period during which the unpaid services referred to in this section are performed, of every limited liability company, shall jointly and severally be personally liable for all debts, wages or salaries due and owing to any of its laborers, servants or employees, for services performed by them for such limited liability company. Before such laborer, servant or employee shall charge such member for such services, he or she shall give notice in writing to such member that he or she intends to hold such member liable under this section. Such notice shall be given within one hundred eighty days after termination of such services. An action to enforce such liability shall be commenced within ninety days after the return of an execution unsatisfied against the limited liability company upon a judgment recovered against it for such services. A member who has paid more than his or her pro rata share under this section shall be entitled to contribution pro rata from the other members liable under this section with respect to the excess so paid, over and above his or her pro rata share, and may sue them jointly or severally or any number of them to recover the amount due from them. Such recovery may be had in a separate action. As used in this subdivision, "pro rata" means in proportion to percentage ownership interest. Before a member may claim contribution from other members under this section, he or she shall give them notice in writing that he or she intends to hold them so liable to him or her.

(d) For the purposes of this section, wages or salaries shall mean all compensation and benefits payable by an employer to or for the account of the employee, servant or laborer, for services performed by them for such limited liability company. These shall specifically include but not be limited to salaries, overtime, vacation, holiday and severance pay; employer contributions to or payments of insurance or welfare benefits; employer contributions to pension or annuity funds; and any other moneys properly due or payable for services rendered by such employee, servant or laborer, including any concomitant liquidated damages, penalties, interest, attorneys' fees or costs.

History: Add, L 1994, ch 576, § 1, eff Oct 24, 1994; L 2014, ch 537, § 11, eff Feb 27, 2015.

CASE ANNOTATIONS

Where a condominium unit owner alleged that a limited liability company (LLC) and its officers damaged its units, its negligence claims survived dismissal because a factual issue existed as to whether the officers participated in the commission of a tort in furtherance of the LLC's business and whether the LLC was a mere alter ego for its individual members. Howard Borress Enters. Inc. v CSJ LLC (2005, Sup) 234 NYLJ 100, affd (2006, 1st Dept) 30 App Div 3d 322, 818 NYS2d 61.

In an action alleging injuries to a minor based on exposure to lead paint and dust in apartments, former members of limited liability companies (LLCs) that owned the apartments could not be held individually liable under N.Y. Ltd. Liab. Co. Law §§ 609, 610 because, inter alia, first member had transferred her ownership interest before the minor became a tenant and second member had presented evidence that she was not the LLCs' de facto owner and manager as second member did not exclusively and completely control the management and operation of the buildings at issue. Matias v Mondo Props. LLC (2007, 1st Dept) 43 App Div 3d 367, 841 NYS2d 279.

In a suit brought by a festival attendee alleging harm after ingesting a harmful substance and sustaining significant injuries, the trial court erred by denying the motion to dismiss of the co-owners of the festival company because the attendee failed to allege any manner in which the co-owners participated in the commission of a tort in furtherance of company business or to benefit the business. Bynum v Keber, 135 A.D.3d 1066, 23 N.Y.S.3d 654 (3d Dep't 2016).

Supreme court properly denied non-sponsors' motion to dismiss because a purchaser's allegations that the non-sponsors were the principal and the managing member of the sponsor, that they executed the certification page of an offering plan, and that they directly participated in the transactions by virtue of their control of the sponsor were sufficient to support the claim that they participated in the commission of a tort and were not insulated from liability. Board of Mgrs. of Beacon Tower Condominium v 85 Adams St., LLC, 136 A.D.3d 680, 25 N.Y.S.3d 233, 2016 N.Y. App. Div. LEXIS 696 (2d Dep't 2016).

Mere fact that non-sponsors were members of the sponsor, a limited liability company, was insufficient to impose liability upon them because the sponsor was a separate legal entity from its members; the purchaser failed to allege facts sufficient to justify piercing the corporate veil with respect to the non-sponsors. Board of Mgrs. of Beacon Tower Condominium v 85 Adams St., LLC, 136 A.D.3d 680, 25 N.Y.S.3d 233, 2016 N.Y. App. Div. LEXIS 696 (2d Dep't 2016).

Attorney A was entitled to summary judgment in a client's malpractice claim because, under the circumstances, the attorney was not individually liable for the work performed by the law firm of which she was a member; attorney B failed to prepare and record the subject deed, resulting in the client's inability to sell the marital residence to satisfy the unpaid equitable distribution award, as intended by the stipulation of settlement. Walker v Kramer, 162 A.D.3d 827, 2018 N.Y. App. Div. LEXIS 4281 (N.Y. App. Div. 2d Dep't 2018).

Order requiring a medical provider to pay part of a successful medical malpractice action plaintiff's attorney fees to a judgment creditor of the plaintiff's first law limited liability company (LLC) counsel was reversed since neither that or second law LLC were the same entity as the plaintiff's third and last law professional corporation (PC)counsel, to whom fees were awarded, just because all three law entities had one lawyer in common, partly based on N.Y. Ltd. Liab. Co. Law § 609, and partly based on the creditor not indicating any relevant relationship between the PC and either LLC, or that there were any other relevant circumstances, such as fraud, to support enforcement of his judgment as against the PC. Irushalmi v Ostroff (2005, A.D., 2d Dept) 795 N.Y.S.2d 752

§ 610. Parties to actions

A member of a limited liability company is not a proper party to proceedings by or against a limited liability company, except where the object is to enforce a member's right against or liability to the limited liability company.

History: Add, L 1994, ch 576, § 1, eff Oct 24, 1994.

CASE ANNOTATIONS

In an action alleging injuries to a minor based on exposure to lead paint and dust in apartments, former members of limited liability companies (LLCs) that owned the apartments could not be held individually liable under N.Y. Ltd. Liab. Co. Law §§ 609, 610 because, inter alia, first member had transferred her ownership interest before the minor became a tenant and second member had presented evidence that she was not the LLCs' de facto owner and manager as second member did not exclusively and completely control the management and operation of the buildings at issue. Matias v Mondo Props. LLC (2007, 1st Dept) 43 App Div 3d 367, 841 NYS2d 279

Where parties' marital residence was owned by a limited liability company, of which the husband was the sole member, he lacked standing in his individual capacity to recover compensatory damages from the wife for her "holdover occupancy" of the premises. Katz v Katz (2008, 2d Dept) 55 App Div 3d 680, 867 NYS2d 100.

Mere fact that non-sponsors were members of the sponsor, a limited liability company, was insufficient to impose liability upon them because the sponsor was a separate legal entity from its members; the purchaser failed to allege facts sufficient to justify piercing the corporate veil with respect to the non-sponsors. Board of Mgrs. of Beacon Tower Condominium v 85 Adams St., LLC, 136 A.D.3d 680, 25 N.Y.S.3d 233, 2016 N.Y. App. Div. LEXIS 696 (2d Dep't 2016).

§ 611. Business transactions of a member with the limited liability company

Except as may be provided in the operating agreement, a member may lend money to, borrow money from, act as a guarantor or surety for, provide collateral for the obligations of and transact other business with the limited liability company and, subject to other applicable law, has the same rights and obligations with respect thereto as a person who is not a member.

History: Add, L 1994, ch 576, § 1, eff Oct 24, 1994.

CASE ANNOTATIONS

Creditor's application to seize the assets of a limited liability company (LLC) was properly granted because, inter alia, although the creditor was a member of the LLC, and the operating agreement barred any member from any act that made it impossible for the LLC to carry on its business, under Limited Liability Company Law § 611, any member who became a creditor had the same rights and obligations with respect thereto as a person who was not a member. Christopher's Partner, LLC v Christopher's of Colonie, LLC (2010, App Div, 3d Dept) 893 NYS2d 689.

ARTICLE VII
DISSOLUTION

History: Add, L 1994, ch 576, § 1, eff Oct 24, 1994.

§ 701. Dissolution

(a) A limited liability company is dissolved and its affairs shall be wound up upon the first to occur of the following:

(1) the latest date on which the limited liability company is to dissolve, if any, provided in the articles of organization, or the time specified in the operating agreement, but if no such date is provided in the articles of organization and if no such time is speci-

fied in the operating agreement, then the limited liability company shall have a perpetual existence;

(2) the happening of events specified in the operating agreement;

(3) subject to any requirement in the operating agreement requiring approval by any greater or lesser percentage in interest of the members or class or classes or group or groups of members, the vote or written consent of at least a majority in interest of the members or, if there is more than one class or group of members, then by at least a majority in interest of each class or group of members;

(4) at any time there are no members, provided that, unless otherwise provided in the operating agreement, the limited liability company is not dissolved and is not required to be wound up if, within one hundred eighty days or such other period as is provided for in the operating agreement after the occurrence of the event that terminated the continued membership of the last remaining member, the legal representative of the last remaining member agrees in writing to continue the limited liability company and to the admission of the legal representative of such member or its assignee to the limited liability company as a member, effective as of the occurrence of the event that terminated the continued membership of the last remaining member; or

(5) the entry of a decree of judicial dissolution under section seven hundred two of this article.

(b) Unless otherwise provided in the operating agreement, the death, retirement, resignation, expulsion, bankruptcy or dissolution of any member or the occurrence of any other event that terminates the continued membership of any member shall not cause the limited liability company to be dissolved or its affairs to be wound up, and upon the occurrence of any such event, the limited liability company shall be continued without dissolution, unless within one hundred eighty days following the occurrence of such event, a majority in interest of all of the remaining members of the limited liability company or, if there is more than one class or group of members, then by a majority in interest of all the remaining members of each class or group of members, vote or agree in writing to dissolve the limited liability company.

(c) A limited liability company whose original articles of organization were filed with the secretary of state and effective prior to the effective date of this subdivision shall continue to be governed by this section as in effect on such date and shall not be governed by this section, unless otherwise provided in the operating agreement.

History: Add, L 1994, ch 576, § 1; amd, L 1995, ch 643, § 11, eff Aug 8, 1995; L 1999, ch 420, § 4, eff Aug 31, 1999.

CASE ANNOTATIONS

Contrary to the contention of a limited liability company (LLC), it was not previously dissolved; there was nothing in the record to indicate that the LLC's affairs were wound up as required by N.Y. Ltd. Liab. Co. Law § 701, that the articles of dissolution were filed with the Secretary of State as required by N.Y. Ltd. Liab. Co. Law § 705, or that, if the LLC had been dissolved and a member had elected to continue the business while he was still alive, that member had served the other member with notice of that election, as required by the LLC's operating agreement. Sealy v Clifton, LLC (2009, App Div, 2d Dept) 890 NYS2d 598.

§ 702. Judicial dissolution

On application by or for a member, the supreme court in the judicial district in which the office of the limited liability company is located may decree dissolution of a limited liability company whenever it is not reasonably practicable to carry on the business in conformity with the articles of organization or operating agreement. A certified copy of the order of dissolution shall be filed by the applicant with the department of state within thirty days of its issuance.

History: Add, L 1994, ch 576, § 1, eff Oct 24, 1994.

CASE ANNOTATIONS

Trial court may, on the petition of any member, decree dissolution of a limited liability company whenever it is not reasonably practicable to carry on the business in conformity with the articles of organization or operating agreement; in an action for the dissolution of a company, the trial court properly found that the managing member had not made any initial capital contribution because the company agreement made no provision for crediting the member's personal services. KSI Rockville, LLC v Eichengrun, 305 A.D.2d 681, 760 N.Y.S.2d 520, 2003 N.Y. App. Div. LEXIS 6010 (N.Y. App. Div. 2d Dep't 2003).

Order for the dissolution of a limited liability company (LLC) was improper because the trial court's refusal to allow a member to withdraw his motion for dissolution was error, and, because plaintiff's resignation was accepted by an attorney purporting to represent the LLC, but the record did not disclose the circumstances under which the attorney came to represent the LLC and whether such representation was authorized by the operating agreement, there was an issue of fact whether plaintiff had standing to seek dissolution. Caplash v Rochester Oral & Maxillofacial Surgery Assoc., LLC, 48 A.D.3d 1139, 851 N.Y.S.2d 769, 2008 N.Y. App. Div. LEXIS 913 (N.Y. App. Div. 4th Dep't 2008).

Judgment in favor of appellant against members in a N.Y. Ltd. Liab. Co. Law § 702 proceeding was error because the settlement document, on which the judgment was based, provided that it would not be enforceable unless executed by all parties; having been signed by only two out of three parties, the document was unenforceable by its own terms. A letter written by the attorney for the party who did not sign the document was not sufficient to render the purported settlement enforceable. Matter of Morse Hill Assoc., LLC, 50 A.D.3d 906, 855 N.Y.S.2d 652, 2008 N.Y. App. Div. LEXIS 3433 (N.Y. App. Div. 2d Dep't 2008).

Plaintiff had standing pursuant to N.Y. Ltd. Liab. Co. Law § 702 to seek dissolution of a limited liability company (LLC), despite his submission of a resignation letter; the LLC was member-managed rather than manager-managed, and since the appointment of company counsel by a member was neither for carrying on the LLC's usual business, nor, as required by the operating agreement, sanctioned by majority vote of the LLC's members, the company counsel was not authorized to represent the company and thus could not have accepted plaintiff's purported resignation letter. Caplash v Rochester Oral & Maxillofacial Surgery Assoc., 63 A.D.3d 1683, 881 N.Y.S.2d 270, 2009 N.Y. App. Div. LEXIS 4740 (N.Y. App. Div. 4th Dep't 2009).

Trial court did not err in granting a first member's application for dissolution of a limited liability company (LLC) under N.Y. Ltd. Liab.

Co. Law § 702 because it was not reasonably practicable for the LLC to continue to operate as continuing the LLC was financially unfeasible. Mizrahi v Cohen, 104 A.D.3d 917, 961 N.Y.S.2d 538, 2013 N.Y. App. Div. LEXIS 2003 (N.Y. App. Div. 2d Dep't 2013).

Trial court did not err in determining that if the assets of the limited liability company (LLC) were to be liquidated, then the capital contributions of the first member were to be treated as loans to the LLC to the extent that those contributions exceeded those made by the second member; although the LLC agreement provided that a member did not have the right to receive any return of capital contributions, the LLC agreement also provided for the repayment of debts of the LLC upon dissolution, and the record, including an affidavit submitted by the second member, established that the parties intended that the capital contributions by the first member were to be treated as loans to the LLC to the extent that those contributions exceeded those made by the second member. In addition, the LLC agreement was silent as to the issue of equalization of capital contributions. Mizrahi v Cohen, 104 A.D.3d 917, 961 N.Y.S.2d 538, 2013 N.Y. App. Div. LEXIS 2003 (N.Y. App. Div. 2d Dep't 2013).

Trial court should have granted, in effect, the first member's application for an order authorizing him to purchase the second member's interest in the limited liability company (LLC) upon its dissolution; the Limited Liability Company Law did not expressly authorize a buyout in a dissolution proceeding, but in certain circumstances, a buyout may be an appropriate equitable remedy upon the dissolution of an LLC, and under the facts of the case, the remedy of a buyout was appropriate. The provisions of the LLC agreement regarding dissolution of the LLC did not preclude an order authorizing a buyout upon the judicial dissolution of the LLC pursuant to N.Y. Ltd. Liab. Co. Law § 702. Mizrahi v Cohen, 104 A.D.3d 917, 961 N.Y.S.2d 538, 2013 N.Y. App. Div. LEXIS 2003 (N.Y. App. Div. 2d Dep't 2013).

Trial court properly dismissed a first brother's action to judicially dissolve a limited liability company (LLC) because the first brother's allegations, if true, would not establish that the LLC's management was unable or unwilling to permit or promote the stated purpose of the LLC or that continuing the LLC was financially unfeasible. Matter of Kassab v Kasab, 137 A.D.3d 1135, 29 N.Y.S.3d 39, 2016 N.Y. App. Div. LEXIS 2086 (N.Y. App. Div. 2d Dep't 2016), app. dismissed, 2017 N.Y. App. Div. LEXIS 5847 (N.Y. App. Div. 2d Dep't July 5, 2017).

Trial court erred in granting a motion by the managing members (the managers) of a limited liability company (LLC) to dismiss a member's cause of action for judicial dissolution of the LLC because neither the operating agreement nor the leases of the property utterly refuted the member's allegation as to the LLC's purpose so as to conclusively establish a defense as a matter of law to the member's dissolution cause of action, the managers did not show that the material fact alleged by the member regarding the LLC's purpose was not a fact at all and that no significant dispute existed regarding it, and the court's determination that the LLC's purpose was simply to acquire and manage property constituted an impermissible factual finding. Mace v Tunick, 153 A.D.3d 689, 60 N.Y.S.3d 314, 2017 N.Y. App. Div. LEXIS 6127 (N.Y. App. Div. 2d Dep't 2017).

Court exercised its discretion and decreed judicial dissolution of a limited liability company as it was not reasonably practicable for the company to carry on its business in conformity with a statutory operating agreement that explicitly required the dissolution and winding up of the company prior to the withdrawal of one of its members. Spires v Lighthouse Solutions, LLC, 778 N.Y.S.2d 259, 4 Misc. 3d 428, 2004 N.Y. Misc. LEXIS 628 (N.Y. Sup. Ct. 2004).

Partner's petition to dissolve a limited liability company (LLC) under N.Y. Ltd. Liab. Co. Law § 702 was dismissed because, given the statutory standard under § 702 for involuntary dissolution of an LLC without an operating agreement, the partner failed to meet his burden to raise a material issue of fact warranting a trial under N.Y. C.P.L.R. 410. As the evidence did not demonstrate that it was not reasonably practicable to carry on the business of the LLC in the circumstances, the court's discretion, conferred by statute only, was not invoked; thus, the court summarily dismissed the partner's petition under N.Y. C.P.L.R. 409(b). Matter of Jeffrey M. Horning v Horning Constr. LLC, 816 N.Y.S.2d 877, 12 Misc. 3d 402, 2006 N.Y. Misc. LEXIS 555 (N.Y. Sup. Ct. 2006).

While the surviving member of a limited liability company (LLC) established a prima facie case for the LLC's dissolution under N.Y. Ltd. Liab. Co. Law § 702, and the doctrine of laches was not estab-

lished, pursuant to N.Y. C.P.L.R. 3225(b), the administrator of the deceased member's estate was entitled to amend her answer to assert a cause of action for slander of title. Sealy v Clifton L.L.C., 933 N.Y.S.2d 805, 34 Misc. 3d 266, 2011 N.Y. Misc. LEXIS 5052 (N.Y. Sur. Ct. 2011), aff'd, 106 A.D.3d 981, 966 N.Y.S.2d 454, 2013 N.Y. App. Div. LEXIS 3592 (N.Y. App. Div. 2d Dep't 2013).

Order granting a petition for dissolution of a limited liability company (LLC) under N.Y. Ltd. Liab. Co. Law § 702 was error because, inter alia, there was no allegation of fraud or frustration of the LCC's purpose, the operating agreement contained no specific provisions relating to dissolution and did not require regular meetings or quorums, the record showed that the managers communicated with each other on a regular basis without the formality of a noticed meeting and there was no showing that the LLC was unable to function as intended or that it was failing financially; the operating agreement was silent as to the issue of manager conflicts and the dispute between the two managers was not shown to be inimical to achieving the LLC's purpose. There was no objection to the quality of construction work being done by one manager's company on the LLC's property, but only to its expense, and beyond complaining about the cost of the work and seeking to withdraw, the petitioning member ratified the manager's unilateral efforts. Matter of 1545 Ocean Ave., LLC, 72 A.D.3d 121, 893 N.Y.S.2d 590, 2010 N.Y. App. Div. LEXIS 674 (N.Y. App. Div. 2d Dep't 2010).

Order granting a petition for dissolution of a limited liability company (LLC) under N.Y. Ltd. Liab. Co. Law § 702 was error because, inter alia, the petitioning member failed to establish, in the context of the terms of the operating agreement, that (1) the management of the LLC was unable or unwilling to reasonably permit or promote the stated purpose of the LLC to be realized or achieved, or (2) continuing the LLC was financially unfeasible; "deadlock" was a basis, in and of itself, for judicial dissolution under N.Y. Bus. Corp. Law § 1104, but no such independent ground for dissolution was available under § 702. Matter of 1545 Ocean Ave., LLC, 72 A.D.3d 121, 893 N.Y.S.2d 590, 2010 N.Y. App. Div. LEXIS 674 (N.Y. App. Div. 2d Dep't 2010).

Corporation's request to dissolve a member pursuant to N.Y. Ltd. Liab. Co. Law § 702 was denied without prejudice because the corporation did not seek summary judgment on a claim or a counterclaim for judicial dissolution, but rather, merely cross-moved for the relief sought, and the preferable way to proceed with judicial dissolution was by petition. Ficus Invs., Inc. v Private Capital Mgmt. LLC, 241 N.Y.L.J. 42, 2009 N.Y. Misc. LEXIS 2391 (N.Y. Sup. Ct. Feb. 23, 2009).

§ 703. Winding up

(a) In the event of a dissolution of a limited liability company, except for a dissolution pursuant to section seven hundred two of this article, unless otherwise provided in the operating agreement, the members may wind up the limited liability company's affairs. Upon cause shown, the supreme court in the judicial district in which the office of the limited liability company is located may wind up the limited liability company's affairs upon application of any member, or his or her legal representative or assignee, and in connection therewith may appoint a receiver or liquidating trustee.

(b) Upon dissolution of a limited liability company, the persons winding up the limited liability company's affairs may, in the name of and for and on behalf of the limited liability company, prosecute and defend suits, whether civil, criminal or administrative, settle and close the limited liability company's business, dispose of and convey the limited liability company's property, discharge the limited liability company's liabilities and distribute to the members any remaining assets of the limited liability company, all without affecting the liability of members including members participating in the winding up of the limited liability company's affairs.

History: Add, L 1994, ch 576, § 1, eff Oct 24, 1994.

CASE ANNOTATIONS

Court exercised its discretion and decreed judicial dissolution of a limited liability company as it was not reasonably practicable for the company to carry on its business in conformity with a statutory operating agreement that explicitly required the dissolution and winding up of the company prior to the withdrawal of one of its members. Spires v Casterline (2004, Sup) 778 N.Y.S.2d 259

Trial court should have dismissed a member's partition claim because, since the properties at issue were owned by a limited liability company (LLC), the member could not have maintained a partition claim in his individual capacity; further, since the member lacked capacity to sue for partition, the judgment demanded was not one that would have affected the title to, or the possession, use, or enjoyment of, real property under N.Y. C.P.L.R. 6501 and the member's notice of pendency should have been cancelled. The member's claim to wind up the LLC's affairs under N.Y. Ltd. Liab. Co. Law § 703(a) likewise did not support a notice of pendency. Sealy v Clifton, LLC (2009, App Div, 2d Dept) 890 NYS2d 598.

Assignee of no-fault benefits, which was a professional service limited liability company (PLLC), could not continue an action under N.Y. Ins. Law § 5102(a) against an insurer because the doctor who was its sole member had been suspended from the practice of medicine; the PLLC was required to go through a disqualification process under N.Y. Limited Liability Company Law §§ 1209 and 1210 but could pursue the claims as part of its winding up under N.Y. Limited Liability Company Law § 703(b), and a stay was ordered under N.Y. C.P.L.R. § 2201 for the appointment of a representative to do so. A.B. Med. Servs. PLLC v Travelers Indem. Co. (2008, Dist Ct) 239 NYLJ 106, 858 NYS2d 574.

§ 704.   Distribution of assets

Upon the winding up of a limited liability company, the assets shall be distributed as follows:

(a) to creditors, including members who are creditors, to the extent permitted by law, in satisfaction of liabilities of the limited liability company, whether by payment or by establishment of adequate reserves, other than liabilities for distributions to members and former members under section five hundred seven or section five hundred nine of this chapter;

(b) except as provided in the operating agreement, to members and former members in satisfaction of liabilities for distributions under section five hundred seven or section five hundred nine of this chapter; and

(c) except as provided in the operating agreement, to members first for the return of their contributions, to the extent not previously returned, and second respecting their membership interests, in the proportions in which the members share in distributions in accordance with section five hundred four of this chapter.

History: Add, L 1994, ch 576, § 1, eff Oct 24, 1994.

Sub (a), amd, L 1995, ch 643, § 12, eff Aug 8, 1995.

CASE ANNOTATIONS

Contrary to the contention of a limited liability company (LLC), it was not previously dissolved; there was nothing in the record to indicate that the LLC's affairs were wound up as required by N.Y. Ltd. Liab. Co. Law § 701, that the articles of dissolution were filed with the Secretary of State as required by N.Y. Ltd. Liab. Co. Law § 705, or that, if the LLC had been dissolved and a member had

elected to continue the business while he was still alive, that member had served the other member with notice of that election, as required by the LLC's operating agreement. Sealy v Clifton, LLC (2009, App Div, 2d Dept) 890 NYS2d 598.

Trial court did not err in determining that if the assets of the limited liability company (LLC) were to be liquidated, then the capital contributions of the first member were to be treated as loans to the LLC to the extent that those contributions exceeded those made by the second member; although the LLC agreement provided that a member did not have the right to receive any return of capital contributions, the LLC agreement also provided for the repayment of debts of the LLC upon dissolution, and the record, including an affidavit submitted by the second member, established that the parties intended that the capital contributions by the first member were to be treated as loans to the LLC to the extent that those contributions exceeded those made by the second member. In addition, the LLC agreement was silent as to the issue of equalization of capital contributions. Mizrahi v Cohen (2013, 2d Dept) 104 App Div 3d 917, 961 NYS2d 538.

§ 705.   Articles of dissolution

(a) Within ninety days following the dissolution and the commencement of winding up of the limited liability company, or at any other time after the expiration of the time period for continuation of the limited liability company without the agreement in writing to continue by the legal representative of the last remaining member under paragraph four of subdivision (a) of section seven hundred one of this article has expired, articles of dissolution shall be filed with the department of state entitled "Articles of dissolution of .... (name of limited liability company) under section seven hundred five of the Limited Liability Company Law"and executed in accordance with section two hundred seven of this chapter. The articles of dissolution shall set forth:

(1) the name of the limited liability company; and if it has been changed, the name under which it was formed;

(2) the date of filing of its articles of organization;

(3) the event giving rise to the filing of the articles of dissolution; and

(4) any other information the persons filing the articles determine.

(b) The cancellation of the articles of organization is effective at the time of filing of the articles of dissolution.

(c) The cancellation of the articles of organization shall not affect the liability of the members during the period of winding up and termination of the limited liability company.

History: Add, L 1994, ch 576, § 1, eff Oct 24, 1994.

Sub (a), opening par, amd, L 1999, ch 420, § 5, eff Aug 31, 1999.

Sub (a), par (2), amd, L 1999, ch 172, § 20, eff July 6, 1999.

ARTICLE VIII
FOREIGN LIMITED LIABILITY
COMPANIES

History: Add, L 1994, ch 576, § 1, eff Oct 24, 1994.

§ 801.   Governing law

Subject to the constitution of this state:

(a) the laws of the jurisdiction under which a foreign limited liability company is formed govern its organization and internal affairs and the liability of its members and managers; and

(b) a foreign limited liability company may not be denied a certificate of authority by reason of any difference between such laws and the laws of this state.

History: Add, L 1994, ch 576, § 1, eff Oct 24, 1994.

CASE ANNOTATIONS

Based on N.Y. Ltd. Liab. Co. Law § 801 and N.Y. P'ship Law § 121-901, a dissolved Texas limited partnership and limited liability company were governed by Texas law with respect to liability of the individual after the dissolution of those entities in an action by a property owner, alleging environmental pollution to its property; where the claim was brought within three years of the dissolution, dismissal of the claim against the limited liability company was error under former Tex. Limited Liability Company Act art 8.12, former Tex. Bus. Corp. Act. Ann. art. 7.12. Treeline 1 OCR, LLC v Nassau County Indus. Dev. Agency (2011, 2d Dept) 82 App Div 3d 748, 918 NYS2d 128.

§ 802.   Application for authority

(a) Before doing business in this state, a foreign limited liability company shall apply for authority to do business in this state by submitting to the department of state (i) a certificate of existence or, if no such certificate is issued by the jurisdiction of formation, a certified copy of the articles of organization of the limited liability company and all subsequent amendments thereto or, if no articles of organization have been filed, a certified copy of the certificate filed as its organizational basis and all amendments thereto (if such certificate or certified copy is in a foreign language, a translation in English thereof under oath of the translator shall be attached thereto) and (ii) an application for authority as a foreign limited liability company entitled "Application for authority of .... (name of foreign limited liability company) under section eight hundred two of the Limited Liability Company Law," signed and setting forth:

(1) the name of the foreign limited liability company and, if a foreign liability company's name is not acceptable for authorization pursuant to section two hundred four of this chapter, the fictitious name under which it proposes to apply for authority and do business in this state, which name shall be in compliance with section two hundred four of this chapter and shall be used by the foreign limited liability company in all its dealings with the department of state and in the conduct of its business in this state. The provisions of section one hundred thirty of the general business law shall not apply to any fictitious name filed by a foreign limited liability company pursuant to this section, and a filing under section one hundred thirty of the general business law shall not constitute the adoption of a fictitious name;

(2) the jurisdiction and date of its organization;

(3) the county within this state in which the office of the foreign limited liability company is to be located or if the foreign limited liability company shall maintain more than one office in this state, the county within the state in which the principal office of the foreign limited liability company is to be located;

(4) a designation of the secretary of state as its agent upon whom process against it may be served and the post office address within or without this state to which the secretary of state shall mail a copy of any process against it served upon him or her;

(5) if it is to have a registered agent, his or her name and address within the state and a statement that the registered agent is to be its agent upon whom process may be served;

(6) the address of the office required to be maintained in the jurisdiction of its formation by the laws of that jurisdiction or, if not so required, of the principal office of the foreign limited liability company;

(7) a statement that the foreign limited liability company is in existence in the jurisdiction of its formation at the time of the filing of such application; and

(8) the name and address of the authorized officer in the jurisdiction of its formation where a copy of its articles of organization is filed or, if no public filing of its articles of organization is required by the law of the jurisdiction of formation, a statement that the foreign limited liability company shall provide, on request, a copy thereof with all amendments thereto (if such documents are in a foreign language, a translation in English thereof under oath of the translator shall be attached thereto), and the name and post office address of the person responsible for providing such copies.

(b)(i) Within one hundred twenty days after the filing of the application for authority with the department of state, a copy of the same or a notice containing the substance thereof shall be published once in each week for six successive weeks, in two newspapers of the county within this state in which the office of the foreign limited liability company is located, one newspaper to be printed weekly and one newspaper to be printed daily, to be designated by the county clerk. When such county is located within a city with a population of one million or more, such designation shall be as though the copy or notice were a notice or advertisement of judicial proceedings. Proof of the publication required by this paragraph, consisting of the certificate of publication of the foreign limited liability company with the affidavits of publication of such newspapers annexed thereto, must be filed with the department of state. Notwithstanding any other provision of law, if the office of the foreign limited liability company is located in a county wherein a weekly or daily newspaper of the county, or both, has not been so designated by the county clerk, then the publication herein required shall be made in a weekly or daily newspaper of any county, or both, as the case may be, which is contiguous to, such county, provided that any such newspaper meets all the other requirements of this paragraph. A copy or notice published in a newspaper other than the newspaper or newspapers designated by the county clerk shall not be deemed to be one of the publications required by this subdivision. The notice shall include: (l) the name of the foreign limited liability company; (2) the date of filing of the application for authority with the department of state; (3) the jurisdiction and date of its organization; (4) the county within this state, in which the office of the foreign limited liability company is located; (4-a) the street address of the principal business location, if any; (5) a statement that the secretary of state has been designated as agent of the foreign limited liability company upon whom process against it may be served and the post office address within or without this state to which the secretary of state shall mail a copy of any process against it served upon him or her; (6) if the foreign limited liability company is to have a registered agent, his or her name and address within this state and a statement that the registered agent is to be the agent of the foreign limited liability company upon whom process against it may be served; (7) the address of the office required to be maintained in the jurisdiction of its organization by the laws of that jurisdiction or, if not so required, of the principal office of the foreign limited liability company; (8) the name and address of the authorized officer in its jurisdiction of organization where a copy of its certificate of organization is filed or, if no public filing of its certificate of organization is required by the law of its jurisdiction of organization, a statement that the foreign limited liability company shall provide, on request, a copy thereof with all amendments thereto (if such documents are in a foreign language, a translation thereof under oath of the translator shall be attached thereto), and the name and post office address of the person responsible for providing such copies; and (9) the character or purpose of the business of such foreign limited liability company. Where, at any time after completion of the first of the six weekly publications required by this paragraph and prior to the completion of the sixth such weekly publication, there is a change in any of the information contained in the copy or notice as published, the foreign limited liability company may complete the remaining publications of the original copy or notice, and the foreign limited liability company shall not be required to publish any further or amended copy or notice. Where, at any time after completion of the six weekly publications required by this paragraph, there is a change to any of the infor-

mation contained in the copy or notice as published, no further or amended publication or republication shall be required to be made. If within one hundred twenty days after the filing of its application for authority with the department of state, proof of such publication, consisting of the certificate of publication of the foreign limited liability company with the affidavits of publication of the newspapers annexed thereto has not been filed with the department of state, the authority of such foreign limited liability company to carry on, conduct or transact any business in this state shall be suspended, effective as of the expiration of such one hundred twenty day period. The failure of a foreign limited liability company to cause such copy or notice to be published and such certificate of publication and affidavits of publication to be filed with the department of state within such one hundred twenty day period or the suspension of such foreign limited liability company's authority to carry on, conduct or transact business in this state pursuant to this paragraph shall not limit or impair the validity of any contract or act of such foreign limited liability company, or any right or remedy of any other party under or by virtue of any contract, act or omission of such foreign limited liability company, or the right of any other party to maintain any action or special proceeding on any such contract, act or omission, or right of such foreign limited liability company to defend any action or special proceeding in this state, or result in any member, manager or agent of such foreign limited liability company becoming liable for the contractual obligations or other liabilities of the foreign limited liability company. If, at any time following the suspension of a foreign limited liability company's authority to carry on, conduct or transact business in this state pursuant to this paragraph, such foreign limited liability company shall cause proof of publication in substantial compliance with the provisions (other than the one hundred twenty day period) of this paragraph, consisting of the certificate of publication of the foreign limited liability company with the affidavits of publication of the newspapers annexed thereto, to be filed with the department of state, such suspension of such foreign limited liability company's authority to carry on, conduct or transact business shall be annulled.

(ii)(1) A foreign limited liability company which was formed and filed its application for authority with the department of state prior to the effective date of this paragraph and complied with the publication and filing requirements of this subdivision as in effect prior to such effective date shall not be required to make any publication or republication or any filing under paragraph (i) of this subdivision, and shall not be subject to suspension pursuant to this subdivision.

(2) Within twelve months after the effective date of this paragraph, a foreign limited liability company which was formed and filed its application for authority with the department of state prior to such effective date and which did not comply with the publica-

tion and filing requirements of this subdivision as in effect prior to such effective date shall publish a copy of its application for authority or a notice containing the substance thereof in the manner required (other than the one hundred twenty day period) by this subdivision as in effect prior to such effective date and file proof of such publication, consisting of the certificate of publication of the foreign limited liability company with the affidavits of publication of the newspapers annexed thereto, with the department of state.

(3) If a foreign limited liability company that is subject to the provisions of subparagraph two of this paragraph fails to file the required proof of publication with the department of state within twelve months after the effective date of this paragraph, its authority to carry on, conduct or transact any business in this state shall be suspended, effective as of the expiration of such twelve month period.

(4) The failure of a foreign limited liability company that is subject to the provisions of subparagraph two of this paragraph to fully comply with the provisions of said subparagraph two or the suspension of such foreign limited liability company's authority to carry on, conduct or transact any business in this state pursuant to subparagraph three of this paragraph shall not impair or limit the validity of any contract or act of such foreign limited liability company, or any right or remedy of any other party under or by virtue of any contract, act or omission of such foreign limited liability company, or the right of any other party to maintain any action or special proceeding on any such contract, act or omission, or right of such foreign limited liability company to defend any action or special proceeding in this state, or result in any member, manager or agent of such foreign limited liability company becoming liable for the contractual obligations or other liabilities of the foreign limited liability company.

(5) If, at any time following the suspension of a foreign limited liability company's authority to carry on, conduct or transact business in this state, pursuant to subparagraph three of this paragraph, such foreign limited liability company shall cause proof of publication in substantial compliance with the provisions (other than the one hundred twenty day period) of paragraph (i) of this subdivision, consisting of the certificate of publication of the foreign limited liability company with the affidavits of publication of the newspapers annexed thereto, to be filed with the department of state, such suspension of such foreign limited liability company's authority to carry on, conduct or transact business shall be annulled.

(6) For the purposes of this paragraph, a foreign limited liability company which was formed and filed its application for authority with the department of state prior to the effective date of this paragraph shall be deemed to have complied with the publication and filing requirements of this subdivision as in effect prior to such effective date if (i) the foreign limited liability company was formed and filed its application for authority with the department of state on or after January first, nineteen hundred ninety-nine and prior to such effective date and the foreign limited liability company filed at least one affidavit of the printer or publisher of a newspaper with the department of state at any time prior to such effective date, or (ii) the foreign limited liability company was formed and filed its application for authority with the department of state prior to January first, nineteen-hundred ninety-nine, without regard to whether the foreign limited liability company did or did not file any affidavit of the printer or publisher of a newspaper with the secretary of state.

(iii) The information in a notice published pursuant to this subdivision shall be presumed to be in compliance with and satisfaction of the requirements of this subdivision.

History: Add, L 1994, ch 576, § 1, eff Oct 24, 1994; amd, L 1995, ch 643, § 13, eff Aug 8, 1995; L 1997, ch 470, § 7, eff Aug 26, 1997 (see 1997 note below); L 1998, ch 375, § 25, eff Aug 13, 1998; L 1999, ch 420, § 6; L 2005, ch 767, § 4; L 2006, ch 44, § 4, eff June 1, 2006.

§ 803. Activities not constituting doing business

(a) Without excluding other activities that may not constitute doing business in this state, a foreign limited liability company shall not be considered to be doing business in this state for the purposes of this chapter, by reason of carrying on in this state any one or more of the following activities:

(1) maintaining or defending any action or proceeding, whether judicial, administrative, arbitrative or otherwise or effecting settlement thereof or the settlement of claims or disputes;

(2) holding meetings of its members or managers;

(3) maintaining bank accounts; or

(4) maintaining offices or agencies only for the transfer, exchange and registration of its membership interests or appointing and maintaining depositaries with relation to its membership interests.

(b) The specification in subdivision (a) of this section does not establish a standard of activities that may subject a foreign limited liability company to service of process under this chapter or any other statute of this state.

History: Add, L 1994, ch 576, § 1, eff Oct 24, 1994.

§ 804. Amendments to application for authority

(a) A foreign limited liability company may amend its application for authority from time to time if the amendments contain only such provisions as might be lawfully contained in an application for authority at the time of making such amendment. To accomplish such amendment, a certificate, entitled "Certificate of amendment of .... (name of foreign limited liability company) under section eight hundred four of the Limited Liability Company Law,"shall be signed by an authorized person and delivered to the department of state. The certificate shall set forth:

(1) the name of the foreign limited liability company as it appears on the index of names of existing domestic and authorized foreign limited liability companies of any type or kind in the department of state, and the fictitious name, if any, the foreign limited liability company has agreed to use in this state pursuant to section eight hundred two of this article;

(2) the jurisdiction of its organization;

(3) the date it was authorized to do business in this state;

(4) each amendment effected thereby; and

(5) if the true name of the foreign limited liability company is to be changed, a statement that the change of name has been effected under the laws of the jurisdiction of its formation and the date the change was so effected.

(b) Every foreign limited liability company that has received a filing receipt entitled "Certificate of authority of............ (name of foreign limited liability company) under section eight hundred five of the Limited Liability Company Law,"evidencing authority as provided herein, shall, within ninety days after it has changed its name in the jurisdiction of its formation, file an amendment to its application with the department of state under subdivision (a) of this section.

History: Add, L 1994, ch 576, § 1, eff Oct 24, 1994; amd, L 1997, ch 470, § 8 (see 1997 note below); L 1998, ch 375, § 26; L 1999, ch 172, § 21, eff July 6, 1999,22, eff July 6, 1999.

§ 804-A.　Certificate of change

(a) A foreign limited liability company may amend its application for authority from time to time to (i) specify or change the location of the limited liability company's office; (ii) specify or change the post office address to which the secretary of state shall mail a copy of any process against the limited liability company served upon him; and (iii) to make, revoke or change the designation of a registered agent, or to specify or change the address of a registered agent. Any one or more such changes may be accomplished by filing a certificate of change which shall be entitled "Certificate of Change of.... (name of limited liability company) under section 804-A of the Limited Liability Company Law"and shall be signed and delivered to the department of state. It shall set forth:

(1) the name of the foreign limited liability company and, if applicable, the fictitious name the limited liability company has agreed to use in this state pursuant to section eight hundred two of this article;

(2) the date its application for authority was filed by the department of state; and

(3) each change effected thereby, [.]*

* The bracketed punctuation has been inserted by the Publisher.

(b) A certificate of change which changes only the post office address to which the secretary of state shall mail a copy of any process against a foreign limited liability company served upon him or the address of the registered agent, provided such address being changed is the address of a person, partnership or corporation whose address, as agent, is the address to be changed or who has been designated as registered agent for such limited liability company may be signed and delivered to the department of state by such agent. The certificate of change shall set forth the statements required under subdivision (a) of this section; that a notice of the proposed change was mailed to the foreign limited liability company by the party signing the certificate not less than thirty days prior to the date of delivery to the department of state and that such foreign limited liability company has not objected thereto; and that the party signing the certificate is the agent of such foreign limited liability company to whose address the secretary of state is required to mail copies of process or the registered agent, if such be the case. A certificate signed and delivered under this subdivision shall not be deemed to effect a change of location of the office of the foreign limited liability company in whose behalf such certificate is filed.

History: Add, L 1998, ch 448, § 4, eff Oct 20, 1998.

§ 805.　Issuance of certificate of authority; effect

(a) Upon filing with the department of state of the application for authority, the department of state shall issue a filing receipt entitled "Certificate of authority of....(name of foreign limited liability company) under section eight hundred five of the Limited Liability Company Law,"and the foreign limited liability company shall be authorized to do business in this state. Such authority shall continue so long as the foreign limited liability company retains its authority to do business in the jurisdiction of its formation and its authority to do business has not been surrendered, suspended or annulled in accordance with the law.

(b) A foreign limited liability company that has received a certificate of authority shall have such powers to conduct business in this state as are permitted by the laws of the jurisdiction in which it was organized but no greater than those of a domestic limited liability company; provided, that this subdivision shall not affect the powers of the foreign limited liability company outside this state; and provided, further, that a foreign related limited liability partnership (i) shall have such powers to conduct business in this state as are permitted by the laws of the jurisdiction whose laws govern the agreement under which such foreign related limited liability partnership operates but no greater than those of a partnership without limited partners operating under an agreement governed by the laws of this state and provided that such foreign related limited liability partnership shall not engage in any profession or professions and (ii) shall be deemed to be a foreign limited liability partnership for purposes of subdivisions (l) and (m) of section 121-1502 of the partnership law which subdivisions shall be applicable to foreign related limited liability partnerships.

History: Add, L 1994, ch 576, § 1, eff Oct 24, 1994.

§ 806. Surrender of certificate of authority

(a) A foreign limited liability company may surrender its certificate of authority by filing with the department of state a certificate entitled "Certificate of surrender of authority of .... (name of foreign limited liability company) under section eight hundred six of the Limited Liability Company Law"signed by an authorized person, or by a trustee, receiver or other person authorized by law to wind up such limited liability company. The authority of the foreign limited liability company to do business in this state shall terminate on such filing of the certificate of surrender of authority. A surrender shall not terminate the authority of the secretary of state to accept service of process on the foreign limited liability company with respect to causes of action arising out of doing business in this state.

(b) The certificate of surrender of authority shall set forth:

(1) the name of the foreign limited liability company as it appears on the index of names of existing domestic and authorized foreign limited liability companies of any type or kind in the department of state, and the fictitious name the foreign limited liability company has agreed to use in this state pursuant to section eight hundred two of this article;

(2) the jurisdiction where it was organized;

(3) the date on which its certificate of authority to do business in this state was filed with the department of state;

(4) that it surrenders its authority to do business in this state;

(5) that it revokes the authority of its registered agent, if any, previously designated, and that it consents that process against it in any action or special proceeding based upon any liability or obligation incurred by it within this state before the filing of the certificate of surrender may be served on the secretary of state in the manner set forth in article three of this chapter; and

(6) a post office address within or without this state to which the secretary of state shall mail a copy of any process against it served upon him or her.

History: Add, L 1994, ch 576, § 1, eff Oct 24, 1994.

Sub (a), amd, L 1998, ch 375, § 27, eff Aug 13, 1998.

§ 807. Termination of existence

When a foreign limited liability company that has received a certificate of authority is dissolved or its authority to conduct its business or existence is otherwise terminated or canceled in the jurisdiction of its formation or when such foreign limited liability company is merged into or consolidated with another foreign limited liability company, (a) a certificate of the secretary of state or official performing the equivalent function as to limited liability company records in the jurisdiction of organization of such limited liability company attesting to the occurrence of any such event or (b) a certified copy of an order or decree of a court of such jurisdiction directing the dissolution of such foreign limited liability company, the termination of its existence or the surrender of its authority shall be delivered to the department of state. The filing of the certificate, order or decree shall have the same effect as the filing of a certificate of surrender of authority under section eight hundred six of this article. The secretary of state shall continue as agent of the foreign limited liability company upon whom process against it may be served in the manner set forth in article three of this chapter, in any action or proceeding based upon any liability or obligation incurred by the foreign limited liability company within this state prior to the filing of such certificate, order or decree. The post office address may be changed by filing with the department of state a certificate of amendment under section eight hundred four of this article.

History: Add, L 1994, ch 576, § 1, eff Oct 24, 1994.

§ 808. Doing business without certificate of authority

(a) A foreign limited liability company doing business in this state without having received a certificate of authority to do business in this state may not maintain any action, suit or special proceeding in any court of this state unless and until such limited liability company shall have received a certificate of authority in this state.

(b) The failure of a foreign limited liability company that is doing business in this state to comply with the provisions of this chapter does not impair the validity of any contract or act of the foreign limited liability company or prevent the foreign limited liability company from defending any action or special proceeding in any court of this state.

(c) A member, manager or agent of a foreign limited liability company is not liable for the contractual obligations or other liabilities of the foreign limited liability company solely by reason of the limited liability company's doing or having done business in this state without having received a certificate of authority.

(d) By doing business in this state without authority, a foreign limited liability company appoints the secretary of state as its agent for service of process with respect to causes of action arising out of doing business in this state. In any such case, process against such foreign limited liability company may be served upon the secretary of state in the manner set forth in article three of this chapter.

History: Add, L 1994, ch 576, § 1, eff Oct 24, 1994.

Sub (a), amd, L 2005, ch 767, § 5, eff June 1, 2006.

CASE ANNOTATIONS

Because an owner's lack of authorization to do business in New York under N.Y. Ltd. Liab. Co. Law § 808(a) did not impair the validity of its ownership of the subject premises or any contracts it might have executed, it was prevented from going forward with a holdover proceeding against an occupant of the premises. RMS Residential Props., LLC v Naaze (2010, Dist Ct) 243 NYLJ 119, 903 NYS2d 729.

§ 809. Action by attorney general

The attorney general shall, upon his or her own motion or upon the motion of proper parties, bring an action to restrain a foreign limited liability company without a certificate of authority from doing any business in this state in violation of this chapter or from doing any business in this state that is prohibited under the laws of this state. The attorney general may bring an action or special proceeding to annul the authority of a foreign limited liability company that is doing any business in this state that is prohibited under the laws of this state. The attorney general shall deliver a certified copy of the order of annulment to the department of state. Upon the filing thereof by the department of state, the certificate of authority of the foreign limited liability company to do business in this state shall be annulled, and the provisions of section eight hundred seven of this article shall thereafter be applicable. The secretary of state shall continue as agent of the foreign limited liability company upon whom process against it may be served in any action, suit or special proceeding based upon any liability or obligation incurred by the foregoing foreign limited liability company within the state prior to the filing of the certified copy of the order of annulment by the department of state.

History: Add, L 1994, ch 576, § 1, eff Oct 24, 1994.

ARTICLE X
MERGERS

History: Add, L 1994, ch 576, § 1, eff Oct 24, 1994.

§ 1001. Merger or consolidation

(a) As used in this article, "merger" means a procedure in which two or more limited liability companies or other business entities merge into a single limited liability company or other business entity that shall be one of the constituent limited liability companies or other business entities, and "consolidation" means a procedure in which two or more limited liability companies or other business entities consolidate into a single limited liability company or other business entity that shall be a new limited liability company or other business entity to be formed pursuant to the consolidation.

(b) Pursuant to an agreement of merger or consolidation and to the extent not expressly prohibited by law, a domestic limited liability company may merge or consolidate with or into one or more domestic limited liability companies or other business entities formed or organized under the laws of this state or any other state or the United States or any foreign country or other foreign jurisdiction, with such domestic limited liability company or other business entity as the agreement shall provide being the surviving or resulting domestic limited liability company or other business entity.

History: Add, L 1994, ch 576, § 1, eff Oct 24, 1994 Ltd. Liab. Co. Law §§ 1001, 1002, 1005, 417 and 509; BCL § 623.

§ 1002. Procedures for merger or consolidation

(a) In connection with a merger or consolidation under this chapter, rights or securities of, or interests in, a limited liability company or other business entity that is a constituent party to the merger or consolidation may be exchanged for or converted into cash, property, rights or securities of, or interests in, the surviving or resulting limited liability company or other business entity or, in addition to or in lieu thereof, may be exchanged for or converted into cash, property, rights or securities of, or interests in, a limited liability company or other business entity that is not the surviving or resulting limited liability company or other business entity in the merger or consolidation.

(b) The members of each domestic limited liability company or other business entity shall adopt (with respect to a domestic limited liability company, in the manner provided in subdivision (c) of this section) an agreement of merger or consolidation, setting forth the terms and conditions of the conversion of the membership interests of the members of the domestic limited liability company into interests in the surviving or resulting limited liability company or other business entity or the cash or other consideration to be paid or delivered in exchange for membership interests in each domestic limited liability company, or a combination thereof.

(c) The agreement of merger or consolidation shall be submitted to the members of each domestic limited liability company who are entitled to vote with respect to a merger or consolidation at a meeting called on twenty days' notice or such greater notice as the operating agreement may provide. Subject to any requirement in the operating agreement requiring approval by any greater or lesser percentage in interest of the members who are entitled to vote with respect to a merger or consolidation, which shall not be less than a majority in interest of those members who are so entitled to vote, the agreement shall be approved on behalf of each domestic limited liability company (i) by such voting interests of the members as shall be required by the operating agreement, or (ii) if no provision is made, by the members representing at least a majority in interest of the members.

(d) Notwithstanding authorization by the members, the agreement of merger or consolidation may be terminated or amended pursuant to a provision for such termination or amendment, if any, contained in the agreement of merger or consolidation.

(e) Any member that is a party to a proposed merger or consolidation who is entitled to vote with respect to such proposed merger or consolidation may, prior to that time of the meeting at which such merger or consolidation is to be voted on, file with the domestic limited liability company written notice of dissent from the proposed merger or consolidation. Such notice of dissent may be withdrawn by the dissenting member at any time prior to the effective date of the merger or consolidation and shall be deemed to be withdrawn if the member casts a vote in favor of the proposed merger or consolidation.

(f) Upon the effectiveness of the merger or consolidation, the dissenting member (referred to in subdivision (e) of this section) of any domestic limited liability company shall not become or continue to be a member of or hold an interest in the surviving or resulting limited liability company or other business entity but shall be entitled to receive in cash from the surviving or resulting domestic limited liability company or other business entity the fair value of his or her membership interest in the domestic limited liability company as of the close of business of the day prior to the effective date of the merger or consolidation in accordance with section five hundred nine of this chapter but without taking account of the effect of the merger or consolidation.

(g) A member of a domestic limited liability company who has a right under this chapter to demand payment for his or her membership interest shall not have any right at law or in equity under this chapter to attack the validity of the merger or consolidation or to have the merger or consolidation set aside or rescinded, except in an action or contest with respect to compliance with the provisions of the operating agreement or subdivision (c) of this section.

(h) A limited liability company whose original articles of organization were filed with the secretary of state and effective prior to the effective date of this subdivision shall continue to be governed by this section as in effect on such date and shall not be governed by this section, unless otherwise provided in the operating agreement.

History: Add, L 1994, ch 576, § 1, eff Oct 24, 1994.

Sub (c), amd, L 1999, ch 420, § 7, eff Aug 31, 1999.

Sub (h), add, L 1999, ch 420, § 7, eff Aug 31, 1999 Ltd. Liab. Co. Law §§ 1001, 1002, 1005, 417 and 509; BCL § 623.

§ 1003. Certificate of merger or consolidation; contents

(a) After approval of the agreement of merger or consolidation by each domestic limited liability company or other business entity merging or consolidating under this article, unless the merger or consolidation is terminated in accordance with subdivision (d) of section ten hundred two of this article, paragraph (b) of section nine hundred three of the business corporation law, or other applicable statute, and the surviving or resulting entity is a limited liability company, foreign limited liability company or other business entity for which the laws of this state do not provide for the filing of a certificate of merger or consolidation with the department of state, a certificate of merger or consolidation, entitled "Certificate of merger (or consolidation) of .... and...................... into .... (names of domestic limited liability companies or other business entities) under section one thousand three of the Limited Liability Company Law," shall be signed on behalf of each domestic limited liability company and other business entity and delivered to the department of state. The certificate of merger or consolidation shall set forth:

(1) the name and jurisdiction of formation or organization of each of the domestic limited liability companies or other business entities that are to merge or consolidate, and if the name of any of them has been changed, the name under which it was formed;

(2) for each domestic limited liability company and domestic other business entity that is to merge or consolidate, the date when its initial articles of organization or formation document, if any, were filed with the department of state;

(3) that an agreement of merger or consolidation has been approved and executed by each of the domestic limited liability companies or other business entities that are to merge or consolidate;

(4) the name of the surviving or resulting limited liability company, foreign limited liability company or other business entity;

(5) the future effective date (which shall be a date certain) of the merger or consolidation in accordance with subdivision (b) of this section, if it is not to be effective upon the filing of the certificate of merger or consolidation;

(6) if a domestic limited liability company is the surviving limited liability company, such changes in

its articles of organization as shall be necessary by reason of the merger;

(7) if a domestic limited liability company is the resulting limited liability company in a consolidation, the matters required to be set forth under subdivision (e) of section two hundred three of this chapter;

(8) if a constituent entity is a foreign limited liability company or foreign other business entity, the jurisdiction and date of filing of its initial articles of organization or formation document, if any, and the date when its application for authority was filed by the department of state or if no such application has been filed, a statement to such effect and (if the constituent foreign limited liability company is the surviving entity) that it is not to do business in this state until an application for such authority shall have been filed with the department of state;

(9) if the surviving or resulting entity is a foreign limited liability company or other business entity, an agreement that the foreign limited liability company or other business entity may be served with process in this state in any action or special proceeding for the enforcement of any liability or obligation of any domestic limited liability company, domestic business corporation or domestic other business entity previously amenable to suit in this state that is to merge or consolidate, and for the enforcement as provided in this chapter, of the right of members of any domestic limited liability company, shareholders of any domestic business corporation or owners of any domestic other business entity to receive payment for their interests against the surviving or consolidated foreign limited liability company;

(10) if the surviving or resulting entity is a foreign limited liability company or other business entity, an agreement that, subject to the provisions of section six hundred twenty-three of the business corporation law, section one thousand five of this article, or any applicable statute, the surviving or resulting foreign limited liability company or other business entity will promptly pay to the shareholders of each constituent domestic business corporation, the members of each domestic limited liability company or owners of any constituent other business entity the amount, if any, to which they shall be entitled under the provisions of the business corporation law, any applicable statute and this chapter relating to the right of shareholders, members and owners to receive payment for their interests;

(11) a designation of the secretary of state as its agent upon whom process against it may be served in the manner set forth in article three of this chapter in any action or special proceeding, and a post office address, within or without this state, to which the secretary of state shall mail a copy of any process served upon him or her. Such post office address shall supersede any prior address designated as the address to which process shall be mailed;

(12) for each foreign limited liability company and foreign other business entity, a statement that such merger or consolidation is permitted by the jurisdiction of organization or formation and is in compliance therewith;

(13) that the agreement of merger or consolidation is on file at a place of business of the surviving or resulting limited liability company or other business entity and shall state the address thereof; and

(14) that a copy of the agreement of merger or consolidation will be furnished by the surviving or resulting limited liability company or other business entity on request and without cost, to any member of any domestic limited liability company or any person holding an interest in any other business entity that is to merge or consolidate.

(b) The merger or consolidation shall be effective upon the filing by the department of state of the certificate, or at such later date not more than thirty days after the date of such filing as the certificate filed may provide.

(c) The surviving or resulting limited liability company or other business entity shall thereafter cause a copy of such certificate, certified by the department of state, to be filed in the office of the clerk of each county in which each office of a constituent corporation is located, and in the office of the official who is the recording officer of each county in this state in which real property of a constituent corporation is situated.

History: Add, L 1994, ch 576, § 1; amd, L 1997, ch 470, § 9, eff Aug 26, 1997,9; L 1998, ch 374, § 6, eff Sept 12, 1998; L 1999, ch 172, § 23, eff July 6, 1999; L 2008, ch 177, § 3, eff July 7, 2008.

§ 1004. Effect of merger or consolidation

(a) When any merger or consolidation shall have become effective under this chapter, for all purposes of the laws of this state, all of the rights, privileges, immunities, powers and purposes of each of the domestic limited liability companies and other business entities that have merged or consolidated, and all property, real, personal and mixed, tangible and intangible, and all debts, obligations, liabilities, penalties and duties of such domestic limited liability companies and other business entities, as well as all other things belonging to each of such domestic limited liability companies and other business entities, shall be vested in the surviving or resulting domestic limited liability company or other business entity, and shall thereafter be the property of the surviving or resulting domestic limited liability company or other business entity as they were of each of the domestic limited liability companies and other business entities that have merged or consolidated, and the title to any real property vested by deed or otherwise, under the laws of this state, in any of such domestic limited liability companies and other business entities, shall not revert or be in any way impaired by reason of this chapter; but all rights of creditors and all liens upon any property of any of such domestic limited liability companies and other business entities shall be preserved unimpaired, and all debts, obligations, liabilities, penalties and duties of each of such domestic limited liability companies and other business entities that have merged or consolidated shall thenceforth attach to the surviving or resulting domestic limited liability company or other business entity and may be enforced against it to the same extent as if such debts, obligations, liabilities, penalties and duties had been incurred or contracted by it.

(b) When any merger or consolidation shall have become effective under this chapter, no action, suit or proceeding, civil or criminal, then pending by or against any constituent limited liability company or other business entity in its common name shall abate or be discontinued by reason of such merger or consolidation, but may be prosecuted by or may proceed against such surviving or resulting domestic limited liability company or other business entity.

(c) Unless otherwise agreed, a merger or consolidation of a domestic limited liability company, including a domestic limited liability company that is not the surviving or resulting entity in the merger or consolidation, shall not require such domestic limited liability company to wind up its affairs under section seven hundred three of this chapter or pay its liabilities and distribute its assets under section seven hundred four of this chapter.

(d) A certificate of merger or consolidation shall act as articles of dissolution for a domestic limited liability company that is not the surviving or resulting entity in the merger or consolidation.

(e) Notwithstanding anything to the contrary contained in an operating agreement, an operating agreement containing a specific reference to this subdivision may provide that an agreement of merger or consolidation approved in accordance with subdivision (c) of section ten hundred two of this article may (i) effect any amendment to the operating agreement or (ii) effect the adoption of a new operating agreement for a domestic limited liability company if it is the surviving or resulting domestic limited liability company in the merger or consolidation. Any amendment to an operating agreement or adoption of a new operating agreement made pursuant to the foregoing sentence shall be effective at the effective time or date of the merger or consolidation. The provisions of this subdivision shall not be construed to limit the accomplishment of a merger or of any of the matters referred to herein by any other means provided for in an operating agreement or other agreement or as otherwise permitted by law, including that the operating agreement of any domestic limited liability company to the merger or consolidation (including a domestic limited liability company formed for the purpose of consummating a merger or consolidation) shall be the operating agreement of the surviving or resulting domestic limited liability company.

History: Add, L 1994, ch 576, § 1, eff Oct 24, 1994.

§ 1005. Payment of interest of dissenting members

(a) Within ten days after the occurrence of an event described in section ten hundred two of this article, the surviving or resulting domestic limited liability company or other business entity shall send to each dissenting former member a written offer to pay in cash the fair value of such former member's membership interest. Payment in cash shall be made to each former member accepting such offer within ten days after notice of such acceptance is received by the surviving or resulting domestic limited liability company or other business entity.

(b) If a former member and the surviving or resulting limited liability company or other business entity fail to agree on the price to be paid for the former member's membership interest within ninety days after the surviving or resulting domestic limited liability company or other business entity shall have made the offer provided for in subdivision (a) of this section, or if the domestic limited liability company or surviving domestic limited liability company or other business entity shall fail to make such an offer within the period provided for in subdivision (a) of this section, the procedure provided for in paragraphs (h), (i), (j) and (k) of section six hundred twenty-three of the business corporation law (or any successor provisions or statute) shall apply, as such paragraphs may be amended from time to time.

(c) A payment under this section shall constitute a return of a member's contribution for the purposes of section five hundred eight of this chapter.

History: Add, L 1994, ch 576, § 1, eff Oct 24, 1994 Ltd. Liab. Co. Law §§ 1001, 1002, 1005, 417 and 509; BCL § 623.

§ 1006. Conversion of partnership or limited partnership to limited liability company

(a) As used in this article, unless the context otherwise requires, the term, "limited partnership" means a limited partnership formed under the laws of this state; and the terms "general partner," "limited partner" and "majority in interest of the limited partners" shall have the meanings assigned to such terms in article eight-A of the partnership law; and the term "partnership" shall have the meaning assigned to such term in article two of the partnership law.

(b) A partnership or limited partnership may be converted to a limited liability company pursuant to this section.

(c) Subject to any requirements in the partnership agreement requiring approval by any lesser percentage in interest of partners, an agreement of conversion setting forth the terms and conditions of a conversion of a partnership to a limited liability company must be approved by all of the partners of the partnership. Subject to any requirement in the partnership agreement requiring approval by any greater or lesser percentage in interest of limited partners, which shall not be less than a majority in interest, the terms and conditions of a conversion of a limited partnership to a limited liability company must be approved (i) by such a vote of general partners as shall be required by the partnership agreement, or, if no provision is made, by all general partners, and (ii) by limited partners representing at least a majority in interest of each class of limited partners. The agreement of conversion shall be submitted to the general partners and limited partners of a limited partnership at a regular or special meeting called on twenty days notice or such other notice as the partnership agreement may provide. A dissenting limited partner shall have the rights provided in article eight-A of the partnership law and shall not be a member of the converted limited liability company. Notwithstanding authorization by the partners of a partnership or general partners or limited partners of a limited partnership, the conversion to a limited liability company may be abandoned pursuant to a provision for such abandonment, if any, contained in the agreement of conversion.

(d) The agreement of conversion shall set forth the terms and conditions of the conversion of the interests of partners of a partnership or general partners and limited partners of a limited partnership, as the case may be, into membership interests in the converted limited liability company or the cash or other consideration to be paid or delivered as a result of the conversion of the interests of such partners, or a combination thereof.

(e) In connection with any conversion approved under subdivision (c) of this section, the partnership or limited partnership shall file with the department of state a signed certificate entitled "Certificate of Conversion of............ (name partnership or limited partnership) to............ (name of limited liability company) under section one thousand six of the Limited Liability Company Law"and shall also satisfy the publication requirements of section two hundred six of this chapter. Such certificate shall include either:

(A) (i) articles of organization for such limited liability company in the same manner as if newly formed pursuant to section two hundred three of this chapter;

(ii) a statement that the partnership or limited partnership was, in accordance with the provisions of this chapter, duly converted to a limited liability company from a partnership or limited partnership, as the case may be; and

(iii) The name of such partnership or limited partnership and in the case of a limited partnership the date its initial certificate was filed with the department of state, or:

(B) where such partnership or limited partnership is being converted into a limited liability company formed pursuant to section two hundred three of this chapter prior to the conversion,

(i) the name of such partnership or limited partnership and in the case of a limited partnership the date its initial certificate was filed with the department of state;

(ii) a statement that the partnership or limited partnership was, in accordance with the provisions of this chapter duly converted to a limited liability company from a partnership or limited partnership, as the case may be; and

(iii) the name of the limited liability company and the date its articles of organization were filed with the department of state.

(f) If the limited partnership is a domestic limited partnership, such domestic limited partnership shall cancel its certificate of limited partnership pursuant to article eight-A of the partnership law. The certificate of cancellation shall include the name of the limited liability company and a statement that the limited partnership will be converted into a limited liability company upon the filing of such certificate.

(g) The conversion takes effect, in the case of a partnership, when the certificate of conversion is filed with the department of state or at any later date specified in the certificate of conversion or, in the case of a limited partnership, when the certificate of limited partnership is canceled.

(h) A partner or, in the case of a limited partnership, a general partner who becomes a member of a limited liability company as a result of a conversion, remains liable as a partner or general partner, as the case may be, for any debt, obligation, liability and penalty incurred by the partnership or limited partnership before the conversion takes effect. A limited partner who becomes a member as a result of a conversion remains liable only as a limited partner for a debt, obligation, liability or penalty incurred by the limited partnership before the conversion takes effect. The partner's, general partner's or limited partner's liability, if any, for a debt, obligation, liability or penalty incurred by the limited liability company after the conversion takes effect is that of a member as provided in this chapter.

(i) A limited liability company whose original articles of organization were filed with the secretary of state and effective prior to the effective date of this subdivision shall continue to be governed by this section as in effect on such date and shall not be governed by this section, unless otherwise provided in the operating agreement.

History: Add, L 1994, ch 576, § 1, eff Oct 24, 1994; amd, L 1997, ch 470, § 10, eff Aug 26, 1997,10; L 1998, ch 375, § 28, eff Aug 13, 1998; L 1999, ch 420, § 8, eff Aug 31, 1999.

CASE ANNOTATIONS

Because a purported conversion of a New York limited partnership into a Delaware limited liability company was ineffective under the limited partnership agreement and N.Y. Ltd. Liab. Co. Law § 1006(c), the trial court properly denied the defendants' motion for summary judgment. Miller v Ross (2007, 1st Dept) 43 App Div 3d 730, 841 NYS2d 586

Plaintiffs were entitled to summary judgment on their cause of action to nullify the conversion of a limited partnership (LP) to a Delaware limited liability company (LLC); the direct conversion to an LLC without the consent of a majority in interest of each class of limited partners was not permitted under N.Y. Ltd. Liab. Co. Law § 1006 or Delaware law. As a "Class Z" limited partner of the LP constituted 100% of Class Z, the LP could not convert to an LLC without the Class Z limited partner's consent. Miller v Ross (2007, Sup) 237 NYLJ 39, later proceeding (2007, NY App Div, 1st Dept) 2007 NY App Div LEXIS 4092, later proceeding (2007, 1st Dept) 43 App Div 3d 730, 841 NYS2d 586

§ 1007. Effect of conversion

(a) A partnership or limited partnership that has been converted pursuant to this chapter is for all purposes the same entity that existed before the conversion.

(b) When a conversion takes effect:

(i) all property, real and personal, tangible and intangible, of the converting partnership or limited partnership remains vested in the converted limited liability company;

(ii) all debts, obligations, liabilities and penalties of the converting partnership or limited partnership continue as debts, obligations, liabilities and penalties of the converted limited liability company;

(iii) any action, suit or proceeding, civil or criminal, then pending by or against the converting partnership or limited partnership may be continued as if the conversion had not occurred; and

(iv) to the extent provided in the agreement of conversion and in this chapter, the partners of a partnership or the general partners and limited partners of a limited partnership shall continue as members in the converted limited liability company.

History: Add, L 1994, ch 576, § 1, eff Oct 24, 1994.

ARTICLE XI
MISCELLANEOUS

History: Add, L 1994, ch 576, § 1, eff Oct 24, 1994.

§ 1101. Fees

Except as otherwise provided, the department of state shall collect the following fees pursuant to this chapter:

(a) For the reservation of a limited liability company name pursuant to section two hundred five of this chapter, twenty dollars.

(b) For the change of address of the post office address to which the secretary of state shall mail a copy of any process against the limited liability company served upon him or her pursuant to section three hundred one of this chapter, twenty dollars.

(c) For the statement of address of the post office address to which the secretary of state shall mail a copy of any process against the limited liability company served upon him or her pursuant to section three hundred one of this chapter, nine dollars. This fee shall not apply to statements submitted through the department of taxation and finance pursuant to paragraph two of subdivision (e) of section three hundred one of this chapter.

(d) For the change of address of a registered agent for service of process by such registered agent pursuant to section three hundred two of this chapter, twenty dollars.

(e) For the resignation of a registered agent for service of process pursuant to section three hundred two of this chapter, twenty dollars.

(f) For filing articles of organization pursuant to section two hundred nine of this chapter, two hundred dollars.

(g) For filing a certificate of amendment pursuant to section two hundred eleven of this chapter, sixty dollars.

(h) For filing articles of dissolution pursuant to section seven hundred five of this chapter, sixty dollars.

(i) For filing restated articles of organization pursuant to section two hundred fourteen of this chapter, sixty dollars.

(j) For filing a judicial dissolution pursuant to section seven hundred two of this chapter, sixty dollars.

(k) For filing an application for authority pursuant to section eight hundred two of this chapter, two hundred fifty dollars.

(l) For filing an amendment to an application for authority pursuant to section eight hundred four of this chapter, sixty dollars.

(m) For filing a certificate of surrender of authority pursuant to section eight hundred six of this chapter, sixty dollars.

(n) For filing a certificate of termination of existence pursuant to section eight hundred seven of this chapter, sixty dollars.

(o) For filing a certificate of merger or consolidation pursuant to section ten hundred three of this chapter, sixty dollars.

(p) For filing an application for cancellation of reservation of name pursuant to section two hundred five of this chapter, twenty dollars.

(q) For filing a certificate of correction pursuant to section two hundred twelve of this chapter, sixty dollars.

(r) For filing a certificate of conversion pursuant to section one thousand six of this chapter, two hundred dollars.

(s) For filing a certificate of publication with affidavits of publication annexed thereto pursuant to section two hundred six, eight hundred two, twelve hundred three or thirteen hundred six of this chapter, fifty dollars.

(t) For filing a certificate of resignation for receipt for process pursuant to section three hundred one-A of this chapter, ten dollars.

(u) For service of process on the secretary of state pursuant to subdivision (e) of section three hundred one-A or pursuant to section three hundred three of this chapter, forty dollars. No fee shall be collected for process served on behalf of a county, city, town or village or other political subdivision of the state.

(v) For filing a certificate of change pursuant to subdivision (a) of section two hundred eleven-A or subdivision (a) of section eight hundred four-A of this chapter, thirty dollars, and for filing a certificate of change pursuant to subdivision (b) of section two hundred eleven-A or subdivision (b) of section eight hundred four-A of this chapter, five dollars.

History: Add, L 1994, ch 576, § 1, eff Oct 24, 1994; amd, L 1995, ch 643, § 14, eff Aug 8, 1995; L 1997, ch 470, § 11, eff Aug 26, 1997; L 1998, ch 448, § 5, eff Oct 20, 1998; L 2005, ch 767, § 6, eff June 1, 2006; L 2015, ch 59, §7 (Part S), eff April 13, 2015.

§ 1102. Records

(a) Each domestic limited liability company shall maintain the following records, which may, but need not, be maintained in this state:

(1) if the limited liability company is managed by a manager or managers, a current list of the full name set forth in alphabetical order and last known mailing address of each such manager;

(2) a current list of the full name set forth in alphabetical order and last known mailing address of each member together with the contribution and the share of profits and losses of each member or information from which such share can be readily derived;

(3) a copy of the articles of organization and all amendments thereto or restatements thereof, together with executed copies of any powers of attorney pursuant to which any certificate or amendment has been executed;

(4) a copy of the operating agreement, any amendments thereto and any amended and restated operating agreement; and

(5) a copy of the limited liability company's federal, state and local income tax or information returns and reports, if any, for the three most recent fiscal years.

(b) Any member may, subject to reasonable standards as may be set forth in, or pursuant to, the operating agreement, inspect and copy at his or her own expense, for any purpose reasonably related to the member's interest as a member, the records referred to in subdivision (a) of this section, any financial statements maintained by the limited liability company for the three most recent fiscal years and other information regarding the affairs of the limited liability company as is just and reasonable.

(c) If provided in the operating agreement, certain members or managers shall have the right to keep confidential from other members for such period of time as such certain members or the managers deem reasonable, any information which such certain members or the managers reasonably believe to be in the nature of trade secrets or other information the disclosure of which such certain members or the managers in good faith believe is not in the best interest of the limited liability company or its business or which the limited liability company is required by law or by agreement with a third party to keep confidential.

(d) A limited liability company may maintain its records in other than a written form if such form is capable of conversion into written form within a reasonable time.

History: Add, L 1994, ch 576, § 1, eff Oct 24, 1994.

CASE ANNOTATIONS

Because a member was a one-third owner of a limited liability company (LLC), and the tax records of the LLC's subsidiary were both necessary and otherwise unavailable for the member's fraud litigation against the LLC and its tax member, pursuant to N.Y. Ltd. Liab. Co. Law § 1102(b), the member was entitled to inspect the tax records of the subsidiary; consequently, the trial court erred in denying the member's motion to compel the company and the tax member to disclose the subsidiary's sales tax records. Sachs v Adeli (2005, A.D., 1st Dept) 804 N.Y.S.2d 731

Trial court's finding that plaintiff was the "sole member" of a limited liability company (LLC) was not supported by the evidence as the determination as to the membership of the LLC should have been based primarily on the LLC's own records; the only evidence that arguably satisfied the requirements of N.Y. Ltd. Liab. Co. Law § 1102(a)(2) consisted of two of the LLC's tax returns, both of which listed defendant as a member having a 25 percent ownership of capital, profit sharing, and loss sharing and plaintiff as the other member, having a 75 percent ownership of capital, profit sharing, and loss sharing. Chiu v Chiu (2007, 2d Dept) 38 App Div 3d 619, 832 NYS2d 89

§ 1103. Transactions of business outside the state

(a) It is the intention of the legislature by the enactment of this chapter that the legal existence of a limited liability company formed under this chapter be recognized beyond the limits of this state and that, subject to any reasonable registration requirements, any such limited liability company transacting business outside this state shall be granted the protection of full faith and credit under section 1 of article IV of the Constitution of the United States.

(b) The provisions of this chapter shall determine the rights and obligations of a domestic limited liability company, organized under this chapter, in commerce with foreign nations and among the several states, except as prohibited by law.

History: Add, L 1994, ch 576, § 1, eff Oct 24, 1994.

§ 1104. Limited liability companies prohibited from interposing defense of usury

(a) No domestic or foreign limited liability company shall hereafter interpose the defense of usury in any action.

(b) The provisions of subdivision (a) of this section shall not apply to a domestic or foreign limited liability company, the principal asset of which is the ownership of a one or two family dwelling, where it appears either that such limited liability company was formed, or that the controlling interest therein was acquired, within a period of six months prior to the execution by such limited liability company of a bond or note evidencing indebtedness, and a mortgage creating a lien for such indebtedness on such one or two family dwelling. Any provision of any contract, or any separate written instrument executed prior to, simultaneously with or within sixty days after the delivery of any moneys to any borrower in connection with such indebtedness, whereby the defense of usury is waived or any such limited liability company estopped from asserting it, is hereby declared to be contrary to public policy and absolutely void.

(c) The provisions of subdivision (a) of this section shall not apply to any action in which a limited liability company interposes a defense of criminal usury as described in section 190.40 of the penal law.

History: Add, L 1994, ch 576, § 1, eff Oct 24, 1994

§ 1105. Limited liability geology company

(a) Prior to the first day of March, two thousand nineteen, the state education department and the department of state shall allow an existing limited liability company organized under article two of this chapter to become a professional service limited liability company as defined in article twelve of this chapter for the purpose of practicing professional geology, provided the limited liability company meet all of the requirements to become a professional service limited liability company, including that the name of a professional service limited liability company shall end with the words "Professional Limited Liability Company" or "Limited Liability Company", or the abbreviations "P.L.L.C.", "PLLC", "L.L.C.", or "LLC" by amending its articles of organization so that it contains the following:

(1) the names and residence addresses of all individuals who are to be the original members and the original managers, if any;

(2) a statement that the professional limited liability company is formed pursuant to section twelve hundred three of the limited liability company law; and

(3) a statement that the amendment shall not effect a dissolution of the limited liability company, but shall be deemed a continuation of its existence, without affecting its then existing property rights or liabilities or the liabilities of its members or officers as such, but thereafter it shall have only such rights, powers and privileges, and be subject only to such other duties and liabilities, as a professional service limited liability company created for the same purposes under this article.

(b) The certificate of amendment shall have attached thereto a certificate or certificates issued by the licensing authority certifying that each of the proposed members and managers listed:

(1) is authorized by law to practice a profession which the professional service limited liability company is organized to practice and, if applicable, that one or more of such individuals is authorized to practice each profession which the professional service limited liability company will be authorized to practice; and

(2) has been deemed to be of good moral character as may be established by the regulations of the commissioner of education.

(c) The certificate of amendment shall also have attached thereto a tax clearance issued by the department of taxation and finance certifying that the existing limited liability company is current with respect to payment of its state tax liabilities.

(d) Notwithstanding any provision of law to the contrary, any company formed under this section shall be required to comply with all applicable laws, rules, or regulations relating to the practice of a profession under title eight of the education law.

History: L 2016, ch 260, § 2, eff Nov 21, 2016; amd, L 2018, ch 302, § 3, eff Oct 1, 2018.

Blackline Showing Effect of 2018 Amendments. — (a) Prior to the first day of March, two thousand ~~eighteen~~ nineteen, the state education department and the department of state shall allow an existing limited liability company organized under article two of this chapter to become a professional service limited liability company as defined in article twelve of this chapter for the purpose of practicing professional geology, provided the limited liability company meet all of the requirements to become a professional service limited liability company, including that the name of a professional service limited liability company shall end with the words "Professional Limited Liability Company" or "Limited Liability Company", or the abbreviations "P.L.L.C.", "PLLC", "L.L.C.", or "LLC" by amending its articles of organization so that it contains the following:

(1) the names and residence addresses of all individuals who are to be the original members and the original managers, if any;

(2) a statement that the professional limited liability company is formed pursuant to section twelve hundred three of the limited liability company law; and

(3) a statement that the amendment shall not effect a dissolution of the limited liability company, but shall be deemed a continuation of its existence, without affecting its then existing property rights or liabilities or the liabilities of its members or officers as such, but thereafter it shall have only such rights, powers and privileges, and be subject only to such other duties and liabilities, as a professional service limited liability company created for the same purposes under this article.

(b) The certificate of amendment shall have attached thereto a certificate or certificates issued by the licensing authority certifying that each of the proposed members and managers listed:

(1) is authorized by law to practice a profession which the professional service limited liability company is organized to practice and, if applicable, that one or more of such individuals is authorized to practice each profession which the professional service limited liability company will be authorized to practice; and

(2) has been deemed to be of good moral character as may be established by the regulations of the commissioner of education.

(c) The certificate of amendment shall also have attached thereto a tax clearance issued by the department of taxation and finance certifying that the existing limited liability company is current with respect to payment of its state tax liabilities.

(d) Notwithstanding any provision of law to the contrary, any company formed under this section shall be required to comply with all applicable laws, rules, or regulations relating to the practice of a profession under title eight of the education law.

ARTICLE XII
PROFESSIONAL SERVICE LIMITED LIABILITY COMPANIES

History: Add, L 1994, ch 576, § 1, eff Oct 24, 1994.

§ 1201. Definitions

As used in this article, unless the context otherwise requires, the term:

(a) "Licensing authority" means the regents of the university of the state of New York or the state education department, as the case may be, in the case of all professions licensed under title eight of the education law, and the appropriate appellate division of the supreme court in the case of the profession of law.

(b) "Profession" includes any practice as an attorney and counselor-at-law, or as a licensed physician, and those professions designated in title eight of the education law.

(c) "Professional" means an individual duly authorized to practice a profession, a professional service corporation, a professional service limited liability company, a foreign professional service limited liability company, a registered limited liability partnership, a foreign limited liability partnership, a foreign professional service corporation or a professional partnership.

(d) "Professional service" means any type of service to the public that may be lawfully rendered by a member of a profession within the purview of his or her profession.

(e) "Professional service corporation" means (i) a corporation organized under article fifteen of the business corporation law and (ii) any other corporation organized under the business corporation law or under any other predecessor statute, which is authorized by, or holds a license, certificate, registration or permit issued by, the licensing authority pursuant to the education law to render professional services within this state.

(f) "Professional service limited liability company" means a limited liability company organized under this article.

(g) "Foreign professional service corporation" has the meaning given to it in subdivision (d) of section fifteen hundred twenty-five of the business corporation law.

(h) "Foreign professional service limited liability company" has the meaning given to it in subdivision (a) of section thirteen hundred one of this chapter.

(i) "Professional partnership" means (1) a partnership without limited partners each of whose partners is a professional authorized by law to render a professional service within this state, (2) a partnership without limited partners each of whose partners is a professional, at least one of whom is authorized by law to render a professional service within this state or (3) a partnership without limited partners authorized by, or holding a license, certificate, registration or permit issued by the licensing authority pursuant to the education law to render a professional service within this state.

History: Add, L 1994, ch 576, § 1, eff Oct 24, 1994.

§ 1202. Limited liability companies organized under other provisions of law

The provisions of this article shall not apply to limited liability companies heretofore or hereafter duly formed under any other provision of law.

History: Add, L 1994, ch 576, § 1, eff Oct 24, 1994.

§ 1203. Formation

(a) Notwithstanding the education law or any other provision of law, one or more professionals each of whom is authorized by law to render a professional service within the state, or one or more professionals, at least one of whom is authorized by law to render a professional service within the state, may form, or cause to be formed, a professional service limited liability company for pecuniary profit under this article for the purpose of rendering the professional service or services as such professionals are authorized to practice. With respect to a professional service limited liability company formed to provide medical services as such services are defined in article 131 of the education law, each member of such limited liability company must be licensed pursuant to article 131 of the education law to practice medicine in this state. With respect to a professional service limited liability company formed to provide dental services as such services are defined in article 133 of the education law, each member of such limited liability company must be licensed pursuant to article 133 of the education law to practice dentistry in this state. With respect to a professional service limited liability company formed to provide veterinary services as such services are defined in article 135 of the education law, each member of such limited liability company must be licensed pursuant to article 135 of the education law to practice veterinary medicine in this state. With respect to a professional service limited liability company formed to provide professional engineering, land surveying, architectural, landscape architectural and/or geological services as such services are defined in article 145, article 147 and article 148 of the education law, each member of such limited liability company must be licensed pursuant to article 145, article 147 and/or article 148 of the education law to practice one or more of such professions in this state. With respect to a professional service limited liability company formed to provide licensed clinical social work services as such services are defined in article 154 of the education law, each member of such limited liability company shall be licensed pursuant to article 154 of the education law to practice licensed clinical social work in this state. With respect to a professional service limited liability company formed to provide creative arts therapy services as such services are defined in article 163 of the education law, each member of such limited liability company must be licensed pursuant to article 163 of the education law to practice creative arts therapy in this state. With respect to a professional service limited liability company formed to provide marriage and family therapy services as such services are defined in article 163 of the education law, each member of such limited liability company must be licensed pursuant to article 163 of the education law to practice marriage and family therapy in this state. With respect to a professional service limited liability company formed to provide mental health counseling services as such services are defined in article 163 of the education law, each member of such limited liability company must be licensed pursuant to article 163 of the education law to practice mental health counseling in this state. With respect to a professional service limited liability company formed to provide psychoanalysis services as such services are defined in article 163 of the education law, each member of such limited liability company must be licensed pursuant to article 163 of the education law to practice psychoanalysis in this state. With respect to a professional service limited liability company formed to provide applied behavior analysis services as such services are defined in article 167 of the education law, each member of such limited liability company must be licensed or certified pursuant to article 167 of the education law to practice applied behavior analysis in this state. In addition to engaging in such profession or professions, a professional service limited liability company may engage in any other business or activities as to which a limited liability company may be formed under section two hundred one of this chapter. Notwithstanding any other provision of this section, a professional service limited liability company (i) authorized to practice law may only engage in another profession or business or activities or (ii) which is engaged in a profession or other business or activities other than law may only engage in the practice of law, to the extent not prohibited by any other law of this state or any rule adopted by the appropriate appellate division of the supreme court or the court of appeals.

(b) The articles of organization of a professional service limited liability company shall meet the requirements of this chapter and (i) shall state the profession or professions to be practiced by such limited liability company and (A) the names and residence addresses of all individuals who are to be the original members and the original managers, if any, of such limited liability company, and (B) the names and residence addresses or, if none, the business address of all shareholders, directors, officers, members, managers and partners of all professional service corporations, foreign professional service corporations, professional service limited liability companies, foreign professional service limited liability companies, registered limited liability partnerships, foreign limited liability partnerships, and professional partnerships who are to be the original members or managers, if any, who are individuals of such limited liability company, (ii) shall have attached thereto a certificate or certificates issued by the licensing authority or by the comparable authority of another state certifying that each of the proposed members and managers, if any, who are individuals is authorized by law to practice a profession that such limited liability company is being formed to practice and, if applicable, that one or more of such individuals are authorized to practice within the state each profession that such limited liability company will be authorized to practice, and (iii) if such proposed member or manager, if any, is a professional service corporation, foreign professional service corporation, professional service limited liability company, foreign professional service limited liability company, registered limited liability partnership, foreign limited liability partnership or professional partnership, (A) such certificate or certificates issued by the licensing authority or by the comparable authority of another state shall certify either (1) that each proposed member or manager is authorized by law to practice a profession that such limited liability company is being formed to practice and, if applicable, that each shareholder, member or partner of such proposed member or manager is authorized by law to render a professional service within the state or (2) that one or more of such proposed members and one or more of such proposed managers, are authorized to practice within the state each profession that such limited liability company will be authorized to practice and that one or more of the shareholders, members or partners of such proposed members or managers are authorized to practice within the state each profession that such limited liability company will be authorized to practice within the state and (B) there shall be attached to the articles of organization of the professional service limited liability company a certificate by an authorized officer of the jurisdiction of its formation that the professional service corporation, foreign professional service corporation, professional service limited liability company, foreign professional service limited liability company, registered limited liability partnership or foreign limited liability partnership is validly existing and, in the case of a foreign professional service corporation, foreign professional service limited liability company or foreign limited liability partnership, a certificate from the secretary of state that such foreign professional service corporation, foreign professional service limited liability company or foreign limited liability partnership is authorized to do business under article fifteen-A of the business corporation law, under article thirteen of this chapter or under article eight-B of the partnership law, as the case may be.

(c) (1) A certified copy of the articles of organization and of each amendment thereto and restatement thereof shall be filed by the professional service limited liability company with the licensing authority within thirty days after the filing of such certificate or amendment with the department of state.

(2) (A) Within one hundred twenty days after the filing of the articles of organization, a copy of the same or a notice containing the substance thereof shall be published once in each week for six successive weeks, in two newspapers of the county in which the office of the professional service limited liability company is located, one newspaper to be printed weekly and one newspaper to be printed daily, to be designated by the county clerk. When such county is located within a city with a population of one million or more, such designation shall be as though the copy or notice were a notice or advertisement of judicial proceedings. Proof of the publication required by this subparagraph, consisting of the certificate of publication of the professional service limited liability company with the affidavits of publication of such newspapers annexed thereto, be filed with the department of state. Notwithstanding any other provision of law, if the office of the professional service limited liability company is located in a county wherein a weekly or daily newspaper of the county, or both, has not been so designated by the county clerk, then the publication herein required shall be made in a weekly or daily newspaper of any county, or both, as the case may be, which is contiguous to, such county, provided that any such newspaper meets all the other requirements of this subparagraph. A copy or notice published in a newspaper other than the newspaper or newspapers designated by the county clerk shall not be deemed to be one of the publications required by this subparagraph. The notice shall include: (i) the name of the professional service limited liability company; (ii) the date of filing of the articles of organization with the department of state; (iii) the county within this state, in which the office of the professional service limited liability company is located; (iii-a) the street address of the principal business location, if any; (iv) a statement that the secretary of state has been designated as agent of the professional service limited liability company upon whom process against it may be served and the post office address within or without this state to which the secretary of state shall mail a copy of any process against it served upon him or her; (v) if the professional service limited liability company is to have a registered agent, his or her name and address within this state and a statement that the registered agent is to be the agent of the professional service limited liability company upon whom process against it may be served; (vi) if the professional service limited liability company is to have a specific date of dissolution in addition to the events of dissolution set forth in section seven hundred one of this chapter, the latest date upon which the professional service limited liability company is to dissolve; and (vii) the character or purpose of the business of such professional service limited liability company. Where, at any time after completion of the first of the six weekly publications required by this subparagraph and prior to the completion of the sixth such weekly publication, there is a change in any of the information contained in the copy or notice as published, the professional service limited liability company may complete the remaining publications of the original copy or notice, and the professional service limited liability company shall not be required to publish any further or amended copy or notice. Where, at any time after completion of the six weekly publications required by this subparagraph, there is a change to any of the information contained in the copy or notice as published, no further or amended publication or republication shall be required to be made. If within one hundred twenty days after its formation, proof of such publication, consisting of the certificate of publication of the professional service limited liability company with the affidavits of publication of the newspapers annexed thereto has not been filed with the department of state, the authority of such professional service limited liability company to carry on, conduct or transact any business in this state shall be suspended, effective as of the expiration of such one hundred twenty day period. The failure of a professional service limited liability company to cause such copy or notice to be published and such certificate of publication and affidavits of publication to be filed with the department of state within such one hundred twenty day period or the suspension of such professional service limited liability company's authority to carry on, conduct or transact business in this state pursuant to this subparagraph shall not limit or impair the validity of any contract or act of such professional service limited liability company, or any right or remedy of any other party under or by virtue of any contract, act or omission of such professional service limited liability company, or the right of any other party to maintain any action or special proceeding on any such contract, act or omission, or right of such professional service limited liability company to defend any action or special proceeding in this state, or result in any member, manager or agent of such professional service limited liability company becoming liable for the contractual obligations or

other liabilities of the professional service limited liability company. If, at any time following the suspension of a professional service limited liability company's authority to carry on, conduct or transact business in this state pursuant to this subparagraph, such professional service limited liability company shall cause proof of publication in substantial compliance with the provisions (other than the one hundred twenty day period) of this subparagraph, consisting of the certificate of publication of the professional service limited liability company with the affidavits of publication of the newspapers annexed thereto, to be filed with the department of state, such suspension of such professional service limited liability company's authority to carry on, conduct or transact business shall be annulled.

(B) (i) A professional service limited liability company which was formed prior to the effective date of this subparagraph and which complied with the publication and filing requirements of this paragraph as in effect prior to such effective date shall not be required to make any publication or republication or any filing under subparagraph (A) of this paragraph, and shall not be subject to suspension pursuant to this paragraph.

(ii) Within twelve months after the effective date of this subparagraph, a professional service limited liability company which was formed prior to such effective date and which did not comply with the publication and filing requirements of this paragraph as in effect prior to such effective date shall publish a copy of its articles of organization or a notice containing the substance thereof in the manner required (other than the one hundred twenty day period) by this paragraph as in effect prior to such effective date and file proof of such publication, consisting of the certificate of publication of the professional service limited liability company with the affidavits of publication of the newspapers annexed thereto, with the department of state.

(iii) If a professional service limited liability company that is subject to the provisions of clause (ii) of this subparagraph fails to file the required proof of publication with the department of state within twelve months after the effective date of this subparagraph, its authority to carry on, conduct or transact any business in this state shall be suspended, effective as of the expiration of such twelve month period.

(iv) The failure of a professional service limited liability company that is subject to the provisions of clause (ii) of this subparagraph to fully comply with the provisions of said clause (ii) or the suspension of such professional service limited liability company's authority to carry on, conduct or transact any business in this state pursuant to clause (iii) of this subparagraph shall not impair or limit the validity of any contract or act of such professional service limited liability company, or any right or remedy of any other party under or by virtue of any contract, act or omission of such professional service limited liability company, or the right of any other party to maintain any action or special proceeding on any such contract, act or omission, or right of such professional service limited liability company to defend any action or special proceeding in this state, or result in any member, manager or agent of such professional service limited liability company becoming liable for the contractual obligations or other liabilities of the professional service limited liability company.

(v) If, at any time following the suspension of a professional service limited liability company's authority to carry on, conduct or transact business in this state, pursuant to clause (iii) of this subparagraph, such professional service limited liability company shall cause proof of publication in substantial compliance with the provisions (other than the one hundred twenty day period) of subparagraph (A) of this paragraph, consisting of the certificate of publication of the professional service limited liability company with the affidavits of publication of the newspapers annexed thereto, to be filed with the department of state, such suspension of such professional service limited liability company's authority to carry on, conduct or transact business shall be annulled.

(vi) For the purposes of this subparagraph, a professional service limited liability company which was formed prior to the effective date of this subparagraph shall be deemed to have complied with the publication and filing requirements of this paragraph as in effect prior to such effective date if (i) the professional service limited liability company was formed on or after January first, nineteen hundred ninety-nine and prior to such effective date and the professional service limited liability company filed at least one affidavit of the printer or publisher of a newspaper with the department of state at any time prior to such effective date, or (ii) the professional service limited liability company was formed prior to January first, nineteen hundred ninety-nine, without regard to whether the professional service limited liability company did or did not file any affidavit of the printer or publisher of a newspaper with the secretary of state.

(C) The information in a notice published pursuant to this paragraph shall be presumed to be in compliance with and satisfaction of the requirements of this paragraph.

(d) A professional service limited liability company, other than a professional service limited liability company authorized to practice law, shall be under the supervision of the regents of the university of the state of New York and be subject to disciplinary proceedings and penalties, and its articles of organization shall be subject to suspension, revocation or annulment for cause, in the same manner and to the same extent as is provided with respect to individuals and their licenses, certificates and registrations in title eight of the education law relating to the applicable profession. Notwithstanding the provisions of this subdivision, a professional service limited liability company authorized to practice medicine shall be subject to the pre-hearing procedures and hearing procedures as are provided with respect to individual physicians and their licenses in Title II-A of article two of the public health law.

(e) A professional service limited liability company authorized to practice law shall be subject to the regulation and control of, and its articles of organization shall be subject to suspension, revocation or annulment for cause by, the appellate division of the supreme court and the court of appeals in the same manner and to the same extent provided in the judiciary law with respect to individual attorneys and counselors-at-law. Such limited liability company need not qualify for any certification under section four hundred sixty-four of the judiciary law, take an oath of office under section four hundred sixty-six of the judiciary law or register under section four hundred sixty-seven of the judiciary law.

(f) The order of suspension, revocation or annulment of the articles of organization of a professional service limited liability company pursuant to subdivisions (d) and (e) of this section shall be effective upon the filing of such order with the department of state.

History: Add, L 1994, ch 576, § 1, eff Oct 24, 1994; L 1995, ch 643, § 15, L 1999, ch 420, § 9, eff Aug 31, 1999, L 2002, ch 420, § 2, L 2002, ch 676, § 13, eff Jan 1, 2005, L 2005, ch 767, § 7, L 2006, ch 44, § 5, eff June 1, 2006, L 2013, ch 554, § 6, eff Jan 10, 2014; L 2014, ch 475, § 21 eff Nov 21, 2016.

CASE ANNOTATIONS

Parents of an infant dental patient properly alleged a negligence claim against dentists' practices, based in part on the Limited Liability Company Law, because issues of fact existed as to whether there was a statutory violation, whether such violation was part of an overall scheme to place maximization of profits over the quality of patient care, and whether causation applied. Matter of Small Smiles Litig., 125 A.D.3d 1287, 4 N.Y.S.3d 412 (4th Dep't 2015).

Healthcare provider was not entitled to receive payment under N.Y. Ins. Law § 5102(a)(2) and N.Y. Comp. Codes R. & Regs. tit. 11, § 65-3.16(a)(12) as the provider performed psychological services in violation of N.Y. Ltd. Liab. Co. Law §§ 1203(b) and 1207 as: (1) the provider's articles of organization stated that the company was to provide psychological services and listed a licensed psychologist as the provider of those services, but the named psychologist testified that the psychologist was never an owner or member of the provider, and that the psychologist never received a stock certificate or any compensation based on an ownership interest, and (2) the provider's ownership had changed since its initial organization, and while certain other health services were added and dropped, the same psychologist continued to be listed as a member and manager of the provider. Multiquest, P.L.L.C. v Allstate Ins. Co. (2007, Sup App T) 17 Misc 3d 37, 844 NYS2d 565.

Limited liability companies generally, as opposed to professional services limited liability companies, may not lawfully practice law in New York. Jacoby & Meyers, LLP v Presiding Justices of the Appellate Div. (2012, SD NY) 847 F Supp 2d 590

§ 1204. Rendering of professional service

(a) No professional service limited liability company may render a professional service except through individuals authorized by law to render such professional service, as individuals, provided, that nothing in this chapter shall authorize a professional service limited liability company to render a professional service in this state except through individuals authorized by law to render such professional service as individuals in this state.

(b) Each final plan and report made or issued by a professional service limited liability company practicing professional engineering, architecture, landscape architecture or land surveying shall bear the name and seal of one or more professional engineers, architects, landscape architects or land surveyors, respectively, who are in responsible charge of such plan or report.

(c) Each report, diagnosis, prognosis and prescription made or issued by a professional service limited liability company practicing medicine, dentistry, podiatry, optometry, ophthalmic dispensing, veterinary medicine, pharmacy, nursing, psychology, physical therapy or chiropractic shall bear the signature of one or more physicians, dentists, podiatrists, optometrists, ophthalmic dispensers, veterinarians, pharmacists, nurses, licensed psychologists, physical therapists or chiropractors, respectively, who are in responsible charge of such report, diagnosis, prognosis or prescription.

(d) Each record, transcript, report and hearing report prepared by a professional service limited liability company practicing certified shorthand reporting shall bear the signature of one or more certified shorthand reporters who are in responsible charge of such record, transcript, report or hearing report.

(e) Each professional service limited liability company practicing public accounting or certified public accounting shall maintain records indicating the identity of each public accountant or certified public accountant, respectively, who was responsible for each report or statement that is issued, prepared or examined by such limited liability company.

(f) Each opinion prepared by a professional service limited liability company practicing law shall bear the signature of one or more attorneys and counselors-at-law who're in responsible charge of such opinion.

(g) In addition to the requirements pursuant to subdivisions (b) through (f) of this section, each document prepared by a professional service limited liability company that under the rules, regulations, laws or customs of the applicable profession is required to bear the signature of an individual in responsible charge of such document, shall be signed by one or more such individuals.

History: Add, L 1994, ch 576, § 1, eff Oct 24, 1994.

§ 1205. Professional relationships and liabilities

(a) Each member, manager, employee or agent of a professional service limited liability company shall be personally and fully liable and accountable for any negligent or wrongful act or misconduct committed by him or her or by any person under his or her direct

Limited Liability Company Law

supervision and control while rendering professional services on behalf of such limited liability company.

(b) Each shareholder, director, officer, employee, member, manager, partner and agent of a professional service corporation, foreign professional service corporation, professional service limited liability company, foreign professional service limited liability company, registered limited liability partnership, foreign limited liability partnership or professional partnership that is a member, manager, employee or agent of a professional service limited liability company shall be personally and fully liable and accountable for any negligent or wrongful act or misconduct committed by him or her or by any person under his or her direct supervision and control while rendering professional services in his or her capacity as a member, manager, employee or agent of such professional service limited liability company.

(c) The relationship of a professional to a professional service limited liability company with which such professional is associated, whether as member, manager, employee or agent, shall not modify or diminish the jurisdiction over such professional of the licensing authority and in the case of an attorney and counselor-at-law, or a professional service corporation, foreign professional service corporation, professional service limited liability company, foreign professional service limited liability company, registered limited liability partnership, foreign limited liability partnership or professional partnership engaged in the practice of law, the courts of this state.

History: Add, L 1994, ch 576, § 1, eff Oct 24, 1994.

CASE ANNOTATIONS

Under N.Y. Ltd. Liab. Co. Law § 1205(b), dentist two could not be held vicariously liable for alleged dental malpractice performed solely by dentist one based on dentist two's status as the sole shareholder of a dental practice that was a limited liability company. Oviedo v Weinstein (2013, 2d Dept) 102 App Div 3d 844, 958 NYS2d 467.

Although N.Y. Ltd. Liab. Co. Law § 1205 did hold shareholders or officers personally liable for certain acts, the provision was simply a reflection of the common law rule that a shareholder was liable for those torts of the corporation in which he was a participant. Individual defendants were not liable for a breach of agreement made with the corporation; therefore, the clients could not hold the attorney personally liable for their first claim, which was based on breach of contract. Galpern v De Vos & Co. PLLC (2011, ED NY) 2011 US Dist LEXIS 117095 (UNPUBLISHED).

§ 1206. Purposes of formation

No professional service limited liability company shall engage in any profession or professions other than those set forth in its articles of organization. A professional service limited liability company may only engage in a profession or professions as to which one or more of its members is authorized by law to render professional services in this state. In addition to engaging in such profession or professions, a professional service limited liability company may carry on, or conduct or transact any other business or other activities as to which a limited liability company may be formed under section two hundred one of this chapter. Notwithstanding any other provision of this section, and subject to the next succeeding

sentence of this section, a professional service limited liability company (i) authorized to practice law may only engage in another profession or other business or activities or (ii) which is engaged in a profession or other business or activities other than law may only engage in the practice of law, to the extent not prohibited by any other law of this state or any rule adopted by the appropriate appellate division of the supreme court or the court of appeals. Any professional service limited liability company may invest its funds in real estate, mortgages, stocks, bonds or any other type of investments.

History: Add, L 1994, ch 576, § 1, eff Oct 24, 1994.

§ 1207. Membership of professional service limited liability companies

(a) A member of a professional service limited liability company shall be only:

(1) A professional, other than a foreign professional service corporation, foreign professional service limited liability company or foreign limited liability partnership, authorized by law to practice in this state a profession that such limited liability company is authorized to practice and who is or has been engaged in the practice of such profession in such limited liability company or a predecessor entity, or who will engage in the practice of such profession in such limited liability company within thirty days of the date such professional becomes a member;

(2) A professional, other than a foreign professional service corporation, foreign professional service limited liability company or foreign limited liability partnership, authorized by law to practice in any foreign jurisdiction a profession that such limited liability company is authorized to practice and who is or has been engaged in the practice of such profession in such limited liability company or a predecessor entity, or who will engage in the practice of such profession in such limited liability company within thirty days of the date such professional becomes a member; or

(3) A foreign professional service corporation, foreign professional service limited liability company or foreign limited liability partnership authorized by law to practice in this state or in any foreign jurisdiction a profession that such limited liability company is authorized to practice and who is or has been engaged in the practice of such profession in such limited liability company or a predecessor entity, or who will engage in the practice of such profession in such limited liability company within thirty days of the date such professional becomes a member.

(b) With respect to a professional service limited liability company formed to provide medical services as such services are defined in article 131 of the education law, each member of such limited liability company must be licensed pursuant to article 131 of the education law to practice medicine in this state. With respect to a professional service limited liability company formed to provide dental services as such services are defined in article 133 of the education law, each member of such limited liability company must be licensed pursuant to article 133 of the education law to practice dentistry in this state. With respect to a professional service limited liability company formed to provide veterinary services as such services are defined in article 135 of the education law, each member of such limited liability company must be licensed pursuant to article 135 of the education law to practice veterinary medicine in this state. With respect to a professional service limited liability company formed to provide professional engineering, land surveying, architectural, landscape architectural and/or geological services as such services are defined in article 145, article 147 and article 148 of the education law, each member of such limited liability company must be licensed pursuant to article 145, article 147 and/or article 148 of the education law to practice one or more of such professions in this state. With respect to a professional service limited liability company formed to provide licensed clinical social work services as such services are defined in article 154 of the education law, each member of such limited liability company shall be licensed pursuant to article 154 of the education law to practice licensed clinical social work in this state. With respect to a professional service limited liability company formed to provide creative arts therapy services as such services are defined in article 163 of the education law, each member of such limited liability company must be licensed pursuant to article 163 of the education law to practice creative arts therapy in this state. With respect to a professional service limited liability company formed to provide marriage and family therapy services as such services are defined in article 163 of the education law, each member of such limited liability company must be licensed pursuant to article 163 of the education law to practice marriage and family therapy in this state. With respect to a professional service limited liability company formed to provide mental health counseling services as such services are defined in article 163 of the education law, each member of such limited liability company must be licensed pursuant to article 163 of the education law to practice mental health counseling in this state. With respect to a professional service limited liability company formed to provide psychoanalysis services as such services are defined in article 163 of the education law, each member of such limited liability company must be licensed pursuant to article 163 of the education law to practice psychoanalysis in this state. With respect to a professional service limited liability company formed to provide applied behavior analysis services as such services are defined in article 167 of the education law, each member of such limited liability company must be licensed or certified pursuant to article 167 of the education law to practice applied behavior analysis in this state.

(c) No member of a professional service limited liability company shall enter into a voting trust agreement, proxy or any other type of agreement vesting in another person, other than another member of such limited liability company or professional who would be eligible to become a member of such limited liability company, the authority to exercise voting power of any or all of the membership interests of such limited liability company. All membership interests or proxies granted or agreements made in violation of this section shall be void.

History: Add, L 1994, ch 576, § 1, eff Oct 24, 1994; amd, L 1995, ch 643, § 16, eff Aug 8, 1995, L 1996, ch 170, § 3, L 2002, ch 420, § 3, L 2002, ch 676, § 14, eff Jan 1, 2005, L 2013, ch 554, § 7, eff Jan 10, 2014; L 2014, ch 475, § 22 eff Nov 21, 2016.

CASE ANNOTATIONS

Healthcare provider was not entitled to receive payment under N.Y. Ins. Law § 5102(a)(2) and N.Y. Comp. Codes R. & Regs. tit. 11, § 65-3.16(a)(12) as the provider performed psychological services in violation of N.Y. Ltd. Liab. Co. Law §§ 1203(b) and 1207 as: (1) the provider's articles of organization stated that the company was to provide psychological services and listed a licensed psychologist as the provider of those services, but the named psychologist testified that the psychologist was never an owner or member of the provider, and that the psychologist never received a stock certificate or any compensation based on an ownership interest, and (2) the provider's ownership had changed since its initial organization, and while certain other health services were added and dropped, the same psychologist continued to be listed as a member and manager of the provider. Multiquest, P.L.L.C. v Allstate Ins. Co. (2007, Sup App T) 17 Misc 3d 37, 844 NYS2d 565.

§ 1208. [Reserved]

History: Add, L 1994, ch 576, § 1, eff Oct 24, 1994.

§ 1209. Disqualification of members, managers and employees

If any member, manager or employee of a professional service limited liability company who has been rendering professional service to the public becomes legally disqualified to practice his, her or its profession within this state, he, she or it shall sever all employment with and financial interests (other than interests as a creditor or vested rights under a bona fide retirement program) in such limited liability company forthwith or as otherwise provided in section twelve hundred ten of this article. All provisions of law regulating the rendering of professional services by a person elected or appointed to a public office shall be applicable to a member, manager or employee of such limited liability company in the same manner and to the same extent as if fully set forth herein. Such legal disqualification to practice such profession within this state shall be deemed to constitute an irrevocable offer by the disqualified member to sell his, her or its membership interest to the professional service limited liability company, pursuant to the provisions of section twelve hundred ten of this article or of the articles of organization or operating agreement, whichever is applicable. Compliance with the terms of such offer shall be specifically enforceable in the courts of this state. A professional service limited liability company's failure to

enforce compliance with this provision shall constitute a ground for its dissolution.

History: Add, L 1994, ch 576, § 1, eff Oct 24, 1994.

Assignee of no-fault benefits, which was a professional service
limited liability company (PLLC), could not continue an action under
N.Y. Ins. Law § 5102(a) against an insurer because the doctor who
was its sole member had been suspended from the practice of
medicine; the PLLC was required to go through a disqualification
process under N.Y. Limited Liability Company Law §§ 1209 and 1210
but could pursue the claims as part of its winding up under N.Y.
Limited Liability Company Law § 703(b), and a stay was ordered
under N.Y. C.P.L.R. § 2201 for the appointment of a representative to
do so. A.B. Med. Servs. PLLC v Travelers Indem. Co. (2008, Dist Ct)
239 NYLJ 106, 858 NYS2d 574.

§ 1210. Death, disqualification or dissolution of members

(a) A professional service limited liability company shall purchase or redeem the membership interest
of a member in case of such member's death or
disqualification pursuant to the provisions of section
twelve hundred nine of this article or in the case of a
member that is a professional service corporation,
foreign professional service corporation, professional
service limited liability company, foreign professional
service limited liability company, registered limited
liability partnership, foreign limited liability partnership or professional partnership, dissolution or
disqualification of such professional service corporation, foreign professional service corporation, professional service limited liability company, foreign
professional service limited liability company, registered limited liability partnership, foreign limited
liability partnership or professional partnership (in
the case of registered limited liability partnership,
foreign limited liability partnership and professional
partnership, other than a dissolution followed by a
reconstitution where at least a majority of the total
interests in the current profits of a successor partnership are held by partners of the predecessor partnership that was a registered limited liability partnership, foreign limited liability partnership or professional partnership who were partners of such predecessor partnership immediately prior to the
dissolution of such predecessor partnership) or the
death, dissolution or disqualification of all of its
shareholders, members or partners, within six
months after the appointment of the executor or
administrator or other legal representative of the
estate of such deceased member, or within six months
after such disqualification or dissolution, at the book
value of such membership interest as of the end of the
month immediately preceding the death, disqualification or dissolution of the member as determined from
the records of such limited liability company in
accordance with its regular method of accounting.
The operating agreement of such limited liability
company may modify this section by providing for a
shorter period of purchase or redemption, or an
alternate method of determining the price to be paid
for the membership interest, or both. If such limited
liability company shall fail to purchase or redeem

such membership interest within the required period,
a successful plaintiff in an action to recover the
purchase price of such membership interest shall also
be awarded reasonable attorneys' fees and costs.
Nothing herein contained shall prevent such limited
liability company from paying pension benefits or
other deferred compensation to or on behalf of a
former or deceased member, manager or employee
thereof, or where such member, manager or employee
is a professional service corporation, foreign professional service corporation, professional service limited
liability company, foreign professional service limited
liability company, registered limited liability partnership, foreign limited liability partnership or professional partnership, on behalf of a former or deceased
shareholder, officer, director, member, manager,
partner, or employee of such professional service
corporation, foreign professional service corporation,
professional service limited liability company, foreign
professional service limited liability company, registered limited liability partnership, foreign limited
liability partnership or professional partnership, as
otherwise permitted by law. The provisions of this
section shall not be deemed to require the purchase of
the membership interest of a disqualified member
where the period of disqualification is for less than six
months and the member again becomes eligible to
practice his or her profession within six months from
the date of disqualification (or, in the case of a disqualified member that is a professional service
corporation, foreign professional service corporation,
professional service limited liability company, foreign
professional service limited liability company, registered limited liability partnership, foreign limited
liability partnership or professional partnership,
where the period of disqualification of such professional service corporation, foreign professional corporation, professional service limited liability company,
foreign professional service limited liability company,
registered limited liability partnership, foreign
limited liability partnership or professional partnership or all shareholders, members or partners of such
professional service corporation, foreign professional
service corporation, professional service limited
liability company, foreign professional service limited
liability company, registered limited liability partnership, foreign limited liability partnership or professional partnership is for less than six months and
such professional service corporation, foreign professional service corporation, professional service limited
liability company, foreign professional service limited
liability company, registered limited liability partnership, foreign limited liability partnership or professional partnership or each such shareholder, member
or partner becomes eligible to practice his or her
profession within six months from the date of disqualification).

(b) Notwithstanding the provisions of subdivision
(a) of this section, the professional service limited
liability company shall not be required to purchase or
redeem the membership interest of a deceased or

disqualified or dissolved member if such membership interest, within the time limit prescribed by subdivision (a) of this section, is sold or transferred to another professional pursuant to the provisions of section twelve hundred eleven of this article.

History: Add, L 1994, ch 576, § 1, eff Oct 24, 1994.

CASE ANNOTATIONS

Assignee of no-fault benefits, which was a professional service limited liability company (PLLC), could not continue an action under N.Y. Ins. Law § 5102(a) against an insurer because the doctor who was its sole member had been suspended from the practice of medicine; the PLLC was required to go through a disqualification process under N.Y. Limited Liability Company Law §§ 1209 and 1210 but could pursue the claims as part of its winding up under N.Y. Limited Liability Company Law § 703(b), and a stay was ordered under N.Y. C.P.L.R. § 2201 for the appointment of a representative to do so. A.B. Med. Servs. PLLC v Travelers Indem. Co. (2008, Dist Ct) 239 NYLJ 106, 858 NYS2d 574.

§ 1211. Transfer of a membership interest

(a) No member of a professional service limited liability company may sell or assign his, her or its membership interest in such limited liability company except to another professional eligible to become a member of such limited liability company or except in trust to another professional who would be eligible to become a member if such professional were employed by such limited liability company.

(b) Nothing contained in subdivision (a) of this section shall be construed to prohibit the assignment of a membership interest by operation of law or by court decree. An assignee of a membership interest by operation of law or court decree shall have the rights of an assignee of a membership interest set forth in section six hundred three of this chapter. Such assignee shall automatically become a member of the professional service limited liability company if such assignee would be eligible to be a member of such limited liability company and, a majority in interest of the members shall fail to redeem the membership interest so transferred, pursuant to section twelve hundred ten of this article, within sixty days of receiving written notice of such transfer.

(c) Any sale or transfer, except by operation of law or court decree or except for a professional service limited liability company having only one member, may be made only after the same shall have been approved by the vote or written consent of such proportion, not less than a majority in interest of the members, exclusive of the interest of the member proposing to sell or transfer such membership interest, as may be provided in the operating agreement of such professional service limited liability company. The voting interest held by the member proposing to sell or transfer his, her or its membership interest may not be voted or counted for any purpose, unless all the members consent that such interests be voted or counted. The professional service limited liability company may provide, in lieu of or in addition to the foregoing provisions, for the alienation of membership interests and may require the redemption or purchase of such membership interests by such limited liability company at prices and in a manner specifically set forth therein. The existence of the restrictions on the sale or transfer of a membership interest, as contained in this article and, if applicable, in the operating agreement, shall be noted conspicuously on the face or back of every certificate representing a membership interest issued by a professional service limited liability company. Any sale or transfer in violation of such restrictions shall be void.

History: Add, L 1994, ch 576, § 1, eff Oct 24, 1994.

§ 1212. Limited liability company name

(a) Notwithstanding any other provision of law, the name of a professional service limited liability company may contain any word that, at the time of formation, could be used in the name of a partnership or professional service corporation practicing a profession that such limited liability company is authorized to practice and may not contain any word that could not be used by such a partnership or professional service corporation; provided, however, the name of a professional service limited liability company may not contain the name of a deceased person unless:

(1) such person's name was part of the name of such limited liability company at the time of such person's death; or

(2) such person's name was part of the name of an existing partnership or professional service corporation and at least two-thirds of such partnership's partners or corporation's shareholders, as the case may be, become members of such limited liability company.

(b) A professional service limited liability company name shall end with the words "Professional Limited Liability Company" or "Limited Liability Company" or the abbreviation "P.L.L.C.", "PLLC", "L.L.C." or "LLC". The provisions of subdivision (a) of section two hundred four of this chapter shall not apply to a professional service limited liability company.

History: Add, L 1994, ch 576, § 1, eff Oct 24, 1994.

§ 1213. Limited liability company act applicable

This chapter, except article eight and article thirteen, shall be applicable to a professional service limited liability company except to the extent that the provisions thereof conflict with this article. A professional service limited liability company may consolidate or merge with another limited liability company formed under this article, a foreign professional service limited liability company authorized to do business under article thirteen of this chapter or other business entity, only if all of the professions practiced by such limited liability company, foreign limited liability company or other business entity could be practiced by a single limited liability company organized under this article.

History: Add, L 1994, ch 576, § 1, eff Oct 24, 1994.

Limited Liability
Company Law

CASE ANNOTATIONS

De facto merger doctrine did not render an attorney liable to an assignee as a successor by merger to the professional service limited liability company (PSLLC) inasmuch as the PSLLC was created pursuant to N.Y. Ltd. Liab. Co. Law art. 12, any merger or consolidation between the attorney and the PSLLC would be governed by that article and the attorney was a "natural person," despite the fact that he practiced law under an assumed name and the fact that his law practice was characterized as a sole proprietorship; thus, even if the attorney and the PSLLC desired to be merged, rather than having such merger imposed upon them by a judicially created doctrine, such a merger could not be accomplished under the Limited Liability Company Law. Hamilton Equity Group, LLC v Juan E. Irene, PLLC (2012, 4th Dept) 101 App Div 3d 1703, 957 NYS2d 527, subsequent app (2012, 4th Dept) 101 App Div 3d 1702, 955 NYS2d 903.

§ 1214. [Reserved]

History: Add, L 1994, ch 576, § 1, eff Oct 24, 1994.

§ 1215. Regulation of professions

This article shall not repeal, modify or restrict any provision of the education law or the judiciary law or any rules or regulations adopted thereunder regulating the professions referred to in the education law or the judiciary law except to the extent in conflict herewith.

History: Add, L 1994, ch 576, § 1, eff Oct 24, 1994.

§ 1216. Mergers and consolidations

Notwithstanding any inconsistent provision of this article, a professional service limited liability company, pursuant to the provisions of article ten of this chapter, may be merged or consolidated with another limited liability company formed pursuant to the provisions of this chapter, a foreign professional service limited liability company authorized to do business under article thirteen of this chapter or other business entity formed or recognized under the laws of this state or any other state, provided that the limited liability company or other business entity that survives or that is formed pursuant thereto is a professional service limited liability company, a foreign professional service limited liability company authorized to do business under article thirteen of this chapter or other business entity practicing the same profession or professions in this state or the state of its formation. The restrictions on the issuance, transfer or sale of membership interests of a professional service limited liability company other than the requirements of the first two sentences of subdivision (c) of section twelve hundred eleven of this chapter, shall be suspended for a period not exceeding thirty days with respect to any issuance, transfer or sale of membership interests made pursuant to such merger or consolidation, provided that (a) no person or business entity who would not be eligible to be a member in the absence of this section shall vote or receive any distribution from such limited liability company; (b) after such merger or consolidation, any professional service limited liability company that survives or that is created thereby shall be subject to all the provisions of this article; and (c) membership interests thereafter may be held only by persons or business entities who are eligible to be a member of such professional service limited liability company.

Nothing herein contained shall be construed as permitting the practice of a profession in this state by a limited liability company that is not formed pursuant to the provisions of this article or authorized to do business in the state pursuant to the provisions of article thirteen of this chapter.

History: Add, L 1994, ch 576, § 1, eff Oct 24, 1994.

CASE ANNOTATIONS

De facto merger doctrine did not render an attorney liable to an assignee as a successor by merger to the professional service limited liability company (PSLLC) inasmuch as the PSLLC was created pursuant to N.Y. Ltd. Liab. Co. Law art. 12, any merger or consolidation between the attorney and the PSLLC would be governed by that article and the attorney was a "natural person," despite the fact that he practiced law under an assumed name and the fact that his law practice was characterized as a sole proprietorship; thus, even if the attorney and the PSLLC desired to be merged, rather than having such merger imposed upon them by a judicially created doctrine, such a merger could not be accomplished under the Limited Liability Company Law. Hamilton Equity Group, LLC v Juan E. Irene, PLLC (2012, 4th Dept) 101 App Div 3d 1703, 957 NYS2d 527, subsequent app (2012, 4th Dept) 101 App Div 3d 1702, 955 NYS2d 903.

ARTICLE XIII
FOREIGN PROFESSIONAL SERVICE LIMITED LIABILITY COMPANIES

History: Add, L 1994, ch 576, § 1, eff Oct 24, 1994.

§ 1301. Definitions

As used in this article, unless the context otherwise requires, the term:

(a) "Foreign professional service limited liability company" means a professional service limited liability company, whether or not denominated as such, organized under the laws of a jurisdiction other than this state, (i) each of whose members and managers, if any, is a professional authorized by law to render a professional service within this state and who is or has been engaged in the practice of such profession in such professional service limited liability company or a predecessor entity, or will engage in the practice of such profession in the professional service limited liability company within thirty days of the date such professional becomes a member, or each of whose members and managers, if any, is a professional at least one of such members is authorized by law to render a professional service within this state and who is or has been engaged in the practice of such profession in such professional service limited liability company or a predecessor entity, or will engage in the practice of such profession in the professional service limited liability company within thirty days of the date such professional becomes a member, or (ii) authorized by, or holding a license, certificate, registration or permit issued by the licensing authority pursuant to, the education law to render a professional service within this state; except that all members and managers, if any, of a foreign professional service limited liability company that provides health services in this state shall be licensed in this state. With respect to a foreign professional service limited liability company which provides veterinary services as such services are defined in article 135 of the education law, each member of such foreign professional service limited liability company shall be licensed pursuant to article 135 of the education law to practice veterinary medicine. With respect to a foreign professional service limited liability company which provides medical services as such services are defined in article 131 of the education law, each member of such foreign professional service limited liability company must be licensed pursuant to article 131 of the education law to practice medicine in this state. With respect to a foreign professional service limited liability company which provides dental services as such services are defined in article 133 of the education law, each member of such foreign professional service limited liability company must be licensed pursuant to article 133 of the education law to practice dentistry in this state. With respect to a foreign professional service limited liability company which provides professional engineering, land surveying, geologic, architectural and/or landscape architectural services as such services are defined in article 145, article 147 and article 148 of the education law, each member of such foreign professional service limited liability company must be licensed pursuant to article 145, article 147 and/or article 148 of the education law to practice one or more of such professions in this state. With respect to a foreign professional service limited liability company which provides licensed clinical social work services as such services are defined in article 154 of the education law, each member of such foreign professional service limited liability company shall be licensed pursuant to article 154 of the education law to practice clinical social work in this state. With respect to a foreign professional service limited liability company which provides creative arts therapy services as such services are defined in article 163 of the education law, each member of such foreign professional service limited liability company must be licensed pursuant to article 163 of the education law to practice creative arts therapy in this state. With respect to a foreign professional service limited liability company which provides marriage and family therapy services as such services are defined in article 163 of the education law, each member of such foreign professional service limited liability company must be licensed pursuant to article 163 of the education law to practice marriage and family therapy in this state. With respect to a foreign professional service limited liability company which provides mental health counseling services as such services are defined in article 163 of the education

law, each member of such foreign professional service limited liability company must be licensed pursuant to article 163 of the education law to practice mental health counseling in this state. With respect to a foreign professional service limited liability company which provides psychoanalysis services as such services are defined in article 163 of the education law, each member of such foreign professional service limited liability company must be licensed pursuant to article 163 of the education law to practice psychoanalysis in this state. With respect to a foreign professional service limited liability company which provides applied behavior analysis services as such services are defined in article 167 of the education law, each member of such foreign professional service limited liability company must be licensed or certified pursuant to article 167 of the education law to practice applied behavior analysis in this state.

(b) "Licensing authority"means the regents of the university of the state of New York or the state education department, as the case may be, in the case of all professions licensed under title eight of the education law, and the appropriate appellate division of the supreme court in the case of the profession of law.

(c) "Profession"includes any practice as an attorney and counselor-at-law, or as a licensed physician, and those professions designated in title eight of the education law.

(d) "Professional"means an individual duly authorized to practice a profession, a professional service corporation, a professional service limited liability company, a foreign professional service limited liability company, a registered limited liability partnership, a foreign limited liability partnership, a foreign professional service corporation or a professional partnership.

(e) "Professional service"means any type of service to the public that may be lawfully rendered by a member of a profession within the purview of his or her profession.

(f) "Professional partnership" means (1) a partnership without limited partners each of whose partners is a professional authorized by law to render a professional service within this state, (2) a partnership without limited partners each of whose partners is a professional, at least one of whom is authorized by law to render a professional service within this state or (3) a partnership without limited partners authorized by, or holding a license, certificate, registration or permit issued by the licensing authority pursuant to the education law to render a professional service within this state; except that all partners of a professional partnership that provides medical services in this state must be licensed pursuant to article 131 of the education law to practice medicine in this state and all partners of a professional partnership that provides dental services in this state must be licensed pursuant to article 133 of the education law to practice dentistry in this state;

except that all partners of a professional partnership that provides veterinary services in this state must be licensed pursuant to article 135 of the education law to practice veterinary medicine in this state; and further except that all partners of a professional partnership that provides professional engineering, land surveying, geologic, architectural, and/or landscape architectural services in this state must be licensed pursuant to article 145, article 147 and/or article 148 of the education law to practice one or more of such professions.

(g) "Professional service corporation"means (i) a corporation organized under article fifteen of the business corporation law and (ii) any other corporation organized under the business corporation law or any predecessor statute, which is authorized by, or holds a license, certificate, registration or permit issued by, the licensing authority pursuant to the education law to render professional services within this state.

(h) "Professional service limited liability company"means a limited liability company organized under article twelve of this chapter.

(i) "Foreign professional service corporation"has the meaning given to it in paragraph (d) of section fifteen hundred twenty-five of the business corporation law.

History: Add, L 1994, ch 576, § 1, eff Oct 24, 1994; amd, L 1995, ch 643, § 17, L 1996, ch 170, § 4, eff June 18, 1996, L 2002, ch 420, § 4, L 2002, ch 676, § 15, eff Jan 1, 2005, L 2013, ch 554, § 8, eff Jan 10, 2014; L 2014, ch 475, § 23 eff Nov 21, 2016.

§ 1302. Rendering of professional service

(a) No foreign professional service limited liability company may render a professional service in this state except through individuals authorized by law to render such professional service as individuals in this state.

(b) Each final plan and report made or issued by a foreign professional service limited liability company practicing professional engineering, geology, architecture, landscape architecture or land surveying shall bear the name and seal of one or more professional engineers, professional geologists, architects, landscape architects, or land surveyors, respectively, who are in responsible charge of such plan or report.

(c) Each report, diagnosis, prognosis and prescription made or issued by a foreign professional service limited liability company practicing medicine, dentistry, podiatry, optometry, ophthalmic dispensing, veterinary medicine, pharmacy, nursing, psychology, physical therapy or chiropractic shall bear the signature of one or more physicians, dentists, podiatrists, optometrists, ophthalmic dispensers, veterinarians, pharmacists, nurses, licensed psychologists, physical therapists or chiropractors, respectively, who are in responsible charge of such report, diagnosis, prognosis or prescription.

(d) Each record, transcript, report and hearing report prepared by a foreign professional service limited liability company practicing certified shorthand reporting shall bear the signature of one or more certified shorthand reporters who are in responsible charge of such record, transcript, report or hearing report.

(e) Each report and statement prepared by a foreign professional service limited liability company practicing public accounting or certified public accounting shall bear the signature of one or more public accountants or certified public accountants, respectively, who are in responsible charge of such report or statement.

(f) Each opinion prepared by a foreign professional service limited liability company practicing law shall bear the signature of one or more attorneys and counselors-at-law who are in responsible charge of such opinion.

(g) In addition to the requirements in subdivisions (b) through (f) of this section, each document prepared by a foreign professional service limited liability company that under the rules, regulations, laws or customs of the applicable profession is required to bear the signature of an individual in responsible charge of such document, shall be signed by one or more such individuals licensed to practice in this state.

History: Add, L 1994, ch 576, § 1, eff Oct 24, 1994; L 2014, ch 475, § 24 eff Nov 21, 2016.

§ 1303. Professional relationships and liabilities

(a) Each member, manager, employee or agent of a foreign professional service limited liability company who performs professional services in this state on behalf of such limited liability company shall be personally and fully liable and accountable for any negligent or wrongful act or misconduct committed by him or her or by any person under his or her direct supervision and control while rendering such professional services in this state and shall bear professional responsibility for compliance by such limited liability company with all laws, rules and regulations governing the practice of a profession in this state.

(b) Each shareholder, director, officer, employee, member, manager, partner or agent of a professional service corporation, foreign professional service corporation, professional service limited liability company, foreign professional service limited liability company, registered limited liability partnership, foreign limited liability partnership or professional partnership that is a member, manager, employee or agent of a foreign professional service limited liability company who performs professional services in this state on behalf of such foreign professional service limited liability company shall be personally and fully liable and accountable for any negligent or wrongful act or misconduct committed by him or her or by any person under his or her direct supervision and control while rendering professional services in this state in his or her capacity as a member, manager, employee or agent of such foreign professional service limited liability company and shall bear professional responsibility for compliance by such limited liability company with all laws, rules and regulations governing the practice of the profession in this state.

(c) The relationship of a professional to a foreign professional service limited liability company with which such professional is associated, whether as a member, manager, employee or agent, shall not modify or diminish the jurisdiction over such professional of the licensing authority and in the case of an attorney and counselor-at-law or a professional service corporation, foreign professional service corporation, professional service limited liability company, foreign professional service limited liability company, registered limited liability partnership, foreign limited liability partnership or professional partnership, engaged in the practice of law, the courts of this state.

History: Add, L 1994, ch 576, § 1, eff Oct 24, 1994.

§ 1304. Foreign professional service limited liability company

No foreign professional service limited liability company shall engage in any profession or carry on, or conduct or transact any other business or activities in this state other than the rendering of the professional services or the carrying on, or conducting or transacting of any other business or activities for which it is formed and is authorized to do business in this state; provided that such limited liability company may invest its funds in real estate, mortgages, stocks, bonds or any other type of investments; provided, further, that a foreign professional service limited liability company (i) authorized to practice law may only engage in another profession or other business or activities in this state or (ii) which is engaged in a profession or other business or activities other than law, may only engage in the practice of law in this state, to the extent not prohibited by any other law of this state or any rule adopted by the appropriate appellate division of the supreme court or the court of appeals.

History: Add, L 1994, ch 576, § 1, eff Oct 24, 1994.

§ 1305. Limited liability company act applicable

Except for the provisions of sections eight hundred two and eight hundred nine of this chapter, this chapter shall be applicable to a foreign professional service limited liability company to the extent that the provisions thereof are not in conflict with the provisions of this article. A foreign professional service limited liability company may practice in this state or may consolidate or merge with another limited liability company or other business entity, only if all of the professions practiced by such limited liability company or other business entity could be practiced by a single professional service limited liability company organized in this state; and, further, only if such foreign professional service limited

liability company is domiciled in a state the laws of which, at the time of application by such limited liability company under section thirteen hundred six of this article, contain a reciprocal provision under which professional service limited liability companies domiciled in this state may similarly apply for the privilege of doing business in any such state or territory.

History: Add, L 1994, ch 576, § 1, eff Oct 24, 1994.

§ 1306. Filing requirements

(a) A foreign professional service limited liability company may apply for authority to do business in this state. An application entitled "Application for authority of .... (name of limited liability company) under section thirteen hundred six of the Limited Liability Company Law," shall be signed by an authorized person for the limited liability company and delivered to the department of state. It shall set forth:

(1) the name of the foreign professional service limited liability company. If the name does not end with the words "Professional Limited Liability Company" or "Limited Liability Company" or the abbreviation "P.L.L.C.", "PLLC", "L.L.C."or "LLC", it shall in addition to the foregoing set forth the name to be used in this state, ending with the words "Professional Limited Liability Company" or "Limited Liability Company" or the abbreviation "P.L.L.C.", "PLLC", "L.L.C."or "LLC";

(2) the jurisdiction and date of its formation;

(3) a statement of the profession or professions to be practiced in this state and a statement that the foreign professional service limited liability company is authorized to practice such profession or professions in the jurisdiction of its formation;

(4) the name, address and, where applicable, license number of each professional within the foreign professional service limited liability company who is licensed to practice the profession or professions in this state;

(5) the city, incorporated village or town and the county within this state in which its office is to be located;

(6) a designation of the secretary of state as its agent upon whom process against it may be served and the post office address within or without this state to which the secretary of state shall mail a copy of any process against it served upon him or her; and

(7) if it is to have a registered agent, his or her name and address within this state and a statement that the registered agent is to be its agent upon whom process against it may be served.

(b) Attached to the application for authority shall be:

(1) a certificate by an authorized officer of the jurisdiction of its formation that the foreign professional service limited liability company is an existing limited liability company;

(2) a certificate or certificates issued by the licensing authority that each professional within such limited liability company who is an individual and intending to practice the profession or professions in this state is licensed to practice said profession or professions in this state and for each such professional that is a professional service corporation, foreign professional service corporation, professional service limited liability company, foreign professional service limited liability company, registered limited liability partnership, foreign limited liability partnership or professional partnership, (A) such certificate or certificates issued by the licensing authority shall certify either (i) that each such professional service corporation, foreign professional service corporation, professional service limited liability company, foreign professional service limited liability company, registered limited liability partnership, foreign limited liability partnership or professional partnership intending to practice a profession in the state is authorized by law to practice in the state the profession that such foreign limited liability company intends to practice in the state and, if applicable, that each shareholder, member or partner of such proposed member or manager is authorized by law to render the professional service that such foreign limited liability company intends to practice in this state or (ii) that one or more of such professional service corporation, foreign professional service corporation, professional service limited liability company, foreign professional service limited liability company, registered limited liability partnership, foreign limited liability partnership or professional partnership, intending to practice a profession in this state is authorized by law to practice in this state the profession that such foreign limited liability company intends to practice and that one or more of the shareholders, members or partners of such proposed members or managers are authorized to practice within this state each profession that such foreign limited liability company will be authorized to practice within this state and (B) there shall be attached to the application for authority a certificate by an authorized officer of the jurisdiction of its formation that the professional service corporation, foreign professional service corporation, professional service limited liability company, foreign professional service limited liability company, registered limited liability partnership or foreign limited liability partnership is validly existing and, in the case of a foreign professional service corporation, foreign professional service limited liability company or foreign limited liability partnership, a certificate from the secretary of state that such foreign professional service corporation, foreign professional service limited liability company or foreign limited liability partnership is authorized to do business under article fifteen-A of the business corporation law, this article or article eight-B of the partnership law, as the case may be. In order to obtain said certificate or certificates, a copy of the

articles of organization shall be furnished to the licensing authority; and

(3) a certificate or certificates, issued by the licensing authority in the case of a foreign professional service limited liability company providing health services, stating that each member or manager of the foreign professional service limited liability company is licensed to practice said profession in this state.

(c) The fee for filing the application for authority shall be two hundred dollars, payable to the department of state, and the fee for a certificate of authority issued by the state education department shall be fifty dollars.

(d) (i) Within one hundred twenty days after the filing of the application for authority with the department of state, a copy of the same or a notice containing the substance thereof shall be published once in each week for six successive weeks, in two newspapers of the county within this state in which the office of the foreign professional service limited liability company is located, one newspaper to be printed weekly and one newspaper to be printed daily, to be designated by the county clerk. When such county is located within a city with a population of one million or more, such designation shall be as though the copy or notice were a notice or advertisement of judicial proceedings. Proof of the publication required by this paragraph, consisting of the certificate of publication of the foreign professional service limited liability company with the affidavits of publication of such newspapers annexed thereto, must be filed with the department of state. Notwithstanding any other provision of law, if the office of the foreign professional service limited liability company is located in a county wherein a weekly or daily newspaper of the county, or both, has not been so designated by the county clerk, then the publication herein required shall be made in a weekly or daily newspaper of any county, or both, as the case may be, which is contiguous to, such county, provided that any such newspaper meets all the other requirements of this paragraph. A copy or notice published in a newspaper other than the newspaper or newspapers designated by the county clerk shall not be deemed to be one of the publications required by this paragraph. The notice shall include: (1) the name of the foreign professional service limited liability company; (2) the date of filing of the application for authority with the department of state; (3) the jurisdiction and date of its organization; (4) the county within this state, in which the office of the foreign professional service limited liability company is located; (4-a) the street address of the principal business location, if any; (5) a statement that the secretary of state has been designated as agent of the foreign professional service limited liability company upon whom process against it may be served and the post office address within or without this state to which the secretary of state shall mail a copy of any process against it served upon him or her; (6) if the foreign professional service limited liability company is to have a registered agent, his or her name and address within this state and a statement that the registered agent is to be the agent of the foreign professional service limited liability company upon whom process against it may be served; (7) the address of the office required to be maintained in the jurisdiction of its organization by the laws of that jurisdiction or, if not so required, of the principal office of the foreign professional service limited liability company; (8) the name and address of the authorized officer in its jurisdiction of organization where a copy of its certificate of organization is filed or, if no public filing of its certificate of organization is required by the law of its jurisdiction of organization, a statement that the foreign professional service limited liability company shall provide, on request, a copy thereof with all amendments thereto (if such documents are in a foreign language, a translation thereof under oath of the translator shall be attached thereto), and the name and post office address of the person responsible for providing such copies; and (9) the character or purpose of the business of such foreign professional service limited liability company. Where, at any time after completion of the first of the six weekly publications required by this paragraph and prior to the completion of the sixth such weekly publication, there is a change in any of the information contained in the copy or notice as published, the foreign professional service limited liability company may complete the remaining publications of the original copy or notice, and the foreign professional service limited liability company shall not be required to publish any further or amended copy or notice. Where, at any time after completion of the six weekly publications required by this paragraph, there is a change to any of the information contained in the copy or notice as published, no further or amended publication or republication shall be required to be made. If within one hundred twenty days after the filing of its application for authority with the department of state, proof of such publication, consisting of the certificate of publication of the foreign professional service limited liability company with the affidavits of publication of the newspapers annexed thereto has not been filed with the department of state, the authority of such foreign professional service limited liability company to carry on, conduct or transact any business in this state shall be suspended, effective as of the expiration of such one hundred twenty day period. The failure of a foreign professional service limited liability company to cause such copy or notice to be published and such certificate of publication and affidavits of publication to be filed with the department of state within such one hundred twenty day period or the suspension of such foreign professional service limited liability company's authority to carry on, conduct or transact business in this state pursuant to this paragraph shall not limit or impair the validity of any contract or act of such foreign professional service limited liability company, or any right or remedy of any other party under or by virtue of any contract, act or

omission of such foreign professional service limited liability company, or the right of any other party to maintain any action or special proceeding on any such contract, act or omission, or right of such foreign professional service limited liability company to defend any action or special proceeding in this state, or result in any member, manager or agent of such foreign professional service limited liability company becoming liable for the contractual obligations or other liabilities of the foreign professional service limited liability company. If, at any time following the suspension of a foreign professional service limited liability company's authority to carry on, conduct or transact business in this state pursuant to this paragraph, such foreign professional service limited liability company shall cause proof of publication in substantial compliance with the provisions (other than the one hundred twenty day period) of this paragraph, consisting of the certificate of publication of the foreign professional service limited liability company with the affidavits of publication of the newspapers annexed thereto, to be filed with the department of state, such suspension of such foreign professional service limited liability company's authority to carry on, conduct or transact business shall be annulled.

(ii) (1) A foreign professional service limited liability company which was formed and filed its application for authority with the department of state prior to the effective date of this paragraph and complied with the publication and filing requirements of this subdivision as in effect prior to such effective date shall not be required to make any publication or republication or any filing under paragraph (i) of this subdivision, and shall not be subject to suspension pursuant to this subdivision.

(2) Within twelve months after the effective date of this paragraph, a foreign professional service limited liability company which was formed and filed its application for authority with the department of state prior to such effective date and which did not comply with the publication and filing requirements of this subdivision as in effect prior to such effective date shall publish a copy of its application for authority or a notice containing the substance thereof in the manner required (other than the one hundred twenty day period) by this subdivision as in effect prior to such effective date and file proof of such publication, consisting of the certificate of publication of the foreign professional service limited liability company with the affidavits of publication of the newspapers annexed thereto, with the department of state.

(3) If a foreign professional service limited liability company that is subject to the provisions of subparagraph two of this paragraph fails to file the required proof of publication with the department of state within twelve months after the effective date of this paragraph, its authority to carry on, conduct or transact any business in this state shall be suspended, effective as of the expiration of such twelve month period.

(4) The failure of a foreign professional service limited liability company that is subject to the provisions of subparagraph two of this paragraph to fully comply with the provisions of said subparagraph two of this paragraph or the suspension of such foreign professional service limited liability company's authority to carry on, conduct or transact any business in this state pursuant to subparagraph three of this paragraph shall not impair or limit the validity of any contract or act of such foreign professional service limited liability company ,or any right or remedy of any other party under or by virtue of any contract, act or omission of such foreign professional service limited liability company, or the right of any other party to maintain any action or special proceeding on any such contract, act or omission, or right of such foreign professional service limited liability company to defend any action or special proceeding in this state, or result in any member, manager or agent of such foreign professional service limited liability company becoming liable for the contractual obligations or other liabilities of the foreign professional service limited liability company.

(5) If, at any time following the suspension of a foreign professional service limited liability company's authority to carry on, conduct or transact business in this state, pursuant to subparagraph three of this paragraph, such foreign professional service limited liability company shall cause proof of publication in substantial compliance with the provisions (other than the one hundred twenty day period) of paragraph (i) of this subdivision, consisting of the certificate of publication of the foreign professional service limited liability company with the affidavits of publication of the newspapers annexed thereto, to be filed with the department of state, such suspension of such foreign professional service limited liability company's authority to carry on, conduct or transact business shall be annulled.

(6) For the purposes of this paragraph, a foreign professional service limited liability company which was formed and filed its application for authority with the department of state prior to the effective date of this paragraph shall be deemed to have complied with the publication and filing requirements of this subdivision as in effect prior to such effective date if (i) the foreign professional service limited liability company was formed and filed its application for authority with the department of state on or after January first, nineteen hundred ninety-nine and prior to such effective date and the foreign professional service limited liability company filed at least one affidavit of the printer or publisher of a newspaper with the department of state at any time prior to such effective date, or (ii) the foreign professional service limited liability company was formed and filed its application for authority with the department of state prior to January first, nineteen hundred ninety-nine, without regard to whether the foreign professional service limited liability company did or did not

file any affidavit of the printer or publisher of a newspaper with the secretary of state.

(iii) The information in a notice published pursuant to this subdivision shall be presumed to be in compliance with and satisfaction of the requirements of this subdivision.

History: Add, L 1994, ch 576, § 1, eff Oct 24, 1994; amd, L 1995, ch 643, § 18; L 1998, ch 375, § 29, eff Aug 13, 1998; L 1999, ch 420, § 10; L 2005, ch 767, § 8; L 2006, ch 44, § 6, eff June 1, 2006.

§ 1307. [Reserved]

History: Add, L 1994, ch 576, § 1, eff Oct 24, 1994.

§ 1308. Regulation of professions

(a) This article shall not repeal, modify or restrict any provision of the education law or the judiciary law or any rules or regulations adopted thereunder regulating the professions referred to in the education law or the judiciary law except to the extent in conflict herewith.

(b) A foreign professional service limited liability company, other than a foreign professional service limited liability company authorized to practice law, shall be under the supervision of the regents of the university of the state of New York and be subject to disciplinary proceedings and penalties, and its authority to do business shall be subject to suspension, revocation or annulment for cause, in the same manner and to the same extent as is provided with respect to individuals and their licenses, certificates and registrations in title eight of the education law relating to the applicable profession. Notwithstanding the provisions of this subdivision, a foreign professional service limited liability company authorized to practice medicine shall be subject to the pre-hearing procedures and hearing procedures as are provided with respect to individual physicians and their licenses in Title II-A of article two of the public health law.

(c) A foreign professional service limited liability company authorized to practice law shall be subject to the regulation and control of, and its authority to do business shall be subject to suspension, revocation or annulment for cause by, the appellate division of the supreme court and the court of appeals in the same manner and to the same extent provided in the judiciary law with respect to individual attorneys and counselors-at-law. Such limited liability company need not qualify for any certification under section four hundred sixty-four of the judiciary law, take an oath of office under section four hundred sixty-six of the judiciary law or register under section four hundred sixty-seven of the judiciary law.

History: Add, L 1994, ch 576, § 1, eff Oct 24, 1994.

§ 1309. Licensing of individuals

No member, manager or employee of a foreign professional service limited liability company who is an individual shall practice his or her profession in this state unless such individual is duly licensed to practice such profession in this state.

History: Add, L 1994, ch 576, § 1, eff Oct 24, 1994.

ARTICLE XIV
SAVINGS CLAUSES; EFFECTIVE DATES

History: Add, L 1994, ch 576, § 1, eff Oct 24, 1994.

§ 1401. Severability

If any provision of this chapter or application thereof to any person or circumstances is held invalid, such invalidity shall not affect other provisions or applications of this chapter that can be given effect without the invalid provision or application, and to this end the provisions of this chapter are declared severable.

History: Add, L 1994, ch 576, § 1, eff Oct 24, 1994.

§ 1402. Statutory construction; references

(a) Unless otherwise stated, all references in this chapter to articles or sections refer to the articles or sections of this chapter, and all references in any section of this chapter to a lettered or numbered subdivision refer to the subdivision so lettered or numbered in such section.

(b) Headings to sections are supplied in this chapter for the purpose of convenient reference and do not constitute part of the law.

(c) As used in this chapter all pronouns and any variations thereof refer to the masculine, feminine or neuter, singular or plural, as the context may require.

History: Add, L 1994, ch 576, § 1, eff Oct 24, 1994.

§ 1403. Effective date

This chapter shall take effect on the ninetieth day after it shall have become a law.

History: Add, L 1994, ch 576, § 1, eff Oct 24, 1994.

PARTNERSHIP LAW

History: Add, L 1919, ch 408, eff Oct 1, 1919, superseding L 1909, ch 44.

ARTICLE 1
SHORT TITLE; DEFINITIONS; CONSTRUCTION

§ 1. Short title
§ 2. General definitions
§ 3. Interpretation of knowledge and notice
§ 4. Rules of construction
§ 5. Rules for cases not provided for in this chapter

History: Add, L 1919, ch 408, eff Oct 1, 1919.

§ 1.   Short title

This chapter shall be known as the "partnership law."

History: Add, L 1919, ch 408; eff Oct 1, 1919.

§ 2.   General definitions

As used in this chapter "court" includes every court and judge having jurisdiction in the case;

"Business" includes every trade, occupation, or profession;

"Person" includes individuals, partnerships, corporations, and other associations;

"Bankrupt" includes bankrupt under the federal bankruptcy act or insolvent under any state insolvent act;

"Conveyance" includes every assignment, lease, mortgage, or encumbrance;

"Real property" includes land and any interest or estate in land.

"Foreign professional service corporation" has the meaning given to it in subdivision (d) of section fifteen hundred twenty-five of the business corporation law.

"Foreign professional service limited liability company" has the meaning given to it in subdivision (a) of section thirteen hundred one of the limited liability company law.

"Foreign limited liability partnership" means (i) any partnership without limited partners operating under an agreement governed by the laws of any jurisdiction, other than this state, each of whose partners is a professional authorized by law to render a professional service within this state and who is or has been engaged in the practice of such profession in such partnership or a predecessor entity, or will engage in the practice of such profession in the foreign limited liability partnership within thirty days of the date of the effectiveness of the notice provided for in subdivision (a) of section 121-1502 of this chapter or each of whose partners is a professional, at least one of whom is authorized by law to render a professional service within this state and who is or has been engaged in the practice of such profession in such partnership or a predecessor entity, or will engage in the practice of such profession in the foreign limited liability partnership within thirty days of the date of the effectiveness of the notice provided for in subdivision (a) of section 121-1502 of this chapter, (ii) any partnership without limited partners operating under an agreement governed by the laws of any jurisdiction, other than this state, authorized by, or holding a license, certificate, registration or permit issued by the licensing authority pursuant to, the education law to render a professional service within this state, which renders or intends to render professional services within this state and which is denominated as a registered limited liability partnership or limited liability partnership under such laws, regardless of any difference between such laws and the laws of this state, or (iii) a foreign related limited liability partnership; except that all partners of a foreign limited liability partnership that provides health, professional engineering, land surveying, geologic, architectural and/or landscape architectural services in this state shall be licensed in this state.

"Licensing authority" means the regents of the university of the state of New York or the state education department, as the case may be, in the case of all professions licensed under title eight of the education law, and the appropriate appellate division of the supreme court in the case of the profession of law.

"New York registered foreign limited liability partnership" means a foreign limited liability partnership which has filed a notice pursuant to subdivision (a) of section 121-1502 of this chapter that has not been withdrawn or revoked and which complies with subdivision (1) of section 121-1502 of this chapter.

"Profession" includes any practice as an attorney and counsellor-at-law or as a licensed physician, and those professions designated in title eight of the education law.

"Professional" means an individual duly authorized to practice a profession, a professional service corporation, a professional service limited liability company, a foreign professional service limited liability company, a registered limited liability partnership, a foreign limited liability partnership, a foreign professional service corporation or a professional partnership.

"Professional partnership" means (1) a partnership without limited partners each of whose partners is a professional authorized by law to render a professional service within this state, (2) a partnership without limited partners each of whose partners is a professional, at least one of whom is authorized by law to render a professional service within this state or (3) a partnership without limited partners authorized by, or holding a license, certificate, registration or permit issued by the licensing authority pursuant to the education law to render a professional service within this state; except that all partners of a professional partnership that provides medical services in this state must be licensed pursuant to article 131 of the education law to practice medicine in this state and all partners of a professional partnership that provides dental services in this state must be licensed pursuant to article 133 of the education law to practice dentistry in this state; and further except that all partners of a professional partnership that provides professional engineering, land surveying, geologic, architectural and/or landscape architectural services in this state must be licensed pursuant to article 145, article 147 and/or article 148 of the education law to practice one or more of such professions in this state.

"Professional service" means any type of service to the public that may be lawfully rendered by a member of a profession within the purview of his or her profession.

"Professional service corporation" means (i) a corporation organized under article fifteen of the business corporation law and (ii) any other corporation organized under the business corporation law or any predecessor statute, which is authorized by, or holds a license, certificate, registration or permit issued by, the licensing authority pursuant to the education law to render professional services within this state.

"Professional service limited liability company" means a limited liability company organized under article twelve of the limited liability company law.

"Registered limited liability partnership" means a partnership without limited partners operating under an agreement governed by the laws of this state, registered under section 121-1500 of this chapter and complying with section 121-1501 of this chapter.

"Foreign related limited liability partnership" means a partnership without limited partners operating under an agreement governed by the laws of any jurisdiction, other than this state, which (i) is denominated as a limited liability partnership or registered limited liability partnership under such laws, (ii) is not a foreign limited liability partnership under

clause (i) or (ii) of the paragraph defining foreign limited liability partnership in this section, (iii) is affiliated with a professional service limited liability company, foreign professional service limited liability company, professional service corporation, foreign professional service corporation, registered limited liability partnership that is a professional partnership under this section or a foreign limited liability partnership under clause (i) or (ii) of the paragraph defining foreign limited liability partnership in this section, and (iv) renders services related or complementary to the professional services rendered by, or provides services or facilities to, such professional service limited liability company, foreign professional service limited liability company, professional service corporation, foreign professional service corporation, registered limited liability partnership or foreign limited liability partnership. For purposes of this paragraph, such a partnership is affiliated with a professional service limited liability company, foreign professional service limited liability company, professional service corporation, foreign professional service corporation, registered limited liability partnership or foreign limited liability partnership if (1) at least a majority of partners in one partnership are partners in the other partnership, (2) at least a majority of the partners in each partnership also are partners, hold interests or are members in a limited liability company or other business entity, and each partnership renders services pursuant to an agreement with such limited liability company or other business entity, or (3) the partnerships or the partnership and such professional service limited liability company, such foreign professional service limited liability company, such professional service corporation, or such foreign professional service corporation are affiliates within the meaning of paragraph (a) of section nine hundred twelve of the business corporation law.

"Related limited liability partnership" means a partnership without limited partners operating under an agreement governed by the laws of this state, which (i) is not a professional partnership under this section, (ii) is affiliated with a professional service limited liability company, foreign professional service limited liability company, professional service corporation, foreign professional service corporation, registered limited liability partnership that is a professional partnership under this section or a foreign limited liability partnership under clause (i) or (ii) of the paragraph defining foreign limited liability partnership in this section, and (iii) renders services related or complementary to the professional services rendered by, or provides services or facilities to, such professional service limited liability company, foreign professional service limited liability company, professional service corporation, foreign professional service corporation, registered limited liability partnership or foreign limited liability partnership. For purposes of this paragraph, such a partnership is affiliated with a professional service limited liability company, foreign professional service limited liability company, professional service corporation, foreign professional service corporation, registered limited liability partnership or foreign limited liability partnership if (1) at least a majority of partners in one partnership are partners in the other partnership, (2) at least a majority of the partners in each partnership also are partners, hold interests or are members in a limited liability company or other business entity, and each partnership renders services pursuant to an agreement with such limited liability company or other business entity, or (3) the partnerships or the partnership and such professional service limited liability company, such foreign professional service limited liability company, such professional service corporation, or such foreign professional service corporation are affiliates within the meaning of paragraph (a) of section nine hundred twelve of the business corporation law.

History: Add, L 1919, ch 408, eff Oct 1, 1919, amd, L 1994, ch 576, § 6, eff Oct 24, 1994, L 1995, ch 643, §§ 19, 20, eff Aug 8, 1995, L 1996, ch 170, § 5, eff June 18, 1996, L 2014, ch 475, § 25, eff Nov 21, 2016.

CASE ANNOTATIONS

In computing unincorporated business taxable income, limited partnership was entitled to a deduction for personal services of a corporate partner actively engaged in the business of partnership. Mutual Mortg. Co. v State Tax Com. (1974, 3d Dept) 44 A.D.2d 273, 354 N.Y.S.2d 448

Business within the meaning of this section will include pooling of joint capital and joint management thereof. Chisholm v Commissioner (1935, CA2) 79 F.2d 14, 35-2 USTC P 9493, 16 AFTR 585, 101 ALR 200, cert den (1935) 296 US 641, 80 L Ed 456, 56 S Ct 174

The word "person" as defined by this section does not give corporations the right to enter into partnerships either with other corporations or with individuals. 1935 Ops Atty Gen 230

Special act creating Charles Hayden Foundation expressly grants to that corporation the powers declared in the will of Charles Hayden, deceased, which include powers to directors or trustees of the corporation to allow a part of the capital of the decedent's estate to remain in the partnership of Hayden, Stone & Co. for a limited time, as limited or special capital. In view of such special grant of authority, the corporation is authorized to become a partner in that firm as a limited partner. 1938 Ops Atty Gen 340

A partnership is authorized to become a partner in a limited partnership. 1972 Ops Atty Gen Dec 15

It is permissible for a County Clerk to accept for filing a Certificate of Limited Partnership in which the general partner is a corporation. 1979 Op Atty Gen July 19 (informal)

A general partnership may engage only in the business authorized by the partnership agreement. A limited partnership may engage only in the business authorized by the certificate filed under section 91 of the Partnership Law. A limited partnership may become a general partner in a new limited partnership. 1980 Op Atty Gen Oct. 28 (informal)

A limited partnership may become a general partner in a general partnership. The partnership with which the limited partnership becomes associated must in its certificate reflect the addition of the limited partnership as a partner. This amended certificate must be executed and acknowledged by the members of the limited partnership; however, a limited partner may designate one of the limited partnerships general partners to execute the amended certificate on his behalf. Ops Atty Gen 84-54

Non-resident limited liability partnerships may not be licensed as insurance brokers in New York State since they are not considered professionals as defined by CLS Partn § 2. Insurance Department, Opinions of General Counsel, Opinion Number 01-04-05

§ 3.   Interpretation of knowledge and notice

1. A person has "knowledge" of a fact within the meaning of this chapter not only when he has actual knowledge thereof, but also when he has knowledge of such other facts as in the circumstances shows bad faith.

2. A person has "notice" of a fact within the meaning of this chapter when the person who claims the benefit of the notice:

(a) States the fact to such person, or

(b) Delivers through the mail, or by other means of communication, a written statement of the fact to such person or to a proper person at his place of business or residence.

History: Add, L 1919, ch 408, eff Oct 1, 1919.

§ 4.   Rules of construction

1. The rule that statutes in derogation of the common law are to be strictly construed shall have no application to this chapter.

2. The law of estoppel shall apply under this chapter.

3. The law of agency shall apply under this chapter.

4. This chapter shall be so interpreted and construed as to effect its general purpose to make uniform the law of those states which enact it.

5. This chapter shall not be construed so as to impair the obligations of any contract existing when the chapter goes into effect, nor to affect any action or proceedings begun or right accrued before this chapter takes effect.

History: Add, L 1919, ch 408, eff Oct 1, 1919.

CASE ANNOTATIONS

Plaintiff could not recover for work performed and materials supplied as against defendant based solely on her status as partner in operation of tavern where plaintiff presented no direct evidence that he was hired by partnership or by landlord in his capacity as partner of defendant, landlord expressly testified that he hired plaintiff in his capacity as landlord/owner of building for purpose of obtaining certificate of occupancy, and work performed and materials supplied by plaintiff were found to be fixtures. Wolensky v Locke (1997, 2d Dept) 244 A.D.2d 546, 664 N.Y.S.2d 355

Partners were not liable for a debt incurred by a debtor, individually, as: (1) partnerships were governed by the laws of agency under N.Y. P'ship Law § 4(3), (2) the partners did not have any communication with a creditor that would give rise to the appearance and reasonable belief that the debtor possessed apparent authority to enter into the loan agreements on their behalf, (3) the creditor's own affidavit revealed that the creditor relied on the creditor's conversations with the debtor and never spoke to the partners, (4) the creditor failed to make reasonable inquiries into the debtor's actual authority, (5) the creditor's claim that the loans were apparently made in the usual course of the business of a public accounting firm and, therefore, binding on the partners was without merit under N.Y. P'ship Law § 20(1), and (6) the partnership agreement did not give the debtor the authority to borrow money on the partnership's behalf, and borrowing money for the purpose of investing in other business ventures was not an act apparently made for the carrying on in the usual way the business of a pubic accounting firm under N.Y. P'ship Law § 20(2). Beizer v Bunsis (2007, 2d Dept) 38 App Div 3d 813, 833 NYS2d 154

Partnership Law

§ 5.   Rules for cases not provided for in this chapter

In any case not provided for in this chapter the rules of law and equity, including the law merchant, shall govern.

History: Add, L 1919, ch 408, eff Oct 1, 1919.

ARTICLE 2
NATURE OF A PARTNERSHIP

§ 10. Partnership defined
§ 11. Rules for determining the existence of a partnership
§ 12. Partnership property

History: Add, L 1919, ch 408, eff Oct 1, 1919.

§ 10.   Partnership defined

1. A partnership is an association of two or more persons to carry on as co-owners a business for profit and includes for all purposes of the laws of this state, a registered limited liability partnership.

2. But any association formed under any other statute of this state, or any statute adopted by authority, other than the authority of this state, is not a partnership under this chapter, unless such association would have been a partnership in this state prior to the adoption of this chapter; but this chapter shall apply to limited partnerships except in so far as the statutes relating to such partnerships are inconsistent herewith.

History: Add, L 1919, ch 408, eff Oct 1, 1919, with substance transferred from § 2.

Sub 1, amd, L 1994, ch 576, § 7, eff Oct 24, 1994.

CASE ANNOTATIONS

1. In general
2. Partnership as separate entity
3. Joint venture
4. Agreements
5. Sharing in profits and losses
6. Management

1. In general

Nonresident junior partner of law firm doing business in New York who receives share of profits, albeit small, in addition to salary and who is also subject to liability for firm losses is subject to New York State income tax as nonresident partner of firm. Weil v Chu (1986, 3d Dept) 120 A.D.2d 781, 501 N.Y.S.2d 515, affd (1987) 70 N.Y.2d 783, 521 N.Y.S.2d 223, 515 N.E.2d 908, app dismd (1988) 485 US 901, 99 L Ed 2d 229, 108 S Ct 1069

In action to determine ownership of race horse, court did not err in refusing to include in its charge to jury provisions of CLS Partn § 10(1), defining term partnership as association of 2 or more persons to carry on business for profit as co-owners, since term "co-owners" in statute refers to business rather than assets used in business, and question of whether parties formed partnership was not relevant. Werronen v Taylor (1992, 3d Dept) 187 A.D.2d 774, 589 N.Y.S.2d 666

In action to recover payment under contingent-fee contract, plaintiff would not be heard to contradict its prior admissions that it was sole proprietorship of its principal individually and that accountant had been retained as its consultant where sole preexisting documentary evidence for plaintiff's new position that it was in partnership with accountant was designation on signature page of contract on which plaintiff's principal wrote "Partner" in blank space for insertion of his title. Milton Weinstein Assocs. v Nynex Corp. (1999, 1st Dept) 266 A.D.2d 138, 699 N.Y.S.2d 23, later proceeding (2000, N.Y. A.D., 1st Dept) 2000 N.Y. A.D. LEXIS 2292 and app den (2000) 95 N.Y.2d 753, 711 N.Y.S.2d 155, 733 N.E.2d 227

In breach of contract action against partnership and individuals, 2 individual defendants were not entitled to summary judgment dismissing complaint insofar as it was asserted against them where there were triable issues of fact as to whether they withdrew from partnership before it entered into construction contract with plaintiffs. Roy McCutcheon, P.C. v Dolgin (1999, 2d Dept) 266 A.D.2d 368, 697 N.Y.S.2d 532, app dismd (2000) 95 N.Y.2d 790, 711 N.Y.S.2d 157, 733 N.E.2d 229

Court properly dismissed causes of action alleging business partnership and seeking dissolution and distribution of its alleged assets where plaintiff did not allege essential express agreement to share both profits and losses of business. Potter v Davie (2000, 4th Dept) 275 A.D.2d 961, 713 N.Y.S.2d 627

No partnership existed between the parties to carry on as co-owners a business for profit, when there was no written partnership agreement between the parties, because, although the party who claimed that a partnership existed contributed skill and knowledge to the business, the parties never shared the intent to enter into a partnership, the other party had sole control and management of the business, and party who claimed that a partnership existed invested no capital and was not liable to creditors. Hammond v Smith, 2017 NY Slip Op 05337, 2017 NY Slip Op 5337, 2017 N.Y. App. Div. LEXIS 5462 (N.Y. App. Div. 4th Dep't 2017).

Where, in suit by one partner against another for alleged fraud in division of proceeds from dissolution of partnership, partners' affairs were really settled and action really involved manner in which funds derived from partnership assets would be divided, formal suit for accounting was not condition precedent to action. Auld v Estridge (1976) 86 Misc. 2d 895, 382 N.Y.S.2d 897

Partner breached his fiduciary duty to fellow partner when, having engineered sale of partnership assets to third party, he concealed total amount of over-the-counter stock shares received in exchange. Auld v Estridge (1976) 86 Misc. 2d 895, 382 N.Y.S.2d 897

Action brought by former member of law firm against current firm must be dismissed for lack of federal jurisdiction, where substantial weight of evidence shows that current firm is organized, treated, and conducted as limited liability partnership as defined in Partn § 10, because plaintiff and one member of current firm share New Jersey citizenship, and diversity is lacking. Cohen v Kurtzman (1999, DC NJ) 45 F. Supp. 2d 423, 44 FR Serv 3d 68

A partnership is authorized to become a partner in a limited partnership. 1972 Ops Atty Gen Dec 15

A general partnership may engage only in the business authorized by the partnership agreement. A limited partnership may engage only in the business authorized by the certificate filed under section 91 of the Partnership Law. A limited partnership may become a general partner in a new limited partnership. 1980 Op Atty Gen Oct. 28 (informal)

A limited partnership may become a general partner in a general partnership. The partnership with which the limited partnership becomes associated must in its certificate reflect the addition of the limited partnership as a partner. This amended certificate must be executed and acknowledged by the members of the limited partnership; however, a limited partner may designate one of the limited partnerships general partners to execute the amended certificate on his behalf. Ops Atty Gen 84-54

2. Partnership as separate entity

A partnership cannot be regarded as a legal entity separate and distinct from the several partners therein. In re Peck (1912) 206 N.Y. 55, 99 N.E. 258

It has long been the rule in this and many other jurisdictions that a partnership is not in the eyes of the law an entity separate from its members. But the legislature and businessmen do so regard a partnership for various purposes. Ruzicka v Rager (1953) 305 N.Y. 191, 111 N.E.2d 878, 39 ALR2d 288, reh den (1953) 305 N.Y. 798, 113 N.E.2d 306

A partnership is not a separate legal entity and the partners are "co-owners." Kaplan v Kaplan (1961) 27 Misc. 2d 596, 213 N.Y.S.2d 178

3. Joint venture

The legal consequences of a joint venture are almost identical with those of a partnership. Pedersen v Manitowoc Co. (1969) 25 N.Y.2d 412, 306 N.Y.S.2d 903, 255 N.E.2d 146

In dispute between joint venturers, court properly looked to partnership law principles, since joint venture is "special combination of 2 or more persons where in some specific venture a profit is jointly sought" and is, in sense, partnership for limited purpose. Gramercy

Equities Corp. v Dumont (1988) 72 N.Y.2d 560, 534 N.Y.S.2d 908, 531 N.E.2d 629

In absence of other indicia that would establish existence of joint venture, assertion of agreement to distribute proceeds of enterprise on percentage basis will not suffice. Davella v Nielsen (1994, 2d Dept) 208 A.D.2d 494, 616 N.Y.S.2d 800 (criticized in Bay Casino, LLC v M/V Royal Empress (1998, ED NY) 1998 US Dist LEXIS 19713)

Plaintiff's failure to allege that he and defendant agreed to distribute burden of any possible losses was fatal to assertion that parties entered into joint venture. Davella v Nielsen (1994, 2d Dept) 208 A.D.2d 494, 616 N.Y.S.2d 800 (criticized in Bay Casino, LLC v M/V Royal Empress (1998, ED NY) 1998 US Dist LEXIS 19713)

Cross motions for summary judgment were precluded by triable issue of fact as to, inter alia, whether parties to joint venture agreement intended to treat plaintiff development company and its affiliates as one entity for purposes of their business dealings where (1) defendant guarantor admitted in letter that he was indebted to another plaintiff "and/or its affiliates," which included development company, (2) guarantor failed to dispute that development company was formed as corporate vehicle for plaintiffs' participation in joint venture, and (3) guarantor made payment to development company's affiliate in what appeared to be partial satisfaction of debt incurred under subject joint venture agreement. Emerald Dev. Corp. v Real Equities, Inc. (1998, 1st Dept) 251 A.D.2d 180, 675 N.Y.S.2d 857

Where all the basic elements of partnership exist in an agreement in which the parties refer to themselves as partners but sometimes describe their association as a partnership and sometimes as a joint venture, the court will treat the parties as partners and determine their rights and duties under the Partnership Law. Napoli v Domnitch (1962) 34 Misc. 2d 237, 226 N.Y.S.2d 908, mod on other grounds (1962, 2d Dept) 18 A.D.2d 707, 236 N.Y.S.2d 549, affd (1964) 14 N.Y.2d 508, 248 N.Y.S.2d 228, 197 N.E.2d 623

A joint venture is a special combination of two or more persons in some specific venture where a profit is jointly sought without any actual partnership or corporate designation, while an indispensable requirement of a partnership is a mutual promise or understanding of the parties to submit to the burden of making good the losses as well as to share in the profits of the business, which relates to a general business of a particular kind; however, insofar as the right to an accounting and concomitant relief is concerned, it is enough that the parties stand in a mutual and confidential relationship to each other and have a joint interest in the result of the venture. Accordingly, where such an analogon of property or interests as would create at least a joint venture between the parties is shown, although it is unclear whether there was an agreement that each party would share the burden of losses, plaintiff is entitled to equitable relief in the form of an accounting in an action arising out of a dispute as to the parties' respective interests in their business even though he has not come to the court with the cleanest of hands, since a court of equity must do equity where both parties are seeking equitable relief. Hanlon v Melfi (1979) 102 Misc. 2d 170, 423 N.Y.S.2d 132

Partnership Law defines a partnership as an "association of two or more persons to carry on as co-owners a business for profit." A joint venture is generally described as an association of two or more persons, in the nature of a partnership to carry out a business enterprise for profit. Wollard v Radl (1952, City Ct) 112 N.Y.S.2d 572

Allegations that plaintiff was to purchase goods from suppliers, resell them to certain customers supplied by defendants at prices specified by defendants, and share in the net profits of such resales, set forth a joint venture relationship, even though plaintiff was not to share in the losses. Montenegro v Roxas (1955, Sup) 141 N.Y.S.2d 681

4. Agreements

If a contract as a whole contemplates an association of two or more persons to carry on as co-owners a business for profit there is a partnership. Martin v Peyton (1927) 246 N.Y. 213, 158 N.E. 77

Complaint based on claim that plaintiff was partner in defendant partnership was properly dismissed on motion for summary judgment where parties' course of dealing and performance under subject agreement contradicted plaintiffs' claim, and there was no objective evidence of manifestation of intent to be bound by terms asserted by plaintiffs, but only their self-serving assertions as to their subjective understanding and private intent. Kantor v Bernstein (1997, 1st Dept) 245 A.D.2d 138, 665 N.Y.S.2d 883

Attorney could not be precluded from being paid his agreed-on retirement income while he continued to practice law where parties' partnership agreement contained unenforceable provision that improperly restricted his practice of law on his retirement and implicated prohibition against sharing legal fees with nonattorneys. Sage v Polansky (1998, 2d Dept) 251 A.D.2d 567, 673 N.Y.S.2d 614

Plaintiff was entitled to indemnification for expenses incurred under parties' partnership agreement where those expenses were incurred in good faith and without gross negligence in furtherance of partnership business interests. Nave v Dunbar Partners (1998, 1st Dept) 255 A.D.2d 159, 679 N.Y.S.2d 582

Court properly dismissed causes of action alleging business partnership and seeking dissolution and distribution of its alleged assets where plaintiff did not allege essential express agreement to share both profits and losses of business. Potter v Davie (2000, 4th Dept) 275 A.D.2d 961, 713 N.Y.S.2d 627

Court properly dismissed cause of action for dissolution of alleged domestic partnership and distribution of its alleged assets where (1) plaintiff expressly linked her claim of domestic partnership to her allegation of common-law marriage, which concept was expressly rejected in Morone v Morone, 50 N.Y.2d 481, (2) plaintiff made no attempt to satisfy Morone's requirement of express agreement, and (3) even if plaintiff's allegations and averments could be construed as referring to express agreement, such agreement would fail for lack of definiteness because it did not specify what contributions and efforts were required of plaintiff and how much defendant was required to pay her in compensation. Potter v Davie (2000, 4th Dept) 275 A.D.2d 961, 713 N.Y.S.2d 627

While the agreement between the parties was not in writing, the existence of a partnership to conduct a rooming house business was indicated by evidence such as exaction of a lease by plaintiff and defendant, contribution of money by plaintiff necessary to take and furnish the premises, sharing of profits and losses between them and filing of partnership income tax returns. The arrangement meets the statutory definition of a partnership. Boxill v Boxill (1952) 201 Misc 386, 111 N.Y.S.2d 33

An oral partnership agreement under which doctors conducted a joint practice, superseded a prior employment agreement, containing a restrictive covenant barring the defendant from practicing urology for a period of five years after termination of employment by the plaintiff, even though parties planned to reduce oral partnership agreement to writing. Keen v Jason (1959) 19 Misc. 2d 538, 187 N.Y.S.2d 825, affd (1960, 2d Dept) 11 A.D.2d 1039, 207 N.Y.S.2d 1001

Where all the basic elements of partnership exist in an agreement in which the parties refer to themselves as partners but sometimes describe their association as a partnership and sometimes as a joint venture, the court will treat the parties as partners and determine their rights and duties under the Partnership Law. Napoli v Domnitch (1962) 34 Misc. 2d 237, 226 N.Y.S.2d 908, mod on other grounds (1962, 2d Dept) 18 A.D.2d 707, 236 N.Y.S.2d 549, affd (1964) 14 N.Y.2d 508, 248 N.Y.S.2d 228, 197 N.E.2d 623

Agreement which two attorneys signed three years before their firm was dissolved showed that they intended to give an attorney who worked for the firm an equity interest in the firm, and the agreement was valid even though it was not filed with the New York Secretary of State. Joachim v Flanzig (2004, Sup) 773 N.Y.S.2d 267

In view of the definition of partnership in subd 1 of this section as an association of two or more persons to carry on a business for profit as co-owners, it would seem to be basic that a partnership agreement is superior to that of any alleged contract for employment of one of the partners by the firm. Foster v United States (1963, SD NY) 221 F. Supp. 291, 63-2 USTC P 9588, 12 AFTR 2d 5212, affd (1964, CA2 NY) 329 F.2d 717, 64-1 USTC P 9362, 13 AFTR 2d 1118

Where each of three original partners entered into separate agreements with other individuals designated as "participants" who were not authorized to act as agents for the partnership and who could transfer their interests with the consent of the partner from whom they made their purchase, such arrangement did not constitute a partnership. Beckerman v Sands (1973, SD NY) 364 F. Supp. 1197, 18 FR Serv 2d 86

5. Sharing in profits and losses

If a contract as a whole contemplates an association of two or more persons to carry on as co-owners a business for profit there is a partnership. Martin v Peyton (1927) 246 N.Y. 213, 158 N.E. 77

A sharing of profits and losses as owners of a business is evidenced within the meaning of this section where it appears from schedules in bankruptcy that each of four persons was the owner of a one-fourth interest in each of four farms, listing identical liabilities relating to operation of the farms in question. A. Sam & Sons Produce Co. v Campese (1961, 4th Dept) 14 A.D.2d 487, 217 N.Y.S.2d 275

Partnership Law

In an action, inter alia, to declare plaintiff a partner in certain business ventures with defendants and for an accounting, plaintiff failed to establish the existence of a joint venture or partnership where, although plaintiff performed services for the business in exchange for a share of profits, plaintiff had no capital invested in the business and never held himself out as a partner or participant in a joint venture, where plaintiff was not personally liable for any of the obligations of the enterprise since it was conducted in the corporate name, and where plaintiff acknowledged that defendant was the principal giving the initial capital to start the enterprise with sole authority to sign checks and with control over issuing invoices and collecting proceeds from customers. Ramirez v Goldberg (1981, 2d Dept) 82 A.D.2d 850, 439 N.Y.S.2d 959

Defendant was not entitled to summary judgment dismissing cause of action for partnership accounting where there was evidence that could support findings that (1) parties had confidential relationship that was in many respects analogous to that of husband and wife, (2) plaintiff reasonably trusted defendant and relied on him to protect her interests, and (3) in reliance on his promises that she would have life use of his home and other financial benefits, she sold her home, moved in with him, and made substantial contributions of money and labor to upkeep and improvement of his house and grounds; oral partnership agreement was not entirely unenforceable merely because it incorporated promises that could not be fully performed within year or lifetime, and there was no merit in defendant's contention that plaintiff's claim was deficient because services purportedly rendered as her contribution to partnership were not "profits." Williams v Lynch (1997, 3d Dept) 245 A.D.2d 715, 666 N.Y.S.2d 749, app dismd without op (1998) 91 N.Y.2d 957, 671 N.Y.S.2d 717, 694 N.E.2d 886

There was not a fact issue as to whether there was a partnership under N.Y. P'ship Law § 10(1) since it was not shown that an attorney and a lawyer shared profits or submitted to the burden of making good the losses. Community Capital Bank v Fischer & Yanowitz (2008, 2d Dept) 47 App Div 3d 667, 850 NYS2d 508.

While the agreement between the parties was not in writing, the existence of a partnership to conduct a rooming house business was indicated by evidence such as exaction of a lease by plaintiff and defendant, contribution of money by plaintiff necessary to take and furnish the premises, sharing of profits and losses between them and filing of partnership income tax returns. The arrangement meets the statutory definition of a partnership. Boxill v Boxill (1952) 201 Misc 386, 111 N.Y.S.2d 33

The fact that there is no written agreement of partnership is not conclusive in determining whether a partnership, which is an association of two or more persons with the mutual promise or understanding to share in the profits of a business and submit to the burden of making good the losses, exists, but it is an element to be taken into serious consideration; where no partnership agreement is executed in writing by the parties, the issue must be determined from the testimony, from the conduct of the parties, and especially from the documentary evidence, and the burden of establishing the existence of such an oral partnership agreement by a fair preponderance of the credible evidence rests upon the party claiming the partnership. Hanlon v Melfi (1979) 102 Misc. 2d 170, 423 N.Y.S.2d 132

An attorney who received his share of his law firm's profits in each of several consecutive years as evidenced by his personal tax returns and partnership tax returns filed by defendants for years in question, and who was held out to the public as a partner in the firm, met his burden of establishing a partnership relationship, notwithstanding the lack of a written agreement between the parties, and was therefore entitled to an accounting of the law practice in connection with a claim that certain fees were improperly excluded from partnership income; a cause of action premised on the failure of defendants, plaintiff's former partners, to use their best efforts to secure law firm business and clients for plaintiff would be dismissed since plaintiff did not have a property right to any clients and could not seek legal redress when clients chose new counsel after the partnership was dissolved. Missan v Schoenfeld (1981, Sup) 111 Misc. 2d 1022, 445 N.Y.S.2d 856

One referred to as a junior partner but who received a fixed salary and shared only in certain profits of the firm and had no authority to participate in the management of the firm was not a co-owner within the definition of a partnership. Peterson v Eppler (1946, Sup) 67 N.Y.S.2d 498

Allegations that plaintiff was to purchase goods from suppliers, resell them to certain customers supplied by defendants at prices specified by defendants, and share in the net profits of such resales, set forth a joint venture relationship, even though plaintiff was not to share in the losses. Montenegro v Roxas (1955, Sup) 141 N.Y.S.2d 681

6. Management

One referred to as a junior partner but who received a fixed salary and shared only in certain profits of the firm and had no authority to participate in the management of the firm was not a co-owner within the definition of a partnership. Peterson v Eppler (1946, Sup) 67 N.Y.S.2d 498

Under §§ 10, 11, 40 there could not be partnership in which whole management was vested in one partner. Wild v Commissioner (1933, CA2) 62 F.2d 777, 3 USTC P 1032, 11 AFTR 1376

§ 11. Rules for determining the existence of a partnership

In determining whether a partnership exists, these rules shall apply:

1. Except as provided by section twenty-seven persons who are not partners as to each other are not partners as to third persons.

2. Joint tenancy, tenancy in common, tenancy by the entireties, joint property, common property, or part ownership does not of itself establish a partnership, whether such co-owners do or do not share any profits made by the use of the property.

3. The sharing of gross returns does not of itself establish a partnership, whether or not the persons sharing them have a joint or common right or interest in any property from which the returns are derived.

4. The receipt by a person of a share of the profits of a business is prima facie evidence that he is a partner in the business, but no such inference shall be drawn if such profits were received in payment:

(a) As a debt by installments or otherwise,

(b) As wages of an employee or rent to a landlord,

(c) As an annuity to a surviving spouse or representative of a deceased partner,

(d) As interest on a loan, though the amount of payment vary with the profits of the business,

(e) As the consideration for the sale of the goodwill of a business or other property by installments or otherwise.

History: Add, L 1919, ch 408, eff Oct 1, 1919.

Sub 4, par (c), amd, L 1976, ch 110, § 4, eff Sept 1, 1976.

CASE ANNOTATIONS

1. In general

If trustees of syndicate act as principals, owners of sums subscribed free from control of subscribers, trust is created and members are not liable for debts incurred by managers but if trustees are subject to control of subscribers as co-owners of business for profit, partnership or joint undertaking exists as to third parties, although otherwise specified as to subscribers among themselves. Brown v Bedell (1934) 263 N.Y. 177, 188 N.E. 641, reh den (1934) 264 N.Y. 453, 191 N.E. 510 and motion den (1934) 264 N.Y. 513, 191 N.E. 541

A farm lease under which the rental was one-half the receipts of the produce does not establish a partnership between the landlord and the tenant. Pestlin v Haxton Canning Co. (1948) 274 A.D. 144, 80 N.Y.S.2d 869, affd (1949) 299 N.Y. 477, 87 N.E.2d 522

In an action by a wife against her husband for an accounting of the partnership assets and liabilities of their farming business, the complaint was properly dismissed at the close of all the evidence where the wife wholly failed to demonstrate that there was a partnership between the parties, as required by Partn Law §§ 10(1), 11. Galbraith v Galbraith (1980, 4th Dept) 78 A.D.2d 770, 433 N.Y.S.2d 651

Defendants were entitled to obtain redacted versions of plaintiff's income tax returns where issue was whether partnership between parties existed, and those returns, which presumably included requisite form K-1 and reflected deductions for plaintiff's share of partnership expenses, might be sole source of positive evidence of partnership's existence. Rosenfeld v Kaplan (1997, 1st Dept) 245 A.D.2d 176, 666 N.Y.S.2d 180

In action to recover payment under contingent-fee contract, plaintiff would not be heard to contradict its prior admissions that it was sole proprietorship of its principal individually and that accountant had been retained as its consultant where sole preexisting documentary evidence for plaintiff's new position that it was in partnership with accountant was designation on signature page of contract on which plaintiff's principal wrote "Partner" in blank space for insertion of his title. Milton Weinstein Assocs. v Nynex Corp. (1999, 1st Dept) 266 A.D.2d 138, 699 N.Y.S.2d 23, later proceeding (2000, N.Y. A.D., 1st Dept) 2000 N.Y. A.D. LEXIS 2292 and app den (2000) 95 N.Y.2d 753, 711 N.Y.S.2d 155, 733 N.E.2d 227

In action alleging that plaintiff and defendant (her former lover) were partners in defendant's glassblowing business, defendant was entitled to summary judgment on ground that no partnership existed as matter of law, where record established that studio property was owned solely by defendant and that plaintiff made no contribution to its purchase and neither made nor assumed responsibility for mortgage payments thereon, her name was never placed on certificate of doing business as partners, no partnership tax returns were ever filed, there was never any sharing of profits or losses, document executed by parties to establish their "financial and personal relationship" characterized plaintiff's financial contributions to business as loans, and plaintiff sought compensation in form of wages for any services she performed for business, thus portraying herself as mere employee. Cleland v Thirion (2000, 3d Dept) 268 A.D.2d 842, 704 N.Y.S.2d 316

Defendant physician, operating as professional corporation, was entitled to summary judgment in action for accounting by associate who claimed to have formed partnership with him, since partnership may not generally exist where business is conducted in corporate form. Berke v Hamby (2001, 2d Dept) 279 A.D.2d 491, 719 N.Y.S.2d 280, subsequent app (2d Dept) 279 A.D.2d 491, 718 N.Y.S.2d 887

An association of farmers formed to construct, at their joint expense, a telephone line connecting their homes with the lines of a telephone company was not a partnership where it was not formed to engage in any business and contemplated no profits to be shared. Branagan v Buckman (1910) 67 Misc 242, 122 N.Y.S. 610, affd (1911) 145 A.D. 950, 130 N.Y.S. 1106, affd (1913) 207 N.Y. 719, 101 N.E. 1095

The fact that title to the partnership property is retained by one of the parties does not destroy the character of the relationship. Fullam v Peterson (1940, Sup) 21 N.Y.S.2d 797

2. Factual question

Whether or not a partnership exists is a question of fact. Palmentola v Morrell (1964, 2d Dept) 21 A.D.2d 828, 251 N.Y.S.2d 479

Court properly denied plaintiff's motion for summary judgment in action to recover money pursuant to written agreement providing for return of money if formal limited partnership agreement were not executed and filed within 90 days, where fact issues existed as to whether plaintiff waived time requirement by reexecuting partnership certificate after time for filing had expired and thereafter accepting benefits from partnership for more than one year. Giusti v Zackheim (1992, 1st Dept) 184 A.D.2d 358, 585 N.Y.S.2d 213

Summary judgment for plaintiff in partnership dissolution action was premature where issue had not yet been joined, and there were issues of fact as to whether attempted reconstitution of partnership and transfer of assets had been completed. Model v Elliman (1997, 1st Dept) 240 A.D.2d 330, 659 N.Y.S.2d 755

Petitioner was not partner with her husband in operation of restaurant, and thus was not person required to collect tax under CLS Tax § 1131(1), where, inter alia, there was no evidence of written partnership agreement, and no evidence to controvert petitioner's characterization of her role in business as hostess of restaurant who did not perform any meaningful role in management of business. N.Y. Tax Appeals Tribunal TSB-D-95(10)S

3. Partnership contract

A partnership results from a contract express or implied and does not arise by operation of law. Martin v Peyton (1927) 246 N.Y. 213, 158 N.E. 77

An attorney was not barred by the statute of frauds from alleging that, pursuant to an oral agreement, he was a partner in a law firm, since a partnership agreement may be oral. Missan v Schoenfeld (1983, 1st Dept) 95 A.D.2d 198, 465 N.Y.S.2d 706, app dismd (1983) 60 N.Y.2d 860

Partnership may only arise by mutual agreement between two or more persons; it exists as to its members where they have agreed to combine their labor, property and skill, or some of them, for purpose of engaging in any lawful trade or business and share profits and losses as such between them. Smith v Maine (1932) 145 Misc 521, 260 N.Y.S. 409, 260 N.Y.S. 425

4. – Construction and requisites

Indispensable essential of contract of co-partnership, either under common-law rule or this section is mutual promise or undertaking of parties to share in profits of business, and submit to burden of making good losses. Reynolds v Searle (1919) 186 A.D. 202, 174 N.Y.S. 137

Agreement for purchase of property from joint funds and for division of property does not constitute partnership where there is no contemplation of sharing profits and losses. Columbian Laundry v Hencken (1922) 203 A.D. 140, 196 N.Y.S. 523

An agreement among certain painters which provided that one S., who supplied the equipment and the capital, procured the business and acted as manager, treasurer and bookkeeper, should receive $5,000 per year and bear all losses up to $5,000 yearly; that the other members of the firm were permitted to draw on the firm's account, but only on a daily or weekly basis, with no withdrawals except for days, weeks or months actually devoted to work for the partnership; and that profits beyond the foregoing items of expense were to be shared, and losses beyond the $5,000 charged to S., borne equally by the partners, did not constitute a partnership. Scott v Miller (1940) 260 A.D. 428, 22 N.Y.S.2d 981, affd (1941) 285 N.Y. 760, 34 N.E.2d 910, motion den (1941) 285 N.Y. 847, 35 N.E.2d 509

Defendants were not general partners where partnership agreement provided that control of partnership rested with 3 individual plaintiffs and that defendants were to have no vote in partnership decisions. Hoffman v Eisenberg (1988, 2d Dept) 140 A.D.2d 306, 527 N.Y.S.2d 814, app den (1988) 72 N.Y.2d 806, 532 N.Y.S.2d 847, 529 N.E.2d 177

Evidence supported determination that parties did not enter into partnership to operate service station where (1) plaintiff testified that partnership was created, but admitted that tax identification number was never applied for, that licenses were never changed to partnership name, and that his name was never added to lease, (2) parties' accountant testified that parties' income tax returns and financial statements drawn up for business were prepared as if business were sole proprietorship, (3) attorney who prepared "partnership agreement" testified that he had drafted earlier agreements between parties which were titled otherwise and were intended to be security agreements to protect loan from plaintiff to defendant, (4) defendant testified that he thought partnership agreement was security agreement, (5) partnership agreement uncharacteristically left all control of business to plaintiff and stated that its primary purpose was to protect parties in case of death or disability of either party, and (6) arrangement after plaintiff left business, whereby defendant paid fixed sum to plaintiff on monthly basis rather than share of profits, was inconsistent with partnership. Kellogg v Kellogg (1992, 3d Dept) 185 A.D.2d 426, 585 N.Y.S.2d 824

In partnership dissolution action, although defendants were judicially estopped from asserting that certain plaintiffs were not presently partners, triable issues of fact existed as to whether those plaintiffs had signed requisite documents for reconstitution of partnership, and whether other plaintiffs had orally resigned, where partnership agreement required unanimous consent of nondissolving partners to reconstitute partnership without winding up partnership affairs. Model v Elliman (1997, 1st Dept) 240 A.D.2d 330, 659 N.Y.S.2d 755

An express contract provision for sharing profits is not essential to the existence of a partnership. If it was the intention of the parties to form a partnership they would become partners and as such would be entitled to share in the profits unless the terms and provisions of the contract are so framed as to leave the partners without any community of interest in the business or in the profits. Fullam v Peterson (1940, Sup) 21 N.Y.S.2d 797

Intention is the leading test of partnership and in determining that question the fact that by contract the parties have characterized their relationship as a partnership, though not conclusive, is entitled to much weight. Fullam v Peterson (1940, Sup) 21 N.Y.S.2d 797

Statements in a contract that no partnership is intended are not conclusive and if as a whole the contract contemplates an association of two or more persons to carry on as co-owners the business for profit there is a partnership. Greenstone v Klar (1947, Sup) 69 N.Y.S.2d 548, mod on other grounds (1947) 272 A.D. 892, 71 N.Y.S.2d 201

Where each of three original partners entered into separate agreements with other individuals designated as "participants" who were not authorized to act as agents for the partnership and who could transfer their interests with the consent of the partner from whom they made their purchase, such arrangement did not constitute a partnership. Beckerman v Sands (1973, SD NY) 364 F. Supp. 1197, 18 FR Serv 2d 86

5. – No written contract

Partnership, if denied, may be proved by production of some written instrument, by testimony as to some conversation, or by circumstantial evidence. Martin v Peyton (1927) 246 N.Y. 213, 158 N.E. 77

Where no partnership agreement is executed in writing by parties, it must be determined from testimony, from conduct of parties, and especially from documentary evidence, whether or not partnership existed. Adamson v Adamson (1937) 249 A.D. 418, 292 N.Y.S. 492

Where a man and woman holding themselves out to the community as husband and wife agreed orally to conduct a farming operation, with joint ownership of some of the properties, management, and equal sharing of profits and loans, there was a partnership and the woman was entitled to a dissolution of the partnership and an accounting with respect to partnership affairs when, after joint operation of the farm for more than five years, the man refused to allow her to participate in the operation of the farm. The trial court improperly relied on a theory of quantum meruit theory in making an award to her for performance of substantial services. Lee v Slovak (1981, 3d Dept) 81 A.D.2d 98, 440 N.Y.S.2d 358, app dismd (1981) 54 N.Y.2d 831

Evidence failed, as matter of law, to establish oral partnership agreement asserted by plaintiff for 1/2 ownership of building where plaintiff's only contribution was to be his supervision in refurbishing building, which was same as work he performed as salaried employee of defendant's company, and plaintiff could not specifically state when and where agreement was made, when it would take effect, or extent of defendant's interest in building. Azoulay v Cassin (1987, 2d Dept) 128 A.D.2d 660, 512 N.Y.S.2d 900

Court properly dismissed action to recover damages for breach of alleged partnership agreement on ground that plaintiff was defendants' employee rather than their partner where (1) parties did not have written partnership agreement, (2) plaintiff did not contribute any capital to enterprise and he apparently was not liable for its losses, (3) money advanced to enterprise by plaintiff was repaid by defendants, and (4) there was no evidence that defendants intended to enter into partnership arrangement with plaintiff; mere fact that certain documents referred to organization as partnership did not make it one. Brodsky v Stadlen (1988, 2d Dept) 138 A.D.2d 662, 526 N.Y.S.2d 478

Alleged partners suing managing partners in firm for accounting were entitled to amend their complaint to include breach of contract claim where new claim was based on same facts and evidence as accounting claim, thus eliminating possibility of prejudice or unfair surprise, and parties apparently had oral contract to effectuate their intent to merge 2 firms by sharing profits in specified percentage, allowing defendants to retain their management responsibilities, and allowing plaintiffs discretion to allocate their profit share among themselves; fact that duration of arrangement was unspecified did not necessarily make agreement too indefinite to enforce. Muhlstock v Cole (1997, 1st Dept) 245 A.D.2d 55, 666 N.Y.S.2d 116, 135 CCH LC ¶ 58396

The fact that there is no written agreement of partnership is not conclusive in determining whether a partnership exists, but is an element to be taken into serious consideration in determining where truth of controversy is. Smith v Maine (1932) 145 Misc 521, 260 N.Y.S. 409, 260 N.Y.S. 425

Mere loose and indefinite talk cannot be made basis of finding that partnership agreement exists. Smith v Maine (1932) 145 Misc 521, 260 N.Y.S. 409, 260 N.Y.S. 425

The fact that there is no written agreement of partnership is not conclusive in determining whether a partnership, which is an association of two or more persons with the mutual promise or understanding to share in the profits of a business and submit to the burden of making good the losses, exists, but it is an element to be taken into serious consideration; where no partnership agreement is executed in writing by the parties, the issue must be determined from the testimony, from the conduct of the parties, and especially from the documentary evidence, and the burden of establishing the existence of such an oral partnership agreement by a fair preponderance of the credible evidence rests upon the party claiming the partnership. Hanlon v Melfi (1979) 102 Misc. 2d 170, 423 N.Y.S.2d 132

6. Intention of parties

Plaintiff was not entitled to summary judgment declaring him to be sole owner of certain property under terms of contract by which he had provided funds for its purchase on condition that property would be forfeited to him if not resold within specific time, where (1) plaintiff contended that contract constituted partnership with defendants, under which property was purchased as joint venture, (2) defendants contended that transaction constituted usurious mortgage loan by plaintiff, and (3) one defendant submitted affidavit raising questions of fact regarding preliminary negotiations between parties, going directly to issue of intent. Boyarsky v Froccaro (1987, 2d Dept) 131 A.D.2d 710, 516 N.Y.S.2d 775

Intention is the leading test of partnership and in determining that question the fact that by contract the parties have characterized their relation as a partnership, though not conclusive, is entitled to much weight. Fullam v Peterson (1940, Sup) 21 N.Y.S.2d 797

An express contract provision for sharing profits is not essential to the existence of a partnership. If it was the intention of the parties to form a partnership they would become partners and as such would be entitled to share in the profits unless the terms and provisions of the contract are so framed as to leave the partners without any community of interest in the business or in the profits. Fullam v Peterson (1940, Sup) 21 N.Y.S.2d 797

Agreement which two attorneys signed three years before their firm was dissolved showed that they intended to give an attorney who worked for the firm an equity interest in the firm, and the agreement was valid even though it was not filed with the New York Secretary of State. Joachim v Flanzig (2004, Sup) 773 N.Y.S.2d 267

7. Community of interest

One of fundamental tests for determination of existence of partnership is existence of community interest inter se for business purposes. Richardson v Hughitt (1879) 76 N.Y. 55

There must be an amalgam of property or interests to create a partnership. Steinbeck v Gerosa (1958) 4 N.Y.2d 302, 175 N.Y.S.2d 1, 151 N.E.2d 170, app dismd (1958) 358 US 39, 3 L Ed 2d 45, 79 S Ct 64 and (criticized in Bay Casino, LLC v M/V Royal Empress (1998, ED NY) 1998 US Dist LEXIS 19713)

Ultimate question in determination of existence of partnership is whether parties have so joined their property, interests, skills, and risks that for the purpose of the particular partnership venture their respective contributions have become as one and the commingled property and interests of the parties have thereby been made subject to each of the associates on the trust and inducement that each would act for the joint benefit of all. Steinbeck v Gerosa (1958) 4 N.Y.2d 302, 175 N.Y.S.2d 1, 151 N.E.2d 170, app dismd (1958) 358 US 39, 3 L Ed 2d 45, 79 S Ct 64 and (criticized in Bay Casino, LLC v M/V Royal Empress (1998, ED NY) 1998 US Dist LEXIS 19713)

An express contract provision for sharing profits is not essential to the existence of a partnership. If it was the intention of the parties to form a partnership they would become partners and as such would be entitled to share in the profits unless the terms and provisions of the contract are so framed as to leave the partners without any community of interest in the business or in the profits. Fullam v Peterson (1940, Sup) 21 N.Y.S.2d 797

8. Sharing profits and earnings

In determining the existence of a partnership and arrangement for sharing profits is to be considered and given its due weight. It is not decisive. It may be merely the method adopted to pay a debt or wages or interest on a loan or for other reasons. Martin v Peyton (1927) 246 N.Y. 213, 158 N.E. 77

The fact that a person was credited on books of company with annual salary for managing business does not sustain argument that he was employee and not partner where at same time he was also credited with one-half the profits as part owner. In re Rosenberg's Will (1929) 251 N.Y. 115, 167 N.E. 190

Indispensable essential of contract of co-partnership, either under common-law rule or this section is mutual promise or undertaking of parties to share in profits of business, and submit to burden of making good losses. Reynolds v Searle (1919) 186 A.D. 202, 174 N.Y.S. 137

Receipt by person of share of profits of business is prima facie evidence that he is partner in business. Cafadaris v Bulow (1930) 138 Misc 301, 244 N.Y.S. 600

Partnership may only arise by mutual agreement between two or more persons; it exists as to its members where they have agreed to combine their labor, property and skill, or some of them, for purpose of engaging in any lawful trade or business and share profits and losses as such between them. Smith v Maine (1932) 145 Misc 521, 260 N.Y.S. 409, 260 N.Y.S. 425

An express contract provision for sharing profits is not essential to the existence of a partnership. If it was the intention of the parties to form a partnership they would become partners and as such would be entitled to share in the profits unless the terms and provisions of the contract are so framed as to leave the partners without any community of interest in the business or in the profits. Fullam v Peterson (1940, Sup) 21 N.Y.S.2d 797

Where members of a so-called partnership had no interest in partnership fund, nor profits, and carried on no business, nor held themselves out as partners, there was no partnership. Schumacher v Davis (1932, DC NY) 1 F. Supp. 959

9. – Debt

In determining the existence of a partnership and arrangement for sharing profits is to be considered and given its due weight. It is not decisive. It may be merely the method adopted to pay a debt or wages or interest on a loan or for other reasons. Martin v Peyton (1927) 246 N.Y. 213, 158 N.E. 77

10. – Wages

In determining the existence of a partnership and arrangement for sharing profits is to be considered and given its due weight. It is not decisive. It may be merely the method adopted to pay a debt or wages or interest on a loan or for other reasons. Martin v Peyton (1927) 246 N.Y. 213, 158 N.E. 77

11. – Interest on loan

In determining the existence of a partnership and arrangement for sharing profits is to be considered and given its due weight. It is not decisive. It may be merely the method adopted to pay a debt or wages or interest on a loan or for other reasons. Martin v Peyton (1927) 246 N.Y. 213, 158 N.E. 77

12. – Miscellaneous

In action to hold respondents as partners in firm doing business as bankers and brokers, where it appears that firm being financially involved it entered into agreement with respondents, expressed in three documents executed as part of one transaction, by terms of which respondents were to loan firm securities to be used by it as collateral and business of firm was to be controlled by trustees representing lenders who were to share in profits until return of securities, upon examination of papers, taken as a whole, it cannot be held that a partnership exists. Martin v Peyton (1927) 246 N.Y. 213, 158 N.E. 77

Agreement for purchase of property from joint funds and for division of property does not constitute partnership where there is no contemplation of sharing profits and losses. Columbian Laundry v Hencken (1922) 203 A.D. 140, 196 N.Y.S. 523

An agreement among certain painters which provided that one S., who supplied the equipment and the capital, procured the business and acted as manager, treasurer and bookkeeper, should receive $5,000 per year and bear all losses up to $5,000 yearly; that the other

members of the firm were permitted to draw on the firm's account, but only on a daily or weekly basis, with no withdrawals except for days, weeks or months actually devoted to work for the partnership; and that profits beyond the foregoing items of expense were to be shared, and losses beyond the $5,000 charged to S., borne equally by the partners, did not constitute a partnership. Scott v Miller (1940) 260 A.D. 428, 22 N.Y.S.2d 981, affd (1941) 285 N.Y. 760, 34 N.E.2d 910, motion den (1941) 285 N.Y. 847, 35 N.E.2d 509

Alleged partners in merged accounting firm were not mere employees where they invested in firm at managing partners' request, indicating joint venture, and although it is not unusual for professional firm to give high-level employees share of profits as part of their salary, such employees do not generally have discretion to decide how profits are allocated among themselves, as plaintiffs did. Muhlstock v Cole (1997, 1st Dept) 245 A.D.2d 55, 666 N.Y.S.2d 116, 135 CCH LC ¶ 58396

Defendant was not entitled to summary judgment dismissing cause of action for partnership accounting where there was evidence that could support findings that (1) parties had confidential relationship that was in many respects analogous to that of husband and wife, (2) plaintiff reasonably trusted defendant and relied on him to protect her interests, and (3) in reliance on his promises that she would have life use of his home and other financial benefits, she sold her home, moved in with him, and made substantial contributions of money and labor to upkeep and improvement of his house and grounds; oral partnership agreement was not entirely unenforceable merely because it incorporated promises that could not be fully performed within year or lifetime, and there was no merit in defendant's contention that plaintiff's claim was deficient because services purportedly rendered as her contribution to partnership were not "profits." Williams v Lynch (1997, 3d Dept) 245 A.D.2d 715, 666 N.Y.S.2d 749, app dismd without op (1998) 91 N.Y.2d 957, 671 N.Y.S.2d 717, 694 N.E.2d 886

No partnership existed between the parties to carry on as co-owners a business for profit, when there was no written partnership agreement between the parties, because the party who claimed that a partnership existed invested no capital, was not liable to creditors, and there was no allegation or evidence that the party received a share of profits. Hammond v Smith, 2017 NY Slip Op 05337, 2017 NY Slip Op 5337, 2017 N.Y. App. Div. LEXIS 5462 (N.Y. App. Div. 4th Dep't 2017).

In a medical malpractice action, there was no basis on which to impose vicarious liability under a partnership theory against one doctor for the acts of a second doctor who orally agreed to perform medical services in the former's office while he was away on vacation using the former's prescription pads, equipment and staff, where the latter retained 70 percent of the fees collected from insured patients and 100 percent from private patients, in that an indispensible requirement to the existence of a partnership is a mutual promise or undertaking of the parties to share in the business profits as well as the burden of making good the losses, and the latter neither had the obligation to bear the burden of any losses that the former's business might suffer nor had she any control over the business or physical aspect of the office. Impastato v De Girolamo (1983, Sup) 117 Misc. 2d 786, 459 N.Y.S.2d 512

Although referred to as a junior partner one who had no voice in the management of the business and received only a fixed salary and a share of certain profits was not a partner. Peterson v Eppler (1946, Sup) 67 N.Y.S.2d 498

There was no partnership under this section and Uniform Partnership Act, where son shared his earnings with his mother, but it was not intended to carry on joint business, and she did not have least direction of his affairs or any part in conduct of his business. Cohan v Comm'r (1930, CA2) 39 F.2d 540, 2 USTC P 489, 8 AFTR 10552 (superseded by statute as stated in Lewis v Commissioner (1977, CA9) 560 F.2d 973, 77-2 USTC P 9673, 40 AFTR 2d 5817) and (superseded by statute as stated in Ellis Banking Corp. v Commissioner (1982, CA11) 688 F.2d 1376, 82-2 USTC P 9630, 50 AFTR 2d 5909) and (superseded by statute as stated in Security Associates Agency Ins. Corp. v Commissioner (1987) TC Memo 1987-317, RIA TC Memo P 87317, 53 CCH TCM 1239) and (superseded by statute as stated in Ellison v Commissioner (1994) TC Memo 1994-437, RIA TC Memo P 94437, 68 CCH TCM 630, 94 TNT 168-10) and (superseded by statute as stated in Beckey v Commissioner (1994) TC Memo 1994-514, RIA TC Memo P 94514, 68 CCH TCM 945, 94 TNT 204-11) and (superseded by statute as stated in Witherspoon v Commissioner (1994) TC Memo 1994-593, RIA TC Memo P 94593, 68 CCH TCM

1333, 94 TNT 237-19) and (superseded by statute as stated in Velinsky v Commissioner (1996) TC Memo 1996-180, RIA TC Memo P 96180, 71 CCH TCM 2766) and (superseded by statute as stated in Rezazadeh v Comm'r (1996) TC Memo 1996-245, RIA TC Memo P 96245, 71 CCH TCM 3113) and (superseded by statute as stated in Hirahara v Commissioner (1997) TC Memo 1997-16, RIA TC Memo P 97016, 73 CCH TCM 1699) and (superseded by statute as stated in Marotte v United States (1997, Ct Fed Cl) 97-2 USTC P 50856, 80 AFTR 2d 7182) and (superseded by statute as stated in Bailey v United States (1997, Ct Fed Cl) 97-2 USTC P 50877, 80 AFTR 2d 6878) and (superseded by statute as stated in Lonsberry v United States (1997, Ct Fed Cl) 97-2 USTC P 50888, 80 AFTR 2d 7125) and (superseded by statute as stated in Hanna v United States (1997, Ct Fed Cl) 97-2 USTC P 50993, 80 AFTR 2d 7077) and (superseded by statute as stated in Rutledge v United States (1997, Ct Fed Cl) 97-2 USTC P 50907, 80 AFTR 2d 7228) and (superseded by statute as stated in Price v United States (1997, Ct Fed Cl) 97-2 USTC P 50999, 80 AFTR 2d 7485) and (superseded by statute as stated in Charron v United States (1997, Ct Fed Cl) 97-2 USTC P 50852, 80 AFTR 2d 6948) and (superseded by statute as stated in Gill v United States (1997, Ct Fed Cl) 97-2 USTC P 50918, 80 AFTR 2d 7384) and (superseded by statute as stated in Jacobs v Commissioner (1998) TC Memo 1998-451, RIA TC Memo P 98451) and (superseded by statute as stated in Wilson v Commissioner (1999) TC Memo 1999-141, RIA TC Memo P 99141, 77 CCH TCM 1923) and (superseded by statute as stated in Kelly v Commissioner (1999) TC Memo 1999-140, RIA TC Memo P 99140, 77 CCH TCM 1920) and (superseded by statute as stated in Taylor v Commissioner (1999) TC Memo 1999-323, 78 CCH TCM 491) and (superseded by statute as stated in Charron v United States (1999, CA FC) 200 F.3d 785, 2000-1 USTC P 50129, 84 AFTR 2d 7473) and (superseded by statute as stated in Aldea v Commissioner (2000) 2000 TC Memo 136) and (superseded by statute as stated in Haeder v Commissioner (2001) TC Memo 2001-7, RIA TC Memo P 54211, 81 CCH TCM 987) and (superseded by statute as stated in Burris v Commissioner (2001) TC Memo 2001-49, RIA TC Memo P 54259, 81 CCH TCM 1227) and (superseded by statute as stated in Xuncax v Comm'r (2001) TC Memo 2001-226, RIA TC Memo P 54461, 82 CCH TCM 455) and (superseded by statute as stated in Olsen v Comm'r (2002) TC Memo 2002-42)

Summary judgment against general partner on issue of whether he and plaintiffs were partners is improper, despite showing of part ownership of property and sharing of its profits, because all elements of relationship must be considered when determining existence of partnership under CLS Partn Law § 11. Bickhardt v Ratner (1994, SD NY) 871 F. Supp. 613, CCH Fed Secur L Rep P 98780

In an action in which a claimed inventor sought a constructive trust over money received by a named inventor in connection with patents describing a novel shape for a diamond, the existence of a partnership between the parties was not implied pursuant to N.Y. P'ship Law § 11(4) because there was no evidence that the claimed inventor received any profits of the named inventor's business or diamond venture. Finkelstein v Mardkha (2007, SD NY) 495 F Supp 2d 329, reconsideration den (2007, SD NY) 2007 US Dist LEXIS 79769

13. Sharing of losses

It is not necessary, before one can be subjected to partnership as to third persons, that he should agree to share in losses of business. Manhattan Brass & Mfg. Co. v Sears (1871) 45 N.Y. 797

Indispensable essential of contract of co-partnership, either under common-law rule or this section is mutual promise or undertaking of parties to share in profits of business, and submit to burden of making good losses. Reynolds v Searle (1919) 186 A.D. 202, 174 N.Y.S. 137

Agreement for purchase of property from joint funds and for division of property does not constitute partnership where there is no contemplation of sharing profits and losses. Columbian Laundry v Hencken (1922) 203 A.D. 140, 196 N.Y.S. 523

An agreement among certain painters which provided that one S., who supplied the equipment and the capital, procured the business and acted as manager, treasurer and bookkeeper, should receive $5,000 per year and bear all losses up to $5,000 yearly; that the other members of the firm were permitted to draw on the firm's account, but only on a daily or weekly basis, with no withdrawals except for days, weeks or months actually devoted to work for the partnership; and that profits beyond the foregoing items of expense were to be shared, and losses beyond the $5,000 charged to S., borne equally by the partners, did not constitute a partnership. Scott v Miller (1940)

260 A.D. 428, 22 N.Y.S.2d 981, affd (1941) 285 N.Y. 760, 34 N.E.2d 910, motion den (1941) 285 N.Y. 847, 35 N.E.2d 509

Members of premerger accounting firm were not partners in merged firm where they had no real say in management and did not agree to share firm's losses. Muhlstock v Cole (1997, 1st Dept) 245 A.D.2d 55, 666 N.Y.S.2d 116, 135 CCH LC ¶ 58396

Partnership may only arise by mutual agreement between two or more persons; it exists as to its members where they have agreed to combine their labor, property and skill, or some of them, for purpose of engaging in any lawful trade or business and share profits and losses as such between them. Smith v Maine (1932) 145 Misc 521, 260 N.Y.S. 409, 260 N.Y.S. 425

Although it may not be determinative, fact that member of firm does not share in losses of firm may indicate that he is not a partner. Peterson v Eppler (1946, Sup) 67 N.Y.S.2d 498

14. Fixed salary

The fact that a person was credited on the books of the company with an annual salary for managing the business does not sustain an argument that he was an employee and not a partner where at the same time he was also credited with one-half the profits as a part owner. In re Rosenberg's Will (1929) 251 N.Y. 115, 167 N.E. 190

An agreement among certain painters which provided that one S., who supplied the equipment and the capital, procured the business and acted as manager, treasurer and bookkeeper, should receive $5,000 per year and bear all losses up to $5,000 yearly; that the other members of the firm were permitted to draw on the firm's account, but only on a daily or weekly basis, with no withdrawals except for days, weeks or months actually devoted to work for the partnership; and that profits beyond the foregoing items of expense were to be shared, and losses beyond the $5,000 charged to S., borne equally by the partners, did not constitute a partnership. Scott v Miller (1940) 260 A.D. 428, 22 N.Y.S.2d 981, affd (1941) 285 N.Y. 760, 34 N.E.2d 910, motion den (1941) 285 N.Y. 847, 35 N.E.2d 509

Evidence failed, as matter of law, to establish oral partnership agreement asserted by plaintiff for 1/2 ownership of building where plaintiff's only contribution was to be his supervision in refurbishing building, which was same as work he performed as salaried employee of defendant's company, and plaintiff could not specifically state when and where agreement was made, when it would take effect, or extent of defendant's interest in building. Azoulay v Cassin (1987, 2d Dept) 128 A.D.2d 660, 512 N.Y.S.2d 900

The circumstance that one party in addition to a share in the profits is to receive a fixed salary does not destroy the character of the partnership relation. Fullam v Peterson (1940, Sup) 21 N.Y.S.2d 797

Although referred to as a junior partner one who had no voice in the management of the business and received only a fixed salary and a share of certain profits was not a partner. Peterson v Eppler (1946, Sup) 67 N.Y.S.2d 498

15. Management and control

Members of premerger accounting firm were not partners in merged firm where they had no real say in management and did not agree to share firm's losses. Muhlstock v Cole (1997, 1st Dept) 245 A.D.2d 55, 666 N.Y.S.2d 116, 135 CCH LC ¶ 58396

Although referred to as a junior partner one who had no voice in the management of the business and received only a fixed salary and a share of certain profits was not a partner. Peterson v Eppler (1946, Sup) 67 N.Y.S.2d 498

Under §§ 10, 11, 40, there cannot be a partnership where the whole management is vested in one partner. Wild v Commissioner (1933, CA2) 62 F.2d 777, 3 USTC P 1032, 11 AFTR 1376

16. Co-ownership and the like

Where an oil lease was held by co-owners as tenants in common and each co-owner was paid individually for his share of the oil run and each then paid his share of expenses out of his own personal funds and no partnership funds were maintained there was no partnership or joint venture. Conkling v First Nat'l Bank (1955) 286 A.D. 537, 145 N.Y.S.2d 682, 5 OGR 224

While a joint purchase of land does not make owners partners, nevertheless, it is well-settled law that partnership may be created by agreement relating to single transaction in sale or purchase of land. Schneider v Brenner (1929) 134 Misc 449, 235 N.Y.S. 55

Where it was alleged that the plaintiff and two others had agreed to purchase realty as owners in common but after the acceptance of the bid the successful bidder refused to recognize plaintiff as the owner of any part thereof, a cause of action to compel conveyance to the plaintiff or a one-third interest in the realty was barred by the statute of frauds in the absence of a showing that a partnership of joint venture existed, or that there was a relationship of confidence and trust between the parties, or that plaintiff had parted with anything. A partnership was not created by the mere existence of a tenancy in common even though the co-owners were to share the profits. Rizika v Kowalsky (1954) 207 Misc 254, 138 N.Y.S.2d 711, affd (1955) 285 A.D. 1009, 139 N.Y.S.2d 299, app den (1955) 285 A.D. 1116, 141 N.Y.S.2d 515

The acquisition of a coproprietary interest in patents or patent rights does not result in the creation of a partnership where the agreement does not provide for a partnership and does not contemplate any of the incidents of one. Mariani v Summers (1944, Sup) 3 Misc. 2d 534, 52 N.Y.S.2d 750, affd (1945, 1st Dept) 269 A.D. 840, 56 N.Y.S.2d 537 and (criticized in Artco, Inc. v Kidde, Inc. (1993, SD NY) 1993 US Dist LEXIS 21227)

17. Burden of proof

Burden of establishing existence of oral partnership by fair preponderance of credible evidence rests upon party claiming partnership. Kahn v Kahn (1957, 1st Dept) 3 A.D.2d 820, 160 N.Y.S.2d 972

Law imposes upon person who alleges existence of partnership burden of proof of that fact. Rizika v Potter (1947, Sup) 72 N.Y.S.2d 372

§ 12.   Partnership property

1. All property originally brought into the partnership stock or subsequently acquired, by purchase or otherwise, on account of the partnership is partnership property.

2. Unless the contrary intention appears, property acquired with partnership funds is partnership property.

3. Any estate in real property may be acquired in the partnership name. Title so acquired can be conveyed only in the partnership name.

4. A conveyance to a partnership in the partnership name, though without words of inheritance, passes the entire estate of the grantor unless a contrary intent appears.

History: Add, L 1919, ch 408, eff Oct 1, 1919.

CASE ANNOTATIONS

1. In general
2. Conditional or limited contributions
3. Good will
4. – Evaluation
5. – Professional partnership
6. Real property
7. – Equitable conversion

1. In general

This statute provides that all property originally brought into the partnership or subsequently acquired is partnership property. In re Estate of Havemeyer (1966) 17 N.Y.2d 216, 270 N.Y.S.2d 197, 217 N.E.2d 26, reh den (1966) 17 N.Y.2d 918

Contingency fee cases pending in law firm are assets subject to distribution in action to dissolve partnership following death of one partner, unless partners have agreed otherwise. Dwyer v Nicholson (1993, 2d Dept) 193 A.D.2d 70, 602 N.Y.S.2d 144, app dismd (1995, 2d Dept) 220 A.D.2d 555, 633 N.Y.S.2d 963, app den (1996) 87 N.Y.2d 808, 641 N.Y.S.2d 830, 664 N.E.2d 896, motion gr, motion den (1996) 88 N.Y.2d 963, 647 N.Y.S.2d 716, 670 N.E.2d 1348

If the activities of an errant joint venturer are in any way traceable to the business or assets of the venture they will be treated as part of the venture. This standard of rigid fair-dealing is especially high when the self-dealing party is manager of the enterprise. In re Kohn's Estate (1952) 26 Misc. 2d 659, 116 N.Y.S.2d 167, affd (1953) 282 A.D. 1045, 126 N.Y.S.2d 897

An individual partner has no fractional right in specific partnership property which he alone can assign. A partner is not the owner of a fractional or undivided interest in each partnership asset. Upon the withdrawal of one partner and death of another and the admission of two new partners there was no transfer of partnership stocks and bonds subject to Federal stamp taxes. Salomon Bros. & Hutzler v Pedrick (1952, SD NY) 105 F. Supp. 210, 52-1 USTC P 9323, 42 AFTR 109

2. Conditional or limited contributions

Where an agreement provided that, upon dissolution, a stock exchange seat which was part of the contribution of one of the partners should be disposed of and the proceeds added to the firm assets, the equitable title was in the partnership. In re Snow (1937) 252 A.D. 369, 299 N.Y.S. 287, affd (1938) 277 N.Y. 660, 14 N.E.2d 208

Where a partner contributed the use of a stock exchange seat under an agreement that the seat should remain his sole property except that it should be deemed a firm asset to the extent necessary for the protection of creditors, the seat was a partnership asset only for the purpose specified and was not subject to repayment of a partner's capital contribution. Chalmers v Weed (1941) 175 Misc 740, 25 N.Y.S.2d 195

3. Good will

Goodwill may be element to be considered in partnership accounting. Mitchell v Read (1881) 84 N.Y. 556

Name of a firm is important part of goodwill and its use may be protected accordingly. Slater v Slater (1903) 175 N.Y. 143, 67 N.E. 224

In absence of contract, express or implied, to the contrary, goodwill of partnership is usually considered part of property and assets of the firm. In re Brown (1926) 242 N.Y. 1, 150 N.E. 581, 44 ALR 510

4. – Evaluation

Unless it is established upon the dissolution accounting the defendant partner appropriated goodwill after termination of copartnership, no allowance for goodwill can be awarded. Kade v Sanitary Fireproofing & Contracting Co. (1929) 227 A.D. 622, 236 N.Y.S. 78, adhered to (1929) 228 A.D. 646, 238 N.Y.S. 858 and mod on other grounds (1931) 257 N.Y. 203, 177 N.E. 421

In a particular case, value of partnership goodwill may be nominal. In re Estate of Spingarn (1956) 5 Misc. 2d 36, 159 N.Y.S.2d 532

5. – Professional partnership

Salable goodwill can exist only in commercial partnership and cannot arise in professional partnership, such as law office. Siddall v Keating (1959, 1st Dept) 8 A.D.2d 44, 185 N.Y.S.2d 630, affd (1959) 7 N.Y.2d 846, 196 N.Y.S.2d 986, 164 N.E.2d 860

Goodwill must always rest upon some principal and tangible thing and never can arise as asset of partnership where members contribute only their professional skill and reputation, however intrinsically valuable these may be. Sheldon v Houghton (1865, CC NY) Fed Cas No. 12748

6. Real property

In an action to compel the determination of a claim to real property a deed to a named company together with testimony that the plaintiff and another individual did business under that name may be sufficient to establish prima facie the existence of a competent grantee. Bendersky v Simmons (1947) 272 A.D. 1024, 73 N.Y.S.2d 781

In a partnership dissolution proceeding, the referee in setting a value of the partnership property erred by aggregating separate values assigned by an appraiser to the property and to fixtures attached to the property, where the proper method was to value the real property as enhanced by the fixtures. Hasnas v Hasnas (1983, 2d Dept) 91 A.D.2d 1058, 459 N.Y.S.2d 288, app dismd (1983) 58 N.Y.2d 1113

The fact that a lease does not recite the interests of the tenants therein and does not recite that it was made or the term granted to them as partners does not preclude one partner from establishing by parol evidence the fact that though title to the real estate or to this lease was taken in their individual names such property is partnership property. In re Allen Street in New York (1933) 148 Misc 488, 266 N.Y.S. 277, affd (1933) 239 A.D. 775, 263 N.Y.S. 942, reh and app den (1933) 239 A.D. 827, 264 N.Y.S. 919

Although any estate in real property may be acquired in the partnership name (sub 3) it does not follow that a managing partner of a rooming house business who, without the knowledge of his partner purchased the rooming house which had been leased to the partnership, would be directed to reform the deed to include the name of his partner as grantee where the grantor was not before the court and the managing partner had made a substantial investment in the house. Boxill v Boxill (1952) 201 Misc 386, 111 N.Y.S.2d 33

7. – Equitable conversion

Under the terms of the Uniform Partnership Act, specific partnership real estate is converted into personal property and on the death of a partner passes to the surviving partner under the partnership

Partnership Law

agreement. In re Estate of Havemeyer (1966) 17 N.Y.2d 216, 270 N.Y.S.2d 197, 217 N.E.2d 26, reh den (1966) 17 N.Y.2d 918

ARTICLE 3
RELATIONS OF PARTNERS TO PERSONS DEALING WITH THE PARTNERSHIP

§ 20. Partner agent of partnership as to partnership business
§ 21. Conveyance of real property of the partnership
§ 22. Partnership bound by admission of partner
§ 23. Partnership charged with knowledge of or notice to partner
§ 24. Partnership bound by partner's wrongful act
§ 25. Partnership bound by partner's breach of trust
§ 26. Nature of partner's liability
§ 27. Partner by estoppel
§ 28. Liability of incoming partner

History: Add, L 1919, ch 408, eff Oct 1, 1919.

§ 20. Partner agent of partnership as to partnership business

1. Every partner is an agent of the partnership for the purpose of its business, and the act of every partner, including the execution in the partnership name of any instrument, for apparently carrying on in the usual way the business of the partnership of which he is a member binds the partnership, unless the partner so acting has in fact no authority to act for the partnership in the particular matter, and the person with whom he is dealing has knowledge of the fact that he has no such authority.

2. An act of a partner which is not apparently for the carrying on of the business of the partnership in the usual way does not bind the partnership unless authorized by the other partners.

3. Unless authorized by the other partners or unless they have abandoned the business, one or more but less than all the partners have no authority to:

(a) Assign the partnership property in trust for creditors or on the assignee's promise to pay the debts of the partnership.

(b) Dispose of the good-will of the business.

(c) Do any other act which would make it impossible to carry on the ordinary business of the partnership.

(d) Confess a judgment.

(e) Submit a partnership claim or liability to arbitration or reference.

4. No act of a partner in contravention of a restriction on his authority shall bind the partnership to persons having knowledge of the restriction.

History: Add, L 1919, ch 408, eff Oct 1, 1919, with substance transferred from § 5.

CASE ANNOTATIONS

1. In general
2. Nature of agency
3. Express or implied authority
4. – Necessity of writing
5. Limitations
6. – Acts outside scope of business
7. – Partnership for special purposes
8. – Acts harmful to business
9. Ratification
10. Authority in particular matters
11. – Contracts of suretyship
12. – Guaranty
13. – Borrowing money or pledging credit
14. – Assignment for benefit of creditors
15. – Confession of judgment
16. – Payment, release or compromise of claim
17. – Arbitration
18. – Assignment in payment of debt
19. – Litigation matters
20. – Negotiable instruments

1. In general

A partnership relationship is sufficient to invoke the application of CPLR 302, subd a and to sustain jurisdiction. Balogh v Rayner-Smith (1968, 1st Dept) 30 A.D.2d 788, 291 N.Y.S.2d 440

This section is not relevant in an action concerned with the liability of the partners or the partnership inter alia but of the partners, inter se. In re Dunham's Will (1966) 52 Misc. 2d 364, 276 N.Y.S.2d 132

Where each of three original partners entered into separate agreements with other individuals designated as "participants" who were not authorized to act as agents for the partnership and who could transfer their interests with the consent of the partner from whom they made their purchase, such arrangement did not constitute a partnership. Beckerman v Sands (1973, SD NY) 364 F. Supp. 1197, 18 FR Serv 2d 86

2. Nature of agency

Each partner acts, as to himself, as a principal having a joint interest in the partnership property, and, as to each other partner, as a general agent. Pringle v Leverich (1884) 97 N.Y. 181

Each member of a partnership acts as to himself as a person having a joint interest in the partnership property and as to each other partner as a general agent but even so far as he acts as general agent of his partners the circumstance that he at the same time acts as principal as to himself may prevent the application of the rules of agency. Caplan v Caplan (1935) 268 N.Y. 445, 198 N.E. 23, 101 ALR 1223 (superseded by statute as stated in People v Morton (1954) 308 N.Y. 96, 123 N.E.2d 790)

Each member of a partnership has actual or apparent authority to bind all the partners by acts in the course of the partnership business and ordinarily all are responsible for torts committed in the course of the joint business. Caplan v Caplan (1935) 268 N.Y. 445, 198 N.E. 23, 101 ALR 1223 (superseded by statute as stated in People v Morton (1954) 308 N.Y. 96, 123 N.E.2d 790)

A member of a partnership or joint venture is ordinarily a general agent of the group for purposes of the venture, and, notwithstanding his authority is limited by a special agreement, one who deals with him without any notice of the limitation upon his authority is entitled to rely upon the general authority of such a member to contract for the group. Smith v Legg (1961, 4th Dept) 15 A.D.2d 15, 222 N.Y.S.2d 55

During the existence of a partnership, each member is deemed to be authorized to transact the whole business for the firm, his acts being treated as the acts of all, and binding on them. In re Kahane (1957) 6 Misc. 2d 575, 160 N.Y.S.2d 252

3. Express or implied authority

The authority of a partner to bind a firm may be expressly stated, either by parole or in writing. Worrall v Munn (1851) 5 N.Y. 229

As to third persons, authority given to a partner may be found in actual agreement of partnership, or through implication in nature of business according to usual and ordinary course in which it is carried on by those engaged in it in the locality which is its seat, or as reasonably necessary or fit for its successful prosecution. First Nat'l Bank v Farson (1919) 226 N.Y. 218, 123 N.E. 490, reh den (1919) 226 N.Y. 703, 123 N.E. 864

The implied powers of a partner are based in the usages and business methods of those conducting commerce and trade, and go out of the necessities of commercial business, but they do not extend broadly to partners and nontrading partnerships. First Nat'l Bank v Farson (1919) 226 N.Y. 218, 123 N.E. 490, reh den (1919) 226 N.Y. 703, 123 N.E. 864

Attorney was properly awarded $189,307.16 in accordance with his retainer agreement with defendant partners where (1) contracting partner had apparent authority to enter into retainer agreement on behalf of other partners, (2) statute of frauds was not issue, because agreement was in writing, (3) agreement was fair, reasonable, and fully understood by partners, and (4) there was no basis for relegating attorney to quantum meruit. Peter A. Dankin, P.C. v North Shore Pshp. (1998, 1st Dept) 255 A.D.2d 207, 680 N.Y.S.2d 91

4. – Necessity of writing

Where individual who was principal of landlord's managing agent and who executed lease of prime tenant on behalf of the landlord was also a partner of the landlord his status as a partner of the landlord and, thus, as its agent during term of the lease had the effect of validating his authority to bind the landlord retroactive to date of execution of the lease; thus, prime tenant could not avoid liability for rent on ground that such individual's authority to act as agent was not in writing and therefore the lease was void under statute of frauds. Fisk Bldg. Associates v Continental American Ins. Co. (1974) 80 Misc. 2d 56, 362 N.Y.S.2d 315

A partner has the authority to bind the partnership and his specific authority to do so need not be in writing. Fisk Bldg. Associates v Continental American Ins. Co. (1974) 80 Misc. 2d 56, 362 N.Y.S.2d 315

A letter written by a partner which clearly conveys the impression that the partnership is assuming liability for the debt and ratifies an arrangement made originally between others binds the other partners; therefore, the partnership is liable for the debt assumed. Blue Print Co. v Ford Marrin Esposito Witmeyer & Bergman (1980) 102 Misc. 2d 1090, 424 N.Y.S.2d 970, affd (1981) 107 Misc. 2d 239, 438 N.Y.S.2d 170

5. Limitations

The principal of agency applies to copartners but it is only when it can be seen that a partner is in fact acting as an agent of his copartners that he binds them. Bienenstok v Ammidown (1898) 155 N.Y. 47, 49 N.E. 321

A partner who is engaged in the perpetration of a fraud is not acting as the agent of his partners, nor is his knowledge ordinarily imputable to them. In re Steinmetz' Estate (1937, Sur) 1 N.Y.S.2d 601

6. – Acts outside scope of business

Each member of a firm is the general agent of the firm in relation to all the business of the firm and can bind it in what he says and does in such business but when one partner has a transaction which is neither apparently nor really within the scope of the partnership business the partnership is not bound by his declaration or acts in the transaction. Union Nat'l Bank v Underhill (1886) 102 N.Y. 336, 7 N.E. 293

Where one partner has a transaction which is neither apparently nor really within the scope of the partnership business, the partnership is not bound by his declaration or acts in the transaction. Iroquois Rubber Co. v Griffin (1919) 226 N.Y. 297, 123 N.E. 369, reh den (1919) 226 N.Y. 702, 123 N.E. 871

In order to determine whether attorney's partners could be held liable for his conversion of client's trust assets, it was necessary to ascertain whether his conduct was within ordinary course of law firm's business, and whether law firm benefited from or ratified his actions. Ottinger v Dempsey (1986, 2d Dept) 122 A.D.2d 125, 504 N.Y.S.2d 517, appeal after remand (1990, 2d Dept) 161 A.D.2d 691, 555 N.Y.S.2d 827

Plaintiff in action for trespass and nuisance was not entitled to partial summary judgment on issue of liability where fact issues remained as to whether actions of defendant's partner were outside ordinary course of partnership business and whether defendant knew of and authorized those actions. Staten Island-Arlington, Inc. v Wilpon (1998, 2d Dept) 251 A.D.2d 650, 676 N.Y.S.2d 469

7. – Partnership for special purposes

Where a partnership is a particular or special one the power of one of the copartners to bind another extends only to acts necessarily connected with the particular enterprise for which the partnership was formed. Macaulay v Palmer (1891) 125 N.Y. 742, 26 N.E. 912

Where a partnership is limited to a particular trade or business, one partner cannot bind his copartner by any contract not relating to such trade or business. Caplan v Caplan (1935) 268 N.Y. 445, 198 N.E. 23, 101 ALR 1223 (superseded by statute as stated in People v Morton (1954) 308 N.Y. 96, 123 N.E.2d 790)

8. – Acts harmful to business

Unless specifically empowered to do so, one partner has no authority to dispose of the capital assets of the partnership. However, where business has been discontinued and both partners were endeavoring to sell the assets neither was required to give notice to the other of

intention to sell. Hapworth v Grievson (1938) 255 A.D. 927, 8 N.Y.S.2d 700

The assent of all partners is necessary in order to dispose of the good will of the business or to do any other act making it impossible to carry on the business. Commissioner v Whitney (1948, CA2) 169 F.2d 562, 48-2 USTC P 9354, 37 AFTR 211, cert den (1948) 335 US 892, 93 L Ed 429, 69 S Ct 246 and cert den (1948) 335 US 892, 93 L Ed 429, 69 S Ct 247 and cert den (1948) 335 US 892, 93 L Ed 429, 69 S Ct 248 and cert den (1948) 335 US 892, 93 L Ed 429, 69 S Ct 249

9. Ratification

Ratification may be by parole or in writing. Worrall v Munn (1851) 5 N.Y. 229

Although one partner cannot bind his associates by a submission to arbitration, they can ratify it. Becker v Boon (1874) 61 N.Y. 317

In order to determine whether attorney's partners could be held liable for his conversion of client's trust assets, it was necessary to ascertain whether his conduct was within ordinary course of law firm's business, and whether law firm benefited from or ratified his actions. Ottinger v Dempsey (1986, 2d Dept) 122 A.D.2d 125, 504 N.Y.S.2d 517, appeal after remand (1990, 2d Dept) 161 A.D.2d 691, 555 N.Y.S.2d 827

The assent of other partners to one of them entering into an order contract might be inferred from the fact that the bill for certain samples furnished under the contract was paid. Stein-Tex, Inc. v Scappatillio (1948) 193 Misc 402, 87 N.Y.S.2d 317, mod (1949) 275 A.D. 749, 88 N.Y.S.2d 270

Where a partner-wife knew of an assignment for the benefit of creditors 4 days after it was made and 12 days before the sale took place, she was estopped from attacking such assignment on the ground that she was not consulted and did not consent to it. In re Kahane (1957) 6 Misc. 2d 575, 160 N.Y.S.2d 252

10. Authority in particular matters

The implied authority granted to a co-partner under this section applies to a matter involving the business of the partnership, as well as to internal differences between the partners themselves. Balogh v Rayner-Smith (1968, 1st Dept) 30 A.D.2d 788, 291 N.Y.S.2d 440

In action for tortious interference with joint venture agreement to convert to cooperative ownership premises owned as tenants in common by coventurer and plaintiff, who had purchased interests of all partners in realty company owning premises except for coventurer's 45 percent interest, sale of premises to defendant by plaintiff's coventurer on behalf of realty company should not have been declared void based on jury's advisory determination that plaintiff was partner in realty company, since coventurer, as sole remaining partner in realty company, was authorized by CLS Partn §§ 20(1) and 21 to make conveyance in partnership name. Bogoni v Friedlander (1994, 1st Dept) 197 A.D.2d 281, 610 N.Y.S.2d 511, related proceeding (1994, 1st Dept) 203 A.D.2d 149, 610 N.Y.S.2d 519 and stay den (1994, N.Y. A.D., 1st Dept) 1994 N.Y. A.D. LEXIS 8275 and motion den (1994) 84 N.Y.2d 803, 617 N.Y.S.2d 137, 641 N.E.2d 158

Plaintiff could not recover for work performed and materials supplied as against defendant based solely on her status as partner in operation of tavern where plaintiff presented no direct evidence that he was hired by partnership or by landlord in his capacity as partner of defendant, landlord expressly testified that he hired plaintiff in his capacity as landlord/owner of building for purpose of obtaining certificate of occupancy, and work performed and materials supplied by plaintiff were found to be fixtures. Wolensky v Locke (1997, 2d Dept) 244 A.D.2d 546, 664 N.Y.S.2d 355

Partners were not bound by 99-year lease of real property constituting partnership's only asset, entered into by remaining partners, even if newly discovered partnership agreements were not merely reflective of CLS Partn § 20(1), and could be fairly construed to preclude partners' interference with contemplated or consummated long-term lease, since agreements, on their face, terminated partnership before contemplated lease would expire. Northmon Inv. Co. v Milford Plaza Assocs. (2001, 1st Dept) 284 A.D.2d 250, 727 N.Y.S.2d 419, app den 97 N.Y.2d 677, 738 N.Y.S.2d 291, 764 N.E.2d 395 and app den, motion gr 97 N.Y.2d 743, 742 N.Y.S.2d 599, 769 N.E.2d 345

Partners lacked authority to enter into 99-year lease of real property constituting partnership's only asset, even if such lease were to be deemed in ordinary course of partnership's business; partners could not impose their decision to enter into lease on remaining partners, and remaining partners' right to interfere with lease or any other contract or prospective contract involving partnership was absolute and privileged, excusable, and justified. Northmon Inv. Co. v Milford Plaza Assocs. (2001, 1st Dept) 284 A.D.2d 250, 727 N.Y.S.2d

419, app den 97 N.Y.2d 677, 738 N.Y.S.2d 291, 764 N.E.2d 395 and app den, motion gr 97 N.Y.2d 743, 742 N.Y.S.2d 599, 769 N.E.2d 345

Tenant was not entitled to dismissal of holdover proceeding on ground that court lacked subject matter jurisdiction by virtue of fact that notice to quit was unaccompanied by proof that landlord was partnership and that signatory of notice was partner with authority to bind landlord, since partnership is legal entity that can function only through acts of individuals comprising its membership, and named general partner, in signing notice in his capacity as general partner, is authorized to act on behalf of and to bind partnership landlord by operation of law; whether landlord was, in fact, partnership and whether signatory was general partner were matters to be proven at trial. Bronx Park South II Assoc. v Aballe (1987, Civ Ct) 136 Misc. 2d 755, 519 N.Y.S.2d 289

Stockholders gave a stock option to a partnership, with one partner as trustee of the stock with the direction that he hold it for the term of the option and vote it for the benefit of the corporation. Under the arrangement, the corporation's financial condition worsened and the trustee and another partner resigned and renounced their right, and sale of the stock was made to another group in good faith. The stockholders, two partners, and the other group were not, under the circumstances, liable to the remaining partner for breach of the option contract. Kravetz v United Artists Corp. (1955, Sup) 143 N.Y.S.2d 539, mod on other grounds (1956, 1st Dept) 1 A.D.2d 992, 151 N.Y.S.2d 36, motion den (1957) 2 N.Y.2d 880, 161 N.Y.S.2d 136, 141 N.E.2d 623

11. – Contracts of suretyship

A partner cannot bind his copartners, without their assent, by signing or endorsing the firm name as surety on a note of a third person. Foot v Sabin (1821) 19 Johns 154

12. – Guaranty

Each partner is impliedly empowered to conduct the business in the usual way to that class of business and thus in making sales of property of the partnership implied authority to guarantee may spring from the usage of the business in which the partnership is engaged. If in that business it is usual to give a guarantee in making the sale the authority to sell carries with it the power of guaranty. First Nat'l Bank v Farson (1919) 226 N.Y. 218, 123 N.E. 490, reh den (1919) 226 N.Y. 703, 123 N.E. 864

In an action by plaintiff bank to recover on a defaulted loan by proceeding on a continuing guaranty made by defendant, a limited partnership, the court improperly denied defendant's motion to dismiss where a general partner of defendant limited partnership was not authorized, under the partnership agreement, to bind the limited partnership on a continuing guaranty to support a loan from plaintiff bank to a corporation, which loan was also supported by a continuing guaranty executed by the general partner personally; similarly when plaintiff made a second loan to the same corporation, which the general partner guaranteed solely in his personal capacity, he had neither actual nor apparent authority to bind the limited partnership thereon. Further, despite a jury finding that the attorney for defendant limited partnership had knowledge of the purported guaranty binding the limited partnership when the second loan was extended, this did not constitute ratification of the unauthorized act of the general partner. Moreover, there was no proof that the limited partnership received or accepted the benefit of the loan or that it was applied to the limited partnership. Chelsea Nat'l Bank v Lincoln Plaza Towers Associates (1983, 1st Dept) 93 A.D.2d 216, 461 N.Y.S.2d 328, affd (1984) 61 N.Y.2d 817, 473 N.Y.S.2d 953, 462 N.E.2d 130

13. – Borrowing money or pledging credit

Whenever a party receives an obligation of the firm in any form, from any partner, in payment for a debt due from that partner only, whether the debt is created at the time or was existent, or by way of settlement or security for a debt or indebtedness, the presumption is that the partner gives this and the creditor receives it in fraud of the partnership. Union Nat'l Bank v Underhill (1886) 102 N.Y. 336, 7 N.E. 293

A member of a nontrading partnership has no authority, actual, implied or apparent, to borrow money and bind the firm by the issuance of a promissory note. Riley v Larocque (1937) 163 Misc 423, 297 N.Y.S. 756

Partners were not liable for a debt incurred by a debtor, individually, as: (1) partnerships were governed by the laws of agency under N.Y. P' ship Law § 4(3), (2) the partners did not have any communication with a creditor that would give rise to the appearance and reasonable belief that the debtor possessed apparent authority to enter into the loan

agreements on their behalf, (3) the creditor's own affidavit revealed that the creditor relied on the creditor's conversations with the debtor and never spoke to the partners, (4) the creditor failed to make reasonable inquiries into the debtor's actual authority, (5) the creditor's claim that the loans were apparently made in the usual course of the business of a public accounting firm and, therefore, binding on the partners was without merit under N.Y. P' ship Law § 20(1), and (6) the partnership agreement did not give the debtor the authority to borrow money on the partnership's behalf, and borrowing money for the purpose of investing in other business ventures was not an act apparently made for the carrying on in the usual way the business of a pubic accounting firm under N.Y. P' ship Law § 20(2). Beizer v Bunsis (2007, 2d Dept) 38 App Div 3d 813, 833 NYS2d 154

14. – Assignment for benefit of creditors

Where partner-wife knew of assignment for the benefit of creditors 4 days after it was made and 12 days before the sale took place, she was estopped from attacking such assignment on the grounds that she was not consulted and did not consent to it. In re Kahane (1957) 6 Misc. 2d 575, 160 N.Y.S.2d 252

15. – Confession of judgment

Confession of judgment made by partner on behalf of partnership is valid only as to partner confessing and can affect only that partner's individual property and his interest in partnership effects. Scanlon v Kuehn (1929) 225 A.D. 256, 232 N.Y.S. 592

Confession of one partner who was joint debtor did not bar action against other joint debtors; other partners of limited partnership were not bound by any fact underlying the confession of judgment by one partner, and there was no collateral estoppel. Rubin v A. C. Kluger & Co. (1976) 86 Misc. 2d 1014, 383 N.Y.S.2d 828

Confession of judgment by one partner was ineffective against limited partnership, being valid only as to private assets of confessing partner and possibly against confessing partner's share of partnership income. Rubin v A. C. Kluger & Co. (1976) 86 Misc. 2d 1014, 383 N.Y.S.2d 828

16. – Payment, release or compromise of claim

A compromise settlement made by less than all of the members of a partnership firm, on behalf of such firm, whereby a smaller sum than the amount due is accepted in liquidation of the entire claim, is binding upon the firm or the other partner. People ex rel. Immerman v Devlin (1909) 63 Misc 363, 118 N.Y.S. 478

Despite absence of a partner, the partners who are available have apparent as well as actual authority to bind partnership in computation and payment of the share of a deceased partner. M. & C. Creditors Corp. v Pratt (1938) 172 Misc 695, 17 N.Y.S.2d 240, affd (1938) 255 A.D. 838, 7 N.Y.S.2d 662, affd (1939) 281 N.Y. 804, 24 N.E.2d 482

17. – Arbitration

Although one partner cannot bind his associates by a submission to arbitration, they can ratify it. Becker v Boon (1874) 61 N.Y. 317

Two architectural firms entered into a contract with a Board of Education for the construction of school buildings. The contract provided that all disputes could be submitted to arbitration at the choice of either party. One of the firms could demand arbitration over objections of both the Board and the other firm even though a partnership existed between the two firms. This section was inapplicable since the contract containing the arbitration clause had been signed by all the partners and the dispute was within the coverage of the arbitration clause. Baker v Board of Education (1956) 309 N.Y. 551, 132 N.E.2d 837

A partner as an agent of a partnership can invoke the arbitration provisions of a contract between the partnership and another in settlement of a dispute under the contract even though the other partner objects to the arbitration. The dispute between the partners is immaterial to the arbitration of the dispute between the partnership and the third parties. Application of Damsker (1954) 283 A.D. 719, 127 N.Y.S.2d 355

Where claimed breach of partnership agreements consisted, in part, of allegations concerning events arising subsequent to time defendant instituted arbitration proceeding which resulted in award denying defendant's claims and also denying respondents' claim that arbitration proceeding had been instituted in bad faith and without reasonable cause, neither direct nor collateral estoppel could be invoked to bar arbitration proceedings instituted by respondents. Steinberg v Steinberg (1975, 1st Dept) 47 A.D.2d 723, 365 N.Y.S.2d 12

Claim that partner's sons condoned and approved acts of their father in instituting arbitration proceedings was subject to arbitration pursuant to provisions of partnership agreement. Steinberg v Steinberg (1975, 1st Dept) 47 A.D.2d 723, 365 N.Y.S.2d 12

This clause does not invalidate an arbitration provision in a contract for the purchase of cloth, signed by one partner only, where that partner has implied authority to enter into such contracts, and the agreement is ratified by the payment of a portion of the bill. Stein-Tex, Inc. v Scappatillio (1948) 193 Misc 402, 87 N.Y.S.2d 317, mod on other grounds (1949) 275 A.D. 749, 88 N.Y.S.2d 270

18. – Assignment in payment of debt

Partners may lawfully make general assignments of their partnership property for the payment of firm debts and may, in such assignment, make such preferences as they deem just and proper. Williams v Whedon (1888) 109 N.Y. 333, 16 N.E. 365

19. – Litigation matters

Copartner cannot individually sue and recover judgment upon partnership claim. Alpaugh v Battles (1932) 235 A.D. 321, 257 N.Y.S. 126

In action against law firm to recover fees paid in connection with services rendered to partnership, law firm was entitled to summary judgment as to claim of certain individual partners, insofar as such claim was asserted on behalf of partnership rather than by individual partners in their own right, where law firm's fees had not been paid by partnership or from partnership funds, but had been paid only out of individual proceeds of each partner's share of sale of partnership asset following consent by majority of partners who had not joined in litigation against law firm. Koppel v Wien, Lane & Malkin (1986, 1st Dept) 125 A.D.2d 230, 509 N.Y.S.2d 327

Plaintiff lacked standing to prosecute claim for breach of recording contract in his individual capacity where partnership agreement between him and his fellow band members clearly evinced partners' intent to divest themselves of their rights under recording contract with defendant record company and to transfer those rights to partnership. Poley v Sony Music Entertainment (1995, 1st Dept) 222 A.D.2d 308, 636 N.Y.S.2d 10

Where an attorney was hired by one partner without the knowledge of the other, and, in fact, the other did not even know of the pendency of the action, the attorney's appearance could not be construed as a general appearance for the individual partner who did not know of the action, but could be an appearance only for the partnership, and for the partner who was personally served with the summons. Harrison Nat'l Bank v Lion Varnish Works (1950, City Ct) 97 N.Y.S.2d 71

20. – Negotiable instruments

Ordinarily, any partner can bind the firm by making, endorsing, and accepting bills and notes within scope of partnership business. Union Nat'l Bank v Underhill (1886) 102 N.Y. 336, 7 N.E. 293

In case of nontrading partnership, authority of one partner to bind firm by issuance of promissory note will not be implied. Riley v Larocque (1937) 163 Misc 423, 297 N.Y.S. 756

In case of commercial or trading partnerships, rule is well settled that each partner has implied authority to issue negotiable instruments in firm name and in its behalf. Bank of Rochester v Monteath (1845) 1 Denio 402

§ 21. Conveyance of real property of the partnership

1. Where title to real property is in the partnership name, any partner may convey title to such property by a conveyance executed in the partnership name; but the partnership may recover such property unless the partner's act binds the partnership under the provisions of subdivision one of section twenty, or unless such property has been conveyed by the grantee or a person claiming through such grantee to a holder for value without knowledge that the partner, in making the conveyance, has exceeded his authority.

2. Where title to real property is in the name of the partnership, a conveyance executed by a partner, in his own name, passes the equitable interest of the partnership, provided the act is one within the

authority of the partner under the provisions of subdivision one of section twenty.

3. Where title to real property is in the name of one or more but not all the partners, and the record does not disclose the right of the partnership, the partners in whose name the title stands may convey title to such property, but the partnership may recover such property if the partners' act does not bind the partnership under the provisions of subdivision one of section twenty, unless the purchaser or his assignee is a holder for value, without knowledge.

4. Where the title to real property is in the name of one or more or all the partners, or in a third person in trust for the partnership, a conveyance executed by a partner in the partnership name, or in his own name, passes the equitable interest of the partnership, provided the act is one within the authority of the partner under the provisions of subdivision one of section twenty.

5. Where the title to real property is in the names of all the partners a conveyance executed by all the partners passes all their rights in such property.

History: Add, L 1919, ch 408, eff Oct 1, 1919.

CASE ANNOTATIONS

Prospective buyer was not entitled to specific performance of contract to sell real property where seller's former partner had previously granted option to purchase property to third party since (1) partnership was in business of investing in real property and former partner had granted option as part of partnership business, and thus former partner's actions bound partnership, and (2) partnership granted option as integral part of transaction in which it conveyed 10-acre parcel, and thus option was supported by consideration. Meisner v Crane (1987, 3d Dept) 131 A.D.2d 934, 516 N.Y.S.2d 801, app den (1987) 70 N.Y.2d 613, 524 N.Y.S.2d 431, 519 N.E.2d 342

In action for tortious interference with joint venture agreement to convert to cooperative ownership premises owned as tenants in common by coventurer and plaintiff, who had purchased interests of all partners in realty company owning premises except for coventurer's 45 percent interest, sale of premises to defendant by plaintiff's coventurer on behalf of realty company should not have been declared void based on jury's advisory determination that plaintiff was partner in realty company, since coventurer, as sole remaining partner in realty company, was authorized by CLS Partn §§ 20(1) and 21 to make conveyance in partnership name. Bogoni v Friedlander (1994, 1st Dept) 197 A.D.2d 281, 610 N.Y.S.2d 511, related proceeding (1994, 1st Dept) 203 A.D.2d 149, 610 N.Y.S.2d 519 and stay den (1994, N.Y. A.D., 1st Dept) 1994 N.Y. A.D. LEXIS 8275 and motion den (1994) 84 N.Y.2d 803, 617 N.Y.S.2d 137, 641 N.E.2d 158

In action to foreclose mortgage executed by 2 general partners of defendant partnership, plaintiffs were properly granted summary judgment and appointment of referee where (1) record did not support partnership's conclusory allegations of fraud, and (2) issues as to scope of power of attorney granted by third partner, and whether general partners exceeded their authority by granting mortgage in first instance, were irrelevant because general partners were acting within scope of partnership agreement when they granted mortgage to plaintiffs in effort to discharge mechanics lien that arose after partnership was unable to pay for work performed and materials provided. Todd Welch Constr. v Peregrine Partners (2000, 3d Dept) 270 A.D.2d 786, 705 N.Y.S.2d 713

In a partnership between the mother and father and their son, the trial court properly granted the son's motion seeking a determination that the conveyance of one third of the partnership property to the executrix by the mother and father prior to dissolution of the partnership was null and void because (1) the transfer of the property effectively made the executrix a partner to the partnership, and it was undisputed that the son did not consent to the transfer of the partnership property; and (2) the transfer of the property to the executrix did not fall within N.Y. Partnership Law § 40(8) because it was not an ordinary matter connected with the partnership business that could be decided by a majority of the partners. Forbes v Six-S Country Club (2004, A.D., 4th Dept) 785 N.Y.S.2d 209

Since there was genuine issue whether decedent partner owned 20 percent interest in land (1) directly, as tenant in common, or (2) indirectly, under N.Y. Partnership Law § 21(3)-(5), as partner in partnership that dissolved at his death under N.Y. Partnership Law § 62(4) (and for which his executors were entitled to an accounting under N.Y. Partnership Law § 74), summary judgment to partition his alleged undivided interest in land was reversed. Facts indicating that partnership was the direct owner included that the decedent (or his executors) (1) reported on income tax returns his share of the partnership's income which, in turn, included his share of the land's tax attributes reported on the partnership's tax returns, (2) reported on his estate tax returns his indirect interest in the partnership's interest in the land but no direct interest in the land. Vick v Albert (2005, A.D., 1st Dept) 793 N.Y.S.2d 413, app withdrawn (2005, N.Y. A.D., 1st Dept) 2005 N.Y. A.D. LEXIS 5470

§ 22. Partnership bound by admission of partner

An admission or representation made by any partner concerning partnership affairs within the scope of his authority as conferred by this chapter is evidence against the partnership.

History: Add, L 1919, ch 408, eff Oct 1, 1919, with substance transferred to § 82.

CASE ANNOTATIONS

Admissions or representations made by a partner concerning partnership affairs within the scope of his authority may be used against the partnership. Vogt v Tully (1981) 53 N.Y.2d 580, 444 N.Y.S.2d 441, 428 N.E.2d 847

In action for declaratory judgment with respect to option to purchase parcel of real property owned by 4 cousins doing business as realty company, which option was signed by one cousin purportedly on behalf of realty company, cousins were not entitled to summary judgment on basis of CLS Partn § 21(5) since issue presented was whether cousin who signed option bound remaining cousins to option agreement, and questions of fact existed as to whether cousins were conducting business as partnership, whether grant of option was business purpose of partnership, whether consideration was tendered for option, and whether option was exercised within reasonable time. Frank v Katz (1988, 2d Dept) 145 A.D.2d 597, 536 N.Y.S.2d 135

§ 23. Partnership charged with knowledge of or notice to partner

Notice to any partner of any matter relating to partnership affairs, and the knowledge of the partner acting in the particular matter, acquired while a partner or then present to his mind, and the knowledge of any other partner who reasonably could and should have communicated it to the acting partner, operate as notice to or knowledge of the partnership, except in the case of a fraud on the partnership committed by or with the consent of that partner.

History: Add, L 1919, ch 408, eff Oct 1, 1919.

CASE ANNOTATIONS

In regard to the making of a demand on one partner as the representative of the firm, the same general principles apply as in the case of a notice given to one member of a partnership. Gates v Beecher (1875) 60 N.Y. 518

Where two members of partnership law firm had authority to act as representatives for interest of all in subscribing to fund raised by certain directors and stockholders to cover impairment of capital of trust company, acting members' knowledge was chargeable to remaining partners precluding partners from repudiating subscription agreement on ground that part of money was wrongfully paid

into company's funds before raising of entire fund. Baumann v Citizens Trust Co. (1936) 248 A.D. 9, 289 N.Y.S. 606, mod (1937) 249 A.D. 369, 293 N.Y.S. 45, affd (1937) 276 N.Y. 623, 12 N.E.2d 608

Notwithstanding that notice given to one person generally will be imputed to another person if an agency relationship exists between the parties, in an action arising out of default payments on an assigned truck lease summary judgment was properly denied, where the papers submitted upon the motion wholly failed to detail the relationship between defendants and therefore notice to one defendant could not be imputed to the others. Mileasing Co. v Hogan (1982, 3d Dept) 87 A.D.2d 961, 451 N.Y.S.2d 211

In action to recover for injuries sustained in construction accident against, inter alia, general partnership that owned property and corporation which was general partner, service of summons with notice on general partner conferred jurisdiction over partnership; there was no need for delivery to general partner of second summons with notice specifically directed to general partnership. Brown v Sagamore Hotel (1992, 3d Dept) 184 A.D.2d 47, 590 N.Y.S.2d 934

Plaintiffs, as limited partners of first partnership, stated fraud cause of action against law firm, even though firm made no representations to plaintiffs, where it was alleged that firm failed to disclose material information to plaintiff, which was tantamount to affirmative misrepresentation given that fiduciary relationship existed between firm and second partnership, of which first partnership was limited partner; moreover, since first partnership's general partners were accused of committing fraud on partnership, their knowledge of material information could not be imputed to plaintiffs. Franco v English (1994, 3d Dept) 210 A.D.2d 630, 620 N.Y.S.2d 156

Notwithstanding attorney two's denial of any knowledge of or consent to the payments made to a lawyer from law firm three's business accounts, attorney one, as a partner, approved such payments, which imputed knowledge thereof to attorney two. Masson v Wiggins & Masson, LLP (2013, 3d Dept) 110 App Div 3d 1402, 974 NYS2d 619.

Where the individual who executed lease with prime tenant on behalf of landlord was a principal of such landlord, a partnership, as well as the executive vice-president of the landlord's corporate managing agent, such pre-existing superior agency relationship demanded that the managing agent be treated as standing in place of landlord and that landlord be charged with constructive knowledge and responsibility for the negligence of the managing agent, which acted as agent for prime tenant in connection with sublease, in failing to promptly notify prime tenant of subtenant's default; landlord was estopped from recovering against prime tenant for nonpayment of rent which it was managing agent's duty to collect. Fisk Bldg. Associates v Continental American Ins. Co. (1974) 80 Misc. 2d 56, 362 N.Y.S.2d 315

If one partner knows that sheep sold by the firm are at the time deceased, this information will be imputed to all the partners in an action against the firm for fraud in the sale of the sheep. Jeffrey v Bigelow (1835) 13 Wend 518

§ 24. Partnership bound by partner's wrongful act

Where, by any wrongful act or omission of any partner acting in the ordinary course of the business of the partnership, or with the authority of his co-partners, loss or injury is caused to any person, not being a partner in the partnership, or any penalty is incurred, the partnership is liable therefor to the same extent as the partner so acting or omitting to act.

History: Add, L 1919, ch 408, eff Oct 1, 1919.

CASE ANNOTATIONS

1. In general
2. Joint and several liability
3. Test of liability
4. Effect of lack of knowledge
5. When liability attaches
6. Action by partner's wife
7. Particular wrongs
8. Breach of fiduciary duty

9. – Fraud and misrepresentation

1. In general

Members of a partnership are treated like other persons who jointly commit a tort, either in person or by the hand of an agent. Caplan v Caplan (1935) 268 N.Y. 445, 198 N.E. 23, 101 ALR 1223 (superseded by statute as stated in People v Morton (1954) 308 N.Y. 96, 123 N.E.2d 790)

Partner may be held liable for wrongful act of copartner only where act is committed in ordinary course of business of partnership. Barnhard v Barnhard (1992, 2d Dept) 179 A.D.2d 715, 578 N.Y.S.2d 615

In personal injury action arising from collapse of ceiling in building owned by defendant partnerships, there was no inconsistency between jury's finding that individual partners were not grossly negligent and its finding of gross negligence of part of owner-partnerships, and thus defendants' motion to set aside verdict in favor of plaintiffs was denied. Bank of New York v Ansonia Assocs. (1997, Sup) 172 Misc. 2d 70, 656 N.Y.S.2d 813

2. Joint and several liability

All the members of a partnership are jointly and severally liable for torts committed in the course of the partnership business by an employee or by a partner. Caplan v Caplan (1935) 268 N.Y. 445, 198 N.E. 23, 101 ALR 1223 (superseded by statute as stated in People v Morton (1954) 308 N.Y. 96, 123 N.E.2d 790)

When a tort is committed by a partnership, the wrong is imputable to all of the partners jointly and severally, and an action may be brought against all or any of them in their individual capacities or against the partnership as an entity. Pedersen v Manitowoc Co. (1969) 25 N.Y.2d 412, 306 N.Y.S.2d 903, 255 N.E.2d 146

N.Y. Partnership Law § 26(b) does not shield a general partner in a registered limited liability partnership from personal liability for breaches of the partnership's or partners' obligations to each other. Ederer v Gursky (2007) 9 NY3d 514, 851 NYS2d 108, 881 NE2d 204, reargument den (2008) 10 NY3d 780, 857 NYS2d 15, 886 NE2d 776.

In a suit brought by a withdrawing partner of a Limited Liability Partnership (LLP) for an accounting and for breach of contract, a trial court order holding the remaining partners liable to the withdrawing partner for an accounting was upheld on appeal as N.Y. Partnership Law § 26(b) did not shield the general partner of the LLP from personal liability for breaches of the partnership's or partners' obligations to each other. Since no formal written agreement existed governing the LLP, the provisions of § 26(b) applied. Ederer v Gursky (2007) 9 NY3d 514, 851 NYS2d 108, 881 NE2d 204, reargument den (2008) 10 NY3d 780, 857 NYS2d 15, 886 NE2d 776.

In the field of tort liability members of a partnership are jointly and severally liable for a tort committed in the course of the partnership business. Payne v Payne (1970, 4th Dept) 34 A.D.2d 375, 313 N.Y.S.2d 312, revd on other grounds (1971) 28 N.Y.2d 399, 322 N.Y.S.2d 238, 271 N.E.2d 220

Partners are jointly and severally liable for torts committed in the course of partnership business. Martinoff v Triboro Roofing Co. (1962, Sup) 228 N.Y.S.2d 139

Appellate court applied New York partnership law to hold that taxpayers who were members of de facto partnerships that orchestrated an evasion of over $6 million in federal gasoline excise taxes were jointly and severally liable to pay the taxes. United States ex rel. Perler v Papandon (2003, CA2 NY) 331 F.3d 52

Partner is not indispensable party in action naming other partners or partnership as parties defendant, but where less than all partners are named, execution of any judgment secured is limited to partnership property and individual property of partners named and summoned. Benvenuto v Taubman (1988, ED NY) 690 F. Supp. 149

Taxpayer failed to make a valid claim for a tax refund under 28 U.S.C.S. § 1346(a)(1) for an overpayment because under both N.Y. Partnership Law § 24 and Cal. Corp. Code § 1630(a), the taxpayer as a general partner was jointly and severally liable for tax liabilities of the partnership so that the Internal Revenue Service was entitled to levy on the taxpayer's personal individual retirement account and was not obligated to enter into a settlement rather than levy. Young v United States IRS (2005, ED NY) 387 F. Supp. 2d 143, 2005-2 USTC P 50608, 96 AFTR 2d 5676

3. Test of liability

A tort for which a partnership is liable makes every member of the firm severally individually liable. Such liability is not dependent upon the personal wrong of the individual member of the partnership against which the liability is asserted. The test of the liability is based upon a determination of the question whether the wrong was committed in behalf of and within the reasonable scope of the business of the partnership. In re Peck (1912) 206 N.Y. 55, 99 N.E. 258

In underlying action by partner whose check for share of dissolved partnership assets was cashed by defendant copartner under forged endorsement, summary judgment dismissing third-party complaint against remaining partners was proper, since defendant's unlawful and unilateral act of forgery was neither within partnership's ordinary course of business nor authorized by third-party defendant partners. Barnhard v Barnhard (1992, 2d Dept) 179 A.D.2d 715, 578 N.Y.S.2d 615

In underlying action by partner whose check for share of dissolved partnership assets was cashed by defendant copartner under forged endorsement, summary judgment dismissing third-party complaint against remaining partners was proper, since defendant's unlawful and unilateral act of forgery was neither within partnership's ordinary course of business nor authorized by third-party defendant partners. Barnhard v Barnhard (1992, 2d Dept) 179 A.D.2d 715, 578 N.Y.S.2d 615

Innocent partners of a firm who had no guilty knowledge and did not knowingly participate in any wrongdoing and were not guilty of actionable negligence were not liable for the torts of other partners, where what was done by those partners was not within the scope of the partnership business. Gerdes v Reynolds (1941, Sup) 28 N.Y.S.2d 622

As to an attorney who was employed by a law firm that another attorney was suing for an alleged failure to compensate him in accordance with an agreement with the law firm, none of the three indicia of partnership applied to defendant; the attorney-employee had no: (1) joint control over the enterprise; (2) profit splitting; or (3) loss sharing. Since the attorney-employee was not a partner of the law firm within the meaning of N.Y. P'ship Law § 24, he could not be held personally liable for any alleged wrongs by the firm or its partners. Zito v Fischbein Badillo Wagner Harding (2006, Sup) 809 NYS2d 444, later proceeding (2006, NY App Div, 1st Dept) 2006 NY App Div LEXIS 3943

Law firm partners could not be held liable pursuant to N.Y. P'ship Law §§ 24, 26, for the alleged legal malpractice conduct of former partners of the law firm where those actions were alleged to have occurred after the law firm disbanded. Green v Conciatori (2006, App Div, 2d Dept) 809 NYS2d 559

Motion to dismiss action by investor in limited partnership against partners for alleged securities violations in connection with investment should be granted to those defendants who became partners subsequent to alleged securities violations since under New York law liability of partner is limited to fraudulent acts occurring while he is partner. Halperin v Edwards & Hanly (1977, ED NY) 430 F. Supp. 121, CCH Fed Secur L Rep P 96028

4. Effect of lack of knowledge

Every member of a partnership is liable for torts committed by one of the members acting in the scope of the firm business, though they do not participate in, ratify, or have knowledge of such torts. Kavanaugh v McIntyre (1914) 210 N.Y. 175, 104 N.E. 135, affd (1916) 242 US 138, 61 L Ed 205, 37 S Ct 38 (superseded by statute as stated in In re Pattison (1991, BC DC NM) 132 BR 449)

Plaintiff in action for trespass and nuisance was not entitled to partial summary judgment on issue of liability where fact issues remained as to whether actions of defendant's partner were outside ordinary course of partnership business and whether defendant knew of and authorized those actions. Staten Island-Arlington, Inc. v Wilpon (1998, 2d Dept) 251 A.D.2d 650, 676 N.Y.S.2d 469

Partners are individually responsible for torts by a firm when acting within the general scope of its business whether they personally participated therein or not and although they had no knowledge of the actions. Guild v Herrick (1944, Sup) 51 N.Y.S.2d 326

5. When liability attaches

In view of evidence that defendant became general partner of brokerage firm after the time that firm allegedly wrongfully manipulated plaintiff's stock, in absence of allegation that defendant represented himself to any person to be partner of the firm, mere assertion that two other partners represented to plaintiff that defendant was a partner at the time in question, absent a showing that such representation was authorized or that defendant had knowledge of it, was not sufficient to make defendant liable. Skillern v Rooks (1974, 1st Dept) 46 A.D.2d 745, 360 N.Y.S.2d 657

Partnership Law

A partner is liable for wrongs of the firm only during the period in which he was a partner. Guild v Herrick (1944, Sup) 51 N.Y.S.2d 326

6. Action by partner's wife

Partners are liable for the acts of a copartner in a business carried on by them jointly only within the field where liability is joint and members of a partnership cannot be held individually liable for injuries to the wife of a partner from the negligent operation of an automobile by her husband in the business of the partnership where the husband is by virtue of the marriage relation himself immune from liability. Caplan v Caplan (1935) 268 N.Y. 445, 198 N.E. 23, 101 ALR 1223 (superseded by statute as stated in People v Morton (1954) 308 N.Y. 96, 123 N.E.2d 790)

Partnership is not liable for personal injuries to wife of partner, suffered while riding in firm automobile operated by her husband, since, under this section partnership is liable only "to the same extent as the partner so acting or omitting to act," and, under common law, which has not been changed by statute, husband cannot be held legally liable for negligently injuring his wife. Wadsworth v Webster (1932) 237 A.D. 319, 261 N.Y.S. 670

Inasmuch as provisions of Domestic Relations Law grants husband or wife right to recover against other in tort, wife may now maintain action against one who is her husband's partner for wrong committed by such partner against her. Jacobs v United States Fidelity & Guaranty Co. (1956) 2 Misc. 2d 428, 152 N.Y.S.2d 128

7. Particular wrongs

Plaintiff held an unsatisfied judgment against two partners, individually and as partners, for personal injuries suffered when he was assaulted by one of them while acting in the course of the partnership business. Plaintiff was entitled to judgment against the defendant-insurer on a public liability policy issued to the two partners individually, for although the policy's exclusion of wilful assaults applied to one partner, the other was not guilty of wilful assault. A policy issued to two individuals contemplates separate and distinct obligations to the various named assured, rather than a single obligation to all of the assured. Morgan v Greater New York Taxpayers Mut. Ins. Ass'n (1953) 305 N.Y. 243, 112 N.E.2d 273

Where record, in action on lease, supported contention that lease had been assigned to and assumed by partnership, and that no individual, but only partnership liability, attached, and where there was no allegation that partnership was insolvent or otherwise unable to pay its obligations, motion to strike complaint as to individual partner defendants and to sever such causes should have been granted since no action would lie against partners individually. Helmsley v Cohen (1977, 1st Dept) 56 A.D.2d 519, 391 N.Y.S.2d 522

Defendants who had complied with plaintiff's discovery demands were nevertheless accountable for codefendant's failure to comply where codefendant was their partner, and thus their answer would be stricken if codefendant failed to satisfy court's order giving him 20 days to respond to discovery demands. Metflex Corp. v Klafter (1986, 2d Dept) 123 A.D.2d 845, 507 N.Y.S.2d 460

In action by worker who was injured in fall from newly constructed loft flooring on leased premises, it was improper to dismiss claims predicated on common-law negligence and violation of CLS Labor § 200 against members of partnership that owned premises, where 2 partners had helped to supervise construction of loft floor and had actual knowledge of dangerous condition, thus creating fact issues as to whether partnership retained control of premises and whether some partners' knowledge of dangerous condition should be imputed to other partners; mere fact that premises were leased did not absolve partners from liability, and conclusory assertion that partnership surrendered control to tenant was insufficient to negate facts showing that it retained right of control. Callari v Pellitieri (1987, 4th Dept) 130 A.D.2d 935, 516 N.Y.S.2d 371

Surrogate properly denied legal fees to 2 law firms of which attorney/drafter was partner, for services rendered in connection with administration of estate, since attorney/drafter's fraudulent scheme occurred while he was partner acting in ordinary course of business of each law firm, and therefore each law firm was liable for misconduct of attorney/drafter to same extent as was he. In re Estate of Klenk (1994, 2d Dept) 204 A.D.2d 640, 612 N.Y.S.2d 220

Plaintiff was properly permitted to amend his age and religious discrimination complaint against law firm in order to add individual partners of firm, despite passage of several years between original complaint and amendment, since partners are jointly and severally liable for wrongful acts of partnership under CLS Partn §§ 24 and 26. Schutz v Finkelstein Bruckman Wohl Most & Rothman (1996, 2d

Dept) 232 A.D.2d 470, 648 N.Y.S.2d 174, subsequent app (1998, 2d Dept) 247 A.D.2d 460, 668 N.Y.S.2d 669

Where the obligation undertaken by a partnership did not arise from the wrongful use of proceeds of the sale of plaintiff's property but rather was an obligation arising upon contract, the breach of which occurred upon failure to account this section did not apply and the partnership obligation was a joint obligation. Salem v Seigel (1953, Sup) 126 N.Y.S.2d 214

Court rejected plaintiff's contention that the fiduciary of a decedent's estate remained liable for any malpractice committed by a law firm after the decedent's withdrawal, as a partner was ordinarily individually liable for the tortious conduct of another member or employee of the firm only if such conduct occurred while that partner was a member of the firm, N.Y. P'ship Law §§ 24, 26(a)(1). Wright v Shapiro (2007, 4th Dept) 37 App Div 3d 1181, 830 NYS2d 627

Dismissal of a claim against a partner based on a lawyer's violation of N.Y. Jud. Ct. Acts Law § 487 was error because the test for liability of partners under N.Y. P'ship Law §§ 24, 26(a)(1) was whether the wrong was committed on behalf of and within reasonable scope of partnership business, not whether the wrongful act was criminal in nature, or whether the other partners condoned the offending partner's actions. Dupree v Voorhees (2009, App Div, 2d Dept) 891 NYS2d 124, subsequent app (2009, App Div, 2d Dept) 891 NYS2d 422.

Alleged acts of partner, in law firm retained by singer, to defraud singer's estate through execution of false legal documents and dissolution and creation of corporations are not, as matter of law, beyond scope of partner's authority so as to relieve partnership of liability for such acts, however, death of singer terminated attorney client relationship, and absent relationship there can be no action for negligence against law firm. Bingham v Zolt (1988, SD NY) 683 F. Supp. 965, later proceeding (1990, SD NY) 1990 US Dist LEXIS 6396, later proceeding (1993, SD NY) 810 F. Supp. 100, RICO Bus Disp Guide (CCH) P 8187, motion den (1993, SD NY) 1993 US Dist LEXIS 7095 and motion den, corrected (1993, SD NY) 823 F. Supp. 1126, RICO Bus Disp Guide (CCH) P 8351, subsequent app (1995, CA2 NY) 66 F.3d 553, RICO Bus Disp Guide (CCH) P 8900, cert den (1996) 517 US 1134, 134 L Ed 2d 543, 116 S Ct 1418, reh den (1996) 517 US 1230, 134 L Ed 2d 967, 116 S Ct 1870 and reh den (1996) 517 US 1240, 135 L Ed 2d 185, 116 S Ct 1891 and (criticized in Klehr v A.O. Smith Corp. (1997) 521 US 179, 138 L Ed 2d 373, 117 S Ct 1984, 97 CDOS 4621, 97 Daily Journal DAR 7638, RICO Bus Disp Guide (CCH) P 9295, 11 FLW Fed S 9)

8. Breach of fiduciary duty

In order to determine whether attorney's partners could be held liable for his conversion of client's trust assets, it was necessary to ascertain whether his conduct was within ordinary course of law firm's business, and whether law firm benefited from or ratified his actions. Ottinger v Dempsey (1986, 2d Dept) 122 A.D.2d 125, 504 N.Y.S.2d 517, appeal after remand (1990, 2d Dept) 161 A.D.2d 691, 555 N.Y.S.2d 827

Court should have dismissed cause of action for breach of fiduciary duty predicated on plaintiff's claim that he was never told of magnitude of potential liability to which he was being exposed on joining real estate development venture, where personal guarantee agreement signed by him clearly disclosed magnitude of his potential liability, and there were no factual allegations to suggest that person of reasonable intelligence could not have discovered, with exercise of reasonable diligence, that he or she could be liable to bank for entire amount of venture's loan obligation. Beltrone v General Schuyler & Co. (1996, 3d Dept) 223 A.D.2d 938, 636 N.Y.S.2d 917, subsequent app (1996, 3d Dept) 229 A.D.2d 857, 645 N.Y.S.2d 914, subsequent app (1998, 3d Dept) 252 A.D.2d 640, 675 N.Y.S.2d 198

Where there is an alleged breach of a general partner's fiduciary duty to the limited partners and claimed wrongful conduct, a representative action will lie in view of the fact the general partners diverted a substantial portion of the partnership funds received upon sale of partnership's real property to their own use or to the use of several codefendants whom they controlled. Alpert v Haimes (1970) 64 Misc. 2d 608, 315 N.Y.S.2d 332

A cause of action will also lie for a breach of fiduciary duties and wrongful conduct by a general partner for conspiring, with several codefendants, to defraud the partnership in the operation and subsequent sale of the partnership's real property. Alpert v Haimes (1970) 64 Misc. 2d 608, 315 N.Y.S.2d 332

9. – Fraud and misrepresentation

Where one of a firm of warehousemen falsely represented to a person who advanced money on the faith of such representation that he had in storage with the firm a certain quantity of grain, the innocent partners were held bound by such representation. Griswold v Haven (1862) 25 N.Y. 595

Generally, each partner is liable for misrepresentations and concealments of others committed while engaged in promoting the enterprise. In re Peck (1912) 206 N.Y. 55, 99 N.E. 258

Fraud by one partner whereby money or property is gained by the partnership renders all partners civilly liable despite the partnership's discharge in bankruptcy. A. Sam & Sons Produce Co. v Campese (1961, 4th Dept) 14 A.D.2d 487, 217 N.Y.S.2d 275

In view of evidence that defendant became general partner of brokerage firm after the time that firm allegedly wrongfully manipulated plaintiff's stock, in absence of allegation that defendant represented himself to any person to be a partner of the firm, mere assertion that two other partners represented to plaintiff that defendant was a partner at the time in question, absent a showing that such representation was authorized or that defendant had knowledge of it, was not sufficient to make defendant liable. Skillern v Rooks (1974, 1st Dept) 46 A.D.2d 745, 360 N.Y.S.2d 657

In action by plaintiffs who allegedly lost substantial investment in restricted shares of common stock of company because of material fraudulent misrepresentations and fraudulent concealment of material information by attorney who helped negotiate sale of stock on behalf of company, claim for punitive damages against defendant attorney's law firm would be sustained even though law partnership may not have explicitly ratified attorney's activities on behalf of their corporate client, as alleged misconduct was conducted within scope of partnership's business and firm could thus be held liable to same extent as individual attorney. Swersky v Dreyer & Traub (1996, 1st Dept) 219 A.D.2d 321, 643 N.Y.S.2d 33, reh den, app gr (1996, 1st Dept) 232 A.D.2d 968, 656 N.Y.S.2d 857 and app withdrawn (1997) 89 N.Y.2d 983, 656 N.Y.S.2d 741, 678 N.E.2d 1357

Defendant was entitled to dismissal of fraud cause of action where (1) statements allegedly made by codefendant regarding their joint and several liability as partners of company that joined with plaintiff to undertake real estate development project were not false when made, and (2) conclusory allegation that various statements made by defendant and others caused plaintiff to enter into real estate partnership agreement, and to suffer financial losses, was insufficient to plead requisite justifiable reliance, especially as plaintiff did not claim that facts allegedly misrepresented were peculiarly within defendant's knowledge or that he had no reasonable means available to ascertain truth. Beltrone v General Schuyler & Co. (1996, 3d Dept) 223 A.D.2d 938, 636 N.Y.S.2d 917, subsequent app (1996, 3d Dept) 229 A.D.2d 857, 645 N.Y.S.2d 914, subsequent app (1998, 3d Dept) 252 A.D.2d 640, 675 N.Y.S.2d 198

Law client adequately stated a cause of action for fraud against a law firm and partner-A, an attorney in the firm, arising from their representation in a personal injury action, because the claim alleged the essential elements of fraud, including that partner-A made knowingly false statements which induced the client into a settlement, and that the client acted to his detriment. Salazar v Sacco & Fillas, LLP (2014, 2d Dept) 114 App Div 3d 745, 980 NYS2d 484

Even a professional partnership will be responsible if partners participated in the wrongdoing, or closed their eyes to a fraud being perpetrated by one of them, where if their conduct, whether by acts of commission or omission, were such as to bind them with the mark of bad faith. Riley v Larocque (1937) 163 Misc 423, 297 N.Y.S. 756

Where plaintiff dealt with a member of a partnership as an individual, and nowhere alleged that he dealt with the member as a representative of the partnership, there can be no basis for holding the partnership liable for the individual's alleged fraud. Weisinger v Rae (1959) 19 Misc. 2d 341, 188 N.Y.S.2d 10

§ 25. Partnership bound by partner's breach of trust

The partnership is bound to make good the loss:

1. Where one partner acting within the scope of his apparent authority receives money or property of a third person and misapplies it; and

2. Where the partnership in the course of its business receives money or property of a third person and the money or property so received is misapplied by any partner while it is in the custody of the partnership.

History: Add, L 1919, ch 408, eff Oct 1, 1919.

CASE ANNOTATIONS

When a tort is committed by a partnership, the wrong is imputable to all of the partners jointly and severally, and an action may be brought against all or any of them in their individual capacities or against the partnership as an entity. Pedersen v Manitowoc Co. (1969) 25 N.Y.2d 412, 306 N.Y.S.2d 903, 255 N.E.2d 146

In consolidated actions for fraud and breach of fiduciary duty, in which plaintiffs sought reimbursement of moneys owed under partnership agreement, individual defendants, as both partners and stockholders, were proper parties to litigation where (1) complaint alleged that partnership was insolvent, and (2) partnership and shareholder's agreements, entered into by individual defendants, provided that stock and partnership interests were to be treated as indivisible units. St. James Plaza v Notey (1990, 2d Dept) 166 A.D.2d 438, 560 N.Y.S.2d 672

Law client adequately stated a cause of action for fraud against a law firm and partner-A, an attorney in the firm, arising from their representation in a personal injury action, because the claim alleged the essential elements of fraud, including that partner-A made knowingly false statements which induced the client into a settlement, and that the client acted to his detriment. Salazar v Sacco & Fillas, LLP (2014, 2d Dept) 114 App Div 3d 745, 980 NYS2d 484

Where partners participating in distribution from brokerage firm's unclaimed dividend account agreed to indemnify firm against any claim by state and subsequently partners, including executors of deceased partner, paid comptroller their proportionate shares of distribution in settlement of claim that distribution should have been delivered to comptroller pursuant to Abandoned Property Law, the debt was that of participants in the distribution and could not properly be set off against decedent's partnership interest; thus, executors were entitled to commissions on total value of partnership interest received and paid by them, including sum paid to comptroller. In re Will of Heming (1975) 83 Misc. 2d 272, 371 N.Y.S.2d 546

Where the obligation undertaken by a partnership did not arise from the wrongful use of proceeds of the sale of plaintiff's property but rather was an obligation arising upon contract, the breach of which occurred upon failure to account, this section did not apply and the partnership obligation was a joint obligation. Salem v Seigel (1953, Sup) 126 N.Y.S.2d 214

General partner of partnership mortgagor is liable personally for rents collected after July 1994, regardless of exculpation clauses in note, mortgage, and assignment exonerating him from personal liability, where court has held that mortgagee is entitled to rents collected by partnership from date of default, and partnership never remitted these funds to mortgagee, because such funds in hands of partner are misappropriated and partner cannot be shielded from personal liability under CLS Partn Law § 25(2) since exoneration clauses have no application to liability for breach of trust. Credit Lyonnais v Getty Square Assocs. (1995, SD NY) 876 F. Supp. 517

§ 26. Nature of partner's liability

(a) Except as provided in subdivision (b) of this section, all partners are liable:

1. Jointly and severally for everything chargeable to the partnership under sections twenty-four and twenty-five.

2. Jointly for all other debts and obligations of the partnership; but any partner may enter into a separate obligation to perform a partnership contract.

(b) Except as provided by subdivisions (c) and (d) of this section, no partner of a partnership which is a registered limited liability partnership is liable or accountable, directly or indirectly (including by way of indemnification, contribution or otherwise), for any debts, obligations or liabilities of, or chargeable to, the registered limited liability partnership or each other, whether arising in tort, contract or otherwise, which are incurred, created or assumed by such partnership while such partnership is a registered limited liability partnership, solely by reason of being such a partner or acting (or omitting to act) in such capacity or rendering professional services or otherwise participating (as an employee, consultant, contractor or otherwise) in the conduct of the other business or activities of the registered limited liability partnership.

(c) Notwithstanding the provisions of subdivision (b) of this section, (i) each partner, employee or agent of a partnership which is a registered limited liability partnership shall be personally and fully liable and accountable for any negligent or wrongful act or misconduct committed by him or her or by any person under his or her direct supervision and control while rendering professional services on behalf of such registered limited liability partnership and (ii) each shareholder, director, officer, member, manager, partner, employee and agent of a professional service corporation, foreign professional service corporation, professional service limited liability company, foreign professional service limited liability company, registered limited liability partnership, foreign limited liability partnership or professional partnership that is a partner, employee or agent of a partnership which is a registered limited liability partnership shall be personally and fully liable and accountable for any negligent or wrongful act or misconduct committed by him or her or by any person under his or her direct supervision and control while rendering professional services in his or her capacity as a partner, employee or agent of such registered limited liability partnership. The relationship of a professional to a registered limited liability partnership with which such professional is associated, whether as a partner, employee or agent, shall not modify or diminish the jurisdiction over such professional of the licensing authority and in the case of an attorney and counsellor-at-law or a professional service corporation, professional service limited liability company, foreign professional service limited liability company, registered limited liability partnership, foreign limited liability partnership, foreign professional service corporation or professional partnership, engaged in the practice of law, the other courts of this state.

(d) Notwithstanding the provisions of subdivision (b) of this section, all or specified partners of a partnership which is a registered limited liability partnership may be liable in their capacity as partners for all or specified debts, obligations or liabilities of a registered limited liability partnership to the extent at least a majority of the partners shall have agreed unless otherwise provided in any agreement between the partners. Any such agreement may be modified or revoked to the extent at least a majority of the part-

ners shall have agreed, unless otherwise provided in any agreement between the partners; provided, however, that (i) any such modification or revocation shall not affect the liability of a partner for any debts, obligations or liabilities of a registered limited liability partnership incurred, created or assumed by such registered limited liability partnership prior to such modification or revocation and (ii) a partner shall be liable for debts, obligations and liabilities of the registered limited liability partnership incurred, created or assumed after such modification or revocation only in accordance with this article and, if such agreement is further modified, such agreement as so further modified but only to the extent not inconsistent with subdivision (c) of this section. Nothing in this section shall in any way affect or impair the ability of a partner to act as a guarantor or surety for, provide collateral for or otherwise be liable for, the debts, obligations or liabilities of a registered limited liability partnership.

(e) Subdivision (b) of this section shall not affect the liability of a registered limited liability partnership out of partnership assets for partnership debts, obligations and liabilities.

(f) Neither the withdrawal or revocation of a registered limited liability partnership pursuant to subdivision (f) or (g), respectively, of section 121-1500 of this chapter nor the dissolution, winding up or termination of a registered limited liability partnership shall affect the applicability of the provisions of subdivision (b) of this section for any debt, obligation or liability incurred, created or assumed while the partnership was a registered limited liability partnership.

History: Add, L 1919, ch 408, with substance transferred from § 6; amd, L 1994, ch 576, § 8, eff Oct 24, 1994.

CASE ANNOTATIONS

1. **In general**
2. **Torts**
3. **Contract**
4. **– Insufficient joint property**
5. **– Deceased partner's estate**
6. **– Effect of partner's withdrawal from firm**
7. **– Assumption of liability by partner**
8. **– Judgments**

1. In general

Where record, in action on lease, supported contention that lease had been assigned to and assumed by partnership, and that no individual, but only partnership liability, attached, and where there was no allegation that partnership was insolvent or otherwise unable to pay its obligations, motion to strike complaint as to individual partner defendants and to sever such causes should have been granted since no action would lie against partners individually. Helmsley v Cohen (1977, 1st Dept) 56 A.D.2d 519, 391 N.Y.S.2d 522

Partner's liability for contractual liabilities of partnership is joint rather than several, and each partner is liable for whole amount of every debt of partnership rather than for proportionate amount. Midwood Dev. Corp. v K 12th Associates (1989, 2d Dept) 146 A.D.2d 754, 537 N.Y.S.2d 237

Pleading rule which requires that cause of action against individual partner allege that partnership is insolvent or unable to pay its debts is inapplicable where partnership is named as party defendant along with individual partners. Beltrone v General Schuyler & Co. (1996, 3d Dept) 223 A.D.2d 938, 636 N.Y.S.2d 917, subsequent app

(1996, 3d Dept) 229 A.D.2d 857, 645 N.Y.S.2d 914, subsequent app (1998, 3d Dept) 252 A.D.2d 640, 675 N.Y.S.2d 198

Dismissal of a withdrawing partner's suit against remaining partners, alleging a breach of the parties' partnership agreement was error because N.Y. P'ship Law § 26(b) did not shield a general partner in a registered limited liability partnership from personal liability for breaches of the partnership's or partners' obligations to each other. Kuslansky v Kuslansky, Robbins, Stechel & Cunningham, LLP (2008, 2d Dept) 50 App Div 3d 1100, 858 NYS2d 213, decision reached on appeal by (2008, 2d Dept) 50 App Div 3d 1101, 858 NYS2d 212.

Liability of members of partnership in quasi or implied contract action based on tortious act is joint and several. State Bank of Binghamton v Bache (1935) 156 Misc 503, 282 N.Y.S. 187

Trial court erred in marking an action to collect money allegedly owed for secretarial services off the calendar upon the death of an attorney; there was an issue as to whether the remaining attorney was the deceased attorney's partner pursuant to N.Y. Partnership Law § 26, and thus as to whether the remaining attorney was liable for the debt pursuant to N.Y. C.P.L.R. 1015. Bon Temps Agency, Ltd. v Hickey (2004, A.D., 1st Dept) 773 N.Y.S.2d 56

Appellate court applied New York partnership law to hold that taxpayers who were members of de facto partnerships that orchestrated an evasion of over $6 million in federal gasoline excise taxes were jointly and severally liable to pay the taxes. United States ex rel. Perler v Papandon (2003, CA2 NY) 331 F.3d 52

Where there is joint liability of partners under §§ 24-26, and all parties are indispensable parties defendant, and 3 out of 5 partners live in plaintiff's state, there is not a controversy wholly between citizens of different states and consequently federal courts are without jurisdiction. Minez v Merrill (1930, DC NY) 43 F.2d 201

2. Torts

A tort for which a partnership is liable makes every member of the firm severally individually liable. Such liability is not dependent upon the personal wrong of the individual member of the partnership against which the liability is asserted. The test of the liability is based upon a determination of the question whether the wrong was committed in behalf of and within the reasonable scope of the business of the partnership. In re Peck (1912) 206 N.Y. 55, 99 N.E. 258

The liability of members of a partnership for a tort committed in the course of its business is joint and several. Caplan v Caplan (1935) 268 N.Y. 445, 198 N.E. 23, 101 ALR 1223 (superseded by statute as stated in People v Morton (1954) 308 N.Y. 96, 123 N.E.2d 790)

Plaintiff held an unsatisfied judgment against two partners, individually and as partners, for personal injuries suffered when he was assaulted by one of them while acting in the course of the partnership business. Plaintiff was entitled to judgment against the defendant-insurer on a public liability policy issued to the two partners individually, for although the policy's inclusion of wilful assaults applied to one partner, the other was not guilty of wilful assault. A policy issued to two individuals contemplates separate and distinct obligations to the various named assured, rather than a single obligation to all of the assured. Morgan v Greater New York Taxpayers Mut. Ins. Ass'n (1953) 305 N.Y. 243, 112 N.E.2d 273

When a tort is committed by a partnership, the wrong is imputable to all of the partners jointly and severally, and an action may be brought against all or any of them in their individual capacities or against the partnership as an entity. Pedersen v Manitowoc Co. (1969) 25 N.Y.2d 412, 306 N.Y.S.2d 903, 255 N.E.2d 146

Board of Trustees of Clients' Security Fund could properly prosecute subrogation claim not only against attorney who engaged in dishonest conduct but also against his former law partner, even though partner was not responsible for attorney's conversion of funds and other unethical behavior, since traditional partnership law provides aggrieved clients with cause of action against partner for attorney's tortious conduct, fund stood in clients' shoes through subrogation agreement executed when clients were reimbursed from fund, and CLS St Fin § 97-t vests fund with broad power to structure reimbursement agreements. Clients' Sec. Fund v Grandeau (1988) 72 N.Y.2d 62, 530 N.Y.S.2d 775, 526 N.E.2d 270

Clients' Security Fund could pursue subrogation claim against law partner of dishonest attorney based on his alleged negligence, as well as his vicarious liability for dishonest attorney's tortious conduct, although CLS St Fin § 97-t allows fund to reimburse clients only for losses attributable to "dishonest conduct"; statute does not prohibit fund from securing more extensive subrogation rights, and reasonable acts undertaken in furtherance of regulatory scheme should be

sustained in view of fund's broad authority to regulate in public interest. Clients' Sec. Fund v Grandeau (1987, 3d Dept) 129 A.D.2d 383, 517 N.Y.S.2d 587, affd, ctfd ques ans (1988) 72 N.Y.2d 62, 530 N.Y.S.2d 775, 526 N.E.2d 270

In lease dispute, liability for intentional infliction of emotional distress could attach to individual partner of partnership-landlord; individual partner is liable for tortious action committed by partnership, and action may be brought against him in his individual capacity. Meyer v Park South Assoc. (1990, 1st Dept) 159 A.D.2d 337, 552 N.Y.S.2d 614

Plaintiff was properly permitted to amend his age and religious discrimination complaint against law firm in order to add individual partners of firm, despite passage of several years between original complaint and amendment, since partners are jointly and severally liable for wrongful acts of partnership under CLS Partn §§ 24 and 26. Schutz v Finkelstein Bruckman Wohl Most & Rothman (1996, 2d Dept) 232 A.D.2d 470, 648 N.Y.S.2d 174, subsequent app (1998, 2d Dept) 247 A.D.2d 460, 668 N.Y.S.2d 669

Because the associate attorneys were individually liable under N.Y. P'ship Law § 26(c)(i) for their negligent or wrongful acts, and because some of the attorneys at the law firm engaged in intentional deceit, in violation of N.Y. Jud. Ct. Acts Law § 487, none of the defendants was entitled to summary judgment in an administrator's legal malpractice action. Scarborough v Napoli, Kaiser & Bern, LLP (2009, 4th Dept) 63 App Div 3d 1531, 880 NYS2d 800.

Law client adequately stated a cause of action for fraud against a law firm and partner-A, an attorney in the firm, arising from their representation in a personal injury action, because the claim alleged the essential elements of fraud, including that partner-A made knowingly false statements which induced the client into a settlement, and that the client acted to his detriment. Salazar v Sacco & Fillas, LLP (2014, 2d Dept) 114 App Div 3d 745, 980 NYS2d 484

In action for injuries sustained by plaintiffs when ceiling of building collapsed, in which jury found that owner-partnerships were grossly negligent, net worth of general partners was relevant to issue of partnerships' net worth for purposes of punitive damages award, even though jury specifically found that general partners were not liable for gross negligence; general partners would be individually liable for payment of any partnership liabilities that could not be paid out of partnership assets, regardless of how jury viewed their individual culpability. Bank of New York v Ansonia Assocs. (1997, Sup) 172 Misc. 2d 70, 656 N.Y.S.2d 813

Release in favor of law firm, which was operated as limited liability partnership, did not release partner who was alleged to have acted negligently in handling of firm escrow account, where partner was not named in release; safe course of partnership that wishes to be certain that all of its partners are released of liability when procuring release is to have all partners specifically named therein. Schuman v Gallet, Dreyer & Berkey, L. L. P. (1999, Sup) 180 Misc. 2d 485, 689 N.Y.S.2d 628

Law firm partners could not be held liable pursuant to N.Y. P'ship Law §§ 24, 26, for the alleged legal malpractice conduct of former partners of the law firm where those actions were alleged to have occurred after the law firm disbanded. Green v Conciatori (2006, App Div, 2d Dept) 809 NYS2d 559

Court rejected plaintiff's contention that the fiduciary of a decedent's estate remained liable for any malpractice committed by a law firm after the decedent's withdrawal, as a partner was ordinarily individually liable for the tortious conduct of another member or employee of the firm only if such conduct occurred while that partner was a member of the firm, N.Y. P'ship Law §§ 24, 26(a)(1). Wright v Shapiro (2007, 4th Dept) 37 App Div 3d 1181, 830 NYS2d 627

Dismissal of a claim against a partner based on a lawyer's violation of N.Y. Jud. Ct. Acts Law § 487 was error because the test for liability of partners under N.Y. P'ship Law §§ 24, 26(a)(1) was whether the wrong was committed on behalf of and within reasonable scope of partnership business, not whether the wrongful act was criminal in nature, or whether the other partners condoned the offending partner's actions. Dupree v Voorhees (2009, App Div, 2d Dept) 891 NYS2d 124, subsequent app (2009, App Div, 2d Dept) 891 NYS2d 422.

Partners in a brokerage firm who became partners after plaintiff made his investment which was allegedly fraudulently induced by the partnership, could not be liable for any securities laws violations occurring before they became partners. Halperin v Edwards & Hanly (1977, ED NY) 430 F. Supp. 121, CCH Fed Secur L Rep P 96028

Subcontractor's claim, based on subcontract agreement, against partner of joint venture that was contractor on bridge project is not dismissed, where actions giving rise to liability may have predated formation of joint venture, because partner may have acted individually and not on behalf of joint venture, and may be liable even if joint venture does not become insolvent. L.K. Comstock & Co. v Perini Corp. (1995, SD NY) 903 F. Supp. 609

Partners in law firm, which was limited liability partnership representing company operating ice cream store in connection with loan made by investor, were not liable to investor under Partn § 26 for alleged breach of fiduciary duty, common-law fraud, civil conspiracy, and negligent misrepresentation, where there was no showing that partners acted negligently or wrongfully while rendering professional services or that any person under their supervision and control so acted. Lewis v Rosenfeld (2001, SD NY) 138 F. Supp. 2d 466, reconsideration gr, claim dismissed (2001, SD NY) 145 F. Supp. 2d 341

3. Contract

In an action to enforce a partnership claim, a counterclaim may not be set up by a defendant to impose a "nonpartnership liability" against the partners (one of them a limited partner) individually. Ruzicka v Rager (1953) 305 N.Y. 191, 111 N.E.2d 878, 39 ALR2d 288, reh den (1953) 305 N.Y. 798, 113 N.E.2d 306

Law firm that represented limited partnership could not collect its fee from individual shareholder of corporate participant in partnership since there was no evidence of enforceable independent promise by individual to pay partnership's obligation, and thus law firm's action was barred by statute of frauds, CLS Gen Oblig § 5-701. Paul, Weiss, Rifkind, Wharton & Garrison v Westergaard (1989) 75 N.Y.2d 755, 551 N.Y.S.2d 896, 551 N.E.2d 97

Where an obligation is joint under subd 2 of this section an action cannot be severed as between a defaulting and an answering partner. Nathan v Zierler (1928) 223 A.D. 355, 228 N.Y.S. 170

In action for breach of employment contract, hearing officer erred in holding company and individual jointly and severally liable since complaint specifically alleged that contract was entered into with company, and plaintiff failed to establish that individual was partner or partner by estoppel, or that partnership was insolvent or otherwise unable to discharge its obligations. Rose v Green (1988, 2d Dept) 145 A.D.2d 618, 536 N.Y.S.2d 822, app dismd (1989) 74 N.Y.2d 836, 546 N.Y.S.2d 343, 545 N.E.2d 633, reconsideration den (1989) 75 N.Y.2d 766, 551 N.Y.S.2d 908, 551 N.E.2d 109, reconsideration den (1990) 75 N.Y.2d 866, 552 N.Y.S.2d 931, 552 N.E.2d 179

Landlord's general partner could not be held individually liable to tenant for injunctive relief, breach of warranty of habitability, or attorney's fees predicated on contractual provisions in lease, where claims arose out of lease and business activities of partnership as sole landlord; no cause of action lies against individual partner for violation of lease by partnership absent allegation that partnership is insolvent or otherwise unable to pay its obligations. Meyer v Park South Assoc. (1990, 1st Dept) 159 A.D.2d 337, 552 N.Y.S.2d 614

Defendant was not entitled to dismissal of breach of contract causes of action arising from obligations allegedly imposed on him as partner of company that had formed partnership with plaintiff to undertake real estate development project, on ground that he was not liable for any loss sustained by plaintiff in paying bank pursuant to terms of personal guarantee of bank's loan because he was not obligated to contribute to partnership capital due to provisions in partnership agreements providing that no contributions to capital would be made by any partner except on agreement of all partners; it could not be said as matter of law at pleading stage that provisions of partnership agreements that governed partners' contributions to capital also limited partners' liability for partnership debts. Beltrone v General Schuyler & Co. (1996, 3d Dept) 223 A.D.2d 938, 636 N.Y.S.2d 917, subsequent app (1996, 3d Dept) 229 A.D.2d 857, 645 N.Y.S.2d 914, subsequent app (1998, 3d Dept) 252 A.D.2d 640, 675 N.Y.S.2d 198

Claim was stated against the members of a workers' compensation group self-insured trust for the trust's cumulative deficit as the complaint alleged that the members were partners in the named entities, which reasonably implied that they were general partners. New York State Workers' Compensation Bd. v Any-time Home Care Inc., 156 A.D.3d 1043, 66 N.Y.S.3d 690, 2017 N.Y. App. Div. LEXIS 8696 (N.Y. App. Div. 3d Dep't 2017).

Landlord was not entitled to amend complaint, in action against partnership for unpaid rent, to assert such causes of action against individual partners where lease amendment, in which parties

expressly continued individual partners' personal guarantee of their personal corporation's lease obligations after partnership had succeeded that corporation as tenant, showed intent to preserve liability cap set forth in guarantee, and thus clear agreement overrode usual rule that partner may be held liable for partnership debts if partnership is insolvent and its assets are insufficient to pay its debts. 111-115 Broadway Ltd. Pshp. v Minter & Gay (2001, 1st Dept) 281 A.D.2d 153, 721 N.Y.S.2d 346

Where a non-managing partner in real estate syndicates cast in the form of general partnerships made partial assignments of portions of his partnership interest, the partial assignees were not partners at all and were not personally liable for the partnership debts. United States v Silverstein (1965, SD NY) 237 F. Supp. 446, 65-1 USTC P 9266, 15 AFTR 2d 283, affd (1965, CA2 NY) 344 F.2d 1016, 65-2 USTC P 9480, 15 AFTR 2d 991, cert den (1965) 382 US 828, 15 L Ed 2d 73, 86 S Ct 65

"At-will" former associate sued a law firm and its partners for breaching an employment contract by firing him for refusing to assist defendants in covering up their wrongful acts. The complaint's allegations that one partner prepared a false affidavit, that another partner tried to induce the associate to sign it, and that the third partner guided every aspect of the firm's operation, sufficiently stated a cause of action against the partners under N.Y. P'ship Law § 26(c)(i). Connolly v Napoli, Kaiser & Bern, LLP (2006, Sup) 12 Misc 3d 530, 817 NYS2d 872, 152 CCH LC P 60181

4. – Insufficient joint property

General partners are personally and individually liable for all obligations of partnership where the joint property is inadequate to pay partnership debts, so that if the partnership assets are insufficient, creditors may look to the separate property of any of the general partners. Stern v Low (1967, 2d Dept) 27 A.D.2d 756, 277 N.Y.S.2d 756

In an action against general partners of a limited partnership which had executed a promissory note payable to plaintiff, judgment would be granted over for indemnification in favor of one defendant against two other defendants where it was undisputed that the limited partnership was without assets to satisfy the debt due to plaintiff. Belgian Overseas Sec. Corp. v Howell Kessler Co. (1982, 1st Dept) 88 A.D.2d 559, 450 N.Y.S.2d 493

In action against general partnership and its individual partners to recover on partnership's guaranty contract, court properly dismissed individual partners' affirmative defenses asserting that plaintiff had effective remedy against general partnership assets without recourse to assets of individual partners because general partnership assets were sufficient to satisfy debt; creditor is not required to affirmatively establish that partnership assets are insufficient before he is permitted to reach individual assets of partners unless he seeks to dispense with joining partnership as party defendant. United States Trust Co. v Bamco 18 (1992, 1st Dept) 183 A.D.2d 549, 585 N.Y.S.2d 186, corrected, on reh (1993, 1st Dept) 189 A.D.2d 689

Only where creditor seeks to dispense with joining partnership as defendant in action on debt need it be affirmatively shown that pursuing claim against partnership would be futile because of its insolvency or inability to pay; where plaintiff has named partnership as party defendant, along with individual partners, it is unnecessary to aver insufficiency of partnership assets to satisfy claim. National Union Fire Ins. Co. v Robert Christopher Assocs. (1999, 1st Dept) 257 A.D.2d 1, 691 N.Y.S.2d 35

Partners are jointly liable with respect to their contractual obligations. The creditors upon such obligations may look primarily to the joint property for their satisfaction but if that is insufficient each partner is liable severally to pay the whole debt of his individual property and this individual liability dates back to the time when the obligation was incurred and arises simultaneously with the joint liability so that with respect to the ultimate rights of the creditor the contractual obligation of a partnership is incurred by all and each. Patrikes v J. C. H. Service Stations, Inc. (1943) 180 Misc 917, 41 N.Y.S.2d 158, affd (1943) 180 Misc 927, 46 N.Y.S.2d 233, app den (1943) 266 A.D. 924, 44 N.Y.S.2d 472

This section did not change the common law. The partnership remains liable jointly only on contract while each partner is liable severally in equity in the event of a need to reach the several estates of each partner. Salem v Seigel (1953, Sup) 126 N.Y.S.2d 214

Although general partners were individually liable for partnership obligations under equitable doctrine of "marshaling assets", resort could be had against them under such principle only if joint or partnership property was insufficient to pay firm debts or it appeared that there could be no effective remedy without resorting to individual property. Wisnouse v Telsey (1973, SD NY) 367 F. Supp. 855, CCH Fed Secur L Rep P 94215

General partners of a limited liability partnership were individually liable for the Comprehensive Environmental Response, Compensation, and Liability Act of 1980 liability, 42 U.S.C.S. § 9607(a), incurred by the partnership because, pursuant to N.Y. Partnership Law § 26, general partners in a limited liability partnership were not protected as individuals from liability incurred by the partnership if the assets of the partnership were insufficient to satisfy the liability. United States v 175 Inwood Assocs. LLP (2004, ED NY) 330 F. Supp. 2d 213

General partners of a limited liability partnership were individually liable for the Comprehensive Environmental Response, Compensation, and Liability Act of 1980 liability, 42 U.S.C.S. § 9607(a), incurred by the partnership because, pursuant to N.Y. Partnership Law § 26, general partners in a limited liability partnership were not protected as individuals from liability incurred by the partnership if the assets of the partnership were insufficient to satisfy the liability. United States v 175 Inwood Assocs. LLP (2004, ED NY) 330 F. Supp. 2d 213, 59 Envt Rep Cas 1211

5. – Deceased partner's estate

A creditor of a firm which has been dissolved by the death of one of the members is not entitled to proceed against the estate of the deceased partner until he has exhausted his remedy against the surviving partner. Leggat v Leggat (1903) 79 A.D. 141, 80 N.Y.S. 327, affd (1903) 176 N.Y. 590, 68 N.E. 1119

An action by a creditor is not maintainable against the estate of a deceased joint venturer without alleging the insolvency or inability to pay on the part of the surviving joint venturers. Friedman v Gettner (1958, 1st Dept) 6 A.D.2d 647, 180 N.Y.S.2d 446, affd (1959) 7 N.Y.2d 764, 194 N.Y.S.2d 35, 163 N.E.2d 141

Where a partnership arose out of a contractual relation and the obligation of the partners is joint and not joint and several, it is necessary to allege and prove inability to collect from the surviving partners in order to enforce the legal liability against the executor of the deceased partner. Georgian Press, Inc. v Hill (1943) 180 Misc 548, 45 N.Y.S.2d 561, affd (1944) 181 Misc 464, 48 N.Y.S.2d 316

Where partners participating in distribution from brokerage firm's unclaimed dividend account agreed to indemnify firm against any claim by state and subsequently partners, including executors of deceased partner, paid comptroller their proportionate shares of distribution in settlement of claim that distribution should have been delivered to comptroller pursuant to Abandoned Property Law, the debt was that of participants in the distribution and could not properly be set off against decedent's partnership interest; thus, executors were entitled to commissions on total value of partnership interest received and paid by them, including sum paid to comptroller. In re Will of Heming (1975) 83 Misc. 2d 272, 371 N.Y.S.2d 546

Plaintiff delivered to a partnership during the lifetime of a deceased partner, certain property which the partnership was to sell on behalf of plaintiff and to account to him for the proceeds after deducting agreed commissions. The property was sold but the partnership did not account. Plaintiff then sued the surviving partner and the estate of deceased partner but upon stipulation between plaintiff and the surviving partner judgment was entered against the latter. The action having been severed, plaintiff then proceeded against the estate of the deceased partner based upon the judgment already entered and upon a second cause of action based upon the original claim. In dismissing the complaint against the estate of the deceased partner, the court held that the obligation of the partnership was joint and that the estate of the deceased partner was entitled to judgment. Salem v Seigel (1953, Sup) 126 N.Y.S.2d 214

6. – Effect of partner's withdrawal from firm

In an action wherein it is alleged that a law firm and one of its partners committed wrongs in connection with the creation and management of an inter vivos trust of which plaintiff was the settlor, sole beneficiary and cotrustee, the law firm representing plaintiff is disqualified, since two of the members of that firm were members of the defendant law firm during the period in which the alleged improprieties took place, and an attorney may not act on behalf of a client in an action where the attorney has a direct interest in the subject matter of the suit; moreover, the members of the firm representing plaintiff who were members of the defendant law firm, are manifestly liable, jointly and severally, for all tortious conduct which might have occurred during their tenure with defendant law firm, and they are named as third-party defendants. As former partners in defendant law firm, the third-party defendants owe a fiduciary obligation to their former law firm similar to that owed by an attorney to his client, and there is a likelihood that information obtained by them in their role as fiduciaries will be used in the pending lawsuit. Greene v Greene (1979) 47 N.Y.2d 447, 418 N.Y.S.2d 379, 391 N.E.2d 1355

N.Y. Partnership Law § 26(b) does not shield a general partner in a registered limited liability partnership from personal liability for breaches of the partnership's or partners' obligations to each other. Ederer v Gursky (2007) 9 NY3d 514, 851 NYS2d 108, 881 NE2d 204, reargument den (2008) 10 NY3d 780, 857 NYS2d 15, 886 NE2d 776.

In a suit brought by a withdrawing partner of a Limited Liability Partnership (LLP) for an accounting and for breach of contract, a trial court order holding the remaining partners liable to the withdrawing partner for an accounting was upheld on appeal as N.Y. Partnership Law § 26(b) did not shield the general partner of the LLP from personal liability for breaches of the partnership's or partners' obligations to each other. Since no formal written agreement existed governing the LLP, the provisions of § 26(b) applied. Ederer v Gursky (2007) 9 NY3d 514, 851 NYS2d 108, 881 NE2d 204, reargument den (2008) 10 NY3d 780, 857 NYS2d 15, 886 NE2d 776.

One who was a member of a partnership when it became a member of a garment makers' association which entered into a collective bargaining agreement with a labor union, although he did not sign the agreement with the association and later withdrew from the firm, was nevertheless bound by the terms but could not be required to arbitrate a charge of operating a nonunion shop as such issue was not within scope of the arbitration agreement. Application of Camhi (1961, 1st Dept) 13 A.D.2d 752, 215 N.Y.S.2d 406

Individual tenant partners were liable for unpaid rent due landlord for time during which neither partnership nor five defendant partners occupied premises where partnership tenant had assigned its interest in lease, which was still effective, to corporation for remainder of lease period with express stipulation stating that partnership was in no way relieved or released from its duties and obligations during remainder of term of leasehold, and where partnership assets were insufficient to pay rent due. Barbro Realty Co. v Newburger (1976, 1st Dept) 53 A.D.2d 34, 385 N.Y.S.2d 68

Absent contrary agreement, individual defendants could not be held liable for rent where defendant partnership did not default on its rent until after they had already resigned from firm. 600 Partners Co. v Berger (1997, 1st Dept) 245 A.D.2d 140, 666 N.Y.S.2d 158

Mere fact that new partners had not signed guarantee did not mean that partnership had less than 8 partners potentially liable thereunder at time of defendants' withdrawal from partnership, within meaning of lease providing that "[a]ny partner of Tenant who retires from the partnership and the estate of any deceased partner shall, upon such partner's retirement or death, be immediately released hereunder and under [the accompanying] guaranty as to any liability with respect to the period after such retirement or death, provided that at least eight (8) partners of Tenant remain liable hereunder and under the guaranty." 600 Partners Co. v Berger (1997, 1st Dept) 245 A.D.2d 140, 666 N.Y.S.2d 158

Partners are personally and individually liable for the obligations of the partnership, including those under contract executed for the partnership by another partner, and a partner's subsequent withdrawal from the partnership does not relieve him of any obligations of the partnership assumed during the time he was a member thereof. Application of Camhi (1960) 28 Misc. 2d 93, 208 N.Y.S.2d 162, 43 CCH LC P 50365, revd on other grounds (1961, 1st Dept) 13 A.D.2d 752, 215 N.Y.S.2d 406

N.Y. P'ship Law § 26(b), limiting the liability of partners of a limited liability partnership, did not exempt such partners from their individual obligations to account to a withdrawing partner under the earlier enacted and unamended N.Y. P'ship Law § 74; moreover, § 26(b) did not exempt the individual limited partners from liability to an attorney for breaches of firm-related agreements between them. Ederer v Gursky (2006, App Div, 1st Dept) 826 NYS2d 210

7. – Assumption of liability by partner

The joint and several liabilities of partners arising out of the partnership relation is subject to the equitable rule in marshaling assets but this rule does not prevent the partner by his individual contract subjecting his individual property in law and equity to payment of partnership debts. In re Peck (1912) 206 N.Y. 55, 99 N.E. 258

In action for real estate brokerage commissions arising from leases, corporation which was member of partnership which owned building in question could not be held liable on assumption theory where (1) contracts pertaining to brokerage commissions were entered into between plaintiff and corporate predecessor of partnership which retained beneficial ownership of property, and (2) corporation never held title to property or assumed obligations under contracts. Cushman & Wakefield, Inc. v Progress Corp., N.V. (1991, 1st Dept) 172 A.D.2d 191, 568 N.Y.S.2d 56

8. – Judgments

A default judgment against parties designated in a complaint as limited partners in consolidated actions arising out of an alleged breach of contract was properly vacated where the limited partners did not authorize an attorney who appeared on their behalf to do so, where the general partner had no actual or apparent authority to subject the personal assets of the limited partners to judgment, though he could bind their interest in the partnership, and where the defense tendered by the limited partners was colorably meritorious. Ward v Kent Properties (1984, 1st Dept) 102 A.D.2d 771, 477 N.Y.S.2d 129, app dismd (1984) 63 N.Y.2d 771

Judgment for partnership debt becomes a lien upon real estate of each of partners with same effect as if it were for the separate debt of such partner. Gomez v Vazquez (1941) 177 Misc 874, 32 N.Y.S.2d 34

A contractual obligation of partners is joint and several but nevertheless creditors may at law satisfy an execution out of separate property of any one or more of debtors. Gomez v Vazquez (1941) 177 Misc 874, 32 N.Y.S.2d 34

Where, in an action against partners on a partnership obligation, one of the partners answers, judgment cannot properly be entered against the other by default while the issues raised by the other partner's answer are still unresolved, and the default judgment against the other partner is subject to motion to vacate. Spencer Kellogg & Sons, Inc. v Bush (1961) 31 Misc. 2d 70, 219 N.Y.S.2d 453

A partner could not impeach a judgment where after a lapse of almost 20 years since the entry of judgment on a partnership obligation, he moved to cancel the sale of his real property which took place in 1951 on the ground that he was not served with the summons and did not authorize the appearance of an attorney which was concededly made on his behalf. Hudson Plush Co. v Romano (1952, Sup) 127 N.Y.S.2d 342

§ 27.   Partner by estoppel

1. When a person, by words spoken or written or by conduct, represents himself, or consents to another representing him to any one, as a partner in an existing partnership or with one or more persons not actual partners, he is liable to any such person to whom such representation has been made, who has, on the faith of such representation, given credit to the actual or apparent partnership, and if he has made such representation or consented to its being made in a public manner he is liable to such person, whether the representation has or has not been made or communicated to such person so giving credit by or with the knowledge of the apparent partner making the representation or consenting to its being made.

(a) When a partnership liability results, he is liable as though he were an actual member of the partnership.

(b) When no partnership liability results, he is liable jointly with the other persons, if any, so consenting to the contract or representation as to incur liability, otherwise separately.

2. When a person has been thus represented to be a partner in an existing partnership, or with one or more persons not actual partners, he is an agent of the persons consenting to such representation to bind them to the same extent and in the same manner as though he were a partner in fact, with respect to persons who rely upon the representation. Where all

the members of the existing partnership consent to the representation, a partnership act or obligation results; but in all other cases it is the joint act or obligation of the person acting and the persons consenting to the representation.

History: Add, L 1919, ch 408, eff Oct 1, 1919.

CASE ANNOTATIONS

Partners who continue to carry on business in firm name, despite private agreement to dissolve partnership, with no manifestation of their dissolution, are estopped to deny liability to party relying on public indicia of partnership for tort committed by partner acting with apparent authority; while partnership by estoppel should not be lightly invoked and generally presents issues of fact, creditor was entitled to summary judgment against law firm where firm's office space, telephone number, telephone book listing, and stationery continued to be used by individual partners, with no discernible sign of dissolution, for nearly 2 years after alleged agreement among partners to dissolve firm, and individual listings of partners in attorney directory did not create issue of fact as to creditor's negligence in failing to investigate further. Royal Bank & Trust Co. v Weintraub, Gold & Alper (1986) 68 N.Y.2d 124, 506 N.Y.S.2d 151, 497 N.E.2d 289

In light of evidence tending to establish that joint venturer in plan to purchase and develop real estate held himself out to attorney as a partner in the project and that attorney performed services in reliance on this representation, joint venturer could be found liable to attorney for legal fees for services performed on behalf of all joint venturers even if he were not actually a member of a partnership. Mulvey v Hamilton (1977, 3d Dept) 57 A.D.2d 995, 394 N.Y.S.2d 318, app dismd (1978) 43 N.Y.2d 646 and app dismd (1978) 43 N.Y.2d 847

Individual defendant could not be held personally liable pursuant to CLS Partn § 27, in action for breach of contract, where defendant and another were purported owners of company known as "Majestic Marine," plaintiff had contracted with company through salesperson for purchase of boat pursuant to preprinted form showing company name "Majestic Marine" at head of front page, and he made payments on contract by checks payable to "Majestic Marine"; since plaintiff did not know that defendant was associated with company prior to execution of agreement, and it was not shown that partnership existed, individual defendant could not have held himself out to plaintiff as member of such partnership. Ranieri v Leavy (1992, 2d Dept) 180 A.D.2d 723, 580 N.Y.S.2d 366

Individual defendant was personally liable for promissory note based on CLS Partn § 27 where it was undisputed that he signed promissory note and modification agreement, and those documents clearly indicated that defendant signed on behalf of defaulting partnership. Fleet Bank NH v Royall (1995, 2d Dept) 218 A.D.2d 727, 630 N.Y.S.2d 559

In law firm's action for determination and enforcement of charging lien, firm was not entitled to amend caption to delete individual's name from firm's title on ground that individual was not partner of firm where firm had included that name in title of action; person who has represented himself to be partner in existing partnership is agent of persons consenting to such representation and binds them to same extent and in same manner as partner in fact with respect to persons relying on representation. Grutman Katz Greene & Humphrey v Goldman (1998, 1st Dept) 251 A.D.2d 7, 673 N.Y.S.2d 649

Doctrine of partnership by estoppel under N.Y. P'ship Law § 27 did not apply as there was no evidence that an attorney made any representations to a client that the attorney and a lawyer were partners, and there was no evidence that the attorney consented to the lawyer representing the attorney as a partner; there was no indication that the client relied on the attorney and the lawyer being partners in retaining the lawyer for legal representation. Community Capital Bank v Fischer & Yanowitz (2008, 2d Dept) 47 App Div 3d 667, 850 NYS2d 508.

There is no retroactive estoppel; representation or conduct relied on must be concurrent with or prior to action party is alleged to have influenced. Hartford Acci. & Indem. Co. v Oles (1934) 152 Misc 876, 274 N.Y.S. 349

In action to recover account claimed to be due for insurance premiums on agency contract entered into between plaintiff insurance company and defendants, allegedly doing business as partnership, plaintiff cannot recover under this section from one of these defendants, where his acts and conduct do not show him to be partner by estoppel and where other defendant, upon selling business and in his income tax returns, stated that he was sole owner. Hartford Acci. & Indem. Co. v Oles (1934) 152 Misc 876, 274 N.Y.S. 349

The service of process upon a corporation which held itself out to be a joint venturer or a partner of several other corporations was sufficient to constitute good and effective service so as to grant the court jurisdiction over the other several corporations. John's, Inc. v Island Garden Center of Nassau, Inc. (1966) 49 Misc. 2d 1086, 269 N.Y.S.2d 231, affd (1967) 53 Misc. 2d 1021, 280 N.Y.S.2d 34

In a medical malpractice action, there would be no basis on which to impose vicarious liability upon one doctor for the acts of a second doctor on a theory of partnership by estoppel, since the first doctor did not represent or hold out the second doctor as his partner. Impastato v De Girolamo (1983, Sup) 117 Misc. 2d 786, 459 N.Y.S.2d 512

By reason of § 11 only those who are partners between themselves may be charged for partnership debts by others with the exception of a situation where, under § 27, the debtor may not deny the claim. Greenstone v Klar (1947, Sup) 69 N.Y.S.2d 548, mod on other grounds (1947) 272 A.D. 892, 71 N.Y.S.2d 201

§ 28. Liability of incoming partner

A person admitted as a partner into an existing partnership is liable for all the obligations of the partnership arising before his admission as though he had been a partner when such obligations were incurred, except that his liability shall be satisfied only out of partnership property.

History: Add, L 1919, ch 408, eff Oct 1, 1919.

CASE ANNOTATIONS

Although provision of partnership law excludes incoming partner from personal liability for preexisting partnership debts, such debts may be satisfied out of partnership property. Barbro Realty Co. v Newburger (1976, 1st Dept) 53 A.D.2d 34, 385 N.Y.S.2d 68

Partnership obligation to pay rent, under lease initially executed by partnership and assigned to corporation with stipulation that partnership was in no way relieved or released from its duties and obligations during remainder of term of leasehold, did not constitute preexisting debt as to persons who were not partners at time lease was executed but who were partners at time of corporation's default in rent payments, and such incoming partners could be held personally liable therefore where partnership assets were insufficient to pay rent due, since rent as debt arose only when it became due. Barbro Realty Co. v Newburger (1976, 1st Dept) 53 A.D.2d 34, 385 N.Y.S.2d 68

Mere fact that new partners had not signed guarantee did not mean that partnership had less than 8 partners potentially liable thereunder at time of defendants' withdrawal from partnership, within meaning of lease providing that "[a]ny partner of Tenant who retires from the partnership and the estate of any deceased partner shall, upon such partner's retirement or death, be immediately released hereunder and under [the accompanying] guaranty as to any liability with respect to the period after such retirement or death, provided that at least eight (8) partners of Tenant remain liable hereunder and under the guaranty." 600 Partners Co. v Berger (1997, 1st Dept) 245 A.D.2d 140, 666 N.Y.S.2d 158

Where partner upon his admission to firm as general partner expressly agreed to be "subject to all the duties and liabilities of General Partners of the firm as expressed in the Articles of Partnership", he was individually liable to plaintiff who had entered into subordination agreement with respect to securities then in his account prior to time defendant in question had become general partner despite Partnership Law § 28 which limits his liability to his interest in the partnership. Wisnouse v Telsey (1973, SD NY) 367 F. Supp. 855, CCH Fed Secur L Rep P 94215

ARTICLE 4
RELATIONS OF PARTNERS TO ONE ANOTHER

§ 40. Rules determining rights and duties of partners

§ 41. Partnership books
§ 42. Duty of partners to render information
§ 43. Partner accountable as a fiduciary
§ 44. Right to an account
§ 45. Continuation of partnership beyond fixed term

History: Add, L 1919, ch 408, eff Oct 1, 1919.

§ 40. Rules determining rights and duties of partners

The rights and duties of the partners in relation to the partnership shall be determined, subject to any agreement between them, by the following rules:

1. Each partner shall be repaid his contributions, whether by way of capital or advances to the partnership property and share equally in the profits and surplus remaining after all liabilities, including those to partners, are satisfied; and except as provided in subdivision (b) of section twenty-six of this chapter, each partner must contribute toward the losses, whether of capital or otherwise, sustained by the partnership according to his share in the profits.

2. Except as provided in subdivision (b) of section twenty-six of this chapter, the partnership must indemnify every partner in respect of payments made and personal liabilities reasonably incurred by him in the ordinary and proper conduct of its business, or for the preservation of its business or property.

3. A partner, who in aid of the partnership makes any payment or advance beyond the amount of capital which he agreed to contribute, shall be paid interest from the date of the payment or advance.

4. A partner shall receive interest on the capital contributed by him only from the date when repayment should be made.

5. All partners have equal rights in the management and conduct of the partnership business.

6. No partner is entitled to remuneration for acting in the partnership business, except that a surviving partner is entitled to reasonable compensation for his services in winding up the partnership affairs.

7. No person can become a member of a partnership without the consent of all the partners.

8. Any difference arising as to ordinary matters connected with the partnership business may be decided by a majority of the partners; but no act in contravention of any agreement between the partners may be done rightfully without the consent of all the partners.

History: Add, L 1919, ch 408, eff Oct 1, 1919.

Sub 1, amd, L 1994, ch 576, § 9, eff Oct 24, 1994.

Sub 2, amd, L 1994, ch 576, § 9, eff Oct 24, 1994.

CASE ANNOTATIONS

1. In general
2. Agreements, generally
3. Termination, withdrawal or expulsion
4. Profits or surplus
5. Losses and expenses
6. Indemnity
7. Return of contributions and capital
8. Interest on capital contributions
9. Interest on advances beyond required contribution

Partnership Law

10. Management and control
11. Rendition of services
12. – Salary or remuneration
13. Consent for new partners

1. In general

In dispute between joint venturers, court properly looked to partnership law principles, since joint venture is "special combination of 2 or more persons where in some specific venture a profit is jointly sought" and is, in sense, partnership for limited purpose. Gramercy Equities Corp. v Dumont (1988) 72 N.Y.2d 560, 534 N.Y.S.2d 908, 531 N.E.2d 629

Where both parties requested an accounting of a leather goods business in which they were concededly partners, in an action for dissolution of partnership and for an accounting, accounting for the leather goods business should have been ordered where the business allegedly was the source, at least in part, of the funds used for the purchase of real estate in which such parties were held to be partners. Gordon v Ginsberg (1964, 2d Dept) 22 A.D.2d 944, 255 N.Y.S.2d 966

If stock options obtained by an attorney from his client were intended to be a part of the compensation to be paid to his firm for services rendered or if the possibility of securing such options might have presented a partnership opportunity, diversion of such options by such partner to himself would be contrary to the fiduciary duty he owed his partner and would make such conduct actionable regardless of disclosure. Weinrauch v Epstein (1965, 1st Dept) 23 A.D.2d 743, 258 N.Y.S.2d 572, motion gr (1965) 16 N.Y.2d 483

In action to cancel allegedly coerced bill of sale and to recover damages, evidence supported determination that defendant conspired to deprive plaintiff of his half interest in partnership and coerced plaintiff into executing a bill of sale by holding a knife in his ribs, judgment awarding plaintiff $3000 as compensatory damages and $7000 as punitive damages would be modified to delete decretal paragraph also setting aside bill of sale. Rosenzweig v Avzar (1970, 2d Dept) 34 A.D.2d 818, 311 N.Y.S.2d 752

Partnership agreement providing that assignments, encumbrances and agreements "as a result of which any person shall become interested with (assignor) in this firm" would not be allowed unless agreed to by majority of partners, "except for members of his immediate family who have attained majority," was intended to limit partner with respect to his right to assign partnership interest to right to profits; thus partners could not transfer full partnership interest to their children, and such children only had rights as assignees to receive share of partnership income and profits of their assignors. Rapoport v 55 Perry Co. (1975, 1st Dept) 50 A.D.2d 54, 376 N.Y.S.2d 147

While action at law will not ordinarily lie against wrongdoing partner or his agents for otherwise lawful acts committed with intent to harm other partners during duration of partnership, wrongdoing partner can be compelled to account in equity. Erlitz v Segal, Liling & Erlitz (1988, 2d Dept) 142 A.D.2d 710, 530 N.Y.S.2d 848

Partnership of medical doctors was entitled to summary judgment in former partner's action for breach of contract and accounting where former partner failed to prove that partnership's offer to settle dispute, which she rejected, constituted requisite "balance struck" or promise to pay which would permit partner's suit against partnership; moreover, partner's claim for incidental benefits of employment did not fall under exception which would permit partner to maintain action at law against partnership when no complex accounting is required or when only one transaction is involved which is fully closed but unadjusted. Giblin v Anesthesiology Assoc. (1991, 2d Dept) 171 A.D.2d 839, 567 N.Y.S.2d 775

Business judgment rule could be applied to action arising out of business decisions made by 2 real estate partnerships since rationale of rule, which is usually applied to actions against corporate directors, is equally applicable to partners acting as fiduciaries for partnership and other partners. Levine v Levine (1992, 1st Dept) 184 A.D.2d 53, 590 N.Y.S.2d 439

Court erred in failing to grant partner's motion to dismiss complaint brought against him by another partner where partnership agreement provided that, except in ordinary course of business, no litigation could be commenced unless there was affirmative vote of 75 percent of partnership interests, and it was undisputed that present action was not commenced in ordinary course of business and was approved by only 55.45 percent of partnership interests. Heritage Co. v LaValle (1993, 4th Dept) 199 A.D.2d 1036, 605 N.Y.S.2d 613

In action brought by limited partner against general partners and assignees of mortgage (limited partnership's only asset), wherein plaintiff claimed that general partners converted mortgage and breached their fiduciary duties by pledging mortgage as collateral for non-partnership obligations, court properly concluded that plaintiff was not suited to represent other limited partners based on, inter alia, (1) statement by limited partner that he was not concerned with vindicating rights of other limited partners, and (2) court's conclusion, predicated on several years of litigation before court, that limited partner was not interested in anything beyond what was due him personally. Cialeo v Mehlman (1994, 1st Dept) 210 A.D.2d 67, 619 N.Y.S.2d 276

In action for accounting and breach of partnership agreement which entitled plaintiff to share only in net profits as of date of his termination, plaintiff was nevertheless entitled to disclosure of financial information for 6-month period immediately following his termination, to cover possibility that income which accrued before termination was deferred until after termination. Shabasson v Max E. Greenberg, Trager, Toplitz & Herbst (2000, 1st Dept) 268 A.D.2d 357, 715 N.Y.S.2d 142

This section is identical with § 18 of the Uniform Partnership Act. Colligan v Caprio (1964) 43 Misc. 2d 897, 252 N.Y.S.2d 571

Plaintiff, after working on behalf of defendants in expectation that proposed joint venture, which never came to fruition, would be established between parties, was entitled to injunction restraining defendants from using trade secrets and inventions, which plaintiff brought to defendants or developed during his association with them and which were imparted to them only on basis that joint venture would be created, was entitled to injunction restraining defendants from using name of corporation owned by plaintiff and could recover profits acquired by defendants through use of such secrets, inventions and name. Ewen v Gerofsky (1976) 86 Misc. 2d 913, 382 N.Y.S.2d 651, 201 USPQ 940

Plaintiff, after working on behalf of defendants in expectation that a proposed joint venture, which would relate to field of telephone interconnective devises and which never came to fruition, would be established between the parties as result of continuing negotiations, was entitled to recover sum, together with interest, representing his cash contributions to capital of the proposed venture and the value of equipment and supplies which he furnished defendants, less amount advanced by defendants as patent lawyer's fee for patent obtained by plaintiff. Ewen v Gerofsky (1976) 86 Misc. 2d 913, 382 N.Y.S.2d 651, 201 USPQ 940

Former partner's action against law firm partnership, for breach of covenant of food faith and fair dealing and breach of fiduciary duties under CLS Partn §§ 42 and 43, was not precluded due to uncertainty of amount of damages, uncertainty of partnership profits, or uncertainty attributable to defendant's conduct. Smith v Brown & Jones (1995, Sup) 167 Misc. 2d 12, 633 N.Y.S.2d 436, later proceeding sub nom Stuart v Lane & Mittendorf (1997, 1st Dept) 235 A.D.2d 294, 652 N.Y.S.2d 951, stay den (1997, NY) 1997 N.Y. LEXIS 371 and app den (1997) 89 N.Y.2d 811, 657 N.Y.S.2d 404, 679 N.E.2d 643

2. Agreements, generally

In the absence of prohibitory provisions of statutes or rules of the common law relating to partnerships or considerations of public policy the partners of either a general or limited partnership, as between themselves, may include in the partnership articles any agreement they wish concerning the sharing of profits and losses, priorities of distribution on winding up of the partnership affairs and other matters. If complete, as between the parties, an agreement so made controls. Lanier v Bowdoin (1939) 282 N.Y. 32, 24 N.E.2d 732, reh den (1940) 282 N.Y. 611, 25 N.E.2d 391

Where one partner wrote other partners informing them that due to high costs, certain increases in rates to be charged partnership for care of its cattle and additional labor charge were necessary, other partners, by responding in letter that cattle should be marketed as soon as possible and that any losses incurred would come "off the top" before sharing of receipts, and by failing to object to institution of rate increase at subsequent partnership meetings, implicitly accepted increased cost modification of partnership agreement. Ben-Dashan v Plitt (1977, 4th Dept) 58 A.D.2d 244, 396 N.Y.S.2d 542

In arbitration proceeding pursuant to partnership agreement which provided that arbitrator's award would be "final and binding" on partners, consent of all partners was required to approve settlement agreement which purported to nullify arbitrator's award since it constituted modification of partnership agreement; thus, absent approval of settlement agreement by all partners, Special Term properly confirmed arbitrator's award. In re Fishman (1987, 2d Dept) 126 A.D.2d 546, 510 N.Y.S.2d 670

Complaint based on claim that plaintiff was partner in defendant partnership was properly dismissed on motion for summary judgment where parties' course of dealing and performance under subject agreement contradicted plaintiffs' claim, and there was no objective evidence of manifestation of intent to be bound by terms asserted by plaintiffs, but only their self-serving assertions as to their subjective understanding and private intent. Kantor v Bernstein (1997, 1st Dept) 245 A.D.2d 138, 665 N.Y.S.2d 883

1986 contract between 25-year law partners, providing for plaintiff's repayment, without interest, of debt to defendant from proceeds of future sales of portions of particular premises, was not vitiated by alleged impossibility of performance, even though subject property was later taken off market in accordance with parties' 1989 letter of intent to include that property in shopping center development, where parties were seasoned attorneys, contract specified no deadline for repayment, property could have remained on market for prolonged period despite existence of letter of intent, and no modification of contract was sought before parties' signed letter of intent, which had only one-year term. Lagarenne v Ingber (2000, 3d Dept) 273 A.D.2d 735, 710 N.Y.S.2d 425

Contract between 25-year law partners, providing for plaintiff's repayment, without interest, of debt to defendant from proceeds of future sales of portions of particular premises, was enforceable despite defendant's claims of lack of consideration and substantial nonperformance, even though plaintiff knew that defendant had personal loan obligations with high rate of interest, where contract settled firm debt between parties that was precipitated by fee dispute with defendant's brother, and plaintiff substantially reduced debt with funds derived from sources other than proceeds of sales from subject property. Lagarenne v Ingber (2000, 3d Dept) 273 A.D.2d 735, 710 N.Y.S.2d 425

Contract between 25-year law partners, providing for plaintiff's repayment, without interest, of debt to defendant from proceeds of future sales of portions of particular premises, was enforceable despite defendant's claims of mutual mistake, unconscionability, and breach of fiduciary duty, where (1) record was bereft of evidence indicating anything other than fair and equitable bargaining position between parties at time of execution, and (2) parties' later disagreement as to meaning of "proceeds," after substantial partial payments had been made without interest or dispute, was insufficient to prove any of defendant's claimed grounds for unenforceability. Lagarenne v Ingber (2000, 3d Dept) 273 A.D.2d 735, 710 N.Y.S.2d 425

In action by one law partner against another for claimed overdraws, defendant partner did not prove existence of oral agreement that if his annual draw were less than specified amount in any year, adjustment would be made to increase his draw where (1) plaintiff and partnership accountant both recalled some discussion of such adjustment but could not recall any specific agreement, and (2) although those discussions took place when 1988 partnership agreement was being drafted, neither that agreement nor later amended agreements included such adjustment provision. Lagarenne v Ingber (2000, 3d Dept) 273 A.D.2d 735, 710 N.Y.S.2d 425

Court properly construed partnership agreement in light of federal tax laws and properly received expert testimony thereon where agreement was plainly drafted with eye to tax consequences. Harber Phila. Ctr. City Office v Tokai Bank (2001, 1st Dept) 281 A.D.2d 179, 721 N.Y.S.2d 519, app den 96 N.Y.2d 713, 729 N.Y.S.2d 440, 754 N.E.2d 200

In action by partners for breach of purchase agreement and wrongful takeover of particular partnership office, plaintiffs were entitled to amend their complaint to assert cause of action for accounting, even though they initially asserted that defendant was employee rather than partner but later stipulated that he was partner, where (1) essential operating facts-existence of parties' purchase agreement and its alleged breach-were all set forth in initial complaint, in response to which defendant answered and asserted counterclaim for accounting, and (2) because defendant knew of pertinent factual allegations from outset, plaintiffs' delay in seeking amendment did not substantially prejudice defendant by hindering his case preparation. Morris v Crawford (2001, 3d Dept) 281 A.D.2d 805, 722 N.Y.S.2d 296

In action by partners for breach of purchase agreement, wrongful takeover of particular partnership office, and accounting, defendant was not entitled to summary judgment on ground that action was premature, despite general rule that partners cannot sue each other at law unless there has been accounting, prior settlement, or adjustment of partnership affairs, where (1) parties had not conducted business as partners since 1992, thus limiting period that accounting would need to cover and obviating need for judicial intervention into daily operations of firm, and (2) dismissal of plaintiffs' causes of action pending completion of separate accounting would not serve interest of judicial economy. Morris v Crawford (2001, 3d Dept) 281 A.D.2d 805, 722 N.Y.S.2d 296

Defendant law firm was entitled to summary judgment declaring that execution of new partnership agreement by majority of firm's partners did not result in termination of prior partnership agreement as between plaintiffs and other partners in firm, although new agreement provided that "all preceding partnership agreements among the parties hereto are hereby terminated and superseded," where plaintiffs never signed new agreement; thus, defendant was not partnership-at-will, subject to dissolution upon withdrawal of any partner, when plaintiffs withdrew from firm on day after meeting at which new partnership agreement was approved. Borgeest v Wilson, Elser, Moskowitz, Edelman & Dicker (2001, 1st Dept) 283 A.D.2d 245, 724 N.Y.S.2d 408

Partners were not bound by 99-year lease of real property constituting partnership's only asset, entered into by remaining partners, even if newly discovered partnership agreements were not merely reflective of CLS Partn § 20(1), and could be fairly construed to preclude partners' interference with contemplated or consummated long-term lease, since agreements, on their face, terminated partnership before contemplated lease would expire. Northmon Inv. Co. v Milford Plaza Assocs. (2001, 1st Dept) 284 A.D.2d 250, 727 N.Y.S.2d 419, app den 97 N.Y.2d 677, 738 N.Y.S.2d 291, 764 N.E.2d 395 and app den, motion gr 97 N.Y.2d 743, 742 N.Y.S.2d 599, 769 N.E.2d 345

Partners lacked authority to enter into 99-year lease of real property constituting partnership's only asset, even if such lease were to be deemed in ordinary course of partnership's business; partners could not impose their decision to enter into lease on remaining partners, and remaining partners' right to interfere with lease or any other contract or prospective contract involving partnership was absolute and privileged, excusable, and justified. Northmon Inv. Co. v Milford Plaza Assocs. (2001, 1st Dept) 284 A.D.2d 250, 727 N.Y.S.2d 419, app den 97 N.Y.2d 677, 738 N.Y.S.2d 291, 764 N.E.2d 395 and app den, motion gr 97 N.Y.2d 743, 742 N.Y.S.2d 599, 769 N.E.2d 345

Under this section, the rules determining rights and duties of partners are expressly "subject to any agreement between them." Napoli v Domnitch (1962) 34 Misc. 2d 237, 226 N.Y.S.2d 908, mod on other grounds (1962, 2d Dept) 18 A.D.2d 707, 236 N.Y.S.2d 549, affd (1964) 14 N.Y.2d 508, 248 N.Y.S.2d 228, 197 N.E.2d 623

Where the parties partnership agreement clearly laid out how to calculate each parties' capital contribution, it was error for the lower court to ignore the agreement and to, instead, apply N.Y. Partnership Law § 40. Sexter v Kimmelman (2005, 1st Dept) 19 A.D. 3d 298, 798 N.Y.S.2d 409

3. Termination, withdrawal or expulsion

The partners may include in the partnership articles any agreement they wish concerning the sharing of profits, and if the agreement is complete as between the parties, it will control. Lanier v Bowdoin (1939) 282 N.Y. 32, 24 N.E.2d 732, reh den (1940) 282 N.Y. 611, 25 N.E.2d 391

Provision of medical partnership agreement authorizing involuntary expulsion of a partner on majority vote of copartners was not unlawful; court could not frustrate intention of the parties by superimposing a good faith requirement on the right of expulsion, at least so long as the provisions for dismissal worked no undue penalty or unjust forfeiture, or invalid overreaching or other violation of public policy. Gelder Medical Group v Webber (1977) 41 N.Y.2d 680, 394 N.Y.S.2d 867, 363 N.E.2d 573, 87 ALR3d 321

It is proper to include in a partnership agreement a provision authorizing withdrawal or expulsion of a partner; while there is no common law or statutory right to expel a member of a partnership, partners may provide for an involuntary dismissal of one of their number, with or without cause. Gelder Medical Group v Webber (1977) 41 N.Y.2d 680, 394 N.Y.S.2d 867, 363 N.E.2d 573, 87 ALR3d 321

Even if bad faith might limit otherwise absolute language of medical partnership agreement authorizing involuntary expulsion, there was no showing of bad faith expulsion of one partner since embarrassing situations developed, affecting the physicians and their patients, as a result of the expelled partner's conduct, however, highly motivated his conduct might have been; it was as important, therefore, in the group's eyes, as anything affecting survival of the group that it be disassociated from the expelled member's conflict-producing conduct. Gelder Medical Group v Webber (1977) 41 N.Y.2d 680, 394 N.Y.S.2d 867, 363 N.E.2d 573, 87 ALR3d 321

In a suit brought by a withdrawing partner of a Limited Liability Partnership (LLP) for an accounting and for breach of contract, a trial court order holding the remaining partners liable to the withdrawing partner for an accounting was upheld on appeal as N.Y. Partnership Law § 26(b) did not shield the general partner of the LLP from personal liability for breaches of the partnership's or partners' obligations to each other. Since no formal written agreement existed governing the LLP, the provisions of § 26(b) applied. Ederer v Gursky (2007) 9 NY3d 514, 851 NYS2d 108, 881 NE2d 204, reargument den (2008) 10 NY3d 780, 857 NYS2d 15, 886 NE2d 776.

N.Y. Partnership Law § 26(b) does not shield a general partner in a registered limited liability partnership from personal liability for breaches of the partnership's or partners' obligations to each other. Ederer v Gursky (2007) 9 NY3d 514, 851 NYS2d 108, 881 NE2d 204, reargument den (2008) 10 NY3d 780, 857 NYS2d 15, 886 NE2d 776.

Where partnership agreement expressly provided for involuntary expulsion of partner, there was no public policy requirement good faith. Gelder Medical Group v Webber (1976, 3d Dept) 53 A.D.2d 994, 385 N.Y.S.2d 867, affd (1977) 41 N.Y.2d 680, 394 N.Y.S.2d 867, 363 N.E.2d 573, 87 ALR3d 321

A partner, who had been constructively removed from an accounting partnership when the other partners dissolved the partnership and formed two different partnerships from which he was excluded, was properly granted summary judgment compensating him for the value of his interest based on the formular governing involuntary removal of a partner in the buy-sell provisions of the partnership agreement, rather than the value of his interest based on the terms of the dissolution agreement, where the terms of the partnership agreement precluded defendants from continuing the partnership's business under the arrangement described without purchasing plaintiff's interest under the buy-sell agreement; however, defendants would be granted a summary judgment dismissing plaintiff partner's causes of action for tortious interference with contract and for the remainder of his salary, since plaintiff's rights were fully protected and satisfied by his action on the partnership buy-out agreement. Curtin v Glazier (1983, 4th Dept) 94 A.D.2d 434, 464 N.Y.S.2d 899

Partnership agreement which provided that, for purposes of determining inventory shares, outgoing partner's share might be "reduced...to reflect the shares of partners admitted to the Firm" during relevant period, but made no mention of partners leaving firm during such period, could not be read to require increase in inventory sharing percentages to account for such departures. Kushner v Winston & Strawn (1993, 1st Dept) 195 A.D.2d 317, 600 N.Y.S.2d 16

Withdrawing partner was entitled to 1/12 of full fiscal year's net income of partnership where partnership agreement unambiguously gave withdrawing partner his proportionate share of partnership's net income, multiplied by percentage of fiscal year completed as of withdrawal from partnership (here 1/12); to construe agreement otherwise would render meaningless clause requiring estimated amount in cases of uncertainty. Rutkowski v Hill, Betts & Nash (1994, 1st Dept) 206 A.D.2d 258

Clause in partnership's by-laws was not anticompetitive in providing that withdrawing partner was entitled to 10 percent of amount that would be due deceased or retiring partner since it did so without reference to whether or not withdrawing partner did work for partnership's former clients or otherwise competed with partnership. Reiner v Townley & Updike (1997, 1st Dept) 243 A.D.2d 338, 663 N.Y.S.2d 168

Court properly concluded that goodwill was not distributable partnership asset where partnership agreement did not specify that goodwill was asset of firm, no consideration was paid for goodwill on admission of partners, no amounts had been paid or given on account of goodwill, and firm's financial statements did not reflect any goodwill. Kaplan v Joseph Schachter & Co. (1999, 2d Dept) 261 A.D.2d 440, 690 N.Y.S.2d 91

In action between former law partners concerning splitting of contingent fee earned after dissolution of their partnership, defendant earned only 6.5 percent "preparation fee," not 12.5 percent "trial fee," and plaintiff was not required to perform any legal services in that case in order to be entitled to whatever remained of fee after defendant's 6.5 percent share, where those results followed from plain terms of parties' fee-sharing agreement and from defendant's own description of his services in connection with case that generated

contingent fee. Friedman v Eisenstein (1999, 1st Dept) 263 A.D.2d 367, 694 N.Y.S.2d 25

Whether a partnership agreement was originally terminable at will or was directed only to a particular undertaking, it is subject to terms of the written agreement entered into as to how one of the partners may withdraw from the partnership and rights of the remaining partners to purchase his interest in case of withdrawal. Napoli v Domnitch (1962) 34 Misc. 2d 237, 226 N.Y.S.2d 908, mod on other grounds (1962, 2d Dept) 18 A.D.2d 707, 236 N.Y.S.2d 549, affd (1964) 14 N.Y.2d 508, 248 N.Y.S.2d 228, 197 N.E.2d 623

Law firm partnership breached partnership's covenant of good faith and fair dealing, inter alia, by denying withdrawing partner any role in compensation process for his final year in firm, by refusing to give him copy of final compensation materials and opportunity to make bonus recommendations as to other partners, by creating new category of client without putting it to partnership vote and recharacterizing one of his largest billing clients as firm client, by refusing to try to settle with him in good faith, and by directing partners to compensate him for only 2/3 of his final year compensation. Smith v Brown & Jones (1995, Sup) 167 Misc. 2d 12, 633 N.Y.S.2d 436, later proceeding sub nom Stuart v Lane & Mittendorf (1997, 1st Dept) 235 A.D.2d 294, 652 N.Y.S.2d 951, stay den (1997, NY) 1997 N.Y. LEXIS 371 and app den (1997) 89 N.Y.2d 811, 657 N.Y.S.2d 404, 679 N.E.2d 643

Amendment of a law firm partnership agreement's withdrawal provisions by a majority vote of partnership shares was valid against partners who withdrew after the vote and did not violate the unanimous consent provisions of N.Y. P'ship Law § 40(8); the agreement provided for majority rule, and 31 previous amendments passed by unanimous consent did not negate its clear and unambiguous terms. Bailey v Fish & Neave (2006, App Div, 1st Dept) 814 NYS2d 104

4. Profits or surplus

Former partners of law firm did not lose all their financial rights in law partnership by reason of their breach of fiduciary duty, and were entitled to recover their respective shares of firm profits accruing until their respecting departures from firm, but they were not entitled to their inventory interest which would have included future profits, where acts that they engaged in after their departure severely damaged firm's ability to operate its trusts and estates department; moreover, the breach was not a substantial cause of the law firm's lost profits, and recovery thereof would be disallowed. Gibbs v Breed, Abbott & Morgan (2000, 1st Dept) 271 A.D.2d 180, 710 N.Y.S.2d 578

Written memorandum to copartnership agreement which provided for payment of two-thirds of net profits of business to partner subscribing to bulk of copartnership capital, with remaining one-third going to defendant, other partner, who had not contributed anything by way of capital, to effect that thereafter parties to agreement were to be "equal partners in the firm," did not in any way change or modify rights and equities theretofore existing between partners beyond modifying original copartnership agreement as to share in profits to be received by each partner, and accordingly, upon accounting, respective contributions of each partner to capital of firm must be considered and repaid before there can be division of remainder of assets and defendant, under memorandum, is not entitled to equal share of net assets of firm. Gillespie v Gillespie (1924) 124 Misc 881, 210 N.Y.S. 303

There is no requirement, in the absence of provision in the partnership agreement, that a partnership business must strip itself of all of its cash and pay out moneys as profits to partners when such payment may wreck the business or keep it from prospering, merely because in the preceding year it had made some money in its operation. Wolchek v Wecher (1946, Sup) 66 N.Y.S.2d 384, affd (1947) 272 A.D. 912, 72 N.Y.S.2d 273

5. Losses and expenses

As between subsidiaries and parent corporations a provision to share partnership losses under an oral partnership agreement in the same ratio as partnership profits would readily be implied, where the only written agreement in evidence referred exclusively only to the subsidiary and in no way bound their parent corporations, and there was an overarching oral partnership agreement among the parent corporations and the parent subsidiaries, in conformity with which the subordinate partnership between the subsidiaries pursuant to their written partnership agreements was the implementing instrumentality. Louis Dreyfus Corp. v ACLI International, Inc. (1980) 52 N.Y.2d 736, 436 N.Y.S.2d 268, 417 N.E.2d 562, reh den (1981) 52 N.Y.2d 1072

In action to recover defendants' alleged proportionate share of plaintiff partnership's negative net worth pursuant to terms of partnership agreement, plaintiff was not entitled to summary judgment, and defendants were entitled to complete discovery, where defendants, who were former partners whose interests were allegedly terminated for failure to meet capital call, asserted (1) that they received their partnership interests due to their status as key employees of corporation, whose principals were their co-partners in partnership at issue, (2) that they were promised that they would be protected from losses, (3) that such promise was fulfilled until they left employ of corporation under hostile circumstances, (4) that underlying capital call was first made in plaintiff's 8-year history, and (5) that capital contributions made by remaining partners in response to capital call were refunded by partnership after defendants' default. Aggen Rd. Citrus Grove v Kousi (1992, 1st Dept) 180 A.D.2d 563, 580 N.Y.S.2d 267

The Partnership Law recognizes the reciprocal obligations of the partners to bear their respective share of the partnership expenses merely as an incident of the partnership relationship and not as a condition to their participation in the benefits and profits to it. Greenstone v Klar (1947, Sup) 69 N.Y.S.2d 548, mod on other grounds (1947) 272 A.D. 892, 71 N.Y.S.2d 201

6. Indemnity

Where one joint venturer, managing business of joint venture, alone commits intentional fraud against third parties resulting in recovery of damages by them, he is not thereafter entitled to be indemnified by other joint venturer, since acts constituting intentional fraud may not be considered to constitute "ordinary and proper conduct" of business under CLS Partn § 40. Gramercy Equities Corp. v Dumont (1988) 72 N.Y.2d 560, 534 N.Y.S.2d 908, 531 N.E.2d 629

Under subd 2 of this section, a partner in a real estate firm was entitled to reimbursement by the partnership for monies paid out to settle an action brought against the partnership based on an instrument which he alone signed as part of the papers closing a real estate deal, notwithstanding that his signing of the particular paper turned out to have been unwise, where his partner had known about and acquiesced for many years in his closing titles without legal assistance. Kraemer v Gallagher (1962, 2d Dept) 18 A.D.2d 676, 235 N.Y.S.2d 874

Payments by a partner in settlement of an action by architects retained by the partnership were incurred in the reasonable operation of the partnership and became a partnership charge for which a second partner became responsible pro rata when the partnership assets were insufficient to satisfy the first partner's claim and the first partner is entitled to indemnity for the sums expended to satisfy the architects' claim. Schuler v Birnbaum (1978, 4th Dept) 62 A.D.2d 461, 405 N.Y.S.2d 351

Defendant former partners of plaintiff were not entitled to summary judgment where plaintiff raised triable issues of fact as to his implied equitable right, as guarantor of partnership debt, to seek reimbursement from them. Tanenbaum v Dolgin (1998, 2d Dept) 251 A.D.2d 492, 673 N.Y.S.2d 1022

Plaintiff was entitled to indemnification for expenses incurred under parties' partnership agreement where those expenses were incurred in good faith and without gross negligence in furtherance of partnership business interests. Nave v Dunbar Partners (1998, 1st Dept) 255 A.D.2d 159, 679 N.Y.S.2d 582

Defendant corporate general partner and its employees were entitled to pay legal fees related to defense of action from assets of restaurant operated by limited partnership where (1) limited partnership agreement specifically provided for defendants' indemnification, including attorney fees that might be "paid as incurred," barring fraud, willful misconduct, or prohibition by law, and (2) plaintiff's unsubstantiated allegations of fraud and misconduct were insufficient to bar indemnification under that provision. Meyerson v Tullman (2001, 1st Dept) 281 A.D.2d 170, 721 N.Y.S.2d 517

Under subd 2 of this section, providing that a partnership must indemnify every partner in respect of payments made and personal liabilities reasonably incurred in ordinary and proper conduct of its business, etc., unless it is established that the claim sued on arises from an isolated transaction and all partners are not joined in the action, the partners should be required to determine their respective claims in an equity action where there can be final settlement of the partnership affairs so that "personal liabilities reasonably incurred" by each partner on behalf of the partnership may be determined. Colligan v Caprio (1964) 43 Misc. 2d 897, 252 N.Y.S.2d 571

7. Return of contributions and capital

In plaintiff's action to recover its initial capital contribution in partnership that was unsuccessful in achieving main purpose for which it was formed, breach of contract claim was properly dismissed where plaintiff was afforded no right under terms of partnership agreement to return of its initial capital contribution, or to recoup expenses incurred in carrying on partnership business. Non-Linear Trading Co. v Braddis Assocs. (1998, 1st Dept) 243 A.D.2d 107, 675 N.Y.S.2d 5

Limited partner had limited obligation to restore deficit in its capital account on dissolution of partnership where (1) provision of partnership agreement increasing general partner's capital account by "the amount of Partnership liabilities for which the General Partner is personally liable following dissolution and winding up of the Partnership" was properly construed, in light of relevant federal tax law, to attribute to general partner assumption by its constituent general partners partnership liability, thus resulting in general partner's having positive capital account on dissolution and thus triggering limited partner's deficit restoration obligation, and (2) immediately following clause of agreement, stating "except to the extent such liabilities are not then legally enforceable against the General Partner," was properly construed to refer to claims discharged in bankruptcy or barred by Statute of Limitations, so as to give both clauses effect. Harber Phila. Ctr. City Office v Tokai Bank (2001, 1st Dept) 281 A.D.2d 179, 721 N.Y.S.2d 519, app den 96 N.Y.2d 713, 729 N.Y.S.2d 440, 754 N.E.2d 200

Partners may agree, as between themselves, that any contribution to the capital of the concern shall be regarded as a loan, but that as to the rest of the world the transaction shall represent a contribution to capital. In re Probst's Estate (1903) 40 Misc 431, 82 N.Y.S. 396

Under provisions of written agreement underlying dissolved partnership, one partner was entitled first to recover advances made to partnership from proceeds of dissolution, and second partner was then entitled to 25% of remainder of such proceeds. Auld v Estridge (1976) 86 Misc. 2d 895, 382 N.Y.S.2d 897

8. Interest on capital contributions

In the absence of an agreement, a partner is not ordinarily entitled to interest on contributions to capital, since he must rely upon the profits of the business to compensate him for his investment. McGibbon v Tarbox (1912) 205 N.Y. 271, 98 N.E. 390

The right to charge interest upon one's share of the partnership funds basically depends upon the contract between the parties. Levy v Leavitt (1931) 257 N.Y. 461, 178 N.E. 758

Defendant kept proceeds from the sale of properties for himself without notifying the other partners or engaging in the allocation of expenses, profits and losses called for by the agreement, and thus there was no date on which repayment of defendant's capital contributions should have been made, and interest never became payable. Sutton v Burdick, 135 A.D.3d 1016, 22 N.Y.S.3d 633 (3d Dep't 2016).

Partnership agreement broadly provided that all of partners were to contribute any capital that they deemed necessary to the operation of the business partnership and could make additional capital contributions if they saw fit, and thus one section of the statute did not apply, and defendant's contention that the referee should have awarded him interest on his capital contributions to certain entities was rejected. Sutton v Burdick, 135 A.D.3d 1016, 22 N.Y.S.3d 633 (3d Dep't 2016).

9. Interest on advances beyond required contribution

Partner who managed the business and who was under no obligation to contribute to its capital was at liberty to finance venture by loans and when he borrowed money on his own behalf and furnished it to venture he was entitled to interest on that money. Levy v Leavitt (1931) 257 N.Y. 461, 178 N.E. 758

To the extent that a partnership agreement fails to impose an obligation upon the partners to furnish capital requisite for the conduct of the business, the parties to the contract must intend that money will be borrowed to carry on the business and that interest will be paid on such money; therefore, where partner pays money to the partnership beyond his partnership obligation, it is a reasonable inference that the parties intended that such payment should be a loan and bear interest. M. & C. Creditors Corp. v Pratt (1938) 172 Misc 695, 17 N.Y.S.2d 240, affd (1938) 255 A.D. 838, 7 N.Y.S.2d 662, affd (1939) 281 N.Y. 804, 24 N.E.2d 482

Under provisions of written agreement underlying dissolved partnership, one partner was entitled first to recover advances made to partnership from proceeds of dissolution, and second partner was then entitled to 25% of remainder of such proceeds. Auld v Estridge (1976) 86 Misc. 2d 895, 382 N.Y.S.2d 897

10. Management and control

Ambiguities on face of 1985 agreement, as well as contemporaneously executed distribution agreement, raised issue of fact as to whether signatories intended to supersede super-majority voting provision of 1978 agreement, which required 60-percent vote of general partners. 187 Concourse Assocs., L.P. v Stonecrest Mgmt. (1997, 1st Dept) 238 A.D.2d 179, 655 N.Y.S.2d 957

Plaintiff, as a general partner, had an equal right to manage and conduct partnership business and an absolute right to see and examine partnership business books, and where he had been denied access to those books and records, he was permitted to examine the defendant, a general partner who had acted as accountant for the partnership. Romeo v Russo (1969, 2d Dept) 31 A.D.2d 935, 299 N.Y.S.2d 7

All partners are fiduciaries of one another; however, in traditional partnership, each partner has absolute and equal statutory right to manage business. People v Zinke (1989, 1st Dept) 147 A.D.2d 106, 541 N.Y.S.2d 986, app den (1989) 74 N.Y.2d 749, 545 N.Y.S.2d 124, 543 N.E.2d 767 and app gr (1989) 74 N.Y.2d 822, 546 N.Y.S.2d 580, 545 N.E.2d 894 and motion gr (1989) 75 N.Y.2d 764, 551 N.Y.S.2d 904, 551 N.E.2d 105 and revd on other grounds (1990) 76 N.Y.2d 8, 556 N.Y.S.2d 11, 555 N.E.2d 263

In action for damages arising from business decisions made by 2 real estate partnerships in which plaintiffs alleged that partnerships breached fiduciary duty to them by freezing them out of decisions which affected all partners equally, defendants were entitled to summary judgment where plaintiffs never sought to be involved in decision making process or to be kept informed but instead relied on one partner (their father) to represent their interests. Levine v Levine (1992, 1st Dept) 184 A.D.2d 53, 590 N.Y.S.2d 439

In action to foreclose mortgage executed by 2 general partners of defendant partnership, plaintiffs were properly granted summary judgment and appointment of referee where (1) record did not support partnership's conclusory allegations of fraud, and (2) issues as to scope of power of attorney granted by third partner, and whether general partners exceeded their authority by granting mortgage in first instance, were irrelevant because general partners were acting within scope of partnership agreement when they granted mortgage to plaintiffs in effort to discharge mechanics lien that arose after partnership was unable to pay for work performed and materials provided. Todd Welch Constr. v Peregrine Partners (2000, 3d Dept) 270 A.D.2d 786, 705 N.Y.S.2d 713

In a partnership between the mother and father and their son, the trial court properly granted the son's motion seeking a determination that the conveyance of one third of the partnership property to the executrix by the mother and father prior to dissolution of the partnership was null and void because (1) the transfer of the property effectively made the executrix a partner to the partnership, and it was undisputed that the son did not consent to the transfer of the partnership property; and (2) the transfer of the property to the executrix did not fall within N.Y. Partnership Law § 40(8) because it was not an ordinary matter connected with the partnership business that could be decided by a majority of the partners. Forbes v Six-S Country Club (2004, A.D., 4th Dept) 785 N.Y.S.2d 209

Under §§ 10, 11, 40, there cannot be a partnership where the whole management is vested in one partner. Wild v Commissioner (1933, CA2) 62 F.2d 777, 3 USTC P 1032, 11 AFTR 1376

11. Rendition of services

Express stipulations for services are not necessary, inasmuch as in the absence of any express agreement to the contrary, a partner is impliedly bound to devote himself reasonably to the advancement of the corporation of which he has become a member. Barclay v Barrie (1913) 209 N.Y. 40, 102 N.E. 602

There is an inherent difference between obligations of a partner to render services in the partnership business and his obligation to provide capital. Levy v Leavitt (1931) 257 N.Y. 461, 178 N.E. 758

Absent express agreement otherwise, plaintiff, as coventurer, had no right to compensation for services rendered in furtherance of joint venture. Levy v Keslow (1997, 1st Dept) 235 A.D.2d 293, 652 N.Y.S.2d 292

12. – Salary or remuneration

In the absence of other agreements profits constitute a partner's reward for services rendered and there is no right to other compensation based on the reasonable value of the services actually rendered

even though they be extraordinary. Levy v Leavitt (1931) 257 N.Y. 461, 178 N.E. 758

The principle that one partner is not entitled to compensation for services rendered by him on behalf of the partnership is relevant only to partnerships where such partner has an equal interest, is equally liable, and equally responsible for the conduct of the partnership business, but the principle does not apply where the interest, liabilities and responsibilities of the general partners and the special partners are not equal. Steinberg v Goodman (1970) 27 N.Y.2d 304, 317 N.Y.S.2d 342, 265 N.E.2d 758

In the absence of agreement a partner is not entitled to compensation for his services in disposing of firm assets after discontinuance of business. Hapworth v Grievson (1938) 255 A.D. 927, 8 N.Y.S.2d 700

A co-partner, in the absence of special agreement, is not entitled to be paid for services rendered in the partnership business and in the absence of a full accounting, cannot maintain an action at law against partners for a claim arising therefrom. Cohen v Erdle (1953) 282 A.D. 569, 126 N.Y.S.2d 32

Coventurer did not have claim in quantum meruit where, by express terms of joint venture agreement governing parties' relationship, coventurer was to provide services to venture and receive in exchange 45 percent to 50 percent of any profits realized on sale of real property that was subject of venture; that extent of services required was unforeseen or underestimated at time of agreement did not entitle coventurer to additional compensation. Levy v Keslow (1997, 1st Dept) 235 A.D.2d 293, 652 N.Y.S.2d 292

Managing partners' reduction of compensation of plaintiff, who was hired as employee but was promised that he would become partner on certain date, was novation that he ratified by remaining at merged accounting firm for 4 months after old agreement was terminated, until he found other employment. Muhlstock v Cole (1997, 1st Dept) 245 A.D.2d 55, 666 N.Y.S.2d 116, 135 CCH LC ¶ 58396

Managing partners were not entitled to setoff against amount of their improper reduction of firm employee's compensation where sum allegedly wrongfully collected by employee while at his subsequent employer for work done at partners' firm was deposited in escrow account awaiting judge's decision. Muhlstock v Cole (1997, 1st Dept) 245 A.D.2d 55, 666 N.Y.S.2d 116, 135 CCH LC ¶ 58396

Attorney could not be precluded from being paid his agreed-on retirement income while he continued to practice law where parties' partnership agreement contained unenforceable provision that improperly restricted his practice of law on his retirement and implicated prohibition against sharing legal fees with nonattorneys. Sage v Polansky (1998, 2d Dept) 251 A.D.2d 567, 673 N.Y.S.2d 614

Partners are not entitled to charge each other, or the firm of which they are members, for services in the care and management of the business of the copartnership unless there is a special agreement to that effect. McDermott v Rossney Contracting Corp. (1928) 131 Misc 759, 228 N.Y.S. 1, mod on other grounds (1928) 225 A.D. 784, 232 N.Y.S. 804

On death of one of partners surviving partner is entitled to reasonable compensation for services in winding up partnership affairs. In re Belden's Estate (1932) 143 Misc 159, 256 N.Y.S. 162

No credit may be allowed surviving partners for their liquidating services where articles of partnership provide for no such compensation. In re Witkind's Estate (1938) 167 Misc 885, 4 N.Y.S.2d 933

Retirement agreement restriction on retiring partner's right to practice law as condition to payment of retirement benefits is legitimate exception to CLS Code of Prof Resorts DR 2-108 prohibition against restricting attorney's right to practice law by agreement among counsel, but restriction ceases to apply if retiree abandons right to benefits under agreement. Graubard Mollen Horowitz Pomeranz & Shapiro v Moskovitz (1990, Sup) 149 Misc. 2d 481, 565 N.Y.S.2d 672, summary judgment den (1994, 1st Dept) 204 A.D.2d 218, 612 N.Y.S.2d 39, affd, ctfd ques ans (1995) 86 N.Y.2d 112, 629 N.Y.S.2d 1009, 653 N.E.2d 1179 (criticized in Champion Titanium Horseshoe v Wyman-Gordon Inv. Castings (1996, SD NY) 925 F. Supp. 188)

Policy of trusts and estates department of defendant law firm, whereby firm partner who acted as executor for estate was required to make up difference to extent of his or her executor's commissions when he or she acted as executor for estate and firm did not collect full amount of its fees for work performed in connection with estate, was not enforceable where stipulation of settlement on estate was less than fee requested on law firm's fee application; if enforced, policy would place plaintiff partner in serious conflict of interest.

Gibbs v Breed, Abbott & Morgan (1996, Sup) 170 Misc. 2d 493, 649 N.Y.S.2d 974

Where neither partner is a surviving partner, neither is entitled to compensation for services in winding up the affairs of the partnership; each partner is entitled to credit for whatever is fair for expenses incurred and reasonable overhead in connection with his services in carrying out the winding up of the partnership business. Geist v Burnstine (1940, Sup) 19 N.Y.S.2d 76

Only partner who is entitled to compensation for winding up the affairs of a partnership, in the absence of a special agreement, is a surviving partner. Geist v Burnstine (1940, Sup) 19 N.Y.S.2d 76

13. Consent for new partners

At the heart of the partnership concept is the principle that partners may choose with whom they wish to be associated. Gelder Medical Group v Webber (1977) 41 N.Y.2d 680, 394 N.Y.S.2d 867, 363 N.E.2d 573, 87 ALR3d 321

In absence of partners' written consent as required by limited partnership agreement, party did not acquire partnership interest by virtue of one partner's assignment to her of right to receive portion of his partnership profits. Whalen v Gerzof (1990) 76 N.Y.2d 914, 563 N.Y.S.2d 46, 564 N.E.2d 656, subsequent app (1994, 3d Dept) 206 A.D.2d 688, 615 N.Y.S.2d 465, app den (1994) 84 N.Y.2d 809, 621 N.Y.S.2d 518, 645 N.E.2d 1218

Under provisions of partnership law, unless parties have agreed otherwise, person cannot become member of partnership without consent of all partners, whereas assignment of partnership interest may be made without consent, but assignee is entitled only to receive profits of assigning partner. Rapoport v 55 Perry Co. (1975, 1st Dept) 50 A.D.2d 54, 376 N.Y.S.2d 147

Where corporation and third person, as joint-adventurers, leased patent machine and formed corporation to operate machine, the obligations of the parties toward each other were similar to those of a partnership, and the assignee of third person was barred from active participation in the enterprise over the objections of the corporation. Schlesinger v Regenstreif (1954) 26 Misc. 2d 604, 135 N.Y.S.2d 858

The discretionary, subjective judgment that necessarily goes into the partnership promotion process of a large law firm, and the application to that process of Partnership Law § 40(7), allowing the unanimous consent of the partners for selection of a new partner, are not limited by the application of Title VII of the Civil Rights Act of 1964 except to preclude factors of race, color, religion, sex, or national origin from being considered in this promotion process. If the Partnership Law is inconsistent with the application of Title VII, Title VII, which expressly pre-empts state law contrary to it, controls. Lucido v Cravath, Swaine & Moore (1977, SD NY) 425 F. Supp. 123, 14 BNA FEP Cas 353, 13 CCH EPD P 11432

Arbitrators did not manifestly disregard the law by concluding that a partner's voting agreement with third parties did not transfer a partnership interest in violation of N.Y. P'ship Law §§ 40(7) and 53(1) as the agreement merely concerned a vote for the retention of an entity as a managing agent, which vote the partner was entitled to cast with or without the agreement; the panel found that there was no claim that the entity sought to become a partner, only that a partner agreed to vote on a specific limited issue, and that invalidating the voting agreement would undermine an option agreement, which furthered the interests of the partnership and continuity of its business. Wien & Malkin LLP v Helmsley-Spear, Inc. (2006) 813 NYS2d 691, 846 NE2d 1201, reported at (2006, NY) 2006 NY LEXIS 270

Children of the original partners in two partnerships were not entitled to full partnership rights because while a partnership was usually dissolved upon the death of a partner under N.Y. P'ship Law § 62(4), the surviving partners, in effect, created a new partnership at will as they continued to operate the business of the former partnerships; because no evidence was presented that defendant partner consented under N.Y. P'ship Law § 40(7) to the bequest or assignment of the original partners' interests to their children, the children were not entitled to an ownership in what was considered a new entity partnership. Sperber v Rubell (2008, Sup) 239 NYLJ 55, app withdrawn (2009, 1st Dept) 63 App Div 3d 479, 879 NYS2d 715.

§ 41. Partnership books

The partnership books shall be kept, subject to any agreement between the partners, at the principal place of business of the partnership, and every partner shall at all times have access to and may inspect and copy any of them.

History: Add, L 1919, ch 408, eff Oct 1, 1919.

CASE ANNOTATIONS

General rule regarding business partnerships is that books should be kept open to inspection of any partner at all reasonable times, even after dissolution, subject, however, to special agreement. Sanderson v Cooke (1931) 256 N.Y. 73, 175 N.E. 518

This section stating that partnership books shall be kept at principal place of business of partnership and every partner shall have access to and may inspect and copy any of them, refers to a going partnership. Sanderson v Cooke (1931) 256 N.Y. 73, 175 N.E. 518

A partner's rights with regard to the partnership books are not absolute, and he may be restrained from using the information gathered from inspecting them for other than partnership purposes; application to examine partnership books may be refused if it is made in bad faith, or if the examination is desired for improper purposes. Sanderson v Cooke (1931) 256 N.Y. 73, 175 N.E. 518

Plaintiff, as a general partner, had an equal right to manage and conduct partnership business and an absolute right to see and examine partnership business books, and where he had been denied access to those books and records, he was permitted to examine the defendant, a general partner who had acted as accountant for the partnership. Romeo v Russo (1969, 2d Dept) 31 A.D.2d 935, 299 N.Y.S.2d 7

In a Grand Jury probe concerning possible tax and other offenses, a motion to quash subpoenas duces tecum was properly denied where the exclusionary rule was not applicable to Grand Jury proceedings, where the secrecy requirements of the Tax Law were not violated in that tax information could be turned over to the Attorney-General for investigation, and where the papers of the husband-and-wife partnership being investigated were not private in that partnership records held by one of the partners were possessed in a representative capacity. In re Grand Jury Proceedings (1982, 2d Dept) 89 A.D.2d 605, 452 N.Y.S.2d 643

Even after removal of minority shareholder from his positions as officer and director of 8 related corporations and partnerships, he retained right to inspect books of those entities in order to determine true value of his shares in response to buy-out offer where he was still partner in partnerships and shareholder in corporations. Berkowitz v Astro Moving & Storage Co. (1997, 2d Dept) 240 A.D.2d 450, 658 N.Y.S.2d 425

Plaintiff's action to recover its initial capital contribution in partnership that was unsuccessful in achieving main purpose for which it was formed sufficiently stated cause of action for accounting, to which plaintiff was absolutely entitled, and for judicial dissolution if parties did not agree to voluntarily dissolve partnership, where record reflected defendant's failure to provide complete information regarding disposition of partnership funds. Non-Linear Trading Co. v Braddis Assocs. (1998, 1st Dept) 243 A.D.2d 107, 675 N.Y.S.2d 5

The books of a partnership belong to all of the partners, and each partner has equal rights thereto unless there is a contrary agreement, express or implied. People v Phillips (1955) 207 Misc 205, 137 N.Y.S.2d 697

In a limited partnership, the limited partners have the right to have the partnership books kept at the principal place of business and to inspect and copy them. United States v Silverstein (1963, CA2 NY) 314 F.2d 789, 63-1 USTC P 9346, 11 AFTR 2d 1025, cert den (1963) 374 US 807, 10 L Ed 2d 1031, 83 S Ct 1696

Where a non-managing partner in real estate syndicates cast in form of general partnerships made partial assignments of portions of his partnership interest, the partial assignees had some property rights in the partnership books and records. United States v Silverstein (1965, SD NY) 237 F. Supp. 446, 65-1 USTC P 9266, 15 AFTR 2d 283, affd (1965, CA2 NY) 344 F.2d 1016, 65-2 USTC P 9480, 15 AFTR 2d 991, cert den (1965) 382 US 828, 15 L Ed 2d 73, 86 S Ct 65

§ 42. Duty of partners to render information

Partners shall render on demand true and full information of all things affecting the partnership to any partner or the legal representative of any deceased partner or partner under legal disability.

History: Add, L 1919, ch 408, eff Oct 1, 1919.

Partnership Law

CASE ANNOTATIONS

The fact that the relations between copartners have become strained does not relieve them from the duties of good faith and disclosure. In re Silkman (1907) 121 A.D. 202, 105 N.Y.S. 872, affd (1908) 190 N.Y. 560, 83 N.E. 1131

Constructive trust would be placed on 1/3 of assets of new partnership where 2 of 3 partners in venture which leased building space to their family business secretly withdrew funds from existing partnership and used them to form new partnership-from which third partner was excluded-purpose of which was to lease additional space to family business; 2 partners' secret conduct constituted breach of their duty to third partner which deprived her of partnership opportunity. Sandler v Fishman (1990, 2d Dept) 157 A.D.2d 708, 549 N.Y.S.2d 808

Plaintiff's action to recover its initial capital contribution in partnership that was unsuccessful in achieving main purpose for which it was formed sufficiently stated cause of action for accounting, to which plaintiff was absolutely entitled, and for judicial dissolution if parties did not agree to voluntarily dissolve partnership, where record reflected defendant's failure to provide complete information regarding disposition of partnership funds. Non-Linear Trading Co. v Braddis Assocs. (1998, 1st Dept) 243 A.D.2d 107, 675 N.Y.S.2d 5

Plaintiff established his entitlement to accounting for partnership funds where both parties testified that they purchased property in question as partners with funds obtained through mortgage given by defendant on his residence, defendant took title to property in his own name although it belonged to partnership, defendant sold property but failed to inform plaintiff of sale or account for its proceeds, and defendant admitted diverting net proceeds to his own use. Chamberlain v Amato (1999, 4th Dept) 259 A.D.2d 1048, 688 N.Y.S.2d 345

Each partner has the right to know all that the other knows, and their connection is one of great confidence. Schneider v Brenner (1929) 134 Misc 449, 235 N.Y.S. 55

Good faith requires not only that every partner should not make any false representations to his partners, but also that he abstain from all concealments which may be injurious to the partnership business. Schneider v Brenner (1929) 134 Misc 449, 235 N.Y.S. 55

Law firm partnership breached its duty under CLS Partn § 42 where, after excluding partner from compensation process for year in which he resigned from partnership, it failed to give him all financial information regarding compensation process when he requested it and when he asked to be made part of process, thereby breaching its obligation to turn over all information pertaining to partnership's finances. Smith v Brown & Jones (1995, Sup) 167 Misc. 2d 12, 633 N.Y.S.2d 436, later proceeding sub nom Stuart v Lane & Mittendorf (1997, 1st Dept) 235 A.D.2d 294, 652 N.Y.S.2d 951, stay den (1997, NY) 1997 N.Y. LEXIS 371 and app den (1997) 89 N.Y.2d 811, 657 N.Y.S.2d 404, 679 N.E.2d 643

§ 43.   Partner accountable as a fiduciary

1. Every partner must account to the partnership for any benefit, and hold as trustee for it any profits derived by him without the consent of the other partners from any transaction connected with the formation, conduct, or liquidation of the partnership or from any use by him of its property.

2. This section applies also to the representatives of a deceased partner engaged in the liquidation of the affairs of the partnership as the personal representatives of the last surviving partner.

History: Add, L 1919, ch 408, eff Oct 1, 1919.

CASE ANNOTATIONS

1. In general
2. When fiduciary relationship begins
3. Duration and termination of relationship
4. Nature of relationship
5. Effect of assignment of interest
6. Particular activities as violation of relationship
7. – Acquisition or renewal of property rights for own benefit
8. – Solicitation of partnership accounts

9. Accounting
1. In general

A partner may not retain for himself alone benefits from the firm relationship or from any act of his which constitutes a breach of duty to the firm. Lord v Hull (1904) 178 N.Y. 9, 70 N.E. 69

Co-adventures are subject to same fiduciary duties and obligations as partners. Endries v Paddock (1934) 241 A.D. 195, 271 N.Y.S. 848, affd (1935) 267 N.Y. 526, 196 N.E. 562

Failure to file a certificate of partnership as required by the Penal Law does not deprive the partnership of its right of action for breach of a fiduciary duty. Frey v St. Lawrence Residence Club, Inc. (1945) 269 A.D. 300, 55 N.Y.S.2d 849

In a Grand Jury probe concerning possible tax and other offenses, a motion to quash subpoenas duces tecum was properly denied where the exclusionary rule was not applicable to Grand Jury proceedings, where the secrecy requirements of the Tax Law were not violated in that tax information could be turned over to the Attorney-General for investigation, and where the papers of the husband-and-wife partnership being investigated were not private in that partnership records held by one of the partners were possessed in a representative capacity. In re Grand Jury Proceedings (1982, 2d Dept) 89 A.D.2d 605, 452 N.Y.S.2d 643

In action for damages arising from business decisions made by 2 real estate partnerships in which plaintiffs alleged that payment of commissions to business owned by defendant partner's children was improper, partnerships were not entitled to summary judgment where it was alleged that business owned by partner's children acted as selling agent for cooperative conversions, that one of partnerships paid all business expenses associated with cooperative sales, and that commissions on cooperative sales were nevertheless paid to business owned by partner's children. Levine v Levine (1992, 1st Dept) 184 A.D.2d 53, 590 N.Y.S.2d 439

In action on bond, defendant partnership failed to raise triable issue of fact as to its offset defense where (1) it claimed that plaintiff was mere nominee of her husband, who was its former managing partner, and that it was entitled to offset because of his mismanagement of partnership, (2) financial schedule allegedly prepared by accounting firm and purporting to show partnership losses due to mismanagement by plaintiff's husband was not verified or certified and thus lacked evidentiary value, and (3) although claim against plaintiff's husband for breach of fiduciary duty was subject of separate, pending lawsuit, no evidence of liability or damages in that case was offered in support of present defense. Spodek v Park Prop. Dev. Assocs. (1999, 2d Dept) 263 A.D.2d 478, 693 N.Y.S.2d 199, 130, 130D motion filed (2000) 94 N.Y.2d 760, 706 N.Y.S.2d 81 and subsequent app (2001, 2d Dept) 279 A.D.2d 467, 719 N.Y.S.2d 109, app gr (2001) 96 N.Y.2d 711, 727 N.Y.S.2d 696, 751 N.E.2d 944 and affd (2001) 96 N.Y.2d 577, 733 N.Y.S.2d 674, 759 N.E.2d 760

Former partners of law firm did not lose all their financial rights in law partnership by reason of their breach of fiduciary duty, and were entitled to recover their respective shares of firm profits accruing until their respecting departures from firm, but they were not entitled to their inventory interest which would have included future profits, where acts that they engaged in after their departure severely damaged firm's ability to operate its trusts and estates department; moreover, the breach was not a substantial cause of the law firm's lost profits, and recovery thereof would be disallowed. Gibbs v Breed, Abbott & Morgan (2000, 1st Dept) 271 A.D.2d 180, 710 N.Y.S.2d 578

If the activities of the errant partner are in anywise traceable to the business or assets of the partnership venture, they will be treated as part of the venture. In re Kohn's Estate (1952) 26 Misc. 2d 659, 116 N.Y.S.2d 167, affd (1953) 282 A.D. 1045, 126 N.Y.S.2d 897

If the activities of an errant joint venturer are in any way traceable to the business or assets of the venture they will be treated as part of the venture. This standard of rigid fair-dealing is especially high when the self-dealing party is manager of the enterprise. In re Kohn's Estate (1952) 26 Misc. 2d 659, 116 N.Y.S.2d 167; affd (1953) 282 A.D. 1045, 126 N.Y.S.2d 897

The general principle that an action at law may not be maintained by one partner against another for any claim arising from partnership business until after an accounting has been had is inapplicable where the partners by their own acts submit to the court what amounts to a substantial account of their respective contributions to the business and the status of its affairs and it appears that the partnership has already ceased operation as a going concern. Fazio v Tracy (1963) 39 Misc. 2d 172, 240 N.Y.S.2d 412

One partner cannot secretly or clandestinely take advantage of his position to better himself at the expense of his copartner. Sorenson v Nielsen (1930, Sup) 240 N.Y.S. 250

Partners are not relieved of fiduciary duties by strained relations between them. Newburger, Loeb & Co. v Gross (1977, CA2 NY) 563 F.2d 1057, 1977, CCH Fed Secur L Rep P 96148, 1977-2 CCH Trade Cases P 61604, 24 FR Serv 2d 42, cert den (1978) 434 US 1035, 54 L Ed 2d 782, 98 S Ct 769 and appeal after remand (1979, CA2 NY) 611 F.2d 423, 28 FR Serv 2d 602

Violation of fiduciary duty to general partner was not excused by allegations that general partner was attempting to use limiting partners for his own purposes, where limited partners were the general partner's sister and secretary and all had a common interest in preventing fraudulent transfer of partnership's assets. Newburger, Loeb & Co. v Gross (1977, CA2 NY) 563 F.2d 1057, 1977, CCH Fed Secur L Rep P 96148, 1977-2 CCH Trade Cases P 61604, 24 FR Serv 2d 42, cert den (1978) 434 US 1035, 54 L Ed 2d 782, 98 S Ct 769 and appeal after remand (1979, CA2 NY) 611 F.2d 423, 28 FR Serv 2d 602

2. When fiduciary relationship begins

Prior to the formation of a partnership, the individuals of which it is to be composed are merely parties to a contract to form the partnership, and do not assume toward each other the fiduciary obligations which characterize the relations of partners. Sivin v Jones (1930) 138 Misc 234, 244 N.Y.S. 541

A person who contemplated forming a partnership was not permitted to appropriate to himself alone the gain from buying property at a low figure and selling it to the partnership at a higher figure, such property being that in which the partnership enterprise was designed to deal. R. C. Gluck & Co. v Tankel (1960) 24 Misc. 2d 841, 199 N.Y.S.2d 12, affd (1961, 1st Dept) 12 A.D.2d 339, 211 N.Y.S.2d 602

3. Duration and termination of relationship

A partnership was legally dissolved when the partners determined to discontinue business and a partner's fiduciary relationship terminated at that time although the partnership affairs had not been wound up. Bayer v Bayer (1926) 215 A.D. 454, 214 N.Y.S. 322

In an action against a trustee and receiver of a partnership in liquidation to impress a trust on real property which had been transferred by the trustee and for an accounting, the trial court properly ruled that plaintiff was only entitled to an accounting for the period of the receivership, and with respect to the period of time after defendant had commenced operation of the incorporated country club plaintiff's remedy was a shareholder's action and not an action against the receiver. Oliner v Bess (1981, 2d Dept) 81 A.D.2d 658, 438 N.Y.S.2d 368, app den (1981) 54 N.Y.2d 610

Court would remove general partner, without compensation, where he was found to have breached his fiduciary duty to his fellow general and limited partners by forcing abandonment of conversion of partnership's primary asset to cooperative ownership at time when it could have netted substantial profits, even though amount of financial harm caused to partnership was not sufficiently proved at trial. Drucker v Mige Assocs. II (1996, 1st Dept) 225 A.D.2d 427, 639 N.Y.S.2d 365, app den (1996) 88 N.Y.2d 807, 647 N.Y.S.2d 164, 670 N.E.2d 448

Until the partnership relation is at a definite factual and judicial end, the legal immunity of one partner from subtle or open attack by the other must remain impregnable. Boxill v Boxill (1952) 201 Misc 386, 111 N.Y.S.2d 33

Although partner's duties to his copartners may be relaxed in relationship that looks to the future of a newly dissolved partnership, a partner's duty of good faith and full disclosure continues as to dealings affecting winding up of the partnership and the proper preservation of partnership assets during that period. Lavin v Ehrlich (1974) 80 Misc. 2d 247, 363 N.Y.S.2d 50

Although the partners had agreed to dissolve, the fiduciary relationship continued and a partner could be required to account for profits from a transaction involving partnership property where the actual dissolution did not take place until a time subsequent to the transaction complained of. Pearlstein v Baff (1945, Sup) 60 N.Y.S.2d 713, revd on other grounds (1946) 270 A.D. 1043, 63 N.Y.S.2d 710, amd on other grounds (1946) 271 A.D. 834, 65 N.Y.S.2d 851, affd (1947) 296 N.Y. 881, 72 N.E.2d 613

Although a managing partner withdrew from the partnership, since, under the partnership agreement, his capital remained in the firm and he continued to share in the partnership's profits and losses, a fiduciary duty was still owed to him. Newburger, Loeb & Co. v Gross (1977, CA2 NY) 563 F.2d 1057, 1977, CCH Fed Secur L Rep P 96148, 1977-2 CCH Trade Cases P 61604, 24 FR Serv 2d 42, cert den

(1978) 434 US 1035, 54 L Ed 2d 782, 98 S Ct 769 and appeal after remand (1979, CA2 NY) 611 F.2d 423, 28 FR Serv 2d 602

4. Nature of relationship

The fiduciary obligation of a partnership usually arises upon the coagulation of property, profits, or other interests with which the parties can then be said to hold jointly and which are made accessible to each other in terms of the confidential relationship existing between joint associates. Steinbeck v Gerosa (1958) 4 N.Y.2d 302, 175 N.Y.S.2d 1, 151 N.E.2d 170, app dismd (1958) 358 US 39, 3 L Ed 2d 45, 79 S Ct 64 and (criticized in Bay Casino, LLC v M/V Royal Empress (1998, ED NY) 1998 US Dist LEXIS 19713)

Good faith requires that no partner make a secret profit out of the undertaking. Schneider v Brenner (1929) 134 Misc 449, 235 N.Y.S. 55

Fiduciary duties owed to a partner are the duties of good faith, fairness, and loyalty in dealings with him regarding partnership business. Newburger, Loeb & Co. v Gross (1977, CA2 NY) 563 F.2d 1057, 1977, CCH Fed Secur L Rep P 96148, 1977-2 CCH Trade Cases P 61604, 24 FR Serv 2d 42, cert den (1978) 434 US 1035, 54 L Ed 2d 782, 98 S Ct 769 and appeal after remand (1979, CA2 NY) 611 F.2d 423, 28 FR Serv 2d 602

In a nondischargeability proceeding, the court noted that the language of N.Y. P'ship Law § 43 was insufficient by itself to establish a fiduciary relationship between the debtor and creditor, who were equal partners in a law firm, for purposes of 11 U.S.C.S. § 523(a)(4). However, as the debtor was in charge of overseeing the expenses of the firm and its books and records, it furthered the creditor's contention that the debtor be held to a high standard of loyalty and that a fiduciary duty existed under New York common law. Cho v Tuan (In re Tuan) (2013, BC DC NJ) 2013 Bankr LEXIS 1932 (UNPUBLISHED).

5. Effect of assignment of interest

Under the rule that an assignment of an interest does not of itself dissolve the partnership a plaintiff's right to hold his partner to his fiduciary duty was not affected by the assignment of his interest to his wife where the business had never been treated as dissolved and the interest had been reassigned prior to the time of the action. Meinhard v Salmon (1928) 249 N.Y. 458, 164 N.E. 545, 62 ALR 1

6. Particular activities as violation of relationship

Uncle, who owned 50 percent of property, owed fiduciary duty to niece and nephew, each of whom owned 25 percent, regardless of whether their business arrangement constituted partnership, joint venture, or tenancy in common, and thus in accounting proceeding court properly ruled that uncle could not charge against property fees paid to his wife for her services in developing property absent full disclosure and assent of niece and nephew; asserted charge against property was for services which uncle was obligated to perform without direct compensation, and his financial relationship with his wife violated precept of undiluted trust at core of his fiduciary responsibilities. Birnbaum v Birnbaum (1989) 73 N.Y.2d 461, 541 N.Y.S.2d 746, 539 N.E.2d 574, reconsideration den (1989) 74 N.Y.2d 843, 546 N.Y.S.2d 559, 545 N.E.2d 873

Where a partner in a law firm received stock options solely as an inducement for him to enter into the employ of a client and the firm as such was fully compensated for its services in the matter by a payment of $25,000, it was held that there was no departure from the high standard of fidelity imposed upon partners and the other partner in such firm was accordingly not entitled to any relief as to such options. Weinrauch v Epstein (1965, 1st Dept) 23 A.D.2d 743, 258 N.Y.S.2d 572, motion gr (1965) 16 N.Y.2d 483

If stock options obtained by an attorney from his client were intended to be a part of the compensation to be paid to his firm for services rendered or if the possibility of securing such options might have presented a partnership opportunity, diversion of such options by such partner to himself would be contrary to the fiduciary duty he owed his partner and would make such conduct actionable regardless of disclosure. Weinrauch v Epstein (1965, 1st Dept) 23 A.D.2d 743, 258 N.Y.S.2d 572, motion gr (1965) 16 N.Y.2d 483

The trial court properly dismissed a cause of action, brought by a limited partner against general partners and their wholly owned corporation, for breach of duty in failing to distribute net profits and maintenance of excessive reserves, where the general partners explained that a cash reserve fund of $5 to $6 million was reasonable, due to the age and physical condition of the building which was the subject of the partnership, necessary repairs ordered by the city, and alterations which often accompany the procurement of new and lucrative tenancies, was reasonable, where plaintiff submitted no evidence to counter their explanation, and where the partnership agreement directed that the general partners were to set up reasonable reserves at their discretion. Weckstein v Breitbart (1985, 1st Dept) 111 A.D.2d 6, 488 N.Y.S.2d 665

Constructive trust would be placed on 1/3 of assets of new partnership where 2 of 3 partners in venture which leased building space to their family business secretly withdrew funds from existing partnership and used them to form new partnership-from which third partner was excluded-purpose of which was to lease additional space to family business; 2 partners' secret conduct constituted breach of their duty to third partner which deprived her of partnership opportunity. Sandler v Fishman (1990, 2d Dept) 157 A.D.2d 708, 549 N.Y.S.2d 808

Plaintiff's action to recover its initial capital contribution in partnership that was unsuccessful in achieving main purpose for which it was formed sufficiently stated cause of action for accounting, to which plaintiff was absolutely entitled, and for judicial dissolution if parties did not agree to voluntarily dissolve partnership, where record reflected defendant's failure to provide complete information regarding disposition of partnership funds. Non-Linear Trading Co. v Braddis Assocs. (1998, 1st Dept) 243 A.D.2d 107, 675 N.Y.S.2d 5

Limited partner defendants assumed fiduciary duty to plaintiff limited partner when they took over control of partnership, and breached that duty when they settled dispute with general partners without contacting plaintiff; measure of plaintiff's damages was amount he would have received had he been party to settlement agreement. Goldwasser v Geller (1999, 1st Dept) 257 A.D.2d 489, 684 N.Y.S.2d 210, motion den, app dismd (1999) 93 N.Y.2d 954, 694 N.Y.S.2d 344, 716 N.E.2d 179 and subsequent app (2001, 1st Dept) 279 A.D.2d 297, 718 N.Y.S.2d 349

In action by former partners of defendant law firm for monies due to them under their partnership agreement, trial court properly determined that plaintiffs breached their fiduciary duty as partners of firm they were about to leave by supplying confidential employee information to firm they were about to join; however, neither plaintiffs' discussion of joint move to another firm, nor taking their desk copies of correspondence with good faith belief that they were entitled to do so, breached any duty to their former firm. Gibbs v Breed, Abbott & Morgan (2000, 1st Dept) 271 A.D.2d 180, 710 N.Y.S.2d 578

The uncompromising hostility of the courts to self dealings can find no better field for application than a situation where, at a time when the venture was first beginning to realize a profit in its dealings, one of the partners took the opportunity to use the firm credit and secure for himself a highly profitable arrangement in connection with the purchase of bonds and securities. In re Kohn's Estate (1952) 26 Misc. 2d 659, 116 N.Y.S.2d 167, affd (1953) 282 A.D. 1045, 126 N.Y.S.2d 897

One who engineered a Russian stamp deal while abroad and sold a one-half interest to plaintiff by representing that the deal involved $250,000, whereas the purchase price was only $125,000, became trustee of any benefit or profit realized by him from formation, conducting, or liquidating the joint venture. R. C. Gluck & Co. v Tankel (1960) 24 Misc. 2d 841, 199 N.Y.S.2d 12, affd (1961, 1st Dept) 12 A.D.2d 339, 211 N.Y.S.2d 602

Law firm partnership breached its fiduciary duty under CLS Partn § 43 by failing to include former partner in compensation process for year in which he resigned from partnership. Smith v Brown & Jones (1995, Sup) 167 Misc. 2d 12, 633 N.Y.S.2d 436, later proceeding sub nom Stuart v Lane & Mittendorf (1997, 1st Dept) 235 A.D.2d 294, 652 N.Y.S.2d 951, stay den (1997, NY) 1997 N.Y. LEXIS 371 and app den (1997) 89 N.Y.2d 811, 657 N.Y.S.2d 404, 679 N.E.2d 643

Trial court erred in granting summary judgment to limited partners who claimed that general partners had breached their fiduciary duty under Partnership Law § 43. If a rental agreement allowed noncollection of rent for periods when a business was experiencing financial difficulties, the general partners had not breached a fiduciary duty. Carella v Scholet (2006, 3d Dept) 34 App Div 3d 915, 824 NYS2d 185

Local managing partner of 2 housing projects that breached partnership agreements requiring general partners to "exercise their responsibilities in a fiduciary capacity," also breached its fiduciary duty under CLS Partn § 43 by benefitting from its dealings with its identity-of-interest companies without consent of supervising partners, entitling supervising partners to accounting with respect to all transactions between partnerships, managing partner and identity-of-interest companies regardless of when entered into. NCAS Realty Mgmt. Corp. v National Corp. for Hous. Pshps. (1998, CA2 NY) 143 F.3d 38

General partner (GP) engaged in self-dealing to the detriment of a "Class Z" limited partner and another limited partner when the GP sought conversion of a limited partnership (LP) to a Delaware limited liability company without disclosure requested by the Class Z limited partner and the other limited partner. The Class Z limited partner's potential loss of interest in the LP justified complete disclosure of the state of the LP's financial affairs. Miller v Ross (2007, Sup) 237 NYLJ 39, later proceeding (2007, NY App Div, 1st Dept) 2007 NY App Div LEXIS 4092, later proceeding (2007, 1st Dept) 43 App Div 3d 730, 841 NYS2d 586

Threat of instituting litigation against one general partner on a meritless claim in order to coerce him into coercing limited partners to approve a transfer of partnership assets was a breach of fiduciary duty. Newburger, Loeb & Co. v Gross (1977, CA2 NY) 563 F.2d 1057, 1977, CCH Fed Secur L Rep P 96148, 1977-2 CCH Trade Cases P 61604, 24 FR Serv 2d 42, cert den (1978) 434 US 1035, 54 L Ed 2d 782, 98 S Ct 769 and appeal after remand (1979, CA2 NY) 611 F.2d 423, 28 FR Serv 2d 602

7. – Acquisition or renewal of property rights for own benefit

A partner may not secretly acquire outstanding title to affirm property and set it up against his copartner. Mitchell v Reed (1874) 61 N.Y. 123

A partner may not obtain a renewal of a partnership lease for his own purposes, to commence after the expiration of the original lease. Mitchell v Reed (1874) 61 N.Y. 123

The limited partners of a partnership were entitled to a partial summary judgment dissolving their partnership with two other partners due to a breach of fiduciary duty by the general partner and another limited partner where defendant partners had individually guaranteed the obligations of a restauranteur on an equipment lease with another partnership composed of the limited partners of the first partnership, the restauranteur defaulted and assigned the equipment lease to the first partnership, and defendant partners caused such partnership to agree to indemnify them for their obligations on the lease and their guarantee to the other partnership, and where the indemnity agreement was clearly detrimental to the first partnership and constituted self-dealing by defendant partners. May v Flowers (1984, 4th Dept) 106 A.D.2d 873, 483 N.Y.S.2d 551, app dismd without op (1985) 64 N.Y.2d 611 and app dismd without op (1985) 65 N.Y.2d 637

Partner that purchased sole partnership property (real estate) from other partner was liable to selling partner for restitutionary damages for breach of contract where selling partner had bargained for contract clause by which purchasing partner represented that it intended to construct new building on premises and would commence "substantial construction activity" within 2 years, but instead conducted only preparatory work, and then sold property to third party at substantial profit. Elmsmere Assoc. v Gladstone (1989, 1st Dept) 153 A.D.2d 501, 545 N.Y.S.2d 136, app den, clarified, in part (1989, 1st Dept) 153 A.D.2d 821, appeal after remand (1991, 1st Dept) 172 A.D.2d 451, 568 N.Y.S.2d 952, app den (1991) 78 N.Y.2d 864, 578 N.Y.S.2d 879, 586 N.E.2d 62

Defendant partner breached his fiduciary responsibility to his fellow general and limited partners where he derailed profitable conversion of partnership's building into cooperative apartment through his unwarranted demands that, if met, would have resulted in him receiving amount of money in excess of what other general partners were going to obtain and would have reduced amount that was left over for limited partners. Drucker v Mige Assocs. II (1996, 1st Dept) 225 A.D.2d 427, 639 N.Y.S.2d 365, app den (1996) 88 N.Y.2d 807, 647 N.Y.S.2d 164, 670 N.E.2d 448

General partner who breached his fiduciary duty to partnership should not have been awarded any management fees and insurance commissions with regard to conversion of partnership building into cooperative apartment where he was completely uninvolved in partnership and his purported exposure, as general partner, to partnership's legal liabilities, as well as arrangement made between original partners, was insufficient basis on which to make such award given circumstances of his conduct which resulted in partnership being forced to forego its efforts to effect conversion. Drucker v Mige Assocs. II (1996, 1st Dept) 225 A.D.2d 427, 639 N.Y.S.2d 365, app den (1996) 88 N.Y.2d 807, 647 N.Y.S.2d 164, 670 N.E.2d 448

Because the former partners had removed funds from the law firm and deposited them into their present partnership account, they breached their fiduciary duty to the old law firm, as those funds were connected with the liquidation of the partnership as envisioned in N.Y. P'ship Law § 43(1); thus, the former partners were jointly and severally liable. If the law firm's remaining partners had made similar deposits of funds involving a former client, they too were subject to joint and several liability to the extent those funds exceeded those owed by the former partners. Sexter v Kimmelman (2007, 1st Dept) 43 App Div 3d 790, 844 NYS2d 183

Attorney's claim that a Chapter 7 debtor who was a partner in a law firm that was dissolved diverted money the firm was owed to himself and a new firm he created was sufficient to survive the debtor's motion to dismiss the attorney's claims that a judgment the attorney obtained in state court was nondischargeable under 11 U.S.C.S. § 523(a)(4) and (a)(6), and that the debtor should be denied a discharge under 11 U.S.C.S. § 727(a)(2)(A), (a)(3), (a)(4)(A), and (a)(5). The debtor was a fiduciary under the New York Partnership Law during the period the law firm was being dissolved. Shiboleth v Yerushalmi (In re Yerushalmi) (2008, BC ED NY) 393 BR 288, 50 BCD 215, judgment entered, cause dismd (2008, BC ED NY) 2008 Bankr LEXIS 2603.

Where some general partners transferred partnership assets to a corporation and in return obtained forgiveness of their capital arrearages, there was self-dealing in violation of the fiduciary duty owed other partners. Newburger, Loeb & Co. v Gross (1977, CA2 NY) 563 F.2d 1057, 1977, CCH Fed Secur L Rep P 96148, 1977-2 CCH Trade Cases P 61604, 24 FR Serv 2d 42, cert den (1978) 434 US 1035, 54 L Ed 2d 782, 98 S Ct 769 and appeal after remand (1979, CA2 NY) 611 F.2d 423, 28 FR Serv 2d 602

8. – Solicitation of partnership accounts

As matter of public policy, preresignation surreptitious "solicitation" of law firm's clients for partner's personal gain is actionable as breach of fiduciary duty owed to firm by partner; such conduct exceeds what is necessary to protect important value of client freedom of choice in legal representation, and thoroughly undermines loyalty owed partners. Graubard Mollen Dannett & Horowitz v Moskovitz (1995) 86 N.Y.2d 112, 629 N.Y.S.2d 1009, 653 N.E.2d 1179 (criticized in Champion Titanium Horseshoe v Wyman-Gordon Inv. Castings (1996, SD NY) 925 F. Supp. 188)

Attorney's actions, on preparing for departure from firm, in secretly attempting to lure law firm clients (even those attorney has brought into firm and personally represented) to new firm, lying to clients about their rights with respect to choice of counsel, lying to partners about plans to leave, and abandoning firm on short notice (taking clients and files), would not be consistent with partner's fiduciary duties. Graubard Mollen Dannett & Horowitz v Moskovitz (1995) 86 N.Y.2d 112, 629 N.Y.S.2d 1009, 653 N.E.2d 1179 (criticized in Champion Titanium Horseshoe v Wyman-Gordon Inv. Castings (1996, SD NY) 925 F. Supp. 188)

Where attorney is dissatisfied with existing association with other attorneys, taking steps to locate alternative space and affiliations would not violate partner's fiduciary duties, and as matter of ethics, departing partners are permitted to inform firm clients with whom they have prior professional relationship about their impending withdrawal and new practice, and to remind client of its freedom to retain counsel of its choice; ideally, such approaches should take place only after notice to firm of partner's plans to leave. Graubard Mollen Dannett & Horowitz v Moskovitz (1995) 86 N.Y.2d 112, 629 N.Y.S.2d 1009, 653 N.E.2d 1179 (criticized in Champion Titanium Horseshoe v Wyman-Gordon Inv. Castings (1996, SD NY) 925 F. Supp. 188)

In action against defendant who breached his fiduciary duty to his former partners, jury improperly computed damages by apparent reference to each plaintiff's percentage of full value of partnership at time of its termination, as partnership was terminable at will and thus defendant could not be held liable for ending his own participation in partnership even if it caused termination of partnership; damages should have been computed solely with reference to then-present value (including opportunities for profit) to partnership of any accounts actually solicited by defendant for his new business during his partnership relationship with plaintiffs and successfully diverted to that new business. Byrne v Keefe (1995, 1st Dept) 217 A.D.2d 529, 629 N.Y.S.2d 764

A partner may not quietly solicit a partnership account for himself to the detriment of the partnership. Sorenson v Nielsen (1930, Sup) 240 N.Y.S. 250

9. Accounting

While action at law will not ordinarily lie against wrongdoing partner or his agents for otherwise lawful acts committed with intent to harm other partners during duration of partnership, wrongdoing partner can be compelled to account in equity. Erlitz v Segal, Liling & Er litz (1988, 2d Dept) 142 A.D.2d 710, 530 N.Y.S.2d 848

In action by alleged partners for accounting and breach of contract against managing partners of merged accounting firm, defendants' counterclaim for breach of fiduciary duty was properly dismissed where plaintiffs were justified in seeking professional association elsewhere after defendants wrongfully reduced plaintiffs' compensation, plaintiffs did not solicit defendants' clients away from their firm, and it would be inequitable to prevent plaintiffs from reacquiring their own former clients. Muhlstock v Cole (1997, 1st Dept) 245 A.D.2d 55, 666 N.Y.S.2d 116, 135 CCH LC ¶ 58396

§ 44.   Right to an account

Any partner shall have the right to a formal account as to partnership affairs:

1. If he is wrongfully excluded from the partnership business or possession of its property by his copartners,

2. If the right exists under the terms of any agreement,

3. As provided by section forty-three,

4. Whenever other circumstances render it just and reasonable.

History: Add, L 1919, ch 408, eff Oct 1, 1919.

CASE ANNOTATIONS

1. In general
2. Accounting as prerequisite to suit at law
3. – Exceptions
4. Parties
5. When action will lie
6. – Agreement
7. – Doctrine of "unclean hands"
8. – Termination, withdrawal, or expulsion
9. Accounting of illegal business
10. Laches
11. Limitation of actions
12. Accountability for profits and earnings
13. Accountability for secret profits
14. Allowance of interest
15. – Compound interest
16. Accounts stated
17. Practice and procedure

1. In general

"Interim accounting" voluntarily rendered by general partners did not provide complete documentary defense to accounting sought by limited partner since (1) "interim accounting" failed to account for any income, or capital of, or loan to partnership, or to allocate any costs it purported to report, (2) general partner had not sworn to its accuracy, and (3) accounting firm that prepared it disclaimed any responsibility for its accuracy and disavowed any suggestion that it certified its truth. CCG Assoc. I v Riverside Assoc. (1990, 1st Dept) 157 A.D.2d 435, 556 N.Y.S.2d 859

Allegation of wrongdoing is not indispensable element of demand for accounting where complaint indicates fiduciary relationship between parties or some other special circumstance warranting equitable relief. Morgulas v J. Yudell Realty, Inc. (1990, 1st Dept) 161 A.D.2d 211, 554 N.Y.S.2d 597

Although proposition that law practice has no good will is consequence of ethical concerns that sale of law practice would necessarily involve disclosure of client confidences, such concerns do not come into play in contexts other than sale, in particular in partnership dissolution. Dawson v White & Case (1995, 1st Dept) 212 A.D.2d 385, 622 N.Y.S.2d 269, reh den (1995, N.Y. A.D., 1st Dept) 1995 N.Y. A.D. LEXIS 5560 and app dismd (1995) 86 N.Y.2d 837, 634 N.Y.S.2d 445, 658 N.E.2d 223 and app gr (1996) 87 N.Y.2d 806, 641 N.Y.S.2d 597, 664 N.E.2d 508 and mod on other grounds, affd, remanded (1996) 88 N.Y.2d 666, 649 N.Y.S.2d 364, 672 N.E.2d 589

Good will was not a distibutable asset of a law firm, where the partners had impliedly so agreed prior to the dissolution of the firm. Dawson v White & Case (1995, 1st Dept) 212 A.D.2d 385, 622 N.Y.S.2d 269, reh den (1995, N.Y. A.D., 1st Dept) 1995 N.Y. A.D. LEXIS 5560 and app dismd (1995) 86 N.Y.2d 837, 634 N.Y.S.2d 445, 658 N.E.2d 223 and app gr (1996) 87 N.Y.2d 806, 641 N.Y.S.2d 597,

664 N.E.2d 508 and mod, affd, remanded (1996) 88 N.Y.2d 666, 649 N.Y.S.2d 364, 672 N.E.2d 589

Absent provision in partnership agreement specifying method of accounting, whether cash or accrual, to be used on dissolution of partnership, accrual method is to be used. McDonald v Fenzel (1996, 1st Dept) 224 A.D.2d 261, 638 N.Y.S.2d 15, motion den, remanded on other grounds (1996, 1st Dept) 233 A.D.2d 219, 650 N.Y.S.2d 9

Court erred when, without hearing, it summarily accepted accounting filed by defendants despite numerous fact issues raised by plaintiff, including whether plaintiff's share was properly determined under application of generally accepted accounting principles, and whether defendants did not account for contingency fees of dissolved law partnership. McDonald v Fenzel (1996, 1st Dept) 233 A.D.2d 219, 650 N.Y.S.2d 9

Where partner, in action for accounting and involuntary dissolution of partnership, alleged demand and failure to account, he established right to accounting. 220-52 Assocs. v Edelman (1997, 1st Dept) 241 A.D.2d 365, 659 N.Y.S.2d 885, later proceeding (1998, 1st Dept) 253 A.D.2d 352, 676 N.Y.S.2d 566, app dismd (1998) 92 N.Y.2d 1026, 684 N.Y.S.2d 490, 707 N.E.2d 445

The liability in equity for the use of the property of another comprehends the gains realized by the converter of property from his use thereof. This principle does not end with the appropriation of property belonging solely to another. It extends as well to the case where the malefactor has an interest in the property. Partners are thus obliged to account to each other; and each is responsible to the other for the fruits of wrongfully appropriated partnership property. Hasday v Barocas (1952) 10 Misc. 2d 22, 115 N.Y.S.2d 209

2. Accounting as prerequisite to suit at law

As a general rule partners cannot sue each other at law for anything relating to the partnership unless there has been an adjustment, settlement or balance struck and promise to pay. Bankers Trust Co. v Dennis (1939) 256 A.D. 495, 10 N.Y.S.2d 710, affd (1940) 282 N.Y. 635, 25 N.E.2d 981

In action for dissolution of partnership and related relief, Special Term was not warranted in severing part of cross-petition seeking damages and setting matter down for immediate trial, since cross-petitioner alleged that parties' financial disputes were caused by petitioner's fraud, conversion, embezzlement, breach of partnership agreement, and breach of fiduciary duty; such claim for damages would require inspection of partnership books, records, and accounts, and thus its validity must be resolved in action for accounting. Kriegsman v Kraus, Ostreicher & Co. (1987, 1st Dept) 126 A.D.2d 489, 511 N.Y.S.2d 17

Where one of two partners accuses the other of having wrecked partnership property and misappropriated partnership assets the cause is one growing out of the partnership business and an action at law may not be maintained until after an accounting. Duncan v Bruce (1943) 179 Misc 992, 43 N.Y.S.2d 447

As a general rule, suits between partners should be brought in equity, particularly for an accounting, and an action at law may not be maintained by one against the other until after an accounting has been had and a balance struck. Squire v Wing (1962) 35 Misc. 2d 287, 230 N.Y.S.2d 42, affd (1962, 2d Dept) 17 A.D.2d 835, 233 N.Y.S.2d 84

Where one partner gives another partner his promissory note, an action at law will lie on that note without a partnership accounting since the note constitutes an acknowledgment of a separate debt and evidences an intent of the parties to segregate the debt from partnership affairs. Thus, where both plaintiff and defendant partners in an action on a promissory note given by one to the other acknowledge that the debt evidenced by the note is purely personal and not a true aspect of the partnership business, a partnership accounting in Supreme Court is not a prerequisite to the action and the affirmative defense stating that equity court is the exclusive forum must be stricken. Katz v Powers (1978) 92 Misc. 2d 892, 401 N.Y.S.2d 720

Partners cannot sue each other at law for any thing relating to their partnership concerns, unless there has been a settlement and balance struck. Coleman v Purtell (1951, Sup) 115 N.Y.S.2d 712

3. – Exceptions

While the ordinary rule is that suits between partners should be brought in equity and that an action at law may not be maintained until after an accounting, where the general partners covenanted that the limited partner was not to be liable as between them for operating losses and agreed to indemnify him from their individual assets there was a distinct obligation on the general partners to make good the contribution of the limited partner from their own assets

and an action at law could be maintained without a previous accounting. Herrick v Guild (1939) 257 A.D. 341, 13 N.Y.S.2d 115

Partner who attempts to dissolve the partnership before the end of the term agreed upon in the partnership articles is liable in an action at law against him by his copartner for breach of the contract. Burnstine v Geist (1939) 257 A.D. 792, 15 N.Y.S.2d 48

In a declaratory judgment action against a partnership to recover damages and for an accounting, the trial court, in treating defendants motion to dismiss as one for summary judgment, improperly dismissed plaintiffs' cause of action to terminate the partnership interest of defendants and fix appropriate compensation, even though it was well established as a rule that an action at law could not be maintained by one partner against another for any claim arising from the partnership until there had been a full accounting, where the partnership agreement provided that the partnership would terminate the interest of any partner convicted of a crime, where each of the defendants had been convicted of a crime, where the well-established rule was inapplicable to cases that sought declaratory relief, where declaratory judgment was a creature of statute unknown to the common law, where the cause of action thus did not constitute an action at law, and where even if the cause of action were an action at law an exception to the rule would apply, in that the plaintiffs sought to enforce a provision of the partnership agreement that would not necessitate an examination of the partnership accounts; the trial court also erred in dismissing causes of action alleging improper receipt of kickbacks and an accounting to determine the actual losses sustained, even though the cause of action for kickbacks was an action at law, where that action could be maintained, in that it involved a claim that was fully closed but unadjusted, there was no danger of premature piecemeal judgments between partners that could later require adjustment when all the business with the partnership was reviewed, and there was ample evidence in the record to establish that defendants were engaged in illegal conduct in connection with their operation of the partnership, and where an action for an accounting can be maintained even if the partnership has not been terminated; a cause of action seeking reimbursement from defendants for salaries received from the partnership during the period of the alleged illegalities was also improperly dismissed, since the record on appeal supported the claim of disloyalty and an employee may forfeit his right to compensation for services rendered by him during periods of disloyalty. St. James Plaza v Notey (1983, 2d Dept) 95 A.D.2d 804, 463 N.Y.S.2d 523, appeal after remand (1985, 2d Dept) 111 A.D.2d 228, 489 N.Y.S.2d 264, later proceeding (1990, 2d Dept) 166 A.D.2d 439, 560 N.Y.S.2d 670, later proceeding (1990, 2d Dept) 166 A.D.2d 438, 560 N.Y.S.2d 672

4. Parties

An equitable cause of action for an accounting cannot be maintained without the presence of all of the parties before the court. Perlman v Perlman (1932) 235 A.D. 313, 257 N.Y.S. 48

Wife of deceased partner, who received his partnership interest upon his death pursuant to partnership agreement, did not lack legal capacity to maintain action for accounting and injunctive relief on her claim that another partner mismanaged and misappropriated partnership assets; partner's death dissolved partnership as matter of law, but partnership business was not thereby terminated. Parnes v Edelman (1987, 2d Dept) 128 A.D.2d 596, 512 N.Y.S.2d 856

In action seeking equitable relief against copartner and other named defendants in form of accounting, reconveyance of real property to partnership, and imposition of constructive trust, joinder of all partners as necessary parties was not required since (1) action specifically concerned isolated and fully closed transaction, (2) plaintiff was not seeking dissolution or formal accounting, (3) relief was sought against only one partner, and (4) there was no claim that any other partner had not consented to action. Agrawal v Razgaitis (1989, 2d Dept) 149 A.D.2d 390, 539 N.Y.S.2d 496

All partners were necessary parties in action for partnership accounting brought by limited and general partner on behalf of themselves against another general partner. Goodwin v MAC Resources, Inc. (1989, 2d Dept) 149 A.D.2d 666, 540 N.Y.S.2d 477

Investor was entitled to intervene as limited partner, even though all statutory requirements for becoming limited partner pursuant to CLS Partn § 114 might not have been met, where (1) complaint alleged improper accounting of funds, mismanagement, and misuse of assets of limited partnership, and (2) at time suit was brought, investor had acquired 3 percent partnership interest and had satisfactorily fulfilled requirements mandated by partnership agreement to effectively become limited partner. Goldberger v Sonn (1992, 1st Dept) 179 A.D.2d 573, 579 N.Y.S.2d 52, related proceeding (1995, 1st Dept) 212 A.D.2d 430, 622 N.Y.S.2d 711

In action for accounting of Iranian family partnership brought by 3 younger brothers who were to divide 20 percent interest in business while defendant older siblings would each own 20 percent share, intervening plaintiffs who were children of older brother killed in Iran in 1979 had standing to sue since (1) action was not for wrongful death or other claims being asserted on behalf of their father's estate and requiring appointment of personal representative pursuant to CLS EPTL § 11-3.2(b), but was being brought in their own names to secure what was allegedly due them as their father's heirs, and (2) causes of action were not alleged to have arisen before father's death and thus did not abate on his death pursuant to CLS EPTL § 11-3.2. Elghanayan v Elghanayan (1993, 1st Dept) 190 A.D.2d 449, 598 N.Y.S.2d 524

Appellate Division's present decision did not allow unmarried plaintiff to obtain relief reserved to spouses, such as maintenance and equitable distribution of parties' assets, where decision merely gave plaintiff opportunity to show her entitlement to much more limited avenues of redress available regardless of marital status, including fraud, constructive trust, and partnership accounting. Williams v Lynch (1997, 3d Dept) 245 A.D.2d 715, 666 N.Y.S.2d 749, app dismd without op (1998) 91 N.Y.2d 957, 671 N.Y.S.2d 717, 694 N.E.2d 886

Defendants were not entitled to summary judgment dismissing action for partnership accounting on ground that plaintiff was not partner of firm, where there was no written partnership agreement and plaintiff submitted, inter alia, tax schedules listing him as partner, affidavit of firm's former bookkeeper that one defendant told her that plaintiff had been made partner and would be receiving draw instead of salary, and his own affidavit attesting to various ways he participated in management of firm. Rosen v Efros (1999, 1st Dept) 258 A.D.2d 333, 685 N.Y.S.2d 205

Where there is an alleged breach of a general partner's fiduciary duty to the limited partners and claimed wrongful conduct, a representative action will lie in view of the fact that the general partners diverted a substantial portion of the partnership funds received upon sale of partnership's real property to their own use or to the use of several codefendants whom they controlled. Alpert v Haimes (1970) 64 Misc. 2d 608, 315 N.Y.S.2d 332

An action for a partnership accounting cannot be maintained by a person claiming to be a partner whose name was not included in a license issued pursuant to a statute requiring full disclosure of the members of a partnership. Orr v Pfohl (1948, Sup) 84 N.Y.S.2d 23

There may be exceptional circumstances where it is impossible to get jurisdiction over a particular partner, and his presence is then not required for a determination of the issue as between the other partners. Gardiner v Hyde (1955, Sup) 144 N.Y.S.2d 426

5. When action will lie

A copartner who alleges that his copartners are denying the relationship in refusing to give him that participation to which he claims to be entitled in copartnership assets and profits brings himself within the principle that a court of equity will entertain an action for accounting where it is necessary so to do in order to compel one partner to carry out his agreement with another one in the transaction of copartnership business, even though a dissolution is not asked for. Bailly v Betti (1925) 241 N.Y. 22, 148 N.E. 776

An accounting between partners cannot ordinarily be had unless the partnership has terminated or dissolution is demanded, or other facts arise to show the right to a legal accounting. Klenoff v Goodstein (1944) 268 A.D. 510, 51 N.Y.S.2d 919

An unlicensed engineer cannot obtain a partnership for accounting for professional fees earned by a consulting and engineering firm. Griffin v Cafarelli (1972, 2d Dept) 38 A.D.2d 847, 330 N.Y.S.2d 110

Plaintiffs did not create joint venture or establish proprietary right in bankrupt company so as to entitle them to accounting or imposition of constructive trust, and thus trial court properly granted defendant's motion for summary judgment, where defendant had provided all funds for purchase of interest in bankrupt company, plaintiffs' contribution of $20,000 was insufficient to permit plaintiffs to participate in joint venture, plaintiffs failed to specifically allege what services, if any, they had contributed to venture, and plaintiffs did not join in contract for purchase of realty, and thus did not expose themselves to any risk. Liberty Moving & Storage Co. v Bay Shore Moving & Storage, Inc. (1989, 2d Dept) 152 A.D.2d 682, 543 N.Y.S.2d 745, app den (1989) 75 N.Y.2d 701, 551 N.Y.S.2d 905, 551 N.E.2d 106

Although plaintiff was entitled to promised consideration following termination of joint venture, she was not entitled to accounting under Partnership Law and payment of value of her 1/3 interest in joint venture as of date it was terminated on formation of corporation combining plaintiff's and defendant co-venturer's assets since, once parties agreed to conduct business as corporation and implemented agreement forming corporation, they ceased to be partners and had only rights, duties and obligations of stockholders; instead, plaintiff was entitled either to impress trust on 1/3 of shares of stock of corporation, or at her option, to receive value of stock as of date of commencement of action. Sanders v Boelke (1991, 4th Dept) 172 A.D.2d 1014, 569 N.Y.S.2d 272

Defendant was not entitled to summary judgment dismissing cause of action for partnership accounting where there was evidence that could support findings that (1) parties had confidential relationship that was in many respects analogous to that of husband and wife, (2) plaintiff reasonably trusted defendant and relied on him to protect her interests, and (3) in reliance on his promises that she would have life use of his home and other financial benefits, she sold her home, moved in with him, and made substantial contributions of money and labor to upkeep and improvement of his house and grounds; oral partnership agreement was not entirely unenforceable merely because it incorporated promises that could not be fully performed within year or lifetime, and there was no merit in defendant's contention that plaintiff's claim was deficient because services purportedly rendered as her contribution to partnership were not "profits." Williams v Lynch (1997, 3d Dept) 245 A.D.2d 715, 666 N.Y.S.2d 749, app dismd without op (1998) 91 N.Y.2d 957, 671 N.Y.S.2d 717, 694 N.E.2d 886

There can be no accounting between the parties unless dissolution is sought, except where the accounting is necessary to compel enforcement of an agreement in transacting the copartnership business or where some special reason exists to make it necessary or where it is required under the Partnership Law. Friedland v Friedland (1958) 12 Misc. 2d 349, 175 N.Y.S.2d 264

An action for dissolution of a partnership and an accounting can be maintained only if it appears factually that a partnership relation exists. Jones v Jones (1958) 15 Misc. 2d 960, 179 N.Y.S.2d 480

Formal accounting to wind up a limited partnership was appropriate under N.Y. P'ship Law § 44 as it was not disputed that the partnership was dissolved by the retirement of one of the limited partners as provided by the partnership agreement. Lai v Gartlan (2007, App Div, 1st Dept) 845 NYS2d 30

Partners can bring an equitable action for an accounting against co-partners for their alleged wrongful acts against their fellow partners during the period of partnership. Newburger, Loeb & Co. v Gross (1973, SD NY) 365 F. Supp. 1364, CCH Fed Secur L Rep P 94190, 1973-2 CCH Trade Cases P 74766

6. – Agreement

Where several persons agree on terms of a partnership, to begin at a future date, and in order to be ready to transact business on the day in question they proceed with the plans necessary for that purpose, the partners who have been authorized to incur liabilities or expend money in making such preparations may bring an action for an accounting against the other members of the partnership and obtain judgment for the proportionate share the other members of the partnership might pay. Sivin v Jones (1932) 236 A.D. 483, 260 N.Y.S. 91

Partner's death terminated original partnership and created partnership at will where original agreement contained no provision covering contingency of partner's death, and new partnership ended when 2 of remaining 3 partners terminated relationship; thus, third remaining partner had no basis on which to enforce terms of original agreement either with respect to accounting or implementation of restrictive covenant contained therein, and remaining partners would be liable to account to third partner only for his share of new partnership profits and assets to date of its termination. Burger, Kurzman, Kaplan & Stuchin v Kurzman (1988, 1st Dept) 139 A.D.2d 422, 527 N.Y.S.2d 15, app dismd without op (1988) 72 N.Y.2d 909, 532 N.Y.S.2d 757, 528 N.E.2d 1230 and app den (1989) 74 N.Y.2d 606, 544 N.Y.S.2d 820, 543 N.E.2d 85

Plaintiff was entitled to summary judgment in action for accounting of assets of law partnership of which her deceased husband was member since there was no written agreement among members of partnership, and alleged oral agreement of partners, which provided that on death of any one of them interest of his estate in partnership would be limited to proceeds of life insurance policy purchased by

Partnership Law

partnership with wife of partner as beneficiary, was void because it could not be performed within lifetime. Cane v Farmelo (1989, 4th Dept) 151 A.D.2d 1023, 543 N.Y.S.2d 775, later proceeding (1989, 4th Dept) 151 A.D.2d 1024, 543 N.Y.S.2d 966

It was error to dismiss action brought by limited partner to compel accounting where partnership agreement provided that accounting was due on sale "of all or substantially all of the Property," and partnership had sold 99.995 percent of its property. CCG Assoc. I v Riverside Assoc. (1990, 1st Dept) 157 A.D.2d 435, 556 N.Y.S.2d 859

As to the property, although the seller alleged that the purchaser had failed to collect rent and other obligations from the tenants and sought an accounting, there was no written partnership agreement that allowed the partners to call for an accounting, Partnership Law § 44, and the record did not establish that the purchaser breached his fiduciary duty to the seller with respect to the partnership or that other circumstances existed that warranted an accounting; moreover, the evidence at trial established that the seller was active in the partnership and its financial affairs, and there was no evidence to suggest that the seller was excluded by the purchaser therefrom. As a result, the seller failed to demonstrate his entitlement to a formal accounting. Mills v Chauvin (2013, 3d Dept) 103 App Div 3d 1041, 962 NYS2d 412.

As to the property, although the seller alleged that the purchaser had failed to collect rent and other obligations from the tenants and sought an accounting, there was no written partnership agreement that allowed the partners to call for an accounting, Partnership Law § § 44, and the record did not establish that the purchaser breached his fiduciary duty to the seller with respect to the partnership or that other circumstances existed that warranted an accounting; moreover, the evidence at trial established that the seller was active in the partnership and its financial affairs, and there was no evidence to suggest that the seller was excluded by the purchaser therefrom. As a result, the seller failed to demonstrate his entitlement to a formal accounting. Mills v Chauvin (2013, 3d Dept) 103 App Div 3d 1041, 962 NYS2d 412.

7. – Doctrine of "unclean hands"

In an action for a partnership accounting in which the plaintiff's evidence revealed that some transactions were in cash and not reported on any tax return the court was in error in dismissing the suit based on the doctrine of unclean hands, since incidental or collateral illegality will not preclude an accounting and the doctrine was only available when the conduct relied upon is directly related to the subject matter in litigation and the party seeking to invoke the doctrine was injured by such conduct. Dinerstein v Dinerstein (1969, 1st Dept) 32 A.D.2d 750, 300 N.Y.S.2d 677

A joint venture is a special combination of two or more persons in some specific venture where a profit is jointly sought without any actual partnership or corporate designation, while an indispensable requirement of a partnership is a mutual promise or understanding of the parties to submit to the burden of making good the losses as well as to share in the profits of the business, which relates to a general business of a particular kind; however, insofar as the right to an accounting and concomitant relief is concerned, it is enough that the parties stand in a mutual and confidential relationship to each other and have a joint interest in the result of the venture. Accordingly, where such an analogon of property or interests as would create at least a joint venture between the parties is shown, although it is unclear whether there was an agreement that each party would share the burden of losses, plaintiff is entitled to equitable relief in the form of an accounting in an action arising out of a dispute as to the parties' respective interests in their business even though he has not come to the court with the cleanest of hands, since a court of equity must do equity where both parties are seeking equitable relief. Hanlon v Melfi (1979) 102 Misc. 2d 170, 423 N.Y.S.2d 132

8. – Termination, withdrawal, or expulsion

Where the plaintiff was the owner of a one-half interest in a partnership which by terms of partnership agreement, had been terminated he was entitled to a full accounting of all the assets belonging to the partnership. But since both sides had stipulated to go to trial at the next term of court, appointment of a receiver pendente lite was not necessary but enough was shown to warrant, for plaintiff's protection, an injunction restraining defendant from wasting or transferring the partnership assets. Mester v Morgenstern (1953) 281 A.D. 967, 120 N.Y.S.2d 817

Justice court's finding in prior action that plaintiff had breached the partnership agreement did not preclude such partner's action for an accounting to recover his interest in the partnership since the

misconduct of a partner does not necessarily deprive him of his right to demand an accounting. Bell v Herzog (1972, 3d Dept) 39 A.D.2d 813, 332 N.Y.S.2d 501

Although a partnership automatically dissolves upon the death of a partner, a surviving partner may still bring an action for an accounting, and the deceased partner's nominee in the partnership can and should be compelled to render such an accounting. Paul v Ascher (1984, 2d Dept) 106 A.D.2d 619, 483 N.Y.S.2d 422

Transferee of partnership interest of deceased partner did not lack standing to seek accounting and injunctive relief against surviving partner who allegedly mismanaged and misappropriated partnership assets; although one partner may not sue another partner in action at law prior to accounting, offending partner may be held to account in action in equity. Parnes v Edelman (1987, 2d Dept) 128 A.D.2d 596, 512 N.Y.S.2d 856

Son-in-law was not entitled to accounting and dissolution of partnership where he expressly conceded in his testimony that he had sold his partnership interest to his partner (father-in-law) in return for father-in-law's promise to make weekly payments to him, parties signed document terminating partnership, father-in-law made agreed payments for some time, and Keogh account was split between them; agreement terminating partnership was not rescinded by father-in-law's failure to continue weekly payments, but son-in-law was entitled to amendment of complaint to conform to proof with new trial on cause of action for breach of contract. Stempel v Rosen (1988, 2d Dept) 140 A.D.2d 326, 527 N.Y.S.2d 825, adhered to, motion den, in part (1988, 2d Dept) 143 A.D.2d 409, 532 N.Y.S.2d 437

Withdrawing law partner should have been granted partial summary judgment to extent of directing accounting where he demonstrated existence of at-will partnership by producing partnership income tax returns and evidence of actual sharing of profits and parties' holding themselves out to public as partners, whereas defendant's averments raised issue not as to formation of partnership but only as to date of its formation. Kirsch v Leventhal (1992, 3d Dept) 181 A.D.2d 222, 586 N.Y.S.2d 330

Exclusion of the plaintiff from participation in the conduct of a corporation set up by partners to carry out the partnership agreement constituted a violation of the agreement and justified an accounting and dissolution. Dow v Beals (1933) 149 Misc 631, 268 N.Y.S. 425

Allegations that subsequent to the dissolution of a partnership the defendant refused to account to the plaintiff with respect to the partnership affairs, profits and loss, were sufficient to entitle the plaintiff to maintain an action for an accounting. Rosenblum v Arbitman (1948, Sup) 81 N.Y.S.2d 478

9. Accounting of illegal business

No proceedings for an accounting will ordinarily be permitted in the case of a partnership organized for the prosecution of an illegal business or one which is contrary to public policy. Woodworth v Bennett (1871) 43 N.Y. 273

Incidental or collateral illegality will not preclude an accounting. Candee v Baker (1909) 131 A.D. 641, 116 N.Y.S. 55

An accounting may be had in the case of a completed illegal partnership. Hebblethwaite v Flint (1918) 185 A.D. 249, 173 N.Y.S. 81, app den (1919) 187 A.D. 959, 175 N.Y.S. 905

Fact that partnership created for transaction of real estate business did not have a real estate broker's license as required by law did not preclude one of the parties from seeking an accounting. Bell v Herzog (1972, 3d Dept) 39 A.D.2d 813, 332 N.Y.S.2d 501

An accounting will be allowed where it appears that the plaintiff partner was not in pari delicto with the defendant. Jennings v Chute (1902) 37 Misc 39, 74 N.Y.S. 739

An accounting of a partnership formed ultra vires by a corporation may be granted. Standard Oil Co. v Scofield (1885) 16 Abb NC 372

10. Laches

Laches and acquiescence of a plaintiff will preclude the adjudication of an accounting of the partnership affairs where the same have worked to the disadvantage of the defendant. Corr v Hoffman (1931) 256 N.Y. 254, 176 N.E. 383

The doctrine of laches is of great importance where persons have agreed to become partners and one of them has unfairly left the other to do all the work and then, there being a profit, comes forward and claims a share of it. Smith v Maine (1932) 145 Misc 521, 260 N.Y.S. 409

11. Limitation of actions

The statute runs against a suit by a retiring partner against a liquidating partner for an accounting, from the date when it was the duty of the latter to have had business in a condition for its complete settlement, and the operation of the statute is not postponed by the fact that he leaves one or more of the partnership obligations unsettled which are subsequently enforced in an action against the retiring partner by which he is compelled to pay the amount thereof; in such cases due consideration is given both to the necessity of reasonable promptness and diligence on the part of the liquidator, having a due regard for the rights of his copartner, and to the fact that the latter must not sleep on his rights and wait until books are lost, or vouchers mislaid, or witness dead, before seeking an accounting in payment. Gilmore v Ham (1894) 142 N.Y. 1, 36 N.E. 826

Running of statute of limitations against action for an accounting cannot always be governed by any rigid or formal rule but must depend upon circumstances; it may begin to run from the date when it is the duty of the accounting partner to have the firm in condition for its complete settlement. Gray v Green (1894) 142 N.Y. 316, 37 N.E. 124

Assuming that an agreement made upon dissolution of a partnership that the partners should continue to be liable for obligations in the same proportions as their interests in the firm constituted an agreement postponing the accrual of a right to an accounting, the right accrued when all obligations had been met and a cause of action for an accounting was barred by the statute of limitations where it was not commenced within ten years. Bankers Trust Co. v Dennis (1939) 256 A.D. 495, 10 N.Y.S.2d 710, affd (1940) 282 N.Y. 635, 25 N.E.2d 981

It was error to dismiss action for accounting under CLS Partn § 74 on ground that it was time barred where fact issue existed as to when, if ever, partnership was dissolved and thus when, if ever, cause of action accrued. Consiglio v Consiglio (1988, 4th Dept) 143 A.D.2d 505, 533 N.Y.S.2d 260

Action commenced in 1989 for partnership accounting arising out of plaintiff's 1982 purchase from defendant of 80 percent interest in thoroughbred for breeding purposes was time-barred by 6-year statute of limitations of CLS CPLR § 213(1), notwithstanding plaintiff's contention that she did not learn that defendant had bred horse and kept fees until 1984, since plaintiff's right to accounting accrued on dissolution of partnership and by selling her interest in horse in 1982, plaintiff manifested unequivocal election to dissolve partnership. Mills v O'Donnell (1992, 3d Dept) 188 A.D.2d 692, 591 N.Y.S.2d 83

In 1990 action for accounting of Iranian family partnership brought by 3 younger brothers who were to divide 20 percent interest in business while defendant older siblings would each own 20 percent share, court erred in dismissing complaint as time-barred under 6-year statute of limitations of CLS CPLR § 213, without reaching issue of dissolution of partnership under either Iranian or New York Law, by finding that cause of action accrued at latest in 1982 when Iranian elders attempted to mediate discord between siblings; while 1982 mediation attempt might constitute binding settlement of parties' dispute up to time of mediation (assuming it was arbitration), plaintiffs had right under CLS Partn § 44 to obtain accounting of partnership business affairs for period following mediation. Elghanayan v Elghanayan (1993, 1st Dept) 190 A.D.2d 449, 598 N.Y.S.2d 524

It was error to grant plaintiff's motion for summary judgment directing accounting as to rights of joint venturers, and to deny defendants' motion for summary judgment based on statute of limitations, where fact issue existed as to when actual dissolution of joint venture took place. Sagus Marine Corp. v Donald G. Rynne & Co. (1994, 1st Dept) 207 A.D.2d 701, 616 N.Y.S.2d 496

The right of the estate of a deceased partner to an accounting of the partnership assets continues until barred by the ten-year statute of limitations. In re Vitelli's Estate (1949) 196 Misc 644, 92 N.Y.S.2d 322

12. Accountability for profits and earnings

An interlocutory agreement rendered in an action between two partners to the effect that neither the plaintiff nor the defendant had any claim against the other with respect to "said premises," merely acknowledged that the partnership no longer had title to certain real estate as a result of the settlement of an earlier partition action and plaintiff's demand that defendant account for the income from the partnership asset was not a claim against the premises, but rather against the proceeds therefrom prior to a partition sale. Gordon v Ginsberg (1970) 26 N.Y.2d 236, 309 N.Y.S.2d 326, 257 N.E.2d 880

Upon death of one partner in 1968 and the initiation of new profit and loss ratio for surviving partners, new partnership independent of 1960 partnership agreement came into existence and, therefore, dissolution provision of the 1960 agreement requiring an accounting of profits as determined on cash basis and distribution of assets in

specified manner was inapplicable to dissolution of the new partnership. Wagner v Etoll (1974, 3d Dept) 46 A.D.2d 990, 362 N.Y.S.2d 278, app dismd (1975) 37 N.Y.2d 795, 375 N.Y.S.2d 107, 337 N.E.2d 612

In an action for an accounting of a law partnership's assets pursuant to an agreement giving each party the right to an accounting from the other of an equal division of the net profits on fees received after a certain date, each party was entitled to deduct from the fees collected a ratable share of his overhead expenses. Nishman v De Marco (1983, 2d Dept) 94 A.D.2d 697, 462 N.Y.S.2d 50, app dismd (1983) 60 N.Y.2d 858, 470 N.Y.S.2d 143, 458 N.E.2d 384 and affd (1984) 62 N.Y.2d 926, 479 N.Y.S.2d 185, 468 N.E.2d 23

In action for accounting arising from dissolution of law partnership, continued distribution of plaintiff's pro rata share of contingent fees was not precluded by provision of partnership agreement which limited partner's annual distribution of partnership assets on dissolution to 50 percent of that partner's "net income for the preceding year"; when read in context, such provision applied to distribution of partnership assets on dissolution, other than income from designated cases, and was intended to protect surviving partner by precluding payment of excessive amounts that would cripple continuing practice by deferring such distributions to following years. Gilbride v Harrison (1995, 2d Dept) 212 A.D.2d 757, 623 N.Y.S.2d 292, app dismd without op (1995) 87 N.Y.2d 896, 640 N.Y.S.2d 879, 663 N.E.2d 921

Plaintiff established his entitlement to accounting for partnership funds where both parties testified that they purchased property in question as partners with funds obtained through mortgage given by defendant on his residence, defendant took title to property in his own name although it belonged to partnership, defendant sold property but failed to inform plaintiff of sale or account for its proceeds, and defendant admitted diverting net proceeds to his own use. Chamberlain v Amato (1999, 4th Dept) 259 A.D.2d 1048, 688 N.Y.S.2d 345

In action for accounting and breach of partnership agreement which entitled plaintiff to share only in net profits as of date of his termination, plaintiff was nevertheless entitled to disclosure of financial information for 6-month period immediately following his termination, to cover possibility that income which accrued before termination was deferred until after termination. Shabasson v Max E. Greenberg, Trager, Toplitz & Herbst (2000, 1st Dept) 268 A.D.2d 357, 715 N.Y.S.2d 142

A former law partner was not entitled to maintain an action for an accounting of a fee received by the firm in a particular matter, where he had cashed a check from the firm for his share in the matter, which check was accompanied by a statement of account. Norton v Tart (1959) 16 Misc. 2d 681, 189 N.Y.S.2d 990

Although both members of a partnership agree to its dissolution as of a certain date, they were equally entitled to share in profits from business being negotiated by one of them prior to the agreed date of dissolution. Bogen v Alston (1961) 33 Misc. 2d 313, 215 N.Y.S.2d 388

In an accounting, a wrongful failure to distribute partnership profits to limited partners is a personal action since the obligation to distribute partnership profits pursuant to the partnership agreement runs from the partnership to the individual limited partners and a failure to fulfil this obligation may be the subject of a class action in that all limited partners are injured in the same manner. Alpert v Haimes (1970) 64 Misc. 2d 608, 315 N.Y.S.2d 332

13. Accountability for secret profits

A member of a partnership is accountable to the other partners for secret profits made during the course of a partnership transaction. R. C. Gluck & Co. v Tankel (1961, 1st Dept) 12 A.D.2d 339, 211 N.Y.S.2d 602

A partner who had full knowledge of, and consented to, all the acts of another partner, may not thereafter complain at law or in equity on the basis that partnership funds were diverted. Gutwirth v Carewell Trading Corp. (1961, 1st Dept) 12 A.D.2d 920, 211 N.Y.S.2d 732

14. Allowance of interest

Where there were no articles of partnership and all that was found with respect to partnership interest was that one of partners was to have one-fifth of profits and was to bear one-fifth of losses, when partnership was dissolved by death of one of partners, there was no basis upon which to predicate claim for interest on capital up to time of final settlement; the fact that in making of previous accounts between the partners, interest had been credited, was not sufficient evidence of usage to dispense with the necessity of proving a special agreement in this regard. In re James (1895) 146 N.Y. 78, 40 N.E. 876

Partnership Law

Generally, in the absence of special agreement or express statute, interest cannot be allowed as between partners on money put in as capital. Rodgers v Clement (1900) 162 N.Y. 422, 56 N.E. 901

General rule appears to be that in absence of agreement to the contrary, interest is not to be allowed on partnership accounts until after a balance is struck. McGibbon v Tarbox (1912) 205 N.Y. 271, 98 N.E. 390

In the absence of an agreement to the contrary, it was error to award interest on partnership account from date of receivership rather than from date of judgment of dissolution only. Berkovits v Hanley (1972, 3d Dept) 40 A.D.2d 921, 338 N.Y.S.2d 339

15. – Compound interest

Ordinarily compound interest is not allowable to the estate of a deceased partner on computing the balance owing to him. Johnson v Hartshorne (1873) 52 N.Y. 173

A surviving partner may be charged with compound interest on sums owing from him to the estate of the deceased partner in cases of bad faith on his part, refusal to account, and private use of the money, and the question of the propriety of charging compound interest in such a case is one of fact for referee or trial court, whose decision is conclusive. Johnson v Hartshorne (1873) 52 N.Y. 173

If a surviving partner who is also the executor of the deceased partner continues the business without making a division of the assets of the deceased partner as he should have done, he may be chargeable with compound interest on the amount due the deceased partner's estate, on the ground of his negligence or wrongdoing. Hannahs v Hannahs (1877) 68 N.Y. 610

16. Accounts stated

After partners have mutually stated and adjusted an account it will not be reopened except for fraud, mistake, or duress. Wahl v Barnum (1889) 116 N.Y. 87, 22 N.E. 280

17. Practice and procedure

Plenary hearing is necessary to determine partner's right to accounting where foundation of right, partnership agreement itself, does not clearly provide for the allocation of pending contingency case fees. Dwyer v Nicholson (1985, 2d Dept) 109 A.D.2d 862, 487 N.Y.S.2d 56, motion gr (1991, Sup) 154 Misc. 2d 123, 583 N.Y.S.2d 738, app dismd, affirmed in part, remanded (1993, 2d Dept) 193 A.D.2d 70, 602 N.Y.S.2d 144, app dismd (1995, 2d Dept) 220 A.D.2d 555, 633 N.Y.S.2d 963, app den (1996) 87 N.Y.2d 808, 641 N.Y.S.2d 830, 664 N.E.2d 896, motion gr, motion den (1996) 88 N.Y.2d 963, 647 N.Y.S.2d 716, 670 N.E.2d 1348

In action by widow of deceased partner for accounting and injunctive relief, court properly refused to dismiss managing partner's affirmative defense denying widow's status as partner where partnership agreement provided for continuation of partnership on death of partner, and fact issues existed as to widows's status as transferee of her husband's interests. Parnes v Edelman (1987, 2d Dept) 128 A.D.2d 596, 512 N.Y.S.2d 856

Defendants were not entitled to jury trial in action for partnership accounting. Homburger v Levitin (1988, 2d Dept) 140 A.D.2d 583, 528 N.Y.S.2d 853, app den (1988) 73 N.Y.2d 701, 535 N.Y.S.2d 595, 532 N.E.2d 101

In action for accounting on dissolution of law partnership, referee did not exceed his authority by ordering disclosure relating to income which partnership received for providing nonlegal services to its clients since order of reference authorized referee "to supervise all discovery proceedings in the instant action" and empowered him to report his findings "with respect to all accounting issues"; further, plaintiffs were not required to obtain interlocutory judgment establishing their right to accounting prior to obtaining disclosure ordered by referee. Marshall v Pappas (1988, 2d Dept) 143 A.D.2d 979, 533 N.Y.S.2d 636

In action for accounting after dissolution of partnership, in which defendant claimed that he was entitled to credit certain sums to his own account on basis that plaintiff had overdrawn their joint account at some time in past, there was insufficient evidence to invoke doctrine of unclean hands since it could not be determined whether defendant's claim was directly related to subject matter of current litigation and harmed defendant. Mehlman v Avrech (1989, 2d Dept) 146 A.D.2d 753, 537 N.Y.S.2d 236

Statute of frauds was not bar to action for accounting wherein it was alleged that plaintiff and defendants orally entered into partnership or joint venture agreement to acquire commercial real property, since plaintiff was not seeking to acquire interest in land but was asserting alleged interest in assets of partnership or joint venture. Walsh v Rechler (1989, 2d Dept) 151 A.D.2d 473, 542 N.Y.S.2d 262

New York County action for accounting brought by plaintiffs, tenants in common of joint venture, was not precluded under CLS CPLR § 3211(a)(4) due to existence of prior Nassau County action for dissolution and partition brought against plaintiffs by remaining tenants in common, notwithstanding that plaintiffs had option of counterclaiming for accounting in Nassau County, and even if dissolution in Nassau County would inevitably lead to accounting, since CLS Part § 74 does not mandate accounting, and sort of accounting desired by plaintiffs was not necessarily same type of accounting available on dissolution in Nassau County even assuming that plaintiffs would not prevail therein. Morgulas v J. Yudell Realty, Inc. (1990, 1st Dept) 161 A.D.2d 211, 554 N.Y.S.2d 597

In action seeking accounting to determine rights of joint venturers, it was error to direct defendants to maintain entire award they obtained in prior litigation in joint venture account where only matter in dispute was plaintiff's entitlement to 1/3 of that amount, minus cost of prior litigation, with amount of setoff to be determined by accounting. Sagus Marine Corp. v Donald G. Rynne & Co. (1994, 1st Dept) 207 A.D.2d 701, 616 N.Y.S.2d 496

In action for defendant's alleged interference with plaintiffs' law practice, plaintiffs were not entitled to summary judgment as to defendant's counterclaims to direct accounting and to appoint appraiser where plaintiffs failed to produce evidence conclusively negating defendant's allegations as to existence of oral partnership agreement. Lynn v Corcoran (1995, 2d Dept) 219 A.D.2d 698, 631 N.Y.S.2d 754

In action to compel accounting following breakup of parties' law partnership, court properly denied defense motion to dismiss complaint on basis that parties had agreed to arbitrate any disputes arising out of dissolution, because existence of arbitration agreement would merely entitle defendant to stay of action, not dismissal, and controversy existed as to whether there was enforceable arbitration agreement, requiring hearing on issue. Weiss v Kozupsky (1997, 2d Dept) 237 A.D.2d 514, 656 N.Y.S.2d 907

Plaintiff's action to recover its initial capital contribution in partnership that was unsuccessful in achieving main purpose for which it was formed sufficiently stated cause of action for accounting, to which plaintiff was absolutely entitled, and for judicial dissolution if parties did not agree to voluntarily dissolve partnership, where record reflected defendant's failure to provide complete information regarding disposition of partnership funds. Non-Linear Trading Co. v Braddis Assocs. (1998, 1st Dept) 243 A.D.2d 107, 675 N.Y.S.2d 5

On finding that partnership was dissolved, court properly directed accounting and held in abeyance declaration of parties' partnership interests pending such accounting. Staines Assocs. v Adler (1999, 1st Dept) 266 A.D.2d 52, 698 N.Y.S.2d 639

As a former equity partner was properly expelled in accordance with the parties' partnership agreement, the former partner was not entitled to a judicial accounting under N.Y. P'ship Law § 44(1) because he failed to allege that the firm and the other partners failed to provide the audits to which the former partner was entitled under the agreement. Altebrando v Gozdziewski (2008, 1st Dept) 47 App Div 3d 520, 849 NYS2d 550.

§ 45.   Continuation of partnership beyond fixed term

1. When a partnership for a fixed term or particular undertaking is continued after the termination of such term or particular undertaking without any express agreement, the rights and duties of the partners remain the same as they were at such termination, so far as is consistent with a partnership at will.

2. A continuation of the business by the partners or such of them as habitually acted therein during the term, without any settlement or liquidation of the partnership affairs, is prima facie evidence of a continuation of the partnership.

History: Add, L 1919, ch 408, eff Oct 1, 1919.

Option clause in written partnership agreement, which partnership to last three years, was continued in existence by mutual oral extension of original agreement of partnership which operated to turn partnership into one at will, for option did not contain any limitation of time and was not inconsistent with such partnership, and, therefore, respondent had right to exercise option if he saw fit at any time prior to dissolution of partnership. Corr v Hoffman (1927) 219 A.D. 278, 219 N.Y.S. 656

Ordinarily, partnership agreement continues in absence of new written agreement after expiration of its term so long as actions of the partners indicate implied consent to continue particular provisions of the partnership relationship, even though some of the provisions of the written agreement are disregarded. Wagner v Etoll (1974, 3d Dept) 46 A.D.2d 990, 362 N.Y.S.2d 278, app dismd (1975) 37 N.Y.2d 795, 375 N.Y.S.2d 107, 337 N.E.2d 612

Absent agreement to the contrary, death of one partner in 1968 resulted in dissolution of partnership which, by terms of partnership agreement, was to expire on December 31, 1961 but which was continued after expiration date without formal written agreement. Wagner v Etoll (1974, 3d Dept) 46 A.D.2d 990, 362 N.Y.S.2d 278, app dismd (1975) 37 N.Y.2d 795, 375 N.Y.S.2d 107, 337 N.E.2d 612

Upon death of one partner in 1968 and initiation of new profit and loss ratio for surviving partners, new partnership independent of 1960 partnership agreement came into existence and, therefore, dissolution provision of the 1960 agreement requiring an accounting of profits as determined on cash basis and distribution of assets in specified manner was inapplicable to dissolution of the new partnership. Wagner v Etoll (1974, 3d Dept) 46 A.D.2d 990, 362 N.Y.S.2d 278, app dismd (1975) 37 N.Y.2d 795, 375 N.Y.S.2d 107, 337 N.E.2d 612

Even if the partnership agreement failed to meet the requirements of the Statute of Frauds, the only effect would be to convert the partnership into one at will, which exists until something is done to dissolve it. Boxill v Boxill (1952) 201 Misc 386, 111 N.Y.S.2d 33

ARTICLE 5
PROPERTY RIGHTS OF A PARTNER

History: Add, L 1919, ch 408, eff Oct 1, 1919.

§ 50.   Extent of property rights of a partner

The property rights of a partner are (a) his rights in specific partnership property, (b) his interest in the partnership, and (c) his right to participate in the management.

History: Add, L 1919, ch 408, eff Oct 1, 1919.

Specific partnership property is all property except a partner's share of the profits and surplus. Geitner v United States Fidelity & Guaranty Co. (1929) 225 A.D. 451, 233 N.Y.S. 378, affd (1929) 251 N.Y. 205, 167 N.E. 222

Under provisions of partnership law, unless parties have agreed otherwise, person cannot become member of partnership without consent of all partners, whereas assignment of partnership interest may be made without consent, but assignee is entitled only to receive profits of assigning partner. Rapoport v 55 Perry Co. (1975, 1st Dept) 50 A.D.2d 54, 376 N.Y.S.2d 147

Partnership agreement providing that assignments, encumbrances and agreements "as a result of which any person shall become interested with (assignor) in this firm" would not be allowed unless agreed to by majority of partners, "except for members of his immediate family who have attained majority," was intended to limit partner with respect to his right to assign partnership interest to right to profits; thus partners could not transfer full partnership interest to their children, and such children only had rights as assignees to receive share of partnership income and profits of their assignors. Rapoport v 55 Perry Co. (1975, 1st Dept) 50 A.D.2d 54, 376 N.Y.S.2d 147

All partners are fiduciaries of one another; however, in traditional partnership, each partner has absolute and equal statutory right to manage business. People v Zinke (1989, 1st Dept) 147 A.D.2d 106, 541 N.Y.S.2d 986, app den (1989) 74 N.Y.2d 749, 545 N.Y.S.2d 124, 543 N.E.2d 767 and app gr (1989) 74 N.Y.2d 822, 546 N.Y.S.2d 580, 545 N.E.2d 894 and motion gr (1989) 75 N.Y.2d 764, 551 N.Y.S.2d 904, 551 N.E.2d 105 and revd on other grounds (1990) 76 N.Y.2d 8, 556 N.Y.S.2d 11, 555 N.E.2d 263

Withdrawing partner was entitled to 1/12 of full fiscal year's net income of partnership where partnership agreement unambiguously gave withdrawing partner his proportionate share of partnership's net income, multiplied by percentage of fiscal year completed as of withdrawal from partnership (here 1/12); to construe agreement otherwise would render meaningless clause requiring estimated amount in cases of uncertainty. Rutkowski v Hill, Betts & Nash (1994, 1st Dept) 206 A.D.2d 258

Court properly concluded that goodwill was not distributable partnership asset where partnership agreement did not specify that goodwill was asset of firm, no consideration was paid for goodwill on admission of partners, no amounts had been paid or given on account of goodwill, and firm's financial statements did not reflect any goodwill. Kaplan v Joseph Schachter & Co. (1999, 2d Dept) 261 A.D.2d 440, 690 N.Y.S.2d 91

It is obvious under §§ 50-52 of this law that a partner's interest in specific partnership property is not subject to estate tax. In re Estate of Finkelstein (1963) 40 Misc. 2d 910, 245 N.Y.S.2d 225

§ 51.   Nature of a partner's right in specific partnership property

1. A partner is co-owner with his partners of specific partnership property holding as a tenant in partnership.

2. The incidents of this tenancy are such that:

(a) A partner, subject to the provisions of this chapter and to any agreement between the partners, has an equal right with his partners to possess specific partnership property for partnership purposes; but he has no right to possess such property for any other purpose without the consent of his partners.

(b) A partner's right in specific partnership property is not assignable except in connection with the assignment of the rights of all the partners in the same property.

(c) A partner's right in specific partnership property is not subject to attachment or execution, except on a claim against the partnership. When partnership property is attached for a partnership debt the partners, or any of them, or the representatives of a deceased partner, cannot claim any right under the homestead or exemption laws.

(d) On the death of a partner his right in specific partnership property vests in the surviving partner or partners, except where the deceased was the last surviving partner, when his right in such property vests in his legal representative. Such surviving partner or partners, or the legal representative of the last surviving partner, has no right to possess the partnership property for any but a partnership purpose.

Partnership Law

(e) A partner's right in specific partnership property is not subject to dower, curtesy, or allowances to surviving spouses, heirs, or next of kin.

History: Add, L 1919, ch 408, eff Oct 1, 1919.

Sub 2, par (e), amd, L 1976, ch 110, § 5, eff Sept 1, 1976.

CASE ANNOTATIONS

1. In general
2. Tenancy in partnership
3. Partition
4. Assignment or transfer
5. Attachment or execution
6. Surviving partners
7. Conjugal rights; heirs and next of kin

1. In general

In an action to enforce a partnership claim, a counterclaim may not be set up by a defendant to impose a "nonpartnership liability" against the partners (one of them a limited partner) individually. Ruzicka v Rager (1953) 305 N.Y. 191, 111 N.E.2d 878, 39 ALR2d 288, reh den (1953) 305 N.Y. 798, 113 N.E.2d 306

General partner cannot be convicted of grand larceny for stealing limited partnership funds, in accordance with common-law rule. People v Zinke (1990) 76 N.Y.2d 8, 556 N.Y.S.2d 11, 555 N.E.2d 263

This section contains no guide to accounting principles to be employed in valuing a partner's interest. Soechtig v Amick (1955) 285 A.D. 701, 140 N.Y.S.2d 85, affd (1956) 309 N.Y. 988, 132 N.E.2d 897

A partner has no personal right in any specific partnership property of which he is a member, and any real estate which the partnership owns is considered personalty. La Russo v Paladino (1951, Sup) 109 N.Y.S.2d 627, affd (1952) 280 A.D. 988, 116 N.Y.S.2d 617, app den (1953) 281 A.D. 753, 118 N.Y.S.2d 557

2. Tenancy in partnership

Distinction between tenancy in common and tenancy in partnership is not always very important when describing holding of property by partners as between themselves, for equity regards the holding as tenancy in partnership while at same time asserting right of survivorship to be in surviving partner. Preston v Fitch (1893) 137 N.Y. 41, 33 N.E. 77

Charge against plaintiff for equitable share of value of use of land, bought with partnership money but used after dissolution, before equities between partners were adjusted, by plaintiff for his own private business, is proper. Plaintiff was not tenant in common but "tenant in partnership" as described in this section. Kraus v Kraus (1928) 250 N.Y. 63, 164 N.E. 743

Under this section partners are co-owners of specific firm property and while partnership is often treated as entity theory has never been adopted by N.Y. law. Rossmoore v Commissioner (1935, CA2) 76 F.2d 520, 35-1 USTC P 9277, 15 AFTR 1178

3. Partition

In absence of any accounting between the copartners or adjustment of the partnership accounts, the real estate cannot be separated from the rest of the copartnership property and made the subject of a separate action in partition so as to defy the same or the proceeds thereof between the parties. Eisner v Eisner (1896) 5 A.D. 117, 38 N.Y.S. 671

Where partnership is formed for the purpose of dealing in real estate, such real estate is deemed merchandise in which copartnership trades, and accordingly parties have impliedly indicated intention to convert realty into personalty and property is considered as such; action for partition could not lie. Broida v Bunnell Associates (1960) 26 Misc. 2d 213, 201 N.Y.S.2d 572

Real estate owned by copartnership was personalty, and did not resume its character of real estate until copartnership creditors were paid and interest of copartners adjusted; being part of partnership property and assets, it could not, in absence of any accounting between the copartners or adjustment of the copartnership accounts, be separated from the rest of the copartnership property and made the subject of a separate action for partition. MacFarlane v MacFarlane (1894) 82 Hun 238, 31 N.Y.S. 272

4. Assignment or transfer

The Partnership Law does not preclude an assignment by one partner to another of a cause of action for specific property theretofore belonging to a partnership of two persons. It merely forbids such an assignment by one partner to a third party or stranger unless it is joined in by all of the other partners or an assignment to a partner not executed by all other partners. Becker v Hercules Foundries, Inc. (1942) 263 A.D. 991, 33 N.Y.S.2d 367, app den (1942, 2d Dept) 264 A.D. 721, 34 N.Y.S.2d 524

Where partners agreed that real property should be held as a partnership asset they became, as to such property, tenants in partnership and as an incident of this tenancy their right in the partnership property was not assignable except in connection with the assignment of the rights of all the partners in the same property. Altman v Altman (1946) 271 A.D. 884, 67 N.Y.S.2d 119, affd (1948) 297 N.Y. 973, 80 N.E.2d 359

Subdivision 2(b) of this section is a codification of the common law and an essential qualification of all partnership agreements binding upon all co-partnerships, but where all the partners execute an agreement in writing which includes, among other things, the right of one of their number to purchase from the estate of one of the others, in the event of the latter's death, decedent's interest in the partnership all consent to such purpose and the agreement supersedes prohibitions of that subdivision. In re Estate of Bennett (1960, Sur) 205 N.Y.S.2d 50

An individual partner has no fractional right in specific partnership property which he alone can assign. A partner is not the owner of a fractional or undivided interest in each partnership asset. Upon the withdrawal of one partner and death of another and the admission of two new partners, there was no transfer of partnership stocks and bonds subject to Federal stamp taxes. Salomon Bros. & Hutzler v Pedrick (1952, SD NY) 105 F. Supp. 210, 52-1 USTC P 9323, 42 AFTR 109

5. Attachment or execution

This section provides merely that partner's interest (not the interest of all partners) in specific partnership property is not subject to attachment or execution, except on claim against partnership. Geitner v United States Fidelity & Guaranty Co. (1929) 251 N.Y. 205, 167 N.E. 222

The difference in the relationship of a partner as such and as an individual to creditors, e.g., the unavailability of partnership assets for execution on individual claims and the priorities of firm and individual creditors upon insolvency, illustrate the general principle that a person who holds membership in a partnership acts, serves and is obligated in two distinct and different capacities. Ruzicka v Rager (1953) 305 N.Y. 191, 111 N.E.2d 878, 39 ALR2d 288, reh den (1953) 305 N.Y. 798, 113 N.E.2d 306

Third party order in proceedings supplementary to execution, which directed examination of bank in which partnership, one of whose members was judgment debtor, deposited their money, to restrain bank from transferring any property belonging to judgment debtor individually or as a copartner, violated subd. 2, paragraph c. Proper procedure was under § 54. Rader v Goldoff (1928) 223 A.D. 455, 228 N.Y.S. 453

The interest of a judgment debtor in the profits of a partnership cannot be reached by means of a third party subpoena served for examination of the partnership in supplementary proceedings. Northeastern Real Estate Sec. Corp. v Goldstein (1944) 267 A.D. 832, 45 N.Y.S.2d 848, app dismd (1944) 292 N.Y. 720, 56 N.E.2d 125

Divorce court erred in restraining and attaching husband's capital account with his law firm for purposes of satisfying his financial obligations. MacDonald v MacDonald (1996, 2d Dept) 226 A.D.2d 596, 641 N.Y.S.2d 349

No statutory authority existed on July 22, 1940, which authorized an attachment prior to judgment of a partner's general interest in the partnership as distinguished from his right in specific partnership property; however, any such levy would now be sustained by reason of Civ. Pr. Act, § 917, as amended by L 1940, c 625, effective September 1, 1940. Dalinda v Abegg (1941) 175 Misc 945, 25 N.Y.S.2d 612

Levy against partnership property was ineffective where the action was brought against defendant both individually and as doing business under the partnership trade name. Saligman v Ginsburg (1950, Sup) 102 N.Y.S.2d 142

6. Surviving partners

The interest of a deceased partner whose estate is being administered in New York in out-of-state real estate which is an asset of the partnership entered into between New York residents in conformity with New York law must be included as a part of his gross taxable estate, and it is immaterial that his interest in the property might also be taxable in the state of its situs. In re Estate of Havemeyer

(1966) 17 N.Y.2d 216, 270 N.Y.S.2d 197, 217 N.E.2d 26, reh den (1966) 17 N.Y.2d 918

Inasmuch as New York partnership law expressly provides for the conversion of real estate into personalty and that on death it shall pass to the surviving partner, the deceased partner's interest in out-of-state realty must be included in his gross estate for tax purposes where the partnership was entered into between New York residents and under the law of that state. In re Estate of Havemeyer (1966) 17 N.Y.2d 216, 270 N.Y.S.2d 197, 217 N.E.2d 26, reh den (1966) 17 N.Y.2d 918

A partner is co-owner with his partners of specific partnership property, holding as a tenant in partnership, and one of the incidents of this tenancy is that upon the death of a partner his right in specific property vests in the surviving partners, except where the deceased was the last surviving partner, in which event his right in the property vests in his legal representatives. In re Estate of Havemeyer (1966) 17 N.Y.2d 216, 270 N.Y.S.2d 197, 217 N.E.2d 26, reh den (1966) 17 N.Y.2d 918

Under the terms of the Uniform Partnership Act, specific partnership real estate is converted into personal property and on the death of a partner passes to the surviving partner under the partnership agreement. In re Estate of Havemeyer (1966) 17 N.Y.2d 216, 270 N.Y.S.2d 197, 217 N.E.2d 26, reh den (1966) 17 N.Y.2d 918

The death of a partner while a claim of the partnership was pending in arbitration did not cause the arbitration proceeding to abate but the claim became vested in the surviving partners. A substitution of the representative of the estate of the deceased partner would not have been proper. First Nat'l Oil Corp. v Arrieta (1956, 2d Dept) 2 A.D.2d 590, 157 N.Y.S.2d 313, reh and app den (1957, 2d Dept) 3 A.D.2d 672, 159 N.Y.S.2d 673, app dismd (1957) 2 N.Y.2d 992, 163 N.Y.S.2d 604, 143 N.E.2d 341 and app dismd without op (1957) 2 N.Y.2d 711

Upon the death of a partner, the right to possession of the books and accounts of the partnership vests in the surviving partner. The executor of the deceased partner was not subject to an order for a discovery and inspection of the books. Goldstein v Kaye (1956, 2d Dept) 2 A.D.2d 889, 156 N.Y.S.2d 238

Action by surviving partner, seeking dissolution of partnership and accounting, was not barred by failure to file claim against deceased partner's estate, which was probated in Florida, as required by Florida statutes, as action did not involve claim against deceased partner's estate; partnership property vested in plaintiff after partner's death, subject to accounting to deceased partner's estate. Blank v Blank (1995, 3d Dept) 222 A.D.2d 851, 634 N.Y.S.2d 886

Where all partnership property, including choses in action, vested in surviving partner upon death of his partners, he is proper party plaintiff under subd. 2, paragraph d, and representatives of deceased partner are not necessary parties to action to recover under fire insurance policies covering partnership property. Gallotti v Continental Ins. Co. (1934) 152 Misc 351, 273 N.Y.S. 29, affd (1934) 241 A.D. 804, 270 N.Y.S. 930

The law is clear that upon the death of a partner, the deceased partner's representative has no legal interest in the assets, but only an equitable interest in the distribution of any surplus remaining after the payment of firm debts. It becomes the duty of the surviving partner to settle the partnership affairs and remit the deceased partner's share to his representative. This obligation, however, and the corresponding right of the estate representative may be affected by the surviving partner's agreement with the decedent or by the provisions of the deceased partner's will. In re Lutz' Will (1952) 202 Misc 903, 112 N.Y.S.2d 640, affd (1953, 1st Dept) 281 A.D. 809, 118 N.Y.S.2d 751

Where the owner of a business took his son into partnership and filed a copy of the certificate of partnership, it was presumed that father and son became partners on the date stated therein and upon death of the father the Surrogate's Court had no jurisdiction to compel delivery of partnership assets to the father's administratrix. The administratrix could recover assets retained by the father by discovery proceedings against the son, but not cash and insurance, determination of the estate's interest in which must await the partnership accounting. In re Palega's Estate (1955) 208 Misc 966, 145 N.Y.S.2d 271

Partnership realty is considered personalty with regard to a partner's rights therein, and a surviving partner is vested with the legal

ownership of the partnership property, hence the deceased partner's administrator has no legal interest therein other than a right to an accounting. In re Sage's Estate (1961) 31 Misc. 2d 715, 221 N.Y.S.2d 414

Upon the death of a partner the partnership is dissolved and the only property right which the survivor of such partner possesses is a claim for an accounting. La Russo v Paladino (1951, Sup) 109 N.Y.S.2d 627, affd (1952) 280 A.D. 988, 116 N.Y.S.2d 617, app den (1953) 281 A.D. 753, 118 N.Y.S.2d 557

Subdivision (d) of this section is a codification of the well-settled principle that, upon death of a member of a partnership, title to partnership property vests in the survivor as legal owner. Virshup v Industrial Bank of Commerce (1959, CA2 NY) 272 F.2d 43

7. Conjugal rights; heirs and next of kin

Where a law partnership agreement provided, among other matters, that upon dissolution of the partnership for any cause other than because of the misconduct of a partner the interest of the retiring, withdrawing, or former partner should consist of "his capital account, which shall be determined upon an accounting," and that where the dissolution of the partnership results from "the misconduct of a partner, the interest of that partner in the partnership shall be determined at arbitration," a proceeding by the representative of a deceased partner, under SCPA § 2103, to discover the extent of the interest of a deceased partner in the partnership and to have money or personal property representing such interest delivered to her would be dismissed since, under the first agreement, until an accounting is had there is no "specific personal property or money which belongs to the estate," possession of which could be obtained through a proceeding pursuant to SCPA § 2103 and, under the second agreement, determination of the deceased partner's interest in event of dissolution because of misconduct of partner was determinable, not by accounting, but by arbitration and in either event, unless and until the nature and extent of the deceased partner's interest in the partnership assets is determined either by arbitration or by an accounting, an SCPA § 2103 proceeding may not properly be instituted, since the purpose of such proceeding is "to obtain the possession of specific personal property or money which belongs to the estate." Estate of Schwartzenberg (1984, 1st Dept) 99 A.D.2d 969, 472 N.Y.S.2d 658

Partners have no personal right in any specific property of partnership, and such property is not subject to conjugal rights. In re Dumarest's Estate (1933) 146 Misc 442, 262 N.Y.S. 450

§ 52. Nature of partner's interest in the partnership

A partner's interest in the partnership is his share of the profits and surplus and the same is personal property.

History: Add, L 1919, ch 408, eff Oct 1, 1919.

CASE ANNOTATIONS

Under the terms of the Uniform Partnership Act, specific partnership real estate is converted into personal property and on the death of a partner passes to the surviving partner under the partnership agreement. In re Estate of Havemeyer (1966) 17 N.Y.2d 216, 270 N.Y.S.2d 197, 217 N.E.2d 26, reh den (1966) 17 N.Y.2d 918

Specific partnership property is all property except a partner's share of the profits and surplus. Geitner v United States Fidelity & Guaranty Co. (1929) 225 A.D. 451, 233 N.Y.S. 378, affd (1929) 251 N.Y. 205, 167 N.E. 222

The interest of a judgment debtor in the profits of a partnership cannot be reached by means of a third party subpoena served for examination of the partnership in supplementary proceedings. Northeastern Real Estate Sec. Corp. v Goldstein (1944) 267 A.D. 832, 45 N.Y.S.2d 848, app dismd (1944) 292 N.Y. 720, 56 N.E.2d 125

Where partners agreed that real property or the interest of the parties therein should be held as a partnership asset, to be applied together with the other assets of the partnership to the payment of partnership debts and any balance found to be due from one partner to another on the winding up of the partnership affairs, to the extent necessary for such purposes the character of the property is deemed changed into personalty. Altman v Altman (1946) 271 A.D. 884, 67 N.Y.S.2d 119, affd (1948) 297 N.Y. 973, 80 N.E.2d 359

Use of death benefit provision in partnership agreement is acceptable method of valuation of interest in law partnership. Douglas v Douglas (2001, 3d Dept) 281 A.D.2d 709, 722 N.Y.S.2d 87

In valuing husband's interest in law partnership for purposes of equitable distribution in divorce action, court properly adopted valuation made by wife's expert, rather than that made by husband's expert, where (1) husband's expert conceded that his methodology, which used withdrawal analysis and death analysis, had never been accepted by any court, that he had never used that method before, that death benefit was not available to husband on demand, that withdrawal benefit was artificially low, that death benefit value was more accurate than withdrawal value, and that "excess earnings" approach was more common method of valuing practice, and (2) wife's expert, using excess earnings method, relied on his previous experience in valuing interests of partners in other large New York City law firms, ascertained compensation level of senior associates in such firms engaged in same area of practice as that of husband, and adjusted their compensation upward to reflect higher hourly billing rate attributable to him. Douglas v Douglas (2001, 3d Dept) 281 A.D.2d 709, 722 N.Y.S.2d 87

Husband's interest in his law partnership's unfunded, nonqualified retirement plan was not too speculative to be valued as marital asset for purposes of equitable distribution in divorce action where (1) partnership historically had been profitable enough to make payments called for by plan to retired partners, (2) there was no indication that husband, who was 50 years old and had more than 10 years as partner in firm, would not continue as partner until retirement, and (3) wife's expert valued husband's interest in plan at $412,700, $460,400, or $479,400, depending on whether husband retired at age 50, 56, or 62. Douglas v Douglas (2001, 3d Dept) 281 A.D.2d 709, 722 N.Y.S.2d 87

In divorce action, there was no merit in husband's claim that court violated "double counting" rules by failing to consider his maintenance and child support obligations when awarding 50 percent of his law practice appreciation and future unfunded retirement benefits to wife where (1) court properly accepted excess earnings method, used by wife's expert, for valuation of law practice, (2) wife's expert first subtracted $538,000 from husband's earnings stream, (3) that adjustment, representing reasonable compensation for senior associate possessing husband's skills, was excluded from calculation of value of appreciation of husband's law practice during marriage and was not used as part of formula to evaluate his law license, and (4) because $538,000 was not capitalized, converted, and distributed as marital asset, it remained available for maintenance payments without impacting rules against double counting. Douglas v Douglas (2001, 3d Dept) 281 A.D.2d 709, 722 N.Y.S.2d 87

Where, according to articles of co-partnership, a partnership was formed to purchase and hold for investment certain real property, and, upon termination of the partnership, an account was to be had and the property divided among the partners after payment of co-partnership liabilities, under this section, property of the partnership was personalty and could not be made the subject of an action for partition. Broida v Bunnell Associates (1960) 26 Misc. 2d 213, 201 N.Y.S.2d 572

A court order providing that the "interests" of two members of a partnership be charged with payment of personal judgment obtained against them individually, and providing for sale of their "partnership interest," refers merely by the words quoted to such interest in the business as they may have under this section, and a purchaser at sale made pursuant to such order could obtain no greater rights. Beckley v Speaks (1963) 39 Misc. 2d 241, 240 N.Y.S.2d 553, affd (1964, 1st Dept) 21 A.D.2d 759, 251 N.Y.S.2d 1015, app dismd (1964) 15 N.Y.2d 481, reported in full (1964) 15 N.Y.2d 546, 254 N.Y.S.2d 362, 202 N.E.2d 906

This section is declaratory of the common law and partner's "interest in the partnership" is personal property. In re Estate of Finkelstein (1963) 40 Misc. 2d 910, 245 N.Y.S.2d 225

As the estate representative of a decedent, plaintiff was entitled under N.Y. P'ship Law §§ 52, 62(4), and 73 to demand an account from the decedent's surviving partners and to receive the decedent's interest in the partnership. Priel v Linarello (2007, App Div, 2d Dept) 843 NYS2d 436

This section does not change the common law. Rossmoore v Anderson (1932, SD NY) 1 F. Supp. 35, 11 AFTR 1140, affd (1933, CA2 NY) 67 F.2d 1009, 13 AFTR 437, cert den (1934) 292 US 630, 78 L Ed 1484, 54 S Ct 640

§ 53.   Assignment of partner's interest

1. A conveyance by a partner of his interest in the partnership does not of itself dissolve the partnership, nor, as against the other partners in the absence of agreement, entitle the assignee, during the continuance of the partnership, to interfere in the management or administration of the partnership business or affairs, or to require any information or account of partnership transactions, or to inspect the partnership books; but it merely entitles the assignee to receive in accordance with his contract the profits to which the assigning partner would otherwise be entitled.

2. In case of a dissolution of the partnership, the assignee is entitled to receive his assignor's interest and may require an account from the date only of the last account agreed to by all the partners.

History: Add, L 1919, ch 408, eff Oct 1, 1919.

CASE ANNOTATIONS

Under the rule that an assignment of an interest does not of itself dissolve the partnership a plaintiff's right to hold his partner to his fiduciary duty was not affected by the assignment of his interest to his wife where the business had never been treated as dissolved and the interest had been reassigned prior to the time of the action. Meinhard v Salmon (1928) 249 N.Y. 458, 164 N.E. 545, 62 ALR 1

A third-party beneficiary contract of partnership providing that "in the event of the death of any partner, his share will be transferred to his wife, with no termination of the partnership" is not invalid as an attempted testamentary disposition. In re Estate of Hillowitz (1968) 22 N.Y.2d 107, 291 N.Y.S.2d 325, 238 N.E.2d 723

Conveyances and assignments of property by two of five partners to persons who had notice of an agreement that the property was to be held as a partnership asset were ineffective to dissolve the tenancy in partnership and the transferees did not become tenants in common and could not compel partition. Altman v Altman (1946) 271 A.D. 884, 67 N.Y.S.2d 119, affd (1948) 297 N.Y. 973, 80 N.E.2d 359

The assignment of an interest in a partnership does not destroy the partnership, but merely entitles the assignee to any profit that the assignor would have received as well as any of the assignor's interest in the partnership upon dissolution. Leon v Glaser (1967, 1st Dept) 28 A.D.2d 833, 281 N.Y.S.2d 441, mod on other grounds (1967, 1st Dept) 28 A.D.2d 835, 282 N.Y.S.2d 923

Under provisions of partnership law, unless parties have agreed otherwise, person cannot become member of partnership without consent of all partners, whereas assignment of partnership interest may be made without consent, but assignee is entitled only to receive profits of assigning partner. Rapoport v 55 Perry Co. (1975, 1st Dept) 50 A.D.2d 54, 376 N.Y.S.2d 147

Partnership agreement providing that assignments, encumbrances and agreements "as a result of which any person shall become interested with (assignor) in this firm" would not be allowed unless agreed to by majority of partners, "except for members of his immediate family who have attained majority," was intended to limit partner with respect to his right to assign partnership interest to right to profits; thus partners could not transfer full partnership interest to their children, and such children only had rights as assignees to receive share of partnership income and profits of their assignors. Rapoport v 55 Perry Co. (1975, 1st Dept) 50 A.D.2d 54, 376 N.Y.S.2d 147

In action by assignee of portion of residual interest held by defendant in certain partnerships, syndicates and proprietorship, alleging that defendant sold partnership equipment at below-market prices, thereby improperly diminishing plaintiff's residual interests, court properly granted plaintiff's motion to compel production of documents relating to sale or disposition of partnership equipment since (1) documents sought by plaintiff were material and necessary in preparation for trial of plaintiff's claims for breach of contract and breach of fiduciary duty, and (2) CLS Partn § 53(1) does not preclude assignee from obtaining information or account of partnership transactions in action by assignee against assignor after dissolution of partnership. Kidder, Peabody & Co. v Condren (1990, 1st Dept) 166 A.D.2d 328, 561 N.Y.S.2d 2

Defendant's letter to plaintiff, which stated "this will acknowledge that you have a 50 percent interest in the 50 percent interest which I hold" in partnership, constituted valid legal assignment, not mere promise to assign in futuro, which did not require consideration, since no special language or form is required for assignment so long as intention to effect present transfer is apparent. Whalen v Gerzof (1994, 3d Dept) 206 A.D.2d 688, 615 N.Y.S.2d 465, app den (1994) 84 N.Y.2d 809, 621 N.Y.S.2d 518, 645 N.E.2d 1218

Validity of defendant's assignment of partnership interest to plaintiff did not depend on plaintiff's exercise of control over partnership where she was not entitled to participate in partnership, but was given right to receive share of profits, as limited by assignment, to which defendant would otherwise have been entitled. Whalen v Gerzof (1994, 3d Dept) 206 A.D.2d 688, 615 N.Y.S.2d 465, app den (1994) 84 N.Y.2d 809, 621 N.Y.S.2d 518, 645 N.E.2d 1218

Fact that plaintiff failed to contribute additional capital to partnership as required of partners did not reduce her partnership interest or affect damages to be awarded in her action to enforce assignment of 50 percent of defendant's partnership interest to her where plaintiff was not partner but only assignee of 1/2 of any distribution of income or profits received from partnership by defendant. Whalen v Gerzof (1994, 3d Dept) 206 A.D.2d 688, 615 N.Y.S.2d 465, app den (1994) 84 N.Y.2d 809, 621 N.Y.S.2d 518, 645 N.E.2d 1218

Defendant partnership was judicially estopped from denying validity of assignment of partnership interest to plaintiffs where partnership, as prevailing party in prior California action brought against it by plaintiffs' assignor, had taken position that assignor lacked standing to enforce his rights as partner because he had assigned his partnership interest. Sunseri v Macro Cellular Partners (1999, 1st Dept) 263 A.D.2d 365, 692 N.Y.S.2d 383

In action against partnership by plaintiffs who claimed right to distribution of certain partnership assets as assignees of partnership interest, validity of assignment was proved by unrefuted documentary evidence that partnership had recognized and ratified assignment. Sunseri v Macro Cellular Partners (1999, 1st Dept) 263 A.D.2d 365, 692 N.Y.S.2d 383

In action in which deceased partner's spouse/executor alleged that defendant managing partner engaged in self-dealing, misappropriated partnership income and violated fiduciary duty of loyalty to his partners, court erred in denying defendants' motion to dismiss complaint for failure to state cause of action, to extent that it sought dissolution of partnership and accounting, where no partnership agreements alleged in or made part of complaint gave transferee spouse any right to participate in partnership, to seek its dissolution or winding up, or to compel accounting of any partner and, further, interest in partnership which she did receive gave her no rights other than to receive profits to which decedent would have been entitled had he lived. Dame v Williams (2001, 3d Dept) 285 A.D.2d 928, 727 N.Y.S.2d 816

An assignment of a partner's interest, made to protect a person advancing funds for his contribution to the firm, which expressly recognized the existence of a partnership and under which his obligation did not arise until termination of the partnership did not affect the assignor's status as a partner. Rosenstein v Weiser (1947, Sup) 73 N.Y.S.2d 402

Under this section a conveyance of a partner's interest gives no interest in the firm assets as such and is ineffective to remove from the transferring partner his income tax burden and subsequent profit. Rossmoore v Anderson (1932, SD NY) 1 F. Supp. 35, 11 AFTR 1140, affd (1933, CA2 NY) 67 F.2d 1009, 13 AFTR 437, cert den (1934) 292 US 630, 78 L Ed 1484, 54 S Ct 640

Where a non-managing partner in real estate syndicates cast in form of general partnerships made partial assignments of portions of his partnership interest, the partial assignees were not personally liable for the partnership debts and under § 53(1) they had no right to interfere in the management or administration of the partnership business or affairs. United States v Silverstein (1965, SD NY) 237 F. Supp. 446, 65-1 USTC P 9266, 15 AFTR 2d 283, affd (1965, CA2 NY) 344 F.2d 1016, 65-2 USTC P 9480, 15 AFTR 2d 991, cert den (1965) 382 US 828, 15 L Ed 2d 73, 86 S Ct 65

Arbitrators did not manifestly disregard the law by concluding that a partner's voting agreement with third parties did not transfer a partnership interest in violation of N.Y. P'ship Law §§ 40(7) and 53(1) as the agreement merely concerned a vote for the retention of an entity as a managing agent, which vote the partner was entitled to cast with or without the agreement; the panel found that there was no claim that the entity sought to become a partner, only that a partner agreed to vote on a specific limited issue, and that invalidating the voting agreement would undermine an option agreement, which furthered the interests of the partnership and continuity of its business. Wien & Malkin LLP v Helmsley-Spear, Inc. (2006) 813 NYS2d 691, 846 NE2d 1201, reported at (2006, NY) 2006 NY LEXIS 270

§ 54.   Partner's interest subject to charging order

1. On due application to a competent court by any judgment creditor of a partner, the court which entered the judgment, order, or decree, or any other court, may charge the interest of the debtor partner with payment of the unsatisfied amount of such judgment debt with interest thereon. Upon such application or upon the granting of an order attaching the interest of the debtor partner before judgment, the court may then or later appoint a receiver of his share of the profits, and of any other money due or to fall due to him in respect of the partnership, and make all other orders, directions, accounts and inquiries which the debtor partner might have made, or which the circumstances of the case may require.

2. The interest charged may be redeemed at any time before foreclosure, or in case of a sale being directed by the court may be purchased without thereby causing a dissolution:

(a) With separate property, by any one or more of the partners, or

(b) With partnership property, by any one or more of the partners with the consent of all the partners whose interests are not so charged or sold.

3. Nothing in this act shall be held to deprive a partner of his right, if any, under the exemption laws, as regards his interest in the partnership.

History: Add, L 1919, ch 408, eff Oct 1, 1919.

Sub 1, amd, L 1962, ch 310, § 298, eff Sept 1, 1963.

CASE ANNOTATIONS

The interest of a judgment debtor in the profits of a partnership cannot be reached by means of a third party subpoena served for examination of the partnership in supplementary proceedings. Northeastern Real Estate Sec. Corp. v Goldstein (1944) 267 A.D. 832, 45 N.Y.S.2d 848, app dismd (1944) 292 N.Y. 720, 56 N.E.2d 125

Section 54 of the Partnership Law does not represent the exclusive method of levy by a judgment creditor upon a partner's interest in a partnership; rather, such an interest can also be reached under CPLR 5201, which in relevant part provides "Where property consists of an interest in a partnership, any partner other than the judgment debtor, on behalf of the partnership, shall be the garnishee." Princeton Bank & Trust Co. v Berley (1977, 2d Dept) 57 A.D.2d 348, 394 N.Y.S.2d 714

A charging order was granted and a receiver appointed of the interest of a purchaser of a going partnership business where more than thirty days after notice of final determination by the New York City Comptroller of the amount of sales tax due from the seller and buyer on a bulk sale, a warrant was docketed in the County Clerk's office as a judgment. New York v Bencivenga (1955) 8 Misc. 2d 29, 169 N.Y.S.2d 515

Defendants were denied summary judgment in an action by judgment creditors of the general partners of a limited partnership to set aside as fraudulent and void, a conveyance by the limited partnership to a corporation shortly prior to the entry of judgment against the

Partnership Law

general partners. The record made out a prima facie case for a decree directing retransfer of title to the limited partnership and defendants failed to establish by documentary evidence that the judgment creditors were not entitled to recover. Central Petroleum Corp. v Korman (1958) 15 Misc. 2d 245, 177 N.Y.S.2d 761, app dismd (1959, 1st Dept) 8 A.D.2d 782, 190 N.Y.S.2d 314

Although property of a partnership is not subject to attachment or execution except as a claim against a partnership, a judgment creditor of any general or limited partner has the statutory right to obtain an order charging his debtor's interest in the partnership with payment of the unsatisfied amount of judgment with interest thereon. Central Petroleum Corp. v Korman (1958) 15 Misc. 2d 245, 177 N.Y.S.2d 761, app dismd (1959, 1st Dept) 8 A.D.2d 782, 190 N.Y.S.2d 314

Plaintiff, who was engaged in a joint venture with a member of a partnership, was not entitled to maintain lis pendens proceeding against property owned by the partnership, where the complaint failed to allege any cause of action against the partnership, which would affect the title of the partnership to the real property. Weisinger v Rae (1959) 19 Misc. 2d 341, 188 N.Y.S.2d 10

Where a judgment creditor of individual members of a partnership obtains a court order for sale of their "partnership interest", the interests to be sold are merely such as the judgment debtors have under § 52 of the Partnership Law and a purchaser at such sale has no status as a member of the partnership and no right to interfere with partnership business or to file an application for renewal of the partnership liquor license. Beckley v Speaks (1963) 39 Misc. 2d 241, 240 N.Y.S.2d 553, affd (1964, 1st Dept) 21 A.D.2d 759, 251 N.Y.S.2d 1015, app dismd (1964) 15 N.Y.2d 481, reported in full (1964) 15 N.Y.2d 546, 254 N.Y.S.2d 362, 202 N.E.2d 906

Judgment creditor of doctor could be satisfied out of retirement profit sharing account established at bank by partnership of which judgment debtor was member, despite judgment debtor's contention that onerous tax consequences and penalties would result from withdrawal of such funds. Lerner v Williamsburg Sav. Bank (1976) 87 Misc. 2d 685, 386 N.Y.S.2d 906

ARTICLE 6
DISSOLUTION AND WINDING UP

History: Add, L 1919, ch 408, eff Oct 1, 1919.

§ 60.   Dissolution defined

The dissolution of a partnership is the change in the relation of the partners caused by any partner ceasing to be associated in the carrying on as distinguished from the winding up of the business.

History: Add, L 1919, ch 408, eff Oct 1, 1919.

CASE ANNOTATIONS

Dissolution takes place when the partners determine to discontinue business although the partnership affairs have not been wound up. Bayer v Bayer (1926) 215 A.D. 454, 214 N.Y.S. 322

Partner had right to continue partnership for purpose of development of plaza where 2 parties had formed partnership for development of factory outlet plaza, other partner decided that he no longer wished to be member of partnership, and partnership agreement contained no provision for duration of partnership. St. Lawrence Factory Stores v Ogdensburg Bridge & Port Auth. (1994, 3d Dept) 202 A.D.2d 844, 609 N.Y.S.2d 370

In partnership at will dissolution thereof may be inferred from circumstances, but when not result of mutual agreement there must be (a) notice by party desiring a dissolution to other, or former's election to terminate partnership, or (b) said election must be manifested by unequivocal acts or circumstances brought to the knowledge of the other party, which signify exercise of will of former that partnership be dissolved. Smith v Maine (1932) 145 Misc 521, 260 N.Y.S. 409

Order of dissolution of Curb Exchange may not be construed as an order requiring liquidation of affairs of partnership. Avery v Moffatt (1945) 187 Misc 576, 55 N.Y.S.2d 215

A provision in a contract for setting up a joint venture, giving one and all of the joint venturers the privilege of retiring upon 90-days' notice, could, in view of the provisions of this section for dissolution of partnerships, have ended contractual relations and resulted in a dissolution and termination of the venture within one year, thus taking the contract out of the statute of frauds. Glenmark, Inc. v Carity (1961) 30 Misc. 2d 1065, 221 N.Y.S.2d 330

Winding up means the process of settling partnership affairs after dissolution. In re Luckenbach's Estate (1965) 45 Misc. 2d 897, 258 N.Y.S.2d 44

Though summary judgment was properly granted to trustees as a result of the complaint of remaindermen to a partnership trust challenging the trustees' conversion of corporate shares to partnership interests being time-barred, the remaindermen were entitled to the relief they sought with regard to compelling partnership accountings and a distribution of partnership assets. Because no partnership agreement existed, N.Y. Partnership Law §§ 62(4), 60, and 73, provided for the remaindermen to receive, as ordinary creditors, an amount equal to the value of their interest in the dissolved partnership when the trust terminated and, therefore, entitled them to an accounting and distribution. Breidbart v Wiesenthal (2004, A.D., 2d Dept) 781 N.Y.S.2d 123

Defendants were not entitled to summary judgment in plaintiffs' action to recover executive search fees because the parties' conflicting allegations raised questions of fact as to whether plaintiffs anticipatorily repudiated their partnership agreement when they sought to withdraw and declare the partnership dissolved before the termination date or whether the purpose of the partnership was frustrated by defendants' failure to comply with their search obligations. Gardiner Int'l, Inc. v J.W. Townsend & Assocs. (2004, A.D., 1st Dept) 788 N.Y.S.2d 312

Circumstances of a former partner's full-time employment with the State Insurance Fund, and his limited work winding up a few pending cases, reflected an express withdrawal from his former partnership and effected its dissolution by operation of law. Conolly v Thuillez (2006, 3d Dept) 26 App Div 3d 720, 810 NYS2d 239

Partnership is dissolved when partner withdraws, not when winding up of partnership affairs is completed; withdrawing partner no longer shares in gains and losses of any continuing entity, and his actions cannot bind continuing partnership or its partners. Estate of Quirk v Commissioner (1991, CA6) 928 F.2d 751, 91-1 USTC P 50148, 67 AFTR 2d 782, on remand (1995) TC Memo 1995-234, RIA TC Memo P 95234, 69 CCH TCM 2746, 95 TNT 106-11

§ 61.   Partnership not terminated by dissolution

On dissolution the partnership is not terminated, but continues until the winding up of partnership affairs is completed.

History: Add, L 1919, ch 408, eff Oct 1, 1919.

CASE ANNOTATIONS

1. In General
2. Winding-up of affairs

1. In General

Dissolution takes place when the partners determine to discontinue business although the partnership affairs have not been wound up. Bayer v Bayer (1926) 215 A.D. 454, 214 N.Y.S. 322

Where a partner ceases to be associated in the carrying on of the business so that the relation of the partners is changed a dissolution is effected for all purposes except liquidation. Patrikes v J. C. H. Service Stations, Inc. (1943) 180 Misc 917, 41 N.Y.S.2d 158, affd (1943) 180 Misc 927, 46 N.Y.S.2d 233, app den (1943) 266 A.D. 924, 44 N.Y.S.2d 472

Order of dissolution of Curb Exchange may not be construed as an order requiring liquidation of affairs of partnership. Avery v Moffatt (1945) 187 Misc 576, 55 N.Y.S.2d 215

In the light of this section, there is no merit in a contention that a partnership cannot be sued because it has dissolved. Emerson Radio & Phonograph Corp. v Eskind (1957) 32 Misc. 2d 1038, 228 N.Y.S.2d 841

A partner's right to require dissolution of the firm does not give him the right, after notifying a copartner that the firm should be dissolved, to organize a rival business and use the firm assets for profit, and partners who pursue such a course are liable to the old firm in the amount of such profit. Hamilton Co. v Hamilton Tile Corp. (1960) 23 Misc. 2d 589, 197 N.Y.S.2d 384

Letter from managing partner to other partners announcing his immediate withdrawal from and dissolution of the partnership did not free managing partner of all fiduciary relationship to the partnership since partnership continues until winding up is completed. Lavin v Ehrlich (1974) 80 Misc. 2d 247, 363 N.Y.S.2d 50

A partner's motion for an order dispensing with the other partner's signature to a certificate of discontinuance was granted, where the requirement of filing the certificate was intended to afford the public information as to the identities of persons conducting the business, where the continuance of the present certificate would have constituted a misrepresentation to the public, and where Partn Law § 61 was not ground for denial of the motion in that the purpose of that section is to continue the partners' liability for predissolution obligations. Reed v Pelley (1982, Sup) 112 Misc. 2d 382, 447 N.Y.S.2d 98

Dissolved New York partnership is not "person" eligible to avail itself of reorganization in Chapter 11 bankruptcy proceeding because Partnership Law prohibits dissolved partnership from engaging in any business other than liquidation. C-TC 9th Ave. Pshp. v Norton Co. (In re C-TC 9th Ave. Pshp.) (1997, CA2 NY) 113 F.3d 1304, 30 BCD 1146, 38 CBC2d 115, CCH Bankr L Rptr P 77410 (criticized in In re Shea & Gould (1997, BC SD NY) 214 BR 739, 38 CBC2d 1453)

Under this section business of firm and firm itself continues from time of dissolution until winding up of partnership affairs is completed. Rossmoore v Commissioner (1935, CA2) 76 F.2d 520, 35-1 USTC P 9277, 15 AFTR 1178

A dissolution of a partnership did not terminate its existence. Jacques Krijn En Zoon v Schrijver (1957, DC NY) 151 F. Supp. 955

Partnership is not terminated on dissolution but continues until winding up of partnership affairs is completed; partnership remains in existence until final settlement of all partnership affairs. Merriman v Town of Colonie (1996, ND NY) 934 F. Supp. 501, affd without op sub nom Merriman v Ye Ole Locksmith Shoppe (1997, CA2 NY) 112 F.3d 504, reported in full (1997, CA2 NY) 1997 US App LEXIS 9852

2. Winding-up of affairs

Tax matters would seem inevitably to be among the "affairs" to be wound up following dissolution of a partnership. Broom v Murphy (1961, 3d Dept) 14 A.D.2d 639, 218 N.Y.S.2d 709

Where record showed that following partners' mutual agreement to dissolve in March, 1973, neither party took initiative to liquidate assets or commence accounting action, where there was never any agreement reached with respect to who would take it upon himself to liquidate remaining assets, and where, even though one partner offered to buy remaining partnership horses from other partner for $5,200, other partner was under no obligation to accept former course of action nor was agreement ever reached on offer, costs for caring and feeding of partnership's horses from March, 1973 until their sale in May, 1974, would be charged to partnership and shared by both

parties. Ben-Dashan v Plitt (1977, 4th Dept) 58 A.D.2d 244, 396 N.Y.S.2d 542

Plaintiff's vested inventory interest was not terminated under terms of partnership agreement when defendant law firm dissolved. Keogh v Breed, Abbott & Morgan (1996, 1st Dept) 224 A.D.2d 180, 637 N.Y.S.2d 124, app den (1996) 88 N.Y.2d 801, 644 N.Y.S.2d 688, 667 N.E.2d 338

Tenant partnership was amenable to action by landlord for rent due under lease where partnership, despite its dissolution, continued to exist at all relevant times for purpose of winding up its affairs, among which was its prolonged and ongoing rent dispute with landlord. 111-115 Broadway Ltd. Pshp. v Minter & Gay (1998, 1st Dept) 255 A.D.2d 192, 680 N.Y.S.2d 12

Partnership had capacity to commence tax certiorari proceedings as part of its obligation to wind up its affairs under CLS Bus Corp § 1005(a) and (b) and CLS Partn §§ 60 et seq. Fox Meadow Partners, Ltd. v Board of Assessment Review (2000, 2d Dept) 273 A.D.2d 472, 710 N.Y.S.2d 610

Winding up means the process of settling partnership affairs after dissolution. In re Luckenbach's Estate (1965) 45 Misc. 2d 897, 258 N.Y.S.2d 44

Because a limited partnership was not terminated upon dissolution but continued for the purpose of winding up under N.Y. P'ship Law § 61 until its affairs, including the sale of its primary asset, were completed, a trial court improperly found that the partners' cash capital accounts were frozen at the moment of dissolution with respect to the distribution of the proceeds of the sale of the partnership's primary asset, the sale of which occurred two years after the partnership dissolved due to the retirement of a limited partner. Lai v Gartlan (2007, App Div, 1st Dept) 845 NYS2d 30

Partner, in completing certain construction work, was merely winding up partnership obligations which were incurred prior to co-partner's death, and all income and expenses derived from such work were properly attributable to partnership, rather than to partner as individual. Re Orsini & Earl, 1983 Dec State Tax Comm, TSB-H-83(127)I, June 13, 1983

Attorney's claim that a Chapter 7 debtor who was a partner in a law firm that was dissolved diverted money the firm was owed to himself and a new firm he created was sufficient to survive the debtor's motion to dismiss the attorney's claims that a judgment the attorney obtained in state court was nondischargeable under 11 U.S.C.S. § 523(a)(4) and (a)(6), and that the debtor should be denied a discharge under 11 U.S.C.S. § 727(a)(2)(A), (a)(3), (a)(4)(A), and (a)(5). The debtor was a fiduciary under the New York Partnership Law during the period the law firm was being dissolved. Shiboleth v Yerushalmi (In re Yerushalmi) (2008, BC ED NY) 393 BR 288, 50 BCD 215, judgment entered, cause dismd (2008, BC ED NY) 2008 Bankr LEXIS 2603.

Only manner in which partnership can be "wound up" is through formal accounting wherein overall financial status may be evaluated. Sitchenko v Di Resta (1981, ED NY) 512 F. Supp. 758

Partnership remained in existence pending accounting, absent contrary court order, and both partners retained equal authority, rights and access as tenants in partnership premises although one partner dissolved partnership, notified ousted partner, and changed office locks; even though retaining partner held lease on premises in her own name, she was not entitled to bar ousted partner from premises. Merriman v Town of Colonie (1996, ND NY) 934 F. Supp. 501, affd without op sub nom Merriman v Ye Ole Locksmith Shoppe (1997, CA2 NY) 112 F.3d 504, reported in full (1997, CA2 NY) 1997 US App LEXIS 9852

§ 62. Causes of dissolution

Dissolution is caused:

1. Without violation of the agreement between the partners,

(a) By the termination of the definite term or particular undertaking specified in the agreement,

(b) By the express will of any partner when no definite term or particular undertaking is specified,

(c) By the express will of all the partners who have not assigned their interests or suffered them to be charged for their separate debts, either before or after the termination of any specified term or particular undertaking,

(d) By the expulsion of any partner from the business bona fide in accordance with such a power conferred by the agreement between the partners;

2. In contravention of the agreement between the partners, where the circumstances do not permit a dissolution under any other provision of this section, by the express will of any partner at any time;

3. By any event which makes it unlawful for the business of the partnership to be carried on or for the members to carry it on in partnership;

4. By the death of any partner;

5. By the bankruptcy of any partner or the partnership;

6. By decree of court under section sixty-three.

History: Add, L 1919, ch 408, eff Oct 1, 1919.

CASE ANNOTATIONS

1. In General
2. Partner's disassociating himself
3. Exclusion or expulsion of partner
4. No fixed term in agreement
5. Expiration of term specified in agreement
6. Purchase of one partner's interest
7. Death of partner
8. – Actions for accounting
9. New partners
10. Litigation; complaints

1. In General

A partnership may be dissolved at any time by any partner. De Martino v Pensavalle (1977, 2d Dept) 56 A.D.2d 589, 391 N.Y.S.2d 461

Partnership's continuing operations and obligations, including lease payments and "sale-leaseback" type arrangements, did not preclude dissolution of partnership, thereby triggering accounting, since transactions cited by defendant general partners did not constitute sale- leaseback agreements, which would have permitted them to avoid accounting pursuant to terms of partnership agreement, and adequate reserves could be maintained to cover any potential liability. CCG Assoc. I v Riverside Assoc. (1990, 1st Dept) 157 A.D.2d 435, 556 N.Y.S.2d 859

Existence of law firm partnership terminated on merger with another law firm, and thus plaintiff was entitled to collect value of his partnership participation as of date of termination, despite remaining partners' contention that majority of partners did not choose to characterize merger as exercise of its option to terminate in event of departure of partners having at least 75 percent participation after partners having at least 50 percent participation formed or joined successor firm, where (1) firm's clients were advised that they would be represented by acquiring firm, (2) firm's assets and obligations were transferred to acquiring firm, (3) all attorneys in firm except plaintiff would practice under name of acquiring firm, (4) firm's telephone number would be answered in name of acquiring firm, (5) firm had vacated its office, and (6) no business would be conducted in firm's name. Wolfson v Rosenthal (1994, 1st Dept) 210 A.D.2d 47, 619 N.Y.S.2d 43, app dismd without op (1995) 85 N.Y.2d 924, 627 N.Y.S.2d 325, 650 N.E.2d 1327

Partner manifested unequivocal election to dissolve partnership where he transferred to himself individually partnership's primary asset, which was residence in which parties lived on separate floors, and encumbered property with mortgage, proceeds of which he alone received. Staines Assocs. v Adler (1999, 1st Dept) 266 A.D.2d 52, 698 N.Y.S.2d 639

Plaintiff partner's service of notice of his election to dissolve at-will partnership, demanding that winding up of partnership affairs commence immediately, accomplished dissolution of partnership, and thus defendant partner's action for judicial dissolution was rendered academic. 220-52 Assocs. v Edelman (1997, 1st Dept) 241 A.D.2d 365, 659 N.Y.S.2d 885, later proceeding (1998, 1st Dept) 253 A.D.2d 352,

676 N.Y.S.2d 566, app dismd (1998) 92 N.Y.2d 1026, 684 N.Y.S.2d 490, 707 N.E.2d 445

Where managing partner instituted and carried out negotiations for building's purchase during vital partnership tenure and completed them after announcing dissolution of partnership but prior to winding up, the purchase opportunity which carried with it continued possession of the good will asset of the business embodied in the location belonged to the partnership and managing partner breached fiduciary duty by appropriating opportunity for himself, with result that he held the building in constructive trust for the partnership. Lavin v Ehrlich (1974) 80 Misc. 2d 247, 363 N.Y.S.2d 50

A partnership can only be dissolved under the statute or within the bounds of the partnership agreement. Clark v Gunn (1954, Sup) 134 N.Y.S.2d 206

Under N.Y. Gen. Oblig. Law § 15-107, if a partnership was dissolved at the time that a partner was released from partnership liability, the release did not benefit co-partners; in the instant foreclosure action, one partner had filed for bankruptcy prior to the agreement, and another partner died prior to the agreement, and under N.Y. Partnership Law § 62(4), (5), both of these events resulted in the dissolution of the partnership, and since the partnership was dissolved at the time of the settlement agreement, settlement agreements between the estates of the bankrupt and dead partners did not relieve a remaining partner and the partnership of liability to a mortgage holder under N.Y. Gen. Oblig. Law § 15-107. NAB Asset Venture IV, L.P. v Orangeburg Equities (2002, A.D., 2d Dept) 751 N.Y.S.2d 41

Trial court's determination that the partnership had dissolved on May 15, 1992 was supported by evidence showing that the partner communicated his desire to dissolve the partnership as early as March 1992, and the parties agreed to enter into negotiations for the partner to take over the operation of one of the offices and acknowledged a transition period beginning Mary 14, 1992. Morris v Crawford (2003, A.D., 3d Dept) 757 N.Y.S.2d 383

New York law is clear that a venture at will can be terminated without liability for breach of contract by any partner at any time by any act which evidences intent to terminate the association. Kidz Cloz, Inc. v Officially for Kids, Inc. (2004, SD NY) 320 F. Supp. 2d 164

2. Partner's disassociating himself

Minority partner violated the partnership agreement when he sought to unilaterally dissolve the partnership because the partnership agreement covered the terms of the dissolution and this section had no application since it would only apply if the agreement did not address the issue. Congel v Malfitano, 31 N.Y.3d 272, 101 N.E.3d 341, 76 N.Y.S.3d 873, 2018 N.Y. LEXIS 496 (N.Y. 2018).

Even though a partnership agreement provides a definite term for duration, the partnership may be dissolved at any time by any partner, thereby putting an end to it but rendering the partner who breaches the agreement subject to a claim for damages for breach of contract by each partner who did not wrongfully cause the dissolution. Napoli v Domnitch (1962, 2d Dept) 18 A.D.2d 707, 236 N.Y.S.2d 549, affd (1964) 14 N.Y.2d 508, 248 N.Y.S.2d 228, 197 N.E.2d 623

No one can be forced to continue as a partner against his will. Napoli v Domnitch (1962, 2d Dept) 18 A.D.2d 707, 236 N.Y.S.2d 549, affd (1964) 14 N.Y.2d 508, 248 N.Y.S.2d 228, 197 N.E.2d 623

In an action for dissolution of a law partnership and for an accounting, in which plaintiff two years after having entered into an oral agreement establishing the partnership, withdrew therefrom, taking with him certain files, furniture, books and equipment without the consent of the other partners, notifying them by phone the next day that he had withdrawn from the partnership, a decree ordering dissolution of the partnership was unwarranted, since a partnership at will, such as the one in question, can be dissolved at any time by the express will of any partner (Partn Law § 62(1)(b), and since plaintiff had already exercised his right to dissolve the partnership by his actions on the date he voluntarily left the firm. Carola v Grogan (1984, 3d Dept) 102 A.D.2d 934, 477 N.Y.S.2d 525

Where a partner ceases to be associated in the carrying on of the business so that the relation of the partners is changed a dissolution is effected for all purposes except liquidation. Patrikes v J. C. H. Service Stations, Inc. (1943) 180 Misc 917, 41 N.Y.S.2d 158, affd (1943) 180 Misc 927, 46 N.Y.S.2d 233, app den (1943) 266 A.D. 924, 44 N.Y.S.2d 472

Partnership is dissolved when partner withdraws, not when winding up of partnership affairs is completed; withdrawing partner no longer shares in gains and losses of any continuing entity, and his actions cannot bind continuing partnership or its partners. Estate of

Quirk v Commissioner (1991, CA6) 928 F.2d 751, 91-1 USTC P 50148, 67 AFTR 2d 782, on remand (1995) TC Memo 1995-234, RIA TC Memo P 95234, 69 CCH TCM 2746, 95 TNT 106-11

Pursuant to the terms of the partnership agreement, the partner's letter providing notice of his intent to dissolve the partnership did not effectuate a dissolution because the letter was not signed by the other partner as required by the terms of the agreement. Under the terms of the agreement, the partnership was not dissolved until the former partner left his employment position with the partnership. Dental Health Assoc. v Zangeneh (2006, 2d Dept) 34 App Div 3d 622, 825 NYS2d 505

3. Exclusion or expulsion of partner

Repudiation by either partner is sufficient to dissolve a partnership, and where partners signed a certificate of dissolution and one partner was excluded from the partnership office, the partnership was dissolved. Niles v Leitman (1951) 278 A.D. 330, 104 N.Y.S.2d 822

A partner cannot recover damages for wrongful expulsion from a firm where he breached the partnership agreement, although § 62 does not make a breach a ground for expulsion and § 63 does make it a ground for a court dissolution which the other partners did not obtain. Schnitzer v Josephthal (1923) 122 Misc 15, 202 N.Y.S. 77, affd (1924) 208 A.D. 769, 202 N.Y.S. 952

Exclusion of the plaintiff from participation in the conduct of a corporation set up by partners to carry out the partnership agreement constituted a violation of the agreement and justified an accounting and dissolution. Dow v Beals (1933) 149 Misc 631, 268 N.Y.S. 425

4. No fixed term in agreement

Partnership was dissolvable at will by either partner under N.Y. P'ship Law § 62(1)(b), and a complaint alleging breach of the oral partnership agreement was properly dismissed, because the agreement did not include a definite term or particular undertaking, and the complaint lacked a fixed, express period during which the enterprise was expected to operate; instead, the complaint alleged a flexible temporal framework: the parties were to solicit investments for an indefinite length of time, conduct an open-ended (possibly two-year) search for an unidentified business in an unknown business sector or industry, secure additional capital investments over the course of an unspecified period, and then buy and operate the enterprise for an indeterminate duration (perhaps four to seven years) until a liquidity event would hopefully occur. Further, when the entire scheme was considered, the alleged sequence of anticipated partnership events detailed in the complaint were too amorphous to meet the statutory "particular undertaking" standard for precluding unilateral dissolution. Gelman v Buehler (2013) 20 NY3d 534, 964 NYS2d 80.

Where an agreement creates a partnership at will but right of one partner to terminate the partnership is subject to the right granted others to purchase his interest, such partner cannot be compelled to remain as a partner and be subject to liabilities which could be imposed upon him by the other partners if they refuse to exercise their option to purchase his interests. Napoli v Domnitch (1962, 2d Dept) 18 A.D.2d 707, 236 N.Y.S.2d 549, affd (1964) 14 N.Y.2d 508, 248 N.Y.S.2d 228, 197 N.E.2d 623

Where a partnership agreement provides for continuing performance by the parties as long as the agreement is in effect but fixes no period for its duration, only a partnership at will is created which is subject to dissolution at any time by either partner without violating the agreement. Malmeth v Schneider (1963, 2d Dept) 18 A.D.2d 1030, 238 N.Y.S.2d 986

A partnership at will was created where the parties agreed to form a partnership but made no provision for the length of that relationship between them; the agreement did not violate the statute of frauds since it is possible to dissolve a partnership at will within one year. Pace v Perk (1981, 2d Dept) 81 A.D.2d 444, 440 N.Y.S.2d 710 (criticized in Philan Ins. v Frank B. Hall & Co. (1996, Sup) 170 Misc. 2d 729, 651 N.Y.S.2d 289)

In an action to interpret the dissolution terms of a joint venture agreement, the court erred when it looked exclusively to the agreement to determine the parties' intent instead of also considering additional agreements between the parties where, although the joint venture agreement provided that it would continue "without limitation as to time," the integration clause of the contract rendered other agreements part of the joint venture agreement, and where a question of fact was presented as to whether the parties intended limitations other than time to determine the duration and whether agreements when read together provided for a specific undertaking.

Hooker Chemicals & Plastics Corp. v International Minerals & Chemical Corp. (1982, 4th Dept) 90 A.D.2d 991, 456 N.Y.S.2d 587

When partner's actions are claimed to constitute requisite "express will" under CLS Partn § 62(1)(b), actions must manifest unequivocal election to dissolve partnership. Alessi v Brozzetti (1996, 3d Dept) 228 A.D.2d 917, 644 N.Y.S.2d 422

Partner's relocation to Florida did not manifest unequivocal intention to dissolve partnership. Alessi v Brozzetti (1996, 3d Dept) 228 A.D.2d 917, 644 N.Y.S.2d 422

Dissolution of partnership did not occur when 2 partners notified third partner that they refused to continue sharing certain management fees with him where there was no evidence that partnership stopped doing business, and third partner continued to receive his share of incentive fee paid to partnership. Alessi v Brozzetti (1996, 3d Dept) 228 A.D.2d 917, 644 N.Y.S.2d 422

Defendant partners' attempt to restructure partners' profit-sharing arrangement did not manifest requisite unequivocal election to dissolve partnership. Alessi v Brozzetti (1996, 3d Dept) 228 A.D.2d 917, 644 N.Y.S.2d 422

Where 3-party partnership had no definite term, it was terminated, without breaching partnership agreement, by actions of 2 partners in giving written notice to third partner that they were dissolving partnership. Teeter v De Lorenzo (2000, 3d Dept) 275 A.D.2d 528, 711 N.Y.S.2d 629

Where partnership agreement provides no specific term of life of partnership, it is a partnership at will to be dissolved at the insistence of any partner. Lavin v Ehrlich (1974) 80 Misc. 2d 247, 363 N.Y.S.2d 50

5. Expiration of term specified in agreement

Ordinarily, partnership agreement continues in absence of new written agreement after expiration of its term so long as actions of the partners indicate implied consent to continue particular provisions of the partnership relationship, even though some of the provisions of the written agreement are disregarded. Wagner v Etoll (1974, 3d Dept) 46 A.D.2d 990, 362 N.Y.S.2d 278, app dismd (1975) 37 N.Y.2d 795, 375 N.Y.S.2d 107, 337 N.E.2d 612

Trial court erred when it denied the motion to dismiss, under N.Y. C.P.L.R. 3211(a)(7). The six-year limitations period in which the owner could have timely brought the breach of contract claim began to run in December 1997 when the joint venture ceased to exist, under N.Y. P'ship Law § 62(2), rendering the action for a breach of contract untimely. Eskenazi v Schapiro (2006, App Div, 1st Dept) 812 NYS2d 474

6. Purchase of one partner's interest

Son-in-law was not entitled to accounting and dissolution of partnership where he expressly conceded in his testimony that he had sold his partnership interest to his partner (father-in-law) in return for father-in-law's promise to make weekly payments to him, parties signed document terminating partnership, father-in-law made agreed payments for some time, and Keogh account was split between them; agreement terminating partnership was not rescinded by father-in-law's failure to continue weekly payments, but son-in-law was entitled to amendment of complaint to conform to proof with new trial on cause of action for breach of contract. Stempel v Rosen (1988, 2d Dept) 140 A.D.2d 326, 527 N.Y.S.2d 825, adhered to, motion den, in part (1988, 2d Dept) 143 A.D.2d 409, 532 N.Y.S.2d 437

Where surviving partner purchased partner's interest and then sold business, partnership dissolved upon such purchase and situation for tax purposes was no other than if former partner had never been a partner at all, except that to extent of one-third of amount realized on sale, his basis was different. Williams v McGowan (1945, CA2 NY) 152 F.2d 570, 46-1 USTC P 9120, 34 AFTR 615, 162 ALR 1036

7. Death of partner

The death of a partner terminated the partnership and also resulted in termination of a joint venture to which the partnership was a party. Silberfeld v Swiss Bank Corp. (1948) 273 A.D. 686, 79 N.Y.S.2d 380, affd (1948) 298 N.Y. 776, 83 N.E.2d 468

Absent agreement to the contrary, death of one partner in 1968 resulted in dissolution of partnership which, by terms of partnership agreement, was to expire on December 31, 1961 but which was continued after expiration date without formal written agreement. Wagner v Etoll (1974, 3d Dept) 46 A.D.2d 990, 362 N.Y.S.2d 278, app dismd (1975) 37 N.Y.2d 795, 375 N.Y.S.2d 107, 337 N.E.2d 612

Upon death of one partner in 1968 and initiation of new profit and loss ratio for surviving partners, new partnership independent of 1960 partnership agreement came into existence and, therefore,

Partnership Law

dissolution provision of the 1960 agreement requiring an accounting of profits as determined on cash basis and distribution of assets in specified manner was inapplicable to dissolution of the new partnership. Wagner v Etoll (1974, 3d Dept) 46 A.D.2d 990, 362 N.Y.S.2d 278, app dismd (1975) 37 N.Y.2d 795, 375 N.Y.S.2d 107, 337 N.E.2d 612

Partner's death terminated original partnership and created partnership at will where original agreement contained no provision covering contingency of partner's death, and new partnership ended when 2 of remaining 3 partners terminated relationship; thus, third remaining partner had no basis on which to enforce terms of original agreement either with respect to accounting or implementation of restrictive covenant contained therein, and remaining partners would be liable to account to third partner only for his share of new partnership profits and assets to date of its termination. Burger, Kurzman, Kaplan & Stuchin v Kurzman (1988, 1st Dept) 139 A.D.2d 422, 527 N.Y.S.2d 15, app dismd without op (1988) 72 N.Y.2d 909, 532 N.Y.S.2d 757, 528 N.E.2d 1230 and app den (1989) 74 N.Y.2d 606, 544 N.Y.S.2d 820, 543 N.E.2d 85

Heirs of deceased partners were not entitled to their predecessors' ownership interest in absence of written agreement by or with deceased partners that heirs would be substituted to receive deceased partners' ownership interests or that business would continue after partners' deaths since (1) partners' deaths effected dissolutions by operation of law, (2) when deceased partners' heirs continued to operate business of former partnership, new partnerships at will were created, and (3) ownership interests of deceased partners in former dissolved partnership did not transfer into new entity. Peirez v Queens P.E.P. Assoc., Corp. (1989, 2d Dept) 148 A.D.2d 596, 539 N.Y.S.2d 61, app dismd without op (1989) 74 N.Y.2d 792, 545 N.Y.S.2d 106, 543 N.E.2d 749 and app den (1990) 75 N.Y.2d 704, 552 N.Y.S.2d 927, 552 N.E.2d 175

Court erred in holding that last survivor of 3 original partners, who in combination with second partner elected to continue business along with deceased partner's husband and executor rather than exercise option in partnership agreement to buy out deceased partner's interest, was entitled along with husband and executor to buy out second partner's interest on his death, since partnership agreement also expressly provided for dissolution of partnership on death of any 2 of partners. Scharff v SS & K Partnership (1992, 2d Dept) 187 A.D.2d 645, 590 N.Y.S.2d 243, app dismd without op (1993) 81 N.Y.2d 954, 597 N.Y.S.2d 939,·613 N.E.2d 971, reconsideration den (1993) 81 N.Y.2d 1068, 601 N.Y.S.2d 586, 619 N.E.2d 664, motion den (1994) 82 N.Y.2d 665, 610 N.Y.S.2d 152, 632 N.E.2d 462

Under an agreement providing that upon the dissolution of a partnership at the expiration of the term, or at any other time, the assets shall be divided and in case of a failure to agree, the dispute shall be settled by arbitration, the representative of a deceased partner may not be compelled to arbitrate. In re Rosenshine's Estate (1950) 199 Misc 984, 102 N.Y.S.2d 3

Although death of one partner dissolves the partnership under subd 4 of this section, it remains in existence and may be continued for a reasonable time by the surviving partners for the purpose of winding up its affairs. Beckley v Speaks (1963) 39 Misc. 2d 241, 240 N.Y.S.2d 553, affd (1964, 1st Dept) 21 A.D.2d 759, 251 N.Y.S.2d 1015, app dismd (1964) 15 N.Y.2d 481, reported in full (1964) 15 N.Y.2d 546, 254 N.Y.S.2d 362, 202 N.E.2d 906

Under this section a partnership terminates on the death of a partner and no decree to that effect is necessary. Sanders v Wyle (1946, Sup) 67 N.Y.S.2d 623

Since there was genuine issue whether decedent partner owned 20 percent interest in land (1) directly, as tenant in common, or (2) indirectly, under N.Y. Partnership Law § 21(3)-(5), as partner in partnership that dissolved at his death under N.Y. Partnership Law § 62(4) (and for which his executors were entitled to an accounting under N.Y. Partnership Law § 74), summary judgment to partition his alleged undivided interest in land was reversed. Facts indicating that partnership was the direct owner included that the decedent (or his executors) (1) reported on income tax returns his share of the partnership's income which, in turn, included his share of the land's tax attributes reported on the partnership's tax returns, (2) reported on his estate tax returns his indirect interest in the partnership's interest in the land but no direct interest in the land. Vick v Albert (2005, A.D., 1st Dept) 793 N.Y.S.2d 413, app withdrawn (2005, N.Y. A.D., 1st Dept) 2005 N.Y. A.D. LEXIS 5470

As a partner's death dissolves the partnership (N.Y. Partnership Law § 62(4), and a partner may not maintain claims for the sale of partnership assets and the distribution of sale proceeds until an accounting has been completed, a count in a complaint seeking to dissolve an alleged oral partnership with a decedent was dismissed, except for that portion that sought an accounting. Gaentner v Benkovich (2005, A.D., 2d Dept) 795 N.Y.S.2d 246

Children of the original partners in two partnerships were not entitled to full partnership rights because while a partnership was usually dissolved upon the death of a partner under N.Y. P'ship Law § 62(4), the surviving partners, in effect, created a new partnership at will as they continued to operate the business of the former partnerships; because no evidence was presented that defendant partner consented under N.Y. P'ship Law § 40(7) to the bequest or assignment of the original partners' interests to their children, the children were not entitled to an ownership in what was considered a new entity partnership. Sperber v Rubell (2008, Sup) 239 NYLJ 55, app withdrawn (2009, 1st Dept) 63 App Div 3d 479, 879 NYS2d 715.

Partnership whose fiscal year expired July 31, 1933, was dissolved by the death of a member in December, 1933, and decedent's taxable income for the calendar year 1933 includes his share of partnership profits from the beginning of the partnership fiscal year on Aug. 1, 1933, to the date of his death in the same year. Guaranty Trust Co. v Commissioner (1938) 303 US 493, 82 L Ed 975, 58 S Ct 673, 38-1 USTC P 9216, 20 AFTR 1043

Although upon death of partner partnership ceased to exist under §§ 60, 62 where the partnership agreement provided for computation of his share at time of his death by giving effect to events happening thereafter income should be prorated according to agreement. Darcy v Commissioner (1933, CA2) 66 F.2d 581, 3 USTC P 1152, 12 AFTR 1284, cert den (1933) 290 US 705, 78 L Ed 606, 54 S Ct 372

A partnership is dissolved for income tax purposes at the date of the partner's death and it was immaterial that the partnership agreement permitted the executor to permit the deceased partner's interest to continue to remain at the risk of the business. Commissioner v Waldman's Estate (1952, CA2) 196 F.2d 83, 52-1 USTC P 9283, 41 AFTR 1160

8. – Actions for accounting

Where a law partnership agreement provided, among other matters, that upon dissolution of the partnership for any cause other than because of the misconduct of a partner the interest of the retiring, withdrawing, or former partner should consist of "his capital account, which shall be determined upon an accounting," and that where the dissolution of the partnership results from "the misconduct of a partner, the interest of that partner in the partnership shall be determined at arbitration," a proceeding by the representative of a deceased partner, under SCPA § 2103, to discover the extent of the interest of a deceased partner in the partnership and to have money or personal property representing such interest delivered to her would be dismissed since, under the first agreement, until an accounting is had there is no "specific personal property or money which belongs to the estate," possession of which could be obtained through a proceeding pursuant to SCPA § 2103 and, under the second agreement, determination of the deceased partner's interest in event of dissolution because of misconduct of partner was determinable, not by accounting, but by arbitration and in either event, unless and until the nature and extent of the deceased partner's interest in the partnership assets is determined either by arbitration or by an accounting, an SCPA § 2103 proceeding may not properly be instituted, since the purpose of such proceeding is "to obtain the possession of specific personal property or money which belongs to the estate." Estate of Schwartzenberg (1984, 1st Dept) 99 A.D.2d 969, 472 N.Y.S.2d 658

Although a partnership automatically dissolves upon the death of a partner, a surviving partner may still bring an action for an accounting, and the deceased partner's nominee in the partnership can and should be compelled to render such an accounting. Paul v Ascher (1984, 2d Dept) 106 A.D.2d 619, 483 N.Y.S.2d 422

While a partnership is not terminated on dissolution, it continues merely for the purpose of winding up the partnership affairs, and the process of winding up is an exclusive obligation and right of the surviving partner. The executors of a dead partner have no right to participate in or interfere with the winding up process by the surviving partner. The only right of the executors of a deceased partner is to demand an accounting from the surviving partner upon completion of the winding up of its affairs. Niagara Mohawk Power Corp. v Silbergeld (1968) 58 Misc. 2d 285, 294 N.Y.S.2d 975

Upon the death of a partner the partnership is dissolved and the only property right which the survivor of such partner possesses is a claim for an accounting. La Russo v Paladino (1951, Sup) 109 N.Y.S.2d 627, affd (1952) 280 A.D. 988, 116 N.Y.S.2d 617, app den (1953) 281 A.D. 753, 118 N.Y.S.2d 557

Since a partnership between relatives had actually been dissolved years earlier when one relative withdrew, a trial court did not exceed its powers in ordering an accounting, despite the fact that the parties had entered into a settlement, where the allegation was that one partner had not complied with the terms of the settlement. Aaron v Aaron (2003, A.D., 3d Dept) 768 N.Y.S.2d 739

Though summary judgment was properly granted to trustees as a result of the complaint of remaindermen to a partnership trust challenging the trustees' conversion of corporate shares to partnership interests being time-barred, the remaindermen were entitled to the relief they sought with regard to compelling partnership accountings and a distribution of partnership assets. Because no partnership agreement existed, N.Y. Partnership Law §§ 62(4), 60, and 73, provided for the remaindermen to receive, as ordinary creditors, an amount equal to the value of their interest in the dissolved partnership when the trust terminated and, therefore, entitled them to an accounting and distribution. Breidbart v Wiesenthal (2004, A.D., 2d Dept) 781 N.Y.S.2d 123

As the estate representative of a decedent, plaintiff was entitled under N.Y. P'ship Law §§ 52, 62(4), and 73 to demand an account from the decedent's surviving partners and to receive the decedent's interest in the partnership. Priel v Linarello (2007, App Div, 2d Dept) 843 NYS2d 436

9. New partners

The induction of two of three members of a partnership into the armed forces dissolved the partnership by operation of law. J. C. H. Service Stations, Inc. v Patrikes (1944) 181 Misc 401, 46 N.Y.S.2d 228

Entrance of new partner into firm is not a cause of dissolution under this section. Helvering v Archbald (1934, CA2) 70 F.2d 720, 4 USTC P 1285, 13 AFTR 1079, cert den (1934) 293 US 594, 79 L Ed 688, 55 S Ct 109

10. Litigation; complaints

Wife of deceased partner, who received his partnership interest upon his death pursuant to partnership agreement, did not lack legal capacity to maintain action for accounting and injunctive relief on her claim that another partner mismanaged and misappropriated partnership assets; partner's death dissolved partnership as matter of law, but partnership business was not thereby terminated. Parnes v Edelman (1987, 2d Dept) 128 A.D.2d 596, 512 N.Y.S.2d 856

Plaintiff stated cause of action for dissolution of partnership and accounting where he alleged that he and his brother entered into business partnership in 1945, that they agreed to share profits and losses equally and invest profits into new businesses, that they made several real estate investments prior to brother's death in 1992, and that disagreements arose between plaintiff and members of his brother's family after his brother's death, which prevented partnership business from proceeding in productive and fruitful manner; fact that some real estate referred to in complaint was owned by corporations formed by partnership, not by partnership itself, did not render complaint insufficient as matter of law. Blank v Blank (1995, 3d Dept) 222 A.D.2d 851, 634 N.Y.S.2d 886

Defendant law firm was entitled to summary judgment declaring that execution of new partnership agreement by majority of firm's partners did not result in termination of prior partnership agreement as between plaintiffs and other partners in firm, although new agreement provided that "all preceding partnership agreements among the parties hereto are hereby terminated and superseded," where plaintiffs never signed new agreement; thus, defendant was not partnership-at-will, subject to dissolution upon withdrawal of any partner, when plaintiffs withdrew from firm on day after meeting at which new partnership agreement was approved. Borgeest v Wilson, Elser, Moskowitz, Edelman & Dicker (2001, 1st Dept) 283 A.D.2d 245, 724 N.Y.S.2d 408

In an action for a dissolution of a partnership pursuant to this section, it was unnecessary for the plaintiff to set forth causes of action for accounting or for any relief relating to the desired dissolution. All the plaintiff had to allege were facts showing the making of a partnership agreement, the terms of conditions of the partnership agreement, the manner in which the partnership had been conducted and the facts showing the grounds for the dissolution. Friedland v Friedland (1958) 12 Misc. 2d 349, 175 N.Y.S.2d 264

Complaint for dissolution of partnership was insufficient where it failed to allege facts that partner seeking dissolution had given notice to co-partner of election to terminate partnership or that election had

been manifested by unequivocable acts or circumstances brought to the knowledge of the co-partner signifying exercise of will of partner seeking dissolution that partnership should be dissolved. Jones v Jones (1958) 15 Misc. 2d 960, 179 N.Y.S.2d 480

Before an action for dissolution of a partnership and an accounting can be maintained and a judgment predicated on the existence of a partnership can be had, it must appear factually that a partnership relation exists. Jones v Jones (1958) 15 Misc. 2d 960, 179 N.Y.S.2d 480

Although death of a partner has the effect of dissolving the partnership, the general rule is that suits between partners can only be brought in equity for an accounting and that an action at law may not be maintained until after an accounting has been had with balance struck; therefore a surviving partner has no right to maintain an action at law against the executor of the estate of the deceased partner for a money judgment in the amount of alleged overdraft by the decedent from partnership funds, without first seeking an accounting in equity. Squire v Wing (1962) 35 Misc. 2d 287, 230 N.Y.S.2d 42, affd (1962, 2d Dept) 17 A.D.2d 835, 233 N.Y.S.2d 84

Since death of a partner effects dissolution of a partnership, running of limitations against a cause of action against a partnership is tolled by death of one of the partners. Pitti v Warshaw (1962) 35 Misc. 2d 875, 231 N.Y.S.2d 310

Where a complaint clearly alleged facts establishing the plaintiff's right to proceed in equity for the dissolution of a partnership, a motion by defendant for judgment on the pleadings should be denied. In such an action, there is no constitutional right to a trial by jury. While the court may in its discretion direct the trial by jury of any of the issues presented, such step is not necessary in the absence of a showing therefor. The verdict of the jury is purely advisory and there is no particular value in having the facts in such a case twice considered. Scherer v Scherer (1953, Sup) 121 N.Y.S.2d 810

Although, as a general matter under New York law, the filing of an individual bankruptcy petition by one partner causes the dissolution of the partnership, the partners could and did contract otherwise, so the bankruptcy filing did not result in dissolution of the partnership. In re Century/ML Cable Venture (2003, BC SD NY) 294 BR 9

Children's clothing manufacturer and other defendants were awarded summary judgment on claims arising from the termination of the manufacturer's relationship with a marketing company, as (1) no partnership or joint venture was established given, inter alia, no evidence of any agreement to share losses and, (2) as there was no written agreement concerning the relationship, any partnership or joint venture would have been terminable at will. Kidz Cloz, Inc. v Officially for Kids, Inc. (2004, SD NY) 320 F. Supp. 2d 164

§ 63.   Dissolution by decree of court

The court shall decree a dissolution.

1. On application by or for a partner whenever:

(a) A partner has been declared incompetent in any judicial proceeding or is shown to be of unsound mind,

(b) A partner becomes in any other way incapable of performing his part of the partnership contract,

(c) A partner has been guilty of such conduct as tends to affect prejudicially the carrying on of the business,

(d) A partner wilfully or persistently commits a breach of the partnership agreement, or otherwise so conducts himself in matters relating to the partnership business that it is not reasonably practicable to carry on the business in partnership with him,

(e) The business of the partnership can only be carried on at a loss,

(f) Other circumstances render a dissolution equitable;

2. On the application of the purchaser of a partner's interest under sections fifty-three or fifty-four:

(a) After the termination of the specified term or particular undertaking,

(b) At any time if the partnership was a partnership at will when the interest was assigned or when the charging order was issued.

History: Add, L 1919, ch 408; amd, L 1936, ch 330, eff April 9, 1936.

Sub 1, par (a), amd, L 1978, ch 550, § 35, eff July 24, 1978.

CASE ANNOTATIONS

1. In general
2. Insanity and the like
3. Breach of agreement
4. Misconduct
5. What constitutes misconduct
6. – Acts affecting management of partnership
7. Alienation or encumbrance of interest
8. Practice and procedure
9. – Adequacy and form of complaint
10. – Summary judgment

1. In general

A price fixed in a partnership "buy-and-sell" agreement did not apply to an accounting upon a judicial dissolution under this section which was not based upon any of the causes of dissolution in the agreement. Goergen v Nebrich (1957, 4th Dept) 4 A.D.2d 526, 167 N.Y.S.2d 491

Judicial dissolution of partnership is inappropriate where no specific provisions of CLS Partn § 63 are applicable and there is no dispute concerning fact or date of dissolution. Mehlman v Avrech (1989, 2d Dept) 146 A.D.2d 753, 537 N.Y.S.2d 236

Limited partners could not force dissolution of partnership and distribution of partnership profits and assets where (1) predecessors to limited partners had owned and sold real property to corporation, (2) when corporation had difficulty making payments on mortgage, parties entered into agreement whereby limited partners were given interest in profits from property, (3) partnership agreement provided that partnership could be terminated if property were disposed of by sale or otherwise, and (4) corporation created new corporation and transferred property to it for purpose of conversion to cooperative apartments; transfer to new corporation was not disposition of property, since original corporation still held property through its interest in new corporation, and agreement was intended to apply only to transfer to separate distinct entity. Savasta v 470 Newport Assoc. (1992, 2d Dept) 180 A.D.2d 624, 579 N.Y.S.2d 167, app gr (1993) 81 N.Y.2d 703, 594 N.Y.S.2d 717, 610 N.E.2d 390 and affd (1993) 82 N.Y.2d 763, 603 N.Y.S.2d 821, 623 N.E.2d 1171, reconsideration den (1993) 82 N.Y.2d 889, 610 N.Y.S.2d 155, 632 N.E.2d 465

Plaintiff's action to recover its initial capital contribution in partnership that was unsuccessful in achieving main purpose for which it was formed sufficiently stated cause of action for accounting, to which plaintiff was absolutely entitled, and for judicial dissolution if parties did not agree to voluntarily dissolve partnership, where record reflected defendant's failure to provide complete information regarding disposition of partnership funds. Non-Linear Trading Co. v Braddis Assocs. (1998, 1st Dept) 243 A.D.2d 107, 675 N.Y.S.2d 5

Action brought by 2 partners of 3-party partnership, seeking dissolution or declaration of dissolution, did not violate provision of partnership agreement that prohibited any partner from making judicial application for dissolution where action was brought only after partnership had been terminated. Teeter v De Lorenzo (2000, 3d Dept) 275 A.D.2d 528, 711 N.Y.S.2d 629

Plaintiff partner's service of notice of his election to dissolve at-will partnership, demanding that winding up of partnership affairs commence immediately, accomplished dissolution of partnership, and thus defendant partner's action for judicial dissolution was rendered academic. 220-52 Assocs. v Edelman (1997, 1st Dept) 241 A.D.2d 365, 659 N.Y.S.2d 885, later proceeding (1998, 1st Dept) 253 A.D.2d 352, 676 N.Y.S.2d 566, app dismd (1998) 92 N.Y.2d 1026, 684 N.Y.S.2d 490, 707 N.E.2d 445

In the absence of any claim of irreparable loss or damage to firm assets appointment of a receiver pending trial of an action for dissolution will be denied. Markowitz v Zadan (1948) 192 Misc 968, 83 N.Y.S.2d 29

Where both members of a partnership expressed a desire to dissolve the partnership as of a specified date, the partnership should be considered dissolved as of that date subject to accounting, termination of partnership affairs, and distribution of assets, if any. Bogen v Alston (1961) 33 Misc. 2d 313, 215 N.Y.S.2d 388

Although both members of a partnership agreed to its dissolution as of a certain date, they were equally entitled to share in profits from business being negotiated by one of them prior to the agreed date of dissolution. Bogen v Alston (1961) 33 Misc. 2d 313, 215 N.Y.S.2d 388

2. Insanity and the like

A court of equity has power to, and will decree the dissolution of, a copartnership because of the incapacity of a partner which materially affects his ability to discharge the duties imposed by his partnership relation and contract. Barclay v Barrie (1913) 209 N.Y. 40, 102 N.E. 602

Incapacity for a period of 3 years and 11 months out of a partnership period of 4 years and 11 months to attend to the duties of the partnership, where the incapacity was occasioned by a stroke of paralysis is ground for dissolution although there has been a progressive recovery and such partner will be practically restored to health by the expiration of the contract period of the partnership. Barclay v Barrie (1913) 209 N.Y. 40, 102 N.E. 602

3. Breach of agreement

The court may decree a dissolution where one partner has willfully and persistently breached the partnership agreement. Cahill v Haff (1928) 248 N.Y. 377, 162 N.E. 288, remittitur amd (1928) 249 N.Y. 509, 164 N.E. 564 and remittitur den (1928) 250 N.Y. 536, 166 N.E. 314

Failure to divide profits as called for by the agreement will warrant dissolution of the partnership. Menihan v Menihan (1930) 231 A.D. 3, 245 N.Y.S. 547

A partner cannot recover damages for wrongful expulsion from a firm where he breached the partnership agreement, although § 62 does not make a breach a ground for expulsion and § 63 does make it a ground for a court dissolution which the other partners did not obtain. Schnitzer v Josephthal (1923) 122 Misc 15, 202 N.Y.S. 77, affd (1924) 208 A.D. 769, 202 N.Y.S. 952

Exclusion of the plaintiff from participation in the conduct of a corporation set up by partners to carry out the partnership agreement constituted a violation of the agreement and justified an accounting and dissolution. Dow v Beals (1933) 149 Misc 631, 268 N.Y.S. 425

A partner's unequivocal notice of election to "dissolve" the partnership, followed by institution of an action to enforce his alleged right to do so, constitutes a breach of the partnership agreement, notwithstanding the absence of any provision as to term of the partnership, where it is in disregard of terms of the agreement prescribing how a partner may withdraw and giving the other partners rights and options to purchase his interest in case of withdrawal. Napoli v Domnitch (1962) 34 Misc 237, 226 N.Y.S.2d 908, mod 18 A.D.2d 707, 236 N.Y.S.2d 549, affd 14 N.Y.2d 508, 248 N.Y.S.2d 228, 197 N.E.2d 623

4. Misconduct

A judicial dissolution of partnership is clearly warranted where one of the partners conducts himself in such fashion as to affect the carrying on of the partnership venture to the damage of the other partner. Copp v Chestnutt (1960) 23 Misc. 2d 457, 196 N.Y.S.2d 752

Misconduct by some general partners was sufficient to entitle another general partner to a decree of dissolution and an accounting. Newburger, Loeb & Co. v Gross (1977, CA2 NY) 563 F.2d 1057, 1977, CCH Fed Secur L Rep P 96148, 1977-2 CCH Trade Cases P 61604, 24 FR Serv 2d 412, cert den (1978) 434 US 1035, 54 L Ed 2d 782, 98 S Ct 769 and appeal after remand (1979, CA2 NY) 611 F.2d 423, 28 FR Serv 2d 602

5. What constitutes misconduct

Dissolution will not ordinarily be decreed except for gross misconduct, lack of good faith, or some cause which is productive of serious impairment and injury to the partnership concerned, or renders it impracticable to carry on the business. Skolny v Richter (1910) 139 A.D. 534, 124 N.Y.S. 152

The question of incapability of a partner within the meaning of a partnership agreement permitted expulsion in case of incompatibility presents question of fact for trial court. Millet v Slocum (1957, 4th Dept) 4 A.D.2d 528, 167 N.Y.S.2d 136, affd (1958) 5 N.Y.2d 734, 177 N.Y.S.2d 716, 152 N.E.2d 672

The limited partners of a partnership were entitled to a partial summary judgment dissolving their partnership with two other partners due to a breach of fiduciary duty by the general partner and another limited partner where defendant partners had individually guaranteed the obligations of a restauranteur on an equipment lease with another partnership composed of the limited partners of the first partnership, the restauranteur defaulted and assigned the equipment lease to the first partnership, and defendant partners caused such partnership to agree to indemnify them for their obligations on the lease and their guarantee to the other partnership, and where the indemnity agreement was clearly detrimental to the first partnership and constituted self-dealing by defendant partners. May v Flowers (1984, 4th Dept) 106 A.D.2d 873, 483 N.Y.S.2d 551, app dismd without op (1985) 64 N.Y.2d 611 and app dismd without op (1985) 65 N.Y.2d 637

Wrecking and misappropriation of partnership assets by one of two partners would entitle the other to a dissolution. Duncan v Bruce (1943) 179 Misc 992, 43 N.Y.S.2d 447

Where a partnership was formed for the purpose of giving investment advice, but defendant partner used $35,000 of the firm's funds to form a "mutual fund" corporation for sale of securities to the public, this constituted an improper use of partnership funds and ground for dissolution. Copp v Chestnutt (1960) 23 Misc. 2d 457, 196 N.Y.S.2d 752

The court may decree a dissolution where one partner has been guilty of fraud in connection with the partnership business. Gianuso v Weis (1922, Sup) 195 N.Y.S. 279

Some general partners were guilty of sufficient misconduct to justify dissolution where they attempted to transfer partnership property to a corporation under their control in violation of limited partners' rights and where they threatened a general partner with litigation on a meritless claim assigned to them for the purpose of coercing the general partner into coercing the limited partners into approving the transfer. Newburger, Loeb & Co. v Gross (1977, CA2 NY) 563 F.2d 1057, 1977, CCH Fed Secur L Rep P 96148, 1977-2 CCH Trade Cases P 61604, 24 FR Serv 2d 42, cert den (1978) 434 US 1035, 54 L Ed 2d 782, 98 S Ct 769 and appeal after remand (1979, CA2 NY) 611 F.2d 423, 28 FR Serv 2d 602

6. – Acts affecting management of partnership

Dissolution will be allowed for misconduct if acts complained of directly affect management of partnership such as where plaintiff and defendant had formed a partnership, for a term of 5 years, to conduct the business of "making productions of operas, extravaganzas, and for general amusement purposes," the plaintiff to be general manager and the defendant stage manager and director, the business was impracticable because plaintiff could not find "sufficient places to promise a remuneration for the outlay," and the defendant, then engaged in a business similar to that contemplated by the partnership, had abandoned his company of singers, unpaid, in a town on the road, and had become "of such ill repute in the business that a successful execution of the contract under him is hopeless for that reason alone." Waite v Aborn (1901) 60 A.D. 521, 69 N.Y.S. 967

Whether a partner who has been convicted of unlawfully receiving unemployment benefits about which there has been newspaper publicity has been guilty of conduct prejudicially affecting the business within the meaning of this section where there is no charge of misconduct in the operation of the business itself must be determined on the evidence in a trial. Markowitz v Zadan (1948) 192 Misc 968, 83 N.Y.S.2d 29

Where, at a time when the partnership agreement was about to expire, one group of partners was attempting to prematurely wind up the partnership and the other group was acting so as to hinder the speedy winding up of affairs, there was conduct prejudicially affecting the business so as to give jurisdiction for court intervention and supervision of the dissolution. Mele v Tory (1947, Sup) 68 N.Y.S.2d 638

Dissolution will be allowed for misconduct if acts complained of directly affect management of partnership, such as where dissention exists between partners and one of them refuses to proceed with business, although term of partnership has not expired. Bishop v Breckles (1840) 1 Hoffm Ch 534

7. Alienation or encumbrance of interest

In proceeding commenced by general partners seeking judicial dissolution of limited partnership, trial court's finding that one general partner breached his fiduciary duty (by causing certain loan to be repaid through related company instead of directly to partnership) supported court's holding that proper remedy was mandatory retirement of all general partners, rather than dissolution, in view of limited partnership agreement whereby all general partners had agreed to tender their resignations if any of them committed "any material breach" of their duties or obligations under agreement, since breach of fiduciary duties by one general partner was necessarily imputed by agreement to all of them. In re New Haven Plaza Associates (1987, 2d Dept) 134 A.D.2d 596, 521 N.Y.S.2d 495, app den (1988) 71 N.Y.2d 802, 527 N.Y.S.2d 768, 522 N.E.2d 1066

Partner manifested unequivocal election to dissolve partnership where he transferred to himself individually partnership's primary asset, which was residence in which parties lived on separate floors, and encumbered property with mortgage, proceeds of which he alone received. Staines Assocs. v Adler (1999, 1st Dept) 266 A.D.2d 52, 698 N.Y.S.2d 639

A conveyance to a stranger by a partner of his moiety of land held as tenants in common with his copartner on which the firm was carrying on a farming business dissolved the partnership and rendered the grantee a tenant in common with the other partner in the partnership property. Mumford v McKay 8 Wend 442

8. Practice and procedure

An action for dissolution of a partnership on the ground that defendant had wrongfully taken partnership assets and profits and otherwise neglected and mismanaged the partnership affairs would be dismissed, where the proof presented sustained none of the grounds alleged in the complaint for dissolution, and where no motion was made to conform the pleadings to the proof in support of any other ground for dissolution. Couch v Langan (1984) 63 N.Y.2d 987, 483 N.Y.S.2d 998, 473 N.E.2d 248

In an action for dissolution of a partnership initiated by an attorney in fact for one of the partners, the trial court properly denied the other partners' motion to dismiss the complaint on the ground that a partner's attorney in fact has no authority to maintain an action to dissolve a partnership, since an attorney in fact is essentially an alter ego of the principal and is authorized to act with respect to any and all matters on behalf of the principal except as to acts which, by their nature, by public policy, or by contract require personal performance, since Gen Oblig Law § 5-1502 authorizes an attorney in fact to assert and to prosecute any cause of action or claim which the principal may have against any individual or partnership, and since the same result is contemplated by Partn Law § 63(1), which directs a court to decree a dissolution upon any appropriate application made "by or for" a partner. Zaubler v Picone (1984, 2d Dept) 100 A.D.2d 620, 473 N.Y.S.2d 580, appeal after remand (1985, 2d Dept) 112 A.D.2d 157, 490 N.Y.S.2d 843

In action for, inter alia, dissolution of partnership, there was no need to issue judgment dissolving partnership since, pursuant to partnership agreement, partnership had already terminated on sale of its only asset. Mehlman v Avrech (1989, 2d Dept) 146 A.D.2d 753, 537 N.Y.S.2d 236

Although proposition that law practice has no good will is consequence of ethical concerns that sale of law practice would necessarily involve disclosure of client confidences, such concerns do not come into play in contexts other than sale, in particular in partnership dissolution. Dawson v White & Case (1995, 1st Dept) 212 A.D.2d 385, 622 N.Y.S.2d 269, reh den (1995, N.Y. A.D., 1st Dept) 1995 N.Y. A.D. LEXIS 5560 and app dismd (1995) 86 N.Y.2d 837, 634 N.Y.S.2d 445, 658 N.E.2d 223 and app gr (1996) 87 N.Y.2d 806, 641 N.Y.S.2d 597, 664 N.E.2d 508 and mod on other grounds, affd, remanded (1996) 88 N.Y.2d 666, 649 N.Y.S.2d 364, 672 N.E.2d 589

Good will was not a distibutable asset of a law firm, where the partners had impliedly so agreed prior to the dissolution of the firm. Dawson v White & Case (1995, 1st Dept) 212 A.D.2d 385, 622 N.Y.S.2d 269, reh den (1995, N.Y. A.D., 1st Dept) 1995 N.Y. A.D. LEXIS 5560 and app dismd (1995) 86 N.Y.2d 837, 634 N.Y.S.2d 445, 658 N.E.2d 223 and app gr (1996) 87 N.Y.2d 806, 641 N.Y.S.2d 597, 664 N.E.2d 508 and mod, affd, remanded (1996) 88 N.Y.2d 666, 649 N.Y.S.2d 364, 672 N.E.2d 589

In action by surviving member of family partnership for dissolution of partnership and accounting, defendant was not entitled to dismissal of complaint as against him although he purportedly had resigned as trustee, where record was silent as to whether any court had granted him permission to resign. Blank v Blank (1995, 3d Dept) 222 A.D.2d 851, 634 N.Y.S.2d 886

Absent provision in partnership agreement specifying method of accounting, whether cash or accrual, to be used on dissolution of partnership, accrual method is to be used. McDonald v Fenzel (1996,

1st Dept) 224 A.D.2d 261, 638 N.Y.S.2d 15, motion den, remanded on other grounds (1996, 1st Dept) 233 A.D.2d 219, 650 N.Y.S.2d 9

Arbitration clause of partnership agreement governed action for judicial dissolution under CLS Partn § 63(1)(c) predicated on alleged breaches of partnership agreement and fiduciary duty, where partnership agreement provided that it governed dissolution but that plaintiff could not seek dissolution prior to April 1, 2002, and defendant claimed that plaintiff violated partnership agreement by seeking dissolution prior to 2002 and demanded that default be cured. Morelli v Dinkes (1998, 1st Dept) 250 A.D.2d 530, 673 N.Y.S.2d 427

On finding that partnership was dissolved, court properly directed accounting and held in abeyance declaration of parties' partnership interests pending such accounting. Staines Assocs. v Adler (1999, 1st Dept) 266 A.D.2d 52, 698 N.Y.S.2d 639

In action for accounting and involuntary dissolution of partnership engaged in business of owning and managing certain real property, plaintiff partner was entitled to depose non-party tenant in order to substantiate his claim that defendant partner diverted tenants' rent monies to himself, since such evidence would be material and relevant to accounting action and it was unlikely that evidence of defendant's alleged self-dealing would be revealed solely in partnership's records. 220-52 Assocs. v Edelman (1997, 1st Dept) 241 A.D.2d 365, 659 N.Y.S.2d 885, later proceeding (1998, 1st Dept) 253 A.D.2d 352, 676 N.Y.S.2d 566, app dismd (1998) 92 N.Y.2d 1026, 684 N.Y.S.2d 490, 707 N.E.2d 445

Before an action for dissolution of a partnership and an accounting can be maintained and a judgment predicated on the existence of a partnership can be had, it must appear factually that a partnership relation exists. Jones v Jones (1958) 15 Misc. 2d 960, 179 N.Y.S.2d 480

9. – Adequacy and form of complaint

Plaintiff stated cause of action for dissolution of partnership and accounting where he alleged that he and his brother entered into business partnership in 1945, that they agreed to share profits and losses equally and invest profits into new businesses, that they made several real estate investments prior to brother's death in 1992, and that disagreements arose between plaintiff and members of his brother's family after his brother's death, which prevented partnership business from proceeding in productive and fruitful manner; fact that some real estate referred to in complaint was owned by corporations formed by partnership, not by partnership itself, did not render complaint insufficient as matter of law. Blank v Blank (1995, 3d Dept) 222 A.D.2d 851, 634 N.Y.S.2d 886

Action for dissolution of partnership and accounting would not be dismissed due to failure to name, as parties, various corporations and partnerships through which subject partnership acted, as it did not appear that unnamed entities would be inequitably affected where plaintiff was only seeking accounting and trying to wind up partnership affairs, which should not involve organizational structure of other entities, and unnamed entities could be joined if need arose. Blank v Blank (1995, 3d Dept) 222 A.D.2d 851, 634 N.Y.S.2d 886

Action by surviving partner, seeking dissolution of partnership and accounting, was not barred by failure to file claim against deceased partner's estate, which was probated in Florida, as required by Florida statutes, as action did not involve claim against deceased partner's estate; partnership property vested in plaintiff after partner's death, subject to accounting to deceased partner's estate. Blank v Blank (1995, 3d Dept) 222 A.D.2d 851, 634 N.Y.S.2d 886

In an action for a dissolution of a partnership pursuant to this section, it was unnecessary for the plaintiff to set forth causes of action for accounting or for any relief relating to the desired dissolution. All the plaintiff had to allege were facts showing the making of a partnership agreement, the terms of conditions of the partnership agreement, the manner in which the partnership had been conducted and the facts showing the grounds for the dissolution. Friedland v Friedland (1958) 12 Misc. 2d 349, 175 N.Y.S.2d 264

Where a complaint clearly alleged facts establishing the plaintiff's right to proceed in equity for the dissolution of a partnership, a motion by defendant for judgment on the pleadings should be denied. In such an action, there is no constitutional right to a trial by jury. While the court may in its discretion direct the trial by jury of any of the issues presented, such step is not necessary in the absence of a showing therefor. The verdict of the jury is purely advisory and there is no particular value in having the facts in such a case twice considered. Scherer v Scherer (1953, Sup) 121 N.Y.S.2d 810

10. – Summary judgment

Defendants were not entitled to summary judgment dismissing action for dissolution of joint venture where fact issue existed as to whether parties entered into binding oral joint venture agreement. Blank v Nadler (1988, 2d Dept) 143 A.D.2d 966, 533 N.Y.S.2d 891

Court properly declared partnership dissolved on search of record, even though plaintiff purported to limit his motion for partial summary judgment to that part of his first cause of action that sought declaration of extent of his interest in partnership, where submissions in connection with his motion and defendant's cross motion for same relief provided ample evidentiary basis for declaration of dissolution. Staines Assocs. v Adler (1999, 1st Dept) 266 A.D.2d 52, 698 N.Y.S.2d 639

In action for accounting and for involuntary dissolution of partnership, court erred in holding cross-motions for summary judgment in abeyance pending completion of discovery, because at-will partnership may be dissolved at any time by any partner and, on dissolution, any partner is entitled to accounting. 220-52 Assocs. v Edelman (1997, 1st Dept) 241 A.D.2d 365, 659 N.Y.S.2d 885, later proceeding (1998, 1st Dept) 253 A.D.2d 352, 676 N.Y.S.2d 566, app dismd (1998) 92 N.Y.2d 1026, 684 N.Y.S.2d 490, 707 N.E.2d 445

§ 64. General effect of dissolution on authority of partner

Except so far as may be necessary to wind up partnership affairs or to complete transactions begun but not then finished, dissolution terminates all authority of any partner to act for the partnership,

1. With respect to the partners:

(a) When the dissolution is not by the act, bankruptcy or death of a partner; or

(b) When the dissolution is by such act, bankruptcy or death of a partner, in cases where section sixty-five so requires.

2. With respect to persons not partners, as declared in section sixty-six.

History: Add, L 1919, ch 408, eff Oct 1, 1919.

CASE ANNOTATIONS

In action for, inter alia, accounting and injunctive relief by several former members of dissolved partnership against one other former member of partnership, defendant was entitled to dismissal of cause of action seeking to restrain him from prosecuting collection action on behalf of partnership since plaintiffs did not contend that defendant had wrongfully dissolved partnership. Yorkes v Ross (1988, 2d Dept) 142 A.D.2d 642, 530 N.Y.S.2d 590

Former law partners had duty to wind up affairs of dissolved partnership following plaintiff's withdrawal from firm where they had no right under partnership agreement or Partnership Law to form new partnership to continue business of dissolved partnership. Shandell v Katz (1995, 1st Dept) 217 A.D.2d 472, 629 N.Y.S.2d 437

Partnership is dissolved when partner withdraws, not when winding up of partnership affairs is completed; withdrawing partner no longer shares in gains and losses of any continuing entity, and his actions cannot bind continuing partnership or its partners. Estate of Quirk v Commissioner (1991, CA6) 928 F.2d 751, 91-1 USTC P 50148, 67 AFTR 2d 782, on remand (1995) TC Memo 1995-234, RIA TC Memo P 95234, 69 CCH TCM 2746, 95 TNT 106-11

§ 65. Right of partner to contribution from copartners after dissolution

Where the dissolution is caused by the act, death or bankruptcy of a partner, each partner is liable to his copartners for his share of any liability created by any partner acting for the partnership as if the partnership had not been dissolved unless

1. The dissolution being by act of any partner, the partner acting for the partnership had knowledge of the dissolution,

2. The dissolution being by the death or bankruptcy of a partner, the partner acting for the partnership had knowledge or notice of the death or bankruptcy, or

3. The liability is for a debt, obligation or liability for which the partner is not liable as provided in subdivision (b) of section twenty-six of this chapter.

History: Add, L 1919, ch 408; amd, L 1994, ch 576, § 10, eff Oct 24, 1994.

Sub 1, amd, L 1994, ch 576, § 10, eff Oct 24, 1994.

Sub 2, amd, L 1994, ch 576, § 10, eff Oct 24, 1994.

Sub 3, add, L 1994, ch 576, § 10, eff Oct 24, 1994.

§ 66.   Power of partner to bind partnership to third persons after dissolution

(1) After dissolution a partner can bind the partnership except as provided in subdivision three

(a) By any act appropriate for winding up partnership affairs or completing transactions unfinished at dissolution;

(b) By any transaction which would bind the partnership if dissolution had not taken place, provided the other party to the transaction

(I) Had extended credit to the partnership prior to dissolution and had no knowledge or notice of the dissolution; or

(II) Though he had not so extended credit, had nevertheless known of the partnership prior to the dissolution, and, having no knowledge or notice of dissolution, the fact of dissolution had not been advertised in a newspaper of general circulation in the place (or in each place if more than one) at which the partnership business was regularly carried on.

2. The liability of a partner under subdivision one, paragraph (b), shall be satisfied out of partnership assets alone when such partner had been prior to dissolution

(a) Unknown as a partner to the person with whom the contract is made; and

(b) So far unknown and inactive in partnership affairs that the business reputation of the partnership could not be said to have been in any degree due to his connection with it.

3. The partnership is in no case bound by any act of a partner after dissolution

(a) Where the partnership is dissolved because it is unlawful to carry on the business, unless the act is appropriate for winding up partnership affairs; or

(b) Where the partner has become bankrupt; or

(c) Where the partner has no authority to wind up partnership affairs, except by a transaction with one who

(I) Had extended credit to the partnership prior to dissolution and had no knowledge or notice of his want of authority; or

(II) Had not extended credit to the partnership prior to dissolution, and, having no knowledge or notice of his want of authority, the fact of his want of authority has not been advertised in the manner provided for advertising the fact of dissolution in subdivision one, paragraph (b), clause (II).

4. Nothing in this section shall affect the liability under section twenty-seven of any person who after dissolution represents himself or consents to another representing him as a partner in a partnership engaged in carrying on business.

History: Add, L 1919, ch 408; amd, L 1936, ch 330, eff April 9, 1936.

CASE ANNOTATIONS

Court erred in granting motion for summary judgment dismissing partnership's action for breach of contract to purchase property where there was question of fact as to whether consummation of sale was "transaction unfinished at dissolution" within meaning of CLS Partn § 66(1)(a), and there was question of fact as to whether composition of partnership was fundamentally altered when one partner withdrew. St. Lawrence Factory Stores v Ogdensburg Bridge & Port Auth. (1994, 3d Dept) 202 A.D.2d 844, 609 N.Y.S.2d 370

The surviving partner becomes possessed of the sole right to liquidate the partnership on the death of his copartner and his right to collect the firm assets and debts due it implies a right to retain counsel therefor. In re Allen Street in New York (1933) 148 Misc 488, 266 N.Y.S. 277, affd (1933) 239 A.D. 775, 263 N.Y.S. 942, reh and app den (1933) 239 A.D. 827, 264 N.Y.S. 919

While partnership property is liable for partnership debts, that rule does not extend to debts contracted, after dissolution, by one of the partners with a third person having knowledge of the dissolution. J. C. H. Service Stations, Inc. v Patrikes (1944) 181 Misc 401, 46 N.Y.S.2d 228

Plaintiff was entitled to charge defendant partnership for merchandise ordered prior to date of actual notice of dissolution. Kaydee Sales Corp. v Feldman (1958) 14 Misc. 2d 793, 183 N.Y.S.2d 151

Partner was not released from liability for partnership debt, on the ground that former partner had assumed debts of partnership, where there was no evidence that former partner had assumed existing obligations of the partnership. Kaydee Sales Corp. v Feldman (1958) 14 Misc. 2d 793, 183 N.Y.S.2d 151

A former law partner was not entitled to maintain an action for an accounting of fee received by firm in a particular matter, where he had cashed a check from the firm for his share in the matter, which check was accompanied by a statement of account. Norton v Tart (1959) 16 Misc. 2d 681, 189 N.Y.S.2d 990

Consent required by Lien Law § 3 to impose liability on owner of property under mechanic's lien is not under terms of above statute within powers of partner after dissolution, where firm is such owner. Forte v Roc Hill Associates, Inc. (1965) 45 Misc. 2d 278, 256 N.Y.S.2d 879

After the dissolution of a partnership authority to charge the property and to create personal liabilities of co-partners is confined to acts incident to winding up. In re Luckenbach's Estate (1965) 45 Misc. 2d 897, 258 N.Y.S.2d 44

Dissolved New York partnership is not "person" eligible to avail itself of reorganization in Chapter 11 bankruptcy proceeding because Partnership Law prohibits dissolved partnership from engaging in any business other than liquidation. C-TC 9th Ave. Pshp. v Norton Co. (In re C-TC 9th Ave. Pshp.) (1997, CA2 NY) 113 F.3d 1304, 30 BCD 1146, 38 CBC2d 115, CCH Bankr L Rptr P 77410 (criticized in In re Shea & Gould (1997, BC SD NY) 214 BR 739, 38 CBC2d 1453)

§ 67.   Effect of dissolution on partner's existing liability

1. The dissolution of the partnership does not of itself discharge the existing liability of any partner.

2. A partner is discharged from any existing liability upon dissolution of the partnership by an agreement to that effect between himself, the partnership creditor and the person or partnership continuing the business; and such agreement may be inferred from the course of dealing between the

Partnership Law

creditor having knowledge of the dissolution and the person or partnership continuing the business.

3. Where a person agrees to assume the existing obligations of a dissolved partnership, the partners whose obligations have been assumed shall be discharged from any liability to any creditor of the partnership who, knowing of the agreement, consents to a material alteration in the nature or time of payment of such obligations.

4. The individual property of a deceased partner shall be liable for those obligations of the partnership incurred while he was a partner and for which he was liable under section twenty-six of this chapter but subject to the prior payment of his separate debts.

History: Add, L 1919, ch 408, eff Oct 1, 1919.

Sub 4, amd, L 1994, ch 576, § 11, eff Oct 24, 1994.

CASE ANNOTATIONS

1. In general
2. Effect of General Obligations Law
3. Retiring partner
4. – Retiring partner as surety
5. Assumption of liability by remaining partner
6. Inferred discharge of liability

1. In general

In action against former members of dissolved partnership for goods sold to partnership, defense set forth in this section is not available to partners unless creditor accepted note of one of partners in substitution for partnership debt and had knowledge of dissolution of partnership. Cameron & Hawn v La Porte (1926) 216 A.D. 579, 215 N.Y.S. 543

Present value of unfunded pension plan benefits payable under dissolved law firm's pension plan were properly excluded as liability of firm where there was evidence to support special referee's findings that pension payments were operating expenses for successor firm contingent on its profitability, in that purported million-dollar liability never appeared in any of firm's financial statements, liability was never assessed against either firm or any of its partners for accounting purposes, and it was only against departing partner that firm sought to impose burden; unfunded plan was, if anything, future liability, and dissolution of firm absolved it of any responsibility for paying such benefits to retiring partners. Dawson v White & Case (1995, 1st Dept) 212 A.D.2d 385, 622 N.Y.S.2d 269, reh den (1995, N.Y. A.D., 1st Dept) 1995 N.Y. A.D. LEXIS 5560 and app dismd (1995) 86 N.Y.2d 837, 634 N.Y.S.2d 445, 658 N.E.2d 223 and app gr (1996) 87 N.Y.2d 806, 641 N.Y.S.2d 597, 664 N.E.2d 508 and mod on other grounds, affd, remanded (1996) 88 N.Y.2d 666, 649 N.Y.S.2d 364, 672 N.E.2d 589

The fact of dissolution does not by itself discharge the existing contractual liability of any partner without an express or implied agreement between himself, the partnership creditor and the partner continuing business or without a novation. Patrikes v J. C. H. Service Stations, Inc. (1943) 180 Misc 917, 41 N.Y.S.2d 158, affd (1943) 180 Misc 927, 46 N.Y.S.2d 233, app den (1943) 266 A.D. 924, 44 N.Y.S.2d 472

A soldier partner's military status does not operate to release from partnership obligations the members of the partners who are not called to service. Patrikes v J. C. H. Service Stations, Inc. (1943) 180 Misc 917, 41 N.Y.S.2d 158, affd (1943) 180 Misc 927, 46 N.Y.S.2d 233, app den (1943) 266 A.D. 924, 44 N.Y.S.2d 472

The fact that a partnership has recently been dissolved does not preclude an action against it on obligations which survive its expiration or termination. Emerson Radio & Phonograph Corp. v Eskind (1957) 32 Misc. 2d 1038, 228 N.Y.S.2d 841

2. Effect of General Obligations Law

Provision of General Obligations Law providing that release of partner from partnership liability shall release his copartners from same liability to creditor giving release, but after partnership has been dissolved, by consent or otherwise, any partner may make separate composition or compromise with any partnership creditor, and such composition or compromise shall discharge from such liability the partner making it, and him only, applies only to situation where partnership has been dissolved by mutual consent of partners and the partnership affairs have been wound up and the partnership business discontinued, but has no application to the situation where the partnership is dissolved but one partner continues the business and assumes the operation. Bank of United States v Moskowitz (1934) 150 Misc 629, 268 N.Y.S. 705

3. Retiring partner

In the absence of notice of withdrawal a retiring partner continues liable for all obligations occurring after as well as before dissolution. Drake v Hodgson (1924) 207 A.D. 783, 202 N.Y.S. 813

Retirement of partner, in absence of proof, pursuant to subd 3 of this section indicating that any creditor of copartnership has knowledge that party remaining in business has assumed existing obligations for dissolved partnership and consents to material alteration in nature or time of payment of such obligations, does not discharge said retiring partner from existing obligations. Advance Rubber Co. v Bershad (1925) 125 Misc 826, 211 N.Y.S. 574

4. – Retiring partner as surety

When a partner transfers his interest in the partnership assets to another and retires from the partnership, he occupies the position of a surety not only as between himself and the continuing partners, but as to all others who have had dealings with the partnership to whom notice of the new contract has been brought. Colgrove v Tallman (1876) 67 N.Y. 95

Creditors are bound to respect the suretyship relations thus existing, and any dealings with the partner assuming to pay the debts must be had with due regard to the rights of the retiring partner as surety, or he will be discharged. Colgrove v Tallman (1876) 67 N.Y. 95

Even as to persons having notice of dissolution, in the absence of facts showing a novation and discharge, the retiring partner continues liable as surety in connection with liabilities accrued at the time of dissolution. Drake v Hodgson (1924) 207 A.D. 783, 202 N.Y.S. 813

A creditor of a dissolved copartnership having knowledge of the dissolution must first pursue his remedy against the partnership assets in the hands of the copartners who assumed responsibility, and the retiring partner stands merely as a surety. Stikeman v Whitman, Requardt & Smith (1947) 272 A.D. 627, 75 N.Y.S.2d 73, 13 CCH LC P 64132, app den (1948) 273 A.D. 827, 76 N.Y.S.2d 537 and app dismd (1948) 297 N.Y. 951, 80 N.E.2d 347

Whether or not the retiring partner has been indemnified by a third party for the payment of any of the firm debts which he may be called upon to make is immaterial, and his position remains only that of a surety for his former partner. Bank of United States v Moskowitz (1934) 150 Misc 629, 268 N.Y.S. 705

5. Assumption of liability by remaining partner

A creditor who joins as a party in the contract whereby another, as purchaser of a partner's interest, assumes to pay firm debts may ordinarily bring suit on the agreement. Barlow v Myers (1876) 64 N.Y. 41

Limited partner had limited obligation to restore deficit in its capital account on dissolution of partnership where (1) provision of partnership agreement increasing general partner's capital account by "the amount of Partnership liabilities for which the General Partner is personally liable following dissolution and winding up of the Partnership" was properly construed, in light of relevant federal tax law, to attribute to general partner assumption by its constituent general partners partnership liability, thus resulting in general partner's having positive capital account on dissolution and thus triggering limited partner's deficit restoration obligation, and (2) immediately following clause of agreement, stating "except to the extent such liabilities are not then legally enforceable against the General Partner," was properly construed to refer to claims discharged in bankruptcy or barred by Statute of Limitations, so as to give both clauses effect. Harber Phila. Ctr. City Office v Tokai Bank (2001, 1st Dept) 281 A.D.2d 179, 721 N.Y.S.2d 519, app den 96 N.Y.2d 713, 729 N.Y.S.2d 440, 754 N.E.2d 200

Upon dissolution of partnership, whereby continuing partner assumes obligations of partnership, retiring partner nevertheless remains surety for his former partner on such obligations, but he is entitled to usual defense against creditor of partnership who, knowing of agreement, consents to material alteration in nature or time of payment of obligations. Bank of United States v Moskowitz (1934) 150 Misc 629, 268 N.Y.S. 705

6. Inferred discharge of liability

Even assuming that the assignment of the general partner's interest amounted to a dissolution, no agreement to discharge the general partners under section 67(2) can be inferred from the conduct of the creditor in acknowledging and accepting the transfer of the partners' interest. County of Oswego Indus. Dev. Agency v Fulton Cogeneration Associates, LP, 2009 US Dist LEXIS 61394 (ND NY July 16, 2009).

§ 68.   Right to wind up

Unless otherwise agreed the partners who have not wrongfully dissolved the partnership or the legal representative of the last surviving partner, not bankrupt, has the right to wind up the partnership affairs; provided, however, that any partner, his legal representative, or his assignee, upon cause shown, may obtain winding up by the court.

History: Add, L 1919, ch 408, eff Oct 1, 1919.

CASE ANNOTATIONS

Upon the death of a partner the partnership was automatically dissolved and the surviving partner had a right to settle the partnership affairs and the partnership assets as such never reached the hands of any executor or trustee of the decedent's estate. Slater v Slater (1924) 208 A.D. 567, 204 N.Y.S. 112, affd (1925) 240 N.Y. 557, 148 N.E. 703

Although there are elements of trust in the position of a liquidating partner, the authority given is only to the limited extent necessary to settle the business and does not create a direct trust. Bankers Trust Co. v Dennis (1939) 256 A.D. 495, 10 N.Y.S.2d 710, affd (1940) 282 N.Y. 635, 25 N.E.2d 981

On the death of one partner a surviving partner has the exclusive right to wind up the affairs of a partnership and representatives of the deceased partner have no legal right to interfere in the administration of the assets. Silberfeld v Swiss Bank Corp. (1948) 273 A.D. 686, 79 N.Y.S.2d 380, affd (1948) 298 N.Y. 776, 83 N.E.2d 468

In action for, inter alia, accounting and injunctive relief by several former members of dissolved partnership against one other former member of partnership, defendant was entitled to dismissal of cause of action seeking to restrain him from prosecuting collection action on behalf of partnership since plaintiffs did not contend that defendant had wrongfully dissolved partnership. Yorkes v Ross (1988, 2d Dept) 142 A.D.2d 642, 530 N.Y.S.2d 590

In action for, inter alia, accounting and injunctive relief by several former members of dissolved partnership against one other former member of partnership, defendant was not entitled to dismissal of cause of action seeking declaration that partnership had wound up its affairs since partners are permitted to seek winding up by court and to seek declaration that partnership's activities have been wound up. Yorkes v Ross (1988, 2d Dept) 142 A.D.2d 642, 530 N.Y.S.2d 590

Limited partners unreasonably delayed their attempt to exercise option to terminate partnership on disposition of partnership property where (1) property owned by partnership was transferred to new entity for conversion to cooperative apartments, (2) limited partners sought to extend partnership so that they might share in profits realized from sale of apartments, and (3) when general partner refused to permit such undeserved windfall, limited partners waited 22 months, while accepting accountings and their share of profits from partnership, and then claimed that there had been disposition of property within meaning of partnership agreement. Savasta v 470 Newport Assoc. (1992, 2d Dept) 180 A.D.2d 624, 579 N.Y.S.2d 167, app gr (1993) 81 N.Y.2d 703, 594 N.Y.S.2d 717, 610 N.E.2d 390 and affd (1993) 82 N.Y.2d 763, 603 N.Y.S.2d 821, 623 N.E.2d 1171, reconsideration den (1993) 82 N.Y.2d 889, 610 N.Y.S.2d 155, 632 N.E.2d 465

Limited partners had waived their right to terminate partnership and were estopped from termination of partnership on basis of disposition of partnership property where (1) property owned by partnership was transferred to new entity for conversion to cooperative apartments, (2) limited partners sought to extend partnership so that they might share in profits realized from sale of apartments, and (3) when general partner refused to permit such undeserved windfall, limited partners waited 22 months, while accepting accountings and

their share of profits from partnership, and then claimed that there had been disposition of property within meaning of partnership agreement. Savasta v 470 Newport Assoc. (1992, 2d Dept) 180 A.D.2d 624, 579 N.Y.S.2d 167, app gr (1993) 81 N.Y.2d 703, 594 N.Y.S.2d 717, 610 N.E.2d 390 and affd (1993) 82 N.Y.2d 763, 603 N.Y.S.2d 821, 623 N.E.2d 1171, reconsideration den (1993) 82 N.Y.2d 889, 610 N.Y.S.2d 155, 632 N.E.2d 465

Tenant partnership was amenable to action by landlord for rent due under lease where partnership, despite its dissolution, continued to exist at all relevant times for purpose of winding up its affairs, among which was its prolonged and ongoing rent dispute with landlord. 111-115 Broadway Ltd. Pshp. v Minter & Gay (1998, 1st Dept) 255 A.D.2d 192, 680 N.Y.S.2d 12

Partnership had capacity to commence tax certiorari proceedings as part of its obligation to wind up its affairs under CLS Bus Corp § 1005(a) and (b) and CLS Partn §§ 60 et seq. Fox Meadow Partners, Ltd. v Board of Assessment Review (2000, 2d Dept) 273 A.D.2d 472, 710 N.Y.S.2d 610

The surviving partner becomes possessed of the sole right to liquidate the partnership on the death of his copartner and his right to collect the firm assets and debts due it implies a right to retain counsel therefor. In re Allen Street in New York (1933) 148 Misc 488, 266 N.Y.S. 277, affd (1933) 239 A.D. 775, 263 N.Y.S. 942, reh and app den (1933) 239 A.D. 827, 264 N.Y.S. 919

As title to partnership assets and property vested in surviving partner, he had right to wind up partnership affairs pursuant to this section, and, therefore, had title to a check, which was partnership asset, and had right to indorse and collect it. Beech-Nut Packing Co. v National City Bank (1933) 149 Misc 682, 268 N.Y.S. 51

Upon the death of a partner the partnership was dissolved and it became the duty of the survivor to settle the partnership affairs and remit the deceased partner's share to his representative. In re Vitelli's Estate (1949) 196 Misc 644, 92 N.Y.S.2d 322

Limited partners had a statutory right to a dissolution and winding up decree of a court and accordingly, such relief with respect to the winding up decree had to be granted, pursuant to N.Y. Partnership Law §§ 68, 99(1)(c), and 105(4)(a). Polner v Monchik Realty Co. (2005, Sup) 9 Misc 3d 755, 803 N.Y.S.2d 370

Plaintiffs New York company and its president could not sell assets unilaterally under N.Y. Partnership Law §§ 68, 69, because they agreed to resolve all disputes in connection with the joint venture with defendant foreign company by arbitration, and the court confirmed the arbitration panel's directive that plaintiffs stop the sale of inventory without the panel's approval. Yonir Techs., Inc. v Duration Sys. (2002, SD NY) 244 F. Supp. 2d 195

§ 69.   Rights of partners to application of partnership property

1. When dissolution is caused in any way, except in contravention of the partnership agreement, each partner, as against his copartners and all persons claiming through them in respect of their interests in the partnership, unless otherwise agreed, may have the partnership property applied to discharge its liabilities, and the surplus applied to pay in cash the net amount owing to the respective partners. But if dissolution is caused by expulsion of a partner, bona fide under the partnership agreement, and if the expelled partner is discharged from all partnership liabilities, either by payment or agreement under section sixty-seven, subdivision two, he shall receive in cash only the net amount due him from the partnership.

2. When dissolution is caused in contravention of the partnership agreement the rights of the partners shall be as follows:

(a) Each partner who has not caused dissolution wrongfully shall have,

(I) All the rights specified in subdivision one of this section, and

(II) The right, as against each partner who has caused the dissolution wrongfully, to damages for breach of the agreement.

(b) The partners who have not caused the dissolution wrongfully, if they all desire to continue the business in the same name, either by themselves or jointly with others, may do so, during the agreed term for the partnership and for that purpose may possess the partnership property, provided they secure the payment by bond approved by the court, or pay to any partner who has caused the dissolution wrongfully, the value of his interest in the partnership at the dissolution, less any damages recoverable under clause (II) of paragraph (a) of subdivision two of this section, and in like manner indemnify him against all present or future partnership liabilities.

(c) A partner who has caused the dissolution wrongfully shall have:

(I) If the business is not continued under the provisions of paragraph (b) of subdivision two of this section all the rights of a partner under subdivision (1), subject to clause (II) of paragraph (a) of subdivision two, of this section.

(II) If the business is continued under paragraph (b) of subdivision two of this section the right as against his copartners and all claiming through them in respect of their interest in the partnership, to have the value of his interest in the partnership, less any damages caused to his copartners by the dissolution, ascertained and paid to him in cash, or the payment secured by bond approved by the court, and to be released from all existing liabilities of the partnership; but in ascertaining the value of the partner's interest the value of the good-will of the business shall not be considered.

History: Add, L 1919, ch 408, eff Oct 1, 1919.

CASE ANNOTATIONS

An interlocutory judgment rendered in an action between two partners to the effect that neither the plaintiff nor the defendant had any claim against the other with respect "to said premises," merely acknowledged that the partnership no longer had title to certain real estate as a result of the settlement of an earlier partition action and plaintiff's demand that defendant account for the income from the partnership asset was not a claim against the premises, but rather against the proceeds therefrom prior to a partition sale. Gordon v Ginsberg (1970) 26 N.Y.2d 236, 309 N.Y.S.2d 326, 257 N.E.2d 880

In an action brought by a partnership seeking damages representing sums demanded from the estate of a deceased partner as additional capital contributions, the case would be remitted with directions for a partnership accounting on the basis that the proper remedy was an equitable action for an accounting, since the capital contributions were not the absolute property of the partners in which the contributing partner had no interest, but were only one element in the complex of rights and liabilities whose net result could result in a judgment in some as yet undetermined way, and since audit statements forming the basis of a referee's findings were not an adequate substitute, in that such statements prepared by professional accountants are prepared to show the financial condition of the enterprise in accordance with the generally accepted accounting principles, whereas the judicial accounting is an action resulting in a final judgment adjudicating the rights and liabilities. Hotel Prince George Affiliates v Maroulis (1984) 62 N.Y.2d 1005, 479 N.Y.S.2d 489, 468 N.E.2d 671

Withdrawing partner was entitled to summary judgment in his action for departure compensation under partnership agreement, even though agreement conditioned payment of earned but uncollected partnership revenues on withdrawing partner's obligation to refrain from practice of law in competition with former firm, and partner nonetheless continued his practice, since condition violated CLS Code of Prof Respons DR 2-108(A) and was thus unenforceable as against public policy. Cohen v Lord, Day & Lord (1989) 75 N.Y.2d 95, 551 N.Y.S.2d 157, 550 N.E.2d 410

Trial court properly reduced the minority partner's share for goodwill because the findings were supported by evidence that there was goodwill value in the partnership. Congel v Malfitano, 31 N.Y.3d 272, 101 N.E.3d 341, 76 N.Y.S.3d 873, 2018 N.Y. LEXIS 496 (N.Y. 2018).

Trial court properly applied a minority discount when valuing the minority partner's share because the minority interest was worth less to anyone buying that interest alone while the remaining interest was ongoing. Congel v Malfitano, 31 N.Y.3d 272, 101 N.E.3d 341, 76 N.Y.S.3d 873, 2018 N.Y. LEXIS 496 (N.Y. 2018).

Any partner may dissolve the partnership at any time, but if he thereby breaches the agreement under which the partnership is organized, he is subject to a claim for damages for breach of contract by the other partners. Napoli v Domnitch (1962, 2d Dept) 18 A.D.2d 707, 236 N.Y.S.2d 549, affd (1964) 14 N.Y.2d 508, 248 N.Y.S.2d 228, 197 N.E.2d 623

As a general rule, in an action upon a partnership debt, a claim of a defendant against an individual partner may not be utilized as a set-off against the debt. Kamer v ITT Life Ins. Co. (1969, 1st Dept) 33 A.D.2d 682, 305 N.Y.S.2d 825, app den (1970) 26 N.Y.2d 612, stay den (1970) 26 N.Y.2d 882

Real estate purchased as partnership property is not within statute of frauds since, for purpose of reconciling equities between partners, real property is said to have been equitably converted to personalty and is to be dealt with as such until needs of partnership are met; accordingly, partner may be permitted to establish, absent writing, that real property which during and prior to formation of partnership was held in names of particular partners is indeed partnership property for dissolution purposes. Johnson v Johnson (1985, 3d Dept) 111 A.D.2d 1005, 490 N.Y.S.2d 324

In Article 75 proceeding to confirm arbitration award regarding dissolution of partnership, it could not be said that arbitrators improperly rewrote parties' partnership agreement by awarding sum to plaintiff which exceeded value of his interest in firm as determined by partnership's accountant since, although partnership agreement contained provision to effect that accountant's calculations would be final and binding in event of termination of association of partner with firm, since such provision was inapplicable as case involved dissolution of partnership rather than termination of partner's association with firm. Levy v Spanier (1989, 2d Dept) 155 A.D.2d 517, 547 N.Y.S.2d 378

In Article 75 proceeding to confirm arbitration award regarding dissolution of partnership, court would modify award to plaintiff of share of certain executor's commissions and legal fees arising from firm's representation of clients so as to include provision limiting plaintiff's recovery to portion of only those commissions and fees which represented work performed prior to arbitration award. Levy v Spanier (1989, 2d Dept) 155 A.D.2d 517, 547 N.Y.S.2d 378

Court properly treated plaintiff's motion for judicial accounting as motion for discovery, and properly denied it, where partnership agreement expressly set forth exclusive method for calculating and distributing partnership assets on dissolution and plaintiff failed to establish that written account previously provided by defendant was prepared contrary to methodology set forth in partnership agreement or contrary to practices followed by partnership for more than 20 years in which plaintiff had acquiesced. Hand v Kenyon & Kenyon (1996, 1st Dept) 227 A.D.2d 137, 641 N.Y.S.2d 307, app den, reargument den (1996, N.Y. A.D., 1st Dept) 1996 N.Y. A.D. LEXIS 8041, app dismd without op (1997, 1st Dept) 237 A.D.2d 996, 655 N.Y.S.2d 737, app dismd (1998, 1st Dept) 246 A.D.2d 446, 667 N.Y.S.2d 245, app den, reargument den (1998, N.Y. A.D., 1st Dept) 1998 N.Y. A.D. LEXIS 4448 and app dismd, in part, app den, in part (1998) 92 N.Y.2d 872, 677 N.Y.S.2d 775, 700 N.E.2d 314

Where judicial sale of assets of partnership under prevailing conditions would be practically confiscation to plaintiff, who stands innocent in transactions, under powers of this section and § 75 court will dispense with judicial sale. Dow v Beals (1933) 149 Misc 631, 268 N.Y.S. 425

While partnership property is liable for partnership debts, that rule does not extend to debts contracted, after dissolution, by one of the partners with a third person having knowledge of the dissolution. J. C. H. Service Stations, Inc. v Patrikes (1944) 181 Misc 401, 46 N.Y.S.2d 228

Where all the parties to a joint venture which was originally to continue for one year, signed an agreement that it should terminate as of a specified date short of the year, this amounted to a dissolution "by the express will of all partners" and, in the absence of other agreement, the members then became entitled to distribution of the profits. Mounteney & Mounteney v H. W. Ringhoff Corp. (1962) 33 Misc. 2d 362, 224 N.Y.S.2d 729

Where one partner serves unequivocal notice of election to "dissolve" the partnership, in disregard of provisions of the partnership agreement prescribing how a partner may withdraw and fixing the rights of other partners in such case, the remaining partners, in an action by the first partner seeking dissolution, are entitled to disregard the formula set up by the agreement in case of withdrawal of a partner and to have the assets distributed pursuant to the provisions of this section. Napoli v Domnitch (1962) 34 Misc. 2d 237, 226 N.Y.S.2d 908, mod (1962, 2d Dept) 18 A.D.2d 707, 236 N.Y.S.2d 549, affd (1964) 14 N.Y.2d 508, 248 N.Y.S.2d 228, 197 N.E.2d 623

Plaintiffs New York company and its president could not sell assets unilaterally under N.Y. Partnership Law §§ 68, 69, because they agreed to resolve all disputes in connection with the joint venture with defendant foreign company by arbitration, and the court confirmed the arbitration panel's directive that plaintiffs stop the sale of inventory without the panel's approval. Yonir Techs., Inc. v Duration Sys. (2002, SD NY) 244 F. Supp. 2d 195

While the trial court properly did not abuse its discretion in using fair market value to determine the value of each partner's interest pursuant to N.Y. P'ship Law § 69(2), it erred in substituting its own determination for that of the parties' experts as to the value of the partnership's equipment and machinery at the time of the dissolution based upon its personal inspection of the partnership's premises. Quick v Quick (2012, App Div, 2d Dept) 953 NYS2d 271.

§ 70.   Rights where partnership is dissolved for fraud, or misrepresentation

Where a partnership contract is rescinded on the ground of the fraud or misrepresentation of one of the parties thereto, the party entitled to rescind is, without prejudice to any other right, entitled,

(a) To a lien on, or right of retention of, the surplus of the partnership property after satisfying the partnership liabilities to third persons for any sum of money paid by him for the purchase of an interest in the partnership and for any capital or advances contributed by him; and

(b) To stand, after all liabilities to third persons have been satisfied, in the place of the creditors of the partnership for any payments made by him in respect of the partnership liabilities; and

(c) To be indemnified by the person guilty of the fraud or making the representation against all debts and liabilities of the partnership.

History: Add, L 1919, ch 408, eff Oct 1, 1919.

CASE ANNOTATIONS

By terms of §§ 10, 40, 71, 98 and 112, the rules there laid down for determining rights and duties of partners and for distribution of assets are applicable only in absence of an agreement between the partners on the same subject matter. Lanier v Bowdoin (1939) 282 N.Y. 32, 24 N.E.2d 732, reh den (1940) 282 N.Y. 611, 25 N.E.2d 391

In the absence of prohibitory provisions of statutes or rules of the common law relating to partnerships or considerations of pubic policy the partners of either a general or limited partnership, as between themselves, may include in the partnership articles any agreement they wish concerning the sharing of profits and losses, priorities of distribution on winding up of the partnership affairs and other matters. If complete, as between the parties, an agreement so made

controls. Lanier v Bowdoin (1939) 282 N.Y. 32, 24 N.E.2d 732, reh den (1940) 282 N.Y. 611, 25 N.E.2d 391

The difference in the relationship to creditors of a partner as such and a partner as an individual, e.g., the unavailablity of partnership assets for execution on individual claims and the priorities of firm and individual creditors upon insolvency, illustrate the general principles that a person who holds membership in a partnership acts, serves and is obliged in two distinct and different capacities. Ruzicka v Rager (1953) 305 N.Y. 191, 111 N.E.2d 878, 39 ALR2d 288, reh den (1953) 305 N.Y. 798, 113 N.E.2d 306

In an action to enforce a partnership claim, a counterclaim may not be set up by a defendant to impose a "nonpartisanship liability" against the partners (one of them a limited partner) individually. Ruzicka v Rager (1953) 305 N.Y. 191, 111 N.E.2d 878, 39 ALR2d 288, reh den (1953) 305 N.Y. 798, 113 N.E.2d 306

Action for dissolution and accounting of joint adventure and partnership may be had in equity but there is a simpler remedy under Part. Law. Davis v Horan (1933) 237 A.D. 761, 263 N.Y.S. 270

Court properly awarded recission of partnership agreement and return of plaintiff's capital investment under CLS Partn § 70 where, during operation of partnership, defendant engaged in conduct tantamount to fraudulent concealment and breach of fiduciary duty. Leibevic v Bronstein (1987, 4th Dept) 134 A.D.2d 891, 522 N.Y.S.2d 56

Liquidation of a partnership dissolved by the death of one of the partners is controlled by the provisions of the partnership agreement and in the absence of such provisions by the Partnership Law. In re Eddy's Estate (1941) 175 Misc 1011, 26 N.Y.S.2d 115, affd (1941) 262 A.D. 1015, 30 N.Y.S.2d 848, app dismd (1942) 288 N.Y. 524, 41 N.E.2d 930 and affd (1943) 290 N.Y. 677, 49 N.E.2d 628

While partnership property is liable for partnership debts, that rule does not extend to debts contracted, after dissolution, by one of the partners with a third person having knowledge of the dissolution. J. C. H. Service Stations, Inc. v Patrikes (1944) 181 Misc 401, 46 N.Y.S.2d 228

This section sanctions a partnership agreement between the owner of a business and an employee who manages it whereby the latter agrees to devote his business ability to the operation but is not required to invest money in it. Graziani v Rohan (1959, Sup) 195 N.Y.S.2d 156, revd on other grounds (1960, 1st Dept) 10 A.D.2d 154, 198 N.Y.S.2d 383, affd (1960) 8 N.Y.2d 967, 204 N.Y.S.2d 346, 169 N.E.2d 8

§ 71.   Rules for distribution

In settling accounts between the partners after dissolution, the following rules shall be observed, subject to any agreement to the contrary:

(a) The assets of the partnership are:

I. The partnership property,

II. The contributions of the partners specified in paragraph (d) of this subdivision.

(b) The liabilities of the partnership shall rank in order of payment, as follows:

I. Those owing to creditors other than partners,

II. Those owing to partners other than for capital and profits,

III. Those owing to partners in respect of capital,

IV. Those owing to partners in respect of profits.

(c) The assets shall be applied in the order of their declaration in clause (a) of this paragraph to the satisfaction of the liabilities.

(d) Except as provided in subdivision (b) of section twenty-six of this section: (1) partners shall contribute, as provided by section forty, subdivision one, the amount necessary to satisfy the liabilities; and (2) if any, but not all, of the partners are insolvent, or, not being subject to process, refuse to contribute, the other partners shall contribute their share of the liabilities, and, in the relative proportions in which they share the profits, the additional amount necessary to pay the liabilities.

(e) An assignee for the benefit of creditors or any person appointed by the court shall have the right to enforce the contributions specified in paragraph (d) of this subdivision.

(f) Any partner or his legal representative shall have the right to enforce the contributions specified in paragraph (d) of this subdivision, to the extent of the amount which he has paid in excess of his share of the liability.

(g) The individual property of a deceased partner shall be liable for the contributions specified in paragraph (d) of this subdivision.

(h) When partnership property and the individual properties of the partners are in the possession of a court for distribution, partnership creditors shall have priority on partnership property and separate creditors on individual property, saving the rights of lien or secured creditors as heretofore.

(i) Where a partner has become bankrupt or his estate is insolvent the claims against his separate property shall rank in the following order:

I. Those owing to separate creditors,

II. Those owing to partnership creditors,

III. Those owing to partners by way of contribution.

History: Add, L 1919, ch 408; amd, L 1994, ch 576, § 12, eff Oct 24, 1994.

Sub (a), amd, L 1994, ch 576, § 12, eff Oct 24, 1994.

Sub (a), par II, amd, L 1994, ch 576, § 12, eff Oct 24, 1994.

Sub (d), amd, L 1994, ch 576, § 12, eff Oct 24, 1994.

CASE ANNOTATIONS

1. In general
2. Assets
3. Liabilities

1. In general

In action brought by estate of deceased partner for dissolution of partnership and for an accounting, in which original interlocutory judgment directed that defendants account for profits up to date of such judgment, August 31, 1970, but defendants did not finally submit their accounting until March 9, 1972, trial court was justified in requiring defendants to account for year 1971, in view of protracted delay occasioned by defendants. Rosen Trust v Rosen (1976, 4th Dept) 53 A.D.2d 342, 386 N.Y.S.2d 491, affd (1977) 43 N.Y.2d 693, 401 N.Y.S.2d 66, 371 N.E.2d 828

In action between partners for accounting on dissolution of partnership, Special Term did not err in setting forth figure for office expenses without holding hearing as to proper amount; no hearing was required where plaintiff failed to raise any factual issue in dispute of amounts claimed by defendant for office expenses. Glanzman v Fischman (1986, 2d Dept) 122 A.D.2d 195, 504 N.Y.S.2d 733

2. Assets

In action for partnership accounting of plaintiff's interest in law firm that was dissolved and then re-formed without plaintiff, goodwill was not distributable asset of partnership where partnership agreement, which reflected binding written expression of terms under which partners assented to associate with each other, evinced their

intention that goodwill be deemed "of no value." Dawson v White & Case (1996) 88 N.Y.2d 666, 649 N.Y.S.2d 364, 672 N.E.2d 589

Where partnership agreement provided that no partner would receive salary for services rendered to partnership, but one of partners was paid management fee without objection from other partners from inception of partnership until death of one of partners, partners altered terms of partnership agreement by their acceptance of such compensation as legitimate expense, and partner performing such services was entitled to compensation for such services during period in which surviving partners carried on business following death of one of partners; however, such partner was not entitled to leasing commissions for such period, in view of fact that performing partner did not receive such compensation prior to death of deceased partner. Rosen Trust v Rosen (1976, 4th Dept) 53 A.D.2d 342, 386 N.Y.S.2d 491, affd (1977) 43 N.Y.2d 693, 401 N.Y.S.2d 66, 371 N.E.2d 828

Where depreciation was deducted in computation of income of partnership business from inception of partnership and each partner had received benefit of depreciation deduction on his personal tax return, and, following death of one of partners, surviving partners received income from partnership's assets unreduced by depreciation and in declaring such income under personal tax returns, surviving partners utilized one-half of permissible depreciation deduction, in applying equitable remedy of accounting, depreciation deduction was properly denied in computing total postdissolution profits of partnership. Rosen Trust v Rosen (1976, 4th Dept) 53 A.D.2d 342, 386 N.Y.S.2d 491, affd (1977) 43 N.Y.2d 693, 401 N.Y.S.2d 66, 371 N.E.2d 828

In action brought by estate of deceased partner for dissolution of partnership and for an accounting, in which plaintiff elected to recover its one-third interest in partnership assets valued as of date of dissolution of partnership, plus one-third of postdissolution profits up to date of judgment, trial court erred in including in determination of postdissolution profits gain realized on postdissolution sale of rental property held by partnership. Rosen Trust v Rosen (1976, 4th Dept) 53 A.D.2d 342, 386 N.Y.S.2d 491, affd (1977) 43 N.Y.2d 693, 401 N.Y.S.2d 66, 371 N.E.2d 828

In dissolution of partnership whose major asset was building containing residential and commercial units, hearing officer properly found highest and best use of property to be use as cooperatives and condominiums, and properly adopted "coop/condominium approach" (based upon sales of comparable coop and condominium units), rather than income or leasehold approach, for purposes of valuing partners' interests; however, valuation of individual partners' interests should be reduced to reflect "net" valuation by allowing for necessary costs and expenses of effectuating conversion of building to cooperative and condominium use, and such costs should be shared equally by partners even though their interests in partnership were not identical. Brandston v Giordano (1987, 1st Dept) 126 A.D.2d 411, 510 N.Y.S.2d 117

Pending contingency fee cases of dissolved law partnership were assets subject to distribution following plaintiff's voluntary withdrawal from partnership where partnership agreement was silent as to treatment of post-dissolution contingency fees. Shandell v Katz (1995, 1st Dept) 217 A.D.2d 472, 629 N.Y.S.2d 437

In action for judicial determination of value of 3 deceased physicians' interests in partnership and corporation that owned and operated hospital, trial court properly held that redemption ratios established at 1982 and 1983 annual meetings of partnership and corporation were valid and controlling. Livack v Central Gen. Hosp. (1997, 2d Dept) 242 A.D.2d 684, 664 N.Y.S.2d 935

In action for judicial determination of value of 3 deceased physicians' interests in partnership and corporation that owned and operated hospital, trial court properly concluded that one physician's interests in hospital were ineligible for inclusion in any computation for quorum and voting purposes, by reason of that physician's felony conviction and stipulation of withdrawal. Livack v Central Gen. Hosp. (1997, 2d Dept) 242 A.D.2d 684, 664 N.Y.S.2d 935

In action for judicial determination of value of 3 deceased physicians' interests in partnership and corporation that owned and operated hospital, trial court employed proper methodology to determine redemption ratios applicable to plaintiffs' interests, where partnership and stockholder agreements, read together, expressly provided for alternative valuation methods. Livack v Central Gen. Hosp. (1997, 2d Dept) 242 A.D.2d 684, 664 N.Y.S.2d 935

Absent contrary agreement, pending contingent fee cases of dissolved partnership are assets subject to distribution. Grant v Heit

Partnership Law

(1999, 1st Dept) 263 A.D.2d 388, 693 N.Y.S.2d 564, app dismd (1999) 93 N.Y.2d 1040, 697 N.Y.S.2d 568, 719 N.E.2d 929

Settlement value of pending contingent fee cases was not tantamount to value to be ascribed to them as assets subject to distribution after dissolution of law partnership; rather, referee had to evaluate efforts undertaken by former law firm on those cases before dissolution date and any other evidence relevant to valuation. Grant v Heit (1999, 1st Dept) 263 A.D.2d 388, 693 N.Y.S.2d 564, app dismd (1999) 93 N.Y.2d 1040, 697 N.Y.S.2d 568, 719 N.E.2d 929

There were errors in the referee's final reconciliation of the entities' assets and the sums to be allocated to the parties; in part, the partnership agreement provided that capital contributions were to be repaid after expenses and before profits and losses were assessed, and the referee erred in calculating a presumptive share of the profit to be received by each partner before making deductions for capital contributions. Sutton v Burdick, 135 A.D.3d 1016, 22 N.Y.S.3d 633 (3d Dep't 2016).

3. Liabilities

In action for partnership accounting of plaintiff's interest in law firm that was dissolved and then re-formed without plaintiff, future pension payments pursuant to firm's unfunded pension plan were properly disallowed as partnership liability where partnership never included unfunded pension plan as liability in firm's financial statements, and partnership provided that pension payments could be made only out of partnership assets and could not exceed 15 percent of profits; pension payments were not liability of firm in dissolution but operating expenses for successor firm contingent on its profitability. Dawson v White & Case (1996) 88 N.Y.2d 666, 649 N.Y.S.2d 364, 672 N.E.2d 589

N.Y. Partnership Law § 26(b) does not shield a general partner in a registered limited liability partnership from personal liability for breaches of the partnership's or partners' obligations to each other. Ederer v Gursky (2007) 9 NY3d 514, 851 NYS2d 108, 881 NE2d 204, reargument den (2008) 10 NY3d 780, 857 NYS2d 15, 886 NE2d 776.

In a suit brought by a withdrawing partner of a Limited Liability Partnership (LLP) for an accounting and for breach of contract, a trial court order holding the remaining partners liable to the withdrawing partner for an accounting was upheld on appeal as N.Y. Partnership Law § 26(b) did not shield the general partner of the LLP from personal liability for breaches of the partnership's or partners' obligations to each other. Since no formal written agreement existed governing the LLP, the provisions of § 26(b) applied. Ederer v Gursky (2007) 9 NY3d 514, 851 NYS2d 108, 881 NE2d 204, reargument den (2008) 10 NY3d 780, 857 NYS2d 15, 886 NE2d 776.

Where partnership agreement made no provision concerning payment or distribution of a partner's loans or capital, alleged loans to partnership made by two of partners, regardless of whether they were denominated as loans or capital contributions, were entitled to repayment before distribution of net assets of partnership, as provided by statutory priority. Rosen Trust v Rosen (1976, 4th Dept) 53 A.D.2d 342, 386 N.Y.S.2d 491, affd (1977) 43 N.Y.2d 693, 401 N.Y.S.2d 66, 371 N.E.2d 828

In determining postdissolution profits of partnership in business of constructing and leasing rental properties, deferred leasing commissions and deferred mortgage expenses were properly allowed as deductions, in view of fact that such expenses were costs of ongoing business. Rosen Trust v Rosen (1976, 4th Dept) 53 A.D.2d 342, 386 N.Y.S.2d 491, affd (1977) 43 N.Y.2d 693, 401 N.Y.S.2d 66, 371 N.E.2d 828

§ 71-a.   Payment of wages by receivers

Upon the appointment of a receiver of a partnership the wages of the employees of such partnership shall be preferred to every other debt or claim.

History: Add, L 1921, ch 23, eff March 3, 1921.

CASE ANNOTATIONS

In proceeding to determine priorities of claims on settlement of account of receiver of nursing home, CLS Partn § 71-a did not support contention of union, which represented employees of nursing home, that its claim for moneys due for fringe benefits took priority over claim by landlord for rent due. D'Guardia v Piffath (1992, 2d Dept) 180 A.D.2d 630, 579 N.Y.S.2d 447

§ 72.   Liability of persons continuing the business in certain cases

1. When any new partner is admitted into an existing partnership, or when any partner retires and assigns (or the representative of the deceased partner assigns) his rights in partnership property to two or more of the partners, or to one or more of the partners and one or more third persons, if the business is continued without liquidation of the partnership affairs, creditors of the first or dissolved partnership are also creditors of the partnership so continuing the business.

2. When all but one partner retire and assign (or the representative of a deceased partner assigns) their rights in partnership property to the remaining partner, who continues the business without liquidation of partnership affairs, either alone or with others, creditors of the dissolved partnership are also creditors of the person or partnership so continuing the business.

3. When any partner retires or dies and the business of the dissolved partnership is continued as set forth in subdivisions one and two of this section, with the consent of the retired partners or the representative of the deceased partner, but without any assignment of his right in partnership property, rights of creditors of the dissolved partnership and of the creditors of the person or partnership continuing the business shall be as if such assignment had been made.

4. When all the partners or their representatives assign their rights in partnership property to one or more third persons who promise to pay the debts and who continue the business of the dissolved partnership, creditors of the dissolved partnership are also creditors of the person or partnership continuing the business.

5. When any partner wrongfully causes a dissolution and the remaining partners continue the business under the provisions of section sixty-nine, paragraph (b) of subdivision two, either alone or with others, and without liquidation of the partnership affairs, creditors of the dissolved partnership are also creditors of the person or partnership continuing the business.

6. When a partner is expelled and the remaining partners continue the business either alone or with others, without liquidation of the partnership affairs, creditors of the dissolved partnership are also creditors of the person or partnership continuing the business.

7. The liability of a third person becoming a partner in the partnership continuing the business under this section to the creditors of the dissolved partnership shall be satisfied out of partnership property only.

8. When the business of a partnership after dissolution is continued under any conditions set forth in

this section the creditors of the dissolved partnership, as against the separate creditors of the retiring or deceased partner or the representative of the deceased partner, have a prior right to any claim of the retired partner or the representative of the deceased partner against the person or partnership continuing the business, on account of the retired or deceased partner's interest in the dissolved partnership or on account of any consideration promised for such interest or for his right in partnership property.

9. Nothing in this section shall be held to modify any right of creditors to set aside any assignment on the ground of fraud.

10. The use by the person or partnership continuing the business of the partnership name, or the name of a deceased partner as part thereof, shall not of itself make the individual property of the deceased partner liable for any debts contracted by such person or partnership.

History: Add, L 1919, ch 408, eff Oct 1, 1919.

CASE ANNOTATIONS

Whether or not a new partnership firm, upon reorganization, took over the accounts and business of the old firm and assumed its obligations is a question of fact. Jamestown Lounge Co. v Kay (1930) 231 A.D. 5, 246 N.Y.S. 136

Two of the four executors of the estate of a deceased partner were entitled to an accounting as a matter of right where the deceased partner, in his last will, requested that the partnership be continued and his executors agree to such a continuance. In re Shubert's Will (1955, 1st Dept) 1 A.D.2d 654, 146 N.Y.S.2d 257, affd (1956) 1 N.Y.2d 914, 154 N.Y.S.2d 969, 136 N.E.2d 913

Defendants, sons of deceased partner who succeeded to his interest, were entitled to summary judgment dismissing action brought by surviving partner seeking indemnification for payment of preexisting partnership debt since CLS Partn § 72 limits an incoming partner's liability to partnership property unless personal liability is expressly assumed, and inasmuch as surviving partner continued partnership business after death of his partner without consent of deceased's representative, surviving partner was required to bear all losses. Kalichman v Beverly Holding Co. (1987, 3d Dept) 130 A.D.2d 327, 520 N.Y.S.2d 255, app den (1988) 70 N.Y.2d 616, 526 N.Y.S.2d 437, 521 N.E.2d 444

Law firm three's (F3) partnership agreement could not defeat its liability to a lawyer for those fees generated by F3 for clients and business matters it continued from law firm one as attorneys one and two could not contract with each other to avoid liability of the partnership to a nonparty to their agreement. Masson v Wiggins & Masson, LLP (2013, 3d Dept) 110 App Div 3d 1402, 974 NYS2d 619.

The purpose of this section is to protect the creditors of a partnership which, dissolved by a change in membership, nevertheless proceeds with its business, and the purpose of subd. 3 is to render available to creditors the share of the deceased partner in the assets of the firm where his representatives have consented to the continuance of the business. M. & C. Creditors Corp. v Pratt (1938) 172 Misc 695, 17 N.Y.S.2d 240, affd (1938) 255 A.D. 838, 7 N.Y.S.2d 662, affd (1939) 281 N.Y. 804, 24 N.E.2d 482

Surrogate's Court was without authority to entertain petition for continuance of a business in which decedent was a copartner rather than the sole owner. In re Estate of Saffioti (1974) 77 Misc. 2d 1052, 355 N.Y.S.2d 709

Former partner in a dental partnership was obligated to observe the restrictions in a covenant not to compete that had been made part of the partnership even when the former partner's termination of employment with the partnership effectively terminated the partnership. The restrictive covenant also applied to the business of the partnership that continued after the dissolution. Dental Health Assoc. v Zangeneh (2006, 2d Dept) 34 App Div 3d 622, 825 NYS2d 505

§ 73.   Rights of retiring or estate of deceased partner when the business is continued

When any partner retires or dies, and the business is continued under any of the conditions set forth in section seventy-two, subdivisions one, two, three, five and six, or section sixty-nine, paragraph (b) of subdivision two, without any settlement of accounts as between him or his estate and the person or partnership continuing the business, unless otherwise agreed, he or his legal representative as against such persons or partnership may have the value of his interest at the date of dissolution ascertained, and shall receive as an ordinary creditor an amount equal to the value of his interest in the dissolved partnership with interest, or, at his option or at the option of his legal representative, in lieu of interest, the profits attributable to the use of his right in the property of the dissolved partnership; provided that the creditors of the dissolved partnership as against the separate creditors, or the representative of the retired or deceased partner, shall have priority on any claim arising under this section, as provided by section seventy-two, subdivision eight of this chapter.

History: Add, L 1919, ch 408, eff Oct 1, 1919.

CASE ANNOTATIONS

1. In general
2. Outgoing partner
3. Deceased partner's estate
4. – Absence of agreement
5. – Right of accounting
6. – Power of surrogate court
7. Interest

1. In general

This section is not retroactive. Germann v Jones (1927) 220 A.D. 5, 221 N.Y.S. 32

Where one partner instituted an accounting action on April 28, 1969, where parties stipulated that partnership would be terminated as of October 25, 1972, and where partnership was evaluated as of December 31, 1973, interest on partner's share should run from the date of dissolution. Hedley v Hedley (1976, 4th Dept) 52 A.D.2d 1077, 384 N.Y.S.2d 298

Where law partnership had no retirement plan, effort of partner who allegedly served as "manager" of partnership to provide such a plan for retiring partner in exchange for retiring partner's interest in partnership was first attempt to make such arrangement with any partner, agreement providing for such exchange was evaluated as of secrecy, and, with respect to other partners, there was confusion as to parties to agreement and lack of knowledge as to its terms, there was no acquiescence or ratification of agreement by remaining partners, and such agreement was invalid as to partnership, and each partner, except partner who negotiated agreement and second partner who participated in negotiations and had detailed knowledge of its terms. Application of Lester (1976) 87 Misc. 2d 717, 386 N.Y.S.2d 509

2. Outgoing partner

In an action by a withdrawing partner for an accounting, it was error to include in the order a provision prohibiting plaintiff from competing with defendants in their business where there was nothing in the partnership agreement which limited the activities of withdrawing partners and the appraisal of plaintiff's interest in the firm was based in part upon the absence of any such provision. Elia v Damianopulos (1965, 4th Dept) 23 A.D.2d 803, 258 N.Y.S.2d 56

In action arising out of dissolution of law partnership, if it were found that medical malpractice case which defendant partner successfully settled after plaintiff partner's withdrawal constituted partnership asset, plaintiff would be entitled to his share in value of case as of date of dissolution, with interest, or at his option, in lieu of interest, profits attributable to use of his right in property of dissolved partnership; plaintiff was not limited to quantum meruit value of his services with respect to case on theory that it was under contingent fee arrangement and had not been disposed of before partnership was dissolved. Kirsch v Leventhal (1992, 3d Dept) 181 A.D.2d 222, 586 N.Y.S.2d 330

Plaintiff who voluntarily withdrew from law partnership was required to account to his former partners on partnership cases he took with him (CLS Partn § 73). Shandell v Katz (1995, 1st Dept) 217 A.D.2d 472, 629 N.Y.S.2d 437

Former partner is only entitled to the value of his interest at the date of dissolution with interest, or, at his option in lieu of interest, the profits attributable to the use of his right in the property of the dissolved partnership, pre-dissolution; in an action for an accounting, a law firm failed to articulate any basis, in support of their burden of proof as accounting fiduciaries, to distinguish between the money a former partner paid in and capital contributions credited to other partners. Liddle, Robinson & Shoemaker v Shoemaker (2003, A.D., 1st Dept) 758 N.Y.S.2d 628

Former partner is only entitled to the value of his interest at the date of dissolution with interest, or, at his option in lieu of interest, the profits attributable to the use of his right in the property of the dissolved partnership, pre-dissolution; in an action for an accounting, a law firm failed to articulate any basis, in support of their burden of proof as accounting fiduciaries, to distinguish between the money a former partner paid in and capital contributions credited to other partners. Liddle, Robinson & Shoemaker v Shoemaker (2003, A.D., 1st Dept) 758 N.Y.S.2d 628

Trial court erred in granting partial summary judgment to defendant partners in an action by trust remaindermen, seeking an accounting and distribution of partnership assets upon the dissolution of various partnerships due to the termination of a trust that held interests in the partnerships, as the settling of a trustee's final accounting with respect to trust assets and the value thereof pursuant to N.Y. P'ship Law § 73 did not prevent the remaindermen from seeking their own accounting; the value was to be computed as of the date of dissolution of the partnerships, but the trustee's account did not disclose the methodology used to compute the values. Breidbart v Wiesenthal (2007, 2d Dept) 44 App Div 3d 982, 844 NYS2d 442, subsequent app (2007, 2d Dept) 44 App Div 3d 985, 843 NYS2d 848

3. Deceased partner's estate

The words "as a general creditor" as used in this section apply to the method of collecting the value of the deceased partner's interest, especially vis-a-vis creditors of the partnership and creditors of the individual partners. Shubert v Lawrence (1967, 1st Dept) 27 A.D.2d 292, 278 N.Y.S.2d 537

Where partnership agreement provided that no partner would receive salary for services rendered to partnership, but one of partners was paid management fee without objection from other partners from inception of partnership until death of one of partners, partners altered terms of partnership agreement by their acceptance of such compensation as legitimate expense, and partner performing such services was entitled to compensation for such services during period in which surviving partners carried on business following death of one of partners; however, such partner was not entitled to leasing commissions for such period, in view of fact that performing partner did not receive such compensation prior to death of deceased partner. Rosen Trust v Rosen (1976, 4th Dept) 53 A.D.2d 342, 386 N.Y.S.2d 491, affd (1977) 43 N.Y.2d 693, 401 N.Y.S.2d 66, 371 N.E.2d 828

Estate of deceased partner was entitled to that portion of partnership's postdissolution profits which corresponded to decedent's equitable percentage share of partnership's total assets as of date of dissolution, in view of fact that provision of partnership agreement providing for equal division of partnership profits or losses did not specifically apply to postdissolution distribution. Rosen Trust v Rosen (1976, 4th Dept) 53 A.D.2d 342, 386 N.Y.S.2d 491, affd (1977) 43 N.Y.2d 693, 401 N.Y.S.2d 66, 371 N.E.2d 828

In action brought by estate of deceased partner for dissolution of partnership and for an accounting, in which plaintiff elected to recover its one-third interest in partnership assets valued as of date of dissolution of partnership, plus one-third of postdissolution profits up to date of judgment, trial court erred in including in determination of postdissolution profits gain realized on postdissolution sale of rental property held by partnership. Rosen Trust v Rosen (1976, 4th Dept) 53 A.D.2d 342, 386 N.Y.S.2d 491, affd (1977) 43 N.Y.2d 693, 401 N.Y.S.2d 66, 371 N.E.2d 828

In action brought by estate of deceased partner for dissolution of partnership and for an accounting, in which original interlocutory judgment directed that defendants account for profits up to date of such judgment, August 31, 1970, but defendants did not finally submit their accounting until March 9, 1972, trial court was justified in requiring defendants to account for year 1971, in view of protracted delay occasioned by defendants. Rosen Trust v Rosen (1976, 4th Dept) 53 A.D.2d 342, 386 N.Y.S.2d 491, affd (1977) 43 N.Y.2d 693, 401 N.Y.S.2d 66, 371 N.E.2d 828

Estate tax appraisals of partnership properties prepared by estate of deceased partner shortly after deceased partner's death were not binding on estate of deceased partner in action for dissolution of partnership and for an accounting. Rosen Trust v Rosen (1976, 4th Dept) 53 A.D.2d 342, 386 N.Y.S.2d 491, affd (1977) 43 N.Y.2d 693, 401 N.Y.S.2d 66, 371 N.E.2d 828

In proceeding by estate of deceased partner against fiduciary who misappropriated estate's interest in partnership, fiduciary was barred by principles of waiver and estoppel from attempting to invoke dissolution provisions of partnership agreement to limit estate's interest in partnership to value of decedent's interest on date of his death where (1) surviving partners abandoned those provisions following decedent's death, just as they had done in earlier instances in which partners died, (2) surviving partners continued partnership, deeming estate to have succeeded to limited partnership interest, and (3) fiduciary also clearly considered that estate had succeeded to limited partnership interest; likewise, CLS Partn § 62 did not operate to establish dissolution of partnership on decedent's death. Birnbaum v Birnbaum (1990, 4th Dept) 157 A.D.2d 177, 555 N.Y.S.2d 982, later proceeding (1991, 4th Dept) 171 A.D.2d 1074, 569 N.Y.S.2d 532, later proceeding (1992, 4th Dept) 177 A.D.2d 170, 582 N.Y.S.2d 853, app dismd without op (1992) 80 N.Y.2d 925, 589 N.Y.S.2d 311, 602 N.E.2d 1127

In proceeding by decedent's estate against fiduciary who misappropriated estate's interest in limited partnership, estate was properly awarded limited partnership interest rather than general partnership interest, although decedent was general partner at time of his death, where surviving partners continued enterprise as limited partnership; representative of deceased partner is not entitled to participate in continuation or winding up of partnership by surviving partners. Birnbaum v Birnbaum (1990, 4th Dept) 157 A.D.2d 177, 555 N.Y.S.2d 982, later proceeding (1991, 4th Dept) 171 A.D.2d 1074, 569 N.Y.S.2d 532, later proceeding (1992, 4th Dept) 177 A.D.2d 170, 582 N.Y.S.2d 853, app dismd without op (1992) 80 N.Y.2d 925, 589 N.Y.S.2d 311, 602 N.E.2d 1127

In action to determine amount owed to estate of attorney on dissolution of law partnership, practice of decedent on prior occasions, when former partners had died, was highly probative of nature of his partnership relationship at time that he died. Dwyer v Nicholson (1993, 2d Dept) 193 A.D.2d 70, 602 N.Y.S.2d 144, app dismd (1995, 2d Dept) 220 A.D.2d 555, 633 N.Y.S.2d 963, app den (1996) 87 N.Y.2d 808, 641 N.Y.S.2d 830, 664 N.E.2d 896, motion gr, motion den (1996) 88 N.Y.2d 963, 647 N.Y.S.2d 716, 670 N.E.2d 1348

In action to determine amount owed to estate of attorney on dissolution of law partnership, estate was entitled to distribution of net income, cash, and other deposits in partnership bank accounts and accounts receivable, but was not entitled to share of evaluated value of contingency fee cases, where (1) partnership agreement only provided for distribution of net income, cash and other deposits in partnership bank accounts and accounts receivable, (2) on prior occasions when former partners of decedent had died, their interests had been calculated so as to not to include value of contingency fee cases, and (3) accountant employed by firm testified that decedent had told him to keep books of firm in same manner as that used in connection with prior firms. Dwyer v Nicholson (1993, 2d Dept) 193 A.D.2d 70, 602 N.Y.S.2d 144, app dismd (1995, 2d Dept) 220 A.D.2d 555, 633 N.Y.S.2d 963, app den (1996) 87 N.Y.2d 808, 641 N.Y.S.2d 830, 664 N.E.2d 896, motion gr, motion den (1996) 88 N.Y.2d 963, 647 N.Y.S.2d 716, 670 N.E.2d 1348

Action by surviving partner, seeking dissolution of partnership and accounting, was not barred by failure to file claim against deceased partner's estate, which was probated in Florida, as required by Florida statutes, as action did not involve claim against deceased partner's estate; partnership property vested in plaintiff after partner's death, subject to accounting to deceased partner's estate. Blank v Blank (1995, 3d Dept) 222 A.D.2d 851, 634 N.Y.S.2d 886

Court erred in determining that executor, on accounting of decedent's partnership interest, was entitled to her choice between value of partnership as of date on decedent's death or its value as of date accounting was rendered where surviving partner with 2/3 partnership interest continued partnership business with executor's implied consent; thus, executor was entitled to value of her partnership interest as of date of decedent's death, date partnership was dissolved, with, at executor's option, either interest on value of her partnership interest as of date of decedent's death, or 1/3 of profits from date of decedent's death, less any money she had received since decedent's death. Ronan v Valley Stream Realty Co. (1998, 2d Dept) 249 A.D.2d 288, 670 N.Y.S.2d 885

Discounts are not barred by N.Y. P'ship Law § 73, which addressed not valuation but the method of collecting the value of the deceased partner's interest vis-a-vis creditors of the partnership and of the individual partners; a trial court correctly concluded that minority lack of control and decreased marketability discounts in valuing the decedent's interests in the partnerships were unavailable, albeit not for the reason stated. Vick v Albert (2008, 1st Dept) 47 App Div 3d 482, 849 NYS2d 250.

Surviving partners are not required to liquidate assets of partnership preliminary to ascertainment of the share due deceased partner's estate. M. & C. Creditors Corp. v Pratt (1938) 172 Misc 695, 17 N.Y.S.2d 240, affd (1938) 255 A.D. 838, 7 N.Y.S.2d 662, affd (1939) 281 N.Y. 804, 24 N.E.2d 482

Depreciation in value of partnership securities intervening between date of death of deceased partner and date of actual payment, does not affect distributable share of deceased partner inasmuch as continuance of the business was at the risk of surviving partners. M. & C. Creditors Corp. v Pratt (1938) 172 Misc 695, 17 N.Y.S.2d 240, affd (1938) 255 A.D. 838, 7 N.Y.S.2d 662, affd (1939) 281 N.Y. 804, 24 N.E.2d 482

Surviving partners and executors of deceased partner have power to make a binding adjustment of partnership affairs on any basis they choose in absence of mistake or fraud. M. & C. Creditors Corp. v Pratt (1938) 172 Misc 695, 17 N.Y.S.2d 240, affd (1938) 255 A.D. 838, 7 N.Y.S.2d 662, affd (1939) 281 N.Y. 804, 24 N.E.2d 482

4. – Absence of agreement

Where there is no written partnership agreement and the partnership business is continued after the death or retirement of a partner, the rights and obligations of the remaining partners and of the retiring partner or the deceased partner's estate are governed by the Partnership Law, which provides that the deceased partner's legal representative shall receive as an ordinary creditor an amount equal to the value of his interest in the dissolved partnership with interest, or, in lieu of interest, the profits attributable to the use of his right in the property of the dissolved partnership. Dreher v Levy (1979, 2d Dept) 67 A.D.2d 438, 415 N.Y.S.2d 658

In plaintiffs' action for accounting against surviving partners of former dissolved partnership, evidence established that plaintiffs had 8 percent interest in profits and assets of new partnerships at will created by operation of law when they continued to operate business of former partnership upon deaths of their predecessors, since they had received tax forms, cash distributions, and accompanying letters setting forth their interests as 8 percent, which proved that they had notice of their ownership interests and circumstantially proved such term of parties' new oral partnership agreements; therefore, plaintiffs' claims for breach of contract or imposition of constructive trust, based on surviving partners' failure to make distributions exceeding 8 percent, would be dismissed. Peirez v Queens P.E.P. Assoc., Corp. (1989, 2d Dept) 148 A.D.2d 596, 539 N.Y.S.2d 61, app dismd without op (1989) 74 N.Y.2d 792, 545 N.Y.S.2d 106, 543 N.E.2d 749 and app den (1990) 75 N.Y.2d 704, 552 N.Y.S.2d 927, 552 N.E.2d 175

Estate of deceased partner was entitled to receive value of decedent's interest determined as of date of dissolution (death) or date of judgment, at election of estate; thus, if estate so chose, it was entitled to present appreciated value of its partnership interests. Birnbaum v Birnbaum (1991, 4th Dept) 171 A.D.2d 1074, 569 N.Y.S.2d 532, later proceeding (1992, 4th Dept) 177 A.D.2d 170, 582 N.Y.S.2d 853, app dismd without op (1992) 80 N.Y.2d 925, 589 N.Y.S.2d 311, 602 N.E.2d 1127

Estate was entitled to present appreciated value of decedent's interest in partnership, notwithstanding that partnership had been corporation at time of decedent's death, since decedent's interest in corporation was easily traceable to interest in partnership. Birnbaum v Birnbaum (1991, 4th Dept) 171 A.D.2d 1074, 569 N.Y.S.2d 532, later proceeding (1992, 4th Dept) 177 A.D.2d 170, 582 N.Y.S.2d 853, app dismd without op (1992) 80 N.Y.2d 925, 589 N.Y.S.2d 311, 602 N.E.2d 1127

Executors of deceased partner are entitled to receive payment of value of their decedent's interest in partnership as of date of his

death, where partnership business was continued without their consent. M. & C. Creditors Corp. v Pratt (1938) 172 Misc 695, 17 N.Y.S.2d 240, affd (1938) 255 A.D. 838, 7 N.Y.S.2d 662, affd (1939) 281 N.Y. 804, 24 N.E.2d 482

If the surviving partner carries on the business without an agreement, the representative of the deceased partner is entitled at his option to receive the profits attributable to the use of his rights in the property of the dissolved partnership or in lieu thereof, interest may be demanded on the value of the deceased partner's interest ascertained as of the date of dissolution. In re Vitelli's Estate (1949) 196 Misc 644, 92 N.Y.S.2d 322

The rights on liquidation of a partnership dissolved by death of a member are controlled by the Partnership Law only in the absence of a particular agreement on the subject made by the partners themselves. Pailthorpe v Tallman (1949, Sup) 87 N.Y.S.2d 822, affd (1949) 276 A.D. 823, 93 N.Y.S.2d 712

5. – Right of accounting

On the death of a partner his estate has the right to call on the survivor to account with reference to his conduct and the partnership assets received by him but has no right to interefere in the administration of the assets or with the right of the surviving partner to wind up the affairs of the partnership. Silberfeld v Swiss Bank Corp. (1948) 273 A.D. 686, 79 N.Y.S.2d 380, affd (1948) 298 N.Y. 776, 83 N.E.2d 468

Two of the four executors of the estate of a deceased partner were entitled to an accounting as a matter of right where the deceased partner, in his last will, requested that the partnership be continued and his executors agree to such a continuance. In re Shubert's Will (1955, 1st Dept) 1 A.D.2d 654, 146 N.Y.S.2d 257, affd (1956) 1 N.Y.2d 914, 154 N.Y.S.2d 969, 136 N.E.2d 913

In an action brought by the administrator of a deceased partner's estate for a partnership accounting, the surviving partners would be directed to account to the administrator where deceased's widow had not been the "legal representative" of deceased for purposes of a release given by her to the surviving partners, and where no actual accounting had taken place inasmuch as a partnership accounting would encompass more than supplying tax returns. Juliano v Rea (1982, 2d Dept) 89 A.D.2d 618, 452 N.Y.S.2d 668, later proceeding (1986, 2d Dept) 120 A.D.2d 643, 502 N.Y.S.2d 97

In proceeding by estate of deceased partner against fiduciary who misappropriated estate's interest in partnership, estate was properly awarded value of decedent's interest in partnership as determined on date of dissolution or date of judgment (at its election) under CLS Partn § 73, since surviving partners continued partnership business after decedent's death, thus breaching their duty to estate to account for decedent's partnership interest. Birnbaum v Birnbaum (1990, 4th Dept) 157 A.D.2d 177, 555 N.Y.S.2d 982, later proceeding (1991, 4th Dept) 171 A.D.2d 1074, 569 N.Y.S.2d 532, later proceeding (1992, 4th Dept) 177 A.D.2d 170, 582 N.Y.S.2d 853, app dismd without op (1992) 80 N.Y.2d 925, 589 N.Y.S.2d 311, 602 N.E.2d 1127

Unless partnership agreement provides otherwise, limited partner is entitled to account of his interest under CLS Partn §§ 73 and 74. Adam v Cutner & Rathkopf (1997, 1st Dept) 238 A.D.2d 234, 656 N.Y.S.2d 753

In order to enlist aid of court of equity in vindicating right to accounting, plaintiff must show not only existence of partnership, its dissolution following transaction of business that produced profits or losses to be accounted for, and demand for accounting, but also failure or refusal by partner with books, records, profits, or other assets of partnership in his possession to account to other partner or partners. Adam v Cutner & Rathkopf (1997, 1st Dept) 238 A.D.2d 234, 656 N.Y.S.2d 753

Doctrine of collateral estoppel did not bar action for accounting based on individual partners' status as escrow agents where adjudication of whether defendant partners fulfilled their fiduciary duties to plaintiff partners was not necessary to prior adjudication of limited partnership as bankrupt. Adam v Cutner & Rathkopf (1997, 1st Dept) 238 A.D.2d 234, 656 N.Y.S.2d 753

Right to accounting is premised on existence of confidential or fiduciary relationship and breach of duty imposed by that relationship respecting property in which party seeking accounting has interest. Adam v Cutner & Rathkopf (1997, 1st Dept) 238 A.D.2d 234, 656 N.Y.S.2d 753

Allegation of wrongdoing is not indispensable element of demand for accounting where complaint indicates fiduciary relationship between parties or some other special circumstance warranting equitable relief. Adam v Cutner & Rathkopf (1997, 1st Dept) 238 A.D.2d 234, 656 N.Y.S.2d 753

Plaintiff partners' failure to defeat defendant partners' motion for judgment summarily dismissing causes of action for negligent and intentional misrepresentation, fraud, conversion, negligence, and breach of contract did not nullify plaintiffs' entitlement to accounting. Adam v Cutner & Rathkopf (1997, 1st Dept) 238 A.D.2d 234, 656 N.Y.S.2d 753

Plaintiff partners' recovery against defendant partners on sole remaining cause of action for accounting would be limited to damages attributable to defendants' failure to apply plaintiffs' deposits to partnership purposes. Adam v Cutner & Rathkopf (1997, 1st Dept) 238 A.D.2d 234, 656 N.Y.S.2d 753

Though summary judgment was properly granted to trustees as a result of the complaint of remaindermen to a partnership trust challenging the trustees' conversion of corporate shares to partnership interests being time-barred, the remaindermen were entitled to the relief they sought with regard to compelling partnership accountings and a distribution of partnership assets. Because no partnership agreement existed, N.Y. Partnership Law §§ 62(4), 60, and 73, provided for the remaindermen to receive, as ordinary creditors, an amount equal to the value of their interest in the dissolved partnership when the trust terminated and, therefore, entitled them to an accounting and distribution. Breidbart v Wiesenthal (2004, A.D., 2d Dept) 781 N.Y.S.2d 123

Vacatur of the default judgment was proper; since the relief sought was equitable in nature, it was beyond the scope of the New York Civil Court's jurisdiction. To the extent that the wife sought to recover her husband's partnership investments, the value of his interest could have been determined only by an accounting, N.Y. Partnership Law § 73. Priel v Linarello (2005, Sup App T) 7 Misc 3d 62, 794 N.Y.S.2d 775

As the estate representative of a decedent, plaintiff was entitled under N.Y. P'ship Law §§ 52, 62(4), and 73 to demand an account from the decedent's surviving partners and to receive the decedent's interest in the partnership. Priel v Linarello (2007, App Div, 2d Dept) 843 NYS2d 436

6. – Power of surrogate court
Surrogate properly ordered fiduciary of estate to reconvey interest in partnership which fiduciary misappropriated from estate, since estate would thereby receive percentage interest of present day value of partnership, reflecting proportion of partnership interest that fiduciary purchased with estate funds; such relief was appropriate, although it was not shown that estate would otherwise have participated in fiduciary's purchase of partnership interest, since purchase was made with funds that belonged to estate. Birnbaum v Birnbaum (1990, 4th Dept) 157 A.D.2d 177, 555 N.Y.S.2d 982, later proceeding (1991, 4th Dept) 171 A.D.2d 1074, 569 N.Y.S.2d 532, later proceeding (1992, 4th Dept) 177 A.D.2d 170, 582 N.Y.S.2d 853, app dismd without op (1992) 80 N.Y.2d 925, 589 N.Y.S.2d 311, 602 N.E.2d 1127

Surrogate's Court was without authority to entertain petition for continuance of a business in which decedent was a copartner rather than the sole owner. In re Estate of Saffioti (1974) 77 Misc. 2d 1052, 355 N.Y.S.2d 709

A surrogate's court is limited as to intervention in partnership affairs and has no jurisdiction to compel a surviving partner to turn over a sum of money alleged to be due a deceased partner's estate where it was not alleged that such surviving partner had made a claim against the estate or that he had any interest therein and he was not the administrator or executor and refused to submit voluntarily to jurisdiction. In re Saxe's Will (1946, Sur) 64 N.Y.S.2d 123

7. Interest
In valuing the dissolved joint venture's property, trial court did not abuse its discretion by pegging the allowance of interest to the adjustable interest rate on the mortgage loan because, inter alia, the interest rate was a reliable indicator of the cost that defendant would have incurred to replace plaintiff's capital investment in the property. Schultz v Sayada, 163 A.D.3d 1218, 2018 N.Y. App. Div. LEXIS 5162 (N.Y. App. Div. 3d Dep't 2018).

§ 74.   Accrual of actions

The right to an account of his interest shall accrue to any partner, or his legal representative, as against the winding up partners or the surviving partners or the person or partnership continuing the business, at the date of dissolution, in the absence of agreement to the contrary.

History: Add, L 1919, ch 408, eff Oct 1, 1919.

CASE ANNOTATIONS

1. **In general**
2. **Agreements to the contrary**
3. **Decedent's representatives**
4. **Doctrine of "unclean hands"**
5. **Partners**
6. **Statute of limitations**

1. In general
In accounting proceeding under CLS Partn § 74, valuation of law firm's goodwill was not subject to blanket prohibition, in absence of ethical concerns, in view of economic realities of contemporary practice of law, illustrated by attorney advertising, internationalization of law firms, and other professional developments. Dawson v White & Case (1996) 88 N.Y.2d 666, 649 N.Y.S.2d 364, 672 N.E.2d 589

Defendant, by virtue of failure to appeal order which implemented accounting, on judicial dissolution of partnership, by directing payment of net cash available for distribution was bound by figures therein and for same reason was limited to contesting distributable shares of assets solely from period not covered by referee, but, in interests of justice, matter would be remitted for hearing to determine propriety of supplemental computations insofar as they did not adopt figures originally used by referee in his accounting. Armitage v Heary (1977, 4th Dept) 58 A.D.2d 995, 397 N.Y.S.2d 35

New York County action for accounting brought by plaintiffs, tenants in common of joint venture, was not precluded under CLS CPLR § 3211(a)(4) due to existence of prior Nassau County action for dissolution and partition brought against plaintiffs by remaining tenants in common, notwithstanding that plaintiffs had option of counterclaiming for accounting in Nassau County, and even if dissolution in Nassau County would inevitably lead to accounting, since CLS Partn § 74 does not mandate accounting, and sort of accounting desired by plaintiffs was not necessarily same type of accounting available on dissolution in Nassau County even assuming that plaintiffs would not prevail therein. Morgulas v J. Yudell Realty, Inc. (1990, 1st Dept) 161 A.D.2d 211, 554 N.Y.S.2d 597

Unless partnership agreement provides otherwise, limited partner is entitled to account of his interest under CLS Partn §§ 73 and 74. Adam v Cutner & Rathkopf (1997, 1st Dept) 238 A.D.2d 234, 656 N.Y.S.2d 753

In order to enlist aid of court of equity in vindicating right to accounting, plaintiff must show not only existence of partnership, its dissolution following transaction of business that produced profits or losses to be accounted for, and demand for accounting, but also failure or refusal by partner with books, records, profits, or other assets of partnership in his possession to account to other partner or partners. Adam v Cutner & Rathkopf (1997, 1st Dept) 238 A.D.2d 234, 656 N.Y.S.2d 753

Doctrine of collateral estoppel did not bar action for accounting based on individual partners' status as escrow agents where adjudication of whether defendant partners fulfilled their fiduciary duties to plaintiff partners was not necessary to prior adjudication of limited partnership as bankrupt. Adam v Cutner & Rathkopf (1997, 1st Dept) 238 A.D.2d 234, 656 N.Y.S.2d 753

Right to accounting is premised on existence of confidential or fiduciary relationship and breach of duty imposed by that relationship respecting property in which party seeking accounting has interest. Adam v Cutner & Rathkopf (1997, 1st Dept) 238 A.D.2d 234, 656 N.Y.S.2d 753

Allegation of wrongdoing is not indispensable element of demand for accounting where complaint indicates fiduciary relationship between parties or some other special circumstance warranting equitable relief. Adam v Cutner & Rathkopf (1997, 1st Dept) 238 A.D.2d 234, 656 N.Y.S.2d 753

Upon dissolution of a partnership the surviving partners are required to close up the partnership affairs, dispose of the assets, pay all creditors, and remit the decedent partner's share to his representatives. M. & C. Creditors Corp. v Pratt (1938) 172 Misc 695, 17 N.Y.S.2d 240, affd (1938) 255 A.D. 838, 7 N.Y.S.2d 662, affd (1939) 281 N.Y. 804, 24 N.E.2d 482

Partnership Law

In respondent partner's suit against appellants, partnerships and partners, seeking an accounting and dissolution of two partnerships, a judicial hearing officer's order striking appellants' answer unless they provided a proper accounting by a set date was not improper even though the partner had not first proved the partner's right to an accounting on the merits, as, pursuant to N.Y. Partnership Law § 74, the parties had entered into a stipulation which entitled the partner to an accounting before dissolution. Halpern v Goldstein & Halpern (2002, A.D., 2d Dept) 742 N.Y.S.2d 372

Former partner's accounting claim, under N.Y. Partnership Law § 74, which the former partner sought to arbitration, was colorable; the issues involved in the accounting claim were appropriate for arbitration, as these issues included whether entitlement to an accounting was waived under the partnership agreement by the manner of the former partner's departure from the firm and whether that departure amounted to simply the termination of a partner or dissolution of the firm. Fuchsberg & Fuchsberg v Fuchsberg (2003, A.D., 1st Dept) 767 N.Y.S.2d 623

2. Agreements to the contrary

Assuming that an agreement made upon dissolution of a partnership that the partners should continue to be liable for obligations in the same proportions as their interests in the firm constituted an agreement postponing the accrual of a right to an accounting; the right accrued when all obligations had been met and a cause of action for an accounting was barred by the statute of limitations where it was not commenced within ten years. Bankers Trust Co. v Dennis (1939) 256 A.D. 495, 10 N.Y.S.2d 710, affd (1940) 282 N.Y. 635, 25 N.E.2d 981

Court properly treated plaintiff's motion for judicial accounting as motion for discovery, and properly denied it, where partnership agreement expressly set forth exclusive method for calculating and distributing partnership assets on dissolution and plaintiff failed to establish that written account previously provided by defendant was prepared contrary to methodology set forth in partnership agreement or contrary to practices followed by partnership for more than 20 years in which plaintiff had acquiesced. Hand v Kenyon & Kenyon (1996, 1st Dept) 227 A.D.2d 137, 641 N.Y.S.2d 307, app den, reargument den (1996, N.Y. A.D., 1st Dept) 1996 N.Y. A.D. LEXIS 8041, app dismd without op (1997, 1st Dept) 237 A.D.2d 996, 655 N.Y.S.2d 737, app dismd (1998, 1st Dept) 246 A.D.2d 446, 667 N.Y.S.2d 245, app den, reargument den (1998, N.Y. A.D., 1st Dept) 1998 N.Y. A.D. LEXIS 4448 and app dismd, in part, app den, in part (1998) 92 N.Y.2d 872, 677 N.Y.S.2d 775, 700 N.E.2d 314

3. Decedent's representatives

Plaintiff cannot sustain her right to an accounting under § 74 where a partnership agreement explicitly states that upon the death of a partner there shall not be a dissolution, since the statute grants such right only as of the date of the dissolution and in the absence of an agreement to the contrary. Hermes v Compton (1940, 2d Dept) 260 A.D. 507, 1027, 23 N.Y.S.2d 126, reargument gr, amd (1940, 2d Dept) 260 A.D. 1027

In an action brought by the administrator of a deceased partner's estate for a partnership accounting, the surviving partners would be directed to account to the administrator where deceased's widow had not been the "legal representative" of deceased for purposes of a release given by her to the surviving partners, and where no actual accounting had taken place inasmuch as a partnership accounting would encompass more than supplying tax returns. Juliano v Rea (1982, 2d Dept) 89 A.D.2d 618, 452 N.Y.S.2d 668, later proceeding (1986, 2d Dept) 120 A.D.2d 643, 502 N.Y.S.2d 97

The right of the estate of a deceased partner to an accounting of the partnership assets continues until barred by the ten-year statute of limitations. In re Vitelli's Estate (1949) 196 Misc 644, 92 N.Y.S.2d 322

Where the owner of a business took his son into partnership and filed a copy of the certificate of partnership, it was presumed that father and son became partners on the date stated therein and upon death of the father the Surrogate's Court had no jurisdiction to compel delivery of partnership assets to the father's administratrix. The Administratrix could recover assets retained by the father by discovery proceedings against the son, but not cash and insurance, determination of the estate's interest in which must await the partnership accounting. In re Palega's Estate (1955) 208 Misc 966, 145 N.Y.S.2d 271

Residuary beneficiary under will of deceased partner was entitled to maintain an action for an accounting from surviving partner, where complaint alleged that sons of deceased partner, who also acted as executors in the estate, held interest of deceased partner in trust for benefit of estate. Peller v Katz (1958) 15 Misc. 2d 1093, 181 N.Y.S.2d 519

Relationship of joint venturers between the parties terminated and was dissolved upon death of one and, at the instance of the estate, the survivor was subject to an accounting. Srybnik v Gibbons (1954, Sup) 129 N.Y.S.2d 483

Since there was genuine issue whether decedent partner owned 20 percent interest in land (1) directly, as tenant in common, or (2) indirectly, under N.Y. Partnership Law § 21(3)-(5), as partner in partnership that dissolved at his death under N.Y. Partnership Law § 62(4) (and for which his executors were entitled to an accounting under N.Y. Partnership Law § 74), summary judgment to partition his alleged undivided interest in land was reversed. Facts indicating that partnership was the direct owner included that the decedent (or his executors) (1) reported on income tax returns his share of the partnership's income which, in turn, included his share of the land's tax attributes reported on the partnership's tax returns, (2) reported on his estate tax returns his indirect interest in the partnership's interest in the land but no direct interest in the land. Vick v Albert (2005, A.D., 1st Dept) 793 N.Y.S.2d 413, app withdrawn (2005, N.Y. A.D., 1st Dept) 2005 N.Y. A.D. LEXIS 5470

4. Doctrine of "unclean hands"

Justice court's finding in prior action that plaintiff had breached the partnership agreement did not preclude an action by such partner for an accounting to recover his interest in the partnership since the misconduct of a partner does not necessarily deprive him of his right to demand an accounting. Bell v Herzog (1972, 3d Dept) 39 A.D.2d 813, 332 N.Y.S.2d 501

5. Partners

In action for partnership accounting of plaintiff's interest in law firm that was dissolved and then re-formed without plaintiff, future pension payments pursuant to firm's unfunded pension plan were properly disallowed as partnership liability where partnership never included unfunded pension plan as liability in firm's financial statements, and partnership provided that pension payments could be made only out of partnership assets and could not exceed 15 percent of profits; pension payments were not liability of firm in dissolution but operating expenses for successor firm contingent on its profitability. Dawson v White & Case (1996) 88 N.Y.2d 666, 649 N.Y.S.2d 364, 672 N.E.2d 589

N.Y. Partnership Law § 26(b) does not shield a general partner in a registered limited liability partnership from personal liability for breaches of the partnership's or partners' obligations to each other. Ederer v Gursky (2007) 9 NY3d 514, 851 NYS2d 108, 881 NE2d 204, reargument den (2008) 10 NY3d 780, 857 NYS2d 15, 886 NE2d 776.

Where partnership between the parties was judicially established, plaintiffs who instituted action to dissolve partnership were entitled to an accounting. De Martino v Pensavalle (1977, 2d Dept) 56 A.D.2d 589, 391 N.Y.S.2d 461

An attorney who withdrew from an at-will law partnership and claimed that the remaining partners excluded him from the winding up of the partnership and misappropriated partnership funds to which he was entitled was entitled to an accounting, where the only manner in which the partnership could be wound up was through an accounting, where the partnership could be terminated at any time, in that it was an at-will arrangement, and where a partner was entitled to an accounting on dissolution of a partnership, but the attorney would not be entitled to the appointment of a temporary receiver, where he had not demonstrated the existence of any danger that any partnership property would be removed from the state, lost, materially injured or destroyed. Shandell v Katz (1983, 1st Dept) 95 A.D.2d 742, 464 N.Y.S.2d 177, appeal after remand (1985, 1st Dept) 112 A.D.2d 102, 491 N.Y.S.2d 658, later proceeding (1990, 1st Dept) 159 A.D.2d 389, 553 N.Y.S.2d 17

When partner's actions are claimed to constitute requisite "express will" under CLS Partn § 62(1)(b), actions must manifest unequivocal election to dissolve partnership. Alessi v Brozzetti (1996, 3d Dept) 228 A.D.2d 917, 644 N.Y.S.2d 422

Partner's relocation to Florida did not manifest unequivocal intention to dissolve partnership. Alessi v Brozzetti (1996, 3d Dept) 228 A.D.2d 917, 644 N.Y.S.2d 422

Dissolution of partnership did not occur when 2 partners notified third partner that they refused to continue sharing certain management fees with him where there was no evidence that partnership stopped doing business, and third partner continued to receive his share of incentive fee paid to partnership. Alessi v Brozzetti (1996, 3d Dept) 228 A.D.2d 917, 644 N.Y.S.2d 422

Defendant partners' attempt to restructure partners' profit-sharing arrangement did not manifest requisite unequivocal election to dissolve partnership. Alessi v Brozzetti (1996, 3d Dept) 228 A.D.2d 917, 644 N.Y.S.2d 422

Plaintiff partners' failure to defeat defendant partners' motion for judgment summarily dismissing causes of action for negligent and intentional misrepresentation, fraud, conversion, negligence, and breach of contract did not nullify plaintiffs' entitlement to accounting. Adam v Cutner & Rathkopf (1997, 1st Dept) 238 A.D.2d 234, 656 N.Y.S.2d 753

Plaintiff partners' recovery against defendant partners on sole remaining cause of action for accounting would be limited to damages attributable to defendants' failure to apply plaintiffs' deposits to partnership purposes. Adam v Cutner & Rathkopf (1997, 1st Dept) 238 A.D.2d 234, 656 N.Y.S.2d 753

Disbarred attorney lacked standing to bring a suit against a former partner, seeking an accounting for the value of equity in the parties' dissolved partnership and legal fees earned, because the claims arose when the partnership dissolved, but the disbarred attorney failed to list those claims as assets in his after-filed bankruptcy proceeding; the claims in the suit were also contradictory to the claims in the bankruptcy petition, and thus judicial estoppel barred the suit. Goldman v Rio (2008, Sup) 19 Misc 3d 384, 853 NYS2d 837, reargument den (2008, Sup) 20 Misc 3d 1131A, 872 NYS2d 690, affd in part and app dismd in part (2009, 2d Dept) 62 App Div 3d 834, 879 NYS2d 199.

As a partner's death dissolves the partnership (N.Y. Partnership Law § 62(4), and a partner may not maintain claims for the sale of partnership assets and the distribution of sale proceeds until an accounting has been completed, a count in a complaint seeking to dissolve an alleged oral partnership with a decedent was dismissed, except for that portion that sought an accounting. Gaentner v Benkovich (2005, A.D., 2d Dept) 795 N.Y.S.2d 246

Action seeking dissolution of a partnership and an accounting was not barred by the statute of limitations, N.Y. C.P.L.R. 213(1), N.Y. Partnership Law § 74, as the actual dissolution of the partnership occurred after the instant action was filed. Sterling v Sterling (2005, 3d Dept) 21 A.D. 3d 663, 800 N.Y.S.2d 463

N.Y. P'ship Law § 26(b), limiting the liability of partners of a limited liability partnership, did not exempt such partners from their individual obligations to account to a withdrawing partner under the earlier enacted and unamended N.Y. P'ship Law § 74; moreover, § 26(b) did not exempt the individual limited partners from liability to an attorney for breaches of firm–related agreements between them. Ederer v Gursky (2006, App Div, 1st Dept) 826 NYS2d 210

Plaintiffs' breach of contract, declaratory judgment, their claim for "damages," and an unnamed claim referring to the alleged breach of a non–disclosure agreement, were properly categorized as legal claims arising between parties to a joint venture that could not be heard prior to an accounting, and accordingly, the claims had to be dismissed (the rights of parties to a joint venture agreement were governed by reference to the principles of the laws of partnership). Kitty Walk Sys. v Midnight Pass, Inc. (2006, ED NY) 431 F Supp 2d 306, motion den (2006, ED NY) 460 F Supp 2d 405

Even though the business of the law firm continued after the former partner left the firm, the partnership itself was dissolved and could not be revived, thus, in valuing his partnership interest as of the date of the partnership dissolution pursuant to N.Y. Partnership Law § 74, the trial court concluded that it should use the liquidation value rather than the fair market/going concern value. Bitetto v F. Chau & Assoc., LLP (2005, Sup) 10 Misc 3d 595, 807 NYS2d 260

6. Statute of limitations

An attorney was not barred by the statute of limitations from bringing suit to establish that he was a partner in a law firm and for an accounting, since the right to an accounting does not accrue until dissolution of the partnership, and since the partnership was dissolved only six months prior to the commencement of the suit. Missan v Schoenfeld (1983, 1st Dept) 95 A.D.2d 198, 465 N.Y.S.2d 706, app dismd (1983) 60 N.Y.2d 860

It was error to dismiss action for accounting under CLS Partn § 74 on ground that it was time barred where fact issue existed as to when, if ever, partnership was dissolved and thus when, if ever, cause of action accrued. Consiglio v Consiglio (1988, 4th Dept) 143 A.D.2d 505, 533 N.Y.S.2d 260

Action by surviving spouse of deceased partner against partnership, seeking accounting and constructive trust on partnership premises, was barred by 6-year limitations period applicable to actions for partnership accounting since (1) partnership agreement did not confer any partnership interest on plaintiff, and thus her only remedy was to demand accounting as administratrix, and (2) plaintiff's time in which to demand partnership accounting, as administratrix, began to run when partnership was dissolved by her husband's death, more than 10 years before action was commenced. Schwartz v Lois Associates (1989, 1st Dept) 149 A.D.2d 307, 539 N.Y.S.2d 360, later proceeding (1990, SD NY) 1990 US Dist LEXIS 7755

It was error to grant plaintiff's motion for summary judgment directing accounting as to rights of joint venturers, and to deny defendants' motion for summary judgment based on statute of limitations, where fact issue existed as to when actual dissolution of joint venture took place. Sagus Marine Corp. v Donald G. Rynne & Co. (1994, 1st Dept) 207 A.D.2d 701, 616 N.Y.S.2d 496

Although the arbitration demand included some claims that dated back as much as 27 years, the claims were timely under N.Y. C.P.L.R. 7502(b), as the facts underlying the breach of contract, conversion, fraud, and breach of fiduciary duty claims were intertwined with and directly related to the former partner's demand for an accounting under N.Y. Partnership Law § 74. Fuchsberg & Fuchsberg v Fuchsberg (2003, A.D., 1st Dept) 767 N.Y.S.2d 623

§ 75.   Continuance of partnership business during action for accounting

In an action brought to dissolve a partnership, or for an accounting between partners, or affecting the continued prosecution of the business, the court may, in its discretion, by order, authorize the partnership business to be continued, during the pendency of the action by one or more of the partners, upon their executing and filing with the clerk an undertaking, in such a sum and with such sureties as the order prescribes, to the effect that they will obey all orders of the court, in the action, and perform all things which the judgment therein requires them to perform. The court may impose such other conditions as it deems proper, and it may in its discretion at any time thereafter require a new undertaking to be given. The court may also ascertain the value of the partnership property, and of the interest of the respective partners by a reference or otherwise, and may direct an accounting between any of the partners; and the judgment may make such provision for the payment to the retiring partners, for their interest, and with respect to the rights of creditors, the title to the partnership property, and otherwise, as justice requires, with or without the appointment of a receiver, or a sale of the partnership property.

History: Add, L 1920, ch 394, eff April 15, 1921, with substance transferred from Code Civ Proc § 1947.

CASE ANNOTATIONS

In an action to dissolve a partnership, until a final decree has been entered, a receiver ought not to be appointed unless there is danger that the partnership property will be removed beyond the jurisdiction of the court, lost, materially injured or destroyed. Cohn v Wahn (1909) 132 A.D. 849, 117 N.Y.S. 633

Where the existence of a partnership is denied and the partnership property cannot be definitely described the issues should be tried and there should be a decision defining the scope of the partnership business and identifying partnership property before the appointment of a receiver. Hannevig & Johnsen, Inc. v Lougheed (1917) 180 A.D. 579, 167 N.Y.S. 785

Partnership Law

In action by one partner to dissolve partnership, pursuant to § 75, the court could have authorized the partnership business to be continued during the pendency of the action. Savio v Del Bello (1944) 267 A.D. 950, 47 N.Y.S.2d 560

Where Appellate Court is unable to determine basis upon which Supreme Court arrived at sum it fixed as amount of undertaking pursuant to CLS Partnership § 75, judgment is modified and matter is remitted to Special Term for hearing on issue. Zaubler v Picone (1985, 2d Dept) 112 A.D.2d 157, 490 N.Y.S.2d 843

In action for dissolution of partnership, winding-up partner was properly directed to maintain partnership assets in interest-bearing account pending accounting action, in view of cross-complaint charging other partner with misconduct. Kriegsman v Kraus, Ostreicher & Co. (1987, 1st Dept) 126 A.D.2d 489, 511 N.Y.S.2d 17

In action for dissolution of partnership and accounting of partnership assets, court did not improvidently exercise its discretion in ordering temporary receiver to take immediate steps to liquidate tangible partnership assets by auction sale since partnership agreement set no definite term for partnership and defendant had already expressly elected to dissolve partnership. Zari v Zari (1989, 2d Dept) 155 A.D.2d 452, 547 N.Y.S.2d 112

Temporary receiver should not have been appointed in law firm dissolution action where plaintiff submitted nothing more than his own affidavit expressing dissatisfaction with defendant's handling of firm's caseload, and that firm's clients suffered serious delay in prosecution of their cases to their extreme prejudice; appointment of receiver is drastic remedy used sparingly in partnership dissolution actions. Harmon v Marks (1991, 1st Dept) 175 A.D.2d 44, 572 N.Y.S.2d 305

Where plaintiff had right to dissolution of partnership but did not show that there was danger, pending final dissolution, that business property would be removed from the state, or lost or materially injured or destroyed, application for appointment of receiver was granted in alternative, and defendant would be permitted to continue partnership business, during pendency of action, on his executing and filing surety undertaking conditioned upon obedience to all orders and judgment of the court in the action. Netburn v Fischman (1975) 81 Misc. 2d 117, 364 N.Y.S.2d 727

In action for dissolution of partnership engaged in retail poultry business, outsider would not be appointed receiver to conduct the business pendente lite, but defendant who is in charge of the business would be permitted to conduct the business pendente lite on filing a surety undertaking, subject to requirement that defendant keep accurate records and not use partnership moneys for his personal use without a court order. Tankleff v Klein (1946, Sup) 66 N.Y.S.2d 81

Ordinarily a receiver will not be appointed in an action for an accounting before dissolution, but where dissolution is inevitable and great damage may result unless the assets are properly cared for such relief may be granted. Wagner v Von Tresckow (1948, Sur) 81 N.Y.S.2d 315

Where a partnership was threatened with dispossess and there was danger that the assets would be lost, removed or destroyed the appointment of a receiver was necessary. Sims v Klein (1948, Sup) 82 N.Y.S.2d 444

Where the assets of a partnership were already in liquidation by agreement of the parties and the situation required prompt action to preserve the leases and equity of the partnership, the strained relations of the partners justify the appointment of a receiver. Corso v Corso (1948, Sup) 82 N.Y.S.2d 645

Where after separation of a husband and wife, the wife and her brother denied the husband's position as a partner with them and their interests were entirely hostile to his and the husband sought dissolution and an accounting, appointment of a receiver was necessary to protect his interest. Heisler v Heisler (1948, Sup) 85 N.Y.S.2d 342

In an action for dissolution of a partnership brought by the executrix and widow of deceased partner, where it appeared that the surviving partner had been in active charge of the business for a long time prior to the death of the deceased partner, he was permitted to conduct the business during the pendency of the action on filing a surety undertaking. Tannenbaum v Rosenbaum (1955, Sup) 141 N.Y.S.2d 708

ARTICLE 7
BUSINESS AND PARTNERSHIP NAMES

History: Add, L 1919, ch 408, eff Oct 1, 1919.

§ 80.   When partnership or business name may be continued

The use of a partnership or a business name may be continued in either of the following cases:

1. Where the business of any firm or partnership in this state, having business relations with foreign countries or which has transacted business in this state or in any other state or territory of the United States continues to be conducted by some or any of the partners, their or any of their assignees, appointees or successors in interest.

2. Where any partnership shall hereafter be formed under the laws of this state it may use the firm or corporate name of any general or limited partnership or of any corporation, domestic or foreign, which may theretofore have carried on its business within this state, where said general or limited partnership or corporation has discontinued or shall be about to discontinue its business within the state, and where a majority of the partners, general or special, in either of such last mentioned copartnerships or of the survivors thereof shall be members of the new copartnership, or where a majority of the members of such copartnership theretofore existing or of the surviving members thereof, or where stockholders holding a majority of the stock of such corporation shall consent in writing to the use of such firm or corporate name by such new copartnership; or

3. Where any resident of this state dies, who at the time of his death and for at least five years immediately prior thereto, conducted and carried on in his sole name, any business in this state, or who at the time of his death, so conducted and carried on any business having relation with other states or foreign countries, the right to use the name of such person, for the purpose of continuing and carrying on such business, shall survive and pass and be disposed of and accounted for as a part of the personal estate of such deceased person, and such business may be continued and carried on under such name by any person who comes into the legal possession thereof.

History: Add, L 1919, ch 408, eff Oct 1, 1919, with substance transferred from § 20.

Sub 1 amd, L 1923, ch 268, L 1937, ch 614, eff May 25, 1937.

Sub 2 amd, L 1938, ch 129, eff March 15, 1938.

CASE ANNOTATIONS

Upon a sale of the good will and assets of a co-partnership in proceedings brought therefor by the executrix of a deceased partner the right to continue the use of the firm name is a firm asset and is subject to sale with the other firm property without condition, restriction or limitation upon the purchaser and the purchaser at such a sale, whether the surviving partner or otherwise, acquires a right to continue the business under the firm name upon complying with the provisions of the Partnership Law. Slater v Slater (1903) 175 N.Y. 143, 67 N.E. 224

A firm name which is solely or predominantly the name of a living man may not be sold against his protest and the effect of this section making names capable of transfer is solely to give approval to what would otherwise be criminal. The statute tells what may be assigned but does not state what must be assigned. In re Brown (1926) 242 N.Y. 1, 150 N.E. 581, 44 ALR 510

Neither partner nor anyone else is entitled to use of partnership name until partnership has been terminated by winding up of partnership affairs. Palu v Lincoln Weather Strip & Screens Corp. (1931) 232 A.D. 647, 251 N.Y.S. 52

A purchaser of the good will and assets of a copartnership is entitled to continue to use the firm name only upon compliance with the statute. Thus an injunction may be granted to restrain a purchaser who has not complied with the statute from listing his telephone and business number under the former firm name. Kram v Shyev (1907) 57 Misc 112, 107 N.Y.S. 539, affd (1908) 125 A.D. 922, 110 N.Y.S. 1134

This section which authorizes a partnership to use the corporate name of a corporation, was not intended to include in the partnership name words or abbreviations which the corporation had used in its corporate name to distinguish it from a natural person or a firm. In re Application of Seigal (1958) 9 Misc. 2d 751, 171 N.Y.S.2d 186

Petitioners, co-partners, as successors of the goodwill and advertising which a corporate name had received, were entitled to file a certificate using the corporate name "Kass-Seigal Interiors" with or without the word "Company" or an abbreviation thereof, but not with the designation "Ltd,". In re Application of Seigal (1958) 9 Misc. 2d 751, 171 N.Y.S.2d 186

The right to continue the use of the firm name becomes the exclusive property of the surviving partner on the death of his co-partner, no provision in the articles of partnership to the contrary. Campbell v Campbell (1891, CP Ct) 16 N.Y.S. 165

Name of limited partnership may not contain word "limited" or abbreviation thereof without any additional indication that entity is organized as limited partnership. Ops Atty Gen 88-61 (Informal)

§ 81.   Certificate to be filed

Whenever a partnership or business name continues to be used as provided by section eighty, the person or persons using such name shall sign and acknowledge or swear to a certificate, declaring the person or persons intending to deal under such name, with their respective places of residence, and file the same in the clerk's office of the county where the principal place of business is located, and cause a copy of such certificate to be published once in each week for four consecutive weeks in a newspaper of the city or town in which such principal place of business is located, or if none be published in such city or town, in the newspaper nearest thereto. A county clerk with whom any such certificate is filed, shall keep a register in which shall be entered in alphabetical order the name of every such partnership and of the partners thereof, and every such business name of a deceased person and the names of the person filing certificates therefor.

History: Add, L 1919, ch 408, with substance transferred from § 21; amd, L 1939, ch 239, L 1939, ch 580, § 1, L 1948, ch 712, § 1, eff July 1, 1948.

CASE ANNOTATIONS

A purchaser of the good will and assets of a copartnership is entitled to continue to use the firm name only upon compliance with the statute. Thus an injunction may be granted to restrain a purchaser who has not complied with the statute from listing his telephone and business number under the former firm name. Kram v Shyev (1907)

57 Misc 112, 107 N.Y.S. 539, affd (1908) 125 A.D. 922, 110 N.Y.S. 1134

Fact that name of plaintiff's decedent did not appear in notices filed in office of clerk of New York County, or in public prints, indicates that he was merely an employee of defendant. Place v Brooks (1943, DC NY) 49 F. Supp. 124

§ 82.   Fictitious firm names prohibited

No person shall hereafter transact business in the name of a partner not interested in his firm, and when the designation "and company," or "and Co." is used, it shall represent an actual partner; but a violation of this section shall not be a defense in an action or proceeding brought by an assignee for the benefit of creditors or by a receiver of the property of or by an executor or administrator of a person who has violated the same.

History: Add, L 1919, ch 408, eff Oct 1, 1919, with substance transferred from § 22.

CASE ANNOTATIONS

1. In general; purpose
2. Construction and application
3. Effect of noncompliance

1. In general; purpose

The purpose of the fictitious names laws is to protect persons giving credit to a fictitious firm on the faith of its designation. Gay v Seibold (1884) 97 N.Y. 472

The section of the former Penal Code providing for filing of a certificate stating intention to conduct a business under an assumed or fictitious name was so not intended to repeal the provisions of the Partnership Law so that thereafter the person might conduct a business under any name, style or title, provided he filed a certificate stating his intention to conduct a business under that name or style or to authorize the commission of acts forbidden by the Partnership Law. Jenner v Shope (1912) 205 N.Y. 66, 98 N.E. 325

The purpose of the fictitious names laws is to provide for public notification as to the name under which a partnership is operating. Weinstein v Welden (1914) 160 A.D. 554, 145 N.Y.S. 772, affd (1917) 220 N.Y. 693, 116 N.E. 1082

Name of limited partnership may not contain word "limited" or abbreviation thereof without any additional indication that entity is organized as limited partnership. Ops Atty Gen 88-61 (Informal)

2. Construction and application

The statutory limitations on the use of fictitious name by a partnership are highly penal and must be strictly construed. Sinnott v German-American Bank of Rochester (1900) 164 N.Y. 386, 58 N.E. 286

This section cannot be invoked by competitor of one who violates section. Wallach Bros. v Wallack (1922) 200 A.D. 169, 192 N.Y.S. 723

Penal Law, § 924, and this section, do not imply that any other designation than "and company", no matter how misleading, is permissible. Application of Birdwell (1945) 268 A.D. 642, 53 N.Y.S.2d 77

A county clerk may refuse to file a certificate for a person "and associates," where he has no associates. Application of Birdwell (1945) 268 A.D. 642, 53 N.Y.S.2d 77

Statute does not apply to foreign enterprises, even if they employ an agent here. Cahn v Gottschalk (1888, CP Ct) 14 Daly 542, 2 N.Y.S. 13

3. Effect of noncompliance

Recovery on the bond of an employee was not defeated by reason of violation of a statute, where at the time it was executed the defendant knew who the real partners were. Gay v Seibold (1884) 97 N.Y. 472

A person doing business under a fictitious name is not precluded thereby from bringing action to recover from a person to whom he has given credit. Kennedy v Budd (1896) 5 A.D. 140, 39 N.Y.S. 81

Mere fact that a person is violating the fictitious name laws will not prevent his recovery either upon an executed or an executory contract. McArdle v Thames Ironworks (1904) 96 A.D. 139, 89 N.Y.S. 485

Partnership Law

Members of a firm maintaining a lawful business but conducting it under a fictitious name in violation of the statutes were held not entitled to recover damages for injury to their business in an action for libel. Williams v New York Herald Co. (1914) 165 A.D. 529, 150 N.Y.S. 838, app dismd (1916) 218 N.Y. 625, 112 N.E. 1079

Violation of this section works neither forfeiture nor disability. Black v New York Life Ins. Co. (1911) 70 Misc 532, 127 N.Y.S. 409

One who transacts business in his own name with addition "& Company" which does not represent any individual may recover upon policy of life insurance assigned to him in his firm name, and prohibition of this section is no defense to action. Black v New York Life Ins. Co. (1911) 70 Misc 532, 127 N.Y.S. 409

Violation of statute by plaintiff was not a defense to an action for goods sold to the defendant, if the latter knew at the time of the purchase who composed the firm and did not deal with it on reliance on the apparent membership of a third party who, in fact, had no interest therein. Donlon v English (1895) 89 Hun 67, 35 N.Y.S. 82

ARTICLE 8
LIMITED PARTNERSHIPS

History: Add, L 1922, ch 640, eff April 13, 1922.

Former Art 8, add, L 1919, ch 408, with substance transferred from prior Art 4; repealed, L 1922, ch 640.

§ 90. Limited partnership defined

A limited partnership is a partnership formed by two or more persons under the provisions of section ninety-one, having as members one or more general partners and one or more limited partners. The limited partners as such shall not be bound by the obligations of the partnership.

History: Add, L 1922, ch 640, § 1, eff April 13, 1922, with substance transferred from §§ 4 and 30.

Former § 90, add, L 1919, ch 408; repealed, L 1922, ch 640, § 1, eff April 13, 1922.

CASE ANNOTATIONS

Choice of the limited partnership organization form is necessarily an election to submit to a greater degree of governmental intervention than would be true of a simple common-law partnership, closely approximating the corporate form. United States v Silverstein (1963, CA2 NY) 314 F.2d 789, 63-1 USTC P 9346, 11 AFTR 2d 1025, cert den (1963) 374 US 807, 10 L Ed 2d 1031, 83 S Ct 1696

A general partner in a number of related limited partnerships wherein he, his son, and his son-in-law are the general partners and the limited partners number from 25 to 147, total capitalization of which is upwards of $5,000,000, cannot resist an internal revenue summons requiring him to produce books and records of the partnerships on the basis of right to protection of the privilege against self incrimination. United States v Silverstein (1963, CA2 NY) 314 F.2d 789, 63-1 USTC P 9346, 11 AFTR 2d 1025, cert den (1963) 374 US 807, 10 L Ed 2d 1031, 83 S Ct 1696

Being strictly a creature of statute, a limited partnership resembles a corporation more closely than it does an ordinary partnership, and the principal-agent relationship which exists between the partners of an ordinary partnership is not present between the limited and general partners of a limited partnership. Lynn v Cohen (1973, SD NY) 359 F. Supp. 565, 17 FR Serv 2d 1295, 30 ALR Fed 576 (criticized in Pilates, Inc. v Pilates Inst. (1995, SD NY) 891 F. Supp. 175)

A partnership is authorized to become a partner in a limited partnership. 1972 Ops Atty Gen Dec 15

A limited partnership may become a general partner in a general partnership. The partnership with which the limited partnership becomes associated must in its certificate reflect the addition of the limited partnership as a partner. This amended certificate must be executed and acknowledged by the members of the limited partnership; however, a limited partner may designate one of the limited partnerships general partners to execute the amended certificate on his behalf. Ops Atty Gen 84-54

Name of limited partnership may not contain word "limited" or abbreviation thereof without any additional indication that entity is organized as limited partnership. Ops Atty Gen 88-61 (Informal)

§ 91. Formation

(1) Two or more persons desiring to form a limited partnership shall

(a) Sign and acknowledge or swear to a certificate, which shall state.*

I. The name of the partnership.

II. The character of the business.

III. The location of the principal place of business.

IV. The name and place of residence of each member; general and limited partners being respectively designated.

V. The term for which the partnership is to exist.

VI. The amount of cash and a description of and the agreed value of the other property contributed by each limited partner.

VII. The additional contributions, if any, agreed to be made by each limited partner and the times at which or events on the happening of which they shall be made.

VIII. The time, if agreed upon, when the contribution of each limited partner is to be returned.

IX. The share of the profits or the other compensation by way of income which each limited partner shall receive by reason of his contribution.

X. The right, if given, of a limited partner to substitute an assignee as contributor in his place, and the terms and conditions of the substitution.

XI. The right, if given, of the partners to admit additional limited partners.

XII. The right, if given, of one or more of the limited partners to priority over other limited partners, as to contributions or as to compensation by way of income, and the nature of such priority.

XIII. The right, if given, of the remaining general partner or partners to continue the business on the death, retirement or insanity of a general partner, and

XIV. The right, if given, of a limited partner to demand and receive property other than cash in return for his contribution.

(b) File the certificate in the office of the county clerk of the county in which the principal office of such partnership is located. Immediately after the filing of the certificate, a copy of the same or a notice containing the substance thereof, shall be published once in each week for six successive weeks, in two newspapers of the county in which such original certificate is filed, to be designated by the county clerk, one of which newspapers shall be a newspaper published in the city or town in which the principal place of business is intended to be located, if a newspaper be published therein; or, if no newspaper is published therein, in the newspaper nearest thereto, and proof of such publication by the affidavit of the printer or publisher of each of such newspapers must be filed with the original certificate.

* So in original.

(2) If there has been substantial compliance in good faith with the requirements of paragraph (a) of subdivision one of this section, a limited partnership is formed and may commence the transaction of business as such upon the filing of its certificate as required by paragraph (b) of subdivision one of this section and the effectuation of the first of the six successive weekly publications required by said paragraph (b); provided, however, that the continued existence of a limited partnership as such shall be conditioned upon completion of the publication requirement contained in said paragraph (b).

History: Add, L 1922, ch 640, § 1, with substance of sub 1 transferred from §§ 31 and 32; amd, L 1939, ch 580, § 2, eff Sept 1, 1939.

Former § 91, add, L 1919, ch 408; repealed, L 1922, ch 640, § 1, eff April 13, 1922.

Sub (1) par (b), amd, L 1948, ch 712, § 2, eff July 1, 1948.

Sub (2), add, L 1980, ch 499, § 1, eff June 24, 1980.

Former sub 2, deleted, L 1980, ch 499, § 1, eff June 24, 1980.

CASE ANNOTATIONS

1. In general
2. Construction
3. Filing and execution of certificate

4. – Publication
5. Liability of limited partners

1. In general

A limited partnership is exclusively statutory. Lanier v Bowdoin (1939) 282 N.Y. 32, 24 N.E.2d 732, reh den (1940) 282 N.Y. 611, 25 N.E.2d 391

In the absence of prejudice or reliance on the signature of a general partner on the certificate of limited partnership, a third party has no standing to object to the failure of said general partner to disclose his authority for signing. Micheli Contracting Corp. v Fairwood Associates (1979, 3d Dept) 68 A.D.2d 460, 418 N.Y.S.2d 164

In view of the fact that a certificate of limited partnership omitted nothing of substance required to be contained therein by statute and there is no claim that anything contained therein is false or that any defects therein misled a third party, there was substantial compliance with the statute and the limited partnership was validly formed. Micheli Contracting Corp. v Fairwood Associates (1979, 3d Dept) 68 A.D.2d 460, 418 N.Y.S.2d 164

Although the publication of a certificate of limited partnership as required by section 91 of the Partnership Law is an essential element of the proper formation of a limited partnership, the failure to file the affidavits of publication in the County Clerk's office is not a fatal defect. Micheli Contracting Corp. v Fairwood Associates (1979, 3d Dept) 68 A.D.2d 460, 418 N.Y.S.2d 164

Limited partnership cannot be created orally. Winter v Beale, Lynch & Co. (1993, 1st Dept) 198 A.D.2d 124, 603 N.Y.S.2d 846, app dismd, in part, app den, in part (1994) 83 N.Y.S.2d 944, 615 N.Y.S.2d 871, 639 N.E.2d 411

Motion to dismiss a breach of contract case alleging that a newspaper charged higher rates to publish legal notices relating to the formation of partnerships, limited liability companies, and other business entities based on geographical location was proper because such was not unlawful; while the various county clerks situated within the city of New York designated the publisher's newspaper as one of two for the publication of the legal notices at issue, the use of the publisher's newspaper as an officially-designated newspaper did not make the resulting absence of choice unconscionable because such designation was pursuant to legislative authority. NCJ Cleaners, LLC v ALM Media, Inc. (2008, 2d Dept) 48 App Div 3d 766, 852 NYS2d 384.

For venue purposes, limited partnership's "principal office" under CLS CPLR § 503 is principal place of business designated in certificate of limited partnership. Mid Valley Discount Mall Associates v Credit Alliance Corp. (1988, Sup) 139 Misc. 2d 271, 528 N.Y.S.2d 302

A corporation has no power, in absence of statutory authority, to become a limited partner. 1943 Ops Atty Gen 433

A general partnership may engage only in the business authorized by the partnership agreement. A limited partnership may engage only in the business authorized by the certificate filed under section 91 of the Partnership Law. A limited partnership may become a general partner in a new limited partnership. 1980 Op Atty Gen Oct. 28 (informal)

A limited partnership may become a general partner in a general partnership. The partnership with which the limited partnership becomes associated must in its certificate reflect the addition of the limited partnership as a partner. This amended certificate must be executed and acknowledged by the members of the limited partnership; however, a limited partner may designate one of the limited partnerships general partners to execute the amended certificate on his behalf. Ops Atty Gen 84-54

Limited partnership may not file certificate of doing business under assumed name pursuant to CLS Gen Bus § 130; however, limited partnership must comply with filing requirements of CLS Partnership § 91. Ops Atty Gen 88-56 (Informal)

2. Construction

The provisions relative to formation of limited partnerships are remedial and will protect those who substantially, in good faith, comply with their essential requirements. White v Eiseman (1892) 134 N.Y. 101, 31 N.E. 276

The requirement for the statement of term in the Certificate of Limited Partnership is not a limiting phrase and a limited partnership may have an indefinite term. 1978 Op Atty Gen April 7

3. Filing and execution of certificate

Failure of firm of stockbrokers to file or even attempt to file its certificate of limited partnership or copy thereof, in county where it maintains branch office, renders member of firm liable as general partner upon transactions through said office, although said certificate has been filed in county where it maintains its home office. O'Connor v Graff (1919) 186 A.D. 116, 173 N.Y.S. 730, affd (1920) 230 N.Y. 552, 130 N.E. 890

Parties were not limited partners where they were not listed in any capacity whatever in certificate of limited partnership. Hoffman v Eisenberg (1988, 2d Dept) 140 A.D.2d 306, 527 N.Y.S.2d 814, app den (1988) 72 N.Y.2d 806, 532 N.Y.S.2d 847, 529 N.E.2d 177

Where a certificate of limited partnership is executed by a general partner or some other person on behalf of a limited partner, pursuant to power of attorney, it is unnecessary to attach the power of attorney to the certificate, but the County Clerk should require that it be produced for his inspection when the certificate is presented for filing. 1961 Ops Atty Gen Feb 2

Acknowledgment of the signatures on a certificate of limited partnership may be in the usual form, notwithstanding some of the signatures are executed by virtue of powers of attorney. 1961 Ops Atty Gen Feb 2

Designation of the nominee of a limited partner in a certificate of limited partnership is not in compliance with the requirements of this section that the name and place of residence of each member must be stated in the certificate. 1961 Ops Atty Gen June 16

Inclusion of an office address of an agent such as an attorney or theatrical agent does not comply with the requirement imposed by § 91 of the Partnership Law that the name and place of residence of each member of a limited partnership be listed on the certificate required to be filed pursuant to that section. 1973 Ops Atty Gen July 9 (informal)

A limited partnership formed for the purpose of owning and operating an apartment complex in Rensselaer County, and whose principals work and reside in New York County, is not required by section 91 of the Partnership Law to file and publish a Certificate of Limited Partnership in Rensselaer County if the partnership's principal office is in New York County. Ops Atty Gen 84-60

4. – Publication

The requirement of publication of the terms of the partnership is satisfied by the publication of the terms of the certificate and an omission to state in the published notice all the details of the partnership agreement is not a failure to comply. Metropolitan Nat'l Bank v Sirret (1884) 97 N.Y. 320

Where the articles of partnership, the certificate, and the order of publication bore a date of October 1 and the certificate was recorded on that day a publication in one newspaper beginning October 6 and in another October 10 substantially complied with the statute requiring publication to be commenced immediately. Manhattan Co. v Phillips (1888) 109 N.Y. 383, 17 N.E. 129

Failure to file in the county clerk's office proof of publication of the certificate and affidavit required by the Partnership Law in the case of a limited partnership does not make the special partner liable as a general partner. Buckle v Iler (1903) 40 Misc 214, 81 N.Y.S. 631

A mistake in one of the two newspapers in which the terms of a limited partnership was published as to the amount of the contribution of the special partner renders him liable as a general partner. Smith v Argall (1844) 6 Hill 479, affd 3 Denio 435

Publication of certificate of limited partnership pursuant to section 91(1)(b) of Partnership Law must be completed prior to limited partnership doing business. Section 114 of Partnership Law does not require publication of certificate of amendment or cancellation of limited partnership. 1978 Op Atty Gen Nov 13

An amendment or cancellation of a limited partnership certificate need not be published. 1981 Op Atty Gen May 1 (informal)

5. Liability of limited partners

Action cannot be maintained against estate of limited partner to recover on claim against partnership on theory that limited partner became general partner because of failure to file copies of certificate in county wherein business out of which claim arose was transacted where it appears that, after death of limited partner, surviving members of partnership, individually and as copartners in firm, were adjudicated bankrupts and trustee asserted that estate of limited partner was liable on theory stated and executors of that estate offered certain amount in settlement of alleged liability, which offer was accepted. Nichols v Emerson (1924) 210 A.D. 281, 206 N.Y.S. 13, affd (1925) 241 N.Y. 531, 150 N.E. 542

Infants may become general partners and a special partner is not liable for their contracts. Continental Nat'l Bank v Strauss (1892) 60 N.Y. Super Ct 151, 17 N.Y.S. 188, affd (1893) 137 N.Y. 148, 32 N.E. 1066

§ 92. Business which may be carried on

A limited partnership may carry on any business which a partnership without limited partners may carry on.

History: Add, L 1922, ch 640, § 1, eff April 13, 1922.

Former § 92, add, L 1919, ch 408; repealed, L 1922, ch 640, § 1, eff April 13, 1922.

CASE ANNOTATIONS

This section does not permit a private nursing home to be operated by a limited partnership, although neither § 35-a of the Social Welfare Law nor the Hospital Code and Regulations specifically so states. Windsor Park Nursing Home v Trussell (1964) 41 Misc. 2d 1015, 247 N.Y.S.2d 189

A partnership is authorized to become a partner in a limited partnership. 1972 Ops Atty Gen Dec 15

A general partnership may engage only in the business authorized by the partnership agreement. A limited partnership may engage only in the business authorized by the certificate filed under section 91 of the Partnership Law. A limited partnership may become a general partner in a new limited partnership. 1980 Op Atty Gen Oct. 28 (informal)

§ 93. Character of limited partner's contribution

The contributions of a limited partner may be cash or other property, but not services.

History: Add, L 1922, ch 640, § 1, eff April 13, 1922.

Former § 93, add, L 1919, ch 408; repealed, L 1922, ch 640, § 1, eff April 13, 1922.

CASE ANNOTATIONS

Parties who concededly contributed only their legal services to partnership could not be found to be limited partners. Hoffman v Eisenberg (1988, 2d Dept) 140 A.D.2d 306, 527 N.Y.S.2d 814, app den (1988) 72 N.Y.2d 806, 532 N.Y.S.2d 847, 529 N.E.2d 177

"Offsetting payables" approach adopted by parties to partnership agreement violated § 93 requiring that capital contributions be made in cash or property and not in services. Thus, substantial portion of "payables" which were offset by the accounts receivable, consisting of fees for services including consulting fees, management fees, finders fees, construction fees, and "overhead" charges for payroll, administration, and data processing services rendered by one of parties, did not qualify as contribution of cash or property to partnership. Bamco 18 v Reeves (1989, SD NY) 717 F. Supp. 143, later proceeding (1989, SD NY) 1989 US Dist LEXIS 13187, subsequent app (1990, CA2 NY) 923 F.2d 842

The salary paid to an employee of a partnership is a deductible business expense even though the employee is also a limited partner. 1953 Ops Atty Gen July 15

§ 94. Name not to contain surname of limited partner; exceptions

(1) The surname of a limited partner shall not appear in the partnership name, unless

(a) It is also the surname of a general partner, or

(b) Prior to the time when the limited partner became such the business had been carried on under a name in which his surname appeared.

(2) A limited partner whose name appears in a partnership name contrary to the provisions of subdivision one of this section is liable as a general partner to partnership creditors who extend credit to

the partnership without actual knowledge that he is not a general partner.

History: Add, L 1922, ch 640, § 1, eff April 13, 1922, with substance transferred from § 35.

Former § 94, add, L 1919, ch 408; repealed, L 1922, ch 640, § 1, eff April 13, 1922.

CASE ANNOTATIONS

Name of limited partnership may not contain word "limited" or abbreviation thereof without any additional indication that entity is organized as limited partnership. Ops Atty Gen 88-61 (Informal)

§ 95. Liability for false statements in certificate

If the certificate contains a false statement, one who suffers loss by reliance on such statement may hold liable any party to the certificate who knew the statement to be false

(a) At the time he signed the certificate, or

(b) Subsequently, but within a sufficient time before the statement was relied upon to enable him to cancel or amend the certificate, or to file a petition for its cancellation or amendment as provided in section one hundred and fourteen of this article.

History: Add, L 1922, ch 640, § 1, eff April 13, 1922, with substance transferred from § 34.

Former § 95, add, L 1919, ch 408; repealed, L 1922, ch 640, § 1, eff April 13, 1922.

CASE ANNOTATIONS

Provision such as this is intended to prevent evasion and fraud, and as a bar to shut out the dishonest, not as a trap to catch the innocent and unwary. White v Eiseman (1892) 134 N.Y. 101, 31 N.E. 276

Certificate and its attached affidavits establish the fact, prima facie, that the statements therein are true, although this creates a mere presumption which can be rebutted by the person attacking the instrument. Hotopp v Huber (1899) 160 N.Y. 524, 55 N.E. 206

Transfer of partnership assets to a corporation without the consent of the limited partners is a violation of Partnership L § 98, subd 1(b), which prohibits acts which make it impossible to carry out the ordinary business of the partnership. Newburger, Loeb & Co. v Gross (1977, CA2 NY) 563 F.2d 1057, 1977, CCH Fed Secur L Rep P 96148, 1977-2 CCH Trade Cases P 61604, 24 FR Serv 2d 42, cert den (1978) 434 US 1035, 54 L Ed 2d 782, 98 S Ct 769 and appeal after remand (1979, CA2 NY) 611 F.2d 423, 28 FR Serv 2d 602

General partners who plotted against limited partners to gain control of partnership assets by forming a corporation and transferring the partnership assets to the corporation without the limited partner's consent, in violation of Partnership L § 98, were guilty of conspiracy. Newburger, Loeb & Co. v Gross (1977, CA2 NY) 563 F.2d 1057, 1977, CCH Fed Secur L Rep P 96148, 1977-2 CCH Trade Cases P 61604, 24 FR Serv 2d 42, cert den (1978) 434 US 1035, 54 L Ed 2d 782, 98 S Ct 769 and appeal after remand (1979, CA2 NY) 611 F.2d 423, 28 FR Serv 2d 602

General partner had standing to recover for breach of fiduciary duty owed him when other general partners transferred partnership assets without consent of limited partners. Newburger, Loeb & Co. v Gross (1977, CA2 NY) 563 F.2d 1057, 1977, CCH Fed Secur L Rep P 96148, 1977-2 CCH Trade Cases P 61604, 24 FR Serv 2d 42, cert den (1978) 434 US 1035, 54 L Ed 2d 782, 98 S Ct 769 and appeal after remand (1979, CA2 NY) 611 F.2d 423, 28 FR Serv 2d 602

General partners' right reserved in partnership agreement to terminate the business did not justify a transfer of partnership assets to a corporation in violation of Partnership L § 98, where the partnership was not dissolved and the limited partners' capital shares were not returned. Newburger, Loeb & Co. v Gross (1977, CA2 NY) 563 F.2d 1057, 1977, CCH Fed Secur L Rep P 96148, 1977-2 CCH Trade Cases P 61604, 24 FR Serv 2d 42, cert den (1978) 434 US

1035, 54 L Ed 2d 782, 98 S Ct 769 and appeal after remand (1979, CA2 NY) 611 F.2d 423, 28 FR Serv 2d 602

There is no exception to Partnership L § 98 in cases where a partnership is in financial distress or where a transfer of partnership assets to a corporation is necessary to enable the partnership to carry on its business. Newburger, Loeb & Co. v Gross (1977, CA2 NY) 563 F.2d 1057, 1977, CCH Fed Secur L Rep P 96148, 1977-2 CCH Trade Cases P 61604, 24 FR Serv 2d 42, cert den (1978) 434 US 1035, 54 L Ed 2d 782, 98 S Ct 769 and appeal after remand (1979, CA2 NY) 611 F.2d 423, 28 FR Serv 2d 602

Where general partners transferred assets to corporation without consent of limited partners, and did not dissolve the partnership or return the limited partner's capital shares, they were guilty of conversion and liable to the limited partners for an accounting. Newburger, Loeb & Co. v Gross (1977, CA2 NY) 563 F.2d 1057, 1977, CCH Fed Secur L Rep P 96148, 1977-2 CCH Trade Cases P 61604, 24 FR Serv 2d 42, cert den (1978) 434 US 1035, 54 L Ed 2d 782, 98 S Ct 769 and appeal after remand (1979, CA2 NY) 611 F.2d 423, 28 FR Serv 2d 602

§ 96. Limited partner not liable to creditors

A limited partner shall not become liable as a general partner unless, in addition to the exercise of his rights and powers as a limited partner, he takes part in the control of the business; and the exercise of the rights and powers granted by subdivision three of section ninety-nine of this chapter shall not constitute taking part in the control of the business. The commencement of or other participation by a limited partner in an action brought pursuant to section one hundred fifteen-a of this article shall not be deemed to be a taking part in the control of the business within the meaning of this section.

History: Add, L 1922, ch 640, § 1, with substance transferred from §§ 7 and 36; amd, L 1968, ch 496, § 1, L 1976, ch 717, § 1, eff July 24, 1976.

Former § 96, add, L 1919, ch 408; repealed, L 1922, ch 640, § 1, eff April 13, 1922.

CASE ANNOTATIONS

1. In general
2. Liable as general partner
3. Not liable as general partner

1. In general

Limited partner who "takes part in the control of" limited partnership's business should not automatically be insulated from individual liability merely by benefit of status as officer and sole owner of corporate general partner; limited partner in such dual capacity bears heavy burden when seeking to elude personal liability and must, at least, prove that any relevant actions taken were performed solely in capacity as officer of general partner. Gonzalez v Chalpin (1990) 77 N.Y.2d 74, 564 N.Y.S.2d 702, 565 N.E.2d 1253, reconsideration den (1991) 77 N.Y.2d 940, 569 N.Y.S.2d 613, 572 N.E.2d 54

Court would decline to incorporate into CLS Partn § 96 requirement that plaintiff seeking to hold limited partner individually liable must prove reliance on limited partner's personal conduct; such qualification on statutorily regulated liability pattern must come from legislature. Gonzalez v Chalpin (1990) 77 N.Y.2d 74, 564 N.Y.S.2d 702, 565 N.E.2d 1253, reconsideration den (1991) 77 N.Y.2d 940, 569 N.Y.S.2d 613, 572 N.E.2d 54

A limited partner has no right to sue in a derivative capacity upon behalf of the partnership, and a limited partner does not become liable as a general partner unless he takes part in the control of the business. Millard v Newmark & Co. (1966, 1st Dept) 24 A.D.2d 333, 266 N.Y.S.2d 254

Partnership statute distinguishes general partners from limited partners only in insulating limited partners from partnership liabilities and barring limited partners from participating in management of partnership. Goldman, Sachs & Co. v Michael (1985, 1st Dept) 113 A.D.2d 326, 496 N.Y.S.2d 427

A creditor's complaint against a limited partner, seeking to impose liability upon him because he has taken part in control of the business, must plead ultimate facts and is insufficient where it merely contains conclusory statements. Bell Sound Studios, Inc. v Enneagram Productions Co. (1962) 36 Misc. 2d 879, 234 N.Y.S.2d 12

If a limited partner chooses to act as a general partner, and does so, under this section he becomes liable as a general partner taking part in the control of the business and must bear the burdens of his choice. Executive Hotel Associates v Elm Hotel Corp. (1964) 41 Misc. 2d 354, 245 N.Y.S.2d 929, affd (1964) 43 Misc. 2d 153, 250 N.Y.S.2d 351

In an action against a partnership a defense by one partner that it was a limited partnership and that her liability was limited to her capital contribution presented an issue of fact and precluded a summary judgment as against her. Standard Factors Corp. v Kreisler (1945, Sup) 53 N.Y.S.2d 871, affd (1945) 269 A.D. 830, 56 N.Y.S.2d 414

2. Liable as general partner

Limited partner was properly denied limited liability protection of CLS Partn § 96, despite his contention that he acted at all times solely in his capacity as officer of corporate general partner when he took part in control of limited partnership's business, where (1) the only evidence he produced consisted of certificate of limited partnership, signed by him on behalf of general partnership, which stated that he was limited partner, and (2) evidence in refutation consisted of limited partnership checks signed by limited partner in his own name which failed to name generalpartnership or to indicate that he was signing in any representative capacity. Gonzalez v Chalpin (1990) 77 N.Y.2d 74, 564 N.Y.S.2d 702, 565 N.E.2d 1253, reconsideration den (1991) 77 N.Y.2d 940, 569 N.Y.S.2d 613, 572 N.E.2d 54

In action by board of managers of condominium against sponsors of condominium project, bank that was limited partner in project was not entitled to dismissal of causes of action against it, notwithstanding contention that bank merely loaned money to provide financing for development and marketing of project, since there was question regarding amount of control that bank exercised in business of sponsor of project. Board of Managers at North Hills Condominium v Fairways at North Hills (1989, 2d Dept) 150 A.D.2d 32, 545 N.Y.S.2d 343, later proceeding (1993, 2d Dept) 193 A.D.2d 322, 603 N.Y.S.2d 867

In action to recover for extensive renovation work performed on apartment building, individual defendant was properly found personally liable for amount awarded to plaintiff, despite his contention that he was only limited partner of defendant partnership and that any part he took in running of partnership business was solely in his role as officer of corporate general partner, since evidence established that he performed extensive role in running of partnership and thereby became personally liable as general partner. Gonzalez v Chalpin (1990, 2d Dept) 159 A.D.2d 553, 552 N.Y.S.2d 419, app gr (1990) 76 N.Y.2d 704, 559 N.Y.S.2d 983, 559 N.E.2d 677 and affd (1990) 77 N.Y.2d 74, 564 N.Y.S.2d 702, 565 N.E.2d 1253, reconsideration den (1991) 77 N.Y.2d 940, 569 N.Y.S.2d 613, 572 N.E.2d 54

Plaintiff was entitled to summary judgment as to defendant's liability to contribute 1/2 of judgment already paid by plaintiff on his behalf in light of prior judicial finding in underlying action that defendant was jointly and severally liable with plaintiff for debt of their defunct limited partnership; defendant could not claim that he was liable only to extent of his interest in limited partnerships where he had admitted personal liability and had jointly exercised control with plaintiff over partnerships' property. Sonnenfeldt v Kyriakoudes (1996, 1st Dept) 226 A.D.2d 286, 641 N.Y.S.2d 289

Plaintiff was entitled to summary judgment as to defendant's liability to contribute 1/2 of judgment already paid by plaintiff on his behalf in light of prior judicial finding in underlying action that defendant was jointly and severally liable with plaintiff for debt of their defunct limited partnership; defendant could not claim that he was liable only to extent of his interest in limited partnerships where he had admitted personal liability and had jointly exercised control with plaintiff over partnerships' property. Sonnenfeldt v Kyriakoudes (1996, 1st Dept) 226 A.D.2d 286, 641 N.Y.S.2d 289

A special partner who buys the entire partnership property and continues the business in his own name on his own account renders himself liable as a general partner. First Nat. Bank v Whitney (1871) 4 Lans 34, affd 53 N.Y. 627

3. Not liable as general partner

Although a partnership may sue or be sued in the partnership name for purposes of pleading, a limited partner, unless he is also a general partner, is not a proper party to proceedings by or against a partnership, except where the object is to enforce a limited partner's right against or liability to the partnership; and when limited partners instituted suit in the partnership name as an entity, they assumed liability as general partners; and when they amended the caption of their action to sue as individuals in a class action, rather than as an entity, they insulated themselves from liability as general partners and could not therefore maintain the action. Riviera Congress Associates v Yassky (1966, 1st Dept) 25 A.D.2d 291, 268 N.Y.S.2d 854, affd (1966) 18 N.Y.2d 540, 277 N.Y.S.2d 386, 223 N.E.2d 876 (superseded by statute as stated in Koppel v 4987 Corp. (1999, SD NY) CCH Fed Secur L Rep P 90640)

Plaintiffs failed to state cause of action against individual partners to recover security deposit on commercial lease where individual defendants were limited partners and thus could not be held liable for obligations of partnership absent allegation that they participated in control of business. Hajar, Inc. v One Peach Assocs. (2001, 2d Dept) 281 A.D.2d 592, 722 N.Y.S.2d 175

The bringing of an action by a special partner to conserve the assets of a firm is not such an interference with the firm management as to make him liable as a general partner. Continental Nat'l Bank v Strauss (1892) 60 N.Y. Super Ct 151, 17 N.Y.S. 188, affd (1893) 137 N.Y. 148, 32 N.E. 1066

Where a non-managing partner's sole participation in real estate syndicates cast in form of general partnerships was to attend three or four meetings when the partnerships were in financial straits to make his views known, such participation, even if he were a limited partner, would not constitute taking "part in the control of the business" so as to make him liable as a general partner. United States v Silverstein (1965, SD NY) 237 F. Supp. 446, 65-1 USTC P 9266, 15 AFTR 2d 283, affd (1965, CA2 NY) 344 F.2d 1016, 65-2 USTC P 9480, 15 AFTR 2d 991, cert den (1965) 382 US 828, 15 L Ed 2d 73, 86 S Ct 65

Where a non-managing partner in real estate syndicates cast in the form of general partnerships made partial assignments of portions of his partnership interest the partial assignees were not partners at all and were not personally liable for the partnership debts. United States v Silverstein (1965, SD NY) 237 F. Supp. 446, 65-1 USTC P 9266, 15 AFTR 2d 283, affd (1965, CA2 NY) 344 F.2d 1016, 65-2 USTC P 9480, 15 AFTR 2d 991, cert den (1965) 382 US 828, 15 L Ed 2d 73, 86 S Ct 65

A special partner may make a loan to the firm without necessarily rendering himself liable as a general partner. Walkenshaw v Perzel (1866) 27 N.Y. Super Ct (4 Robt) 426, 32 How Pr 233

§ 97.　　Admission of additional limited partners

After the formation of a limited partnership, additional limited partners may be admitted upon filing an amendment to the original certificate in accordance with the requirements of section one hundred and fourteen.

History: Add, L 1922, ch 640, § 1, eff April 13, 1922.

Former § 97, add, L 1919, ch 408; repealed, L 1922, ch 640, § 1, eff April 13, 1922.

§ 98.　　Rights, powers and liabilities of a general partner

(1) A general partner shall have all the rights and powers and be subject to all the restrictions and liabilities of a partner in a partnership without limited partners, except that without the written consent or ratification of the specific act by all the limited partners, a general partner or all of the general partners have no authority to

(a) Do any act in contravention of the certificate.

(b) Do any act which would make it impossible to carry on the ordinary business of the partnership.

(c) Confess a judgment against the partnership.

(d) Possess partnership property, or assign their rights in specific partnership property, for other than a partnership purpose.

(e) Admit a person as a general partner.

(f) Admit a person as a limited partner, unless the right so to do is given in the certificate.

(g) Continue the business with partnership property on the death, retirement or insanity of a general partner, unless the right so to do is given in the certificate.

History: Add, L 1922, ch 640, § 1, eff April 13, 1922, with substance transferred from § 37.

Former § 98, add, L 1919, ch 408; repealed, L 1922, ch 640, § 1, eff April 13, 1922.

CASE ANNOTATIONS

1. In general
2. Agreements
3. Powers and liabilities; construction
4. Actions undertaken without authority

1. In general

Management of the property and business is vested exclusively in the general partners. Durant v Abendroth (1884) 97 N.Y. 132

An infant who becomes a general partner is responsible for all partnership engagements until he elects to set up the plea of infancy and therefore the fact that one partner is an infant does not affect the liability of the special partner. Continental Nat'l Bank v Strauss (1893) 137 N.Y. 148, 32 N.E. 1066

Partnership statute distinguishes general partners from limited partners only in insulating limited partners from partnership liabilities and barring limited partners from participating in management of partnership. Goldman, Sachs & Co. v Michael (1985, 1st Dept) 113 A.D.2d 326, 496 N.Y.S.2d 427

Although in some respects a limited partner does have some resemblance to a creditor of the partnership, in the main, a limited partner is more like a shareholder. Klebanow v New York Produce Exchange (1965, CA2 NY) 344 F.2d 294, 1965 CCH Trade Cases P 71413, 9 FR Serv 2d 17B.3, Case 1 (superseded by statute as stated in Koppel v 4987 Corp. (1999, SD NY) CCH Fed Secur L Rep P 90640)

One who is merely a limited partner has no authority to act for or bind the partnership for the general partners. Berman v Herrick (1964, ED Pa) 231 F. Supp. 918, affd (1965, CA3 Pa) 346 F.2d 116, cert den (1965) 382 US 892, 15 L Ed 2d 150, 86 S Ct 185

2. Agreements

In the absence of prohibitory provisions of statutes or rules of the common law relating to partnerships or considerations of public policy the partners of either a general or limited partnership, as between themselves, may include in the partnership articles any agreement they wish concerning the sharing of profits and losses, priorities of distribution on winding up of the partnership affairs and other matters. If complete, as between the parties, an agreement so made controls. Lanier v Bowdoin (1939) 282 N.Y. 32, 24 N.E.2d 732, reh den (1940) 282 N.Y. 611, 25 N.E.2d 391

A cause of action alleging breach of a limited partnership agreement should have been dismissed, where there was not the slightest indication that the limited partnership agreement was meant to govern the internal affairs of the corporate general partner, where a restriction on the sale of shares in the corporate general partner was nowhere to be found in the agreement or the private placement documents prepared by the individual defendants, where such a provision could not be implied due to the merger clause in the partnership agreement, where there was no alteration of tax benefits to limited partners occasioned by the sale of the corporate partner's shares to a third party, and thus no intrinsic logic to a prohibition against alienation of the corporation's shares, and where, therefore, there was no breach of the partnership agreement and the individual who purchased the corporate shares could not liable for inducement

to breach that contract. Goldfeld v Mattoon Communications Corp. (1984, 1st Dept) 99 A.D.2d 711, 472 N.Y.S.2d 6, app dismd (1984) 62 N.Y.2d 802

Nothing in this section establishes a public policy which prevents persons entering into a limited partnership agreement from agreeing, and being bound by such agreement, that the general partners shall have the right to convey partnership property for purposes therein specified. Mist Properties, Inc. v Fitzsimmons Realty Co. (1962, Sup) 228 N.Y.S.2d 406

Local managing partner of 2 housing projects that breached partnership agreements requiring general partners to "exercise their responsibilities in a fiduciary capacity," also breached its fiduciary duty under CLS Partn § 43 by benefitting from its dealings with its identity-of-interest companies without consent of supervising partners, entitling supervising partners to accounting with respect to all transactions between partnerships, managing partner and identity-of-interest companies regardless of when entered into. NCAS Realty Mgmt. Corp. v National Corp. for Hous. Pshps. (1998, CA2 NY) 143 F.3d 38

General partner exceeded his authority under CLS Partn L § 98 in exchanging properties without consent or ratification of limited partners, in that exchange violated terms of partnership agreement and certificate and destroyed character of partnership's business. Shlomchik v Richmond 103 Equities Co. (1986, SD NY) 662 F. Supp. 365, amd, in part, on other grounds, adhered to, in part (1991, SD NY) 763 F. Supp. 732, CCH Fed Secur L Rep P 96124

3. Powers and liabilities; construction

An interest in a limited partnership, even a partnership that deals in real estate, is personalty, not realty; individuals who contributed to the partnership acquires no title to the real property which is acquired by the partnership; they merely acquire a pro rata share in the partnership profits and surplus, which is personalty. Reiter v Greenberg (1968) 21 N.Y.2d 388, 288 N.Y.S.2d 57, 235 N.E.2d 118

Subdivision 1 of this section is to be construed in connection with subd 2 of § 26, under which liability of partners is joint, and thus any action by a creditor of a limited partnership against the limited partners must include the general partner or partners. Bell Sound Studios, Inc. v Enneagram Productions Co. (1962) 36 Misc. 2d 879, 234 N.Y.S.2d 12

Where one who had been one of the limited partners in a limited partnership became the sole general partner and proceeded to act as such, he had no authority, under this section, and without consent of the limited partners, to do anything which would make it impossible to carry on the ordinary business or to assign away specific partnership property for other than a partnership purpose and his conduct in violating these prohibitions was so conflicting with his fiduciary obligation to the other partners as to preclude his assertion of validity of the action taken by him. Executive Hotel Associates v Elm Hotel Corp. (1964) 41 Misc. 2d 354, 245 N.Y.S.2d 929, affd (1964) 43 Misc. 2d 153, 250 N.Y.S.2d 351

The provision of the above statute as to the liabilities of a general partner, applied. Riviera Congress Associates v Yassky (1965) 48 Misc. 2d 282, 264 N.Y.S.2d 624, mod on other grounds (1966, 1st Dept) 25 A.D.2d 291, 268 N.Y.S.2d 854, affd (1966) 18 N.Y.2d 540, 277 N.Y.S.2d 386, 223 N.E.2d 876 (superseded by statute as stated in Koppel v 4987 Corp. (1999, SD NY) CCH Fed Secur L Rep P 90640)

As a matter of law, a limited partner does not individually have a cause of action to recover for the loss of his partnership investment resulting from the acts of his general partners. Blattberg v Weiss (1969) 61 Misc. 2d 564, 306 N.Y.S.2d 88

Transfer of partnership assets to a corporation without the consent of the limited partners is a violation of Partnership L § 98, subd 1(b), which prohibits acts which make it impossible to carry out the ordinary business of the partnership. Newburger, Loeb & Co. v Gross (1977, CA2 NY) 563 F.2d 1057, 1977, CCH Fed Secur L Rep P 96148, 1977-2 CCH Trade Cases P 61604, 24 FR Serv 2d 42, cert den (1978) 434 US 1035, 54 L Ed 2d 782, 98 S Ct 769 and appeal after remand (1979, CA2 NY) 611 F.2d 423, 28 FR Serv 2d 602

General partner had standing to recover for breach of fiduciary duty owed him when other general partners transferred partnership assets without consent of limited partners. Newburger, Loeb & Co. v Gross (1977, CA2 NY) 563 F.2d 1057, 1977, CCH Fed Secur L Rep P 96148, 1977-2 CCH Trade Cases P 61604, 24 FR Serv 2d 42, cert den (1978) 434 US 1035, 54 L Ed 2d 782, 98 S Ct 769 and appeal after remand (1979, CA2 NY) 611 F.2d 423, 28 FR Serv 2d 602

There is no exception to Partnership L § 98 in cases where a partnership is in financial distress or where a transfer of partnership assets to a corporation is necessary to enable the partnership to carry on its business. Newburger, Loeb & Co. v Gross (1977, CA2 NY) 563 F.2d 1057, 1977, CCH Fed Secur L Rep P 96148, 1977-2 CCH Trade Cases P 61604, 24 FR Serv 2d 42, cert den (1978) 434 US 1035, 54 L Ed 2d 782, 98 S Ct 769 and appeal after remand (1979, CA2 NY) 611 F.2d 423, 28 FR Serv 2d 602

4. Actions undertaken without authority

A general partner of a limited partnership breaches its fiduciary duty and violates section 98 (subd [1], par [d]) of the Partnership Law, which provides that a general partner shall have no authority to possess partnership property, or assign his rights in specific partnership property, without the written consent or ratification by all the limited partners, where it indorses and sells negotiable notes to a bank that were given to it as a capital contribution by the limited partners of the limited partnership, these notes to become due in the future, and deposits the proceeds of the sale in its own corporate account; the silence of the limited partners upon their discovery of the sale does not constitute ratification of the general partner's act where there is nothing to show that the limited partners had any reason to suspect that the bank held the notes other than for an indebtedness of the limited partnership in furtherance of its business, and the limited partners have a valid defense to the enforcement of the notes held by the bank where the bank is not a holder in due course. (Uniform Commercial Code, § 3-306.) Accordingly, where the bank had notice that the general partner was negotiating the partnership's notes for its own corporate purpose in breach of its fiduciary duty to the limited partners, the bank is a not a holder in due course and, as a nonholder in due course, takes the notes subject to this defense and cannot recover on the notes from the limited partners. Chemical Bank of Rochester v Haskell (1979, 4th Dept) 68 A.D.2d 347, 417 N.Y.S.2d 541, 26 UCCRS 952, revd on other grounds (1980) 51 N.Y.2d 85, 432 N.Y.S.2d 478, 411 N.E.2d 1339, 29 UCCRS 1529, reh den (1980) 51 N.Y.2d 1009 and reh den (1980) 51 N.Y.2d 1009 and reh den (1980) 51 N.Y.2d 1009

Partnership was entitled to summary judgment dismissing action by limited partner for judgment declaring conveyance of partnership property to be void, despite contention of limited partner that limited partners had not agreed to sale and that sale made it impossible for partnership to carry on business, where (1) partnership agreement gave general partner right to sell property with consent of at least 51 percent of limited partners, (2) partnership presented consents from 75 percent of limited partners, and (3) all limited partners except plaintiff had accepted distribution of proceeds of sale. Alexandru v Berritt (1990, 2d Dept) 168 A.D.2d 472, 562 N.Y.S.2d 712

Successor general partner of limited partnership was duly qualified to act on behalf of partnership where partnership agreement granted power of attorney to "the General Partner, or any successor individual General Partner," and amendment to certificate of partnership was signed by successor as attorney-in-fact for limited partners, although not signed by withdrawing general partner or any limited partners; successor gained legal status as general partner when limited partners voted him in, not when amended certificate was filed, and thus had power of attorney under partnership agreement to execute amended certificate. Marsh v Brady (1991, Sup) 152 Misc. 2d 990, 579 N.Y.S.2d 813

General partners who plotted against limited partners to gain control of partnership assets by forming a corporation and transferring the partnership assets to the corporation without the limited partner's consent, in violation of Partnership L § 98, were guilty of conspiracy. Newburger, Loeb & Co. v Gross (1977, CA2 NY) 563 F.2d 1057, 1977, CCH Fed Secur L Rep P 96148, 1977-2 CCH Trade Cases P 61604, 24 FR Serv 2d 42, cert den (1978) 434 US 1035, 54 L Ed 2d 782, 98 S Ct 769 and appeal after remand (1979, CA2 NY) 611 F.2d 423, 28 FR Serv 2d 602

General partners' right reserved in partnership agreement to terminate the business did not justify a transfer of partnership assets to a corporation in violation of Partnership L § 98, where the partnership was not dissolved and the limited partners' capital shares were not returned. Newburger, Loeb & Co. v Gross (1977, CA2 NY) 563 F.2d 1057, 1977, CCH Fed Secur L Rep P 96148, 1977-2 CCH Trade Cases P 61604, 24 FR Serv 2d 42, cert den (1978) 434 US 1035, 54 L Ed 2d 782, 98 S Ct 769 and appeal after remand (1979, CA2 NY) 611 F.2d 423, 28 FR Serv 2d 602

Where general partners transferred assets to corporation without consent of limited partners, and did not dissolve the partnership or return the limited partner's capital shares, they were guilty of

conversion and liable to the limited partners for an accounting. Newburger, Loeb & Co. v Gross (1977, CA2 NY) 563 F.2d 1057, 1977, CCH Fed Secur L Rep P 96148, 1977-2 CCH Trade Cases P 61604, 24 FR Serv 2d 42, cert den (1978) 434 US 1035, 54 L Ed 2d 782, 98 S Ct 769 and appeal after remand (1979, CA2 NY) 611 F.2d 423, 28 FR Serv 2d 602

Where a nonmanaging partner's sole participation in real estate syndicates cast in form of general partnerships was to attend three or four meetings when the partnerships were in financial straits to make his views known such participation, even if he were a limited partner, would not constitute taking "part in the control of the business" so as to make him liable as a general partner. United States v Silverstein (1965, SD NY) 237 F. Supp. 446, 65-1 USTC P 9266, 15 AFTR 2d 283, affd (1965, CA2 NY) 344 F.2d 1016, 65-2 USTC P 9480, 15 AFTR 2d 991, cert den (1965) 382 US 828, 15 L Ed 2d 73, 86 S Ct 65

Despite fact that execution of transfer agreement by which assets of brokerage partnership were sold to newly formed corporation was in violation of law in that the transaction was consummated without written consent of all partners, rescission was unwarranted within context of case and damages would be adequate remedy. Newburger, Loeb & Co. v Gross (1973, SD NY) 365 F. Supp. 1364, CCH Fed Secur L Rep P 94190, 1973-2 CCH Trade Cases P 74766

§ 99.   Rights of a limited partner

(1) A limited partner shall have the same rights as a general partner to

(a) Have the partnership books kept at the principal place of business of the partnership, and at all times to inspect and copy any of them.

(b) Have on demand true and full information of all things affecting the partnership, and a formal account of partnership affairs whenever circumstances render it just and reasonable, and

(c) Have dissolution and winding up by decree of court.

(2) A limited partner shall have the right to receive a share of the profits or other compensation by way of income, and to the return of his contribution as provided in sections one hundred and four and one hundred and five of this article.

(3) When the limited partnership is qualified as an investment company under the Investment Company Act of 1940, the limited partner shall have the right to vote: (a) in the election of directors or trustees of the investment company; (b) to approve or terminate investment advisory or underwriting contracts; (c) for approval of auditors; and (d) any other matters that the Investment Company Act of 1940 requires to be approved by the holders of beneficial interests in the investment company.

History: Add, L 1922, ch 640, § 1, eff April 13, 1922, with substance transferred from § 37.

Former § 99, add, L 1919, ch 408; repealed, L 1922, ch 640, § 1, eff April 13, 1922.

Sub (3), add, L 1976, ch 717, § 2, eff July 24, 1976.

CASE ANNOTATIONS

1. In general
2. Nature of limited partner's status
3. Access to books and information
4. Dissolution
5. Accounting
6. Other kinds of actions against partnership

1. In general

An infant who becomes a general partner is responsible for all partnership engagements until he elects to set up the plea of infancy and therefore the fact that one partner is an infant does not affect the liability of the special partner. Continental Nat'l Bank v Strauss (1893) 137 N.Y. 148, 32 N.E. 1066

In the absence of prohibitory provisions of statutes or rules of the common law relating to partnerships or considerations of public policy the partners of either a general or limited partnership, as between themselves, may include in the partnership articles any agreement they wish conserning the sharing of profits and losses, priorities of distribution on winding up of the partnership affairs and other matters. If complete, as between the parties, an agreement so made controls. Lanier v Bowdoin (1939) 282 N.Y. 32, 24 N.E.2d 732, reh den (1940) 282 N.Y. 611, 25 N.E.2d 391

Special partner in limited partnership does not make breach of his copartnership obligation so as to warrant dissolution by becoming special partner in another limited partnership conducting similar or competing business if there be no actual fraud or deceit on his part. However, that it would be act of bad faith for general partner to engage in competing business without consent of or against objections of his copartners. Skolny v Richter (1910) 139 A.D. 534, 124 N.Y.S. 152

Section 115 of the Partnership Law does not restrict or limit the rights enumerated in § 88 of that law. Millard v Newmark & Co. (1966, 1st Dept) 24 A.D.2d 333, 266 N.Y.S.2d 254

Partnership statute distinguishes general partners from partnership liabilities and barring limited partners only in insulating limited partners from partnership liabilities and barring limited partners from participating in management of partnership. Goldman, Sachs & Co. v Michael (1985, 1st Dept) 113 A.D.2d 326, 496 N.Y.S.2d 427

Limited partners did not state cause of action against partnership's brokers for failure to return partners' uninvested capital contributions where brokers returned $23.6 million to partnership for distribution to limited partners, which represented $18.5 million of uninvested capital plus certain expenses and 9 percent interest, and factual allegations neither met basic requirements of CLS CPLR § 3013 nor supported assertion that $30-$32 million should have been returned. Broome v ML Media Opportunity Partners L.P. (2000, 1st Dept) 273 A.D.2d 63, 709 N.Y.S.2d 59

In action by corporation against another corporation and its employees who were formerly employed by plaintiff corporation, defendant's counterclaim alleging that its capital was to remain in the business for thirty months during which time it was to be paid whatever its capital earned, and that defendant received no accounting, was sufficient. Union Circulation Co. v Hardel Publishers Service, Inc. (1957) 6 Misc. 2d 340, 164 N.Y.S.2d 435

2. Nature of limited partner's status

A New York limited partnership resembles sufficiently the nature of a corporation so that limited partners may be considered stockholders or members within § 44(a) of the Bankruptcy Act, and as such ineligible to vote for a trustee. In re Ira Haupt & Co. (1965, CA2 NY) 343 F.2d 726, cert den (1965) 382 US 890, 15 L Ed 2d 148, 86 S Ct 182

Although in some respects a limited partner does have some resemblance to a creditor of the partnership, in the main, a limited partner is more like a shareholder. Klebanow v New York Produce Exchange (1965, CA2 NY) 344 F.2d 294, 1965 CCH Trade Cases P 71413, 9 FR Serv 2d 17B.3, Case 1 (superseded by statute as stated in Koppel v 4987 Corp. (1999, SD NY) CCH Fed Secur L Rep P 90640)

3. Access to books and information

A limited partner has a right of full and free access to information contained in the partnership books, and to all things affecting the partnership, as well as a right to a formal accounting. A limited partner also has a right to dissolution in addition to his right as an individual against third parties. Millard v Newmark & Co. (1966, 1st Dept) 24 A.D.2d 333, 266 N.Y.S.2d 254

In limited partner's action for accounting and injunctive relief, court properly struck general partner's answer where he engaged in willful and contumacious conduct for some 2 years in failing to provide documentary confirmation of partnership's alleged expenditures involving separate legal action against third party; absence of express determination by court that general partner's noncompliance was deliberate did not detract from validity of order to strike where record clearly supported inference that conduct was willful and that court so concluded. Homburger v Levitin (1987, 2d Dept) 130 A.D.2d

715, 515 N.Y.S.2d 825, app dismd without op (1987) 70 N.Y.2d 795, 522 N.Y.S.2d 112, 516 N.E.2d 1225

Where a non-managing partner in real estate syndicates cast in form of general partnerships made partial assignments of portions of his partnership interest the partial assignees had some property rights in the partnership books and records. United States v Silverstein (1965, SD NY) 237 F. Supp. 446, 65-1 USTC P 9266, 15 AFTR 2d 283, affd (1965, CA2 NY) 344 F.2d 1016, 65-2 USTC P 9480, 15 AFTR 2d 991, cert den (1965) 382 US 828, 15 L Ed 2d 73, 86 S Ct 65

4. Dissolution

An action for dissolution may be brought by a special partner to prevent waste of funds by the general partners. Continental Nat'l Bank v Strauss (1893) 137 N.Y. 148, 32 N.E. 1066

A limited partner has a right of full and free access to information contained in the partnership books, and to all things affecting the partnership, as well as a right to a formal accounting. A limited partner also has a right to dissolution in addition to his right as an individual against third parties. Millard v Newmark & Co. (1966, 1st Dept) 24 A.D.2d 333, 266 N.Y.S.2d 254

Where plaintiffs alleged a breach of fiduciary duty, a formal accounting of the partnership affairs prior to dissolution is just and reasonable under Partnership Law § 99. Alpert v Haimes (1970) 64 Misc. 2d 608, 315 N.Y.S.2d 332

Limited partners had a statutory right to a dissolution and winding up decree of a court and accordingly, such relief with respect to the winding up decree had to be granted, pursuant to N.Y. Partnership Law §§ 68, 99(1)(c), and 105(4)(a). Polner v Monchik Realty Co. (2005, Sup) 9 Misc 3d 755, 803 N.Y.S.2d 370

When general partners proposed transfer of partnership assets to a corporation, limited partners were under no obligation to consent, and were entitled to insist that the partnership be dissolved. Newburger, Loeb & Co. v Gross (1977, CA2 NY) 563 F.2d 1057, 1977, CCH Fed Secur L Rep P 96148, 1977-2 CCH Trade Cases P 61604, 24 FR Serv 2d 42, cert den (1978) 434 US 1035, 54 L Ed 2d 782, 98 S Ct 769 and appeal after remand (1979, CA2 NY) 611 F.2d 423, 28 FR Serv 2d 602

5. Accounting

A limited partner has a right of full and free access to information contained in the partnership books, and to all things affecting the partnership, as well as a right to a formal accounting. A limited partner also has a right to dissolution in addition to his right as an individual against third parties. Millard v Newmark & Co. (1966, 1st Dept) 24 A.D.2d 333, 266 N.Y.S.2d 254

Although limited partners, who were not liable as general partners, could not maintain an action against the partnership and the general partners for alleged rent due, their interest in the partnership constituted personal property and gave them a right to a formal accounting. Riviera Congress Associates v Yassky (1966, 1st Dept) 25 A.D.2d 291, 268 N.Y.S.2d 854, affd (1966) 18 N.Y.2d 540, 277 N.Y.S.2d 386, 223 N.E.2d 876 (superseded by statute as stated in Koppel v 4987 Corp. (1999, SD NY) CCH Fed Secur L Rep P 90640)

It was error to dismiss action brought by limited partner to compel accounting where partnership agreement provided that accounting was due on sale "of all or substantially all of the Property," and partnership had sold 99.995 percent of its property. CCG Assoc. I v Riverside Assoc. (1990, 1st Dept) 157 A.D.2d 435, 556 N.Y.S.2d 859

"Interim accounting" voluntarily rendered by general partners did not provide complete documentary defense to accounting sought by limited partner since (1) "interim accounting" failed to account for any income, or capital of, or loan to partnership, or to allocate any costs it purported to report, (2) general partner had not sworn to its accuracy, and (3) accounting firm that prepared it disclaimed any responsibility for its accuracy and disavowed any suggestion that it certified its truth. CCG Assoc. I v Riverside Assoc. (1990, 1st Dept) 157 A.D.2d 435, 556 N.Y.S.2d 859

In action by general partner alleging that limited partner improperly assigned its right to receive partnership distributions, court properly granted protective order striking limited partner's notice of discovery and inspection of partnership records, since (1) limited partner's alleged assignment constituted sufficient misconduct to bar it from viewing records at such stage of proceeding, and (2) limited partner could not seek through discovery ultimate relief sought on merits of its counterclaim for accounting. Macklowe v 42nd Street Dev. Corp. (1990, 1st Dept) 157 A.D.2d 566, 550 N.Y.S.2d 309

In action arising from purchase and sale of limited partnership interests in general partnership, there was no basis for court to order accounting to resolve dispute concerning whether partnership made improper charges against income, where record was silent as to whether or not accounting was ever demanded. McMahan & Co. v Bass (1998, 1st Dept) 250 A.D.2d 460, 673 N.Y.S.2d 19, app den (1998, N.Y. A.D., 1st Dept) 1998 N.Y. A.D. LEXIS 9429, motion to strike den (1998, 1st Dept) 255 A.D.2d 238, 680 N.Y.S.2d 238 and app den, in part, app dismd, in part (1998) 92 N.Y.2d 1013, 684 N.Y.S.2d 484, 707 N.E.2d 439, app dismd (1999, 1st Dept) 258 A.D.2d 975, 685 N.Y.S.2d 567 and later proceeding (1999, N.Y. A.D., 1st Dept) 1999 N.Y. A.D. LEXIS 7539, related proceeding (2001, CA11 Fla) 256 F.3d 1120, 14 FLW Fed C 944 (criticized in BDO Seidman, LLP v British Car Auctions, Inc. (2001, Fla App D4) 802 So 2d 366, 26 FLW D 2593)

Plaintiff was entitled to summary judgment on cause of action seeking accounting with respect to limited partnership where plaintiff was successor in interest to decedent, defendant general partner was collaterally estopped to deny that decedent was trustee of portion of trust, and trust held interest in limited partnership. Fischer v Levy (1999, 1st Dept) 260 A.D.2d 291, 689 N.Y.S.2d 48

Where plaintiffs alleged a breach of fiduciary duty, a formal accounting of the partnership affairs prior to dissolution is just and reasonable under Partnership Law § 99. Alpert v Haimes (1970) 64 Misc. 2d 608, 315 N.Y.S.2d 332

Limited partners were statutorily entitled to a formal accounting upon the winding up of the partnership, pursuant to N.Y. Partnership Law § 99(1)(b). Polner v Monchik Realty Co. (2005, Sup) 9 Misc 3d 755, 803 N.Y.S.2d 370

A special partner may compel general partners to account. Van Voorhis v Webster (1895) 85 Hun 591, 33 N.Y.S. 121

The statutory duty of a partnership to provide a formal account of partnership affairs whenever just and reasonable requires that any claims existing which have genuine likelihood of reducing a withdrawing partner's interest in a limited partnership as computed by certified public accountants be disclosed to the withdrawing partner. Rosenthal v Emanuel, Deetjen & Co. (1975, CA2 NY) 516 F.2d 325

Where general partners transferred assets to corporation without consent of limited partners, and did not dissolve the partnership or return the limited partner's capital shares, they were guilty of conversion and liable to the limited partners for an accounting. Newburger, Loeb & Co. v Gross (1977, CA2 NY) 563 F.2d 1057, 1977, CCH Fed Secur L Rep P 96148, 1977-2 CCH Trade Cases P 61604, 24 FR Serv 2d 42, cert den (1978) 434 US 1035, 54 L Ed 2d 782, 98 S Ct 769 and appeal after remand (1979, CA2 NY) 611 F.2d 423, 28 FR Serv 2d 602

6. Other kinds of actions against partnership

Limited partners, although not permitted to interfere in any manner with the conduct of the partnership business, may bring a class action on behalf of others similarly situated based upon alleged mismanagement of the partnership property by the general partners resulting in impairment of the rate of return on the investment of the limited partners. Lichtyger v Franchard Corp. (1966) 18 N.Y.2d 528, 277 N.Y.S.2d 377, 223 N.E.2d 869

Although limited partners, who were not liable as general partners, could not maintain an action against the partnership and the general partners for alleged rent due, their interest in the partnership constituted personal property and gave them a right to a formal accounting. Riviera Congress Associates v Yassky (1966, 1st Dept) 25 A.D.2d 291, 268 N.Y.S.2d 854, affd (1966) 18 N.Y.2d 540, 277 N.Y.S.2d 386, 223 N.E.2d 876 (superseded by statute as stated in Koppel v 4987 Corp. (1999, SD NY) CCH Fed Secur L Rep P 90640)

Limited partner was properly elevated to status of general partner in general partner's stead in order to preserve leasehold (which was principal asset of partnership) where (1) in limited partner's action for accounting and injunctive relief, general partner's answer was properly struck following his willful refusal to disclose financial information relating to partnership, (2) limited partner, in his action, had initially requested appointment of receiver of partnership assets, and (3) leasehold was subject to termination at option of lessor on appointment of receiver. Homburger v Levitin (1987, 2d Dept) 130 A.D.2d 715, 515 N.Y.S.2d 825, app dismd without op (1987) 70 N.Y.2d 795, 522 N.Y.S.2d 112, 516 N.E.2d 1225

Where plaintiffs alleged a breach of fiduciary duty, a formal accounting of the partnership affairs prior to dissolution is just and reasonable under Partnership Law § 99. Alpert v Haimes (1970) 64 Misc. 2d 608, 315 N.Y.S.2d 332

A limited partner has no property interest in the partnership assets and cannot maintain an action under the Trading with the Enemy Act for recovery of the property. Alley v Clark (1947, DC NY) 71 F. Supp. 521

§ 100. Status of person erroneously believing himself a limited partner

A person who has contributed to the capital of a business conducted by a person or partnership erroneously believing that he has become a limited partner in a limited partnership is not, by reason of his exercise of the rights of a limited partner, a general partner with the person or in the partnership carrying on the business, or bound by the obligations of such person or partnership; provided that on ascertaining the mistake he promptly renounces his interest in the profits of the business, or other compensation by way of income.

History: Add, L 1922, ch 640, § 1, eff April 13, 1922.

Former § 100, add, L 1919, ch 408; repealed, L 1922, ch 640, § 1, eff April 13, 1922.

§ 101. One person both general and limited partner

(1) A person may be a general partner and a limited partner in the same partnership at the same time.

(2) A person who is a general, and also at the same time a limited partner, shall have all the rights and powers and be subject to all the restrictions of a general partner; except that, in respect to his contributions, he shall have the rights against the other members which he would have had if he were not also a general partner.

History: Add, L 1922, ch 640, § 1, eff April 13, 1922.

Former § 101, add, L 1919, ch 408; repealed, L 1922, ch 640, § 1, eff April 13, 1922.

§ 102. Loans and other business transactions with limited partner

(1) A limited partner also may loan money to and transact other business with the partnership, and, unless he is also a general partner, receive on account of resulting claims against the partnership, with general creditors, a pro rata share of the assets. No limited partner shall in respect to any such claim

(a) Receive or hold as collateral security any partnership property, or,

(b) Receive from a general partner or the partnership any payment, conveyance or release from liability, if at the time the assets of the partnership are not sufficient to discharge partnership liabilities to persons not claiming as general or limited partners.

(2) The receiving of collateral security, or a payment, conveyance or release in violation of the provisions of subdivision one is a fraud on the creditors of the partnership.

History: Add, L 1922, ch 640, § 1, eff April 13, 1922.

Former § 102, add, L 1919, ch 408; repealed, L 1922, ch 640, § 1, eff April 13, 1922.

Under the above statute and §§ 105 and 112, a limited partner is not entitled to payment either on account of his capital contribution, as a return thereon or as a creditor, before creditors who are not partners are paid in full or until full payment to them is assured. Nexsen v New York Stock Exchange (1965, 2d Dept) 24 A.D.2d 514, 261 N.Y.S.2d 780

The salary paid to an employee of a partnership is a deductible business expense even though the employee is also a limited partner. 1953 Ops Atty Gen July 15

§ 103. Relation of limited partners inter se

Where there are several limited partners the members may agree that one or more of the limited partners shall have a priority over other limited partners as to the return of their contributions, as to their compensation by way of income, or as to any other matter. If such an agreement is made it shall be stated in the certificate, and in the absence of such a statement all the limited partners shall stand upon equal footing.

History: Add, L 1922, ch 640, § 1, eff April 13, 1922.

§ 104. Compensation of limited partner

A limited partner may receive from the partnership the share of the profits or the compensation by way of income stipulated for in the certificate; provided, that after such payment is made, whether from the property of the partnership or that of a general partner, the partnership assets are in excess of all liabilities of the partnership except liabilities to limited partners on account of their contributions and to general partners.

History: Add, L 1922, ch 640, § 1, eff April 13, 1922.

CASE ANNOTATIONS

The principle that one partner is not entitled to compensation for services rendered by him on behalf of the firm is relevant only to partnerships where each partner has an equal interest, is equally liable, and equally responsible for the conduct of the partnership business but the principle does not apply where the interests, liabilities and responsibilities of the general partners and the special partners are not equal. Steinberg v Goodman (1970) 27 N.Y.2d 304, 317 N.Y.S.2d 342, 265 N.E.2d 758

The salary paid to an employee of a partnership is a deductible business expense even though the employee is also a limited partner. 1953 Ops Atty Gen July 15

§ 105. Withdrawal or reduction of limited partner's contribution

(1) A limited partner shall not receive from a general partner or out of partnership property any part of his contribution until

(a) All liabilities of the partnership, except liabilities to general partners and to limited partners on account of their contributions, have been paid or there remains property of the partnership sufficient to pay them.

(b) The consent of all members is had, unless the return of the contribution may be rightfully demanded under the provisions of subdivision two, and

(c) The certificate is cancelled or so amended as to set forth the withdrawal or reduction.

(2) Subject to the provisions of subdivision one, a limited partner may rightfully demand the return of his contribution

(a) On the dissolution of a partnership, or,

(b) When the date specified in the certificate for its return has arrived, or,

(c) After he has given six months' notice in writing to all other members, if no time is specified in the certificate either for the return of the contribution or for the dissolution of the partnership.

(3) In the absence of any statement in the certificate to the contrary or the consent of all members, a limited partner, irrespective of the nature of his contribution, has only the right to demand and receive cash in return for his contribution.

(4) A limited partner may have the partnership dissolved and its affairs wound up when

(a) He rightfully but unsuccessfully demands the return of his contribution, or,

(b) The other liabilities of the partnership have not been paid, or the partnership property is insufficient for their payment and the limited partner would otherwise be entitled to the return of his contribution.

History: Add, L 1922, ch 640, § 1, eff April 13, 1922, with substance transferred from § 39.

CASE ANNOTATIONS

Drawing interest monthly on capital invested was not a violation of a former analogous section. Metropolitan Nat'l Bank v Sirret (1884) 97 N.Y. 320

Special partner may not receive any part of his capital contribution until all liabilities of partnership, except liabilities to general partners and to limited partners on account of their contributions, have been paid or there remains property of partnership sufficient to pay them. Kittredge v Langley (1930) 252 N.Y. 405, 169 N.E. 626, 67 ALR 1087, reh den (1930) 253 N.Y. 555, 171 N.E. 780

Allegation that debts and liabilities of partnership have been paid is a condition precedent to plaintiff's right to maintain an action at law on the convenant of the general partners to protect plaintiff from loss on his capital contribution. Herrick v Guild (1939) 257 A.D. 341, 13 N.Y.S.2d 115

Under the above statute, a limited partner who is entitled under the partnership agreement to a return of the securities contributed by him to the firm capital upon tendering cash in lieu thereof, is not entitled to enforce such agreement so long as creditors who are not partners have not been paid in full and the partnership assets are insufficient to discharge the liabilities to such creditors. Nexsen v New York Stock Exchange (1965, 2d Dept) 24 A.D.2d 514, 261 N.Y.S.2d 780

In an action for specific performance of an agreement providing that general partners would repurchase all or any part of the interest of limited partners, the complaint was insufficient in the absence of allegations that all liabilities of the partnership, other than those owed to general and limited partners on account of their contributions, had been paid or that there remained sufficient property of the partnership to pay them in the event plaintiffs were granted relief. Stern v Low (1967, 2d Dept) 27 A.D.2d 756, 277 N.Y.S.2d 756

Subdivision (4) of section 106 of the Partnership Law, which provides that a limited partner is liable to a partnership for the return to him of any sum not in excess of his capital contribution with interest, necessary to discharge its liabilities to all creditors whose claims arose before the return of such contribution is an independent remedy, not merely a remedy for the violation of section 105 (subd [1], par [a]) of the Partnership Law, which precludes a limited partner from receiving any part of his contribution from a general partner until all liabilities of the partnership have been paid or there remains property of the partnership sufficient to pay them; moreover, although the liability of the limited partner runs to the limited partnership under the terms of section 106, creditors succeed to the equity thus established in the partnership. Accordingly, where a return of capital contribution to limited partners is affected by a direct distribution of stock in the acquiring corporation to the limited partners in exchange for their partnership interests, although section 105 would not, on its face, apply, since their contributions were not received from either the partnership or a general partner, subdivision (4) of section 106 provides a remedy for an unsatisfied judgment creditor of the partnership to recover against the limited partners to the extent of their returned capital contributions. Whitley v Klauber (1979, 1st Dept) 69 A.D.2d 99, 417 N.Y.S.2d 959, stay den (1979) 48 N.Y.2d 882 and affd (1980) 51 N.Y.2d 555, 435 N.Y.S.2d 568, 416 N.E.2d 569

Limited partners had a statutory right to a dissolution and winding up decree of a court and accordingly, such relief with respect to the winding up decree had to be granted, pursuant to N.Y. Partnership Law §§ 68, 99(1)(c), and 105(4)(a). Polner v Monchik Realty Co. (2005, Sup) 9 Misc 3d 755, 803 N.Y.S.2d 370

Successors to a limited partner's interest were not limited to the partner's initial investment, as the terms of the partnership agreement were controlling over statutory provisions and over the partnership certificate, and the agreement did not provide such a limitation, pursuant to N.Y. Partnership Law § 105(2) and 112(2); accordingly, a summary judgment motion by other partners, seeking to limit the amount that the limited partners could recoup on the initial investment, was denied. Polner v Monchik Realty Co. (2005, Sup) 9 Misc 3d 755, 803 N.Y.S.2d 370

Notes given upon dissolution or termination to a special partner do not constitute a withdrawal of capital. George v Carpenter (1893) 73 Hun 221, 25 N.Y.S. 1086, affd (1895) 147 N.Y. 686, 42 N.E. 723

§ 106. Liability of limited partner to partnership

(1) A limited partner is liable to the partnership

(a) For the difference between his contribution as actually made and that stated in the certificate as having been made, and

(b) For any unpaid contributions which he agreed in the certificate to make in the future at the time and on the conditions stated in the certificate.

(2) A limited partner holds as trustee for the partnership

(a) Specific property stated in the certificate as contributed by him, but which was not contributed or which has been wrongfully returned, and

(b) Money or other property wrongfully paid or conveyed to him on account of his contribution.

(3) The liabilities of a limited partner as set forth in this section can be waived or compromised only by the consent of all members; but a waiver or compromise shall not affect the right of a creditor of a partnership, who extended credit or whose claim arose after the filing and before a cancellation or amendment of the certificate, to enforce such liabilities.

(4) When a contributor has rightfully received the return in whole or in part of the capital of his contribution, he is nevertheless liable to the partnership for any sum, not in excess of such return with interest, necessary to discharge its liabilities to all creditors who extended credit or whose claims arose before such return.

History: Add, L 1922, ch 640, § 1, eff April 13, 1922.

CASE ANNOTATIONS

Members of either general or limited partnership, as between themselves, may include in partnership articles any agreement they wish for sharing of profits and losses, priorities of distribution on winding up of partnership affairs and other matters, in absence of prohibitory provisions of statutes, common law rules, or considerations of public policy, and agreement so controls, if complete, as between partners. Lanier v Bowdoin (1939) 282 N.Y. 32, 24 N.E.2d 732, reh den (1940) 282 N.Y. 611, 25 N.E.2d 391

Managing or general partner of limited partnership is bound in fiduciary relationship with limited partners, and latter are therefore cestuis que trustent. Riviera Congress Associates v Yassky (1966) 18 N.Y.2d 540, 277 N.Y.S.2d 386, 223 N.E.2d 876 (superseded by statute as stated in Koppel v 4987 Corp. (1999, SD NY) CCH Fed Secur L Rep P 90640)

Limited partner only incurs limited liability and is only permitted limited, if any, voice in administration of partnership. Sloan v Clark (1966) 18 N.Y.2d 570, 277 N.Y.S.2d 411, 223 N.E.2d 893

In an action by an unsatisfied judgment creditor of a former limited partnership against the former limited partners, the limited partners were responsible to the judgment creditor to the extent of their capital contributions that were withdrawn where, as part of the plan to dispose of the assets of the limited partnership, all of the general and limited partners sold their interests in the partnership to a corporation in exchange for stock of the purchaser's parent corporation and, in so doing, received a return on their partnership capital within the meaning of Partn Law § 106(4). Whitley v Klauber (1980) 51 N.Y.2d 555, 435 N.Y.S.2d 568, 416 N.E.2d 569

Plaintiff creditor who pursued available remedies against both a judgment debtor partnership and its sole general partner, a corporation, and cannot satisfy the judgment thereby procured against either, may seek equitable relief against the limited partners of the partnership, pursuant to subdivision (4) of section 106 of the Partnership Law, to the extent of capital contributions returned to them, where the claim arose prior to such return. Accordingly, plaintiff creditor need not first proceed against individual stockholders of the corporate general partner, which proceeding would require proof sufficient to warrant piercing the corporate veil of the general partner, where no basis for such an action appears, or against the general manager of the partnership, since the statutory provision does not so restrict the liability of limited partners; nor is plaintiff precluded by the fact that he pursued his remedy against the corporation which bought all of the partners' interests in the partnership after the claim arose, and recovered a portion of the amount owing to him in that corporation's bankruptcy proceeding. Whitley v Klauber (1979, 1st Dept) 69 A.D.2d 99, 417 N.Y.S.2d 959, stay den (1979) 48 N.Y.2d 882 and affd (1980) 51 N.Y.2d 555, 435 N.Y.S.2d 568, 416 N.E.2d 569

Where it is clear that limited partners received what was, to all intents and purposes, a return of their capital contribution as a result of the acquisition of the partnership by a third-party corporation and where plaintiff's entitlement to a finder's fee and the limited partnership's liability for such fee, which arose prior to the acquisition, have already been established in prior litigation between plaintiff, the partnership and its general partner, considerations as to whether acquisition of the partnership was with a fraudulent purpose are not relevant to the issue of the limited partners' liability to the unsatisfied judgment creditor of the partnership, to the extent of the capital contributions returned, under subdivision (4) of section 106 of the Partnership Law; nor does the fact that the limited partners received a return of their original investment directly from the acquiring corporation in the form of stock in that corporation, in lieu of formal disposition from the partnership, change the nature of the payment to the limited partners or enable them to avoid their liability to judgment creditors of the partnership. Whitley v Klauber (1979, 1st Dept) 69 A.D.2d 99, 417 N.Y.S.2d 959, stay den (1979) 48 N.Y.2d 882 and affd (1980) 51 N.Y.2d 555, 435 N.Y.S.2d 568, 416 N.E.2d 569

Subdivision (4) of section 106 of the Partnership Law, which provides that a limited partner is liable to a partnership for the return to him of any sum not in excess of his capital contribution with interest, necessary to discharge its liabilities to all creditors whose claims arose before the return of such contribution is an independent remedy, not merely a remedy for the violation of section 105 (subd [1], par [a]) of the Partnership Law, which precludes a limited partner from receiving any part of his contribution from a general partner until all liabilities of the partnership have been paid or there remains property of the partnership sufficient to pay them; moreover, although the liability of the limited partner runs to the limited partnership under the terms of section 106, creditors succeed to the equity thus established in the partnership. Accordingly, where a return of capital contribution to limited partners is affected by a direct distribution of stock in the acquiring corporation to the limited partners in exchange for their partnership interests, although section 105 would not, on its face, apply, since their contributions were not received from either the partnership or a general partner, subdivision (4) of section 106 provides a remedy for an unsatisfied judgment creditor of the partnership to recover against the limited partners to the extent of their returned capital contributions. Whitley v Klauber (1979, 1st Dept) 69 A.D.2d 99, 417 N.Y.S.2d 959, stay den (1979) 48 N.Y.2d 882 and affd (1980) 51 N.Y.2d 555, 435 N.Y.S.2d 568, 416 N.E.2d 569

Plaintiff was entitled to summary judgment as to defendant's liability to contribute 1/2 of judgment already paid by plaintiff on his behalf in light of prior judicial finding in underlying action that defendant was jointly and severally liable with plaintiff for debt of their defunct limited partnership; defendant could not claim that he was liable only to extent of his interest in limited partnerships where he had admitted personal liability and had jointly exercised control with plaintiff over partnerships' property. Sonnenfeldt v Kyriakoudes (1996, 1st Dept) 226 A.D.2d 286, 641 N.Y.S.2d 289

Plaintiff was entitled to summary judgment as to defendant's liability to contribute 1/2 of judgment already paid by plaintiff on his behalf in light of prior judicial finding in underlying action that defendant was jointly and severally liable with plaintiff for debt of their defunct limited partnership; defendant could not claim that he was liable only to extent of his interest in limited partnerships where he had admitted personal liability and had jointly exercised control with plaintiff over partnerships' property. Sonnenfeldt v Kyriakoudes (1996, 1st Dept) 226 A.D.2d 286, 641 N.Y.S.2d 289

Special proceeding under CLS CPLR § 5227 was summarily dismissed as against limited partners of debtor partnership due to lack of competent evidence that they actually owed any debt to partnership, where petitioner sought to compel general and limited partners to pay over funds "owed" to partnership in amount of negative balance in each of their capital accounts as reflected in partnership's federal partnership return (Form 1065) and partners' K-2 schedules, but it appeared that deficit reflected in Form 1065 and K-2 schedules resulted from net loss for tax year, and petitioner submitted no expert testimony or other aid in interpreting documents or evidence that otherwise would support inference that "paper" deficit in partners' capital accounts was caused by failure to make required capital contributions or withdrawal of contributions previously made. Trustco Bank NA v Strong (1999, 3d Dept) 261 A.D.2d 25, 699 N.Y.S.2d 805

Only the limited partnership, not one of its creditors, can institute an action against a limited partner for failure to make his agreed contribution to the capital of the partnership. Bell Sound Studios, Inc. v Enneagram Productions Co. (1962) 36 Misc. 2d 879, 234 N.Y.S.2d 12

§ 107.   Nature of interest in partnership

A limited partner's interest in the partnership is personal property.

History: Add, L 1922, ch 640, § 1, eff April 13, 1922.

CASE ANNOTATIONS

An interest in a limited partnership, even a partnership that deals solely in real estate, is personalty, not realty. Reiter v Greenberg (1968) 21 N.Y.2d 388, 288 N.Y.S.2d 57, 235 N.E.2d 118

Although limited partners, who were not liable as general partners, could not maintain an action against the partnership and the general partners for alleged rent due, their interest in the partnership constituted personal property and gave them a right to a formal accounting. Riviera Congress Associates v Yassky (1966, 1st Dept) 25 A.D.2d 291, 268 N.Y.S.2d 854, affd (1966) 18 N.Y.2d 540, 277 N.Y.S.2d 386, 223 N.E.2d 876 (superseded by statute as stated in Koppel v 4987 Corp. (1999, SD NY) CCH Fed Secur L Rep P 90640)

Interest of a deceased partner in limited partnership governed by L 1919 c 408, among whose assets are buildings and land, is interest in surplus of assets with right to accounting-a chose in action. It is intangible property subject to succession tax in state of his domicile. Blodgett v Silberman (1928) 277 US 1, 72 L Ed 749, 48 S Ct 410, 8 AFTR 10243

§ 108.   Assignment of interest

(1) A limited partner's interest is assignable.

(2) A substituted limited partner is a person admitted to all the rights of a limited partner who has died or has assigned his interest in a partnership.

(3) An assignee, who does not become a substituted limited partner, has no right to require any information or account of the partnership transactions or to inspect the partnership books; he is only entitled to receive the share of the profits or other compensation by way of income, or the return of his contribution, to which his assignor would otherwise be entitled.

(4) An assignee shall have the right to become a substituted limited partner if all the members, except the assignor, consent thereto or if the assignor, being thereunto empowered by the certificate, gives the assignee that right.

(5) An assignee becomes a substituted limited partner when the certificate is appropriately amended in accordance with section one hundred and fourteen of this article.

(6) The substituted limited partner has all the rights and powers, and is subject to all the restrictions and liabilities of his assignor, except those liabilities of which he was ignorant at the time he became a limited partner and which could not be ascertained from the certificate.

(7) The substitution of the assignee as a limited partner does not release the assignor from liability to the partnership under sections ninety-five and one hundred and six.

History: Add, L 1922, ch 640, § 1, eff April 13, 1922.

CASE ANNOTATIONS

The trial court properly granted a former wife, who was the receiver in sequestration of three limited partnerships in which her former husband had an interest, access to the books, records and accounts of these limited partnerships in order for her to determine their financial condition, where the former husband had failed to make the required alimony and child support payments and the wife had obtained a substantial judgment against him. Klein v Klein (1981, 1st Dept) 81 A.D.2d 775, 439 N.Y.S.2d 1

Plaintiff who purchased partner's right to receive distributions and losses from partnership business could not maintain action against partnership or partners for alleged conflict of interest, breach of fiduciary duty, and breach of alleged obligation to refinance mortgage on partnership property within specified time, since (1) decision to refinance mortgage involved business judgment, to be exercised within procedures set forth in partnership agreement, (2) partnership and participation agreements specifically disclaimed extension of fiduciary obligations beyond partners or parties substituted for partners pursuant to procedures set forth in partnership agreement, and (3) complaint did not allege fraud; under participation agreement, partners' liability was limited to gross negligence or willful misconduct, and participant could not convey greater rights to plaintiff than he himself possessed. Levine v Murray Hill Manor Co. (1988, 1st Dept) 143 A.D.2d 298, 532 N.Y.S.2d 130, app dismd without op (1989) 73 N.Y.2d 995, 540 N.Y.S.2d 1006, 538 N.E.2d 358

In action to recover interest on sums awarded by Surrogate's Court pursuant to stipulation of settlement, defendant was entitled to

Partnership Law

summary judgment to extent of dismissing complaint except for cause of action asserted on behalf of plaintiff individually, where original action was commenced by plaintiff individually and as representative of certain limited partnerships, plaintiff had assigned his interest in partnerships to trust before commencing action for interest, and there was nothing to suggest that trust became substituted limited partner in subject partnerships; thus, neither plaintiff individually nor trust he created could act for partnerships and bring action to recover interest on their behalf. Cohen v Estate of Cohen (1997, 2d Dept) 242 A.D.2d 358, 661 N.Y.S.2d 1002

Provisions of partnership agreement prohibiting limited partner from substituting assignee "as contributor in her place" did not apply to assignment of loan indebtedness, as distinguished from limited partner's right to assign her claim for contributions made to the partnership capital. Myerson v Lampl (1959) 19 Misc. 2d 206, 191 N.Y.S.2d 599

A certificate of amendment of a limited partnership certificate is not required to be executed by a retired general partner. 1962 Ops Atty Gen May 28

§ 109. Effect of retirement, death or insanity of a general partner

The retirement, death or insanity of a general partner dissolves the partnership, unless the business is continued by the remaining general partners

(a) Under a right so to do stated in the certificate, or,

(b) With the consent of all members.

History: Add, L 1922, ch 640, § 1, eff April 13, 1922.

§ 110. Death of limited partner

(1) On the death of a limited partner his executor or administrator shall have all the rights of a limited partner for the purpose of settling his estate, and such power as the deceased had to constitute his assignee a substituted limited partner.

(2) The estate of a deceased limited partner shall be liable for all his liabilities as a limited partner.

History: Add, L 1922, ch 640, § 1, eff April 13, 1922, with substance transferred from § 41.

Former § 110, add, L 1919, ch 408; renumbered § 125, L 1922, ch 640, § 2.

CASE ANNOTATIONS

Insured partnership may not use CLS Partn Law § 110 to defeat diversity jurisdiction in recovery action by Pennsylvania insurer, where Pennsylvania limited partner died prior to commencement of insured's action, because that statute only gives partner's estate those rights of limited partner for purpose of settling his estate United Nat'l Ins. Co. v Waterfront N.Y. Realty Corp. (1995, SD NY) 907 F. Supp. 663, amd on other grounds, summary judgment gr, in part, motion den (1996, SD NY) 948 F. Supp. 263

§ 111. Rights of creditors of limited partner

(1) On due application to a court of competent jurisdiction by any judgment creditor of a limited partner, the court may charge the interest of the indebted limited partner with payment of the unsatisfied amount of the judgment debt; and may appoint a receiver, and make all other orders, directions, and inquiries which the circumstances of the case may require.

(2) The interest may be redeemed with the separate property of any general partner, but may not be redeemed with partnership property.

(3) The remedies conferred by subdivision one of this section shall not be deemed exclusive of others which may exist.

(4) Nothing in this act shall be held to deprive a limited partner of his statutory exemption.

History: Add, L 1922, ch 640, § 1, eff April 13, 1922.

Former § 111, add, L 1919, ch 408; renumbered § 126, L 1922, ch 640, § 2.

CASE ANNOTATIONS

The trial court properly granted a former wife, who was the receiver in sequestration of three limited partnerships in which her former husband had an interest, access to the books, records and accounts of these limited partnerships in order for her to determine their financial condition, where the former husband had failed to make the required alimony and child support payments and the wife had obtained a substantial judgment against him. Klein v Klein (1981, 1st Dept) 81 A.D.2d 775, 439 N.Y.S.2d 1

Although property of a partnership is not subject to attachment or execution except as a claim against a partnership, a judgment creditor of any general or limited partner has the statutory right to obtain an order charging his debtor's interest in the partnership with payment of the unsatisfied amount of judgment with interest thereon. Central Petroleum Corp. v Korman (1958) 15 Misc. 2d 245, 177 N.Y.S.2d 761, app dismd (1959, 1st Dept) 8 A.D.2d 782, 190 N.Y.S.2d 314

Defendants were denied summary judgment in an action by judgment creditors of the general partners of a limited partnership to set aside as fraudulent and void, a conveyance by the limited partnership to a corporation shortly prior to the entry of judgment against the general partners. The record made out prima facie case for a decree directing transfer of title to the limited partnership and defendants failed to establish by documentary evidence that the judgment creditors were not entitled to recover. Central Petroleum Corp. v Korman (1958) 15 Misc. 2d 245, 177 N.Y.S.2d 761, app dismd (1959, 1st Dept) 8 A.D.2d 782, 190 N.Y.S.2d 314

§ 112. Distribution of assets

(1) In settling accounts after dissolution the liabilities of the partnership shall be entitled to payment in the following order:

(a) Those to creditors, in the order of priority as provided by law, except those to limited partners on account of their contributions, and to general partners.

(b) Those to limited partners in respect to their share of the profits and other compensation by way of income on their contributions.

(c) Those to limited partners in respect to the capital of their contributions.

(d) Those to general partners other than for capital and profits.

(e) Those to general partners in respect to profits.

(f) Those to general partners in respect to capital.

(2) Subject to any statement in the certificate or to subsequent agreement, limited partners share in the partnership assets in respect to their claims for capital, and in respect to their claims for profits or for compensation by way of income on their contributions respectively, in proportion to the respective amounts of such claims.

History: Add, L 1922, ch 640, § 1, eff April 13, 1922, with substance transferred from § 42.

CASE ANNOTATIONS

Claims of creditors shall have priority over those of special partners for capital contributions, though claims of special partners are to have priority over those of their associates. Kittredge v Langley (1930) 252 N.Y. 405, 169 N.E. 626, 67 ALR 1087, reh den (1930) 253 N.Y. 555, 171 N.E. 780

In the absence of prohibitory provisions of statutes or rules of the common law relating to partnerships or considerations of public policy the partners of either a general or limited partnership, as between themselves, may include in the partnership articles any agreement they wish concerning the sharing of profits and losses, priorities of distribution on winding up of the partnership affairs and other matters. If complete, as between the parties, an agreement so made controls. Lanier v Bowdoin (1939) 282 N.Y. 32, 24 N.E.2d 732, reh den (1940) 282 N.Y. 611, 25 N.E.2d 391

Although limited partners are creditors of the partnership, under § 112 of the Partnership Law, their rights are subordinate to those of the partnership's general creditors. Sloan v Clark (1966) 18 N.Y.2d 570, 277 N.Y.S.2d 411, 223 N.E.2d 893

Allegation that debts and liabilities of partnership have been paid is a condition precedent to plaintiff's right to maintain an action at law on the covenant of the general partners to protect plaintiff from loss on his capital contribution. Herrick v Guild (1939) 257 A.D. 341, 13 N.Y.S.2d 115

Under §§ 102 and 105 and the above statute, a limited partner is not entitled to payment either on account of his capital contribution, as a return thereon or as a creditor, before creditors who are not partners are paid in full or until full payment to them is assured. Nexsen v New York Stock Exchange (1965, 2d Dept) 24 A.D.2d 514, 261 N.Y.S.2d 780

In the absence of an agreement to the contrary, it was error to award interest on partnership account from date of receivership rather than from date of judgment of dissolution only. Berkovits v Hanley (1972, 3d Dept) 40 A.D.2d 921, 338 N.Y.S.2d 339

Determination as to net worth of limited partnership was properly based on receiver's report which, although not completely accurate, was the only competent evidence of net worth, and was inaccurate due to defendant partner's failure to co-operate in computing net worth. Berkovits v Hanley (1972, 3d Dept) 40 A.D.2d 921, 338 N.Y.S.2d 339

Where an agreement provided that if the partnership was not renewed the partners were to recover back the assets originally contributed, the partner contributing the least premises was entitled to possession and he notified his partner that the agreement would not be renewed. Pierce v De Rothermann (1948, Sup) 82 N.Y.S.2d 837

Successors to a limited partner's interest were not limited to the partner's initial investment, as the terms of the partnership agreement were controlling over statutory provisions and over the partnership certificate, and the agreement did not provide such a limitation, pursuant to N.Y. Partnership Law § 105(2) and 112(2); accordingly, a summary judgment motion by other partners, seeking to limit the amount that the limited partners could recoup on the initial investment, was denied. Polner v Monchik Realty Co. (2005, Sup) 9 Misc 3d 755, 803 N.Y.S.2d 370

A New York limited partnership resembles sufficiently the nature of a corporation so that limited partners may be considered stockholders or members within § 44(a) of the Bankruptcy Act, and as such ineligible to vote for a trustee. In re Ira Haupt & Co. (1965, CA2 NY) 343 F.2d 726, cert den (1965) 382 US 890, 15 L Ed 2d 148, 86 S Ct 182

Although in some respects a limited partner does have some resemblance to a creditor of the partnership, in the main, a limited partner is more like a shareholder. Klebanow v New York Produce Exchange (1965, CA2 NY) 344 F.2d 294, 1965 CCH Trade Cases P 71413, 9 FR Serv 2d 17B.3, Case 1 (superseded by statute as stated in Koppel v 4987 Corp. (1999, SD NY) CCH Fed Secur L Rep P 90640)

§ 113.   Certificate cancelled or amended

(1) The certificate shall be cancelled when the partnership is dissolved or all limited partners cease to be such.

(2) A certificate shall be amended when

(a) There is a change in the name of the partnership or in the amount or character of the contribution of any limited partner,

(b) A person is substituted as a limited partner,

(c) An additional limited partner is admitted,

(d) A person is admitted as a general partner,

(e) A general partner retires, dies or becomes mentally ill, and the business is continued under section one hundred and nine,

(f) There is a change in the character of the business of the partnership, or a change in the location of the principal place of business,

(g) There is a false or erroneous statement in the certificate,

(h) There is a change in the time as stated in the certificate for the dissolution of the partnership or for the return of a contribution,

(i) A time is fixed for the dissolution of the partnership, or the return of a contribution, no time having been specified in the certificate, or,

(j) The members desire to make a change in any other statement in the certificate in order that it shall accurately represent the agreement between them.

History: Add, L 1922, ch 640, § 1, eff April 13, 1922.

Sub (2), amd, L 1947, ch 316, § 1, eff Sept 1, 1947.

Sub (2), par (e), amd, L 1978, ch 550, § 36, eff July 24, 1978.

CASE ANNOTATIONS

Successor general partner of limited partnership was duly qualified to act on behalf of partnership where partnership agreement granted power of attorney to "the General Partner, or any successor individual General Partner," and amendment to certificate of partnership was signed by successor as attorney-in-fact for limited partners, although not signed by withdrawing general partner or any limited partners; successor gained legal status as general partner when limited partners voted him in, not when amended certificate was filed, and thus had power of attorney under partnership agreement to execute amended certificate. Marsh v Brady (1991, Sup) 152 Misc. 2d 990, 579 N.Y.S.2d 813

A limited partnership may become a general partner in a general partnership. The partnership with which the limited partnership becomes associated must in its certificate reflect the addition of the limited partnership as a partner. This amended certificate must be executed and acknowledged by the members of the limited partnership; however, a limited partner may designate one of the limited partnerships general partners to execute the amended certificate on his behalf. Ops Atty Gen 84-54

§ 114.   Requirements for amendment or cancellation

(1) The writing to amend a certificate shall

(a) Conform to the requirements of subdivision one-a of section ninety-one of this article, as far as necessary to set forth clearly the change in the certificate which it is desired to make, and

(b) Be signed and acknowledged or sworn to by all members, except that a writing making a change in the statement of the place of residence of any member shall be signed and acknowledged by such member

Partnership Law

only. An amendment substituting a limited partner or adding a limited or general partner shall be signed also by the member to be substituted or added, and when a limited partner is to be substituted, the amendment shall also be signed by the assigning limited partner.

(2) The writing to cancel a certificate shall be signed by all members.

(3) A person desiring the cancellation or amendment of a certificate, if any person designated in subdivisions one and two of this section as a person who must execute the writing refuses to do so, may petition the supreme court to direct a cancellation or amendment thereof.

(4) If the court finds that the petitioner has a right to have the writing executed by a person who refuses to do so, it shall order the county clerk of the county where the certificate is filed to file the cancellation or amendment of the certificate; and where the certificate is to be amended, the court shall also cause to be filed in said office a certified copy of its decree setting forth the amendment.

(5) A certificate is amended or cancelled when there is filed in the office of the county clerk where the certificate is filed. [:] *

(a) A writing in accordance with the provisions of subdivisions one and two of this section, or,

(b) A certified copy of the order of court in accordance with the provisions of subdivision four thereof

Provided, however, that in the case of an amendment made where there is a change to another county of the location of the principal place of business, a certificate is not amended until a certified copy of the certificate and certified copies of all writings or certified copies of orders amending the certificate are also filed in the office of the county clerk of the county to which the location of the principal place of business is changed.

* The bracketed punctuation has been inserted by the Publisher.

(6) After the certificate is duly amended in accordance with this section, the amended certificate shall thereafter be for all purposes the certificate provided for by this article, and when the certificate has been amended by reason of a change to another county of the location of the principal place of business, the county in which a certified copy of the amended certificate was last filed shall thereafter be deemed to be the county where the certificate is filed.

History: Add, L 1922, ch 640, § 1; amd, L 1939, ch 580, § 3, L 1947, ch 316, § 2, eff Sept 1, 1947.

Sub 4, amd, L 1948, ch 712, § 3, eff July 1, 1948.

Sub 5, amd, L 1948, ch 712, § 3, eff July 1, 1948.

Sub 6, amd, L 1948, ch 712, § 3, eff July 1, 1948.

CASE ANNOTATIONS

Successor general partner of limited partnership was duly qualified to act on behalf of partnership where partnership agreement granted power of attorney to "the General Partner, or any successor individual General Partner," and amendment to certificate of partnership was signed by successor as attorney-in-fact for limited partners, although not signed by withdrawing general partner or any limited partners; successor gained legal status as general partner when limited partners voted him in, not when amended certificate was filed, and thus had power of attorney under partnership agreement to execute amended certificate. Marsh v Brady (1991, Sup) 152 Misc. 2d 990, 579 N.Y.S.2d 813

A certificate of amendment of the articles of a limited partnership, upon withdrawal of a limited partner, must be executed by all partners including the withdrawing partner. 1961 Ops Atty Gen Feb 2

Publication of certificate of limited partnership pursuant to section 91(1)(b) of Partnership Law must be completed prior to limited partnership doing business. Section 114 of Partnership Law does not require publication of certificate of amendment or cancellation of limited partnership. 1978 Op Atty Gen Nov 13

A general partnership may engage only in the business authorized by the partnership agreement. A limited partnership may engage only in the business authorized by the certificate filed under section 91 of the Partnership Law. A limited partnership may become a general partner in a new limited partnership. 1980 Op Atty Gen Oct. 28 (informal)

An amendment or cancellation of a limited partnership certificate need not be published. 1981 Op Atty Gen May 1 (informal)

§ 115. Parties to actions

A contributor, unless he is a general partner, is not a proper party to proceedings by or against a partnership, except where the object is to enforce a limited partner's right against or liability to the partnership, and except in cases provided for in section one hundred fifteen-a of this article.

History: Add, L 1922, ch 640, § 1, with substance transferred from § 38; amd, L 1968, ch 496, § 2, eff June 5, 1968.

CASE ANNOTATIONS

1. In general
2. Jurisdiction
3. Derivative actions

1. In general

For the purposes of pleading, there is good reason for regarding a limited partnership as an entity distinct from its members. Limited partnerships are unknown to the common law and, like corporations, are creatures of statute. Statutes permitting limited partnerships are intended to encourage investment in business enterprise by affording to a limited partner a position analogous to that of a corporate shareholder. Hence, in a suit by a limited partnership, the individual partners, whether general or limited, ought not to be subject to counterclaims against them upon causes of action unrelated to partnership affairs. Ruzicka v Rager (1953) 305 N.Y. 191, 111 N.E.2d 878, 39 ALR2d 288, reh den (1953) 305 N.Y. 798, 113 N.E.2d 306

The purpose of this statute is solely to restrain limited partners from interfering with the rights of the general partners to carry on the business of the partnership. Riviera Congress Associates v Yassky (1966) 18 N.Y.2d 540, 277 N.Y.S.2d 386, 223 N.E.2d 876 (superseded by statute as stated in Koppel v 4987 Corp. (1999, SD NY) CCH Fed Secur L Rep P 90640)

Section 115 of the Partnership Law does not restrict or limit the rights enumerated in § 88 of that law. Millard v Newmark & Co. (1966, 1st Dept) 24 A.D.2d 333, 266 N.Y.S.2d 254

Although limited partners, who were not liable as general partners, could not maintain an action against the partnership and the general partners for alleged rent due, their interest in the partnership constituted personal property and gave them a right to a formal accounting. Riviera Congress Associates v Yassky (1966, 1st Dept) 25 A.D.2d 291, 268 N.Y.S.2d 854, affd (1966) 18 N.Y.2d 540, 277 N.Y.S.2d 386, 223 N.E.2d 876 (superseded by statute as stated in Koppel v 4987 Corp. (1999, SD NY) CCH Fed Secur L Rep P 90640)

Although a partnership may sue or be sued in the partnership name for purposes of pleading, a limited partner, unless he is also a general partner, is not a proper party to proceedings by or against a partnership, except where the object is to enforce a limited partner's right against or liability to the partnership; and when limited partners instituted suit in the partnership name as an entity, they assumed liability as general partners; and when they amended the caption of their action to sue as individuals in a class action, rather than as an entity, they insulated themselves from liability as general partners and could not therefore maintain the action. Riviera Congress Associates v Yassky (1966, 1st Dept) 25 A.D.2d 291, 268 N.Y.S.2d 854, affd (1966) 18 N.Y.2d 540, 277 N.Y.S.2d 386, 223 N.E.2d 876 (superseded by statute as stated in Koppel v 4987 Corp. (1999, SD NY) CCH Fed Secur L Rep P 90640)

In action which involved interpretation of partnership agreement and which sought accounting of partnership, defendants were entitled to joinder of limited partners, notwithstanding contention that such joinder would require inappropriate active participation by limited partners in affairs of partnership; dispute was not proceeding by or against partnership and was, instead, dispute over interpretation of rights and obligations under partnership agreement, and involvement of all general and limited partners was appropriate and necessary. TESCO Properties, Inc. v Troy Rehabilitation & Improv. Project, Inc. (1990, 3d Dept) 166 A.D.2d 839, 562 N.Y.S.2d 827

Limited partners lacked standing to assert individual or class action claims for breach of contract and breach of fiduciary duty against partnership, general partner, and entities controlling general partner, based on wrongful deferral of management fees and payment of such fees from proceeds of sale of partnership assets, where complaint alleged only derivative claims of mismanagement and diversion of assets and did not implicate any injury to limited partners distinct from harm to partnership. Broome v ML Media Opportunity Partners L.P. (2000, 1st Dept) 273 A.D.2d 63, 709 N.Y.S.2d 59

Limited partners had standing to sue general partner for breach of provision in partnership agreement requiring return of capital contributions to limited partners if those funds were not invested by April 1990. Broome v ML Media Opportunity Partners L.P. (2000, 1st Dept) 273 A.D.2d 63, 709 N.Y.S.2d 59

Plaintiffs failed to state cause of action against individual partners to recover security deposit on commercial lease where individual defendants were limited partners and thus could not be held liable for obligations of partnership absent allegation that they participated in control of business. Hajar, Inc. v One Peach Assocs. (2001, 2d Dept) 281 A.D.2d 592, 722 N.Y.S.2d 175

The owners of real estate condemned by the state, who formed a partnership, assigned their interest in the land to the partnership, and functioned as the general partners, were entitled to file claims in their individual names against the state, but those partners designated as investing partners, who were in a legal sense limited partners, were not proper parties to the claim and their inclusion as claimants would have been erroneous. The court also noted that the five general partners could have filed the claim in the partnership name, but were not required to do so since CPLR 1025 is permissive and not mandatory. Arlen of Nanuet, Inc. v State (1967) 52 Misc. 2d 1009, 277 N.Y.S.2d 560

Individual denominated "managing partner" was not proper party plaintiff, and action ostensibly commenced by limited partnership would be dismissed in absence of motion to amend, since defect was not mere misnomer where petition did not allege name of partnership or names of other partners; due process requires that real party in interest be named in caption or in other appropriate documents to protect one being sued from having to defend against same claim second time because someone else was owner of claim and therefore entitled to sue. Patel v MacArthur (1987, City Ct) 137 Misc. 2d 104, 519 N.Y.S.2d 769

Limited partners who were assessed by IRS for underpayment of taxes plus interest had standing to sue accounting firm, which had been hired exclusively by limited partnership itself to conduct annual audits and prepare partnership returns, for breach of duty owed directly to limited partners since relationship between parties was so close as to approach privity, in view of allegations regarding delivery of firm's letters and forms to limited partners. Ackerman v Price Waterhouse (1992, Sup) 156 Misc. 2d 865, 591 N.Y.S.2d 936, affd (1993, 1st Dept) 198 A.D.2d 1, 604 N.Y.S.2d 721, motion gr (1993, N.Y. A.D., 1st Dept) 1993 N.Y. A.D. LEXIS 11715, app gr (1994, NY) 1994 N.Y. LEXIS 433 and app gr (1994, 1st Dept) 200 A.D.2d 951, 608 N.Y.S.2d 69 and revd on other grounds (1994) 84 N.Y.2d 535, 620 N.Y.S.2d 318, 644 N.E.2d 1009, motion den (1995) 85 N.Y.2d 836, 624 N.Y.S.2d 364, 648 N.E.2d 783, subsequent app (1995, 1st Dept) 216 A.D.2d 123, 629 N.Y.S.2d 5, subsequent app (1998, 1st Dept) 252 A.D.2d 179, 683 N.Y.S.2d 179, motion den (1999, N.Y. A.D., 1st Dept) 1999 N.Y. A.D. LEXIS 1068 and related proceeding (2000, 1st Dept) 270 A.D.2d 150, 704 N.Y.S.2d 590

Limited partners of a New York partnership in dissolution can sue on its behalf for damages claimed to have been inflicted on it by conduct proscribed by federal anti-trust laws, when partnership and liquidating partner allegedly have rendered themselves unable to sue and their delegate is claimed to be unwilling to do so because of affiliations with defendants. Klebanow v New York Produce Exchange (1965, CA2 NY) 344 F.2d 294, 1965 CCH Trade Cases P 71413, 9 FR Serv 2d 17B.3, Case 1 (superseded by statute as stated in Koppel v 4987 Corp. (1999, SD NY) CCH Fed Secur L Rep P 90640)

2. Jurisdiction

The fact that a New York securities dealer partnership had a limited partner in Delaware would not defeat diversity jurisdiction in a suit against the partnership by a Delaware corporation, since under New York law a limited partner is not a proper party to a proceeding by or against a partnership, except where the object of the action is to enforce a limited partner's right against or liability to the partnership. Colonial Realty Corp. v Bache & Co. (1966, CA2 NY) 358 F.2d 178, cert den (1966) 385 US 817, 17 L Ed 2d 56, 87 S Ct 40 and (disapproved as stated in Curley v Brignoli, Curley & Roberts Assoc. (1990, CA2 NY) 915 F.2d 81, 17 FR Serv 3d 1460) and (criticized in Advanced Magnetics v Bayfront Partners (1996, SD NY) CCH Fed Secur L Rep P 99036)

Oklahoma resident who invested in limited partnership which was producing movies in New York did not by reason of such investment transact business in New York by reason of the fact that he became an agent of the corporation so as to subject him to personal jurisdiction of New York courts. Lynn v Cohen (1973, SD NY) 359 F. Supp. 565, 17 FR Serv 2d 1295, 30 ALR Fed 576 (criticized in Pilates, Inc. v Pilates Inst. (1995, SD NY) 891 F. Supp. 175)

Diversity jurisdiction of District Court is not defeated by citizenship of limited partner who is not proper party to proceeding by or against partnership. Gilbert Switzer & Associates v National Housing Partnership, Ltd. (1986, DC Conn) 641 F. Supp. 150

3. Derivative actions

A limited partner has no right to sue in a derivative capacity upon behalf of the partnership, and a limited partner does not become liable as a general partner unless he takes part in the control of the business. Millard v Newmark & Co. (1966, 1st Dept) 24 A.D.2d 333, 266 N.Y.S.2d 254

Plaintiff lacked standing to bring derivative action challenging defendant partnership's business decision to retain and compensate defendant law firm, despite characterizing himself as beneficiary of trust relationship in which defendants breached their fiduciary obligations to him, since he was bound by terms of his written "participation agreement," which strictly limited his rights to fixed share of net income generated by partnership arrangement (ordinary contractual obligation) and limited target of his legal remedies to named agent of partnership who transferred interest to him. Studley v Empire State Bldg. Assocs. (1998, 1st Dept) 249 A.D.2d 7, 670 N.Y.S.2d 839, app den (1998) 92 N.Y.2d 809, 678 N.Y.S.2d 595, 700 N.E.2d 1231 and related proceeding (2000, 1st Dept) 276 A.D.2d 350, 719 N.Y.S.2d 218, app den (2001) 96 N.Y.2d 710, 726 N.Y.S.2d 373, 750 N.E.2d 75

§ 115-a. Limited partners' derivative action brought in the right of a limited partnership to procure a judgment in its favor

1. An action may be brought in the right of a limited partnership to procure a judgment in its favor, by a limited partner, additional limited partner, or substituted limited partner.

2. In any such action, it shall be made to appear that at least one plaintiff is such a limited partner, additional limited partner or substituted limited partner at the time of bringing the action, and that he was such at the time of the transaction of which he complains, or that his status as substituted limited partner devolved upon him by operation of law or

Partnership Law

pursuant to the terms of the certificate of limited partnership or written partnership agreement in effect at the time of the transaction of which he complains.

3. In any such action, the complaint shall set forth with particularity the efforts of the plaintiff to secure the initiation of such action by the general partner or partners, or the reasons for not making such effort.

4. Such action shall not be discontinued, compromised or settled, without the approval of the court having jurisdiction of the action. If the court shall determine that the interests of the limited partners, additional limited partners or substituted limited partners, will be substantially affected by such discontinuance, compromise or settlement, the court, in its discretion, may direct that notice, by publication or otherwise, shall be given to the limited, additional or substituted limited partners whose interests it determines will be so affected; if notice is so directed to be given, the court may determine which one or more of the parties to the action shall bear the expense of giving the same, in such amount as the court shall determine and find to be reasonable in the circumstances, and the amount of such expense shall be awarded as special costs of the action and recoverable in the same manner as statutory taxable costs.

5. If the action on behalf of the limited partnership was successful, in whole or in part, or if anything was received by the plaintiff or plaintiffs or a claimant or claimants as a result of a judgment, compromise or settlement of an action or claim, the court may award the plaintiff or plaintiffs, claimant or claimants, reasonable expenses, including reasonable attorneys' fees, and shall direct him or them to account to the partnership for the remainder of the proceeds so received by him or them. This paragraph shall not apply to any judgment rendered for the benefit of injured limited, additional or substituted limited partners only and limited to a recovery of the loss or damage sustained by them.

History: Add L 1968, ch 496, § 3, eff June 5, 1968.

CASE ANNOTATIONS

1. In general
2. Direct action
3. Miscellaneous

1. In general

In action against limited partnership, asserted by plaintiff as class action on behalf of participants in partnership and their assignees, derivative causes of action against partnership and general partners should have been dismissed, since plaintiff lacked standing to sue on behalf of partnership because he was neither limited partner, additional partner, or substituted limited partner. Levine v Murray Hill Manor Co. (1988, 1st Dept) 143 A.D.2d 298, 532 N.Y.S.2d 130, app dismd without op (1989) 73 N.Y.2d 995, 540 N.Y.S.2d 1006, 538 N.E.2d 358

Plaintiff lacked standing to bring derivative action challenging defendant partnership's business decision to retain and compensate defendant law firm, despite characterizing himself as beneficiary of trust relationship in which defendants breached their fiduciary obligations to him, since he was bound by terms of his written "participation agreement," which strictly limited his rights to fixed

share of net income generated by partnership arrangement (ordinary contractual obligation) and limited target of his legal remedies to named agent of partnership who transferred interest to him. Studley v Empire State Bldg. Assocs. (1998, 1st Dept) 249 A.D.2d 7, 670 N.Y.S.2d 839, app den (1998) 92 N.Y.2d 809, 678 N.Y.S.2d 595, 700 N.E.2d 1231 and related proceeding (2000, 1st Dept) 276 A.D.2d 350, 719 N.Y.S.2d 218, app den (2001) 96 N.Y.2d 710, 726 N.Y.S.2d 373, 750 N.E.2d 75

As a matter of law, a limited partner does not individually have a cause of action at law to recover for the loss of his partnership investment resulting from the acts of his general partners. Blattberg v Weiss (1969) 61 Misc. 2d 564, 306 N.Y.S.2d 88

Where the cause of action is derivative, limited partners must bring suit pursuant to the Partnership Law and may not bring a class action and although the word "may" appears in the statute, the Legislature's intent was not to allow limited partners a choice between the two types of action but was to give limited partners the procedural right to bring a derivative action, which right had not been available before. Alpert v Haimes (1970) 64 Misc. 2d 608, 315 N.Y.S.2d 332

Party to action other than a governmental unit must be an actual person or corporation except as provided specifically by law for partnerships and unincorporated associations. Little Shoppe Around the Corner v Carl (1975) 80 Misc. 2d 717, 363 N.Y.S.2d 784

In order for limited partner to be able to maintain action on behalf of the general partnership, the limited partner need not show that general partners' refusal to initiate the action was improper or that there was a general concensus among the partners that the action should be brought or that the general partners actually consent thereto or are unable to bring the action. Wien v Chelsea Theater Center (1977) 91 Misc. 2d 226, 397 N.Y.S.2d 865, 1979, 96 BNA LRRM 2330, 1979-1 CCH Trade Cases P 62626, revd on other grounds (1978, 1st Dept) 66 A.D.2d 741, 411 N.Y.S.2d 316, 101 BNA LRRM 2206, 86 CCH LC P 11505, app dismd (1979) 47 N.Y.2d 763, 417 N.Y.S.2d 465, 391 N.E.2d 301, 103 BNA LRRM 2306

2. Direct action

In limited partners' action under CLS Partn § 115-a, particular cause of action which asserted direct, rather than derivative, action would be dismissed since complaint showed that partners actually sought to recover funds belonging to limited partnership in which they were limited partners, which was derivative action despite some language in complaint stating otherwise. Re v Weksel (1987, 2d Dept) 130 A.D.2d 640, 515 N.Y.S.2d 568, app den (1988) 71 N.Y.2d 803, 527 N.Y.S.2d 769, 522 N.E.2d 1068

Partnership Law § 115-a applies only to limited partners' derivative suits; since complaint on its face, to extent it alleges claims in name of partnership, appears to have been brought by partnership itself, § 115-a does not apply. Navigator Group Funds v Shearson Hayden Stone, Inc. (1980, SD NY) 487 F. Supp. 416

3. Miscellaneous

It was proper for partial remaindermen of two trusts to commence a proceeding in the Surrogate's Court to remove trustees for alleged violations of fiduciary duty and to seek an assessment of damages for alleged diversion or waste of trust assets against general partners of a limited partnership in which the trust had a 50 percent limited partnership interest. Even though the Surrogate's Court is a court of limited jurisdiction, allegations relating to impairment of the value of the trust corpus by waste and diversion of partnership assets, and the failure of the trustees to sue on the behalf of the trust, formed a sufficient nexus to the operation of the partnership to justify jurisdiction by the Surrogate's Court over the entire matter, including management of the partnership. In re Estate of Brandt (1981, 1st Dept) 81 A.D.2d 268, 440 N.Y.S.2d 189

In a derivation action under § 115-a, surrogate may submit defendant's supplement proposal to partners over objection of representative plaintiff where there is indication that plaintiff has some personal stake in outcome of litigation going beyond representation of partnership, and may approve proposed settlement where most responses received are favorable and hearing is ordered to give objectors opportunity to show cause why proposal should not be approved. Cohen v Reed (1986, 2d Dept) 120 A.D.2d 480, 501 N.Y.S.2d 685, app dismd without op (1986) 68 N.Y.2d 807 and app dismd without op (1987) 69 N.Y.2d 1038, 517 N.Y.S.2d 1031, 511 N.E.2d 90 and app dismd (1987) 70 N.Y.2d 899, 524 N.Y.S.2d 427, 519 N.E.2d 338 and app den (1989) 74 N.Y.2d 614, 547 N.Y.S.2d 848, 547 N.E.2d 103 and cert den (1990) 494 US 1031, 108 L Ed 2d 618, 110 S Ct 1481

Individual plaintiffs, as limited partners of first partnership, had standing to bring action on behalf of second partnership where, at time transactions complained of occurred, first partnership itself was limited partner of second partnership, and thus was vested with authority under CLS Partn § 155-a(1) to bring derivative action on behalf of second partnership for loss of its assets due to acts of second partnership's general partner. Franco v English (1994, 3d Dept) 210 A.D.2d 630, 620 N.Y.S.2d 156

In action to recover interest on sums awarded by Surrogate's Court pursuant to stipulation of settlement, defendant was entitled to summary judgment to extent of dismissing complaint except for cause of action asserted on behalf of plaintiff individually, where original action was commenced by plaintiff individually and as representative of certain limited partnerships, plaintiff had assigned his interest in partnerships to trust before commencing action for interest, and there was nothing to suggest that trust became substituted limited partner in subject partnerships; thus, neither plaintiff individually nor trust he created could act for partnerships and bring action to recover interest on their behalf. Cohen v Estate of Cohen (1997, 2d Dept) 242 A.D.2d 358, 661 N.Y.S.2d 1002

As a limited partner's rights and interests in litigation involving, inter alia, an option agreement were derivative under N.Y. Partnership Law §§ 115-a, 121-1002, the partner could not claim that it was not bound by a forum selection clause because it was not a signatory to the option agreement. Harry Casper, Inc. v Pines Assoc., L.P. (2008, 3d Dept) 53 App Div 3d 764, 861 NYS2d 820.

By alleging money due and owing the partnership pursuant to a leasing agreement and failure by a limited partner to complete payment to the partnership of his capital contribution under the terms of the partnership agreement, the defendants' obligations run directly to the partnership and not to the limited partners and as such are derivative in nature and being derivative actions, the limited partners have failed to allege sufficient facts to state a cause of action. Alpert v Haimes (1970) 64 Misc. 2d 608, 315 N.Y.S.2d 332

Settlement of attorney's fees which reduced by 10 percent the amount originally due from limited partnership under contingent fee contract for representation of general partners in their action against limited partners was approved where efforts of counsel were successful, and award obtained for client was largest sum ever awarded in commercial case administered by American Arbitration Association, and such fee was not required to be reduced by extent of limited partners' interests as both "debtors" and "creditors". Rodgers v Sound of Music Co. (1972) 74 Misc. 2d 699, 343 N.Y.S.2d 672

Although Partnership Law § 115-a sets forth no standard for passing on proposed settlement of derivative actions, eight guiding principles evolve from a study of the authorities: (1) The benefits in the agreement of settlement, as against the likelihood of recovery after trial; (2) the general rule that courts favor settlements; (3) whether sharply contested and dubious issues are present, the determination of which would be obviated by the settlement; (4) the expense of going to trial; (5) the likelihood of success at the trial; (6) whether the settlement is the result of good faith negotiation at arms' length, or of collusion, chicanery, fraud; (7) the position of the parties to the litigation concerning the settlement; the opposition, if any, to the settlement; (8) whether in the court's judgment, the settlement is fair and reasonable under all the circumstances. Rodgers v Sound of Music Co. (1972) 74 Misc. 2d 699, 343 N.Y.S.2d 672

Complaint which alleged that limited partner had demanded in writing that general partner institute suit against union and had been advised in writing of the general partner's refusal to take such action was sufficient to show that limited partner had taken action to secure the initiation of the action by the general partner and thus to give the limited partner standing to maintain the action on behalf of the partnership. Wien v Chelsea Theater Center (1977) 91 Misc. 2d 226, 397 N.Y.S.2d 865, 1979, 96 BNA LRRM 2330, 1979-1 CCH Trade Cases P 62626, revd on other grounds (1978, 1st Dept) 66 A.D.2d 741, 411 N.Y.S.2d 316, 101 BNA LRRM 2206, 86 CCH LC P 11505, app dismd (1979) 47 N.Y.2d 763, 417 N.Y.S.2d 465, 391 N.E.2d 301, 103 BNA LRRM 2306

Plaintiff, limited partner in both partnership formed to develop urban renewal site and limited partnership set up by original partnership to build luxury townhouses on site, was not entitled to attorneys' fees in derivative action against general partners alleging that they arranged loan by original partnership to townhouse partnership in order to avert default and thus to avoid liability on their personal guarantees, since repayment of loan by townhouse partnership rendered plaintiff's action moot, and therefore not "successful" as required for recovery of attorneys' fees under CLS Partn § 115-a(5). Site 35 Redevelopment Assoc. No. 1 v Kretchmer (1989, Sup) 148 Misc. 2d 89, 559 N.Y.S.2d 911

Complaint brought by a former limited liability company (LLC) member asserting self-dealing and other claims against the remaining members was dismissed since the former member lacked standing to bring suit due to no longer being a member. Further, the complaint asserted harm to the detriment of the LLC, not individual harm and was, therefore, derivative in nature. Billings v Bridgepoint Partners, LLC (2008, Sup) 21 Misc 3d 535, 240 NYLJ 66, 863 NYS2d 591.

Trial court erred in granting defendants' summary judgment motion as to a claim brought by the limited partners on behalf of the partnership, that the general partners wrongfully allowed their business to remain in the partnership's building despite its failure to pay rent; the claim was derivative only and it was improperly dismissed pending an accounting under N.Y. Partnership Law § 115-a. Carella v Scholet (2004, A.D., 3d Dept) 773 N.Y.S.2d 763

§ 115-b.   Security for expenses in limited partners' derivative action brought in the right of the limited partnership to procure a judgment in its favor

In any action specified in section one hundred fifteen-a of this article, unless the contributions of or allocable to plaintiff or plaintiffs to partnership property amount to five percent or more of the contributions of all limited partners, in their status as limited partners, or such contributions of or allocable to such plaintiff or plaintiffs have a fair value in excess of fifty thousand dollars, the limited partnership in whose right such action is brought shall be entitled at any stage of the proceedings before final judgment to require the plaintiff or plaintiffs to give security for the reasonable expenses, including attorneys' fees, which may be incurred by it in connection with such action and by the other parties defendant in connection therewith for which the limited partnership may become liable under this article under any contract or otherwise under law, to which the limited partnership shall have recourse in such amount as the court having jurisdiction of such action shall determine upon the termination of such action. The amount of such security may thereafter from time to time be increased or decreased in the discretion of the court having jurisdiction of such action upon showing that the security provided has or may become inadequate or excessive.

History: Add, L 1968, ch 496, § 4, eff June 5, 1968.

CASE ANNOTATIONS

As a matter of law, a limited partner does not individually have a cause of action at law to recover for the loss of his partnership investment resulting from the acts of his general partners. Blattberg v Weiss (1969) 61 Misc. 2d 564, 306 N.Y.S.2d 88

By alleging money due and owing the partnership pursuant to a leasing agreement and failure by a limited partner to complete payment to the partnership of his capital contribution under the terms of the partnership agreement, the defendants' obligations run directly to the partnership and not to the limited partners and as such are derivative in nature and being derivative actions, the limited partners have failed to allege sufficient facts to state a cause of action. Alpert v Haimes (1970) 64 Misc. 2d 608, 315 N.Y.S.2d 332

Where the cause of action is derivative, limited partners must bring suit pursuant to the Partnership Law and may not bring a class action and although the word "may" appears in the statute, the

Legislature's intent was not to allow limited partners a choice between the two types of action but was to give limited partners the procedural right to bring a derivative action, which right had not been available before. Alpert v Haimes (1970) 64 Misc. 2d 608, 315 N.Y.S.2d 332

§ 115-c. Indemnification of general partner in actions in the right of a limited partnership to procure a judgment in its favor

1. No provision made to indemnify general partners for the defense of any action brought pursuant to section one hundred fifteen-a of this article, whether contained in the articles of limited partnership, agreement or otherwise, nor any award of indemnification by a court, shall be valid unless consistent with this section.

2. A limited partnership may indemnify any general partner, made a party to an action in the right of a limited partnership to procure a judgment in its favor by reason of the fact that he, his testator or intestate was a general partner in the limited partnership, against the reasonable expenses, including attorneys' fees, actually and necessarily incurred by him in connection with the defense of such action, or in connection with an appeal therein, except in relation to matters as to which such general partner is adjudged to have breached his duty to the limited partnership.

3. The indemnification authorized under subdivision two of this section shall in no case include

(a) amounts paid in settling or otherwise disposing of a threatened action, or pending action with or without court approval, or

(b) expenses incurred in defending a threatened action, or pending action which is settled or otherwise disposed of without court approval.

4. A general partner who has been wholly successful on the merits or otherwise in the defense of an action of the character described in subdivision two of this section shall be entitled to indemnification as authorized in subdivisions two and three of this section.

5. Except as provided in subdivision four of this section, any indemnification under subdivision two, unless ordered by a court under subdivision six, shall be made by the limited partnership only if authorized in the specific case

(a) by a majority of all the general partners, excluding any partners who are parties to such action, upon a finding that the general partner to be indemnified has met the standard of conduct set forth in subdivision two, or,

(b) if a majority of general partners who are not parties to such action is not obtainable with due diligence by the general partner or partners, upon the opinion of independent legal counsel that indemnification is proper in the circumstances because the standard of conduct set forth in subdivision two has been met by the general partner to be indemnified.

6. (a) Notwithstanding the failure of the limited partnership to provide indemnification, and despite any contrary determination by the general partners, indemnification shall be awarded by a court to the extent authorized under subdivisions two and four of this section. Application therefor may be made, in every case, either

(i) in the action in which the expenses were incurred or other amounts were paid, or

(ii) to the supreme court in a separate proceeding, in which case the application shall set forth the disposition of any previous application made to any court for the same relief and also reasonable cause for the failure to make application for such relief in the action in which the expenses were incurred or other amounts were paid.

(b) The application shall be made in such manner and form as may be required by the applicable rules of court or, in the absence thereof, by direction of a court to which it is made. Such application shall be on notice to the limited partnership, given through a general partner, if any, other than the general partner making the application. The court may also direct that notice be given at the expense of the limited partnership, to the limited partners and such other persons as it may designate in such manner as it may require. When there is no general partner other than those making the application, notice shall be given, as herein provided, to the limited partners.

(c) When indemnification is sought by judicial action, the court may allow a general partner such reasonable expenses, including attorneys' fees, during the pendency of the litigation as are necessary in connection with his defense therein, if the court shall find that the defendant has by his pleadings or during the course of the litigation raised genuine issues of fact or law.

7. Expenses incurred in defending an action of the character described in subdivision two of this section may be paid voluntarily by the limited partnership in advance of the final disposition of such action if authorized under subdivision five of this section.

8. All expenses incurred in defending an action which are allowed by the court under subdivisions six or seven of this section shall be repaid in case the general partner receiving such advancement or allowance is ultimately found, under the procedure set forth in this section, not to be entitled to indemnification or, where indemnification is granted, to the extent the expenses so advanced by the general partnership or allowed by the court exceed the indemnification to which he is entitled.

9. No indemnification, advancement or allowance shall be made under this section in any circumstance where it appears

(a) that indemnification would be inconsistent with a provision of the certificate of limited partnership, agreement, partnership resolution or other proper partnership action, in effect at the time of accrual of the alleged cause of action asserted in the threatened or pending action in which the expenses were incurred or other amounts were paid, which prohibits or otherwise limits indemnification; or

(b) if there has been a settlement approved by the court, that the indemnification would be inconsistent with any condition with respect to indemnification expressly imposed by the court in approving the settlement.

History: Add, L 1968, ch 496, § 5, eff June 5, 1968.

CASE ANNOTATIONS

As a matter of law, a limited partner does not individually have a cause of action at law to recover for the loss of his partnership investment resulting from the acts of his general partners. Blattberg v Weiss (1969) 61 Misc. 2d 564, 306 N.Y.S.2d 88

Where the cause of action is derivative, limited partners must bring suit pursuant to the Partnership Law and may not bring a class action and although the word "may" appears in the statute, the Legislature's intent was not to allow limited partners a choice between the two types of action but was to give limited partners the procedural right to bring a derivative action, which right had not been available before. Alpert v Haimes (1970) 64 Misc. 2d 608, 315 N.Y.S.2d 332

By alleging money due and owing the partnership pursuant to a leasing agreement and failure by a limited partner to complete payment to the partnership of his capital contribution under the terms of the partnership agreement, the defendants' obligations run directly to the partnership and not to the limited partners and as such are derivative in nature and being derivative actions, the limited partners have failed to allege sufficient facts to state a cause of action. Alpert v Haimes (1970) 64 Misc. 2d 608, 315 N.Y.S.2d 332

In unsuccessful derivative action brought by plaintiff, limited partner in both partnership formed to develop urban renewal site and limited partnership set up by original partnership to build luxury townhouses on site, alleging that defendant general partners improperly diverted partnership funds by having arranged fully repaid loan by original partnership to townhouse partnership in order to avert default and thus avoid liability on their personal guarantees, defendants were entitled to indemnification for their counsel fees under CLS Partn § 115-c(4) since, in opinion of independent legal counsel, loan was for proper partnership purpose of preventing catastrophic foreclosure. Site 35 Redevelopment Assoc. No. 1 v Kretchmer (1989, Sup) 148 Misc. 2d 89, 559 N.Y.S.2d 911

§ 116.   Short title

This article shall be known and may be cited as the uniform limited partnership act.

History: Add, L 1922, ch 640, § 1, eff April 13, 1922.

§ 117.   Rules of construction

(1) The rule that statutes in derogation of the common law are to be strictly construed shall have no application to this article.

(2) This article shall be so interpreted and construed as to effect its general purpose.

(3) This article shall not be so construed as to impair the obligations of any contract existing when this article takes effect, nor to affect any action or proceeding begun or right accrued before this article takes effect.

History: Add, L 1922, ch 640, § 1, eff April 13, 1922.

§ 118.   Rules for cases not covered

In any case not provided for in this article the rules of law and equity, including the law merchant, shall govern.

History: Add, L 1922, ch 640, § 1, eff April 13, 1922.

§ 119.   Existing limited partnerships

(1) A limited partnership formed under any statute of this state prior to the adoption of this article may become a limited partnership under this article by complying with the provisions of section ninety-one, provided the certificate sets forth

(a) The amount of the original contribution of each limited partner, and the time when the contribution was made, and

(b) That the property of the partnership exceeds the amount sufficient to discharge its liabilities to persons not claiming as general or limited partners by an amount greater than the sum of the contributions of its limited partners.

(2) The provisions of this article, or the repeal of article eight of this chapter, shall not affect or impair any act done or right accrued, acquired or established by a limited partnership formed under any statute of this state prior to its adoption, until or unless it becomes a limited partnership in accordance with the provisions of this article, and the same may be conducted in the same manner and to the same extent as if this article had not been passed.

History: Add, L 1922, ch 640, § 1, eff April 13, 1922.

———

ARTICLE 8-A
REVISED LIMITED PARTNERSHIP ACT

Partnership Law

History: Add, L 1990, ch 950, 1, eff July 1, 1991.

Former Article 8-A (§§ 120-120-l), add, L 1979, ch 519, § 1; repealed, L 1990, ch 950, § 1, eff July 1, 1991.

§§ 120, 120-a.   [Repealed]

History: Add, L 1979, ch 519, § 1; repealed, L 1990, ch 950, § 1, eff July 1, 1991.

§ 120-b.   [Repealed]

History: Add, L 1979, ch 519, § 1; amd, L 1981, ch 181, § 1; repealed, L 1990, ch 950, § 1, eff July 1, 1991.

§§ 120-c—120-l.   [Repealed]

History: Add, L 1979, ch 519, § 1; repealed, L 1990, ch 950, § 1, eff July 1, 1991.

§ 121-101. Definitions

As used in this article, unless the context otherwise requires:

(a) "Certificate of limited partnership" means the certificate referred to in section 121-201 of this article, and the certificate as amended.

(a-1) "Affidavit of publication" means the affidavit of the printer or publisher of a newspaper in which a publication pursuant to sections 121-201 and 121-902 of this article has been made. The affidavit of publication shall be in a form substantially as follows:

"Affidavit of Publication Under Section (specify applicable section) of the Partnership Law

State of New York,

County _____, ss.:

The undersigned is the printer (or publisher) of _____ (name of newspaper), a _____ (daily or weekly) newspaper published in _____, New York. A notice regarding _____ (name of limited partnership) was published in said newspaper once in each week for six successive weeks, commencing on _____ and ending on _____. The text of the notice as published in said newspaper is as set forth below, or in the annexed exhibit. This newspaper has been designated by the Clerk of _____ County for this purpose.

_____ (signature)

_____ (printed name),

_____ (jurat)"

The text of the notice set forth in or annexed to each affidavit of publication shall: (i) include only the text of the published notice, (ii) be free of extraneous marks, and (iii) if submitted in paper form be printed on paper of such size, weight and color, and in ink of such color, and in such font, and be in such other qualities and form not inconsistent with any other provision of law as, in the judgment of the secretary of state, will not impair the ability of the department of state to include a legible and permanent copy thereof in its official records. Nothing in this subdivision shall be construed as requiring the department of state to accept for filing a document submitted in electronic form.

(a-2) "Certificate of publication" means a certificate presented on behalf of the applicable limited partnership to the department of state together with the affidavits of publication pursuant to section 121-201 or 121-902 of this article. The certificate of publication shall be in a form substantially as follows:

"Certificate of Publication of _____ (name of limited partnership) Under Section _____ (Specify applicable section) of the Partnership Law

The undersigned is the _____ (title) of _____ (name of limited partnership). The published notices described in the annexed affidavits of publication contain all of the information required by the above-mentioned section of the partnership law. The newspapers described in such affidavits of publication satisfy the requirements set forth in the partnership law and the designation made by the county clerk. I certify the foregoing statements to be true under penalties of perjury.

Partnership Law

_____ Date

_____ Signature

_____ Printed Name"

(b) "Contribution" means any cash, property, services rendered, or a promissory note or other binding obligation to contribute cash or property or to render services, which a partner contributes to a limited partnership in his capacity as a partner.

(c) "Distribution" means the transfer of property by a limited partnership to one or more of its partners in his capacity as a partner.

(d) "Event of withdrawal of a general partner" means an event that causes a person to cease to be a general partner as provided in section 121-402 of this article.

(e) "Foreign limited partnership" means a partnership formed under the laws of any jurisdiction, including any foreign country, other than the laws of this state and having as partners one or more general partners and one or more limited partners.

(f) "General partner" means a person who has been admitted to a limited partnership as a general partner in accordance with the partnership agreement and, if required by the law of the jurisdiction under which the limited partnership or foreign limited partnership, as the case may be, is organized, is so named in the certificate of limited partnership or similar instrument.

(g) "Limited partner" means a person who has been admitted to a limited partnership as a limited partner in accordance with the partnership agreement or as otherwise provided by the law of the jurisdiction under which the limited partnership or foreign limited partnership, as the case may be, is organized.

(h) "Limited partnership" and "domestic limited partnership" mean, unless the context otherwise requires, a partnership (i) formed by two or more persons pursuant to this article or which complies with subdivision (a) of section 121-1202 of this article and (ii) having one or more general partners and one or more limited partners.

(i) "Majority in interest of the limited partners" and "two-thirds in interest of the limited partners" mean limited partners whose aggregate share of the current profits of the partnership constitute more than one-half or two-thirds, respectively, of the aggregate shares of all limited partners.

(j) "Office of limited partnership" means the office of the location of which is stated in the certificate of limited partnership of a domestic limited partnership, or in the application for authority of a foreign limited partnership or any amendment thereof. Such office need not be a place where business activities are conducted by such limited partnership.

(j-1) "Other business entity" means any person other than a natural person, general partnership (including any registered limited liability partnership or registered foreign limited liability partnership) or domestic limited partnership.

(k) "Partner" means a limited or general partner.

(l) "Partnership agreement" means any written agreement of the partners as to the affairs of a limited partnership and the conduct of its business.

(m) "Partnership interest" means : (i) a partner's share of the profits and losses of a limited partnership; and (ii) a partner's right to receive distributions.

(n) "Person" means a natural person, partnership, limited partnership (domestic or foreign), limited liability company (domestic or foreign), trust, estate, custodian, nominee, association, corporation or any other individual or entity in its own or any representative capacity.

(o) "Process" means judicial process and all orders, demands, notices or other papers required or permitted by law to be personally served on a limited partnership (domestic or foreign), for the purpose of acquiring jurisdiction of such limited partnership in any action or proceeding, civil or criminal, whether judicial, administrative, arbitrative or otherwise, in this state or in the federal courts sitting in or for this state.

(p) "State" means a state, territory, or possession of the United States, the District of Columbia, or the Commonwealth of Puerto Rico.

History: Add, L 1990, ch 950, § 1, eff July 1, 1991; amd, L 1994, ch 576, § 2, eff Oct 24, 1994; L 1998, ch 374, § 7, eff Sept 12, 1998; L 2005, ch 767, §§ 9, 10, eff June 1, 2006; L 2006, ch 44, § 7, eff June 1, 2006.

§ 121-102. Partnership name

The name of each limited partnership as set forth in its certificate of limited partnership:

(a) (1) shall contain without abbreviation the words "Limited Partnership" or the abbreviation "L.P.";

(2) (A) shall be such as to distinguish it from the name of (i) any limited partnership as defined in subdivision (h) of section 121-101 of this article, or (ii) any foreign limited partnership authorized to do business as a foreign limited partnership in this state;

(B) shall be such as to distinguish it from (i) the names of domestic business corporations, domestic not-for-profit corporations and other domestic corporations of any type or kind that are formed by a filing in the department of state, (ii) the names of authorized foreign business corporations, authorized foreign not-for-profit corporations and other authorized foreign corporations of any type or kind that are authorized to do business or conduct activities in this state by reason of a filing in the department of state, (iii) the fictitious names of authorized foreign business corporations, authorized foreign not-for-profit corporations and other authorized foreign corporations of any type or kind that are authorized to do business or conduct activities in this state by reason of a filing in the department of

Partnership Law

state, (iv) the names of domestic limited liability companies, (v) the names of authorized foreign limited liability companies, or (vi) the fictitious names of authorized foreign limited liability companies, in each case, as such names appear on the index of names of existing domestic and authorized foreign corporations of any type or kind, including fictitious names of authorized foreign corporations of any type or kind, in the department of state, or on the index of names of existing domestic or authorized foreign limited liability companies, including fictitious names of authorized foreign limited liability companies, in the department of state, or names the rights to which are reserved; provided, however, that no limited partnership that was formed prior to the effective date of this subparagraph and no foreign limited partnership that was qualified to do business in this state prior to such effective date shall be required to change the name or fictitious name it had on such effective date solely by reason of such name or fictitious name being indistinguishable from the name or fictitious name of any domestic or authorized foreign corporation or limited liability company or from any name the right to which is reserved by or on behalf of any domestic or foreign corporation or limited liability company;

(3) (A) may not contain the following phrases or any abbreviation or derivative thereof:

board of trade	state trooper
chamber of commerce	tenant relocation
community renewal	urban development
state police	urban relocation

Every certificate of limited partnership in which the name of the proposed limited partnership includes the terms: "school," "education," "elementary," "secondary," "kindergarten," "prekindergarten," "preschool," "nursery school," "museum," "history," "historical," "historical society," "arboretum," "library," "college," "university" or other term restricted by section two hundred twenty-four of the education law; "conservatory," "academy," or "institute," or any abbreviation or derivative of such terms, shall have endorsed thereon or annexed thereto the consent of the commissioner of education.

(B) may not contain the following words, or any abbreviation or derivative thereof:

acceptance	indemnity
annuity	insurance
assurance	investment
bank	lawyer
benefit	loan
bond	mortgage
casualty	savings
doctor	surety
endowment	title
fidelity	trust
finance	underwriter
guaranty	

unless the approval of the superintendent of financial services is attached to the certificate of limited partnership; or unless the word "doctor" or "lawyer"

or an abbreviation or derivative thereof is used in a context which clearly denotes a purpose other than the practice of law or medicine.

(C) shall not, unless the approval of the state department of social services is attached to the certificate of limited partnership or application for authority or amendment thereof, contain the word "blind" or "handicapped". Such approval shall be granted by the state department of social services if in its opinion the word "blind" or "handicapped" as used in the limited partnership name proposed will not tend to mislead or confuse the public into believing that the limited partnership is organized for charitable or nonprofit purposes related to the blind or the handicapped.

(D) shall not, unless the approval of the attorney general is attached to the certificate of limited partnership or application for authority or amendment thereof, contain the word "exchange" or any abbreviation or derivative thereof. Such approval shall not be granted by the attorney general if in his or her opinion the use of the word "exchange" in the proposed limited partnership name would falsely imply that the limited partnership conducts its business at a place where trade is carried on in securities or commodities by brokers, dealers or merchants.

(b) shall, unless the limited partnership or foreign limited partnership shall have complied with the provisions of section one hundred thirty of the general business law be the name used by the limited partnership in its conduct of business.

(c) notwithstanding paragraphs one and two of subdivision (a) of this section, a limited partnership organized under the laws of this state prior to the effective date of this article which shall file a certificate under section 121-1202 of this article within one year of the effective date of this article may file under its name as provided in its certificate of limited partnership on the effective date of this article and thereafter may continue to use such name and a foreign limited partnership which has been authorized to do business in this state prior to the effective date of this article may continue to use the name under which it has heretofore done business in this state.

History: Add, L 1990, ch 950, § 1, eff July 1, 1991; amd, L 1991, ch 264, § 1, eff July 1, 1991, L 2004, ch 344, § 3, eff Aug 10, 2004, L 2005, ch 316, § 7, eff Jan 1, 2006, L 2011, ch 62, § 104 (Part A), eff Oct 3, 2011, L 2012, ch 155, § 65, eff July 18, 2012.

§ 121-103. Reservation of partnership name

(a) Subject to section 121-102 of this article, the exclusive right to the use of a name may be reserved by:

(1) Any person intending to organize a domestic limited partnership under this article;

(2) Any domestic limited partnership or any foreign limited partnership authorized to do business in this state intending to change its name;

(3) Any foreign limited partnership intending to apply for authority to do business in this state and to adopt that name; and

(4) Any person intending to organize a foreign limited partnership and intending to have it apply for authority to do business in this state.

(b) A fictitious name for use pursuant to section 121-902 of this article may be reserved by:

(1) Any foreign limited partnership intending to apply for authority to do business in this state pursuant to subdivision (a) of section 121-902 of this article.

(2) Any authorized foreign limited partnership intending to change its fictitious name under which it does business in this state.

(3) Any authorized foreign limited partnership which has changed its name in its jurisdiction, such new name not being available in this state.

(c) Application to reserve a limited partnership name shall be delivered to the department of state. It shall set forth the name and address of the applicant, the name to be reserved, and a statement of the basis for the application under subdivision (a) or (b) of this section. The secretary of state may require that there be included in the application a statement as to the nature of the business to be conducted by the limited partnership. If the name is available for limited partnership use, the department of state shall reserve the name for the use of the applicant for a period of sixty days and issue a certificate of reservation. The restrictions and qualifications set forth in section 121-102 of this article are not waived by the issuance of a certificate of reservation. The certificate of reservation shall include the name of the applicant, the name reserved, and the date of reservation. The certificate of reservation (or in lieu thereof an affidavit by the applicant or by his or her agent or attorney that the certificate of reservation has been lost or destroyed) shall accompany the certificate of limited partnership or the application for authority when either is delivered to the department of state.

(d) The secretary of state may extend the reservation for additional periods of not more than sixty days each, upon the written request of the applicant or his or her attorney or agent delivered to the department of state, to be filed before expiration of the reservation period then in effect. Such request shall have attached to it the certificate of reservation of name. No more than two such extensions shall be granted.

History: Add, L 1990, ch 950, § 1, eff July 1, 1991.

Sub (c), add, L 1991, ch 264, § 2, eff July 1, 1991.

Former sub (c), repealed, L 1991, ch 264, § 2, eff July 1, 1991.

Sub (d), add, L 1991, ch 264, § 2, eff July 1, 1991.

§ 121-104. Statutory designation of secretary of state as agent for service of process

(a) The secretary of state shall be the agent for every domestic limited partnership which has filed with the secretary of state a certificate making such designation and every foreign limited partnership upon whom process may be served pursuant to this article.

(b) No domestic or foreign limited partnership may be organized or authorized to do business in this state under this article unless in its certificate of limited partnership or application for authority it designates the secretary of state as such agent.

(c) Any designated post office address to which the secretary of state shall mail a copy of process served upon him as agent of a domestic limited partnership or foreign limited partnership shall continue until the filing of a certificate under this article directing the mailing to a different post office address.

(d) The change authorized by subdivision (c) of this section may be accomplished by filing a certificate pursuant to this chapter, which shall be executed by a general partner.

History: Add, L 1990, ch 950, § 1, eff July 1, 1991.

Sub (a), amd, L 1990, ch 951, § 1, eff July 1, 1991.

Sub (d), add, L 1991, ch 264, § 3; amd, L 1998, ch 448, § 6, eff Oct 20, 1998.

§ 121-104-A. Resignation for receipt of process

(a) The party (or his/her legal representative) whose post office address has been supplied by a domestic limited partnership or foreign limited partnership as its address for process may resign. A certificate entitled "Certificate of Resignation for Receipt of Process under Section 121-104-A of the Revised Limited Partnership Act" shall be signed by such party and delivered to the department of state. It shall set forth:

(1) the name of the limited partnership and the date that its articles of organization or application for authority was filed by the department of state.

(2) that the address of the party has been designated by the limited partnership as the post office address to which the secretary of state shall mail a copy of any process served on the secretary of state as agent for such limited partnership, and that such party wishes to resign.

(3) that sixty days prior to the filing of the certificate of resignation with the department of state the party has sent a copy of the certificate of resignation for receipt of process by registered or certified mail to the address of the registered agent of the designated limited partnership, if other than the party filing the certificate of resignation, for receipt of process, or if the resigning limited partnership has no registered agent, then to the last address of the designated limited partnership, known to the party, specifying the address to which the copy was sent. If there is no registered agent and no known address of the designating limited partnership the party shall attach an affidavit to the certificate stating that a diligent but unsuccessful search was made by the party to locate

the limited partnership, specifying what efforts were made.

(4) that the designated limited partnership is required to deliver to the department of state a certificate of amendment or change providing for the designation by the limited partnership of a new address and that upon its failure to file such certificate, its authority to do business in this state shall be suspended.

(b) Upon the failure of the designating limited partnership to file a certificate of amendment or change providing for the designation by the limited partnership of the new address after the filing of a certificate of resignation for receipt of process with the secretary of state, its authority to do business in this state shall be suspended.

(c) The filing by the department of state of a certificate of amendment or change providing for a new address by a designating limited partnership shall annul the suspension and its authority to do business in this state shall be restored and continued as if no suspension had occured [occurred] *.

* The bracketed word has been inserted by the Publisher.

(d) The resignation for receipt of process shall become effective upon the filing by the department of state of a certificate of resignation for receipt of process.

(e) (1) In any case in which a limited partnership suspended pursuant to this section would be subject to the personal or other jurisdiction of the courts of this state under article three of the civil practice law and rules, process against such limited partnership may be served upon the secretary of state as its agent pursuant to this section. Such process may be issued in any court in this state having jurisdiction of the subject matter.

(2) Service of such process upon the secretary of state shall be made by personally delivering to and leaving with him or his deputy, or with any person authorized by the secretary of state to receive such service, at the office of the department of state in the city of Albany, a copy of such process together with the statutory fee, which fee shall be a taxable disbursement. Such service shall be sufficient if notice thereof and a copy of the process are:

(i) delivered personally within or without this state to such limited partnership by a person and in a manner authorized to serve process by law of the jurisdiction in which service is made, or

(ii) sent by or on behalf of the plaintiff to such limited partnership by registered or certified mail with return receipt requested to the last address of such limited partnership known to the plaintiff.

(3) (i) Where service of a copy of process was effected by personal service, proof of service shall be by affidavit of compliance with this section filed, together with the process, within thirty days after such service, with the clerk of the court in which the action or special proceeding is pending. Service of process shall be complete ten days after such papers are filed with the clerk of the court.

(ii) Where service of a copy of process was effected by mailing in accordance with this section, proof of service shall be by affidavit of compliance with this section filed, together with the process, within thirty days after receipt of the return receipt signed by the limited partnership, or other official proof of delivery or of the original envelope mailed. If a copy of the process is mailed in accordance with this section, there shall be filed with the affidavit of compliance either the return receipt signed by such limited partnership, or other official proof of delivery, if acceptance was refused by it, the original envelope with a notation by the postal authorities that acceptance was refused. If acceptance was refused a copy of the notice and process together with notice of the mailing by registered or certified mail and refusal to accept shall be promptly sent to such limited partnership at the same address by ordinary mail and the affidavit of compliance shall so state. Service of process shall be complete ten days after such papers are filed with the clerk of the court. The refusal to accept delivery of the registered or certified mail or to sign the return receipt shall not affect the validity of the service and such limited partnership refusing to accept such registered or certified mail shall be charged with knowledge of the contents thereof.

(4) Service made as provided in this section without the state shall have the same force as personal service made within this state.

(5) Nothing in this section shall affect the right to service process in any other manner permitted by law.

History: Add, L 1998, ch 448, § 7, eff Oct 20, 1998.

§ 121-105. Registered agent

(a) In addition to the designation of the secretary of state, each limited partnership or authorized foreign limited partnership may designate a registered agent upon whom process against the limited partnership may be served. The agent must be (i) a natural person who is a resident of this state or has a business address in this state, or (ii) a domestic corporation or a foreign corporation authorized to do business in this state.

(b) [Repealed]

(c) The registered agent of a limited partnership may resign as such agent. The registered agent shall file a certificate with the department of state entitled, "Certificate of resignation of registered agent .... (name of designating limited partnership) under subdivision (c) of section 121-105 of the Revised Limited Partnership Act which shall be executed by such registered agent. It shall set forth:

(1) The name of the limited partnership, and if it has been changed, the name under which it was organized. A foreign limited partnership must set

forth its name and the fictitious name the foreign limited partnership has agreed to use in this state pursuant to section 121-902 of this article.

(2) The date the certificate of limited partnership or certificate of application for authority of the limited partnership was filed by the department of state.

(3) That he resigns as registered agent for the limited partnership.

(4) That he as sent a copy of the certificate of resignation by registered mail to the limited partnership at the post office address on file in the department of state specified for the mailing of process or if such address is the address of the registered agent, then to the office of the designating limited partnership and the jurisdiction of its organization.

(d) The designation of a registered agent shall terminate thirty days after the filing by the department of state of the certificate of resignation. A certificate designating a new registered agent may be delivered to the department of state by the limited partnership within the thirty days or thereafter.

History: Add, L 1990, ch 950, § 1, eff July 1, 1991.

Sub (b), repealed, L 1999, ch 172, § 31, eff July 6, 1999.

§ 121-106. Records

(a) Each domestic limited partnership shall maintain the following records, which may, but need not, be maintained in this state:

(1) a current list of the full name and last known mailing address of each partner set forth in alphabetical order together with the contribution and the share in profits and losses of each partner or information from which such share can be readily derived;

(2) a copy of the certificate of limited partnership and all amendments thereto, together with executed copies of any powers of attorney pursuant to which any certificate or amendment has been executed;

(3) a copy of the partnership agreement, any amendments thereto and any amended and restated partnership agreements; and

(4) a copy of the limited partnership's federal, state, and local income tax or information returns and reports, if any, for the three most recent fiscal years.

(b) Any partner may, subject to reasonable standards as may be set forth in the partnership agreement or otherwise established by the general partners, inspect and copy at his own expense for any purpose reasonably related to the partner's interest as a partner the records referred to in subdivision (a) of this section, any financial statements maintained by the limited partnership for the three most recent fiscal years and other information regarding the affairs of the limited partnership as is just and reasonable.

History: Add, L 1990, ch 950, § 1, eff July 1, 1991.

§ 121-107. Nature of business

A limited partnership may carry on any business that a partnership without limited partners may carry on except as prohibited by law.

History: Add, L 1990, ch 950, § 1, eff July 1, 1991.

§ 121-108. Business transactions of partner with the partnership

Except as may be provided in the partnership agreement, a partner may lend money to, borrow money from, act as a guarantor or surety for, provide collateral for the obligations of, and transact other business with the limited partnership, and, subject to other applicable law, has the same rights and obligations with respect thereto as a person who is not a partner.

History: Add, L 1990, ch 950, § 1, eff July 1, 1991.

§ 121-109. Service of process on limited partnerships

(a) Service of process on the secretary of state as agent of a domestic or authorized foreign limited partnership shall be made as follows:

(1) By personally delivering to and leaving with him or his deputy, or with any person authorized by the secretary of state to receive such service, at the office of the department of state in the city of Albany, duplicate copies of such process together with the statutory fee, which fee shall be a taxable disbursement.

(2) The service on the limited partnership is complete when the secretary of state is so served.

(3) The secretary of state shall promptly send one of such copies by certified mail, return receipt requested, addressed to the limited partnership at the post office address, on file in the department of state, specified for that purpose.

(b) In any case in which a non-domiciliary would be subject to the personal or other jurisdiction of the courts of this state under article three of the civil practice law and rules, a foreign limited partnership not authorized to do business in this state is subject to a like jurisdiction. In any such case, process against such foreign limited partnership may be served upon the secretary of state as its agent. Such process may issue in any court in this state having jurisdiction of the subject matter. Service of process upon the secretary of state shall be made by personally delivering to and leaving with him or his deputy, or with any person authorized by the secretary of state to receive such service, at the office of the department of state in the city of Albany, a copy of such process together with the statutory fee, which fee shall be a taxable disbursement. Such service shall be sufficient if notice thereof and a copy of the process are:

(1) Delivered personally without this state to such foreign limited partnership by a person and in the manner authorized to serve process by law of the jurisdiction in which service is made, or

(2) Sent by or on behalf of the plaintiff to such foreign limited partnership by registered mail with return receipt requested, at the post office address specified for the purpose of mailing process, on file in the department of state, or with any official or body performing the equivalent function, in the jurisdiction of its creation, or if no such address is specified, to its registered or other office there specified, or if no such office is specified, to the last address of such foreign limited partnership known to the plaintiff.

(3) Where service of a copy of process was effected by personal service, proof of service shall be by affidavit of compliance with this section filed, together with the process, within thirty days after such service with the clerk of the court in which the action or special proceeding is pending. Service of process shall be complete ten days after such papers are filed with the clerk of the court.

(4) Where service of a copy of process was effected by mailing in accordance with this section proof of service shall be by affidavit of compliance with this section filed, together with the process, within thirty days after receipt of the return receipt signed by the foreign limited partnership, or other official proof of delivery or of the original envelope mailed. If a copy of the process is mailed in accordance with this section, there shall be filed with the affidavit of compliance either the return receipt signed by such foreign limited partnership or other official proof of delivery or, if acceptance was refused by it, the original envelope with a notation by the postal authorities that acceptance was refused. If acceptance was refused a copy of the notice and process together with notice of the mailing by registered mail and refusal to accept shall be promptly sent to such foreign limited partnership at the same address by ordinary mail and the affidavit of compliance shall so state. Service of process shall be complete ten days after such papers are filed with the clerk of the court. The refusal to accept delivery of the registered mail or to sign the return receipt shall not affect the validity of the service and such foreign limited partnership refusing to accept such registered mail shall be charged with knowledge of the contents thereof.

(5) Service made as provided in this section shall have the same force as personal service made within this state.

(c) The secretary of state shall keep a record of all process served upon him under this section and shall record therein the date of such service and his action with reference thereto.

(d) Nothing contained in this section shall limit or affect the right to serve any process required or permitted by law to be served upon the limited partnership in any other manner now or hereafter permitted by law or applicable rules of procedure.

History: Add, L 1990, ch 950, § 1, eff July 1, 1991; amd, L 1999, ch 341, § 3, eff July 27, 1999.

§ 121-110. The partnership agreement

(a) The partnership agreement shall be signed by all general partners, in person or by attorneys in fact, and may, but need not, be signed by the limited partners.

(b) A limited partnership shall have a written partnership agreement. Except as provided in sections 121-702 and 121-705 of this article, no person shall have any rights, or be subject to the liabilities, of a general partner who has not signed the partnership agreement in person or by attorney in fact.

(c) The partnership agreement of a limited partnership may be amended from time to time as provided therein; provided, however, that, except as may be provided otherwise in the partnership agreement, without the written consent of each partner adversely affected thereby, no amendment of the partnership agreement shall be made which (i) increases the obligations of any limited partner to make contributions, (ii) alters the allocation for tax purposes of any items of income, gain, loss, deduction or credit, (iii) alters the manner of computing the distributions of any partner, (iv) alters, except as provided in subdivision (a) of section 121-302 of this article, the voting or other rights of any limited partner, (v) allows the obligation of a partner to make a contribution to be compromised by consent of fewer than all partners or (vi) alters the procedures for amendment of the partnership agreement.

History: Add, L 1990, ch 950, § 1, eff July 1, 1991.

Sub (a), amd, L 1990, ch 951, § 2, eff July 1, 1991.

CASE ANNOTATIONS

Plaintiffs were not entitled to specific performance of partnership agreement, removing defendant as general partner and substituting new general partner, where record established that plaintiffs did not own requisite 95 percent or more of aggregate limited partners' interests, and neither partnership agreement nor Partnership Law precluded defendant from voting its limited partnership units to prevent its removal as general partner. DKS Assocs. v Tampa Pipeline Corp. (1994, 4th Dept) 203 A.D.2d 963, 611 N.Y.S.2d 80, remanded (1995, 4th Dept) 217 A.D.2d 928, 629 N.Y.S.2d 892

Action by limited partner, seeking to require general partner to buy his units in partnership pursuant to option provision of partnership agreement, was properly dismissed as limited partner relinquished any prior partnership right to exercise such option by taking part in settlement of investors' class action against general partner and agreeing to broad terms of release; due process did not require further explanation of effects of release provision, in addition to clear meaning of words of release. Mosberg v National Prop. Analyst, Inc. (1995, 1st Dept) 217 A.D.2d 482, 630 N.Y.S.2d 50

In action for breach of partnership agreements, plaintiff was estopped from claiming that he did not approve of terms of disbursement agreement where he had executed power of attorney expressly authorizing third person to execute disbursement agreement that would be binding on plaintiff. Alizio v Perpignano (1997, 2d Dept) 245 A.D.2d 477, 666 N.Y.S.2d 39

§ 121-201. Certificate of limited partnership

(a) In order to form a limited partnership the general partners shall execute a partnership agreement, and a certificate of limited partnership shall be executed in accordance with section 121-204 of this article. The certificate, entitled "Certificate of limited partnership of .... (name of limited partnership) under section 121-201 of the Revised Limited Partnership Act," shall be filed with the department of state in accordance with section 121-206 of this article and shall set forth:

(1) the name of the limited partnership;

(2) the county within this state, in which the office of the limited partnership is to be located;

(3) a designation of the secretary of state as agent of the limited partnership upon whom process against it may be served and the post office address within or without this state to which the secretary of state shall mail a copy of any process against it served upon him;

(4) if the limited partnership is to have a registered agent, his name and address within this state and a statement that the registered agent is to be the agent of the limited partnership upon whom process against it may be served;

(5) the name and the business or residence street address of each general partner;

(6) the latest date upon which the limited partnership is to dissolve; and

(7) any other matters the general partners determine to include therein.

(b) A limited partnership is formed at the time of the filing of the initial certificate of limited partnership with the department of state or at any later time not to exceed sixty days from the date of filing specified in the certificate of limited partnership. The filing of the certificate shall, in the absence of actual fraud, be conclusive evidence of the formation of the limited partnership as of the time of filing or effective date if later, except in an action or special proceeding brought by the attorney general.

(c) (i) Within one hundred twenty days after the filing of the initial certificate, a copy of the same or a notice containing the substance thereof shall be published once in each week for six successive weeks, in two newspapers of the county in which the office of the limited partnership is located, one newspaper to be printed weekly and one newspaper to be printed daily, to be designated by the county clerk. When such county is located within a city with a population of one million or more, such designation shall be as though the copy or notice were a notice or advertisement of judicial proceedings. Proof of the publication required by this paragraph, consisting of the certificate of publication of the limited partnership with the affidavits of publication of such newspapers annexed thereto, must be filed with the department of state. Notwithstanding any other provision of law, if the office of the limited partnership is located in a county wherein a weekly or daily newspaper of the county, or both, has not been so designated by the county clerk, then the publication herein required shall be made in a weekly or daily newspaper of any county, or both, as the case may be, which is contiguous to, such county, provided that any such newspaper meets all the other requirements of this paragraph. A copy or notice published in a newspaper other than the newspaper or newspapers designated by the county clerk shall not be deemed to be one of the publications required by this paragraph. The notice shall include: (1) the name of the limited partnership; (2) the date of filing of the certificate of limited partnership with the department of state; (3) the county within this state, in which the office of the limited partnership is9 located; (3-a) the street address of the principal business location, if any; (4) a statement that the secretary of state has been designated as agent of the limited partnership upon whom process against it may be served and the post office address within or without this state to which the secretary of state shall mail a copy of any process against it served upon him or her; (5) if the limited partnership is to have a registered agent, his or her name and address within this state and a statement that the registered agent is to be the agent of the limited partnership upon whom process against it may be served; (6) a statement that the names and the business or residence street address of each general partner is available from the secretary of state; (7) the latest date upon which the limited partnership is to dissolve; and (8) the character or purpose of the business of such partnership. Where, at any time after completion of the first of the six weekly publications required by this subdivision and prior to the completion of the sixth such weekly publication, there is a change in any of the information contained in the copy or notice as published, the limited partnership may complete the remaining publications of the original copy or notice, and the limited partnership shall not be required to publish any further or amended copy or notice. Where, at any time after completion of the six weekly publications required by this paragraph, there is a change to any of the information contained in the copy or notice as published, no further or amended publication or republication shall be required to be made. If within one hundred twenty days after its formation, proof of such publication, consisting of the certificate of publication of the limited partnership with the affidavits of publication of the newspapers annexed thereto has not been filed with the department of state, the authority of such limited partnership to carry on, conduct or transact any business in this state shall be suspended, effective as of the expiration of such one hundred twenty day period. The failure of a limited partnership to cause such copy or notice to be published and such certificate of publication and affidavits of publication to be filed with the department of state within such one hundred twenty day period or the suspension of such limited partnership's authority to carry on, conduct or transact business in this state pursuant to this paragraph shall not limit or impair the validity of any contract or act of such limited partnership, or any right or remedy of any other party under or by virtue of any contract, act or omission of such limited partnership, or the right of any other party to maintain any action or special proceeding on any such contract, act or omission, or right of such limited partnership to defend any action or special proceeding in this state, or result in any partner or agent of such limited partnership becoming liable for the contractual obligations or other liabilities of the limited partnership. If, at any time following the suspension of a limited partnership's authority to carry on, conduct or transact business in this state pursuant to this paragraph, such limited partnership shall cause proof of publication in substantial compliance with the provisions (other than the one hundred twenty day period) of this paragraph, consisting of the certificate of publication of the limited partnership with the affidavits of publication of the newspapers annexed thereto, to be filed with the department of state, such suspension of such limited partnership's authority to carry on, conduct or transact business shall be annulled.

(ii) (1) A limited partnership which was formed prior to the effective date of this paragraph and which complied with the publication and filing requirements of this subdivision as in effect prior to such effective date shall not be required to make any publication or republication or any filing under paragraph (i) of this subdivision, and shall not be subject to suspension pursuant to this subdivision.

(2) Within twelve months after the effective date of this paragraph, a limited partnership which was formed prior to such effective date and which did not comply with the publication and filing requirements of this subdivision as in effect prior to such effective date shall publish a copy of its certificate or a notice containing the substance thereof in the manner required (other than the one hundred twenty day period) by this subdivision as in effect prior to such effective date and file proof of such publication, consisting of the certificate of publication of the limited partnership with the affidavits of publication of the newspapers annexed thereto, with the department of state.

(3) If a limited partnership that is subject to the provisions of subparagraph two of this paragraph fails to file the required proof of publication with the department of state within twelve months after the effective date of this paragraph, its authority to carry on, conduct or transact any business in this state shall be suspended, effective as of the expiration of such twelve month period.

(4) The failure of a limited partnership that is subject to the provisions of subparagraph two of this paragraph to fully comply with the provisions of said subparagraph two or the suspension of such limited partnership's authority to carry on, conduct or transact any business in this state pursuant to subparagraph three of this paragraph shall not impair or limit the validity of any contract or act of such limited partnership, or any right or remedy of any other party under or by virtue of any contract, act or omission of such limited partnership, or the right of any other party to maintain any action or special proceeding on any such contract, act or omission, or

right of such limited partnership to defend any action or special proceeding in this state, or result in any partner or agent of such limited partnership becoming liable for the contractual obligations or other liabilities of the limited partnership.

(5) If, at anytime following the suspension of a limited partnership's authority to carry on, conduct or transact business in this state, pursuant to subparagraph three of this paragraph, such limited partnership shall cause proof of publication in substantial compliance with the provisions (other than the one hundred twenty day period) of paragraph (i) of this subdivision, consisting of the certificate of publication of the limited partnership with the affidavits of publication of the newspapers annexed thereto, to be filed with the department of state, such suspension of such limited partnership's authority to carry on, conduct or transact business shall be annulled.

(6) For the purposes of this paragraph, a limited partnership which was formed prior to the effective date of this paragraph shall be deemed to have complied with the publication and filing requirements of this subdivision as in effect prior to such effective date if (A) the limited partnership was formed on or after January first, nineteen hundred ninety-nine and prior to such effective date and the limited partnership filed at least one affidavit of the printer or publisher of a newspaper with the department of state at any time prior to such effective date, or (B) the limited partnership was formed prior to January first, nineteen hundred ninety-nine, without regard to whether the limited partnership did or did not file any affidavit of the printer or publisher of a newspaper with the secretary of state.

(iii) The information in a notice published pursuant to this subdivision shall be presumed to be in compliance with and satisfaction of the requirements of this subdivision.

History: Add, L 1990, ch 950, § 1; amd, L 1991, ch 33, §§ 1, 2; L 1991, ch 264, § 4, eff July 1, 1991; L 1999, ch 172, § 32; L 1999, ch 420, § 11, eff Aug 31, 1999; L 2005, ch 767, § 11, eff June 1, 2006; L 2006, ch 44, § 8, eff June 1, 2006.

CASE ANNOTATIONS

In action against limited partnership to foreclose mortgage, plaintiff was entitled to deficiency judgment against general partner, although general partnership interest had been transferred to another party before issuance of mortgage loan, where certificate of limited partnership was not amended to reflect any change in composition of partnership. Arno Management Corp. v 115 East 69th Assoc. (1991, 1st Dept) 173 A.D.2d 258, 569 N.Y.S.2d 656

Court should have granted seller's motion to dismiss action for specific performance of real estate sales contract since buyer, limited partnership, was not in existence at time contract was executed, and was not validly created by time of scheduled closing; moreover, buyer failed to strictly comply with statutory publication requirements (CLS Partn § 121-201(c)). Bay Shore Family Partners, L.P. v Foundation of Jewish Philanthropies of the Jewish Fed'n (1997, 2d Dept) 239 A.D.2d 373, 658 N.Y.S.2d 326, app den (1997) 91 N.Y.2d 803, 668 N.Y.S.2d 558, 691 N.E.2d 630 and later proceeding (2000, 2d Dept) 270 A.D.2d 374, 704 N.Y.S.2d 631, app den (2000) 95 N.Y.2d 756, 712 N.Y.S.2d 447, 734 N.E.2d 759

§ 121-202. Amendment of the certificate of limited partnership

(a) A certificate of limited partnership is amended by filing with the department of state a certificate of amendment thereto entitled "Certificate of amendment of the certificate of limited partnership of .... (name of limited partnership) under section 121-202 of the Revised Limited Partnership Act," and executed in accordance with section 121-204 of this article. The certificate of amendment shall set forth:

(1) The name of the limited partnership and, if it has been changed, the name under which it was formed;

(2) The date of filing its certificate of limited partnership;

(3) Each amendment effected thereby, setting forth the subject matter of each provision of the certificate of limited partnership which is to be amended or eliminated and the full text of the provision or provisions, if any, which are to be substituted or added; and

(4) If the amendment reflects the admission or withdrawal of one or more general partners, the name and business or residence street address of such general partner or partners and the date or dates of admission or withdrawal.

(b) No later than ninety days after the happening of any of the following events, an amendment to a certificate of limited partnership reflecting the occurrence of the event or events shall be filed by a general partner:

(1) the admission of a general partner;

(2) the withdrawal of a general partner;

(3) the continuation of the partnership under section 121-801 of this article after an event of withdrawal of a general partner; or

(4) a change in the name of the limited partnership, or a change in the post office address to which the secretary of state shall mail a copy of any process against the limited partnership served on him, or a change in the name or address of the registered agent, if such change is made other than pursuant to section 121-104 or 121-105 of this article.

(c) A general partner who becomes aware that any statement in a certificate of limited partnership was false in any material respect when made or that a matter described has changed, making the certificate inaccurate in any material respect, shall amend the certificate within ninety days of becoming aware of such fact.

(d) A certificate of limited partnership may be amended at any time for any other proper purpose which the general partners may determine.

(e) Unless otherwise provided in this article, a certificate of amendment shall be effective at the time of its filing with the department of state.

History: Add, L 1990, ch 950, § 1, eff July 1, 1991.

Sub (a), par (4), amd, L 1999, ch 172, § 33, eff July 6, 1999.

Sub (b), par (4), amd, L 1994, ch 576, § 14-a, eff Oct 24, 1994.

CASE ANNOTATIONS

Limited partnership was proper party to maintain summary nonpayment petition against rent-stabilized tenant under CLS RPAPL § 721(1) following death of general partner. 390 W. End Assocs. v Raiff (1995, Sup App T) 166 Misc. 2d 730, 636 N.Y.S.2d 965

Partnership's failure to file a certificate of amendment reflecting the transfer within the 90-day period required under N.Y. Partnership Law § 121-202(b) did not affect the legal status of the partnership, and it did not affect the new general partner's authority to execute the sublease agreement on behalf of the partnership. Orange County - Poughkeepsie MSA, Ltd. P'ship v Communications Concepts of N.Y. (2003, A.D., 2d Dept) 753 N.Y.S.2d 850

§ 121-202-A. Certificate of change

(a) A certificate of limited partnership may be changed by filing with the department of state a certificate of change entitled "Certificate of Change of .... (name of limited partnership) under Section 121-202-A of the Revised Limited Partnership Act" and shall be signed and delivered to the department of state. A certificate of change may (i) specify or change the location of the limited partnership's office; (ii) specify or change the post office address to which the secretary of state shall mail a copy of process against the limited partnership served upon him; and (iii) make, revoke or change the designation of a registered agent, or to specify or change the address of its registered agent. It shall set forth:

(1) the name of the limited partnership, and if it has been changed, the name under which it was formed;

(2) the date its certificate of limited partnership was filed by the department of state; and

(3) each change effected thereby.

(b) A certificate of change which changes only the post office address to which the secretary of state shall mail a copy of any process against a limited partnership served upon him or the address of the registered agent, provided such address being changed is the address of a person, partnership or corporation whose address, as agent, is the address to be changed or who has been designated as registered agent for such limited partnership shall be signed and delivered to the department of state by such agent. The certificate of change shall set forth the statements required under subdivision (a) of this section; that a notice of the proposed change was mailed to the domestic limited partnership by the party signing the certificate not less than thirty days prior to the date of delivery to the department of state and that such domestic limited partnership has not objected thereto; and that the party signing the certificate is the agent of such limited partnership to whose address the secretary of state is required to mail copies of process or the registered agent, if such be the case. A certificate signed and delivered under this subdivision shall not be deemed to effect a change of location of the office of the limited partnership in whose behalf such certificate is filed.

§ 121-203. Cancellation of certificate

(a) Within ninety days following the dissolution and the commencement of winding up of the limited partnership, or at any other time there are no limited partners, a certificate of cancellation shall be filed with the department of state entitled, "Certificate of cancellation of .... (name of limited partnership) under section 121-203 of the Revised Limited Partnership Act" and executed in accordance with section 121-204 of this article. The certificate of cancellation shall set forth:

(1) the name of the limited partnership; and if it has been changed, the name under which it was formed;

(2) the date of filing of its certificate of limited partnership and each subsequent amendment thereto;

(3) the event giving rise to the filing of the certificate; and

(4) any other information the persons filing the certificate determine.

(b) The cancellation of the certificate of limited partnership is effective at the time of the filing of the certificate of cancellation.

(c) The cancellation of the certificate of limited partnership shall not affect the liability of the limited partners during the period of winding up and termination of the partnership.

History: Add, L 1990, ch 950, § 1, eff July 1, 1991.

§ 121-204. Execution of certificates

(a) Each certificate required by this article to be filed with the department of state shall be executed in the following manner:

(1) an initial certificate of limited partnership must be signed by all general partners named therein;

(2) a certificate of amendment must be signed by at least one general partner and by each other general partner designated in the certificate of amendment as a new general partner;

(3) a certificate of cancellation must be signed by all general partners or, if there is no general partner, unless otherwise provided in the partnership agreement, by a majority in interest of the limited partners; and

(4) all other certificates must be signed by at least one general partner.

(b) Any person may sign any certificate by an attorney in fact. Powers of attorney relating to the signing of a certificate by an attorney in fact need not be filed with the department of state nor provided as evidence of authority by the person filing, but must be retained among the records of the partnership.

(c) Each certificate must be signed.

(d) Each certificate must include the name and capacity of each signer.

History: Add, L 1990, ch 950, § 1, eff July 1, 1991.

Sub (c), amd, L 1998, ch 375, § 51, eff Aug 13, 1998.

Sub (d), amd, L 1998, ch 375, § 51, eff Aug 13, 1998.

§ 121-205. Execution, amendment or cancellation by judicial act

(a) If a person required by section 121-204 of this article to execute a certificate fails or refuses to do so, any partner, and any permitted assignee of a partnership interest, who is adversely affected by the failure or refusal may petition the supreme court in the judicial district in which the office of the limited partnership is located to direct the execution of the certificate. If the court finds that the certificate should be executed and that such person has failed or refused to execute the certificate, it shall order such person to file an appropriate certificate.

(b) If a person contractually obligated to execute as a limited partner a partnership agreement of an existing partnership, or any amendment thereto, fails or refuses to do so, any partner, and any assignee of a partnership interest, who is adversely affected by the failure or refusal may petition the supreme court in the judicial district referred to in subdivision (a) of this section to direct the execution of the partnership agreement or amendment. If the court finds that such person has breached a contractual obligation binding upon him to execute the agreement or amendment, it shall enter an order granting appropriate relief.

History: Add, L 1990, ch 950, § 1, eff July 1, 1991.

§ 121-206. Filing with the department of state

A signed certificate of limited partnership and any signed certificates of amendment or other certificates filed pursuant to this article or of any judicial decree of amendment or cancellation shall be delivered to the department of state. If the instrument which is delivered to the department of state for filing complies as to form with the requirements of law and the filing fee required by any statute of this state in connection therewith has been paid, the instrument shall be filed and indexed by the department of state.

History: Add, L 1990, ch 950, § 1, July 1, 1991.

§ 121-207. Liability for false statement in certificate

(a) If any certificate of limited partnership, certificate of amendment, or other certificate filed pursuant to this article contains a materially false statement, one who suffers loss by reasonable reliance on the statement may recover damages for the loss from:

(1) any person who executes the certificate, or causes another to execute it on his behalf, and knew, and any general partner who knew of the filing of such certificate and who knew or should have known with the exercise of reasonable care and diligence, the

statement to be false in any material respect at the time the certificate was executed; and

(2) any general partner who thereafter knows of the filing of such certificate and who knows or should have known with the exercise of reasonable care and diligence that any arrangement or other fact described in the certificate has changed, making the statement false in any material respect, if that general partner had ninety days to amend or cancel the certificate, or to file a petition for its amendment or cancellation before the statement was relied upon.

(b) No person shall have any liability for failing to cause the amendment or cancellation of a certificate to be filed or failing to file a petition for its amendment or cancellation, if the certificate or petition is filed within ninety days of the time when that person knew or should have known that the statement in the certificate was false in any material respect.

History: Add, L 1990, ch 950, § 1, eff July 1, 1991.

§ 121-208. Restated certificate of limited partnership

(a) A limited partnership may restate in a single certificate the text of its certificate of limited partnership, without making any amendment thereby. Alternatively, a limited partnership may restate in a single certificate the text of its certificate of limited partnership and as amended thereby to effect any one or more of the amendments authorized by this article.

(b) If the restated certificate of limited partnership merely restates and integrates but does not amend or further amend the certificate of limited partnership, it shall be executed by a general partner. If the restated certificate also amends or further amends the certificate of limited partnership, it shall be executed in accordance with section 121-204 of this article.

(c) The restated certificate shall be filed with the department of state in accordance with section 121-206 of this article and shall set forth:

(1) the name of the limited partnership and, if it has been changed, the name under which it was formed;

(2) the date of filing of its certificate of limited partnership;

(3) if the restated certificate restates the text of the certificate of limited partnership without making any amendments, then a statement that the text of the certificate of limited partnership is thereby restated without amendment to read as therein set forth in full; or

(4) if the restated certificate restates the text of the certificate of limited partnership, and is amended thereby, then a statement that the certificate of limited partnership is amended to effect one or more of the amendments authorized by this article, specifying each such amendment and that the text of the certificate of limited partnership is thereby restated as amended to read as therein set forth in full.

(d) Any amendments effected in connection with the restatement of the certificate of limited partnership shall be subject to any other provision of this article which would apply if a separate certificate of amendment were filed to effect such amendment.

History: Add, L 1990, ch 950, § 1, eff July 1, 1991.

§ 121-301. Admission of limited partners

(a) A person becomes a limited partner on the later of:

(1) the effective date of the original certificate of limited partnership; or

(2) the date as of which the person becomes a limited partner pursuant to the partnership agreement; provided, however, that if such date is not ascertainable, the date stated in the records of the limited partnership.

(b) After the effective date of a limited partnership's original certificate of limited partnership, a person may be admitted as a limited partner:

(1) in the case of a person acquiring a partnership interest directly from the limited partnership, upon compliance with the partnership agreement or, if the partnership agreement does not so provide, upon the written consent of all partners; and

(2) in the case of an assignee of a partnership interest of a partner who has the power, as provided in section 121-704 of this article, to grant the assignee the right to become a limited partner, upon the exercise of that power and compliance with any conditions limiting the grant or exercise of the power.

History: Add, L 1990, ch 950, § 1, eff July 1, 1991.

§ 121-302. Classes and voting by limited partners

(a) A partnership agreement may provide for classes or groups of limited partners having such relative rights and powers as the partnership agreement may provide, and may make provision for the future creation in the manner provided in the partnership agreement of additional classes of limited partners having such relative rights and powers as may from time to time be established pursuant to the partnership agreement including rights and duties senior to existing classes of limited partners. The partnership agreement may grant to or withhold from all or one or more classes of limited partners the right to vote, on a per capita, class or other basis, upon any matter.

(b) A partnership agreement which grants a right to vote may set forth provisions relating to notice of the time, place or purpose of any meeting at which any matter is to be voted on by any limited partners, waiver of any such notice, action by consent without a meeting, the establishment of a record date, quorum requirements, voting in person or by proxy, or any other matter with respect to the exercise of any such right to vote.

History: Add, L 1990, ch 950, § 1, eff July 1, 1991.

Partnership Law

§ 121-303. Liability to third parties

(a) Except as provided in subdivision (d) of this section, a limited partner is not liable for the contractual obligations and other liabilities of a limited partnership unless he is also a general partner or, in addition to the exercise of his rights and powers as a limited partner, he participates in the control of the business. However, if the limited partner does participate in the control of the business, he is liable only to persons who transact business with the limited partnership reasonably believing, based upon the limited partner's conduct, that the limited partner is a general partner.

(b) A limited partner does not participate in the control of the business within the meaning of subdivision (a) of this section by virtue of doing one or more of the following:

(1) being a contractor for or transacting business with, including being a contractor for, or an agent or employee of the limited partnership or of a general partner or an officer, director or shareholder of a corporate general partner, or a member, manager or agent of a limited liability company that is a general partner of the limited partnership, or a partner of a partnership that is a general partner of the limited partnership, or a trustee, administrator, executor, custodian or other fiduciary or beneficiary of an estate or trust which is a general partner, or a trustee, officer, advisor, shareholder or beneficiary of a business trust which is a general partner, or acting in such capacity;

(2) consulting with and advising or rendering professional services to a general partner with respect to any matter, including the business of the limited partnership;

(3) acting as surety or endorser for the limited partnership, or guaranteeing or providing security for or lending money to or assuming one or more debts of the limited partnership;

(4) approving or disapproving an amendment to the partnership agreement, or calling, requesting, or participating in any meeting of general and limited partners or limited partners;

(5) taking any action to bring, prosecute, or terminate any derivative action brought in the right of the limited partnership;

(6) proposing, approving, disapproving, or voting on any one or more of the following matters:

(A) the amendment of the partnership agreement or certificate of limited partnership;

(B) the dissolution and winding up of the limited partnership;

(C) the sale, exchange, lease, mortgage, assignment, pledge, or other transfer of, or granting of a security interest in, any asset or assets of the limited partnership;

(D) the merger or consolidation of the limited partnership or election to continue the business of the limited partnership;

(E) the incurrence, renewal, refinancing or payment or other discharge of indebtedness by the limited partnership;

(F) a change in the nature of the business;

(G) the admission or removal of a partner;

(H) a transaction or other matter involving an actual or potential conflict of interest;

(I) in respect of a limited partnership which is registered as an investment company under an act of Congress entitled Investment Company Act of 1940, any matter required by said Investment Company Act of 1940, or the rules and regulations promulgated thereunder, to be approved by holders of beneficial interests in an investment company;

(J) such other matters as are required for submission to limited partners by federal or state securities laws or rules or regulations thereunder, or rules of self-regulatory bodies governing the trading of limited partnership interests;

(K) the indemnification of any partner or other person; or

(L) such other matters as are stated in the partnership agreement to be subject to approval, disapproval or vote by the limited partners;

(7) consulting with or advising, or being an officer, director, shareholder, partner, member, manager, agent or employee of, or being a fiduciary for, any person in which the limited partnership has an interest;

(8) winding up the limited partnership pursuant to section 121-803 of this article; or

(9) exercising any right or power permitted to limited partners under this article and not specifically enumerated in this subdivision.

(c) The enumeration in subdivision (b) of this section does not mean that the possession or exercise of any other powers by a limited partner constitutes participation by him in the control of the business of the limited partnership.

(d) A limited partner who expressly consents in writing to his name being used in the name of the limited partnership is liable to creditors who extend credit to the limited partnership without actual knowledge that the limited partner is not a general partner.

(e) A limited partner does not participate in the control of the business within the meaning of subdivision (a) of this section regardless of the nature, extent, scope, number or frequency of the limited partner's possessing or, regardless of whether or not the limited partner has the rights or powers, exercising or attempting to exercise one or more of the rights or powers or having or, regardless of whether or not the limited partner has the rights or powers, acting or attempting to act in one or more of the capacities which are permitted under this section.

History: Add, L 1990, ch 950, § 1; amd, L 1990, ch 951, § 3, eff July 1, 1991; L 1994, ch 576, § 4, eff Oct 24, 1994.

§ 121-304. Person erroneously believing himself a limited partner

(a) Except as provided in subdivision (b) of this section, a person who makes a contribution to a limited partnership and erroneously but in good faith believes that he has become a limited partner in the limited partnership is not a general partner in the limited partnership and is not bound by its obligations by reason of making the contribution, receiving distributions from the limited partnership or exercising any rights of a limited partner, if, on ascertaining the mistake, he:

(1) causes an accurate certificate of limited partnership or a certificate of amendment to be executed and filed; or

(2) withdraws from the partnership by executing and delivering to the limited partnership a written notice declaring withdrawal under this section.

(b) A person who makes a contribution of the kind described in subdivision (a) of this section is liable as a general partner to any third party who transacts business with the limited partnership (i) before the person withdraws and an appropriate certificate is filed to show withdrawal, or (ii) before an appropriate certificate is filed to show that he is not a general partner, but in either case only if the third party reasonably believed, based upon the limited partner's conduct, that the limited partner was a general partner and extended credit to the partnership in reasonable reliance on the credit of such person.

History: Add, L 1990, ch 950, § 1, eff July 1, 1991.

§ 121-401. Admission of additional general partners

After the effective date of the original certificate of limited partnership, additional general partners may be admitted as provided in the partnership agreement, or if the partnership agreement does not provide for the admission of additional general partners, with the written consent of all partners.

History: Add, L 1990, ch 950, § 1, eff July 1, 1991.

CASE ANNOTATIONS

Limited partners were within their rights under partnership agreement when they refused to consent to admission of new general partner, regardless of whether refusal was unreasonable, where partnership agreement provided (1) that general partner could transfer partnership interest with consent of limited partners, which consent could not be unreasonably withheld, (2) that any person who acquired interest of general partner would not be general partner, and (3) that person who acquired interest of general partner could become general partner only with consent of limited partners. Brodsky v Central Trust Co. (1993, 4th Dept) 195 A.D.2d 1028, 600 N.Y.S.2d 398

§ 121-402. Events of withdrawal of a general partner

A person ceases to be a general partner of a limited partnership upon the happening of any of the following events:

(a) the general partner withdraws from the limited partnership as provided in section 121-602 of this article;

(b) the general partner ceases to be a general partner as provided in section 121-702 of this article;

(c) the general partner is removed as a general partner as may be provided in the partnership agreement;

(d) unless otherwise provided in the partnership agreement or approved by all partners, the general partner (i) makes an assignment for the benefit of creditors, (ii) is the subject of an order for relief under Title 11 of the United States Code, (iii) files a petition or answer seeking for himself any reorganization, arrangement, composition, readjustment, liquidation, dissolution, or similar relief under any statute, law, or regulation, (iv) files an answer or other pleading, admitting or failing to contest the material allegations of a petition filed against him in any proceeding of this nature, or (v) seeks, consents to, or acquiesces in the appointment of a trustee, receiver, or liquidator of the general partner or of all or any substantial part of his properties;

(e) unless otherwise provided in the partnership agreement or approved by all partners, (i) if within one hundred twenty days after the commencement of any proceeding against the general partner seeking reorganization, arrangement, composition, readjustment, liquidation, dissolution, or similar relief under any statute, law, or regulation, the proceeding has not been dismissed or stayed, or within ninety days after the expiration of any such stay, the proceeding has not been dismissed, or (ii) if within ninety days after the appointment without his consent or acquiescence of a trustee, receiver, or liquidator of the general partner or of all or any substantial part of his properties, the appointment is not vacated or stayed, or within ninety days after the expiration of any such stay, the appointment is not vacated;

(f) in the case of a general partner who is a natural person, (i) his death or (ii) the entry of a judgment by a court of competent jurisdiction adjudicating him incompetent to manage his person or his property;

(g) in the case of a general partner who is acting as a general partner by virtue of being a trustee of a trust, the termination of the trust (but not merely the substitution of a new trustee);

(h) in the case of a general partner that is a partnership, unless the partnership agreement of such partnership provides for the right of any one or more of the partners of such partnership to continue the

Partnership Law

business of such partnership and such partnership is so continued, the dissolution and commencement of winding up of such partnership;

(i) in the case of a general partner that is a corporation, the filing of a certificate of dissolution, or its equivalent, for the corporation or the revocation of its charter;

(j) in the case of a general partner that is an estate, the distribution by the fiduciary of the estate's entire interest in the limited partnership; or

(k) in the case of a general partner that is a limited liability company, unless the operating agreement of such limited liability company provides for the right of any member of such limited liability company to continue the limited liability company and such limited liability company is so continued, the dissolution and commencement of winding up of such limited liability company.

History: Add, L 1990, ch 950, § 1, eff July 1, 1991.

Sub (i), amd, L 1994, ch 576, § 5, eff Oct 24, 1994.

Sub (j), amd, L 1994, ch 576, § 5, eff Oct 24, 1994.

Sub (k), add, L 1994, ch 576, § 5, eff Oct 24, 1994.

CASE ANNOTATIONS

Court would remove general partner, without compensation, where he was found to have breached his fiduciary duty to his fellow general and limited partners by forcing abandonment of conversion of partnership's primary asset to cooperative ownership at time when it could have netted substantial profits, even though amount of financial harm caused to partnership was not sufficiently proved at trial. Drucker v Mige Assocs. II (1996, 1st Dept) 225 A.D.2d 427, 639 N.Y.S.2d 365, app den (1996) 88 N.Y.2d 807, 647 N.Y.S.2d 164, 670 N.E.2d 448

§ 121-403. General powers and liabilities

(a) Except as provided in this article or in the partnership agreement, a general partner of a limited partnership has the rights and powers and is subject to the restrictions of a partner in a partnership without limited partners.

(b) Except as provided in this article, a general partner of a limited partnership has the liabilities of a partner in a partnership without limited partners to persons other than the limited partnership and the other partners.

(c) Except as provided in this article or in the partnership agreement, a general partner of a limited partnership has the liabilities of a partner in a partnership without limited partners to the limited partnership and to the other partners.

History: Add, L 1990, ch 950, § 1, eff July 1, 1991.

CASE ANNOTATIONS

Existence of dispute as to whether defendant made alleged oral promises, including promise of 8 percent return on plaintiffs' investment in real estate development partnership, did not create triable issue fact on fraud claim, even assuming that defendant intended to induce plaintiffs' reliance on those promises, because plaintiffs could not show that their alleged reliance was justified where they were relatively sophisticated investors who should have understood risks of investing in such venture without conducting "due diligence" investigation or consulting their lawyers and accountants, and one plaintiff did not even read investment prospec-

tus. Stuart Silver Assocs. v Baco Dev. Corp. (1997, 1st Dept) 245 A.D.2d 96, 665 N.Y.S.2d 415

Discrepancies between appraisal, commissioned by defendants, and offering materials given to investors in real estate development partnership, regarding projected cost of and income from venture, were legally insufficient to support inference that offering materials were intentionally falsified where discrepancies were largely based on different assumptions about available square footage at sites, and appraiser did not give defendants his report until after plaintiffs had received offering materials and had made their initial investment; thus, appraisal provided no support for plaintiffs' claim that defendants' projections in offering materials were contradicted by information then in their possession. Stuart Silver Assocs. v Baco Dev. Corp. (1997, 1st Dept) 245 A.D.2d 96, 665 N.Y.S.2d 415

Plaintiffs who invested as limited partners in real estate development venture failed to raise triable issue of fact as to whether general partners who solicited their investments owed them fiduciary duty where (1) plaintiffs easily could have obtained background information about Harlem real estate market by consulting legal and financial advisors who had guided their previous investment decisions, (2) they could have requested supporting documentation for project summaries, investigated project site and its existing leases, reviewed construction contract, and asked for more information about terms and success rate of defendants' similar ventures, and (3) difference in business expertise between plaintiffs and defendants was not so great as to raise fiduciary duty to suggest that plaintiffs perform due diligence before investing. Stuart Silver Assocs. v Baco Dev. Corp. (1997, 1st Dept) 245 A.D.2d 96, 665 N.Y.S.2d 415

Even if there were fiduciary relationship between defendant general partners and plaintiffs who invested as limited partners in real estate development venture, there was no triable issue of fact as to breach of that duty where plaintiffs showed no basis for their fraud claim, and business judgment rule shielded defendants from liability in absence of bad faith, conflict of interest, or personal bias. Stuart Silver Assocs. v Baco Dev. Corp. (1997, 1st Dept) 245 A.D.2d 96, 665 N.Y.S.2d 415

Plaintiffs who invested as limited partners in real estate development venture had no viable claim for punitive damages where that claim was based on their fraud claim, as to which defendant general partners were entitled to summary judgment. Stuart Silver Assocs. v Baco Dev. Corp. (1997, 1st Dept) 245 A.D.2d 96, 665 N.Y.S.2d 415

§ 121-404. Contributions by a general partner

A general partner of a limited partnership shall make contributions to the limited partnership and share in the profits and losses of, and in distributions from, the limited partnership as a general partner. A person who is a general partner also may make contributions and share in profits, losses, and distributions as a limited partner. A person who is both a general partner and a limited partner has the rights and powers, and is subject to the restrictions and liabilities, of a general partner and, except as provided in the partnership agreement, also has the rights and powers, and is subject to the restrictions, of a limited partner to the extent of his participation in the partnership as a limited partner.

History: Add, L 1990, ch 950, § 1, eff July 1, 1991.

§ 121-405. Classes and voting by general partners

(a) A partnership agreement may provide for classes or groups of general partners having such relative rights and powers as the partnership agreement may provide, and may make provision for the future creation in the manner provided in the partnership agreement of additional classes of general partners having such relative rights and powers as may from time to time be established pursuant to the partnership agreement including rights and powers senior to existing classes of general partners. The partnership agreement may grant to all or to one or more classes of general partners the right to vote, on a per capita, class or other basis, upon any matter.

(b) A partnership agreement may set forth provisions relating to notice of the time, place or purpose of any meeting at which any matter is to be voted on by any general partners, waiver of any such notice, action by consent without a meeting, the establishment of a record date, quorum requirements, voting in person or by proxy, or any other matter with respect to the exercise of any such right to vote.

History: Add, L 1990, ch 950, § 1, eff July 1, 1991.

§ 121-501. Form of contribution

The contribution of a partner may be in cash, property, or services rendered, or a promissory note or other obligation to contribute cash or property or to render services.

History: Add, L 1990, ch 950, § 1, eff July 1, 1991.

§ 121-502. Liability for contributions

(a) Except as provided in the partnership agreement, a partner is obligated to perform any promise, to contribute cash or property or to perform services which is otherwise enforceable in accordance with applicable law, even if he is unable to perform because of death, disability or any other reason. Except as provided in the partnership agreement, if a partner does not make any required contribution of property or services, he is obligated at the option of the limited partnership to contribute cash equal to that portion of the value, as stated in the partnership records if so stated, of the contribution that has not been made. The foregoing option shall be in addition to, and not in lieu of, any other rights, including the right to specific performance, that the limited partnership may have against such partner under the partnership agreement or applicable law.

(b) Unless otherwise provided in the partnership agreement and except as provided in section 121-705 of this article, the obligation of a partner to make a contribution or to return money or other property paid or distributed in violation of this article may be compromised only by consent of all the partners. Notwithstanding the compromise, a creditor of a limited partnership who extends credit in reliance on that obligation may enforce the original obligation to the extent he reasonably relied on such obligation.

(c) A partnership agreement may provide that the interest of any partner who fails to make any required contribution shall be subject to specified consequences of such failure. Such consequences may take the form of reducing or eliminating the defaulting partner's interest in the limited partnership, subordinating his partnership interest to that of nondefaulting partners, a forced sale of his partnership interest, the lending by other partners of the amount necessary to meet his commitment, a fixing of the value of his partnership interest by appraisal or by formula and redemption or sale of his partnership interest at such value, or other consequences.

History: Add, L 1990, ch 950, § 1, eff July 1, 1991.

§ 121-503. Sharing of profits and losses

The profits and losses of a limited partnership shall be allocated among the partners, and among the classes of partners, in the manner provided in the partnership agreement. If the partnership agreement does not so provide, profits and losses shall be allocated on the basis of the value, as stated in the records of the limited partnership if so stated, of the contributions, but not including defaulted obligations to make contributions, of each partner to the extent they have been received by or promised to the limited partnership and have not been returned.

History: Add, L 1990, ch 950, § 1, eff July 1, 1991.

§ 121-504. Sharing of distributions

Distributions of cash or other assets of a limited partnership shall be allocated among the partners, and among classes of partners, in the manner provided in the partnership agreement which may, among other things, establish record dates for distributions. If the partnership agreement does not so provide, distributions shall be allocated on the basis of the value, as stated in the records of the limited partnership, if so stated, of the contributions, but not including defaulted obligations to make contributions, of each partner to the extent they have been received by or promised to the limited partnership and have not been returned.

History: Add, L 1990, ch 950, § 1, eff July 1, 1991.

§ 121-601. Interim distributions

Except as provided in this article, a partner is entitled to receive distributions from a limited partnership before his withdrawal from the limited partnership and before the dissolution and winding up thereof to the extent and at the times or upon the happening of the events specified in the partnership agreement.

History: Add, L 1990, ch 950, § 1, eff July 1, 1991.

§ 121-602. Withdrawal of a general partner

A general partner may withdraw from a limited partnership at any time by giving written notice to the other partners, but if the withdrawal violates the partnership agreement, the limited partnership may recover from the withdrawing general partner damages for breach of the partnership agreement, which may be determined as set forth in the partnership agreement, and offset the damages against the amount otherwise distributable to him.

History: Add, L 1990, ch 950, § 1, eff July 1, 1991.

Partnership Law

§ 121-603. Withdrawal of a limited partner

(a) A limited partner may withdraw from a limited partnership at the time or upon the happening of events specified in the partnership agreement and in accordance with the partnership agreement. Notwithstanding anything to the contrary under applicable law, unless a partnership agreement provides otherwise, a limited partner may not withdraw from a limited partnership prior to the dissolution and winding up of the limited partnership. Notwithstanding anything to the contrary under applicable law, a partnership agreement may provide that a partnership interest may not be assigned prior to the dissolution and winding up of the limited partnership.

(b) A limited partnership whose original certificate of limited partnership was filed with the secretary of state and effective prior to the effective date of this subdivision shall continue to be governed by this section as in effect on such date and shall not be governed by this section, unless otherwise provided in the partnership agreement.

History: Sub (a), formerly entire section, add, L 1990, ch 950, § 1; so designated sub (a) and amd, L 1999, ch 420, § 12, eff Aug 31, 1999.

Sub (b), add, L 1999, ch 420, § 12, eff Aug 31, 1999.

CASE ANNOTATIONS

Limited partner was bound by forum selection clause contained in restated limited partnership agreement where neither original agreement nor restated agreement provided for withdrawal of limited partner, and restated agreement was approved by requisite percentage of limited partners before limited partner's resignation became effective. In re Cantor Fitzgerald, L.P. (1996, 2d Dept) 228 A.D.2d 591, 645 N.Y.S.2d 36

§ 121-604. Right to distribution upon withdrawal

Except as provided in this article upon withdrawal any withdrawing partner is entitled to receive any distribution to which he is entitled under the partnership agreement and, if not otherwise provided in the partnership agreement, he is entitled to receive, within a reasonable time after withdrawal, the fair value of his interest in the limited partnership as of the date of withdrawal based upon his right to share in distributions from the limited partnership.

History: Add, L 1990, ch 950, § 1, eff July 1, 1991.

§ 121-605. Distribution in kind

Except as provided in the partnership agreement, a partner, regardless of the nature of his contribution, has no right to demand and receive any distribution from a limited partnership in any form other than cash. Except as provided in the partnership agreement, a partner may not be compelled to accept a distribution of any asset in kind from a limited partnership to the extent that the percentage of the asset distributed to him exceeds a percentage of that asset which is equal to the percentage in which he shares in distributions from the limited partnership.

History: Add, L 1990, ch 950, § 1, eff July 1, 1991.

§ 121-606. Right to distribution

Subject to sections 121-607 and 121-804 of this article, at the time a partner becomes entitled to receive a distribution, he has the status of, and is entitled to all remedies available to, a creditor of the limited partnership with respect to the distribution.

History: Add, L 1990, ch 950, § 1, eff July 1, 1991.

§ 121-607. Limitations on distribution

(a) A limited partnership shall not make a distribution to a partner to the extent that, at the time of the distribution, after giving effect to the distribution, all liabilities of the limited partnership, other than liabilities to partners on account of their partnership interests and liabilities for which recourse of creditors is limited to specified property of the limited partnership, exceed the fair market value of the assets of the limited partnership, except that the fair market value of property that is subject to a liability for which the recourse of creditors is limited shall be included in the assets of the limited partnership only to the extent that the fair value of that property exceeds that liability.

(b) A limited partner who receives a distribution in violation of subdivision (a) of this section, and who knew at the time of the distribution that the distribution violated subdivision (a) of this section, shall be liable to the limited partnership for the amount of the distribution. A limited partner who receives a distribution in violation of subdivision (a) of this section, and who did not know at the time of the distribution that the distribution violated subdivision (a) of this section, shall not be liable for the amount of the distribution. Subject to subdivision (c) of this section, this subdivision shall not affect any obligation or liability of a limited partner under a partnership agreement or other applicable law for the amount of a distribution.

(c) Unless otherwise agreed, a limited partner who receives a wrongful distribution from a limited partnership shall have no liability under this article or other applicable law for the amount of the distribution after the expiration of three years from the date of the distribution.

History: Add, L 1990, ch 950, § 1, eff July 1, 1991.

CASE ANNOTATIONS

Because the three-year statute of limitations contained in N.Y. P'ship Law § 121-607(c) was applicable to a successor liquidating trustee's claims and it was uncontested that none of the claims fell within the three-year period of limitations, the limited partners' motions to dismiss the complaint on that ground should have been granted. Williamson v Culbro Corp. Pension Fund (2007, 1st Dept) 41 App Div 3d 229, 838 NYS2d 524.

Trial court properly granted a limited partner's motion for summary judgment in a judgment creditor's action to collect a transfer of the limited partnership's tax refund to the manager and then to the limited partner because the claim was barred by the three-year statute of limitations, the transaction had been upheld after trial as non-fraudulent, which barred the judgment creditor's claim against the limited partner, but did not preclude the limited partner from presenting proof to establish that the transfer, despite being filtered through the manager's account, was really a partnership distribution where the assignment was of a partnership interest made in exchange for consideration, payment of which was delayed. Peckar & Abramson, P.C. v Lyford Holdings, Ltd., 20 N.Y.S.3d 41, 2015 N.Y. App. Div. LEXIS 8466 (N.Y. App. Div. 1st Dep't 2015).

§ 121-701. Nature of partnership interest

An interest in a limited partnership is personal property and a partner has no interest in specific partnership property.

History: Add, L 1990, ch 950, § 1, eff July 1, 1991.

§ 121-702. Assignment of partnership interest

(a) Except as provided in the partnership agreement,

(1) A partnership interest is assignable in whole or in part;

(2) An assignment of a partnership interest does not dissolve a limited partnership or entitle the assignee to become or to exercise any rights or powers of a partner;

(3) The only effect of an assignment is to entitle the assignee to receive, to the extent assigned, the distributions and allocations of profits and losses to which the assignor would be entitled; and

(4) A partner ceases to be a partner and to have the power to exercise any rights or powers of a partner upon assignment of all of his partnership interest. Unless otherwise provided in the partnership agreement, the pledge of, or the granting of a security interest, lien or other encumbrance in or against, any or all of the partnership interest of a partner shall not cause the partner to cease to be a partner or to have the power to exercise any rights or powers of a partner.

(b) The partnership agreement may provide that a limited partner's interest may be evidenced by a certificate issued by the partnership and may also provide for the assignment or transfer of any of the interest represented by such a certificate. A limited partner's interest may be a certificated security or an uncertificated security within the meaning of section 8-102 of the uniform commercial code if the requirements of 8-103(c) are met, and if the requirements are not met shall be deemed to be a general intangible.

(c) Unless otherwise provided in a partnership agreement and except to the extent assumed by agreement, until an assignee of a partnership interest becomes a partner, the assignee shall have no liability as a partner solely as a result of the assignment.

History: Add, L 1990, ch 950, § 1, eff July 1, 1991.

Sub (a), par (4), amd, L 1990, ch 951, § 4, eff July 1, 1991.

Sub (b), amd, L 1997, ch 566, § 24, eff Oct 10, 1997.

§ 121-703. Rights of creditor

On application to a court of competent jurisdiction by any judgment creditor of a partner, the court may charge the partnership interest of the partner with payment of the unsatisfied amount of the judgment with interest. To the extent so charged, the judgment creditor has only the rights of an assignee of the partnership interest. This article does not deprive any partner of the benefit of any exemption laws applicable to his partnership interest.

History: Add, L 1990, ch 950, § 1, eff July 1, 1991.

§ 121-704. Right of assignee to become limited partner

(a) An assignee of a partnership interest, including an assignee of a general partner, may become a limited partner if (i) the assignor gives the assignee that right in accordance with authority granted in the partnership agreement, or (ii) all partners consent in writing, or (iii) to the extent that the partnership agreement so provides.

(b) An assignee who has become a limited partner has, to the extent assigned, the rights and powers, and is subject to the restrictions and liabilities, of a limited partner under the partnership agreement and this article. Notwithstanding the foregoing, unless otherwise provided in the partnership agreement, an assignee who becomes a limited partner is liable for the obligations of his assignor to make contributions as provided in section 121-502 of this article, but shall not be liable for the obligations of his assignor under sections 121-603 and 121-607 of this article. However, the assignee is not obligated for liabilities, including the obligations of his assignor to make contributions as provided in section 121-502 of this article, unknown to the assignee at the time he becomes a limited partner.

History: Add, L 1990, ch 950, § 1, eff July 1, 1991.

Sub (a), amd, L 1990, ch 951, § 5, eff July 1, 1991.

§ 121-705. Liability upon assignment

(a) The assignor of a partnership interest is not released from any liability under this article or the partnership agreement, except liabilities which arise after the effectiveness of the assignment and are pursuant to section 121-207 of this article, section 121-607 of this article or, in the event the assignee becomes a limited partner, unless otherwise provided in the partnership agreement, section 121-502 of this article.

(b) An assignee who becomes a limited partner is liable for the obligations to make contributions and return distributions as provided for in this article, provided, however, that the assignee is not obligated for liabilities unknown to the assignee at the time he became a limited partner and which could not be ascertained from the partnership agreement and provided, further, that the assignee is not obligated for any accrued liabilities of the assignor at the time of assignment unless the assignee specifically assumes such liabilities.

History: Add, L 1990, ch 950, § 1, eff July 1, 1991.

§ 121-706. Power of estate of deceased or incompetent partner

Subject to subdivision (f) of section 121-402 of this article, if a partner who is an individual dies or a court of competent jurisdiction adjudges him to be incompetent to manage his person or his property, the partner's executor, administrator, guardian, conservator or other legal representative may exercise all of the partner's rights for the purpose of settling his estate or administering his property, including any power under the partnership agreement of an assignee to become a limited partner. If a partner is a corporation, trust, or other entity and is dissolved or terminated, the powers of that partner may be exercised by its legal representative or successor.

History: Add, L 1990, ch 950, § 1, eff July 1, 1991.

§ 121-801. Nonjudicial dissolution

A limited partnership is dissolved and its affairs shall be wound up upon the happening of the first to occur of the following:

(a) at the time, if any, provided in the certificate of limited partnership;

(b) at the time or upon the happening of events specified in the partnership agreement;

(c) subject to any requirement in the partnership agreement requiring approval by any greater or lesser percentage of limited partners and general partners, upon the written consent (1) of all of the general partners and (2) of a majority in interest of each class of limited partners;

(d) an event of withdrawal of a general partner unless (1) at the time there is at least one other general partner and the partnership agreement permits the business of the limited partnership to be carried on by the remaining general partner and that partner does so, or (2) unless the partnership agreement provides otherwise, if within ninety days after the withdrawal of the last general partner, not less than a majority in interest of the limited partners agree in writing to continue the business of the limited partnership and to the appointment, effective as of the date of withdrawal, of one or more additional general partners if necessary or desired; or

(e) entry of a decree of judicial dissolution under section 121-802 of this article.

(f) a limited partnership whose original certificate of limited partnership was filed with the secretary of state and effective prior to the effective date of this subdivision shall continue to be governed by this section as in effect on such date and shall not be governed by this section, unless otherwise provided in the partnership agreement.

History: Add, L 1990, ch 950, § 1, eff July 1, 1991.

Sub (c), amd, L 1990, ch 951, § 6, L 1999, ch 420, § 13, eff Aug 31, 1999.

Sub (d), amd, L 1991, ch 264, § 5, L 1999, ch 420, § 13, eff Aug 31, 1999.

Sub (f), add, L 1999, ch 420, § 13, eff Aug 31, 1999.

§ 121-802. Judicial dissolution

On application by or for a partner, the supreme court in the judicial district in which the office of the limited partnership is located may decree dissolution of a limited partnership whenever it is not reasonably practicable to carry on the business in conformity with the partnership agreement. A certified copy of the order of dissolution shall be filed by the applicant with the department of state within thirty days of its issuance.

History: Add, L 1990, ch 950, § 1, eff July 1, 1991.

§ 121-803. Winding up

(a) In the event of a dissolution of a limited partnership, except for a dissolution pursuant to section 121-802 of this article, unless otherwise provided in the partnership agreement, the general partners who have not wrongfully dissolved a limited partnership or, if none, the limited partners, may wind up the limited partnership's affairs; upon cause shown, the supreme court in the judicial district in which the office of the limited partnership is located may wind up the limited partnership's affairs upon application of any partner, his legal representative, or assignee, and in connection therewith may appoint a receiver or liquidating trustee.

(b) Upon dissolution of a limited partnership, the persons winding up the limited partnership's affairs may, in the name of, and for and on behalf of, the limited partnership prosecute and defend suits, whether civil, criminal or administrative, settle and close the limited partnership's business, dispose of and convey the limited partnership's property, discharge the limited partnership's liabilities, and distribute to the partners any remaining assets of the limited partnership, all without affecting the liability of limited partners including limited partners participating in the winding up of the limited partnership's affairs.

History: Add, L 1990, ch 950, § 1, eff July 1, 1991.

§ 121-804. Distribution of assets

Upon the winding up of a limited partnership, the assets shall be distributed as follows:

(a) to creditors, including partners who are creditors, to the extent permitted by law, in satisfaction of liabilities of the limited partnership, whether by payment or by establishment of adequate reserves, other than liabilities for distributions to partners under section 121-601 or 121-604 of this article;

(b) except as provided in the partnership agreement, to partners and former partners in satisfaction of liabilities for distributions under section 121-601 or 121-604 of this article; and

(c) except as provided in the partnership agreement, to partners first for the return of their contri butions, to the extent not previously returned, and secondly respecting their partnership interests, in the proportions in which the partners share in distributions in accordance with section 121-504 of this article.

History: Add, L 1990, ch 950, § 1, eff July 1, 1991.

CASE ANNOTATIONS

In action for law partnership accounting, sole distributable assets of partnership were its contingency-fee files, which were distributed to parties in accordance with their partnership agreement through self-help methods. Cohen v Katz (1997, 1st Dept) 242 A.D.2d 448, 662 N.Y.S.2d 40

In action for law partnership accounting, plaintiff's claims that defendant breached partnership agreement by taking files without first obtaining client consents and that plaintiff was entitled to share of any proceeds realized on files that were distributed to defendant were defeated by plaintiff's admissions that he retained for his own benefit partnership money and fees that he collected on files that were distributed to him; in view of plaintiff's breach of his own fiduciary duties to defendant, doctrine of unclean hands barred any right that plaintiff might otherwise have had to accounting. Cohen v Katz (1997, 1st Dept) 242 A.D.2d 448, 662 N.Y.S.2d 40

§ 121-901. Law governing

Subject to the constitution of this state, the laws of the jurisdiction under which a foreign limited partnership is organized govern its organization and internal affairs and the liability of its limited partners.

History: Add, L 1990, ch 950, § 1, eff July 1, 1991.

CASE ANNOTATIONS

Based on N.Y. Ltd. Liab. Co. Law § 801 and N.Y. P'ship Law § 121-901, a dissolved Texas limited partnership and limited liability company were governed by Texas law with respect to liability of the individual after the dissolution of those entities in an action by a property owner, alleging environmental pollution to its property; where the claim was brought within three years of the dissolution, dismissal of the claim against the limited liability company was error under former Tex. Limited Liability Company Act art 8.12, former Tex. Bus. Corp. Act. Ann. art. 7.12. Treeline 1 OCR, LLC v Nassau County Indus. Dev. Agency (2011, 2d Dept) 82 App Div 3d 748, 918 NYS2d 128.

In a dispute over the proper distribution of the assets of a dissolved limited partnership, the court determined, as a Delaware limited partnership, Delaware law applied. Mizrahi v Chanel, Inc. (2001, Sup) 746 N.Y.S.2d 878

§ 121-902. Application for authority, contents

(a) Before doing business in this state, a foreign limited partnership shall apply for authority to do business in this state by submitting to the department of state (i) a certificate of existence or, if no such certificate is issued by the jurisdiction of organization, a certified copy of a restated certificate of limited partnership and all subsequent amendments thereto or, if no restated certificate has been filed, a certified copy of the certificate filed as its organizational basis and all amendments thereto (if such certificate or certified copy is in a foreign language, a translation thereof under oath of the translator shall be attached thereto) and (ii) an application for authority as a foreign limited partnership entitled "Application for authority of .... (name of limited partnership) under Section 121-902 of the Revised Limited Partnership Act," signed by a general partner and setting forth:

(1) the name of the foreign limited partnership and, if a foreign limited partnership's name is not acceptable for authorization pursuant to section 121-102 of this article, the fictitious name under which it proposes to apply for authority and do business in this state, which name shall be in compliance with section 121-102 of this article and shall be used by the foreign limited partnership in all its dealings with the department of state and in the conduct of its business in this state. (The provisions of section one hundred thirty of the general business law shall not apply to any fictitious name filed by a foreign limited partnership pursuant to this section, and a filing under section one hundred thirty of the general business law shall not constitute the adoption of a fictitious name.);

(2) the jurisdiction and date of its organization;

(3) the county within this state in which the office of the limited partnership is to be located;

(4) a designation of the secretary of state as its agent upon whom process against it may be served and the post office address within or without this state to which the secretary of state shall mail a copy of any process against it served upon him;

(5) if it is to have a registered agent, his name and address within the state and a statement that the registered agent is to be its agent upon whom process may be served;

(6) the address of the office required to be maintained in the jurisdiction of its organization by the laws of that jurisdiction or, if not so required, of the principal office of the foreign limited partnership;

(7) a list of the names and business or residence addresses of all general partners;

(8) a statement that the foreign limited partnership is in existence in the jurisdiction of its organization at the time of the filing of such application; and

(9) the name and address of the authorized officer in its jurisdiction of its organization where a copy of its certificate of limited partnership is filed and, if no public filing of its certificate of limited partnership is required by the law of its jurisdiction of organization, a statement that the limited partnership shall provide, on request, a copy thereof with all amendments thereto (if such documents are in a foreign language, a translation thereof under oath of the translator shall be attached thereto), and the name and post office address of the person responsible for providing such copies.

(b) Without excluding other activities which may not constitute doing business in this state, a foreign limited partnership shall not be considered to be doing business in this state for the purposes of this article, by reason of carrying on in this state any one or more of the following activities:

(1) maintaining or defending any action or proceeding, whether judicial, administrative, arbitrative

or otherwise, or effecting settlement thereof or the settlement of claims or disputes;

(2) holding meetings of its partners, general or limited;

(3) maintaining bank accounts; or

(4) maintaining offices or agencies only for the transfer, exchange and registration of its partnership interests, or appointing and maintaining depositaries with relation to its partnership interests.

(c) The specification in subdivision (b) of this section does not establish a standard for activities which may subject a foreign limited partnership to service of process under this article or any other statute of this state.

(d) (i) Within one hundred twenty days after the filing of the application for authority, a copy of the same or a notice containing the substance thereof shall be published once in each week for six successive weeks, in two newspapers of the county within this state in which the office of the foreign limited partnership is located, one newspaper to be printed weekly and one newspaper to be printed daily, to be designated by the county clerk. When such county is located within a city with a population of one million or more, such designation shall be as though the copy or notice were a notice or advertisement of judicial proceedings. Proof of the publication required by this paragraph, consisting of the certificate of publication of the foreign limited partnership with the affidavits of publication of such newspapers annexed thereto, must be filed with the department of state. Notwithstanding any other provision of law, if the office of the foreign limited partnership is located in a county wherein a weekly or daily newspaper of the county, or both, has not been so designated by the county clerk, then the publication herein required shall be made in a weekly or daily newspaper of any county, or both, as the case may be, which is contiguous to, such county, provided that any such newspaper meets all the other requirements of this paragraph. A copy or notice published in a newspaper other than the newspaper or newspapers designated by the county clerk shall not be deemed to be one of the publications required by this subdivision. The notice shall include: (1) the name of the foreign limited partnership and the fictitious name under which it applied for authority to do business in this state, if any; (2) the date of filing of the application for authority with the department of state; (3) the jurisdiction and date of its organization; (4) the county within this state in which the office of the foreign limited partnership is located; (4-a) the street address of the principal business location, if any; (5) a statement that the secretary of state has been designated as its agent upon whom process against it may be served and the post office address within or without this state to which the secretary of state shall mail a copy of any process against it served upon him or her; (6) if it has a registered agent, his or her name and address within the state and a statement that the registered agent is

its agent upon whom process may be served; (7) the address of the office required to be maintained in the jurisdiction of its organization by the laws of that jurisdiction or, if not so required, of the principal office of the foreign limited partnership; (8) a statement that the list of the names and business or residence addresses of all general partners is available from the secretary of state; (9) the name and address of the authorized officer in its jurisdiction of organization where a copy of its certificate of limited partnership is filed and, if no public filing of its certificate of limited partnership is required by the law of its jurisdiction of organization, a statement that the limited partnership shall provide, on request, a copy thereof with all amendments thereto (if such documents are in a foreign language, a translation thereof under oath of the translator shall be attached thereto), and the name and post office address of the person responsible for providing such copies; and (10) the character or purpose of the business of such partnership. Where, at any time after completion of the first of the six weekly publications required by this paragraph and prior to the completion of the sixth such weekly publication, there is a change in any of the information contained in the copy or notice as published, the foreign limited partnership may complete the remaining publications of the original copy or notice, and the foreign limited partnership shall not be required to publish any further or amended copy or notice. Where, at any time after completion of the six weekly publications required by this paragraph, there is a change to any of the information contained in the copy or notice as published, no further or amended publication or republication shall be required to be made. If within one hundred twenty days after the filing of application for authority with the department of state, proof of such publication, consisting of the certificate of publication of the foreign limited partnership with the affidavits of publication of the newspapers annexed thereto has not been filed with the department of state, the authority of such foreign limited partnership to carry on, conduct or transact any business in this state shall be suspended, effective as of the expiration of such one hundred twenty day period. The failure of a foreign limited partnership to cause such copy or notice to be published and such certificate of publication and affidavits of publication to be filed with the department of state within such one hundred twenty day period or the suspension of such foreign limited partnership's authority to carry on, conduct or transact business in this state pursuant to this paragraph shall not limit or impair the validity of any contract or act of such foreign limited partnership, or any right or remedy of any other party under or by virtue of any contract, act or omission of such foreign limited partnership, or the right of any other party to maintain any action or special proceeding on any such contract, act or omission, or right of such foreign limited partnership to defend any action or special proceeding in this state, or result in any partner or agent of such foreign limited partnership becoming liable for the contractual obligations or other liabilities of the foreign limited partnership. If, at any time following the suspension of a foreign limited partnership's authority to carry on, conduct or transact business in this state pursuant to this paragraph, such foreign limited partnership shall cause proof of publication in substantial compliance with the provisions (other than the one hundred twenty day period) of this paragraph, consisting of the certificate of publication of the foreign limited partnership with the affidavits of publication of the newspapers annexed thereto, to be filed with the department of state, such suspension of such foreign limited partnership's authority to carry on, conduct or transact business shall be annulled.

(ii) (1) A foreign limited partnership which was formed and filed its application for authority with the department of state prior to the effective date of this paragraph and complied with the publication and filing requirements of this subdivision as in effect prior to such effective date shall not be required to make any publication or republication or any filing under paragraph (i) of this subdivision, and shall not be subject to suspension pursuant to this subdivision.

(2) Within twelve months after the effective date of this paragraph, a foreign limited partnership which was formed and filed its application for authority with the department of state prior to such effective date and which did not comply with the publication and filing requirements of this subdivision as in effect prior to such effective date shall publish a copy of its application for authority or a notice containing the substance thereof in the manner required (other than the one hundred twenty day period) by this subdivision as in effect prior to such effective date and file proof of such publication, consisting of the certificate of publication of the foreign limited partnership with the affidavits of publication of the newspapers annexed thereto, with the department of state.

(3) If a foreign limited partnership that is subject to the provisions of subparagraph two of this paragraph fails to file the required proof of publication with the department of state within twelve months after the effective date of this paragraph, its authority to carry on, conduct or transact any business in this state shall be suspended, effective as of the expiration of such twelve month period.

(4) The failure of a foreign limited partnership that is subject to the provisions of subparagraph two of this paragraph to fully comply with the provisions of said subparagraph two or the suspension of such foreign limited partnership's authority to carry on, conduct or transact any business in this state pursuant to subparagraph three of this paragraph shall not impair or limit the validity of any contract or act of such foreign limited partnership, or any right or remedy of any other party under or by virtue of any contract, act or omission of such foreign limited partnership, or the right of any other party to maintain any action or special proceeding on any such contract, act or omission, or right of such foreign limited partnership to defend any action or special proceeding in this state, or result in any partner or agent of such foreign limited partnership becoming liable for the contractual obligations or other liabilities of the foreign limited partnership.

(5) If, at any time following the suspension of a foreign limited partnership's authority to carry on, conduct or transact business in this state, pursuant to subparagraph three of this paragraph, such foreign limited partnership shall cause proof of publication in substantial compliance with the provisions (other than the one hundred twenty day period) of paragraph (i) of this subdivision, consisting of the certificate of publication of the foreign limited partnership with the affidavits of publication of the newspapers annexed thereto, to be filed with the department of state, such suspension of such foreign limited partnership's authority to carry on, conduct or transact business shall be annulled.

(6) For the purposes of this paragraph, a foreign limited partnership which was formed and filed its application for authority with the department of state prior to the effective date of this paragraph shall be deemed to have complied with the publication and filing requirements of this subdivision as in effect prior to such effective date if (A) the foreign limited partnership was formed and filed its application for authority with the department of state on or after January first, nineteen hundred ninety-nine and prior to such effective date and the foreign limited partnership filed at least one affidavit of the printer or publisher of a newspaper with the department of state at any time prior to such effective date, or (B) the foreign limited partnership was formed and filed its application for authority with the department of state prior to January first, nineteen hundred ninety-nine, without regard to whether the foreign limited partnership did or did not file any affidavit of the printer or publisher of a newspaper with the secretary of state.

(iii) The information in a notice published pursuant to this subdivision shall be presumed to be in compliance with and satisfaction of the requirements of this subdivision.

History: Add, L 1990, ch 950, § 1, eff July 1, 1991; amd, L 1990, ch 952, § 2; L 1991, ch 33, § 3; L 1991, ch 264, § 6,7; L 1999, ch 172, §§ 35-37, eff July 6, 1999; L 1999, ch 420, § 14, eff Aug 31, 1999; L 2005, ch 767, § 12, eff June 1, 2006; L 2006, ch 44, § 9, eff June 1, 2006.

§ 121-903. Certificate of amendment

(a) A foreign limited partnership may amend its application for authority from time to time if the amendments contain only such provisions as might be lawfully contained in an application for authority at the time of making such amendment. To accomplish such amendment, a certificate, entitled "Certificate of amendment of .... (name of limited partnership) under section 121-903 of the Revised Limited Partnership Act," shall be signed and delivered to the department of state. It shall set forth:

(1) the name of the foreign organization as it appears on the index of names of existing domestic and authorized foreign limited partnerships of any type or kind in the department of state, and the fictitious name, if any, the foreign limited partnership has agreed to use in this state pursuant to section 121-902 of this article;

(2) the jurisdiction of its organization;

(3) the date it was authorized to do business in this state;

(4) each amendment effected thereby; and

(5) if the true name of the foreign limited partnership is to be changed, a statement that the change of name has been effected under the laws of the jurisdiction of its organization and the date the change was so effected.

(b) Every foreign limited partnership which has received a filing receipt evidencing authority as provided herein, shall, within ninety days after it has changed its name in the jurisdiction of its formation file an amendment to its application with the department of state under subdivision (a) of this section.

History: Add, L 1990, ch 950, § 1, eff July 1, 1991; amd, L 1999, ch 172, § 38, eff July 6, 1999,39, eff July 6, 1999,40, eff July 6, 1999.

§ 121-903-A.   Certificate of change

(a) A foreign limited partnership may change its application for authority by filing with the department of state a certificate of change entitled "Certificate of Change of .... (name of limited partnership) under Section 121-903-A of the Revised Limited Partnership Act" and shall be signed and delivered to the department of state. A certificate of change may (i) change the location of the limited partnership's office; (ii) change the post office address to which the secretary of state shall mail a copy of process against the limited partnership served upon him; and (iii) make, revoke or change the designation of a registered agent, or to specify or change the address of its registered agent. It shall set forth:

(1) the name of the foreign limited partnership and, if applicable, the fictitious name the foreign limited partnership has agreed to use in this state pursuant to section 121-902 of this article;

(2) the date its application for authority was filed by the department of state; and

(3) each change effected thereby.

(b) A certificate of change which changes only the post office address to which the secretary of state shall mail a copy of any process against a foreign limited partnership served upon him or the address of the registered agent, provided such address being changed is the address of a person, partnership or corporation whose address, as agent, is the address to be changed or who has been designated as registered agent for such foreign limited partnership shall be signed and delivered to the department of state by such agent. The certificate of change shall set forth the statements required under subdivision (a) of this section; that a notice of the proposed change was mailed to the foreign limited partnership by the party signing the certificate not less than thirty days prior to the date of delivery to the department of state and that such foreign limited partnership has not objected thereto; and that the party signing the certificate is the agent of such foreign limited partnership to whose address the secretary of state is required to mail copies of process or the registered agent, if such be the case. A certificate signed and delivered under this subdivision shall not be deemed to effect a change of location of the office of the limited partnership in whose behalf such certificate is filed.

History: Add, L 1998, ch 448, § 7, eff Oct 20, 1998.

§ 121-904.   Application for authority; effect

(a) Upon filing by the department of state of the application for authority the foreign limited partnership shall be authorized to do business in this state. Such authority shall continue so long as it retains its authority to do business in the jurisdiction of its formation and its authority to do business has not been surrendered, suspended or annulled in accordance with the law.

(b) A foreign limited partnership which has received a certificate of authority shall have such powers to conduct business in this state as are permitted by the laws of the jurisdiction in which it was organized but no greater than those of a domestic limited partnership; provided, that this subdivision shall not affect the powers of the foreign limited partnership outside this state.

History: Add, L 1990, ch 950, § 1, eff July 1, 1991.

Sub (b), amd, L 1990, ch 951, § 7, eff July 1, 1991.

§ 121-905.   Surrender of certificate of authority

(a) A foreign limited partnership may surrender its certificate of authority by filing with the department of state a certificate entitled, " Certificate of surrender of authority of .... (name of limited partnership)" signed by a general partner, or by a trustee, receiver or other person authorized by law to wind up such partnership. The authority of the foreign limited partnership to do business in this state shall terminate on such filing of the certificate of surrender of authority. A surrender shall not terminate the authority of the secretary of state to accept service of process on the foreign limited partnership with respect to causes of action arising out of doing business in this state.

(b) The certificate of surrender of authority shall state:

(1) the name of the foreign limited partnership as it appears on the index of names of existing domestic and authorized foreign limited partnerships of any type or kind in the department of state, and the fictitious name the foreign limited partnership has agreed to use in this state pursuant to section 121-902 of this article;

(2) the jurisdiction where it was organized;

(3) the date on which its certificate of authority to do business in this state was filed with the department of state;

(4) that it surrenders its authority to do business in this state;

(5) that it revokes the authority of its registered agent, if any, previously designated, and that it consents that process against it in any action or special proceeding based upon any liability or obligation incurred by it within this state before the filing of the certificate of surrender may be served on the secretary of state in the manner set forth in section 121-109 of this article; and

(6) a post office address within or without this state to which the secretary of state shall mail a copy of any process against it served upon him.

History: Add, L 1990, ch 950, § 1, eff July 1, 1991.

Sub (a), amd, L 1999, ch 172, § 41, eff July 6, 1999.

§ 121-906. Termination of existence

When a foreign limited partnership which has received a certificate of authority is dissolved or its authority to conduct its business or existence is otherwise terminated or cancelled in the jurisdiction of its organization or when such foreign limited partnership is merged into or consolidated with another foreign limited partnership, (i) a certificate of the secretary of state, or official performing the equivalent function as to limited partnership records, in the jurisdiction of organization of such limited partnership attesting to the occurrence of any such event, or (ii) a certified copy of an order or decree of a court of such jurisdiction directing the dissolution of such foreign limited partnership, the termination of its existence or the surrender of its authority, shall be delivered to the department of state. The filing of the certificate, order or decree shall have the same effect as the filing of a certificate of surrender of authority under section 121-905 of this article. The secretary of state shall continue as agent of the foreign limited partnership upon whom process against it may be served in the manner set forth in section 121-109 of this article, in any action or proceeding based upon any liability or obligation incurred by the foreign limited partnership within this state prior to the filing of such certificate, order or decree. The post office address may be changed by filing with the department of state a certificate of amendment under section 121-903 or a certificate of change under section 121-903-A of this article.

History: Add, L 1990, ch 950, § 1; amd, L 1999, ch 172, § 42, eff July 6, 1999.

§ 121-907. Doing business without certificate of authority

(a) A foreign limited partnership doing business in this state without having received a certificate of authority to do business in this state may not maintain any action, suit or special proceeding in any court of this state unless and until such partnership shall have received a certificate of authority in this state.

(b) The failure of a foreign limited partnership that is doing business in this state to comply with the provision of this article does not impair the validity of any contract or act of the foreign limited partnership or prevent the foreign limited partnership from defending any action or special proceeding in any court of this state.

(c) A limited partner of a foreign limited partnership is not liable as a general partner of the foreign limited partnership solely by reason of the limited partnership's doing or having done business in this state without having received a certificate of authority.

(d) A foreign limited partnership by doing business in this state without authority appoints the secretary of state as its agent for service of process with respect to causes of action arising out of doing business in this state. In any such case, process against such foreign limited partnership may be served upon the secretary of state in the manner set forth in section 121-109 of this article.

History: Add, L 1990, ch 950, § 1, eff July 1, 1991.

Sub (a), amd, L 1994, ch 576, § 13, eff Oct 24, 1994.

Sub (a), amd, L 2005, ch 767, § 13, eff June 1, 2006.

§ 121-908. Violations

The attorney general shall, upon his own motion or upon the motion of proper parties, bring an action to restrain a foreign limited partnership without a certificate of authority from doing any business in this state in violation of this article, or from doing any business in this state which is prohibited under the laws of this state. The attorney general may bring an action or special proceeding to annul the authority of a foreign limited partnership which is doing any business in this state which is prohibited under the laws of this state. The attorney general shall deliver a certified copy of the order of annulment to the department of state. Upon the filing thereof by the department of state the certificate of authority of the foreign limited partnership to do business in this state shall be annulled, and the provisions of section 121-906 of this article shall thereafter be applicable. The secretary of state shall continue as agent of the foreign limited partnership upon whom process against it may be served in any action, suit or special proceeding based upon any liability or obligation incurred by the foregoing foreign limited partnership within the state prior to the filing of the certified copy of the order of annulment by the department of state.

History: Add, L 1990, ch 950, § 1, eff July 1, 1991.

§ 121-1001. Parties to actions

A limited partner, unless he is also a general partner, is not a proper party to proceedings by or against a partnership, except where the object is to enforce a limited partner's right against or liability to the partnership and except in cases provided for in section 121-1002 of this article.

History: Add, L 1990, ch 950, § 1, eff July 1, 1991.

CASE ANNOTATIONS

In libel suit by public figure, motion to join limited partner of newspaper as party defendant, on grounds that he hired defendant journalist with knowledge of journalist's penchant for twisting and slanting truth, would be denied for failure to establish any basis on which partner could be held to account for libel under First Amendment. Doe v Daily News, L.P. (1995, Sup) 167 Misc. 2d 1, 632 N.Y.S.2d 750, complaint dismd, application den (1997, Sup) 173 Misc. 2d 321, 660 N.Y.S.2d 604, reported in full (1997, N.Y. Sup) 25 Media L R 1673

§ 121-1002. Limited partners' derivative action

(a) A limited partner may bring an action in the right of a limited partnership to recover a judgment in its favor if all general partners with authority to do so have refused to bring the action or if an effort to cause those general partners to bring the action is not likely to succeed.

(b) In a derivative action, at least one plaintiff must be a limited partner at the time of bringing the action and (i) at the time of the transaction of which he complains, or (ii) his status as a limited partner had devolved upon him by operation of law or in accordance with the terms of the partnership agreement from a person who was a partner at the time of the transaction of which he complains.

(c) In a derivative action, the complaint shall set forth with particularity the efforts of the plaintiff to secure the initiation of such action by a general partner, or the reasons for not making such effort.

(d) A derivative action shall not be discontinued, compromised or settled without the approval of the court having jurisdiction of the action. If the court shall determine that the interests of the limited partners will be substantially affected by such discontinuance, compromise or settlement, the court, in its discretion, may direct that notice, by publication or otherwise, shall be given to the limited partners whose interests it determines will be so affected. If notice is so directed to be given, the court may determine which one or more of the parties to the action shall bear the expenses of giving the same, in such amount as the court shall determine and find to be reasonable in the circumstances, and the amount of such expense shall be awarded as special costs of the action and recoverable in the same manner as statutory taxable costs.

(e) If the derivative action on behalf of the limited partnership is successful, in whole or in part, or if anything is received by the plaintiff or plaintiffs or a claimant or claimants as a result of a judgment, compromise or settlement of an action or claim, the court may award the plaintiff or plaintiffs, claimant or claimants reasonable expenses, including reasonable attorneys' fees, and shall direct him or them to account to the limited partnership for the remainder of the proceeds so received by him or them. This subdivision shall not apply to any judgment rendered for the benefit of injured limited partners only and limited to a recovery of the loss or damage sustained by them.

History: Add, L 1990, ch 950, § 1, eff July 1, 1991.

CASE ANNOTATIONS

Limited partners had standing to commence derivative action on behalf of partnership against law firm whose partner had previously served as partnership's escrow agent where limited partners proffered unrebutted evidence that both oral and written demands to commence suit were made on partnership's general partner, that such demands were not acted on, and that demands were in conformity with partnership agreement and were stated with particularity in complaint. E. Daskal Corp. v New City Ventures LP-1 (1996, 2d Dept) 225 A.D.2d 653, 639 N.Y.S.2d 473

As a limited partner's rights and interests in litigation involving, inter alia, an option agreement were derivative under N.Y. Partnership Law §§ 115-a, 121-1002, the partner could not claim that it was not bound by a forum selection clause because it was not a signatory to the option agreement. Harry Casper, Inc. v Pines Assoc., L.P. (2008, 3d Dept) 53 App Div 3d 764, 861 NYS2d 820.

Because a co-general partner's N.Y. P'ship Law § 121-1002(d) complaint improperly sought to vindicate both the personal rights of the co-general partner in the co-general partner's individual capacity and the derivative claims of the limited partnership, the causes of action were dismissed. Wallace v Perret (2010, Sup) 244 NYLJ 6, 903 NYS2d 888.

§ 121-1003. Security for expenses

In a derivative action, brought pursuant to section 121-1002 of this article, unless the contributions of or allocable to the plaintiff or plaintiffs amount to five percent or more of the contributions of all limited partners, in their status as limited partners, or such contributions of or allocable to such plaintiff or plaintiffs have a fair value in excess of fifty thousand dollars, the limited partnership in whose right such action is brought shall be entitled at any stage of the proceedings before final judgment to require the plaintiff or plaintiffs to give security for the reasonable expenses, including attorney's fees, which may be incurred by it in connection with such action and by the other parties defendant in connection therewith for which the limited partnership may become liable under this article or under any contract or otherwise under law. The limited partnership shall have recourse to such security in such amount as the court having jurisdiction of such action shall determine upon the termination of such action. Notwithstanding the first sentence of this section, the amount of any security may from time to time be determined in the discretion of the court having jurisdiction of such action, even if the five percent of contributions or fifty thousand dollar value test is met, upon a showing of the need therefor.

History: Add, L 1990, ch 950, § 1, eff July 1, 1991.

§ 121-1004. Indemnification of general partner

(a) No provision made to indemnify general partners for the defense of a derivative action, brought pursuant to section 121-1002 of this article, whether contained in the partnership agreement or otherwise, nor any award of indemnification by a court, shall be valid unless consistent with this section. Nothing contained in this section shall affect any rights to indemnification to which limited partners, employees and agents of the limited partnership who are not general partners may be entitled by contract or otherwise under law.

(b) A limited partnership may indemnify, and may advance expenses to, any general partner, including a general partner made a party to an action in the right of a limited partnership to procure a judgment in its favor by reason of the fact that he, his testator or intestate, is or was a general partner in the limited partnership, provided that no indemnification may be made to or on behalf of any general partner if a judgment or other final adjudication adverse to the general partner establishes that his acts were committed in bad faith or were the result of active and deliberate dishonesty and were material to the cause of action so adjudicated, or that he personally gained in fact a financial profit or other advantage to which he was not legally entitled.

History: Add, L 1990, ch 950, § 1, eff July 1, 1991.

§ 121-1101. Merger and consolidation of limited partnerships

One or more limited partnerships formed under this article or which complies with subdivision (a) of section 121-1202 of this article may merge with, or consolidate into, a limited partnership formed under this article or which complies with subdivision (a) of such section or under the law of any other state. Whenever used in this article, "merger" shall mean a procedure in which two or more limited partnerships merge into a single limited partnership which shall be one of the constituent limited partnerships and "consolidation" shall mean a procedure in which two or more limited partnerships consolidate into a single limited partnership which shall be a new limited partnership to be formed pursuant to the consolidation.

History: Add, L 1990, ch 950, § 1, eff July 1, 1991.

§ 121-1102. Procedure for merger or consolidation

(a) The general partners of each constituent limited partnership shall adopt an agreement of merger or consolidation, setting forth the partnership agreement of the surviving or consolidated limited partnership and the terms and conditions of the conversion of the interests of general and limited partners of the constituent limited partnerships into general and limited partnership interests in the surviving or resulting limited partnership or the cash or other consideration to be paid or delivered in exchange for interests in a constituent limited partnership, or a combination thereof. The agreement shall be submitted to the partners of each constituent limited partnership at a regular or special meeting called on twenty days notice or such greater notice as the partnership agreement may provide. Subject to any requirement in the partnership agreement requiring approval by any greater or lesser, which shall not be less than a majority in interest, percentage of limited partners, the agreement shall be approved on behalf of each constituent limited partnership (i) by such vote of general partners as shall be required by the partnership agreement, or, if no provision is made, by all general partners, and (ii) by limited partners representing a majority in interest of each class of limited partners. Notwithstanding authorization by the partners, the plan of merger or consolidation may be abandoned pursuant to a provision for such abandonment, if any, contained in the plan of merger or consolidation.

(b) Any limited partner of a limited partnership which is a party to a proposed merger or consolidation may, prior to that time of the meeting at which such merger or consolidation is to be voted on, file with the limited partnership written notice of dissent from the proposed merger or consolidation. Such notice of dissent may be withdrawn by the dissenting limited partner at any time prior to the effective date of the merger or consolidation and shall be deemed to be withdrawn if the limited partner casts a vote in favor of the proposed merger or consolidation.

(c) Upon the effectiveness of the merger or consolidation the dissenting limited partner of any constituent limited partnership shall not become or continue to be a limited partner of the surviving or resulting limited partnership, but shall be entitled to receive in cash from the surviving or resulting limited partnership the fair value of his interest in the limited partnership as of the close of business of the day prior to the effective date of the merger or consolidation in accordance with section 121-604 of this article, but without taking account of the effect of the merger or consolidation.

(d) A limited partner of a constituent limited partnership who has a right under this article to demand payment for his partnership interest shall not have any right at law or in equity under this article to attack the validity of the merger or consolidation, or to have the merger or consolidation set aside or rescinded, except in an action or contest with respect to compliance with the provisions of the partnership agreement or subdivision (a) of this section.

(e) A limited partnership whose original certificate of limited partnership was filed with the secretary of state and effective prior to the effective date of this subdivision shall continue to be governed by this section as in effect on such date and shall not be governed by this section, unless otherwise provided in the partnership agreement.

History: Add, L 1990, ch 950, § 1, eff July 1, 1991.

Sub (a), amd, L 1999, ch 420, § 15, eff Aug 31, 1999.

Sub (d), amd, L 1990, ch 951, § 8, eff July 1, 1991.

Sub (e), add, L 1999, ch 420, § 15, eff Aug 31, 1999.

CASE ANNOTATIONS

Trial court's order was reversed, defendants' motion to dismiss was granted, and complaint was dismissed as under N.Y. P'ship Law § 121-1102(d), since no limited partner (LP) exercised rights under § 121-1102(b) and (c), subsequent action by LPs in law or equity to attack validity of merger, or to have merger set aside or rescinded, was barred; the LPs' invitation to rewrite the statute and graft the fraud exception of N.Y. Bus. Corp. Law § 623(k) onto an otherwise clear legislative pronouncement was rejected.. Appleton Acquisition, LLC v National Hous. Partnership (2006, 1st Dept) 34 App Div 3d 339, 826 NYS2d 7

§ 121-1103. Certificate of merger or consolidation; contents

(a) After adoption of the plan of merger or consolidation by the partners of each constituent limited partnership, unless the merger or consolidation is abandoned in accordance with subdivision (a) of section 121-1102 of this article, a certificate of merger or consolidation, entitled "Certificate of merger (or consolidation) of .... and .... into .... (names of limited partnership) under Section 121-1103 of the Revised Limited Partnership Act", shall be signed on behalf of each constituent limited partnership and delivered to the department of state. The certificate of merger or consolidation shall set forth:

(1) The name of each constituent limited partnership, and if the name has been changed, the name under which it was formed; and the name of the surviving limited partnership, or the name of the consolidated limited partnership;

(2) If a constituent is a domestic limited partnership, the date when its certificate of limited partnership was filed with the department of state under this article, or the date when and the county in which its original certificate of limited partnership was filed under article eight of this chapter;

(3) If a constituent is a foreign limited partnership the jurisdiction and date of filing of its original certificate of limited partnership and the date when its application for authority was filed by the department of state or if no such application has been filed, a statement to such effect and (if the constituent foreign limited partnership is the survivor) that it is not to do business in this state until an application for such authority shall have been filed by the department of state;

(4) If a domestic limited partnership is the surviving limited partnership, such changes in its certificate of limited partnership as shall be necessary by reason of merger;

(5) If a domestic limited partnership is the resulting limited partnership in a consolidation, the matters required to be set forth under section 121-201 of this article;

(6) If the surviving or resulting limited partnership is a foreign limited partnership: An agreement that the surviving or consolidated foreign limited partnership may be served with process in this state in any action or special proceeding for the enforcement of any liability or obligation of any domestic limited partnership or of any foreign limited partnership previously amenable to suit in this state which is a constituent limited partnership in such merger or consolidation, and for the enforcement as provided in this article, of the right of partners of any domestic limited partnership to receive payment for their interest against the surviving or consolidated limited partnership; and

(7) A designation of the secretary of state as its agent upon whom process against it may be served in the manner set forth in section 121-109 of this article in any action or special proceeding, and a post office address, within or without this state, to which the secretary of state shall mail a copy of any process served upon him. Such post office address shall supersede any prior address designated as the address to which process shall be mailed.

(b) The merger or consolidation shall be effective upon the filing thereof by the department of state of the certificate, or at such later date not more than thirty days after the date of such filing as the certificates filed may provide.

History: Add, L 1990, ch 950, § 1, eff July 1, 1991.

Sub (a), opening par, amd, L 1999, ch 172, § 43, eff July 6, 1999.

§ 121-1104. Effect of merger or consolidation

When such merger or consolidation has been effected:

(a) all the property, real and personal, tangible and intangible, of each constituent limited partnership shall vest in the surviving or resulting limited partnership;

(b) to the extent provided in the plan of merger or consolidation, the partners of each constituent limited partnership shall continue or become partners in the surviving or resulting limited partnership with such interest as the agreement of merger or consolidation shall provide;

(c) the surviving or resulting limited partnership shall be liable for all debts, obligations, liabilities and penalties of each constituent limited partnership as though each such debt, obligation, liability or penalty had been originally incurred by such surviving or resulting limited partnership; and

(d) no action, suit or proceeding, civil or criminal, then pending by or against any such constituent limited partnership in its common name shall abate or be discontinued by reason of such merger or consolidation, but may be prosecuted by or proceed against such surviving or resulting limited partnership.

History: Add, L 1990, ch 950, § 1, eff July 1, 1991.

§ 121-1105. Payment for interest of dissenting limited partners

(a) Within ten days after the occurrence of an event described in section 121-1102 of this article, the surviving or resulting limited partnership shall send to each dissenting former limited partner a written offer to pay in cash the fair value of such former partner's interest. Payment in cash shall be made to each former limited partner accepting such offer within ten days after notice of such acceptance is received by the surviving or resulting limited partnership.

(b) If a former limited partner and the surviving or resulting limited partnership fail to agree on the price to be paid for the former limited partner's partnership interest within ninety days after the surviving or resulting limited partnership shall have made the offer provided for in subdivision (a) of this section, or if the limited partnership or surviving limited partnership shall fail to make such an offer within the period provided for in subdivision (a) of this section, the procedure provided for in paragraphs (h)-(k) of section six hundred twenty-three of the business corporation law shall apply, as they may be amended from time to time.

(c) A payment under this section shall constitute a return of a partner's contribution for the purposes of section 121-607 of this article.

History: Add, L 1990, ch 950, § 1, eff July 1, 1991.

§ 121-1106. Mergers and consolidations involving other business entities

One or more domestic limited partnerships formed under this article or which comply with subdivision (a) of section 121-1202 of this article may merge with, or consolidate into, one or more other business entities formed under the law of this state or the law of any other state, in each case with the surviving or resulting entity being a limited partnership or a domestic or foreign other business entity; provided that (i) any limited partnership so merging or consolidating complies with the provisions of this chapter so far as applicable to it and as applicable to any surviving or resulting limited partnership and (ii) any such other business entity so merging or consolidating complies with the applicable provisions of the statute governing such other business entity. With respect to adoption of an agreement of merger or consolidation pursuant to section 121-1102 of this article, the general partners of each constituent limited partnership shall adopt an agreement of merger or consolidation (to be submitted to the partners of the limited partnership as provided in subdivision (a) of section 121-1102) setting forth the terms and conditions of the conversion of the inter-

ests of the general and limited partners of such constituent limited partnerships into interests in the surviving or resulting entity or the cash or other consideration to be paid or delivered in exchange for interests in such constituent limited partnerships, or a combination thereof. The rights of any dissenting limited partner of any constituent limited partnership shall be as provided in this chapter whether the surviving or resulting entity is a limited partnership or a domestic or foreign other business entity. The certificate of merger or consolidation required pursuant to section 121-1103 of this article shall include the information required by paragraphs one, two, three and six of subdivision (a) of such section (as applicable) as to the constituent other business entities. The provisions of section 121-1104 of this article shall govern the effect of the merger or consolidation with respect to the property of, debts, obligations, liabilities and penalties of, and actions, suits and proceedings by or against, the constituent limited partnership if the survivor or resultant entity therefrom is a limited partnership. A certificate of merger or consolidation shall be filed with the department of state pursuant to the law applicable to such surviving or resulting entity. If the surviving or resulting entity is an other business entity for which the laws of this state do not provide for the filing of a certificate of merger or consolidation, suchcertificate shall be filed pursuant to this section.

History: Add, L 1994, ch 576, § 14; amd, L 1998, ch 374, § 8, eff Sept 12, 1998.

Amd, L 2008, ch 177, § 4, eff July 7, 2008.

Section heading, amd, L 1998, ch 374, § 8, eff Sept 12, 1998.

§ 121-1201. Existing limited partnership

(a) All limited partnerships formed on or after the effective date of this article shall be governed by this article.

(b) Except as provided in section 121-1202 of this article, all domestic limited partnerships formed under the laws of this state prior to the effective date of this article shall continue to be governed by article eight of this chapter, as amended, in the same manner as if this article had not been enacted.

(c) All foreign limited partnerships which have authority to do business in New York on such effective date shall be deemed to have received authority under this article and such foreign limited partnerships shall not be required to take any action with respect thereto.

History: Add, L 1990, ch 950, § 1, eff July 1, 1991.

§ 121-1202. Adoption by previously formed limited partnerships

(a) A limited partnership formed under the laws of this state prior to the effective date of this article may adopt and thereafter be governed by this article by filing with the department of state a certificate of limited partnership conforming to the requirements of section 121-201 of this article. Such certificate (i) shall be entitled "Certificate of adoption of Revised Limited Partnership Act of .... (name of limited partnership) under Section 121-1202 of the Revised Limited Partnership Act", and (ii) shall state the date and the county in which its original certificate of limited partnership was filed, as well as the name of the limited partnership as provided in such original certificate, if different. Simultaneously, such limited partnership shall file a notice with the county clerk of the county in which its prior certificate was filed stating that it has filed a certificate under this article in the department of state.

(b) On and after the effective date of this article, any limited partnership formed under the laws of the state prior to the effective date of this article which does not elect to be governed by this article which would be required under article eight to amend its certificate of limited partnership or wishes to amend its certificate of limited partnership shall file such amendment with the department of state, together with a certificate of adoption as described in subdivision (a) of this section. Such amendment shall (i) contain a caption that such amendment is filed pursuant to this subdivision and (ii) shall state (A) the date on which and the county in which its original certificate of limited partnership was filed as well as the name of the limited partnership as provided in such original certificate, if different; and (B) if the principal place of business stated in such original certificate of limited partnership has been changed to another county and an amendment thereto filed with the county clerk of the county in which such principal place of business was changed, the date on and the county in which such amendment was filed. Simultaneously, such limited partnership shall file a notice with the county clerk of the county in which its prior certificate was filed stating that it has filed an amendment to its certificate under this section. Following the filing of an initial notice to such clerks of the county no further notice of any additional amendments need be filed with such clerks of the county.

(c) Notwithstanding the provisions of section 121-102 of this article, any limited partnership not electing to be governed by this article may continue to use the name under which it has heretofore done business in this state. A limited partnership electing not to be governed by this article upon filing the amendments provided for in subdivision (b) of this section shall thereafter be governed by this article and not by the law previously applicable to it.

(d) Unless otherwise provided in the partnership agreement of the limited partnership organized prior to the effective date of this article, the general partners of such limited partnership shall have the power and authority to elect whether at any time such limited partnership shall be governed by this article.

History: Add, L 1990, ch 950, § 1, eff July 1, 1991.

Sub (b), amd, L 1990, ch 951, § 9, L 1991, ch 264, § 8, eff July 1, 1991.

Sub (c), amd, L 1991, ch 264, § 9, eff July 1, 1991.

§ 121-1300. Fees

Except as otherwise provided, the department of state shall collect the following fees and deposit such fees in the corporations, state records and uniform commercial code account pursuant to this article:

(a) For the reservation of a limited partnership name pursuant to section 121-103 of this article, twenty dollars.

(b), (c) [Repealed]

(d) For the resignation of a registered agent for service of process pursuant to subdivision (c) of section 121-105 of this article, twenty dollars.

(e) For filing a certificate of limited partnership pursuant to section 121-201 of this article, two hundred dollars.

(f) For filing a certificate of publication with affidavits of publication annexed thereto pursuant to either section 121-201 or 121-902 of this article, fifty dollars.

(g) For filing a certificate of amendment pursuant to section 121-202 of this article, sixty dollars.

(h) For filing a certificate of cancellation pursuant to section 121-203 of this article, sixty dollars.

(i) For filing a restated certificate of limited partnership pursuant to section 121-208 of this article, sixty dollars.

(j) For filing a judicial dissolution pursuant to section 121-802 of this article, sixty dollars.

(k) For filing an application for authority pursuant to section 121-902 of this article, two hundred dollars.

(l) For filing an amendment to an application for authority pursuant to section 121-903 of this article, sixty dollars.

(m) For filing a certificate of surrender of authority pursuant to section 121-905 of this article, sixty dollars.

(n) For filing a certificate of termination of existence pursuant to section 121-906 of this article, sixty dollars.

(o) For filing a certificate of merger or consolidation pursuant to section 121-1103 of this article, sixty dollars.

(p) For filing a certificate of adoption pursuant to section 121-1202 of this article, two hundred dollars.

(q) For filing a certificate of resignation for receipt for process pursuant to section 121-104-A of this article, ten dollars.

(r) For service of process on the secretary of state pursuant to section 121-104-A or section 121-109 of this article, forty dollars. No fee shall be collected for process served on behalf of a county, city, town or village or other political subdivision of the state.

(s) For filing a certificate of change pursuant to subdivision (a) of section 121-202-A or subdivision (a) of section 121-903-A of this article, thirty dollars, and for filing a certificate of change pursuant to subdivision (b) of section 121-202-A or subdivision (b) of section 121-903-A of this article, five dollars.

History: Add, L 1990, ch 950, § 1, eff July 1, 1991; amd, L 1991, ch 264, § 10, eff July 1, 1991,10, eff July 1, 1991; L 1994, ch 170, § 404; L 1996, ch 309, § 168, eff July 13, 1996; L 1998, ch 448, § 8, eff Oct 20, 1998; L 1999, ch 172, § 44, eff July 6, 1999; L 2005, ch 767, § 14, eff June 1, 2006.

ARTICLE 8-B
REGISTERED LIMITED LIABILITY PARTNERSHIPS

History: Add, L 1994, ch 576, § 15, eff Oct 24, 1994.

§ 121-1500. Registered limited liability partnership

(a) (I) Notwithstanding the education law or any other provision of law, (i) a partnership without limited partners each of whose partners is a professional authorized by law to render a professional service within this state and who is or has been engaged in the practice of such profession in such partnership or a predecessor entity, or will engage in the practice of such profession in the registered limited liability partnership within thirty days of the date of the effectiveness of the registration provided for in this subdivision or a partnership without limited partners each of whose partners is a professional, at least one of whom is authorized by law to render a professional service within this state and who is or has been engaged in the practice of such profession in such partnership or a predecessor entity, or will engage in the practice of such profession in the registered limited liability partnership within thirty days of the date of the effectiveness of the registration provided for in this subdivision, (ii) a partnership without limited partners authorized by, or holding a license, certificate, registration or permit issued by the licensing authority pursuant to the education law to render a professional service within this state, which renders or intends to render professional services within this state, or (iii) a related limited liability partnership may register as a registered limited liability partnership by filing with the department of state a registration which shall set forth:

(1) the name of the registered limited liability partnership;

(2) the address of the principal office of the partnership without limited partners;

(3) the profession or professions to be practiced by such partnership without limited partners and a statement that it is eligible to register as a registered limited liability partnership pursuant to subdivision (a) of this section;

(4) a designation of the secretary of state as agent of the partnership without limited partners upon whom process against it may be served and the post office address within or without this state to which the secretary of state shall mail a copy of any process against it or served upon it;

(5) if the partnership without limited partners is to have a registered agent, its name and address in this state and a statement that the registered agent is to be the agent of the partnership without limited partners upon whom process against it may be served;

(6) that the partnership without limited partners is filing a registration for status as a registered limited liability partnership;

(7) if the registration of the partnership without limited partners is to be effective on a date later than the time of filing, the date, not to exceed sixty days from the date of such filing, of such proposed effectiveness;

(8) if all or specified partners of the registered limited liability partnership are to be liable in their capacity as partners for all or specified debts, obligations or liabilities of the registered limited liability partnership as authorized pursuant to subdivision (d) of section twenty-six of this chapter, a statement that all or specified partners are so liable for such debts, obligations or liabilities in their capacity as partners of the registered limited liability partnership as authorized pursuant to subdivision (d) of section twenty-six of this chapter; and

(9) any other matters the partnership without limited partners determines to include in the registration.

(II) (A) Within one hundred twenty days after the effective date of the registration, a copy of the same or a notice containing the substance thereof shall be published once in each week for six successive weeks, in two newspapers of the county in which the principal office of the registered limited liability partnership is located in this state, one newspaper printed weekly and one newspaper to be printed daily, to be designated by the county clerk. When such county is located within a city with a population of one million or more, such designation shall be as though the copy or notice were a notice or advertisement of judicial proceedings. Proof of the publication required by this subparagraph, consisting of the certificate of publication of the registered limited liability partnership with the affidavits of publication annexed thereto, must be filed, with a fee of fifty dollars, with the department of state. Notwithstanding any other provision of law, if the office of the registered limited liability partnership is located in a county wherein a weekly or daily newspaper of the county, or both, has not been so designated by the county clerk, then the publication herein required shall be made in a weekly or daily newspaper of any county, or both, as the case may be, which is contiguous to, such county, provided that any such newspaper meets all the other requirements of this subparagraph. A copy or notice published in a newspaper other than the newspaper or newspapers designated by the county clerk shall not be deemed to be one of the publications required by this paragraph. The notice shall include: (1) the name of the registered limited liability partnership; (2) the date of filing of the registration with the department of state; (3) the county within this state, in which the principal office of the registered limited liability partnership is located; (3-a) the street address of the principal business location, if any; (4) a statement that the secretary of state has been designated as agent of the registered limited liability partnership upon whom process against it may be served and the post office address within or without this state to which the secretary of state shall mail a copy of any process against it served upon him or her; (5) if the registered limited liability partnership is to have a registered agent, his or her name and address within this state and a statement that the registered agent is to be the agent of the registered limited liability partnership upon whom process against it may be served; (6) if the registered limited liability partnership is to have a specific date of dissolution in addition to the events of dissolution set forth in section sixty-two of this chapter, the latest date upon which the registered limited liability partnership is to dissolve; and (7) the character or purpose of the business of such registered limited liability partnership. Where, at any time after completion of the first of the six weekly publications required by this subparagraph and prior to the completion of the sixth such weekly publication, there is a change in any of the information contained in the copy or notice as published, the registered limited liability partnership may complete the remaining publications of the original copy or notice, and the registered limited liability partnership shall not be required to publish any further or amended copy or notice. Where, at any time after completion of the six weekly publications required by this subparagraph, there is a change to any of the information contained in the copy or notice as published, no further or amended publication or republication shall be required to be made. If within one hundred twenty days after its formation, proof of such publication, consisting of the certificate of publication of the registered limited liability partnership with the affidavits of publication of the newspapers annexed thereto has not been filed with the department of state, the authority of such registered limited liability partnership to carry on, conduct or transact any business in this state shall be suspend-

ed, effective as of the expiration of such one hundred twenty day period. The failure of a registered limited liability partnership to cause such copy or notice to be published and such certificate of publication and affidavits of publication to be filed with the department of state within such one hundred twenty day period or the suspension of such registered limited liability partnership's authority to carry on, conduct or transact business in this state pursuant to this subparagraph shall not limit or impair the validity of any contract or act of such registered limited liability partnership, or any right or remedy of any other party under or by virtue of any contract, act or omission of such registered limited liability partnership, or the right of any other party to maintain any action or special proceeding on any such contract, act or omission, or right of such registered limited liability partnership to defend any action or special proceeding in this state, or result in any partner or agent of such registered limited liability partnership becoming liable for the contractual obligations or other liabilities of the registered limited liability partnership. If, at any time following the suspension of a registered limited liability partnership's authority to carry on, conduct or transact business in this state pursuant to this subparagraph, such registered limited liability partnership shall cause proof of publication in substantial compliance with the provisions (other than the one hundred twenty day period) of this subparagraph, consisting of the certificate of publication of the registered limited liability partnership with the affidavits of publication of the newspapers annexed thereto, to be filed with the department of state, such suspension of such registered limited liability partnership's authority to carry on, conduct or transact business shall be annulled.

(B) (1) A registered limited liability partnership which was formed prior to the effective date of this subparagraph and which complied with the publication and filing requirements of this paragraph as in effect prior to such effective date shall not be required to make any publication or republication or any filing under subparagraph (A) of this paragraph, and shall not be subject to suspension pursuant to this paragraph.

(2) Within twelve months after the effective date of this subparagraph, a registered limited liability partnership which was formed prior to such effective date and which did not comply with the publication and filing requirements of this paragraph as in effect prior to such effective date shall publish a copy of its registration or a notice containing the substance thereof in the manner required (other than the one hundred twenty day period) by this paragraph as in effect prior to such effective date and file proof of such publication, consisting of the certificate of publication of the registered limited liability partnership with the affidavits of publication of the newspapers annexed thereto, with the department of state.

(3) If a registered limited liability partnership that is subject to the provisions of clause two of this

subparagraph fails to file the required proof of publication with the department of state within twelve months after the effective date of this subparagraph, its authority to carry on, conduct or transact any business in this state shall be suspended, effective as of the expiration of such twelve month period.

(4) The failure of a registered limited liability partnership that is subject to the provisions of clause two of this subparagraph to fully comply with the provisions of said clause two or the suspension of such registered limited liability partnership's authority to carry on, conduct or transact any business in this state pursuant to clause three of this subparagraph shall not impair or limit the validity of any contract or act of such registered limited liability partnership, or any right or remedy of any other party under or by virtue of any contract, act or omission of such registered limited liability partnership, or the right of any other party to maintain any action or special proceeding on any such contract, act or omission, or right of such registered limited liability partnership to defend any action or special proceeding in this state, or result in any partner or agent of such registered limited liability partnership becoming liable for the contractual obligations or other liabilities of the registered limited liability partnership.

(5) If, at any time following the suspension of a registered limited liability partnership's authority to carry on, conduct or transact business in this state, pursuant to clause three of this subparagraph, such registered limited liability partnership shall cause proof of publication in substantial compliance with the provisions (other than the one hundred twenty day period) of subparagraph (A) of this paragraph, consisting of the certificate of publication of the registered limited liability partnership with the affidavits of publication of the newspapers annexed thereto, to be filed with the department of state, such suspension of such registered limited liability partnership's authority to carry on, conduct or transact business shall be annulled.

(6) For the purposes of this subparagraph, a registered limited liability partnership which was formed prior to the effective date of this subparagraph shall be deemed to have complied with the publication and filing requirements of this paragraph as in effect prior to such effective date if (A) the registered limited liability partnership was formed on or after January first, nineteen hundred ninety-nine and prior to such effective date and the registered limited liability partnership filed at least one affidavit of the printer or publisher of a newspaper with the department of state at any time prior to such effective date, or (B) the registered limited liability partnership was formed prior to January first, nineteen hundred ninety-nine, without regard to whether the registered limited liability partnership did or did not file any affidavit of the printer or publisher of a newspaper with the secretary of state.

(C) The information in a notice published pursuant to this paragraph shall be presumed to be in compliance with and satisfaction of the requirements of this paragraph.

(b) The registration shall be executed by one or more partners of the partnership without limited partners.

(c) The registration shall be accompanied by a fee of two hundred dollars.

(d) A partnership without limited partners is registered as a registered limited liability partnership at the time of the payment of the fee required by subdivision (c) of this section and the filing of a completed registration with the department of state or at the later date, if any, specified in such registration, not to exceed sixty days from the date of such filing. A partnership without limited partners that has been registered as a registered limited liability partnership is for all purposes the same entity that existed before the registration and continues to be a partnership without limited partners under the laws of this state. The status of a partnership without limited partners as a registered limited liability partnership shall not be affected by changes in the information stated in the registration after the filing of the registration. If a partnership without limited partners that is a registered limited liability partnership dissolves, a partnership without limited partners which is the successor to such registered limited liability partnership (i) shall not be required to file a new registration and shall be deemed to have filed the registration filed by the registered limited liability partnership pursuant to subdivision (a) of this section, as well as any withdrawal notice filed pursuant to subdivision (f) of this section, any statement or certificate of consent filed pursuant to subdivision (g) of this section or any certificate of amendment filed pursuant to subdivision (j) of this section and (ii) shall be bound by any revocation of registration pursuant to subdivision (g) of this section and any annulment thereof of the dissolved partnership without limited partners that was a registered limited liability partnership. For purposes of this section, a partnership without limited partners is a successor to a partnership without limited partners that was a registered limited liability partnership if a majority of the total interests in the current profits of such successor partnership without limited partners are held by partners of the predecessor partnership without limited partners that was a registered limited liability partnership who were partners of such predecessor partnership immediately prior to the dissolution of such predecessor partnership.

(e) If the signed registration delivered to the department of state for filing complies as to form with the requirements of law and the filing fee required by any statute of this state has been paid, the registration shall be filed and indexed by the department of state.

Partnership Law

(f) A registration may be withdrawn by filing with the department of state a written withdrawal notice executed by one or more partners of the registered limited liability partnership, with a filing fee of sixty dollars. A withdrawal notice must include: (i) the name of the registered limited liability partnership (and if it has been changed since registration, the name under which it was registered); (ii) the date the registration was filed with the department of state pursuant to subdivision (a) of this section; (iii) the address of the registered limited liability partnership's principal office; (iv) if the withdrawal of the registered limited liability partnership is to be effective on a date later than the time of filing, the date, not to exceed sixty days from the date of such filing, of such proposed effectiveness; (v) a statement acknowledging that the withdrawal terminates the partnership's status as a registered limited liability partnership; and (vi) any other information determined by the registered limited liability partnership. A withdrawal notice terminates the status of the partnership as a registered limited liability partnership as of the date of filing the notice or as of the later date, if any, specified in the notice, not to exceed sixty days from the date of such filing. The termination of registration shall not be affected by errors in the information stated in the withdrawal notice. If a registered limited liability partnership is dissolved, it shall within thirty days after the winding up of its affairs is completed file a withdrawal notice pursuant to this subdivision.

(g) Each registered limited liability partnership shall, within sixty days prior to the fifth anniversary of the effective date of its registration and every five years thereafter, furnish a statement to the department of state setting forth: (i) the name of the registered limited liability partnership, (ii) the address of the principal office of the registered limited liability partnership, (iii) the post office address within or without this state to which the secretary of state shall mail a copy of any process accepted against it served upon him or her, which address shall supersede any previous address on file with the department of state for this purpose, and (iv) a statement that it is eligible to register as a registered limited liability partnership pursuant to subdivision (a) of this section. The statement shall be executed by one or more partners of the registered limited liability partnership. The statement shall be accompanied by a fee of twenty dollars if submitted directly to the department of state. The commissioner of taxation and finance and the secretary of state may agree to allow registered limited liability partnerships to provide the statement specified in this subdivision on tax reports filed with the department of taxation and finance in lieu of statements filed directly with the secretary of state and in a manner prescribed by the commissioner of taxation and finance. If this agreement is made, starting with taxable years beginning on or after January first, two thousand sixteen, each registered limited liability partnership required to file the

statement specified in this subdivision that is subject to the filing fee imposed by paragraph three of subsection (c) of section six hundred fifty-eight of the tax law shall provide such statement annually on its filing fee payment form filed with the department of taxation and finance in lieu of filing a statement under this subdivision with the department of state. However, each registered limited liability partnership required to file a statement under this section must continue to file a statement with the department of state as required by this section until the registered limited liability partnership in fact has filed a filing fee payment form with the department of taxation and finance that includes all required information. After that time, the registered limited liability partnership shall continue to provide annually the statement specified in this subdivision on its filing fee payment form in lieu of the statement required by this subdivision. The commissioner of taxation and finance shall deliver the completed statement specified in this subdivision to the department of state for filing. The department of taxation and finance must, to the extent feasible, also include in such delivery the current name of the registered limited liability partnership, department of state identification number for such registered limited liability partnership, the name, signature and capacity of the signer of the statement, name and street address of the filer of the statement, and the email address, if any, of the filer of the statement. If a registered limited liability partnership shall not timely file the statement required by this subdivision, the department of state may, upon sixty days' notice mailed to the address of such registered limited liability partnership as shown in the last registration or statement or certificate of amendment filed by such registered limited liability partnership, make a proclamation declaring the registration of such registered limited liability partnership to be revoked pursuant to this subdivision. The department of state shall file the original proclamation in its office and shall publish a copy thereof in the state register no later than three months following the date of such proclamation. This shall not apply to registered limited liability partnerships that have filed a statement with the department of state through the department of taxation and finance. Upon the publication of such proclamation in the manner aforesaid, the registration of each registered limited liability partnership named in such proclamation shall be deemed revoked without further legal proceedings. Any registered limited liability partnership whose registration was so revoked may file in the department of state a statement required by this subdivision. The filing of such statement shall have the effect of annulling all of the proceedings theretofore taken for the revocation of the registration of such registered limited liability partnership under this subdivision and (1) the registered limited liability partnership shall thereupon have such powers, rights, duties and obligations as it had on the date of the publication of the proclamation, with the same force and effect as if such proclamation had not been made or published and (2) such publication shall not affect the applicability of the provisions of subdivision (b) of section twenty-six of this chapter to any debt, obligation or liability incurred, created or assumed from the date of publication of the proclamation through the date of the filing of the statement with the department of state . If, after the publication of such proclamation, it shall be determined by the department of state that the name of any registered limited liability partnership was erroneously included in such proclamation, the department of state shall make appropriate entry on its records, which entry shall have the effect of annulling all of the proceedings theretofore taken for the revocation of the registration of such registered limited liability partnership under this subdivision and (A) such registered limited liability partnership shall have such powers, rights, duties and obligations as it had on the date of the publication of the proclamation, with the same force and effect as if such proclamation had not been made or published and (B) such publication shall not affect the applicability of the provisions of subdivision (b) of section twenty-six of this chapter to any debt, obligation or liability incurred, created or assumed from the date of publication of the proclamation through the date of the making of the entry on the records of the department of state. Whenever a registered limited liability partnership whose registration was revoked shall have filed a statement pursuant to this subdivision or if the name of a registered limited liability partnership was erroneously included in a proclamation and such proclamation was annulled, the department of state shall publish a notice thereof in the state register.

(h) The filing of a withdrawal notice by a registered limited liability partnership pursuant to subdivision (f) of this section, a revocation of registration pursuant to subdivision (g) of this section and the filing of a certificate of amendment pursuant to subdivision (j) of this section shall not affect the applicability of the provisions of subdivision (b) of section twenty-six of this chapter to any debt, obligation or liability incurred, created or assumed while the partnership was a registered limited liability partnership. After a withdrawal or revocation of registration, the partnership without limited partners shall for all purposes remain the same entity that existed during registration and continues to be a partnership without limited partners under the laws of this state.

(i) The department of state shall remove from its active records the registration of a registered limited liability partnership whose registration has been withdrawn or revoked.

(j) A registration or statement filed with the department of state under this section may be amended or corrected by filing with the department of state a certificate of amendment executed by one or more partners of the registered limited liability partnership. No later than ninety days after (i) a change in the name of the registered limited liability partnership or (ii) a partner of the registered limited liability partnership becomes aware that any statement in a registration or statement was false in any material respect when made or that an event has occurred which makes the registration or statement inaccurate in any material respect, the registered limited liability partnership shall file a certificate of amendment. The filing of a certificate of amendment shall be accompanied by a fee of sixty dollars. The certificate of amendment shall set forth: (i) the name of the limited liability partnership and, if it has been changed, the name under which it was registered and (ii) the date of filing its initial registration or statement.

(j-1) A certificate of change which changes only the post office address to which the secretary of state shall mail a copy of any process against a registered limited liability partnership served upon him or the address of the registered agent, provided such address being changed is the address of a person, partnership or corporation whose address, as agent, is the address to be changed or who has been designated as registered agent for such registered limited liability partnership shall be signed and delivered to the department of state by such agent. The certificate of change shall set forth: (i) the name of the registered limited liability partnership and, if it has been changed, the name under which it was originally filed with the department of state; (ii) the date of filing of its initial registration or notice statement; (iii) each change effected thereby; (iv) that a notice of the proposed change was mailed to the limited liability partnership by the party signing the certificate not less than thirty days prior to the date of delivery to the department of state and that such limited liability partnership has not objected thereto; and (v) that the party signing the certificate is the agent of such limited liability partnership to whose address the secretary of state is required to mail copies of process or the registered agent, if such be the case. A certificate signed and delivered under this subdivision shall not be deemed to effect a change of location of the office of the limited liability partnership in whose behalf such certificate is filed. The certificate of change shall be accompanied by a fee of five dollars.

(k) The filing of a certificate of amendment pursuant to subdivision (j) of this section with the department of state shall not alter the effective date of the registration being amended or corrected.

(l) Except as otherwise provided in any agreement between the partners, the decision of a partnership without limited partners to file, withdraw or amend a registration pursuant to subdivision (a), (f) or (j), respectively, of this section is an ordinary matter connected with partnership business under subdivision eight of section forty of this chapter.

(m) A registered limited liability partnership, other than a registered limited liability partnership authorized to practice law, shall be under the supervision of the regents of the university of the state of New York and be subject to disciplinary proceedings and penalties in the same manner and to the same extent as is provided with respect to individuals and their licenses, certificates and registrations in title eight of the education law relating to the applicable profession. Notwithstanding the provisions of this subdivision, a registered limited liability partnership authorized to practice medicine shall be subject to the pre-hearing procedures and hearing procedures as are provided with respect to individual physicians and their licenses in title two-A of article two of the public health law. In addition to rendering the professional service or services the partners are authorized to practice in this state, a registered limited liability partnership may carry on, or conduct or transact any other business or activities as to which a partnership without limited partners may be formed. Notwithstanding any other provision of this section, a registered limited liability partnership (i) authorized to practice law may only engage in another profession or business or activities or (ii) which is engaged in a profession or other business or activities other than law may only engage in the practice of law, to the extent not prohibited by any other law of this state or any rule adopted by the appropriate appellate division of the supreme court or the court of appeals. Any registered limited liability partnership may invest its funds in real estate, mortgages, stocks, bonds or any other types of investments.

(n) No registered limited liability partnership may render a professional service except through individuals authorized by law to render such professional service as individuals, provided, that nothing in this chapter shall authorize a registered limited liability partnership to render a professional service in this state except through individuals authorized by law to render such professional service as individuals in this state.

(o) This section shall not repeal, modify or restrict any provision of the education law or the judiciary law or any rules or regulations adopted thereunder regulating the professions referred to in the education law or the judiciary law except to the extent in conflict herewith.

(p) A certified copy of the registration and of each certificate of amendment shall be filed by the registered limited liability partnership with the licensing authority within thirty days after the filing of such registration or amendment with the department of state.

(q) Each partner of a registered limited liability partnership formed to provide medical services in this state must be licensed pursuant to article 131 of the education law to practice medicine in this state and each partner of a registered limited liability partnership formed to provide dental services in this state must be licensed pursuant to article 133 of the education law to practice dentistry in this state. Each partner of a registered limited liability partnership

formed to provide veterinary services in this state must be licensed pursuant to article 135 of the education law to practice veterinary medicine in this state. Each partner of a registered limited liability partnership formed to provide professional engineering, land surveying, geological services, architectural and/or landscape architectural services in this state must be licensed pursuant to article 145, article 147 and/or article 148 of the education law to practice one or more of such professions in this state. Each partner of a registered limited liability partnership formed to provide licensed clinical social work services in this state must be licensed pursuant to article 154 of the education law to practice clinical social work in this state. Each partner of a registered limited liability partnership formed to provide creative arts therapy services in this state must be licensed pursuant to article 163 of the education law to practice creative arts therapy in this state. Each partner of a registered limited liability partnership formed to provide marriage and family therapy services in this state must be licensed pursuant to article 163 of the education law to practice marriage and family therapy in this state. Each partner of a registered limited liability partnership formed to provide mental health counseling services in this state must be licensed pursuant to article 163 of the education law to practice mental health counseling in this state. Each partner of a registered limited liability partnership formed to provide psychoanalysis services in this state must be licensed pursuant to article 163 of the education law to practice psychoanalysis in this state. Each partner of a registered limited liability partnership formed to provide applied behavior analysis service in this state must be licensed or certified pursuant to article 167 of the education law to practice applied behavior analysis in this state.

History: Add, L 1994, ch 576, § 15, eff Oct 24, 1994; amd, L 1995, ch 643, § 21, eff Aug 8, 1995, L 1997, ch 470, § 12, L 1998, ch 448, § 9, eff Oct 20, 1998, L 1999, ch 172, §§ 45, 46, eff July 6, 1999, L 1999, ch 420, § 16, eff Aug 31, 1999, L 2002, ch 420, § 5, eff Sept 1, 2004, L 2002, ch 676, § 16, eff Jan 1, 2005, L 2005, ch 767, §§ 15, 16, eff June 1, 2006, L 2006, ch 44, § 10, eff June 1, 2006, L 2013, ch 554, § 9, eff Jan 10, 2014; L 2014, ch 475, § 26 eff Nov 21, 2016; L 2015, ch 59, §8 (Part S), eff April 13, 2015.

CASE ANNOTATIONS

Agreement which two attorneys signed three years before their firm was dissolved showed that they intended to give an attorney who worked for the firm an equity interest in the firm, and the agreement was valid even though it was not filed with the New York Secretary of State. Joachim v Flanzig (2004, Sup) 773 N.Y.S.2d 267

Non-resident limited liability partnerships may not be licensed as insurance brokers in New York State since they are not considered professionals as defined by CLS Partn § 2. Insurance Department, Opinions of General Counsel, Opinion Number 01-04-05

Law firm and an affiliate lacked standing to seek a declaration that N.Y. R. Prof. Conduct 5.4 (N.Y. Comp. Codes R. & Regs. tit. 22, § 1200.0) was unconstitutional because it prohibited non-lawyer equity investment in law practices, as invalidating the rule would not have redressed the claimed injury. The law firm was a limited

Partnership Law

liability partnership, and it could not continue to operate in that form if it allowed a non-lawyer to own an equity interest. Jacoby & Meyers, LLP v Presiding Justices of the Appellate Div. (2012, SD NY) 847 F Supp 2d 590

§ 121-1501. Name of registered limited liability partnership

The name of each registered limited liability partnership shall contain without abbreviation the words "Registered Limited Liability Partnership" or "Limited Liability Partnership" or the abbreviations "R.L.L.P.", "RLLP", "L.L.P." or "LLP"; provided, however, the partnership may use any such words or abbreviation, without limitation, in addition to its registered name.

History: Add, L 1994, ch 576, § 15, eff Oct 24, 1994.

§ 121-1502. New York registered foreign limited liability partnership

(a) In order for a foreign limited liability partnership to carry on or conduct or transact business or activities as a New York registered foreign limited liability partnership in this state, such foreign limited liability partnership shall file with the department of state a notice which shall set forth: (i) the name under which the foreign limited liability partnership intends to carry on or conduct or transact business or activities in this state; (ii) the date on which and the jurisdiction in which it registered as a limited liability partnership; (iii) the address of the principal office of the foreign limited liability partnership; (iv) the profession or professions to be practiced by such foreign limited liability partnership and a statement that it is a foreign limited liability partnership eligible to file a notice under this chapter; (v) a designation of the secretary of state as agent of the foreign limited liability partnership upon whom process against it may be served and the post office address within or without this state to which the secretary of state shall mail a copy of any process against it or served upon it; (vi) if the foreign limited liability partnership is to have a registered agent, its name and address in this state and a statement that the registered agent is to be the agent of the foreign limited liability partnership upon whom process against it may be served; (vii) a statement that its registration as a limited liability partnership is effective in the jurisdiction in which it registered as a limited liability partnership at the time of the filing of such notice; (viii) a statement that the foreign limited liability partnership is filing a notice in order to obtain status as a New York registered foreign limited liability partnership; (ix) if the registration of the foreign limited liability partnership is to be effective on a date later than the time of filing, the date, not to exceed sixty days from the date of filing, of such proposed effectiveness; and (x) any other matters the foreign limited liability partnership determines to include in the notice. Such notice shall be accompanied by either (1) a copy of the last registration or renewal registration (or similar filing), if

any, filed by the foreign limited liability partnership with the jurisdiction where it registered as a limited liability partnership or (2) a certificate, issued by the jurisdiction where it registered as a limited liability partnership, substantially to the effect that such foreign limited liability partnership has filed a registration as a limited liability partnership which is effective on the date of the certificate (if such registration, renewal registration or certificate is in a foreign language, a translation thereof under oath of the translator shall be attached thereto). Such notice shall also be accompanied by a fee of two hundred fifty dollars.

(b) Without excluding other activities which may not constitute the carrying on or conducting or transacting of business or activities in this state, for purposes of determining whether a foreign limited liability partnership is required to file a notice pursuant to subdivision (a) of this section, a foreign limited liability partnership shall not be considered to be carrying on or conducting or transacting business or activities in this state by reason of carrying on in this state any one or more of the following activities:

(i) maintaining or defending any action or proceeding, whether judicial, administrative, arbitrative or otherwise, or effecting settlement thereof or the settlement of claims or disputes;

(ii) holding meetings of its partners; or

(iii) maintaining bank accounts.

The specification in this subdivision does not establish a standard for activities which may subject a foreign limited liability partnership to service of process under this article or any other statute of this state. The filing of a notice pursuant to subdivision (a) of this section by a foreign limited liability partnership shall not by itself be deemed to be evidence that such foreign limited liability partnership is carrying on or conducting or transacting business or activities in this state.

(c) A notice shall be executed by one or more partners of the foreign limited liability partnership.

(d) If a signed notice delivered to the department of state for filing complies as to form with the requirements of law and the filing fee required by any statute of this state has been paid, the notice shall be filed and indexed by the department of state. If a foreign limited liability partnership that is a New York registered foreign limited liability partnership dissolves, a foreign limited liability partnership which is the successor to such New York registered foreign limited liability partnership (i) shall not be required to file a new notice and shall be deemed to have filed the notice filed by the New York registered foreign limited liability partnership pursuant to subdivision (a) of this section, as well as any withdrawal notice filed pursuant to subdivision (e) of this section, any statement or certificate of consent filed pursuant to subdivision (f) of this section and any notice of amendment filed pursuant to subdivision (i) of this section and (ii) shall be bound by any revocation of status pursuant to subdivision (f) of this section and any annulment thereof of the dissolved foreign limited liability partnership that was a New York registered foreign limited liability partnership. For purposes of this section, a foreign limited liability partnership is a successor to a foreign limited liability partnership that was a New York registered foreign limited liability partnership if a majority of the total interests in the current profits of such successor foreign limited liability partnership are held by partners of the predecessor foreign limited liability partnership that was a New York registered foreign limited liability partnership who were partners of such predecessor partnership immediately prior to the dissolution of such predecessor partnership.

(e) A notice may be withdrawn by filing with the department of state a written withdrawal notice executed by one or more partners of the New York registered foreign limited liability partnership, with a filing fee of sixty dollars. A withdrawal notice must include: (i) the name or names under which the New York registered foreign limited liability partnership carried on or conducted or transacted business or activities in this state (and if it has been changed since the filing of the notice, the name under which it filed such notice); (ii) the date a notice was filed with the department of state pursuant to subdivision (a) of this section; (iii) the address of the New York registered foreign limited liability partnership's principal office and the jurisdiction in which it is registered as a limited liability partnership; (iv) if the withdrawal of the New York registered foreign limited liability partnership is to be effective on a date later than the time of such filing, the date, not to exceed sixty days from the date of such filing, of such proposed effectiveness; (v) a statement acknowledging that the withdrawal terminates the foreign limited liability partnership's status as a New York registered foreign limited liability partnership; and (vi) any other information determined by the New York registered foreign limited liability partnership. A withdrawal notice terminates the status of the foreign limited liability partnership as a New York registered foreign limited liability partnership as of the date of filing of the notice or as of the later date, if any, specified in the notice, not to exceed sixty days from the date of such filing. The termination of status shall not be affected by errors in the information stated in the withdrawal notice. If a New York registered foreign limited liability partnership ceases to be denominated as a registered limited liability partnership or limited liability partnership under the laws of the jurisdiction governing the agreement under which such New York registered foreign limited liability partnership operates, it shall within thirty days after the occurrence of such event file a withdrawal notice pursuant to this subdivision.

(f) (I) Each New York registered foreign limited liability partnership shall, within sixty days prior to the fifth anniversary of the effective date of its notice

and every five years thereafter, furnish a statement to the department of state setting forth:

(i) the name under which the New York registered foreign limited liability partnership is carrying on or conducting or transacting business or activities in this state, (ii) the address of the principal office of the New York registered foreign limited liability partnership, (iii) the post office address within or without this state to which the secretary of state shall mail a copy of any process accepted against it served upon him or her, which address shall supersede any previous address on file with the department of state for this purpose, and (iv) a statement that it is a foreign limited liability partnership. The statement shall be executed by one or more partners of the New York registered foreign limited liability partnership. The statement shall be accompanied by a fee of fifty dollars if submitted directly to the department of state. The commissioner of taxation and finance and the secretary of state may agree to allow New York registered foreign limited liability partnerships to provide the statement specified in this paragraph on tax reports filed with the department of taxation and finance in lieu of statements filed directly with the secretary of state and in a manner prescribed by the commissioner of taxation and finance. If this agreement is made, starting with taxable years beginning on or after January first, two thousand sixteen, each New York registered foreign limited liability partnership required to file the statement specified in this paragraph that is subject to the filing fee imposed by paragraph three of subsection (c) of section six hundred fifty-eight of the tax law shall provide such statement annually on its filing fee payment form filed with the department of taxation and finance in lieu of filing a statement under this paragraph directly with the department of state. However, each New York registered foreign limited liability partnership required to file a statement under this section must continue to file a statement with the department of state as required by this section until the New York registered foreign limited liability partnership in fact has filed a filing fee payment form with the department of taxation and finance that includes all required information. After that time, the New York registered foreign limited liability partnership shall continue to provide annually the statement specified in this paragraph on its filing fee payment form in lieu of filing the statement required by this paragraph directly with the department of state. The commissioner of taxation and finance shall deliver the completed statement specified in this paragraph to the department of state for filing. The department of taxation and finance must, to the extent feasible, also include in such delivery the current name of the New York registered foreign limited liability partnership, department of state identification number for such New York registered foreign limited liability partnership, the name, signature and capacity of the signer of the statement, name and street address of the filer of the statement, and the email address, if any, of the filer of the statement. If a New York registered foreign limited liability partnership shall not timely file the statement required by this subdivision, the department of state may, upon sixty days' notice mailed to the address of such New York registered foreign limited liability partnership as shown in the last notice or statement or certificate of amendment filed by such New York registered foreign limited liability partnership, make a proclamation declaring the status of such New York registered foreign limited liability partnership to be revoked pursuant to this subdivision. This shall not apply to New York registered foreign limited liability partnerships that have filed a statement with the department of state through the department of taxation and finance. The department of state shall file the original proclamation in its office and shall publish a copy thereof in the state register no later than three months following the date of such proclamation. Upon the publication of such proclamation in the manner aforesaid, the status of each New York registered foreign limited liability partnership named in such proclamation shall be deemed revoked without further legal proceedings. Any New York registered foreign limited liability partnership whose status was so revoked may file in the department of state a statement required by this subdivision. The filing of such statement shall have the effect of annulling all of the proceedings theretofore taken for the revocation of the status of such New York registered foreign limited liability partnership under this subdivision and (1) the New York registered foreign limited liability partnership shall thereupon have such powers, rights, duties and obligations as it had on the date of the publication of the proclamation, with the same force and effect as if such proclamation had not been made or published and (2) such publication shall not affect the applicability of the laws of the jurisdiction governing the agreement under which such New York registered foreign limited liability partnership is operating (including laws governing the liability of partners) to any debt, obligation or liability incurred, created or assumed from the date of publication of the proclamation through the date of the filing of the statement with the department of state. If, after the publication of such proclamation, it shall be determined by the department of state that the name of any New York registered foreign limited liability partnership was erroneously included in such proclamation, the department of state shall make appropriate entry on its records, which entry shall have the effect of annulling all of the proceedings theretofore taken for the revocation of the status of such New York registered foreign limited liability partnership under this subdivision and (1) such New York registered foreign limited liability partnership shall have such powers, rights, duties and obligations as it had on the date of the publication of the proclamation, with the same force and effect as if such proclamation had not been made or published and (2) such publication shall not affect the applicability of the laws of the

jurisdiction governing the agreement under which such New York registered foreign limited liability partnership is operating (including laws governing the liability of partners) to any debt, obligation or liability incurred, created or assumed from the date of publication of the proclamation through the date of the making of the entry on the records of the department of state. Whenever a New York registered foreign limited liability partnership whose status was revoked shall have filed a statement pursuant to this subdivision or if the name of a New York registered foreign limited liability partnership was erroneously included in a proclamation and such proclamation was annulled, the department of state shall publish a notice thereof in the state register.

(II) (A) Within one hundred twenty days after the effective date of the notice filed under subdivision (a) of this section, a copy of the same or a notice containing the substance thereof shall be published once in each week for six successive weeks, in two newspapers of the county within this state in which the principal office of the foreign limited liability partnership is located, one newspaper to be printed weekly and one newspaper to be printed daily, to be designated by the county clerk. When such county is located within a city with a population of one million or more, such designation shall be as though the copy or notice were a notice or advertisement of judicial proceedings. Proof of the publication required by this subparagraph, consisting of the certificate of publication of the foreign limited liability partnership with the affidavits of publication of such newspapers annexed thereto, must be filed with the department of state, with a filing fee of fifty dollars. Notwithstanding any other provision of law, if the office of the foreign limited liability partnership is located in a county wherein a weekly or daily newspaper of the county, or both, has not been so designated by the county clerk, then the publication herein required shall be made in a weekly or daily newspaper of any county, or both, as the case may be, which is contiguous to, such county, provided that any such newspaper meets all the other requirements of this subparagraph. A copy or notice published in a newspaper other than the newspaper or newspapers designated by the county clerk shall not be deemed to be one of the publications required by this subparagraph. The notice shall include: (l) the name of the foreign limited liability partnership; (2) the date of filing of such notice with the department of state; (3) the jurisdiction and date of its organization; (4) the county within this state, in which the principal office of the foreign limited liability partnership is located; (4-a) the street address of theprincipal business location, if any; (5) a statement that the secretary of state has been designated as agent of the foreign limited liability partnership upon whom process against it may be served and the post office address within or without this state to which the secretary of state shall mail a copy of any process against it served upon him or her; (6) if the foreign limited liability partnership is to have a registered agent, his or her name and address within this state and a statement that the registered agent is to be the agent of the foreign limited liability partnership upon whom process against it may be served; (7) the address of the office required to be maintained in the jurisdiction of its organization by the laws of that jurisdiction or, if not so required, of the principal office of the foreign limited liability partnership; (8) the name and address of the authorized officer in its jurisdiction in which it registered as a limited liability partnership where a copy of its registration is filed or, if no public filing of its registration is required by the law of its jurisdiction of organization, a statement that the foreign limited liability partnership shall provide, on request, a copy thereof with all amendments thereto (if such documents are in a foreign language, a translation thereof under oath of the translator shall be attached thereto), and the name and post office address of the person responsible for providing such copies; or (9) the character or purpose of the business of such foreign limited liability partnership. Where, at any time after completion of the first of the six weekly publications required by this subparagraph and prior to the completion of the sixth such weekly publication, there is a change in any of the information contained in the copy or notice as published, the foreign limited liability partnership may complete the remaining publications of the original copy or notice, and the foreign limited liability partnership shall not be required to publish any further or amended copy or notice. Where, at any time after completion of the six weekly publications required by this subparagraph, there is a change to any of the information contained in the copy or notice as published, no further or amended publication or republication shall be required to be made. If within one hundred twenty days after the effective date of the notice required to be filed under subdivision (a) of this section, proof of such publication, consisting of the certificate of publication of the foreign limited liability partnership with the affidavits of publication of the newspapers annexed thereto has not been filed with the department of state, the authority of such foreign limited liability partnership to carry on, conduct or transact any business in this state shall be suspended, effective as of the expiration of such one hundred twenty day period. The failure of a foreign limited liability partnership to cause such copy or notice to be published and such certificate of publication and affidavits of publication to be filed with the department of state within such one hundred twenty day period or the suspension of such foreign limited liability partnership's authority to carry on, conduct or transact business in this state pursuant to this subparagraph shall not limit or impair the validity of any contract or act of such foreign limited liability partnership, or any right or remedy of any other party under or by virtue of any contract, act or omission of such foreign limited liability partnership, or the right of any other party to maintain any action

or special proceeding on any such contract, act or omission, or right of such foreign limited liability partnership to defend any action or special proceeding in this state, or result in any partner or agent of such foreign limited liability partnership becoming liable for the contractual obligations or other liabilities of the foreign limited liability partnership. If, at any time following the suspension of a foreign limited liability partnership's authority to carry on, conduct or transact business in this state pursuant to this subparagraph, such foreign limited liability partnership shall cause proof of publication in substantial compliance with the provisions (other than the one hundred twenty day period) of this subparagraph, consisting of the certificate of publication of the foreign limited liability partnership with the affidavits of publication of the newspapers annexed thereto, to be filed with the department of state, such suspension of such foreign limited liability partnership's authority to carry on, conduct or transact business shall be annulled.

(B) (1) A foreign limited liability partnership which was formed and filed the notice required to be filed under subdivision (a) of this section prior to the effective date of this subparagraph, and which filed a notice and complied with the publication and filing requirements of this paragraph as in effect prior to such effective date shall not be required to make any publication or republication or any filing under subparagraph (A) of this paragraph, and shall not be subject to suspension pursuant to this paragraph.

(2) Within twelve months after the effective date of this subparagraph, a foreign limited liability partnership which was formed and filed the notice required to be filed under subdivision (a) of this section prior to such effective date and which did not comply with the publication and filing requirements of this paragraph as in effect prior to such effective date shall publish a copy of its notice or a notice containing the substance thereof in the manner required (other than the one hundred twenty day period) by this paragraph as in effect prior to such effective date and file proof of such publication, consisting of the certificate of publication of the foreign limited liability partnership with the affidavits of publication of the newspapers annexed thereto, with the department of state.

(3) If a foreign limited liability partnership that is subject to the provisions of clause two of this subparagraph fails to file the required proof of publication with the department of state within twelve months after the effective date of this subparagraph, its authority to carry on, conduct or transact any business in this state shall be suspended, effective as of the expiration of such twelve month period.

(4) The failure of a foreign limited liability partnership that is subject to the provisions of clause two of this subparagraph to fully comply with the provisions of said clause two or the suspension of such foreign limited liability partnership's authority to

carry on, conduct or transact any business in this state pursuant to clause three of this subparagraph shall not impair or limit the validity of any contract or act of such foreign limited liability partnership, or any right or remedy of any other party under or by virtue of any contract, act or omission of such foreign limited liability partnership, or the right of any other party to maintain any action or special proceeding on any such contract, act or omission, or right of such foreign limited liability partnership to defend any action or special proceeding in this state, or result in any partner or agent of such foreign limited liability partnership becoming liable for the contractual obligations or other liabilities of the foreign limited liability partnership.

(5) If, at any time following the suspension of a foreign limited liability partnership's authority to carry on, conduct or transact business in this state, pursuant to clause three of this subparagraph, such foreign limited liability partnership shall cause proof of publication in substantial compliance with the provisions (other than the one hundred twenty day period) of subparagraph (A) of this paragraph, consisting of the certificate of publication of the foreign limited liability partnership with the affidavits of publication of the newspapers annexed thereto, to be filed with the department of state, such suspension of such foreign limited liability partnership's authority to carry on, conduct or transact business shall be annulled.

(6) For the purposes of this subparagraph, a foreign limited liability partnership which was formed and filed the notice required to be filed under subdivision (a) of this section prior to the effective date of this subparagraph shall be deemed to have complied with the publication and filing requirements of this paragraph as in effect prior to such effective date if (A) the foreign limited liability partnership was formed and filed the notice required to be filed under subdivision (a) of this section on or after January first, nineteen hundred ninety-nine and prior to such effective date and the foreign limited liability partnership filed at least one affidavit of the printer or publisher of a newspaper with the department of state at any time prior to such effective date, or (B) the foreign limited liability partnership was formed and filed the notice required to be filed under subdivision (a) of this section prior to January first, nineteen hundred ninety-nine, without regard to whether the foreign limited liability partnership did or did not file any affidavit of the printer or publisher of a newspaper with the secretary of state.

(C) The information in a notice published pursuant to this paragraph shall be presumed to be in compliance with and satisfaction of the requirements of this paragraph.

(g) The filing of a withdrawal notice by a New York registered foreign limited liability partnership pursuant to subdivision (e) of this section, a revocation of status pursuant to subdivision (f) of this section and the filing of a notice of amendment pursuant to subdivision (i) of this section shall not affect the applicability of the laws of the jurisdiction governing the agreement under which such foreign limited liability partnership is operating (including laws governing the liability of partners) to any debt, obligation or liability incurred, created or assumed while the foreign limited liability partnership was a New York registered foreign limited liability partnership. After a withdrawal or revocation of registration, the foreign limited liability partnership shall for all purposes continue to be a foreign partnership without limited partners under the laws of this state.

(h) The department of state shall remove from its active records the notice of any New York registered foreign limited liability partnership whose notice has been withdrawn or revoked.

(i) A notice or statement filed with the department of state under this section may be amended or corrected by filing with the department of state a notice of amendment executed in accordance with subdivision (c) of this section. No later than ninety days after (i) a change in the name of the New York registered foreign limited liability partnership or (ii) a partner of the New York registered foreign limited liability partnership becomes aware that any statement in a notice or statement was false in any material respect when made or that an event has occurred which makes the notice or statement inaccurate in any material respect, the New York registered foreign limited liability partnership shall file a notice of amendment. The filing of a notice of amendment shall be accompanied by a fee of sixty dollars. The certificate of amendment shall set forth: (i) the name of the limited liability partnership and, if it has been changed, the name under which it originally filed a notice under this section and (ii) the date of filing its initial registration or statement.

(i-1) A certificate of change which changes only the post office address to which the secretary of state shall mail a copy of any process against a New York registered foreign limited liability partnership served upon him or the address of the registered agent, provided such address being changed is the address of a person, partnership or corporation whose address, as agent, is the address to be changed or who has been designated as registered agent of such registered foreign limited liability partnership shall be signed and delivered to the department of state by such agent. The certificate of change shall set forth: (i) the name of the New York registered foreign limited liability partnership; (ii) the date of filing of its initial registration or notice statement; (iii) each change effected thereby; (iv) that a notice of the proposed change was mailed to the limited liability partnership by the party signing the certificate not less than thirty days prior to the date of delivery to the department of state and that such limited liability partnership has not objected thereto; and (v) that the party signing the certificate is the agent of such limited liability partnership to whose address the secretary of state is required to mail copies of process or the registered agent, if such be the case. A certificate signed and delivered under this subdivision shall not be deemed to effect a change of location of the office of the limited liability partnership in whose behalf such certificate is filed. The certificate of change shall be accompanied by a fee of five dollars.

(j) The filing of a notice of amendment pursuant to subdivision (i) of this section with the department of state shall not alter the effective date of the notice being amended or corrected.

(k) Each foreign limited liability partnership carrying on or conducting or transacting business or activities in this state shall use a name which contains without abbreviation the words "Registered Limited Liability Partnership" or "Limited Liability Partnership" or the abbreviations "R.L.L.P.", "RLLP", "P.L.L.", "PLL", "L.L.P." or "LLP"; provided, however, the partnership may use any such words or abbreviation, without limitation, in addition to its registered name.

(l) Subject to the constitution of this state, the laws of the jurisdiction that govern a foreign limited liability partnership shall determine its internal affairs and the liability of partners for debts, obligations and liabilities of, or chargeable to, the foreign limited liability partnership; provided that (i) each partner, employee or agent of a foreign limited liability partnership who performs professional services in this state on behalf of such foreign limited liability partnership shall be personally and fully liable and accountable for any negligent or wrongful act or misconduct committed by him or her or by any person under his or her direct supervision and control while rendering such professional services in this state and shall bear professional responsibility for compliance by such foreign limited liability partnership with all laws, rules and regulations governing the practice of a profession in this state and (ii) each shareholder, director, officer, member, manager, partner, employee or agent of a professional service corporation, foreign professional service corporation, professional service limited liability company, foreign professional service limited liability company, registered limited liability partnership, foreign limited liability partnership or professional partnership that is a partner, employee or agent of a foreign limited liability partnership who performs professional services in this state on behalf of such foreign limited liability partnership shall be personally and fully liable and accountable for any negligent or wrongful act or misconduct committed by him or her or by any person under his or her direct supervision and control while rendering professional services in this state in his or her capacity as a partner, employee or agent of such foreign limited liability partnership and shall bear professional responsibility for compliance by such foreign limited liability partnership with all laws, rules and regulations governing the practice of a profession in this state. The relationship of a professional to a foreign limited liability partnership with which such professional is associated, whether as a partner, employee or agent, shall not modify or diminish the

jurisdiction over such professional of the licensing authority and, in the case of an attorney and counsellor-at-law or a professional service corporation, foreign professional service corporation, professional service limited liability company, foreign professional service limited liability company, registered limited liability partnership, foreign limited liability partnership or professional partnership engaged in the practice of law, the courts of this state. A limited partnership formed under the laws of any jurisdiction, other than this state, which is denominated as a registered limited liability partnership or limited liability partnership under such laws shall be recognized in this state as a foreign limited partnership but not as a foreign limited liability partnership or a New York registered foreign limited liability partnership. Except to the extent provided in article eight of the limited liability company law, a partnership without limited partners operating under an agreement governed by the laws of any jurisdiction, other than this state, which is denominated as a registered limited liability partnership or a limited liability partnership under such laws, but is not a foreign limited liability partnership, shall be recognized in this state as a foreign partnership without limited partners, but not as a foreign limited liability partnership or a New York registered foreign limited liability partnership.

(m) A foreign limited liability partnership carrying on or conducting or transacting business or activities in this state without having filed a notice pursuant to subdivision (a) of this section may not maintain any action, suit or special proceeding in any court of this state unless and until such foreign limited liability partnership shall have filed such notice and paid all fees that it would have been required to pay had it filed a notice pursuant to subdivision (a) of this section before carrying on or conducting or transacting business or activities as a New York registered foreign limited liability partnership in this state and shall have filed proof of publication pursuant to subdivision (f) of this section. The failure of a foreign limited liability partnership that is carrying on or conducting or transacting business or activities in this state to comply with the provisions of this section does not impair the validity of any contract or act of the foreign limited liability partnership or prevent the foreign limited liability partnership from defending any action or special proceeding in any court of this state.

(n) A foreign limited liability partnership, other than a foreign limited liability partnership authorized to practice law, shall be under the supervision of the regents of the university of the state of New York and be subject to disciplinary proceedings and penalties in the same manner and to the same extent as is provided with respect to individuals and their licenses, certificates and registrations in title eight of the education law relating to the applicable profession. Notwithstanding the provisions of this subdivision, a foreign limited liability partnership authorized to practice medicine shall be subject to the pre-hearing procedures and hearing procedures as are provided with respect to individual physicians and their licenses in title two-A of article two of the public health law. No foreign limited liability partnership shall engage in any profession or carry on, or conduct or transact any other business or activities in this state other than the rendering of the professional services or the carrying on, or conducting or transacting of any other business or activities for which it is formed and is authorized to do business in this state; provided that such foreign limited liability partnership may invest its funds in real estate, mortgages, stocks, bonds or any other type of investments; provided, further, that a foreign limited liability partnership (i) authorized to practice law may only engage in another profession or other business or activities in this state or (ii) which is engaged in a profession or other business or activities other than law may only engage in the practice of law in this state, to the extent not prohibited by any other law of this state or any rule adopted by the appropriate appellate division of the supreme court or the court of appeals.

(o) No foreign limited liability partnership may render a professional service in this state except through individuals authorized by law to render such professional service as individuals in this state.

(p) This section shall not repeal, modify or restrict any provision of the education law or the judiciary law or any rules or regulations adopted thereunder regulating the professions referred to in the education law or the judiciary law except to the extent in conflict herewith.

(q) Each partner of a foreign limited liability partnership which provides medical services in this state must be licensed pursuant to article 131 of the education law to practice medicine in the state and each partner of a foreign limited liability partnership which provides dental services in the state must be licensed pursuant to article 133 of the education law to practice dentistry in this state. Each partner of a foreign limited liability partnership which provides veterinary service in the state shall be licensed pursuant to article 135 of the education law to practice veterinary medicine in this state. Each partner of a foreign limited liability partnership which provides professional engineering, land surveying, geological services, architectural and/or landscape architectural services in this state must be licensed pursuant to article 145, article 147 and/or article 148 of the education law to practice one or more of such professions. Each partner of a foreign limited liability partnership which provides licensed clinical social work services in this state must be licensed pursuant to article 154 of the education law to practice licensed clinical social work in this state. Each partner of a foreign limited liability partnership which provides creative arts therapy services in this state must be licensed pursuant to article 163 of the education law to practice creative arts therapy in this state. Each partner of a foreign limited liability partnership which provides marriage and family therapy services

in this state must be licensed pursuant to article 163 of the education law to practice marriage and family therapy in this state. Each partner of a foreign limited liability partnership which provides mental health counseling services in this state must be licensed pursuant to article 163 of the education law to practice mental health counseling in this state. Each partner of a foreign limited liability partnership which provides psychoanalysis services in this state must be licensed pursuant to article 163 of the education law to practice psychoanalysis in this state. Each partner of a foreign limited liability partnership which provides applied behavior analysis services in this state must be licensed or certified pursuant to article 167 of the education law to practice applied behavior analysis in this state.

History: Add, L 1994, ch 576, § 15, eff Oct 24, 1994; amd, L 1995, ch 643, § 22, eff Aug 8, 1995, L 1997, ch 470, §§ 13-15, eff Aug 26, 1997, L 1998, ch 448, § 10, eff Oct 20, 1998, L 1999, ch 172, § 47, eff July 6, 1999, L 1999, ch 420, § 17, eff Aug 31, 1999, L 2002, ch 676, § 17, eff Jan 1, 2005, L 2004, ch 230, § 29, eff July 27, 2004, L 2004, ch 230, § 30, eff Jan 1, 2005, L 2005, ch 767, § 17, eff June 1, 2006, L 2006, ch 44, § 11, eff June 1, 2006, L 2013, ch 554, § 10, eff Jan 10, 2014; L 2014, ch 475, § 27 eff Nov 21, 2016; L 2015, ch 59, §9 (Part S), eff April 13, 2015.

CASE ANNOTATIONS

Non-resident limited liability partnerships may not be licensed as insurance brokers in New York State since they are not considered professionals as defined by CLS Partn § 2. Insurance Department, Opinions of General Counsel, Opinion Number 01-04-05

§ 121-1503. Transaction of business outside the state

(a) It is the intent of the legislature that the registration of a partnership without limited partners as a registered limited liability partnership under this article shall be recognized beyond the limits of this state and that such registered limited liability partnership may conduct its business or activities, carry on its operations, and have and exercise the powers granted by this article in any state, territory, district or possession of the United States or in any foreign country and that, subject to any reasonable registration requirements any such registered limited liability partnership transacting business outside this state and the laws of this state governing such registered limited liability partnership shall be granted the protection of full faith and credit under section 1 of article IV of the Constitution of the United States.

(b) It is the policy of this state that the internal affairs of a partnership without limited partners registered as a registered limited liability partnership under this article and the liability of partners in a registered limited liability partnership for debts, obligations and liabilities of, or chargeable to, the registered limited liability partnership shall be subject to and governed by the laws of this state, including the provisions of this article.

Partnership Law

History: Add, L 1994, ch 576, § 15, eff Oct 24, 1994.

§ 121-1504. Foreign related limited liability partnership

Any foreign related limited liability partnership that has filed a certificate of authority under and satisfied all the requirements of section eight hundred two of the limited liability company law shall be deemed to have filed a notice pursuant to section 121-1502 of this chapter until the fifth anniversary of filing its application for such certificate of authority, at which time the foreign related limited liability partnership shall file a notice pursuant to section 121-1502 of this chapter.

History: Add, L 1995, ch 643, § 23, eff Aug 8, 1995.

§ 121-1505. Service of process

(a) Service of process on the secretary of state as agent of a registered limited liability partnership under this article shall be made by personally delivering to and leaving with the secretary of state or a deputy, or with any person authorized by the secretary of state to receive such service, at the office of the department of state in the city of Albany, duplicate copies of such process together with the statutory fee, which fee shall be a taxable disbursement. Service of process on such registered limited liability partnership shall be complete when the secretary of state is so served. The secretary of state shall promptly send one of such copies by certified mail, return receipt requested, to such registered limited liability partnership, at the post office address on file in the department of state specified for such purpose.

(b) As used in this article, process shall mean judicial process and all orders, demands, notices or other papers required or permitted by law to be personally served on a registered limited liability partnership, for the purpose of acquiring jurisdiction of such registered limited liability partnership in any action or proceeding, civil or criminal, whether judicial, administrative, arbitrative or otherwise, in this state or in the federal courts sitting in or for this state.

(c) Nothing in this section shall affect the right to serve process in any other manner permitted by law.

History: Add, L 1997, ch 470, § 16, eff Aug 26, 1997.

§ 121-1506. Resignation for receipt of process

(a) A registered agent may resign as such agent. A certificate entitled "Certificate of resignation of registered agent of .... (name of limited liability partnership) under section 121-1506 of the Partnership Law" shall be signed and delivered to the department of state. It shall set forth:

(1) That he resigns as registered agent for the designated limited liability partnership.

(2) The date the certificate of registration of the designated limited liability partnership was filed by the department of state.

(3) That he has sent a copy of the certificate of resignation by registered mail to the designating limited liability partnership at the post office address on file in the department of state specified for the mailing of process or if such address is the address of the registered agent, then to the office of the designating limited liability partnership in the jurisdiction of its formation.

(b) The party (or the party's legal representative) whose post address [post office address] * has been supplied by a limited liability partnership as its address for process may resign. A certificate entitled "Certificate of Resignation for Receipt of Process under Section 121-1506(b) of the Partnership Law" shall be signed by such party and delivered to the department of state. It shall set forth:

(1) The name of the limited liability partnership and the date that its certificate of registration was filed by the department of state.

(2) That the address of the party has been designated by the limited liability partnership as the post office address to which the secretary of state shall mail a copy of any process served on the secretary of state as agent for such limited liability partnership and that such party wishes to resign.

(3) That sixty days prior to the filing of the certificate of resignation with the department of state the party has sent a copy of the certificate of resignation for receipt of process by registered or certified mail to the address of the registered agent of the designated limited liability partnership, if other than the party filing the certificate of resignation, for receipt of process, or if the resigning limited liability partnership has no registered agent, then to the last address of the designated limited liability partnership, known to the party, specifying the address to which the copy was sent. If there is no registered agent and no known address of the designating limited liability partnership the party shall attach an affidavit to the certificate stating that a diligent but unsuccessful search was made by the party to locate the limited liability partnership, specifying what efforts were made.

(4) That the designated limited liability partnership is required to deliver to the department of state a certificate of amendment providing for the designation by the limited liability partnership of a new address and that upon its failure to file such certificate, its authority to do business in this state shall be suspended.

* The bracketed words have been inserted by the Publisher.

(c) Upon the failure of the designating limited liability partnership to file a certificate of amendment providing for the designation by the limited liability partnership of the new address after the filing of a certificate of resignation for receipt of process with the secretary of state, its authority to do business in this state shall be suspended.

(d) The filing by the department of state of a certificate of amendment or the filing of a statement providing for a new address by a designating limited liability partnership shall annul the suspension and its authority to do business in this state shall be restored and continued as if no suspension had occurred.

(e) The resignation for receipt of process shall become effective upon the filing by the department of state of a certificate of resignation for receipt of process.

(f) (1) In any case in which a limited liability partnership suspended pursuant to this section would be subject to the personal or other jurisdiction of the courts of this state under article three of the civil practice law and rules, process against such limited liability partnership may be served upon the secretary of state as its agent pursuant to this section. Such process may be issued in any court in this state having jurisdiction of the subject matter.

(2) Service of such process upon the secretary of state shall be made by personally delivering to and leaving with him or his deputy, or with any person authorized by the secretary of state to receive such service, at the office of the department of state in the city of Albany, a copy of such process together with the statutory fee, which fee shall be a taxable disbursement. Such service shall be sufficient if notice thereof and a copy of the process are:

(i) delivered personally within or without this state to such limited liability partnership by a person and in the manner authorized to serve process by law of the jurisdiction in which service is made, or

(ii) sent by or on behalf of the plaintiff to such limited liability partnership by registered or certified mail with return receipt requested to the last address of such limited liability partnership known to the plaintiff.

(3) (i) Where service of a copy of process was effected by personal service, proof of service shall be by an affidavit of compliance with this section filed, together with the process, within thirty days after such service, with the clerk of the court in which the action or special proceeding is pending. Service of process shall be complete ten days after such papers are filed with the clerk of the court.

(ii) Where service of a copy of process was effected by mailing in accordance with this section, proof of service shall be by affidavit of compliance with this section filed, together with the process, within thirty days after receipt of the return receipt signed by the limited liability partnership, or other official proof of delivery or of the original envelope mailed. If a copy of the process is mailed in accordance with this section, there shall be filed with the affidavit of compliance either the return receipt signed by such limited liability partnership or other official proof of delivery, if acceptance was refused by it, the original envelope with a notation by the postal authorities that acceptance was refused. If acceptance was refused a copy of the notice and process together with notice of the mailing by registered or certified mail and refusal to accept shall be promptly sent to such limited liability partnership at the same address by ordinary mail and the affidavit of compliance shall so state. Service of process shall be complete ten days after such papers are filed with the clerk of the court. The refusal to accept delivery of the registered or certified mail or to sign the return receipt shall not affect the validity of the service and such limited liability partnership refusing to accept such registered or certified mail shall be charged with knowledge of the contents thereof.

(4) Service made as provided in this section without the state shall have the same force as personal service made within this state.

(5) Nothing in this section shall affect the right to serve process in any other manner permitted by law.

(g) The filing of a certificate of resignation of a registered agent pursuant to subdivision (a) of this section shall be accompanied by the fee of ten dollars, and the filing of a certificate of resignation for receipt of process pursuant to subdivision (b) of this section shall be accompanied by the fee of ten dollars.

History: Add, L 1998, ch 448, § 11, eff Oct 20, 1998; amd, L 1999, ch 172, §§ 48-52, eff July 6, 1999; L 2015, ch 59, § 10 (Part S), eff April 13, 2015.

§ 121-1507. Definitions

For purposes of this article:

(a) "Partnership interest" means: (i) a partner's share of the profits and losses of a registered limited liability partnership; and (ii) the partner's right to receive distributions of a registered limited liability partnership.

(b) "Affidavit of publication" means the affidavit of the printer or publisher of a newspaper in which a publication required to be filed pursuant to sections 121-1500 and 121-1502 of this article has been made. The affidavit of publication shall be in a form substantially as follows:

"Affidavit of Publication Under Section _____(specify applicable section) of the Partnership Law State of New York, County of _____, ss.:

The undersigned is the printer (or publisher) of _____ (name of newspaper), a_____ (daily or weekly) newspaper published in _____, New York. A notice regarding _____ (name of limited liability partnership) was published in said newspaper once in each week for six successive weeks, commencing on _____ and ending on _____. The text of the notice as published in said newspaper is as set forth below, or in the annexed exhibit. This newspaper has been designated by the Clerk of _____County for this purpose.

_____ (signature)

_____ (printed name),

_____ (jurat)"

The text of the notice set forth in or annexed to each affidavit of publication shall: (i) include only the text of the published notice, (ii) be free of extraneous marks, and (iii) if submitted in paper form, be printed on paper of such size, weight and color, and in ink of such color, and in such fonts, and be in such other qualities and form not inconsistent with any other provision of law as, in the judgment of the secretary of state, will not impair the ability of the department of state to include a legible and permanent copy thereof in its official records. Nothing in this subdivision shall be construed as requiring the department of state to accept for filing a document submitted in electronic form.

(c) "Certificate of publication" means a certificate presented on behalf of the applicable limited liability partnership to the department of state together with the affidavits of publication pursuant to section 121-1500 or 121-1502 of this article. The certificate of publication shall be in a form substantially as follows:

"Certificate of Publication of _____ (name of limited partnership) Under Section (specify applicable section) of the Partnership Law

The undersigned is the _____ (title) of _____ (name of limited liability partnership). The published notices described in the annexed affidavits of publication contain all of the information required by the above-mentioned section of the partnership law. The newspapers described in such affidavits of publication satisfy the requirements set forth in the partnership law and the designation made by the county clerk. I certify the foregoing statements to be true under penalties of perjury.

_____ Date

_____ Signature

_____ Printed Name"

History: Add, L 2005, ch 767, § 18, eff June 1, 2006; amd, L 2006, ch 44, § 12, eff June 1, 2006.

Sub (b), first undesignated par, amd, L 2006, ch 44, § 12, eff June 1, 2006.

ARTICLE 9
LAWS REPEALED; WHEN TO TAKE EFFECT

§ 125. Laws repealed
§ 126. When to take effect.

History: Add, L 1919, ch 408, eff Oct 1, 1919.

§ 125. Laws repealed

Chapter forty-four of the laws of nineteen hundred and nine and all other acts or parts of acts inconsistent with this chapter are hereby repealed.

History: Formerly § 110, add, L 1919, ch 408; redesignated § 125, L 1922, ch 640, § 1.

§ 126. When to take effect

This chapter shall take effect October first, nineteen hundred and nineteen.

History: Formerly § 111, add, L 1919, ch 408; redesignated § 126, L 1922, ch 640, § 1.

NOT-FOR-PROFIT CORPORATION LAW

History: Add, L 1969, ch 1066, eff Sept 1, 1970.

ARTICLE 1
SHORT TITLE; DEFINITIONS; APPLICATION; CERTIFICATES; MISCELLANEOUS

History: Add, L 1969, ch 1066, § 1; amd, L 1970, ch 847, § 1, eff Sept 1, 1970.

Article heading, amd, L 1970, ch 847, § 1, eff Sept 1, 1970.

§ 101.   Short title

This chapter shall be known as the "Not-for-Profit Corporation Law" and may be cited as "N-PCL".

History: Add, L 1969, ch 1066, § 1, eff Sept 1, 1970.

§ 102.   Definitions

(a) As used in this chapter, unless the context otherwise requires, the term:

(1) "Bonds" includes secured and unsecured bonds, debentures, and notes.

(2) "By-laws" means the code or codes of rules adopted for the regulation or management of the affairs of the corporation irrespective of the name or names by which such rules are designated.

(3) "Certificate of incorporation" includes (A) the original certificate of incorporation or any other instrument filed or issued under any statute to form a domestic or foreign corporation, as amended, supplemented or restated by certificates of amendment, merger or consolidation or other certificates or instruments filed or issued under any statute; or (B) a special act or charter creating a domestic or foreign corporation, as amended, supplemented or restated.

(3-a) "Charitable corporation" means any corporation formed, or for the purposes of this chapter, deemed to be formed, for charitable purposes

(3-b) "Charitable purposes" of a corporation means one or more of the following purposes: charitable, educational, religious, scientific, literary, cultural or for the prevention of cruelty to children or animals.

(4) "Conducting of activities" of a corporation means the operations for the conduct of which such corporation is formed and may constitute "doing of business" or "transaction of business" as those terms are used in the statutes of this state.

(5) "Corporation" or "domestic corporation" means a corporation (1) formed under this chapter, or existing on its effective date and theretofore formed under any other general statute or by any special act of this state, exclusively for a purpose or purposes, not for pecuniary profit or financial gain, for which a corporation may be formed under this chapter, and (2) no part of the assets, income or profit of which is distributable to, or enures to the benefit of, its members, directors or officers except to the extent permitted under this statute.

(6) "Director" means any member of the governing board of a corporation, whether designated as director, trustee, manager, governor, or by any other title. The term "board" means "board of directors" or any other body constituting a "governing board" as defined in this section.

(6-a) "Entire board" means the total number of directors entitled to vote which the corporation would have if there were no vacancies. If the by-laws of the corporation provide that the board shall consist of a fixed number of directors, then the "entire board" shall consist of that number of directors. If the by-laws of any corporation provide that the board may consist of a range between a minimum and maximum number of directors, and the number within that range has not been fixed in accordance with paragraph (a) of section seven hundred two of this chapter, then the "entire board" shall consist of the number of directors within such range that were elected or appointed as of the most recently held election of directors, as well as any directors whose terms have not yet expired.

(7) "Foreign corporation" means a corporation formed under laws other than the statutes of this state, which, if formed under the statutes of this state, would be within the term "corporation or domestic corporation" as herein defined. "Authorized", when used with respect to a foreign corporation, means having authority under Article 13 (Foreign Corporations) to conduct activities of the corporation in this state.

(7-a) "Infant" or "minor" means any person who has not attained the age of eighteen years.

(8) "Insolvent" means being unable to pay debts as they become due in the usual course of the debtor's business.

(9) "Member" means one having membership rights in a corporation in accordance with the provisions of its certificate of incorporation or by-laws.

(9-a) "Non-charitable corporation" means any corporation formed under this chapter, other than a charitable corporation, including but not limited to one formed for any one or more of the following non-pecuniary purposes: civic, patriotic, political, social, fraternal, athletic, agricultural, horticultural, or animal husbandry, or for the purpose of operating a professional, commercial, industrial, trade or service association.

(10) "Not-for-profit corporation" means a corporation as defined in subparagraph (5).

(11) "Office of a corporation" means the office the location of which is stated in the certificate of incorporation of a domestic corporation, or in the application for authority of a foreign corporation or an amendment thereof. Such office need not be a place where activities are conducted by such corporation.

(12) "Process" means judicial process and all orders, demands, notices or other papers required or permitted by law to be personally served on a domestic or foreign corporation, for the purpose of acquiring jurisdiction of such corporation in any action or proceeding, civil or criminal, whether judicial, administrative, arbitrative or otherwise, in this state or in the federal courts sitting in or for this state.

(13) [Repealed]

(14) [Repealed]

(15) "Governing board" means the body responsible for the management of a corporation or of an institutional fund.

(16) "Historic dollar value" means the aggregate fair value in dollars of (i) an endowment fund at the time it became an endowment fund, (ii) each subsequent donation to the fund at the time it is made, and (iii) each accumulation made pursuant to a direction in the applicable gift instrument at the time the accumulation is added to the fund. The determination

of historic dollar value made in good faith by the corporation is conclusive.

(17) [Repealed]

(18) "Authorized person" means a person, whether or not a member, officer, or director, who is authorized to act on behalf of a corporation or foreign corporation.

(19) An "affiliate" of a corporation means any entity controlled by, or in control of, such corporation.

(20) "Independent auditor" means any certified public accountant performing the audit of the financial statements of a corporation required by subdivision one of section one hundred seventy-two-b of the executive law.

(21) "Independent director" means a director who: (i) is not, and has not been within the last three years, an employee or a key person of the corporation or an affiliate of the corporation, and does not have a relative who is, or has been within the last three years, a key person of the corporation or an affiliate of the corporation; (ii) has not received, and does not have a relative who has received, in any of the last three fiscal years, more than ten thousand dollars in direct compensation from the corporation or an affiliate of the corporation; (iii) is not a current employee of or does not have a substantial financial interest in, and does not have a relative who is a current officer of or has a substantial financial interest in, any entity that has provided payments, property or services to, or received payments, property or services from, the corporation or an affiliate of the corporation if the amount paid by the corporation to the entity or received by the corporation from the entity for such property or services, in any of the last three fiscal years, exceeded the lesser of ten thousand dollars or two percent of such entity's consolidated gross revenues if the entity's consolidated gross revenue was less than five hundred thousand dollars; twenty-five thousand dollars if the entity's consolidated gross revenue was five hundred thousand dollars or more but less than ten million dollars; one hundred thousand dollars if the entity's consolidated gross revenue was ten million dollars or more; or (iv) is not and does not have a relative who is a current owner, whether wholly or partially, director, officer or employee of the corporation's outside auditor or who has worked on the corporation's audit at any time during the past three years. For purposes of this subparagraph, the terms: "compensation" does not include reimbursement for expenses reasonably incurred as a director or reasonable compensation for service as a director as permitted by paragraph (a) of section 202 (General and special powers) of this chapter; and "payment" does not include charitable contributions, dues or fees paid to the corporation for services which the corporation performs as part of its nonprofit purposes, or payments made by the corporation at fixed or non-negotiable rates or amounts for services received, provided that such services by and to the corporation are available to individual mem-

bers of the public on the same terms, and such services received by the corporation are not available from another source.

(22) "Relative" of an individual means (i) his or her spouseor domestic partner as defined in section twenty-nine hundred ninety-four-a of the public health law; (ii) his or her ancestors, brothers and sisters (whether whole or half blood), children (whether natural or adopted), grandchildren, great-grandchildren; or (iii) the spouse or domestic partner of his or her brothers, sisters, children, grandchildren, and great-grandchildren.

(23) "Related party" means (i) any director, officer or key person of the corporation or any affiliate of the corporation; (ii) any relative of any individual described in clause (i) of this subparagraph; or (iii) any entity in which any individual described in clauses (i) and (ii) of this subparagraph has a thirty-five percent or greater ownership or beneficial interest or, in the case of a partnership or professional corporation, a direct or indirect ownership interest in excess of five percent.

(24) "Related party transaction" means any transaction, agreement or any other arrangement in which a related party has a financial interest and in which the corporation or any affiliate of the corporation is a participant, except that a transaction shall not be a related party transaction if: (i) the transaction or the related party's financial interest in the transaction is de minimis, (ii) the transaction would not customarily be reviewed by the board or boards of similar organizations in the ordinary course of business and is available to others on the same or similar terms, or (iii) the transaction constitutes a benefit provided to a related party solely as a member of a class of the beneficiaries that the corporation intends to benefit as part of the accomplishment of its mission which benefit is available to all similarly situated members of the same class on the same terms.

(25) "Key person" means any person, other than a director or officer, whether or not an employee of the corporation, who (i) has responsibilities, or exercises powers or influence over the corporation as a whole similar to the responsibilities, powers, or influence of directors and officers; (ii) manages the corporation, or a segment of the corporation that represents a substantial portion of the activities, assets, income or expenses of the corporation; or (iii) alone or with others controls or determines a substantial portion of the corporation's capital expenditures or operating budget.

History: Add, L 1969, ch 1066, § 1, with substance derived from Gen Corp Law § 3, subd 11, 12, 13, 15, 16, 17, and Mem Corp Law § 2; amd, L 1970, ch 847, § 2, eff Sept 1, 1970; L 1974, ch 901, § 1, eff Sept 1, 1974; L 1978, ch 690, § 1, eff July 25, 1978; L 1998, ch 375, § 30, eff Aug 13, 1998; L 2005, ch 726, § 1, eff April 9, 2006; L 2006, ch 434, § 1, eff July 26, 2006; L 2010, ch 490, § 2, eff Sept 17, 2010; L 2013, ch

549, § 29, eff July 1, 2014; L 2014, ch 23, § 2, eff July 1, 2014; L 2015, ch 555, § 1, eff Dec 11, 2015; L 2016, ch 466, § 1, eff May 27, 2017.

CASE ANNOTATIONS

1. Generally

Plaintiff was entitled to summary judgment declaring null and void certain deeds conveying certain properties from plaintiff to defendant where (1) plaintiff was not-for-profit corporation whose board of directors never authorized challenged conveyances, (2) defendant's claim that plaintiff's then-president conveyed properties in order to satisfy his personal debt to defendant did nothing to advance, and even undermined, legitimacy of transactions, because no part of not-for-profit corporation's assets may inure to benefit of its members, and (3) no triable issue of fact was raised as to president's apparent authority, because sole evidence thereof was president's own representations at time of transactions. Stand Up Harlem Inc. v Miller (2001, 1st Dept) 286 A.D.2d 644, 730 N.Y.S.2d 437

Holders' claims under the N.Y. Not-for-Profit Corporation Law challenging a board of trade merger were not viable because N.Y. Not-for-Profit Corporation Law § 102(a)(9) expressly delegated to the board of trade the right to designate members in its certificate of incorporation or by-laws, and the board of trade's by-laws clearly provided that the holders did not have any of the rights or privileges of members under the N.Y. Not-for-Profit Corporation Law. Altman v New York Bd. of Trade, Inc. (2008, 1st Dept) 52 App Div 3d 396, 860 NYS2d 94.

Parishioners lacked standing to challenge the sale of a church's property as they were not members of the religious corporation; the church was managed by a five-member board of trustees consisting of the diocesan bishop, the vicar general of the diocese, the rector of the church and two laypersons selected by the other trustees, and the custody and control of the religious corporation's real property was vested in the board of trustees. Citizens for St. Patrick's v Saint Patrick's Church of W. Troy, 117 A.D.3d 1213, 985 N.Y.S.2d 743, 2014 NY Slip Op 3314, 2014 N.Y. App. Div. LEXIS 3259 (N.Y. App. Div. 3d Dep't 2014).

A charitable bequest made to petitioner nonprofit hospital under a 1924 will, presently valued at $850,000, "to be used by said hospital to endow charity beds... and for charitable purposes only," as a memorial to decedent and his sister would be an endowment under Not for Profit Corporation Law § 102(a)(13) in view of decedent's clear intent to bestow upon petitioner a permanent fund as memorial and, as such, would be governed by Not for Profit Corporation Law § 102(a)(16) requiring the governing board of the corporation to at all times retain the "historic dollar value" of the gift, representing principal payments received by petitioner between 1926 and 1962, and petitioner would be entitled to expend any amount in excess of the "historic dollar value" of the endowment for such hospital purposes as would be deemed prudent by its board of trustees under Not for Profit Corporation Law § 513(c) where the will specifically stated that the fund was to be used for charity beds "and for charitable purposes," there no longer being a need for charity beds; since the very nature of petitioner's operation is charitable, any expenditure that is necessary to further its operation is within the framework of the "charitable purposes" intended by the testator. In re Estate of McKenna (1982, Sur) 114 Misc. 2d 304, 451 N.Y.S.2d 617

Business improvement district that was organized as a non-profit entity but operated a taxi service was not immune from suit by a customer who claimed that the district's employees acted negligently when they established a taxi dispatch area near a defect in a roadway, and the trial court denied the district's motion for summary judgment on the customer's claim that she was injured when she stepped off a curb to enter a taxi because the customer raised issues of fact about whether the district knew or should have known about the condition which caused her injury. Hendryx v City of New York (2004, Sup) 3 Misc 3d 512, 776 N.Y.S.2d 763

2. Under former Membership Corporations Law § 2

Since above statute limits membership corporations to those not organized for pecuniary profit and Insurance Law § 250 provides for organization of membership corporations for purpose of issuing medical expense indemnity policies, such corporations organized under that statute cannot operate for profit. Shapira v United Medical Service, Inc., 15 N.Y.2d 200, 257 N.Y.S.2d 150, 205 N.E.2d 293, 1965 N.Y. LEXIS 1581 (N.Y. 1965).

A corporation created by special statute and not organized under this law is not governed by its provisions. Petition of Sousa, 12 A.D.2d 956, 211 N.Y.S.2d 204, 1961 N.Y. App. Div. LEXIS 12759 (N.Y. App. Div. 2d Dep't), rev'd, 10 N.Y.2d 68, 217 N.Y.S.2d 58, 176 N.E.2d 77, 1961 N.Y. LEXIS 1167 (N.Y. 1961).

Mandamus will not issue to compel the respondent to accept an executed certificate of consolidation of a corporation created under provisions of the Stock Corporation Law with one created under provisions of the Membership Corporation Law, since that writ will only issue to compel performance of a prescribed act to which the petitioner had a clear legal right. Debs Memorial Radio Fund, Inc. v Lomenzo, 50 Misc. 2d 51, 269 N.Y.S.2d 632, 1966 N.Y. Misc. LEXIS 2253 (N.Y. Sup. Ct. 1966).

Fact that certain town fire corporations were legalized and other fire corporations created under general law made subject to the statute's provisions did not make the Firemen's Benevolent Fund Association of the City of Mount Vernon a membership corporation, for purpose of determining effectiveness of 1930 amendment to certificate of incorporation changing membership requirements, since the Association was created by special law. Crohn v Firemen's Benevolent Fund Ass'n, 79 Misc. 2d 536, 359 N.Y.S.2d 599, 1973 N.Y. Misc. LEXIS 1279 (N.Y. Sup. Ct. 1973).

3. —Engaging in business for profit

The test of whether a corporation is engaged in business for a pecuniary profit cannot rest upon the financial results of its operations, retrospectively or currently or even prospectively; the court rather must regard the nature rather than the results of its activities. Kubik v American Composers Alliance, Inc., 54 N.Y.S.2d 764, 1945 N.Y. Misc. LEXIS 1763 (N.Y. Sup. Ct. 1945).

A membership corporation made up of the composers of serious music, which takes assignments of performing rights to the compositions of its members and licenses such rights for a consideration, thereby producing some income for distribution to the members, is engaged in an activity for pecuniary profit which is not permitted to a membership corporation. Kubik v American Composers Alliance, Inc., 54 N.Y.S.2d 764, 1945 N.Y. Misc. LEXIS 1763 (N.Y. Sup. Ct. 1945).

4. — —Right to own productive property

A membership corporation is not prohibited from owning productive property if the income is devoted to legitimate purposes of the corporation. Burton Potter Post v Epstein, 219 N.Y.S.2d 224, 1961 N.Y. Misc. LEXIS 3635 (N.Y. Sup. Ct. 1961).

5. —Membership corporations; generally

A corporation which has no authorization either in its certificate of incorporation or by statute to connect it with a business for profit or to distribute profits among its stockholders, and whose certificates are not transferable and can only be assigned to another member of the corporation, and in case of the death of the member are purchasable by the corporation at their issued value, so that a member can in no case realize a profit, is a membership corporation within the meaning of this section rather than a stock corporation within the meaning of General Corporation Law § 3. Stationers' & Publishers' Board of Trade v Flynn, 226 A.D. 496, 235 N.Y.S. 58, 1929 N.Y. App. Div. LEXIS 8759 (N.Y. App. Div. 1929).

The American Society for Prevention of Cruelty to Animals is not a membership corporation. Bailey v American Soc. for Prevention of Cruelty to Animals, 282 A.D. 502, 125 N.Y.S.2d 18, 1953 N.Y. App. Div. LEXIS 4503 (N.Y. App. Div. 1953), aff'd, 307 N.Y. 679, 120 N.E.2d 853, 307 N.Y. (N.Y.S.) 679, 1954 N.Y. LEXIS 1423 (N.Y. 1954).

A corporation formed for "benevolent, charitable, literary and scientific purposes and mutual improvement of religious knowledge" is a membership corporation and its character as such is not affected by an insertion in the certificate of incorporation that "the amount of the capital stock of the said association is $ 20,000 and is divided into 2,000 shares at $ 10 each." Bartlett v Lily Dale Assembly, 249 N.Y.S. 482, 139 Misc. 338, 1931 N.Y. Misc. LEXIS 1248 (N.Y. Sup. Ct. 1931).

6. — —Effect of issuance of stock

A corporation formed for educational purposes, and in which shares of stock have been issued, is not a membership corporation within the meaning of this section. Rye Country Day School v Lynch, 239 A.D. 614, 269 N.Y.S. 761, 1934 N.Y. App. Div. LEXIS 10902 (N.Y. App. Div. 1934), aff'd, 266 N.Y. 549, 195 N.E. 194, 266 N.Y. (N.Y.S.) 549, 1935 N.Y. LEXIS 1438 (N.Y. 1935).

7. — —Effect of excessive solicitor's commissions

The certificate of incorporation of a membership corporation will be revoked where it appears from an investigation of the Attorney General that 40 per cent of the sums collected ostensibly in the form of contributions by the organization to advance its charitable purposes, actually was used for the payment of solicitor's commissions, thereby violating the provision of this section that membership corporations must be operated for purposes other than pecuniary gain. Bennett v American-Canadian Ambulance Corps, 37 N.Y.S.2d 470, 179 Misc. 21, 1942 N.Y. Misc. LEXIS 2047 (N.Y. Sup. Ct. 1942).

8. — —Right to maintain action for slander

A membership corporation, which is not permitted to engage in any business for pecuniary profit cannot maintain an action for slander in the absence of an allegation of special damages, since its credit could not be affected, and no pecuniary injury could be occasioned to it. Electrical Board of Trade v Sheehan, 214 A.D. 712, 210 N.Y.S. 127, 1925 N.Y. App. Div. LEXIS 6950 (N.Y. App. Div. 1925).

9. — —Tax liability

The liability of a social club for tax, under the Revenue Act, on the sale of tickets to an amusement place depends on whether the club is the agent of its members in procuring theatre tickets for which a service charge is made, and this is a matter of intention between the parties, as manifested by their acts and by all surrounding circumstances. Columbia University Club v Higgins, 23 F. Supp. 572, 1938 U.S. Dist. LEXIS 2228 (S.D.N.Y. 1938).

A social club is not liable for tax where the relationship of agent and principal existed between club and member where the member controlled the purchase of tickets, with respect to time, location and price, and had the final say as to whether it would accept those which the club was able to obtain although the ticket broker billed the club monthly for the tickets purchased. Columbia University Club v Higgins, 23 F. Supp. 572, 1938 U.S. Dist. LEXIS 2228 (S.D.N.Y. 1938).

Since the certificate of incorporation states one purpose which is not within section 420 of the Real Property Tax Law, real property owned by the corporation would not be exempt from taxation. 1967 Ops St Compt No. 67-872.

10. —Bankruptcy proceedings

A country club which operates a golf course for the pleasure of its members, and which was organized under this section, cannot be the object of involuntary proceedings in bankruptcy. In re Elmsford Country Club, 50 F.2d 238, 1931 U.S. Dist. LEXIS 1383 (D.N.Y. 1931).

11. —Right of action of member

Minority members of a membership corporation could not complain that corporation had, by illegally adopting by-laws in 1900 and 1907, usurped excessive powers and made board of directors self perpetuating by permitting the then board to elect their successors and permitting further changes in by-laws without their consent. The 1900 and 1907 irregularities had been affirmed and ratified by the members, and in any event, by-laws of such a corporation organized for non-profit purposes permitting self-perpetuation of board of directors did not infringe on any property right or enforceable right of ordinary members. Bailey v American Soc. for Prevention of Cruelty to Animals, 307 N.Y. 679, 120 N.E.2d 853, 307 N.Y. (N.Y.S.) 679, 1954 N.Y. LEXIS 1423 (N.Y. 1954).

A member of a membership corporation, who has actively participated in activities of the corporation designed to promote pecuniary gain, is not thereby estopped from asserting the illegality of the activities of the corporation. Kubik v American Composers Alliance, Inc., 54 N.Y.S.2d 764, 1945 N.Y. Misc. LEXIS 1763 (N.Y. Sup. Ct. 1945).

12. —Miscellaneous

An order granted on affidavits alone, without trial permanently enjoining a local non-profit trading association from using a name was not justified where respondent's affidavit alleged circumstances indicating good faith and a right to use the name. Association of Contracting Plumbers, Inc. v Contracting Plumbers Ass'n, 302 N.Y. 495, 99 N.E.2d 542, 302 N.Y. (N.Y.S.) 495, 1951 N.Y. LEXIS 709 (N.Y. 1951).

A membership corporation conducting a collection agency for charitable hospitals is not a charitable corporation so as to exempt it from the prohibition against the practice of law by corporations. Hospital Credit Exchange, Inc. v Shapiro, 59 N.Y.S.2d 812, 186 Misc. 658, 1946 N.Y. Misc. LEXIS 1790 (N.Y. Mun. Ct. 1946).

§ 103. Application

(a) Except as otherwise provided in this section, this chapter applies to every domestic corporation as herein defined, and to every foreign corporation as herein defined which is authorized to conduct or which conducts any activities in this state. This chapter also applies to any other domestic corporation or foreign corporation of any kind to the extent, if any, provided under this chapter or any law governing such corporation and, if no such provision for application is made, to the extent, if any, that the membership corporations law applied to such corporation as of the effective date of this chapter. A corporation formed by a special act of this state which has as its principal purpose an education purpose and which is a member of the university of the state of New York, is an "education corporation" under section two hundred sixteen-a of the education law.

To the extent that the membership corporations law or the general corporation law applied to it as of the effective date of this chapter, the corresponding provisions of this chapter apply to a corporation heretofore formed by or pursuant to a special act of this state other than a religious corporation or an "education corporation" under clause (b) of subdivision one of section two hundred sixteen-a of the education law, if (1) its principal purpose is a religious, charitable or education purpose, and (2) it is operated, supervised or controlled by or in connection with a religious organization. Any such corporation may at any time after the effective date of this chapter file a restated certificate of incorporation under section 805 [restated certificate of incorporation] including a statement that it elects to have this chapter apply in all respects to it. The restated certificate of incorporation shall conform with the requirements of section 402 [certificate of incorporation; contents] for new corporations. Upon the filing of such certificate by the department of state, this chapter shall apply in all respects to such corporation.

This chapter also applies to any other corporation of any kind, formed not-for-profit under any other chapter of the laws of this state except a chapter of the consolidated laws, to the extent that provisions of this chapter do not conflict with the provisions of such unconsolidated law. If an applicable provision of such unconsolidated law relates to a matter embraced in this chapter but is not in conflict therewith, both provisions shall apply. Any corporation to which this chapter is made applicable by this paragraph shall be treated as a "corporation" or "domestic corporation" as such terms are used in this chapter, except that the purposes of any such corporation formed or formable under such unconsolidated law shall not thereby be extended. For the purpose of this paragraph, the effective date of this chapter as to corporations to which this chapter is made applicable by this paragraph shall be September one, nineteen hundred seventy-three.

(b) The general corporation law does not apply to a corporation of any kind to which this chapter applies. A reference in any statute of this state which makes a provision of the general corporation law applicable to a corporation of any kind to which this chapter is applicable or a reference in any statute of this state, other than the membership corporations law, which makes a provision of the membership corporations law applicable to a corporation of any kind shall be deemed and construed to refer to and make applicable the corresponding provision, if any, of this chapter.

(c) If any provision in articles one to thirteen inclusive of this chapter conflicts with a provision of any subsequent articles or of any special act under which a corporation to which this chapter applies is formed, the provision in such subsequent article or special act prevails. A provision of any such subsequent article or special act relating to a matter referred to in articles one to thirteen inclusive and not in conflict therewith is supplemental and both shall apply. Whenever the board of a corporation, formed under a special act, reasonably makes an interpretation as to whether a provision of the special act or this chapter prevails, or both apply, such interpretation shall govern unless and until a court determines otherwise, if such board has acted in good faith for a purpose which it reasonably believes to be in the best interests of the corporation, provided however, that such interpretation shall not bind any governmental body or officer.

(d) A corporation whose formation under this chapter is authorized by another corporate law is, unless otherwise provided by such corporate law, subject to all the provisions of this chapter that are applicable to a charitable corporation formed under this chapter.

(e) This chapter applies to commerce with foreign nations and among the several states, and to corporations formed by or under any act of congress, only to the extent permitted under the constitution and laws of the United States.

(f) The enactment of this chapter shall not affect the duration of a corporation which is existing on the effective date of this chapter. Any such existing corporation, its members, directors and officers shall have the same rights and be subject to the same limitations, restrictions, liabilities and penalties as a corporation formed under this chapter, its members, directors and officers.

(g) This chapter shall not affect any cause of action, liability, penalty or action or special proceeding, which on the effective date of this chapter, is accrued, existing, incurred or pending but the same may be asserted, enforced, prosecuted or defended as if this chapter had not been enacted.

History: Add, L 1969, ch 1066, § 1 eff Sept 1, 1970, with substance derived in part from Mem Corp Law § 3; amd, L 1969, ch 1067, L 1970, ch 847, § 3, L 1971, ch 955, § 1, L 1971, ch 956, § 1, L 1972, ch 901, § 6, L 1972, ch 961, § 1, eff Sept 1, 1972, L 1973, ch 807, § 1, eff Sept 1, 1973, L 2013, ch 549, § 30, eff July 1, 2014, L 2014, ch 23, §§ 3, 4, eff July 1, 2014.

CASE ANNOTATIONS

Where a religious society did not follow its own by-law procedures and the trustees were considered "directors" under the Not-For-Profit Law and where neither N.Y. Relig. Corp. Law § 2-b(1)(a) nor NY. Not-For-Profit Corp. Law § 103(c) contained inconsistent provisions, they clearly did not preclude the removal of the trustees, the trial court erred in denying the members' petition to remove the trustees, invalidate the new by-laws, and appoint a referee. Venigalla v Alagappan (2003, A.D., 2d Dept) 763 N.Y.S.2d 765

There is no requirement that multiple employer welfare association (MEWA) be non-profit organization. Insurance Department, Opinions of General Counsel, Opinion Number 03-11-07

§ 104.   Certificates; requirements, signing, filing, effectiveness

(a) Every certificate or other instrument relating to a domestic or foreign corporation which is delivered to the department of state for filing under this chapter, other than a certificate of existence under section 1304 (Application for authority; contents), shall be in the English language, except that the corporate name may be in another language if written in English letters or characters.

(b) [Repealed]

(c) Whenever such instrument is required to set forth the date of incorporation or the date when a certificate of incorporation was filed, the original certificate of incorporation is meant. This requirement shall be satisfied, in the case of a corporation created by special act, by setting forth the chapter number and year of passage of such act.

(d) Every such certificate required under this chapter to be signed and delivered to the department of state shall, except as otherwise specified in the section providing for such certificate, be signed either by an officer, director, attorney-in-fact or duly authorized person and include the name and the capacity in which such person signs such certificate.

(e) If an instrument which is delivered to the department of state for filing complies as to form with the requirements of law and there has been attached to it the consent or approval of the supreme court justice, governmental body or officer, or, other person or body, if any, whose consent to or approval of such instrument or the filing thereof is required by any statute of this state and the filing fee and tax, if any, required by any statute of this state in connection therewith have been paid, the instrument shall be filed and indexed by the department of state. No

certificate of authentication or conformity or other proof shall be required with respect to any verification, oath or acknowledgment of any instrument delivered to the department of state under this chapter, if such verification, oath or acknowledgment purports to have been made before a notary public, or person performing the equivalent function, of one of the states, or any subdivision thereof, of the United States or the District of Columbia. Without limiting the effect of section four hundred three of this chapter, filing and indexing by the department of state shall not be deemed a finding that a certificate conforms to law, nor shall it be deemed to constitute an approval by the department of state of the name of the corporation or the contents of the certificate, nor shall it be deemed to prevent any person with appropriate standing from contesting the legality thereof in an appropriate forum.

(f) Except as otherwise provided in this chapter, such instrument shall become effective upon the filing thereof by the department of state.

(g) The department shall make, certify and transmit electronically a copy of each such instrument to the clerk of the county in which the office of the domestic or foreign corporation is or is to be located. The county clerk shall file and index such copy.

History: Add, L 1969, ch 1066, § 1, eff Sept 1, 1970, with substance derived from Gen Corp Law § 8; amd, L 1982, ch 833, § 1, eff Oct 25, 1982, L 1998, ch 375, §§ 31, 32, eff Aug 13, 1998, L 2014, ch 57, § 2 (Part O), eff March 31, 2014.

CASE ANNOTATIONS

1. Generally
2-5. [Reserved for future use]
6. Under former Membership Corporations Law §
7. Under former General Corporation Law § 8

1. Generally
The Not-For-Profit Corporation Law mandates the Secretary of State to accept for filing a certificate of incorporation which meets the formal requirements of the statute and sets forth corporate purposes that are lawful. Gay Activists Alliance v Lomenzo (1973) 31 N.Y.2d 965, 341 N.Y.S.2d 108, 293 N.E.2d 255

Filing of an amendatory certificate of incorporation commences the effective date of the amendment; approval of a Supreme Court justice is a mere condition precedent to the right to file the amendment and is not conclusive on either the public or Secretary of State; however, such approval indicates that the purpose of the amendment is lawful and an acceptance by the Secretary enforces such view. Crohn v Firemen's Benevolent Fund Asso. (1973) 79 Misc. 2d 536, 359 N.Y.S.2d 599

2-5. [Reserved for future use]
6. Under former Membership Corporations Law §
An incorporated fire company may purchase with its own funds and retain ownership of fire apparatus and equipment although it is located in a fire district. 1955 Ops St Compt File #7480

7. Under former General Corporation Law § 8
Mere execution of a certificate of incorporation does not create a de facto corporation if the incorporators have not complied with this section and, therefore, where the incorporators, prior to any attempt made in good faith to comply with this section, transfer all the stock of the proposed corporation in exchange for certain rights under alleged contracts owned by a third party, the transfer is without consideration and it is error to dismiss a complaint of a judgment creditor seeking to sequester the assets of the corporation and to

recover on the personal liability of the stockholders. Stevens v Episcopal Church History Co. (1910) 140 A.D. 570, 125 N.Y.S. 573

A corporation which had failed to comply with the requirements of this section was not a corporation authorized to do business nor a de facto corporation and the Secretary of State was not justified in refusing to file the certificate of another corporation on the grounds of similarity of name. Brooks Clothing of California, Ltd. v Flynn (1931) 232 A.D. 346, 250 N.Y.S. 69

Where a company went out of existence as a result of merger and no new corporation was formed under § 85 of the Stk. Corp. Law, this section does not apply. O'Donnell v Milling & Lighting Co. (1937) 163 Misc 860, 298 N.Y.S. 9

Article 78 of the Civil Practice Act is not available to review an alleged erroneous filing of a certificate of incorporation, for the statutory authority "to review a determination" relates only to the determination of a body or an officer exercising quasi-judicial functions and in receiving a certificate authorized for filing the Department of State is acting in a ministerial capacity, except where there is some conflict of names. Where the certificate is in conformity with law there is a duty to receive and file it. New York State Soc. of Professional Engineers, Inc. v Department of State (1940) 174 Misc 173, 20 N.Y.S.2d 62

Filing of an amendatory certificate of incorporation commences the effective date of the amendment; approval of a Supreme Court justice is a mere condition precedent to the right to file the amendment and is not conclusive on either the public or Secretary of State; however, such approval indicates that the purpose of the amendment is lawful and an acceptance by the Secretary enforces such view. Crohn v Firemen's Benevolent Fund Asso. (1973) 79 Misc. 2d 536, 359 N.Y.S.2d 599

The existence of a corporation is not affected by the fact that no stock was ever actually issued, if its certificate of incorporation was duly filed and payment of the tax and filing fee was made. Gale-Hasslacher Corp. v Carmen Contracting Corp. (1961, Sup) 219 N.Y.S.2d 212

A certificate with no statement of duration of corporation shall not be filed. 1926 Ops Atty Gen 128

§ 104-A. Fees

Except as otherwise provided, the department of state shall collect the following fees pursuant to this chapter:

(a) [Repealed]

(b) For the reservation of a corporate name pursuant to section three hundred three of this chapter, ten dollars.

(c) For the resignation of a registered agent for service of process pursuant to section three hundred five of this chapter, thirty dollars.

(d) For service of process on the secretary of state pursuant to section three hundred six or three hundred seven of this chapter, forty dollars. If the service is in an action brought solely to recover a sum of money not in excess of two hundred dollars and the process is so endorsed, or the process is served on behalf of a county, city, town or village or other subdivision of the state, ten dollars.

(e) For filing a certificate of incorporation pursuant to section four hundred two of this chapter, seventy-five dollars.

(f) For filing a certificate of amendment pursuant to section eight hundred three of this chapter, thirty dollars.

(g) For filing a certificate of change pursuant to section eight hundred three-A of this chapter, twenty dollars.

(h) For filing a restated certificate of incorporation pursuant to section eight hundred five of this chapter, thirty dollars.

(i) For filing a certificate of merger or consolidation pursuant to section nine hundred four of this chapter, thirty dollars.

(j) For filing a certificate of merger or consolidation of domestic and foreign corporations pursuant to section nine hundred six of this chapter, thirty dollars.

(k) For filing a certified copy of an order of approval of the supreme court pursuant to section nine hundred seven of this chapter, thirty dollars.

(l) For filing a certificate of dissolution pursuant to section one thousand three of this chapter, thirty dollars.

(m) For filing a certificate of annulment of dissolution pursuant to section one thousand twelve of this chapter, thirty dollars.

(n) For filing an application by a foreign corporation for authority to do business in New York state pursuant to section thirteen hundred four of this chapter, one hundred thirty-five dollars.

(o) For filing a certificate of amendment of an application for authority by a foreign corporation pursuant to section thirteen hundred nine of this chapter, thirty dollars.

(p) For filing a certificate of change of application for authority by a foreign corporation pursuant to section thirteen hundred ten of this chapter, twenty dollars.

(q) For filing a certificate of surrender of authority pursuant to section thirteen hundred eleven of this chapter, thirty dollars.

(r) For filing a statement of the termination of existence of a foreign corporation pursuant to section thirteen hundred twelve of this chapter, thirty dollars. There shall be no fee for the filing by an authorized officer of the jurisdiction of incorporation of a foreign corporation of a certificate that the foreign corporation has been dissolved or its authority or existence has been otherwise terminated or cancelled in the jurisdiction of its incorporation.

(s) For filing any other certificate or instrument, thirty dollars.

History: Add, L 1982, ch 591, § 2, eff Sept 20, 1982; amd, L 1991, ch 166, § 271, eff June 12, 1991, L 1984, ch 198, § 3, eff June 12, 1984, L 2013, ch 549, § 31, eff July 1, 2014.

§ 105. Certificates; corrections

(a) *Corrections prior to filing by department of state.* Any certificate or other instrument relating to a domestic or foreign corporation submitted to the department of state under this chapter may be corrected with respect to any typographical, or similar non-material error apparent on the face of the

Not-For-Profit Corporation Law

certificate or instrument, prior to the filing of such certificate or instrument by the department of state. Such correction shall be effected by the department of state upon authorization in writing by the incorporator in a form acceptable to the department. Such authorization may be delivered by mail or sent by electronic mail to the department .

(b) *Corrections following incorporation.* Any certificate or other instrument relating to a domestic or foreign corporation filed by the department of state under this chapter may be corrected with respect to any typographical or similar non-material error apparent on the face or defect in the execution thereof including the deletion of any matter not permitted to be stated therein. A certificate, entitled "Certificate of correction of . . . . (correct title of certificate and name of corporation)" shall be signed and delivered to the department of state by mail or electronic mail . It shall set forth the name of the corporation, the date the certificate to be corrected was filed by the department of state, the provision in the certificate as corrected or eliminated and if the execution was defective, the proper execution. The filing of the certificate by the department of state shall not alter the effective time of the instrument being corrected, which shall remain as its original effective time, and shall not affect any right or liability accrued or incurred before such filing.

(c) A corporate name may not be changed or corrected under this section other than to correct any typographical or similar non-material error.

History: Add, L 1969, ch 1066, § 1, with substance derived from Gen Corp Law § 10; amd, L 1999, ch 172, § 24, eff July 6, 1999, L 2013, ch 549, § 32, eff July 1, 2014, L 2014, ch 23, § 5, eff July 1, 2014.

CASE ANNOTATIONS

1-5. [Reserved for future use]
6. Under former Membership Corporations Law § 10

1-5. [Reserved for future use]
6. Under former Membership Corporations Law § 10

Membership corporations may amend their charter under this section so as to truly set forth the object and purpose of the corporation. In re Creditors' Audit & Adjustment Ass'n (1911) 72 Misc 461, 131 N.Y.S. 263

A certificate of a membership corporation may not be amended, without the approval of the state board of social welfare, to delete a condition set forth in the certificate. 1941 Ops Atty Gen Feb 18

The failure of a membership corporation to obtain the necessary approval of the Board of Social Welfare to a certificate of extension of corporate existence is a defect which cannot be corrected by an amendatory certificate or by the Board's nunc pro tunc approval. However, a remedy lies in the filing of a certificate of revival of corporate existence pursuant to General Corporation Law § 49. 1952 Ops Atty Gen Feb 15

§ 106.   Certificates as evidence

(a) Any certificate or other instrument filed by the department of state relating to a domestic or foreign corporation and containing statements of fact required or permitted by law to be contained therein, shall be received in all courts, public offices and official bodies as prima facie evidence of such facts and of the execution of such instrument.

(b) Whenever by the laws of any jurisdiction other than this state, any certificate by any officer in such jurisdiction or a copy of any instrument certified or exemplified by any such officer may be received as prima facie evidence of the incorporation, existence or capacity of any foreign corporation incorporated in such jurisdiction, or claiming so to be, such certificate when exemplified, or such copy of such instrument when exemplified shall be received in all courts, public offices and official bodies of this state, as prima facie evidence with the same force as in such jurisdiction. Such certificate or certified copy of such instrument shall be so received, without being exemplified, if it is certified by the secretary of state, or official performing the equivalent function as to corporate records, of such jurisdiction.

History: Add, L 1969, ch 1066, § 1, eff Sept 1, 1970, with substance derived from Gen Corp Law § 12.

§ 107.   Corporate seal as evidence

The presence of the corporate seal on a written instrument purporting to be executed by authority of a domestic or foreign corporation shall be prima facie evidence that the instrument was so executed.

History: Add, L 1969, ch 1066, § 1, eff Sept 1, 1970, with substance derived from Gen Corp Law § 14(2).

§ 108.   When notice or lapse of time unnecessary; notices dispensed with when delivery is prohibited

(a) Whenever, under this chapter or the certificate of incorporation or by-laws of any corporation or by the terms of any agreement or instrument, a corporation or the board or any committee thereof is authorized to take any action after notice to any person or persons or after the lapse of a prescribed period of time, such action may be taken without notice and without the lapse of such period of time, if at any time before or after such action is completed the person or persons entitled to such notice or entitled to participate in the action to be taken or, in the case of a member, by his attorney-in-fact, submit a signed waiver of notice of such requirements.

(b) Whenever any notice or communication is required to be given to any person by this chapter, the certificate of incorporation or by-laws, or by the terms of any agreement or instrument, or as a condition precedent to taking any corporate action and communication with such person is then unlawful under any statute of this state or of the United States or any regulation, proclamation or order issued under said statutes, then the giving of such notice or communication to such person shall not be required and there shall be no duty to apply for license or other permission to do so. Any affidavit, certificate or other instrument which is required to be made or filed as proof of the giving of any notice or communication required under this chapter shall, if such notice or communication to any person is dispensed with under this paragraph, include a statement that such notice or communication was not given to any person with whom communication is unlawful. Such affidavit, certificate or other instrument shall be as effective for all purposes as though such notice or communication had been personally given to such person.

(c) Whenever any notice or communication is required or permitted by this chapter to be given by mail, it shall, except as otherwise expressly provided in this chapter, be mailed to the person to whom it is directed at the address designated by him for that purpose or, if none is designated, at his last known address. Such notice or communication is given when deposited, with postage thereon prepaid, in a post office or official depository under the exclusive care and custody of the United States post office department. Such mailing shall be by first class mail except where otherwise required by this chapter.

History: Add, L 1969, ch 1066, § 1, eff Sept 1, 1970, with substance derived from Gen Corp Law §§ 31, 32.

§ 109.   Reservation of power

The legislature reserves the right, at pleasure, to alter, amend, suspend or repeal in whole or in part this chapter, or any certificate of incorporation or any authority to do business in this state, of any domestic or foreign corporation, whether or not existing or authorized on the effective date of this chapter.

History: Add, L 1969, ch 1066, eff Sept 1, 1970, with substance derived from Gen Corp Law § 5.

§ 110.   Effect of invalidity of part of chapter; severability

If any provision of this chapter or application thereof to any person or circumstances is held invalid, such invalidity shall not affect other provisions or applications of this chapter which can be given effect without the invalid provision or application, and to this end the provisions of this chapter are declared severable.

History: Add, L 1969, ch 1066, § 1, eff Sept 1, 1970.

§ 111.   References

Unless otherwise stated, all references in this chapter to articles or sections refer to the articles or sections of this chapter, and all references in any section of this chapter to a lettered or numbered paragraph or subparagraph refer to the paragraph or subparagraph so lettered or numbered in such section.

History: Add, L 1969, ch 1066, § 1; amd, L 1970, ch 847, § 4, eff Sept 1, 1970.

§ 112.   Actions or special proceedings by attorney-general

(a) The attorney-general may maintain an action or special proceeding:

(1) To annul the corporate existence or dissolve a corporation that has acted beyond its capacity or power or to restrain it from carrying on unauthorized activities;

(2) To annul the corporate existence or dissolve any corporation that has not been duly formed;

(3) To restrain any person or persons from acting as a domestic or foreign corporation within this state without being duly incorporated or from exercising in this state any corporate rights, privileges or franchises not granted to them by the law of the state;

(4) To procure a judgment removing a director of a corporation for cause under section 706 (Removal of directors);

(5) To dissolve a corporation under article 11 (Judicial dissolution);

(6) To restrain a foreign corporation or to annul its authority to carry on activities in this state under section 1303 (Violations).

(7) To enforce any right given under this chapter to members, a director or an officer of a charitable corporation. The attorney-general shall have the same status as such members, director or officer.

(8) To compel the directors and officers, or any of them, of a charitable corporation which has been dissolved under section 1011 (Dissolution for failure to file certificate of type of Not-for-Profit Corporation Law under section 113) to account for the assets of the dissolved corporation.

(9) Upon application, ex parte, for an order to the supreme court at a special term held within the judicial district where the office of the corporation is located, and if the court so orders, to enforce any right given under this chapter to members, a director or an officer of a non-charitable corporation. For such purpose, the attorney-general shall have the same status as such members, director or officer.

(10) To enjoin, void or rescind any related party transaction, seek damages and other appropriate remedies, in law or equity, in addition to any actions pursuant to section 715 (Related party transactions) of this chapter.

(b) In an action or special proceeding brought by the attorney-general under any of the provisions of this chapter:

(1) If an action, it is triable by jury as a matter of right.

(2) The court may confer immunity in accordance with the provisions of section six hundred nineteen-c of the code of criminal procedure.

(3) A temporary restraining order to restrain the commission or continuance of the unlawful acts which form the basis of the action or special proceeding may be granted upon proof, by affidavit, that the defendant or defendants have committed or are about to commit such acts. Application for such restraining

Not-For-Profit
Corporation Law

order may be made ex parte or upon such notice as the court may direct.

(4) If the action or special proceeding is against a foreign corporation, the attorney-general may apply to the court at any stage thereof for the appointment of a temporary receiver of the assets in this state of such foreign corporation, whenever it has assets or property of any kind whatsoever, tangible or intangible, within this state.

(5) When final judgment in such action or special proceeding is rendered against the defendant or defendants, the court may direct the costs to be collected by execution against any or all of the defendants or by order of attachment or other process against the person of any director of officer of a corporate defendant.

(6) In connection with any such proposed action or special proceeding, the attorney-general may take proof and issue subpoenas in accordance with the civil practice law and rules.

(c) In any such action or special proceeding against a foreign corporation which has not designated the secretary of state as its agent for service of process under section 304 (Statutory designation of secretary of state as agent for service of process), any of the following acts in this state by such foreign corporation shall constitute the appointment by it of the secretary of state as its agent upon whom process against such foreign corporation may be served.

(1) As used in this paragraph the term "resident" shall include individuals, domestic corporations of any kind and foreign corporations of any kind authorized to do business or carry on activities in the state.

(2) Any act done, or representation made as part of a course of the solicitation of orders, or the issuance, or the delivery of contracts for, or the sale of, property, or the performance of services to residents which involves or promotes a plan or scheme to defraud residents in violation of the laws or the public policy of the state.

(3) Any act done as part of a course of conduct of business or activities in the solicitation of orders from residents for property, goods or services, to be delivered or rendered within this state to, or on their behalf, where the orders or contracts are executed by such residents within this state and where such orders or contracts are accompanied or followed by an earnest money deposit or other down payment or any installment payment thereon or any other form of payment, which payment is either delivered in or transmitted from the state.

(4) Any act done as part of the conduct of a course of business or activities with residents which defrauds such residents or otherwise involves or promotes an attempt by such foreign corporation to circumvent the laws of this state.

(d) Paragraphs (b), (c), (d) and (e) of section 307 (Service of process of unauthorized foreign corpora-

tion) shall apply to process served under paragraph (c).

History: Add, L 1969, ch 1066, § 1, eff Sept 1, 1970, with substance derived from Gen Corp Law §§ 61, 83, 84, 85, 91, 93, 94, 95, 219; amd, L 1970, ch 992, § 1; L 1971, ch 1058, § 1, eff Sept 1, 1971; L 2013, ch 549, §§ 33, 34, eff July 1, 2014; L 2015, ch 358, § 1, eff Sept 25, 2015.

CASE ANNOTATIONS

The Attorney-General, purporting to represent the ultimate beneficiaries of a charitable organization, which is the donee of an unconditional gift of corporate stock, does not have standing pursuant to EPTL 8-1.1 (subd [f]), which provides that the Attorney-General shall represent the beneficiaries of dispositions of property for religious, charitable, educational or benevolent purposes and it shall be his duty to enforce the rights of such beneficiaries, to sue the corporation to compel both the declaration and payment of dividends and the payment of market value of those shares repurchased from the donee corporation at less than market value, since although the Attorney-General's powers of representation and enforcement are not limited to express trusts, but encompass those charitable dispositions where property has been donated for a specific purpose, this does not mean that the Attorney-General has standing to represent those who might eventually reap the benefit of gifts made without a specified purpose to charitable organizations; in such cases, the charity implicitly receives the gift for its own uses, consistent with its charitable purposes and there are no beneficiaries, legally cognizable, apart from the donee, and the charity may use the gift as it sees fit, in accordance with the laws of its creation. Where there has been a completed, unconditional, irrevocable gift of stock to a charity, there is neither any intention of the donor for the Attorney-General to protect, nor any beneficiaries to represent. Furthermore, the Not-For-Profit Corporation Law (§ 112, subd [a], par [7]; §§ 719, 720), which authorizes the Attorney-General to bring an action against the directors and officers of a charitable corporation for certain specified types of misconduct and to enforce any right afforded under the statute to members, a director or an officer of a charitable corporation, does not provide the Attorney-General with standing. Lefkowitz v Lebensfeld (1979, 1st Dept) 68 A.D.2d 488, 417 N.Y.S.2d 715, affd (1980) 51 N.Y.2d 442, 434 N.Y.S.2d 929, 415 N.E.2d 919

Religious organization and its founder would be compelled to comply with subpoena issued by Attorney General in connection with investigation of fraudulent charitable solicitations since (1) religious corporations are subject to provisions of Not-for-Profit Corporation Law, (2) while not required to register with and report annually to Attorney General under CLS EPTL § 8-1.4(b)(3), religious corporations are within Attorney General's subpoena power, and (3) investigation in question was not being conducted in bad faith or in manner disruptive to respondents' religious activity. Abrams v Temple of Lost Sheep, Inc. (1990, Sup) 148 Misc. 2d 825, 562 N.Y.S.2d 322, dismd, motion den (1990, ED NY) 1990 US Dist LEXIS 13699, affd (1991, CA2 NY) 930 F.2d 178, cert den (1991) 502 US 866, 116 L Ed 2d 153, 112 S Ct 193

Subpoena issued by Attorney General in connection with investigation of fraudulent charitable solicitations, requiring religious organization and its founder to produce corporate books and records, would not be quashed on Fourth Amendment grounds since documents sought were not overly broad, burdensome or irrelevant to proper inquiry. Abrams v Temple of Lost Sheep, Inc. (1990, Sup) 148 Misc. 2d 825, 562 N.Y.S.2d 322, dismd, motion den (1990, ED NY) 1990 US Dist LEXIS 13699, affd (1991, CA2 NY) 930 F.2d 178, cert den (1991) 502 US 866, 116 L Ed 2d 153, 112 S Ct 193

Religious organization and its founder could not refuse to comply with subpoena, issued by Attorney General in connection with investigation of fraudulent charitable solicitations, on ground that compliance with subpoena would deprive them of Fifth Amendment right against self-incrimination since neither religious organization nor its officers have Fifth Amendment rights against production of corporate records pursuant to lawful judicial order. Abrams v Temple of Lost Sheep, Inc. (1990, Sup) 148 Misc. 2d 825, 562 N.Y.S.2d 322, dismd, motion den (1990, ED NY) 1990 US Dist LEXIS 13699, affd

(1991, CA2 NY) 930 F.2d 178, cert den (1991) 502 US 866, 116 L Ed 2d 153, 112 S Ct 193

In action by Attorney-General under CLS N-PCL § 112(a)(1) and CLS EPTL Art 8 to obtain injunctive relief against Long Island Society for the Prevention of Cruelty to Children (LISPCC), venue was properly in New York County where Charities Bureau of Attorney-General was located, and where LISPCC was required to annually file its financial reports or exemptions from filing. Koppell ex rel. People v Long Island Soc'y for the Prevention of Cruelty to Children (1994, Sup) 163 Misc. 2d 654, 621 N.Y.S.2d 762

Attorney-General has legal capacity to commence action to preserve cemetery's assets by seeking injunctive relief to restrain defendants from invading principal of cemetery's "permanent maintenance trust fund" and "perpetual care trust fund," and from borrowing money from its "perpetual care income fund" or otherwise carrying on unauthorized activities. People by Vacco v Woodlawn Cemetery (1997, Sup) 173 Misc. 2d 846, 662 N.Y.S.2d 369

In action under CLS N-PCL § 112(a)(1) to restrain cemetery from invading principal of its permanent maintenance trust fund and perpetual care trust fund, and from borrowing money from its perpetual care income fund, Attorney General's failure to have followed every possible administrative procedure before commencing action did not warrant dismissal of complaint; when Attorney General or Cemetary Board are not challenging agency determinations, they are not bound to exhaust all of their own procedures before commencing actions to quell wrongdoing by entities they oversee. People by Vacco v Woodlawn Cemetery (1997, Sup) 173 Misc. 2d 846, 662 N.Y.S.2d 369

CLS N-PCL § 513(c) does not override CLS N-PCL § 1507 restrictions on invading principal and thus, in action under CLS N-PCL § 112(a)(1), defendants were preliminarily enjoined from invading principal of cemetery's permanent maintenance trust fund or perpetual care trust fund, and from borrowing money from its perpetual care income fund (without prejudice to them if they applied for judicial approval under § 1507(a)), because (1) borrowing money that probably cannot be repaid is extra-statutory means of removing monies from funds without seeking court approval, (2) there would be continued invasion and arguably irreparable harm if injunction was not issued, and (3) balancing of equities favored issuance of preliminary injunction. People by Vacco v Woodlawn Cemetery (1997, Sup) 173 Misc. 2d 846, 662 N.Y.S.2d 369

Trial court declined to issue an order on the Attorney General's request that the trial court do so to allow the Attorney General to bring his four claims against the stock exchange chairman involving his alleged receipt of unreasonable compensation; the trial court had already denied the stock exchange chairman's motion to dismiss the four claims and, thus, an ex parte order was unnecessary. People v Grasso (2006, Sup) 12 Misc 3d 384, 816 NYS2d 863, 38 EBC 1221, stay gr (2006, NY App Div, 1st Dept) 2006 NY App Div LEXIS 10785, motion den (2006, Sup) 13 Misc 3d 1214A, 236 NYLJ 56, 824 NYS2d 757, motion gr, in part, motion den, in part, claim dismissed, summary judgment gr, in part, summary judgment den, in part (2006, Sup) 13 Misc 3d 1227A, 236 NYLJ 80, 25 BNA IER Cas 349, later proceeding (2006, NY App Div, 1st Dept) 2006 NY App Div LEXIS 13192 and stay gr (2006, NY App Div, 1st Dept) 2006 NY App Div LEXIS 14716

Owner cited no authority for the proposition that any entity other than the attorney general had the right to take action against a not-for-profit foundation based upon a claimed violation of its legal obligations; neither the foundation's tax status nor case law allowing charities unique enforcement rights for charitable subscriptions gave the owner any rights. Thome v Alexander & Louisa Calder Found. (2009, App Div, 1st Dept) 890 NYS2d 16.

§ 113.   [Repealed]

History: Add, L 1969, ch 1066, § 1, eff Sept 1, 1970; amd, L 1970, ch 847, § 5, L 1973, ch 1008, § 1, L 1974, ch 415, §§ 1-3, eff May 23, 1974, amd, L 1971, ch 1058, § 2, L 1984, ch 438, § 1, eff Aug 18, 1984, L 1998, ch 375, §§ 33, 34, eff Aug 13, 1998; repealed, L 2013, ch 549, § 35, eff July 1, 2014.

§ 114.   Visitation of supreme court

Charitable corporations, whether formed under general or special laws, with their books and vouchers, shall be subject to the visitation and inspection of a justice of the supreme court, or of any person appointed by the court for that purpose. If it appears by the verified petition of a member, director, officer or creditor of any such corporation, that it, or its directors, officers, members, key persons or agents, have misappropriated any of the funds or property of the corporation, or diverted them from the purpose of its incorporation, or that the corporation has acquired property in excess of the amount which it is authorized by law to hold, or has engaged in any business other than that stated in its certificate of incorporation, the court may order that notice of at least eight days, with a copy of the petition, be served on the corporation, the attorney general and the persons charged with misconduct, requiring them to show cause at a time and place specified, why they should not be required to make and file an inventory and account of the property, effects and liabilities of such corporation with a detailed statement of its transactions during the twelve months next preceding the granting of such order. On the hearing of such application, the court may make an order requiring such inventory, account and statement to be filed, and proceed to take and state an account of the property and liabilities of the corporation, or may appoint a referee for that purpose. When such account is taken and stated, after hearing all the parties to the application, the court may enter a final order determining the amount of property so held by the corporation, its annual income, whether any of the property or funds of the corporation have been misappropriated or diverted to any other purpose than that for which such corporation was incorporated, and whether such corporation has been engaged in any activity not covered by its certificate of incorporation. An appeal may be taken from the order by any party aggrieved to the appellate division of the supreme court, and to the court of appeals, as in a civil action. No corporation shall be required to make and file more than one inventory and account in any one year, nor to make a second account and inventory, while proceedings are pending for the statement of an account under this section.

History: Add, L 1970, ch 847, § 6, eff Sept 1, 1970; amd, L 2013, ch 549, § 36, eff July 1, 2014; L 2016, ch 466, § 2, eff May 27, 2017.

CASE ANNOTATIONS

Petitioner, who was a resident and taxpayer of town and who made annual charitable contributions to nursing home organized pursuant to Not-For-Profit Corporation Law, but who was not a manager thereof under any of four tests specified by Law and who was not an officer or director and had no beneficial interest in corporation, had no right to inspect records of corporation. Getman v Mohawk Valley Nursing Home, Inc., 44 A.D.2d 392, 355 N.Y.S.2d 508, 1974 N.Y. App. Div. LEXIS 4990 (N.Y. App. Div. 4th Dep't 1974).

Not-For-Profit Corporation Law

The Court has authority to intervene in corporate proceedings in matters of compliance with the corporation's charter and by-laws where the need for such intervention is clearly demonstrated. Santos v Chappell, 65 Misc. 2d 559, 318 N.Y.S.2d 570, 1971 N.Y. Misc. LEXIS 1875 (N.Y. Sup. Ct. 1971).

§ 115. Power to solicit contributions for charitable purposes

(a) No corporation required to obtain approval or provide notice of formation pursuant to section 404 [Approvals, notices and consents] of this chapter may solicit contributions for any purpose requiring such approval or notice unless and until such corporation [1] obtains and submits any approval or notice required thereunder, and [2] is in compliance with the registration and reporting requirements of article seven-A of the executive law and section 8-1.4 of the estates, powers and trusts law.

(b) The attorney general may maintain an action or proceeding pursuant to the provisions of subparagraph one of paragraph (a) of section one hundred twelve of this article against any corporation that solicits contributions in violation of paragraph [a] of this section. Such an action may also be maintained in relation to a corporation hereinafter incorporated if the name, purposes, objects or the activities of such corporation may, in any manner, lead to the belief that the corporation possesses or may exercise any of such purposes.

History: Add, L 1977, ch 669, § 7, eff Oct 1, 1977; amd, L 2013, ch 549, § 37, eff July 1, 2014.

ARTICLE 2
CORPORATE PURPOSES AND POWERS

History: Add, L 1969, ch 1066, § 1, eff Sept 1, 1970.

§ 201. Purposes

(a) A corporation, as defined in paragraph (a) of § 102 (Definitions), may be formed under this chapter as a charitable corporation or a non-charitable corporation unless it may be formed under any other corporate law of this state, in which event it may not be formed under this chapter unless such other corporate law expressly so provides.

(b) A corporation formed under this chapter on or after July first, two thousand fourteen shall either be a charitable corporation or a non-charitable corporation. Any corporation formed for both charitable purposes and non-charitable purposes shall be deemed a charitable corporation for purposes of this chapter. A type A not-for-profit corporation formed prior to July first, two thousand fourteen shall be deemed a non-charitable corporation under this chapter. Any submission or filing by such corporation to any person or entity shall be deemed to have been submitted or filed by a non-charitable corporation, and any reference in any such filing or submission referring to the status of such corporation as a type A corporation shall be deemed to refer to a non-charitable corporation.

(c) A type B or C not-for-profit corporation formed prior to July first, two thousand fourteen shall be deemed a charitable corporation for all purposes under this chapter. Any submission or filing by such corporation to any person or entity shall be deemed to have been submitted or filed by a charitable corporation, and any reference in any such filing or submission referring to the status of such corporation as a type B or type C corporation shall be deemed to refer to a charitable corporation.

(d) A type D not-for-profit corporation formed prior to July first, two thousand fourteen for charitable purposes shall be deemed a charitable corporation. Any submission or filing by such corporation to any person or entity shall be deemed to have been submitted or filed by a charitable corporation, and any reference in any such filing or submission referring to the status of such corporation as a type D corporation shall be deemed to refer to a charitable corporation. Any other type D not-for-profit corporations formed prior to July first, two thousand fourteen shall be deemed a non-charitable corporation. Any submission or filing by such corporation to any person or entity shall be deemed to have been submitted or filed by a non-charitable corporation, and any reference in any such filing or submission referring to the status of such corporation as a type D corporation shall be deemed to refer to a non-charitable corporation.

History: Add, L 1969, ch 1066, § 1, eff Sept 1, 1970, with substance derived from Mem Corp Law § 10; amd, L 1970, ch 847, § 7, eff Sept 1, 1970, L 1971, ch 1058, § 3, eff Sept 1, 1971, L 2013, ch 549, § 38, eff July 1, 2014, L 2014, ch 23, § 6, eff July 1, 2014.

CASE ANNOTATIONS

1. Generally
2-10. [Reserved for future use]
11. Under former Membership Corporations Law § 10
12. – Vague and indefinite purpose clause
13. – Existence of organization for similar purpose
14. – Particular purposes
15. – – Religious
16. – – Rehabilitation of prisoners
17. – – Aid to displaced children
18. – – Foreign birth or ancestry
19. – – Mutual assistance
20. – – Legal action; aid to lawyers
21. – – Transportation
22. – – Military
23. – Powers
24. – Miscellaneous
25. Under former Membership Corporation Law § 20

1. Generally

Where formal requirements for filing a certificate of incorporation were complied with and the purposes for which corporation was to be formed offended against no law, secretary of state lacked authority to label those purposes (namely, furthering of homosexual's rights), violative of "public policy," and secretary's refusal to accept certificate was arbitrary. Gay Activists Alliance v Lomenzo (1973) 31 N.Y.2d 965, 341 N.Y.S.2d 108, 293 N.E.2d 255

Each certificate of incorporation for a not-for-profit corporation must be evaluated on the nature of proposed activities and not merely on the results, no matter how laudatory, to determine whether the proposed corporation would be a business purpose or nonbusiness purpose not-for-profit corporation. Bodell v Ghezzi (1975, 3d Dept) 50 A.D.2d 674, 375 N.Y.S.2d 426

Despite the fact that buildings and improvements which proposed not-for-profit corporation proposed to construct for purposes of leasing, selling or giving would be so leased, sold, or given exclusively to voluntary agencies which were exempt from taxation under the Internal Revenue Code, the sale and lease of real property, without restriction, could only be considered a business purpose so that Secretary of State properly refused to accept proposed certificate of incorporation which stated that the proposed corporation would be a nonbusiness purpose not-for-profit corporation rather than a business purpose not-for-profit corporation. Bodell v Ghezzi (1975, 3d Dept) 50 A.D.2d 674, 375 N.Y.S.2d 426

An application for approval of a certificate of incorporation pursuant to the Not-For-Profit Corporation Law, setting forth the purposes of the corporation as being "to print, mail, disseminate, Roman Catholic information ... to conduct prayer vigils, and with divine guidance keep the knowledge of God and His plan for peace and security in the hearts of all mankind", brings the proposed corporation within the definition of an incorporated church making it subject to the provisions of the Religious Corporations Law as well as the Not-For-Profit Corporation Law, and, as such, the application must be denied for failure to conform to the specific provisions of the Religious Corporations Law which govern the incorporation of groups associated with the Roman Catholic Church, including the requirement of an execution and acknowledgment by certain specific officials of that church. In re Lueken (Our Lady of Roses) (1978) 97 Misc. 2d 201, 410 N.Y.S.2d 793

Judicial approval of certificate of incorporation for proposed type B not-for-profit corporation would be withheld as unnecessary since proposed corporation was type A not-for-profit corporation, for which no judicial approval was necessary, where proposed corporation did not have charitable purpose but was intended for specific benefit of 3 named persons, and no provision was made for using any portion of funds raised for benefit of public or any class of public. In re Application of Howard Beach Appeal Fund, Inc. (1988, Sup) 141 Misc. 2d 735, 534 N.Y.S.2d 341

In action against organization which operated residence for young single working women, there was nothing inconsistent in organization's claim to exemption from rent stabilization code, as charity, and to exemption from Human Rights Law, as religious institution, since entity may have different status under different statutes, and organization was religious order engaged in charitable work. Priolo v Saint Mary's Home for Working Girls (1993, Sup) 157 Misc. 2d 494, 597 N.Y.S.2d 890, mod on other grounds, affd (1994, 1st Dept) 207 A.D.2d 664, 616 N.Y.S.2d 36

Life insurer's claim against a purported beneficiary on grounds of an improper assignment should not have been dismissed because the insurer had raised litigable issues as to whether the assignee beneficiary was in fact the type of religious organization, Type B religious charitable corporation under N.Y. Not-for-Profit Corp. Law § 201, that could have been an assignee under N.Y. Ins. Law § 3205(b)(3) as it was constituted at that time. Am. Mayflower Life Ins. Co. v Moskowitz (2005, A.D., 1st Dept) 794 N.Y.S.2d 32

A village may not form a not-for-profit corporation and convey to it title to unused reservoir property for the purposes of avoiding real estate taxes. 1979 Op Atty Gen August 16 (informal)

A subsidiary of the Urban Development Corporation may incorporate under the Business Corporation Law without forfeiting its public status. The subsidiary may not pay profits to private investors, and upon dissolution of the corporation, the assets belong to the State. 1980 Op Atty Gen Oct. 20

The possession and rehabilitation of wildlife, as well as the restoration of wildlife to their natural habitat, are governed exclusively by the Environmental Conservation Law. Agents or officers of an incorporated society for the prevention of cruelty to animals or other humane societies may not engage in such activities, except in accordance with the procedures set forth in that statute. Ops Atty Gen 82-78

A central school district may not convey a building no longer needed for district purposes to a not-for-profit corporation for a nominal consideration. 1975 Ops St Compt File #1230

An incorporated volunteer fire company performing services in a fire protection district may set aside part of the payment received each year under the contract to accumulate money for a new fire truck. 1979 Op St Compt File #648

It was not necessary for out-of-state non-profit 501(c)(3) corporation, licensed as debt management company without physical presence in New York, to become licensed under Banking Law in order to receive payments directly from debtor who had relocated to New York. Banking Department, Legal Opinion (1/27/00)

Purchase of condominium unit by petitioner, tax-exempt not-for-profit corporation, would be subject to real estate transfer tax; further, since petitioner was required to pay grantor's obligation for transfer tax as condition of contract, such payment of tax would be deemed to be additional consideration for real property. N.Y. Adv Op Comm T & F TSB-A-90-(3)R

If petitioner, tax-exempt not-for-profit corporation about to execute mortgage with lending institution, was organization that had established exemption under Internal Revenue Code § 501(a), petitioner would be exempt from portion of mortgage recording tax representing special additional tax, but would be subject to basic tax, additional tax, and tax on mortgages recorded in cities having population of one million or more. N.Y. Adv Op Comm T & F TSB-A-90-(3)R

If college is type B corporation under CLS N-PCL § 201(b), it may procure life insurance under CLS Ins § 3205(b)(3). Insurance Department, Opinions of General Counsel, Opinion Number 03-05-01

Certificate of incorporation for museum formed under CLS N-PCL § 201(b) should be reviewed to determine purpose or purposes for which it was organized, and if one of purposes is charitable or educational, exception provided under CLS Ins § 3205(b)(3) would apply. Insurance Department, Opinions of General Counsel, Opinion Number 03-08-13

2-10. [Reserved for future use]

11. Under former Membership Corporations Law § 10

Where a certificate of incorporation under this section provides for the holding of the annual meeting on Sunday, it will not be approved for the reason that transaction of secular business on Sunday is contrary to public policy. In re Hakehiloth (1896) 18 Misc 717, 42 N.Y.S. 985

A corporation may not be incorporated under this law if it may be incorporated under any other general law. Hence, an organization basically religious in nature had to be incorporated under the Religious Corporations Law. Application of Basilio Scientific Spiritist Cult Asso. (1958) 9 Misc. 2d 389, 170 N.Y.S.2d 679

A proposed corporation which has for its object the conduct of religious services may not be granted a certificate of incorporation under this section, inasmuch as a corporation organized for religious purposes must be organized under the Religious Corporations Law. Application for Temple of Joy (1949, Sup) 86 N.Y.S.2d 678

12. – Vague and indefinite purpose clause

Court approval of an application to incorporate under the Membership Corporations Law for the objectives of promoting and fostering public understanding of insurance, insurance claims, policies, etc., was denied on the ground that the purposes stated were too general and vague, might invade the professional field of practice of law, failure to state necessity for incorporation under this act, and lack of any indication that applicants had the facilities or ability to attain their stated objectives. In re Policyholders Information Office (1960) 23 Misc. 2d 1093, 206 N.Y.S.2d 897

Approval was refused of a proposed certificate of incorporation of a membership corporation, to be known as "Aid Foundation," the vague purpose of which was to obtain funds to be distributed to worthwhile charitable and philanthropic endeavors, upon the ground that such an organization would merely duplicate the efforts of charities already in existence. In re Aid Foundation, Inc. (1960) 27 Misc. 2d 314, 210 N.Y.S.2d 165

An application for judicial approval of a certificate of incorporation was insufficient to enable the court to exercise its function of "judicial scrutiny" where it merely stated the proposed name of the organization and that its purpose was "to develop a program to meet the cultural, physical, mental and community needs of the individual." In re Fraternidad Hispana Americana (1963) 39 Misc. 2d 106, 240 N.Y.S.2d 110

Application for certificate of incorporation of membership corporation was denied where the purposes of the said corporation were too generalized and vague to warrant approval thereof. Re Council for Small Business, Inc. (1956, Sup) 155 N.Y.S.2d 530

The secretary of state must refuse to file a certificate of incorporation which contains a vague and indefinite purpose clause. 1940 Ops Atty Gen May 14

A proposed certificate of incorporation which is so vague and general as to purposes that it cannot be determined therefrom what the corporation proposes to do should not be filed by the Secretary of State, notwithstanding it bears indorsement of court approval and the Attorney General's acknowledgment of notice. 1963 Ops Atty Gen Apr 4

13. – Existence of organization for similar purpose

A certificate of incorporation will not be granted to an organization which has for its purpose the perpetuation of the name of the late President Roosevelt, the proposed organization to be called the F.D.R. Social and Civic Club, in view of the fact that existing membership corporations are adequate for the laudable purposes sought to be attained, and in view of the danger that the unrestricted use of the name of the late president would lead to confusion and create the impression that the corporation has official sanction, and could readily result in unauthorized and uncontrolled solicitation of funds. Application of F. D. R. Social & Civic Club (1945) 185 Misc 1015, 58 N.Y.S.2d 549

An application for incorporation of a proposed membership corporation, designed to substantially duplicate the functions of an already well established organization, will not be looked upon with favor by the courts since the public interest will not be served by the economic waste and loss of efficiency which would result from approval. In re Boy Explorers of America, Inc. (1946) 21 Misc. 2d 114, 67 N.Y.S.2d 108

A proposed certificate of incorporation may not be approved where the objects of the new corporation are listed as helping soldiers in need of money, food and clothing, and sending them packages of food, cigarettes and books, since the present agencies are adequate to accomplish these purposes, and incorporation would mean the solicitation and collection of funds in competition with already existing organizations. In re East Flatbush Victory Club, Inc. (1943, Sup) 42 N.Y.S.2d 351

An organization will not be incorporated for the purpose of fostering friendship and good will among returning service men and women and their families and to engage in social events and patriotic rallies, parades, etc., since there are already many organizations doing this kind of work which need more money than they have been able to secure and the objects specified are obviously the basis of an appeal for funds. In re Victory Committee of Greenpoint of Patriotic, Social & Fraternal Club, Inc. (1945, Sup) 59 N.Y.S.2d 546

Application for approval of proposed certificate of incorporation was denied where proposed rabbinic corporation would merely lead to confusion and misunderstanding and tend to impair the work presently carried on by long established and well known rabbinic organizations. Application of Knesseth Harabonim D'America, Inc. (1954, Sup) 131 N.Y.S.2d 543

Court denied application for approval of proposed amended certificate of incorporation for membership corporation where the papers failed to show that any purpose could be achieved by the sponsors, or that they would not merely duplicate work done by other organizations. Application of Howard Memorial Fund (1956, Sup) 155 N.Y.S.2d 126

Application for approval of proposed certificate of incorporation was denied where the existing agency with the same purpose was sufficient. In re Certificate of Incorporation of Humanity Club (1956, Sup) 155 N.Y.S.2d 210

14. – Particular purposes

There is nothing unlawful in stated purposes of a corporation to promote rights of individual freedom of choice and association and the individual right to associate with only those persons with whom he desires to associate, to investigate the problems involved, assist in elimination of barriers to individual freedom of choice, etc., and an individual judge of the Supreme Court, on application for his approval of such a certificate, lacks power to deny the application. Association for Preservation of Freedom of Choice, Inc. v Shapiro (1961) 9 N.Y.2d 376, 214 N.Y.S.2d 388, 174 N.E.2d 487, remittitur

den (1961) 9 N.Y.2d 909, reh den (1962) 11 N.Y.2d 720 and reh den (1962) 11 N.Y.2d 662, 225 N.Y.S.2d 740, 180 N.E.2d 898

The Secretary of State may properly refuse to file a certificate of incorporation of an alleged membership corporation which is executed under this section, where the certificate states that the purpose or object of the corporation is to make loans out of the common funds of the corporation and to collect the same together with dues, assessments and other contributions. The certificate, as drawn, violates Stk. Corp. Law, § 5. A corporation for that purpose should be formed under the Bank. Law. Bernstein v Moses (1928) 133 Misc 513, 231 N.Y.S. 669

Where the affidavit submitted in connection with an application to the Supreme Court for approval of a proposed certificate of incorporation contained repeated references to underbidding as one of the purposes of the proposed corporation, contrary to public policy as declared in General Business Law § 340, the court, in exercise of its discretion, declined to approve the proposed certificate. In re Application of Excavating Machine Owners Asso. (1960, Sup) 208 N.Y.S.2d 364

The Secretary of State cannot be compelled to file a certificate of incorporation as a social club, when its objects are, in fact, of a business nature. People ex rel. Davenport v Rice (1893) 68 Hun 24, 22 N.Y.S. 631

Formation of a corporation to engage in the practice of medicine is possible only under the provisions of § 11. 1934 Ops Atty Gen 240

A membership corporation cannot be formed for purposes essentially of a business nature, such as ownership, maintenance, improvement and operation of common utility systems of heat, water, electricity, etc. for the mutual benefit of individual owners of housing units. 1951 Ops Atty Gen Oct 17

15. – – Religious

Certificates of incorporation must be denied to a proposed corporation organized for the purpose of changing the religious beliefs of a specified religious group, in this case the object being to convert persons of the Jewish faith to Christianity. In re American Jewish Evangelization Soc. (1944) 183 Misc 634, 50 N.Y.S.2d 236

16. – – Rehabilitation of prisoners

A certificate of incorporation will be granted under this section to a corporation organized to solicit, receive and apply funds "for the moral betterment, religious advancement, temporal improvement and rehabilitation of inmates of prisons or penal institutions", where the fund in question was the result of publicity attendant upon the construction by prisoners of Clinton Prison at Dannemora of a church within the walls of the prison. In re Good Thief Foundation, Inc. (1944, Sup) 47 N.Y.S.2d 511

17. – – Aid to displaced children

A certificate of incorporation for a charitable organization to be known as "German Jewish Children's Aid, Incorporated," submitted to the court for approval, pursuant to this section, will be approved where the certificate recites that the purposes of the corporation are, to facilitate the entry into the U.S. from Nazi Germany of German children of Jewish extraction, to give to the secretary of labor and others such bonds and undertakings as may be necessary without charge and without indemnity, to aid and care for such children, and to perform matters incidental to the foregoing purposes, all without profit to the corporation, its members or officers. The objects of the corporation are charitable. In re German Jewish Children's Aid, Inc. (1934) 151 Misc 834, 272 N.Y.S. 540

18. – – Foreign birth or ancestry

A certificate of incorporation will be denied for an organization, the incorporators of which are naturalized citizens, which has for its object to "instill in its members a double patriotic love for both their country of origin, Italy, and for their adopted country, the great and free United States of America" since there can be no dual citizenship or double patriotic love for both a country of origin and the United States. In re Societa Fra-E Nate-Di Torre-Faro, Inc. (1940) 175 Misc 373, 22 N.Y.S.2d 688

Approval by the court of an application to form a membership corporation of "all New York City Transit System employees of Italian extraction" will be withheld, because there is no necessity for this membership corporation and because its existence under certain circumstances might prove embarrassing to its membership or to New York city. In re Columbia Ass'n of New York City Transit System, Inc. (1940) 175 Misc 876, 24 N.Y.S.2d 901

A corporate body composed of city employees of one nationality formed "to promote unity," one of the objects of the proposed corporation, would not aid the orderly administration of a city's affairs. In re

Columbia Ass'n of New York City Transit System, Inc. (1940) 175 Misc 876, 24 N.Y.S.2d 901

Incorporation will be granted to an organization of German and Austria-Hungarian war veterans whether or not the members thereof were to be veterans of the armed forces of the United States or of the armies of Germany and Austria-Hungary in the late war, where the purposes specified in the certificate are laudable and patriotic, provided, however, the court is satisfied that the organization is not being used as a front for a bund, semi-military in character, secretly supporting Hitlerian views. In re German & Austrian-Hungarian War Veterans Post (1939, Sup) 13 N.Y.S.2d 207

A certificate of incorporation for an organization to be known as the "Voters Alliance for Americans of German Ancestry, Inc." will not be approved where the purposes of the proposed corporation are the political education of Germans seeking or granted naturalization as American citizens since the court is not convinced of any need of politically educating Americans of German ancestry, and the other purposes set forth are adequately accomplished by the Steuben Society, and further the name is provocative of a notion that the organization is intended to unite persons resentful of the victory of the United States over Germany at a time when United States forces are in occupation of Germany and German leaders are on trial as war criminals. In re Voters Alliance for Americans of German Ancestry, Inc. (1946, Sup) 64 N.Y.S.2d 298

19. – – Mutual assistance

Notwithstanding grave concern expressed by the court as to the legality of purposes expressed by 21 milk distributors seeking to organize for mutual assistance in the milk industry field, the proposed certificate of incorporation was approved, following admonitions of the Court of Appeals as to the extent of the functions of a Supreme Court justice in passing upon approval applications, provided a clause relating to elimination of unfair competition was deleted. In re Wholesale Milk Distributors Asso. (1963) 39 Misc. 2d 738, 241 N.Y.S.2d 944

Organizations for aid by voluntary assistance dependent upon dues or assessments of members have not been looked upon with favor unless they are subject to some supervision by a public authority such as the Insurance Department of the State of New York. In re Gold Star Parents Ass'n (1946, Sup) 67 N.Y.S.2d 73

20. – – Legal action; aid to lawyers

Incorporation will be refused to an organization which has for its purpose to sponsor amendments to the United States Constitution and the constitutions of the various states which would bar from citizenship, from offices of trust and from old age benefits and unemployment insurance or other benefits persons advocating overthrow of the government by force or who knowingly circulates literature advocating such overthrow, and the deportation of naturalized citizens advocating such overthrow, since such amendments as outlined would be so drastic and sweeping as to be contrary to democratic principles. In re Patriotic Citizenship Ass'n (1945) 26 Misc. 2d 995, 53 N.Y.S.2d 595

The application for a certificate of incorporation of the "Committee for the Preservation of the Constitutional Rights to Trial by Jury," was granted. In re Application of "Committee for Preservation, etc." (1956) 1 Misc. 2d 548, 151 N.Y.S.2d 1005

A certificate of incorporation will be granted to an organization having among its objectives the advancement of knowledge and understanding of the law and research in jurisprudence, the promotion of a sound administration of justice and a grant of aid to members of the bar who may find themselves in need because of ill health, physical disability, or misfortune. In re Certificate of Incorporation of New York County Lawyers' Ass'n Fund, Inc. (1948, Sup) 81 N.Y.S.2d 724

21. – – Transportation

A corporation having for its purpose the ownership and operation of motor vehicles upon public highways for transportation of persons may not be organized under the Membership Corporations Law even though the corporation be not organized for profit and the persons transported be limited to members of the corporation. 1942 Ops Atty Gen July 20

22. – – Military

A membership corporation may not be formed for "the purpose of organizing, equipping and maintaining a voluntary local guard of citizen soldiers... subject at all times to the laws and general rules and regulations of the United States and of the state of New York." In

re Proposed Incorporation of L. B. Defense Guards, Inc. (1917) 100 Misc 584, 166 N.Y.S. 459

A proposed certificate of incorporation for a membership corporation is not entitled to judicial approval where one of its recited purposes is the training of young persons "in military tactics, procedure and discipline," notwithstanding consents of various state executive officers are annexed to the proposed certificate, as authority for formation of military forces rests with the legislative bodies of the State and National Government. In re Bronx County Cadet Corps, Inc. (1963) 40 Misc. 2d 3, 242 N.Y.S.2d 669

23. – Powers

In view of provision of the General Corporation Law § 14 subd 3, that every corporation has power to acquire property for corporate purposes by devise, a membership corporation whose certificate of incorporation specified that it may "own and acquire land" falls within the exception to Decedent's Estate Law § 12 permitting corporation expressly authorized by its charter or by statute to take by devise. In re Battles' Estate (1965) 45 Misc. 2d 348, 257 N.Y.S.2d 91

Where membership corporation is formed for research purposes it obviously has implied power to solicit and collect funds from public since nature of research is such as to make it financially unproductive and corporation cannot carry out its authorized purposes without getting money from some source. Waldemar Medical Research Foundation, Inc. v Margolies (1965) 45 Misc. 2d 887, 257 N.Y.S.2d 991, affd (1966, 2d Dept) 25 A.D.2d 444, 267 N.Y.S.2d 483

The conduct of fund-raising activities by volunteer firemen is within the purposes stated in the usual charter provisions of a volunteer fire corporation. 1955 Ops St Compt File #7124

24. – Miscellaneous

New York Soccer Association could not enjoin National Soccer Association from registering players of a league which was not a member or affiliated with the New York Association. New York State Soccer Football Asso. v United States Soccer Football Asso. (1957) 8 Misc. 2d 729, 166 N.Y.S.2d 319

Trial court denied the stock exchange chairman's motion to dismiss, as the Attorney General had the statutory responsibility to protect investors, had the authority to pursue the stock exchange chairman under the doctrine of parens patriae because they could not protect themselves from the allegedly unreasonable compensation that the New York Stock Exchange, a type A not-for-profit corporation, allowed him to receive, and the Attorney General stated four viable claims against him: for imposition of a constructive trust and for restitution for ultra vires payments allegedly received, for payment had and received, for violation of N.Y. Not-for-Profit Corp. Law § 715 for benefits he received that were improperly approved, and for violation of N.Y. Not-for-Profit Corp. Law for his allegedly receiving improper loans. People v Grasso (2006, Sup) 12 Misc 3d 384, 816 NYS2d 863, 38 EBC 1221, stay gr (2006, NY App Div, 1st Dept) 2006 NY App Div LEXIS 10785, motion den (2006, Sup) 13 Misc 3d 1214A, 236 NYLJ 56, 824 NYS2d 757, motion gr, in part, motion den, in part, claim dismissed, summary judgment gr, in part, summary judgment den, in part (2006, Sup) 13 Misc 3d 1227A, 236 NYLJ 80, 25 BNA IER Cas 349, later proceeding (2006, NY App Div, 1st Dept) 2006 NY App Div LEXIS 13192 and stay gr (2006, NY App Div, 1st Dept) 2006 NY App Div LEXIS 14716

Plaintiff lacked standing to bring a declaratory judgment suit alleging discrimination in unmet housing needs, municipal services, and lack of representation on the planning and zoning boards on behalf of its shareholders as plaintiff, which was formed to assert the objectives of the shareholders, could not do so as a for-profit corporation under N.Y. Bus. Corp. Law § 201(a); plaintiff's claims were maintainable under N.Y. Not-for-Profit Corp. Law § 201(b). United Fairness, Inc. v Town of Woodbury (2011, Sup) 932 NYS2d 895.

25. Under former Membership Corporation Law § 20

The Secretary of State should not accept for filing a certificate of incorporation which includes as a stated purpose matters of a business nature within the purview of the Federal Export Trade Act. 1955 Ops Atty Gen Jan. 12

§ 202.   General and special powers

(a) Each corporation, subject to any limitations provided in this chapter or any other statute of this state or its certificate of incorporation, shall have power in furtherance of its corporate purposes:

(1) To have perpetual duration.

(2) To sue and be sued in all courts and to participate in actions and proceedings, whether judicial, administrative, arbitrative or otherwise, in like cases as natural persons.

(3) To have a corporate seal, and to alter such seal at pleasure, and to use it by causing it or a facsimile to be affixed or impressed or reproduced in any other manner.

(4) To purchase, receive, take by grant, gift, devise, bequest or otherwise, lease, or otherwise acquire, own, hold, improve, employ, use and otherwise deal in and with, real or personal property, or any interest therein, wherever situated.

(5) To sell, convey, lease, exchange, transfer or otherwise dispose of, or mortgage or pledge, or create a security interest in, all or any of its property, or any interest therein, wherever situated.

(6) To purchase, take, receive, subscribe for, or otherwise acquire, own, hold, vote, employ, sell, lend, lease, exchange, transfer, or otherwise dispose of, mortgage, pledge, use and otherwise deal in and with, bonds and other obligations, shares, or other securities or interests issued by others, whether engaged in similar or different business, governmental, or other activities.

(7) To make capital contributions or subventions to other not-for-profit corporations.

(8) To accept subventions from other persons or any unit of government.

(9) To make contracts, give guarantees and incur liabilities, borrow money at such rates of interest as the corporation may determine, issue its notes, bonds and other obligations, and secure any of its obligations by mortgage or pledge of all or any of its property or any interest therein, wherever situated.

(10) To lend money, invest and reinvest its funds, and take and hold real and personal property as security for the payment of funds so loaned or invested.

(11) To conduct the activities of the corporation and have offices and exercise the powers granted by this chapter in any jurisdiction within or without the United States.

(12) To elect or appoint officers, employees and other agents of the corporation, define their duties, fix their reasonable compensation and the reasonable compensation of directors, and to indemnify corporate personnel. Such compensation shall be commensurate with services performed.

(13) To adopt, amend or repeal by-laws, including emergency by-laws made pursuant to subdivision seventeen of section twelve of the state defense emergency act, relating to the activities of the corporation, the conduct of its affairs, its rights or powers or the rights or powers of its members, directors or officers.

(14) To make donations, irrespective of corporate benefit, for the public welfare or for community fund, hospital, charitable, educational, scientific, civic or similar purposes, and in time of war or other national emergency in aid thereof.

(15) To be a member, associate or manager of other non-profit activities or to the extent permitted in any other jurisdiction to be an incorporator of other corporations, and to be a partner in a redevelopment company formed under the private housing finance law.

(16) To have and exercise all powers necessary to effect any or all of the purposes for which the corporation is formed.

(b) If any general or special law heretofore passed, or any certificate of incorporation, shall limit the amount of property a corporation may take or hold, or the yearly income from the corporate assets or any part thereof, such corporation may take and hold property of the value of fifty million dollars or less, or the yearly income derived from which shall be six million dollars or less, or may receive yearly income from such corporate assets of six million dollars or less, notwithstanding any such limitations. In computing the value of such property, no increase in value arising otherwise than from improvements made thereon shall be taken into account.

(c) When any corporation shall have sold or conveyed any part of its real property, the supreme court, notwithstanding a restriction in any general or special law, may authorize it to purchase and hold from time to time other real property, upon satisfactory proof that the value of the property so purchased does not exceed the value of the property so sold and conveyed within the three years next preceding the application.

(d) A corporation formed under general or special law to provide parks, playgrounds or cemeteries, or buildings and grounds for camp or grove meetings. Sunday school assemblies, cemetery purposes, temperance, missionary, educational, scientific, musical and other meetings, subject to the ordinances and police regulations of the county, city, town, or village in which such parks, playgrounds, cemeteries, buildings and grounds are situated, may appoint from time to time one or more special police officers, with power to remove the same at pleasure. Such special police officers shall preserve order in and about such parks, playgrounds, cemeteries, buildings and grounds, and the approaches thereto, and to protect the same from injury, and shall enforce the established rules and regulations of the corporation. Every police officer so appointed shall within fifteen days after his or her appointment and before entering upon the duties of his or her office, take and subscribe the oath of office prescribed in the thirteenth article of the constitution of the state of New York, which oath shall be filed in the office of the county clerk of the county where such grounds are situated. A police officer appointed under this section when on duty shall wear conspicuously a metallic shield with the name of the corporation which appointed him or her inscribed thereon. The compensation of police officers appointed under this section shall be paid by the corporation by which they are appointed.

(e) Any wilful trespass in or upon any of the parks, playgrounds, buildings or grounds provided for the purposes mentioned in the preceding paragraph, or upon the approaches thereto, and any wilful injury to any of the said parks, playgrounds, building or grounds, or to any trees, shrubbery, fences, fixtures or other property thereon or pertaining thereto, and any wilful disturbance of the peace thereon by intentional breach of the rules and regulations of the corporation, is a misdemeanor.

(f) No corporation shall conduct activities in New York state under any name, other than that appearing in its certificate of incorporation, without compliance with the filing provisions of section one hundred thirty of the general business law governing the conduct of business under an assumed name.

(g) Every corporation receiving any kind of state funding shall ensure the provision on any form required to be completed at application or recertification for the purpose of obtaining financial assistance pursuant to this chapter, that the application form shall contain a check-off question asking whether the applicant or recipient or a member of his or her family served in the United States military, and an option to answer in the affirmative. Where the applicant or recipient answers in the affirmative to such question, the not-for-profit corporation shall ensure that contact information for the state division of veterans' affairs is provided to such applicant or recipient in addition to any other materials provided.

History: Add, L 1969, ch 1066, § 1, eff Sept 1, 1970; amd, L 1970, ch 847, § 8; L 1971, ch 246, § 4, eff May 11, 1971; L 1971, ch 1097, § 70; L 1972, ch 961, § 2; L 1978, ch 693, eff Jan 1, 1979; L 1980, ch 843, § 191, eff Sept 1, 1980; L 1984, ch 757, § 1, eff Aug 3, 1984; L 2016, ch 407, § 2, eff Jan 3, 2017; L 2018, ch 476, § 233, eff Dec 28, 2018.

Blackline Showing Effect of 2018 Amendments. — (a) Each corporation, subject to any limitations provided in this chapter or any other statute of this state or its certificate of incorporation, shall have power in furtherance of its corporate purposes:

(1) To have perpetual duration.

(2) To sue and be sued in all courts and to participate in actions and proceedings, whether judicial, administrative, arbitrative or otherwise, in like cases as natural persons.

(3) To have a corporate seal, and to alter such seal at pleasure, and to use it by causing it or a facsimile to be affixed or impressed or reproduced in any other manner.

(4) To purchase, receive, take by grant, gift, devise, bequest or otherwise, lease, or otherwise acquire, own, hold, improve, employ, use and otherwise deal in and with, real or personal property, or any interest therein, wherever situated.

(5) To sell, convey, lease, exchange, transfer or otherwise dispose of, or mortgage or pledge, or create a security interest in, all or any of its property, or any interest therein, wherever situated.

(6) To purchase, take, receive, subscribe for, or otherwise acquire, own, hold, vote, employ, sell, lend, lease, exchange, transfer, or otherwise dispose of, mortgage, pledge, use and otherwise deal in and with, bonds and other obligations, shares, or other securities or interests issued by others, whether engaged in similar or different business, governmental, or other activities.

(7) To make capital contributions or subventions to other not-for-profit corporations.

(8) To accept subventions from other persons or any unit of government.

(9) To make contracts, give guarantees and incur liabilities, borrow money at such rates of interest as the corporation may determine, issue its notes, bonds and other obligations, and secure any of its obligations by mortgage or pledge of all or any of its property or any interest therein, wherever situated.

(10) To lend money, invest and reinvest its funds, and take and hold real and personal property as security for the payment of funds so loaned or invested.

(11) To conduct the activities of the corporation and have offices and exercise the powers granted by this chapter in any jurisdiction within or without the United States.

(12) To elect or appoint officers, employees and other agents of the corporation, define their duties, fix their reasonable compensation and the reasonable compensation of directors, and to indemnify corporate personnel. Such compensation shall be commensurate with services performed.

(13) To adopt, amend or repeal by-laws, including emergency by-laws made pursuant to subdivision seventeen of section twelve of the state defense emergency act, relating to the activities of the corporation, the conduct of its affairs, its rights or powers or the rights or powers of its members, directors or officers.

(14) To make donations, irrespective of corporate benefit, for the public welfare or for community fund, hospital, charitable, educational, scientific, civic or similar purposes, and in time of war or other national emergency in aid thereof.

(15) To be a member, associate or manager of other non-profit activities or to the extent permitted in any other jurisdiction to be an incorporator of other corporations, and to be a partner in a redevelopment company formed under the private housing finance law.

(16) To have and exercise all powers necessary to effect any or all of the purposes for which the corporation is formed.

(b) If any general or special law heretofore passed, or any certificate of incorporation, shall limit the amount of property a corporation may take or hold, or the yearly income from the corporate assets or any part thereof, such corporation may take and hold property of the value of fifty million dollars or less, or the yearly income derived from which shall be six million dollars or less, or may receive yearly income from such corporate assets of six million dollars or less, notwithstanding any such limitations. In computing the value of such property, no increase in value arising otherwise than from improvements made thereon shall be taken into account.

(c) When any corporation shall have sold or conveyed any part of its real property, the supreme court, notwithstanding a restriction in any general or special law, may authorize it to purchase and hold from time to time other real property, upon satisfactory proof that the value of the property so purchased does not exceed the value of the property so sold and conveyed within the three years next preceding the application.

(d) A corporation formed under general or special law to provide parks, playgrounds or cemeteries, or buildings and grounds for camp or grove meetings. Sunday school assemblies, cemetery purposes, temperance, missionary, educational, scientific, musical and other meetings, subject to the ordinances and police regulations of the county, city, town, or village in which such parks, playgrounds, cemeteries, buildings and grounds are situated, may appoint from time to time one or more special ~~policemen~~ police officers, with power to remove the same at pleasure. Such special ~~policemen~~ police officers shall preserve order in and about such parks, playgrounds, cemeteries, buildings and grounds, and the approaches thereto, and to protect the same from injury, and shall enforce the established rules and regulations of the corporation. Every ~~policeman~~ police officer so appointed shall within fifteen days after his or her appointment and before entering upon the duties of his or her office, take and subscribe the oath of office prescribed in the thirteenth article of the constitution of the state of New York, which oath shall be filed in the office of the county clerk of the county where such grounds are situated. A ~~policeman~~ police officer appointed under this section when on duty shall wear conspicuously a metallic shield with the name of the corporation which appointed him ~~or her~~ inscribed thereon. The compensation of ~~policemen~~ police officers appointed under this section shall be paid by the corporation by which they are appointed.

(e) Any wilful trespass in or upon any of the parks, playgrounds, buildings or grounds provided for the purposes mentioned in the preceding paragraph, or upon the approaches thereto, and any wilful injury to any of the said parks, playgrounds, building or grounds, or to any trees, shrubbery, fences, fixtures or other property thereon or pertaining thereto, and any wilful disturbance of the peace thereon by intentional breach of the rules and regulations of the corporation, is a misdemeanor.

(f) No corporation shall conduct activities in New York state under any name, other than that appearing in its certificate of incorporation, without compliance with the filing provisions of section one hundred thirty of the general business law governing the conduct of business under an assumed name.

(g) Every corporation receiving any kind of state funding shall ensure the provision on any form required to be completed at application or recertification for the purpose of obtaining financial assistance pursuant to this chapter, that the application form shall contain a check-off question asking whether the applicant or recipient or a member of his or her family served in the United States military, and an option to answer in the affirmative. Where the applicant or recipient answers in the affirmative to such question, the not-for-profit corporation shall ensure that contact information for the state division of veterans' affairs is provided to such applicant or recipient in addition to any other materials provided.

CASE ANNOTATIONS

1. **Generally**
2. **Under former General Corporation Law § 13**
3. **Under former General Corporation Law § 14**
4. **–Right to acquire property**
5. **–Meaning of take and hold**
6. **–Right to use or dispose of property**
7. **–Miscellaneous**
8. **Under former General Corporation Law § 15**
9. **Under former General Corporation Law § 34**

1. Generally

Tribal social service agency incorporated under District of Columbia Nonprofit Corporation Act and qualified to do business in New York under Nonprofit Corporation Act did not waive its common-law tribal sovereign immunity by virtue of reference in its corporate charter to statutory authority to sue and be sued where tribe itself had not explicitly consented in agency's charter, or by any ordinance or resolution, to waive its sovereign immunity, to submit corporate disputes to jurisdiction of New York courts, or to be bound by such judgment. Ransom v St. Regis Mohawk Educ. & Community Fund, 86 N.Y.2d 553, 635 N.Y.S.2d 116, 658 N.E.2d 989, 1995 N.Y. LEXIS 3551 (N.Y. 1995).

Tribal social service agency incorporated under District of Columbia Nonprofit Corporation Act and qualified to do business in New York under Nonprofit Corporation Act did not waive its common-law tribal sovereign immunity by virtue of reference in its corporate charter to statutory authority to sue and be sued where tribe itself had not explicitly consented in agency's charter, or by any ordinance or resolution, to waive its sovereign immunity, to submit corporate disputes to jurisdiction of New York courts, or to be bound by such judgment. Ransom v St. Regis Mohawk Educ. & Community Fund, 86 N.Y.2d 553, 635 N.Y.S.2d 116, 658 N.E.2d 989, 1995 N.Y. LEXIS 3551 (N.Y. 1995).

Tribal social service agency incorporated under District of Columbia Nonprofit Corporation Act and qualified to do business in New York under Nonprofit Corporation Act did not waive its common-law tribal sovereign immunity by virtue of reference in its corporate charter to statutory authority to sue and be sued where tribe itself had not explicitly consented in agency's charter, or by any ordinance or resolution, to waive its sovereign immunity, to submit corporate disputes to jurisdiction of New York courts, or to be bound by such judgment. Ransom v St. Regis Mohawk Educ. & Community Fund, 86 N.Y.2d 553, 635 N.Y.S.2d 116, 658 N.E.2d 989, 1995 N.Y. LEXIS 3551 (N.Y. 1995).

Blue Cross has authority to enter into contracts, and contract with pharmacists is in furtherance of function to provide subscribers with prepaid prescription benefits; upon finding that corporation did not exceed its powers by offering agreement, its rationality is not proper subject for judicial inquiry. Pharmacists' Asso. of Western New York, Inc. v Blue Cross of Western New York, Inc., 112 A.D.2d 728, 492 N.Y.S.2d 221 (4th Dept 1985).

Article 78 proceeding was appropriate vehicle to challenge not-for-profit corporation's determination to terminate employee where it was claimed that corporation violated its own rules set forth in employee manual. De Petris v Union Settlement Ass'n, 209 A.D.2d 180, 618 N.Y.S.2d 276, 1994 N.Y. App. Div. LEXIS 10865 (N.Y. App. Div. 1st Dep't 1994), aff'd, 86 N.Y.2d 406, 633 N.Y.S.2d 274, 657 N.E.2d 269, 1995 N.Y. LEXIS 3555 (N.Y. 1995).

Under N-PCL § 202, subd 11, act of not for profit general bridge corporation in sanctioning and organizing membership districts wholly within Canada was not ultra vires where certificate of incorporation did not specifically limit the corporation's activities to the territorial boundaries of the United States. Central New York Bridge Asso. v American Contract Bridge League, Inc., 72 Misc. 2d 271, 339 N.Y.S.2d 438 (1972).

Grant of special use permit to college to renovate buildings and lease them to not for profit corporation for purposes of offering community instruction in art courses was proper under zoning ordinance authorizing use for bona fide educational purposes despite fact that school would not be approved by board of regents. Imbergamo v Barclay, 77 Misc. 2d 188, 352 N.Y.S.2d 337, 1973 N.Y. Misc. LEXIS 1215 (N.Y. Sup. Ct. 1973).

Vehicle owned by county Society for Prevention of Cruelty to Children, and operated by society employee, was not "police vehicle" under CLS Veh & Tr § 132-a for purposes of claiming exemption from enforcement of traffic laws under CLS Veh & Tr § 1104 since society is not equivalent to state or public authority by virtue of its limited powers under CLS N-PCL § 1403, and is not authorized to maintain law enforcement unit under CLS N-PCL § 202. People v Ellman, 135 Misc. 2d 1010, 517 N.Y.S.2d 664, 1987 N.Y. Misc. LEXIS 2351 (N.Y. City Ct. 1987).

Trial court denied the stock exchange chairman's motion to dismiss, as the Attorney General had the statutory responsibility to protect investors, had the authority to pursue the stock exchange chairman under the doctrine of parens patriae because they could not protect themselves from the allegedly unreasonable compensation that the New York Stock exchange allowed him to receive, and the Attorney General stated four viable claims against him: for imposition of a constructive trust and for restitution for ultra vires payments allegedly received, for payment had and received, for violation of N.Y. Not-for-Profit Corp. Law § 715 for benefits he received that were improperly approved, and for violation of N.Y. Not-for-Profit Corp. Law for his allegedly receiving improper loans. People v Grasso, 816 N.Y.S.2d 863, 2006 NY Slip Op 26095, 12 Misc. 3d 384, 235 N.Y.L.J. 54, 2006 N.Y. Misc. LEXIS 484 (N.Y. Sup. Ct. 2006), rev'd, 42 A.D.3d 126, 836 N.Y.S.2d 40, 2007 NY Slip Op 3990, 2007 N.Y. App. Div. LEXIS 5719 (N.Y. App. Div. 1st Dep't 2007).

Through application of N.Y. Not-for-Profit Corp. Law § 202(a)(2) and N.Y. Educ. Law §§ 2853(1) and 216-a(4), charter schools had the capacity to sue, as natural persons, the State and its comptroller to challenge the constitutionality of statutes requiring the comptroller to audit the charter schools. Matter of New York Charter Schools Assn. v DiNapoli, 857 N.Y.S.2d 450 (Sup 2008).

State attorney general's complaint against stock exchange chairman was not properly removed where contrary to the chairman's argument, the complaint did not seek to hold him liable for the manner in which he enforced federal securities laws, but rather the state attorney general sought to hold the chairman liable for what the complaint alleged was the receipt of excessive and improperly determined compensation under N.Y. Not-for-Profit Corp. Law § 202(a)(12) and the validity of this claim did not depend on whether the chairman's enforcement of federal securities laws or of the exchange rules was proper or not. New York v Grasso, 350 F. Supp. 2d 498, 2004 U.S. Dist. LEXIS 25044 (S.D.N.Y. 2004).

2. Under former General Corporation Law § 13

A cemetery corporation organized under the membership corporation law has a general power to convey its property under this section even gratuitously, except when limitations are imposed by statute. Application of Kensico Cemetery, 83 N.Y.S.2d 73, 193 Misc. 479, 1948 N.Y. Misc. LEXIS 3287 (N.Y. Sup. Ct. 1948), rev'd, 275 A.D. 681, 86 N.Y.S.2d 737, 1949 N.Y. App. Div. LEXIS 4009 (N.Y. App. Div. 2d Dep't 1949).

Mere issuance of registration certificates by a department will not confer a power on a corporation not set forth in its certificate of incorporation. John B. Waldbillig, Inc. v Gottfried, 43 Misc. 2d 664, 251 N.Y.S.2d 991, 1964 N.Y. Misc. LEXIS 1536 (N.Y. Sup. Ct.), rev'd, 22 A.D.2d 997, 254 N.Y.S.2d 924, 1964 N.Y. App. Div. LEXIS 2450 (N.Y. App. Div. 3d Dep't 1964).

Board of governors of public hospital has no power to contract indebtedness to obtain funds for hospital purposes. It does have authority to employ professional fund raisers. 1965 Ops St Compt File #452.

3. Under former General Corporation Law § 14

This section is apparently inapplicable to impose power to acquire and dispose of real property on an educational corporation whose powers in such matters are controlled by the Education Law. Board of Education v Board of Cooperative Educational Services, 41 Misc. 2d 699, 246 N.Y.S.2d 48, 1964 N.Y. Misc. LEXIS 2192 (N.Y. Sup. Ct. 1964).

A cemetery association did not dedicate lands to the cemetery use where the land has not been surveyed or plotted for burial purposes, nor has it either been set apart for the burial of the dead, or marked and distinguished from the adjoining ground as a place of burial, and, as a result, it could sell the land. Diamond v Foote, 109 N.Y.S.2d 831, 1952 N.Y. Misc. LEXIS 2365 (N.Y. City Ct. 1952).

4. –Right to acquire property

A membership corporation duly incorporated has power under this section to take property by bequest. In re McQuirk's Estate, 224 N.Y.S. 431, 130 Misc. 336, 1927 N.Y. Misc. LEXIS 1138 (N.Y. Sur. Ct. 1927), aff'd, 224 A.D. 724, 229 N.Y.S. 880, 1928 N.Y. App. Div. LEXIS 10714 (N.Y. App. Div. 1928).

Subordinate post of Veterans of Foreign Wars which has filed certificate required by Benevolent Orders Law § 2, subd 38-b and final unnumbered paragraph, has power under terms of §§ 3 and 3-a of such law and those of General Corporation Law § 14, subd 3, to receive property by devise or bequest. And authority conferred by above statutes is sufficient to bring such post within exception to Decedent's Estate Law § 12 for corporations expressly authorized by statute to take by devise. In re Battles' Estate, 45 Misc. 2d 348, 257 N.Y.S.2d 91, 1965 N.Y. Misc. LEXIS 2197 (N.Y. Sur. Ct. 1965).

Power to acquire property by gift conferred on corporations generally by subd 3 of above statute includes power to solicit gifts. Waldemar Medical Research Foundation, Inc. v Margolies, 45 Misc. 2d 887, 257 N.Y.S.2d 991, 1965 N.Y. Misc. LEXIS 2155 (N.Y. Sup. Ct. 1965), aff'd, 25 A.D.2d 444, 267 N.Y.S.2d 483, 1966 N.Y. App. Div. LEXIS 5165 (N.Y. App. Div. 2d Dep't 1966).

Fire district may acquire real estate for fire house purposes upon condition that the property be used for such purposes and will revert to donor on breach of such condition. The condition of such deed may provide that fire district shall remove the building in the event of breach of condition. The fire house upon such property so acquired may be financed by issuance of serial bonds. 1947 Ops St Compt 225.

5. –Meaning of take and hold

The words take and hold, as used in § 15, do not mean taking by devise when taking by such method is not authorized, but such words refer to all methods by which a corporation can acquire property set forth in § 14 so that a hospital corporation was entitled to take and hold real and personal property devised and bequeathed to it, the amount of which was within the limitations of § 15. In re Clark's Estate, 7 N.Y.S.2d 299, 1938 N.Y. Misc. LEXIS 2044 (N.Y. Sur. Ct. 1938), aff'd, 257 A.D. 982, 14 N.Y.S.2d 157, 1939 N.Y. App. Div. LEXIS 8798 (N.Y. App. Div. 1939).

6. –Right to use or dispose of property

A soldiers' monument corporation was permitted to sell its real property where before closing, a majority of the whole number of directors authorized the sale under the terms contained in the contract. The evidence established the adequacy of the consideration and that the interests of the corporation would be promoted by the sale. Application of Staten Island War Memorial Asso., 286 A.D. 887, 143 N.Y.S.2d 100, 1955 N.Y. App. Div. LEXIS 4441 (N.Y. App. Div.), app. denied, 286 A.D. 1017, 145 N.Y.S.2d 318, 1955 N.Y. App. Div. LEXIS 5023 (N.Y. App. Div. 1955).

A cemetery corporation organized under the membership corporation law has a general power to convey its property under this section even gratuitously, except when limitations are imposed by statute. Application of Kensico Cemetery, 83 N.Y.S.2d 73, 193 Misc. 479, 1948

N.Y. Misc. LEXIS 3287 (N.Y. Sup. Ct. 1948), rev'd, 275 A.D. 681, 86 N.Y.S.2d 737, 1949 N.Y. App. Div. LEXIS 4009 (N.Y. App. Div. 2d Dep't 1949).

A village fire department may convey for a consideration less than actual value, a parcel of real estate purchased by it with its own funds. Such conveyance must be in accordance with applicable law and the by-laws of the department. 1955 Ops St Compt File #7747.

7. –Miscellaneous

A religious corporation could not remove the pastor of a Baptist church on the theory that the power to appoint given in subd 4 of this section includes the power to remove, where the rules and regulations of that denomination show that the pastor is an officer of the religious society of the church and not of the religious corporation. Walker Memorial Baptist Church v Saunders, 285 N.Y. 462, 35 N.E.2d 42, 285 N.Y. (N.Y.S.) 462, 1941 N.Y. LEXIS 1487 (N.Y.), reh'g denied, 286 N.Y. 607, 35 N.E.2d 944, 286 N.Y. (N.Y.S.) 607, 1941 N.Y. LEXIS 2155 (N.Y. 1941).

A chamber of commerce, although not specifically granted the power by its charter to own real property, had such power under either the Membership Corporations Law or the General Corporation Law, it being incorporated as a membership corporation. Corning Chamber of Commerce v Bohoy, 139 N.Y.S.2d 503, 207 Misc. 789, 1955 N.Y. Misc. LEXIS 3459 (N.Y. County Ct. 1955).

8. Under former General Corporation Law § 15

A missionary society, incorporated by a special act under which it might take, receive, hold and enjoy by gift, devise or bequest any real estate or personal property within state "provided the annual value of such real estate . . . shall not exceed sum of ten thousand dollars," by reason of this section is entitled to hold and enjoy real and personal property, value of which would produce an income of not more than $ 2,000,000 yearly. In re Dooper's Will, 212 N.Y.S. 616, 125 Misc. 909, 1925 N.Y. Misc. LEXIS 1142 (N.Y. Sur. Ct. 1925).

The words take and hold, as used in § 15, do not mean taking by devise where taking by such method is not authorized, but such words refer to all methods by which a corporation can acquire property set forth in § 14 so that a hospital corporation was entitled to take and hold real and personal property devised and bequeathed to it, the amount of which was within the limitations of § 15. In re Clark's Estate, 7 N.Y.S.2d 299, 1938 N.Y. Misc. LEXIS 2044 (N.Y. Sur. Ct. 1938), aff'd, 257 A.D. 982, 14 N.Y.S.2d 157, 1939 N.Y. App. Div. LEXIS 8798 (N.Y. App. Div. 1939).

A cemetery association did not dedicate lands to cemetery use where the land has not been surveyed or plotted for burial purposes, nor has it either been set apart for the burial of the dead, or marked and distinguished from the adjoining ground as a place of burial, and, as a result, it could sell the land. Diamond v Foote, 109 N.Y.S.2d 831, 1952 N.Y. Misc. LEXIS 2365 (N.Y. City Ct. 1952).

9. Under former General Corporation Law § 34

A fire corporation organized under the Membership Corporations Law may make a gift of money to a fire district to be used to purchase fire apparatus. 1947 Ops St Compt 61.

§ 203. Defense of ultra vires

(a) No act of a corporation and no transfer of real or personal property to or by a corporation, otherwise lawful, shall, if duly approved or authorized by a judge, court or administrative department or agency as required, be invalid by reason of the fact that the corporation was without capacity or power to do such act or to make or receive such transfer, but such lack of capacity or power may be asserted:

(1) In an action by a member against the corporation to enjoin the doing of any act or the transfer of real or personal property by or to the corporation. If the unauthorized act or transfer sought to be enjoined is being, or is to be, performed or made under any contract to which the corporation is a party, the court may, if all of the parties to the contract are parties to the action and if it deems the same to be equitable,

Not-For-Profit Corporation Law

set aside and enjoin the performance of such contract, and in so doing may allow to the corporation or to the other parties to the contract, as the case may be, such compensation as may be equitable for the loss or damage sustained by any of them from the action of the court in setting aside and enjoining the performance of such contract; provided that anticipated profits to be derived from the performance of the contract shall not be awarded by the court as a loss or damage sustained.

(2) In an action by or in the right of the corporation to procure a judgment in its favor against an incumbent or former officer or director of the corporation for loss or damage due to his unauthorized act.

(3) In an action or special proceeding by the attorney-general to annul or dissolve the corporation or to enjoin it from the carrying on of unauthorized activities.

History: Add, L 1969, ch 1066, § 1, eff Sept 1, 1970.

CASE ANNOTATIONS

The trial court erred in failing to grant summary judgment to the purchasers of real property from a not-for-profit corporation on their claim that the seller should bear the loss due to fire damage to the property where the parties' agreement provided that seller would bear the risk of loss until closing, that closing would occur by a certain date, but that the contract was subject to court approval, where purchasers took possession of the property on the date set for closing and three days later the property was damaged by fire, and where the deed was not recorded until several days later, after the transaction was approved by the court. Caulfield v Improved Risk Mutuals, Inc. (1985, 4th Dept) 107 A.D.2d 1013, 486 N.Y.S.2d 531, revd (1985) 66 N.Y.2d 793, 497 N.Y.S.2d 903, 488 N.E.2d 833

Town supervisor lacked standing to maintain action alleging that both Not-for-Profit Corporation Law and defendant not-for-profit corporation's charter precluded it from leasing site owned by Army Corps of Engineers to house homeless single mothers and their children since (1) corporation was not subject to town's zoning laws, in that land owned by United States or any agency thereof for purposes authorized by Congress is immune from local laws in contravention thereof, (2) supervisor did not have authority under Not-for-Profit Corporation Law to challenge corporation's authority because he was not member of corporation or party to proposed lease, (3) supervisor was not within Not-for-Profit Corporation Law's zone of interest, since statute was enacted to protect corporation and its members rather than supervisor, and (4) CLS Town § 65 did not confer standing on supervisor to protect town residents. Pellegrini v Rockland Community Action Council, Inc. (1993, 3d Dept) 190 A.D.2d 881, 593 N.Y.S.2d 131

Trial court denied the stock exchange chairman's motion to dismiss, as the Attorney General had the statutory responsibility to protect investors, had the authority to pursue the stock exchange chairman under the doctrine of parens patriae because they could not protect themselves from the allegedly unreasonable compensation that the New York Stock Exchange, a type A not-for-profit corporation, allowed him to receive, and the Attorney General stated four viable claims against him: for imposition of a constructive trust and for restitution for ultra vires payments allegedly received, for payment had and received, for violation of N.Y. Not-for-Profit Corp. Law § 715 for benefits he received that were improperly approved, and for violation of N.Y. Not-for-Profit Corp. Law for his allegedly receiving improper loans. People v Grasso (2006, Sup) 12 Misc 3d 384, 816 NYS2d 863, 38 EBC 1221, stay gr (2006, NY App Div, 1st Dept) 2006 NY App Div LEXIS 10785, motion den (2006, Sup) 13 Misc 3d 1214A, 236 NYLJ 56, 824 NYS2d 757, motion gr, in part, motion den, in part, claim dismissed, summary judgment gr, in part, summary judgment den, in part (2006, Sup) 13 Misc 3d 1227A, 236 NYLJ 80, 25 BNA IER Cas 349, later proceeding (2006, NY App Div, 1st Dept) 2006 NY App Div LEXIS 13192 and stay gr (2006, NY App Div, 1st Dept) 2006 NY App Div LEXIS 14716

§ 204.   Limitation on activities

Notwithstanding any other provision of this chapter or any other general law, a corporation of any kind to which this chapter applies shall conduct no activities for pecuniary profit or financial gain, whether or not in furtherance of its corporate purposes, except to the extent that such activity supports its other lawful activities then being conducted.

History: Add, L 1969, ch 1066, § 1, eff Sept 1, 1970; amd, L 2013, ch 549, § 39, eff July 1, 2014.

CASE ANNOTATIONS

A multiple listing service of a real estate brokers' trade association was held not a permissible activity under the Not-for-Profit Corporation Law where the substantial receipts of the Multiple Listing Service of the organization were devoted to continued promotion and generation of real estate sales through the Multiple Listing Service and in expanding the scope and effectiveness of that service. Santos v Chappell (1971) 65 Misc. 2d 559, 318 N.Y.S.2d 570

It was not necessary for out-of-state non-profit 501(c)(3) corporation, licensed as debt management company without physical presence in New York, to become licensed under Banking Law in order to receive payments directly from debtor who had relocated to New York. Banking Department, Legal Opinion (1/27/00)

§ 205.   Conveyance of real property to members for dwelling houses

A not-for-profit corporation, if its by-laws so provide, and pursuant to the provisions thereof, and without leave of the court, may convey to a member of the corporation a portion of its real property for the erection thereupon of a cottage or other dwelling-house with suitable outbuildings. When so conveyed the title to such portion, together with the buildings thereon, shall continue in such member and on his death pass to his heirs or devisees, but the land shall not be alienable except to the corporation or to a member thereof.

History: Add, L 1971, ch 1058, § 4, eff July 2, 1971, deemed eff on and after September 1, 1970.

ARTICLE 3
CORPORATE NAME AND SERVICE OF PROCESS

History: Add, L 1969, ch 1066, eff Sept 1, 1970.

§ 301.   Corporate name; general

(a) Except as otherwise provided in this chapter, the name of a domestic or foreign corporation:

(1) Shall, unless the corporation is formed for charitable or religious purposes, or for purposes for which the approval of the commissioner of social

services or the public health and health planning council is required, or is a bar association, contain the word "corporation", "incorporated" or "limited" or an abbreviation of one of such words; or, in the case of a foreign corporation, it shall, for use in this state, add at the end of its name one of such words or an abbreviation thereof.

(2) (A) Shall be such as to distinguish it from the names of corporations of any kind, or a fictitious name of an authorized foreign corporation filed pursuant to article thirteen of this chapter, as such names appear on the index of names of existing domestic and authorized foreign corporations of any kind, including fictitious names of authorized foreign corporations filed pursuant to article thirteen of this chapter, in the department of state, division of corporations, or a name the right to which is reserved.

(B) Shall be such as to distinguish it from (i) the names of domestic limited liability companies, (ii) the names of authorized foreign limited liability companies, (iii) the fictitious names of authorized foreign limited liability companies, (iv) the names of domestic limited partnerships, (v) the names of authorized foreign limited partnerships, or (vi) the fictitious names of authorized foreign limited partnerships, in each case, as such names appear on the index of names of existing domestic and authorized foreign limited liability companies, including fictitious names of authorized foreign limited liability companies, in the department of state, or on the index of names of existing domestic or authorized foreign limited partnerships, including fictitious names of authorized foreign limited partnerships, in the department of state, or names the rights to which are reserved; provided, however, that no corporation that was formed prior to the effective date of this clause and no foreign corporation that was qualified to conduct activities in this state prior to such effective date shall be required to change the name or fictitious name it had on such effective date solely by reason of such name or fictitious name being indistinguishable from the name or fictitious name of any domestic or authorized foreign limited liability company or limited partnership or from any name the right to which is reserved by or on behalf of any domestic or foreign limited liability company or limited partnership.

(3) Shall not contain any word or phrase, or any abbreviation or derivative thereof, the use of which is prohibited or restricted by section 404 (Approvals, notices and consents) or any other statute of this state, unless in the latter case the restrictions have been complied with.

(4) Shall not contain any word or phrase, or any abbreviation or derivative thereof, in a context which indicates or implies that the corporation, if domestic, is formed or, if foreign, is authorized for any purpose or is possessed in this state of any power other than a purpose for which, or a power with which, the domes-

tic corporation may be and is formed or the foreign corporation is authorized.

(5) (A) Shall not contain any of the following phrases, or any abbreviation or derivative thereof:

> state police
> state trooper

(B) Shall not contain any of the following words, or any abbreviation or derivative thereof:

acceptance	fidelity	mortgage
annuity	finance	savings
assurance	guaranty	surety
bank	indemnity	title
bond	insurance	trust
casualty	investment	underwriter
doctor	lawyer	
endowment	loan	

unless the approval of the superintendent of financial services is attached to the certificate of incorporation, or application for authority or amendment thereof; or that the word "doctor", "lawyer", or the phrase "state police" or "state trooper" or an abbreviation or derivation thereof, may be used in the name of a corporation the membership of which is composed exclusively of doctors, lawyers, state police officers or state troopers, respectively.

(6) Shall not contain any words or phrases, or any abbreviation or derivative thereof in a context which will tend to mislead the public into believing that the corporation is an agency or instrumentality of the United States or the state of New York or a subdivision thereof or is a public corporation.

(7) Shall not contain the word "cooperative" or an abbreviation, contraction or derivative thereof.

(8) Shall not contain any word or phrase, or any abbreviation or derivation thereof, which, separately, or in context, shall be indecent or obscene or shall ridicule or degrade any person, group, belief, business or agency of government or indicate or imply any unlawful activity.

(9) Notwithstanding any other provision of this chapter, may, in the case of a foundation organized for the sole purpose of publishing the literary works of a deceased person, include the word "doctor" or any abbreviation or derivative thereof as part of its name if such word, abbreviation or derivative is used to identify the person whose works are to be published.

History: Add, L 1969, ch 1066, § 1, eff Sept 1, 1970; amd, L 1970, ch 847, § 9; L 1971, ch 1057, § 1; L 1971, ch 1058, § 5; L 1973, ch 961, § 2; L 1974, ch 750, § 2, eff June 7, 1974; L 1977, ch 669, § 8, eff Oct 1, 1977; L 1978, ch 497, § 1; L 1982, ch 227, § 1, eff June 15, 1982; L 1982, ch 590, § 12; L 1982, ch 833, §§ 2, 3; L 1983, ch 9, § 2, eff March 18, 1983; L 1999, ch 172, §§ 25, 26, eff July 6, 1999; L 2004, ch 344, § 4, eff Aug 10, 2004; L 2010, ch 58, § 78 (Part A), eff Dec 1, 2010; L 2011, ch 62, § 104 (Part A), eff Oct 3, 2011; L 2012, ch 155, § 64, eff July 18, 2012; L 2013, ch 549, § 40, eff July 1, 2014; L 2018, ch 476, § 234, eff Dec 28, 2018.

Blackline Showing Effect of 2018 Amendments. — (a) Except as otherwise provided in this chapter, the name of a domestic or foreign corporation:

(1) Shall, unless the corporation is formed for charitable or religious purposes, or for purposes for which the approval of the commissioner of social services or the public health and health planning council is required, or is a bar association, contain the word "corporation", "incorporated" or "limited" or an abbreviation of one of such words; or, in the case of a foreign corporation, it shall, for use in this state, add at the end of its name one of such words or an abbreviation thereof.

(2) (A) Shall be such as to distinguish it from the names of corporations of any kind, or a fictitious name of an authorized foreign corporation filed pursuant to article thirteen of this chapter, as such names appear on the index of names of existing domestic and authorized foreign corporations of any kind, including fictitious names of authorized foreign corporations filed pursuant to article thirteen of this chapter, in the department of state, division of corporations, or a name the right to which is reserved.

(B) Shall be such as to distinguish it from (i) the names of domestic limited liability companies, (ii) the names of authorized foreign limited liability companies, (iii) the fictitious names of authorized foreign limited liability companies, (iv) the names of domestic limited partnerships, (v) the names of authorized foreign limited partnerships, or (vi) the fictitious names of authorized foreign limited partnerships, in each case, as such names appear on the index of names of existing domestic and authorized foreign limited liability companies, including fictitious names of authorized foreign limited liability companies, in the department of state, or on the index of names of existing domestic or authorized foreign limited partnerships, including fictitious names of authorized foreign limited partnerships, in the department of state, or names the rights to which are reserved; provided, however, that no corporation that was formed prior to the effective date of this clause and no foreign corporation that was qualified to conduct activities in this state prior to such effective date shall be required to change the name or fictitious name it had on such effective date solely by reason of such name or fictitious name being indistinguishable from the name or fictitious name of any domestic or authorized foreign limited liability company or limited partnership or from any name the right to which is reserved by or on behalf of any domestic or foreign limited liability company or limited partnership.

(3) Shall not contain any word or phrase, or any abbreviation or derivative thereof, the use of which is prohibited or restricted by section 404 (Approvals, notices and consents) or any other statute of this state, unless in the latter case the restrictions have been complied with.

(4) Shall not contain any word or phrase, or any abbreviation or derivative thereof, in a context which indicates or implies that the corporation, if domestic, is formed or, if foreign, is authorized for any purpose or is possessed in this state of any power other than a purpose for which, or a power with which, the domestic corporation may be and is formed or the foreign corporation is authorized.

(5) (A) Shall not contain any of the following phrases, or any abbreviation or derivative thereof:

state police
state trooper

(B) Shall not contain any of the following words, or any abbreviation or derivative thereof:

acceptance	fidelity	mortgage
annuity	finance	savings
assurance	guaranty	surety
bank	indemnity	title
bond	insurance	trust
casualty	investment	underwriter
doctor	lawyer	
endowment	loan	

unless the approval of the superintendent of financial services is attached to the certificate of incorporation, or application for authority or amendment thereof; or that the word "doctor", "lawyer", or the phrase "state police" or "state trooper" or an abbreviation or derivative thereof, may be used in the name of a corporation the membership of which is composed exclusively of doctors, lawyers, state ~~policemen~~ police officers or state troopers, respectively.

(6) Shall not contain any words or phrases, or any abbreviation or derivative thereof in a context which will tend to mislead the public into believing that the corporation is an agency or instrumentality of the United States or the state of New York or a subdivision thereof or is a public corporation.

(7) Shall not contain the word "cooperative" or an abbreviation, contraction or derivative thereof.

(8) Shall not contain any word or phrase, or any abbreviation or derivation thereof, which, separately, or in context, shall be indecent or obscene or shall ridicule or degrade any person, group, belief, business or agency of government or indicate or imply any unlawful activity.

(9) Notwithstanding any other provision of this chapter, may, in the case of a foundation organized for the sole purpose of publishing the literary works of a deceased person, include the word "doctor" or any abbreviation or derivative thereof as part of its name if such word, abbreviation or derivative is used to identify the person whose works are to be published.

CASE ANNOTATIONS

1. Generally
2-5. [Reserved for future use]
6. Under former General Corporation Law § 9
7. Under former General Corporation Law § 9a
8. Under former Membership Corporations Law § 10
9. – Name
10. – – Undignified or frivolous
11. – – Generic
12. – – Political; political party
13. – – Foreign political hero
14. – Injunction against use of name

1. Generally

Where the formal requirements for incorporation were complied with and the purposes for which the corporation was to be formed, i.e., to promote an understanding and tolerance of the homosexual, etc., offended no law, the Secretary of State lacked the authority to label the purposes violative of public policy and did not possess the power to reject the certificate on the ground that the proposed corporate name was not appropriate. Gay Activists Alliance v Lomenzo (1973) 31 N.Y.2d 965, 341 N.Y.S.2d 108, 293 N.E.2d 255

The name "Gay Activists Alliance" was not inappropriate. Owles v Lomenzo (1972, 3d Dept) 38 A.D.2d 981, 329 N.Y.S.2d 181, affd (1973) 31 N.Y.2d 965, 341 N.Y.S.2d 108, 293 N.E.2d 255

An order directing a reference to determine the nature of plaintiff's corporate status would be reversed and defendants' motion to dismiss plaintiff's action based upon constructive eviction would be denied where defendant did not establish that plaintiff violated the provisions of N-PCL § 301 dealing with representations as to purpose in a corporate name in such a manner as would preclude plaintiff from maintaining its action by using a letterhead describing plaintiff as "non-profit organization" which allegedly implied that plaintiff was organized under the Not-For-Profit Corporation Law when, in fact, it was not, and by using the phrase "Not-For-Profit Corporation" twice during the proceeding in that the use of the phrase on the letterhead did not form part of the corporate name and the use of the phrase during the proceeding was attributable to either an erroneous or colloquial use of language by plaintiff's attorney, which might be remedied on the appropriate motion by striking the misleading and ambiguous phrase from the complaint. Grand Cent. Art Galleries, Inc. v Milstein (1982, 1st Dept) 89 A.D.2d 178, 454 N.Y.S.2d 839

Any corporation using an assumed name prior to January 1, 1979, or seeking to now use an assumed name, is now required to file a certificate with the Secretary of State pursuant to Section 130 of the General Business Law. A corporation which is listed as a partner on a certificate filed with the county clerk prior to January 1, 1979, must register with the Secretary of State if it is doing business under any name other than its corporate name. 1979 Op Atty Gen Mar 14. (Informal)

2-5. [Reserved for future use]

6. Under former General Corporation Law § 9

A foreign co-operative corporation may be authorized to do business in this State even though its name does not include the word "co-operative." 1948 Ops Atty Gen Sept 25

A hospital service corporation formed pursuant to Membership Corporations Law as provided under the cited article of the Insurance

Law is a moneyed corporation and may use the word "Insurance" as part of its corporate name. 1965 Ops Atty Gen May 12

7. Under former General Corporation Law § 9a

The state board of standards and appeals, under this section and Mem. Corp. Law, § 11, subd. 1-a (as both were amended by L 1937 c 820), may approve or disapprove a proposed certificate of incorporation of a corporation having for its purpose the formation of an organization of groups of working men and women, depending on whether or not the corporation is one that is consistent in all respects with provisions of Labor Law, §§ 700 to 716, as added by L 1937 c 443. Campbell v Picard (1937) 165 Misc 148, 300 N.Y.S. 515

The purpose specified in the proposed certificate of incorporation for "Hotel Roosevelt Employees Welfare Association," that the corporation was designed to promote the well-being of employees, brings the proposed corporation within § 9-a and Mem. Corp. Law, § 11, subd. 1-a. Breen v Picard (1938) 167 Misc 561, 4 N.Y.S.2d 301, 3 BNA LRRM 797

The use of the word "purpose" in this section means the purpose as stated in the certificate and should be construed in the same manner in this respect as subd. 1a of § 11 of the Membership Corporations Law. Wilson v Picard (1940) 173 Misc 788, 20 N.Y.S.2d 119

The word "union" as used in this section was intended to refer to its generally accepted meaning as a labor union or organization of workers and a corporation which admittedly was not such an organization was properly denied the right to use such a name. Tool Owners Union v Roberts (1947) 190 Misc 577, 76 N.Y.S.2d 239

8. Under former Membership Corporations Law § 10

Application for approval of a certificate of incorporation is denied, where it is obvious that use of the name proposed would lead to confusion, misunderstanding and mistaken belief on the part of the public. In re World's Fair Information & Service Club (1937) 164 Misc 180, 297 N.Y.S. 922

The statute did not apply to a certificate of change of name where the name of the political party had been part of petitioner's corporate name since its incorporation. Powhatan Democratic Club, Etc v Curran (1954) 206 Misc 960, 138 N.Y.S.2d 15

9. – Name

A certificate of incorporation must be denied for a proposed organization to be known as the Boy Explorers of America in view of the possibility of confusion in the public mind with explorer scouting, an activity carried on by the Boy Scouts of America, and which has as its function a program similar to that outlined for the proposed new corporation. In re Boy Explorers of America, Inc. (1946) 21 Misc. 2d 114, 67 N.Y.S.2d 108

The name "New York State Voters League, Inc." was not approved since it gave the impression that the society was an official function and arm of the state. In re New York State Voters League, Inc. (1956) 3 Misc. 2d 979, 157 N.Y.S.2d 210

Where a proposed organization was not military in character and its membership would not conceivably come within any of the other lexicon definitions of "cadet", use by a group of name "cadet" would be misleading; and in view of a local connotation of the term, as having reference to one living illicitly with a woman and subsisting on her earnings or procuring and seducing for offensive purposes, use of term would offend dignity and good taste. Hence, an application for approval of a certificate of incorporation of the "United Cadet Association, Inc." was denied. Application of United Cadet Asso. (1958) 13 Misc. 2d 957, 178 N.Y.S.2d 479

An application for approval of a certificate of incorporation under the name "International Sports Foundation, Inc." was denied, the court being convinced that the activities of the proposed corporation would merely lead to confusion and misunderstanding in view of the numerous organizations already in the same field. Application of International Sports Foundation, Inc. (1960) 24 Misc. 2d 23, 203 N.Y.S.2d 399

The name "Gold Star Parents" which is the title of a proposed membership corporation conflicts with American Gold Star Mothers of World Wars, Inc. In re Gold Star Parents Ass'n (1946, Sup) 67 N.Y.S.2d 73

10. – – Undignified or frivolous

Application for approval of a proposed certificate of incorporation of the "Jiggs Nut Club, Inc." must be denied, since the name proposed is not one that would appeal to the spirit of good taste of the country, would reflect upon the dignity of the empire state, and is neither appropriate nor dignified. In re Jiggs Nut Club, Inc. (1932) 142 Misc 762, 256 N.Y.S. 273

11. – – Generic

No group will be permitted to incorporate "We Americans" as their exclusive designation. In re We Americans, Inc. (1938) 166 Misc 167, 2 N.Y.S.2d 235

12. – – Political; political party

Where "the Regular Democratic Organization of the Rockaways Inc.," was originally organized with the consent of the Democratic County Chairman, but was dissolved in 1952 by proclamation of the Secretary of State, and in 1955 dissolution was annulled but without the consent of the Chairman of the Democratic County Committee or Executive Member of the district, a temporary injunction was issued to restrain the corporation from using the words "Regular Democratic Organization" in promoting the candidacy of a Republican candidate for justice of the Municipal Court. Dixon v Corrigan (1955) 208 Misc 911, 145 N.Y.S.2d 222

In an application for approval of a certificate of incorporation pursuant to this section, it was found that the use of the word "political" is objectionable. While in its literal sense the word "political" might be defined as pertaining to the science of government, when used in connection with a club or party, in the common accepted sense it is more limited and pertains to an organization composed of persons holding similar beliefs on certain public questions who strive to get control of the government in order to put their beliefs in effect, and an organization of this type should be organized under the Election Law. Application of Stillwell Political Club, Inc. (1951) 26 Misc. 2d 931, 109 N.Y.S.2d 331

Propriety of withholding consent to use of the name of a political party in the name of a proposed membership corporation is to be tested by the danger of confusion which may arise from the existence of such a named organization and its stated objectives and scope of activities. Application of Coles (1961) 27 Misc. 2d 789, 211 N.Y.S.2d 751

13. – – Foreign political hero

A corporation composed of residents of Brooklyn of Italian descent, designed to foster an appreciation of musical arts, to sponsor musical productions, concerts, etc., and to encourage musical education among underprivileged children as well as to perpetuate 100 per cent Americanism cannot be incorporated under the name Mazzini Cultural Center, Mazzini being the name of a great Italian political leader, but rather should be named for an eminent American, or possibly a famous Italian musician. In re Mazzini Cultural Center, Inc. (1945) 185 Misc 1031, 58 N.Y.S.2d 529

14. – Injunction against use of name

The possession of a corporate name by a corporation is not conclusive evidence of the right to use such name and accordingly a membership corporation may, under proper circumstances, be restrained from using a name previously adopted and used by an unincorporated association. Democratic Organization of County of Richmond v Democratic Organization of County of Richmond, Inc. (1938) 253 A.D. 820, 1 N.Y.S.2d 349

Summary proceedings may be brought to enjoin misuse of political party name where there is intent to mislead the public. William J. Sheldrick Asso. v Robert B. Blaikie Regular Democratic Organization, Inc. (1954) 17 Misc. 2d 238, 134 N.Y.S.2d 218

§ 302.   Corporate name; exceptions

(a) Any reference to a corporation in this section except as otherwise provided herein shall include both domestic and foreign corporations.

(b) The provisions of section 301 (Corporate name; general):

(1) Shall not require any corporation, existing or authorized under any statute on the effective date of this chapter, to add to, modify or otherwise change its corporate name.

(2) Shall not prevent a corporation with which another corporation is merged, or which is formed by the consolidation of one or more other corporations

from having the same name as any of such corporations if at the time such other corporation was authorized or existing under any statute of this state.

(3) Shall not prevent a foreign corporation from being authorized under a name which is similar to the name of a corporation of any kind existing or authorized under any statute, if the department of state finds, upon proof by affidavit or otherwise as it may determine, that a difference between such names exists in the terms or abbreviations indicating corporate character or otherwise, that the applicant has conducted activities as a corporation under its said name for not less than ten consecutive years immediately prior to the date of its application, that the activities to be conducted in this state are not the same or similar to the business or activities conducted by the corporation with whose name it may conflict and that the public is not likely to be confused or deceived, and if the applicant shall agree in its application for authority to use with its corporate name, in this state, to be placed immediately under or following such name, the words "a -------- (name of jurisdiction of incorporation) corporation".

History: Add, L 1969, ch 1066, § 1, eff Sept 1, 1970, with substance derived from Gen Corp Law §§ 9, 9-b, 9-c, and Mem Corp Law § 10; amd, L 1970, ch 847, § 10, eff Sept 1, 1970, L 1971, ch 1058, § 6, eff Sept 1, 1971, L 2013, ch 549, § 41, eff July 1, 2014.

§ 303. Reservation of name

(a) A corporate name may be reserved by:

(1) Any person intending to form a domestic corporation.

(2) Any domestic corporation intending to change its name.

(3) Any foreign corporation intending to apply for authority to conduct activities in this state.

(4) Any authorized foreign corporation intending to change its name.

(5) Any person intending to incorporate a foreign corporation and to have it apply for authority to conduct activities in this state.

(6) Any domestic corporation intending to file the consent of the attorney general to reinstate such corporation pursuant to section 1014 of this chapter.

(b) A fictitious name for use pursuant to section 1301 of this chapter may be reserved by:

(1) Any foreign corporation intending to apply for authority to do business in this state, pursuant to paragraph (d) of section 1301 of this chapter.

(2) Any authorized foreign corporation intending to change its fictitious name under which it conducts activities in this state.

(3) Any authorized foreign corporation which has changed its corporate name in its jurisdiction, which new corporate name is not available in this state.

(c) Application to reserve a corporate name shall be delivered to the department of state. It shall set forth the name and address of the applicant, the name to be reserved and a statement of the basis under paragraph (a) or (b) for the application. The secretary of state may require the applicant to set forth in his application the nature of the activities to be conducted by the corporation. If the name is available for corporate use, the department of state shall reserve the name for the use of the applicant for a period of sixty days and issue a certificate of reservation. The prohibitions, restrictions and qualifications set forth in section 301 (Corporate name; general), section 302 (Corporate name; exceptions) and section 404 (Approvals, notices and consents) are not waived by the issuance of a certificate of reservation. The certificate of reservation shall include the name of the applicant, the name reserved and the date of the reservation. The certificate of reservation (or in lieu thereof an affidavit by the applicant or by his agent or attorney that the certificate of reservation has been lost or destroyed) shall accompany the certificate of incorporation or the application for authority when either is delivered to the department of state.

(d) The secretary of state may extend the reservation for additional periods of not more than sixty days each, upon the written request of the applicant, his attorney or agent delivered to the department of state, to be filed before the expiration of the reservation period then in effect. Such request shall have attached to it the certificate of reservation of name. Not more than two such extensions shall be granted.

(e) Upon the request of the applicant, delivered to the department of state before the expiration of the reserved period, together with the certificate of reservation, the department shall cancel the reservation.

(f) Any application or request under this section shall be signed by the applicant, his attorney or agent.

History: Add, L 1969, ch 1066, § 1, eff Sept 1, 1970, with substance derived from Gen Corp Law §§ 40, 215; amd, L 1982, ch 590, §§ 13, 14, eff Oct 20, 1982, L 1984, ch 241, § 2, eff June 19, 1984, L 2006, ch 434, § 3, eff July 26, 2006, L 2013, ch 549, § 42, eff July 1, 2014.

§ 304. Statutory designation of secretary of state as agent of domestic corporations formed under article four of this chapter and authorized foreign corporations for service of process

(a) The secretary of state shall be the agent of every domestic corporation formed under article four of this chapter and every authorized foreign corporation upon whom process against the corporation may be served.

(b) Any designation by a domestic corporation formed under article four of this chapter or foreign corporation of the secretary of state as such agent, which designation is in effect on the effective date of this chapter, shall continue. Every domestic corporation formed under article four of this chapter or foreign corporation, existing or authorized on the effective date of this chapter, which has not designated the secretary of state as such agent, shall be deemed to have done so.

(c) Any designation by a domestic corporation formed under article four of this chapter or foreign corporation of an agent other than the secretary of state which is in effect on the effective date of this chapter shall continue in effect until changed or revoked as provided in this chapter.

(d) Any designated post-office address to which the secretary of state shall mail a copy of process served upon him or her as agent of a domestic corporation formed under article four of this chapter or foreign corporation, shall continue until the filing of a certificate under this chapter directing the mailing to a different post-office address.

History: Add, L 1969, ch 1066, § 1, with substance derived from Gen Corp Law §§ 213, 214a, and Mem Corp Law §§ 51, 52; amd, L 1981, ch 564, § 1; L 1982, ch 168, § 1, eff June 8, 1982; L 2013, ch 549, § 43 (repealed by L 2014, ch 23, § 7, eff July 1, 2014), eff July 1, 2014; L 2015, ch 358, § 2, eff Sept 25, 2015.

§ 305. Registered agent for service of process

(a) Every domestic corporation or authorized foreign corporation may designate a registered agent in this state upon whom process against such corporation may be served. The agent shall be a natural person who is a resident of or has a business address in this state or a domestic corporation or foreign corporation of any kind formed, or authorized to do business in this state, under this chapter or under any other statute of this state.

(b) Any such designation of a registered agent may be made, revoked or changed as provided in this chapter.

(c) A registered agent may resign as such agent. A certificate, entitled "Certificate of resignation of registered agent of .... (name of designating corporation) under section 305 of the Not-for-Profit Corporation Law", shall be signed by him and delivered to the department of state. It shall set forth:

(1) That he resigns as registered agent for the designating corporation.

(2) The date the certificate of incorporation or the application for authority of the designating corporation was filed by the department of state.

(3) That he has sent a copy of the certificate of resignation by registered mail to the designating corporation at the post-office address on file in the department of state specified for the mailing of process or if such address is the address of the registered agent, then to the office of the designating corporation in the jurisdiction of its formation or incorporation.

(d) The designation of a registered agent shall terminate thirty days after the filing by the department of state of a certificate of resignation or a certificate containing a revocation or change of the designation, whichever is filed earlier. A certificate designating a new registered agent may be delivered to the department of state by the corporation within the thirty days or thereafter.

History: Add, L 1969, ch 1066, § 1, eff Sept 1, 1970, with substance derived from Gen Corp Law § 213; amd, L 1985, ch 131, § 2, eff May 28, 1985, L 1998, ch 375, § 35, eff Aug 13, 1998, L 2013, ch 549, § 44, eff July 1, 2014.

§ 306. Service of process

(a) Service of process on a registered agent may be made in the manner provided by law for the service of a summons, as if the registered agent was a defendant.

(b) Service of process on the secretary of state as agent of a domestic corporation formed under article four of this chapter or an authorized foreign corporation shall be made by personally delivering to and leaving with the secretary of state or his or her deputy, or with any person authorized by the secretary of state to receive such service, at the office of the department of state in the city of Albany, duplicate copies of such process together with the statutory fee, which fee shall be a taxable disbursement. Service of process on such corporation shall be complete when the secretary of state is so served. The secretary of state shall promptly send one of such copies by certified mail, return receipt requested, to such corporation, at the post office address, on file in the department of state, specified for the purpose. If a domestic corporation formed under article four of this chapter or an authorized foreign corporation has no such address on file in the department of state, the secretary of state shall so mail such copy to such corporation at the address of its office within this state on file in the department.

(c) If an action or special proceeding is instituted in a court of limited jurisdiction, service of process may be made in the manner provided in this section if the office of the domestic corporation formed under article four of this chapter or foreign corporation is within the territorial jurisdiction of the court.

(d) Nothing in this section shall affect the right to serve process in any other manner permitted by law.

History: Add, L 1969, ch 1066, § 1, eff Sept 1, 1970, with substance derived from Gen Corp Law § 213; amd, L 1985, ch 131, § 2, eff May 28, 1985, L 1998, ch 375, § 35, eff Aug 13, 1998, § 45, eff July 1, 2014, L 2014, ch 23, § 8, eff July 1, 2014.

CASE ANNOTATIONS

1-10. [Reserved for future use]
11. Under former General Corporation Law § 217
12. – Service of process on secretary of state

13. – – Notice to corporation of service
14. – Jurisdiction obtained by service
15. – Statutory fees
16. – Miscellaneous

1-10. [Reserved for future use]
11. Under former General Corporation Law § 217

An action brought in the justice court on a policy of insurance issued within the state, service having been effected on the superintendent of insurance pursuant to § 59 of the Insurance Law, is within the jurisdiction of such a court even though the defendant insurance company has no office within the jurisdiction and service was not made upon the Secretary of State under this section. Jackson v National Grange Mut. Liability Co. (1948) 274 A.D. 330, 83 N.Y.S.2d 602, app gr (1949) 274 A.D. 1076, 85 N.Y.S.2d 330 and app dismd (1949) 299 N.Y. 333, 87 N.E.2d 283

In a personal injury action arising out of an accident in another state, service of summons on a foreign corporation authorized to do business in the state must be made under the provisions of § 217; service made in accordance with Veh. & Traf. Law § 52 is ineffectual. Schlago v Seaboard Freight Lines, Inc. (1946) 187 Misc 732, 65 N.Y.S.2d 369

Where foreign corporation maintained regular and established place of business in New York within jurisdiction of N.Y. Fed. Dist. Ct. and had obtained license to do business in New York, and designated Secretary of State of New York as its agent to receive process in New York, such service is valid. American Blower Corp. v B. F. Sturtevant Co. (1945, DC NY) 61 F. Supp. 756, 66 USPQ 278

12. – Service of process on secretary of state

Section 217, as amended by L 1941 c 538, permits service on the secretary of state of process of court of limited territorial jurisdiction if the cause of action arose and stated office of the defendant is within such territorial jurisdiction. Pohlers v Exeter Mfg. Co. (1944) 293 N.Y. 274, 56 N.E.2d 582

Where the agent appointed to receive service of process died and no new agent had been appointed the federal district court in New York obtained jurisdiction where service was made on the secretary of state even though it was a foreign cause of action. Cohen v American Window Glass Co. (1942, CA2 NY) 126 F.2d 111

Process issued under this section may only be made upon the secretary of state or a deputy secretary of state. 1933 Ops Atty Gen 288

13. – – Notice to corporation of service

Where a foreign corporation licensed to do business in this state has filed an instrument with the Secretary of State designating him as agent for service of process and specifying the address of its office within New York State, and this section is complied with in serving the Secretary of State, a default judgment obtained against the corporation is not subject to being set aside on the ground that the corporation inadvertently failed to provide the Secretary of State with its full address and accordingly did not receive the notice of service forwarded to it by the Secretary of State. General Crane Service, Inc. v Whiting-Turner Contracting Co. (1960) 27 Misc. 2d 403, 208 N.Y.S.2d 244

Administrative reclassification of title of assistant, senior and associate corporation examiners to titles of attorney, senior attorney and associate attorney will not affect their authority to receive process against corporations served upon the Secretary of State pursuant to these sections. 1954 Ops Atty Gen Aug 20

14. – Jurisdiction obtained by service

Jurisdiction in rem is obtained by the city court of New York by attachment levy in an action against a foreign corporation served with summons and complaint within thirty days after the granting of the warrant by service on the secretary of state at Albany. Swedosh v Belding Hosiery Mills, Inc. (1938) 168 Misc 673, 6 N.Y.S.2d 532

Municipal court of New York city has no jurisdiction to enter a judgment against a foreign corporation which has been authorized to do business in this state and has designated the secretary of state to receive process, where the corporation was served by serving the secretary of state at Albany under § 217, because § 217 cannot extend the territorial jurisdiction of the municipal court beyond the territorial limits of New York city. McCulloch v American Carrier Corp. (1939) 172 Misc 450, 15 N.Y.S.2d 566, app den (1940) 260 A.D. 933, 24 N.Y.S.2d 129

15. – Statutory fees

Superintendent of insurance, when acting as liquidator, is not exempt from payment of filing fees provided for in § 217. 1939 Ops Atty Gen 225

State insurance fund is not exempt from the payment of the fees prescribed by § 217 or Stk. Corp. Law, § 25. 1942 Ops Atty Gen June 11

16. – Miscellaneous

Under former § 16 where a foreign corporation doing business in this state had designated a person as agent upon whom process against the corporation might be served, the agency of such person was not limited to actions which arose out of business transacted in this state. Bagdon v Philadelphia & Reading Coal & Iron Co. (1916) 217 N.Y. 432, 111 N.E. 1075

Under former § 15 where a foreign corporation was authorized to do business in the state and had officers residing here and had a local bank account, its certificate never having been revoked, it was presumed to be subject to service of summons in this state in the absence of clear and convincing proof on its part that it was not transacting business here. Burke v Galveston, H. & H. R. Co. (1916) 173 A.D. 221, 159 N.Y.S. 379

Under former § 16 where a foreign corporation had designated a person on whom process might be served process might be served on such person although the cause of action arose outside the state. Smolik v Philadelphia & Reading Coal & Iron Co. (1915, DC NY) 222 F 148

§ 307.   Service of process on unauthorized foreign corporation

(a) In any case in which a non-domiciliary would be subject to the personal or other jurisdiction of the courts of this state under article three of the civil practice law and rules, a foreign corporation not authorized to conduct activities in this state is subject to a like jurisdiction. In any such case, process against such foreign corporation may be served upon the secretary of state as its agent. Such process may issue in any court in this state having jurisdiction of the subject matter.

(b) Service of such process upon the secretary of state shall be made by personally delivering to and leaving with him or his deputy, or with any person authorized by the secretary of state to receive such service, at the office of the department of state in the city of Albany, a copy of such process together with the statutory fee, which fee shall be a taxable disbursement. Such service shall be sufficient if notice thereof and a copy of the process are:

(1) Delivered personally without this state to such foreign corporation by a person and in the manner authorized to serve process by law of the jurisdiction in which service is made, or

(2) Sent by or on behalf of the plaintiff to such foreign corporation by registered mail with return receipt requested, at the post office address specified for the purpose of mailing process, on file in the department of state, or with any official or body performing the equivalent function, in the jurisdiction of its incorporation, or if no such address is there specified, to its registered or other office there specified, or if no such office is there specified, to the last address of such foreign corporation known to the plaintiff.

(c) (1) Where service of a copy of process was effected by personal service, proof of service shall be by affidavit of compliance with this section filed, together with the process, within thirty days after such service, with the clerk of the court in which the action or special proceeding is pending. Service of process shall be complete ten days after such papers are filed with the clerk of the court.

(2) Where service of a copy of process was effected by mailing in accordance with this section, proof of service shall be by affidavit of compliance with this section filed, together with the process, within thirty days after receipt of the return receipt signed by the foreign corporation, or other official proof of delivery or of the original envelope mailed. If a copy of the process is mailed in accordance with this section, there shall be filed with the affidavit of compliance either the return receipt signed by such foreign corporation or other official proof of delivery or, if acceptance was refused by it, the original envelope with a notation by the postal authorities that acceptance was refused. If acceptance was refused, a copy of the notice and process together with the notice of the mailing by registered mail and refusal to accept shall be promptly sent to such foreign corporation at the same address by ordinary mail and the affidavit of compliance shall so state. Service of process shall be complete ten days after such papers are filed with the clerk of the court. The refusal to accept delivery of the registered mail or to sign the return receipt shall not affect the validity of the service and such foreign corporation refusing to accept such registered mail shall be charged with knowledge of the contents thereof.

(d) Service made as provided in this section shall have the same force as personal service made within this state.

(e) Nothing in this section shall affect the right to serve process in any other manner permitted by law.

History: Add, L 1969, ch 1066, § 1, eff Sept 1, 1970; amd, L 1970, ch 847, § 11, eff Sept 1, 1970; L 1971, ch 1058, § 7, eff Sept 1, 1971.

§ 308.   Records and certificates of department of state

The department of state shall keep a record of each process served upon the secretary of state under this chapter, including the date of service. It shall, upon request made within ten years of such service, issue a certificate under its seal certifying as to the receipt of the process by an authorized person, the date and place of such service and the receipt of the statutory fee. Process served upon the secretary of state under this chapter shall be destroyed by him after a period of ten years from such service.

History: Add, L 1969, ch 1066, § 1, eff Sept 1, 1970.

§ 309.   Personal jurisdiction and service of process on non-domiciliary resident director, officer, key person or agent.

A person, by becoming a director, officer, key person or agent of a corporation is subject to the personal jurisdiction of the supreme court of the state of New York, and in an action or proceeding by the attorney general under this chapter process may be served upon such person as provided in section three hundred thirteen of the civil practice law and rules.

History: Add, L 2013, ch 549, § 46, eff July 1, 2014; amd, L 2016, ch 466, § 3, eff May 27, 2017.

ARTICLE 4
FORMATION OF CORPORATIONS

History: Add, L 1969, ch 1066, § 1, eff Sept 1, 1970.

§ 401.   Incorporators

One or more natural persons at least eighteen years of age may act as incorporators of a corporation to be formed under this chapter.

History: Add, L 1969, ch 1066, § 1, deriving from Gen Corp Law § 7 and Mem Corp Law § 10; amd, L 1970, ch 847, § 12, L 1974, ch 901, § 2, eff Sept 1, 1974.

CASE ANNOTATIONS

1. Generally
2-5. [Reserved for future use]
6. Under former General Corporation Law § 7
7. Under former Membership Corporations Law § 10

1. Generally

A village may not form a not-for-profit corporation and convey to it title to unused reservoir property for the purposes of avoiding real estate taxes. 1979 Op Atty Gen August 16 (informal)

A town may not form a not-for-profit corporation to operate and manage town marinas and dockage facilities. However, a town, by local law, may authorize a contract with any entity for the management and operation of such facilities. 1981 Op St Compt File #81-151

2-5. [Reserved for future use]

6. Under former General Corporation Law § 7

Recitation of facts is not a statement of them, and requirement of this section that certificate of incorporation shall state certain facts is not satisfied by recitation of them in certificate. In re Wendover Athletic Ass'n (1911) 70 Misc 273, 128 N.Y.S. 561

It is not essential that all incorporators shall make an affidavit as to age, citizenship and residence of incorporators for the purpose of showing that this section has been followed. In re Daughters of Israel Orphan Aid Soc. (1925) 125 Misc 217, 210 N.Y.S. 541 (disapproved on other grounds by Association for Preservation of Freedom of Choice, Inc. v Shapiro (1961) 9 N.Y.2d 376, 214 N.Y.S.2d 388, 174 N.E.2d 487)

7. Under former Membership Corporations Law § 10

One may not be designated as a director of an organization seeking to be incorporated who is not listed as a member in the certificate of incorporation. In re Victory Committee of Greenpoint of Patriotic, Social & Fraternal Club, Inc. (1945, Sup) 59 N.Y.S.2d 546

Discussion of procedure for incorporation of volunteer fire company and the beneficial effect of a corporate status to simplify matters concerning the management of affairs and ownership of assets. 1967 Ops St Compt File #786

§ 402. Certificate of incorporation; contents

(a) A certificate, entitled "Certificate of Incorporation of............ (name of corporation), under section 402 of the Not-for-Profit Corporation Law," shall be signed by each incorporator with his name and address included in such certificate and delivered to the department of state. It shall set forth:

(1) The name of the corporation.

(2) That the corporation is a corporation as defined in subparagraph (5) of paragraph (a) of section 102 (Definitions).

(2-a) the purpose or purposes for which it is formed, it being sufficient to state that the purpose of the corporation is any purpose for which corporations may be organized under this chapter as a charitable or non-charitable corporation, and whether it is a charitable corporation or a non-charitable corporation under section 201 (Purposes). Any corporation may also set forth any activities that it intends to carry out in furtherance of such purpose or purposes; provided that this subparagraph shall not be interpreted to require that the certificate of incorporation set forth such activities or otherwise state how the corporation's purposes will be achieved.

(2-b) If it is not formed to engage in any activity or for any purpose requiring consent or approval of any state official, department, board, agency or other body, a statement that no such consent or approval is required. Such statement shall be deemed conclusive for purposes of filing by the department of state. If subsequent to submitting the certificate of incorporation for filing, the corporation plans to engage in any activity requiring consent or approval pursuant to section 404 (approvals, notices and consents) of this chapter, the corporation shall obtain such consent or approval and accordingly amend its certificate of incorporation pursuant to article eight of this chapter.

(3) The county within the state in which the office of the corporation is to be located. It may also set forth the post office address of an office without the state, at which, pursuant to section 621 (Books and records; right of inspection; prima facie evidence), the books and records of account of the corporation shall be kept.

(4) The names and addresses of the initial directors.

(5) The duration of the corporation if other than perpetual.

(6) A designation of the secretary of state as agent of the corporation upon whom process against it may be served and the post office address within or without this state to which the secretary of state shall mail a copy of any process against it served upon him.

(7) If the corporation is to have a registered agent, his name and address within this state and a statement that the registered agent is to be the agent of the corporation upon whom process against it may be served.

(8) The statements, if any, with respect to special not-for-profit corporations required under article 14 (Special not-for-profit corporations).

(b) If the certificate is for the incorporation of an existing unincorporated association or group it shall have annexed thereto an affidavit of the subscribers of such certificate stating that they constitute a majority of the members of a committee duly authorized to incorporate such association or group.

(c) The certificate of incorporation may set forth any provision, not inconsistent with this chapter or any other statute of the state, which provision is (1) for the regulation of the internal affairs of the corporation, including types or classes of membership and the distribution of assets on dissolution or final liquidation, or (2) required by any governmental body or officer or other person or body as a condition for giving the consent or approval required for the filing of such certificate of incorporation.

History: Add, L 1969, ch 1066, § 1, eff Sept 1, 1970, with substance derived from Gen Corp Law § 13(2) and Mem Corp Law §§ 10, 11; amd, L 1970, ch 847, § 13, eff Sept 1, 1970, L 1972, ch 961, eff Sept 1, 1972, L 1981, ch 564, § 3, L 1983, ch 145, § 1, L 1985, ch 132, § 1, eff May 28, 1985, L 1985, ch 499, § 3, eff Oct 22, 1985, L 1985, ch 679, § 1, eff Nov 29, 1985, L 1998, ch 375, § 36, eff Aug 13, 1998, L 2013, ch 549, § 47, eff July 1, 2014, L 2014, ch 23, § 9, eff July 1, 2014.

CASE ANNOTATIONS

1. Generally
2-5. [Reserved for future use]
6. Under former Membership Corporations Law § 10

1. Generally

If nonprofit hospital seeking some special advantage separately incorporates for such advantage, separate corporation cannot thereafter be classified as "voluntary nonprofit hospital corporation" for purpose of seeking relief from imposition of mortgage tax. St. Joseph's Health Center Properties, Inc. v State Tax Com. (1977, 3d Dept) 55 A.D.2d 484, 391 N.Y.S.2d 16, app den (1977) 41 N.Y.2d 804

Although a temple's certificate of incorporation failed to fully comport with N.Y. Relig. Corp. Law § 180, summary judgment for defendants for lack of standing was improper because the certificate was, in effect, a hybrid of the relevant criteria of both the Religious Corporations Law and the Not-For-Profit Corporation Law regarding corporation formation and the temple was a "de facto" religious corporation; the temple was intended to be a religious corporation and, in fact, carried on under the assumption that it was a religious corporation, was a place of worship and did not receive any money in the form of stock or otherwise, and regularly solicited and received donations in the donation boxes. Further, there were unresolved fact issues as to whether the individual plaintiffs constituted the temple's validly appointed board of trustees. Temple-Ashram v Satyanandji (2011, 2d Dept) 84 App Div 3d 1158, 923 NYS2d 664.

Application for certificate of incorporation pursuant to Not For Profit Corporation L § 402 was refused organization which had as its purpose the advising of students, parents, and the general public as to means of improving the school system and where the proposed name of the organization implied professional legal advice which would not in fact be available. In re Application of Queens Lay Advocate Service, Inc. (1972) 71 Misc. 2d 33, 335 N.Y.S.2d 583

The Camillus Volunteer Fire Department may, without public bidding, purchase an ambulance with its own funds and then donate the ambulance to the village. But, any purchase made with village funds must meet the requirements of public bidding. 1979 Op St Compt File #666

Under Sections 10-1000 et seq. of the Village Law, a village fire department is a corporation consisting of members of all the fire, hose, protective and hook and ladder companies of a village; it is administered by a board of fire commissioners or, where no board of fire commissioners has been appointed, by the village board of trustees and the council of the fire department. Fire companies in a village are associations or corporations, which must operate in accordance with their certificates of incorporation, bylaws, and statutes; and, although fire companies are separate and distinct from the village, the statutes do permit village authorities to exercise a certain degree of control over their organization, incorporation, governance, and membership, including residency for membership. A fire company must consent to a contract for the provision of fire protection outside the village and the fire chief of the village fire department cannot consent on behalf of members of the company. 1990 Op St Compt 90-19

Certificate of incorporation for museum formed under CLS N-PCL § 201(b) should be reviewed to determine purpose or purposes for which it was organized, and if one of purposes is charitable or educational, exception provided under CLS Ins § 3205(b)(3) would apply. Insurance Department, Opinions of General Counsel, Opinion Number 03-08-13

2-5. [Reserved for future use]

6. Under former Membership Corporations Law § 10

A certificate of incorporation, as provided by this section, contains no reference to the number of memberships or the capital of the corporation and creditors are not put upon notice as to either. Keeler v New York Hide Exchange, Inc. (1931) 231 A.D. 450, 247 N.Y.S. 482

The fact that none of the corporation papers on file contained a statement that the hospital was incorporated as a "charitable corporation" did not negate the actuality that the hospital was a charitable institution within the purport of § 189 of the Lien Law. The court pointed out there was no general charitable corporation statute in New York, and that the law contemplated, with respect to hospitals, that charitable pursuits may be pursued by an entity functioning under the Membership Corporation Law. Gonzalez v New York City Transit Authority (1967, 2d Dept) 27 A.D.2d 744, 277 N.Y.S.2d 527

A proposed certificate of incorporation was fatally defective in that it omitted to state the county in which the proposed corporation's office was to be located. In re Daughters of Bilitis, Inc. (1967) 52 Misc. 2d 1075, 277 N.Y.S.2d 709

A membership corporation may not include in its charter purposes power to act as a trustee. 1936 Ops Atty Gen 206

§ 403. Certificate of incorporation; effect

Upon the filing of the certificate of incorporation by the department of state, the corporate existence shall begin, and such certificate shall be conclusive evidence that all conditions precedent have been fulfilled and that the corporation has been formed under this chapter, except in an action or special proceeding brought by the attorney-general. Where the certificate is for the incorporation of an unincorporated association or group, the members of such association or group shall be members of the corporation so created, and all property owned by or held for it shall belong to and vest in the corporation, subject to all existing incumbrances and claims as if incorporation had not taken place. Where the certificate is for the reincorporation of a corporation created by special law for purposes for which a corporation may be formed under this chapter, such reincorporation shall not effect a dissolution of the corporation but shall be a continuation of its corporate existence,

without affecting its then existing property rights or liabilities, or the liabilities of its members or officers as such, but thereafter it shall have only such rights, powers and privileges, and be subject to such other duties and liabilities as a corporation formed for the same purposes under this chapter.

History: Add, L 1969, ch 1066, § 1, eff Sept 1, 1970, with substance derived from Gen Corp Law §§ 8, 12 and Mem Corp Law §§ 12, 13.

CASE ANNOTATIONS

1. Generally
2-5. [Reserved for future use]
6. Under former Membership Corporations Law § 10
7. Under former Membership Corporations Law § 12

1. Generally

The Westchester Society for the Prevention of Cruelty to Children did not have standing to maintain a proceeding to annul and vacate the certificate of the Yonkers Society for the Prevention of Cruelty to children, which had been duly filed and judicially approved pursuant to N-PCL § 403, notwithstanding the fact that N-PCL § 1403 prohibited more than one society for the prevention of cruelty to children in a single county; an action for the involuntary judicial dissolution of a corporation formed pursuant to the Not-For-Profit Corporation Law can be maintained only by the Attorney-General (N-PCL § 1101) or upon specified conditions by a certain number of members or directors of the corporation (N-PCL § 1102). The use of the permissive word "may" in N-PCL § 1101 does not support the argument that a dissolution action can be maintained by private individuals. Westchester County S.P.C.C. v Pisani (1984, 2d Dept) 105 A.D.2d 793, 481 N.Y.S.2d 735

Town lacked standing to file N.Y. C.P.L.R. art. 78 proceeding since: (1) it was not an established corporation, since it had filed no incorporation papers with the New York Department of State under N.Y. Bus. Corp. Law § 403 and N.Y. Not-for-Profit Corp. Law §§ 403 and 904(a), (2) the state's highest court had not recognized it as a corporation, or as the governing body of the town, (3) the town failed to show that it was the successor corporation to the original incorporated proprietors of the town, (4) a municipal corporation was a political subdivision of the State having only the authority delegated to it by the State under N.Y. Const. art. IX, § 2, and (5) another town specifically included the town, and was a legitimate municipal corporation with the authority to govern the town under N.Y. Town Law § 2. Matter of Town of Montauk, Inc. v Pataki (2007, 2d Dept) 40 App Div 3d 772, 835 NYS2d 447, motion den (2007, 2d Dept) 40 App Div 3d 772, 834 NYS2d 661.

2-5. [Reserved for future use]

6. Under former Membership Corporations Law § 10

Five weeks delay after court approval of political membership corporation before filing certificate with secretary of state was not abandonment thereof. Archinal v Reuss (1965) 46 Misc. 2d 428, 260 N.Y.S.2d 78

Mandamus is the proper remedy upon refusal of the Secretary of State to file a certificate. People ex rel. New York Phonograph Co. v Rice (1890) 57 Hun 486, 11 N.Y.S. 249, affd (1891) 128 N.Y. 591, 28 N.E. 251

7. Under former Membership Corporations Law § 12

A notice of a meeting of an unincorporated association at which authorization was given to incorporate, is inadequate, in the absence of any provision in the association's bylaws or constitution in regard thereto, where notice was mailed but two days before the meeting was held, and it does not appear that the notice was sent to all the members of the association insofar as they were known or could have been identified. Heights Democratic Club, Inc. v Brewer (1947) 272 A.D. 1009, 74 N.Y.S.2d 243

Where an unincorporated association has no constitution or by-laws, it will be assumed that a vote of the majority of the members of the club at a meeting duly called and held will be sufficient to authorize an application for incorporation. Heights Democratic Club, Inc. v Brewer (1947) 272 A.D. 1009, 74 N.Y.S.2d 243

Where a general committee with an executive committee, adopted a name, conducted a campaign, and erected a hospital, the general committee was, to all intents and purposes an unincorporated association which subsequently became incorporated. Tioga County General Hospital v Tidd (1937) 164 Misc 273, 298 N.Y.S. 460

Former members of an unincorporated association, who resigned or were expelled, have no right to the assets of the association upon subsequent incorporation thereof under the Membership Corporation Law. Community Volunteer Fire Co. v City Nat'l Bank (1939) 171 Misc 1027, 14 N.Y.S.2d 306

The remedy of interpleader is available to determine the ownership of a bank deposit as between a membership corporation and certain of its former members prior to incorporation, even though the bank has made no showing of a reasonable foundation for the adverse claim. Community Volunteer Fire Co. v City Nat'l Bank (1939) 171 Misc 1027, 14 N.Y.S.2d 306

§ 404.   Approvals, notices and consents

(a) Every certificate of incorporation which includes among its purposes the formation of a trade or business association shall have endorsed thereon or annexed thereto the consent of the attorney-general.

(b) (1) Every certificate of incorporation which includes among its purposes the care of destitute, delinquent, abandoned, neglected or dependent children; the establishment or operation of any adult care facility, or the establishment or operation of a residential program for victims of domestic violence as defined in subdivision four of section four hundred fifty-nine-a of the social services law, or the placing-out or boarding-out of children or a home or shelter for unmarried mothers, excepting the establishment or maintenance of a hospital or facility providing health-related services as those terms are defined in article twenty-eight of the public health law and a facility for which an operating certificate is required by articles sixteen, nineteen, twenty-two and thirty-one of the mental hygiene law; or the solicitation of contributions for any such purpose or purposes, shall have endorsed thereon or annexed thereto the approval of the commissioner of the office of children and family services or with respect to any adult care facility, the commissioner of health.

(2) A corporation whose statement of purposes specifically includes the establishment or operation of a child day care center, as that term is defined in section three hundred ninety of the social services law, shall mail a certified copy of the certificate of incorporation, each amendment thereto, and any certificate of merger, consolidation or dissolution involving such corporation to the office of children and family services within thirty days after receipt of confirmation of the filing of such certificate, amendment, merger, consolidation or dissolution with the department of state. This requirement shall also apply to any foreign corporation filing an application for authority under section thirteen hundred four of this chapter, any amendments thereto, and any surrender of authority or termination of authority in this state of such corporation.

(c) Every certificate of incorporation which includes among the purposes of the corporation, the establishment, maintenance and operation of a hospital service or a health service or a medical expense indemnity plan or a dental expense indemnity plan as permitted in article forty-three of the insurance law, shall have endorsed thereon or annexed thereto the approval of the superintendent of financial services and the commissioner of health.

(d) Every corporation whose certificate of incorporation includes among its purposes the operation of a school; a college, university or other entity providing post secondary education; a library; or a museum or historical society shall have endorsed thereon or annexed thereto the approval of the commissioner of education, or in the case of a college or a university, the written authorization of the Regents of the university of the state of New York. Any other corporation the certificate of incorporation of which includes a purpose for which a corporation might be chartered by the regents of the university of the State of New York shall mail a certified copy of the certificate of incorporation to the commissioner of education within thirty days after receipt of confirmation of filing.

(e) Every certificate of incorporation of a cemetery corporation, except those within the exclusionary provisions of section 1503 (Cemetery corporations) shall have endorsed thereon or annexed thereto the approval of the cemetery board.

(f) Every certificate of incorporation of a fire corporation shall have endorsed thereon or annexed thereto the approval, signed and acknowledged, of the authorities of each city, village, town or fire district in which the corporation proposes to act. Such authorities shall be: in a city, the mayor; in a village, a majority of the trustees; in a town, a majority of the members of the town board; in a fire district, a majority of the fire commissioners. The members of the town board of a town, or the trustees of a village, shall not consent to the formation of a fire corporation as hereinbefore provided, until such board shall have held a public hearing on the question of whether the fire company should be incorporated. The notice shall be published at least once in each week for two successive weeks in the official newspaper published in the county in which such fire corporation intends to locate, prior to the regular meeting of such board designated by the chairman of the board to consider the matter. Such notice shall contain the name of the proposed company, the names of the persons signing the certificate of incorporation, a brief description of the territory to be protected by the fire company and that all persons interested shall be heard. If no newspaper is published in the county the publication of the notice shall be in a newspaper in an adjoining county selected by the chairman of such board. All expenses in connection with such publication shall be borne by the parties making the application and paid before the hearing.

(g) Every certificate of incorporation of a corporation for prevention of cruelty to animals shall have endorsed thereon or annexed thereto the approval of the American Society for the Prevention of Cruelty to

Animals, or, if such approval be withheld thirty days after application therefor, a certified copy of an order of a justice of the supreme court of the judicial district in which the office of the corporation is to be located, dispensing with such approval, granted upon eight days' notice to such society.

(h) Every certificate of incorporation of a Young Men's Christian Association shall have endorsed thereon or annexed thereto the approval of the chairman of the national board of Young Men's Christian Associations.

(i) Every certificate of incorporation which indicates that the proposed corporation is to solicit funds for or otherwise benefit the armed forces of the United States or of any foreign country, or their auxiliaries, or of this or any other state or any territory, shall have endorsed thereon or annexed thereto the approval of the adjutant general. The department of state, in conjunction with the division of military and naval affairs, shall establish and maintain on the department's website a public listing of all approved not-for-profit corporations soliciting funds for or otherwise benefiting the armed forces of the United States or of any foreign country, or their auxiliaries, or of this or any other state or territory.

(j) Every certificate of incorporation which includes among its purposes the organization of wage-earners for their mutual betterment, protection and advancement; the regulation of hours of labor, working conditions, or wages; or the performance, rendition or sale of services as labor consultant, labor-management advisor, negotiator, arbitrator, or specialist; and every certificate of incorporation in which the name of the proposed corporation includes "union", "labor", "council" or "industrial organization", or any abbreviation or derivative thereof in a context that indicates or implies that the corporation is formed for any of the above purposes, shall have endorsed thereon or annexed thereto the approval of the industrial board of appeals. The board shall make such inquiry into the purposes of the proposed corporation as it shall deem advisable and shall order a hearing if necessary to determine whether or not such purposes are in all respects consistent with public policy and the labor law. Notice of the time and place of hearing shall be given to the applicants and such other persons as the board may determine.

(k) Every certificate of incorporation for a corporation which has as its exclusive purpose the promotion of the interests of savings bank life insurance or the promotion of the interests of member banks may, if the approval of the superintendent of financial services is endorsed thereon or annexed thereto, use as a part of the corporate name any of the words or phrases, or any abbreviation or derivative thereof, set forth in subparagraph (5) of paragraph (a) of section 301 (Corporate name; general).

(l) Every certificate of incorporation for a corporation which has as its exclusive purpose the creation of an association of licensed insurance agents, licensed insurance brokers, or licensed insurance underwriters and every application for authority of a foreign corporation which is an independent laboratory engaged in testing for public safety, or which has as its purpose the advancement of corporate, governmental, and institutional risk and insurance management, or which has as its exclusive purpose the creation of an association of insurers, each of which is duly licensed in this state or, if it does no business or is not licensed in this state, is duly licensed in another state or foreign jurisdiction may, if the approval of the superintendent of financial services is endorsed thereon or annexed thereto, use as a part of the corporate name any of the words or phrases, or any abbreviation or derivative thereof, set forth in subparagraph (5) of paragraph (a) of section 301 (Corporate name; general).

(m) Every certificate of incorporation in which the name of the proposed corporation includes the name of a political party shall have endorsed thereon or annexed thereto the consent of the chairman of the county committee of such political party of the county in which the office of the corporation is to be located, except in cases where the supreme court finds that the withholding of such consent of the county chairman is unreasonable.

(n) Every certificate of incorporation in which the name of the proposed corporation includes the words "American Legion," shall have endorsed thereon or annexed thereto the approval of the Department of New York, the American Legion, duly acknowledged by its commander or adjutant.

(o) Every certificate of incorporation which includes among its corporate purposes or powers the establishment or maintenance of any hospital, as defined in article twenty-eight of the public health law, or the solicitation of contributions for any such purpose, or purposes, shall have endorsed thereon or annexed thereto the approval of the public health and health planning council.

(p) Every certificate of incorporation of a medical corporation as defined in article forty-four of the public health law and organized pursuant thereto and pursuant to this chapter, shall have endorsed thereon or annexed thereto the consent of the commissioner of health and the approval of the public health and health planning council.

(q) Every certificate of incorporation which includes among its corporate purposes or powers the establishment, or operation of a facility for which an operating certificate from the commissioner of mental health is required by article thirty-one of the mental hygiene law, or the solicitation of contributions for any such purpose, shall have endorsed thereon or annexed thereto the approval of the commissioner of mental health.

(r) Every certificate of incorporation of a health maintenance organization as defined in article forty-four of the public health law and organized pursuant thereto and pursuant to this chapter, shall have endorsed thereon or annexed thereto the consent of the commissioner of health.

(s) [Repealed]

(t) Every certificate of incorporation which includes among its purposes and powers the establishment or maintenance of a hospital or facility providing health related services, as those terms are defined in article twenty-eight of the public health law, or the solicitation of contributions for any such purpose or two or more of such purposes, shall have endorsed thereon the approval of the public health and health planning council.

(u) Every certificate of incorporation which includes among the purposes of the corporation, the establishment or operation of a substance abuse, substance dependence, alcohol abuse, alcoholism, or chemical abuse or dependence program, or the solicitation of contributions for any such purpose, shall have endorsed thereon or annexed thereto the consent of the commissioner of the office of alcoholism and substance abuse services to its filing by the department of state.

(v) Every certificate of incorporation which includes among the purposes of the corporation, the establishment, maintenance and operation of a nonprofit property/casualty insurance company, pursuant to article sixty-seven of the insurance law, shall have endorsed thereon or annexed thereto the approval of the superintendent of financial services.

History: Add, L 1969, ch 1066, § 1; amd, L 1970, ch 617, §§ 13, 14; amd, L 1970, ch 847, § 14; L 1971, ch 1058, § 9; L 1971, ch 1139, § 12; L 1972, ch 961, § 4; L 1973, ch 1036, § 1; L 1974, ch 168, § 1; L 1974, ch 527, § 1; L 1975, ch 498, § 1; L 1976, ch 72, § 10; L 1976, ch 436, §§ 5, 6; L 1976, ch 938, § 1; L 1977, ch 450, § 5; L 1977, ch 669, §§ 9, 11, 12; L 1978, ch 162, § 1; L 1978, ch 555, §§ 62, 63, eff July 24, 1978; L 1981, ch 173, § 1; L 1981, ch 601, § 13; L 1984, ch 805, § 45; L 1985, ch 99, § 2; L 1985, ch 804, § 4; L 1985, ch 856, § 5; L 1987, ch 838, § 9; L 1988, ch 141, § 7; L 1990, ch 526, § 1; L 1992, ch 17, § 1; L 1993, ch 139, § 1; L 1993, ch 201, § 3; L 1993, ch 431, § 1, eff Aug 20, 1993; L 1997, ch 468, § 1, eff Sept 25, 1997; L 1999, ch 558, § 23, eff Oct 5, 1999; L 2000, ch 598, § 6, eff Dec 20, 2000; L 2005, ch 316, § 6, eff Jan 1, 2006; L 2006, ch 58, § 4 (Part D), eff April 12, 2006; L 2010, ch 58, § 79 (Part A), eff Dec 31, 2010; L 2010, ch 198, § 2, eff July 15, 2010; L 2011, ch 62, § 104 (Part A), eff Oct 3, 2011; L 2013, ch 549, §§ 48, 49, eff July 1, 2014; L 2014, ch 23, § 10, eff July 1, 2014; L 2015, ch 358, § 3, eff Sept 25, 2015; L 2016, ch 134, § 1, eff July 21, 2016; L 2017, ch 405, § 2, eff Jan 1, 2019.

Laws 2017, ch 405, § 3 , eff Jan 1, 2019, provides:

§ 3. This act shall take effect January 1, 2019 (Amd, L 2018, ch 24, § 1, eff April 18, 2018).

CASE ANNOTATIONS

1. Generally
2-10. [Reserved for future use]
11. Under former Membership Corporations Law § 10
12. – Court approval of certificate of incorporation
13. – – As exercise of judicial function
14. – – Discretion of court
15. – – Conclusiveness of approval
16. – – Constitutionality of requirement
17. – Other requirements; notice to attorney general
18. – – Incorporation of political club
19. – – Incorporation of fire company
20. Under former Membership Corporation Law § 11
21. – Required prior consent of various state agencies
22. – – Commissioner of education; board of regents
23. – – Board of standards and appeals
24. – – Board of social welfare
25. – – Board of charities
26. – Court approval
27. – Incorporation and powers of particular corporations
28. – – Practice of medicine; practice of optometry
29. – – Bar association; aid to lawyers
30. – – Labor union
31. – – Fire company
32. – – Prevention of cruelty to animals
33. – Tax liability
34. – Miscellaneous

1. Generally

The name "Gay Activists Alliance" was not inappropriate. Owles v Lomenzo (1972, 3d Dept) 38 A.D.2d 981, 329 N.Y.S.2d 181, affd (1973) 31 N.Y.2d 965, 341 N.Y.S.2d 108, 293 N.E.2d 255

In a proceeding to review determinations of a town board of appeals granting a special use permit for a private boarding school to a not-for-profit corporation and its agent, the board erred in granting a permit to the agent where he was merely the nominal head of the school and where it was undisputed that the corporation did not have authorization as required by law to operate the school. McLain Street Area Asso. v Board of Appeals (1981, 2d Dept) 82 A.D.2d 834, 439 N.Y.S.2d 668

Commissioner of Education properly determined that foreign nonprofit corporation had no authority to operate a private school in New York under N-PCL §§ 404, subd d, 1301, and 1304, subd c where said school, although in existence prior to passage of N-PCL, had never been authorized to do business here within the meaning of N-PCL § 1302. Green Valley School, Inc. v Nyquist (1972) 72 Misc. 2d 889, 340 N.Y.S.2d 234

An application for approval of a certificate of incorporation pursuant to the Not-For-Profit Corporation Law, setting forth the purposes of the corporation as being "to print, mail, disseminate, Roman Catholic information... to conduct prayer vigils, and with divine guidance keep the knowledge of God and His plan for peace and security in the hearts of all mankind", brings the proposed corporation within the definition of an incorporated church making it subject to the provisions of the Religious Corporations Law as well as the Not-For-Profit Corporation Law, and, as such, the application must be denied for failure to conform to the specific provisions of the Religious Corporations Law which govern the incorporation of groups associated with the Roman Catholic Church, including the requirement of an execution and acknowledgment by certain specific officials of that church. In re Lueken (Our Lady of Roses) (1978) 97 Misc. 2d 201, 410 N.Y.S.2d 793

Although the Attorney-General failed to appear on two occasions when the court was to consider an amendment to the certificate of incorporation of petitioner not-for-profit corporation, petitioner may not compel the Attorney-General to respond to petitioner's application by a CPLR article 78 proceeding in the nature of mandamus since mandamus does not lie in the absence of a showing that the Attorney-General failed to perform a duty enjoined upon him by law and there is no statute or other requirement obligating the Attorney-General to furnish a waiver or consent in connection with the approval of an amendment to the certificate of incorporation of a not-for-profit corporation; the applicable statutes (Not-For-Profit Corporation Law, § 804, subd [a]; § 404, subd [a]) require only that the Attorney-General be given notice that a not-for-profit corporation is applying to an appropriate Justice to amend its certificate of incorporation, and the failure of the Attorney-General to appear after proper service of the notice should result in the court's approval of the application in the absence of an apparent defect in the certificate. Electrical Industry Ass'n v State (1979) 102 Misc. 2d 494, 423 N.Y.S.2d 576

Judicial approval of certificate of incorporation for proposed type B not-for-profit corporation would be withheld as unnecessary since proposed corporation was type A not-for-profit corporation, for which no judicial approval was necessary, where proposed corporation did not have charitable purpose but was intended for specific benefit of 3 named persons, and no provision was made for using any portion of funds raised for benefit of public or any class of public. In re Application of Howard Beach Appeal Fund, Inc. (1988, Sup) 141 Misc. 2d 735, 534 N.Y.S.2d 341

The State Board of Social Welfare has legal authority to approve the physical facility and the certificate of incorporation of a not-for-profit corporation to be formed for the purpose of operating, with federal funds, a multi-service halfway house residential facility for adult female ex-offenders and their children. 1977 Op Atty Gen March 9

A subsidiary of the Urban Development Corporation may incorporate under the Business Corporation Law without forfeiting its public status. The subsidiary may not pay profits to private investors, and upon dissolution of the corporation, the assets belong to the State. 1980 Op Atty Gen Oct. 20

In constructing a firehouse to be utilized for fire fighting or fire prevention, a fire corporation in a fire district need not comply with town zoning and building regulations. Ops Atty Gen 83-33

2-10. [Reserved for future use]

11. Under former Membership Corporations Law § 10

Under former § 41 from which this section is derived the approval of a justice of the supreme court of a certificate of incorporation was an indispensable requisite to the creation of a membership corporation. People v Smith (1923) 121 Misc 338, 200 N.Y.S. 863

12. – Court approval of certificate of incorporation

Public policy of the state is not violated where the purposes of a proposed corporation are lawful, and the grant of a charter should not be granted or denied on the basis of the personal notion of the justice of what is contrary to public policy or injurious to the community. Association for Preservation of Freedom of Choice, Inc. v Shapiro (1961) 9 N.Y.2d 376, 214 N.Y.S.2d 388, 174 N.E.2d 487, remittitur den (1961) 9 N.Y.2d 909, reh den (1962) 11 N.Y.2d 720 and reh den (1962) 11 N.Y.2d 662, 225 N.Y.S.2d 740, 180 N.E.2d 898

This section, stripped of technical requirements and certain exceptions, authorizes five or more persons to become a membership corporation "for any lawful purpose," but requires that the certificate of incorporation be approved by a justice of the Supreme Court, thus setting up practically no standards to guide exercise of judicial power; and it would seem logical to assume that the function of judicial scrutiny as intended by the Legislature was merely to ascertain whether the proposed incorporation was for a lawful purpose. Association for Preservation of Freedom of Choice, Inc. v Shapiro (1961) 9 N.Y.2d 376, 214 N.Y.S.2d 388, 174 N.E.2d 487, remittitur den (1961) 9 N.Y.2d 909, reh den (1962) 11 N.Y.2d 720 and reh den (1962) 11 N.Y.2d 662, 225 N.Y.S.2d 740, 180 N.E.2d 898

There is no basis for the view that this section authorizes a Supreme Court justice, for whose approval a membership corporation certificate is submitted, to grant or deny the application on his personal notion of what is contrary to public policy or injurious to the community, the basic test of whether the application is entitled to judicial approval being whether the stated purposes of the corporation are lawful. Association for Preservation of Freedom of Choice, Inc. v Shapiro (1961) 9 N.Y.2d 376, 214 N.Y.S.2d 388, 174 N.E.2d 487, remittitur den (1961) 9 N.Y.2d 909, reh den (1962) 11 N.Y.2d 720 and reh den (1962) 11 N.Y.2d 662, 225 N.Y.S.2d 740, 180 N.E.2d 898

The fact that the aims of a proposed membership corporation are lawful is not alone sufficient for judicial sanction as a matter of course. In re Boy Explorers of America, Inc. (1946) 21 Misc. 2d 114, 67 N.Y.S.2d 108

Mere legality of aims is not sufficient for judicial sanction of a certificate of incorporation as a matter of course. Application of United Cadet Asso. (1958) 13 Misc. 2d 957, 178 N.Y.S.2d 479

13. – – As exercise of judicial function

The approval of a Supreme Court Justice as required by this section does not involve simply the performance of a ministerial act but the exercise of a judicial function to decide whether the special privilege of a corporate charter should be granted under all the circumstances surrounding the application. Hence, an application for approval of a proposed certificate of incorporation was denied an organization seeking the establishment of a hospital in Israel where the proposed corporation would merely lead to confusion and misunderstanding and tend greatly to impair the work now being carried on by long established and well-known agencies. Application of United Winograder Medical Center (1953) 21 Misc 27, 125 N.Y.S.2d 279

The approval of a justice of the supreme court as required by this section does not simply involve the performance of a ministerial act, but the exercise of a judicial function to decide whether the special privilege of a corporate charter should be granted or conferred under all the circumstances surrounding the application. In re Boy Explorers of America, Inc. (1946) 21 Misc. 2d 114, 67 N.Y.S.2d 108

The approval by a justice of the Supreme Court required by this section does not involve simply the performance of a ministerial act, but the exercise of a judicial function, to decide whether the special franchise of a corporate charter should be granted or conferred under all the circumstances surrounding the application. Application of Council of Orthodox Rabbis, Inc. (1958) 10 Misc. 2d 62, 171 N.Y.S.2d 664

14. – – Discretion of court

A justice before approving an application for incorporation as a membership corporation as required by this section must draw freely on his own knowledge and experience as well as whatever sources of information may be available to him in determining whether the proper exercise of judicial discretion dictates approval or disapproval in any particular case. In re Boy Explorers of America, Inc. (1946) 21 Misc. 2d 114, 67 N.Y.S.2d 108

By reason of the ex parte nature of the application for approval of a certificate of incorporation, it is incumbent upon a justice considering it to draw freely upon his own knowledge and experience as well as other sources of information available to assist him in proper exercise of his discretion. Application of United Cadet Asso. (1958) 13 Misc. 2d 957, 178 N.Y.S.2d 479

The duty imposed upon the Justice of the Supreme Court to whom a certificate for leave to file articles of incorporation is presented is not clerical or ministerial, but requires exercise of judgment and discretion, the questions to be determined being whether objects of the corporation violate public policy, whether approval will permit irresponsible or unequipped citizens to operate under a corporate charter, and whether the proposed corporation will duplicate or conflict with existing corporations. In re Application of Excavating Machine Owners Asso., Inc. (1960) 25 Misc. 2d 419, 205 N.Y.S.2d 265

A justice who rules on the certificate of a trade association is exercising a semi-administrative discretion as a separate and distinct step in the procedure for incorporation, and in no sense merely reviewing the decision of the Attorney General; therefore, the court is not limited to matter presented by the applicant but may consider extraneous facts, including such facts as may be presented for its consideration by the Attorney General after his own investigation has been made. In re Application of Excavating Machine Owners Asso., Inc. (1960) 25 Misc. 2d 419, 205 N.Y.S.2d 265

15. – – Conclusiveness of approval

Approval of a judge is not conclusive upon the Secretary of State as to the regularity of a certificate. People ex rel. Blossom v Nelson (1871) 46 N.Y. 477 (questioned in Clara C. v William L. (2001) 96 N.Y.2d 244, 727 N.Y.S.2d 20, 750 N.E.2d 1068)

The consent and approbation of a Justice of the Supreme Court, required as one of the conditions precedent to right to file a certificate of incorporation as a membership corporation of the types dealt with in §§ 10 and 11 of the Membership Corporation Law, is cumulative to the other requisites of the act, but decides nothing, and is not conclusive either upon the public or the Secretary of State. In re Application of Excavating Machine Owners Asso., Inc. (1960) 25 Misc. 2d 419, 205 N.Y.S.2d 265

16. – – Constitutionality of requirement

Neither § 10 of the Membership Corporation Law, nor subd. 2 of § 212 of the General Corporation Law, is unconstitutional in making an application for a certificate to do business in this state as a membership corporation subject to approval of a justice of the Supreme Court, and mandamus will not issue to compel the Secretary of State to accept and file such a certificate without the required judicial approval. Association for Preservation of Freedom of Choice, Inc. v Simon (1960) 22 Misc. 2d 1016, 201 N.Y.S.2d 135, app dismd (1960) 8 N.Y.2d 909, 204 N.Y.S.2d 150, 168 N.E.2d 826 and affd

(1960, 1st Dept) 11 A.D.2d 927, 206 N.Y.S.2d 532, affd (1961) 9 N.Y.2d 376, 214 N.Y.S.2d 388, 174 N.E.2d 487, remittitur den (1961) 9 N.Y.2d 909, reh den (1962) 11 N.Y.2d 720 and reh den (1962) 11 N.Y.2d 662, 225 N.Y.S.2d 740, 180 N.E.2d 898

17. – Other requirements; notice to attorney general

The purpose of the 1958 amendment of this section, requiring the giving of five days' written notice of the application to the Attorney General where it relates to certain types of corporations, was to permit him to present to the court relevant facts at his disposal rather than to authorize him to make any independent ruling or determination on the application. In re Application of Excavating Machine Owners Asso., Inc. (1960) 25 Misc. 2d 419, 205 N.Y.S.2d 265

Where a certificate of incorporation specifies as a purpose of the proposed corporation maintenance and support of a centennial celebration for the benefit of village citizens, the purpose is charitable and five days' written notice of application for approval should be given to the Attorney General. 1962 Ops Atty Gen July 31

Judicial approval of the certificate of incorporation of a membership corporation requires five days' notice to the Attorney General and is not ex parte. 1963 Ops Atty Gen Nov 27

18. – – Incorporation of political club

This section confers a qualified veto power on county chairman in permitting the use of the word descriptive of a political party. The policy of this section has in some cases been extended to cover certain unincorporated associations on the theory that they are de facto corporations. However, the statute does not extend to every unincorporated association which may use the descriptive word or the name of a political party. So, a temporary injunction granted against 5 unincorporated associations of Republicans which prohibited them from using the word "Republican" in their organizational name was modified by permitting the use of the word "Republican" and also to use the party emblems and the initials "G. O. P." so long as it was clear that the 5 associations were opposed to the regular organization. Mele v Ryder (1959, 1st Dept) 8 A.D.2d 390, 188 N.Y.S.2d 446, 122 USPQ 350, app gr (1959, 1st Dept) 9 A.D.2d 608, 191 N.Y.S.2d 132 and motion gr (1959) 7 N.Y.2d 759, 193 N.Y.S.2d 881, 163 N.E.2d 39 and app dismd (1960) 7 N.Y.2d 1027, 200 N.Y.S.2d 69, 166 N.E.2d 859

An unincorporated association formed for political purposes with offices, stationery, and the name of the club on office windows, is a de facto corporation and therefore subject to the prohibition of this section against the use of the name of a political party without the consent of the county chairman of that party. Gerlach v Good Government Republican Club (1953) 16 Misc. 2d 1050, 123 N.Y.S.2d 902, mod on other grounds (1953, 2d Dept) 282 A.D. 830, 123 N.Y.S.2d 641

Republican county chairman could withhold consent to use of name "Metropolitan Republican Club, Inc." where the incorporators intended to appeal to all individuals. In re Application of Roosevelt (1957) 9 Misc. 2d 205, 160 N.Y.S.2d 747, affd (1957, 1st Dept) 3 A.D.2d 988, 163 N.Y.S.2d 403, app gr (1957) 3 N.Y.2d 709 and affd (1958) 4 N.Y.2d 19, 171 N.Y.S.2d 841, 148 N.E.2d 895

Where the persons seeking to incorporate an organization to be known as the "7th Ward Democratic Club" of a particular city are, in the majority, not residents of that ward, are of undetermined residence and not even enrolled members of the party in the county, such danger of confusion exists as to warrant the county party chairman in withholding consent to incorporation of the organization. Application of Coles (1961) 27 Misc. 2d 789, 211 N.Y.S.2d 751

Subdivision 8 of this section recognizes the necessity of propriety of control, albeit a limited control, by the party chairman where the name of the proposed corporation includes the name of a political party, and only when the exercise of such power by the county chairman is patently unreasonable should the Supreme Court veto his withholding of consent. Application of Coles (1961) 27 Misc. 2d 789, 211 N.Y.S.2d 751

Secretary of state properly received certificate of incorporation of membership corporation with name containing name of political party where endorsement of county chairman was made when encumbent had resigned but still held office and certificate was approved by court before resignation of chairman took effect. Archinal v Reuss (1965) 46 Misc. 2d 428, 260 N.Y.S.2d 78

An affidavit attached to an application for approval of a certificate of incorporation of a political club, stating that the county chairman has refused to give his consent because the leader of the assembly district in which the proposed club is to operate objects, does not take the place of the indorsement of consent required by this section, and

approval must be withheld until the county chairman is given an opportunity to be heard before the court so that there may be a determination as to whether the withholding of consent is unreasonable. In re Independent Republican Club (1945, Sup) 58 N.Y.S.2d 162

Where county chairman is deceased and rules of county committee authorize first vice-chairman to perform the duties of and exercise the powers of chairman in his absence, approval of first vice-chairman and acting chairman to incorporation of membership corporation containing name of political party is sufficient compliance with requirements of this section. 1954 Ops Atty Gen Sept 2

19. – – Incorporation of fire company

Incorporation of a fire company requires approval of a justice of the Supreme Court and consent of the Town Board after public hearing. 1964 Ops St Compt #176

20. Under former Membership Corporation Law § 11

The purposes stated in Soc. Wel. Law, § 35, subd. 1, are purposes for which a corporation must be formed under the provisions of the Membership Corporations Law. 1941 Ops Atty Gen Apr 15

Public hearing may not be held under this section until after expiration of 14 days from first publication of notice of such hearing. 1955 St Compt File #7248

21. – Required prior consent of various state agencies

Above statute providing for special prior consents from variety of State agencies for numerous activities affected with public interest, contains no such requirement as to solicitation of funds. Waldemar Medical Research Foundation, Inc. v Margolies (1965) 45 Misc. 2d 887, 257 N.Y.S.2d 991, affd (1966, 2d Dept) 25 A.D.2d 444, 267 N.Y.S.2d 483

22. – – Commissioner of education; board of regents

The Commissioner of Education has no power to approve the incorporation of an educational organization known as the "Human Engineering Laboratory, Inc.", in view of the provisions of § 1461 of the Education Law which provides that the word "engineers" or "engineering" shall not be used in the title of any such corporation except a nonprofit group composed exclusively of professional engineers. New York State Soc. of Professional Engineers, Inc. v Education Dep't of New York (1941) 262 A.D. 602, 31 N.Y.S.2d 305

Where the Commissioner of Education has improperly approved a certificate of incorporation and the Board of Regents has refused to correct the mistake, the courts will order such correction where the refusal to act is unfair, arbitrary or capricious. New York State Soc. of Professional Engineers, Inc. v Education Dep't of New York (1941) 262 A.D. 602, 31 N.Y.S.2d 305

Under subd. 2 of this section, a certificate of incorporation for a membership corporation to establish professional standards for training and research in the field of psychoanalysis and to arrange lectures and discussions pertaining to relationship between that field and other fields of science and education clearly required the consent of the Commissioner of Education. National Psychological Asso. for Psychoanalysis, Inc. v Allen (1961, 3d Dept) 14 A.D.2d 190, 217 N.Y.S.2d 893, motion gr (1962) 11 N.Y.2d 642

The purposes referred to in subd. 2 of this section, requiring consent of the Commissioner of Education, are those found in § 216 of the Education Law. National Psychological Asso. for Psychoanalysis, Inc. v Allen (1961, 3d Dept) 14 A.D.2d 190, 217 N.Y.S.2d 893, motion gr (1962) 11 N.Y.2d 642

The Secretary of State was entitled to refuse to file a certificate of incorporation without express consent of the Commissioner of Education where one of the stated purposes of the corporation was "to promote and develop facilities for training and study for its members." Association for Psychoanalysis, Inc. v Simon (1964, 3d Dept) 21 A.D.2d 209, 250 N.Y.S.2d 253

Prior acceptance for filing by the Secretary of State of the certificate of organization of a membership corporation, without requiring consent of the Commissioner of Education pursuant to subd 2 of this section, did not mandate similar action in a later incident under pain of being charged with arbitrary conduct. Association for Psychoanalysis, Inc. v Simon (1964, 3d Dept) 21 A.D.2d 209, 250 N.Y.S.2d 253

Where the purposes enumerated in a certificate of incorporation of a membership corporation constituted no basis for incorporation by the Board of Regents, the Secretary of State improperly refused to file a certificate without the endorsement of consent of the Commissioner of Education. Lunderman v De Sapio (1957) 9 Misc. 2d 322, 173 N.Y.S.2d 158

The Secretary of State was not required to file the certificate of incorporation of a group organized "to advise, encourage and assist local area (areas) in obtaining a betterment of methods, means, facilities, and operations in education matters" without the consent of the Commissioner of Education, since such an association could be incorporated by the Regents of the University. Lunderman v De Sapio (1958) 19 Misc. 2d 679, 196 N.Y.S.2d 250, affd (1959, 3d Dept) 9 A.D.2d 803, 193 N.Y.S.2d 1022

A certificate of incorporation which includes some primary educational features can be granted pursuant to the Mem. Corp. Law with the consent of the board of regents, and the approval of a justice of supreme court and the state board of charities. 1915 Ops Atty Gen 300

Where the purposes of a proposed corporation are to investigate the present educational system, to disseminate information thereon, to stimulate public interest in securing improvement, such purposes constitute the "promotion" of "education" under Education Law § 216 so as to require the consent of the commissioner of education before the certificate may be filed. 1957 Ops Atty Gen July 8

23. – – Board of standards and appeals

The Board of Standards and Appeals may not refuse approval of a proposed certificate of incorporation of a labor organization because it disapproves of provisions in a tentative contract which may be offered to the employers by the proposed corporation. McNair v Picard (1941) 262 A.D. 927, 29 N.Y.S.2d 18, 8 BNA LRRM 1102

The purpose specified in a proposed certificate of incorporation for the "Hotel Roosevelt Employees Welfare Association", that the corporation was designed to promote the well-being of the employees, brings the proposed corporation within subd. 1-a of this section and Gen. Corp. Law, § 9-a. Breen v Picard (1938) 167 Misc 561, 4 N.Y.S.2d 301, 3 BNA LRRM 797

The Board of Standards and Appeals may not refuse to approve the incorporation as a membership corporation of a formerly unincorporated association consisting of public employees, where the purpose of the organization set forth in its certificate is to benefit and advance the welfare and interest of the employees of the Park Department of the City of New York. Hagan v Picard (1939) 171 Misc 475, 12 N.Y.S.2d 873, 4 BNA LRRM 852, affd (1939) 258 A.D. 771, 14 N.Y.S.2d 706, 5 BNA LRRM 949

The power vested by the statute and the Board of Standards and Appeals to approve or disapprove certificates of incorporation of organizations of workingmen is ministerial, and does not authorize action on the basis of some policy which the Board thinks should be followed by the state, and it is not competent for the Board to withhold approval because it is not in sympathy with the purposes of the corporation. Hagan v Picard (1939) 171 Misc 475, 12 N.Y.S.2d 873, 4 BNA LRRM 852, affd (1939) 258 A.D. 771, 14 N.Y.S.2d 706, 5 BNA LRRM 949

An application for a certificate of incorporation which enumerates the following purposes: "To further the social and economic conditions of its members and to take over, carry on, and continue the affairs, property, obligations, business and objectives of the unincorporated association" needs no approval by the Board of Standards and Appeals, since the certificate contains no statement that the members of the corporation, whose social and economic ambitions are to be furthered, are workingmen or women or wage earners, as required by subdivision 1-a of this section. Wilson v Picard (1940) 173 Misc 788, 20 N.Y.S.2d 119

A certificate of incorporation stating a purpose to assume the affairs, business and objects of the unincorporated Yard Workers Association and not disclosing what those affairs, business and objects were, and disclosing other purposes authorizing incorporation under § 10, may be accepted for filing without approval of the board of standards and appeals under subd 1-a of this section, if the clause disclosing the purpose to assume the affairs, business and objects of the unincorporated association is deleted. 1940 Ops Atty Gen May 14

24. – – Board of social welfare

Where the Board of Social Welfare has refused to permit a membership corporation to amend its certificate of incorporation to permit it to operate a hospital, the court should not substitute its judgment for that of the Board where it clearly appears that there was no arbitrary or malicious exercise of power. Italian Hospitalization Soc. v State Department of Social Welfare (1942) 178 Misc 183, 34 N.Y.S.2d 385

Where a proposed certificate of incorporation states in its purpose clause that it is formed to give financial and other help, aid and assistance to existing institutions or organizations established for the care and treatment of the sick, needy and infirm, such proposed certificate does not require the approval of the state board of social welfare. 1940 Ops Atty Gen Nov 8

It is permissible in stating the powers of a membership corporation subject to the jurisdiction of the state department of social welfare to attach a condition to the effect that any institution which if incorporated separately under a general law would require the approval of the state board of social welfare, shall not be established or maintained in this state unless the written approval of such state board shall first have been obtained; and such a certificate may not be amended, without the approval of the state board of social welfare, to delete the condition set forth in the certificate. 1941 Ops Atty Gen Feb 18

Before a foreign corporation organized to maintain a home for the aged may take title to realty in this State it must obtain approval of the State Board of Social Welfare and file statement and designation with Secretary of State. 1955 Ops Atty Gen Apr 20 (informal)

25. – – Board of charities

A hospital should be organized under the provisions of the Membership Corporations Law rather than under the Business Corporations Law, and the State Board of Charities is not authorized to approve certificates for incorporation under the latter statute. 1911 Ops Atty Gen 191

The functions of public health authorities in considering the location of a new hospital as a public health matter are entirely different from those of the state board of charities in the same premises. The latter cannot base its refusal to approve the certificate of incorporation upon the grounds involved in a determination already made by the former. 1927 Ops Atty Gen 331

26. – Court approval

The consent and approbation of a Justice of the Supreme Court, required as one of the conditions precedent to right to file a certificate of incorporation as a membership corporation of the types dealt with in §§ 10 and 11 of the Membership Corporation Law, is cumulative to the other requisites of the act, but decides nothing, and is not conclusive either upon the public or the Secretary of State. In re Application of Excavating Machine Owners Asso., Inc. (1960) 25 Misc. 2d 419, 205 N.Y.S.2d 265

The duty imposed upon the Justice of the Supreme Court to whom a certificate for leave to file articles of incorporation is presented is not clerical or ministerial, but requires exercise of judgment and discretion, the questions to be determined being whether objects of the corporation violate public policy, whether approval will permit irresponsible or unequipped citizens to operate under a corporate charter, and whether the proposed corporation will duplicate or conflict with existing corporations. In re Application of Excavating Machine Owners Asso., Inc. (1960) 25 Misc. 2d 419, 205 N.Y.S.2d 265

27. – Incorporation and powers of particular corporations

Where the great council of New York was not given the power, by its charter, to erect and maintain a home for aged members, this section does not give it such power in the absence of a change in its charter to that effect. Kiowa Council, etc. v Great Council of New York, etc. (1928) 132 Misc 106, 228 N.Y.S. 256

Approval of certificate of incorporation under name "National Foundation for Diarrheal Diseases, Inc." was denied where the organization sought generally to foster, promote, and disseminate information. In re National Foundation for Diarrheal Diseases (1957) 8 Misc. 2d 12, 164 N.Y.S.2d 177

A hospital service corporation formed pursuant to Membership Corporations Law as provided under the cited article of the Insurance Law is a moneyed corporation and may use the word "Insurance" as part of its corporate name. 1965 Ops Atty Gen May 12

28. – – Practice of medicine; practice of optometry

Formation of a corporation to engage in the practice of medicine is possible only under the provisions of this section. 1934 Ops Atty Gen 240

A corporation other than one to organize a hospital or similar institution may not lawfully be formed, under the Mem. Corp. Law, for the purpose of engaging in the practice of optometry. 1935 Ops Atty Gen 373

29. – – Bar association; aid to lawyers

Activity of bar association in conducting poll of membership to determine fitness of candidates for judicial office and expending funds to support judicial candidates found to be fit was not ultra vires under this section. Pecora v Queens County Bar Asso. (1965) 46 Misc. 2d 530, 260 N.Y.S.2d 116

Not-For-Profit Corporation Law

A certificate of incorporation will be granted to an organization having among its objectives the advancement of knowledge and understanding of the law and research in jurisprudence, the promotion of a sound administration of justice and a grant of aid to members of the bar who may find themselves in need because of ill health, physical disability, or misfortune. In re Certificate of Incorporation of New York County Lawyers' Ass'n Fund, Inc. (1948, Sup) 81 N.Y.S.2d 724

30. – – Labor union

The Secretary of State may properly refuse to approve a certificate of incorporation of a labor union where it appears that the union seeking incorporation is or will be dominated by the employer and therefor approval would be in conflict with the public policy of the state as set forth in the Labor Law. Campbell v Picard (1937) 165 Misc 148, 300 N.Y.S. 515

31. – – Fire company

The certificate of incorporation of a volunteer fire company may be amended so as to include a fire district within the territory in which the fire company proposes to act. 1955 Ops St Compt File #7319

A town board may, in its discretion, consent to the incorporation of a fire company which will have its headquarters in and protect against fires in a fire protection district which is presently being served pursuant to contract with another fire company situated in the fire protection district. 1955 Ops St Compt File #7736

The members of a volunteer fire company organized and incorporated in an area of a town not within a village or fire district will be covered under a county self-insurance plan. The cost of this coverage is included as part of the town's apportionate share. 1958 Ops St Compt File #366

Discussion of procedure for incorporation of volunteer fire company and the beneficial effect of a corporate status to simplify matters concerning the management of affairs and ownership of assets. 1967 Ops St Compt File #786

The board of fire commissioners of a fire district may organize, operate, maintain and equip additional fire companies in the fire district. The board of fire commissioners may consent to the formation of a fire corporation which intends to operate within the territory of such fire district. In either case, either the fire company or the district could purchase and own real property and equipment. 1968 Ops St Compt File #926

32. – – Prevention of cruelty to animals

The approval of the National Association for the Prevention of Cruelty to Animals as a condition precedent to incorporation of a county society may be dispensed with upon evidence that the public interest required approval of the proposed certificate of incorporation. In re Warren County Soc. for Prevention of Cruelty to Animals, Inc. (1953, Sup) 123 N.Y.S.2d 419

33. – Tax liability

A membership corporation was entitled to exemption from real property taxes where its membership was open to the public as a little theater corporation and no officer, member or employee other than production directors received money. Little Theatre of Watertown, Inc. v Hoyt (1956) 7 Misc. 2d 907, 165 N.Y.S.2d 292, affd (1957, 4th Dept) 4 A.D.2d 853, 167 N.Y.S.2d 240

34. – Miscellaneous

The fact that none of the corporation papers on file contained a statement that the hospital was incorporated as a "charitable corporation" did not negate the actuality that the hospital was a charitable institution within the purport of § 189 of the Lien Law. The court pointed out there was no general charitable corporation statute in New York, and that the law contemplated, with respect to hospitals, that charitable pursuits may be pursued by an entity functioning under the Membership Corporation Law. Gonzalez v New York City Transit Authority (1967, 2d Dept) 27 A.D.2d 744, 277 N.Y.S.2d 527

A will directing that a memorial to testator's wife be maintained, and setting aside from the remainder a certain sum for perpetual care, for the maintenance and exhibition of valuable art objects, and for which purpose a nonprofit corporation had been formed, will be given effect and the testator's intention will be determined as having established a charitable and educational bequest with a devise of the real property and improvements thereon to the corporation. In re Klauber's Will (1951) 201 Misc 839, 106 N.Y.S.2d 264

§ 405. Organization meeting

(a) After the corporate existence has begun, an organization meeting of the initial directors, or, if directors are not designated in the certificate of incorporation, of the incorporator or incorporators, shall be held within or without this state, for the purpose of adopting by-laws, electing directors to hold office as provided in the certificate of incorporation or the by-laws, and the transaction of such other business as may come before the meeting. The meeting may be held at the call of any director or, if directors are not designated in the certificate of incorporation, any incorporator who shall give at least five days' notice thereof by mail to each other director or incorporator, which notice shall set forth the time and place of the meeting. Notice need not be given to any director or incorporator who submits a signed waiver of notice before or after the meeting, or who attends the meeting without protesting, prior thereto or at its commencement, the lack of notice to him. If there are more than two directors or incorporators, a majority shall constitute a quorum and the act of the majority of those present at a meeting at which a quorum is present shall be the act of the directors or incorporators. For the purposes of this section an incorporator or director may act in person or by proxy signed by him or his attorney in fact.

(b) Any action permitted to be taken at an organization meeting may be taken without a meeting if each director or, if directors are not designated in the certificate of incorporation, each incorporator or his attorney-in-fact signs an instrument setting forth the action so taken.

(c) If a designated director or an incorporator dies or is for any reason unable to act, the other or others may act. If there is no designated director or incorporator able to act, any person for whom an incorporator is acting as agent may act in his stead, or if such other person also dies or is for any reason unable to act, his legal representative may act.

History: Add, L 1969, ch 1066, § 1, eff Sept 1, 1970.

§ 406. Private foundation, as defined in the United States internal revenue code of 1954: provisions included in the certificate of incorporation

(a) The following provisions are hereby included in the certificate of incorporation of every domestic corporation, heretofore or hereafter formed, to which this chapter applies in whole or in part, and which is a "private foundation" as defined in section 509 of the United States internal revenue code of 1954 ("code"):

(1) The corporation shall distribute such amounts for each taxable year at such time and in such manner as not to subject the corporation to tax on undistributed income under section 4942 of the code.

(2) The corporation shall not engage in any act or self-dealing which is subject to tax under section 4941 of the code.

(3) The corporation shall not retain any excess business holdings which are subject to tax under section 4943 of the code.

(4) The corporation shall not make any investments in such manner as to subject the corporation to tax under section 4944 of the code.

(5) The corporation shall not make any taxable expenditures which are subject to tax under section 4945 of the code.

Except as provided in paragraph (b), this paragraph applies notwithstanding any other provision of the certificate of incorporation or any direction in a gift instrument.

(b) Paragraph (a) shall not apply to the extent that it conflicts with any mandatory direction in a gift instrument executed prior to the effective date of this section unless such conflicting direction is removed as impracticable under article eight of the estates, powers and trusts law or in any other manner provided by law. The absence of a specific provision in the gift instrument for the current use of the principal of the fund, or the presence in such an instrument of a provision, as to the principal of a fund, limited to the principal's being held, invested and reinvested, is not such a conflicting mandatory direction.

(b-1) A domestic, not-for-profit corporation that is a "private foundation" as defined in section 509 of the code and that is required by section 6104(d) of the code to make available for public inspection its annual return shall publish notice of the availability of such return for inspection. Such notice shall be published, not later than the day prescribed for filing such annual return (determined with regard to any extension of time for filing), in a newspaper designated by the clerk of the county in which the principal office of the private foundation is located, having general circulation in that county. When such county is located within a city with a population of one million or more, such designation shall be as though such notice were a notice of judicial proceedings. The notice shall state that the annual return of the private foundation is available at its principal office for inspection during regular business hours by any citizen who requests it within one hundred eighty days after the date of such publication, and shall state the address and the telephone number of the private foundation's principal office and the name of its principal manager. A copy or notice published in a newspaper other than the newspaper or newspapers designated by the county clerk shall not be deemed to be one of the publications required by this paragraph.

(c) All references in this section to sections of the code shall be to such sections as amended from time to time, or to corresponding provisions of subsequent internal revenue laws.

(d) Nothing in this section shall impair the rights and powers of the courts or the attorney-general of this state.

(e) For purposes of this section, the term gift instrument shall have the meaning set forth in section 551 (Definitions).

History: Add, L 1971, ch 331, § 1, eff June 1, 1971; amd, L 2000, ch 242, § 2, eff Jan 1, 2001, L 2005, ch 767, § 21, eff June 1, 2006, L 2006, ch 44, § 14, eff June 1, 2006, L 2010, ch 490, §§ 3, 4, eff Sept 17, 2010.

ARTICLE 5
CORPORATE FINANCE

History: Add, L 1969, ch 1066, § 1, eff Sept 1, 1970.

Schedule of sections, amd, L 1970, ch 847, § 15, eff Sept 1, 1970.

§ 501.   Stock and shares prohibited; membership certificates authorized

A corporation shall not have stock or shares or certificates for stock or for shares, but may issue non-transferable membership certificates or cards to evidence membership, whether or not connected with any financial contribution to the corporation, as provided in section 601 (Members). The fact that the corporation is a not-for-profit corporation, and that the membership certificate or card is non-transferable shall be noted conspicuously on the face or back of each such certificate or card.

History: Add, L 1969, ch 1066, § 1; amd, L 1970, ch 847, § 16, eff Sept 1, 1970.

CASE ANNOTATIONS

Non-profit corporation was statutorily prohibited from issuing shares, so a "shareholder's" assertion that she had acquired the shares of another member, giving her 50 percent of the shares in the corporation and creating a voting deadlock between herself and the corporation's directors, was incorrect. Spencer v Petrone (2002, A.D., 2d Dept) 747 N.Y.S.2d 569.

2003 amended by-laws of a non-profit corporation that owned an apartment building violated N.Y. Not-for-Profit Corp. Law § 602(f) and 611(e) because no shares could be issued pursuant to N.Y. Not-for-Profit Corp. Law § 501 and each member could have only one vote; it was improper to give petitioner families entitlement to an additional vote because they possessed an additional unit. Matter of Thakur v 210 Forsyth St. Hous. Dev. Fund Corp. (2007, Sup) 844 NYS2d 686.

Because plaintiff's "equity interest" in defendant corporation was a forbidden "stock or share" in a not-for-profit corporation, the agreement was therefore invalid; plaintiff therefore did not allege the existence of a valid contract to support a claim for breach of contract, and its complaint was properly dismissed. IDT Corp. v Touro College (2010, CA3 NJ) 2010 US App LEXIS 7627 (UNPUBLISHED).

§ 502.   Members' capital contributions

(a) The certificate of incorporation may provide that members, upon or subsequent to admission, shall make capital contributions in the amount specified therein. The requirement of a capital contribution may apply to all members, or to the members of a single class, or to members of different classes in different amounts or proportions.

(b) A member's capital contribution shall consist of money or other property, tangible or intangible, or labor or services actually received by or performed for the corporation or for its benefit or in its formation or reorganization, or a combination thereof. In the absence of fraud in the transaction, the judgment of the board as to the value of the consideration received by the corporation shall be conclusive.

(c) Neither obligations of the member for future payments nor future services shall constitute payment or part payment of a member's capital contribution.

(d) A member's capital contribution shall be evidenced by a capital certificate which shall be nontransferable, except that the certificate of incorporation of a non-charitable corporation may provide that its capital certificates, or some of them, may be transferable to other members with the consent of the corporation upon specified terms and conditions.

(e) A member's capital contribution shall not be repaid or redeemed by the corporation except upon dissolution of the corporation or upon redemption of the capital certificate as provided in this chapter. A corporation may provide in its certificate of incorporation that its capital certificates, or some of them, shall be redeemable, in whole or in part, at the option of the corporation only, at such price or prices (not to exceed the amount of the capital contribution), within such period or periods, and on such terms and conditions, not inconsistent with this chapter, as are stated in the certificate of incorporation.

History: Add, L 1969, ch 1066, § 1, eff Sept 1, 1970; amd, L 1971, ch 1058, § 10, L 1971, ch 1057, § 2, eff Sept 1, 1971, L 2013, ch 549, § 50, eff July 1, 2014.

§ 503.   Capital certificates

(a) Each capital certificate shall be signed by the chairman or vice-chairman of the board or the presi-

dent or a vice-president and the secretary or an assistant secretary or the treasurer or an assistant treasurer of the corporation, and may be sealed with the seal of the corporation or a facsimile thereof. The signatures of the officers upon a certificate may be facsimiles if the certificate is countersigned by a transfer agent or registered by a registrar other than the corporation itself or its employee. In case any officer who has signed or whose facsimile signature has been placed upon a certificate shall have ceased to be such officer before such certificate is issued it may be issued by the corporation with the same effect as if he were such officer at the date of issue.

(b) Each capital certificate shall when issued state upon the face thereof:

(1) The name of the member to whom issued.

(2) The amount of the member's capital contribution evidenced by such certificate.

(3) If appropriate, that the corporation is a non-charitable corporation, and that its certificate of incorporation provides that the capital certificate is transferable to other members with the consent of the corporation.

(4) The fact that the corporation is a not-for-profit corporation, and that the capital certificate is non-transferable or is transferable to other members, with the consent of the corporation, shall be noted conspicuously on the face or back of each such certificate.

(c) [Redesignated]

History: Add, L 1969, ch 1066, § 1, eff Sept 1, 1970; amd, L 1970, ch 847, § 17, eff Sept 1, 1970, L 2013, ch 549, § 51, eff July 1, 2014.

CASE ANNOTATIONS

Complaint against defendants was properly dismissed due to plaintiff's lack of standing to bring derivative action on behalf of not-for-profit cemetery corporation; plaintiff was not capital certificate holder under CLS N-PCL § 623(a) based on his status as land share certificate holder under CLS N-PCL § 1511(b) in that definition of capital certificates (CLS N-PCL § 503) does not include land share certificates, and land share certificates are not equivalent of capital certificates as they represent debt rather than equity. Harris v Lyke (1995, 4th Dept) 217 A.D.2d 982, 629 N.Y.S.2d 911, app den (1995) 87 N.Y.2d 801, 637 N.Y.S.2d 688, 661 N.E.2d 160

§ 504.   Subventions

(a) The certificate of incorporation may provide that the corporation shall be authorized by resolution of the board to accept subventions from members or non-members on terms and conditions not inconsistent with this chapter, and to issue certificates therefor. Subvention certificates shall be nontransferable unless such resolution provides that they shall be transferable, either at will or subject to specified restrictions.

(b) A subvention shall consist of money or other property, tangible or intangible, actually received by the corporation or expended for its benefit or for its formation or reorganization, or a combination thereof. In the absence of fraud in the transaction, the judgment of the board as to the value of the consideration received by the corporation shall be conclusive.

(c) The rights of holders of subvention certificates shall at all times be subordinate to the rights of creditors of the corporation.

(d) The resolution of the board may provide that holders of subvention certificates shall be entitled to a fixed or contingent periodic payment out of the corporate assets equal to a percentage of the original amount or value of the subvention, but such payment shall not exceed two-thirds of the maximum interest rate authorized pursuant to section 5-501 of the general obligations law.

(e) The resolution of the board may provide that a subvention shall be redeemable, in whole or in part, at the option of the corporation at such price or prices (not to exceed the original amount or value of the subvention plus any periodic payments due or accrued thereon), within such period or periods, and on such terms and conditions, not inconsistent with this chapter, as are stated in the resolution.

(f) The resolution of the board may provide that holders of all or some subvention certificates shall have the right to require the corporation after a specified period of time to redeem such certificates, in whole or in part, at a price or prices that do not exceed the original amount or value of the subvention plus any periodic payments due or accrued thereon, upon an affirmative showing that the financial condition of the corporation will permit the required payment to be made without impairment of its operations or injury to its creditors. The right to require redemption may in addition be conditioned upon the occurrence of a specified event. For the purpose of enforcing their rights under this paragraph, holders of subvention certificates shall be entitled to inspect the books and records of the corporation.

(g) Holders of subvention certificates, upon dissolution of the corporation, shall be entitled, after the claims of creditors have been satisfied, to a repayment of the original amount or value of the subvention plus any periodic payments due or accrued thereon, unless a lesser sum is specified in the certificate of incorporation or the resolution of the board concerning such subvention.

History: Add, L 1969, ch 1066, § 1, eff Sept 1, 1970.

§ 505.   Subvention certificates

(a) Each subvention certificate shall be signed by the chairman or a vice-chairman of the board or the president or a vice-president and the secretary or an assistant secretary or the treasurer or an assistant treasurer of the corporation, and may be sealed with the seal of the corporation or a facsimile therof. The signatures of the officers upon a certificate may be facsimiles if the certificate is countersigned by a transfer agent or registered by a registrar other than the corporation itself or its employees. In case any officer who has signed or whose facsimile signature

has been placed upon a certificate shall have ceased to be such officer before such certificate is issued, it may be issued by the corporation with the same effect as if he were such officer at the date of issue.

(b) Each subvention certificate shall when issued state upon the face thereof:

(1) The name of the person or persons to whom issued.

(2) The amount of the subvention evidenced by such certificate.

(3) The amount of the periodic payment thereon, if any, authorized by the resolution of the board.

(4) If appropriate, that the certificate is redeemable and a summary of the conditions for redemption at the option of the corporation or of the holder.

(5) If appropriate, that the certificate is transferable, either at will or subject to specified restrictions.

(6) [Redesignated]

(c) The fact that the corporation is a not-for-profit corporation and, where appropriate, that the certificate is transferable at will or subject to restrictions, shall be noted conspicuously on the face or back of each such certificate.

History: Add, L 1969, ch 1066, § 1, eff Sept 1, 1970; amd, L 1970, ch 847, § 18, eff Sept 1, 1970, L 2013, ch 549, § 52, eff July 1, 2014.

§ 506.   Bonds and security interests

(a) No corporation shall issue bonds except for money or other property, tangible or intangible, or labor or services actually received by or performed for the corporation or for its benefit or in its formation or reorganization, or a combination thereof. In the absence of fraud in the transaction, the judgment of the board as to the value of the consideration received by the corporation shall be conclusive.

(b) A corporation may pay reasonable interest on its bonds, may issue its bonds at a reasonable discount and may pay a reasonable premium for the redemption thereof prior to maturity, but the holders of its bonds shall not be entitled at any time to receive any part of the income or profit of the corporation nor at maturity to receive more than the principal sum thereof plus interest due and accrued thereon. In the absence of fraud in the transaction, the judgment of the board as to the reasonableness of any such interest, discount or premium shall be conclusive. However, with respect to bonds not a part of a public offering, notwithstanding the terms of the instrument, no member of a corporation shall be entitled to receive, directly or indirectly, as a holder or beneficiary of such bond, prior to maturity or redemption, more than simple interest thereon at a rate equal to the higher of (1) the maximum interest authorized pursuant to section 5-501 of the general obligations law or (2) one percent over the prime rate of interest generally prevailing on the interest due date in the Federal Reserve District of New York, nor at maturity or redemption, more than the principal sum thereof plus any interest, not exceeding the maximum interest herein specified, due and accrued thereon.

(c) A corporation may, in its certificate of incorporation or by-laws, confer upon the holders of any bonds issued or to be issued by the corporation, rights to inspect the corporate books and records and, upon default of interest or principal, to vote in the election of directors. The certificate of incorporation or the by-laws may apportion the number of votes that may be cast with respect to bonds on the basis of the amount of bonds held.

(d) The board may authorize any mortgage or pledge of, or the creation of a security interest in, all or any part of the corporation's personal property, or any interest therein. Unless the certificate of incorporation provides otherwise, no vote or consent of the members shall be required to approve such action by the board.

History: Add, L 1969, ch 1066, § 1, eff Sept 1, 1970.

Par (b), amd, L 1970, ch 847, § 19, L 1971, ch 1058, § 11, eff Sept 1, 1971.

Par (c), amd, L 1971, ch 1057, § 3, L 1971, ch 1058 § 11, eff Sept 1, 1971.

§ 507.   Fees, dues and assessments; fines and penalties

(a) If authorized by its certificate of incorporation or by-laws and subject to any limitations stated therein a corporation may levy initiation fees, dues and assessments on its members, whether or not they are voting members, and may impose reasonable fines or other penalties upon its members for violations of its rules and regulations.

(b) Initiation fees, dues or assessments may be levied on all classes of members alike or in different amounts or proportions for different classes of members, as the certificate of incorporation or the by-laws may provide, but in all cases the fees, dues and assessments payable by members of one class shall be determined upon the same basis.

(c) The certificate of incorporation or the by-laws may contain such provisions as are deemed necessary to enforce the collection of fees, dues, assessments, fines or other penalties, including provisions for the termination of membership, upon reasonable notice, for non-payment of such fees, dues, assessments, fines or other penalties, and provisions for reinstatement of membership.

(d) Subject to the provisions of this chapter, the certificate of incorporation may provide that members paying initiation fees, dues or assessments shall, upon dissolution of the corporation, have distributive rights in its assets. The distributive rights may be different for different classes of members, but in all cases the rights of members of one class shall be the same.

History: Add, L 1969, ch 1066, § 1, eff Sept 1, 1970, with substance derived from Mem Corp Law § 20; amd, L 1970, ch 847, § 20, eff Sept 1, 1970.

CASE ANNOTATIONS

1. Generally
2-5. [Reserved for future use]
6. Under former Membership Corporations Law § 21

1. Generally

Automatic suspension provided by a not-for-profit corporation's by-laws was unenforceable because it violated N.Y. Not-for-Profit Corp. Law § 507(c); it was undisputed that no notice was given to the members that had not paid dues, and, thus, pursuant to § 507(c), the votes of members who had not paid dues could not have been disqualified from voting an amendments to the by-laws based solely on that basis. Abraham v Diamond Dealers Club, Inc. (2010, Sup) 27 Misc 3d 663, 896 NYS2d 848, affd, motion den (2011, NY App Div, 1st Dept) 2011 NY Slip Op 92, 2011 NY App Div LEXIS 98.

Low balance surcharge and insufficient fund penalty imposed by not-for-profit corporation organized to provide for collective management of many of business and administrative responsibilities of individual chapters of college fraternities and sororities, which were imposed upon members who failed to contribute to or maintain designated minimum balance in fund set up to pay for goods and services, were properly imposed upon members as penalties authorized by Not-For-Profit Corporation Law § 507(a), where money collected from imposition of such penalties was not retained by corporation but was distributed among members in accordance with their participation in fund. Sigma Phi Soc. v Rensselaer Fraternity Managers Ass'n (1985, 3d Dept) 114 A.D.2d 711, 494 N.Y.S.2d 532

Townhouse developer was not collaterally estopped from challenging validity of foreclosure judgment for maintenance and special assessments entered against it following its voluntary filing for bankruptcy where central issue before Bankruptcy Court was motion of townhouse owners' association to lift stay of foreclosure sale, and parties did not litigate validity of association's underlying lien for assessments, which Bankruptcy Court simply presumed valid for purposes of resolving stay issue. Roxrun Estates, Inc. v Roxbury Run Village Asso. (1988, 3d Dept) 136 A.D.2d 162, 526 N.Y.S.2d 633, app den (1988) 72 N.Y.2d 808, 533 N.Y.S.2d 57, 529 N.E.2d 425

Automatic suspension provided by a not-for-profit corporation's by-laws was unenforceable because it violated N.Y. Not-for-Profit Corp. Law § 507(c); it was undisputed that no notice was given to the members that had not paid dues, and, thus, pursuant to § 507(c), the votes of members who had not paid dues could not have been disqualified from voting on amendments to the by-laws based solely on that basis. Abraham v Diamond Dealers Club, Inc. (2010, Sup) 896 NYS2d 848.

Supreme Court properly imposed reduced assessment on townhouse developer for maintenance of its unimproved lots (as compared to full rate which individual townhouse owners were required to pay for their improved lots) under rules of owners' association in which developer and individual owners were members as same class, even though CLS N-PCL § 507(b) requires that assessments payable by members must be determined on same basis, since rates were based on actual cost of maintaining properties. Roxrun Estates, Inc. v Roxbury Run Village Asso. (1988, 3d Dept) 136 A.D.2d 162, 526 N.Y.S.2d 633, app den (1988) 72 N.Y.2d 808, 533 N.Y.S.2d 57, 529 N.E.2d 425

Financial Industry Regulatory Authority, Inc. had sufficient authority under state corporation law to impose penalties on its members. Fiero v Fin. Indus. Regulatory, Auth., Inc. (2009, SD NY) 606 F Supp 2d 500.

2-5. [Reserved for future use]

6. Under former Membership Corporations Law § 21

A bylaw imposing a fine upon members of a milk association for not furnishing a certain quantity of milk is void. Monroe Dairy Ass'n v Webb (1899) 40 A.D. 49, 57 N.Y.S. 572

An attempt to enforce an involuntary payment of moneys by depriving members of certain privileges, under a levied "assessment," is not the collection of dues or fees authorized by this section. Kiowa Council, etc. v Great Council of New York, etc. (1928) 132 Misc 106, 228 N.Y.S. 256

An amendment to the bylaws of a membership corporation assessing each of the members thereof a certain sum for the purchase, equipment and maintenance of a home for aged members, is of no effect, where the power to purchase and maintain such a home was not granted under the original certificate of incorporation, and there has been no amendment of such certificate or legislative authorization of the proposed additional activity. Kiowa Council, etc. v Great Council of New York, etc. (1928) 132 Misc 106, 228 N.Y.S. 256

An assessment does not fall within the terms "dues" or "fees" as used in this section. In re Monroe Chapter, O. E. S. (1928) 132 Misc 109, 228 N.Y.S. 248

While the defendant contends that a by-law authorizing an assessment and providing that "there shall be an annual assessment due and payable on April first, which assessment shall be determined upon a vote of the club on the report made at the annual meeting by the Treasurer," assumed to provide for an assessment without authority in law, it is clear that this so-called assessment was to cover the expenses for the ensuing year and not to cover expenses already incurred, and consequently constitutes "fees" or "dues," which the plaintiff is authorized to levy. Rainbow Falls Fish & Game Club, Inc. v Clute (1941) 177 Misc 71, 29 N.Y.S.2d 948

The word "dues" with reference to membership corporations means the obligation to pay a sum to be fixed, usually by bylaws, at recurring intervals for maintenance of the organization, and dues so fixed become a debt by the member to the club. Associated General Contractors of America v Lapardo Bros. Excavating Contractors, Inc. (1964) 43 Misc. 2d 825, 252 N.Y.S.2d 486

A membership corporation may raise its dues in the discretion of the body authorized to make its bylaws and has a right to adopt a bylaw that no member may withdraw from membership unless by resignation in writing accompanied by all outstanding dues. Associated General Contractors of America v Lapardo Bros. Excavating Contractors, Inc. (1964) 43 Misc. 2d 825, 252 N.Y.S.2d 486

Where an organization under this law did not provide for enforcible regular assessments but made an extraordinary assessment in one year to pay for repairs and replacements without the usual reference to suspension of members for nonpayment of indebtedness, such an assessment was taxable under the meaning of 26 USC § 1712(a). City Athletic Club v United States (1957, CA2 NY) 242 F.2d 43, 57-1 USTC P 9485, 50 AFTR 1787

§ 508. Income from corporate activities

A corporation whose lawful activities involve among other things the charging of fees or prices for its services or products shall have the right to receive such income and, in so doing, may make an incidental profit. All such incidental profits shall be applied to the maintenance, expansion or operation of the lawful activities of the corporation, and in no case shall be divided or distributed in any manner whatsoever among the members, directors, or officers of the corporation.

History: Add, L 1969, ch 1066, § 1; amd, L 1970, ch 847, § 21, eff Sept 1, 1970.

CASE ANNOTATIONS

Grant of special use permit to college to renovate buildings and lease them to not for profit corporation for purposes of offering community instruction in art courses was proper under zoning ordinance authorizing use for bona fide educational purposes despite fact that school would not be approved by board of regents. Imbergamo v Barclay (1973) 77 Misc. 2d 188, 352 N.Y.S.2d 337

A subsidiary of the Urban Development Corporation may incorporate under the Business Corporation Law without forfeiting its public status. The subsidiary may not pay profits to private investors, and upon dissolution of the corporation, the assets belong to the State. 1980 Op Atty Gen Oct. 20

§ 509. Purchase, sale, mortgage and lease of real property

(a) No corporation shall purchase real property unless such purchase is authorized by the vote of a majority of directors of the board or of a majority of a committee authorized by the board, provided that if such property would, upon purchase thereof, constitute all, or substantially all, of the assets of the corporation, then the vote of two-thirds of the entire board shall be required, or, if there are twenty-one or more directors, the vote of a majority of the entire board shall be sufficient.

(b) No corporation shall sell, mortgage, lease, exchange or otherwise dispose of its real property unless authorized by the vote of a majority of directors of the board or of a majority of a committee authorized by the board; provided that if such property constitutes all, or substantially all, of the assets of the corporation, then the vote of two-thirds of the entire board shall be required, or, if there are twenty-one or more directors, the vote of a majority of the entire board shall be sufficient.

(c) If a corporation authorizes a committee to act pursuant to paragraphs (a) and (b) of this section, the committee shall promptly report any actions taken to the board, and in no event after the next regularly scheduled meeting of the board.

History: Add, L 1969, ch 1066, § 1, with substance derived from Mem Corp Law §§ 21, 22; amd, L 1991, ch 145, § 2, eff Jan 1, 1992, L 2013, ch 549, § 53, eff July 1, 2014.

CASE ANNOTATIONS

1. Generally
2. Evidence
3-10. [Reserved for future use]
11. Under former Membership Corporations Law § 21
12. – Authority to purchase, lease, or sell; directors, trustees
13. – – President
14. – – Members
15. – Actions involving lease or sale
16. – Miscellaneous
17. Under former Membership Corporations Law § 22

1. Generally

In mortgage foreclosure action arising from loans made by plaintiff bank to member of defendant not-for-profit corporation who falsely represented that he was acting on behalf of and with authorization from defendant when he repeatedly borrowed money in defendant's name, court properly dismissed complaint and vacated mortgages following nonjury trial where (1) corporate resolutions on which plaintiff relied in granting loans were patently fraudulent and invalid, (2) member's fraudulent transactions were made without defendant's knowledge, (3) plaintiff made no factual showing that defendant was responsible for appearance of authority to conduct such transactions, and (4) plaintiff failed to take even minimal steps to discover actual scope of member's authority. Fleet Bank v Consola, Riccitello, Squadere Post No. 17 Inc. (2000, 3d Dept) 268 A.D.2d 627, 701 N.Y.S.2d 182

In real estate broker's action for sale commission, not-for-profit corporation could not invoke provisions of N-PCL § 509 to avoid contract where statute did not prohibit corporate officers from contracting with brokers to procure a purchaser, where corporate committee responsible for selling property had authority under N-PCL § 712 to act on board's behalf, and where, under general agency principles, committee had apparent authority to bind corporation. Shear v National Rifle Asso. (1979) 196 US App DC 344, 606 F.2d 1251

A religious corporation must obtain leave of court to sell any of its real estate or any interest therein to a municipality for a public purpose. 1982 Op Atty Gen Feb 19 (informal)

New York City Public Development Corporation does not have authority to delegate approval of real property transactions to executive committee or another standing committee of board of directors. 1988 Op Atty Gen no.88-35 (Informal)

2. Evidence

Two members of a limited liability company (LLC) were not entitled to summary judgment on a claim under this statute by the estate of a third member of the LLC, seeking a distribution upon withdrawal, because the only evidence supporting the members' claim that they offered the estate the fair value of the decedent's interest in the LLC as of the date of withdrawal was their attorney's affirmation, which had no probative or evidentiary value. Deerin v Ocean Rich Foods, LLC, 2018 N.Y. App. Div. LEXIS 820 (N.Y. App. Div. 2d Dep't 2018).

3-10. [Reserved for future use]

11. Under former Membership Corporations Law § 21

Compliance with the statute is absolutely necessary to the validity of any mortgage of real estate which corporations of the class described therein shall execute and deliver. Dudley v Congregation of Third Order of St. Francis (1893) 138 N.Y. 451, 34 N.E. 281

This section merely imposes a limitation on the power of a cemetery corporation organized under the Membership Corporations Law to convey away its property, and is in no sense to be considered a grant of power not previously enjoyed by such a corporation. Application of Kensico Cemetery (1948) 193 Misc 479, 83 N.Y.S.2d 73, revd on other grounds (1949) 275 A.D. 681, 86 N.Y.S.2d 737, affd (1949) 299 N.Y. 752, 87 N.E.2d 670

A chamber of commerce, although not specifically granted the power by its charter to own real property, had such power under either the Membership Corporations Law or the General Corporation Law, it being incorporated as a membership corporation. Corning Chamber of Commerce v Bohoy (1955) 207 Misc 789, 139 N.Y.S.2d 503

An agricultural society may lease real estate for a term not greater than five years, without leave of court, under former § 13 from which this section is derived and leasing is not violation of this section. 1911 Ops Atty Gen 432

While a membership corporation may acquire real property for its corporate purposes, it may not use such property, as by way of lease, for a purpose essentially of a business nature for profit. 1953 Ops Atty Gen May 14 (informal)

12. – Authority to purchase, lease, or sell; directors, trustees

A soldiers' monument corporation was permitted to sell its real property where, before title closing, a majority of the directors authorized the sale under the terms contained in the contract. The evidence established the adequacy of the consideration and that the interests of the corporation would be promoted by the sale. Application of Staten Island War Memorial Asso. (1955) 286 A.D. 887, 143 N.Y.S.2d 100, app den (1955) 286 A.D. 1017, 145 N.Y.S.2d 318 and resettlement den (1955) 286 A.D. 966, 146 N.Y.S.2d 474

The majority of directors of a membership corporation may authorize a sale of real estate, and provisions of Gen. Corp. Law, § 71, in regard to a two-thirds vote are inapplicable. In re Application of Diocesan Auxiliary (1922) 119 Misc 610, 197 N.Y.S. 750

A buyer is entitled to inquire into the question of whether the required number of trustees approved the sale to the buyer, since this is a matter peculiarly within the knowledge of the seller. Bounding Home Corp. v Chapin Home for Aged & Infirm. (1959) 19 Misc. 2d 653, 191 N.Y.S.2d 722

13. – – President

Resolutions adopted by the directors of a membership corporation to the effect that the president "be empowered to take charge of the fiscal affairs of the corporation" and that he "has authority to sign and execute all documents," standing alone and without other evidence, are not sufficient to authorize him to enter into an agreement for the purchase of real property by the corporation. Catholic Foreign Mission Soc. v Oussani (1915) 215 N.Y. 1, 109 N.E. 80

14. – – Members

A corporation could impose further requirements in its bylaws regarding the leasing of real property than those imposed by this section. So where a membership corporation's bylaws limited the powers of its directors to a great degree and required a majority vote of the members themselves on almost every conceivable problem, a lease of real property without membership approval never had a valid inception. In re Trapasso Oldsmobile, Inc. (1958) 4 N.Y.2d 133, 173 N.Y.S.2d 10, 149 N.E.2d 515

15. – Actions involving lease or sale

A member of a membership corporation composed of the property holders of a certain community, which corporation performs many of the functions ordinarily performed by a municipal government, has the right to maintain an action in equity to restrain a contemplated sale of all the real property of the corporation to a business corporation in exchange for shares in the business corporation which are to be divided among the members of the membership corporation. Richter v Sea Gate Asso. (1923) 207 A.D. 573, 202 N.Y.S. 68

In an action for breach of an implied warranty of authority by the president and treasurer of a membership corporation to execute a lease for five years with a two year renewal and also a purchase option, the complaint must allege facts showing that the contract is one which the law would enforce against the principal, and the facts required by this section and Gen. Corp. Law, § 50. Yorkville Square Club, Inc. v Lichtenberger (1931) 140 Misc 348, 250 N.Y.S. 571

16. – Miscellaneous

The commissioners of a fire district may lease a firehouse owned by a volunteer fire company. 1945 Ops St Compt 584

A town may sell a portion of its property to an incorporated fire company for the construction of a firehouse and subsequently lease space therein for town purposes. 1953 Ops St Compt File #6153

17. Under former Membership Corporations Law § 22

A membership corporation could convey portions of its real property to members of the corporation, but it could not give more than is authorized by law, and a power reserved to change restrictions could not be exercised to make certain substantial alterations. Resnick v Croton Park Colony, Inc. (1955) 3 Misc. 2d 109, 151 N.Y.S.2d 328

§ 510.   Disposition of all or substantially all assets

(a) A sale, lease, exchange or other disposition of all, or substantially all, the assets of a corporation may be made upon such terms and conditions and for such consideration, which may consist in whole or in part of cash or other property, real or personal, including shares, bonds or other securities of any other domestic or foreign corporation or corporations of any kind, as may be authorized in accordance with the following procedure:

(1) If there are members entitled to vote thereon, the board shall adopt a resolution recommending such sale, lease, exchange or other disposition. The resolution shall specify the terms and conditions of the proposed transaction, including the consideration to be received by the corporation and the eventual disposition to be made of such consideration, together with a statement that the dissolution of the corporation is or is not contemplated thereafter. The resolution shall be submitted to a vote at a meeting of members entitled to vote thereon, which may be either an annual or a special meeting. Notice of the meeting shall be given to each member and each holder of subvention certificates or bonds of the corporation, whether or not entitled to vote. At such meeting by two-thirds vote as provided in paragraph (c) of section 613 (Vote of members) the members may approve the proposed transaction according to the terms of the resolution of the board, or may approve such sale, lease, exchange or other disposition and

may authorize the board to modify the terms and conditions thereof.

(2) If there are no members entitled to vote thereon, such sale, lease, exchange or other disposition shall be authorized by the vote of at least two-thirds of the entire board, provided that if there are twenty-one or more directors, the vote of a majority of the entire board shall be sufficient.

(3) If the corporation is, or would be if formed under this chapter, classified as a charitable corporation under section 201 (Purposes) such sale, lease, exchange or other disposition shall in addition require approval of the attorney general or the supreme court in the judicial district or of the county court of the county in which the corporation has its office or principal place of carrying out the purposes for which it was formed in accordance with section 511 (Petition for court approval) or section 511-a (Petition for attorney general approval) of this article.

(b) After such authorization the board in its discretion may abandon such sale, lease, exchange or other disposition of assets, subject to the rights of third parties under any contract relating thereto, without further action or approval.

History: Add, L 1969, ch 1066, § 1, eff Sept 1, 1970, with substance derived from Mem Corp Law § 21; amd, L 1970, ch 847, § 22, eff Sept 1, 1970, L 1972, ch 961, § 5, eff Sept 1, 1972, L 2013, ch 549, § 54, eff July 1, 2014.

CASE ANNOTATIONS

1. Generally
2-5. [Reserved for future use]
6. Under former Membership Corporations Law § 21

1. Generally
Charitable foundation's sale of 34 acres of land to defendants fell within ambit of CLS N-PCL §§ 510 and 511 where property in question was foundation's largest, most significant and single most valuable possession, and its sale for inadequate consideration severely hampered foundation's ability to carry out its mission of constructing and operating senior citizens' center thereon; accordingly, contract of sale and deed were null and void where transaction was never subjected to requisite judicial scrutiny, and there was no proof that it was approved by foundation's membership or board of trustees. Rose Ocko Found., Inc. v Lebovits (1999) 93 N.Y.2d 997, 696 N.Y.S.2d 107, 718 N.E.2d 412

Prior arbitration proceeding before rabbinical panel and subsequent proceeding to confirm arbitration award were not res judicata to proceeding under CLS Relig Corp § 12 and CLS N-PCL § 511 since prior proceedings did not address issue of whether proposed sale of religious organization's real property met requirements of Religious Corporations Law and Not-for-Profit Corporation Law, and CLS Relig Corp § 12 and CLS N-PCL §§ 510 and 511 expressly make authorization by Supreme Court or County Court condition precedent to sale of property, so that rabbinical panel had no authority to give such authorization. Agudist Council of Greater New York v Imperial Sales Co. (1990, 2d Dept) 158 A.D.2d 683, 551 N.Y.S.2d 955, app den (1990) 76 N.Y.2d 707, 560 N.Y.S.2d 989, 561 N.E.2d 889

Where a not-for-profit seller had not met the requirements of N.Y. Not-For-Profit Corp. Law §§ 510(a), 511(d) by, inter alia, obtaining leave of court to sell certain property, a buyer could not obtain specific performance of a real property sale contract; therefore, the buyer's N.Y. C.P.L.R. 3215 motion for a default judgment was denied. Century 2000 Custom Home Builders & Developers, LLC. v United Muslim Org. of N.Y., Inc. (2003, Sup) 1 Misc 3d 890, 772 N.Y.S.2d 186

When a court was asked to approve the sale of the assets of a not-for-profit corporation, under N.Y. Not-for-Profit Corp. Law § 510(3), it also had to review, in the same proceeding, termination payment clauses or similar damages or reimbursement provisions in the sales contract under the standard in N.Y. Not-for-Profit Corp. Law § 511(d) of fairness, reasonableness and furtherance of corporate purpose, as provisions of this type could be valuable to not-for-profits but judicial scrutiny would protect not-for-profits against board actions that might be adverse to the entity's well-being. 64th Assocs., L.L.C. v Manhattan Eye, Ear & Throat Hosp. (2004) 2 NY3d 585, 780 N.Y.S.2d 746, 813 N.E.2d 887

2-5. [Reserved for future use]
6. Under former Membership Corporations Law § 21
Where a membership corporation leased a hall to be used as a theater and later relying upon the lease, the building was completely remodeled, the court would not void the lease on the ground that it was entered by the trustees improvidently by reason of their inexperience in business affairs and that the rent reserved in the lease was inadequate where no claim of fraud is made even though the provisions of this section was not followed in that no approval of the lease was obtained from the supreme court. Application of Norbury Theatre Corp. (1952) 279 A.D. 827, 109 N.Y.S.2d 291

A lease executed by a membership corporation for a term of more than five years is not void even though it is not confirmed by a court and it may be confirmed in a proceeding under this section. Application of Trapasso Oldsmobile, Inc. (1956, 4th Dept) 2 A.D.2d 166, 153 N.Y.S.2d 753

A lease from a membership corporation for a term of five years, but not effective until a future date, is a lease "for more than five years" and is subject to court approval. Application of Trapasso Oldsmobile, Inc. (1956, 4th Dept) 2 A.D.2d 166, 153 N.Y.S.2d 753

A lease of cemetery lands for mining purposes is not only ultra vires but is in contravention of former § 13 from which this section is derived and inconsistent with the objects and purposes for which the lessor was organized, and the court is without power to sanction such a lease without explicit legislative authority. Briggs v Bloomingdale Cemetery Ass'n (1920) 113 Misc 685, 185 N.Y.S. 348, affd (1924) 208 A.D. 761, 202 N.Y.S. 918

In a proceeding under this section to confirm two mortgages executed by a membership corporation, since dissolved initially organized to provide a school building for special guidance of mentally and emotionally handicapped children on a nonprofit basis, the mortgages in question were confirmed on the basis of authorization by the Board of Trustees and court approval and findings that the corporation was not insolvent when the mortgages were executed. Application of Eleven Bros. Realty Corp. (1961) 28 Misc. 2d 201, 213 N.Y.S.2d 1004

This section does not require that a copy of the proposed mortgage be presented to the court and approved by it. Harper v Larchmont Yacht Club (1942, Sup) 38 N.Y.S.2d 505

A proposed twelve-year lease of lands owned by a membership corporation and used as a park and playground area to private individuals for the construction of a swimming pool could not be made without leave of the Supreme Court which could be obtained only after satisfactory proof that the transaction is legal and to the advantage of the corporation. Such approval would have the effect of a visitation of the Supreme Court with respect to that transaction. Petition of Moss (1952, Sup) 114 N.Y.S.2d 314

A religious corporation must obtain leave of court to sell any of its real estate or any interest therein to a municipality for a public purpose. 1982 Op Atty Gen Feb 19 (informal)

A membership corporation with leave of the Supreme Court may convey its real property to a town without consideration. 1947 Ops St Compt 156

Conveyance of property of cemetery associations to a town should be made only after prior judicial approval. 1954 Ops St Compt File #6779

Permission of the Court must be obtained by a religious corporation or a membership corporation before it may grant an easement in its real property. 1955 Ops St Compt File #7735

A fire company may, under certain conditions, lease a portion of its real property to a fire district in which the property is located for parking of vehicles of members and residents of the fire district while in attendance at social functions at the district fire house. Where the rent under any such lease does not exceed the amount of carrying, maintenance and depreciation charges, the leased portion may remain or become tax exempt. 1968 Ops St Compt File #252

§ 511. Petition for court approval

(a) To obtain court approval to sell, lease, exchange or otherwise dispose of all or substantially all its assets, a corporation shall present a verified petition to the supreme court of the judicial district, or the county court of the county, wherein the corporation has its office or principal place of carrying out the purposes for which it was formed. The petition shall set forth:

1. The name of the corporation, the law under or by which it was incorporated.

2. The names of its directors and principal officers, and their places of residence.

3. The activities of the corporation.

4. A description, with reasonable certainty, of the assets to be sold, leased, exchanged, or otherwise disposed of, or a statement that it is proposed to sell, lease, exchange or otherwise dispose of all or substantially all the corporate assets more fully described in a schedule attached to the petition; and a statement of the fair value of such assets, and the amount of the corporation's debts and liabilities and how secured.

5. The consideration to be received by the corporation and the disposition proposed to be made thereof, together with a statement that the dissolution of the corporation is or is not contemplated thereafter.

6. That the consideration and the terms of the sale, lease, exchange or other disposition of the assets of the corporation are fair and reasonable to the corporation, and that the purposes of the corporation, or the interests of its members will be promoted thereby, and a concise statement of the reasons therefor.

7. That such sale, lease, exchange or disposition of corporate assets, has been recommended or authorized by vote of the directors in accordance with law, at a meeting duly called and held, as shown in a schedule annexed to the petition setting forth a copy of the resolution granting such authority with a statement of the vote thereon.

8. Where the consent of members of the corporation is required by law, that such consent has been given, as shown in a schedule annexed to the petition setting forth a copy of such consent, if in writing, or of a resolution giving such consent, adopted at a meeting of members duly called and held, with a statement of the vote thereon.

9. A request for court approval to sell, lease, exchange or otherwise dispose of all or substantially all the assets of the corporation as set forth in the petition.

(b) Upon presentation of the petition, the court shall direct that a minimum of fifteen days notice be given by mail or in person to the attorney general, and in its discretion may direct that notice of the application be given, personally or by mail, to any person interested therein, as member, officer or creditor of the corporation. The court shall have authority to shorten the time for service on the attorney general upon a showing of good cause. The notice shall specify the time and place, fixed by the court, for a hearing upon the application. Any person interested, whether or not formally notified, may appear at the hearing and show cause why the application should not be granted.

(c) If the corporation be insolvent, or if its assets be insufficient to liquidate its debts and liabilities in full, the application shall not be granted unless all the creditors of the corporation shall have been served, personally or by mail, with a notice of the time and place of the hearing.

(d) If it shall appear, to the satisfaction of the court, that the consideration and the terms of the transaction are fair and reasonable to the corporation and that the purposes of the corporation or the interests of the members will be promoted, it may authorize the sale, lease, exchange or other disposition of all or substantially all the assets of the corporation, as described in the petition, for such consideration and upon such terms as the court may prescribe. The order of the court shall direct the disposition of the consideration to be received thereunder by the corporation.

History: Add, L 1969, ch 1066, § 1, eff Sept 1, 1970, with substance derived from Gen Corp Law §§ 50, 51, 52, 53; amd, L 1970, ch 847, § 23, L 1972, ch 961, eff Sept 1, 1972, L 1985, ch 102, § 1, eff May 21, 1985, L 2013, ch 549, § 55, eff July 1, 2014.

CASE ANNOTATIONS

1. Generally
2-10. [Reserved for future use]
11. Under former General Corporation Law § 50
12. – Authority to act for corporation
13. – Petition for approval of sale
14. – – Decision of court
15. – Proceeding to confirm unauthorized sale
16. – Stockholder action to set aside sale
17. – Specific performance of contract of sale
18. – Miscellaneous
19. Under former General Corporation Law § 52

1. Generally

Charitable foundation's sale of 34 acres of land to defendants fell within ambit of CLS N-PCL §§ 510 and 511 where property in question was foundation's largest, most significant and single most valuable possession, and its sale for inadequate consideration severely hampered foundation's ability to carry out its mission of constructing and operating senior citizens' center thereon; accordingly, contract of sale and deed were null and void where transaction was never subjected to requisite judicial scrutiny, and there was no proof that it was approved by foundation's membership or board of trustees. Rose Ocko Found., Inc. v Lebovits (1999) 93 N.Y.2d 997, 696 N.Y.S.2d 107, 718 N.E.2d 412

Plaintiff is not entitled to specific performance of a contract to sell real property owned by defendant and upon which its church edifice was erected where, despite the fact that the contract was fair and reasonable when made, the conveyance would be detrimental to the purpose of defendant corporation and the interests of its members. Church of God v Fourth Church of Christ, Scientist (1980, 2d Dept) 76 A.D.2d 712, 431 N.Y.S.2d 834, affd (1981) 54 N.Y.2d 742, 442 N.Y.S.2d 986, 426 N.E.2d 480

In action by prospective purchasers for specific performance of religious corporation's contract to sell property, defended by religious corporation on ground that its trustees had not approved sale as required by CLS Relig Corp § 12 and CLS N-PCL § 511, prospective purchasers could not be bound by findings of rabbinical court (acting as arbitrator of internal dispute among trustees over issue of whether approval had been given) where prospective purchasers were not parties to arbitration and thus had no opportunity to litigate issue; accordingly, religious corporation was not entitled to dismissal of complaint, since "legitimate question" still existed as to whether trustees had validly voted to authorize sale. Levovitz v Yeshiva Beth Henoch, Inc. (1986, 2d Dept) 120 A.D.2d 289, 508 N.Y.S.2d 196, later proceeding (1988, BC ED NY) 86 BR 755, 17 BCD 1162, CCH Bankr L Rptr P 72371

At trial of action by prospective purchasers for specific performance of religious corporation's contract to sell property, it would not be necessary to litigate questions of fairness of contract's terms and its promotion of interests of religious corporation (as required by CLS N-PCL § 511), since such questions had been determined by prior Supreme Court order approving sale of property, and that order had never been challenged by parties. Levovitz v Yeshiva Beth Henoch, Inc. (1986, 2d Dept) 120 A.D.2d 289, 508 N.Y.S.2d 196, later proceeding (1988, BC ED NY) 86 BR 755, 17 BCD 1162, CCH Bankr L Rptr P 72371

In determining whether to approve religious corporation's sale of real property under CLS Relig Corp § 12 and CLS N-PCL § 511, court must consider whether bargain was fair and reasonable at time it was entered into and whether sale of property would presently benefit religious corporation (church) and promote best interests of its members, who were real parties in interest. Rende & Esposito Consultants, Inc. v St. Augustine's Roman Catholic Church (1987, 2d Dept) 131 A.D.2d 740, 516 N.Y.S.2d 959

Prior arbitration proceeding before rabbinical panel and subsequent proceeding to confirm arbitration award were not res judicata to proceeding under CLS Relig Corp § 12 and CLS N-PCL § 511 since prior proceedings did not address issue of whether proposed sale of religious organization's real property met requirements of Religious Corporations Law and Not-for-Profit Corporation Law, and CLS Relig Corp § 12 and CLS N-PCL §§ 510 and 511 expressly make authorization by Supreme Court or County Court condition precedent to sale of property, so that rabbinical panel had no authority to give such authorization. Agudist Council of Greater New York v Imperial Sales Co. (1990, 2d Dept) 158 A.D.2d 683, 551 N.Y.S.2d 955, app den (1990) 76 N.Y.2d 707, 560 N.Y.S.2d 989, 561 N.E.2d 889

Religious corporation cannot invalidate ultra vires, but otherwise lawful, transfer of property if transfer was duly approved or authorized by judge; religious corporation's remedy is to sue its misbehaving corporate officers. Congregation Yetev Lev D'Satmar v 26 Adar N.B. Corp. (1996, 2d Dept) 219 A.D.2d 186, 641 N.Y.S.2d 680, app den (1996) 88 N.Y.2d 808, 647 N.Y.S.2d 713, 670 N.E.2d 1345 and related proceeding (1999, 2d Dept) 265 A.D.2d 360, 696 N.Y.S.2d 496, 28 Media L R 1126

In action brought by plaintiff, religious organization, seeking, inter alia, to rescind sale of its property on ground that agreement with buyer, which made substantial changes to terms of court-approved sale, was not court-approved, and to void mortgages on property, court erred in dismissing counterclaims alleging that plaintiff negligently failed to inform mortgagee of agreement and that had he been informed of agreement he would not have made loans to buyer since fact issue existed as to whether mortgagee's reliance on plaintiff's negligent misrepresentation was justified. Salesian Soc'y, Inc. v Nutmeg Partners Ltd. (2000, 2d Dept) 271 A.D.2d 671, 706 N.Y.S.2d 459

Not-for-profit hospitals and not-for-profit corporations that sought to affiliate under newly created common parent corporation, which would assume certain statutory powers under Not-For-Profit Corporation Law including power to appoint and/or remove directors and approve amendments to respective certificates of incorporation and bylaws, were properly granted summary judgment declaring that proposed affiliation did not require notification to Attorney General and court approval under CLS N-PCL §§ 510, 511, 804 and 805. Nathan Littauer Hosp. Ass'n v Spitzer (2001, 3d Dept) 287 A.D.2d 202, 734 N.Y.S.2d 671, motion gr (NY) 2002 N.Y. LEXIS 942 and app den (NY) 2002 N.Y. LEXIS 940

In determining pursuant to N-PCL § 511 whether a church had leave of court to sell a building, the court determined that the consideration in terms of the transactions were fair and reasonable to the church at the time the contract was made where the fair market value of the building at that time was $2,000,000 and the amended contract price was $2,200,000. In re Church of St. Francis de Sales (1981, Sup) 110 Misc. 2d 511, 442 N.Y.S.2d 741

A contract for the sale of real property owned by defendant, a nonprofit organization of fraternal lodges, which was properly executed by the corporation president but never delivered to plaintiff purchaser, would not be a valid contract, since the mere signing of the instrument by the parties, not in each other's presence, without more, did not evince the necessary intent, since the failure to satisfy an express condition precedent conditioning the sale upon a final determination of a pending action brought by a faction of defendant's organization opposed to the sale rendered the contract void, since the court had not approved of the sale, which represented substantially all the assets of the corporation, as required by N-PCL § 511, and since the proposed sale would not benefit the corporation or promote the best interests of its members at the present time. Manhattan Theatre Club, Inc. v Bohemian Benevolent & Literary Asso. (1983, Sup) 120 Misc. 2d 1094, 467 N.Y.S.2d 143, affd (1984, 1st Dept) 102 A.D.2d 788, 478 N.Y.S.2d 274, affd (1985) 64 N.Y.2d 1069, 489 N.Y.S.2d 877, 479 N.E.2d 222

Prospective purchaser of church property is not properly interested person under CLS N-PCL § 511 and purchaser's due process rights are not violated by failure to give purchaser notice of hearing at which court disapproves contract on basis of inadequate consideration or to allow purchaser to otherwise participate in hearing. Wolkoff v Church of St. Rita (1986, Sup) 132 Misc. 2d 464, 505 N.Y.S.2d 327, affd (1987, 2d Dept) 133 A.D.2d 267, 518 N.Y.S.2d 1020

Court denied CLS N-PCL § 511 application to approve sale of acute care specialty teaching hospital to for-profit hospital which would open breast cancer facility and to real estate developer which planned to use remaining real estate for apartment building, as (1) transaction could not be deemed "fair and reasonable," even if real estate was fairly valued, where petitioner's board of directors failed to account for significant value of hospital as going concern, (2) proposed sale did not promote "purposes of the corporation," in absence of reasoned and studied determination that there was lack of need for hospital or that financial difficulties made it impossible to ensure hospital's survival, and (3) board failed to properly consider various alternatives which would have preserved hospital's mission. Manhattan Eye, Ear & Throat Hosp. v Spitzer (1999, Sup) 186 Misc. 2d 126, 715 N.Y.S.2d 575

Article 78 proceeding, challenging sale and proposed demolition of building of cultural and historical significance based on respondents' alleged noncompliance with CLS N-PCL § 511 and CLS PHRPL § 14.09(c), was dismissed as premature where new owner had neither applied for nor received any demolition permit. Historic Dist. Council, Inc. v Spitzer (2000, Sup) 187 Misc. 2d 455, 722 N.Y.S.2d 687

Where a not-for-profit seller had not met the requirements of N.Y. Not-For-Profit Corp. Law §§ 510(a), 511(d) by, inter alia, obtaining leave of court to sell certain property, a buyer could not obtain specific performance of a real property sale contract; therefore, the buyer's N.Y. C.P.L.R. 3215 motion for a default judgment was denied. Century 2000 Custom Home Builders & Developers, LLC. v United Muslim Org. of N.Y., Inc. (2003, Sup) 1 Misc 3d 890, 772 N.Y.S.2d 186

When a court was asked to approve the sale of the assets of a not-for-profit corporation, under N.Y. Not-for-Profit Corp. Law § 510(3), it also had to review, in the same proceeding, termination payment clauses or similar damages or reimbursement provisions in the sales contract under the standard in N.Y. Not-for-Profit Corp. Law § 511(d) of fairness, reasonableness and furtherance of corporate purpose, as provisions of this type could be valuable to not-for-profits but judicial scrutiny would protect not-for-profits against board actions that might be adverse to the entity's well-being. 64th Assocs., L.L.C. v Manhattan Eye, Ear & Throat Hosp. (2004) 2 NY3d 585, 780 N.Y.S.2d 746, 813 N.E.2d 887

Deeds used by respondent-appellant to purportedly take title to certain property were null and void because respondent-appellant did not provide evidence showing that the putative grantors had an interest in the property that could be conveyed to respondent-appellant, and no evidence showed the putative grantors of the deed ever had legal title to the property. Furthermore, the conveyance of the property from the former owner/mortgagor religious not-for-profit corporation was ineffective because neither judicial consent nor consent from the state attorney general was obtained for the sale as required under N.Y. Relig. Corp. Law § 12 and N.Y. Not-for-Profit Corp. Law § 511. Wiggs v Williams (2007, 1st Dept) 36 App Div 3d 570, 828 NYS2d 397.

Proceeding to authorize the sale of real property pursuant to N.Y. Not-For-Profit Corp. Law § 511 was remitted for a hearing to determine whether the premises' authorized sale would meet the principles of protecting the beneficiaries of a charitable organization from loss through unwise bargains and from perversion of the use of its property. Matter of Prospect Hgts. Hous. Dev. Fund Corp. (2007, 2d Dept) 38 App Div 3d 781, 833 NYS2d 132

A religious corporation must obtain leave of court to sell any of its real estate or any interest therein to a municipality for a public purpose. 1982 Op Atty Gen Feb 19 (informal)

2-10. [Reserved for future use]

11. Under former General Corporation Law § 50

A mere exchange of a member's right to share in the property of a membership corporation for a stock interest in a realty corporation to be formed, which interest would be less than the share in the property of the membership corporation, is not a "sale" within the contemplation of this section. Richter v Sea Gate Ass'n (1923) 120 Misc 307, 199 N.Y.S. 303, affd (1923) 207 A.D. 573, 202 N.Y.S. 68

This section merely imposes a limitation on the power of a cemetery corporation organized under the membership corporation law to convey away its property, and is in no sense to be considered a grant of power previously not enjoyed by such a corporation. Application of Kensico Cemetery (1948) 193 Misc 479, 83 N.Y.S.2d 73, revd on other grounds (1949) 275 A.D. 681, 86 N.Y.S.2d 737, affd (1949) 299 N.Y. 752, 87 N.E.2d 670

12. – Authority to act for corporation

For an extension of a lease to be the act of a corporation, the person signing for the corporation must be authorized to do the act of the corporation, and whether or not he has been so authorized must be determined according to the general corporate law and is not affected by the General Obligations Law. Once it is determined that the signer was authorized to sign for the corporation, the corporation has signed and the statute is satisfied. Commission on Ecumenical Mission & Relations of United Presbyterian Church v Roger Gray, Ltd. (1970, 1st Dept) 34 A.D.2d 94, 309 N.Y.S.2d 225

A buyer is entitled to enquire into the question of whether the required number of seller's trustees approved of the sale to the buyer, since this is a matter peculiarly within the knowledge of the seller. Bounding Home Corp. v Chapin Home for Aged & Infirm. (1959) 19 Misc. 2d 653, 191 N.Y.S.2d 722

13. – Petition for approval of sale

Even though a church's deed of property to a minister was invalid due to the fact that the church did not seek court approval of the transfer, nor was the New York Attorney General notified of the transfer, the minister, as the owner of record, was properly notified of a tax foreclosure proceeding. Matter of City of Hudson (2014, 3d Dept) 114 App Div 3d 1106, 981 NYS2d 225, app dismd (2014) 23 NY3d 984, 990 NYS2d 462, 13 NE3d 1048.

Petition for approval of church conveyance did not comply with this section, where the secretary's certificate did not show that the sale was authorized by a vote of at least two thirds of the board of directors, and also failed to state, that the interests of the church corporation was promoted by the sale. Application of Margolin (1959) 16 Misc. 2d 961, 183 N.Y.S.2d 36

The facts required to be set forth in a petition under this section are those facts which exist at the time of the presentment of the petition. Wilson v Ebenezer Baptist Church, Inc. (1959) 17 Misc. 2d 607, 187 N.Y.S.2d 861

14. – – Decision of court

The court in determining whether a sale of real property by a religious corporation is in the best interest of the corporation will take into consideration the circumstances surrounding the transaction. Sun Assets Corp. v English Evangelical Lutheran Church of Ascension (1959) 19 Misc. 2d 187, 185 N.Y.S.2d 695

15. – Proceeding to confirm unauthorized sale

Where at the time of the sale of real property by a religious corporation, the corporation failed to obtain the permission of the court to sell the property, proceedings for confirmation of the conveyance were referred to a referee to inquire into whether it was for the best interest of the corporation to sell, the reasons for the sale, whether the corporation was solvent, whether consideration was adequate and how the proceeds were to be used, and the oral consent of the religious corporation's attorney was not sufficient. In re Application of Barusek (1956) 1 Misc. 2d 950, 149 N.Y.S.2d 420

16. – Stockholder action to set aside sale

A stockholder's derivative action to set aside a conveyance of real property by the corporation on the ground that it was not made with unanimous approval of the directors and stockholders because plaintiff, one of them, had not consented to the sale, was properly dismissed on the merits where it appeared that plaintiff attended the closing and participated in the sale, her conduct being tantamount to formal approval of the sale. Bradley v East Williston Shopping Center, Inc. (1961, 2d Dept) 15 A.D.2d 560, 222 N.Y.S.2d 943

17. – Specific performance of contract of sale

The court cannot bypass the submission of a petition under this section and grant specific performance of a contract of sale of church property contrary to the determination by the trustees that it would be against the best interests of the church to convey title. Empire Ralph Corp. v Moving Picture Operators Union (1956) 17 Misc. 2d 601, 155 N.Y.S.2d 76, 38 BNA LRRM 2108, 38 BNA LRRM 2185

Complaint for specific performance of a contract for the sale of church property, where no prior approval thereof has been obtained from the court, must plead the essential facts required by this section. Wilson v Ebenezer Baptist Church, Inc. (1959) 17 Misc. 2d 669, 185 N.Y.S.2d 1018

18. – Miscellaneous

Library trustees may not loan trust funds of the library to a religious corporation. 1958 Ops Atty Gen Jan 24 (informal)

19. Under former General Corporation Law § 52

A contemplated sale is illegal where it appears that a membership corporation is to dispose of all its real property without any consideration which can be applied to its corporate purposes of municipal government, as interests of the corporation will not be promoted by the sale as required by § 50 and this section. Richter v Sea Gate Asso. (1923) 207 A.D. 573, 202 N.Y.S. 68

A soldiers' monument corporation was permitted to sell its real property where, before title closing, a majority of the directors authorized the sale under the terms contained in the contract. The evidence established the adequacy of the consideration and that the interests of the corporation would be promoted by the sale. Application of Staten Island War Memorial Asso. (1955) 286 A.D. 887, 143 N.Y.S.2d 100, app den (1955) 286 A.D. 1017, 145 N.Y.S.2d 318 and resettlement den (1955) 286 A.D. 966, 146 N.Y.S.2d 474

Where at the time of the sale of real property by a religious corporation, the corporation failed to obtain the permission of the court to sell the property, proceedings for confirmation of the conveyance were referred to a referee to inquire into whether it was for the best interest of the corporation to sell, the reasons for the sale, whether the corporation was solvent, whether consideration was adequate and how the proceeds were to be used, and the oral consent of the religious corporation's attorney was not sufficient. In re Application of Barusek (1956) 1 Misc. 2d 950, 149 N.Y.S.2d 420

A petition for sale of hospital property must be approved by the court where it clearly appears that the terms of sale are fair and that the sale will be in the best interests of the corporation. Application of St. Luke's Hospital (1962) 33 Misc. 2d 888, 228 N.Y.S.2d 25

§ 511-a.   Petition for attorney general approval

(a) In lieu of obtaining court approval under section 511 (Petition for court approval) of this article to sell, lease, exchange or otherwise dispose of all or substantially all of its assets, the corporation may alternatively seek approval of the attorney general by verified petition, except in the following circumstances: (1) the corporation is insolvent, or would become insolvent as a result of the transaction, and must proceed on notice to creditors pursuant to paragraph (c) of section 511 of this article; or (2) the attorney general, in his or her discretion, concludes that a court should review the petition and make a determination thereon.

(b) The verified petition to the attorney general shall set forth (1) all of the information required to be included in a verified petition to obtain court approval pursuant to subparagraphs one through nine of paragraph (a) of section 511 of this article; (2) a statement that the corporation is not insolvent and will not become insolvent as a result of the transaction; and (3) a statement as to whether any persons have raised, or have a reasonable basis to raise, objections to the sale, lease, exchange or other disposition that is the subject of the petition, including a statement setting forth the names and addresses of such persons, the nature of their interest, and a description of their objections. The attorney general, in his or her discretion, may direct the corporation to provide notice of such petition to any interested person, and the corporation shall provide the attorney general with a certification that such notice has been provided.

(c) If it shall appear, to the satisfaction of the attorney general that the consideration and the terms of the transaction are fair and reasonable to the corporation and that the purposes of the corporation or the interests of the members will be promoted, the attorney general may authorize the sale, lease, exchange or other disposition of all or substantially all the assets of the corporation, as described in the petition, for such consideration and upon such terms as the attorney general may prescribe. The authorization of the attorney general shall direct the disposition of the consideration to be received thereunder by the corporation.

(d) At any time, including if the attorney general does not approve the petition, or if the attorney general concludes that court review is appropriate, the petitioner may seek court approval on notice to the attorney general pursuant to section 511 (Petition for court approval) of this article.

History: Add, L 2013, ch 549, § 56, eff July 1, 2014.

§ 512.   Repealed

History: Add, L 1978, ch 690, § 2, eff July 25, 1978; repealed, L 2010, ch 490, § 2, eff Sept 17, 2010.

§ 513.   Administration of assets received for specific purposes

(a) A corporation which is, or would be if formed under this chapter, a charitable corporation shall hold full ownership rights in any assets consisting of funds or other real or personal property of any kind, that may be given, granted, bequeathed or devised to or otherwise vested in such corporation in trust for, or with a direction to apply the same to, any purpose specified in its certificate of incorporation, and shall not be deemed a trustee of an express trust of such assets. Any other corporation subject to this chapter may similarly hold assets so received, unless otherwise provided by law or in the certificate of incorporation.

(b) Except as may be otherwise permitted under article eight of the estates, powers and trusts law or section 555 (Release or modification of restrictions on management, investment, or purpose), the governing board shall apply all assets thus received to the purposes specified in the gift instrument as defined in section 551 (Definitions) and to the payment of the reasonable and proper expenses of administration of such assets. The governing board shall cause accurate accounts to be kept of such assets separate and apart from the accounts of other assets of the corporation. Unless the terms of the particular gift instrument provide otherwise, the treasurer shall make an annual report to the members (if there be members) or to the governing board (if there be no members) concerning the assets held under this section and the use made of such assets and of the income thereof.

(c), (d) [Repealed]

History: Add, L 1969, ch 1066, § 1; amd, L 1970, ch 847, § 24, eff Sept 1, 1970, L 1972, ch 961, § 7, L 1978, ch 690, §§ 3, 4, eff July 25, 1978, L 2010, ch 490, §§ 2, 5, eff Sept 17, 2010, L 2013, ch 549, § 57, eff July 1, 2014.

CASE ANNOTATIONS

A charitable bequest made to petitioner nonprofit hospital under a 1924 will, presently valued at $850,000, "to be used by said hospital to endow charity beds... and for charitable purposes only," as a memorial to decedent and his sister would be an endowment under Not for Profit Corporation Law § 102(a)(13) in view of decedent's clear intent to bestow upon petitioner a permanent fund as memorial and, as such, would be governed by Not for Profit Corporation Law § 102(a)(16) requiring the governing board of the corporation to at all times retain the "historic dollar value" of the gift, representing principal payments received by petitioner between 1926 and 1962, and petitioner would be entitled to expend any amount in excess of the "historic dollar value" of the endowment for such hospital purposes as would be deemed prudent by its board of trustees under Not for Profit Corporation Law § 513(c) where the will specifically stated that the fund was to be used for charity beds "and for charitable purposes," there no longer being a need for charity beds; since the very nature of petitioner's operation is charitable, any expenditure that is necessary to further its operation is within the framework of the "charitable purposes" intended by the testator. In re Estate of McKenna (1982, Sur) 114 Misc. 2d 304, 451 N.Y.S.2d 617

CLS N-PCL § 513(c) does not override CLS N-PCL § 1507 restrictions on invading principal and thus, in action under CLS N-PCL § 112(a)(1), defendants were preliminarily enjoined from invading principal of cemetery's permanent maintenance trust fund or perpetual care trust fund, and from borrowing money from its perpetual care income fund (without prejudice to them if they applied for judicial approval under § 1507(a)), because (1) borrowing money that probably cannot be repaid is extra-statutory means of removing monies from funds without seeking court approval, (2) there would be continued invasion and arguably irreparable harm if injunction was not issued, and (3) balancing of equities favored issuance of preliminary injunction. People by Vacco v Woodlawn Cemetery (1997, Sup) 173 Misc. 2d 846, 662 N.Y.S.2d 369

§ 514.   Delegation of investment management

(a) Except as otherwise provided by the applicable gift instrument as defined in section 551 (Definitions), the governing board may delegate to its committees, officers or employees of the corporation or the fund the authority to act in place of the governing board in investment and reinvestment of institutional funds as defined in section 551 (Definitions). Each contract, if any, pursuant to which authority is so delegated shall provide that it may be terminated by the governing board at any time, without penalty, upon not more than sixty days' notice. Section 554 (Delegation of management and investment functions) shall govern external delegation.

(b) The governing board shall exercise the standard of care required by section 717 (Duty of directors and officers) in the selection of persons to whom authority is delegated or with whom contracts are made under paragraph (a) of this section and in the continuation or termination of such delegation or contracts. The governing board shall be relieved of all liability for the investment and reinvestment of institutional funds by, and for the other acts or omissions of, persons to whom authority is so delegated or with whom contracts are so made.

History: Add, L 1978, ch 690, § 5, eff July 25, 1978; amd, L 2010, ch 490, § 6, eff Sept 17, 2010.

§ 515.   Dividends prohibited; certain distributions of cash or property authorized

(a) A corporation shall not pay dividends or distribute any part of its income or profit to its members, directors, or officers.

(b) A corporation may pay compensation in a reasonable amount to members, directors, or officers, for services rendered, and may make distributions of cash or property to members upon dissolution or final liquidation as permitted by this chapter. No person who may benefit from such compensation may be present at or otherwise participate in any board or committee deliberation or vote concerning such person's compensation; provided that nothing in this section shall prohibit the board or authorized committee from requesting that a person who may benefit from such compensation present information as background or answer questions at a committee or board meeting prior to the commencement of deliberations or voting relating thereto. Nothing in this section or in paragraph (h) of section seven hundred fifteen of this chapter shall be construed to prohibit a director from deliberating or voting concerning compensation for service on the board that is to be made available or provided to all directors of the corporation on the same or substantially similar terms.

(c) A corporation may confer benefits upon members or nonmembers in conformity with its purposes, may redeem its capital certificates or subvention certificates, and may make other distributions of cash or property to its members or former members, directors, or officers prior to dissolution or final liquidation, as authorized by this article, except when the corporation is currently insolvent or would thereby be made insolvent or rendered unable to carry on its corporate purposes, or when the fair value of the corporation's assets remaining after such conferring of benefits, or redemption, or other distribution would be insufficient to meet its liabilities.

History: Add, L 1969, ch 1066, § 1, eff Sept 1, 1970; amd, L 1970, ch 847, § 26, eff Sept 1, 1970; L 2013, ch 549, § 58, eff July 1, 2014; L 2015, ch 555, § 2, eff Dec 11, 2015.

CASE ANNOTATIONS

The Town of Hempstead Local Development Corporation is authorized to compensate its directors by reason of rendering services in effecting its corporate purposes. 1977 Op Atty Gen March 29

A subsidiary of the Urban Development Corporation may incorporate under the Business Corporation Law without forfeiting its public status. The subsidiary may not pay profits to private investors, and upon dissolution of the corporation, the assets belong to the State. 1980 Op Atty Gen Oct. 20

§ 516.   Distributions to members upon termination of membership

(a) Except as provided in this chapter or the certificate of incorporation or the by-laws, the interest of a member in the property of a corporation shall terminate upon the termination of his membership, whether by expiration of the term of membership, or by the death, voluntary withdrawal, or expulsion of the member, or otherwise. Such termination shall be without prejudice to his rights, if any, as holder of a capital or subvention certificate.

(b) In the event of a termination of membership, whether voluntary or involuntary, and subject to any restrictions contained in this chapter or the certificate of incorporation or the by-laws, a corporation may at its option thereafter call for redemption any capital certificate or certificates held by such former member, and redeem the same upon payment of a sum of money equal to the redemption price thereof if such certificates are by their terms redeemable, or upon payment of a sum of money equal to the amount of the capital contribution evidenced by such certificates if they are not by their express terms redeemable.

(c) If a member who would upon dissolution of the corporation have distributive rights in its assets under paragraph (d) of section 507 (Fees, dues and assessments; fines and penalties) is expelled other than for cause pursuant to a provision of the certificate of incorporation or by-laws authorizing such expulsion, and the corporation is dissolved within a period of five years after the date of such expulsion, the expelled member shall be entitled to share in the distribution of assets in the same manner as other members of the same class entitled to share at that time, except that his share shall be charged with any arrearages and all dues and assessments which he would have paid if he had remained a member, plus interest on all such items.

(d) Nothing in this section shall authorize a corporation to make a distribution of cash or property to a former member in contravention of the provisions of section 515 (Dividends prohibited; certain distributions of cash or property authorized).

History: Add, L 1969, ch 1066, eff Sept 1, 1970. Derived from; amd, L 1969, ch 1066, § 1, eff Sept 1, 1970, with substance derived from Mem Corp Law § 40; L 1970, ch 847, § 27, eff Sept 1, 1970.

§ 517. Liabilities of members

(a) The members of a corporation shall not be personally liable for the debts, liabilities or obligations of the corporation.

(b) A member shall be liable to the corporation only to the extent of any unpaid portion of the initiation fees, membership dues or assessments which the corporation may have lawfully imposed upon him, or for any other indebtedness owed by him to the corporation. No action shall be brought by any creditor of the corporation to reach and apply any such liability to any debt of the corporation until after final judgment shall have been rendered against the corporation in favor of the creditor and execution thereon returned unsatisfied, or the corporation shall have been adjudged bankrupt, or a receiver shall have been appointed with power to collect debts, and which receiver, on demand of a creditor to bring suit thereon, has refused to sue for such unpaid amount, or the corporation shall have been dissolved or ceased its activities leaving debts unpaid. No such action shall be brought more than three years after the happening of any one of such events.

History: Add, L 1969, ch 1066, § 1, eff Sept 1, 1970.

§ 518. [Repealed]

History: Add, L 1969, ch 1066, § 1, with substance derived from Mem Corp Law § 25; repealed, L 1990, ch 87, § 2, eff July 12, 1990.

§ 519. Annual report of directors

(a) The board shall present at the annual meeting of members a report, verified by the president and treasurer or by a majority of the directors, or certified by an independent public or certified public accountant or a firm of such accountants selected by the board, showing in appropriate detail the following:

(1) The assets and liabilities, including the trust funds, of the corporation as of the end of a twelve month fiscal period terminating not more than six months prior to said meeting.

(2) The principal changes in assets and liabilities, including trust funds, during said fiscal period.

(3) The revenue or receipts of the corporation, both unrestricted and restricted to particular purposes during said fiscal period.

(4) The expenses or disbursements of the corporation, for both general and restricted purposes, during said fiscal period.

(5) The number of members of the corporation as of the date of the report, together with a statement of increase or decrease in such number during said fiscal period, and a statement of the place where the names and places of residence of the current members may be found.

(b) The annual report of directors shall be filed with the records of the corporation and either a copy or an abstract thereof entered in the minutes of the proceedings of the annual meeting of members.

(c) The board of a corporation having no members shall direct the president and treasurer to present at the annual meeting of the board a report in accordance with paragraph (a), but omitting the requirement of subparagraph (5). This report shall be filed with the minutes of the annual meeting of the board.

History: Add, L 1969, ch 1066, § 1, eff Sept 1, 1970, with substance derived from Mem Corp Law §§ 26, 46; amd, L 1970, ch 847, § 28; L 1971, ch 1058 § 12, eff Sept 1, 1971; L 1974, ch 213, eff July 1, 1974.

CASE ANNOTATIONS

1. Generally
2-5. [Reserved for future use]
6. Under former Membership Corporations Law § 46

1. Generally

Where purported accounting by nonprofit church corporation failed to comply with statutory requirement, church corporation was ordered to render an accounting of its assets and financial transactions for the period from October 1, 1974, to the date of the judgment. Anthony v Cardin (1977) 91 Misc. 2d 506, 398 N.Y.S.2d 215

2-5. [Reserved for future use]

6. Under former Membership Corporations Law § 46

A bylaw of a membership corporation which precludes any and all access to the corporate records of lists of guild membership on the say-so of the guild council is so far inconsistent with the letter and spirit of § 46 as to be wholly void and without effect. Davids v Sillcox (1948) 297 N.Y. 355, 79 N.E.2d 440, reh den (1948) 298 N.Y. 618, 81 N.E.2d 353

This section specifically excludes a corporation promoting or maintaining the principles of a political party from the mandate of the law requiring a corporation to provide a member with a copy of the membership list upon demand. Avallon v Riverside Democrats, Inc. (1966, 1st Dept) 25 A.D.2d 378, 269 N.Y.S.2d 573, app dismd (1966) 18 N.Y.2d 714, 274 N.Y.S.2d 151, 220 N.E.2d 798

This section does not require directors to file an account; the report required is limited to the information described in the statute, whereas an accounting is without limitation. Hamilton v Patrolmen's Benov. Ass'n (1949) 202 Misc 848, 88 N.Y.S.2d 683

A director of a membership corporation has the unqualified right to inspect the books and records of the corporation. Javits v Investors League, Inc. (1949, Sup) 92 N.Y.S.2d 267

This section does not make it necessary to furnish a copy of the membership list of the corporation to a director, since the names and addresses of those admitted to membership during the preceding year may be verified by the president and treasurer or by a majority of the directors. Javits v Investors League, Inc. (1949, Sup) 92 N.Y.S.2d 267

Where a director of a membership corporation seeks to inspect the membership list of the corporation for the purpose of enabling him to communicate his views to the members, and it appears that there are grounds for suspicion that the director is seeking to establish a new corporation in opposition to that of which he is a director, he will be allowed to inspect such records, but will be allowed to make no copies thereof and he will be required to submit correspondence to the corporation for transmission to the members. Javits v Investors League, Inc. (1949, Sup) 92 N.Y.S.2d 267

§ 519-a. Annual reports for certain transactions required

(a) A condominium created pursuant to the real property law or a cooperative housing corporation created pursuant to the business corporation law, shall, at least once each year:

(1) require that each director, as defined in paragraph six of subdivision (a) of section one hundred

two of this chapter, receive a copy of section seven hundred fifteen of this chapter; and

(2) provide an annual report to the members or to the governing board, if there are no members, which shall be signed by each such director, containing information on any contracts made, entered into, or otherwise voted on by the board of directors that were considered a related party transaction pursuant to section seven hundred fifteen of this chapter.

(b) The annual report required by subdivision (a) of this section shall include, but not be limited to, the following:

(1) a list of all contracts voted on by the board of directors, including information on the contract recipient, contract amount, and the purpose of entering into the contract;

(2) the record of each meeting including director attendance, voting records for contracts, and how each director voted on such contracts; and

(3) the date of each vote on each contract, and the date the contract would be and remain valid.

(c) If the annual report required by paragraph two of subdivision (a) of this section would, notwithstanding the requirements of this section, contain no information because of the absence of any actions taken by the board that would otherwise qualify for inclusion in such annual report, then the board shall instead submit to the members or to the governing board, if there are no members, a document, signed by each director, indicating: "No actions taken by the board were subject to the annual report required pursuant to section 519-a of the Not-for-Profit Corporation Law".

History: Add, L 2017, ch 305, § 1, eff Jan 1, 2018; amd, L 2018, ch 9, § 1, eff Jan 1, 2018.

Laws 2017, ch 305, § 3, eff Jan 1, 2018, provides:

§ 3. This act shall take effect on the first of January next succeeding the date on which it shall have become a law.

Laws 2018 ch 9, § 3, eff January 1, 2018, provides:

§ 3. This act shall take effect on the same date and in the same manner as a chapter of the laws of 2017, amending the not-for-profit corporation law and the business corporation law, relating to conflicts of interests for condominium and cooperative housing, as proposed in legislative bills numbers S.6652-A and A.8261-A, takes effect.

Blackline Showing Effect of 2018 Amendments. — (a) ~~Every condominium or cooperative housing corporation, incorporated pursuant to this chapter, shall, at least once each year~~ A condominium created pursuant to the real property law or a cooperative housing corporation created pursuant to the business corporation law, shall, at least once each year:

(1) require that each director, as defined in paragraph six of subdivision (a) of section one hundred two of this chapter, receive a copy of section seven hundred fifteen of this chapter; and

(2) provide an annual report to the members or to the governing board, if there are no members, which shall be signed by each such director, containing information on any contracts made, entered into, or otherwise voted on by the board of directors that were considered a related party transaction pursuant to section seven hundred fifteen of this chapter.

(b) The annual report required by subdivision (a) of this section shall include, but not be limited to, the following:

(1) a list of all contracts voted on by the board of directors, including information on the contract recipient, contract amount, and the purpose of entering into the contract;

(2) the record of each meeting including director attendance, voting records for contracts, and how each director voted on such contracts; and

(3) the date of each vote on each contract, and the date the contract would be and remain valid.

(c) If the annual report required by paragraph two of subdivision (a) of this section would, notwithstanding the requirements of this section, contain no information because of the absence of any actions taken by the board that would otherwise qualify for inclusion in such annual report, then the board shall instead submit to the members or to the governing board, if there are no members, a document, signed by each director, indicating: "No actions taken by the board were subject to the annual report required pursuant to section 519-a of the Not-for-Profit Corporation Law".

§ 520.   Reports of corporation

Each domestic corporation, and each foreign corporation authorized to conduct activities in this state, shall from time to time file such reports on its activities as may be required by the laws of this state. All registration and reporting requirements pursuant to article seven-A of the executive law, and section 8-1.4 of the estates, powers and trusts law, or related successor provisions, are, without limitation on the foregoing, expressly included as reports required by the laws of this state to be filed within the meaning of this section. Willful failure of a corporation to file a report as required by law shall constitute a breach of the directors' duty to the corporation and shall subject the corporation, at the suit of the attorney-general, to an action or special proceeding for dissolution under article 11 (Judicial dissolution) in the case of a domestic corporation, or under section 1303 (Violations) in the case of a foreign corporation.

History: Add, L 1969, ch 1066, § 1; amd, L 1970, ch 847, § 29, L 1981, ch 58, § 1, eff July 5, 1981; L 2013, ch 549, § 59, eff July 1, 2014.

§ 521.   Liability for failure to disclose required information

Failure of the corporation to comply in good faith with the notice or disclosure or reporting provisions of section 501 (Stock and shares prohibited; membership certificates authorized), or paragraph (c) of section 503 (Capital certificates), or paragraph (c) of section 505 (Subvention certificates), or paragraph (b) of section 513 (Administration of assets received for specific purposes), or section 518 (Reports to comptroller), or section 519 (Annual report of directors), or section 520 (Reports of corporation), shall make the corporation liable for any damage sustained by any person in consequence thereof.

History: Add, L 1969, ch 1066, § 1; amd, L 1970, ch 847, § 30, L 1978, ch 690, § 6, eff July 25, 1978.

§ 522.   [Repealed]

History: Add, L 1978, ch 690, § 7, eff July 25, 1978; amd, L 1982, ch 165, § 1, eff June 8, 1982; repealed, L 2010, ch 490, § 2, eff Sept 17, 2010.

ARTICLE 5-A
PRUDENT MANAGEMENT OF
INSTITUTIONAL FUNDS ACT

§ 550.   Short title

This article may be known and may be cited as the "New York prudent management of institutional funds act".

History: Add, L 2010, ch 490, § 1, eff Sept 17, 2010.

§ 551.   Definitions

As used in this article:

(a) "Charitable purpose" means the relief of poverty, the advancement of education or religion, the promotion of health, the promotion of a governmental purpose, or any other purpose the achievement of which is beneficial to the community including any purpose that is charitable under the laws of the state of New York.

(a-1) "Donor" means the person who grants or transfers property to an institution pursuant to a gift instrument, or a person designated in the applicable gift instrument to act in the place of the donor, but does not otherwise include the person's executors, heirs, successors, assigns, transferees, or distributees.

(b) "Endowment fund" means an institutional fund or part thereof that, under the terms of a gift instrument, is not wholly expendable by the institution on a current basis. The term does not include assets that an institution may designate as an endowment fund for its own use, consistent with the terms of the applicable gift instrument.

(c) "Gift instrument" means a record or records, including an institutional solicitation, under which property is granted to, transferred to, or held by an institution as an institutional fund.

(d) "Institution" means: (1) a person, other than an individual, organized and operated exclusively for charitable purposes; (2) a trust that had both charitable and noncharitable interests, after all noncharita-ble interests have terminated; or (3) any corporation described in subparagraph five of paragraph (a) of section 102 (Definitions). Whenever any provision of this article imposes any obligation on, or requires any action to be taken by, an institution, such obligation is imposed on, and such action shall be authorized by, the governing board of such institution.

(e) "Institutional fund" means a fund held by an institution. This term shall not include: (1) program-related assets; (2) a fund held for an institution by a trustee that is not an institution; or (3) a fund in which a beneficiary that is not an institution has an interest, other than an interest that could arise upon violation or failure of the purposes of the fund.

(f) "Notice" means information given by an institution as required by this article. An institution will be considered to have given notice if notice is given personally in writing or sent to the recipient's last known address on record with the institution, or, if no address is on record with the institution, if the institution makes reasonable efforts to attempt to find and notify the recipient. If the notice is mailed, such notice is given when deposited in the United States mail, with postage thereon prepaid. If the notice is delivered by electronic means, such as via facsimile or email, such notice is given when the notice is sent.

(g) "Person" means an individual, corporation, business trust, estate, trust, partnership, limited liability company, association, joint venture, or any other legal entity.

(h) "Program-related asset" means an asset held by an institution not for investment under the terms of the gift instrument, but primarily to accomplish a programmatic purpose of the institution.

(i) "Record" means information that is inscribed on a tangible medium or that is stored in an electronic or other medium and is retrievable in perceivable form.

(j) A donor is "available" if such donor (1) is living or, if the donor is not a natural person, is in existence and conducting activities; and (2) can be identified and located with reasonable efforts.

(k) "External agent" means an independent investment advisor, investment counsel or manager, bank, or trust company.

History: Add, L 2010, ch 490, § 1, eff Sept 17, 2010.

§ 552.   Standard of conduct in managing and investing an institutional fund

(a) Subject to the intent of a donor expressed in a gift instrument, an institution, in managing and investing an institutional fund, shall consider the purposes of the institution and the purposes of the institutional fund.

(b) In addition to complying with the duty of loyalty imposed by law other than this article, each person responsible for managing and investing an institutional fund shall manage and invest the fund in good faith and with the care an ordinarily prudent person in a like position would exercise under similar circumstances.

(c) In managing and investing an institutional fund, an institution consistent with section 717 (Duty of Directors and Officers):

(1) may incur only costs that are appropriate and reasonable in relation to the assets, the purposes of the institution, and the skills available to the institution; and

(2) shall make a reasonable effort to verify facts relevant to the management and investment of the fund.

(d) An institution may pool two or more institutional funds for purposes of management and investment.

(e) Except as otherwise provided by a gift instrument, the following rules apply:

(1) In managing and investing an institutional fund, the following factors, if relevant, must be considered: (A) general economic conditions; (B) the possible effect of inflation or deflation; (C) the expected tax consequences, if any, of investment decisions or strategies; (D) the role that each investment or course of action plays within the overall investment portfolio of the fund; (E) the expected total return from income and the appreciation of investments; (F) other resources of the institution; (G) the needs of the institution and the fund to make distributions and to preserve capital; and (H) an asset's special relationship or special value, if any, to the purposes of the institution.

(2) Management and investment decisions about an individual asset must be made not in isolation but rather in the context of the institutional fund's portfolio of investments as a whole and as a part of an overall investment strategy having risk and return objectives reasonably suited to the fund and to the institution.

(3) Except as otherwise provided by law other than this article, an institution may invest in any kind of property or type of investment consistent with this article.

(4) An institution shall diversify the investments of an institutional fund unless the institution prudently determines that, because of special circumstances, the purposes of the fund are better served without diversification. An institution shall review a decision not to diversify as frequently as circumstances require, but at least annually.

(5) Within a reasonable time after receiving property, an institution shall make and carry out decisions concerning the retention or disposition of the property or to rebalance a portfolio, in order to bring the institutional fund into compliance with the purposes, terms, and distribution requirements of the institution as necessary to meet other circumstances of the institution and the requirements of this article.

(6) A person that has special skills or expertise, or is selected in reliance upon the person's representation that the person has special skills or expertise, has a duty to use those skills or that expertise in managing and investing institutional funds.

(f) Each institution shall adopt a written investment policy setting forth guidelines on investments and delegation of management and investment functions in accord with the standards of this article.

History: Add, L 2010, ch 490, § 1, eff Sept 17, 2010.

§ 553. Appropriation for expenditure or accumulation of endowment fund; rules of construction

(a) Subject to the intent of a donor expressed in the gift instrument, an institution may appropriate for expenditure or accumulate so much of an endowment fund as the institution determines is prudent for the uses, benefits, purposes, and duration for which the endowment fund is established. Unless stated otherwise in the gift instrument, the assets in an endowment fund are donor-restricted assets until appropriated for expenditure by the institution. In making a determination to appropriate or accumulate, the institution shall act in good faith, with the care that an ordinarily prudent person in a like position would exercise under similar circumstances, and shall consider, if relevant, the following factors:

(1) the duration and preservation of the endowment fund;

(2) the purposes of the institution and the endowment fund;

(3) general economic conditions;

(4) the possible effect of inflation or deflation;

(5) the expected total return from income and the appreciation of investments;

(6) other resources of the institution;

(7) where appropriate and circumstances would otherwise warrant, alternatives to expenditure of the endowment fund, giving due consideration to the effect that such alternatives may have on the institution; and

(8) the investment policy of the institution.

For each determination to appropriate for expenditure, the institution shall keep a contemporaneous record describing the consideration that was given by the governing board to each of the factors enumerated in this paragraph.

(b) To limit the authority to appropriate for expenditure or accumulate under paragraph (a) of this section, a gift instrument must specifically state the limitation. Terms in a gift instrument setting forth a specific spending level, rate, or amount, or explicitly modifying or overriding the provisions of paragraph (a) of this section, will limit the authority of the institution to appropriate for expenditure or accumulate under paragraph (a) of this section.

(c) Terms in a gift instrument designating a gift as an endowment, or a direction or authorization in the gift instrument to use only "income," "interest," "dividends," or "rents, issues, or profits," or "to preserve the principal intact," or words of similar import:

(1) create an endowment fund of permanent duration unless other language in the gift instrument limits the duration or purpose of the fund; and

(2) do not otherwise limit the authority to appropriate for expenditure or accumulate under paragraph (a) of this section.

(d) A rebuttable presumption of imprudence shall apply to gift instruments executed upon or after the effective date of this article as follows: The appropriation for expenditure in any year of an amount greater than seven percent of the fair market value of an endowment fund, calculated on the basis of market values determined at least quarterly and averaged over a period of not less than five years immediately preceding the year in which the appropriation for expenditure is made, creates a rebuttable presumption of imprudence. For an endowment fund in existence for fewer than five years, the fair market value of the endowment fund must be calculated for the period the endowment fund has been in existence. This subsection does not:

(1) apply to an appropriation for expenditure permitted under law other than the chapter of the laws of 2010 that enacted this article or by the gift instrument; or

(2) create a presumption of prudence for an appropriation for expenditure of an amount less than or equal to seven percent of the fair market value of the endowment fund.

(e)(1) With respect to a gift instrument executed by the donor before the effective date of this article an institution must provide ninety days notice to the donor, if the donor is then available, before applying paragraph (a) of this section for the first time, during which time the donor may clarify or amend the gift instrument to prohibit the application of paragraph (a) of this section. Such notice shall include a form for use by the donor, which shall contain language substantially as follows:

Attention, Donor:
Please check Box #1 or #2 below and return to the address shown above.
( ) #1 The institution may spend as much of my gift as may be prudent.
( ) #2 The institution may not spend below the original dollar value of my gift.
If you check Box #1 above, the institution may spend as much of your endowment gift (including all or part of the original value of your gift) as may be prudent under the criteria set forth in Article 5-A of the Not-for-Profit Corporation Law (The Prudent Management of Institutional Funds Act).
If you check Box #2 above, the institution may not spend below the original dollar value of your endowment gift but may spend the income and the appreciation over the original dollar value if it is prudent to do so. The criteria for the expenditure of endowment funds set forth in Article 5-A of the Not-for-Profit Corporation Law (The Prudent Management of Institutional Funds Act) will not apply to your gift.

If the donor does not respond within ninety days from the date notice was given, paragraphs (a), (b), and (c) of this section shall be applied.

(2) This paragraph shall not apply if: (A) the gift instrument permits appropriation for expenditure from the endowment fund without regard for the fund's historic dollar value; (B) the gift instrument limits the institution's authority to appropriate for expenditure in accordance with paragraph (b) of this section; or (C) the gift consists of funds received as a result of an institutional solicitation without a separate statement by the donor expressing a restriction on the use of funds.

(f) When an institution acts pursuant to paragraph (a) or (e) of this section, it shall keep a record of such action.

History: Add, L 2010, ch 490, § 1, eff Sept 17, 2010.

§ 554.   Delegation of management and investment functions

(a) Subject to any specific limitation set forth in a gift instrument or in law other than this article, an institution may delegate to an external agent the management and investment of an institutional fund to the extent that an institution could prudently delegate under the circumstances. An institution shall act in good faith, with the care that an ordinarily prudent person in a like position would exercise under similar circumstances as required by section seven hundred seventeen of this chapter, in:

(1) selecting, continuing or terminating an agent, including assessing the agent's independence including any conflicts of interest such agent has or may have;

(2) establishing the scope and terms of the delegation, including the payment of compensation, consistent with the purposes of the institution and the institutional fund; and

(3) monitoring the agent's performance and compliance with the scope and terms of the delegation.

(b) In performing a delegated function, an agent owes a duty to the institution to exercise reasonable care, skill and caution to comply with the scope and terms of the delegation.

(c) An institution that complies with paragraph (a) of this section is not liable for the decisions or actions of an agent to which the function was delegated.

(d) By accepting delegation of a management or investment function from an institution that is subject to the laws of this state, an agent submits to the jurisdiction of the courts of this state in all proceedings arising from or related to the delegation or the performance of the delegated function.

(e) Each contract, if any, pursuant to which authority is so delegated shall provide that it may be terminated by the institution at any time, without penalty, upon not more than sixty days notice.

(f) An institution may delegate management and investment functions to its committees, officers, or employees as authorized by the laws of this state other than this article, as set forth in, inter alia, section 514 (Delegation of investment management).

(g) Nothing in this article shall impair the operation of section 717 (Duty of directors and officers).

History: Add, L 2010, ch 490, § 1, eff Sept 17, 2010.

§ 555. Release or modification of restrictions on management, investment, or purpose

(a) If the donor consents in a record, an institution may release or modify, in whole or in part, a restriction contained in a gift instrument on the management, investment, or purpose of an institutional fund. A release or modification may not allow a fund to be used for a purpose other than a charitable purpose of the institution.

(b) A court, upon application of an institution, may modify a restriction contained in a gift instrument regarding the management or investment of an institutional fund if the restriction has become impracticable or wasteful, if it impairs the management or investment of the fund, or if, because of circumstances not anticipated by the donor, a modification of a restriction will further the purposes of the fund. The institution shall notify the donor, if available, and the attorney general of the application, and the attorney general and such donor must be given an opportunity to be heard. To the extent practicable, any modification must be made in accordance with the donor's probable intention.

(c) If a particular purpose or a restriction contained in a gift instrument on the use of an institutional fund becomes unlawful, impracticable, impossible to achieve, or wasteful, the court, upon application of an institution, may modify the purpose of the fund or the restriction on the use of the fund in a manner consistent with the purposes expressed in the gift instrument. The institution shall notify the donor, if available, and the attorney general of the application, and the attorney general and such donor must be given an opportunity to be heard.

(d) (1) If an institution determines that a restriction contained in a gift instrument on the management, investment, or purpose of an institutional fund is unlawful, impracticable, impossible to achieve, or wasteful, the institution, ninety days after notification to the attorney general, may release or modify the restriction, in whole or part, if:

(A) the institutional fund subject to the restriction has a total value of less than one hundred thousand dollars;

(B) more than twenty years have elapsed since the fund was established; and

(C) the institution uses the property in a manner consistent with the purposes expressed in the gift instrument.

(2) Notice to the attorney general shall contain: (A) an explanation of (i) the institution's determination that the restriction meets the requirements set forth in subparagraph one of this paragraph and (ii) the proposed release or modification; (B) a copy of a record of the institution approving the release or modification; and (C) a statement of the proposed use of the institutional fund after such release or modification.

(3) If the attorney general does not notify the institution within ninety days, the institution may proceed with the release or modification.

(4) Notice shall also be given to the donor, as defined in paragraph (a-1) of section 551 (Definitions), if available, provided, however, that such notice shall not be required for funds described in clause (B) of subparagraph two of paragraph (e) of section 553 (Appropriation for expenditure or accumulation of endowment fund; rules of construction).

(e) For purposes of this section, an institution may apply to the following courts to release or modify a restriction contained in a gift instrument:

(1) to the supreme court of the judicial district wherein the institution has its office or principal place of carrying out the purposes for which it was formed; or

(2) where the applicable gift instrument is a will, to the surrogate's court in which such will is probated.

(f) This chapter shall not limit the application of the doctrines of cy pres and deviation.

History: Add, L 2010, ch 490, § 1, eff Sept 17, 2010; amd, L 2013, ch 549, § 60, eff July 1, 2014.

§ 556. Reviewing compliance

Compliance with this article shall be determined in light of the facts and circumstances existing at the time a decision is made or action is taken, and not retrospectively.

History: Add, L 2010, ch 490, § 1, eff Sept 17, 2010.

§ 557.   Application to existing institutional funds

This article shall apply to institutional funds existing on or established after the effective date of this article. As applied to institutional funds existing on the effective date of this article, this article shall govern only decisions made or actions taken on or after that date.

History: Add, L 2010, ch 490, § 1, eff Sept 17, 2010.

§ 558.   Relation to Electronic Signatures in Global and National Commerce Act

This article modifies, limits, and supersedes the Electronic Signatures in Global and National Commerce Act, 15 U.S.C. Section 7001 et seq., but does not modify, limit, or supersede Section 101 of that act, 15 U.S.C. Section 7001(a), or authorize electronic delivery of any of the notices described in Section 103 of that act, 15 U.S.C. Section 7003(b).

History: Add, L 2010, ch 490, § 1, eff Sept 17, 2010.

ARTICLE 6
MEMBERS

History: Add, L 1969, ch 1066, § 1, eff Sept 1, 1970.

§ 601.   Members

(a) A corporation shall have one or more classes of members, or, in the case of a charitable corporation, may have no members, in which case any such provision for classes of members or for no members shall be set forth in the certificate of incorporation or the by-laws. Corporations, joint-stock associations, unincorporated associations and partnerships, as well as any other person without limitation, may be members, provided however, that effective July first, two thousand nineteen, no corporation except a corporation that has no members, shall have a membership comprised of fewer than three persons. A corporation may have a corporation, joint-stock association, unincorporated association or partnership as a sole member, if such corporation, joint-stock association, unincorporated association or partnership is owned or controlled by no fewer than three persons.

(b) If the corporation has two or more classes of members, the designation and characteristics of each class and the qualifications and rights of, and limitations upon, the members of each class may be set forth in the certificate of incorporation, the by-laws or, if the by-laws so provide, a resolution of the board.

(c) If the corporation has members, membership may be effected and evidenced by:

(1) Signature on the certificate of incorporation.

(2) Designation in the certificate of incorporation or the by-laws.

(3) Membership certificate or card or capital certificate.

(4) Such method, including but not limited to the foregoing, as is prescribed by the certificate of incorporation or the by-laws.

(d) Membership certificates or cards shall not be transferable. If the certificate of incorporation or by-laws permits transfer of membership, upon each such transfer the certificate or card issued to a former member shall be surrendered, and a new certificate or card shall be issued to the new member.

(e) Except as otherwise provided in this chapter or the certificate of incorporation or the by-laws, membership shall be terminated by death, resignation, expulsion, expiration of a term of membership or dissolution and liquidation under articles 10 and 11.

History: Add, L 1969, ch 1066, § 1, eff Sept 1, 1970; amd, L 1970, ch 847, § 31, eff Sept 1, 1970; L 1971, ch 1058, § 13, eff Sept 1, 1971; L 2013, ch 549, § 61, eff July 1, 2014; L 2018, ch 411, § 1, eff Dec 21, 2018.

Blackline Showing Effect of 2018 Amendments. — (a) A corporation shall have one or more classes of members, or, in the case of a charitable corporation, may have no members, in which case any such provision for classes of members or for no members shall be set forth in the certificate of incorporation or the by-laws. Corporations, joint-stock associations, unincorporated associations and partnerships, as well as any other person without limitation, may be members, <u>provided however, that effective July first, two thousand nineteen, no corporation except a corporation that has no members, shall have a membership comprised of fewer than three persons. A corporation may have a corporation, joint-stock association, unincorporated association or partnership as a sole member, if such corpora-</u>

tion, joint-stock association, unincorporated association or partnership is owned or controlled by no fewer than three persons.

(b) If the corporation has two or more classes of members, the designation and characteristics of each class and the qualifications and rights of, and limitations upon, the members of each class may be set forth in the certificate of incorporation, the by-laws or, if the by-laws so provide, a resolution of the board.

(c) If the corporation has members, membership may be effected and evidenced by:

(1) Signature on the certificate of incorporation.

(2) Designation in the certificate of incorporation or the by-laws.

(3) Membership certificate or card or capital certificate.

(4) Such method, including but not limited to the foregoing, as is prescribed by the certificate of incorporation or the by-laws.

(d) Membership certificates or cards shall not be transferable. If the certificate of incorporation or by-laws permits transfer of membership, upon each such transfer the certificate or card issued to a former member shall be surrendered, and a new certificate or card shall be issued to the new member.

(e) Except as otherwise provided in this chapter or the certificate of incorporation or the by-laws, membership shall be terminated by death, resignation, expulsion, expiration of a term of membership or dissolution and liquidation under articles 10 and 11.

CASE ANNOTATIONS

1. **Generally**
2-10. **[Reserved for future use]**
11. **Under former Membership Corporations Law § 20**
12. **– Reduction of membership**
13. **– Voluntary withdrawal of member**
14. **– Power to discipline, suspend, or expel**
15. **– – Grounds**
16. **– Procedure for expulsion**
17. **– – Notice of charges**
18. **– Readmission of expelled member**
19. **– Miscellaneous**
20. **Under former Membership Corporations Law § 40**
21. **– Applicant for membership**
22. **– Reduction of membership**
23. **– Voluntary withdrawal of member**
24. **– Power to discipline or expel**
25. **– Procedure for expulsion**
26. **– – Notice of meeting to consider expulsion**
27. **– – Notice of charges**
28. **– – Waiver of notice**
29. **– Remedy for improper expulsion**
30. **– Readmission of expelled member**
31. **– Membership as property**
32. **– Miscellaneous**

1. Generally

Petitioner, who was a resident and taxpayer of town and who made annual charitable contributions to nursing home organized pursuant to Not-For-Profit Corporation Law, but who was not a manager thereof under any of four tests specified by Law and who was not an officer or director and had no beneficial interest in corporation, had no right to inspect records of corporation. Getman v Mohawk Valley Nursing Home, Inc. (1974, 4th Dept) 44 A.D.2d 392, 355 N.Y.S.2d 508

Under corporate trade association's bylaw providing that "Upon receipt at the principal place of business of the cooperative of a notice of intention to resign, the Secretary of the corporation shall mark such receipt in the records of the corporation, and sixty days after such receipt such resignation shall become effective, relieving the member of all liability and responsibility for assessments thereafter," secretary's marking the receipt of notice of intention to resign from membership in association on records of association was not a condition precedent to a valid resignation. New York New Jersey Producer Dealers Cooperative, Inc. v Mocker (1977, 3d Dept) 59 A.D.2d 970, 399 N.Y.S.2d 280

Conflict between definition of "member" as used in restrictive covenants in deeds of subdivision to include an "entity" and the definition of membership in the by-laws of association incorporated under the Not-For-Profit Corporation Law must be governed by by-laws and would be construed to preclude corporation from membership in the Association. Procopio v Fisher (1981, 4th Dept) 83 A.D.2d 757, 443 N.Y.S.2d 492

Complaint was properly dismissed due to plaintiff's lack of standing to bring derivative action on behalf of not-for-profit cemetery corporation where plaintiff was not member of corporation as set forth in its certificate or incorporation, and he did not otherwise come within categories of members defined by its by-laws; fact that plaintiff was land share certificate holder, and thus had voting rights under corporation's by-laws, was irrelevant where enumeration in by-laws of "members" did not include land share certificate holders. Harris v Lyke (1995, 4th Dept) 217 A.D.2d 982, 629 N.Y.S.2d 911, app den (1995) 87 N.Y.2d 801, 637 N.Y.S.2d 688, 661 N.E.2d 160

Petitioner's expulsion from country club violated CLS N-PCL § 601 where board of governors failed to strictly comply with provision of club by-laws which required notifying petitioner, in writing, of charges against him and action that might be taken on those charges. Capossela v Wykagyl Country Club (1999, 2d Dept) 258 A.D.2d 522, 685 N.Y.S.2d 275

In Article 78 proceeding in which "inactive" members of respondent not-for-profit corporation involved in presentation of "Tony" Awards challenged respondent's decision to amend its bylaws to prevent inactive members from participating in Tony awards, respondent was directed to provide its official membership list of Tony award voters for season in question and to create such list if it did not already exist, as petitioners' disclosure demand was not frivolous or intended to harass, in light of issues presented. Wells v League of Am. Theatres & Producers, Inc. (2000, Sup) 183 Misc. 2d 915, 706 N.Y.S.2d 599

There is prima facie validity to any provision of a not-for-profit corporation by-law restricting right of member to withdraw voluntarily. Leon v Chrysler Motors Corp. (1973, DC NJ) 358 F. Supp. 877, affd without op (1973, CA3 NJ) 474 F.2d 1340

By-laws of not-for-profit corporation which required each member to agree not to withdraw from the association without the consent of a majority of all members were valid despite fact that members were in effect locked into the association unless they could persuade a majority of the members to vote against their own economic interests to release them. Leon v Chrysler Motors Corp. (1973, DC NJ) 358 F. Supp. 877, affd without op (1973, CA3 NJ) 474 F.2d 1340

A volunteer member of a fire company may be removed in accordance with the constitution and by-laws of the company. Ops Atty Gen 85-17

2-10. [Reserved for future use]

11. Under former Membership Corporations Law § 20

The Medical Society of County of New York has jurisdiction to try a member on charges which, if proved, would show that he had committed acts unfavorably affecting the dignity, character and interests of the medical profession, of the society and its members, although the acts do not directly involve the relations of the member as such to the society. Ewald v Medical Soc. of New York County (1911) 144 A.D. 82, 128 N.Y.S. 886

Where the bylaws and the constitution of a membership corporation provide for the determination of claims involving members, and a member voluntarily submits his case to the arbitration committee thereof and has appealed from the arbitration award, he cannot then dispute the authority of the arbitration committee to consider and pass upon the claim on the ground that the adversary party is not a member of the association. National League of Com. Merchants v Hornung (1911) 148 A.D. 355, 132 N.Y.S. 871, appeal after remand (1912) 153 A.D. 937, 138 N.Y.S. 1131, affd (1914) 211 N.Y. 575, 105 N.E. 1091

This section provides that bylaws of a membership corporation may make provisions not inconsistent with law or its certificate of incorporation regulating admission and voluntary withdrawal of members, their dues, and termination of membership on nonpayment of dues or otherwise, and a member of such a corporation makes its valid bylaws part of his contract of membership and becomes bound by them. Associated General Contractors of America v Lapardo Bros. Excavating Contractors, Inc. (1964) 43 Misc. 2d 825, 252 N.Y.S.2d 486

In the absence of provisions in the bylaws to the contrary, members of one faction in a club may solicit and induct into membership, new members for the purpose of gaining their support in a forthcoming election. Petition of Serenbetz (1943, Sup) 46 N.Y.S.2d 475, affd (1944) 267 A.D. 836, 46 N.Y.S.2d 127

Where an association incorporated pursuant to former § 8 from which this section is derived sets up a private tribunal to determine whether a member has forfeited his rights of membership, the courts will interfere to keep such tribunals within its jurisdiction, and inquire into whether action was taken in bad faith, or in violation of law, but will not investigate the merits of the tribunal's decision. Stevenson v Holstein-Friesian Ass'n (1929, CA2 NY) 30 F.2d 625

This section regulates admission, voluntary withdrawal, censure, suspension and expulsion of members. 1963 Ops Atty Gen Feb 21

The by-laws of an incorporated volunteer fire department may provide for provisional appointment of new members for a probationary period. 1955 Ops St Compt File #7411

12. – Reduction of membership

The number of members of a membership corporation may be reduced by an amendment in respect thereto to the bylaws, in the absence of a provision in the certificate of incorporation fixing the membership. Keeler v New York Hide Exchange, Inc. (1931) 231 A.D. 450, 247 N.Y.S. 482

13. – Voluntary withdrawal of member

A by-law of a membership corporation which states that any withdrawal must be approved by the board, and, if not so approved, the member may still have the benefit of his contract for a period of two years by continuing to receive service and pay for it, at the end of which period, automatically, his withdrawal shall become final is not invalid as arbitrary. Associated Press v Emmett (1942, DC Cal) 45 F. Supp. 907

14. – Power to discipline, suspend, or expel

Where the bylaws of a society provide for the expulsion of a member for two specific offenses, and further recite that as to other infractions, the directing board has discretion to impose "disciplinary measures and punishments", the term disciplinary measures and punishments does not include the power of expulsion. Pepe v Missanellese Soc. of Mut. Aid (1930) 141 Misc 7, 252 N.Y.S. 70

A membership corporation has no right to impose a fine on one of its members under a provision of its bylaws giving the corporation the right to expel, suspend or discipline a member for any violation of the bylaws of the corporation or any agreement made thereby. Merchants' Ladies Garment Ass'n v Coat House of William M. Schwartz, Inc. (1934) 152 Misc 130, 273 N.Y.S. 317

The power of expulsion, unless it appears by the most express and unambiguous language that such power has been transferred to the governing body of the organization, either in the bylaws or by the constitution, is in the membership of the organization as a whole. Weinberg v Carton (1949) 196 Misc 74, 90 N.Y.S.2d 398

Where the bylaws of a membership corporation whose membership consisted of commercial discount companies provided that each member should inform the secretary of the organization of unusual or suspicious transactions involving clients, and the bylaws further provided for the punishment of a member failing to comply with such bylaws, the sole recourse of a member who feels that he has been injured by another member's nonobservance of the bylaw is by seeking the punishment of the offending member in the manner and to the extent authorized by the bylaws, and such member has no action either in breach of contract or in tort, even though such bylaws constitute a contract not only with the association and its members, but also between the members inter sese. Weissman v Birn (1945, Sup) 56 N.Y.S.2d 269, affd (1946) 270 A.D. 757, 59 N.Y.S.2d 917

15. – – Grounds

A membership corporation has the natural right of self-preservation and the inherent power to expell its members for disloyalty in joining or forming rival organizations. So, a complaint by members of a national society of decorators in their action for a judgment declaring illegal a resolution terminating their membership in the society if they did not resign from a competitive society, was dismissed. Bockman v American Institute of Decorators (1959, 1st Dept) 7 A.D.2d 495, 184 N.Y.S.2d 381, affd (1959) 7 N.Y.2d 850, 196 N.Y.S.2d 988, 164 N.E.2d 862

Nothing in this section precludes the inclusion of a provision in the by-laws of a membership corporation, which is a trade organization composed of persons and entities engaged in the retail furniture business in New York State, automatically suspending any member who files a bankruptcy petition or makes an assignment for benefit of creditors and further provides for expulsion from membership in such case, nor is such a by-law in violation of general law or of federal law relating to bankruptcy. Schlossmans, Inc. v Associated Furniture Dealers, Inc. (1961) 31 Misc. 2d 938, 221 N.Y.S.2d 872

A local membership corporation is bound by the rules and decisions of the parent organization and the power to suspend or expel members is "for cause" when such conduct is destructive of the purpose of the organization. Paglia v Staten Island Little League, Inc. (1971) 66 Misc. 2d 626, 322 N.Y.S.2d 37, revd on other grounds (1971, 2d Dept) 38 A.D.2d 575, 328 N.Y.S.2d 224

16. – Procedure for expulsion

Where a bylaw provides that in order to expel a member, there must be a hearing at a regular meeting and the person charged must be found guilty by a two-thirds vote of the members present, the directors, or the governing body of the association, have no power to conduct a hearing, and expel a member at a directors' meeting. Weinberg v Carton (1949) 196 Misc 74, 90 N.Y.S.2d 398

In the absence of any provision in the bylaws or constitution of an organization as to procedure regulating the filing of charges and subsequent preliminary procedure before trial of one charged with an offense which if proved would result in expulsion, such charges must be filed with the members of the association as a body at a meeting of the association, and they, as such body, must prescribe the preliminary procedure. Weinberg v Carton (1949) 196 Misc 74, 90 N.Y.S.2d 398

17. – – Notice of charges

A bylaw permitting expulsion of a member without notice of charges and an opportunity to be heard is invalid. Briggs v Technocracy, Inc. (1948, Sup) 85 N.Y.S.2d 735

Expulsion of a member of a membership corporation without notice or a statement of charges or an opportunity to be heard is illegal, notwithstanding the fact that the bylaws of the corporation make no express provision for a hearing. Briggs v Technocracy, Inc. (1948, Sup) 85 N.Y.S.2d 735

18. – Readmission of expelled member

Where the bylaws of a union provided for readmission of members "on such terms as a local union or Executive Board... may determine upon a two-thirds vote of the members present at a meeting of the local or its executive or membership committee" an applicant for readmission cannot be considered to have been readmitted where no official action was taken by the union upon the application. Felman v Fur Dressers' Union (1941, Sup App T) 29 N.Y.S.2d 174

19. – Miscellaneous

So long as it is so authorized by the by-laws of a fire company incorporated under the village law or the membership corporations law, an active village fireman may receive compensation for his services as Secretary-Treasurer of the fire department. 1960 Ops Atty Gen July 25 (informal)

20. – Under former Membership Corporations Law § 40

A bylaw restricting membership is valid. Matthews v Associated Press of State (1893) 136 N.Y. 333, 136 N.Y. 662, 32 N.E. 981

The language of this section compels the conclusion that where the sole method of termination has not been employed, membership would appear still to exist. In re Mt. Sinai Hospital (1926) 128 Misc 476, 219 N.Y.S. 505, affd (1928) 223 A.D. 836, 228 N.Y.S. 855, affd (1928) 250 N.Y. 103, 164 N.E. 871, 62 ALR 564

A member upon joining a membership corporation accepts and agrees to abide by the bylaws of the corporation and the duly adopted amendments thereto; the by-laws are a contract between the corporation and the member. Buffalo Ass'n of Fire Underwriters v Noxsel-Dimick Co. (1931) 141 Misc 333, 253 N.Y.S. 40, revd on other grounds (1932) 235 A.D. 92, 256 N.Y.S. 263, affd (1932) 260 N.Y. 678, 184 N.E. 142

Each person admitted to membership in a membership corporation pursuant to law or its bylaws shall be a member until his membership shall terminate by death, resignation or otherwise. Associated General Contractors of America v Lapardo Bros. Excavating Contractors, Inc. (1964) 43 Misc. 2d 825, 252 N.Y.S.2d 486

The by-laws of an incorporated volunteer fire department may provide for provisional appointment of new members for a probationary period. 1955 Ops St Compt File #7411

21. – Applicant for membership

There is no rule of law which gives power to a court to compel a membership corporation or a voluntary association to accept an applicant as a member. Simons v Berry (1924) 210 A.D. 90, 205 N.Y.S. 442

Where one who is a member of a suspended and subsequently dissolved local union and who is a party to such dissolution, seeks to join the international union of which the former local was affiliated, his status is that of an applicant for membership, not that of one seeking reinstatement, and upon rejection of his application, he cannot claim to have been improperly expelled. Simons v Berry (1924) 210 A.D. 90, 205 N.Y.S. 442

22. – Reduction of membership

The number of members of a membership corporation may be reduced by an amendment in respect thereto to the bylaws, in the absence of a provision in the certificate of incorporation fixing the membership. Keeler v New York Hide Exchange, Inc. (1931) 231 A.D. 450, 247 N.Y.S. 482

A membership corporation may use its capital funds for the purchase of an outstanding certificate of membership, even though such a purchase reduces the outstanding membership of the corporation and such reduction increases the burden of assessment for operating expenses upon each of the remaining members. Keeler v New York Hide Exchange, Inc. (1931) 231 A.D. 450, 247 N.Y.S. 482

A creditor cannot complain of a reduction of membership resulting from the purchase by a membership corporation of an outstanding certificate of membership, at least in the absence of a provision in the certificate of incorporation fixing the number of members. Keeler v New York Hide Exchange, Inc. (1931) 231 A.D. 450, 247 N.Y.S. 482

23. – Voluntary withdrawal of member

By-law of membership corporation which states that any withdrawal must be approved by the board, and, if not so approved, the member may still have the benefit of his contract for a period of two years by continuing to receive service and pay for it, at the end of which period, automatically, his withdrawal shall become final is not invalid as arbitrary. Associated Press v Emmett (1942, DC Cal) 45 F. Supp. 907

24. – Power to discipline or expel

Where the bylaws of a society provide for the expulsion of a member for two specific offenses, and further recite that as to other instances, the directing board has discretion to impose "disciplinary measures and punishments", the term disciplinary measures and punishments does not include the power of expulsion. Pepe v Missanellese Soc. of Mut. Aid (1930) 141 Misc 7, 252 N.Y.S. 70

In the absence of an express provision in the constitution or bylaws of the society, the power of expulsion belongs to the association, that is, to the membership at large. Weinberg v Carton (1949) 196 Misc 74, 90 N.Y.S.2d 398

A member cannot be expelled for failure to comply with a bylaw which conflicts with the statute or the constitution. People ex rel. Doyle v New York Benevolent Soc. of Operative Masons (1875, NY) 3 Hun 361

25. – Procedure for expulsion

Where the bylaws of a membership corporation provide that the nonpayment of dues shall render the delinquent member liable to expulsion, the latter retains his membership until corporate action is taken. Davis v Congregation Beth Tephilas Israel (1899) 40 A.D. 424, 57 N.Y.S. 1015

Where a bylaw provides that in order to expel a member, there must be a hearing at a regular meeting and the person charged must be found guilty by a two-thirds vote of the members present, the directors or the governing body of the association, have no power to conduct a hearing and expel a member at a directors' meeting. Weinberg v Carton (1949) 196 Misc 74, 90 N.Y.S.2d 398

In the absence of any provision in the bylaws or constitution of an organization as to procedure regulating the filing of charges and subsequent preliminary procedure before trial of one charged with an offense which if proved would result in expulsion, such charges must be filed with the members of the association as a body at a meeting of an association, and they, as such body, must prescribe the preliminary procedure. Weinberg v Carton (1949) 196 Misc 74, 90 N.Y.S.2d 398

26. – – Notice of meeting to consider expulsion

Where the bylaws of an organization provide for the participation of the entire membership of the society in a vote for the expulsion of a member, or such bylaws omit to provide for the notice to the members of a meeting at which such a vote is to be taken, proper notice of the meeting and of the right of the members to participate in the trial and the vote for expulsion must nevertheless be given to the members; such notice should properly be given by mail, preferably by registered mail. Weinberg v Carton (1949) 196 Misc 74, 90 N.Y.S.2d 398

An article in the newspaper of a society which merely reports that expulsion proceedings against certain delegates or directors who are unnamed, are scheduled at a delegate's meeting and inviting rank and file members to attend, does not constitute notice to the members of such a meeting, where the bylaws provided that the expulsion of

any member must be by a vote at a meeting of the entire membership. Weinberg v Carton (1949) 196 Misc 74, 90 N.Y.S.2d 398

27. – – Notice of charges

A member cannot be expelled without fair, adequate and sufficient notice, and an opportunity of meeting the accusation. People ex rel. Bartlett v Medical Soc. of County of Erie (1865) 32 N.Y. 187

A bylaw permitting the expulsion of a member without notice of charges and an opportunity to be heard is invalid. Briggs v Technocracy, Inc. (1948, Sup) 85 N.Y.S.2d 735

Expulsion of a member of a membership corporation without notice or a statement of charges or an opportunity to be heard is illegal, notwithstanding the fact that the bylaws of the corporation make no express provisions for a hearing. Briggs v Technocracy, Inc. (1948, Sup) 85 N.Y.S.2d 735

28. – – Waiver of notice

Where a notice of an extraordinary meeting called to consider the expulsion of a member fails to recite the object thereof, but the member whose expulsion was to be considered attended the meeting and raised no question in that regard nor was any objection made by other persons, the member must be deemed to have waived the defect in the notice. Pepe v Missanellese Soc. of Mut. Aid (1930) 141 Misc 7, 252 N.Y.S. 70

29. – Remedy for improper expulsion

While the remedy of mandamus is available to a member who is improperly expelled, the remedies provided by the constitution and bylaws of the corporation should be first exhausted. Lafond v Deems (1880) 81 N.Y. 507

If a member is improperly expelled his remedy is by mandamus. People ex rel. Doyle v New York Benevolent Soc. of Operative Masons (1875, NY) 3 Hun 361

30. – Readmission of expelled member

Where the bylaws of a union provide for readmission of members "on such terms as a local union or Executive Board... may determine upon a two-thirds vote of the members present at a meeting of the local or its executive or membership committee" an applicant for readmission cannot be considered to have been readmitted where no official action was taken by the union upon the application. Felman v Fur Dressers' Union (1941, Sup App T) 29 N.Y.S.2d 174

31. – Membership as property

It has been generally held that, to the extent that an exchange seat or membership includes rights which are transferable and is subject to purchase and sale, it constitutes property, and the proceeds should be applied in payment of the debt of an insolvent debtor. Ulmann v Thomas (1931) 255 N.Y. 506, 175 N.E. 192

The membership of a judgment debtor in a produce exchange, though having a market value, is not property of which a receiver may be appointed to take possession, where the judgment debtor is in a foreign state and beyond the jurisdiction of the court, and the membership is represented by a certificate also beyond the reach of the court which, by the bylaws of the exchange, represents the sole means of transferring or assigning the membership. Ulmann v Thomas (1931) 255 N.Y. 506, 175 N.E. 192

32. – Miscellaneous

Where in an action to recover dues and assessments alleged to be due from incorporation as a member of a membership corporation it is made to appear that the defendant under former § 41 from which the present § 10 is derived could not legally become a member of the plaintiff, the complaint will be dismissed. Doll & Stuffed Toy Mfg. Ass'n v Ideal Novelty & Toy Co. (1922) 119 Misc 63, 195 N.Y.S. 71

In an action to recover the face amount of certificates of indebtedness together with accrued interest thereon, where the certificates provided that no interest should be payable except as declared by the governors and in no event in excess of 6 percent per year, the holders were entitled to no more than the face amount of their certificates less any indebtedness which they might owe the club. Whatever remained after sale of the club would belong to the members. Kendall v Oakland Golf Club (1953, Sup) 123 N.Y.S.2d 907, affd (1953) 282 A.D. 1057, 126 N.Y.S.2d 379, affd (1954) 307 N.Y. 753, 121 N.E.2d 554

§ 602.   By-laws

(a) The initial by-laws of a corporation may be adopted by its incorporators at the organization meeting and, if not so adopted by the incorporators, by its board. Any reference in this chapter to a "by-law adopted by the members" includes a by-law adopted by the incorporators.

(b) Subject to section 612 (Limitations on right to vote), the by-laws may be adopted, amended or repealed by the members at the time entitled to vote in the election of directors and, unless otherwise provided in the certificate of incorporation or the by-laws adopted by the members, by the board.

(c) Any by-law adopted by the board may be amended or repealed by the members and, unless otherwise provided in the certificate of incorporation or the by-laws adopted by the members, any by-law adopted by the members may be amended or repealed by the board.

(d) In the case of a corporation which is subject, under any other law of this state, to regulation or control by a governmental body or officer, such body or officer may, to the extent provided in such other law, in furtherance of its or his authority to regulate or control:

(1) Adopt, amend or repeal by-laws.

(2) Amend or repeal any by-law adopted by the members or the board.

(e) If any by-law regulating an impending election of directors is adopted, amended or repealed by the board, there shall be set forth in the notice of the next meeting of the members for the election of directors the by-law so adopted, amended or repealed, together with a concise statement of the changes made.

(f) The by-laws may contain any provision relating to the business of the corporation, the conduct of its affairs, its rights or powers or the rights or powers of its members, directors or officers, not inconsistent with this chapter or any other statute of this state or the certificate of incorporation.

History: Add, L 1969, ch 1066, § 1, eff Sept 1, 1970, with substance derived from Gen Corp Law §§ 14, 27 and Mem Corp Law § 20.

Par (d), opening par, amd, L 1970, ch 847, § 32, eff Sept 1, 1970.

CASE ANNOTATIONS

1. Generally
2-5. [Reserved for future use]
6. Under former Membership Corporations Law § 20

1. Generally

In a proceeding by a member of a not-for-profit corporation providing free ambulance services in which the member sought to annul a determination expelling her for removing and copying a trip sheet from the corporate headquarters, the member would be reinstated where her conduct violated no rule of the corporation and constituted no breach of any obligation to the corporation. Ames v Central Oneida County Volunteer Ambulance Corps. (1981, 4th Dept) 81 A.D.2d 1035, 440 N.Y.S.2d 122

Where original constitution of not-for-profit corporation provided that all officers should be elected for term of one year and that no officer should succeed himself for more than two successive years for same office, and term of office was increased to two years but it was neglected to amend time provided for succession, period of one year would be construed to mean "one term" in order to give meaning to constitutional provision on succession. In re Election of Officers & Directors of F.I.G.H.T., Inc. (1974) 79 Misc. 2d 655, 360 N.Y.S.2d 564

Where, though irregularities appeared to have taken place, there was no showing of fraud or wrongdoing and it appeared that, even if some delegates to convention of not-for-profit corporation members were barred, their vote or presence would not have changed results of election of officers, new election was denied. In re Election of Officers & Directors of F.I.G.H.T., Inc. (1974) 79 Misc. 2d 655, 360 N.Y.S.2d 564

In a personal injury action defendant ski club's motion for summary judgment would be denied, where, although an exculpatory clause contained in the by-laws of the ski club purporting to exempt the club from liability for "claims of any kind... including claims resulting from the negligence of an... employee of... the Club... arising out of the use of any of the Club's facilities" by a member or the member's family was sufficiently clear and unambiguous as to include within its scope the injuries sustained by plaintiff, the wife of a club member while using the club's chair lift, such exculpatory clause was nonetheless unenforceable against either plaintiff or her husband on his derivative claim, where plaintiff who was a nonmember of the club did not agree to indemnification nor was she apprised of the existence of the exculpatory clause and her husband never received the by-laws and had no notice of the exculpatory clause until after institution of the suit, where defendant club offered no proof that the exculpatory clause was properly enacted by the membership after sufficient notice had been sent to the members as required by N-PCL § 602, and where, in any event, the exculpatory clause was invalid under Gen Oblig Law § 5-326 which deems void as against public policy any agreement exempting a place of amusement or recreation or similar establishment from liability for damages caused by or resulting from its own negligence and defendant, at the time of the accident, was a "place of... recreation" within the plain meaning of the statute. Blanc v Windham Mountain Club, Inc. (1982, Sup) 115 Misc. 2d 404, 454 N.Y.S.2d 383, affd (1983, 1st Dept) 92 A.D.2d 529, 459 N.Y.S.2d 447

Automatic suspension provided by a not-for-profit corporation's by-laws was unenforceable because it violated N.Y. Not-for-Profit Corp. Law § 507(c); it was undisputed that no notice was given to the members that had not paid dues, and, thus, pursuant to § 507(c), the votes of members who had not paid dues could not have been disqualified from voting on amendments to the by-laws based solely on that basis. Abraham v Diamond Dealers Club, Inc. (2010, Sup) 896 NYS2d 848.

Automatic suspension provided by a not-for-profit corporation's by-laws was unenforceable because it violated N.Y. Not-for-Profit Corp. Law § 507(c); it was undisputed that no notice was given to the members that had not paid dues, and, thus, pursuant to § 507(c), the votes of members who had not paid dues could not have been disqualified from voting an amendments to the by-laws based solely on that basis. Abraham v Diamond Dealers Club, Inc. (2010, Sup) 27 Misc 3d 663, 896 NYS2d 848, affd, motion den (2011, NY App Div, 1st Dept) 2011 NY Slip Op 92, 2011 NY App Div LEXIS 98.

There is prima facie validity to any provision of a not-for-profit corporation by-law restricting right of member to withdraw voluntarily. Leon v Chrysler Motors Corp. (1973, DC NJ) 358 F. Supp. 877, affd without op (1973, CA3 NJ) 474 F.2d 1340

By-laws of not-for-profit corporation which required each member to agree not to withdraw from the association without the consent of a majority of all members were valid despite fact that members were in effect locked into the association unless they could persuade a majority of the members to vote against their own economic interests to release them. Leon v Chrysler Motors Corp. (1973, DC NJ) 358 F. Supp. 877, affd without op (1973, CA3 NJ) 474 F.2d 1340

A fire company may adopt a bylaw providing that only firemen who attend at least 15 percent of all fire calls during the year may vote in an election of line officers of the fire company. 1982 Op Atty Gen March 5 (informal)

An incorporated volunteer fire company may amend its by-laws and constitution to require that members of the company attend at least three meetings annually as a qualification to vote for company officers. 1983 Op St Compt File #83-65

Under Sections 10-1000 et seq. of the Village Law, a village fire department is a corporation consisting of members of all the fire, hose, protective and hook and ladder companies of a village; it is administered by a board of fire commissioners or, where no board of fire commissioners has been appointed, by the village board of trustees and the council of the fire department. Fire companies in a village are associations or corporations, which must operate in accordance with their certificates of incorporation, bylaws, and statutes; and, although fire companies are separate and distinct from the village, the statutes do permit village authorities to exercise a certain degree of control over their organization, incorporation, governance, and membership, including residency for membership. A fire company must consent to a contract for the provision of fire protection outside the village and the fire chief of the village fire department cannot consent on behalf of members of the company. 1990 Op St Compt 90-19

2003 amended by-laws of a non-profit corporation that owned an apartment building violated N.Y. Not-for-Profit Corp. Law § 602(f) and 611(e) because no shares could be issued pursuant to N.Y. Not-for-Profit Corp. Law § 501 and each member could have only one vote; it was improper to give petitioner families entitlement to an additional vote because they possessed an additional unit. Matter of Thakur v 210 Forsyth St. Hous. Dev. Fund Corp. (2007, Sup) 844 NYS2d 686.

2-5. [Reserved for future use]

6. Under former Membership Corporations Law § 20

Bylaws must be reasonable. Matthews v Associated Press of State (1893) 136 N.Y. 333, 662, 136 N.Y. 662, 32 N.E. 981

An amendment to the bylaws of a membership corporation organized for charitable purposes which permits amendments to the bylaws without notice to the members of the corporation may be unwise and contrary to the corporation's best interests, but it is not so unreasonable or unfair that it is beyond the power of the members to adopt, especially where no member has objected. In re Flushing Hospital & Dispensary (1942) 288 N.Y. 125, 41 N.E.2d 917, remittitur amd (1942) 288 N.Y. 735, 43 N.E.2d 356 and remittitur den (1942) 289 N.Y. 654, 44 N.E.2d 626

Where amended bylaws were adopted without proper notice, but for seven years had gone unchallenged by the membership of the corporation and the affairs of the corporation have been conducted in accordance therewith, there has been a waiver of the irregularity and the bylaws are valid. In re Flushing Hospital & Dispensary (1942) 288 N.Y. 125, 41 N.E.2d 917, remittitur amd (1942) 288 N.Y. 735, 43 N.E.2d 356 and remittitur den (1942) 289 N.Y. 654, 44 N.E.2d 626

Under § 20 the bylaws of a New York membership corporation may not make provisions inconsistent with law. Davids v Sillcox (1948) 297 N.Y. 355, 79 N.E.2d 440, reh den (1948) 298 N.Y. 618, 81 N.E.2d 353

Where the bylaws do not state whether they may be amended by a vote of the directors, or by a vote of electors and delegates, or by a vote of the members, the directors have no power to change the bylaws of a society which governs eligibility to membership. Croughan v New York Mut. Benevolent Soc. (1917) 179 A.D. 211, 166 N.Y.S. 161

A member of a membership corporation makes the by-laws thereof a part of his contract of membership and becomes bound by them. Cabana v Holstein-Friesian Ass'n (1921) 196 A.D. 842, 188 N.Y.S. 277, affd (1922) 233 N.Y. 644, 135 N.E. 953

A purported election will be set aside where such election was not in accord with the corporation's bylaws. Brunone v Societa' Mutuo Soccorso, etc. (1938) 254 A.D. 753, 4 N.Y.S.2d 305

The bylaws of a corporation when legally adopted, which are reasonable and fair in character, have the force of law within the corporate body. In re Flushing Hospital & Dispensary (1941, Sup) 27 N.Y.S.2d 207, affd (1941) 262 A.D. 749, 28 N.Y.S.2d 155, mod (1942) 288 N.Y. 125, 41 N.E.2d 917, remittitur amd (1942) 288 N.Y. 735, 43 N.E.2d 356 and remittitur den (1942) 289 N.Y. 654, 44 N.E.2d 626

The membership application, the constitution and by-laws of membership corporations are the contract by which each member is bound. Associated Press v Emmett (1942, DC Cal) 45 F. Supp. 907

§ 603.   Meetings of members

(a) Meetings of members may be held at such place, within or without this state, as may be fixed by or under the by-laws or, if not so fixed, at the office of the corporation in this state.

(b) A meeting of the members shall be held annually for the election of directors and the transaction of other business on a date fixed by or under the by-laws. Failure to hold the annual meeting on the date so fixed or to elect a sufficient number of directors to

conduct the business of the corporation shall not work a forfeiture or give cause for dissolution of the corporation, except as provided in paragraph (a) of section 1102 (Judicial dissolution; petition by directors or members; petition in case of deadlock among directors or members).

(c) Special meetings of the members may be called by the board and by such person or persons as may be authorized by the certificate of incorporation or the by-laws. In any case, such meetings may be convened by the members entitled to cast ten per cent of the total number of votes entitled to be cast at such meeting, who may, in writing, demand the call of a special meeting specifying the date and month thereof, which shall not be less than two nor more than three months from the date of such written demand. The secretary of the corporation upon receiving the written demand shall promptly give notice of such meeting, or if he fails to do so within five business days thereafter, any member signing such demand may give such notice. The meeting shall be held at the place fixed in the by-laws or, if not so fixed, at the office of the corporation.

(d) A corporation may provide in its certificate of incorporation or by-laws adopted by the members for the election of representatives or delegates, who, when assembled within or without the state as directed by the certificate of incorporation or the by-laws, shall have and may exercise all of the powers, rights and privileges of members at an annual meeting. When so exercising the powers, rights and privileges of members, such representatives or delegates shall be subject in all respects to the provisions of this chapter governing members.

History: Add, L 1969, ch 1066, § 1, eff Sept 1, 1970, with substance derived from Gen Corp Law §§ 21, 26 and Mem Corp Law §§ 42, 44.

Par (c), amd, L 1971, ch 1058 § 14, L 1972, ch 961, § 8, eff Sept 1, 1972.

CASE ANNOTATIONS

1. Generally
2-5. [Reserved for future use]
6. Under former General Corporation Law § 21
7. Under former Membership Corporations Law § 44
8. Under former Membership Corporations Law § 45

1. Generally

Defendants' counterclaim to compel plaintiff church to call a special membership meeting for the purpose of voting on a proposed amendment to the church's by-laws that was submitted by an individual defendant church member at a parish meeting would be dismissed where the proposed resolution was not submitted in accordance with N-PCL Law § 603(c), which requires a written demand by 10 percent of the members eligible to vote to compel church officials to call such a meeting when the church charter or by-laws do not provide therefor. Rector, Church Wardens & Vestrymen etc. v Committee to Preserve St. Bartholomew's Church, Inc. (1981, 1st Dept) 84 A.D.2d 516, 443 N.Y.S.2d 233

N-PCL § 603(3) is not in conflict with Relig Corps Law § 5, inasmuch as the Relig Corp L makes no provision for convening a special meeting of parishioners to vote on a proposed amendment to the Church's by-laws. Rector, Church Wardens & Vestrymen etc. v Committee to Preserve St. Bartholomew's Church, Inc. (1981, 1st Dept) 84 A.D.2d 516, 443 N.Y.S.2d 233

2-5. [Reserved for future use]

6. Under former General Corporation Law § 21

Where plaintiff was elected as a member of the board of directors of the Jamaica Community Corporation for a term of one year commencing in June of 1967 and continued to serve as director until receiving a letter on October 4, 1968 which purported to terminate his membership; plaintiff was entitled to a preliminary injunction to enjoin the defendant chairman of the board from conducting meetings unless and until plaintiff was permitted to participate, where no successor had been elected to his position on the board. The court held that General Corporation Law § 21 must be deemed controlling to preserve plaintiff's position until his successor was elected. Ming v Simpkins (1968) 59 Misc. 2d 853, 300 N.Y.S.2d 805

7. Under former Membership Corporations Law § 44

A provision in the bylaws of a lodge that any number of delegates may be held to constitute a quorum at a "second call meeting" is void since it violates the provisions of § 20 and this applies equally to meetings of delegates, even though this section contains no statement as to what constitutes a quorum. Di Silvestro v Sons of Italy Grand Lodge (1927) 130 Misc 494, 223 N.Y.S. 791

8. Under former Membership Corporations Law § 45

A purported election will be set aside where such election was not in accord with the corporation's bylaws. Brunone v Societa' Mutuo Soccorso, etc. (1938) 254 A.D. 753, 4 N.Y.S.2d 305

This section is inapplicable to a membership corporation created by special law. Petition of Sousa (1961, 2d Dept) 12 A.D.2d 956, 211 N.Y.S.2d 204, revd on other grounds (1961) 10 N.Y.2d 68, 217 N.Y.S.2d 58, 176 N.E.2d 77, stay den (1961) 9 N.Y.2d 1015 and remittitur amd (1961) 10 N.Y.2d 886, reported in full (1961) 10 N.Y.2d 812, 221 N.Y.S.2d 515, 178 N.E.2d 230 and stay gr (1961) 10 N.Y.2d 885

In the absence of provision in the bylaws to the contrary, members of one faction of a club may solicit and induct into membership new members for the purpose of gaining their support in a forthcoming election. Petition of Serenbetz (1943, Sup) 46 N.Y.S.2d 475, affd (1944) 267 A.D. 836, 46 N.Y.S.2d 127

If a bylaw for the election of directors has not been adopted, a valid election may be held under the General Corporation Law on the call of any member of the corporation. In re David Jones Co. (1893) 67 Hun 360, 22 N.Y.S. 318

§ 604.   Special meeting for election of directors

(a) If, for a period of one month after the date fixed by or under the by-laws for the annual meeting of members or, if no date has been so fixed, for a period of thirteen months after the formation of the corporation or the last annual meeting, there is a failure to elect a sufficient number of directors to conduct the business of the corporation, the board shall call a special meeting for the election of directors. If such special meeting is not called by the board within two weeks after the expiration of such period or if it is so called but there is a failure to elect such directors for a period of two months after the expiration of such period, members entitled to cast one hundred votes or ten per cent of the total number of votes entitled to be cast in an election of directors, whichever is lesser, may, in writing, demand the call of a special meeting for the election of directors specifying the date and month thereof, which shall not be less than two nor more than three months from the date of such written demand. The secretary of the corporation upon receiving the written demand shall promptly give notice of such meeting or, if he fails to do so within five business days thereafter, any member signing such demand may give such notice.

The meeting shall be held at the place fixed in the by-laws or, if not so fixed, at the office of the corporation.

(b) At any such special meeting called on the demand of members, notwithstanding section 608 (Quorum of members), the members attending, in person or by proxy, and entitled to vote in an election of directors shall constitute a quorum for the purpose of electing directors, but not for the transaction of any other business.

History: Add, L 1969, ch 1066, § 1, eff Sept 1, 1970, with substance derived from Gen Corp Law §§ 22, 23.

CASE ANNOTATIONS

1. Generally

2-5. [Reserved for future use]

6. Under former General Corporation Law § 22

1. Generally

Defendants were entitled to summary judgment declaring that they were proper officers, directors and trustees of plaintiff nonprofit corporation where they established that "special annual membership meeting" at which those in attendance voted to remove them as members of board of trustees, and to elect new board, had been called without requisite notice and in violation of other sections of applicable by-laws. Residents for Equitable & Affordable Permanent Shelter v Lawrence (1997, 2d Dept) 236 A.D.2d 382, 654 N.Y.S.2d 575

2-5. [Reserved for future use]

6. Under former General Corporation Law § 22

The provisions of General Corporation Law § 22 are applicable where there is a claim failure to elect directors of a membership corporation. In re Election of Directors of FDR-Woodrow Wilson Democrats, Inc. (1968) 57 Misc. 2d 743, 293 N.Y.S.2d 463

Where due notice was given of annual membership meeting of membership corporation but directors of corporation were not elected on such date, subsequent election of directors at membership meeting, notice of which was insufficient in accordance with statute and by-laws was void. In re Election of Directors of FDR-Woodrow Wilson Democrats, Inc. (1968) 57 Misc. 2d 743, 293 N.Y.S.2d 463

This section is applicable to a membership corporation since its provisions are not in conflict with any provision of the Membership Corporation Law. Application of Atwater (1948, Sup) 85 N.Y.S.2d 738, affd (1950) 277 A.D. 766, 97 N.Y.S.2d 541, app den (1950) 277 A.D. 1104, 101 N.Y.S.2d 731

Where, under the conditions in the case, any member of a membership corporation could call a meeting pursuant to this section, petitioning members of such a corporation were not entitled to an order to compel the directors to call a meeting for the purpose of electing officers and directors. Application of Atwater (1948, Sup) 85 N.Y.S.2d 738, affd (1950) 277 A.D. 766, 97 N.Y.S.2d 541, app den (1950) 277 A.D. 1104, 101 N.Y.S.2d 731

§ 605.   Notice of meeting of members

(a) Whenever under the provisions of this chapter members are required or permitted to take any action at a meeting, written notice shall state the place, date and hour of the meeting and, unless it is an annual meeting, indicate that it is being issued by or at the direction of the person or persons calling the meeting. Notice of a special meeting shall also state the purpose or purposes for which the meeting is called. A copy of the notice of any meeting shall be given, personally, by mail, or by facsimile telecommunications or by electronic mail, to each member entitled to vote at such meeting. If the notice is given personally, by first class mail or by facsimile telecommunications or by electronic mail, it shall be given not less than ten nor more than fifty days before the date of the meeting; if mailed by any other class of mail, it shall be given not less than thirty nor more than sixty days before such date. If mailed, such notice is given when deposited in the United States mail, with postage thereon prepaid, directed to the member at his address as it appears on the record of members, or, if he shall have filed with the secretary of the corporation a written request that notices to him be mailed to some other address, then directed to him at such other address. If sent by facsimile telecommunication or mailed electronically, such notice is given when directed to the member's fax number or electronic mail address as it appears on the record of members, or, to such fax number or other electronic mail address as filed with the secretary of the corporation. Notwithstanding the foregoing, such notice shall not be deemed to have been given electronically (1) if the corporation is unable to deliver two consecutive notices to the member by facsimile telecommunication or electronic mail; or (2) the corporation otherwise becomes aware that notice cannot be delivered to the member by facsimile telecommunication or electronic mail. An affidavit of the secretary or other person giving the notice or of a transfer agent of the corporation that the notice required by this section has been given shall, in the absence of fraud, be prima facie evidence of the facts therein stated. Whenever a corporation has more than five hundred members, the notice may be served by publication in a newspaper published in the county in the state in which the principal office of the corporation is located, once a week for three successive weeks next preceding the date of the meeting, provided that the corporation shall also prominently post notice of such meeting on the homepage of any website maintained by the corporation continuously from the date of publication through the date of the meeting. A corporation shall send notice of meetings by first class mail to any member who requests in writing that such notices be delivered by such method.

(b) When a meeting is adjourned to another time or place, it shall not be necessary, unless the by-laws require otherwise, to give any notice of the adjourned meeting if the time and place to which the meeting is adjourned are announced at the meeting at which the adjournment is taken, and at the adjourned meeting any business may be transacted that might have been transacted on the original date of the meeting. However, if after the adjournment the board fixes a new record date for the adjourned meeting, a notice of the adjourned meeting shall be given to each member of record on the new record date entitled to notice under paragraph (a).

History: Add, L 1969, ch 1066, § 1, eff Sept 1, 1970, with substance derived from Mem Corp Law §§ 42, 43; amd, L 1971, ch 1058 § 15, eff Sept 1, 1971, L 2013, ch 549, § 62, eff July 1, 2014.

CASE ANNOTATIONS

1. Generally

2-5. [Reserved for future use]
6. Under former Membership Corporations Law § 20
7. Under former Membership Corporations Law § 42
8. Under former Membership Corporations Law § 43

1. Generally
Congregation had the authority to discharge members of a not-for-profit corporation's board of directors because (1) N.Y. Not-for-Profit Corp. Law § 703(b) and the corporation's bylaws only let the board increase the board's number, (2) the congregation, as the corporation's sole member, could not be denied the right to vote except by the congregation's removal or resignation, under N.Y. Not-for-Profit Corp. Law §§ 612 and 605(a), so bylaw amendments denying that right had no effect, (3) the bylaws in effect let the congregation veto the board's bylaw amendments, and (4) the congregation vetoed amendments denying the congregation the rights to vote, remove directors, and adopt, amend, or repeal bylaws. Gluck v Chevre Liady Nusach Hoary (2012, 2d Dept) 97 App Div 3d 787, 949 NYS2d 149

Congregation had the authority to discharge members of a not-for-profit corporation's board of directors without notice because (1) the congregation was the corporation's sole member, (2) N.Y. Not-for-Profit Corp. Law § 605(a) only entitled members to notice, and (3) the corporation's certificate of incorporation and bylaws did not require notice. Gluck v Chevre Liady Nusach Hoary (2012, 2d Dept) 97 App Div 3d 787, 949 NYS2d 149

Where, though irregularities appeared to have taken place, there was no showing of fraud or wrongdoing and it appeared that, even if some delegates to convention of not-for-profit corporation members were barred, their vote or presence would not have changed results of election of officers, new election was denied. In re Election of Officers & Directors of F.I.G.H.T., Inc. (1974) 79 Misc. 2d 655, 360 N.Y.S.2d 564

Meeting of delegates of public employee labor union organized as not-for-profit corporation was nullity, and all actions taken at meeting were void, where union's constitution provided that each local chapter elect delegates who were, in effect, representatives of union rank and file, but only notice of meeting sent to all such delegates failed to set forth time and place of meeting and thus failed to comply with CLS N-PCL § 605. Simoni v Civil Service Employees Asso., Local 1000, etc. (1986, Sup) 133 Misc. 2d 1, 507 N.Y.S.2d 371

2-5. [Reserved for future use]
6. Under former Membership Corporations Law § 20
Where the bylaws of a corporation provide for the expulsion of members by the rank and file members, after a hearing held at a regular meeting of members, the chance presence of certain members at a directors' meeting, and participation by them in a vote along with the directors present, resulting in a purported expulsion, does not lend validity to the proceedings. Weinberg v Carton (1949) 196 Misc 74, 90 N.Y.S.2d 398

Where the bylaws of an organization provide for the participation of the entire membership of the society in a vote for the expulsion of a member, but such bylaws omit to provide for notice to the members of a meeting at which such a vote is to be taken, proper notice of the meeting and of the right of the members to participate in the trial and the vote for expulsion must nevertheless be given to the members; such notice should properly be given by mail, preferably by registered mail. Weinberg v Carton (1949) 196 Misc 74, 90 N.Y.S.2d 398

An article in the newspaper of a society which merely reports that expulsion proceedings against certain delegates or directors who are unnamed are scheduled at a delegates' meeting, and inviting rank and file members to attend, does not constitute notice to the members of such a meeting, where the bylaws provided that the expulsion of any member must be by a vote at a meeting of the entire membership. Weinberg v Carton (1949) 196 Misc 74, 90 N.Y.S.2d 398

7. Under former Membership Corporations Law § 42
Where there is no provision in the constitution or the bylaws of an unincorporated association specifying the time or manner of giving notice of a meeting, such notice must be given a reasonable time before the date of the meeting at which authorization is given to incorporate the association. Heights Democratic Club, Inc. v Brewer (1947) 272 A.D. 1009, 74 N.Y.S.2d 243

A notice of a meeting of an unincorporated association at which authorization was given to incorporate, is inadequate in the absence of any provision in the association's bylaws or constitution in regard thereto, where notice was mailed but two days before the meeting was held, and it does not appear that the notice was sent to all the-members of the association insofar as they were known or could have been identified. Heights Democratic Club, Inc. v Brewer (1947) 272 A.D. 1009, 74 N.Y.S.2d 243

8. Under former Membership Corporations Law § 43

Although the votes cast at a meeting of a membership corporation in favor of the consolidation with another membership corporation were not by at least 2/3 of its members entitled to vote thereon and the notice of meeting might have been defective in that it was not given at least 10 days before the meeting and was not signed by an executive officer, former treasurer of one of the consolidated clubs could not claim that consolidation should be upset on those grounds in the light of the fact that he took no steps to litigate his claim until after a lapse of almost a year after said meeting and seven months after the court approved the certificate of consolidation. Liberal Civic Club, Inc. v Poli (1954) 284 A.D. 1057, 135 N.Y.S.2d 814

Where there was a substantial controversy between parties, and moving papers were voluminous, motion for injunction pendente lite was denied. Sorokin v Young Israel of Kings Bay (1954, Sup) 133 N.Y.S.2d 242

§ 606.   Waivers of notice

Notice of meeting need not be given to any member who submits a waiver of notice, in person or by proxy, whether before or after the meeting. Waiver of notice may be written or electronic. If written, the waiver must be executed by the member or the member's authorized officer, director, employee, or agent by signing such waiver or causing his or her signature to be affixed to such waiver by any reasonable means, including, but not limited to facsimile signature. If electronic, the transmission of the waiver must be sent by electronic mail and set forth, or be submitted with, information from which it can reasonably be determined that the transmission was authorized by the member. The attendance of any member at a meeting, in person or by proxy, without protesting prior to the conclusion of the meeting the lack of notice of such meeting, shall constitute a waiver of notice by him or her.

History: Add, L 1969, ch 1066, § 1, eff Sept 1, 1970, with substance derived from Gen Corp Law § 31; amd, L 2013, ch 549, § 63, eff July 1, 2014; L 2015, ch 358, § 4, eff Sept 25, 2015.

CASE ANNOTATIONS

Where, though irregularities appeared to have taken place, there was no showing of fraud or wrongdoing and it appeared that, even if some delegates to convention of not-for-profit corporation members were barred, their vote or presence would not have changed results of election of officers, new election was denied. In re Election of Officers & Directors of F.I.G.H.T., Inc. (1974) 79 Misc. 2d 655, 360 N.Y.S.2d 564

Under evidence, members of not-for-profit corporation acquiesced in action of previous convention in adopting constitutional amendment, and failure to question validity of amendment prior to application to court following election at 1974 convention constituted waiver of claim that improper notice had been given as to amendment. In re Election of Officers & Directors of F.I.G.H.T., Inc. (1974) 79 Misc. 2d 655, 360 N.Y.S.2d 564

There could be no waiver, under CLS N-PCL § 606, of notice of special meeting of delegates of public employee labor union organized as not-for- profit corporation where delegate submitted affidavit stating that he did not attend meeting because of lack of notice, and no evidence was produced that such delegate received proper notice of meeting, leaving no factual dispute on issue. Simoni v Civil Service Employees Asso., Local 1000, etc. (1986, Sup) 133 Misc. 2d 1, 507 N.Y.S.2d 371

§ 607.   List or record of members at meetings

A list or record of members entitled to vote, certified by the corporate officer responsible for its preparation or by a transfer agent, shall be produced at any meeting of members upon the request therefor of any member who has given written notice to the corporation that such request will be made at least ten days prior to such meeting. If the right to vote at any meeting is challenged, the inspectors of election, or the person presiding thereat, shall require such list or record of members to be produced as evidence of the right of the persons challenged to vote at such meeting, and all persons who appear from such list or record to be members entitled to vote thereat may vote at such meeting.

History: Add, L 1969, ch 1066, § 1, with substance deriving from Mem Corp Law, § 41; amd, L 1970, ch 847, § 33, eff Sept 1, 1970.

CASE ANNOTATIONS

Where, though irregularities appeared to have taken place, there was no showing of fraud or wrongdoing and it appeared that, even if some delegates to convention of not-for-profit corporation members were barred, their vote or presence would not have changed results of election of officers, new election was denied. In re Election of Officers & Directors of F.I.G.H.T., Inc. (1974) 79 Misc. 2d 655, 360 N.Y.S.2d 564

§ 608.   Quorum at meeting of members

(a) Members entitled to cast a majority of the total number of votes entitled to be cast thereat shall constitute a quorum at a meeting of members for the transaction of any business, provided that when a specified item of business is required to be voted on by a class of members, voting as a class, members entitled to cast a majority of the total number of votes entitled to be cast by such class shall constitute a quorum for the transaction of such specified items of business.

(b) The certificate of incorporation or the by-laws may provide for any lesser quorum not less than the members entitled to cast one hundred votes or one-tenth of the total number of votes entitled to be cast, whichever is lesser, and may, under section 615 (Greater requirement as to quorum and vote of members), provide for a greater quorum.

(c) Action to amend the certificate of incorporation or by-laws to conform to paragraph (b) may be taken at a special meeting of members at which the quorum requirements applicable to the corporation immediately prior to the effective date of this chapter are fulfilled, but action may be taken only once under this paragraph.

(d) The members present may adjourn the meeting despite the absence of a quorum.

(e) If for any reason it has proved to be impractical or impossible for a corporation to obtain a quorum in order to conduct a meeting of its members in the manner prescribed by its certificate or by-laws or by statute, then upon the petition of a director, officer or member to the supreme court in the judicial district where the office of the corporation is or was located on notice to the attorney general or by the attorney general, the supreme court may in its discretion dispense with the requirement as to quorums that would otherwise be imposed by the corporation's certificate of incorporation or by-laws or by statute. The petition shall set forth the reasonable efforts the corporation has made to obtain a quorum, including the manner in which the corporation provided notice to its members of prior meetings. The supreme court shall, in an order issued pursuant to this section, provide for a method of notice reasonably designed to give actual notice to all persons who would be entitled to notice of a meeting held pursuant to the certificate of incorporation or by-laws or the statute, whether or not the method results in actual notice to all such persons or conforms to the notice requirements that would otherwise apply. In a proceeding under this section the court may determine who are the members of the corporation.

(f) For purposes of this section "person" means any association, corporation, joint stock company, estate, general partnership (including any registered limited liability partnership or foreign limited liability partnership), limited association, limited liability company (including a professional service limited liability company), foreign limited liability company (including a foreign professional service limited liability company), joint venture, limited partnership, natural person, real estate investment trust, business trust or other trust, custodian, nominee or any other individual or entity in its own or any representative capacity.

History: Add, L 1969, ch 1066, § 1, eff Sept 1, 1970, with substance derived from Gen Corp Law § 14 and Mem Corp Law § 20; amd, L 1971, ch 1058 § 16; L 1972, ch 961, § 9, eff Sept 1, 1972; L 2005, ch 726, § 2, eff April 9, 2006; L 2006, ch 434, § 2, eff July 26, 2006.

CASE ANNOTATIONS
1. Generally
2-5. [Reserved for future use]
6. Under former Membership Corporations Law § 20

1. Generally

Because the quorum provision in a society's revised bylaws was inconsistent with N.Y. Not-for-Profit Corp. Law § 608(a), the trial court properly determined that the bylaws were null and void and enjoined the society from exercising any powers or taking any action pursuant to the bylaws relating to the removal of the officers and directors. Sealey v American Socy. of Hypertension, Inc. (2006, App Div, 1st Dept) 810 NYS2d 48

2-5. [Reserved for future use]

6. Under former Membership Corporations Law § 20

A provision in the by-laws of a lodge that any number of delegates may be held to constitute a quorum at a "second call meeting" is void since it violates the provisions of the Mem. Corp. Law of 1909, § 8 (now this section). Mem. Corp. Law of 1909, § 8 controls although there is no statement in the Mem. Corp. Law of 1909, § 44 (now the Mem. Corp. Law of 1926, § 44) as to number of delegates necessary to constitute a quorum, where the meeting is held by delegates instead of by members. Di Silvestro v Sons of Italy Grand Lodge (1927) 130 Misc 494, 223 N.Y.S. 791

Where the membership of a membership corporation had dwindled to less than thirty persons, an event in which the bylaws of the corporation through an oversight failed to indicate what constituted a quorum, and where at least nine members were present and voted at

a duly called meeting, election of officers at such a meeting is a valid act. Application of Havender (1943) 181 Misc 989, 44 N.Y.S.2d 213, affd (1944) 267 A.D. 860, 47 N.Y.S.2d 114, reh and app den (1944) 267 A.D. 901, 48 N.Y.S.2d 325

§ 609.   Proxies

(a) Except as otherwise provided in the certificate of incorporation or the by-laws:

(1) Every member entitled to vote at a meeting of members or to express consent or dissent without a meeting may authorize another person or persons to act for him by proxy.

(2) No proxy shall be valid after the expiration of eleven months from the date thereof unless otherwise provided in the proxy. Every proxy shall be revocable at the pleasure of the member executing it, except as otherwise provided in this section.

(3) The authority of the holder of a proxy to act shall not be revoked by the incompetence or death of the member who executed the proxy unless, before the authority is exercised, written notice of an adjudication of such incompetence or of such death is received by the corporate officer responsible for maintaining the list or record of members.

(4) Except when other provision shall have been made by written agreement between the parties, the record holder of capital certificates which he holds as pledgee or otherwise as security or which belong to another, shall issue to the pledgor or to such owner of such capital certificates, upon demand therefor and payment of necessary expenses thereof, a proxy to vote or take other action thereon.

(5) A member shall not sell his vote or issue a proxy to vote to any person for any sum of money or anything of value, except as authorized in this section and section 619 (Agreements as to voting).

(6) A proxy which is entitled "irrevocable proxy" and which states that it is irrevocable is irrevocable when it is held by any of the following or a nominee of any of the following:

(A) A pledgee.

(B) A person who has purchased or agreed to purchase the capital certificates.

(C) A creditor or creditors of the corporation who extend or continue credit to the corporation in consideration of the proxy if the proxy states that it was given in consideration of such extension or continuation of credit, the amount thereof, and the name of the person extending or continuing credit.

(D) A person who has contracted to perform services as an officer of the corporation, if a proxy is required by the contract of employment, if the proxy states that it was given in consideration of such contract of employment, the name of the employee and the period of employment contracted for.

(E) A person designated by or under an agreement under section 619.

(7) Notwithstanding a provision in a proxy, stating that it is irrevocable, the proxy becomes revocable after the pledge is redeemed, or the debt of the

corporation is paid, or the period of employment provided for in the contract of employment has terminated, or the agreement under section 619 has terminated; and, in a case provided for in subparagraphs (6)(C) or (D), becomes revocable three years after the date of the proxy or the end of the period, if any, specified therein, whichever period is less, unless the period of irrevocability is renewed from time to time by the execution of a new irrevocable proxy as provided in this section. This paragraph does not affect the duration of a proxy under subparagraph (2).

(8) A proxy may be revoked, notwithstanding a provision making it irrevocable, by a purchaser of capital certificates without knowledge of the existence of the provision unless the existence of the proxy and its irrevocability is noted conspicuously on the face or back of the capital certificate.

(b) Without limiting the manner in which a member may authorize another person or persons to act for him as proxy pursuant to paragraph (a) of this section, the following shall constitute a valid means by which a member may grant such authority:

(1) A member may execute a writing authorizing another person or persons to act for him as proxy. Execution may be accomplished by the member or the member's authorized officer, director, employee or agent signing such writing or causing his or her signature to be affixed to such writing by any reasonable means including, but not limited to, by facsimile signature.

(2) A member may authorize another person or persons to act for the member as proxy by providing such authorization by electronic mail to the person who will be the holder of the proxy or to a proxy solicitation firm, proxy support service organization or like agent duly authorized by the person, provided that any such authorization by electronic mail shall either set forth information from which it can be reasonably determined that the authorization by electronic mail was authorized by the member. If it is determined that such authorization by electronic mail is valid, the inspectors or, if there are no inspectors, such other persons making that determination shall specify the nature of the information upon which they relied.

(c) Any copy, facsimile telecommunication or other reliable reproduction of the writing or electronic mail created pursuant to paragraph (b) of this section may be substituted or used in lieu of the original writing or transmission for any and all purposes for which the original writing or transmission could be used, provided that such copy, facsimile telecommunication or other reproduction shall be a complete reproduction of the entire original writing or transmission.

History: Add, L 1969, ch 1066, § 1, with substance deriving from Gen Corp Law § 19 and Mem Corp Law § 41; amd, L 1970, ch 847, § 34, eff Sept 1, 1970, L 1999, ch 186, §§ 1, 2, eff July 6, 1999, L 2013, ch 549, § 64, eff July 1, 2014.

CASE ANNOTATIONS

1. Generally
2-5. [Reserved for future use]
6. Under former Membership Corporations Law § 20
7. Under former Membership Corporations Law § 41

1. Generally
Unless provided in certificate of incorporation or bylaws, proxy voting by members of religious corporation is not authorized except for limited purposes set forth in CLS Relig Corp § 207. Holler v Goldberg (1995, Sup) 163 Misc. 2d 1075, 623 N.Y.S.2d 512

2-5. [Reserved for future use]

6. Under former Membership Corporations Law § 20
Bylaws of a membership corporation which deprive members of the privilege of registering proxy votes are invalid as in conflict with the express provisions of § 41 of the Membership Corporation Law. Flynn v Kendall (1949) 195 Misc 221, 88 N.Y.S.2d 299

7. Under former Membership Corporations Law § 41
The right to vote by proxy, specifically conferred by this section, is not abridged by the failure of the bylaws of a membership corporation to provide for voting by proxy. Flynn v Kendall (1949) 195 Misc 221, 88 N.Y.S.2d 299

A provision of the bylaws of a membership corporation, that the board shall be elected by the vote of members present at the meeting, does not restrict the right to vote by proxy expressly conferred by this section. Flynn v Kendall (1949) 195 Misc 221, 88 N.Y.S.2d 299

Directors cannot vote by proxy. Craig Medicine Co. v Merchants' Bank of Rochester (1891) 59 Hun 561, 14 N.Y.S. 16

§ 610.   Selection of inspectors at meeting of members; duties

(a) If the by-laws require inspectors at any meeting of members, such requirement is waived unless compliance therewith is requested by a member present in person or by proxy and entitled to vote at such meeting. Unless otherwise provided in the by-laws, the board, in advance of any meeting of members, may appoint one or more inspectors to act at the meeting or any adjournment thereof. If inspectors are not so appointed, the person presiding at a meeting of members may, and on the request of any member entitled to vote thereat shall, appoint one or more inspectors. In case any person appointed fails to appear or act, the vacancy may be filled by appointment made by the board in advance of the meeting or at the meeting by the person presiding thereat. Each inspector, before entering upon the discharge of his duties, shall take and sign an oath faithfully to execute the duties of inspector at such meeting with strict impartiality and according to the best of his ability.

(b) The inspectors shall determine the number of membership certificates or cards and capital certificates outstanding and the voting power of each, the certificates and cards represented at the meeting, the existence of a quorum, the validity and effect of proxies, and shall receive votes, ballots or consents, hear and determine all challenges, and questions arising in connection with the right to vote, count and tabulate all votes, ballots or consents, determine the result, and do such acts as are proper to conduct the election or vote with fairness to all members. On request of the person presiding at the meeting or any members entitled to vote thereat, the inspectors shall make a report in writing of any challenge, question or matter determined by them and execute a certificate of any fact found by them. Any report or certificate made by them shall be prima facie evidence of the facts stated and of the vote as certified by them.

History: Add, L 1969, ch 1066, § 1, eff Sept 1, 1970, with substance derived from Gen Corp Law §§ 23, 24.

§ 611.   Qualification of voters; fixing record date to determine eligibility to vote; voting entitlement

(a) The by-laws may provide or, in the absence of such provision, the board may fix, in advance, a date as the record date for the purpose of determining the members entitled to notice of any meeting of members or any adjournment thereof. Such record date shall not be more than fifty nor less than ten days before the date of the meeting.

(b) Any member in good standing, otherwise eligible to vote, is entitled to vote at any meeting of members, except that, if the certificate of incorporation or the by-laws so provide, the by-laws may provide or, in the absence of such provision, the board may fix a date as the record date for the purpose of determining the members entitled to vote at any meeting of members or any adjournment thereof, or to express consent to or dissent from any proposal without a meeting, or for the purpose of determining members entitled to receive any distribution or the allotment of any rights, or for the purpose of any other action by the members. Such record date shall not be more than fifty nor less than ten days before the date of the meeting.

(c) If the certificate of incorporation or the by-laws provide for a record date, as authorized by paragraph (b), and no record date is fixed:

(1) The record date for the determination of members entitled to vote at a meeting of members shall be at the close of business on the day next preceding the day on which notice is given, or, if no notice is given, the day on which the meeting is held.

(2) The record date for determining members for any purpose other than that specified in subparagraph (1) shall be at the close of business on the day on which the resolution of the board relating thereto is adopted.

(d) When a determination of members of record entitled to notice of or to vote at any meeting of members has been made as provided in this section, such determination shall apply to any adjournment thereof, unless the board fixes a new record date under this section for the adjourned meeting.

(e) In any case in which a member is entitled to vote, he shall have no more than, nor less than, one vote; except that if a corporation has an organization as a member, the certificate of incorporation or by-laws may provide that such organization shall be entitled to votes substantially proportionate to its membership.

History: Add, L 1969, ch 1066, § 1, with substance deriving from Mem Corp Law §§ 20, 41; amd, L 1970, ch 847, § 35, eff Sept 1, 1970; L 1971, ch 1057 § 4, eff Sept 1, 1971; L 1971, ch 1058 § 17.

CASE ANNOTATIONS

1. Generally
2-5. [Reserved for future use]
6. Under former Membership Corporations Law § 20
7. Under former Membership Corporations Law § 41

1. Generally

By-law of not-for-profit corporation which provided for issuance of membership certificate for each lot owned in subdivision and permitted member to have one vote for each membership certificate issued violated statutory proscription providing that "members shall have no more than, nor less than, one vote" and was therefore invalid. Procopio v Fisher (1981, 4th Dept) 83 A.D.2d 757, 443 N.Y.S.2d 492

Townhouse developer possessed "class A" membership in owners' association (which provided same single-vote rights as those exercised by individual owners), not "class B" membership (which gave predecessor sponsor-developer 3 votes per lot), where class B membership expired in 1979 by virtue of amended certificate of incorporation by which sponsor turned over management of association to owners, and, despite reference to current developer's "class B sites" in 1985 amendment to association's declaration of covenants, conditions and restrictions, neither 1979 nor 1985 amendment recreated class B membership. Roxrun Estates, Inc. v Roxbury Run Village Asso. (1988, 3d Dept) 136 A.D.2d 162, 526 N.Y.S.2d 633, app den (1988) 72 N.Y.2d 808, 533 N.Y.S.2d 57, 529 N.E.2d 425

Townhouse developer was entitled to only one vote as member of owners' association, regardless of number of units developer owned, where developer was member of same voting class as other individual owners; power in not-for-profit corporation is more appropriately shared between members on equivalent basis rather than on degree of investment. Roxrun Estates, Inc. v Roxbury Run Village Asso. (1988, 3d Dept) 136 A.D.2d 162, 526 N.Y.S.2d 633, app den (1988) 72 N.Y.2d 808, 533 N.Y.S.2d 57, 529 N.E.2d 425

2003 amended by-laws of a non-profit corporation that owned an apartment building violated N.Y. Not-for-Profit Corp. Law § 602(f) and 611(e) because no shares could be issued pursuant to N.Y. Not-for-Profit Corp. Law § 501 and each member could have only one vote; it was improper to give petitioner families entitlement to an additional vote because they possessed an additional unit. Matter of Thakur v 210 Forsyth St. Hous. Dev. Fund Corp. (2007, Sup) 844 NYS2d 686.

2-5. [Reserved for future use]

6. Under former Membership Corporations Law § 20

Where a membership corporation is formed for charitable and benevolent purposes and for the fostering of spiritualism a bylaw declaring the unit of voting strength as a membership corporation to be measured by each share of stock held by the members thereof is void. Bartlett v Lily Dale Assembly (1931) 139 Misc 338, 249 N.Y.S. 482

7. Under former Membership Corporations Law § 41

Where Membership Corporation Law § 41 and bylaws of Girl Scout Council provided by implication that only active members had a right to vote, failure to give notice of a meeting in which active members voted to consolidate Girl Scout Councils to associate members did not invalidate the action. Armstrong v White Plains Council of Girl Scouts, Inc. (1968, 2d Dept) 30 A.D.2d 818, 292 N.Y.S.2d 813, affd (1969) 24 N.Y.2d 748, 299 N.Y.S.2d 846, 247 N.E.2d 662

Where a membership corporation is formed for charitable and benevolent purposes and for the fostering of spiritualism a bylaw declaring the unit of voting strength as a membership corporation to be measured by each share of stock held by the members thereof is void. Bartlett v Lily Dale Assembly (1931) 139 Misc 338, 249 N.Y.S. 482

Insofar as voting rights and election of officers of a charitable corporation are governed by special statute chartering the corporation, and amendments thereof, the provisions of the Membership Corporations Law are inapplicable. Petiton of Sousa (1960) 26 Misc. 2d 474, 203 N.Y.S.2d 3, affd (1961, 2d Dept) 12 A.D.2d 956, 211

N.Y.S.2d 204, revd on other grounds (1961) 10 N.Y.2d 68, 217 N.Y.S.2d 58, 176 N.E.2d 77, stay den (1961) 9 N.Y.2d 1015 and remittitur amd (1961) 10 N.Y.2d 886, reported in full (1961) 10 N.Y.2d 812, 221 N.Y.S.2d 515, 178 N.E.2d 230 and stay gr (1961) 10 N.Y.2d 885

The fact that a member may be restricted from voting in a membership corporation in no way diminishes his standing as a member, and plaintiffs, who were members, had standing to bring a derivative action on behalf of the membership corporation, notwithstanding the lack of voting rights or the fact plaintiffs were not members when the transactions complained of occurred. Atwell v. Bide-A-Wee Home Asso. (1969) 59 Misc. 2d 321, 299 N.Y.S.2d 40

§ 612.   Limitations on right to vote

The certificate of incorporation or the by-laws may provide, either absolutely or contingently, that the members of any class shall not be entitled to vote, or it may limit or define the matters on, and the circumstances in, which a member or a class of members shall be entitled to vote, and, except as otherwise provided in this chapter, such provisions of the certificate of incorporation or the by-laws shall prevail, according to their tenor, in all elections and in all proceedings, over the provisions of this chapter which authorize any action by the members, but no such denial, limitation or definition of voting rights shall be effective unless at the time one or more classes of members, singly or in the aggregate, are entitled to full voting rights.

History: Add, L 1969, ch 1066, § 1, with substance deriving from Mem Corp Law § 20, amd, L 1971, ch 1058, § 18, L 1971, ch 1057, § 5, both eff Sept 1, 1971.

CASE ANNOTATIONS

Congregation had the authority to discharge members of a not-for-profit corporation's board of directors because (1) N.Y. Not-for-Profit Corp. Law § 703(b) and the corporation's bylaws only let the board increase the board's number, (2) the congregation, as the corporation's sole member, could not be denied the right to vote except by the congregation's removal or resignation, under N.Y. Not-for-Profit Corp. Law §§ 612 and 605(a), so bylaw amendments denying that right had no effect, (3) the bylaws in effect let the congregation veto the board's bylaw amendments, and (4) the congregation vetoed amendments denying the congregation the rights to vote, remove directors, and adopt, amend, or repeal bylaws. Gluck v Chevre Liady Nusach Hoary (2012, 2d Dept) 97 App Div 3d 787, 949 NYS2d 149

§ 613.   Vote of members

(a) Except as otherwise required by this chapter or by the certificate of incorporation or the by-laws as permitted by this chapter, directors shall be elected by a plurality of the votes cast at a meeting of members by the members entitled to vote in the election.

(b) Whenever any corporate action, other than the election of directors, is to be taken under this chapter by vote of the members, it shall, except as otherwise required by this chapter or by the certificate of incorporation or by by-laws as permitted by this chapter, be authorized by a majority of the votes cast at a meeting of members by the members entitled to vote thereon.

(c) Except as provided in paragraph (b), any reference in this chapter to corporate action at a meet-ing of members by "majority vote" or "two-thirds vote" shall require the action to be taken by such proportion of the votes cast at such meeting, provided that the affirmative votes cast in favor of any such action shall be at least equal to the quorum. Blank votes or abstentions shall not be counted in the number of votes cast.

History: Add, L 1969, ch 1066, § 1, eff Sept 1, 1970.

CASE ANNOTATIONS

A fire company may adopt a bylaw providing that only firemen who attend at least 15 percent of all fire calls during the year may vote in an election of line officers of the fire company. 1982 Op Atty Gen. March 5 (informal)

§ 614.   Action by members without a meeting

(a) Whenever, under this chapter, members are required or permitted to take any action by vote, such action may be taken without a meeting upon the consent of all of the members entitled to vote thereon, which consent shall set forth the action so taken. Such consent may be written or electronic. If written, the consent must be executed by the member or the member's authorized officer, director, employee or agent by signing such consent or causing his or her signature to be affixed to such consent by any reasonable means including but not limited to facsimile signature. If electronic, the transmission of the consent must be sent by electronic mail and set forth, or be submitted with, information from which it can reasonably be determined that the transmission was authorized by the member. This paragraph shall not be construed to alter or modify any provision in a certificate of incorporation not inconsistent with this chapter under which the written consent of less than all of the members is sufficient for corporate action.

(b) Written or electronic consent thus given by all members entitled to vote shall have the same effect as a unanimous vote of members and any certificate with respect to the authorization or taking of any such action which is delivered to the department of state shall recite that the authorization was by unanimous written consent.

(c) When there are no members of record, such action may be taken on the written consent signed by a majority in interest of the subscribers for capital certificates whose subscriptions have been accepted or their successors in interest or, if no subscription has been accepted, on the written consent signed by the incorporator or a majority of the incorporators. When there are two or more incorporators, if any dies or is for any reason unable to act, the other or others may act. If there is no incorporator able to act, any person for whom an incorporator was acting as agent may act in his or her stead, or if such other person also dies or is for any reason unable to act, his or her legal representative may act.

Not-For-Profit Corporation Law

History: Add, L 1969, ch 1066, § 1, eff Sept 1, 1970; amd, L 2013, ch 549, § 65, eff July 1, 2014; L 2015, ch 358, § 5, eff Sept 25, 2015.

§ 615.   Greater requirement as to quorum and vote of members

(a) The certificate of incorporation or a by-law adopted by the members may contain provisions specifying either or both of the following:

(1) That the proportion of members, or of a class thereof, who shall be present in person or by proxy at any meeting of members, including a special meeting for election of directors under section 604 (Special meeting for election of directors), in order to constitute a quorum for the transaction of any business or of any specified item of business, including amendments to the certificate of incorporation, shall be greater than the proportion prescribed by this chapter in the absence of such provision.

(2) That the proportion of votes of the members, or of a class thereof, that shall be necessary at any meeting of members for the transaction of any business or of any specified item of business, including amendments to the certificate of incorporation, shall be greater than the proportion prescribed by this chapter in the absence of such provision.

(b) An amendment of the certificate of incorporation or a by-law adopted by the members which adds a provision permitted by this section or which changes or strikes out such a provision, shall be authorized at a meeting of members by vote of the members entitled to cast two-thirds of the total number of votes entitled to be cast thereon, or of such greater proportion of such total number of votes or the total number of votes of a class, as may be provided specifically in the certificate of incorporation or a by-law adopted by the members for adding, changing or striking out a provision permitted by this section.

(c) If the certificate of incorporation or a by-law adopted by the members contains a provision authorized by this section, the existence of such provision shall be noted conspicuously on the face or back of every membership certificate or card or capital certificate issued by such corporation.

History: Add, L 1969, ch 1066, § 1, with substance deriving from Mem Corp Law § 20; amd, L 1970, ch 847, § 36, eff Sept 1, 1970.

§ 616.   Voting by class of members

(a) The certificate of incorporation or the by-laws may contain provisions specifying that any class or classes of members shall vote as a class in connection with the transaction of any business or of any specified item of business at a meeting of members, including amendments to the certificate of incorporation.

(b) Where voting as a class is provided in the certificate of incorporation or the by-laws, it shall be by the proportionate vote so provided or, if no proportionate vote is provided, in the election of directors, by a plurality of the votes cast at such meeting by the members of such class entitled to vote in the election, or for any other corporate action, by a majority of the votes cast at such meeting by the members of such class entitled to vote thereon.

(c) Such voting by class shall be in addition to any other vote, including vote by class, required by this chapter or by the certificate of incorporation or the by-laws as permitted by this chapter.

History: Add, L 1969, ch 1066, § 1, eff Sept 1, 1970.

§ 617.   Cumulative voting

The certificate of incorporation or the by-laws of any corporation may provide that in all elections of directors of such corporation each member shall be entitled to as many votes as shall equal the number of votes which, except for such provisions as to cumulative voting, he would be entitled to cast for the election of directors multiplied by the number of directors to be elected, and that he may cast all of such votes for a single director or may distribute them among the number to be voted for, or for any two or more of them, as he may see fit, which right, when exercised, shall be termed cumulative voting.

History: Add, L 1969, ch 1066, § 1, eff Sept 1, 1970.

§ 618.   Power of supreme court respecting elections

Upon the petition of any member aggrieved by an election and upon notice to the persons declared elected thereat, the corporation and such other persons as the court may direct, the supreme court at a special term held within the judicial district where the office of the corporation is located shall forthwith hear the proofs and allegations of the parties, and confirm the election, order a new election, or take such other action as justice may require.

History: Add, L 1969, ch 1066, § 1, eff Sept 1, 1970, with substance derived from Gen Corp Law § 25

CASE ANNOTATIONS

1. Generally
2-10. [Reserved for future use]
11. Under former General Corporation Law § 25
12. – Purpose of section
13. – – Exclusiveness of remedy
14. – – As authorizing mandamus
15. – – Stay of subsequent election
16. – Proceeding to determine validity of election; parties
17. – – Who is party "aggrieved" by election
18. – – Petition
19. – – Limitations and laches
20. – – Nature and conduct of proceeding
21. – Power of court; confirm or order new election
22. – – Determination of other issues
23. – Decision on election; confirming
24. – – Setting aside
25. – Miscellaneous

1. Generally

A challenge by a candidate for the office of president of a union was not untimely for failure to exhaust his remedy within the union by filing a protest by a certain date where there was no evidence that such a deadline was properly adopted by the board of directors of the union and, assuming it was so adopted, a candidate should not be charged with knowledge of a deadline which does not appear in the election rules and regulations or the election timetable. Accordingly, said candidate, having exhausted his internal union remedies, was improperly barred from raising objections to the election. Wenzl v Civil Service Employees Asso. (1978, 3d Dept) 62 A.D.2d 82, 404 N.Y.S.2d 426

The Supreme Court properly declared a winner in an election for the position of editor-in-chief of a student publication, rather than ordering a new election, after disallowing proxy votes in the election pursuant to the publication's bylaws, which stated that the editor-in-chief would be elected at each annual meeting by "the members present" and that "[no] proxy votes may be counted," since N-PCL § 618 provides that the Supreme Court may "confirm the election, order a new election, or take such other action as justice may require," and since the votes that had been cast in person had already been fairly alloted and there was no claim of fraud or irregularity. In re Application of Kachic (1983, 4th Dept) 98 A.D.2d 965, 470 N.Y.S.2d 60

In a proceeding pursuant to Not-for-Profit Corp Law § 618 to compel a church to hold a membership meeting to elect officers and trustees, which dispute arose out of the alleged failure to hold a membership meeting pursuant to the church's bylaws, under the church's certificate of incorporation relating to membership, dues, active parishioners, and the governance of the church, the trial court properly found the church to have subjected itself to the heirarchial ecclesiastical authority, together with the right of the church to determine the qualifications of membership, so that the bishop had the power to determine who in fact was a member in good standing, and therefore the proceeding was properly dismissed as the matter of when there was to be a new meeting had to await the action of the bishop in determining membership issues. Kissel v Russian Orthodox Greek Catholic Holy Trinity Church (1984, 2d Dept) 103 A.D.2d 830, 478 N.Y.S.2d 68

Court would dismiss petition to declare church elections of trustees and officers to be null and void and to require new elections pursuant to CLS Relig Corp § 182 since petition was not filed within 4-month period mandated by CLS CPLR § 217. In re Uranian Phalanstery 1st New York Gnostic Lyceum Temple (1989, 1st Dept) 155 A.D.2d 302, 547 N.Y.S.2d 63

Court did not improperly interfere with internal affairs of petitioner not-for-profit corporation when it declared that petitioner had no authority to limit number of nominees for elective office, where petitioner had initially commenced proceeding to restrain respondents from engaging in disruptive and violent behavior at nomination meetings, and obtained such relief, and then invoked CLS N-PCL § 618 (which provides for judicial intervention in election matters) by specifically seeking judicial oversight of nomination meeting and extension of executive committee's authority until nominations and elections were completed. Sun Wei Ass'n v Wong (1995, 1st Dept) 222 A.D.2d 203, 634 N.Y.S.2d 475

New election for president of dental society was required, under by-law requiring new election if result "could have been affected by the extra ballots," where 4 extra votes were cast, and margin of victory was only 3 votes; it did not matter that, when extra ballots were examined, they would not have changed result of election, because test was not whether outcome was changed but whether it "could have" been affected by number of excess votes. Jackson v First Dist. Dental Soc'y (1997, 1st Dept) 240 A.D.2d 265, 659 N.Y.S.2d 14

In special proceeding under CLS N-PCL § 618 to set aside results of election to parish council of church, injunctive relief would be granted against individuals purportedly elected to council where church's constitution and bylaws gave bishop authority to rule on challenges to election within 60 days, which he did by setting aside election results for irregularities and directing new election. Ionescu v Barbu (1998, 2d Dept) 255 A.D.2d 584, 680 N.Y.S.2d 653, app den (1999) 93 N.Y.2d 809, 694 N.Y.S.2d 631, 716 N.E.2d 696

Petition under CLS N-PCL § 618 to set aside petitioner's removal from not-for-profit corporation's board of trustees lacked merit to extent that it was based on claim that proceedings were tainted by "fraud" where (1) petitioner was present at and participated in challenged election and was fully able to communicate her views to other board members, (2) her mother's statement that petitioner no longer represented her family was prompted by petitioner's es-

trangement from her family, and (3) even if certain memoranda previously adopted by board and relied on by petitioner were enforceable, her removal complied with them. Nesbeda v Edna McConnell Clark Found. (1999, 1st Dept) 266 A.D.2d 72, 698 N.Y.S.2d 627

Proceeding to annul action of stockholders in removing director was not the forum for approving an express agreement that director was to be retained as long as he or his designee was a stockholder. Teperman v Atcos Baths, Inc. (1957) 6 Misc. 2d 162, 163 N.Y.S.2d 221, affd (1959, 2d Dept) 7 A.D.2d 854, 182 N.Y.S.2d 765

In an action challenging, inter alia, the election of a religious corporation's board of directors and board of trustees, the court converted the action under N.Y. C.P.L.R. § 103(c) to a special proceeding under N.Y. Not-for-Profit Corporation Law § 618 as the allegations that synagogue members who failed to pay their dues were allowed to vote in contravention of the corporation's bylaws did not involve ecclesiastical matters and the special proceeding was the exclusive remedy for challenging the validity of the election of a director or trustee. Esformes v Brinn (2008, 2d Dept) 52 App Div 3d 459, 860 NYS2d 547.

In passing upon election of officers of not-for-profit corporation, court sits as court of equity, and should not interfere in internal affairs of such corporation unless clear showing is made to warrant such action. In re Election of Officers & Directors of F.I.G.H.T., Inc. (1974) 79 Misc. 2d 655, 360 N.Y.S.2d 564

Where, though irregularities appeared to have taken place, there was no showing of fraud or wrongdoing and it appeared that, even if some delegates to convention of not-for-profit corporation members were barred, their vote or presence would not have changed results of election of officers, new election was denied. In re Election of Officers & Directors of F.I.G.H.T., Inc. (1974) 79 Misc. 2d 655, 360 N.Y.S.2d 564

Court in passing upon election of officers of not-for-profit corporation has broad equitable powers and may direct new election where election under review is so clouded with doubt and tainted with questionable circumstances that standards of fair dealing require new, clear and adequate expression. In re Election of Officers & Directors of F.I.G.H.T., Inc. (1974) 79 Misc. 2d 655, 360 N.Y.S.2d 564

Where original constitution of not-for-profit corporation provided that all officers should be elected for term of one year and that no officer should succeed himself for more than two successive years for same office, and term of office was increased to two years but it was neglected to amend time provided for succession, period of one year would be construed to mean "one term" in order to give meaning to constitutional provision on succession. In re Election of Officers & Directors of F.I.G.H.T., Inc. (1974) 79 Misc. 2d 655, 360 N.Y.S.2d 564

Petitioner's election to board of directors of her cooperative was not invalid on ground that she was delinquent on her carrying charges for August and September 1988 and thus ineligible under cooperative's by-laws to have her name placed in nomination on September 13, 1988 since (1) by allowing petitioner to make late payments of 3 to 4 weeks each month over past year without notifying her that future rent had to be paid on first of month, cooperative waived its right to enforce provision of by-laws that tenant nominated to run for directorship not be delinquent in payment of carrying charges at time of nomination, and (2) uncontroverted evidence established that petitioner's August carrying charge check was, through no fault of petitioner, incorrectly refused payment by her bank. Smith v Ellerbe (1988, Sup) 141 Misc. 2d 699, 534 N.Y.S.2d 100

New York City Civil Court lacked jurisdiction over action to enjoin not-for-profit organization and its executive committee from transferring power pursuant to recent elections and expending assets of organization, as such matters are reserved for Supreme Court. Koshy v Thomas (2000, Civ Ct) 185 Misc. 2d 102, 712 N.Y.S.2d 727

Member of New York Mercantile Exchange who leased all her seats to obtain income therefrom is not granted injunction allowing her to reclaim right to vote, where member had been without vote for 2 years but waited until 3 weeks prior to election to seek relief, because (1) member did not show irreparable injury, and (2) member had adequate remedy at law in form of CLS N-PCL § 618 which provides judicial authority to overturn or modify results of improper election. Blanksteen v New York Mercantile Exch. (1995, SD NY) 879 F. Supp. 363, 1995-1 CCH Trade Cases ¶ 70939

When competing members of a religious community sought the validation of their election of the community's board of directors and the invalidation of rival members' election, such a decision could not be made by reference to neutral principles of law, and the tangential issues that would have to be decided required the impermissible application of ecclesiastical doctrine or law, so the competing petitions were dismissed. Congregation Yetev Lev DSatmar v Kahan (2004, Sup) 5 Misc 3d 1023A, 799 N.Y.S.2d 159

2-10. [Reserved for future use]

11. Under former General Corporation Law § 25

The provisions of this section are not limited to stock corporations. In re Empire State Supreme Lodge D. of H. (1907) 118 A.D. 616, 103 N.Y.S. 1124

A federal savings and loan association is subject to this section although an agency of the federal government. In re Election of Directors of Baldwinsville Federal Sav. & Loan Ass'n (1944) 268 A.D. 414, 51 N.Y.S.2d 816

12. – Purpose of section

The purpose of this section is to provide a summary review of a contested election, free from the procedural complications of a plenary proceeding. In re William Faehndrich, Inc. (1957) 2 N.Y.2d 468, 161 N.Y.S.2d 99, 141 N.E.2d 597 (superseded by statute as stated in In re Schmidt (1983, 2d Dept) 97 A.D.2d 244, 468 N.Y.S.2d 663)

This section was enacted to give the court power to test in a summary manner the title of corporate officers without resorting to the cumbersome action of quo warranto. In re Lake Placid Co. (1948) 274 A.D. 205, 81 N.Y.S.2d 36

13. – – Exclusiveness of remedy

If an election of directors by board of directors is illegal, petitioner's only remedy is to proceed under this section to have the election set aside and a new election ordered, and not by motion to reinstate him as director on the ground that he was illegally removed, since by force of the annual election, if that election is legal, he is not entitled to be reinstated as director. In re Moscowitz (1923) 206 A.D. 289, 200 N.Y.S. 630

In an action by a corporation to restrain defendants who claimed to be directors from interfering with directors previously elected, remedy must be sought under Civil Practice Act, § 1208 or under this section. Merchants' Loan & Inv. Corp. v Abramson (1925) 214 A.D. 252, 212 N.Y.S. 193, affd (1926) 242 N.Y. 587, 152 N.E. 438

The remedy afforded by this section is not exclusive and does not preclude an application for injunction against use of proxies allegedly obtained by defendants through fraud in connection with an election of directors. Segal v Bresnick (1952) 30 Misc. 2d 569, 222 N.Y.S.2d 768

This section has been referred to as a somewhat quicker method of determining right to corporate office than an action at law in the nature of quo warranto, but either remedy is available for such a purpose. Application of Porea (1961) 29 Misc. 2d 48, 215 N.Y.S.2d 881

The remedy provided by this section is not exclusive for determining validity of election as director. Tabulating Card Co. v Leidesdorf (1961) 32 Misc. 2d 720, 223 N.Y.S.2d 652

14. – – As authorizing mandamus

This section does not authorize mandamus. People ex rel. Putzel v Simonson (1891) 61 Hun 338, 16 N.Y.S. 118

15. – – Stay of subsequent election

Tenant-owners of a cooperative apartment building brought a proceeding to set aside a 1956 election of its directors upon the ground of fraud allegedly perpetrated by the management, which was under the control of a former owner under a 10-year contract. During the course of the litigation, the time for the 1957 election approached, and the tenant-owners obtained a stay thereof. It was conceded that a new election would render the issues at bar moot and academic. However, similar issues might easily arise concerning the new election. In view of the nature of this corporation and the relationship of the parties, the court was justified in granting such a stay until a determination of partially tried issues could be had, although it should not have enjoined the solicitation of proxies for the prospective election. Ohrbach v Kirkeby (1957, 1st Dept) 3 A.D.2d 269, 161 N.Y.S.2d 371

16. – Proceeding to determine validity of election; parties

In a proceeding under this section brought to set aside an election of directors, the corporation itself is a necessary party defendant. In re P. F. Keogh, Inc. (1920) 192 A.D. 624, 183 N.Y.S. 408

Under this section the corporation itself may complain of an illegal election of directors at directors' meeting. In re Election of Directors of Hammond Light & Power Co. (1928) 131 Misc 747, 228 N.Y.S. 70, affd (1928) 224 A.D. 684, 229 N.Y.S. 865

Petitioner, in order to set aside election which has been held in accordance with proper authority and upon due notice, must show only that he has been aggrieved by it, but where alleged election was illegal in that it was unauthorized or insufficient notice of it was given, no further showing is required. In re Green Bus Lines, Inc. (1937) 166 Misc 800, 2 N.Y.S.2d 556

Only an aggrieved party may institute a proceeding under this section to determine validity of a concluded corporate election; such a proceeding may not be brought by the corporation. Veverka v Suffolk County Patrolemen's Benevolent Asso. (1963, Sup) 236 N.Y.S.2d 917

17. – – Who is party "aggrieved" by election

One who was a candidate for election and thus was directly affected by the outcome of an election was an aggrieved member within the meaning of this section. In re Workmen's Ben. Fund (1942) 265 A.D. 176, 38 N.Y.S.2d 429, app den (1943) 265 A.D. 991, 39 N.Y.S.2d 990

Voting in a previous election and in the election complained of, knowing that no provision had been made for classification of directors as required by the charter, did not constitute such ratification of an illegal act that the petitioner was not an aggrieved person, particularly where he objected at the election and was assured that the directors would be classified after the election. In re Election of Directors of Baldwinsville Federal Sav. & Loan Ass'n (1944) 268 A.D. 414, 51 N.Y.S.2d 816

Unless a petitioner has been injured by the proceedings he is not a party "aggrieved" by the election; and in order to have it set aside he must show that fact. Such a showing must amount to either an inequitable result or proof that the irregularity complained of would, if corrected, produce a different result. In re Workmen's Ben. Fund (1942, Sup) 36 N.Y.S.2d 662, app dismd (1942) 265 A.D. 176, 38 N.Y.S.2d 429, app den (1943) 265 A.D. 991, 39 N.Y.S.2d 990

18. – – Petition

There are no grounds for ordering a new corporate election under this section where there was no allegation of fraud as to the original election, which was conducted by an impartial committee composed of supporters of both candidates and whose decision regarding a certain disputed proxy upon which the election turned could not be said to be arbitrary. Burke v Wiswall (1948) 193 Misc 14, 85 N.Y.S.2d 187

Petition for order annulling action of corporation whereby petitioner was removed as director was sufficient as a matter of pleading and the motion to dismiss was denied. Teperman v Atcos Baths, Inc. (1956) 4 Misc. 2d 738, 158 N.Y.S.2d 391, later proceeding (1957) 6 Misc. 2d 162, 163 N.Y.S.2d 221, affd (1959, 2d Dept) 7 A.D.2d 854, 182 N.Y.S.2d 765

19. – – Limitations and laches

The four-month limitation period is inapplicable to a proceeding under this section and no statute or principle of equity precludes maintenance of proceeding where respondents were not injured by delay in commencement. Wyatt v Armstrong (1945) 186 Misc 216, 59 N.Y.S.2d 502

20. – – Nature and conduct of proceeding

A proceeding under this section is summary in nature and does not lend itself to the delays entailed by taking of depositions. In re Scharf (1961) 28 Misc. 2d 869, 216 N.Y.S.2d 775, mod on other grounds (1961, 2d Dept) 15 A.D.2d 563, 223 N.Y.S.2d 307

This statute does not prescribe that the court hearing the application shall take oral proof; it is clearly within the power of the parties to agree on proof in written form; no statutory provision is made for trying the issue of fact by a jury. Petition of Serenbetz (1943, Sup) 46 N.Y.S.2d 475, affd (1944) 267 A.D. 836, 46 N.Y.S.2d 127

21. – Power of court; confirm or order new election

The court has no power to supervise an election which it has ordered. In re Flushing Hospital & Dispensary (1942) 289 N.Y. 654, 44 N.E.2d 626

In a proceeding under this section, the court is not authorized to vacate a corporate election without ordering a new one. In re William Faehndrich, Inc. (1957) 2 N.Y.2d 468, 161 N.Y.S.2d 99, 141 N.E.2d 597 (superseded by statute as stated in In re Schmidt (1983, 2d Dept) 97 A.D.2d 244, 468 N.Y.S.2d 663)

In a proceeding under this section, the court sits as a court of equity which may order a new election "as justice may require." Gearing v Kelly (1962) 11 N.Y.2d 201, 227 N.Y.S.2d 897, 182 N.E.2d 391, reh den (1962) 11 N.Y.2d 1016

The supreme court has no authority, to act in advance of an annual election of a religious corporation to determine qualifications of voters or to supervise proceedings at an election to be thereafter held, but the limit of the court's authority is to pass upon the validity of an election that has been held and to confirm it or to order a new election. In re Trustees of Washington Ave. Baptist Church (1926) 215 A.D. 529, 214 N.Y.S. 259

This section gives the court discretionary power to confirm an election or to order a new one, as justice may require. Application of Kaminsky (1937) 251 A.D. 132, 295 N.Y.S. 989, reh den (1937) 251 A.D. 795, 298 N.Y.S. 171 and affd (1938) 277 N.Y. 524, 13 N.E.2d 456

The power of a court under this section is to confirm an election or order a new election, as justice may require, and it has no authority to go beyond this by setting aside an election already held and ordering a new election where there is a deadlock in control and no possibility of a change in result. Jacobs v Ostow & Jacobs, Inc. (1960, 1st Dept) 12 A.D.2d 613, 209 N.Y.S.2d 37

The court's powers under this section are limited to confirming an election or ordering a new election as justice may require. Burke v Wiswall (1948) 193 Misc 14, 85 N.Y.S.2d 187

The court refused to undertake to substitute itself for the tellers of an election of directors where the claims of the adversary parties were in sharp conflict. Juster v Morrison (1956) 15 Misc. 2d 998, 182 N.Y.S.2d 940

22. – – Determination of other issues

A summary proceeding to determine which of two slates of directors were validly elected was inappropriate to the determination of questions properly triable by plenary action such as the actual or equitable ownership of stock. In re Bruder's Estate (1950) 302 N.Y. 52, 96 N.E.2d 84

While this section confers ample authority upon court to determine any question relating to election of trustees, including such as are merely incidental thereto, if necessarily involved in controversy, proceeding is summary in its nature, and does not permit decision of equitable claims, or extraneous matters not necessarily involved in determination of primary question itself. Application of Kaminsky (1937) 251 A.D. 132, 295 N.Y.S. 989, reh den (1937) 251 A.D. 795, 298 N.Y.S. 171 and affd (1938) 277 N.Y. 524, 13 N.E.2d 456

Under this section, the court was limited to confirming an election of directors or ordering a new one and had no authority to pass on other issues, such as questions of stock ownership. Unbekant v Bohl Tours Travel Agency, Inc. (1964, 3d Dept) 21 A.D.2d 317, 250 N.Y.S.2d 397, app dismd (1964) 14 N.Y.2d 959, 253 N.Y.S.2d 996, 202 N.E.2d 377

Proceeding to annul action of stockholders in removing director was not the forum for approving an express agreement that director was to be retained as long as he or his designee was a stockholder. Teperman v Atcos Baths, Inc. (1957) 6 Misc. 2d 162, 163 N.Y.S.2d 221, affd (1959, 2d Dept) 7 A.D.2d 854, 182 N.Y.S.2d 765

23. – Decision on election; confirming

Where the constitution of a fraternal benefit association consisting of subordinate councils, grand councils, and supreme council, provides that each grand council is entitled to send two representatives to meetings of the supreme council, and that subordinate councils shall have no representation in the supreme council, members of subordinate council are precluded from questioning the validity of election of officers at a meeting of the supreme council, in proceeding under this section where they acquiesced in the provisions of the constitution excluding them by failing to send representatives to the meeting and by not making a demand for representation. In re Triennial Election of Catholic R. & B. Ass'n (1911) 142 A.D. 307, 127 N.Y.S. 143

In proceeding under § 25 to confirm claimed election of petitioner and others as duly elected officers and directors of membership corporation and to set aside claimed wrongful election of respondents as such officers and directors, where election meeting conducted by respondents was regularly called and members duly warned thereof, change of place of meeting from hotel suite announced in notice of meeting to another suite in same hotel, by notice posted at original suite, did not prejudice any of petitioner's group, all of whom attended meeting, or mislead any other member or deprive her of a vote. Application of Havender (1943) 181 Misc 989, 44 N.Y.S.2d 213, affd (1944) 267 A.D. 860, 47 N.Y.S.2d 114, reh and app den (1944) 267 A.D. 901, 48 N.Y.S.2d 325

Election of a particular person as a director of a membership corporation would not be set aside, because of informality in the manner in which the election was held, upon petition of one who, up to that meeting, had personally dominated the affairs of the corporation, making the corporation a vehicle for his own personal use or abuse. Hungarian Freedom Fighters Federation, Inc. v Samson (1961) 30 Misc. 2d 354, 219 N.Y.S.2d 348

Since this section commands that the court confirm the election or order a new election, "as justice may require," an election will not be set aside merely because of informality in convening the meeting where all of those in active interest were present and took part. Hungarian Freedom Fighters Federation, Inc. v Samson (1961) 30 Misc. 2d 354, 219 N.Y.S.2d 348

Elections are not vitiated for mere irregularity; there must be fraud involved or such a degree of irregularity as to effect the result in a material respect. In re Workmen's Ben. Fund (1942, Sup) 36 N.Y.S.2d 662, app dismd (1942) 265 A.D. 176, 38 N.Y.S.2d 429, app den (1943) 265 A.D. 991, 39 N.Y.S.2d 990

24. – – Setting aside

Where amendments adopted at the annual meeting were void, an election which followed thereunder must be set aside. In re Flushing Hospital & Dispensary (1942) 288 N.Y. 125, 41 N.E.2d 917, remittitur amd (1942) 288 N.Y. 735, 43 N.E.2d 356 and remittitur den (1942) 289 N.Y. 654, 44 N.E.2d 626

An election of directors of a membership corporation will be set aside and a new election ordered, where it appears that a small portion of the membership in attendance at an annual meeting separated from the main body and held an election of directors in strict accordance with their legal rights, but said election was contrary to long-continued, though illegal, practice of electing directors. In re Bogart (1925) 215 A.D. 45, 213 N.Y.S. 137

Where a certificate of incorporation provided for unanimous vote or consent of all stockholders for transaction of corporate business, election of a board of directors by a plurality vote, pursuant to a by-law of the corporation was invalid, since the provision in the certificate took priority over the by-law. In re Election of Directors of Radiant Knitting Mills, Inc. (1959) 20 Misc. 2d 915, 194 N.Y.S.2d 232

25. – Miscellaneous

Even though directors and officers were illegally elected, they were nonetheless de facto directors and officers who could call a meeting required by the by-laws. Petition of Weinstein (1953) 203 Misc 975, 119 N.Y.S.2d 457

§ 619.   Agreements by members as to voting

An agreement between two or more members, if in writing and signed by the parties thereto, may provide that in exercising their voting rights as members they shall vote as therein provided, or as they may agree, or as determined in accordance with a procedure agreed upon by them.

History: Add, L 1969, ch 1066, § 1; amd, L 1970, ch 847, § 37, eff Sept 1, 1970.

§ 620.   Preemptive rights

There shall be no preemptive rights in relation to membership certificates or cards, capital certificates, subvention certificates, or bonds. In the case of bonds having lawful voting rights, this section shall not invalidate otherwise valid contract provisions designed to protect such voting rights.

History: Add, L 1969, ch 1066, § 1, with substance deriving from Mem Corp Law § 26, amd, L 1971, ch 1058 § 19, eff Sept 1, 1971

Section heading, amd, L 1971, ch 1058 § 19, eff Sept 1, 1971

§ 621.   Books and records; right of inspection; prima facie evidence

(a) Except as otherwise provided herein, every corporation shall keep, at the office of the corporation, correct and complete books and records of account and minutes of the proceedings of its members, board and executive committee, if any, and shall keep at such office or at the office of its transfer agent or registrar in this state, a list or record containing the names and addresses of all members, the class or classes of membership or capital certificates and the number of capital certificates held by each and the dates when they respectively became the holders of record thereof. A corporation may keep its books and records of account in an office of the corporation without the state, as specified in its certificate of incorporation. Any of the foregoing books, minutes and records may be in written form or in any other form capable of being converted into written form within a reasonable time.

(b) Any person who shall have been a member of record of a corporation for at least six months immediately preceding his demand, or any person holding, or thereunto authorized in writing by the holders of, at least five percent of any class of the outstanding capital certificates, upon at least five days written demand shall have the right to examine in person or by agent or attorney, during usual business hours, its minutes of the proceedings of its members and list or record of members and to make extracts therefrom.

(c) An inspection authorized by paragraph (b) may be denied to such member or other person upon his refusal to furnish to the corporation, its transfer agent or registrar an affidavit that such inspection is not desired and will not be used for a purpose which is in the interest of a business or object other than the business of the corporation and that he has not within five years given, sold or offered for sale any list or record of members of any domestic or foreign corporation or aided or abetted, or attempted or offered to aid or abet, any person in procuring any such list or record of members for any such purpose.

(d) Upon refusal by the corporation or by an officer or agent of the corporation to permit an inspection of the minutes of the proceedings of its members or of the list or record of members, as herein provided, the person making the demand for inspection may apply to the supreme court in the judicial district where the office of the corporation is located, upon such notice as the court may direct, for an order directing the corporation, its officer or agent to show cause why an order should not be granted permitting such inspection by the applicant. Upon the return day of the order to show cause, the court shall hear the parties summarily, by affidavit or otherwise, and if it appears that the applicant is qualified and entitled to such inspection, the court shall grant an order compelling such inspection and awarding such further relief as to the court may seem just and proper.

(e) Upon the written request of any person who shall have been a member of record for at least six months immediately preceding his request, or of any person holding, or thereunto authorized in writing by the holders of, at least five percent of any class of the outstanding capital certificates, the corporation shall provide to such member an annual balance sheet and

profit and loss statement or a financial statement performing a similar function for the preceding fiscal year, and, if any interim balance sheet or profit and loss or similar financial statement has been distributed to its members or otherwise made available to the public, the most recent such interim balance sheet or profit and loss or similar financial statement. The corporation shall be allowed a reasonable time to prepare such annual balance sheet and profit and loss or similar financial statement.

(e-1) In addition to those documents described in paragraph (e) of this section, members of a homeowners association incorporated pursuant to the provisions of this chapter shall also be entitled to review, upon request to the homeowners association's governing board, invoices, ledgers, bank accounts, reconciliations, contracts, and any documents related to the expenditure of homeowners association dues.

(f) Nothing herein contained shall impair the power of courts to compel the production for examination of the books and records of a corporation.

(g) The books and records specified in paragraph (a) shall be prima facie evidence of the facts therein stated in favor of the plaintiff in any action or special proceeding against such corporation or any of its officers, directors or members.

(h) Nothing in this chapter shall require an employee organization certified or recognized for any collective negotiating unit of an employer pursuant to article fourteen of the civil service law to disclose the home address of any member or former member of such organization.

History: Add, L 1969, ch 1066, § 1; amd, L 1970, ch 847, § 38, eff Sept 1, 1970; amd, L 1984, ch 27, § 1, eff March 20, 1984, and applicable to any request made pursuant to the not-for-profit corporation law for which there is no final determination, including judicial review; amd, L 2013, ch 549, § 66, eff July 1, 2014; L 2017, ch 343, § 1, eff Oct 23, 2017.

CASE ANNOTATIONS

1. **Generally**
2. **Beneficial interest**
3. **Good faith**
4-10. **[Reserved for future use]**
11. **Under former Membership Corporation Law § 26**
12. – **Order appointing referee to investigate for court**
13. – – **Right to appeal order**
14. – **Order requiring inventory and accounting**
15. – – **Provision restraining sale of property**
16. – **Investigation or attack by others; city**
17. – – **Nonmembers**
18. – **Bylaw precluding access to membership list**

1. Generally

When asserting a common-law right of access to corporate books and records the shareholder must plead and prove that inspection is desired for a proper purpose. Crane Co. v Anaconda Co. (1976) 39 N.Y.2d 14, 382 N.Y.S.2d 707, 346 N.E.2d 507

The manner of communication selected by stockholder desiring to discuss aspects of tender offer with fellow stockholders should be within the judgment of the shareholder. Crane Co. v Anaconda Co. (1976) 39 N.Y.2d 14, 382 N.Y.S.2d 707, 346 N.E.2d 507

Qualified stockholder may inspect corporation's stock register to ascertain the identity of fellow stockholders for the avowed purpose of informing them directly of its exchange offer and soliciting tenders of stock. Crane Co. v Anaconda Co. (1976) 39 N.Y.2d 14, 382 N.Y.S.2d 707, 346 N.E.2d 507

It was overly broad for petitioner to request "the corporate books, records, papers and contracts, including minute books, any and all cancelled checks, bills, bank statements, vouchers, correspondence, and any other documents or data which deal in any way with any entry on the books and records of said corporation." Mathews v Onondaga County Deputy Sheriff's Benevolent Ass'n (1996, 4th Dept) 225 A.D.2d 1048, 639 N.Y.S.2d 613

Petitioner was not entitled under common-law principles to compel not-for-profit corporation to make available to petitioner certain financial records and documents he sought where petition alleged nothing more than disagreement with corporation's officers as to expenditure of some of corporation's funds. Mathews v Onondaga County Deputy Sheriff's Benevolent Ass'n (1996, 4th Dept) 225 A.D.2d 1048, 639 N.Y.S.2d 613

Dismissal of a member's cause of action seeking to compel production of a church's books and records was error because the issue of whether the member, who sought to enforce a statutory right, was entitled to the production, could have been determined by resort to neutral principles of law; although the action was not brought as a special proceeding pursuant to N.Y. Not-for-Profit Corporation Law § 621, it was appropriate to convert the action. Tae Hwa Yoon v New York Hahn Wolee Church, Inc. (2008, 2d Dept) 56 App Div 3d 752, 870 NYS2d 42.

Although plaintiff did not cross move for summary judgment, in action seeking to enjoin defendants from paying any salary or other sums to executive director of corporation and to direct complete disclosure of names and addresses of all members and books of account of corporation, the trial court would grant plaintiff's request for complete disclosure where appropriate demand for production was made, there was sufficient showing that inspection was not desired and would not be used for purpose which was in interest of business or object other than business of corporation, and there was no proof that plaintiff had otherwise failed to comply with provisions of Not-for-Profit Corporation Law. Hoffert v Dank (1976) 86 Misc. 2d 384, 382 N.Y.S.2d 421, mod (1976, 1st Dept) 55 A.D.2d 518, 389 N.Y.S.2d 101

Phrase "by one or more of the members," in statute providing that actions against corporate directors and officers for mismanagement, waste of corporate assets and unlawful conduct may be brought by one or more of its members, does not relate back to provisions of general statutory provision requiring that derivative action be instituted by at least five percent of members of corporation, but instead, authorizes bringing of such actions against corporate directors and officers by one or more of members; such construction gives effect to entire statute and gives recognition to apparent legislative intent to differentiate actions against officers and directors for misconduct or misfeasance in office from other derivative actions. Hoffert v Dank (1976) 86 Misc. 2d 384, 382 N.Y.S.2d 421, mod (1976, 1st Dept) 55 A.D.2d 518, 389 N.Y.S.2d 101

A candidate for vice-president of a union was entitled, under Not-For-Profit Corp Law § 621, to inspect and copy the membership list of the union, notwithstanding the federal preemption argument, since the Labor Management Reporting Disclosure Act requires yielding to more favorable remedies under State law. Frankland v Independent Asso. of Publishers' Employees, Inc. (1981, Sup) 110 Misc. 2d 732, 442 N.Y.S.2d 951

Right of "inactive" members of not-for-profit corporation to inspect its books and records, in connection with their challenge to its decision to amend its bylaws, was not as broad as disclosure permitted under CLS CPLR § 3101; better statute to compare to CLS N-PCL § 621 was CLS Bus Corp § 624 (describing for-profit corporation's obligation to shareholders who demand inspection of corporate books, records and minutes). Wells v League of Am. Theatres & Producers, Inc. (2000, Sup) 183 Misc. 2d 915, 706 N.Y.S.2d 599

2. Beneficial interest

Provision of Not-For-Profit Corporation Law reserving to court right to authorize inspection of corporate documents authorizes court to grant right to one entitled thereto on common-law principles, to a pledgee of stock, to a holder of a voting trust certificate, to an executor of a deceased stockholder, and to directors of corporation, but does not authorize court to grant such right to persons who have no beneficial interest in corporation and who are not officers or directors thereof. Getman v Mohawk Valley Nursing Home, Inc. (1974, 4th Dept) 44 A.D.2d 392, 355 N.Y.S.2d 508

Petitioner, who was a resident and taxpayer of town and who made annual charitable contributions to nursing home organized pursuant to Not-For-Profit Corporation Law, but who was not a manager thereof under any of four tests specified by Law and who was not an officer or director and had no beneficial interest in corporation, had no right to inspect records of corporation. Getman v Mohawk Valley Nursing Home, Inc. (1974, 4th Dept) 44 A.D.2d 392, 355 N.Y.S.2d 508

Petitioners were not precluded from inspecting books and records of respondent not-for-profit corporation involved in presentation of Antoinette Perry ("Tony") Awards, on ground that their application was not made in good faith and for proper purpose; fact that petitioners were "inactive" members of respondent corporation, and had some personal interest in challenging its decision to amend its bylaws so as to prevent inactive members from participating in Tony awards process, did not preclude there being legitimate corporate interest involved in their claims. Wells v League of Am. Theatres & Producers, Inc. (2000, Sup) 183 Misc. 2d 915, 706 N.Y.S.2d 599

3. Good faith

In an Article 78 proceeding to inspect and copy certain minutes, reports and membership lists of a not-for-profit cemetery corporation from which petitioner had purchased a burial plot, a hearing to determine the good faith of petitioner in seeking the inspection was required, where the president of the corporation, in an affidavit in opposition to petitioner's application, averred that petitioner was an attorney employed by a law firm representing a former employee of the corporation in various actions against the corporation, that these actions had been based on charges of waste and conversion of corporate assets by the corporation's directors and that these charges had been investigated by the attorney general's office, the cemetery board and the county grand jury and in each instance no impropriety or wrongdoing was found and that the request to inspect was made in bad faith and for the improper purpose of aiding the former employee's continuing harassment of the corporation. De Paula v Memory Gardens, Inc. (1982, 3d Dept) 90 A.D.2d 886, 456 N.Y.S.2d 522, appeal after remand (1983, 3d Dept) 96 A.D.2d 641, 465 N.Y.S.2d 73

In proceeding under CLS N-PCL § 621(d) against not-for-profit corporation to inspect and copy various of its records, corporation properly raised issue as to bad faith of petitioners, who were residential members of corporation involved in long and bitter dispute with corporation regarding rent control status of residence units, and hearing was necessary to determine good faith of petitioners in their request; although ill will and desire to change corporation's management and policies did not render request improper, request would be improper if driving motive was personal gain. Mayer v National Arts Club (1993, 3d Dept) 192 A.D.2d 863, 596 N.Y.S.2d 537

Although petitioner in action seeking inspection of corporation's membership lists filed the affidavit required by Not-For-Profit Corp L § 621, the court could, where the question was raised, go beyond the face of the affidavit to determine whether in fact the inspection was sought in good faith. Application of Santuccio (1972) 70 Misc. 2d 587, 334 N.Y.S.2d 67

Because of the special relationship between the N.R.A. and The American Rifleman the fiduciary obligations of the association's directors and officers, as imposed by N.P.C.L. § 717, applied with equal vigor to the operation of The American Rifleman to the effect that the Board could not refuse to publish advertisements of candidates for N.R.A. directorships in order that they might retain control of the association for themselves; refusal of the Board to furnish a membership list to candidates and to publish a request for monetary support for a candidate raised the issue of directors' bad faith. Fitzgerald v National Rifle Asso. (1974, DC NJ) 383 F. Supp. 162

4-10. [Reserved for future use]

11. Under former Membership Corporation Law § 26

The power of visitation vested in the supreme court by former § 16 from which this section is derived and other statutes where the word "visitation" is used confers no power to do anything other than as specifically stated in former § 16. In re Norton (1916) 97 Misc 289, 161 N.Y.S. 710

This section may not be invoked for the investigation of the affairs of a religious corporation. Taylor v Day Star Baptist Church, Inc. (1949) 196 Misc 449, 92 N.Y.S.2d 206

Not-For-Profit Corporation Law

Where there has been a demand for relief in the form of an inventory and account with a detailed statement of transactions by a membership corporation, under this section, and the pleadings allege that one of the directors caused moneys to be paid to himself without the concurring vote of two-thirds of the Board of Directors as required by § 47 of the Membership Corporations Law, the court before granting such relief will direct a trial of the issues raised. Application of Atwater (1948, Sup) 85 N.Y.S.2d 738, affd (1950) 277 A.D. 766, 97 N.Y.S.2d 541, app den (1950) 277 A.D. 1104, 101 N.Y.S.2d 731

12. – Order appointing referee to investigate for court

An order appointing a referee to conduct the investigation in a proceeding instituted under former § 16 from which the section is derived to make visitation and inquiry into the affairs of a membership corporation should contain only the statutory provisions defining the scope and method of the referee's investigation and nothing in the way of adjudication upon the merits. People v Horowitz (1915) 216 N.Y. 637, 110 N.E. 1046

13. – – Right to appeal order

An order appointing a referee to conduct the investigation in a proceeding instituted under former § 16 from which this section is derived to make visitation and inquiry into the affairs of a membership corporation, is not appealable to the appellate division. People v Horowitz (1915) 216 N.Y. 637, 110 N.E. 1046

14. – Order requiring inventory and accounting

Under former § 16 from which this section is derived the supreme court had power to make an order requiring an inventory and account of the property, effects and liabilities of a cemetery corporation, with a detailed statement of its transactions during the twelve months next preceding the granting of said order. In re Norton (1916) 97 Misc 289, 161 N.Y.S. 710

Directors of a membership corporation organized chiefly for charitable purposes were directed to file inventory, accounting and statement of transactions during 12 months next preceding the granting of the order, where it appeared that the members of the corporation, under the guise of voting compensation to themselves for past services, sought to divide the assets among themselves. Distribution of the assets of a membership corporation whose purposes were charitable among the membership, even on dissolution, would be improper. It was also immaterial that the petitioner, a member of the corporation, might be estopped to object to the resolution for payment of compensation since the supreme court may act on its own motion. In re Green (1957) 10 Misc. 2d 557, 177 N.Y.S.2d 933

15. – – Provision restraining sale of property

In an order granted under former § 16 from which this section is derived, providing for visitation by the supreme court of a cemetery corporation and directing the filing of an inventory and account, a provision in the nature of an injunction restraining the sale of the property of such corporation is unauthorized. In re Greene (1912) 153 A.D. 8, 138 N.Y.S. 95

16. – Investigation or attack by others; city

Where city is entitled to net revenues of membership corporation it has power to investigate the finances thereof under General City Law § 20, subds 19 and 21, although books and vouchers of such corporation are subject to visitation and inspection of justice of the Supreme Court or of any person appointed by such court under above statute. New York World's Fair 1964-1965 Corp. v Beame (1965) 45 Misc. 2d 683, 257 N.Y.S.2d 543, affd (1965, 1st Dept) 22 A.D.2d 611, 257 N.Y.S.2d 747, affd (1965) 16 N.Y.2d 570, 260 N.Y.S.2d 841, 208 N.E.2d 785

17. – – Nonmembers

No procedure is afforded in law for an attack upon a budget regularly adopted by the directors of a membership corporation by one who is not a member of the corporation and has not taken advantage of opportunities to become a member. Sea Gate Asso. v Fleischer (1960, Sup) 211 N.Y.S.2d 767

Persons who bought property in a private community with knowledge that its facilities, such as police protection, street repair, sewage disposal, and the like, were, and for many years had been, handled through a membership corporation open to all property owners on an annual assessment basis, having refused to pay such assessments and not having become members of the corporation, had no standing, in an action to collect service assessments, to attack the assessments as excessive or because they were denied use of certain facilities by reason of nonpayment. Sea Gate Asso. v Fleischer (1960, Sup) 211 N.Y.S.2d 767

18. – Bylaw precluding access to membership list

A bylaw of a membership corporation which precludes all access to the corporate record of lists of its members on the say-so of its governing body is so far inconsistent with the letter and spirit of section 46 of the Membership Corporations Law as to be wholly void and without effect. Davids v Sillcox (1948) 297 N.Y. 355, 79 N.E.2d 440, reh den (1948) 298 N.Y. 618, 81 N.E.2d 353

§ 622.   Infant members

(a) If the certificate of incorporation or the by-laws provide that a member shall be of full age:

(1) A corporation may treat an infant who holds a membership certificate or card or capital certificate or a bond of such corporation as having capacity to receive and to empower others to receive payments or distributions, to vote or express consent or dissent, in person or by proxy, and to make elections and exercise rights relating to such certificates or bonds, unless, in the case of membership certificates or cards or capital certificates, the corporate officer responsible for maintaining the list or record of members or the transfer agent of the corporation or, in the case of bonds, the treasurer or paying officer or agent has received written notice that such holder is an infant.

(2) An infant holder of a membership certificate or card or capital certificate or a bond of a corporation who has received or empowered others to receive payments or distributions, voted or expressed consent or dissent, or made an election or exercised a right relating thereto, shall have no right thereafter to disaffirm or avoid, as against the corporation, any such act on his part, unless prior to such receipt, vote, consent, dissent, election or exercise, as to membership certificates or cards or capital certificates, the corporate officer responsible for maintaining the list or record of members or its transfer agent or, in the case of bonds, the treasurer or paying officer or agent had received written notice that such holder was an infant.

History: Add, L 1969, ch 1066, § 1, with substance deriving from Gen Corp Law § 12-a; amd, L 1970, ch 847, § 39, eff Sept 1, 1970.

CASE ANNOTATIONS

If permitted in the by-laws or the certificate of incorporation of a not-for-profit corporation, minors may be members and hold office in the corporation. Ops Atty Gen 84-64

§ 623.   Members' derivative action brought in the right of the corporation to procure a judgment in its favor

(a) An action may be brought in the right of a domestic or foreign corporation to procure a judgment in its favor by five percent or more of any class of members or by such percentage of the holders of capital certificates or of the owners of a beneficial interest in the capital certificates of such corporation.

(b) In any such action, it shall be made to appear that each plaintiff is such a member, holder or owner at the time of bringing the action.

(c) In any such action, the complaint shall set forth with particularity the efforts of the plaintiff or plaintiffs to secure the initiation of such action by the board of the reason for not making such effort.

(d) Such action shall not be discontinued, compromised or settled without the approval of the court having jurisdiction of the action. If the court shall determine that the interests of the members or of any class or classes thereof will be substantially affected by such discontinuance, compromise or settlement, the court, in its discretion, may direct that notice, by publication or otherwise, shall be given to the members or class or classes thereof whose interests it determines will be so affected; if notice is so directed to be given, the court may determine which one or more of the parties to the action shall bear the expense of giving the same, in such amount as the court shall determine and find to be reasonable in the circumstances, and the amount of such expense shall be awarded as special costs of the action and recoverable in the same manner as statutory taxable costs.

(e) If the action on behalf of the corporation was successful, in whole or in part, or if anything was received by the plaintiff or plaintiffs or a claimant or claimants as the result of a judgment, compromise or settlement of an action or claim, the court may award the plaintiff or plaintiffs, claimant or claimants, reasonable expenses, including reasonable attorney's fees, and shall direct him or them to account to the corporation for the remainder of the proceeds so received by him or them. This paragraph shall not apply to any judgment rendered for the benefit of injured members or non-record owners only and limited to a recovery of the loss or damage sustained by them.

History: Add, L 1969, ch 1066, § 1, eff Sept 1, 1970, with substance derived from Gen Corp Law §§ 60, 61; amd, L 1971, ch 1058, § 20, eff Sept 1, 1971.

CASE ANNOTATIONS

1. **Generally**
2. **Standing**
3. **Demand on board**
4. **Defenses**
5. **Procedure**

1. Generally

Not-for-profit cemetery corporation did not owe fiduciary duty to plaintiff on basis that land share agreement between corporation and development corporation from which plaintiff obtained his land share certificates provided that proceeds from sale of cemetery lots would be placed into land purchase fund for distribution to land share certificate holders, and thus derivative action against defendants was properly dismissed where plaintiff's claim of standing was based on his fiduciary relationship with corporation; land purchase fund merely was account in which proceeds from sale of cemetery lots were placed until time when contractually-determined payments for sales were disbursed to land share certificate holders, and cemetery corporation merely acted as collector and disburser of land purchase funds. Harris v Lyke, 217 A.D.2d 982, 629 N.Y.S.2d 911, 1995 N.Y. App. Div. LEXIS 8420 (N.Y. App. Div. 4th Dep't), app. denied, 87 N.Y.2d 801, 637 N.Y.S.2d 688, 661 N.E.2d 160, 1995 N.Y. LEXIS 4931 (N.Y. 1995).

2. Standing

An individual bringing a derivative action against directors or officers of a corporation for misconduct must meet requirement for standing by representing five percent or more of the membership of the corporation. Hoffert v Dank, 55 A.D.2d 518, 389 N.Y.S.2d 101, 1976 N.Y. App. Div. LEXIS 15153 (N.Y. App. Div. 1st Dep't 1976).

Phrase "one or more of the members thereof," within statute governing a member's derivative action brought in right of corporation to procure a judgment in its favor by one or more of the members thereof, does not eliminate requirement for standing in preceding statute that plaintiff represent five percent or more of the members. Hoffert v Dank, 55 A.D.2d 518, 389 N.Y.S.2d 101, 1976 N.Y. App. Div. LEXIS 15153 (N.Y. App. Div. 1st Dep't 1976).

An individual bringing a derivative action on behalf of a corporation with a membership of 20 or less would meet the statutory requirement for standing that he represent five percent or more of the members. Hoffert v Dank, 55 A.D.2d 518, 389 N.Y.S.2d 101, 1976 N.Y. App. Div. LEXIS 15153 (N.Y. App. Div. 1st Dep't 1976).

Cause of action advancing derivative claim seeking to recover for alleged misconduct of board of governors of country club was properly dismissed since plaintiff did not represent 5 percent or more of any class of members of country club and therefore lacked standing. Bernbach v Bonnie Briar Country Club, 144 A.D.2d 610, 534 N.Y.S.2d 695, 1988 N.Y. App. Div. LEXIS 12353 (N.Y. App. Div. 2d Dep't 1988), app. dismissed, 74 N.Y.2d 715, 543 N.Y.S.2d 401, 541 N.E.2d 430, 1989 N.Y. LEXIS 798 (N.Y. 1989).

Complaint was properly dismissed due to plaintiff's lack of standing to bring derivative action on behalf of not-for-profit cemetery corporation where plaintiff was not member of corporation as set forth in its certificate or incorporation, and he did not otherwise come within categories of members defined by its by-laws; fact that plaintiff was land share certificate holder, and thus had voting rights under corporation's by-laws, was irrelevant where enumeration in by-laws of "members" did not include land share certificate holders. Harris v Lyke, 217 A.D.2d 982, 629 N.Y.S.2d 911, 1995 N.Y. App. Div. LEXIS 8420 (N.Y. App. Div. 4th Dep't), app. denied, 87 N.Y.2d 801, 637 N.Y.S.2d 688, 661 N.E.2d 160, 1995 N.Y. LEXIS 4931 (N.Y. 1995).

Complaint against defendants was properly dismissed due to plaintiff's lack of standing to bring derivative action on behalf of not-for-profit cemetery corporation; plaintiff was not capital certificate holder under CLS N-PCL § 623(a) based on his status as land share certificate holder under CLS N-PCL § 1511(b) in that definition of capital certificates (CLS N-PCL § 503) does not include land share certificates, and land share certificates are not equivalent of capital certificates as they represent debt rather than equity. Harris v Lyke, 217 A.D.2d 982, 629 N.Y.S.2d 911, 1995 N.Y. App. Div. LEXIS 8420 (N.Y. App. Div. 4th Dep't), app. denied, 87 N.Y.2d 801, 637 N.Y.S.2d 688, 661 N.E.2d 160, 1995 N.Y. LEXIS 4931 (N.Y. 1995).

Land share certificate holder did not have standing, on public policy grounds, to bring derivative action on behalf of not-for-profit cemetery corporation based on his claim that he had strong interest in policing corporate management, and thus complaint against defendants was properly dismissed; land share certificate holders such as plaintiff have other available remedies for management delinquency, plaintiff had already complained of corporate wrongdoing to district attorney's office and state's Division of Cemeteries which investigated matter and decided not to pursue it, and court had permitted plaintiff to commence new action under "contract theory." Harris v Lyke, 217 A.D.2d 982, 629 N.Y.S.2d 911, 1995 N.Y. App. Div. LEXIS 8420 (N.Y. App. Div. 4th Dep't), app. denied, 87 N.Y.2d 801, 637 N.Y.S.2d 688, 661 N.E.2d 160, 1995 N.Y. LEXIS 4931 (N.Y. 1995).

Plaintiff did not have standing, in equity, to bring derivative action on behalf of not-for-profit cemetery corporation based on corporation's alleged fiduciary obligation to him due to his status as land share certificate holder, and thus complaint against defendants was properly dismissed; action was derivative, not equitable, and record did not establish any relationship that would make corporation trustee or agent for plaintiff. Harris v Lyke, 217 A.D.2d 982, 629 N.Y.S.2d 911, 1995 N.Y. App. Div. LEXIS 8420 (N.Y. App. Div. 4th Dep't), app. denied, 87 N.Y.2d 801, 637 N.Y.S.2d 688, 661 N.E.2d 160, 1995 N.Y. LEXIS 4931 (N.Y. 1995).

Dismissal of a member's causes of action, pursuant to N.Y. Not-for-Profit Corp. Law § 720, to compel the a church's pastor and trustees to account for certain alleged misconduct, and for a judgment

Not-For-Profit
Corporation Law

declaring that the pastor and the trustees had engaged in certain unlawful conduct, was proper because, inasmuch as the member sought to vindicate the church's rights by asserting those claims, they had to have been, but were not, asserted in the context of a derivative action brought by at least 5 percent of the church's members pursuant to N.Y. Not-for-Profit Corp. Law § 623(a); further, the complaint failed to set forth the member's efforts to secure the initiation of a derivative action or the reason for not making such effort. Therefore, the member lacked standing to bring the claims. Tae Hwa Yoon v New York Hahn Wolee Church, Inc., 56 A.D.3d 752, 870 N.Y.S.2d 42, 2008 N.Y. App. Div. LEXIS 9041 (N.Y. App. Div. 2d Dep't 2008).

Trial court properly found that an owner had standing to sue the homeowners association for violation of the declaration of covenants because the declaration specifically provided that any owner had the right to enforce the provisions of the declaration, and N.Y. Not-for-Profit Corp. Law § 623(a) did not operate to take away individual standing derived from other sources. In the Matter of St. Denis v Queensbury Baybridge Homeowners Assn., Inc., 100 A.D.3d 1326, 955 N.Y.S.2d 263, 2012 N.Y. App. Div. LEXIS 8168 (N.Y. App. Div. 3d Dep't 2012).

Lot owners lacked standing to assert any derivative claims on behalf of the homeowners' association (HOA) because the owners sought to vindicate the HOA's rights and recover damages on behalf of the HOA, and, as such, the owners' breach of contract cause of action had to be, but was not, asserted in the context of a derivative action brought by at least 5 percent of the HOA members. Schaefer v Chautauqua Escapes Assn., Inc., 158 A.D.3d 1186, 71 N.Y.S.3d 244, 2018 N.Y. App. Div. LEXIS 702 (N.Y. App. Div. 4th Dep't), reh'g denied, app. denied, 160 A.D.3d 1507, 72 N.Y.S.3d 854, 2018 N.Y. App. Div. LEXIS 3023 (N.Y. App. Div. 4th Dep't 2018), app. denied, 2018 N.Y. LEXIS 2523 (N.Y. Sept. 6, 2018).

Lot owners lacked standing to assert any derivative claims on behalf of the homeowners' association (HOA) because the owners sought to vindicate the HOA's rights and recover damages on behalf of the HOA, and, as such, the owners' breach of contract cause of action had to be, but was not, asserted in the context of a derivative action brought by at least 5 percent of the HOA members. Schaefer v Chautauqua Escapes Assn., Inc., 158 A.D.3d 1186, 71 N.Y.S.3d 244, 2018 N.Y. App. Div. LEXIS 702 (N.Y. App. Div. 4th Dep't), reh'g denied, app. denied, 160 A.D.3d 1507, 72 N.Y.S.3d 854, 2018 N.Y. App. Div. LEXIS 3023 (N.Y. App. Div. 4th Dep't 2018), app. denied, 2018 N.Y. LEXIS 2523 (N.Y. Sept. 6, 2018).

Plaintiff failed to meet 5 percent standing requirement of CLS N-PCL § 623, warranting dismissal of derivative action against not-for-profit corporation, where he failed to name in complaint individuals who constituted requisite "5 percent or more of any class of members"; standing under § 623 must be shown to exist at time of bringing action. Segal v Powers, 180 Misc. 2d 57, 687 N.Y.S.2d 589, 1999 N.Y. Misc. LEXIS 96 (N.Y. Sup. Ct. 1999).

3. Demand on board

Derivative action, seeking to nullify sale of nonprofit organization's headquarters, was properly dismissed where plaintiffs alleged that unsuccessful demands were made on board of directors to initiate legal action but complaint provided no indication as to who made demands, when they were made, which board members they were made to, content of demands or why board refused to take action; nor did court err in denying plaintiffs' motion to amend complaint to allege contradictory claim that no demand was made on board because it would have been futile, as plaintiffs' conclusory allegation that board was not functionally constituted was plainly without merit in light of documentary evidence. Tomczak v Trepel, 283 A.D.2d 229, 724 N.Y.S.2d 737, 2001 N.Y. App. Div. LEXIS 4804 (N.Y. App. Div. 1st Dep't), app. denied, 96 N.Y.2d 930, 733 N.Y.S.2d 365, 759 N.E.2d 364, 2001 N.Y. LEXIS 3085 (N.Y. 2001).

Derivative action against not-for-profit corporation was dismissed under CLS CPLR § 3211(a)(3) due to lack of adequate demand on board of governors, where complaint merely alleged that plaintiff asked current president (who was one of 22 board members) to obtain board's authorization to initiate action, and that "this request has been denied"; complaint alleged that president failed to present issue to board, not that board considered demand and rejected it, and there was no showing that demand to board would have been futile. Segal v Powers, 180 Misc. 2d 57, 687 N.Y.S.2d 589, 1999 N.Y. Misc. LEXIS 96 (N.Y. Sup. Ct. 1999).

4. Defenses

Dissident fraternity members failed to establish prima facie case of bad faith or fraud in a derivative action under N.Y. Not-for-Profit Corp. Law § 623 to protest the sale of a fraternity house to a university by the fraternity board because the evidence showed that the board obtained an independent appraisal and exacted significant concessions from the university and the board was thus protected by the business judgment rule. Sanford v Colgate Univ., 36 A.D.3d 1060, 828 N.Y.S.2d 633, 2007 N.Y. App. Div. LEXIS 254 (N.Y. App. Div. 3d Dep't 2007).

Directors and officers were entitled to summary judgment on a corporation's cause of action pursuant to N.Y. Not-for-Profit Corp. Law §§ 623, 720, asserting the improper transfer of real property because the claim was asserted in a prior action which was resolved by a stipulation, and, contrary to the corporation's claim, the identity requirement of res judicata was satisfied; however, although the issue of improper assessment of membership dues was raised in the prior action, any losses occasioned by assessments made after the discontinuance of that action constituted separate injuries for which recovery could not have been obtained in the prior action, and the stipulation did not prevent the corporation from asserting claims that accrued after the stipulation came into effect. Pawling Lake Prop. Owners Assn., Inc. v Greiner, 72 A.D.3d 665, 897 N.Y.S.2d 729, 2010 N.Y. App. Div. LEXIS 2868 (N.Y. App. Div. 2d Dep't 2010).

5. Procedure

Because a factual dispute existed as to whether the first director possessed standing to sue under N.Y. Not-for-Profit Corp. Law § 623(a), 720, a cross-motion by the second director and a non-profit corporation to dismiss the complaint for lack of standing to sue was properly denied. Brach v Harmony Servs., Inc., 93 A.D.3d 748, 940 N.Y.S.2d 652, 2012 N.Y. App. Div. LEXIS 2054 (N.Y. App. Div. 2d Dep't 2012).

ARTICLE 7
DIRECTORS AND OFFICERS

History: Add, L 1969, ch 1066, § 1, eff Sept. 1, 1970.

Schedule of sections, amd, L 1970, ch 847, § 40, eff Sept 1, 1970.

§ 701.   Board of directors

(a) Except as otherwise provided in the certificate of incorporation, a corporation shall be managed by its board of directors. Each director shall be at least eighteen years of age; provided, however, that a member of the board of directors of any girl scout council chartered by Girl Scouts of the United States of America, Inc., or any Camp Fire Girls club member serving as a member of the board of directors on the National Board and National Council of Camp Fire Girls, Inc. or on the local board of the Camp Fire Girls, Inc. or any member of Aspira of America Inc. or Aspira of New York Inc. serving on the board of directors, shall be at least sixteen years of age. Notwithstanding the above, a corporation organized for educational purposes primarily for the benefit of individuals below eighteen years of age may include one director below eighteen years of age who is at least sixteen years of age. Further, a corporation organized for recreational or youth development and delinquency prevention purposes primarily for the benefit of individuals below eighteen years of age may include one or more directors, the number of which shall not exceed one-half of the total number of directors for a quorum for the transaction of business, who are at least sixteen years of age but not over eighteen years of age. The certificate of incorporation or the by-laws may prescribe other qualifications for directors, provided, however, any corporation organized for recreation or youth development and delinquency prevention purposes, when increasing the number of directors between the ages of sixteen and eighteen years old to more than one, shall prescribe in its certificate of incorporation the number of such directors not to exceed the limitations of this paragraph.

(b) If the certificate of incorporation vests the management of the corporation, in whole or in part, in one or more persons other than the board, individually or collectively, such other person or persons shall be subject to the same obligations and the same liabilities for managerial acts or omissions as are imposed upon directors by this chapter.

History: Add, L 1969, ch 1066, § 1, with substance deriving from Gen Corp Law §§ 27, 28; amd, L 1970, ch 847, § 41; L 1972, ch 437, eff Sept 1, 1972; L 1972, ch 961, § 10; L 1973, ch 875, § 1; L 1975, ch 266, § 1; L 1980, ch 154, § 1; L 1980, ch 502, § 1; L 1983, ch 730, § 1, eff July 27, 1983.

CASE ANNOTATIONS

1. Generally
2-10. [Reserved for future use]
11. Under former General Corporation Law § 27
12. – Bylaws; relating to vote of stockholders
13. – – Relating to quorum of directors
14. – Management of corporation by board of directors
15. – – Veto of litigation instituted by president
16. – – Authorization of bankruptcy
17. – Directors meeting; required notice
18. – – Action by majority of quorum

19. Under former Membership Corporations Law § 46

1. Generally

Business judgment rule prohibits judicial inquiry into actions of corporate directors taken in good faith and in exercise of honest judgment in lawful and legitimate furtherance of corporate purposes; so long as directors have not breached their fiduciary obligation to corporation, exercise of their powers for common and general interests of corporation may not be questioned, even if results show that what they did was unwise or inexpedient. Levandusky v One Fifth Ave. Apartment Corp. (1990) 75 N.Y.2d 530, 554 N.Y.S.2d 807, 553 N.E.2d 1317, later proceeding (1991, 1st Dept) 171 A.D.2d 590, 567 N.Y.S.2d 662 and (criticized in Mulligan v Panther Valley Prop. Owners Ass'n (2001, NJ Super Ct A.D.) 766 A2d 1186)

Action by board of directors of corporation that comes within business judgment rule cannot be characterized as arbitrary and capricious, or abuse of discretion, for purpose of Article 78 proceeding. Levandusky v One Fifth Ave. Apartment Corp. (1990) 75 N.Y.2d 530, 554 N.Y.S.2d 807, 553 N.E.2d 1317, later proceeding (1991, 1st Dept) 171 A.D.2d 590, 567 N.Y.S.2d 662 and (criticized in Mulligan v Panther Valley Prop. Owners Ass'n (2001, NJ Super Ct A.D.) 766 A2d 1186)

The business of corporations shall be managed by the board of directors, the only exception being a provision contrary to the rule in its charter. Weiss v Opportunities for Cortland County, Inc. (1972, 3d Dept) 40 A.D.2d 45, 337 N.Y.S.2d 409

Members of board of cooperative residential association were not entitled to summary judgment in shareholder's derivative action brought by board member, despite business judgment doctrine which bars judicial inquiry into actions of corporate directors, where triable issues of fact were raised regarding good faith of board's actions including, inter alia, whether voting proxies were improperly used, whether one member was coerced into voting certain way, and whether remodeling application at issue was evaluated in good faith. Van Camp v Sherman (1987, 1st Dept) 132 A.D.2d 453, 517 N.Y.S.2d 152

Under CLS N-PCL § 701, public employee labor union organized as not- for-profit corporation was to be managed by its board of directors despite provision in union's constitution that board's authority to transact business of union was "subject to the power and authority of the delegates at meetings of the Association," and any attempt by delegates to place general management responsibility in another person without so specifying in certificate of incorporation would be violation of § 701; however, if delegates desired to limit management authority of board of directors by amending certificate of incorporation, they could, after proper notice, vote to do so at general or special meeting, and if delegates believed board of directors, either individually or as group, failed to abide by union's constitution and bylaws, they could, after proper notice, vote to remove board of directors in whole or in part. Simoni v Civil Service Employees Asso., Local 1000, etc. (1986, Sup) 133 Misc. 2d 1, 507 N.Y.S.2d 371

Resolutions passed by board of directors of public employee labor union organized as not-for-profit corporation, by which board reorganized union's staff in manner inconsistent with union president's organizational plan, were in conflict with provision of union's bylaws stating that "President shall be responsible for the organization and direction of the staff of the Association," constituted attempt to usurp authority given by members to president, and were therefore void. Simoni v Civil Service Employees Asso., Local 1000, etc. (1986, Sup) 133 Misc. 2d 1, 507 N.Y.S.2d 371

Because not-for-profit corporations were given statutory authority to exercise all powers necessary to affect their purposes, and this power could be curtailed only if restricted by another statute or its own certificate of incorporation or bylaws, unless there was a specific prohibition in the documents or another statute, the corporation could act in any appropriate way in pursuit of its purposes. Suburban Scholastic Council v Section 2 of N.Y. State Pub. High School Athletic Assn., Inc. (2005, A.D., 3d Dept) 803 N.Y.S.2d 270

If permitted in the by-laws or the certificate of incorporation of a not-for-profit corporation, minors may be members and hold office in the corporation. Ops Atty Gen 84-64

Under Sections 10-1000 et seq. of the Village Law, a village fire department is a corporation consisting of members of all the fire, hose, protective and hook and ladder companies of a village; it is

Not-For-Profit Corporation Law

administered by a board of fire commissioners or, where no board of fire commissioners has been appointed, by the village board of trustees and the council of the fire department. Fire companies in a village are associations or corporations, which must operate in accordance with their certificates of incorporation, bylaws, and statutes; and, although fire companies are separate and distinct from the village, the statutes do permit village authorities to exercise a certain degree of control over their organization, incorporation, governance, and membership, including residency for membership. A fire company must consent to a contract for the provision of fire protection outside the village and the fire chief of the village fire department cannot consent on behalf of members of the company. 1990 Op St Compt 90-19

2-10. [Reserved for future use]

11. Under former General Corporation Law § 27

Vacancies on a Board of Directors are to be filled as the by-laws of the corporation may provide, subject to statutory limitations. Gearing v Kelly (1961, 1st Dept) 15 A.D.2d 219, 222 N.Y.S.2d 474, affd (1962) 11 N.Y.2d 201, 227 N.Y.S.2d 897, 182 N.E.2d 391, reh den (1962) 11 N.Y.2d 1016

The court would not entertain a petition for an order setting aside a special meeting of the board of directors of a corporation, and vacating the removal of a corporate officer. Heller v Clark Merchandisers, Inc. (1955) 9 Misc. 2d 106, 154 N.Y.S.2d 150

12. – Bylaws; relating to vote of stockholders

A by-law requiring unanimous vote of stockholders for any action by them is invalid as contrary to decree of § 27. Benintendi v Kenton Hotel, Inc. (1945) 294 N.Y. 112, 60 N.E.2d 829, 159 ALR 280 (superseded by statute as stated in Application of Burkin (1956) 1 N.Y.2d 570, 154 N.Y.S.2d 898, 136 N.E.2d 862, 64 ALR2d 638) and (superseded by statute as stated in Sutton v Sutton (1994) 84 N.Y.2d 37, 614 N.Y.S.2d 369, 637 N.E.2d 260)

13. – – Relating to quorum of directors

By § 27 every corporation is given privilege of enacting a by-law fixing its own quorum requirement at any fraction not less than one-third, nor more than a majority, of its directors. Benintendi v Kenton Hotel, Inc. (1945) 294 N.Y. 112, 60 N.E.2d 829, 159 ALR 280 (superseded by statute as stated in Application of Burkin (1956) 1 N.Y.2d 570, 154 N.Y.S.2d 898, 136 N.E.2d 862, 64 ALR2d 638) and (superseded by statute as stated in Sutton v Sutton (1994) 84 N.Y.2d 37, 614 N.Y.S.2d 369, 637 N.E.2d 260)

Reading together § 27 and § 28 and examining their legislative history, court concluded that there never was legislative intent so to change common-law rule as to quorums as to authorize a by-law requiring unanimous vote of directors. Benintendi v Kenton Hotel, Inc. (1945) 294 N.Y. 112, 60 N.E.2d 829, 159 ALR 280 (superseded by statute as stated in Application of Burkin (1956) 1 N.Y.2d 570, 154 N.Y.S.2d 898, 136 N.E.2d 862, 64 ALR2d 638) and (superseded by statute as stated in Sutton v Sutton (1994) 84 N.Y.2d 37, 614 N.Y.S.2d 369, 637 N.E.2d 260)

This section and § 28 do not forbid a bylaw requiring a two-thirds' vote of a quorum of directors. In re Lake Placid Co. (1948) 274 A.D. 205, 81 N.Y.S.2d 36

A by-law provision that a "majority of the directors shall constitute a quorum" is ambiguous as to whether the reference is to a majority of the remaining directors in case of a vacancy or to a majority of the authorized number of members, but where other by-law provisions indicate a distinction between action which can only be taken by a majority of the "whole" board, or by a certain fraction of the whole board, it can be implied that in instances where the whole board is not called for the "board" consists of the directors actually in office. Gearing v Kelly (1961, 1st Dept) 15 A.D.2d 219, 222 N.Y.S.2d 474, affd (1962) 11 N.Y.2d 201, 227 N.Y.S.2d 897, 182 N.E.2d 391, reh den (1962) 11 N.Y.2d 1016.

14. – Management of corporation by board of directors

Directors have power to manage the corporation only when acting as a board. Acting singly the directors cannot bind the corporation. Knapp v Rochester Dog Protective Ass'n (1932) 235 A.D. 436, 257 N.Y.S. 356

The directors of a corporation may not be bound by an agreement requiring that any question involving removal be submitted to a board of arbitrators, nor may their authority be delegated to others. In re Allied Fruit & Extract Co. (1934) 243 A.D. 52, 276 N.Y.S. 153

15. – – Veto of litigation instituted by president

Any actual or implied authority which the president of a corporation may have to institute litigation is terminated when the board of directors refuses to sanction it, the management of a corporation

being in its board of directors. Sterling Industries, Inc. v Ball Bearing Pen Corp. (1949) 298 N.Y. 483, 84 N.E.2d 790, 10 ALR2d 694

16. – – Authorization of bankruptcy

A petition in bankruptcy, in order to justify adjudication in voluntary bankruptcy and consequent transfer of all property of the corporation, real and personal, to a trustee, should at least allege and show corporate action by the board of directors authorizing the petition and its execution by an officer signing the name of the corporation thereto. In re Jefferson Casket Co. (1910, DC NY) 182 F 689

17. – Directors meeting; required notice

The provision of this section that a majority of the Board of Directors at a meeting "duly assembled" shall constitute a quorum infer that each director shall receive proper notice of the meeting unless he waives it. Cirrincione v Polizzi (1961, 4th Dept) 14 A.D.2d 281, 220 N.Y.S.2d 741

18. – – Action by majority of quorum

It appears to be the legislative intent that a board of directors can act by a majority of a quorum, irrespective of the number of other directors who may merely be present at the meeting. Crowley v Commodity Exchange, Inc. (1944, CA2 NY) 141 F.2d 182

19. Under former Membership Corporations Law § 46

The authority of directors of a membership corporation are similar to those of directors of other corporations, except that the authority of the directors of membership corporations to deal with property is restricted by § 21. Van Campen v Olean General Hospital (1924) 210 A.D. 204, 205 N.Y.S. 554, affd (1925) 239 N.Y. 615, 147 N.E. 219 ·

The directors of a hospital incorporated under this law may deprive a physician of the privilege of treating his patients in the hospital, the latter not being within the definition of a public corporation even though it is sustained in part by charitable gifts. Van Campen v Olean General Hospital (1924) 210 A.D. 204, 205 N.Y.S. 554, affd (1925) 239 N.Y. 615, 147 N.E. 219

In a membership corporation the power of control is vested in the board of directors and stockholders cannot bind the corporation by contract. Clifford v Firemen's Mut. Benevolent Ass'n (1931) 232 A.D. 260, 249 N.Y.S. 713, affd (1932) 259 N.Y. 547, 182 N.E. 175

The Board of Directors cannot impose an obligation on a corporation long after their term of office, and accordingly a contract to pay a former president a salary for life cannot be enforced. Clifford v Firemen's Mut. Benevolent Ass'n (1931) 232 A.D. 260, 249 N.Y.S. 713, affd (1932) 259 N.Y. 547, 182 N.E. 175

The indebtedness of a membership corporation for rent is not contracted, within the meaning of former § 11 from which this section is derived, when the lease is made, but when the instalments of rent come due. Dunn v Neustadtl (1911) 72 Misc 1, 129 N.Y.S. 161

§ 702.   Number of directors

(a) The number of directors constituting the entire board shall be not less than three. Subject to such limitation, such number may be fixed by the by-laws or by action of the members or of the board under the specific provisions of a by-law allowing such action, or by any number within a range set forth in the by-laws. If not otherwise fixed under this paragraph, the number shall be three.

(b) The number of directors may be increased or decreased by amendment of the by-laws or by action of the members, or of the board under the specific provisions of a by-law, subject to the following limitations:

(1) If the board is authorized by the by-laws to change the number of directors, whether by amending the by-laws or by taking action under the specific provisions of a by-law, such amendment or action shall require the vote of a majority of the entire board.

(2) No decrease shall shorten the term of any incumbent director.

History: Add, L 1969, ch 1066, § 1, eff Sept 1, 1970, with substance derived from Mem Corp Law § 20; amd, L 2013, ch 549, § 67, eff July 1, 2014; L 2015, ch 555, § 3, eff Dec 11, 2015.

§ 703. Election and term of office of directors; alternates

(a) A corporation may provide in its certificate of incorporation or by-laws for directors to be elected or appointed at large, or by special districts or membership sections, or by virtue of their office or former office in the corporation or other entity, public or private, or by bondholders pursuant to paragraph (c) of section 506 (Bonds and security interests) voting as a class, or any combination thereof.

(b) Directors shall be elected or appointed in the manner and for the term of office provided in the certificate of incorporation or the by-laws. The term of office of directors, other than those elected or appointed by virtue of their office or former office in the corporation or other entity, public or private, shall not exceed five years; and, if the board is classified under section 704 (Classification of directors), such term shall not exceed a number of years equal to the number of classes into which the board is classified. In the absence of a provision fixing the term, it shall be one year.

(c) Each director shall hold office until the expiration of the term for which he is elected or appointed, and until his successor has been elected or appointed and qualified.

(d) If the certificate of incorporation or by-laws so provide, a special district or membership section entitled to elect or appoint one or more directors may elect or appoint an alternate for each such director. In the absence of a director from a meeting of the board, his alternate may, upon written notice to the secretary of the corporation, attend such meeting and exercise therein the rights, powers, and privileges of the absent director. When so exercising the rights, powers, and privileges of the absent director, such alternate shall be subject in all respects to the provisions of this chapter governing directors.

History: Add, L 1969, ch 1066, § 1, eff Sept 1, 1970, with substance derived from Gen Corp Law § 21 and Mem Corp Law §§ 20, 45.

Par (a), amd, L 1970, ch 847, § 42, eff Sept 1, 1970.

Par (b), amd, L 1970, ch 847, § 42, L 1972, ch 961, § 11, eff Sept 1, 1972.

CASE ANNOTATIONS

1. Generally
2-5. [Reserved for future use]
6. Under former Membership Corporations Law § 45

1. Generally
Congregation had the authority to discharge members of a not-for-profit corporation's board of directors because (1) N.Y. Not-for-Profit Corp. Law § 703(b) and the corporation's bylaws only let the board increase the board's number, (2) the congregation, as the corpora-

tion's sole member, could not be denied the right to vote except by the congregation's removal or resignation, under N.Y. Not-for-Profit Corp. Law §§ 612 and 605(a), so bylaw amendments denying that right had no effect, (3) the bylaws in effect let the congregation veto the board's bylaw amendments, and (4) the congregation vetoed amendments denying the congregation the rights to vote, remove directors, and adopt, amend, or repeal bylaws. Gluck v Chevre Liady Nusach Hoary (2012, 2d Dept) 97 App Div 3d 787, 949 NYS2d 149.

Directors of not-for-profit corporation did not abandoned their duties by their involvement with a separate not-for-profit group where, the directors did not surrender their positions in writing, were not replaced by the not-for-profit corporation and did not regard themselves as having abandoned their roles. Machne Menachem, Inc. v Hershkop (2002, ED NY) 237 F. Supp. 2d 227, motion gr, claim dismissed, motion den (2003, ED NY) 2003 US Dist LEXIS 2804

The terms "special district" and "improvement district" are synonomous and are used interchangeably in the statutes. The provisions of Public Officers Law § 36 for removal of town, village, improvement district or fire district officers are applicable to officers of what the Nassau County Civil Divisions Act refers to as "special districts" including removal of a commissioner of the Port Washington Police District. 1980 Op Atty Gen April 14 (informal)

2-5. [Reserved for future use]
6. Under former Membership Corporations Law § 45
The office of director confers certain responsibilities of management and control upon such officers, but they are merely representatives of their associates, and their action is subject to fair criticism by any such associate. People ex rel. Ward v Uptown Ass'n (1898) 26 A.D. 297, 49 N.Y.S. 881

The provisions of this section providing that directors of such corporations need not be members is permissive rather than mandatory and the by-laws may require that directors be members. Thus, a non-member of a hospital corporation which required payment of dues as a condition of membership could not be elected to the office of director where the by-laws limited such offices to members. In re Tri-County Memorial Hospital (1957, 4th Dept) 4 A.D.2d 304, 165 N.Y.S.2d 590

Members of a charitable membership corporation have no vested right to choose its directors, nor is "self-perpetuation" of the board of such a corporation per se invalid in the absence of clear showing that it violates fundamental principles of justice. Petition of Sousa (1961, 2d Dept) 12 A.D.2d 956, 211 N.Y.S.2d 204, revd on other grounds (1961) 10 N.Y.2d 68, 217 N.Y.S.2d 58, 176 N.E.2d 77, stay den (1961) 9 N.Y.2d 1015 and remittitur amd (1961) 10 N.Y.2d 886, reported in full (1961) 10 N.Y.2d 812, 221 N.Y.S.2d 515, 178 N.E.2d 230 and stay gr (1961) 10 N.Y.2d 885

Where a cemetery corporation has elected an entire slate of six directors but has failed to specify the terms of such directors, and the bylaws of the corporation as well as a statute in effect at the time of the election, provided that one-third of the directors were to be elected each year, upon agreement of the elected directors that the terms of two of them were to expire at the end of the first year, at the first subsequent annual election only two new directors are to be elected, rather than an entire new slate as urged upon the theory that the original election was invalid. In re Washington Cemetery (1930) 135 Misc 763, 238 N.Y.S. 664

Directors cannot vote by proxy. Craig Medicine Co. v Merchants' Bank of Rochester (1891) 59 Hun 561, 14 N.Y.S. 16

By-laws of membership corporation may provide for an executive committee of the board of directors. Requirement that at least five members of executive committee be chosen from directors of another corporation not proper. 1955 Ops Atty Gen Mar 21

§ 704. Classification of directors

(a) The certificate of incorporation or a by-law adopted by the members may provide that directors elected or appointed at large shall be divided into either two, three, four or five classes for the purpose of staggering their terms of office and that all or some of the directors elected or appointed otherwise than at large shall be divided into the same or a different number of classes, not exceeding five, for the same purpose. All classes of each type shall be as nearly equal in number as possible and, if provision has been made for cumulative voting under section 617 (Cumulative voting), no class shall include less than three directors.

(b) The terms of office of the directors initially classified shall be as follows: that of the first class shall expire at the next annual meeting of members if there be members, or of the board if there be no members, the second class at the second succeeding annual meeting, the third class, if any, at the third succeeding annual meeting, the fourth class, if any, at the fourth succeeding annual meeting and the fifth class, if any, at the fifth succeeding annual meeting. After such initial classification, directors to replace those whose terms expire at each annual meeting shall be elected or appointed at such meeting to hold office for a full term in accordance with such classification.

(c) If directors are classified and the number of directors is thereafter changed by action of the board:

(1) Any newly created directorships or any decrease in directorships shall be so apportioned among the classes as to make all classes as nearly equal in number as possible.

(2) If newly created directorships are filled by the board in a corporation having members, there shall be no classification of the additional directors until the next annual meeting of members.

History: Add, L 1969, ch 1066, § 1, eff Sept 1, 1970, with substance derived from Mem Corp Law § 20.

Par (a), amd, L 1970, ch 847, § 43, eff Sept 1, 1970.

Par (b), amd, L 1970, ch 847, § 43, eff Sept 1, 1970.

§ 705. Newly created directorships and vacancies

(a) Newly created directorships resulting from an increase in the number of directors elected or appointed at large, and vacancies among such directors for any reason, may be filled by vote of a majority of the directors then in office, regardless of their number, unless the certificate of incorporation or the by-laws provide that such newly created directorships or vacancies shall be filled by vote of the members.

(b) Vacancies among directors elected or appointed by special districts or membership sections, or by bondholders voting as a class, shall be filled by action of the persons entitled to vote thereon; except that, if a vacancy remains unfilled for six months after it occurs, and by reason of the absence, illness, or other inability of one or more of the remaining directors a quorum of the board cannot be obtained, the remaining directors, or a majority of them, may appoint a director to fill such vacancy.

(c) A director elected or appointed to fill a vacancy shall hold office until the next annual meeting at which the election of directors is in the regular order of business, and until his successor is elected or appointed and qualified.

History: Add, L 1969, ch 1066, § 1, eff Sept 1, 1970, with substance derived from Mem Corp Law § 45.

CASE ANNOTATIONS

The terms "special district" and "improvement district" are synonomous and are used interchangeably in the statutes. The provisions of Public Officers Law § 36 for removal of town, village, improvement district or fire district officers are applicable to officers of what the Nassau County Civil Divisions Act refers to as "special districts" including removal of a commissioner of the Port Washington Police District. 1980 Op Atty Gen April 14 (informal)

§ 706. Removal of directors

(a) Except as limited in paragraph (c), any or all of the directors may be removed for cause by vote of the members, or by vote of the directors provided there is a quorum of not less than a majority present at the meeting of directors at which such action is taken.

(b) Except as limited in paragraph (c), if the certificate of incorporation or the by-laws so provide, any or all of the directors may be removed without cause by vote of the members.

(c) The removal of directors, with or without cause, as provided in paragraphs (a) and (b) is subject to the following:

(1) In the case of a corporation having cumulative voting, no director may be removed when the votes cast against his removal would be sufficient to elect him if voted cumulatively at an election at which the same total number of votes were cast and the entire board, or the entire class of directors of which he is a member, were then being elected; and

(2) When by the provisions of the certificate of incorporation or the by-laws the members of any class or group, or the holders of bonds, voting as a class, are entitled to elect one or more directors, any director so elected may be removed only by the applicable vote of the members of that class or group, or the holders of such bonds, voting as a class.

(d) An action to procure a judgment removing a director for cause may be brought by the attorney-general or by ten percent of the members whether or not entitled to vote. The court may bar from re-election any director so removed for a period fixed by the court.

History: Add, L 1969, ch 1066, § 1, eff Sept 1, 1970, with substance derived from Gen Corp Law §§ 60, 136.

CASE ANNOTATIONS

Board of governors of not-for-profit corporation had inherent power to remove directors for cause where they had commenced personal injury action against corporation and searched its records for confidential information as to nature and extent of its insurance coverage; directors acted in breach of their fiduciary obligation to corporation and contrary to its interest. Davidson v James (1991, 1st Dept) 172 A.D.2d 323

Congregation had the authority to discharge members of a not-for-profit corporation's board of directors without cause because N.Y. Not-for-Profit Corp. Law § 706(b) and the corporation's bylaws allowed a discharge without cause. Gluck v Chevre Liady Nusach Hoary (2012, 2d Dept) 97 App Div 3d 787, 949 NYS2d 149

Where a religious society did not follow its own by-law procedures and the trustees were considered "directors" under the Not-For-Profit Law and where neither N.Y. Relig. Corp. Law § 2-b(1)(a) nor NY. Not-For-Profit Corp. Law § 103(c) contained inconsistent provisions, they clearly did not preclude the removal of the trustees, the trial court erred in denying the members' petition to remove the trustees, invalidate the new by-laws, and appoint a referee. Venigalla v Alagappan (2003, A.D., 2d Dept) 763 N.Y.S.2d 765

In a proceeding to remove a religious society's board of trustees, newly-elected trustees were properly directed to assume their duties upon the signing of the judgment because findings that the society failed to comply with by-laws providing for election of trustees constituted the law of the case and could not be challenged; an appeal from the denial of a motion for an order rejecting the interim report of the court-appointed referee was dismissed. Matter of Venigalla v Nori (2007, 2d Dept) 41 App Div 3d 725, 840 NYS2d 365, app gr (2007) 9 NY3d 815

A volunteer member of a fire company may be removed in accordance with the constitution and by-laws of the company. Ops Atty Gen 85-17

§ 707.   Quorum of directors

Unless a greater proportion is required by this chapter or by the certificate of incorporation or by a by-law adopted by the members, a majority of the entire board shall constitute a quorum for the transaction of business or of any specified item of business, except that the certificate of incorporation or the by-laws may fix the quorum at less than a majority of the entire board, provided that in the case of a board of fifteen members or less the quorum shall be at least one-third of the entire number of members and in the case of a board of more than fifteen members the quorum shall be at least five members plus one additional member for every ten members (or fraction thereof) in excess of fifteen.

History: Add, L 1969, ch 1066, § 1, with substance deriving from Gen Corp Law § 27 and Mem Corp Law § 20; amd, L 1970, ch 847, § 44, L 1971, ch 1058 § 21, eff Sept 1, 1971.

§ 708.   Action by the board

(a) Except as otherwise provided in this chapter, any reference in this chapter to corporate action to be taken by the board shall mean such action at a meeting of the board.

(b) Unless otherwise restricted by the certificate of incorporation or the by-laws, any action required or permitted to be taken by the board or any committee thereof may be taken without a meeting if all members of the board or the committee consent to the adoption of a resolution authorizing the action. Such consent may be written or electronic. If written, the consent must be executed by the director by signing such consent or causing his or her signature to be affixed to such consent by any reasonable means including, but not limited to, facsimile signature. If electronic, the transmission of the consent must be sent by electronic mail and set forth, or be submitted

with, information from which it can reasonably be determined that the transmission was authorized by the director. The resolution and the written consents thereto by the members of the board or committee shall be filed with the minutes of the proceedings of the board or committee.

(c) Unless otherwise restricted by the certificate of incorporation or the by-laws, any one or more members of the board or of any committee thereof who is not physically present at a meeting of the board or a committee may participate by means of a conference telephone or similar communications equipment or by electronic video screen communication. Participation by such means shall constitute presence in person at a meeting as long as all persons participating in the meeting can hear each other at the same time and each director can participate in all matters before the board, including, without limitation, the ability to propose, object to, and vote upon a specific action to be taken by the board or committee.

(d) Except as otherwise provided in this chapter, the vote of a majority of the directors present at the time of the vote, if a quorum is present at such time, shall be the act of the board. Directors who are present at a meeting but not present at the time of a vote due to a conflict of interest or related party transaction shall be determined to be present at the time of the vote for purposes of this paragraph.

History: Add, L 1969, ch 1066, § 1, eff Sept 1, 1970, with substance derived from Gen Corp Law § 28; amd, L 1975, ch 173, § 1, eff Sept 1, 1975; L 1977, ch 314, § 1, eff June 21, 1977; L 1983, ch 92, § 1, eff May 17, 1983; L 2007, ch 211, § 1, eff July 3, 2007; L 2013, ch 549, § 68, eff July 1, 2014; L 2015, ch 555, § 4, eff Dec 11, 2015.

CASE ANNOTATIONS

1-5. [Reserved for future use]
6. Under former General Corporation Law § 28

1-5. [Reserved for future use]
6. Under former General Corporation Law § 28

Reading together § 27 and § 28 and examining their legislative history, court concluded that there never was legislative intent so to change common-law rule as to quorums as to authorize a by-law requiring unanimous vote of directors. Benintendi v Kenton Hotel, Inc. (1945) 294 N.Y. 112, 60 N.E.2d 829, 159 ALR 280 (superseded by statute as stated in Application of Burkin (1956) 1 N.Y.2d 570, 154 N.Y.S.2d 898, 136 N.E.2d 862, 64 ALR2d 638) and (superseded by statute as stated in Sutton v Sutton (1994) 84 N.Y.2d 37, 614 N.Y.S.2d 369, 637 N.E.2d 260)

This section and § 27 do not forbid a bylaw requiring a two-thirds' vote of a quorum of directors. In re Lake Placid Co. (1948) 274 A.D. 205, 81 N.Y.S.2d 36

The court would not entertain a petition for an order setting aside a special meeting of the board of directors, and vacating the removal of a corporate officer by a majority vote of the board. Heller v Clark Merchandisers, Inc. (1955) 9 Misc. 2d 106, 154 N.Y.S.2d 150

Court vacated determination of respondent not-for-profit corporation which found petitioner guilty of inappropriate behavior at its recreational club and suspended his membership privileges for 6 weeks where (1) petitioner was not provided any written notice of date, time and place of hearing, he was not afforded opportunity to testify, submit evidence, call witness or examine any complaining witness, and (2) informal meetings between club president and petitioner did not satisfy fundamental due process requirement of Not-For-Profit Corporation Law or "substantially" comply with club's by-laws and rules. Anderson v Board of Dirs. of the Powelton Club (1999, Sup) 183 Misc. 2d 200, 702 N.Y.S.2d 762

Failure to notify library trustees of a meeting in accordance with the Education Law was such a defect as could be cured or waived by the actual presence of the trustees at the meeting. Kahn v Blinn (1946, Sup) 60 N.Y.S.2d 413

Corporation which had been dissolved could not maintain action for specific performance of alleged undertaking to effectuate a lien on realty. Dieselcraft Corp. v Joca Realty Corp. (1957, Sup) 161 N.Y.S.2d 761

It appears to be the legislative intent that a board of directors can act by a majority of a quorum, irrespective of the number of other directors who may merely be present at the meeting. Crowley v Commodity Exchange, Inc. (1944, CA2 NY) 141 F.2d 182

§ 709.   Greater requirement as to quorum and vote of directors

(a) The certificate of incorporation or a by-law adopted by the members may contain provisions specifying either or both of the following:

(1) That the proportion of directors that shall constitute a quorum for the transaction of business or of any specified item of business shall be greater than the proportion prescribed by this chapter in the absence of such provision.

(2) That the proportion of votes of directors that shall be necessary for the transaction of business or of any specified item of business shall be greater than the proportion prescribed by this chapter in the absence of such provision.

(b) An amendment by the members of the certificate of incorporation or of the by-laws which adds a provision permitted by this section or which changes or strikes out such a provision, shall be authorized by vote of two-thirds of the members entitled to vote or of such greater proportion as may be provided specifically in the certificate of incorporation or the by-law for adding, changing or striking out a provision permitted by this section.

(c) If there are no members, an amendment by the board of directors of the certificate of incorporation or the by-law which adds a provision permitted by this section or which changes or strikes out such a provision, shall be authorized at a meeting by vote of two-thirds of the entire board, or of such greater proportion as may be provided specifically in the certificate of incorporation or the by-law for adding, changing or striking out a provision permitted by this section.

History: Add, L 1969, ch 1066, § 1, with substance deriving from Gen Corp Law § 28, amd, L 1970, ch 847, § 45, eff Sept 1, 1970.

§ 710.   Place and time of meetings of the board

(a) Meetings of the board, annual, regular or special, may be held at any place within or without this state, unless otherwise provided by the certificate of incorporation or the by-laws.

(b) The time and place for holding annual or regular meetings of the board shall be fixed by or under the by-laws, or, if not so fixed, by the board.

(c) A special meeting may be called at any time by the president or other corporate officer as provided in the by-laws or as determined by the board; and, in the case of a corporation without members, by any director upon written demand of not less than one-fifth of the entire board.

History: Add, L 1969, ch 1066, § 1; amd, L 1971, ch 1058, § 22, eff Sept 1, 1971.

Section heading, amd, L 1971, ch 1058, § 22, eff Sept 1, 1971.

Par (c), add, L 1971, ch 1058, § 22, eff Sept 1, 1971 atthew Bender) ¶ 710.01.

§ 711.   Notice of meetings of the board

(a) Unless otherwise provided by the by-laws, regular meetings of the board may be held without notice if the time and place of such meetings are fixed by the by-laws or the board. Special meetings of the board shall be held upon notice to the directors.

(b) The by-laws may prescribe what shall constitute notice of meeting of the board. A notice, or waiver of notice, need not specify the purpose of any regular or special meeting of the board, unless required by the by-laws.

(c) Notice of a meeting need not be given to any alternate director, nor to any director who submits a waiver of notice whether before or after the meeting, or who attends the meeting without protesting, prior thereto or at its commencement, the lack of notice to him. Such waiver of notice may be written or electronic. If written, the waiver must be executed by the director signing such waiver or causing his or her signature to be affixed to such waiver by any reasonable means including but not limited to facsimile signature. If electronic, the transmission of the waiver must be sent by electronic mail and set forth, or be submitted with, information from which it can reasonably be determined that the transmission was authorized by the director.

(d) A majority of the directors present, whether or not a quorum is present, may adjourn any meeting to another time and place. If the by-laws so provide, notice of any adjournment of a meeting of the board to another time or place shall be given to the directors who were not present at the time of the adjournment and, unless such time and place are announced at the meeting, to the other directors.

History: Add, L 1969, ch 1066, § 1, eff Sept 1, 1970, with substance derived from Gen Corp Law §§ 28, 31; amd, L 1970, ch 847, § 46, eff Sept 1, 1970; L 2013, ch 549, § 69, eff July 1, 2014; L 2015, ch 358, § 6, eff Sept 25, 2015.

CASE ANNOTATIONS

By failing to object to propriety of notice of meeting or any other defect regarding regularity of meeting at which hospital board of trustees authorized its takeover by another hospital, plaintiff waived any objection to board's action. Union Hosp. Ass'n ex rel. Shumofsky v Carty (1992, 1st Dept) 185 A.D.2d 787, 586 N.Y.S.2d 798

§ 712. Executive committee and other committees

(a) The certificate of incorporation, the by-laws, or the board may create committees of the board, each consisting of three or more directors. The board shall appoint the members of such committee of the board, except that in the case of any executive committee or similar committee however denominated, the appointment shall be made by a majority of the entire board, provided that in the case of a board of thirty members or more, the appointment shall be made by at least three-quarters of the directors present at the time of the vote, if a quorum is present at that time. In addition, the by-laws may provide that directors who are the holders of certain positions in the corporation shall be ex-officio members of specific committees. Each such committee shall have the authority of the board to the extent provided in a board resolution or in the certificate of incorporation or by-laws, except that no committee of any kind shall have authority as to the following matters:

(1) The submission to members of any action requiring members' approval under this chapter.

(2) The filling of vacancies in the board of directors or in any committee.

(3) The fixing of compensation of the directors for serving on the board or on any committee.

(4) The amendment or repeal of the by-laws or the adoption of new by-laws.

(5) The amendment or repeal of any resolution of the board which by its terms shall not be so amendable or repealable.

(6) The election or removal of officers and directors.

(7) The approval of a merger or plan of dissolution.

(8) The adoption of a resolution recommending to the members action on the sale, lease, exchange or other disposition of all or substantially all the assets of a corporation or, if there are no members entitled to vote, the authorization of such transaction.

(9) The approval of amendments to the certificate of incorporation.

(b) The board may designate one or more directors as alternate members of any committee, who may replace any absent member or members at any meeting of such committee.

(c) [Repealed]

(d) Each committee of the board shall serve at the pleasure of the board. The designation of any such committee and the delegation thereto of authority shall not alone relieve any director of his duty to the corporation under section 717 (Duty of directors and officers).

(e) Committees, other than committees of the board, whether created by the board or by the members, shall be committees of the corporation. No such committee shall have the authority to bind the board. Members of such committees of the corporation, who may be non-directors, shall be elected or appointed in the manner set forth in the by-laws, or if not set forth in the by-laws, in the same manner as officers of the corporation.

History: Add, L 1969, ch 1066, § 1, eff Sept 1, 1970, with substance derived from Mem Corp Law § 20; amd, L 1971, ch 1057 § 6; L 1971, ch 1058 § 23; L 1972, ch 961, § 12, eff Sept 1, 1972; L 2013, ch 549, §§ 70, 71, eff July 1, 2014; L 2015, ch 555, § 5, eff Dec 11, 2015; L 2016, ch 466, § 4, eff May 27, 2017.

CASE ANNOTATIONS

1. Generally

1. Generally

In real estate broker's action for sale commission, not-for-profit corporation could not invoke provisions of N-PCL § 509 to avoid contract where statute did not prohibit corporate officers from contracting with brokers to procure a purchaser, where corporate committee responsible for selling property had authority under N-PCL § 712 to act on board's behalf, and where, under general agency principles, committee had apparent authority to bind corporation. Shear v NRA, 606 F.2d 1251, 196 U.S. App. D.C. 344, 1979 U.S. App. LEXIS 12492 (D.C. Cir. 1979).

§ 712-a. Audit oversight

(a) The board, or a designated audit committee of the board comprised solely of independent directors, of any corporation required to file an independent certified public accountant's audit report with the attorney general pursuant to subdivision one of section one hundred seventy-two-b of the executive law shall oversee the accounting and financial reporting processes of the corporation and the audit of the corporation's financial statements. The board or designated audit committee shall annually retain or renew the retention of an independent auditor to conduct the audit and, upon completion thereof, review the results of the audit and any related management letter with the independent auditor.

(b) The board, or a designated audit committee of the board comprised solely of independent directors, of any corporation required to file an independent certified public accountant's audit report with the attorney general pursuant to subdivision one of section one hundred seventy-two-b of the executive law and that in the prior fiscal year had or in the current fiscal year reasonably expects to have annual revenue in excess of one million dollars shall, in addition to those duties set forth in paragraph (a) of this section:

(1) review with the independent auditor the scope and planning of the audit prior to the audit's commencement;

(2) upon completion of the audit, review and discuss with the independent auditor: (A) any material risks and weaknesses in internal controls identified

by the auditor; (B) any restrictions on the scope of the auditor's activities or access to requested information; (C) any significant disagreements between the auditor and management; and (D) the adequacy of the corporation's accounting and financial reporting processes;

(3) annually consider the performance and independence of the independent auditor; and

(4) if the duties required by this section are performed by an audit committee, report on the committee's activities to the board.

(c) [Repealed]

(d) If a corporation controls a group of corporations, the board or designated audit committee of the board of the controlling corporation may perform the duties required by this section for one or more of the controlled corporations and, if independent directors, directors from one or more of such controlled corporations may serve on any designated audit committee of the board of such controlling corporation, and perform the duties required by this section for each corporation and any controlled corporations.

(e) Only independent directors may participate in any board or committee deliberations or voting relating to matters set forth in this section, provided that nothing in this paragraph shall prohibit the board or designated audit committee from requesting that a person with an interest in the matter present information as background or answer questions at a committee or board meeting prior to the commencement of deliberations or voting relating thereto.

(f) Any corporation that is a state authority or a local authority as defined in section two of the public authorities law and that has complied substantially with sections twenty-eight hundred two and twenty-eight hundred twenty-four of such law shall be deemed in compliance with this section.

History: Add, L 2013, ch 549, § 72, eff July 1, 2014; amd, L 2015, ch 555, § 6, eff Dec 11, 2015; L 2016, ch 466, § 5, eff May 27, 2017; L 2018, ch 468, § 1, eff Dec 28, 2018.

Blackline Showing Effect of 2018 Amendments. — (a) The board, or a designated audit committee of the board comprised solely of independent directors, of any corporation required to file an independent certified public accountant's audit report with the attorney general pursuant to subdivision one of section one hundred seventy-two-b of the executive law shall oversee the accounting and financial reporting processes of the corporation and the audit of the corporation's financial statements. The board or designated audit committee shall annually retain or renew the retention of an independent auditor to conduct the audit and, upon completion thereof, review the results of the audit and any related management letter with the independent auditor.

(b) The board, or a designated audit committee of the board comprised solely of independent directors, of any corporation required to file an independent certified public accountant's audit report with the attorney general pursuant to subdivision one of section one hundred seventy-two-b of the executive law and that in the prior fiscal year had or in the current fiscal year reasonably expects to have annual revenue in excess of one million dollars shall, in addition to those duties set forth in paragraph (a) of this section:

(1) review with the independent auditor the scope and planning of the audit prior to the audit's commencement;

(2) upon completion of the audit, review and discuss with the independent auditor: (A) any material risks and weaknesses in internal controls identified by the auditor; (B) any restrictions on the scope of the auditor's activities or access to requested information; (C) any significant disagreements between the auditor and management; and (D) the adequacy of the corporation's accounting and financial reporting processes;

(3) annually consider the performance and independence of the independent auditor; and

(4) if the duties required by this section are performed by an audit committee, report on the committee's activities to the board.

(c) [Repealed]

(d) If a corporation controls a group of corporations, the board or designated audit committee of the board of the controlling corporation may perform the duties required by this section for one or more of the controlled corporations and, if independent directors, directors from one or more of such controlled corporations may serve on any designated audit committee of the board of such controlling corporation, and perform the duties required by this section for each corporation and any controlled corporations.

(e) Only independent directors may participate in any board or committee deliberations or voting relating to matters set forth in this section, provided that nothing in this paragraph shall prohibit the board or designated audit committee from requesting that a person with an interest in the matter present information as background or answer questions at a committee or board meeting prior to the commencement of deliberations or voting relating thereto.

(f) Any corporation that is a state authority or a local authority as defined in section two of the public authorities law and that has complied substantially with sections twenty-eight hundred two and twenty-eight hundred twenty-four of such law shall be deemed in compliance with this section.

§ 713. Officers

(a) The board may elect or appoint a chair or president, or both, one or more vice-presidents, a secretary and a treasurer, and such other officers as it may determine, or as may be provided in the by-laws. These officers may be designated by such alternate titles as may be provided in the certificate of incorporation or the by-laws. Any two or more offices may be held by the same person, except the offices of president and secretary, or the offices corresponding thereto.

(b) The certificate of incorporation or a by-law adopted by the members may provide that all officers or that specified officers shall be elected by the members instead of by the board, or it may authorize the president to appoint the other officers, or some of them, subject to approval by the board.

(c) Each officer shall hold office for the term for which he is elected or appointed, and until his successor has been elected or appointed and qualified. Unless otherwise provided in the certificate of incorporation or the by-laws, all officers shall be elected or appointed annually.

(d) The certificate of incorporation or the by-laws may provide that any one or more officers shall be ex-officio members of the board, with voting rights unless specified otherwise.

(e) All officers as between themselves and the corporation shall have such authority and perform such duties in the management of the corporation as may be provided in the by-laws or, to the extent not so provided, by the board. The board may require any officer to give security for the faithful performance of his duties.

(f) No employee of the corporation shall serve as chair of the board or hold any other title with similar responsibilities, unless the board approves such employee serving as chair of the board by a two-thirds vote of the entire board and contemporaneously documents in writing the basis for the board approval; provided, however, that no such employee shall be considered an independent director for the purposes of this chapter.

History: Add, L 1969, ch 1066, § 1, eff Sept 1, 1970, with substance derived from Mem Corp Law §§ 20, 45; amd, L 1970, ch 847, § 47; L 1971, ch 1058, § 24, eff Sept 1, 1971; L 2013, ch 549, § 73, eff July 1, 2014; L 2016, ch 466, § 6, eff Jan 1, 2017.

CASE ANNOTATIONS

1. Generally
2. Under former Membership Corporations Law § 20
3. Under former Membership Corporations Law § 45

1. Generally

Resolutions passed by board of directors of public employee labor union organized as not-for-profit corporation, by which board reorganized union's staff in manner inconsistent with union president's organizational plan, were in conflict with provision of union's bylaws stating that "President shall be responsible for the organization and direction of the staff of the Association," constituted attempt to usurp authority given by members to president, and were therefore void. Simoni v Civil Service Employees Ass'n, Local 1000, etc., 133 Misc. 2d 1, 507 N.Y.S.2d 371, 1986 N.Y. Misc. LEXIS 2958 (N.Y. Sup. Ct. 1986).

Because a union's bylaws complied with N.Y. Not-for-Profit Corp. Law § 713(b), (e), its officers could suspend a police officer for refusing to relinquish an assignment that violated the colletive bargaining agreement; thus, the officer's N.Y. C.P.L.R. art. 78 reinstatement petition was properly dismissed for failing to state a cause of action. Matter of Berich v Ithaca Police Benevolent Assn., Inc., 23 A.D.3d 904, 804 N.Y.S.2d 833, 2005 NY Slip Op 8812, 2005 N.Y. App. Div. LEXIS 13137 (N.Y. App. Div. 3d Dep't 2005).

Under Sections 10-1000 et seq. of the Village Law, a village fire department is a corporation consisting of members of all the fire, hose, protective and hook and ladder companies of a village; it is administered by a board of fire commissioners or, where no board of fire commissioners has been appointed, by the village board of trustees and the council of the fire department. Fire companies in a village are associations or corporations, which must operate in accordance with their certificates of incorporation, bylaws, and statutes; and, although fire companies are separate and distinct from the village, the statutes do permit village authorities to exercise a certain degree of control over their organization, incorporation, governance, and membership, including residency for membership. A fire company must consent to a contract for the provision of fire protection outside the village and the fire chief of the village fire department cannot consent on behalf of members of the company. 1990 Op St Compt 90-19.

2. Under former Membership Corporations Law § 20

An election of officers will be set aside and a new election ordered where by amending the bylaws of a membership corporation organized for charitable purposes certain of the members thereof overthrew the long established custom of the corporation to elect only candidates for office who had been nominated in advance, thereby unfairly depriving the members of the corporation in effect of their right to vote in the election, inasmuch as under the pre-existing bylaws few of the members attended such meetings. In re Flushing Hospital & Dispensary, 288 N.Y. 125, 41 N.E.2d 917, 288 N.Y. (N.Y.S.) 125, 1942 N.Y. LEXIS 1064 (N.Y. 1942).

An election of officers will be set aside and a new election ordered where by amending the bylaws of a membership corporation organized for charitable purposes certain of the members thereof overthrew the long established custom of the corporation to elect only candidates for office who had been nominated in advance, thereby

unfairly depriving the members of the corporation in effect of their right to vote in the election, inasmuch as under the pre-existing bylaws few of the members attended such meetings. In re Flushing Hospital & Dispensary, 288 N.Y. 125, 41 N.E.2d 917, 288 N.Y. (N.Y.S.) 125, 1942 N.Y. LEXIS 1064 (N.Y. 1942).

A bylaw of a corporation fixing the salary of its president may be validly modified by an agreement whereby the president accepts a lower salary in consideration of being continued in office. Bowler v American Box Strap Co., 49 N.Y.S. 153, 22 Misc. 335, 1898 N.Y. Misc. LEXIS 32 (N.Y. App. Term 1898).

A provision of a union constitution which would suppress the protests of members against the actions of their officers which such members regard as improper or opposed to their best interests, would be illegal and unenforceable. Schrank v Brown, 80 N.Y.S.2d 452, 192 Misc. 80, 1948 N.Y. Misc. LEXIS 2586 (N.Y. Sup. Ct. 1948).

Where bylaws make no provision for filling the office of president, in the event of the resignation of the president and certain other officers designated to be in succession for the office, one who becomes head of the organization by the action of its members is the de facto president with the powers and duties of that office. Petition of Serenbetz, 46 N.Y.S.2d 475, 1943 N.Y. Misc. LEXIS 2788 (N.Y. Sup. Ct. 1943), aff'd, 267 A.D. 836, 46 N.Y.S.2d 127, 1944 N.Y. App. Div. LEXIS 5031 (N.Y. App. Div. 1944).

In the absence of any bylaw provision relating thereto, in the event of the resignation of an officer of a club, where the members refuse to accept such resignation, the officer, whether he knows it or not, continues to hold office. Petition of Serenbetz, 46 N.Y.S.2d 475, 1943 N.Y. Misc. LEXIS 2788 (N.Y. Sup. Ct. 1943), aff'd, 267 A.D. 836, 46 N.Y.S.2d 127, 1944 N.Y. App. Div. LEXIS 5031 (N.Y. App. Div. 1944).

Any attempt in the by-laws of a membership corporation to invest its Board of Trustees or anyone else with power to void an election of officers would contravene the provisions of this section. Veverka v Suffolk County Patrolemen's Benevolent Asso., 236 N.Y.S.2d 917 (N.Y. Sup. Ct. 1963).

If a bylaw for the election of directors has not been adopted, a valid election may be held under the General Corporation Law on the call of any member of the corporation. In re David Jones Co., 22 N.Y.S. 318, 67 Hun 360 (1893).

3. Under former Membership Corporations Law § 45

A national union may not prevent the directors of an incorporated local union affiliated with the national organization from removing the president of the local in accordance with the bylaws thereof. Kunze v Weber, 197 A.D. 319, 188 N.Y.S. 644, 1921 N.Y. App. Div. LEXIS 7459 (N.Y. App. Div. 1921).

Where the bylaws of a membership corporation failed to define a quorum where the membership of the corporation consisted of less than thirty members, in view of the provisions of § 20 of the Membership Corporation Law a meeting at which nine members participated had a quorum, and an election of officers at such meeting was valid. Application of Havender, 44 N.Y.S.2d 213, 181 Misc. 989, 1943 N.Y. Misc. LEXIS 2935 (N.Y. Sup. Ct. 1943).

An officer of a membership corporation may not be held criminally liable for the violation of a penal statute by the corporation. People v Smith, 74 N.Y.S.2d 845, 190 Misc. 871, 1947 N.Y. Misc. LEXIS 3319 (N.Y. Magis. Ct. 1947).

Where the bylaws make no provision for filling the office of president, in the event of the resignation or incapacity of the president and certain other officers designated to be in succession for the office, one who becomes head of the organization by the action of its members is the de facto president with powers and duties of that office. Petition of Serenbetz, 46 N.Y.S.2d 475, 1943 N.Y. Misc. LEXIS 2788 (N.Y. Sup. Ct. 1943), aff'd, 267 A.D. 836, 46 N.Y.S.2d 127, 1944 N.Y. App. Div. LEXIS 5031 (N.Y. App. Div. 1944).

In the absence of any bylaw provision relating thereto, in the event of the resignation of an officer of a club, where the members refuse to accept such resignation, the officer whether he knows it or not continues to hold office. Petition of Serenbetz, 46 N.Y.S.2d 475, 1943 N.Y. Misc. LEXIS 2788 (N.Y. Sup. Ct. 1943), aff'd, 267 A.D. 836, 46 N.Y.S.2d 127, 1944 N.Y. App. Div. LEXIS 5031 (N.Y. App. Div. 1944).

Activity of certain officers of a membership corporation information, and as members, of an allegedly competing and hostile organization, could not bar them from examining its books and records as long as no action had been taken to remove them from office. Pino v United Democratic Regular Organization, 195 N.Y.S.2d 860 (N.Y. Sup. Ct. 1959).

§ 714.   Removal of officers

(a) Any officer elected or appointed by the board may be removed by the board with or without cause. An officer elected by the members or a class of members may be removed, with or without cause, only by the vote of the members or such class of members, but his authority to act as an officer may be suspended by the board for cause.

(b) The removal of an officer without cause shall be without prejudice to his contract rights, if any. The election or appointment of an officer shall not of itself create contract rights.

(c) An action to procure a judgment removing an officer for cause may be brought by the attorney-general, by any director, by ten percent of the members, whether or not entitled to vote, or by the holders of ten percent of the face value of the outstanding capital certificates, subvention certificates or bonds having voting rights. The court may bar from re-election or reappointment any officer so removed for a period fixed by the court.

History: Add, L 1969, ch 1066, § 1, eff Sept 1, 1970, with substance derived from Gen Corp Law §§ 60, 136.

CASE ANNOTATIONS

Employee's N.Y. Not-for-Profit Corp. Law § 714 claim that alleged that an employee's supervisor improperly removed the employee from his position as an officer of an employer was moot as the board of directors later removed the employee from his position as an officer of the employer. Waddell v Boyce Thompson Inst. for Plant Research, Inc. (2012, 3d Dept) 92 App Div 3d 1172, 940 NYS2d 331, 33 BNA IER Cas 900.

A volunteer member of a fire company may be removed in accordance with the constitution and by-laws of the company. Ops Atty Gen 85-17

The attorney general or one or more members of the Medina Firemen's Benevolent Association having standing to bring an action to challenge improper disbursements by this not-for-profit corporation. 1979 Op St Compt File #238-A

§ 715.   Related party transactions

(a) No corporation shall enter into any related party transaction unless the transaction is determined by the board, or an authorized committee thereof, to be fair, reasonable and in the corporation's best interest at the time of such determination. Any director, officer or key person who has an interest in a related party transaction shall disclose in good faith to the board, or an authorized committee thereof, the material facts concerning such interest.

(b) With respect to any related party transaction involving a charitable corporation and in which a related party has a substantial financial interest, the board of such corporation, or an authorized committee thereof, shall:

(1) Prior to entering into the transaction, consider alternative transactions to the extent available;

(2) Approve the transaction by not less than a majority vote of the directors or committee members present at the meeting; and

(3) Contemporaneously document in writing the basis for the board or authorized committee's approv-

al, including its consideration of any alternative transactions.

(c) The certificate of incorporation, by-laws or any policy adopted by the board may contain additional restrictions on related party transactions and additional procedures necessary for the review and approval of such transactions, or provide that any transaction in violation of such restrictions shall be void or voidable.

(d) Unless otherwise provided in the certificate of incorporation or the by-laws, the board shall have authority to fix the compensation of directors for services in any capacity.

(e) The fixing of compensation of officers, if not done in or pursuant to the by-laws, shall require the affirmative vote of a majority of the entire board unless a higher proportion is set by the certificate of incorporation or by-laws.

(f) The attorney general may bring an action to enjoin, void or rescind any related party transaction or proposed related party transaction that violates any provision of this chapter or was otherwise not reasonable or in the best interests of the corporation at the time the transaction was approved, or to seek restitution, and the removal of directors or officers, or seek to require any person or entity to:

(1) Account for any profits made from such transaction, and pay them to the corporation;

(2) Pay the corporation the value of the use of any of its property or other assets used in such transaction;

(3) Return or replace any property or other assets lost to the corporation as a result of such transaction, together with any income or appreciation lost to the corporation by reason of such transaction, or account for any proceeds of sale of such property, and pay the proceeds to the corporation together with interest at the legal rate; and

(4) Pay, in the case of willful and intentional conduct, an amount up to double the amount of any benefit improperly obtained.

(g) The powers of the attorney general provided in this section are in addition to all other powers the attorney general may have under this chapter or any other law.

(h) No related party may participate in deliberations or voting relating to a related party transaction in which he or she has an interest; provided that nothing in this section shall prohibit the board or authorized committee from requesting that a related party present information as background or answer questions concerning a related party transaction at a board or committee meeting prior to the commencement of deliberations or voting relating thereto.

(i) In an action by any person or entity other than the attorney general, it shall be a defense to a claim of violation of any provisions of this section that a transaction was fair, reasonable and in the corporation's best interest at the time the corporation approved the transaction.

(j) In an action by the attorney general with respect to a related party transaction not approved in accordance with paragraphs (a) or (b) of this section at the time it was entered into, whichever is applicable, it shall be a defense to a claim of violation of any provisions of this section that (1) the transaction was fair, reasonable and in the corporation's best interest at the time the corporation approved the transaction and (2) prior to receipt of any request for information by the attorney general regarding the transaction, the board has: (A) ratified the transaction by finding in good faith that it was fair, reasonable and in the corporation's best interest at the time the corporation approved the transaction; and, with respect to any related party transaction involving a charitable corporation and in which a related party has a substantial financial interest, considered alternative transactions to the extent available, approving the transaction by not less than a majority vote of the directors or committee members present at the meeting; (B) documented in writing the nature of the violation and the basis for the board's or committee's ratification of the transaction; and (C) put into place procedures to ensure that the corporation complies with paragraphs (a) and (b) of this section as to related party transactions in the future.

History: Add, L 1969, ch 1066, § 1, with substance deriving from Mem Corp Law § 47; amd, L 1970, ch 847, § 48, eff Sept 1, 1970; L 1971, ch 1057, § 7, eff July 2, 1971; L 2013, ch 549, § 74, eff July 1, 2014; L 2015, ch 555, § 7, eff Dec 11, 2015; L 2016, ch 466, § 7, eff May 27, 2017.

CASE ANNOTATIONS

1. Generally
2. Under former Membership Corporations Law § 47

1. Generally

Attorney general could not challenge the compensation of the former chairman of the New York Stock Exchange as not being approved in accordance with N.Y. Not-for-Profit Corp. Law § 715(f) as § 715 provided that only the non-profit corporation had the power to avoid contracts or transactions between the corporation and its officers or directors. People v Grasso, 11 N.Y.3d 64, 862 N.Y.S.2d 828, 2008 NY Slip Op 5770, 893 N.E.2d 105, 2008 N.Y. LEXIS 1821 (N.Y. 2008).

Dismissal of petitioner's action seeking rescission of management fees for a non-profit was reversed because that cause of action was dependent upon resolution of issues of fact related to whether respondents engaged in improper related party transactions or otherwise transferred the senior living facility's surplus to benefit the non-profit and its other affiliates. Matter of The People of The State of New York v The Lutheran Care Network, Inc., 2018 N.Y. App. Div. LEXIS 8666 (N.Y. App. Div. 3d Dep't 2018).

Trial court denied the stock exchange chairman's motion to dismiss, as the Attorney General had the statutory responsibility to protect investors, had the authority to pursue the stock exchange chairman under the doctrine of parens patriae because they could not protect themselves from the allegedly unreasonable compensation that the New York Stock Exchange, a type A not-for-profit corporation, allowed him to receive, and the Attorney General stated four viable claims against him: for imposition of a constructive trust and for restitution for ultra vires payments allegedly received, for payment had and received, for violation of N.Y. Not-for-Profit Corp.

Law § 715 for benefits he received that were improperly approved, and for violation of N.Y. Not-for-Profit Corp. Law for his allegedly receiving improper loans. People v Grasso, 816 N.Y.S.2d 863, 2006 NY Slip Op 26095, 12 Misc. 3d 384, 235 N.Y.L.J. 54, 2006 N.Y. Misc. LEXIS 484 (N.Y. Sup. Ct. 2006), rev'd, 42 A.D.3d 126, 836 N.Y.S.2d 40, 2007 NY Slip Op 3990, 2007 N.Y. App. Div. LEXIS 5719 (N.Y. App. Div. 1st Dep't 2007).

2. Under former Membership Corporations Law § 47

Where the plaintiff was a director and an officer of the defendant membership corporation, she should be denied a recovery on a lease under this section, for the by-laws of the defendant do not authorize the making of a contract with any officer or director, and it is not claimed that any such authority was given by resolution of the board which was concurred in by two-thirds of the directors. Knapp v Rochester Dog Protective Ass'n, 235 A.D. 436, 257 N.Y.S. 356, 1932 N.Y. App. Div. LEXIS 7981 (N.Y. App. Div. 1932).

Directors of a membership corporation organized chiefly for charitable purposes were directed to file inventory, account and statement of transactions during 12 months next preceding the granting of the order, where it appeared that the members of the corporation, under the guise of voting compensation to themselves for past services, sought to divide the assets among themselves. Distribution of the assets of a membership corporation whose purposes were charitable among the membership, even on dissolution, would be improper. It was also immaterial that the petitioner, a member of the corporation, might be estopped to object to the resolution for payment of compensation since the supreme court, may act on its own motion. In re Green, 10 Misc. 2d 557, 177 N.Y.S.2d 933, 1957 N.Y. Misc. LEXIS 2680 (N.Y. Sup. Ct. 1957).

§ 715-a. Conflict of interest policy

(a) Except as provided in paragraph (d) of this section, the board shall adopt, and oversee the implementation of, and compliance with, a conflict of interest policy to ensure that its directors, officers and key persons act in the corporation's best interest and comply with applicable legal requirements, including but not limited to the requirements set forth in section seven hundred fifteen of this article.

(b) The conflict of interest policy shall include, at a minimum, the following provisions:

(1) a definition of the circumstances that constitute a conflict of interest;

(2) procedures for disclosing a conflict of interest or possible conflict of interest to the board or to a committee of the board, and procedures for the board or committee to determine whether a conflict exists;

(3) a requirement that the person with the conflict of interest not be present at or participate in board or committee deliberation or vote on the matter giving rise to such conflict, provided that nothing in this section shall prohibit the board or a committee from requesting that the person with the conflict of interest present information as background or answer questions at a committee or board meeting prior to the commencement of deliberations or voting relating thereto;

(4) a prohibition against any attempt by the person with the conflict to influence improperly the deliberation or voting on the matter giving rise to such conflict;

(5) a requirement that the existence and resolution of the conflict be documented in the corporation's

records, including in the minutes of any meeting at which the conflict was discussed or voted upon; and

(6) procedures for disclosing, addressing, and documenting related party transactions in accordance with section seven hundred fifteen of this article.

(c) The conflict of interest policy shall require that prior to the initial election of any director, and annually thereafter, such director shall complete, sign and submit to the secretary of the corporation or a designated compliance officer a written statement identifying, to the best of the director's knowledge, any entity of which such director is an officer, director, trustee, member, owner (either as a sole proprietor or a partner), or employee and with which the corporation has a relationship, and any transaction in which the corporation is a participant and in which the director might have a conflicting interest. The policy shall require that each director annually resubmit such written statement. The secretary of the corporation or the designated compliance officer shall provide a copy of all completed statements to the chair of the audit committee or, if there is no audit committee, to the chair of the board.

(d) A corporation that has adopted and possesses a conflict of interest policy pursuant to federal, state or local laws that is substantially consistent with the provisions of paragraph (b) of this section shall be deemed in compliance with provisions of this section. In addition, any corporation that is a state authority or a local authority as defined in section two of the public authorities law, and that has complied substantially with section twenty-eight hundred twenty-four and subdivision three of section twenty-eight hundred twenty-five of such law, shall be deemed in compliance with this section.

(e) Nothing in this section shall be interpreted to require a corporation to adopt any specific conflict of interest policy not otherwise required by this section or any other law or rule, or to supersede or limit any requirement or duty governing conflicts of interest required by any other law or rule.

History: Add, L 2013, ch 549, § 75, eff July 1, 2014; amd, L 2015, ch 555, §§ 8, 9, eff Dec 11, 2015; L 2016, ch 466, §§ 8, 9, eff May 27, 2017.

§ 715-b. Whistleblower policy

(a) Except as provided in paragraph (c) of this section, the board of every corporation that has twenty or more employees and in the prior fiscal year had annual revenue in excess of one million dollars shall adopt, and oversee the implementation of, and compliance with, a whistleblower policy to protect from retaliation persons who report suspected improper conduct. Such policy shall provide that no director, officer, employee or volunteer of a corporation who in good faith reports any action or suspected action taken by or within the corporation that is illegal, fraudulent or in violation of any adopted policy of the corporation shall suffer intimidation, harassment, discrimination or other retaliation or, in the case of employees, adverse employment consequence.

(b) The whistleblower policy shall include the following provisions:

(1) Procedures for the reporting of violations or suspected violations of laws or corporate policies, including procedures for preserving the confidentiality of reported information;

(2) A requirement that an employee, officer or director of the corporation be designated to administer the whistleblower policy and to report to the board or an authorized committee thereof, except that directors who are employees may not participate in any board or committee deliberations or voting relating to administration of the whistleblower policy;

(3) A requirement that the person who is the subject of a whistleblower complaint not be present at or participate in board or committee deliberations or vote on the matter relating to such complaint, provided that nothing in this subparagraph shall prohibit the board or committee from requesting that the person who is subject to the complaint present information as background or answer questions at a committee or board meeting prior to the commencement of deliberations or voting relating thereto; and

(4) A requirement that a copy of the policy be distributed to all directors, officers, employees and to volunteers who provide substantial services to the corporation. For purposes of this subdivision, posting the policy on the corporation's website or at the corporation's offices in a conspicuous location accessible to employees and volunteers are among the methods a corporation may use to satisfy the distribution requirement.

(c) A corporation that has adopted and possesses a whistleblower policy pursuant to federal, state or local laws that is substantially consistent with the provisions of paragraph (b) of this section shall be deemed in compliance with provisions of this section. In addition, any corporation that is a state authority or local authority as defined in section two of the public authorities law, and that has complied substantially with section twenty-eight hundred twenty-four of such law and is subject to the provisions of section twenty-eight hundred fifty-seven of such law, shall be deemed in compliance with the provisions of this section.

(d) Nothing in this section shall be interpreted to relieve any corporation from any additional requirements in relation to internal compliance, retaliation, or document retention required by any other law or rule.

History: Add, L 2013, ch 549, § 75, eff July 1, 2014; amd, L 2015, ch 555, § 10, eff Dec 11, 2015; L 2016, ch 466, §§ 10, 11, eff May 27, 2017.

§ 716. Loans to directors and officers

No loans, other than through the purchase of bonds, debentures, or similar obligations of the type customarily sold in public offerings, or through ordinary deposit of funds in a bank, shall be made by a corporation to its directors or officers, or to any other corporation, firm, association or other entity in which one or more of its directors or officers are directors or officers or hold a substantial financial interest, except a loan by one charitable corporation to another charitable corporation. A loan made in violation of this section shall be a violation of the duty to the corporation of the directors or officers authorizing it or participating in it, but the obligation of the borrower with respect to the loan shall not be affected thereby.

History: Add, L 1969, ch 1066, § 1; amd, L 1970, ch 847, § 49, L 1971, ch 644, eff Sept 1, 1971, L 2013, ch 549, § 76, eff July 1, 2014.

§ 717. Duty of directors and officers

(a) Directors and officers shall discharge the duties of their respective positions in good faith and with the care an ordinarily prudent person in a like position would exercise under similar circumstances. The factors set forth in subparagraph one of paragraph (e) of section 552 (Standard of conduct in managing and investing an institutional fund), if relevant, must be considered by a governing board delegating investment management of institutional funds pursuant to section 514 (Delegation of investment management)[.] For purposes of this paragraph, the term institutional fund is defined in section 551 (Definitions).

(b) In discharging their duties, directors and officers, when acting in good faith, may rely on information, opinions, reports or statements including financial statements and other financial data, in each case prepared or presented by: (1) one or more officers or employees of the corporation, whom the director believes to be reliable and competent in the matters presented, (2) counsel, public accountants or other persons as to matters which the directors or officers believe to be within such person's professional or expert competence or (3) a committee of the board upon which they do not serve, duly designated in accordance with a provision of the certificate of incorporation or the bylaws, as to matters within its designated authority, which committee the directors or officers believe to merit confidence, so long as in so relying they shall be acting in good faith and with that degree of care specified in paragraph (a) of this section. Persons shall not be considered to be acting in good faith if they have knowledge concerning the matter in question that would cause such reliance to be unwarranted. Persons who so perform their duties shall have no liability by reason of being or having been directors or officers of the corporation.

History: Add, L 1969, ch 1066, § 1, eff Sept 1, 1970; amd, L 1978, ch 690, § 8, eff July 25, 1978, L 1988, ch 734, § 1, eff Dec 16, 1988, L 2010, ch 490, § 7, eff Sept 17, 2010.

Editor's note. The bracketed period in (a) was inserted by the publisher.

CASE ANNOTATIONS

1. Generally
2. Fiduciary duty
3. Business judgment rule
4. Summary judgment

1. Generally

Board of not-for-profit residential cooperative corporation owes its duty of loyalty to cooperative—that is, it must act for benefit of residents collectively and, so long as board acts for purposes of cooperative, within scope of its authority and in good faith, courts will not substitute their judgment for board's; unless resident who is challenging board's action is able to demonstrate breach of duty, judicial review is unavailable. Levandusky v One Fifth Ave. Apartment Corp., 75 N.Y.2d 530, 554 N.Y.S.2d 807, 553 N.E.2d 1317, 1990 N.Y. LEXIS 753 (N.Y. 1990).

Proprietary lessee failed to show that board of not-for-profit residential cooperative corporation acted improperly in issuing "stop-work" order in response to renovation work in which lessee relocated certain heating pipes, and thus his Article 78 petition to have order set aside was properly dismissed, even though lessee claimed that he had relied on board's initial approval of his plans and that, in any case, no harm was done to building, where lessee failed to comply with provisions either of alteration agreement or of renovation guidelines which required explicit written notice to board of any proposed changes in building's heating system, board promptly consulted its engineer when it learned of lessee's intent, and board notified lessee that it would not depart from its policy of refusing to permit movement of pipes. Levandusky v One Fifth Ave. Apartment Corp., 75 N.Y.2d 530, 554 N.Y.S.2d 807, 553 N.E.2d 1317, 1990 N.Y. LEXIS 753 (N.Y. 1990).

CLS N-PCL § 717 did not prohibit church from expending sums necessary to renovate existing landmark building, and thus did not require granting of "hardship exception" under Landmarks Law (NYC Admin Code §§ 207-4.0 and 207-8.0, redesignated NYC Admin Code § 25-309) that would permit replacement of existing building with commercial office tower, since § 717 does no more than impose on church fiduciary duty of care to manage congregation's money in prudent and responsible fashion, and would be implicated only if expenditures in question unacceptably impaired church's financial condition. Rector, Wardens, & Members of Vestry of St. Bartholomew's Church v New York, 914 F.2d 348, 1990 U.S. App. LEXIS 16005 (2d Cir. N.Y. 1990), cert. denied, 499 U.S. 905, 111 S. Ct. 1103, 113 L. Ed. 2d 214, 1991 U.S. LEXIS 1447 (U.S. 1991).

2. Fiduciary duty

Yacht club member failed to sufficiently plead a breach of fiduciary duty claim against the club's board of directors because the complaint did not allege that the board failed to act in good faith on behalf of the club or its members' collective interests, but merely alleged that the board failed to act in the individual member's personal best interest. Nachbar v Cornwall Yacht Club, 160 A.D.3d 972, 75 N.Y.S.3d 494, 2018 N.Y. App. Div. LEXIS 2744 (N.Y. App. Div. 2d Dep't 2018).

District court had ample evidence indicating that the sole beneficiary of a choreographer breached his fiduciary duty to a dance school and a dance center. There was evidence that the beneficiary ignored questions that surfaced from several sources about his ownership of the choreographer's dances, sets, and costumes, and made assertions regarding ownership of these items to the center's board of directors and to third parties; moreover, the court had ample evidence that the beneficiary sought to register as unpublished works in his own name works that he knew to be published and to belong to the center. Martha Graham Sch. & Dance Found., Inc. v Martha Graham Ctr. of Contemporary Dance, Inc., 380 F.3d 624, 2004 U.S. App. LEXIS 17452 (2d Cir. N.Y. 2004), amended, reprinted, 2004 U.S. App. LEXIS 20904 (2d Cir. N.Y. Aug. 18, 2004), cert. denied, 544 U.S. 1060, 125 S. Ct. 2518, 161 L. Ed. 2d 1110, 2005 U.S. LEXIS 4372 (U.S. 2005).

Because of the special relationship between the N.R.A. and The American Rifleman the fiduciary obligations of the association's directors and officers, as imposed by N.P.C.L. § 717, applied with equal vigor to the operation of The American Rifleman to the effect that the Board could not refuse to publish advertisements of candidates for an N.R.A. directorships in order that they might retain

Not-For-Profit Corporation Law

control of the association for themselves; refusal of the Board to furnish a membership list to candidates and to publish a request for monetary support for a candidate raised the issue of directors' bad faith. Fitzgerald v National Rifle Asso., 383 F. Supp. 162, 1974 U.S. Dist. LEXIS 6646 (D.N.J. 1974).

3. Business judgment rule

Business judgment rule prohibits judicial inquiry into actions of corporate directors taken in good faith and in exercise of honest judgment in lawful and legitimate furtherance of corporate purposes; so long as directors have not breached their fiduciary obligation to corporation, exercise of their powers for common and general interests of corporation may not be questioned, even if results show that what they did was unwise or inexpedient. Levandusky v One Fifth Ave. Apartment Corp., 75 N.Y.2d 530, 554 N.Y.S.2d 807, 553 N.E.2d 1317, 1990 N.Y. LEXIS 753 (N.Y. 1990).

Action by board of directors of corporation that comes within business judgment rule cannot be characterized as arbitrary and capricious, or abuse of discretion, for purpose of Article 78 proceeding. Levandusky v One Fifth Ave. Apartment Corp., 75 N.Y.2d 530, 554 N.Y.S.2d 807, 553 N.E.2d 1317, 1990 N.Y. LEXIS 753 (N.Y. 1990).

Nonstatutory claims for, inter alia, constructive trust against the former chairman of the New York Stock Exchange (NYSE) regarding his compensation could not be pursued by the attorney general as those claims required a lower burden of proof as knowledge or good faith did not have to be shown as in the statutory claims pursuant to N.Y. Not-for-Profit Corp. Law § 720(a)(b); directors and officers of a non-profit corporation, such as the NYSE, were provided with the protection of the business judgment rule under N.Y. Not-for-Profit Corp. Law § 717. People v Grasso, 11 N.Y.3d 64, 862 N.Y.S.2d 828, 893 N.E.2d 105, 2008 N.Y. LEXIS 1821 (N.Y. 2008).

Director and the officers were entitled to summary judgment in an N.Y. Not-for-Profit Corp. Law § 720(a)(1) proceeding because they established, inter alia, that payments made by the director and the officers to a law firm to dissolve the corporation were either authorized or made in good faith and the attorney general failed to raise a triable fact issue in opposition; because officers of a not-for-profit corporation are protected by the business judgment rule, N.Y. Not-for-Profit Corp. Law § 717, liability pursuant to N.Y. Not-for-Profit Corp. Law § 720(a)(1) required a showing that the officer or director lacked good faith in executing his or her duties. The absence of a majority vote of all members to dissolve the corporation, did not demonstrate a lack of good faith because, pursuant to N-PCL 1102(a)(2), ten percent of the total number of members may commence a proceeding for judicial dissolution of a corporation under certain circumstances, and thus a minority interest had the power to dissolve a corporation. People v Lawrence, 74 A.D.3d 1705, 903 N.Y.S.2d 618, 2010 N.Y. App. Div. LEXIS 4940 (N.Y. App. Div. 4th Dep't 2010).

Corporations which determined eligibility for nomination for annual "Tony" awards concerning excellence in theatre could not be held liable in damages for their refusal to categorize comedian's one-man theatrical comedy show as "play" eligible for award where they complied with their internal, published threshold requirements as to eligibility, within scope of their broad discretionary authority; in absence of any evidence of bad faith or discriminatory enforcement of rules, business judgment rule precluded court from inquiring into wisdom of such corporate action. Mason v American Theatre Wing, 165 Misc. 2d 432, 627 N.Y.S.2d 539, 1995 N.Y. Misc. LEXIS 241 (N.Y. Sup. Ct. 1995).

It is improper to dismiss a suit at the motion to dismiss stage on the basis of the business judgment rule if the plaintiff's pleadings allege that directors or officers did not act in good faith. Levy v Young Adult Inst., Inc., 103 F. Supp. 3d 426, 2015 U.S. Dist. LEXIS 57216 (S.D.N.Y. 2015).

4. Summary judgment

In action for injunction prohibiting townhouse homeowners' association from enforcing rule restricting parking on private streets of development, association was entitled to summary judgment since (1) bylaws of association gave broad discretion to board of directors to enact reasonable regulations governing use of development property, (2) business judgment rule applied to review of regulations, and (3) there was no evidence that parking restriction was unreasonable or enacted in bad faith. Gillman v Pebble Cove Home Owners Ass'n, 154 A.D.2d 508, 546 N.Y.S.2d 134, 1989 N.Y. App. Div. LEXIS 12778 (N.Y. App. Div. 2d Dep't 1989).

In action by homeowners' association and individual homeowners against construction company and individuals for breach of contract and warranties regarding quality of workmanship and materials, individual defendants were not entitled to summary judgment where it had been established that they were officers of construction company as well as directors of homeowners' association, and that they failed to disclose and failed to take steps to correct purported misconduct by construction company. Pebble Cove Homeowners' Ass'n v Shoratlantic Dev. Co., 191 A.D.2d 544, 595 N.Y.S.2d 92, 1993 N.Y. App. Div. LEXIS 2339 (N.Y. App. Div. 2d Dep't), app. dismissed, 82 N.Y.2d 802, 604 N.Y.S.2d 559, 624 N.E.2d 697, 1993 N.Y. LEXIS 3878 (N.Y. 1993).

Because the chairman of a compensation committee might not have effectively communicated a former chief executive officer's compensation to the board of directors, and his recommendations might not have been in the best interest of the New York Stock Exchange, the chairman was not entitled to summary judgment as the chairman did not establish that the chairman fulfilled the chairman's obligations under N.Y. Not-for-Profit Corp. Law § 717. People v Grasso, 50 A.D.3d 535, 858 N.Y.S.2d 23, 2008 N.Y. App. Div. LEXIS 3592 (N.Y. App. Div. 1st Dep't), app. dismissed, 53 A.D.3d 403, 859 N.Y.S.2d 563, 2008 N.Y. App. Div. LEXIS 5846 (N.Y. App. Div. 1st Dep't 2008), app. dismissed, 53 A.D.3d 404, 859 N.Y.S.2d 564, 2008 N.Y. App. Div. LEXIS 5850 (N.Y. App. Div. 1st Dep't 2008).

With respect to a cause of action alleging breach of fiduciary duty by the former CEO of the New York Stock Exchange under N.Y. Not-for-Profit Corp. Law § 717(b), the trial court improperly decided a disputed issue of fact as to the compensation committee's and board's knowledge of the extent of the CEO's supplemental executive retirement plan (SERP) benefit. People v Grasso, 54 A.D.3d 180, 861 N.Y.S.2d 627, 2008 N.Y. App. Div. LEXIS 5853 (N.Y. App. Div. 1st Dep't 2008).

§ 718.   List of directors and officers

(a) If a member or creditor of a corporation, in person or by his attorney or agent, or a representative of the district attorney or of the secretary of state, the attorney general, or other state official, makes a written demand on a corporation to inspect a current list of its directors and officers, the corporation shall, within two business days after receipt of the demand and for a period of one week thereafter, make the list available for such inspection at its office during usual business hours.

(b) Upon refusal by the corporation to make a current list of its directors and officers available, as provided in paragraph (a) of this section, the person making a demand for such list may apply, ex parte, to the supreme court at a special term held within the judicial district where the office of the corporation is located for an order directing the corporation to make such list available. The court may grant such order or take such other action as it may deem just and proper.

History: Add, L 1969, ch 1066, § 1, eff Sept 1, 1970; amd, L 1970, ch 992, eff Sept 1, 1970, L 2013, ch 549, § 77, eff July 1, 2014.

CASE ANNOTATIONS

Although plaintiff did not cross move for summary judgment, in action seeking to enjoin defendants from paying any salary or other sums to executive director of corporation and to direct complete disclosure of names and addresses of all members and books of account of corporation, the trial court would grant plaintiff's request for complete disclosure where appropriate demand for production was made, there was sufficient showing that inspection was not desired and would not be used for purpose which was in interest of business or object other than business of corporation, and there was no proof that plaintiff had otherwise failed to comply with provisions of Not-for-Profit Corporation Law. Hoffert v Dank (1976) 86 Misc. 2d 384,

382 N.Y.S.2d 421, mod (1976, 1st Dept) 55 A.D.2d 518, 389 N.Y.S.2d 101

§ 719. Liability of directors in certain cases

(a) Directors of a corporation who vote for or concur in any of the following corporate actions shall be jointly and severally liable to the corporation for the benefit of its creditors or members or the ultimate beneficiaries of its activities, to the extent of any injury suffered by such persons, respectively, as a result of such action, or, if there be no creditors or members or ultimate beneficiaries so injured, to the corporation, to the extent of any injury suffered by the corporation as a result of such action:

(1) The distribution of the corporation's cash or property to members, directors or officers, other than a distribution permitted under section 515 (Dividends prohibited; certain distributions of cash or property authorized).

(2) The redemption of capital certificates, subvention certificates or bonds, to the extent such redemption is contrary to the provisions of section 502 (Member's capital contributions), section 504 (Subventions), or section 506 (Bonds and security interests).

(3) The payment of a fixed or contingent periodic sum to the holders of subvention certificates or of interest to the holders or beneficiaries of bonds to the extent such payment is contrary to the provisions of section 504 or section 506.

(4) The distribution of assets in violation of section 1002-a (Carrying out the plan of dissolution and distribution of assets) or without paying or adequately providing for all known liabilities of the corporation, excluding any claims not filed by creditors within the time limit set in a notice given to creditors under articles 10 (Non-judicial dissolution) or 11 (Judicial dissolution).

(5) The making of any loan contrary to section 716 (Loans to directors and officers).

(b) A director who is present at a meeting of the board, or any committee thereof, at which action specified in paragraph (a) is taken shall be presumed to have concurred in the action unless his dissent thereto shall be entered in the minutes of the meeting, or unless he shall submit his written dissent to the person acting as the secretary of the meeting before the adjournment thereof, or shall deliver or send by registered mail such dissent to the secretary of the corporation promptly after the adjournment of the meeting. Such right to dissent shall not apply to a director who voted in favor of such action. A director who is absent from a meeting of the board, or any committee thereof, at which such action is taken shall be presumed to have concurred in the action unless he shall deliver or send by registered mail his dissent thereto to the secretary of the corporation or shall cause such dissent to be filed with the minutes of the proceedings of the board or committee within a reasonable time after learning of such action.

(c) Any director against whom a claim is successfully asserted under this section shall be entitled to contribution from the other directors who voted for or concurred in the action upon which the claim is asserted.

(d) Directors against whom a claim is successfully asserted under this section shall be entitled, to the extent of the amounts paid by them to the corporation as a result of such claims:

(1) Upon reimbursement to the corporation of any amount of an improper distribution of the corporation's cash or property, to be subrogated to the rights of the corporation against members, directors or officers who received such distribution with knowledge of facts indicating that it was not authorized by this chapter, in proportion to the amounts received by them respectively.

(2) Upon reimbursement to the corporation of an amount representing an improper redemption of a capital certificate, subvention or bond, to have the corporation rescind such improper redemption and recover the amount paid, for their benefit but at their expense, from any member or holder who received such payment with knowledge of facts indicating that such redemption by the corporation was not authorized by this chapter.

(3) Upon reimbursement to the corporation of an amount representing all or part of an improper payment of a fixed or contingent periodic sum to the holder of a subvention certificate, or of interest to the holder or beneficiary of a bond, to have the corporation recover the amount so paid, for their benefit but at their expense, from any holder or beneficiary who received such payment with knowledge of facts indicating that such payment by the corporation was not authorized by this chapter.

(4) Upon payment to the corporation of the claim of the attorney general or of any creditor by reason of a violation of subparagraph (a)(4), to be subrogated to the rights of the corporation against any person who received an improper distribution of assets.

(5) Upon reimbursement to the corporation of the amount of any loan made contrary to section 716 (Loans to directors and officers), to be subrogated to the rights of the corporation against a director or officer who received the improper loan.

(e) A director or officer shall not be liable under this section if, in the circumstances, he discharged his duty to the corporation under section 717 (Duty of directors and officers).

(f) This section shall not affect any liability otherwise imposed by law upon any director or officer.

History: Add, L 1969, ch 1066, § 1, eff Sept 1, 1970, with substance derived from Mem Corp Law § 46.

Not-For-Profit Corporation Law

Par (a), subpar (4), amd, L 1970, ch 847, § 50, eff Sept 1, 1970.

Par (a), subpar (4), amd, L 2005, ch 726, § 3, eff April 9, 2006.

CASE ANNOTATIONS

1. Generally
2-5. [Reserved for future use]
6. Under former Membership Corporations Law § 46

1. Generally

New York Not-for-Profit-Corporation Law (N-PCL) forbade the New York Attorney General from suing a chief executive officer (CEO) of a non-profit corporation on four non-statutory causes of action, as the N-PCL delineated the specific circumstances under which he could sue officers or directors, and he could not use his parens patriae-based authority to avoid the N-PCL's requirement that he prove fault on the CEO's part. People of the State of New York, by Eliot Spitzer, the Attorney Gen. of the State of New York v Grasso (2007, 1st Dept) 42 App Div 3d 126, 836 NYS2d 40

2-5. [Reserved for future use]
6. Under former Membership Corporations Law § 46

The office of director confers certain responsibilities of management and control upon such officers, but they are merely representatives of the associates, and their action is subject to fair criticism by any of such associates. People ex rel. Ward v Uptown Ass'n (1898) 26 A.D. 297, 49 N.Y.S. 881

Where, in an action to enforce the liability of a director of a membership corporation, under former § 11 from which this section is derived, the plaintiff for a first cause of action alleges all necessary jurisdictional facts, and states that the defendant was a director at the time the debt was contracted, and for a second cause of action repeats the same facts, but instead of stating that the defendant was a director, alleges that the defendant and his codefendants were held out by the corporation with the permission and consent of the defendants as being the directors of said corporation, and the credit for the indebtedness mentioned and described in a certain paragraph was extended by said plaintiff on the belief and reliance of the fact and the holding out thereof to the public, the second cause of action is insufficient under the statue and does not contain the necessary allegations for an action based upon fraud or misrepresentation, since the allegations of "holding out" are mere conclusions and there are no averments that the representations were false. Edward Davis, Inc. v Albee (1916) 172 A.D. 414, 158 N.Y.S. 623

Where a membership corporation is organized under this law, the treasurer of a subordinate branch, called a "court," which is not incorporated, but which consists of more than seven persons, is not entitled to sue to recover moneys alleged to be due to the local court, for the title to the money and the right of action is in the corporation itself, there being nothing to show that the subordinate court has any derivative rights. Conboy v Mathews (1916) 174 A.D. 523, 160 N.Y.S. 538

Directors of a membership corporation who were active in the promulgation of a prospectus designed to interest investors in purchasing the notes of the corporation, which prospectus contained statements which the directors knew or should have known to be false, are liable for the loss occasioned to investors resulting therefrom. First Nat'l Bank v Level Club, Inc. (1934) 241 A.D. 433, 272 N.Y.S. 273

The scope of this section is imprecise, but its basic purpose is clearly to charge directors in circumstances of "fraud or bad faith" with a liability which they would otherwise escape because it was exclusively a corporate liability, but where the same cause of action lies against both the corporation and against its directors personally, the statute would seem needless and should therefore be interpreted as inapplicable. Faulk v Milton (1966, 1st Dept) 25 A.D.2d 314, 268 N.Y.S.2d 844, affd (1967) 20 N.Y.2d 894, 285 N.Y.S.2d 864, 232 N.E.2d 860

A complaint in an action to enforce the liability of a trustee of a club upon a note given by such club is sufficient, although it does not state when the debt for which the note was given was contracted; it must be assumed that the debt was contracted simultaneously with the giving of the note. Straus v Sage (1894) 10 Misc 118, 30 N.Y.S. 905

Directors are jointly and severally liable, and the plaintiff may sue one, any or all. Kugelman v Hirschman (1898) 22 Misc 533, 49 N.Y.S. 1012, affd (1898) 23 Misc 773, 53 N.Y.S. 1107

The appointment of a permanent receiver of a dissolved membership corporation neither vests in him the personal right of its creditors to enforce the liability of directors under former § 11 from which this section is derived nor does it enable him to assert or enforce the rights of the corporation under Gen. Fordham v Poor (1919) 109 Misc 187, 179 N.Y.S. 367

An officer of a membership corporation may not be held criminally liable for the violation of a penal statute by the corporation. People v Smith (1947) 190 Misc 871, 74 N.Y.S.2d 845

Directors cannot vote by proxy. Craig Medicine Co. v Merchants' Bank of Rochester (1891) 59 Hun 561, 14 N.Y.S. 16

§ 720.   Actions against directors, officers and key persons

(a) An action may be brought against one or more directors, officers, or key persons of a corporation to procure a judgment for the following relief:

(1) To compel the defendant to account for his official conduct in the following cases:

(A) The neglect of, or failure to perform, or other violation of his duties in the management and disposition of corporate assets committed to his charge.

(B) The acquisition by himself, transfer to others, loss or waste of corporate assets due to any neglect of, or failure to perform, or other violation of his duties.

(2) To set aside an unlawful conveyance, assignment or transfer of corporate assets, where the transferee knew of its unlawfulness.

(3) To enjoin a proposed unlawful conveyance, assignment or transfer of corporate assets, where there are reasonable grounds for belief that it will be made.

(b) An action may be brought for the relief provided in this section and in paragraph (a) of section 719 (Liabilities of directors in certain cases) by the attorney general, by the corporation, or, in the right of the corporation, by any of the following:

(1) A director or officer of the corporation.

(2) A receiver, trustee in bankruptcy, or judgment creditor thereof.

(3) Under section 623 (Members' derivative action brought in the right of the corporation to procure a judgment in its favor), by one or more of the members thereof.

(4) If the certificate of incorporation or the by-laws so provide, by any holder of a subvention certificate or any other contributor to the corporation of cash or property of the value of $ 1,000 or more.

(c) In a corporation having no members, an action may be brought by a director against third parties to obtain a judgment in favor of the corporation. The complaint shall set forth with particularity the efforts of the plaintiff to secure the initiation of such action by the board or the reason for not making such efforts. The court in its discretion shall determine whether it is in the interest of the corporation that the action be maintained, and if the action is successful in whole or in part, what reimbursement if any should be made out of the corporate treasury to the plaintiff for his reasonable expenses including attorney's fees, incurred in the prosecution of the action.

History: Add, L 1969, ch 1066, § 1, eff Sept 1, 1970, with substance derived from Gen Corp Law §§ 60, 61; amd, L 1971, ch 1058, § 25, eff Sept 1, 1971; L 2013, ch 549, § 78, eff July 1, 2014; L 2016, ch 466, § 12, eff May 27, 2017.

CASE ANNOTATIONS

1. Generally

Assuming plaintiff to be trustee or officer of not-for-profit corporation, her removal without validly called meeting was nullity, and her right of action against other officers and directors of corporation could not be challenged for lack of standing; thus, court properly denied motion to dismiss her complaint for breach of fiduciary duty and for declaration of her status as officer and director. Chang v Fa-Yun, 265 A.D.2d 265, 697 N.Y.S.2d 31, 1999 N.Y. App. Div. LEXIS 10886 (N.Y. App. Div. 1st Dep't 1999).

Directors and officers were entitled to summary judgment on a corporation's cause of action pursuant to N.Y. Not-for-Profit Corp. Law §§ 623, 720, asserting the improper transfer of real property because the claim was asserted in a prior action which was resolved by a stipulation, and, contrary to the corporation's claim, the identity requirement of res judicata was satisfied; however, although the issue of improper assessment of membership dues was raised in the prior action, any losses occasioned by assessments made after the discontinuance of that action constituted separate injuries for which recovery could not have been obtained in the prior action, and the stipulation did not prevent the corporation from asserting claims that accrued after the stipulation came into effect. Pawling Lake Prop. Owners Assn., Inc. v Greiner, 72 A.D.3d 665, 897 N.Y.S.2d 729, 2010 N.Y. App. Div. LEXIS 2868 (N.Y. App. Div. 2d Dep't 2010).

Phrase "by one or more of the members," in statute providing that actions against corporate directors and officers for mismanagement, waste of corporate assets and unlawful conduct may be brought by one or more of its members, does not relate back to provisions of general statutory provision requiring that derivative action be instituted by at least five percent of members of corporation, but instead, authorizes bringing of such actions against corporate directors and officers by one or more of members; such construction gives effect to entire statute and gives recognition to apparent legislative intent to differentiate actions against officers and directors for misconduct or misfeasance in office from other derivative actions. Hoffert v Dank, 86 Misc. 2d 384, 382 N.Y.S.2d 421, 1976 N.Y. Misc. LEXIS 2452 (N.Y. Sup. Ct.), modified, 55 A.D.2d 518, 389 N.Y.S.2d 101, 1976 N.Y. App. Div. LEXIS 15153 (N.Y. App. Div. 1st Dep't 1976).

While pending statutory claims against, inter alia, the former CEO of the New York Stock Exchange (NYSE) were not completely extinguished by virtue of N.Y. Bus. Corp. Law § 906(b)(3) following the NYSE's merger into a for-profit entity from a non-profit corporation as the NYSE could bring the claims itself, the public policy concerns supporting the state attorney general's authority under N.Y. Not-for-Profit Corp. § 720(b) to bring the claims no longer existed as the public interest was not involved in the NYSE as a private corporation. People v Grasso, 54 A.D.3d 180, 861 N.Y.S.2d 627, 2008 N.Y. App. Div. LEXIS 5853 (N.Y. App. Div. 1st Dep't 2008).

2. Actions by attorney general

Nonstatutory claims for, inter alia, constructive trust against the former chairman of the New York Stock Exchange (NYSE) regarding his compensation could not be pursued by the attorney general as those claims required a lower burden of proof as knowledge or good faith did not have to be shown as in the statutory claims pursuant to N.Y. Not-for-Profit Corp. Law § 720(a)(b); directors and officers of a non-profit corporation, such as the NYSE, were provided with the protection of the business judgment rule under N.Y. Not-for-Profit Corp. Law § 717. People v Grasso, 11 N.Y.3d 64, 862 N.Y.S.2d 828, 893 N.E.2d 105, 2008 N.Y. LEXIS 1821 (N.Y. 2008).

The Attorney-General, purporting to represent the ultimate beneficiaries of a charitable organization, which is the donee of an unconditional gift of corporate stock, does not have standing pursuant to EPTL 8-1.1 (subd [f]), which provides that the Attorney-General shall represent the beneficiaries of dispositions of property for religious, charitable, educational or benevolent purposes and it shall be his duty to enforce the rights of such beneficiaries, to sue the corporation to compel both the declaration and payment of dividends and the payment of market value of those shares repurchased from the donee corporation at less than market value, since although the Attorney-General's powers of representation and enforcement are not limited to express trusts, but encompass those charitable dispositions where property has been donated for a specific purpose, this does not mean that the Attorney-General has standing to represent those who might eventually reap the benefit of gifts made without a specified purpose to charitable organizations; in such cases, the charity implicitly receives the gift for its own uses, consistent with its charitable purposes and there are no beneficiaries, legally cognizable, apart from the donee, and the charity may use the gift as it sees fit, in accordance with the laws of its creation. Where there has been a completed, unconditional, irrevocable gift of stock to a charity, there is neither any intention of the donor for the Attorney-General to protect, nor any beneficiaries to represent. Furthermore, the Not-For-Profit Corporation Law (§ 112, subd [a], par [7]; §§ 719, 720), which authorizes the Attorney-General to bring an action against the directors and officers of a charitable corporation for certain specified types of misconduct and to enforce any right afforded under the statute to members, a director or an officer of a charitable corporation, does not provide the Attorney-General with standing. Lefkowitz v Lebensfeld, 68 A.D.2d 488, 417 N.Y.S.2d 715, 1979 N.Y. App. Div. LEXIS 10968 (N.Y. App. Div. 1st Dep't 1979), aff'd, 51 N.Y.2d 442, 434 N.Y.S.2d 929, 415 N.E.2d 919, 1980 N.Y. LEXIS 2739 (N.Y. 1980).

New York Not-for-Profit-Corporation Law (N-PCL) forbade the New York Attorney General from suing a chief executive officer (CEO) of a non-profit corporation on four non-statutory causes of action, as the N-PCL delineated the specific circumstances under which he could sue officers or directors, and he could not use his parens patriae-based authority to avoid the N-PCL's requirement that he prove fault on the CEO's part. People v Grasso, 42 A.D.3d 126, 836 N.Y.S.2d 40, 2007 N.Y. App. Div. LEXIS 5719 (N.Y. App. Div. 1st Dep't 2007), aff'd, 11 N.Y.3d 64, 862 N.Y.S.2d 828, 893 N.E.2d 105, 2008 N.Y. LEXIS 1821 (N.Y. 2008).

Serious constitutional questions under N.Y. Const. art. VII, § 8(1), regarding state subsidization of a nongovernmental entity, would be raised if N.Y. Not-for-Profit Corp. Law § 720(b) were construed to permit the continued prosecution of statutory claims by the state attorney general against, inter alia, the former CEO of the New York Stock Exchange after the Exchange was involved in a merger converting it from a non-profit corporation into a for-profit entity. People v Grasso, 54 A.D.3d 180, 861 N.Y.S.2d 627, 2008 N.Y. App. Div. LEXIS 5853 (N.Y. App. Div. 1st Dep't 2008).

Term "constituent corporation" under N.Y. Bus. Corp. Law § 901(b)(3) plainly excluded an entity such as a non-profit subsidiary of the New York Stock Exchange (NYSE) that was created at the time of or after the merger of the NYSE from a non-profit corporation into a for-profit entity; thus, the state attorney general did not have the authority to pursue claims against the former CEO of the NYSE under N.Y. Not-for-Profit Corp. Law § 720(b). People v Grasso, 54 A.D.3d 180, 861 N.Y.S.2d 627, 2008 N.Y. App. Div. LEXIS 5853 (N.Y. App. Div. 1st Dep't 2008).

When the Attorney General sued a non-profit corporation's executive and board members, under N.Y. Not-For-Profit Corp. Law § 720(a) and (b), for, inter alia, various breaches of fiduciary duty, a six year limitations period applied, under N.Y. C.P.L.R. § 213(7), as the action was on behalf of the corporation to recover damages for waste or injury to property. Spitzer v Schussel, 792 N.Y.S.2d 798, 7 Misc. 3d 171, 233 N.Y.L.J. 18, 2005 N.Y. Misc. LEXIS 83 (N.Y. Sup. Ct. 2005).

3. Standing

An individual bringing a derivative action against directors or officers of a corporation for misconduct must meet requirement for standing by representing five percent or more of the membership of the corporation. Hoffert v Dank, 55 A.D.2d 518, 389 N.Y.S.2d 101, 1976 N.Y. App. Div. LEXIS 15153 (N.Y. App. Div. 1st Dep't 1976).

An individual bringing a derivative action on behalf of a corporation with a membership of 20 or less would meet the statutory requirement for standing that he represent five percent or more of the members. Hoffert v Dank, 55 A.D.2d 518, 389 N.Y.S.2d 101, 1976 N.Y. App. Div. LEXIS 15153 (N.Y. App. Div. 1st Dep't 1976).

Dismissal of a member's causes of action, pursuant to N.Y. Not-for-Profit Corp. Law § 720, to compel the a church's pastor and trustees to account for certain alleged misconduct, and for a judgment declaring that the pastor and the trustees had engaged in certain unlawful conduct, was proper because, inasmuch as the member sought to vindicate the church's rights by asserting those claims, they had to have been, but were not, asserted in the context of a derivative action brought by at least 5 percent of the church's members pursuant to N.Y. Not-for-Profit Corp. Law § 623(a); further, the complaint failed to set forth the member's efforts to secure the initiation of a derivative action or the reason for not making such effort. Therefore, the member lacked standing to bring the claims. Tae Hwa Yoon v New York Hahn Wolee Church, Inc., 56 A.D.3d 752, 870 N.Y.S.2d 42, 2008 N.Y. App. Div. LEXIS 9041 (N.Y. App. Div. 2d Dep't 2008).

Because a factual dispute existed as to whether the first director possessed standing to sue under N.Y. Not-for-Profit Corp. Law § 623(a), 720, a cross-motion by the second director and a non-profit corporation to dismiss the complaint for lack of standing to sue was properly denied. Brach v Harmony Servs., Inc., 93 A.D.3d 748, 940 N.Y.S.2d 652, 2012 N.Y. App. Div. LEXIS 2054 (N.Y. App. Div. 2d Dep't 2012).

4. Pleadings

While the attorney general had the authority to pursue a claim that alleged that certain advance payments from a supplemental retirement plan for the former chairman of the New York Stock Exchange constituted an improper loan under N.Y. Not-for-Profit Corp. Law § 716, the claim pleaded disregarded the knowledge element that other statutory claims under N.Y. Not-for-Profit Corp. Law §§ 719(3) and 720(a)(2) had to allege and, thus, had to be dismissed. People v Grasso, 11 N.Y.3d 64, 862 N.Y.S.2d 828, 893 N.E.2d 105, 2008 N.Y. LEXIS 1821 (N.Y. 2008).

5. Under former General Corporation Law § 60

Under an agreement whereby the corporate defendant agreed to employ plaintiff as an officer, plaintiff had a right of action for specific performance and damages. He also might have a right of action for fraud, but the court was without power to intervene in the management of the corporation and set aside the action of the board of directors in dismissing plaintiff. Heller v Clark Merchandisers, Inc., 9 Misc. 2d 106, 154 N.Y.S.2d 150, 1955 N.Y. Misc. LEXIS 2316 (N.Y. Sup. Ct. 1955).

Officers of a membership corporation could not be barred from examining its books and records because of their participation in formation of an allegedly competing and hostile organization, and membership therein, as long as they had not been removed from office or resigned their existing positions. Pino v United Democratic Regular Organization, 195 N.Y.S.2d 860 (N.Y. Sup. Ct. 1959).

This section applies to a foreign corporation and an action under it may be tried in a federal court. Schwarz v Artcraft Silk Hosiery Mills, Inc., 110 F.2d 465, 1940 U.S. App. LEXIS 4569 (2d Cir. N.Y. 1940).

6. –Cause of action

This section does not create any new cause of action except as to removal or suspension of directors. Rights and remedies conferred are cumulative but not exlcusive rights. Bailey v Colleen Products Corp., 198 N.Y.S. 418, 120 Misc. 297, 1923 N.Y. Misc. LEXIS 790 (N.Y. Sup. Ct. 1923).

A cause of action pursuant to this action and § 61 may be maintained only by a judgment creditor. Kendall v Oakland Golf Club, 123 N.Y.S.2d 907, 1953 N.Y. Misc. LEXIS 2067 (N.Y. Sup. Ct.), aff'd, 282 A.D. 1057, 126 N.Y.S.2d 379, 1953 N.Y. App. Div. LEXIS 5809 (N.Y. App. Div. 1953).

7. – –Transfer of assets

The transfer of assets of a debtor corporation, made by an officer subsequent to the date when the plaintiff secured a judgment against the corporation, such transfers whether made to another corporation, without consideration, or to select creditors in preference to others at a time when he knew the corporation to be insolvent, all fall within the prohibition of this section. Beol, Inc. v Dorf, 22 Misc. 2d 798, 193 N.Y.S.2d 394, 1959 N.Y. Misc. LEXIS 2530 (N.Y. Sup. Ct. 1959), aff'd, 12 A.D.2d 459, 209 N.Y.S.2d 267, 1960 N.Y. App. Div. LEXIS 7135 (N.Y. App. Div. 1st Dep't 1960).

Where a judgment creditor sued the debtor corporation, its secretary, her mother, and others and proved a conspiracy to fraudulently convey, conceal, and dispose of the assets of the corporation by means of a fraudulent chattel mortgage and foreclosure, bills of sale, disregard of the corporate entity and other acts, the intent to defraud creditors was actual and affirmative, and the plaintiff established causes of action under the fraudulent conveyance statute and Art 6 of this chapter. Lazar v Towne House Restaurant Corp., 142 N.Y.S.2d 315, 1955 N.Y. Misc. LEXIS 2796 (N.Y. Sup. Ct. 1955), aff'd, 5 A.D.2d 794, 171 N.Y.S.2d 334, 1958 N.Y. App. Div. LEXIS 7167 (N.Y. App. Div. 2d Dep't 1958).

8. – –Waste of assets

Under §§ 60 and 61, a creditor may maintain an action if any misconduct has resulted in waste of any money or property of the corporation even though the money or property comes out of surplus, but general creditors have no right to rely on the assumption that all of the surplus assets of the corporation have in the past been fully conserved. New York Credit Men's Ass'n v Harris, 11 N.Y.S.2d 435, 170 Misc. 988, 1939 N.Y. Misc. LEXIS 1744 (N.Y. Sup. Ct. 1939), aff'd, 262 A.D. 826, 29 N.Y.S.2d 505, 1941 N.Y. App. Div. LEXIS 6052 (N.Y. App. Div. 1941).

9. – –Accounting

The plaintiff is not entitled to an accounting personally but only to an accounting by the defendants to the corporation. Wangrow v Wangrow, 211 A.D. 552, 207 N.Y.S. 132, 1924 N.Y. App. Div. LEXIS 9918 (N.Y. App. Div. 1924).

In New York, an action brought under this section is in equity and in the nature of an action for an accounting, rather than a legal action for damages. Chambers v Blickle Ford Sales, Inc., 313 F.2d 252, 1963 U.S. App. LEXIS 6345 (2d Cir. Conn. 1963).

10. – –Removal of officers

The attorney-general cannot proceed under this section and § 136 to remove vestrymen and church wardens from their office on the ground of violation of their official duties, in view of § 130. Fiske v Beaty, 206 A.D. 349, 201 N.Y.S. 441, 1923 N.Y. App. Div. LEXIS 7209 (N.Y. App. Div. 1923), aff'd, 238 N.Y. 598, 144 N.E. 907, 238 N.Y. (N.Y.S.) 598, 1924 N.Y. LEXIS 778 (N.Y. 1924).

Subd 4 of § 60 deals with the removal by the corporation of its officers. But by the precise words of § 130, § 60 does not apply to religious corporations. Walker Memorial Baptist Church, Inc. v Saunders, 17 N.Y.S.2d 842, 173 Misc. 455, 1940 N.Y. Misc. LEXIS 1463 (N.Y. Sup. Ct.), aff'd, 259 A.D. 1010, 21 N.Y.S.2d 512, 1940 N.Y. App. Div. LEXIS 7748 (N.Y. App. Div. 1940).

11. – –Cause of action as bar to voluntary dissolution

Where a corporation and its creditors have an apparent cause of action against the officers and directors of the corporation for maladministration of its affairs, a petition for voluntary dissolution should be denied. In re Great Northern Trading Co., 168 A.D. 536, 153 N.Y.S. 213, 1915 N.Y. App. Div. LEXIS 8232 (N.Y. App. Div. 1915).

12. –Parties; plaintiff

The property of a corporation is a trust fund in the hands of its directors for payment of its debts and an action at law cannot be brought against an officer or director under this section. An action brought pursuant to said section is maintainable only in equity and must be brought in a representative capacity for the benefit of the plaintiff and all other creditors similarly situated. Schwartzreich v Bauman, 183 N.Y.S. 440, 112 Misc. 464, 1920 N.Y. Misc. LEXIS 1588 (N.Y. App. Term 1920).

A single stockholder may not, under this section, maintain an individual proceeding against officers and directors for misconduct. In re Tama, 137 N.Y.S.2d 248, 1954 N.Y. Misc. LEXIS 2530 (N.Y. Sup. Ct. 1954).

In an action by a judgment creditor for himself and on behalf of all other creditors of a corporation, since under Debtor and Creditor Law § 278 the action may be maintained only by a creditor in his own right and since under General Corporation Law § 133 the court need not make an order requiring all creditors to prove their claims, the court granted judgment to plaintiff only as an individual and not as a representative of other creditors. Lazar v Towne House Restaurant Corp., 142 N.Y.S.2d 315, 1955 N.Y. Misc. LEXIS 2796 (N.Y. Sup. Ct. 1955), aff'd, 5 A.D.2d 794, 171 N.Y.S.2d 334, 1958 N.Y. App. Div. LEXIS 7167 (N.Y. App. Div. 2d Dep't 1958).

13. – –Defendant

Liability of directors in an action brought under this section is several, and plaintiff may proceed against one or more of them without joining all. Buckley v United Cloak & Suit Co., 155 A.D. 735, 140 N.Y.S. 953, 1913 N.Y. App. Div. LEXIS 5184 (N.Y. App. Div. 1913), aff'd, 214 N.Y. 679, 108 N.E. 1090, 214 N.Y. (N.Y.S.) 679, 1915 N.Y. LEXIS 1391 (N.Y. 1915).

Where an action is brought against defendant officers, and the complaint states no cause of action against the corporation itself, it states but a single cause of action, although the corporation is properly made party defendant to whom the individual defendants will be directed to account and pay over. Higgins v Applebaum, 183 A.D. 527, 170 N.Y.S. 228, 1918 N.Y. App. Div. LEXIS 5006 (N.Y. App. Div. 1918).

14. –Pleadings; complaint

While subd 1 of this section permits an action to be brought to compel a director or officer to account to plaintiff for official conduct, including negligence or misconduct in management and disposition of funds, a complaint which merely alleges a discrepancy in the corporate books over a two-month period for which, it is asserted, only the president of the corporation can be responsible, fails to state a cause of action. Cirrincione v Polizzi, 14 A.D.2d 281, 220 N.Y.S.2d 741, 1961 N.Y. App. Div. LEXIS 8260 (N.Y. App. Div. 4th Dep't 1961).

Dismissal of petitioner's action seeking rescission of management fees for a non-profit was reversed because that cause of action was dependent upon resolution of issues of fact related to whether respondents engaged in improper related party transactions or otherwise transferred the senior living facility's surplus to benefit the non-profit and its other affiliates. Matter of The People of The State of New York v The Lutheran Care Network, Inc., 2018 N.Y. App. Div. LEXIS 8666 (N.Y. App. Div. 3d Dep't 2018).

A complaint in an action by a trustee in bankruptcy, which is brought to compel former officers and directors of the bankrupt to account for funds misappropriated, is insufficient in failing to allege that there were any creditors in existence at the time of the alleged misconduct or that misappropriation was for the purpose of defrauding creditors then existing and for whom the plaintiff is now acting, or in furtherance of a scheme to defraud subsequent creditors. Garrison v Pope, 223 N.Y.S. 737, 130 Misc. 290, 1927 N.Y. Misc. LEXIS 1026 (N.Y. Sup. Ct. 1927).

Complaint, in action brought under § 60, which alleges merely that the assets of the corporation were misappropriated, but does not allege that these assets constituted the capital stock of the corporation and also does not allege any fraudulent transfer as against subsequent creditors, is insufficient and must be dismissed in absence of an allegation that there were creditors in existence at time of alleged unlawful transaction, who are still creditors. New York Credit Men's Ass'n v Harris, 11 N.Y.S.2d 435, 170 Misc. 988, 1939 N.Y. Misc. LEXIS 1744 (N.Y. Sup. Ct. 1939), aff'd, 262 A.D. 826, 29 N.Y.S.2d 505, 1941 N.Y. App. Div. LEXIS 6052 (N.Y. App. Div. 1941).

15. – –Counterclaim

In an action by a director of a corporation in which it is alleged that the defendant, president, treasurer and manager of the corporation, mismanaged its business and appropriated and wasted its assets, it seems that the defendant is not entitled to counterclaim for moneys loaned and advanced to the corporation. Burgess v Stevens, 266 N.Y.S. 79, 148 Misc. 450, 1933 N.Y. Misc. LEXIS 1229 (N.Y. Sup. Ct. 1933).

In an action by a corporation against a former officer and director for an accounting, a money judgment for funds allegedly converted, and other relief, defendant's counterclaim against the corporation and another officer and director would substantially change the litigation to a stockholder's derivative suit, and the counterclaim was therefore dismissed without prejudice to new action because a derivative action is a class suit and in many respects is in a technical class by itself. Orto Theatres Corp. v Newins, 138 N.Y.S.2d 550, 207 Misc. 414, 1955 N.Y. Misc. LEXIS 2641 (N.Y. Sup. Ct. 1955).

16. – –Defenses

In an action under this section brought on the theory that the directors of the corporation were guilty of negligence and waste in conveying all the assets without other security than exaction from the grantee of a covenant to assume debts and pay them, held, there was no breach of duty since the plaintiff had assented and concurred in the breach of trust or had subsequently acquiesced in it. Darcy v Brooklyn & N. Y. Ferry Co., 196 N.Y. 99, 89 N.E. 461, 196 N.Y. (N.Y.S.) 99, 1909 N.Y. LEXIS 803 (N.Y. 1909).

In an action by directors of a corporation to compel defendant directors to restore to said defendant corporation moneys and assets which were allegedly wasted or fraudulently transferred at grossly inadequate prices, it was not a defense that the plaintiffs were estopped because they might have participated in or ratified said wrongs. Williams v Robinson, 9 Misc. 2d 774, 169 N.Y.S.2d 811, 1957 N.Y. Misc. LEXIS 2107 (N.Y. Sup. Ct. 1957), aff'd, 5 A.D.2d 823, 170 N.Y.S.2d 991, 1958 N.Y. App. Div. LEXIS 6927 (N.Y. App. Div. 1st Dep't 1958).

Ratification is not a defense to acts of directors which are unequivocally prohibited by law. Cowin v Jonas, 43 N.Y.S.2d 468, 1943 N.Y. Misc. LEXIS 2249 (N.Y. Sup. Ct. 1943), aff'd, 267 A.D. 947, 48 N.Y.S.2d 460, 1944 N.Y. App. Div. LEXIS 5647 (N.Y. App. Div. 1944).

17 –Service of process

The only valid method of affecting service on a foreign corporation which was the subject of a stockholder's derivative action and had surrendered its authority to do business in the State by a certificate in which it consented that process in any action on a liability incurred before filing of the certificate might be served on the Secretary of State, was by such service on the Secretary of State. The wrongs complained of occurred before the corporation surrendered its authority, and jurisdiction was properly secured. Herold v Wills, 110 N.Y.S.2d 321, 201 Misc. 114, 1952 N.Y. Misc. LEXIS 2412 (N.Y. Sup. Ct. 1952).

18. –Statute of limitations

In an action for waste where the profits obtained by officers and directors do not exceed the losses to the corporation the legal remedy is adequate and the action is governed by the three year statute of limitations. Corash v Texas Co., 264 A.D. 292, 35 N.Y.S.2d 334, 1942 N.Y. App. Div. LEXIS 4134 (N.Y. App. Div. 1942).

The gravamen of the cause of action, not the prayer for relief, determines the statute of limitations applicable. The fact that the action is in equity and equitable relief is demanded does not make the ten year statute of limitations applicable. Corash v Texas Co., 264 A.D. 292, 35 N.Y.S.2d 334, 1942 N.Y. App. Div. LEXIS 4134 (N.Y. App. Div. 1942).

Action by judgment creditors under §§ 60, 61, and 70, because of alleged waste committed by individual defendants, as directors of a corporation against which plaintiffs held an unsatisfied judgment were actions at law and having come into being in favor of judgment creditors perforce the statute, under Civ. Pr. Act, § 48, subd 2, six-year statute of limitations (since reduced to three years) is applicable to them. Luke v Polstein, 268 A.D. 921, 51 N.Y.S.2d 427, 1944 N.Y. App. Div. LEXIS 4258 (N.Y. App. Div. 2d Dep't 1944), aff'd, 294 N.Y.

896, 63 N.E.2d 27, 294 N.Y. (N.Y.S.) 896, 1945 N.Y. LEXIS 1074 (N.Y. 1945).

The three year statute of limitations applies to actions for corporate waste where the individual directors have not profited personally through the transaction. Purdy v Humphrey, 82 N.Y.S.2d 92, 192 Misc. 309, 1947 N.Y. Misc. LEXIS 3805 (N.Y. Sup. Ct. 1947), aff'd, 274 A.D. 841, 82 N.Y.S.2d 388, 1948 N.Y. App. Div. LEXIS 3578 (N.Y. App. Div. 1948).

The six year period of limitations applies to actions for waste of corporate funds where the director has profited by the transaction. Purdy v Humphrey, 82 N.Y.S.2d 92, 192 Misc. 309, 1947 N.Y. Misc. LEXIS 3805 (N.Y. Sup. Ct. 1947), aff'd, 274 A.D. 841, 82 N.Y.S.2d 388, 1948 N.Y. App. Div. LEXIS 3578 (N.Y. App. Div. 1948).

The six year statute of limitations applies to actions against directors and officers of a corporation for an accounting for misfeasance in office. Baker v Cohn, 42 N.Y.S.2d 159, 1942 N.Y. Misc. LEXIS 2396 (N.Y. Sup. Ct. 1942), modified, 266 A.D. 715, 40 N.Y.S.2d 623, 1943 N.Y. App. Div. LEXIS 4025 (N.Y. App. Div. 1943).

Since, under New York law, an action in behalf of the corporation against its directors is an equitable one, in the nature of one to require an accounting, the tort statute of limitations is inapplicable and the longer period of limitations on time to seek an accounting is applicable. Chambers v Blickle Ford Sales, Inc., 313 F.2d 252, 1963 U.S. App. LEXIS 6345 (2d Cir. Conn. 1963).

19. – –Accrual of cause of action

Where an action is brought under this section no cause of action accrues to a creditor with certain exceptions until judgment has been obtained and execution returned unsatisfied. The statute of limitations does not commence to run until the cause of action is accrued to the creditor. Buttles v Smith, 281 N.Y. 226, 22 N.E.2d 350, 281 N.Y. (N.Y.S.) 226, 1939 N.Y. LEXIS 1003 (N.Y. 1939).

An action by a creditor to secure an accounting for losses caused by the wrongful acts of the defendant can be maintained, pursuant to this section, only after entry of judgment in return of execution unsatisfied and therefore the statute of limitations does not commence to run until entry of judgment and return of execution unsatisfied. Hastings v H. M. Byllesby & Co., 38 N.Y.S.2d 201, 1942 N.Y. Misc. LEXIS 2167 (N.Y. Sup. Ct. 1942).

20. –Burden of proof

In an action by a trustee in bankruptcy against officers, directors and stockholders of a corporation who disposed of the corporate assets at an auction sale, held without notice to creditors and without compliance with any statutory procedure designed to protect the rights of creditors, the burden of showing that full value was realized, and that the creditors therefor did not sustain a loss by virtue of the defendant's unilateral action, is upon the defendants, and they must account and respond in damages for the amount, if any, by which less than full value was realized upon the sale. New York Credit Men's Adjustment Bureau, Inc. v Weiss, 278 A.D. 501, 105 N.Y.S.2d 604, 1951 N.Y. App. Div. LEXIS 3848 (N.Y. App. Div. 1951), aff'd, 305 N.Y. 1, 110 N.E.2d 397, 305 N.Y. (N.Y.S.) 1, 1953 N.Y. LEXIS 844 (N.Y. 1953).

21. –Right to and questions for jury

Order setting issues to be tried by jury in an action brought under this section against officers for neglect and misconduct, which is alleged to have consisted in wrongfully excluding plaintiff from participating in management of corporation, jury should not be allowed to determine damage to corporation caused by such acts as it is wholly a matter of speculation. Momand v Landers, 174 A.D. 227, 160 N.Y.S. 1053, 1916 N.Y. App. Div. LEXIS 7707 (N.Y. App. Div. 1916).

Defendants were entitled to a jury trial of causes of action at law contained in a complaint for an accounting under §§ 60, 61. Duane Jones Co. v Burke, 280 A.D. 889, 115 N.Y.S.2d 529, 1952 N.Y. App. Div. LEXIS 4041 (N.Y. App. Div. 1952).

In an action by a director of a corporation against other directors of same corporation for damages for negligent transactions, the question whether the plaintiff-director acquiesced in and ratified the transactions complained of is a question for the jury. Kehaya v Axton, 30 F. Supp. 838, 1940 U.S. Dist. LEXIS 3658 (D.N.Y. 1940).

22. –Liability of officers and directors

In an action under this section, where it has been adjudged that one of the defendants has misappropriated a stated sum, his refusal to pay the receiver of the corporation does not entitle the plaintiff, as a matter of law, to an order committing such defendant for contempt, where no specific fund has been directed to be paid over and it does not appear that the money cannot be collected by execution. Nelson v

Hirsch, 264 N.Y. 316, 190 N.E. 653, 264 N.Y. (N.Y.S.) 316, 1934 N.Y. LEXIS 1433 (N.Y. 1934).

Officers and directors of a solvent corporation who, confronted with unfavorable business conditions, sold all the corporate property at public auction without notice to creditors, are prima facie liable to creditors for waste of the corporate assets if the proceeds of the property at the auction were less than its full value. New York Credit Men's Adjustment Bureau, Inc. v Weiss, 305 N.Y. 1, 110 N.E.2d 397, 305 N.Y. (N.Y.S.) 1, 1953 N.Y. LEXIS 844 (N.Y. 1953).

Corporate assets constitute a trust fund for payment of corporate debts, and when two directors of a stock corporation transfer all corporate property to a third director for nominal consideration they commit a breach of duty toward creditors, and become personally liable for existing claims. Cullen v Friedland, 152 A.D. 124, 136 N.Y.S. 659, 1912 N.Y. App. Div. LEXIS 8493 (N.Y. App. Div. 1912).

Directors of a defunct corporation, who distribute all of its assets among themselves without formal dissolution proceeding and notice to creditors of the corporation, are not liable to such creditors on the ground that they have wrongfully and unlawfully distributed assets of the corporation, where it does not appear that the creditors would have been entitled to payment of their claims if the corporation had been regularly dissolved, and there is no proof of fraud or bad faith. Curran v Oppenheimer, 164 A.D. 746, 150 N.Y.S. 369, 1914 N.Y. App. Div. LEXIS 8513 (N.Y. App. Div. 1914), aff'd, 222 N.Y. 615, 118 N.E. 1055, 222 N.Y. (N.Y.S.) 615, 1918 N.Y. LEXIS 1496 (N.Y. 1918).

Action by judgment creditors of corporate debtor to set aside transfers made by corporation to another corporation, money judgment against individual defendants who were officers and directors of both corporations sustained as a breach of their duties as directors of corporate debtor. Thorne Neale & Co. v New York Southern Coal Terminal Corp., 270 A.D. 816, 59 N.Y.S.2d 833, 1946 N.Y. App. Div. LEXIS 4085 (N.Y. App. Div.), aff'd, 295 N.Y. 977, 68 N.E.2d 56, 295 N.Y. (N.Y.S.) 977, 1946 N.Y. LEXIS 1114 (N.Y. 1946).

Diversion of corporate funds by a director-officer of a corporation to his personal use is in flagrant dereliction of his duty and violation of his trust, rendering him liable to a trustee in bankruptcy of the corporation. Newfield v Ettlinger, 22 Misc. 2d 769, 194 N.Y.S.2d 670, 1959 N.Y. Misc. LEXIS 2554 (N.Y. Sup. Ct. 1959), app. dismissed, 10 A.D.2d 947, 205 N.Y.S.2d 908, 1960 N.Y. App. Div. LEXIS 9529 (N.Y. App. Div. 1st Dep't 1960).

Where the individual defendant, an officer in the debtor corporation, controlled and dominated the corporation, the individual defendant was liable to a judgment-creditor for the money and value of the corporate debtor's assets disbursed by him with knowledge of its actual or impending insolvency. This liability includes, but is not limited to, the preferential repayments of loans made by the individual defendant to the debtor corporation or to the corporation's customers in behalf of the debtor corporations. Beol, Inc. v Dorf, 22 Misc. 2d 798, 193 N.Y.S.2d 394, 1959 N.Y. Misc. LEXIS 2530 (N.Y. Sup. Ct. 1959), aff'd, 12 A.D.2d 459, 209 N.Y.S.2d 267, 1960 N.Y. App. Div. LEXIS 7135 (N.Y. App. Div. 1st Dep't 1960).

In an action by a judgment creditor attacking the transfer of assets of a debtor corporation, where the evidence established that the secretary of the corporation and others fraudulently transferred the corporation's assets and also that the secretary fraudulently transferred her interest in certain real estate, such transfer of title was vitiated and the secretary's interest in the property was made subject to the lien of the judgment. Lazar v Towne House Restaurant Corp., 142 N.Y.S.2d 315, 1955 N.Y. Misc. LEXIS 2796 (N.Y. Sup. Ct. 1955), aff'd, 5 A.D.2d 794, 171 N.Y.S.2d 334, 1958 N.Y. App. Div. LEXIS 7167 (N.Y. App. Div. 2d Dep't 1958).

Although New York law holds directors liable for misappropriations of assets and provides a remedy to require them to account, it does not go so far as to make them actual trustees of the corporate assets, even in liquidation. Chambers v Blickle Ford Sales, Inc., 313 F.2d 252, 1963 U.S. App. LEXIS 6345 (2d Cir. Conn. 1963).

23. –Appointment of receiver pendente lite

A receiver pendente lite cannot be appointed in the absence of any allegation in the complaint that the corporation is insolvent or that insolvency threatens. Lichtenstadter v Lichtenstadter Bros., Inc., 224 N.Y.S. 459, 130 Misc. 772, 1927 N.Y. Misc. LEXIS 1144 (N.Y. Sup. Ct. 1927).

24. Under former General Corporation Law § 61

An action by corporate directors and stockholders against other directors and the corporation for an accounting was a representative suit. Handler v Belmare Lighting Co., 8 Misc. 2d 687, 168 N.Y.S.2d 288, 1957 N.Y. Misc. LEXIS 2331 (N.Y. Sup. Ct. 1957).

An action against officers of a corporation for waste and breach of fiduciary duty can only be maintained by the corporation or in its behalf. Hyde v Everett Van Kleeck & Co., 17 Misc. 2d 375, 190 N.Y.S.2d 914, 1959 N.Y. Misc. LEXIS 4092 (N.Y. Sup. Ct. 1959).

Waste, mismanagement and inference with the corporation's business are wrongs to the corporation, and such wrongs must be redressed by means of a suit by, or in behalf of the corporation. It gives no rise to a cause of action in favor of the individual stockholders. Weinstein v Behn, 65 N.Y.S.2d 536, 1946 N.Y. Misc. LEXIS 2874 (N.Y. Sup. Ct. 1946), aff'd, 272 A.D. 1045, 75 N.Y.S.2d 284, 1947 N.Y. App. Div. LEXIS 4875 (N.Y. App. Div. 1947).

25. –Action by corporation

Plaintiff membership corporations may assert a cause of action for an accounting (§§ 60, 61). Kang Jai Ass'n, Inc. v Poon Gee Datt, 279 A.D. 872, 110 N.Y.S.2d 424, 1952 N.Y. App. Div. LEXIS 5154 (N.Y. App. Div. 1952).

Where causes of action against directors and officers for breach of contract or fiduciary duties are sought to be enforced by the corporation directly, they are not controlled by limitations prescribed by this section with respect to maintenance of derivative actions. Platt Corp. v Platt, 21 A.D.2d 116, 249 N.Y.S.2d 75, 1964 N.Y. App. Div. LEXIS 3973 (N.Y. App. Div. 1st Dep't 1964), aff'd, 15 N.Y.2d 705, 256 N.Y.S.2d 335, 204 N.E.2d 495, 1965 N.Y. LEXIS 1699 (N.Y. 1965).

26. –Stockholder's derivative action

In a stockholder's derivative action, the corporation is an indispensable party. The corporation cannot be made a party simply by act of the defendant in inserting the name of the corporation in his answer as an additional defendant. Thus, a motion to dismiss a counter-claim seeking an accounting by the plaintiff was granted with leave to file an amended answer after compelling the plaintiff to join the corporation as a party defendant. Meier v Holmes, 282 A.D. 1030, 126 N.Y.S.2d 655, 1953 N.Y. App. Div. LEXIS 5726 (N.Y. App. Div. 1953).

Action by stockholder of co-operative corporation to obtain order requiring officers to call a meeting for election of directors or that a meeting to consider his charges be held, was a representative action. Lazar v Knolls Cooperative Section No. 2, Inc., 130 N.Y.S.2d 407, 205 Misc. 748, 1954 N.Y. Misc. LEXIS 2044 (N.Y. Sup. Ct. 1954).

27. – –Complaint

A complaint in a stockholder's derivative suit that "plaintiff brings this action derivately in the right and for the benefit of" the designated corporation is sufficient to fully apprise all parties of plaintiff's position. Abramson v Blakeley, 25 Misc. 2d 967, 202 N.Y.S.2d 586, 1960 N.Y. Misc. LEXIS 2997 (N.Y. Sup. Ct. 1960).

A complaint in a stockholders' derivative suit is insufficient to state a cause of action against individual directors and officers of the corporation for alleged mismanagement and wasting of the corporate funds where its allegations are wholly conclusory, vague and general, and fail to allege when the acts complained of occurred. Arvonio v Arvonio, 31 Misc. 2d 5, 219 N.Y.S.2d 635, 1961 N.Y. Misc. LEXIS 2754 (N.Y. Sup. Ct. 1961).

28. –Action by officer or director

Under § 61 third persons to whom property was transferred are properly joined in such action and a director of a corporation may bring an action without prior demand that the corporation bring the action. Katz v Braz, 66 N.Y.S.2d 722, 188 Misc. 581, 1946 N.Y. Misc. LEXIS 3126 (N.Y. Sup. Ct. 1946), aff'd, 271 A.D. 970, 69 N.Y.S.2d 324, 1947 N.Y. App. Div. LEXIS 5447 (N.Y. App. Div. 1947).

This section expressly authorizes an action by a director of a corporation against its officers for an accounting. Wyckoff v Sagall, 16 Misc. 2d 630, 56 N.Y.S.2d 392, 1945 N.Y. Misc. LEXIS 1461 (N.Y. Sup. Ct. 1945).

An officer or director of a corporation may maintain an action to compel other officers or directors to account for their conduct in management of the corporation. Scott v Funaroff, 84 N.Y.S.2d 144, 1948 N.Y. Misc. LEXIS 3527 (N.Y. Sup. Ct. 1948).

Under § 61 a director of a foreign corporation may bring an action against such corporation for misconduct of other directors. Kehaya v Axton, 32 F. Supp. 266, 1940 U.S. Dist. LEXIS 3343 (D.N.Y. 1940).

29. – –Complaint

It is not necessary for a director of a corporation, bringing an action under this section, to state in the title of the action that he sues in a representative capacity if complaint itself alleges that he is a director. Higgins v Applebaum, 183 A.D. 527, 170 N.Y.S. 228, 1918 N.Y. App. Div. LEXIS 5006 (N.Y. App. Div. 1918).

An action under this section only lies when the plaintiff is a director at the time of commencement of the action, which fact he should allege specifically, or by an allegation of other facts which by necessary inference will show him to be such. Rothbart v Star Wet Wash Laundry Co., 185 A.D. 807, 174 N.Y.S. 76, 1919 N.Y. App. Div. LEXIS 5797 (N.Y. App. Div. 1919).

Under the provisions of this section permitting an action by an officer or director, an allegation that the plaintiff is and has been treasurer of the corporation is sufficient to enable him to maintain an action for conversion and misappropriation of corporate property in his own name. Peets v Manhasset Civil Engineers, Inc., 68 N.Y.S.2d 335, 1946 N.Y. Misc. LEXIS 3364 (N.Y. Sup. Ct. 1946).

30. – –Defense

In an action by directors of a corporation to compel defendant directors to restore to said defendant corporation moneys and assets which were allegedly wasted or fraudulently transferred at grossly inadequate prices, it was not a defense that the plaintiffs were estopped because they might have participated in or ratified said wrongs to the corporation. Williams v Robinson, 9 Misc. 2d 774, 169 N.Y.S.2d 811, 1957 N.Y. Misc. LEXIS 2107 (N.Y. Sup. Ct. 1957), aff'd, 5 A.D.2d 823, 170 N.Y.S.2d 991, 1958 N.Y. App. Div. LEXIS 6927 (N.Y. App. Div. 1st Dep't 1958).

31. – –Abatement

An action by a director of a corporation against other directors does not abate when the plaintiff ceases to be a director of the corporation and the action which is one for the benefit of the corporation may be continued in the director's name after he ceases to be such. Manix v Fantl, 209 A.D. 756, 205 N.Y.S. 174, 1924 N.Y. App. Div. LEXIS 8730 (N.Y. App. Div. 1924).

The fact that the plaintiff was illegally ousted as a director of the corporation after commencement of an action under this section does not abate the action. Wangrow v Wangrow, 211 A.D. 552, 207 N.Y.S. 132, 1924 N.Y. App. Div. LEXIS 9918 (N.Y. App. Div. 1924).

Action commenced by director of corporate defendant to compel individual defendants, directors and officers of corporate defendant, to account for and to set aside certain corporate transactions did not abate the cause, after commencement of action, plaintiff ceased to be a director. Tenney v Rosenthal, 6 A.D.2d 510, 179 N.Y.S.2d 728, 1958 N.Y. App. Div. LEXIS 4130 (N.Y. App. Div. 1st Dep't 1958), aff'd, 6 N.Y.2d 204, 189 N.Y.S.2d 158, 160 N.E.2d 463, 1959 N.Y. LEXIS 1134 (N.Y. 1959).

An illegal attempted removal of an officer or director would not prevent his maintaining an action as such. Wyckoff v Sagall, 16 Misc. 2d 630, 56 N.Y.S.2d 392, 1945 N.Y. Misc. LEXIS 1461 (N.Y. Sup. Ct. 1945).

Director who commenced an action against other directors of corporation for negligence and waste under § 60, could not continue to maintain action after he was ousted as a director. Kehaya v Axton, 32 F. Supp. 266, 1940 U.S. Dist. LEXIS 3343 (D.N.Y. 1940).

32. –Action by judgment creditor

Suit by creditor to recover moneys misappropriated by directors or other officers of corporation, should be brought by plaintiff in a representative capacity. Davis v Wilson, 150 A.D. 704, 135 N.Y.S. 825, 1912 N.Y. App. Div. LEXIS 7197 (N.Y. App. Div. 1912).

Judgment creditor of a corporation may maintain an individual action against directors who have caused the assets of the corporation to be transferred to another corporation without providing for payment of plaintiff's claim, if the rights of no other creditors are involved. Buckley v United Cloak & Suit Co., 155 A.D. 735, 140 N.Y.S. 953, 1913 N.Y. App. Div. LEXIS 5184 (N.Y. App. Div. 1913), aff'd, 214 N.Y. 679, 108 N.E. 1090, 214 N.Y. (N.Y.S.) 679, 1915 N.Y. LEXIS 1391 (N.Y. 1915).

A creditor of a corporation seeking to hold liable its trustees in dissolution for alleged wrongful distribution of assets of the corporation must not only proceed under §§ 60, 61, but must be a judgment creditor. Bristol Mfg. Corp. v Elk Textile Co., 200 N.Y.S. 860, 121 Misc. 138, 1923 N.Y. Misc. LEXIS 1553 (N.Y. Sup. Ct. 1923), aff'd, 209 A.D. 95, 204 N.Y.S. 427, 1924 N.Y. App. Div. LEXIS 8559 (N.Y. App. Div. 1924).

A creditor who is not a judgment creditor may not maintain an action against corporate directors to compel them to account for their official conduct. Levy v Paramount Publix Corp., 266 N.Y.S. 271, 149 Misc. 129, 1933 N.Y. Misc. LEXIS 1260 (N.Y. Sup. Ct. 1933), aff'd, 241 A.D. 711, 269 N.Y.S. 997, 1934 N.Y. App. Div. LEXIS 9067 (N.Y. App. Div. 1934).

Not-For-Profit Corporation Law

To maintain an action either under § 276 of the Debtor and Creditor Law or § 61 of the General Corporation Law, the plaintiff must have status as a creditor, and he cannot maintain such an action after his claim has been fully paid. Lazar v Libby, 28 Misc. 2d 131, 219 N.Y.S.2d 362, 1960 N.Y. Misc. LEXIS 2142 (N.Y. Sup. Ct. 1960).

A cause of action pursuant to this section and § 60 may be maintained by a judgment creditor. Kendall v Oakland Golf Club, 123 N.Y.S.2d 907, 1953 N.Y. Misc. LEXIS 2067 (N.Y. Sup. Ct.), aff'd, 282 A.D. 1057, 126 N.Y.S.2d 379, 1953 N.Y. App. Div. LEXIS 5809 (N.Y. App. Div. 1953).

In an action by a judgment creditor for himself and on behalf of all other creditors of a corporation, since under Debtor and Creditor Law § 278 the action may be maintained only by a creditor in his own right and since under General Corporation Law § 133 the court need not make an order requiring all creditors to prove their claims, the court granted judgment to plaintiff only as an individual and not as a representative of other creditors. Lazar v Towne House Restaurant Corp., 142 N.Y.S.2d 315, 1955 N.Y. Misc. LEXIS 2796 (N.Y. Sup. Ct. 1955), aff'd, 5 A.D.2d 794, 171 N.Y.S.2d 334, 1958 N.Y. App. Div. LEXIS 7167 (N.Y. App. Div. 2d Dep't 1958).

33. –Action by receiver for corporation

The receiver of corporation, appointed on application of one creditor may recover in an action to recover the value of property alleged to have been illegally transferred to certain directors thereby denuding the corporation and defeating and impairing the rights of creditors. Hitz v Garfinkel, 246 A.D. 728, 283 N.Y.S. 872, 1935 N.Y. App. Div. LEXIS 9952 (N.Y. App. Div. 1935).

A receiver appointed in supplementary proceedings has the same power as a general receiver and may maintain an action against officers and directors of a corporation to recover property wrongfully conveyed and dividends improperly declared. Klages v Cohen, 146 F.2d 641, 1945 U.S. App. LEXIS 3101 (2d Cir. N.Y. 1945).

34. –Action by attorney general

An action for the removal of the officers and directors of a corporation may be brought only by the attorney general. Purdy v Humphrey, 82 N.Y.S.2d 92, 192 Misc. 309, 1947 N.Y. Misc. LEXIS 3805 (N.Y. Sup. Ct. 1947), aff'd, 274 A.D. 841, 82 N.Y.S.2d 388, 1948 N.Y. App. Div. LEXIS 3578 (N.Y. App. Div. 1948).

35. – –Complaint

A complaint by the attorney general, which alleges matters concerning the internal management of a corporation as between itself and its stockholders or individuals with whom private contractual rights are involved, might be sustainable as a derivative action under §§ 60 and 61 but could not be sustained as affecting the public interest under § 134. People v Singer, 85 N.Y.S.2d 727, 193 Misc. 976, 1949 N.Y. Misc. LEXIS 1693 (N.Y. Sup. Ct. 1949).

36. –Right to jury trial

Defendants were entitled to a jury trial of causes of action at law contained in a complaint which also alleged a cause of action for an accounting under §§ 60, 61. Duane Jones Co. v Burke, 280 A.D. 889, 115 N.Y.S.2d 529, 1952 N.Y. App. Div. LEXIS 4041 (N.Y. App. Div. 1952).

§ 720-a. Liability of directors, officers and trustees

Except as provided in sections seven hundred nineteen and seven hundred twenty of this chapter, and except any action or proceeding brought by the attorney general or, in the case of a charitable trust, an action or proceeding against a trustee brought by a beneficiary of such trust, no person serving without compensation as a director, officer or trustee of a corporation, association, organization or trust described in section 501(c)(3) of the United States internal revenue code shall be liable to any person other than such corporation, association, organization or trust based solely on his or her conduct in the execution of such office unless the conduct of such director, officer or trustee with respect to the person asserting liability constituted gross negligence or was intended to cause the resulting harm to the person asserting such liability. For purposes of this section,

such a director, officer or trustee shall not be considered compensated solely by reason of payment of his or her actual expenses incurred in attending meetings or otherwise in the execution of such office.

History: Add, L 1986, ch 220, § 11, eff June 28, 1986, applicable to causes of action arising on or after June 28, 1986.

CASE ANNOTATIONS

Board of governors of country club is not entitled to qualified immunity conferred upon uncompensated officials of not-for-profit corporations pursuant to CLS CPLR § 3211 (a)(11) and CLS N-PCL § 720-a since those provisions only grant qualified immunity to tax exempt organizations which are largely charitable or otherwise socially beneficial in nature. Bernbach v Bonnie Briar Country Club (1988, 2d Dept) 144 A.D.2d 610, 534 N.Y.S.2d 695, app dismd without op (1989) 74 N.Y.2d 715, 543 N.Y.S.2d 401, 541 N.E.2d 430

Cause of action for allegedly defamatory remarks made by members of board of governors of country club was improperly dismissed on ground that plaintiff failed to overcome qualified immunity of board of governors since country club was not organization entitled to qualified immunity pursuant to CLS CPLR § 3211 (a)(11) and CLS N-PCL § 720-a. Bernbach v Bonnie Briar Country Club (1988, 2d Dept) 144 A.D.2d 610, 534 N.Y.S.2d 695, app dismd without op (1989) 74 N.Y.2d 715, 543 N.Y.S.2d 401, 541 N.E.2d 430

Trustees and officers of religious corporation were not entitled to dismissal of action under CLS CPLR § 3211(a)(11) where (1) they did not present affidavit of chief financial officer as to their uncompensated status, and (2) it was alleged that certain individual defendant, who had nearly absolute authority over church, its trustees and officers, its membership, and related churches, raped, sodomized, and sexually abused infant plaintiffs while they were under his religious guidance. Karen S. v Streitferdt (1991, 1st Dept) 172 A.D.2d 440, 568 N.Y.S.2d 946

CLS CPLR § 3211(a)(11) motion to dismiss complaint must be made before service of answer, and inclusion of statutory defense in answer neither preserves nor extends time within which to make dismissal motion. Woodford v Benedict Community Health Center (1991, 3d Dept) 176 A.D.2d 1115, 575 N.Y.S.2d 415

In defamation action against directors of not-for-profit corporation by plaintiffs who were removed from their positions as executive director and treasurer of corporation due to alleged fiscal improprieties, where defendants sought dismissal under CLS CPLR § 3211(a)(11) on ground that they were immune from liability under CLS N-PCL § 720-a, plaintiffs were required to come forward with evidentiary proof showing fair likelihood that they would be able to prove that defendants were grossly negligent or intended to cause resulting harm. Rabushka v Marks (1996, 3d Dept) 229 A.D.2d 899, 646 N.Y.S.2d 392

Unpaid directors of California not-for-profit organization were immune from suit under CLS N-PCL § 720-a and CLS CPLR § 3211(a)(11), absent allegations of their gross negligence or intention to cause harm. Pontarelli v Shapero (1996, 1st Dept) 231 A.D.2d 407, 647 N.Y.S.2d 185

Uncompensated trustee defendants were entitled to summary judgment dismissing employee's cause of action for fraud where those defendants were immune from liability under CLS N-PCL § 720-a. Goldsmith v Fight for Sight, Inc. (1998, 1st Dept) 251 A.D.2d 120, 674 N.Y.S.2d 649

Defendants were not entitled to dismissal of action on ground that they had immunity under CLS N-PCL § 720-a as uncompensated directors of not-for-profit corporation where plaintiff, not-for-profit religious corporation, alleged in detail that defendants formed second not-for-profit corporation so as to assist in deceptive scheme to appropriate property for themselves; such allegation came within statutory exception for intentional misconduct. American Baptist Churches v Galloway (2000, 1st Dept) 271 A.D.2d 92, 710 N.Y.S.2d 12

Individual defendants are not liable for federal copyright infringements under CLS N-PCL § 720-a, where photographer does not prove that their actions in posting 2 of his photographs on corporation's Internet site were grossly negligent or intended to cause him harm, because § 720-a provides that individual director of not-for-profit corporation can only be held liable for act undertaken as director if that person's act "constituted gross negligence or was intended to cause resulting harm to person asserting such liability." Scanlon v Kessler (1998, SD NY) 11 F. Supp. 2d 444, 47 USPQ2d 1692, costs/fees proceeding (1998, SD NY) 23 F. Supp. 2d 413, 48 USPQ2d 1794

A village can be held vicariously liable for Dram Shop Act violations committed by volunteer firefighters during fundraising events, but not for misconduct during social activities. Atty Ops Gen I90-64

Appellate court found that tax returns and other financial documents which plaintiff requested from defendant in her lawsuit alleging sexual discrimination, negligent supervision, and breach of contract were relevant to defendant's claim that he was entitled to qualified immunity, pursuant to N.Y. Not-for-Profit Corp. Law § 720-a, and held that defendant's claim of qualified immunity under § 720-a should be stricken if he did not provide those documents. Samide v Roman Catholic Diocese of Brooklyn (2004, A.D., 2d Dept) 773 N.Y.S.2d 116

Both this section and CPLR § 3211 (a)(11) provide qualified immunity to members of volunteer, not-for-profit organizations from liability absent a showing of gross negligence. Plaintiffs, asserting a cause of action against a tenants' association for negligence, breach of contract, and misrepresentation, have failed to plead a cause of action for "gross negligence." Kofin v Court Plaza, 2009 NY Slip Op 50876U (NY Cty Sup Ct April 9, 2009).

Complaint could not proceed against the individual defendants, who were entitled to qualified immunity pursuant to N.Y. Not-for-Profit Corp. Law § 720-a, in view of the affidavit by the foundation's chairman and director establishing that they served without compensation, and because, as provided by N.Y. C.P.L.R. 3211(a)(11), there was no "reasonable probability" that their conduct constituted gross negligence or was intended to cause harm; although the chairman was not the chief financial officer (CFO) of the foundation, the Civil Practice Law and Rules did not require that it be the CFO who submitted a letter, but, rather, stated only that the evidence "may consist" of a letter from the CFO. Thome v Alexander & Louisa Calder Found. (2009, App Div, 1st Dept) 890 NYS2d 16.

§ 721. Nonexclusivity of statutory provisions for indemnification of directors and officers

The indemnification and advancement of expenses granted pursuant to, or provided by, this article shall not be deemed exclusive of any other rights to which a director or officer seeking indemnification or advancement of expenses may be entitled, whether contained in the certificate of incorporation or the by-laws or, when authorized by such certificate of incorporation or by-laws, (a) a resolution of members, (b) a resolution of directors, or (c) an agreement providing for such indemnification, provided that no indemnification may be made to or on behalf of any director or officer if a judgment or other final adjudication adverse to the director or officer establishes that his acts were committed in bad faith or were the result of active and deliberate dishonesty and were material to the cause of action so adjudicated, or that he personally gained in fact a financial profit or other advantage to which he was not legally entitled. Nothing contained in this article shall affect any rights to indemnification to which corporate personnel other than directors and officers may be entitled by contract or otherwise under law.

History: Add, L 1969, ch 1066, § 1; amd, L 1987, ch 368, § 1, eff July 23, 1987.

Section heading, amd, L 1987, ch 368, § 1, eff July 23, 1987.

§ 722. Authorization for indemnification of directors and officers

(a) A corporation may indemnify any person, made, or threatened to be made, a party to an action or proceeding other than one by or in the right of the corporation to procure a judgment in its favor, whether civil or criminal, including an action by or in the right of any other corporation of any kind, domestic or foreign, or any partnership, joint venture, trust, employee benefit plan or other enterprise, which any director or officer of the corporation served in any capacity at the request of the corporation, by reason of the fact that he, his testator or intestate, was a director or officer of the corporation, or served such other corporation, partnership, joint venture, trust, employee benefit plan or other enterprise in any capacity, against judgments, fines, amounts paid in settlement and reasonable expenses, including attorneys' fees actually and necessarily incurred as a result of such action or proceeding, or any appeal therein, if such director or officer acted, in good faith, for a purpose which he reasonably believed to be in, or, in the case of service for any other corporation or any partnership, joint venture, trust, employee benefit plan or other enterprise, not opposed to, the best interests of the corporation and, in criminal actions or proceedings, in addition, had no reasonable cause to believe that his conduct was unlawful.

(b) The termination of any such civil or criminal action or proceeding by judgment, settlement, conviction or upon a plea of nolo contendere, or its equivalent, shall not in itself create a presumption that any such director or officer did not act, in good faith, for a purpose which he reasonably believed to be in, or, in the case of service for any other corporation or any partnership, joint venture, trust, employee benefit plan or other enterprise, not opposed to, the best interests of the corporation or that he had reasonable cause to believe that his conduct was unlawful.

(c) A corporation may indemnify any person made, or threatened to be made, a party to an action by or in the right of the corporation to procure a judgment in its favor by reason of the fact that he, his testator or intestate, is or was a director or officer of the corporation, or is or was serving at the request of the corporation as a director or officer of any other corporation of any kind, domestic or foreign, of any partnership, joint venture, trust, employee benefit plan or other enterprise, against amounts paid in settlement and reasonable expenses, including attorneys' fees, actually and necessarily incurred by him in connection with the defense or settlement of such action, or in connection with an appeal therein, if such director or officer acted, in good faith, for a purpose which he reasonably believed to be in, or, in the case of service for any other corporation or any partnership, joint venture, trust, employee benefit plan or other enterprise, not opposed to, the best interests of the corporation, except that no indemnification under this paragraph shall be made in respect of (1) a threatened action, or a pending action which is settled or otherwise disposed of, or (2) any claim, issue or matter as to which such person shall have been adjudged to be liable to the corporation, unless and only to the extent that the court in which the action was brought, or, if no action was brought, any court of competent jurisdiction, determines upon application that, in view of all the circumstances of the case, the person is fairly and reasonably entitled to indemnity for such portion of the settlement amount and expenses as the court deems proper.

(d) For the purpose of this section, a corporation shall be deemed to have requested a person to serve an employee benefit plan where the performance by such person of his duties to the corporation also imposes duties on, or otherwise involves services by, such person to the plan or participants or beneficiaries of the plan; excise taxes assessed on a person with respect to an employee benefit plan pursuant to applicable law shall be considered fines; and action taken or omitted by a person with respect to an employee benefit plan in the performance of such person's duties for a purpose reasonably believed by such person to be in the interest of the participants and beneficiaries of the plan shall be deemed to be for a purpose which is not opposed to the best interests of the corporation.

History: Formerly § 723, add, L 1969, ch 1066, § 1, with substance derived from Gen Corp Law § 63; amd, L 1970, ch 847, § 51, L 1977, ch 299, § 2; renumbered § 722 and amd, L 1987, ch 368, §§ 2, 3, eff July 23, 1987; amd, L 2013, ch 549, § 79, eff July 1, 2014.

CASE ANNOTATIONS
1. Generally
2-5. [Reserved for future use]
6. Under former § 722
7. Under former General Corporation Law § 63

1. Generally

Director was not entitled to the advancement of fees under this statute because the documentation presented by the director lacked probative value, the director did not provide any affirmed statement that he acted in good faith, and the director did not make any showing whatsoever as to irreparable harm. Kaloyeros v Fort Schuyler Mgt. Corp., 157 A.D.3d 1152, 69 N.Y.S.3d 739, 2018 N.Y. App. Div. LEXIS 359 (N.Y. App. Div. 3d Dep't 2018).

Director was not entitled to the advancement of fees under this statute because the documentation presented by the director lacked probative value, the director did not provide any affirmed statement that he acted in good faith, and the director did not make any showing whatsoever as to irreparable harm. Kaloyeros v Fort Schuyler Mgt. Corp., 2018 N.Y. App. Div. LEXIS 359 (N.Y. App. Div. 3d Dep't 2018).

CLS N-PCL § 722, regarding corporate indemnification of director or officer, must be construed with corporation's bylaws to determine if bylaws permit indemnification and whether such indemnification would be authorized if director or officer acted in good faith. Vacco v Diamandopoulos (1998, Sup) 185 Misc. 2d 724, 715 N.Y.S.2d 269

Union officers vindicated against charges by union nevertheless cannot recover attorney's fees and expenses, where union is unincorporated association, because, inter alia, N-PCL §§ 722-726 and Bus Corp §§ 724-726 do not apply to union. Doyle v Turner (2000, SD NY) 90 F. Supp. 2d 311, 165 BNA LRRM 2968, affd sub nom Hughley v Local 1199, Drug, Hosp. and Health Care Emples. Union (2000, CA2 NY) 231 F.3d 889, 165 BNA LRRM 2987, later proceeding (2001, SD

NY) 167 BNA LRRM 2839, 144 CCH LC P 11082, later proceeding (2001, SD NY) 2001 US Dist LEXIS 9758

2-5. [Reserved for future use]

6. Under former § 722

Neither section 17 nor section 18 of the Public Officers Law covers officers and directors of Safe Affordable Housing, Inc., a not-for-profit community development corporation organized by the Division of Housing and Community Renewal, even though the officers and directors are also officers and employees of the division. The corporation is authorized to indemnify its officers and directors. 1982 Op Atty Gen July 13 (formal)

7. Under former General Corporation Law § 63

This section, changing the common-law rule that each party pays his own lawyer, is to be construed strictly. Diamond v Diamond (1954) 307 N.Y. 263, 120 N.E.2d 819

As to assessment of attorney's fees against a corporation for legal services in successfully defending an officer of the corporation against charges of misconduct, although some of the language in § 68 might indicate that the attorney is entitled to apply directly for the assessment, the implication from § 63 and other sections of this article is that the assessment and allowance can only be made by way of indemnity or reimbursement to the officer charged with the allegedly objectionable conduct, and that the application must be in his name notwithstanding both he and the attorney are residents of New York. Buchman & Buchman v Lanston Industries, Inc. (1960) 25 Misc. 2d 818, 200 N.Y.S.2d 445

The statute which provides for the reimbursement of litigation expenses of corporation officials in a suit, action or proceeding to which the official is made a party by reason of the fact that he is such a corporation official does not apply to criminal actions. Petition of Schwarz (1950, DC NY) 94 F. Supp. 129

A certificate of incorporation which excepts only cases wherein a director, etc., is adjudged "guilty of wilful misfeasance or malfeasance in the performance of his duties" violates this section which excepts all cases wherein it is adjudged that the director, etc., is "liable for negligence or misconduct in the performance of his duties". 1953 Ops Atty Gen Dec 31

A certificate of incorporation may provide for the indemnification of a director officer or employee for expenses if an action brought against him as such as been settled with the approval of a court. But a certificate which provides for indemnification upon settlement without court approval does not comply with the statute and should be refused filing. 1953 Ops Atty Gen Dec 31

§ 723. Payment of indemnification other than by court award

(a) A person who has been successful, on the merits or otherwise, in the defense of a civil or criminal action or proceeding of the character described in section 722 shall be entitled to indemnification as authorized in such section.

(b) Except as provided in paragraph (a), any indemnification under section 722 or otherwise permitted by section 721, unless ordered by a court under section 724 (Indemnification of directors and officers by a court), shall be made by the corporation, only if authorized in the specific case:

(1) By the board acting by a quorum consisting of directors who are not parties to such action or proceeding upon a finding that the director or officer has met the standard of conduct set forth in section 722 or established pursuant to section 721, as the case may be, or,

(2) If a quorum under subparagraph (1) is not obtainable or, even if obtainable, a quorum of disinterested directors so directs:

(A) By the board upon the opinion in writing of independent legal counsel that indemnification is proper in the circumstances because the applicable standard of conduct set forth in such sections has been met by such director or officer, or

(B) By the members upon a finding that the director or officer has met the applicable standard of conduct set forth in such sections.

(c) Expenses incurred in defending a civil or criminal action or proceeding may be paid by the corporation in advance of the final disposition of such action or proceeding upon receipt of an undertaking by or on behalf of such director or officer to repay such amount as, and to the extent, required by paragraph (a) of section 725.

History: Formerly § 724, add, L 1969, ch 1066, § 1; renumbered § 723 and amd, L 1987, ch 368, §§ 2, 4, eff July 23, 1987; L 1987, ch 368, § 4, eff July 23, 1987.

§ 724.   Indemnification of directors and officers by a court

(a) Notwithstanding the failure of a corporation to provide indemnification, and despite any contrary resolution of the board or of the members in the specific case under section 723 (Payment of indemnification other than by court award), indemnification shall be awarded by a court to the extent authorized under section 722 (Authorization for indemnification of directors and officers), and paragraph (a) of section 723 (Payment of indemnification other than by court award). Application therefor shall be made on notice to the attorney general and may be made, in every case, either:

(1) In the civil action or proceeding in which the expenses were incurred or other amounts were paid, or

(2) To the supreme court in a separate proceeding, in which case the application shall set forth the disposition of any previous application made to any court for the same or similar relief and also reasonable cause for the failure to make application for such relief in the action or proceeding in which the expenses were incurred or other amounts were paid.

(b) The application shall be made in such manner and form as may be required by the applicable rules of court or, in the absence thereof, by direction of a court to which it is made. Such application shall be upon notice to the corporation. The court may also direct that notice be given at the expense of the corporation to the members and such other persons as it may designate in such manner as it may require.

(c) Where indemnification is sought by judicial action, the court may allow a person such reasonable expenses, including attorneys' fees, during the pendency of the litigation as are necessary in connection with his defense therein, if the court shall find that the defendant has by his pleadings or during the course of the litigation raised genuine issues of fact or law.

History: Formerly § 725, add, L 1969, ch 1066, with substance derived from Gen Corp Law §§ 64, 65, 66; amd, L 1970, ch 847, § 52; renumbered § 724 and amd, L 1987, ch 368, §§ 2, 5, eff July 23, 1987; amd, L 2013, ch 549, § 80, eff July 1, 2014.

CASE ANNOTATIONS

1. Generally
2-10. [Reserved for future use]
11. Under former General Corporation Law § 64
12. – Construction and constitutionality
13. – Common law right to reimbursement
14. – Right of individual defendant to reimbursement
15. – – Absence of adjudication of negligence or misconduct
16. – – Conviction on plea of nolo contendere
17. – Action or proceeding
18. – – Martin Act proceeding
19. – – Joinder of causes of action
20. – – Effect of severance
21. – Jurisdiction of United States District Court
22. Under former General Corporation Law § 65
23. Under former General Corporation Law § 66
24. Under former General Corporation Law § 67
25. Under former General Corporation Law § 68

1. Generally

Director was not entitled to the advancement of fees under this statute because the documentation presented by the director lacked probative value, the director did not provide any affirmed statement that he acted in good faith, and the director did not make any showing whatsoever as to irreparable harm. Kaloyeros v Fort Schuyler Mgt. Corp., 157 A.D.3d 1152, 69 N.Y.S.3d 739, 2018 N.Y. App. Div. LEXIS 359 (N.Y. App. Div. 3d Dep't 2018).

Director was not entitled to the advancement of fees under this statute because the documentation presented by the director lacked probative value, the director did not provide any affirmed statement that he acted in good faith, and the director did not make any showing whatsoever as to irreparable harm. Kaloyeros v Fort Schuyler Mgt. Corp., 2018 N.Y. App. Div. LEXIS 359 (N.Y. App. Div. 3d Dep't 2018).

Former university trustees were not entitled to advance indemnification by university for cost of their legal defense in action brought by Attorney General where Board of Regents, in its investigation, found that trustees had engaged in grossly negligent conduct and extreme breaches of fiduciary duties in, inter alia, awarding compensation package to trustee as university president, and permitting conflicts of interest in purchasing goods and services for university. Vacco v Diamandopoulos (1998, Sup) 185 Misc. 2d 724, 715 N.Y.S.2d 269

2-10. [Reserved for future use]
11. Under former General Corporation Law § 64

This section was not applicable to a consolidated action brought in the right of an insurance society by nine out of its more than 1,750,000 policy holders. Imberman v Alexander (1952) 203 Misc 576, 116 N.Y.S.2d 609, affd (1952) 281 A.D. 656, 117 N.Y.S.2d 682, affd (1953) 305 N.Y. 820, 113 N.E.2d 560

This section was not controlling with respect to a petition of attorneys for allowance of fees and expenses against a corporation whose trustees in bankruptcy sued their clients, directors of the corporation, to recover damages for alleged breach of duties owed to the corporation. The question whether allowances could or should be made depended on the Bankruptcy Act. Le Boeuf v Austrian (1957, CA4 Va) 240 F.2d 546, cert den (1957) 353 US 965, 1 L Ed 2d 914, 77 S Ct 1049

12. – Construction and constitutionality

This section, being in derogation of both the common law and the contract rights of the parties, must be strictly construed. Schwarz v General Aniline & Film Corp. (1953) 305 N.Y. 395, 113 N.E.2d 533

Former section 61-a provided for the assessment of the plaintiff's expenses against the corporation and the amount of such expenses could not be added to the amount of the recovery and the entire amount charged to the individual defendants. Masholie v Salvator

(1944) 182 Misc 523, 46 N.Y.S.2d 596, mod on other grounds (1945) 269 A.D. 846, 55 N.Y.S.2d 395

The purpose of § 64 was to broaden the scope of former § 61-a in order to make it consistent with former § 27-a, which was amended and renumbered as § 63. Tichner v Andrews (1949) 193 Misc 1050, 85 N.Y.S.2d 760, app dismd (1949) 275 A.D. 749, 90 N.Y.S.2d 920

Nothing in the legislative history of Section 61-b indicates the intention of the Legislature to make co-extensive Section 61-b and this section. Imberman v Alexander (1952) 203 Misc 576, 116 N.Y.S.2d 609, affd (1952) 281 A.D. 656, 117 N.Y.S.2d 682, affd (1953) 305 N.Y. 820, 113 N.E.2d 560

Enactments awarding attorney's fees and including them in the classification of costs are valid exercises of the police power and are immune from attack upon the ground that they are unconstitutional legislation. Hayman v Morris (1942, Sup) 37 N.Y.S.2d 884, settled (1942) 179 Misc 265, 38 N.Y.S.2d 782

Former section 61-a was not invalid as being extraterritorial legislation as applied to a foreign corporation. Hayman v Morris (1942, Sup) 37 N.Y.S.2d 884, settled (1942) 179 Misc 265, 38 N.Y.S.2d 782

Former section 61-a was constitutional. Shielcrawt v Moffett (1944, Sup) 49 N.Y.S.2d 64, affd (1944) 268 A.D. 352, 51 N.Y.S.2d 188, revd on other grounds (1945) 294 N.Y. 180, 61 N.E.2d 435, 159 ALR 971, reh den (1945) 294 N.Y. 840, 62 N.E.2d 392

13. – Common law right to reimbursement

Directors have no common law right to reimbursement for expenses. Bailey v Bush Terminal Co. (1943, Sup) 46 N.Y.S.2d 877, affd (1944) 267 A.D. 899, 48 N.Y.S.2d 324, affd (1944) 293 N.Y. 735, 56 N.E.2d 739

14. – Right of individual defendant to reimbursement

The court-mandated reimbursement under this article can never be had as to expenses of one defending himself against criminal charges. Schwarz v General Aniline & Film Corp. (1953) 305 N.Y. 395, 113 N.E.2d 533

An officer, director, employee and substantial stockholder of a corporation could not be reimbursed for his litigation expenses from his corporation in a damage action against the corporation and the officer as an individual where the proof showed that the officer could be liable only if he participated as an individual. Spring v Moncrieff (1958) 10 Misc. 2d 731, 173 N.Y.S.2d 86

Directors named as defendants purely for procedural reasons are not entitled to attorney fees under this section. Warnecke v Forty Wall Street Bldg., Inc. (1959) 16 Misc. 2d 467, 183 N.Y.S.2d 925, affd (1961, 1st Dept) 13 A.D.2d 630, 215 N.Y.S.2d 720, reh den (1961, 1st Dept) 13 A.D.2d 760, 216 N.Y.S.2d 674, affd (1962) 11 N.Y.2d 679, 225 N.Y.S.2d 755, 180 N.E.2d 909 and (superseded by statute as stated in Schmidt v Magnetic Head Corp. (1983, 2d Dept) 97 A.D.2d 151, 468 N.Y.S.2d 649)

If a defendant seeks to impose upon a corporation the responsibility of meeting the expenses of contesting an action against him, it is an indispensable condition that the corporation have been a party defendant to the action by reason of his being or having been a director or officer or employee of the corporation. People v Uran Mining Corp. (1960) 26 Misc. 2d 957, 206 N.Y.S.2d 455, affd (1961, 4th Dept) 13 A.D.2d 419, 216 N.Y.S.2d 985

Under this section providing for and authorizing reimbursement and compensation, there is no reason why the successful defendants in a derivative stockholders' action should not have the benefit of this enactment even though an award was also made to plaintiffs or their counsel. Cohn v Columbia Pictures Corp. (1952, Sup) 117 N.Y.S.2d 809

15. – – Absence of adjudication of negligence or misconduct

The words "negligence or misconduct" as used in this section refer back to sections 60 and 61, setting up civil actions by or on behalf of corporations against their officers or directors who have injured the corporation by wrongdoing or inattention to duty. Schwarz v General Aniline & Film Corp. (1953) 305 N.Y. 395, 113 N.E.2d 533

This section, read in conjunction with § 61-b, authorizes assessment of "reasonable expenses, including attorney's fees, actually and necessarily incurred in connection with the defense of" a stockholder's derivative suit by an individual defendant where there has been no adjudication rendering him liable for negligence or misconduct, and such a defendant is accordingly entitled to apply for such an assessment where the action has been dismissed by reason of plaintiff's failure to give security for expenses pursuant to an order under § 61-b. Tyler v Gas Consumers Asso. (1962) 35 Misc. 2d 801, 231 N.Y.S.2d 15

16. – – Conviction on plea of nolo contendere

A conviction upon a plea of nolo contendere was an adjudication that the director was liable for misconduct in the performance of his duties within the statute. Schwarz v General Aniline & Film Corp. (1951) 198 Misc 1046, 102 N.Y.S.2d 325, affd (1952) 279 A.D. 996, 112 N.Y.S.2d 146, affd (1953) 305 N.Y. 395, 113 N.E.2d 533

17. – Action or proceeding

Section 65, the complement of this section, being thus limited to a basic civil action or proceeding, the legislative intention, therefore, clearly was to limit similarly this section to a civil action or proceeding. Schwarz v General Aniline & Film Corp. (1953) 305 N.Y. 395, 113 N.E.2d 533

18. – – Martin Act proceeding

The fact alone that a petitioner, seeking to recover reasonable expenses, including attorney's fees, incurred in defending Martin Act proceedings involving his acts as a director and officer of a corporation, was successful in defending the underlying suit, it not sufficient to require granting of his petition, as against the receiver who was not a party. People v Uran Mining Corp. (1961, 4th Dept) 13 A.D.2d 419, 216 N.Y.S.2d 985

In connection with an application by an officer and director of a corporation for reimbursement of expenses, under this section, incurred in defending Martin Act proceedings against the corporation, a Referee's finding that petitioner was only a truck driver who was hired to operate and maintain motor vehicles would not aid his position where he was likewise an officer and director at the scene of field operations which were the subject of the Martin Act proceeding, knew or should have known what was going on, and lent his name and activities to fraudulent operations of the corporation. People v Uran Mining Corp. (1961, 4th Dept) 14 A.D.2d 481, 216 N.Y.S.2d 992

19. – – Joinder of causes of action

Sections 61-b, 64, apply where the complaint alleges several causes of action for the benefit of the corporation notwithstanding the fact that some causes of action alleged in the complaint appear to be personal to the plaintiff. Sherman v P & Q Shops, Inc. (1949) 275 A.D. 788, 87 N.Y.S.2d 759

20. – – Effect of severance

Upon severance of an action each cause of action becomes a separate action and terminates in a distinct judgment and this must be considered in the award of reasonable expenses under this section. Diamond v Davis (1945, Sup) 62 N.Y.S.2d 175

21. – Jurisdiction of United States District Court

The United States District Court had no jurisdiction of an application under this article for expenses and attorney's fees incurred by them in the defense of an action brought by the trustees of a corporation in reorganization although the petitioners successfully defended themselves in that court for their conduct as stockholders, officers and directors. The award of allowances was exclusively for the reorganization court. Austrian v Williams (1954, CA2 NY) 216 F.2d 278, cert den (1955) 348 US 953, 99 L Ed 745, 75 S Ct 441

22. Under former General Corporation Law § 65

The court-mandated reimbursement under this article can never be had as to expenses of one defending himself against criminal charges. Schwarz v General Aniline & Film Corp. (1953) 305 N.Y. 395, 113 N.E.2d 533

This section, the complement of section 64, being thus limited to a basic civil action or proceeding, the legislative intention therefore clearly was to limit similarly section 64 to a civil action or proceeding. Schwarz v General Aniline & Film Corp. (1953) 305 N.Y. 395, 113 N.E.2d 533

Assessment and award to stockholders of reasonable expenses incurred in prosecution of actions on behalf of the corporation is incidental to the action and is properly applied for therein. The rule that a proceeding to fix attorney's fees is a special proceeding does not apply to such actions. Smith v Bradlee (1942, Sup) 37 N.Y.S.2d 512, mod on other grounds (1942) 265 A.D. 931, 38 N.Y.S.2d 379

The statute which provides for the reimbursement of litigation expenses of corporation officials in a suit, action or proceeding to which the official is made a party by reason of the fact that he is such a corporation official does not apply to criminal actions. Petition of Schwarz (1950, DC NY) 94 F. Supp. 129

No assessment of expenses could be effected under former § 61-a without approval of the court. 1942 Ops Atty Gen Feb 10

23. Under former General Corporation Law § 66

This section does not offend the due process clause of the national and state constitution in failing to provide for the giving of notice to the corporation, or for opportunity to be properly represented and heard. Hayman v Morris (1942, Sup) 37 N.Y.S.2d 884, settled (1942) 179 Misc 265, 38 N.Y.S.2d 782

24. Under former General Corporation Law § 67

Where there is doubt as to whether the judgments against the individual defendants will be substantially or wholly collected the fixation of the allowance for the plaintiff's attorney should be deferred until it can be determined if the corporation has benefited. Masholie v Salvator (1945) 269 A.D. 846, 55 N.Y.S.2d 395

Plaintiffs who create fund for benefit of corporation are entitled to their expenses and reasonable attorneys' and accountants' fees out of fund; former § 61-a was declaratory in this respect. Neuberger v Barrett (1942) 180 Misc 222, 39 N.Y.S.2d 575

To warrant assessment of expenses against corporations pursuant to former § 61-a, corporations must have been benefited. Masholie v Salvator (1944) 182 Misc 523, 46 N.Y.S.2d 596, mod on other grounds (1945) 269 A.D. 846, 55 N.Y.S.2d 395

Former § 61-a was intended to reward, out of corporate treasury, those who either brought money to the treasury or prevented others from taking money out of it. Drivas v Lekas (1944) 182 Misc 567, 48 N.Y.S.2d 785

A successful party was entitled to allowance of expenses under former § 61-a regardless of specific demand therefor in complaint on principle that those sharing benefits should share expenses of producing benefit. Gildener v Lynch (1945) 184 Misc 427, 54 N.Y.S.2d 827

A vindication on the merits is not a condition precedent to granting an application for assessment of expenses allowed by § 64. A dismissal of an action for failure to furnish security for cost is a sufficient determination that the defendant has been successful in whole or in part as required by § 67. Tichner v Andrews (1949) 193 Misc 1050, 85 N.Y.S.2d 760, app dismd (1949) 275 A.D. 749, 90 N.Y.S.2d 920

Since this section permits a party to be reimbursed for expenses where successful either "in whole or in part," the fact that he has only been partially successful at the stage of trial when plaintiff is required to give security pursuant to § 61-b, and has been ordered to account with respect to certain matters, will not entitle plaintiff to an order cancelling a prior order requiring the posting of security pursuant to § 61-b. Sorin v Shahmoon Industries, Inc. (1962) 34 Misc. 2d 1008, 231 N.Y.S.2d 6

Under this section the only test for the granting of allowances is that of success in the prosecution or defense of the action. The creation or production of a fund is not a prerequisite for an award of compensation for services. Bysheim v Miranda (1943, Sup) 45 N.Y.S.2d 473

A certificate of incorporation may provide for the indemnification of a director, officer or employee for expenses if an action brought against him as such has been settled with the approval of a court. But a certificate which provides for indemnification upon settlement without court approval does not comply with the statute and should be refused filing. 1953 Ops Atty Gen Dec 31

25. Under former General Corporation Law § 68

As to assessment of attorney's fees against a corporation for legal services in successfully defending an officer of the corporation against charges of misconduct, although some of the language in § 68 might indicate that the attorney is entitled to apply directly for the assessment, the implication from § 63 and other sections of this article is that the assessment and allowance can only be made by way of indemnity or reimbursement to the officer charged with the allegedly objectionable conduct, and that the application must be in his name notwithstanding both he and the attorney are residents of New York. Buchman & Buchman v Lanston Industries, Inc. (1960) 25 Misc. 2d 818, 200 N.Y.S.2d 445

§ 725.   Other provisions affecting indemnification of directors and officers

(a) All expenses incurred in defending a civil or criminal action or proceeding which are advanced by the corporation under paragraph (c) of section 723 (Payment of indemnification other than by court award) or allowed by a court under paragraph (c) of section 724 (Indemnification of directors and officers by a court) shall be repaid in case the person receiv-

ing such advancement or allowance is ultimately found, under the procedure set forth in this article, not to be entitled to indemnification or, where indemnification is granted, to the extent the expenses so advanced by the corporation or allowed by the court exceed the indemnification to which he is entitled.

(b) No indemnification, advancement or allowance shall be made under this article in any circumstance where it appears:

(1) That the indemnification would be inconsistent with the law of the jurisdiction of incorporation of a foreign corporation which prohibits or otherwise limits such indemnification; or

(2) That the indemnification would be inconsistent with a provision of the certificate of incorporation, a by-law, a resolution of the board or of the members, an agreement or other proper corporate action, in effect at the time of the accrual of the alleged cause of action asserted in the threatened or pending action or proceeding in which the expenses were incurred or other amounts were paid, which prohibits or otherwise limits indemnification; or

(3) If there has been a settlement approved by the court, that the indemnification would be inconsistent with any condition with respect to indemnification expressly imposed by the court in approving the settlement.

(c) If any expenses or other amounts are paid by way of indemnification, otherwise than by court order or action by the members, the corporation shall prepare a statement specifying the persons paid, the amounts paid, and the nature and status at the time of such payment of the litigation or threatened litigation, and

(1) Not later than the next annual meeting of members, unless such meeting is held within three months from the date of such payment, and, in any event, within fifteen months of the date of such payment, shall mail the statement to its members of record entitled at the time to vote for the election of directors; or

(2) If the corporation has no members, shall include the statement in the records of the corporation open to public inspection, or

(3) If the corporation is a cemetery corporation, as defined in paragraph (a) of section 1502 (Definitions), which term, for the purposes of this section, shall include a religious corporation having members, (i) by including the statement required by this paragraph or paragraph (d) of section 726 (Insurance for indemnification of directors and officers), as the case may be in the records of the corporation open to public inspection; (ii) by including the information required by the statement in any notice published pursuant to the provisions of section 605 (Notice of meeting of members), except as otherwise provided by law; (iii) by enclosing the statement with the notice of annual meeting if such notice is in fact mailed to the mem-

bers; and (iv) by raising the issue for approval at the next annual meeting of the members.

(d) If any action with respect to indemnification of directors and officers is taken by way of amendment of the by-laws, resolution of directors, or by agreement, then the corporation shall, not later than the next annual meeting of members, unless such meeting is held within three months from the date of such action, and, in any event, within fifteen months from the date of such action, mail to its members of record at the time entitled to vote for the election of directors a statement specifying the action taken. If the corporation has no members, the statement shall be included in the records of the corporation open to public inspection.

(e) The provisions of this article relating to indemnification of directors and officers and insurance therefor shall apply to domestic corporations and foreign corporations conducting activities in this state, except as provided in section 1321 (Exemption from certain provisions).

History: Formerly § 726, add, L 1969, ch 1066, with substance derived from Gen Corp Law §§ 63, 67, 68; renumbered § 725 and amd, L 1987, ch 368, §§ 2, 6, eff July 23, 1987; L 1970, ch 847, § 53; L 1987, ch 368, § 6, eff July 23, 1987; L 1988, ch 389, § 1, eff July 29, 1988,2, eff July 29, 1988.

§ 726.   Insurance for indemnification of directors and officers

(a) Subject to paragraph (b), a corporation shall have power to purchase and maintain insurance:

(1) To indemnify the corporation for any obligation which it incurs as a result of the indemnification of directors and officers under the provisions of this article, and

(2) To indemnify directors and officers in instances in which they may be indemnified by the corporation under the provisions of this article, and

(3) To indemnify directors and officers in instances in which they may not otherwise be indemnified by the corporation under the provisions of this article provided the contract of insurance covering such directors and officers provides, in a manner acceptable to the superintendent of insurance, for a retention amount and for co-insurance.

(b) No insurance under paragraph (a) may provide for any payment, other than cost of defense, to or on behalf of any director or officer:

(1) if a judgment or other final adjudication adverse to the insured director or officer establishes that his acts of active and deliberate dishonesty were material to the cause of action so adjudicated, or that he personally gained in fact a financial profit or other advantage to which he was not legally entitled, or

(2) in relation to any risk the insurance of which is prohibited under the insurance law of this state.

(c) Insurance under any or all subparagraphs of paragraph (a) may be included in a single contract or supplement thereto. Retrospective rated contracts are prohibited.

(d) The corporation shall, within the time and to the persons provided in paragraph (c) of section 725 (Other provisions affecting indemnification of directors and officers), mail a statement in respect to any insurance it has purchased or renewed under this section, specifying the insurance carrier, date of the contract, cost of the insurance, corporate positions insured, and a statement explaining all sums, not previously reported in a statement to members, paid under any indemnification insurance contract. Notwithstanding any other provision of law, a cemetery corporation or a religious corporation having members which purchases or renews any insurance under this section after the effective date of the act which added this sentence to this paragraph, which corporation had two hundred fifty or more interments in the calendar year preceding such purchase or renewal, shall mail the statement required by this section to every person to whom a care notice or solicitation for services has been sent during such calendar year and to every person to whom a notice of annual meeting was mailed during such calendar year, but in no event to less than ten per centum of the lot owners of record during such calendar year. Such corporation shall not be required to mail such statement during any subsequent year, unless such corporation elects to mail notices of annual meeting to its members in which event the statement shall be enclosed as provided in clause (iii) of paragraph (c)(3) of section 725 (Other provisions affecting indemnification of directors and officers). A corporation having less than two hundred fifty interments in the calendar year preceding such purchase or renewal shall not be required to mail such statement unless such corporation elects to mail notices of annual meeting to its members in which event the statement shall be enclosed as provided in clause (iii) of paragraph (c)(3) of section 725 (Other provisions affecting indemnification of directors and officers).

(e) This section is the public policy of this state to spread the risk of corporate management, notwithstanding any other general or special law of this state or of any other jurisdiction, including the federal government.

History: Formerly § 727, add, L 1970, ch 847, § 54; renumbered § 726 and amd, L 1987, ch 368, § 2, eff July 23, 1987; L 1987, ch 368, § 7; L 1988, ch 389, § 3, eff July 29, 1988; L 2011, ch 62, § 104 (Part A), eff Oct 3, 2011.

CASE ANNOTATIONS

Neither section 17 nor section 18 of the Public Officers Law covers officers and directors of Safe Affordable Housing, Inc., a not-for-profit community development corporation organized by the Division of Housing and Community Renewal, even though the officers and directors are also officers and employees of the division. The corporation is authorized to indemnify its officers and directors. 1982 Op Atty Gen July 13 (formal)

§ 727.   [Renumbered]

History: Add, L 1970, ch 847, § 54; renumbered § 726, L 1987, ch 368, § 2, eff July 23, 1987

ARTICLE 8
AMENDMENTS AND CHANGES

History: Add, L 1969, ch 1066, § 1, eff Sept 1, 1970.

§ 801.   Right to amend certificate of incorporation

(a) A corporation may amend its certificate of incorporation, from time to time, in any and as many respects as may be desired, if such amendment contains only such provisions as might be lawfully contained in an original certificate of incorporation filed at the time of making such amendment.

(b) In particular, and without limitation upon such general power of amendment, a corporation may amend its certificate of incorporation, from time to time, so as:

(1) To change its corporate name.

(2) To enlarge, limit or otherwise change its corporate purposes.

(3) To strike out, change or add any provision not inconsistent with this chapter or any other statute relating to the affairs of the corporation, its rights or powers or the rights or powers of its members, directors or officers, including any provision required or permitted to be set forth in the by-laws.

(4) To extend its duration, or revive its existence if it has ceased to exist because of the expiration of its period of duration. A corporation may not however reduce its corporate duration.

(5) To specify, change or revoke the voting rights of its directors or members or of any class of members.

(6) To specify or change the location of the office of the corporation.

(7) To specify or change the post office address to which the secretary of state shall mail a copy of any process against the corporation served upon him.

(8) To make, revoke or change the designation of a registered agent, or to specify or change the address of its registered agent.

(9) To authorize the issuance of capital certificates and to fix the face value and terms of such certificates and the rights and privileges of their holders and the manner in which the terms, rights and privileges may be amended and to confer upon the holders of such certificates the right to vote in the election of directors and upon any other matters as may be set forth.

(c) A corporation created by special act may accomplish any or all amendments permitted in this article, in the manner and subject to the conditions provided in this article.

History: Add, L 1969, ch 1066, § 1, eff Sept 1, 1970, with substance derived from Gen Corp Law §§ 40, 45, 49, and Mem Corp Law § 30.

Par (b), subpar (7), amd, L 1984, ch 438, § 2, eff Aug 18, 1984.

CASE ANNOTATIONS

1-5. [Reserved for future use]
6. Under former Membership Corporations Law § 30
7. Under former General Corporation Law § 40
8. Under former General Corporation Law § 49
1-5. [Reserved for future use]
6. Under former Membership Corporations Law § 30

The vested rights of members are not violated by an amendment to the certificate of incorporation. In re Walker (1937) 276 N.Y. 567, 12 N.E.2d 579

Firemen's Benevolent Fund Association of the City of Mount Vernon, which is a domestic corporation created in 1894 by special act, constitutes a membership corporation by virtue of the General Corporation Law as it existed before and after the Association's creation and, thus, Association was authorized to amend its certificate of incorporation in 1930 to restrict membership to volunteer firemen. Crohn v Firemen's Benevolent Fund Asso. (1973) 79 Misc. 2d 536, 359 N.Y.S.2d 599

By changing its membership requirements from members of any fire company to volunteer members the Firemen's Benevolent Fund Association of the City of Mount Vernon did not unlawfully discriminate against professional firemen individually or as a class. Crohn v Firemen's Benevolent Fund Asso. (1973) 79 Misc. 2d 536, 359 N.Y.S.2d 599

A corporation incorporated under the Mem Corp Law, having for its principal objects the establishment and maintenance of a hospital and home for treatment, care, support, maintenance and education of crippled and atypical children, is not entitled, under this section, to eliminate some objects of the present charter. 1911 Ops Atty Gen 460

A corporation, existing under the provisions of the Mem Corp Law, other than a hospital or similar corporation, may not, by amendment of its charter pursuant to this section acquire authority to engage in the practice of medicine as a corporation other than a hospital or similar corporation. 1935 Ops Atty Gen 229. See also 1935 Ops Atty Gen 373

A membership corporation may not include in its charter purposes the power to act as a trustee. 1936 Ops Atty Gen 206

An agricultural and horticultural corporation must comply with the provisions of the Stock Corporation Law in order to amend its certificate of incorporation so as to eliminate the authorization for issuance of capital stock entitling shareholders to dividends, as distinguished from non-dividend bearing stock. 1950 Ops Atty Gen Sept 27

The conduct of fund-raising activities by volunteer firemen is within the purposes stated in the usual charter provisions of a volunteer fire corporation. 1955 Ops St Compt File #7124

The certificate of incorporation of a volunteer fire company may be amended so as to include a fire district within the territory in which the fire company proposes to act. 1955 Ops St Compt File #7319

7. Under former General Corporation Law § 40

Use of a similar name to that of another corporation cannot be denied where a corporation desires to reincorporate under the same name which it has theretofore borne. People ex rel. United States Grand Lodge of O. B. A. v Payn (1899) 28 Misc 275, 59 N.Y.S. 851, affd (1899) 43 A.D. 621, 60 N.Y.S. 1146, affd (1900) 161 N.Y. 229, 55 N.E. 849

Not-For-Profit Corporation Law

The absence of any element of fraud in the use of the proposed new name bearing similarity to the name of another corporation is not controlling; if there are reasonable grounds to conclude that the granting of the change will result in injury to the complaining corporation it should be denied. In re United States Mortg. Co. (1895) 83 Hun 572, 32 N.Y.S. 11

A corporation does not die or "cease to exist" merely because of a change of name pursuant to this section. Williams Grain Co. v Leval & Co. (1960, CA8 Ark) 277 F.2d 213, 3 FR Serv 2d 474

8. Under former General Corporation Law § 49

The failure of a membership corporation to obtain the necessary approval of the Board of Social Welfare to a certificate of extension of corporate existence is a defect which cannot be corrected by an amendatory certificate or by the Board's nunc pro tunc approval. However, a remedy lies in the filing of a certificate of revival of corporate existence pursuant to General Corporation Law § 49. 1952 Ops Atty Gen Feb 15

§ 802. Authorization of amendment or change, class vote

(a) Amendment or change of the certificate of incorporation shall be authorized:

(1) If there are members entitled to vote thereon, by majority vote of such members at a meeting as provided in paragraph (c) of section 613 (Vote of members).

(2) If there are no members entitled to vote thereon, by vote of a majority of the entire board.

(b) Notwithstanding any provision in the certificate of incorporation or by-laws, members of a class shall be entitled to vote and to vote as a class upon the authorization of an amendment and, in addition to the authorization of the amendment required by paragraph (a)(1), the amendment shall be authorized by majority vote of the members of the class, when the proposed amendment would exclude or limit their right to vote on any matter except as such right may be limited by voting rights given to members of an existing class or of a new class.

(c) Any one or more of the following changes may be authorized by or pursuant to authorization of the board:

(1) To specify or change the location of the office of the corporation.

(2) To specify or change the post office address to which the secretary of state shall mail a copy of any process against the corporation served upon him.

(3) To make, revoke or change the designation of a registered agent, or to specify or change the address of its registered agent.

(d) This section shall not alter the vote required under any other section for the authorization of an amendment referred to therein, nor alter the authority of the board to authorize amendments under any other section.

History: Add, L 1969, ch 1066, § 1, with substance deriving from Gen Corp Law §§ 40, 45, 49 and Mem Corp Law § 30; amd, L 1970, ch 847, § 55, eff Sept 1, 1970; L 1971, ch 1058, § 26, eff Sept 1, 1971; L 1972, ch 961, § 13, eff Sept 1, 1972; L 1983, ch 186, § 5, eff June 30, 1983.

§ 803. Certificate of amendment; contents

(a) To accomplish any amendment, a certificate of amendment entitled "Certificate of amendment of the certificate of incorporation of............ (name of corporation) under section 803 of the Not-for-Profit Corporation Law" shall be signed and delivered to the department of state. It shall set forth:

(1) The name of the corporation and, if it has been changed, the name under which it was formed.

(2) The date its certificate of incorporation was filed by the department of state and the law under which it was formed.

(3) That the corporation is a corporation as defined in subparagraph (a) (5) of section 102 (Definitions).

(4) Each amendment effected thereby, setting forth the subject matter of each provision of the certificate of incorporation which is to be amended or eliminated and the full text of the provision or provisions, if any, which are to be substituted or added.

(5) The manner in which the amendment of the certificate of incorporation was authorized.

(6) A designation of the secretary of state as agent of the corporation upon whom process against it may be served and the post office address within or without this state to which the secretary of state shall mail a copy of any process against it served upon the secretary.

(b) Any number of amendments or changes may be included in one certificate under this section. Such certificate may also include any amendments or changes permitted by other sections and in that case the certificate shall set forth any additional statement required by any other section specifying the contents of a certificate to effect such amendment or change.

History: Add, L 1969, ch 1066, § 1, eff Sept 1, 1970, with substance derived from Gen Corp Law §§ 40, 45, 49 and Mem Corp Law § 30; amd, L 1970, ch 847, § 56, L 1971, ch 1058 § 27, L 1972, ch 961, § 14, L 1973, ch 176, L 1981, ch 564, § 4, L 1982, ch 168, § 3, eff June 8, 1982, L 1983, ch 145, § 2, eff May 23, 1983, L 1985, ch 101, § 2, eff May 21, 1985, L 1998, ch 375, § 37, eff Aug 13, 1998, L 2013, ch 549, § 81, eff July 1, 2014, L 2014, ch 23, § 11, eff July 1, 2014.

§ 803-A. Certificate of change; contents

(a) Any one or more of the changes authorized by paragraph (c) of section 802 (Authorization of amendment or change, class vote) may be accomplished by filing a certificate of change which shall be entitled "Certificate of Change of............ (name of corporation) under section 803-A of the Not-for-Profit Corporation Law" and shall be signed and delivered to the department of state. It shall set forth:

(1) The name of the corporation and if it has been changed, the name under which it was formed.

(2) The date its certificate of incorporation was filed by the department of state.

(3) Each change effected thereby.

(4) The manner in which the change was authorized.

(b) A certificate of change which changes only the post office address to which the secretary of state shall mail a copy of any process against the corporation served upon him or the address of the registered agent, provided such address being changed is the address of a person, partnership or other corporation whose address, as agent, is the address to be changed or who has been designated as registered agent for such corporation, may be signed and delivered to the department of state by such agent. The certificate of change shall set forth the statements required under subparagraphs (1), (2) and (3) of paragraph (a) of this section; that a notice of the proposed change was mailed to the corporation by the party signing the certificate not less than thirty days prior to the date of delivery to the department and that such corporation has not objected thereto; and that the party signing the certificate is the agent of such corporation to whose address the secretary of state is requried to mail copies of any process against the corporation served upon him or the registered agent, if such be the case. A certificate signed and delivered under this paragraph shall not be deemed to effect a change of location of the office of the corporation in whose behalf such certificate is filed.

History: Add, L 1971, ch 1058 § 28, eff Sept 1, 1971; amd, L 1983, ch 186, § 6; L 1984, ch 438, § 3; L 1998, ch 375, § 38, eff Aug 13, 1998; L 1999, ch 172, § 27, eff July 6, 1999.

§ 804.   Approvals, notices and effect

(a) (i) A certificate of amendment shall not be filed if the amendment adds, changes or eliminates a purpose, power or provision the inclusion of which in a certificate of incorporation requires consent or approval of a governmental body or officer or any other person or body, or if the amendment changes the name of a corporation whose certificate of incorporation had such consent or approval endorsed thereon or annexed thereto, unless such consent or approval is no longer required or is endorsed on or annexed to the certificate of amendment. A certificate of amendment adding, changing or eliminating a purpose, power or provision the inclusion of which in a certificate of incorporation requires the incorporator to send such certificate to a governmental body or officer or any other person or body, or if the amendment changes the name of a corporation whose certificate of incorporation was required to be delivered by the incorporator to a governmental body or officer or any other person or body, shall be delivered by the person or entity filing the certificate of amendment within thirty business days after the corporation receives confirmation from the depart-

ment of state that the certificate has been accepted for filing.

(ii) Every certificate of amendment of a charitable corporation which seeks to change or eliminate a purpose or power enumerated in the corporation's certificate of incorporation, or to add a power or purpose not enumerated therein, shall have endorsed thereon or annexed thereto the approval of either (A) the attorney general, or (B) a justice of the supreme court of the judicial district in which the office of the corporation is located. At any time, including if the attorney general does not approve a certificate of amendment submitted pursuant to clause (A) of this subparagraph, or if the attorney general concludes that court review is appropriate, the corporation may apply for approval of the amendment to a justice of the supreme court of the judicial district in which the office of the corporation is located. Any application for approval of a certificate of amendment by the supreme court pursuant to this paragraph shall be on ten days' written notice to the attorney general.

(b) The department of state shall not file a certificate of amendment reviving the existence of a corporation unless the consent or approval of a governmental body or officer or any other person or body required to be endorsed on or annexed to the certificate of incorporation of a corporation formed for similar purposes, is attached thereto, or, if notice to the attorney-general was required prior to the filing of its certificate of incorporation, the certificate of amendment should indicate that such notice has been given as required by law.

(c) The department of state shall not file a certificate of amendment reviving the existence of a corporation if the name of the corporation being revived is not available under section 301 (Corporate name; general) for use by a corporation then being formed under this chapter, unless the certificate of amendment shall change the name to one which is available for such use.

(d) No amendment or change shall affect any existing cause of action in favor of or against the corporation, or any pending suit to which it shall be a party, or the existing rights of persons other than members; and in the event the corporate name shall be changed, no suit brought by or against the corporation under its former name shall abate for that reason.

(e) Notwithstanding any law to the contrary, a certificate of amendment of a corporation whose statement of purposes specifically includes the establishment or operation of a child day care center, as that term is defined in section three hundred ninety of the social services law, shall provide a certified copy of such certificate to the office of children and family services within thirty days after the filing of such certificate with the department of state.

History: Add, L 1969, ch 1066, § 1, eff Sept 1, 1970, with substance derived from Gen Corp Law § 40 and Mem Corp Law § 30; amd, L 1971, ch 1058 § 29, eff Sept 1, 1971, L 1972, ch 961, § 15, L 1993, ch 139, § 2, eff Aug 20, 1993, L 2006, ch 58, § 5 (Part D), eff April 12, 2006, L 2010, ch 198, § 3, eff July 15, 2010, L 2013, ch 549, § 82, eff July 1, 2014.

CASE ANNOTATIONS

1. Generally
2-5. [Reserved for future use]
6. Under former Membership Corporations Law § 30

1. Generally

Because The Not-For Profit Corporation Law Provisions governing Type B corporations, expressly incorporates a quasi-cy pres principle with respect to both the administration and use of assets (N-PCL §§ 513(6), 522) and the transfer of assets on dissolution (N-PCL §§ 1005(a)(3)(A), 1008(a)(15)), N-PCL § 804, which permits amendment of the certificate of incorporations of such corporation, cannot be construed to authorize an amendment inconsistent with the purposes for which funds were given to the corporation without compliance with such quasi-cy pres principles. Thus, the amendment of the certificate of incorporation of defendant The Knapp Foundation, a Type B not-for-profit corporation, authorizing its trustees "in their absolute discretion" to transfer its assets to another foundation for the purpose of furthering the good works of that organization without the Supreme Court passing upon said quasi-cy pres considerations, was improper. Alco Gravure, Inc. v Knapp Foundation (1985) 64 N.Y.2d 458, 490 N.Y.S.2d 116, 479 N.E.2d 752, motion den (1986) 67 N.Y.2d 717, 499 N.Y.S.2d 942, 490 N.E.2d 861

Not-for-profit hospitals and not-for-profit corporations that sought to affiliate under newly created common parent corporation, which would assume certain statutory powers under Not-For-Profit Corporation Law including power to appoint and/or remove directors and approve amendments to respective certificates of incorporation and bylaws, were properly granted summary judgment declaring that proposed affiliation did not require notification to Attorney General and court approval under CLS N-PCL §§ 510, 511, 804 and 805. Nathan Littauer Hosp. Ass'n v Spitzer (2001, 3d Dept) 287 A.D.2d 202, 734 N.Y.S.2d 671, motion gr (NY) 2002 N.Y. LEXIS 942 and app den (NY) 2002 N.Y. LEXIS 940

Delineation of nonprofit corporate powers was not an addition of powers triggering review and approval procedures; Reservation of enumerated powers to sole corporate member did not change, eliminate or add to corporate powers warranting judicial intervention. Nathan Littauer Hosp. Ass'n v Spitzer (2001, 3d Dept) 287 A.D.2d 202, 734 N.Y.S.2d 671, motion gr (2002, NY) 2002 N.Y. LEXIS 942 and app den (2002, NY) 2002 N.Y. LEXIS 940

Although the Attorney-General failed to appear on two occasions when the court was to consider an amendment to the certificate of incorporation of petitioner not-for-profit corporation, petitioner may not compel the Attorney-General to respond to petitioner's application by a CPLR article 78 proceeding in the nature of mandamus since mandamus does not lie in the absence of a showing that the Attorney-General failed to perform a duty enjoined upon him by law and there is no statute or other requirement obligating the Attorney-General to furnish a waiver or consent in connection with the approval of an amendment to the certificate of incorporation of a not-for-profit corporation; the applicable statutes (Not-For-Profit Corporation Law, § 804, subd [a]; § 404, subd [a]) require only that the Attorney-General be given notice that a not-for-profit corporation is applying to an appropriate Justice to amend its certificate of incorporation, and the failure of the Attorney-General to appear after proper service of the notice should result in the court's approval of the application in the absence of an apparent defect in the certificate. Electrical Industry Ass'n v State (1979) 102 Misc. 2d 494, 423 N.Y.S.2d 576

New York Attorney General must be given notice of any application for approval to dilute the influence of a college and its president on the governance of a not-for-profit foundation, in effect transforming the foundation into an independent entity unaccountable to the college. Herbert H. Lehman College Found., Inc. v Fernandez (2002, 1st Dept) 292 A.D.2d 227, 739 N.Y.S.2d 375

A subsidiary of the Urban Development Corporation may incorporate under the Business Corporation Law without forfeiting its public status. The subsidiary may not pay profits to private investors, and upon dissolution of the corporation, the assets belong to the State. 1980 Op Atty Gen Oct. 20

2-5. [Reserved for future use]
6. Under former Membership Corporations Law § 30

Where the original certificate of incorporation as a membership corporation was such as to require the consent of the Commissioner of Education under subd 2 of § 1, as specifying a purpose of establishing training and research in the field of psychoanalysis, an amendment of the certificate, under this section, which made it a purpose of the corporation to maintain an institution of learning for instruction of students in psychoanalysis and related subjects, would still require approval of the Board of Regents under § 224. National Psychological Asso. for Psychoanalysis, Inc. v Allen (1961, 3d Dept) 14 A.D.2d 190, 217 N.Y.S.2d 893, motion gr (1962) 11 N.Y.2d 642

An increase of the board of a membership corporation did not become legally effective until the filing of the certificate in the proper offices required by former § 14 from which this section is in part derived. Cabana v Holstein-Friesian Ass'n (1920) 112 Misc 262, 182 N.Y.S. 658, mod (1921) 196 A.D. 842, 188 N.Y.S. 277, affd (1922) 233 N.Y. 644, 135 N.E. 953

The statute of limitations runs from the time an application for a proposed amended certificate of incorporation is denied rather than from the date of a subsequent hearing granted as a matter of courtesy by the Board of Social Welfare at which the original decision was adhered to, and accordingly an application for an order under Civil Practice Act §§ 1283 et seq. annulling the determination which was made more than four months after the original disapproval is barred. Italian Hospitalization Soc. v State Department of Social Welfare (1942) 178 Misc 183, 34 N.Y.S.2d 385

Where the Board of Social Welfare has refused to permit a membership corporation to amend its certificate of incorporation to permit it to operate a hospital, the court should not substitute its judgment for that of the Board where it clearly appears that there was no arbitrary or malicious exercise of power. Italian Hospitalization Soc. v State Department of Social Welfare (1942) 178 Misc 183, 34 N.Y.S.2d 385

When the statute refers to "each public office", what is meant is the office of the Secretary of State and the office of the clerk of the county in which the corporation is located as specified in its certificate of incorporation. In re Daughters of Bilitis, Inc. (1967) 52 Misc. 2d 1075, 277 N.Y.S.2d 709

§ 805. Restated certificate of incorporation

(a) A corporation, when authorized by the board, may restate in a single certificate the text of its certificate of incorporation without making any amendment or change thereby, except that it may include any one or more of the amendments or changes which may be authorized by the board without a vote of members under this chapter. Alternatively, a corporation may restate in a single certificate the text of its certificate of incorporation as amended thereby to effect any one or more of the amendments or changes authorized by this chapter, when authorized as required by section 802 (Authorization of amendment or change, class vote).

(b) A restated certificate of incorporation, entitled "Restated certificate of incorporation of............ (name of corporation) under section 805 of the Not-for-Profit Corporation Law", shall be signed and delivered to the department of state. It shall set forth:

(1) The name of the corporation and, if it has been changed, the name under which it was formed.

(2) The date its certificate of incorporation was filed by the department of state.

(3) If the restated certificate restates the text of the certificate of incorporation without making any amendment or change, then a statement that the text

of the certificate of incorporation is thereby restated without amendment or change to read as therein set forth in full.

(4) If the restated certificate restates the text of the certificate of incorporation as amended or changed thereby, then a statement that the certificate of incorporation is amended or changed to effect one or more of the amendments or changes authorized by this chapter, specifying each such amendment or change and that the text of the certificate of incorporation is thereby restated as amended or changed to read as therein set forth in full.

(5) The manner in which the restatement of the certificate of incorporation was authorized.

(c) A restated certificate need not include statements as to the incorporator or incorporators, or the first directors.

(d) Any amendment or change under this section shall be subject to any other section, not inconsistent with this section, which would be applicable if a separate certificate were filed to effect such amendment or change.

(e) Notwithstanding that the corporation would be required by any statute to secure from any supreme court justice, governmental body or officer, or other person or body, any consent or approval to the filing of its certificate of incorporation or a certificate of amendment, such consent or approval shall not be required with respect to the restated certificate if such certificate makes no amendment and if any previously required consent or approval had been secured.

(f) Upon filing by the department, the original certificate of incorporation shall be superseded and the restated certificate of incorporation, including any amendments and changes made thereby, shall be the certificate of incorporation of the corporation.

History: Add, L 1969, ch 1066, eff Sept 1, 1970; amd, L 1971, ch 1058 § 30, eff Sept 1, 1971; L 1981, ch 210, § 4, eff June 9, 1981,5, eff June 9, 1981,6, eff June 9, 1981; L 1998, ch 375, § 39, eff Aug 13, 1998.

CASE ANNOTATIONS

Not-for-profit hospitals and not-for-profit corporations that sought to affiliate under newly created common parent corporation, which would assume certain statutory powers under Not-For-Profit Corporation Law including power to appoint and/or remove directors and approve amendments to respective certificates of incorporation and bylaws, were properly granted summary judgment declaring that proposed affiliation did not require notification to Attorney General and court approval under CLS N-PCL §§ 510, 511, 804 and 805. Nathan Littauer Hosp. Ass'n v Spitzer (2001, 3d Dept) 287 A.D.2d 202, 734 N.Y.S.2d 671, motion gr (NY) 2002 N.Y. LEXIS 942 and app den (NY) 2002 N.Y. LEXIS 940

Not-for-profit hospitals and not-for-profit corporations that sought to affiliate under newly created common parent corporation, which would assume certain statutory powers under Not-For-Profit Corporation Law including power to appoint and/or remove directors and approve amendments to respective certificates of incorporation and bylaws, were properly granted summary judgment declaring that proposed affiliation did not require notification to Attorney General and court approval under CLS N-PCL §§ 510, 511, 804 and 805.

Nathan Littauer Hosp. Ass'n v Spitzer (2001, 3d Dept) 287 A.D.2d 202, 734 N.Y.S.2d 671, motion gr (NY) 2002 N.Y. LEXIS 942 and app den (NY) 2002 N.Y. LEXIS 940

ARTICLE 9
MERGER OR CONSOLIDATION

History: Add, L 1969, ch 1066, § 1, eff Sept 1, 1970.

§ 901.   Power of merger or consolidation

(a) Two or more domestic corporations may, as provided in this chapter:

(1) Merge into a single corporation which shall be one of the constituent corporations; or

(2) Consolidate into a single corporation which shall be a new corporation to be formed pursuant to the consolidation.

(b) Whenever used in this article:

(1) "Merger" means a procedure of the character described in subparagraph (a)(1).

(2) "Consolidation" means a procedure of the character described in subparagraph (a)(2).

(3) "Constituent corporation" means an existing corporation that is participating in the merger or consolidation with one or more other corporations.

(4) "Surviving corporation" means the constitutent corporation into which one or more other constituent corporations are merged.

(5) "Consolidated corporation" means the new corporation in which two or more constituent corporations are consolidated.

History: Add, L 1969, ch 1066, § 1, eff Sept 1, 1970, with substance derived from Mem Corp Law § 50.

CASE ANNOTATIONS

1-5. [Reserved for future use]
6. Under former Membership Corporations Law § 50

1-5. [Reserved for future use]
6. Under former Membership Corporations Law § 50
Where a consolidation agreement does not comply with the requirements of the Religious Corporation Law § 12 or with Membership Corporations Law § 7, it is ultra vires, and a single dissenting member of either corporation may maintain an action to set aside the agreement. Davis v Congregation Beth Tephilas Israel (1899) 40 A.D. 424, 57 N.Y.S. 1015

Not-For-Profit
Corporation Law

A Young Women's Association of a city, incorporated pursuant to L 1848 c 319, may, by permission of the court, consolidate with the Young Women's Christian Association of the city, incorporated under this law, although the latter corporation is to consist of persons conforming to Protestant evangelical denominations while some of the members of the former corporation do not adhere to a "Protestant" religion. In re Young Women's Ass'n (1915) 169 A.D. 734, 155 N.Y.S. 838

Mandamus will not issue to compel the respondent to accept an executed certificate of consolidation of a corporation created under provisions of the Stock Corporation Law with one created under provisions of the Membership Corporation Law, since that writ will only issue to compel performance of a prescribed act to which the petitioner had a clear legal right. Debs Memorial Radio Fund, Inc. v Lomenzo (1966) 50 Misc. 2d 51, 269 N.Y.S.2d 632

An application by seven incorporated domestic membership corporations for an order approving an agreement for consolidation was granted, notwithstanding opposition by respondents relative to the alleged non-exchange of audited financial statements and statements of contingent liabilities, where the court found that by incorporation by reference of various exhibits to the moving petition the property and the manner in which it was held, all liabilities, and the amount and sources of the annual income of each member corporation had been adequately disclosed. Sackerah Path Girl Scout Council, Inc. v Armstrong (1966) 50 Misc. 2d 883, 272 N.Y.S.2d 34, affd (1966, 2d Dept) 25 A.D.2d 956, 271 N.Y.S.2d 191

An order consolidating membership corporations should be filed with the secretary of state, under Gen Corp Law, § 9. 1912 Ops Atty Gen 353

§ 902.   Plan of merger or consolidation

(a) The board of each corporation proposing to participate in a merger or consolidation under section 901 (Power of merger or consolidation) shall adopt a plan of merger or consolidation, setting forth:

(1) The name of each constituent corporation and if the name of any of them has been changed, the name under which it was formed, and the name of the surviving corporation, or the name or the method of determining it, of the consolidated corporation.

(2) As to each constituent corporation, a description of the membership and holders of any certificates evidencing capital contributions or subventions, including their number, classification, and voting rights, if any.

(3) The terms and conditions of the proposed merger or consolidation, including the manner and basis of converting membership or other interest in each constituent corporation into membership or other interest in the surviving or consolidated corporation, or the cash or other consideration to be paid or delivered in exchange for membership or other interest in each constituent corporation, or a combination thereof.

(4) In case of merger, a statement of any amendments or changes in the certificate of incorporation of the surviving corporation to be effected by such merger; in case of consolidation, all statements required to be included in a certificate of incorporation for a corporation formed under this chapter, except statements as to facts not available at the time the plan of consolidation is adopted by the board.

(5) In case of a merger or consolidation under section 906 (Merger or consolidation of domestic and foreign corporations), a statement of any agreements

required by subparagraph (2)(D) of paragraph (d) thereof.

History: Add, L 1969, ch 1066, § 1, eff Sept 1, 1970, with substance derived from Mem Corp Law § 52.

§ 903.   Approval of plan

(a) The board of each constituent corporation, upon approving such plan of merger or consolidation shall submit such plan to a vote of the members in accordance with the following:

(1) Notice of meeting shall be given to each member whether or not entitled to vote. A copy of the plan of merger or consolidation or an outline of the material features of the plan shall accompany such notice.

(2) The plan of merger or consolidation shall be approved at a meeting of the members by two-thirds vote as provided in paragraph (c) of section 613 (Vote of members).

(3) If any merging or consolidating corporation has no members entitled to vote thereon, a plan of merger or consolidation shall be deemed approved by the members of the corporation when it is adopted by the board of such corporation pursuant to section 902 (Plan of merger or consolidation).

(b) Notwithstanding authorization as provided herein, at any time prior to the filing of the certificate of merger or consolidation, the plan of merger or consolidation may be abandoned pursuant to a provision for such abandonment, if any, contained in the plan of merger or consolidation.

History: Add, L 1969, ch 1066, § 1, eff Sept 1, 1970, with substance derived from Mem Corp Law § 50.

CASE ANNOTATIONS

1-5. [Reserved for future use]
6. Under former Membership Corporations Law § 50
1-5. [Reserved for future use]
6. Under former Membership Corporations Law § 50

Although the votes cast at a meeting of a membership corporation in favor of the consolidation with another membership corporation were not by at least 2/3 of its members entitled to vote thereon and the notice of meeting might have been defective in that it was not given at least 10 days before the meeting and was not signed by an executive officer, former treasurer of one of the consolidated clubs could not claim that consolidation should be upset on those grounds in the light of the fact that he took no steps to litigate his claim until after a lapse of almost a year after said meeting and seven months after the court approved the certificate of consolidation. Liberal Civic Club, Inc. v Poli (1954) 284 A.D. 1057, 135 N.Y.S.2d 814

§ 904.   Certificate of merger or consolidation; contents

(a) After approval of the plan of merger or consolidation unless the merger or consolidation is abandoned in accordance with paragraph (b) of section 903 (Approval of plan) a certificate of merger or consolidation, entitled "Certificate of merger (or consolidation) of............ and............ into (names of corporations) under section 904 of the Not-for-Profit Corporation Law," shall be signed on behalf of each constituent corporation and delivered to the department of state. It shall set forth:

(1) The statements required by subparagraphs (a)(1), (2), and (4) of section 902 (Plan of merger or consolidation).

(2) The effective date of the merger or consolidation if other than the date of filing of the certificate of merger or consolidation by the department of state.

(3) In the case of consolidation, any statement required to be included in a certificate of incorporation formed under this chapter but which was omitted under subparagraph (a)(4) of section 902.

(4) The date when the certificate of incorporation of each constituent corporation was filed by the department of state or, in the case of constituent corporations created by special law, the chapter number and year of passage of such law.

(5) The manner in which the merger or consolidation was authorized with respect to each constituent corporation.

(b) The surviving or consolidated corporation shall thereafter cause a copy of such certificate certified by the department of state, to be filed in the office of the clerk of each county in which the office of a constituent corporation, other than the surviving corporation, is located, and in the office of the official who is the recording officer of each county in this state in which real property of a constituent corporation, other than the surviving corporation, is situated.

History: Add, L 1969, ch 1066, § 1, eff Sept 1, 1970, with substance derived from Mem Corp Law § 50; amd, L 1971, ch 1058 § 31, eff Sept 1, 1971; L 1971, ch 1058, § 31, eff Sept 1, 1971; L 1971, ch 1058 § 31, eff Sept 1, 1971; L 1971, ch 1058, § 31, eff Sept 1, 1971; L 1971, ch 1058 § 31, eff Sept 1, 1971; L 1998, ch 375, § 40, eff Aug 13, 1998.

CASE ANNOTATIONS

Town lacked standing to file N.Y. C.P.L.R. art. 78 proceeding since: (1) it was not an established corporation, since it had filed no incorporation papers with the New York Department of State under N.Y. Bus. Corp. Law §§ 403 and N.Y. Not-for-Profit Corp. Law §§ 403 and 904(a), (2) the state's highest court had not recognized it as a corporation, or as the governing body of the town, (3) the town failed to show that it was the successor corporation to the original incorporated proprietors of the town, (4) a municipal corporation was a political subdivision of the State having only the authority delegated to it by the State under N.Y. Const. art. IX, § 2, and (5) another town specifically included the town, and was a legitimate municipal corporation with the authority to govern the town under N.Y. Town Law § 2. Matter of Town of Montauk, Inc. v Pataki (2007, 2d Dept) 40 App Div 3d 772, 835 NYS2d 447, motion den (2007, 2d Dept) 40 App Div 3d 772, 834 NYS2d 661

§ 905. Effect of merger or consolidation

(a) Upon the filing of the certificate of merger and consolidation by the department of state or on such date subsequent thereto, not to exceed thirty days, as shall be set forth in such certificate, the merger or consolidation shall be effected.

(b) When such merger or consolidation has been effected:

(1) Such surviving or consolidated corporation shall thereafter, consistently with its certificate of incorporation as altered or established by the merger or consolidation, possess all the rights, privileges, immunities, powers and purposes of each of the constituent corporations.

(2) All the property, real and personal, including causes of action and every other asset of each of the constituent corporations, shall vest in such surviving or consolidated corporation without further act or deed, except as otherwise provided in paragraph (b) of section 907 (Approval by the Supreme Court). Except as the court may otherwise direct, as provided in section 8-1.1 of the Estates, Powers and Trusts Law, any disposition made in the will of a person dying domiciled in this state or in any other instrument executed under the laws of this state, taking effect after such merger or consolidation, to or for any of the constituent corporations shall inure to the benefit of the surviving or consolidated corporation. So far as is necessary for that purpose, or for the purpose of a like result with respect to a disposition governed by the law of any other jurisdiction, the existence of each constituent domestic corporation shall be deemed to continue in and through the surviving or consolidated corporation.

(3) The surviving or consolidated corporation shall assume and be liable for all the liabilities, obligations and penalties of each of the constituent corporations. No liability or obligation due or to become due, claim or demand for any cause existing against any such corporation, or any member, officer or director thereof, shall be released or impaired by such merger or consolidation. No action or proceeding, whether civil or criminal, then pending by or against any such constituent corporation, or any member, officer or director thereof, shall abate or be discontinued by such merger or consolidation, but may be enforced, prosecuted, settled or comprised as if such merger or consolidation had not occurred, or such surviving or consolidated corporation may be substituted in such action or special proceeding in place of any constituent corporation.

(4) In the case of a merger, the certificate of incorporation of the surviving corporation shall be automatically amended to the extent, if any, that changes in its certificate of incorporation are set forth in the plan of merger; and, in the case of a consolidation, the statements set forth in the certificate of consolidation and which are required or permitted to be set forth in a certificate of incorporation of a corporation formed under this chapter shall be its certificate of incorporation.

History: Add, L 1969, ch 1066, § 1, eff Sept 1, 1970, with substance derived from Mem Corp Law § 53.

Not-For-Profit Corporation Law

Par (b), subpar (1), amd, L 1970, ch 847, § 57, eff Sept 1, 1970.

Par (b), subpar (2), amd, L 1973, ch 357, eff Sept 1, 1973.

CASE ANNOTATIONS

1. In General
2-5. [Reserved for future use]
6. Under former Membership Corporations Law § 53
1. In General

When the operator of a children's hospital's simply amended its corporate name and purpose after the hospital's assets and facilities were purchased by medical centers, N.Y. Not-for-Profit Corp. Law §§ 1005 and 905 did not apply to a bequest under a charitable trust because the hospital had not been formally dissolved and because there had not been a merger. Matter of Hummel (2006, App Div, 3d Dept) 817 NYS2d 424

2-5. [Reserved for future use]
6. Under former Membership Corporations Law § 53

Where a testatrix provided for a legacy of $5,000 to the Hahnemann Hospital of the City of New York and prior to her death, that hospital merged with a second hospital to form a single corporation known as the Fifth Avenue Hospital, such consolidation being ratified by appropriate order of the supreme court of New York County, and the new corporation has continued the general policy and methods of the named legatee, the legacy is payable to the consolidated corporation. In re Doane's Estate (1925) 124 Misc 663, 208 N.Y.S. 320

A trust created for the benefit of a membership corporation by a will executed in 1927 will not cease upon the subsequent merger of the beneficiary with another membership corporation, in view of the express provisions of this section. In re Hoaglund's Estate (1947) 194 Misc 803, 74 N.Y.S.2d 156, affd (1947) 272 A.D. 1040, 74 N.Y.S.2d 911, affd (1948) 297 N.Y. 920, 79 N.E.2d 746

A gift to a hospital under a 1906 will vested in the consolidated corporation where the named hospital and other hospitals consolidated in 1938. In re Estate of Doughty (1959) 24 Misc. 2d 625, 194 N.Y.S.2d 50

A bequest made to a constituent corporation later consolidated with another corporation passes to the successor by consolidation. In re Morris' Will (1962) 36 Misc. 2d 1094, 234 N.Y.S.2d 122

Plan of merger between 2 not-for-profit health providers, one of which was controlled by California health care provider, was approved by court subject to condition that Attorney General be given notice of future nonmerger transfers of operational or managerial control, and that courts be given authority to approve or reject such transfers consistent with goals set forth in CLS N-PCL § 907(e) to assure that interests of constituent corporations and public would not be adversely affected by merger or consolidation. In re Kaiser Found. Health Plan (1999, Sup) 185 Misc. 2d 110, 713 N.Y.S.2d 108

§ 906. Merger or consolidation of domestic and foreign corporations

(a) One or more foreign corporations and one or more domestic corporations may be merged or consolidated into a corporation of this state or of another jurisdiction, if such merger or consolidation is permitted by the laws of the jurisdiction under which each such foreign corporation is incorporated. With respect to such merger or consolidation, any reference in paragraph (b) of section 901 (Power of merger or consolidation) to a corporation shall, unless the context otherwise requires, include both domestic and foreign corporations.

(b) With respect to procedure, including the requirement of approval by members, each domestic corporation shall comply with the provisions of this chapter relating to merger or consolidation of domestic corporations, and each foreign corporation shall comply with the applicable provisions of the law of the jurisdiction under which it is incorporated.

(c) if the surviving or consolidated corporation is, or is to be, a domestic corporation, a certificate of merger or consolidation shall be signed, verified and delivered to the department of state as provided in section 904 (Certificate of merger or consolidation; contents). In addition to the matters specified in such section, the certificate shall set forth as to each constituent foreign corporation the jurisdiction and date of its incorporation and the date when its application for authority to conduct activities in this state was filed by the department of state, and its fictitious name used in this state pursuant to article thirteen of this chapter, if applicable, or, if no such application has been filed, a statement to such effect.

(d) If the surviving or consolidated corporation is, or is to be, formed under the law of any jurisdiction other than this state:

(1) It shall comply with the provisions of this chapter relating to foreign corporations if it is to conduct activities in this state.

(2) It shall deliver to the department of state a certificate, entitled "Certificate of merger (or consolidation) of .... and .... into .... (names of corporations) under section 906 of the Not-for-Profit Corporation Law", which shall be signed on behalf of each constituent domestic and foreign corporation. It shall set forth:

(A) The statements required by subparagraphs (a)(1) and (2) of section 902 (Plan of merger or consolidation).

(B) The jurisdiction and date of incorporation of the surviving or consolidated foreign corporation, the date when its application for authority to conduct activities in this state was filed by the department of state, and its fictitious name used in this state pursuant to article thirteen of this chapter, if applicable, or, if no such application has been filed, a statement to such effect and that it is not to conduct activities in this state until an application for such authority shall have been filed by such department.

(C) The date when the certificate of incorporation of each constituent domestic corporation was filed by the department of state and the jurisdiction and date of incorporation of each constituent foreign corporation, other than the surviving or consolidated foreign corporation, and; in the case of each such corporation authorized to conduct activities in this state, the date when its application for authority was filed by the department of state.

(D) An agreement that the surviving or consolidated foreign corporation may be served with process in this state in any action or special proceeding for the enforcement of any liability or obligation of any domestic corporation or of any foreign corporation, previously amenable to suit in this state, which is a constituent corporation in such merger or consolidation, and an agreement that the surviving or consoli dated foreign corporation may be sued in this state in respect of any property transferred or conveyed to it as provided in paragraph (c) of section 907 (Approval by the supreme court), or the use made of such property, or any transaction in connection therewith.

(E) A designation of the secretary of state as its agent upon whom process against it may be served in the manner set forth in paragraph (b) of section 306 (Service of process), in any action or special proceeding described in subparagraph (D) and a post office address, within or without this state, to which the secretary of state shall mail a copy of the process in such action or special proceeding.

(F) The manner in which the plan of merger or consolidation was approved with respect to each constituent domestic corporation and that the merger or consolidation is permitted by the laws of the jurisdiction of each constituent foreign corporation and is in compliance therewith.

(G) The effective date of the merger or consolidation if other than the date of filing of the certificate of merger or consolidation by the department of state.

(e) Upon the filing of the certificate of merger or consolidation by the department of state or on such date subsequent thereto, not to exceed thirty days as shall be set forth in such certificate, the merger or consolidation shall be effected.

(f) The surviving or consolidated domestic or foreign corporation shall thereafter cause a copy of such certificate, certified by the department of state, to be filed in the office of the clerk of each county in which the office of a constituent corporation, other than the surviving corporation, is located, and in the office of the official who is the recording officer of each county in this state in which real property of a constituent corporation, other than the surviving corporation, is situated.

(g) If the surviving or consolidated corporation is, or is to be, formed under the law of this state, the effect of such merger or consolidation shall be the same as in the case of the merger or consolidation of domestic corporations under section 905 (Effect of merger or consolidation). If the surviving or consolidated corporation is, or is to be, incorporated under the law of any jurisdiction other than this state, the effect of such merger or consolidation shall be the same as in the case of the merger or consolidation of domestic corporations, except in so far as the law of such other jurisdiction provides otherwise.

History: Add, L 1969, ch 1066, § 1, eff Sept 1, 1970, with substance derived from Mem Corp Law § 51; amd, L 1970, ch 847, § 58, eff Sept 1, 1970; L 1971, ch 1058 § 32, eff Sept 1, 1971; L 1971, ch 1058, § 32, eff Sept 1, 1971; L 1971, ch 1058 § 32, eff Sept 1, 1971; L 1971, ch 1058, § 32, eff Sept 1, 1971; L 1982, ch 590, § 15, eff Oct 20, 1982,16, eff Oct 20, 1982; L 1998, ch 375, § 41, eff Aug 13, 1998.

§ 907.   Approval by the supreme court or attorney general

Where any constituent corporation or the consolidated corporation is, or would be if formed under this chapter, a charitable corporation under section 201 (Purposes) of this chapter, no certificate shall be filed pursuant to section 904 (Certificate of merger or consolidation; contents) or section 906 (Merger or consolidation of domestic and foreign corporations) until (a) the supreme court has granted an order approving the plan of merger or consolidation and authorizing the filing of the certificate, as provided in section 907-a (Application for approval of the supreme court) of this article or (b) the attorney general has approved the plan of merger or consolidation and authorized the filing of the certificate, as provided in section 907-b (Application for approval of the attorney general) of this article.

History: Add, L 1969, ch 1066, § 1, eff Sept 1, 1970, with substance derived from Mem Corp Law § 52; amd, L 2013, ch 549, § 83, eff July 1, 2014.

CASE ANNOTATIONS

1-5. [Reserved for future use]
6. Under former Membership Corporations Law § 52
1-5. [Reserved for future use]
6. Under former Membership Corporations Law § 52

An application by seven incorporated domestic membership corporations for an order approving an agreement for consolidation was granted, notwithstanding opposition by respondents relative to the alleged non-exchange of audited financial statements and statements of contingent liabilities, where the court found that by incorporation by reference of various exhibits to the moving petition the property and the manner in which it was held, all liabilities, and the amount and sources of the annual income of each member corporation had been adequately disclosed. Sackerah Path Girl Scout Council, Inc. v Armstrong (1966) 50 Misc. 2d 883, 272 N.Y.S.2d 34, affd (1966, 2d Dept) 25 A.D.2d 956, 271 N.Y.S.2d 191

Plan of merger between 2 not-for-profit health providers, one of which was controlled by California health care provider, was approved by court subject to condition that Attorney General be given notice of future nonmerger transfers of operational or managerial control, and that courts be given authority to approve or reject such transfers consistent with goals set forth in CLS N-PCL § 907(e) to assure that interests of constituent corporations and public would not be adversely affected by merger or consolidation. In re Kaiser Found. Health Plan (1999, Sup) 185 Misc. 2d 110, 713 N.Y.S.2d 108

§ 907-a.   Application for approval of the supreme court

(a) Application for an order approving the plan of merger and authorizing the filing of the certificate may be made in the judicial district in which the principal office of the surviving or consolidated corporation is to be located, or in which the office of one of the domestic constituent corporations is located. The application shall be made by all the constituent corporations jointly and shall set forth by affidavit: (1) the plan of merger or consolidation, (2) the approval required by section 903 (Approval of plan) or paragraph (b) of section 906 (Merger or consolidation of domestic and foreign corporations) of this article for each constituent corporation, (3) the objects and purposes of each such corporation to be promoted by the merger or consolidation, (4) a statement of all property, and the manner in which it is held, and of all liabilities and of the amount and sources of the annual income of each such corporation, (5) whether any votes against adoption of the resolution approving the plan of merger or consolidation were cast at the meeting at which the resolution was adopted by each constituent corporation, and (6) facts showing that the consolidation is authorized by the laws of the jurisdictions under which each of the constituent corporations is incorporated.

(b) Upon the filing of the application the court shall fix a time for hearing thereof and shall direct that notice thereof be given to such persons as may be interested, including the attorney general, any governmental body or officer and any other person or body whose consent or approval is required by section 909 (Consent to filing) of this article, in such form and manner as the court may prescribe. If no votes against adoption of the resolution approving the plan of merger or consolidation were cast at the meeting at which the resolution was adopted by any constituent corporation the court may dispense with notice to anyone except the attorney-general, any governmental body or officer and any other person or body whose consent or approval is required by section 909 (Consent to filing) of this article. Any person interested may appear and show cause why the application should not be granted.

(c) If the court shall find that any of the assets of any of the constituent corporations are held for a charitable purpose or are legally required to be used for a particular purpose, but not upon a condition requiring return, transfer or conveyance by reason of the merger or consolidation, the court may, in its discretion, direct that such assets be transferred or conveyed to the surviving or consolidated corporation subject to such purpose or use, or that such assets be transferred or conveyed to the surviving or consolidated corporation or to one or more other domestic or foreign corporations or organizations engaged in substantially similar activities, upon an express trust the terms of which shall be approved by the court.

(d) If the court shall find that the interests of non-consenting members are or may be substantially prejudiced by the proposed merger or consolidation, the court may disapprove the plan or may direct a modification thereof. In the event of a modification, if the court shall find that the interests of any members may be substantially prejudiced by the proposed merger or consolidation as modified, the court shall direct that the modified plan be submitted to vote of the members of the constituent corporations, or if the court shall find that there is not such substantial prejudice, it shall approve the agreement as so modified without further approval by the members. If the court, upon directing a modification of the plan of merger or consolidation, shall direct that a further approval be obtained from members of the constituent corporations or any of them, such further approval shall be obtained in the manner specified in section

903 (Approval of plan) or paragraph (b) of section 906 (Merger or consolidation of domestic and foreign corporations) of this article.

(e) If it shall appear, to the satisfaction of the court, that the provisions of this section have been complied with, and that the interests of the constituent corporations and the public interest will not be adversely affected by the merger or consolidation, it shall approve the merger or consolidation upon such terms and conditions as it may prescribe.

(f) A certified copy of such order shall be annexed to the certificate of merger or consolidation.

History: Add, 2013, ch 549, § 84, eff July 1, 2014.

§ 907-b. Application for approval of the attorney general

(a) In lieu of obtaining an order approving the plan of merger or consolidation and authorizing the filing of the certificate, the corporation may alternatively make an application to the attorney general for approval, except where the attorney general, in his or her discretion, concludes that a court should review the application and make a determination thereon.

(b) The application to the attorney general shall be made by all the constituent corporations jointly and shall set forth by affidavit: (i) all of the information required to be included in an application to obtain court approval pursuant to section 907-a (Application for approval of the supreme court) of this article, (ii) all consents and approvals required by section 909 (Consent to filing), and (iii) a statement as to whether any persons have raised, or have a reasonable basis to raise, objections to the merger or consolidation that is the subject of the application, including a statement setting forth the names and addresses of such persons, the nature of their interest, and a description of their objections.

(c) Upon the filing of the application, the attorney general, in his or her discretion, may direct that the constituent corporations provide notice to such persons as may be interested, including any governmental body or officer and any other person or body that is required either to give consent or be notified under section 404 (Approvals, notices and consents) of this article or 909 (Consent to filing) of this article. The constituent corporations shall provide the attorney general with a certification that such notice has been provided.

(d) If any assets of any of the constituent corporations are held for a charitable purpose or are assets received for a specific purpose and legally required to be used for a particular purpose, but not upon a condition requiring return, transfer or conveyance by reason of the merger or consolidation, the attorney general may, in his or her discretion, direct that such assets be transferred or conveyed to the surviving or consolidated corporation subject to such purpose or use.

(e) If the attorney general shall find that the interests of non-consenting members are or may be substantially prejudiced by the proposed merger or consolidation, the attorney general may disapprove of the application or may condition approval of the application upon modification of the plan of merger or consolidation in accordance with this chapter and any other law or rule.

(f) If it shall appear, to the satisfaction of the attorney general, that the provisions of this section have been complied with, and that the interests of the constituent corporations and the public interest will not be adversely affected by the merger or consolidation, the attorney general shall approve the merger or consolidation upon such terms and conditions as it may prescribe.

(g) The approval of the attorney general shall be annexed to the certificate of merger or consolidation.

(h) At any time, including if the attorney general does not approve the application, or if the attorney general concludes that court review is appropriate, the constituent corporations may seek court approval on notice to the attorney general pursuant to section 907-a (Application for approval of the supreme court) of this article.

History: Add L 2013, ch 549, § 85, eff July 1, 2014.

§ 908. Merger or consolidation of business and not-for-profit corporations

(a) One or more domestic or foreign corporations which is, or would be if formed under this chapter, a non-charitable corporation, or any corporation formed as a type A corporation prior to July first, two thousand fourteen, may be merged or consolidated into a domestic or foreign corporation which is, or would be if formed under the laws of this state, a corporation formed under the business corporation law of this state if such merger or consolidation is not contrary to the law of the state of incorporation of any constituent corporation. With respect to such merger or consolidation, any reference in paragraph (b) of section 901 (Power of merger or consolidation) of this article or paragraph (b) of section 901 (Power of merger or consolidation) of the business corporation law to a corporation shall, unless the context otherwise requires, include both domestic and foreign corporations.

(b) With respect to procedure including authorization by shareholders or approval by members, each domestic business corporation shall comply with the business corporation law, each domestic not-for-profit corporation shall comply with the provisions of this chapter and each foreign corporation shall comply with the applicable provisions of the law of the jurisdiction under which it is incorporated.

(c) The plan of merger or consolidation shall set forth all matter required by section 902 of the business corporation law or section 902 of this chapter and the terms and conditions of the proposed merger

or consolidation, including the manner and basis of converting shares, membership or other interest in each constituent corporation into shares, bonds or other securities of the surviving or consolidated corporation, or the cash or other consideration to be paid or delivered in exchange for shares, membership or other interest in each constituent corporation, or a combination thereof.

(d) After adoption of the plan of merger or consolidation by the board and members or shareholders of each constituent corporation, unless the merger or consolidation is abandoned in accordance with paragraph (b) of section 903 (Approval by members) and paragraph (b) of section 903 (Authorization by shareholders) of the business corporation law, a certificate of merger or consolidation, entitled "Certificate of merger (or consolidation) of .... and ...... into .... (names of corporations) under section 908 of the Not-for-Profit Corporation Law", shall be signed on behalf of each constituent corporation and delivered to the department of state.

(1) If the surviving or consolidated corporation is, or is to be, a domestic corporation such certificate shall set forth the statements required by section 904(a) of the business corporation law or section 904(a) of this chapter and, as to each constituent foreign corporation the jurisdiction and date of its incorporation and the date when its application for authority to conduct activities or do business in this state was filed by the department of state or, if no such application has been filed, a statement to such effect.

(2) If the surviving or consolidated corporation is, or is to be formed under the law of any jurisdiction other than this state such certificate shall set forth:

(A) The statements required by subparagraphs (a)(1) and (2) of section 902 of the business corporation law or subparagraphs (a)(1) and (2) of section 902 (Plan of merger or consolidation) of this chapter, and the manner in which the merger or consolidation was authorized with respect to each constitutent domestic corporation.

(B) The jurisdiction and date of incorporation of the surviving or consolidated foreign corporation, the date when its application for authority to do business in this state was filed by the department of state or, if no such application has been filed, a statement to such effect and that it is not to do business in this state until an application for such authority shall have been filed by such department.

(C) The date when the certificate of incorporation of each constituent domestic corporation was filed by the department of state and the jurisdiction and date of incorporation of each constituent foreign corporation, other than the surviving or consolidated foreign corporation, and, in the case of each such corporation authorized to do business or conduct activities in this state, the date when its application for authority was filed by the department of state.

(D) An agreement that the surviving or consolidated foreign corporation may be served with process in this state in any action or special proceeding for the enforcement of any liability or obligation of any domestic corporation or of any foreign corporation, previously amenable to suit in this state, which is a constituent corporation in such merger or consolidation, and for the enforcement, as provided in the business corporation law, of the rights of shareholders of any constituent domestic business corporation to receive payment for their shares against the surviving or consolidated corporation.

(E) An agreement that, subject to the provisions of section 623 of the business corporation law, the surviving or consolidated foreign corporation will promptly pay to the shareholders of each constituent domestic business corporation the amount, if any, to which they shall be entitled under the provisions of the business corporation law relating to the right of shareholders to receive payment for their shares.

(F) A designation of the secretary of state as his agent upon whom process against it may be served in the manner set forth in paragraph (b) of section 306 (Service of process), in any action or special proceeding described in subparagraph (D) and a post office address, within or without the state, to which the secretary of state shall mail a copy of the process in such action or special proceeding.

(e) The department of state shall not file a certificate delivered to it under subparagraph (d)(2) unless the consent of the state tax commission to the merger or consolidation is attached thereto.

(f) [Repealed]

(g) Upon the filing of the certificate of merger or consolidation by the department of state or on such dates subsequent thereto, not to exceed thirty days, as shall be set forth in such certificate, the merger or consolidation shall be effected.

(h) The surviving or consolidated domestic or foreign corporation shall thereafter cause a copy of such certificate, certified by the department of state, to be filed in the office of the clerk of each county in which the office of a constituent corporation, other than the surviving corporation, is located, and in the office of the official who is the recording officer of each county in this state in which real property of a constituent corporation, other than the surviving corporation, is situated.

(i) When such merger or consolidation has been effected:

(A) If the surviving or consolidated corporation is, or is to be, formed under the law of this state, it shall be subject to the business corporation law and the effect of such merger or consolidation shall be the same as in the case of the merger or consolidation of domestic corporations under section 906 (Effect of merger or consolidation) of the business corporation

law, except that in subparagraph (b)(3) of such section the word "shareholder" shall be read to include the word "member" as the latter is defined in this chapter.

(B) If the surviving or consolidated corporation is, or is to be, incorporated under the law of any jurisdiction other than this state, the effect of such merger or consolidation shall be as provided in subparagraph (A), except insofar as the law of such other jurisdiction provides otherwise.

History: Add, L 1969, ch 1066, § 1, eff Sept 1, 1970; amd, L 1971, ch 1058 § 33, eff Sept 1, 1971, L 1998, ch 375, § 42, eff Aug 13, 1998, L 2013, ch 549, §§ 85-a, 86, eff July 1, 2014.

§ 909. Consent to filing; notices

(a) If the purposes of any constituent or consolidated corporation would require the approval or consent of any governmental body or officer or any other person or body under section 404 (Approvals, notices and consents) of this chapter no certificate of merger or consolidation shall be filed pursuant to this article unless such approval or consent is endorsed thereon or annexed thereto. A corporation whose statement of purposes specifically includes the establishment or operation of a child day care center, as that term is defined in section three hundred ninety of the social services law, shall mail a certified copy of any certificate of merger or consolidation involving such corporation to the office of children and family services within thirty days after receipt of confirmation of the filing of such merger or consolidation with the department of state.

(b) If the purposes of any constituent or consolidated corporation would require the certificate of incorporation or any other notice to be delivered to any person or entity under section 404 (Approvals, notices and consents) of this chapter, the corporation shall provide to such person or entity a certified copy of the certificate of incorporation within thirty days after the corporation receives confirmation from the department of state that the certificate has been accepted for filing.

History: Add, L 1969, ch 1066, § 1, eff Sept 1, 1970, with substance derived from Mem Corp Law § 50; amd, L 2006, ch 58, § 6 (Part D), eff April 12, 2006; L 2013, ch 549, § 87, eff July 1, 2014; L 2015, ch 358, § 7, eff Sept 25, 2015.

§ 910. Merger or consolidation of corporations formed under the religious corporations law and certain other corporations formed for religious purposes

(a) One or more corporations formed under the religious corporations law and one or more corporations formed for religious purposes to which the not-for-profit corporation law applies by virtue of paragraph (a) of section one hundred three of this chapter may be merged or consolidated pursuant to section nine hundred one, with the effect provided in section nine hundred one and paragraph (b) of section nine hundred five of this chapter.

(b) Each corporation which is a party to such merger or consolidation shall comply with the provisions of this section and of sections 902, 903, 904 and 907 of this chapter and, if and to the extent applicable, sections 906 and 909 of this chapter.

(c) If the surviving corporation or consolidated corporation is a domestic or authorized foreign corporation not formed under the religious corporations law, then, a certificate of merger or consolidation shall be filed with the department of state, and the surviving or consolidated corporation shall thereafter cause a copy of such certificate, certified by the department of state, to be filed in the office of the clerk of the county in which each constituent corporation other than the surviving corporation is located, the county in which the certificate of incorporation of each constituent domestic corporation or application for authority of each constituent authorized foreign corporation, other than the surviving corporation, is filed and the office of the official who is the recording officer of such county in this state in which real property of a constituent corporation other than the surviving corporation, is located.

(d) If the surviving corporation or consolidated corporation is a corporation formed under the religious corporations law, then, the certificate of merger or consolidation shall be filed with the office of the official in which the certificate of incorporation of the surviving or consolidated corporation was filed, and the surviving or consolidated corporation shall thereafter cause a copy of such certificate, certified by such office, to be filed in the office in which the certificate of incorporation of each constituent domestic corporation or application for authority of each authorized foreign corporation other than the surviving corporation was filed, and in the office of the official who is the recording officer of each county in this state in which real property of a constituent corporation, other than the surviving or consolidated corporation, is located.

(e) Such merger or consolidation shall become effective with respect to each constituent corporation upon the filing of a certificate of merger or consolidation or certified copy thereof pursuant to paragraph (c) or paragraph (d) of this section with the appropriate state or county official therein specified. With respect to the surviving corporation, such merger may become effective on such date subsequent thereto, not to exceed thirty days, as shall be set forth in such certificate. The filing of a certified copy with the office of a recording officer of a county in which real property is located shall not be a condition precedent to such merger or consolidation becoming effective.

History: Add, L 1992, ch 623, § 1, eff July 24, 1992.

ARTICLE 10
NON-JUDICIAL DISSOLUTION

History: Add, L 1969, ch 1066, § 1, eff Sept 1, 1970.

§ 1001.   Plan of dissolution and distribution of assets

(a) The board shall adopt a plan for the dissolution of the corporation and the distribution of its assets. Such plan shall implement any provision in the certificate of incorporation prescribing the distributive rights of members.

(b) If the corporation is a charitable corporation and has no assets to distribute and no liabilities at the time of dissolution, the plan of dissolution shall include a statement to that effect.

(c) If the corporation has no assets to distribute, other than a reserve not to exceed twenty-five thousand dollars for the purpose of paying ordinary and necessary expenses of winding up its affairs including attorney and accountant fees, and liabilities not in excess of ten thousand dollars at the time of adoption of the plan of dissolution, the plan of dissolution shall include a statement to that effect.

(d) If the corporation has assets to distribute or liabilities, the plan of dissolution shall contain:

(1) a description with reasonable certainty of the assets of the corporation and their fair value, and the total amount of debts and other liabilities incurred or estimated by the corporation, including the total amount of any accounting and legal fees incurred or estimated, in connection with the dissolution procedure.

(2) a statement as to whether any gifts or other assets are legally required to be used for a particular purpose.

(3) if there are assets received and held by the corporation either for a charitable purpose or which are legally required to be used for a particular purpose, a statement that the assets owned by the

corporation, subject to any unpaid liabilities of the corporation, shall be distributed as required by any gift instrument or to a charitable corporation or organization or organizations exempt from taxation pursuant to federal and state laws and engaged in activities substantially similar to those of the dissolved corporation. Each such recipient organization shall be identified and the governing instrument and amendments thereto of each of the proposed recipient organizations shall be annexed to such statement, along with the most recent financial report of each recipient organization and a sworn affidavit from a director and officer of each recipient organization stating the purposes of the organization, and that it is currently exempt from federal income taxation.

(4) if any of the assets of the corporation are to be distributed to a recipient for a particular legally required purpose, an agreement by the recipient to apply the assets received only for such purpose shall be included.

History: Add, L 1969, ch 1066, § 1; amd, L 1970, ch 847, § 59, eff Sept 1, 1970, L 1971, ch 1057 § 8, eff Sept 1, 1971, L 2005, ch 726, § 4, eff April 9, 2006, L 2006, ch 434, § 4, eff July 26, 2006, L 2013, ch 549, § 88, eff July 1, 2014.

§ 1002. Authorization of plan

(a) Upon adopting a plan of dissolution and distribution of assets, the board shall submit it to a vote of the members, if any, and such plan shall be approved at a meeting of members by two-thirds vote as provided in paragraph (c) of section 613 (Vote of members) of this chapter; provided, however, that if the corporation is a charitable corporation, other than a corporation incorporated pursuant to article 15 (Public cemetery corporations) of this chapter, the vote required by the corporation's board of directors for adoption of the plan of dissolution of such a corporation or by the corporation's members for the authorization thereof shall be:

(1) In the case of a vote by the board of directors:

(i) the number of directors required under the certificate of incorporation, by-laws, this chapter and any other applicable law; or

(ii) if the number of directors actually holding office as such at the time of the vote to adopt the plan is less than the number required to constitute a quorum of directors under the certificate of incorporation, the by-laws, this chapter or any other applicable law, the remaining directors unanimously;

(2) In the case of a vote by the members, (i) the number of members required under the certificate of incorporation, by-laws, this chapter and any other applicable law; or (ii) by the vote of members authorized by an order of the supreme court pursuant to section 608 (Quorum at meeting of members) of this chapter permitting the corporation to dispense with the applicable quorum requirement.

Notice of a special or regular meeting of the board of directors or of the members entitled to vote on adoption and authorization or approval of the plan of dissolution shall be sent to all the directors and members of record entitled to vote. Unless otherwise directed by order of the supreme court pursuant to section 608 (Quorum at meeting of members) of this chapter, the notice shall be sent by certified mail, return receipt requested, to the last known address of record of each director and member not fewer than thirty, and not more than sixty days before the date of each meeting provided, however, that if the last known address of record of any director or member is not within the United States, the notice to such director shall be sent by any other reasonable means.

(b) If there are no members entitled to vote on the dissolution of the corporation, the plan of dissolution and distribution of assets shall be deemed authorized upon its adoption by the board.

(c) Whenever a statute creating, or authorizing the formation of, a corporation requires approval by a governmental body or officer for the formation of such corporation, dissolution shall not be authorized without the approval of such body or officer.

(d) (1) The plan of dissolution and distribution of assets shall have annexed thereto the approval of the attorney general in the case of a charitable corporation, and in the case of any non-charitable corporation which at the time of dissolution holds assets legally required to be used for a particular purpose.

(2) Application to the attorney general for such approval shall be by verified petition, with the plan of dissolution and distribution of assets and certified copies of the consents prescribed by this section annexed thereto.

(3) The attorney general may approve the petition if the corporation has adopted a plan in accordance with the requirements of section 1001 (Plan of dissolution and distribution of assets) of this article, and any other requirements imposed by law or rule. At any time, including if the attorney general does not approve the petition, or the attorney general concludes, in his or her discretion, that court review of the petition is appropriate, the corporation may apply for approval to the supreme court in the judicial district in which the principal office of the corporation is located, or in which the office of one of the domestic constituent corporations is located, for an order dissolving the corporation. Application to the supreme court for an order for such approval shall be by verified petition upon ten days written notice to the attorney general, and shall include all information required to be included in the application to the attorney general pursuant to this section.

History: Add, L 1969, ch 1066, § 1, eff Sept 1, 1970, with substance derived from Gen Corp Law § 101 and Mem Corp Law § 55; amd, L 1971, ch 1058 § 34, L 1971, ch 1057 § 9, eff Sept 1, 1971, L 2005, ch 726, § 5, eff April 9, 2006, L 2006, ch 434, § 5, eff July 26, 2006, L 2013, ch 549, § 89, eff July 1, 2014.

§ 1002-a. Carrying out the plan of dissolution and distribution of assets

Prior to filing the certificate of dissolution with the department of state, a corporation, as applicable, shall:

(a) Carry out the plan of dissolution and distribution of assets, pay its liabilities and distribute its assets in accordance therewith within two hundred seventy days from the date the plan of dissolution and distribution of assets shall have been (1) authorized as provided in section 1002 (Authorization of plan) of this article, (2) approved by any governmental body or officer whose approval is required pursuant to paragraph (c) of section 1002 (Authorization of plan) of this article, and (3) approved by either the attorney general or a justice of the supreme court pursuant to paragraph (d) of section 1002 (Authorization of plan) of this article. Evidence of the disposition of its assets and payment of its liabilities pursuant to the plan of dissolution and distribution of assets shall be submitted by the corporation to the attorney general and any other governmental body or officer, as required under applicable laws. If the plan of dissolution and distribution of assets cannot be carried out within the prescribed time, the attorney general may upon good cause shown extend such time, or any extended period of time, by not fewer than thirty days nor more than one year;

(b) Pursuant to the plan of dissolution and distribution of assets, fulfill or discharge its contracts, collect and sell its assets for cash at public or private sale, discharge or pay its liabilities, and do all other acts appropriate to liquidate its business;

(c) Distribute the assets of the corporation that remain after paying or adequately providing for the payment of its liabilities, in the following manner:

(1) assets received and held by the corporation either for a charitable purpose or which are legally required to be used for a particular purpose, shall be distributed to one or more domestic or foreign corporations or other organizations engaged in activities substantially similar to those of the dissolved corporation pursuant to the plan of dissolution and distribution or, if applicable, as approved by the attorney general or ordered by the supreme court pursuant to section 1002 (Authorization of plan) of this article. Any disposition of assets contained in a will or other instrument, in trust or otherwise, made before or after the dissolution, to or for the benefit of any corporation so dissolved shall inure to or for the benefit of the corporation or organization acquiring such assets of the dissolved corporation as provided in this section, and so far as is necessary for that purpose the corporation or organization acquiring such disposition shall be deemed a successor to the dissolved corporation with respect to such assets; provided, however, that such disposition shall be devoted by the acquiring corporation or organization to the purposes intended by the testator, donor or grantor.

(2) assets other than those described by subparagraph one of this paragraph, if any, shall be distributed in accordance with the specifications of the plan of dissolution and distribution of assets or, to the extent that the certificate of incorporation prescribes the distributive rights of members, or of any class or classes of members, as provided in such certificate;

(d) Within six months from the date fixed for the payment of the final liquidating distribution pursuant to paragraph (a) of this section, pay any assets distributable to a creditor or member who is unknown or cannot be found, to the state comptroller pursuant to the abandoned property law;

(e) Distribute assets that are not subject to subparagraph one of paragraph (c) of this section under a plan of distribution, in accordance with the following order of priorities:

(1) holders of certificates of subvention.

(2) holders of capital certificates.

(3) members, if permitted by law.

History: Add, L 2005, ch 726, § 6, eff April 9, 2006; amd, L 2006, ch 434, § 6, eff July 26, 2006, L 2013, ch 549, § 90, eff July 1, 2014.

§ 1003. Certificate of dissolution; contents; approval

(a) After the plan of dissolution and distribution of assets has been adopted, authorized, approved and carried out pursuant to the terms of the plan within the time period set forth pursuant to section 1002-a (Carrying out the plan of dissolution and distribution of assets), a certificate of dissolution, entitled "Certificate of dissolution of . . . . (name of corporation) under section 1003 of the Not-for-Profit Corporation Law" shall be signed and, if required pursuant to subparagraph two of paragraph (b) of this section, after the attorney general has affixed thereon his or her consent to the dissolution, such certificate of dissolution shall be delivered to the department of state. It shall set forth:

(1) The name of the corporation and, if its name has been changed, the name under which it was formed.

(2) The date its certificate of incorporation was filed by the department of state.

(3) The name and address of each of its officers and directors.

(4) A statement as to whether the corporation is a charitable corporation or a non-charitable corporation.

(5) A statement as to whether or not the corporation holds assets at the time of authorization of its plan of dissolution and distribution of assets as provided in section 1002 of this article (Authorization of plan) which are legally required to be used for a particular purpose.

(6) That the corporation elects to dissolve.

(7) The manner in which the dissolution was authorized. If the dissolution of the corporation is authorized by a vote of the directors and/or members of the corporation that is less than that ordinarily required by the certificate of incorporation, the by-laws, this chapter or any other applicable law, as permitted by paragraph (a) of section 1002 (Authorization of plan) of this article, then the certificate of dissolution shall so state.

(8) A statement that prior to delivery of such certificate of dissolution to the department of state for filing, the plan of dissolution and distribution of assets has been approved by the attorney general or by a justice of the supreme court, if such approval is required pursuant to section 1002 (Authorization of plan) of this article. A copy of the approval of the attorney general or of the court order shall be attached to the certificate of dissolution. In the case of a corporation, other than a corporation incorporated pursuant to article 15 (Public cemetery corporations), having no assets to distribute, or having no assets to distribute other than a reserve not to exceed twenty-five thousand dollars for the purpose of paying ordinary and necessary expenses of winding up its affairs including attorney and accountant fees, and liabilities not in excess of ten thousand dollars at the time of dissolution, a statement that a copy of the plan of dissolution which contains the statement prescribed by paragraph (b) of section 1001 (Plan of dissolution and distribution of assets) has been duly filed with the attorney general, if required.

(b) Such certificate of dissolution shall have endorsed thereon or annexed thereto the approval of the dissolution:

(1) By a governmental body or officer, if such approval is required. A corporation whose statement of purposes specifically includes the establishment or operation of a child day care center, as that term is defined in section three hundred ninety of the social services law, shall provide a certified copy of any certificate of dissolution involving such corporation to the office of children and family services within thirty days after the filing of such dissolution with the department of state.

(2) By the attorney general in the case of a charitable corporation, or any other corporation that holds assets at the time of dissolution legally required to be used for a particular purpose.

(c) The application to the attorney general for approval of the certificate of dissolution pursuant to paragraph (b) of this section shall be by verified petition and shall include a final financial report showing disposition of all of the corporation's assets and liabilities, the requisite governmental approvals and the appropriate fees, if any, accompanied by the certificate of dissolution.

History: Add, L 1969, ch 1066, § 1, eff Sept 1, 1970, with substance derived from Mem Corp Law § 55; amd, L 1971, ch 1057 § 10, eff Sept 1, 1971; L 1971, ch 1058 § 35; L 1998, ch 375, § 43, eff Aug 13, 1998; L 2005, ch 726, § 7, eff April 9, 2006; L 2006, ch 58, § 7 (Part D), eff April 9, 2006; L 2006, ch 434, § 7, eff July 26, 2006; L 2013, ch 549, § 91, eff July 1, 2014; L 2015, ch 358, § 8, eff Sept 25, 2015.

CASE ANNOTATIONS

In view of the special circumstances relating to the block of stock in the trust, requiring protracted arrangements for its sale or disposition, there was no reason to disapprove a plan of dissolution and distribution of charitable trust assets merely because liquidation required a step by step process. In re Martin Foundation, Inc. (1972) 73 Misc. 2d 985, 343 N.Y.S.2d 518, affd (1973, 1st Dept) 41 A.D.2d 905, 342 N.Y.S.2d 643

§ 1004. Certificate of dissolution; filing; effect

(a) The department of state shall not file a certificate of dissolution unless the consent of the state department of taxation and finance to the dissolution is attached thereto. Upon filing the certificate, the corporation is dissolved.

(b) Notwithstanding paragraph (a) of this section, with respect to any corporation that has done business in the city of New York and incurred liability for any tax or charge under chapter six, seven, eight, ten, eleven, twelve, thirteen, fourteen, fifteen, twenty-one, twenty-four, twenty-five or twenty-seven of title eleven of the administrative code of the city of New York, the department of state shall not file a certificate of dissolution unless the consent of the commissioner of finance of the city of New York to the dissolution is also attached thereto.

History: Add, L 1969, ch 1066, § 1, eff Sept 1, 1970, with substance derived from Mem Corp Law § 55.

Amd, L 2009, ch 201, § 75, eff Oct 1, 2009.

§ 1005. [Repealed]

History: Add, L 1969, ch 1066, § 1, eff Sept 1, 1970, with substance derived from Gen Corp Law § 29 and Mem Corp Law §§ 55, 56; amd, L 1970, ch 847, § 60, eff Sept 1, 1970; repealed, L 2005, ch 726, § 8, eff April 9, 2006.

§ 1006. Corporate action and survival of remedies after dissolution

(a) After dissolution, a corporation shall not commence any new activities. A dissolved corporation, its directors, officers and members may continue to function for the purpose of winding up the affairs of the corporation in the same manner as if the dissolution had not taken place, except as otherwise provided in this chapter or by court order. In particular and without limiting the generality of the foregoing:

(1) The directors of a dissolved corporation shall not be deemed to be trustees of its assets; title to such assets shall not vest in them, but shall remain in the corporation until transferred by it in its corporate name.

(2) Dissolution shall not change quorum or voting requirements for the board or members, or provisions regarding election, appointment, resignation or removal of, or filling vacancies among, directors or

officers, or provisions regarding amendment or repeal of by-laws or adoption of new by-laws.

(3) Capital certificates may be transferred and determination of members for any purpose may be made without closing the record of members until such time, if any, as such record may be closed, and either the board or the members may close it.

(4) The corporation may sue or be sued in all courts and participate in actions and proceedings, whether judicial, administrative, arbitrative or otherwise, in its corporate name, and process may be served by or upon it.

(b) The dissolution of a corporation shall not affect any remedy available to or against such corporation, its directors, officers or members, for any right or claim existing or any liability incurred before such dissolution, except as provided in sections 1007 (Notice to creditors; filing or barring claims) or 1008 (Jurisdiction of supreme court to supervise dissolution and liquidation.)

History: Add, L 1969, ch 1066, § 1, eff Sept 1, 1970, with substance derived from Gen Corp Law § 29 and Mem Corp Law §§ 55, 56.

Par (a), opening par, amd, L 2005, ch 726, § 9, eff April 9, 2006.

Par (b), amd, L 1970, ch 847, § 61, eff Sept 1, 1970.

CASE ANNOTATIONS

1-5. [Reserved for future use]
6. Under former Membership Corporations Law § 56
1-5. [Reserved for future use]
6. Under former Membership Corporations Law § 56

This section relates to but does not conflict with § 29 of the General Corporation Law which provides in part that "upon the dissolution of a corporation for any cause and whether voluntary or involuntary its corporate existence shall continue for the purpose of collecting its assets and it may sue and be sued in its corporate name." In re Mohr's Estate (1941) 175 Misc 706, 24 N.Y.S.2d 977

Two societies adjudged to be successors of a dissolved membership corporation were entitled to share equally in funds which might fall to the dissolved corporation under will probated after dissolution. Application of Richmond County Soc. for Prevention of Cruelty to Children (1957) 8 Misc. 2d 123, 165 N.Y.S.2d 861, app dismd (1960, 2d Dept) 11 A.D.2d 236, 204 N.Y.S.2d 707, app gr (1960) 8 N.Y.2d 710 and motion gr (1961) 9 N.Y.2d 689, remittitur amd (1961) 9 N.Y.2d 750, 214 N.Y.S.2d 454, 174 N.E.2d 535, amd (1961) 9 N.Y.2d 792, 215 N.Y.S.2d 503, 175 N.E.2d 163, amd (1961) 9 N.Y.2d 966, 218 N.Y.S.2d 50, 176 N.E.2d 504, cert den and app dismd (1961) 368 US 33, 7 L Ed 2d 91, 82 S Ct 147 and remittitur amd (1961) 9 N.Y.2d 1015 and affd (1961) 9 N.Y.2d 913, 217 N.Y.S.2d 86, 176 N.E.2d 97, remittitur amd (1961) 10 N.Y.2d 750 and remittitur amd (1961) 10 N.Y.2d 746, 219 N.Y.S.2d 415, 176 N.E.2d 920, cert den and app dismd (1961) 368 US 290, 7 L Ed 2d 336, 82 S Ct 375

Where a membership Corporation prayed for the exoneration and discharge of its officers, directors, trustees and members, as authorized by subdivision 3 of this section, the corporation would be directed to file an accounting within 30 days of the entry of the order therefor and for the purpose of passing on such accounting, the matter would be referred to a referee to take and state such account. Application of Italian Benevolent Institute (1953, Sup) 127 N.Y.S.2d 396

An Italian benevolent institute, formed for one of the purposes described in § 11(1) of the Membership Corporation Law and thereafter dissolved, as indicated by the certificate of the secretary of state, was entitled to petition for the relief prescribed by subdivision 5

of this section. Application of Italian Benevolent Institute (1953, Sup) 127 N.Y.S.2d 396

Where a charitable society, which was remainderman under a testamentary trust, was dissolved prior to the death of the life beneficiary, the remainder gift vested irrevocably in the society upon the death of the testatrix. The trustee was directed to make inquiry and join in the proceeding for judicial settlement of his accounts the successors in interest or surviving directors of such society. In re Tapper's Will (1954, Sur) 139 N.Y.S.2d 110

§ 1007. Notice to creditors by corporations intending to dissolve; filing or barring claims

(a) At any time after the plan of dissolution and distribution of assets shall have been (1) authorized as provided in section 1002 of this article (Authorization of plan), (2) approved by any governmental body or officer whose approval is required pursuant to paragraph (c) of section 1002 of this article, and (3) approved by either by the attorney general or a justice of the supreme court pursuant to paragraph (d) of section 1002 of this article, and prior to filing the certificate of dissolution, the corporation may give a notice requiring all creditors and claimants, including any with unliquidated or contingent claims and any with whom the corporation has unfulfilled contracts, to present their claims in writing and in detail at a specified place and by a specified day, which shall not be less than six months after the first publication of such notice. Such notice shall be published at least once a week for two successive weeks in a newspaper of general circulation in the county in which the office of the corporation was located at the date of authorization of its plan of dissolution and distribution of assets as provided in section 1002 of this article (Authorization of plan). On or before the date of the first publication of such notice, the corporation shall mail a copy thereof, postage prepaid, to each person believed to be a creditor of or claimant against the corporation whose current name and address are known to or can with due diligence be ascertained by the corporation. The giving of such notice shall not constitute a recognition that any person is a proper creditor or claimant, and shall not revive or make valid, or operate as a recognition of the validity of, or a waiver of any defense or counterclaim in respect of any claim against the corporation, its assets, directors, officers or members, which has been barred by any statute of limitations or become invalid by any cause, or in respect of which the corporation, its directors, officers or members, has any defense or counterclaim.

(b) Any claims which shall have been filed as provided in such notice and which shall be disputed by the corporation may be submitted for determination to the supreme court under section 1008 (Jurisdiction of supreme court to supervise dissolution and liquidation) or pursuant to article 11 (Judicial dissolution). A claim filed by the trustee or paying agent for the holders of bonds or coupons shall have the same effect as if filed by the holder of any such bonds or coupons.

Any person whose claim is, at the date of the first publication of such notice, barred by any statute of limitations is not a creditor or claimant entitled to any notice under this section or such section 1008. The claim of any such person and all other claims which are not timely filed as provided in such notice except claims which are the subject of litigation on the date of the first publication of such notice and all claims which are so filed but are disallowed by the court under such section 1008, shall be forever barred as against the corporation, its assets, directors, officers and members, except to such extent, if any, as the court may allow them against any remaining assets of the corporation in the case of a creditor who shows satisfactory reason for failure to file a claim as so provided. If the court requires a further notice under such section 1008, any reference to a notice in this section shall, to the extent that the court so orders, mean such further notice, except that a claim which has been filed in accordance with a notice under this section need not be refiled under such further notice.

(c) Notwithstanding this section and section 1008 (Jurisdiction of supreme court to supervise dissolution and liquidation), tax claims and other claims of this state, of the United States and of the department of finance of the city of New York shall not be required to be filed under those sections, and such claims shall not be barred because not so filed, and distribution of the assets of the corporation, or any part thereof, may be deferred until determination of any such claims.

(d) Laborer's wages shall be preferred claims and entitled to payment before any other creditors out of the assets of the corporation in excess of valid prior liens or encumbrances.

History: Add, L 1969, ch 1066, § 1, eff Sept 1, 1970, with substance derived from Gen Corp Law § 133 and Mem Corp Law § 56; amd, L 1970, ch 847, § 62, eff Sept 1, 1970, L 1971, ch 1058 § 36, eff Sept 1, 1971, L 2005, ch 726, § 10, eff April 9, 2006, L 2006, ch 434, § 8, eff July 26, 2006, L 2009, ch 201, § 76, eff Oct 1, 2009, L 2013, ch 549, § 92, eff July 1, 2014.

§ 1008. Jurisdiction of supreme court to supervise dissolution and liquidation

(a) At any time after the filing of a certificate of dissolution under this article, the supreme court in the judicial district where the office of the corporation was located at the date of its dissolution, in a special proceeding instituted under this section, upon the petition of the corporation or, in a situation approved by the court, upon the petition of a creditor, claimant, director, officer, member, subscriber for capital certificates, incorporator or the attorney general, may suspend or annul the dissolution or continue the liquidation of the corporation under the supervision of the court and may make all such orders as it may deem proper in all matters in connection with the dissolution or the winding up of the affairs of the corporation, and in particular, and without limiting

the generality of the foregoing, in respect of the following:

(1) The determination of the validity of the authorization of the dissolution of the corporation and of the execution and delivery of the certificate of dissolution under this article.

(2) The adequacy of the notice given to creditors and claimants and, if it is determined to have been inadequate, the requirement of such further notice as the court may deem proper.

(3) The determination of the validity and amount of invalidity of any claims which have been presented to the corporation.

(4) The barring of all creditors and claimants who have not timely filed claims as provided in any such notice, or whose claims have been disallowed by the court, as against the corporation, its assets, directors, officers and members.

(5) The determination and enforcement of the liability of any director, officer, member or subscriber for capital certificates, to the corporation or for the liabilities of the corporation.

(6) The presentation and filing of intermediate and final accounts of the directors, the hearing thereon, the allowance or disallowance thereof, and the discharge of the directors, or any of them, from their liabilities.

(7) The administration of any trust, or the disposition of any property held in trust by or for the corporation.

(8) The adequacy of a plan of distribution.

(9) The payment, satisfaction or compromise of claims against the corporation, the retention of assets for such purpose, and the determination of the adequacy of provisions made for payment of the liabilities of the corporation.

(10) The disposition or destruction of records, documents and papers of the corporation.

(11) The appointment and removal of a receiver under article 12 (Receivership) who may be a director, officer or member of the corporation.

(12) The issuance of injunctions for one or more of the purposes and as provided in section 1113 (Injunction).

(13) The return of subscription payments to subscribers for capital certificates, and the making of distributions, in cash or in kind or partly in each, to the members.

(14) The payment to the state comptroller, as abandoned property, of assets under paragraph (d) of section 1002-a (Carrying out the plan of dissolution and distribution of assets).

(15) Where assets were received and held by the corporation either for a charitable purpose or legally required to be used for a particular purpose, the distribution of such assets to one or more domestic or foreign corporations or other organizations engaged in activities substantially similar to those of the

dissolved corporation, on notice to the attorney general and to such other persons, and in such manner, as the court may deem proper.

(b) No order annulling a dissolution shall be made under this section if the name of the corporation whose dissolution is to be annulled is no longer available for use by such corporation, unless such corporation submits with its petition for the annulment of the dissolution a certificate of reservation of another available name.

(c) Orders under this section may be entered ex parte, except that if such special proceeding was not instituted upon petition of the corporation, notice shall be given to the corporation in such manner as the court may direct. Notice shall be given to other persons interested, and in such manner, as the court may deem proper, of any hearings and of the entry of any orders on such matters as the court shall deem proper. All orders made by the court under this section shall be binding upon the attorney-general, the corporation, its directors, officers, members, subscribers for capital certificates, incorporators, creditors and claimants.

History: Add, L 1969, ch 1066, § 1, eff Sept 1, 1970, with substance derived from Mem Corp Law § 56; amd, L 2005, ch 726, § 11, eff April 9, 2006, L 2013, ch 549, § 93, eff July 1, 2014.

CASE ANNOTATIONS

1. Generally
2-5. [Reserved for future use]
6. Under former Membership Corporations Law § 56

1. Generally

Where certificate of dissolution which is required as a condition for court supervision of liquidation had not been filed, court lacked jurisdiction to appoint referee to aid it in supervision of liquidation of foundation. Martin Foundation, Inc. v Ginsburg (1973, 1st Dept) 41 A.D.2d 824, 342 N.Y.S.2d 726

In ordering distribution under the dissolution statutes, the Supreme Court is not concerned with the directions or intentions of the creator or testator but only that the funds be transferred to a charitable recipient having similar purposes to the dissolved charitable corporation. In re Will of Goehringer (1972) 69 Misc. 2d 145, 329 N.Y.S.2d 516

2-5. [Reserved for future use]

6. Under former Membership Corporations Law § 56

The Special Term has inherent power to permit the filing of a claim after the expiration of the time fixed therefor in an order obtained pursuant to the statute. New York World's Fair 1964-1965 Corp. v De Rijdt (1968, 2d Dept) 30 A.D.2d 928, 294 N.Y.S.2d 80

§ 1009. Applicability to dissolution under other provisions

The provisions of paragraphs (c), (d) and (e) of section 1002-a of this article (Carrying out the plan of dissolution and distribution of assets), sections 1006 (Corporate action and survival of remedies after dissolution), 1007 (Notice to creditors; filing or barring claims) and 1008 (Jurisdiction of supreme court to supervise dissolution and liquidation) shall apply to a corporation dissolved by proclamation pursuant to section 1014 (Dissolution of domestic corporations by proclamation), by expiration of its period of dura-

tion or under section 203-a of the tax law, or to an incorporated firemen's benevolent association created by act of the legislature if such act is subsequently repealed.

History: Add, L 1969, ch 1066, § 1; amd, L 1970, ch 847, § 63, eff Sept 1, 1970; L 1984, ch 275, § 1, eff June 25, 1984; L 2005, ch 726, § 12, eff April 9, 2006; L 2006, ch 434, § 10, eff July 26, 2006.

§ 1010. Revocation of voluntary dissolution proceedings

(a) At any time prior to the filing of a certificate of dissolution by the department of state, a corporation may revoke the action taken to dissolve the corporation in the following manner:

(1) If there are members entitled to vote thereon:

(A) Unless the certificate of incorporation dispenses with dissolution action by the board, the board shall adopt a resolution recommending that the voluntary dissolution proceedings be revoked and directing submission of the proposed revocation to a vote of the members entitled to vote thereon.

(B) Revocation of the voluntary dissolution proceedings shall be authorized by two-thirds vote as provided in paragraph (c) of section 613 (Vote of members).

(2) If there are no members entitled to vote thereon, revocation of the voluntary dissolution proceedings shall be authorized by the vote of a majority of the directors then in office.

(3) If approval of the dissolution of a corporation by a governmental body or officer is required, as provided in paragraph (c) of section 1002 (Authorization of plan), and such approval has been given, revocation of the voluntary dissolution proceedings shall not be authorized without approval thereof by such body or officer.

History: Add, L 1969, ch 1066, § 1, eff Sept 1, 1970.

§ 1011. [Repealed]

History: Amd, L 1970, ch 847, § 64; repealed, L 1974, ch 415, § 4, eff May 23, 1974.

§ 1012. Certificate of annulment of dissolution and reinstatement of corporate existence

(a) Any corporation dissolved under former section 57 of the membership corporations law may, at any time after the effective date of this chapter, deliver to the department of state a signed certificate which shall be entitled, "certificate of annulment of dissolution and reinstatement of corporate existence of.................(name of corporation) pursuant to section 1012 of the Not-for-Profit Corporation Law", and shall set forth:

(1) The name of the corporation and, if it has been changed, the name under which it was formed.

(2) The date of the filing of its certificate of incorporation by the department of state.

(3) The law under which it was formed.

(4) That it failed to deliver to the department of state a certificate, as required by subdivision 1 of section 57 of the membership corporations law.

(5) That it elects to be reinstated and to continue its corporate existence.

(6) That it is a charitable corporation or a noncharitable corporation, as applicable.

(b) Notwithstanding subparagraph one of paragraph (a) of section 1006 (Corporate action and survival of remedies after dissolution), the directors of a corporation whose dissolution is annulled under this section shall be deemed trustees of its assets, unless such assets have been distributed pursuant to section 1002-a (Carrying out the plan of dissolution and distribution of assets).

(c) The filing of such certificate by the department of state shall have the effect of annulling all of the proceedings theretofore taken for the dissolution of such corporation, and it shall thereafter have such corporate powers, rights, privileges, immunities, duties and liabilities as it had on the date of publication of the proclamation of dissolution, as if such proclamation had not been made and published.

(d) The department of state shall not file a certificate of annulment of dissolution and reinstatement of corporate existence if the name of the corporation being reinstated is not available under section 301 (Corporate name; general) for use by a corporation then being formed under this chapter, unless such certificate shall change the name to one which is available for such use.

(e) If, after the publication of the proclamation of dissolution, it shall appear that the name of any corporation was erroneously included therein, the secretary of state shall make an appropriate entry on the records of the department of state, which entry shall have the effect of annulling all of the proceedings theretofore taken for the dissolution of the corporation under this section, and it shall have such corporate powers, rights, privileges, immunities, duties and liabilities as it had on the date of such publication of the proclamation, as if such proclamation had not been made and published.

(f) Whenever a corporation has complied with paragraph (a) or the action specified in paragraph (e) has been taken, the secretary of state shall publish a notice thereof in the state advertising bulletin and shall send a copy of such bulletin to the clerk of the county in which the office of the corporation is located. The county clerk shall file such copy and make appropriate entry on his record without charge.

(g) Nothing in this section shall be deemed to extend the duration of any corporation as stated in its certificate of incorporation.

(h) The fee of the secretary of state for filing a certificate under this section shall be ten dollars.

History: Add, L 1969, ch 1066, § 1, eff Sept 1, 1970, with substance derived from Mem Corp Law § 57; amd, L 1970, ch 847, § 65, eff Sept 1, 1970, L 1974, ch 415, § 5, eff May 23, 1974, L 1998, ch 375, § 44, eff Aug 13, 1998, L 2005, ch 726, § 13, eff April 9, 2006, L 2013, ch 549, § 94, eff July 1, 2014.

§ 1013.   Dissolution of certain firemen's benevolent associations

(a) An incorporated firemen's benevolent association created by act of the legislature may dissolve in accordance with the provisions of this article.

(b) Any such corporation authorized to have paid to it foreign fire insurance premium taxes imposed under sections 9104 and 9105 of the insurance law shall, in addition to any other requirements of this article, file with the superintendent of insurance a copy of the certificate of dissolution. Moneys then due and owing to the corporation under said sections, and moneys thereafter otherwise payable to the corporation pursuant to such authorization, shall be distributed as provided in said sections.

History: Add, L 1984, ch 275, § 2, eff June 25, 1984.

Par (b), amd, L 1988, ch 293, § 3, eff Jan 1, 1989.

§ 1014.   Dissolution of domestic corporations by proclamation

Every corporation incorporated pursuant to this chapter, other than a corporation incorporated pursuant to article 15 (Public cemetery corporations), and registered or required to be registered pursuant to article 7-A of the executive law or article 8 of the estates, powers and trusts law shall be subject to dissolution for failure to register or to file annual financial reports in accordance with the following procedures:

(a) On or before the last day of March, June, September and December in each calendar year, the attorney general may certify and transmit to the department of state a list containing the names of any or all corporations formed pursuant to this chapter and registered or required to register pursuant to article 7-A of the executive law or article 8 of the estates, powers and trusts law that have not filed annual financial reports for each of the five years immediately preceding the date of such certification. This section shall not be applicable to corporations that filed reports deemed by the attorney general to be incomplete, erroneous or otherwise deficient.

(b) No corporation shall be included in any list prepared pursuant to paragraph (a) of this section unless (1) in each of the last two years during which such corporation failed to file its annual report, the attorney general has sent to such corporation by certified mail return receipt requested notice that the corporation has failed to file and has three months from the date of such notice to file all delinquent reports and complete all registration requirements, provided, however, that if the last known address of record of the corporation is not within the United States, the notice to such corporation shall be sent by any other reasonable means, (2) the second such notice was sent at least six months prior to the date of the certification required by paragraph (a) of this section and (3) the attorney general used reasonable diligence to identify a current address for the corporation.

(c) If the secretary of state, upon comparing the names so certified with his or her records, shall discover error, he or she may return the list to the attorney general for correction.

(d) The secretary of state shall make a proclamation under his or her hand and seal of office as to each list received from the attorney general declaring any corporations whose names are included in such list to be dissolved and their certificates of incorporation to be forfeited. The secretary shall file the original proclamation in his or her office and shall publish a copy thereof in the state register no later than three months following receipt of the list by him or her.

(e) Upon the publication of such proclamation in the manner proscribed in paragraph (d) of this section, each corporation named therein shall be deemed dissolved without further legal proceedings.

(f) The secretary of state shall mail a copy of the state register containing such proclamation to the clerk of each county in the state. The county clerk shall file the copy without charge but need not record it.

(g) The names of all corporations so dissolved shall be reserved for a period of one year immediately following the publication of the proclamation, and during such period no domestic business corporation, not-for-profit corporation, limited liability company or limited partnership shall be formed under a name the same as any name so reserved or which may not be distinguished from any name so reserved, nor shall any foreign business corporation, not-for-profit corporation, limited liability company or limited partnership, within such period, be authorized to do business or conduct activities in this state under a name the same as any name so reserved or which may not be distinguished from such any name so reserved.

(h) Any corporation so dissolved may file in the department of state a written consent by the attorney general to the reinstatement of the corporation. Such written consent shall be given if the attorney general shall have received all annual financial reports and fees required by article 7-A of the executive law and article 8 of the estates, powers and trusts law and penalties and interest charges related thereto have been paid or waived. The filing of such consent shall have the effect of annulling all of the proceedings theretofore taken under the provisions of this section for the dissolution of such corporation with the same force and effect as if such proclamation had not been made or published. The fee of the secretary of state for filing such consent shall be fifty dollars. No such consent shall be filed if the name of a domestic not-for-profit corporation, business corporation, not-for-profit corporation, limited liability company or limited partnership formed later than one year after the publication of the proclamation of dissolution, or the name or fictitious name or of a foreign business corporation, not-for-profit corporation, limited liability company or limited partnership which has obtained authority to do business or conduct activities in the state later than one year after such proclamation, or name which has been reserved later than one year after such proclamation, is the same as or may not be distinguished from the name of the corporation filing such consent unless such corporation simultaneously files in the department of state a certificate of amendment to change the name of such corporation. Such certificate of amendment shall be executed in like manner as if such corporation had not been dissolved.

(i) If, after the publication of such proclamation, it shall appear that the name of any corporation was erroneously included therein, the attorney general shall so certify to the secretary of state, and the secretary of state shall make appropriate entry on the records of the department of state, which entry shall have the effect of annulling all of the proceedings theretofore taken under the provisions of this section for the dissolution of such corporation with the same force and effect as if such proclamation had not been made or published.

(j) Whenever a corporation shall have complied with paragraph (h) of this section or whenever the procedures specified in paragraph (i) of this section shall have been taken, the secretary of state shall publish a notice thereof in the state register and shall send a copy of such notice to the county clerk of the county in which, according to his or her records, the office of the corporation is located. Such county clerk shall file such copy and make appropriate entry on his or her records without charge.

(k) If, after the dissolution of any corporation, assets of the corporation are located, the attorney general shall act with respect to such assets in accordance with this article and article 11 (Judicial dissolution).

History: Add, L 2005, ch 726, § 17, eff April 9, 2006; amd, L 2006, ch 434, § 11, eff July 26, 2006.

ARTICLE 11
JUDICIAL DISSOLUTION

§ 1106.   Referee
§ 1107.   Hearing and decision
§ 1108.   Application for final order
§ 1109.   Judgment or final order of dissolution
§ 1110.   Venue
§ 1111.   Preservation of assets; appointment of receiver
§ 1112.   Certain sales, transfers, security interests and judgments void
§ 1113.   Injunction
§ 1114.   Discontinuance of action or special proceeding
§ 1115.   Applicability of other provisions

History: Add, L 1969, ch 1066, § 1, eff Sept 1, 1970.

§ 1101.   Attorney-general's action for judicial dissolution

(a) The attorney-general may bring an action for the dissolution of a corporation upon one or more of the following grounds:

(1) That the corporation procured its formation through fraudulent misrepresentation or concealment of a material fact.

(2) That the corporation has exceeded the authority conferred upon it by law, or has violated any provision of law whereby it has forfeited its charter, or carried on, conducted or transacted its business in a persistently fraudulent or illegal manner, or by the abuse of its powers contrary to public policy of the state has become liable to be dissolved.

(b) An action under this section is triable by jury as a matter or [of]* right.

* The bracketed word has been inserted by the Publisher.

(c) The enumeration in paragraph (a) of grounds for dissolution shall not exclude actions or special proceedings by the attorney-general or other state officials for the annulment or dissolution of a corporation for other causes as provided in this chapter or in any other statute of this state.

History: Add, L 1969, ch 1066, § 1, eff Sept 1, 1970, with substance derived from Gen Corp Law §§ 83, 90, 91, 92, 94.

CASE ANNOTATIONS

1. Generally
2-10. [Reserved for future use]
11. Under former General Corporation Law § 90
12. Under former General Corporation Law § 91
13. – Dissolution of corporation on action of attorney general
14. – – Pendency of voluntary dissolution as bar
15. – Requirement of, and application for, leave of court
16. – – Order granting leave; revocation
17. – – Appeal from order
18. – Elements of cause of action
19. – Statute of limitations
20. – Right to intervene
21. – Grounds for forfeiture
22. – – Construction of "violation of any provision" of law
23. – – Waiver
24. – Effect of action on corporate cause of action
25. Under former General Corporation Law § 92

1. Generally

It was error to summarily dismiss proceeding brought by Attorney General under CLS N-PCL § 1101(a) to dissolve corporation where, inter alia, there were facts lending support to claim that corporation was actually being controlled by another organization and that

charitable contributions were being funneled to that organization by corporation. People v Zymurgy, Inc. (1996, 1st Dept) 233 A.D.2d 178, 649 N.Y.S.2d 662

Mootness doctrine did not bar appeal from dismissal of proceeding brought by Attorney General under CLS N-PCL § 1101(a) to dissolve corporation, despite legislative dissolution of corporation, where petition for dissolution requested various other relief, and to extent that any issues on appeal were moot, they nevertheless warranted invocation of exception to mootness doctrine. People v Zymurgy, Inc. (1996, 1st Dept) 233 A.D.2d 178, 649 N.Y.S.2d 662

2-10. [Reserved for future use]

11. Under former General Corporation Law § 90

The provisions of this statute apply only to domestic corporations. Wilkinson v North River Constr. Co. (1884) 66 How Pr 423

12. Under former General Corporation Law § 91

This section is simply a rule of procedure and in no way determines or enlarges corporate liability. It merely fixes and enumerates the classes of cases in which, if liability exists, an action may be maintained by the attorney general. People v Atlantic A. R. Co. (1891) 125 N.Y. 513, 26 N.E. 622

This section has no application to the dissolution of a state bank for insolvency. Hagmayer v Alten (1901) 36 Misc 59, 72 N.Y.S. 623

13. – Dissolution of corporation on action of attorney general

A provision of a statute that a corporation forfeits its charter or forfeits the rights acquired thereby unless certain acts are performed does not ipso facto dissolve the corporation or deprive it of its corporate existence, but simply exposes it to proceedings on behalf of the state to enforce the forfeiture. In re Brooklyn E. R. Co. (1891) 125 N.Y. 434, 26 N.E. 474

An action can be maintained only by the state under this statute and not by a private individual. In re Brooklyn E. R. Co. (1891) 125 N.Y. 434, 26 N.E. 474

An action under this section should be brought in the name of the people by the attorney general without a relator. People v Buffalo Stone & Cement Co. (1892) 131 N.Y. 140, 29 N.E. 947

An action to rescind the charter of the American Society for the Prevention of Cruelty to Animals for not performing the functions for which it was organized and preventing violation of § 195-a of the Penal Law, dealing with docking of horses' tails, could only be brought by the Attorney General, and the complaint must be dismissed where the Attorney General declined to proceed. People ex rel. Vivisection Investigation League v American Soc. for Prevention of Cruelty to Animals (1964, 1st Dept) 20 A.D.2d 762, 247 N.Y.S.2d 487, affd (1964) 15 N.Y.2d 511, 254 N.Y.S.2d 116, 202 N.E.2d 561

Under section 91 of the General Corporation Law the Attorney General can annul the existence of a corporation which is existing or operating illegally, but the rightfulness of the existence of the corporation can be questioned only by the state and cannot be raised in a collateral proceeding, therefore the owners and operators of pharmacies within the city have no standing to raise the issue of the legality of the existence of the H.I.P. Drug Plan, Inc. as a non-profit membership corporation. Bank v Allen (1970, 3d Dept) 35 A.D.2d 245, 315 N.Y.S.2d 323

14. – – Pendency of voluntary dissolution as bar

The pendency of a proceeding for the voluntary dissolution of a corporation will not constitute a bar to an action instituted by the attorney general for the purpose of securing the dissolution of such corporation. People v Seneca Lake Grape & Wine Co. (1889) 52 Hun 174, 5 N.Y.S. 136, affd (1891) 126 N.Y. 631, 27 N.E. 410

15. – Requirement of, and application for, leave of court

An action under this section may be maintained only with the leave of the court. People ex rel. Hearst v Ramapo Water Co. (1900) 51 A.D. 145, 64 N.Y.S. 532

Under §§ 91 and 134 of this act of the Attorney-General, upon leave granted, may bring an action against a corporation organized under New York law to vacate its charter upon enumerated grounds, such as abuse of powers, but is required to apply for leave to bring the action showing that he has reason to believe the action can be maintained and that the public interests require it. Accordingly, the Attorney-General must determine in the first instance that it is his duty to bring the action, but the court is then required to exercise discretion whether or not to grant leave. People v B. C. Associates, Inc. (1959) 22 Misc. 2d 43, 194 N.Y.S.2d 353

Application for leave to bring an action pursuant to this section must be in writing. In re Central Stamping Co. (1894) 79 Hun 369, 29 N.Y.S. 449

16. – – Order granting leave; revocation

Granting of leave to bring an action under this section is discretionary with the court and is to be determined upon the circumstances of each case. People v Bleecker S. & F. F. R. Co. (1910) 140 A.D. 611, 125 N.Y.S. 1045, affd (1911) 201 N.Y. 594, 95 N.E. 1136

While a court which grants leave for an action under this section may revoke it, it will be done only in extreme cases. People v Boston, H. T. & W. R. Co. (1882, NY) 27 Hun 528

17. – – Appeal from order

An order granting leave to maintain an action under this section will not be reviewed upon appeal except in extreme cases. People v Boston, H. T. & W. R. Co. (1882, NY) 27 Hun 528

18. – Elements of cause of action

To sustain an action by the people to dissolve a corporation for violation of law or abuse of its powers, two things must be shown; first, that the defendant corporation has exceeded its powers; and second, that the excesses or abuses threatened or harmed the public welfare. People v North River Sugar Refining Co. (1890) 121 N.Y. 582, 24 N.E. 834

Under this section it must be shown that a cause of forfeiture exists, that it involves a public interest and that the court has authorized the action. People v Ulster & D. R. Co. (1891) 128 N.Y. 240, 28 N.E. 635

19. – Statute of limitations

An action to compel forfeiture, under § 91, is covered by the two-year period of limitation in Civil Pr Act, § 50, subd 2. People v Society of St. Joseph Palo Del Colle, Inc. (1941) 177 Misc 419, 30 N.Y.S.2d 551

20. – Right to intervene

The lessee of a railway company whose charter is sought to be annulled under this section is entitled to be made a party defendant. People v Albany & V. R. Co. (1879) 77 N.Y. 232

21. – Grounds for forfeiture

The failure of a manufacturing corporation to file an annual report is a ground of forfeiture at the suit of the attorney general, independently of the liability of the directors. People v Buffalo Stone & Cement Co. (1892) 131 N.Y. 140, 29 N.E. 947

Where a corporation has never exercised its powers and franchises, but its sole business is to fix the market price of which a commodity shall be bought and sold, and its nonuser was wilful and without justification, it is proper for the attorney general to bring an action for its dissolution. People v Milk Exchange, Ltd. (1892) 133 N.Y. 565, 30 N.E. 850

Where consolidation have taken place affecting the welfare of the people the attorney general may sue for annulment. People v Milk Exchange, Ltd. (1895) 145 N.Y. 267, 39 N.E. 1062

A combination of milk dealers and creamery men to fix and control the prices they should pay for milk is unlawful and a judgment annulling the corporation in an action in the name of the people is proper. People v Milk Exchange, Ltd. (1895) 145 N.Y. 267, 39 N.E. 1062

A corporate charter may be annulled where a corporation engages in the insurance business contrary to statute. People v Standard Plate Glass & Salvage Co. (1916) 174 A.D. 501, 156 N.Y.S. 1012

A corporation which represents property owners before commissioners of taxes and assessments is practicing law in violation of Penal Law and its charter will be revoked. 1916 Ops Atty Gen 455

22. – – Construction of "violation of any provision" of law

The provisions of subd 2 of this section authorizing forfeiture of a corporate charter for "violation of any provision" of law must be read more broadly than as a mere reference to violation of one or more of the list of statutory provisions governing corporate organization and functioning. People v Abbott Maintenance Corp. (1960, 1st Dept) 11 A.D.2d 136, 201 N.Y.S.2d 895, app den (1960) 8 N.Y.2d 710, reported in full (1960) 8 N.Y.2d 1120, 209 N.Y.S.2d 800, 171 N.E.2d 883 and motion gr (1961) 9 N.Y.2d 687, 212 N.Y.S.2d 422, 173 N.E.2d 241 and affd (1961) 9 N.Y.2d 810, 215 N.Y.S.2d 761, 175 N.E.2d 341

23. – – Waiver

Causes for forfeiture may be waived. In re Petition of New York E. R. Co. (1877) 70 N.Y. 327

24. – Effect of action on corporate cause of action

An action brought by the people to effect the dissolution of a corporation does not of itself divest the title of the corporation to a cause of action for tort, but the corporation may sue upon the action at any time before the final judgment dissolving the corporation, and making the receiver permanent. The receiver may assign such action with the assets of the corporation so as to allow the purchaser to be substituted in the action. Mutual Brewing Co. v New York & C. P. Ferry Co. (1897) 16 A.D. 149, 45 N.Y.S. 101

25. Under former General Corporation Law § 92

When the Attorney General, pursuant to this section, is granted leave to institute an action to vacate corporation charters and to annul existence of the corporations, initial interest of the people in whether the charters of defendants should be continued is judicially established. People v Abbott Maintenance Corp. (1960, 1st Dept) 11 A.D.2d 136, 201 N.Y.S.2d 895, app den (1960) 8 N.Y.2d 710, reported in full (1960) 8 N.Y.2d 1120, 209 N.Y.S.2d 800, 171 N.E.2d 883 and motion gr (1961) 9 N.Y.2d 687, 212 N.Y.S.2d 422, 173 N.E.2d 241 and affd (1961) 9 N.Y.2d 810, 215 N.Y.S.2d 761, 175 N.E.2d 341

In a proceeding by the Attorney General under § 92 of the General Corporation Law, seeking judicial permission to bring proceedings for dissolution of two corporations for conduct contrary to § 91 of the General Corporation Law, the record was sufficient to make out a prima facie case for vacating the first corporation's charter and the case should not have been dismissed as to it. People v Abbott Maintenance Corp. (1960, 1st Dept) 11 A.D.2d 136, 201 N.Y.S.2d 895, app den (1960) 8 N.Y.2d 710, reported in full (1960) 8 N.Y.2d 1120, 209 N.Y.S.2d 800, 171 N.E.2d 883 and motion gr (1961) 9 N.Y.2d 687, 212 N.Y.S.2d 422, 173 N.E.2d 241 and affd (1961) 9 N.Y.2d 810, 215 N.Y.S.2d 761, 175 N.E.2d 341

A subpoena duces tecum issue by the Attorney General under § 91 will not be quashed on application of the person or corporation to whom it is directed where its purpose is to ascertain whether there has been a violation of § 396 of the General Business Law which will support an application for leave to file proceedings for annulment of charter. Lawrence Aluminum Industries, Inc. v Lefkowitz (1960) 20 Misc. 2d 739, 196 N.Y.S.2d 844

Authorization for the Attorney-General to take proof and make a determination of the relevant facts is presumably to enable him to make the required showing upon application under § 91 to a court for leave to bring the action contemplated by that section. Goodyear Aluminum Products, Inc. v State (1960) 21 Misc. 2d 725, 203 N.Y.S.2d 256, revd on other grounds (1960, 3d Dept) 12 A.D.2d 692, 207 N.Y.S.2d 904

Failure to give notice is no objection to the proceedings where the court directed no notice in its order. People v Boston, H. T. & W. R. Co. (1882, NY) 27 Hun 528

§ 1102. Judicial dissolution; petition by directors or members; petition in case of deadlock among directors or members

(a) A petition for the judicial dissolution of a corporation may be presented:

(1) By a majority of the directors then in office, or by the members, or such of them as are designated for such purpose, when authorized to do so by a resolution adopted by majority vote as provided in paragraph (c) of section 613 (Vote of members) (provided that, notwithstanding any provision of the certificate of incorporation or the by-laws, a members' meeting to consider such a resolution may be called, no more often than once in any period of twelve consecutive months, by ten percent of the members entitled to vote thereon or by such lesser percentage or number of members as may be provided in the certificate of incorporation or by-laws), in the following cases:

(A) The assets of the corporation are not sufficient to discharge its liabilities.

(B) Dissolution will be beneficial to the members.

(2) By ten percent of the total number of members or by any director, in the following cases:

(A) The directors are so divided respecting the management of the corporation's affairs that the votes required for action by the board cannot be obtained.

(B) The members are so divided that the votes required for the election of directors cannot be obtained.

(C) There is internal dissension and two or more factions of members are so divided that dissolution would be beneficial to the members.

(D) The directors or members in control of the corporation have looted or wasted the corporate assets, have perpetuated the corporation solely for their personal benefit, or have otherwise acted in an illegal, oppressive or fraudulent manner.

(E) The corporation is no longer able to carry out its purposes.

(b) In any proceeding for judicial dissolution the attorney-general shall be a necessary party.

History: Add, L 1969, ch 1066, § 1, eff Sept 1, 1970, with substance derived from Gen Corp Law §§ 101, 102, 103.

Par (a), subpar (1), amd, L 1970, ch 847, § 66, eff Sept 1, 1970.

Par (a), subpar (2), cl (C), amd, L 1970, ch 847, § 67, eff Sept 1, 1970.

CASE ANNOTATIONS

1. **Generally**
2-10. [Reserved for future use]
11. **Under former General Corporation Law § 101**
12. – **Jurisdiction of court; venue**
13. – – **Notice of application for dissolution to attorney general**
14. – **Who may file petition**
15. – – **Meeting of directors as prerequisite**
16. – – **Verification**
17. – **Effect of filing petition**
18. – **Finding of insufficient assets**
19. **Under former General Corporation Law § 102**
20. **Under former General Corporation Law § 103**
21. – **Effect on jurisdiction of failure to serve attorney general**
22. – **Petition for dissolution on grounds of deadlock**
23. – **Requirements for dissolution**
24. – **Order granting examination of individual defendants; appeal**
25. – **Appointment of referee**
26. – **Costs and expenses**

1. Generally

Even if some of the expenditures made by incorporated building and trade association for secretarial service and to directors for meetings attended were excessive, in absence of bad faith, a remedy short of dissolution of the corporation on such ground would be in order. John Luther & Sons Co. v Geneva Builders & Trade Asso. (1976, 4th Dept) 52 A.D.2d 737, 381 N.Y.S.2d 934

A complaint by the Attorney-General seeking dissolution of the Richmond County Society for the Prevention of Cruelty to Children on the grounds that it had not engaged in any activity since 1977 and was no longer able to carry out the purpose for which it was formed (N-PCL § 1102(a)(2)(E)) stated a cause of action, since public policy dictates that such a society, vested with extraordinary powers, (see N-PCL § 1403), be effective and active, and the Attorney-General had standing to maintain this action (N-PCL § 112(a)(7)); in addition, the allegation that defendant had failed to file the financial reports required of a charitable organization (EPTL § 8-1.4) stated a cause of action, since defendant obtained a Federal income tax exemption as a charitable organization and it could not now refute its status as such, nor did the fact that defendant became statutorily exempt from filing requirements in 1982 release defendant from its culpability for failing to file the requisite reports from 1976 to 1982. Abrams v Richmond County S.P.C.C. (1984, Sup) 125 Misc. 2d 530, 479 N.Y.S.2d 624

Allegations that a homeowner's association failed to comply with corporate formalities and never served a useful purpose did not fall within any of the enumerated grounds for a judicial dissolution, and a review of the pleadings, affidavits, and exhibits revealed that residents failed to raise any triable issues of fact that warranted a trial; the evidence did not show that the homeowner's association engaged in oppressive or illegal actions, or that there was internal dissension to warrant a dissolution, and the dismissal of two causes of action seeking dissolution was affirmed. Korotun v Laurel Place Homeowner's Ass'n (2004, A.D., 2d Dept) 775 N.Y.S.2d 568, subsequent app (2004, A.D., 2d Dept) 775 N.Y.S.2d 567

In a judicial dissolution of a non-profit educational corporation under N.Y. Not-for-Profit Corp. Law § 1102, where donors imposed limitations on the use of the assets, those limitations must be honored in the dissolution, because New York's policy honoring donors' restrictions on the use of donated property has greater weight than the claims of creditors. Matter of Friends for Long Island's Heritage (2010, App Div, 2d Dept) 911 NYS2d 412.

Where a non-profit educational corporation is dissolving, if the purpose behind the donation of a charitable asset may be maintained even with a sale to satisfy, or partially satisfy, the claims of creditors, nothing in the law requires that the asset be distributed without charge. Matter of Friends for Long Island's Heritage (2010, App Div, 2d Dept) 911 NYS2d 412.

Where a non-profit educational corporation was dissolving, the trial court could allow the sale of a donated collection to an entity engaged in activities substantially similar to those of the corporation, as long as the sale was conditioned on the entity's agreeing to be bound, to the extent practical, to the terms of the original gift agreement. Matter of Friends for Long Island's Heritage (2010, App Div, 2d Dept) 911 NYS2d 412.

2-10. [Reserved for future use]

11. Under former General Corporation Law § 101

The method of effecting corporate dissolution prescribed by statute is exclusive. In re Importers' & Grocers' Exchange (1892) 132 N.Y. 212, 30 N.E. 401

An action for equitable dissolution of a corporation could be maintained even though remedies other than equitable dissolution might be available against corporate directors. Gilbert v Hamilton (1970, 1st Dept) 35 A.D.2d 715, 315 N.Y.S.2d 92, affd (1971) 29 N.Y.2d 842, 327 N.Y.S.2d 855, 277 N.E.2d 787

In a proceeding under this Article for voluntary dissolution of a corporation the court must find its authority in the statute without recourse to its authority in the statute without recourse to its ordinary equity powers. Gutwirth & Errante Homes, Inc. v Jacobowitz (1948, Sup) 81 N.Y.S.2d 607

12. – Jurisdiction of court; venue

While this section provides that an action or a special proceeding for dissolution of a corporation shall be brought in the Supreme Court and judicial district in which the office of the corporation is located, failure to comply with this requirement is not a jurisdictional defect and involves only a question of venue which is waived if objection thereto is not timely raised by the parties. Application of Elishewitz Hat Co. (1964) 42 Misc. 2d 51, 247 N.Y.S.2d 806

13. – – Notice of application for dissolution to attorney general

It is necessary that service be made upon the attorney-general of the state of notice of application for an order to show cause under this section to give the supreme court jurisdiction of a special proceeding instituted to dissolve a membership benevolent corporation. In re Society of Justice (1922) 233 N.Y. 691, 135 N.E. 972

Notice of an application for voluntary dissolution must be given to the Attorney General whether the corporation is solvent or insolvent. In re Board of Directors of Broadway Ins. Co. (1897) 23 A.D. 282, 48 N.Y.S. 299

14. – Who may file petition

The petition may be presented by the proper officers who are not required to resign, the action is instituted by them in their individual capacity. Zeltner v Henry Zeltner Brewing Co. (1903) 174 N.Y. 247, 66 N.E. 810

De facto directors may join in a petition for voluntary dissolution. In re Manoca Temple Ass'n (1908) 128 A.D. 796, 113 N.Y.S. 172

A majority of the board of directors may file a petition for dissolution under this section irrespective of any provisions of section 103. In re McLoughlin (1917) 176 A.D. 653, 163 N.Y.S. 547

An action for the equitable dissolution of a corporation could be maintained as a class action even though the plaintiff class consisted of only five persons. Gilbert v Hamilton (1970, 1st Dept) 35 A.D.2d 715, 315 N.Y.S.2d 92, affd (1971) 29 N.Y.2d 842, 327 N.Y.S.2d 855, 277 N.E.2d 787

A petition for a dissolution of a corporation was dismissed where the application was made by only one of the three directors of the corporation. Application of Ades (1958) 12 Misc. 2d 915, 177 N.Y.S.2d 574

15. – – Meeting of directors as prerequisite

A meeting of the board of directors is not a prerequisite to a petition by a majority of the board under this section. Application of Gail Kiddie Clothes, Inc. (1945, Sup) 56 N.Y.S.2d 117

16. – – Verification

The petition must be verified by a majority of the directors in strict compliance with the statute. In re Dolgeville Electric Light & Power Co. (1899) 160 N.Y. 500, 55 N.E. 287

17. – Effect of filing petition

The court acquires jurisdiction of the property of the corporation upon presentation of a petition for voluntary dissolution as provided in this title. In re Christian Jensen Co. (1891) 128 N.Y. 550, 28 N.E. 665

Officers and managing agents are not stripped of their power by the mere filing of a petition or the appointment of a temporary receiver, and service of process on a managing agent after such appointment is valid. Garibaldi v Yonkers (1949) 198 Misc 1100, 102 N.Y.S.2d 200, affd (1951) 278 A.D. 571, 102 N.Y.S.2d 426

18. – Finding of insufficient assets

The provision of this section for a finding that the assets are insufficient to discharge the liabilities means that the corporation is unable to pay its debts in the ordinary course of business. Application of Gail Kiddie Clothes, Inc. (1945, Sup) 56 N.Y.S.2d 117

19. Under former General Corporation Law § 102

A bylaw, that no resolution shall be adopted except by unanimous vote of the stockholders, is inconsistent with the law and therefore invalid. (Gen Corp Law, §§ 102, 103; Stk Corp Law, §§ 35, 37, 55, 86, 105). Benintendi v Kenton Hotel, Inc. (1943) 181 Misc 897, 45 N.Y.S.2d 705, affd (1944) 268 A.D. 857, 50 N.Y.S.2d 843, mod on other grounds (1945) 294 N.Y. 112, 60 N.E.2d 829, 159 ALR 280 (superseded by statute as stated in Application of Burkin (1956) 1 N.Y.2d 570, 154 N.Y.S.2d 898, 136 N.E.2d 862, 64 ALR2d 638) and (superseded by statute as stated in Sutton v Sutton (1994) 84 N.Y.2d 37, 614 N.Y.S.2d 369, 637 N.E.2d 260)

20. Under former General Corporation Law § 103

In liquidation proceedings the court must find its authority·in the statute, without recourse to its ordinary equity powers. Gutwirth & Errante Homes, Inc. v Jacobowitz (1948, Sup) 81 N.Y.S.2d 607

Under § 29 the directors are authorized to settle the corporate affairs of a corporation undergoing dissolution, but where the directors are evenly divided, making agreement on conduct impossible, the court has implied power to appoint a liquidator. Gutwirth & Errante Homes, Inc. v Jacobowitz (1948, Sup) 81 N.Y.S.2d 607

21. – Effect on jurisdiction of failure to serve attorney general

In a dissolution proceeding, full and complete adherence to the statute is indispensable to give the court jurisdiction, and thus failure to serve papers on the Attorney General in connection with proceedings under this section as required by § 137 is fatal to jurisdiction. In re Petition of Clemente Bros., Inc. (1959) 32 Misc. 2d 665, 228 N.Y.S.2d 320

22. – Petition for dissolution on grounds of deadlock

A petition stating that dissolution is sought upon the claim that the corporation has an equal number of directors who are equally divided regarding management of the affairs of the corporation sufficient. In re Gotham Tissue Corp. (1945) 269 A.D. 922, 57 N.Y.S.2d 550

A petition for the voluntary dissolution of a corporation under § 103 is insufficient in the absence of a showing of equal division among directors or of an attempt and failure to elect directors. Application of Landau (1944) 183 Misc 876, 51 N.Y.S.2d 651

A petition praying for dissolution of a corporation fails to meet the requirements of this section where it does not state the name and place of residence of creditors, details as to indebtedness, and contains no inventory of all property of the corporation, likewise does not set forth sufficient facts to satisfy the court that it would be beneficial to dissolve the corporation. Coucounas v Coucounas (1961, Sup) 222 N.Y.S.2d 592

A petition would not lie for voluntary dissolution of a corporation under this section by reason of a deadlock in management where it appeared that the corporation was set up to have an odd number of directors and there was nothing in the petition to explain how a deadlock could exist in view of the terms of the agreement under which it was organized. Dissolution of Roanoke Homes, Inc. (1962, Sup) 234 N.Y.S.2d 109

23. – Requirements for dissolution

An order granting a motion to have the court entertain a petition for dissolution under this section was reversed where it appeared from argument of counsel on appeal that the parties had agreed to sale of the corporation as a going business under judicial supervision, with case remitted to Special Term for reconsideration. Application for Dissolution of Venice Amusement Corp. (1961, 1st Dept) 14 A.D.2d 742, 220 N.Y.S.2d 47

A deadlock allegedly resulting because of three directors of a corporation who were in military service was not sufficient, under this section, to empower one of the directors to petition for dissolution. Application of Ades (1958) 12 Misc. 2d 915, 177 N.Y.S.2d 574

An application for the dissolution of a corporation rests in the sound discretion of the court, and unless facts are shown establishing a complete deadlock and irreconcilable and discordant interests so as to prevent efficient management, dissolution would constitute an improvident exercise of discretion. Application of George W. Anderson, Inc. (1951, Sup) 104 N.Y.S.2d 184, affd (1951) 279 A.D. 594, 107 N.Y.S.2d 556

Where corporations each had two directors who opposed each other and stalemate existed between stockholders, and it was shown that it would be beneficial to all that corporations be dissolved, motions for dissolution of both corporations were granted. Application of Stutman (1954, Sup) 132 N.Y.S.2d 538

24. – Order granting examination of individual defendants; appeal

Corporations are not necessary or proper parties in a proceeding for the examination of individual defendants upon the dissolution of a corporation because of a deadlock in its management. Hence, an appeal taken by the corporation from an order granting the examination should be dismissed. In re Guaranteed Pictures Co. (1953) 282 A.D. 1028, 126 N.Y.S.2d 526

25. – Appointment of referee

Appointment of a referee ex parte in a proceeding to dissolve a corporation is an abuse of discretion; compulsory reference is permissible but not without opportunity for persons interested to express objections. Application of Audio-Scriptions, Inc. (1947) 272 A.D. 50, 69 N.Y.S.2d 27

A referee should be appointed in a proceeding under this section only in cases where the factual situation is so intricate and ascertainment of the facts will be so time consuming that a substantial saving of court time would be expected to result. A determination of facts made by a referee in such a proceeding is binding on the court and since the court has the responsibility of the decision, it should hear, in the first instance, a matter where the facts are not unduly complicated. Application of 3260 Perry Ave. Realty Corp. (1954) 285 A.D. 71, 135 N.Y.S.2d 551, resettlement den (1955) 285 A.D. 882, 140 N.Y.S.2d 506

Special terms had discretion to entertain an application for a reference and to appoint a referee where papers submitted upon a motion for the reference in a proceeding for a voluntary dissolution of a corporation indicated on their face that there was a deadlock in the management of the corporation's affairs and that dissolution would be noninjurious to the public and beneficial to the stockholders. In re Sahara Beach Club, Inc. (1957, 2d Dept) 3 A.D.2d 933, 163 N.Y.S.2d 315

26. – Costs and expenses

An application for the voluntary dissolution of a corporation is a special proceeding and therefore, insofar as the costs and expenses thereof are concerned, is governed by provisions of the Civil Practice Act applicable to such proceedings. The court is without power to make an allowance for attorney's fees. In re Stoll-Meyer Woodcrafters, Inc. (1948, Sup) 84 N.Y.S.2d 757

§ 1103.   Contents of petition for judicial dissolution

A petition for dissolution shall specify the section, and the subparagraph or subparagraphs thereof, under which it is authorized and state the reasons why the corporation should be dissolved. It shall be verified by the petitioner or by one of the petitioners.

History: Add, L 1969, ch 1066, § 1, eff Sept 1, 1970, with substance derived from Gen Corp Law § 104.

CASE ANNOTATIONS

1-5. [Reserved for future use]
6. Under former General Corporation Law § 104

1-5. [Reserved for future use]
6. Under former General Corporation Law § 104
A technical or accidental omission in the inventory which does not show a lack of good faith may be obviated by the evidence. In re Majority of Trustees of Santa Eulalia Silver Min. Co. (1889) 115 N.Y. 657, 21 N.E. 1119

This section should be construed to mean that a petition must show that the case is one of those specified in §§ 101 and 103; that is to say, it need not be shown that case comes within §§ 101 and 103, for the word "and" as used in said clause should be construed to mean "or." In re McLoughlin (1917) 176 A.D. 653, 163 N.Y.S. 547

Where a complaint praying for dissolution of a corporation fails to state the facts required by §§ 103 and 104 of the General Corporation Law, and the application is not brought on by petition and order to show cause approved by the court, it cannot be granted. Coucounas v Coucounas (1961, Sup) 222 N.Y.S.2d 592

The petition should contain a full and complete inventory of the property. Re Dubois (1857) 15 How Pr 7

§ 1104.   Order to show cause; issuance; publication, service, filing

(a) Upon the presentation of such a petition, the court shall make an order requiring the corporation and all persons interested in the corporation to show cause before it, or before a referee designated in the order, at a time and place therein specified, not less than four weeks after the granting of the order, why the corporation should not be dissolved. In connection therewith, the court may order the corporation, its officers and directors, to furnish the court with a schedule of all information, known or ascertainable with due diligence by them, deemed pertinent by the court, including a statement of the corporate assets and liabilities, and the name and address of each member and of each creditor and claimant, including any with unliquidated or contingent claims and any with whom the corporation has unfulfilled contracts.

(b) A copy of the order to show cause shall be published as prescribed therein, at least once in each of the three weeks before the time appointed for the hearing thereon, in one or more newspapers, specified in the order, of general circulation in the county in which the office of the corporation is located at the date of the order.

(c) A copy of the order to show cause shall be served upon the state tax commission and the corporation and upon each person named in the petition, or in any schedule provided for in paragraph (a), as a member, creditor or claimant, except upon a person whose address is stated to be unknown and cannot with due diligence be ascertained by the corporation. The service shall be made personally, at least ten days before the time appointed for the hearing, or by mailing a copy of the order, postage prepaid, at least twenty days before the time so appointed, addressed to the person to be served at his last known address.

(d) A copy of the order to show cause and the petition shall be filed, within ten days after the order is entered, with the clerk of the county where the office of the corporation is located at the date of the order. A copy of each schedule furnished to the court under this section shall, within ten days thereafter, be filed with such clerk.

(e) Publication, service and filing provided for in this section shall be effected by the corporation or such other persons as the court may order.

History: Add, L 1969, ch 1066, § 1, eff Sept 1, 1970, with substance derived from Gen Corp Law §§ 106, 107, 108, 109.

CASE ANNOTATIONS

1-5. [Reserved for future use]
6. Under former General Corporation Law § 106
7. Under former General Corporation Law § 107
8. Under former General Corporation Law § 108

1-5. [Reserved for future use]
6. Under former General Corporation Law § 106
An order requiring persons interested to show cause why the prayer of the petition should not be granted substantially complies with the section and is sufficient although served without a copy of the petition. In re Christian Jensen Co. (1891) 128 N.Y. 550, 28 N.E. 665

Although an order to show cause does not contain a direction in accordance with this section requiring publication. Such defect does not render the appointment of a temporary receiver void and may be remedied by amendment. In re Christian Jensen Co. (1891) 128 N.Y. 550, 28 N.E. 665

Where the petition for the dissolution of a corporation does not indicate a necessity therefor, i.e., that it will be beneficial to the stockholders and not injurious to the public, there was no need for a reference or for the taking of proof under this section and § 113. In re Radom & Neidorff, Inc. (1954) 307 N.Y. 1, 119 N.E.2d 563, motion den (1954) 307 N.Y. 701, 120 N.E.2d 865

Purely formal defect in the order to show cause may be corrected by entry of an order nunc pro tunc. In re Lenox Corp. (1901) 57 A.D. 515, 68 N.Y.S. 103, affd (1901) 167 N.Y. 623, 60 N.E. 1115

This proceeding is purely statutory and the provisions of the statute must be followed and the authority of the court is limited to that given by the statute itself. In re Seneca Oil Co. (1912) 153 A.D. 594, 138 N.Y.S. 78, affd (1913) 208 N.Y. 545, 101 N.E. 1121

The court has power, on resignation of a referee appointed under this section, to appoint a new referee upon notice, and direct him to attend at the time and place specified in the original order for return thereof and to adjourn the reference to be thereafter held in office of new referee to a time to be designated by said referee on adjournment, where no rights of any one interested in corporation will thereby be impaired. Application of Baumann (1922) 201 A.D. 136, 194 N.Y.S. 243, affd (1922) 234 N.Y. 555, 138 N.E. 444

Appointment of a referee ex parte in a proceeding to dissolve a corporation is an abuse of discretion; compulsory reference is permissible but not without opportunity for persons interested to express objections. Application of Audio-Scriptions, Inc. (1947) 272 A.D. 50, 69 N.Y.S.2d 27

A proceeding for the dissolution of a corporation under this article is a special proceeding to which CPA § 308 is applicable and hence, special term had the power, in its discretion, to permit an examination before trial in the proceeding. In re Sahara Beach Club, Inc. (1957, 2d Dept) 3 A.D.2d 933, 163 N.Y.S.2d 315

Where the parties to a proceeding seeking dissolution of a corporation stipulated to waive notice of hearing and for adoption of a plan of liquidation and dissolution under an impartial management involving the election of specified directors, but one of the specified directors refused to accept the position, and the contemplated independent management could not be put into effect as agreed upon, petitioner should be permitted to withdraw her consent to the plan and given an opportunity to litigate her right to dissolution and the appointment of a receiver. In re Venice Amusement Corp. (1962, Sup) 235 N.Y.S.2d 54

The order to show cause is in the nature of a process for bringing interested persons before the court and such order must be in strict compliance with the statute. In re Pyrolusite Manganese Co. (1883, NY) 29 Hun 429

7. Under former General Corporation Law § 107

After hearing objections against any proposed reference, if the court determine that a referee should be appointed, it is not necessary to publish and serve notice again. Application of Audio-Scriptions, Inc. (1947) 272 A.D. 50, 69 N.Y.S.2d 27

8. Under former General Corporation Law § 108

Service of the order to show cause on creditors does not require them to take notice of all further proceedings; notice of an accounting by the temporary receiver should be served on the creditors. In re Simonds Mfg. Co. (1899) 39 A.D. 576, 57 N.Y.S. 776

§ 1105.   Amending papers

At any stage, before final order, the court may grant an order amending the petition or any other paper filed in the action or special proceeding, with like effect as though originally filed as amended, or otherwise as the court may direct.

History: Add, L 1969, ch 1066, § 1, eff Sept 1, 1970, with substance derived from Gen Corp Law § 115.

Failure to annex the affidavit required by section 105 to the schedules may be remedied at any time before final order. In re Greenwald (1936) 248 A.D. 590, 287 N.Y.S. 362

§ 1106.   Referee

If a referee was not designated in the order to show cause, the court, in its discretion, may appoint a referee when or after the order is returnable. The court may at any time appoint a successor referee.

History: Add, L 1969, ch 1066, § 1, eff Sept 1, 1970, with substance derived from Gen Corp Law § 112.

§ 1107.   Hearing and decision

At the time and place specified in the order to show cause, or at any other time and place to which the hearing is adjourned, the court or the referee shall hear the allegations and proofs of the parties and determine the facts. The decision of the court or the report of the referee shall be made and filed with the clerk of the court with all convenient speed.

History: Add, L 1969, ch 1066, § 1, eff Sept 1, 1970, with substance derived from Gen Corp Law §§ 113, 114.

Where the petition for the dissolution of a corporation does not indicate a necessity therefor, i.e., that it will be beneficial to the stockholders and not injurious to the public, there was no need for a reference or for the taking of proof under this section and § 106. In re Radom & Neidorff, Inc. (1954) 307 N.Y. 1, 119 N.E.2d 563, motion den (1954) 307 N.Y. 701, 120 N.E.2d 865

§ 1108.   Application for final order

When the hearing is before a referee, a motion for a final order must be made to the court upon notice to each party to the action or special proceeding who has appeared therein. The notice of motion may be served as prescribed for the service of papers upon an attorney in an action in such court. When the hearing is before the court, a motion for a final order may be made at the hearing or at such time and upon such notice as the court prescribes.

History: Add, L 1969, ch 1066, § 1, eff Sept 1, 1970, with substance derived from Gen Corp Law § 116.

In proceedings for voluntary dissolution of a corporation, the facts must be determined by a referee or by the court itself and then a separate motion must be made, on the referee's report or on the court's decision of the facts, for a determination by the court of the law question of whether the facts as found justify a dissolution. The court's order of reference, regardless of its form, is controlled by § 113 under which any reference was for a determination of facts. Hence, the review of facts as found by a referee and of the laws pronounced by the court upon those facts is for the Appellate Division and Special Term therefore had no power to reject the findings of an official referee that the shareholders would not benefit from a dissolution. Such finding was conclusive upon the Special Term and all the court could do after that was to make an order denying dissolution as a matter of law. If there was to be a reversal on the facts, that is for the Appellate Division. In re Seamerlin Operating Co. (1954) 307 N.Y. 407, 121 N.E.2d 392

§ 1109.   Judgment or final order of dissolution

(a) In an action or special proceeding under this article if, in the court's discretion, it shall appear that the corporation should be dissolved, it shall make a judgment or final order dissolving the corporation.

(b) In making its decision, the court shall take into consideration the following criteria:

(1) In an action brought by the attorney-general, the interest of the public is of paramount importance.

(2) In a special proceeding brought by directors or members, the benefit to the members of a dissolution is of paramount importance.

(c) If the judgment or final order shall provide for a dissolution of the corporation, the court may, in its discretion, provide therein for the distribution of the property of the corporation to those entitled thereto according to their respective rights. Any property of

Not-For-Profit Corporation Law

the corporation described in subparagraph one of paragraph (c) of section 1002-a (Carrying out the plan of dissolution and distribution of assets) shall be distributed in accordance with that section.

(d) The clerk of the court or such other person as the court may direct shall transmit certified copies of the judgment or final order of dissolution to the department of state and to the clerk of the county in which the office of the corporation was located at the date of the judgment or order. Upon filing by the department of state, the corporation shall be dissolved.

(e) The corporation shall promptly thereafter transmit a certified copy of the judgment or final order to the clerk of each other county in which its certificate of incorporation was filed.

History: Add, L 1969, ch 1066, § 1, eff Sept 1, 1970, with substance derived from Gen Corp Law §§ 77, 80, 96, 97, 117.

Par (c), amd, L 2005, ch 726, § 14, eff April 9, 2006.

CASE ANNOTATIONS

1. Generally
2-5. [Reserved for future use]
6. Under former General Corporation Law § 77
7. Under former General Corporation Law § 97
8. Under former General Corporation Law § 117

1. Generally
The alleged internal dissension between members of incorporated building and trade association was not ground for dissolution of the corporation in absence of showing that dissolution would be beneficial to the members of the corporation as required by the Not-For-Profit Corporation Law. John Luther & Sons Co. v Geneva Builders & Trade Asso. (1976, 4th Dept) 52 A.D.2d 737, 381 N.Y.S.2d 934

2-5. [Reserved for future use]
6. Under former General Corporation Law § 77
All creditors are entitled to share equally in the distribution. Home Bank v J. B. Brewster & Co. (1897) 15 A.D. 338, 44 N.Y.S. 54, appeal after remand (1898) 33 A.D. 330, 53 N.Y.S. 867, app dismd (1899) 159 N.Y. 526, 53 N.E. 1126

The judgment should provide for an accounting and distribution of the fund among the creditors in full or proportionately. Hallett v Metropolitan Messenger Co. (1902) 69 A.D. 258, 74 N.Y.S. 639

Acts done by sole stockholder on behalf of corporation, resulting in corporate liability stemming solely therefrom, did not establish individual liability of stockholder for overcharge by corporation. Multiple Products, Inc. v Seaboard Nat'l Distribution Center, Inc. (1970, 1st Dept) 34 A.D.2d 919, 311 N.Y.S.2d 346

Irrespective of the statute the court has power to distribute the funds in accordance with the best interests of all concerned. Smith v Danzig (1883) 3 N.Y. Civ Proc 127

7. Under former General Corporation Law § 97
Publishing substance and effect of judgments of dissolution is sufficient. 1914 Ops Atty Gen 169

8. Under former General Corporation Law § 117
A petition for dissolution was not subject to dismissal, on the ground, that there was pending and undetermined two actions for money damages by petitioner against the corporation. Application of Pivot Punch & Die Corp. (1959) 15 Misc. 2d 713, 182 N.Y.S.2d 459, mod on other grounds (1959, 4th Dept) 9 A.D.2d 861, 193 N.Y.S.2d 34

In connection with a receivership imposed upon an insolvent corporation in voluntary proceedings for its dissolution, there should ordinarily be a ratable distribution of whatever sum is available for payment to creditors of a particular class, regardless of the order in which they file and prove their claims. Application of Lyding (1962) 33 Misc. 2d 561, 226 N.Y.S.2d 12

Where, in proceedings for voluntary dissolution of an insolvent corporation, the court appoints a receiver, the receiver's fees and expenses and disbursements incidental to a reference made for

hearing in relation to the receivership are to be paid before all other claims, including pre-existing liens. Application of Lyding (1962) 33 Misc. 2d 561, 226 N.Y.S.2d 12

The court would not dispense with a receiver where it was impossible to determine in some instances who was entitled to distribution, and further, where it was evident that some difficulty would be encountered in determining the persons entitled to distribution and in determining the interest of the Department of Welfare. In re Application of St. Luke Stockholders, Inc. (1954, Sup) 133 N.Y.S.2d 457

§ 1110.   Venue

An action or special proceeding under this article shall be brought in the supreme court in the judicial district in which the office of the corporation is located at the time of the service on the corporation of a summons in such action or of the presentation to the court of the petition in such special proceeding.

History: Add, L 1969, ch 1066, § 1, eff Sept 1, 1970, with substance derived from Gen Corp Law §§ 101, 138, 139.

§ 1111.   Preservation of assets; appointment of receiver

At any stage of an action or special proceeding under this article, the court may, in its discretion, make all such orders as it may deem proper in connection with preserving the property and carrying on the business of the corporation, including the appointment and removal of a receiver under article 12 (Receivership), who may be a director, officer or member of the corporation.

History: Add, L 1969, ch 1066, § 1, eff Sept 1, 1970, with substance derived from Gen Corp Law §§ 29, 74, 93, 110, 118, 150.

CASE ANNOTATIONS

1-5. [Reserved for future use]
6. Under former General Corporation Law § 110

1-5. [Reserved for future use]
6. Under former General Corporation Law § 110
Where a temporary receiver is continued as permanent receiver the creditors may require him to account for everything received by him as temporary receiver. In re Simonds Mfg. Co. (1899) 39 A.D. 576, 57 N.Y.S. 776

A temporary receiver may be authorized by the courts to finish and complete the outstanding contracts of the corporation. Nason Mfg. Co. v Garden (1900) 52 A.D. 363, 65 N.Y.S. 147

A temporary receiver should not be authorized to sell property except where for most cogent reasons. In re Malcom Brewing Co. (1903) 78 A.D. 592, 79 N.Y.S. 1057

A temporary receiver of property of a corporation may be appointed only when it appears that the corporation is insolvent. In re Greenwald (1936) 248 A.D. 590, 287 N.Y.S. 362

Occupation of the premises by a temporary receiver creates no personal liability. Metropolitan Life Ins. Co. v Sanborn (1901) 34 Misc 531, 69 N.Y.S. 1009

A temporary receiver will not be appointed where the corporation is not shown to be insolvent. In re Kaufman Circle Express Co. (1941) 177 Misc 106, 29 N.Y.S.2d 264

A court cannot appoint a temporary receiver where the corporation is solvent. Garibaldi v Yonkers (1949) 198 Misc 1100, 102 N.Y.S.2d 200, affd (1951) 278 A.D. 571, 102 N.Y.S.2d 426

§ 1112.   Certain sales, transfers, security interests and judgments void

A sale, mortgage, conveyance or other transfer of, or the creation of a security interest in any property of a corporation made, without prior approval of the court, after service upon the corporation of a summons in an action, or of an order to show cause in a special proceeding, under this article in payment of or as security for an existing or prior debt or for any other or for no consideration, or a judgment thereafter rendered against the corporation by confession or upon the acceptance of any offer, shall be void as against such persons and, to such extent, if any, as the court shall determine.

History: Add, L 1969, ch 1066, § 1, eff Sept 1, 1970, with substance derived from Gen Corp Law § 119.

§ 1113. Injunction

(a) At any stage of an action or special proceeding under this article, the court may, in its discretion, grant an injunction, effective during the pendency of the action or special proceeding or such shorter period as it may specify in the injunction, for one or more of the following purposes:

(1) Restraining the corporation and its directors and officers from conducting any unauthorized activities and from exercising any corporate powers, except by permission of the court.

(2) Restraining the corporation and its directors and officers from collecting or receiving any debt or other property of the corporation, and from paying out or otherwise transferring or delivering any property of the corporation, except by permission of the court.

(3) Restraining the creditors of the corporation from beginning any action against the corporation, or from taking any proceedings in an action theretofore commenced, except by permission of the court. Such injunction shall have the same effect and be subject to the same provisions of law as if each creditor upon whom it is served was named therein.

History: Add, L 1969, ch 1066, § 1, eff Sept 1, 1970, with substance derived from Gen Corp Law §§ 73, 95, 111, 132, 135.

CASE ANNOTATIONS

1-5. [Reserved for future use]
6. Under former General Corporation Law § 73
7. Under former General Corporation Law § 111
8. Under former General Corporation Law § 135

1-5. [Reserved for future use]
6. Under former General Corporation Law § 73
The injunction provided by this section does not work a dissolution of the corporation. Kincaid v Dwinelle (1875) 59 N.Y. 548

It was improper to enjoin the defendant from acting as manager and director of defendant corporation where the corporation was in receivership and there was no fear that he would reduce the corporate assets. Sandfield v Goldstein (1970, 3d Dept) 33 A.D.2d 376, 308 N.Y.S.2d 25, affd (1971) 28 N.Y.2d 794, 321 N.Y.S.2d 904, 270 N.E.2d 723

7. Under former General Corporation Law § 111
An action to foreclose a lien upon property pledged or upon realty is not an action to recover "a sum of money," within the meaning of this section conferring authority on the court in dissolution proceedings to enjoin certain actions. In re French (1918) 181 A.D. 719, 168 N.Y.S. 988, affd (1918) 224 N.Y. 555, 120 N.E. 863

This section expressly provides that creditors may be enjoined only where a receiver is legally appointed. In re Greenwald (1936) 248 A.D. 590, 287 N.Y.S. 362

Officers and managing agents are not stripped of their power by the mere filing of a petition or the appointment of a temporary receiver, and service of process on a managing agent after such appointment is valid. Garibaldi v Yonkers (1949) 198 Misc 1100, 102 N.Y.S.2d 200, affd (1951) 278 A.D. 571, 102 N.Y.S.2d 426

8. Under former General Corporation Law § 135
The notice of an application for an injunction required by this section may be given by means of an order to show cause. Goss v Warp Twisting-In Mach. Co. (1909) 133 A.D. 122, 117 N.Y.S. 228

Where two directors of a corporation claim to be the only persons interested in it, and assert that the third director is a mere dummy put forward by them because the statute required three directors, a clause contained in an order to show cause why the third director should not be permitted to examine corporate books, staying defendants from removing him pending proceeding, is not an injunction within the meaning of this section. People ex rel. Stauffer v Bonwit Bros. (1910) 69 Misc 70, 125 N.Y.S. 958

It may be seriously questioned whether an ex parte order temporarily enjoining defendants from continuing their business is valid to the extent that it suspends the business of the corporation or restrains the officers and directors from exercising their powers and duties. However, a court had the power, ex parte or otherwise, to restrain specific corporate acts to preserve status quo. People v Borg-Johnson (1958) 11 Misc. 2d 928, 176 N.Y.S.2d 167

This section, in declaring void the ex parte grant of an injunction suspending "the general and ordinary business of a corporation or restraining a director thereof from the exercise of the powers," does not prohibit an ex parte restraint of a power of a director which does not interfere with the general and ordinary business of the corporation, the word "power" as here employed not being synonymous with the word "right." United Democratic Regular Organization of Sixteenth Assembly Dist., Inc. v Lewis (1959) 21 Misc. 2d 822, 194 N.Y.S.2d 225

§ 1114. Discontinuance of action or special proceeding

An action or special proceeding for the dissolution of a corporation may be discontinued at any stage when it is established that the cause for dissolution did not exist or no longer exists. In such event, the court shall dismiss the action or special proceeding and direct any receiver to redeliver to the corporation all its remaining property.

History: Add, L 1969, ch 1066, § 1, eff Sept 1, 1970.

§ 1115. Applicability of other provisions

(a) Subject to the provisions of this article, the provisions of sections 1006 (Corporate action and survival of remedies after dissolution), 1007 (Notice to creditors; filing or barring claims) and 1008 (Jurisdiction of supreme court to supervise dissolution and liquidation) shall apply to a corporation dissolved under this article.

(b) Any orders provided for in section 1008, may be made at any stage of an action or special proceeding for dissolution of a corporation under this article, and if the corporation is dissolved under this article, the court may retain jurisdiction for the purpose of making such orders, after the dissolution, in such action or special proceeding. The court may also make such orders in separate special proceedings, as provided in section 1008.

Not-For-Profit Corporation Law

(c) Notice to creditors and claimants, provided for in section 1007, may also be given, by order of the court, at any stage of an action or special proceeding for dissolution of a corporation under this article.

History: Add, L 1969, ch 1066, § 1; amd, L 1970, ch 847, § 68, eff Sept 1, 1970.

Par (a), amd, L 2005, ch 726, § 15, eff April 9, 2006.

ARTICLE 12
RECEIVERSHIP

History: Add, L 1969, ch 1066, § 1, eff Sept 1, 1970.

§ 1201.   Action by judgment creditor for sequestration

Where final judgment for a sum of money has been rendered against a corporation, and an execution issued thereupon to the sheriff of the county where the corporation conducts its activities, or where its office is located, has been returned wholly or partly unsatisfied, the judgment creditor may maintain an action to procure a judgment sequestrating the property of the corporation and providing for a distribution thereof.

History: Add, L 1969, ch 1066, § 1, eff Sept 1, 1970, with substance derived from Gen Corp Law § 70.

CASE ANNOTATIONS

1-10. [Reserved for future use]
11. Under former General Corporation Law § 70
12. – Action by judgment creditor for sequestration
13. – – Accrual of cause of action
14. – – Requirement of insolvency
15. – – Effect of action on status of corporation
16. – Statute of limitations
17. – Parties
18. – – Defendant
19. – Relief granted
20. – – Setting aside fraudulent or preferential transfers
21. – – Determination of rights of purchaser from corporation

1-10. [Reserved for future use]
11. Under former General Corporation Law § 70
This section has no application to foreign corporations. Dreyfus v Charles Seale & Co. (1899) 37 A.D. 351, 55 N.Y.S. 1111

Although this section does not apply to foreign corporations a court of equity has power to protect the property of a foreign corporation within this state and secure its equitable distribution among its creditors. Dreyfus v Charles Seale & Co. (1899) 37 A.D. 351, 55 N.Y.S. 1111

Although this section applies only to domestic corporations, the fact that the corporation is a foreign corporation may be waived by the consent of the parties; and having been so waived an administration of the property by the court may not be interfered with by a third party who has consented. Horton v Thomas McNally Co. (1913) 155 A.D. 322, 140 N.Y.S. 357

12. – Action by judgment creditor for sequestration
The action provided by this section is purely statutory but is equitable in character. Proctor v Sidney Sash, Blind & Furniture Co. (1896) 8 A.D. 42, 40 N.Y.S. 454

The statute does not apply to an ordinary equitable action by a judgment creditor to set aside a fraudulent judgment. Easton Nat'l Bank v Buffalo Chemical Works (1888) 48 Hun 557, 1 N.Y.S. 250

13. – – Accrual of cause of action
In a judgment creditor's action to sequester the assets of a corporation the plaintiff is not entitled to judgment where he began his action before his rights under assignment had accrued even though the rights had become absolute at the time of trial. A court of equity can mold its relief to fit the circumstances at the time of the decree but the plaintiff must have a right to some relief at the time of commencement of the action. Wappler v Woodbury Co. (1927) 246 N.Y. 152, 158 N.E. 56

The remedy of sequestration may not be pursued as provided by this section until the remedy by execution has been exhausted. Buttles v Smith (1939) 281 N.Y. 226, 22 N.E.2d 350

14. – – Requirement of insolvency
In an action under this section there is no specific requirement that proof of insolvency need be alleged or shown but if such proof is necessary, the allegation of the return of the execution nulla bona is sufficient. Buttles v Smith (1939) 281 N.Y. 226, 22 N.E.2d 350

This statute does not apply where the corporation has sufficient property in the county where it transacts its business or has its office to satisfy the judgment even though the corporation be insolvent. National Broadway Bank v Wessell Metal Co. (1891) 59 Hun 470, 13 N.Y.S. 744

15. – – Effect of action on status of corporation
A sequestration action does not dissolve the corporation. People v Troy Steel & Iron Co. (1894) 82 Hun 303, 31 N.Y.S. 337

16. – Statute of limitations
Action by judgment creditors under §§ 60, 61 and 70 because of alleged waste committed by individual defendants, as directors of a corporation against which plaintiffs held an unsatisfied judgment were actions at law and having come into being in favor of judgment creditors perforce the statute, under Civ Pr Act, § 48, subd 2, six-year statute of limitations (since reduced to three years) is applicable to them. Luke v Polstein (1944) 268 A.D. 921, 51 N.Y.S.2d 427, affd 294 N.Y. 896, 63 N.E.2d 27

17. – Parties
Parties whose presence is necessary to complete the determination of the controversy may be brought in. Woodard v Holland Medicine Co. (1891, Super Ct) 15 N.Y.S. 128

An action pursuant to this section may not be maintained by a director as such, but only indirectly by arrangement with a judgment creditor. National Broadway Bank v Wessell Metal Co. (1891) 59 Hun 470, 13 N.Y.S. 744

18. – – Defendant
An action under this section lies not only against the corporation as a defendant, but against those having possession of the corporate assets. Proctor v Sidney Sash, Blind & Furniture Co. (1896) 8 A.D. 42, 40 N.Y.S. 454

The corporation is a proper defendant in an action by a receiver appointed on sequestration to set aside the corporation's fraudulent conveyance. Hubbell v Merchants' Nat'l Bank (1886, NY) 42 Hun 200

19. – Relief granted
A bankruptcy court may stay an action to set aside a fraudulent transfer. This section and § 73 confer no greater rights upon a judgment creditor than may be exercised on behalf of such creditor by

a trustee in bankruptcy. In re Suffolk Airways, Inc. (1933, DC NY) 3 F. Supp. 815

20. - - Setting aside fraudulent or preferential transfers

Fraudulent transfers may be set aside in an action under this section in order to reach the property sought to be sequestered but other creditors will be entitled to share in the distribution. Home Bank v J. B. Brewster & Co. (1897) 15 A.D. 338, 44 N.Y.S. 54, appeal after remand (1898) 33 A.D. 330, 53 N.Y.S. 867, app dismd (1899) 159 N.Y. 526, 53 N.E. 1126

An action under this section may not be used to set aside a transfer of property intended to create a preference in favor of one creditor over another, unless such intent is clearly shown, and such property cannot be reached in such action without showing that when the transfers were made the corporation knew of the existence of the plaintiff's claim. Abrams v Manhattan Consumers' Brewing Co. (1911) 142 A.D. 392, 126 N.Y.S. 844

21. - - Determination of rights of purchaser from corporation

In an action under this section the right of one who had purchased property from the defendant corporation and retained part of the purchase price to discharge liens to retain such money could not be determined summarily on a motion for the appointment of a receiver. Savoy-Reeland Printing Corp. v Cove Theatres, Inc. (1930) 228 A.D. 504, 240 N.Y.S. 229

§ 1202.   Appointment of receiver of property of a domestic or foreign corporation

(a) A receiver of the property of a corporation can be appointed only by the court, and in one of the following cases:

(1) An action or special proceeding brought under article 10 (Non-judicial dissolution) or 11 (Judicial dissolution).

(2) An action under section 1201 (Action by judgment creditor for sequestration).

(3) An action brought by the attorney-general under section 112 (Actions or special proceedings by attorney-general), or brought by the attorney-general or by a member to preserve the assets of a corporation, which has no officer within this state qualified to administer them.

(4) An action to preserve the assets in this state, of any kind, tangible or intangible, of a foreign corporation which has been dissolved, nationalized or its authority or existence otherwise terminated or cancelled in the jurisdiction of its incorporation or which has ceased to conduct its activities, brought by any creditor or member of such corporation or by one on whose behalf an order of attachment against the property of such corporation has been issued.

(5) An action brought for the foreclosure of a mortgage upon property of the corporation, where the mortgage debt or the interest thereon has remained unpaid for at least thirty days after payment demanded and where either the income of the property is specifically mortgaged or the property itself appears to be insufficient to pay the mortgage debt. A receiver appointed under this subparagraph shall be receiver only of the property upon which the mortgage is being foreclosed.

(6) An application of the regents of the university, in aid of the liquidation of a corporation whose dissolution they contemplate or have decreed; or on the application of the trustees of such a corporation, on notice to the regents.

(b) A receiver shall be subject to the control of the court at all times and may be removed by the court at any time.

(c) All actions or special proceedings brought by or against a receiver shall have a preference upon the calendars of all courts next in order to actions or special proceedings brought by the people of the state of New York.

History: Add, L 1969, ch 1066, § 1, eff Sept 1, 1970, with substance derived from Gen Corp Law §§ 74, 140, 150, 154, 161.

Par (a), subpar (3), amd, L 1970, ch 847, § 69, eff Sept 1, 1970.

Par (a), subpar (5), amd, L 1970, ch 847, § 69 eff Sept 1, 1970.

CASE ANNOTATIONS

1-5. [Reserved for future use]
6. Under former General Corporation Law § 150

1-5. [Reserved for future use]
6. Under former General Corporation Law § 150

Although supplementary proceedings may be maintained against domestic corporations by judgment creditors, such right does not authorize appointment of a receiver. Boucker Contracting Co. v W. H. Callahan Contracting Co. (1916) 218 N.Y. 321, 113 N.E. 257

The provisions of this section and § 151 for appointment of receivers of property of corporations do not apply to the appointment of a receiver of rents and profits of mortgaged premises, owned by the corporation, in connection with an action to foreclose a mortgage. New York Title & Mortg. Co. v Polk Arms, Inc. (1933) 262 N.Y. 21, 186 N.E. 35; Home Title Ins. Co. v Isaac Scherman Holding Corp. (1934) 240 A.D. 851, 267 N.Y.S. 84

A receiver should not be appointed under this section on the grounds that there are no officers qualified to hold the assets of the corporation where, although three of the five directors have been removed, the two remaining directors are prima facie qualified to act in that they are apparently duly elected and one of them has the powers of the president who was ousted. Ehret v George Ringler & Co. (1911) 144 A.D. 480, 129 N.Y.S. 551, app dismd 204 N.Y. 638, 98 N.E. 1102

A receivership will be terminated when the parties applying for receivership have not brought themselves within any of the provisions of this section. Schindler v George Ringler & Co. (1923) 206 A.D. 217, 200 N.Y.S. 692

Under this section a receiver cannot be appointed in an action brought to foreclose a mortgage upon property of a corporation, where the requirement of the statutes as to default, demand and failure to pay have not been complied with, and there is no allegation in the moving papers that parties liable for the debt are insolvent, or proof that the mortgaged premises are inadequate security for debt. Manufacturers' Trust Co. v Roerich Museum (1932) 236 A.D. 76, 258 N.Y.S. 284, app dismd 260 N.Y. 562, 184 N.E. 93

Where it does not appear that the plaintiff ever demanded payment of any installment of principal or interest or taxes, or that thirty days had elapsed since any of such items fell due, or that the income of the property was specifically mortgaged, or that the property is insufficient to pay the amounts claimed, the plaintiff is not entitled to appointment of a receiver of rents of the property of a corporate mortgagor. Emigrant Industrial Sav. Bank v Fairdeal Holding Corp. (1933) 238 A.D. 850, 262 N.Y.S. 992

Plaintiff, in an action to foreclose a mortgage, is entitled to an order appointing a receiver of property covered by a mortgage and of rents and profits where the mortgage by its terms permits appointment of a receiver and there has been default in the obligations to be performed by the mortgagor. Moreover, the application is within the meaning of subd 2 of this section since property of the corporation is involved in foreclosure action and mortgage debt, or interest thereon, has remained unpaid for thirty days and payment has been duly demanded. Greisman v Albany Malleable Iron Co. (1930) 138 Misc 763, 246 N.Y.S. 25

The court may in supplementary proceedings appoint a receiver of property of a foreign corporation not doing business within this state, and having no business or fiscal agency, or agency for transfer of its stock within this state. Davis v Pneumatic Cushion Mfg. Corp. (1933) 146 Misc 578, 261 N.Y.S. 684

Supreme court has jurisdiction of a claim of United States government for deficiencies in income taxes of corporation, all of the property of which is in exclusive possession and control of receivers appointed by the court under § 150 in action to foreclose mortgage on property of said corporation, which receivers operated all of property and filed income tax returns. Guaranty Trust Co. v New York & Q.C.R. Co. (1938) 167 Misc 795, 4 N.Y.S.2d 532

§ 1203.   Temporary and permanent receiver

(a) At any stage before final judgment or final order in an action or special proceeding brought under this article, the court may appoint one or more receivers of the property of the corporation or of the property in this state of a foreign corporation against which an action has been brought under subparagraph (4) of paragraph (a) of section 1202 of this article. Notice of an application shall be given to the attorney-general, to each governmental body or officer whose consent is required for the dissolution of such corporation, and to such other persons and in such manner as the court directs. The determination by the court of the necessity or advisability of appointing a receiver or an attorney for a receiver, and the allowance of expenses, commissions or compensation to the receiver or such attorney, shall be subject to review on appeal. This provision shall not affect any other right to review on appeal.

(b) A receiver appointed by or under a final judgment or order in an action or special proceeding, or a temporary receiver who is continued by the final judgment or order, is a permanent receiver. The court may confer upon a temporary receiver the powers, and subject the temporary receiver to the duties of a permanent receiver, or so much thereof as it deems proper.

History: Add, L 1969, ch 1066, § 1, eff Sept 1, 1970, with substance derived from Gen Corp Law §§ 162, 163; amd, L 2013, ch 549, § 95, eff July 1, 2014.

CASE ANNOTATIONS

1-5. [Reserved for future use]
6. Under former General Corporation Law § 162
7. Under former General Corporation Law § 163

1-5. [Reserved for future use]
6. Under former General Corporation Law § 162

A temporary receiver appointed pursuant to § 162 is merely a custodian and agent of the court. He does not supersede the corporation in the exercise of its corporate powers except as to the particular property confided to him, with title to its property remaining in the corporation. He had no power to bring an action to recover legal fees allegedly wrongfully paid by the corporation. Cohen v Sherman (1952) 279 A.D. 939, 111 N.Y.S.2d 439

Where a temporary receiver is appointed pursuant to this section, his commissions are governed by General Corporation Law § 192 and not by Civil Practice Act § 1547. La Vin v La Vin (1953) 281 A.D. 888, 119 N.Y.S.2d 573

Only a permanent receiver in dissolution has title. Garibaldi v Yonkers (1949) 198 Misc 1100, 102 N.Y.S.2d 200, affd (1951) 278 A.D. 571, 102 N.Y.S.2d 426

Because of waste, misconduct, misappropriation and mismanagement of retail stores operated by two separate corporations and one partnership, the court ordered the appointment of a receiver for each store though the corporations were solvent businesses. Nadrich v Nagelberg (1957) 8 Misc. 2d 339, 165 N.Y.S.2d 166

On a motion for appointment of a temporary receiver of corporations, the attorney general must be given notice of the application. Leonard v Soufoul (1957) 13 Misc. 2d 659, 172 N.Y.S.2d 11

A temporary receiver appointed to liquidate local assets of an Austrian corporation under § 977b of the Civil Practice Act does not obtain title to the property involved under this section and therefore is not entitled to such assets as against the Alien Property Custodian, who was the authorized repository of all Austrian property in the United States. Clark v Propper (1948, CA2 NY) 169 F.2d 324, affd (1949) 337 US 472, 93 L Ed 1480, 69 S Ct 1333, reh den (1949) 338 US 841, 94 L Ed 514, 70 S Ct 33 and reh den (1952) 342 US 907, 96 L Ed 679, 72 S Ct 289

By virtue of his appointment as a receiver under this section, plaintiff was authorized to receive property of the corporation to be held subject to the order of the court and to maintain suit to obtain possession of such property. That being so, he could maintain such a suit in a foreign jurisdiction and the order of appointment by virtue of which his authority to sue was conferred could not be attacked collaterally. Cohen v La Vin (1954, CA2 Conn) 210 F.2d 550

7. Under former General Corporation Law § 163

Appointment of a permanent receiver of local assets of a foreign corporation is ineffective to give the receiver title to the property involved when these assets were subject to an executive order preventing unlicensed transfers issued prior to the appointment of the receiver. Clark v Propper (1948, CA2 NY) 169 F.2d 324, affd (1949) 337 US 472, 93 L Ed 1480, 69 S Ct 1333, reh den (1949) 338 US 841, 94 L Ed 514, 70 S Ct 33 and reh den (1952) 342 US 907, 96 L Ed 679, 72 S Ct 289

§ 1204.   Oath and security

A receiver, before entering upon his or her duties, shall:

(a) Take and subscribe an oath that he or she will faithfully, honestly and impartially discharge the trust committed to him or her, and the oath shall be filed with the clerk of the court in which the action or special proceeding is pending.

(b) File with the clerk of such court a bond to the people, with at least two sufficient sureties or a bond executed by any fidelity or surety company authorized by the laws of this state to transact business, in a penalty fixed by the court appointing him or her, conditioned for the faithful discharge of his or her duties as receiver. The court may at any time direct a receiver to give a new bond with new sureties and with like condition.

History: Add, L 1969, ch 1066, § 1, eff Sept 1, 1970, with substance derived from Gen Corp Law §§ 153, 154, 164; amd, L 2013, ch 549, § 95, eff July 1, 2014.

§ 1205.   Designation of depositories by court

All orders appointing a receiver of a corporation shall designate therein one or more places of deposit, wherein all funds of the corporation not needed for immediate disbursement shall be deposited and no other deposits and no investment of such funds shall be made, except upon the order of the court.

History: Add, L 1969, ch 1066, § 1, eff Sept 1, 1970, with substance derived from Gen Corp Law § 152.

§ 1206. Powers of permanent receiver

(a) A permanent receiver, upon qualifying under section 1204 (Oath and security), shall be vested with title to all the property of the corporation wherever situated or of the property in this state of a foreign corporation against which an action or special proceeding has been brought under subparagraph (a)(4) of section 1202 (Appointment of receiver of property of a domestic or foreign corporation), for the benefit of the creditors and members of the corporation.

(b) A permanent receiver shall have the power:

(1) To sue in his own name or otherwise for the recovery of the property, debts and causes of action of the corporation. No set-off or counterclaim shall be allowed in any such action for any demand unless it was owing by the corporation to the defendant before the commencement of the action or special proceeding in which the receiver was appointed or unless it shall have been incurred by the receiver subsequent to his appointment.

(2) To sell at public or private sale all the property vested in the permanent receiver, in such manner and on such terms and conditions as the court shall direct, and to make necessary transfers and conveyances thereof.

(3) To examine on oath, to be administered by the permanent receiver, any person concerning any matter pertaining to or affecting the receivership.

(4) To settle or compound any demands by or against the receivership.

(c) When more than one receiver is appointed, all provisions in this article in reference to one receiver shall apply to them.

(d) When more than one receiver is appointed, the debts and property of the corporation may be collected and received by any of them; when more than two receivers are appointed, the powers and rights conferred on them may be exercised by any two.

(e) When more than one receiver is appointed, the survivor or survivors of such receivers shall have all the powers and rights of the receivers.

History: Add, L 1969, ch 1066, § 1, eff Sept 1, 1970, with substance derived from Gen Corp Law §§ 165, 166, 167, 168, 169, 170, 171, 179; amd, L 1971, ch 1058 § 37, eff Sept 1, 1971, L 2013, ch 549, § 96, eff July 1, 2014.

CASE ANNOTATIONS

1-5. [Reserved for future use]
6. Under former General Corporation Law § 168
7. Under former General Corporation Law § 169
8. – Powers of receiver
9. – – Action against officer or director
10. – – Action to set aside transfer; vacate judgment
11. – – Subpoena witnesses
12. – Sale by receiver

1-5. [Reserved for future use]
6. Under former General Corporation Law § 168
The receiver's title is not subject to a judgment obtained after he was appointed. Attorney Gen. v Atlantic Mut. Ins. Co. (1885) 100 N.Y. 279, 3 N.E. 193

Upon security being filed the receiver's title relates back to the time of his appointment. In re Lenox Corp. (1901) 57 A.D. 515, 68 N.Y.S. 103, affd (1901) 167 N.Y. 623, 60 N.E. 1115

The receiver's rights are subject to those of prior judgment creditors, prior attaching creditors, prior assignees, or purchasers of property at previous judicial sales. National Park Bank v Clark (1904) 92 A.D. 262, 87 N.Y.S. 185

A temporary receiver is merely a custodian and agent of the court, to take and hold possession without title and has no authority to continue or discontinue the authority of any officer or agent. Garibaldi v Yonkers (1949) 198 Misc 1100, 102 N.Y.S.2d 200, affd (1951) 278 A.D. 571, 102 N.Y.S.2d 426

Permanent receiver had no title to cause of action against corporation's former officers to recover for an alleged preferential transfer but could plead a conversion cause of action. Hubsch v Insler (1954, Sup) 129 N.Y.S.2d 619

Appointment of a permanent receiver of local assets of a foreign corporation is ineffective to give the receiver title to the property involved when these assets were subject to an executive order preventing unlicensed transfers issued prior to the appointment of the receiver. Clark v Propper (1948, CA2 NY) 169 F.2d 324, affd (1949) 337 US 472, 93 L Ed 1480, 69 S Ct 1333, reh den (1949) 338 US 841, 94 L Ed 514, 70 S Ct 33 and reh den (1952) 342 US 907, 96 L Ed 679, 72 S Ct 289

A temporary receiver appointed to liquidate local assets of an Austrian corporation under § 977b of the Civil Practice Act does not obtain title to the property involved under this section and therefore is not entitled to such assets as against the Alien Property Custodian, who was the authorized repository of all Austrian property in the United States. Clark v Propper (1948, CA2 NY) 169 F.2d 324, affd (1949) 337 US 472, 93 L Ed 1480, 69 S Ct 1333, reh den (1949) 338 US 841, 94 L Ed 514, 70 S Ct 33 and reh den (1952) 342 US 907, 96 L Ed 679, 72 S Ct 289

7. Under former General Corporation Law § 169
A receiver cannot be sued without permission of the courts. In re Commercial Bank (1898) 35 A.D. 224, 54 N.Y.S. 722

Receiver may not be appointed to sue on contract made after existence of corporation has been terminated for failure to pay franchise taxes. In re Solomon (1939, Sup) 16 N.Y.S.2d 472

8. – Powers of receiver
A receiver has the power to collect notes and judgments. Higgins v Herrmann (1897) 23 A.D. 420, 48 N.Y.S. 244

A receiver may recover corporate funds improperly paid under court order. Mills v Ross (1899) 39 A.D. 563, 57 N.Y.S. 680, affd (1901) 168 N.Y. 673, 61 N.E. 1131

The receiver may maintain an action to determine the validity of bonds issued by the corporation. Hubbell v Syracuse Iron Works (1886, NY) 42 Hun 182

9. – – Action against officer or director
A receiver may enforce the liability of officers or directors for losses sustained by their misapplication of corporate assets. Mason v Henry (1897) 152 N.Y. 529, 46 N.E. 837

A receiver may sue an officer of a corporation to recover moneys received from a third person to procure the election of certain directors. McClure v Law (1899) 161 N.Y. 78, 55 N.E. 388

A receiver may sue the directors for negligence. Kelly v Dolan (1916, CA3 Pa) 233 F 635

10. – – Action to set aside transfer; vacate judgment
A receiver may maintain an action to vacate a judgment against the corporation on the ground that it was obtained by collusion with the officers. Whittlesey v Delaney (1878) 73 N.Y. 571

A receiver may maintain an action to set aside fraudulent transfer. Attorney Gen. v Guardian Mut. Life Ins. Co. (1879) 77 N.Y. 272

A receiver may move to vacate a judgment against corporate property. Yorkville Bank v Henry Zeltner Brewing Co. (1903) 80 A.D. 578, 80 N.Y.S. 839, app dismd (1904) 178 N.Y. 572, 70 N.E. 1111

Not-For-Profit Corporation Law

11. – – Subpoena witnesses

Subpoenas issued by the attorney for a permanent receiver must be vacated, where it appears that the subpoenas, which were issued under this section commanded witnesses to appear before the receiver at his office to testify and give evidence in a proceeding for dissolution of the corporation. While said section authorizes a receiver to examine a person under oath, there is no authority given him to subpoena witnesses. In re Klein (1930) 138 Misc 282, 245 N.Y.S. 486

12. – Sale by receiver

A sale by a receiver of a leasehold subject to a claim for rent does not prevent the landlord who purchased at the receiver's sale from asserting this claim for rent accruing while the receiver was in possession. Schwartz v Cahill (1917) 220 N.Y. 174, 115 N.E. 451

All sales made by receivers of corporate property are subject to liens thereon. Mayer v Burr (1909) 133 A.D. 604, 118 N.Y.S. 203

§ 1207.　　Duties of receiver upon appointment

(a) Upon appointment and qualification, a receiver shall have the following duties:

(1) To give immediate notice of his or her appointment by publication once a week for two successive weeks in two newspapers of general circulation in the county where the office of the corporation is located or, in the case of a foreign corporation against which an action has been brought under subparagraph (4) of paragraph (a) of section 1202 (Appointment of receiver of property of a domestic or foreign corporation), in a newspaper of general circulation as directed by the court, requiring:

(A) All persons indebted to the corporation to render an account of all debts owing by them to the corporation and to pay the same to the receiver at a specified place and by a specified day.

(B) All persons having in their possession any property of the corporation to deliver the same to the receiver at the specified place and by the specified day.

(C) All creditors and claimants, including any with unliquidated or contingent claims and any with whom the corporation has unfulfilled contracts, to present their claims to the receiver in writing and in detail at a specified place and by a specified day, which shall not be less than six months after the first publication of such notice. Whenever a receiver is appointed in dissolution proceedings under article 10 (Non-judicial dissolution) or article 11 (Judicial dissolution), section 1007 (Notice to creditors by corporations intending to dissolve; filing or barring claims) of this chapter shall apply and shall control the giving of notice to creditors and claimants and the filing and barring of claims.

(2) To call a general meeting of the creditors of the corporation within four months from the date of his appointment by a notice to be published as directed in subparagraph (a)(1), setting forth the time and place of such meeting, which time shall be not more than two months, nor less than one month after the first publication of such notice. At such meeting, or at an adjournment thereof, the receiver shall present a statement of all accounts and demands for and against the corporation, its subsisting contracts, and the money and other assets in his hands.

(3) To keep true books of account of all moneys received and expended by him as receiver, which books shall be open for inspection at reasonable times by creditors or other persons interested therein. On or before the first day of February in each year, for the preceding calendar year, and at such other times as the court shall direct, the receiver shall file with the clerk of the court by which he was appointed a verified statement showing the assets received, the disposition thereof, the money on hand, all payments made, specifying the persons to whom paid and the purpose of the payments, the amount necessary to be retained to meet necessary expenses and claims against the receiver, and the distributive share in the remainder of each person interested therein. A copy of such statement shall be served by the receiver upon the attorney-general within five days after the filing thereof.

History: Add, L 1969, ch 1066, § 1, eff Sept 1, 1970, with substance derived from Gen Corp Law §§ 171, 172, 174, 177, 178; amd, L 1970, ch 847, § 70, eff Sept 1, 1970, L 2013, ch 549, § 97, eff July 1, 2014.

CASE ANNOTATIONS

1-5. [Reserved for future use]
6. Under former General Corporation Law § 174

1-5. [Reserved for future use]
6. Under former General Corporation Law § 174

A receiver appointed in an action to foreclose a corporate mortgage covering all of the property and income of corporation, who has collected money for services rendered by the corporation and for rent which had become due to it prior to his appointment, should proceed under this section and §§ 180, 181 of this chapter to ascertain general creditors and pay their claims in order of priority. No other receiver can or need be appointed. State Bank of Williamson v Lamoka Power Corp. (1935) 269 N.Y. 1, 198 N.E. 609

Claims against a corporation in receivership, filed with the referee after the time stated in the notice to creditors and which claims are not barred by the statute of limitations under Civil Practice Act, § 48, should be heard by referee, where payment of the final dividend has not been made. People v S. W. Straus & Co. (1936) 158 Misc 186, 222, 285 N.Y.S. 648, mod on other grounds 248 A.D. 785, 289 N.Y.S. 209, and affd 248 A.D. 785, 290 N.Y.S. 423

§ 1208.　　Penalty for concealing property from receiver

Any persons having possession of property belonging to the corporation, who shall wrongfully withhold such property from the receiver after the day specified in the notice given under section 1207 (Duties of receiver upon appointment), shall forfeit to the receiver double the value of such property, and the same may be recovered in an action by the receiver.

History: Add, L 1969, ch 1066, § 1, eff Sept 1, 1970, with substance derived from Gen Corp Law § 176.

§ 1209.　　Recovery of assets

(a) Whenever a receiver, by verified petition to the supreme court at a special term held in the judicial district in which the receiver was appointed, shall show that he or she has good reason to believe that any person has in his or her possession or under his or her control, or has wrongfully concealed, withheld or disposed of, any property of the corporation, or that any person can testify concerning such facts, the court, with or without notice, shall make an order requiring such person to appear before the court or a referee, at a time and place designated, and submit to an examination concerning such facts. In such order, or at any time thereafter, in its discretion, the court may enjoin and restrain such person from disposing of any property of the corporation in his or her possession or under his or her control.

(b) In any examination under such order, the court may confer immunity in accordance with the provisions of section six hundred nineteen-c of the code of criminal procedure; provided that no immunity shall be conferred except upon twenty-four hours prior written notice to the appropriate district attorney having an official interest therein.

(c) A person so ordered to appear shall be entitled to the same fees and mileage, to be paid at the time of serving the order, as are allowed by law to witnesses subpoenaed to attend and testify in an action in the supreme court, and shall be subject to the same penalties upon failure to appear and testify in obedience to such order as are provided by law in the case of witnesses who fail to obey a subpoena to appear and testify in an action.

(d) A person appearing for examination in obedience to such order shall be sworn, and shall be entitled to be represented on such examination by counsel, and may be cross-examined, or may make a voluntary statement in his own behalf concerning the subject of his examination.

(e) The testimony taken under such order shall be signed and sworn to by the person examined, and be filed in the office of the clerk of the county where the action or proceeding is pending. If it shall appear that any person is wrongfully concealing or withholding, or has in his or her possession or under his or her control, any property of the corporation, on notice to such person, the court may make an order requiring such person forthwith to deliver it to the receiver, subject to the further order of the court.

History: Add, L 1969, ch 1066, § 1, eff Sept 1, 1970, with substance derived from Gen Corp Law § 170; amd, L 2013, ch 549, § 98, eff July 1, 2014.

CASE ANNOTATIONS

1-5. [Reserved for future use]
6. Under former General Corporation Law § 170

1-5. [Reserved for future use]
6. Under former General Corporation Law § 170
A receiver appointed in sequestration proceedings is not entitled to an order summarily directing a bank to turn over the amount of a deposit account of an insolvent corporation, the entire amount of which had been paid out on checks of the depositor, even where part of it had been held subject to the order of the court in prior supplementary proceedings. Re Delaney (1931) 256 N.Y. 315, 176 N.E. 407

A receiver of a corporation or of its property not appointed as such by supreme court of this state cannot invoke this section in order to procure examination concerning property of such corporation. Statute expressly limits such examination to receivers not only appointed by

New York court, whether primary or ancillary, but appointed pursuant to §§ 150, et seq. Re Myerberg, (1936) 249 A.D. 149, 291 N.Y.S. 519

Before an order may be made directing a defendant in a proceeding under § 170 to deliver to the receiver property allegedly wrongfully concealed or withheld, the court should direct the defendant to appear before the court or referee and submit to an examination concerning the facts recited in the petition. Petition of Horowitz (1940) 260 A.D. 879, 22 N.Y.S.2d 946

A receiver of property of a corporation having been appointed, under the general equity jurisdiction of the court, and not under § 150, this section cannot be invoked by him for the purpose of permitting examination of third person concerning property of the corporation as a judgment debtor. Howell v German Theater, Inc. (1909) 64 Misc 110, 117 N.Y.S. 1124

In a proceeding by receivers of defendant, a Russian bank, under § 170, for discovery of assets, in which an order was granted for examination of a trust company which had an account containing large sums of money in name of defendant, which receivers were endeavoring to reach, examination of witnesses was permissible and they could be required to produce documentary evidence since § 170 should be given a broad and liberal interpretation. Smith v Russo-Asiatic Bank (1939) 170 Misc 408, 10 N.Y.S.2d 10

The right of a receiver of a corporation to examine persons claimed to possess assets of the corporation or to have knowledge of their whereabouts is not defeated by their claim or affidavits that they do not have such knowledge or assets. Talmon v Societates Romana Pentru Industria De Bumbac (1954) 206 Misc 449, 132 N.Y.S.2d 776

§ 1210.　Order of payment by receiver

(a) Laborers' wages shall be preferred claims and entitled to payment before any other creditors out of the assets of the corporation in excess of valid prior liens or encumbrances.

(b) The receiver shall subject to any prior liens or encumbrances distribute the residue of the moneys in his hands, among the creditors whose claims have been proved and allowed, as follows:

(1) All debts due by such corporation to the United States, and all debts entitled to a preference under the laws of the United States.

(2) All debts that may be owing by the corporation as trustee.

(3) Judgments against the corporation, to the extent of the value of the real property on which they are liens.

(4) All other creditors in proportion to their respective demands, without preference to specialty debts.

History: Add, L 1969, ch 1066, § 1, eff Sept 1, 1970, with substance derived from Gen Corp Law §§ 180, 181.

CASE ANNOTATIONS

1. Generally
2-5. [Reserved for future use]
6. Under former General Corporation Law § 180

1. Generally
In proceeding to determine priorities of claims on settlement of account of receiver of nursing home, CLS Bus Corp § 1210 did not support contention of union, which represented employees of nursing home, that its claim for moneys due for fringe benefits took priority over claim by landlord for rent due. D'Guardia v Piffath (1992, 2d Dept) 180 A.D.2d 630, 579 N.Y.S.2d 447

In proceeding to determine priorities of claims on settlement of account of receiver of nursing home, CLS N-PCL § 1210 did not support contention of union, which represented employees of nursing home, that its claim for moneys due for fringe benefits took priority over claim by landlord for rent due. D'Guardia v Piffath (1992, 2d Dept) 180 A.D.2d 630, 579 N.Y.S.2d 447

In proceeding to determine priorities of claims on settlement of account of receiver of nursing home, CLS Partn § 71-a did not support contention of union, which represented employees of nursing home, that its claim for moneys due for fringe benefits took priority over claim by landlord for rent due. D'Guardia v Piffath (1992, 2d Dept) 180 A.D.2d 630, 579 N.Y.S.2d 447

In proceeding to determine priorities of claims on settlement of account of receiver of nursing home, CLS Pub Health § 2810 did not support contention of union, which represented employees of nursing home, that its claim for moneys due for fringe benefits took priority over claim by landlord for rent due since statute granted no such priority and in fact mandated that receiver honor all existing leases. D'Guardia v Piffath (1992, 2d Dept) 180 A.D.2d 630, 579 N.Y.S.2d 447

In proceeding to determine priorities of claims on settlement of account of receiver of nursing home, CLS Soc Serv § 461-f did not support contention of union, which represented employees of nursing home, that its claim for moneys due for fringe benefits took priority over claim by landlord for rent due since statute granted no such priority and in fact mandated that receiver honor all existing leases. D'Guardia v Piffath (1992, 2d Dept) 180 A.D.2d 630, 579 N.Y.S.2d 447

In proceeding to determine priorities of claims on settlement of account of receiver of nursing home, law of case did not entitle union, which represented employees of nursing home on claim for fringe benefits, to priority over claim of landlord for rent due, notwithstanding that earlier judgment based on arbitration granted first priority to union's claim since (1) landlord was not party to arbitration or proceeding to confirm arbitration award, and therefore was not impeded from seeking relitigation of matters decided therein, (2) fact that landlord may have had actual notice of pendency of union's motion to confirm arbitration award did not make him proper party to motion, and (3) fact that landlord had his own motion for priority pending at time union's motion was decided did not mean that landlord's papers were actually considered by court in making judgment in favor of union. D'Guardia v Piffath (1992, 2d Dept) 180 A.D.2d 630, 579 N.Y.S.2d 447

2-5. [Reserved for future use]

6. Under former General Corporation Law § 180

Under Labor Law, § 9 (L 1909, ch 36) prior to its repeal by L 1921, ch 50, § 474, sales agent for corporation was not "employee" entitled to be preferred creditor, for § 2 defined "employee" as "mechanic, workingman or laborer who works for another for hire" and, therefore, such sales agent became general creditor under this section. De Vries v Alsen Cement Co. (1923, CA2 NY) 290 F 746

Where claimant was head of department in the defendant's dry goods store, and as such bought goods and was responsible for sales of that department, and was under written contract for a monthly salary plus percentage of sales, his claim was not entitled to priority under this section. MacGregor v Johnson-Cowdin-Emmerrich, Inc. (1928, CA2 NY) 26 F.2d 311

§ 1211. Final distribution by receiver

(a) If there remains property of the corporation after the first distribution, the receiver shall, within one year thereafter, make a final distribution among the creditors entitled thereto. Notice that such distribution will be the final distribution to creditors shall be published once a week for two consecutive weeks in a newspaper of general circulation in the county where the office of the corporation is located and posted prominently and continuously for two consecutive weeks on the homepage of any website maintained by the corporation.

(b) A creditor or claimant who failed to prove his claim before the first distribution and who proves it before the final one shall receive the sum he would have been entitled to on the first distribution before

any further distribution shall be made to other creditors or claimants.

(c) Unless the court shall otherwise direct, no other distribution shall be made thereafter to creditors, except to those having pending actions against the corporation or the receiver.

(d) After the final distribution to creditors, the receiver shall not be answerable to any creditor or claimant, unless his claim shall have been proved before or at the time specified in the notice of the final distribution.

History: Add, L 1969, ch 1066, § 1, eff Sept 1, 1970, with substance derived from Gen Corp Law §§ 182, 183, 187; amd, L 2013, ch 549, § 99, eff July 1, 2014.

§ 1212. Disposition of moneys retained; surplus; unclaimed distributions

(a) When any action pending at the time of final distribution shall be terminated, the receiver shall apply the moneys retained by the receiver to the payment of the amount recovered, and the receiver's necessary charges and expenses incurred therein.

(b) After the final distribution to creditors and after deducting the receiver's charges and expenses, the receiver shall distribute any surplus in the manner prescribed in section 1002-a of this chapter or, if dissolution of the corporation is not involved, in such manner as the court shall order.

History: Add, L 1969, ch 1066, § 1, eff Sept 1, 1970, with substance derived from Gen Corp Law §§ 184, 185, 186; amd, L 1970, ch 847, § 71, eff Sept 1, 1970, L 2005, ch 726, § 16, eff April 9, 2006, L 2013, ch 549, § 100, eff July 1, 2014.

§ 1213. Omission or default of receiver

Upon notice to the attorney-general and upon such notice to creditors or others interested as the court shall direct, the court may, in the furtherance of justice, relieve a receiver from any omission or default, on such conditions as may be imposed, and, on compliance therewith, confirm the receiver's action.

History: Add, L 1969, ch 1066, § 1, eff Sept 1, 1970, with substance derived from Gen Corp Law § 173; amd, L 2013, ch 549, § 101, eff July 1, 2014.

§ 1214. Application by attorney-general for removal of receiver and to close receivership

(a) Whenever he or she deems it to be to the advantage of the members, creditors or other persons interested in the assets of any corporation for which a receiver has been appointed, the attorney-general may move:

(1) For an order removing the receiver and appointing another receiver;

(2) To compel the receiver to account;

(3) For such other and additional orders as may facilitate the closing of the receivership.

History: Add, L 1969, ch 1066, § 1, eff Sept 1, 1970, with substance derived from Gen Corp Law § 156; amd, L 2013, ch 549, § 101, eff July 1, 2014.

§ 1215. Resignation by receiver; filling any vacancy

(a) A receiver may petition the appointing court for an order to show cause why he or she should not be permitted to resign.

(b) The petition shall be accompanied by a verified account of all the assets of the corporation received by the receiver, of all payments or other disposition thereof made by the receiver, of the remaining assets of the corporation in respect to which the receiver was appointed receiver and the situation of the same, and of all his or her transactions as receiver. Thereupon, the court shall grant an order directing notice to be given to the sureties on his or her official bond and to all persons interested in the property of the corporation to show cause, at a time and place specified, why the receiver should not be permitted to resign. Such notice shall be published once in each week for six successive weeks in one or more newspapers as the court shall direct. If it shall appear that the proceedings of the receiver in the discharge of his or her trust have been fair and honest and that there is no good cause to the contrary, the court shall make an order permitting such receiver to resign. Thereupon the receiver shall be discharged and his or her powers as receiver shall cease, but he or she shall remain subject to any liability incurred prior to the making of such order. The court, in its discretion, may require the expense of such proceeding to be paid by the receiver presenting the petition.

(c) Any vacancy created by resignation, removal, death or otherwise, may be filled by the court, and the property of the receivership shall be delivered to the remaining receivers or, if there are none, to the successor appointed by the court. The court may summarily enforce delivery by order in the action or special proceeding in which the receiver was appointed.

History: Add, L 1969, ch 1066, § 1, eff Sept 1, 1970, with substance derived from Gen Corp Law §§ 157, 158, 167; amd, L 2013, ch 549, § 101, eff July 1, 2014.

§ 1216. Final accounting; notice; duty of attorney-general

(a) Within one year after qualifying, the receiver shall apply to the court for a final settlement of his accounts and for an order for distribution, or, upon notice to the attorney-general and to any governmental body or officer whose consent is required for the dissolution of the corporation, for an extension of time, setting forth the reasons therefor. If the receiver has not so applied for a settlement of his accounts or for such extension of time, the attorney-general or any creditor or member may apply for an order that the receiver show cause why an accounting and distribution should not be had, and after the expiration of eighteen months from the time the receiver qualified, it shall be the duty of the attorney-general to apply for such an order on notice to the receiver.

(b) Before presenting a final account, the receiver shall give notice of his intention to file it by publication, under subparagraph (a)(1) of section 1207 (Duties of receiver upon appointment), setting forth the time and place of filing and presentation to the court. The receiver shall also give not less than eight days' written notice to the sureties on his official bond.

(c) Upon presentation of such account, the court shall hear the allegations, objections and proofs of all parties interested and allow or disallow such account, in whole or in part, and make a final order. The court may refer the account and the hearing, in whole or in part, to a referee who shall report thereon to the court.

History: Add, L 1969, ch 1066, § 1, eff Sept 1, 1970, with substance derived from Gen Corp Law §§ 155, 188, 189, 190.

§ 1217. Commissions

(a) A receiver shall be entitled, in addition to his necessary expenses, to such commissions upon the sums received and disbursed as may be allowed by the court, as follows:

(1) On the first twenty thousand dollars, not exceeding five percent;

(2) On the next eighty thousand dollars, not exceeing two and one-half percent; and

(3) On the remainder, not exceeding one percent.

(b) If the commissions of the receiver so computed do not amount to one hundred dollars, the court in its discretion may allow such sum not exceeding one hundred dollars as shall be reasonable.

(c) When more than one receiver shall be appointed, the compensation herein provided shall be divided between them, as the court directs.

History: Add, L 1969, ch 1066, § 1, eff Sept 1, 1970, with substance derived form Gen Corp Law §§ 191, 192.

CASE ANNOTATIONS

1-5. [Reserved for future use]
6. Under former General Corporation Law § 192
7. Under former General Corporation Law § 226

1-5. [Reserved for future use]
6. Under former General Corporation Law § 192

A receiver may not continue a pre-existing arrangement for compensation in excess of the statutory commissions. Salmon v Schenectady Mason Supply Corp. (1951) 278 A.D. 609, 102 N.Y.S.2d 91

Where a temporary receiver is appointed pursuant to General Corporation Law § 162, his commissions are governed by this section and not by Civil Practice Act § 1547. La Vin v La Vin (1953) 281 A.D. 888, 119 N.Y.S.2d 573

Not-For-Profit Corporation Law

Computation of fees and allowances of a receiver in a foreclosure proceeding was properly based on § 1547 of the CPA, instead of this section, even though the principal mortgagor was a corporation, since the character of the mortgagor in a foreclosure proceeding is immaterial. Murphy v Pfeiffer Glass, Inc. (1958) 15 Misc. 2d 214, 180 N.Y.S.2d 639, mod on other grounds (1960, 4th Dept) 11 A.D.2d 902, 202 N.Y.S.2d 937

7. Under former General Corporation Law § 226

Court refused extraterritorial recognition to foreign order granting intervenor appointed for foreign corporation under foreign law control of litigation here pertaining to assets in this jurisdiction, and granted order substituting attorneys selected by corporation's president for attorneys designated by intervenor. Mann v Compania Petrolera Trans-Cuba, S. A. (1962) 32 Misc. 2d 790, 223 N.Y.S.2d 900

In action by stockholder of foreign corporation for appointment of permanent receiver of its assets in this state, court refused to give extraterritorial effect to foreign order appointing intervenor to control litigation on behalf of foreign corporation, since to do so would deprive the stockholders and directors of a corporation of the power to manage its affairs in this state. Mann v Compania Petrolera Trans-Cuba, S. A. (1962) 32 Misc. 2d 790, 223 N.Y.S.2d 900

§ 1218. Special provisions relating to actions or special proceedings against foreign corporations

(a) In any action or special proceeding brought against a foreign corporation under this article, the following provisions shall apply:

(1) Service of the summons in such action may be made personally within the state of New York, by delivery of the same to any officer or director of the corporation, or by publication pursuant to an order obtained as hereinafter provided.

(2) An order directing service by publication of the summons shall be made upon application of a plaintiff in any such action and shall be founded upon a verified complaint, alleging that the defendant is a foreign corporation and has or may have or may be entitled to assets, credits, choses in action or other property, tangible or intangible within the state and that such corporation has been dissolved, nationalized or that its authority or existence has been terminated or cancelled in the jurisdiction of its incorporation, or that it has ceased to conduct its activities, and upon an affidavit reciting that personal service of the summons cannot be effected within the state with due diligence and that a temporary receiver of its property within the state of New York has been appointed pursuant to this article in such action and that a copy of the order appointing the receiver has been served personally by or on behalf of such receiver upon a person, firm or corporation holding property, tangible or intangible, of the said foreign corporation, or against whom a claim or demand in favor of such foreign corporation exists and that demand therefor has been made upon such person, firm or corporation by or on behalf of such receiver.

(3) The order directing service of the summons shall require the publication thereof in a newspaper published in the state of New York in the English language at least once a week for four successive weeks, and shall also require the mailing on or before the date of the first publication of a copy of the summons, complaint and order to the corporation at its last known principal or head office in the state or country of its incorporation.

(4) In any such action, the summons shall be served personally or an order directing service thereof by publication shall be obtained and the first publication thereof made within sixty days after the appointment of the temporary receiver, and if served by publication, the service shall be made complete by the continuance thereof.

(5) If served by publication, service of the summons shall be deemed complete on the date of the last publication. The action shall be deemed commenced upon the issuance of the summons. The order appointing the receiver and the papers upon which the same is granted shall be filed in the office of the clerk of the court where the action is triable within ten days after the order is made.

(6) In the event that the defendant defaults in answering, or if after a trial the court is satisfied that the defendant has ceased to conduct its activities by reason of any thing or matter whatsoever, or that it has been dissolved, nationalized, or its authority or existence has been otherwise terminated or cancelled, the court shall thereupon direct judgment, appointing a permanent receiver and directing the receiver to liquidate the assets, credits, choses in action and property, tangible and intangible, in the state of New York of the said defendant, in the manner provided in this article.

(7) The time between the cessation of its activities by the corporation or its dissolution or nationalization or the termination or cancellation of its authority or existence and the appointment of a receiver in this state pursuant to this article, whichever time is longer, plus three years after such appointment, shall not be a part of the time limited by domestic or foreign laws for the commencement of an action or for the assertion of a claim therein by or on behalf of or against said corporation or by or against said receiver, whether or not said action or claim has heretofore been barred by any statute of limitations of this state or of any other state or country.

(8) The existence of and causes of action of or against such corporation existing at the time of its dissolution, nationalization, or the termination or cancellation of its authority or existence, or arising thereafter, shall not be deemed ended, abated or affected thereby, nor shall actions brought by or against such corporation or a receiver appointed hereunder or any remedy therein be deemed to have ended or abated or to have been affected by reason of such dissolution, nationalization, or termination or cancellation of its authority or existence. This provision shall apply to all property, tangible and intangible, debts, demands, and choses in action of such corporation within the state of New York, and to all litigation heretofore or hereafter brought in the courts of the state or of the United States to which the corporation or the receiver of said corporation appointed pursuant to the provisions of this article is

a party. Any receiver appointed pursuant to the provisions of this article may be substituted for such corporation in any action or proceeding pending in the courts of the state or of the United States to which such corporation is a party and may intervene in any action or proceeding which relates to or affects any of the assets or claims of the corporation and revive any action which shall have heretofore or which may hereafter have abated, and such dissolution, nationalization, or termination or cancellation of its authority or existence in the jurisdiction of its incorporation, or any confiscatory law or decree thereof, shall not be deemed to have any extraterritorial effect or validity as to the property, tangible or intangible, debts, demands or choses in action of such corporation within the state or any debts or obligations owing to such corporation from persons, firms or corporations residing, sojourning or doing business in the state. Nothing contained in this subdivision shall be deemed to validate claims for or causes of action or actions to recover property located in or moneys payable in the jurisdiction of incorporation which are unenforceable under the laws of such jurisdiction.

(9) If any receiver or trustee has heretofore been appointed in this state for such corporation or its property in any action or proceeding, either before or supplementary to judgment, otherwise than in an action brought pursuant to this article, such receiver or trustee may be appointed or continued as the receiver in any action brought pursuant to the provisions of this article.

(10) The appointment of a receiver or the pendency of an action for the appointment of such receiver, shall until such receiver shall be discharged or until such action shall have terminated, be a bar to any subsequent application or action for the appointment of a receiver of the assets of the same corporation.

(11) An action shall be commenced within three years from the discovery by the plaintiff or his predecessor in interest, of any asset of said corporation in the state of New York.

History: Add, L 1969, ch 1066, § 1, eff Sept 1, 1970, with substance derived from Gen Corp Law § 226.

Par (a), subpar (8), amd, L 1971, ch 1058 § 38, eff Sept 1, 1971.

ARTICLE 13
FOREIGN CORPORATIONS

History: Add, L 1969, ch 1066, § 1, eff Sept 1, 1970.

Article heading, amd, L 1970, ch 847, § 72, eff Sept 1, 1970.

§ 1301.   Authorization of foreign corporations

(a) A foreign corporation shall not conduct activities in this state until it has been authorized to do so as provided in this article. A foreign corporation may be authorized to conduct in this state any activities which may be conducted lawfully in this state by a domestic corporation, to the extent that it is authorized to conduct such activities in the jurisdiction of its incorporation, but no other activities.

(b) Without excluding other acts which may not constitute conducting activities in this state, a foreign corporation shall not be considered to be conducting activities in this state, for the purposes of this chapter, by reason of doing in this state any one or more of the following acts:

(1) Maintaining or defending any action or proceeding, whether judicial, administrative, arbitrative or otherwise, or effecting settlement thereof or the settlement of claims or disputes.

(2) Holding meetings of its directors or its members.

(3) Maintaining bank accounts.

(4) Maintaining offices or agencies only for the transfer, exchange and registration of its securities, or appointing and maintaining trustees or depositaries with relation to its securities.

(5) Granting funds.

(6) Distributing information to its members.

(c) The specification in paragraph (b) does not establish a standard for activities which may subject a foreign corporation to service of process under this chapter or any other statute of this state.

(d) A foreign corporation whose corporate name is not acceptable for authorization pursuant to sections 301 and 302 of this chapter, may submit in its application for authority pursuant to section thirteen hundred four of this chapter, a fictitious name under which it shall do business in this state. A fictitious name submitted pursuant to this section shall be subject to the provisions of subparagraphs 2 through

9 of paragraph (a) of section 301 and section 302 of this chapter. A foreign corporation authorized to conduct activities in this state under a fictitious name pursuant to this section, shall use such fictitious name in all of its dealings with the secretary of state and in the conduct of its activities in this state. The provisions of section one hundred thirty of the general business law shall not apply to any fictitious name filed by a foreign corporation pursuant to this section.

History: Add, L 1969, ch 1066, § 1, eff Sept 1, 1970, with substance derived from Gen Corp Law §§ 210, 211.

Par (d), add, L 1982, ch 590, § 17, eff Oct 20, 1982.

CASE ANNOTATIONS

1. Generally
2-10. [Reserved for future use]
11. Under former General Corporation Law § 210
12. – Authorization to do business in state
13. – – Requirement that name indicate applicant is corporation
14. – Designation of secretary of state for service of process
15. – – Service on secretary of state
16. – – Constitutionality of requirement
17. – – Revocation of designation
18. – Designation of agent as consent to be sued in federal courts
19. – – Jurisdiction of federal court in absence of designation
20. – – Venue of action against airline
21. – What constitutes "doing business" within state
22. – – Regular and continuous business conduct
23. – – Investing in, or subletting of, leased property
24. – – Solicitation of orders
25. – – Selling through commission salesman
26. – – Presence of agents
27. – – Mailing of executed contract to state
28. – Unauthorized foreign corporation
29. – – Right to maintain action
30. – – Action involving insurance policy
31. – – Right to enforce arbitration agreement
32. – – Venue of action against corporation
33. Under former General Corporation Law § 211

1. Generally

A dismissal by the Appellate Division of a petition by a foreign not-for-profit corporation seeking to dispense with the approval of the New York Society for the Prevention of Cruelty to Children, which normally was required before a corporation could conduct in New York all the activities of a domestic society, would be reversed and remanded for redetermination, even though the determination of the Appellate Division was correct as the matter stood before it, where the litigation had proceeded on the assumption that the corporation sought to conduct in New York all the activities of a domestic society, and where in fact the corporation sought to conduct only those activities that it was authorized to conduct under the laws of its incorporating state. Re American Soc. for Prevention of Cruelty to Children (1983) 58 N.Y.2d 1071, 462 N.Y.S.2d 634, 449 N.E.2d 414

Commissioner of Education properly determined that foreign nonprofit corporation had no authority to operate a private school in New York under N-PCL §§ 404, subd d, 1301, and 1304, subd c where said school, although in existence prior to passage of the N-PCL, had never been authorized to do business here within the meaning of N-PCL § 1302. Green Valley School, Inc. v Nyquist (1972) 72 Misc. 2d 889, 340 N.Y.S.2d 234

Court set aside resolution whereby regional chapter of non-for-profit California corporation ("Sierra Club") suspended petitioner ("New York City Group") from its organization without requisite notice and meaningful opportunity to be heard, where regional chapter did not adhere to national Sierra Club's bylaws and standing rules, its e-mail communications to its own board of governance and

"other interested parties" did not fulfill notice requirements, and only evidence of notification addressed to petitioners' members consisted of notifications informing them of their suspension. Lane v Sierra Club (2000, Sup) 183 Misc. 2d 944, 706 N.Y.S.2d 577

2-10. [Reserved for future use]

11. Under former General Corporation Law § 210

This section and § 212 circumscribe official action to be taken by secretary of state under § 9. Barber Co. v Department of State (1938) 277 N.Y. 55, 12 N.E.2d 790, 115 ALR 1236

Sections 210 and 218 of the General Corporation Law do not apply to corporations "exclusively engaged in interstate or foreign commerce." Munoz v American Stevedores, Inc. (1960, 2d Dept) 10 A.D.2d 963, 201 N.Y.S.2d 640

A foreign corporation, concededly not qualified under the laws of this state at the time certain land owned by it in this state was taken by proceedings under § 30 of the Highway Law, was not "doing business" within the state so as to require it to qualify under § 218. Wm. G. Roe & Co. v State (1964) 43 Misc. 2d 417, 251 N.Y.S.2d 151

Above statute does not apply to national banking association because it is "moneyed corporation" within meaning of exception contained in such statute. State Nat'l Bank v Laura (1965) 45 Misc. 2d 430, 256 N.Y.S.2d 1004

A municipality may or may not require a foreign corporation to comply with § 210, supra, as a condition precedent to the award of a public contract required by § 103, supra, to be let by public bidding. Notice of such requirement should be given to all prospective bidders in advance of the submission of bids. 1967 Ops Atty Gen Feb 26

12. – Authorization to do business in state

A foreign corporation may be licensed to do business in this state without any requirement that it possess property within this jurisdiction. Colgate Palmolive Peet Co. v Planet Service Corp. (1939) 173 Misc 494, 15 N.Y.S.2d 558

Granting of certificate to do business constitutes a true contract with state, and secretary of state was true agent of corporation, and the actions in which he was to represent the corporation were not limited. Trounstine v Bauer, Pogue & Co. (1942, DC NY) 44 F. Supp. 767, affd (1944, CA2 NY) 144 F.2d 379, cert den (1944) 323 US 777, 89 L Ed 621, 65 S Ct 190

A foreign business corporation can engage only in business that a similar corporation organized in this state is permitted to do. 1921 Ops Atty Gen 307

Before a foreign corporation organized to maintain a home for the aged may take title to realty in this State it must obtain approval of the State Board of Social Welfare and file statement and designation with Secretary of State. 1955 Ops Atty Gen Apr 20 (informal)

13. – – Requirement that name indicate applicant is corporation

Where the name of a foreign corporation does not "clearly indicate" that it is a corporation and it is unwilling to use "in this state such an affix or prefix" as will indicate the necessary distinction, the secretary of state may deny its application authorizing it to do business within the state. People ex rel. United Verde Copper Co. v Hugo (1917) 181 A.D. 149, 168 N.Y.S. 80

14. – Designation of secretary of state for service of process

A foreign corporation which has obtained a license to do business in New York and designated a person in this state upon whom process in actions against it may be served cannot limit the causes of action upon which it may be sued. Sukosky v Philadelphia & Reading Coal & Iron Co. (1919) 189 A.D. 689, 179 N.Y.S. 23

Designation of the secretary of state upon whom process might be served in New York was a consent to be sued there, and a waiver of any claim of want of jurisdiction over the person of the corporation. Trounstine v Bauer, Pogue & Co. (1942, DC NY) 44 F. Supp. 767, affd (1944, CA2 NY) 144 F.2d 379, cert den (1944) 323 US 777, 89 L Ed 621, 65 S Ct 190

Failure to actually do business within the state does not vitiate an unwithdrawn designation pursuant to this section. Aaron v Ag-wilines, Inc. (1948, DC NY) 75 F. Supp. 604, 14 CCH LC P 64339

15. – – Service on secretary of state

Service on the secretary of state at Albany as duly designated agent of a foreign corporation is proper but does not confer jurisdiction in personam. Swedosh v Belding Hosiery Mills, Inc. (1938) 168 Misc 673, 6 N.Y.S.2d 532

Where a foreign corporation is doing business in this state, jurisdiction of a transitory cause of action arising in another state may be obtained by service on the secretary of state as the agent designated pursuant to this section. Where the plaintiff is a resident of this state such an action is not a burden on interstate commerce. Karius v All States Freight, Inc. (1941) 176 Misc 155, 26 N.Y.S.2d 738

A foreign corporation, by obtaining a certificate of authority to do business in this state, is required to designate the Secretary of State as agent upon whom process in any action or proceeding against it within the state may be served, and accordingly a subpoena issued in connection with supplementary proceedings involving such corporation may be served upon the Secretary of State and such service is valid and effective. Nesbitt v Nesbitt (1963) 39 Misc. 2d 855, 241 N.Y.S.2d 611

16. – – Constitutionality of requirement

A state may constitutionally require a foreign corporation, as a condition of doing local business, to designate an agent upon whom service of process may be made. Neirbo Co. v Bethlehem Shipbuilding Corp. (1939) 308 US 165, 84 L Ed 167, 60 S Ct 153, 128 ALR 1437 (questioned in Cognitronics Imaging Sys. v Recognition Research Inc. (2000, ED Va) 83 F. Supp. 2d 689)

17. – – Revocation of designation

Where a corporation which has done business in this state and designated the Secretary of State as an agent to receive process, has surrendered its authority to do business in this state and revoked its designation of the Secretary of State, process cannot thereafter be effectively served upon the Secretary of State, even though the corporation continues to do business in the state. Green v Clark (1959, DC NY) 173 F. Supp. 233

18. – Designation of agent as consent to be sued in federal courts

A designation by a foreign corporation, as a condition of doing business within a state, of an agent upon whom service of process may be made is an effective consent to be sued in the federal courts of that state. Neirbo Co. v Bethlehem Shipbuilding Corp. (1939) 308 US 165, 84 L Ed 167, 60 S Ct 153, 128 ALR 1437 (questioned in Cognitronics Imaging Sys. v Recognition Research Inc. (2000, ED Va) 83 F. Supp. 2d 689)

Designation of an agent for service of process by a foreign corporation under this section results in a waiver of its right to be sued in a Federal district of which it is an inhabitant, in an action brought under the Fair Labor Standards Act, in the enforcement of which state and Federal courts have concurrent jurisdiction. Roger v A. H. Bull & Co. (1948, CA2 NY) 170 F.2d 664, 15 CCH LC P 64835

A consent filed under this section constitutes a waiver of objection to the venue provisions of section 51 of the Judicial Code and in a suit based upon diversity of citizenship a motion to quash service and dismiss the action must be denied where service has been made within the state of New York pursuant to the statutory designation of an agent to accept service on the part of a foreign corporation. Detachable Bit Co. v Timken Roller Bearing Co. (1940, DC NY) 31 F. Supp. 632, 44 USPQ 643

A foreign corporation filing a certificate designating the secretary of state as the person upon whom process might be served may be sued in the federal court in this state by service of process upon the secretary of state. American Blower Corp. v B. F. Sturtevant Co. (1945, DC NY) 61 F. Supp. 756, 66 USPQ 278

A foreign corporation's designation of an agent for service of process pursuant to this section constitutes a consent to be sued in the federal courts in this state even where jurisdiction is founded on non-diversity grounds. Aaron v Agwilines, Inc. (1948, DC NY) 75 F. Supp. 604, 14 CCH LC P 64339

When a foreign corporation domesticated itself under this statute whereby it designated an agent for the service of process within this state, the Federal district court had jurisdiction of an action brought under the Federal Antitrust Laws though the defendant was served with process in another Federal district and even though the foreign corporation did no business in the district in which it was sued. Bertha Bldg. Corp. v National Theatres Corp. (1952, DC NY) 106 F. Supp. 489

19. – – Jurisdiction of federal court in absence of designation

Even though it does sufficient business within the state so that it should file a consent to be sued pursuant to § 210 a foreign corporation which does not file such a consent is not a resident within the meaning of the federal statute providing that where federal jurisdiction is based on diversity of citizenship suit may be brought only in the district of the residence of the plaintiff or defendant. Moss v Atlantic C. L. R. Co. (1945, CA2 NY) 149 F.2d 701

A foreign corporation which has not filed a consent to be sued pursuant to this section does not waive the venue provisions of § 51 of the Judicial Code even though it is doing such a business within this state that it is violating this section in not filing such a consent. Donahue v M. A. Henry Co. (1948, DC NY) 78 F. Supp. 91

20. – – Venue of action against airline

Principal place of business of an airline is the location it designates in its application for a certificate of authority to do business and in the event that no certificate has been procured, the location of its principal place of business may be a question of fact. Kibler v Transcontinental & Western Air, Inc. (1945, DC NY) 63 F. Supp. 724

Rule that a railroad is a resident of every county where it operates, where it has a place of business, etc., for purposes of venue, is also applicable to airlines. Kibler v Transcontinental & Western Air, Inc. (1945, DC NY) 63 F. Supp. 724

The United States District Court for the Southern District of New York was an improper forum for an action against an airline, a Delaware corporation, which at the time the action was instituted had not obtained a certificate of authority to do business in New York nor had it filed a designation of an agent for the service of process. Maryland use of Brandt v Eastern Air Lines, Inc. (1948, DC NY) 120 F. Supp. 745

21. – What constitutes "doing business" within state

A foreign corporation having its principal office in Chicago could not be considered as doing business in New York with respect to certain promissory notes sued upon as obligations of a New York dealer under a financing arrangement merely because the notes were dated at a named location in New York where they were actually signed in his behalf at the Chicago office of the plaintiff under a general authorization to sign such instruments as part of the financing arrangement, or because it often sent employees into New York State to check on wholesalers and retailers of its products doing business there. Samuels v Mott (1960) 29 Misc. 2d 705, 211 N.Y.S.2d 242

A credit corporation, set up as a subsidiary of a manufacturing corporation, the latter doing no business with dealers and the former having its principal office in Chicago and being organized under the laws of Delaware, was not doing business in New York within the meaning of this section where it merely, through the home office in Chicago, arranged to finance a dealer in New York through trust receipt financing, but had no personal contacts with the dealer. Samuels v Mott (1960) 29 Misc. 2d 705, 211 N.Y.S.2d 242

Each case involving the question of what constitutes "doing business" within the state is to be determined in the light of its own particular facts. Berkshire Engineering Corp. v Scott-Paine (1961) 29 Misc. 2d 1010, 217 N.Y.S.2d 919

Foreign corporations maintaining exhibits at New York World's Fair are not doing business in this state so as to be subject to taxation or require qualification. 1938 Ops Atty Gen 331

22. – – Regular and continuous business conduct

Whether local activities by an unauthorized corporation sufficiently make out transaction of business in this state must be determined on the particular facts of each case, a showing of business conduct, regular and continuous, being essential to bring a foreign corporate plaintiff within its operative provisions. Conklin Limestone Co. v Linden (1964, 3d Dept) 22 A.D.2d 63, 253 N.Y.S.2d 578

There was ample evidence to support a conclusion that plaintiff foreign corporation was doing business in New York without authority where it was engaged for several years in crushing limestone at a plant in Connecticut the major portion of which was sold in bulk and transported in special vehicles equipped with a spreading device for spreading as fertilizer on farmlands, and, in 1960, received 351 orders directly from customers in New York or New York retail dealers and delivered about 30% of its total sales in that state, though it maintained no salesmen there nor any offices. Conklin Limestone Co. v Linden (1964, 3d Dept) 22 A.D.2d 63, 253 N.Y.S.2d 578

"Doing business in this state" implies corporate continuity of conduct in doing of regular business in customary way with a place of business of some kind in New York. McDowell v Starobin Electrical Supply Co. (1918) 104 Misc 596, 172 N.Y.S. 221

Regular and long-continued practice of buying instead of selling is doing business within state. Merchandise Reporting Co. v L. Oransky & Sons (1929) 133 Misc 890, 234 N.Y.S. 83

The maintenance of an office for transaction of business in New York was not essential to "doing business" in New York by a foreign corporation which has engaged in a series of extensive and persistent transactions in this state over varying periods of time signifying intention to establish a permanent business situs here. Berkshire Engineering Corp. v Scott-Paine (1961) 29 Misc. 2d 1010, 217 N.Y.S.2d 919

A Massachusetts corporation was engaged in doing business in New York where, over a two and one-half year period, it had been engaged in erecting houses and general building construction work in New York where its employees resided for varying periods of time while working on such contracts and where its machinery and equipment was stationed for weeks and sometimes months. Berkshire Engineering Corp. v Scott-Paine (1961) 29 Misc. 2d 1010, 217 N.Y.S.2d 919

23. – – Investing in, or subletting of, leased property

The provision in this section requiring every foreign stock corporation doing business in this state to obtain a certificate, has relation to the regular and customary business for which the corporation was organized, and not to investment in real estate that is leased, unless the company is organized for the immediate purpose of taking title to or leasing land. Singer Mfg. Co. v Granite Spring Water Co. (1910) 66 Misc 595, 123 N.Y.S. 1088

Subletting to different tenants, of a building in city of New York leased to a foreign corporation under a lease delivered in this state, constitutes "doing business in this state." Cassidy's, Ltd. v Rowan (1917) 99 Misc 274, 163 N.Y.S. 1079

24. – – Solicitation of orders

A plaintiff, soliciting orders within the state to be filled outside of the state through a nonsalaried representative who receives messages through telephone message service, is not doing business within the state under §§ 210, 218. National Tool Salvage Co. v National Tool Salvage Industries, Inc. (1946) 186 Misc 833, 60 N.Y.S.2d 308, 68 USPQ 118

Merely soliciting orders within the state which are accepted outside the state does not constitute doing business within the state, nor placing of a name on an office door or listing of a name in a telephone directory or keeping of samples not evidence that one is doing business within state. National Tool Salvage Co. v National Tool Salvage Industries, Inc. (1946) 186 Misc 833, 60 N.Y.S.2d 308, 68 USPQ 118

The solicitation of business alone by the representative of a foreign corporation for the performance of services, or manufacture or sale of goods where such services are performed and the goods manufactured in, or originate in, another state, cannot be prohibited by this state. A foreign corporation can send its agents to this state to make contracts for the sale and manufacture of goods without falling into the inhibitions of this state. In re Dennin's Will (1942, Sur) 37 N.Y.S.2d 725

Where Connecticut corporation solicited orders in New York for goods purchased in Connecticut and shipped therefrom in interstate commerce, and corporation was not subject to New York's franchise tax, the corporation was not "doing business" in New York within the meaning of General Corporation Law § 218. National Folding Box Co. v Bisceglia Bros. Wines Corp. (1950, Sup) 147 N.Y.S.2d 361, app dismd (1951) 278 A.D. 711, 103 N.Y.S.2d 836

25. – – Selling through commission salesman

A foreign corporation is not doing business in New York where such corporation sells 7 per cent of its total product in New York City through a commission salesman, who also represents eight other firms, and where such salesman is not an employee or managing agent of the corporation. New York Automatic Canteen Corp. v Keppel & Ruof, Inc. (1949) 195 Misc 526, 90 N.Y.S.2d 454

26. – – Presence of agents

Unless a foreign corporation is engaged in business within the state it is not brought within the state by presence of its agents. But there is no precise test of the nature or extent of business that must be done. All that is requisite is that enough be done to enable the court to say that the corporation is here, and when once it is here it may be served. Jurisdiction does not fail because the cause of action sued upon has no relation in its origin to business here transacted. Finley v Atlantic Transport Co. (1917) 220 N.Y. 249, 115 N.E. 715

27. – – Mailing of executed contract to state

The execution of a contract by a foreign corporation and the mailing thereof to defendant within this state without securing a certificate to do business within this state as required by this section is not doing business within the state in violation of this section.

Whitney v Dudley (1943, Sup) 40 N.Y.S.2d 838, affd (1943) 266 A.D. 1056, 45 N.Y.S.2d 725

28. – Unauthorized foreign corporation

A foreign corporation not regularly engaged in business here may file a notice of mechanic's lien under § 9 of the Lien Law with respect to work and materials involved in an isolated transaction, and the notice of lien is not invalid for failure to state the corporation's "principal place of business within the state," and, instead, giving the actual principal place of business of the corporation elsewhere. Garden State Brickface Co. v Artcourt Realty Corp. (1963) 40 Misc. 2d 712, 243 N.Y.S.2d 733

Failure of a corporation to obtain consent of the secretary of state to do business in N.Y. should not invalidate a mortgage executed by said corporation. In re Heffron Co. (1914, DC NY) 216 F 642

29. – – Right to maintain action

Where, after a foreign corporation, which had never complied with this section, entered into a contract within this state for sale and delivery of merchandise, the receivers of the corporation completed the contract by delivery of merchandise, complaint, in an action by assignees of the receivers to recover the agreed price, is properly dismissed because of failure of the corporation to comply with this section. Meyers v Spangenberg & McLean Co. (1909) 65 Misc 475, 120 N.Y.S. 174

Where the plaintiff, a foreign corporation serving as collection agency, having office facilities in N.Y. and entering about fifty contracts annually in this state, entered into a N.Y. contract under which the defendant made the initial payment by check, turned over acceptance card to plaintiff's representative here, and check was deposited in plaintiff's bank account in N.Y. city bank, performance of the contract not entailing interstate commerce, complaint of plaintiff, doing business here without complying with this section and Tax Law, § 181, will be dismissed. American Sec. Credit Co. v Empire Properties Corp. (1935) 154 Misc 191, 276 N.Y.S. 970

The claim of a foreign trucking corporation for property damage caused by alleged negligence in maintaining state highways which accrued on March 20, 1963, was not barred by legislation that provided that an unauthorized foreign corporation could not maintain any action in the state of New York until it obtained authority to do business in this state, which became effective on April 1, 1963, notwithstanding that suit was instituted on June 14, 1963, since the Act had been amended and the effective date extended to September 1, 1963. Tetreault v State (1966) 50 Misc. 2d 170, 269 N.Y.S.2d 812

Plaintiff, a foreign corporation, could sue here for the foreclosure of a chattel mortgage notwithstanding the fact that it had not obtained a certificate of doing business. Plaintiff was doing business in this state at the time the contract was made and, moreover, since it was an assignee, the contract was not one "made by it" in this state. Landerton Co. v Sy-Jo Luncheonette, Inc. (1953, Sup) 118 N.Y.S.2d 478

Where verified complaint, and supporting affidavits, gave prima facie proof that plaintiff's assignor was not doing business in the state within the prohibition of the statute, and that the contract in question involved interstate commerce, the complaint was not dismissed. Nicolich v E. Muniz Ferreira & Cia (1956, Sup) 149 N.Y.S.2d 662

30. – – Action involving insurance policy

A foreign corporation which had issued insurance policies at the instance of a New York insurance broker under § 122 of the Insurance Law, although unauthorized to do business in New York, is entitled to maintain in New York a declaratory judgment action seeking to establish its nonliability on a particular policy without alleging compliance with this section. Empire Mut. Ins. Co. v International Tram-Po-Line Mfrs., Inc. (1963) 39 Misc. 2d 810, 242 N.Y.S.2d 28

A foreign insurance company not authorized to do business in New York but which has issued a policy through a New York broker under § 122 of the Insurance Law may maintain an action with respect to the policy in New York courts without pleading or proving facts bringing it within this section, subject to right of defendant to set up noncompliance herewith as a defense. Empire Mut. Ins. Co. v International Tram-Po-Line Mfrs., Inc. (1963) 39 Misc. 2d 810, 242 N.Y.S.2d 28

31. – – Right to enforce arbitration agreement

Although a foreign corporation cannot maintain an action in this State upon a contract made by it in this State unless, before the making of the contract, it has obtained a certificate of authority from the Secretary of State, it may institute a special proceeding to enforce an arbitration agreement. Terminal Auxiliar Maritima v Cocotos S.S. Co. (1957) 11 Misc. 2d 697, 178 N.Y.S.2d 298 (superseded by statute as stated in In re Knoll N. Am., Inc. (1993, Sup) 158 Misc. 2d 227, 601 N.Y.S.2d 224)

32. – – Venue of action against corporation

In an action to recover transportation charges for goods carried from Washington D. C. to Brooklyn, the venue of the action may be in New York although the contract was made in Washington D. C. and although the foreign corporation defendant had not filed or registered with the Secretary of State. Brooks Transp. Co. v Hillcrea Export & Import Corp. (1951, Sup) 106 N.Y.S.2d 868

33. Under former General Corporation Law § 211

A foreign co-operative corporation may be authorized to do business in this State even though its name does not include the word "co-operative." 1948 Ops Atty Gen Sept 25

§ 1302. Application to existing authorized foreign corporations

Every foreign corporation which on the effective date of this chapter is authorized to conduct activities in this state under a certificate of authority heretofore issued to it by the secretary of state shall continue to have such authority. Such foreign corporation, its members, directors, and officers shall have the same rights, franchises, and privileges and shall be subject to the same limitations, restrictions, liabilities, and penalties as a foreign corporation authorized under this chapter, its members, directors, and officers respectively. A foreign corporation may by amendment to its certificate of authority set forth whether it is a charitable corporation or a non-charitable corporation and in the absence of such amendment an authorized foreign corporation shall be a charitable corporation. Reference in this chapter to an application for authority shall, unless the context otherwise requires, include the statement and designation and any amendment thereof required to be filed by the secretary of state under prior statutes to obtain a certificate of authority.

History: Add, L 1969, ch 1066, § 1, with substance deriving from Gen Corp § 213, amd, L 1970, ch 847, § 73, eff Sept 1, 1970; amd, L 2013, ch 549, § 102, eff July 1, 2014.

CASE ANNOTATIONS

1. Generally
2-5. [Reserved for future use]
6. Under former General Corporation Law § 213

1. Generally

Commissioner of Education properly determined that foreign nonprofit corporation had no authority to operate a private school in New York under N-PCL §§ 404, subd d, 1301, and 1304, subd c where said school, although in existence prior to passage of the N-PCL, had never been authorized to do business here within the meaning of N-PCL § 1302. Green Valley School, Inc. v Nyquist (1972) 72 Misc. 2d 889, 340 N.Y.S.2d 234

2-5. [Reserved for future use]
6. Under former General Corporation Law § 213

Where the designated agent for service of process upon a foreign corporation authorized to do business in this state dies, and the corporation designates no other person in his place, service of summons upon the secretary of state in an action against said corporation upon a liability arising without this state is futile, where the defendant is not shown to have property in this state, and on motion will be set aside. Eastern Products Corp. v Tennessee C., I. & R. Co. (1918) 102 Misc 557, 170 N.Y.S. 100

Service of summons by the plaintiff, a resident of this state, upon the secretary of state as agent for the defendant, a Florida corporation, based upon a transitory cause of action arising in Florida, was invalid, under this section, since service upon the agent designated solely by statute of the state wherein suit is brought, is valid only in respect to cause of action originating in that state. Powell v Home Seekers' Realty Co. (1928) 131 Misc 590, 228 N.Y.S. 131

A non-stock corporation, although doing business within the meaning of § 218, could, by reason of § 213, maintain an action where it had obtained authority to do business as a business corporation prior to the extension of the prohibition against action by corporations not organized to do business in this state to non-stock corporations. Vilter Mfg. Co. v Dairymen's League Co-op. Ass'n (1948, Sup) 84 N.Y.S.2d 445, affd (1949) 275 A.D. 706, 88 N.Y.S.2d 248, resettled (1949, 1st Dept) 275 A.D. 769, 88 N.Y.S.2d 902 and motion den (1949, 1st Dept) 275 A.D. 769, 88 N.Y.S.2d 903 and reh and app den (1949, 1st Dept) 275 A.D. 769, 88 N.Y.S.2d 903

Where the agent appointed to receive service of process died and no new agent had been appointed the federal district court in New York obtained jurisdiction where service was made on the Secretary of State even though it was a foreign cause of action. Cohen v American Window Glass Co. (1942, CA2 NY) 126 F.2d 111

Section 213 should be read in connection with Civil Pr. Act, § 229(2). Cohen v American Window Glass Co. (1941, DC NY) 41 F. Supp. 48, mod on other grounds (1942, CA2 NY) 126 F.2d 111

§ 1303. Violations

The attorney-general may bring an action to restrain a foreign corporation from conducting in this state without authority any activities for the conduct of which it is required to be authorized in the state, or from conducting in this state any activities not set forth in its application for authority or certificate of amendment filed by the department of state. The attorney-general may bring an action or special proceeding to annul the authority of a foreign corporation to conduct in this state any activities not set forth in its application for authority or certificate of amendment or the authority of which was obtained through fraudulent misrepresentation or concealment of a material fact or to enjoin or annul the authority of any foreign corporation which within this state contrary to law has done or omitted any act which if done by a domestic corporation would be a cause for its dissolution under section 1101 (Attorney-general's action for judicial dissolution) or to annul the authority of a foreign corporation that has been dissolved or has had its authority or existence otherwise terminated or cancelled in the jurisdiction of its incorporation. The attorney-general shall deliver a certified copy of the order of annulment to the department of state. Upon the filing thereof by the department of state the authority of the foreign corporation to conduct activities in this state shall be annulled. The secretary of state shall continue as agent of the foreign corporation upon whom process against it may be served in any action or special proceeding based upon any liability or obligation incurred by the foreign corporation within the state prior to the filing of the certified copy of the order of annulment by the department of state.

History: Add, L 1969, ch 1066, § 1, with substance deriving from Gen Corp Law § 219; amd, L 1970, ch 847, § 74, L 1984, ch 198, § 4, eff June 12, 1984.

Not-For-Profit Corporation Law

CASE ANNOTATIONS

1-5. [Reserved for future use]
6. Under former General Corporation Law § 219

1-5. [Reserved for future use]
6. Under former General Corporation Law § 219

Merely soliciting orders within the state which are accepted outside the state does not constitute doing business within the state, nor does placing of a name on an office door or listing of a name in a telephone directory or the keeping of samples constitute evidence that one is doing business within the state. National Tool Salvage Co. v National Tool Salvage Industries, Inc. (1946) 186 Misc 833, 60 N.Y.S.2d 308

§ 1304. Application for authority; contents

(a) A foreign corporation may apply for authority to conduct activities in this state by filing an application entitled "Application for authority of............ (name of corporation) under section 1304 of the Not-for-Profit Corporation Law." The application shall be signed and delivered to the department of state. It shall set forth:

(1) The name of the foreign corporation.

(2) The fictitious name the corporation agrees to use in this state pursuant to section 1301 of this chapter, if applicable.

(3) The jurisdiction and date of its incorporation.

(4) That the corporation is a foreign corporation as defined in subparagraph (7) of paragraph (a) of section 102 (Definitions) of this chapter, whether it would be a charitable corporation or noncharitable corporation if formed in this state; a statement of its purposes to be pursued in this state and of the activities which it proposes to conduct in this state; and a statement that it is authorized to conduct those activities in the jurisdiction of its incorporation.

(5) The county within this state in which its office is to be located.

(6) A designation of the secretary of state as its agent upon whom process against it may be served and the post office address within or without this state to which the secretary of state shall mail a copy of any process against it served upon him.

(7) If it is to have a registered agent, the name and address of the agent within this state and a statement that the registered agent is to be its agent upon whom process against it may be served.

(8) A statement that the foreign corporation has not, since its incorporation or since the date its authority to conduct activities in this state was last surrendered, done any act in this state, except as set forth in paragraph (b) of section 1301 (Authorization of foreign corporations); or in lieu of such statement the consent of the state tax commission to the filing of the application shall be attached thereto.

(9) Any provision required by any governmental body or officer or other person or body as a condition for giving the consent or approval required for the filing of such application for authority, provided such provision is not inconsistent with this chapter or any other statute of this state. A corporation whose statement of purposes to be conducted in this state specifically includes the establishment or operation of a child day care center, as that term is defined in section three hundred ninety of the social services law, shall provide a certified copy of any application for authority and any amendment thereto involving such corporation to the office of children and family services within thirty days after receipt of confirmation of the filing of such application or amendment with the department of state.

(b) Attached to the application for authority shall be a certificate by an authorized officer of the jurisdiction of its incorporation that the foreign corporation is an existing corporation. If such certificate is in a foreign language, a translation thereof under oath of the translator shall be attached thereto.

(c) If the application for authority sets forth any purpose or activity for which a domestic corporation could be formed only with the consent or approval of any governmental body or officer, or other person or body under section 404 (Approvals, notices and consents) of this chapter, such consent or approval shall be endorsed thereon or annexed thereto.

(d) If the application for authority sets forth any purpose or activity requiring a domestic corporation to provide notice of the filing of a certificate of incorporation to any person or entity under section 404 (Approvals, notices and consents) of this chapter, then the corporation shall send by certified mail, return receipt requested, a certified copy of the certificate of authority to such person or entity within ten business days after the corporation receives confirmation from the department of state that the certificate has been accepted for filing.

History: Add, L 1969, ch 1066, § 1, eff Sept 1, 1970, with substance derived from Gen Corp Law § 210; amd, L 1970, ch 847 § 75; L 1972, ch 961, § 16; L 1982, ch 590, § 18, eff Oct 20, 1982; L 1984, ch 39, § 1, eff April 3, 1984; L 1985, ch 499, § 4, eff Oct 22, 1985; L 1998, ch 375, § 45, eff Aug 13, 1998; L 2006, ch 58, § 8 (Part D), eff April 12, 2006; L 2013, ch 549, §§ 103, 104, eff July 1, 2014; L 2015, ch 358, § 9, eff Sept 25, 2015.

CASE ANNOTATIONS

A dismissal by the Appellate Division of a petition by a foreign not-for-profit corporation seeking to dispense with the approval of the New York Society for the Prevention of Cruelty to Children, which normally was required before a corporation could conduct in New York all the activities of a domestic society, would be reversed and remanded for redetermination, even though the determination of the Appellate Division was correct as the matter stood before it, where the litigation had proceeded on the assumption that the corporation sought to conduct in New York all the activities of a domestic society, and where in fact the corporation sought to conduct only those activities that it was authorized to conduct under the laws of its incorporating state. Re American Soc. for Prevention of Cruelty to Children (1983) 58 N.Y.2d 1071, 462 N.Y.S.2d 634, 449 N.E.2d 414

Commissioner of education properly determined that foreign non-profit corporation had no authority to operate a private school in New York under N-PCL §§ 404, subd d, 1301, and 1304, subd c where said school, although in existence prior to passage of the N-PCL, had never been authorized to do business here within the meaning of N-PCL § 1302. Green Valley School, Inc. v Nyquist (1972) 72 Misc. 2d 889, 340 N.Y.S.2d 234

§ 1305.   Application for authority; effect

Upon filing by the department of state of the application for authority the foreign corporation shall be authorized to conduct in this state any activities set forth in the application. Such authority shall continue so long as the corporation retains its authority to conduct such activities in the jurisdiction of its incorporation and its authority to conduct activities in this state has not been surrendered, suspended or annulled in accordance with law.

History: Add, L 1969, ch 1066, § 1, eff Sept 1, 1970, with substance derived from Gen Corp Law § 212.

CASE ANNOTATIONS

1. Generally
2-5. [Reserved for future use]
6. Under former General Corporation Law § 212

1. Generally

Real property of a foreign nonprofit corporation, which corporation has filed for authority to conduct activities in New York, is entitled to exemption pursuant to section 420 of the Real Property Tax Law, provided the requirements of that section are satisfied. 7 Op Counsel SBEA #18 (1980, Aug 6)

2-5. [Reserved for future use]
6. Under former General Corporation Law § 212

The authorization to do business in this state upon issuance of a certificate of authority does not affect the requirement in § 10 of the Membership Corporation Law that an application by such a corporation to do business in New York is subject to approval of a justice of the Supreme Court. Association for Preservation of Freedom of Choice, Inc. v Simon (1960) 22 Misc. 2d 1016, 201 N.Y.S.2d 135, app dismd (1960) 8 N.Y.2d 909, 204 N.Y.S.2d 150, 168 N.E.2d 826 and affd (1960, 1st Dept) 11 A.D.2d 927, 206 N.Y.S.2d 532, affd (1961) 9 N.Y.2d 376, 214 N.Y.S.2d 388, 174 N.E.2d 487, remittitur den (1961) 9 N.Y.2d 909, reh den (1962) 11 N.Y.2d 720 and reh den (1962) 11 N.Y.2d 662, 225 N.Y.S.2d 740, 180 N.E.2d 898

An application by a corporation organized under the laws of the Territory of Virgin Islands to do business in New York was properly denied by the Secretary of State where the applicant's corporate name included the word "psychology," in view of art. 153 of the Education Law. Industrial Psychology, Inc. v Simon (1960) 27 Misc. 2d 879, 211 N.Y.S.2d 256

Upon compliance with §§ 212 and 218 of the General Corporation Law, a foreign corporation is in no different position from a domestic corporation and is not subject to a claim of ultra vires as bar to a claim for services rendered. New York Factors, Inc. v Yam K. Seid (1961) 28 Misc. 2d 753, 213 N.Y.S.2d 294

§ 1306.   Powers of authorized foreign corporations

An authorized foreign corporation shall have such powers as are permitted by the laws of the jurisdiction of its incorporation but no greater powers than those of a domestic corporation formed for the purposes set forth in the application for authority.

History: Add, L 1969, ch 1066, § 1, eff Sept 1, 1970.

CASE ANNOTATIONS

It was not arbitrary and capricious for regional chapter of non-for-profit California corporation ("Sierra Club") to suspend petitioner ("New York City Group") from its organization for engaging in direct-mail fundraising in violation of national Sierra Club's rules and petitioner's own bylaws, where suspension of petitioner was business judgment call inspired by regional chapter's attempt to rectify difficult internal problem, and was within limits of its discretion. Lane v Sierra Club (2000, Sup) 183 Misc. 2d 944, 706 N.Y.S.2d 577

§ 1307.   Tenure of real property

A foreign corporation may acquire and hold real property in this state in furtherance of its corporate purposes and may convey the same by deed or otherwise in the same manner as a domestic corporation.

History: Add, L 1969, ch 1066, § 1, eff Sept 1, 1970, with substance derived from Gen Corp Law § 221.

CASE ANNOTATIONS

1-5. [Reserved for future use]
6. Under former General Corporation Law § 221

1-5. [Reserved for future use]
6. Under former General Corporation Law § 221

A mortgage is a conveyance within the meaning of this section. Re Heffron Co. (1914, DC NY) 216 F 642

Before a foreign corporation organized to maintain a home for the aged may take title to realty in this State it must obtain approval of the State Board of Social Welfare and file statement and designation with Secretary of State. 1955 Ops Atty Gen Apr 20 (informal)

§ 1308.   Amendments or changes

(a) An authorized foreign corporation may amend or change its application for authority from time to time in any and as many of the following respects as may be desired if the amendments contain only such provisions as might be lawfully contained in an application for authority at the time of making such amendment:

(1) To change its corporate name if such change has been effected under the laws of the jurisdiction of its incorporation.

(2) To change its fictitious name filed pursuant to paragraph (d) of section 1301 of this chapter, to another fictitious name, if its true corporate name is not available for use in this state.

(3) To delete its fictitious name filed pursuant to paragraph (d) of section 1301 of this chapter, if its true corporate name is now available for use in this state.

(4) To adopt a fictitious name when the corporate name is changed and is not available in this state.

(5) To enlarge, limit or otherwise change the activities which it proposes to conduct in this state.

(6) To change the location of its office in this state.

(7) To specify or change the post office address to which the secretary of state shall mail a copy of any process against it served upon him.

(8) To make, revoke or change the designation of a registered agent or to specify or change his address.

History: Add, Add, L 1969, ch 1066, § 1, eff Sept 1, 1970, with substance derived from Gen Corp Law §§ 214, 214-a, 215; amd, redesignated par (a), subpar (5), L 1983, ch 186, § 7, eff June 30, 1983; L 1982, ch 590, § 19, eff Oct 20, 1982; L 1983, ch 186, § 7, eff June 30, 1983.

§ 1309.   Certificate of amendment; contents, effect

(a) To accomplish such amendment a certificate, entitled "Certificate of amendment of application for authority of .... (name of corporation) under section 1309 of the Not-for-Profit Corporation Law," shall be signed and delivered to the department of state. It shall set forth:

(1) The name of the foreign corporation as it appears on the index of names of existing domestic and authorized foreign corporations of any kind in the department of state and the fictitious name the corporation has agreed to use in this state pursuant to paragraph (d) of section 1301 of this article.

(2) The jurisdiction of its incorporation.

(3) The date it was authorized to conduct activities in this state.

(4) Each amendment effected thereby.

(5) If the true corporate name of the foreign corporation is to be changed, a statement that the change of name has been effected under the laws of the jurisdiction of its incorporation and the date the change was so effected.

(6) If the activities it proposes to conduct in this state are to be enlarged, limited or otherwise changed, a statement that it is authorized to conduct in the jurisdiction of its incorporation the activities which it proposes to conduct in this state.

(b) If an authorized foreign corporation has changed its name in the jurisdiction of its incorporation, it shall deliver to the department of state within twenty days after the change became effective in that jurisdiction a certificate of amendment under paragraph (a). Upon its failure to deliver such certificate, its authority to conduct activities in this state shall upon the expiration of said twenty days be suspended. The filing by the department of state of a certificate of amendment changing the corporation name within one hundred twenty days after the effective date of the change of name in the jurisdiction of its incorporation shall annul the suspension and its authority to conduct activities in this state shall be restored and continue as if no suspension had occurred. The secretary of state shall continue, during such suspension, as agent of the foreign corporation upon whom process against the foreign corporation may be served in the manner set forth in paragraph (b) of section 306 (Service of process).

(c) A certificate of amendment of application for authority shall not be filed, if the amendment adds, changes or eliminates a purpose, power or provision the inclusion of which in an application for authority requires consent or approval of any governmental body or officer or other person or body, or if the amendment changes the name of a corporation whose application for authority had such consent or approval endorsed thereon or annexed thereto, unless such consent or approval is endorsed on or annexed to the certificate of amendment of application for authority.

History: Add, L 1969, ch 1066, § 1, eff Sept 1, 1970, with substance derived from Gen Corp Law §§ 214, 214-a, 215; amd, L 1970, ch 847, § 76, eff Sept 1, 1970, L 1972, ch 961, §§ 1, 2, 17, L 1973, ch 176, L 1982, ch 590, § 20, L 1983, ch 186, § 8, eff June 30, 1983, L 1984, ch 39, § 2, eff April 3, 1984, L 1998, ch 375, § 46, eff Aug 13, 1998, L 2013, ch 549, § 105, eff July 1, 2014.

§ 1310.   Certificate of change; contents

(a) In lieu of a certificate of amendment, an authorized foreign corporation, upon compliance with this section, may make any or all of the following changes in its application for authority:

(1) To change the location of its office in this state.

(2) To specify or change the post office address to which the secretary of state shall mail a copy of any process against it served upon him.

(3) To make, revoke or change the designation of a registered agent or specify or change his address.

(b) To accomplish such change, a certificate entitled "Certificate of change of application for authority of .... (name of corporation) under section 1310 of the Not-for-Profit Corporation Law" shall be signed and delivered to the department of state. It shall set forth:

(1) The name of the foreign corporation as it appears on the index of names of existing domestic and authorized foreign corporations of any kind in the department of state and the fictitious name the corporation has agreed to use in this state pursuant to paragraph (d) of section 1301 of this article.

(2) The jurisdiction of its incorporation.

(3) The date it was authorized to conduct activities in this state.

(4) Each change effected thereby.

(c) A certificate of change of application for authority which changes only the post office address to which the secretary of state shall mail a copy of any process against an authorized foreign corporation served upon him or which changes the address of its registered agent, provided such address is the address of a person, partnership or other corporation whose address, as agent, is the address to be changed or who has been designated as registered agent for such authorized foreign corporation, may be signed and delivered to the department of state by such agent. The certificate of change of application for authority shall set forth the statements required under subparagraphs (1), (2), (3) and (4) of paragraph (b) of this section; that a notice of the proposed change was mailed by the party signing the certificate to the authorized foreign corporation not less than thirty days prior to the date of delivery to the department and that such corporation has not objected thereto; and that the party signing the certificate is the agent of such foreign corporation to whose address the secretary of state is required to mail copies of process or the registered agent, if such be the case. A certificate signed and delivered under this paragraph shall not be deemed to effect a change of location of the office of the corporation in whose behalf such certificate is filed.

History: Add, L 1969, ch 1066, § 1, eff Sept 1, 1970, with substance derived from Gen Corp Law § 214-a(2); amd, L 1982, ch 590, § 21, L 1983, ch 186, § 9, eff June 30, 1983, L 1998, ch 375, § 47, eff Aug 13, 1998, L 1999, ch 172, § 28, eff July 6, 1999, L 2013, ch 549, § 106, eff July 1, 2014.

§ 1311. Surrender of authority

(a) An authorized foreign corporation desiring to surrender its authority shall deliver to the department of state a certificate entitled "Certificate of surrender of authority of............ (name of corporation) under section 1311 of the Not-for-Profit Corporation Law." The certificate shall be signed. It shall set forth:

(1) The name of the foreign corporation as it appears on the index of names of existing domestic and authorized foreign corporations of any kind in the department of state and the fictitious name the corporation has agreed to use in this state pursuant to paragraph (d) of section 1301 of this article.

(2) The jurisdiction of its incorporation.

(3) The date it was authorized to conduct activities in this state.

(4) That it surrenders its authority to conduct activities in this state.

(5) That it revokes the authority of its registered agent, if any, previously designated and consents that process against it in any action or special proceeding based upon any liability or obligation incurred by it within this state before the filing of the certificate of surrender may be served on the secretary of state after the filing thereof in the manner set forth in paragraph (b) of section 306 (Service of process).

(6) A post office address within or without this state to which the secretary of state shall mail a copy of any process against it served upon him.

(b) The department shall not file such certificate unless the consent of the state tax commission to the surrender of authority is attached thereto.

(c) The authority of the foreign corporation to conduct activities in this state shall terminate on the filing by the department of state of the certificate of surrender of authority.

(d) The post office address specified under subparagraph (a) (6) may be changed by delivering to the department of state a certificate, entitled "Certificate of amendment of certificate of surrender of authority of .... (name of corporation) under section 1311 of the Not-for-Profit Corporation Law." The certificate shall be signed. It shall set forth:

(1) The name of the foreign corporation.

(2) The jurisdiction of its incorporation.

(3) The date its certificate of surrender of authority was filed by the department of state.

(4) The changed post office address, within or without this state, to which the secretary of state shall mail a copy of any process against it served upon him.

History: Add, L 1969, ch 1066, § 1, eff Sept 1, 1970, with substance derived from Gen Corp Law § 216; amd, L 1982, ch 590, § 22, L 1983, ch 186, § 10, eff June 30, 1983, L 1998, ch 375, § 48, eff Aug 13, 1998, L 2013, ch 549, § 107, eff July 1, 2014.

CASE ANNOTATIONS

1-10. [Reserved for future use]
11. Under former General Corporation Law § 216
12. – Continuation of amenability to process
13. – – Service of process on secretary of state
14. – Complaint
15. – Accrual of cause of action; incurred within state
16. – What constitutes liability or obligation incurred within state
17. – – Stockholder's derivative action
18. – – Martin Act violation
19. – – Sherman Act violation
20. – – Violation of federal criminal statute

1-10. [Reserved for future use]

11. Under former General Corporation Law § 216

The fact that this section provides, in more specific terms, for continuation of designations made by foreign corporations, other than moneyed corporations, cannot change the construction placed upon Bank Law, former § 180, subd 3 (now § 200), for no reason exists why a banking corporation should be placed on any different footing in this respect. Society Milion Athena, Inc. v National Bank of Greece (1937) 166 Misc 190, 2 N.Y.S.2d 155, affd (1938) 253 A.D. 650, 3 N.Y.S.2d 677 and affd (1938) 254 A.D. 728, 4 N.Y.S.2d 1004

Though a Delaware corporation, against which an action for accounting was brought, ceased to exist under Delaware laws, yet, it may be still existent in New York so that the winding up of its business and administration of the assets may be carried on in New York where it did its business and where the controversy in suit arose. Trounstine v Bauer, Pogue & Co. (1942, DC NY) 44 F. Supp. 767, affd (1944, CA2 NY) 144 F.2d 379, cert den (1944) 323 US 777, 89 L Ed 621, 65 S Ct 190

12. – Continuation of amenability to process

Where causes of action for breach of implied warranty of merchantability and fitness of an electronic safety device and for common-law negligence accrued against a foreign corporation at a time when it had authority to do business in New York under the above statute, the subsequent filing of a certificate thereunder does not affect such causes of action since subdivision 2 thereof provides for the continuance of such a corporation's amenability to process upon any liability or obligation incurred within the state before such filing. Munn v Security Controls, Inc. (1965, 4th Dept) 23 A.D.2d 813, 258 N.Y.S.2d 475

The filing of a certificate is irrevocable as to any cause of action arising within the state while the corporation was doing business therein. Mid-Continent Petroleum Corp. v Universal Oil Products Co. (1950) 198 Misc 1073, 102 N.Y.S.2d 74, affd (1951) 278 A.D. 564, 102 N.Y.S.2d 451

Even though a corporation informally surrendered its right to do business in this state, under this section, it is still subject to process in any action or proceeding against it upon any liability or obligation incurred within the state before the filing of the formal surrender of its right to do business. General Motors Overseas Operations Div. v The Lichtenstein (1954, DC NY) 126 F. Supp. 395

13. – – Service of process on secretary of state

Where a foreign corporation procures a certificate of authority to transact business within this state, and has a person designated upon

Not-For-Profit Corporation Law

whom service may be made, and thereafter files a surrender of its certificate of authority and revocation of the designation of the person upon whom service of process may be made, an action against it, based on a liability arising in this state prior to filing of surrender of its certificate of authority, may be commenced by service of a summons upon the secretary of state. Saxe v Sugarland Mfg. Co. (1919) 189 A.D. 204, 178 N.Y.S. 454

Where a cause of action for personal injuries arose prior to the dissolution of a foreign corporation, but the action was not commenced until after the corporation had filed a certificate of surrender of authority to do business here, service of summons on one who had been vice-president and resided in this state should be set aside, since, upon the filing of the certificate of surrender, service of process is to be made on the secretary of state. Cappello v Union Carbide & Carbon Corp. (1950) 276 A.D. 277, 95 N.Y.S.2d 36

Where a corporation which has done business in this state and designated the Secretary of State as an agent to receive process, has surrendered its authority to do business in this state and revoked its designation of the Secretary of State, process cannot thereafter be effectively served upon the Secretary of State, even though the corporation continues to do business in the state. Green v Clark (1959, DC NY) 173 F. Supp. 233

14. – Complaint

Where a foreign corporation has filed a certificate of surrender of authority to do business in this state, in order to sustain service of process on the secretary of state the complaint must show that the liability was incurred within this state and prior to the surrender of authority to do business. Hexter v Day-Elder Motors Corp. (1920) 192 A.D. 394, 182 N.Y.S. 717

Where a complaint by a trustee in bankruptcy alleges that the sole stockholder of a corporation licensed to do business in this state, prior to its surrender of its license, transferred assets of the corporation to his personal estate in fraud of the rights of creditors and that the corporation was a party to such transfer, the action is predicated on a liability or obligation incurred within the state within the meaning of this section. Irving Trust Co. v Miss L. Brogan, Inc. (1936) 247 A.D. 275, 287 N.Y.S. 423

15. – Accrual of cause of action; incurred within state

A liability or obligation is incurred immediately upon the commission of an act whereby the corporation is caused to suffer damage and, in the case of foreign corporations licensed to do business in this state, is incurred within the state if the defendants liable are residents of the state and subject to the jurisdiction of the courts of the state. Druckerman v Harbord (1940) 174 Misc 1077, 22 N.Y.S.2d 595

16. – What constitutes liability or obligation incurred within state

Where a foreign corporation has surrendered its authority to do business in New York and has consented to service on Secretary of State in accordance with subd e of above statute, instrument executed by it in New York while authorized to do business here guaranteeing obligation of third party under sublease of business property in Massachusetts which later resulted in declaratory judgment there that specified sum of money was due upon such guarantee and an action on the Massachusetts judgment was brought in New York for such sum, such action was on liability or obligation incurred in this state within meaning of such subdivision. Jay's Stores, Inc. v Ann Lewis Shops, Inc. (1965) 15 N.Y.2d 141, 256 N.Y.S.2d 600, 204 N.E.2d 638

The act of a corporation in refusing to redress wrongs against it constitutes a liability or obligation incurred within the state within the meaning of this section. Druckerman v Harbord (1940) 174 Misc 1077, 22 N.Y.S.2d 595

The words "any liability or obligation incurred within this state" as used in this section, when the plaintiff is a resident of the state, means that the acts out of which liability or obligation arises occurred while the corporation was licensed to do business in the state, regardless of whether the acts were committed within this state. Carlton Properties, Inc. v 328 Properties, Inc. (1955) 208 Misc 776, 143 N.Y.S.2d 140

17. – – Stockholder's derivative action

A stockholder's derivative action to recover property of the corporation allegedly misappropriated prior to the surrender of its certificate of authority to do business in this state is an action on an obligation incurred within the state prior to filing of its certificate surrendering authority to do business within the meaning of this section. Thorne v Brand (1938) 277 N.Y. 212, 14 N.E.2d 42

A stockholder's derivative action constitutes a liability of the corporation, within the meaning of this section which arises from refusal of the corporation to bring action to secure redress for wrongful acts damaging it; it is a liability incurred "within this state" when the persons against whom redress may be sought are subject to suit in this state. Devlin v Webster (1946) 188 Misc 891, 66 N.Y.S.2d 464, affd (1947) 272 A.D. 793, 71 N.Y.S.2d 706

In a stockholder's derivative action based on misfeasance of officers and directors, the liability of the corporation arises from its failure to fulfill its obligations to bring suit against the offending officers and directors and is an obligation incurred within the state within the meaning of this section regardless of where the wrongful acts of the officers and directors took place. Lissauer v Brown (1941, Sup) 86 N.Y.S.2d 35, affd (1941) 262 A.D. 723, 28 N.Y.S.2d 722

Where a foreign corporation which had surrendered its license to do business in this state could have, while licensed in this state, maintained an action against an officer for misconduct, a stockholder's derivative action to recover for such misconduct was an action based on a liability or obligation incurred within the state prior to surrender of authority within the meaning of this section and service of process on the secretary of state was valid. Spielberger v Textron Inc. (1949, CA2 NY) 172 F.2d 85

18. – – Martin Act violation

A proceeding pursuant to provisions of Martin Act (Gen Bus Law, Art 23-A) may be regarded as a "liability or obligation incurred" within the state so that service of summons and complaint on the secretary of state may be made under subd 1, par e of this section. People v Bankers' Capital Corp. (1930) 137 Misc 293, 241 N.Y.S. 693

19. – – Sherman Act violation

A proceeding brought against a defendant for an alleged previous violation of Sherman Act is an action or proceeding "upon any liability or obligation" within the meaning of this section. In re Grand Jury Subpoenas Duces Tecum, etc. (1947, DC NY) 72 F. Supp. 1013

20. – – Violation of federal criminal statute

Violation of Federal criminal statutes is one of the "obligations or liabilities" for satisfaction and discharge of which the New York law continues the existence of a corporation after voluntary dissolution. United States v Brakes, Inc. (1958, DC NY) 157 F. Supp. 916

§ 1312. Termination of existence

When an authorized foreign corporation is dissolved or its authority or existence is otherwise terminated or cancelled in the jurisdiction of its incorporation or when such foreign corporation is merged into or consolidated with another foreign corporation, a certificate of the secretary of state, or official performing the equivalent function as to corporate records, of the jurisdiction of incorporation of such foreign corporation attesting to the occurrence of any such event or a certified copy of an order or decree of a court of such jurisdiction directing the dissolution of such foreign corporation, the termination of its existence or the cancellation of its authority shall be delivered to the department of state. The filing of the certificate, order or decree shall have the same effect as the filing of a certificate of surrender of authority under section 1311 (Surrender of authority). The secretary of state shall continue as agent of the foreign corporation upon whom process against it may be served in the manner set forth in paragraph (b) of section 306 (Service of process), in any action or special proceeding based upon any liability or obligation incurred by the foreign corporation within this state prior to the filing of such certificate, order or decree and he shall promptly cause a copy of any such process to be mailed by registered mail, return receipt requested, to such foreign corporation at the post office address on file in his office specified for such purpose. The post office address may be changed by signing and delivering to the department of state a certificate of change setting forth the statements required under section 1310 (Certificate of change, contents) to effect a change in the post office address under subparagraph (a) (4) of section 1308 (Amendments or changes).

History: Add, L 1969, ch 1066, § 1; amd, L 1998, ch 375, § 49, eff Aug 13, 1998.

§ 1313. Actions or special proceedings by unauthorized foreign corporations

(a) A foreign corporation conducting activities in this state without authority shall not maintain any action or special proceeding in this state unless and until such corporation has been authorized to conduct activities in this state and it has paid to the state all fees, penalties and franchise taxes, if any, for the years or parts thereof during which it conducted activities in this state without authority. This prohibition shall apply to any successor in interest of such foreign corporation.

(b) The failure of a foreign corporation to obtain authority to conduct activities in this state shall not impair the validity of any contract or act of the foreign corporation or the right of any other party to the contract to maintain any action or special proceeding thereon, and shall not prevent the foreign corporation from defending any action or special proceeding in this state.

History: Add, L 1969, ch 1066, § 1, eff Sept 1, 1970, with substance derived from Gen Corp Law § 218.

CASE ANNOTATIONS

1. Generally
2-10. [Reserved for future use]
11. Under former General Corporation Law § 218
12. – Prohibition against action by foreign corporation
13. – – Effective date
14. – – Application to foreign or interstate commerce
15. – – What is a "foreign corporation"
16. – – Holder in due course as subject to prohibition
17. – – Waiver of statute
18. – What constitutes "doing business" within state
19. – – Regular and continuous business conduct
20. – – Business for which corporation organized
21. – – Extent of local activity
22. – – Selling through others
23. – – Solicitation of orders
24. – Presumption as to doing business
25. – Contracts made by corporation
26. – – Made in this state
27. – – Made outside state
28. – – Time of making contract
29. – Validity of contract
30. – – Right to enforce in federal court
31. – Actions or proceedings subject to prohibition
32. – – Contract
33. – – Foreclosure of mechanic's lien
34. – – Tort
35. – – Injunction against use of name
36. – – Conversion
37. – – Condemnation
38. – – Arbitration
39. – Pleadings; complaint by corporation

40. – – Answer
41. – – Dismissal of complaint
42. – Corporation's right to counterclaim
43. – Examination before trial

1. Generally

Fact that national association of opticians held occasional meetings in State of New York, sent publications into New York, received dues from New York members, and occasionally handled orders for nonoptical products which were sold and shipped by others and for which it received no compensation did not mean that the association, a not-for-profit corporation, was "conducting activities" in the State of New York, and thus it would not be precluded, on ground it was an unauthorized foreign corporation, from bringing action against state opticians' association for alleged infringement of service marks. Opticians Asso. of America v Guild of Prescription Opticians, Inc. (1975) 49 A.D.2d 370, 374 N.Y.S.2d 451

Any actions transacted in New York by national opticians' association, a not-for-profit corporation, which received dues from New York members, which sent publications into New York, which held occasional meetings in New York, and which occasionally handled orders for products which were advertised in its publications but which were sold or shipped by others fell within interstate commerce so as to remove the association, with regard to those acts, from the operation of statute requiring authorization of a foreign not-for-profit corporation before it may maintain suit in New York. Opticians Asso. of America v Guild of Prescription Opticians, Inc. (1975) 49 A.D.2d 370, 374 N.Y.S.2d 451

Fact that, prior to 1962, national association of opticians did conduct activities within the state such as would bring it within requirement of Not-for-Profit Corporation Law to be authorized in order to bring suit in New York would not preclude the not-for-profit corporation from bringing suit in 1974 in New York where provision of the Not-for-Profit Law requiring authorization was not adopted until 1970; provision was not to be retroactively applied to activities before its effective date. Opticians Asso. of America v Guild of Prescription Opticians, Inc. (1975) 49 A.D.2d 370, 374 N.Y.S.2d 451

2-10. [Reserved for future use]

11. Under former General Corporation Law § 218

The purpose of this section is to regulate and control the business of foreign stock corporations in this state, for the protection of citizens of the state against any unlawful business of a foreign stock corporation and, if they are doing business in this state, to render them equally accessible to process with domestic corporations; compliance with the statute is a condition precedent to the right of a foreign stock corporation to do business in the state, and the penalty for failure to comply with the statute is prohibition to maintain any action in this state upon any contract made by it within state. Bradford Co. v Dunn (1919) 188 A.D. 454, 176 N.Y.S. 834

Upon compliance with §§ 212 and 218 of the General Corporation Law, a foreign corporation is in no different position from a domestic corporation and is not subject to a claim of ultra vires as bar to a claim for services rendered. New York Factors, Inc. v Yam K. Seid (1961) 28 Misc. 2d 753, 213 N.Y.S.2d 294

12. – Prohibition against action by foreign corporation

A foreign corporation, doing business in this state, may not maintain an action on the basis of contract made with defendant in this state, where it has not, prior to making of such contract, obtained a certificate of authority to do business here. American Middle East Corp. v Barouk (1961, 1st Dept) 13 A.D.2d 919, 215 N.Y.S.2d 843

This section applies only when a foreign corporation is doing business in New York and the contract is made therein. McDowell v Starobin Electrical Supply Co. (1918) 104 Misc 596, 172 N.Y.S. 221

To bring plaintiff within prohibition of this section, it must affirmatively appear not only that it is a foreign corporation, but also that it is doing business within state and that contract sued upon was made in this state. Hedges & Bro. v Busch (1931) 141 Misc 493, 252 N.Y.S. 693

As a general rule, the prohibition contained in this section is the only penalty imposed against a foreign corporation for doing business without the required authority. Wm. G. Roe & Co. v State (1964) 43 Misc. 2d 417, 251 N.Y.S.2d 151

This section which prohibits actions by foreign corporations doing business in this state upon any contract made by it in this state unless it has obtained a certificate of authority is inapplicable where the plaintiff neither does business here nor was the contract made here. John Dirkmaat Co. v Pruyser (1947, Sup) 72 N.Y.S.2d 797

In action by seller against guarantor upon guaranty contract, court was satisfied from the evidence that plaintiff, a foreign corporation, did not do business in the state within the meaning of this section. F. C. Russell Co. v Kaye (1954, Sup) 129 N.Y.S.2d 585, app dismd (1954) 284 A.D. 1037, 137 N.Y.S.2d 819

Before a foreign corporation is disqualified from maintaining an action in New York, under this section, without a certificate of authority to do business, (1) it must be "doing business in this state," (2) the action must be upon contract, and (3) the contract must be made by it in this state. Max Factor & Co. v Janel Sales Corp. (1962, CA2 NY) 298 F.2d 511

13. – – Effective date

The claim of a foreign trucking corporation for property damage caused by negligence in maintaining state highways which accrued on March 20, 1963, was not barred by legislation that provided that an unauthorized foreign corporation could not maintain any action in the state of New York until it obtained authority to do business in this state, which became effective on April 1, 1963, notwithstanding that suit was instituted on June 14, 1963, since the Act had been amended and the effective date extended to September 1, 1963. Tetreault v State (1966) 50 Misc. 2d 170, 269 N.Y.S.2d 812

14. – – Application to foreign or interstate commerce

Where the plaintiff foreign corporation, engaged in the business of giving instruction by correspondence, has no place of business within this state but agents only, whose sole duty is to solicit pupils whose applications for membership must be sent to the home office for acceptance, no contracts being closed here and no instruction given in this state, subscribers receiving their instruction from text books, papers and letters sent from the home office, such corporation is engaged in interstate commerce and is not within the purview of this section, nor is it within the prohibition of Tax Law, § 181. International Text-Book Co. v Tone (1917) 220 N.Y. 313, 115 N.E. 914, 3 AFTR 3296

If the business of a corporation be interstate, it is beyond state interference. To come within this section, a foreign corporation must do more than make a single contract, engage in an isolated piece of business, or occasional undertaking; it must maintain and carry on business with some continuity of act and purpose. International Fuel & Iron Corp. v Donner Steel Co. (1926) 242 N.Y. 224, 151 N.E. 214

If a corporation was engaged in foreign commerce, this section is not applicable. Stephenson v Wiltsee (1928) 223 A.D. 41, 227 N.Y.S. 230

A defense that the plaintiff was doing business in this state, within the meaning of this section without authority from the secretary of state was not good, where even though the plaintiff was doing business in this state, the polices upon which action was brought were incidental to foreign commerce. Ruby S.S. Corp. v American Merchant Marine Ins. Co. (1928) 224 A.D. 531, 231 N.Y.S. 503, 513, affd (1929) 250 N.Y. 573, 166 N.E. 329

Sections 210 and 218 of the General Corporation Law do not apply to corporations "exclusively engaged in interstate or foreign commerce." Munoz v American Stevedores, Inc. (1960, 2d Dept) 10 A.D.2d 963, 201 N.Y.S.2d 640

A Canadian corporation by contract made in New York agreed to carry those participating in the annual outing of the defendant company from Niagara Falls to Erie Beach, Canada, and return for a certain sum of money. The plaintiff had a legal right to enter New York and maintain therein an office for transaction of business in interstate commerce, and the fact that it never procured the certificate required by this section and never paid any license tax as required by Tax Law, § 181, did not preclude recovery upon cause of action. Erie Beach Amusements, Ltd. v Spirella Co. (1918) 105 Misc 170, 173 N.Y.S. 626

In an action by a foreign stock corporation for breach of contract of shipment from one state to another, no question under this section is properly in the case. Publicker Commercial Alcohol Co. v Roberts (1921) 114 Misc 551, 187 N.Y.S. 178

The power of the state to exclude a foreign corporation from doing business in this state is subject to the limitation that freedom of interstate commerce is not to be impaired, and this section must be construed in subordination to that principle. Pittsburgh & Shawmut Coal Co. v State (1922) 118 Misc 50, 192 N.Y.S. 310

This section is not applicable where it is clear that the contracts are transactions in interstate commerce and any activities in connection therewith, performed within the state, were incidental to

the contracts. Eatonton Cotton Mills, Inc. v Goodyear Tire & Rubber Co. (1924) 124 Misc 211, 208 N.Y.S. 218, affd (1925) 212 A.D. 885, 208 N.Y.S. 857

Where a foreign corporation has been continuously doing business out of its New York office for a considerable length of time, without having a license to engage in New York business, this section can be invoked by way of defense against an action by it to collect for goods sold, notwithstanding the particular transaction was in interstate commerce. Talbot Mills, Inc. v Benezra (1962) 35 Misc. 2d 924, 231 N.Y.S.2d 229

Where a plaintiff ships products from its warehouse in another state to a defendant in New York, such importation is not an intrastate transaction, but a transaction in interstate commerce and the activities in connection therewith are incidental to such commerce and this section has no application, nor would the result be any different if a series of sales were made through selling agents by means of orders directed to the foreign corporation in its own state where the goods are delivered to a common carrier of that state under the terms of the contract, for a foreign corporation has a right to send its agents into a state for the purpose of making contracts for the purchase or sale of goods without falling within the inhibition of this section. M. M. Mades Co. v Gassman (1948, City Ct) 77 N.Y.S.2d 236

15. – – What is a "foreign corporation"

A business trust is not a "foreign corporation". Burgoyne v James (1935) 156 Misc 859, 282 N.Y.S. 18, affd (1935) 246 A.D. 605, 284 N.Y.S. 977

Since a credit union is a moneyed corporation, its contracts are not rendered unenforceable by this section. Walsh v Mazzariello (1947) 189 Misc 433, 71 N.Y.S.2d 806

Above statute does not apply to national banking association because it is "moneyed corporation" within meaning of exception contained in such statute. State Nat'l Bank v Laura (1965) 45 Misc. 2d 430, 256 N.Y.S.2d 1004

Since national bank is brought into existence under federal legislation, it does not come within above statute limiting the right of foreign corporations to sue. Were contrary construction to be given to this statute, in case of national banking corporation, it would be clearly unconstitutional. State Nat'l Bank v Laura (1965) 45 Misc. 2d 430, 256 N.Y.S.2d 1004

A non-stock corporation, although doing business within the meaning of § 218, could, by reason of § 213, maintain an action where it had obtained authority to do business as a business corporation prior to the extension of the prohibition against action by corporations not organized to do business in this state to non-stock corporations. Vilter Mfg. Co. v Dairymen's League Co-op. Ass'n (1948, Sup) 84 N.Y.S.2d 445, affd (1949) 275 A.D. 706, 88 N.Y.S.2d 248, resettled (1949, 1st Dept) 275 A.D. 769, 88 N.Y.S.2d 902 and motion den (1949, 1st Dept) 275 A.D. 769, 88 N.Y.S.2d 903 and reh and app den (1949, 1st Dept) 275 A.D. 769, 88 N.Y.S.2d 903

16. – – Holder in due course as subject to prohibition

Neither the word "assignee" nor the words "any person claiming under such foreign corporation" were intended to cover a holder in due course. Allison Hill Trust Co. v Sarandrea (1932) 236 A.D. 189, 258 N.Y.S. 299

Failure of a corporation to comply with conditions precedent with respect to doing business as prescribed by statute cannot be set up as a defense against a holder in due course of a negotiable note. Household Discount Corp. v Gleasman (1964) 42 Misc. 2d 344, 247 N.Y.S.2d 981

17. – – Waiver of statute

A provision in a contract guaranteeing indebtedness of a foreign corporation that the agreement shall be deemed to have been made, entered into, executed and delivered at Detroit, Michigan does not, of itself establish as matter of law that the benefit of this section has been waived. Allen Industries, Inc. v Exquisite Form Brassiere, Inc. (1962, 1st Dept) 15 A.D.2d 760, 224 N.Y.S.2d 579

18. – What constitutes "doing business" within state

Where it appears upon the face of the complaint that a foreign corporation employs in this state a district manager to take charge of its ordinary and usual business of selling portraits without limitation as to territory, it is to be assumed, in the absence of allegations to the contrary, that the corporation transacts business here and is doing business within this state. Chicago Crayon Co. v Slattery (1910) 68 Misc 148, 123 N.Y.S. 987

It is not necessary that a foreign corporation maintain an office in this state in order to transact business here. Woodridge Heights Const. Co. v Gippert (1915) 92 Misc 204, 155 N.Y.S. 363

A foreign corporation which had neither capital invested in this state, nor an office for transaction of business therein was entitled to maintain an action for goods sold and delivered by one conducting a commission business in this state and who was plaintiff's selling agent under an agreement terminable by either party on sixty days' notice. Lederwerke v Capitelli (1915) 92 Misc 260, 155 N.Y.S. 651

The phrase, "doing business in this state" implied such continuity of corporate activity as is evidenced by investment of capital within the state, with maintenance of an office for transaction of business and such other incidental circumstances which attest corporate intent to avail itself of privilege to conduct business. Eatonton Cotton Mills, Inc. v Goodyear Tire & Rubber Co. (1924) 124 Misc 211, 208 N.Y.S. 218, affd (1925) 212 A.D. 885, 208 N.Y.S. 857

A foreign corporation is doing business in this state within the meaning of this section where it maintains its principal office within the state and conducts within the state a factory for manufacture of certain commodities. Foreman & Clark Mfg. Co. v Bartle (1925) 125 Misc 759, 211 N.Y.S. 602

In an action by a foreign corporation upon a promissory note, in which the proof shows that an agent for the corporation took a lease of office space in his own name and caused bills for telephone and watchman's services to be made out in his own name, fact that there is nothing to show an investment of capital within this state or maintenance of an office, and those incidental circumstances which attest corporate intent to avail itself of privilege to carry on a business, warrants finding that corporation is not doing business here. Ideal Werke A. G. Fur Drahtlose Telephonie v Roos (1931) 140 Misc 298, 250 N.Y.S. 481

While a foreign corporation may be considered as present in this state for the purpose of obtaining jurisdiction over it such a determination does not carry with it the conclusion that the corporation is doing business here to the extent that the state may demand compliance with this section. M. M. Mades Co. v Gassman (1948, City Ct) 77 N.Y.S.2d 236

19. -- Regular and continuous business conduct

Whether local activities by an unauthorized corporation sufficiently make out transaction of business in this state must be determined on the particular facts of each case, a showing of business conduct, regular and continuous, being essential to bring a foreign corporate plaintiff within its operative provisions. Conklin Limestone Co. v Linden (1964, 3d Dept) 22 A.D.2d 63, 253 N.Y.S.2d 578

The fact that the plaintiff maintained a bank account in N.Y. is not conclusive on the question of doing business in the absence of proof of a continuity of its corporate activity in New York. Lebanon Mill Co. v Kuhn (1932) 145 Misc 918, 261 N.Y.S. 172

20. -- Business for which corporation organized

Doing business within the meaning of this section relates to ordinary business which the corporation was organized to do. It has no relation to an incidental contract of a foreign corporation with a domestic corporation, such as insuring its property. Kline Bros. & Co. v German Union Fire Ins. Co. (1911) 147 A.D. 790, 132 N.Y.S. 181, affd (1913) 210 N.Y. 534, 103 N.E. 1125

A foreign corporation was not doing business in this state by taking out an insurance policy in this state, where the property insured was in a foreign state in which it transacted its general business, where insured did no business here when the insurance was taken and whatever books it had within this state were sent to the foreign state prior to the contract of insurance. Kline Bros. & Co. v German Union Fire Ins. Co. (1911) 147 A.D. 790, 132 N.Y.S. 181, affd (1913) 210 N.Y. 534, 103 N.E. 1125

Procuring subscriptions to capital stock of a foreign corporation and issuing stock to subscribers is not doing business within the meaning of this section. Southworth v Morgan (1910) 71 Misc 214, 128 N.Y.S. 598, affd (1911) 143 A.D. 648, 128 N.Y.S. 196, revd (1912) 205 N.Y. 293, 98 N.E. 490

Effecting insurance in New York on single item of property is not "doing business." Richmond Cedar Works v Buckner (1910, CCD NY) 181 F 424

21. -- Extent of local activity

One sale within the state does not constitute "doing business in this state" within the meaning of this section. Spiegel May Stern Co. v Mitchell (1925) 125 Misc 604, 211 N.Y.S. 495

A foreign corporation is doing business in this state within the proscription of this section, when its local activity transcends the ambit of transient, occasional, noncontinuous sphere, and becomes attended with an appreciable measure of volume, continuity and regularity. Lebanon Mill Co. v Kuhn (1932) 145 Misc 918, 261 N.Y.S. 172

A foreign corporation was not doing business within this state by proof of a few previous sales to defendant where there is no proof of similar sales to others in New York. Lebanon Mill Co. v Kuhn (1932) 145 Misc 918, 261 N.Y.S. 172

It was not established that a Georgia corporation was doing business in New York State within the meaning of this section merely by showing that it had an office-showroom and a sales manager in New York, where it was undisputed that it did not maintain a bank account in New York and that all orders had to be approved by the Georgia office and shipments made from its Georgia mill. James Talcott, Inc. v J. J. Delaney Carpet Co. (1961) 28 Misc. 2d 600, 213 N.Y.S.2d 354, affd (1961, 1st Dept) 14 A.D.2d 866, 222 N.Y.S.2d 312

Whether or not a single transaction constitutes doing business within the state depends upon whether it constitutes a part of a general attempt to transact business in violation of the statute, and, if it does, the first transaction is as illegal as the second, third, or twentieth. Franklin Enterprises Corp. v Moore (1962) 34 Misc. 2d 594, 226 N.Y.S.2d 527

A foreign corporation was precluded by this section from maintaining an action in New York to collect for goods sold, because it was doing business in New York without a license, where it maintained an office and bank account here, was listed in the New York telephone directory, its stationery indicated that its main office was in New York, and it continuously sold and accepted payment for goods through the New York office. Talbot Mills, Inc. v Benezra (1962) 35 Misc. 2d 924, 231 N.Y.S.2d 229

22. -- Selling through others

A foreign stock corporation manufacturing goods in another state and having no office for transaction of business here is not doing business within this state merely because it consigns its manufactured products to a commission merchant doing business here, authorizing him to sell, receive the proceeds and remit the same. Under such circumstances it is the commission merchant who does business here, not the foreign corporation. Brookford Mills, Inc. v Baldwin (1913) 154 A.D. 553, 139 N.Y.S. 195

Plaintiff, foreign corporation, is not doing business in this state where it appeared that the order for the goods in question was taken by a firm of commission merchants in the city of N.Y. who represented a number of foreign corporations including the plaintiff; that the plaintiff had nothing whatever to do with the running of the N.Y. office or its expenses and contributed nothing towards its maintenance; that the only goods of the plaintiff in possession of the commission merchant were samples which had nominal value only; that the order taken by the commission merchant was subject to approval of the plaintiff and that plaintiff never had any stock of merchandise in this state nor any bank account, nor any office, nor did it keep any books within the state. Eagle Mfg. Co. v Arkell & Douglas, Inc. (1921) 197 A.D. 788, 189 N.Y.S. 140, affd (1922) 234 N.Y. 573, 138 N.E. 451

A foreign corporation was not doing business in this State where its primary contact was a domestic corporation acting as sales representative. William L. Bonnell Co. v Katz (1960) 23 Misc. 2d 1028, 196 N.Y.S.2d 763

23. -- Solicitation of orders

A foreign corporation is entitled to recover the purchase price of books shipped to a resident of this state from a foreign state on an order taken by a traveling salesman who exhibited samples in this state, when the order was sent by mail to the foreign state and there accepted and the corporation had no place of business or bank account in this state. Under the circumstances it was not doing business here. L. C. Page & Co. v Sherwood (1911) 146 A.D. 618, 131 N.Y.S. 322

Taking by a foreign corporation of orders for goods in this state by traveling salesman is not doing business in the state. L. C. Page Co. v Sherwood (1910) 65 Misc 543, 120 N.Y.S. 837

That salesmen solicit business in New York is not in itself "doing business in this state." McDowell v Starobin Electrical Supply Co. McDowell v Starobin Electrical Supply Co. (1918) 104 Misc 596, 172 N.Y.S. 221

Where for several years claimant had maintained a sales office in Buffalo in charge of its vice-president and general manager, who had no authority to bind claimant, and the only acts of claimant within the state of New York were solicitation of orders for coal from customers by letter, wire or personal interviews. Such orders were transmitted to the home office in the state of Pennsylvania for approval, and if approved were filled by shipment to the purchaser from mines in that state. Held, that such acts did not constitute "doing business in this state." Pittsburgh & Shawmut Coal Co. v State (1922) 118 Misc 50, 192 N.Y.S. 310

Merely soliciting orders within the state which are accepted outside the state does not constitute doing business within the state, nor does placing of a name on an office door or listing of a name in a telephone directory or the keeping of samples constitute evidence that one is doing business within the state. National Tool Salvage Co. v National Tool Salvage Industries, Inc. (1946) 186 Misc 833, 60 N.Y.S.2d 308, 68 USPQ 118

A plaintiff, soliciting orders within the State to be filled outside of the State through a nonsalaried representative who receives message through telephone message service, is not doing business within the State under §§ 210, 218. National Tool Salvage Co. v National Tool Salvage Industries, Inc. (1946) 186 Misc 833, 60 N.Y.S.2d 308, 68 USPQ 118

Pennsylvania corporation which merely solicited orders in New York, and did not have a bank account in New York, a telephone or other means of communication, was not "doing business" in New York within the meaning of this section. Suss v Durable Knit Corp. (1955) 4 Misc. 2d 666, 147 N.Y.S.2d 363

Where Connecticut corporation solicited orders in New York for goods purchased in Connecticut and shipped therefrom in interstate commerce, and corporation was not subject to New York's franchise tax, the corporation was not "doing business" within the meaning of this section. National Folding Box Co. v Bisceglia Bros. Wines Corp. (1950, Sup) 147 N.Y.S.2d 361, app dismd (1951) 278 A.D. 711, 103 N.Y.S.2d 836

24. – Presumption as to doing business

There is a presumption that a foreign corporation is doing business in its own state and not in this State. William L. Bonnell Co. v Katz (1960) 23 Misc. 2d 1028, 196 N.Y.S.2d 763

25. – Contracts made by corporation

In respect to all contracts, except those made in this state, a foreign corporation has the same rights in our courts as a domestic corporation. Eclipse Silk Mfg. Co. v Hiller (1911) 145 A.D. 568, 129 N.Y.S. 879

Where a contract between one foreign corporation and another foreign corporation was made within this state, and payments thereunder were to be made at the plaintiff's office in New York City, it is a condition precedent to maintainence of the action that this section should have been complied with prior to entering into the contract. East Coast Oil Co. v Hollins (1918) 183 A.D. 67, 170 N.Y.S. 576

It is no defense to an action by a foreign corporation against its surety, to allege that plaintiff has not been licensed to do business in this state. Statutory prohibition placed upon foreign corporations relates to negotiated contracts which become binding by consent or voluntary action of the foreign corporation, and not to contracts inuring to its benefit by implications of law, such as an undertaking on an attachment with respect to which it had no volition. Fairmount Film Corp. v New Amsterdam Casualty Co. (1919) 189 A.D. 246, 178 N.Y.S. 525

An order which dismissed an action by a subcontractor to foreclose a mechanic's lien on the theory that the plaintiff did not have legal capacity to sue was reversed, and it was held that § 218 of the General Corporation Law, which was concededly the applicable statute, was applicable only where the contract sued upon was made by the plaintiff in New York and it did not appear from the papers submitted that the contract between the plaintiff and the general contractor had been made in this state. Kosson & Sons v Carleton (1966, 2d Dept) 26 A.D.2d 582, 272 N.Y.S.2d 81

An implied obligation by the defendant to repay a foreign corporation, the plaintiff, for money had and received in a fiduciary capacity was not a contract made by the foreign corporation in this State within the meaning of this section. Evyan Perfumes, Inc. v Hamilton (1959) 20 Misc. 2d 950, 195 N.Y.S.2d 869

Plaintiff, a foreign corporation, could sue here for the foreclosure of a chattel mortgage notwithstanding the fact that it had not obtained a certificate of doing business. Plaintiff was doing business in this state at the time the contract was made and, moreover, since it was an assignee, the contract was not one "made by it" in this state.

Landerton Co. v Sy-Jo Luncheonette, Inc. (1953, Sup) 118 N.Y.S.2d 478

26. – – Made in this state

Where residents of this state ordered a cash register from a foreign corporation, the order being given here, and the purchaser paid twenty-five dollars on account, which was to be refunded in this state if the corporation did not accept the contract, the balance of the purchase price to be paid here, the contract was one "made in this state." American Case & Register Co. v Griswold (1911) 143 A.D. 807, 128 N.Y.S. 206

This section relates only to actions upon contracts made in this state. Bremer v Ringe (1911) 146 A.D. 724, 131 N.Y.S. 487

Unless the contract was made in this state, § 218 has no application. Bertolf Bros., Inc. v Leuthardt (1941) 261 A.D. 981, 26 N.Y.S.2d 114

An unauthorized Connecticut corporation lacked capacity to sue where obligations in litigation first arose in New York because the work and services creating a contract implied in fact occurred here and the contract sued upon was made in this state. Albini Constr. Co. v Montgomery Ward & Co. (1968, 3d Dept) 30 A.D.2d 1006, 294 N.Y.S.2d 109

This section does not preclude a foreign corporation from maintaining an action upon all contracts, but the prohibition relates only to contracts made by it within the state. Sterling Mfg. Co. v National Surety Co. (1916) 94 Misc 604, 159 N.Y.S. 979

27. – – Made outside state

In an action by plaintiff, as assignee of a Georgia stock corporation, to recover for goods sold and delivered by such corporation to defendant, plaintiff's action was not subject to dismissal under this section where it clearly appeared that the contracts in question were made in Georgia, not in New York. James Talcott, Inc. v J. J. Delaney Carpet Co. (1961) 28 Misc. 2d 600, 213 N.Y.S.2d 354, affd (1961, 1st Dept) 14 A.D.2d 866, 222 N.Y.S.2d 312

A foreign corporation is not precluded from suing in New York by lack of authority to do business in that state where all sales made by it in New York are subject to confirmation at the corporation's home office in another state and the contract on which it sues is not made within this state, defendant having the burden of proving that plaintiff was transacting business within the state without authority. La Mar Hosiery Mills, Inc. v Credit & Commodity Corp. (1961) 28 Misc. 2d 764, 216 N.Y.S.2d 186

A foreign corporation is not precluded from seeking an injunction against a New York retailer for violating "fair trade" price stipulations where defendant is not a signatory of the fair trade price stipulation agreement and the original contract by which prices were fixed was signed in California by plaintiff after being signed by the New York retailer, that contract not being one "made" in New York. Max Factor & Co. v Janel Sales Corp. (1962, CA2 NY) 298 F.2d 511

The fact that a contract was modified at a meeting in New York did not alter the result that where the contract was not made in New York and the plaintiff was not doing business in New York, the New York statute of limitations did not apply. Franklin Research & Development Corp. v Swift Electrical Supply Co. (1964, SD NY) 236 F. Supp. 992, affd (1964, CA2 NY) 340 F.2d 439

28. – – Time of making contract

A contract made by a foreign corporation before it commenced business in this state is not within the meaning of § 218. In re Scheftel's Estate (1937) 275 N.Y. 135, 9 N.E.2d 809

It is only upon a contract made at a time when the corporation is actually doing business here without having secured a certificate, that it is precluded from maintaining an action thereon. Stephenson v Wiltsee (1928) 223 A.D. 41, 227 N.Y.S. 230

This section was not a bar to an action to disaffirm a contract and recover bank moneys paid where the contract was made prior to the time the plaintiff, a foreign corporation, did business in the state. Hanley Co. v Bradley (1927) 145 Misc 285, 259 N.Y.S. 278

29. – Validity of contract

The only penalty which is prescribed by this section for a disregard of this provision is that no such corporation "shall maintain any action in this state upon any contract made by it in this state, unless prior to making of such contract it shall have procured such certificate." This section does not wholly invalidate a contract the only infirmity in which a disability on the part of a foreign corporation to sue thereon in this state. Mahar v Harrington Park Villa Sites (1912) 204 N.Y. 231, 97 N.E. 587

30. – – Right to enforce in federal court

A foreign corporation which has failed to qualify to do business pursuant to state law may not maintain an action in a federal court on a contract entered into in the state where the state statutes provide in effect that such a corporation failing to comply with the requirements for doing business shall not be permitted to bring or maintain an action or suit in the courts of the state. Woods v Interstate Realty Co. (1949) 337 US 535, 93 L Ed 1524, 69 S Ct 1235 (criticized as stated in Stock West, Inc. v Confederated Tribes of Colville Reservation (1989, CA9 Wash) 873 F.2d 1221) and (criticized in McKenzie v Hawaii Permanente Med. Group, Inc. (1998, DC Hawaii) 29 F. Supp. 2d 1174)

The provision that no foreign stock corporation doing business in N.Y. shall maintain an action in this state upon a contract made by it in this state if it had not obtained certificate from the secretary of state that it had complied with requirements to authorize it to do business in this state prior to making the contract does not make the contract void but prevents its enforcement in a state court; federal courts may entertain an action on such a contract. Johnson v New York Breweries Co. (1910, CA2 NY) 178 F 513

Non-compliance with § 210 does not make contracts void nor close federal courts to actions arising under those contracts. Richmond Cedar Works v Buckner (1910, CCD NY) 181 F 424

Contracts made in New York by a foreign corporation which has not complied with the requirements of this statute are not rendered void. The corporation is denied right to seek redress in the courts of N.Y. but not in courts of other states or in federal court of N.Y. Wing v McCallum (1926, DC Mass) 16 F.2d 645, affd (1929, CA1 Mass) 30 F.2d 505, reh den (1929, CA1 Mass) 31 F.2d 940

Where plaintiff is a foreign corporation, which has not filed its certificate, its business being purely interstate, unfair competition with it by anyone, provided proper jurisdiction is obtained, may be passed upon by federal court for eastern district of New York. United Drug Co. v Parodney (1928, DC NY) 24 F.2d 577

A foreign corporation was entitled to sue in United States district court in New York on a contract executed, delivered, and partly performed in the state, notwithstanding the corporation had not procured a certificate of authority to do business in the state. Bamberger Broadcasting Service, Inc. v William Irving Hamilton, Inc. (1940, DC NY) 33 F. Supp. 273

Where the answer in a state action raises an issue of the plaintiff's right to maintain an action, the plaintiff cannot bring an action in the District Court pending determination of state action. Maxwell Co. v Central Hanover Bank & Trust Co. (1943, DC NY) 48 F. Supp. 408

31. – Actions or proceedings subject to prohibition

Filing of a claim by a foreign corporation, doing business within this state, with court of claims constitutes an attempt to "maintain an action in this state" within the meaning of this section. Amos D. Bridge's Sons, Inc. v State (1919) 188 A.D. 500, 177 N.Y.S. 3, affd (1921) 231 N.Y. 532, 132 N.E. 876

The word "action" includes a claim in the court of claims. Pittsburgh & Shawmut Coal Co. v State (1922) 118 Misc 50, 192 N.Y.S. 310

32. – – Contract

Prior to September 1, 1963 an unauthorized foreign corporation was precluded from maintaining an action on a contract made in this state unless it had obtained a certificate of authority for making the contract, but this section did not apply to contracts made outside the state. Garden State Brickface & Stone Co. v Oradell Constr. Corp. (1964) 44 Misc. 2d 22, 252 N.Y.S.2d 790

This section is not inapplicable to an action for accounting under a contract for the sale of coal on the ground that the action was not one for breach of contract in view of the fact that a fiduciary relationship upon which the accounting action was predicated was created by the contract itself. Knight Products, Inc. v Donnen-Fuel Co. (1940, Sup) 20 N.Y.S.2d 135

33. – – Foreclosure of mechanic's lien

A corporation doing business in this state without filing a certificate of authority cannot acquire a mechanic's lien under a contract made in this state. Furthermore, such a corporation, though made party defendant to a foreclosure of a mechanic's lien, cannot enforce any claim predicated upon the lien filed by it. Italian Mosaic & Marble Co. v Niagara Falls (1928) 131 Misc 281, 227 N.Y.S. 64

Where there was sufficient evidence to establish that plaintiff foreign corporation, seeking to foreclose a mechanic's lien, had been engaged for a considerable period of time in construction work in New York without being licensed to do business here, it could not foreclose a mechanic's lien growing out of such a construction contract in a New York court where it was further shown that the contract was initiated while it was performing certain work in New York, and, following certain correspondence, the contract for the work in question was concluded at the home of defendant in New York by acceptance there of a written proposal offered by plaintiff. Berkshire Engineering Corp. v Scott-Paine (1961) 29 Misc. 2d 1010, 217 N.Y.S.2d 919

34. – – Tort

The prohibition of General Corporation Law § 218 cannot be a defense to a cause of action which does not lie in contract, but rather seeks to set aside allegedly fraudulent conveyances. St. Regis Paper Co. v Bellin (1966, 1st Dept) 25 A.D.2d 523, 267 N.Y.S.2d 311

The statute only prohibits a foreign corporation from maintaining any action upon any contract made by it in this state and does not interdict any action purely ex delicto. Meisel Tire Co. v Mar-Bel Trading Co. (1935) 155 Misc 664, 280 N.Y.S. 335

An action by a foreign corporation, not licensed to do business in New York, to enjoin price cutting on its products under the Fair Trade law (Gen. Bus. § 369-a et seq.), is not within the scope of this section, first, because such an action rests upon tort rather than contract, but, even assuming the action to be based upon contract, this section is inapplicable in the absence of a showing that the corporation was doing business in New York and that the contract was made there. Max Factor & Co. v Janel Sales Corp. (1962, CA2 NY) 298 F.2d 511

A foreign corporation is not precluded by this section from bringing an action in New York based on violation of § 369 of the General Business Law and charging defendant with "unfair competition" in violating "fair trade" prices in sale of plaintiff's product, since the cause of action is not based upon contract. Max Factor & Co. v Janel Sales Corp. (1962, CA2 NY) 298 F.2d 511

35. – – Injunction against use of name

A foreign corporation may maintain suit to enjoin use of its trade name by another upon grounds that such use constitutes unfair competition, although at the time of bringing the action it was not licensed to do business in this state. This, because such suit is not an action upon a contract, nor is it to obtain relief by reason of any business transacted by the corporation in this state. Hoevel Sand-Blast Mach. Co. v Hoevel (1915) 167 A.D. 548, 153 N.Y.S. 35

The provisions of this section did not prevent a foreign corporation doing business in this state without a certificate from bringing an action under Penal L § 964 to restrain the respondent from using the similar name to that of petitioner. Dunkin' Donuts of America, Inc. v Dunkin Donuts, Inc. (1958) 12 Misc. 2d 380, 176 N.Y.S.2d 915, affd (1959, 3d Dept) 8 A.D.2d 228, 188 N.Y.S.2d 132, 122 USPQ 220

The fact that a foreign corporation has not taken out a license to do business in N.Y. and has transacted business there unlawfully does not incapacitate it from maintaining a suit in the state courts to enjoin a N.Y. corporation for tortious use of its corporate name. United States Light & Heating Co. v United States Light & Heating Co. (1910, CCD NY) 181 F 182

A foreign corporation can restrain the use by a domestic corporation of a trade name similar to its own when the name is chosen by a domestic corporation with knowledge of name and business of the foreign corporation although it has obtained no authorization to do business in N.Y. Mutual Export & Import Corp. v Mutual Export & Import Corp. (1917, DC NY) 241 F 137

36. – – Conversion

While this section would not be available as a defense to an action by a foreign corporation which has been doing business in New York without a certificate of authority to do so, based upon conversion of money belonging to plaintiff, an action for conversion will not lie where the right of action clearly rests upon a contract entered into in this state, which is annexed to the complaint and contains no provision justifying an allegation that monies advanced were received and held in trust by defendant for plaintiff. American Middle East Corp. v Barouk (1961, 1st Dept) 13 A.D.2d 919, 215 N.Y.S.2d 843

If a foreign corporation doing business in this state without a license can state a cause of action against defendant based on conversion of funds by defendant, this section provides no defense, notwithstanding the basis for the claim of conversion arises out of the terms of a contract under which defendant has agreed to hold certain funds in trust for plaintiff. American Middle East Corp. v Barouk (1961) 31 Misc. 2d 823, 226 N.Y.S.2d 874

37. – – Condemnation

The provisions of this section are limited strictly to contract actions, and a foreign corporation need not qualify under this section in order to be entitled to seek damages for appropriation of land owned by it in New York or by related condemnation proceedings. Wm. G. Roe & Co. v State (1964) 43 Misc. 2d 417, 251 N.Y.S.2d 151

38. – – Arbitration

Section 218 does not prevent a foreign corporation, which has not obtained a certificate of authority to do business in the state, from participating in arbitration proceedings, in regard to a dispute involving materials sold by one party to the other. Tugee Laces v Mary Muffet, Inc. (1948) 297 N.Y. 914, 79 N.E.2d 744

An arbitration proceeding comes within the purview of § 218; this section is mandatory and self-executing; the bar set up by this section does not concern itself with jurisdiction, but rather with right to invoke jurisdiction of the court; amendment to Civil Practice Act (§ 1450) did not repeal § 218 as to arbitration agreements. In re Vanguard Films, Inc. (1947) 188 Misc 796, 67 N.Y.S.2d 893

Foreign corporation, which had its principal place of business in New York City, and which had a certificate of authority, could maintain an action in the Supreme Court of New York County for enforcement of arbitration provision contained in a charter party, where charter party was entered into between the parties in New York State and provided for arbitration in the City of New York. T. J. Stevenson & Co. v International Coal Corp. (1953) 15 Misc. 2d 904, 185 N.Y.S.2d 599

Although a foreign corporation cannot maintain an action in this State upon a contract made by it in this State unless, before the making of the contract, it has obtained a certificate of authority from the Secretary of State, it may institute a special proceeding to enforce an arbitration agreement. Terminal Auxiliar Maritima v Cocotos S.S. Co. (1957) 11 Misc. 2d 697, 178 N.Y.S.2d 298 (superseded by statute as stated in In re Knoll N. Am., Inc. (1993, Sup) 158 Misc. 2d 227, 601 N.Y.S.2d 224)

A foreign corporation doing business in this state without a license at the time a contract containing an arbitration clause was entered into was prohibited by this section from initiating or prosecuting arbitration proceedings in this state. Application of Levys (1947, Sup) 73 N.Y.S.2d 801, affd (1950) 276 A.D. 953, 94 N.Y.S.2d 924

Whether or not a foreign corporation could compel performance of an agreement to arbitrate entered into in this state, in the absence of filing a certificate of doing business, one who seeks to bar such a proceeding on the basis of this section has the burden of establishing that the foreign corporation was doing business within this state and that the contract in question was made here, and § 1450 of the Civil Practice Act, as amended makes no provision for staying a demand for arbitration, the remedy being statutory rather than an "action." General Knitting Mills, Inc. v Rudd Plastic Fabrics Corp. (1961, Sup) 212 N.Y.S.2d 783 (superseded by statute as stated in In re Knoll N. Am., Inc. (1993, Sup) 158 Misc. 2d 227, 601 N.Y.S.2d 224)

39. – Pleadings; complaint by corporation

Where the complaint in an action by a foreign corporation to recover on a contract of sale contains no allegation that the contract was made here, or that the plaintiff is doing business in this state, it is not necessary to allege that at the time the contract was made the plaintiff had procured a certificate to do business here, or, in the alternative, that it was not doing business within this state. Eclipse Silk Mfg. Co. v Hiller (1911) 145 A.D. 568, 129 N.Y.S. 879

Where a foreign corporation brings suit in the courts of this state and sets out a good cause of action it will be assumed that it is rightfully in the state and properly in court until the contrary is made to appear. Eclipse Silk Mfg. Co. v Hiller (1911) 145 A.D. 568, 129 N.Y.S. 879

A complaint in an action by a foreign corporation is not demurrable for failure to allege compliance with this section unless it appears on its face that the foreign corporation was doing business in this state, and that it made the contract sued upon in this state. Frick Co. v Pultz (1914) 162 A.D. 209, 147 N.Y.S. 732

Failure to allege compliance with this section rendered complaint demurrable. East Coast Oil Co. v Hollins (1918) 183 A.D. 67, 170 N.Y.S. 576

An allegation in a complaint in an action by a foreign corporation that the plaintiff "was then and still is duly authorized to do business in the state of New York" sufficiently alleges the plaintiff's compliance with this section. United Bldg. Material Co. v Odell (1910) 67 Misc 584, 123 N.Y.S. 313, affd (1910) 141 A.D. 921, 125 N.Y.S. 1148

Where the allegation of a complaint in an action on a contract, that the plaintiff is a foreign corporation and duly authorized to do business in this state, is specifically denied by the answer, it will be assumed that the plaintiff is a stock corporation, in the absence of an allegation and proof on the point, and the plaintiff cannot recover without both pleading and proving its compliance with this and following sections. E. A. Strout Farm Agency v Hunter (1914) 85 Misc 476, 148 N.Y.S. 924

Where the complaint of a foreign stock corporation in an action on a contract fails to allege that prior to making of the alleged contract the plaintiff procured a certificate of its compliance with all requirements of law to authorize it to do business in New York, complaint should be dismissed. Dan Talmage's Sons Co. v American Dock Co. (1916) 93 Misc 535, 157 N.Y.S. 445

Where a foreign corporation suing upon a contract made in this state, failed to allege in its complaint that it had obtained a certificate of authority to do business in this state, pursuant to this section, a statement of the secretary of state, annexed to the moving papers, reciting that the plaintiff had authority to do business here prior to the date of contract on which the action is based is sufficient to show compliance with the statute. Western Felt Works v Modern Carpet Cleaning & Storage Corp. (1931) 141 Misc 495, 252 N.Y.S. 696

40. – – Answer

Where the complaint in an action by a foreign corporation to recover the purchase price of goods sold in this state does not allege that the plaintiff is a foreign stock corporation "doing business" in this state, and does not show upon its face that it comes within the provisions of this section, it is the duty of the defendants, if they wish to rely upon the statutory defense, to plead the necessary facts. Angldile Computing Scale Co. v Gladstone (1914) 164 A.D. 370, 149 N.Y.S. 807

This section must be pleaded to be effective. Barney & Smith Car Co. v E. W. Bliss Co. (1917) 100 Misc 21, 164 N.Y.S. 800, affd (1917) 178 A.D. 919, 165 N.Y.S. 1076

A defense to an action founded upon contract cannot be based upon this section without affirmatively alleging that plaintiff is doing business within this state and that the contract sued upon was made in this state. Fleet-Wing Corp. v Pease Oil Co. (1961) 29 Misc. 2d 437, 212 N.Y.S.2d 871, mod on other grounds (1961, 4th Dept) 14 A.D.2d 728, 218 N.Y.S.2d 533

A defense based on an alleged violation of this section must clearly set forth the contract and dealings between the parties, since "a foreign corporation may transact some kinds of business within the state without procuring a certificate or submitting to control..." Gindy Mfg. Corp. v Fishman (1959, Sup) 189 N.Y.S.2d 56

41. – – Dismissal of complaint

It is error to dismiss a complaint, before evidence is taken, in an action on a promissory note brought by a foreign corporation against a domestic corporation on the ground that there is no allegation that the plaintiff was authorized to do business in this state, although the note set forth was payable at a bank in this state, if there be no allegation of the time and place of its delivery, consideration, or where the transaction out of which it arose took place, or that plaintiff is doing business in this state or has any office therein. Alpha Portland Cement Co. v Schratwieser Fireproof Const. Co. (1911) 146 A.D. 571, 131 N.Y.S. 142

Where, in an action by foreign corporation for goods sold in another state, neither complaint nor answer alleges that plaintiff was doing business in this state, or that goods were sold or delivered therein, dismissal of complaint, on ground that plaintiff was doing business within state and had not obtained certificate required by this section is error. E. H. Stafford Mfg. Co. v Newman (1912) 75 Misc 636, 133 N.Y.S. 1073

A defense, in an action on a promissory note, which alleges that the plaintiff is a foreign corporation and that the note was made and delivered in this state at a time when plaintiff had not obtained a certificate to do business here, as required by this section raises a question of fact, which cannot be disposed of upon motion. J. H. Balmer Co. v Mallamo (1931) 142 Misc 100, 253 N.Y.S. 37

A complaint based upon a contract by a foreign corporation could not be dismissed for failure to comply with this statute where neither the contract nor the complaint indicated that the contract was executed in New York State. Even though a plaintiff may be a foreign corporation and doing business here, the provisions of this section do not apply unless a contract in a suit is a New York contract. National Merchandising Corp. v Powers (1957) 8 Misc. 2d 881, 168 N.Y.S.2d 507

A motion to dismiss a complaint by a foreign corporation on the ground that it lacks capacity to sue because the contract in suit was made in this state and plaintiff is doing business here without a license, cannot succeed merely on the basis of a showing that the corporation has a telephone listing and maintains a bank account in New York and its president maintains an office here. Ascher Corp. v Horvath (1962) 35 Misc. 2d 375, 231 N.Y.S.2d 676

Under this section, a foreign corporation may sue in this state in like manner and subject to the same regulations as a domestic corporation except as otherwise specially prescribed by law. But if it appears on the face of the complaint that a foreign corporation doing business in this state is not authorized to maintain an action for its failure to obtain a certificate of doing business here, the defendant may move to dismiss the complaint on the ground that it fails to state a cause of action. Maple Motor Co. v Beales (1951, Co Ct) 110 N.Y.S.2d 623

Where. verified complaint, and supporting affidavits, gave prima facie proof that plaintiff's assignor was not doing business in the state within the prohibition of the statute, and that the contract in question involved interstate commerce, the complaint was not dismissed. Nicolich v E. Muniz Ferreira & Cia (1956, Sup) 149 N.Y.S.2d 662

42. – Corporation's right to counterclaim

This section does not prohibit assertion of a counterclaim by a foreign corporation sued in this state, where it has not complied with said section. James Howden & Co. v American Condenser & Engineering Corp. (1920) 194 A.D. 164, 185 N.Y.S. 159, affd (1921) 231 N.Y. 627, 132 N.E. 915

Although a foreign stock corporation, other than a moneyed corporation, cannot maintain an action on a contract made in New York unless it alleges and proves that it has complied with this and next succeeding sections, yet, if sued in New York, it can counterclaim any cause arising out of the transaction, although it has not complied with this section, as amended by L 1917, ch 594. Rolle v Rolle (1922) 201 A.D. 698, 194 N.Y.S. 661

Where, in an action for goods sold and delivered to a foreign corporation doing business in this state, the answer pleads two counterclaims, one of which arose out of a contract sued on and the other did not, failure of the defendant to comply with this section is not a defense to the first counterclaim, but the defendant's failure to comply with Tax Law, § 181, providing for payment of a license tax by a foreign corporation engaged in business in this state, is a defense to both counterclaims. American Ink Co. v Riegel Sack Co. (1913) 79 Misc 421, 140 N.Y.S. 107

A contention that a carrier could not assert a contract set forth in receipt given to vendor of goods shipped by said carrier, because its answer did not allege that it had complied with this section was without merit, since the carrier was entitled to litigate any question affecting not only its liability but the amount to which vendee might be entitled by reason of such contract. Jones v Wells Fargo Express Co. (1914) 83 Misc 508, 145 N.Y.S. 601

Plaintiff, a domestic corporation, brought an action against a Canadian corporation having a place of business in this state, to recover the balance due under a contract for the sale and delivery of machinery and apparatus for air-conditioning and installation of same upon the premises of the defendant, and for a stipulated bonus of $100 a day for each day apparatus was ready for operation previous to the time mentioned in the contract as to be completed, and for certain extra materials mentioned in the contract. Held, that though the defendant was not duly licensed to do business in this state it might plead as a counterclaim and a separate defense a cause of action based upon loss of profits alleged to have been sustained by it because of certain failures on the part of the plaintiff to complete installation of various portions of equipment; such counterclaim arises out of the same transaction as that which forms the basis of the plaintiff's suit. Carrier Engineering Corp. v International Mfg. Co. (1918) 104 Misc 191, 171 N.Y.S. 641

There is nothing in this section preventing an unlicensed foreign corporation from enforcing, by means of a counterclaim, a cause of action based upon a contract made in this state by its assignor, a domestic corporation. Conoley v Distileria Serralles, Inc. (1944, City

Ct) 48 N.Y.S.2d 11, affd (1946) 270 A.D. 1003, 63 N.Y.S.2d 827, app den (1946) 271 A.D. 784, 67 N.Y.S.2d 719

Where, in an action against a foreign corporation, the plaintiff discontinued his action on trial putting the corporation to proof on its counterclaim the status of the defendant corporation was not changed to that of plaintiff so as to preclude it from maintaining its counterclaim because of noncompliance with this section prohibiting suits by foreign corporations without certificates from the Secretary of State. Bellak v Bon Specialty Co. (1948, Sup App T) 80 N.Y.S.2d 248

The New York Law in respect to the status of defendant foreign corporation in asserting its counterclaim, does not control. Air King Products Co. v Hazeltine Research, Inc. (1950, DC NY) 94 F. Supp. 85, 87 USPQ 315

43. – Examination before trial

Defendant is entitle to examination before trial of plaintiff, an assignee of foreign corporation, as to whether plaintiff's assignor has been and is doing business in New York without having obtained certificate of authority required under this section. Stevens v Silverman (1935) 157 Misc 381, 283 N.Y.S. 744

§ 1314. Actions or special proceedings by foreign corporations

An action or special proceeding may be maintained by a foreign corporation, in like manner and subject to the same limitations, as an action or special proceeding brought by a domestic corporation, except as otherwise prescribed by statute.

History: Add, L 1969, ch 1066, § 1, eff Sept 1, 1970, with substance derived from Gen Corp Law § 223.

CASE ANNOTATIONS

1-5. [Reserved for future use]
6. Under former General Corporation Law § 223

1-5. [Reserved for future use]
6. Under former General Corporation Law § 223

The courts of this state give or deny effect of law to decrees or acts of foreign governmental establishment in accordance with our own public policy; our courts are open or closed to foreign corporations according to our public policy, and in determining our public policy in these matters common sense and justice must be consideration of weight. Russian Reinsurance Co. v Stoddard (1925) 240 N.Y. 149, 147 N.E. 703, reh den 240 N.Y. 682, 148 N.E. 757

In an action to compel return to the plaintiffs of securities and moneys deposited by the plaintiff insurance company with the defendant trust company, as capital of said insurance company in this state for protection of policyholders and creditors in U. S., where the defendant resists the plaintiffs' claim solely on the ground that plaintiffs fail to establish ownership or right of possession to the exclusion of others who might demand the property hereafter, pointing out that at the present time the plaintiff corporation is no longer in existence or, if in existence, has no capacity to sue, until the time comes when a government which we recognize rules in Russia or until the plaintiff is able to re-establish itself there courts should not take jurisdiction of this action. Both justice and common sense require us to give effect to conditions existing in Russia, though those conditions are created by a force which we are not ready to acknowledge as entitled to recognition as a state or government. Russian Reinsurance Co. v Stoddard (1925) 240 N.Y. 149, 147 N.E. 703, reh den 240 N.Y. 682, 148 N.E. 757

The plaintiff, a foreign corporation, may sue on a note executed by the defendant corporation in Florida, bearing eight per cent interest. It is not a defense to the action that the plaintiff is a foreign corporation not licensed to do business in this state and that the instrument sued upon is one that a N.Y. corporation is forbidden by the laws of this state to make, and that, therefore, the cause of action is not maintainable because of the prohibition in this section. City Nat. Bank v Lake Const. Co. (1929) 227 A.D. 85, 237 N.Y.S. 58

This section permits an action by a foreign corporation against a nonresident in the courts of this state on a cause of action which arose outside the state. John Dirkmaat Co. v Pruyser (1947, Sup) 72 N.Y.S.2d 797

Under this section, a foreign corporation may sue in this state in like manner and subject to the same regulations as a domestic corporation except as otherwise specially prescribed by law. But if it appears on the face of the complaint that a foreign corporation doing business in this state is not authorized to maintain an action for its failure to obtain a certificate of doing business here, the defendant may move to dismiss the complaint on the ground that it fails to state a cause of action. Maple Motor Co. v Beales (1951, Co Ct) 110 N.Y.S.2d 623

§ 1315.   Actions or special proceedings against foreign corporations

(a) An action or special proceeding against a foreign corporation may be maintained by a resident of this state or by a domestic corporation of any kind for any cause of action.

(b) Except as otherwise provided in this article, an action or special proceeding against a foreign corporation may be maintained by another foreign corporation of any kind or by a nonresident in the following cases only:

(1) Where the action is brought to recover damages for the breach of a contract made or to be performed within this state, or relating to property situated within this state at the time of the making of the contract.

(2) Where the subject matter of the litigation is situated within this state.

(3) Where the cause of action arose within this state, except where the object of the action or special proceeding is to affect the title of real property situated outside this state.

(4) Where, in any case not included in the preceding subparagraphs, a non-domiciliary would be subject to the personal jurisdiction of the courts of this state under section three hundred two of the civil practice law and rules.

(5) Where the defendant is a foreign corporation conducting activities or authorized to conduct activities in this state.

(c) Paragraph (b) does not apply to a corporation which was formed under the laws of the United States and which maintains an office in this state.

History: Add, L 1969, ch 1066, § eff Sept 1, 1970, with substance derived from Gen Corp Law §§ 224, 225; amd, L 1970, ch 847, § 77, eff Sept 1, 1970. L 2013, ch 549, § 108, eff July 1, 2014.

CASE ANNOTATIONS

1. Generally

In Article 78 proceeding to set aside resolution by regional chapter of non-for-profit California corporation ("Sierra Club") which, inter alia, suspended petitioner ("New York City Group") from its organization, court would not decline jurisdiction on forum non convenience grounds where regional chapter was headquartered in New York and controversy solely involved New York residents, acts complained of took place in New York, immediate and substantial impact of outcome of litigation (although resonating in California and elsewhere) would be felt primarily in New York, and facts did not suggest that litigation in California would be better aligned with interests of litigants and public. Lane v Sierra Club (2000, Sup) 183 Misc. 2d 944, 706 N.Y.S.2d 577

2-10. [Reserved for future use]

11. Under former General Corporation Law § 224

This section, in permitting a resident of New York to maintain an action against a foreign corporation for any cause of action, states an elemental policy of jurisdiction in the courts of New York which cannot be neglected in the absence of some overriding policy consideration. Fuss v French Nat. Railroads (1962) 35 Misc. 2d 680, 231 N.Y.S.2d 57, affd without op 17 A.D.2d 941, 233 N.Y.S.2d 1013

If the Legislature intended this section to apply to fiduciaries, it would have so stated. Henshaw v Lewis (1953) 118 N.Y.S.2d 360, affd Kane v Lewis (1953) 282 A.D. 529, 125 N.Y.S.2d 544

12. – Exercise of jurisdiction over action arising outside state

Courts of this state may entertain jurisdiction of negligence case arising in another state where plaintiff is a resident or non-resident of this state. As to non-residents courts may, in exercise of their discretion, refuse to entertain jurisdiction but as to residents of this state courts have no discretion in matter and are without power to dismiss complaint because tort happened in a foreign state and was governed somewhat by the statutes of that state. Gregonis v Philadelphia & Reading Coal & Iron Co. (1923) 235 N.Y. 152, 139 N.E. 223, 32 ALR 1

13. – – Where plaintiff is resident

Transitory causes of action arising outside of the state are within the general jurisdiction of the courts of the state when brought by a resident of the state even though the defendant be a foreign corporation and the plaintiff be the assignee of a person not himself a resident of the state. Banque De France v Supreme Court of New York (1942) 287 N.Y. 483, 41 N.E.2d 65, cert den 316 US 646, 86 L Ed 1730, 62 S Ct 1279

Courts of this state have jurisdiction of transitory actions brought by residents of this state against non-residents who appear generally, and if discretion were to be exercised there is no reason to decline jurisdiction. Re Hamburg-American Line (1930) 135 Misc 715, 238 N.Y.S. 331, affd without op 228 A.D. 802, 239 N.Y.S. 914

General jurisdiction of courts of this state extends to transitory actions against foreign corporation where the subject of the action is a tort committed outside of the state, if the plaintiffs were residents of the state at the time the action was commenced. Rojzenblitt v Polish Trans-Atlantic Shipping Co. (1936) 162 Misc 251, 293 N.Y.S. 79

The mere fact that a cause of action in favor of a resident of New York State against a foreign corporation arose outside the state is not sufficient ground for a New York court to close its doors to one of its residents. Fuss v French Nat. Railroads (1962) 35 Misc. 2d 680, 231 N.Y.S.2d 57, affd without op 17 A.D.2d 941, 233 N.Y.S.2d 1013

A New York court will assume jurisdiction of an action brought by a resident of New York against a French railroad corporation where it appears that such corporation is doing a substantial amount of business in New York and that plaintiff is physically and financially unable to maintain such an action in France. Fuss v French Nat. Railroads (1962) 35 Misc. 2d 680, 231 N.Y.S.2d 57, affd without op 17 A.D.2d 941, 233 N.Y.S.2d 1013

14. – – Where plaintiff is nonresident

The general jurisdiction of the courts of this state extends to transitory causes of action arising in another jurisdiction, even though the plaintiff may not have been a resident of this state at the time the cause of action arose, and although the defendant is a foreign corporation. Silberfeld v Swiss Bank Corp. (1944) 268 A.D. 884, 50 N.Y.S.2d 841

State court refused to exercise its discretion and entertain jurisdiction of suit for damages by citizen of Israel, a passenger on an Israel vessel, against Israel corporation, owner of the vessel, where contract of passage provided, that all disputes in connection with the passage should be litigated in courts of Israel, since contract provision was reasonable. Schwartz v Zim Israel Navigation Co. (1958) 15 Misc. 2d 576, 181 N.Y.S.2d 283

15. – – As burden on commerce

Motion by a foreign railroad corporation to set aside service of summons on the ground that litigation would tend to burden interstate commerce must be denied, for, while the action, which is based on an injury to perishable property, arose out of the state, still this section authorizes an action against a foreign corporation by a resident of this state. It cannot be said that maintenance of an action in this state constitutes an unreasonable burden upon interstate commerce. Johnston v Atlantic C. L. R. Co. (1926) 128 Misc 82, 217 N.Y.S. 758

An action for damages by a New York resident against a French railroad corporation is not precluded by Art. I § 8, cl. 3 of the Federal Constitution, giving Congress exclusive power to regulate commerce with foreign nations, etc., unless it imposes an undue burden upon such commerce to such extent that it will be unreasonable for a New York court to take jurisdiction. Fuss v French Nat. Railroads (1962) 35 Misc. 2d 680, 231 N.Y.S.2d 57, affd without op 17 A.D.2d 941, 233 N.Y.S.2d 1013

16. – Action against foreign corporation; by resident

Failure of a plaintiff to state in his original papers that he is a resident of the state is not a fatal defect which cannot be cured. Cantor v Mutual Trimming & Binding Co. (1940, City Ct) 23 N.Y.S.2d 429

17. – – Who is resident

Where a member of a partnership came from another state to New York, intending to remain indefinitely, he acquired a New York residence which he retained until he took up residence elsewhere so that, under this section authorizing an action by a resident against a foreign corporation on any cause of action, he could maintain an action against a foreign corporation not doing business in this state. Randolph v American Packing Corp. (1947) 273 A.D. 105, 75 N.Y.S.2d 187, reh den 273 A.D. 807, 76 N.Y.S.2d 266

The mere fact that a Czechoslovakian citizen arrived in New York under a temporary visa was not enough to prevent him from becoming a resident of the state so as to maintain an action under § 224. Greiner v Bank of Adelaide (1941) 176 Misc 315, 26 N.Y.S.2d 515

Czechoslovakian citizen in this state under a temporary visa may, under §§ 224 and 225, maintain an action against an Australian banking corporation. Greiner v Bank of Adelaide (1941) 176 Misc 315, 26 N.Y.S.2d 515

A foreign corporation cannot be a resident even though it is licensed to do business within the state. Schwartz v Zim Israel Navigation Co. (1958) 15 Misc 576, 181 N.Y.S.2d 283

A plaintiff, in order to qualify as a resident, within the meaning of this section, must establish (1) his intent to make this state his permanent home, or (2) that he has no present intent to establish or have a permanent home elsewhere; to the extent that Greiner v Bank of Adelaide (1941) 176 Misc 315, 26 N.Y.S.2d 515, and Von Petersdorff v Insurance Co. of North America (1944) 181 Misc 907, 46 N.Y.S.2d 651, are to the contrary, they will not be followed. Schwartz v Zim Israel Navigation Co. (1958) 15 Misc. 2d 576, 181 N.Y.S.2d 283

18. – – By resident assignee

Assignment of a claim may be made by a foreign corporation to a resident of this state even though the assignment is made solely to enable an action to be brought here, whether the assignor could or could not bring it himself. Severnoe Secur. Corp. v Westminster Bank, Ltd. (1925) 214 A.D. 14, 210 N.Y.S. 629

The rule that a foreign corporation cannot maintain an action against another foreign corporation in the courts of this state upon a contract made without the state, can be circumvented by an assignment of cause of action to a resident of this state, even though it be without consideration. McCauley v Georgia Railroad Bank (1924) 122 Misc 632, 203 N.Y.S. 550, affd without op 209 A.D. 886, 205 N.Y.S. 935, and affd without op 239 N.Y. 514, 147 N.E. 175

Where assignment of a cause of action to a resident of this state is not colorable merely, court has jurisdiction of subject-matter under this section. Hewitt v Canadian P. R. Co. (1924) 124 Misc 186, 207 N.Y.S. 797, affd without op 212 A.D. 815, 207 N.Y.S. 851

A complaint in an action by a resident assignee of a foreign corporation against other foreign corporations for damage to merchandise transported by defendants, common carriers, from Italy to Montreal, will not be dismissed for lack of jurisdiction, for this section specifically gives a resident of this state the right of action against any foreign corporation for any cause of action. Ball v Nippon Yusen (Kabushki Kaisha) (1931) 142 Misc 201, 253 N.Y.S. 260, affd 143 Misc 243, 256 N.Y.S. 298

This section in so far as it authorizes a suit by a resident assignee of a cause of action accruing to a non-resident against non-resident interstate carrier for damage to merchandise is unconstitutional. Miele v Chicago, M., S. P. & P. R. Co. (1934) 151 Misc 137, 270 N.Y.S. 788

19. – – By domestic corporation

A domestic corporation may maintain an action against a foreign corporation for any cause of action and when such action is begun and jurisdiction properly obtained its retention is compulsory even though the action is brought on a claim assigned by a nonresident. Commission for Polish Relief, Ltd. v Banca Nationala A Romaniei (1941) 176 Misc 1064, 27 N.Y.S.2d 377, affd 288 N.Y. 332, 43 N.E.2d 345

A New York corporation can maintain an action against a nonresident partnership where the partnership, under terms of a distributor franchise agreement, has appointed an agent for service of process in this state. Emerson Radio & Phonograph Corp. v Eskind (1957) 32 Misc. 2d 1038, 228 N.Y.S.2d 841

Court has jurisdiction of tort action for conversion brought by domestic corporation against foreign banking corporation. Newtown Jackson Co. v Barclays Bank (1954, Sup) 133 N.Y.S.2d 726

20. – Jurisdictional requirement; doing business in state

Although this section provides that an action against a foreign corporation may be maintained by a resident of the state, or by a domestic corporation, for any cause of action, it is nonetheless an essential to acquiring jurisdiction over the foreign corporation that it be "doing business" in this state. Simonson v International Bank (1962) 16 A.D.2d 55, 225 N.Y.S.2d 392, affd 14 N.Y.2d 281, 251 N.Y.S.2d 433, 200 N.E.2d 427; Emerson Radio & Phonograph Corp. v Eskind (1957) 32 Misc. 2d 1038, 228 N.Y.S.2d 841

Pursuant to this section service of summons on the president of a foreign corporation, in an action on a contract of employment, must be vacated and set aside, where it appears that said corporation has no place for transaction of business in this state and has failed to file a certificate to do business here. Kohn v Wilkes-Barre Dry Goods Co. (1930) 139 Misc 116, 246 N.Y.S. 425

In an action between a resident of Poland and a Russian corporation, neither authorized to do business or doing business in this state, to recover damages for breach of contract to deposit rubles made in Russia and relating to property situated in Russia at time of making of contract which was breached in Russia, the plaintiff does not come within the provisions of this section and § 225, and the supreme court cannot assume jurisdiction of the action. Rzeszotarski v Co-operative Ass'n Kasa Polska (1931) 139 Misc 400, 247 N.Y.S. 471

Service may not be sustained, under this section, where proof fails to show that defendant is engaged in doing business within this state. Trautman v Taylor-Adams Co. (1931) 141 Misc 500, 252 N.Y.S. 701

21. – – What constitutes doing business

A Pennsylvania corporation, having its office and principal place of business in that state and having no bank account, office, resident manager or representative within this state, and employing no salesmen or conducting no meetings of directors or stockholders in this state, is not doing business in this state within the meaning of this section and § 225, notwithstanding that it purchased merchandise within this state, and that its president, secretary, and treasurer are residents of and live with their families within city of New York. Scheinman v Bonwit Teller & Co. (1928) 132 Misc 311, 229 N.Y.S. 783

Where it appears that a foreign corporation since its incorporation has been controlled, directed and managed by its officers from their office in N.Y. where they regularly and systematically transact substantial portion of corporate business with a fair measure of permanency and continuity, the corporation must be regarded as doing business in this state and service of summons on the president thereof in New York City, where he performed his duties was valid. Stark v Howe Sound Co. (1931) 141 Misc 148, 252 N.Y.S. 233, affd 234 A.D. 904, 254 N.Y.S. 959

A foreign corporation doing business of about $100,000 annually in the state through the efforts of its sole representative, which represented itself as having an office in New York City by permitting its name to be listed on the door and directory of the building in which the sole representative maintained an office, and also permitted itself to be listed in the telephone directory, was conducting business within the state. Murry v J. P. Ward Co. (1959) 15 Misc. 2d 944, 181 N.Y.S.2d 216

A Colorado corporation owning a department store in Denver, though it sold nothing in New York but only bought merchandise there, was held to have such contacts and presence in New York as to require it to defend an action brought against it in New York by a New York manufacturer for the price of goods sold to it by him, where, with other out-of-town stores, it had joined in organizing and sharing expenses of a New York corporation which maintained a buying office in New York City managed by an office manager and used by store buyers when they came to New York, and the Colorado corporation's name was listed on the office door, in the building lobby, and in the Manhattan telephone directory. Kimberly Knitwear, Inc. v Mid-West Pool Car Asso. (1959) 21 Misc. 2d 730, 191 N.Y.S.2d 347

22. – – Attachment of funds

Plaintiff may maintain an action against a defendant foreign corporation not doing business in this state by attachment of funds of the defendant in N.Y. bank under this section. Madsen v Baltimore Mail S.S. Co. (1935) 244 A.D. 809, 279 N.Y.S. 766, cert den 298 US 675, 80 L Ed 1396, 56 S Ct 939

23. – – Consent to jurisdiction

This section and § 225 concern jurisdiction over subject-matter, and, in actions between foreign parties plaintiff and a foreign corporation defendant, jurisdiction is either not conferred upon or expressly denied to our courts, unless foreign corporation is "doing business in this state," and if that fact be absent, jurisdiction cannot be conferred even by consent of defendants. Davis v Julius Kessler & Co. (1922) 118 Misc 292, 194 N.Y.S. 9, affd without op 202 A.D. 798, 194 N.Y.S. 927

24. Under former General Corporation Law § 225

Where the plaintiff and defendant are both foreign corporations and the cause of action did not arise in this state, did not concern property here and the defendant was not doing business in this state, the court does not have jurisdiction of the cause of action under this section. Swift & Co. v Karline (1927) 245 N.Y. 570, 157 N.E. 861

An action by a nonresident against a foreign corporation can come within the classes of cases specified in this section. Gonzalez v Industrial Bank (of Cuba) (1960) 10 A.D.2d 624, 196 N.Y.S.2d 926, affd 9 N.Y.2d 623, 210 N.Y.S.2d 227, 172 N.E.2d 80

Section 225 was held inapplicable to an action brought pursuant to a supervisory order of the alien property custodian. Yokohama Specie Bank, Ltd. v National City Bank (1944) 183 Misc 610, 52 N.Y.S.2d 97

If the Legislature intended this section to apply to fiduciaries, it would have so stated. Henshaw v Lewis (1953, Sup) 118 N.Y.S.2d 360, affd 282 A.D. 529, 125 N.Y.S.2d 544

Under this section, suits may be maintained in New York courts by one foreign corporation against another foreign corporation only in four cases, jurisdiction cannot be conferred by consent on a New York court in other instances, and, if the only possible basis on which a particular action can be sustained is that the defendant is doing business in New York, plaintiff has the burden of proof as to that point. Electric Race Patrol, Inc. v National Trailer Convoy, Inc. (1961, DC NY) 191 F. Supp. 364

25. – Exercise of jurisdiction over action

An action by one foreign corporation against another foreign corporation can only be brought in New York State if the cause of action arose in New York State. Cala v Luis De Ridder Ltda., S. A. (1962) 17 A.D.2d 729, 232 N.Y.S.2d 284

In an action by a Massachusetts corporation against a Connecticut corporation, doing business in this state, the court has no discretion, under this section to refuse jurisdiction on the ground of expense and inconvenience in bringing witness here from without the state. Crane, H & Co. v New York, N. H. & H. R. Co. (1927) 131 Misc 71, 225 N.Y.S. 775

Subdivision 4 of this section which permits the maintenance of an action by a non-resident against a foreign corporation doing business in this State is permissive and not mandatory and our courts may or may not accept jurisdiction as a matter of discretion. Yesuvida v Pennsylvania R. Co. (1951) 200 Misc 815, 111 N.Y.S.2d 417

An action may be maintained by a foreign corporation against another foreign corporation where the latter is doing business within this state. However, it is discretionary with the court as to whether, in such case, it will entertain or refuse jurisdiction. Generally where the action is for tort based upon acts which occurred outside the state, jurisdiction will be refused. Where the controversy is of a commercial or contractual nature, jurisdiction will ordinarily be retained where public policy will not be violated. Rederiet Ocean Aktieselskab v W. A. Kirk & Co. (1944, Sup) 51 N.Y.S.2d 565

State courts can take jurisdiction of actions between two foreign corporations, wherever defendant was doing business within the state, but they are not required to assume jurisdiction merely because the defendant was engaged in business in the state if the cause of action did not arise therein. Heydemann v Westinghouse Electric Mfg. Co. (1936, CA2 NY) 80 F.2d 837

26. – – As burden on commerce

Subd 4 of this section is unconstitutional when construed to subject an interstate carrier to necessity of defending suits, other than tort actions, in courts of this State, as imposing an unreasonable burden upon carrier, in violation of U.S. Const., Art. I, § 8, subd 3. N. V. Brood en Beschuitfabriek V/H John Simons v Aluminum Co. of America (1931) 231 A.D. 693, 248 N.Y.S. 460

Contention that § 225, subd 4, is invalid under the commerce clause of the Constitution (U.S. Const. Art. I, § 8) is rejected. Williamson v Palmer (1943) 181 Misc 610, 43 N.Y.S.2d 532

Construction of this section to permit suit by a non-resident against a foreign corporation doing business in this state on a cause of action which arises in another state and is entirely unconnected with business done in this state would impose unreasonable burdens on interstate commerce and violate the commerce clause, and thus courts of this state have no jurisdiction. Panstwowe Zaklady Graviozne v Automobile Ins. Co. (1928, DC NY) 36 F.2d 504

27. – Tort actions

Where securities of a non-resident were deposited in New York with a bank organized under the laws of another country and the bank, in purported compliance with an invalid decree of that country, sent them to that country where they were confiscated, the bank was guilty of conversion in New York so that an action could be maintained here under this section permitting actions between non-residents where the cause of action arose here. Plesch v Banque Nationale De La Republique D'Haiti (1948) 273 A.D. 224, 77 N.Y.S.2d 43, affd 298 N.Y. 573, 81 N.E.2d 106

In an action for personal injuries by non-resident plaintiffs against non-resident trustees of a foreign corporation authorized to do business in this state the court may accept or decline jurisdiction as a matter of discretion. Williamson v Palmer (1943) 181 Misc 610, 43 N.Y.S.2d 532

28. – – Tort committed outside state

Courts of this state in their discretion will exercise jurisdiction in an action by a resident of the state of Connecticut against an Illinois corporation doing business in this state to recover for negligence of defendant growing out of an accident which occurred in state of Oklahoma; where no fraud or collusion is alleged and nothing is shown to indicate an imposition on the courts of this state. Richter v Chicago R. I. & P. R. Co. (1924) 123 Misc 234, 205 N.Y.S. 128

The court in the exercise of its discretion (§ 22, subd 4) refuses to entertain actions brought by residents of Pennsylvania to recover damage for personal injuries sustained as passengers in a train involved in a collision in Ohio, although defendant, a Pennsylvania corporation, is doing business in New York. Yesuvida v Pennsylvania R. Co. (1951) 200 Misc 815, 111 N.Y.S.2d 417

This section does not require the state court to accept jurisdiction in a tort action between non-residents where the tort occurred in some other state; the court may exercise its discretion. Gilbert v Gulf Oil Corp. (1945, DC NY) 62 F. Supp. 291, revd on other grounds (CA2 NY) 153 F.2d 883, 170 ALR 319, which is revd on other grounds 330 US 501, 91 L Ed 1055, 67 S Ct 839

29. – – Action under federal statute

The courts of this state exercise their discretion in all other cases where a tort action is brought by one non-resident against another and, therefore, may refuse, in their discretion, to entertain jurisdiction over a cause of action arising out of a tort committed in a sister state, where both plaintiff and defendant are non-residents, even though the action be brought under Federal Employers' Liability Act. A litigant who brings his action under that act stands before the court in the same attitude as a litigant who brings an action under a statute of a sister state; he may not be cast out because he is suing under an act of Congress and he may not enforce his rights merely because he is suing under such an act. Murnan v Wabash R. Co. (1927) 246 N.Y. 244, 158 N.E. 508, 54 ALR 1522

In an action by a non-resident seaman to recover under the Jones Act for injuries sustained on the defendant's vessel, where the defendant has an office in New York and there is no proof that it is not doing business in this state, the case comes within the purview of this section and the court may accept or decline jurisdiction as a matter of discretion. Seeley v Waterman S. S. Corp. (1947, Sup) 73 N.Y.S.2d 80, revd on other grounds 274 A.D. 934, 83 N.Y.S.2d 502

The Federal district court in N.Y. refused to exercise jurisdiction of an action under the Jones Act against a foreign corporation doing business in N.Y. by a non-resident of N.Y. for a tort committed on the high seas. Summerall v United Fruit Co. (1935, DC NY) 11 F. Supp. 963, affd (CA2 NY) 80 F.2d 1020, cert den 298 US 658, 80 L Ed 1384, 56 S Ct 680

30. – Commercial or contractual actions

New York courts should not decline jurisdiction of an action by an Ohio corporation to compel a New York stockholder to submit its stock certificates for endorsement in accord with charter and by-law amendments allegedly made under Ohio law, where defendant could not be served in Ohio but argued that validity of amendments could be decided only in Ohio. Royal China, Inc. v Regal China Corp. (1952) 304 N.Y. 309, 107 N.E.2d 461, revg 279 A.D. 515, 110 N.Y.S.2d 718, and op withdrawn 280 A.D. 921, 116 N.Y.S.2d 926

A contract made in New York is a proper subject of an action under subd 1 of this section. N. V. Tonerde Maatschappij Voor Montaan-Chemie v Great Lakes Coal & Coke Co. (1935) 243 A.D. 640, 276 N.Y.S. 895

A foreign corporation or its assignee may sue a foreign interstate carrier doing business within the state of N.Y. for failure to deliver in N.Y. shipment from another state. Jacobson v Baltimore & O. R. Co. (1936) 161 Misc 268, 291 N.Y.S. 628

A foreign corporation may sue another foreign corporation in this state on a contract executed here. Distillers Factors Corp. v Country Distillers Products, Inc. (1947) 189 Misc 497, 71 N.Y.S.2d 654

Court had no jurisdiction of action by a non-resident against a foreign corporation not doing business in the state for breach of employment contract where the contract was not made in New York and none of its terms or conditions were to be performed in New York. Fidan v Austral American Trading Corp. (1957) 8 Misc. 2d 598, 168 N.Y.S.2d 27

In an action by a foreign corporation, most of whose stockholders reside in New York, against a Canadian bank concerning a contract made in, and to be performed in, Canada, the New York court need not decline to take jurisdiction under the doctrine of forum non conveniens where retention of jurisdiction will work no injury and the balance is not so strongly in favor of defendant's contention as to warrant exercise of discretion in its favor. Plasticos Industriales Extrusos, A. A. v Bank of Nova Scotia (1963) 38 Misc. 2d 9, 237 N.Y.S.2d 802, affd 19 A.D.2d 592, 240 N.Y.S.2d 934

An action for breach of contract brought by a non-resident plaintiff against a foreign corporation admittedly doing business in this state was within the purview of this section and where the details of the contract were negotiated in New York and the defendant did not show that the convenience of the witnesses would be served by granting the motion, a motion to dismiss the complaint as a matter of discretion was denied. Mackenzie v Climax Industries, Inc. (1947, Sup) 73 N.Y.S.2d 504

In a contract action under this section, the courts of this state may not in their discretion refuse to entertain jurisdiction, as they may in tort actions. Panstwowe Zaklady Graviozne v Automobile Ins. Co. (1928, DC NY) 36 F.2d 504

31. – When cause of action arises in state

A cause of action arises against a foreign corporation in New York where the foreign corporation does, in New York, an act which it should not have done and which violates the implied agreement between the parties. Gonzalez v Industrial Bank (of Cuba) (1962) 12 N.Y.2d 33, 234 N.Y.S.2d 210, 186 N.E.2d 410, reh den 12 N.Y.2d 835, 236 N.Y.S.2d 611, 187 N.E.2d 465

32. – – Contract executed in state

A Cuban refugee's cause of action against a Cuban bank for interfering with payment of a draft drawn by the Cuban bank on a New York bank, payable to the refugee plaintiff, by directing the New York bank not to pay the draft, for which plaintiff had paid the Cuban bank in full, was based upon a cause of action arising in New York, warranting an action against the foreign bank here under subd 3 of this section. Gonzalez v Industrial Bank (of Cuba) (1962) 12 N.Y.2d 33, 234 N.Y.S.2d 210, 186 N.E.2d 410, reh den 12 N.Y.2d 835, 236 N.Y.S.2d 611, 187 N.E.2d 465

The question of whether a particular contract was made within the State of New York, so as to subject the foreign corporation which is a party to the contract to an action for damages in New York for breach of it, is not determinable under modern Conflict of Laws rules relating to "grouping of contracts." Fremay, Inc. v Modern Plastic Machinery Corp. (1961) 15 A.D.2d 235, 222 N.Y.S.2d 694

With respect to right to institute an action in a New York court against a foreign corporation, the provision that such an action may be brought to recover damages for breach of a contract "made within the state," relates to the time and place when the last act necessary for formulation of the contract is done, and where that last act is signing of the contract by the defendant corporation in another state, the contract is not one made within the State of New York. Fremay, Inc. v Modern Plastic Machinery Corp. (1961) 15 A.D.2d 235, 222 N.Y.S.2d 694

In regard to the defendant's contention that a resolution promulgated in Washington was an acceptance of plaintiff's bid and the plaintiff's contention that there was no contract until the documents were signed in New York, the court found that the contract was made in New York. Merritt-Chapman & Scott Corp. v Public Utility Dist. (1965, DC NY) 237 F. Supp. 985

33. – – Contract provision governing place of execution

A written contract between plaintiff, non-resident, and defendant, a foreign corporation, executed in the state of New York, contained the following provision: "First. It is agreed that while for convenience this agreement is signed by the parties in New York City, United States of America, it should be considered and held to be as one duly made and executed in London, England." Under this section the supreme court of the state of New York has jurisdiction of an action and a levy under a warrant of attachment of defendant's interest in certain options on oil properties in foreign country will be upheld. Stagg v British Controlled Oilfields, Ltd. (1921) 117 Misc 474, 192 N.Y.S. 596

Under this section, a foreign corporation authorized to do business in New York was entitled to sue another foreign corporation in a New York court for breach of contract which was not only clearly executed in New York but which expressly provided that it was to be deemed as made in that state and to be interpreted in accordance with New York law. National Equipment Rental, Ltd. v Graphic Art Designers, Inc. (1962) 36 Misc. 2d 442, 234 N.Y.S.2d 61

34. – Venue

In an action to recover transportation charges for goods carried from Washington D.C. to Brooklyn, the venue of the action may be in New York although the contract was made in Washington D.C. and although the foreign corporation defendant had not filed or registered with the Secretary of State. Brooks Transp. Co. v Hillcrea Export & Import Corp. (1951, Sup) 106 N.Y.S.2d 868

35. – Plaintiff; foreign corporation or nonresident

A foreign corporation does not have a right, under this section, to maintain action against another foreign corporation on a contract not made here, where it is not doing business in this state. Gano-Moore Coal Mining Co. v W. E. Deegans Coal Co. (1929) 214 A.D. 634, 213 N.Y.S. 54

In an action between a resident of Poland and a Russian corporation, neither authorized to do business or doing business in this state, to recover damages for breach of a contract to deposit rubles in Russia, relating to property situated in Russia at the time of making the contract which was breached in Russia, the plaintiff is not within the provisions of sections 224 and 225 and the court cannot assume jurisdiction of the action. Rzeszotarski v Co-operative Ass'n Kasa Polska (1931) 139 Misc 400, 247 N.Y.S. 471

A Czechoslovakian citizen in this state under a temporary visa may, under §§ 224 and 225, maintain an action against an Australian banking corporation. Greiner v Bank of Adelaide (1941) 176 Misc 315, 26 N.Y.S.2d 515

An action by a non-resident against a foreign corporation for damage to merchandise which passed through this State will be entertained, where a defendant is doing business in this State. The action places no undue burden on interstate commerce. The assignment of the action by the non-resident to a resident is disregarded and the action treated as one by a non-resident. Cincis v Seaboard A. L. Ry. (1952) 201 Misc 887, 113 N.Y.S.2d 29

Under subd 4 of this section, a New York court has jurisdiction of the subject matter of an action brought by a foreign corporation, almost all of whose stockholders are here, where there is likewise nothing to indicate that defendant is a foreign corporation or nonresident. Plasticos Industriales Extrusos, A. A. v Bank of Nova Scotia (1963) 38 Misc. 2d 9, 237 N.Y.S.2d 802, affd 19 A.D.2d 592, 240 N.Y.S.2d 934

A resident of this state as assignee of a cause of action may maintain the action in the courts of this state even though the assignment was made for the sole purpose of bringing an action in the courts of New York by an assignor who under this section could not itself bring the action in our courts. Segal Lock & Hardware Co. v Markey (1953, Sup) 124 N.Y.S.2d 181

36. – Defendant; foreign corporation doing business in state

The provision of this section that a foreign corporation or nonresident may maintain an action against another foreign corporation "where a foreign corporation is doing business within this state," seems to be a limitation upon power of a foreign corporation to maintain an action here as matter of right. Emerson Quiet Kool Corp. v Eskind (1957) 32 Misc. 2d 1037, 1039, 228 N.Y.S.2d 839

The municipal court of New York did not have jurisdiction over an action brought by a citizen of Connecticut, as assignee of a foreign corporation against another foreign corporation to recover for cargo from Winnipeg to London, where defendant's activities in state of New York were confined to international commerce. Ball v Canadian Pacific S. S., Ltd. (1937, Mun Ct) 6 N.Y.S.2d 877, affd without op 276 N.Y. 650, 12 N.E.2d 804

Under this section the court may retain jurisdiction where the defendant is found to be doing business here. McCaskell Filters, Inc. v Goslin-Birmingham Mfg. Co. (1948, Sup) 81 N.Y.S.2d 309, affd without op 274 A.D. 761, 79 N.Y.S.2d 925

37. – – Foreign corporation not doing business

An action against a foreign corporation which did no business in the state except to enter into, in New York, the particular contract upon which suit was based, could not be subjected to New York court jurisdiction by personal service on one of its directors in New York in 1960 and prior to effective date of § 302 of the new CPLR. Simonson v International Bank (1964) 14 N.Y.2d 281, 251 N.Y.S.2d 433, 200 N.E.2d 427

A foreign corporation is not subject to suit in New York State on the ground that it is doing business within the state merely because the contract upon which the suit is brought has significant contacts within New York State, making the law of that state applicable in determining its construction and validity under modern principles of the law of Conflicts of Laws. Fremay, Inc. v Modern Plastic Machinery Corp. (1961) 15 A.D.2d 235, 222 N.Y.S.2d 694

This section provides the circumstances in which an action may be maintained against a foreign corporation by another foreign corporation or by a nonresident, but, in order to acquire jurisdiction over the foreign corporation defendant, it must further appear that it was

doing business in New York State. Simonson v International Bank (1962) 16 A.D.2d 55, 225 N.Y.S.2d 392, affd 14 N.Y.2d 281, 251 N.Y.S.2d 433, 200 N.E.2d 427

In an action by a Maryland corporation against a Swedish steamship corporation for breach of a contract made in Sweden for transportation of goods from that country to Baltimore, the defendant may not question the jurisdiction of the city court of New York, because it does no business here, where it answered on the merits and did not move to dismiss the complaint. Baltimore Pub. Co. v Swedish-American Mexico Line, Ltd. (1932) 143 Misc 229, 256 N.Y.S. 284

38. – – Effect to be given defendant's consent to jurisdiction

Sections 224 and 225 concern jurisdiction over the subject-matter, and, in actions between foreign parties plaintiff and a foreign corporation defendant, jurisdiction is either not conferred or expressly denied to our courts, unless the foreign corporation is doing business in this state, and if that fact be absent, jurisdiction cannot be conferred even by consent of the defendant. Davis v Julius Kessler & Co. (1922) 118 Misc 292, 194 N.Y.S. 9, affd 202 A.D. 798, 194 N.Y.S. 927

Consent given by a nonresident partnership, not doing business in New York, to exercise of jurisdiction over it by a New York court because of its action in appointing an agent for service of process under the terms of a distributor franchise agreement, was ineffectual under the language of this section. Emerson Quiet Kool Corp. v Eskind (1957) 32 Misc. 2d 1037, 1039, 228 N.Y.S.2d 839

39. – – Federal corporation

A motion to dismiss the complaint in an action by a nonresident brought under the Merchant Marine Act of 1920 to recover damages for injuries suffered in Manila, which motion is made on the ground that the court has no jurisdiction of the defendant, a federal corporation having an office in this state, must be denied, for under this section the defendant is a domestic corporation for the purposes of the action, and since it had an office within this state, the court acquired jurisdiction of it. Jacobsen v United States Shipping Board Emergency Fleet Corp. (1926) 128 Misc 138, 217 N.Y.S. 856

40. – What constitutes doing business

A foreign corporation is not doing business in New York so as to be suable under subd 4 of this section in New York unless it falls within the classic "presence" test set forth in leading cases. Fremay, Inc. v Modern Plastic Machinery Corp. (1961) 15 A.D.2d 235, 222 N.Y.S.2d 694

Even a complex of incidents and facts will not necessarily suffice to show that a foreign corporation is doing business in New York, so as to be subject to suit here, and the fact that certain transactions have occurred in New York will not suffice to establish that the corporation is subject to suit under this section. Fremay, Inc. v Modern Plastic Machinery Corp. (1961) 15 A.D.2d 235, 222 N.Y.S.2d 694

In determining whether a foreign corporation is doing business in New York so as to be subject to suit here, the fact that some of its officers reside here is of no particular moment, or that they use their own offices, largely devoted to other businesses, for incidental transactions affecting the particular corporation, nor is existence of a corporate bank account in New York of itself sufficient, or that it makes use of a local New York attorney or solicits buyers here to whom goods will be shipped from outside the state on contracts made elsewhere. Fremay, Inc. v Modern Plastic Machinery Corp. (1961) 15 A.D.2d 235, 222 N.Y.S.2d 694

The fact that the president of a corporation lived within this state and wrote letters to bring about settlement of business of the corporation did not bring the defendant within this state and engage in "doing business" here, within the meaning of this section, so as to subject it to valid service of process which would give the courts of this state jurisdiction. Western Hair Goods Co. v B. R. Haberkorn Co. (1928) 131 Misc 930, 229 N.Y.S. 273

A Pennsylvania corporation having its office and principal place of business in that state and having no bank account, office, resident manager or representative within this state, and employing no salesmen or conducting no meetings of directors or stockholders in this state, is not doing business in this state within the meaning of §§ 224 and 225, notwithstanding it purchased merchandise within the state and its president, secretary and treasurer are New York residents. Scheinman v Bonwit Teller & Co. (1928) 132 Misc 311, 229 N.Y.S. 783

41. – – Maintenance of office and telephone facilities

Where a corporation organized under the laws of the State of Connecticut and owning and operating a factory in that state has no office or place of business in New York and does not now nor has it ever carried on business within this state, nor has it ever taken out a certificate to do business, nor applied for such certificate, and has no bank account, no money or property of any kind within the state, it is not doing business within the meaning of this section even though its selling agent maintains an office in city of New York and has placed respondent's name on door and listed it in telephone directory. Hamlin v G. E. Barrett & Co. (1927) 246 N.Y. 554, 159 N.E. 648

A national bank with its principal place of business in California was not doing business in this state, within the meaning of this section in the absence of proof showing that it performed any banking function within this state; the fact that it maintained offices in the city of New York for a vice-president, whose duty was to solicit business and to gather information, does not in itself establish that it was doing business in New York. Raiola v Los Angeles First Nat. Trust & Sav. Bank, (1929) 133 Misc 630, 233 N.Y.S. 301

A foreign corporation is doing business in this state to an extent sufficient to authorize our courts to take jurisdiction of actions instituted against it, where it appears that said corporation is maintaining desk room and telephone facilities in an office in this state, and in accepting orders and executing contracts therein. Madison Distributing Co. v Phoenix Piece Dye Works (1930) 135 Misc 543, 239 N.Y.S. 176

42. – – Solicitation of business

Although mere solicitation of business within this state may not be sufficient, such solicitation plus some additional activity is sufficient to make a foreign corporation amenable to our process. Hence, a foreign railroad corporation, with freight solicitation offices in this state, was doing business here where its New York City office was listed in the telephone directory as "executive office" and in the "Official Guide of Railroads" as "general offices". The New York office also accepted tenders for certain corporation bond issues and one of the four annual directors' meetings was held in this state. Elish v St. Louis S. R. Co. (1953) 305 N.Y. 267, 112 N.E.2d 842, reh den 305 N.Y. 824, 113 N.E.2d 561

43. – – Inference from license to do business

In an action against a foreign corporation to recover damages for breach of a London contract for sale and delivery of steel rails in Baltimore payable in New York on presentation of shipping documents in which the defendant contends that it is not subject to the jurisdiction of the court, the fact that the defendant was authorized to do business in this state as a foreign corporation justifies an inference that it was doing business here within the meaning of subd 4 of this section. L. B. Foster Co. v Koppel Industrial Car & Equipment Co. (1926) 127 Misc 51, 215 N.Y.S. 214

An action against a foreign corporation may be maintained by a nonresident where the foreign corporation is doing business within the state and where a foreign corporation has been licensed to do business within the state the court may infer that it was doing such business within the meaning of this section. Hamilton v Berwind-White Coal Mining Co. (1945, Sup) 60 N.Y.S.2d 561

44. – – Effect of withdrawal from state

A complaint by a resident of California against a Delaware corporation, for personal injuries arising from the plaintiff's use of the defendant's hair dye preparation, will be dismissed where it appears that the plaintiff purchased the preparation in California when defendant was authorized to do business in this state, but that this action was not commenced until a year after the defendant withdrew from this state and filed with the secretary of state a certificate surrendering its authority to do business here, pursuant to this section, and where it further appears that seven days after commencement of this action similar action was brought by the plaintiff against the defendant in the state of Delaware. Simons v Inecto, Inc. (1934) 242 A.D. 275, 275 N.Y.S. 501

Subd 4 of this section appears to contemplate that an action by a non-resident against a foreign corporation may be maintained as a matter of right only while the foreign corporation is doing business in this state, and not thereafter. Simons v Inecto, Inc. (1934) 242 A.D. 275, 275 N.Y.S. 501

Where a foreign corporation doing business in this state withdraws therefrom its former managing agent or its entire staff of representatives, the corporation, for the purpose of sustaining jurisdiction of the state courts over it in regard to controversies affecting the corporation activities in this state, initiated prior to the period of withdrawal, is still doing business in this state, and where

on the day service of summons in an action was made on an officer of the corporation withdrawal of the defendant from doing business in this state was not complete, service is valid and a motion to set aside same will be denied. Smith v Compania Litografica De La Habana (1923) 121 Misc 368, 201 N.Y.S. 65

45. – Service of process

A foreign corporation must be doing some substantial part of its main business in this state to justify service of process upon its representative. Holzer v Dodge Bros. (1922) 233 N.Y. 216, 135 N.E. 268

Service of process upon an Illinois corporation was attempted by serving an officer of a Delaware corporation doing business in this State and owned by the Illinois corporation. A new hearing was directed on the question whether the acts of the Delaware corporation constituted doing business by the Illinois corporation. Donner v Weinberger's Hair Shops Inc. (1952) 280 A.D. 67, 111 N.Y.S.2d 310

46. – – On foreign insurance corporation

Insurance Law § 59-a, providing for service of process on foreign insurance companies, when interpreted in conformity with this section subjects the foreign company to jurisdiction of this state for performing even a single enumerated act. Zacharakis v Bunker Hill Mut. Ins. Co. (1953) 281 A.D. 487, 120 N.Y.S.2d 418, app gr 281 A.D. 1019, 121 N.Y.S.2d 271

A foreign corporation, doing business in this state, may maintain an action in the courts of this state against another foreign corporation, under subd 4 of this section. Accordingly, the N.Y. supreme court has jurisdiction of an action brought by a Delaware corporation for fire loss suffered in Pennsylvania, covering property located in that state, against a foreign insurance corporation doing business in this state, and service of summons on the insurance corporation, made upon the superintendent of insurance, in accordance with Insur. Law, § 30 is valid and will not be set aside. Bisbee Linseed Co. v Fireman's Fund Ins. Co. (1927) 128 Misc 851, 220 N.Y.S. 309

47. – Attachment of assets

A plaintiff, a non-resident, in an action for rent against a foreign corporation, was entitled to an attachment on a verified complaint and accompanying affidavit, for the court granting it had jurisdiction of the subject-matter under this section, where it appears that a certificate of the secretary of state, annexed to the affidavit recited that the defendant had authority to do business in this state on November 3, 1925, since said court might properly infer that a foreign corporation which obtained a certificate entitling it to do business in this state at that time, paying appropriate fees and taxes involved in that act, was doing business within the state seven months later when the attachment was granted. Bloom v Wrought Iron Novelty Corp. (1926) 128 Misc 460, 219 N.Y.S. 92

48. – Jurisdiction of federal court

Even though it does sufficient business within the state so that it should file a consent to be sued pursuant to § 210 a foreign corporation which does not file such a consent is not a resident within the meaning of the federal statute providing that where federal jurisdiction is based on diversity of citizenship suit may be brought only in the district of the residence of the plaintiff or defendant. Moss v Atlantic C. L. R. Co. (1945, CA2 NY) 149 F.2d 701

United States District Court has jurisdiction of an action by residents of California against a defendant corporation organized and existing under the laws of Pennsylvania having tracks within New York, where the cause of action arose in Washington, D. C., and where the New York Supreme Court had jurisdiction. Cohn v Pennsylvania R. Co. (1942, DC NY) 45 F. Supp. 243

§ 1316.   Record of members

(a) Any resident of this state who shall have been a member of record, for at least six months immediately preceding his demand, of a foreign corporation conducting activities in this state, or any resident of this state authorized in writing by at least five percent of the members, entitled to vote, of the foreign corporation, upon at least five days' written demand may require such foreign corporation to produce a record of its members setting forth the names and addresses of all members, the number and class of capital certificates held by each and the dates when they respectively became the owners of record thereof, and shall have the right to examine in person or by agent or attorney at the office of the foreign corporation in this state or at the office of its transfer agent or registrar in this state or at such other place in any county in this state in which the foreign corporation is conducting activities as may be designated by the foreign corporation during the usual business hours, a record of members or an exact copy of the record of members certified as correct by the corporate officer or agent responsible for keeping or producing such record and to make extracts therefrom. In the case of a foreign corporation having shares, a record of shareholders shall for the purpose of this section be regarded as a record of members, and holders of voting trust certificates representing such shares shall for the purpose of this section be regarded as members.

(b) An examination authorized by paragraph (a) may be denied to such member or other person upon his refusal to furnish to the foreign corporation or its transfer agent or registrar an affidavit that such inspection is not desired for a purpose which is in the interests of a business or object other than the activities of the foreign corporation and that such member or other person has not within five years sold or offered for sale any list or record of members of any corporation of any kind, whether or not formed under the laws of this state, or aided or abetted any person in procuring any such list or record of members for any such purpose.

(c) Upon refusal by the foreign corporation or by an officer or agent of the foreign corporation to produce for examination or to permit an examination of the record of members as herein provided, the person making the demand for production and examination may apply to the supreme court in the judicial district where the office of the foreign corporation within this state is located, upon such notice as the court may direct, for an order directing the foreign corporation, its officer or agent, to show cause why an order should not be granted directing such production and permitting such examination by the applicant. Upon the return day of the order to show cause, the court shall hear the parties summarily, by affidavit or otherwise, and if it appears that the applicant is qualified and entitled to such examination, the court shall grant an order compelling such production for examination and awarding such further relief as to the court may seem just and proper.

(d) Nothing herein contained shall impair the power of courts to compel the production for examination of the books of a foreign corporation. The record of members specified in paragraph (a) shall be prima facie evidence of the facts therein stated in favor of the plaintiff in any action or special proceeding against such foreign corporation or any of its officers, directors or members.

History: Add, L 1969, ch 1066, § 1, eff Sept 1, 1970; amd, L 1970, ch 847, § 78, eff Sept 1, 1970, L 2013, ch 549, § 109, eff July 1, 2014.

§ 1317.　Voting trust records

(a) A voting trustee, appointed under a voting trust agreement to vote the shares of a foreign corporation conducting activities in this state, who either has an office in this state or has designated a transfer agent within this state, shall produce for examination and permit to be examined in this state, at the office of the foreign corporation or at his office or at the office of such transfer agent, a record of voting trust certificate holders setting forth their names, alphabetically arranged, and addresses, the number and class of shares represented by the certificates held by them respectively and the dates when they respectively became the owners thereof, upon the written demand of any resident of this state who shall have been a voting trust certificate holder or a shareholder of the foreign corporation for at least six months immediately preceding his demand, or of any resident of this state holding, or thereunto authorized in writing by the holders of, at least five percent of any class of the outstanding shares of such foreign corporation, either directly or as holders of voting trust certificates for such shares, subject to the same terms and conditions set forth with respect to the right of examination of the record of members of the foreign corporation in section 1316 (Record of members).

(b) The voting trustee shall deposit an exact copy of the voting trust agreement with the foreign corporation at its office in this state or at the office of the transfer agent in this state.

(c) The copy of the voting trust agreement shall be subject to the same right of examination by voting trust certificate holders and by shareholders of the foreign corporation as is the record of members of a corporation under section 621 (Books and records; right of inspection, prima facie evidence).

(d) Upon refusal by a voting trustee or his transfer agent to produce for examination or to permit an examination of the record of voting trust certificate holders or of such copy of the voting trust agreement as herein provided, the person making the demand may apply to the supreme court, upon such notice as the court may direct, for an order directing the voting trustee or his transfer agent to show cause why an order should not be granted directing such production and permitting such examination. Upon the return day of the order to show cause, the court shall hear the parties summarily, by affidavit or otherwise, and if it appears that the applicant is entitled to such examination, the court shall grant an order compelling such production for examination and awarding such further relief as to the court may seem just and proper.

(e) Where the voting trust agreement shall vest in the voting trustee the right to vote the shares of a foreign corporation which has an office in this state for conducting activities and either the principal activity of which is conducted within this state or the greater part of its property is located within this state, the voting trust agreement is an express trust created under the laws of this state and the supreme court upon the petition of a voting trust certificate holder may exercise such power over the trustee named therein as is granted to the court by section 7-2.6 of the estates, powers and trusts law.

History: Add, L 1969, ch 1066, § 1, eff Sept 1, 1970.

§ 1318.   Liabilities of directors and officers of foreign corporations

(a) Except as otherwise provided in this chapter, the directors and officers of a foreign corporation conducting activities in this state are subject, to the same extent as directors and officers of a domestic corporation, to the provisions of:

(1) Section 719 (Liability of directors in certain cases) except subparagraph (a)(4) thereof, and

(2) Section 720 (Action against directors and officers for misconduct).

(b) Any liability imposed by paragraph (a) may be enforced in, and such relief granted by, the courts in this state, in the same manner as in the case of a domestic corporation.

History: Add, L 1969, ch 1066, § 1, eff Sept 1, 1970.

Par (a), subpar (1), amd, L 1970, ch 847, § 79, eff Sept 1, 1970.

§ 1319.   Liability of foreign corporations for failure to disclose required information

A foreign corporation conducting activities in this state shall, in the same manner as a domestic corporation, disclose to its members of record who are residents of this state the information required under Article 5 and shall be liable as provided in section 521 (Liability for failure to disclose required information) for failure to comply in good faith with these requirements.

History: Add, L 1969, ch 1066, § 1, eff Sept 1, 1970.

§ 1320.   Applicability of other provisions

(a) In addition to articles 1 (Short title; definitions; application; certificates; miscellaneous) and 3 (Corporate name and service of process) and the other sections of article 13, the following provisions, to the extent provided therein, shall apply to a foreign corporation conducting activities in this state, its directors, officers and members:

(1) Section 623 (Members' derivative action brought in the right of the corporation to procure a judgment in its favor).

(2) Sections 721 (Exclusivity of statutory provisions for idemnification of directors and officers) through 727 (Insurance for idemnification of directors and officers), inclusive.

(3) Section 906 (Merger or consolidation of domestic and foreign corporations).

History: Add, L 1969, ch 1066, § 1, eff Sept 1, 1970.

Par (a), subpar (2), amd, L 1970, ch 847, § 80, eff Sept 1, 1970.

§ 1321.   Exemption from certain provisions

(a) Notwithstanding any other provision of this chapter, a foreign corporation conducting activities in this state which is authorized under this article, its directors, officers and members, shall be exempt from the provisions of paragraph (e) of section 1317 (Voting trust records), subparagraph (1) of paragraph (a) of section 1318 (Liabilities of directors and officers of foreign corporations), and subparagraph (2) of paragraph (a) of section 1320 (Applicability of other provisions) of this article if such provision would otherwise apply:

(1) The corporation is a non-charitable corporation under this chapter; its principal activities are conducted outside this state; the greater part of its property is located outside this state; and less than one third of its members are residents of this state; or

(2) The corporation is a charitable corporation under this chapter; its principal activities are conducted outside this state; the greater part of its property is located outside this state; and less than ten per cent of its annual revenues is derived from solicitation of funds within this state.

History: Add, L 1969, ch 1066, § 1, eff Sept 1, 1970; amd, L 1970, ch 847, § 81, eff Sept 1, 1970, L 2013, ch 549, § 110, eff July 1, 2014.

ARTICLE 14
SPECIAL NOT-FOR-PROFIT CORPORATIONS

History: Add, L 1969, ch 1066, § 1, eff Sept 1, 1970.

§ 1401.   Private and family cemetery corporations

(a) Private cemetery corporation. Seven or more persons may become a private cemetery corporation by setting off for a private cemetery enclosed real property, to the extent of not more than three acres, and by electing at a meeting of the owners of the property so set off, at which not less than seven shall be present, three of their number to be directors, to hold office for five years. The chairman and secretary of such meeting shall make, sign and acknowledge, and file in the office of the clerk of the county in which such real property is situated, a certificate containing the name of the corporation, a description of the lands so purchased or set apart, and the names of the directors. No such cemetery shall be located within one hundred rods of any dwelling-house without the written consent of the owner thereof. Additional lands not exceeding three acres may be acquired by a private cemetery corporation; but no additional lands so purchased or otherwise acquired shall be used for the purpose of burial within three hundred feet of any dwelling without the written consent of the owner thereof.

(b) Removal of remains from private cemeteries to other cemeteries. The supervisor of any town containing a private cemetery may remove any body interred in such cemetery to any other cemetery within the town, if the owners of such cemeteries and the next of kin of the deceased consent to such removal. The owners of a private cemetery may remove the bodies interred therein to any other cemetery within such town, or to any cemetery designated by the next of kin of the deceased. Notice of such removal shall be given within twenty days before such removal personally or by certified mail to the next of kin of the deceased if known and to the clerk and historian of the county in which such real property is situated and notice shall be given to the New York state department of state, division of cemeteries. If any of the deceased are known to be veterans, the owners shall also notify the division of veterans' affairs. In the absence of the next of kin, the county clerk, county historian or the division of veterans' affairs may act as a guardian to ensure proper reburial.

(c) Family cemetery corporations. Any person, by deed or devise, may dedicate land to be used exclusively for a family cemetery. The executors, administrators or trustees of a deceased person, with the written authority of all of his surviving heirs, next of kin, devisees and legatees, executed in person or by an attorney, or if infants, by legal guardian, may dedicate lands of such deceased person exclusively for a family cemetery, or may purchase with the funds of the estate, suitable lands therefor. The land so dedicated shall not exceed three acres, not be located within one hundred rods of a dwelling-house, without the consent of the owner, unless such land, at the time of dedication, is in actual use for burial or cemetery purposes within the limits of a city. The instrument dedicating such land shall describe the same, may appoint directors to manage such cemetery, prescribe, or provide for making rules, directions or by-laws for such management, direct the manner of choosing successors to the directors, specify their qualifications, and grant to them and their successors money or personal property as a fund for maintaining, improving and embellishing the cemetery, in accordance with the deed or will, or the written authority of the heirs, next of kin, devisees and legatees. The instrument dedicating land for a family cemetery, together with the authority, if any, of the heirs, next of kin, devisees and legatees of the deceased person, shall be filed in the office of the county clerk of each county in which the cemetery is to be situated. The directors before entering on their duties, shall file in the office of the county clerk of each such county, a written acceptance of their appointment; and thereupon they and their successors shall constitute a corporation under the name designated in such instrument. A fund created by will for the purpose of maintaining, improving and embellishing such a cemetery shall not exceed ten per centum of the net value of the estate of the testator. Such corporation before receiving any property, money or funds for improving, maintaining and embellishing the cemetery, shall execute to the surrogate of the county in which such real property is situated, a bond with sureties, or the bond of a surety company, approved by him, in a penalty of twice the principal sum of the fund placed in charge of the corporation, conditioned for the faithful preservation and application thereof according to the rules, directions or by-laws prescribed in the instrument under which the appointment of such directors was made, and renew such bond or execute a new bond whenever required so to do by such surrogate. At least once in each year and oftener if required by the surrogate the corporation shall file with him a verified account of its receipts and expenditures on account of the funds in its hands, or under its control, together with vouchers for all disbursements. Any person may bequeath or transfer to, and any such corporation may take, money or personal property by will, deed or other transfer, upon trust, to hold and apply to dispose of the same for the purpose of maintaining, improving and embellishing any lot, plot or portion of such cemetery, either according to the discretion of the directors, or for such time and upon such terms and conditions, if any, as to the application, investment and reinvestment of the principal and income and otherwise as shall be stated in the instrument creating the trust as agreed upon, but no such trust fund created by will shall exceed ten per centum of the net value of the estate of the testator. The corporation shall give security and account for such money or personal property as hereinbefore provided.

If security is furnished by a surety company bond, the reasonable expense thereof shall be a charge against the funds of the corporation.

(d) Type of corporation. A family or private cemetery corporation is a charitable corporation under this chapter.

(e) Private and family cemetery corporations; prohibitions.

(1) No private or family cemetery corporation shall, directly or indirectly:

(i) sell, or have, enter into or perform a lease of any of its real property to a funeral entity, or use any of its property for location of a funeral entity;

(ii) commingle its funds with a funeral entity;

(iii) direct or carry on its business or affairs with a funeral entity;

(iv) authorize control of its business or affairs by a funeral entity;

(v) engage in any sale or cross-marketing of goods or services with a funeral entity;

(vi) have, enter into or perform a management or service contract for cemetery operations with a funeral entity; or

(vii) have, enter into or perform a management contract with any entity, other than a not-for-profit cemetery corporation.

(2) Only the provisions of subparagraphs (i) and (ii) of subdivision one of this paragraph shall apply to cemetery corporations with thirty acres or less of real property dedicated to cemetery purposes, and only to the extent the sale or lease is of real property dedicated to cemetery purposes, and such cemeteries shall not engage in the sale of funeral home goods or services, except if such goods and services are otherwise permitted to be sold by cemeteries.

(3) For the purposes of this paragraph, "funeral entity" means a person, partnership, corporation, limited liability company or other form of business organization providing funeral home services, or owning, controlling, conducting or affiliated with a funeral home, any subsidiary thereof or an officer, director or stockholder having a ten per centum or greater proprietary, beneficial, equitable or credit interest in a funeral home.

History: Add, L 1977, ch 871, § 1, eff Aug 11, 1977.

Former § 1401, add, L 1969, ch 1066, § 1; amd, L 1970, ch 221, L 1970, ch 847, §§ 82-86, L 1971, ch 458,§ 1, L 1971, ch 738, § 1, L 1971, ch 1058, § 39, L 1971, ch 1118, § 1, L 1972, ch 960, § 1, L 1974, ch 901, § 3, L 1976, ch 653; repealed, L 1977, ch 871, § 1; amd, L 1977, ch 872 § 2, L 1980, ch 565, § 1, eff June 26, 1980, L 1998, ch 560, § 2, eff Sept 4, 1998, L 2004, ch 675, § 1, eff Nov 3, 2004, L 2013, ch 549, § 111, eff July 1, 2014.

CASE ANNOTATIONS

1. Generally
2-5. [Reserved for future use]
6. Under former § 1401
7. Under former Membership Corporations Law § 70
8. Under former Membership Corporations Law § 71
9. Under former Membership Corporations Law § 71-a
10. Under former Membership Corporations Law § 71-b
11. Under former Membership Corporations Law § 72
12. Under former Membership Corporations Law § 73
13. Under former Membership Corporations Law § 74
14. Under former Membership Corporations Law § 75
15. Under former Membership Corporations Law § 76
16. Under former Membership Corporations Law § 78
17. Under former Membership Corporations Law § 79-a
18. Under former Membership Corporations Law § 80
19. Under former Membership Corporations Law § 81
20. Under former Membership Corporations Law § 87
21. – Public policy
22. – Purchase of land by cemetery
23. – – Determination of fair and reasonable value
24. – Proceeds from sale of individual lots
25. – – Maintenance fund
26. – – Payment of purchase price
27. – Relationship between certificate holders and cemetery
28. – Right to accounting; certificate holder
29. – – Lot owner
30. – Condemnation proceeding; right to be heard
31. – – Condemnation award
32. Under former Membership Corporations Law § 88
33. Under former Membership Corporations Law § 89
34. – Jurisdiction of court to order removal
35. – – As dependent upon ownership of cemetery
36. – Application for disinterment
37. – – Discretion of court
38. – Policy as to removal
39. – – Removal from consecrated to unhallowed ground
40. – Effect of particular circumstances; decedent's wishes
41. – – Consent to burial given under strain
42. – – Delay in seeking removal
43. – – Objection of owner of plot
44. – – Objection of estranged widow
45. – – Objection of cemetery
46. – Reason for removal
47. – – Reburial in family plot
48. – – Reburial in cemetery of religious affiliation
49. – – Determine existence of desecration
50. – – Cremation
51. Under former Membership Corporations Law § 82
52. – Contracts relating to operation of cemetery
53. – – As subject to changes in law
54. – – As subject to rate changes approved by state board
55. – Rules and regulations
56. – – Amendment or change
57. – – Restrictions on interment
58. – – Monument quality standards
59. – Regulation of charges; by secretary of state
60. – – Determination of reasonableness
61. – – Price of plaques
62. – – Charges for services of outside commercial gardeners
63. Under former Membership Corporations Law § 84
64. – Agreement for purchase of lot
65. – – Necessity of deed
66. – Rights acquired by purchase of lot
67. – – On purchase by decedent's estate
68. – – Right to erect and protect monument
69. – – Injunction against interference with rights
70. – Succession to rights of owner
71. – Right to burial in lot
72. – – Surviving spouse
73. – – Designee of owner
74. Under former Membership Corporations Law § 85
75. Under former Membership Corporations Law § 86
76. Under former Membership Corporations Law § 86-a
77. Under former Membership Corporations Law § 90
78. Under former Membership Corporations Law § 91
79. Under former Membership Corporations Law § 92
80. Under former Membership Corporations Law § 95

Not-For-Profit Corporation Law

81. Under former Membership Corporations Law § 97

82. Under former Membership Corporations Law § 106

83. Under former Membership Corporations Law § 108

84. Under former Membership Corporations Law § 108-a

1. Generally

Daughter of deceased mother failed to show good and substantial reasons why her father's remains should be moved so that he would buried next to mother where (1) when brother died, father purchased burial plot and interred him there, (2) when he died, father was buried next to brother, apparently in accordance with his wishes, and (3) when mother died 26 years later, brother's widow refused to permit her to be buried in plot with father and brother; although daughter asserted that father and mother wished to be buried together, father also wished to buried with brother, and mother had made no plans to be buried in same plot. Isola v Siani (1991, 2d Dept) 178 A.D.2d 599, 577 N.Y.S.2d 486

Petitioner could not bring Article 78 proceeding to compel New York State Division of Cemeteries to further investigate and prosecute complaint alleging misconduct by cemetery since petitioner failed to file protest with Cemetery Board prior to seeking judicial review (19 NYCRR § 200.2(e)). Lichtman v New York State Div. of Cemeteries (1996, 2d Dept) 226 A.D.2d 641, 641 N.Y.S.2d 561, app den 88 N.Y.2d 814, 651 N.Y.S.2d 15, 673 N.E.2d 1242

Petitioners in Article 78 proceeding were entitled to order compelling cemetery to issue and register plot deeds in their names where cemetery's counsel indicated in letter that cemetery would abide by whatever direction court gave in matter, and individual respondents filed stipulation in Appellate Division indicating that they took no position on issue of requested deeds. Turkewitz v Congregation Kehilath Isr. (1999, 1st Dept) 263 A.D.2d 371, 691 N.Y.S.2d 775

A decision of the Federal Circuit Court of Appeals which, for Federal estate tax purposes, disallowed a charitable bequest to a nonprofit cemetery corporation in the absence of any proof that the subject cemetery operated exclusively for "charitable purposes" within the meaning of section 2055 (subd [a], par [2]) of the Internal Revenue Code (US Code, tit 26, § 2055, subd [a], par [2]) is not decisive of the allowance of such a bequest for New York estate tax purposes, since the final Federal judicial determination has been shown by a preponderance of the evidence to be inimical to the statutory laws of this State (Tax Law, § 961) which clearly express the legislative intent that nonprofit cemetery corporations (Not-For-Profit Corporation Law, § 1401, subd [d]; § 1501) be deemed to operate exclusively for charitable purposes (see, also, EPTL 8-1.5) in that, in the absence of sufficient funds, the cost of preservation and maintenance of cemeteries would descend upon the public. Re Estate of Watson (1978) 96 Misc. 2d 327, 409 N.Y.S.2d 357

Common sense, logic and reasoning dictate that bequests to five nonprofit cemetery corporations (Not-For-Profit Corporation Law, § 1401, subd [d]) be deemed to be deductible charitable bequests under the New York Tax Law since, had the bequests been to cemeteries having a religious affiliation, they would be considered appropriate deductions for both Federal and State estate tax purposes. Making religious affiliation a point of demarcation for the charitable aspects of a cemtery would be discriminatory and irrational, representing a denial of equal protection of the laws. Re Estate of Watson (1978) 96 Misc. 2d 327, 409 N.Y.S.2d 357

Cemetery association breached contracts to beautify 2 graves by planting grass and providing perpetual care where for 3 years no grass was planted on graves for 3 years, and they were left covered in white sand and pebbles while surrounding graves were lush and green. Yochim v Mount Hope Cemetery Ass'n (1994, City Ct) 163 Misc. 2d 1054, 623 N.Y.S.2d 80

Cemetery associations are authorized to act as trustees and to establish trusts for perpetual care of burial plots. Yochim v Mount Hope Cemetery Ass'n (1994, City Ct) 163 Misc. 2d 1054, 623 N.Y.S.2d 80

Failure of cemetery association to plant grass and to deliver law care services was so complete over 3-year period that rescission of perpetual care agreements was justified, despite fact that cemetery association finally installed grass after commencement of action. Yochim v Mount Hope Cemetery Ass'n (1994, City Ct) 163 Misc. 2d 1054, 623 N.Y.S.2d 80

In action against cemetery association for failure to plant grass and provide care for graves of plaintiff's parents, plaintiff would be awarded damages in amount paid by plaintiff in consideration of perpetual care agreements and related contracts, and for distress and

mental anguish in amount of $300 ($50 per visit). Yochim v Mount Hope Cemetery Ass'n (1994, City Ct) 163 Misc. 2d 1054, 623 N.Y.S.2d 80

Operation of cemetery by cemetery association is impressed with public interest, is considered in nature of pious and public use, and is subject to police power of state for protection of public health. Yochim v Mount Hope Cemetery Ass'n (1994, City Ct) 163 Misc. 2d 1054, 623 N.Y.S.2d 80

Right of owner of grave to beautify, adorn and improve resting place of beloved dead cannot be interfered with by cemetery. Yochim v Mount Hope Cemetery Ass'n (1994, City Ct) 163 Misc. 2d 1054, 623 N.Y.S.2d 80

2-5. [Reserved for future use]

6. Under former § 1401

Cemetery corporation which owned 2,000 acres of real property, a portion of which was not exempt from taxation, would be enjoined from interring bodies on taxed parcels, since corporation's ownership of land in excess of 250 acres was in contravention of statutes. Pinelawn Cemetery v Cesare (1977) 90 Misc. 2d 736, 395 N.Y.S.2d 984, revd (1978, 2d Dept) 64 A.D.2d 607, 406 N.Y.S.2d 862

Where cemetery corporation was formed in 1902 as result of consolidation of 11 corporations, order of consolidation could not be interpreted as court approval of cemetery corporation's holding more than 2,000 acres of land, in view of fact that law in existence at that time barred cemetery corporation from holding more than 200 acres, and town's subsequent conveyance of additional property to cemetery corporation did not constitute an approval of cemetery corporation's holdings, since town could not confer rights in excess of those authorized by legislature. Pinelawn Cemetery v Cesare (1977) 90 Misc. 2d 736, 395 N.Y.S.2d 984, revd (1978, 2d Dept) 64 A.D.2d 607, 406 N.Y.S.2d 862

Service on Cemetery Board in condemnation proceeding which affects cemetery corporation. 1971 Ops Atty Gen Jan 15

Where a cemetery association owns a cemetery which is located partly in one town and partly in the adjoining town, either town, or both towns jointly, may accept a conveyance of such property. 1971 Ops St Compt File #663

7. Under former Membership Corporations Law § 70

A burial lot is real property, but the purchaser of such a lot acquires, not a title in fee simple thereto, but only the right to hold the lot for burial purposes. Daniell v Hopkins (1931) 257 N.Y. 112, 177 N.E. 390, 76 ALR 1367

A cemetery refererd to in this section means a place for burial of the dead, not necessarily a grave in the ground or in a mausoleum or vault, but in any other receptacle. Moore v United States Cremation Co. (1937) 275 N.Y. 105, 9 N.E.2d 795, 113 ALR 1124, reh den (1937) 275 N.Y. 544, 11 N.E.2d 743, 113 ALR 1128

Article 9 applies to a cemetery corporation incorporated under an act repealed by the Membership Corporations Law. In re Bauer (1902) 68 A.D. 212, 74 N.Y.S. 155

A crematory is not a cemetery, and the statute recognizes that the disposition of a dead body by burial or by cremation are entirely different. Moore v United States Cremation Co. (1936) 249 A.D. 637, 291 N.Y.S. 289, revd on other grounds (1937) 275 N.Y. 105, 9 N.E.2d 795, 113 ALR 1124, reh den (1937) 275 N.Y. 544, 11 N.E.2d 743, 113 ALR 1128

A cemetery corporation is not a "subdivider" within the meaning of Art. 9-A of the Real Property Law and that article is not applicable to it. Mt. Hope Cemetery Ass'n v Department of State (1943) 182 Misc 599, 45 N.Y.S.2d 249

A corporation may not be formed under the Stk. Corp. Law for the purpose of conducting a mausoleum. 1929 Ops Atty Gen 114

A corporation may not be formed under the Stk. Corp. Law for purpose of engaging in the business of buying and selling cemetery lots. 1929 Ops Atty Gen 118

8. Under former Membership Corporations Law § 71

In view of the provisions of § 71, the permission of the Board of Supervisors of Erie County is not necessary to permit a religious corporation to purchase additional lands and use such lands for cemetery purposes. Wojtkowiak v Evangelical Lutheran St. John's Church (1932) 236 A.D. 411, 259 N.Y.S. 481, affd (1933) 261 N.Y. 656, 185 N.E. 779

This section applies to a corporation incorporated under the Membership Corporations Law, even though some of the objects for which the organization was incorporated are of a religious nature. In re Drozda (1943) 266 A.D. 498, 43 N.Y.S.2d 610

On the basis of the history and the expressed legislation intention in the 1949 revision of this article, this section was intended to exempt only such religious corporations as owned their own cemeteries, and not those which, together with other organizations or individuals, merely hold plots in cemeteries owned by unrelated cemetery corporations. Jewish Center of Mt. Vernon, Inc. v Mt. Eden Cemetery Asso. (1961, 2d Dept) 15 A.D.2d 94, 222 N.Y.S.2d 644, mod (1962) 12 N.Y.2d 773, 234 N.Y.S.2d 720, 186 N.E.2d 567

This section excludes only such religious corporations as own their own cemeteries, and not those who have entered into contracts with cemetery corporations for maintenance by the cemetery corporation, from having the charges fixed by the agreement subject to change at the instance of the cemetery corporation with the approval of the State Cemetery Board, except in the instances covered by § 92. Jewish Center of Mt. Vernon, Inc. v Mt. Eden Cemetery Asso. (1961, 2d Dept) 15 A.D.2d 94, 222 N.Y.S.2d 644, mod (1962) 12 N.Y.2d 773, 234 N.Y.S.2d 720, 186 N.E.2d 567

Villages are governed by those provisions of the Membership Corporations Law which pertain to cemetery corporations only in the matter of perpetual care funds. 1961 Ops St Compt #719

A town has no authority to transfer town cemetery property to a corporation organized under the Religious Corporations Law. 1968 Ops St Compt File #333

9. Under former Membership Corporations Law § 71-a

Whether a cemetery regulation fixing a standard of quality for monuments is or is not reasonable is a question of fact for the determination of the Cemetery Board. 1966 Ops Atty Gen Jan 10

10. Under former Membership Corporations Law § 71-b

The Director of the Division of Cemeteries may accept appointment to the Advisory Committee for Funeral Directors without forfeiting his office as Director of the Division of Cemeteries. 1958 Ops Atty Gen Jul 2

11. Under former Membership Corporations Law § 72

Under former § 65 from which this section is derived a cemetery corporation had to procure the consent of the board of aldermen of New York city for maintenance of a cemetery in Bronx county. People ex rel. Hirsch v Department of Health (1925) 126 Misc 122, 212 N.Y.S. 680

Any state policy declared by Membership Corporations Law §§ 72, 73, and 75, permitting the acquisition of lands for cemetery purposes, is subject to reasonable regulations or restrictions adopted by the municipality as to the location and use of such land, such policy being in general terms, not prescribing a definite procedure or locating the exact site for the cemetery, thus not being violated by local town ordinances requiring a permit from the board of appeals of the town, for such use. Holy Sepulchre Cemetery v Greece (1947) 191 Misc 241, 79 N.Y.S.2d 683, affd (1948) 273 A.D. 942, 79 N.Y.S.2d 863

12. Under former Membership Corporations Law § 73

Where the notice required by the statute was not published in the two newspapers having the largest circulation in the county, and it appeared that the entire time between the first publication and the time of making the application to the Board of Supervisors was only 38 days, the Board of Supervisors has no jurisdiction to grant the consent sought; an owner of the land in the vicinity of a proposed cemetery, whose property will be depreciated in value by the establishment of the cemetery, may maintain an action in equity to restrain the acquisition of lands of such cemetery where the conditions of the statute have not been complied with. Palmer v Hickory Grove Cemetery (1903) 84 A.D. 600, 82 N.Y.S. 973

Although the present county of Nassau was carved out of the county of Queens by L 1898 c 588, a cemetery association cannot maintain a cemetery in the former county without first obtaining the consent of the board of supervisors as required by former § 42 from which this section is ultimately derived. Baylis v Rosemount Cemetery Ass'n (1909) 134 A.D. 251, 118 N.Y.S. 947

Action of a board of supervisors under former § 62 from which this section is derived was not judicial but legislative, and is not subject to review by a writ of certiorari. People ex rel. Baylis v Board of Supervisors (1916) 176 A.D. 888, 162 N.Y.S. 1138

This section has no application to a cemetery belonging to a religious or municipal corporation. Wojtkowiak v Evangelical Lutheran St. John's Church (1932) 236 A.D. 411, 259 N.Y.S. 481, affd (1933) 261 N.Y. 656, 185 N.E. 779

That former § 62 from which this section is derived required the consent of "the board of aldermen of New York city," for the acquisi-

tion of cemetery lands in the counties of Kings and Queens, does not relieve a cemetery corporation from the duty of procuring the consent of the board of aldermen of New York city with respect to lands located in Bronx county. People ex rel. Hirsch v Department of Health (1925) 126 Misc 122, 212 N.Y.S. 680

Any state policy declared by Membership Corporations Law §§ 72, 73 and 75, permitting the acquisition of lands for cemetery purposes, is subject to reasonable regulations or restrictions adopted by the municipality as to the location and use of such land, such policy being in general terms, not prescribing a definite procedure or locating the exact site for the cemetery, thus not being violated by local town ordinances requiring a permit from the board of appeals of the town, for such use. Holy Sepulchre Cemetery v Greece (1947) 191 Misc 241, 79 N.Y.S.2d 683, affd (1948) 273 A.D. 942, 79 N.Y.S.2d 863

This section merely imposes a limitation on the power of a cemetery corporation organized under the Membership Corporations Law to convey away its property, and is in no sense to be considered a grant of power previously not enjoyed by such a corporation. Application of Kensico Cemetery (1948) 193 Misc 479, 83 N.Y.S.2d 73, revd on other grounds (1949) 275 A.D. 681, 86 N.Y.S.2d 737, affd (1949) 299 N.Y. 752, 87 N.E.2d 670

This section is designed to limit the quantity of land which may be taken for cemetery purposes in certain counties and has no application to a proposed transfer of land already designated for cemetery purposes from one cemetery corporation to another. Application of Kensico Cemetery (1948) 193 Misc 479, 83 N.Y.S.2d 73, revd on other grounds (1949) 275 A.D. 681, 86 N.Y.S.2d 737, affd (1949) 299 N.Y. 752, 87 N.E.2d 670

A cemetery corporation, which failed to secure the consent of the County of Queens to operate in the county, was not entitled to a tax exemption, since its operation was illegal. United States Columbarium Co. v Tax Com. of New York (1959) 19 Misc. 2d 256, 187 N.Y.S.2d 602

13. Under former Membership Corporations Law § 74

Each member or group may vote once for each lot owned in full by him or by it, and a member owning a lot or lots in full may vote once for each such lot or lots, and may also participate as a member of a group owning a lot in choosing a vote for that group. In re Fentonville Cemetery Ass'n (1933) 238 A.D. 491, 264 N.Y.S. 790

A cemetery corporation, which contracted with its vendors pursuant to § 87 of the Membership Corporations Law to sell its cemetery property to lot owners entitled to vote at its meetings and subject to the right to assess them for funds for maintenance, is not authorized to convey land in which there have been no burials to another cemetery corporation, since the latter as a corporate body could not be a member of the former corporation and would not be subject to assessment. Application of Kensico Cemetery (1949) 275 A.D. 681, 86 N.Y.S.2d 737, affd (1949) 299 N.Y. 752, 87 N.E.2d 670

14. Under former Membership Corporations Law § 75

Lands acquired by a cemetery association are held in fee simple. Buffalo City Cemetery v Buffalo (1871) 46 N.Y. 503

The lands of a cemetery association organized under Laws 1847, ch 133, under § 10 of such act are exempt from taxation the moment they are acquired by the association and continue exempt so long as the corporation exists, although no dead body is buried thereon and although by a valid ordinance passed after its incorporation by a city within whose limits its lands lie, the burial of the dead therein is forbidden. People ex rel. Oak Hill Cemetery Ass'n v Pratt (1891) 129 N.Y. 68, 29 N.E. 7

This section is to be construed as part of a general system of legislation dealing with the acquisition of real property by cemetery corporations. Springfield L. I. Cemetery Soc. v New York (1936) 271 N.Y. 66, 2 N.E.2d 48

The exemption from taxation or assessment of "land actually used and occupied for cemetery purposes" as authorized by Real Property Law § 450 does not extend to "additional real property" held by a cemetery corporation "for the purposes of the convenient transaction of its business," no portion of which is used for the purposes of a cemetery, as provided for in this section. Springfield L. I. Cemetery Soc. v New York (1936) 271 N.Y. 66, 2 N.E.2d 48

The right of a corporation or association to acquire lands whereon to construct and operate a crematory or columbarium is governed by the provisions of law relating to cemetery associations and the acquisition of land for cemetery purposes. Moore v United States

Cremation Co. (1937) 275 N.Y. 105, 9 N.E.2d 795, 113 ALR 1124, reh den (1937) 275 N.Y. 544, 11 N.E.2d 743, 113 ALR 1128

It was competent for the Legislature to deprive a cemetery corporation of its right to secure lands for cemetery purposes even after the cemetery corporation had begun the publication of a notice of an application to the Board of Supervisors for its consent to acquire such lands by enacting the above section. Palmer v Hickory Grove Cemetery (1903) 84 A.D. 600, 82 N.Y.S. 973

The power of any corporation, be it a religious, municipal, or one organized under the Membership Corporations Law to take and hold real property for cemetery purposes, is subject to the exercise of the police power of the state, and a cemetery which is so situated that it endangers life or health, by corrupting the surrounding atmosphere or the water of wells or springs or otherwise, may easily become a nuisance which can be abeyed by a court of equity. Wojtkowiak v Evangelical Lutheran St. John's Church (1932) 236 A.D. 411, 259 N.Y.S. 481, affd (1933) 261 N.Y. 656, 185 N.E. 779

Any state policy declared by Membership Corporations Law §§ 72, 73 and 75, permitting the acquisition of lands for cemetery purposes, is subject to reasonable regulations or restrictions adopted by the municipality as to the location and use of such land, such policy being in general terms, not prescribing a definite procedure or locating the exact site for the cemetery, thus not being violated by local town ordinances requiring a permit from the board of appeals of the town, for such use. Holy Sepulchre Cemetery v Greece (1947) 191 Misc 241, 79 N.Y.S.2d 683, affd (1948) 273 A.D. 942, 79 N.Y.S.2d 863

Property acquired by a cemetery corporation prior to enactment of this section in counties in which property ownership by cemeteries is restricted, is not subject to a limitation that "no portion... shall be used for the purposes of a cemetery", and, therefore, since the property may be used for actual interment, it is not subject to taxation even though it may be temporarily used as a service yard in connection with the maintenance of the cemetery proper. People ex rel. Woodlawn Cemetery v Chambers (1949, Sup) 91 N.Y.S.2d 774

15. Under former Membership Corporations Law § 76

The trial term properly dismissed a complaint on merit where the plaintiff sought to revoke the transfer of a fund to the defendant cemetery under a written "form for perpetual care" of a lot which provided for the investment and application of income to maintanance, repair and care; an agreement or trust for such a purpose is valid and enforceable. French v Kensico Cemetery (1943) 291 N.Y. 77, 50 N.E.2d 551

It is the public policy of the state that cemeteries and structures thereon shall be kept in proper condition and appearance. French v Kensico Cemetery (1942) 264 A.D. 617, 35 N.Y.S.2d 826, affd (1943) 291 N.Y. 77, 50 N.E.2d 551

Disposition by a testatrix of her entire residuary estate for the purchase of a cemetery plot, the erection of a mausoleum, and its perpetual care, is sufficiently explicit as to the use of the entire residuary estate as to be valid, and no trust was created except one for perpetual care. In re Baeuchle's Will (1950) 276 A.D. 925, 94 N.Y.S.2d 582, affd (1950) 301 N.Y. 582, 93 N.E.2d 491

Where a testator's will contains no direction as to how the property given to a cemetery corporation is to be expended, it must be assumed that the gift is made for and limited to corporate purposes, and is therefore valid. In re Pearsall's Estate (1925) 125 Misc 634, 211 N.Y.S. 841

A bequest of a residuary estate to a cemetery corporation, with a direction that corporation is at all times to keep the lot and monument of the testator in good condition, is a valid bequest which the corporation has the power to receive, and it is a bequest of property absolute and not in trust, made for the general purposes of the cemetery association as provided by law. In re Pearsall's Estate (1925) 125 Misc 634, 211 N.Y.S. 841

A cemetery corporation may accept a gift in trust of real and personal property under a will. In re Johnson's Estate (1933) 148 Misc 218, 265 N.Y.S. 395

In view of the specifically stated powers of cemetery corporations concerning the investment of trust funds, the 1950 amendment, which liberally enlarges the investment powers of fiduciaries generally, has no application to such corporations. 1950 Ops Atty Gen July 10

16. Under former Membership Corporations Law § 78

Under this section acquisition of real property in the county of Nassau for the construction and operation of crematory and columbarium is prohibited. Moore v United States Cremation Co. (1937)

275 N.Y. 105, 9 N.E.2d 795, 113 ALR 1124, reh den (1937) 275 N.Y. 544, 11 N.E.2d 743, 113 ALR 1128

Former § 85 from which this section is derived was not unconstitutional, for the legislature has power to control the question of new and additional cemeteries. Baylis v Van Nostrand (1917) 176 A.D. 396, 162 N.Y.S. 831

Former § 85 from which this section is derived applied only to cemeteries established after its passage and did not apply to existing unincorporated cemetery associations; such associations may incorporate under this law. Baylis v Van Nostrand (1917) 176 A.D. 396, 162 N.Y.S. 831

Under former § 85 as amended in 1916, although an unincorporated cemetery association at Elmont, Nassau county, which had been inexistence for many years, could lawfully incorporate in the year 1914, it was prohibited from acquiring any additional contiguous land for cemetery purposes, not being an existing corporation prior to 1913. Baylis v Van Nostrand (1917) 176 A.D. 396, 162 N.Y.S. 831

17. Under former Membership Corporations Law § 79-a

The power of a cemetery corporation to sell property acquired for burial purposes is limited to sales of lots to individuals, except when the conveyance is made to a city or village or the corporation has no liabilities and there are no burials in the parcel involved (under former § 81). Application of Kensico Cemetery (1949) 275 A.D. 681, 86 N.Y.S.2d 737, affd (1949) 299 N.Y. 752, 87 N.E.2d 670

A cemetery corporation may convey to a town a cemetery situated partly within and partly without a village. 1953 Ops St Compt File #6140

Conveyance of property of cemetery associations to a town should be made only after prior judicial approval. 1954 Ops St Compt File #6779

A village may accept a cemetery conveyed to it by a membership corporation and administer the assets transferred subject to all conditions and agreements with lot owners. 1955 Ops St Compt File #7078

A town may not appropriate moneys to assist in the care of a cemetery which is controlled by a cemetery corporation. 1957 Ops St Compt File #207

Where the lands and money of a cemetery corporation are transferred to a town, the money is subject to all trust agreements and restrictions upon its use which obtained prior to transfer. 1963 Ops St Compt #146

Unrestricted cash assets of a cemetery association whose cemetery has been transferred to a town may be applied to care of municipal cemeteries other than the cemetery so transferred. 1963 Ops St Compt #374

There is no provision for any state aid specifically for the care and maintenance of cemeteries located in a town. 1967 Ops St Compt File #706

The town board is under a duty to care for all cemeteries located in the town except those presently controlled by an existing board or corporate body. 1967 Ops St Compt File #706

The term abandoned cemetery means one for which there no longer exists any board or corporate body or trust fund or endowment to maintain it. 1967 Ops St Compt File #706

A village may not contribute to the maintenance of a cemetery owned by a private cemetery association, but it may accept a conveyance of the property by the association, or may purchase it and maintain it as a village cemetery. 1968 Ops St Compt File #993

18. Under former Membership Corporations Law § 80

The power of a cemetery corporation to sell property acquired for burial purposes is limited to sales of lots to individuals, except when the conveyance is made to a city or village or the corporation has no liabilities and there are no burials in the parcel involved (under former § 81). Application of Kensico Cemetery (1949) 275 A.D. 681, 86 N.Y.S.2d 737, affd (1949) 299 N.Y. 752, 87 N.E.2d 670

19. Under former Membership Corporations Law § 81

The fact that lands have been previously devoted to cemetery purposes does not place them beyond the power of eminent domain, and in the absence of an express statutory prohibition, land devoted to a private cemetery may be condemned under a general statute for the condemnation of land for a public use. In re Board of Street Openings & Improv., etc. (1892) 133 N.Y. 329, 31 N.E. 102

An order directing the receiver of a cemetery corporation to sell so much of the lands acquired by the cemetery pursuant to former § 70, from which present § 87 is derived, as may be necessary to produce sufficient moneys to satisfy a judgment in a judgment creditor's action, is unauthorized. In re Chauncey (1920) 191 A.D. 359, 181 N.Y.S. 653

Even when interments had occurred, if the bodies had been afterwards removed, cemetery land could be sold by the court on notice to all parties including the cemetery association, and even for unpaid lot taxes, a sale may be had of such portion of a single burial lot as has not been occupied as well for unpaid expenses of restoring a lot after the removal of a body. Johnson v Ocean View Cemetery (1921) 198 A.D. 854, 191 N.Y.S. 128

A cemetery corporation which contracted with its vendors pursuant to § 87 of the Membership Corporation Law to sell its cemetery property to lot owners entitled to vote at its meetings and subject to the right to assess them for funds for maintenance, is not authorized to convey land in which there have been no burials to another cemetery corporation, since the latter as a corporate body could not be a member of the former corporation and would not be subject to assessment. Application of Kensico Cemetery (1949) 275 A.D. 681, 86 N.Y.S.2d 737, affd (1949) 299 N.Y. 752, 87 N.E.2d 670

A lease of cemetery lands for mining purposes is not only ultra vires, but is in contravention of former § 13 from which present § 21 is derived and is inconsistent with the objects and purposes for which the lessor was organized, and the court is without power to sanction such a lease without explicit legislative authority. Briggs v Bloomingdale Cemetery Ass'n (1920) 113 Misc 685, 185 N.Y.S. 348, affd (1924) 208 A.D. 761, 202 N.Y.S. 918

A village Board of Cemetery Commissioners may accept the conveyance of a church cemetery which is to become part of the village cemetery, provided the conveyance by the church is authorized by appropriate court order. 1947 Ops St Compt 395

Conveyance of property of cemetery associations to a town should be made only after prior judicial approval. 1954 Ops St Compt File #6779

20. Under former Membership Corporations Law § 87
The provisions of this section are intended to benefit the lot owners and insure payment to the land share owners. Application of Kensico Cemetery (1949) 275 A.D. 681, 86 N.Y.S.2d 737, affd (1949) 299 N.Y. 752, 87 N.E.2d 670

No provision is made by this section for a change in the source of moneys to be received by a cemetery corporation, provision being made only for a change in the price of lots. Application of Kensico Cemetery (1949) 275 A.D. 681, 86 N.Y.S.2d 737, affd (1949) 299 N.Y. 752, 87 N.E.2d 670

There is no statutory provision permitting the parties or the Supreme Court to modify agreements authorized by this section. Application of Kensico Cemetery (1949) 275 A.D. 681, 86 N.Y.S.2d 737, affd (1949) 299 N.Y. 752, 87 N.E.2d 670

21. – Public policy
The 1949 Act, in amending this section to provide that where a vendor, by agreement, is being paid a share of his vendee's burial lot sale proceeds, the vendor's share is to be figured not on net burial lot price but on that price reduced by prior deduction of 25% for the maintenance fund, means just what it says and is not unconstitutional as applied to a contract entered into in 1910, as state policy has historically been to regard funds derived from sale of cemetery lots as dedicated to public use and held in trust, with disposal subject to regulation under the police power. Grove Hill Realty Co. v Ferncliff Cemetery Asso. (1960) 7 N.Y.2d 403, 198 N.Y.S.2d 287, 165 N.E.2d 858

It is the public policy of the state that cemeteries and structures thereon shall be kept in proper condition and appearance. French v Kensico Cemetery (1942) 264 A.D. 617, 35 N.Y.S.2d 826, affd (1943) 291 N.Y. 77, 50 N.E.2d 551

22. – Purchase of land by cemetery
Where property is to be paid for not at a flat price, but by giving to the vendor a certain proportion of the amount received from the sale of lots and plots, fifty percent only of the proceeds can be applied to the purchase price; however, when a flat price is agreed upon, it is legal for the association to pay all or any part of the proceeds derived from the sale of lots to the purchase price of the land. In re Norton (1916) 97 Misc 289, 161 N.Y.S. 710

23. – – Determination of fair and reasonable value
Under subd 3 of this section, in fixing the fair and reasonable value of land to be purchased by a cemetery corporation, the court may take into consideration the method by which the purchase price is to be paid and, where no mortgage or other security may be given

by the corporation, the only method available for consummation of the transaction is by issuance of certificates of indebtedness. Application of Jordan Cemetery Asso. (1962) 33 Misc. 2d 274, 225 N.Y.S.2d 303, revd on other grounds (1963, 2d Dept) 19 A.D.2d 540, 240 N.Y.S.2d 944

With respect to a proposal for a cemetery corporation to issue $10,000,000 in certificates of indebtedness at two percent interest, to finance purchase of additional land, upon review of the evidence it was held that fair and reasonable value of the property, if paid in cash, was $1,000,000 and, where paid by certificates of indebtedness, over a period of from 50 to 90 years, would not be more than $8,000,000 with interest at the rate of .0063%. Application of Jordan Cemetery Asso. (1962) 33 Misc. 2d 274, 225 N.Y.S.2d 303, revd on other grounds (1963, 2d Dept) 19 A.D.2d 540, 240 N.Y.S.2d 944

24. – Proceeds from sale of individual lots
This section in effect provides that not more than one-half of the proceeds of the sale shall be applied to the payment of the purchase price, while the remainder is to be used for the preservation, embellishment and improvement of the cemetery. Reese v Pinelawn Cemetery (1934) 243 A.D. 165, 276 N.Y.S. 381

25. – – Maintenance fund
Subdivision 2 of § 87 and § 86-a, requiring cemetery corporations to set up maintenance funds from proceeds of sale of each lot, properly declared to be valid and constitutional. Grove Hill Realty Co. v Ferncliff Cemetery Asso. (1958, 2d Dept) 7 A.D.2d 736, 180 N.Y.S.2d 767, affd (1960) 7 N.Y.2d 403, 198 N.Y.S.2d 287, 165 N.E.2d 858

26. – – Payment of purchase price
The phrase "one-half of the proceeds," as used in this section, entitles certificate holders to only one-half of the net proceeds of the sales. Reese v Pinelawn Cemetery (1934) 243 A.D. 165, 276 N.Y.S. 381

Holders of purchase money certificates, issued by a cemetery corporation, are not entitled to have the entire land purchase fund, comprising 70 per cent of the proceeds from the sale of cemetery land, applied to the redemption of their certificates since this section prohibits the payment of more than 50 per cent of the cemetery's net proceeds to the vendors of land. Jackson v Elmont Cemetery, Inc. (1949) 275 A.D. 544, 90 N.Y.S.2d 521, affd (1949) 300 N.Y. 526, 89 N.E.2d 250

Purchase money certificates, issued by a cemetery corporation providing that more than 50 per cent of the proceeds were to go for the redemption of the certificates, are issued in violation of this section and are not certificates of indebtedness. Jackson v Elmont Cemetery, Inc. (1949) 275 A.D. 544, 90 N.Y.S.2d 521, affd (1949) 300 N.Y. 526, 89 N.E.2d 250

Membership Corporation Law §§ 86-a and 87 do not impair a cemetery corporation's obligation under a contract whereby, in consideration of land conveyed to it, it agreed to pay the vendor one-half the proceeds of the sale of each plot. Grove Hill Realty Co. v Ferncliff Cemetery Asso. (1957) 9 Misc. 2d 47, 167 N.Y.S.2d 675, affd (1958, 2d Dept) 7 A.D.2d 736, 180 N.Y.S.2d 767, affd (1960) 7 N.Y.2d 403, 198 N.Y.S.2d 287, 165 N.E.2d 858

27. – Relationship between certificate holders and cemetery
Certificate holders in a cemetery corporation have a direct interest in a specific fund, and a cemetery association or corporation as to them is either a trustee or agent in the management of that fund. Mitchell v Pinelawn Cemetery (1942, Sup) 37 N.Y.S.2d 207

28. – Right to accounting; certificate holder
Where the allegations of the complaint in an action by the holder of certificates of indebtedness of a cemetery corporation contains allegations sufficient to found a request for an accounting and the defendant corporation is well aware of plaintiff's desire for such an accounting, the omission of a request for such relief is immaterial. Jackson v Elmont Cemetery, Inc. (1948, Sup) 80 N.Y.S.2d 407

29. – – Lot owner
A plot owner in a cemetery may not maintain an action in his own behalf or in behalf of other owners similarly situated for an accounting of the proceeds of sales of lots. Mitchell v Pinelawn Cemetery (1942, Sup) 37 N.Y.S.2d 207

30. – Condemnation proceeding; right to be heard
Where a cemetery corporation, pursuant to power conferred by the act under which it was incorporated, purchased land and gave back "land shares" to the grantor, whereby it agreed to pay her one-half of

all moneys received from the sale of cemetery lots made from the land, the holders of the shares have a right to be heard upon a proceeding by New York city to condemn land for its water supply. In re Bensel (1911) 144 A.D. 751, 129 N.Y.S. 682

31. – – Condemnation award

Where a cemetery associations' land, which had been purchased under an agreement that the vendors were to receive one-half of the proceeds of sale of lots, was condemned after 1949, the vendors were entitled to one-half of the condemnation award remaining after the deduction of sales expenses, 10% for a permanent maintenance fund and 15% for a current maintenance fund. Keith v Maple Grove Cemetery Asso. (1955) 208 Misc 217, 145 N.Y.S.2d 198, app dismd (1955, 1st Dept) 1 A.D.2d 665, 149 N.Y.S.2d 702

32. Under former Membership Corporations Law § 88

Burial of a widow in a lot of which her husband died possessed cannot be denied by the husband's executor; the fact that a widow thought that her burial by the side of her husband might be denied is no justification for the removal of her husband's remains to another lot and the charge of the expense thereof against the husband's estate. In re Caldwell (1907) 188 N.Y. 115, 80 N.E. 663

Former § 71 from which this section is derived did not apply to cemeteries belonging to religious or municipal corporations. In re Cohen (1902) 76 A.D. 401, 78 N.Y.S. 417

The mere fact of a husband's burial in a lot does not establish that he has "an estate or right of burial therein" nor is such a right automatically conferred upon his widow. In re Steiner (1943) 179 Misc 962, 43 N.Y.S.2d 556

The widow of a predeceased husband is not entitled to interment in the same lot with the remains of her husband irrespective of the consent of any person claiming to be the owner or having an interest in such lot. In re Steiner (1943) 179 Misc 962, 43 N.Y.S.2d 556

33. Under former Membership Corporations Law § 89

Bodies may not be removed without the permission of the cemetery from a burial plot which was purchased subject to the rules of the cemetery printed on the face of the deed, one of which provided that no disinterment would be allowed without such permission. Smith v Green-Wood Cemetery (1940) 173 Misc 215, 17 N.Y.S.2d 706

34. – Jurisdiction of court to order removal

Section 89 of the Membership Corporation Law governs the disinterment or removal of bodies and where the heirs of a deceased person do not consent to the removal of his remains the removal can only be accomplished if the County Court or Supreme Court grants permission. Evergreen Cemetery Asso. v Jurgensen (1970, 3d Dept) 34 A.D.2d 709, 309 N.Y.S.2d 847

35. – – As dependent upon ownership of cemetery

Section 71 from which this section is derived authorizing the removal of a body from a cemetery does not apply to a cemetery corporation incorporated prior to the enactment of the Membership Corporations Law, under a special act, which was not repealed by such law. In re Owens (1903) 79 A.D. 236, 79 N.Y.S. 1114

A religious corporation, organized to teach the Hebrew religion, which also maintains a cemetery with burial lots for its members, did not come within former § 71 from which this section is derived, so as to authorize the court to consent to the removal of a body buried in such cemetery, where the corporation refused to consent thereto; it is only in the instance of a membership corporation that the court's consent can be substituted for that of the corporation. Application of Bleistift (1920) 193 A.D. 477, 184 N.Y.S. 296

A county court has jurisdiction under this section where a corporation owning cemetery is a membership corporation and not a religious corporation within terms of § 71. In re Drozda (1943) 266 A.D. 498, 43 N.Y.S.2d 610

36. – Application for disinterment

An application by decedent's widow to remove his body from Westchester County cemetery to a New Jersey cemetery was granted. Application of Sherman (1952) 304 N.Y. 745, 108 N.E.2d 613

Absent the consent of the cemetery corporation, the owners of the burial plot, and of the surviving spouse, parents of the deceased, and adult children for the removal and reinterment elsewhere of a human body, an order of court is required for this purpose. Application of McEvilly (1967) 54 Misc. 2d 602, 283 N.Y.S.2d 293

37. – – Discretion of court

An application made under this section for the removal of a body buried in a cemetery under authority granted by a cemetery corporation to a benevolent association should be granted by the supreme court, notwithstanding a bylaw of the benevolent association, having control of the plot in which such body was buried, that no removal of

a corpse from such plot should be permitted for reinterment in another burial ground. In re Bauer (1902) 68 A.D. 212, 74 N.Y.S. 155

The question of disinterment of a body is dependent upon the exercise of discretion or equitable jurisdiction and in either event, the effect of legal title is merely a reason to be considered by the court. Evergreen Cemetery Asso. v Jurgensen (1970, 3d Dept) 34 A.D.2d 709, 309 N.Y.S.2d 847

Upon an application under this section for disinterment of the remains of the wife and the son of the petitioner from consecrated ground and to bury them in a private family plot in the same cemetery, also in consecrated ground, where neither the petitioner's version of his wife's wishes nor the association's version that the wife meant to be buried only "in the same cemetery" as her son, meets the condition of Hebrew law under which a body may be disinterred, the right to disinter will be determined on equitable grounds in the court's discretion. Application of Glasser (1942) 180 Misc 311, 41 N.Y.S.2d 733

38. – Policy as to removal

The dead are to rest where they have been laid unless reason of substance is brought forward for disturbing their repose. Yome v Gorman (1926) 242 N.Y. 395, 152 N.E. 126, 47 ALR 1165

39. – – Removal from consecrated to unhallowed ground

Only some rare emergency could move a court of equity to take a body from its grave in consecrated ground and put it in ground unhallowed if there is good reason to suppose that the conscience of the deceased were he alive would be outraged by the change. Yome v Gorman (1926) 242 N.Y. 395, 152 N.E. 126, 47 ALR 1165

40. – Effect of particular circumstances; decedent's wishes

The wish of the deceased has at least a large significance especially when the wish has its origin in a tense religious feeling. Yome v Gorman (1926) 242 N.Y. 395, 152 N.E. 126, 47 ALR 1165

A petition to remove the deceased from a mausoleum and rebury her in an adjoining plot will be granted where deceased's original hope in being interred in the mausoleum was that her children would be laid to rest beside her and the children no longer plan on being interred in the mausoleum and the petitioner is the son of the deceased and the only party opposing the disinterment is the cemetery corporation. Application of Currier (1949) 275 A.D. 933, 91 N.Y.S.2d 624, affd (1949) 300 N.Y. 162, 90 N.E.2d 18, 21 ALR2d 465

A husband will be permitted to disinter the body of his wife from ground consecrated in accordance with Jewish law to a family plot, also in consecrated ground, where it appears that, inasmuch as the relatives of the deceased were negotiating for such a family plot at the time of the burial, and that the deceased requested burial in a family plot during her lifetime, the original interment was intended to be temporary, and that accordingly, such disinterment and reburial was not in conflict with Jewish law, although conflict did exist between eminent rabbis in such matters. In re Katz (1938) 167 Misc 301, 3 N.Y.S.2d 754

The wishes of the deceased in the matter of the disposition of his body are paramount to all other considerations. In re Harlam (1945, Sup) 57 N.Y.S.2d 103

41. – – Consent to burial given under strain

Where widow consented to the burial of her deceased husband in a plot owned by the husband's sister while under mental strain and in reliance on the understanding that she would be buried next to her husband, and thereafter the widow's confidence in that eventuality was disturbed, the consent given by the widow did not bar an application for an order permitting disinterment and reburial. Teitman v Elmwier Cemetery Asso. (1956) 3 Misc. 2d 143, 148 N.Y.S.2d 159

42. – – Delay in seeking removal

A daughter will not be granted permission to remove the remains of her deceased father where the deceased has been buried for thirty years and the daughter has had the plot to which the deceased is sought to be removed for a period of at least five years, but apparently waited until her mother, by reason of her mental condition, is unable to express her desire as to the disposition of the remains of the decedent. Petition of Guggenheim (1936) 249 A.D. 653, 291 N.Y.S. 467

43. – – Objection of owner of plot

Petition of widow for disinterment of her husband's body from grave owned by decedent's brother so that she would be assured that upon her death her body would be interred in same grave as her husband's, denied upon condition that owner of the plot in which the husband's body was interred would make and deliver to petitioner, without expense to her and in proper form, a deed to that plot, and, upon failure to comply with such condition, the application would be granted. Application of McEvilly (1967) 54 Misc. 2d 602, 283 N.Y.S.2d 293

While it is within the power of the court to allow disinterment under certain circumstances even without the consent of all the owners of a plot, where disinterment of the deceased and her reburial in a concrete vault would certainly take up a larger portion of the plot, it should not be permitted over the objection of one of the co-owners of the plot since the usage of more space for the reburial would work to the disadvantage of the other co-owners. Application of Cabot (1968) 55 Misc. 2d 742, 286 N.Y.S.2d 598

Sister of decedent, was entitled to an order removing decedent's body from plot owned by nephew of decedent to plot owned by sister in the same cemetery, where the evidence showed, that the sister and the decedent were very close in life and nephew was only interested in getting money out of decedent's estate. Application of Wechsler (1959, Sup) 191 N.Y.S.2d 870

44. – – Objection of estranged widow

The father of the deceased may remove the body of the deceased from one plot to another in a cemetery, over the objections of the wife of the deceased, where it appears that the deceased and his wife were not living together at the time of his death. Petition of Forrisi (1939) 170 Misc 649, 10 N.Y.S.2d 888

45. – – Objection of cemetery

A defense by an association that the defendant offered to consent to a disinterment and removal of the remains of the decedent upon plaintiff's obtaining such other consents as were required by this section, is entirely proper and should not be stricken from the answer. Henry v Vintschger (1932) 234 A.D. 593, 256 N.Y.S. 581, app dismd (1932) 260 N.Y. 578, 184 N.E. 100

Upon application of the husband and two of the children of a decedent for an order under this section authorizing disinterment of the decedent's remains from a burial plot in the cemetery of a particular religious congregation, for burial in a private family plot in a different cemetery, to which all the remaining children of the decedent consented in writing and only the congregation objected by reason of customs and usages of the particular religious body, as to which there was considerable conflict of authority, the desires and motivations of the decedent and surviving relatives should be accorded paramount consideration. Petition of Davis (1959) 21 Misc. 2d 825, 192 N.Y.S.2d 174

Petition by husband, joined in by all children, for an order authorizing and permitting the husband to remove the body of his deceased wife from the present cemetery plot to a plot in another cemetery was granted, where it appeared that the cemetery corporation was the only opponent and the petition was for reasonable and laudable purposes. Petition of Morochnick (1962) 35 Misc. 2d 71, 229 N.Y.S.2d 880

A request for disinterment consented to by all of the known relatives of the deceased and opposed only by the cemetery association was granted. Petition of Brogan (1965) 47 Misc. 2d 315, 262 N.Y.S.2d 724

Permission to disinter a body and remove it to another cemetery will be granted when all the children of deceased join in motion therefor, over claim of congregation cemetery that disinterment violates tenets of Jewish faith, and over claim of second wife of deceased who did not live with deceased for eleven years preceding his death. In re Mushel (1953, Sup) 125 N.Y.S.2d 130

46. – Reason for removal

Burial of a widow in a lot of which her husband died possessed cannot be denied by the husband's executor; the fact that a widow thought that her burial by the side of her husband might be denied is no justification for the removal of her husband's remains to another lot and the charge of the expense thereof against the husband's estate. In re Caldwell (1907) 188 N.Y. 115, 80 N.E. 663

On application, made by seven of eight children, under this section, for permission to remove the bodies of their parents from the cemetery lot in which they are buried and which is now owned by one not a member of the family to lot in another cemetery purchased by some of the children, as a result of differences with said owner, who objects to the size and nature of the monument selected by said children for erection on that lot, consent to such removal is granted, but only on condition that the owner of said lot refuses to allow the erection thereon of such monument and headstones as the children believe suitable in memory of their father and mother and as meets the approval of the directors of the said cemetery, since it appears that the parents, who owned no lot, had expressed a desire to be buried where they are. In re Winters (1937) 165 Misc 226, 300 N.Y.S. 853

Where in his lifetime a decedent had the remains of his friend buried in his family plot, those remains would not be disinterred upon application of the decedent's surviving widow and two children, notwithstanding their desire to be buried in the family plot and the fact that only two graves remained therein. Application of Von Gross (1968) 56 Misc. 2d 275, 288 N.Y.S.2d 308

The petition of a surviving wife to remove the body of her deceased husband's first wife so that she and a deceased daughter might be buried beside the husband was not a sufficient reason to grant the application, where during his lifetime the husband exhibited no interest in removing the remains of his first wife. Brand v Elmwier Cemetery Asso. (1968) 59 Misc. 2d 408, 299 N.Y.S.2d 573

A wife will not be granted permission to remove the remains of her husband from a burial plot owned by her adopted daughter's husband merely because differences have arisen between the wife and daughter and son-in-law, where it appears that the deceased approved of and intended to be buried in the plot in question, provided that the son-in-law shall provide, in accordance with the regulations of the cemetery, an instrument insuring to the wife the right of burial next to her husband in the lot, and giving the wife the right to erect and maintain a joint monument or headstone at the head of the two graves with such inscription thereon as she may dictate. Petition of Costa (1947, Sup) 83 N.Y.S.2d 65, affd (1948) 274 A.D. 872, 83 N.Y.S.2d 226

47. – – Reburial in family plot

A husband will be granted permission to remove the body of his deceased wife to a private family plot in the same cemetery, where all the members of his family may be buried, where all the children consented to the removal and the only objector to the disinterment was the cemetery society. In re Schechter (1941) 261 A.D. 926, 25 N.Y.S.2d 434

An application of a wife to remove the remains of her deceased husband from a burial plot owned by a society of which neither husband nor wife was a member, to a subsequently acquired family plot in another cemetery where all the other members of the family may be buried, where the consent of the two minor children of the deceased has been obtained, though such consent is unnecessary under this section, and the only objector to the disinterment is the cemetery society. Application of Bobrowsky (1943) 266 A.D. 849, 42 N.Y.S.2d 36

A liberal view has been adopted by the courts in permitting disinterment at the request of all of the nearest of kin for the purpose of reburial in after-acquired family plots. In re Herskovits (1944) 183 Misc 411, 48 N.Y.S.2d 906

The only surviving child is entitled to remove the bodies of his parents to a family plot, where the only opposition thereto comes from a cemetery association on the ground that disinterment is prohibited by the tenets of the Hebrew faith, and that prior to his death, the plaintiff's father had requested an Orthodox Hebrew burial. Dickstein v First Strussower Sick & Support Ass'n (1947) 188 Misc 642, 68 N.Y.S.2d 758

The decedent was interred in a church owned cemetery. Thereafter, the family purchased a family burial lot in a private cemetery. The church refused to give its consent to the removal of the decedent's body from the church cemetery to the private cemetery. Held: since there was a conflict of Rabbinical authority in the matter, and since the family desired to make the removal in order that all members of the family could be buried in the same place, the petition for removal was granted. Petition of Davis (1959) 21 Misc. 2d 825, 192 N.Y.S.2d 174

Disinterment of a body from a cemetery lot for reburial in a later-acquired family plot is permissible when all members of the family agree and the only objector is the society owning the cemetery, and an application to the court for permission to remove the remains for reburial should not be conditioned upon delivery by the applicant and other relatives of a general release in favor of the cemetery association. Application of Stanton (1961) 28 Misc. 2d 966, 216 N.Y.S.2d 384

A husband will be permitted to remove the body of his wife from one Jewish cemetery to another where the children of the petitioner and the deceased have consented thereto, and the purpose of the removal is to place the remains in a family burial plot which cannot be located in the first cemetery because of lack of room, and the only opposition offered is by the society which owns land in both of the cemeteries on the ground that disinterment is contrary to the spirit and principle of Judaism. In re Plancher (1942, Sup) 37 N.Y.S.2d 87

The only surviving children may, upon giving bond, remove the bodies of their parents from an Orthodox Jewish cemetery to a family plot in a second Jewish cemetery, where the sole objection thereto is offered by the Jewish congregation from whom burial rights were purchased for the original interment, on the ground that such disinterment is contrary to Jewish ecclesiastical law, and that such removal would desecrate the adjoining graves and the remainder of the cemetery. Raisler v Krakauer Simon Schreiber Congregation (1944, Sup) 47 N.Y.S.2d 938

A surviving husband is entitled to remove his wife's remains to a family burial plot, over the objection of the society which owned the burial rights to the original burial plot, all the relatives of the decedent who have attained their majority consenting, where the decedent expressed a desire to be buried in a family plot, and where desire was unfulfilled because of her sudden death. Silver v Mt. Hebron Cemetery (1946, Sup) 64 N.Y.S.2d 274

48. – – Reburial in cemetery of religious affiliation
The petitioner, owner of a lot in a cemetery of a congregation organized under the Membership Corporations Law is properly authorized to remove the body of her husband to a cemetery of their religious affiliation by the county court under § 89. In re Drozda (1943) 266 A.D. 498, 43 N.Y.S.2d 610

49. – – Determine existence of desecration
An application by a petitioner to open a grave to remove the bodies of his parents and to determine whether there had been a despoilment and desecration in removing them from metal caskets in which they were originally interred, will be granted, pursuant to this section, on consent of the cemetery corporation and without the written consent of the actual owners of the lot, where it appears that the petitioner had purchased from the cemetery corporation a plot on which to erect a mausoleum and wherein there were later entombed the bodies of his mother and father, and that during his absence for some years someone representing himself as being the petitioner sold the mausoleum, removing the bodies of the petitioner's father and mother and placing them in a grave purchased in the name of the petitioner. Dispenza v St. John's Cemetery, Inc. (1939) 173 Misc 560, 17 N.Y.S.2d 533

50. – – Cremation
A wife will not be permitted to disinter the body of her husband after it has been buried for more than three months for purposes of cremation which, the wife alleges, is in accordance with the expressed wish of the decedent, where the body has been buried in a family plot with the consent of the petitioning wife, and there is no positive evidence that the decedent in fact wished to be cremated; disinterment and cremation both being against the tenets of the Hebrew faith, the lot owners, the sisters of the deceased, object thereto. In re Herskovits (1944) 183 Misc 411, 48 N.Y.S.2d 906

The surviving children will not be permitted to disinter their father's remains from a Jewish cemetery for purposes of cremation, pursuant to the request of their mother prior to her death, where the evidence indicates that the father had expressed no desire for cremation, that his grave had been left undisturbed for over 20 years, that disinterment was contrary to the tenets of the Hebrew faith and disinterment was opposed by the Jewish cemetery corporation which owned the plot in which the remains were buried. In re Harlam (1945, Sup) 57 N.Y.S.2d 103

51. Under former Membership Corporations Law § 82
The provisions of subds 1 and 3 of this section are clear and unambiguous and must be given effect as written, not as a public officer charged with administering the law may think they should have been written. May v Washington Cemetery (1961) 29 Misc. 2d 1046, 217 N.Y.S.2d 897, affd (1962, 2d Dept) 16 A.D.2d 931, 230 N.Y.S.2d 671

52. – Contracts relating to operation of cemetery
Where a deficit would result in operating a cemetery by a membership corporation, if it were required to abide by service charges fixed in agreements with lot owners prior to the 1949 revision of this article, it is not clear that the deficit could be made up by charging the other lot owners enough more to make ends meet. Jewish Center of Mt. Vernon, Inc. v Mt. Eden Cemetery Asso. (1961, 2d Dept) 15 A.D.2d 94, 222 N.Y.S.2d 644, mod (1962) 12 N.Y.2d 773, 234 N.Y.S.2d 720, 186 N.E.2d 567

53. – – As subject to changes in law
Since it is well settled that operation of a cemetery is impressed with a public purpose and that any contract relating to its operations implicitly contains a clause making it subject to changes in the law, a religious corporation which owned only a portion of a cemetery owned and operated by a membership corporation could not rely on a 1939 agreement with the cemetery corporation as to service charges for the particular portion of the cemetery as against liability for subsequent charges approved by the Cemetery Board following the 1949 revision of this article. Jewish Center of Mt. Vernon, Inc. v Mt. Eden Cemetery Asso. (1961, 2d Dept) 15 A.D.2d 94, 222 N.Y.S.2d 644, mod (1962) 12 N.Y.2d 773, 234 N.Y.S.2d 720, 186 N.E.2d 567

The Cemetery Law was enacted in exercise of the state's police power to impress the operation of a cemetery with public interest so that any contract, relating to its operation, is subject to changes made in the law. Silver Mt. Cemetery Asso. v Simon (1962) 36 Misc. 2d 792, 231 N.Y.S.2d 909, revd on other grounds (1963, 1st Dept) 18 A.D.2d 801, 237 N.Y.S.2d 507

54. – – As subject to rate changes approved by state board
A religious corporation, which merely owns, for the benefit of its members, part of a cemetery owned and operated by a cemetery corporation organized under the Membership Corporations Law, is subject to reasonable rate charges for services approved by the State Cemetery Board, regardless of a previous agreement between the religious corporation and the cemetery corporation on what charges for services could be made by the latter against the former, particularly where the earlier agreement had no specified period of duration. Jewish Center of Mt. Vernon, Inc. v Mt. Eden Cemetery Asso. (1961, 2d Dept) 15 A.D.2d 94, 222 N.Y.S.2d 644, mod (1962) 12 N.Y.2d 773, 234 N.Y.S.2d 720, 186 N.E.2d 567

55. – Rules and regulations
Rules adopted pursuant to this section, with penalties attached for their violation, do not apply to a person not a member nor the owner of a lot, who works in the cemetery under the direction of certain lot owners. Johnstown Cemetery Ass'n v Parker (1899) 45 A.D. 55, 60 N.Y.S. 1015

Rules filed by a cemetery corporation do not become rules of the Cemetery Board upon approval by that Board, and accordingly need not be filed with the Department of State. 1962 Ops Atty Gen July 16

56. – – Amendment or change
After a cemetery has filed rules with the State Cemetery Board, which have been approved by the Board, the cemetery cannot amend or change such rules without approval of the Board. Cemetery Board v Evergreens Cemetery (1962, 1st Dept) 16 A.D.2d 60, 225 N.Y.S.2d 104

57. – – Restrictions on interment
An injunction would not issue against closing of respondent's cemetery grounds for interment on Saturdays, at the instance of the State Cemetery Board, where the rules and regulations of that board asserted to have been violated by the burial restrictions imposed by the respondent cemeteries did not explicitly command that such cemeteries be open on Saturdays for interments. Cemetery Board of State v Evergreens Cemetery (1962) 33 Misc. 2d 60, 224 N.Y.S.2d 636, affd (1962, 1st Dept) 16 A.D.2d 60, 225 N.Y.S.2d 104

Interments may be restricted to persons of a particular religious faith. People ex rel. Coppers v Trustees of St. Patrick's Cathedral (1880, NY) 21 Hun 184

58. – – Monument quality standards
Whether a cemetery regulation fixing a standard of quality for monuments is or is not reasonable is a question of fact for the determination of the Cemetery Board. 1966 Ops Atty Gen Jan 10

59. – Regulation of charges; by secretary of state
This section gives the Secretary of State ample power to regulate cemetery charges in order to promote the public welfare, and, where such determinations are not arbitrary, capricious, unreasonable or illegal, they must be upheld. Silver Mt. Cemetery Asso. v Simon (1962) 36 Misc. 2d 792, 231 N.Y.S.2d 909, revd on other grounds (1963, 1st Dept) 18 A.D.2d 801, 237 N.Y.S.2d 507

60. – – Determination of reasonableness
The State Cemetery Board acted in disregard of the mandate to consider fair and reasonable cost and expense of rendering services and performing work in connection with which a cemetery corporation sought leave to increase its charges to lot owners, where the board merely took into consideration the report of its senior accountant, who admittedly had not gone into the cost and expense aspects of the particular services but only the overall needs of the cemetery. Pinelawn Cemetery v Simon (1961) 30 Misc. 2d 654, 220 N.Y.S.2d

198, app dismd (1962, 1st Dept) 16 A.D.2d 765, 228 N.Y.S.2d 460, app gr (1962) 12 N.Y.2d 644 and app dismd (1963) 12 N.Y.2d 1103, 240 N.Y.S.2d 167, 190 N.E.2d 538

In determining whether a schedule of charges for which a cemetery corporation seeks approval from the State Cemetery Board is fair and reasonable, the State Board can take into consideration proceeds from land sales only to the extent that the petitioner receives such proceeds in its own right, excluding amounts required to be deposited in the permanent and current maintenance funds. Pinelawn Cemetery v Simon (1961) 30 Misc. 2d 654, 220 N.Y.S.2d 198, app dismd (1962, 1st Dept) 16 A.D.2d 765, 228 N.Y.S.2d 460, app gr (1962) 12 N.Y.2d 644 and app dismd (1963) 12 N.Y.2d 1103, 240 N.Y.S.2d 167, 190 N.E.2d 538

61. – – Price of plaques

The State Cemetery Board has power to control the price of plaques sold by a cemetery corporation to lot owners, where they are not sold as merchandise, but as incidental to service of providing and installing memorials. Pinelawn Cemetery v Simon (1961) 30 Misc. 2d 654, 220 N.Y.S.2d 198, app dismd (1962, 1st Dept) 16 A.D.2d 765, 228 N.Y.S.2d 460, app gr (1962) 12 N.Y.2d 644 and app dismd (1963) 12 N.Y.2d 1103, 240 N.Y.S.2d 167, 190 N.E.2d 538

62. – – Charges for services of outside commercial gardeners

Although this section authorizes the directors of a cemetery corporation to fix and make reasonable "charges," it does not authorize the imposition of a charge by such corporations for services performed by outside commercial gardeners who were retained by certain lot owners to service cemetery plots in the corporation's cemetery. Wunderlin v Lutheran Cemetery (1967, 2d Dept) 27 A.D.2d 861, 278 N.Y.S.2d 544

If a cemetery corporation wishes to raise funds for improving the cemetery and for perpetual care and maintenance of lots and graves, it should establish a maintenance fund under § 86-a and may further resort to taxing lot owners under § 90, and it has no authority to proceed indirectly to create such a fund by imposing a fixed charge on commercial gardeners caring for graves and lots under contract with the owners. May v Washington Cemetery (1961) 29 Misc. 2d 1046, 217 N.Y.S.2d 897, affd (1962, 2d Dept) 16 A.D.2d 931, 230 N.Y.S.2d 671

The power vested by this section in a cemetery corporation to promulgate reasonable rules and regulations for care, management and protection of the property and the various lots and plots does not include power to assess a charge upon outside gardeners of two dollars per grave per annum for the purpose of operating commercially under contracts with individual plot owners to care for and maintain their graves and plots. May v Washington Cemetery (1961) 29 Misc. 2d 1046, 217 N.Y.S.2d 897, affd (1962, 2d Dept) 16 A.D.2d 931, 230 N.Y.S.2d 671

63. Under former Membership Corporations Law § 84

This section merely imposes a limitation on the power of a cemetery corporation organized under the membership corporation law to convey away its property, and is in no sense to be considered a grant of power previously not enjoyed by such a corporation. Application of Kensico Cemetery (1948) 193 Misc 479, 83 N.Y.S.2d 73, revd on other grounds (1949) 275 A.D. 681, 86 N.Y.S.2d 737, affd (1949) 299 N.Y. 752, 87 N.E.2d 670

The sale of unused and undeveloped cemetery land from one cemetery corporation to another is not prohibited by this section. Application of Kensico Cemetery (1948) 193 Misc 479, 83 N.Y.S.2d 73, revd on other grounds (1949) 275 A.D. 681, 86 N.Y.S.2d 737, affd (1949) 299 N.Y. 752, 87 N.E.2d 670

64. – Agreement for purchase of lot

An oral agreement made at the time of the purchase of an 8-grave burial lot which required the defendants, who were co-owners with plaintiff of the lot, to designate two graves for the interment of the plaintiff and his family was not an assignment or surrender of an easement and was not within the statute of frauds. Hampar v Hampar (1955) 285 A.D. 1053, 139 N.Y.S.2d 478

An agreement for the purchase of a lot must be in writing. In re O'Rourke (1895, Sur) 12 Misc 248, 1 Gibbons 270, 34 N.Y.S. 45

65. – – Necessity of deed

The execution of a deed is not essential. Conger v Treadway (1888) 50 Hun 451, 3 N.Y.S. 152, affd (1892) 132 N.Y. 259, 30 N.E. 505

66. – Rights acquired by purchase of lot

Cemetery lots, after a burial therein, are inalienable, but, if no burial has been made, the lot may be sold by the owner with the consent of the cemetery corporation. Daniell v Hopkins (1931) 257 N.Y. 112, 177 N.E. 390, 76 ALR 1367

While the purchaser of a cemetery lot does not acquire a title thereto in fee simple, he becomes possessed with a property right therein which the law protects from invasion; he has an easement for burial purposes therein, in accordance with the usual custom prevailing in the locality which carries with it the right to erect tombstones and monuments and to protect them from injury or spoliation. Oatka Cemetery Ass'n v Cazeau (1934) 242 A.D. 415, 275 N.Y.S. 355

The purchaser of a burial plot does not acquire a title in fee simple but ordinarily is regarded as acquiring only an easement or license to make interments in the lot purchased so long as it remains a cemetery. Sockel v Degel Yehudo Cemetery Corp. (1944) 268 A.D. 207, 49 N.Y.S.2d 176

It seems, that an agreement by a decedent for a conveyance of the right of interment would be inhibited by this section. In re Marshall's Estate (1933) 146 Misc 601, 262 N.Y.S. 528, affd (1933) 239 A.D. 768, 263 N.Y.S. 936

A wife, who held a burial lot as a tenant in common with her husband, could not convey the lot, after her husband's burial therein, to persons not related to her. In re Appelbaum's Ex'rs (1933) 146 Misc 603, 262 N.Y.S. 503

The purchaser of a cemetery plot acquires no title to the soil but merely an easement or right of burial, and in so far as this has not been exhausted by the purchaser himself, it descends pursuant to Rel. In re Rosen (1940) 173 Misc 433, 17 N.Y.S.2d 794

The title or right which a lot owner obtains by his purchase from a cemetery association is an incorporeal hereditament rather than the land itself. Mt. Hope Cemetery Ass'n v Department of State (1943) 182 Misc 599, 45 N.Y.S.2d 249

Purported conveyances by proprietor of burial lot in municipal cemetery of individual graves are ineffective to convey rights. 1954 Ops St Compt File #6685

67. – – On purchase by decedent's estate

Where decedent's distributees were his widow and sister, and his estate was less than $10,000, the widow was entitled to the whole. The payment by the estate to decedent's brother-in-law for decedent's grave did not entitle decedent's sister to be registered as a distributee on the cemetery receipt. In re Kandolian's Estate (1956) 3 Misc. 2d 711, 157 N.Y.S.2d 121

If the claim of a funeral director for money paid by him to a cemetery for a new grave for the decedent was paid by the executor to the funeral director out of funds in the executor's hands, it would be in effect a purchase of a burial lot, and this section would become applicable. The widow, although she would have a statutory right of interment in the grave, took no interest in the burial lot as a residuary legatee or devisee under the decedent's will. In re McDonald's Estate (1955, Sur) 139 N.Y.S.2d 386

68. – – Right to erect and protect monument

The common-law rule is that, if a tombstone at the grave of a deceased person has been defaced or removed, he who originally erected it has a cause of action against the guilty party for the resulting injury, and after his death the right to maintain such an action passes to the heirs at law of him in whose honor and memory the monument was erected. Oatka Cemetery Ass'n v Cazeau (1934) 242 A.D. 415, 275 N.Y.S. 355

The children of a co-owner of a cemetery lot were entitled to have names of third parties removed from a monument, which was erected on the lot pursuant to the will of one of the co-owners of the lot, where the will expressly provided that the monument was to bear only the family name of the co-owners of the lot. Fromer v Shientag (1959) 16 Misc. 2d 953, 189 N.Y.S.2d 937

69. – – Injunction against interference with rights

An injunction may be procured by one of several owners in common of the right to maintain a cemetery lot and of the right of way thereto, to restrain interference with such rights, without joining with the other owners. Mitchell v Thorne (1892) 134 N.Y. 536, 32 N.E. 10

A contractor is entitled to an injunction restraining a cemetery corporation from interference with the erection of a mausoleum where the structure when completed will not be unsightly, and is erected pursuant to contract with the owner of the lot, and the objections of the cemetery corporation appear to be totally unreasonable. Tonella v Fishkill Rural Cemetery (1929) 135 Misc 81, 236 N.Y.S. 663, affd (1930) 229 A.D. 732, 241 N.Y.S. 851, affd (1931) 255 N.Y. 617, 175 N.E. 338

70. – Succession to rights of owner

In the absence of a specific devise of a cemetery plot by the owner, the ownership of the plot would descend to the son, the father's only child, and in the absence of an objection filed by the father during his lifetime, the son would have had a right to burial in the plot during his father's lifetime. Saulia v Saulia (1969) 25 N.Y.2d 80, 302 N.Y.S.2d 775, 250 N.E.2d 197, reh den (1969) 25 N.Y.2d 959

Heirs and devisees of the original owners of lots in a cemetery association succeed to the rights of their ancestors and devisors. In re Fentonville Cemetery Ass'n (1933) 238 A.D. 491, 264 N.Y.S. 790

Cemetery plots may be specifically devised. Saulia v Saulia (1968, 2d Dept) 31 A.D.2d 640, 295 N.Y.S.2d 980, mod on other grounds (1969) 25 N.Y.2d 80, 302 N.Y.S.2d 775, 250 N.E.2d 197, reh den (1969) 25 N.Y.2d 959

An administratrix, as such, possesses no rights with respect to a decedent's burial plot. In re Rosen (1940) 173 Misc 433, 17 N.Y.S.2d 794

Testator's interest in a mausoleum passed to his widow where his will made no reference thereto, and his adopted stepson as his sole surviving descendant had agreed not to participate in testator's estate. In re Estate of Paschkes (1956) 2 Misc. 2d 677, 151 N.Y.S.2d 303, affd (1956, 1st Dept) 2 A.D.2d 877, 156 N.Y.S.2d 1002

Upon the death of the surviving spouse who had jointly owned with her predeceased husband a 20-grave burial plot in which there were no interments, the burial rights to the cemetery plot passed to her heirs at law and the administratrices of the estate had no rights with respect to the disposition of this ground. In re Turkish's Estate (1965) 48 Misc. 2d 600, 265 N.Y.S.2d 888

71. – Right to burial in lot

Son of deceased cemetery plot owner would have had a right to be buried in the father's plot had he predeceased his father, or had its ownership passed by intestacy. Saulia v Saulia (1969) 25 N.Y.2d 80, 302 N.Y.S.2d 775, 250 N.E.2d 197, reh den (1969) 25 N.Y.2d 959

The next of kin of the original purchaser of a cemetery plot are entitled to its use. O'Shaughnessy v John J. Barrett, Inc. (1946) 186 Misc 1040, 66 N.Y.S.2d 4

Although the owner of a burial lot is entitled to designate, in his will, who shall be buried in the lot, a devise of all his estate to his wife does not authorize her to designate who shall be buried in the lot for lack of mention of the burial lot in the will. If, however, the husband declared in his lifetime that she was entitled to be buried in the lot, she, herself, would have the right to be buried there. Hammerstein v Woodlawn Cemetery (1960) 21 Misc. 2d 42, 194 N.Y.S.2d 385

72. – – Surviving spouse

A widow does not forfeit her right to interment in a cemetery lot owned by her husband under subd. 7 of this section because she has been separated from him for about one year prior to his death, and an expression of desire in her will that she be buried in the husband's cemetery lot should predominate as against a proceeding by a child by a former marriage of the deceased husband to require disinterment of her remains. Froehlich v Woodlawn Cemetery (1962) 37 Misc. 2d 1025, 236 N.Y.S.2d 693

Subdivision 7 of this section confers on the owner of a cemetery lot only the power to control the number of persons he wishes to be interred in the lot, and only when each grave in the lot is used to full capacity can his widow be excluded from burial therein. Froehlich v Woodlawn Cemetery (1962) 37 Misc. 2d 1025, 236 N.Y.S.2d 693

A surviving wife of the deceased owner of a cemetery lot, though she is his second wife, has the right to be interred in that lot provided all burial space has not been designated by him for interment of others in manner and form as provided in subd 9 of this section. Froehlich v Woodlawn Cemetery (1962) 37 Misc. 2d 1025, 236 N.Y.S.2d 693

A surviving spouse's right to be interred in a grave in a cemetery plot owned by her husband at the time of his death accrued at such time, and the fact that she remarried and was widowed for a second time is of no consequence in determining her status on the date of the death of her first husband. Honig v Elmont Cemetery, Inc. (1966) 49 Misc. 2d 1069, 269 N.Y.S.2d 336

73. – – Designee of owner

The only meaning that can be attributed to subd 9 of this section, dealing with designations by the owner of a cemetery lot of who shall be entitled to burial therein, is that such designation must be made by instrument executed, acknowledged and filed by the lot owner during his lifetime, or by will. Froehlich v Woodlawn Cemetery (1962) 37 Misc. 2d 1025, 236 N.Y.S.2d 693

Expressions of desire by the owner of a cemetery lot that not more than one person be placed in each of the first five graves cannot supersede the right of his widow to be buried wherever space is available in the lot. Froehlich v Woodlawn Cemetery (1962) 37 Misc. 2d 1025, 236 N.Y.S.2d 693

There is no designation of who shall be buried in a cemetery lot by the owner of such lot such as to defeat the right of his surviving spouse to interment therein where the lot owner, though he had drawn up a plan of the lots and indicated thereon who should be buried in the various grave sites, had failed to acknowledge the document or have it filed in his lifetime. Froehlich v Woodlawn Cemetery (1962) 37 Misc. 2d 1025, 236 N.Y.S.2d 693

74. Under former Membership Corporations Law § 85

A cemetery lot in which there have been no burials is subject to sale by the executors of the lot owner for the purpose of paying his debts. Daniell v Hopkins (1931) 257 N.Y. 112, 177 N.E. 390, 76 ALR 1367

Executors may sell a burial lot selected by the testator before a burial thereon, and buy one more in keeping with the financial condition of the estate. Daniell v Hopkins (1931) 257 N.Y. 112, 177 N.E. 390, 76 ALR 1367

This section, as enacted by ch 533 of the Laws of 1949, was intended to put an end to the shocking abuses perpetrated by bulk sales of cemetery plots to favored individuals for re-sale at pressure prices and to place cemeteries upon a non-profit basis, including parcels already sold, at time of its enactment, with right of re-sale. Diamant v Mt. Pleasant Westchester Cemetery Corp. (1960, 2d Dept) 10 A.D.2d 404, 201 N.Y.S.2d 861, reh den (1960, 2d Dept) 11 A.D.2d 702, 205 N.Y.S.2d 861

Since ch 533 of the Laws of 1949 was designed to put a stop to the abuses mentioned in its introductory provisions, it is clear that restrictions in re-sale of burial rights in cemetery plots, enacted by that law, apply to all burial rights in cemetery lands, whenever acquired. Diamant v Mt. Pleasant Westchester Cemetery Corp. (1960, 2d Dept) 10 A.D.2d 404, 201 N.Y.S.2d 861, reh den (1960, 2d Dept) 11 A.D.2d 702, 205 N.Y.S.2d 861

With the exception of religious or membership corporations, or unincorporated associations or societies which provide burial benefits for their members, under this section as it now stands only the cemetery corporation has the unrestricted power to sell burial lots. Diamant v Mt. Pleasant Westchester Cemetery Corp. (1960, 2d Dept) 10 A.D.2d 404, 201 N.Y.S.2d 861, reh den (1960, 2d Dept) 11 A.D.2d 702, 205 N.Y.S.2d 861

The purpose of former § 69 from which this section is derived was to prevent the replatting or changing of the map of the property of the cemetery association, and there was no intent to convey a cemetery lot to be used for speculation by the purchaser through division and which would be sold in competition with the association. Du Bois v Fantinekill Cemetery Ass'n (1921) 118 Misc 37, 192 N.Y.S. 145

A wife, who had a burial lot as a tenant in common with her husband, could not convey the lot after her husband's burial therein to persons not related to her. In re Appelbaum's Ex'rs (1933) 146 Misc 603, 262 N.Y.S. 503

75. Under former Membership Corporations Law § 86

A provision of former § 69-a, from which this section is derived, giving the owners or proprietors of a lot held in inalienable form the right to revoke the designation of persons in whose favor interments had been restricted applied not to inalienable lots as referred to in present § 85 but rather to lots "held in the inalienable form," that is, lots so conveyed that upon each conveyance thereof, or after there shall have been an interment therein, such lots are to be forever thereafter inalienable. Hegeman v Woodlawn Cemetery (1927) 219 A.D. 573, 220 N.Y.S. 379

Under former § 69-a from which this section is derived, where one made a declaration in writing and under seal declaring that the remains of certain named persons be interred in a mausoleum erected upon his cemetery lot, and provided further that the instrument was to bind the maker and his heirs, the instrument was more than a designation or revocable license, and could not be revoked by an heir of the maker, even assuming that former § 69-a applied to inalienable lots. Hegeman v Woodlawn Cemetery (1927) 219 A.D. 573, 220 N.Y.S. 379

76. Under former Membership Corporations Law § 86-a

Subdivision 2 of § 87 and § 86-a, requiring cemetery corporations to set up maintenance funds from proceeds of sale of each lot, properly declared to be valid and constitutional. Grove Hill Realty Co. v Ferncliff Cemetery Asso. (1958, 2d Dept) 7 A.D.2d 736, 180 N.Y.S.2d 767, affd (1960) 7 N.Y.2d 403, 198 N.Y.S.2d 287, 165 N.E.2d 858

Since a seller of burial rights is required by § 85 of this act to offer the property to the Cemetery Corporation at the price paid, plus interest at 2% per annum, before he can re-sell to another, this section cannot be considered as requiring him to pay to the Cemetery Corporation 25% of the sale proceeds where the corporation takes up the offer. Diamant v Mt. Pleasant Westchester Cemetery Corp. (1960, 2d Dept) 10 A.D.2d 404, 201 N.Y.S.2d 861, reh den (1960, 2d Dept) 11 A.D.2d 702, 205 N.Y.S.2d 861

With respect to valuing the portion of cemetery property expropriated, since a cemetery corporation, under this section, is under a statutory duty to make certain dispositions of the gross proceeds of sale of every cemetery lot by depositing not less than 10% in a permanent maintenance fund and an additional 15% in a current maintenance fund, and the current maintenance fund is to be transferred into the permanent fund when all burial rights have been conveyed, both the required 10% and the required 15% deductions are to be taken into consideration in valuing the property taken. Mt. Hope Cemetery Asso. v State (1960, 3d Dept) 11 A.D.2d 303, 203 N.Y.S.2d 415, adhered to (1960, 3d Dept) 12 A.D.2d 705, 208 N.Y.S.2d 737, affd (1961) 10 N.Y.2d 752, 219 N.Y.S.2d 606, 177 N.E.2d 49

Where a cemetery association's land, which had been purchased under an agreement that the vendors were to receive one-half of the proceeds of the sale of lots, was condemned after 1949, the vendors were entitled to one-half of the condemnation award remaining after the deduction of sales expenses and 10% for a permanent maintenance fund and 15% for a current maintenance fund. Keith v Maple Grove Cemetery Asso. (1955) 208 Misc 217, 145 N.Y.S.2d 198, app dismd (1955, 1st Dept) 1 A.D.2d 665, 149 N.Y.S.2d 702

Membership Corporation Law §§ 86-a and 87 do not impair a cemetery corporation's obligation under a contract whereby, in consideration of land conveyed to it, it agreed to pay the vendor one-half the proceeds of the sale of each plot. Grove Hill Realty Co. v Ferncliff Cemetery Asso. (1957) 9 Misc. 2d 47, 167 N.Y.S.2d 675, affd (1958, 2d Dept) 7 A.D.2d 736, 180 N.Y.S.2d 767, affd (1960) 7 N.Y.2d 403, 198 N.Y.S.2d 287, 165 N.E.2d 858

A cemetery corporation, desiring to establish permanent and current maintenance funds, should do so under this section, and possibly by taxing lot owners as provided in § 90, and has no authority to raise the money by imposing a charge of so much per grave per annum on commercial gardeners caring for graves and plots under contracts with the owners. May v Washington Cemetery (1961) 29 Misc. 2d 1046, 217 N.Y.S.2d 897, affd (1962, 2d Dept) 16 A.D.2d 931, 230 N.Y.S.2d 671

In view of the specifically stated powers of cemetery corporations concerning the investment of trust funds, the 1950 amendment, which liberally enlarges the investment powers of fiduciaries generally, has no application to such corporations. 1950 Ops Atty Gen July 10

77. Under former Membership Corporations Law § 90

A cemetery corporation which contracted with its vendors pursuant to § 87 of the Membership Corporations Law to sell its cemetery property to lot owners entitled to vote at its meetings and subject to the right to assess them for funds for maintenance, is not authorized to convey land in which there have been no burials to another cemetery corporation, since the latter as a corporate body could not be a member of the former corporation and would not be subject to assessment. Application of Kensico Cemetery (1949) 275 A.D. 681, 86 N.Y.S.2d 737, affd (1949) 299 N.Y. 752, 87 N.E.2d 670

Where it was virtually undisputed that the funds of the Cemetery were wholly inadequate to properly service and maintain the grounds, a tax for the benefit of all plot owners so designed as to compel every plot owner to pay his fair proportionate share is legally valid, but the exaction of $50 annual fee from each outside gardener as a supervision fee was not valid. Wunderlin v Lutheran Cemetery (1967, 2d Dept) 27 A.D.2d 861, 278 N.Y.S.2d 544

78. Under former Membership Corporations Law § 91

The trial term properly dismissed a complaint on the merits where the plaintiff sought to revoke the transfer of a fund to the defendant cemetery under a written "form for perpetual care" of a lot which provided for the investment and application of income to maintenance, repair and care; an agreement of trust for such a purpose is valid and enforceable. French v Kensico Cemetery (1943) 291 N.Y. 77, 50 N.E.2d 551

It is the public policy of the state that cemeteries and structures thereon shall be kept in proper condition and appearance. French v Kensico Cemetery (1942) 264 A.D. 617, 35 N.Y.S.2d 826, affd (1943) 291 N.Y. 77, 50 N.E.2d 551

Disposition by testatrix of her entire residuary estate for the purchase of a cemetery plot, the erection of a mausoleum, and its perpetual care, is sufficiently explicit as to the use of the entire residuary estate as to be valid, and no trust was created except one for perpetual care. In re Baeuchle's Will (1950) 276 A.D. 925, 94 N.Y.S.2d 582, affd (1950) 301 N.Y. 582, 93 N.E.2d 491

Where it appears that the administration of a cemetery trust under a will is impractical and that the corpus thereof is insufficient for full accomplishment of the expressed purposes, upon renunciation of such trusteeship by the trustee, the executors are authorized to enter into a suitable agreement for perpetual care with a cemetery, subject to the approval of the surrogate pursuant to the provisions of this section. In re Allen's Estate (1943, Sur) 45 N.Y.S.2d 699

A perpetual improvement fund may not attach to its acceptance of a bequest a condition which would constitute a deviation from the provisions of the will or of the statute. In re Ross' Estate (1948, Sur) 81 N.Y.S.2d 662

The perpetual care of burial lots is part of the reasonable funeral expenses of the decedent within the meaning of § 216 of the Surrogate's Court Act which directs that such expenses be paid from the first moneys received and be preferred to all debts and claims against the deceased. In re Ross' Estate (1948, Sur) 81 N.Y.S.2d 662

A reasonable expenditure by the executors for renovation and repairs of a testator's plot and mausoleum to place them in condition and for their future maintenance and perpetual care is within the authority granted by § 314, subd 3 of the Surrogate's Court Act. In re Ross' Estate (1948, Sur) 81 N.Y.S.2d 662

79. Under former Membership Corporations Law § 92

This section expressly prohibits different use of any part of the principal recieved by a cemetery association for perpetual care, and a court is powerless to require trustees of a cemetery association and the executors of the estate of a decedent to enter into any agreement to the contrary, even though authorized by will of a decedent. In re Estate of Cohen (1961) 30 Misc. 2d 122, 214 N.Y.S.2d 955

In view of the specifically stated powers of cemetery corporations concerning the investment of trust funds, the 1950 amendment, which liberally enlarges the investment powers of fiduciaries generally, has no application to such corporations. 1950 Ops Atty Gen July 10

A village board of cemetery commissioners and the county treasurer may accept and administer perpetual care funds for cemetery purposes. 1947 Ops St Compt 395

Villages are governed by those provisions of the Membership Corporation Law which pertain to cemetery corporations only in the matter of perpetual care funds. 1961 Ops St Compt #719

Assets of a cemetery corporation which have been conveyed to a town and are held as perpetual care funds may not be used by the town for acquisition of additional land for the cemetery. 1963 Ops St Compt #281

80. Under former Membership Corporations Law § 95

The prohibitions of this section are against public authorities proposing to lay out roads and not against cemetery associations, for whose benefit the statute was enacted. Thus, this section did not prohibit a cemetery from condemning land separated from the existing cemetery by a public highway. Westerlo Rural Cemetery Asso. v Hotaling (1957, 3d Dept) 3 A.D.2d 884, 161 N.Y.S.2d 925

In this action for an injunction against construction of a public highway through the lands of a cemetery association devoted to cemetery purposes, alleged to be contrary to this section, the appearance by the cemetery association in proceedings to condemn the right-of-way through the cemetery without raising any objection or interposing any answer constitutes a waiver of the right to an injunction. Catskill Rural Cemetery Ass'n v Greene (1935) 155 Misc 492, 280 N.Y.S. 598

A complaint by a rural cemetery corporation against the state for wrongful taking of cemetery property for highway purposes was sufficient to state a cause of action where it alleged that all acts of the county and state in taking over part of the cemetery land and using it for highway purposes were "in contravention" of this section and without complying with its requirements. Nyack Rural Cemetery, Inc. v State (1962) 32 Misc. 2d 828, 225 N.Y.S.2d 815

A rural cemetery corporation may waive the protective provisions of the above statute not only by an appearance and subsequent neglect to raise a failure of conditions precedent but also by a failure to appear at all until some 28 years have passed. Nyack Rural Cemetery, Inc. v State (1965) 46 Misc. 2d 1025, 261 N.Y.S.2d 797, affd (1967, 3d Dept) 27 A.D.2d 762, 277 N.Y.S.2d 53

81. Under former Membership Corporations Law § 97

The statute of limitations runs against certificates from the time a sufficient sum is collected from the sale of lots to pay them. Thacher v Hope Cemetery Ass'n (1891) 126 N.Y. 507, 27 N.E. 1040

A certificate of indebtedness cannot create an obligation for the payment of money by the cemetery corporation at a definite date, upon which an action at law can be maintained and execution issued. Sullivan v Mt. Carmel Cemetery Ass'n (1927) 244 N.Y. 294, 155 N.E. 580

An action at law upon a certificate of indebtedness may not be maintained; the remedy of the holder of such a certificate is an action in equity for an accounting. Sullivan v Mt. Carmel Cemetery Ass'n (1927) 244 N.Y. 294, 155 N.E. 580

Purchase money certificates issued for the purchase of land by a cemetery corporation which provided for a fund of 70 per cent of the gross proceeds of the sale of the land and application of five-sevenths of the fund to the payment of the certificates and two-sevenths to the payment of a mortgage, are not certificates of indebtedness so as to fall within this section as they were not issued as the result of the funding of a debt and also the certificates had no maturity date as would be required if they were certificates of indebtedness. Jackson v Elmont Cemetery, Inc. (1949) 275 A.D. 544, 90 N.Y.S.2d 521, affd (1949) 300 N.Y. 526, 89 N.E.2d 250

Nothing prevents a vendor of real property to a cemetery corporation from giving part or all of the certificates, issued to him in exchange for the real property, to any one he wishes or from agreeing in advance to do so; and therefore, the agreement of vendors to give a mortgagee of property one-half of the certificates of indebtedness issued to them in order that the mortgagee should refrain from foreclosing his mortgages and should release from the lien of his mortgages the cemetery lots as they were sold, is valid. United Disner Benevolent Ass'n v Springfield, L. I. Cemetery Soc. (1939) 171 Misc 498, 13 N.Y.S.2d 45

In an action by a corporate purchaser of cemetery lots on behalf of all other lot holders similarly situated, the members of which corporate purchaser are lot and certificate holders, to cancel the remaining unpaid certificates issued by the cemetery corporation pursuant to this section in payment of real estate purchased by it and to recover back from the certificate holders the sums which had been paid to them on their certificates on the ground that the certificates are illegal and void, as fraudulently issued, judgment must be granted in favor of the defendants where the plaintiff fails to show that it or any other lot owner has suffered damage. United Disner Benevolent Ass'n v Springfield, L. I. Cemetery Soc. (1939) 171 Misc 498, 13 N.Y.S.2d 45

A petition, under this section, for a grant of authority to a cemetery association to issue certificates of indebtedness to persons furnishing the purchase price for land which it desires to purchase is premature where it does not appear that the corporation has yet become indebted for the lands in question or that the State Cemetery Board has approved the purchase price. Application of Jordan Cemetery Asso. (1962) 33 Misc. 2d 274, 225 N.Y.S.2d 303, revd on other grounds (1963, 2d Dept) 19 A.D.2d 540, 240 N.Y.S.2d 944

The issuance of certificates to pay all corporate liabilities made without fraud or dishonesty was valid even though the requirements of this section were not complied with. People v Hults (1950, Sup) 103 N.Y.S.2d 546

82. Under former Membership Corporations Law § 106

The proper procedure to be followed where a particular cemetery wishes to adopt a rule against Saturday interments, or the like, is to file the rule with the State Cemetery Board, and, if the Board refuses to approve the rule, and its conclusion is considered arbitrary or capricious, seek review of the adverse determination by a proceeding under art. 78 of the Civil Practice Act. Cemetery Board v Evergreens Cemetery (1962, 1st Dept) 16 A.D.2d 60, 225 N.Y.S.2d 104

If the State Cemetery Board arbitrarily refuses to authorize issuance of certificates of indebtedness to finance purchase of additional land by a cemetery corporation, its determination is subject to review by the Supreme Court in an art. Application of Jordan Cemetery Asso. (1962) 33 Misc. 2d 274, 225 N.Y.S.2d 303, revd on other grounds (1963, 2d Dept) 19 A.D.2d 540, 240 N.Y.S.2d 944

83. Under former Membership Corporations Law § 108

Proper exercise of judicial power required denial for a petition by the State Cemetery Board to enjoin certain cemeteries from closing their grounds to Saturday interments without prior consent or approval of the Board. Cemetery Board v Evergreens Cemetery (1962, 1st Dept) 16 A.D.2d 60, 225 N.Y.S.2d 104

When the State Cemetery Board approved certain rules filed by certain cemeteries with respect to days and hours on which interments could be made, such rules could not thereafter be changed without approval of the Board. Cemetery Board v Evergreens Cemetery (1962, 1st Dept) 16 A.D.2d 60, 225 N.Y.S.2d 104

To the extent that a cemetery board order conditioned board approval of service charge increases upon the association's compliance with other particular directions designed to improve the association's financial condition, imposition of the conditions was not justified. Silver Mt. Cemetery Asso. v Simon (1963, 1st Dept) 18 A.D.2d 801, 237 N.Y.S.2d 507

Whether a cemetery regulation fixing a standard of quality for monuments is or is not reasonable is a question of fact for the determination of the Cemetery Board. 1966 Ops Atty Gen Jan 10

84. Under former Membership Corporations Law § 108-a

In view of the provisions of this section, the State Cemetery Board was acting in conformity with its authority in seeking to intervene in an action brought by two cemetery lot owners against a named cemetery to require defendant to permit plaintiffs to maintain and care for their own lots without paying the service charges prescribed by the State Cemetery Board, challenging the validity of such charges, and the State Board was granted leave to intervene. May v Washington Cemetery (1961, Sup) 212 N.Y.S.2d 679

§ 1402.   Fire corporations

(a) Certificate of incorporation; additional contents.

In addition to the requirements of section 402 (Certificate of incorporation; contents), the certificate of incorporation of a fire corporation shall state the precise boundaries of the territory in which the corporation intends to operate.

(b) Type of corporation.

A fire corporation is a charitable corporation under this chapter.

(c) Appointment of firefighters.

(1) A person shall not be eligible to be named in the certificate of incorporation of a fire corporation unless he shall be at least eighteen years of age and a resident of a city, village, fire district, or town outside of villages and fire districts, where the fire corporation intends to operate.

(2) If the fire corporation becomes part of the fire department of a city, village or fire district, a person shall not be eligible to be elected as a member or to continue as a member except as provided by law for volunteer members of the fire companies in such city, village or fire district.

(3) In towns outside of villages and fire districts, the consent of a majority of the members of the town board to the formation of a fire corporation shall constitute an appointment of the persons named in the certificate of incorporation as town firefighters. Thereafter, other eligible persons may be elected as members pursuant to the by-laws of the fire corpora-

tion, but the election of a member must be approved by the town board of each town which consented to the formation of the fire corporation. Such a person shall be a resident of the territory specified in the certificate of incorporation or of territory outside such boundaries which is afforded fire protection by the fire corporation pursuant to a contract for fire protection under which a cash consideration is received by the corporation or for which negotiations for renewal of such a contract are pending. The membership of any volunteer member shall terminate when he or she ceases to be a resident of such inside or outside territory, except that the corporation may authorize his or her continued membership where he or she notifies the secretary of the fire corporation (a) that he or she plans to change his or her residence to a territory which is not in such inside or outside territory, and (b) that by reason of his or her residence in the vicinity or his or her usual occupation he or she will be available to render active service as a volunteer firefighter in either such inside or such outside territory. Voting for such authorization shall be pursuant to the by-laws. Such authorization shall not become effective unless approved by resolution of the town board of each town which consented to the formation of the corporation. Any membership so continued shall terminate when the member can no longer meet the requirements of this subparagraph. A person who cannot meet the residence requirements of this subparagraph may be elected to membership as a volunteer member if by reason of his or her residence in the vicinity or his or her usual occupation he or she will be available to render active service as a volunteer firefighter in such inside or outside territory. Voting for such election shall be pursuant to the by-laws. Such election shall not become effective unless approved by resolution of the town board of each town which consented to the formation of the corporation. Such membership shall terminate when the member can no longer meet the requirements of this subparagraph. The election or continuance of any person as a member shall be deemed to have been approved by the town board pursuant to this subparagraph in the event that no action is taken by the town board, either approving or disapproving, within forty days in the case of residents of the territory specified in the certificate of incorporation or of outside contract territory, and within seventy days in the case of all others, after service of written notice of such election or continuance of membership shall have been made by the secretary of the corporation upon the town clerk, either personally or by mail. The membership of any volunteer firefighter shall not be continued pursuant to this subparagraph, and persons who do not reside in the territory specified in the certificate of incorporation or in territory protected pursuant to a contract for fire protection shall not be elected to membership, if, by so doing, the percentage of such nonresident members in the fire corporation would exceed forty-

five per centum of the actual membership thereof, provided, however, that the forty-five percent limit on non-resident members shall not apply to the membership of the Huguenot Fire Company, Inc., within the town of Deerpark, Orange county, to the membership of the Prospect Terrace Fire Company, Inc., within the town of Dickinson, Broome county, to membership of the Hopewell Volunteer Fire Department, Inc., to membership of the Wales Center Volunteer Fire Company, Inc., within the town of Wales, Erie county, to the membership of the Nedrow Fire Department, within the town of Onondaga, Onondaga county, to the membership of the Pleasant Square Fire Company, Inc. within the town of Johnstown, Fulton county, or to membership of the fire departments within the town of Fleming, Cayuga county. Nonresidents of the territory specified in the certificate of incorporation whose volunteer membership has been authorized or continued pursuant to this subparagraph may be elected or appointed to any office in the fire corporation and shall have all the powers, duties, immunities, and privileges of resident volunteer members except a non-resident of this state whose membership has been continued pursuant to this subparagraph, or who was elected to membership pursuant to this subparagraph, shall not be considered to be performing any firefighting duty, or to be engaged in any firefighting activity, as a member of the fire company while he or she is outside of this state unless and until he or she has first reported to the officer or firefighter in command of his or her fire department, or any company, squad or other unit thereof, engaged or to be engaged in rendering service outside this state, or has received orders or authorization from an officer of the fire department or fire company to participate in or attend authorized activities outside of this state in the same manner as resident members of the fire company. A person shall not be eligible to volunteer membership in any other fire corporation or fire company at one time. The provisions of this subparagraph shall not be deemed to authorize the election or the continuance of any person as a member of the corporation if such election or continuance of membership shall be contrary to the by-laws, rules or regulations of the fire corporation.

(4) A person who has been convicted of arson in any degree shall not be eligible to be named in the certificate of incorporation of a fire corporation, or to be elected or appointed as a volunteer member of a fire corporation. The membership of any volunteer member of a fire corporation shall immediately terminate if he is convicted of arson in any degree while a member of a fire corporation.

(5) Upon application by any person for membership in a fire corporation operating pursuant to this section, the fire chief shall cause the applicant's background to be checked pursuant to section eight hundred thirty-seven-o of the executive law for a criminal history involving a conviction for arson and

conviction of a crime which requires the person to register as a sex offender under article six-C of the correction law. Where such criminal history information includes conviction of a crime which requires the person to register as a sex offender under article six-C of the correction law, a fire company shall determine whether or not such person shall be eligible to be elected or appointed as a volunteer member of such fire company. Such determination shall be made in accordance with the criteria established in sections seven hundred fifty-two and seven hundred fifty-three of the correction law.

(d) Incorporation of fire corporations in towns legalized.

Any fire, hose, protective or hook and ladder corporation heretofore organized under any general law with the consent of the town board in the territory served by such corporation is hereby legalized and confirmed, notwithstanding the omission of any town board to appoint or confirm the members of such corporations as town firefighters. Any such corporation shall hereafter be subject to the provisions of this section.

(e) Powers.

(1) A fire, hose, protective or hook and ladder corporation heretofore incorporated under any general law or a fire corporation hereafter incorporated under this section shall be under the control of the city, village, fire district or town authorities having, by law, control over the prevention or extinguishment of fires therein. Such authorities may adopt rules and regulations for the government and control of such corporations. Notwithstanding the provisions of any such local law, a person who has been convicted of arson in any degree shall not be eligible for nomination, election or appointment to any office of the corporation, nor may such person serve as director of the corporation. Any fire corporation officer or director who is convicted of arson in any degree during his term of office shall be disqualified from completing such term of office.

(2) Where a fire corporation formed outside of a city, village or fire district furnishes fire protection to territory outside of the boundaries specified in its certificate of incorporation, the fire corporation and the members thereof shall be under the exclusive control of the town board of the town in which the fire corporation maintains its apparatus.

(3) The emergency relief squad of a fire corporation incorporated under this section or subject to the provisions thereof shall have power to furnish general ambulance service when duly authorized under the provisions of section two hundred nine-b of the general municipal law.

(4) Any fire company incorporated under this section or subject to the provisions thereof shall have power to engage in fund raising activities pursuant to section two hundred four-a of the general municipal law.

(5) Any fire company incorporated under this section or subject to the provisions thereof shall have power, subject to the approval or authorization of the town board, to attend a funeral.

(6) Fire, hose, protective or hook and ladder corporations heretofore incorporated under any general law or fire corporations hereafter incorporated under this section or volunteer fire companies or fire departments as defined in section three of the volunteer firefighters' benefits [benefit]* law are hereby authorized to enter into contracts among themselves and among municipal corporations for the joint purchase of goods, supplies and services. Provided that the provisions of article five-A of the general municipal law shall be controlling for any proposed joint purchase between such fire corporation, company, or department and a municipal corporation. For the purposes of this subparagraph the term "municipal corporation" shall mean a county, city, town, village, fire district, or ambulance district.

* The bracketed word has been inserted by the Publisher.

(f) Directors to file report.

It shall be the duty of the directors of all fire, hose, protective or hook and ladder corporations incorporated under a general law or of a fire corporation formed under this section in territory outside of cities or villages, or a majority of them, on or before the fifteenth day of January in each year, to make and file in the county clerk's office, where the certificate of incorporation is filed a verified certificate, stating the names of the directors and officers of the corporation, containing an inventory of its property, a statement of its liabilities and that the corporation has not engaged, directly or indirectly, in any business other than that set forth in its certificate of incorporation.

(g) Firefighters' exemption.

Every active firefighter who shall be a member of a corporation subject to the provisions of this section shall be entitled to all the rights granted by law to volunteer firefighters and every such active firefighter who shall meet the requirements of section two hundred of the general municipal law shall be entitled to the additional rights granted by law to exempt volunteer firefighters.

(h) Legalization of membership of fire corporations in towns outside villages and fire districts.

(1) Any person:

(A) who was recognized prior to the first day of July, nineteen hundred fifty-four, as a volunteer member of a fire corporation subject to the provisions of this section located in a town outside villages and fire districts by the town board or by the officers and members of the fire corporation, and

(B) who rendered active service with such fire corporation prior to such date, and

(C) who was, at the time of his or her election to membership, a resident of the territory specified in the certificate of incorporation or of territory outside such boundaries which was afforded fire protection by the fire corporation pursuant to a contract for fire protection, shall for all purposes in law be considered to have been duly elected and confirmed as a member in such fire corporation as of the date of such confirmation, if any, and, if none, then as of the date of such election; notwithstanding that there may have been some legal defect in such election, or the proceedings precedent thereto, or a failure of the town board to confirm such member, as provided by the law in force at the time of such election, and the status of such person as a volunteer firefighter as of the date of such confirmation or election is hereby legalized, validated and confirmed. This subparagraph shall not apply to a person, if any, whose volunteer membership in a fire corporation was declared invalid by a court of competent jurisdiction prior to the first day of January, nineteen hundred fifty-five.

(2) Any person:

(A) who was recognized on or after the first day of July, nineteen hundred fifty-four and prior to the first day of January, two thousand eleven as a volunteer member of a fire corporation subject to the provisions of this section located in a town outside villages and fire districts by the town board or by the officers and members of the fire corporation, and

(B) who rendered active service with such fire corporation between such dates, and

(C) who was, at the time of his or her election to membership, a resident of the territory specified in the certificate of incorporation or of territory outside such boundaries which was afforded fire protection by the fire corporation pursuant to a contract for fire protection, or who was a nonresident elected to membership or who was continued as a member, pursuant to the provisions of subparagraph (A) shall for all purposes in law be considered to have been duly elected and confirmed, or continued, as a member in such fire corporation as of the date of such confirmation, if any, and, if none, then as of the date of such election or, in the case of a continuance, as of the date of approval, if any, by the town board and, if none, as of the date of authorization of continuance by the fire corporation; notwithstanding that there may have been some legal defect in such election, or the proceedings thereto, or a failure of the town board to confirm the election, or approve the continuance, of membership, of such member, as provided by the law in force at the time of such election or continuance, and the status of such person as a volunteer firefighter as of such date is hereby legalized, validated and confirmed. This subparagraph shall not apply to a person, if any, whose volunteer membership in a fire corporation was declared invalid by a court of competent jurisdiction prior to the first day of January, two thousand eleven.

(i) Discrimination because of race, color, creed or national origin prohibited.

(1) It shall be an unlawful discriminatory practice for any volunteer fire department, fire company or fire corporation, through any member or members thereof, directors, officers, members of a town board, board of fire commissioners or other body or office having power of appointment of volunteer firefighters in any fire department, fire company or fire corporation pursuant to this section, because of the race, creed, color, national origin, sex or marital status of any individual, to exclude or to expel from its volunteer membership such individual, or to discriminate against any of its members because of the race, creed, color, national origin, sex or marital status of such volunteer members.

(2) Any person claiming to be aggrieved by an unlawful discriminatory practice pursuant to this paragraph may by himself or his attorney at law make, sign and file with the state division of human rights, a verified complaint which shall set forth the particulars of the alleged unlawful discriminatory practice and contain such other information as the division of human rights may require. The division shall thereupon cause to be made an investigation and disposition of the charges pursuant to the provisions of article fifteen of the executive law.

History: Add, L 1969, ch 1066, § 1, eff Sept 1, 1970; amd, L 1970, ch 847, §§ 87, 88; L 1971, ch 914, § 1; L 1971, ch 1058, § 40; L 1974, ch 901, § 4, eff Sept 1, 1974; L 1976, ch 273, § 3; L 1978, ch 215, § 3, eff Sept 1, 1978; L 1980, ch 133, § 3, eff May 16, 1980; L 1980, ch 307, § 4, eff June 19, 1980; L 1984, ch 185, § 2; L 1985, ch 719, §§ 1, 2, eff Aug 1, 1985; L 1999, ch 423, § 5, eff April 1, 2000; L 2000, ch 351, § 3, eff Aug 23, 2000; L 2003, ch 393, §§ 8, 9, eff Aug 19, 2003; L 2010 ch 276, § 1, eff July 30, 2010; L 2011, ch 373, §§ 8, 9, eff Aug 3, 2011; L 2011, ch 472, § 1, eff Aug 17, 2011; L 2012, ch 407, § 1, eff Aug 17, 2012; L 2013, ch 505, § 1, eff Nov 13, 2013; L 2013, ch 549, § 112, eff July 1, 2014; L 2014, ch 149, § 1, eff Aug 21, 2014; L 2014, ch 198, § 4, eff Dec 2, 2014; L 2016, ch 276, § 1, eff Aug 19, 2016; L 2018, ch 476, § 235, eff Dec 28, 2018; L 2018, ch 500, § 1, eff Dec 28, 2018; L 2018, ch 513, § 1, eff Dec 28, 2018.

Blackline Showing Effect of 2018 Amendments. — (a) Certificate of incorporation; additional contents.

In addition to the requirements of section 402 (Certificate of incorporation; contents), the certificate of incorporation of a fire corporation shall state the precise boundaries of the territory in which the corporation intends to operate.

(b) Type of corporation.

A fire corporation is a charitable corporation under this chapter.

(c) Appointment of ~~firemen~~ firefighters.

(1) A person shall not be eligible to be named in the certificate of incorporation of a fire corporation unless he shall be at least eighteen years of age and a resident of a city, village, fire district, or town outside of villages and fire districts, where the fire corporation intends to operate.

(2) If the fire corporation becomes part of the fire department of a city, village or fire district, a person shall not be eligible to be elected as a member or to continue as a member except as provided by law

for volunteer members of the fire companies in such city, village or fire district.

(3) In towns outside of villages and fire districts, the consent of a majority of the members of the town board to the formation of a fire corporation shall constitute an appointment of the persons named in the certificate of incorporation as town firefighters. Thereafter, other eligible persons may be elected as members pursuant to the by-laws of the fire corporation, but the election of a member must be approved by the town board of each town which consented to the formation of the fire corporation. Such a person shall be a resident of the territory specified in the certificate of incorporation or of territory outside such boundaries which is afforded fire protection by the fire corporation pursuant to a contract for fire protection under which a cash consideration is received by the corporation or for which negotiations for renewal of such a contract are pending. The membership of any volunteer member shall terminate when he or she ceases to be a resident of such inside or outside territory, except that the corporation may authorize his or her continued membership where he or she notifies the secretary of the fire corporation (a) that he or she plans to change his or her residence to a territory which is not in such inside or outside territory, and (b) that by reason of his or her residence in the vicinity or his or her usual occupation he or she will be available to render active service as a volunteer firefighter in either such inside or such outside territory. Voting for such authorization shall be pursuant to the by-laws. Such authorization shall not become effective unless approved by resolution of the town board of each town which consented to the formation of the corporation. Any membership so continued shall terminate when the member can no longer meet the requirements of this subparagraph. A person who cannot meet the residence requirements of this subparagraph may be elected to membership as a volunteer member if by reason of his or her residence in the vicinity or his or her usual occupation he or she will be available to render active service as a volunteer firefighter in such inside or outside territory. Voting for such election shall be pursuant to the by-laws. Such election shall not become effective unless approved by resolution of the town board of each town which consented to the formation of the corporation. Such membership shall terminate when the member can no longer meet the requirements of this subparagraph. The election or continuance of any person as a member shall be deemed to have been approved by the town board pursuant to this subparagraph in the event that no action is taken by the town board, either approving or disapproving, within forty days in the case of residents of the territory specified in the certificate of incorporation or of outside contract territory, and within seventy days in the case of all others, after service of written notice of such election or continuance of membership shall have been made by the secretary of the corporation upon the town clerk, either personally or by mail. The membership of any volunteer firefighter shall not be continued pursuant to this subparagraph, and persons who do not reside in the territory specified in the certificate of incorporation or in territory protected pursuant to a contract for fire protection shall not be elected to membership, if, by so doing, the percentage of such nonresident members in the fire corporation would exceed forty-five per centum of the actual membership thereof, provided, however, that the forty-five percent limit on non-resident members shall not apply to the membership of the Huguenot Fire Company, Inc., within the town of Deerpark, Orange county, to the membership of the Prospect Terrace Fire Company, Inc., within the town of Dickinson, Broome county, to membership of the Hopewell Volunteer Fire Department, Inc., to membership of the Wales Center Volunteer Fire Company, Inc., within the town of Wales, Erie county, to the membership of the Nedrow Fire Department, within the town of Onondaga, Onondaga county, to the membership of the Pleasant Square Fire Company, Inc. within the town of Johnstown, Fulton county, or to membership of the fire departments within the town of Fleming, Cayuga county. Nonresidents of the territory specified in the certificate of incorporation whose volunteer membership has been authorized or continued pursuant to this subparagraph may be elected or appointed to any office in the fire corporation and shall have all the powers, duties, immunities, and privileges of resident volunteer members except a non-resident of this state whose membership has been continued pursuant to this subparagraph, or who was elected to membership pursuant to this subparagraph, shall not be considered to be performing any firefighting duty, or to be engaged in any firefighting activity, as a member of the fire company while he or she is outside of this state unless and until he or she has first reported to the officer or firefighter in command of his or her fire

department, or any company, squad or other unit thereof, engaged or to be engaged in rendering service outside this state, or has received orders or authorization from an officer of the fire department or fire company to participate in or attend authorized activities outside of this state in the same manner as resident members of the fire company. A person shall not be eligible to volunteer membership in any other fire corporation or fire company at one time. The provisions of this subparagraph shall not be deemed to authorize the election or the continuance of any person as a member of the corporation if such election or continuance of membership shall be contrary to the by-laws, rules or regulations of the fire corporation.

(4) A person who has been convicted of arson in any degree shall not be eligible to be named in the certificate of incorporation of a fire corporation, or to be elected or appointed as a volunteer member of a fire corporation. The membership of any volunteer member of a fire corporation shall immediately terminate if he is convicted of arson in any degree while a member of a fire corporation.

(5) Upon application by any person for membership in a fire corporation operating pursuant to this section, the fire chief shall cause the applicant's background to be checked pursuant to section eight hundred thirty-seven-o of the executive law for a criminal history involving a conviction for arson and conviction of a crime which requires the person to register as a sex offender under article six-C of the correction law. Where such criminal history information includes conviction of a crime which requires the person to register as a sex offender under article six-C of the correction law, a fire company shall determine whether or not such person shall be eligible to be elected or appointed as a volunteer member of such fire company. Such determination shall be made in accordance with the criteria established in sections seven hundred fifty-two and seven hundred fifty-three of the correction law.

(d) Incorporation of fire corporations in towns legalized.

Any fire, hose, protective or hook and ladder corporation heretofore organized under any general law with the consent of the town board in the territory served by such corporation is hereby legalized and confirmed, notwithstanding the omission of any town board to appoint or confirm the members of such corporations as town ~~firemen~~ firefighters. Any such corporation shall hereafter be subject to the provisions of this section.

(e) Powers.

(1) A fire, hose, protective or hook and ladder corporation heretofore incorporated under any general law or a fire corporation hereafter incorporated under this section shall be under the control of the city, village, fire district or town authorities having, by law, control over the prevention or extinguishment of fires therein. Such authorities may adopt rules and regulations for the government and control of such corporations. Notwithstanding the provisions of any such local law, a person who has been convicted of arson in any degree shall not be eligible for nomination, election or appointment to any office of the corporation, nor may such person serve as director of the corporation. Any fire corporation officer or director who is convicted of arson in any degree during his term of office shall be disqualified from completing such term of office.

(2) Where a fire corporation formed outside of a city, village or fire district furnishes fire protection to territory outside of the boundaries specified in its certificate of incorporation, the fire corporation and the members thereof shall be under the exclusive control of the town board of the town in which the fire corporation maintains its apparatus.

(3) The emergency relief squad of a fire corporation incorporated under this section or subject to the provisions thereof shall have power to furnish general ambulance service when duly authorized under the provisions of section two hundred nine-b of the general municipal law.

(4) Any fire company incorporated under this section or subject to the provisions thereof shall have power to engage in fund raising activities pursuant to section two hundred four-a of the general municipal law.

(5) Any fire company incorporated under this section or subject to the provisions thereof shall have power, subject to the approval or authorization of the town board, to attend a funeral.

(6) Fire, hose, protective or hook and ladder corporations heretofore incorporated under any general law or fire corporations hereafter incorporated under this section or volunteer fire companies or fire departments as defined in section three of the volunteer firefighters' benefits law are hereby authorized to enter into contracts among themselves and among municipal corporations for the joint purchase

of goods, supplies and services. Provided that the provisions of article five-A of the general municipal law shall be controlling for any proposed joint purchase between such fire corporation, company, or department and a municipal corporation. For the purposes of this subparagraph the term "municipal corporation" shall mean a county, city, town, village, fire district, or ambulance district.

(f) Directors to file report.

It shall be the duty of the directors of all fire, hose, protective or hook and ladder corporations incorporated under a general law or of a fire corporation formed under this section in territory outside of cities or villages, or a majority of them, on or before the fifteenth day of January in each year, to make and file in the county clerk's office, where the certificate of incorporation is filed a verified certificate, stating the names of the directors and officers of the corporation, containing an inventory of its property, a statement of its liabilities and that the corporation has not engaged, directly or indirectly, in any business other than that set forth in its certificate of incorporation.

(g) ~~Firemen's~~ Firefighter's exemption.

Every active ~~fireman~~ firefighter who shall be a member of a corporation subject to the provisions of this section shall be entitled to all the rights granted by law to volunteer ~~firemen~~ firefighters and every such active ~~fireman~~ firefighter who shall meet the requirements of section two hundred of the general municipal law shall be entitled to the additional rights granted by law to exempt volunteer ~~firemen~~ firefighters.

(h) Legalization of membership of fire corporations in towns outside villages and fire districts.

(1) Any person:

(A) who was recognized prior to the first day of July, nineteen hundred fifty-four, as a volunteer member of a fire corporation subject to the provisions of this section located in a town outside villages and fire districts by the town board or by the officers and members of the fire corporation, and

(B) who rendered active service with such fire corporation prior to such date, and

(C) who was, at the time of his or her election to membership, a resident of the territory specified in the certificate of incorporation or of territory outside such boundaries which was afforded fire protection by the fire corporation pursuant to a contract for fire protection, shall for all purposes in law be considered to have been duly elected and confirmed as a member in such fire corporation as of the date of such confirmation, if any, and, if none, then as of the date of such election; notwithstanding that there may have been some legal defect in such election, or the proceedings precedent thereto, or a failure of the town board to confirm such member, as provided by the law in force at the time of such election, and the status of such person as a volunteer ~~fireman~~ firefighter as of the date of such confirmation or election is hereby legalized, validated and confirmed. This subparagraph shall not apply to a person, if any, whose volunteer membership in a fire corporation was declared invalid by a court of competent jurisdiction prior to the first day of January, nineteen hundred fifty-five.

(2) Any person:

(A) who was recognized on or after the first day of July, nineteen hundred fifty-four and prior to the first day of January, two thousand eleven as a volunteer member of a fire corporation subject to the provisions of this section located in a town outside villages and fire districts by the town board or by the officers and members of the fire corporation, and

(B) who rendered active service with such fire corporation between such dates, and

(C) who was, at the time of his or her election to membership, a resident of the territory specified in the certificate of incorporation or of territory outside such boundaries which was afforded fire protection by the fire corporation pursuant to a contract for fire protection, or who was a nonresident elected to membership or who was continued as a member, pursuant to the provisions of subparagraph (A) shall for all purposes in law be considered to have been duly elected and confirmed, or continued, as a member in such fire corporation as of the date of such confirmation, if any, and, if none, then as of the date of such election or, in the case of a continuance, as of the date of approval, if any, by the town board and, if none, as of the date of authorization of continuance by the fire corporation; notwithstanding that there may have been some legal defect in such

election, or the proceedings thereto, or a failure of the town board to confirm the election, or approve the continuance of membership, of such member, as provided by the law in force at the time of such election or continuance, and the status of such person as a volunteer ~~fireman~~ firefighter as of such date is hereby legalized, validated and confirmed. This subparagraph shall not apply to a person, if any, whose volunteer membership in a fire corporation was declared invalid by a court of competent jurisdiction prior to the first day of January, two thousand eleven.

(i) Discrimination because of race, color, creed or national origin prohibited.

(1) It shall be an unlawful discriminatory practice for any volunteer fire department, fire company or fire corporation, through any member or members thereof, directors, officers, members of a town board, board of fire commissioners or other body or office having power of appointment of volunteer ~~firemen~~ firefighters in any fire department, fire company or fire corporation pursuant to this section, because of the race, creed, color, national origin, sex or marital status of any individual, to exclude or to expel from its volunteer membership such individual, or to discriminate against any of its members because of the race, creed, color, national origin, sex or marital status of such volunteer members.

(2) Any person claiming to be aggrieved by an unlawful discriminatory practice pursuant to this paragraph may by himself or his attorney at law make, sign and file with the state division of human rights, a verified complaint which shall set forth the particulars of the alleged unlawful discriminatory practice and contain such other information as the division of human rights may require. The division shall thereupon cause to be made an investigation and disposition of the charges pursuant to the provisions of article fifteen of the executive law.

CASE ANNOTATIONS

1. **Generally**
2. **Control of city, town, village or fire district**
3. **Discrimination**
4. **Fundraising activities**
5. **Membership**
6. **Offices**
7. **Powers**
8. **Territory**
9-10. **[Reserved for future use]**
11. **Under former Membership Corporation Law § 110**
12. **– Municipal consent; incorporation of voluntary fire company**
13. **– – To operation outside limits**
14. **– Ownership of fire apparatus and equipment**
15. **– Insurance; purchase by town board**
16. **– – County self-insurance plan**
17. **– Membership in fire company**
18. **– – Women**
19. **– – Nonresidents**
20. **– Liability for torts of firemen**
21. **Under former Membership Corporation Law § 111**
22. **Under former Membership Corporation Law § 112**
23. **– Village control of voluntary fire company**
24. **– – Fire company located in village**
25. **– Contract; between incorporated fire company and village**
26. **– – To provide fire protection outside village**
27. **– – Money received under contract**
28. **– Powers of board of fire commissioners**
29. **– – Organize fire company**
30. **– – Require physical examination of firemen**
31. **– Power of municipality to acquire and house equipment**
32. **– Eligibility for membership in fire company**
33. **– Dual village office holding**
34. **Under former Membership Corporation Law § 113**
35. **Under former Membership Corporation Law § 114**
36. **Under former Membership Corporation Law § 115**

1. Generally

In action by plaintiff who was injured in accident involving vehicle driven by volunteer firefighter responding to fire alarm, fire company incorporated under CLS N-PCL § 1402 was properly granted summary judgment on ground that it was not proper party to action, where town had chosen to establish "fire protection district" (which, unlike "fire district," is not political subdivision independent of town), fire company provided fire protection services within fire protection district pursuant to contract with town, and town retained complete control over fire company and ultimate responsibility for fire protection pursuant to § 1402. Miller v Savage (1997, 3d Dept) 237 A.D.2d 695, 654 N.Y.S.2d 215

In constructing a firehouse to be utilized for fire fighting or fire prevention, a fire corporation in a fire district need not comply with town zoning and building regulations. Ops Atty Gen 83-33

A fire district in which a fire company is located is a necessary party to a fire protection contract under which such company provides protection to a fire protection district, notwithstanding the fact that the fire company owns all the buildings and equipment necessary in connection with such fire protection contract. 1978 Op St Compt File #300

A village may not transfer title to its real property without consideration to an incorporated fire company. 1978 Op St Compt File #451

A town may not make an outright gift or transfer of moneys to the emergency rescue and first aid squad of a volunteer fire department or fire company. 1980 Op St Compt File #271

The Hewlett Fire Department of the Hewlett Bay Fire District as presently constituted, in terms of its corporate status, is a fire department rather than a fire company and it is the Fire Department of the Hewlett Bay Fire District. However, for purposes of Article 11 of the Town Law, the Hewlett Fire Department should be considered a fire company. 1981 Op St Compt File #81-53

Under Sections 10-1000 et seq. of the Village Law, a village fire department is a corporation consisting of members of all the fire, hose, protective and hook and ladder companies of a village; it is administered by a board of fire commissioners or, where no board of fire commissioners has been appointed, by the village board of trustees and the council of the fire department. Fire companies in a village are associations or corporations, which must operate in accordance with their certificates of incorporation, bylaws, and statutes; and, although fire companies are separate and distinct from the village, the statutes do permit village authorities to exercise a certain degree of control over their organization, incorporation, governance, and membership, including residency for membership. A fire company must consent to a contract for the provision of fire protection outside the village and the fire chief of the village fire department cannot consent on behalf of members of the company. 1990 Op St Compt 90-19

By operation of law, mere existence of fire companies in village results in corporation known as village fire department. 1994 Op St Compt No. 94-18

2. Control of city, town, village or fire district

In actions arising out of an automobile collision in which it was alleged that the accident was caused by the negligence of a volunteer fireman who, while operating his own automobile, was answering a mutual aid call, causes of action are stated against the town which established a fire protection district and which entered into a contract with the volunteer fire department of which the volunteer fireman was a member. By the terms of section 1402 (subd [e], par 1) of the Not-for-Profit Corporation Law the volunteer fire department is under the control of the town which has control over fire prevention and extinguishment and, consequently, the town can be held liable for the acts of the volunteer firemen. Cuddy v Amsterdam (1978) 62 A.D.2d 119, 403 N.Y.S.2d 590

Volunteer fire company, which is private not-for-profit corporation, is not liable to plaintiff for damages sustained to his business property allegedly caused by negligence of fire company, since company was discharging public function over which municipality exercised control. Helman v County of Warren (1985, 3d Dept) 114 A.D.2d 573, 494 N.Y.S.2d 188

Fire company could not be held vicariously liable for alleged negligence of firefighter in operating her vehicle in response to emergency since, under statute, (1) fire district, not fire company, employs, supervises and controls individual firefighters, (2) district is responsible for prevention and extinguishment of fires, (3) district possesses virtually total supervision and control over all aspects of creation and staffing of fire companies as well as over rules and regulations governing firefighting practices and procedures, and (4) district is answerable for negligence of its firefighters committed in course of

their duties. Knapp v Union Vale Fire Co. (1988, 2d Dept) 141 A.D.2d 509, 529 N.Y.S.2d 132

In negligence action by homeowners whose residence was destroyed by rekindling of fire after fire chief had assured them that earlier fire had been extinguished, defendant town was not entitled to summary judgment on basis that fire company was independent contractor over which it exercised no control, since CLS N-PCL § 1402(e) specifies that fire company incorporated under statute is under control of town authorities having, by law, control over prevention or extinguishment of fires, and town's concession that it had established fire protection district pursuant to CLS Town § 184(1) made it responsible for providing fire protection. Miller v Morania Oil, O.C.P. (1993, 2d Dept) 194 A.D.2d 770, 599 N.Y.S.2d 303

A volunteer fire company located entirely within city limits would be held covered under the city's excess liability policy in an action to recover for personal injuries sustained in an automobile accident while plaintiff was a passenger in a car owned and operated by a volunteer fireman responding to a fire in the city, since, although the city's three volunteer fire companies were otherwise independent corporations free to carry on their internal affairs without interference by the city, once a fire alarm sounded, the fire chief, a paid civil service employee of the city, by virtue of the city charter assumed command of the city's volunteer companies to coordinate and direct the firefighting efforts (see also, N-PCL § 1402[e][1]; Gen Mun Law § 209-l), thus making the volunteer company a "named insured" as an organization under the "control and management" of the city during a fire; such holding is consistent with the rule that fire districts may be held liable for the negligence of volunteer fireman while operating privately-owned vehicles in responding to an alarm; even if the volunteer company were not a "named insured," it would nevertheless be entitled to coverage as an insured under the city's primary policy. Cook v Geneva (1985) 127 Misc. 2d 261, 485 N.Y.S.2d 497

When the entire unincorporated area of a town comprises a fire protection district and is served by several volunteer fire companies within the district by contract with the town, the town board may require volunteer firemen to have physical examinations before the town board approves them as members of the fire companies. 1980 Op St Compt File #325

Village must be party to any contract for fire protection provided by volunteer fire company situated within the village. 1987 Op St Compt No 87-73

In general, a board of fire commissioners, or if there is no board of fire commissioners, the village board of trustees and the council of the fire department, has control of the external affairs of a fire company within the village, and the constitution and by-laws of the fire company regulate the internal affairs of the company. In addition, the by-laws of a fire company within the village should not be inconsistent with the rules and regulations enacted by the board of fire commissioners, or the village board of trustees and the council of the fire department. There is, however, no statutory requirement that the latter approve the by-laws of the fire company. 1990 Op St Compt 90-19

While there is no statute requiring fire company which constitutes village fire department to submit its books and records pertaining to receipt and expenditure of proceeds from fire protection contracts and fund raising to village board for audit, village board may make such requirement condition to entering into fire protection contracts for outside service or to allowing company to undertake fund raising activities; financial information concerning fire department may also be obtained under provisions of CLS Not-For-Profit Corporation Law and Freedom of Information Law; board of fire commissioners or, if there is no board of fire commissioners, board of trustees of village may require submission of report by chief of fire department. Ops St Compt 88-55

3. Discrimination

By changing its membership requirements from members of any fire company to volunteer members the Firemen's Benevolent Fund Association of the City of Mount Vernon did not unlawfully discriminate against professional firemen individually or as a class. Crohn v Firemen's Benev. Fund Asso. (1973) 79 Misc. 2d 536, 359 N.Y.S.2d 599

By-law provisions for the admission of members of volunteer fire companies which provide that three negative votes or black balls will defeat election to membership appear to be valid but if they are used in a manner contrary to the Constitutions of the United States or of the State of New York or the anti-discrimination statutes of the state, such a by-law would be invalid. 1977 Op Atty Gen May 9

A woman may be admitted to membership in a volunteer fire company to participate in all firemanic activities. 1974 Ops St Compt File #1171

Whether a woman may be excluded from membership in a volunteer fire company, in the face of a claim of unconstitutional discrimination, is a matter for judicial determination. 1974 Ops St Compt File #1171

4. Fundraising activities

City was entitled to summary judgment dismissing consolidated actions for personal injuries and wrongful death arising out of alcohol-related automobile accident which occurred after intoxicated driver consumed beer at fund-raising event to benefit volunteer fire companies, although city was vested with authority to control activities of its volunteer fire company under CLS N-PCL § 1402(e)(1) and CLS Gen Mun § 204-a(6)(b), since participation by volunteer firefighters in fund-raising activities was not deemed to constitute "duty as volunteer firemen" within meaning § 204-a(7); moreover, city submitted evidentiary proof that it had not received prior written notice of fire company's fund-raising activities as required by § 204-a(8)(a). Haskell v Chautauqua County Fireman's Fraternity, Inc. (1992, 4th Dept) 184 A.D.2d 12, 590 N.Y.S.2d 637, app dismd without op 81 N.Y.2d 954

A village can be held vicariously liable for Dram Shop Act violations committed by volunteer firefighters during fundraising events, but not for misconduct during social activities. Atty Ops Gen I90-64

5. Membership

Where denial of membership would work an irreparable injury an action will lie to compel a membership corporation or a voluntary association to accept an applicant. Crohn v Firemen's Benev. Fund Asso. (1973) 79 Misc. 2d 536, 359 N.Y.S.2d 599

A volunteer fireman may not be a member of a fire company within New York State and a volunteer fire company located out of New York State at the same time. 1975 Ops Atty Gen Feb 24

When a volunteer fireman is removed from membership in a volunteer fire company by vote of the members themselves based on the company's constitution and bylaws, rather than by village fire authorities, then the village may not provide a legal defense to the fire department when sued by the discharged fireman for wrongful removal. 1980 Op St Compt File #366

A volunteer firefighter may not simultaneously be a member of 2 fire companies, regardless of whether the companies are part of the same fire department or different fire departments. 1991 Op St Compt No. 91-23

There is no statutory prohibition on individual becoming member of fire company and member of volunteer ambulance corps at same time. 1997 Op St Compt No. 97-23

6. Offices

An alien may not be a fire district officer; an alien may not vote in a fire district election; an alien may be a volunteer fireman; an alien may be appointed fire chief or assistant fire chief and may be elected to fire company corporate office. 1980 Op Atty Gen Feb 6 (informal)

Establishment of qualifications to hold line offices in fire department of fire district are established solely by board of fire commissioners of fire district. 1997 Ops Atty Gen I 97-49

An individual may be appointed or elected to any office in a volunteer fire company located in a fire protection district if he is a member of the volunteer fire company and a resident of the State. In the area of towns outside of villages and fire districts, election of a member to the volunteer fire company must be approved by the town board of each town which consented to formation of the fire corporation. 1983 Op St Compt File #83-60

An incorporated volunteer fire company may amended its by-laws and constitution to require that members of the company attend at least three meetings annually as a qualification to vote for company officers. 1983 Op St Compt File #83-65

7. Powers

A fire district has no authority to pay the cost of construction of a memorial monument in memory of deceased volunteer firemen. 1980 Op Atty Gen Jun 11 (informal)

Debts incurred by an incorporated fire company are the responsibility of such corporation and a municipality would not be liable therefor in the event of default by the corporation. 1978 Op St Compt File #451

An incorporated volunteer fire company performing services in a fire protection district may set aside part of the payment received each year under the contract to accumulate money for a new fire truck. 1979 Op St Compt File #648

Competitive bidding would not be required if volunteer fire company expended moneys received from donations and membership dues to improve village fire hall and then made gift of improvement to village. 1987 Op St Compt No. 87-87

8. Territory

A volunteer fire department may not secede or separate itself from the village in which it is located. 1983 Op Atty Gen Mar 24 (informal)

The exclusive firefighting jurisdiction of a village fire department does not automatically expand upon annexation by the village of territory in a neighboring fire district; an agreement by which a village fire department would provide services to the annexed portion of a fire district is possible under Town Law § 176(22). 1990 Ops Atty Gen I90-59

(1) A village fire department or a volunteer fire company serving territory outside a village may respond to a call for assistance to a fire outside its designated area even if the call is not made pursuant to a mutual aid agreement. However, there is no authority to respond to a fire outside the area usually served when no call for assistance is made. (2) A village fire department or volunteer fire company has no authority to contract to provide fire protection to a business establishment or school located outside its designated area. 1979 Op St Compt File #568

9-10. [Reserved for future use]

11. Under former Membership Corporation Law § 110

Fact that certain town fire corporations were legalized and other fire corporations created under general law made subject to the statute's provisions did not make the Firemen's Benevolent Fund Association of the City of Mount Vernon a membership corporation, for purpose of determining effectiveness of 1930 amendment to certificate of incorporation changing membership requirements, since the Association was created by special law. Crohn v Firemen's Benev. Fund Asso. (1973) 79 Misc. 2d 536, 359 N.Y.S.2d 599

12. – Municipal consent; incorporation of voluntary fire company

There may be two volunteer fire companies in the same town, and the town board may consent to the incorporation of an additional volunteer fire company. 1956 Ops Atty Gen Mar 1 (informal)

An unincorporated fire company with its headquarters in a village may, with the consent of the village board, incorporate as a village fire company. The persons named in the certificate of incorporation should be residents of the village. 1968 Ops St Compt File #635

13. – – To operation outside limits

There appears to be no statutory prohibition against a town board consenting to the formation of a volunteer fire company which proposes to operate in a territory already served by a volunteer fire department where the territory is outside the limits of a village or fire district. 1954 Ops Atty Gen Oct 16 (informal)

The fire department of the village of Bergen may operate outside of the village limits only if the village has authorized such operation. The town of Bergen may contract with the village of Bergen for the furnishing of fire protection outside of the village limits only if a fire protection or fire alarm district has been established. 1947 Ops St Compt 441

14. – Ownership of fire apparatus and equipment

An incorporated fire company may purchase with its own funds and retain ownership of fire apparatus and equipment although it is located in a fire district. 1955 Ops St Compt File #7480

15. – Insurance; purchase by town board

Where there is no fire district in a town and no tax for fire protection purposes is levied, the town board may not expend town funds for the purchase of public liability insurance upon a truck owned by and licensed in the name of an unincorporated volunteer fire company furnishing fire protection services in the town. The town board may, however, expend town fund for the purchase of insurance indemnifying the town against any loss by reason of the liability imposed by § 205 of the General Municipal Law. 1945 Ops St Compt 176

16. – – County self-insurance plan

The members of a volunteer fire company organized and incorporated in an area of a town not within a village or fire district will be covered under a county self-insurance plan. The cost of this coverage is included as part of the town's apportionate share. 1958 Ops St Compt File #366

17. – Membership in fire company

A volunteer fireman may not be a member of two volunteer fire companies on or after July 1, 1954. 1954 Ops St Compt File #6669

18. – – Women

Women may be elected to membership in an incorporated fire company, if the by-laws do not prohibit such membership and if their election is approved by the board of fire commissioners or town board. 1955 Ops St Compt File #7128

19. – – Nonresidents

For a general explanation of Chapter 699 of Laws of 1954 in relation to non-resident members of volunteer fire departments see 1954 Ops St Compt File #7063

Admission of non-resident volunteer members in fire district fire department discussed. 1955 Ops St Compt File #7275

A fire company may not restrict the powers, duties, immunities and privileges of a nonresident member to a greater extent than is provided by statute. 1956 Ops St Compt File #7850

20. – Liability for torts of firemen

A town which contracts on behalf of a fire protection district for fire protection is liable for injuries to a third person caused by the negligent act of a member of an incorporated fire company located within the fire protection district, in answering an alarm pursuant to contract. However, if the tort was committed by a member of a village fire company under contract, located outside the fire protection district, the village would be liable. 1956 Ops St Compt File #7984

A municipality or district being aided by an outside fire company is not liable to third parties for torts of firemen rendering assistance where such firemen are not under the control of the officials of the municipality or district being aided. 1956 Ops St Compt File #7984

21. Under former Membership Corporation Law § 111

The term "fire district" as used in § 205-b of the General Municipal Law, referring to liability for negligence of fire district and volunteer firemen, has a specific meaning in law and does not include fire companies. Heifetz v Rockaway Point Volunteer Fire Department (1953, Sup) 124 N.Y.S.2d 257, affd 282 A.D. 1062, 126 N.Y.S.2d 604

22. Under former Membership Corporation Law § 112

A fire corporation organized under the Membership Corporations Law may make a gift of money to a fire district to be used to purchase fire apparatus. 1947 Ops St Compt 61

The funds of a fire corporation are under the exclusive control of the directors of such corporation. 1959 Ops St Compt File #665

23. – Village control of voluntary fire company

A village fire company, under the direction of the chief, may respond to emergency calls from outside the area regularly protected, until such outside service is restricted by action of the governing board of the village. 1957 Ops Atty Gen Oct 4 (informal)

Incorporation of a volunteer fire company of a village will not affect the control which the village exercises over the fire company, nor will it affect the duties and liabilities of the village in regard to its volunteer firemen. 1947 Ops St Compt 414

The village board of fire commissioners is not required to include in its annual report moneys raised by an incorporated volunteer fire company constituting the fire department of the village. 1953 Ops St Compt File #6225

24. – – Fire company located in village

Incorporated fire companies situated within a village are under the control of village authorities having control over prevention and extinguishment of fires therein. 1945 Ops St Compt 215

An incorporated fire company located in a village is subject to the control of the village authorities irrespective of the fact it existed before incorporation of the village. Such fire company may not contract to furnish fire protection outside the village independently of the village board. 1953 Ops St Compt File #6358

An incorporated fire company located in a village is subject to control of the village board of fire commissioners. 1961 Ops St Compt File #266

25. – Contract; between incorporated fire company and village

The making of a contract between an incorporated fire company and village will not operate to make the fire company a paid fire company. 1947 Ops St Compt 414

26. – – To provide fire protection outside village

An incorporated fire company of a village cannot contract to furnish fire protection outside of the village independently of the village board of trustees. 1947 Ops St Compt 414; 1953 Ops St Compt #6358

A village must be a party to all contracts to provide fire protection outside the limits of said village between a fire company, located in said village, and those desiring fire protection outside said village. 1956 Ops St Compt File #7934

27. – – Money received under contract

Both village and fire department or fire company should be parties to contract to furnish fire protection outside of village. Village may retain moneys received pursuant to such contract or pay over a portion to the fire department or fire company. 1954 Ops St Compt File #6769

28. – Powers of board of fire commissioners

Where a volunteer fire company has purchased apparatus for corporate purposes from company funds, such apparatus remains the property of the company. Board of Fire Commissioners has no control over expenditure of fire company moneys. 1955 Ops Atty Gen Apr 28 (informal)

A fire district created pursuant to former § 38 of the County Law must function through a board of fire commissioners, which shall have the management and control of all of the property and affairs of such district, including control of the activities of all fire companies situated within such district. 1945 Ops St Compt 196

For a discussion re control of board of fire commissioners over "jeep" purchased with fire company funds, see 1953 Ops St Compt File #6388

29. – – Organize fire company

The board of fire commissioners may not disband an incorporated fire company constituting the fire department of the district, but may organize other companies. 1953 Ops St Compt File #6282

30. – – Require physical examination of firemen

A Board of Fire Commissioners may require volunteer firemen of the district to undergo physical examinations at expense of the district. 1963 Ops St Compt #849

31. – Power of municipality to acquire and house equipment

A city is empowered to acquire fire apparatus by gift or otherwise, to pay the cost of maintenance and operation thereof, to pay rent for housing such apparatus and to have volunteer firemen fight fires. A contract may be made for such fire-fighting force to serve an area in another city. 1947 Ops St Compt 445

A town may sell a portion of its property to an incorporated fire company for the construction of a firehouse and subsequently lease space therein for town purposes. 1953 Ops St Compt File #6153

A village may construct an addition to the village owned firehouse for the purpose of housing fire equipment, owned by the incorporated fire company and to be used outside of the village. Providing the arrangement is provident for the village, rental need not be charged the fire company for such use. 1965 Ops St Compt File #320

32. – Eligibility for membership in fire company

If a member of a volunteer fire company located within fire district moves outside such district, he is no longer a member of such company unless there is compliance with provisions of subdivision 24 of Section 176 of Town Law. 1947 Ops St Compt 317

A person is eligible for membership in a fire corporation organized outside a city, village or fire district if he resides either (1) in the territory specified in the certificate of incorporation of the corporation or (2) in an area furnished fire protection by the corporation pursuant to contract. 1953 Ops St Compt File #6442

33. – Dual village office holding

The offices of village trustee and chief engineer of the village fire department may not be held by the same person at the same time. 1964 Ops Atty Gen Sept 25

34. Under former Membership Corporation Law § 113

Fire apparatus and equipment purchased by an incorporated fire company is its own property and not the property of the village. 1955 Ops St Compt File #7135

The funds of a fire corporation are under the exclusive control of the directors of such corporation. 1959 Ops St Compt File #665

The fact that a fire corporation undertakes to render fire protection to an area located in another county does not require it, or the Secretary of State, to file a copy of its certificate of incorporation in such other county. 1962 Ops St Compt #575

35. Under former Membership Corporation Law § 114

Where there is no proof that a city employee, upon his dismissal May 15, 1935, had qualified as an exempt volunteer fireman under Gen Mun Law, § 200, he cannot invoke this section, because this section (as amended by L 1935, ch 771, eff May 6), adopts requirements of Gen Mun Law, § 200. Brown v Stephan (1935) 245 A.D. 552, 284 N.Y.S. 403

A village employee who had qualified as an exempt volunteer fireman under this section, although he had not so qualified under Gen Mun Law, § 200, was entitled to a hearing under Civil Ser Law, § 22 upon his summary dismissal April 2, 1935. Brown v Stephan (1935) 245 A.D. 588, 283 N.Y.S. 31

A member of a volunteer fire company which has not been incorporated, is not entitled to a hearing upon his removal from a civil service position, where he had not served for a five year period, even though had the company been incorporated he would have been entitled under this section to such a hearing in spite of his failure to serve for five years. Mahan v Bacon (1935) 154 Misc 291, 277 N.Y.S. 390, affd 154 Misc 535, 277 N.Y.S. 393

A volunteer fireman in a fire company subject to this section is not entitled to a hearing prior to his removal, where he has not served the five year "term required by law" under Civil Ser Law, § 22, subd. 1, and Gen Mun Law, § 200. Huber v Stephan (1935) 156 Misc 131, 282 N.Y.S. 154

36. Under former Membership Corporation Law § 115

Petitioner was reinstated to the position of Principal Park Superintendent and should not have been dismissed from employment except for incompetency or misconduct found after a hearing where evidence showed that he secured a certificate after his dismissal that he was an exempt volunteer fireman and the affidavits of the fire company's officer past and present left no room for triable issue of fact as to whether he was honorably discharged or whether he was not in good standing at the time he applied for his certificate. Badman v Falk (1957) 4 A.D.2d 149, 163 N.Y.S.2d 570, affd 4 N.Y.2d 839, 173 N.Y.S.2d 813, 150 N.E.2d 240

A person who claims membership in a fire company, the home territory of which is a fire protection district located in two towns, is protected by the Volunteer Firemen's Benefit Law although one town has not confirmed his membership by proper resolution, if his membership has been legalized under this section. 1963 Ops St Compt #391

§ 1403. Corporations for the prevention of cruelty

(a) Prohibition of new corporations in certain counties.

(1) A corporation for the prevention of cruelty to animals shall not hereafter be incorporated for the purpose of conducting its operations in the counties of New York, Kings, Queens, Richmond, Rensselaer, or Westchester outside of the city of Yonkers; or in any other county if thereby two or more such corporations would exist in such county except as provided in subparagraph three hereof. Any corporation for the prevention of cruelty to animals may exercise its powers and conduct its operations in any adjacent county in which no such corporation exists until the establishment of such a corporation therein.

(1-a) No corporation for the prevention of cruelty to children, or for the dual purpose of prevention of cruelty to children and cruelty to animals shall be incorporated on or after November first, nineteen hundred eighty-nine. Any such corporations, incorporated prior to November first, nineteen hundred eighty-nine, may exercise their powers and conduct their operation in any adjacent county in which no such corporations exist until the establishment of such corporations therein prior to November first, nineteen hundred eighty-nine. The Brooklyn society for the prevention of cruelty to children may exercise all its powers in the county of Nassau until a society for the prevention of cruelty to children shall be incorporated prior to November first, nineteen hundred eighty-nine, and located therein, and may exercise all its powers in the county of Suffolk until such a corporation is incorporated prior to November first, nineteen hundred eighty-nine, and located therein.

(2) In addition to the requirements of section 402, a certificate of incorporation under which an additional corporation is formed in the City of Yonkers must designate such city as the place where its operations are to be conducted.

(3) In any county having a population of one hundred thousand or less, where there is already in existence a corporation duly incorporated for the prevention of cruelty to animals and where it appears that the functions of such corporation are confined to a local area in such county and where it further appears that part of such county is not served by the existing corporation, an application may be made for the incorporation of a second such corporation in such county. If it appears to the satisfaction of the court that such existing corporation does not serve the area from which the application for incorporation of a new corporation is made, the court shall approve the proposed certificate of incorporation.

(b) Special powers.

(1) A corporation formed for the purpose of preventing cruelty to children, when represented by an attorney duly admitted to the practice of law, may prosecute a complaint before any court, tribunal or magistrate having jurisdiction, for the violation of any law enacted to prevent (i) the abuse, maltreatment or neglect of a child, as those terms are defined in section four hundred twelve of the social services law and section one thousand twelve of the family court act, or (ii) the exploitation of or harm to a child at the hands of an adult that would constitute a violation of article one hundred twenty, one hundred thirty, one hundred thirty-five, two hundred sixty or two hundred sixty-three of the penal law, and may aid in presenting the law and facts to such court, tribunal or magistrate in any proceeding therein.

(2) A corporation formed for the purpose of preventing cruelty to animals may prefer a complaint before any court, tribunal or magistrate having jurisdiction, for the violation of any law relating to or affecting the prevention of cruelty to animals, and may aid in presenting the law and facts to such court, tribunal or magistrate in any proceeding therein.

(3) A corporation for the prevention of cruelty to children may be appointed guardian of the person of a minor child during its minority by a court of record, or a judge thereof, and may receive and retain any child at its own expense on commitment by a court or magistrate.

(4) All magistrates, peace officers, acting pursuant to their special duties and police officers shall aid such a corporation, its officers, agents and members

in the enforcement of laws enacted to prevent (i) the abuse, maltreatment or neglect of a child, as those terms are defined in section four hundred twelve of the social services law and section one thousand twelve of the family court act, or (ii) the exploitation of or harm to a child at the hands of an adult that would constitute a violation of article one hundred twenty, one hundred thirty, one hundred thirty-five, two hundred sixty or two hundred sixty-three of the penal law, and for the prevention of cruelty to animals.

(c) Type of corporation.

A corporation for the prevention of cruelty is a charitable corporation under this chapter.

History: Add, L 1969, ch 1066, § 1, eff Sept 1, 1970, with substance derived from Mem Corp Law §§ 120, 121; amd, L 1970, ch 847, § 89, L 1980, ch 843, § 192, L 1983, ch 207, § 1, L 1989, ch 618, § 1, eff Nov 1, 1989, L 1993, ch 201, § 4, eff July 6, 1993, L 2013, ch 549, § 113, eff July 1, 2014.

CASE ANNOTATIONS

1. Generally
2-5. [Reserved for future use]
6. Under former Membership Corporations Law § 120
7. Under former Membership Corporations Law § 121

1. Generally

A dismissal by the Appellate Division of a petition by a foreign not-for-profit corporation seeking to dispense with the approval of the New York Society for the Prevention of Cruelty to Children, which normally was required before a corporation could conduct in New York all the activities of a domestic society, would be reversed and remanded for redetermination, even though the determination of the Appellate Division was correct as the matter stood before it, where the litigation had proceeded on the assumption that the corporation sought to conduct in New York all the activities of a domestic society, and where in fact the corporation sought to conduct only those activities that it was authorized to conduct under the laws of its incorporating state. Re American Soc. for Prevention of Cruelty to Children (1983) 58 N.Y.2d 1071, 462 N.Y.S.2d 634, 449 N.E.2d 414

In initiating and prosecuting child protective proceeding, not-for-profit corporation for prevention of cruelty to children may represent itself-appearing by individual who is not attorney-and need not be represented by counsel of record. Re Sharon B. (1988) 72 N.Y.2d 394, 534 N.Y.S.2d 124, 530 N.E.2d 832

The Westchester Society for the Prevention of Cruelty to Children did not have standing to maintain a proceeding to annul and vacate the certificate of the Yonkers Society for the Prevention of Cruelty to children, which had been duly filed and judicially approved pursuant to N-PCL § 403, notwithstanding the fact that N-PCL § 1403 prohibited more than one society for the prevention of cruelty to children in a single county; an action for the involuntary judicial dissolution of a corporation formed pursuant to the Not-For-Profit Corporation Law can be maintained only by the Attorney-General (N-PCL § 1101) or upon specified conditions by a certain number of members or directors of the corporation (N-PCL § 1102). The use of the permissive word "may" in N-PCL § 1101 does not support the argument that a dissolution action can be maintained by private individuals. Westchester County S.P.C.C. v Pisani (1984, 2d Dept) 105 A.D.2d 793, 481 N.Y.S.2d 735

Nonattorney officer of Society for Prevention of Cruelty to Children was not authorized to represent society in child abuse proceeding by virtue of CLS Jud §§ 478 and 484, which provide that prohibitions against practice of law by nonattorneys do not apply to officers of societies for prevention of cruelty when exercising special powers conferred by CLS N-PCL § 1403, since (1) § 1403 states that societies for prevention of cruelty may prefer complaints before courts and "may aid in" presenting law and facts therein, suggesting that legislature did not intend to permit nonattorneys to represent those societies in litigated proceedings, and (2) under CLS CPLR § 321,

societies for prevention of cruelty are not excepted from legislative mandate that corporations "shall appear by attorney"; statutes in question may be harmonized by requiring society to have attorney of record who may be assisted in presentation of case by officer of society to secure best interests of child. Re Sharon B. (1987, 2d Dept) 127 A.D.2d 761, 512 N.Y.S.2d 154, app gr 71 N.Y.2d 803, 527 N.Y.S.2d 769, 522 N.E.2d 1067

CLS N-PCL § 1403 does not expressly or impliedly prohibit incorporation of more than one society for prevention of cruelty to children in Nassau County. Long Island Soc. for Prevention of Cruelty to Children, Inc. v Abrams (1989, 2d Dept) 154 A.D.2d 536, 547 N.Y.S.2d 244

CLS N-PCL § 1403 does not expressly or impliedly prohibit incorporation of more than one society for prevention of cruelty to children in Kings County. Society for Prevention of Cruelty to Children, Inc. v Abrams (1989, 2d Dept) 154 A.D.2d 540, 546 N.Y.S.2d 161

Application for pre-action disclosure, seeking unredacted copy of complaint in order to identify person who reported to respondent that petitioner was abusing his donkeys, was properly denied on ground that public interest in preventing cruelty to animals outweighed petitioner's interest in obtaining name of complainant in order to seek civil redress. LaBarbera v Ulster County SPCA (2000, 3d Dept) 277 A.D.2d 672, 716 N.Y.S.2d 421

In a Family Court proceeding to determine whether respondent had violated the terms of an order of protection, in which proceeding a guardian ad litem from the Society for the Prevention of Cruelty to Children (SPCC) had been appointed, it was not improper for the SPCC to question those persons testifying, since the SPCC is specifically exempted from the provisions of the Judiciary Law which state who may appear in court proceedings, and the SPCC representative need not be an attorney admitted to practice in New York when exercising the special powers conferred by the Not-For-Profit Corporation Law (see Judiciary Law, §§ 478, 484); under section 1403 (subd [b], par [1]) of the Not-For-Profit Corporation Law, a corporation formed for the purpose of preventing cruelty to children may aid the court in presenting the law and the facts, and the only reasonable construction of this language is that SPCC, as guardian ad litem, may question any parties or witnesses testifying at a hearing. Accordingly, respondent's motion to set aside the finding that he violated the order of protection is denied. Rapp v Rapp (1979) 101 Misc. 2d 375, 438 N.Y.S.2d 154

A complaint by the Attorney-General seeking dissolution of the Richmond County Society for the Prevention of Cruelty to Children on the grounds that it had not engaged in any activity since 1977 and was no longer able to carry out the purpose for which it was formed (N-PCL § 1102(a)(2)(E)) stated a cause of action, since public policy dictates that such a society, vested with extraordinary powers, (see N-PCL § 1403), be effective and active, and the Attorney-General had standing to maintain this action (N-PCL § 112(a)(7)); in addition, the allegation that defendant had failed to file the financial reports required of a charitable organization (EPTL § 8-1.4) stated a cause of action, since defendant obtained a Federal income tax exemption as a charitable organization and it could not now refute its status as such, nor did the fact that defendant became statutorily exempt from filing requirements in 1982 release defendant from its culpability for failing to file the requisite reports from 1976 to 1982. Abrams v Richmond County S.P.C.C. (1984) 125 Misc. 2d 530, 479 N.Y.S.2d 624

Employee of Society for Prevention of Cruelty to Children was not exempt from provisions of vehicle and traffic laws under public policy exception for police officers in performance of their duties, on ground that he was peace officer "acting pursuant to his special duties" and thus was "police officer" within meaning of CLS Veh & Tr § 132; distinctions between police and peace officers should be maintained, as matter of public policy, in view of peace officers' lack of screening, police training, and police department accountability. People v Ellman (1987) 135 Misc. 2d 1010, 517 N.Y.S.2d 664

Vehicle owned by county Society for Prevention of Cruelty to Children, and operated by society employee, was not "police vehicle" under CLS Veh & Tr § 132-a for purposes of claiming exemption from enforcement of traffic laws under CLS Veh & Tr § 1104 since society is not equivalent to state or public authority by virtue of its limited powers under CLS N-PCL § 1403, and is not authorized to maintain law enforcement unit under CLS N-PCL § 202. People v Ellman (1987) 135 Misc. 2d 1010, 517 N.Y.S.2d 664

Court would approve incorporation of Society for the Prevention of Cruelty to Children (SPCC) located in Nassau county, despite existence of another SPCC in same county, since society's fitness to engage in activities on behalf of children was unquestioned and CLS N-PCL § 1403 does not expressly prohibit operation of 2 societies in county with population of more than 100,000; it would be illogical to hold that only counties with fewer than 100,000 people may have 2 or more societies under statute. Re Society for Prevention of Cruelty to Children (1987) 137 Misc. 2d 271, 520 N.Y.S.2d 506, later proceeding (App Div, 2d Dept) 547 N.Y.S.2d 244

In action by Attorney-General under CLS N-PCL § 112(a)(1) and CLS EPTL Art 8 to obtain injunctive relief against Long Island Society for the Prevention of Cruelty to Children (LISPCC), venue was properly in New York County where Charities Bureau of Attorney-General was located, and where LISPCC was required to annually file its financial reports or exemptions from filing. Koppell ex rel. People v Long Island Soc'y for the Prevention of Cruelty to Children (1994, Sup) 163 Misc. 2d 654, 621 N.Y.S.2d 762

In action under CLS N-PCL § 112(a) and CLS EPTL Art 8 to obtain injunctive relief against Long Island Society for the Prevention of Cruelty to Children (LISPCC), Attorney-General established that LISPCC misrepresented that it was state or police agency where (1) LISPCC offices and vehicles displayed state shield and used word "Police," (2) LISPCC vehicles used red bar and flashing lights in plain violation of provisions of Vehicle and Traffic Law which limit such items to emergency vehicles, and (3) LISPCC agents used official license plates that were not authorized for use by private not-for-profit corporation vehicles. Koppell ex rel. People v Long Island Soc'y for the Prevention of Cruelty to Children (1994, Sup) 163 Misc. 2d 654, 621 N.Y.S.2d 762

Neither society for prevention of cruelty to animals nor its agents or officers is authorized to issue appearance tickets, summon, or arrest person for violating any provisions of CLS Agr & M Art 26, or to seize lost, stolen, strayed, homeless, abandoned, or improperly confined animals as set forth in CLS Agr & M § 373, within adjacent county that is served by its own duly incorporated society. 2001 Ops Atty Gen I 2001-4

The possession and rehabilitation of wildlife, as well as the restoration of wildlife to their natural habitat, are governed exclusively by the Environmental Conservation Law. Agents or officers of an incorporated society for the prevention of cruelty to animals or other humane societies may not engage in such activities, except in accordance with the procedures set forth in that statute. Ops Atty Gen 82-78

2-5. [Reserved for future use]

6. Under former Membership Corporations Law § 120

Where the record did not show that the existing corporation did not serve the area from which the application for incorporation of a new corporation was made, the application for a second incorporation was denied. In re Incorporation of Columbia County Soc. for Prevention of Cruelty to Animals, Inc. (1954, Sup) 133 N.Y.S.2d 748

7. Under former Membership Corporations Law § 121

A New York society for the prevention of cruelty to children is not subject to visitation by the State Board of Charities. People ex rel. State Board of Charities v New York Soc. for Prevention of Cruelty to Children (1900) 161 N.Y. 233, 55 N.E. 1063, reh den (1900) 162 N.Y. 429, 56 N.E. 1004

A humane society may constitutionally be authorized to seize and destroy unlicensed dogs, but a statute which provides for the payment of license fees for such dogs to a humane society is unconstitutional. Fox v Mohawk & H. R. Humane Soc. (1901) 165 N.Y. 517, 59 N.E. 353

The New York Society for the Prevention of Cruelty to Children, though one-half of the society's income is contributed by the City of New York, is not a governmental instrumentality or agent of the City of New York. Lindsay v Bowers (1927, SD NY) 17 F.2d 264, 6 AFTR 6505

Fire district commissioners have authority to install a radio in a fire company truck and also have the authority to permit a fire company pumper truck to be garaged in a fire district firehouse. A fire company may own its own pumper truck even when it is under jurisdiction of a fire district. 1964 Ops Atty Gen Oct 8 (informal)

§ 1404. Christian associations

(a) Certificate of incorporation; additional contents.

In addition to the requirements of section 402, the certificate of incorporation of a Young Men's or a Young Women's Christian Association shall state the qualifications of active membership; and may name, in addition to the directors, six trustees and shall divide such trustees into three classes to hold office for one, two and three years respectively, or until their successors are elected by the board of directors.

(b) Type of corporation.

A christian association is a charitable corporation under this chapter.

(c) Directors and trustees.

(1) The trustees of a corporation organized for the purposes of a young men's christian association or a young women's christian association, with the president of the corporation shall be a board of trustees thereof, and hold and control the real property of the corporation and all gifts and bequests of money to be held in trust. They or the directors if there is no board of trustees shall pay the income of such property to the treasurer of the corporation so long as the income shall be expended by the directors thereof for the purposes for which the corporation was formed. Such association may, by amendment to its certificate of incorporation, in the manner provided by law, eliminate its board of trustees, in which case the real property, gifts, bequests and other grants held in trust by such trustee shall be transferred to its board of directors which shall hold and control the real property of the corporation and all gifts and bequests of money to be held in trust.

(2) The real property of such corporation shall not be liable for any debt or obligation contracted without the approval of the board of trustees.

(3) In all proceedings for the purchase, sale, mortgage and lease of real property, the board of trustees of such a corporation shall perform the functions of the board of directors.

(4) The board of directors shall have the management and control of the property and affairs of the corporation, except as such management and control is vested by law in the board of trustees.

(5) A young men's christian association incorporated prior to eighteen hundred and eighty-seven may create a board of trustees possessing the qualifications and divided into classes, and such board shall have the powers set forth in this paragraph.

(6) A young men's christian association incorporated prior to nineteen hundred and eight may divide its trustees into classes.

(d) Dissolution.

Whenever any young men's christian association subject to this section shall cease to carry out the objects set forth in its certificate of incorporation, according to the general rules and regulations of the national board of young men's christian associations, or shall abandon or discontinue for one year the use of any of its property for such objects, then upon the verified petition of a majority of the directors of such association upon fourteen days' notice to the national board by service thereof upon its chairman and secretary or in the event of the failure of such directors to act, upon the verified petition of the national board of young men's christian associations, upon fourteen days' notice to such association by service thereof upon its president or any director thereof, and upon one of the trustees thereof, and upon notice to the attorney general, the supreme court, upon satisfactory proof by affidavit or otherwise of such failure or abandonment, must make a final order dissolving such corporation. Upon the entry of such order, the corporation shall be dissolved, and thereupon the national board of young men's christian associations may take possession of the property of the corporation and manage the same, or if authorized by the concurring vote of two-thirds of the members of the national board may sell or lease the same and apply the proceeds thereof after the payment of the debts, if any, of the corporation solely to such purposes as those for which the corporation was organized.

(e) Incorporation of county committees.

(1) Five or more men resident in any county of this state, appointed by the national board of Young Men's Christian Associations, to act as the county committee of Young Men's Christian Associations for such county, may form a corporation under the provisions of this chapter under the name of "The County Committee of the Young Men's Christian Association of ---- County," (the blank space being filled by the name of the county in which the incorporators reside.)

(2) The management and control of the property and affairs of such corporation shall be vested in its members and their successors in office, except that the powers and duties of the trustees thereof shall be those specified in paragraph (a); and the successors of such members shall be elected annually at a meeting of the Young Men's Christian Associations of the county for which such committee has been appointed, at which meeting each association may be represented by one delegate for each ten active members of such association. A plurality vote of the delegates present, and voting at such meeting, shall be sufficient to elect. If any vacancy in the membership of such corporation shall occur during the interim between the regular elections, it may be filled by the remaining members.

(3) The officers of the corporation shall consist of a chairman, treasurer and secretary, and such other officers as the members may decide; and shall be elected annually by such members from their own number.

History: Add, L 1969, ch 1066, § 1, eff Sept 1, 1970, with substance derived from Mem Corp Law §§ 11(6), 140, 141, 142; amd, L 1971, ch 1058, § 41, eff Sept 1, 1971, L 1977, ch 702, § 1, eff Aug 5, 1977, L 2013, ch 549, § 114, eff July 1, 2014.

CASE ANNOTATIONS

1. Generally
2-5. [Reserved for future use]
6. Under former Membership Corporations Law § 140

1. Generally

Cemetery association breached its fiduciary duty to plaintiff when it failed to plant grass or provide care for graves of plaintiff's parents after accepting monies from plaintiff and issuing trust certificates. Yochim v Mount Hope Cemetery Ass'n (1994, City Ct) 163 Misc. 2d 1054, 623 N.Y.S.2d 80

2-5. [Reserved for future use]

6. Under former Membership Corporations Law § 140

Whether a proposed Y.W.C.A. building was a membership club within the meaning of a zoning ordinance providing for a special use in favor of "golf clubs, country clubs and other membership clubs not operated for profit" was a question of fact for the zoning board to determine, and action of the board granting a variance to permit the construction of such building in a residence district was valid. Von Kohorn v Morrell (1961) 9 N.Y.2d 27, 210 N.Y.S.2d 525, 172 N.E.2d 287

§ 1405.   Soldiers' monument corporations

(a) Property; erection of monuments.

A corporation formed for the purpose of erecting and maintaining a monument or memorial, including a memorial hall or building to perpetuate the memory of persons who served in the armed forces of the United Colonies or of the United States in the Revolutionary War, the Civil War, or in any other war in which the United States has been engaged may acquire and hold real property necessary for its corporate purposes, and may erect any such monument, monuments or memorial upon any public street, square or ground of any town, city or village, with the consent of the proper officers thereof, or may purchase or accept the donation of land suitable for that purpose; and may take and hold the property given, devised or bequeathed to it in trust, to apply the same or the income or proceeds thereof for the erection, improvement, embellishment, preservation, repair, renewal, care and maintenance of such monument, monuments or memorial, or of any structure, fences or walks upon its lands, or for planting or cultivating trees, shrubs, flowers and plants, in and around or upon its lands, or for improving or embellishing the same in any manner consistent with the design and purposes of the association, according to the terms of such grant, devise or bequest. It may take by gift or purchase any lots or lands in any cemetery to be used and occupied exclusively for the burial of honorably discharged members of the armed forces who served in any of such wars, and for the erection of suitable monuments or memorials therein.

(b) Type of corporation.

A soldiers' monument corporation is a charitable corporation.

(c) Town and village aid.

The town clerk of a town or the board of trustees of a village, upon the petition of twenty-five resident taxpayers, shall submit to a biennial town meeting or village election, as the case may be, a proposition to raise by taxation a sum stated therein, not exceeding five hundred dollars in any one year, to be spent during the fiscal year for which such tax is to be levied, for the purpose of erecting such a monument, or contributing to the expense of such a monument, erected by a corporation specified in this article, or for repairing, improving and maintaining the same and the grounds thereof; and such tax shall be levied in the manner prescribed by law for levying general taxes in such town or village, and when raised shall be applied to the purposes specified in such proposition.

(d) Exemptions.

The property of a corporation specified in this section or of a corporation formed under the laws of eighteen hundred and sixty-six, chapter two hundred and seventy-three, as amended by laws of eighteen hundred and eighty-eight, chapter two hundred and ninety-nine, shall be exempt from levy and sale on execution, and from all public taxes, rates and assessments, and no street, road, avenue or thoroughfare shall be laid through the lands of such association held for the purposes aforesaid without the consent of the trustees of such corporation, except by special permission of the legislature of the state.

(e) Improvement taxes.

A tax may be levied and collected on the taxable property in a town, village or city in which such monument, monuments or other memorial may be erected, for the purpose of repairing or improving the same and the grounds thereof; and such tax shall be levied in the manner prescribed by law for levying general taxes in such town, village or city.

(f) Transfer of property from unincorporated association.

Any unincorporated association organized solely for one or more of the purposes set forth in paragraph (a) by a majority vote of all its members present at a meeting thereof, called as in this section provided, may transfer to and vest in any incorporated association created by general or special law having like objects any or all money or other property which it shall have accumulated for such objects, but the property so transferred shall be used exclusively for one or more of the purposes mentioned in such paragraph. A vote upon the question of transferring the funds or property of such unincorporated association shall be had only at a meeting of such association called for that purpose by the president or secretary or other managing officer thereof, upon notice stating the object of the meeting of at least ten days before the time fixed for such meeting, served personally or by mail on each member of the association within the United States whose residence or post office address is known.

History: Add, L 1969, ch 1066, § 1, eff Sept 1, 1970, with substance derived from Mem Corp Law §§ 160, 161, 162, 163, 164; amd, L 2013, ch 549, § 115, eff July 1, 2014.

1. Generally
2-5. [Reserved for future use]
6. Under former Membership Corporations Law § 160
7. Under former Membership Corporations Law § 162

1. Generally
County, city, town or village may, in accordance with pertinent statutory requirements, contribute public funds to veterans memorial committee for purpose of erecting memorial monument. Ops St Compt 88-74

2-5. [Reserved for future use]

6. Under former Membership Corporations Law § 160
Corporation organized under this section is not entitled to summary judgment cancelling tax assessments where property was acquired two years previously for purpose of constructing monument but is still vacant and no unequivocal proof is available as to construction. Callahan-Kelly Post Memorial Ass'n v New York (1953, Sup) 124 N.Y.S.2d 261

7. Under former Membership Corporations Law § 162
The legislature, by the enactment of this section, intended to exempt real property acquired and utilized by an authorized corporation for purposes of a soldier's memorial. Legislature did not intend that land be kept vacant and withheld indefinitely from the tax roles. Plaintiff should not be granted summary judgment in action to cancel tax assessments where property was acquired two years previously, is still vacant and no definite building plans are shown. Callahan-Kelly Post Memorial Ass'n v New York (1953, Sup) 124 N.Y.S.2d 261

§ 1406.   Medical societies

(a) Medical societies heretofore formed.

Any medical society now existing in any of the counties of the state set apart prior to or since the passage of the act entitled "An act to incorporate medical societies for the purpose of regulating the practice of physic and surgery in this state," passed April tenth, eighteen hundred and thirteen, and not heretofore duly incorporated under the provisions of said act shall, upon complying with the provisions of this section enjoy the same privileges and possess the same powers as the societies incorporated by virtue of such act now enjoy and possess, but subject, nevertheless, to the provisions of any acts or parts of acts heretofore passed in relation to medical societies or to regulate the practice of physic and surgery in this state.

(b) Type of corporation.

A medical society is a non-charitable corporation under this chapter.

(c) Certificate of incorporation, additional contents.

In addition to the requirements of section 402, the certificate of incorporation of a medical society shall state: (1) the name of such society; (2) the date of its organization; (3) the names and residences of its members; and (4) that such society, by a majority vote of its members, has elected to become and be a body corporate under and by virtue of the Act described in paragraph (a), and be subject to the provisions of any acts or parts of acts heretofore enacted and now in force, in relation to such societies or the practice of medicine or surgery in this state.

(d) Regulations for county medical societies.

Not-For-Profit Corporation Law

It shall be lawful for any county medical society in this state, entitled to representation in the medical society of the state of New York, or in the homeopathic medical society of the state of New York, to establish such rules and regulations, not inconsistent with the laws of the state, for the government of its members as such county society may deem fit, provided such action receives the sanction of the state medical society in which such county medical society is represented. Such county medical society may fix the amount of the annual dues and assessments to be collected from its members.

(e) Enforcement of discipline; appeal.

Every county medical society shall have full power and authority to enforce discipline among its members and obedience to its rules and regulations and to expel or otherwise discipline its members as it may deem for the best interests of the society. Any member of such a society who has been disciplined or an applicant for membership therein, who has been refused membership, feeling aggrieved at the action of the society, shall have the right to appeal to the medical society of the state of New York, in which such county medical society is represented.

(f) Power to acquire property.

It shall be lawful for any county medical society heretofore or hereafter incorporated and for the medical society of the state of New York and for the homeopathic medical society of the state of New York to acquire and hold for its corporate purposes real and personal property without limitation of amount or value, notwithstanding any limitation heretofore existing.

History: Add, L 1969, ch 1066, § 1, eff Sept 1, 1970, with substance derived from Mem Corp Law §§ 160, 161, 162, 163, 164; amd, L 1970, ch 847, § 90, eff Sept 1, 1970, L 2013, ch 549, § 116, eff July 1, 2014.

CASE ANNOTATIONS

1. Generally
2-5. [Reserved for future use]
6. Under former Membership Corporations Law Art 14
7. Under former Membership Corporations Law § 173
8. Under former Membership Corporations Law § 174

1. Generally
Under evidence that physician who had written book commenced suit against publisher to cease use of physician's photograph on book, finding by judicial council of state medical society that physician had violated medical society's bylaw forbidding physician to permit his photograph to be published was unjustified. Atkins v Medical Soc. of County of New York (1975) 50 A.D.2d 751, 376 N.Y.S.2d 156

Disciplinary determination of board of directors of county medical society must be based on substantial evidence. Atkins v Medical Soc. of County of New York (1975) 50 A.D.2d 751, 376 N.Y.S.2d 156

2-5. [Reserved for future use]
6. Under former Membership Corporations Law Art 14
A county medical society of a county established prior to April 10, 1813 may not be incorporated under the cited article which applies only to medical societies organized in counties established since that date. 1950 Ops Atty Gen July 10

7. Under former Membership Corporations Law § 173
Medical society could make such regulations as it deemed fit, not inconsistent with the laws of New York, and exclusion of one trained as osteopath from membership was proper in the absence of an

allegation of monopoly. Kurk v Medical Soc. of County of Queens, Inc. (1965, 2d Dept) 24 A.D.2d 897, 264 N.Y.S.2d 859, affd (1966) 18 N.Y.2d 928, 276 N.Y.S.2d 1007, 223 N.E.2d 499

8. Under former Membership Corporations Law § 174
Where rule attacked is void for any reason, appeal to state society would not be mandatory and direct resort to courts would be permissible. Kurk v Medical Soc. of County of Queens, Inc. (1965) 46 Misc. 2d 790, 260 N.Y.S.2d 520, revd on other grounds (1965, 2d Dept) 24 A.D.2d 897, 264 N.Y.S.2d 859, affd (1966) 18 N.Y.2d 928, 276 N.Y.S.2d 1007, 223 N.E.2d 499

Osteopath was not required by this section first to appeal to New York State Medical Society from his rejection by local society while local society's rule against osteopaths had been authorized by state society. Kurk v Medical Soc. of County of Queens, Inc. (1965) 46 Misc. 2d 790, 260 N.Y.S.2d 520, revd on other grounds (1965, 2d Dept) 24 A.D.2d 897, 264 N.Y.S.2d 859, affd (1966) 18 N.Y.2d 928, 276 N.Y.S.2d 1007, 223 N.E.2d 499

A district dental society, as a component part of the state dental society, functions as an agent of the state, and a code of ethics adopted by the district society providing it would be unethical for any member to publish or broadcast any manuscript or talk to the lay public without securing the society's approval therefor, which authorized the suspension or expulsion of any member guilty of violating the code, was an unconstitutional interference with the right of free speech. Firestone v First Dist. Dental Soc. (1969) 59 Misc. 2d 362, 299 N.Y.S.2d 551

§ 1407.   Alumni corporations

(a) Alumni may be incorporated.

The alumni of any college or university, or of one or more colleges or schools of any university, may be incorporated by executing and filing a certificate pursuant to article 4 of this chapter.

(b) Type of corporation.

An alumni corporation is a charitable corporation.

(c) Powers.

An alumni corporation may create, manage and control a fund, to be known as the alumni fund, and for that purpose acquire and hold real and personal property. The principal of such fund, or the income derived therefrom, may be transferred to the college or university with which such corporation is identified, or used for and applied to such object or objects connected with such college or university as such alumni corporation shall direct.

(d) Alumni fund.

The directors of an alumni corporation shall have the custody and management of the alumni fund but shall not dispose of the whole or any part of the principal of any invested fund except as authorized by a two-thirds vote of the members of such corporation, present at an annual meeting thereof.

History: Add, L 1969, ch 1066, § 1, eff Sept 1, 1970, with substance derived from Mem Corp Law §§ 180, 182, 183; amd, L 2013, ch 549, § 117, eff July 1, 2014; L 2015, ch 555, § 11, eff Dec 11, 2015.

§ 1408.   Historical societies

(a) Historical societies may hold property.

Any incorporated historical society of this state is hereby authorized to have and hold for the purposes of inclosure, preservation and the erection of monuments, but not for business purposes, the sites of old forts, battlegrounds and other historic sites, not exceeding six acres in any one locality, which shall be exempt from taxation; and to receive donations of articles of historic interest on the condition that in case of its dissolution or inability to pay its debts otherwise than from its effects, such articles shall revert to the donors or their heirs. Fees may be charged by any such society for the exhibition of its property or collections only to the extent that the proceeds thereof are used for the preservation, maintenance and development of such property or collections.

(b) Type of corporation.

An historical society is a charitable corporation under this chapter.

(c) Acquisition.

The acquisition by any such historical society of this state of any real property for the purpose of inclosure, preservation and the erection of monuments, is hereby declared to be for a public use. Such property may be acquired in the manner prescribed by the eminent domain procedure law.

History: Add, L 1969, ch 1066, § 1, eff Sept 1, 1970, with substance derived from Mem Corp Law §§ 190, 191; amd, L 1977, ch 840, § 65, eff July 1, 1978, L 2013, ch 549, § 118, eff July 1, 2014.

CASE ANNOTATIONS

The Historic Track at Goshen, Inc. is not entitled to an exemption from taxation pursuant to either section 1408 of the Not-For-Profit Corporations Law or section 450 of the Real Property Tax Law. It is a factual issue as to whether it is organized or conducted exclusively for educational or historical purposes and whether all or a portion of its property is used exclusively for such purposes so as to entitle some or all of its property to an exemption pursuant to section 420 of the Real Property Tax Law. 6 Op Counsel SBEA #101 (1980 March 25)

§ 1409.   Agricultural and horticultural corporations

(a) Definition.

An agricultural or horticultural corporation or society is a corporation formed under or by a general or special law for promoting agriculture, horticulture and the mechanic arts.

(b) Type of corporation.

Type of corporation. An agricultural or horticultural corporation is a non-charitable corporation under this chapter, except that any such corporation which has received moneys from the state or has acted as agent for the state under paragraph (c) of this section, or has acquired or does acquire real property by condemnation is or becomes a charitable corporation under this chapter.

(c) Condemnation.

In case any agricultural or horticultural corporation or any other agricultural society which has received moneys from the state for premiums paid for improving the breed of cattle, sheep and horses, or has acted as agent for the state in disbursing moneys for such purpose can not acquire real property needed

for its corporate purposes upon satisfactory terms, it may acquire such real property by condemnation. Any real property acquired by condemnation, or otherwise, shall not be subject to condemnation by any other private corporation except a railroad corporation.

(d) Report of corporation receiving aid; disposition of property.

Any county agricultural corporation receiving after May tenth, nineteen hundred and twenty, money from any county shall, through its secretary, make annually to the board of supervisors a detailed statement with vouchers showing the disbursement during the year of all moneys so received. If such a corporation shall cease to exist, or without satisfactory reason shall fail or neglect to hold its annual exhibitions or fairs for a period of two years, the board of supervisors on notice to the corporation may petition the supreme court of the judicial district or the county court of the county to declare a forfeiture to the county of the real and personal property of the corporation in whole or in part or to confer on the county a lien upon such property, whereupon such court may make a decree determining the legal or equitable rights of the county in such property subject to the rights of creditors of the corporation.

(e) Restrictions on the formation of corporations.

There shall be but one county corporation in a county, and but one town corporation in a town, except that a second corporation may be formed if it is to be the surviving corporation under a plan of merger with the existing corporation, in which event, the certificate of incorporation of such second corporation shall have endorsed thereon or annexed thereto the approval of a justice of the supreme court of the judicial district in which the office of such corporation is to be located. Ten days written notice of the application for such approval, accompanied by a copy of the proposed certificate, shall be given to the attorney general. Whenever a new county shall be or shall have been erected out of a part of an existing county in which a county corporation existed at the time of the erection of such new county, the existing corporation may at its option be continued as the county corporation of both counties. The determination of an existing corporation to be continued as a county corporation for both counties shall be evidenced by a certificate thereof, signed and acknowledged by a majority of the directors, and filed in the office of the secretary of state and in the office of the clerk of each of such counties. A town corporation may be formed for several towns, but the formation of such corporation shall not prevent the formation of a separate town corporation for any such town.

(f) Annual fairs and premiums.

Every agricultural or horticultural corporation, the American institute in the city of New York, and the New York state agricultural society, shall hold annual fairs and exhibitions, and distribute premiums. Such corporations and societies shall regulate and award premiums on such articles, productions and improvements as they deem best calculated to promote the agricultural, horticultural, mechanic and domestic arts of the state, having special reference to the net profits which accrue or are likely to accrue from the mode of raising crops, or stock, or fabricating the articles exhibited, so that the award be made to the most economical or profitable mode of production. A county or town corporation, by a two–thirds vote of the members present and voting at a regular meeting or at a special meeting, duly called for that purpose, may fix the place where the annual fair and exhibition of the corporation shall be held.

(g) Regulation of shows on exhibition grounds.

Any agricultural or horticultural corporation, or the executive committee of such board, may regulate or prevent all kinds of theatrical, or circus, exhibitions and shows, huckstering and traffic in fruits, goods, wares and merchandise, of whatever description, and shall prevent all kinds of mountebank exhibitions or shows for gain on the fair days on such fair grounds, and also within a distance of two hundred yards of the fair grounds of the corporation, if it shall determine that they obstruct or interfere with the free and uninterrupted use of the highways around and approaching such fair grounds.

(h) Capital stock.

An agricultural or horticultural corporation may have capital stock aggregating not less than five thousand dollars, divided into shares of not less than ten dollars each, and may issue such certificates at not less than the par value thereof to raise money for its corporate purposes, if provision therefor is made in its certificate of incorporation or in a certificate filed pursuant to section 803 (Certificate of amendment; contents). An agricultural or horticultural corporation, which has issued or shall hereafter issue capital stock, entitling its shareholders to dividends from the profits of the corporation, shall be subject to the business corporation law and not to the provisions of this chapter in conflict therewith.

(i) Annual report.

On or before December fifteenth in each year, the directors of every agricultural or horticultural corporation shall make a verified report to the commissioner of agriculture and markets of the transactions of the corporation for the preceding twelve months giving full details of the receipts and expenditures thereof, with a list of premiums awarded and to whom and for what awarded.

(j) Membership in state society.

The presidents of the county agricultural corporations, or delegates to be chosen by such corporations annually, shall be ex officio members of the New York state agricultural society.

(k) Exhibitions and entertainments on fair grounds to be exempt from license.

The provisions of any special or local law or municipal ordinance, requiring the payment of a license fee for exhibitions or entertainments or requiring that an approval be obtained from any local government except an approval required to protect the safety, health and well-being of persons, shall not apply to any exhibition or entertainment held on the grounds of a town or county corporation whether or not the corporation derives a pecuniary profit from such exhibition or entertainment by the lease of its grounds for such purpose and the provisions of any special or local law or municipal ordinance shall not be construed or applied to unreasonably prohibit or restrict any agricultural or horticultural corporation receiving reimbursement pursuant to article twenty-four of the agriculture and markets law from the construction, improvement, renovation, relocation or demolition of all or any of such agricultural or horticultural corporation grounds, buildings and facilities.

History: Add, L 1969, ch 1066, § 1, eff Sept 1, 1970, with substance derived from Mem Corp Law §§ 200-209; amd, L 1970, ch 847, § 91, L 1971, ch 1057 § 11, eff July 2, 1971, L 1971, ch 1058 § 42, eff Sept 1, 1971, L 1976, ch 4, § 1, eff Feb 9, 1976, L 2006, ch 726, § 1, eff Sept 13, 2006, L 2013, ch 549, § 119, eff July 1, 2014; L 2014, ch 488, § 2 eff Dec 17, 2014.

CASE ANNOTATIONS

1. Generally
2-5. [Reserved for future use]
6. **Under former Membership Corporations Law § 200**
7. **Under former Membership Corporations Law § 201**
8. **Under former Membership Corporations Law § 204**
9. **Under former Membership Corporations Law § 206**
10. **Under former Membership Corporations Law § 209**

1. Generally

Zoning ordinance was not inapplicable to agricultural society, a not-for-profit corporation, on ground that society possessed authority to condemn which, if used, could be restricted by ordinance. Union Agricultural Soc. v Sheldon (1974) 79 Misc. 2d 818, 361 N.Y.S.2d 598

The conduct of county fairs by agricultural society does not come within definition of "public use." Union Agricultural Soc. v Sheldon (1974) 79 Misc. 2d 818, 361 N.Y.S.2d 598

Town may not impose licensing fee for concerts to be held on county fairgrounds during running of fair, even if property on which fair is held is not owned by agricultural corporation which runs fair. 1992 Op St Compt No. 92-20

2-5. [Reserved for future use]

6. Under former Membership Corporations Law § 200

Tax Law, § 180 applies to stock issued by agricultural societies under this section. 1909 Ops Atty Gen 315

An agricultural league may be formed under this section for the purpose of establishing a farm bureau. 1912 Ops Atty Gen 486

7. Under former Membership Corporations Law § 201

Where a corporation having the right to condemn real property under this section has alleged that right in its petition for condemnation of land, the allegation is traversable and the answer admits proof that the petitioner has lost the right to condemn by issuing capital stock "entitling its shareholders to dividends." Rensselaer County Agricultural & Horticultural Soc. v Weatherwax (1931) 255 N.Y. 329, 174 N.E. 699

In the absence of proof to the contrary the right to condemn remains. Rensselaer County Agricultural & Horticultural Soc. v Weatherwax (1931) 255 N.Y. 329, 174 N.E. 699

8. Under former Membership Corporations Law § 204

Where a society is a non-stock or membership corporation and has not paid dividends, and no provision is made in its charter for the payment thereof, and its only business, except an occasional and temporary renting of buildings, is the holding of agricultural fairs or exhibitions, which the law requires it to hold, it is not employing workmen in hazardous employment in a trade, business or occupation carried on by it for pecuniary gain. Finkell v Cobleskill Agricultural Soc. (1927) 220 A.D. 429, 222 N.Y.S. 70

Where a county agricultural society has conveyed certain lands to a village "excepting and reserving the right and privilege to use such premises for county fair purposes" the village is not entitled to an injunction preventing the agricultural society from having automobile races as one of the attractions at the fair. Owego v Tioga County Agricultural Soc. (1934) 152 Misc 544, 273 N.Y.S. 828

9. Under former Membership Corporations Law § 206

Under the provisions of this section, agricultural or horticultural corporations become "subject to the stock corporation law" only where capital stock is issued "entitling its shareholders to dividends from the profits of the corporation." Rensselaer County Agricultural & Horticultural Soc. v Weatherwax (1931) 255 N.Y. 329, 174 N.E. 699

Where a corporation having the right to condemn real property under § 201 has alleged that right in its petition for condemnation of land, the allegation is traversable and the answer admits proof that the petitioner had lost the right to condemn by issuing capital stock "entitling its shareholders to dividends." Rensselaer County Agricultural & Horticultural Soc. Rensselaer County Agricultural & Horticultural Soc. v Weatherwax (1931) 255 N.Y. 329, 174 N.E. 699

Agricultural societies, associations or corporations are exempt from general taxation on their property and from payment of an annual franchise tax to the state whether such corporations are stock corporations or membership corporations. 1929 Ops Atty Gen 132

An agricultural and horticultural corporation must comply with the provisions of the Stock Corporation Law in order to amend its certificate of incorporation so as to eliminate the authorization for issuance of capital stock entitling shareholders to dividends, as distinguished from non-dividend bearing stock. 1950 Ops Atty Gen Sept 27

10. Under former Membership Corporations Law § 209

Where a county agricultural society has conveyed certain lands to a village "excepting and reserving the right and privilege to use such premises for county fair purposes" the village is not entitled to an injunction preventing the agricultural society from having automobile races as one of the attractions at the fair. Owego v Tioga County Agricultural Soc. (1934) 152 Misc 544, 273 N.Y.S. 828

Vending machines, used in conjunction with the operation of a fair by an agricultural society, are not subject to taxation by the town in which the fairground is located. 1960 Ops St Compt File #374

A town may not adopt an ordinance to license side shows and various kinds of amusement enterprises using the county fair grounds during the holding of the annual fair and harness racing season. 1961 Ops St Compt File #292

A village may not impose a license requirement upon automobile racing conducted on the property of a county agricultural society. 1962 Ops St Compt #525

§ 1410. Boards of trade and chambers of commerce

(a) Definitions.

(1) A board of trade is a corporation formed for the purpose of fostering trade and commerce, or the interests of those having a common trade, business, financial or professional interest, to reform abuses relative thereto, to secure freedom from unjust or unlawful exactions, to diffuse accurate and reliable information as to the standing of merchants and other matters, to procure uniformity and certainty in the customs and usages of trade and commerce, and of those having a common trade, business, financial or professional interest; to settle and adjust differences between its members and others and to promote a more enlarged and friendly intercourse among business people; to advance the civic, commercial, industrial and agricultural interests of the territory

where the corporation is situate; to promote the general welfare and prosperity of such territory and to stimulate public sentiment to these ends; and to provide such civic, commercial, industrial, agricultural and social features as will promote these purposes.

(2) A chamber of commerce is a corporation, the members of which are in diverse lines of business, membership in which is not restricted to, nor in practice consists primarily of, persons, partnerships or corporations engaged in or carrying on the same, allied or interdependent lines of business, and which is formed for the purpose of fostering trade and commerce, or the interests of those carrying on such trade and commerce; to promote the general welfare and prosperity of the state, territory or community in which such corporation is situate; to reform abuses involving business, professional or financial interests, to secure freedom from unjust or unlawful exactions, to diffuse accurate and reliable information as to the standing of merchants and other matters, to procure uniformity and certainty in the customs and usages of trade and commerce; to settle and adjust differences between its members and others, and to promote a more enlarged and friendly intercourse among businessmen; to advance the civic, commercial, industrial and agricultural interests of the territory where the corporation is situate; to provide such features as will promote these purposes, and to stimulate public sentiment to these ends. A corporation formed before the first day of January, eighteen hundred seventy-five, the purposes and activities of which are those of a chamber of commerce as herein defined, shall be a chamber of commerce regardless of its name, and shall not be required to change its existing name by reason of this subparagraph.

(b) Type of corporation.

A board of trade or a chamber of commerce is a non-charitable corporation under this chapter.

(c) Special powers.

(1) A board of trade or a chamber of commerce organized for the purposes set forth in paragraph (a), shall have the power to be appointed and to act under the order or appointment of any court of competent jurisdiction as receiver or trustee of the property or estate of any person or corporation in insolvency and bankruptcy proceedings, and to act as assignee or trustee for the benefit of creditors in any case in which a member or members of such board of trade or a chamber of commerce are creditors of such insolvent or bankrupt estate; or of such assignor for the benefit of creditors; or in any other instance where the purposes of the corporation might reasonably be involved.

(2) A board of trade or chamber of commerce organized for the purposes set forth in paragraph (a) may make loans to its members, directors or officers, or to any other corporation, firm, association or other entity in which one or more of its members, directors

or officers are directors or officers or hold a financial interest, in any case where its board of directors finds that the making of such loan will be in furtherance of its corporate purposes and for a lawful public or quasi-public objective.

(3) A board of trade organized for the purposes set forth in paragraph (a) of this section may make distributions of cash or property to, or confer other benefits upon, its members, or former members, prior to dissolution or final liquidation in any case where the board of directors of such corporation finds that such cash, property or other benefit is not required for the conduct of its corporate purposes; provided, however, that no such action shall be taken when the corporation is currently insolvent or would thereby be made insolvent or rendered unable to carry on its corporate purposes, or when the fair value of the corporation's assets remaining after the taking of such action would be insufficient to meet its liabilities.

(4) A board of trade organized for the purposes set forth in paragraph (a) of this section may provide in its certificate of incorporation or by-laws that the members or any class of members shall, with respect to any matter on which the members of such class are entitled to vote, have more than, or less than, one vote.

History: Add, L 1969, ch 1066, § 1, eff Sept 1, 1970, with substance derived from Mem Corp Law §§ 220, 221; amd, L 1970, ch 847, § 92, eff Sept 1, 1970, L 1972, ch 741, § 1, L 1976, ch 72, § 11, eff Sept 1, 1976, L 1977, ch 869, eff Aug 11, 1977, L 2013, ch 549, § 120, eff July 1, 2014.

CASE ANNOTATIONS

1-5. [Reserved for future use]
6. Under former Membership Corporations Law § 220
1-5. [Reserved for future use]
6. Under former Membership Corporations Law § 220
A Chamber of Commerce organized for the purpose of fostering local business and trade does not qualify for real property tax exemption. 1957 Ops Atty Gen April 5 (informal)

§ 1411. Local development corporations

(a) Purposes.

This section shall provide an additional and alternate method of incorporation or reincorporation of not-for-profit corporations for any of the purposes set forth in this paragraph and shall not be deemed to alter, impair or diminish the purposes, rights, powers or privileges of any corporation heretofore or hereafter incorporated under this section or under the stock or business corporation laws. Corporations may be incorporated or reincorporated under this section as not-for-profit local development corporations operated for the exclusively charitable or public purposes of relieving and reducing unemployment, promoting and providing for additional and maximum employment, bettering and maintaining job opportunities, instructing or training individuals to improve or develop their capabilities for such jobs, carrying on scientific research for the purpose of aiding a community or

geographical area by attracting new industry to the community or area or by encouraging the development of, or retention of, an industry in the community or area, and lessening the burdens of government and acting in the public interest, and any one or more counties, cities, towns or villages of the state, or any combination thereof, or the New York job development authority in exercising its power under the public authorities law to encourage the organization of local development corporations, may cause such corporations to be incorporated by public officers or private individuals or reincorporated upon compliance with the requirements of this section, and it is hereby found, determined and declared that in carrying out said purposes and in exercising the powers conferred by paragraph (b) such corporations will be performing an essential governmental function.

(b) Type of corporation.

A local development corporation is a charitable corporation under this chapter.

(c) Powers.

In furtherance of its purposes set forth in paragraph (a) but not for any other purposes, a local development corporation incorporated or reincorporated under this section shall have the following powers: to construct, acquire, rehabilitate and improve for use by others industrial or manufacturing plants in the territory in which its operations are principally to be conducted, to assist financially in such construction, acquisition, rehabilitation and improvement, to maintain such plants for others in such territory, to disseminate information and furnish advice, technical assistance and liaison with federal, state and local authorities with respect thereto, to acquire by purchase, lease, gift, bequest, devise or otherwise real or personal property or interests therein, to borrow money and to issue negotiable bonds, notes and other obligations therefor, and notwithstanding section 510 (Disposition of all or substantially all assets) without leave of the court, to sell, lease, mortgage or otherwise dispose of or encumber any such plants or any of its real or personal property or any interest therein upon such terms as it may determine and, in connection with loans from the New York job development authority, to enter into covenants and agreements and to comply with all the terms, conditions and provisions thereof, and otherwise to carry out its corporate purposes and to foster and encourage the location or expansion of industrial or manufacturing plants in the territory in which the operations of such corporation are principally to be conducted, provided, however, that no such corporation shall attempt to influence legislation by propaganda or otherwise, or participate or intervene, directly or indirectly, in any political campaign on behalf of or in opposition to any candidate for public office.

(d) Purchase or lease of real property owned by a county, city, town or village.

(1) The local legislative body of a county, city, town or village or, if there is a board of estimate in a city, then the board of estimate, may by resolution determine that specifically described real property owned by the county, city, town or village is not required for use by such county, city, town or village and authorize the county, city, town or village to sell or lease such real property to a local development corporation incorporated or reincorporated under this article; provided, however, that title to such land be not declared inalienable as a forest preserve or a parkland.

(2) Notwithstanding the provisions of any general, special or local law, charter or ordinance to the contrary, such sale or lease may be made without appraisal, public notice, (except as provided in subparagraph (4)) or public bidding for such price or rental and upon such terms as may be agreed upon between the county, city, town or village and said local development corporation; provided, however, that in case of a lease the term may not exceed ninety-nine years and provided, further, that in cities having a population of one million or more, no such sale or lease shall be made without the approval of a majority of the members of the borough improvement board of the borough in which such real property is located.

(3) Before any sale or lease to a local development corporation incorporated or reincorporated under this article shall be authorized, a public hearing shall be held by the local legislative body, or by the board of estimate, as the case may be, to consider the proposed sale or lease.

(4) Notice of such hearing shall be published at least ten days before the date set for the hearing in such publication and in such manner as may be designated by the local legislative body, or the board of estimate as the case may be.

(5) A local development corporation, incorporated or reincorporated under this section, which purchases or leases real property from a county, city, town or village, shall not, without the written approval of the county, city, town or village, use such real property for any purpose except the purposes set forth in the certificate of incorporation or reincorporation of said local development corporation. In the event such real property is used in violation of the restrictions of this paragraph, the attorney-general may bring an action or special proceeding to enjoin the unauthorized use.

(e) Certificate of incorporation.

In addition to the requirements of section 402 (Certificate of incorporation; contents) the certificate of incorporation or reincorporation of a local development corporation incorporated or reincorporated under this article shall state (1) that all income and earnings of such corporation shall be used exclusively for its corporate purposes or accrue and be paid to the New York job development authority, (2) that no part of the income or earnings of such corporation shall inure to the benefit or profit of, nor shall any distribution of its property or assets be made to any member or private person, corporate or individual, or any other private interest, except that the certificate of incorporation or reincorporation may authorize the repayment of loans and may also authorize the repayment of contributions (other than dues) to the local development corporation but only if and to the extent that any such contribution may not be allowable as a deduction in computing taxable income under the internal revenue code of nineteen hundred fifty-four, (3) that if such corporation accepts a mortgage loan or loans from the New York job development authority, such corporation shall be dissolved in accordance with the provisions of paragraph (g) upon the repayment or other discharge in full by such corporation of all such loans.

(f) Exemption of income from taxation.

The income and operations of corporations incorporated or reincorporated under this section shall be exempt from taxation.

(g) Dissolution.

Upon the dissolution of any local development corporation incorporated or reincorporated under this section no member or private person, corporate or individual, or other private interest, shall be entitled to any distribution or division of its remaining funds and other property and rights and interests in property, and the balance thereof, after the payment of all debts and liabilities of the corporation of whatsoever kind and nature, (including the payment of loans and contributions the repayment of which has been authorized in its certificate of incorporation or reincorporation) shall be distributed to one or more counties, cities, towns or villages within the territory designated in its certificate of incorporation or reincorporation as the territory in which its operations are principally to be conducted, for furtherance of the purposes set forth in paragraph (a), or to the New York job development authority, as shall be provided by said corporation or by order of the supreme court of the state of New York pursuant to section 1008 (Jurisdiction of supreme court to supervise dissolution and liquidation).

(h) Corporations heretofore incorporated.

Any corporation heretofore incorporated under the membership corporations law or this chapter, or under the stock or business corporation law for any of the purposes set forth in paragraph (a) of this section may amend its certificate of incorporation and be reincorporated as a local development corporation organized under this section by making and filing in the office of the secretary of state a certificate, stating the name of such corporation, and, if it has been changed, the name under which it was originally incorporated, the date of its incorporation, the names and post-office addresses of its members or of the holders of record of all of the outstanding shares of such corporation entitled to vote with relation to the proceedings provided for in the certificate and that such corporation has elected to become and be a local development corporation organized and operated under and by virtue of this section. Such certificate shall be either (1) subscribed in person or by proxy by all of the members or the holders of record of all of the outstanding shares of such corporation entitled to vote with relation to such proceedings and shall have annexed an affidavit of the secretary or an assistant secretary that the persons who have executed the certificate, in person or by proxy, constitute all of the members or the holders of record of all of the outstanding shares of the corporation entitled to vote with relation to the proceedings provided for in the certificate, or (2) subscribed by the president or a vice president and the secretary or an assistant secretary and shall have annexed an affidavit of such officers stating that they have been authorized to execute and file such certificate by the votes, cast in person or by proxy, of all of the members or of the holders of record of all of the outstanding shares of such corporation entitled to vote with relation to such proceedings at the meeting at which such votes were cast, and that such votes were cast at a meeting of members or stockholders held on a date specified, upon notice pursuant to section 605 (Notice of meeting of members) or to section 605 of the Business Corporation Law. Every certificate filed under this paragraph shall have endorsed thereon or annexed thereto the approval of a justice of the supreme court of the judicial district in which the office of the corporation is to be located. A reincorporation pursuant to this paragraph shall not effect a dissolution of the corporation, but shall be deemed a continuation of its corporate existence, without affecting its then existing property rights or liabilities, or the liabilities of its members or officers as such, but thereafter it shall have only such rights, powers and privileges, and be subject only to such other duties and liabilities, as a corporation created for the same purposes under this article.

(i) Effect of section.

Corporations incorporated or reincorporated under this section shall be organized and operated exclusively for the purposes set forth in paragraph (a), shall have, in addition to the powers otherwise conferred by law, the powers conferred by paragraph (c) and shall be subject to all the restrictions and limitations imposed by paragraph (e) and paragraph (g). In so far as the provisions of this section are inconsistent with the provisions of any other law, general or special, the provisions of this section shall be controlling as to corporations incorporated or reincorporated hereunder.

History: Add, L 1969, ch 1066, § 1, eff Sept 1, 1970, with substance derived from Mem Corp Law §§ 230-236; amd, L 1970, ch 847, § 93, eff Sept 1, 1970, L 1981, ch 179, § 1, eff June 2, 1981, L 1999, ch 172, § 29, eff July 6, 1999, L 2013, ch 549, § 121, eff July 1, 2014.

CASE ANNOTATIONS

1. Generally
2-5. [Reserved for future use]
6. Under former Membership Corporations Law § 231

1. Generally

The Town of Hempstead Local Development Corporation is authorized to compensate its directors by reason of rendering services in effecting its corporate purposes. 1977 Op Atty Gen March 29

Positions of town attorney and director of local development corporation are compatible; office of town board member also is compatible with director position. 1998 Ops Atty Gen I 98-23

Many of local development corporation's records would remain subject to Freedom of Information Law, even if corporation were not itself subject to that statute as not-for-profit corporation, where corporation performed government function and several members of its board served due to their status as city officials. Comm on Open Gov't FOIL-AO-12386

Board of local development corporation would be deemed "public body" for purposes of Open Meetings Law where (1) it was entity for which quorum was required pursuant to provisions of Not-for-Profit Corporation Law, (2) it consisted of more than 2 members, and (3) based on language of CLS N-PCL § 1411(a), it conducted public business and performed governmental function for public corporation (city). Comm on Open Gov't FOIL-AO-12386

Local development corporation (LDC) would be required to comply with Freedom of Information Law, notwithstanding its status as not-for-profit corporation, if there is significant government control, i.e., if majority of LDC's board of directors consists of or is designated by government. Comm on Open Gov't FOIL-AO-12401

If town official acting in his or her capacity as town official serves on local development corporation (LDC) board, records that he or she produces or receives in that capacity would be town records subject to rights conferred by Freedom of Information Law. Comm on Open Gov't FOIL-AO-12401

Petitioner, membership corporation whose sole member was Town of Clifton Park Water Authority, public benefit corporation, was not supplying water under CLS Tax § 186, and was not subject to franchise tax imposed under that section, where petitioner's activities consisted of leasing of all of its facilities and assets to Authority, under lease agreement with Authority, whereby petitioner relinquished its possession and control of facilities and assets to Authority; further, petitioner was not selling water or furnishing water service for purposes of CLS Tax § 186-a, and thus was not subject to excise tax imposed thereunder. N.Y. Adv Op Comm T & F TSB-A-00-(6)C

Petitioner was not subject to franchise tax imposed under CLS Tax Law Art 9-A since petitioner was reincorporated as not-for-profit local development corporation under CLS N-PCL § 1411 with its exclusive purpose to lessen burdens of government and act in public interest. N.Y. Adv Op Comm T & F TSB-A-00-(6)C

Mortgages given to or by petitioner, not-for-profit local development corporation, were exempt from mortgage recording taxes since petitioner was reincorporated under CLS N-PCL § 1411, and CLS N-PCL § 1411(f) provided that income and operations of corporations incorporated or reincorporated under such section shall be exempt from taxation. N.Y. Adv Op Comm T & F TSB-A-93-(13)R

Construction loan mortgages recorded by Greater Syracuse Business Development Corporation (petitioner) were exempt from mortgage recording tax, even if mortgages were or might be assigned immediately after recording to private lender for duration of construction phase of project, but then reassigned to petitioner after completion of construction phase for remainder of their term, since petitioner was reincorporated under CLS N-PCL § 1411, and CLS N-PCL § 1411(f) provides that income and operations of corporations incorporated or reincorporated under such section shall be exempt from taxation. N.Y. Adv Op Comm T & F TSB-A-95-(16)R

2-5. [Reserved for future use]

6. Under former Membership Corporations Law § 231

Where the County Board of Supervisors has been abolished and succeeded by a County Legislature upon the adoption of a County Charter, the simultaneous holding of the elective town office of Town Supervisor and the appointed office of Executive Director of a County Area Development Corporation are not incompatible, as any conflict of duties in the performance of the normal and regular functions in each office is extremely remote and unusual and does not invalidate the simultaneous holding of dual positions nor constitute incompatibility. 1967 Ops St Compt File #263

§ 1412. University faculty practice corporations

(a) Organization. Notwithstanding any other provision of law, one or more individuals who are duly authorized by law to render the same professional service, which shall be the practice of medicine, the practice of dentistry, the practice of chiropractics, the practice of physical therapy or the practice of optometry, and who are members of the faculty of the same accredited medical school, dental school, chiropractic college, college or university with an accredited doctor of physical therapy program or optometry college, as applicable, in the state of New York may organize, or cause to be organized, a university faculty practice corporation under this article (1) for the purpose of supporting the educational mission of such school by providing clinical instruction and supervision of students of such school, interns and residents and, incident thereto, rendering professional services and (2) which shall be operated in compliance with (A) section 501(c)(3) of the United States internal revenue code and (B) the faculty practice plan with which members of the faculty of such school are required to comply, as amended from time to time.

(b) Definition. "University faculty practice corporation" means a corporation organized or reincorporated under this section.

(c) Certificate of incorporation. The certificate of incorporation of a university faculty practice corporation shall meet the requirements of this chapter and shall have attached thereto a certificate or certificates issued by the licensing authority certifying that each of the proposed members, if any, directors and officers is authorized by law to practice the profession which the corporation is being organized to practice. The certificate shall also state (1) the name of the medical school, dental school, chiropractic college, college or university with an accredited doctor of physical therapy program or optometry college, as applicable, in the state of New York of which the proposed members, if any, directors and officers are faculty and (2) that such corporation shall operate in compliance with (A) section 501(c)(3) of the United States internal revenue code and (B) the faculty practice plan with which members of the faculty of such school are required to comply, as amended from time to time.

(d) Type. A university faculty practice corporation is a charitable corporation under this chapter.

(e) Applicability of laws; members, directors and officers. This chapter shall be applicable to a university faculty practice corporation except to the extent that the provisions thereof conflict with this section. A university faculty practice corporation may consolidate or merge only with another university faculty practice corporation. The following provisions of article fifteen of the business corporation law shall be applicable to a university faculty practice corporation except that each reference in such provisions to a "shareholder" shall be deemed to be a reference to a "member" and each reference in such provisions to "shareholders" shall be deemed a reference to "members": paragraphs (a), (b), (c) and (e) of section fifteen hundred one; paragraphs (b), (c) and (d) of section fifteen hundred three; paragraphs (a), (c) and (g) of section fifteen hundred four; section fifteen hundred five; section fifteen hundred nine except to the extent such section refers to section fifteen hundred ten; paragraph (a) of section fifteen hundred twelve; section fifteen hundred fourteen; and section fifteen hundred fifteen. No individual may be a member, director or officer of a university faculty practice corporation unless such individual is authorized by law to practice in this state the profession which such corporation is authorized to practice and is a member of the faculty of the medical school, dental school, chiropractic college, college or university with an accredited doctor of physical therapy program or optometry college which such corporation is organized to support.

(f) Corporations heretofore incorporated. Any corporation heretofore incorporated under article fifteen of the business corporation law and operated in compliance with the requirements of section 501(c)(3) of the United States internal revenue code may amend its certificate of incorporation and be reincorporated as a university faculty practice corporation organized under this section by making and filing in the office of the secretary of state a certificate entitled "Certificate of Reincorporation of....(name of incorporation) under section 1412 of the Not-for-Profit Corporation Law."

(1) Such reincorporation certificate shall contain the provisions required, and any other provisions permitted, by section 402 of this chapter and shall also set forth (A) a statement that such corporation is filing such reincorporation certificate under this section, (B) if the name of such corporation has been changed, the name under which such corporation was originally incorporated, (C) the date of incorporation of such corporation, (D) the names and post-office addresses of the holders of record of all of the outstanding shares of such corporation entitled to vote, (E) a statement that such corporation has elected to become and be a university faculty practice corporation organized and operated under by virtue of this section and (F) the statements required by paragraph (c) of this section.

(2) Such reincorporation certificate shall be either (A) subscribed in person or by proxy by all of the holders of record of all of the outstanding shares of such corporation entitled to vote and shall have annexed an affidavit of the secretary or an assistant secretary that the persons who have executed the certificate, in person or by proxy, constitute all of the holders of record of all of the outstanding shares of

the corporation entitled to vote or (B) subscribed by the president or a vice president and the secretary or an assistant secretary and shall have annexed an affidavit of such officers stating that they have been authorized to execute and file such reincorporation certificate by the votes, cast in person or by proxy, of all of the holders of record of all of the outstanding shares of such corporation entitled to vote at the meeting at which such votes were cast, and that such votes were cast at a meeting of shareholders held on a date specified, upon notice pursuant to section six hundred five of the business corporation law.

(3) A reincorporation pursuant to this paragraph shall not effect a dissolution of such corporation, but shall be deemed a continuation of its corporate existence, without affecting its then-existing property rights or liabilities, or the liabilities of its shareholders, directors or officers as such, but thereafter it shall have only such rights, powers and privileges, and it and such shareholders, directors and officers shall be subject only to such other duties and liabilities, as a university faculty practice corporation and members, directors and officers thereof.

(4) Upon the filing of a reincorporation certificate in the office of the secretary of state, (A) any issued and outstanding shares of such corporation shall be purchased by such corporation at a purchase price equal to the price for which such shares were originally issued, or such other price as such corporation shall agree to, such price to be paid out of the surplus of the corporation, whereupon such shares shall be deemed cancelled as of the date of such filing and (B) such reincorporation certificate shall be deemed to replace the certificate of incorporation of such corporation. The department of state shall not file such certificate of reincorporation unless the consent of the commissioner of taxation and finance is attached thereto. Such certificate of consent shall only be given if the commissioner of taxation and finance ascertains that all taxes imposed under article nine-A of the tax law, as well as penalties and interest charges related thereto, accrued against the corporation have been paid.

(g) Effect of section. University faculty practice corporations incorporated or reincorporated under this section shall be organized and operated exclusively for the purposes set forth in paragraph (a) of this section and shall be subject to the restrictions and limitations imposed by or pursuant to paragraphs (a) and (e) of this section. Notwithstanding anything to the contrary in article twenty-eight of the public health law or the regulations adopted pursuant thereto, no corporation organized under this section shall be deemed to be establishing or operating a hospital, diagnostic center and/or treatment center requiring establishment or construction approval solely by reason of being organized as a not-for-profit corporation. Insofar as the provisions of this section are inconsistent with the provisions of any other law, general or special, the provisions of this section shall be controlling as to the corporations incorporated or reincorporated hereunder.

History: Add, L 1993, ch 555, § 1, eff July 28, 1993; amd, , L 1993, ch 555, § 16, eff Aug 20, 1993, L 1998, ch 158, § 1, L 1999, ch 253, §§ 1-3, eff July 13, 1999, L 1998, ch 375, § 50, L 1999, ch 172, § 30, eff July 6, 1999, L 2012, ch 323, § 1, eff Aug 1, 2012, L 2013, ch 549, § 122, eff July 1, 2014.

ARTICLE 15
PUBLIC CEMETERY CORPORATIONS

History: Add, L 1977, ch 871, § 2, eff Aug 11, 1977.

§ 1501.　Declaration of policy

The people of this state have a vital interest in the establishment, maintenance and preservation of public burial grounds and the proper operation of the corporations which own and manage the same. This article is determined an exercise of the police powers of this state to protect the well-being of our citizens, to promote the public welfare and to prevent cemeteries from falling into disrepair and dilapidation and becoming a burden upon the community, and in furtherance of the public policy of this state that cemeteries shall be conducted on a non-profit basis for the mutual benefit of plot owners therein.

History: Add, L 1977, ch 871, § 2, eff Aug 11, 1977.

CASE ANNOTATIONS

Town zoning board properly denied cemetery corporation's application for use variance to permit certain mausoleum complex to be built on corporation's newly acquired addition to cemetery, based on project's effect on character of locality; town's zoning ordinance, which provided that cemetery was not permitted use in any district, but that it was nonconforming use which could be continued if existing at time of passage of ordinance, was not unconstitutional as applied to corporation since state law regarding cemetery regulation does not preempt local zoning law, and zoning board's disapproval of specific mausoleum complex did not preclude subsequent applications for projects having lesser impact on area. Beverly Hills Cemetery Corp. v Putnam Valley (1988, 2d Dept) 136 A.D.2d 669, 524 N.Y.S.2d 47, app dismd, app den 72 N.Y.2d 828, 530 N.Y.S.2d 547, 526 N.E.2d 38

New York State Cemetery Board properly denied non-for-profit cemetery corporation's application to lease 3-acre parcel to for-profit funeral home for purpose of constructing and operating funeral home and related businesses where Board determined that proposal had potential adverse financial repercussions for cemetery corporation in that duration of lease (40 years with 4 10-year options to renew) would preclude future alternatives, cemetery corporation did not present sufficient proof that it adequately sought offers from other entities, nature and duration of relationship between cemetery corporation and funeral home was deemed significant as source of potential conflict with interests of lot owners, and Board found proposed construction inappropriate when viewed in light of public policy concerns underpinning statutorily mandated not-for-profit status of cemeteries (19 NYCRR § 201.16(c)(5), CLS N-PCL § 1501). Poughkeepsie Rural Cemetery v Treadwell (1998, 3d Dept) 252 A.D.2d 903, 676 N.Y.S.2d 338

New York State Cemetery Board's comprehensive report indicating its opposition to relationships between funeral homes and not-for-profit cemeteries did not constitute unlawful rule-making since such declaration did not constitute mandatory procedure applied without discretion but was limited to factual circumstances of particular contractual relationship in question. Poughkeepsie Rural Cemetery v Treadwell (1998, 3d Dept) 252 A.D.2d 903, 676 N.Y.S.2d 338

A decision of the Federal Circuit Court of Appeals which, for Federal estate tax purposes, disallowed a charitable bequest to a nonprofit cemetery corporation in the absence of any proof that the subject cemetery operated exclusively for "charitable purposes" within the meaning of section 2055 (subd [a], par [2]) of the Internal Revenue Code (US Code, tit 26, § 2055, subd [a], par [2]) is not decisive of the allowance of such a bequest for New York estate tax purposes, since the final Federal judicial determination has been shown by a preponderance of the evidence to be inimical to the statutory laws of this State (Tax Law, § 961) which clearly express the legislative intent that nonprofit cemetery corporations (Not-For-Profit Corporation Law, § 1401, subd [d]; § 1501) be deemed to operate exclusively for charitable purposes (see, also, EPTL 8-1.5) in that, in the absence of sufficient funds, the cost of preservation and maintenance of cemeteries would descend upon the public. Re Estate of Watson (1978) 96 Misc. 2d 327, 409 N.Y.S.2d 357

A town which accepts a conveyance of a cemetary and perpetual trust fund from an unincorporated cemetary association may later convey what is received to a not-for-profit cemetary corporation, but it is doubtful whether the town could make such a conveyance to an unincorporated association. 1981 Op St Compt File #80-810

§ 1502. Definitions

As used in this article:

(a) The term "cemetery corporation" means any corporation formed under a general or special law for the disposal or burial of deceased human beings, by cremation or in a grave, mausoleum, vault, columbarium or other receptacle but does not include a family cemetery corporation or a private cemetery corporation.

(b) The term "lot owner" or "owner of a lot" means any person having a lawful title to the use of a niche, crypt, lot, plot or part thereof, in a cemetery, mausoleum or columbarium.

(c) The term "cemetery board" means the cemetery board in the division of cemeteries in the department of state.

(d) A public mausoleum, crematory or columbarium shall be included within the term "cemetery".

(e) The sale of a lot, plot or part thereof, grave, niche or crypt shall mean the sale of the right of use thereof for burial purposes.

(f) The term "monuments" means a memorial erected in a cemetery on a lot, plot or part thereof, except private mausoleums.

(g) The term "interment" means the permanent disposition of human remains by inurnment, entombment or ground burial.

(h) The term "cremation" means the technical process, using heat and flame, that reduces human remains to ashes and other residue. "Cremation" shall include the processing, and may include the pulverization, of such ashes and other residue.

(i) The term "cremains" means ashes and other residue recovered after the completion of cremation, which may include residue of foreign matter that may have been cremated with the human remains.

(j) The term "alternative container" or "external wrappings" means a nonmetal receptacle or enclosure, without ornamentation or a fixed interior lining, which is designed for the encasement of human remains and which is made of cardboard, pressed wood, composite materials (with or without an outside covering), or pouches of canvas or other material.

(k) The term "casket" means a rigid container that is designed for the encasement of human remains and customarily ornamented and lined with fabric.

(l) The term "crematory" means a facility or portion of a building in which the remains of deceased human beings are processed by cremation.

(m) The term "holding facility" or "temporary storage facility" means an area that (i) is designated for the retention of human remains prior to cremation; (ii) complies with all applicable public health laws, (iii) preserves the health and safety of the crematory personnel; and (iv) is secure from access by anyone other than authorized persons. The interior of such facility shall not be visible from any area accessible to the general public.

(n) The term "cremation permit" means the burial and removal permit required pursuant to section forty-one hundred forty-five of the public health law that is annotated for disposition of the remains of a deceased human being by cremation.

(o) The term "cremation authorization" means the crematory form authorizing a cremation which is signed by the next of kin or authorizing agent. This crematory form must be a separate document and cannot be a part of another form or document.

(p) The term "authorizing agent" shall mean the person with the right to control the disposition of the decedent pursuant to section forty-two hundred one of the public health law.

(q) The term "pet cremated remains" means ashes and/or other residue recovered after the completion of cremation of any domestic animal that has been adapted or tamed to live in intimate association with people where such cremation has occurred at a pet crematorium as defined in section seven hundred fifty-a of the general business law.

(r) The term "nonsectarian burial society" means a corporation or unincorporated association or society having among its activities or its former activities the provision of burial benefits for its members and not supervised or controlled by a religious corporation.

(s) The term "religious burial society" means a corporation or unincorporated association or society having among its activities or its former activities the provision of burial benefits for its members and supervised or controlled by a religious corporation.

History: Add, L 1977, ch 871, § 2, eff Aug 11, 1977; amd, L 1985, ch 608, § 1, eff Sept 1, 1985; L 2006, ch 579, § 1, eff Oct 15, 2006 (see 2006 note below); L 2016, ch 330, §1, eff Sept 26, 2016; L 2017, ch 442, § 1, eff Nov 29, 2017.

§ 1503.   Application

(a) [As amended, L 2006, ch 579, § 2 and ch 580, § 1] Except as otherwise provided in paragraph (b) of this section, paragraph (c) of section fifteen hundred seven and paragraph (m) of section fifteen hundred ten, this article does not apply to (1) a religious corporation, (2) a municipal corporation, (3) a cemetery corporation owning a cemetery operated, supervised or controlled by or in connection with a religious corporation or (4) a cemetery belonging to a religious or a municipal corporation, or operated, supervised or controlled by or in connection with a religious corporation unless any officer, member or employee of any such corporation shall receive or may be lawfully entitled to receive any pecuniary profit from the operations thereof, other than reasonable compensation for services in effecting one or more of the purposes of such corporation or as proper beneficiaries of its strictly charitable purposes or unless the organization of any such corporation for any of its avowed purposes be a guise or pretense for directly or indirectly making any other pecuniary profit for such corporation, or for any of its officers, members or employees, and unless any such corporation is not, in good faith, organized or conducted exclusively for one or more of its stated purposes.

(b) All crematories shall be subject to inspection by the division of cemeteries. Upon inspection, the crematory may be asked to produce any and all records for the operation and maintenance of the crematory. These records may include but not be limited to cremation authorizations, rules and regulations of the crematory, procedures as set forth in section fifteen hundred seventeen of this article, and the written procedure of the identification of remains.

History: Add, L 1977, ch 871, § 2; amd, L 1993, ch 169, § 1, eff June 28, 1993; L 2006, ch 579, § 2, eff Oct 15, 2006; L 2006, ch 580, § 1, eff Feb 12, 2007.

§ 1504.   Cemetery board and general administration

(a) A cemetery board is hereby created within the division of cemeteries in the department of state, subject to the following requirements: (1) The members of such board shall be the secretary of state, the attorney general and the commissioner of health, who shall serve without additional compensation. (2) The secretary of state, attorney general and commissioner of health may each, by official order filed in the office of his respective department and in the office of the board, designate a deputy or other representative in his department to perform any or all of the duties under this section of the department head making such designation, as may be provided in such order. Such designation shall be deemed temporary only and shall not affect the civil service or retirement rights of any person so designated. Such designees shall serve without additional compensation. (3) The secretary of state shall be chairman of such board, provided that in his absence at any meeting of the board the attorney general or the commissioner of health, in such order, if either or both be present, shall act as chairman. When designees of such officers, in the absence of all such officers, are present at any meeting of the board, the designee of the secretary of state, if present, and in his absence one of the other designees present, in the same order of preference as provided for the officer appointing him, shall act as chairman. (4) Technical, legal or other services shall be performed in so far as practicable by personnel of the departments of state, law and health without additional compensation but the board may employ and compensate within appropriations available therefor such assistants and employees as may be necessary to carry out the provisions of this section and may prescribe their powers and duties. (5) Two members of the board shall constitute a quorum to transact the business of the board at both regular and special meetings. (6) The board shall meet at least once a month, shall keep a record of all its proceedings and shall determine the rules of its own proceedings. (7) Special meetings may be called by the chairman upon his initiative, and must be called by him upon receipt of a written request therefor signed by another member of the board. Written notice of the time and place of such special meeting shall be delivered to the office of each member of the board. (8) The board shall have the duty of administering the provisions of this chapter which deal with cemetery corporations other than the cemeteries and cemetery corporations enumerated in section fifteen hundred three and shall have all the powers herein provided and such other powers and duties as may be otherwise prescribed by law.

(b) Director of the division of cemeteries. The cemetery board shall appoint a director of the division of cemeteries who shall hold his office for a term of six years. He shall receive an annual salary to be fixed by the board within the appropriations available to the board. Subject to the supervision, direction and control of the board, the director of the division of cemeteries shall be responsible for the administration of this article and he shall exercise and perform such duties and functions of the board as it may assign or delegate to him from time to time.

(c) Powers and duties of the cemetery board. With respect to any cemetery or cemetery corporation, the cemetery board shall have the following duties and powers:

(1) To adopt such reasonable rules and regulations as the cemetery board shall deem necessary for the proper administration of this article.

(2) To order any cemetery corporation to do such acts as may be necessary to comply with the provisions of this article or any rule or regulation adopted by the cemetery board or to refrain from doing any act in violation thereof.

(2-a) To adopt reasonable rules and regulations to exempt those cemetery corporations from the provisions of paragraph (h) of section fifteen hundred ten of this chapter which because of a limited number of paid employees or appropriate resources are unable to carry out such provisions.

(2-b) To adopt reasonable rules and regulations to extend the time period mandated by the provisions of paragraph (h) of section fifteen hundred ten of this chapter when necessary because compliance by a cemetery corporation within such time period is impossible.

(3) To enforce its orders by mandamus or injunction in a summary proceeding or otherwise. In connection with such action or proceeding, the attorney general is authorized to take proof, issue subpoenas and administer oaths in the manner provided in the civil practice law and rules.

(4) To impose a civil penalty upon a cemetery corporation not exceeding one thousand dollars, after conducting an adjudicatory hearing pursuant to the provisions of the state administrative procedure act, for a violation of or a failure to comply with any provisions contained in this article or any regulation, directive or order of the board, and without the need to maintain a civil action pursuant to subdivision five of this paragraph.

(5) To maintain a civil action in the name of the people of the state to recover a judgment for a money penalty imposed under the provisions of this article.

(d) Judicial review. Any order or determination of the cemetery board made pursuant to this article shall be subject to review by the supreme court in the manner provided by article seventy-eight of the civil practice law and rules; provided, however, that an application for review of such order or determination must be made within one hundred twenty days from the date of the filing of such order or determination, and provided further that no stay shall be granted pending the determination of the matter except on notice to the cemetery board and for a period not exceeding thirty days. Proceedings to review such order shall be entitled to a preference.

History: Add, L 1977, ch 871, § 2, eff Aug 11, 1977; amd, L 1977, ch 872; L 1980, ch 565, § 1, eff June 26, 1980,2, eff Oct 15, 2006 (see 2006 note below); L 1981, ch 255, § 1, eff June 15, 1981; L 1985, ch 557, § 1, eff July 26, 1985.

CASE ANNOTATIONS

1. **Generally**
2-5. **[Reserved for future use]**
6. **Under former § 1401**

1. Generally

New York State Cemetery Board properly denied non-for-profit cemetery corporation's application to lease 3-acre parcel to for-profit funeral home for purpose of constructing and operating funeral home and related businesses where Board determined that proposal had potential adverse financial repercussions for cemetery corporation in that duration of lease (40 years with 4 10-year options to renew) would preclude future alternatives, cemetery corporation did not present sufficient proof that it adequately sought offers from other entities, nature and duration of relationship between cemetery corporation and funeral home was deemed significant as source of potential conflict with interests of lot owners, and Board found proposed construction inappropriate when viewed in light of public policy concerns underpinning statutorily mandated not-for-profit status of cemeteries (19 NYCRR § 201.16(c)(5), CLS N-PCL § 1501). Poughkeepsie Rural Cemetery v Treadwell (1998, 3d Dept) 252 A.D.2d 903, 676 N.Y.S.2d 338

New York State Cemetery Board's comprehensive report indicating its opposition to relationships between funeral homes and not-for-profit cemeteries did not constitute unlawful rule-making since such declaration did not constitute mandatory procedure applied without discretion but was limited to factual circumstances of particular contractual relationship in question. Poughkeepsie Rural Cemetery v Treadwell (1998, 3d Dept) 252 A.D.2d 903, 676 N.Y.S.2d 338

2-5. [Reserved for future use]

6. Under former § 1401

Where cemetery corporation bound itself to pay purchase price of $7 million for land in certificates of indebtedness, and also to satisfy vendors' purchase obligations of $800,000, and certificates required that $800,000 obligation be satisfied out of cemetery's land purchase fund rather than out of unrestricted funds, State Cemetery Board had ample authority, under CLS Not-For-Profit Corporations Law § 1401, subds zz(2) and z(2), to issue order suspending payments to holders of certificates until amounts paid on $800,000 obligation were recovered from land purchase fund. Reed v Knollwood Park Cemetery, Inc. (1977, DC NY) 441 F. Supp. 1144

§ 1505.   Special requirements of incorporation

(a) Certificate of incorporation; additional contents. In addition to the requirements of section four hundred two (Certificate of incorporation; contents), the certificate of incorporation of a cemetery corporation shall be filed in the office of the clerk of each county in which any part of the cemetery is proposed to be, or is, situated, and shall state: (1) each city, village or town, and county, in which any part of the cemetery is or is proposed to be situated; and (2) the time of the annual meeting.

(b) Cemetery board endorsement. Every certificate of incorporation of a cemetery corporation, except those within the exclusionary provisions of section fifteen hundred three, shall have endorsed thereon or annexed thereto the approval of the cemetery board as required in subdivision (e) of section four hundred four of this chapter.

Not-For-Profit Corporation Law

(c) Type of corporation. A cemetery corporation is a charitable corporation under this chapter.

(d) Lot owners in unincorporated cemeteries may incorporate. (1) Not less than three owners of lots in an unincorporated cemetery may cause a notice to be posted in at least six conspicuous places in the city, town or village in which such cemetery is located, and to be published once in each week for three successive weeks in a newspaper, if any, published in such municipality, stating that at a time and place specified, a meeting of the lot owners will be held to determine whether such cemetery shall be incorporated, pursuant to this chapter. (2) The meeting shall be held at a convenient place in the city, town or village in which the cemetery is located, not less than twenty-five nor more than thirty days after the first posting and publication of the notice of the meeting. At such meeting every lot owner shall be entitled to one vote in person or by proxy for each lot owned by him. The persons entitled to vote at such meeting shall select a chairman and secretary, and determine by ballot whether or not the lot owners shall incorporate pursuant to this chapter. (3) If a majority of the ballots are in favor of incorporation, the persons entitled to vote at such meeting shall select three lot owners to incorporate and the provisions of this chapter shall be applicable, except that three persons may incorporate, and the corporation shall not be required to have more than three directors. Upon such incorporation, the lot owners shall be members of the corporation, and it shall be vested with the title to such cemetery and the personal property appertaining thereto. If the title to the cemetery has prior to such incorporation vested in the town, pursuant to section two hundred and ninety-one of the town law of section one of title seven of chapter eleven of part one of the revised statute, the supervisor of such town shall on request of the directors of such corporation, execute to it a deed of such cemetery lands releasing all interest of the town therein, and thereafter the title shall be vested in the corporation.

History: Add, L 1977, ch 871, § 2, eff Aug 11, 1977; amd, L 2013, ch 549, § 123, eff July 1, 2014.

§ 1505-a. Additional requirements for incorporation of crematories

(a) Approval. A cemetery corporation seeking the approval to operate a crematory must submit for approval by the cemetery board the following: (1) a list of the directors, employees, and certificate holders of the cemetery corporation; (2) a certified survey of the site and location within the county it will be situated; (3) a business plan for the operation of the crematory to include, but not be limited to, number of expected cremations per year, number of cremation units, manufacture, capital costs, financing, anticipated number of employees, types of services provided, pricing thereof; (4) a description of the impact of the proposed crematory on other crematories within the county or whether the crematory will have an adverse impact on the surrounding community; (5) plans,

designs, and costs of any structures to be erected or retrofitted for the crematory use; (6) a description of any approvals or permits required by state or local law. No crematory shall be approved until such other approvals or permits have been obtained. Any board approval of a crematory shall be so conditioned.

(b) Further information. Within thirty-five days following receipt of the information required by paragraph (a) of this section, the cemetery board or the division of cemeteries may request from the cemetery corporation any additional information or documentation and technical assistance deemed necessary to review such information. Such information shall not be deemed complete until the requested additional information has been received. If no such request is made, the submission shall be deemed complete on the thirty-fifth day after its receipt by the division.

(c) Determination. The cemetery board shall approve or deny the proposed crematory within ninety days of the completed submission.

(d) Notification. The cemetery board shall provide written notice of its determination to the cemetery corporation. If a negative determination is made, such notice shall state the reasons therefor. Notice shall be made by registered or certified mail addressed to the corporation at its principal office.

Add, L 2006, ch 579, § 3, eff Oct 15, 2006.

§ 1506. Cemetery lands

(a) Purchase of land; notice to cemetery board. No cemetery corporation, in purchasing real property hereafter, shall pay or agree to pay more than the fair and reasonable market value thereof. The terms of the purchase, including the price to be paid and the method of payment, shall be subject to notice and approval of the cemetery board. In determining the fair and reasonable market value, the cemetery board may take into consideration the method by which the purchase price is to be paid.

(b) Consent of local authorities.

(1) No cemetery shall hereafter be located in any city or village without the consent of the local legislative body of such city, or the board of trustees of such village.

(2) No cemetery shall hereafter be located in any town, outside of an incorporated village in Suffolk county, without the consent of the town board of such town.

(c) Cemeteries in Kings, Queens, Rockland, Westchester, Nassau, Suffolk, Putnam and Erie counties. A cemetery corporation shall not take by deed, devise or otherwise any land in the counties of Kings, Queens, Rockland, Westchester, Nassau, Suffolk, Putnam or Erie for cemetery purposes, or set apart any ground therefor in any of such counties, unless the consent of the board of supervisors or legislative body thereof, or of the city council of the city of New York, in respect to Kings or Queens county, be first obtained. Such consent may be granted upon such conditions and under such regulations and restrictions as the public health and welfare may require. Notice of application for such consent shall be published, once a week for six weeks, in the newspapers designated to publish the session laws and in such other newspapers published in the county as such board or body may direct, stating the time when the application will be made, a brief description of the lands proposed to be acquired, their location and the area thereof. Any person interested therein may be heard on such presentation. If such consent is granted the corporation may take and hold the lands designated therein. The consent shall not authorize any one corporation to take or hold more than two hundred and fifty acres of land. Nothing contained in this subdivision shall prevent any religious corporation in existence on April fifteenth, eighteen hundred fifty-four, in any of said counties from using as heretofore any burial ground then belonging to it within such county. Such board or body, from time to time, may make such regulation as to burials in any cemetery in the county as the public health may require.

(d) Limitation on the acquisition of land by rural cemetery corporations. It shall not be lawful for any rural cemetery corporation hereafter to acquire or take by deed, devise or otherwise, any land in any county within the state of New York, having a population of between one hundred and seventy-five thousand and two hundred thousand, according to the federal census of nineteen hundred, or set apart any ground for cemetery purposes therein, where there has already been set apart in any such county, five hundred acres of land for rural cemetery purposes, and the consent of the board of supervisors of any such county shall not be granted where there has already been granted five hundred acres of land, or upwards, within such county, to rural cemetery corporations. But nothing herein contained shall affect any lawful consent or grant hitherto made by the board of supervisors of any such county.

(e) Limitations on the acquisition of land for cemetery purposes in certain counties.

(1) It shall not be lawful for any corporation, association or person hereafter to set aside or use for cemetery purposes any lands in any county within the state erected on and after January first, eighteen hundred ninety, adjoining a city of the first class and having a population of between eighty thousand and eighty-five thousand according to the federal census of nineteen hundred ten; but nothing herein contained shall prevent cemetery corporations formed prior to January first, nineteen hundred seventeen, which own in such county a cemetery in which burials have been made prior to such date, from setting apart and using for burial purposes lands lying contiguous or adjacent to such cemetery which lands have been heretofore acquired by a recorded deed of conveyance made to such a cemetery corporation either for burial purposes, or for the purposes of the convenient transaction of its general business, which lands shall have been acquired with the consent of the board of supervisors; nor to prohibit the dedication or use of land within such county for a family cemetery as provided in subdivision (c) of section fourteen hundred one of this chapter.

(2) The provisions of this paragraph shall not operate to prevent any such cemetery corporation located in Nassau county from using for burial purposes contiguous or adjacent land acquired by it provided that such use shall be consented to by the Nassau county legislature.

(f) Conveyance by religious corporations or by trustees. A cemetery corporation may accept a conveyance of real property held by a religious corporation for burial purposes, or by trustees for such purposes if all such trustees living and residing in this state unite in the conveyance, subject to all trusts, restrictions and conditions upon the title or use. Lots previously sold and grants for burial purposes shall not be affected by any such conveyance; nor shall any grave, monument or other erection, or any remains, be disturbed or removed without the consent of the lot owner, or if there be no such owner, without the consent of the heirs of the persons whose remains are buried in such grave.

(g) Certain conveyances to cemetery corporations authorized. Upon approval of the cemetery board first having been obtained, a cemetery corporation which maintains and operates a cemetery may accept a conveyance of title to the fee of or to burial rights in lands within the confines of said cemetery and it shall be lawful for any cemetery or business corporation to make such conveyances. Lots previously sold and grants previously made for burial purposes shall not be affected by such conveyance. The cemetery corporation, in consideration of the conveyance to it of burial rights in lands within the confines of said cemetery, may, with the approval of the cemetery board, issue participating certificates of the kind and nature provided for in paragraph three of subdivision (e) of section fifteen hundred eleven of this article. In making its determination the cemetery board shall consider and may condition its approval on the purposes of this section.

(h) Acquisition of property by condemnation. If the certificate of incorporation or by-laws of a cemetery corporation do not exclude any person, on equal terms with other persons, from the privilege of purchasing a lot or of burial in its cemetery, such corporation may, from time to time, acquire by condemnation, exclusively for the purposes of a cemetery, not more than two hundred acres of land in the aggregate, forming one continuous tract, wholly or partly within the county in which its certificate of incorporation is filed or recorded, except as in this section otherwise provided as to the counties of Erie, Nassau, Suffolk, Putnam, Kings, Queens, Rockland

and Westchester. A cemetery corporation may acquire by condemnation, exclusively for the purposes of a cemetery, any real property or any interest therein necessary to supply water for the uses of such cemetery, and the right to lay, relay, repair and maintain conduits and water pipes with connections and fixtures, in, through or over the lands of others and the right to intercept and divert the flow of waters from the lands of riparian owners, and from persons owning or interested in any waters. But no such cemetery corporation shall have power to take or use water from any of the canals of this state, or any canal reservoirs as feeders, or any streams which have been taken by the state for the purpose of supplying the canals with water. A cemetery corporation may acquire, otherwise than by condemnation, real property as aforesaid and additional real property, not exceeding in value two hundred thousand dollars, for the purposes of the convenient transactions of its business, no portion of which shall be used for the purposes of a cemetery.

(i) Sale or disposition of cemetery lands. (1) No cemetery corporation may sell or dispose of the fee of all or any part of its lands dedicated to cemetery use, unless it shall prove to the satisfaction of the supreme court in the district where any portion of the cemetery lands is located or the cemetery board, that either: (A) all bodies have been removed from each and every part of the cemetery, that all the lots in the entire cemetery have been reconveyed to the corporation and are not used for burial purposes, and that it has no debts and liabilities, or (B) the land to be sold or disposed of is not used or is not physically adaptable for burial purposes and that the sale or disposition will benefit the cemetery corporation and the owners of plots and graves in the cemetery, and (C) the sale or disposition is not to a funeral entity as defined in paragraph (c) of section fifteen hundred six-a of this article. (2) If the sale or disposition is made pursuant to subparagraph (A) of subdivision one of this paragraph, the cemetery shall satisfy the court or the cemetery board that it is in the public interest to dispose of such cemetery land in the manner proposed; that the subject land is not suitable for cemetery purposes or is no longer needed by the community for such cemetery uses or purposes; and that the subject land is being sold for its current market value. (3) If the sale or disposition of the land is made pursuant to subparagraph (B) of subdivision one of this paragraph, the court or cemetery board shall order that the consideration received by the cemetery corporation, less the necessary expenses incurred, shall be deposited into the permanent maintenance fund established by the cemetery corporation pursuant to paragraph (a) of section fifteen hundred seven of this article. (4) Notice of any application hereunder shall be given in addition to the cemetery board, to the holders of certificates of indebtedness and land shares of the cemetery corporation, to any person having informed the cemetery board by petition or notice of interest in the proceeding and to any person interested in the proceeding pursuant to section five hundred eleven of this chapter (Petition for leave of court).

(j) Conveyance by cemetery corporation to city or village. A cemetery corporation may convey and transfer its real property held for burial purposes, together with its other assets, to a city having a population of less than one million inhabitants in which such real property is located, or to a village, provided such real property is located within such village or wholly within three miles of the boundaries thereof, or to a town, in which such real property is located, if all the directors and trustees of such cemetery corporation living and residing in the state of New York unite in the conveyance and transfer. Such conveyance and transfer shall be subject to all agreements as to lots sold and all trusts, restrictions and conditions upon the title or use of such real property and assets. Lots previously sold and grants previously made for burial purposes shall not be affected by such conveyance, nor shall any grave, monument or other erection be disturbed or removed except in accordance with law. No such conveyance shall be effective unless and until the legislative body of such city, town or village shall by ordinance or resolution accept the same subject to the conditions and restrictions hereinabove imposed, which ordinance or resolution said legislative body is hereby authorized and empowered to adopt by a majority vote of such body. Upon such conveyance and transfer such property shall be and become a municipal cemetery of such city, town or village and such property and assets so conveyed and transferred shall be administered as any other municipal cemetery of such city, town or village and the said cemetery corporation shall be dissolved by the recording of such conveyance and transfer.

(k) Streets or highways not to be laid out through certain cemetery lands. So long as the lands of a rural cemetery corporation organized under the act entitled "An act authorizing the incorporation of rural cemetery associations," constituting chapter one hundred thirty-three of the laws of eighteen hundred forty-seven, and the acts amendatory thereof, shall remain dedicated to the purpose of a cemetery, no street, road, avenue or public thoroughfare shall be laid out through such cemetery, or any part of the lands held by such association for the purposes aforesaid, without the consent of the trustees of such association and the cemetery board.

(l) Exclusive right of cemetery corporation to provide annual care services. Notwithstanding any provision of this article to the contrary, it shall be the right of each cemetery corporation, at its option, to exclusively provide all annual care services to be performed for consideration on all or any part of its lands at rates to be reviewed by the cemetery board. In the event that the cemetery board determines that an excessive, unauthorized or improper charge has been made for such services or that the services have not been properly performed, he or she may direct the cemetery corporation to pay to the person from whom such charge was collected a sum equivalent to three times the excess as determined by the cemetery board, or in the case of work not properly performed, it may direct the cemetery corporation to perform the work properly. Every cemetery corporation that chooses to provide, on an exclusive basis, such annual care services shall include in any contract for the sale of any part of its lands the following notice, in at least ten point bold type:

Notice

The .... (name of cemetery corporation), pursuant to state law, provides annual care services on an exclusive basis. Therefore, the purchaser of the plot or lot being transferred by this agreement may not contract with any outside party for such annual care services. For purposes of this paragraph, the term "annual care" shall mean the maintenance of a lot, plot or part thereof, and may include care of lawns, trees, shrubs, monuments and markers within the plot. The provisions of this paragraph shall not be construed to prohibit a lot owner from placing, or arranging to place, floral or similar arrangements on such cemetery lots or plots.

(m) Prohibition of stand-alone mausoleum and columbarium. No application for the construction of a mausoleum or columbarium to be located in any city, town or village shall be approved by the cemetery board when such mausoleum or columbarium shall be the only form of interment offered by a cemetery corporation, unless a management contract has been entered into with an existing cemetery corporation regulated under this article, that will provide operational management of the mausoleum or columbarium, and the owner of the mausoleum or columbarium has reserved interment space and secured interment services in a cemetery regulated under this article, in order to assure continued perpetual care of the remains contained in the mausoleum or columbarium should such mausoleum or columbarium become abandoned or choose to cease operations.

History: Add, L 1977, ch 871, § 2, eff Aug 11, 1977; amd, L 1998, ch 548, § 1, eff Sept 4, 1998; L 1998, ch 560, § 3; L 1999, ch 292, § 1, eff July 20, 1999; L 2014, ch 392, § 1, eff Sept 23, 2014; L 2015, ch 539, § 1, eff Dec 11, 2015; L 2018, ch 296, § 1, eff Oct 1, 2018.

Blackline Showing Effect of 2018 Amendments. — (a) Purchase of land; notice to cemetery board. No cemetery corporation, in purchasing real property hereafter, shall pay or agree to pay more than the fair and reasonable market value thereof. The terms of the purchase, including the price to be paid and the method of payment, shall be subject to notice and approval of the cemetery board. In determining the fair and reasonable market value, the cemetery board may take into consideration the method by which the purchase price is to be paid.

(b) Consent of local authorities.

(1) No cemetery shall hereafter be located in any city or village without the consent of the local legislative body of such city, or the board of trustees of such village.

(2) No cemetery shall hereafter be located in any town, outside of an incorporated village in Suffolk county, without the consent of the town board of such town.

(c) Cemeteries in Kings, Queens, Rockland, Westchester, Nassau, Suffolk, Putnam and Erie counties. A cemetery corporation shall not take by deed, devise or otherwise any land in the counties of Kings, Queens, Rockland, Westchester, Nassau, Suffolk, Putnam or Erie for cemetery purposes, or set apart any ground therefor in any of such counties, unless the consent of the board of supervisors or legislative body thereof, or of the city council of the city of New York, in respect to Kings or Queens county, be first obtained. Such consent may be granted upon such conditions and under such regulations and restrictions as the public health and welfare may require. Notice of application for such consent shall be published, once a week for six weeks, in the newspapers designated to publish the session laws and in such other newspapers published in the county as such board or body may direct, stating the time when the application will be made, a brief description of the lands proposed to be acquired, their location and the area thereof. Any person interested therein may be heard on such presentation. If such consent is granted the corporation may take and hold the lands designated therein. The consent shall not authorize any one corporation to take or hold more than two hundred and fifty acres of land. Nothing contained in this subdivision shall prevent any religious corporation in existence on April fifteenth, eighteen hundred fifty-four, in any of said counties from using as heretofore any burial ground then belonging to it within such county. Such board or body, from time to time, may make such regulation as to burials in any cemetery in the county as the public health may require.

(d) Limitation on the acquisition of land by rural cemetery corporations. It shall not be lawful for any rural cemetery corporation hereafter to acquire or take by deed, devise or otherwise, any land in any county within the state of New York, having a population of between one hundred and seventy-five thousand and two hundred thousand, according to the federal census of nineteen hundred, or set apart any ground for cemetery purposes therein, where there has already been set apart in any such county, five hundred acres of land for rural cemetery purposes, and the consent of the board of supervisors of any such county shall not be granted where there has already been granted five hundred acres of land, or upwards, within such county, to rural cemetery corporations. But nothing herein contained shall affect any lawful consent or grant hitherto made by the board of supervisors of any such county.

(e) Limitations on the acquisition of land for cemetery purposes in certain counties.

(1) It shall not be lawful for any corporation, association or person hereafter to set aside or use for cemetery purposes any lands in any county within the state erected on and after January first, eighteen hundred ninety, adjoining a city of the first class and having a population of between eighty thousand and eighty-five thousand according to the federal census of nineteen hundred ten; but nothing herein contained shall prevent cemetery corporations formed prior to January first, nineteen hundred seventeen, which own in such county a cemetery in which burials have been made prior to such date, from setting apart and using for burial purposes lands lying contiguous or adjacent to such cemetery which lands have been heretofore acquired by a recorded deed of conveyance made to such a cemetery corporation either for burial purposes, or for the purposes of the convenient transaction of its general business, which lands shall have been acquired with the consent of the board of supervisors; nor to prohibit the dedication or use of land within such county for a family cemetery as provided in subdivision (c) of section fourteen hundred one of this chapter.

(2) The provisions of this paragraph shall not operate to prevent any such cemetery corporation located in Nassau county from using for burial purposes contiguous or adjacent land acquired by it provided that such use shall be consented to by the Nassau county legislature.

(f) Conveyance by religious corporations or by trustees. A cemetery corporation may accept a conveyance of real property held by a religious corporation for burial purposes, or by trustees for such purposes if all such trustees living and residing in this state unite in the conveyance, subject to all trusts, restrictions and conditions upon the title or use. Lots previously sold and grants for burial purposes shall not be affected by any such conveyance; nor shall any grave, monument or other erection, or any remains, be disturbed or removed without the consent of the lot owner, or if there be no such owner, without the consent of the heirs of the persons whose remains are buried in such grave.

(g) Certain conveyances to cemetery corporations authorized. Upon approval of the cemetery board first having been obtained, a cemetery corporation which maintains and operates a cemetery may accept a conveyance of title to the fee of or to burial rights in lands within the confines of said cemetery and it shall be lawful for any cemetery or business corporation to make such conveyances. Lots previously sold and grants previously made for burial purposes shall not be affected by such conveyance. The cemetery corporation, in consideration of the conveyance to it of burial rights in lands within the confines of said cemetery, may, with the approval of the cemetery board, issue participating certificates of the kind and nature provided for in paragraph three of subdivision (e) of section fifteen hundred eleven of this article. In making its determination the cemetery board shall consider and may condition its approval on the purposes of this section.

(h) Acquisition of property by condemnation. If the certificate of incorporation or by-laws of a cemetery corporation do not exclude any person, on equal terms with other persons, from the privilege of purchasing a lot or of burial in its cemetery, such corporation may, from time to time, acquire by condemnation, exclusively for the purposes of a cemetery, not more than two hundred acres of land in the aggregate, forming one continuous tract, wholly or partly within the county in which its certificate of incorporation is filed or recorded, except as in this section otherwise provided as to the counties of Erie, Nassau, Suffolk, Putnam, Kings, Queens, Rockland and Westchester. A cemetery corporation may acquire by condemnation, exclusively for the purposes of a cemetery, any real property or any interest therein necessary to supply water for the uses of such cemetery, and the right to lay, relay, repair and maintain conduits and water pipes with connections and fixtures, in, through or over the lands of others and the right to intercept and divert the flow of waters from the lands of riparian owners, and from persons owning or interested in any waters. But no such cemetery corporation shall have power to take or use water from any of the canals of this state, or any canal reservoirs as feeders, or any streams which have been taken by the state for the purpose of supplying the canals with water. A cemetery corporation may acquire, otherwise than by condemnation, real property as aforesaid and additional real property, not exceeding in value two hundred thousand dollars, for the purposes of the convenient transactions of its business, no portion of which shall be used for the purposes of a cemetery.

(i) Sale or disposition of cemetery lands. (1) No cemetery corporation may sell or dispose of the fee of all or any part of its lands dedicated to cemetery use, unless it shall prove to the satisfaction of the supreme court in the district where any portion of the cemetery lands is located or the cemetery board, that either: (A) all bodies have been removed from each and every part of the cemetery, that all the lots in the entire cemetery have been reconveyed to the corporation and are not used for burial purposes, and that it has no debts and liabilities, or (B) the land to be sold or disposed of is not used or is not physically adaptable for burial purposes and that the sale or disposition will benefit the cemetery corporation and the owners of plots and graves in the cemetery, and (C) the sale or disposition is not to a funeral entity as defined in paragraph (c) of section fifteen hundred six-a of this article. (2) If the sale or disposition is made pursuant to subparagraph (A) of subdivision one of this paragraph, the cemetery shall satisfy the court or the cemetery board that it is in the public interest to dispose of such cemetery land in the manner proposed; that the subject land is not suitable for cemetery purposes or is no longer needed by the community for such cemetery uses or purposes; and that the subject land is being sold for its current market value. (3) If the sale or disposition of the land is made pursuant to subparagraph (B) of subdivision one of this paragraph, the court or cemetery board shall order that the consideration received by the cemetery corporation, less the necessary expenses incurred, shall be deposited into the permanent maintenance fund established by the cemetery corporation pursuant to paragraph (a) of section fifteen hundred seven of this article. (4) Notice of any application hereunder shall be given in addition to the cemetery board, to the holders of certificates of indebtedness and land shares of the cemetery corporation, to any person having informed the cemetery board by petition or notice of interest in the proceeding and

to any person interested in the proceeding pursuant to section five hundred eleven of this chapter (Petition for leave of court).

(j) Conveyance by cemetery corporation to city or village. A cemetery corporation may convey and transfer its real property held for burial purposes, together with its other assets, to a city having a population of less than one million inhabitants in which such real property is located, or to a village, provided such real property is located within such village or wholly within three miles of the boundaries thereof, or to a town, in which such real property is located, if all the directors and trustees of such cemetery corporation living and residing in the state of New York unite in the conveyance and transfer. Such conveyance and transfer shall be subject to all agreements as to lots sold and all trusts, restrictions and conditions upon the title or use of such real property and assets. Lots previously sold and grants previously made for burial purposes shall not be affected by such conveyance, nor shall any grave, monument or other erection be disturbed or removed except in accordance with law. No such conveyance shall be effective unless and until the legislative body of such city, town or village shall by ordinance or resolution accept the same subject to the conditions and restrictions hereinabove imposed, which ordinance or resolution said legislative body is hereby authorized and empowered to adopt by a majority vote of such body. Upon such conveyance and transfer such property shall be and become a municipal cemetery of such city, town or village and such property and assets so conveyed and transferred shall be administered as any other municipal cemetery of such city, town or village and the said cemetery corporation shall be dissolved by the recording of such conveyance and transfer.

(k) Streets or highways not to be laid out through certain cemetery lands. So long as the lands of a rural cemetery corporation organized under the act entitled "An act authorizing the incorporation of rural cemetery associations," constituting chapter one hundred thirty-three of the laws of eighteen hundred forty-seven, and the acts amendatory thereof, shall remain dedicated to the purpose of a cemetery, no street, road, avenue or public thoroughfare shall be laid out through such cemetery, or any part of the lands held by such association for the purposes aforesaid, without the consent of the trustees of such association and the cemetery board.

(l) Exclusive right of cemetery corporation to provide annual care services. Notwithstanding any provision of this article to the contrary, it shall be the right of each cemetery corporation, at its option, to exclusively provide all annual care services to be performed for consideration on all or any part of its lands at rates to be reviewed by the cemetery board. In the event that the cemetery board determines that an excessive, unauthorized or improper charge has been made for such services or that the services have not been properly performed, he or she may direct the cemetery corporation to pay to the person from whom such charge was collected a sum equivalent to three times the excess as determined by the cemetery board, or in the case of work not properly performed, it may direct the cemetery corporation to perform the work properly. Every cemetery corporation that chooses to provide, on an exclusive basis, such annual care services shall include in any contract for the sale of any part of its lands the following notice, in at least ten point bold type:

Notice

The (name of cemetery corporation), pursuant to state law, provides annual care services on an exclusive basis. Therefore, the purchaser of the plot or lot being transferred by this agreement may not contract with any outside party for such annual care services. For purposes of this paragraph, the term "annual care" shall mean the maintenance of a lot, plot or part thereof, and may include care of lawns, trees, shrubs, monuments and markers within the plot. The provisions of this paragraph shall not be construed to prohibit a lot owner from placing, or arranging to place, floral or similar arrangements on such cemetery lots or plots.

(m) Prohibition of stand-alone mausoleum and columbarium. No application for the construction of a mausoleum or columbarium to be located in any city, town or village shall be approved by the cemetery board when such mausoleum or columbarium shall be the only form of interment offered by a cemetery corporation, unless a management contract has been entered into with an existing cemetery corporation regulated under this article, that will provide operational management of the mausoleum or columbarium, and the owner of the mausoleum or columbarium has reserved interment space and secured interment services in a cemetery regulated under this article, in order to assure continued perpetual care of the remains contained in the mauseoleum or columbarium should such mauseoleum or columbarium become abandoned or choose to cease operations.

CASE ANNOTATIONS

County's general power of eminent domain did not empower it to acquire cemetery land for purpose of widening road in proceeding under CLS EDPL § 402, even though lands devoted to cemetery purposes are not entirely beyond reach of power of eminent domain, since, in enacting CLS N-PCL § 1506, legislature "practically promised" that cemetery grounds should be put to no other use without consent of trustees of cemetery association and its board, requisite consent was not obtained, and any rule excluding widening of existing highways from consent requirement would defeat intent of legislature. County of Suffolk v Pinelawn Cemetery (1987, 2d Dept) 130 A.D.2d 575, 515 N.Y.S.2d 294

In condemnation proceeding in which Metropolitan Transportation Authority (MTA) sought permission pursuant to CLS EDPL § 402 to file acquisition map, court properly rejected objection interposed by cemetery that MTA lacked authority to condemn property because it had not obtained consent, under CLS N-PCL § 1506, as prerequisite to building access road on cemetery land since (1) cemetery had failed to challenge MTA's determination and findings after public hearing, by way of appellate review, and (2) in any case, CLS N-PCL § 1506 was inapplicable in absence of evidentiary support for cemetery's conclusory allegation that MTA intended to construct access road, which was refuted by affidavit of MTA official denying that MTA's present plans included construction of access road. Metropolitan Transp. Authority v Pinelawn Cemetery (1987, 2d Dept) 135 A.D.2d 686, 522 N.Y.S.2d 586

Town zoning board properly denied cemetery corporation's application for use variance to permit certain mausoleum complex to be built on corporation's newly acquired addition to cemetery, based on project's effect on character of locality; town's zoning ordinance, which provided that cemetery was not permitted use in any district, but that it was nonconforming use which could be continued if existing at time of passage of ordinance, was not unconstitutional as applied to corporation since state law regarding cemetery regulation does not preempt local zoning law, and zoning board's disapproval of specific mausoleum complex did not preclude subsequent applications for projects having lesser impact on area. Beverly Hills Cemetery Corp. v Putnam Valley (1988, 2d Dept) 136 A.D.2d 669, 524 N.Y.S.2d 47, app dismd, app den 72 N.Y.2d 828, 530 N.Y.S.2d 547, 526 N.E.2d 38

Court approved sale of portion of cemetery land where cemetery (1) estimated that parcel would not be needed for at least 1,000 years due to availability of many unused acres of cemetery land, and (2) demonstrated that sale would benefit cemetery and owners of plots and graves because portion of proceeds would be used to better maintain cemetery, and because house built on land would serve as buffer zone between railroad tracks and cemetery. In re Prospect Lawn Cemetery Ass'n (1998, Sup) 176 Misc. 2d 909, 675 N.Y.S.2d 516

§ 1506-a. Cemetery corporations; restrictions

(a) No cemetery corporation shall, directly or indirectly:

(1) sell, or have, enter into or perform a lease of any of its real property to a funeral entity, or use any of its property for location of a funeral entity;

(2) commingle its funds with a funeral entity;

(3) direct or carry on its business or affairs with a funeral entity;

(4) authorize control of its business or affairs by a funeral entity;

(5) engage in any sale or cross-marketing of goods or services with a funeral entity;

(6) have or enter into or perform a management or service contract for cemetery operations with a funeral entity; or

(7) have, enter into or perform a management contract with any entity other than a not-for-profit cemetery corporation; provided, however, that a not-for-profit cemetery corporation may enter into or perform a management contract with a private cemetery corporation for the operational management of a mauseoleum or columbarium by such private cemetery corporation provided such contract shall have first been authorized by the board of the not-for-profit cemetery corporation.

(b) Only the provisions of subdivisions one and two of paragraph (a) of this section shall apply to cemetery corporations with thirty acres or less of real property dedicated to cemetery purposes, and only to the extent the sale or lease is of real property dedicated to cemetery purposes, and such cemeteries shall not engage in the sale of funeral home goods or services, except if such goods and services are otherwise permitted to be sold by cemeteries, nor shall a majority of the members of the board of directors or trustees of such cemeteries be made up of the representatives of a funeral entity.

(c) For the purposes of this section, "funeral entity" means a person, partnership, corporation, limited liability company or other form of business organization providing funeral home services, or owning, controlling, conducting or affiliated with a funeral home, any subsidiary thereof or an officer, director or stockholder having a ten per centum or greater proprietary, beneficial, equitable or credit interest in a funeral home.

History: Add, L 1998, ch 560, § 4, eff Sept 4, 1998; amd, L 2018, ch 296, § 2, eff Oct 1, 2018.

Blackline Showing Effect of 2018 Amendments. — (a) No cemetery corporation shall, directly or indirectly:

(1) sell, or have, enter into or perform a lease of any of its real property to a funeral entity, or use any of its property for location of a funeral entity;

(2) commingle its funds with a funeral entity;

(3) direct or carry on its business or affairs with a funeral entity;

(4) authorize control of its business or affairs by a funeral entity;

(5) engage in any sale or cross-marketing of goods or services with a funeral entity;

(6) have or enter into or perform a management or service contract for cemetery operations with a funeral entity; or

(7) ~~have, enter into or perform a management contract with any entity other than a not-for-profit cemetery corporation~~ have, enter into or perform a management contract with any entity other than a not-for-profit cemetery corporation; provided, however, that a not-for-profit cemetery corporation may enter into or perform a management contract with a private cemetery corporation for the operational management of a mauseoleum or columbarium by such private cemetery corporation provided such contract shall have first been authorized by the board of the not-for-profit cemetery corporation.

(b) Only the provisions of subdivisions one and two of paragraph (a) of this section shall apply to cemetery corporations with thirty acres or less of real property dedicated to cemetery purposes, and only to the extent the sale or lease is of real property dedicated to cemetery purposes, and such cemeteries shall not engage in the sale of funeral home goods or services, except if such goods and services are otherwise permitted to be sold by cemeteries, nor shall a majority of the members of the board of directors or trustees of such cemeteries be made up of the representatives of a funeral entity.

(c) For the purposes of this section, "funeral entity" means a person, partnership, corporation, limited liability company or other form of business organization providing funeral home services, or owning, controlling, conducting or affiliated with a funeral home, any subsidiary thereof or an officer, director or stockholder having a ten per centum or greater proprietary, beneficial, equitable or credit interest in a funeral home.

CASE ANNOTATIONS

New York State Cemetery Board properly denied non-for-profit cemetery corporation's application to lease 3-acre parcel to for-profit funeral home for purpose of constructing and operating funeral home and related businesses where Board determined that proposal had potential adverse financial repercussions for cemetery corporation in that duration of lease (40 years with 4 10-year options to renew) would preclude future alternatives, cemetery corporation did not present sufficient proof that it adequately sought offers from other entities, nature and duration of relationship between cemetery corporation and funeral home was deemed significant as source of potential conflict with interests of lot owners, and Board found proposed construction inappropriate when viewed in light of public policy concerns underpinning statutorily mandated not-for-profit status of cemeteries (19 NYCRR § 201.16(c)(5), CLS N-PCL § 1501). Poughkeepsie Rural Cemetery v Treadwell (1998, 3d Dept) 252 A.D.2d 903, 676 N.Y.S.2d 338

§ 1506-b. Transfer of lands of Valley View Rural Cemetery

Notwithstanding any other provision of law to the contrary, the board of trustees of the Valley View Rural Cemetery Association in the town of Dover Plains, New York, may by resolution of such board, sell, lease or transfer any portion of the lands of Valley View Rural Cemetery to the parish of St. Charles Borromeo in the town of Dover Plains, New York, for cemetery purposes for the adjoining and contiguous cemetery of the parish of St. Charles Borromeo.

History: Add, L 2000, ch 581, § 1, eff Dec 8, 2000.

§ 1506-c. Abandoned cemetery maintenance by cemetery corporations

(a) Upon application and approval by the cemetery board, a cemetery corporation may assume management and maintenance of an abandoned cemetery. For the purposes of this section, abandoned cemetery means a cemetery which was previously owned by a cemetery corporation organized pursuant to this chapter or existing by virtue of the membership corporation law, for which there no longer exists any corporate board or body to maintain it, and for which there is no sufficient trust fund or endowment to provide ordinary and necessary care and maintenance. Provided, however, that in no event shall the cemetery board approve the assumption of the management and maintenance of an abandoned cemetery under this section if the abandoned cemetery was affiliated with any religious denomination or tradition or if the majority of the persons whose bodies were interred in such cemetery were affiliated with any religious denomination or tradition unless the cemetery assuming the management and maintenance of such abandoned cemetery follows the customs and practices of the same religious denomination or tradition.

(b) A cemetery corporation assuming management and maintenance of an abandoned cemetery shall make application for funds pursuant to para-

graph (h) of section fifteen hundred seven of this article and section ninety-seven-r of the state finance law for maintenance of abandoned cemeteries. Within sixty days of submission of a completed application, the cemetery board shall approve or deny such application.

(c) Monies disbursed under such assumption shall be used exclusively for the purpose of the management and maintenance of an abandoned cemetery such as the ordinary and necessary care of a cemetery, including the removal of grass and weeds, the refilling of graves, and the preservation, care, and fencing of a cemetery, and also including the care of crypts, niches, grave sites, monuments, and memorials paid for by means of the general fund or special fund or the income applied from the permanent maintenance fund, perpetual care fund, monument maintenance fund, general fund, or a special fund of the abandoned cemetery.

(d) Any residual funds disbursed to a cemetery corporation after the maintenance of an abandoned cemetery has been performed must be returned to the cemetery board for redeposit into the state cemetery vandalism restoration, monument repair or removal and administration fund established by section ninety-seven-r of the state finance law.

(e) Within ninety days of its receipt of disbursements, the cemetery corporation shall make a report to the cemetery board setting forth details of the maintenance and clean-up undertaken and the amount of funds, if any, to be redeposited into the fund. If the maintenance and clean-up have not been completed, or necessary equipment has not been purchased, the reasons therefor shall be set forth, and the anticipated date for a subsequent, final report shall be disclosed.

History: Add, L 2009, ch 363, § 1, eff Oct 25, 2009.

§ 1507. Trust funds

(a) Maintenance and preservation; permanent maintenance fund; current maintenance fund. Subject to rules and regulations of the cemetery board: (1) Every cemetery corporation shall maintain and preserve the cemetery, including all lots, plots and parts thereof. For the sole purpose of such maintenance and preservation, every cemetery corporation shall establish and maintain (A) a permanent maintenance fund, and (B) a current maintenance fund. At the time of making the sale of a lot, plot or part thereof, the cemetery corporation shall deposit not less than ten per centum of the gross proceeds of the sale into the permanent maintenance fund. An additional fifteen per centum of the gross proceeds of the sale shall be deposited in the current maintenance fund. In addition to the foregoing, at the time the cemetery corporation receives payment for the performance of an interment or inurnment, the cemetery corporation shall collect and deposit into the permanent maintenance fund the sum of thirty-five dollars. (2) The permanent maintenance fund is hereby declared to be and shall be held by the corporation as a trust fund, for the purpose of maintaining and preserving the cemetery, including all lots, crypts, niches, plots, and parts thereof. The principal of such fund shall be invested in such securities as are permitted for the investment of trust funds by section 11-2.3 of the estates, powers and trusts law. The income in the form of interest and ordinary dividends therefrom shall be used solely for the maintenance and preservation of the cemetery grounds. In addition, the governing board of the corporation may appropriate for expenditure solely for the maintenance and preservation of the cemetery grounds a portion of the net appreciation, in the fair market value of the principal of the trust, as is prudent under the standard established by article five-A of this chapter, the prudent management of institutional funds act. In the event that a cemetery corporation seeks to appropriate any percentage of its net appreciation in its permanent maintenance fund in accordance with this subparagraph, the cemetery corporation shall provide notice of such proposed appropriation by certified mail to the cemetery board not less than sixty days in advance of such proposed appropriation and shall disclose such appropriation as part of and in addition to their annual reporting requirements as defined in section fifteen hundred eight of this article, setting forth the amount of funds to be appropriated for such expenditure and its effect on the permanent maintenance fund. Such proposed appropriation shall become effective sixty days after receipt of such notice, unless the cemetery board within such sixty-day period notifies the cemetery corporation that the board objects to the proposed appropriation. Notwithstanding the foregoing provisions of this subparagraph, all principal of the permanent maintenance fund shall remain inviolate, except that, upon application to the supreme court in a district where a portion of the cemetery grounds is located, the court may make an order permitting the principal or a part thereof to be used for the purpose of current maintenance and preservation of the cemetery or otherwise. Such application may be made by the cemetery board on notice to the corporation or by the corporation on notice to the cemetery board. Unless the cemetery can clearly demonstrate that it lacks sufficient future revenue to make repayment, any such allowance from the permanent maintenance fund shall be in the form of a loan, and the court shall determine the method for repayment of such a loan by the cemetery to the fund. (3) The current maintenance fund shall be used and applied for the sole purpose of ordinary and necessary expenses of the care and maintenance of the cemetery. When all burial rights in the cemetery have been conveyed, the fund remaining on deposit or to the credit of the current maintenance fund shall be transferred into the permanent maintenance fund. (4) The percentage of the proceeds of sales required to be deposited in the permanent maintenance fund or current maintenance fund by a particular cemetery corporation may be increased or diminished by order of the supreme court in a district where any portion of the cemetery is located. Such application may be made by the cemetery board on notice to the corporation or by the corporation on notice to the cemetery board.

(b) Perpetual care of lots. (1) Upon the application of a prospective purchaser of any lot, plot or part thereof and upon payment of the purchase price and the amount fixed as a reasonable charge for the perpetual care of any lot, plot or part thereof, every cemetery corporation shall include with the deed of conveyance an agreement perpetually to care for such lot, plot, or part thereof, to the extent that the income derived by the corporation from such amount will permit. (2) Such corporation also, upon the application of an owner or of the executor or administrator of a deceased owner of any lot and upon the payment of the amount fixed as a reasonable charge for the perpetual care of such lot, shall, and upon the application of any other person and the payment of such amount, may enter into a like agreement with him. Such agreement shall be executed and may be recorded in the same manner as a deed. (3) Any corporation organized under or subject to the provisions of this section may enter into an agreement in writing with any executor or executors, trustee or trustees, under a last will and testament to whom there has heretofore been, or may hereafter be, bequeathed a sum for the perpetual care of any lot, plot or part thereof in any such cemetery or with any administrator or administrators with the will annexed under any such will perpetually to care for such lot, plot or part thereof under the provisions of the terms of such last will and testament, and subject in all cases to the approval of the surrogate's court having jurisdiction over such trust estate. Such approval may be evidenced by the written endorsement of the surrogate on a duplicate original of such agreement filed in the surrogate's court. In case the surrogate shall approve such agreement any such executor, trustee or administrator with the will annexed thereupon shall pay over to the treasurer of such perpetual care fund of such cemetery corporation any moneys remaining or being in his hands belonging to such trust, and upon making such payment and accounting therefore to the surrogate's court may be discharged from said trust as such executor, trustee or administrator with the will annexed.

(c) Perpetual care fund. (1) Every cemetery corporation and every religious corporation having charge and control of a cemetery which heretofore has been or which hereafter may be used for burials, shall keep separate and apart from its other funds, all moneys and property received by it, whether by contract, in trust or otherwise, for the perpetual care and maintenance of any lot, plot or part thereof in its cemetery, and all such moneys or property so received by any such corporation are hereby declared to be, and shall be held by the corporation as trust funds. Any moneys and property so received, unless otherwise provided in the instrument under which such moneys or property were received, shall be kept in a separate fund to be known as the perpetual care fund. (2) The principal of such funds, whether kept in the perpetual care fund or otherwise, and unless already so invested when received, shall be invested within a reasonable time after receipt thereof, and kept invested, in such securities as are permitted for the investment of trust funds by sections 11-2.2 and 11-2.3 of the estates, powers and trusts law. The income arising therefrom shall be used solely for the perpetual care and maintenance of the lot or plots or parts thereof for which such income has been provided. In addition, the governing board of the corporation may appropriate for expenditure solely for the perpetual care and maintenance of the lot or plots or parts thereof for which such income has been provided, a portion of the net appreciation in the fair market value of the principal of the trust as is prudent under the standard established by article five-A of this chapter, the prudent management of institutional funds act. In the event that a cemetery corporation seeks to appropriate any percentage of its net appreciation in its perpetual care fund in accordance with this subparagraph, the cemetery corporation shall provide notice of such appropriation to the cemetery board not less than sixty days in advance of such proposed appropriation and shall disclose such appropriation as part of and in addition to their annual reporting requirements as defined in section fifteen hundred eight of this article setting forth the amount of funds appropriated for such expenditure and its effect on the perpetual care funds. Such proposed appropriation shall become effective sixty days after receipt of such notice, unless the cemetery board within such sixty day period notifies the cemetery corporation that the board objects to the proposed appropriation. (3) The corporation may, for the purpose of investing and reinvesting such funds, add the same to any similar trust fund or funds and apportion shares or interest to each trust fund, showing upon its records at all times every share or interest. (4) The corporation may accept in trust for the perpetual care of a lot, plot or part thereof in its cemetery, property not made eligible for the investment of trust funds under the foregoing provisions of this subdivision and may retain such property in the form in which received, separate and apart from the perpetual care fund, if directed so to do by the instrument under which such property is received, so long as such property remains in the form in which it was received; but whenever such property is sold or otherwise disposed of, the proceeds of such sale or other disposition shall be invested in the manner heretofore provided in this subdivision for the investment of trust funds. The exchange of stock or evidences of indebtedness issued by a corporation for stock or evidences of indebtedness of the same corporation, or for stock, evidences of indebtedness, war-

rants or script received as a result of merger, consolidation or reorganization of such corporation, or the receipt of additional stock or evidences of indebtedness of such corporation, as a distribution by such corporation, shall not be deemed to be a disposition of the property originally received in trust, and such exchanged or additional property may be retained in place and stead of the property originally received, and under the same conditions. The corporation shall keep accurate accounts of all funds for the perpetual care and maintenance of cemetery lots, plots or parts thereof, separate and apart from its other funds. A copy of the record pertaining to each such perpetual care fund shall be at all times available at the office of the corporation during usual business hours, for inspection and copy by any owner of an endowed lot or his representative.

(d) Perpetual care fund; allocation of income and cost of care and maintenance. On or before the fifteenth day of March in each calendar year the officers of every cemetery corporation shall fix and determine that portion of the income on the investment of the principal of the perpetual care fund during the calendar or fiscal year immediately preceding, to be apportioned to each separate lot or part thereof for which a perpetual care agreement has been made. The cost during such previous calendar or fiscal year of the care of each lot or part thereof shall be allocated and charged against the income so apportioned to it. Any excess of the income so apportioned over and above the allocated cost of the care and maintenance of such lot or part thereof shall be credited to such lot or part thereof, to be used in any future years to make up the deficiency if the income apportioned to such lot or part thereof should, in any year since September first, nineteen hundred forty-nine, or in any future year, fall, or have fallen, below the cost of care thereof.

(e) Designation of fiduciary corporation by directors or trustees of cemetery corporation to act as custodians of funds. Notwithstanding the provisions of any other law, the directors or trustees of cemetery corporations are hereby authorized to designate a bank or trust company to act as custodian and trustee of any or all of the respective funds of such cemetery corporation received by it for the perpetual care of lots in the cemetery thereof pursuant to paragraph (b), of this section, the permanent maintenance of such cemetery pursuant to paragraph (a) of this section, and for special purposes pursuant to paragraph (f) of this section. Such corporate trustee shall be designated by a resolution duly adopted by the board of directors or trustees and approved by a justice of the supreme court of the judicial district in which the cemetery of said corporation is located or the cemetery board; and the directors or trustees of such cemetery corporation may, with the approval of the justice of the supreme court, revoke such trust, and either take over such trust fund or name another trustee to handle the same, but if not so revoked, such trust shall be perpetual. Any bank or trust company accepting any such cemetery fund shall keep the same separate from all other funds, except that it may, irrespective of any provision contained in this article invest the same in a legal common trust fund or in shares of a mutual trust investment company organized under the banking law, and shall pay over the net income to the directors or trustees of the cemetery corporation by whom it shall be expended and applied to the purpose for which such trust fund was paid to the cemetery corporations and accounted for in accordance with such paragraphs (a), (b) and (f) of this section.

(e-1) Monument maintenance fund.

(1) A cemetery corporation may, subject to the approval of the cemetery board, establish and maintain a monument maintenance fund. Such a fund is hereby declared to be and shall be held by the cemetery corporation as a trust fund, for the purpose of providing notice if such monuments are damaged or defaced by an act of vandalism and for the restoration of such monuments. Two or more cemetery corporations may establish a joint monument maintenance fund.

(2) The principal of the fund shall be invested in securities permitted for the investment of trust funds by sections 11-2.2 and 11-2.3 of the estates, powers and trusts law. The principal of such fund shall remain inviolate, except that upon application to the cemetery board, which may make an order permitting the principal or a part thereof to be used for the purpose of restoring monuments damaged or defaced by an act of vandalism. The income arising from such investment shall be used solely for the costs and expenses resulting from an act of vandalism against monuments in such cemetery.

(3) The fund shall be financed by a charge levied at the time of each interment at a rate established by each cemetery creating such a fund, subject to cemetery board approval pursuant to section fifteen hundred nine of this article. Such a charge shall be levied in addition to the approved rates for interment. The fund may also accept gifts, donations and bequests.

(4) Each cemetery creating such a fund shall promulgate rules and regulations to administer the fund, subject to cemetery board approval pursuant to section fifteen hundred nine of this article. Such rules shall include the conditions under which the income from such fund may be properly expended.

(5) The cemetery corporation shall keep accurate accounts of all moneys for the fund, separate and apart from its other funds.

(f) Acquisition of property for special purposes and in trust. (1) A cemetery corporation may acquire, otherwise than by condemnation, real or personal property, absolutely or in trust, in perpetuity or otherwise, and shall use the same or the income therefrom in pursuance of the terms of the instru-

ment by which it was acquired, for the following purposes only: (i) The improvement or embellishment, but not the enlargement, of its cemetery; (ii) The construction, preservation or replacement of any building, structure, fence, wall, or walk therein; (iii) The erection, renewal or preservation of any tomb, monument, stone, fence, wall, railing or other erection or structure on or around its cemetery or any lot or plot therein; (iv) The planting or cultivation of trees, grass, shrubs, flowers or plants in or about its cemetery or any lot or plot therein; (v) The construction, operation, maintenance, repair and replacement of a crematory or columbarium or both in its cemetery; (vi) The care, keeping in order and embellishment of any lot, plot or part thereof or the structures thereon, in its cemetery, as prescribed in the instrument transferring such property to the cemetery corporation, or by the person or persons from time to time having possession, care and control of such lot, plot or part thereof, as the case may be. (2) All moneys and property received by a cemetery corporation in trust under this subdivision, unless otherwise provided in the instrument under which such moneys or property were received and unless already so invested when received, shall be invested within a reasonable time after the receipt thereof, and kept invested in such securities as are permitted for the investment of trust funds by sections 11-2.2 and 11-2.3 of the estates, powers and trusts law. The corporation may, for the purpose of investing and reinvesting such funds, add the same to any similar trust fund or funds and apportion shares or interests to each trust fund, showing upon its records at all times every share or interest. The cemetery corporation shall maintain a record for each such trust fund. Such record shall be at all times available at the office of the corporation during usual business hours, for inspection and copy by any owner of an endowed lot or his representative.

(g) Trust for the care of burial ground. A cemetery corporation, incorporated under or by a general or special law, may receive tangible property, securities or funds in trust, and hold and invest the same and apply the principal or income thereof, in accordance with the terms of the trust, for the purpose of repairing, maintaining, improving or embellishing a burial ground, not constituting a part of the cemetery of such cemetery corporation, and located outside of a city of more than one million inhabitants and within ten miles of the cemetery of the corporation accepting such trust. The directors of such corporation, or a majority of them and the treasurer, shall annually within sixty days after the close of each calendar or fiscal year, make, sign and shall file at the office of the corporation a detailed accounting and report of such trust funds held under this subdivision and the use made of such funds or of the income thereof for the preceding calendar or fiscal year, which shall include among other things, properly itemized, the securities in which the same is then invested, and any purchases, sales or other changes made therein during the period covered by such report. Such accounting and report shall be at all times available at the office of the corporation, during usual business hours, for inspection and copy by any lot owner or any contributor to such trust fund.

(h) Vandalism, abandonment and monument repair or removal.

(1) Cemeteries incorporated under this article shall contribute to a fund created pursuant to section ninety-seven-r of the state finance law for the maintenance of abandoned cemeteries, including the construction of cemetery fences, placement of cemetery lights and replacement of cemetery doors and locks, for the restoration of property damaged by acts of vandalism, and for the repair or removal of monuments or other markers not owned by the cemetery corporation that have fallen into disrepair or dilapidation so as to create a dangerous condition. Such fund shall be administered by a board of trustees comprised of the secretary of state, the attorney general and the commissioner of health, or their designees, who shall serve without additional compensation.

(2) The fund shall be financed by contributions by the cemetery corporations of not more than five dollars ($ 5.00) per interment or cremation in a manner to be determined by the New York state cemetery board. No contributions shall be collected upon the interment of the cremains of a deceased person where a contribution was collected upon cremations.

(3) The moneys of the fund shall be expended equally for the maintenance of abandoned cemeteries previously owned by a corporation incorporated pursuant to this chapter or the membership corporations law and the repair of cemetery vandalism damage and the repair or removal of monuments or other markers not owned by the cemetery corporation, provided, however, that the cemetery board may determine that circumstances necessitate an unequal distribution due to specific needs and may provide for such distribution. For purposes of this section, the maintenance of abandoned cemeteries may include the construction of cemetery fences, placement of cemetery lights and replacement of cemetery doors and locks.

(4) Authorization for payments by the fund for maintenance of an abandoned cemetery shall be made by the secretary of state only upon approval by the cemetery board of an application by a municipality or other solvent not-for-profit cemetery corporation for fair and reasonable expenses required to be made by the municipality or other solvent not-for-profit cemetery corporation for maintenance of an abandoned cemetery; provided, however, that the cemetery board shall not approve any such application unless the municipality or other solvent not-for-profit cemetery corporation acknowledges that the respon-

sibility for restoration and future care, preservation, and maintenance of such cemetery has been assumed by the municipality or other solvent not-for-profit cemetery corporation. For the purposes of this paragraph, such cemetery shall always be deemed an abandoned cemetery.

(5) Authorization for payments by the fund for the repair of vandalism damage shall be made by the secretary of state only on approval by the New York state cemetery board which shall determine:

(i) that an act of vandalism to the extent described by the cemetery corporation did take place;

(ii) that either a written report of the vandalism was filed with the local police or sheriff's department, or, that the cemetery, upon consent of the division, made a determination not to file the report because the publicity generated by filing the report would have adverse consequences for the cemetery;

(iii) that the cost of repairs is fair and reasonable; and

(iv) that the cemetery corporation has been unable to obtain funds from the lot owner, his spouse, devisees or descendants within a reasonable period of time nor are there adequate funds in the cemetery corporations monument maintenance fund, if such a fund has been established by the cemetery.

(6) Authorization for payments by the fund for the repair or removal of monuments or other markers not owned by the cemetery corporation shall be made by the secretary of state only on approval by the New York state cemetery board on application by the cemetery corporation showing:

(i) that the monuments or markers are so badly out of repair or dilapidated as to create a dangerous condition;

(ii) that the cost of remedying the condition is fair and reasonable;

(iii) that the cemetery corporation has given not less than sixty days notice to the last known owner to repair or remove the monument or other marker and the said owner has failed to do so within the time prescribed in said notice.

(7) The New York state cemetery board shall promulgate rules defining standards of maintenance, as well as what type of vandalism or out of repair or dilapidated monuments or other markers shall qualify for payment of repair or removal by the fund and the method and amount of payment of contributions described in subparagraph two of this paragraph upon the recommendation of the state cemetery board citizens advisory council created by section fifteen hundred seven-a of this article (State cemetery board citizens advisory council).

(8) Nothing contained in this paragraph is to be construed as giving a cemetery corporation an "insurable interest" in monuments or other embellishments on a plot, lot or part thereof, nor is it meant to imply that the cemetery corporation has any responsibility for repairing vandalism damage not covered by this

fund, nor for repairing or removing out of repair or dilapidated monuments or other markers not owned by the cemetery corporation, nor shall it constitute the doing of an insurance business.

History: Add, L 1977, ch 871, § 2, eff Aug 11, 1977; amd, L 1985, ch 608, § 2, eff Sept 1, 1985; L 1988, ch 494, § 2 (see 1988 note below); L 1988, ch 495, § 1, eff Nov 29, 1988; L 1990, ch 779, § 1, eff July 25, 1990; L 1990, ch 895, § 2; L 1992, ch 117, § 1, eff June 1, 1992; L 1993, ch 200, § 1; L 2000, ch 111, § 1,2, eff Jan 1, 2001,3, eff Jan 1, 2001,4, eff Jan 1, 2001; L 2000, ch 380, § 1, eff Sept 29, 2000; L 2001, ch 517, § 1, eff Nov 28, 2001; L 2004, ch 679, § 1, eff Jan 1, 2005; L 2009, ch 363, § 2, eff Oct 25, 2009; L 2014, ch 509, § § 1, 2, eff Dec 17, 2014; L 2015, ch 539, § 2, eff Dec 11, 2015.

CASE ANNOTATIONS

In a proceeding pursuant to N-PCL § 1507, the trial court improperly granted a petition by a cemetery association for permission to withdraw monies from its permanent maintenance fund to pay attorney fees and dispursements, where the phrase "or otherwise" in the provision in § 1507 allowing the withdrawal of part of the principal of the trust for the purpose of current maintenance and preservation of the cemetery is limited to that purpose by the principle of ejusdem generis, in that the legislative history of § 1507 bore out the conclusion that the trust fund was to be limited to the maintenance and preservation of the cemetery, and none of the legal proceedings for which the attorney fees were incurred could seriously be said to have been occasioned by a necessity to preserve the cemetery proper. Re Memory Gardens, Inc. (1983, 3d Dept) 91 A.D.2d 1163, 458 N.Y.S.2d 737

Zoning board of appeals did not err in determining that a crematory was not a part of an existing nonconforming cemetery use; however, it erred in refusing to grant a variance under General City Law § 81-b[3][b] based on its inaccurate findings that the cemetery was not experiencing financial hardship based on income from its statutorily required trust fund and that the crematory would alter the character of the neighborhood. Matter of White Plains Rural Cemetery Assn. v City of White Plains, 2019 N.Y. App. Div. LEXIS 605 (N.Y. App. Div. 2d Dep't 2019).

CLS N-PCL § 513(c) does not override CLS N-PCL § 1507 restrictions on invading principal and thus, in action under CLS N-PCL § 112(a)(1), defendants were preliminarily enjoined from invading principal of cemetery's permanent maintenance trust fund or perpetual care trust fund, and from borrowing money from its perpetual care income fund (without prejudice to them if they applied for judicial approval under § 1507(a)), because (1) borrowing money that probably cannot be repaid is extra-statutory means of removing monies from funds without seeking court approval, (2) there would be continued invasion and arguably irreparable harm if injunction was not issued, and (3) balancing of equities favored issuance of preliminary injunction. People by Vacco v Woodlawn Cemetery (1997, Sup) 173 Misc. 2d 846, 662 N.Y.S.2d 369

§ 1507-a. State cemetery board citizens advisory council

(a) There is hereby created a state cemetery board citizens advisory council, to study, investigate, monitor and make recommendations with respect to the maintenance and operation of the state cemetery vandalism restoration, monument repair or removal and administration fund. Such advisory council shall study and investigate incidents of cemetery abandonment, vandalism and desecration, monitor the administration of such fund and recommend changes to improve the management of and expenditures from the state cemetery vandalism restoration, monument repair or removal and administration fund.

(b) The advisory council shall be composed of a member designated by the secretary of state, a member designated by the attorney general, a member designated by the commissioner of health, a member designated by the comptroller and a member designated by the commissioner of taxation and finance. The appointees to the advisory council shall not be employees of the department of state, department of law, department of health, department of audit and control or department of taxation and finance. Each of the members shall serve for a term of two years, provided, however, that the first appointments by the comptroller and commissioner of taxation and finance shall serve for a term of one year. Vacancies occurring other than by expiration of term shall be filled in the same manner as the original appointments for the balance of the unexpired term. Persons designated or appointed to the advisory council shall have demonstrated a long-standing interest, knowledge and experience in the care and preservation of gravesites. One member shall be elected chairman of the advisory council by a majority vote of the members of such council.

(c) The members of the advisory council shall receive no compensation for their services but shall be reimbursed for travel expenses incurred in the performance of their duties.

(d) The advisory council shall meet at least quarterly at the call of the chairman.

(e) The advisory council may request and shall receive from any department, division, board, bureau, commission, agency, public authority of the state or any political subdivision thereof such assistance and data as will enable it properly to carry out its activities hereunder and effectuate the purposes set forth herein.

History: Add, L 1990, ch 895, § 1, eff Nov 27, 1990.

Par (a), amd, L 2000, ch 380, § 2, eff Sept 29, 2000.

§ 1508.   Reports by cemeteries

(a) Annual report. Each cemetery corporation shall, on or before the fifteenth day of March after the end of its calendar year, or if on a fiscal year the seventy-fifth day after the close of such year, file with the cemetery board (1) a statement as to the condition of the permanent maintenance trust fund and a schedule of the assets of such fund. (2) a statement as to the condition of the perpetual care fund and a schedule of the assets of such fund. (3) a statement as to the condition of the moneys and properties received by the cemetery corporation in trust under the provisions of subdivisions (f) and (g) of section fifteen hundred seven of this article. (4) a statement of the gross proceeds of the sale of plots, lots and parts thereof, graves, niches and crypts showing the disposition of such proceeds and (5) a statement of changes in the number and amount of certificates of indebtedness in accordance with the provisions of paragraph three of subdivision (a) of section fifteen hundred eleven of this article. (6) a statement as to the condition of the monument maintenance fund, if any, and a schedule of the assets of such fund.

(b) Additional reports. The cemetery board may address to any cemetery corporations or its officers or any person any inquiry in relation to the transactions or conditions of the cemetery corporation or any matter connected therewith, and may require that a reply be verified. Failure to submit such reply within the time designated by the cemetery board shall subject the corporation, officer or person so addressed to the penalties provided in subdivision (d) hereof.

(c) Cemetery payment for administration. To defray the expenses of examination and administration, each cemetery corporation shall not later than March fifteenth in each calendar year, pay to the cemetery board the sum of three dollars per interment and cremation in excess of fifteen interments or cremations for the preceding calendar year. No contribution shall be collected upon the interment of the cremains of a deceased person where a contribution was collected upon cremation.

(d) Failure to file report. Any cemetery corporation or individual failing to file any report or any schedule of rules, regulations and charges required by this article shall forfeit to the people of the state the sum of one hundred dollars for each day that each such report shall be delayed or withheld, except that the cemetery board may extend the time for filing any such report and may waive payment of any penalty or part thereof provided herein.

History: Add, L 1977, ch 871, § 2, eff Aug 11, 1977.

Par (a), subpar (6), add, L 1985, ch 608, § 3, eff Sept 1, 1985.

§ 1509. Cemetery rules and regulations; charges and lot tax assessments

(a) Rules and regulations. The directors of a cemetery corporation shall make reasonable rules and regulations for the use, care, management and protection of the property of the corporation and of all lots, plots and parts thereof; for regulating the dividing marks between the lots, plots and parts thereof; for prohibiting or regulating the erection of structures upon such lots, plots or parts thereof; for preventing unsightly monuments, effigies and structures within the cemetery grounds, and for the removal thereof; for regulating the introduction and care of plants, trees and shrubs within such grounds; for the prevention of the burial in a lot, plot or part thereof, of a body not entitled to burial therein; for regulating or preventing disinterments; for regulating the conduct of persons while within the cemetery grounds; for excluding improper persons and preventing improper

assemblages therein. The directors may prescribe penalties for the violation of any such rule or regulation, not exceeding twenty–five dollars for each violation, which shall be recoverable by the corporation in a civil action.

(b) Charges for services. The directors of a cemetery corporation shall fix and make reasonable charges for any acts and services ordered by the owner and rendered by the corporation in connection with the use, care, including perpetual, annual and special care, management and protection of lots, plots and parts thereof. In determining said charges the directors shall consider the propriety and the fair and reasonable cost and expense of rendering the services or performing the work for which such charges are made.

(c) Cemetery board approval. (1) A cemetery corporation's rules, regulations and original charges shall not become effective unless and until approved by the cemetery board as hereinafter provided. (2) The directors of any cemetery corporation, organized on or before August thirty–first, nineteen hundred forty–nine, shall file in the office of the cemetery board the name and address of the corporation together with its rules, regulations and charges, and a statement showing the basis upon which they were made, within ninety days after the time this section as hereby amended takes effect. The directors of any cemetery corporation organized on or after September first, nineteen hundred forty–nine, shall file in the office of the cemetery board the name and address of the corporation together with its rules, regulations and charges, and a statement showing the basis on which they were made, within ninety days after the date of the filing of the certificate of incorporation in the department of state. (3) Within six months after the date of such filing, the cemetery board shall make and file in its office an order approving, disapproving or amending such rules, regulations and original charges in whole or part. Such rules, regulations and charges, if approved with or without amendment, shall become effective as approved upon the filing of such order by the cemetery board in its office. The cemetery board shall notify the directors of the action taken by it and its reasons therefor by registered mail addressed to the corporation at its principal office. In making its determination as to the schedule of charges the cemetery board shall consider the propriety and the fair and reasonable cost and expense of rendering the services or performing the work for which such charges are made. In passing upon the rules and regulations, the cemetery board shall consider the interests of the members of the corporation and the public interest in the proper maintenance and operation of burial grounds. (4) The rules, regulations and charges of any cemetery corporation existing on or before August thirty–first, nineteen hundred forty–nine, shall remain in effect until the cemetery board files in its office an order pursuant to the provisions of subdivision three hereof. A cemetery corporation organized on or after September first, nineteen hundred forty–nine, may enforce the rules, regulations and charges filed by it in the office of the cemetery board until the cemetery board files in its office an order pursuant to the provisions of subdivision three hereof.

(d) Services not in list of charges. In the event that a cemetery corporation provides any services not included in the list of charges, and for which a charge cannot reasonably be fixed in advance, the charges made therefor shall be reviewable by the cemetery board. In the event that the cemetery board determines that an excessive, unauthorized or improper charge has been made for such services or that the services have not been properly performed, it may direct the cemetery corporation to pay to the person from whom such charge was collected a sum equivalent to three times the amount of the excess as determined by the cemetery board, or in the case of work not properly performed, it may direct the cemetery corporation to perform the work properly.

(e) Amendment and modification. (1) The rules and regulations of a cemetery corporation may be amended or added to by the corporation by filing such proposed amendments or additions in the office of the cemetery board but no such amendment or addition shall be effective unless and until an order approving such amendments or additions is made by the cemetery board and filed in its office in the same manner as that applicable to the original filing of the rules, regulations and charges of the cemetery corporation. (2) The charges of a cemetery corporation may be amended or added to by the corporation by filing an application containing such proposed amendment or addition in the office of the division of cemeteries and shall be processed in accordance with subparagraph three of this paragraph. The cemetery board shall consider the propriety and the fair and reasonable costs and expense of rendering the services or performing the work for which such charges are made. The effective rules, regulations or charges of a cemetery corporation may be amended, modified or vacated by the cemetery board at any time. The cemetery board shall notify the directors of the action taken by it and its reasons therefor by registered or certified mail addressed to the corporation at its principal office. In amending, modifying or vacating any rule, regulation or charge, the cemetery board shall be guided by the standards set forth in subparagraph three of paragraph (c) of this section. (3) Any application setting forth the proposed amendment of, or addition to, the charges of a cemetery corporation as provided for by subparagraph two of this paragraph shall be processed in accordance either with clauses A, B and C of this subparagraph or in accordance with clause D of this subdivision.

A. Within thirty–five days following receipt of the application, the board or the division may request from the cemetery corporation any additional information or documentation deemed necessary to complete such application, and such application shall not be complete for the purposes of compliance with this subparagraph until the requested information has been received. If no such request is made, the application shall be deemed to be complete on the thirty–fifth day after its receipt by the division.

B. An application setting forth the proposed amendment of, or addition to, the charges of a cemetery corporation shall be deemed to be approved for any cemetery corporation holding, including unrestricted funds, cash and investments totalling less than four hundred thousand dollars, if the board does not object to the proposed charges within sixty days following: (i) the date on which the application shall have been deemed to be complete or (ii) the date on which the requested information necessary to complete the application shall have been received, whichever is later. If the board objects to the proposed charges, it shall notify the directors in writing with the reasons therefor, such notice to be mailed by registered or certified mail to the corporation at its principal office, not less than three business days before the end of such sixty day period. If the board approves such amendment of or addition to the charges, it shall do so by order.

C. An application setting forth the proposed amendment of, or addition to, the charges of a cemetery corporation shall be deemed to be approved for any cemetery corporation holding, including unrestricted funds, cash and investments totalling more than four hundred thousand dollars, if the board does not object to the proposed charges within ninety days following: (i) the date on which the application shall have been deemed to be complete or (ii) the date on which the requested information necessary to complete the application shall have been received, whichever is later. If the board objects to the proposed charges, it shall notify the directors in writing with the reasons therefor, such notice to be mailed by registered or certified mail to the corporation at its principal office, not less than three business days before the end of such ninety day period. If the board approves such amendment of or addition to the charges, it shall do so by order.

D. A cemetery may apply to the cemetery board for an increase in any or all of its approved charges by submitting a schedule to the cemetery board showing its currently approved charges and the proposed charges after applying the employment cost index to said charges as it appears in the United States Department of Labor, Bureau of Labor Statistics, Series ECU10001A, not seasonally adjusted, total compensation, civilian, twelve month percent change for all workers schedule or any subsequent schedule that may be adopted by the United States Department of Labor, Bureau of Labor Statistics, as a replacement for the aforementioned schedule. Any application by a cemetery under this subparagraph will prohibit application under subparagraph two of this paragraph for one year from the effective date of the approved increase under this subparagraph. An application setting forth the proposed changes in charges shall be deemed to be approved if the board does not object to the proposed charges within sixty–days following the date on which the application is submitted by a cemetery. If the board objects to the proposed charges, it shall notify the directors in writing with the reasons therefore, such notice to be mailed to the corporation at its principal office, not less than three business days before the end of such sixty day period. If the board approves such amendment of or addition to the charges, it shall do so by order. The cemetery board shall not approve application by a cemetery under this subparagraph if (i) the proposed percentage increases exceed the employment cost index percentages as provided in this subparagraph; (ii) there have been invasions of the permanent maintenance fund by the cemetery that have not been repaid or are not currently being repaid; (iii) the cemetery is currently not in compliance with any court order or any cemetery board order that is not under judicial review under paragraph (d) of section 1504; (iv) the cemetery has not filed in a timely manner its annual reports with the division of cemeteries as required under section 1508 (Reports by cemeteries); (v) all assessments as required under paragraph (c) of section 1508 (Reports by cemeteries) and vandalism fund payments as required under subparagraph two of paragraph (h) of section 1507 (Trust funds) have not been paid.

(f) Lot tax assessment. (1) If the funds of a cemetery corporation applicable to the improvement and care of its cemetery, or applicable to the construction of a receiving vault therein for the common use of lot owners, be insufficient for such purposes, the directors of the corporation, not oftener than once in any year and for such purposes only, may, upon the prior approval of the cemetery board, which shall determine the necessity and propriety thereof, levy a tax on some basis to be determined by the directors of such corporation, but no such tax shall exceed two dollars on any one lot, except that with the written consent of two–thirds of the lot owners or by the vote of a majority of the lot owners present at an annual meeting, or at a special meeting duly called for such purpose, such tax may be for an amount which shall not exceed a total of five dollars per annum per lot, and the tax on any one lot shall not exceed five dollars per annum but the taxes may be levied upon each lot in the first instance for a sum sufficient for the improvement and care of the lot, but no greater sum than five dollars shall be collected in any one year. The whole tax levied may be collected in sums of five dollars in successive years in the manner herein provided. (2) Notice of such tax shall be served on the lot owners or where two or more persons are owners of the same lot, on one of them, either personally, or by leaving it at his residence, with a person of mature age and discretion, or by mail, if he resides in a city, town or village where the office of the corpora-

tion is not located, or in case the residence or whereabouts of the owner cannot be ascertained, by publication once a week for four successive weeks in a newspaper published in the town where such cemetery is located, or if no newspaper is published in such town then in some newspaper published in the county where such cemetery is located. (3) If such tax remain unpaid for more than thirty days after the service of such notice, the president and secretary of the corporation may issue a warrant to the treasurer of the corporation, requiring him to collect such tax in the same manner as school collectors are required to collect school taxes; and such treasurer shall have the same power and be subject to the same liabilities in executing such warrant as a collector of school taxes has or is subject to by law in executing a warrant for the collection of school taxes. (4) If the taxes so levied remain unpaid for five years after the levying of such tax the amount thereof with interest shall be a lien on the unused portion of the lot which is subject to such tax, and no portion of the lot so taxed shall be used by the owner thereof for burial purposes, while any such tax remains unpaid. (5) If at the expiration of five years from the date of the service of the first notice of assessment as herein provided, any such assessment or the interest thereon shall remain unpaid, the corporation may sell the unused portion of such lot at public auction upon the cemetery grounds, in the following manner: If the person owning such lot resides within the state, a written notice, under the seal of such cemetery corporation, if it have a seal, and the hand of the president or secretary thereof, stating the amount of such tax or taxes unpaid and that such unused portion of such lot will be sold at a time therein to be specified, not less than twenty days from the date of the service of such notice, shall be personally served upon such owner; if such owner is not a resident of the state, or if the place of his residence cannot with due diligence be ascertained, or if, for any other reason satisfactory to the court, personal service cannot with due diligence be made upon such owner, such cemetery corporation, or any of its officers, may present a duly verified petition stating the facts to the county court of the county in which such cemetery lands are situated, or to the supreme court, and such court may upon satisfactory proof, by its order, direct the service of such notice in the manner provided by the civil practice law and rules for the substituted service of a summons. The president or secretary of such corporation, or any suitable and proper person appointed by it or by the court, upon filing proof of publication and service of such notice as provided by section three hundred fourteen of the surrogate's court procedure act may make such sale, and such sale may be adjourned from time to time for the accommodation of the parties or for other proper reasons. Previous notice of such sale shall be posted at the main entrance of the cemetery. Prior to such sale such corporation shall cause such lot to be resurveyed and replotted showing the part thereof not used for burial purposes and only such unused portion shall be sold. The cemetery corporation may at any such sale purchase any such lots or parts of lots. The surplus remaining after paying all assessments, interest, cost and charges shall be set aside by the corporation, as a fund for the care and improvement of the portion of such lot that has been used for burial purposes. In case the proceeds of such sale shall amount to more than thirty dollars the person making it shall make his report, under oath, to the court, of the proceedings and shall state the amount for which such lot was sold and that it was sold to the highest responsible bidder, together with the names of the purchasers, and the court may and in a proper case shall, by order, confirm the sale; in all other cases the person making such sale shall file in the office of the county clerk of the county in which the cemetery lands are situated a like report duly verified; on the filing of such order of confirmation or such report, as the case may be, the ownership of the unoccupied portion of such lot shall vest in the purchaser thereof. (6) The directors of any such corporation may make a contract with a lot owner which shall provide for the payment by him of an agreed gross sum in lieu of further taxes and assessments and that upon the payment of such gross sum the lot of such owner shall be thereafter exempt from taxes and assessments.

(g) Purchases through office of general services. Notwithstanding the provisions of any general, special or local law, any officer or agent of a cemetery corporation subject to the provisions of this article authorized to make purchases of commodities and services may make such purchases through the office of general services subject to such rules as may be established from time to time pursuant to section one hundred sixty-three of the state finance law; provided that any such purchase shall exceed five hundred dollars and that the cemetery corporation for which such officer or agent acts shall accept sole responsibility for any payment due the vendor. All purchases shall be subject to audit and inspection by the cemetery corporation for which made. Two or more cemetery corporations may join in making purchases pursuant to this section and, for the purposes of this section, such groups shall be deemed a cemetery corporation.

History: Add, L 1977, ch 871, § 2, eff Aug 11, 1977; amd, L 1991, ch 426, § 1, eff Jan 1, 1992, L 1992, ch 16, § 1, eff March 13, 1992, L 1992, ch 151, § 1, eff June 16, 1992, L 2006, ch 709, § 1, eff Nov 12, 2006, L 2012, ch 55, § 23 (Part L), eff March 30, 2012.

Laws 2012, ch 55, § 39 (Part L), eff. March 30, 2012, provides as follows:

§ 39. This act shall take effect immediately, provided, however, that procurement contracts for which bid solicitations have been issued prior to the effective date of this act shall be subject to the provisions of law in effect at the time of issuance; provided, however, that the amendments made to section 163 of the state finance law by sections two, three, four, five, seven, nine, ten, twelve and thirty-six of this act shall not affect the repeal of such section and shall be deemed to be repealed therewith; and provided, however, that the amendments to section 104 of the general municipal law made by section six of this act shall be subject to the expiration and reversion of such section pursuant to section 9 of subpart A of part C of chapter 97 of the laws of 2011, when upon such date the provisions of section twenty-seven of this act shall take effect; and provided, however, that the amendments to paragraph a of subdivision 5 of section 355 of the education law made by section thirty-one of this act shall be subject to the expiration and reversion of such subdivision pursuant to section 4 of subpart B of part D of chapter 58 of the laws of 2011, when upon such date the provisions of section thirty-two of this act shall take effect; and provided that the amendments to subdivision a of section 6218 of the education law made by section thirty-three of this act shall be subject to the expiration and reversion of such subdivision pursuant to section 4 of subpart B of part D of chapter 58 of the laws of 2011, as amended, when upon such date the provisions of section thirty-four of this act shall take effect.

CASE ANNOTATIONS

New York State Cemetery Board properly denied non-for-profit cemetery corporation's application to lease 3-acre parcel to for-profit funeral home for purpose of constructing and operating funeral home and related businesses where Board determined that proposal had potential adverse financial repercussions for cemetery corporation in that duration of lease (40 years with 4 10-year options to renew) would preclude future alternatives, cemetery corporation did not present sufficient proof that it adequately sought offers from other entities, nature and duration of relationship between cemetery corporation and funeral home was deemed significant as source of potential conflict with interests of lot owners, and Board found proposed construction inappropriate when viewed in light of public policy concerns underpinning statutorily mandated not-for-profit status of cemeteries (19 NYCRR § 201.16(c)(5), CLS N-PCL § 1501). Poughkeepsie Rural Cemetery v Treadwell (1998, 3d Dept) 252 A.D.2d 903, 676 N.Y.S.2d 338

New York State Cemetery Board's comprehensive report indicating its opposition to relationships between funeral homes and not-for-profit cemeteries did not constitute unlawful rule-making since such declaration did not constitute mandatory procedure applied without discretion but was limited to factual circumstances of particular contractual relationship in question. Poughkeepsie Rural Cemetery v Treadwell (1998, 3d Dept) 252 A.D.2d 903, 676 N.Y.S.2d 338

§ 1510. Cemetery duties

(a) Posting and distribution of rules, regulations, charges and prices. The rules, regulations, charges, and prices of lots, plots or parts thereof shall be suitably printed and shall be conspicuously posted by the corporation in each of its offices. A printed copy of prices of lots, plots or parts thereof shall be made available upon request by any person for up to the actual price of the printing of the copy. For each day in which the corporation fails to post the rules, regulations, charges and prices the corporation shall be subject to a penalty of twenty-five dollars which may be recovered in a civil action by the cemetery board. For each instance in which the corporation fails to make available a copy of the prices of lots, plots, or parts thereof, to a person who request [requests]* such copy, the corporation shall be subject to a penalty of twenty-five dollars which may be recovered in a civil action by the cemetery board. The cemetery board may waive the payment of the penalty or any part thereof.

    * The bracketed word has been inserted by the Publisher.

    (b) Surveys and maps of cemetery. (1) Every cemetery corporation, from time to time, as land in its cemetery may be required for burial purposes, shall survey and subdivide such lands and make and file in the office of the corporation a map thereof, open to public inspection, delineating the lots or plots, avenues, paths, alleys and walks and their respective designations; a true copy thereof shall upon its written request, be filed with the cemetery board. Any unsold lots, plots or parts thereof, in which there are no remains, by order of the directors, may be resurveyed and altered in shape or size, and properly designated on such map. (2) Every cemetery corporation shall provide reasonable access to every lot, plot and grave. This provision shall not be applicable where on September first, nineteen hundred forty-nine such access cannot be provided without the disinterment of a body or bodies. A cemetery corporation shall not permit or allow a body to be interred hereafter in a path, alley, avenue or walk shown on the cemetery maps or actually in existence. Nothing herein contained, however, shall prevent a cemetery corporation in special cases from enlarging a lot by selling to the owner thereof the access space next to such lot, and permitting interments therein, provided reasonable access to such lot and to adjoining lots is not thereby eliminated, and provided the approval of the cemetery board shall have first been obtained.

    (c) Record of burials or cremations. A record shall be kept of every burial in the cemetery of a cemetery corporation, showing the date of burial, the name, age, and place of birth of the person buried, when these particulars can be conveniently obtained, and the lot, plot, or part thereof, in which such burial was made. A copy of such record, duly certified by the secretary of such corporation, shall be furnished on demand and payment of such fees therefor as are allowed the county clerk for certified copies of records. Notwithstanding any other provision of this section, all cemetery corporations which conduct cremations shall maintain permanent records of the name of the deceased human being, the funeral home from which the remains were received, the receipt of delivery of the deceased human remains, the authorizing agent for the cremation, and the manner of disposition of the cremains. Such records may be reviewed by the division of cemeteries at any time.

    (d) When burial not to be refused. No cemetery corporation shall refuse or deny the right of burial and the privileges incidental thereto in any lot, plot

or part thereof to those otherwise lawfully entitled to be buried therein, for any reason except for the nonpayment of interment charges and the purchase price of the lot, plot or part thereof, in accordance with the terms of the contract of purchase or except as provided in subdivision (f) of section fifteen hundred nine of this article.

    (e) Removals. A body interred in a lot in a cemetery owned or operated by a corporation incorporated by or under a general or special law may be removed therefrom, with the consent of the corporation, and the written consent of the owners of the lot, and of the surviving wife, husband, children, if of full age, and parents of the deceased. If the consent of any such person or of the corporation can not be obtained, permission by the county court of the county, or by the supreme court in the district, where the cemetery is situated, shall be sufficient. Notice of application for such permission must be given, at least eight days prior thereto, personally, or, at least sixteen days prior thereto, by mail, to the corporation or to the persons not consenting, and to every other person or corporation on whom service of notice may be required by the court.

    (f) Expenses of improving vacant lot. Whenever a person having a lot in a cemetery shall vacate the same by a removal of all the bodies therefrom, and leave such lot in an unsightly condition for one month, the corporation may grade, cut, fill or otherwise change the surface thereof, without reducing the area of the lot. The expense, not exceeding ten dollars, shall be chargeable to the lot. If the owners of such lot, within six months after such expense has been incurred, shall not repay such expense, the corporation may sell the lot at public auction upon the cemetery grounds, previous notice of such sale having been posted at the main entrance of the cemetery, and mailed to the owners of such lot at their last-known post office address, at least ten days prior to the day of sale, and shall pay the surplus, if any, on demand to the owners of such lot.

    (g) Removal or correction of dangerous conditions in cemetery lots. Any plant life, fencing or embellishment or structure other than a mausoleum, monument or mound, in a lot, plot or part thereof which becomes so worn, neglected, broken or deteriorated that its continued existence is a danger to persons or property within the cemetery grounds may be removed, repaired or corrected by the cemetery corporation at its own cost and expense, provided it first gives not less than fifteen days notice by registered or certified mail to the last known owner at his last known address to repair or remove such object and the said owner shall fail to repair or remove the object within the time provided in said notice. In the event of such removal, correction or repair by the cemetery corporation it shall, within twenty days thereafter, notify the lot owner, by registered or certified mail addressed to him at his last known address, of the action taken by the cemetery corporation. Nothing herein contained shall be construed to affect, supersede or impair any contract, rule or regulation duly approved by the cemetery board, or right or obligation of the cemetery corporation, nor shall it be construed as placing any legal duty or obligation to exercise any right authorized by this subdivision.

(h) Repair or notice as to non-dangerous damage or defacement. Except as otherwise provided by rule or regulation of the cemetery board pursuant to subparagraph two-a of paragraph (c) of section fifteen hundred four of this article, in the event a lot, plot or part thereof is substantially damaged or defaced which does not present a dangerous condition to persons or property, or in the event a mausoleum, monument or mound in a lot, plot or part thereof is substantially damaged or defaced, and the correction of such condition is not subject to the provisions of paragraph (g) of this section or section fifteen hundred ten-a of this article, the cemetery corporation within thirty days of the discovery of this condition may at its own cost and expense repair the damage or defacement, or if it determines not to do so, the corporation shall within such thirty day period notify the owner, his or her distributee or the person filing an affidavit with such corporation pursuant to the provisions of paragraph (e) of section fifteen hundred twelve of this article of such condition at the last address of such owner, distributee or person appearing on the books and records of the corporation. The notice shall be sent by first class mail and a certificate of mailing shall be obtained. Nothing herein contained shall be construed as establishing any right of damages not otherwise provided by law, rule or contract in any person against the cemetery corporation for failure to repair any condition described or give notice thereof as provided for in this paragraph.

(i) Record of inscriptions to be filed. Whenever, under any general or special law, any cemetery is abandoned or is taken for a public use, the town board of the town or the governing body of the city in which such cemetery is located, shall cause to be made, at the time of the removal of the bodies interred therein, an exact copy of all inscriptions on each headstone, monument, slab or marker erected on each lot or plot in such cemetery and shall cause the same to be duly certified and shall file one copy thereof in the office of the town or city clerk of the town or city in which such cemetery was located and one copy in the office of the state historian and chief of the division of history in the department of education at Albany. In addition to such inscriptions, such certificate shall state the name and location of the cemetery so abandoned or taken for a public use, the cemetery in which each such body was so interred and the disposition of each such headstone, monument, slab or marker.

(j) Grave markers. No cemetery corporation, which provides for the burial of persons of the Jewish faith, shall promulgate any rule or regulation prohibiting the use of cement beds as a means of demarcating a specific grave area. Such cemetery corporations shall provide this service to all persons of the Jewish faith requesting this method of marking a grave when such grave area is provided through the agency of a membership or religious corporation or unincorporated association or society which provides burial benefits for the members. Subject to the rules and regulations promulgated by the cemetery board, such cemetery corporations shall establish the schedule of charges to be assessed for installation and maintenance of cement beds. The schedule of charges shall be filed with and approved by the cemetery board. Such regulation may require the payment of the cost of perpetual care as a condition to such installation and maintenance. The charges assessed shall be paid by the person requesting the service. The provisions of this paragraph shall only be applicable within the counties contained within the first, second, tenth and eleventh judicial districts as such districts are arranged pursuant to section one hundred forty of the judiciary law.

(k) Notice and restoration as to damage and defacement due to vandalism. In the event a monument is damaged or defaced by an act of vandalism, the cemetery corporation shall, within thirty days of the discovery of such damage, notify the owner, his distributee or the person filing an affidavit with such corporation pursuant to the provisions of paragraph one of subdivision (e) of section fifteen hundred twelve of this article of such damage in the manner provided in subdivision (h) of this section. The cost and expense of such notice may be provided from the fund where such fund exists. If a fund has been established, the cemetery corporation shall restore the monument with moneys from such fund. If such a fund has not been established or where such fund is inadequate to restore the monument, the cemetery corporation may restore such monument at its own cost and expense. Nothing herein contained shall be construed as establishing any right of damages not otherwise provided by law, rule or contract in any person against the cemetery corporation for failure to restore any monument if no monument maintenance fund exists or if such fund is inadequate to restore such monument.

(l) Removal of monument. No person or organization shall remove a monument without authorization in the form of a court order from a court of competent jurisdiction, or without the written authorization of the owner of a burial plot, or the lineal descendants of the deceased, if such owner or lineal descendants are known, and without obtaining written approval from a duly incorporated cemetery association, which association shall keep a record of all such written approvals. The provisions of this section shall not prohibit the removal, in accordance with rules and regulations promulgated by the secretary of state, of a monument for the purpose of repair, nonpayment or adding inscriptions as authorized by a cemetery association or as permitted in this article. A violation of any provision of this paragraph shall be punishable by a fine not to exceed five hundred dollars.

(m) Use of construction and demolition debris for burial. No cemetery corporation or religious corporation having charge and control of a cemetery which heretofore has been or which hereafter may be used for burials, shall use construction and demolition debris, as that term is defined in 6 NYCRR 360-1.2, for the purpose of burying human remains.

(n) Interment of pet cremated remains. The interment of pet cremated remains in a cemetery corporation shall be available to a lot owner only in those circumstances where the interment is incidental to the burial of human remains and where authorization has been provided in a written statement from the cemetery corporation. The cemetery corporation shall provide a list of approved charges for the interment of such remains. All payments received for interment of such remains shall be deposited in the cemetery corporation's permanent maintenance fund. Pet cremated remains must be disposed of by placing them in a grave, crypt, or niche. Nothing in this section shall obligate a cemetery corporation to allow interment of such cremated pet remains where prior approval at the time of sale or in advance of need has not been received. The provisions of this section shall not apply to an incorporated or unincorporated cemetery operated, supervised or controlled by a religious corporation or a lot, plot or part thereof whose record owner is an incorporated or unincorporated religious association or society.

History: Add, L 1977, ch 871, § 2, eff Aug 11, 1977; amd, L 1977, ch 872; L 1980, ch 565 § 4, eff June 26, 1980; L 1980, ch 565, §§ 3, 4, eff June 26, 1980; L 1981, ch 874, § 1; L 1981, ch 875, § 1, eff July 31, 1981; L 1985, ch 608, § 4, eff Sept 1, 1985; L 1992, ch 821, § 1, eff Nov 1, 1992; L 1993, ch 169, § 2, eff June 28, 1993; L 2000, ch 380, § 4, eff Sept 29, 2000; L 2006, ch 254, § 1, eff Oct 24, 2006; L 2006, ch 579, § 5, eff Oct 15, 2006; L 2016, ch 330, §2, eff Sept 26, 2016.

CASE ANNOTATIONS

1. Generally
2. Application to disinter
3. —Jurisdiction
4. —Procedural matters
5. —Standing
6. —Evidence
7. —Grant of application
8. —Denial of application
9. Wrongful disinterment
10. Exhumation

1. Generally

CLS N-PCL § 1510(m) is violated when cemetery permits burials on site which contains construction and demolition debris, even where such material is first covered by 10 to 12 feet of topsoil. People v Cypress Hills Cemetery, 208 A.D.2d 247, 622 N.Y.S.2d 300, 1995 N.Y. App. Div. LEXIS 1049 (N.Y. App. Div. 2d Dep't 1995).

2. Application to disinter

Supreme Court was foreclosed from granting application to disinter decedent's body and remove and reinter it in different cemetery plot where there was no proof that they obtained consent of cemetery corporation and owner of cemetery lot, or that these entities were given notice of application. Dutcher v Paradise, 217 A.D.2d 774, 629 N.Y.S.2d 501, 1995 N.Y. App. Div. LEXIS 7786 (N.Y. App. Div. 3d Dep't 1995).

Where all necessary parties do not consent to disinterment of body, court has discretion to determine whether good and substantial reasons have been shown for disinterment based on equitable principles, with due consideration given to expressed wishes of decedent and those most closely bound to him by ties of love and affection. Weinstein v Mintz, 148 Misc. 2d 820, 562 N.Y.S.2d 917, 1990 N.Y. Misc. LEXIS 580 (N.Y. Sup. Ct. 1990).

Request for exhumation or disinterment of body pursuant to CLS N-PCL § 1510 should be carefully scrutinized to determine if there is legitimate basis to conduct further autopsy, especially taking into account overriding concern of surviving next of kin that those laid to rest should be permitted to rest in peace. People v Radtke, 152 Misc. 2d 744, 578 N.Y.S.2d 827, 1991 N.Y. Misc. LEXIS 724 (N.Y. Sup. Ct. 1991).

When considering an application to disinter a widow's husband buried in a plot erroneously sold to the widow, as it had previously been sold to someone else, the court was to exercise benevolent discretion and consider factors such as (1) the religious convictions of the deceased; (2) who chose the burial site; (3) the desires and motives of those of close kinship to the deceased, especially a spouse, in prompting a change of location; and (4) the sanctity of the burial ground. Corp. of the Roslyn Presbyterian Church & Congregation v Perlman, 193 Misc. 2d 60, 747 N.Y.S.2d 304, 2002 N.Y. Misc. LEXIS 1144 (N.Y. Sup. Ct. 2002).

3. —Jurisdiction

Widow's failure to consent to the disinterment of her deceased husband, who had been buried in a plot erroneously sold to the widow, as it had been previously sold to someone else, allowed judicial intervention under N.Y. Not-For-Profit Corp. Law § 1510(e). Corp. of the Roslyn Presbyterian Church & Congregation v Perlman, 193 Misc. 2d 60, 747 N.Y.S.2d 304, 2002 N.Y. Misc. LEXIS 1144 (N.Y. Sup. Ct. 2002).

4. —Procedural matters

Trial court erred by not holding a hearing on the disinterment of an archbishop because the trial court did not give adequate consideration to a monsignor's affidavit and too narrowly defined the inquiry into the archbishop's wishes, but instead improperly deferred to the family's wishes, without a full exploration of the archbishop's desires; any inquiry into whether the archbishop would be canonized a saint called for undue speculation. Matter of Cunningham v Trustees of St. Patrick's Cathedral, 159 A.D.3d 161, 72 N.Y.S.3d 29, 2018 N.Y. App. Div. LEXIS 806 (N.Y. App. Div. 1st Dep't 2018).

Trial court erred by not holding a hearing on the disinterment of an archbishop because the trial court did not give adequate consideration to a monsignor's affidavit and too narrowly defined the inquiry into the archbishop's wishes, but instead improperly deferred to the family's wishes, without a full exploration of the archbishop's desires; any inquiry into whether the archbishop would be canonized a saint called for undue speculation. Matter of Cunningham v Trustees of St. Patrick's Cathedral, 2018 N.Y. App. Div. LEXIS 806 (N.Y. App. Div. 1st Dep't 2018).

Proceeding under CLS N-PCL § 1510(e) to reinter decedent's remains was not jurisdictionally defective due to lack of service of summons and complaint, since statute requires only "application" upon notice, which may be given by ordinary mail. In re Elman, 152 Misc. 2d 656, 578 N.Y.S.2d 95, 1991 N.Y. Misc. LEXIS 686 (N.Y. Sup. Ct. 1991).

5. —Standing

Decedent's girlfriend, as owner of cemetery lot in which decedent's body was buried, had standing to object to petition brought by decedent's estranged wife seeking permission to disinter his body; further, inasmuch as decedent's wishes are factor to be considered whenever court is asked to sanction disinterment, girlfriend would have standing to represent those wishes since wife was unable to secure all consents needed to obtain disinterment without court approval. In re Estate of Conroy, 138 A.D.2d 212, 530 N.Y.S.2d 653, 1988 N.Y. App. Div. LEXIS 7237 (N.Y. App. Div. 3d Dep't), app. dismissed, 73 N.Y.2d 810, 537 N.Y.S.2d 497, 534 N.E.2d 335, 1988 N.Y. LEXIS 3379 (N.Y. 1988).

Decedent's sisters, his sole surviving next of kin, had standing under CLS N-PCL § 1510(e) to seek permission to reinter his remains in newly purchased family plot since there was no surviving relative whose consent to disinterment was required. In re Elman, 152 Misc. 2d 656, 578 N.Y.S.2d 95, 1991 N.Y. Misc. LEXIS 686 (N.Y. Sup. Ct. 1991).

6. —Evidence

Formal evidentiary rule embodied in Dead Man's Statute under CLS CPLR § 4519 was inapplicable to proceeding brought by decedent's estranged wife seeking to disinter his body under CLS N-PCL § 1510; thus, decedent's girlfriend, who objected to disinterment, could offer proof of statements made by decedent regarding his burial wishes. In re Estate of Conroy, 138 A.D.2d 212, 530 N.Y.S.2d 653, 1988 N.Y. App. Div. LEXIS 7237 (N.Y. App. Div. 3d Dep't), app. dismissed, 73 N.Y.2d 810, 537 N.Y.S.2d 497, 534 N.E.2d 335, 1988 N.Y. LEXIS 3379 (N.Y. 1988).

In proceeding under CLS N-PCL § 1510(e) to reinter decedent's remains, allegations of decedent's nephew as to "expressed wishes" of decedent would not be disregarded as mere hearsay, since decedent's wishes were important factor to be considered and it would be counterproductive to exclude evidence thereof due to formal evidentiary objections. In re Elman, 152 Misc. 2d 656, 578 N.Y.S.2d 95, 1991 N.Y. Misc. LEXIS 686 (N.Y. Sup. Ct. 1991).

In proceeding under CLS N-PCL § 1510(e) in which husband requested that remains of his deceased wife be moved from plot next to her mother to another plot at same cemetery where he and their children would be buried, respondent's claim that deceased had expressed wish to be buried with her mother was not determinative, where respondent failed to provide affidavits or other evidence to buttress her claim that she overheard deceased (who was her sister) express such wish, deceased's alleged wish was neither recent nor expressed in causa mortis but rather was expressed in emotional tide of her mother's death, and respondent did not allege that deceased knew that burial next to her mother would necessarily exclude interment of her spouse with her by virtue of number of unreserved spaces left. Viscomi v McGuire, 169 Misc. 2d 713, 647 N.Y.S.2d 397, 1996 N.Y. Misc. LEXIS 329 (N.Y. Sup. Ct. 1996).

While CLS N-PCL § 1510(e) is special proceeding to which hearsay principles and Dead Man's Statute (CLS CPLR § 4519) normally apply, facts that statute not only designates request to court for disinterment as "application," but allows for service of any required notice by mere regular mail, indicates legislative intent to informalize proceeding and relax rules of evidence so as to allow deceased's expressed wish to be buried with her mother to become part of record. Viscomi v McGuire, 169 Misc. 2d 713, 647 N.Y.S.2d 397, 1996 N.Y. Misc. LEXIS 329 (N.Y. Sup. Ct. 1996).

7 —Grant of application

Because the paramount concern of a husband's deceased wife was that he be buried beside her, and because he was unable to obtain assurances from relatives who owned interests in the cemetery plot that he would be buried in a grave adjoining hers, the trial court properly granted the husband's N.Y. Not-for-Profit Corp. Law § 1510(e) petition to disinter the remains of his wife. Matter of Pring v Cemetery, 54 A.D.3d 766, 863 N.Y.S.2d 730, 2008 N.Y. App. Div. LEXIS 6665 (N.Y. App. Div. 2d Dep't 2008).

Application for disinterment of deceased husband's body and its reburial in plot next to that of his wife would be granted over objection of one of his children where clear intention of both decedents was that their final resting place be together. Weinstein v Mintz, 148 Misc. 2d 820, 562 N.Y.S.2d 917, 1990 N.Y. Misc. LEXIS 580 (N.Y. Sup. Ct. 1990).

Husband was permitted to move remains of his deceased wife from plot next to her mother to another plot at same cemetery where he and their children would be buried, although he had originally acceded to have her buried next to her mother where, inter alia, it was not shown that he was fully aware in his grief that, by virtue of fact that she was being buried in last unreserved space of her mother's 6-grave plot, he was thereby excluding himself from ever reposing with her. Viscomi v McGuire, 169 Misc. 2d 713, 647 N.Y.S.2d 397, 1996 N.Y. Misc. LEXIS 329 (N.Y. Sup. Ct. 1996).

Court granted husband's request to move remains of his wife from plot next to her mother to another plot at same cemetery where he and their children would be buried, over objections of his wife's sister, who asserted that her deceased sister's marriage was "difficult" for 10 years prior to her death, where husband conceded 9-month separation that occurred after more than 30 years of marriage, but reconcil-

iation was honestly accomplished as he and his wife stayed together for 12 more years prior to her unexpected demise at age 58. Viscomi v McGuire, 169 Misc. 2d 713, 647 N.Y.S.2d 397, 1996 N.Y. Misc. LEXIS 329 (N.Y. Sup. Ct. 1996).

Because the decedent died without having designated a representative pursuant to a validly executed written instrument, without a surviving spouse, and with a child under 18 years of age, the rights to the remains unequivocally belonged to the decedent's parents; therefore, pursuant to N.Y. Not-for-Profit Corp. Law § 1510(e), N.Y. Pub. Health Law § 4201(2)(a), and N.Y. C.P.L.R. art. 4, the parents could disinter and relocate the decedent's remains. Bochnik v Gate of Heaven Cemetery, 927 N.Y.S.2d 739, 32 Misc. 3d 269, 2011 N.Y. Misc. LEXIS 2223 (N.Y. Sup. Ct. 2011).

Where the legal and equitable owner of a burial plot did nothing to create the plot's wrongful resale to someone else or the burial of a stranger to the owner in the plot, and no religious or personal convictions of the deceased precluding his disinterment were set forth, the equities required that the disinterment of the deceased be ordered, along with his re-interment, all at the expense of the religious corporation which wrongfully sold the same burial plot to two people. Corp. of the Roslyn Presbyterian Church & Congregation v Perlman, 193 Misc. 2d 60, 747 N.Y.S.2d 304, 2002 N.Y. Misc. LEXIS 1144 (N.Y. Sup. Ct. 2002).

8. —Denial of application

Need to ascertain cause of death is not good and substantial reason required to justify disinterment where cause of death has already been determined by jury after full trial. In re Band, 117 A.D.2d 597, 498 N.Y.S.2d 67, 1986 N.Y. App. Div. LEXIS 52872 (N.Y. App. Div. 2d Dep't 1986).

Wife was not entitled to have her husband's body disinterred and moved to another cemetery where she failed to show that she had requested consents of cemetery corporation, lot owner, and decedent's children prior to requesting judicial approval, as required by CLS N-PCL § 1510, or that she served statutory notice (if those parties did not consent); CLS Pub Health § 4213—relied on by wife—refers to claiming of body by friend or relative prior to burial, not to disinterment. In re Estate of Conroy, 129 A.D.2d 849, 513 N.Y.S.2d 873, 1987 N.Y. App. Div. LEXIS 45545 (N.Y. App. Div. 3d Dep't 1987).

It was abuse of discretion to summarily grant application by decedent's estranged wife to disinter his body even though all family members agreed to such action and despite absence of decedent's contractual arrangement for place of burial or religious beliefs to contrary, where decedent's girlfriend had objected to disinterment on ground that burial arrangements she made following his death were those expressly requested by him after learning of his terminal illness. In re Estate of Conroy, 138 A.D.2d 212, 530 N.Y.S.2d 653, 1988 N.Y. App. Div. LEXIS 7237 (N.Y. App. Div. 3d Dep't), app. dismissed, 73 N.Y.2d 810, 537 N.Y.S.2d 497, 534 N.E.2d 335, 1988 N.Y. LEXIS 3379 (N.Y. 1988).

Court did not err by summarily dismissing application to disinter decedent's body from Roman Catholic cemetery at which his mother would someday be buried, and to remove and reinter it in plot in unconsecrated cemetery, where record clearly established that decedent (who was Roman Catholic) wished to be buried with his mother in Roman Catholic cemetery and there was no convincing proof from petitioners creating material issue of fact. Dutcher v Paradise, 217 A.D.2d 774, 629 N.Y.S.2d 501, 1995 N.Y. App. Div. LEXIS 7786 (N.Y. App. Div. 3d Dep't 1995).

Only "circumstances of extreme exigency" supported by a "strong case" and no light reasons will suffice to justify disinterment upon equitable grounds (Not-For-Profit Corporation Law, § 1510, subd [e]) taking into account the feeling of the next of kin as survivors, the request and consent of all of decedent's next of kin and "all those promptings and emotions that men and women hold sacred in the disposition of their dead" particularly "that those united during lifetime shall not be divided after their death"; accordingly, in light of the resistance of decedent's daughters to the removal of her remains by petitioner association to the grave lot actually purchased because of their intense sentiment and religious beliefs and the fact that petitioner association made the mistake in burying decedent in the wrong grave, petitioner association has the duty and responsibility to resolve the situation without disturbing decedent's remains. Rabeni Mendel Hager Zablotower K. U. V. v Mt. Zion Cemetery, 98 Misc. 2d

77, 413 N.Y.S.2d 106, 1979 N.Y. Misc. LEXIS 2044 (N.Y. Sup. Ct. 1979).

Defendant charged with killing his 6-day-old son failed to show good and substantial reasons for exhuming body under CLS N-PCL § 1510 for purpose of conducting new autopsy to determine if body parts had been cut by sharp instrument or by animal in absence of substantiating proof challenging findings of original autopsy that cause of death was skull fracture, that body had been dismembered, and that body parts were fed to family dog. People v Radtke, 152 Misc. 2d 744, 578 N.Y.S.2d 827, 1991 N.Y. Misc. LEXIS 724 (N.Y. Sup. Ct. 1991).

Petitioner, who sought to establish standing to contest probate of will, was not entitled to order to exhume body of decedent for purpose of conducting DNA test to establish that he was petitioner's father since (1) CLS EPTL § 4-1.2(a)(2)(D) provides for establishment of paternity of decedent only where blood genetic test "had" been administered to father during his lifetime, (2) insofar as petitioner sought exhumation in order to gather evidence for trial, she failed to show actual need or real and legitimate basis to overcome objections of family members, and (3) petitioner's experts acknowledged that there might be insufficient DNA material to perform traditional and accepted tests. In re Estate of Janis, 157 Misc. 2d 999, 600 N.Y.S.2d 416, 1993 N.Y. Misc. LEXIS 246 (N.Y. Sur. Ct. 1993), aff'd, 210 A.D.2d 101, 620 N.Y.S.2d 342, 1994 N.Y. App. Div. LEXIS 12666 (N.Y. App. Div. 1st Dep't 1994).

9. Wrongful disinterment

Court properly dismissed claim that disinterment was procured by fraud based on grandson's allegation that cemetery required approval of 2 rabbis before it could consent to disinterment and that defendant misrepresented this approval to cemetery, in view of affidavit of cemetery's president stating that cemetery did not rely on any representations made by defendant, but itself consulted rabbi before consenting to disinterment; although court is generally required to accept allegations set forth in complaint as true when considering motion to dismiss for failure to state cause of action, when movant submits affidavits which discredit facts on which complaint relies, complaint may nevertheless be subject to such motion. Orlin v Torf, 126 A.D.2d 252, 513 N.Y.S.2d 870, 1987 N.Y. App. Div. LEXIS 41224 (N.Y. App. Div. 3d Dep't), app. denied, 70 N.Y.2d 605, 519 N.Y.S.2d 1029, 513 N.E.2d 1309, 1987 N.Y. LEXIS 18231 (N.Y. 1987).

Grandson was not proper party to allege that his grandparents' disinterment was procured by fraud, based on his claim that cemetery required approval of 2 rabbis before it could consent to disinterment and that defendant misrepresented this approval to cemetery, since any representation made by defendant concerning rabbinical approval was made to cemetery, not grandson, and grandson did not allege that he relied on such representation in any way. Orlin v Torf, 126 A.D.2d 252, 513 N.Y.S.2d 870, 1987 N.Y. App. Div. LEXIS 41224 (N.Y. App. Div. 3d Dep't), app. denied, 70 N.Y.2d 605, 519 N.Y.S.2d 1029, 513 N.E.2d 1309, 1987 N.Y. LEXIS 18231 (N.Y. 1987).

Disinterment will be permitted so long as required consents are obtained pursuant to CLS N-PCL § 1510, which requires consent of cemetery, lot owners, and surviving spouse, children and parents of deceased, and court approval is necessary only when required consents have not been obtained; accordingly, judicial scrutiny was not available to review propriety of disinterment based on grandson's contention that those parties consenting to his grandparents' disinterment did not respect grandparents' intentions concerning their final resting place. Orlin v Torf, 126 A.D.2d 252, 513 N.Y.S.2d 870, 1987 N.Y. App. Div. LEXIS 41224 (N.Y. App. Div. 3d Dep't), app. denied, 70 N.Y.2d 605, 519 N.Y.S.2d 1029, 513 N.E.2d 1309, 1987 N.Y. LEXIS 18231 (N.Y. 1987).

Common-law cause of action for wrongful disinterment does not exist in New York in view of existence of CLS N-PCL § 1510, which sets forth requirements for disinterment without court approval; moreover, Supreme Court is without jurisdiction to order disinterment in absence of specific statutory authority. Orlin v Torf, 126 A.D.2d 252, 513 N.Y.S.2d 870, 1987 N.Y. App. Div. LEXIS 41224 (N.Y. App. Div. 3d Dep't), app. denied, 70 N.Y.2d 605, 519 N.Y.S.2d 1029, 513 N.E.2d 1309, 1987 N.Y. LEXIS 18231 (N.Y. 1987).

Decedent's son failed to state a claim for a N.Y. Not-for-Profit Corp. Law § 1510(e) violation or negligent infliction of emotional distress as there was no allegation that the decedent's body was mishandled in any way by anyone during a disinterment or reinterment, to allow the decedent to be buried in a family plot. Estate of

LaMore v Sumner, 46 A.D.3d 1262, 848 N.Y.S.2d 754, 2007 N.Y. App. Div. LEXIS 13240 (N.Y. App. Div. 3d Dep't 2007).

Because a decedent's body, which always remained in the casket, was not mishandled or in any way desecrated during the process of removing it from one crypt to the other, because the removal did not arise from malice or wantonness, and because the parties' contract unambiguously provided that any negligence by the cemetery did not give rise to a claim for emotional damages, the cemetery was properly granted summary judgment in the family's action for breach of contract and violations of N.Y. Pub. Health Law §§ 4216, 4218, and N.Y. Not-for-Profit Corp. Law § 1510(e). Brandenburg v St. Michael's Cemetery, 92 A.D.3d 631, 938 N.Y.S.2d 159, 2012 N.Y. App. Div. LEXIS 968 (N.Y. App. Div. 2d Dep't 2012).

10. Exhumation

Where there was no indication that plaintiff mother, on behalf of her child, had made any efforts to secure the requisite consent for exhumation, there was no reasonable likelihood that such consent would have been granted if sought, nor any good and substantial reasons offered for disinterment, the court rejected the mother's argument that the deceased wage earner's body could have been exhumed to recover genetic material to prove paternity for purposes of receiving surviving child insurance benefits under the Social Security Act, 42 U.S.C.S. § 401 et seq. Howell v Barnhart, 265 F. Supp. 2d 268, 2003 U.S. Dist. LEXIS 8964 (S.D.N.Y. 2003).

§ 1510-a. Repair or removal of monuments

(a) Cemetery corporations may repair or remove any monuments or other markers not owned by the cemetery corporation that have fallen into disrepair or dilapidation so as to create a dangerous condition, provided that the cemetery corporation has given not less than sixty days notice by registered or certified mail to the last known owner at that person's last known address to repair or remove the monument or other marker and the said owner has failed to do so within the time provided in said notice.

(b) In the event that the last known owner cannot be found, the notice may be given by publishing the same once each week for three consecutive weeks in a newspaper published or circulated in the county in which the cemetery is located. Such notice shall be addressed to the last known owner and to all persons having or claiming any interest in or to the burial lot on which the monument or other marker is located. The notice shall date from the date of mailing such notice by registered or certified mail, or the date of the third publication in the newspaper.

(c) Any monument or other marker that is removed as provided for in this section shall be replaced with a flush bronze or granite marker suitably inscribed if replacement is appropriate for identification purposes.

(d) Nothing contained herein shall be construed as establishing any right of damages not otherwise provided by law, rule or contract in any person against the cemetery corporation for failure to repair or remedy any condition described or give notice thereof as provided for in this section.

History: Add, L 2000, ch 380, § 3, eff Sept 29, 2000.

§ 1510-b. Availability for interment on six-day basis

Every cemetery corporation shall be available for interments at least six days per week, excluding legal holidays, as set forth in the cemetery's regulations or in accordance with its practices. Any cemetery which maintains and designates a burial section for persons of a particular religious belief must remain available for grave openings and interments Sunday through Friday or other six-day period in accordance with the religious and/or ethnic traditions of the persons interred in said religious section. Nothing in this section shall require a cemetery to provide grave openings and/or interments if they are otherwise unable to do so as to direct consequence of severe weather conditions or other similar conditions.

Add, L 2006, ch 580, § 2, eff Feb 12, 2007.

§ 1511. Cemetery indebtedness

(a) Certificates of indebtedness. (1) If a cemetery corporation be indebted for lands purchased for cemetery purposes, or for services rendered or materials furnished in connection with the necessary and proper preservation or improvement of its cemetery or for moneys borrowed exclusively for payment of such services or materials, the directors, by the concurring vote of a majority of their whole number, with the consent of the creditor to whom such indebtedness is owing, may issue certificates under the corporate seal, signed by the president and secretary, for such amount, payable at the times and at the rate of interest agreed upon but not to exceed six per centum per annum; provided, however, that there be first obtained from the cemetery board an order approving the issuance of such certificates. In the case of certificates of indebtedness issued for moneys borrowed exclusively for payment for services rendered or materials furnished in connection with the necessary and proper preservation or improvement of its cemetery the consent of the creditor to whom such indebtedness is owing shall not be required. (2) Such approval shall be given by the cemetery board only if it determines that the amount of the certificates proposed to be issued does not exceed the fair and reasonable value of the services rendered or materials furnished or the purchase price of real property as fixed in accordance with subdivision (b) of this section. No certificate issued shall be valid or enforceable unless there has first been issued by the cemetery board an order of approval as herein provided. No certificate shall be for less than one hundred dollars. The certificate shall be transferable by delivery, unless therein otherwise provided. (3) The directors shall keep an account of the number and amount of such certificates, the persons to whom issued, the date of maturity, the rate of interest and the purpose for which the same were issued. Each cemetery corporation shall file with the cemetery board a verified statement setting forth all changes in such account during the previous calendar or fiscal year. (4) The directors shall set aside from the proceeds of sales of lots, plots and parts thereof such sums to pay such certificates at maturity as they deem necessary.

Until the certificates are paid the holders thereof shall be entitled at all meetings of the corporation, to one vote for each one hundred dollars of indebtedness remaining unpaid, except that those certificates of indebtedness issued for moneys borrowed exclusively for payment of services or materials shall have no voting power. The certificates shall not be a lien upon any lot, plot or part thereof belonging to a lot owner.

(b) Application of proceeds of sales of lots. (1) At least one-half of the proceeds of sales of lots or the use thereof remaining after the deductions for the portion thereof required to be deposited in the permanent maintenance fund and current maintenance fund together with the expenses of sale shall be applied by a cemetery corporation to the payment of the purchase price of the real property acquired by it. The remainder of such proceeds shall be applied by the corporation to preserving, improving and embellishing the cemetery grounds and the avenues and roads leading thereto, and to defraying its expenses and discharging its liabilities. After the payment of such purchase price, and the expense of surveying and laying out the cemetery, all the proceeds of such sales shall be applied to the improvement, preservation and embellishment of the cemetery and to such expenses and liabilities. (2) Where a corporation has agreed with a person from whom any such lands were purchased to pay therefor a specified share not exceeding one-half of the proceeds of sales of lots therein or the use thereof, such corporation may continue to make payments as so agreed, provided however that there be first deducted from said proceeds of sales the amount required to be deposited in the permanent maintenance fund and current maintenance fund as aforesaid together with the expenses of sale. The balance of such proceeds shall continue to be applied by the corporation to the preservation, improvement and embellishment of the cemetery, and the expenses and liabilities of the corporation. Where the corporation has heretofore agreed to pay a specified share of the proceeds as aforesaid in payment of the purchase price of land, the prices of lots or the use thereof in force when such purchase was made, shall not be changed, while the purchase price remains unpaid, without the written consent of a majority in interest of the persons from whom the lands were purchased or their legal representatives. (3) A corporation which has heretofore issued certificates of land shares which entitle the owner to a specified share in the proceeds of the sale of lots, may purchase such certificates with its surplus or reserve funds and hold such certificates for the benefit of its surplus or reserve funds, but such certificates may not thereafter be sold or reissued.

(c) Certificates of stock formerly issued. If a cemetery corporation, incorporated under a law repealed by the membership corporations law, prior to September first, eighteen hundred ninety-five, converted its outstanding indebtedness or certificates of indebtedness into certificates of stock, in pursuance of law, no interest shall accrue to the holders of such stock, but they shall receive annually or semi-annually a dividend thereon for their proportional part of the entire surplus or net receipts of the corporation over and above current expenses; or if the proportion of the net receipts or surplus which stockholders shall be entitled to receive shall have been fixed by agreement at the time of issuing such stock, such stockholders shall be entitled to receive dividends in accordance with such agreement. Such certificates of stock shall be transferable only on the books of the corporation on the surrender of the certificate, unless otherwise provided on the face thereof, and on every such surrender a new certificate of stock shall be issued to the person to whom the same has been transferred; and the holders of such stock shall be entitled, in person or by proxy, to one vote for every share thereof, at each meeting of the corporation. A register of the stock issued by the corporation shall be kept by its directors showing the date of issue, the number of shares, the par value thereof, the name of each person to whom issued, the number of the certificates therefor; and all transfers of such stock shall be noted and entered in such register, and the certificates surrendered shall be deemed canceled by the issue of a new certificate, and the surrendered certificate shall be destroyed. Any director may become the holder or transferee of such stock for his own individual use or benefit. No such stock shall be a lien on the lot of any individual lot owner within the cemetery limits; and no other or greater liability of the corporation issuing such stock shall be created or deemed to exist than may be necessary to enforce the faithful application of the surplus or net receipts of the corporation to and among the holders of the stock in the manner hereinbefore specified. A cemetery which has heretofore issued such certificates of stock is a membership corporation and not a stock corporation.

(d) Retirement of certificates of stock of certain cemetery corporations. If a cemetery association, incorporated under a law repealed by chapter five hundred fifty-nine of the laws of eighteen hundred ninety-five has changed certificates of indebtedness into certificates of stock, pursuant to chapter one hundred seven of the laws of eighteen hundred seventy-nine, and such stock remains unimpaired, such association may retire such stock and issue in exchange therefor certificates of indebtedness representing the par value of such stock, such certificates of indebtedness to bear interest at a rate not exceeding six per centum per annum from the date of the last preceding dividend payment; provided, however, the exchange of such stock for certificates of indebtedness shall be authorized at a duly called meeting of such association by the affirmative vote of at least two-thirds of the stock issued and outstanding and of at least two-thirds of all votes cast at such meeting in favor of such exchange. Any holder of such stock not voting in favor of the exchange of such stock for

certificates of indebtedness may at any time prior to the vote upon such exchange, or if notice of the meeting to vote upon such exchange was not mailed to him at least twenty days prior to the taking of such vote, then within twenty days after the mailing of such notice, object to such exchange and demand payment for his stock and thereupon such stockholder or the corporation shall have the right, subject to the same conditions and provisions contained in section six hundred twenty-three of the business corporation law, to have such stock appraised and paid for as provided in such section. Such objection and demand must be in writing and filed with the corporation. The provisions of this section relating to certificates of indebtedness and the rights of the holders thereof shall apply to certificates of indebtedness issued as provided in this subdivision. The stocks so retired shall not be reissued by such association and it shall have no right thereafter to issue any certificates of stock.

(e) Purchase, retirement and exchange of stock. (1) A cemetery corporation which has issued certificates of stock, pursuant to chapter one hundred seven of the laws of eighteen hundred seventy-nine, or chapter two hundred sixty-seven of the laws of eighteen hundred ninety-four, may purchase such certificates of stock with its surplus or reserve funds, and hold such certificates for the benefit of its surplus or reserve funds, but such certificates of stock so purchased may not thereafter be sold or reissued. (2) A cemetery corporation which has issued certificates of stock may also effect the retirement of such stock as follows: The board of directors of such corporation shall adopt by vote of a majority of the entire number of such directors a plan for such retirement which shall include the fixing of a price which the corporation will pay for all shares of stock then outstanding, which price shall, in the opinion of such directors, represent the fair value of such stock. The said plan shall be submitted to a duly called meeting of the members of such corporation and, if approved by the affirmative vote of at least two-thirds of all votes cast at such meeting, including the affirmative vote of the holders of record of at least two-thirds of all shares of stock issued and then outstanding exclusive of any shares of stock held by the corporation, shall become binding upon all stockholders, and they shall proceed to transfer and surrender to the corporation their certificates of stock and to receive payment therefor in accordance with the terms of such plan. Any holder of shares of such stock not voting in favor of such plan may at any time prior to the vote approving such plan, or if notice of the meeting to vote upon such plan was not mailed to him at least twenty days prior to the taking of such vote, then within twenty days after the mailing of such notice, but in any event within ten days after the taking of such vote, by written notice filed with such corporation, object to such plan and demand appraisal of his shares. Thereupon, such stockholder or the corporation shall have the right, subject to the same conditions and provisions contained in section six hundred twenty-three of the business corporation law, to have such stock appraised and paid for as provided in such section. (3) A cemetery corporation which has issued certificates of stock may also effect the exchange of such stock as follows: The board of directors of such corporation shall adopt by a vote of a majority of the entire number of such directors a plan for the exchange of all shares of stock then outstanding for a like number of participating certificates. Such participating certificates shall entitle the owners to a specified share not exceeding, collectively, one-half of the proceeds of sales of lots therein or the use thereof after first deducting from such proceeds of sale the amount required to be deposited in the permanent maintenance fund and current maintenance fund as provided in and pursuant to subdivision (a) of section fifteen hundred seven of this article, together with the expenses of sale. Such plan shall then be submitted to the cemetery board for its approval. In making its determination the cemetery board shall consider and may condition its approval on the purposes of this section. Thereafter, if the cemetery board approves such plan, or in the event the cemetery board conditioned its approval and the conditions imposed have been accepted by a vote of a majority of the entire board of directors of the corporation, such plan shall be submitted to a duly called meeting of the members of such corporation, and, if approved by the affirmative vote of at least two-thirds of all votes cast at such meeting, including the affirmative vote of the holders of record of at least ninety per centum of all shares of stock issued and then outstanding exclusive of any shares of stock held by the corporation, shall become binding upon all stockholders. The stockholders shall then proceed to transfer and surrender to the corporation their shares of stock and to receive in exchange therefor participating certificates in accordance with the terms of such plan. Any holder of shares of such stock not voting in favor of such plan may at any time prior to the vote approving such plan, or if notice of the meeting to vote upon such plan was not mailed to him at least twenty days prior to the taking of such vote, then within twenty days after the mailing of such notice, but in any event within ten days after the taking of such vote, by written notice filed with such corporation, object to such plan and demand appraisal of his shares. Thereupon, such stockholder or the corporation shall have the right, subject to the same conditions and provisions contained in section six hundred twenty-three of the business corporation law, to have such stock appraised and paid for as provided in such section. Each such participating certificate issued in exchange for a share of stock shall entitle the holder thereof to one vote for each certificate at all meetings of the corporation. The prices of lots or the use thereof at the time when such exchange is made shall not be changed, while such participating certificates remain outstanding, without the written consent of a majority in interest of the holders thereof except as now or hereafter authorized by law. The shares of stock so exchanged shall not be reissued by such corporation and it shall have no right thereafter to issue any shares of stock.

(f) Exchange of certificates for shares. The directors of a cemetery corporation, which has issued certificates for shares, from time to time by resolution, may fix the value of each of such shares and authorize the acceptance by the corporation of such certificates at the value so fixed in payment for land. All certificates so accepted shall be immediately cancelled and shall not be again issued.

History: Add, L 1977, ch 871, § 2, eff Aug 11, 1977.

CASE ANNOTATIONS

1. Generally
2-5. [Reserved for future use]
6. Under former § 1401
7. Under former Membership Corporations Law § 87

1. Generally

Complaint against defendants was properly dismissed due to plaintiff's lack of standing to bring derivative action on behalf of not-for-profit cemetery corporation; plaintiff was not capital certificate holder under CLS N-PCL § 623(a) based on his status as land share certificate holder under CLS N-PCL § 1511(b) in that definition of capital certificates (CLS N-PCL § 503) does not include land share certificates, and land share certificates are not equivalent of capital certificates as they represent debt rather than equity. Harris v Lyke (1995, 4th Dept) 217 A.D.2d 982, 629 N.Y.S.2d 911, app den 87 N.Y.2d 801, 637 N.Y.S.2d 688, 661 N.E.2d 160

Land share certificate holder did not have standing, on public policy grounds, to bring derivative action on behalf of not-for-profit cemetery corporation based on his claim that he had strong interest in policing corporate management, and thus complaint against defendants was properly dismissed; land share certificate holders such as plaintiff have other available remedies for management delinquency, plaintiff had already complained of corporate wrongdoing to district attorney's office and state's Division of Cemeteries which investigated matter and decided not to pursue it, and court had permitted plaintiff to commence new action under "contract theory." Harris v Lyke (1995, 4th Dept) 217 A.D.2d 982, 629 N.Y.S.2d 911, app den 87 N.Y.2d 801, 637 N.Y.S.2d 688, 661 N.E.2d 160

Plaintiff did not have standing, in equity, to bring derivative action on behalf of not-for-profit cemetery corporation based on corporation's alleged fiduciary obligation to him due to his status as land share certificate holder, and thus complaint against defendants was properly dismissed; action was derivative, not equitable, and record did not establish any relationship that would make corporation trustee or agent for plaintiff. Harris v Lyke (1995, 4th Dept) 217 A.D.2d 982, 629 N.Y.S.2d 911, app den 87 N.Y.2d 801, 637 N.Y.S.2d 688, 661 N.E.2d 160

Not-for-profit cemetery corporation did not owe fiduciary duty to plaintiff on basis that land share agreement between corporation and development corporation from which plaintiff obtained his land share certificates provided that proceeds from sale of cemetery lots would be placed into land purchase fund for distribution to land share certificate holders, and thus derivative action against defendants was properly dismissed where plaintiff's claim of standing was based on his fiduciary relationship with corporation; land purchase fund merely was account in which proceeds from sale of cemetery lots were placed until time when contractually-determined payments for sales were disbursed to land share certificate holders, and cemetery corporation merely acted as collector and disburser of land purchase funds. Harris v Lyke (1995, 4th Dept) 217 A.D.2d 982, 629 N.Y.S.2d 911, app den 87 N.Y.2d 801, 637 N.Y.S.2d 688, 661 N.E.2d 160

2-5. [Reserved for future use]

6. Under former § 1401

Where cemetery corporation bound itself to pay purchase price of $7,000,000 for land in certificates of indebtedness and also to satisfy vendors' purchase obligations of $800,000, thereby in effect agreeing to pay for land twice, to permit cemetery corporation to satisfy $800,000 obligation out of unrestricted portion of proceeds from sale of cemetery lots, while devoting entire other half of such proceeds to payment of certificate holders, would constitute approval of expenditure of greater than one-half of lot proceeds for payment of real estate costs; construction of certificates of indebtedness to require such disposition of proceeds was barred by former § 87 of Membership Corporations Law and by [former] § 1401, subd z(2) of Not-for-Profit Corporation Law. Reed v Knollwood Park Cemetery, Inc. (1977, DC NY) 441 F. Supp. 1144

Where proceeds of cemetery lot sales were divided between land purchase fund and unrestricted funds, clause in certificate of indebtedness issued by cemetery corporation, providing that whenever land purchase fund shall have accumulated an amount in excess of $10,000, after setting aside amount' necessary to purchase and pay for certain land, such excess shall be used to pay certificates of indebtedness, contemplated that moneys for purchase of land were to be set aside out of land purchase fund. Reed v Knollwood Park Cemetery, Inc. (1977, DC NY) 441 F. Supp. 1144

Although CLS Not-for-Profit Corporation Law § 1401, subd z(2) diminished fund from which holders of certificates of indebtedness issued by cemetery corporation were to be paid, and might ultimately prevent any recovery on certificates bearing high serial numbers, it did not deprive plaintiff certificate holder of due process. Reed v Knollwood Park Cemetery, Inc. (1977, DC NY) 441 F. Supp. 1144

CLS Not-for-Profit Corporation Law § 1401, subd z, requirement that unrestricted funds of cemetery corporation be applied to preservation, improvement and embellishment of cemetery grounds and that such funds not be diminished by more than approximately 12 1/2 percent in order to maintain effective functioning of cemetery, did not unconstitutionally impair contract rights of holders of certificates of indebtedness issued by cemetery corporation. Reed v Knollwood Park Cemetery, Inc. (1977, DC NY) 441 F. Supp. 1144

Although CLS Not-For-Profit Corporation Law § 1401, subd z(2) diminished fund from which holders of certificates of indebtedness issued by cemetery corporation were to be paid, resulting impairment of contract rights under certificates was not unconstitutional, since establishment of maintenance funds under statute was a reasonable and necessary means of correcting serious abuses in operation of cemeteries. Reed v Knollwood Park Cemetery, Inc. (1977, DC NY) 441 F. Supp. 1144

Where cemetery corporation bound itself to pay purchase price of $7 million for land in certificates of indebtedness, and also to satisfy vendors' purchase obligations of $800,000, and certificates required that $800,000 obligation be satisfied out of cemetery's land purchase fund rather than out of unrestricted funds, State Cemetery Board had ample authority, under CLS Not-For-Profit Corporations Law § 1401, subds zz(2) and z(2), to issue order suspending payments to holders of certificates until amounts paid on $800,000 obligation were recovered from land purchase fund. Reed v Knollwood Park Cemetery, Inc. (1977, DC NY) 441 F. Supp. 1144

7. Under former Membership Corporations Law § 87

Where cemetery corporation bound itself to pay purchase price of $7,000,000 for land in certificates of indebtedness and also to satisfy vendors' purchase obligations of $800,000, thereby in effect agreeing to pay for land twice, to permit cemetery corporation to satisfy $800,000 obligation out of unrestricted portion of proceeds from sale of cemetery lots, while devoting entire other half of such proceeds to payment of certificate holders, would constitute approval of expenditure of greater than one-half of lot proceeds for payment of real estate costs; construction of certificates of indebtedness to require such disposition of proceeds was barred by former § 87 of Membership Corporations Law and by [former] § 1401, subd z(2) of Not-for-Profit Corporation Law. Reed v Knollwood Park Cemetery, Inc. (1977, DC NY) 441 F. Supp. 1144

§ 1512.   Rights of lot owners

(a) Lots; indivisible and inalienable. All lots, plots or parts thereof, the use of which has been conveyed as a separate lot, shall be indivisible, except with the consent of the lot owner or lot owners and the corporation, or as in this section provided. After a burial therein, the same shall be inalienable, except as otherwise provided.

(b) Interest of deceased lot owner. Upon the death of an owner or co-owner of any lot, plot or part thereof, unless the same shall be held in joint tenancy, or tenancy by the entirety, the interest of the deceased lot owner shall pass to the devises of such lot owner, but, if such interest be not effectually devised, then to his or her descendants then surviving, and if there be none, then to the surviving spouse, and if there be none, then to those entitled to take the real and personal property of the deceased lot owner pursuant to article four of the estates, powers and trust law provided, however, that no interest in any lot, plot or part thereof shall pass by any residuary or other general clause in a will and such interest shall pass by will only if the lot, plot or part thereof sought to be devised is specifically referred to in such will. The surviving spouse of a deceased lot owner during his or her life and the owners from time to time of the deceased lot owner's lot, plot or part thereof, shall have in common the possession, care and control of such lot, plot or part thereof.

(c) Purchase for burial of decedent. Whenever a lot, plot or part thereof shall be purchased by the executor, administrator or representative of a decedent from estate funds for the burial of the decedent, the surviving spouse of the decedent shall have the right of interment therein, and the deed shall run to the names of the distributees, other than the surviving spouse, of the decedent, or to "The distributees, other than the surviving spouse, of -----, deceased", if there be such surviving spouse, otherwise to "The distributees of -----, deceased." If the deed shall run to "The distributees, other than the surviving spouse of -----, deceased," or to "The distributees of -----, deceased," the executor, administrator or representative shall, at the time of delivery of the deed to such lot, plot or part thereof, file with the corporation an affidavit setting forth the names and places of residence of all the decedent's distributees, and the corporation shall be entitled to rely upon the truth of the statements contained in such affidavit.

(d) Right of interment. A deceased person shall have the right of interment in any lot, plot or part thereof of which he or she was the owner or co-owner at the time of his or her death, or in any tomb erected thereon. The surviving spouse shall have the right of interment for his or her body in a lot or tomb in which the deceased spouse was an owner or co-owner at the time of his or her death, except where all the available burial spaces in a lot or tomb have been designated for the interment of persons other than the surviving spouse, pursuant to subdivision (f) of this section, and a right to have his or her body remain permanently interred or entombed therein, except, that such body may be removed therefrom as provided in subdivision (e) of section fifteen hundred ten of this article. Such right may be enforced and protected by his or her personal representatives. The remains of a spouse, parent or child of a person who is an owner or co-owner thereof may be interred in such lot or tomb without the consent of any person claiming any interest therein, subject, however, to the following rules and exceptions: (A) The place of interment in such lot shall be subject to the reasonable determination by a majority of the co-owners or in the absence of such determination by the cemetery corporation or its officer or agent having immediate charge of interments. (B) Any husband or wife living separate from the other and owning a lot in which the other, but for this section, would have no right of burial, at least thirty days before the death of the other, may file with the cemetery corporation a written objection to the interment of the other, and thereupon there shall be no right of interment under this subdivision. (C) A parent or child owning a lot in which the other would have no right of burial but for this section, at least thirty days before the death of the other, may file with the cemetery corporation a written objection to the interment of the other, and thereupon there shall be no right of interment under this subdivision. In such case, if the parent or child so excluded from burial in such lot shall die without having any place of interment, then the person filing such objection shall at once provide for the other a suitable place of burial in a convenient cemetery. The cost of such place of interment shall be chargeable to the decedent's estate, if any. (D) This section shall not permit a burial in any ground or place contrary to or in violation of any precept, rule, regulation or usage of any church or religious society, association or corporation restricting burial therein. This subdivision shall not limit any existing right of burial under other provisions of law, nor shall it limit or curtail the right of alienation, under the rules of the cemetery corporation wherein such lot is situated, by the owner of a lot before the death of the person for whose remains the right of burial is provided herein, and there shall be no right of burial in any lot sold by its owner, before the death of the person for whose remains the right of burial is provided herein.

(e) More than one person entitled to possession and control. (1) At any time when more than one person is entitled to the possession, care and control of such lot, any of the persons so entitled thereto may file with the corporation an affidavit setting forth the names and places of residence of all the persons entitled to the possession, care and control of such lot, and the corporation shall be entitled to rely upon the truth of the statements contained in such affidavit. The corporation shall be entitled to collect a reasonable fee for filing and recording such affidavit and other documents filed in its office. (2) At any time when more than one person is entitled to the possession, care or control of such lot, plot or part thereof, the persons so entitled thereto shall file with the corporation a designation of a person who shall represent the lot, plot or part thereof, and so long as they shall fail to designate, the corporation may make such designation. A distributee may release his or her interest in a lot, plot or part thereof, to the other distributees, and a joint owner may release or devise to the other joint owners, his or her right in the lot, plot or part thereof, on conditions specified in the release or will, the original or certified copy of which shall be filed in the office of the corporation. The surviving spouse not excluded from the right of burial under the provisions of subdivision (d) of this section, at any time may release his or her right in such lot, plot or part thereof, but no conveyance or devise by any other person shall deprive him or her of such right.

(f) Designation of persons who may be interred. At any time all the owners of a lot, and any surviving spouse having a right of interment therein, may execute, acknowledge and file with the corporation an instrument, and the sole owner of a lot may, in a testamentary instrument admitted to probate, make a provision, which may (A) designate the person or persons or class of persons who may thereafter be interred in said lot or in a tomb in such lot and the places of their interment; (B) direct that upon the interment of certain named persons, the lot or tomb in such lot shall be closed to further interments; (C) direct that the title of the lot shall upon the death of any one or more of the owners, descend in perpetuity to his, her or their distributees, unaffected by any devise. In any case in which an irrevocable designation of a person, persons or class of persons who may be interred in any lot or tomb has been made pursuant to this subdivision and in which the designated person or persons, or all of the known class of designated persons, have died and have not been buried in the places designated in said lot or tomb, or have by a written instrument duly signed and acknowledged and filed with the corporation, renounced the right of interment pursuant to such designation, then, and in any such event, the then owner or owners of said lot or tomb and any surviving spouse having the right of interment therein, may designate another person or persons or class of persons who may thereafter be interred in said lot or in a tomb in said lot, and the places of their interment, unless the original designation clearly indicated not only that it was irrevocable, but also that no further designations were to be made. Any designation provided for by this subdivision except a designation by testamentary instrument, shall be deemed revocable unless such instrument provides otherwise. In the event an owner or co-owner of a lot is under the age of eighteen years, any designation provided for by this subdivision, except a designation by testamentary instrument, may be executed and acknowledged by the parent or general or testamentary guardian for and on behalf of such owner or co-owner, provided, however, that no such designation may be made unless a place of interment shall remain available in said lot or in a tomb in such lot for the interment of each owner or co-owner of the lot under the age of eighteen years, and any designation so made may be revoked by the owner or co-owner upon reaching the age of eighteen years except with respect to burials effected before that time. A designation made by a parent or guardian on behalf of an infant owner or co-owner who is over the age of fourteen years must contain the written consent of such infant owner or co-owner.

(g) Lot owner voting. Each owner of full age of a lot in the cemetery of the corporation, as shown in the records of the cemetery at the time of the purchase of the lot from the corporation, or if there be two or more owners, then one of them designated in writing by a majority of them, may cast, in person or by proxy, one vote at meetings of the corporation in respect to each such lot so owned. At such meetings, each owner of a certificate of stock heretofore lawfully issued shall be entitled to one vote for each share of stock owned by him and each owner of a certificate of indebtedness shall be entitled to one vote for each one hundred dollars of such indebtedness remaining unpaid. No lot owner shall be entitled to vote unless all assessments against the lot of such owner shall have been paid. A quorum for the transaction of business, unless the certificate of incorporation or by-laws otherwise provide, shall be five members entitled to vote at the meeting. In the event a lot owner has executed a proxy which has been in effect for five or more years, the cemetery corporation shall not honor such proxy unless it is presented with proof that the lot owner has been sent a written notice at the address listed in the records of the corporation at least thirty days prior to the meeting at which the proxy is to be exercised advising the lot owner that the proxy is still effective. The notice shall identify the date, time and place of such meeting, and the name of the person holding the proxy and shall state that it may, unless the proxy provides otherwise, be terminated at any time. Such notice need not be mailed more frequently than every fifth year.

(h) Plots owned by religious corporations, unincorporated associations, or other entities that provide burial benefits for its members. With respect to any lot, plot or part thereof owned by a membership or religious corporation or unincorporated association or other entity that provides burial benefits for its members, and requires the cemetery to obtain a burial authorization from the membership, religious corporation, unincorporated association, or other entity, the following rules shall apply:

(1) If a cemetery receives a request to bury an individual who was a member of a membership, religious corporation, unincorporated association, or other entity that owns the lot, plot or part thereof in which the burial would be made, and despite reasonable efforts on the part of the family of the deceased, the funeral home, and/or the cemetery, no representative of the membership, religious corporation, unincorporated association, or other entity that owns the lot, plot or part thereof in which the burial would be made can be located to authorize the burial, the cemetery may, at its discretion, proceed with the interment provided that documentary evidence indicating a specific grave reservation in the lot, plot or part thereof, for the deceased individual is provided to the cemetery and further that the cemetery has recorded such reservation on its books and in its records;

(2) If the decedent is within the first degree of consanguinity to an individual already interred in the lot, plot or part thereof, or the spouse of the decedent is already interred in the lot, plot or part thereof, the cemetery may, at its discretion, proceed with the interment, provided some form of documentary evidence is provided to the cemetery as to the decedent's right of burial in the lot, plot or part thereof;

(3) The right of memorialization shall, under the circumstances described in this paragraph, pass to the person with the right of possession of the body at the time of burial; and

(4) Neither the cemetery nor the funeral director shall be liable for any claims, in law or equity, relating to the failure to obtain authorization from the membership, religious corporation, unincorporated association, or other entity for the use of the plot, lot, or portion thereof provided that the requirements of this paragraph have been met.

History: Add, L 1977, ch 871, § 2, eff Aug 11, 1977.

Sub (g), amd, L 1991, ch 426, § 2, eff Jan 1, 1992.

Sub (h), add, L 2004, ch 645, § 1, eff Nov 25, 2004.

CASE ANNOTATIONS

Although construction of burial contract prohibiting burial of persons other than Jewish persuasion, mandates unfortunate result for plaintiff's family, result is not contrary to public policy where there is countervailing public policy supporting enforcement of restrictions limiting burial in cemetery to persons of particular religious faith under CLS Not For Profit Corporation Law § 1512. Seligman v Mt. Ararat Cemetery, Inc. (1985, 2d Dept) 112 A.D.2d 928, 492 N.Y.S.2d 445

§ 1513.   Sale of burial rights

(a) Conveyance of lots. (1) Except as otherwise provided in this subdivision the right to use any lot, plot or part thereof may be sold or conveyed only by the cemetery corporation. (2) It shall be unlawful for any person, firm or corporation to purchase or for a cemetery corporation to sell a lot, plot or part thereof for the purpose of resale. This provision, however, shall not prohibit the sale to its members of lots, plots or parts thereof, or the right to use any lot, plot or part thereof, by a membership or religious corporation or unincorporated association or society which provides burial benefits for its members. (3) It shall be unlawful for a cemetery corporation to pay or offer to pay, or for any person, firm or corporation to receive, directly or indirectly, a commission, bonus, rebate or other things of value for, or in connection with, the sale of any lot, plot or part thereof, or the sale of space in a public mausoleum, or the furnishing by or through the cemetery corporation of any service, merchandise, wares, goods or articles. The provisions of this paragraph shall not apply to a person regularly employed and supervised by the cemetery corporation. (4) A violation of this subdivision shall constitute a misdemeanor and shall be punishable by a fine of not more than five hundred dollars or not more than six months imprisonment or both. Each violation shall constitute a separate offense.

(b) Prices for burial rights and instruments of conveyance. (1) The directors must fix and determine the prices of the burial lots, plots or parts thereof, and keep a plainly printed copy of the schedules of such prices conspicuously posted in each of the offices of the corporation, open at all reasonable times to inspection, and shall file a schedule of such prices in the office of the cemetery board. (2) Unless its certificate of incorporation or by-laws otherwise provide, and subject to its rules and regulations, the corporation shall sell and convey to any person the use of the lots, plots or parts thereof designated on the map filed in the office of the corporation, on payment of the prices so fixed and determined, but need not sell and convey more than one lot, plot or part thereof to any one person. Conveyances of lots, plots and parts thereof shall be signed by the president or vice-president and treasurer or assistant treasurer of the corporation. A written contract for the sale or use of a lot, plot or part thereof shall have attached thereto and made a part thereof a copy of the rules and regulations of the cemetery corporation or such parts of such rules and regulations as relate to the size and placement of monuments, restrictions on plot usage, warranties, obligations of the cemetery corporation and financial obligations and duties of the lot owner. If a lot, plot or part thereof is sold without a written contract, the corporation shall, before any part of the purchase price is paid by the purchaser, deliver to the purchaser a copy of the rules and regulations or such parts thereof as would be required to be attached to a written contract. Nothing in this subdivision shall prevent the subsequent amendment of such rules and regulations to increase the charges for services rendered by the corporation or in other particulars by or with the consent of the cemetery board under section fifteen hundred nine of this article. (3) A cemetery corporation that shall sell a lot, plot or part thereof, in excess of the price shown on the schedule filed in the office of the cemetery board, and any person acting for or on behalf of the cemetery corporation in connection with such sale, shall each forfeit to the people of the state of New York a sum equivalent to three times the excess amount so paid. Such penalty may be recovered in a civil action by the cemetery board. (4) The instrument of conveyance of any burial lot, plot or part thereof shall include the actual amount paid therefor and a description showing the dimensions of the property conveyed, and the plot number, section and block number as they appear on the cemetery map.

(c) Resale by lot owner. Before any burial shall have been made in any such lot, plot or part thereof, or, if all the bodies therein have been lawfully removed, the lot owner may sell or convey such lot, plot or part thereof upon notice to the cemetery. Such sale shall only occur in those instances where the owner of such lot, plot or part thereof shall have offered it to the cemetery corporation within one year prior to the sale, in writing by registered or certified mail, at the price paid therefor by said lot owner, together with simple interest at the rate of four per centum per annum, and the cemetery corporation shall have failed to accept such offer within thirty days after the making thereof. Subsequent to the receipt of notice of sale of such lot, plot or part thereof, the secretary of the cemetery corporation shall file and record in its books all instruments of transfer. An owner may convey or devise to the corporation his right and title in and to any such lot, plot or part thereof.

(d) Lots held in inalienable form. (1) No portion of the cemetery of a cemetery corporation which any person other than the corporation is entitled to use for burial purposes, or in which bodies have been buried and not removed, shall be sold, mortgaged or leased by the corporation. A cemetery corporation may convey any lot so that upon such conveyance, or after an interment therein, such lot shall be forever inalienable, and upon the death of the lot owner shall pass to such person or persons as may be designated in the conveyance or if no such designation be made, shall descend as provided in section fifteen hundred twelve of this article. Any one or more of the owners of such a lot may release or devise to any other owner of the lot his interest therein on such conditions as shall be specified in the release or will. (2) Any person who is the sole owner of the burial rights in a cemetery lot, plot or any part thereof, in which a burial has been made, may give his entire interest, or, if not prohibited by the rules and regulations of the cemetery corporation, any portion thereof to any person within the third degree of consanguinity to the owner, or, in the event that no such person exists, within the fourth degree of consanguinity to such owner. Such conveyance shall be made subject to the right of interment of the spouse of any deceased owner, which right said spouse may release at any time, but no conveyance or devise by any other person shall deprive the surviving spouse of such right. Burial rights shall not be conveyed pursuant to the provisions of this subparagraph more frequently than once in any ten-year period. (3) A cemetary corporation may take and hold any lot conveyed or devised to it by the lot owner so that thereafter it will be inalienable, and the interments therein shall be restricted to such person or class of persons as may be designated in the conveyance or devise. (4) The title of a lot owner shall not be affected by the dissolution of the corporation, by non-user of its corporate rights and franchises by any act of forfeiture on its part, by any alienation of its property or by incumbrance thereon made or suffered by it.

History: Add, L 1977, ch 871, § 2, eff Aug 11, 1977; amd, L 1978, ch 154, § 1, eff June 16, 1978; L 2015, ch 539, § 3, eff Dec 11, 2015.

CASE ANNOTATIONS

CLS N-PCL § 1513(c), regulating the sale of cemetery plots, is not unconstitutional, despite contention by owners of plots in Jewish cemeteries who wished to sell the lots at market value contended that the statutory requirement that the lots first be offered to the cemetery at original purchase price plus interest was unconstitutional, because the statute is a valid exercise of police power since the legislature could have rationally believed it necessary to prevent commercial exploitation of cemetery plots intended to be devoted to eleemosynary purposes. Warschauer Sick Support Soc v New York (1991, ED NY) 754 F. Supp. 305

Cemetery corporation may sell cemetery plots, for purpose of resale, to membership or religious corporation or unincorporated association or society which provides burial benefits for its members. 1998 Ops Atty Gen F 98-9

§ 1513-a. Reacquisition of a lot, plot or part thereof by a cemetery corporation

A cemetery corporation may, upon application and approval by the cemetery board, reacquire, resubdivide, and resell a lot, plot or part thereof under the following circumstances:

(a) (i) If the records of the corporation demonstrate that the lot, plot or part thereof was purchased more than seventy-five years prior to the application of the corporation; and (ii) if no burials have been made in the lot, plot or part thereof or all the bodies therein have been lawfully removed; and (iii) if neither the owner or owners of the lot, plot or part thereof nor any person having a credible claim to ownership who has visited, made payments in respect of or engaged in any other proprietary activities with respect to the lot, plot or part thereof can be identified after a reasonable search conducted by the cemetery corporation, it shall be conclusively presumed that the owner or owners of the lot, plot or part thereof have abandoned their burial rights. A reasonable search consists of a search of: (1) all cemetery records to determine the name of the owner or owners of the lot, plot or part thereof, their last known addresses and all information available to the cemetery relating to any person buried in the lot, plot or part thereof and the names and last known addresses of any persons making inquiry about or visiting the lot, plot or part thereof; (2) a search for the death certificates and the probated wills of the owner or owners of the lot, plot or part thereof; (3) the posting of notice by the cemetery at the entrance to the cemetery and in the cemetery office, if any, of its intention to declare the lot, plot or part thereof abandoned; (4) the mailing of such notice certified mail with return receipt requested to the owner or owners of the lot, plot or part thereof and each person identified during the reasonable search at their last known addresses; (5) publication of such notice once in each week for three successive weeks, in two newspapers of regular commercial circulation by subscription and/or newsstand sale, to be designated by the county clerk of the

county where the cemetery is located which in his or her judgement, given the ethnic, religious, geographic or other related demographic characteristics of the owner or owners of the lot, plot or part thereof and each person identified through the reasonable search and the predominant readership of such newspapers are best calculated to inform the owner or owners of the lot, plot or part thereof and each person identified through the reasonable search of any application pursuant to the provisions of this section; and (6) the preparation of an affidavit describing the steps taken by the cemetery corporation to ascertain the identity of and to contact the current owner or owners of the lot, plot or part thereof or next-of-kin thereof or any other persons identified in the course of the reasonable search who might have relevant information and the results of such steps. After the filing with the cemetery board of proof of compliance with the above requirements in form and substance reasonably satisfactory to such board and upon approval by the cemetery board, the lot, plot or part thereof may be resold by the cemetery to any party in compliance with the cemetery rules and regulations provided, however, that any monument subsequently placed on such lot, plot or part thereof shall conform to the general appearance of any existing monuments in said section of lots, plots or parts thereof, if any.

(b) If (i) the circumstances described in paragraph (a) of this section exist except that one or more burials have been made in a lot, and the last burial was made more than seventy-five years prior to the application, (ii) the lot, plot or part thereof can be subdivided to create new graves, (iii) the bodies have not been lawfully removed, and (iv) the cemetery submits an application to the cemetery board which complies with the requirements set forth in paragraph (a) of this section, it shall be conclusively presumed that the lot owner has abandoned the right to make further burials in the lot, the lot may be subdivided, and the resubdivided lot, plot or parts thereof which do not contain the remains of the deceased persons may be resold by the cemetery corporation as provided in this section. Nothing in this section shall permit a cemetery corporation to declare abandoned a lot, plot or part thereof, where such lot, plot or part thereof was purchased for multiple depth burials and where one or more burials has occurred or authorized a cemetery corporation to remove a monument or other embellishment to facilitate the resale of such lot, plot or part thereof, except as provided by section fifteen hundred ten of this article.

(c) If the owner or owners of a lot, plot or part thereof can be identified, the cemetery corporation, with the consent of the owner or owners of the lot, plot or part thereof, the lot, plot or part thereof may be resubdivided, and the resubdivided lot, plot or part thereof which does not contain the remains of deceased persons may be resold by the cemetery corporation, provided, however, if no burial has been made in the lot, plot or part thereof, in the twenty-five year period preceding such application, the owner of a lot, plot or part thereof has notified his or her parents, spouse, issue, brothers, sisters, grandparents, and grandchildren, if any, of the application to the cemetery board, and provided further, however, if a burial has been made in this lot, plot or part thereof during such twenty-five year period, the spouse and issue of such deceased person are also notified, and provided further, in either case the owner of the lot, plot or part thereof satisfies the cemetery board that none of the persons notified have agreed within forty-five days of notification to purchase the lot, plot or part thereof at the price provided under paragraph (c) of section fifteen hundred thirteen of this article.

(d) Upon the sale of a lot, plot or part thereof reacquired by the corporation under the provisions of paragraph (a), (b), or (c) of this section, thirty-five percent of the net proceeds shall be placed in the permanent maintenance fund and sixty-five percent shall be placed in the current maintenance fund. Provided, however, that if their property was reacquired under paragraph (i) of this section, thirty-five percent of the net proceeds shall be placed in the permanent maintenance fund, fifty percent shall be placed in the current maintenance fund and fifteen percent shall be placed in a perpetual care fund which the cemetery shall establish in the name of the defunct society for the exclusive purpose of maintenance of the grounds on which the graves were reacquired.

(e) If the owner of the lot, plot or part thereof is subsequently identified, the cemetery corporation shall: (i) return all unsold lots, plots or parts thereof if any, to the owner if so requested; and (ii) with respect to any lots, plots or parts thereof that have been sold pursuant to this section, at the option of the owner of the lot, plot or part thereof; either (1) provide the owner, at no cost to the owner, with a lot, plot or part thereof comparable to any lot, plot or part thereof that was sold by the cemetery corporation or (2) provide the owner with the proceeds from the sale of the lot, plot or part thereof reacquired under this section with interest thereon from the date of the sale at six percent per annum.

(f) The provisions of this section shall not apply to a lot, plot or part thereof whose record owner is a religious burial society.

(g) The provisions of this section shall not violate the burial requirements of sectarian sections of cemetery corporations.

(h) Monuments to be erected on a lot, plot or parts thereof, following the resale of a lot, plot or part thereof, shall conform to the rules and regulations or other requirements of the cemetery corporation and shall conform to the size, style and type of monuments in the section of the cemetery where such resale occurs.

(i) A cemetery corporation may, upon application and approval by the cemetery board, reacquire, resubdivide, and resell a lot, plot or part thereof formerly owned by a nonsectarian burial society under the following circumstances:

(1) If the cemetery corporation has received a request to make a burial on the grounds of a nonsectarian burial society and the provisions of paragraph (h) of section fifteen hundred twelve of this article had to be invoked to make the burial then the cemetery corporation may, at its discretion, commence the process of reacquiring the unused graves on the grounds of the nonsectarian burial society, except that any graves that have been reserved for individuals where such reservations have been recorded on the books and records of the cemetery corporation shall be exempt from reclamation; or

(2) If routine mailings or proxy mailings are sent to the officers of record of a nonsectarian burial society and such mailings are returned by the post office, the cemetery corporation may, at its discretion, make a second mailing by certified mail return receipt requested to each officer of record of the nonsectarian burial society as recorded on the cemetery's books and records and, if each of these mailings is returned by the post office, the cemetery corporation may, at its discretion, commence the process of reacquiring the unused graves on the grounds of the nonsectarian burial society, except that any graves that have been reserved for individuals where such reservations have been recorded on the books and records of the cemetery corporation shall be exempt from reacquisition.

(j) If a cemetery corporation has decided to commence the process of reacquiring graves owned by a nonsectarian burial society it shall:

(1) send by certified mail return receipt requested to each individual who has engaged in proprietary activities in connection with graves on the grounds of a nonsectarian burial society, seeking the names and addresses of any current officers of the nonsectarian burial society and informing those individuals of the cemetery corporation's intentions of reacquiring the unused graves on the grounds of the nonsectarian burial society;

(2) send by certified mail return receipt requested to each individual who has a grave reserved or deeded to them a letter seeking the names and addresses of any current officers of the nonsectarian burial society and informing such individuals of the cemetery corporation's intentions or reacquiring the unused graves on the grounds of the nonsectarian burial society;

(3) post a notice as provided in clause three of subparagraph (iii) of paragraph (a) of this section;

(4) publish a notice as provided in clause five of subparagraph (iii) of paragraph (a) of this section;

(5) prepare and submit an affidavit as provided in clause six of subparagraph (iii) of paragraph (a) of this section; and

(6) upon the sale of any grave or graves on the grounds of the nonsectarian burial society which have been reacquired by the cemetery corporation, the cemetery corporation shall distribute the net proceeds of the sale as provided in paragraph (d) of this section.

(k) The cemetery corporation shall delay the sale of ten percent of the graves it reacquires from the nonsectarian burial society for twenty years as a reserve in the event an individual or individuals are identified who have a valid claim for burial on the grounds of the nonsectarian burial society.

(l) At the time the graves that have been reacquired by a cemetery corporation from a nonsectarian burial society are sold, the contract of sale shall contain a clause in bold type which specifies that the monuments to be erected on such lot, plot or part thereof, shall conform to the size, style and type of monuments in the section of the cemetery where such graves are located.

History: Add, L 2003, ch 478, § 1, eff Nov 8, 2003; amd, L 2017, ch 442, § 2, eff Nov 29, 2017.

§ 1514.   Misdemeanor; general penalty

Wherever under the provisions of this article a person violating any part thereof is deemed to be guilty of a misdemeanor and no specific penalty is provided, the penalty for each separate violation shall be imprisonment for not more than six months or a fine of not more than five hundred dollars, or both.

History: Add, L 1977, ch 871, § 2, eff Aug 11, 1977.

§ 1515.   Actions affecting cemetery corporations

In any action or proceeding affecting or instituted by any cemetery corporation the cemetery board shall be served with notice thereof in the same manner as any necessary party and shall take such steps in the action or proceeding as it may deem necessary to protect the public interest.

History: Add, L 1977, ch 871, § 2, eff Aug 11, 1977.

§ 1516.   Sale of monuments

(a) No cemetery corporation shall engage in the sale of monuments, not including flush bronze markers, nor shall such monuments be displayed for sale on the property of a cemetery corporation.

(b) No cemetery corporation shall authorize or permit any employee or director thereof to advertise or make known his or her relationship to such corporation while engaged in the sale of monuments outside of his or her employment by the cemetery corporation.

(c) With regard to the sale of flush granite markers, the cemetery board shall adopt reasonable rules

and regulations to exempt cemetery corporations from the provisions of paragraph (a) of this section where a practice for the sale of such flush granite markers was established with the knowledge and approval of the cemetery board prior to the effective date of this section.

History: Add, L 1998, ch 560, § 5, eff Sept 4, 1998.

§ 1517.   Crematory operations

Cemetery corporations that operate a crematory shall have the following duties and obligations:

(a) Maintenance and privacy. (1) A crematory facility shall be maintained in a clean, orderly, and sanitary manner, with adequate ventilation and shall have a temporary storage area available to store the remains of deceased human beings pending disposition by cremation, the interior of which shall not be accessible to the general public.

(2) Entrances and windows of the crematory facility shall be maintained at all times to secure privacy, including (i) doors shall be tightly closed and rigid; (ii) windows shall be covered; and (iii) entrances shall be locked and secured when not actively attended by authorized crematory personnel.

(b) Cremation process. (1) The cremation process shall be conducted in privacy. No person except authorized persons shall be admitted into the retort area, holding facility, or the temporary storage facility while the remains of deceased human beings are being cremated. Authorized persons, on admittance, shall comply with all rules of the crematory corporation and not infringe upon the privacy of the remains of deceased human beings.

(2) The following are authorized persons: (i) licensed, registered funeral directors, registered residents, and enrolled students of mortuary science; (ii) officers and trustees of the cemetery corporation; (iii) authorized employees or their authorized agents of the cemetery corporation; (iv) public officers acting in the discharge of their duties; (v) authorized instructors of funeral directing schools; (vi) licensed physicians or nurses; and (vii) members of the immediate family of the deceased and their authorized agents and designated representatives.

(c) Identification of deceased human beings. (1) No crematory shall cremate the remains of any deceased human being without the accompanying cremation permit, required pursuant to section four thousand one hundred forty-five of the public health law which permit shall constitute presumptive evidence of the identity of the said remains. In addition, all crematories situated outside the city of New York, must comply with paragraph (b) of subdivision two of section four thousand one hundred forty-five of the public health law pertaining to the receipt for the deceased human being. From the time of such delivery to the crematory, until the time the crematory delivers the cremains as directed, the crematory shall be responsible for the remains of the deceased human being. Further, a cremation authorization form must accompany the permit required in section four thousand one hundred forty-five of the public health law. This form, provided or approved by the crematory, must be signed by the next of kin or authorizing agent attesting to the permission for the cremation of the deceased, and disclosing to the crematory that such body does not contain a battery, battery pack, power cell, radioactive implant, or radioactive device, if any, and that these materials were removed prior to the cremation process.

(2) Upon good cause being shown rebutting the presumption of the identity of such remains, the cremation shall not commence until reasonable confirmation of the identity of the deceased human being is made. This proof may be in the form of, but not limited to, a signed affidavit from a licensed physician, a member of the family of the deceased human being, the authorizing agent or a court order from the state supreme court within the county of the cemetery corporation. Such proof shall be provided by the authorizing agent.

(3) The crematory shall have a written plan to assure that the identification established by the cremation permit accompanies the remains of the deceased human being through the cremation process and until the identity of the deceased is accurately and legibly inscribed on the container in which the cremains are placed.

(d) Opening of container holding the remains of the deceased human being. (1) The casket, alternative container, or external wrappings holding the remains of the deceased human being shall not be opened after delivery to the crematory unless there exists good cause to confirm the identity of the deceased, or to assure that no material is enclosed which might cause injury to employees or damage to crematory property, or upon reasonable demand by members of the immediate family or the authorized agent.

(2) In such instances in which the casket, alternative container, or wrappings are opened after delivery to the crematory, such action shall only be conducted by the licensed funeral director or registered resident delivering the remains of the deceased human being and if necessary, with the assistance of crematory personnel and a record shall be made, which shall include the reason for such action, the signature of the person authorizing the opening thereof, and the names of the person opening the container and the witness thereto, which shall be retained in the permanent file of the crematory. The opening of the container shall be conducted in the presence of the witness and shall comply with all rules and regulations intended to protect the health and safety of crematory personnel.

(e) Ceremonial casket cremation disclosure. In those instances in which the remains of deceased human beings are to be delivered to a crematory in a casket that is not to be cremated with the deceased, timely disclosure thereof must be made by the person making the funeral arrangements to the crematory that prior to cremation the remains of the deceased human being shall be transferred to an alternative container. Such signed acknowledgement of the authorizing person, that the timely disclosure has been made, shall be retained by the crematory in its permanent records.

(f) Transferring remains. (1) The remains of a deceased human being shall not be removed from the casket, alternative container, or external wrappings in which it is delivered to the crematory unless explicit, signed authorization is provided by the person making funeral arrangements or by a public officer discharging his or her statutory duty, which signed authorization shall be retained by the crematory in its permanent records.

(2) When the remains of a deceased human being are to be transferred to an alternative container, the transfer shall be conducted in privacy with dignity and respect and by the licensed funeral director or registered resident who delivered those remains and if necessary, with the assistance of crematory personnel. The transferring operation shall comply with all rules and regulations intended to protect the health and safety of crematory personnel.

(g) Commingling human remains. The cremation of remains of more than one deceased human being in a retort at any one time is unlawful, except upon the explicit, signed authorization provided by the persons making funeral arrangements and the signed approval of the crematory, which shall be retained by the crematory in its permanent records.

(h) Processing of cremains. (1) Upon the completion of the cremation of the remains of a deceased human being, the interior of the retort shall be thoroughly swept so as to render the retort reasonably free of all matter. The contents thereof shall be placed into an individual container and not commingled with other cremains. The cremation permit shall be attached to the individual container preparatory to final processing.

(2) A magnet and sieve, or other appropriate method of separation, may be used to divide the cremains from unrecognizable incidental or foreign material.

(3) The incidental and foreign material of the cremation process shall be disposed of in a safe manner in compliance with all sanitary rules and regulations as byproducts.

(4) The cremains shall be pulverized until no single fragment is recognizable as skeletal tissue.

(5) The pulverized cremains shall be transferred to a sealable container or containers whose inside dimension shall be of suitable size to contain the entire cremains of the person who was cremated.

(6) The prescribed sealable container or containers shall be accurately and legibly labeled with the identification of the human being whose cremains are

contained therein, in a manner acceptable to the division of cemeteries.

(i) Disposition of cremains. The authorizing agent shall be responsible for the final disposition of the cremains. Cremains must be disposed of by placing them in a grave, crypt, or niche, by scattering them in a designated scattering garden or area, or in any manner whatever on the private property of a consenting owner or by delivery to the authorizing agent or a person specifically designated by the authorizing agent. Upon completion of the cremation process, if the cemetery corporation has not been instructed to arrange for the interment, entombment, inurnment or scattering of the cremains, the cemetery corporation shall deliver the cremains to the individual specified on the cremation authorization form or the funeral firm of record. The delivery may be made in person or by registered mail. Upon receipt of the cremains, the individual receiving them may transport them in any manner in the state without a permit, and may dispose of them in accordance with this section. After delivery, the cemetery corporation shall be discharged from any legal obligation or liability concerning the cremains. If, after a period of one hundred twenty days from the date of the cremation, the authorizing agent has not instructed the cemetery corporation to arrange for the final disposition of the cremains or claimed the cremains, the cemetery corporation may dispose of the cremains in any manner permitted by this section. The cemetery corporation, however, shall keep a permanent record identifying the site of final disposition. The authorizing agent shall be responsible for reimbursing the cemetery corporation for all reasonable expenses incurred in disposing of the cremains. Upon disposing of the cremains, the cemetery corporation shall be discharged from any legal obligation or liability concerning the cremains. Except with the express written permission of the authorizing agent, no person shall:

(1) dispose of cremains in a manner or in a location so that the cremains are commingled with those of another person. This prohibition shall not apply to the scattering of cremains at sea, by air, or in an area located in a cemetery and used exclusively for those purposes; and

(2) place cremains of more than one person in the same temporary container or urn.

(j) Crematory operation certification. Any employee of a crematory whose function is to conduct the daily operations of the cremation process shall be certified by an organization approved by the division of cemeteries. Proof of such certification must be posted in the crematory and available for inspection at any time. Any new employees of a crematory required to be certified under this section shall be certified within one year of their employment. Any employees of a crematory required to be certified under this section and retained prior to the effective date of this paragraph shall be certified within one year of such effective date. Renewal of such certifica-

tion shall be completed every five years from the date of certification.

History: Add, L 2006, ch 579, § 6, eff Oct 15, 2006.

ARTICLE 16
LAND BANKS

§ 1600. Short title.

This article shall be known and may be cited as the "land bank act".

History: Add, L 2011, ch. 257.

§ 1601. Legislative intent.

The legislature finds and declares that New York's communities are important to the social and economic vitality of the state. Whether urban, suburban, or rural, many communities are struggling to cope with vacant, abandoned, and tax-delinquent properties.

There exists a crisis in many cities and their metro areas caused by disinvestment in real property and resulting in a significant amount of vacant and abandoned property. For example, Cornell Cooperative Extension Association of Erie county estimates that the city of Buffalo has thirteen thousand vacant parcels, four thousand vacant structures and an estimated twenty-two thousand two hundred ninety vacant residential units. This condition of vacant and abandoned property represents lost revenue to local governments and large costs ranging from demolition, effects of safety hazards and spreading deterioration of neighborhoods including resulting mortgage foreclosures. The need exists to strengthen and revitalize the economy of the state and its local units of government by solving the problems of vacant and abandoned property in a coordinated manner and to foster the development of such property and promote economic growth. Such problems may include multiple taxing jurisdictions lacking common policies, ineffective property inspection, code enforcement and property rehabilitation support, lengthy and/or inadequate foreclosure proceedings and lack of coordination and resources to support economic revitalization.

There is an overriding public need to confront the problems caused by vacant, abandoned and tax-delinquent properties through the creation of new tools to be available to communities throughout New York enabling them to turn vacant spaces into vibrant places.

Land banks are one of the tools that can be utilized by communities to facilitate the return of vacant, abandoned, and tax-delinquent properties to productive use. The primary focus of land bank operations is the acquisition of real property that is tax delinquent, tax foreclosed, vacant, abandoned, and the use of tools authorized in this article to eliminate the harms and liabilities caused by such properties.

History: Add, L 2011, ch. 257.

§ 1602. Definitions.

The following words and phrases when used in this article shall have the meanings given to them in this section unless the context clearly indicates otherwise:

(a) "board of directors" or "board" shall mean the board of directors of a land bank;

(b) "land bank" shall mean a land bank established as a charitable not-for-profit corporation under this chapter and in accordance with the provisions of this article and pursuant to this article;

(c) "foreclosing governmental unit" shall mean "tax district" as defined in subdivision six of section eleven hundred two of the real property tax law;

(d) "municipality" shall mean a city, village, town or county other than a county located wholly within a city;

(e) "school district" shall mean a school district as defined under the education law; and

(f) "real property" shall mean lands, lands under water, structures and any and all easements, air rights, franchises and incorporeal hereditaments and every estate and right therein, legal and equitable, including terms for years and liens by way of judgment, mortgage or otherwise, and any and all fixtures and improvements located thereon.

History: Add, L 2011, ch. 257; amd, L 2013, ch 549, § 124, eff July 1, 2014.

§ 1603. Creation and existence.

(a) Any foreclosing governmental unit may create a land bank by the adoption of a local law, ordinance, or resolution as appropriate to such foreclosing governmental unit which action specifies the following:

(1) the name of the land bank;

(2) the number of members of the board of directors, which shall consist of an odd number of members, and shall be not less than five members nor more than fifteen members;

(3) the initial individuals to serve as members of the board of directors, and the length of terms for which they are to serve;

(4) the qualifications, manner of selection or appointment, and terms of office of members of the board; and

(5) the articles of incorporation for the land bank, which shall be filed with the secretary of state in accordance with the procedures set forth in this chapter.

(b) Two or more foreclosing governmental units may enter into an intergovernmental cooperation agreement which creates a single land bank to act on behalf of such foreclosing governmental units, which agreement shall be authorized by and be in accordance with the provisions of paragraph (a) of this section. Such intergovernmental agreement shall include provisions for dissolution of such land bank.

(c) Any foreclosing governmental units and any municipality may enter into an intergovernmental cooperation agreement which creates a single land bank to act on behalf of such foreclosing governmental unit or units and municipality, which agreement shall be authorized by and be in accordance with the provisions of paragraph (a) of this section. Such intergovernmental agreement shall include provisions for dissolution of such land bank.

(d) Except when a land bank is created pursuant to paragraph (b) or (c) of this section, in the event a county creates a land bank, such land bank shall have the power to acquire real property only in those portions of such county located outside of the geographical boundaries of any other land bank created by any other foreclosing governmental unit located partially or entirely within such county.

(e) A school district may participate in a land bank pursuant to an intergovernmental cooperation agreement with the foreclosing governmental unit or units that create the land bank, which agreement shall specify the membership, if any, of such school district on the board of directors of the land bank, or the actions of the land bank which are subject to approval by the school district.

(f) Each land bank created pursuant to this act shall be a charitable corporation, and shall have permanent and perpetual duration until terminated and dissolved in accordance with the provisions of section sixteen hundred thirteen of this article.

(g) Nothing in this article shall be construed to authorize the existence of more than thirty-five land banks located in the state at one time, provided further that each foreclosing governmental unit or units proposing to create a land bank shall submit such local law, ordinance or resolution as required by paragraph (a) of this section, to the urban development corporation, for its review and approval. The creation of a land bank shall be conditioned upon approval of the urban development corporation.

Not-For-Profit
Corporation Law

(h) The office of the state comptroller shall have the authority to audit any land bank pursuant to this article.

History: Add, L 2011, ch 257, § 1, eff July 29, 2011; amd, L 2013, ch 372, § 1, eff Sept 27, 2013; L 2013, ch 549, § 125, eff July 1, 2014; L 2014, ch 106, § 1, eff July 22, 2014; L 2017, ch 55, § 1 (Part DD), eff April 20, 2017; L 2018, ch 508, § 1, eff Dec 28, 2018.

Blackline Showing Effect of 2018 Amendments. — (a) Any foreclosing governmental unit may create a land bank by the adoption of a local law, ordinance, or resolution as appropriate to such foreclosing governmental unit which action specifies the following:

(1) the name of the land bank;

(2) the number of members of the board of directors, which shall consist of an odd number of members, and shall be not less than five members nor more than fifteen members;

(3) the initial individuals to serve as members of the board of directors, and the length of terms for which they are to serve;

(4) the qualifications, manner of selection or appointment, and terms of office of members of the board; and

(5) the articles of incorporation for the land bank, which shall be filed with the secretary of state in accordance with the procedures set forth in this chapter.

(b) Two or more foreclosing governmental units may enter into an intergovernmental cooperation agreement which creates a single land bank to act on behalf of such foreclosing governmental units, which agreement shall be authorized by and be in accordance with the provisions of paragraph (a) of this section. Such intergovernmental agreement shall include provisions for dissolution of such land bank.

(c) Any foreclosing governmental units and any municipality may enter into an intergovernmental cooperation agreement which creates a single land bank to act on behalf of such foreclosing governmental unit or units and municipality, which agreement shall be authorized by and be in accordance with the provisions of paragraph (a) of this section. Such intergovernmental agreement shall include provisions for dissolution of such land bank.

(d) Except when a land bank is created pursuant to paragraph (b) or (c) of this section, in the event a county creates a land bank, such land bank shall have the power to acquire real property only in those portions of such county located outside of the geographical boundaries of any other land bank created by any other foreclosing governmental unit located partially or entirely within such county.

(e) A school district may participate in a land bank pursuant to an intergovernmental cooperation agreement with the foreclosing governmental unit or units that create the land bank, which agreement shall specify the membership, if any, of such school district on the board of directors of the land bank, or the actions of the land bank which are subject to approval by the school district.

(f) Each land bank created pursuant to this act shall be a charitable corporation, and shall have permanent and perpetual duration until terminated and dissolved in accordance with the provisions of section sixteen hundred thirteen of this article.

(g) Nothing in this article shall be construed to authorize the existence of more than ~~twenty-five~~ thirty-five land banks located in the state at one time, provided further that each foreclosing governmental unit or units proposing to create a land bank shall submit such local law, ordinance or resolution as required by paragraph (a) of this section, to the urban development corporation, for its review and approval. The creation of a land bank shall be conditioned upon approval of the urban development corporation.

(h) The office of the state comptroller shall have the authority to audit any land bank pursuant to this article.

§ 1604. Applicability of New York law.

This article shall apply only to land banks created pursuant to this article.

History: Add, L 2011, ch. 257.

§ 1605. Board of directors.

(a) (1) The initial size of the board shall be determined in accordance with section sixteen hundred three of this article. Unless restricted by the actions or agreements specified in section sixteen hundred three of this article, the provisions of this section shall apply.

(2) The size of the board may be adjusted in accordance with by-laws of the land bank.

(b) In the event that a land bank is created pursuant to an intergovernmental agreement in accordance with section sixteen hundred three of this article, such intergovernmental cooperation agreement shall specify matters identified in paragraph (a) of section sixteen hundred three of this article; provided, however, that each foreclosing governmental unit shall have at least one appointment to the board.

(c) Any public officer shall be eligible to serve as a board member and the acceptance of the appointment shall neither terminate nor impair such public office. For purposes of this section, "public officer" shall mean a person who is elected to a municipal office. Any municipal employee or appointed officer shall be eligible to serve as a board member.

(d) The members of the board of directors shall select annually from among themselves a chairman, a vice-chairman, a treasurer, and such other officers as the board may determine, and shall establish their duties as may be regulated by rules adopted by the board.

(e) The board shall establish rules and requirements relative to the attendance and participation of members in its meetings, regular or special. Such rules and regulations may prescribe a procedure whereby, should any member fail to comply with such rules and regulations, such member may be disqualified and removed automatically from office by no less than a majority vote of the remaining members of the board, and that member's position shall be vacant as of the first day of the next calendar month. Any person removed under the provisions of this paragraph shall be ineligible for reappointment to the board, unless such reappointment is confirmed unanimously by the board.

(f) A vacancy on the board shall be filled in the same manner as the original appointment.

(g) Board members shall serve without compensation, shall have the power to organize and reorganize the executive, administrative, clerical, and other departments of the land bank and to fix the duties, powers, and compensation of all employees, agents, and consultants of the land bank. The board may reimburse any member for expenses actually incurred in the performance of duties on behalf of the land bank.

(h) The board shall meet in regular session according to a schedule adopted by the board, and also shall meet in special session as convened by the chairman or upon written notice signed by a majority of the members.

(i) A majority of the members of the board, not including vacancies, shall constitute a quorum for the conduct of business. All actions of the board shall be approved by the affirmative vote of a majority of the members of that board present and voting; provided, however, no action of the board shall be authorized on the following matters unless approved by a majority of the total board membership:

(1) adoption of by-laws and other rules and regulations for conduct of the land bank's business;

(2) hiring or firing of any employee or contractor of the land bank. This function may, by majority vote of the total board membership, be delegated to a specified officer or committee of the land bank, under such terms and conditions, and to the extent, that the board may specify;

(3) the incurring of debt;

(4) adoption or amendment of the annual budget; and

(5) sale, lease, encumbrance, or alienation of real property, improvements, or personal property.

(j) Members of a board shall not be liable personally on the bonds or other obligations of the land bank, and the rights of creditors shall be solely against such land bank.

(k) Vote by proxy shall not be permitted. Any member may request a recorded vote on any resolution or action of the land bank.

(l) Each director, officer and employee shall be a state officer or employee for the purposes of sections seventy-three and seventy-four of the public officers law.

History: Add, L 2011, ch. 257.

§ 1606. Staff.

A land bank may employ a secretary, an executive director, its own counsel and legal staff, and such technical experts, and such other agents and employees, permanent or temporary, as it may require, and may determine the qualifications and fix the compensation and benefits of such persons. A land bank may also enter into contracts and agreements with municipalities for staffing services to be provided to the land bank by municipalities or agencies or departments thereof, or for a land bank to provide such staffing services to municipalities or agencies or departments thereof.

History: Add, L 2011, ch. 257.

§ 1607. Powers.

(a) A land bank shall constitute a charitable not-for-profit corporation under New York law, which powers shall include all powers necessary to carry out and effectuate the purposes and provisions of this article, including the following powers in addition to those herein otherwise granted:

(1) adopt, amend, and repeal bylaws for the regulation of its affairs and the conduct of its business;

(2) sue and be sued in its own name and plead and be impleaded in all civil actions, including, but not limited to, actions to clear title to property of the land bank;

(3) to adopt a seal and to alter the same at pleasure;

(4) to make contracts, give guarantees and incur liabilities, borrow money at such rates of interest as the land bank may determine;

(5) to issue negotiable revenue bonds and notes according to the provisions of this article;

(6) to procure insurance or guarantees from the state of New York or federal government of the payments of any debts or parts thereof incurred by the land bank, and to pay premiums in connection therewith;

(7) to enter into contracts and other instruments necessary to the performance of its duties and the exercise of its powers, including, but not limited to, intergovernmental agreements under section one hundred nineteen-o of the general municipal law for the joint exercise of powers under this article;

(8) to enter into contracts and other instruments necessary to the performance of functions by the land bank on behalf of municipalities or agencies or departments of municipalities, or the performance by municipalities or agencies or departments of municipalities of functions on behalf of the land bank;

(9) to make and execute contracts and other instruments necessary to the exercise of the powers of the land bank; and any contract or instrument when signed by the chairman or vice-chairman of the land bank, or by an authorized use of their facsimile signatures, and by the secretary or assistant secretary, or, treasurer or assistant treasurer of the land bank, or by an authorized use of their facsimile signatures, shall be held to have been properly executed for and on its behalf;

(10) to procure insurance against losses in connection with the real property, assets, or activities of the land bank;

(11) to invest money of the land bank, at the discretion of the board of directors, in instruments, obligations, securities, or property determined proper by the board of directors, and name and use depositories for its money;

(12) to enter into contracts for the management of, the collection of rent from, or the sale of real property of the land bank;

(13) to design, develop, construct, demolish, reconstruct, rehabilitate, renovate, relocate, and otherwise improve real property or rights or interests in real property;

Not-For-Profit Corporation Law

(14) to fix, charge, and collect rents, fees and charges for the use of real property of the land bank and for services provided by the land bank;

(15) to grant or acquire a license, easement, lease (as lessor and as lessee), or option with respect to real property of the land bank;

(16) to enter into partnership, joint ventures, and other collaborative relationships with municipalities and other public and private entities for the ownership, management, development, and disposition of real property;

(17) to inventory vacant, abandoned and tax foreclosed properties;

(18) to develop a redevelopment plan to be approved by the foreclosing governmental unit or units;

(19) to be subject to municipal building codes and zoning laws;

(20) to enter in agreements with a foreclosing governmental unit for the distribution of revenues to the foreclosing governmental unit and school district;

(21) to organize a subsidiary for a project or projects which the land bank has the power to pursue under this article when the primary reason for which the subsidiary shall be organized shall be to limit the potential liability impact of the subsidiary's project or projects on the land bank or because state or federal law requires that the purpose of a subsidiary be undertaken through a specific corporate or business structure. All real property of a subsidiary organized under this article shall be maintained on the inventory lists required in this article of the land bank of which it is a subsidiary and the subsidiary shall make all reports and other disclosures as are required of land banks under this article and as local public authorities, unless the subsidiary's operations and finances are consolidated with those of the land bank of which it is a subsidiary. Subsidiaries organized under this article shall be established in the form of a New York charitable not-for-profit corporation or a New York single member limited liability company. Subsidiaries shall not have the authority to issue bonds, notes or other debts, provided, however, that such subsidiaries may issue notes or other debt to the land bank of which it is a subsidiary. The organizational documents filed to create a subsidiary under this article shall state that the land bank is organizing the subsidiary for the purposes set forth in this article and the name of the subsidiary shall be reasonably related to the name of the land bank of which it is a subsidiary. The real property of a subsidiary organized under this article and its income and operations are exempt from all taxation by the state of New York and by any of its political subdivisions; and

(22) to do all other things necessary to achieve the objectives and purposes of the land bank or other laws that relate to the purposes and responsibility of the land bank.

(b) A land bank shall neither possess nor exercise the power of eminent domain.

History: Add, L 2011, ch 257, § 1, eff July 29, 2011; amd, L 2013, ch 549, § 126, eff July 1, 2014; L 2016, ch 338, §1, eff Sept 29, 2016.

§ 1608.   Acquisition of property.

(a) The real property of a land bank and its income and operations are exempt from all taxation by the state of New York and by any of its political subdivisions. The real property of a land bank shall be exempt from: (i) all special ad valorem levies and special assessments as defined in section one hundred two of the real property tax law; (ii) sewer rent imposed under article fourteen-F of the general municipal law; and (iii) any and all user charges imposed by any municipal corporation, special district or other political subdivisions of the state, provided, however, that real property of a land bank for which such land bank receives rent, fees, or other charges for the use of such real property shall not be exempt from subparagraphs (ii) and (iii) of this paragraph. Such exempt status shall be effective upon the date of transfer of title to a land bank, notwithstanding the applicable taxable status date. Notwithstanding any other general, special or local law relating to fees of clerks, no clerk shall charge or collect a fee for filing, recording or indexing any paper, document, map or proceeding filed, recorded or indexed for a land bank, or an officer thereof acting in an official capacity, nor for furnishing a transcript, certification or copy of any paper, document, map or proceeding to be used for land bank purposes.

(b) The land bank may acquire real property or interests in real property by gift, devise, transfer, exchange, foreclosure, purchase, or otherwise on terms and conditions and in a manner the land bank considers proper.

(c) The land bank may acquire real property by purchase contracts, lease purchase agreements, installment sales contracts, land contracts, and may accept transfers from municipalities upon such terms and conditions as agreed to by the land bank and the municipality. Notwithstanding any other law to the contrary, any municipality may transfer to the land bank real property and interests in real property of the municipality on such terms and conditions and according to such procedures as determined by the municipality.

(d) The land bank shall maintain all of its real property in accordance with the laws and ordinances of the jurisdiction in which the real property is located.

(e) The land bank shall not own or hold real property located outside the jurisdictional boundaries of the foreclosing governmental unit or units which created the land bank; provided, however, that a land bank may be granted authority pursuant to an intergovernmental cooperation agreement with another municipality to manage and maintain real property located within the jurisdiction of such other municipality.

(f) Notwithstanding any other provision of law to the contrary, any municipality may convey to a land bank real property and interests in real property on such terms and conditions, form and substance of consideration, and procedures, all as determined by the transferring municipality in its discretion.

(g) The acquisition of real property by a land bank pursuant to the provisions of this article, from entities other than political subdivisions, shall be limited to real property that is tax delinquent, tax foreclosed, vacant or abandoned; provided, however, that a land bank shall have authority to enter into agreements to purchase other real property consistent with an approved redevelopment plan.

(h) The land bank shall maintain and make available for public review and inspection a complete inventory of all property received by the land bank. Such inventory shall include: the location of the parcel; the purchase price, if any, for each parcel received; the current value assigned to the property for purposes of real property taxation; the amount, if any, owed to the locality for real property taxation; the identity of the transferor; and any conditions or restrictions applicable to the property.

(i) All parcels received by the land bank shall be listed on the received inventory established pursuant to paragraph (h) of this section within one week of acquisition and shall remain in such inventory for one week prior to disposition.

(j) Failure to comply with the requirements in paragraphs (h) and (i) of this section with regard to any particular parcel shall cause such acquisition by the land bank to be null and void.

History: Add, L 2011, ch 257, § 1, eff July 29, 2011; amd, L 2015, ch 407, § 1, eff Oct 26, 2015; L 2016, ch 441, § 1, eff Nov 14, 2016; L 2017, ch 349, § 1, eff Oct 23, 2017; L 2018, ch 483, § 1, eff Dec 28, 2018.

Blackline Showing Effect of 2018 Amendments. — (a) The real property of a land bank and its income and operations are exempt from all taxation by the state of New York and by any of its political subdivisions. The real property of a land bank shall be exempt from: (i) all special ad valorem levies and special assessments as defined in section one hundred two of the real property tax law; (ii) sewer rent imposed under article fourteen-F of the general municipal law; and (iii) any and all user charges imposed by any municipal corporation, special district or other political subdivisions of the state, provided, however, that real property of a land bank for which such land bank receives rent, fees, or other charges for the use of such real property shall not be exempt from subparagraphs (ii) and (iii) of this paragraph. Such exempt status shall be effective upon the date of transfer of title to a land bank, notwithstanding the applicable taxable status date. Notwithstanding any other general, special or local law relating to fees of clerks, no clerk shall charge or collect a fee for filing, recording or indexing any paper, document, map or proceeding filed, recorded or indexed for a land bank, or an officer thereof acting in an official capacity, nor for furnishing a transcript, certification or copy of any paper, document, map or proceeding to be used for land bank purposes.

(b) The land bank may acquire real property or interests in real property by gift, devise, transfer, exchange, foreclosure, purchase, or otherwise on terms and conditions and in a manner the land bank considers proper.

(c) The land bank may acquire real property by purchase contracts, lease purchase agreements, installment sales contracts, land contracts, and may accept transfers from municipalities upon such terms and conditions as agreed to by the land bank and the municipality. Notwithstanding any other law to the contrary, any municipality may transfer to the land bank real property and interests in real property of the municipality on such terms and conditions and according to such procedures as determined by the municipality.

(d) The land bank shall maintain all of its real property in accordance with the laws and ordinances of the jurisdiction in which the real property is located.

(e) The land bank shall not own or hold real property located outside the jurisdictional boundaries of the foreclosing governmental unit or units which created the land bank; provided, however, that a land bank may be granted authority pursuant to an intergovernmental cooperation agreement with another municipality to manage and maintain real property located within the jurisdiction of such other municipality.

(f) Notwithstanding any other provision of law to the contrary, any municipality may convey to a land bank real property and interests in real property on such terms and conditions, form and substance of consideration, and procedures, all as determined by the transferring municipality in its discretion.

(g) The acquisition of real property by a land bank pursuant to the provisions of this article, from entities other than political subdivisions, shall be limited to real property that is tax delinquent, tax foreclosed, vacant or abandoned; provided, however, that a land bank shall have authority to enter into agreements to purchase other real property consistent with an approved redevelopment plan.

(h) The land bank shall maintain and make available for public review and inspection a complete inventory of all property received by the land bank. Such inventory shall include: the location of the parcel; the purchase price, if any, for each parcel received; the current value assigned to the property for purposes of real property taxation; the amount, if any, owed to the locality for real property taxation; the identity of the transferor; and any conditions or restrictions applicable to the property.

(i) All parcels received by the land bank shall be listed on the received inventory established pursuant to paragraph (h) of this section within one week of acquisition and shall remain in such inventory for one week prior to disposition.

(j) Failure to comply with the requirements in paragraphs (h) and (i) of this section with regard to any particular parcel shall cause such acquisition by the land bank to be null and void.

§ 1609. Disposition of property.

(a) The land bank shall hold in its own name, or in the name of a lawfully organized subsidiary, all real property acquired by the land bank irrespective of the identity of the transferor of such property.

(a-1) This section governing the disposition of property by land banks shall supersede section twenty-eight hundred ninety-seven of the public authorities law in the governance of property dispositions by land banks and, as such, notwithstanding any other general, special or local law to the contrary, section twenty-eight hundred ninety-seven of the public authorities law shall not apply to land banks.

(b) The land bank shall maintain and make available for public review and inspection a complete inventory of all real property dispositions by the land bank. Such inventory shall include a complete copy of the sales contract including all terms and conditions including, but not limited to, any form of compensation received by the land bank or any other party which is not included within the sale price.

(c) The land bank shall determine and set forth in policies and procedures of the board of directors the general terms and conditions for consideration to be received by the land bank for the transfer of real property and interests in real property, which consideration may take the form of monetary payments and secured financial obligations, covenants and conditions related to the present and future use of the property, contractual commitments of the transferee, and such other forms of consideration as are consistent with state and local law.

(d) The land bank may convey, exchange, sell, transfer, lease as lessor, grant, release and demise, pledge any and all interests in, upon or to real property of the land bank.

(e) A foreclosing governmental unit may, in its local law, resolution or ordinance creating a land bank, or, in the case of multiple foreclosing governmental units creating a single land bank in the applicable intergovernmental cooperation agreement, establish a hierarchical ranking of priorities for the use of real property conveyed by a land bank including but not limited to:

(1) use for purely public spaces and places;

(2) use for affordable housing;

(3) use for retail, commercial and industrial activities;

(4) use as wildlife conservation areas; and

(5) such other uses and in such hierarchical order as determined by the foreclosing governmental unit or units.

(f) A foreclosing governmental unit may, in its local law, resolution or ordinance creating a land bank, or, in the case of multiple foreclosing governmental units creating a single land bank in the applicable intergovernmental cooperation agreement, require that any particular form of disposition of real property, or any disposition of real property located within specified jurisdictions, be subject to specified voting and approval requirements of the board of directors. Except and unless restricted or constrained in this manner, the board of directors may delegate to officers and employees the authority to enter into and execute agreements, instruments of conveyance and all other related documents pertaining to the conveyance of real property by the land bank.

(g) All property dispositions shall be listed on the property disposition inventory established pursuant to paragraph (b) of this section within one week of disposition. Such records shall remain available for public inspection in the property disposition inventory indefinitely.

(h) Failure to comply with the requirements in paragraph (g) of this section shall subject the land bank to a civil penalty of one hundred dollars per violation up to a maximum of ten thousand dollars for each parcel, recoverable in an action brought by the attorney general or district attorney. The attorney general or district attorney may also seek rescission of the real property transaction.

History: Add, L 2011, ch 257, § 1, eff July 29, 2011; L 2015, ch 407, §2, eff Oct 26, 2015; amd, L 2016, ch 338, §2, eff Sept 29, 2016.

§ 1610. Financing of land bank operations.

(a) A land bank may receive funding through grants and loans from the foreclosing governmental unit or units which created the land bank, from other municipalities, from the state of New York, from the federal government, and from other public and private sources.

(b) A land bank may receive and retain payments for services rendered, for rents and leasehold payments received, for consideration for disposition of real and personal property, for proceeds of insurance coverage for losses incurred, for income from investments, and for any other asset and activity lawfully permitted to a land bank under this article.

(c) Upon the adoption of a local law, ordinance, or resolution by municipality, school district or any taxing district, fifty percent of the real property taxes collected on any specific parcel of real property identified by such municipality, school district or any taxing jurisdiction may be remitted to the land bank, in accordance with procedures established by regulations promulgated by the department of taxation and finance. Such allocation of real property tax revenues shall commence with the first taxable year following the date of conveyance and shall continue for a period of five years.

History: Add, L 2011, ch. 257.

§ 1611. Borrowing and issuance of bonds.

(a) A land bank shall have power to issue bonds for any of its corporate purposes, the principal and interest of which are payable from its revenues generally. Any of such bonds may be secured by a pledge of any revenues, including grants or contributions from the state of New York, the federal government, or any agency, and instrumentality thereof, or by a mortgage of any property of the land bank.

(b) The bonds issued by a land bank are hereby declared to have all the qualities of negotiable instruments under New York state law.

(c) The bonds of a land bank created under the provisions of this article and the income therefrom shall at all times be free from taxation for the state of New York or local purposes under any provision of New York law.

(d) Bonds issued by the land bank shall be authorized by resolution of the board and shall be limited obligations of the land bank; the principal and interest, costs of issuance, and other costs incidental thereto shall be payable solely from the income and revenue derived from the sale, lease, or other disposition of the assets of the land bank. In the discretion of the land bank, the bonds may be additionally secured by mortgage or other security device covering all or part of the project from which the revenues so pledged may be derived. Any refunding bonds issued shall be payable from any source described above or from the investment of any of the proceeds of the refunding bonds and shall not constitute an indebtedness or pledge of the general credit of any foreclosing governmental unit or municipality within the meaning of any constitutional or statutory limitation of indebtedness and shall contain a recital to that effect. Bonds of the land bank shall be issued in such form, shall be in such denominations, shall bear interest, shall mature in such manner, and be executed by one or more members of the board as provided in the resolution authorizing the issuance thereof. Such bonds may be subject to redemption at the option of and in the manner determined by the board in the resolution authorizing the issuance thereof.

(e) Bonds issued by the land bank shall be issued, sold, and delivered in accordance with the terms and provisions of a resolution adopted by the board. The board may sell such bonds in such manner, either at public or at private sale, and for such price as it may determine to be in the best interests of the land bank. The resolution issuing bonds shall be published in a newspaper of general circulation within the jurisdiction of the land bank and posted prominently and continuously on the homepage of any website maintained by the land bank.

(f) Neither the members of a land bank nor any person executing the bonds shall be liable personally on any such bonds by reason of the issuance thereof. Such bonds or other obligations of a land bank shall not be a debt of any municipality or of the state of New York, and shall so state on their face, nor shall any municipality or the state of New York nor any revenues or any property of any municipality or of the state of New York be liable therefor.

History: Add, L 2011, ch. 257; amd, L 2013, ch 549, § 127, eff July 1, 2014.

§ 1612.   Public records and public meetings.

(a) The board shall cause minutes and a record to be kept of all its proceedings. Except as otherwise provided in this section, the land bank shall be subject to the open meetings law and the freedom of information law.

(b) A land bank shall hold a public hearing prior to financing or issuance of bonds. The land bank shall schedule and hold a public hearing and solicit public comment. After the conclusion of the public hearing and comments, the land bank shall consider the results of the public hearing and comments with respect to the proposed actions. Such consideration by the land bank shall include the accommodation of the public interest with respect to such actions; if such accommodation is deemed in the best interest of the community proposed actions shall include such accommodation.

(c) In addition to any other report required by this chapter, the land bank, through its chairperson, shall annually deliver, in oral and written form, a report to the municipality. Such report shall be presented by March fifteenth of each year to the governing body or board of the municipality. The report shall describe in detail the projects undertaken by the land bank during the past year, the monies expended by the land bank during the past year, and the administrative activities of the land bank during the past year. At the conclusion of the report, the chairperson of the land bank shall be prepared to answer the questions of the municipality with respect to the projects undertaken by the authority during the past year, the monies expended by the municipality during the past year, and the administrative activities of the municipality during the past year.

History: Add, L 2011, ch 257, § 1, eff July 29, 2011.

§ 1613.   Dissolution of land bank.

A land bank may be dissolved as a charitable not-for-profit corporation sixty calendar days after an affirmative resolution approved by two-thirds of the membership of the board of directors. Sixty calendar days advance written notice of consideration of a resolution of dissolution shall be given to the foreclosing governmental unit or units that created the land bank, shall be published in a local newspaper of general circulation, and posted prominently and continuously on the homepage of any website maintained by the land bank, and shall be sent certified mail to the trustee of any outstanding bonds of the land bank. Upon dissolution of the land bank all real property, personal property and other assets of the land bank shall become the assets of the foreclosing governmental unit or units that created the land bank. In the event that two or more foreclosing governmental units create a land bank in accordance with section sixteen hundred three of this article, the withdrawal of one or more foreclosing governmental units shall not result in the dissolution of the land bank unless the intergovernmental agreement so provides, and there is no foreclosing governmental unit that desires to continue the existence of the land bank.

History: Add, L 2011, ch. 257; amd, L 2013, ch 549, § 128, eff July 1, 2014.

§ 1614.   Conflicts of interest.

No member of the board or employee of a land bank shall acquire any interest, direct or indirect, in real property of the land bank, in any real property to be acquired by the land bank, or in any real property to be acquired from the land bank. No member of the board or employee of a land bank shall have any interest, direct or indirect, in any contract or proposed contract for materials or services to be furnished or used by a land bank. The board may adopt supplemental rules and regulations addressing potential conflicts of interest and ethical guidelines for members of the board and land bank employees.

History: Add, L 2011, ch 257, § 1, eff July 29, 2011.

§ 1615.   Construction, intent and scope.

The provisions of this article shall be construed liberally to effectuate the legislative intent and the purposes as complete and independent authorization for the performance of each and every act and thing authorized by this article, and all powers granted shall be broadly interpreted to effectuate the intent and purposes and not as a limitation of powers. Except as otherwise expressly set forth in this article, in the exercise of its powers and duties under this article and its powers relating to property held by the land bank, the land bank shall have complete control as fully and completely as if it represented a private property owner and shall not be subject to restrictions imposed by the charter, ordinances, or resolutions of a local unit of government.

History: Add, L 2011, ch 257, § 1, eff July 29, 2011.

§ 1616.   Delinquent property tax enforcement.

The municipality may enter into a contract to sell some or all of the delinquent tax liens held by it to a land bank, subject to the following conditions:

(a) The consideration to be paid may be more or less than the face amount of the tax liens sold.

(b) Property owners shall be given at least thirty days advance notice of such sale in the same form and manner as is provided by subdivision two of section eleven hundred ninety of the real property tax law. Failure to provide such notice or the failure of the addressee to receive the same shall not in any way affect the validity of any sale of a tax lien or tax liens or the validity of the taxes or interest prescribed by law with respect thereto.

(c) The municipality shall set the terms and conditions of the contract of sale.

(d) The land bank must thirty days prior to the commencement of any foreclosure action provide to the municipality a list of liens to be foreclosed. The municipality may, at its sole option and discretion, repurchase a lien or liens on the foreclosure list from the land bank. The repurchase price shall be the amount of the lien or liens plus any accrued interest and collection fees incurred by the land bank. The land bank shall provide the foreclosure list to the municipality, along with the applicable repurchase price of each lien, by certified mail, and the municipality shall have thirty days from receipt to notify the land bank of its option to purchase one or more of the liens. If the municipality opts to purchase the lien, it shall provide payment within thirty days of receipt of the repurchase price of said lien or liens. If the municipality shall fail to opt to repurchase the lien or

liens the land bank shall have the right to commence a foreclosure action immediately.

(e) The sale of a tax lien pursuant to this article shall not operate to shorten the otherwise applicable redemption period or change the otherwise applicable interest rate.

(f) Upon the expiration of the redemption period prescribed by law, the purchaser of a delinquent tax lien, or its successors or assigns, may foreclose the lien as in an action to foreclose a mortgage as provided in section eleven hundred ninety-four of the real property tax law. The procedure in such action shall be the procedure prescribed by article thirteen of the real property actions and proceedings law for the foreclosure of mortgages. At any time following the commencement of an action to foreclose a lien, the amount required to redeem the lien, or the amount received upon sale of a property, shall include reasonable and necessary collection costs, attorneys' fees, legal costs, allowances, and disbursements.

(g) The provisions of title five of article eleven of the real property tax law shall apply so far as is practicable to a contract for the sale of tax liens pursuant to this article.

(h) If the court orders a public sale pursuant to section eleven hundred thirty-six of the real property tax law, and the purchaser of the property is the land bank, then the form, substance, and timing of the land bank's payment of the sales price may be according to such agreement as is mutually acceptable to the plaintiff and the land bank. The obligation of the land bank to perform in accordance with such agreement shall be deemed to be in full satisfaction of the tax claim which was the basis for the judgment.

(i) Notwithstanding any other provision of law to the contrary, in the event that no municipality elects to tender a bid at a public sale pursuant to the provisions of section eleven hundred sixty-six of the real property tax law or sale pursuant to the provisions of a county charter, city charter, administrative code, or special law when applicable under section eleven hundred four of the real property tax law, the land bank may tender a bid at such sale in an amount equal to the total amount of all municipal claims and liens which were the basis for the judgment. In the event of such tender by the land bank the property shall be deemed sold to the land bank regardless of any bids by any other third parties. The bid of the land bank shall be paid as to its form, substance, and timing according to such agreement as is mutually acceptable to the plaintiff and the land bank. The obligation of the land bank to perform in accordance with such agreement shall be deemed to be in full satisfaction of the municipal claim which was the basis for the judgment. The land bank, as purchaser at such public sale or sale pursuant to the provisions of a county charter, city charter, administrative code, or special law when applicable under section eleven hundred four of the real property tax law, shall take and forever thereafter have, an absolute title to the property sold, free and discharged of all tax and municipal claims, liens, mortgages, charges and estates of whatsoever kind. The deed to the land bank shall be executed, acknowledged and delivered within thirty days of the sale. Alternatively, the land bank can assign all rights resulting from the land bank's successful tender for the property to the foreclosing governmental unit, which would allow the property to be deeded directly to the foreclosing governmental unit. All land bank acquisitions pursuant to this paragraph shall comply with section sixteen hundred eight of this article and all dispositions of property acquired pursuant to this paragraph shall comply with section sixteen hundred nine of this article.

History: Add, L 2011, ch 257, § 1, eff July 29, 201; amd, L 2013, ch 372, § 2, eff Sept 27, 2013; L 2016, ch 341, §1, eff Sept 29, 2016.

§ 1617. Contracts.

(a) The land bank may, in its discretion, assign contracts for supervision and coordination to the successful bidder for any subdivision of work for which the land bank receives bids. Any construction, demolition, renovation and reconstruction contract awarded by the land bank shall contain such other terms and conditions as the land bank may deem desirable. The land bank shall not award any construction, demolition, renovation and reconstruction contract greater than ten thousand dollars except to the lowest bidder who, in its opinion, is qualified to perform the work required and who is responsible and reliable. The land bank may, however, reject any or all bids or waive any informality in a bid if it believes that the public interest will be promoted thereby. The land bank may reject any bid, if, in its judgment, the business and technical organization, plant, resources, financial standing, or experience of the bidder justifies such rejection in view of the work to be performed.

(b) For the purposes of article fifteen-A of the executive law only, the land bank shall be deemed a state agency as that term is used in such article, and all contracts for procurement, design, construction, services and materials shall be deemed state contracts within the meaning of that term as set forth in such article.

History: Add, L 2011, ch 257, § 1, eff July 29, 2011.

Not-For-Profit
Corporation Law

COOPERATIVE CORPORATIONS LAW

History: Add, L 1951, ch 712, eff April 11, 1951.

ARTICLE 1
SHORT TITLE; POLICY; DEFINITIONS

History: Add, L 1951, ch 712, with substance transferred from former Article 1.

§ 1.   Short title

This chapter shall be known as the "cooperative corporations law."

History: Add, L 1951, ch 712, eff April 11, 1951, with substance transferred from former § 1.

§ 2.   Declaration of policy

It is the declared policy of this state, as one means of improving the economic welfare of its people, particularly those who are producers, marketers or consumers of food products, to encourage their effective organization in cooperative associations for the rendering of mutual help and service.

History: Add, L 1951, ch 712, eff April 11, 1951.

CASE ANNOTATIONS

In action by cooperative housing corporation against the corporation's sponsors, the decision of the Federal Housing Authority approving the lease and construction agreements of the project did not protect the sponsors against suit based on alleged excess rent charges and construction contract price. Knolls Cooperative Section No. 1, Inc. v Hennessy (1955) 1 Misc. 2d 1001, 148 N.Y.S.2d 669, affd (1956, 1st Dept) 1 A.D.2d 945, 151 N.Y.S.2d 600, affd (1957) 2 N.Y.2d 514, 161 N.Y.S.2d 404, 141 N.E.2d 802

Former section 18 barred the use of the word "cooperative" by any other than a corporation of the character defined in § 3 and classified in former § 2. 1938 Ops Atty Gen 283

The word "co-operative" in the name "Co-operative College" may not be used. 1938 Ops Atty Gen 283

§ 3.   Definitions

(a) The term "agricultural product" means any product of cultivating land, and includes floricultural, horticultural, viticultural, forestry, nut, dairy, livestock, poultry, bee and any farm products or by-products thereof.

(b) The terms "feed," "food," and "food products" mean any substance capable of human, animal or poultry consumption, including all articles of drink, confectionery or condiment, whether simple, mixed or compound, and all substances or ingredients added to food for any purpose.

(c) The terms "cooperative," "cooperative association" and "cooperative corporation" mean a corporation organized under this chapter, or heretofore organized under any special or general law of this state, for the cooperative rendering of mutual help and service to its members. A cooperative shall be either a general cooperative, a membership cooperative, an agricultural cooperative as defined in article six of this chapter or a worker cooperative as defined in section eighty-one of this chapter.

(d) A cooperative corporation shall be classed as a non-profit corporation, since its primary object is not to make profits for itself as such, or to pay dividends on invested capital, but to provide service and means whereby its members may have the economic advantage of cooperative action, including a reasonable and fair return for their product and service.

(e) The term "member" means the holder of a membership in a cooperative, whether evidenced by a certificate of membership or by a certificate of stock or by other authorized means of identification. The term includes a member association or corporation as provided in this chapter.

(f) The term "person" includes an individual, a partnership, a corporation, an association, or two or more individuals acting together.

(g) The term "net margins" or "net retained proceeds" means the amount by which the undistributed receipts from operations exceed the expenses thereof.

(h) The term "patron" refers to persons, partnerships, associations and corporations who transact business with the cooperative either as producers or purchasers, whether members or not.

(i) A cooperative corporation does not include any corporation which is formed or may be formed under the banking law, the insurance law, the railroad law or the transportation corporations law. Except as otherwise expressly provided in this chapter, no cooperative corporation shall do any business for which a corporation may be formed under any such law; but the lawful operations of a cooperative credit corporation as authorized in this chapter shall not be deemed banking or violation of any provisions of law as to banking.

(j) The term "cooperative," "cooperation" or any abbreviation, variation or similitude thereof, shall not be used as or in a name except by a corporation defined in this chapter. Any cooperative corporation may sue for an injunction against such prohibited use of the term. A violation of this prohibition is a misdemeanor, punishable by a fine of not more than five hundred dollars.

(k) A membership cooperative is a non-stock cooperative which admits only natural persons to membership, which provides services only to its members and which makes no distribution of net retained proceeds other than to its members on the basis of their patronage.

(l) The terms "buying, selling or leasing homes for its members" and "conducting housing" shall include but not be limited to, the purposes and uses of residential facilities for the mentally disabled licensed by the office of mental health or the office of mental retardation and developmental disabilities.

History: Add, L 1951, ch 712, eff April 11, 1951 with substance transferred from former § 3.

Sub (c), amd, L 1978, ch 158, § 1, L 1985, ch 805, § 2, eff Aug 2, 1985.

Sub (j), amd, L 1984, ch 805, § 12, eff Sept 1, 1984.

Sub (k), add, L 1978, ch 158, § 2, eff May 23, 1978.

Sub (l), add, L 1987, ch 225, § 4, eff July 7, 1987.

CASE ANNOTATIONS

Interest in cooperative apartment is sui generis in modern property law, and requires case-by-case assessment as to whether real property or personal property rules should apply, since interest is represented by shares of stock, which are personal property, yet in reality what is owned is not interest in ongoing business enterprise but instead right to possess real property. In re Estate of Carmer (1988) 71 N.Y.2d 781, 530 N.Y.S.2d 88, 525 N.E.2d 734

Cooperative corporation is-in fact and function-a corporation, acting through management of its board of directors, and subject to Business Corporation Law. Levandusky v One Fifth Ave. Apartment Corp. (1990) 75 N.Y.2d 530, 554 N.Y.S.2d 807, 553 N.E.2d 1317, later proceeding (1991, 1st Dept) 171 A.D.2d 590, 567 N.Y.S.2d 662 and (criticized in Mulligan v Panther Valley Prop. Owners Ass'n (2001, NJ Super Ct A.D.) 766 A2d 1186)

In a negligence action to recover damages for personal injuries, incurred when the 18-month-old son of a cooperative apartment building's superintendent swallowed some caustic cleaning solvent, which had been left unattended in the basement area by the father, against the cooperative corporation and against the manufacturer of the cleaning solvent and, subsequently, against all of the shareholder-tenants who resided at or owned the premises, defendant shareholders' motion to dismiss the complaint as against them was properly granted. Suit against the shareholder-tenants was instituted on the belief that plaintiff could recover a settlement or verdict in excess of the $500,000 insurance coverage on the building. The complaint, however, did not adequately state a cause of action against the shareholders. Merely because the shareholder defendants, as an incident of their stock ownership, were entitled to occupy their apartments under a proprietary lease and thereby use the apartment in a personal way did not render the corporate structure a sham. The cooperative corporation laws of New York are structured so that shareholders may personally benefit from their membership in the cooperative where there were no allegations that the shareholders ignored, circumvented or perverted the corporate form nor allegations of fraud or misrepresentation, the benefits which flowed to the shareholders, including the limitations on their personal liability, in no way impaired the independent existence of the corporation. Perez v One Clark Street Housing Corp. (1985, 2d Dept) 108 A.D.2d 844, 485 N.Y.S.2d 346

By virtue of their fundamentally dissimilar purposes and powers, a cooperative corporation may not consolidate with a business corporation. 1961 Ops Atty Gen Dec 7

A proposed business corporation to be known as "Tire Supply at Coop City" does not violate the prohibition of § 3(j) of the Cooperative Corporations Law against the use of the word "cooperative" or derivatives thereof in the name of a corporation other than a cooperative corporation organized under the Cooperative Corporations Law. Accordingly, the Secretary of State may accept and file the certificate of incorporation of the proposed business corporation. 1970 Ops Atty Gen Feb 20

§ 4. Applicability

This chapter applies to (a) every corporation heretofore or hereafter formed under this chapter, or under any other general statute or special act of this state, which would, if it were to be formed currently under the laws of this state, be formed under this chapter, and (b) every corporation formed under laws other than the statutes of this state to the extent provided in section five and section seventy-six of this chapter.

History: Add, L 1966, ch 664, § 1, eff Sept 1, 1967.

§ 5. Applicability of business corporation law to cooperative corporations

1. The business corporation law applies to every corporation heretofore or hereafter formed under this chapter, or under any other statute or special act of this state, or under laws other than the statutes of this state, which has as its purpose or among its purposes the cooperative rendering of mutual help and service to its members and which, if formed under laws other than the statutes of this state, would, if it were to be formed currently under the laws of this state, be formed under this chapter except a membership cooperative as defined in section three of this chapter, to which the not-for-profit corporation law shall apply. Any corporation to which the business corporation law is made applicable by this section shall be treated as a "corporation," "domestic corporation," or "foreign corporation," as such terms are used in the business corporation law; provided, however, that neither the purposes for which any such corporation may be formed under this chapter nor its classification as a non-profit corporation shall thereby be extended or affected. Any corporation to which the not-for-profit corporation law is made applicable by this section shall be a type D not-for-profit corporation.

(a) If any provision of the business corporation law conflicts with any provision of this chapter, the provision of this chapter shall prevail, and the conflicting provision of the business corporation law shall not apply in such case. If any provision of this chapter relates to a matter embraced in the business corporation law but is not in conflict therewith, both provisions shall apply.

(b) The following provisions of the business corporation law shall not apply to cooperative corporations: section two hundred one (a), section four hundred three, the final clause of section five hundred one (a) which reads "and no limitation or definition of dividend or liquidation rights shall be effective unless at the time one or more classes of outstanding shares, singly or in the aggregate, are entitled to unlimited dividend and liquidation rights", section five hundred five, section five hundred eighteen (c), section six hundred eight (a) and (b), section six hundred nine, section six hundred fourteen (a), section six hundred eighteen, section six hundred twenty-one, section six hundred twenty-two, section six hundred thirty (a) (except as provided in section forty-seven of this chapter), section seven hundred three (a), section seven hundred four, and section eight hundred three (a).

(c) In applying the business corporation law to non-stock cooperative corporations, unless the context requires otherwise, the terms "shareholder" and "holder of shares" shall mean "member," and the terms "shareholders" and "holders of shares" shall mean "members".

(d) In applying the business corporation law to corporations subject to this chapter, unless the context requires otherwise, references to the holders of a stated percentage or fraction of "all outstanding shares," "all outstanding shares entitled to vote thereon," "the shares entitled to vote," and "the outstanding shares, whether or not entitled to vote," shall mean the stated percentage or fraction of the members or delegates present and voting; provided, however, that this paragraph shall not apply to shares of stock not evidencing membership.

2. For the purpose of this section and elsewhere in this chapter, the effective date of the business corporation law shall be September first, nineteen hundred sixty-seven.

3. Sections five hundred eight and five hundred fifteen of the not-for-profit corporation law notwithstanding, a membership cooperative shall be permitted to distribute any portion or all of its net retained proceeds to its members pro rata on the basis of their patronage.

History: Add, L 1966, ch 664, § 1, eff Sept 1, 1967.

Sub 1, opening par, amd, L 1978, ch 158, § 3, eff May 23, 1978.

Sub 1, par (b), amd, L 1968, ch 618, § 1, eff June 16, 1968.

Sub 3, add, L 1978, ch 158, § 4, eff May 23, 1978.

CASE ANNOTATIONS

Cooperative corporation is-in fact and function-a corporation, acting through management of its board of directors, and subject to Business Corporation Law. Levandusky v One Fifth Ave. Apartment Corp. (1990) 75 N.Y.2d 530, 554 N.Y.S.2d 807, 553 N.E.2d 1317, later proceeding (1991, 1st Dept) 171 A.D.2d 590, 567 N.Y.S.2d 662 and (criticized in Mulligan v Panther Valley Prop. Owners Ass'n (2001, NJ Super Ct A.D.) 766 A2d 1186)

In action for breach of fiduciary duty against cooperative corporation and its directors, plaintiffs' conclusory allegation that defendants impeded plaintiffs' efforts to sell their shares in order to enable board member to purchase shares at below-market price, was insufficient to defeat summary judgment where defendants submitted uncontradicted evidence that their actions were protected by business judgment rule. Cooper v 6 West 20th St. Tenants Corp. (1999, 1st Dept) 258 A.D.2d 362, 685 N.Y.S.2d 245

Since plaintiff tenant never informed defendant co-operative apartment corporation, in writing, of his intention to leave the co-operative as required by the co-operative's by-laws, he could not assign his lease and dispose of his stock in the co-operative without affording defendant the first option to purchase his shares and he is, therefore, not entitled to the return of a $2,000 "waiver of option" fee paid to defendant in return for defendant's waiver of its right to purchase plaintiff's shares; moreover, the "waiver of option" fee is a valid exercise of the power of defendant's board of directors (Cooperative Corporations Law, § 5; Business Corporation Law, § 701) and the complaint must, therefore, be dismissed. Jamil v Southridge Cooperative, Section No. 4, Inc. (1979) 102 Misc. 2d 404, 425 N.Y.S.2d 905, affd (1980) 77 A.D.2d 822, 429 N.Y.S.2d 340, cert den (1981) 450 US 919, 67 L Ed 2d 346, 101 S Ct 1366, reh den (1981) 450 US 1050, 68 L Ed 2d 247, 101 S Ct 1771

A transfer fee imposed by a cooperative board of directors on shares of stock in the cooperative corporation was valid when the authority to impose such a fee is conferred by the corporations's by-laws, the Cooperative Corporations Law, and the Business Corporation Law, and a court will not upset an act of a cooperative board of directors when it is undertaken in good faith, for legitimate corporate purposes, and not in violation of the board's fiduciary duty to stockholders. Mayerson v 3701 Tenants Corp. (1984, Sup) 123 Misc. 2d 235, 473 N.Y.S.2d 123

ARTICLE 2
FORMATION AND DISSOLUTION OF COOPERATIVE CORPORATIONS; CLASSES; POWERS; BY-LAWS

History: Add, L 1951, ch 712, eff April 11, 1951.

§ 10.   Classes of corporations

A cooperative corporation shall be either stock or non-stock. A stock cooperative shall issue to members shares of stock evidencing membership and may issue, to members or others, shares of stock of a different class or classes not evidencing membership.

History: Add, L 1951, ch 712, with substance transferred from § 2; amd, L 1966, ch 664, § 2, eff Sept 1, 1967.

§ 11.   [Certificate of incorporation]*

* So in original. Section heading supplied by the editor.

Five or more persons may form a corporation, under this chapter, by making, acknowledging and filing a certificate of incorporation which shall state:

1. Its name. The name shall include the word "Cooperative."

2. Its purposes, as permitted by this chapter.

3. Its duration.

4. The city, village or town and the county in which its office is to be located.

5. The names and post office addresses of its incorporators.

6. The number of its directors, or that the number of directors shall be within a stated minimum and maximum as the by-laws may from time to time provide. In either case, the number shall be not less than five.

7. The names and post office addresses of the directors until the first annual meeting.

8. Whether organized with or without capital stock. If organized with stock, the total amount thereof, the total number, if any, of the shares without par value, and the total number and par value of any shares having a par value. If the shares are to be classified, the number of shares to be included in each class and all of the designations, preferences, privileges, and voting rights or restrictions and qualifications of the shares of each class.

9. That all of the subscribers are of full age; that at least two-thirds of them are citizens of the United States; that at least one of them is a resident of the state of New York; and that of the persons named as directors at least one is a citizen of the United States and a resident of the state of New York.

10. A designation of the secretary of state as agent of the corporation upon whom process against it may be served and the post office address within or without this state to which the secretary of state shall mail a copy of any process against it served upon him.

11. If the corporation is to have a registered agent, his name and address within this state and a statement that the registered agent is to be the agent of the corporation upon whom process against it may be served.

History: Add, L 1951, ch 712, eff April 11, 1951, with substance transferred from § 10.

Sub 8, amd, L 1966, ch 664, § 3, eff Sept 1, 1967.

Sub 10, add, L 1969, ch 97, eff March 25, 1969.

Sub 11, add, L 1969, ch 97, eff March 25, 1969.

CASE ANNOTATIONS

The provisions of this section requiring that the names of incorporators and directors be stated in the certificate implies that directors so named are intended to act only until such time as the stockholders are able to elect directors. A stockholder, therefore, was entitled to an order compelling a meeting for the election of directors where the existing directors did not hold the first annual meeting within a reasonable time. Lazar v Knolls Cooperative Section No. 2, Inc. (1954) 205 Misc 748, 130 N.Y.S.2d 407

A foreign co-operative corporation may be authorized to do business in this State even though its name does not include the word "co-operative." 1948 Ops Atty Gen Sept 25

§ 12. Amendments to certificate of incorporation

The certificate of incorporation of any cooperative corporation may be amended as approved by the affirmative vote of two-thirds of the members voting thereon at any regular or special meeting, or, if the corporation permits its members to vote on the basis of patronage, by the affirmative vote of a majority of the members and of two-thirds of the patronage, voting thereon, provided that the certificate as amended be authorized by the provisions of this chapter applicable to such corporation. A written or printed notice of the proposed amendment and of the time and place of the meeting to vote thereon shall be delivered to each member, or mailed to his last known address as shown by the books of the corporation, or published in a periodical issued by the corporation and mailed to all members, at least twenty days prior to any such meeting. If the amendment adversely affects the preferential rights of any outstanding shares, any holder of such shares not voting in favor of such change may object to it at or before such meeting by filing his written objection with the secretary of the corporation and demanding payment for his shares of stock at their fair value as provided in section six hundred twenty-three of the business corporation law. No amendment affecting the preferential rights of any member or class of members, or any shareholder or class of shareholders, as set forth in the certificate of incorporation, shall be adopted until the written consent of the holders of two-thirds of such preferential rights has been obtained and filed with the corporation. In the case of a cooperative corporation which has adopted the delegate plan of voting at a convention, the vote to be taken as provided herein may be taken at a convention meeting and the required vote shall be two-thirds of the delegates present and voting. The amended certificate shall be subscribed and acknowledged by the president or a vice-president and the secretary or an assistant secretary, who shall annex an affidavit stating that they have been authorized to execute and file such certificate by the votes required by this section and in the manner herein prescribed.

History: Add, L 1951, ch 712, with substance transferred from § 11; amd, L 1966, ch 664, § 4, eff Sept 1, 1967.

CASE ANNOTATIONS

A certificate of incorporation of a non-stock cooperative corporation may be amended so as to authorize issuance of shares of stock. 1954 Ops Atty Gen Dec. 16

§ 13. Purposes for which general cooperative corporations may be formed

Purposes for which general cooperative corporations may be formed. A cooperative corporation may be created under this chapter primarily for mutual help, not conducted for profit, for the purposes of assisting its members, including other cooperatives with which it is affiliated, by performing services connected with the purchase, financing, production, manufacture, warehousing, cultivating, harvesting, preservation, drying, processing, cleansing, canning, blending, packing, grading, storing, handling, utilization, shipping, marketing, merchandising, selling, financing or otherwise disposing of the agricultural and food products of its members or of any by-products thereof, including livestock waste or other organic agricultural wastes and the capture of methane and other gases for the generation and use or sale of energy, as defined in section 1-103 of the energy law, or connected with the acquisition for its members of labor, supplies and articles of common use, including livestock, equipment, machinery, food products, family or other household and personal supplies, to be used or consumed by the members, their families or guests, or for carrying on any other household operation or educational work in home economics and cooperation by or for its members, or for buying, selling or leasing homes or farms for its members, or building or conducting housing or eating places cooperatively, or for furnishing medical expense indemnity, dental expense indemnity, or hospital services to persons who become subscribers under contracts with such corporations in the manner provided in article forty-three of the insurance law, or for the purpose of organizing agency or credit corporations as provided in article seven of this chapter, but a corporation so organized as a credit corporation shall not have power to engage in any other activities. A certificate of incorporation, which includes the purpose of carrying on educational work, shall have attached thereto the consent of the commissioner of education. A worker cooperative may be formed for any lawful business purpose and may be conducted for profit.

History: Add, L 1951, ch 712, with substance transferred from § 16; amd, L 1984, ch 805, § 13, L 1985, ch 805, § 3, L 1998, ch 103, § 1, eff June 9, 1998.

Amd, L 2005, ch 569, § 1, eff Aug 23, 2005.

CASE ANNOTATIONS

In an action by a cooperative corporation seeking a declaration that persons who made cash payments toward cooperative apartments had no legal right or interest in the corporation, summary judgment would be denied to the corporation where the corporation had been formed in order to convert certain school property to residential apartments, where one of its incorporators had accepted payments from persons, allegedly agreeing with them to form a partnership with respect to the development of the school property, and where questions of fact existed as to the incorporator's authority to act as agent for the corporation, notwithstanding the fact that the incorporator had not been a party to the action. Old East Hill School Housing Cooperative, Inc. v Fritschler (1982, 3d Dept) 91 A.D.2d 696, 457 N.Y.S.2d 953

A non-profit co-operative corporation organized pursuant to Art 13-A of former Ch 35 (now Ch 77) is a "business corporation" within the meaning of the Bankruptcy Act and may be declared a bankrupt. In re South Shore Co-operative Asso. (1933, DC NY) 4 F. Supp. 772

§ 14. General powers

In addition to the powers and rights set out in the business corporation law or, in the case of a membership cooperative, the not-for-profit corporation law and subject thereto and subject to the provisions of this chapter, a cooperative corporation shall have the following additional specific powers to be exercised for the furtherance of its lawful purposes and business:

(a) To define or limit its activities as set forth in its certificate of incorporation or in its by-laws.

(b) To handle the products of non-members, except that, in the case of a producers' cooperative corporation, such non-member products handled in any year must not exceed the total of similar products handled for its own members.

(c) To make advance payments or loans to members.

(d) To act as the agent or representative of any member, including other cooperatives with which it is affiliated in any of the activities of the member or other cooperative.

(e) To acquire, own, sell, transfer or pledge shares of capital stock or bonds or other securities of any corporation or association engaged in any directly related activity or in the warehousing, handling or marketing of any of the products handled by the corporation.

(f) To establish reserves, and to invest the funds thereof in bonds or in such other property as may be provided in the by-laws.

(g) To establish, secure, own and develop patents, trademarks and copyrights.

(h) To set forth in its certificate of incorporation, by-laws or member contracts the number, qualifications, classifications, obligations and relative rights of its members; and general rules as to the property and funds of the corporation, the property rights, voting rights and interests of members and of its several classes of members, the admission of new members, the resignation or removal of members, the transfer, suspension, termination, forfeiture, retirement and purchase of membership and membership certificates (including shares of stocks), the methods thereof, the distribution to members, the making of contracts with its members and with others, the holding of meetings and elections, the establishment of voting districts, and the election of delegates to represent the members in such districts or to represent affiliated corporations or associations.

(i) To adopt and amend by-laws, consistent with law and the certificate of incorporation, including emergency by-laws made pursuant to subdivision seventeen of section twelve of the state defense emergency act, relative to the foregoing subjects, the conduct and management of the affairs of the corporation, the calling and conduct of meetings, the amount of stock or the number or proportion of members or delegates which must be represented at meetings of the shareholders, members or delegates to constitute a quorum, the manner of voting, the election, appointment, removal, powers, duties, terms and compensation of its officers, directors and committees, and the fixing of procedures and liabilities in case of violations of the by-laws or of the obligations of members, officers or directors.

(j) To become a member of any other cooperative corporation with such rights, powers and representations as may be prescribed in the certificate of incorporation or the by-laws of the latter corporation.

(k) To act as agent for a non-member in the performance of such services as are permitted under this chapter for its members.

(l) To enter into all proper contracts and agreements with any other cooperative corporation for the cooperative and more economical carrying on of its business or any portion thereof, or for the employment of common facilities or agencies.

(m) To act as an agency for, or subsidiary of, any other cooperative corporation or corporations.

(n) To act as a holding corporation for the properties of any other cooperative corporation or corporations.

(o) To borrow money and contract debts, when necessary for the exercise of its corporate rights and purposes; to issue and dispose of its obligations for any amount so borrowed; and to pledge its property and franchises to secure the payment of its debts.

(p) To limit the amount of indebtedness which may be incurred by it or on its behalf.

(q) To possess and exercise all powers, rights and privileges, including the acquisition of real property, necessary, suitable or incidental to the purposes or activities for which the corporation is organized or in which it is engaged.

History: Add, L 1951, ch 712, eff April 11, 1951, with substance transferred from § 19.

Opening par, amd, L 1966, ch 664, § 5, L 1978, ch 158, eff May 23, 1978.

Sub (i), amd, L 1966, ch 664, § 6, eff Sept 1, 1967.

Sub (q), formerly sub (r), so designated, L 1966, ch 664, § 7, eff Sept 1, 1967.

Former sub (q), repealed, L 1966, ch 664, § 7, eff Sept 1, 1967.

Sub (r), redesignated sub (q), L 1966, ch 664, § 7, eff Sept 1, 1967.

CASE ANNOTATIONS

1. In general
2. Liability of cooperative corporation
3. Transfer or reallocation of shares

1. In general

Contract rider whereby cooperative corporation imposed maintenance surcharge on dentist in event he brought in associate, although not included in contract or proprietary lease for another dentist occupying office in building, did not violate requirement of CLS Bus Corp § 501(c) that "each share shall be equal to every other share of the same class," since other dentist's agreement with board might well have been reached under different market conditions, and was in form of consent to sublet that required credit and other references from proposed subtenants. Cohen v 120 Owners Corp. (1994, 1st Dept) 205 A.D.2d 394, 613 N.Y.S.2d 615

Requirement imposed by New York City Housing Authority (NYCHA) that cooperative corporation as well as proprietary lease owner execute federal Section 8 documentation before sublease to Section 8 participant in cooperative building would be approved was reasonable where (1) lack of privity of contract between corporation and subtenant meant that subtenant could only hold lease owner responsible for habitability problems even if they were caused by corporation, (2) lease owner could control only condition of interior of unit, (3) corporation maintained common areas and provided many services listed in federal Housing Quality Standards, and (4) thus, NYCHA's decision to secure compliance of corporation forestalled many foreseeable problems and assured necessary cooperation between corporation and lease owner in providing subtenant with safe, sanitary, and affordable housing. Malek v Franco (1999, 1st Dept) 263 A.D.2d 427, 693 N.Y.S.2d 584, related proceeding (1999,

N.Y. A.D., 1st Dept) 1999 N.Y. A.D. LEXIS 12577 and app den (2000) 94 N.Y.2d 762, 707 N.Y.S.2d 622, 729 N.E.2d 341

Cooperative corporation was entitled to partial summary judgment on issue of liability for shareholder's maintenance obligations, brought against bank that had lent shareholder money used to buy shares in cooperative corporation, even though bank had secured loan by perfecting security interest in those shares, where (1) shares of cooperative corporation are "securities" governed by CLS UCC Art 8, (2) CLS UCC § 8-209 provides that "[a] lien in favor of an issuer upon a certificated security is valid against a purchaser only if the right of the issuer of the lien is noted conspicuously on the security certificate, (3) legend on stock certificates stated that corporation "shall" at all times have "first lien" on shares of stock for any unpaid maintenance charges, and (4) thus, corporation had lien, enforceable against bank, on subject shares for any unpaid maintenance charges. Berkowners, Inc. v Dime Sav. Bank of N.Y., FSB. (2001, 2d Dept) 286 A.D.2d 695, 730 N.Y.S.2d 339

A regulation imposing a monthly charge of $2.00 for using washing machines previously installed by member-tenants in their apartments in a cooperatively owned and occupied apartment house was reasonable and enforceable but a regulation adopted imposing a late charge of $2.00 for each month that a member might be in default in payment of any sum due to the corporation was unreasonable and unenforceable as applied to a default in payment of the monthly charge for use of washing machines. Vernon Manor Cooperative Apartments Section 1, Inc. v Salatino (1958) 15 Misc. 2d 491, 178 N.Y.S.2d 895

The owner of a cooperative apartment was entitled to recover the money she paid the cooperative corporation as a "flip tax" of 15 percent of her profits on the sale of her apartment where, after she entered into the sales agreement, the tax was authorized by the board in violation of provisions of the proprietary lease forbidding retroactive changes in rent and charges, where neither the corporate bylaws nor the proprietary lease authorized imposition of the tax, and where the tax was not within the board's power to collect expenses incidental to the transfer of an apartment. McIntyre v Royal Summit Owners, Inc. (1984, Sup App T) 126 Misc. 2d 930, 487 N.Y.S.2d 474

Where a co-operative milk association entered into a contract to sell a certain minimum quantity of milk to distributors each month or upon failure to furnish such minimum to make up the damage suffered by the distributor, deductions from milk checks sent to the producers for such damages were improper. Fietz v Central Milk Producers Co-op. Ass'n (1941, Sup) 32 N.Y.S.2d 574

Tenant/shareholder was entitled to partial summary judgment declaring that residential cooperative could not specially assess her for portion of cost of total roof replacement apportionable to portion of roof to which she had right of exclusive use, although offering plan obligated her to repair and maintain portion of roof to which she had right of exclusive use, because roof replacement (as opposed to repair and maintenance of section of roof) constituted major improvement inuring to benefit of all shareholders. Peckolick v 135 West 17 th St. Tenant's Corp. (2000, 1st Dept) 268 A.D.2d 339, 701 N.Y.S.2d 421

2. Liability of cooperative corporation

Cooperative corporation was entitled to summary judgment dismissing cause of action alleging that it tortiously induced contract vendor to breach its contract to sell cooperative apartment to plaintiffs where contract vendor did not breach that contract; rather, cooperative board did not approve sale. Pober v Columbia 160 Apts. Corp. (1999, 1st Dept) 266 A.D.2d 6, 697 N.Y.S.2d 619

Cooperative corporation that operated dual-purpose residence and hotel was entitled to summary judgment dismissing minority shareholders' causes of action for breach of contract and breach of fiduciary duty where (1) plaintiffs did not rebut strong presumption that corporation, which was owned by its resident shareholders, acted in good faith and in exercise of honest judgment and did not discriminate against plaintiffs, who owned transient units for investment purposes, (2) classification of claim as one for "breach of contract" did not defeat operation of business judgment rule, (3) testimony of plaintiffs' experts did now show discrimination or breach of any specific duty but only that hotel could have been operated more profitably, and (4) parties' past dealings indicated that corporation fully protected and advanced plaintiffs' interests. Sherry Assocs. v Sherry-Netherland, Inc. (2000, 1st Dept) 273 A.D.2d 14, 708 N.Y.S.2d 105

Residential cooperative and its managing agent were entitled to summary judgment dismissing tenant/shareholder's cause of action for breach of covenant of quiet enjoyment where there was neither actual nor constructive eviction. Jacobs v 200 E. 36th Owners Corp. (2001, 1st Dept) 281 A.D.2d 281, 722 N.Y.S.2d 137, reargument den (2001, N.Y. A.D., 1st Dept) 2001 N.Y. A.D. LEXIS 7150

Residential cooperative and its managing agent were entitled to summary judgment dismissing tenant/shareholder's causes of action for harassment where New York does not recognize such action. Jacobs v 200 E. 36th Owners Corp. (2001, 1st Dept) 281 A.D.2d 281, 722 N.Y.S.2d 137, reargument den (2001, N.Y. A.D., 1st Dept) 2001 N.Y. A.D. LEXIS 7150

Residential cooperative and its managing agent were entitled to summary judgment dismissing tenant/shareholder's cause of action based on cooperative's promulgation of rule prohibiting deliveries of food by placing food packages on floor of elevator and sending elevator to residents' floors and requiring residents to pick up food deliveries in lobby, absent evidence that rule was not in furtherance of legitimate concerns for safety and cleanliness. Jacobs v 200 E. 36th Owners Corp. (2001, 1st Dept) 281 A.D.2d 281, 722 N.Y.S.2d 137, reargument den (2001, N.Y. A.D., 1st Dept) 2001 N.Y. A.D. LEXIS 7150

Residential cooperative and its managing agent were entitled to summary judgment dismissing tenant/shareholder's cause of action for intentional infliction of emotional distress, based on cooperative's failure to unscrew light bulb in tenant's apartment for 4 days, where that claim did not allege conduct so extreme and outrageous as to be beyond all possible bounds of decency. Jacobs v 200 E. 36th Owners Corp. (2001, 1st Dept) 281 A.D.2d 281, 722 N.Y.S.2d 137, reargument den (2001, N.Y. A.D., 1st Dept) 2001 N.Y. A.D. LEXIS 7150

Residential cooperative and its managing agent were entitled to summary judgment dismissing tenant/shareholder's cause of action for fraud, based on alleged statements by cooperative's board members concerning noise in building and building's water pressure made during their interview of tenant in connection with her purchase application, absent evidence that statements were known to be false. Jacobs v 200 E. 36th Owners Corp. (2001, 1st Dept) 281 A.D.2d 281, 722 N.Y.S.2d 137, reargument den (2001, N.Y. A.D., 1st Dept) 2001 N.Y. A.D. LEXIS 7150

Residential cooperative and its managing agent were entitled to summary judgment dismissing tenant/shareholder's cause of action for punitive damages for breach of warranty of habitability, based on defendants' refusal to enforce house rules and to remedy noise, low water pressure, and other unpleasant living conditions, where such conduct was not so morally reprehensible as to warrant punitive damages. Jacobs v 200 E. 36th Owners Corp. (2001, 1st Dept) 281 A.D.2d 281, 722 N.Y.S.2d 137, reargument den (2001, N.Y. A.D., 1st Dept) 2001 N.Y. A.D. LEXIS 7150

3. Transfer or reallocation of shares

Defendant cooperative housing corporation's reallocation of shares appurtenant to professional units in building, other than plaintiff tenant-shareholder's, constituted proper exercise of its business judgment in light of enhanced market value attributable to plaintiff's access to certain building amenities not shared by other tenant-shareholders; marketability was proper standard, inasmuch as fair market value was criterion established by defendant's by-laws. Cohen v 120 Owners Corp. (1994, 1st Dept) 205 A.D.2d 394, 613 N.Y.S.2d 615

Absent evidence of self-dealing, there was no basis for judicial interference with cooperative board's denial of contract vendees' application to buy shares in cooperative corporation allocated to cooperative apartment sought by them. Pober v Columbia 160 Apts. Corp. (1999, 1st Dept) 266 A.D.2d 6, 697 N.Y.S.2d 619

Bank, as cooperative apartment lessee's lender, was entitled to summary judgment declaring that it was entitled to transfer of shares of stock allocated to lessee's apartment by residential cooperative's board, and board was properly directed to execute and deliver all documents necessary to complete transfer, where, according to Proprietary Lease and Recognition Agreement, board's approval of such transfer was not required in event of lessee's default. Bankers Trust Co. of Cal., N.A. v W. Shore Apt. Corp. (2001, 1st Dept) 281 A.D.2d 351, 722 N.Y.S.2d 165, app den (2001) 97 N.Y.2d 638, 735 N.Y.S.2d 494, 760 N.E.2d 1290

Bank, as cooperative apartment lessee's lender, was entitled to award of maintenance charges that it had paid since date when transfer to it of shares of stock allocated to lessee's apartment by residential cooperative's board should have been, but was not, effectuated. Bankers Trust Co. of Cal., N.A. v W. Shore Apt. Corp. (2001, 1st Dept) 281 A.D.2d 351, 722 N.Y.S.2d 165, app den (2001) 97 N.Y.2d 638, 735 N.Y.S.2d 494, 760 N.E.2d 1290

Executrix of decedent's estate was bound by provision in decedent's propriety lease with cooperative corporation, stating that lease could not be assigned without corporation's written consent, where executrix was not precluded from disposing of estate asset, because corporation's board of directors owed fiduciary duty to its shareholder lessees and had to act in good faith and not arbitrarily; thus, there was no reason to create special rule exempting executors from restrictions applicable to other holders of proprietary leases. Cavanagh v 133-22nd St. Jackson Heights (1997, 2d Dept) 245 A.D.2d 481, 666 N.Y.S.2d 702

Conveyance of shares in cooperative housing corporation (petitioner), as allocated to each apartment, was subject to real property transfer tax, even though petitioner could not grant proprietary leases per se in building, since it did afford membership in petitioner entitling each member to apartment in building for which member was required to pay monthly maintenance charges; such right to occupancy was same right that would be afforded lessee under proprietary lease, conditional on payment of monthly maintenances charges. N.Y. Adv Op Comm T & F TSB-A-90-(7)R

§ 15. Filing certificate

No certificate of incorporation, and no amendment thereof, and no certificate of merger or consolidation shall take effect until it has been filed with the secretary of state. The secretary of state shall provide copies of such certificates or amendments to the commissioner of agriculture and markets or his or her designee upon request by corporation name.

History: Add, L 1951, ch 712; amd, L 1966, ch 664, § 8, L 1994, ch 435, § 1, L 1997, ch 358, § 3, eff Aug 5, 1997.

Section heading, amd, L 1997, ch 358, § 3, eff Aug 5, 1997.

§ 16. By-laws

The by-laws may provide for their amendment by the board of directors; but any amendment adopted by the board shall be reported to the annual meeting of the corporation and, if not affirmatively approved thereat, shall cease to be in effect. By-laws may be adopted, repealed or amended on the affirmative vote of two-thirds of the members, stockholders or delegates voting thereon at a meeting held after due written notice setting forth the proposed action and the purpose of the meeting.

History: Add, L 1951, ch 712, eff April 11, 1951, with substance transferred from § 67.

CASE ANNOTATIONS

In consolidated actions for judgment declaring rights of parties with respect to condominium unit, plaintiffs' causes of action challenging formation of condominium, validity of certain by-law provisions, and whether Board of Managers was validly constituted were barred by collateral estoppel where plaintiffs, who were defendants in prior action for foreclosure of common-charge lien, had full and fair opportunity to present those claims. Cornwall Warehousing v Town of New Windsor (1997, 2d Dept) 238 A.D.2d 370, 656 N.Y.S.2d 329

Specific requirements of bylaws providing for specific manner in which member of Board of Managers was to be removed overrode general provisions of bylaws allowing unit owners to act without meeting. Cruz v Gentner (1997, 2d Dept) 240 A.D.2d 406, 658 N.Y.S.2d 1010

Contract vendees were not entitled to specific performance and declaratory judgment requiring contract vendor to transfer to them proprietary lease and shares of cooperative corporation allocated to cooperative apartment where they failed to obtain cooperative board's approval, which was condition precedent to sale. Pober v Columbia 160 Apts. Corp. (1999, 1st Dept) 266 A.D.2d 6, 697 N.Y.S.2d 619

Mere contract vendee of condominium units lacked standing to enforce condominium bylaws. Soho Bazaar, Inc. v Board of Managers of Soho Int'l Arts Condo. (1999, 1st Dept) 266 A.D.2d 65, 698 N.Y.S.2d 626

Contract vendee of condominium units was not entitled to preliminary injunction against sale of those units by condominium's board where board had purchased units under right of first refusal provision in condominium bylaws, and board's actions were taken in good faith to further legitimate interest of condominium corporation, especially given corporation's start-up financial status. Soho Bazaar, Inc. v Board of Managers of Soho Int'l Arts Condo. (1999, 1st Dept) 266 A.D.2d 65, 698 N.Y.S.2d 626

In action by shareholders and proprietary lessees who sought to recover sublet fee based on cooperative corporation's nondisclosure of sublet fee provision of amended bylaws at time they purchased their shares from previous owner, complaint would be dismissed for failure to state cause of action as corporation had no duty to inform buyers of letter which notified previous owner-shareholder of changes to bylaws and proprietary lease concerning subletting and sublet fees; any duty concerning notice was to shareholders at time of transaction. Rakowsky v Excelsior 57th Corp. (1995, Civ Ct) 167 Misc. 2d 476, 635 N.Y.S.2d 920

Cooperative corporation's authority to impose sublet fee, pursuant to amended bylaws and proprietary lease, was established by documentary evidence although proprietary lease and bylaws were not physically amended, where correspondence had been sent to each shareholder setting forth content of amendments; thus, corporation was entitled to dismissal of action by shareholders and proprietary lessees to recover sublet fee. Rakowsky v Excelsior 57th Corp. (1995, Civ Ct) 167 Misc. 2d 476, 635 N.Y.S.2d 920

§ 17. Voluntary dissolution

A cooperative corporation may, at any meeting and upon due and express notice previously given, by vote of two-thirds of all of the members or stockholders voting thereon, discontinue its operations and settle its affairs.

Thereupon it shall designate a committee of three members who shall, on behalf of the corporation and within a time fixed in their designation or any extension thereof, liquidate its assets, pay its debts and expenses, and divide the net assets among the members, patrons or stockholders, as they may be entitled under the certificate of incorporation or by-laws. Upon final settlement by such committee, the corporation shall be deemed dissolved. The committee shall make a report in duplicate of the proceedings had under this section, which shall be signed by its members, acknowledged by them before an officer duly authorized to administer oaths in this state, and filed in the offices in which its certificate of incorporation is filed.

In the case of a cooperative corporation which has adopted the delegate plan of voting at a convention, as provided in this chapter, the vote to be taken as provided herein may be taken at a convention meeting and the required vote shall be two-thirds of the delegates present and voting.

After the payment of the corporation's debts and after provision has been made for the retirement of its capital stock outstanding, if any, at par, or other stated dissolution value, and accruals thereon, and other fixed obligations, if any, held by members, the net assets remaining may be distributed to members and/or patrons by distribution based on dollar volume of purchases by members or patrons or other unit of measure or on products marketed as shown by its

books of account over the preceding six fiscal years or in case the estimated cost of making distribution by the foregoing method shall, in the opinion of the committee, approximate fifty per centum of the amount available for distribution, the corporation may dispose of its net assets by pricing its inventory downward or raising its advances to members or both to the extent deemed desirable to finally wind up its affairs in the current fiscal year.

History: Add, L 1951, ch 712, with substance transferred from § 22; amd, L 1966, ch 664, § 9, eff Sept 1, 1967.

CASE ANNOTATIONS

The members of a co-operative corporation, organized under former Art. 5 of the Co-operative Corporations Law, whose certificate of incorporation and by-laws contain no provision relating to the distribution of assets upon dissolution, have no proprietary interest in the corporate assets and no right to the distribution thereof upon dissolution. Attinson v Consumer-Farmer Milk Co-op. (1950) 197 Misc 336, 94 N.Y.S.2d 891

A co-operative corporation, whose purpose in purchasing, processing, and selling milk is to establish a "yardstick" for the industry with respect to the price the farmer receives and the price the consumer pays, is a charitable corporation, and, upon dissolution, its assets must be distributed in accordance with the doctrine of cy pres. Attinson v Consumer-Farmer Milk Co-op. (1950) 197 Misc 336, 94 N.Y.S.2d 891

An injunction to prevent the adoption of a by-law providing for the distribution of assets upon dissolution is not appropriate where no dissolution is threatened or contemplated. Attinson v Consumer-Farmer Milk Co-op. (1950) 197 Misc 336, 94 N.Y.S.2d 891

A plan for the liquidation of a co-operative corporation whereby its merchandise would be liquidated by scrip to be issued to members in a sum equal to amount of stock held and to be used by members at private (for numbers only) auction as half payment for merchandise bought, was illegal under this section because a plan permitted each stockholder to redeem at expense of a nonbidding stockholder and at the expense of corporation's creditors. Application of Luff (1951) 201 Misc 22, 109 N.Y.S.2d 54

§ 18. Jurisdiction of the supreme court

In the case of a corporation dissolving as provided in this chapter, the supreme court, upon the petition of the committee or a majority of them, or in a proper case, upon the petition of a creditor or member, or upon the petition of the attorney-general, upon notice to all of the committee and to such other interested persons as the court may specify from time to time may order and adjudge in respect to the following matters:

1. The giving of notice by publication or otherwise of the time and place for the presentation of all claims and demands against the corporation, which notice may require all creditors of and claimants against the corporation to present in writing and in detail at the place specified their respective accounts and demands to the committee by a day therein specified, which shall not be less than forty days from the service or first publication of such notice.

2. The payment or satisfaction in whole or in part of claims and demands against the corporation, or the retention of moneys for such purpose.

3. The presentation and filing of intermediate and final accounts of the committee, the hearing thereon, the allowance and disallowance thereof, and

the discharge of the committee or any of them, from their duties and liabilities.

4. The administration of any trust or the disposition of any property held in trust by or for the corporation.

5. The sale and disposition of any remaining property of the corporation and the distribution of such property or its proceeds among the members or persons entitled thereto.

6. Such matters as justice may require.

All orders and judgments shall be binding upon the corporation, its property and assets, its committee, members, creditors and all claimants against it.

History: Add, L 1951, ch 712, eff April 11, 1951, with substance transferred from § 23.

§ 19. [Repealed]

History: Add, L 1951, ch 712, with substance transferred from § 27; amd, L 1994, ch 435, § 2; repealed, L 1997, ch 358, § 1, eff Aug 5, 1997.

ARTICLE 3
MEMBERS AND MEETINGS

History: Add, L 1951, ch 712, eff April 11, 1951.

§ 40. Certificate of membership

Every corporation shall issue to each member, upon full payment therefor, a certificate of membership (whether evidenced by stock or otherwise) which shall not be transferable otherwise than as may be prescribed in this chapter, the certificate of incorporation and by-laws. The corporation may accept as full or partial payment a member's promissory note, but shall hold the certificate as security for payment, without, however, affecting the member's right to vote unless such note is past due.

History: Add, L 1951, ch 712, eff April 11, 1951, with substance transferred from § 68.

CASE ANNOTATIONS

In a declaratory judgment action for a determination as to whether plaintiff husband, who signed the lease and paid the rent but who did not reside in the apartment, or defendant wife, who resided in the apartment, had the right to purchase shares allogated to the apartment under a co-operative conversion plan, plaintiff husband, as the signer of the lease, was the tenant and occupancy by his wife and children as permitted by the lease was occupancy by the tenant husband even though he did not himself physically occupy the premises. According to the applicable provision of the city rent stablization code, the right of the lessee of record to purchase was protected even though he had subleased and his sublessee was in actual possession and the position of the wife was essentially no different as respects her husband than that of a subtenant. Burns v

500 East 83rd Street Corp. (1983) 59 N.Y.2d 784, 464 N.Y.S.2d 728, 451 N.E.2d 475

§ 41. Representation of members

If a member be other than a natural person, such member may be represented by any individual duly authorized in writing filed with the corporation.

History: Add, L 1951, ch 712, eff April 11, 1951, with substance transferred from § 17.

§ 42. Forfeiture of membership

In accordance with provisions therefor in the by-laws, any person shall forfeit his membership upon proof that he has ceased to be engaged in the occupation or occupations for the servicing of which the corporation was formed, or has ceased to have the qualifications requisite for membership; and shall upon such notice and terms as may be prescribed in the by-laws, surrender his membership certificate or his shares of stock upon payment of the par or otherwise designated value thereof and of any accrued dividends thereon, as may appear in the accounting at the end of the current fiscal year.

History: Add, L 1951, ch 712, eff April 11, 1951, with substance transferred from § 32.

§ 43. Resignation of members

Any member of a non-stock corporation may, subject to fulfilling the liability, contractural [contractual] * or otherwise, then incurred by him as a member of such corporation, resign and withdraw from such corporation, in accordance with provisions therefor in the by-laws.

* The bracketed word has been inserted by the Publisher.

History: Add, L 1951, ch 712, eff April 11, 1951.

§ 44. Voting by members

Except as otherwise provided in this chapter and section two hundred fifty-eight-l of the agriculture and markets law, each member shall be entitled to one vote only. Vote by proxy shall be permitted only to the extent provided by the by-laws which are consistent with the provisions of this chapter, provided, however, vote by proxy may not be utilized where the certificate of incorporation permits proportionate or unequal voting. Except as otherwise required by this chapter or by the by-laws, directors shall be elected by a plurality of the votes cast at a meeting by the members entitled to vote in the election.

History: Add, L 1951, ch 712; amd, L 1966, § 10, eff Sept 1, 1967.

§ 45. Voting by delegates

A cooperative corporation may, by by-law, provide for a method of voting for the election of a delegate or delegates from each of its designated districts or local associations, and for voting by such delegates. As provided in the by-laws, each delegate may have one vote in the affairs of the corporation; or one vote for each member in his designated district or local association; or one vote for each member who was present and voted in person at meetings in the respective districts or local associations; or the number of votes may be apportioned according to patronage.

History: Add, L 1951, ch 712, eff April 11, 1951.

§ 46. Proportionate voting

A corporation incorporated under this chapter may provide in its certificate of incorporation for proportionate or unequal voting rights of all its members, based upon the patronage of said members, which shall be exercised when and as provided in the by-laws of the corporation, except that no members shall be entitled to more than one vote in any case in which a statute requires the affirmative vote of a majority or more of the members. The certificate of incorporation shall state the method by which such proportionate voting rights shall be determined and fixed.

History: Add, L 1951, ch 712; amd, L 1966, ch 664, § 11, eff Sept 1, 1967.

CASE ANNOTATIONS

Sponsor of co-operative corporation may hold majority of votes of board of directors only during initial 5-year period; after 5 years, sponsor cannot use its voting rights to elect majority of directors nominated or designated by it. Sherbansky v 117 West 81st St. Tenants Corp. (1997, 1st Dept) 238 A.D.2d 246, 657 N.Y.S.2d 14

§ 47. Liability of members

1. Members of a cooperative corporation shall not be personally liable for its debts, unless otherwise provided in its certificate of incorporation; provided, however, that each member and director shall jointly and severally be personally liable for all debts due to any of its laborers, servants or employees, other than contractors, for services performed by them for it as defined by section six hundred thirty (b) of the business corporation law. The liability imposed by this paragraph shall be subject to the notice and limitation of action provisions, set out in section six hundred thirty (a) of the business corporation law, and shall be subject to section six hundred thirty (c) of such law.

2. Every contract, made by the corporation with third parties, for the sale or other disposition of products which the corporation has contracted with members or non-members to market for them, shall in all respects be deemed to be the obligation of the corporation, whether the corporation made such contract as principal or as agent.

History: Add, L 1951, ch 712, eff April 11, 1951, with substance transferred from §§ 69, 116.

Sub 1, amd, L 1966, ch 664, § 12, eff Sept 1, 1957.

CASE ANNOTATIONS

No action is maintainable by a trustee in bankruptcy to recover on the basis of a liability which by a by-law of the bankrupt was imposed upon stockholders in favor of creditors. Huntington v Waldorff (1939) 257 A.D. 1025, 13 N.Y.S.2d 783, affd (1939) 281 N.Y. 746, 23 N.E.2d 554

A counterclaim by a member to recover money paid to a trustee in bankruptcy on an assessment against him under a by-law of the corporation is without merit in equity even though the trustee could not have enforced payment inasmuch as the trustee will apply the money in payment of those persons who under the by-law or former § 69 could have enforced payment. Huntington v Waldorff (1939) 257 A.D. 1025, 13 N.Y.S.2d 783, affd (1939) 281 N.Y. 746, 23 N.E.2d 554

Roofing company that contracted with cooperative corporation to install new roof on building was entitled to summary judgment dismissing complaint by cooperative shareholders alleging that work was done in such manner that leak occurred, prompting them to move bed to prevent it from being damaged, and that one plaintiff sustained personal injury as consequence of physical effort of moving bed, since cooperative shareholders were not in privity with defendant roofing company, and policy considerations did not warrant imposing tort duty on defendant under circumstances of case. Raffa v Louis A. Stilloe Roofing & Siding, Inc. (1992, 3d Dept) 182 A.D.2d 901, 581 N.Y.S.2d 888

Former section 69 created no right of action in favor of a corporation or its trustee in bankruptcy. In re South Shore Co-operative Asso. (1938, DC NY) 23 F. Supp. 743, affd (1939, CA2 NY) 103 F.2d 336

The meaning of the scheme of former § 69 and of a by-law adopted under Mem. Corp. Law, former § 207, was to make each member liable to the co-operative association directly and not directly to a creditor or creditors of the association, at least not until the association had failed to act or perform its duty to marshal its assets and enforce the members' liability under the by-law for the purpose of paying its debts. In re South Shore Co-operative Asso. (1938, DC NY) 23 F. Supp. 743, affd (1939, CA2 NY) 103 F.2d 336

The fact that the statute of limitations has run as against any liability of the members of a co-operative corporation does not give the members the right to recover payments made to a trustee in bankruptcy of the corporation under the claim of a mistake of law since the liability continues and the statute merely creates a bar to the remedy which is waived unless claimed. In re South Shore Co-operative Asso. (1938, DC NY) 23 F. Supp. 743, affd (1939, CA2 NY) 103 F.2d 336

ARTICLE 4
DIRECTORS, OFFICERS AND EMPLOYEES

History: Add, L 1951, ch 712, eff April 11, 1951.

§ 60. Directors; terms; election; duties

Except as otherwise provided in this chapter, the board of directors shall be divided, as nearly equally as practicable, into three classes. At the first annual meeting, the members shall elect from themselves a director or directors of the first class for a term of one year; of the second class for a term of two years; and of the third class for a term of three years. At the expiration of the respective terms, successors shall be elected for terms of three years. Successor directors of corporations to which this chapter applies, which were formed under the stock corporation law prior to January first, nineteen hundred fifty-four, need not be members.

History: Add, L 1951, ch 712; amd, L 1968, ch 618, § 2, eff June 16, 1968.

CASE ANNOTATIONS

Business judgment rule prohibits judicial inquiry into actions of corporate directors taken in good faith and in exercise of honest judgment in lawful and legitimate furtherance of corporate purposes; so long as directors have not breached their fiduciary obligation to corporation, exercise of their powers for common and general interests of corporation may not be questioned, even if results show that what they did was unwise or inexpedient. Levandusky v One Fifth Ave. Apartment Corp. (1990) 75 N.Y.2d 530, 554 N.Y.S.2d 807, 553 N.E.2d 1317, later proceeding (1991, 1st Dept) 171 A.D.2d 590, 567 N.Y.S.2d 662 and (criticized in Mulligan v Panther Valley Prop. Owners Ass'n (2001, NJ Super Ct A.D.) 766 A2d 1186)

Board of not-for-profit residential cooperative corporation owes its duty of loyalty to cooperative-that is, it must act for benefit of residents collectively and, so long as board acts for purposes of cooperative, within scope of its authority and in good faith, courts will not substitute their judgment for board's; unless resident who is challenging board's action is able to demonstrate breach of duty, judicial review is unavailable. Levandusky v One Fifth Ave. Apartment Corp. (1990) 75 N.Y.2d 530, 554 N.Y.S.2d 807, 553 N.E.2d 1317, later proceeding (1991, 1st Dept) 171 A.D.2d 590, 567 N.Y.S.2d 662 and (criticized in Mulligan v Panther Valley Prop. Owners Ass'n (2001, NJ Super Ct A.D.) 766 A2d 1186)

Proprietary lessee failed to show that board of not-for-profit residential cooperative corporation acted improperly in issuing "stop-work" order in response to renovation work in which lessee relocated certain heating pipes, and thus his Article 78 petition to have order set aside was properly dismissed, even though lessee claimed that he had relied on board's initial approval of his plans and that, in any case, no harm was done to building, where lessee failed to comply with provisions either of alteration agreement or of renovation guidelines which required explicit written notice to board of any proposed changes in building's heating system, board promptly consulted its engineer when it learned of lessee's intent, and board notified lessee that it would not depart from its policy of refusing to permit movement of pipes. Levandusky v One Fifth Ave. Apartment Corp. (1990) 75 N.Y.2d 530, 554 N.Y.S.2d 807, 553 N.E.2d 1317, later proceeding (1991, 1st Dept) 171 A.D.2d 590, 567 N.Y.S.2d 662 and (criticized in Mulligan v Panther Valley Prop. Owners Ass'n (2001, NJ Super Ct A.D.) 766 A2d 1186)

Action by board of directors of corporation that comes within business judgment rule cannot be characterized as arbitrary and capricious, or abuse of discretion, for purpose of Article 78 proceeding. Levandusky v One Fifth Ave. Apartment Corp. (1990) 75 N.Y.2d 530, 554 N.Y.S.2d 807, 553 N.E.2d 1317, later proceeding (1991, 1st Dept) 171 A.D.2d 590, 567 N.Y.S.2d 662 and (criticized in Mulligan v Panther Valley Prop. Owners Ass'n (2001, NJ Super Ct A.D.) 766 A2d 1186)

Although cooperative housing corporation has exceedingly broad discretion in admissions decisions, it has fiduciary duty to treat its shareholders fairly and evenly, and must discharge that duty with good faith and scrupulous honesty; any departure from uniform treatment of shareholders must be in furtherance of justifiable and bona fide business purpose. Smolinsky v 46 Rampasture Owners (1996, 1st Dept) 230 A.D.2d 620, 646 N.Y.S.2d 110

In action against cooperative housing corporation for withholding consent to assignment of shareholders' proprietary lease and shares to third party, jury might rationally have determined that cooperative board's asserted grounds for denying consent to transfer of proprietary lease and shares were pretextual, that denial was instead based on cooperative board's anger over litigation and failure to obtain waiver of third party's future sublet rights, and that these grounds for refusal were unreasonable and lacked bona fide business purpose. Smolinsky v 46 Rampasture Owners (1996, 1st Dept) 230 A.D.2d 620, 646 N.Y.S.2d 110

Cooperative board was entitled, under business judgment rule, to summary judgment dismissing plaintiffs' action to compel board to decrease number of shares assigned to their unit where complaint failed to allege any fraud, self-dealing, breach of fiduciary obligation or unequal treatment of shareholders in board's denial of such relief, and plaintiffs were aware of share allocation for unit (which was owned by plaintiffs' father and father-in-law for many years, prior to purchase by plaintiffs). Glassmeyer v 310 Lexington Owners Corp. (1996, 1st Dept) 232 A.D.2d 229, 647 N.Y.S.2d 784

In consolidated actions for judgment declaring rights of parties with respect to condominium unit, plaintiffs' causes of action challenging formation of condominium, validity of certain by-law provisions, and whether Board of Managers was validly constituted were barred by collateral estoppel where plaintiffs, who were defendants in prior action for foreclosure of common-charge lien, had full and fair opportunity to present those claims. Cornwall Warehousing v Town of New Windsor (1997, 2d Dept) 238 A.D.2d 370, 656 N.Y.S.2d 329

Fact that cooperative corporation's board of directors might have taken action that deliberately singled out individuals for harmful treatment did not, ipso facto, expose individual board members to liability where proposed cause of action against them ascribed no independent tortious conduct to any individual director. Konrad v 136 E. 64th St. Corp. (1998, 1st Dept) 246 A.D.2d 324, 667 N.Y.S.2d 354

A stockholder is entitled to an order compelling a meeting for the election of directors where the existing directors do not hold the first annual meeting within a reasonable time. Lazar v Knolls Cooperative Section No. 2, Inc. (1954) 205 Misc 748, 130 N.Y.S.2d 407

In an action to set aside the election of directors of co-operative apartments on the ground that one of the elected directors, who became a co-operative member five days prior to the election, was ineligible to serve on the board by virtue of his failure to comply with a co-operative by-law prohibiting the transfer of membership within 10 days preceding the annual stockholders' meeting, petitioner has waived his right to contest the election by his participation as a director in numerous board meetings during which respondent was sitting as a voting and active member of the board, and more particularly, by petitioner's accepting respondent's seconding motions made by petitioner; in addition, petitioner's request that the board be discharged would necessitate vacating all actions on which the board has given its approval subsequent to the election and would be highly disruptive and prejudicial to the election and to the interests of the co-operators; furthermore, neither section 604 of the Business Corporation Law, which provides for the fixing of a record date to establish shareholder ownership for the purpose of determining shareholder eligibility to notice or to vote, nor section 60 of the Cooperative Corporations Law, which requires directors of a co-operative corporation to be elected from among its members, prohibits a person who is a member of a co-operative as of the date of board elections from being an eligible candidate for a directorship; moreover, the by-law in question, which forbids membership transfer within 10 days preceding the annual meeting, imposes only a technical restriction and furthermore is not concerned with board membership. In re Willoughby Walk Cooperative Apartments, Inc. (1980) 104 Misc. 2d 477, 428 N.Y.S.2d 574

§ 61. Directors from districts

The by-laws may provide for the use of one or more of the following: (a) that the territory in which the corporation has members shall be divided into designated districts, and that directors shall be nominated or elected therefrom in a designated number and manner, either by the members therein or by district delegates elected by such members or by the membership at large; (b) that primary nominations or elections shall be held in each district to nominate the directors apportioned to such districts and that the result of all such primary elections may be ratified by the next regular meeting of the corporation or may be considered final as to the corporation; (c) that, in the case of a corporation having local associations, incorporated or otherwise, affiliated with it or a member of it, election of a designated number of directors may be by the members of such local association at a meeting thereof, followed by transmission of the ballots and of a certified canvass thereof to the annual meeting of the corporation; (d) that one or more directors may be appointed by any public official or commission or by the other directors. Directors so appointed shall represent primarily the interest of the general public in such corporation;

need not be members of the corporation; and shall not constitute more than one-fifth of the entire number of directors.

History: Add, L 1951, ch 712, eff April 11, 1951.

§ 62. Salaries

The corporation may provide a fair remuneration for its officers and directors and for members of its executive committee. No officer or director or member of the executive committee shall be a party to a contract for profit with the corporation which in substance shall differ in any way from similar contracts by it with members or with others, or which shall vary from terms generally current in the district.

History: Add, L 1951, ch 712, eff April 11, 1951.

§ 63. Removal of directors

Any member may bring charges against a director by filing them in writing with the secretary, together with a petition signed by five per centum of the members, requesting removal. The corporation may thereupon remove the director by the affirmative vote of three-fourths of the members voting thereon at a meeting promptly held after due notice in writing setting forth accurately the purpose for which such meeting is called, provided that at such meeting not less than ten per centum of the entire membership vote, personally or by mail. The director involved shall be given a copy of the charges reasonably in advance of the meeting, and he and the complainant shall have an opportunity at the meeting to be heard in person or by counsel and to present and cross examine witnesses.

In case the by-laws provide for election of directors by districts with primary elections in each district, then the petition for removal of a director must be signed by twenty per centum of the members residing in the district from which he was elected. The board of directors must call a special meeting of the members residing in that district to consider the removal of the director in the manner above provided; and, by a concurrent vote of a majority of the members of that district voting thereon, such director shall be removed from office.

History: Add, L 1951, ch 712, eff April 11, 1951.

§ 64. Officers

The officers of every corporation shall include a president, one or more vice-presidents, secretary and treasurer who shall be elected annually by the board of directors. The president and a first vice-president shall be members of the corporation or of a member corporation, and shall be elected from among the directors. Other officers need not be directors or members of the corporation. The offices of secretary and treasurer may be combined.

History: Add, L 1951, ch 712, eff April 11, 1951.

§ 65. Officers and employees to be bonded

Before handling funds or securities of the corporation, amounting to one thousand dollars or more in any one year, the officer or employees shall be covered by an adequate bond to be approved by the board of directors.

History: Add, L 1951, ch 712, eff April 11, 1951.

ARTICLE 5
MISCELLANEOUS PROVISIONS

History: Add, L 1951, ch 712, eff April 11, 1951.

§ 70. Marketing contract

1. The certificate of incorporation or the by-laws may obligate the members to sell all or any part of their specified commodities exclusively to or through the corporation or any facilities created by it, during any designated period of time, subject to the right of any member to be released at a designated period in each year, by giving a prescribed notice.

2. The certificate or by-laws or the marketing contract may fix specific sums to be paid by the member, or contracting non-member, as liquidated damages upon a breach of the marketing obligation, which sums shall not be regarded as penalties; and may further provide that such member pay all the costs, premiums for bonds, expenses and fees in case the corporation recovers judgment therefor.

3. In the event of a breach or threatened breach by a member, or contracting non-member, of such marketing obligation, the corporation shall be entitled to an injunction to prevent any further breach and to a decree of specific performance; and, upon filing of a verified complaint showing such breach and of a bond approved by the court, the corporation shall be entitled to a temporary restraining order.

4. The marketing contract may provide that the corporation may sell or resell the products delivered by its members, with or without taking title thereto; and may pay over to its members the resale-price, or the pool price in case of pooling of sales, after deducting all necessary selling, overhead and other costs and expenses, including interest or distribution on stock, not exceeding six per centum per annum, and any other deductions authorized by the by-laws or marketing contract.

History: Add, L 1951, ch 712, eff April 11, 1951 with substance transferred from §§ 37, 95, 119, 120.

Cooperative
Corporations Law

An action to recover the price of milk delivered and a counterclaim for liquidated damages was properly brought at law, and a provision for liquidated damages is legal in a contract providing for pooling returns on all milk products sold and for the division thereof among all the members of a co-operative corporation on an equal basis. Parker v Dairymen's League Co-op. Ass'n (1927) 222 A.D. 341, 226 N.Y.S. 226

§ 71. Purchasing business of other corporations or persons

Whenever a corporation shall purchase the business of another corporation or person, it may make payment wholly or partly by the issue of shares or other securities to an amount which at par value would equal the fair market value of the business so purchased; and such securities shall thereupon be deemed fully paid for.

History: Add, L 1951, ch 712, eff April 11, 1951.

§ 72. Reserves, net margins, net retained proceeds, distributions, and patronage refunds

The directors shall periodically set aside reasonable sums for reserves. The net margins or net retained proceeds may, in the discretion of the directors, be distributed at least once every twelve months to members or patrons, by uniform distribution and calculated on such bases as the by-laws or marketing contract may prescribe. Distributions may be credited on account of the issuance to members or patrons of capital stock or other securities of the corporation. In the case of cooperatives with capital stock, dividends shall not exceed twelve per centum per annum on any class of stock.

History: Add, L 1951, ch 712, with substance transferred from §§ 17, 18, 19, 93, 116; amd, L 1980, ch 121, § 1, eff May 13, 1980.

§ 73. Misdemeanor to spread false reports about the finances or management thereof

Any person who maliciously and knowingly spreads false reports about the finances or management or activity of any cooperative corporation incorporated under or subject to this chapter or organized under a similar statute of another state, and operating in this state under due authority, shall be guilty of a misdemeanor and be subject to a fine of not less than one hundred dollars and not more than one thousand dollars for each such offense; and shall be liable to the corporation aggrieved in a civil suit in the penal sum of five hundred dollars for each such offense.

History: Add, L 1951, ch 712, eff April 11, 1951, with substance transferred from § 20.

Inasmuch as a violation of this section is a crime punishable by the imposition of a fine and the recovery of a penalty it must be strictly construed. Dairymen's League Co-operative Ass'n v Brockway Co. (1940) 173 Misc 183, 18 N.Y.S.2d 551

A newspaper report that a corporation subject to this law was making overtures toward the settlement of a strike did not constitute "false reports about the finances or management or activity" of the plaintiff by which it was "aggrieved" within the meaning of this section. Dairymen's League Co-operative Ass'n v Brockway Co. (1940) 173 Misc 183, 18 N.Y.S.2d 551

§ 74. Liability for damages for encouraging or permitting delivery of products in violation of marketing agreements

Any person, firm or corporation who solicits or persuades or aids or abets any member of any cooperative corporation incorporated under or subject to this chapter to breach his marketing contract with the corporation by accepting or receiving such member's products for sale, marketing, manufacturing or processing thereof contrary to the terms of any marketing agreement of which said person or any officer or manager of the said corporation has knowledge or notice, shall be liable in the penal sum of one hundred dollars for each contract, to the cooperative corporation aggrieved in a civil suit for damages; and such cooperative corporation shall be entitled to an injunction against such person, firm or corporation to prevent further breaches.

History: Add, L 1951, ch 712, eff April 11, 1951, with substance transferred from § 21.

§ 75. Audit and annual report

Immediately after the close of each fiscal year, every cooperative corporation shall cause an audit to be made of its operations for such fiscal year. A written report of the audit, including a statement of services rendered by the corporation, with total amount of business transacted, balance sheet, income and expenses shall be submitted to the annual meeting of the corporation and shall at all times be available for inspection by any member. Such audit shall be made by an experienced bookkeeper or accountant or firm of accountants not regularly employed by the corporation, provided that in the case of a cooperative corporation, the annual business of which amounts to less than one hundred thousand dollars, the audit may be made by an auditing committee of three members or stockholders of the corporation who shall not be directors, officers, or employees thereof. Any person violating or failing to comply with the provisions of this section shall be deemed guilty of a misdemeanor.

History: Add, L 1951, ch 712, with substance transferred from §§ 22, 26, 124; amd, L 1981, ch 923, § 2, L 1983, ch 140, § 1, L 1994, ch 435, § 3, L 1997, ch 358, § 3, eff Aug 5, 1997.

Closing par, add, L 1973, ch 487, § 1; amd, L 1984, ch 581, § 1; deleted, L 1994, ch 435, § 3, eff July 20, 1994.

§ 76. Foreign corporations

Any cooperative corporation organized as such under the laws of another state, or any foreign corporation of any type or kind which has as its purpose or among its purposes the cooperative rendering of mutual help and services to its members and which would, if it were to be formed currently under the laws of this state, be formed under this chapter, may, in furtherance of such purposes as are permitted by this chapter, do business, and make and enforce contracts, in this state upon compliance with all the applicable provisions of this chapter and of the laws applicable to foreign corporations desiring to do business in this state.

History: Add, L 1951, ch 712; amd, L 1966, ch 664, § 13, L 1994, ch 435, § 4, L 1997, ch 358, § 3, eff Aug 5, 1997.

§ 77.   Annual license fee

1. Each cooperative corporation organized, with or without capital stock, for the purpose of cooperative marketing of agricultural products or for the purpose of making loans to its members producing agricultural products or for the purpose of purchasing food products for sale to its members, such a purchasing cooperative corporation having gross receipts from such sales of less than five hundred thousand dollars in a calendar year, shall pay to the commissioner of taxation and finance an annual fee of ten dollars, in lieu of all franchise or license or corporation taxes.

2. Each cooperative corporation organized without capital stock, with federal internal revenue code section 501(c)12 status, for the purpose of producing and/or distributing district heating and/or cooling service solely for the use of its members where:(a) the heating or cooling facility of such cooperative corporation is located in a city with a population of more than two hundred thousand and less than three hundred thousand and (b) either (i) at least thirty-five percent of such heating and/or cooling service as measured by relative thermal usage is distributed to and used by members which qualify as organizations described in paragraph one, two or four of subdivision (a) of section eleven hundred sixteen of the tax law, or which qualify as cooperative corporations organized without capital stock with federal internal revenue code section 501(c)12 status, or (ii) is a member of a cooperative corporation organized without capital stock which satisfies the requirements of clause (a) and item (i) of clause (b) of this subdivision shall pay to the commissioner of taxation and finance an annual fee of ten dollars, in lieu of all franchise, license or corporation taxes, or the tax imposed under section one hundred eighty-six-a of the tax law.

3. Such annual fee shall be paid for each calendar year on the fifteenth day of March next succeeding the close of such calendar year.

History: Add, L 1951, ch 712, with substance transferred from § 130; amd, L 1959, ch 593; L 1979, ch 420, § 1; L 1988, ch 152, § 1; L 1992, ch 429, § 1, eff July 17, 1992; L 1994, ch 708, § 1; L 1997, ch 330, § 1, eff Jan 1, 1998.

ARTICLE 5-A
WORKER COOPERATIVE CORPORATIONS

History: Add, L 1985, ch 805, § 4, eff Aug 2, 1985.

§ 80.   Legislative findings

The legislature hereby finds and declares that it is the policy of this state to promote the creation of worker cooperatives. Worker cooperatives provide a means by which enterprises may be democratically controlled and operated by their own workers. It is expected that such cooperative ownership will result in increased job satisfaction and increased productivity and will enable workers to receive the fullest economic benefits from their endeavors. It is also expected that the establishment of cooperatives under this article will result in the creation of new jobs in all economic sectors, will offer greater economic stability in the communities of this state and will discourage the movement of capital and jobs out of this state.

History: Add, L 1985, ch 805, § 4, eff Aug 2, 1985.

CASE ANNOTATIONS

By-law provision, whereby petitioners' membership shares in worker cooperative corporation were automatically deemed transferred to corporation on termination of their work in corporation, was consistent with intent of CLS Co-op Corp § 80 that worker cooperative enterprises be democratically controlled and operated by their own workers. In re Judicial Dissolution of Good Co. Gen. Store Coop. (1998, Sup) 178 Misc. 2d 210, 679 N.Y.S.2d 230

§ 81.   Definitions

As used in this article the following words shall, unless the context clearly requires otherwise, have the following meanings:

1. "Worker cooperative," a corporation which has elected to be governed by the provisions of this article.

2. "Member," a natural person who has been accepted in and owns a membership share issued by a worker cooperative.

3. "Patronage", the amount of work performed as a member of a worker cooperative, measured in

accordance with the certificate of incorporation and by-laws.

4. "Written notice of allocation", a written instrument which discloses to a member the stated dollar amount of such member's patronage allocation and the terms for payment of the amount by the worker cooperative.

5. "Paid-in capital", money or other property, exclusive of the membership fee, contributed by a member to a worker cooperative.

History: Add, L 1985, ch 805, § 4, eff Aug 2, 1985.

Sub 3, add, L 1985, ch 806, § 1, eff Aug 2, 1985.

Sub 4, add, L 1985, ch 806, § 1, eff Aug 2, 1985.

Sub 5, add, L 1985, ch 806, § 1, eff Aug 2, 1985.

§ 82. Corporations organized under the business corporation law; election to be governed as worker cooperative

Any corporation organized under the business corporation law may elect to be governed as a worker cooperative under the provisions of this article, by so stating in its certificate of incorporation filed in accordance with article four of the business corporation law or amendments to its certificate of incorporation filed in accordance with article eight of the business corporation law.

History: Add, L 1985, ch 805, § 4, eff Aug 2, 1985.

§ 83. Status as profit-making corporation

Notwithstanding any inconsistent provisions of this chapter, no worker cooperative shall be classed as a non-profit or not-for-profit corporation.

History: Add, L 1985, ch 805, § 4, eff Aug 2, 1985.

§ 84. Applicability of the business corporation law

1. A corporation electing to be governed as a worker cooperative in accordance with section eighty-two of this article shall be governed by all provisions of the business corporation law, except as otherwise provided in this article.

2. Notwithstanding the provisions of paragraph (b) of subdivision (1) of section five of this chapter, the following sections of the business corporation law shall apply to worker cooperatives, except where otherwise provided in this article: section four hundred three, section five hundred five, paragraph (c) of section five hundred eighteen, paragraph (a) of section six hundred eight, paragraph (a) of section seven hundred three, section seven hundred four and paragraph (a) of section eight hundred three.

3. The following sections of the business corporation law shall not apply to membership shares in a worker cooperative as defined in section eighty-one of this article: section five hundred three, section five hundred four, section five hundred nine, paragraph (c) of section five hundred twelve, section six hundred twelve, section six hundred seventeen, section six hundred twenty-two, section six hundred twenty-

three, section six hundred twenty-five and section six hundred twenty-eight.

History: Add, L 1985, ch 805, § 4, eff Aug 2, 1985.

Sub 2, amd, L 1985, ch 806, § 2, eff Aug 2, 1985.

Sub 3, amd, L 1985, ch 806, § 2, eff Aug 2, 1985.

CASE ANNOTATIONS

Terminated members of worker cooperative corporation were not holders of 20 percent or more of outstanding membership shares of defendant company, and thus lacked standing to commence judicial dissolution proceeding under CLS Bus Corp § 1104-a, where their membership shares were automatically deemed transferred to corporation on termination of their work in corporation. In re Judicial Dissolution of Good Co. Gen. Store Coop. (1998, Sup) 178 Misc. 2d 210, 679 N.Y.S.2d 230

§ 85. Applicability of the cooperative corporations law

Except where limited or excluded in this article, all provisions of this chapter shall apply to worker cooperatives. The following sections of the cooperative corporations law shall not apply to worker cooperatives: paragraph (e) of section three, section eleven, section twelve, section fifteen, section sixteen, section seventeen, section eighteen, section forty-six, section seventy, section seventy-one, section seventy-two, section seventy-four, section seventy-five, section seventy-six and section seventy-seven.

History: Add, L 1985, ch 805, § 4; amd, L 1985, ch 806, § 3, L 1986, ch 165, § 1, L 1997, ch 358, § 2, eff Aug 5, 1997.

§ 86. Revocation of election

A worker cooperative may revoke its election under section eighty-two of this article by a vote of two-thirds of the members and through a certificate of amendment filed in accordance with article eight of the business corporation law.

History: Add, L 1985, ch 805, § 4, eff Aug 2, 1985.

§ 87. Corporate name

A worker cooperative shall include the word "cooperative", "corporation", "incorporated" or "limited" in its corporate name, or an abbreviation of one of such words, notwithstanding inconsistent provisions in this chapter or in article three of the business corporation law.

History: Add, L 1985, ch 805, § 4, eff Aug 2, 1985.

§ 88. Members; membership shares; fees; rights and responsibilities

1. The certificate of incorporation or the by-laws shall establish qualifications and the method of acceptance and termination of members. Upon completion of his or her probationary period, all regular full-time or part-time employees shall be offered membership in the worker cooperative. Acceptance as a member in a worker cooperative shall be evidenced by a membership share, which shall be issued for a fee to be paid in such terms and conditions as are provided in the by-laws.

2. A worker cooperative shall issue a class of voting stock designated as "membership shares". Each member shall own only one such membership share, and only members may own such shares.

3. Notwithstanding section forty of this chapter acceptance as a member in a worker cooperative shall be evidenced by a membership share, which shall be issued for a fee to be paid in such terms and conditions as are provided in the by-laws.

4. The redemption price of membership shares may be determined by reference to internal capital accounts as defined in section ninety-two of this article, notwithstanding section six hundred twenty-three of the business corporation law.

5. The stockholders in a worker cooperative shall have all the rights and responsibilities of stockholders of a corporation formed under the provisions of the business corporation law, except as otherwise provided in this article and chapter.

History: Add, L 1985, ch 805, § 4, eff Aug 2, 1985.

Sub 1, amd, L 1985, ch 806, § 4, eff Aug 2, 1985.

Sub 3, amd, L 1985, ch 806, § 4, eff Aug 2, 1985.

CASE ANNOTATIONS

Terminated members of worker cooperative corporation were not holders of 20 percent or more of outstanding membership shares of defendant company, and thus lacked standing to commence judicial dissolution proceeding under CLS Bus Corp § 1104-a, where their membership shares were automatically deemed transferred to corporation on termination of their work in corporation. In re Judicial Dissolution of Good Co. Gen. Store Coop. (1998, Sup) 178 Misc. 2d 210, 679 N.Y.S.2d 230

Terminated members of worker cooperative corporation were entitled to termination distributions to extent that company bylaws provided therefor. In re Judicial Dissolution of Good Co. Gen. Store Coop. (1998, Sup) 178 Misc. 2d 210, 679 N.Y.S.2d 230

§ 89. Voting shares; by-laws; amendment of certificate of incorporation

1. No capital stock other than membership shares shall be given voting power in a worker cooperative, except as otherwise provided in this article.

2. In accordance with section six hundred one of the business corporation law, the power to amend or repeal by-laws of a worker cooperative shall be in the members only, except to the extent the directors are authorized to amend or repeal the by-laws in accordance with said section six hundred one.

3. The provisions of article eight of the business corporation law shall be construed to limit voting on any amendment of the certificate of incorporation of a worker cooperative to the members, except that non-member stockholders shall participate in such voting in accordance with section eight hundred three of the business corporation law where a proposed amendment would adversely affect the rights of such non-member stockholders as provided in subparagraphs two and three of paragraph (a) and paragraph (b) of section eight hundred four of such law.

History: Add, L 1985, ch 805, § 4, eff Aug 2, 1985.

§ 90. Net retained proceeds or losses; distribution and payment

1. The net retained proceeds or losses of a worker cooperative shall be apportioned and distributed at such times and in such manner as the certificate of incorporation or by-laws shall specify. Net retained proceeds declared as patronage allocations with respect to a period of time, and paid or credited to members, shall be apportioned among the members in accordance with the ratio which each member's patronage during the period involved bears to total patronage by all members during that period. As used in this article, "patronage" means the amount of work performed as a member of a worker cooperative, measured in accordance with the certificate of incorporation and by-laws.

2. The apportionment, distribution and payment of net retained proceeds required by subdivision one of this section may be in cash, credits, written notices of allocation, or capital stock issued by the worker cooperative.

History: Add, L 1985, ch 805, § 4, eff Aug 2, 1985.

§ 91. Directors; officers

1. The by-laws of a worker cooperative shall provide for the election, terms, classifications, if any, and removal of directors and officers in accordance with the provisions of this chapter or the provisions of the business corporation law.

2. Non-members may serve as directors or officers of a worker cooperative but at no time shall there be a majority of non-member directors.

3. Notwithstanding section sixty-four of this chapter, non-members may serve as president and first vice-president of a worker cooperative.

4. Vacancies in director positions resulting from death, resignation or removal shall be filled by vote of the member directors.

History: Add, L 1985, ch 805, § 4, eff Aug 2, 1985.

Sub 4, add, L 1985, ch 806, § 5, eff Aug 2, 1985.

§ 92. Internal capital accounts; recall or redemption of shares; interest; collective reserve account

1. Any worker cooperative may establish through its certificate of incorporation or by-laws a system of internal capital accounts, to reflect the book value and to determine the redemption price of membership shares, capital stock and written notices of allocation. As used in this article, "written notice of allocation" means a written instrument which discloses to a member the stated dollar amount of such member's patronage allocation and the terms for payment of that amount by the worker cooperative.

2. The certificate of incorporation or by-laws of a worker cooperative may permit the periodic redemption of written notices of allocation and capital stock, and must provide for recall and redemption of the membership share upon termination of membership

in the cooperative. No redemption shall be made if such redemption would result in the liability of any director or officer of the worker cooperative under section seven hundred nineteen and section seven hundred twenty of the business corporation law.

3. The certificate of incorporation or by-laws may provide for the worker cooperative to pay or credit interest on the balance in each member's internal capital account.

4. The certificate of incorporation or by-laws may authorize assignment of a portion of net retained proceeds and net losses to a collective reserve account. Net retained proceeds assigned to the collective reserve account may be used for any and all corporate purposes as determined by the board of directors.

History: Add, L 1985, ch 805, § 4, eff Aug 2, 1985.

CASE ANNOTATIONS

Terminated members of worker cooperative corporation were entitled to termination distributions to extent that company bylaws provided therefor. In re Judicial Dissolution of Good Co. Gen. Store Coop. (1998, Sup) 178 Misc. 2d 210, 679 N.Y.S.2d 230

§ 93. Internal capital account cooperatives

1. A worker cooperative may provide in its by-laws that it shall operate as an internal capital account cooperative. An internal account cooperative is a worker cooperative whose entire net book value is reflected in internal capital accounts, one for each member, and a collective reserve account, and in which no persons other than members own capital stock. In an internal capital account cooperative, each member shall have one and only one vote in any matter requiring voting by stockholders.

2. An internal capital account cooperative shall credit the paid-in membership fee and additional paid-in capital of a member to the member's internal capital account, and shall also record the apportionment of net retained proceeds or net losses to the members in accordance with patronage by appropriately crediting or debiting the internal capital accounts of members. The collective reserve account in an internal capital account cooperative shall reflect any paid-in capital, net losses and net retained proceeds not allocated to individual members.

3. In an internal capital account cooperative, the balances in all the individual internal capital accounts and collective reserve account, if any, shall be adjusted at the end of each accounting period so that the sum of the balances is equal to the net book value of the worker cooperative.

4. Section six hundred twenty-three of the business corporation law shall not apply to an internal capital account cooperative.

History: Add, L 1985, ch 805, § 4, eff Aug 2, 1985.
Sub 1, amd, L 1985, ch 806, § 6, eff Aug 2, 1985.

§ 94. Conversion of membership shares and internal capital accounts upon revocation of election; consolidation or merger

When any worker cooperative revokes its election in accordance with section eighty-six of this article, an amendment of the certificate of incorporation shall provide for conversion of membership shares and internal capital accounts or their conversion to securities or other property in a manner consistent with the provisions of the business corporation law.

History: Formerly sub 1, add, L 1985, ch 805, § 4; redesignated as entire section, L 1985, ch 806, § 7, eff Aug 2, 1985.

Sub 2, deleted, L 1985, ch 806, § 7, eff Aug 2, 1985.

ARTICLE 6
AGRICULTURAL COOPERATIVE CORPORATION

§ 110. Declaration of policy
§ 111. Definitions
§ 112. Incorporation
§ 113. Reserves
§ 114. [Repealed]

History: Add, L 1951, ch 712, eff April 11, 1951, with substance transferred from Article 4.

§ 110. Declaration of policy

It is the declared policy of this state to promote the effective production and merchandising of agricultural commodities by providing the means by which farmers may act together in manufacturing, processing, preparing for market, handling and/or marketing their farm products and by enabling farmers to act together in purchasing, testing, grading, processing, distributing and/or furnishing farm supplies and/or farm business services through cooperatives operated for the mutual benefit of the members thereof as producers and purchasers.

History: Add, L 1951, ch 712, eff April 11, 1951.

§ 111. Definitions

For the purposes of this article:

(a) the term "agricultural cooperative" means a cooperative, either stock or non-stock, operated for the mutual benefit of the members in which (1) no member is allowed more than one vote because of the amount of stock or membership capital he or she may own therein, and (2) the cooperative does not pay dividends on stock or membership capital in excess of twelve per centum per annum, and (3) the cooperative does not deal in farm products, agricultural waste products or agricultural compost, farm supplies, farm business services and the capture of methane and other gases for the generation and use or sale of energy, as defined in section 1-103 of the energy law with or for non-members in an amount greater in value than the total amount of such business transacted by it with or for members.

Only persons engaged in the production of agricultural products, or cooperative corporations of such producers organized under the laws of this or any other state, shall be eligible for membership in any agricultural marketing or purchasing corporation formed or operated under the provisions of this article. The terms and conditions of membership shall be prescribed in the by-laws. The board of directors shall be chosen at the time and place and for terms fixed by the by-laws, but at least one-fourth of the directors must be elected annually.

The by-laws may provide for their amendment by the board of directors; but any amendment adopted by the board which affects the preferential rights or obligations of the members or stockholders shall be reported to the next annual meeting of the corporation, and if not affirmatively approved thereat shall cease to be in effect. Such by-laws reported to the annual meeting may be adopted, repealed or amended on the affirmative vote of two-thirds of the members, stockholders or delegates voting thereon at a meeting held after due written notice setting forth the proposed action and the purpose of the meeting.

(b) The term "agricultural products" shall mean horticultural, viticultural, dairy, livestock, poultry, bee and any other farm products.

(c) The terms "feed", "food", and "food products" mean any substance, capable of human, animal or poultry consumption, whether simple, mixed or compound, and all substances or ingredients added to food for such purpose.

(d) The term "agricultural waste products" means livestock manure and crop residues.

(e) The term "agricultural compost" means organic waste derived principally from farm operations and which has been subjected to aerobic, thermophilic decomposition to produce a stable, humus-like material.

History: Add, L 1951, ch 712, with substance transferred from § 2; amd, L 1980, ch 121, § 1; L 1998, ch 103, § 2, eff June 9, 1998; L 2005, ch 569, § 2, eff Aug 23, 2005.

§ 112. Incorporation

Five or more producers of agricultural products may form a cooperative agricultural corporation with or without capital stock, under this article. If the principal activities of such a corporation are connected with the marketing, processing, manufacture, sale or other dispositions of agricultural products, agricultural waste product, or agricultural compost including the capture of methane and other gases for the generation and use or sale of energy, as defined in section 1-103 of the energy law, it may be termed a cooperative marketing corporation and incorporated as such. If its principal activities relate to the purchase of supplies for producers of agricultural prod-

ucts, it may be termed a cooperative purchasing association and incorporated as such, but in either case such a corporation may engage in both such lines of activity. Nothing in this section or article shall be deemed to prohibit the incorporation of a cooperative corporation under article two of this chapter or affect the existing powers of any existing cooperative corporation not within section one hundred eleven of this article.

History: Add, L 1951, ch 712, with substance transferred from § 31; amd, L 1998, ch 103, § 3, eff June 9, 1998.

Amd, L 2005, ch 569, § 3, eff Aug 23, 2005.

§ 113. Reserves

In addition to reserves for depreciation, depletion, obsolescence and bad debts, agricultural cooperatives shall create and maintain minimum general purpose reserves. Such reserves shall be set aside periodically until or unless they total an aggregate minimum amount computed in accordance with one of the following optional methods.

The aggregate minimum amount of such general purpose reserve shall be computed and equal either (1) at least two per centum of the average annual gross receipts of the preceding five years to be accumulated at a rate of not less than two-fifths of one per centum of the gross receipts per annum or such part thereof as may be necessary to establish and maintain such reserves, or (2) at least the total amount of paid up capital stock or membership capital contributed to the corporation accumulated at a rate of not less than ten per centum of the net margins in each year or such part thereof as may be necessary to establish and to maintain such reserve, or (3) at least an amount necessary to establish a sixty per centum net worth wherein the paid in capital and surplus (including the general purpose reserve) shall equal sixty per centum of the total assets of the cooperative. Such a reserve shall be accumulated at a rate of not less than ten per centum of the net margins in each year or such part thereof as may be necessary to establish and to maintain such reserves.

The general purpose reserve created, accumulated and maintained in accordance with this article six shall be deemed to be a required statutory reserve for each agricultural cooperative as defined in this article.

History: Add, L 1951, ch 712, eff April 11, 1951.

§ 114. [Repealed]

History: Add, L 1994, ch 435, § 5; repealed, L 1997, ch 358, § 1, eff Aug 5, 1997.

ARTICLE 7
PROVISIONS AS TO CREDIT AND AGENCY CORPORATIONS

§ 122.   Purchase of stock, assets or business of other corporations
§ 123.   Credit and agency corporations; ownership of voting common stock; directors

History: Add, L 1951, ch 712, eff April 11, 1951, with substance transferred from Article 8-A.

§ 120. Organization

A cooperative corporation may be organized as an agency, subsidiary or holding corporation to assist, further and finance other cooperative corporations in their corporate purposes and activities. A credit corporation may be organized solely for the purpose of acting as an agency to enable cooperative corporations, organized or operating under this chapter and the members or stockholders thereof, to obtain loans from the federal intermediate credit bank under and pursuant to an act of congress approved March fourth, nineteen hundred and twenty-three, known as the agricultural credits act of nineteen hundred and twenty-three, same being chapter eight title twelve of the code of laws of the United States as adopted by congress June thirtieth, nineteen hundred and twenty-six, and amendments thereto. A credit corporation may also be organized by a cooperative corporation for the purpose of financing the ordinary crop operations of the members of such cooperative corporation, through funds obtained by loans from any sources or through the issue and sale of common or preferred stock, bonds, debentures or other obligations of the credit corporation, and the payment of such loans or obligations may be guaranteed by the cooperative corporation whose members are being so financed.

History: Add, L 1951, ch 712, with substance transferred from § 131; amd, L 1959, ch 592, eff April 20, 1959.

§ 121. Special powers

Any credit corporation organized under this chapter may make loans to members of a cooperative corporation owning in whole or in part the stock of the credit corporation; and no loans shall be otherwise made. No loans shall be made for more than ten years; nor for other than the agricultural, dairy, or horticultural purposes of the borrower. In all cases, there shall be a written statement by the borrower in the note, collateral agreement or signed application to the effect that the loan will be used only for such purposes; and such statement may be relied upon by the credit corporation. The credit corporation may discount or pledge such note with a federal intermediate credit bank, or other banks or banking institutions, with its guaranty or endorsement, if required.

A credit corporation may invest its capital funds in bonds or obligations of the United States or of any state or municipality, or such other bonds as are authorized for investment by a savings bank or in federal intermediate credit bank obligations, and may deposit or hypothecate such securities with a federal intermediate credit bank, or other banks or banking institutions, as security for notes discounted by it.

History: Add, L 1951, ch 712, with substance transferred from § 137; amd, L 1959, ch 592, eff April 20, 1959.

§ 122. Purchase of stock, assets or business of other corporations

An agency corporation organized under this article may purchase stock or property or any interest in any property of any person, firm, corporation or association, and may discharge the obligations so incurred wholly or in part, by exchanging for the acquired interest shares of its preferred capital stock to an amount which at par value would equal the fair market value of the stock or interest so purchased as determined by the board of directors.

A corporation organized under the provisions of this article shall have the right to hold, own and exercise all rights of ownership in, and to sell, transfer or pledge, shares of capital stock or bonds of any other corporation engaged in any related activity including, but not as a limitation, the warehousing, handling or marketing, in whole or in part, of any of the products handled by the corporation.

History: Add, L 1951, ch 712, eff April 11, 1951, with substance transferred from § 135.

§ 123. Credit and agency corporations; ownership of voting common stock; directors

All the voting common stock of a cooperative credit or agency corporation must be owned by one or more cooperative corporations organized or operating under the provisions of this chapter. The directors must be members or stockholders of one or more of the cooperative corporations which own the voting common stock.

History: Add, L 1951, ch 712, with substance transferred from § 137; amd, L 1959, ch 592, eff April 20, 1959.

ARTICLE 8
REPEALS AND SAVINGS CLAUSES

History: Add, L 1951, ch 712, eff April 11, 1951, with substance transferred from Article 9.

§ 130. Constitutionality

If any portion of this chapter shall be declared unconstitutional for any reason, the remaining portions shall not be affected thereby.

History: Add, L 1951, ch 712, eff April 11, 1951, with substance transferred from § 140.

§ 131. Laws repealed

Chapter two hundred and thirty-one of the laws of nineteen hundred and twenty-six, entitled "An act

Cooperative Corporations Law

relating to cooperative corporations, constituting chapter seventy-seven of the consolidated laws," and all acts amendatory thereof, are hereby repealed.

History: Add, L 1951, ch 712, eff April 11, 1951.

§ 132. Existing actions

Any action or proceeding begun before this chapter takes effect, under or pursuant to any section, article or act repealed by this chapter, may be conducted and completed in the manner provided thereby.

History: Add, L 1951, ch 712, eff April 11, 1951, with substance transferred from § 141.

§ 133. Existing cooperative corporations or associations

A cooperative corporation or association heretofore formed under or subject to a law repealed by this chapter or under article three of the business corporations law heretofore repealed, shall continue under and be subject to the provisions of this chapter as if incorporated hereunder; but all rights of property and by contract, which accrued before this chapter took effect, shall continue to be governed by the law under which such rights accrued. Also it may continue to use existing name, type of operations, by-laws, forms of marketing contracts, methods of financing and requirements as to reserves in so far as valid under prior laws unless expressly contrary to the provisions of this chapter.

History: Add, L 1951, ch 712, eff April 11, 1951, with substance transferred from § 142.

§ 134. When to take effect

This act shall take effect immediately.

History: Add, L 1951, ch 712, eff April 11, 1951, with substance transferred from § 143.

RELIGIOUS CORPORATIONS LAW

History: Add, L 1909, ch 53, eff Feb 17, 1909.

ARTICLE 1
SHORT TITLE AND DEFINITIONS

History: Add, L 1909, ch 53.

§ 1.   Short title

This chapter shall be known as the "Religious Corporations Law."

History: Add, L 1909, ch 53, eff Feb 17, 1909.

CASE ANNOTATIONS

Courts should not interfere with ecclesiastical matters in which temporal rights are not involved and the courts may only take cognizance of ecclesiastical doctrine when necessary to determine property rights. Re First Methodist Church (1970) 62 Misc. 2d 129, 306 N.Y.S.2d 969

Religious corporations are governed by the same general rules of law and equity as other corporations. Crest Chimney Cleaning Co. v Ahi Ezer Congregation (1970) 62 Misc. 2d 1040, 310 N.Y.S.2d 217

If a religious society is incorporated, its corporate activities are governed by this law, and, whether or not incorporated, there exists within the church structure two separate entities, one of which is the corporate entity and the other the ecclesiastical entity. Hayes v Board of Trustees (1962, Sup) 225 N.Y.S.2d 316

§ 2.   Definitions

A "Religious Corporations Law corporation" is a corporation created for religious purposes to which this chapter applies under section two-a of this chapter. Unless the context otherwise requires, whenever "religious corporation" or "corporation" is used in this chapter, such term shall mean a "Religious Corporations Law corporation".

An "incorporated church" is a religious corporation created to enable its members to meet for divine worship or other religious observances.

An "unincorporated church" is a congregation, society, or other assemblage of persons who are accustomed to statedly meet for divine worship or other religious observances, without having been incorporated for that purpose.

The term "clergyman" and the term "minister" include a duly authorized pastor, rector, priest, rabbi, pandit, swami, guru, granthi, imam, moulvi, maulana and a person having authority from, or in accordance with, the rules and regulations of the governing ecclesiastical body of the denomination or order, if any, to which the church belongs, or otherwise from the church or synagogue to preside over and direct the spiritual affairs of the church or synagogue.

The term "funeral entity" means a person, partnership, corporation, limited liability company or other form of business organization providing funeral home services, or owning, controlling, conducting or affiliated with a funeral home, any subsidiary thereof or an officer, director or stockholder having a ten per centum or greater proprietary, beneficial, equitable or credit interest in a funeral home.

History: Add, L 1909, ch 53; amd, L 1947, ch 674, eff Apr 5, 1947; L 1973, ch 329, eff Sept 1, 1973; L 1998, ch 560, § 6, eff Sept 4, 1998; L 2015, ch 468, § 1, eff Nov 20, 2015.

CASE ANNOTATIONS

School lacked standing to argue that a lease was invalid pursuant to N.Y. Relig. Corp. Law § 12(1), which was intended to protect the members of religious corporations from loss through unwise bargains and from perversion of the use of the property; the lease was voidable at the owner's option and the school lacked standing to challenge it. The owner was incorporated solely as a "seminary of learning" and, assuming without deciding that it was a "religious corporation," it did not meet the definition of an incorporated church. Female Academy of

The Sacred Heart v Doane Stuart School (2012, 3d Dept) 91 App Div 3d 1254, 937 NYS2d 682.

Summary judgment declaring that the parties' marriage was null and void was error because, although a void marriage could not have been retroactively validated by estoppel, plaintiff failed to meet his burden of showing that the minister who performed the ceremony lacked authority under N.Y. Dom. Rel. Law § 11 to solemnize the marriage; plaintiff's own submissions established that the officiant was ordained a minister of the church when the ceremony took place, and plaintiff did not present proof assailing the officiant's authority to conduct the church's spiritual affairs. While plaintiff stressed the unconventional nature of the church's method in selecting its ministers in an ostensible attempt to undermine the legitimacy of authority bestowed upon its ministers, judicial involvement was permitted only when the issue can be resolved by application of neutral principles of law and it was not the role of the courts to question the church's membership requirements or the method by which it selected its ministers. Oswald v Oswald (2013, 3d Dept) 107 App Div 3d 45, 963 NYS2d 762.

This section is to be read in conjunction with Domestic Relations Law § 11, subd 1, to determine the authority of "ministers." Re Silverstein's Estate (1947) 190 Misc 745, 75 N.Y.S.2d 144

The proposed corporate name "New York Soul Clinic, Inc." did not indicate adequately that the society was created for religious purposes or that it was a church and was therefore inappropriate. Nor did the purpose of incorporation stated as the founding and continuing of one or more free churches adequately state the religious doctrine proposed to be expounded and taught. Re Application of New York Soul Clinic, Inc. (1955) 208 Misc 612, 144 N.Y.S.2d 543

Marriage performed by mail-order minister was voidable under Dom Rel L § 11 where person solemnizing marriage did not come within the definition of "minister" or "clergyman" contained in Relig L § 2, and that the Universal Life Church issuing "Credentials of Ministry" was not a "governing ecclesiastical body of denomination or order", and there was no actual congregation which could vest said person with the power to perform the marriage ceremony. Ravenal v Ravenal (1972) 72 Misc. 2d 100, 338 N.Y.S.2d 324

A society incorporated under the Religious Corporations Law, which denied existence of God and relied solely on human reason, was not entitled to exemption from property tax under Real Property Tax Law § 420, subd 1(a). Re Religious Soc. of Families (1973) 73 Misc. 2d 923, 343 N.Y.S.2d 159

A defendant whose contract was terminated by the board of trustees of the temple by which he was employed as a cantor was properly convicted of criminal trespass in the third degree when he returned to the temple after he had received three correspondences informing him of the board's decision and two days after he had been informed that if he failed to restrict himself to the public areas of the temple he would be arrested; a cantor does not come within the definition of "minister" in section 2 of the Religious Corporations Law and, therefore, is not an official whose removal is beyond the power of the board of trustees pursuant to section 200 of the Religious Corporations Law; accordingly, the board's action was proper and the order to leave the temple was valid. In addition, the requisite intent was established. People v Tuchinsky (1979) 100 Misc. 2d 521, 419 N.Y.S.2d 843

Parties' failure to obtain marriage license did not render their marriage void, where they were married in accordance with dictates of Hindu religion and neither party contested validity of Hindu religion. Persad v Balram (2001, Sup) 187 Misc. 2d 711, 724 N.Y.S.2d 560

A clergyman duly ordained according to his faith is authorized to perform marriages in this state without any further license or governmental authorization. The term "clergyman" and the term "minister" include a duly authorized pastor, rector, priest, rabbi and any person having authority from or in accordance with the rules and regulations of the governing ecclesiastical body of the denomination or order, if any, to which the church belongs, or otherwise from the church or synagogue to preside over and direct the spiritual affairs of the church or synagogue. 1959 Ops Atty Gen Aug. 31 (informal)

A clergyman or minister of any religion having authority of his denomination, order, church or synagogue may solemnize marriages in this state whether or not ordained, a resident of this state, or occupying a pulpit. There is no statutory provision relative to the age at which one may solemnize a marriage. 1969 Ops Atty Gen Nov 18 (informal)

Statutory requirements noted: as to form of ceremony in solemnizing a marriage; as to registration for solemnizing marriages in New York City; as to necessity of clergymen being presented a marriage license, as to the necessity of clergymen having no knowledge that either party is legally incompetent to contract matrimony; and as to the return of marriage licenses to the issuing clerk. 1974 Ops Atty Gen Apr 23

There is no statutory restriction limiting the authority to solemnize marriages in New York State to clergymen resident therein. 1955 Ops St Compt 336

§ 2-a. Application

This chapter applies (a) to every corporation heretofore or hereafter formed under this chapter, and (b) to every corporation formed under any other statute or special act of this state which would, if it were to be formed currently under the laws of this state, be formed under this chapter, and (c) to every corporation formed under laws other than the statutes of this state which is authorized to conduct or which conducts activities in this state and which would, if it were to be formed currently under the laws of this state, be formed under this chapter.

History: Add, L 1971, ch 956, eff Sept 1, 1972.

§ 2-b. Applicability of not-for-profit corporation law

1. The not-for-profit corporation law applies to every corporation to which this chapter applies, provided that:

(a) If any provision of the not-for-profit corporation law conflicts with any provision of this chapter, the provision of this chapter shall prevail and the conflicting provision of the not-for-profit corporation law shall not apply in such case. If any provision of this chapter relates to a matter embraced in the not-for-profit corporation law but is not in conflict therewith, both provisions shall apply.

(b) A corporation to which the not-for-profit corporation law is made applicable by this section shall be treated as a "corporation", "domestic corporation", or "foreign corporation" as such terms are used in the not-for-profit corporation law, except that the purposes for which any such corporation has been or may be formed under this chapter shall not thereby be extended.

(c) The following provisions of the not-for-profit corporation law shall not apply to religious corporations: subparagraphs (7) and (8) of paragraph (a) of section one hundred twelve, section one hundred fourteen, section two hundred one, section three hundred three, section three hundred four, section three hundred five, section three hundred six, article four except section four hundred one, section five hundred fourteen, that portion of section five hundred fifty-five (b) and section five hundred fifty-five (c) which reads "The institution shall notify the donor, if available, and the attorney general of the application, and the attorney general and such donor must be given an opportunity to be heard", section six hundred five, section six hundred seven, section six hundred nine, section eight hundred four, article nine except section nine hundred ten, article ten except as provided in section eleven hundred fifteen, section eleven hundred two, and article fifteen except paragraph (c) of section fifteen hundred seven.

(d) Any reference in the not-for-profit corporation law to the delivery of any certificate or other instrument to the department of state for filing refers to the filing or recording thereof in the office of the clerk of the county in which the corporation has its principal office or place of worship or otherwise as provided in this chapter.

(d-1) Notwithstanding any provision of this chapter or the not-for-profit corporation law, any church referred to in subdivision two, three, four, five, five-a, five-b, five-c, or six of section twelve of this chapter shall not be required to give notice to the attorney general of any application required by subdivision one of section twelve of this chapter or any application or petition required under section five hundred ten or section five hundred eleven of the not-for-profit corporation law.

(e) No action shall be taken by the trustees of an incorporated Roman Catholic church, or of a Ruthenian Greek Catholic church, under section five hundred fifty-five of the not-for-profit corporation law (Release or modification of restrictions on management, investment, or purpose) without the consent of the archbishop or bishop of the diocese to which such church belongs or in case of their absence or inability to act, without the consent of the vicar general or administrator of such diocese.

2. Every corporation to which the not-for-profit corporation law is made applicable by this section is a charitable corporation as defined in paragraph (a) of section one hundred two (Definitions) of the not-for-profit corporation law for all purposes of that law.

3. From and after the effective date of this section the general corporation law shall not apply to any corporation to which this chapter applies.

4. For the purpose of this section and elsewhere in this chapter the effective date of the not-for-profit corporation law as to corporations to which the not-for-profit corporation law is made applicable by this section shall be September first, nineteen hundred seventy-two.

History: Add, L 1971, ch 956, eff Sept 1, 1972; amd, L 1978, ch 690, §§ 9, 10, eff July 25, 1978, L 1981, ch 244, §§ 1, 2, eff Sept 13, 1981, L 1981, ch 564, § 5, eff Sept 13, 1981, L 1982, ch 168, § 4, eff June 8, 1982, L 1985, ch 193, § 1, eff July 11, 1985, L 1992, ch 623, § 2, eff July 24, 1992, L 2010, ch 490, § 8, eff Sept 17, 2010, L 2013, ch 549, §§ 22, 23, eff July 1, 2014.

CASE ANNOTATIONS

Where purported accounting by nonprofit church corporation failed to comply with statutory requirement, church corporation was ordered to render an accounting of its assets and financial transactions for the period from October 1, 1974, to the date of the judgment. Anthony v Cardin (1977) 91 Misc. 2d 506, 398 N.Y.S.2d 215

Religious organization and its founder would be compelled to comply with subpoena issued by Attorney General in connection with investigation of fraudulent charitable solicitations since (1) religious

corporations are subject to provisions of Not-for-Profit Corporation Law, (2) while not required to register with and report annually to Attorney General under CLS EPTL § 8-1.4(b)(3), religious corporations are within Attorney General's subpoena power, and (3) investigation in question was not being conducted in bad faith or in manner disruptive to respondents' religious activity. Abrams v Temple of Lost Sheep, Inc. (1990) 148 Misc. 2d 825, 562 N.Y.S.2d 322

Subpoena issued by Attorney General in connection with investigation of fraudulent charitable solicitations, requiring religious organization and its founder to produce corporate books and records, would not be quashed on Fourth Amendment grounds since documents sought were not overly broad, burdensome or irrelevant to proper inquiry. Abrams v Temple of Lost Sheep, Inc. (1990) 148 Misc. 2d 825, 562 N.Y.S.2d 322

Religious organization and its founder could not refuse to comply with subpoena, issued by Attorney General in connection with investigation of fraudulent charitable solicitations, on ground that compliance with subpoena would deprive them of Fifth Amendment right against self-incrimination since neither religious organization nor its officers have Fifth Amendment rights against production of corporate records pursuant to lawful judicial order. Abrams v Temple of Lost Sheep, Inc. (1990) 148 Misc. 2d 825, 562 N.Y.S.2d 322

Delivery of summons and complaint to Secretary of State under CLS Bus Corp § 307 was not sufficient to confer jurisdiction over defendant religious corporation, and thus plaintiff's motion for default judgment was denied. Schoenthal v Beth Jacob Teachers Seminary of Am. (1998, Sup) 176 Misc. 2d 958, 675 N.Y.S.2d 756

Requirements that certain churches notify Attorney General when seeking leave of court to sell, mortgage or lease real property (CLS Relig Corp §§ 12 and 2-b(1)(d-1) do not violate either Establishment Clause or Free Exercise Clause. Greek Orthodox Archdiocese of N. & S. Am. v Abrams (1994, Sup) 162 Misc. 2d 850, 618 N.Y.S.2d 504

Requirements that certain churches notify Attorney General when seeking leave of court to sell, mortgage or lease real property, while exempting other churches which are hierarchically structured (CLS Relig Corp §§ 12 and 20b(1)(d-1)), do not unlawfully discriminate between religious denominations since (1) they meet compelling state interests of safeguarding potentially substantial proceeds from sales of property, and ensure that proceeds are properly disbursed, and (2) statutory obligations are narrowly tailored to meet objectives. Greek Orthodox Archdiocese of N. & S. Am. v Abrams (1994, Sup) 162 Misc. 2d 850, 618 N.Y.S.2d 504

Where a religious society did not follow its own by-law procedures and the trustees were considered "directors" under the Not-For-Profit Law and where neither N.Y. Relig. Corp. Law § 2-b(1)(a) nor NY. Not-For-Profit Corp. Law § 103(c) contained inconsistent provisions, they clearly did not preclude the removal of the trustees, the trial court erred in denying the members' petition to remove the trustees, invalidate the new by-laws, and appoint a referee. Venigalla v Alagappan (2003, A.D., 2d Dept) 763 N.Y.S.2d 765

Although N.Y. Not-for-Profit Corp. Law § 511(b) and N.Y. Relig. Corp. Law § 2-b(1)(d-1) did not require the Attorney General be made a party to a foreclosure action, the Attorney General should be given an opportunity to express an interest in the mortgagee's foreclosure proceeding. The Park Ave. Bank v Cong. & Yeshiva Ohel Yehoshea (2010, Sup) 907 NYS2d 571.

A religious corporation must obtain leave of court to sell any of its real estate or any interest therein to a municipality for a public purpose. 1982 Op Atty Gen Feb 19 (informal)

ARTICLE 2
GENERAL PROVISIONS

History: Add, L 1909, ch 53.

§ 3. Filing and recording certificates of incorporation of religious corporations

The certificate of incorporation of a religious corporation shall be acknowledged or proved before an officer authorized to take the acknowledgment or proof of deeds or conveyances of real estate, to be recorded in the county in which the principal office or place of worship of said corporation is or is intended to be situated, and shall be filed and recorded in the office of the clerk of said county. If there is not, or is not intended to be, any such office or place of worship, the certificate shall be filed and recorded in the office of the secretary of state. Where a religious corporation removes to another county within the state a duplicate copy of its certificate of incorporation together with a statement of such removal duly signed and acknowledged by the directors and officers of said corporation may be filed in the office of the clerk of said county to which it has removed.

The recording of any certificate of a religious corporation organized under provisions of "An act to provide for the incorporation of religious societies,"

passed April fifth, eighteen hundred and thirteen, and of the acts amending the same, in the office of a clerk of a county prior to the passage of chapter thirty-five of the laws of eighteen hundred and ninety-seven, instead of in the office of the register of such county, shall be regarded and construed and such recording is hereby declared to be of the same validity, force and effect as would have been the recording of such certificate in the proper office. And every act, deed, matter and thing done or performed by every such religious society or corporation since the recording of its certificate in the office of said county clerk is hereby ratified, confirmed and declared to be as valid in all respects as if the said certificate had been properly and appropriately recorded in the office of the register of the county in which said religious society or corporation was organized; but this section shall not affect any suit or proceeding already commenced arising out of such original mistake.

History: Add, L 1909, ch 53, amd, L 1921, ch 131, eff July 1, 1921.

First par, amd, L 1953, ch 757, eff Apr 16, 1953.

CASE ANNOTATIONS

In dispute concerning ownership of real property which had remained in possession and control of local church after it voted to disaffiliate itself from national church and diocese, plaintiffs (bishop and trustees of diocese) were entitled to summary judgment based on proof that local church and each of its predecessors was incorporated in accordance with canons and constitution of national church, which established that church property was held solely for benefit of national church and its dioceses. Trustees of the Diocese of Albany v Trinity Episcopal Church (1999, 3d Dept) 250 A.D.2d 282, 684 N.Y.S.2d 76

Evidence established that parish was incorporated into the Russian Orthodox Greek Catholic Church of America, the Metropolia, rather than the Synod of Bishops of the Russian Church in Exile and thus that the former remained as the supreme ecclesiastical body to govern the parish. Russian Church of Our Lady of Kazan v Dunkel (1971) 67 Misc. 2d 1032, 326 N.Y.S.2d 727, affd in part and mod in part on other grounds (2d Dept) 41 A.D.2d 746, 341 N.Y.S.2d 148, affd 33 N.Y.2d 456, 354 N.Y.S.2d 631, 310 N.E.2d 307

§ 4. Property of unincorporated society transferred by its incorporation

All the temporalities and property of an unincorporated church, or of any unincorporated religious society, body, association or congregation, shall, on the incorporation thereof, become the temporalities and property of such corporation, whether such temporalities or property be given, granted or devised directly to such unincorporated church, society, body, association or congregation, or to any other person for the use or benefit thereof.

History: Add, L 1909, ch 53, eff Feb 17, 1909.

CASE ANNOTATIONS

Under §§ 4 and 63, the legislature may vest an incorporated church with property of an unincorporated church although the incorporation organized by a majority vote of the members of the congregation was against the protest of the minority. Westminster Presbyterian Church v Trustees of Presbytery (1911) 142 A.D. 855, 127 N.Y.S. 836, app dismd 202 N.Y. 581, 96 N.E. 1134 and later app 152 A.D. 949, 137 N.Y.S. 1148

Nothing in this section or in plaintiff's certificate of incorporation would support plaintiff's claim of title to certain real property based merely upon its incorporation, in the absence of proof of compliance with § 190 et seq. and the parent church's assertion of title in designated trustees as set forth in a recorded "instrument of correction." Church of God of Prophecy v Ferris (1963, 3d Dept) 19 A.D.2d 934, 244 N.Y.S.2d 279

§ 4-a. Age qualifications of voters

To vote at a corporate meeting of a corporation to which this chapter applies, persons, otherwise qualified to vote, shall be of full age unless (1) the age qualifications for voting at corporate meetings are fixed by or pursuant to an applicable provision in articles three through nineteen of this chapter, or (2) in the absence of such provision, the certificate of incorporation or a by-law adopted by the members of such corporation specifies an age, less than full age but not less than the age of sixteen years, at which persons otherwise qualified to vote at corporate meetings, shall be entitled to vote for all purposes or as to particular types or classes of matters to be acted on at such meetings.

History: Add, L 1971, ch 201, eff Sept 1, 1971.

§ 5. General powers and duties of trustees of religious corporations

The trustees of every religious corporation shall have the custody and control of all the temporalities and property, real and personal, belonging to the corporation and of the revenues therefrom, and shall administer the same in accordance with the discipline, rules and usages of the corporation and of the ecclesiastical governing body, if any, to which the corporation is subject, and with the provisions of law relating thereto, for the support and maintenance of the corporation, or, providing the members of the corporation at a meeting thereof shall so authorize, of some religious, charitable, benevolent or educational object conducted by said corporation or in connection with it, or with the denomination, if any, with which it is connected; and they shall not use such property or revenues for any other purpose or divert the same from such uses. They may transfer all or any part of the real or personal estate of such corporation to such bank, trust company, savings bank or savings and loan association organized or existing under the laws of the state of New York, or to a national banking association, federal savings bank or federal savings and loan association having a principal, branch or trust office located in the state of New York as may be designated by them or to a holding company, organized under the laws of the state of New York, of the same religious denomination, such property to be held in trust or in safekeeping or custody, to collect the income thereof and pay over the same to the trustees of such religious corporation at such times and in such manner as shall be agreed upon, and they may also, in their discretion, delegate and grant to the trustee or custodian designated by them all or any portion of the powers, responsibilities and discretionary authority possessed by them with respect to the retention and the investment and reinvestment of such property or any part thereof, and may from time to time modify such powers delegated by them or designate successor or different trustees or custodians within the limits and subject to the regulations and restrictions contained in this section. The trustees of an incorporated Roman Catholic Church, or of a Ruthenian Greek Catholic Church, shall not transfer any property as herein provided without the consent of the archbishop or bishop of the diocese to which such church belongs or in case of their absence or inability to act, without the consent of the vicar general or administrator of such diocese. By-laws may be adopted or amended, by a two-thirds vote of the qualified voters present and voting at the meeting for incorporation or at any subsequent meeting, after written notice, embodying such by-laws or amendment, has been openly given at a previous meeting, and also in the notices of the meeting at which such proposed by-laws or amendment is to be acted upon. By-laws thus adopted or amended shall control the action of the trustees. But this section does not give to the trustees of an incorporated church, any control over the calling, settlement, dismissal or removal of its minister, or the fixing of his salary; or any power to fix or change the times, nature or order of the public or social worship of such church.

History: Add, L 1909, ch 53, amd, L 1925, ch 459, amd, L 1955, ch 90, eff Mar 14, 1955.

Amd, L 2005, ch 82, § 5, eff June 7, 2005.

CASE ANNOTATIONS

1. In general
2. Relationship with rules of governing church body
3. Power and authority of trustees, generally
4. Expulsion of members
5. Selection or removal of minister
6. Legality of particular activities and uses of funds
7. Merger or secession of congregations

1. In general

Resolution by court of internal dispute between church and parishioners, who sought declaratory judgment determining that church had spent funds in violation of CLS Relig Corp § 5, did not violate First Amendment prescription that religious bodies be left free to decide church matters for themselves uninhibited by state interference, because case could be decided on basis of statutory interpretation and common-law precedent without reference to matters of religious belief or dogma. Morris v Scribner (1987) 69 N.Y.2d 418, 515 N.Y.S.2d 424, 508 N.E.2d 136, reconsideration den 70 N.Y.2d 694, 512 N.E.2d 556

The Newark Annual Conference of the Methodist Church was properly awarded proceeds of a condemnation award made when church lands deeded in trustees of church in 1872 were appropriated. Successor to original trustees claimed award on theory church was independent and had not surrendered control to a religious denomination. History of particular church and the Methodist Episcopal Church showed that original grant implied a trust for the benefit of the present annual conference. Conklin v State (1954) 284 A.D. 193, 130 N.Y.S.2d 618

The proper church judiciary of an ecclesiastical body in which one holds membership and under whose tutelage one exercises religious functions is the proper forum for determination of questions affecting objects and interests of the moral and spiritual side of ecclesiastical discipline. Fairchild v Tillotson (1922) 118 Misc 639, 195 N.Y.S. 39

An allegation in a complaint alleging the breach of an executory accord by a religious organization that the offer of the defendant was made at a meeting duly called and duly held in accordance with the constitution and by-laws of the religious organization was a satisfactory allegation of compliance with the Religious Corporations Law.

Harbater v Congregation Beth Israel, Inc. (1953) 204 Misc 83, 119 N.Y.S.2d 700

Religious corporation law held liable for work and labor performed under purported contract even though there had been no specific resolution, enactment or authorization of the board for such work. Crest Chimney Cleaning Co. v Ahi Ezer Congregation (1970) 62 Misc. 2d 1040, 310 N.Y.S.2d 217

The objective of the statute is to provide an orderly method of administering the property and temporalities of religious groups and to protect them from exploitation by those who would divert them from the beneficiaries of the trust. Russian Church of Our Lady of Kazan v Dunkel (1971) 67 Misc. 2d 1032, 326 N.Y.S.2d 727, affd in part and mod in part on other grounds (2d Dept) 41 A.D.2d 746, 341 N.Y.S.2d 148, affd 33 N.Y.2d 456, 354 N.Y.S.2d 631, 310 N.E.2d 307

Evidence established that parish was incorporated into the Russian Orthodox Greek Catholic Church of America, the Metropolia, rather than the Synod of Bishops of the Russian Church in Exile and thus that the former remained as the supreme ecclesiastical body to govern the parish. Russian Church of Our Lady of Kazan v Dunkel (1971) 67 Misc. 2d 1032, 326 N.Y.S.2d 727, affd in part and mod in part on other grounds (2d Dept) 41 A.D.2d 746, 341 N.Y.S.2d 148, affd 33 N.Y.2d 456, 354 N.Y.S.2d 631, 310 N.E.2d 307

Statutory right of religious corporation to determine qualifications of membership could not be used as shield by Jewish Center against its contractual obligations to minority of congregation to allow it to utilize lower area of Center for separate Orthodox services for fee. Park Slope Jewish Center v Stern (1985) 128 Misc. 2d 909, 491 N.Y.S.2d 958

In action to recover for labor and services rendered by plaintiff at church, defendant religious corporation and church's pastor were not entitled to summary judgment on ground that church's board of trustees never expressly authorized work which plaintiff performed, as question of fact existed as to whether current work was constructively authorized by parties' prior practice and course of conduct, such as paying plaintiff for work previously performed by him at express request of pastor, who was also president of board of trustees. Butler v Sacred Heart of Jesus English Rite Catholic Church (1998, Civ Ct) 178 Misc. 2d 851, 680 N.Y.S.2d 909

Statute transferring control of church property from one rival group of members to another cannot be saved from invalidity under constitutional guaranty of freedom of religion on ground that legislature applied cy pres doctrine to trust in which property is held; in determining disposition or use of church property, civil courts are controlled by church rule when property right follows as incident from decisions of church custom or law on ecclesiastical issues; this necessarily follows from constitutional guaranty of freedom of religion. Kedroff v St. Nicholas Cathedral of Russian Orthodox Church (1952) 344 US 94, 97 L Ed 120, 73 S Ct 143

2. Relationship with rules of governing church body

The members of a religious association form the legal entity resulting from its incorporation, and the trustees are not the corporation and their powers of control are limited by § 5 to administration of the temporalities and properties of the corporation and the revenue therefrom "in accordance with the discipline, rules and usages of the corporation and of the ecclesiastical governing body, if any, to which the corporation is subject." Walker Memorial Baptist Church v Saunders (1941) 285 N.Y. 462, 35 N.E.2d 42, reh den 286 N.Y. 607, 35 N.E.2d 944

On motion for summary judgment, members of incorporated Protestant Episcopal Church were entitled to judgment declaring that church trustees had no authority, under church bylaws, to spend church funds on real estate development without first obtaining approval of majority of qualified voters, where (1) bylaws forbad trustees to "undertake the sale, mortgage, lease or other disposition of... property owned by the Church," (2) trustees nevertheless entered into contract with developer to construct office tower on church property, which was "undertaking" designed to dispose of property due to terms of lease with developer, (3) trustees never submitted terms of contract to parish for consideration and vote, and (4) trustees had already spent over $1,000,000 to date in compliance with contract; furthermore, members were entitled to preliminary injunction enjoining trustees from making further expenditures on real estate development. Morris v Scribner (1986, 1st Dept) 121 A.D.2d 912, 505 N.Y.S.2d 121

Under this section the property of a parish church must be administered according to the discipline, rules and usages of the governing church body. Fiske v Beaty (1922) 120 Misc 1, 198 N.Y.S. 358, mod on

other grounds 206 A.D. 349, 201 N.Y.S. 441, affd 238 N.Y. 598, 144 N.E. 907

The sections of the Religious Corporation Law applicable to the Roman Catholic Church must be read in conjunction with the Code of Canon Law of that church. Filetto v St. Mary of Assumption Church (1969) 61 Misc. 2d 278, 305 N.Y.S.2d 403

3. Power and authority of trustees, generally

The Religious Corporations Law entitles the Trustees of Presbytery to possession of property of a dissolved congregation since neither the former congregation, nor the trustees of the church have property rights in lands of the corporation dedicated in perpetuity to religious and charitable uses. Westminster Presbyterian Church v Trustees of Presbytery (1911) 142 A.D. 855, 127 N.Y.S. 836, app dismd 202 N.Y. 581, 96 N.E. 1134 and later app 152 A.D. 949, 137 N.Y.S. 1148

The Board of Trustees of a Baptist Church may commence legal action without the consent of a corporate meeting where it is necessary for the care and preservation of the corporate property. Calvary Baptist Church, Inc. v Williams (1972, 2d Dept) 38 A.D.2d 970, 331 N.Y.S.2d 792

Church members failed to demonstrate their entitlement to preliminary injunction allowing them to continue to use property owned by defendant religious corporation for religious services over defendant's objections, where they failed to show that they had legitimate claims to temporal control over property on which church was located, which was owned and controlled by defendant. Islamic Ctr. v Islamic Science Found. (1995, 2d Dept) 216 A.D.2d 357, 628 N.Y.S.2d 179

Because a meeting purportedly electing the successor trustees was not noticed in accordance with N.Y. Relig. Corp. Law § 162, the successor trustees were enjoined from exercising authority or control over the church's temporalities and property pursuant to N.Y. Relig. Corp. Law § 5. Trustees of Gallilee Pentecostal Church, Inc. v Williams (2009, 2d Dept) 65 App Div 3d 1221, 885 NYS2d 525.

The trustees of a religious corporation having a congregational form of government have no power to initiate proceedings to sell or mortgage the real property of corporation without the consent of its members. Re Beth Israel of Brownsville (1921) 114 Misc 582, 187 N.Y.S. 36

The trustees of a Congregational church have no authority to lease or mortgage church property without consent of its members. Bank of Manhattan Trust Co. v Twenty-One Sixty-Six Broadway Corp. (1932) 142 Misc 910, 256 N.Y.S. 553, affd 236 A.D. 781, 258 N.Y.S. 1046

An individual trustee of a religious corporation is not empowered to hire an attorney in behalf of the corporation. Krehel v Eastern Orthodox Catholic Church (1959) 22 Misc. 2d 522, 195 N.Y.S.2d 334, affd (1st Dept) 12 A.D.2d 465, 207 N.Y.S.2d 93, affd 10 N.Y.2d 831, 221 N.Y.S.2d 724, 178 N.E.2d 428

The powers of trustees of any church organization or religious society are subject to the control of courts of equity as far as are necessary. Crest Chimney Cleaning Co. v Ahi Ezer Congregation (1970) 62 Misc. 2d 1040, 310 N.Y.S.2d 217

Where a church's certificate of incorporation directed that annual elections were required in order to elect trustees, which were admittedly never held by the church but rather, the trustees assumed their positions by appointment, the court found that under N.Y. Relig. Corp. Law art. 10, §§ 193 and 194, the trustees were improperly in their positions and accordingly, it had not basis for affirming a pastor's position because there were no legally elected corporate officers of the church; additionally, pursuant to N.Y. Relig. Corp. Law art. 2, § 5, there were no duly elected trustees to assume "custody and control" of the church corporation's property. St. Matthew Church of Christ Disciples of Christ, Inc. v Creech (2003, Sup) 196 Misc. 2d 843, 768 N.Y.S.2d 111

When competing members of a religious community sought the validation of their election of the community's board of directors and the invalidation of rival members' election, such a decision could not be made by reference to neutral principles of law, and the tangential issues that would have to be decided required the impermissible application of ecclesiastical doctrine or law, so the competing petitions were dismissed. Congregation Yetev Lev DSatmar v Kahan (2004, Sup) 5 Misc 3d 1023A, 799 N.Y.S.2d 159

4. Expulsion of members

A member of a church who is expelled from membership must exhaust his administrative remedies within the church before making an application to the civil courts for redress. Rodyk v Ukrainian Autocephalic Orthodox Church (1968, 2d Dept) 31 A.D.2d

659, 296 N.Y.S.2d 496, affd 29 N.Y.2d 898, 328 N.Y.S.2d 685, 278 N.E.2d 917

A bylaw reading as follows: "Any member of this church who is found, after a hearing, to be a loyal student, follower, supporter or adherent of one who has been expelled from membership in the mother church by the Christian Science board of directors may be dropped from membership in the church by a two-thirds vote of the board of trustees.... Under this section of by-laws no admonition shall be necessary," was fully authorized by this section. Fairchild v Tillotson (1922) 118 Misc 639, 195 N.Y.S. 39

5. Selection or removal of minister

Trustees have no control "over the calling, settlement, dismissal or removal of its minister, or the fixing of his salary" nor may they "fix or change the times, nature or order of the public or social worship of such church." Walker Memorial Baptist Church v Saunders (1941) 285 N.Y. 462, 35 N.E.2d 42, reh den 286 N.Y. 607, 35 N.E.2d 944

A judgment dismissing plaintiffs' complaint was affirmed in suit to restrain defendants, trustees of a Greek Catholic church, selected in accordance with the corporate bylaws, giving them control of all "temporalities and property" belonging to the corporation from interfering with the occupancy and control by a pastor, selected by the bishop, of the parish house, church edifice and other property, where it appeared that this Greek Catholic congregation had incorporated under the Membership Corporations Law; that the bishop of the Greek Catholic Church united with Rome had selected a pastor approved by the plaintiffs, while the defendants, following a vote by the congregation, had selected another, and that nothing had been proven which affected the right of the church and congregation to continue as it began, an independent Greek Catholic church without affiliation with Rome or with successor or successors of the Russian Synod. Drozda v Bassos (1940) 260 A.D. 544, 23 N.Y.S.2d 544, app den 261 A.D. 864, 25 N.Y.S.2d 1013

A minister is not removable by the trustees of an incorporated church but by voting members at a corporate meeting, called and governed according to the discipline of the religious denomination with which the church is connected. Beulah Wesleyan Methodist Church v Henry (1946) 187 Misc 502, 62 N.Y.S.2d 297

6. Legality of particular activities and uses of funds

The defendants dressed in the garb of a nun would sit in public places and receive coins from the public in a metal cup held in their lap. Each defendant was in possession of a written certificate of authority to make collections in behalf of a duly organized religious corporation They acted under an agreement with the corporation whereby each defendant delivered $2.50 a day to the corporation and retained the remainder as personal compensation. Held: the main objective of the solicitation was personal gain and the defendants were guilty of obtaining money by false pretenses in violation of Penal Law § 934. People v Le Grande (1956) 309 N.Y. 420, 131 N.E.2d 712

Church's expenditure of funds to pursue plan for development of high-rise commercial office tower on portion of church property was reasonably incidental to "support and maintenance" of church within meaning of CLS Relig Corp § 5 where it was directed towards assuring that spiritual needs of church would be met; power to invest church funds in income-producing property would be implied from trustees' duty to preserve religious corporation's funds and court would not interfere in process in absence of allegations that trustees acted dishonestly or unfairly, or that they abandoned church purposes in favor of commercial enterprise. Morris v Scribner (1987) 69 N.Y.2d 418, 515 N.Y.S.2d 424, 508 N.E.2d 136, reconsideration den 70 N.Y.2d 694, 512 N.E.2d 556

The use of church funds in an effort to bring a community organizer to promote and encourage good housing standards and good citizenship and to provide social and recreational facilities in an underprivileged and impoverished area of Buffalo did not constitute a violation of § 5 of the Religious Corporations Law, where such usage had been passed upon and approved by the highest governing body of the church. Knight v Presbytery of Western New York (1966, 4th Dept) 26 A.D.2d 19, 270 N.Y.S.2d 218, affd 18 N.Y.2d 868, 276 N.Y.S.2d 120, 222 N.E.2d 738

A religious corporation engaged in making candle sticks for the purpose of maintaining its secular classes was not acting outside the scope of this section nor engaged in "profit making." Beth Jacob of Boro Park v Morgen Appliances (1949) 196 Misc 677, 94 N.Y.S.2d 398

The investment of church funds in income-producing realty for the purpose of producing revenue to accomplish the corporate objectives

is a legitimate use thereof; and there is not statutory limitation restricting investments to legals. Bowman v Bloomfield Management (1950) 197 Misc 523, 99 N.Y.S.2d 66

An action to recover realty brokerage commissions was improperly dismissed on the ground that the prospective purchaser, a religious corporation, had no legal right to invest its funds in income-producing realty. Bowman v Bloomfield Management (1950) 197 Misc 523, 99 N.Y.S.2d 66

A religious corporation may not distribute a specified sum to each of its members out of its general cash fund. Re Application of Congregation Beth David Anshey Roman (1954) 206 Misc 600, 133 N.Y.S.2d 589

A trust set up under this section by a religious corporation in personal property, as to which the church is the only person beneficially interested, may be revoked by the church pursuant to § 23 of the Personal Property Law. Re Gustavus Adolphus Evangelical Lutheran Church's Trust (1960) 26 Misc. 2d 644, 204 N.Y.S.2d 659

7. Merger or secession of congregations

When a congregation secedes, it cannot free itself from the rules of its denomination since no unjust enrichment from succession of denomination to beneficial use of church property on secession of congregation should be allowed and as to ownership of property, the rules of governing the denomination are controlling. Harlem Church of Seventh Day Adventists v Greater New York Corp. of Seventh Day Adventists (1935) 245 A.D. 292, 280 N.Y.S. 828, mod on other grounds 269 N.Y. 18, 198 N.E. 615

In the absence of a provision in church discipline forbidding secession, state law so forbidding, governs. Crawford v Freeman (1947) 189 Misc 882, 72 N.Y.S.2d 781

Where two Roman Catholic churches merged, it was irrelevant that some of the funds accumulated over the years by one church corporation were, in the minds of the parishioners, hopefully intended for construction of a new church edifice. Filetto v St. Mary of Assumption Church (1969) 61 Misc. 2d 278, 305 N.Y.S.2d 403

In light of the duty of trustees of religious corporations to administer the temporalities in accordance with the church discipline regardless of the wishes of the majority of the members, attempt by ad hoc committee of church which entered into a different ecclesiastical hierarchy to amend the parish bylaws to remove the parish from control of hierarchy was fruitless so long as a member of the parish professed allegience to such hierarchy, as the rebellion or secession could not terminate the relationship between the parish and the hierarchy. Russian Church of Our Lady of Kazan v Dunkel (1971) 67 Misc. 2d 1032, 326 N.Y.S.2d 727, affd in part and mod in part on other grounds (2d Dept) 41 A.D.2d 746, 341 N.Y.S.2d 148, affd 33 N.Y.2d 456, 354 N.Y.S.2d 631, 310 N.E.2d 307

§ 5-a. Investment of funds

Subject to the discipline, rules and usages of the corporation and of the ecclesiastical governing body, if any, to which the corporation is subject and subject to the limitations and conditions contained in any gift, devise or bequest, and subject to any applicable provisions of law with respect to the investment of funds for the perpetual care and maintenance of cemetery lots, the trustees of every religious corporation, created by or under a general or special law, may invest the funds of such corporation in such securities, investments or other property, real or personal, located within or without the state of New York, as to them shall seem advisable without being restricted to those classes of securities which are lawful for the investment of trust funds under the laws of this state. The trustees of an incorporated Roman Catholic church, or of a Ruthenian Greek Catholic church, shall not invest its funds as in this subdivision provided without the consent of the archbishop or bishop of the diocese to which such church belongs or in case of their absence or inability to act, without the consent of the vicar general or administrator of such diocese.

History: Add, L 1950, ch 225, amd, L 1954, ch 154, eff Mar 23, 1954.

Section heading add, L 1954, ch 154, eff Mar 23, 1954.

CASE ANNOTATIONS

The investment of church funds in income-producing realty for the purpose of producing revenue to accomplish the corporate objectives is a legitimate use thereof. Bowman v Bloomfield Management, Inc. (1949) 197 Misc 523, 99 N.Y.S.2d 66

An action to recover realty brokerage commissions was improperly dismissed on the ground that the prospective purchaser, a religious corporation, had no legal right to invest its funds in income-producing realty. Bowman v Bloomfield Management (1950) 197 Misc 523, 99 N.Y.S.2d 66

The investment of surplus funds of a religious corporation in business or for speculative purposes is not within the powers granted religious corporations under this law. Bowman v Bloomfield Management (1950) 197 Misc 523, 99 N.Y.S.2d 66, revg 195 Misc 192, 87 N.Y.S.2d 857

§ 5-b. [Application to prior investments]

Any investment of the funds of any religious corporation heretofore made by the trustees thereof shall not be deemed to have been restricted to securities which are lawful for the investment of trust funds.

History: Add, L 1950, ch 225, eff Mar 28, 1950.

§ 6. Acquisition of property by religious corporations for branch institutions; establishment, maintenance and management thereof

Any religious corporation may acquire property for associate houses, church buildings, chapels, mission-houses, school-houses for Sunday or parochial schools, or dispensaries of medicine for its ministers, their wives, husbands and dependent children and for the poor, or property for the residence of its ministers, their wives, husbands and dependent children, teachers or employees, or property for a home for the aged or nursery school or day care center. The persons attending public worship in any such associate house, mission-house, church building, or chapel connected therewith shall not by reason thereof have any rights as members of the parent corporation. The persons statedly worshiping in any such house, mission-house, church building or chapel may, with the consent of the trustees of such corporation, become separately incorporated as a church, and the parent corporation may, in pursuance of the provisions of law regulating the disposition of real property by religious corporations, rent or convey to the new corporation, with or without consideration, any such associate house, church building, chapel, mission-house, school-house or dispensary and the lot connected therewith, subject to such regulations as the trustees of the parent corporation may make. Any religious corporation shall have power to establish, maintain and manage by its trustees or other officers as a part of its religious purpose a home for the aged or nursery school or day care center, and may take and hold by conveyance, donation, bequest or devise real and personal property for such purpose, and may

purchase and may erect suitable buildings therefor. Any such corporation may take and hold any grant, donation, bequest or devise of real or personal property heretofore or hereafter made upon trust, and apply the same, or the income thereof, under the direction of its trustees or other officers, for the purpose of establishing, maintaining and managing such a home, school or center and for the erection, preservation, repair or extension of any building or buildings for such purpose.

History: Add, L 1909, ch 53, amd, L 1953, ch 330, L 1972, ch 606, eff May 24, 1972.

CASE ANNOTATIONS

Determination by town zoning board of appeals that proposed use of land did not fall within broad definition of "religious use" under local zoning ordinance was neither arbitrary nor capricious where petitioner, not-for-profit corporation which operated private school for Jewish children, was seeking permit to change use of premises from one-family residence to center for study of Nazi persecution of Jews, for despite flexible standard for interpreting religious uses under local zoning ordinances, that flexibility is directed to ancillary or accessory functions of religious institutions whose principal use is place of worship, and mere affiliation with or supervision by religious organizations does not, per se, transform institutions into religious ones. Yeshiva & Mesivta Toras Chaim v Rose (1988, 2d Dept) 136 A.D.2d 710, 523 N.Y.S.2d 907

Church members failed to demonstrate their entitlement to preliminary injunction allowing them to continue to use property owned by defendant religious corporation for religious services over defendant's objections, where they failed to show that they had legitimate claims to temporal control over property on which church was located, which was owned and controlled by defendant. Islamic Ctr. v Islamic Science Found. (1995, 2d Dept) 216 A.D.2d 357, 628 N.Y.S.2d 179

§ 7. Acquisition of property by religious corporations for cemetery purposes; management thereof

A religious corporation may take and hold, by purchase, grant, gift or devise, real property for the purposes of a cemetery; or such lot or lots in any cemetery connected with it, as may be conveyed or devised to it, with or without provisions limiting interments therein to particular persons or classes of persons; and may take and hold any property granted, given, devised or bequeathed to it in trust to apply the same or the income or proceeds thereof, under the direction of the trustees of the corporation, for the improvement or embellishment of such cemetery or any lot therein, including the erection, repair, preservation or removal of tombs, monuments, gravestones, fences, railings or other erections, or the planting or cultivation of trees, shubs, plants, or flowers in or around any such cemetery or cemetery lots.

A religious corporation may erect upon any property held by it for cemetery purposes, a suitable building for religious services for the burial of the dead, or for the use of the keepers or other persons employed in connection therewith, and may sell and convey lots in such cemetery for burial purposes, subject to such conditions and restrictions as may be imposed by the instrument by which the same was acquired, or by the rules and regulations adopted by such corporation. Every such conveyance of a lot or plat for burial purposes, signed, sealed and acknowledged in the same manner as a deed to be recorded, may be recorded in like manner and with like effect as a deed of real property.

Notwithstanding the provisions of section four hundred fifty-one of the real property law or any other provision of law to the contrary, a religious corporation that prior to January first, nineteen hundred eighty-four received a special permit from the zoning board of appeals for the use of certain real property as a cemetery and which actually used such real property for cemetery purposes, may use such real property for cemetery purposes without the consent of the county legislative body for the county in which such real property is situated.

No religious corporation owning, managing or controlling a cemetery shall, directly or indirectly:

(a) sell, or have, enter into or perform a lease of any of its real property dedicated to cemetery purposes or adjacent thereto to a funeral entity, or use any of its property for locating a funeral entity;

(b) commingle its funds with a funeral entity;

(c) direct or carry on its cemetery related business or affairs with a funeral entity;

(d) authorize control of its cemetery related business or affairs by a funeral entity;

(e) engage in any sale or cross-marketing of goods or services with a funeral entity;

(f) have, enter into or perform a management or service contract for cemetery operations with a funeral entity; or

(g) have, enter into or perform a management contract with any entity other than a not-for-profit cemetery or religious corporation.

Only the provisions of subparagraphs (a) and (b) of the previous paragraph shall apply to religious corporations with thirty acres or less of real property dedicated to cemetery purposes, and only to the extent the sale or lease is of real property dedicated to cemetery purposes, and such cemeteries shall not engage in the sale of funeral home goods or services, except if such goods and services are otherwise permitted to be sold by cemeteries. No religious corporation shall approve or authorize the construction of a mausoleum or columbarium on property owned by the religious corporation where such mausoleum or columbarium shall be the only form of interment offered for cemetery purposes unless a management contract has been entered into with an existing cemetery corporation regulated under article fifteen of the not-for-profit corporation law, that will provide operational management of the mausoleum or columbarium, and the owner of the mausoleum or columbarium has reserved interment space and secured interment services in a cemetery regulated under this article, in order to assure continued perpetual care of the remains contained in the mausoleum or columbarium should such mausoleum or

columbarium become abandoned or choose to cease operations.

History: Add, L 1909, ch 53, eff Feb 17, 1909; amd, L 1993, ch 712, § 1, eff Aug 6, 1993; L 1998, ch 560, § 7, eff Sept 4, 1998; L 2018, ch 296, § 3, eff Oct 1, 2018.

Blackline Showing Effect of 2018 Amendments. — A religious corporation may take and hold, by purchase, grant, gift or devise, real property for the purposes of a cemetery; or such lot or lots in any cemetery connected with it, as may be conveyed or devised to it, with or without provisions limiting interments therein to particular persons or classes of persons; and may take and hold any property granted, given, devised or bequeathed to it in trust to apply the same or the income or proceeds thereof, under the direction of the trustees of the corporation, for the improvement or embellishment of such cemetery or any lot therein, including the erection, repair, preservation or removal of tombs, monuments, gravestones, fences, railings or other erections, or the planting or cultivation of trees, shubs, plants, or flowers in or around any such cemetery or cemetery lots.

A religious corporation may erect upon any property held by it for cemetery purposes, a suitable building for religious services for the burial of the dead, or for the use of the keepers or other persons employed in connection therewith, and may sell and convey lots in such cemetery for burial purposes, subject to such conditions and restrictions as may be imposed by the instrument by which the same was acquired, or by the rules and regulations adopted by such corporation. Every such conveyance of a lot or plat for burial purposes, signed, sealed and acknowledged in the same manner as a deed to be recorded, may be recorded in like manner and with like effect as a deed of real property.

Notwithstanding the provisions of section four hundred fifty-one of the real property law or any other provision of law to the contrary, a religious corporation that prior to January first, nineteen hundred eighty-four received a special permit from the zoning board of appeals for the use of certain real property as a cemetery and which actually used such real property for cemetery purposes, may use such real property for cemetery purposes without the consent of the county legislative body for the county in which such real property is situated.

No religious corporation owning, managing or controlling a cemetery shall, directly or indirectly:

(a) sell, or have, enter into or perform a lease of any of its real property dedicated to cemetery purposes or adjacent thereto to a funeral entity, or use any of its property for locating a funeral entity;

(b) commingle its funds with a funeral entity;

(c) direct or carry on its cemetery related business or affairs with a funeral entity;

(d) authorize control of its cemetery related business or affairs by a funeral entity;

(e) engage in any sale or cross-marketing of goods or services with a funeral entity;

(f) have, enter into or perform a management or service contract for cemetery operations with a funeral entity; or

(g) have, enter into or perform a management contract with any entity other than a not-for-profit cemetery or religious corporation.

Only the provisions of subparagraphs (a) and (b) of the previous paragraph shall apply to religious corporations with thirty acres or less of real property dedicated to cemetery purposes, and only to the extent the sale or lease is of real property dedicated to cemetery purposes, and such cemeteries shall not engage in the sale of funeral home goods or services, except if such goods and services are otherwise permitted to be sold by cemeteries. No religious corporation shall approve or authorize the construction of a mausoleum or columbarium on property owned by the religious corporation where such mausoleum or columbarium shall be the only form of interment offered for cemetery purposes unless a management contract has been entered into with an existing cemetery corporation regulated under article fifteen of the not-for-profit corporation law, that will provide operational management of the mausoleum or columbarium, and the owner of the mausoleum or columbarium has reserved interment space and secured interment services in a cemetery regulated under this article, in order to assure continued perpetual care of the remains contained in the mausoleum or columbarium should such mausoleum or columbarium become abandoned or choose to cease operations.

Religious Corporations Law

CASE ANNOTATIONS

A contention that the statute under which defendant was organized (L 1801 c 79) and this section, authorize defendant to hold and use its land for cemetery purposes and that, consequently, it is excepted from the prohibition of Real Property Law, § 451, § 1539-a of the city charter, by neither of which statutes is the right of a religious corporation to take and hold land for burial purposes expressly repealed, cannot be sustained. Moritz v United Brethrens Church (1935) 269 N.Y. 125, 199 N.E. 29

A contention that, as this section has not been expressly repealed, it should not be treated as repealed by implication, cannot be upheld. Where the intent of the legislature is clear, and a later local statute covers the whole subject so far as local territory is concerned, the local statute is treated as intended as a substitute for, and repeal pro tanto of, an earlier general statute. The intent by amendment of the local statute to except Richmond county from the general provisions of the general law is unmistakable and such intent must be given effect by holding that the local statute excepts Richmond county from the general provisions of this section. Moritz v United Brethrens Church (1935) 269 N.Y. 125, 199 N.E. 29

A religious corporation which maintains a cemetery under authority of this section is not liable in damages to relatives of decedent whose body was stolen from its grave in the cemetery by unknown persons, on the theory that it was negligent in failing properly to protect the grave. Coleman v St. Michael's Protestant Episcopal Church (1915) 170 A.D. 658, 155 N.Y.S. 1036

Under this section a religious corporation which has entered into a contract for the purchase of additional lands in Erie county to be used in connection with its present cemetery, is not required as a prerequisite to such use of lands to procure permission of the board of supervisors, notwithstanding the provisions of the Membership Corporations Law, § 73. Wojtkowiak v Evangelical Lutheran St. John's Church (1932) 236 A.D. 411, 259 N.Y.S. 481, affd 261 N.Y. 656, 185 N.E. 779

Cemetery lands are exempt from general taxation and assessment for local improvements. St. Stanislaus Church Soc. v Erie County (1934) 153 Misc 511, 275 N.Y.S. 84

This section will not protect church trustees from tort liability for acts done in connection with a cemetery adjoining church property unless the cemetery is a church, as contrasted with a public, cemetery and owned and controlled by the church. Conn v Boylan (1962, Sup) 224 N.Y.S.2d 823

Where neither the existing church, nor any of its predecessor church bodies, ever had title to the land comprising a cemetery adjoining the church site, the cemetery could not be considered a church cemetery within the provisions of this section. Conn v Boylan (1962, Sup) 224 N.Y.S.2d 823

A village board of cemetery commissioners may accept the conveyance of a church cemetery which is to become part of a village cemetery, provided the conveyance by the church is authorized by appropriate court order. The village board of cemetery commissioners and county treasurer may accept and administer perpetual care funds for cemetery purposes. 1947 Ops Compt 395

§ 7-a. Deeds for cemetery purposes; presumption

Every deed of conveyance of real property to a religious corporation used for cemetery purposes, whether heretofore or hereafter recorded, shall be presumptive evidence that the conveyance vested in the grantee and its successors a fee simple absolute in the premises therein described, subject to the limitations and conditions therein prescribed, and that all proceedings prior thereto, including the consent of the court, if required, were regular and in accordance with all the provisions of law relating thereto. At the expiration of twenty years from the date of record of any such conveyance, heretofore or hereafter recorded, such presumption shall be conclusive.

History: Add, L 1929, ch 604, eff Apr 12, 1929.

§ 8. Lot owner's rights

Lots in such cemeteries shall be held indivisible, and upon the decease of a proprietor of such lot the title thereto shall descend to his heirs-at-law or devisees, subject, however, to the following limitations and conditions: If he leaves a widow and children, they shall have in common the possession, care and control of such lot during her life. If he leaves a widow and no children, she shall have the possession, care and control of such lot during her life. If he leaves children and no widow, they, or the survivor of them, shall in common have the possession, care and control of such lot during the life of the survivor of them. The parties having such possession, care and control of such lot during the term thereof, may erect a monument and make other permanent improvements thereon. The widow shall have the right of interment, for her own body in such lot, or in a tomb in such lot and a right to have her body remain permanently interred or entombed therein, except that her body may be removed therefrom to some other family lot or tomb with the consent of her heirs. At any time when more than one person is entitled to the possession, care or control of such lot, the persons so entitled thereto shall designate in writing to the religious corporation which of their number shall represent the lot, and on their failure to designate, the board of trustees or directors of the corporation shall enter of record which of said parties shall represent the lot, while such failure continues. The widow may at any time release her right in such lot, but no conveyance or devise by any other person shall deprive her of such right.

History: Add, L 1909, ch 53, eff Feb 17, 1909.

CASE ANNOTATIONS

An administratrix, as such, possesses no rights with respect to decedent's burial plot. Re Rosen (1940) 173 Misc 433, 17 N.Y.S.2d 794

The purchaser of a cemetery plot acquires no title to the soil but merely an easement or right of burial, and in so far as this has not been exhausted by the purchaser himself, it descends pursuant to the Religious Corporations Law, § 8, Membership Corporations Law, § 84, and General Municipal Law, § 163. Re Rosen (1940) 173 Misc 433, 17 N.Y.S.2d 794

The next of kin of the original purchaser of a cemetery plot are entitled to its use. O'Shaughnessy v John J. Barrett, Inc. (1946) 186 Misc 1040, 66 N.Y.S.2d 4

Since this section makes the title to cemetery lots descend to the heirs at law of the owner, and, under §§ 47-c and 83 of the Decedent Estate Law "heirs" includes children of deceased children, the latter are indispensable parties to an action for declaratory judgment by the owner's surviving child as to his right to designate whose remains may be interred in the remaining graves. Heymann v Union Temple of Brooklyn (1962) 38 Misc. 2d 225, 239 N.Y.S.2d 556

Although N.Y. Relig. Corp. Law § 8 provides for the designation of a representative for a burial plot that has more than one owner, nothing in the statute gives the person so designated any greater rights of possession, care, or control than his or her co-owners; thus, although a trial court properly found that the nephew and spouse of a decedent jointly owned a burial plot purchased by the decedent's father, it erred when it found that the spouse had the exclusive right to possession and control of the lot based on her status as the family representative. Bergman v Feinberg (2004, A.D., 3d Dept) 776 N.Y.S.2d 611

The term widow under N.Y. Relig. Corp. Law § 8 clearly refers back to that of the "proprietor." Bergman v Feinberg (2004, A.D., 3d Dept) 776 N.Y.S.2d 611

A religious corporation may not construct a church structure over a portion of a church cemetery owned by such religious corporation, though no burials have been made since 1912 and no excavation or disturbance of the graves will occur. 1955 St Compt File #7247

§ 8-a. Reacquisition of a lot, plot or part thereof by a cemetery

A religious cemetery corporation may, upon application and approval by a supreme court, reacquire, resubdivide, and resell a lot, plot or part thereof under the following circumstances:

(a)(i) If the records of the corporation demonstrate that the lot, plot or part thereof was purchased more than seventy-five years prior to the application of the corporation; and (ii) if no burials have been made in the lot, plot or part thereof or all the bodies therein have been lawfully removed; and (iii) if neither the owner or owners of the lot, plot or part thereof nor any person having a credible claim to ownership who has visited, made payments in respect of or engaged in any other proprietary activities with respect to the lot, plot or part thereof can be identified after a reasonable search conducted by the religious cemetery corporation, it shall be conclusively presumed that the owner or owners of the lot, plot or part thereof have abandoned their burial rights. A reasonable search consists of a search of: (1) all cemetery records to determine the name of the owner or owners of the lot, plot or part thereof, their last known addresses and all information available to the cemetery relating to any person buried in the lot, plot or part thereof and the names and last known addresses of any persons making inquiry about or visiting the lot, plot or part thereof; (2) a search for the death certificates and the probated wills of the owner or owners of the lot, plot or part thereof; (3) the posting of notice by the cemetery at the entrance to the cemetery, at the site of the lot, plot or part thereof to be reacquired and in the cemetery office, if any, of its intention to declare the lot, plot or part thereof abandoned; (4) the mailing of such notice certified mail with return receipt requested to the owner or owners of the lot, plot or part thereof and each person identified during the reasonable search at their last known addresses; (5) publication of such notice once in each week for three successive weeks, in two newspapers of regular commercial circulation by subscription and/or newsstand sale, to be designated by the county clerk of the county where the cemetery is located which in his or her judgment, given the ethnic, religious, geographic or other related demographic characteristics of the owner or owners of the lot, plot or part thereof and each person identified through the reasonable search and the predominant readership of such newspapers are best calculated to inform the owner or owners of the lot, plot or part thereof and each person identified through the reasonable search of any application pursuant to the provisions of this section; and (6) the preparation of an affidavit describing the steps taken by the religious cemetery corporation to ascertain the identity of and to contact the current owner or owners of the lot, plot or part thereof or next-of-kin thereof or any other persons identified in the course of the reasonable search who might have relevant information and the results of such steps. After the filing with the supreme court of proof of compliance with the above requirements in form and substance reasonably satisfactory to such supreme court and upon approval by the supreme court, the lot, plot or part thereof may be resold by the cemetery to any party in compliance with the cemetery rules and regulations provided, however, that any monument subsequently placed on such lot, plot or part thereof shall conform to the general appearance of any existing monuments in said section of lots, plots or parts thereof, if any.

(b) If (i) the circumstances described in subdivision (a) of this section exist except that one or more burials have been made in a lot, and the last burial was made more than seventy-five years prior to the application, (ii) the lot, plot or part thereof can be subdivided to create new graves, (iii) the bodies have not been lawfully removed, and (iv) the cemetery submits an application to the supreme court which complies with the requirements set forth in subdivision (a) of this section, it shall be conclusively presumed that the lot owner has abandoned the right to make further burials in the lot, the lot may be subdivided, and the resubdivided lot, plot or parts thereof which do not contain the remains of the deceased persons may be resold by the religious cemetery corporation as provided in this section. Nothing in this section shall permit a religious cemetery corporation to declare abandoned a lot, plot or part thereof, where such lot, plot or part thereof was purchased for multiple depth burials and where one or more burials has occurred or authorized a religious cemetery corporation to remove a monument or other embellishment to facilitate the resale of such lot, plot or part thereof.

(c) If the owner or owners of a lot, plot or part thereof can be identified, the religious cemetery corporation, with the consent of the owner or owners of the lot, plot or part thereof, the lot, plot or part thereof may be resubdivided, and the resubdivided lot, plot or part thereof which does not contain the remains of deceased persons may be resold by the religious cemetery corporation, provided, however, if no burial has been made in the lot, plot or part hereof, in the twenty-five year period preceding such application, the owner of a lot, plot or part thereof has notified his or her parents, spouse, issue, brothers, sisters, grandparents, and grandchildren, if any, of the application to the supreme court, and provided further, however, if a burial has been made in this lot, plot or part thereof during such twenty-five year period, the spouse and issue of such deceased person are also notified, and provided further, in either case the owner of the lot, plot or part thereof satisfies the supreme court that none of the persons notified have agreed within forty-five days of notification to purchase the lot, plot or part thereof at the price which the religious cemetery corporation shall certify under penalty of law shall be the price at which the lot, plot or part thereof shall be sold for after reacquisition. Any persons notified pursuant to this subdivision by the identified owner or owners of the lot, plot or part thereof must agree to erect a monument of reasonable uniformity to the immediately surrounding monuments as provided in subdivision (f) of this section before the persons notified may enter into an agreement to purchase the lot, plot or part thereof.

(d) Upon the sale of a lot, plot or part thereof reacquired by a religious cemetery corporation under the provisions of subdivision (a), (b), or (c) of this section, the net proceeds shall be placed in a trust designated to provide future maintenance of the cemetery.

(e) If the owner of the lot, plot or part thereof is subsequently identified, the religious cemetery corporation shall: (i) return all unsold lots, plots or parts thereof if any, to the owner if so requested; and (ii) with respect to any lots, plots or parts thereof that have been sold pursuant to this section, at the option of the owner of the lot, plot or part thereof, either (1) provide the owner, at no cost to the owner, with a lot, plot or part thereof comparable to any lot, plot or part thereof that was sold by the religious cemetery corporation or (2) provide the owner with the proceeds from the sale of the lot, plot or part thereof reacquired under this section with interest thereon from the date of the sale at six percent per annum.

(f) Monuments to be erected on a lot, plot or part thereof, following the resale of a lot, plot or part thereof, shall conform to the rules and regulations or other requirements of the religious cemetery corporation and shall conform to the size, style, and type of monuments in the section of the cemetery where such resale occurs.

(g) No corporation shall utilize the reacquisition provisions of this section in violation of such corporation's sectarian burial requirements.

History: L 2015, ch 547, § 1, eff Jan 10, 2016.

§ 9. Removal of human remains from one cemetery of a religious corporation to another cemetery owned by it

A religious corporation, notwithstanding the restrictions contained in any conveyance or devise to it, may remove the human remains buried in a cemetery owned by it, or when such church corporation is situated within or outside of a city in the grounds surrounding the church belonging to such corporation, to another cemetery owned by it, or to a plot or lot acquired by it in any other cemetery located in the same county, or in any town adjoining the town or city in which the cemetery wherein such human remains are buried is located, if the trustees thereof so determine, and if either three-fourths of the members of such corporation, qualified to vote at its corporate meetings, sign and acknowledge and cause to be recorded in the office of the clerk of the county in which such cemetery or a part thereof is situated, a written consent thereto, or if approval thereof be given by the vote of three-fourths of those members of such corporation qualified to vote, who shall be present and vote thereon, at a corporate meeting of such corporation, specially called for that purpose, a quorum of at least eight qualified voters being present. Provided, however, that in lieu of such removal by such religious corporation it shall be lawful for the surviving spouse or any heir of any decedent, upon obtaining permission of the county court of the county, or of the supreme court in the district, where the cemetery from which the removal is proposed, is situated, at his own expense to cause the removal of such remains and tombstones, monuments or other erections and the reinterment of such remains and the replacement of such tombstones, monuments or other erections in some other cemetery selected by the applicant, the notice of which application for permission to be given in the manner and to those designated by the court. But if such corporation be a church, previous notice of the object of such meeting shall be published once each week for at least four successive weeks in a newspaper of the town, village or city in which the cemetery from which the removal is proposed, is situated, or if no newspaper is published therein, then in a newspaper designated by the county judge of such county. Such removal shall be made in an appropriate manner and in accordance with such directions as to the manner thereof, as may be given by the board of health of the town, village or city in which the cemetery from which the removal is made, is situated. All tombstones, monuments or other erections at or upon any grave from which any remains are removed, shall be properly replaced or raised at the grave where the remains are reinterred. Such religious corporation may, in its discretion, erect one or more tombstones, monuments or other suitable markers appropriately inscribed as a memorial for all those decedents whose remains shall not be found for removal or reinterment, but the said religious corporation shall make a certificate setting forth an exact copy of all inscriptions on each tombstone, monument, or other erection which shall not be replaced or raised because of failure to find remains for removal and reinterment, and shall file the same in the cemetery office or in the office of the town or city clerk of the town or city in which the cemetery from which removal is proposed, is situated; all tombstones, monuments or other erections not so replaced or raised shall be disposed of by such religious corporation as it shall determine and such certificate, in addition to such inscriptions, shall state the disposition so made.

History: Add, L 1909, ch 53, amd, L 1950, ch 224, eff Mar 28, 1950.

§ 10. Acquisition of property by two or more religious corporations for a common parsonage

Two or more religious corporations may acquire such real property as may be necessary for use as a parsonage, and the right, title and interest of each corporation therein shall be in proportion to its contribution to the cost of such property. The trustees of each corporation shall, from time to time, appoint one of their number to be a trustee of such common parsonage property, to hold office during the pleasure of the appointing trustees or until his successor be appointed. The trustees so appointed shall have the care and management of such property and may make such improvements thereupon as they deem necessary, and determine the proportion of the expense of the maintenance thereof which each corporation shall bear. If at any time either of such corporations acquires or desires to acquire for its own exclusive use as a parsonage other real property, it may, in pursuance of the provisions of law, relating to the disposition of real property by religious corporations, sell and convey its interest in such common parsonage property to any one or more of the other corporations having an interest therein.

History: Add, L 1909, ch 53, eff Feb 17, 1909.

§ 11. Correction and confirmation of conveyances to religious corporations

If, in a conveyance of real property, or in any instrument intended to operate as such, heretofore or hereafter made to a religious corporation, its corporate name is not stated or is not correctly stated, but such conveyance or instrument indicates the intention of the grantor therein to convey such property to such corporation, and such corporation has entered into possession and occupation of such property, any officer of the corporation authorized so to do by its trustees may record in the office where such conveyance or instrument is recorded a statement, signed and acknowledged by him or proved, setting forth the date of such conveyance or instrument, the date of record and the number and page of the book of record thereof, the name of the grantor, a description of the property conveyed or intended to be conveyed, the name of the grantee as expressed in such conveyance or instrument, the correct name of such corporation, the fact of authorization by the trustees of the corporation, to make and record such statement, and that the grantor in such conveyance or instrument intended thereby to convey such property to such corporation as the said officer verily believes, with the reason for such belief. Such statement so signed and acknowledged or proved shall be recorded with the records of deeds in such office, and indexed as a deed from the grantee as named in such instrument or in such conveyance to such corporation. The register or clerk, as the case may be, shall note the recording of such statement on the margin of the record of such conveyance, and for his services shall be entitled to receive the fees allowed for recording deeds. Such statement so recorded shall be presumptive evidence that such matters therein stated are true, and that such corporation was the grantee in the original instrument or conveyance. All conveyances heretofore made, or by any instrument intended to be made, to a religious corporation of real property appropriated to the use of such corporation, or entitled to be so appropriated, are hereby confirmed and declared valid and effectual, notwithstanding any defect in the form of the conveyance or the description of the grantee therein.

History: Add, L 1909, ch 53, eff Feb 17, 1909.

§ 12. Sale, mortgage and lease of real property of religious corporations

1. A religious corporation shall not sell, mortgage or lease for a term exceeding five years any of its real property without applying for and obtaining leave of the court or the attorney general therefor pursuant to section five hundred eleven of the not-for-profit corporation law as that section is modified by paragraph (d-1) of subdivision one of section two-b of this chapter or section five hundred eleven-a of the not-for-profit corporation law, except that a religious corporation may execute a purchase money mortgage or a purchase money security agreement creating a security interest in personal property purchased by it without obtaining leave of the court therefor.

2. The trustees of an incorporated Protestant Episcopal church shall not vote upon any resolution or proposition for the sale, mortgage or lease of its real property, unless the rector of such church, if it then has a rector, shall be present, and shall not make application to the court for leave to sell or mortgage any of its real property without the consent of the bishop and standing committee of the diocese to which such church belongs, or execute and deliver a lease of any of its real property for a term exceeding five years without similar consent of the bishop and standing committee of the diocese to which such church belongs; but in case the see be vacant, or the bishop be absent or unable to act, the consent of the standing committee with their certificate of the vacancy of the see or of the absence or disability of the bishop shall suffice.

3. The trustees of an incorporated Roman Catholic church shall not make application to the court for leave to mortgage, lease or sell any of its real property without the consent of the archbishop or bishop of the diocese to which such church belongs or in case of their absence or inability to act, without the consent of the vicar-general or administrator of such diocese.

4. The trustees of an incorporated Ruthenian Catholic church of the Greek rite shall not make application to the court for leave to mortgage, lease or sell any of its real property without the consent in writing of the Ruthenian Greek Catholic bishop of the diocese to which such church belongs, or, in case of his absence or inability to act, without the consent of

the vicar-general of such bishop or of the administrator of such diocese.

5. The trustees of an incorporated African Methodist Episcopal Zion church shall not make application to the court for leave to mortgage, lease or sell any of its real property without the consent of the bishop of the diocese to which said church belongs, or in case of his absence or inability to act, without the consent of the annual conference having jurisdiction over such church.

5-a. The trustees of an incorporated Presbyterian church in connection with the General Assembly of the Presbyterian Church (U.S.A.) shall not make application to the court for leave to mortgage, lease or sell any of its real property without the consent in writing of the particular Presbytery with which said church is connected.

5-b. The trustees of an incorporated United Methodist church shall not make application to the court for leave to mortgage, lease, or sell any of its real property without the written consents of the district superintendent and the preacher in charge and the authorization of the charge conference by a majority of those present and voting at a meeting of the charge conference, provided that not less than ten days' notice of such meeting and proposed action shall have been given from the pulpit of the charge, or, if no regular services are held, by mail to the members of the charge conference.

5-c. The trustees of an incorporated Reformed Church in connection with the General Synod of the Reformed Church in America, shall not make application to the court for leave to mortgage, lease or sell any of its real property without the consent in writing of the trustees of the Classis with which said church is connected.

6. The petition of the trustees of an incorporated Protestant Episcopal church or Roman Catholic church shall, in addition to the matters required by article five of the not-for-profit corporation law to be set forth therein, set forth that this section has also been complied with. The petition of the trustees of an incorporated African Methodist Episcopal Zion church shall in addition to the matters required by article five of the not-for-profit corporation law to be set forth therein, set forth that this section has also been complied with. The petition of the trustees of an incorporated Presbyterian church in connection with the General Assembly of the Presbyterian Church (U.S.A.), shall, in addition to the matters required by article five of the not-for-profit corporation law to be set forth therein, set forth that this section has also been complied with. The petition of the trustees of an incorporated United Methodist church shall, in addition to the matters required by article five of the not-for-profit corporation law to be set forth therein, set forth that this section has also been complied with.

7. Lots, plots or burial permits in a cemetery owned by a religious corporation may, however, be sold, also all or part of such cemetery may be conveyed to a cemetery corporation, without applying for or obtaining leave of the court. No cemetery lands of a religious corporation shall be mortgaged while used for cemetery purposes.

8. Except as otherwise provided in this chapter in respect to a religious corporation of a specified denomination, any solvent religious corporation may, by order of the court, obtained as above provided in proceedings to sell, mortgage or lease real property, convey the whole or any part of its real property to another religious corporation, or to a membership, educational, municipal or other nonprofit corporation, for a consideration of one dollar or other nominal consideration, and for the purpose of applying the provisions of article five of the general corporation law, a proposed conveyance for such consideration shall be treated as a sale, but it shall not be necessary to show, in the petition or otherwise, nor for the court to find that the pecuniary or proprietary interest of the grantor corporation will be promoted thereby; and the interests of such grantor shall be deemed to be promoted if it appears that religious or charitable objects generally are conserved by such conveyance, provided, however, that such an order shall not be made if tending to impair the claim or remedy of any creditor.

9. If a sale, mortgage or lease for a term exceeding five years of any real property of any such religious corporation has been heretofore or shall be hereafter made and a conveyance or mortgage executed and delivered without the authority of a court of competent jurisdiction, obtained as required by law, or not in accordance with its directions, the court may, thereafter, upon the application of the corporation, or of the grantee or mortgagee in any such conveyance or mortgage or of any person claiming through or under any such grantee or mortgagee upon such notice to such corporation, or its successor, and such other person or persons as may be interested in such property, as the court may prescribe, confirm said previously executed conveyance or mortgage, and order and direct the execution and delivery of a confirmatory deed or mortgage, or the recording of such confirmatory order in the office where deeds and mortgages are recorded in the county in which the property is located; and upon compliance with the said order such original conveyance or mortgage shall be as valid and of the same force and effect as if it had been executed and delivered after due proceedings had in accordance with the statute and the direction of the court. But no confirmatory order may be granted unless the consents required in the first part of this section for a Protestant Episcopal, Roman Catholic, Presbyterian church or an incorporated African Methodist Episcopal Zion church or an incorporated United Methodist church have first been given by the prescribed authority thereof, either upon the original application or upon the application for the confirmatory order.

10. The provisions of this section shall not apply to real property heretofore or hereafter acquired on a sale in an action or proceeding for the foreclosure of a mortgage owned by a religious corporation or held by a trustee for or in behalf of a religious corporation or to real property heretofore or hereafter acquired by a religious corporation or held by a trustee for or in behalf of a religious corporation by deed in lieu of the foreclosure of a mortgage owned, either in whole or in part, whether in certificate form or otherwise, by a religious corporation.

History: Add, L 1909, ch 53, eff Feb 17, 1909; amd, L 1942, ch 524, eff Apr 25, 1942; L 1943, ch 368, and L 1949, ch 660; L 1953, ch 772; amd, L 1954, ch 476, § 1; L 1954, ch 578, § 1, 2, eff Apr 8, 1954,3; L 1958, ch 600; L 1960, ch 489, eff Apr 12, 1960; L 1962, ch 552; amd, L 1969, ch 962, § 1, eff May 26, 1969,2,3, eff May 26, 1969; L 1971, ch 956, Sub 1; L 1971, ch 956, eff Sept 1, 1972; amd, L 1973, ch 715, eff Sept 1, 1973; L 1981, ch 244, § 3, eff Sept 13, 1981; L 1985, ch 193, § 2, eff July 11, 1985; L 1985, ch 381, § 1, eff July 19, 1985,2, eff July 19, 1985; L 2015, ch 555, § 17, eff Dec 11, 2015.

CASE ANNOTATIONS

1. **In general**
2. **Requirement of court approval**
3. **Determination of denominational relationship**
4. **Specific performance**
5. **Recovery of property**

1. In general

This section does not require a foreign religious corporation to obtain permission of the court before conveying its real property in this state as is required of a domestic corporation. Muck v Hitchcock (1914) 212 N.Y. 283, 106 N.E. 75

Although approval of the court, under this section, is necessary for the conveyance of property of a religious corporation, such approval is not necessary when the agreement is one restricting the use of the premises to religious purposes. Second Reformed Protestant (Dutch) Church v Trustees of Reformed Protestant Dutch Church. (1927) 220 A.D. 244, 221 N.Y.S. 396

At trial of action by prospective purchasers for specific performance of religious corporation's contract to sell property, it would not be necessary to litigate questions of fairness of contract's terms and its promotion of interests of religious corporation (as required by CLS N-PCL § 511), since such questions had been determined by prior Supreme Court order approving sale of property, and that order had never been challenged by parties. Levovitz v Yeshiva Beth Henoch, Inc. (1986, 2d Dept) 120 A.D.2d 289, 508 N.Y.S.2d 196

In determining whether to approve religious corporation's sale of real property under CLS Relig Corp § 12 and CLS N-PCL § 511, court must consider whether bargain was fair and reasonable at time it was entered into and whether sale of property would presently benefit religious corporation (church) and promote best interests of its members, who were real parties in interest. Rende & Esposito Consultants, Inc. v St. Augustine's Roman Catholic Church (1987, 2d Dept) 131 A.D.2d 740, 516 N.Y.S.2d 959

Purported lease of church property which had agreed term of 5 years and provided option to renew for additional 5 years resulted in overall term of 10 years, and thus brought lease within purview of CLS Relig Corp § 12. Soho Center for Arts & Education v Church of St. Anthony of Padua (1989, 1st Dept) 146 A.D.2d 407, 541 N.Y.S.2d 396

Fixing of reasonable attorney's fees is integral component of court's statutory power over sale, mortgage, and lease of real property of religious corporation under CLS Relig Corp § 12; however, it was error for court to grant attorney's application for counsel fees in sum of $8,000 without holding hearing to ascertain reasonableness of fees where attorney alleged that he was retained by religious congregation and performed various services in connection with sale of its property,

but member of congregation challenged attorney's factual allegations, asserting that his services were limited to typing, serving, and filing legal papers. Re Congregation Ahavath Israel (1989, 1st Dept) 149 A.D.2d 333, 539 N.Y.S.2d 910

Court properly found that transfer of certain property from diocese to church was invalid because of failure to comply with statutory requirement that notice of transfer be given to Attorney General (CLS Relig Corp § 12, CLS N-PCL § 511), because person purporting to execute deed was not authorized to do so, and because at least one of conditions under deed had not been met. St. Andrey Bulgarian Eastern Orthodox Cathedral Church, Inc. v Bosakov (2000, 1st Dept) 272 A.D.2d 55, 707 N.Y.S.2d 95

School lacked standing to argue that a lease was invalid pursuant to N.Y. Relig. Corp. Law § 12(1), which was intended to protect the members of religious corporations from loss through unwise bargains and from perversion of the use of the property; the lease was voidable at the owner's option and the school lacked standing to challenge it. The owner was incorporated solely as a "seminary of learning" and, assuming without deciding that it was a "religious corporation," it did not meet the definition of an incorporated church. Female Academy of The Sacred Heart v Doane Stuart School (2012, 3d Dept) 91 App Div 3d 1254, 937 NYS2d 682.

This section relates solely to voluntary sales or dispositions by religious corporations of their real property and an action lies for partition and sale of property jointly owned by two religious corporations. New York Home Missionary Soc. v First Freewill Baptist Church (1911) 73 Misc 128, 130 N.Y.S. 879

If statutory proceedings for the consolidation of religious corporations had been followed, the property of the corporations would have been vested in a new or consolidated corporation without further act or deed under § 12 and the Membership Corporations Law, §§ 50 and 51. Agoodash Achim of Ithaca, Inc. v Temple Beth-El, Inc. (1933) 147 Misc 405, 263 N.Y.S. 81

The sale of property under execution and by operation of law is not prohibited by this section, and real property of a religious corporation may be sold to satisfy a judgment against it. Rector, Churchwardens & Vestrymen of the Church of Nativity v Fleming (1940) 174 Misc 473, 20 N.Y.S.2d 597, affd 260 A.D. 930, 23 N.Y.S.2d 46, affd 285 N.Y. 706, 34 N.E.2d 485

Appellate court refused to accord retroactive judicial approval under N.Y. Relig. Corp. Law § 12(9) to a transfer of one-half of defendant congregation's interest in a cemetery for a nominal consideration to plaintiff congregation as plaintiff congregation failed to show that the transfer was intended to promote the interests of defendant congregation by furthering a religious or charitable object generally; the appellate court restored the status quo ante as the expulsion of an individual from defendant congregation and his execution of a deed transferring the interest in the cemetery were part of a struggle for the overall leadership of the religious community. Congregation Yetev Lev D'Satmar of Kiryas Joel, Inc. v Congregation Yetev Lev D'Satmar, Inc. (2006, 2d Dept) 31 App Div 3d 480, 820 NYS2d 69

Because the failure to notify the Attorney General of a court-ordered transfer of church property did not render the order void under N.Y. Relig. Corp. Law § 12(9), and because the church did not set forth the alleged fraud with the specificity required by N.Y. C.P.L.R. 3016(b), no ground existed under N.Y. C.P.L.R. 5015 for relief from the court order; therefore, the transferee was properly granted summary judgment in the church's action to set aside the transfer. True Zion Gospel Temple, Inc. v Roberson (2007, 2d Dept) 39 App Div 3d 850, 835 NYS2d 299

Library trustees may not loan trust funds of the library to a religious corporation. 1958 Ops Atty Gen Jan. 24 (informal)

2. Requirement of court approval

The Supreme Court under this section and Real Property Law § 113 may only validate nunc pro tunc a mortgage executed by an incorporated religious association. Thus, an order validating a mortgage executed by an unincorporated religious association without the consent of the court was improper and void even though the association was later incorporated. Re Yancey (1954) 307 N.Y. 858, 122 N.E.2d 746

A motion to vacate a default judgment in a foreclosure action under CPLR § 5015, was properly denied where no valid excuse for such default had been forthcoming. Contrary to Special Term's interpretation, Relig Corp Law § 12 requires a religious corporation to apply for and obtain the court's permission in order to mortgage any of its property and the duration of the mortgage does not affect this requirement. Berlin v New Hope Holiness Church of God, Inc. (1983, 2d Dept) 93 A.D.2d 798, 460 N.Y.S.2d 961

Prior arbitration proceeding before rabbinical panel and subsequent proceeding to confirm arbitration award were not res judicata to proceeding under CLS Relig Corp § 12 and CLS N-PCL § 511 since prior proceedings did not address issue of whether proposed sale of religious organization's real property met requirements of Religious Corporations Law and Not-for-Profit Corporation Law, and CLS Relig Corp § 12 and CLS N-PCL §§ 510 and 511 expressly make authorization by Supreme Court or County Court condition precedent to sale of property, so that rabbinical panel had no authority to give such authorization. Agudist Council of Greater New York v Imperial Sales Co. (1990, 2d Dept) 158 A.D.2d 683, 551 N.Y.S.2d 955, app den 76 N.Y.2d 707, 560 N.Y.S.2d 989, 561 N.E.2d 889

Court properly disapproved sale of religious corporation's senior citizen center where (1) corporation's certificate of incorporation expressly stated that one of its corporate purposes was to conduct activities for senior citizens, and (2) it was clearly demonstrated that, despite initial assurances by third party that relocation of senior citizen's center was possible, and despite concerted investigations of alternative sites, no suitable alternative site could be found to house center, meaning that center would have to be dissolved if contract between parties were specifically enforced. Agudist Council of Greater New York v Imperial Sales Co. (1990, 2d Dept) 158 A.D.2d 683, 551 N.Y.S.2d 955, app den 76 N.Y.2d 707, 560 N.Y.S.2d 989, 561 N.E.2d 889

Judicial approval requirement of CLS Relig Corp § 12(1) requires such approval only in case of sale, mortgage or lease of real property in excess of 5 years, and accordingly does not apply to option to purchase real property in future. Bais Yaakov v Temple Emanu-el (1994, 2d Dept) 202 A.D.2d 534, 609 N.Y.S.2d 274

In action brought by plaintiff, religious organization, seeking, inter alia, to rescind sale of its property on ground that agreement with buyer, which made substantial changes to terms of court-approved sale, was not court-approved, and to void mortgages on property, court erred in dismissing counterclaims alleging that plaintiff negligently failed to inform mortgagee of agreement and that had he been informed of agreement he would not have made loans to buyer since fact issue existed as to whether mortgagee's reliance on plaintiff's negligent misrepresentation was justified. Salesian Soc'y, Inc. v Nutmeg Partners Ltd. (2000, 2d Dept) 271 A.D.2d 671, 706 N.Y.S.2d 459

Even though a church's deed of property to a minister was invalid due to the fact that the church did not seek court approval of the transfer, nor was the New York Attorney General notified of the transfer, the minister, as the owner of record, was properly notified of a tax foreclosure proceeding. Matter of City of Hudson (2014, 3d Dept) 114 App Div 3d 1106, 981 NYS2d 225, app dismd (2014) 23 NY3d 984, 990 NYS2d 462, 13 NE3d 1048

Where at the time of the sale of real property by a religious corporation, the corporation failed to obtain the permission of the court to sell the property, proceedings for confirmation of the conveyance were referred to a referee to inquire into whether it was for the best interest of the corporation to sell, the reasons for the sale, whether the corporation was solvent, whether consideration was adequate and how the proceeds were to be used, and the oral consent of the religious corporation's attorney was not sufficient. Re Application of Barusek (1956) 1 Misc. 2d 950, 149 N.Y.S.2d 420

Petition for approval of church conveyance did not comply with § 50 of the General Corporation Law, where the secretary's certificate did not show that the sale was authorized by a vote of at least two-thirds of the board of directors, and also failed to state that the interests of the church corporation was promoted by the sale. Application of Margolin (1959) 16 Misc. 2d 961, 183 N.Y.S.2d 36

This section does not, as a matter of law, bar a sale of a church property, on the ground that a court has not approved the sale, since a religious corporation may enter into a contract of sale of its property with a condition that the conveyance can only be made with the consent of a court, and even if there is no such provision in the contract, a court will read such a provision into the contract. Sun Assets Corp. v English Evangelical Lutheran Church of Ascension (1959) 19 Misc. 2d 187, 185 N.Y.S.2d 695

Where leave of the court has not been obtained in accordance with the statute, the mortgage is invalid. Bernstein v Friedlander (1968) 58 Misc. 2d 492, 296 N.Y.S.2d 409

Diocesan missionary and church extension society of the Protestant Episcopal Church in the diocese of New York was exempt from that provision of the Religious Corporations Law prohibiting a religious corporation from selling any of its real property without applying for and obtaining leave of the court, since the aforesaid church society was created by a special legislative act which, though subjecting its power to acquire and hold property to the restrictions prescribed by law with regard to charitable corporations organized under the general laws of New York, imposed no similar restrictions on the society's power to dispose of its real and personal property. Bush v Bush (1977) 91 Misc. 2d 389, 398 N.Y.S.2d 16

In determining pursuant to N-PCL § 511 whether a church had leave of court to sell a building, the court determined that the consideration in terms of the transactions were fair and reasonable to the church at the time the contract was made where the fair market value of the building at that time was $2,000,000 and the amended contract price was $2,200,000. Re Church of St. Francis de Sales (1981) 110 Misc. 2d 511, 442 N.Y.S.2d 741

Prospective purchaser of church property is not properly interested person under CLS N-PCL § 511 and purchaser's due process rights are not violated by failure to give purchaser notice of hearing at which court disapproves contract on basis of inadequate consideration or to allow purchaser to otherwise participate in hearing. Wolkoff v Church of St. Rita (1986) 132 Misc. 2d 464, 505 N.Y.S.2d 327

Requirement of court approval under CLS Relig Corp § 12(1) applies to sale, mortgage or lease of any real property by religious corporation, not merely to property used as place of worship; § 12(1) also applies to agreement to modify price to be paid on original contract. Greek Orthodox Archdiocese of N. & S. Am. v Abrams (1994, Sup) 162 Misc. 2d 850, 618 N.Y.S.2d 504

Requirements that certain churches notify Attorney General when seeking leave of court to sell, mortgage or lease real property (CLS Relig Corp §§ 12 and 2-b(1)(d-1) do not violate either Establishment Clause or Free Exercise Clause. Greek Orthodox Archdiocese of N. & S. Am. v Abrams (1994, Sup) 162 Misc. 2d 850, 618 N.Y.S.2d 504

Requirements that certain churches notify Attorney General when seeking leave of court to sell, mortgage or lease real property, while exempting other churches which are hierarchically structured (CLS Relig Corp §§ 12 and 20b(1)(d-1)), do not unlawfully discriminate between religious denominations since (1) they meet compelling state interests of safeguarding potentially substantial proceeds from sales of property, and ensure that proceeds are properly disbursed, and (2) statutory obligations are narrowly tailored to meet objectives. Greek Orthodox Archdiocese of N. & S. Am. v Abrams (1994, Sup) 162 Misc. 2d 850, 618 N.Y.S.2d 504

Religious corporation cannot invalidate ultra vires, but otherwise lawful, transfer of property if transfer was duly approved or authorized by judge; religious corporation's remedy is to sue its misbehaving corporate officers. Congregation Yetev Lev D'Satmar v 26 Adar N.B. Corp. (1996, 2d Dept) 219 A.D.2d 186, 641 N.Y.S.2d 680, app den 88 N.Y.2d 808, 647 N.Y.S.2d 713, 670 N.E.2d 1345

Deeds used by respondent-appellant to purportedly take title to certain property were null and void because respondent-appellant did not provide evidence showing that the putative grantors had an interest in the property that could be conveyed to respondent-appellant, and no evidence showed the putative grantors of the deed ever had legal title to the property. Furthermore, the conveyance of the property from the former owner/mortgagor religious not-for-profit corporation was ineffective because neither judicial consent nor consent from the state attorney general was obtained for the sale as required under N.Y. Relig. Corp. Law § 12 and N.Y. Not-for-Profit Corp. Law § 511. Wiggs v Williams (2007, 1st Dept) 36 App Div 3d 570, 828 NYS2d 397

A religious corporation must obtain leave of court to sell any of its real estate or any interest therein to a municipality for a public purpose. 1982 Op Atty Gen Feb 19 (informal)

Permission of the Court must be obtained by a religious corporation or a membership corporation before it may grant an easement in its real property 1955 Ops St Compt File #7735

3. Determination of denominational relationship

Under the Religious Corporations Law a church which has been affiliated with and a constituent part of the Presbyterian Church in the United States of America, and as such has acquired property, cannot by secession terminate its relationship and thereby avoid supervision and control of the denominational organization at large. Trustees of Presbytery v Westminster Presbyterian Church (1917) 222 N.Y. 305, 118 N.E. 800

A religious corporation, covering many churches in the State and representing a national organization, is not entitled to a summary judgment prohibiting the defendant, a former member church of the religious corporation that withdrew, from transferring its assets to another church where substantial questions of fact exist concerning the extent of defendant's involvement and participation in the ecclesiastical and spiritual activities of the parent structure, i.e., the national organization, and whether said affiliation was such as to subject it to the hierarchical control of the religious corporation as mere involvement by the defendant in the ecclesiastical affairs of the religious corporation and the national organization does not necessarily subject defendant to the control of that body insofar as its property matters may be concerned. Acknowledgment of a higher church authority may be limited to ecclesiastical authority and therefore not inconsistent with local autonomy in property matters as it is not only the extent of the involvement which must be studied but the extent to which the parent body controls the affairs of the local church. New York Dist. of Assemblies of God v Calvary Assembly of God (1978, 3d Dept) 64 A.D.2d 311, 409 N.Y.S.2d 842

4. Specific performance

In an action for specific performance of a contract for sale of real property owned by a religious corporation, judicial consent (Relig Corp Law § 12) was properly withheld where the contemplated sale would not have promoted the purposes of the religious corporation or the interests of the members of its congregation. Church of God v Fourth Church of Christ, Scientist (1981) 54 N.Y.2d 742, 442 N.Y.S.2d 986, 426 N.E.2d 480

In action by prospective purchasers for specific performance of religious corporation's contract to sell property, defended by religious corporation on ground that its trustees had not approved sale as required by CLS Relig Corp § 12 and CLS N-PCL § 511, prospective purchasers could not be bound by findings of rabbinical court (acting as arbitrator of internal dispute among trustees over issue of whether approval had been given) where prospective purchasers were not parties to arbitration and thus had no opportunity to litigate issue; accordingly, religious corporation was not entitled to dismissal of complaint, since "legitimate question" still existed as to whether trustees had validly voted to authorize sale. Levovitz v Yeshiva Beth Henoch, Inc. (1986, 2d Dept) 120 A.D.2d 289, 508 N.Y.S.2d 196

Church was entitled to summary judgment in tenant's action for specific performance of purported lease agreement made with church pastor where agreement's term exceeded 5 years and tenant presented no evidence that church bishop ever gave consent to lease premises; agreement was void ab initio under CLS Relig Corp § 12. Soho Center for Arts & Education v Church of St. Anthony of Padua (1989, 1st Dept) 146 A.D.2d 407, 541 N.Y.S.2d 396

If a church repudiates contract of sale, a buyer is entitled to recover money expended in reliance upon the contract of sale. Wilson v Ebenezer Baptist Church, Inc. (1959) 17 Misc. 2d 607, 187 N.Y.S.2d 861

The court cannot by-pass the submission of a petition under § 50 of the General Corporation Law and grant specific performance of a contract of sale of church property contrary to the determination by the trustees that it would be against the best interests of the church to convey title. Wilson v Ebenezer Baptist Church, Inc. (1959) 17 Misc. 2d 607, 187 N.Y.S.2d 861

Complaint for specific performance of a contract for the sale of church property, where no prior approval thereof has been obtained from the court, must set forth the essential facts which are required to be stated in the verified petition, as provided by § 50 of the General Corporation Law. Wilson v Ebenezer Baptist Church, Inc. (1959) 17 Misc. 2d 669, 185 N.Y.S.2d 1018

5. Recovery of property

Action by diocese officials, seeking declaratory and injunctive relief as to ownership of church property in possession of defendant church after it voted to disaffiliate itself from diocese, was justiciable although dispute arose when diocese refused to ordain church's deacon-in-charge as priest, where controversy could be resolved by neutral principles of law without resort to judicial intrusion into matters of religious doctrine. Trustees of the Diocese of Albany v Trinity Episcopal Church (1999, 3d Dept) 250 A.D.2d 282, 684 N.Y.S.2d 76

Religious corporation that owned church was entitled to possession of church where church was occupied by corporation's congregation under license from corporation, license was revocable at will, and there was no evidence that congregation had changed its position with respect to premises or expended any funds in excess of ordinary maintenance and repairs, which it was required to pay in lieu of rent.

Faith United Christian Church, Inc. v United Christian Church, Inc. (1999, 2d Dept) 266 A.D.2d 428, 698 N.Y.S.2d 874

Religious corporation's decision to sell church was not breach of any duty owed to its congregation; governing body of religious corporation has authority to discontinue work at church, even in disregard of wishes of congregation. Faith United Christian Church, Inc. v United Christian Church, Inc. (1999, 2d Dept) 266 A.D.2d 428, 698 N.Y.S.2d 874

Where a defendant religious corporation executed a deed of certain premises to a similar corporation, and the parties agreed that plaintiff would convey the premises to defendant in the event that plaintiff ceased to use them for religious purposes, such agreement was not invalid under this section. Second Reformed Protestant Church v Trustees of Reformed Protestant Dutch Church (1926) 127 Misc 498, 216 N.Y.S. 616, affd 220 A.D. 244, 221 N.Y.S. 396

A religious corporation is entitled to recover possession of a burial plot from another such corporation claiming title as successor to plaintiff by reason of alleged consolidation of religious corporations where the statutory provisions were not complied with, since the agreement did not effect a transfer of title to the property of plaintiff, and plaintiff is not estopped to deny such transfer under this section and Membership Corporations Law, §§ 50 and 51. Agoodash Achim of Ithaca, Inc. v Temple Beth-El, Inc. (1933) 147 Misc 405, 263 N.Y.S. 81

In light of several facially valid petitions, supporting documentation, court orders, and public records of property ownership, religious corporation could not, many years after transactions were consummated, contend that transactions were never properly authorized by statutorily mandated number of trustees and congregants. Congregation Yetev Lev D'Satmar v 26 Adar N.B. Corp. (1996, 2d Dept) 219 A.D.2d 186, 641 N.Y.S.2d 680, app den 88 N.Y.2d 808, 647 N.Y.S.2d 713, 670 N.E.2d 1345

Religious corporation that waited 12 years to challenge transfer of its property, about which it knew or had every reason to know, either ratified conveyance or was barred by doctrine of laches from contesting it, particularly in light of palpable detriment to several innocent, bona fide purchasers and encumbrancers for value. Congregation Yetev Lev D'Satmar v 26 Adar N.B. Corp. (1996, 2d Dept) 219 A.D.2d 186, 641 N.Y.S.2d 680, app den 88 N.Y.2d 808, 647 N.Y.S.2d 713, 670 N.E.2d 1345

§ 13.   Consolidation or merger of incorporated churches

Two or more incorporated churches may enter into an agreement, under their respective corporate seals, for the consolidation or merger of such corporations, setting forth the name of the proposed new corporation or surviving corporation, the denomination, if any, to which it is to belong, and if the churches of such denomination have more than one method of choosing trustees, by which of such methods the trustees are to be chosen, the number of such trustees, the names of the persons to be the first trustees of the new corporation, and the date of its first annual corporate meeting. Such an agreement shall not be valid for United Methodist churches unless proposed by a majority vote of the charge conference of each church and approved by the superintendent or superintendents of the district or districts in which the consolidating churches are located, and by the majority of the members of each of such churches, over the age of twenty-one years, present and voting at a meeting thereof held in the usual place of public worship and called for the purpose of considering such agreement by announcement made at public service in such churches on two Sundays, the first not less than ten days next preceding the date of such meeting. Such agreement shall not be valid unless approved in the case of Protestant Episcopal churches by the bishop and standing committee of the diocese in which such churches are situated and in the case of churches of other denominations by the governing body of the denomination, if any, to which each church belongs, having jurisdiction over such church. Each corporation shall thereupon make a separate petition to the supreme court for an order consolidating or merging the corporations, setting forth the denomination, if any, to which the church belongs, that the consent of the governing body to the consolidation or merger, if any, of that denomination having jurisdiction over such church has been obtained, the agreement therefor, and a statement of all the property and liabilities and the amount and sources of the annual income of such petitioning corporation. In its discretion the court may direct that notice of the hearing of such petition be given to the parties interested therein in such manner and for such time as it may prescribe. After hearing all the parties interested, present and desiring to be heard, the court may make an order for the consolidation or merger of the corporations on the terms of such agreement and such other terms and conditions as it may prescribe, specifying the name of such new or surviving corporation and the trustees thereof, and the method by which their successors shall be chosen and the date of its first or next annual corporate meeting. When such order is made and duly entered, the persons constituting such consolidated or merged corporations shall be or become an incorporated church by, and said petitioning churches shall become consolidated or merged under, the name designated in the order, and the trustees therein named shall be the trustees thereof, and the future trustees thereof shall be chosen by the method therein designated, and all the estate, rights, powers and property of whatsoever nature belonging to either corporation shall without further act or deed be vested in and transferred to the new or surviving corporation as effectually as they were vested in or belonging to the former corporations; and the said new or surviving corporation shall be liable for all the debts and liabilities of the former corporations in the same manner and as effectually as if said debts or liabilities had been contracted or incurred by the new or surviving corporation. A certified copy of such order shall be recorded in the book for recording certificates of incorporation in each county clerk's office in which the certificate of incorporation of each consolidating or merging church was recorded; or if no such certificate was so recorded, then in the clerk's office of the county in which the principal place of worship or principal office of the new or surviving corporation is, or is intended to be, situated.

History: Add, L 1909, ch 53, amd, L 1949, ch 660, L 1970, ch 705, eff May 12, 1970, L 2013, ch 549, § 24, eff July 1, 2014.

CASE ANNOTATIONS

Court properly determined that church was entitled to withdraw from larger religious organization (defendant), and take back church building and parsonage it had contributed to affiliation, where (1) minutes of meeting held to effect joinder, authored by defendant's district superintendent, unequivocally showed condition permitting church to withdraw its property within 3 years if it was dissatisfied with affiliation, and (2) defendant's district superintendent had actual or apparent authority to make such commitment, or if he did not have such authority, there was no meeting of minds, with result that no affiliation contract was entered into. New York Annual Conference of Methodist Church v Nam Un Cho (1989, 2d Dept) 156 A.D.2d 511, 548 N.Y.S.2d 577, app dismd without op 75 N.Y.2d 947, 555 N.Y.S.2d 694, 554 N.E.2d 1282

Church was not entitled to setting aside of tax deed to property it claimed to own where notices of tax sale had been sent to record titleholder-church with which it had allegedly merged-but it failed to submit proof that merger had been effected in compliance with CLS Relig Corp § 13, and thus its due process rights had not been violated. St. John's Episcopal Church v Cochrane (2001, 2d Dept) 279 A.D.2d 515, 718 N.Y.S.2d 877

Where a testator created a trust, the income to be used to purchase coal for the named church upon consolidation of the named church with another, a trustee will be directed to pay the income to the consolidated church. Re Mills' Will (1935) 156 Misc 473, 282 N.Y.S. 25

Where two Roman Catholic churches merged, it was irrelevant that some of the funds accumulated over the years by one church corporation were, in the minds of the parishioners, hopefully intended for construction of a new church edifice. Filetto v St. Mary of Assumption Church (1969) 61 Misc. 2d 278, 305 N.Y.S.2d 403

The sections of the Religious Corporation Law applicable to the Roman Catholic Church must be read in conjunction with the Code of Canon Law of that church. Filetto v St. Mary of Assumption Church (1969) 61 Misc. 2d 278, 305 N.Y.S.2d 403

Where two churches voted to merge, the fact that three of the five trustees of one of the churches were also trustees of the other church and the same became true of the five trustees of the consolidated church does not render illegal the union of the two original churches or make invalid the transfer of their properties to the new religious corporation. Filetto v St. Mary of Assumption Church (1969) 61 Misc. 2d 278, 305 N.Y.S.2d 403

Consolidation ordered upon evidence that study of a proposed union of the two churches commenced over 6 years prior to the institution of the action; approval of the consolidation agreement was given by each congregation after much planning and consideration; the proposed consolidation was ratified by the higher authorities of each church; and there had been a de facto consolidation for over 2 years. Re First Methodist Church (1970) 62 Misc. 2d 129, 306 N.Y.S.2d 969

§ 14. Judicial investigation of amount of property of religious corporations

The supreme court at a special term, held in the judicial district in which the principal place of worship or of holding corporate meetings of a religious corporation is situated, may require such corporation to make and file an inventory of its property, verified by its trustees or a majority of them, on the written application of the attorney-general, stating that, from his knowledge, or on information and belief, the value of the property held by such corporation exceeds the amount authorized by law. On presentation of such application, the court shall order that a notice of at least eight days, together with a copy of the application, be served upon the trustees of the corporation, requiring them to show cause at a time and place therein specified why they should not make and file such inventory and account. If, on the hearing of such application, no good cause is shown to the contrary, the court may make an order requiring such inventory or account to be filed, and may also proceed to take and state the amount of property held by the corporation, and may appoint a referee for that purpose; and when such account is taken and stated, after hearing all the parties appearing on the application, the court may enter an order determining the amount of property so held by the corporation and its annual income, from which order an appeal may be taken by any party aggrieved as from a judgment of the supreme court in an action tried therein before a court without a jury. No corporation shall be required to make and file more than one inventory and account in any one year, or to make a second account and inventory while proceedings are pending for the statement of an account under this section.

History: Add, L 1909, ch 53, eff Feb 17, 1909.

CASE ANNOTATIONS

This section is not exclusive. It seems to be directed, not to testing the question of the power of a corporation to take by devise or bequest, but rather the right to hold the property which it already has and which it may have acquired by purchase or gift and not necessarily by devise or bequest. Re Dooper's Will (1925) 125 Misc 909, 212 N.Y.S. 616

A petition alleging incorporation under the Religious Corporations Law is insufficient in law when respondent corporation was incorporated under the Membership Corporations Law, since the two laws are entirely separate, the former being devoted to the organization and government of various denominational churches and the latter applicable to benevolent, charitable, philanthropic and missionary organization. Taylor v Day Star Baptist Church, Inc. (1949) 196 Misc 449, 92 N.Y.S.2d 206

§ 15. Corporations with governing authority over, or advisory relations with, churches or synods, or both

1. An unincorporated diocesan convention, presbytery, classis, synod unless otherwise provided, annual or biennial conference or convention, or other governing or advisory body having jurisdiction over or relations with several or a number of churches or synods, or synods and churches, some or all of which are located in this state, may at a meeting thereof duly held, determine to become incorporated by a designated name, and may by a plurality vote, elect not less than three nor more than fifteen persons to be the first trustees of such corporation. The presiding officer and clerk of such governing or advisory body shall execute and acknowledge a certificate stating that such proceedings were duly taken as herein provided, the name by which such corporation is to be known, and the names of such first trustees. On filing such certificate the members of such governing or advisory body and their successors shall be a corporation by the name stated in the certificate, and the persons named as trustees therein shall be the first trustees thereof.

The trustees of every incorporated governing or advisory body and their successors shall hold their offices during the pleasure of such body, which may remove them and fill vacancies in accordance with its rules and regulations. Such corporation may hold its meetings and elect its trustees annually or biennially, and may hold its first and any other meetings outside this state if any of the churches or synods governed or advised by it are located outside of this state. Such corporation may take, administer and dispose of real and personal property in and outside this state for the benefit of such governing or advisory body or of any parish, congregation, society, church, mission, synod, religious, benevolent, charitable or educational institution existing or acting under or related to it, or of any religious work or activity. Such corporation may elect the members of unincorporated or incorporated boards to carry on particular lines of religious work or activity. Such corporation may have in addition to its by-laws, a constitution; and such constitution may be adopted or amended in such manner as the corporation will determine.

2. The trustees of every incorporated governing body of the Protestant Episcopal church in the state of New York, shall consist of the bishop of the diocese, who shall be ex-officio president of the corporation; the bishop coadjutor, should there be one, who shall be ex-officio vice-president of the corporation; and not less than three nor more than nine other persons, residents of the diocese, to be elected by the diocesan convention, and who shall hold their office for such term as shall be decided by the said convention.

Vacancies in the board of trustees, occurring by reason of death, resignation, or removal from the diocese, may be filled by the remaining trustees, until the next diocesan convention.

3. The trustees, who shall constitute the governing body of the Federated Orthodox Greek Catholic Primary Jurisdictions in America, shall consist of the ecclesiastical administrative heads, also known as the hierarchs, of the four constituent primary jurisdictions together with the dean of the preceptorial council, the chancellor and the secretary of said federation and not more than eight additional trustees, communicants of the Orthodox Greek Catholic Church, who are to be elected or appointed by said four constituent primary jurisdictions.

The term Federated Orthodox Greek Catholic Primary Jurisdictions in America, as used herein, is restricted to apply only

(a) to the jurisdiction of the Orthodox Oecumenical Patriarchate of Constantinople exercised in the Americas and all the territorial possessions and/or dependencies or protectorates of the United States of America, by its duly authorized exarch, metropolitan, archbishop or bishop,

(b) to the jurisdiction of the apostolic Orthodox Patriarchate of Antioch, exercised in the Americas and all the territorial possessions and/or dependencies or protectorates of the United States of America, by its duly authorized exarch, metropolitan, archbishop or bishop,

(c) to the jurisdiction of the Patriarchate of Moscow exercised in the Americas and all the territorial possessions and/or dependencies or protectorates of the United States of America, by its duly authorized exarch, metropolitan, archbishop or bishop,

(d) to the jurisdiction of the Patriarchate of Serbia (Jugoslavia) exercised in the Americas and all the territorial possessions and/or dependencies or protectorates of the United States of America, by its duly authorized exarch, metropolitan, archbishop or bishop.

All other Orthodox Greek Catholic jurisdictions, bishoprics, dioceses and missions, officially and canonically in communion with and acknowledged by all four of said primary jurisdictions, if certified by the secretariat thereof as affiliated with the Federated Orthodox Greek Catholic Primary Jurisdictions in America, may incorporate or re-incorporate under this section as affiliates thereof.

4. The trustees of every incorporated governing body of the four primary jurisdictions, respectively, specified in subdivision three of this section, or of any of the affiliates of said jurisdictions, shall consist of the hierarch or ecclesiastical administrator, who shall be ex-officio president of the corporation, the chancellor of the archdiocese, the dean of the archdiocesan theological faculty or one of the members thereof, and the secretary of the archdiocese, who are to be appointed by said hierarch and to serve at his pleasure and, in addition, not less than three nor more than nine other persons, communicants of the Orthodox Church, to be elected by said governing body or by the diocesan convention; the term of such elective first trustees shall be one-third for one year, one-third for two years, and one-third for three years, respectively, and the term of office of their successors shall be three years.

5. The trustees of every incorporated governing body of the Evangelical Lutheran Church in America shall consist of not less than three nor more than thirty persons. If the constitution or by-laws of such governing body so provides, the Bishop or president, vice-president, treasurer and secretary of such governing body shall be ex-officio trustees of such governing body. The remaining trustees shall be elected by the annual or other regular convention of such governing body if it does not meet annually, and shall hold their office for such term as shall be decided by the said convention. Vacancies in the board of trustees, occurring by reason of death, resignation or other cause, may be filled by the remaining trustees as provided in the constitution and by-laws of such governing body.

History: Add, L 1909, ch 53, amd, L 1943, ch 145, eff Mar 20, 1943.

Sub 1, opening par, amd, L 1977, ch 154, eff May 20, 1977.

Sub 5, add, L 1954, ch 29, eff Feb 22, 1954.

Sub 5, amd, L 1987, ch 70, § 1, eff May 16, 1987.

CASE ANNOTATIONS

A decree of dissolution of a church in the county of New York issued by the ecclesiastical governing body to which it was subject extends only to the spiritual side of the church. The governing body has no power in that county to dissolve the corporation, considered as a legal entity. Westminster Presbyterian Church v Trustees of Presbytery (1914) 211 N.Y. 214, 105 N.E. 199, reh den 212 N.Y. 552, 106 N.E. 1044

A religious corporation, covering many churches in the State and representing a national organization, is not entitled to a summary judgment prohibiting the defendant, a former member church of the religious corporation that withdrew, from transferring its assets to another church where substantial questions of fact exist concerning the extent of defendant's involvement and participation in the ecclesiastical and spiritual activities of the parent structure, i.e., the national organization, and whether said affiliation was such as to subject it to the hierarchical control of the religious corporation as mere involvement by the defendant in the ecclesiastical affairs of the religious corporation and the national organization does not necessarily subject defendant to the control of that body insofar as its property matters may be concerned. Acknowledgment of a higher church authority may be limited to ecclesiastical authority and therefore not inconsistent with local autonomy in property matters as it is not only the extent of the involvement which must be studied but the extent to which the parent body controls the affairs of the local church. New York Dist. of Assemblies of God v Calvary Assembly of God (1978, 3d Dept) 64 A.D.2d 311, 409 N.Y.S.2d 842

Religious corporation that owned church was entitled to possession of church where church was occupied by corporation's congregation under license from corporation, license was revocable at will, and there was no evidence that congregation had changed its position with respect to premises or expended any funds in excess of ordinary maintenance and repairs, which it was required to pay in lieu of rent. Faith United Christian Church, Inc. v United Christian Church, Inc. (1999, 2d Dept) 266 A.D.2d 428, 698 N.Y.S.2d 874

Religious corporation's decision to sell church was not breach of any duty owed to its congregation; governing body of religious corporation has authority to discontinue work at church, even in disregard of wishes of congregation. Faith United Christian Church, Inc. v United Christian Church, Inc. (1999, 2d Dept) 266 A.D.2d 428, 698 N.Y.S.2d 874

The secretary of state should not file a certificate for a proposed religious corporation which does not show that the persons executing such certificate are of full age, two-thirds of them citizens of the United States, and at least one a resident of the state. 1912 Ops Atty Gen 393

§ 15-a. Consolidation of incorporated presbyteries

1. Two or more incorporated presbyteries may enter into an agreement for the consolidation or merger of such corporations and such corporations may be consolidated or merged so as to form a single corporation which may be either a new corporation or one of the constituent corporations. Said agreement shall set forth the name of the proposed new corporation or the name of the existing corporation if it is to become the consolidated or merged corporation, the method of choosing trustees, the names of the persons to be the first trustees of the new corporation if the consolidated or merged corporation is to be a new corporation and the date of the first annual corporate meeting.

2. Such agreement must be authorized and approved by a majority vote of the members of each contracting presbytery taken at a meeting at which a quorum is present duly called in accordance with the form of government of the Presbyterian Church (U.S.A.) and the notice of such meeting shall state the purpose of the meeting.

3. Before such agreement is approved as aforesaid, such consolidation or merger must be directed and approved by the Synod of the Northeast and the General Assembly of the Presbyterian Church (U.S.A.).

4. Each presbytery shall thereafter join in a petition to the supreme court for an order consolidating or merging the corporation, setting forth the agreement of the contracting presbyteries, the direction and approval of the bodies as set forth in subdivision

three of this section, a statement of all the property and liabilities and the sources of the annual income of each presbytery and a description of any property held by such presbyteries in trust for specific purposes. In its discretion the court may direct that notice of the hearing of such petition be given to the parties interested therein in such manner as it may prescribe.

5. After hearing all the parties interested, present and desiring to be heard, the court may make an order for the consolidation or merger of the presbyteries on the terms of such agreement and such other terms and conditions as it may prescribe, specifying the name of the new corporation or the name the continuing corporation will have if one of the constituent corporations is to become the consolidated or merged corporation, the first trustees thereof if a new corporation is to be created and the method by which their successors shall be chosen and the date of the first annual corporate meeting if a new corporation is to be created.

6. When such order is made and duly entered, the persons constituting such corporate presbyteries shall become one incorporated consolidated or merged presbytery by, and said petitioning presbyteries shall become consolidated or merged under, the name designated in the order, and the trustees therein named, if it is a new corporation, shall be the first trustees thereof, and if it is a new corporation the trustees thereof shall be chosen by the method therein designated, and all the estate, rights, powers and property of whatsoever nature, belonging to either corporation shall without further act or deed be vested in and/or transferred to the new corporation as effectually as they were vested in or belonging to the former corporations, and the new or continuing corporations shall be liable for all the debts and liabilities of the former corporations in the same manner and as effectually as if said debts or liabilities had been contracted or incurred by the new corporation.

7. The order or a certified copy thereof shall be recorded in the book for recording certificates of incorporation in each county clerk's office in which the certificate of incorporation of each constituent presbytery was recorded.

8. Such consolidated or merged presbytery shall have all the powers and responsibilities conferred upon presbyteries by the constitution and form of government of the Presbyterian Church (U.S.A.).

History: Add, L 1965, ch 108, eff Apr 26, 1965; amd, L 1985, ch 381, § 3, eff July 19, 1985, L 2013, ch 549, § 25, eff July 1, 2014.

§ 15-b. Consolidation or merger of incorporated Presbyterian and Lutheran synods

1. (a) Presbyterian. One or more foreign religious synods and one or more domestic religious synods may merge into a single religious corporation of this state, which shall be one of the constituent corporations or may consolidate into a single religious corporation of this state which shall be a new corporation to be formed pursuant to the consolidation, if such merger or consolidation is permitted by the laws of the jurisdiction under which each such foreign religious corporation is incorporated.

(b) Lutheran. One or more foreign religious synods and one or more domestic religious synods may merge into a single religious corporation formed in this state or outside this state, which shall be one of the constituent corporations or may consolidate into a single religious corporation formed in this state or outside this state, which shall be a new corporation to be formed pursuant to the consolidation, if such merger or consolidation is permitted by the laws of the jurisdiction under which each such foreign religious corporation is incorporated.

2. Whenever used in this section:

(a) "Constituent Corporation" means an existing foreign or domestic religious corporation that is participating in the merger or consolidation with one or more other foreign or domestic religious corporations.

(b) "Surviving Corporation" means the constituent religious corporation into which one or more other domestic or foreign constituent religious corporations are merged.

(c) "Consolidated Corporation" means the new religious corporation in which two or more foreign or domestic constituent religious corporations are consolidated.

(d) "Synod" means

(i) a foreign or domestic religious corporation formed by the Presbyterian church that consists of ministers and ruling elders of not fewer than three presbyteries within a specified geographical region, or

(ii) a foreign or domestic religious corporation formed by the Lutheran church under a religious corporations law or a not-for-profit corporation law.

3. The constituent corporations shall enter into an agreement for the consolidation or merger of such corporations. Said agreement shall set forth the name of the proposed new corporation if a consolidation or the name of the surviving corporation if a merger, the method of choosing trustees, the names of the persons to be the first trustees of the new corporation if a consolidation or of the surviving corporation if a merger and the date of the first annual corporate meeting if a consolidation or of the annual corporate meeting if a merger.

4. Such agreement must be authorized and approved by a two-thirds vote of the board of trustees or governing body of each domestic synod and in the case of a foreign religious synod by such vote or approval as required by the laws of the jurisdiction under which it is incorporated at a meeting where a quorum is present, duly called in accordance with the form of government of the Presbyterian Church

Religious Corporations Law

(U.S.A.) or the Evangelical Lutheran Church in America, as applicable, and the notice of such meeting shall state the purpose of the meeting.

5. Before such agreement is approved as aforesaid, such consolidation or merger must be directed and approved by the General Assembly of the Presbyterian Church (U.S.A.) or the Churchwide Assembly of the Evangelical Lutheran Church in America.

6. Each synod, whether it be a foreign or a domestic religious corporation, shall thereafter join in a petition to the supreme court for an order consolidating or merging the constituent corporations. The petition shall set forth the following: agreement of the contracting synods; the direction and approval of the body as set forth in subdivision five; a statement of all the assets and liabilities and the sources of the annual income of each synod; a description of real property and a description of any property held by such synod in trust for specific purposes for property to be transferred and conveyed to the consolidated or merged corporation. Where required by the law of the state of incorporation of each constituent corporation, notice of the hearing of such petition shall be given to the secretary of state of this state and to the secretary of state of the state in which each foreign religious corporation is incorporated in such manner as the court may prescribe, and the court may, in its discretion, direct that notice of the hearing of such petition to the other parties interested therein shall be given in such manner as the court may prescribe.

7. After hearing all the parties interested, present and desiring to be heard, the court may make an order for the consolidation or merger of the foreign and domestic synods on the terms of such agreement and such other terms and conditions as it may prescribe, specifying the name of the new corporation, if a consolidation, or the name of the surviving corporation, if a merger, the names of the first trustees thereof, if a new corporation is to be created, and the method by which their successors shall be chosen, the date of the first annual corporate meeting, if a consolidation, or the date of the annual corporate meeting, if a merger, and the court may authorize the filing of a certificate of consolidation or merger of the religious corporations with the secretary of state for the consolidated or merged religious corporation.

8. After approval of the petition and when such order is made and duly entered by the court, a certificate of consolidation or merger, entitled "Certificate of consolidation (or merger) of ---- and ---- into (name of religious corporation) under section fifteen-b of the 'Religious Corporations Law'", shall be signed and verified on behalf of each constituent corporation and delivered to the county clerk in which the principal office of said consolidated or merged corporation is or is intended to be situated and shall be filed and recorded in the office of the clerk of said county. If there is no such principal office or there is none intended to be, the certificate of consolidation or

merger shall be filed and recorded in the office of the secretary of state. It shall set forth:

(a) The date when the certificate of incorporation of each constituent domestic corporation was filed by the department of state, or, in the case of constituent domestic corporations created by special law, the chapter number and year of passage of such law. In the case of each constituent foreign corporation, the certificate shall set forth the jurisdiction and date of its incorporation.

(b) A certified copy of the order from the Supreme Court authorizing and approving the merger or consolidation of the foreign and domestic religious corporations.

(c) The name of each constituent corporation and if the name of any of them has been changed, the name under which it was formed, and the name and purposes of the surviving or consolidated corporation.

(d) A description of the membership, officers, and trustees, including their number, classification, and voting rights, if any.

(e) In case of merger, a statement of any amendments or changes in the certificate of incorporation of the surviving corporation to be affectuated by such merger; in case of consolidation, all statements required to be included in a certificate of incorporation for a religious corporation, except statements as to facts not available at the time the agreement of consolidation is adopted.

(f) The effective date of the merger or consolidation, if other than the date of filing of the certificate of merger or consolidation by the department of state.

(g) The manner in which the merger or consolidation was authorized with respect to each constituent religious corporation.

9. The surviving or consolidated corporation shall thereafter cause a copy of such certificate certified by the clerk of the county or the secretary of state, as the case may be, in whose office the certificate of merger or consolidation is filed and recorded, to be filed in the office of the clerk of each county in which the office of a constituent domestic corporation, other than the surviving corporation, is located, in the office of the secretary of state of the jurisdiction where each one of the constituent foreign corporations is incorporated, and in the office of the official who is the recording officer of each county in this state and in foreign states in which real property of a constituent corporation, other than the surviving corporation, is situated.

10. Upon the filing of the certificate of merger or consolidation as aforesaid or on such date subsequent thereto, not to exceed thirty days, as shall be set forth in such certificate, the merger or consolidation shall be effected. When such merger or consolidation has been effected:

(a) Such surviving or consolidated religious corporation shall thereafter, consistently with its certificate of incorporation as altered or established by the merger or consolidation, possess all the rights, privileges, immunities, powers and purposes of each of the constituent religious corporations.

(b) All the property, real and personal, including causes of action and every other asset of each of the constituent religious corporations, shall vest in such surviving or consolidated religious corporation without further act or deed. Except as the court may otherwise direct, as provided in section 8-1.1 of the Estates, Powers and Trusts Law, any disposition made in the Will of a person dying domiciled in this state or in any other instrument executed under the laws of this state, taking effect after such consolidation, to or for any of the constituent religious corporations shall inure to the benefit of the surviving or consolidated religious corporation. So far as is necessary for that purpose, or for the purpose of a like result with respect to a disposition governed by the law of any other jurisdiction, the existence of each constituent religious corporation shall be deemed to continue in and through the surviving or consolidated religious corporation.

(c) The surviving or consolidated religious corporation shall assume and be liable for all the liabilities, obligations and penalties of each of the constituent religious corporations. No liability or obligation due or to become due, claim or demand for any cause existing against any such corporation, or any member, officer or trustee thereof, shall be released or impaired by such merger or consolidation. No action or proceeding, whether civil or criminal, then pending by or against any such constituent corporation, or any member, officer or trustee thereof, shall abate or be discontinued by such merger or consolidation, but may be enforced, prosecuted, settled or comprised as if such merger or consolidation had not occurred, or such surviving or consolidated corporation may be substituted in such action or special proceeding in place of any constituent corporation.

(d) In the case of a merger, the certificate of incorporation of the surviving corporation shall be automatically amended to the extent, if any, that changes in its certificate of incorporation are set forth in the plan of merger; and, in the case of a consolidation, the statements set forth in the certificate of consolidation and which are required or permitted to be set forth in a certificate of incorporation of a religious corporation formed under this section shall be its certificate of incorporation.

11. Such consolidated or merged synod shall have all the powers and responsibilities conferred upon synods by the constitution and form of government of the Presbyterian Church (U.S.A.) or the Evangelical Lutheran Church in America.

12. This section shall apply to consolidation or merger of incorporated foreign and domestic presbyteries as described in section fifteen-a of this chapter.

13. Such consolidated or merged synod may, at a meeting thereof, duly held, determine that its board of trustees and its mission council be merged into a unicameral board which shall be know as the synod mission council, and that the membership of such unicameral board consist of not less than fifteen members but shall not be restricted as to the maximum number of members.

History: Add, L 1974, ch 610, eff May 30, 1974; amd, L 1977, ch 154, eff May 20, 1977; L 1985, ch 381, § 4, eff July 19, 1985; L 1987, ch 70, § 2, eff May 16, 1987.

§ 16. Property of extinct churches

Such incorporated governing body may decide that a church, parish or society in connection with it or over which it has ecclesiastical jurisdiction, has become extinct, if it has failed for two consecutive years next prior thereto, to maintain religious service according to the discipline, customs and usages of such governing body, or has had less than thirteen resident attending members paying annual pew rent, or making annual contributions towards its support, or in case of a United Methodist church, if such action have the consent of the presiding bishop and of a majority of the district superintendents of the annual conference and of the district board of church location and building of the district in which the action is contemplated, or in case of a parish of the Protestant Episcopal Church, if such parish has ceased for two consecutive years next prior thereto, to have a sufficient number of men qualified to elect or to serve as wardens and vestrymen therein, and may take possession of the temporalities and property belonging to such church, parish or religious society, and manage the same; or may, in pursuance of the provisions of law relating to the disposition of real property by religious corporations, sell or dispose of the same and apply the proceeds thereof to any of the purposes to which the property of such governing religious body is devoted, and it shall not divert such property to any other object. And for the purpose of obtaining a record title to the land and the church edifice, or other buildings thereon, by such incorporated governing body, the surviving trustee or trustees of said extinct church, or if there be no surviving trustee then a surviving member of said extinct church, may, without a consideration being paid therefor by such incorporated governing body, convey to it said land and church edifice, or other buildings thereon, subject, however, to an order of the supreme or county court based upon a petition reciting that said church has become extinct; the names of its surviving trustee or trustees, and the names of its members, who must have given their consent to the making of said conveyance. Upon the recital of said facts in said petition the court shall have jurisdiction to grant an order allowing said conveyance to be made without a consideration; and should there be no surviving members, as well as no surviving trustees of said extinct church, said petition may be made by an officer of such incorporated governing body, in which event the court, upon a recital of said fact, shall have jurisdiction to appoint a suitable person as trustee for the purpose of making said conveyance. And in case of a Reformed Church of America, Dutch Reformed Church, or Reformed Dutch Church in the United States of America or the United Reformed Dutch and Lutheran Church of America or a parish of the Protestant Episcopal Church, a Universalist Church or Society, an incorporated United Methodist Church, or an incorporated church of the United Church of Christ, or an incorporated Congregational Christian Church, should either of such surviving members or such surviving trustee of said extinct church refuse to act and sign said petition after request by an officer of said governing body of said last-named churches personally made by such officer, then said petition may be made by an officer of such incorporated governing body and in that event the court shall have jurisdiction and may appoint a suitable person as trustee for the purpose of making said conveyance. And in the case of said last-named Reformed churches, or of a parish of the Protestant Episcopal Church, a Universalist Church or Society, an incorporated United Methodist Church, or of an incorporated church of the United Church of Christ or of an incorporated Congregational Christian Church, the trustees of any such extinct church, the treasurer thereof or any person acting in either of said capacities may be required to show cause before the supreme court at a special term thereof held in the judicial district in which said church shall be located why they should not be required to give an account of all moneys and property of said church which they shall have in their hands or under their control and in case of their failure to show such causes they be required to account before said court for all the properties and moneys of the said church which shall be in their hands or under their control, and after the payment of all the claims against such church, if any, and the expenses of such proceeding, if it shall further appear that none of such property in the hands of said persons is required for the further support or maintenance of said church, said money and proceeds thereof shall be directed to be paid and turned over to said governing religious body to apply to the purposes to which the property of such governing body is devoted. An application or such order to show cause shall be made by a verified petition, which petition may be made by said governing body of said church or any officer thereof. Where a proceeding is instituted under this section for the sale of the real property of an extinct religious corporation, a compliance with paragraphs five, six, seven and eight of section five hundred eleven of the not-for-profit corporation law shall be unnecessary, and such proceedings shall be in all respects valid without a compliance with said subdivisions. Any gift, legacy, devise, annuity, or other benefit to a United Methodist Church that accrues or becomes available after said church has become extinct shall be and become the property of the trustees of the annual conference within whose jurisdiction the said extinct church was located. Any gift, legacy, devise, annuity or other benefit to a Universalist Church or Society that accrues or becomes available after said church or society has become extinct shall be and become the property of the New York State Convention of Universalists, as the governing religious body of every active, extinct or disbanded Universalist church or society within the bounds of the State of New York. The New York conference of the United Church of Christ, Inc. shall be deemed the governing religious body of every extinct or disbanded church of the United Church of Christ and of any extinct or disbanded Congregational Christian Church which is a member of the New York Conference of the United Church of Christ, Inc. within the meaning of this section. The provisions of this section shall not apply to any Presbyterian church in connection with the General Assembly of the Presbyterian Church (U.S.A.).

History: Add, L 1909, ch 53, amd, L 1949, ch 660, L 1954, ch 476, § 2, L 1955, ch 88, L 1960, ch 489, L 1969, ch 962, § 4, L 1972, ch 900, eff Sept. 1, 1972.

Amd, L 1985, ch 381, § 5, eff July 19, 1985.

CASE ANNOTATIONS

The provision of this section has no application to a case where the governing body unlawfully took possession of the corporate property and thus enforced nonuser. Westminster Presbyterian Church v Trustees of Presbytery (1914) 211 N.Y. 214, 105 N.E. 199, reh den 212 N.Y. 552, 106 N.E. 1044

Under the Religious Corporations Law a church which has been affiliated with and a constituent part of the Presbyterian Church in United States of America, and as such has acquired property, cannot by secession terminate its relationship and thereby avoid supervision and control of the denominational organization at large. Trustees of Presbytery v Westminster Presbyterian Church (1917) 222 N.Y. 305, 118 N.E. 800

After the Religious Corporations Law was so amended as to recognize denominational control by constituted authorities existing under ecclesiastical law of the Presbyterian church, and allowed consolidation of Presbyterian churches only with consent of Presbytery, two churches consolidating pursuant to such consent lose their original powers, and, as a single corporation, become subject to the laws in force at the time of consolidation, although as constituent corporations they would not have been subject thereto. Westminster Presbyterian Church v Trustees of Presbytery (1911) 142 A.D. 855, 127 N.Y.S. 836, app dismd 202 N.Y. 581, 96 N.E. 1134 and later app 152 A.D. 949, 137 N.Y.S. 1148

Under this section the Trustees of Presbytery, on dissolving a congregation of an incorporated Presbyterian church so that it has neither members nor trustees of its own, is entitled to possession of the church property as against the church corporation, or its former members who, by ecclesiastical law, are under duty of accepting letters of dismission and to become communicants of some other congregation of that denomination. Westminster Presbyterian Church v Trustees of Presbytery (1911) 142 A.D. 855, 127 N.Y.S. 836, app dismd 202 N.Y. 581, 96 N.E. 1134 and later app 152 A.D. 949, 137 N.Y.S. 1148

The trustees of Presbytery are an incorporated governing body of Presbyterian churches within its territory, within the contemplation of this section, although said trustees were not incorporated under the provisions of § 15, but by L 1867 c 206 special act. And the trustees, as an incorporated body, have the same authority to declare the congregation of a Presbyterian church extinct as if they had been incorporated under § 15. Westminster Presbyterian Church v Trustees of Presbytery (1911) 142 A.D. 855, 127 N.Y.S. 836, app dismd 202 N.Y. 581, 96 N.E. 1134 and later app 152 A.D. 949, 137 N.Y.S. 1148

The Newark Annual Conference of the Methodist Church was properly awarded proceeds of a condemnation award made when church lands deeded in trustees of church in 1872 were appropriated. Successor to original trustees claimed award on theory church was independent and had not surrendered control to a religious denomination. History of particular church and the Methodist Episcopal

Church showed that original grant implied a trust for the benefit of the present annual conference. Conklin v State (1954) 284 A.D. 193, 130 N.Y.S.2d 618

Amendment to this section by ch 660 of the Laws of 1949 cannot be given retroactive application. Re Estate of Aker (1964, 3d Dept) 21 A.D.2d 935, 251 N.Y.S.2d 144

The compulsory provisions of the statute which govern divestiture of title to real estate and other temporalities have application only to those churches or church denominations and organizations as are therein expressly specified. The amendment to this section by L 1928 c 489, which added the provision that "The New York Congregational Conference, Inc., shall be deemed governing religious body of every extinct or disbanded Congregational church within meaning of this section," is to be read only in connection with the fore part of such section which has to do with the voluntary disposition of title to real estate standing in name of an extinct Congregational church. Rollins v Middlebrook (1936) 159 Misc 816, 289 N.Y.S. 963

§ 17. Property of extinct Free Baptist churches

The property both real and personal, belonging to or held in trust for any Free Baptist church, or Free Baptist religious society organized under the laws of the state of New York, that has become, or shall become extinct, shall vest in and become the property of the Central association existing under the laws of the state of New York, and its successors and assigns; provided that this section shall not affect the reversionary interests of any person in such property, nor the interests of any incorporated association; and any Free Baptist church or Free Baptist religious society becoming extinct or about to disband or disorganize may, by a vote of two-thirds of its members present and voting therefor at a meeting regularly called for that purpose assign, transfer, grant and convey all its temporalities to and place the same in the possession of the Central association existing under the laws of the state of New York.

A Free Baptist church or Free Baptist religious society which has failed for two consecutive years next prior thereto to maintain religious services according to the custom and usages of Free Baptist churches, or has less than thirteen resident attending members, paying annual pew rental or making annual contributions towards its support, may be declared extinct in the following manner, viz.: Upon such notice as the court may prescribe, and upon application made by petition, stating fully the facts in the case, and on evidence being furnished that the said Free Baptist church or Free Baptist religious society has ceased to hold religious services in and use said property for religious worship or service for a term of two years previous to such application, the supreme court, at a term thereof held in the judicial district where such property is situated, may grant an order declaring such church or society extinct, and thereon direct that all its temporalities shall be transferred to, and thereupon shall be taken possession of by the Central association of the state of New York, or directing that the same be sold in the manner directed by said order, and that the proceeds thereof, after the payment of the debts of such church or society, be paid over to the Central association of the state of New York. All property and proceeds from the sale of property so transferred to said association shall be used and applied for the purposes for which said Central association of the state of New York was organized and shall not be directed to any other purpose.

The First Free Will Baptist church of the city of New York, located in the borough of Manhattan, shall in no way be amenable to the provisions of this section.

History: Add, L 1909, ch 53, eff Feb 17, 1909.

§ 17-a. Property of extinct Seventh Day Baptist churches and Seventh Day Baptist religious societies

1. All property, both personal and real, belonging to or held in trust for any Seventh Day Baptist church or any Seventh Day Baptist religious society that has or shall become extinct shall vest in and become the property of the Seventh Day Baptist missionary society and its successors and assigns; provided that this section shall not affect the reversionary interest of any person or corporation in said property or any valid lien thereon.

2. Any Seventh Day Baptist church or any Seventh Day Baptist religious society in this state which has ceased or failed, or which shall cease or fail, to maintain religious worship or services, or to use its property for religious worship or services, according to the tenets, usages and customs of Seventh Day Baptist churches which are members of the Seventh Day Baptist general conference, for the space of two consecutive years immediately prior to application to the supreme court of the state for an order dissolving said church or society as herein provided, or whose membership has so diminished or shall so diminish in numbers or in financial strength as to render it impossible or impracticable for such church or society to maintain religious worship or services or to protect its property from exposure to waste or dilapidation, or to fulfill the purpose for which it was incorporated, shall be deemed and taken to be extinct, and may, by order of the supreme court of the state, be so declared and thereupon dissolved, and the property of such church or society may, by said order, be transferred to, and the title and possession thereof vested in, said Seventh Day Baptist missionary society.

3. An application for such an order and disposition of property may be made by any member, trustee, or officer of said Seventh Day Baptist missionary society, or any member of such church or society, when duly authorized thereto by the board of trustees of said Seventh Day Baptist missionary society, upon a verified petition setting forth the facts authorizing such order and disposition of property. Upon the presentation of such petition to the supreme court of the state, such court may proceed in a summary manner after such notice as the court may prescribe, to inquire into the merits of such application, and if, upon examination by the court, it shall satisfactorily appear that the making of the order and the disposition of property applied for is necessary and proper, for any of the causes mentioned in subdivision two of

this section, such court shall make a final order declaring such church or society extinct and dissolving the same and transferring any property and the title and possession thereof, which may belong to such church or society, to and vesting the same in said Seventh Day Baptist missionary society, it being the purpose and intent of this section to preserve to the Seventh Day Baptist denomination all property owned by or held in trust for any such church or society for religious purposes.

History: Add, L 1943, ch 349, eff Apr 7, 1943.

§ 17-b. Property of extinct Presbyterian churches in connection with the General Assembly of the Presbyterian Church (U.S.A.)

Whenever the presbytery having jurisdiction over a particular church in connection with the General Assembly of the Presbyterian Church (U.S.A.) dissolves or declares extinct the particular church, upon petition by the presbytery to the supreme or county court and upon satisfactory proof of the facts leading to said dissolution, the court shall have jurisdiction to grant an order to the effect that all property of whatever kind which may have belonged to, or have been held by, said church shall vest in the presbytery of jurisdiction in as full and ample a manner as the same shall theretofore have been vested in the church so declared to be dissolved and extinct. The stated clerk of the presbytery of jurisdiction shall record in the office of the county clerk, in which the church is located, a certified copy of the resolution of the presbytery declaring such church extinct and the court order transferring the title of the church property; and the recording of such a resolution and court order shall be proof of the vesting of the title of the real property of such church in the presbytery of jurisdiction.

History: Add, L 1954, ch 476, § 3, amd, L 1960, ch 489, L 1962, ch 53, eff Feb 27, 1962.

Amd, L 1985, ch 381, § 6, eff July 19, 1985.

Section heading, amd, L 1985, ch 381, § 6, eff July 19, 1985.

CASE ANNOTATIONS

The denial of motion to vacate an order dissolving a church and vesting its property and assets in the Presbytery was proper and constitutionally enforceable by the court and the court had jurisdiction by virtue of § 17-b of the Religious Corporations Law, which interferes neither with the control of ecclesiastical Polity nor church doctrine. Re Presbytery of Albany (1970, 3d Dept) 35 A.D.2d 252, 315 N.Y.S.2d 428, affd 28 N.Y.2d 772, 321 N.Y.S.2d 377, 269 N.E.2d 918, app dismd 404 US 803, 30 L Ed 2d 35, 92 S Ct 80

There was no violation of the Fourteenth Amendment inherent in the statute that the property involved is deemed to be under the jurisdiction of the General Church, as the very act of becoming a part of a hierarchial church, which respondent church was deemed to do, has a consequence the voluntary relinquishment of dominion and control over church property which precluded any future claim that there was a divesting of property rights or that the statute was retroactive and since the respondent church has been declared extinct, the property and assets vested in the General Church. Application of Presbytery of Albany (1970) 63 Misc. 2d 791, 312 N.Y.S.2d 505, affd (3d Dept) 35 A.D.2d 252, 315 N.Y.S.2d 428, affd 28

N.Y.2d 772, 321 N.Y.S.2d 377, 269 N.E.2d 918, app dismd 404 US 803, 30 L Ed 2d 35, 92 S Ct 80

A A civil court has jurisdiction, without violation of First Amendment of United States Constitution when it decides church property disputes without interferring with or attempting to resolve underlying controversies over religious doctrine and practice, and without duplicating secular interests in matters of purely ecclesiastical concern. Application of Presbytery of Albany (1970) 63 Misc. 2d 791, 312 N.Y.S.2d 505, affd (3d Dept) 35 A.D.2d 252, 315 N.Y.S.2d 428, affd 28 N.Y.2d 772, 321 N.Y.S.2d 377, 269 N.E.2d 918, app dismd 404 US 803, 30 L Ed 2d 35, 92 S Ct 80

§ 17-c. Property of Lutheran congregations

1. Congregations of the Lutheran Church in America. The synod having jurisdiction over a particular congregation of the Lutheran Church in America, may declare defunct any congregation, belonging to the synod, which has disbanded, or has ceased or failed to maintain religious worship or services according to the tenets and usages of the Lutheran Church, or whose membership has so diminished in numbers as to render it impossible or impracticable for such congregation to fulfill the purposes for which it was organized or to protect its property from waste and deterioration, or having departed from membership in the Lutheran Church in America, without the consent of a convention of the synod.

Whenever the synod having jurisdiction over a particular congregation of the Lutheran Church in America, declares defunct the particular congregation, upon petition to the supreme court, and upon satisfactory proof of the facts leading to said declaration, the court shall have jurisdiction to grant an order to the effect that all property of whatever kind which may have belonged to, or having been held by, said congregation shall vest in the synod of jurisdiction in as full and ample a manner as the same shall theretofore, have been vested in the congregation so declared defunct.

The secretary of the synod of jurisdiction shall record in the office of the county clerk, in which the congregation is located, a certified copy of the resolution of the synod, declaring such congregation defunct and the court order transferring the title of the congregation's property; and the recording of such resolution and court order shall be proof of the vesting of the title of the real property of such congregation in the synod of jurisdiction.

2. Congregations of the Evangelical Lutheran Church in America.

(a) The relationship between a congregation of the Evangelical Lutheran church in America and the church may be terminated in one of the following ways:

(i) The congregation takes action to dissolve;

(ii) The congregation ceases to exist;

(iii) The membership of the congregation becomes so scattered or diminished in numbers as to make it impracticable for such congregation to fulfill the purposes for which it was organized. In such case, the synod in order to protect the property from waste and deterioration, through the synod council or trustees appointed by it, may take charge and control of the property of the congregation to hold, manage, and convey the same on behalf of the synod. The congregation shall have the right to appeal the decision to the synod assembly;

(iv) The congregation is no longer recognized by the church under the disciplinary provisions of the Evangelical Lutheran Church in America; or

(v) The congregation terminates its relationship according to the procedure outlined in paragraph (b) of this subdivision.

(b) A congregation may terminate its relationship with the church by the following procedure:

(i) A resolution indicating desire to terminate its relationship must be adopted at a legally called and conducted special meeting of the congregation by a two-thirds majority of the voting members present;

(ii) The secretary of the congregation shall submit a copy of the resolution to the synodical bishop and shall mail a copy of the resolution to voting members of the congregation. This notice shall be submitted within ten days after the resolution has been adopted;

(iii) The bishop of the synod shall consult with the congregation during a period of at least ninety days;

(iv) If the congregation, after consultation, still desires to terminate its relationship, such action may be taken at a legally called and conducted special meeting of the congregation by a two-thirds majority of the voting members present, at which meeting the synodical bishop or an authorized representative shall be present. Notice of the meeting shall be mailed to all voting members at least ten days in advance of the meeting;

(v) A certified copy of the resolution to terminate its relationship shall be sent to the synodical bishop, at which time the relationship between the congregation and this church shall be terminated;

(vi) Notice of termination shall be forwarded by the synodical bishop to the secretary of the church and published in the periodical of the church; and

(vii) Congregations which had been members of the Lutheran Church in America shall be required, in addition to the foregoing provisions, to receive synodical approval before terminating their membership in the church.

(c) Subject to the provisions of the governing documents of congregations recognized at the establishment of the Evangelical Lutheran Church in America, the following shall govern the ownership of property by congregations of the Evangelical Lutheran Church in America:

(i) Title to property shall reside in the congregation. The congregation may dispose of its property as it determines, subject to any self-accepted indebtedness or other self-accepted restrictions;

(ii) Title to the undisposed property of a congregation that ceases to exist by virtue of subparagraph (i), (ii) or (iii) of paragraph (a) of this subdivision,

shall pass to the synod of this church to which the congregation is related;

(iii) Title to the property of a congregation that is no longer recognized by this church as a result of discipline shall continue to reside in the congregation;

(iv) Title to the property of a congregation that has acted to terminate its relationship with this church by the provisions of paragraph (b) of this subdivision and to relate to another Lutheran church body shall continue to reside in the congregation; and

(v) Title to the property of a congregation that has acted to terminate its relationship with this church by the provisions of paragraph (b) of this subdivision and to become independent or to relate to a non-Lutheran church body shall continue to reside in the congregation only with the consent of the Synod Council. The Synod Council, after consultation with the congregation by an established synodical process, may give approval to the request to become independent or to relate to a non-Lutheran church body, in which case title shall remain with the majority of the congregation. If the Synod Council fails to give such approval, title shall remain with those members who desire to continue as a congregation of this church.

History: Add, L 1974, ch 980, eff June 13, 1974; amd, L 1987, ch 70, § 3, eff May 16, 1987.

CASE ANNOTATIONS

Regional synod of national church organization was properly granted summary judgment declaring that it was entitled to all right, title and interest in property and assets of local church, including fire insurance proceeds, under provisions of constitutional documents of local church, constitution of national church organization, and CLS Relig Corp § 17-c authorizing synod to take control of congregation's property where necessary to protect it from waste, where evidence showed that endowment fund of local church had been completely exhausted, that local church was $26,000 in debt, that gas and electric service to property had been terminated for nonpayment, that national church organization and synod had provided considerable financial assistance in effort to save church, that synod had paid premium for property and liability insurance on premises, and that before fire church had discontinued worship services. Upstate New York Synod of Evangelical Lutheran Church v Christ Evangelical Lutheran Church (1992, 4th Dept) 185 A.D.2d 693, 585 N.Y.S.2d 919

In action by regional synod of national church organization seeking declaration that it was entitled to all right, title and interest in property and assets of local church under both provisions of church constitutional documents and CLS Relig Corp § 17-c authorizing synod to take control of congregation's property where necessary to protect it from waste, synod was entitled to summary judgment dismissing local church's counterclaim alleging that synod breached fiduciary duty in failing to provide church with efficient pastors, since civil courts should not intervene in ecclesiastical matters such as church governance even if rights to church property may be affected incidentally. Upstate New York Synod of Evangelical Lutheran Church v Christ Evangelical Lutheran Church (1992, 4th Dept) 185 A.D.2d 693, 585 N.Y.S.2d 919

§ 18. Dissolution of religious corporations

Whenever any religious corporation shall cease to act in its corporate capacity and keep up the religious services; it shall be lawful for the supreme court of this state, upon the application of a majority of the trustees thereof, in case said court shall deem it proper so to do, to order and decree a dissolution of such religious corporation, and for that purpose to order and direct a sale and conveyance of any and all property belonging to such corporation, and after providing for the ascertaining and payment of the debts of such corporation, and the necessary costs and expenses of such sale and proceedings for dissolution, so far as the proceeds of such sale shall be sufficient to pay the same; such court may order and direct any surplus of such proceeds remaining after paying such debts, costs and expenses, to be devoted and applied to any such religious, benevolent, or charitable objects or purposes as the said trustees may indicate by their petition and the said court may approve.

Such application to said court shall be made by petition, duly verified by said trustees, which petition shall state the particular reason or causes why such sale and dissolution are sought; the situation, condition and estimated value of the property of said corporation, and the particular object or purposes to which it is proposed to devote any surplus of the proceeds of such property; and such petition shall, in all cases, be accompanied with proof that notice of the time and place of such intended application to said court, has been duly published once in each week for at least four weeks successively, next preceding such application, in a newspaper published in the county where such corporation is located.

In case there shall be no trustees of such religious corporation residing in the county in which such corporation is located, such application may be made, and such proceedings taken, by a majority of the members of such religious corporation residing in such county.

In case such corporation is under the jurisdiction of an incorporated ecclesiastical governing body such application may be made and such proceedings taken by such incorporated ecclesiastical governing body, provided the trustees or other officers or surviving members of the local church shall refuse to act after request has been duly made by the governing body, and in such case the proceeds shall be turned over to said governing body.

History: Add, L 1909, ch 53, amd, L 1932, ch 152, eff Mar 15, 1932.

CASE ANNOTATIONS

The state may take away a charter of a religious corporation in an equity action where there has been a disregard or perversion of its corporate purpose, although no statutory authority to dissolve such corporation exists. People v Volunteer Rescue Army, Inc. (1941) 262 A.D. 237, 28 N.Y.S.2d 994

Where church constitution provided that, in the event of disbanding, title to property should vest in a synod or its successors and assigns, and where church did disband, trial court properly directed that surplus remaining after payment of debts be transferred to successor to the synod referred to in the constitution even though the church had petitioned for order directing that the surplus be transferred to an orphans' school. German Evangelical Lutheran St. Johannes Church v Metropolitan New York Synod of Lutheran Church (1975, 2d Dept) 47 A.D.2d 904, 366 N.Y.S.2d 214

Church association which qualified neither as trustee nor as member of inactive church lacked authority to seek judicial dissolution of church and transfer of its property under CLS Relig Corp § 18. Community Bible Church, Inc. v Pine Woods Union Church Asso. (1987, 3d Dept) 131 A.D.2d 965, 516 N.Y.S.2d 546, app dismd 70 N.Y.2d 794, 522 N.Y.S.2d 107, 516 N.E.2d 1220

Courts are extremely loath to interfere with the conduct of temporal affairs of religious corporations at the instance of a small number of dissatisfied members. Only in a most extreme case do courts say that an honest and deliberate determination of governing body and of majority of membership of religious corporations in refusing to sue upon claim for past wrongs is so palpably and inexcusably negligent as to be tantamount to a breach of duty and so to justify judicial interference at the instance of a dissenting member. Koch v Estes (1933) 146 Misc 249, 262 N.Y.S. 23, affd 240 A.D. 829, 266 N.Y.S. 1008, affd 264 N.Y. 480, 191 N.E. 525

§ 19. Corporations for organizing and maintaining mission churches and Sunday schools

Ten or more members of two or more incorporated churches may become a corporation for the purpose of organizing and maintaining mission churches and Sunday schools, and of acquiring property therefor, by executing a certificate stating the name of such corporation, the city in which its principal office or church or school is or is intended to be located; the number of trustees to manage its affairs, which shall be three, six or nine, and the names of the trustees for the first year of its existence, which certificate shall be acknowledged or proved and filed as hereinbefore provided. Whenever a mission church established by such corporation becomes self-sustaining, such mission church may become incorporated and shall be governed under the provisions of this chapter for the incorporation and government of a church of the religious denomination to which such mission church belongs, and thereon such parent corporation may convey to such incorporated church the property connected therewith.

History: Add, L 1909, ch 53, eff Feb 17, 1909.

§ 20. Corporations for acquiring parsonages for district superintendents and camp-meeting grounds

The district superintendent and a majority of the district stewards residing within a district erected by an annual conference of The United Methodist Church, may become incorporated for the purposes of acquiring, maintaining and improving real property to be used either as a parsonage for the district superintendent of such district or as a camp ground for camp-meeting purposes, or for both of such objects by executing, acknowledging and filing a certificate stating the name and object of the corporation to be formed, the name of such annual conference, and of such district, the names, residences and official relations to such district of the signers thereof, the number of trustees of such corporation, which shall be three or some multiple of three not more than twenty-one, the names of such trustees, designating one-third to hold office for three years, one-third to hold office for two years, and one-third to hold office for one year. On filing such certificate the district superintendent and all the stewards of such district by virtue of their respective offices, shall be a corporation by the name and for the purposes therein stated, and the persons therein named shall be the first trustees thereof. The district superintendent and stewards of any other adjoining districts, in this or any other state, may become members of any such corporation, at the time of its formation or any time thereafter, with the consent of such corporation, which has for its sole object, or for one of its objects, the acquiring, maintaining and improving of real property as a camp ground for camp-meeting purposes, if such district superintendent and a majority of such stewards sign, acknowledge and cause to be filed in the office of the secretary of state, a certificate stating such object, the name of such adjoining district, and the names, residences and official relations to such district of the signers thereof, with the consent of the original corporation indorsed thereon.

If such a corporation, which has for its sole object or one of its objects, the acquisition and maintenance of camp grounds for camp-meeting purposes, is composed of the district superintendent and the district stewards of more than one district, the number of such trustees shall be apportioned equally, as near as may be, between the different districts, and the district superintendent and district stewards of such district shall elect the number of trustees so apportioned to such district, and the remainder, if any, over an equal division of the trustees, shall be elected by all the members of the corporation.

A person holding property in trust for the purposes of a parsonage for the district superintendent of a district, and his successors in office, or for camp-meeting purposes, for The United Methodist Church, may convey the same to a corporation formed for the purpose of acquiring such property within the district in which the property is situated. Meetings held under the direction of such a corporation upon camp grounds owned by it shall be deemed religious meetings, within the provisions of law relating to disturbances of religious meetings. Whenever such a corporation or any camp ground association owns land bordering upon any navigable waters, to be used for camp-meeting purposes only, such corporation or association may regulate or prohibit the landing of persons or vessels at the wharves, piers or shores upon such grounds during the holding of religious service thereon.

If the trustees of any such corporation heretofore incorporated have not been classified, so that the terms of office of one-third of their number expire each year, the trustees of such corporation shall be elected annually by the members thereof; but if the trustees of any such corporation have been so classified, one-third of the total number of trustees shall be elected annually to hold office for three years. Such a corporation heretofore incorporated may, by a majority vote, at an annual meeting, or at a special meeting duly called therefor, determine to change the number of its trustees to three, or some multiple thereof, not more than twenty-one. On such determination a majority of the trustees shall sign, acknowledge and file in the offices where the original certificate of such corporation is filed, a supplemental certificate, specifying such reduction or increase; and thereon the number of trustees shall be the number stated in such certificate. If the number of trustees is increased, the corporation shall elect, at its next annual meeting, a sufficient number of trustees to hold office for one, two and three years, respectively, so that the terms of office of one-third of the whole number of trustees of such corporation shall expire at each annual meeting thereafter. If the number is reduced, the corporation shall thereafter elect at its annual meetings one-third of the number of trustees specified in such supplemental certificate, but the trustees in office when such certificate is filed shall continue in office until the expiration of their terms, respectively.

History: Add, L 1909, ch 53, amd, L 1924, ch 517, L 1969, ch 962, § 5, eff May 26, 1969.

Third unnumbered par, amd, L 1980, ch 843, § 193, eff Sept 1, 1980.

§ 21. Corporations for acquiring camp-meeting grounds for the Reformed Methodist denomination

The visiting elder of a visiting elder's district, erected by an annual conference of the Reformed Methodist denomination, and three members or more in good and regular standing of three or more churches of such denomination, may become incorporated for the purposes of acquiring, maintaining and improving real property, to be used as a camp ground for camp-meeting purposes, by executing, acknowledging and filing a certificate stating the name and object of the corporation to be formed, the name of such annual conference, and of such visiting elder's district, the names, residences and particular church membership of the signers thereof, the number of trustees of such corporation, which shall be three, or some multiple of three, not more than twenty-one, the names of such trustees, designating one-third to hold office for three years, one-third to hold office for two years, and one-third to hold office for one year. On filing such certificate, the visiting elder and the trustees named therein, and their successors in office, shall be a corporation by the name and for the purposes therein stated. A person holding property in trust for camp-meeting purposes for the Reformed Methodist denomination, may convey the same to a corporation formed for the purpose of acquiring such property within the visiting elder's district where the property is situated. Meetings held under the direction of such a corporation upon camp grounds owned by it, shall be deemed religious meetings within the religious law, relating to the disturbance of religious meetings. Whenever such a corporation, or any camp ground association of the Reformed Methodist denomination, owns land bordering upon any navigable waters to be used for camp-meeting purposes only, such corporation or association may regulate or prohibit the landing of persons or vessels at the wharves, piers or shores upon such grounds during the holding of religious services thereon.

History: Add, L 1909, ch 53, eff Feb 17, 1909.

Religious Corporations Law

Amd, L 1980, ch 843, § 194, eff Sept 1, 1980.

§ 21-a. Corporations for acquiring lands for parsonage or camp-meeting purposes for the Free Methodist denomination

The district elder and a majority of the stewards residing in the district elder's district, elected by an annual conference of the Free Methodist Church denomination, may become incorporated, for the purpose of acquiring, maintaining and improving real property, to be used for the purpose of a district elder's parsonage or for camp-meeting purposes, or for both such purposes, by acknowledging and filing a certificate, stating the name and object of the corporation, the name of such annual conference, and of such district elder's district, the names, residences and official relations to such district of the signers thereof, the number of trustees of said incorporation, which shall be three, or some multiple of three, not to exceed twelve, the names of such trustees, designating one-third to hold office for three years, one-third to hold office for two years and one-third to hold office for one year.

On filing such certificate, the district elder and all the stewards of such district, by virtue of their respective offices, shall be a corporation by the name, and for the purposes therein stated, and the persons therein named as trustees shall be the first trustees thereof.

A person holding property in trust for the purpose of a parsonage for the district elder of the district, or for camp meeting purposes, and his successors in office, for the Free Methodist church denomination, may convey the same to a corporation organized for this purpose of acquiring property within the district in which such property is situated.

Meetings held under the direction of such corporation, upon camp grounds owned by such corporation, shall be deemed to be religious meetings, within the provisions of the law relating to the disturbance of religious meetings.

When such corporation or camp ground association owns land bordering on any navigable waters to be used for camp meeting purposes only, such corporation or association may regulate or prohibit the landing of persons or vessels at the wharves, piers or shores upon such ground during the holding of religious services thereon.

History: Add, L 1915, ch 209, eff Apr 5, 1915.

Fourth unnumbered par, amd, L 1980, ch 843, § 195, eff Sept, 1980.

§ 22. Establishing and maintaining a home for aged poor

An incorporated church or congregation in this state, either by itself or in conjunction with other incorporated churches or congregations, shall have power to establish and maintain by its or their trustees or other officers, as part of its or their regular church and charitable work, a home for the aged poor of its or their membership or congregation and may take and hold as joint tenants, tenants in common or otherwise, by conveyance, donation, bequest or devise, real and personal property for such purpose, and may purchase or erect suitable buildings therefor. Any such church or congregation, either by itself or in conjunction with other incorporated churches or congregations may take and hold any grant, donation, bequest or devise of real or personal property heretofore made, upon trust, and apply the same or the income thereof under the direction of the trustees or other officers having charge of the temporalities of such church, or churches, or congregation, or congregations, for the purpose of establishing or maintaining such a home, and for the erection, preservation, repair or extension of any buildings for such purpose, upon such terms and conditions and subject to such conditions, limitations and restrictions as shall be contained in the deed, will or other instrument or conveyance by which the property is given, transferred or conveyed.

History: Add, L 1909, ch 53, eff Feb 17, 1909.

§ 23. Powers of churches created by special laws

If a church be incorporated by special law, it and its trustees shall have, in addition to the powers conferred on it by such law, all the powers and privileges conferred on incorporated churches and the trustees thereof respectively by the provisions of this article, and also all the powers and privileges conferred by this chapter on churches of the same denomination or of the like character, and on the trustees thereof respectively.

History: Add, L 1909, ch 53, eff Feb 17, 1909.

§ 24. Government of churches incorporated prior to January first, eighteen hundred and twenty-eight

Any provision of this chapter shall not be deemed to apply to any church incorporated under any general or special law, prior to January first, eighteen hundred and twenty-eight, if such provision is inconsistent with or in derogation of any of the rights and privileges of such corporation as they existed under the law by or pursuant to which such corporation was formed, unless such corporation subsequent to such date, shall have lawfully reincorporated under a law enacted since the first day of January, eighteen hundred and twenty-eight, or unless the trustees of such corporation shall, by resolution, determine that the provisions of this chapter applying to churches of the same denomination and to the trustees thereof shall apply to such church, and unless such resolution shall be submitted to the next ensuing annual meeting of such church, and ratified by a majority of the votes of the qualified voters present and voting thereon. Notice of the adoption of such resolution and of the proposed submission thereof for ratification, shall be given with the notice of such annual meeting, and in addition thereto, mailed to each member of such church corporation at his last known post-office address, at least two weeks prior to such annual meeting, and published once a week for two successive weeks immediately preceding such meeting in a newspaper, if any, published in the city, village or town in which the principal place of worship of such corporation is located, and otherwise in a newspaper published in an adjoining town. If such resolution is so ratified, the trustees of such church shall cause a certificate setting forth a copy of such resolution, its adoption by the board of trustees and its due ratification by the members of such corporation, to be filed in the office of the clerk of the county in which the principal place of worship of such corporation is located. Such county clerk shall cause such certificate to be recorded in the book in which certificates of incorporation of religious corporations are recorded in pursuance of law.

History: Add, L 1909, ch 53, eff Feb 17, 1909.

§ 25. Pastoral relation

No provision of this chapter authorizes the calling, settlement, dismissal or removal of a minister, or the fixing or changing of his salary, and a meeting of a church corporation for any such purpose shall be called, held, moderated, conducted, governed and notice of such meeting given and person to preside thereat ascertained and the qualification of voters thereat determined, not as required by any provision of this chapter but only according to the aforesaid laws and regulations, practice, discipline, rules and usages of the religious denomination or ecclesiastical governing body, if any, with which the church corporation is connected.

History: Add, L 1909, ch 53, eff Feb 17, 1909.

CASE ANNOTATIONS

The provisions of Canon Law in respect of the requisite quorum for vestry meetings and not the quorum rules of Religious Corporation Law § 42 applied to the election of a new rector. Church of Holy Trinity v Melish (1957) 3 N.Y.2d 476, 168 N.Y.S.2d 952, 146 N.E.2d 685

Church pastor removed by vote of congregation was afforded due process where he was served with charges of alleged misconduct and given proper notice of meeting and opportunity to defend, and his removal would not be invalidated simply because he chose not to respond to charges or attend meeting. Robinson v Davis (1987, 2d Dept) 126 A.D.2d 715, 511 N.Y.S.2d 311

Court properly dismissed action for judgment declaring invalidity of special meeting at which temple members decided not to renew plaintiff's contract as rabbi where (1) temple's constitution and by-laws specifically provided for manner in which special meetings were to be called and held, and thus failure to renew plaintiff's contract could only be judged in terms of whether temple's constitution and by-laws were complied with, and (2) record established that special meeting had been called and held in accordance with temple's constitution and by-laws. Feldbin v Temple Beth-El (1994, 2d Dept) 210 A.D.2d 374, 620 N.Y.S.2d 113

A minister is not removable by the trustees of an incorporated church but by the voting members at a corporate meeting, called and governed according to the discipline of the religious denomination with which the church is connected. Beulah Wesleyan Methodist Church v Henry (1946) 187 Misc 502, 62 N.Y.S.2d 297

Under section of Religious Corporations Law providing that no provision of the chapter authorizes the calling, settlement, dismissal or removal of a minister, court could not direct Protestant Episcopal Church corporation to elect a rector; temporal courts are required to

keep hands off such matters. Anthony v Cardin (1977) 91 Misc. 2d 506, 398 N.Y.S.2d 215

§ 26. Worship

No provision of this chapter authorizes the fixing or changing of the times, nature or order of public or social or other worship of any church, in any other manner or by any other authority than in the manner and by the authority provided in the laws, regulations, practice, discipline, rules and usages of the religious denomination or ecclesiastical governing body, if any, with which the church corporation is connected.

History: Add, L 1909, ch 53, eff Feb 17, 1909.

§ 27. Reservation as to Baptist churches, churches of the United Church of Christ and Congregational Christian churches

Sections twenty-five and twenty-six are not applicable to a Baptist church, a church of the United Church of Christ, a Congregational Christian church or to any other religious corporation having a congregational form of government.

History: Add, L 1909, ch 53, amd, L 1972, ch 900, eff Sept 1, 1972.

Section heading, amd, L 1972, ch 900, eff Sept 1, 1972.

CASE ANNOTATIONS

Deacons of Baptist church were entitled to lifetime tenure based on constitution of church and church custom; however, members of board of trustees were not entitled to lifetime tenure since board controlled temporalities of church and were required to be subject to control of church membership. Ward v Jones (1992, Sup) 154 Misc. 2d 597, 587 N.Y.S.2d 94

§ 28. [Repealed]

History: Add, L 1981, ch 76, § 1, eff Aug 19, 1981; repealed, L 1995, ch 398, § 5, eff Oct 31, 1995.

Former § 28, add, L 1970, ch 692, renumbered § 49, L 1972, ch 900, eff Sept 1, 1972.

ARTICLE 3
PROTESTANT EPISCOPAL PARISHES OR CHURCHES

History: Add, L 1909, ch 53.

§ 40. Meeting for incorporation

Notice of a meeting for the purpose of incorporating an unincorporated Protestant Episcopal parish or congregation, and of electing the first churchwardens and vestrymen thereof, shall specify the object, time and place of such meeting, and shall be made public for at least two weeks prior to such meeting, either by open reading of such notice in time of divine service, at the usual place of worship of such parish or congregation, or by posting the same conspiciously [conspicuously] * on the outer door of such place of worship. Only persons of full age who have been regular attendants at the worship of such parish or congregation and contributors to the support thereof for one year next prior to such meeting, or since the establishment of such parish or congregation, shall be qualified to vote at such meeting. The presence of at least six persons qualified to vote thereat shall be necessary to constitute a quorum of such meeting. The action of the meeting upon any matter or question shall be decided by a majority of the qualified voters voting thereon, a quorum being present. The officiating minister, or if there be none, or he shall be necessarily absent, any other person qualified to vote at the meeting, who is called to the chair, shall preside thereat. Such presiding officer shall receive the votes, be the judge of the qualifications of voters, and declare the result of the votes cast at such meeting. The polls of the meeting shall remain open for one hour or longer, in the discretion of the presiding officer, or if required by a vote of the majority of the voters present. The meeting shall decide whether such unincorporated parish or congregation shall become incorporated. If such decision be in favor of incorporation, such meeting shall decide upon the name of the proposed corporation; what day, either a Sunday or a secular day, shall be the date of the regular annual election; whether the vestrymen thereof shall be three, six, nine, twelve, fifteen, eighteen, twenty-one or twenty-four; and shall elect by ballot from the persons qualified to be voters thereat, who have been baptized, one-third of the number of vestrymen so decided upon to hold office until the first annual election to be held thereafter, one-third of such number, to hold office until one year after such annual election, and one-third of such number to hold office until two years after such annual election; and shall elect from such qualified voters who are communicants in the Protestant Episcopal church, two persons to be churchwardens thereof, one to hold office until such annual election, and one to hold office until one year after such annual election.

* So in original. Probably should read "conspicuously".

History: Add, L 1909, ch 53, amd, L 1971, ch 643, L 1974, ch 171, eff April 9, 1974.

§ 41. Certificate of incorporation

If such meeting shall decide in favor of incorporation and comply with the next preceding section, the presiding officer of such meeting and at least two other persons present and voting thereat, shall execute and acknowledge a certificate of incorporation setting forth:

1. The fact of the calling and holding of such meeting;

2. The name of the corporation as decided upon thereat;

3. The county, and the town, city or village, in which its principal place of worship is, or is intended to be located;

4. The day, either on Sunday or a secular day, upon which the annual election shall be held;

5. The number of vestrymen decided upon at such meeting;

6. The names of the vestrymen elected at such meeting and the term of office of each;

7. The names of the churchwardens elected at such meeting and the term of office of each.

Such certificate, when accompanied by a certificate of the bishop of the diocese within which the principal place of worship of the proposed corporation is, or is intended to be located, to the effect that he consents to the incorporation of such church, shall be filed in the office of the clerk of the county specified in the certificate of incorporation; but in case the see be vacant, or the bishop be absent or unable to act, the consent of the standing committee, with their certificate of the vacancy of the see or of the absence or disability of the bishop, shall suffice.

On filing such certificate in the office of the clerk of the county so specified therein the churchwardens and vestrymen so elected and their successors in office, together with the rector, when there is one, shall form a vestry and shall be the trustees of such church or congregation; and they and their successors shall thereupon, by virtue of this chapter, be a body corporate by the name or title expressed in such certificate, and shall have power, from time to time to adopt by-laws for its government. Such corporation shall be an incorporated church, and may be termed also an incorporated parish.

History: Add, L 1909, ch 53, amd, L 1917, ch 201, L 1971, ch 643, eff June 22, 1971.

CASE ANNOTATIONS

The rector of an incorporated Protestant Episcopal church is a member of the body corporate and cannot be removed by a vote of the vestry, nor can the vestry exclude him from the church edifice. Ackley v Irwin (1911) 71 Misc 239, 130 N.Y.S. 841

"Rector, Wardens and Members of the Vestry" of Protestant Episcopal Church was proper party to litigate constitutionality of encumbrances placed on church property since, under CLS Relig Corp § 41, church was corporate body placed in trusteeship of its church wardens and vestrymen; individual parishioners and organized group of parishioners opposed to actions of church wardens and vestrymen would be denied intervention since, as members of parish, they enjoyed only right to vote in election of wardens and vestrymen. Rector, Wardens, & Members of Vestry of St. Bartholomew's Church v New York (1990, CA2 NY) 914 F.2d 348, cert den (US) 59 USLW 3598

§ 42. Corporate trustees, vestry; powers and duties thereof

No meeting of the vestry or trustees of any incorporated Protestant Episcopal parish or church shall be held unless either all the members thereof are present, or three days' notice thereof shall be given to each member thereof, by the rector in writing either personally or by mail, or, if there be no rector or he be incapable of acting, by one of the churchwardens; except that twenty-four hours' notice of the first meeting of the vestry or trustees after an annual election shall be sufficient, provided such meeting be held within three days after the election. In the event of the rector of a parish or church refusing or neglecting to call a meeting of the vestry or trustees of any incorporated Protestant Episcopal church, on the written request of two-thirds of all the wardens and vestrymen of the parish, the clerk of the vestry shall call a meeting of the same by giving at least fifteen days' written notice to be served on each member of the vestry personally; if personal service cannot be had, then upon such member by mailing the notice to his last known place of residence. To constitute a quorum of the vestry or board of trustees, there must be present either:

1. The rector and at least a majority of the whole number of wardens and vestrymen, or

2. One churchwarden and one more than a majority of the vestrymen or both churchwardens and a majority of the vestrymen, or

3. If the rector be absent from the diocese and shall have been so absent for over four calendar months, or if the meeting be called by the rector and he be absent therefrom or be incapable of acting, one churchwarden and a majority of the vestrymen, or both churchwardens and one less than a majority of the vestrymen. But if there be a rector of the parish, no measure shall be taken, in his absence, in any case, for effecting the sale or disposition of the real property of the corporation, nor for the sale or disposition of the capital or principal of the personal property of the corporation, nor shall any act be done which shall impair the rights of such rector. The presiding officer of the vestry or trustees shall be the rector, or if there be none, or he be absent, the churchwarden who shall be called to the chair by a majority of the votes, if both the churchwardens be present; or the churchwarden present, if but one be present. At each meeting of the vestry or trustees each member thereof shall be entitled to one vote. The vestry shall have power to fill a vacancy occurring in the office of a churchwarden or vestryman by death, resignation or otherwise than by expiration of term, until the next annual election, at which, if such vacancy would continue thereafter, it shall be filled for the remainder of the unexpired term. If vacancies exist in the offices of churchwardens or vestrymen in such number that a quorum of the vestry or board of trustees is not in office at any time, the rector shall forthwith call a special election for the filling of such vacancies. If there be no rector, the churchwarden longest in office shall call such special election. Notice of such special election shall be read by the rector, or if there be none, or he be absent, by the officiating minister or by one of the churchwardens, on the Sunday next preceding such election, in the time of divine service. If for any reason the usual place of worship of the parish be not open for divine service on such Sunday such notice shall be posted conspicuously on the outer door of the place of worship for one week next preceding the election. Such notice shall conform to that required for an annual election. The provisions of section forty-three of this chapter relating to annual elections shall apply to such special election, except as inconsistent herewith. Such vacancies shall be filled at such election for the remainder of the unexpired terms. The vestry may, subject to the canons of the Protestant Episcopal church in the United States, and of the diocese in which the parish or church is situated, by a majority vote, elect a rector to fill a vacancy occurring in the rector-ship of the parish, and may fix the salary or compensation of the rector.

History: Add, L 1909, ch 53, amd, L 1919, ch 267, eff May 3, 1919.

CASE ANNOTATIONS

The provisions of Canon Law in respect of the requisite quorum for vestry meetings and not the quorum rules of Religious Corporation Law § 42 applied to the election of a new rector. Church of Holy Trinity v Melish (1957) 3 N.Y.2d 476, 168 N.Y.S.2d 952, 146 N.E.2d 685

The vestry of a Protestant Episcopal church may not by resolution dispense with the services of its rector and discharge him from office, without the action of a superior ecclesiastical authority of diocese. Ackley v Irwin (1910) 69 Misc 56, 125 N.Y.S. 672

Under this law, the vestry of an Episcopal Church, namely the rector, wardens, and vestrymen, are the trustees of the church property. Stanton v United States (1960, ED NY) 186 F. Supp. 393, affd (CA2 NY) 287 F.2d 876

§ 42-a. Additional powers of the corporate trustees and vestry

Notwithstanding and in addition to the provisions of section five of this chapter, and subject always to the trust in which all real and personal property is held for the Protestant Episcopal Church and the Diocese thereof in which the parish, mission or congregation is located, the vestry or trustees of any incorporated Protestant Episcopal parish or church, the trustees of every incorporated governing body of the Protestant Episcopal Church and each diocese are authorized to administer the temporalities and property, real and personal, belonging to the corporation, for the support and maintenance of the corporation and, provided it is in accordance with the discipline, rules and usages of the Protestant Episcopal Church and with the provisions of law relating thereto, for the support and maintenance of other religious, charitable, benevolent or educational objects whether or not conducted by the corporation or in connection with it or with the Protestant Episcopal Church.

Religious Corporations Law

History: Add, L 1991, ch 600, § 1, eff July 23, 1991.

§ 43. Annual election and special meetings of incorporated Protestant Episcopal parishes

1. The annual election of a Protestant Episcopal parish, hereafter incorporated, shall be held on the day, either a Sunday or a secular day, designated in its certificate of incorporation.

2. The annual election of an incorporated Protestant Episcopal parish or church heretofore incorporated shall be held on the day fixed for such annual election, by or in pursuance of law, or if no such date be so fixed, then on such day, either a Sunday or a secular day, as may be determined by vote of the vestry.

3. Special meetings of any Protestant Episcopal parish or church heretofore or hereafter incorporated may be held on any Sunday or secular day fixed by the vestry.

4. Notice of such annual election or special meeting shall be read by the rector of the parish, or if there be none, or he be absent, by the officiating minister or by a church warden thereof, on each of the two Sundays next preceding such election or special meeting, in the time of divine service, or if, for any reason, the usual place of worship of the parish be not open for divine service, the notice shall be posted conspicuously on the outer door of the place of worship for two weeks next preceding the election or special meeting. Such notice shall specify the place, day and hour of holding the election or special meeting. The notice of the annual election shall also specify the number and terms of office of each church warden and the vestrymen whose terms of office shall then expire, or whose office shall then be vacant for any cause, and the office for which each such officer is to be then elected. The notice of a special meeting shall specify the matter or question to be brought before such meeting and no matter or question not specified in such notice shall be acted on at such meeting.

5. The presiding officer of such annual or special meeting shall be the rector of the parish, if there be one, or if there be none, or he be absent, one of the church wardens elected for the purpose by a majority of the duly qualified voters present, or if no church warden be present, a vestryman elected in like manner. Such presiding officer shall be the judge of the qualifications of the voters; shall receive the votes cast; and shall declare the result of the votes cast. The presiding officer of such annual or special meeting shall enter the proceedings of the meeting in the book of the minutes of the vestry, sign his name thereto, and offer the same to as many qualified voters present as he shall think fit, to be also signed by them.

6. Persons of full age belonging to the parish, who have been baptized and are regular attendants at its worship and contributors to its support for at least twelve months prior to such election or special meeting or since the establishment of such parish, shall be qualified voters at any such election or special meeting. Whenever so permitted by the canons of the diocese, persons of less than full age, but of the age of eighteen years or more, and having like qualifications except as to age, may vote at the annual elections and special meetings of any parish of such diocese, whenever such parish shall so determine in the manner provided in said section forty-six.

7. The action of an annual or special meeting upon any matter or question shall be decided by a majority of the qualified voters voting thereon. The polls of an election shall continue open for one hour and longer, in the discretion of the presiding officer, or if required by a vote of a majority of the qualified voters present and voting. The church wardens and vestrymen shall be elected by ballot from persons qualified to vote at such election, and no person shall be eligible for election as church-warden, unless that person be also a confirmed communicant in the Protestant Episcopal church, nor be eligible for election as vestryman, unless that person shall have been baptized. Whenever so permitted by the canons of the diocese persons of less than full age but of the age of eighteen years or more and having like qualifications except as to age, shall be eligible for election as church warden or vestryman in any parish, whenever such parish shall so determine in the manner provided in said section forty-six.

8. At each annual election of an incorporated Protestant Episcopal parish hereafter incorporated, one church warden shall be elected to hold office for two years; and one-third of the total number of vestrymen of the parish shall be elected to hold office for three years.

9. At each annual election of an incorporated Protestant Episcopal parish or church heretofore incorporated, two church wardens and the total number of its vestrymen shall be elected to hold office for one year thereafter, unless the term of office of but one church warden or of but one-third of its vestrymen shall then expire, in which case one church warden shall be elected to hold office for two years, and one-third of the total number of its vestrymen shall be elected to hold office for three years.

10. Each church warden and vestryman shall hold office after the expiration of his term until his successor shall be chosen.

History: Add, L 1909, ch 53; amd, L 1935, ch 140, eff Mar 16, 1935; L 1957, ch 908; L 1970, ch 692; L 1971, ch 643, eff June 22, 1971; L 1971, ch 792, eff Jan 1, 1972; L 1972, ch 900, eff Sept 1, 1972; L 1974, ch 171, eff April 9, 1974; L 1986, ch 424, § 1, eff July 21, 1986.

CASE ANNOTATIONS

A committee of church members seeking to set aside a church election authorizing the sale of certain church property would not be permitted to raise the contention, for the first time after the election, that the procedures employed violated Relig Corp Law § 43(6), where the election was conducted in accordance with a ruling of the Justice of the Supreme Court, which ruling the parties had actively sought, had agreed to abide by, and had in fact adopted as the operative guidelines with respect to the election at issue. Rector, Church Wardens & Vestrymen of St. Bartholomew's Church v Committee to Preserve St. Bartholomew's Church, Inc. (1982) 56 N.Y.S.2d 71, 451 N.Y.S.2d 39, 436 N.E.2d 489

It is not necessary that members of a corporation of a church and all its trustees should be communicants of the Protestant Episcopal Church, or members of a religious society of the specific church; a member of the religious society is not necessarily a member of the corporation since ordinarily only persons entitled to vote are males of full age who are regular attendants and contributors. Fiske v Beaty (1923) 206 A.D. 349, 201 N.Y.S. 441, affd 238 N.Y. 598, 144 N.E. 907

A committee to preserve a church would not be able to challenge the outcome of a vote by which the church membership approved a plan to sell church property, where the committee participated in the formulation of the rules by a Supreme Court Justice establishing the qualifications of those church members who would be allowed to vote under Relig Corp Law § 43(6), even if the Justice erred in his interpretation of who was allowed to vote. St. Bartholomew's Church v Committee to Preserve St. Batholomew's Church, Inc., (1982, 1st Dept) 85 A.D.2d 425, 448 N.Y.S.2d 155, affd Rector, Church Wardens & Vestrymen of St. Bartholomew's Church v Committee to Preserve St. Bartholomew's Chuch, Inc. (1982) 56 N.Y.2d 71

In an action brought by a committee of church members to impugn the election by which the church membership approved a plan to sell a portion of the church realty for the construction of a high-rise office building, although the court may have erred in its construction of who was entitled to vote, under Relig Corp Law § 43(6), it endeavored to carry out its purposes and the committee could not be heard to complain about the outcome of the vote, where, following the original proposal to sell the realty, a conference was held in the chambers of a Supreme Court Justice, pursuant to the request of church officials and the committee to preserve the church, voting procedures were discussed, and it was agreed that the court would interpret the governing statute with respect to the qualification of such parishioners who would be allowed to vote and that the court would supervise the actual vote. Rector, Church Wardens & Vestrymen of St. Bartholomew's Church v Committee to Preserve St. Bartholomew's Church, Inc. (1982, 1st Dept) 85 A.D.2d 425, 448 N.Y.S.2d 155, affd 56 N.Y.2d 71, 451 N.Y.S.2d 39, 436 N.E.2d 489

A meeting, called by a self appointed committee within the church for the purpose of hearing charges against nine vestrymen, has no validity where the vestry did not fix the time for holding the meeting. Church of Holy Trinity v Melish (1949) 194 Misc 1006, 88 N.Y.S.2d 764, affd 276 A.D. 1088, 96 N.Y.S.2d 496, app dismd 301 N.Y. 679, 95 N.E.2d 43

Rector was not "absent" within the meaning of this section, where opposing faction through force prevented rector from performing his functions, since the term "absent," as used in this subdivision, means a remaining away induced, not by force or strategy, but by the exercise of one's free choice. Church of Holy Trinity v Manufacturers Trust Co. (1959) 18 Misc. 2d 761, 184 N.Y.S.2d 876, affd (2d Dept) 9 A.D.2d 932, 196 N.Y.S.2d 561, app den (2d Dept) 10 A.D.2d 628, 196 N.Y.S.2d 562

Meeting of vestry which was not called by rector but was called by faction opposing rector and, who had been successful in the lower court, was invalid and resolution disposing of church securities was of no force and effect when the Appellate Division thereafter reversed the lower court and held that rector was duly installed, since church was a party to the proceeding and vestrymen were bound by the decision of the Appellate Division. Church of Holy Trinity v Manufacturers Trust Co. (1959) 18 Misc. 2d 761, 184 N.Y.S.2d 876, affd (2d Dept) 9 A.D.2d 932, 196 N.Y.S.2d 561, app den (2d Dept) 10 A.D.2d 628, 196 N.Y.S.2d 215

Where church members had admittedly reduced their weekly contributions in the year before parish meeting from $1.50 per week to ten cents per week, members had placed themselves in the position of giving a perfunctory, de minimus contribution which did not aid the church in performing its functions and, therefore, church did not act arbitrarily or capriciously in ruling that the members were not eligible to vote at a parish meeting. Anthony v Cardin (1977) 91 Misc. 2d 506, 398 N.Y.S.2d 215

"Rector, Wardens and Members of the Vestry" of Protestant Episcopal Church was proper party to litigate constitutionality of encumbrances placed on church property since, under CLS Relig Corp § 41, church was corporate body placed in trusteeship of its church wardens and vestrymen; individual parishioners and organized group of parishioners opposed to actions of church wardens and vestrymen would be denied intervention since, as members of parish, they enjoyed only right to vote in election of wardens and vestrymen. Rector, Wardens, & Members of Vestry of St. Bartholomew's Church v New York (1990, CA2 NY) 914 F.2d 348, cert den (US) 59 USLW 3598

§ 44. Changing the number of vestrymen of Protestant Episcopal parishes hereafter incorporated

If the vestry of a Protestant Episcopal parish, hereafter incorporated, shall, by resolution, recommend that the number of vestrymen of such parish be changed to either three, six, nine, twelve, fifteen, eighteen, twenty-one or twenty-four vestrymen, notice of such recommendation shall be included in the notice of the next annual election of such parish, or in the notice of a special meeting to be held not less than six months before the time fixed for holding the next annual election thereafter, and be submitted to such annual or special meeting. If such recommendation be ratified by such meeting, the presiding officer thereof, and at least two qualified voters present thereat, shall execute and acknowledge a certificate setting forth such resolution of the vestry, the fact that notice thereof had been given with the notice of such annual election, or with the notice of such special meeting as the case may be; that the meeting had ratified the same; and the number of vestrymen so decided on. Such certificate shall be filed in the office of the clerk of the county in which the original certificate of incorporation is filed and recorded, and such change in the number of vestrymen shall take effect at the time of the next annual election thereafter. If the number of vestrymen be thereby increased, then, in addition to the number of vestrymen to be elected at such annual election, one-third of such increased number of vestrymen shall be elected to hold office for one year thereafter, one-third of such increased number shall be elected to hold office for two years thereafter, and one-third of such increased number shall be elected to hold office for three years thereafter. If the number of vestrymen by such change be reduced, such reduction shall not affect the term of office of any vestryman duly elected, and at such next annual election and at each annual election thereafter, one-third of such reduced number of vestrymen shall be elected to hold office for three years.

History: Add, L 1909, ch 53, eff Feb 17, 1909.

§ 45. Changing date of annual election, number and terms of office of vestrymen and terms of office of churchwardens in Protestant Episcopal churches heretofore incorporated

If the vestry of a Protestant Episcopal parish, heretofore incorporated, shall by resolution, recommend that the date of the annual election be changed to another day, either a Sunday or a secular day, or that the number of vestrymen be changed to three, six, nine, twelve, fifteen, eighteen, twenty-one or twenty-four, and that the terms of office of the churchwardens be changed so that one warden shall be elected annually, notice of such recommendation shall be included in the notice of the next annual election of such parish, or in the notice of a special meeting to be held not less than six months before the time fixed for holding the next annual election thereafter, and be submitted to such annual or special meeting. If such recommendation be ratified by such meeting, the presiding officer thereof and at least two qualified voters present thereat, shall execute and acknowledge a certificate setting forth such resolution of the vestry; the fact that notice thereof had been given with the notice of the annual election, or with the notice of the special meeting, as the case may be; that such meeting had ratified the same; the date determined upon for the annual election of the parish; the number of vestrymen so decided on; and the fact that the meeting determined to thereafter elect churchwardens, so that the term of one warden shall expire annually. Such certificate shall be filed in the office of the clerk of the county in which the original certificate of incorporation is filed and recorded. If the meeting determine to change the date of the annual election, the next annual election shall be held on the day determined on at such meeting, and the terms of the vestrymen and churchwardens which, pursuant to law, would expire at the next annual election shall expire and their successors shall be elected on such day. If the meeting determine to change the number of vestrymen and manner of electing wardens and vestrymen, there shall be elected at the first annual election thereafter, one-third of the number of vestrymen so determined on, to hold office for three years; one-third thereof to hold office for two years; and one-third thereof to hold office for one year; and one churchwarden to hold office for one year, and one to hold for two years; and thereafter at the annual election there shall be elected one-third of the number of vestrymen determined on at such meeting and one churchwarden. Any Protestant Episcopal parish, heretofore incorporated, which has changed the number of its vestrymen and the manner of electing wardens and vestrymen pursuant to the provisions of this section, may make further changes in the number of its vestrymen in the manner provided in section forty-four of this chapter.

History: Add, L 1909, ch 53, amd, L 1919, ch 267, L 1971, ch 643, L 1972, ch 900, eff Sept 1, 1972.

§ 46. Changing the qualifications of voters and the qualifications of wardens and vestrymen

If the vestry of a Protestant Episcopal parish heretofore incorporated shall by resolution recommend that the qualifications of voters and the qualifications of wardens and vestrymen be changed to conform in both cases to the requirements of section forty-three of this chapter, notice of such recommendation shall be included in the notice of the next

annual election of such parish, and be submitted to the meeting. If such recommendation be ratified by such meeting the presiding officer thereof and at least two qualified voters present thereat shall execute and acknowledge a certificate setting forth such resolution of the vestry, the fact that notice thereof had been given with the notice of such annual election, and that the meeting had ratified the same. Such certificate shall be filed in the office of the clerk of the county in which the original certificate of incorporation is filed and recorded.

History: Add, L 1909, ch 53, eff Feb 17, 1909.

CASE ANNOTATIONS

Where a resolution of the vestry of a parish church recommending that the privilege of voting be extended to women was ratified, not at an annual meeting as required by this section, but at a special meeting, notice for which did not, as required by § 43, specify that such action was to be taken, the voting of women at the special meeting called to elect new wardens and vestrymen was illegal. Fiske v Beaty (1922) 120 Misc 1, 198 N.Y.S. 358, mod on other grounds 206 A.D. 349, 201 N.Y.S. 441, affd 238 N.Y. 598, 144 N.E. 907

§ 47. Free churches in communion with the Protestant Episcopal church

Whenever the trustees of any free church in communion with the Protestant Episcopal church heretofore or hereafter organized under the provisions of article nine of this act shall desire to change the management of its affairs and the form of government of the corporation by substituting a vestry in place of such trustees, such change may be made in the following manner: The trustees of any free church having first obtained the written consent of the ecclesiastical authority of the diocese to such change may by an affirmative vote of not less than two-thirds determine by resolution reciting the consent of such ecclesiastical authority and duly recorded in the minutes of such church to change the management of its affairs by substituting a vestry in place of such trustees to manage the affairs of such corporation and free church with the same powers, duties and privileges as are now possessed and exercised by churchwardens and vestrymen in churches of the Protestant Episcopal church organized under this article, but subject to the provisions of section one hundred and eighty-three of this chapter and for the purposes set forth in the certificate of incorporation of such free church and for no other purposes; such resolution shall fix the day, either a Sunday or a secular day, upon which the annual election shall be held, the number to constitute such vestry which shall be two churchwardens and either three, six, nine, twelve, fifteen, eighteen, twenty-one or twenty-four vestrymen as may be determined, and shall also designate the persons to be such churchwardens, and vestrymen, to act until the annual election, and copies of such resolution, together with a statement of the vote of the trustees adopting the same certified under the seal of the corporation and verified by the president and secretary thereof, shall be filed in the office of the secretary of state and also in the office of the clerk of the county in which such church or corporation is located. Upon and after the filing of such certificate, the churchwardens and vestrymen named in said resolution and their successors in office, together with the rector when there shall thereafter be one, shall form the vestry and shall be the vestry and shall constitute the corporation; and at the first annual election the churchwardens and vestrymen shall be divided into classes and their respective terms of office fixed and shall be elected by the persons qualified to vote for the churchwardens and vestrymen in churches or congregations of the Protestant Episcopal church and the provisions of this article shall govern such election and all future elections and all acts of such vestry, subject to the provisions of section one hundred and eighty-three of this chapter.

History: Add, L 1915, ch 247, amd, L 1919, ch 267, amd, L 1972, ch 900, eff Sept 1, 1972.

§ 48. Legacies

Any devise or bequest of real or personal property to an unincorporated parish, mission, congregation, chapel or religious society under the jurisdiction of or in communion with the Protestant Episcopal Church, for the purposes of such gift, may be taken, held and administered for the benefit of such devisee or legatee by the diocesan corporation of the diocese in which such devisee or legatee is situate, and such diocesan corporation shall have the power, subject to the provisions of article five of the not-for-profit corporation law and of section twelve of this chapter, to lease, improve, mortgage, sell, convey and transfer any property so held.

History: Add, L 1953, ch 83, amd, L 1971, ch 956, eff Sept 1, 1972.

§ 49. Eligibility of certain minors as lay delegates and to vote and hold office

Whenever the constitution or canons of a diocese of the Protestant Episcopal church in the state of New York so permits, persons of less than full age but of the age of eighteen years or more shall be eligible to serve as lay delegates to and to vote at any convention of the diocese, when duly chosen by the parish or mission and shall also be eligible for election to or appointment to any lay office of the diocese.

History: Formerly § 28, add, L 1970, ch 692, renumbered § 49 and amd, L 1972, ch 900, eff Sept 1, 1972.

ARTICLE 3-A
APOSTOLIC EPISCOPAL PARISHES OR CHURCHES

History: Add, L 1932, ch 597.

§ 50. Application for incorporation

An unincorporated Apostolic Episcopal Church, or a congregation acknowledging the historic apostolic eastern confession and order in this state, may apply to the bishop who is the ecclesiastical administrator of Metropolitan Synod Apostolic Episcopal Church for permission and sanction to incorporate such church. When such permission aforesaid has been obtained in writing over the signature and seal of such bishop, such church may become an incorporated church by executing, acknowledging and filing a certificate of incorporation as hereinafter provided.

Any religious order, biblical seminary for the preparation of candidates for the ministry, leading to ordination and the granting of credentials of ecclesiastical degrees of orders in sacred theology, or religious society established for evangelical efforts or the relief of the poor and needy, which is intended to be an auxiliary organization of the Apostolic Episcopal Church, where a chapel for the conduct of worship is provided, shall be deemed a congregation to all intents and purposes, and may be incorporated in the manner prescribed in this article as a congregation of the Apostolic Episcopal Church.

History: Add, L 1932, ch 597, amd, L 1933, ch 127, eff Apr 3, 1933.

§ 51. Notice of meeting for incorporation

Notice of a meeting for the purpose of incorporating an unincorporated Apostolic Episcopal Church, or congregation acknowledging the apostolic eastern confession and order, shall be given as follows:

1. The notice shall be in writing and shall state in substance that a meeting of such unincorporated church or congregation will be held at its usual place of worship at a specific day and hour, for the purpose of incorporating such church or congregation, electing laymen trustees thereof and selecting a corporate name therefor.

2. The notice shall also state that the bishop who is the ecclesiastical administrator aforesaid has given sanction and permission in writing to proceed with the incorporation of such church.

3. The notice must be signed by at least six persons of full age, who are baptised, have statedly by worshipped with such church or congregation and have regularly contributed to its support, according to its usages, for at least one year or since it was formed.

4. A copy of such notice shall be publicly read at a regular meeting of such unincorporated church for public worship, on the two successive Sundays immediately preceding the meeting, by the minister

Religious Corporations Law

in charge of such church, or by any one of the persons qualified to sign such notice.

History: Add, L 1932, ch 597, eff Apr 1, 1932.

§ 52. Provisions governing meetings for incorporation

1. At the meeting for incorporation, held in pursuance of such notice, the qualified voters, until otherwise decided as hereinafter provided, shall be all persons of full age who have statedly worshipped with such church and have regularly contributed to its support, according to its usages, for at least one year or since it was formed.

2. At such meeting the presence of a majority of such qualified voters, at least six in number, shall be necessary to constitute a quorum, and all matters or questions shall be decided by a majority of the qualified voters voting thereon.

3. The meeting shall be called to order by one of the signers of the call. There shall be elected at such meeting from the qualified voters then present, a presiding officer, a clerk to keep the record of the proceedings of the meeting and two inspectors of election to receive the ballots cast. The presiding officer and the inspectors shall decide the result of the ballots cast on any matter and shall be the judges of the qualifications of the voters.

4. If the meeting shall decide that such unincorporated church or congregation shall become incorporated, the meeting shall also decide upon the name of the proposed corporation, the number of laymen trustees thereof, which shall be three, six or nine, and the date, not more than fifteen months thereafter, on which the first annual election of the laymen trustees shall be held; and it may, by a two-thirds vote, decide that all members of the unincorporated church, of full age, in good and regular standing, who have statedly worshipped with such church, but who have not contributed to the financial support thereof, shall also be qualified voters at such meeting; and that such church members, who for one year next preceding any subsequent corporate meeting, shall have statedly worshipped with such church and have been members thereof in good and regular standing, but have not regularly contributed to the financial support thereof, shall be qualified voters at such corporate meetings.

5. Such meetings shall thereupon elect by ballot from the persons qualified to vote thereat one-third of the number of the laymen trustees so decided on, who shall hold office until the first annual election of laymen trustees thereof, one-third of the number of such laymen trustees who shall hold office until the second annual election of trustees thereafter, and one-third of such number of laymen trustees who shall hold office until the third annual election of trustees thereafter, or until the respective successors of such laymen trustees shall be elected.

6. Such meeting shall also elect by ballot a clerk of the corporation, who shall hold office until the close of the next annual meeting.

7. Such meeting shall also designate by a vote by ballot two of the laymen trustees so elected, who shall be wardens of the church, whose terms of office as wardens shall be one year or until their respective successors are elected from among the remaining laymen trustees.

History: Add, L 1932, ch 597, eff Apr 1, 1932.

§ 53. Resolution to be adopted at incorporation meeting

At such meeting held for the incorporation of such parish, church or congregation as an Apostolic Episcopal Church, by whatever corporate name said church shall take, the following resolution shall be passed by a majority of the qualified voters of such meeting, to wit:

"Resolved, that whereas, it has been decided by a majority vote to incorporate said church under the name of (here give the corporate name by which such church is to be known) as a congregation of the Apostolic Episcopal Church and under the spiritual jurisdiction of metropolitan synod of such denomination; we likewise, by a majority vote of the duly qualified voters at this meeting, held for the incorporation of said church, now decide that the clergymen trustees of this said church shall be the bishop who is the ecclesiastical administrator, the vicar-general and the chancellor of the aforesaid metropolitan synod and the rector or vicar of this church, and their successors in office, shall by virtue of their offices, be the clergymen trustees of this church, which said four officers together with the --- laymen trustees elected at this incorporation meeting, shall constutute the trustees thereof. Said clergymen trustees' term of office shall continue until their successors in said office are elected by the Metropolitan Synod Apostolic Episcopal Church, and said laymen trustees term of office shall be that fixed by statute."

History: Add, L 1932, ch 597, eff Apr 1, 1932.

§ 54. Certificate of incorporation

1. If the meeting shall decide that such unincorporated church shall become an incorporated church or congregation of the Apostolic Episcopal Church, a certificate of incorporation therefor shall be executed and acknowledged by the bishop who is the ecclesiastical administrator, the vicar-general and the chancellor of Metropolitan Synod Apostolic Episcopal Church, the rector or vicar of the church or congregation and by the laymen trustees that have been elected, and by the clerk of the corporation, and the said certificate of incorporation shall contain the following:

(a) The name of the proposed corporation;

(b) The number of laymen trustees thereof, the names of the persons elected as laymen trustees, the terms of office for which they were respectively elected as laymen trustees;

(c) An exact copy of the resolution which provides for the clerical trustees by virtue of their offices;

(d) The county and town, city or village in which the principal place of worship is or is intended to be located.

2. On filing such certificate in the office of the county clerk of the county in which such church is or is intended to be located, such church shall be a corporation by the name stated in the certificate, and the persons therein stated to be elected clerical and laymen trustees of such church shall be the trustees therefor for their respective terms and until their successors are elected.

History: Add, L 1932, ch 597, eff Apr 1, 1932.

§ 55. Annual and special corporate meetings

1. The annual corporate meeting of every church or congregation incorporated under this article shall be held at the time and place fixed by its by-laws, or if no time and place is so fixed, then at a time and place to be fixed by its trustees, but to be changed only by a by-law adopted at an annual meeting; or if not otherwise fixed, such annual corporate meeting shall be held on the date said certificate of incorporation was executed, unless the same fall due on a Sunday or legal holiday in any year, in which case said annual corporate meeting shall be held the day following.

2. A special corporate meeting of any such church may be called by the trustees thereof, on their own motion, and shall be called on the written request of at least ten qualified voters of such church.

3. The trustees shall cause notice of the time and place of its annual corporate meeting, and the names of any trustees whose successors are to be elected thereat, and if a special meeting, of the business to be transacted thereat, to be publicly read by the minister of such church or any of the trustees thereof at a regular meeting of the church for public worship, on the two successive Sundays immediately preceding such meeting.

4. The annual corporate meeting shall be governed with respect to its organization and election of laymen trustees, clerk of the corporation and qualifications of voters (except with respect to age qualifications of voters as provided in section four-a) by the same provisions as set forth in this article for the incorporation of said church, except, that the duly ordained and regularly appointed rector or vicar shall preside, or if there be a vacancy in such office, one of the wardens shall preside, the congregation in such case voting by ballot for its presiding officer.

5. The same provisions shall apply to a special corporate meeting.

6. At the annual corporate meeting the trustees shall cause to be prepared and read thereat a budget giving the approximate amount of money needed for the maintenance of worship, the administration of the temporal affairs of the church and for the care of the property, and such other regular and special items as shall be brought to the attention of the meeting, which budget shall be discussed and decided upon, ratified or amended by the said meeting by majority vote, with ample provision made to raise such funds by whatever usages the church shall elect.

7. In the event that a quorum shall not be present at any annual corporate meeting and no election of officers shall be accordingly had thereat, the rector, vicar, or minister in charge of the church or congregation is authorized to and shall call a special meeting (which may be referred to as an adjourned annual corporate meeting) at a time and place to be fixed by him. Notice of such meeting shall be given in the same manner as provided for any special meeting. If such special meeting be not called by such rector, vicar or minister within two weeks following the date for such annual meeting, the bishop is authorized to and shall call such special meeting and notice thereof shall be given in like manner. The election of officers and any other business required or scheduled to have been had or conducted at the annual corporate meeting may be had and conducted at such special meeting. In the event that a quorum shall not be present at such special meeting and no election of officers shall be accordingly had thereat, the rector, vicar or minister in charge of the church or congregation, with the approval of the bishop, not more than sixty days thereafter, is authorized to and shall appoint the laymen trustees, wardens and other lay officers to the offices not filled by election at such annual corporate meeting or such special meeting, and they shall hold office as such until the next succeeding annual meeting. If such rector, vicar or minister shall fail to make such appointments, the bishop is authorized to and shall make such appointments, with like force and effect.

History: Add, L 1932, ch 597, eff Apr 1, 1932.

Sub 4, amd, L 1971, ch 201, § 2, eff Sept 1, 1971.

Sub 7 add, L 1947, ch 522, eff Apr 1, 1947.

§ 56. Changing date of annual corporate meetings

An annual corporate meeting of an incorporated church to which this article is applicable may, by a majority vote of the duly qualified voters at such meeting, change the date of its annual meeting thereafter. If such date as so changed shall next thereafter occur less than six months after the annual meeting at which such change is made the next annual meeting shall be held one year from such next recurring date. For the purpose of determining the terms of office of trustees, the period of time elapsing between the date of the annual meeting at which such change is made and the next annual meeting thereafter shall be reckoned as one year.

History: Add, L 1932, ch 597, eff Apr 1, 1932.

§ 57.　Changing number of laymen trustees

An incorporated church to which this article is applicable may, by a majority vote of the duly qualified voters at an annual corporate meeting, change the number of its laymen trustees to three, six or nine, and classify them so that the terms of one-third of such number so changed expire each year. No such change shall affect the terms of the laymen trustees then in office, and if the change reduces the number of laymen trustees, it shall not take effect until the number of laymen trustees whose terms of office continue for one or more years after an annual election of trustees, is less than the number determined upon. Whenever the number of laymen trustees so holding over is less than the number so determined, sufficient laymen trustees shall be elected, in addition to those so holding over, to make the number of laymen trustees for the ensuing year equal to the number so determined. The laymen trustees so elected up to and including one-third of the number so determined shall hold office for a term of three years, the remainder up to and including one-third of the number so determined, for two years and the remainder, for one year.

History: Add, L 1932, ch 597, eff Apr 1, 1932.

§ 58.　Meetings of trustees

Meetings of the trustees of such incorporated church shall be called by giving at least three days' notice thereof in writing, served personally or by mail to all the trustees, unless, by a regularly adopted standing resolution a fixed date for such meeting is the approved order, in which case a written notice may be dispensed with. To duly constitute such regular or special meeting of the trustees for the transaction of business, at any meeting lawfully convened, there shall be present a majority of the laymen trustees, the rector or vicar of the church, the clerk of the corporation and either the bishop who is the ecclesiastical administrator, the vicar-general or the chancellor of the Metropolitan Synod Apostolic Episcopal Church. But if the church has no rector or vicar, at least one of the trustees who is a warden must be present. If either the bishop, vicar-general or the chancellor cannot be present, the bishop who is the ecclesiastical administrator may send his proxy to one of the laymen trustees. No act or procedure other than regular routine matters in regard to the administration of the temporal affairs of the church and for the care of the property of the corporation, as included in the budget items, shall be valid without the sanction of the bishop and ecclesiastical administrator of the synod or diocese to which the church belongs; nor shall the trustees, without the consent of the corporate meeting incur debts for items not provided in the adopted budget. Trustees of such incorporated church shall have no power to call, settle or remove a minister or to fix his salary; or to fix, change the time, nature or order of the public or social worship, rites and religious observances of such church which are or shall be established by the governing ecclesiastical body.

History: Add, L 1932, ch 597, eff Apr 1, 1932.

§ 58-a.　Vacancies among trustees

If any trustee of any such incorporated church declines to act, resigns or dies, or ceases to be a qualified voter at a corporate meeting thereof, his office shall be vacant; and such vacancy may be filled by the remaining trustees until the next annual corporate meeting of such church; at which meeting the vacancy shall be filled for the unexpired term.

History: Add, L 1933, ch 127, eff Apr 3, 1933.

§ 59.　Rector; vicar; ministers; their appointment, removal and compensation

The rector or vicar or other ministers of any such church, by whatever title they are called in ecclesiastical language, shall be called, settled or removed and their salaries fixed, only by the vote of a majority of the members of such corporation duly qualified to vote at elections present and voting at a meeting of such corporation specifically called for that purpose, subject to the consent of the bishop who is the ecclesiastical administrator of Metropolitan Synod Apostolic Episcopal Church, given in writing. A rector or vicar or other minister so called, with the sanction of the bishop in writing, shall be deemed settled definitely in such church, when he has accepted such call in writing. Unless there is sufficient cause to terminate the relationship of such clergyman and such church such relationship shall be deemed permanent and governed entirely by the rules and usages of the Apostolic Episcopal Church, subject to the bishop and metropolitan synod.

History: Add, L 1932, ch 597, eff Apr 1, 1932.

§ 59-a.　Additional qualifications of voters at annual and special corporate meetings

Duly qualified voters at any annual or special corporate meeting of any such incorporated church shall be baptised persons, who have been admitted to the full communion relations of such church according to its usages, and who are qualified in the other respects prescribed by this article.

History: Add, L 1932, ch 597, eff Apr 1, 1932.

§ 59-b.　Transfer of property of extinct parishes and churches

The Metropolitan Synod Apostolic Episcopal Church may decide that a parish or church in connection with it or over which it has ecclesiastical jurisdiction, and to which this article is applicable, has become extinct, if it has failed for two consecutive years next prior thereto, to maintain religious services according to the discipline, customs and usages of such synod, or has had less than ten resident attending members making annual or regular contributions towards its support, and may take possession of the temporalities and property belonging to such church or parish and manage the same; or may, in pursuance of the provisions of this chapter relating to the disposition of real property, sell or dispose of the same and apply the proceeds thereof to any of the purposes to which the property of such synod is devoted, and it shall not divert such property to any other object. For the purpose of obtaining a record title to the land and the church edifice, or other buildings thereon, by such synod, the surviving trustee or trustees of said extinct church or if there be no surviving trustee, then a surviving member of said extinct church, may, without a consideration being paid therefor by such synod, convey to it said land and church edifice, or other buildings thereon, subject, however, to an order of the supreme or county court based upon a petition reciting that said church has become extinct; the name of its surviving trustee or trustees; and the names of its members (who must have given their consent to the making of said conveyance). Upon the recital of said facts in said petition, the court shall have jurisdiction to grant an order allowing said conveyance to be made without a consideration; and should there be no surviving members, as well as no surviving trustee of said extinct church, said petition may be made by an officer of said synod, in which event the court, upon the recital of said fact, shall have jurisdiction to appoint a suitable person as trustee for the purpose of making said conveyance.

History: Add, L 1932, ch 597, eff Apr 1, 1932.

ARTICLE 3-B
PARISHES OR CHURCHES OF THE HOLY ORTHODOX CHURCH IN AMERICA

History: Add, L 1936, ch 105.

The sections comprising this article, §§ 50-aa-50-mm were enacted out of numerical order.

§ 50-aa.   Application for incorporation

An unincorporated congregation of the Holy Orthodox Church in America, or a congregation acknowledging the historic apostolic eastern confession and order in this state, may apply to the archbishop who is the ecclestiastical [ecclesiastical] administrator of Metropolitan Synod, Holy Orthodox Church in America for permission and sanction to incorporate such church. When such permission aforesaid has been obtained in writing over the signature and seal of such archbishop, such church may become an incorporated church by executing, acknowledging and filing a certificate of incorporation as hereinafter provided.

Any religious order, biblical seminary for the preparation of candidates for the ministry, leading to ordination and the granting of credentials of ecclesiastical degrees of orders in sacred theology, or religious society established for evangelical efforts or the relief of the poor and needy, which is intended to be an auxiliary organization of the Holy Orthodox Church in America, where a chapel for the conduct of worship is provided, shall be deemed a congregation to all intents and purposes, and may be incorporated in the manner prescribed in this article as a congregation of the Holy Orthodox Church in America.

History: Add, L 1936, ch 105, eff Mar 16, 1936.

§ 50-bb.   Notice of meeting for incorporation

Notice of a meeting for the purpose of incorporating an unincorporated Holy Orthodox Church in America, parish or congregation acknowledging the apostolic eastern confession and order, shall be given as follows:

1. The notice shall be in writing and shall state in substance that a meeting of such unincorporated church or congregation will be held at its usual place of worship at a specific day and hour, for the purpose of incorporating such church or congregation, electing laymen trustees thereof and selecting a corporate name therefor.

2. The notice shall also state that the archbishop who is the ecclesiastical administrator aforesaid has given sanction and permission in writing to proceed with the incorporation of such church.

3. The notice must be signed by at least six persons of full age, who are baptised, have statedly worshipped with such church or congregation and have regularly contributed to its support, according to its usages, for at least one year or since it was formed.

4. A copy of such notice shall be publicly read at a regular meeting of such unincorporated church for public worship, on the two successive Sundays immediately preceding the meeting, by the minister in charge of such church, or by any one of the persons qualified to sign such notice.

History: Add, L 1936, ch 105, eff Mar 16, 1936.

§ 50-cc. Provisions governing meetings for incorporation

1. At the meeting for incorporation, held in pursuance of such notice, the qualified voters, until otherwise decided as hereinafter provided, shall be all persons of full age who have statedly worshipped with such church and have regularly contributed to its support, according to its usages, for at least one year or since it was formed.

2. At such meeting the presence of a majority of such qualified voters, at least six in number, shall be

necessary to constitute a quorum, and all matters or questions shall be decided by a majority of the qualified voters voting thereon.

3. The meeting shall be called to order by one of the signers of the call. There shall be elected at such meeting from the qualified voters then present, a presiding officer, a clerk to keep the record of the proceedings of the meeting and two inspectors of election to receive the ballots cast. The presiding officer and the inspectors shall decide the result of the ballots cast on any matter and shall be the judges of the qualifications of the voters.

4. If the meeting shall decide that such unincorporated church or congregation shall become incorporated, the meeting shall also decide upon the name of the proposed corporation, the number of laymen trustees thereof, which shall be three, six or nine, and the date, not more than fifteen months thereafter, on which the first annual election of the laymen trustees shall be held; and it may, by a two-thirds vote, decide that all members of the unincorporated church, of full age, in good and regular standing, who have statedly worshipped with such church, but who have not contributed to the financial support thereof, shall also be qualified voters at such meeting; and that such church members, who for one year next preceding any subsequent corporate meeting, shall have statedly worshipped with such church and have been members thereof in good and regular standing, but have not regularly contributed to the financial support thereof, shall be qualified voters at such corporate meeting.

5. Such meeting shall thereupon elect by ballot from the persons qualified to vote thereat one-third of the number of the laymen trustees so decided on, who shall hold office until the first annual election of laymen trustees thereof, one-third of the number of such laymen trustees who shall hold office until the second annual election of trustees thereafter, and one-third of such number of laymen trustees who shall hold office until the third annual election of trustees thereafter, or until the respective successors of such laymen trustees shall be elected.

6. Such meeting shall also elect by ballot a clerk of the corporation, who shall hold office until the close of the next annual meeting.

7. Such meeting shall also designate by a vote by ballot two of the laymen trustees so elected, who shall be wardens of the church, whose terms of office as wardens shall be one year or until their respective successors are elected from among the remaining laymen trustees.

History: Add, L 1936, ch 105, eff Mar 16, 1936.

§ 50-dd. Resolution to be adopted at incorporation meeting

At such meeting held for the incorporation of such parish, church or congregation as of the Holy Orthodox Church in America, by whatever corporate name said church shall take, the following resolution shall be passed by a majority of the qualified voters of such meeting, to wit:

"Resolved, that whereas, it has been decided by a majority vote to incorporate said church under the name of (here give the corporate name by which such church is to be known) as a congregation of the Holy Orthodox Church in America and under the spiritual jurisdiction of Metropolitan Synod of such denomination; we likewise, by a majority vote of the duly qualified voters at this meeting, held for the incorporation of said church, now decide that the clergymen trustees of this said church shall be the archbishop who is the ecclesiastical administrator, the vicar-general and the chancellor of the aforesaid Metropolitan Synod and the rector or vicar of this church, and their successors in office, shall by virtue of their offices, be the clergymen trustees of this church, which said four officers together with the --- laymen trustees elected at this incorporation meeting, shall constitute the trustees thereof. Said clergymen trustees' term of office shall continue until their successors in said office are elected by the Metropolitan Synod Holy Orthodox Church in America, and said laymen trustees term of office shall be that fixed by statute."

History: Add, L 1936, ch 105, eff Mar 16, 1936.

§ 50-ee. Certificate of incorporation

1. If the meeting shall decide that such unincorporated church shall become an incorporated church or congregation of the Holy Orthodox Church in America, a certificate of incorporation therefor shall be executed and acknowledged by the archbishop who is the ecclesiastical administrator, the vicar-general and the chancellor of Metropolitan Synod Holy Orthodox Church in America, the rector or vicar of the church or congregation and by the laymen trustees that have been elected, and by the clerk of the corporation, and the said certificate of incorporation shall contain the following:

(a) The name of the proposed corporation;

(b) The number of laymen trustees thereof, the names of the persons elected as laymen trustees, the terms of office for which they were respectively elected as laymen trustees;

(c) An exact copy of the resolution which provides for the clerical trustees by virtue of their offices;

(d) The county and town, city or village in which the principal place of worship is or is intended to be located.

2. On filing such certificate in the office of the county clerk of the county in which such church is or is intended to be located, such church shall be a corporation by the name stated in the certificate, and the persons therein stated to be elected clerical and laymen trustees of such church shall be the trustees therefor for their respective terms and until their successors are elected.

History: Add, L 1936, ch 105, eff Mar 16, 1936.

§ 50-ff.   Annual and special corporate meetings

1. The annual corporate meeting of every church or congregation incorporated under this article shall be held at the time and place fixed by its by-laws, or if no time and place is so fixed, then at a time and place to be fixed by its trustees, but to be changed only by a by-law adopted at an annual meeting; or if not otherwise fixed, such annual corporate meeting shall be held on the date said certificate of incorporation was executed, unless the same fall due on a Sunday or legal holiday in any year, in which case said annual corporate meeting shall be held the day following.

2. A special corporate meeting of any such church may be called by the trustees thereof, on their own motion, and shall be called on the written request of at least ten qualified voters of such church.

3. The trustees shall cause notice of the time and place of its annual corporate meeting, and the names of any trustees whose successors are to be elected thereat, and if a special meeting, of the business to be transacted thereat, to be publicly read by the minister of such church or any of the trustees thereof at a regular meeting of the church for public worship, on the two successive Sundays immediately preceding such meeting.

4. The annual corporate meeting shall be governed with respect to its organization and election of laymen trustees, clerk of the corporation and qualifications of voters (except with respect to age qualifications of voters as provided in section four-a) by the same provisions as set forth in this article for the incorporation of said church, except, that the duly ordained and regularly appointed rector or vicar shall preside, or if there be a vacancy in such office, one of the wardens shall preside, the congregation in such case voting by ballot for its presiding officer.

5. The same provisions shall apply to a special corporate meeting.

6. At the annual corporate meeting the trustees shall cause to be prepared and read thereat a budget giving the approximate amount of money needed for the maintenance of worship, the administration of the temporal affairs of the church and for the care of the property, and such other regular and special items as shall be brought to the attention of the meeting, which budget shall be discussed and decided upon, ratified or amended by the said meeting by majority vote, with ample provision made to raise such funds by whatever usages the church shall elect.

History: Add, L 1936, ch 105, eff Mar 16, 1936.

Sub 4, amd, L 1971, ch 201, § 3, eff Sept 1, 1971.

§ 50-gg.   Changing date of annual corporate meetings

An annual corporate meeting of an incorporated church to which this article is applicable may, by a majority vote of the duly qualified voters at such meeting, change the date of its annual meeting thereafter. If such date as so changed shall next thereafter occur less than six months after the annual meeting at which such change is made the next annual meeting shall be held one year from such next recurring date. For the purpose of determining the terms of office of trustees, the period of time elapsing between the date of the annual meeting at which such change is made and the next annual meeting thereafter shall be reckoned as one year.

History: Add, L 1936, ch 105, eff Mar 16, 1936.

§ 50-hh.   Changing number of laymen trustees

An incorporated church to which this article is applicable may, by a majority vote of the duly qualified voters at an annual corporate meeting, change the number of its laymen trustees to three, six or nine, and classify them so that the terms of one-third of such number so changed expire each year. No such change shall affect the terms of the laymen trustees then in office, and if the change reduces the number of laymen trustees, it shall not take effect until the number of laymen trustees whose terms of office continue for one or more years after an annual election of trustees, is less than the number determined upon. Whenever the number of laymen trustees so holding over is less than the number so determined, sufficient laymen trustees shall be elected, in addition to those so holding over, to make the number of laymen trustees for the ensuing year equal to the number so determined. The laymen trustees so elected up to and including one-third of the number so determined shall hold office for a term of three years, the remainder up to and including one-third of the number so determined, for two years and the remainder, for one year.

History: Add, L 1936, ch 105, eff Mar 16, 1936.

§ 50-ii.   Meetings of trustees

Meetings of the trustees of such incorporated church shall be called by giving at least three days' notice thereof in writing, served personally or by mail to all of the trustees, unless, by a regularly adopted standing resolution a fixed date for such meeting is the approved order, in which case a written notice may be dispensed with. To duly constitute such regular or special meeting of the trustees for the transaction of business, at any meeting lawfully convened, there shall be present a majority of the laymen trustees, the rector or vicar of the church, the clerk of the corporation and either the archbishop who is the ecclesiastical administrator, the vicar-general or the chancellor of the Metropolitan Synod Holy Orthodox Church of America. But if the church has no rector or vicar, at least one of the trustees who is a warden must be present. If either the archbishop, vicar-general or the chancellor cannot be present, the archbishop who is the ecclesiastical administrator may send his proxy to one of the laymen trustees. No act or procedure other than regular routine matters in regard to the administration of the temporal affairs of the church and for the care of the property of the corporation, as included in the budget items, shall be valid without the sanction of the archbishop and ecclesiastical administrator of the synod or diocese to which the church belongs; nor shall the trustees, without the consent of the corporate meeting incur debts for items not provided in the adopted budget. Trustees of such incorporated church shall have no power to call, settle or remove a minister or to fix his salary; or to fix, change the time, nature or order of the public or social worship, rites and religious observances of such church which are or shall be established by the governing ecclesiastical body.

History: Add, L 1936, ch 105, eff Mar 16, 1936.

§ 50-jj.   Vacancies among trustees

If any trustee of any such incorporated church declines to act, resigns or dies, or ceases to be a qualified voter at a corporate meeting thereof, his office shall be vacant; and such vacancy may be filled by the remaining trustees until the next annual corporate meeting of such church; at which meeting the vacancy shall be filled for the unexpired term.

History: Add, L 1936, ch 105, eff Mar 16, 1936

§ 50-kk.   Rector; vicar; ministers; their appointment, removal and compensation

The rector or vicar or other ministers of any such church, by whatever title they are called in ecclesiastical language, shall be called, settled or removed and their salaries fixed, only by the vote of a majority of the members of such corporation duly qualified to vote at elections present and voting at a meeting of such corporation specifically called for that purpose, subject to the consent of the archbishop who is the ecclesiastical administrator of Metropolitan Synod Holy Orthodox Church in America, given in writing. A rector or vicar or other minister so called, with the sanction of the archbishop in writing, shall be deemed settled definitely in such church, when he has accepted such call in writing. Unless there is sufficient cause to terminate the relationship of such clergyman and such church such relationship shall be deemed permanent and governed entirely by the rules and usages of the Holy Orthodox Church in America, subject to the archbishop and Metropolitan Synod.

History: Add, L 1936, ch 105, eff Mar 16, 1936.

§ 50-ll.   Additional qualifications of voters at annual and special corporate meetings

Duly qualified voters at any annual or special corporate meeting of any such incorporated church shall be baptised persons, who have been admitted to the full communion relations of such church according to its usages, and who are qualified in the other respects prescribed by this article.

History: Add, L 1936, ch 105, eff Mar 16, 1936.

§ 50-mm.   Transfer of property of extinct parishes and churches

The Metropolitan Synod Holy Orthodox Church in America may decide that a parish or church in connection with it or over which it has ecclesiastical jurisdiction, and to which this article is applicable, has become extinct, if it has failed for two consecutive years next prior thereto, to maintain religious services according to the discipline, customs and usages of such synod, or has had less than ten resident attending members making annual or regular contributions towards its support, and may take possession of the temporalities and property belonging to such church or parish and manage the same; or may, in pursuance of the provisions of this chapter relating to the disposition of real property, sell or dispose of the same and apply the proceeds thereof to any of the purposes to which the property of such synod is devoted, and it shall not divert such property to any other object. For the purpose of obtaining a record title to the land and the church edifice, or other buildings thereon, by such synod, the surviving trustee or trustees of said extinct church or if there be no surviving trustee, then a surviving member of said extinct church, may, without a consideration being paid therefor by such synod, convey to it said land and church edifice, or other buildings thereon, subject, however, to an order of the supreme or county court based upon a petition reciting that said church has become extinct; the name of its surviving trustee or trustees; and the names of its members (who must have given their consent to the making of said conveyance). Upon the recital of said facts in said petition, the court shall have jurisdiction to grant an order allowing said conveyance to be made without a consideration; and should there be no surviving members, as well as no surviving trustee of said extinct church, said petition may be made by an officer of said synod, in which event the court, upon the recital of said fact, shall have jurisdiction to appoint a suitable person as trustee for the purpose of making said conveyance.

History: Add, L 1936, ch 105, eff Mar 16, 1936.

ARTICLE III-C
PARISHES OR CHURCHES OF THE AMERICAN PATRIARCHAL ORTHODOX CHURCH

History: Add, L 1940, ch 604.

§ 51-a.   Application for incorporation

An unincorporated congregation of the Holy Orthodox Church in America, or a congregation acknowledging the historic apostolic eastern confession and order in this state, may apply to the ecclesiastical administrator of American Patriarchal Synod, Holy Orthodox Church for permission and sanction to incorporate such church. When such permission aforesaid has been obtained in writing over the signature and seal of such patriarch, such church may become an incorporated church by executing, acknowledging and filing a certificate of incorporation as hereinafter provided.

Any religious order, biblical, seminary for the preparation of candidates for the ministry, leading to ordination and the granting of credentials of ecclesiastical degrees of orders in sacred theology, or religious society established for evangelical efforts or the relief of the poor and needy, which is intended to be an auxiliary organization of the Holy Orthodox Church of the American Patriarchate, where a chapel for the conduct of worship is provided, shall be deemed a congregation to all intents and purposes, and may be incorporated in the manner prescribed in this article as a congregation of the American Patriarchal Orthodox Church.

History: Add, L 1940, ch 604, eff Apr 18, 1940.

This section was enacted out of numerical order.

§ 52-a.   Notice of meeting for incorporation

Notice of meeting for the purpose of incorporating an unincorporated parish or congregation acknowledging the apostolic eastern confession and order, shall be given as follows:

1. The notice shall be in writing and shall state in substance that a meeting of such unincorporated church or congregation will be held at its usual place of worship at a specific day and hour, for the purpose of incorporating such church or congregation, electing laymen trustees thereof and selecting a corporate name therefor.

2. The notice shall also state that the archbishop who is the ecclesiastical administrator aforesaid has given sanction and permission in writing to proceed with the incorporation of such church.

3. The notice must be signed by at least six persons of full age, who are baptised, have statedly worshipped with such church or congregation and have regularly contributed to its support, according to its usages, for at least one year or since it was formed.

4. A copy of such notice shall be publicly read at a regular meeting of such unincorporated church for public worship, on the two successive Sundays immediately preceding the meeting, by the minister in charge of such church, or by any one of the persons qualified to sign such notice.

History: Add, L 1940, ch 604, eff Apr 18, 1940.

This section was enacted out of numerical order.

§ 53-a.   Provisions governing meetings for incorporation

1. If the meeting shall decide that such unincorporated church shall become an incorporated church or congregation of the American Patriarchal Ortho-

dox Church, a certificate of incorporation therefor shall be executed and acknowledged by the archbishop who is the ecclesiastical administrator, the vicar-general and the chancellor of Patriarchal Synod, the rector or vicar of the church or congregation and by the laymen trustees that have been elected, and by the clerk of the corporation, and the said certificate of incorporation shall contain the following:

(a) The name of the proposed corporation;

(b) The number of laymen trustees thereof, the names of the persons elected as laymen trustees, the terms of office for which they were respectively elected as layman trustees;

(c) An exact copy of the resolution which provides for the clerical trustees by virtue of their offices;

(d) The county and town, city or village in which the principal place of worship is or is intended to be located.

2. On filing such certificate in the office of the county clerk of the county in which such church is or is intended to be located, such church shall be a corporation by the name stated in the certificate, and the persons therein stated to be elected clerical and laymen trustees of such church shall be the trustees therefor for their respective terms and until their successors are elected.

History: Add, L 1940, ch 604, eff Apr 18, 1940.

This section was enacted out of numerical order.

§ 54-a.   Rector; vicar; ministers; their appointment, removal and compensation

The rector or vicar or other ministers of any such church, by whatever title they are called in ecclesiastical language, shall be called, settled or removed and their salaries fixed, only by the vote of a majority of the members of such corporation duly qualified to vote at elections present and voting at a meeting of such corporation specifically called for that purpose, subject to the consent of the ecclesiastical administrator of Patriarchal Synod, given in writing. A rector or vicar or other minister so called, with the sanction of the archbishop in writing, shall be deemed settled definitely in such church, when he has accepted such call in writing. Unless there is sufficient cause to terminate the relationship of such clergyman and such church such relationship shall be deemed permanent and governed entirely by the rules and usages of the American Patriarchal Orthodox Church, subject to the patriarch.

History: Add, L 1940, ch 604, eff Apr 18, 1940.

This section was enacted out of numerical order.

ARTICLE 4
PRESBYTERIAN CHURCHES

History: Add, L 1909, ch 53.

§ 60.   Application of this article

This article applies only to a Presbyterian church in connection with the General Assembly of the Presbyterian Church (U.S.A.).

History: Add, L 1909, ch 53, amd, L 1960, ch 489, eff Apr 12, 1960.

Amd, L 1985, ch 381, § 7, eff July 19, 1985.

§ 61.   Creation and termination of pastoral relation

The election, calling, settlement, installation, dismissal, removal, translation, constituting or dissolving of the pastoral relation, or fixing or changing of the salary of a minister or pastor of a Presbyterian church in connection with the General Assembly of the Presbyterian Church (U.S.A.), or taking any action for or toward any such purpose, and the calling and conduct of a meeting of any such church for any such purpose, and the qualification of voters at any such meeting, are not authorized or regulated or controlled by any provision of this chapter, but the same shall be in all respects, done, and regulated, and any meeting therefor called, conducted, and controlled, only in accordance with the constitution of the Presbyterian Church (U.S.A.).

History: Add, L 1909, ch 53, amd, L 1960, ch 489, L 1962, ch 53, eff Feb 27, 1962.

Amd, L 1985, ch 381, § 7, eff July 19, 1985.

§ 62.   Worship

Nothing in this chapter contained shall authorize the fixing or changing of the times, nature or order of public worship of any particular Presbyterian church in any other manner, or by any other authority than in the manner and by the authority provided in the constitution of the Presbyterian Church (U.S.A.).

History: Add, L 1909, ch 53, amd, L 1962, ch 53, eff Feb 27, 1962.

Amd, L 1985, ch 381, § 8, eff July 19, 1985.

§ 63.   Incorporation of unincorporated Presbyterian churches and decision as to system of incorporation and government

A meeting for the purpose of incorporation of an unincorporated Presbyterian church in connection with the Presbyterian Church (U.S.A.), must be called and held in pursuance of the provisions of this article.

1. The notice and call of such meeting shall be in writing, and shall state in substance, that a meeting of such unincorporated church will be held at its usual place of worship at a specified day and hour for the purpose of incorporating such church and designating the trustees thereof. The notice must be signed by at least six persons of full age who are then members in good and regular standing of such church by admission into full communion or membership therewith, in accordance with the constitution of the Presbyterian Church (U.S.A.). Such notice shall be publicly read at each of the two next preceding regular meetings of such unincorporated church for public worship, at least one week apart, at morning service, if such service be held on Sunday, by the first named of the following persons who is present thereat, to wit: The pastor of such church or the officiating minister thereof.

2. At the meeting for incorporation held in pursuance of such notice, the following persons, and no others, shall be qualified voters, to wit: All persons of full age, who are then members, in good and regular standing of such church by admission into full communion or membership therewith, in accordance with the constitution of the Presbyterian Church (U.S.A.). The presence of twenty per cent of such qualified voters, at least six in number, shall be necessary to constitute a quorum of such meeting. The action of the meeting upon any matter or question shall be decided by a majority of the qualified voters present.

3. The pastor of the church or the officiating minister thereof shall preside at the meeting for incorporation. The presiding officer of the meeting shall receive the votes, be the judge of the qualifications of voters, and declare the result of the votes cast on any matter. Nothing contained in this section, or in this chapter, shall prevent the qualified voters at any such meeting, from choosing another person, a qualified voter, to preside at such meeting, other than the person or officer above designated.

4. The first business of such meeting after its organization, shall be to determine whether such church shall be incorporated, and if so, the name of such church, and whether its temporalities shall be managed by the spiritual officers of such church as the trustees thereof, or whether its temporalities shall be managed by trustees to be elected by the church.

5. If such meeting shall determine that such church shall be incorporated and its temporalities managed by the spiritual officers of such church as the trustees thereof, then the meeting shall also determine whether by virtue of their office, the board of deacons only of such church, or the session with the board of deacons of such church, or the session only of such church shall manage its temporalities, and be the trustees of such corporation.

6. If such meeting shall determine that such church shall be incorporated and its temporalities managed by trustees to be elected by the church, it shall further determine the number of trustees of such church, which shall not be less than three nor

more than twenty-four, and shall further determine the date not more than fifteen months thereafter on which the first annual election of the trustees thereof after such meeting shall be held, and such meeting shall elect from the persons qualified to vote at such meeting, one-third of the number of trustees so decided on who shall hold office until the first annual election of trustees thereafter, one-third of such number of trustees to hold office until the second annual election of trustees thereafter, and one-third of such number of trustees to hold office until the third annual election of trustees thereafter. The nomination and election of trustees shall be conducted as provided in the constitution of the Presbyterian Church (U.S.A.).

7. If any such meeting shall determine that such church shall incorporate in pursuance of this article, the presiding officer and at least two other persons present at such meeting, shall execute, acknowledge and cause to be filed and recorded, as provided in this chapter, a certificate of incorporation. Such certificate of incorporation shall state the name of the proposed corporation; the county and town, city or village, where its principal place of worship is or is intended to be located; the fact that a meeting of such church duly called decided that such church be incorporated, also the determination of such meeting of all the matters required in this article to be determined by such meeting, and, as the case shall be, the names of the persons elected as trustees, and the term for which each was elected, or the names of the spiritual officers and their offices, who, by the determination of such meeting, are by virtue of their office to be trustees of such corporation. On filing such certificate such church shall be a corporation by the name stated therein, and the officers determined upon by the meeting for incorporation and their successors in office, by virtue of their offices, if they be spiritual officers of such church, shall be the trustees of such corporation, or if by said meeting it was determined that the trustees should be elected as such, then such as were so elected by said meeting as trustees, and their successors in office shall be the trustees of such corporation.

History: Add, L 1909, ch 53; amd, L 1920, ch 28, eff Mar 3, 1920; amd, L 1960, ch 489; L 1962, ch 53, eff Feb 27, 1962; L 1985, ch 381, § 10, eff July 19, 1985.

§ 64. Changing system of trustees

1. If the trustees of an incorporated Presbyterian church in connection with the Presbyterian Church (U.S.A.) shall at any time be elective as trustees and not trustees by virtue of being spiritual officers, the church may, at an annual corporate meeting if notice thereof be given with the notice of such meeting, determine that the board of deacons thereof, or the session with the board of deacons thereof, or the session thereof shall thereafter constitute the trustees thereof, and thereupon the presiding officer of such meeting and at least two other persons present

thereat shall sign, acknowledge and cause to be filed and recorded a certificate stating the fact of such determination, the names of the officers determined upon to be the ex officio trustees thereof and thereon the terms of office of such elective trustees shall cease, and the officers determined upon by such corporate meeting and their successors in office shall, by virtue of their respective offices, be the trustees of such church.

2. If, at any time, the spiritual officers of an incorporated Presbyterian church in connection with the Presbyterian Church (U.S.A.), which officers by virtue of their offices constitute the trustees thereof, shall determine to submit to a meeting of such church corporation the question whether the trustees of such church shall be thereafter elective as such trustees, they shall cause a special corporate meeting of such church to be called and held in the manner provided in section sixty-five of this chapter, and such corporate meeting shall determine whether the trustees of such church shall thereafter be elective in pursuance of this article and also whether the number of such trustees shall be three, six, nine, twelve, fifteen, eighteen, twenty-one, or twenty-four and the date of the annual corporate meeting of the church. If such meeting shall determine that such trustees shall thereafter be elective as such trustees, the number of such trustees and the date of the first annual corporate meeting of the church, the presiding officer thereof and at least two other persons present and voting thereat shall sign, acknowledge and cause to be filed and recorded in the office of the clerk of the county in which the certificate of incorporation of such church is filed a certificate of such determination of such meeting; thereafter the trustees of such church shall be elective in pursuance of this article. At the next annual corporate meeting after the filing of such certificate, one-third of the number of trustees so determined on shall be elected to hold office for one year, one-third for two years and one-third for three years, the officers of such church who by virtue of their offices have been trustees of such church shall then cease to be such trustees and thereafter the trustees of such church and their successors shall be elective as such trustees as in this article provided. At each subsequent annual corporate meeting of such church, one-third of the number of trustees so determined on shall be elected to hold office for three years. The nomination and election of trustees shall be conducted as provided in the constitution of the Presbyterian Church (U.S.A.).

History: Add, L 1909, ch 53; amd, L 1920, ch 28, eff Mar 3, 1920; amd, L 1960, ch 489; L 1962, ch 53, eff Feb 27, 1962; L 1985, ch 381, § 10, eff July 19, 1985.

§ 65. Corporate meetings

1. In every incorporated church to which this article applies and in which the turstees thereof as such are elective, there shall be held an annual corporate meeting. Such annual corporate meeting of every

incorporated church to which this article is applicable shall be held at the time and place fixed by or in pursuance of law therefor, if such time and place be so fixed, and otherwise at a time and place to be fixed by its trustees and in accordance with the constitution of the Presbyterian Church (U.S.A.).

2. A special corporate meeting of any such church may be called by trustees thereof on their own motion, and must be so called on the written request of at least ten qualified voters of such church, or on the request of the session thereof, and shall be called and notice thereof given in the same manner as for an annual corporate meeting.

3. The trustees shall cause notice of the time and place of its corporate meetings to be given at a regular meeting of the church for public worship, at morning service, if such service be held, on each of the two successive Sundays next preceding such meeting, if public worship be had thereon, or otherwise on each of two days, at least one week apart, next preceding such meeting; or if no such public worship be held during such period, by conspicuously posting such notice, in writing, upon the outer entrance to the principal place of worship of such church. Such notice shall be given by the minister of the church, if there be one, or by the officiating minister thereof, if there be one, or by any officer of such church. If such notice be of an annual corporate meeting it shall specify the names of the trustees whose successors are to be elected thereat; if such notice be of a special corporate meeting, it shall specify the particular business to be transacted thereat, and no other business shall be transacted at such special corporate meeting.

4. Whenever in any such incorporated church, by virtue of their offices, any of the spiritual officers thereof are the trustees thereof, they may in their discretion call special corporate meetings of such incorporated church; and in such case such meetings shall be called by the same notice published or posted in the same manner as herein provided for the notice of such a meeting by the trustees of such a church elected as such; and in each such case such notice must specify the particular business to be transacted at such meeting, and no other business shall be transacted at such special corporate meeting.

History: Add, L 1909, ch 53, eff Feb 17, 1909; amd, L 1962, ch 53, eff Feb 27, 1962; L 1985, ch 381, § 10, eff July 19, 1985.

§ 66. Organization and conduct of corporate meetings; qualifications of voters thereat

1. At a corporate meeting of an incorporated church to which this article is applicable the following persons and no others shall be qualified voters, to wit: All persons who are then members in good and regular standing of such church by admission into full communion and membership therewith, in accordance with the constitution of the Presbyterian Church (U.S.A.).

2. The presence at any corporate meeting of an incorporated church of at least six communicant members of full age shall be necessary to constitute a quorum. The action of the meeting upon any matter or question shall be decided by a majority of the qualified voters present.

3. At any corporate meeting of an incorporated church to which this article is applicable, the pastor of such church, the officiating minister thereof, or the president of the board of trustees shall preside thereat.

4. Nothing contained in this article shall prevent the qualified voters at any meeting held pursuant to this article from choosing a person to preside at any corporate meeting of any incorporated church, other than the person or officer designated in this article to preside thereat, and when such other person shall be chosen he shall exercise all the powers in this article conferred upon the presiding officer of such meeting.

5. The presiding officer of a corporate meeting shall receive the votes, be the judge of the qualifications of voters, and declare the result of the votes cast on any matter. The polls of an annual corporate meeting shall continue open until all qualified voters present shall have had a full opportunity to vote.

6. At each annual corporate meeting successors to those trustees whose terms of office then expire shall be elected from the qualified voters by ballot for a term of three years thereafter. The nomination and election of trustees shall be conducted as provided in the constitution of the Presbyterian Church (U.S.A.).

History: Add, L 1909, ch 53, eff Feb 17, 1909; amd, L 1962, ch 53, eff Feb 27, 1962; L 1985, ch 381, § 10, eff July 19, 1985.

§ 67. Changing date of annual corporate meetings

An annual corporate meeting of an incorporated church to which this article is applicable, may change the date of its annual meeting thereafter. If such date shall next thereafter occur less than six months after the annual meeting at which such change is made the next annual meeting shall be held one year from such next recurring date. For the purpose of determining the terms of office of trustees, the time between the annual meeting at which such change is made, and the next annual meeting thereafter shall be reckoned as one year.

History: Add, L 1909, ch 53, eff Feb 17, 1909.

§ 68. Changing number of trustees

An incorporated church to which this article is applicable, may, at an annual corporate meeting, change the number of its trustees to three, six, nine, twelve, fifteen, eighteen, twenty-one or twenty-four, and classify them so that the terms of one-third expire each year. No such change shall affect the terms of the trustees then in office, and if the change reduces the number of trustees it shall not take effect until the number of trustees whose terms of office continue for one or more years after an annual election, is less than the number determined upon. Whenever the number of trustees so holding over is less than the number so determined on, trustees shall be elected in addition to those so holding over sufficient to make the number of trustees for the ensuing year equal to the number so determined on. The trustees so elected up to and including one-third of the number so determined on, shall be elected for three years, the remainder up to and including one-third of the number so determined on for two years and the remainder for one year.

History: Add, L 1909, ch 53, amd, L 1920, ch 28, amd, L 1957, ch 130, § 2, eff Mar 23, 1957.

§ 69. Trustees, their meetings, vacancies and filling thereof, their powers

1. Two trustees of an incorporated church, to which this article is applicable, may call a meeting of such trustees by giving at least twenty-four hours' notice thereof personally or by mail to the other trustees. A majority of the trustees lawfully convened shall constitute a quorum for the transaction of business. In case of a tie vote at a meeting of the trustees, the presiding officer of such meeting shall, notwithstanding he has voted once, have an additional casting vote.

2. If any trustee of an incorporated church to which this article is applicable, declines to act, resigns or dies, or ceases to be such member, his office shall be vacant. Such vacancy may be filled at a duly called special meeting of the corporation.

3. Subject to the authority of the session, the trustees of an incorporated church to which this article is applicable shall have the custody and control of all the temporalities and property belonging to the corporation and of the revenues from such property and shall administer the same in accordance with the constitution of the Presbyterian Church (U.S.A.), and with the provisions of law relating thereto, for the support and maintenance of the church corporation or, providing the members thereof at a corporate meeting thereof shall so authorize, of some religious, charitable, benevolent or educational object conducted by such church or connected with it or with the denomination with which it is connected, and they shall not use such property or revenue for any other purpose or divert the same from such uses.

4. The words "temporalities," "property," "revenue" and "revenues," as used in this section, or elsewhere in this article, shall not be construed to include the contributions in such church or elsewhere for benevolent or other purposes, which shall be contributed and paid to the pastor or pastors, ruling elders, the church session, or the deacons of any such church, either in the church services or otherwise, to be distributed, or used, or administered, by them, or any, or either of them, nor to any funds or property devised, bequeathed or contributed, to be administered or expended by such pastor or pastors, ruling elders, church session, deacons or other spiritual officers of such church.

5. The trustees of any such church shall have no power, without the consent of a corporate meeting, to incur debts beyond what is necessary for the care of the property of the corporation.

History: Add, L 1909, ch 53, eff Feb 17, 1909; amd, L 1962, ch 53, eff Feb 7, 1962; L 1962, ch 53, eff Feb 27, 1962; L 1985, ch 381, § 10, eff July 19, 1985.

CASE ANNOTATIONS

Under the Religious Corporations Law a church which has been affiliated with, and a constituent part of the Presbyterian Church in United States of America, and as such has acquired property, cannot by secession terminate its relationship and thereby avoid supervision and control of the denominational organization at large. Trustees of Presbytery v Westminister Presbyterian Church (1917) 222 N.Y. 305, 118 N.E. 800

In an action by a local church organization against its parent organization arising out of a disagreement over the latter's financial support of radical political groups and individuals, in which the local church group sought a declaration of its independent status and a permanent injunction preventing the parent organization from interfering with its use and enjoyment of the local church property, an order of the trial court granting injunctive relief was proper, since, insofar as the complaint sought to enjoin the parent organization from interfering with the local organization's use of the local church property the matter was properly before the courts, under the circumstances presented, which indicated that at the time suit was brought, the parent group had not yet appointed a commission to replace the governing body of the local organization and the local organization had terminated its relations with the parent organization, that the local organization held record title to the property free from any competing interests, and that the constitution of the denominational church contained no provision creating an express trust in favor of the parent organization, and Rel Corp Law § 69(3), which requires that trustees of a local church govern property in accordance with the constitution of the parent organization was inapplicable, as was the doctrine of implied trust. First Presbyterian Church v United Presbyterian Church (1984) 62 N.Y.2d 110, 476 N.Y.S.2d 86, 464 N.E.2d 454

Where a Presbyterian church was dissolved so that it ceased to belong to the Presbyterian denomination, a petition by such church, continuing as a secular corporation, for permission to sell its lands will not be granted where the Presbytery of New York has intervened claiming that the lands belong to the Presbyterian denomination, and there are actions pending involving the right to possession and control of the property. Re Westminster Presbyterian Church (1910) 137 A.D. 301, 121 N.Y.S. 1039

§ 70. Definitions

The words "spiritual officers," as used in this article, include the pastor or pastors, the ruling elders, and the deacons, of any church to which this article is applicable.

History: Add, L 1909, ch 53, eff Feb 17, 1909.

ARTICLE 5
ROMAN CATHOLIC CHURCHES

History: Add, L 1909, ch 53. Heading amd, L 1942, ch 228.

§ 90. Incorporation of Roman Catholic churches

An unincorporated Roman Catholic church in this state may become incorporated as a church by executing, acknowledging and filing a certificate of incorporation, stating the corporate name by which such church shall be known and the county, town, city or village where its principal place of worship is, or is intended to be, located.

A certificate of incorporation of an unincorporated Roman Catholic church shall be executed and acknowledged by the Roman Catholic archbishop or bishop, and the vicar-general of the diocese in which its place of worship is, and by the rector of the church, and by two laymen, members of such church who shall be selected by such officials, or by a majority of such officials.

On filing such certificate such church shall be a corporation by the name stated in the certificate.

History: Add, L 1909, ch 53, amd, L 1942, ch 228, eff Mar 29, 1942.

CASE ANNOTATIONS

An application for approval of a certificate of incorporation pursuant to the Not-For-Profit Corporation Law, setting forth the purposes of the corporation as being "to print, mail, disseminate, Roman Catholic information * * * to conduct prayer vigils, and with divine guidance keep the knowledge of God and His plan for peace and security in the hearts of all mankind", brings the proposed corporation within the definition of an incorporated church making it subject to the provisions of the Religious Corporations Law as well as the Not-For-Profit Corporation Law, and, as such, the application must be denied for failure to conform to the specific provisions of the Religious Corporations Law which govern the incorporation of groups associated with the Roman Catholic Church, including the requirement of an execution and acknowledgment by certain specific officials of that church. Re Lueken (Our Lady of Roses) (1978) 97 Misc. 2d 201, 410 N.Y.S.2d 793

§ 91. Government of incorporated Roman Catholic churches

The archbishop or bishop and the vicar-general of the diocese to which any incorporated Roman Catholic church belongs, the rector of such church, and their successors in office shall, by virtue of their offices, be trustees of such church. Two laymen, members of such incorporated church, selected by such officers or by a majority of them, shall also be trustees of such incorporated church, and such officers and such laymen trustees shall together constitute the board of trustees thereof. The two laymen signing the certificate of incorporation of an incorporated Roman Catholic church shall be the two laymen trustees thereof during the first year of its corporate existence. The term of office of the two laymen trustees of an incorporated Roman Catholic church shall be one year. Whenever the office of any such layman trustee shall become vacant by expiration of term of office or otherwise, his successor shall be appointed from members of the church, by such officers or a majority of them. No act or proceeding of the trustees of any such incorporated church shall be valid without the sanction of the archbishop or bishop of the diocese to which such church belongs, or in case of their absence or inability to act, without the sanction of the vicar-general or of the administrator of such diocese.

History: Add, L 1909, ch 53, amd, L 1942, ch 228, eff Mar 29, 1942.

CASE ANNOTATIONS

The sections of the Religious Corporation Law applicable to the Roman Catholic Church must be read in conjunction with the Code of Canon Law of that church. Filetto v St. Mary of Assumption Church (1969) 61 Misc. 2d 278, 305 N.Y.S.2d 403

§ 92. Division of Roman Catholic parish; disposition of property

Wherever a Roman Catholic parish has been heretofore or shall hereafter be duly divided by the Roman Catholic bishop having jurisdiction over said parish, and the original Roman Catholic church corporation is given one part of the old parish, and a new or second Roman Catholic church corporation is given the remaining part of the old parish, and it further appears that by reason of the said division the original Roman Catholic church corporation holds title to real property situate within the part of the old parish that was given to the new or second Roman Catholic church corporation, then the said Roman Catholic bishop or his successor shall have the right and power, of himself, independently of any action or consent on the part of the trustees of the original Roman Catholic church corporation, to transfer the title of the said real property, with or without valuable consideration, to the said new or second Roman Catholic church corporation. Said transfer shall be made by the said Roman Catholic bishop or his successor after having complied with the requirements of this chapter in the same manner as the trustees of any religious corporation are compelled to do before making a transfer of church property. If a valuable consideration is paid for the transfer the same shall be received by the said Roman Catholic bishop or his successor and distributed between the said original Roman Catholic church corporation and the new or second Roman Catholic church corporation in such proportions as in the discretion of the said bishop or his successor may seem proper.

History: Add, L 1909, ch 53, amd, L 1962, ch 310, § 409, eff Sept 1, 1963.

ARTICLE 5-A
CHRISTIAN ORTHODOX CATHOLIC CHURCHES OF THE EASTERN CONFESSION

History: Formerly Art 5-B, renumbered, L 1943, ch 145.

Former Art 5-A, add, L 1917, ch 353, renumbered Art 5-B, L 1943, ch 145.

§ 95. Incorporation of Christian Orthodox Catholic churches of the Eastern Confession

An unincorporated Christian Orthodox Catholic church of the Eastern Confession in this state may become incorporated as a church by executing, acknowledging and filing a certificate of incorporation, stating the corporate name by which such church shall be known and the county, town, city or village where its principal place of worship is, or is intended to be located.

A certificate of incorporation of an unincorporated Christian Orthodox Catholic church of the Eastern Confession shall be executed and acknowledged by six lay members of such church.

On filing such certificate such church shall be a corporation by the name stated in the certificate.

History: Add, L 1942, ch 228, eff Mar 29, 1928.

§ 96. Government of incorporated Christian Orthodox Catholic churches of the Eastern Confession

The six lay members of every incorporated Christian Orthodox Catholic church of the Eastern Confession in this state, incorporated on or after April ninth, nineteen hundred twenty-three, signing the certificate of incorporation, and the rector shall be the trustees of such church for the first year or until their successors are selected according to the by-laws of such church or the rules and usages of the denomination to which such church belongs. The trustees of every such church incorporated before April ninth, nineteen hundred twenty-three, shall consist of the rector and such other persons as may be selected according to the by-laws of such church or the rules and usages of the denomination to which such church belongs.

History: Add, L 1942, ch 228, eff Mar 29, 1928.

ARTICLE 5-B
RUTHENIAN GREEK CATHOLIC CHURCHES

History: Formerly, Art 5-A, renumbered, L 1943, ch 145.

Former Art 5-B, add, L 1942, ch 228, renumbered Art 5-A, L 1943, ch 145.

§ 100. Incorporation of Ruthenian Greek Catholic churches

An unincorporated Ruthenian Greek Catholic church of the Greek rite in this state may become incorporated as a church by executing, acknowledging and filing a certificate of incorporation, stating the corporate name by which said church shall be known, and the county, town, city or village where its principal place of worship is or is intended to be located.

A certificate of incorporation of an unincorporated Ruthenian Greek Catholic church shall be executed and acknowledged by the Ruthenian Catholic bishop, appointed by the pope of Rome to have supervision over Ruthenian Catholics of the Greek rite in the United States, or in case of a vacancy in the office of bishop by reason of death, resignation or otherwise, the Ruthenian administrator of the Ruthenian Catholic diocese duly appointed and recognized by the apostolic delegate in the United States, and the chancellor of the diocese in which its place of worship is, and by the pastor of the church and by two laymen, members of such church, who shall be elected by such officers or by a majority of such officers. On filing such certificate, said church shall be a corporation by the name stated in the certificate.

History: Add, L 1917, ch 353, eff May 3, 1917.

CASE ANNOTATIONS

Ejectment action instituted by plaintiff as record owner of certain real property dismissed upon a showing the plaintiff had failed to furnish pastoral service to defendants, defendants had accepted the pastoral services of another denomination and had held the Church in open hostility to the plaintiff for more than 20 years. Saint Nicholas Ruthenian Ukrainian Greek Catholic Church v Kapsho (1952) 202 Misc 893, 114 N.Y.S.2d 27

§ 101. Government of incorporated Ruthenian Greek Catholic churches

The bishop, or in case of vacancy in the office of the bishop, then the administrator, the chancellor of the diocese to which any incorporated Ruthenian Greek Catholic church belongs, together with the pastor of said church, shall by virtue of their office be trustees of such church; two laymen members of such incorporated church selected by such officers, or by a majority of them, shall also be trustees of such incorporated church, and such officers, pastor and such laymen trustees shall together constitute the board of trustees thereof. The two laymen signing the certificate of incorporation of a Ruthenian Greek Catholic church shall be the two laymen trustees thereof during the first year of its corporate existence. The term of office of the two laymen trustees of an incorporated Ruthenian Greek Catholic church shall be one year. Whenever the office of any such layman trustee shall become vacant by expiration of term of office or otherwise his successor shall be appointed from members of the church by such officers or a majority of them. No act or proceeding of the trustees of any such incorporated church shall be valid without the sanction or approval in writing of the bishop of the diocese to which said church belongs, or, in case of his absence or disability to act, of his vicar-general or of the administrator of such diocese.

History: Add, L 1917, ch 353, eff May 3, 1917.

§ 102. Transfer of other religious organizations to Ruthenian Greek Catholic church; disposition of property

Any religious organization or organizations incorporated under and by virtue of any law of this state, whether incorporated under article five of the religious corporations law, or otherwise, shall be and they are hereby authorized to organize under the provisions of this act relating to incorporation of Ruthenian Greek Catholic churches of the Greek rite, and upon the filing of a certificate to be signed by the trustees of such existing association or organization or a majority of them, consenting to such organization or incorporation, under this act, all the right, title and interest of such association or corporation in any estate, real or personal, shall, with all franchises and charter rights, be vested in said body corporate and politic so created under this act and the original incorporation of such association or organization shall then be null and void.

History: Add, L 1917, ch 353, eff May 3, 1917.

CASE ANNOTATIONS

Where it appears that a certificate of reincorporation filed under this section two days before the election of trustees was not signed by the required number of persons and that it is manifestly incomplete in many other respects, it cannot have the effect to validate reincorporation. Re Trustees of Ruthenian Greek Catholic Church (1928) 224 A.D. 113, 229 N.Y.S. 520, affd 249 N.Y. 607, 164 N.E. 602

ARTICLE 5-C
CHURCHES OF THE ORTHODOX CHURCH IN AMERICA

§ 105. Definitions
§ 106. Incorporation of churches of Orthodox Church in America
§ 107. Government of incorporated churches of Orthodox Church in America; powers and duties of trustees
§ 108. Reincorporation of existing corporations

History: Add, L 1945, ch 693.

Title, amd, L 1971, ch 578, eff June 17, 1971.

Schedule of sections, amd, L 1971, ch 578, eff June 17, 1971.

§ 105. Definitions

The "Orthodox Church in America", as that term is used anywhere in this article, refers to that group of churches, cathedrals, chapels, congregations, societies, parishes, committees and other religious organizations of the Eastern Confesion (Eastern Orthodox or Greek Catholic Church) which were known as (a) Russian American Mission of the Russian Orthodox Church from in or about seventeen hundred ninety-three to in or about eighteen hundred seventy; (b) Diocese of Alaska and the Aleutian Islands of the Russian Orthodox Church from in or about eighteen hundred seventy to in or about nineteen hundred four; (c) Diocese of North America and the Aleutian Islands (or Alaska) of the Russian Orthodox Church from in or about nineteen hundred four to in or about nineteen hundred twenty-four; (d) Russian Orthodox Greek Catholic Church of North America (or America) from in or about nineteen hundred twenty-four to October nineteen hundred seventy; and (e) Orthodox Church in America since October nineteen hundred seventy; and were subject to the administrative jurisdiction of the Most Sacred Governing Synod in Moscow until in or about nineteen hundred seventeen, later the Patriachate of Moscow, thereafter constituted an administratively autonomous metropolitan district, but now constitute an autocephalous church of the Eastern Confession (Eastern Orthodox or Greek Catholic Church) by virtue of a proclamation of autocephaly made on April tenth, nineteen hundred seventy by the Patriarch of Moscow and All Russia and the Holy Synod of the Russian Orthodox Church.

An "American Orthodox church", as that term is used anywhere in this article, is a church, cathedral, chapel, congregation, society, parish, committee or other religious organization founded and established for the purpose and with the intent of adhering to, and being subject to the administrative jurisdiction of said mission, diocese, autonomous metropolitan district or autocephalous church hereinabove defined as the Orthodox Church in America.

History: Add, L 1945, ch 693, amd, L 1948, ch 711, amd, L 1971, ch 578, eff June 17, 1971.

CASE ANNOTATIONS

After the United States Supreme Court had declared this article unconstitutional as a violation of the 14th amendment of the federal constitution, the case was remanded to the court of appeals which thereupon ordered a new trial for the exercise of the discretionary power of the Supreme Court over the conduct of trustees and for the determination as to whether the proper administration of the Cathedral trust required a determination as to whether the archbishop of the North American metropolitan district or the appointee of the Moscow patriarchate was to be put into possession of the Cathedral. Saint Nicholas Cathedral of Russian Orthodox Church v Kedroff (1954) 306 N.Y. 38, 114 N.E.2d 197, reh den 306 N.Y. 572, 115 N.E.2d 681

The statutes do not indicate a legislative intent to accomplish a transfer of the property of all Russian Orthodox churches in this country to the use of the newly organized "Russian Church in America." St. Nicholas Cathedral of Russian Orthodox Church v Fedchenkoff (1948) 192 Misc 327, 77 N.Y.S.2d 333, affd 276 A.D. 309, 94 N.Y.S.2d 453, revd on other grounds 302 N.Y. 1, 96 N.E.2d 56, remittitur amd 302 N.Y. 689, 98 N.E.2d 485 and revd on other grounds 344 US 94, 97 L Ed 120, 73 S Ct 143

Where § 107 provides for the dedication and use of property of Russian Orthodox churches for the benefit of and at the direction of the Russian Church of America it is limited by the definition in § 105 which defines a Russian Orthodox church as one founded and established for the purpose and with the intent of adhering to and being subject to the administrative jurisdiction of the Russian Church of America so that when St. Nicholas Cathedral was founded and established there could have been neither purpose nor intent to adhere and to be subject to the Russian Church in America since it was not then factually in existence. St. Nicholas Cathedral of Russian Orthodox Church v Fedchenkoff (1948) 192 Misc 327, 77 N.Y.S.2d 333, affd 276 A.D. 309, 94 N.Y.S.2d 453, revd on other grounds 302 N.Y. 1, 96 N.E.2d 56, remittitur amd 302 N.Y. 689, 98 N.E.2d 485 and revd on other grounds 344 US 94, 97 L Ed 120, 73 S Ct 143

This article is unconstitutional because it violated the Fourteenth Amendment of the United States Constitution by prohibiting in this country the free exercise of religion. Kedroff v St. Nicholas Cathedral of Russian Orthodox Church (1952) 344 US 94, 97 L Ed 120, 73 S Ct 143

The legislature had no power to make a determination that the "Russian Church of America" is the one which was the trustee which may be relied upon to carry out more effectively and faithfully the purposes of the religious trust by reason of the changed situation of the patriarchate in Russia. Kedroff v St. Nicholas Cathedral of Russian Orthodox Church (1952) 344 US 94, 97 L Ed 120, 73 S Ct 143, revg 302 N.Y. 1, 96 N.E.2d 56

§ 106. Incorporation of churches of Orthodox Church in America

An unincorporated American Orthodox church in this state may be incorporated by executing, acknowledging and filing a certificate of incorporation, stating the corporate name by which such church shall be known and the county, town, city or village where its principal place of worship is or is intended to be located. There shall be attached to such certificate the permission to incorporate signed by the metropolitan archbishop or other primate or hierarch of the Orthodox Church in America, or by the locum tenens acting in his place. Such certificate of incorporation shall be executed and acknowledged by six lay members of such church.

On filing such certificate such church shall be a corporation by the name stated in the certificate.

History: Add, L 1945, ch 693, amd, L 1971, ch 578, eff June 17, 1971.

Section heading, amd, L 1971, ch 578, eff June 17, 1971.

CASE ANNOTATIONS

Since St. Nicholas Cathedral in New York does not fall within any of the categories set out in these statutes, it follows that its use is not subject to the direction of the Russian Church in America St. Nicholas Cathedral of Russian Orthodox Church v Fedchenkoff (1948) 192 Misc 327, 77 N.Y.S.2d 333, affd 276 A.D. 309, 94 N.Y.S.2d 453, revd on other grounds 302 N.Y. 1, 96 N.E.2d 56, remittitur amd 302 N.Y. 689, 98 N.E.2d 485 and revd on other grounds 344 US 94, 97 L Ed 120, 73 S Ct 143

§ 107. Government of incorporated churches of Orthodox Church in America; powers and duties of trustees

1. Every American Orthodox church in this state, whether incorporated before or after the said proclamation of autocephaly, and whether incorporated or reincorporated pursuant to this article or any other article of the religious corporations law, or any general or private law, shall recognize and be and remain subject to the jurisdiction and authority of the general council, metropolitan archbishop or other primate or hierarch, the council of bishops, the executive council and other governing bodies and authorities of the Orthodox Church in America, pursuant to the statute for the government thereof, and any amendments thereto and any other statutes or rules adopted by a general council of the Orthodox Church in America and shall in all other respects conform to, maintain and follow the faith, doctrine, ritual, communion, discipline, canon law, traditions and usages of the Eastern Confession (Eastern Orthodox or Greek Catholic Church); provided, however, that the provisions of this section shall not be applicable to any church incorporated in this state which was excluded from the autocephaly of the Orthodox Church in America by said proclamation of

autocephaly, namely, St. Nicholas Cathedral of the Russian Orthodox Church in North America and St. Mark Chapel, both of the County of New York, City of New York, St. John the Baptist Chapel, County of Bronx, City of New York, Church of St. George the Great Martyr, County of Queens, City of New York, Church of All Saints Glorified in the Russian Land, Village of Pine Bush, County of Orange, House Chapel of St. Seraphim of Sarov, Village of Westtown, County of Orange, and Church of St. George the Great Martyr, City of Buffalo, County of Erie, unless any such church shall reincorporate pursuant to this article and the certificate therefor shall set forth, in addition to the other statements required to be set forth therein, that the corporation is being reincorporated pursuant to this article with the permission of the governing authority of the Russian Orthodox Church.

2. The six lay members of every church incorporated pursuant to this article signing the certificate of incorporation and the rector shall be the trustees of such church for the first year or until their successors are selected according to the by-laws of such church or the rules and usages of the Orthodox Church in America.

3. The trustees of every American Orthodox church shall have the custody and control of all temporalities and property, real and personal, belonging to such church and of the revenues therefrom and shall administer the same in accordance with the by-laws of such church, and any amendments thereto and all other rules, statutes, regulations and usages of the Orthodox Church in America.

History: Add, L 1945, ch 693, amd, L 1948, ch 711, L 1971, ch 578, eff June 17, 1971.

Section heading, amd, L 1971, ch 578, eff June 17, 1971.

CASE ANNOTATIONS

Since St. Nicholas Cathedral in New York does not fall within any of the categories set out in these statutes, it follows that its use is not subject to the direction of the Russian Church in America. St. Nicholas Cathedral of Russian Orthodox Church v Fedchenkoff (1948) 192 Misc 327, 77 N.Y.S.2d 333, affd 276 A.D. 309, 94 N.Y.S.2d 453, revd on other grounds 302 N.Y. 1, 96 N.E.2d 56, remittitur amd 302 N.Y. 689, 98 N.E.2d 485 and revd on other grounds 344 US 94, 97 L Ed 120, 73 S Ct 143

Where this section provides for the dedication and use of property of Russian Orthodox churches for the benefit of and at the direction of the Russian Church of America it is limited by the definition in § 105 which defines a Russian Orthodox church as one founded and established for the purpose and with the intent of adhering to and being subject to the administrative jurisdiction of the Russian Church of America so that when St. Nicholas Cathedral was founded and established there could have been neither purpose nor intent to adhere and to be subject to the Russian Church in America since it was not then factually in existence. St. Nicholas Cathedral of Russian Orthodox Church v Fedchenkoff (1948) 192 Misc 327, 77 N.Y.S.2d 333, affd 276 A.D. 309, 94 N.Y.S.2d 453, revd on other grounds 302 N.Y. 1, 96 N.E.2d 56, remittitur amd 302 N.Y. 689, 98 N.E.2d 485 and revd on other grounds 344 US 94, 97 L Ed 120, 73 S Ct 143

Constitutional guaranty of freedom of religion would be violated by determination that, by reason of domination of patriarch of Moscow by secular authority of Union of Soviet Socialist Republics, his appointee could not under common law of New York validly exercise right to occupy cathedral of his faith. St. Nicholas Cathedral of

Russian Orthodox Church v Kreshik (1960) 363 US 190, 4 L Ed 2d
1140, 80 S Ct 1037, reh den 364 US 855, 5 L Ed 2d 79, 81 S Ct 35 and
motion gr 8 N.Y.2d 1124, 209 N.Y.S.2d 809, 171 N.E.2d 890

§ 108. Reincorporation of existing corporations

Any heretofore incorporated American Orthodox
church may reincorporate under the provisions of this
article, by filing in the office of the county clerk in the
county in which its principal place of worship is
located, a certificate, signed by the trustees in office
at the time of such reincorporation, or by the majority
of them, setting forth that they desire to reincorporate under the provisions of this article, the corporate
name by which such church shall be known, the
county, town, city or village where its principal place
of worship is located and the number and the names
of the trustees who are to hold office until the next
annual meeting of said church. Immediately upon the
filing of such certificate all the right, title, equity and
interest of such church in any estate, real or personal,
together with all franchise and charter rights, shall
be vested in the body corporate and politic so created
under this article and the original incorporation of
such church shall be null and void.

History: Add, L 1945, ch 693, amd, L 1971, ch
578, eff June 17, 1971.

CASE ANNOTATIONS

Since St. Nicholas Cathedral in New York does not fall within any
of the categories set out in these statutes, it follows that its use is not
subject to the direction of the Russian Church in America. St.
Nicholas Cathedral of Russian Orthodox Church v Kedroff (1950) 302
N.Y. 1, 96 N.E.2d 56, remittitur amd 302 N.Y. 689, 98 N.E.2d 485
and revd on other grounds 344 US 94, 97 L Ed 120, 73 S Ct 143

ARTICLE 6
REFORMED DUTCH, REFORMED
PRESBYTERIAN AND LUTHERAN
CHURCHES

History: Add, L 1909, ch 53.

§ 110. Decision by a Reformed Dutch or Re-
formed Presbyterian church as to system
of incorporation and government

The minister or ministers, if there be any, and
the elders and deacons of an unincorporated church
in connection with the Reformed church in America,
the true Reformed Dutch church in the United States
of America, or with the Reformed Presbyterian
church, may determine to incorporate such church in

pursuance of this article, or to call a meeting of such
unincorporated church for the purpose of deciding
whether such church shall be incorporated in pursuance of article ten of this chapter, entitled "Special
provisions for the incorporation and government of
churches of other denominations."

If such ministers, elders and deacons determine
to call such meeting for such purpose, then such
church may be incorporated and shall be governed
after its incorporation in pursuance of the provisions
of article ten of this chapter, except such provisions
thereof as are applicable to churches of a single
denomination only, and except that the notice of the
meeting for incorporation shall be signed by such
ministers, elders and deacons or a majority of them,
and no other signatures thereto shall be necessary to
its validity; and, if it be a Reformed church in America, it shall, after incorporation, be governed by such
of the provisions of this article as relates to its consistory and to the choice of its minister.

History: Add, L 1909, ch 53, eff Feb 17, 1909.

§ 111. Decision by Lutheran church as to sys-
tem of incorporation and government

A meeting for the purpose of incorporating an unincorporated Evangelical Lutheran church must be
called and held in pursuance of the provisions of
article ten of this chapter, except that the first business of such meeting after its organization, shall be to
determine whether such church shall be incorporated
and governed in pursuance of this article, or in
pursuance of article ten of this chapter. If such
meeting determines that such church shall be incorporated and governed in pursuance of this article,
then no further proceedings shall be taken in pursuance of article ten, and such church may be incorporated and shall be governed after its incorporation in
pursuance of the provisions of the following sections
of this article, except such provisions as are applicable only to churches of a different denomination; and
the certificate of incorporation shall recite such
determination of such meeting. If such meeting
determine that such church shall be incorporated and
governed in pursuance of article ten of this chapter,
then this article shall not be applicable thereto, but
such church may be incorporated and shall be governed after its incorporation in pursuance of the
provisions of article ten of this chapter, except such
provisions as are applicable to churches of a single
religious denomination only.

History: Add, L 1909, ch 53, eff Feb 17, 1909.

§ 112. Incorporation of Reformed Dutch, Re-
formed Presbyterian and Evangelical Lu-
theran churches under this article

If any unincorporated church in connection with
the Reformed church in America, the true Reformed
Dutch church in the United States of America, the
Reformed Presbyterian church, or with the Evangelical Lutheran church, determine to incorporate in
pursuance of this article, the minister or ministers

and the elders and deacons thereof shall execute, acknowledge and cause to be filed and recorded, a certificate in pursuance of this article. The deacons of a Reformed Presbyterian church may alone sign such certificate if authorized so to do by such church. Such certificate of incorporation shall state the name of the proposed corporation, the county and town, city or village where its principal place of worship is or is intended to be located, and, if it be an Evangelical Lutheran church, the fact that a meeting of such church duly called decided that it be incorporated under this article. If it be signed by the deacons of a Reformed Presbyterian church, it shall state that they were authorized so to do by such church. On filing such certificate such church shall be a corporation by the name stated therein, and the minister or ministers, if any, and the elders and deacons of such church shall by virtue of their offices be the trustees of such corporation, except that if it be a Reformed Presbyterian church, the certificate of incorporation of which shall have been, in pursuance of law, signed by its deacons only, the deacons of such church shall, by virtue of their offices, be the trustees of such corporation.

History: Add, L 1909, ch 53, eff Feb 17, 1909.

§ 113. Consistory of a Reformed church in America; minister, how chosen

Any church in connection with the Reformed church in America, the choice or election of the members of whose consistory is not subject to the ecclesiastical rules or jurisdiction of such Reformed church in America, shall, if the consistory so determine, be subject to such rules and jurisdiction; and thereafter the choice of the members of the consistory shall be in accordance with such rules and practices.

If any such church be incorporated under article ten of this chapter, or if its trustees be elective in pursuance of such article, its board of trustees and its consistory shall act concurrently in the choice of its minister.

History: Add, L 1909, ch 53, eff Feb 17, 1909.

§ 114. Reformed churches in America, changing system of choosing trustees; minister, how chosen

If the ministers, elders and deacons who, at any time, by virtue of their offices, constitute the trustees of any Reformed church in America, or of any true Reformed Dutch church in the United States of America, determine that the trustees of such church shall thereafter be elective in pursuance of article ten of this chapter, and shall determine whether the number of such trustees shall be three, six or nine, and the date of the annual corporate meeting of the church, they may sign, acknowledge and cause to be filed and recorded in the office of the clerk of the county in which the certificate of incorporation of such church is filed or recorded, a certificate of such determinations. Thereafter the trustees of such church shall be elective in pursuance of the provisions

of article ten of this chapter, relating to the election of trustees of incorporated churches. At the next annual corporate meeting after the filing of such certificate, one-third of the number of trustees so determined on shall be elected to hold office for one year, one-third for two years and one-third for three years, and the minister, elders and deacons shall cease to be the trustees of such church. At each subsequent annual corporate meeting of such church, one-third of the number of trustees so determined on shall be elected to hold office for three years. If the trustees of an incorporated Reformed church in America or of a true Dutch Reformed church in the United States of America are at any time elective, in pursuance of article ten of this chapter, or otherwise, the board of trustees and the consistory thereof may concurrently determine that the minister or ministers, if any, and the elders and deacons of such church shall constitute the trustees thereof. Thereon the president and clerk of the consistory and the president and clerk of the board of trustees shall sign and acknowledge and cause to be filed and recorded in the office of the clerk of the county in which the original certificate of incorporation is filed or recorded, a certificate of such determination, stating the names of such ministers, elders and deacons. On so filing and recording such certificate, such board of trustees shall be dissolved, and the minister or ministers, and elders and deacons of such church, and their successors in office shall constitute the trustees of such church.

History: Add, L 1909, ch 53, eff Feb 17, 1909.

§ 115. Reformed Presbyterian churches, changing system of choosing trustees; pew rents and minister's salary

If any incorporated Reformed Presbyterian church, at a meeting of the church or congregation, determine that the deacons of such church shall be the trustees thereof, then the deacons of such church actively engaged in the exercise of their offices therein, and their successors in office, shall, by virtue of their respective offices, be the trustees of such church. The salary of the minister and the pew rents in any such church shall be fixed by the vote of the congregation, and the trustees shall not fix or change the same.

History: Add, L 1909, ch 53, eff Feb 17, 1909.

§ 116. Evangelical Lutheran church, changing system of electing trustees

If the trustees of an incorporated Evangelical Lutheran church shall at any time be elective in pursuance of article ten of this chapter, the church may, at an annual corporate meeting, if notice thereof be given with the notice of such meeting determine that the minister or ministers and elders and deacons thereof shall thereafter constitute the trustees thereof, and thereon the trustees of such church shall sign, acknowledge and cause to be filed and recorded, a certificate stating the fact of such determination, and the name of the minister or ministers, if any, and of the elders and deacons of such church; and thereon the terms of office of such elective trustees shall cease, and the minister or ministers and the elders and deacons of such church, and their successors in office shall, by virtue of their respective offices, be the trustees of such church. If, at any time, the officers of an incorporated Evangelical Lutheran church which officers by virtue of their offices constitute the trustees thereof shall determine to submit to a meeting of such church corporation, the question whether the trustees of such church shall be thereafter elective in pursuance of article ten of this chapter, they shall cause a corporate meeting of such church to be called and held in the manner provided in sections one hundred and ninety-four and one hundred and ninety-five of this chapter, and such corporate meeting shall determine whether the trustees of such church shall thereafter be elective in pursuance of article ten of this chapter, and also whether the number of such trustees shall be three, six or nine, and the date of the annual corporate meeting of the church. If such meeting shall determine that such trustees shall thereafter be elective, the presiding officer thereof and at least two other persons present and voting thereat, shall sign, acknowledge and cause to be filed and recorded in the office of the clerk of the county in which the certificate of incorporation of such church is filed, a certificate of such determination of such meeting; and thereafter the trustees of such church shall be elective in pursuance of article ten of this chapter. At the next annual corporate meeting after the filing of such certificate, one-third of the number of trustees so determined on shall be elected to hold office for one year, one-third for two years, and one-third for three years, and the officers of such church who by virtue of their offices have been trustees of such church, shall then cease to be such trustees, and thereafter article ten of this chapter shall apply to such church. At each subsequent annual corporate meeting of such church, one-third of the number of trustees so determined on shall be elected to hold office for three years.

History: Add, L 1909, ch 53, eff Feb 17, 1909.

ARTICLE 7
BAPTIST CHURCHES

History: Add, L 1909, ch 53.

§ 130. Notice of meeting for incorporation

Notice of a meeting for the purpose of incorporating an unincorporated Baptist church shall be given as follows: The notice shall be in writing, and shall state, in substance, that a meeting of such unincorporated church will be held at its usual place of worship at a specified day and hour, for the purpose of incorporating such church, electing trustees thereof, and selecting a corporate name therefor. The notice must be signed by at least six persons of full age, who are then members in good and regular standing of such church by admission into full communion or membership therewith. A copy of such notice shall be publicly read at a regular meeting of such unincorporated church for public worship, on the two successive Sundays immediately preceding the meeting, by the minister of such church, or a deacon thereof or by any person qualified to sign such notice.

History: Add, L 1909, ch 53, eff Feb 17, 1909.

CASE ANNOTATIONS

Where it could not be determined from the papers whether the plaintiffs, as members of the Board of Trustees of a certain Baptist Church, would ultimately be successful in obtaining a declaration that they were the legal and authorized officers of the church whose performance of duties as such was allegedly being interfered with by defendants, a temporary injunction was nevertheless issued to preserve status quo pending determination of fact issues. Farmer v Norton (1962, Sup) 236 N.Y.S.2d 906

§ 131. The meeting for incorporation

At the meeting for incorporation, held in pursuance of such notice, the qualified voters, until otherwise decided as hereinafter provided, shall be all persons of full age, who are then members, in good and regular standing of such church, by admission into full communion or membership therewith. At such meeting the presence of a majority of such qualified voters, at least six in number, shall be necessary to constitute a quorum, and all matters or questions shall be decided by a majority of the qualified voters voting thereon. There shall be elected at said meeting from the qualified voters then present, a presiding officer, a clerk to keep the record of the proceedings of the meeting and two inspectors of election to receive the ballots cast. The presiding officer and the inspectors shall declare the result of the ballots cast on any matter, and shall be the judges of the qualifications of voters. If the meeting shall decide that such unincorporated church shall become incorporated, the meeting shall also decide upon the name of the proposed corporation, the number of the trustees thereof, which shall be three, six, nine, twelve or eighteen, and the date, not more than fifteen months thereafter, on which the first annual election of the trustees thereof shall be held, and shall decide also whether those who, from the time of the formation of such church or during the year preceding the meeting for incorporation, have statedly worshipped with such church and have regularly contributed to the financial support thereof, shall be qualified voters at such meeting for incorporation, and whether those who during the year preceding the subsequent corporate meetings of the church shall have statedly worshipped with such church and shall have regularly contributed to the financial support thereof, shall be qualified voters at such corporate meetings. Such meeting shall thereupon elect by ballot from the persons qualified to vote thereat one-third of the number of trustees so decided on, who shall hold office until the first annual election of trustees thereafter, and one-third of such number of trustees who shall hold office until the second annual election of trustees thereafter, and one-third of such number of trustees who shall hold office until the third annual election of trustees thereafter, or until the respective successors of such trustees shall be elected.

History: Add, L 1909, ch 53, amd, L 1913, ch 397, L 1966, ch 503, eff June 7, 1966.

§ 132. The certificate of incorporation

If the meeting shall decide that such unincorporated church shall become incorporated, the presiding officer of such meeting and the two inspectors of election shall execute a certificate setting forth the name of the proposed corporation, the number of the trustees thereof, the names of the persons elected as trustees and the terms of office for which they were respectively elected and the county and town, city or village in which its principal place of worship is or is intended to be located. On the filing and recording of such certificate after it shall have been acknowledged or proved as hereinbefore provided, the persons qualified to vote at such meeting and those persons who shall thereafter, from time to time, be qualified voters at the corporate meetings thereof, shall be a corporation by the name stated in such certificate, and the persons therein stated to be elected trustees of such church shall be the trustees thereof, for the terms for which they were respectively elected and until their respective successors shall be elected.

History: Add, L 1909, ch 53, eff Feb 17, 1909.

§ 133. Time, place and notice of corporate meetings

The annual corporate meeting of every incorporated Baptist church shall be held at the time and place fixed by or in pursuance of law therefor, if such time and place be so fixed, and otherwise, at a time and place to be fixed by its trustees. A special corporate meeting of any such church may be called by the board of trustees thereof, on its own motion, and shall be called on the written request of at least ten qualified voters of such church. The trustees shall cause notice of the time and place of its annual corporate meeting, and of the names of any trustees whose successors are to be elected thereat; and, if a special meeting, of the business to be transacted thereat, to be publicly read by the minister of such church or any trustee thereof at a regular meeting of the church for public worship, on the two successive Sundays immediately preceding such meeting; or if no such

meeting for public worship shall have been held during such period, by conspicuously posting such notice, in writing, upon the outer entrance of the principal place of worship of such church and by mailing a copy of such notice to each member of such church in a securely sealed envelope, postage prepaid, addressed to his last known place of residence, at least two weeks before such meeting.

History: Add, L 1909, ch 53, amd, L 1914, ch 10, eff Feb 26, 1914.

CASE ANNOTATIONS

Compliance with this section is necessary to order to call a special meeting of the congregation, and where notice of special meeting was read by secretary, rather than a trustee or a deacon, such notice was a nullity. Hayes v Brantley (1967) 53 Misc. 2d 1040, 280 N.Y.S.2d 291

The removal of the trustees of a Baptist church corporation was invalid where their conduct was not "inexcusable or contumacious" and where the quarterly meetings of the corporation were not given notice of, as required by statute. Petition of Hayes (1942, Sup) 38 N.Y.S.2d 66

§ 134. Organization and conduct of corporate meetings; qualifications of voters thereat

At a corporate meeting of an incorporated Baptist church the qualified voters shall be all persons who are then members of such church in good and regular standing by admission into full communion or membership therewith, or who have statedly worshiped with such church and have regularly contributed to the financial support thereof during the year next preceding such meeting; but any incorporated Baptist church may at any annual corporate meeting thereof, if notice of the intention so to do has been given with the notice of such meeting, decide that thereafter only members of such church in good and regular standing by admission into full communion or membership therewith shall be qualified voters at the corporate meetings. At such corporate meetings the presence of at least six persons qualified to vote thereat shall be necessary to constitute a quorum, and all matters or questions shall be decided by a majority of the qualified voters voting thereon. There shall be elected at said meeting from the qualified voters then present, a presiding officer, a clerk to keep the records of the proceedings of the meeting and two inspectors of election to receive the ballots cast. The presiding officer and the inspectors of election shall declare the result of the ballots cast on any matter and shall be the judge of the qualifications of voters. At each annual corporate meeting, successors to those trustees whose terms of office then expire, shall be elected by ballot from the qualified voters, for a term of three years thereafter, and until their successors shall be elected.

History: Add, L 1909, ch 53, amd, L 1971, ch 201, § 4, eff Sept 1, 1971.

CASE ANNOTATIONS

Membership in the ecclesiastical body ipso facto allows the church member to vote at a meeting of the religious corporation. Walker Memorial Baptist Church v Saunders (1941) 285 N.Y. 462, 35 N.E.2d 42, reh den 286 N.Y. 607, 35 N.E.2d 944

Call for a meeting under this section was invalid where two of the ten signers of the notice were only 12 years old. Miles v Wilson (1958) 16 Misc. 2d 1085, 181 N.Y.S.2d 585

This section does not provide for the removal of living trustees. Miles v Wilson (1958) 16 Misc. 2d 1085, 181 N.Y.S.2d 585

July letter issued to protesting members of Baptist church, which removed them from active membership, violated church bylaws where bylaws called for determination of active memberships at end of year following financial report, and therefore protesting members could not be excluded from vote for board of trustees. Ward v Jones (1992, Sup) 154 Misc. 2d 597, 587 N.Y.S.2d 94

§ 135. Changing date of annual corporate meetings

An annual corporate meeting of an incorporated Baptist church may change the date of its annual meeting thereafter. If the date fixed for the annual meeting shall be less than six months after the annual meeting at which such change is made, the next annual meeting shall be held one year from the date so fixed. For the purpose of determining the terms of office of trustees, the time between the annual meeting at which such change is made and the next annual meeting thereafter shall be reckoned as one year.

History: Add, L 1909, ch 53, eff Feb 17, 1909.

§ 136. Changing number of trustees

An incorporated Baptist church may, at an annual corporate meeting, change the number of its trustees to not less than three, nor more than eighteen, or classify them so that the terms of one-third expire each year, provided that notice of such intended change or classification be included in the notice of such annual corporate meeting. No such change shall affect the terms of the trustees then in office, and if the change reduces the number of trustees, elections shall not be held to fill vacancies caused by the expiration of the terms of trustees until the number of trustees equals the number to which the trustees were reduced. Whenever the number of trustees in office is less than the number so determined on, sufficient additional trustees shall be elected to make the number of trustees equal to the number so determined on. The trustees so elected up to and including one-third of the number so determined on, shall be elected for three years, the remainder up to and including one-third of the number so determined on for two years, and the remainder for one year.

History: Add, L 1909, ch 53, amd, L 1913, ch 397, L 1966, ch 503, eff June 7, 1966.

Amd, L 1994, ch 65, § 1, eff April 18, 1994.

§ 137. Meetings of trustees

Meetings of the trustees of an incorporated Baptist church shall be called by giving at least twenty-four hours' notice thereof personally or by mail to all the trustees and such notice may be given by two of the trustees, but by the unanimous consent of the trustees a meeting may be held without previous notice thereof. A majority of the whole number of trustees shall constitute a quorum for the transaction of business at any meeting lawfully convened.

History: Add, L 1909, ch 53, eff Feb 17, 1909.

§ 138. The creation and filling of vacancies among trustees of such churches

If any trustee of an incorporated Baptist church declines to act, resigns or dies, or having been a member of such church ceases to be such member, or not having been a member of such church, ceases to be a qualified voter at a corporate meeting thereof, his office shall be vacant, and such vacancy may be filled by the remaining trustees until the next annual corporate meeting of such church, at which meeting the vacancy shall be filled for the unexpired term.

History: Add, L 1909, ch 53, eff Feb 17, 1909.

CASE ANNOTATIONS

This section does not provide for the removal of living trustees. Miles v Wilson (1958) 16 Misc. 2d 1085, 181 N.Y.S.2d 585

§ 139. Control of trustees by corporate meetings of such churches; salary of minister

The trustees of an incorporated Baptist church shall have no power to settle or remove a minister or to fix his salary or, without the consent of a corporate meeting, to incur debts beyond what is necessary for the administration of the temporal affairs of the church and for the care of the property of the corporation; or to fix or change the time, nature or order of the public or social worship of such church. The temporal affairs and property of an incorporated Baptist church shall be administered by its trustees in accordance with and subject to its lawfully adopted by-laws and to the general or special rules, regulations, or resolutions lawfully adopted by the church at its annual or other regular corporate meeting or at any duly called special corporate meeting.

History: Add, L 1909, ch 53, amd, L 1940, ch 490, eff Apr 14, 1940.

CASE ANNOTATIONS

The minister of a Baptist church, under the rules and regulations of that denomination, is an officer of the religious society of the church and is not an officer of the religious corporation, and hence the corporation has no power to discharge a minister from his position. Walker Memorial Baptist Church v Saunders (1941) 285 N.Y. 462, 35 N.E.2d 42, reh den 286 N.Y. 607, 35 N.E.2d 944

The Board of Trustees of a Baptist Church may commence legal action without the consent of a corporate meeting where it is necessary for the care and preservation of the corporate property. Calvary Baptist Church, Inc. v Williams (1972, 2d Dept) 38 A.D.2d 970, 331 N.Y.S.2d 792

While this section expressly prohibits removal of a Baptist minister by the Board of Trustees, the Religious Corporations Law contains no mandate as to procedure or method for legally discharging such a minister and, accordingly, his removal is a function of the spiritual entity of the church only and cannot be validly effected by temporal officers. Evans v Criss (1963) 39 Misc. 2d 314, 240 N.Y.S.2d 517

Deacons of Baptist church were entitled to lifetime tenure based on constitution of church and church custom; however, members of board of trustees were not entitled to lifetime tenure since board controlled temporalities of church and were required to be subject to control of church membership. Ward v Jones (1992, Sup) 154 Misc. 2d 597, 587 N.Y.S.2d 94

The removal of a Sunday school teacher was a spiritual matter, which was subject to the authority of the group of communicants of a religious society, as distinct from the church corporation, which had jurisdiction over the property and temporal affairs of the church.

Metropolitan Baptist Church, Inc. v Braxton (1954, Sup) 137 N.Y.S.2d 294, affd 285 A.D. 1044, 141 N.Y.S.2d 509

Since this section prohibits removal of a pastor by the Board of Trustees, his discharge is a function of the spiritual entity. Hayes v Board of Trustees (1962, Sup) 225 N.Y.S.2d 316

Discharge of a pastor can be effected by failure to elect him at a meeting held for that purpose. Hayes v Board of Trustees (1962, Sup) 225 N.Y.S.2d 316

Although there is no mandate in the Religious Corporations Law as to the method or procedure to be followed in discharging a pastor, if his removal is sought by reason of alleged misconduct the procedure must be in strict accordance with accepted and honored customs, policies and usage, including the right to be apprised of the alleged misconduct and given an oportunity to defend. Hayes v Board of Trustees (1962, Sup) 225 N.Y.S.2d 316

Where the acquisition or ownership of stock in a national bank was never authorized, consented to or ratified by a corporate meeting of the church, the church is not liable on stock assessment. Haight v First Baptist Church (1942, DC NY) 42 F. Supp. 925

§ 140. Transfer of property to Baptist corporations

Any incorporated Baptist church, created by or existing under the laws of the state of New York, having its principal office or place of worship in the state of New York, or whose last place of worship was within the state of New York, is hereby authorized and empowered, by a vote of two-thirds of its qualified voters present and voting therefor, at a meeting regularly called for that purpose, to transfer and convey any of its property, real or personal, which it now has or may hereafter acquire, to any religious, charitable or missionary corporation connected with the Baptist denomination and incorporated by or organized under any law or laws of the state of New York, either solely, or among other purposes, to establish or maintain, or to assist in establishing or maintaining churches, schools, or mission stations or to erect, or assist in the erection of such buildings as may be necessary for any of such purposes, and on or without the payment of any money or other consideration therefor, and upon such transfer or conveyance being made, the title to and the ownership and right of possession of the property so transferred and conveyed shall be vested in and conveyed to such grantee; and also any membership corporation incorporated by or organized under any special or general law or laws of the state of New York, either solely, or among other purposes, for religious, charitable, missionary or educational objects connected with or for the aid of the Baptist denomination or any church or churches thereof or for the erection or maintenance of any building therefor, is hereby authorized and empowered, by the vote of at least two-thirds of the whole number of its directors, or by the vote of at least a majority thereof if such whole number of directors is twenty or more, at any regularly called or regularly held meeting of such directors, to transfer and convey any of its property, real or personal, which it now has or may hereafter acquire, to any incorporated Baptist church within the state of New York, and on or without the payment of any money or other consideration therefor, and upon such transfer or conveyance being made, the title to and the ownership and right of possession of the property

so transferred and conveyed shall be vested in and conveyed to such grantee; provided, however, that nothing herein contained shall impair or affect in any way, any existing claim upon or lien against any property so transferred or conveyed, or any action at law or legal proceeding, and subject, in respect to the amount of property the said grantee may take and hold, to the restrictions and limitations of existing laws.

History: Add, L 1909, ch 53, amd, L 1936, ch 273, eff Apr 6, 1936.

ARTICLE 8
CHURCHES OF THE UNITED CHURCH OF CHRIST, CONGREGATIONAL CHRISTIAN AND INDEPENDENT CHURCHES

History: Add, L 1909, ch 53. Article title, amd, L 1972, ch 900, eff Sept 1, 1972.

§ 160. Notice of meeting for incorporation

Notice of a meeting for the purpose of incorporating an unincorporated church of the United Church of Christ or Independent church shall be given as follows: The notice shall be in writing, and shall state, in substance, that a meeting of such unincorporated church will be held at its usual place of worship at a specified day and hour, for the purpose of incorporating such church, electing trustees thereof, and selecting a corporate name therefor. The notice must be signed by at least six persons of full age, who have statedly worshiped with such church and have regularly contributed to its support, according to its usages, for at least one year or since it was formed. A copy of such notice shall be publicly read at a regular meeting of such unincorporated church for public worship, on the two successive Sundays immediately preceding the meeting, by the minister of such church, or a deacon thereof or by any person qualified to sign such notice.

History: Add, L 1909, ch 53, amd, L 1972, ch 900, eff Sept 1, 1972.

§ 161. The meeting for incorporation

At the meeting for incorporation, held in pursuance of such notice, the qualified voters, until otherwise decided as hereinafter provided, shall be all persons of full age who have stately worshiped with such church and have regularly contributed to its support, according to its usages, for at least one year or since it was formed. At such meeting the presence of a majority of such qualified voters, in person, or by proxy duly authorized in writing, at least six in number, shall be necessary to constitute a quorum, and all matters or questions shall be decided by a majority of the qualified voters voting thereon. The meeting shall be called to order by one of the signers of the call. There shall be elected at such meeting, from the qualified voters then present, a presiding officer, a clerk to keep the record of the proceedings of the meeting and two inspectors of election to receive the ballots cast. The presiding officer and the inspectors shall decide the result of the ballots cast on any matter, and shall be the judges of the qualifications of the voters. If the meeting shall decide that such unincorporated church shall become incorporated, the meeting shall also decide upon the name of the proposed corporation, the number of the trustees thereof, which shall be three, six or nine, and the date, not more than fifteen months thereafter, on which the first annual election of the trustees thereof shall be held; and it may, by a two-thirds vote, decide that all members of the unincorporated church, of full age, in good and regular standing who have stately worshiped with such church but who have not contributed to the financial support thereof, shall also be qualified voters at such meeting, and that such church members, who, for one year next preceding any subsequent corporate meeting, shall have stately worshiped with such church and have been members thereof in good and regular standing, but have not regularly contributed to the financial support thereof, shall be qualified voters at such corporate meetings. Such meetings shall thereupon elect by ballot from the persons qualified to vote thereat one-third of the number of trustees so decided on, who shall hold office until the first annual election of trustees thereafter, one-third of such number of trustees who shall hold office until the second annual election of trustees thereafter, and one-third of such number of trustees who shall hold office until the third annual election of trustees thereafter, or until the respective successors of such trustees shall be elected. Such meeting shall also elect by ballot a clerk of the corporation, who shall hold his office until the close of the next annual meeting.

History: Add, L 1909, ch 53, amd, L 1922, ch 201, eff Mar 23, 1922.

§ 162. The certificate of incorporation

If the meeting shall decide that such unincorporated church shall become incorporated, the presiding officer of such meeting and the two inspectors of election shall execute a certificate setting forth the name of the proposed corporation, the number of trustees thereof, the names of the persons elected as trustees, the terms of office for which they were respectively elected and the county and town, city or

village in which its principal place of worship is or is intended to be located. On the filing and recording of such certificate, after it shall have been acknowledged or proved as hereinbefore provided, the persons qualified to vote at such meeting and those persons who shall thereafter, from time to time, be qualified voters at the corporate meetings thereof, shall be a corporation by the name stated in such certificate, and the persons therein stated to be elected trustees of such church shall be the trustees thereof for the terms for which they were respectively elected and until their respective successors shall be elected.

History: Add, L 1909, ch 53, eff Feb 17, 1909.

CASE ANNOTATIONS

Because a meeting purportedly electing the successor trustees was not noticed in accordance with N.Y. Relig. Corp. Law § 162, the successor trustees were enjoined from exercising authority or control over the church's temporalities and property pursuant to N.Y. Relig. Corp. Law § 5. Trustees of Gallilee Pentecostal Church, Inc. v Williams (2009, 2d Dept) 65 App Div 3d 1221, 885 NYS2d 525.

§ 163. Time, place and notice of corporate meetings

The annual corporate meeting of every church incorporated under this article shall be held at the time and place fixed by its by-laws, or if no time and place be so fixed, then at a time and place to be first fixed by its trustees, but to be changed only by a by-law adopted at an annual meeting. A special corporate meeting of any such church may be called by the board of trustees thereof, on its own motion, and shall be called on the written request of at least ten qualified voters of such church. The trustees shall cause notice of the time and place of its annual corporate meeting, and of the names of any trustees whose successors are to be elected thereat, and if a special meeting, of the business to be transacted thereat, to be publicly read by the minister of such church or any trustees thereof at a regular meeting of the church for public worship, on the two successive Sundays immediately preceding such meeting.

History: Add, L 1909, ch 53, eff Feb 17, 1909.

CASE ANNOTATIONS

In action to recover damages for conversion based upon alleged usurpation of management and control of church, court's directive declaring church election invalid, vacating various offices of church, and requiring that new election be held did not exceed scope of relief requested by pleadings and was warranted by proof adduced at trial. Caldwell v Brown (1976, 2d Dept) 53 A.D.2d 657, 384 N.Y.S.2d 876

Special meeting of church corporation's membership was properly called where there were written requests for such meeting signed by at least 10 members predating notice of meeting, and that notice, which referred to previous meeting at which motion to dismiss pastor had been defeated, and which stated that "conduct of the Board of Trustees" was on agenda, sufficiently apprised members of business to be transacted. Rock Church, Inc. v Milani (1998, 1st Dept) 256 A.D.2d 255, 682 N.Y.S.2d 196

§ 164. Organization and conduct of corporate meetings; qualifications of voters

At every corporate meeting of a church to which this article is applicable the following persons, and no others shall be qualified voters, to wit: all persons who are then members in good and regular standing of such church by admission into full communion or membership therewith in accordance with the by-laws thereof, provided that if the by-laws so provide, persons who have statedly worshiped with such church and have regularly contributed to its financial suppport for not less than one year preceding such meeting shall also be qualified voters.

At such corporate meetings, the presence of at least six persons qualified to vote thereat shall be necessary to constitute a quorum; and all matters or questions shall be decided by a majority of the quali-fied voters voting thereon, except that by-laws can be adopted or amended only by a two-thirds vote. The clerk of the corporation shall call the meeting to order; and under his supervision the qualified voters then present shall choose a presiding officer and two inspectors of election to receive the ballots cast. The presiding officer and the inspectors of election shall declare the result of the ballots cast on any matter and shall be the judges of the qualifications of voters. At each annual corporate meeting, successors to those trustees whose terms of office then expire shall be elected by ballot from the qualified voters, for a term of three years thereafter, and until their successors shall be elected. A clerk of the corporation shall be elected by ballot, who shall hold office until the closing of the next annual meeting, and until his successor shall be elected.

History: Add, L 1909, ch 53, amd, L 1971, ch 201, § 5, eff Sept 1, 1971.

First par repealed and new first paragraph add, L 1972, ch 900, eff Sept 1, 1972.

CASE ANNOTATIONS

In action to recover damages for conversion based upon alleged usurpation of management and control of church, court's directive declaring church election invalid, vacating various offices of church, and requiring that new election be held did not exceed scope of relief requested by pleadings and was warranted by proof adduced at trial. Caldwell v Brown (1976, 2d Dept) 53 A.D.2d 657, 384 N.Y.S.2d 876

§ 165. Changing date of annual corporate meetings

An annual corporate meeting of any church in-corporated under this article may change the date of its subsequent annual meetings. If the date fixed for the annual meeting shall be less than six months after the annual meeting at which such change is made, the next annual meeting shall be held one year from the date so fixed. For the purpose of determining the terms of office of trustees, the time between the annual meeting at which such change is made and the next annual meeting thereafter shall be reckoned as one year.

History: Add, L 1909, ch 53, eff Feb 17, 1909.

§ 166. Changing number of trustees

Any such incorporated church may, at an annual corporate meeting, change the number of its trustees to three, six, nine, twelve or fifteen, classifying them so that the terms of one-third expire each year,

provided that notice of such intended change be included in the notice of such annual corporate meeting. No such change shall affect the terms of the trustees then in office; and if the change reduces the number of trustees, elections shall not be held to fill the vacancies caused by the expiration of the terms of trustees, until the number of trustees equals the number to which the trustees were reduced. Whenev-er the number of trustees in office is less than the number so determined on, sufficient additional trustees shall be elected to make the number of trustees equal to the number so determined on. The trustees so elected, up to and including one-third of the number so determined on, shall be elected for three years, the remainder up to and including one-third of the number so determined on for two years, and the remainder for one year.

History: Add, L 1909, ch 53, amd, L 1926, ch 381, eff Apr 15, 1926.

§ 167. Meetings of trustees

Meetings of the trustees of any such incorporated church shall be called by giving at least twenty-four hours' notice thereof personally or by mail to all the trustees; and such notice may be given by two of the trustees; but by the unanimous consent of the trus-tees, a meeting may be held without previous notice thereof. A majority of the whole number of trustees shall constitute a quorum for the transaction of business, at any meeting lawfully convened.

History: Add, L 1909, ch 53, eff Feb 17, 1909.

§ 168. Vacancies among trustees

If any trustee of any such incorporated church declines to act, resigns or dies, or ceases to be a qualified voter at a corporate meeting thereof, his office shall be vacant; and such vacancy may be filled by the remaining trustees until the next annual corporate meeting of such church; at which meeting the vacancy shall be filled for the unexpired term.

History: Add, L 1909, ch 53, eff Feb 17, 1909.

§ 169. Limitation of powers of trustees

The trustees of any such incorporated church shall have no power to call, settle or remove a minis-ter or to fix his salary, nor without the consent of a corporate meeting, to incur debts, beyond what is necessary for the administration of the temporal affairs of the church and for the care of the property of the corporation; or to fix or change the time, nature or order of the public or social worship of such church.

History: Add, L 1909, ch 53, eff Feb 17, 1909.

CASE ANNOTATIONS

Even if church corporation's board of trustees had authorized retainer of attorney and establishment of "unlimited" legal defense fund, such action was invalid since board had no authority to incur debts beyond those necessary for administration of church without approval of membership. Rock Church, Inc. v Milani (1998, 1st Dept) 256 A.D.2d 255, 682 N.Y.S.2d 196

The expression "incur debts," as used in this section limiting the powers of trustees, includes entering into a mortgage. Bank of

Manhattan Trust Co. v Twenty-One Sixty-Six Broadway Corp. (1932) 142 Misc 910, 256 N.Y.S. 553, affd 236 A.D. 781, 258 N.Y.S. 1046

§ 170. Election and salary of ministers

The ministers of any such church shall be called, settled or removed and their salaries fixed, only by the vote of a majority of the members of such corporation duly qualified to vote at elections present and voting at a meeting of such corporation specially called for that purpose, in the manner hereinbefore provided for the call of special meetings; and any such corporation may, by its by-laws, make the call, settlement or removal of its ministers dependent upon a concurrent vote of the unincorporated church connected with such corporation; and in that case the concurrence of a majority of the members of such unincorporated church, present and voting at a meeting thereof, called for that purpose, shall be necessary to the call, settlement or removal of such ministers.

History: Add, L 1909, ch 53, eff Feb 17, 1909.

§ 171. Transfer of property

Any incorporated church of the United Church of Christ and any incorporated Congregational Christian church which is a member of the New York Conference of the United Church of Christ, created by or existing under the laws of the state of New York, having its principal office or place of worship in the state of New York, or whose last place of worship was within the state of New York, is hereby authorized and empowered, by the concurrent vote of two-thirds of its qualified voters present and voting therefor, at a meeting regularly called for that purpose, and of two-thirds of all its trustees, to direct the transfer and conveyance of any of its property, real or personal, which it now has or may hereafter acquire, to any religious, charitable or missionary corporation connected with the United Church of Christ and incorporated by or organized under any law of the state of New York, either solely, or among other purposes, to establish or maintain, or to assist in establishing or maintaining churches, schools or mission stations, or to erect or assist in the erection of such buildings as may be necessary for any of such purposes, with or without the payment of any money or other consideration therefor; and upon such concurrent votes being given, the trustees shall execute such transfer or conveyance; and upon the same being made, the title to and the ownership and right of possession of the property so transferred and conveyed shall be vested in and conveyed to such grantee; provided, however, that nothing herein contained shall impair or affect in any way any existing claim upon or lien against any property so transferred or conveyed, or any action at law or legal proceeding; and such transfer shall be subject, in respect to the amount of property the said grantee may take and hold, to the restrictions and limitations of all laws then in force.

History: Add, L 1909, ch 53, amd, L 1972, ch 900, eff Sept 1, 1972.

Where voluntary unrestricted contributions were made to the General Council of Congregational Churches for a general charitable and religious purpose, no proprietary or beneficial interest was shown authorizing court interference in their expenditure so long as such use did not violate charter of General Council. Hence, church which dissented to proposed union of Congregational Churches with Evangelical and Reformed Church could not restrain union.on ground that General Council's funds were being diverted. Cadman Memorial Congregational Soc. v Kenyon (1953) 306 N.Y. 151, 116 N.E.2d 481, reh den 306 N.Y. 851, 118 N.E.2d 909

Where entry into a proposed union of Congregational Christian Churches with the Evangelical and Reformed Church depended on voluntary action freely taken by independent autonomous churches and no power existed to compel nonassenting churches to join union, no ecclesiastical question was presented and complaint of dissenting church for a declaratory judgment and to restrain union was properly dismissed. Cadman Memorial Congregational Soc. v Kenyon (1953) 306 N.Y. 151, 116 N.E.2d 481, reh den 306 N.Y. 851, 118 N.E.2d 909

The court will not entertain an action for declaratory judgment of the rights of plaintiffs with respect to funds and assets held by the corporate societies and agencies at least in the absence of such corporate societies and agencies. Cadman Memorial Congregational Soc. v Kenyon (1953) 306 N.Y. 151, 116 N.E.2d 481, reh den 306 N.Y. 851, 118 N.E.2d 909

§ 172. Application of this article

This article applies only to churches of the United Church of Christ, Congregational Christian churches, whether or not part of the United Church of Christ, and Independent churches.

History: Add, L 1972, ch 900, eff Sept 1, 1972.

The mere act by a church of incorporating under article 10 of the Religious Corporations Law is not determinative of the issue of whether said church is independent or hierarchical as it cannot be said that if a church intended to become an independent church it would have incorporated under article 8, in that it is erroneous to read the words "Independent church" in said article to mean independent church in the sense that it is not connected to a parent body. New York Dist. of Assemblies of God v Calvary Assembly of God (1978, 3d Dept) 64 A.D.2d 311, 409 N.Y.S.2d 842

ARTICLE 8-A
CHURCHES OF THE UKRAINIAN ORTHODOX CHURCHES OF AMERICA

History: Add, L 1938, ch 663.

Sections 169-a-169-e have been enacted out of numerical order. Sections 170-172 are to be found in Art. 8.

§ 169-a.   Application for incorporation

Any Ukrainian Orthodox church of the Greek rite may become incorporated in this state as a church of the Ukrainian Orthodox Church of America by executing, acknowledging and filing a certificate of incorporation as hereinafter provided.

History: Add, L 1938, ch 663, eff Apr 12, 1938.

§ 169-b. Notice of meeting for incorporation and provisions governing meetings for incorporation

1. Notice of a meeting for the purpose of incorporating an unincorporated Ukrainian Orthodox church of the Greek rite shall be in writing and shall state in substance that a meeting of such unincorporated church will be held at its usual place of worship at a specified day and hour, for the purpose of incorporating such a church and selecting a name therefor and electing trustees thereof.

2. Such notice shall be publicly read at a regular service of such unincorporated church on a Sunday next preceding such meeting and a copy of such notice shall be sent by mail postpaid at least ten days prior to the date fixed for such meeting to each member of such church in good and regular standing at his last known address as same appears in the church record.

3. At the meeting for incorporation held in pursuance of such notice, all persons of full age, who are then members in good and regular standing of such church, shall be qualified voters. All the duly qualified voters present at such meeting, at least six in number, shall constitute a quorum, and all matters or questions shall be decided by a majority of the qualified voters voting thereon.

4. There shall be elected at such meeting from the qualified voters then present a presiding officer and a clerk to keep the records of the proceedings of the meeting. The presiding officer shall decide the results of the votes cast on any matter and shall be the judge of the qualifications of the voters.

5. If the meeting shall decide that such unincorporated church shall become incorporated, the meeting shall also decide upon the name of the proposed corporation, the number of trustees thereof which shall be either three, five or seven, and the date, not more than fifteen months thereafter, on which the first annual election of the trustees shall be held.

6. Such meeting shall thereupon elect from the persons qualified to vote thereat the trustees who shall hold office until the first annual election of the trustees thereafter, or until their successors are elected and take office.

History: Add, L 1938, ch 663, eff Apr 12, 1938.

§ 169-c. Certification* of incorporation

* So in original; does not agree with Article analysis.

1. The presiding officer of such meeting and at least two other persons present and voting thereat shall execute and acknowledge a certificate of incorporation which shall set forth the following:

(a) The name of the proposed corporation.

(b) The number of trustees thereof.

(c) The names of the trustees elected for the first year.

(d) The county and town, city or village in which the principal place of worship is or is intended to be located.

(e) The date of its annual meeting for the election of trustees.

2. On filing such certificate in the office of the county clerk of the county in which such church is or is intended to be located, such church shall be a corporation by the name stated in the certificate of incorporation.

History: Add, L 1938, ch 663, eff Apr 12, 1938.

§ 169-d. Government; powers and duties of the trustees

1. Every Ukrainian Orthodox church incorporated pursuant to this article shall recognize and be subject to the jurisdiction of the duly appointed bishop or archbishop of the Ukrainian Orthodox Church of America, or his lawful successor in office, and shall conform to and adopt the faith, doctrine, discipline, canons and constitution of the said church.

2. The trustees of every such incorporated church shall have the custody and control of all the temporalities and property, real and personal, belonging to the corporation and the revenues therefrom, and shall administer the same strictly in accordance with the by-laws of the corporation and the rules, regulations and usages of the governing diocesan council of the said Ukrainian Orthodox Church of America.

History: Add, L 1938, ch 663, eff Apr 12, 1938.

§ 169-e. Reincorporation of existing corporations

Any Ukrainian Orthodox church of the Greek rite heretofore incorporated, other than those incorporated under the provisions of article five of the religious corporations law, may reincorporate under the provisions of this article, by filing in the county clerk's office in the county in which its principal place of worship is located, a certificate, signed by the trustees in office at the time of such reincorporation, or by the majority of them, setting forth that they desire to reincorporate under the provisions of this act, the corporate name by which such church shall be known, the county, town, city or village where its place of worship is or is intended to be located, and the number and the names of the trustees who are to hold office until the next annual meeting of said corporation. If the bishop or archbishop having ecclesiastical jurisdiction over such church is not one of the trustees signing the certificate of reincorporation, such certificate shall not be valid until said bishop or archbishop has given his assent in writing to such reincorporation and the same is made a part of the certificate. Immediately upon the filing of such certificate all the right, title and interest of such organization or corporation in any estate, real or personal, shall, with all franchise and charter rights, be vested in said body corporate and politic so created

Religious Corporations Law

under this act and the original incorporation of such organization shall be null and void.

The incorporation of a new church or reincorporation of an old church under this article shall not be valid until the same has been approved by a justice of the supreme court.

History: Add, L 1938, ch 663, eff Apr 12, 1938.

ARTICLE 8-B
CHURCHES OF THE HOLY UKRAINIAN AUTOCEPHALIC ORTHODOX CHURCH IN EXILE

History: Add, L 1961, ch 800, eff Apr 22, 1961.

§ 175. Application for incorporation

Any Ukrainian Orthodox church may become incorporated in this state as a church of the Holy Ukrainian Autocephalic Orthodox Church in Exile by executing, acknowledging and filing a certificate of incorporation as hereinafter provided.

History: Add, L 1961, ch 800, eff Apr 22, 1961.

§ 176. Notice of meeting for incorporation and provisions governing meetings for incorporation

1. Notice of a meeting for the purpose of incorporating an unincorporated Ukrainian Orthodox church under this article shall be in writing and shall state in substance that a meeting of such unincorporated church will be held at its usual place of worship at a specified day and hour, for the purpose of incorporating such a church and selecting a name therefor and electing trustees thereof.

2. Such notice shall be publicly read at a regular service of such unincorporated church on a Sunday next preceding such meeting and a copy of such notice shall be sent by mail postpaid at least ten days prior to the date fixed for such meeting to each member of such church in good and regular standing at his last known address as same appears in the church record.

3. At the meeting for incorporation held in pursuance of such notice, all persons of full age, who are then members in good and regular standing of such church, shall be qualified voters. All the duly qualified voters present at such meeting, at least six in number, shall constitute a quorum, and all matters or questions shall be decided by a majority of the qualified voters voting thereon.

4. There shall be elected at such meeting from the qualified voters then present a presiding officer and a clerk to keep the records of the proceedings of the meeting. The presiding officer shall decide the results

of the votes cast on any matter and shall be the judge of the qualifications of the voters.

5. If the meeting shall decide that such unincorporated church shall become incorporated, the meeting shall also decide upon the name of the proposed corporation, the number of trustees thereof which shall be either three, five or seven, and the date, not more than fifteen months thereafter, on which the first annual election of the trustees shall be held.

6. Such meeting shall thereupon elect from the persons qualified to vote thereat the trustees who shall hold office until the first annual election of the trustees thereafter, or until their successors are elected and take office.

History: Add, L 1961, ch 800, eff Apr 22, 1961.

§ 177. Certificate of incorporation

1. The presiding officer of such meeting and at least two other persons present and voting thereat shall execute and acknowledge a certificate of incorporation which shall set forth the following:

(a) The name of the proposed corporation.

(b) The number of trustees thereof.

(c) The names of the trustees elected for the first year.

(d) The county and town, city or village in which the principal place of worship is or is intended to be located.

(e) The date of its annual meeting for the election of trustees.

2. On filing such certificate in the office of the county clerk of the county in which such church is or is intended to be located, such church shall be a corporation by the name stated in the certificate of incorporation.

History: Add, L 1961, ch 800, eff Apr 22, 1961.

§ 178. Government; powers and duties of the trustees

1. Every Ukrainian Orthodox church incorporated pursuant to this article shall recognize and be subject to the jurisdiction of the duly appointed bishop or archbishop of the Holy Ukrainian Autocephalic Orthodox Church in Exile, or his lawful successor in office, and shall conform to and adopt the faith, doctrine, discipline, canons and constitution of the said church.

2. The trustees of every such incorporated church shall have the custody and control of all the temporalities and property, real and personal, belonging to the corporation and the revenues therefrom, and shall administer the same strictly in accordance with the by-laws of the corporation and the rules, regulations and usages of the governing diocesan council of the said Holy Ukrainian Autocephalic Orthodox Church in Exile.

History: Add, L 1961, ch 800, eff Apr 22, 1961.

§ 179. Reincorporation of existing corporations

Any Ukrainian Orthodox church heretofore incorporated, other than those incorporated under the provisions of article five of the religious corporations law, may reincorporate under the provisions of this article, by filing in the county clerk's office in the county in which its principal place of worship is located, a certificate, signed by the trustees in office at the time of such reincorporation, or by the majority of them, setting forth that they desire to reincorporate under the provisions of this article, the corporate name by which such church shall be known, the county, town, city or village where its place of worship is or is intended to be located, and the number and the names of the trustees who are to hold office until the next annual meeting of said corporation. If the bishop or archbishop having ecclesiastical jurisdiction over such church is not one of the trustees signing the certificate of reincorporation, such certificate shall not be valid until said bishop or archbishop has given his assent in writing to such reincorporation and the same is made a part of the certificate. Immediately upon the filing of such certificate all the right, title and interest of such organization or corporation in any estate, real or personal, shall, with all franchise and charter rights, be vested in said body corporate and politic so created under this article and the original incorporation of such organization shall be null and void.

The incorporation of a new church or reincorporation of an old church under this article shall not be valid until the same has been approved by a justice of the supreme court.

History: Add, L 1961, ch 800, eff Apr 22, 1961.

ARTICLE 9
FREE CHURCHES

§ 180. Corporation, how formed
§ 181. Rights, powers and limitations
§ 182. Vacancies in boards of trustees
§ 182-a. Increasing number of trustees
§ 183. Seats and pews to be free

History: Add, L 1909, ch 53.

§ 180. Corporation, how formed

Any seven or more persons of full age, citizens of the United States, and a majority of them being residents of this state, who shall associate themselves for the purpose of founding and continuing one or more free churches, may make, sign and acknowledge, before any officer authorized to take the acknowledgment of deeds of land to be recorded in this state, and may file in the office of the secretary of state, and also of the clerk of the county in which any such church is to be established, and record as provided in section three of this chapter, a certificate in writing, in which shall be stated the name or title by which such society shall be known in the law, the purpose of its organization, and the names of seven trustees, of whom not less than five shall be persons who are not ministers of the gospel or priests of any denomination, to manage the same; but such certificate shall not be filed, unless with the written consent and approbation of a justice of the supreme court of the district in which any such church shall be intended to be established, to be indorsed on such certificate.

History: Add, L 1909, ch 53, eff Feb 17, 1909.

CASE ANNOTATIONS

Because the bylaws of a religious society, organized under N.Y. Religious Corporations Law art. 9, had been abandoned, and because the provisions of the bylaws that called for the election of trustees by the general body contradicted N.Y. Religious Corporations Law §§ 180, 182, the society did not have to conduct an election of a new board of trustees. Matter of Venigalla v Nori (2008) 11 NY3d 55, 862 NYS2d 457, 892 NE2d 850.

Although a temple's certificate of incorporation failed to fully comport with N.Y. Relig. Corp. Law § 180, summary judgment for defendants for lack of standing was improper because the certificate was, in effect, a hybrid of the relevant criteria of both the Religious Corporations Law and the Not-For-Profit Corporation Law regarding corporation formation and the temple was a "de facto" religious corporation; the temple was intended to be a religious corporation and, in fact, carried on under the assumption that it was a religious corporation, was a place of worship and did not receive any money in the form of stock or otherwise, and regularly solicited and received donations in the donation boxes. Further, there were unresolved fact issues as to whether the individual plaintiffs constituted the temple's validly appointed board of trustees. Temple-Ashram v Satyanandji (2011, 2d Dept) 84 App Div 3d 1158, 923 NYS2d 664.

A certificate of incorporation of a free church under the name of "Long Island Church of Aphrodite" was approved by the court, under § 180, where it appeared that the proposed corporation was not organized for any purpose other than a religious conception of love, beauty and harmony, and that its precepts and practices would not tend to glorify any qualities which are in opposition to the almost universal conception of religion. Re Long Island Church of Aphrodite (1939) 172 Misc 668, 14 N.Y.S.2d 762

The proposed corporate name "New York Soul Clinic, Inc." did not indicate adequately that the society was created for religious purposes or that it was a church and it was therefore inappropriate. Further, the purpose of incorporation stated as the founding and continuing of one or more free churches did not adequately state the religious doctrine proposed to be expounded and taught. Re Application of New York Soul Clinic, Inc. (1955) 208 Misc 612, 144 N.Y.S.2d 543

A proposed amendment to a religious corporation's certificate could not be approved where the powers enumerated in the amendment did not conform with limitations on the holding of real and personal property and on the amount which the corporation could take by devise or bequest, and the amendment did not contain a statement that not less than five of the seven trustees should not be priests or ministers. The refusal to approve the amendment did not constitute a violation of Article I § 3 of the State Constitution. Amendment of Certificate of Incorporation of St. of God in Christ, Inc. (1959) 20 Misc. 2d 532, 194 N.Y.S.2d 339

A justice of the Supreme Court is not required to approve a certificate of incorporation merely because its subscribers wish to establish a church. There must be some statement of the nature of the religious doctrine or dogma that the proposed free church intends to expound and teach. Re Jesus Sobre Las Aguas (1960) 21 Misc. 2d 937, 197 N.Y.S.2d 804

Before approving an application for certificate of incorporation for the "First Temple of the House of David (Hebrew Catholic Faith), Inc.," the court stated that it would have to know the complete meaning of the title as well as the meaning of "benevolent functions" and "to teach and practice the brotherhood of man under God" used in the application, also the identity of each of the subscribers, their age, marital status, and residence, and whether any of them had a criminal record of any kind. Re Application of First Temple of House of David (1959, Sup) 195 N.Y.S.2d 588

§ 181. Rights, powers and limitations

Upon the filing of such certificate the persons named therein as trustees, and their successors, being citizens of the United States and residents of this state, shall be a body politic and corporate, with all the rights, powers and duties, and subject to all the restrictions and obligations and other provisions, so far as the same may be applicable and consistent with this article, specified and contained in the act entitled "An act for the incorporation of benevolent, charitable, scientific and missionary societies," passed April twelfth, eighteen hundred and forty-eight, and the act amending the same, passed April seventh, eighteen hundred and forty-nine, except that the limitation in the first of the said acts of the value of real estate that may be held by any society in the city or county of New York, incorporated under this article, shall not be applicable to any church edifice erected or owned by such society, or the lot of ground on which the same may be built; and except that the provision in the first of the said acts, in relation to the personal liability of the trustees, shall be applicable only to the trustees who shall have assented to the creation of any debt.

History: Add, L 1909, ch 53, eff Feb 17, 1909.

§ 182. Vacancies in boards of trustees

Any vacancies occurring in the said board of trustees shall be supplied by the remaining trustees at any legal meeting of the members; but there shall always be at least five members of the board who are not ministers of the gospel or priests of any denomination.

History: Add, L 1909, ch 53, eff Feb 17, 1909.

CASE ANNOTATIONS

Because the bylaws of a religious society, organized under N.Y. Religious Corporations Law art. 9, had been abandoned, and because the provisions of the bylaws that called for the election of trustees by the general body contradicted N.Y. Religious Corporations Law §§ 180, 182, the society did not have to conduct an election of a new board of trustees. Matter of Venigalla v Nori (2008) 11 NY3d 55, 862 NYS2d 457, 892 NE2d 850.

Court would dismiss petition to declare church elections of trustees and officers to be null and void and to require new elections pursuant to CLS Relig Corp § 182 since petition was not filed within 4-month period mandated by CLS CPLR § 217. Re Uranian Phalanstery 1st New York Gnostic Lyceum Temple (1989, 1st Dept) 155 A.D.2d 302, 547 N.Y.S.2d 63

§ 182-a. Increasing number of trustees

The number of trustees may be increased to not exceeding eleven by said board of trustees at any legal meeting of the members, whereupon a certificate of such increase shall be made, signed, acknowledged and filed by the existing trustees in the manner provided by section one hundred and eighty for the execution and filing of the certificate of incorporation, except that the consent and approbation of a justice of the supreme court shall not be necessary to the filing of such certificate. The additional trustees authorized by such increase shall be supplied in the same manner as vacancies in the original board of trustees; but there shall always be at least a majority

of the board who are not ministers of the gospel or priests of any denomination.

History: Add, L 1929, ch 11, eff Feb 11, 1929. No effective date having been specified by L 1929 ch 11, this section became effective the twentieth day after becoming law, on Feb. 11, 1929.

CASE ANNOTATIONS

Court would dismiss petition to declare church elections of trustees and officers to be null and void and to require new elections pursuant to CLS Relig Corp § 182 since petition was not filed within 4-month period mandated by CLS CPLR § 217. Re Uranian Phalanstery 1st New York Gnostic Lyceum Temple (1989, 1st Dept) 155 A.D.2d 302, 547 N.Y.S.2d 63

§ 183. Seats and pews to be free

The seats and pews in every church, building or edifice, owned or occupied by any corporation organized under this article, shall be forever free for the occupation and use, during public worship, of all persons choosing to occupy the same, and conducting themselves with propriety, and no rent, charge or exaction shall ever be made or demanded for such occupation or use.

History: Add, L 1909, ch 53, eff Feb 17, 1909.

ARTICLE IX-A
CHURCHES OF CHRIST, SCIENTIST

History: Add, L 1918, ch 332.

§ 184. Application of this article

This article applies only to Churches of Christ, Scientist and Christian Science Societies, which are branches of The First Church of Christ, Scientist, in Boston, Massachusetts. Any such church or society heretofore incorporated shall hereafter be governed by the provisions of this article so far as applicable except that no person, who shall, when this article takes effect, be a duly qualified voter in any such previously incorporated church or society, shall be deprived of the right to vote at its corporate meetings by any provision of this article.

History: Add L 1918, ch 332, amd, L 1944, ch 290, eff Mar 23, 1944.

§ 185. Notice of meeting for incorporation

Notice of a meeting for the purpose of incorporating an unincorporated Church of Christ, Scientist or Christian Science Society, shall be given as follows: The notice shall be in writing, and shall state, in substance, that a meeting of such unincorporated church or society will be held at its usual place of worship at a specified day and hour, for the purpose of incorporating such church or society, electing trustees thereof, and selecting a corporate name therefor.

The notice must be signed by at least six persons of full age who are then members in good and regular standing of such church or society by admission into full membership therewith, in accordance with the rules and regulations of such church or society. A copy of such notice shall be publicly read at each regular service of such unincorporated church or society on the two successive Sundays next preceding such meeting by the person acting as first reader, and a copy of such notice shall be sent by mail post paid at least ten days prior to the date fixed for such meeting to each member of such church or society in good and regular standing at his last known address as same appears in the church or society records.

History: Add, L 1918, ch 332, amd, L 1944, ch 290, eff Mar 23, 1944.

§ 186. Meeting for incorporation

At the meeting for incorporation held in pursuance of such notice, the following persons, and no others, shall be qualified voters, to wit: All persons of full age, who are then members in good and regular standing of such church or society by admission into full membership therewith, in accordance with the rules and regulations thereof.

At such meeting, the presence of a majority of such qualified voters, at least six in number, shall be necessary to constitute a quorum. The action of the meeting upon any matter or question shall be decided by a majority of the qualified voters voting thereon, a quorum being present. The meeting shall be called to order by one of the signers of the call. There shall be elected at such meeting, from the qualified voters then present, a presiding officer, a clerk to keep the record of the proceedings, of the meeting and two inspectors of election to receive the ballots cast. The presiding officer of the meeting and the inspectors shall decide the results of the ballots cast on any matter, and shall be the judges of the qualifications of voters.

Such meeting shall decide whether such unincorporated church or society shall become incorporated. If such decision shall be in favor of incorporation such meeting shall decide upon the name of the proposed corporation which shall be "Church of Christ, Scientist," prefixed by "First," "Second," "Third" or other numerical designation, or "Christian Science Society" as the case may be, and followed by the name of the place where it shall be located; the meeting also shall decide the number of the trustees of such church or society, which shall be any number from three to twelve, and shall determine the date, not more than fifteen months thereafter, on which the first annual election of the trustees thereof after such meeting shall be held. Such meeting shall thereupon elect by ballot, from the persons qualified to vote thereat, one-third of the number of trustees as nearly as possible so decided upon who shall hold office until the first annual election of trustees thereafter, one-third of such number of trustees as nearly as possible who shall hold office until the second annual election of trustees thereafter, and the remainder of such trustees who shall hold office until the third annual election of trustees thereafter, or until the respective successors of such trustees shall be elected and take office.

History: Add, L 1918, ch 332, amd, L 1944, ch 290, amd, L 1962, ch 12, eff Feb 13, 1962.

§ 187. Certificate of incorporation

If the meeting shall decide that such unincorporated church or society shall become incorporated, the presiding officer of such meeting and the two inspectors of election, shall execute and acknowledge a certificate of incorporation, setting forth the name of the proposed corporation, the number of trustees thereof, the names of the persons elected as trustees, the terms of office for which they were respectively elected and the county and town, city or village in which its principal place of worship is, or is intended to be located. On the filing and recording of such certificate, as hereinbefore provided in this chapter, the persons qualified to vote at such meeting and those persons who shall thereafter, from time to time be qualified voters at the corporate meetings thereof, shall be a corporation by the name stated in such certificate, and the persons therein stated to be elected trustees of such church or society shall be the trustees thereof for the terms for which they were respectively so elected, or until their respective successors shall be elected and take office.

History: Add, L 1918, ch 332, amd, L 1944, ch 290, eff Mar 23, 1944.

§ 188. Time, place and notice of corporate meetings

The annual corporate meeting of every incorporated church or society to which this article is applicable shall be held at the time and place fixed by its by-laws. A special corporate meeting of any such church or society may be called by the board of trustees thereof, on its own motion, and shall be called on the written request of at least ten qualified voters of such church or society. The trustees shall cause written notice of the time and place of any corporate meeting, therein specifying, if an annual meeting, the names of any trustees whose successors are to be elected thereat, and, if a special meeting, specifying the business to be transacted thereat, to be served, either personally or by mail, upon each qualified voter of the church or society entitled to vote at the meeting, not less than ten nor more than forty days before the meeting. If mailed, the notice shall be directed to each qualified voter entitled to notice at his address as it appears on the books or records of the church or society.

History: Add, L 1918, ch 332, amd, L 1944, ch 290, L 1946, ch 249.

§ 189.　Organization and conduct of corporate meetings; qualifications of voters thereat

At a corporate meeting of every incorporated church or society to which this article is applicable, the following persons, and no others, shall be qualified voters, to wit: All persons who are then members in good and regular standing of such church or society by admission into full membership therewith. The presence at such meetings of at least six persons qualified to vote threat shall be necessary to constitute a quorum, provided that any church or society to which this article is applicable may by its by-laws fix the number of members necessary to constitute a quorum. The action of the meeting upon any matter or question shall be decided by a majority of the qualified voters voting thereon, a quorum being present, except that by-laws may provide specifically for action being taken upon any matter or question by more than a majority vote, in which event such by-law provisions shall govern any such action; and further excepted that by-laws can be adopted or amended only by a two-thirds vote, as hereinbefore provided by this chapter. The clerk of the church or society shall call the meeting to order, and then turn it over to a presiding officer chosen by the qualified voters then present or to the one designated under the provisions of the by-laws; and if an election is to be held at such meeting, two inspectors of election shall be chosen by the qualified voters then present, unless otherwise designated under the provisions of the by-laws. The presiding officer and the inspectors of election shall receive the votes, shall be the judges of the qualifications of voters and shall decide the result of the votes cast at any election. The polls of an annual corporate meeting shall remain open for such time as may be determined by a majority of the qualified voters present. At each annual corporate meeting successors to those trustees whose terms of office then expire, shall be elected from the qualified voters by ballot, for a term of three years thereafter, and until their successors shall be elected and take office.

History: Add, L 1918, ch 332, amd, L 1944, ch 290, L 1962, ch 12, L 1971, ch 201 § 6, eff Sept 1, 1971.

CASE ANNOTATIONS

Where both by this section and by the corporate by-laws of a religious corporation it is provided that action shall be decided by a majority vote of the qualified voters voting thereon, a resolution of removal carried by majority vote is sufficient, even though the by-laws provided that certain "rules of order," stating that removal from office must be by two-thirds vote, should govern at meetings where not in conflict with the by-laws. Re Koch (1931) 257 N.Y. 318, 178 N.E. 545

§ 189-a.　Changing date of annual corporate meetings

Any incorporated church or society to which this article is applicable, at any annual meeting may change the date of its subsequent annual meetings. If the date fixed for the annual meeting shall be less than six months after the annual meeting at which such change is made, the next annual meeting shall be held one year from the date so fixed. For the purpose of determining the terms of office of trustees and officers, the time between the annual meeting at which such change is made and the next annual meeting thereafter shall be reckoned as one year.

History: Add, L 1918, ch 332, amd, L 1944, ch 290, eff Mar 23, 1944.

§ 189-b.　Changing number of trustees

Any incorporated church or society to which this article is applicable may, at an annual corporate meeting, change the number of its trustees to any number from three to twelve and classify them so that the terms of one-third as nearly as possible expire each year, provided that notice of such intended change be included in the notice of such annual corporate meeting. No such change shall affect the terms of the trutees then in office, and if the change reduces the number of trustees, election shall not be held to fill the vacancies caused by the expiration of the terms of trustees, until the number of trustees equals the number to which the trustees were reduced. Whenever the number of trustees in office is less than the number so determined on, sufficient additional trustees shall be elected to make the number of trustees for the ensuing year equal to the number so determined on. The trustees so elected up to and including as nearly as possible one-third of the number so determined on, shall be elected for three years, the remainder up to and including as nearly as possible one-third of the number so determined on for two years and the remainder for one year.

History: Add, L 1918, ch 332, amd, L 1944, ch 290, L 1962, ch 12, eff Feb 13, 1962.

§ 189-c.　Meetings of trustees

The chairman of the board of trustees of any incorporated church or society to which this article is applicable or any two members of such board may call a meeting of such trustees by giving at least twenty-four hours' notice thereof, personally or by mail, to all the other trustees, but by the unanimous consent of the trustees a meeting may be held without previous notice thereof. A majority of the trustees lawfully convened shall constitute a quorum for the transaction of business. In case of a tie vote at the meeting of the trustees the presiding officer of such meeting shall, notwithstanding he had voted once, have an additional casting vote. In case of a vacancy in the office of trustee the remaining trustees may fill such vacancy until the next annual corporate meeting when the vacancy shall be filled for the unexpired term.

History: Add, L 1918, ch 332, amd, L 1944, ch 290, eff Mar 23, 1944.

ARTICLE 10
OTHER DENOMINATIONS

History: Add, L 1909, ch 53.

§ 190. Application of this article

This article is not applicable to a Baptist church, a Congregational Christian church, whether or not a part of the United Church of Christ, a church of the United Church of Christ incorporated after September first, nineteen hundred seventy-one, an Independent church, a United Methodist church, a Protestant Episcopal church, a Roman Catholic church, a Presbyterian church in connection with the General Assembly of the Presbyterian Church in the United States of America, a Christian Orthodox Catholic church of the Eastern Confession, a Ruthenian Greek Catholic church, or a Church of Christ, Scientist. No provision of this article is applicable to a reformed church in America, a True Reformed Dutch church in the United States of America, a Reformed Presbyterian church, or to an Evangelical Lutheran church, incorporated after October first, eighteen hundred and ninety-five, except as declared to be so applicable by article six of this chapter; this article is applicable to an Evangelical Lutheran church incorporated before October first, eighteen hundred ninety-five, if the trustees thereof were then elective as such and so long as they continue to be elective as

such. Article six of this chapter is applicable to an Evangelical Lutheran church incorporated before October first, eighteen hundred and ninety-five, if its trustees were not then elective as such and so long as its trustees continue not to be elective as such. This article is applicable to churches of all other denominations.

History: Add, L 1909, ch 53, amd, L 1949, ch 660, L 1969, ch 962, § 6, L 1972, ch 900, eff Sept 1, 1972.

CASE ANNOTATIONS

The mere act by a church of incorporating under article 10 of the Religious Corporations Law is not determinative of the issue of whether said church is independent or hierarchical as it cannot be said that if a church intended to become an independent church it would have incorporated under article 8, in that it is erroneous to read the words "Independent church" in said article to mean independent church in the sense that it is not connected to a parent body. New York Dist. of Assemblies of God v Calvary Assembly of God (1978, 3d Dept) 64 A.D.2d 311, 409 N.Y.S.2d 842

Where religious corporation named as legatee had ceased to function prior to death of testatrix, but no certificate of dissolution had been filed, and another corporation had succeeded to the congregant's ministry and was of the same type, cy pres doctrine applied. Re Olmsted's Will (1954, Sur) 133 N.Y.S.2d 197

§ 191. Notice of meeting for incorporation

Notice of a meeting for the purpose of incorporating an unincorporated church, to which this article is applicable, shall be given as follows:

The notice shall be in writing, and shall state, in substance, that a meeting of such unincorporated church will be held at its usual place of worship at a specified day and hour, for the purpose of incorporating such church and electing trustees thereof.

The notice must be signed by at least six persons of full age, who are then members in good and regular standing of such church by admission into full communion or membership therewith, in accordance with the rules and regulations of such church, and of the governing ecclesiastical body of the denomination or order, if any, to which the church belongs, or who have statedly worshiped with such church and have regularly contributed to the financial support thereof during the year next prior thereto, or from the time of the formation thereof.

A copy of such notice shall be posted conspicuously on the outside of the main entrance to such place of worship, at least fifteen days before the day so specified for such meeting, and shall be publicly read at each of the two next preceding regular meetings of such unincorporated church for public worship, at least one week apart, at morning service, if such service be held, on Sunday, if Sunday be the day for such regular meetings, by the first named of the following persons who is present thereat, to wit: The minister of such church, the officiating minister thereof, the elders thereof in the order of their age beginning with the oldest, the deacons of the church in the order of their age beginning with the oldest, any person qualified to sign such notice.

History: Add, L 1909, ch 53, eff Feb 17, 1909.

Religious Corporations Law

§ 192. The meeting for incorporation

At the meeting for incorporation held in pursuance of such notice, the following persons, and no others, shall be qualified voters, to wit: All persons of full age, who are then members in good and regular standing of such church by admission into full communion or membership therewith, in accordance with the rules and regulations thereof, and of the governing ecclesiastical body, if any, of the denomination or order, to which the church belongs, or who have statedly worshiped with such church and have regularly contributed to the financial support thereof during the year next preceding such meeting, or from the time of the formation thereof.

The presence of a majority of such qualified voters, at least six in number, shall be necessary to constitute a quorum of such meeting. The action of the meeting upon any matter or question shall be decided by a majority of the qualified voters voting thereon, a quorum being present.

The first named of the following persons who is present at such meeting shall preside thereat, to wit: The minister of the church, the officiating minister thereof, the elders thereof in the order of their age, beginning with the oldest, the deacons thereof in the order of their age, beginning with the oldest, any qualified voter elected to preside. The presiding officer of the meeting shall receive the votes, be the judge of the qualifications of voters and declare the result of the votes cast on any matter. The polls of the meeting shall remain open for one hour, and longer, in the discretion of the presiding officer, or if required by a majority of the voters present.

Such meeting shall decide whether such unincorporated church shall become incorporated. If such decision shall be in favor of incorporation such meeting shall decide upon the name of the proposed corporation, the number of the trustees thereof, which shall be three, six or nine, and shall determine the date, not more than fifteen months thereafter, on which the first annual election of the trustees thereof after such meeting shall be held. Such meeting shall elect from the persons qualified to vote at such meeting, one-third of the number of trustees so decided on who shall hold office until the first annual election of trustees thereafter, one-third of such number of trustees to hold office until the second annual election of trustees thereafter, and one-third of such number of trustees to hold office until the third annual election of trustees thereafter.

History: Add, L 1909, ch 53, eff Feb 17, 1909.

§ 193. The certificate of incorporation

The presiding officer of such meeting and at least two other persons present and voting thereat, shall execute and acknowledge a certificate of incorporation, setting forth the matters so determined at such meeting, the trustees elected thereat and the terms of office for which they were respectively elected and the county, town, city or village in which its principal place of worship is or is intended to be located. On filing such certificate the members of such church and the persons qualified to vote at such meeting and who shall thereafter, from time to time, be qualified voters, at the corporate meetings thereof, shall be a corporation by the name stated in such certificate, and the persons therein stated to be elected trustees of such church shall be the trustees thereof, for the terms for which they were respectively so elected.

History: Add, L 1909, ch 53, eff Feb 17, 1909.

CASE ANNOTATIONS

Where a church's certificate of incorporation directed that annual elections were required in order to elect trustees, which were admittedly never held by the church but rather, the trustees assumed their positions by appointment, the court found that under N.Y. Relig. Corp. Law art. 10, §§ 193 and 194, the trustees were improperly in their positions and accordingly, it had not basis for affirming a pastor's position because there were no legally elected corporate officers of the church; additionally, pursuant to N.Y. Relig. Corp. Law art. 2, § 5, there were no duly elected trustees to assume "custody and control" of the church corporation's property. St. Matthew Church of Christ Disciples of Christ, Inc. v Creech (2003, Sup) 196 Misc. 2d 843, 768 N.Y.S.2d 111

A certificate of incorporation of a religious corporation should show compliance with the statutory requirement of a preliminary meeting. 1962 Ops Atty Gen May 23

§ 194. Time, place and notice of corporate meetings

The annual corporate meeting of every incorporated church to which this article is applicable, shall be held at the time and place fixed by or in pursuance of law therefor, if such time and place be so fixed, and otherwise, at a time and place to be fixed by its trustees. A special corporate meeting of any such church may be called by the board of trustees thereof, on its own motion or on the written request of at least ten qualified voters of such church. The trustees shall cause notice of the time and place of its annual corporate meeting, therein specifying the names of any trustees, whose successors are to be elected thereat, and, if a special meeting, specifying the business to be transacted thereat, to be given at a regular meeting of the church for public worship, at morning service, if such service be held, on each of the two successive Sundays next preceding such meeting, if Sunday be the regular day for such public worship, and public worship be had thereon, or otherwise at a regular meeting of such church for public worship on each of two days, at least one week apart, next preceding such meeting, or if no such public worship be held during such period, by conspicuously posting such notice, in writing, upon the outer entrance to the principal place of worship of such church. Such notice shall be given by the minister of the church, if there be one, or if not, by the officiating minister thereof, if there be one, or if not, or if any such minister refuse to give such notice, by any officer of such church. But a special corporate meeting of an incorporated Presbyterian church, to elect a pastor of such church or to take action in reference to the dissolution of the relations of the pastor and the church, may be called only by the session of such church. They may call such meeting whenever they deem it advisable to do so, or upon the request to them, by petition, of a majority of the qualified voters of such corporation, they must call such meeting. They shall give notice of such meeting in either case, in the manner in this section provided in a notice of a special meeting.

History: Add, L 1909, ch 53, eff Feb 17, 1909.

CASE ANNOTATIONS

An ecclesiastical corporation will not be compelled by mandamus to call a new meeting for the election of trustees on the sole ground that notice of a prior meeting which was in accordance with this section also contained notice that a class meeting would be held on the same day in connection with the meeting for the election of trustees, there being nothing to show that the rights of any persons entitled to attend were affected. People ex rel. Wilson v African Wesleyan M. E. Church (1913) 156 A.D. 386, 141 N.Y.S. 394

The failure to comply with the requirements of this section and § 195 and the by-laws of the corporation constitutes ground for vacating an election. Application of Kaminsky (1937) 251 A.D. 132, 295 N.Y.S. 989, reh den 251 A.D. 795, 298 N.Y.S. 171 and affd 277 N.Y. 524, 13 N.E.2d 456

Failure to comply with provisions of this section and § 196 in calling annual meeting at a date different than that set forth in original certificate made any action taken at the meeting open to question. Horodeckyi v Horodniak (1958) 16 Misc. 2d 865, 182 N.Y.S.2d 280

Where the bylaws of a religious corporation contain no provisions as to the manner of calling special meetings of the congregation, this section requires two announcements at religious services or the posting of a notice at the place of worship, and notice to members merely sent out by post cards does not meet the requirements and leaves any action taken at the special meeting without force and a nullity. Kupperman v Congregation Nusach Sfard (1963) 39 Misc. 2d 107, 240 N.Y.S.2d 315

Where a church's certificate of incorporation directed that annual elections were required in order to elect trustees, which were admittedly never held by the church but rather, the trustees assumed their positions by appointment, the court found that under N.Y. Relig. Corp. Law art. 10, §§ 193 and 194, the trustees were improperly in their positions and accordingly, it had not basis for affirming a pastor's position because there were no legally elected corporate officers of the church; additionally, pursuant to N.Y. Relig. Corp. Law art. 2, § 5, there were no duly elected trustees to assume "custody and control" of the church corporation's property. St. Matthew Church of Christ Disciples of Christ, Inc. v Creech (2003, Sup) 196 Misc. 2d 843, 768 N.Y.S.2d 111

§ 195. Organization and conduct of corporate meetings; qualification of voters thereat

At a corporate meeting of an incorporated church to which this article is applicable the following persons, and no others, shall be qualified voters, to wit: All persons who are then members in good and regular standing of such church by admission into full communion or membership therewith in accordance with the rules and regulations thereof, and of the governing ecclesiastical body, if any, of the denomination or order to which the church belongs, or who have been stated attendants on divine worship in such church and have regularly contributed to the financial support thereof during the year next preceding such meeting; and any other church incorporated under this article, may at any annual corporate meeting thereof, or any corporate meeting called pursuant to the provisions of this

article, if notice of the intention so to do has been given with the notice of such meeting, determine that thereafter only members of such church shall be qualified voters at corporate meetings thereof. The presence at such meetings of at least six persons qualified to vote thereat shall be necessary to constitute a quorum. The action of the meeting upon any matter or question shall be decided by a majority of the qualified voters voting thereon, a quorum being present. The first named of the following persons who is present at such meeting shall preside thereat, to wit: The minister of such church, the officiating minister thereof; the officers thereof in the order of their age beginning with the oldest, any qualified voters elected therefor at the meeting. The presiding officer of the meeting shall receive the votes, be the judge of qualifications of voters and declare the result of the votes cast on any matter. The polls of an annual corporate meeting shall continue open for one hour, and longer in the discretion of the presiding officer, or if required by a majority of the qualified voters present. At each annual corporate meeting, successors to those trustees whose terms of office then expire, shall be elected from the qualified voters by ballot, for a term of three years thereafter.

History: Add, L 1909, ch 53, amd, L 1949, ch 660, L 1971, ch 201 § 7, eff Sept 1, 1971.

CASE ANNOTATIONS

A church has the right to determine the qualifications for membership, and whether one is a member in good standing is a matter of ecclesiastical nature relating to government and discipline of the church, and its decision is binding on the courts. Application of Kaminsky (1937) 251 A.D. 132, 295 N.Y.S. 989, reh den 251 A.D. 795, 298 N.Y.S. 171 and affd 277 N.Y. 524, 13 N.E.2d 456

Individual plaintiffs, who attended and contributed their time and money, constituted members of Islamic Cultural Center of New York under CLS Relig Corp § 195. Islamic Ctr. of Harrison, Inc. v Islamic Science Found., Inc. (1999, 2d Dept) 262 A.D.2d 362, 692 N.Y.S.2d 94, app den 94 N.Y.2d 752, 700 N.Y.S.2d 426, 722 N.E.2d 506

Although subd. 15 of § 3 of the General Corporation Law and § 195 of the Religious Corporations Law contain certain definitions of membership, an allegation of membership in a religious corporation is sufficient, without more, to sustain a complaint against the trustee of a religious corporation to compel them to call a meeting of members for adoption of by-laws and to render an accounting where it is alleged that there is no functioning church organization and no rules or regulations governing membership. Eisenberg v Fauer (1960) 25 Misc. 2d 98, 200 N.Y.S.2d 749

§ 196. Changing date of annual corporate meetings

An annual corporate meeting of an incorporated church to which this article is applicable, may change the date of its annual meeting thereafter. If such date shall next thereafter occur less than six months after the annual meeting at which such change is made, the next annual meeting shall be held one year from such next recurring date. For the purpose of determining the terms of office of trustees, the time between the annual meeting at which such change is made and the next annual meeting thereafter shall be reckoned as one year.

History: Add, L 1909, ch 53, eff Feb 17, 1909.

Religious Corporations Law

§ 197. Changing number of trustees

An incorporated church to which this article is applicable, may, at an annual corporate meeting, change the number of its trustees to three, six, nine, twelve, fifteen, eighteen, twenty-one or twenty-four, or classify them so that the terms of one-third expire each year. No such change shall affect the terms of the trustees then in office, and if the change reduces the number of trustees, it shall not take effect until the number of trustees whose terms of office continue for one or more years after an annual election is less than the number determined on. Whenever the number of trustees so holding over is less than the number so determined on, trustees shall be elected in addition to those so holding over, sufficient to make the number of trustees for the ensuing year equal to the number so determined on. The trustees so elected up to and including one-third of the number so determined on, shall be elected for three years, the remainder up to and including one-third of the number so determined on for two years, and the remainder for one year.

History: Add, L 1909, ch 53, amd, L 1935, ch 220, eff Mar 25, 1935.

§ 198. Meetings of trustees

Two of the trustees of an incorporated church, to which this article is applicable, may call a meeting of such trustees, by giving at least twenty-four hours' notice thereof personally or by mail to the other trustees. A majority of the trustees lawfully convened shall constitute a quorum for the transaction of business. In case of a tie vote at a meeting of the trustees, the presiding officer of such meeting shall, notwithstanding he has voted once, have an additional casting vote.

History: Add, L 1909, ch 53, eff Feb 17, 1909.

§ 199. Vacancies among trustees

If any trustee of an incorporated church to which this article is applicable, declines to act, resigns or dies, or having been a member of such church, ceases to be such member, or not having been a member of such church, ceases to be a qualified voter at a corporate meeting thereof, his office shall be vacant, and such vacancy may be filled by the remaining trustees until the next annual corporate meeting of such church, at which meeting the vacancy shall be filled for the unexpired term.

History: Add, L 1909, ch 53, eff Feb 17, 1909.

CASE ANNOTATIONS

A judicial declaration that a trustee was not a member of the defendant church had the effect of simultaneously declaring his office vacant. Krehel v Eastern Orthodox Catholic Church (1959) 22 Misc. 2d 522, 195 N.Y.S.2d 334, affd (1st Dept) 12 A.D.2d 465, 207 N.Y.S.2d 93, affd 10 N.Y.2d 831, 221 N.Y.S.2d 724, 178 N.E.2d 428

§ 200. Control of trustees by corporate meetings; salaries of ministers

A corporate meeting of an incorporated church, whose trustees are elective as such, may give directions, not inconsistent with law, as to the manner in which any of the temporal affairs of the church shall be administered by the trustees thereof; and such directions shall be followed by the trustees. The trustees of an incorporated church to which this article is applicable, shall have no power to settle or remove or fix the salary of the minister, or without the consent of a corporate meeting, to incur debts beyond what is necessary for the care of the property of the corporation; or to fix or charge [change] the time, nature or order of the public or social worship of such church, except when such trustees are also the spiritual officers of such church.

History: Add, L 1909, ch 53, eff Feb 17, 1909.

CASE ANNOTATIONS

Board of trustees of Jewish center did not affirmatively terminate rabbi's employment where his termination occurred solely because employment contract expired; thus, board did not usurp authority of congregation members, even though board's actions indicated its desire not to continue rabbi's employment. Saffra v Rockwood Park Jewish Ctr. (1997, 2d Dept) 239 A.D.2d 507, 658 N.Y.S.2d 43, app den 90 N.Y.2d 805, 662 N.Y.S.2d 431, 685 N.E.2d 212, motion gr (NY) 1997 N.Y. LEXIS 2679, subsequent app (2d Dept) 249 A.D.2d 480, 671 N.Y.S.2d 668

This section prohibits the trustees of an incorporated church from selecting or removing a rabbi, to accomplish which action of the corporate congregation is required. Kupperman v Congregation Nusach Sfard (1963) 39 Misc. 2d 107, 240 N.Y.S.2d 315

A defendant whose contract was terminated by the board of trustees of the temple by which he was employed as a cantor was properly convicted of criminal trespass in the third degree when he returned to the temple after he had received three correspondences informing him of the board's decision and two days after he had been informed that if he failed to restrict himself to the public areas of the temple he would be arrested; a cantor does not come within the definition of "minister" in section 2 of the Religious Corporations Law and, therefore, is not an official whose removal is beyond the power of the board of trustees pursuant to section 200 of the Religious Corporations Law; accordingly, the board's action was proper and the order to leave the temple was valid. In addition, the requisite intent was established. People v Tuchinsky (1979) 100 Misc. 2d 521, 419 N.Y.S.2d 843

§ 201. [Repealed]

History: Add, L 1909, ch 53, repealed, L 1969, ch 962, § 7, eff May 26, 1969.

§ 201-a. Incorporation of the Religious Society of Friends

An unincorporated meeting of the Religious Society of Friends in this state may be incorporated by executing, acknowledging and filing a certificate of incorporation, stating the corporate name by which such meeting shall be known, and the county, town, city or village where its principal place of worship or principal office is or is intended to be located. Such certificate of incorporation shall be executed and acknowledged by the clerk of such meeting, and shall have attached thereto a statement, duly executed and acknowlecged by the secretary, assistant clerk or such person as shall have the duty of recording the transactions of business sessions of meetings of such meeting, certifying that at a business session or meeting of such meeting, duly held and upon not less than thirty days notice, to the members thereof, as hereinafter provided, by a minute of the proceedings thereat, duly approved according to the usage and custom of such meeting, the clerk of such meeting was authorized and directed to execute and file such certificate of incorporation. Such notice shall be in writing, shall be given by mail addressed to the last known address of each member of such meeting according to the records thereof, and shall state in substance that a meeting of such unincorporated meeting will be held at its usual place of convening at a specified date and hour for the purpose of incorporating such meeting. On the filing of such certificate in accordance with the provisions of this chapter, such meeting shall be a corporation by the name stated in the certificate.

History: Add, L 1959, ch 619, amd, L 1974, ch 326, eff May 13, 1974.

Section heading, amd, L 1974, ch 326, ch 326, eff May 13, 1974.

§ 202. Trusts for Shakers and Friends

All deeds or declarations of trust of real or personal property, executed and delivered before January first, eighteen hundred and thirty, or since May fifth, eighteen hundred and thirty-nine, to any person in trust for any United Society of Shakers, or heretofore executed and delivered to any person or persons in trust for any meeting of the Religious Society of Friends, or any of the purposes thereof, and the legal estates, interests and trusts purported to be conveyed, created or declared thereby, shall be valid. Trusts of real or personal property, for the benefit and use of the members of any United Society of Shakers, or of any meeting of the Religious Society of Friends, or any of the purposes thereof, may hereafter be created, according to the religious constitution of such society of Shakers, or the regulations and rules of discipline of such Society of Friends. Such deeds or declarations of trust, heretofore or hereafter executed and delivered, shall vest in the trustees the legal estates and interests purported to be conveyed or declared thereby, to and for the uses and purposes declared therein; and such legal estates and trusts, and all legal authority with which the original trustees were vested by virtue of their appointment and conferred powers, shall descend to their successors in office or trust, who may be chosen in conformity to the constitution of such society, or the directions of such meeting. In case of the death of all the trustees of any trust for the benefit of any meeting of the Religious Society of Friends or any of the purposes thereof, heretofore appointed, or who may be hereafter appointed by virtue of this section, any such meeting may appoint a trustee or trustees in place of such person or persons, and the person or persons thus appointed by such meeting shall succeed to, and be invested with, all the powers, rights and duties conferred by this section and the deed or declaration of trust upon the trustee or trustees. In case of the consolidation of two or more meetings of the Religious Society of Friends into one meeting, all real and personal property held in trust for either or any of the meetings so consolidated, or any of the purposes

thereof, shall continue to be vested in the trustees holding the same at the time of such consolidation, until their successors shall be chosen as above provided. Such consolidated meeting shall have the same rights, powers and duties in respect to such property, estates and trusts and in respect to the appointment of such trustees and their successors as the meetings so consolidated or either of them previously had. This section does not impair or diminish the rights of any person, meeting or association claiming to be a meeting of the Religious Society of Friends, which such person, meeting, or association claiming to be a meeting, had to any real or personal property held in trust for the use and benefit of any meeting of such society, before the division of such society which took place at the annual meeting held in the city of New York in May, eighteen hundred and twenty-eight. An incorporated or unincorporated society or meeting of Shakers or the Religious Society of Friends may take and hold property of the value or yearly income permitted by statute to a corporation other than a stock corporation. No person shall be a trustee at the same time of more than one society of Shakers or meeting of Friends. A society of Shakers includes all persons of the religious belief of the people called Shakers, resident within the same county.

History: Add, L 1909, ch 53, amd, L 1952, ch 466, eff Apr 3, 1952.

CASE ANNOTATIONS

An unincorporated religious association had power to authorize its trustees to transfer the society's funds to a bank to be held in trust, the income and interest therefrom to be used and applied in the care and maintenance of cemetery ground. Lincoln Rochester Trust Co. v Smith (1956) 4 Misc. 2d 304, 158 N.Y.S.2d 367

§ 203. Conveyance or incumbrance of trust property of Friends

The trustee or trustees, or survivor of any trustees, of any meeting of the Religious Society of Friends, appointed pursuant to the last preceding section, may sell, convey and grant, mortgage, or demise any or all of the trust property described in said trust deed or declaration of trust, to any person absolutely or in trust for such meeting, whenever any meeting of said society by resolution so directs. Any conveyance or mortgage of real estate or property so held in trust by any meeting of the Religious Society of Friends, which is hereafter made in pursuance of a resolution of such meeting as provided herein, shall be as valid and effectual for the conveyance or mortgage of the title of any real estate so held in trust, as if the heirs of any trustee who has died prior to the passage of such resolution had joined in the execution of such conveyance, mortgage or demise. Any instrument for the sale, mortgage, or demise of such property shall embody such resolution, and be executed and acknowledged by such trustee or trustees; and in such acknowledgment such trustee or trustees shall make an affidavit that the person or persons executing such conveyance, mortgage or demise are the trustee or trustees of the trust property, and that the

Religious Corporations Law

resolution embodied in such conveyance, mortgage or demise was duly passed by such meeting. Such affidavit shall be prima facie evidence of the facts therein stated.

History: Add, L 1909, ch 53, amd, L 1924, ch 125, eff Apr 12, 1924.

§ 204. [Repealed]

History: Add, L 1909, ch 53, repealed, L 1949, ch 660, eff July 1, 1949.

§ 204-a. [Repealed]

History: Add, L 1941, ch 238, amd, L 1942, ch 163, repealed, L 1949, ch 660, eff July 1, 1949.

§ 204-b. Change of name of churches and affiliated and subsidiary organizations of the church of the United Brethren in Christ and the Evangelical Church

Notwithstanding any provision of this chapter or of any general, special or local law, the two denominations known as the Church of the United Brethren in Christ and the Evangelical Church having united under the name of the Evangelical United Brethren Church, all existing corporations, institutions, unincorporated boards, societies, associations, churches or administrative agencies formerly affiliated either with the Church of the United Brethren in Christ or the Evangelical Church, and all societies, conferences, boards, associations, corporations or organizations directly connected therewith or subsidiary thereto, shall be known as the Evangelical United Brethren Church or an affiliate thereof and all such churches, corporations, unincorporated associations, and other organizations shall hereafter be known by such names as changed and amended by this section.

The changes in names provided for by this section shall not in any respect change the identity of or affect, abate, defeat, alter or amend any of the rights, privileges, powers, property, rights, obligations, liabilities, or duties of any of said churches, corporations, organizations, or unincorporated associations aforesaid, all of which shall remain in full force and effect as though their respective names had not been so changed.

All churches, corporations, organizations, or unincorporated associations using the changed names as provided in this section shall continue to have and be possessed of all the interest, property, and rights to which they are or may become entitled under their former corporate names or other respective designations.

History: Add, L 1949, ch 391, eff Apr 5, 1949.

§ 205. Presiding officer

Nothing contained in this article shall prevent the qualified voters at any meeting held pursuant to this article or in this article described, from choosing a person to preside at any such meeting, other than the person or officer designated in this article to preside thereat, and when such other person shall be chosen he shall exercise all the powers in this article conferred upon the presiding officer of such meeting.

History: Add, L 1909, ch 53, eff Feb 17, 1909.

§ 206. Termination and dissolution of churches of the General Assembly of the Christian Church (Disciples of Christ), Inc. whose churches are individually known as "Christian Church (Disciples of Christ)" or "Church of Christ (Disciples of Christ)" and affiliated religious societies and the disposition of the real and personal property of such churches and/or affiliated religious societies

1. Any incorporated or unincorporated church of the "General Assembly of the Christian Church (Disciples of Christ), Inc." whose individual churches are known as either "Church of Christ (Disciples of Christ)" or "Christian Church (Disciples of Christ)" and any religious society or organization affiliated with the "General Assembly of the Christian Church (Disciples of Christ), Inc." or a "Christian Church (Disciples of Christ)" or "Church of Christ (Disciples of Christ)" desiring to disband, disorganize and become extinct and if incorporated, to dissolve the corporate entity, shall accomplish the above objectives by an affirmative vote of two-thirds of the members present and voting at a special meeting called for the specific purpose of accomplishing one or more of the above objectives, namely, the extinction of the church and/or religious society and the disbandment of the church and/or religious society and the dissolution of the corporate entity, if the church and/or religious society is incorporated.

2. Any incorporated or unincorporated church of the "General Assembly of the Christian Church (Disciples of Christ), Inc." whose affiliated individual churches are known as either "Church of Christ (Disciples of Christ)" or "Christian Church (Disciples of Christ)" and any religious society or organization affiliated with the "General Assembly of the Christian Church (Disciples of Christ), Inc." or an affiliated "Church of Christ (Disciples of Christ)" or a "Christian Church (Disciples of Christ)" shall be considered extinct when such church or society has not held religious services and/or conducted activities according to the customs and usages of the "General Assembly of the Christian Church (Disciples of Christ), Inc." of which said church or religious society is affiliated for a period of six consecutive months or has less than twenty-five active members attending regular weekly or monthly meetings and making regular weekly or monthly contributions toward the support of said church or religious society.

3. (a) Upon such notice as the supreme court in the judicial district where the church property or the religious society property is situated, may prescribe and upon application made by petition of the officers or the board of trustees or five members of such church or religious society, stating fully the facts in

the case and on evidence being furnished, including but not limited to appropriate affidavits that the conditions as set forth in subdivision one or two above have been established and are currently existing, upon satisfactory proof of the facts leading to said application, the court shall have jurisdiction to grant an order declaring the church or society extinct and the corporate entity dissolved if the petitioner is a religious corporation and said order shall direct the transfer of both real and personal property of the petitioner to the CHRISTIAN CHURCH (DISCIPLES OF CHRIST)-NORTHEASTERN REGION, INC. or direct that the real property and personal property be sold and that the proceeds be paid over to the CHRISTIAN CHURCH (DISCIPLES OF CHRIST)-NORTHEASTERN REGION, INC. after the full payment of all liens on the real property and of all of the outstanding debts of the petitioners.

(b) Such order shall operate to transfer the interest of such extinct church and/or religious society in such property or proceeds to the CHRISTIAN CHURCH (DISCIPLES OF CHRIST)-NORTHEASTERN REGION, INC.

(c) The order shall also direct that the real property and personal property or the proceeds obtained from the sale thereof after the payment of all of the debts, obligations and liabilities of the petitioner, shall be used by the CHRISTIAN CHURCH (DISCIPLES OF CHRIST)-NORTHEASTERN REGION, INC. exclusively for the purpose or purposes for which the CHRISTIAN CHURCH (DISCIPLES OF CHRIST)-NORTHEASTERN REGION, INC. was organized and incorporated.

4. Nothing in this section, however, shall be construed to impair or in any way effect any existing claim upon or lien against any property so transferred or conveyed to the CHRISTIAN CHURCH (DISCIPLES OF CHRIST-NORTHEASTERN REGION, INC. or any action or legal proceedings that may be pending at the time of the transfer referred to herein.

5. (a) The use of proxy or absentee ballots shall not be used relative to any resolution involving matters set forth in subdivisions one and two of this section unless the use of such proxy or absentee ballots is authorized in the constitution and by-laws of the church or religious society proceeding under the provisions of subdivisions one and two of this section.

(b) The relief sought in subdivisions one and two of this section must be accomplished by formal action taken at a special meeting of the congregation of the church or of the members of the religious society called for such purpose. (See Article 10 Section 194-"Time, Place and Notice of Corporate Meetings".)

(c) To vote at any meeting held to accomplish the purposes of subdivisions one and two of this section, persons otherwise qualified to vote must be at least eighteen years of age.

History: Add, L 1984, ch 147, § 1, eff May 25, 1984.

Former § 206, repealed, L 1984, ch 147, § 1 eff May 25, 1984.

§ 207. The number of trustees of Jewish congregations and voting by proxy at certain meetings thereof

A congregation of the Jewish faith may at any general or special corporate meeting thereof change the number of its trustees to not more than seventy-two and classify them so that the terms of one-third shall expire each year and the trustees elected shall hold office for three years. Whenever the number of trustees in office is less than the number determined on, sufficient additional trustees shall be elected to make the total number of trustees equal to the number determined on. The additional trustees so to be elected shall be classified and hold office for such terms, not exceeding three years each, so that the terms of one-third of the total number of trustees shall expire each year, and thereafter for a term of three years each. The right of the members of such congregation to vote at meetings thereof shall be fixed by its by-laws, but every member of such congregation entitled to vote at any meeting thereof may vote by proxy on any proposition to sell, mortgage or lease any of its property or for its consolidation with one or more other religious corporations of the Jewish faith, or, in a city having a population of one million or more according to the latest federal census, in any election of trustees or officers. Every proxy must be executed in writing by the member conferring the same and shall not be given to any person other than a member of the congregation. No proxy shall be valid after the expiration of one year from the date of its execution. Every proxy shall be revocable at the pleasure of the person executing it.

History: Add, L 1926, ch 486, amd, L 1938, ch 246, amd, L 1953, ch 331, L 1954, ch 102, L 1962, ch 520, L 1970, ch 255, L 1971, ch 1107, eff Sept 1, 1971.

CASE ANNOTATIONS

In an action to declare a certain lease of plaintiff's temple auditorium for use as a catering establishment and assembly hall void, the authority for the granting of the lease is governed by the bylaws of the religious organization. Congregation Petach Tikvah v Septimus (1950) 276 A.D. 913, 94 N.Y.S.2d 210

Where a religious corporation has been organized but is not functioning and no by-laws have been adopted, this section will sustain an action in the nature of mandamus to compel calling a meeting of members and adoption of by-laws. Eisenberg v Fauer (1960) 25 Misc. 2d 98, 200 N.Y.S.2d 749

CLS Relig Corp § 207 did not apply to permit proxy voting by members of synagogue at special meeting to decide whether to rehire rabbi, even though question presented at meeting regarded "confidence with the officers and trustees" and that vote of "no confidence" would mean that all officers and trustees would resign and be replaced by temporary committee and that rabbi would be rehired; essence of meeting was whether to rehire rabbi, with board merely stating its position that board members would immediately resign if membership of synagogue voted to rehire rabbi. Holler v Goldberg (1995, Sup) 163 Misc. 2d 1075, 623 N.Y.S.2d 512

Procedure employed by synagogue of providing proxy voting on issue of whether to provide proxy voting was improper and of no effect. Holler v Goldberg (1995, Sup) 163 Misc. 2d 1075, 623 N.Y.S.2d 512

Unless provided in certificate of incorporation or bylaws, proxy voting by members of religious corporation is not authorized except for limited purposes set forth in CLS Relig Corp § 207. Holler v Goldberg (1995, Sup) 163 Misc. 2d 1075, 623 N.Y.S.2d 512

Ruling of court-recommended referee presiding over general membership meeting of synagogue, that proxy votes would not be counted in resolving whether issue of rabbi's tenure should be resubmitted for final determination by panel of rabbis, was within referee's authority and thus binding on parties, who had agreed that referee would make rulings on issues of parliamentary procedure, and was correct in view of fact that proxy voting had never been utilized or permitted at any past congregational meetings. Frankel v Kissena Jewish Center (1989) 144 Misc. 2d 548, 544 N.Y.S.2d 955

§ 208. Consolidation

Any two or more religious corporations of the Jewish faith, incorporated under or by general or special laws, may enter into an agreement for the consolidation or merger of such corporations, setting forth the terms and conditions of consolidation, the name of the proposed or surviving corporation, the number of its trustees, the time of the annual election and the names of the persons to be its trustees until the first or next annual meeting. Each corporation may petition the supreme court for an order consolidating or merging the corporations, setting forth the agreement for consolidation or merger and a statement of its real property and of its liabilities. Before the presentation of the petition to the court the agreement and petition must be approved by two-thirds of the votes cast in person or by proxy at a meeting of the members of each corporation called for the purpose of considering the proposed consolidation or merger in the manner prescribed by section six hundred five of the not-for-profit corporation law. An affidavit by the president and the secretary of each corporation stating that such approval has been given shall be annexed to the petition. On presentation to the court of such petition and agreement for consolidation or merger and on such notice as the court may direct, the court after hearing all the parties interested desiring to be heard, may make an order approving the consolidation or merger. When such order is made and duly entered and a certified copy thereof filed with the secretary of state and in the offices of the clerks of the counties in which the certificates of incorporation of the several constituent corporations were recorded, or if no such certificate was recorded, then in the office of the clerk of the county in which the principal place of worship of the new or surviving corporation is intended to be situated, such corporations shall become one corporation by the name designated in the order and the trustees named in the agreement for consolidation or merger shall be the trustees of the consolidated corporation.

History: Add, L 1927, ch 117, eff Mar 11, 1927; amd, L 2013, ch 549, § 26, eff July 1, 2014.

CASE ANNOTATIONS

Where there was a substantial controversy between parties, and moving papers were voluminous, motion for injunction pendente lite was denied. Sorokin v Young Israel of Kings Bay (1954, Sup) 133 N.Y.S.2d 242

Because a member of a religious corporation did not identify anything in a N.Y. Relig. Corp. Law § 208 consolidation petition that was not known by the congregations before a vote of approval was taken, and because the member did not identify any procedural rule that was violated, the member's motion to vacate the order of consolidation was denied. Matter of Midway Jewish Ctr. (2007, Sup) 16 Misc 3d 607, 838 NYS2d 879

§ 209. Effect of consolidation

The consolidated or merged corporation shall possess all the powers of the constituent corporations and shall have the power and be subject to the duties and obligations of a congregation of the Jewish faith formed for like purposes under the religious corporations law. All the rights, privileges and interests of each of the constituent corporations, all the property, real, personal and mixed, and all the debts due on whatever account to either of them, and all things in action, belonging to either of them, shall be deemed to be transferred to and vested in such new corporation without further act or deed; and all claims, demands, property, and every other interest, belonging to the several constituent corporations, shall be as effectually the property of the new corporation as they were of the constituent corporations, and the title to all real property, held or taken by deed or otherwise under the laws of this state, vested in the several constituent corporations shall not be deemed to revert or to be in any way impaired by reason of the consolidation but shall be vested in the new corporation. Any devise, bequest, gift, grant, or declaration of trust, contained in any deed, will, or other instrument, in trust or otherwise, made before or after such consolidation, or merger to or for any of the constituent corporations, shall inure to the benefit of the consolidated or merged corporation. The consolidated corporation shall be deemed to have assumed and shall be liable for all debts and obligations of the constituent corporations in the same manner as if such new corporation had itself incurred such debts or obligations.

History: Add, L 1927, ch 117, eff Mar 11, 1927; amd, L 2013, ch 549, § 27, eff July 1, 2014.

CASE ANNOTATIONS

Where there was a substantial controversy between parties, and moving papers were voluminous, motion for injunction pendente lite was denied. Sorokin v Young Israel of Kings Bay (1954, Sup) 133 N.Y.S.2d 242

§ 210. Incorporation of church connected with supreme council of Independent Associated Spiritualists

A meeting for incorporating or reincorporating a church in connection with the supreme council of the Independent Associated Spiritualists, Incorporated, shall be held in pursuance of the preceding provisions of this article. Such meeting shall be held and such church shall be subject to the following provisions:

1. Notice of meeting for incorporation. Notice of the meeting must have attached thereto the endorsement and consent of the supreme council of the Independent Associated Spiritualists;

2. The meeting for incorporation. The meeting shall be called to order by a person delegated to do so by the supreme councilor or his representative;

3. The certificate of incorporation. The certificate of incorporation shall have attached thereto the endorsement and consent of the supreme council of the Independent Associated Spiritualists and the name of such church as adopted shall thereafter have affixed "In connection with the supreme council of the Independent Associated Spiritualists, Incorporated," or "Affiliated with the supreme council of the Independent Associated Spiritualists, Incorporated," as the case may be;

4. Rules and regulations. A church incorporated or reincorporated under the provisions of this section shall be subject to the rules and regulations of the supreme council of the Independent Associated Spiritualists;

5. Trustees. The trustees of a church incorporated under this section shall also be the spiritual officers of such church;

6. Election of ministers. No church may engage or retain a minister not certified as in good standing by the supreme council;

7. Licenses and certificates. Only persons holding a minister's license or a certificate of proficiency from the supreme council shall conduct services or classes in any church, incorporated under this section.

History: Add, L 1928, ch 487, eff Mar 21, 1928.

§ 211. Incorporation of church in connection with Spiritual Science Mother Church, Inc

A meeting for incorporating or reincorporating a church in connection with Spiritual Science Mother Church, Inc., shall be held in pursuance of the preceding provisions of this article. Such meeting shall be held and such church shall be subject to the following provisions:

1. Notice of meeting for incorporation. Notice of the meeting must have attached thereto the endorsement and consent of Spiritual Science Mother Church, Inc.

2. The meeting for incorporation. The meeting shall be called to order by an authorized delegate of the board of directors of Spiritual Science Mother Church, Inc., the supreme ecclesiastical council governing Spiritual Science Mother Church and its branch churches.

3. The certificate of incorporation. The certificate of incorporation shall have attached thereto the endorsement and consent of the board of directors of Spiritual Science Mother Church, Inc., and the name of such church as adopted shall thereafter have affixed: "Branch Church of Spiritual Science Mother Church, Inc., of New York."

4. Rules and regulations. A church incorporated or reincorporated under the provisions of this section shall be subject to the rules and regulations of the

board of directors of Spiritual Science Mother Church, Inc.

5. Trustees. The trustees of such branch church incorporated under this section shall also be the spiritual officers of such church.

6. Election of ministers. No branch church of Spiritual Science may engage or retain, under this section, any minister not certified as in good standing by Spiritual Science Mother Church board of directors.

7. Licenses and certificates. Only persons holding a minister's license or a certificate of proficiency from the ecclesiastical council of Spiritual Science Mother Church, Inc., shall conduct services in any church incorporated under this section.

8. Recording of licenses. Such license or certificate shall be made a matter of public record either in the office of the county clerk or such other place as by law may be provided for such record.

History: Add, L 1934, ch 537, eff May 12, 1934.

ARTICLE 11
UNION CHURCHES

History: Add, L 1909, ch 53.

§ 220. Joint meeting for the purposes of incorporation

Two or more unincorporated churches, which separately agree on a plan of union and determine to meet together for the purpose of being incorporated as a union church, may be incorporated as a union church in pursuance of the provisions of article ten, and thereafter such union church shall be governed by the general provisions of such article, as near as may be, except as otherwise provided in this article. A notice of such joint meeting shall be given to the congregation of each church, in pursuance of the provisions of article ten of this chapter, relating to notice of meeting for incorporations, in every respect as if it were a notice of a meeting for the separate incorporation of such church under such article, except that the notice shall state in substance that a joint meeting of such unincorporated churches, which shall be specified in the notice, will be held for the purpose of incorporating such churches as a union church, and electing trustees thereof at a time and place specified in the notice, which place may be the usual place of worship of either of such churches or any other reasonably convenient place. Such notice must be signed by at least six persons from each of such churches who would be authorized to sign a notice for the meeting of each church, respectively, for the purpose of incorporating it under such article.

The provisions of article ten hereof shall be applicable to the organization and conduct of such meeting, the matters to be determined upon and the certificate of incorporation to be executed and filed accordingly, except that the presiding officer of such joint meeting shall be the oldest person present at such meeting who would be entitled to preside at a meeting of either of such churches singly for the purposes of incorporation in pursuance of such article. All persons who would be qualified to vote at such meeting of either of such churches held singly, shall be qualified voters at such joint meeting, and the number of trustees of the union church after incorporation, to be selected from each such church, may be agreed on by such unincorporated churches, and the trustees shall be selected by each of such churches accordingly.

The certificate of incorporation shall set forth the plan of union agreed on and the number of trustees of the incorporated union church to be selected by each unincorporated church.

History: Add, L 1909, ch 53, eff Feb 17, 1909.

§ 221. Government of incorporated union churches

Any union church or society having a common place of worship or holding property belonging jointly to the several societies composing the same, but the sole right of occupancy of which is reserved to each of them in proportion to their interest in such property, or the money originally paid therefor by each, or in accordance with their plan of union agreed on, may, if any one or more of the churches or societies comprising such union church or society has ceased to exist, on the request of such remaining churches or society, redistribute and divide the time of occupancy among such remaining societies in proportion to their contributions to such property respectively, or in accordance with a new plan of union agreed on by them. Such redistribution shall be made by the trustees of said union church or society on written notice to the societies which it is alleged have ceased to exist; but no such society shall be deemed to have ceased to exist unless it has failed or neglected for a period of five consecutive years next preceding such request for redistribution, to hold meetings and have a clerk or secretary, and keep a list or registry of its members, or to have preaching, prayer or conference meetings, or other religious services in keeping with the usages of the denomination to which it belongs.

Any one of the societies composing a union church or society, which shall have built a church edifice in the same village or neighborhood in which it holds its religious services, shall not thereby lose or forfeit in any way any of its rights or privileges in such union society, and the maintaining of divine worship, or contributing to its support in its own building, shall be regarded the same as if it held its meetings in the church building of such union society. Any notice for the election of trustees of the union society or for any other purpose which the law requires to be read or given at the time of divine service, may be read or given in the church edifice so built by any one of such societies, if at the time religious services are not held in the church edifice of such union society. But such

notice must be posted on the outer door of such union church edifice at least fifteen days before the meeting. If any society composing any such church union or society has a greater interest in the occupancy of the church building than others, unless the several churches composing the union church or society have agreed otherwise, the number of trustees shall be odd, and the trustees shall be elected from such societies in proportion to their respective interests in the union, church or society, as nearly as may be. Any society composing such union church or society, which has built for itself a church edifice and become incorporated, may sell its interest and right of occupancy in such union society, and convey the same, when authorized so to do by two-thirds vote of the voters thereof qualified to vote for union trustees, at a special meeting called for that purpose. The proceeds of such sale shall be used for the benefit of its church property.

History: Add, L 1909, ch 53, eff Feb 17, 1909.

ARTICLE 11-A
FREE METHODIST CHURCHES

History: Add, L 1923, ch 270.

§ 225. Application of this article

This article applies only to churches, societies, districts, conferences, and such other authorized religious organizations of the Free Methodist Church of North America as are or shall be situated in the state of New York.

History: Add, L 1923, ch 270, eff Apr 24, 1923.

§ 225-a. Organization of a free Methodist church

It shall be lawful for any number of persons, not less than six, with the consent of the district superintendent of the district in which the proposed church is to be located, to organize a free Methodist church and to procure its incorporation. Said church, when so organized, shall be subject in all matters of church government and ecclesiastical polity to the discipline, rules, usages and ministerial appointments of the Free Methodist Church of North America, as from time to time authorized and declared by the general conference of said church and the annual conference within the bounds of which such church may be situated.

History: Add, L 1923, ch 270, amd, L 1953, ch 389, § 1, eff Apr 2, 1953.

§ 225-b.　Meeting for incorporation

1. Notice of a meeting for the purpose of incorporating an unincorporated free Methodist church shall be in writing and shall state in substance, that a meeting of such unincorporated church will be held at its usual place of worship at a specified day and hour, for the purpose of incorporating such a church and selecting a name therefor and electing trustees thereof.

2. Such notice must be signed by at least six members, either in full connection or on probation, of the local society of full age and in good and regular standing. This notice shall be publicly read at a regular meeting of such unincorporated church for public worship, at least ten days, and not more than thirty days, before the date of such meeting upon Sunday, if such service be held on Sunday, by the pastor or by one of the signers thereof; and a copy of such notice shall be posted conspicuously on the outside of the main entrance to such place of worship at least fifteen days before the date of such meeting.

3. At the meeting for incorporation held in pursuance of such notice, the following persons, and no others, shall be qualified voters, to wit: all persons of full age, who are then members of such church, either in full connection or on probation, and in good and regular standing. The presence of the majority of such qualified voters, at least six in number, shall be necessary to constitute a quorum of such meeting, without which no action can be taken. Each action of the meeting upon any matter or question shall be decided by a majority of the qualified voters present and voting thereon. At such meeting the pastor shall preside, or in the absence of a pastor or in case of his declining to preside, any qualified voter may be elected to preside. The presiding officer shall be the judge of the qualifications of voters, subject to appeal to the vote of the members present whose qualifications as voters are not challenged, and shall receive the votes cast and declare the result of the same.

4. If such meeting shall decide to incorporate such unincorporated church, it shall also decide upon the name of the proposed incorporation, the number of trustees thereof, which shall be three, six or nine. Such meeting shall elect by ballot the number of trustees decided upon, at least two-thirds of whom shall be members in full connection of the free Methodist church and in good and regular standing. One-third of these shall hold office until the first annual election of trustees thereafter, one-third until the second annual election, and one-third until the third annual election.

5. The first annual meeting for the election of trustees shall be held at the date fixed for the annual society meeting which shall be within three months prior to the session of the annual conference.

History: Add, L 1923, ch 270, eff Apr 24, 1923.

§ 225-c.　Certificate of incorporation

1. The presiding officer of such a meeting and at least two other persons present and voting thereat shall be appointed by such meeting to execute and acknowledge, before any person authorized to take acknowledgment of deeds, a certificate of incorporation whereby they shall agree to be governed by the discipline, rules and usages of the Free Methodist Church of North America. To such certificate of incorporation there shall be attached a certificate signed by the district superintendent of the district in which said church is to be located, stating that the said church is incorporated by and with the consent of said district superintendent.

2. This certificate of incorporation shall contain the following items: The name of said church; the township, village or city, and the county in which said church shall be located; an agreement to worship and labor together according to the discipline, rules and usages of the Free Methodist Church of North America; the statement that there were six or more qualified voters present at the meeting where they were elected and this act of incorporation was authorized; the names and respective periods of office of the trustees elected; the place and date of said meeting for incorporation; and the signatures and residences of those authorized to execute and acknowledge this certificate of incorporation.

3. This certificate of incorporation shall be executed in duplicate. One of such duplicate copies shall be retained by such corporation and one copy shall be recorded in the office of the county clerk of the county where such corporation is formed. On filing such certificate the members either in full connection or on probation of such church qualified to vote at such meeting and who shall thereafter, from time to time, be qualified voters at the corporate meetings thereof shall be a corporation by the name stated in such certificate, and the persons therein stated to be elected trustees of such church shall be the trustees thereof, for the terms for which they were respectively elected, and until their successors are elected.

History: Add, L 1923, ch 270, eff Apr 24, 1923.

Sub 1, amd, L 1953, ch 389, § 2, eff Apr 2, 1953.

§ 225-d. Amendment of articles of incorporation

1. It shall be lawful for any incorporated church coming under the provisions of this article, by a two-thirds vote of the members present and voting at a regularly called society meeting, to alter or amend its articles of incorporation in any manner not inconsistent with the provisions of this article, or the book of discipline of the Free Methodist Church of North

America; and such alteration or amendment shall become operative when said society shall execute and acknowledge said amended articles of incorporation as provided for in section two hundred and twenty-five-c of this article, and with an attached certificate of consent by the district superintendent as provided in said section.

2. Every free Methodist church organized and incorporated in the state of New York, after this article takes effect, shall be organized and incorporated under its provisions and be subject thereto.

History: Add, L 1923, ch 270, eff Apr 24 1923.

Sub 1, amd, L 1953, ch 389, § 3, eff Apr 2, 1953.

§ 225-e.   Effect upon existing corporations

Every free Methodist church heretofore incorporated in the state of New York shall, three months after this article takes effect, automatically come under its provisions, unless in the meantime it shall elect by a two-thirds vote of all its members in full connection to remain under the provisions of the general or special law applicable thereto at such time. A certificate of such vote shall be filed in the office of the clerk of the county in which the principal place of worship of such corporation is located and shall be recorded by such clerk in the book in which certificates of religious corporations are recorded pursuant to law.

History: Add, L 1923, ch 270, eff Apr 24, 1923.

§ 225-f.   Annual election of trustees

1. Trustees of an incorporated free Methodist church shall be elected at the annual society meeting held within three months prior to the session of the annual conference to which the society belongs. Notice of such meeting shall be publicly announced at a regular meeting of such incorporated church for public worship upon Sunday, if such service be held on Sunday, and at least ten days, and not more than thirty days, before said meeting shall be held. This notice shall be given by the pastor, the officiating minister or an officer of the church. At the said annual society meeting the pastor shall preside, or in the absence of a pastor or in case of his declining, any qualified voter therein may be elected to preside. During the election of the trustees the following persons, and no others, shall be qualified voters, to wit: all persons who are then members in full connection or on probation of such church in good and regular standing. Said election shall be by ballot and on a majority vote, and at least six persons qualified to vote thereat shall be necessary to constitute a quorum. The trustees shall be so elected that the office of one-third of them shall continue for three years, one-third for two years, and one-third for one year. At least two-thirds of said trustees shall be members in full connection of the free Methodist church in good and regular standing. All trustees shall hold their office until their successors are elected, unless their office shall terminate as provided

for in section two hundred and twenty-five-h of this article.

2. A special corporate meeting of any such church may be called by the trustees thereof on their own motion, and must be called upon the written request of at least six qualified voters of such church, and shall be called and notice thereof given in the same manner as for an annual corporate meeting.

History: Add, L 1923, ch 270, eff Apr 24, 1923.

Sub 1, amd, L 1971, ch 208 § 8, eff Sept 1, 1971.

§ 225-g.   Changing number of trustees

An incorporated church may, at its annual meeting where trustees are elected, by vote change the number of its trustees to three, six or nine by adding more trustees, one-third of which shall be elected for three years, one-third for two years, and one-third for one year; or by voting to discontinue the offices of certain specified trustees as they expire, one-third of said offices to be discontinued each year, until the number left is the number decided upon. Such changes in the board of trustees shall always provide that at least two-thirds of the trustees shall be members in full connection of the free Methodist church in good and regular standing. No such change shall affect the terms of the trustees then in office, but each shall hold office until his full term has expired, unless his office is terminated according to section two hundred and twenty-five-h of this article.

History: Add, L 1923, ch 270, eff Apr 24, 1923.

§ 225-h.   Vacancies in board of trustees

If any trustee of such incorporated church declines to act, resigns, or dies; or, having been a member of such church, ceases to be a member; or removes beyond the bounds of the circuit in which he is elected, his office shall be vacant and a special corporate meeting may be called to fill that vacancy until the next annual society meeting of such church when trustees are elected, at which meeting the vacancy shall be filled for the unexpired term.

History: Add, L 1923, ch 270, eff Apr 24, 1923.

§ 225-i.   Trustee meetings

1. Meetings of the trustees of an incorporated free Methodist church shall be called by giving at least forty-eight hours' notice thereof personally or by mail to all the trustees, and such notice may be given by the pastor, the secretary of the board of trustees or by any two of the trustees, but by the unanimous consent of the trustees a meeting may be held without previous notice thereof. The pastor may preside at a trustee meeting and in his absence the senior trustee in service, or some member, the board of trustees elects for that purpose, shall be chairman. A majority of the whole number of trustees shall constitute a quorum for the transaction of business at any meeting lawfully convened.

2. The effect of a tie vote creating a deadlock shall be to carry the question involved (with all pending

questions appertaining thereto) over to the next sitting or meeting of the board. In case of such a deadlock extending beyond three successive sittings or meetings of the board of trustees, the whole matter involved shall be settled in a meeting of the corporate society.

History: Add, L 1923, ch 270, eff Apr 24, 1923.

§ 225-j. Powers of incorporated societies

1. An incorporated free Methodist church may, under restrictions hereinafter provided, sell, mortgage, or otherwise dispose of or encumber its real estate, but not for current expenses.

2. Said corporation shall at all times permit such ministers belonging to the free Methodist church as shall from time to time be duly authorized by the general conference of said church or by the annual conference, within whose bounds the said corporation may be, to preach and expound God's Holy Word therein; and shall permit pastors and district superintendents duly appointed, to execute the discipline of said free Methodist church and to administer the sacraments therein.

History: Add, L 1923, ch 270, eff Apr 24, 1923.

Sub 2, amd, L 1953, ch 389, § 4, eff Apr 2, 1953.

§ 225-k. Powers and duties of the trustees

1. The trustees shall have the custody of all the temporalities and property, real and personal, belonging to the corporation and of the revenues therefrom, and shall administer the same in accordance with the discipline, rules and usages of the corporation and of the Free Methodist Church of North America; but shall have no control of funds raised for pastoral support, benevolent enterprises or any other purpose save those directly connected with the property of the church.

2. A society meeting of an incorporated free Methodist church whose trustees are elective as such, may give direction, not inconsistent with law, as to the manner in which any of the temporal affairs of the church shall be administered by the trustees thereof; and such directions shall be followed by the trustees. The trustees shall have no power, without the consent of such a society meeting, to incur debts beyond what is necessary for the care of the property of the corporation.

History: Add, L 1923, ch 270, eff Apr 24, 1923.

§ 225-l. Conveyance of property

Whenever it may become necessary or advisable to mortgage or dispose of any church property, the trustees may mortgage or sell and convey the same by first securing the authority of the society for such sale or mortgage and the approval of the district superintendent of the district in which the church is located, and obtaining leave of the supreme or county court therefor pursuant to the provisions of this chapter; provided that in all cases the proceeds of such sale or mortgage shall be used either for the payment of debts or for the purchase or improvement of property for the same uses and deeded to the same corporation; or if not so used, shall be held subject to the order of the annual conference in whose territory such property may be situated. Provided however that, if the deed of the property to be sold shall convey the property to the local corporate society to be held in trust for the use and benefit of the membership of the Free Methodist Church of North America, it shall also be necessary for the trustees to secure the consent of the free Methodist general conference of North America, or in the intervals of its sessions, of such person or persons as are authorized by said general conference to grant such permission, in order to mortgage or sell and convey such property.

History: Add, L 1923, ch 270, amd, L 1953, ch 389, § 5, eff Apr 2, 1953.

§ 225-m. Property of extinct churches

1. Any incorporated annual conference or other governing body of the free Methodist church may decide that a church society in connection with it or over which it has ecclesiastical jurisdiction, has become extinct, if it has failed for two consecutive years next prior thereto, to maintain religious services according to the discipline, customs and usages of such governing body, or has had less than ten resident attending members making annual or regular contributions towards its support, and may take possession of the temporalities and property belonging to such church, or religious society, and manage the same; or may, in pursuance of the provisions of this act relating to the disposition of real property by free Methodist corporations, sell or dispose of the same and apply the proceeds thereof to any of the purposes to which the property of such governing religious body is devoted, and it shall not divert such property to any other object. For the purpose of obtaining a record title to the land and the church edifice, or other buildings thereon, by such incorporated governing body, the surviving trustee or trustees of said extinct church or if there be no surviving trustee, then a surviving member of said extinct church, may, without a consideration being paid therefor by such incorporated governing body, convey to it said land and church edifice, or other buildings thereon, subject, however, to an order of the supreme or county court based upon a petition reciting that said church has become extinct; the name of its surviving trustee or trustees; and the names of its members (who must have given their consent to the making of said conveyance). Upon the recital of said facts in said petition, the court shall have jurisdiction to grant an order allowing said conveyance to be made without a consideration; and should there be no surviving members, as well as no surviving trustee of said extinct church, said petition may be made by an officer of said incorporated governing body, in which event the court, upon the recital of said fact, shall

have jurisdiction to appoint a suitable person as trustee for the purpose of making said conveyance.

History: Add, L 1923, ch 270, eff Apr 24, 1923..

§ 225-n. Corporations for acquiring property for special religious purposes

1. An annual conference, a district quarterly conference, a circuit consisting of two or more organized churches or any other regularly organized free Methodist body may incorporate for the purpose of carrying on special religious enterprises. Notice of such intention shall be signed by at least six members of such organized body of full age and mailed to all the churches existing under the jurisdiction of or directly interested in said organized body at least ten days before the date set for such incorporation. If the meeting so called shall decide to incorporate, it shall also decide upon the name of the proposed corporation and the number of trustees thereof, which shall be three or some multiple of three not more than twenty-one. One-third of said trustees shall hold office for three years, one-third for two years, and one-third for one year. All trustees of such corporations shall hold office until their successors are elected, and always at least two-thirds of said trustees shall be members in full connection of the free Methodist church, in good and regular standing.

2. The presiding officer and at least two other persons present and voting thereat shall be appointed by such meeting to execute and acknowledge a certificate of incorporation whereby they shall agree to be governed by the discipline, rules and usages of the Free Methodist Church of North America.

3. The trustees of such a corporation shall thereafter be elected annually at a regular meeting, notice of which shall have been mailed by the secretary, or some other officer of the board of trustees, to all the churches existing under the jurisdiction of or directly interested in said corporation at least ten days before the date set for said meeting.

4. All members of and regular voters in such an organized and incorporated free Methodist body shall be entitled to vote for trustees, providing they are in good and regular standing in that organization.

5. Such an incorporated free Methodist body may acquire property for churches, parsonages, missions, Sunday schools, denominational educational institutions (subject to the consent of the University of New York), residences of church workers, dispensaries of medicine for the poor, rescue homes, homes for the aged or for needy and orphan children, property for cemeteries, camp grounds or for other religious purposes. Such a corporation shall have power to establish, maintain and manage by its trustees or other officers such institutions as a part of its religious purpose, and may take and hold by conveyance, donation, bequest or devise real and personal property for such purposes, and may purchase and may erect suitable buildings therefor. Any such corporation may take and hold any grant, donation, bequest or devise of real or personal property heretofore or hereafter made upon trust, and apply the same, or the income thereof, under the direction of its trustees or other officers. Such trustees or other officers shall have power to mortgage or sell and convey any property under their care, when directed so to do by the corporation that elected them, having first secured the approval of the district superintendent of the district in which the property is located and obtained leave of the supreme or county court therefor pursuant to the provisions of this chapter; provided that in all cases the proceeds of such sale or mortgage shall be used either for the payment of debts or for the purchase or improvement of property for the same uses and deeded to the same corporation; or if not used, shall be held subject to the order of the annual conference in whose territory such property may be situated. Provided, however, that if the deed of the property to be sold conveys the property to the local corporation to be held in trust for the use and benefit of the membership of the Free Methodist Church of North America incorporated under the name of "Free Methodist General Conference of North America," it shall also be necessary to secure the consent of the Free Methodist General Conference of North America, or in the intervals of its sessions, of such person or persons as are authorized by said general conference to grant such permission, in order to mortgage or sell and convey such property.

6. Vacancies occurring in the board of trustees of any such corporation holding property for special religious purposes, during the intervals between its regular meetings, may be filled by the remaining trustees until the next regular meeting of said corporation, at which meeting the vacancy shall be filled for the unexpired term.

7. In case any such corporation holding property for religious purposes shall have failed to function, in the purposes for which it was incorporated, for two consecutive years next prior thereto, the governing free Methodist body having ecclesiastical jurisdiction over it may declare such corporation extinct, and taking possession of its property manage or dispose of the same according to the provisions made for extinct churches in section two hundred and twenty-five-m of this article.

8. Such corporations for special religious purposes shall be governed in all respects not provided for in this section according to the other provisions of this article.

History: Add, L 1923, ch 270, eff Apr 24, 1923.

Sub 4, amd, L 1971, ch 201 § 9, eff Sept 1, 1971.

Sub 5, amd, L 1953, ch 389, eff Apr 2, 1953.

§ 225-o. Saving clause

Article ten of this chapter is not applicable to corporations of the free Methodist church incorporated under the provisions of this article.

History: Add, L 1923, ch 270, eff Apr 24, 1923.

ARTICLE 12
LAWS REPEALED; WHEN TO TAKE EFFECT

§ 260. Laws repealed
§ 261. When to take effect

History: Add, L 1909, ch 53

§ 260. Laws repealed

Of the laws enumerated in the schedule hereto annexed, that portion specified in the last column is hereby repealed.

History: Add, L 1909, ch 53, eff Feb. 17, 1909.

§ 261. When to take effect

This chapter shall take effect immediately.

History: Add, L 1909, ch 53, eff Feb. 17, 1909.

ARTICLE 13
SPIRITUALIST CHURCHES

§ 262. [Application]
§ 263. Incorporation of unincorporated Spiritualist churches and system of incorporation and government
§ 264. [Meeting for incorporation; qualifications of voters]
§ 265. The certificate of incorporation
§ 266. Time, place and notice of corporate meetings
§ 267. Organization and conduct of corporate meetings; qualifications of voters
§ 268. Election and salary of ministers
§ 269. Duties of ministers, et cetera
§ 270. Reincorporation of present incorporated Spiritualist churches
§ 271. [Regulations]
§ 272. [Definition of church]

History: Add, L 1914, ch 485.

§ 262. [Application]

This article applies only to a Spiritualist church in connection with the General Assembly of Spiritualists.

History: Add, L 1914, ch 485, eff Apr 22, 1914.

§ 263. Incorporation of unincorporated Spiritualist churches and system of incorporation and government

A meeting for the purpose of incorporating an unincorporated Spiritualist church in connection with the General Assembly of Spiritualists must be called and held in pursuance of the provisions of this article:

1. The notice and call of such meeting shall be in writing and shall state in substance, that a meeting of such unincorporated church will be held at its usual place of worship at a specified day and hour for the purpose of incorporating such church and designating trustees thereof.

2. The notice must be signed at least by seven persons of full age who are then members in good and regular standing of such church by admission into full membership therewith, in accordance with the rules and regulations of such church, and who have in good faith expressed in open meeting their belief in the tenets of faith adopted by the General Assembly of Spiritualists.

3. The notice must have endorsed thereon the approval of the body of the General Assembly of Spiritualists governing the admission of churches.

4. A copy of such notice with the approval endorsed thereon shall be publicly read at a regular meeting of such unincorporated church for public worship, on the two successive Sundays immediately preceding the meeting by any person qualified to sign such notice.

History: Add, L 1914, ch 485, eff Apr 22, 1914.

CASE ANNOTATIONS

Permitting those exercising the right of worshipping as Spiritualists, as a religion, the right to incorporate, does not give any license to pretend to tell fortunes. People v Plaskett (1939) 171 Misc 563, 13 N.Y.S.2d 682

§ 264. [Meeting for incorporation; qualifications of voters]

At the meeting for incorporation, held in pursuance to such notice, the qualified voters unless otherwise decided as hereinafter provided shall all be persons of full age who have worshipped with such church, and have regularly contributed to its support according to its usages, for at least one year or since it was formed, and who have in good faith in open meeting expressed their belief in the tenets of faith adopted by the General Assembly of Spiritualists. At such meeting the presence of a majority of such qualified voters, at least seven in number, shall be necessary to constitute a quorum, and all matters or questions shall be decided by a majority of the qualified voters voting thereon. The meeting shall be called to order by a person delegated so to do by the president of the General Assembly of Spiritualists. There shall be elected at such meeting, from the qualified voters then present a presiding officer, a clerk to keep the records of the proceedings of the meeting and two inspectors of election to receive the ballots cast. The presiding officer and the inspectors shall decide the result of the ballots cast on any matter, and shall be the judges of the qualifications of the voters. If the meeting shall decide that such unincorporated church shall become incorporated, the meeting shall also decide upon the name of the proposed corporation, the number of the trustees thereof, which shall be three, six or nine, and the date, not more than fifteen months thereafter, on which the first annual election of the trustees thereof shall be held; and it may, by a two-thirds vote, decide that all members of the unincorporated church, of full age, in good and regular standing, who have worshipped with such church but who have not contributed to the financial support thereof, shall also be qualified voters at such meeting. Such meeting shall thereupon elect by ballot from the persons qualified to vote thereat, of the number of trustees so decided on who shall hold office until the first annual election of trustees thereafter, one-third of such number of trustees who shall hold office until the second annual election of trustees thereafter, and one-third of such number of trustees who shall hold office until the third annual election of trustees thereafter, or until the respective successors of such trustees shall be elected. Such meeting shall also elect by ballot a clerk or secretary of the corporation, who shall hold his office until the close of the next annual meeting.

History: Add, L 1914, ch 485, eff Apr 22, 1914.

CASE ANNOTATIONS

Permitting those exercising the right of worshipping as Spiritualists, as a religion, the right to incorporate, does not give any license to pretend to tell fortunes. People v Plaskett (1939) 171 Misc 563, 13 N.Y.S.2d 682

§ 265. The certificate of incorporation

If the meeting shall decide that such unincorporated church shall become incorporated, the presiding officer of such meeting and the two inspectors of election shall execute a certificate setting forth the name of the proposed corporation, the number of trustees thereof, the names of the persons elected as trustees, the terms of office for which they were respectively elected, and the county or town, city or village in which its principal place of worship is, or is intended to be located. The name of such church as adopted shall bear the words "in connection with the General Assembly of Spiritualists." On the filing and recording of such certificate, after it shall have been acknowledged or proved as hereinbefore provided, the persons qualified to vote at such meeting and those persons who shall thereafter, from time to time be qualified voters at the corporate meetings thereof, shall be a corporation by the name stated in such certificate, and the persons therein stated to be elected trustees of such church shall be the trustees thereof for the terms for which they were respectively elected and until their respective successors shall be elected.

History: Add, L 1914, ch 485, eff Apr 22, 1914.

CASE ANNOTATIONS

Permitting those exercising the right of worshipping as Spiritualists, as a religion, the right to incorporate, does not give any license to pretend to tell fortunes. People v Plaskett (1939) 171 Misc 563, 13 N.Y.S.2d 682

§ 266. Time, place and notice of corporate meetings

The annual corporate meeting of every church incorporated under this article shall be held at the time and place fixed by its by-laws, or if no time and place be so fixed then at a time and place to be first fixed by its trustees, but to be changed only by a by-law adopted at an annual meeting. A special corporate meeting shall be called by the board of trustees thereof, on its own motion, and shall be called on the written request of at least seven qualified voters of such church. The trustees shall cause notice of the time and place of its annual corporate meeting, and of the names of any trustees whose successors are to be

elected thereat, and if a special meeting, of the business to be transacted thereat, to be publicly read by the presiding officer of such church or any trustees thereof at a regular meeting of the church for public worship, on the two successive Sundays immediately preceding such meeting.

History: Add, L 1914, ch 485, eff Apr 22, 1914.

§ 267. Organization and conduct of corporate meetings; qualifications of voters

At every corporate meeting of a church incorporated under this article all persons who for one year next preceding such meeting have worshipped with such church and have regularly contributed to its financial support, according to its usages, shall be qualified voters; but, if so decided, by a two-thirds vote at the original meeting or at any annual corporate meeting thereof, after notice of such meeting all members of such church in good and regular standing, by admission to membership therewith, who have worshipped with such church for one year next preceding the meeting at which they vote, may also be admitted as qualified voters at corporate meetings. At such corporate meetings, the presence of at least seven persons qualified to vote thereat shall be necessary to constitute a quorum; and all matters or questions shall be decided by a majority of the qualified voters voting thereon, except that by-laws can only be adopted or amended by a two-thirds vote. The clerk or secretary of the corporation shall call the meeting to order; and under his supervision the qualified voters then present shall choose a presiding officer and two inspectors of election to receive the ballots cast. The presiding officer and the inspectors of election shall declare the result of the ballots cast on any matter and shall be the judges of the qualifications of the voters. At such annual corporate meeting, successors to those trustees whose terms of office then expire shall be elected by ballot from the qualified voters, for a term of three years thereafter, and until their successors shall be elected. A clerk or secretary of the corporation shall be elected by ballot, who shall hold office until the close of the next annual meeting, and until his successor shall be elected.

History: Add, L 1914, ch 485, amd, L 1971, ch 201, § 10, eff Sept 1, 1971.

§ 268. Election and salary of ministers

The ministerial and clerical attendants of any such church shall be called, elected and removed and their salaries fixed as such corporation in its by-laws shall provide, but no such church shall call, or elect any such person to perform any of the duties of minister or clerical attendant who has not been regularly commissioned so to act by the General Assembly of Spritualists [Spiritualists] * according to its rules, after examination into the character and qualifications of such person by its committees regularly appointed, nor shall any such church retain any person as its minister or clerical attendant after it has been regularly notified that such person has been suspended or removed according to the rules and regulations of the General Assembly of Spiritualists covering such matters.

    * So in original. Probably meant to read "Spiritualists".

History: Add, L 1914, ch 485, eff Apr 22, 1914.

§ 269. Duties of ministers, et cetera

Ministers and clerical attendants shall perform such duties as the by-laws shall direct in accordance with the rules and regulations of the General Assembly of Spiritualists.

History: Add, L 1914, ch 485, eff Apr 22, 1914.

§ 270. Reincorporation of present incorporated Spiritualist churches

Any Spiritualist church heretofore incorporated may reincorporate under the provisions of this article by filing in the county clerk's office of the county in which its principal place of worship is located, a certificate that at a special meeting held pursuant to the provisions of section two hundred and sixty-six of this article, that such church had by two-thirds vote of the members present and qualified to vote, duly voted to reincorporate under the provisions hereof. Such certificate shall be signed by the presiding officer and two inspectors of election acting thereat and shall be acknowledged, and shall bear the indorsement and consent of the body of the General Assembly of Spiritualists governing admission of churches. The name of such church shall thereafter have affixed the words "in connection with the General Assembly of Spiritualists."

History: Add, L 1914, ch 485, eff Apr 22, 1914.

§ 271. [Regulations]

Any church incorporating or reincorporating under this article shall be subject to the rules and regulations of the General Assembly of Spiritualists relating to affiliated churches.

History: Add, L 1914, ch 485, eff Apr 22, 1914.

CASE ANNOTATIONS

Under this section a Spiritualist church is subject to the rules and regulations of the general assembly of Spiritualists. Re Glasser (1934) 150 Misc 207, 268 N.Y.S. 624, mod on other grounds 246 A.D. 565, 283 N.Y.S. 1009

§ 272. [Definition of church]

The word church as used herein shall mean any church or society organized for the purpose of worshipping as Spiritualists as a religion.

History: Add, L 1914, ch 485, eff Apr 22, 1914.

CASE ANNOTATIONS

Art. 13, which permits those exercising the right of worshipping as Spiritualists as a religion the right to incorporate, does not give any license to pretend to tell fortunes. People v Plaskett (1939) 171 Misc 563, 13 N.Y.S.2d 682

ARTICLE XIV
CHURCHES OF THE NAZARENE

History: Add, L 1923, ch 515.

§ 273. Application of article

This article applies only to churches of the Nazarene in connection with the general assembly of the church of the Nazarene.

History: Add, L 1923, ch 515, eff May 21, 1923.

Another § 273, add, L 1914, ch 485, eff Apr 22, 1914, merely enacted the effective date of §§ 263 et seq.

§ 274. Incorporation

An unincorporated church of the Nazarene may become incorporated as a church, by executing, acknowledging and filing a certificate of incorporation, stating the corporate name by which such church shall be known, and the county, town, city or village where its principal place of worship is or is intended to be located.

A certificate of incorporation of unincorporated churches of the Nazarene, shall be executed and acknowledged by the district superintendent of the district in which its principal place of worship is located, or in case of his absence or inability to act, by one of the general superintendents of the church of the Nazarene of the United States, and by the laymen, members of such church, who shall be selected as the first trustees thereof by said official.

In filing the said certificate, said church shall be a corporation by the name stated in the certificate.

History: Add, L 1923, ch 515, eff May 21, 1923.

§ 275. Government

The district superintendent of the district to which any incorporated church of the Nazarene belongs, and his successor in office, shall be by virtue of his office, a trustee of said church; and the laymen, members of such church who signed said certificate of incorporation shall together constitute the first board of trustees thereof. The term of office of the laymen trustees of the incorporated church of the Nazarene, shall be one year; the number of laymen trustees shall be three, six or nine. Whenever the office of any such laymen trustees shall become vacant by expiration of term of office or otherwise, his successor shall be elected by a majority vote of the duly qualified members of said church. No act or proceedings of the trustees of any incorporated church shall be valid, without the sanction of the district superintendent of the district to which such church belongs, or in case of his absence or inability to act, without the sanction of one of the general superintendents of the church of the Nazarene of the United States.

History: Add, L 1923, ch 515, eff May 21, 1923.

§ 276. Reincorporation of present incorporated churches of the Nazarene

Any church of the Nazarene heretofore incorporated may reincorporate under the provisions of this article, by filing in the county clerk's office in the county in which its principal place of worship is located, a certificate, signed by the district superintendent of the district in which its principal place of worship is located, or in case of his absence or inability to act, by one of the general superintendents of the church of the Nazarene of the United States, and by all the trustees in office at the time of such reincorporation, setting forth that they desire to reincorporate under the provisions of this act, the corporate name by which such church shall be known, and the county, town, city or village where its principal place of worship is or is intended to be located; the number and the names of the laymen trustees who are to hold office until the next annual meeting of said corporation. Immediately upon the filing of such certificate, the board of trustees of said church, shall consist of the district superintendent of the district in which the principal place of worship is located, and the laymen trustees selected as above provided, and the office of the trustees of said church heretofore appointed or selected shall become vacant and cease to exist.

History: Add, L 1923, ch 515, eff May 21, 1923.

§ 277. Rules and regulations

Any church incorporated or reincorporated under this article, shall be subject to the rules and regulations of the general assembly of the church of the Nazarene.

History: Add, L 1923, ch 515, eff May 21, 1923.

§ 278. Corporations for acquiring camp meeting grounds for camp meeting purposes

The district superintendent and the members of the camp meeting board duly elected by a district assembly of the Church of the Nazarene may become incorporated for the purposes of acquiring, maintaining and improving real property to be used as a camp ground for camp meeting purposes, by executing, acknowledging and filing a certificate stating the name and object of the corporation, the name of such district assembly and of such district, the names and residences of the signers thereof, the number of trustees of such corporation, which shall be three, or some multiple of three, not more than twenty-one, the names of such trustees, designating one-third to hold office for one year, one-third to hold office for two years and one-third to hold office for three years. On filing such a certificate the district superintendent and the members of such camp meeting board shall be a corporation by the name and for the purposes therein stated and the trustees therein named shall be the first trustees thereof.

A person holding property in trust for camp meeting purposes or other religious purposes for the Church of the Nazarene may convey the same to a corporation organized for the purpose of acquiring such property within the district in which the property is situated.

Meetings held under the direction of such a corporation upon grounds owned by it shall be deemed religious meetings within the provisions of the law relating to disturbance of religious meetings.

History: Add, L 1940, ch 416, eff Apr 12, 1940.

Closing par, amd, L 1980, ch 843, § 196, eff Sept 1, 1980.

§ 279. Incorporation of advisory board of a district of the Church of the Nazarene

1. The district superintendent and the members of the advisory board duly elected by a district assembly of the Church of the Nazarene may incorporate for the purpose of advancing the development of the Churches of Nazarene in such district.

2. The certificate of incorporation shall state the object of the corporation, the name of such district assembly and of such district, the names and residences of the signers thereof, the number of trustees which shall be not less than three or more than five, designating them to hold office for one year. On executing, acknowledging and filing such certificate the advisory board of such district shall be a corporation and the trustees therein stated shall be the first trustees thereof.

3. Such corporation may acquire property for churches, parsonages, missions, Sunday schools, denominational educational institutions (subject to the consent of the university of New York), residences of church workers, dispensaries of medicine for the poor, rescue homes, homes for the aged or for needy and orphan children, subject to the consent of the state board of social welfare, and property for cemeteries, camp grounds or for other religious purposes. Such a corporation shall have power to establish, maintain and manage by its trustees or other officers such institutions as a part of its religious purpose, and may take and hold by conveyance, donation, bequest or devise real and personal property for such purposes, and may purchase and may erect suitable buildings therefor. Any such corporation may take and hold any grant, donation, bequest or devise of real or personal property heretofore or hereafter

made upon trust, and apply the same, or the income thereof, under the direction of its trustees or other officers. Such trustees or other officers shall have power to mortgage or sell and convey any property under the care, when directed so to do by the corporation that elected them, having first obtained leave of the supreme or county court therefor pursuant to the provisions of this chapter; provided that in all cases the proceeds of such sale or mortgage shall be used either for the payment of debts or for the purchase or improvement of property for the same uses and deeded to the same corporation; or if not used, shall be held subject to the order of the annual assembly of the district.

History: Add, L 1950, ch 816, eff Mar 20, 1950.

ARTICLE XV
[FEDERATED ORTHODOX GREEK CATHOLIC PRIMARY JURISDICTIONS IN AMERICA]

History: Add, L 1943, ch 145.

§ 290. Application of article

1. This article applies to all churches, congregations, societies, parishes, committees and other local organizations governed by jurisdictions, bishoprics, dioceses, missions of any Orthodox Patriarchate, Synod or national church of the Orthodox Greek Catholic (Eastern Orthodox) Church, recognized by the apostolic historic Orthodox Patriarchates of Constantinople, Antioch, Moscow and Serbia (Jugoslavia), respectively, through their four primary Orthodox Greek Catholic jurisdictions in America as specified in subdivisions three and four of section fifteen of this chapter; also to any churches, parishes, congregations, societies or committees of the Christian Orthodox Catholic Churches of the Eastern Confession which are included under article five-a of said chapter and in general to all churches, parishes, congregations, committees or religious organizations founded or established with the intent and for the purpose of adhering to and maintaining the apostolic and historic communion, doctrine, discipline, canon law, tradition, worship and unity of the Eastern Confession known as the Orthodox Greek Catholic (Eastern Orthodox) Church.

2. This article does not apply to the following churches, which are autogenic, to wit: American Catholic Church, Old Catholic Church, Western Orthodox Church, Orthodox Old Catholic Church, American Catholic Orthodox Church, Apostolic Episcopal Church, Holy Orthodox Church in America, American Patriarchal Orthodox Church, African Orthodox Church or any other organization, church, society or establishment by whatever name, title or description designated, whose names, titles or descriptions allude, relate or refer to the said Orthodox Greek Catholic (Eastern Orthodox) Church but which are not recognized or accepted by said apostolic and historic Orthodox Greek Catholic Patriarchates.

History: Add, L 1943, ch 145, eff Mar 20, 1943.

§ 291. Application for incorporation

An unincorporated congregation, church, parish or society may apply to the appropriate hierarch, bishop or administrator for permission to incorporate under this article.

When such permission or sanction for incorporation has been given, in writing, over the seal and signature of the appropriate hierarch, bishop or administrator and has been certified by the secretariat of the Federated Orthodox Greek Catholic Primary Jurisdictions in America, it shall be attached to a certificate of incorporation; and said certificate shall be executed, acknowledged and filed, as hereinafter provided, and thereupon such congregation, parish, church, society or committee shall become a corporation under this article.

History: Add, L 1943, ch 145, eff Mar 20, 1943.

§ 292. Notice of meeting for incorporation

Notice of a meeting for the purpose of incorporating an unincorporated parish, congregation, church, society or committee to which this article is applicable shall be given as follows:

1. The notice shall be in writing and shall state in substance that a meeting of the members of such church, congregation, parish, society or committee will be held at a stated place, date and hour for the purpose of incorporating, electing trustees and selecting a corporate name.

2. The notice shall also state that the appropriate ecclesiastical authority has given sanction and permission, required under this article, for the incorporation.

3. The notice must be signed by at least six persons of legal age who, either from the time of the formation of said church or for a period of at least one year have been communicants in canonical standing within the Eastern Orthodox communion and are resident members of the parish, church, society or committee which proposes to incorporate.

4. Such notice shall be publicly read, by the minister in charge of such church or by one of the members signing the same, at two successive regular meetings for public worship or at special meetings of said parish or society on the two Sundays immediately preceding the meeting for incorporation; and at least fifteen days before the meeting for incorporation, a copy of such notice shall be posted at the place of worship or at the place where such special meetings are to be held.

History: Add, L 1943, ch 145, eff Mar 20, 1943.

§ 293. Provisions governing meetings for incorporation and resolutions to be adopted thereat

1. At the meeting for incorporation, held in pursuance of such notice, qualified voters shall be those qualified under the by-laws of such unincorporated church, congregation, parish, society or committee, or in the absence of such by-laws, the persons qualified to vote in parish meetings in accordance with the rules and regulations or general usages of that jurisdiction of the Orthodox Greek Catholic (Eastern Orthodox) Church to which the proposed corporation is to adhere.

2. The meeting shall be called to order by the priest in charge of the parish, congregation, society, or committee or, in his absence, by one of the signers of the notice and shall elect the customarily required officers to conduct the meeting. In order to incorporate under this article the meeting shall adopt the following resolution by a majority of its qualified voters, present and voting, to wit:

Whereas, this (congregation, parish, church, society or committee) was founded and established, and thereby a permanent trust was created, for the purpose and intent of adhering to, maintaining and promoting religious worship and teaching according to the communion, doctrine, discipline, rite, canon law, traditions and usages of the Orthodox Greek Catholic (Eastern Orthodox) Church; and

Whereas, such purpose and intent and the trust thereby created can be fully effected and safeguarded only in complete canonical unity with Orthodox jurisdictions and in obedience to Orthodox Greek Catholic bishops acknowledged and certified by the Federated Orthodox Greek Catholic Primary Jurisdictions in America; and

Whereas, the signers hereof are the trustees, duly elected as such at a meeting duly held on the --- day of ----, nineteen hundred -, in accordance with article fifteen of the religious corporations law; and

Whereas, by a majority vote the said meeting has determined to incorporate under said article as a (parish, society or committee) of the Orthodox Greek Catholic (Eastern Orthodox) Church under the name of ---- (here give the corporate name by which such church, society or committee is to be known); and

Whereas, permission and sanction for such incorporation has been given and certified in accordance with the provisions of said article by (here name the appropriate hierarch, bishop or administrator) to whose jurisdiction and authority this corporation shall adhere,

Therefore it is hereby

Resolved, that this (congregation, parish, church, society or committee) shall become and remain an incorporated (parish, society or committee) of the aforesaid jurisdiction in full unity of communion,

faith and discipline with the Federated Orthodox Greek Catholic Primary Jurisdictions in America.

History: Add, L 1943, ch 145, eff Mar 20, 1943.

§ 294. Certificate of incorporation

1. A certificate of incorporation for a church, society, or committee, to which this article is applicable shall be executed and acknowledged by the trustees who sign the resolution for incorporation.

The said certificate of incorporation shall contain the following:

(a) the name by which the proposed corporation shall be known.

(b) the number of trustees thereof; the names and addresses of the persons elected as trustees; and the term of office for which they were respectively elected.

(c) the name of county, town, city or village in which the principal place of worship or office is or is intended to be located.

(d) the purpose and intent for which said corporation is created, to be set forth as follows:

"The purpose and intent of this corporation is to maintain, propagate, practice and forever perpetuate religious worship, services, sacraments and teaching in full accordance and unity with the doctrine, ritual, canon law, faith, practice, discipline, and traditions and usages of the Orthodox Greek Catholic (Eastern Orthodox) Church; and for the carrying out of said purpose and intent, to form and maintain a religious organization or church adherent and obedient to the Orthodox ecclesiastical jurisdiction and authority, and to the Orthodox hierarch, bishop or administrator, selected by the members applying for incorporation, and certified by the Orthodox Greek Catholic Primary Jurisdictions in America, through the secretariat thereof, as canonical and appropriate for the Orthodox communicant members comprising this corporation."

(e) In the certificate of incorporation of societies or organizations, other than parishes, special purposes, additional to the above, may be set forth.

2. On filing such certificate in the office of the county clerk of the county in which the place of worship or office of such corporation is or is intended to be located, such church, society or committee shall be a corporation by the name stated in the certificate and the persons therein declared to be trustees of such corporation shall be trustees until their successors are elected.

History: Add, L 1943, ch 145, eff Mar 20, 1943.

§ 295. Government: powers and duties of trustees

1. Every church, parish, congregation, society, or committee incorporated or re-incorporated, pursuant to this article, shall recognize and be and remain subject to the jurisdiction and authority of the duly appointed and canonical hierarch, bishop or other administrator, certified through the secretariat of the

Federated Orthodox Greek Catholic Primary Juris-dictions in America, as appropriate for its members, or his successor in office whose authority is likewise certified; shall accept, secure or receive the sacramen-tal, pastoral, or ministerial services of such clergy only as are so certified to be of lawful and canonical status or authority in the Orthodox Greek Catholic (Eastern Orthodox) Church; and shall retain or secure as pastors only such clergy as have, in addi-tion, the permission of the hierarch, bishop or admin-istrator certified to be appropriate; and shall in all other respects conform to, maintain, and follow the faith, doctrine, ritual, communion, discipline, canon law, traditions and usages of the Orthodox Greek Catholic (Eastern Orthodox) Church.

2. Any action of the trustees or parish committees regarding the calling, appointment, removal or compensation of parish clergy shall be subject to approval, in writing, by the appropriate bishop or administrator exercising jurisdiction.

3. The trustees of every such incorporated or re-incorporated church, society or committee shall have the custody and control of all the temporalities and property, real and personal, belonging to the corpora-tion, and of all the revenues therefrom; and shall administer the same strictly in accordance with the by-laws of the corporation and the rules, regulations and usages of the orthodox jurisdiction or ecclesiasti-cal governing body to which such church, society or committee is subject.

4. The number of first trustees shall be a multiple of three; one-third of such first trustees to hold office for three years; one-third thereof to hold office for two years; and one-third thereof to hold office for one year from the first election following the incorporation; and thereafter at each annual election there shall be elected for a term of three years one-third of the number of trustees.

History: Add, L 1943, ch 145, eff Mar 20, 1943.

§ 296. Re-incorporation of existing corpora-tions

Any heretofore incorporated church, congrega-tion, parish, society, or committee, to which this article is applicable, may re-incorporate under the provisions of this article by the same procedure hereinbefore set forth for incorporation substituting, at appropriate places, the word "re-incorporate" for "incorporate" and filing the certificate of re-incorporation in the office of the county clerk in the county in which its principal place of worship or office is located. Immediately upon the filing of such certifi-cate all the right, title, equity and interest of such organization or corporation in any estate, real or personal, together with all franchise and charter rights, shall be vested in the corporation so created under this article, and the original corporation shall be null and void.

History: Add, L 1943, ch 145, eff Mar 20, 1943.

ARTICLE XVI
SPIRITUALIST CHURCHES CONNECTED WITH THE NATIONAL SPIRITUALIST ASSOCIATION

§ 300.   Application of article
§ 301.   Application for incorporation
§ 302.   Notice of meeting for incorporation
§ 303.   Incorporation meeting
§ 304.   Certificate of incorporation
§ 305.   Pastor
§ 306.   Re-incorporation

History: Add, L 1947, ch 791.

§ 300. Application of article

This article shall apply only to Spiritualist churches in connection with the National Spiritualist Association.

History: Add, L 1947, ch 791, eff Apr 11, 1947.

§ 301. Application for incorporation

An unincorporated Spiritualist church may apply to the National Spiritualist Association for permis-sion to incorporate under this article, which written permission granted by the board of trustees of the National Spiritualist Association shall be attached to and become a part of the certificate of incorporation.

History: Add, L 1947, ch 791, eff Apr 11, 1947.

§ 302. Notice of meeting for incorporation

A notice of meeting for the purpose of incorporat-ing an unincorporated Spiritualist church in connec-tion with the National Spiritualist Association shall be given as follows:

1. The notice shall be in writing and shall state in substance that a meeting of the members of such church will be held at a stated place, date and hour for the purpose of incorporating, electing officers and trustees and selecting a corporate name.

2. The notice shall also state that written permis-sion has been granted by the board of trustees of the National Spiritualist Association.

3. The notice shall be signed by at least fifteen persons of legal age who are in good and regular standing of such church, in accordance with the rules and regulations of such church, and who have in good faith expressed in open meeting their belief in the tenets and the declaration of principles adopted by the National Spiritualist Association.

4. The notice shall be publicly read at a regular meeting of such unincorporated church for public worship on two successive Sundays immediately preceding the meeting by any person qualified to sign such notice.

History: Add, L 1947, ch 791, eff Apr 11, 1947.

§ 303. Incorporation meeting

1. At the incorporation meeting, held in pursu-ance of such notice, the qualified voters shall be all persons of legal age who are in good and regular

standing in such church in accordance with the rules and regulations of such church and who have in good faith in open meeting expressed their belief in the tenets of faith and the declaration of principles adopted by the National Spiritualist Association. At such meeting the presence of a majority of the qualified voters, at least eight in number, shall be necessary to constitute a quorum, and all matters or questions shall be decided by a majority of the qualified voters voting thereon.

2. The meeting shall be called to order by the minister of such church, or in his absence, by one of the signers of the notice and shall elect from the qualified voters, a chairman, a secretary and two inspectors of election. The chairman and the inspectors of election shall decide the qualifications of the voters and the result of the ballots cast on any matter.

3. If the meeting shall decide that such church shall become incorporated, the meeting shall also decide upon the name of the proposed corporation, the number and term of officers and trustees, and the name of the county and the city, town or village in which the principal place of worship is or is intended to be located. The meeting shall also elect the officers and trustees. The meeting may also adopt by-laws for the government of the church.

History: Add, L 1947, ch 791, eff Apr 11, 1947.

§ 304. Certificate of incorporation

The certificate of incorporation shall contain:

1. The name by which the proposed corporation shall be known.

2. The names and addresses of the officers and trustees elected at the incorporation meeting, together with the respective terms of said officers and trustees.

3. The name of the county and the city, town or village in which the proposed place of worship is or is intended to be located.

4. The purpose and intent for which the corporation is created to be set forth as follows:

"The purpose and intent of this religious corporation is to promote the science and promulgate the philosophy and religion of Spiritualism, as adopted and practiced by the National Spiritualist Association.

This corporation is subject to the constitution and by-laws of the National Spiritualist Association, a religious body incorporated under the laws of the District of Columbia, to the extent that they may not be inconsistent with the laws of the United States or of this state."

The certificate shall be executed and acknowledged by the duly elected officers and trustees and, together with the written permission to incorporate granted by the board of trustees of the National Spiritualist Association, shall be filed in the office of the county clerk of the county in which the place of

worship is or is intended to be located. On such filing the church shall be a corporation and the persons so elected to be officers and trustees shall be such officers and trustees.

History: Add, L 1947, ch 791, eff Apr 11, 1947.

§ 305. Pastor

The pastor of the church shall be called, settled or removed and his or her salary fixed, only by the vote of a majority of the members of the corporation duly qualified to vote at elections present and voting at a meeting of such corporation called for that purpose, subject to the written consent of the board of trustees of the National Spiritualist Association.

History: Add, L 1947, ch 791, eff Apr 11, 1947.

§ 306. Re-incorporation

Any heretofore incorporated Spiritualist church in connection with the National Spiritualist Association, may re-incorporate under the provisions of this article by the same procedure hereinbefore set forth for incorporation, substituting at the appropriate place the word "re-incorporate" for "incorporate" and filing the certificate of re-incorporation in the office of the county clerk in the county in which its principal place of worship is located.

History: Add, L 1947, ch 791, eff Apr 11, 1947.

ARTICLE 17
METHODIST CHURCHES

History: Add, L 1949, ch 660, eff July 1, 1949.

§ 320. Application of article

This article applies only to Methodist churches and to affiliated and subsidiary organizations.

History: Add, L 1949, ch 660, eff July 1, 1949.

§ 321. Change of name of churches and affiliated and subsidiary organizations

1. Notwithstanding any provisions of this chapter or of any general, special or local law, the three denominations formerly known as the Methodist

Episcopal Church, the Methodist Protestant Church and the Methodist Episcopal Church South having united into one under the name of The Methodist Church, all religious corporations or churches heretofore authorized to use, or be known by the names "Methodist Episcopal Church," "Methodist Protestant Church," or "Methodist Episcopal Church South" and all societies, conferences, boards, associations, corporations or other organizations directly connected therewith or subsidiary thereto shall eliminate from their respective names the word or words "Episcopal," "Protestant" or "South," as the case may be, and all such churches, corporations and other organizations shall hereafter be known by such names as changed and amended by this section.

2. The changes in names provided for by this section shall not in any respect change the identity of or affect, abate, defeat, alter or annul any of the rights, privileges, powers, property rights, obligations, liabilities or duties of any of said churches or corporations aforesaid, all of which shall remain in full force and effect as though their respective names had not been so changed.

3. All churches or other corporations using the changed names as provided in this section shall continue to have and be possessed of all of the interest, property and rights to which they are or may become entitled under their former corporate names.

4. The provisions of this section shall be deemed continuous of the provisions of chapter three hundred twenty-seven of the laws of nineteen hundred forty, and laws amendatory thereof, and shall be construed to have been in existence since April tenth, nineteen hundred forty, the time of the enactment of such chapter.

History: Add, L 1949, ch 660, eff July 1, 1949.

§ 321-a. Use of certain names by religious corporations

1. Notwithstanding any provisions of this chapter or of any general, special or local law, the two denominations formerly known as The Methodist Church and The Evangelical United Brethren Church having united into one under the name of The United Methodist Church, all religious corporations or churches heretofore authorized to use or be known by the names Methodist Church or Evangelical United Brethren Church, and all societies, conferences, boards, associations, corporations or other organizations duly connected therewith or subsidiary thereto shall eliminate from their respective names the word or words The Methodist Church or Evangelical United Brethren or add The United Methodist Church, as the case may be and all such churches, corporations and other organizations shall hereinafter be known by such names as changed and amended by this section.

2. The changes and names provided for by this section shall not in any respect change the identity or affect, abate, defeat, alter or annul any of the rights,

privileges, property rights, obligations, liabilities or duties of any of said churches or corporations aforesaid, all of which shall remain in full force and effect as though their respective names had not been so changed.

3. All churches, corporations, organizations or unincorporated associations using the changed names as provided in this section shall continue to have and be possessed of all of the interest, property and rights to which they are or may become entitled under their former corporate names or other respective designations.

History: Add, L 1969, ch 962, § 8, eff May 26, 1969.

§ 322. Meeting for incorporation

1. Notice of a meeting for the purpose of incorporating an unincorporated United Methodist church shall be in writing and shall state in substance, that a meeting of such unincorporated church will be held at its usual place of worship at a specified day and hour, for the purpose of incorporating such a church and selecting a name therefor and electing trustees thereof.

2. Such notice must be signed by at least six full members of the church who are all of full age and in good and regular standing. This notice shall be publicly read at each of the two next preceding regular meetings of such unincorporated church for public worship, at least one week apart, at morning service, if such service be held, on Sunday, if Sunday be the day for such regular meetings by the pastor or by one of the signers thereof.

3. At the meeting for incorporation held in pursuance of such notice, the following persons, and no others, shall be qualified voters, to wit: all persons of full age who are then full members in good and regular standing in such church. The presence of at least six persons qualified to vote thereat shall be necessary to constitute a quorum of such a meeting. Each action of the meeting upon any matter or question shall be decided by a majority of the qualified voters present and voting thereon. At such a meeting the district superintendent or the pastor shall preside, or in the absence of both or in case of either or both declining to preside, any qualified voter may be elected to preside. The presiding officer shall be the judge of the qualifications of voters, subject to appeal to the vote of the members present whose qualifications as voters are not challenged, and shall receive the votes cast and declare the result of the same.

4. If such meeting shall decide to incorporate such unincorporated church, it shall also decide upon the name of the proposed incorporation, the number of trustees thereof, which shall be three, six or nine, and shall determine the date, not more than fifteen months thereafter, on which the first annual election

of the trustees thereof after such meeting shall be held. Such meeting shall elect by ballot the number of trustees decided upon, which trustees shall be of full age and two-thirds of whom shall be members of The United Methodist Church. One-third of these shall be elected to hold office until the first annual election of trustees thereafter, one-third until the second annual election, and one-third until the third annual election.

History: Add, L 1949, ch 660, eff July 1, 1949.

Sub 1, amd, L 1969, ch 962, § 9, eff May 6, 1969.

Sub 4, amd, L 1969, ch 962, § 9, May 26, 1969.

§ 323. Certificate of incorporation

The presiding officer of such a meeting and at least two other persons present and voting thereat shall be appointed at such a meeting to execute and acknowledge, before any person authorized to take acknowledgment of deeds, a certificate of incorporation which shall have been submitted to and approved by such meeting. Such certificate shall set forth: the place and date of said meeting for incorporation; the name of said church; the township, village or city, and the county in which said church shall be located; the statement that there were six or more qualified voters present at the meeting where this act of incorporation was authorized; the names and respective periods of office of the trustees elected; the signatures and residences of those authorized to execute and acknowledge the certificate of incorporation; the approval of the district superintendent of the district in which the church is located; and a statement that the corporation shall support the doctrine and shall be subject to the laws, usages and ministerial appointments of The United Methodist Church as from time to time established, made and declared by the lawful authority of said church. On the filing of such certificate in the office of the county clerk of the county in which such church shall be located the members of such church qualified to vote at such meeting and those who shall thereafter, from time to time, be qualified voters, at the corporate meetings thereof, shall be a corporation by the name stated in such certificate, and the persons therein stated to be elected trustees of such church shall be the trustees thereof, for the terms for which they were respectively elected, and until their successors are elected.

History: Add, L 1949, ch 660, amd, L 1969, ch 962, § 10, eff May 26, 1969.

§ 324. Amendment of certificate of incorporation

It shall be lawful for any incorporated United Methodist church, by a two-thirds vote of the members present and voting at a regularly called meeting of the corporation, to alter or amend its certificate of incorporation in any manner not inconsistent with the provisions of this chapter or the discipline of The United Methodist church; and such alteration or amendment shall become operative when the amended certificate of incorporation shall have been executed, acknowledged and filed as provided for in section three hundred twenty-three of this article.

History: Add, L 1949, ch 660, amd, L 1969, ch 962, § 10, eff May 26, 1969.

§ 325. Corporate meetings

1. The trustees of an incorporated United Methodist church shall be elected at the annual corporate meeting which shall be held at the time and place fixed by the by-laws, if such time and place be so fixed, and otherwise at a time and place to be fixed by its trustees. A special corporate meeting of any such church may be called by the board of trustees thereof, on its own motion or on the written request of at least ten qualified voters of such church. The trustees shall cause notice of the time and place of the annual corporate meeting therein specifying the name of any trustees, whose successors are to be elected thereat, and, if a special meeting, specifying the business to be transacted thereat, to be given at each of the two next preceding regular meetings of such incorporated church for public worship, at least one week apart, at morning service, if such service be held, on Sunday, if Sunday be the day for such regular meetings, or if no such public worship be held during such period, by conspicuously posting such notice in writing upon the outer entrance to the principal place of worship of such church. Such notice shall be given by the district superintendent, the pastor, the officiating minister or an officer of the church.

2. At such a corporate meeting the following persons, and no other, shall be qualified voters for the election of trustees, to wit: all persons who are full members of such church in good and regular standing. The members present at any duly announced meeting shall constitute a quorum. Each action of the meeting upon any matter or question shall be decided by a majority of the qualified voters present and voting thereon. At such a meeting the district superintendent or the pastor shall preside, or in the absence of both or in case of either or both declining to preside, any qualified voter may be elected to preside. The presiding officer of the meeting shall receive the votes, be the judge of qualifications of voters subject to appeal to the vote of the members present whose qualifications as voters are not challenged, and declare the result of the votes cast on any matter.

3. Election of trustees at the annual corporate meeting shall be by written individual ballot and on a majority vote. Such trustees shall be of full age and each election shall provide that at least two-thirds of the board of trustees shall be members of The United Methodist Church. The trustees shall be elected for a term of three years or until their successors have been duly elected, provided that one-third shall be elected each year.

History: Add, L 1949, ch 660, amd, L 1969, ch 962, § 10, eff May 26, 1969.

Sub 2, amd, L 1971, ch 201, § 11, eff Sept 1, 1971.

§ 326. Changing number of trustees

An incorporated United Methodist church may, at its annual corporate meeting where trustees are elected, by vote change the number of its trustees to three, six or nine by adding more trustees, one-third of which shall be elected for three years, one-third for two years and one-third for one year; or by voting to discontinue the offices of certain specified trustees as they expire, one-third of said offices to be discontinued each year, until the number left is the number decided upon. Such changes in the board of trustees shall always provide that at least two-thirds of the trustees shall be members of The United Methodist church. No such changes shall affect the terms of the trustees then in office, but each shall hold office until his full term has expired unless his office shall terminate as provided for elsewhere in this article.

History: Add, L 1949, ch 660, amd, L 1969, ch 962, § 10, eff May 26, 1969.

§ 327. Vacancies in board of trustees

If any trustee of such incorporated United Methodist church declines to act, resigns, dies, or has his trusteeship terminated by any other means, his office shall be vacant and the quarterly conference of the church in any regular or a special session may fill the vacancy until the next annual corporate meeting when trustees are elected at which meeting the vacancy shall be filled for the unexpired term.

History: Add, L 1949, ch 660, amd, L 1969, ch 962, § 10, eff May 26, 1969.

§ 328. Meetings of trustees

Meetings of the trustees of an incorporated United Methodist church may be held at stated intervals or may be called by giving at least twenty-four hours notice thereof personally or by mail to all trustees and such meeting may be called and such notice given by the pastor, the secretary of the board of trustees, or by any two of the trustees, but by the unanimous consent of the trustees a meeting may be held without previous notice thereof. Some member of the board of trustees elected for that purpose shall be president or chairman, or the pastor may preside without vote. A majority of the whole number of trustees shall constitute a quorum for the transaction of business at any meeting lawfully convened. In case of a tie vote at a meeting of the trustees, the presiding officer of such meeting, if he be a trustee, shall, notwithstanding he has voted once, have an additional casting vote, or, if the presiding officer be the pastor, the secretary of the board shall have the additional casting vote.

History: Add, L 1949, ch 660, amd, L 1969, ch 962, § 10, eff May 26, 1969.

§ 329. Change of date of annual corporate meetings

An annual corporate meeting of an incorporated United Methodist church may change the date of its annual meeting thereafter. If such a date shall next thereafter occur less than six months after the annual meeting at which such change is made, the next annual meeting shall be held one year from such next recurring date. For the purpose of determining the terms of office of trustees, the time between the annual meeting at which such change is made and the next annual meeting thereafter shall be reckoned as one year.

History: Add, L 1949, ch 660, amd, L 1969, ch 962, § 10, eff May 26, 1969.

§ 330. Powers and duties of trustees

1. The trustees of an incorporated United Methodist church shall have the custody and control of all the temporalities and property belonging to the corporation and of the revenues from such property, and shall administer the same in accordance with the discipline, rules and usages of The United Methodist Church, and with the provisions of law relating thereto, for the support and maintenance of the corporation or providing the members thereof at a corporate meeting thereof shall so authorize, of some religious, charitable or benevolent object, conducted by such church, or connected with it, or with The United Methodist Church, and they shall not use such property for any other purpose or divert the same from such uses.

2. The trustees shall be responsible to the charge conference of the church in a manner not inconsistent with any directions of a corporate meeting, and shall annually make a written report to the charge conference which report shall include the items required by the discipline of The United Methodist Church.

3. The trustees shall not prevent or interfere with the pastor or other duly authorized ministers of The United Methodist Church in the use of said property for religious services or other proper meetings recognized by the law and usage of The United Methodist Church.

History: Add, L 1949, ch 660, amd, L 1969, ch 962, § 10, eff May 26, 1969.

§ 331. Control of trustees by corporate meetings

A corporate meeting of an incorporated United Methodist church, whose trustees are elective as such, may give directions, not inconsistent with law or with the discipline of The United Methodist Church, as to the manner in which any of the temporal affairs of the church shall be administered by the trustees thereof; and such directions shall be followed by the trustees.

History: Add, L 1949, ch 660, amd, L 1969, ch 962, § 10, eff May 26, 1969.

§ 332. Conveyance of property

The trustees of an incorporated United Methodist church may sell, mortgage, lease or convey church property by following the provisions of section twelve of article two of this chapter except that in no case shall trustees mortgage or encumber real estate on which a church or parsonage is located for the current expense of a charge, nor shall the principal of the proceeds of the sale of such property be so used.

History: Add, L 1949, ch 660, amd, L 1969, ch 962, § 10, eff May 26, 1969.

§ 333. Conveyance of property for church, school or missionary purposes

Any church or society of The United Methodist Church created by or existing under the laws of the state of New York, having its principal office or place of worship in the state of New York, or whose place of worship was within the state of New York, is hereby authorized and empowered by the concurrent vote of two-thirds of its qualified voters present and voting therefor, at a meeting regularly called for that purpose, and of two-thirds of all its trustees and by the written consent of the resident bishop and the district superintendent, to direct the transfer and conveyance of any of its property, real or personal, which it now has or may hereafter acquire, to any religious, charitable or missionary corporation connected with The United Methodist denomination and incorporated by or organized under any law of the state of New York, either solely, or among other purposes, to establish or maintain, or to assist in establishing or maintaining churches, schools or mission stations, or to erect or assist in the erection of such buildings as may be necessary for any such purposes, with or without the payment of any money or other consideration therefor; and upon such concurrent votes being given, the trustees shall execute such transfer or conveyance; and upon the same being made, the title to and the ownership and right of possession of the property so transferred and conveyed shall be vested in and conveyed to such grantee; provided, however, that nothing herein contained shall impair or affect in any way any existing claim or lien against any property so transferred or conveyed, or any action at law or legal proceeding; and such transfer shall be subject, in respect to the amount of property the said grantee may take and hold, to the restrictions and limitations of all laws then in force.

History: Add, L 1949, ch 660, amd, L 1969, ch 962, § 10, eff May 26, 1969.

§ 334. Bequests

Any bequest of real or personal property to an unincorporated United Methodist church may be taken and held by the incorporated annual conference which has jurisdiction over said church and administered for the benefit of said church.

History: Add, L 1949, ch 660, amd, L 1969, ch 962, § 10, eff May 26, 1969.

§ 335. Powers of certain existing corporations to conform charter to article

A corporation heretofore created in this state by special act or under general law for purposes for which a corporation may be created under this article and other applicable provisions of this chapter, may, by the procedure herein provided, amend its charter or certificate of incorporation to conform to the provisions of this article with the same corporate name and for the same corporate purposes and any additional purposes permitted by this article; but such amendment shall not affect then existing property rights or liabilities.

History: Add, L 1949, ch 660, eff July 1, 1949.

ARTICLE XVIII
CHURCHES OF THE BYELORUSSIAN AUTOCEPHALIC ORTHODOX CHURCH IN AMERICA

History: Add, L 1961, ch 757, eff Apr 22, 1961.

§ 336. Definitions

1. The "Byelorussian Autocephalic Orthodox Church in America," as that term is used anywhere in this article, refers to the churches, cathedrals, chapels, congregations, societies, parishes, committees and other religous organizations of the Eastern Orthodox Church which are subject to ecclesiastical and administrative jurisdiction and authority of the archbishop, or bishop, who is the ecclesiastical administrator of the American diocese of the Byelorussian Autocephalic Orthodox Church created pursuant to resolutions adopted at a diocesan convention (sobor) of said diocese held at Brooklyn, New York, on May twenty-eighth and twenty-ninth, nineteen hundred sixty and subject to the ecclesiastical jurisdiction of the metropolitan archbishop, or other primate, or the locum tenens acting in his place and the council of bishops of the Byelorussian Autocephalic Orthodox Church.

2. Every church, parish, congregation, society, or committee incorporated or reincorporated, pursuant to this article, shall in all respects conform to, maintain, and follow the faith, doctrine, ritual, commun-

ion, discipline, canon law, traditions and usages of the Eastern Orthodox Church as such are determined by the governing ecclesiastical body of the Byelorussian Autocephalic Orthodox Church, and shall recognize and be and remain subject to the jurisdiction and authority of the duly appointed archbishop, bishop or other administrator of the American Diocese of the Byelorussian Autocephalic Orthodox Church, hereinafter called Byelorussian Autocephalic Orthodox Church in America, or his successor in office, and shall accept, secure or receive the sacramental, pastoral, or ministerial services of such clergy only as are so certified to be of lawful and canonical status or authority in the Byelorussian Autocephalic Orthodox Church in America, and retain or secure as pastors only such clergy as have, in addition, the permission of the said archbishop, bishop, or administrator of the Byelorussian Autocephalic Orthodox Church in America.

History: Add, L 1961, ch 757, eff Apr 22, 1961.

§ 337. Application for incorporation

Any number of persons of full age, not less than ten, who are communicants in canonical standing within the Eastern Orthodox Church may associate themselves for the purpose of founding and continuing a congregation acknowledging, conforming to and promoting the faith, doctrine, discipline, rite, canons, traditions, usages and constitution of the Byelorussian Autocephalic Orthodox Church in America and apply to the archbishop or bishop, who is the ecclesiastical administrator of said church, for permission and sanction to incorporate such congregation. When such permission aforesaid has been obtained in writing over the signature and seal of such archbishop or bishop, such congregation may become an incorporated church by executing, acknowledging and filing a certificate of incorporation as hereinafter provided.

Any religious order, theological seminary for the preparation of candidates for ministry, or religious society established for evangelical efforts or the relief of the poor and needy, which is intended to be an auxiliary organization of the Byelorussian Autocephalic Orthodox Church in America, where a chapel for the conduct of worship is provided shall be deemed a congregation to all intents and purposes, and may be incorporated in the manner prescribed in this article.

History: Add, L 1961, ch 757, eff Apr 22, 1961.

§ 338. Notice of a meeting for incorporation

Notice of a meeting for the purpose of incorporating a congregation, to which this article is applicable, shall be given as follows:

1. The notice shall be in writing and shall state in substance that a meeting of the members of such congregation will be held at a stated place, date and hour for the purpose of incorporating such congregation, electing laymen trustees thereof and selecting a corporate name thereof.

2. The notice shall also state that the appropriate ecclesiastical authority has given sanction and permission, required under this article, for the incorporation.

3. The notice must be signed by at least six persons of full age who are then members in good and regular standing of such congregation by admission into full communion and membership therewith, in accordance with the rules and regulations thereof, and of the governing ecclesiastical body of the Byelorussian Autocephalic Orthodox Church and who have statedly worshipped with such congregation and have regularly contributed to its financial support, according to its usages, for at least one year or since it was formed.

4. Such notice shall be publicly read at two successive regular meetings for public worship or at special meetings of such congregation on the two Sundays immediately preceding the meeting for incorporation; and at least fifteen days before the meeting for incorporation, by the first named of the following persons who is present thereat, to wit: The minister in charge of such congregation, officiating minister thereof, or one of the persons qualified to sign such notice in the order of their age beginning with the oldest.

5. A copy of such notice shall be posted conspicuously on the outside of the main entrance to the usual place of worship, or at the place where the special meetings are to be held, at least fifteen days before the meeting for incorporation.

6. A copy of such notice shall be sent by mail postpaid at least ten days prior to the date set for the meeting for incorporation to each member in good and regular standing by admission into full communion and membership therewith, in accordance with the rules and regulations thereof, and of the Byelorussian Autocephalic Orthodox Church, at his last known address as same appears in the records of the congregation.

History: Add, L 1961, ch 757, eff Apr 22, 1961.

§ 339. The meeting for incorporation

1. At the meeting for incorporation, held in pursuance of such notice, the qualified voters, until otherwise decided as hereinafter provided, shall be all persons of full age, who are then members in good and regular standing of such congregation by admission into full communion and membership therewith, in accordance with the rules and regulations thereof, and of the governing ecclesiastical body of the Byelorussian Autocephalic Orthodox Church.

2. At such meeting, the presence of a majority of such qualified voters, at least six in number, shall be necessary to constitute a quorum and all matters or questions shall be decided by a majority of the qualified voters voting thereon.

3. The meeting shall be called to order by the first named of the following persons who is present thereat, to wit: The minister in charge of such congrega-

tion, or the officiating minister thereat, or one of the persons qualified to sign the notice of the meeting for incorporation in the order of their age beginning with the oldest.

4. There shall be elected at such meeting from the qualified voters there present, a presiding officer, a clerk to keep the record of the proceedings of the meeting and two inspectors of election to receive the ballots cast. The presiding officer and the inspector shall decide the result of the ballots cast on any matter and shall be the judges of the qualifications of the voters, subject to appeal to the vote of the members present whose qualifications as voters are not challenged.

5. If the meeting shall decide that such congregation shall become an incorporated church, the meeting shall also decide upon the name of the proposed corporation, the number of laymen trustees thereof, which shall be a multiple of three, and the date, not more than fifteen months thereafter, on which the first annual election of the laymen trustees thereof shall be held, and shall decide also whether those who, from the time of the formation of such congregation or during the year preceding the meeting for incorporation, have stately worshipped with such congregation and have regularly contributed to the financial support thereof, shall be qualified voters at such meeting for incorporation, and that those who during the year preceding the subsequent corporate meetings of the church shall have stately worshipped with such church and shall have regularly contributed to the financial support thereof, shall be qualified voters at such corporate meetings.

6. Such meetings shall thereupon elect by ballot from the persons qualified to vote thereat one-third of the number of trustees so decided on, who shall hold office until the first annual election of trustees thereafter, and one-third of such number of trustees who shall hold office until the second annual election for trustees thereafter, and one-third of such number of trustees who shall hold office until the third annual election thereafter, or until the respective successors of such trustees shall be elected.

7. Such meeting shall also elect by ballot a clerk of the corporation, who shall hold office until the close of the next annual meeting.

History: Add, L 1961, ch 757, eff Apr 22, 1961.

§ 340. Resolutions to be adopted at the meeting for incorporation

In order to incorporate under this article, the meeting shall adopt the following resolution by a majority of its qualified voters, present and voting, to wit:

Whereas, this congregation was founded and established, and thereby a permanent trust was created, for the purpose and intent of adhering to, maintaining and promoting religious worship and teaching according to the communion, doctrine, discipline, rite, canon law, traditions and usages of the Byelorussian Autocephalic Orthodox Church; and

Whereas, such purpose and intent and the trust thereby created can be fully effected and safeguarded only in complete canonical unity with jurisdictions and in obedience to bishops acknowledged and certified by the Byelorussian Autocephalic Orthodox Church in America; and

Whereas, the signors thereof are the trustees, duly elected as such at a meeting duly held on the ---- day of ----, nineteen hundred ----, in accordance with article eighteen of the religious corporations law; and

Whereas, by a majority vote the said meeting has determined to incorporate as a Church of the Byelorussian Autocephalic Orthodox Church in America under the name of (here give the corporate name by which such church is to be known); and

Whereas, permission and sanction for such incorporation has been given and certified in accordance with the provisions of said article by (here name the appropriate archbishop, bishop or administrator) to whose jurisdiction and authority this corporation shall adhere.

Therefore it is hereby resolved, that this congregation shall become and remain an incorporated church of the aforesaid jurisdiction in full unity of communion, faith and discipline with the Byelorussian Autocephalic Orthodox Church in America and that the clergymen trustees of this said church shall be the archbishop, or bishop, who is the administrator of the Byelorussian Autocephalic Orthodox Church in America and rector of this church, and their successors in office, shall by virtue of their offices, be the clergymen trustees of this church, which said two officers together, with the --- laymen trustees elected at this incorporation meeting, shall constitute the trustees thereof. Said clergymen trustees' term of office shall continue until their successors in said office are elected by the governing ecclesiastical body of the Byelorussian Autocephalic Orthodox Church, and said laymen trustees' term of office shall be that fixed by statute.

History: Add, L 1961, ch 757, eff Apr 22, 1961.

§ 341. Certificate of incorporation

1. If the meeting shall decide that such congregation shall become an incorporated church of the Byelorussian Autocephalic Orthodox Church in America, a certificate of incorporation therefor shall be executed and acknowledged by the archbishop, or bishop, who is administrator of the Byelorussian Autocephalic Orthodox Church in America, the rector of the congregation and by the laymen trustees that have been elected, and by the clerk of the corporation, and the said certificate of incorporation shall contain the following:

(a) The name by which the proposed corporation shall be known;

(b) The number of laymen trustees thereof; the names and addresses of the persons elected as trustees; and the term of office for which they were respectively elected;

(c) An exact copy of the resolution which provides for the clerical trustees by virtue of their offices;

(d) The name of county, town, city or village in which the principal place of worship or office is or is intended to be located;

(e) The purpose and intent for which said corporation is created, to be set forth as follows:

"The purpose and intent of this corporation is to maintain, propagate, practice and forever perpetuate religious worship, services, sacraments and teaching in full accordance and unity with the doctrine, ritual, canon law, faith, practice, discipline, and traditions and usages of the Holy Orthodox Church; and for carrying out of said purpose and intent, to form and maintain a religious organization of church adherent and obedient to the ecclesiastical jurisdiction and authority of the archbishop, or bishop, or administrator of the Byelorussian Autocephalic Orthodox Church in America and certified by the governing ecclesiastical body of the Byelorussian Autocephalic Orthodox Church, as canonical and duly appointed."

(f) In the certificate of incorporation of societies or organizations, other than churches, special purposes, additional to the above, may be set forth.

2. On filing such certificate in the office of the county clerk of the county in which such church is or is intended to be located, such church shall be a corporation by the name stated in the certificate, and the persons therein stated to be elected clerical and laymen trustees of such church shall be trustees therefor for their respective terms and until their successors are elected.

History: Add, L 1961, ch 757, eff Apr 22, 1961.

§ 342. Reincorporation of existing corporations

Any heretofore incorporated church, to which this article is applicable, may reincorporate under the provisions of this article by the same procedure hereinbefore set forth for incorporation substituting, at appropriate places, the word "reincorporate" for "incorporate" and filing the certificate of reincorporation in the office of the county clerk in the county in which its principal place of worship is located. Immediately upon the filing of such certificate all the right, title, equity and interest of such corporation in any estate, real or personal, together with all franchise and charter rights, shall be vested in the corporation so created under this article, and the original corporation shall be null and void.

History: Add, L 1961, ch 757, eff Apr 22, 1961.

§ 343. Time, place and notice of corporate meetings

1. The annual corporate meeting of every church incorporated under this article shall be held at the time and place fixed by its by-laws, or if no time and place be so fixed, then at a time and place to be first fixed by its trustees, but to be changed only by a by-law adopted at an annual meeting.

2. A special corporate meeting of any such church may be called by the board of trustees thereof, on its own motion, and shall be called on the written request of at least ten qualified voters of such church.

3. The trustees shall cause notice of the time and place of such annual corporate meeting, therein specifying the names of any trustees, whose successors are to be elected thereat and the business to be transacted thereat, and, if a special meeting, specifying business to be transacted thereat, to be publicly read at two successive regular meetings for public worship or at special meetings of such church on the two Sundays immediately preceding the annual or special corporate meeting, by the rector of such church or if there be none or he be necessarily absent, by the officiating minister thereof, if there be one, or if not, or if any such minister refuse to give such notice, by any officer of such church. If no public worship be held during said period, or if it be the notice of special corporate meeting, a copy of such notice shall be posted conspicuously on the outside of the main entrance to the usual or principal place of worship at least fifteen days before such meeting and a copy of such notice shall be sent by mail postpaid at least ten days prior to the date set for such meeting to each member of such church in good and regular standing by admission into full communion and membership therewith, in accordance with the rules and regulations thereof, and of the governing ecclesiastical body of the Byelorussian Autocephalic Orthodox Church, and who has been stated attendant at divine worship in such church and has regularly contributed to the financial support thereof during the year next preceding such meeting, at his last known address as same appears in the records of the church.

History: Add, L 1961, ch 757, eff Apr 22, 1961.

§ 344. Organization and conduct of corporate meetings; qualifications of voters

1. At a corporate meeting of an incorporated church to which this article is applicable, the following persons, and no others, shall be qualified voters, to wit: All persons who are then members in good and regular standing of such church by admission into full communion or membership therewith in accordance with the rules and regulations thereof, and of the governing ecclesiastical body of the Byelorussian Autocephalic Orthodox Church, and who have been stated attendants on divine worship in such church and have regularly contributed to the financial support thereof during the year next preceding such meeting.

2. The annual corporate meeting shall be governed with respect to its organization and election of laymen trustees and the clerk of the corporation by the same provisions as set forth in this article for the incorporation of said church, except if there be no rector or he be necessarily absent or if he refuses to call such meeting to order, the chairman of the board of trustees shall do so.

3. The same provisions shall apply to a special corporate meeting.

4. At the annual corporate meeting the trustees shall cause to be prepared and read thereat a budget giving the approximate amount of money needed for the maintenance of worship, the administration of the temporal affairs of the church and for the care of the property, and such other regular and special items as shall be brought to the attention of the meeting, which budget shall be discussed and decided upon, ratified or amended by the said meeting by majority vote, with ample provision made to raise such funds by whatever usages the church shall elect.

5. In the event that a quorum shall not be present at any annual corporate meeting and no election of the trustees and officers shall be accordingly had thereat, the board of trustees shall call a special meeting (which may be referred to as an adjourned annual corporate meeting) at a time and place to be fixed by it. Notice of such meeting shall be given in the same manner as provided for any special meeting. If such special meeting be not called by the board of trustees within two weeks following the date for such annual meeting, the rector is authorized to and shall call such special meeting and notice thereof shall be given in like manner. The election of officers and any other business required or scheduled to have been had or conducted at the annual corporate meeting may be had and conducted at such special meeting. In the event that a quorum shall not be present at such special meeting and no election of officers shall be accordingly had thereat, the rector, vicar or minister in charge of the church or congregation, with the approval of the bishop, not more than sixty days thereafter, is authorized to and shall appoint the laymen trustees, and other lay officers to the offices not filled by election at such annual corporate meeting or such special meeting, and they shall hold office as such until the next succeeding annual meeting. If such rector, vicar or minister shall fail to make such appointments, the bishop is authorized to and shall make such appointments, with like force and effect.

History: Add, L 1961, ch 757, eff Apr 22, 1961.

Sub 1, amd, L 1971, ch 201 § 12, eff Sept 1, 1971.

§ 345. Change of date of annual corporate meetings

An annual corporate meeting of an incorporated church to which this article is applicable may, by a majority vote of the duly qualified voters at such meeting, change the date of the annual meeting thereafter. If such date as so changed shall next thereafter occur less than six months after the annual meeting at which such change is made, the next annual meeting shall be held one year from such next recurring date. For the purpose of determining the terms of office of trustees, the period of time elapsing between the date of the annual meeting at which such change is made and the next annual meeting thereafter shall be reckoned as one year.

History: Add, L 1961, ch 757, eff Apr 22, 1961.

§ 346. Changing number of laymen trustees

An incorporated church to which this article is applicable may, at its annual corporate meeting where trustees are elected, by a majority vote of the duly qualified voters at such meeting, change the number of its trustees by adding more trustees, one-third of which shall be elected for three years, one-third for two years and one-third for one year; or by voting to discontinue the offices of certain specified trustees as they expire, one-third of said offices to be discontinued each year, until the number left is the number decided upon. No such changes shall affect the terms of the trustees then in office, but each shall hold office until his full term has expired unless his office shall terminate as provided for elsewhere in this article.

History: Add, L 1961, ch 757, eff Apr 22, 1961.

§ 347. The powers and duties of trustees

1. The trustees of an incorporated church to which this article is applicable shall have the custody and control of all the temporalities and property, real or personal, belonging to the corporation and of all the revenues therefrom and shall administer the same strictly in accordance with the discipline, rules, usages, laws and constitution of the Byelorussian Autocephalic Orthodox Church in America, and with the provisions of law relating thereto, for the support and maintenance of the church corporation or providing the members thereof at a corporate meeting thereof shall so authorize, of some religious, charitable, benevolent or educational object, conducted by such church, or connected with it, or the governing ecclesiastical body of the Byelorussian Autocephalic Orthodox Church in America, and they shall not use such property or revenue for any other purpose or divert the same from such uses.

2. By-laws or directions adopted at any corporate meeting of any such incorporated church shall control the subsequent action of its trustees, as to the temporalities and property or revenues therefrom, and as to the care thereof, and changes in either thereof and disposition thereof.

3. The trustees of any such church shall have no power, without the consent of a corporate meeting, to incur debts beyond what is necessary for the care of the property of the corporation.

4. The trustees shall not prevent or interfere with the rector or other duly authorized ministers in the use of said property for religious services or other proper meetings recognized by the law and usages of the Byelorussian Autocephalic Orthodox Church in America.

5. The trustees of an incorporated church to which this article is applicable, shall have no power to settle or remove or fix the salary of the minister. The trustees shall also have no power to fix or change the time, nature or order of the public or social worship of such church, except when such trustees are also the spiritual officers of such church.

6. The trustees of any such church shall be responsible to the diocesan council or the convention (sobor) of the diocese within bounds of which such church is situated in accordance with the discipline, rules, usages, laws and constitution of the Byelorussian Autocephalic Orthodox Church in America and shall make reports to said diocesan council or convention (sobor) which reports shall include all the items required.

History: Add, L 1961, ch 757, eff Apr 22, 1961.

§ 348. Meetings of trustees

1. Meetings of the trustees of an incorporated church to which this article is applicable may be held at stated intervals, or shall be called by the chairman of the board of trustees on his own motion, or upon request of one of the clergymen trustees or any two of the laymen trustees by giving at least twenty-four hours notice thereof personally or by mail to all trustees, but by the unanimous consent of the trustees a meeting may be held without previous notice thereof.

2. To duly constitute such regular or special meeting of the trustees for the transaction of business, at any meeting lawfully convened, there shall be present a majority of the laymen trustees, the archbishop, or bishop, who is administrator of the Byelorussian Autocephalic Orthodox Church in America, the rector of the church, unless there is no rector at that time, or he shall be necessarily absent, and the clerk of the corporation. If the archbishop, or bishop, cannot be present, he may send his proxy to one of the laymen trustees.

3. The chairman of the board of trustees shall preside or if he shall be necessarily absent, the rector shall preside at the meeting.

4. No act or procedure other than regular routine matters in regard to the administration of the temporal affairs of the church and for the care of the property of the corporation, as included in the budget items, shall be valid without the sanction of the archbishop, or bishop, who is administrator of the Byelorussian Autocephalic Orthodox Church in America.

5. The effect of a tie vote creating a deadlock shall be to carry the question involved (with all pending questions appertaining thereto) over to the next meeting of the board. In case of such a deadlock extending beyond three successive meetings of the board of trustees, the whole matter involved shall be settled in a meeting of the corporate society.

History: Add, L 1961, ch 757, eff Apr 22, 1961.

§ 349. Vacancies among layman trustees

If any layman trustee of an incorporated church to which this article is applicable declines to act, resigns or dies, or ceases to be a qualified voter at a corporate meeting thereof, or has his trusteeship terminated by any other means, his office shall be vacant; and such vacancy may be filled by the remaining trustees until the next annual corporate meeting of such church; at which meeting the vacancy shall be filled for the unexpired term.

History: Add, L 1961, ch 757, eff Apr 22, 1961.

§ 350. Pastoral relations

The election, calling, settlement, installation, dismissal, removal, translation, constituting or dissolving of the pastoral relation, or fixing or changing of the salary of a minister, or taking any action for or toward any such purpose, and the calling and conduct of a meeting of any such church for any such purpose, and the qualification of voters at any such meeting are not authorized or regulated or controlled by any provision of this chapter, but the same shall be in all respects, done, and regulated, and any meeting therefor called, conducted, and controlled, only in accordance with the laws, regulations, practice, discipline, books of government, rules and usages of the ecclesiastical governing body of the Byelorussian Autocephalic Orthodox Church, except that the salary of any such minister may be increased at any corporate meeting of any such church.

History: Add, L 1961, ch 757, eff Apr 22, 1961.

§ 351. Conveyance of property

Whenever it may become necessary or advisable to mortgage or dispose of any church property, the trustees may mortgage or sell and convey the same by first securing the authority of the society for such sale or mortgage and the approval of the archbishop, or bishop, who is administrator of the Byelorussian Autocephalic Orthodox Church in America, and obtaining leave of the supreme or county court therefor pursuant to the provisions of this chapter; provided that in all cases the proceeds of such sale or mortgage shall be used either for the payment of debts or for the purchase or improvement of property for the same uses and deeded to the same corporation; or if not so used, shall be held subject to the order of the diocesan council of the Byelorussian Autocephalic Orthodox Church in America which has ecclesiastical jurisdiction over such church.

History: Add, L 1961, ch 757, eff Apr 22, 1961.

§ 352. Property of extinct churches

The diocesan council of the Byelorussian Autocephalic Orthodox Church in America may decide that a church in connection with it or over which it has ecclesiastical jurisdiction, and to which this article is applicable, has become extinct, if it has failed for two consecutive years next prior thereto, to maintain religious services according to the discipline, customs and usages of the Byelorussian Autocephalic Orthodox Church, or has had less than ten resident attending members making annual or regular contributions towards its support, and may take possession of the temporalities and property belonging to such church or parish and manage the same; or may, in pursuance of the provisions of this chapter relating to the disposition of real property sell or dispose of the same and apply the proceeds thereof to any of the purposes to which the property of such diocesan council is devoted, and it shall not divert such property to any other object. For the purpose of obtaining a record title to the land and the church edifice, or other buildings thereon, by such diocesan council, the surviving trustee or trustees of said extinct church or if there be no surviving trustee, then a surviving member of said extinct church, may, without a consideration being paid therefor by such diocesan council, convey to it said land and church edifice, or other buildings thereon, subject, however, to an order of the supreme or county court based upon a petition reciting that said church has become extinct; the name of its surviving trustee or trustees; and the names of its members (who must have given their consent to the making of said conveyance). Upon the recital of said facts in said petition, the court shall have jurisdiction to grant an order allowing said conveyance to be made without a consideration; and should there be no surviving members, as well as no surviving trustee of said extinct church, said petition may be made by an officer of said diocesan council, in which event the court, upon the recital of said fact, shall have jurisdiction to appoint a suitable person as trustee for the purpose of making said conveyance.

History: Add, L 1961, ch 757, eff Apr 22, 1961.

ARTICLE 19
UNITARIAN AND UNIVERSALIST SOCIETIES

History: Add, L 1968, ch 763, eff June 16, 1968.

§ 400. Application of article

1. This article applies to religious societies which are members of the Unitarian Universalist Association at the time of incorporation under this article.

The term "society" includes churches and fellowships.

2. Incorporation under this article does not confer any ecclesiastical or denominational authority upon the Unitarian Universalist Association in respect to the societies so incorporated.

3. The general provisions of this chapter shall be applicable only in those circumstances where the provisions of this article do not apply.

History: Add, L 1968, ch 763, eff June 16, 1968.

§ 401. Incorporation of an unincorporated society

Any five members of an unincorporated religious society, who are of full age, may call a meeting for the purpose of incorporating such society under this article. The notice of such meeting shall be mailed at least fourteen days prior to the date of the meeting. The notice shall state in substance that a meeting of the unincorporated society will be held at a specified place, day and hour for the purpose of incorporating the society, electing trustees and selecting a corporate name.

History: Add, L 1968, ch 763, eff June 16, 1968.

§ 402. Meeting for incorporation of unincorporated society

At a meeting for incorporation held pursuant to section four hundred one, the qualified voters, until otherwise decided as hereafter provided, shall be all persons of full age who are members of the unincorporated society, according to its rules or usages, for at least one year prior to the meeting or since it was formed.

At such meeting the presence of a majority of such qualified voters, in person, at least six in number, shall be necessary to constitute a quorum, and all matters or questions shall be decided by a majority of the qualified voters voting thereon. The meeting shall be called to order by one of the signers of the call. There shall be elected at such meeting, from the qualified voters then present, a presiding officer, a clerk to keep the record of the proceedings of the meeting and two inspectors of election to receive the ballots cast. The presiding officer and the inspectors shall decide the result of the ballots cast on any matter, and shall be the judges of the qualifications of the voters.

If the meeting shall decide that such unincorporated society shall become incorporated, the meeting shall also decide upon the name of the proposed corporation, the number of the trustees thereof, which shall be not less than three and not more than twelve, and the date, not more than fifteen months thereafter, on which the first annual election of the trustees thereof shall be held.

Such meeting shall also adopt by-laws and then elect by ballot trustees in accordance with the provisions of such by-laws.

Thereafter, the officers of the corporation shall be elected in accordance with the by-laws.

History: Add, L 1968, ch 763, eff June 16, 1968.

§ 403. Certificate of incorporation

(a) If the meeting held pursuant to section four hundred two shall decide that the unincorporated society shall become incorporated, the presiding officer of such meeting and the two inspectors of election shall execute a certificate entitled "Certificate of Incorporation pursuant to article nineteen of the Religious Corporations Law." This certificate shall state:

(1) the name of the proposed corporation,

(2) a statement that it is a member of the Unitarian Universalist Association,

(3) the number of trustees thereof or that the number of trustees shall not be less than a stated minimum nor more than a stated maximum,

(4) the names and residences of the trustees until the first annual meeting,

(5) the terms of office for which the trustees were respectively elected,

(6) the county, town, city or village in which the principal place of worship or office is or is intended to be located.

(b) On the filing and recording of such certificate the persons qualified to vote at such meeting and those persons who shall thereafter from time to time be qualified voters at the corporate meetings thereof shall be a corporation by the name stated in such certificate and the persons therein stated to be elected trustees of such society shall be the trustees thereof for the terms for which they were respectively elected and until their respective successors shall be elected.

History: Add, L 1968, ch 763, eff June 16, 1968.

§ 404. Formation of a new society

Five or more persons of full age may form a corporation under this article by holding a meeting for incorporation in accordance with section four hundred two hereof, at which all of them shall be qualified voters. If the majority of those attending such meeting decide in favor of incorporation, a certificate of incorporation may be filed in accordance with section four hundred three hereof.

History: Add, L 1968, ch 763, eff June 16, 1968.

§ 405. Re-incorporation of existing corporation

Any previously incorporated society, to which this article is applicable, may re-incorporate it under the provisions of this article by the same procedure set forth for incorporation, substituting at appropriate places the word "re-incorporate" for "incorporate" and by filing the certificate of incorporation in the office of the county clerk in the county in which its principal place of worship or office is located. Notwithstanding the provisions of section four hundred two of this article, the requirements for a quorum for the general transaction of business as set forth in the by-laws of the existing corporation, shall determine the requirements for a quorum at a meeting for re-incorporation pursuant to this section, unless there shall be no such provision in the said by-laws, in which case the requirements for a quorum set forth in section four hundred two shall govern.

The re-incorporated corporation shall be deemed a continuation of the previously organized corporation, but thereafter it shall have only such rights and powers and be subject only to such obligations as any other corporation created under this article nineteen, provided, however, that all property rights and liabilities of the previously organized corporation shall be vested in and assumed by the re-incorporated corporation. The corporate by-laws and officers of the re-incorporated corporation shall be the same as those of its predecessor until changed pursuant to the said by-laws.

History: Add, L 1968, ch 763, amd, L 1972, ch 109, eff April 5, 1972.

§ 406. Time, place and notice of corporate meetings

(a) The annual corporate meeting of every society incorporated under this article shall be held at the time and place fixed by its by-laws, or if no time and place be so fixed, then at a time and place to be first fixed by its trustees, but to be changed only by a by-law adopted at an annual meeting.

A special corporate meeting of any such society may be called by the board of trustees thereof, on its own motion, and shall be called on the written request of at least ten qualified voters of such society and in such other manner as the by-laws may prescribe.

(b) The notices of any annual or special meeting shall state the time and place where it is to be held and shall be mailed to each member entitled to vote not less than ten nor more than fifty days before the meeting. Notices shall be mailed to each member at the address which appears on the books or records of the corporation. The by-laws may provide for additional methods of giving notice.

(c) Notice of any special meeting shall state the purpose or purposes for which the meeting is called and no business shall be transacted at such special meeting except that contained in such notice.

(d) Any provision in the statute or a by-law that a particular action can be taken only at a meeting "called for that purpose" shall be deemed to require notice of such purpose as provided in this section four hundred six. This does not preclude the transaction of other business at the same meeting if the notice so states.

History: Add, L 1968, ch 763, eff June 16, 1968.

§ 407. Qualifications of members and voters

(a) Each person admitted to membership pursuant to the by-laws shall be a member of the corporation until his membership shall terminate by death, resignation or as otherwise provided in the by-laws.

(b) Every member of the society shall be entitled to vote unless otherwise provided in the by-laws. Every voting member shall be entitled to one vote. Voting shall be in person only and not by proxy.

History: Add, L 1968, ch 763, eff June 16, 1968.

Religious Corporations Law

§ 408. Trustees

(a) The society shall be administered by its trustees. The trustees shall be responsible to the members.

(b) The by-laws shall provide for the term of office of the trustees and may provide for the division of the trustees into classes.

History: Add, L 1968, ch 763, eff June 16, 1968.

§ 409. Ministers

Any minister shall be called or removed and the salary fixed or changed by a vote of the majority of the members present and voting at a meeting of such corporation called for that purpose, unless the by-laws provide otherwise.

History: Add, L 1968, ch 763, eff June 16, 1968.

§ 410. By-laws

(a) The initial by-laws of a society shall be adopted at the meeting for incorporation. By-laws may thereafter be amended, repealed or adopted as provided in the by-laws. But in the absence of such provision, by-laws may be amended, repealed or adopted by a vote of two-thirds of the members present and voting at a meeting of the members called for that purpose.

(b) The substance of any proposed by-law change shall be stated in the notice to members of the meeting.

(c) The by-laws may contain any provision relating to the business of the society, the conduct of its affairs and the rights or powers of its members, trustees and officers, not inconsistent with this article or any other applicable statute, or the certificate of incorporation.

History: Add, L 1968, ch 763, eff June 16, 1968.

§ 411. Real estate

(a) A society shall not sell or mortgage any of its real property without applying for and obtaining leave of the court therefor pursuant to the provisions of article five of the not-for-profit corporation law.

(b) If a sale or mortgage of any real property of any such society has been heretofore or shall be hereafter made and a conveyance or mortgage executed and delivered without the authority of a court of competent jurisdiction, obtained as required by law, or not in accordance with its directions, the court may, thereafter, upon the application of the corporation, or of the grantee or mortgagee in any such conveyance or mortgage or of any person claiming through or under any such grantee or mortgagee upon such notice to such corporation, or its successor, and such other person or persons as may be interested in such property, as the court may prescribe, confirm said previously executed conveyance or mortgage, and order and direct the execution and delivery of a confirmatory deed or mortgage, or the recording of such confirmatory order in the office

where deeds and mortgages are recorded in the county in which the property is located; and upon compliance with the said order such original conveyance or mortgage shall be as valid and of the same force and effect as if it has been executed and delivered after due proceedings had in accordance with the statute and the direction of the court.

(c) The provisions of this section shall not apply to real property heretofore or hereafter acquired on a sale in an action or proceeding for the foreclosure of a mortgage owned by a society or held by a trustee for or in behalf of a society or to real property heretofore or hereafter acquired by a society or held by a trustee for or in behalf of a society by deed in lieu of the foreclosure of a mortgage owned, either in whole or in part, whether in certificate form or otherwise, by a society.

History: Add, L 1968, ch 763, eff June 16, 1968.

Par (a), amd, L 1971, ch 956, eff Sept 1, 1972.

§ 412. Merger and consolidation

A. (a) Two or more societies incorporated under this article may enter into an agreement for consolidation or merger. No such agreement shall be valid unless approved by a vote of two-thirds of the members of each constituent society present and voting at a meeting called for that purpose.

(b) Any such agreement of merger or consolidation shall contain all the terms and conditions under which the constituent societies are to be merged or consolidated.

(c) After approval of the agreement of merger or consolidation by the members of the constituent societies, a certificate of merger or consolidation, entitled "Certificate of Merger (or Consolidation) of --- and ---- into ---- (names of societies) under section four hundred twelve of the Religious Corporations Law" shall be signed and verified in behalf of each constituent society and shall be filed in the office of the county clerk in the county in which the certificate of incorporation of each constituent society was originally filed. Such certificate shall set forth:

(1) The agreement of merger or consolidation, and, in the case of consolidation, any statement required to be in a certificate of incorporation filed pursuant to section four hundred three of this article which is not contained in such agreement.

(2) The date and place of filing of the certificate of incorporation of each constituent society.

(3) A statement as to due compliance with the provisions of sub-section (a) of this section as to approval of the agreement by the members of the constituent societies.

(d) The merger or consolidation shall be effected upon the filing of the certificate described in subsection (c) above. When such merger or consolidation has been effected:

(1) Such surviving or consolidated corporation shall thereafter, in accordance with its certificate of incorporation as altered or established by the merger or consolidation, possess all the powers of each of the constituent societies.

(2) All the property of each of the constituent societies shall vest in such surviving or consolidated society without further act or deed.

(3) The surviving or consolidated society shall assume and be liable for all the obligations of each of the constituent societies. No obligation due or to become due, claim or demand for any cause existing against any such society shall be released or impaired by such merger or consolidation. Any action or proceeding then pending by or against any such constituent society may be enforced, prosecuted, settled or compromised as if such merger or consolidation had not occurred, or such surviving of consolidated society may be substituted in such action or special proceeding in place of any constituent society.

(4) In the case of a merger, the certificate of incorporation of the surviving society shall be automatically amended to the extent, if any, that changes in its certificate of incorporation are set forth in the plan of merger; and, in the case of a consolidation, the statements set forth in the certificate of consolidation and which are required or permitted to be set forth in a certificate of incorporation of a society under this article shall be its certificate of incorporation.

B. If a society, incorporated under this article, desires to consolidate with a religious corporation organized under any other article of this chapter, section thirteen of this chapter shall apply, provided, however, that the Unitarian Universalist Association shall be given notice of the petition to the supreme court made in this connection, and shall have the privilege of appearing in the proceedings, although its consent to the consolidation shall not be required.

History: Add, L 1968, ch 763, eff June 16, 1968.

§ 413. Dissolution

(a) Whenever two-thirds of the voting members of the society, present at a meeting called for that purpose, decide to dissolve the corporation, they may, by its duly elected officers or trustees or such agents as may be elected at such meeting, make a petition to the supreme court for an order of dissolution.

(b) Such petition shall state:

(1) The particular reasons or causes why dissolution is sought.

(2) The location, extent and estimated value of the property of the society.

(3) The particular object or purposes to which it is proposed to devote any surplus of the proceeds of such property, such purposes to be consistent with the general purposes of the Unitarian Universalist Association.

(4) The due compliance with the provisions of this section as to the authorization of the filing of the certificate of amendment.

(c) Copy of the petition shall be mailed to all members of the corporation and shall be published at least once in a newspaper of general circulation in the county where the society is located.

(d) A copy of the petition shall also be mailed, by registered mail, to the Unitarian Universalist Association. The dissolution shall not require the consent of the Unitarian Universalist Association, but the Unitarian Universalist Association shall have a right to be heard in the proceedings.

(e) Proof of the notices required by subdivisions (c) and (d) hereof shall be filed with the supreme court and no hearing on the petition shall be held by the supreme court until four weeks have elapsed after the giving of all such notices.

(f) Upon consideration of the petition presented to the court, and after any hearing which the court may in its discretion deem to be necessary or appropriate to determine any facts pertinent to the relief requested in the petition, the court may order the dissolution of the society, and for that purpose and upon such terms and conditions deemed appropriate order and direct a sale and conveyance of any and all property belonging to such society. After providing for the ascertaining and payment of the debts of the society and the necessary costs and expenses of such sale and proceedings for dissolution, the court may direct any surplus of the proceeds of such sale remaining after paying such debts, costs and expenses, to be devoted and applied to any such religious, benevolent, educational or charitable objects or purposes consistent with the general purposes of the Unitarian Universalist Association as the petitioners may suggest and the court may approve.

History: Add, L 1968, ch 763, eff June 16, 1968.

§ 414. Amendment

A society may amend its certificate of incorporation at any time, provided that such amendment contains only such provisions as might be properly contained in an original certificate of incorporation filed at the time of making such amendment. Any such amendment must be authorized by vote of two-thirds of the members of the society present and voting at a meeting called for that purpose. A certificate amending the certificate of incorporation shall be signed and verified by the president or chairman of the board of trustees, shall be filed in the same manner as an original certificate of incorporation and shall contain the following:

(1) The name of the society and, if it has been changed, the name under which it was originally incorporated.

(2) The date and place of filing of the original certificate of incorporation and any subsequent amendments thereto.

Religious Corporations Law

(3) Each amendment effected thereby.

(4) A statement as to due compliance with the provisions in this section as to the authorization of the filing of the certificate of amendment.

History: Add, L 1968, ch 763, eff June 16, 1968.

ARTICLE 20
ASSEMBLIES OF GOD CHURCHES

History: Add, L 1984, ch 154, § 1, eff June 28, 1984.

§ 420. Application

1. This article applies to any unincorporated church, church school, seminary or other organization affiliated with the New York district of the Assemblies of God or with the general council of the Assemblies of God with headquarters at Springfield, Missouri, and to any heretofore incorporated church or body, so affiliated, which desires to reincorporate pursuant to this article.

2. Nothing hereinafter provided shall prevent or prohibit any heretofore incorporated church or body, affiliated with the New York district of the Assemblies of God or with the general council of the Assemblies of God, from maintaining and continuing the relationship which such church or body enjoyed at the time of the effective date of this article should such church or body determine not to reincorporate pursuant to this article.

History: Add, L 1984, ch 154, § 1, eff June 28, 1984.

§ 421. Assemblies of God schools; seminaries and agencies of social relief

1. Any church school, biblical seminary for the preparation of candidates for the ministry leading to ordination and the granting of credentials of ecclesiastical degrees in theology, other than those authorized by the rules of the board of regents, or association established for evangelical efforts or for the relief of the poor and the socially needy, which is intended to be an auxiliary organization of the Assemblies of

God and where a chapel for the conduct of worship is provided, shall be deemed a church to all intents and purposes and be subject thereby to all the provisions of this article, except where otherwise indicated, and may be incorporated or reincorporated in the manner prescribed in this article as a church of the Assemblies of God.

2. Such church school, biblical seminary or association, shall be required to adopt a constitution and by-laws not inconsistent with the provisions of this article. The constitution and by-laws must be submitted to the New York district of the Assemblies of God for approval in writing, and become effective and binding only upon receipt of such approval. All future amendments to the constitution and by-laws shall not be inconsistent with the provisions of this article.

3. In any case where such church school, biblical seminary or association does not have within its organization the positions of a minister or officiating minister and where the provisions of any section of this article designate such person or persons to fulfill any function pertaining to incorporation or corporate affairs, there shall be substituted therefor the names of whatever persons or positions are designated in the organization's duly approved constitution and by-laws to fulfill functions of leadership.

History: Add, L 1984, ch 154, § 1, eff June 28, 1984.

§ 422. Approval for incorporation

Any unincorporated church wishing to incorporate as an Assemblies of God church under this article shall first apply to the presbytery of the New York district of the Assemblies of God for written approval. Upon receipt of such approval, the applying church may become an incorporated church by executing, acknowledging and filing a certificate of incorporation as hereinafter provided. There shall be attached to such certificate the written permission to incorporate by the New York district of the Assemblies of God, or their successor.

History: Add, L 1984, ch 154, § 1, eff June 28, 1984.

§ 423. Qualification of voters

1. The following persons and no others shall be qualified voters for all purposes under this article, except as set forth in subdivision two of this section. All persons sixteen years of age or over who are members in good and regular standing of the church or body by admission into membership therewith, in accordance with the standard for membership in the local church as determined by the local church itself, or with the standard set by agreement with the New York district of the Assemblies of God.

2. In the case of a church school, biblical seminary or association of the type set forth in subdivision one of section four hundred twenty-one of this article the by-laws and constitution of such body shall determine the qualifications of voters, providing such

constitution and by-laws have received the written approval of the New York district of the Assemblies of God, as provided in subdivision two of section four hundred twenty-one of this article.

History: Add, L 1984, ch 154, § 1, eff June 28, 1984.

§ 424. Notice of meeting for incorporation

Notice of a meeting for the purpose of incorporating an unincorporated church shall be given as follows:

1. The notice shall be in writing and shall state, in substance, that a meeting of such unincorporated church will be held at its usual place of worship at a specified day and hour for the purpose of incorporating such church and electing any multiple of three trustees thereof but not to exceed twenty-four.

2. The notice must by signed by at least six qualified voters. A copy of such notice shall be publicly read at each of the two consecutive Sunday mornings, or main worship services of such unincorporated church preceding the meeting to incorporate, by the first named of the following persons who is present thereat, to wit: the minister of such church, the officiating minister thereof, the members of the church in the order of their age beginning with the oldest, or any person qualified to sign such notice.

3. In the case where a church school, biblical seminary or association of the type set forth in subdivision one of section four hundred twenty-one of this article does not hold regular Sunday worship services, written notice of the time and place of the meeting for incorporation shall be delivered or read according to the manner prescribed by the duly approved constitution and by-laws of such body intending to incorporate.

History: Add, L 1984, ch 154, § 1, eff June 28, 1984.

§ 425. Meeting for incorporation

1. At the meeting for incorporation held in pursuance of such notice, only qualified voters shall be eligible to vote.

2. The presence of a majority of such qualified voters, at least six in number, shall be necessary to constitute a quorum of such meeting. The action of the meeting upon any matter or question shall be decided by a majority of the qualified voters thereon. The quorum shall not be less than six persons.

3. The first named of the following persons who is present at such meeting shall preside thereat, to wit: Any executive officer of the New York district of the Assemblies of God or delegated representative thereof, the minister of the church or the officiating minister thereof. The meeting shall be called to order by the presiding officer. There shall be elected to such meeting a clerk to keep the record of the proceedings of the meeting, and two inspectors of election to receive the ballots cast.

4. The presiding officer of the meeting shall be the judge of the qualifications of voters. The presiding officer and the inspectors of election shall decide the results of the ballots cast on any matter.

5. Such meeting shall decide whether such unincorporated church shall become incorporated. If such decision shall be in favor of incorporation, such meeting shall decide upon the name of the proposed corporation, the names of the first three trustees thereof, and shall determine the date, not more than fifteen months thereafter, on which the first annual election of the trustees thereof after such meeting shall be held. Such meeting shall elect from the persons qualified to vote at such meeting one trustee who shall hold office until the first annual election of trustees thereafter, a second trustee to hold office until the second annual election of trustees thereafter, and a third trustee to hold office until the third annual election of trustees thereafter. The trustees shall hold office until their successors are elected.

6. At the meeting for incorporation a constitution and by-laws may be adopted except it shall not conflict with: (a) the duly adopted constitution and by-laws of the general council of the Assemblies of God, (b) the duly adopted constitution and by-laws of the New York district of the Assemblies of God, and (c) the provisions of this article or this chapter.

History: Add, L 1984, ch 154, § 1, eff June 28, 1984.

§ 426. Certificate of incorporation

1. If at the meeting for incorporation it shall be decided that such unincorporated church shall become incorporated, the presiding officer of such meeting and the two inspectors of election shall execute and acknowledge a certificate of incorporation, in which shall be stated the name or title by which such body shall be known in the law; the purpose of its organization; the names and addresses of the trustees elected thereat and the terms of office for which they were respectively elected; the county, town or city in which its principal place of worship is or is intended to be located; and a statement that the corporation shall support the doctrine and be subject to the constitution and by-laws of and be in conformity with the principles of the general council of the Assemblies of God and the New York district of the Assemblies of God as from time to time established, made and declared by the lawful authority of said general council of the Assemblies of God and New York district of the Assemblies of God.

2. On filing such certificate in the office of the county clerk of the county in which such corporate body is or is intended to be located, such church shall be a corporation by the name stated in the certificate of incorporation; but such certificate shall not be filed, unless there is affixed thereto the written permission of the New York district of the Assemblies of God to incorporate, pursuant to section four hundred twenty-two of this article.

3. The certificate of incorporation shall further contain a provision that, in the event of dissolution of the corporation, all the remaining assets and property of the corporation shall, after necessary expenses thereof, be distributed to either the New York district of the Assemblies of God, or to the general council of the Assemblies of God, their successors and assigns, and that in the event said New York district of the Assemblies of God or general council of the Assemblies of God or if their successor is not in existence at the time of dissolution, then such assets are to be distributed to such other Assemblies of God organizations as shall qualify under section 501 (c) (3) of the Internal Revenue Code of 1954, as amended, to be used in such manner as in the judgment of a justice of the supreme court shall best accomplish the general purposes for which the corporation was formed.

History: Add, L 1984, ch 154, § 1, eff June 28, 1984.

§ 427. Reincorporation of present incorporated churches

Any church heretofore incorporated may, subject to restrictions and limitations of existing laws, reincorporate under the provisions of this article, by filing in the county clerk's office in the county in which its principal place of worship is located, a certificate, signed and acknowledged by the district superintendent of the New York district of the Assemblies of God, and signed and acknowledged by all the trustees of said church in office at the time of such reincorporation, setting forth that the said church by majority vote desires to reincorporate under the provision of this article, the corporate name by which such church shall be known, the county, town, city or village where its principal place of worship is or is intended to be located and the names and addresses of the trustees who are to hold office until the next annual meeting of said corporation. Such certificate shall not be filed unless endorsed thereon is the written consent of the New York district of the Assemblies of God.

History: Add, L 1984, ch 154, § 1, eff June 28, 1984.

§ 428. Time; place and notice of corporate meetings

1. The annual corporate meeting of every incorporated church or body to which this article is applicable shall be held at the time and place fixed by its by-laws.

2. Notice of the time and place of the annual corporate meeting containing therein the number of any trustees whose terms of office shall expire and whose successors are to be elected thereat, shall be posted and given by means of a public reading of such notice at all services on at least two consecutive Sundays preceding such meetings of the church or body, by the first named of the following persons who are present thereat, to wit: the minister of such church, the

officiating minister thereof, if there be one, or by any corporate officer of such church or body.

3. In the event of the absence of Sunday worship services, written notice of the time and place of the annual corporate meeting shall be given by the board of trustees, either personally or by mail, to each qualified voter not less than ten nor more than twenty days before such meeting.

4. A special corporate meeting of the church or body may be called by the minister of such church or body, the board of trustees, or on the written application of at least twenty percent of the qualified voters, but in no event by less than five qualified voters.

5. Written notice of the time and place of the special meeting, together with a statement of the business to be transacted thereat, shall be given by the board of trustees either by posting a public announcement at all services on at least two consecutive Sundays preceding such meeting or by mail, upon each qualified voter, not less than ten nor more than twenty days before the special meeting.

History: Add, L 1984, ch 154, § 1, eff June 28, 1984.

§ 429. Corporate meetings

1. Each church shall determine the requirements for a quorum in their by-laws.

2. The action of the meeting upon any matter or question shall be decided in a manner provided by the by-laws.

3. The first named of the following persons who are present at such meeting shall preside thereat: the minister of such church, a qualified voter designated by the minister, or voter elected thereto at the meeting. The presiding officer of the meeting shall receive the votes, be the judge of qualifications of voters and declare the result of the votes cast on any matter.

4. At each annual corporate meeting, successors to those trustees whose terms of office then expires, shall be elected from the qualified voters for a term of three years thereafter.

5. If at any meeting of the church the actions of the minister are to be voted upon because of disagreements with the congregation, or a change in his teachings from the doctrines of the Assemblies of God, or his conduct, the minister shall not chair such meeting. A district official is to be invited to chair such a meeting. The minister, being a member of said congregation, may speak at such meeting.

6. Only the members of the church at its annual meeting, or at a special meeting called for that purpose, have the power to call or remove its pastor.

History: Add, L 1984, ch 154, § 1, eff June 28, 1984.

§ 430. Ownership of property

1. The trustees of every such incorporated or reincorporated church shall have the custody and control of all the temporalities and property, real and

personal, belonging to the corporation and the revenues therefrom, and shall administer the same strictly in accordance with the by-laws of the corporation and the rules, regulations and usages of the New York district of the Assemblies of God.

2. The certificate of incorporation or reincorporation under this article shall contain the following provisions:

(a) That in the event that any church shall make a final decision to sever its affiliation with the general council of the Assemblies of God, the trustees shall be deemed to hold title and retain ownership of all corporate property, both real and personal, for the use and benefit of any members whose teaching and practice is in accord with the articles and tenets of faith set forth in the constitution of the general council of the Assemblies of God, as from time to time amended; or

(b) That in the event that any church shall make a final decision to sever its affiliation with the general council of the Assemblies of God, the trustees shall be deemed to hold title and retain ownership of all corporate property, both real and personal, for the use and benefit of the majority of its membership.

3. Any church incorporated or reincorporated under this article shall provide in its certificate of incorporation or reincorporation, that prior to any final decision by the church to sever its affiliation with the general council of the Assemblies of God, the pastor and/or the church council shall invite the officiary of the New York district of the Assemblies of God or its successor, to participate in a specially called business meeting for the express purpose of giving the district officiary the opportunity to present the case for continued general council affiliation.

4. In the event that members of a body incorporated or reincorporated under this article shall commence or advocate a doctrinal teaching or a religious or social activity which contravenes the accepted teaching and practices of the general council of the Assemblies of God, and should serious and apparently irreconcilable differences within the local body result therefrom, and if the local corporate body is unable to resolve the dispute, and there is need to determine which faction of such dispute is in accord with the provisions of the constitution of the general council, either side of the dispute may appeal in writing to the superintendent of the New York district of the Assemblies of God, or its successor. Upon receipt of such appeal, or by invitation of the pastor and/or the church council, in accordance with the general council constitution and by-laws provisions, the district superintendent shall form a board of arbiters consisting of five in number and serve as chairman of such board. The board of arbiters shall consist of one representative chosen by each side of the dispute and two representatives of the presbytery. A fifth member shall be a neutral pastor appointed by the district superintendent and approved by the other four members of the board of arbiters.

The chairman is not to have a vote on the board of arbiters. The first duty of the board shall be to effect a reconciliation of the dispute. If such reconciliation cannot be effected, the board shall proceed to make a determination concerning the appeal, and issue a written resolution thereon. Such resolution shall be by majority vote of the board. The decision of the board of arbiters shall be final subject only to the right of appeal afforded by the general council by-laws right of appeal. Enforcement and fulfillment of such decisions shall rest with the district presbyters.

5. The trustees of the church shall not purchase, sell, mortgage, or lease for a term exceeding five years any of its real property without the approval of a majority of its members present and voting at a duly called business meeting.

History: Add, L 1984, ch 154, § 1, eff June 28, 1984.

§ 431. Property of extinct Assemblies of God churches

1. All property, both real and personal, belonging to or held in trust for any Assemblies of God church, incorporated or reincorporated or supervisory under this article, that has or shall become extinct, shall at the option of the New York district of the Assemblies of God, vest in and become the property of the New York district of the Assemblies of God and its successors and assigns; provided that this section shall not affect the reversionary interests of any person or corporation in such property or any valid lien thereon.

2. An Assemblies of God church, incorporated or reincorporated under this article, which fails to hold regular worship services, such services being distinguished from committee or business meetings, for a period of six months, may be declared by the New York district of the Assemblies of God to be dissolved and extinct, said New York district of the Assemblies of God being the immediate supervisory body over the local church within this state.

3. Whenever the New York district of the Assemblies of God dissolves or declares extinct a particular church under this section; upon petition by the New York district of the Assemblies of God to the supreme or county court and upon satisfactory proof of the facts leading to such dissolution, the court shall have jurisdiction to grant an order to the effect that all property of whatever kind which may have belonged to or have been held by said church shall vest in the New York district of the Assemblies of God in as full and ample a manner as the same shall theretofore have been vested in the church so declared to be dissolved and extinct. There shall be recorded in the office of the clerk of the county in which the church is located, a certified copy of the resolution of the New York district of the Assemblies of God declaring such church extinct and the court order transferring the title of the church property; and the recording of such a resolution and court order shall be proof of the

vesting of title of the real property of such church in the New York district of the Assemblies of God.

History: Add, L 1984, ch 154, § 1, eff June 28, 1984.

§ 432. Church council and church management

Any incorporated church or body to which this article applies shall have its affairs managed by a church council. Such council shall consist of the pastor, the trustees of the corporation as well as any others, such as corporate secretary and treasurer, who may be designated as church council members by the by-laws. If the local church or body has a pastor, he shall be president of the corporation and be a member of such council and serve as presiding officer of its meetings. In the absence of a pastor, the by-laws shall provide for the manner of selecting a presiding officer. The by-laws shall further set forth the time and manner of notice for such meetings.

History: Add, L 1984, ch 154, § 1, eff June 28, 1984.

§ 433. Right of self government

Each church shall have the right of self government under Jesus Christ, its living head, and shall have the power to choose, call or dismiss its minister, establish the minister's salary, elect its trustees and other officials, and transact all other business pertaining to its life as a local unit.

History: Add, L 1984, ch 154, § 1, eff June 28, 1984.

§ 434. Right of affiliation; relationships between churches, district corporations and the general council of the Assemblies of God

Churches shall be deemed to be sovereign, autonomous, self governing and self determining bodies. The affiliation of each church with the general council of the Assemblies of God and the New York district of the Assemblies of God shall be in matters of doctrine and conduct. In the event determination of disaffiliation with the general council of the Assemblies of God is under consideration by an affiliated assembly, the pastor and/or the church council shall invite the district officiary to participate in a special called church meeting for the express matter of giving the district officiary the opportunity to present the case for continued general council affiliation. Final disposition of the matter may then proceed in accordance with the by-laws of the local church not inconsistent with this article.

History: Add, L 1984, ch 154, § 1, eff June 28, 1984.

§ 435. District corporation

1. The present corporation acting within the territorial limits of New York, the New York district of the Assemblies of God, may reorganize by the formation of a new corporation which may have as many trustees as there are regional sections within the state, plus district officers, and others so designated by its constitution and by-laws.

2. Said corporation shall have jurisdiction over all churches to which this article applies, in conformity with the principles of voluntary cooperative fellowship as set forth in the constitution of the general council of the Assemblies of God. It shall also have the right to hold real property for district purposes, including district offices, Bible conference grounds, camps and educational institutions, homes, missions, as well as properties for local unincorporated missions or churches.

3. The said district corporation shall be vested with title to all property within the state now held in the name of the New York district of the Assemblies of God. The said corporation may convey any property without a court order, notwithstanding the provisions of section twelve of this chapter or article five of the not-for-profit corporation law, to a local church under all of the following conditions:

(a) Title was acquired by the district on behalf of the local church before the local church was incorporated.

(b) The local church has been in possession and has had the use of the premises.

(c) Premises had been acquired for and on behalf of the local church, the district corporation holding title merely in the nature of a trust.

(d) The right of creditors will not be affected by such transfer.

History: Add, L 1984, ch 154, § 1, eff June 28, 1984.

§ 436. District government

1. (a) There shall be a district council for the election of trustees, officers and for the general government as hereinafter set forth. The district council shall be the parent body and shall control the rights, duties and prerogatives of all its officers and subdivisions, in conformity with the constitution and by-laws of the district, and the constitution and by-laws of the general council of the Assemblies of God, with headquarters in Springfield, Missouri.

(b) The district council in session shall consist of all ordained and licensed ministers of the district, other individual members as may be provided for by the constitution and by-laws of the district corporation and such delegates as may be elected by assemblies to represent them and who are present in the meetings of the district council. Delegates shall be elected upon a basis of representation as may be agreed upon by the district council, and as fixed by the by-laws of the said district.

2. The district corporation shall designate territorial limits of the regional sections within this state. Each section is entitled to one trustee on the board of trustees of the district corporation.

3. The government of the district between district council sessions shall be vested in a board designated district presbytery. The district presbytery shall consist of the district superintendent, district assistant superintendent, the district secretary and the treasurer, the last two offices may be combined, the general presbyters and the presbyters of the district sections, and others as may be provided for by the constitution and by-laws of the district corporation.

4. The above named officers and presbyters shall constitute the board of trustees of the corporation.

5. All officers shall be elected by the district council according to the constitution and by-laws of the New York district of the Assemblies of God or its successor corporation. In the event that a trustee moves outside the territorial limits of the section from which he was first elected, resigns or is removed, his office shall be declared vacant and the remaining trustees of the district shall according to the rules and regulations of the constitution and by-laws of the New York district of the Assemblies of God or its successor corporation, elect a trustee to fill such unexpired term.

6. In addition to said trustees, said corporation shall have the following officers: president, vice president, secretary, treasurer, the last two officers may be combined, and such other officers as may be provided for by the constitution and by-laws.

7. The prerogatives and limitations placed upon the district board of trustees, shall be according to the authorization granted in the district council constitution and by-laws. In the interim between district council sessions, the district trustees acting as the presbytery shall be empowered to conduct the business of the district council according to the constitution and by-laws. The presbytery shall give a report and be accountable to the district council in its regular session or special session.

History: Add, L 1984, ch 154, § 1, eff June 28, 1984.

§ 437. District superintendent

The district superintendent shall by virtue of his office be designated the president and presiding officer of the district corporation. He shall exercise such powers as are granted him by the constitution and by-laws.

History: Add, L 1984, ch 154, § 1, eff June 28, 1984.

ARTICLE 21
COPTIC ORTHODOX CHURCHES

§ 455. Disposition of property

History: Add, L 1990, ch 912, § 1, eff Aug 29, 1990.

§ 450. Application

1. This article applies to any unincorporated church, church school, seminary or other organization affiliated with the Coptic Orthodox Church and to any heretofore incorporated church or body, so affiliated, which desires to reincorporate pursuant to this article.

2. Nothing hereinafter provided shall prevent or prohibit any heretofore incorporated church or body, affiliated with the Coptic Orthodox Church from maintaining and continuing the relationship with such church or body enjoyed at the time of the effective date of this article should such church or body determine not to reincorporate pursuant to this article.

History: Add, L 1990, ch 912, § 1, eff Aug 29, 1990.

§ 451. Definitions

As used in this article, the following terms shall have the following meanings:

1. "Coptic Orthodox Church" refers to the Apostolic Church presided over by His Holiness, the Pope of Alexandria (Egypt) and the Patriarch of the See of St. Mark, the legislative body of which is known as the Holy Synod. The Coptic Orthodox Church is a hierarchical church.

2. "Holy Synod" is the highest legislative and executive authority in the Coptic Orthodox Church, presided over by His Holiness, the Pope of Alexandria and the Patriarch of the See of St. Mark and is more formally known as "The Holy Synod for the Coptic Orthodox Church of Alexandria and the See of St. Mark."

3. "The Synodical Committee for the Coptic Churches in Immigration" is, according to the constitution and bylaws of the Holy Synod, formed and presided over by His Holiness, the Pope of Alexandria and the Patriarch of the See of St. Mark from among the members of the Holy Synod, to assist him in marshalling the affairs of the churches abroad.

4. "Unincorporated Coptic Orthodox Church" in this state and a "Coptic Orthodox Church" heretofore incorporated in this state refers to a church, cathedral, chapel or other religious organization founded and established for the purpose of and with the intent of adhering to, and being subject to the administrative jurisdiction of the Synodical Committee for the Coptic Churches in Immigration.

5. A "Bishop of the Coptic Orthodox Diocese" refers to that person who is serving as such bishop pursuant to the authority of and in accordance with the rules and regulations of Synodical Committee for the Coptic Churches in Immigration. In accordance with the laws of the Holy Synod, the Pope of Alexandria (Egypt) is the presiding bishop of any new diocese during the foundation period and until a bishop is ordained for such diocese. Likewise, and pursuant to such laws, the

Pope of Alexandria (Egypt) is the presiding bishop of any existing diocese which has no bishop.

History: Add, L 1990, ch 912, § 1, eff Aug 29, 1990; amd, L 1992, ch 624, § 1, eff July 24, 1992, deemed eff Aug 29, 1990.

§ 452. Incorporation of Coptic Orthodox Churches

An unincorporated Coptic Orthodox Church in this state may become incorporated as a church by executing, acknowledging and filing a certificate of incorporation, stating the corporate name by which such church shall be known and the county, town, city or village where its principal place of worship is, or is intended to be located. A certificate of incorporation of an unincorporated Coptic Orthodox Church shall be executed and acknowledged by the bishop of the Coptic Orthodox Diocese in which its place of worship is located and by two or more persons who shall be appointed by the bishop from among the priests and deacons of such church. Upon filing such certificate such church shall be a corporation by the name stated in the certificate.

History: Add, L 1990, ch 912, § 1, eff Aug 29, 1990.

§ 453. Reincorporation of existing corporations

Any Coptic Orthodox Church heretofore incorporated in this state, with the consent of the bishop of the Coptic Orthodox Diocese in which its place of worship is located, may reincorporate under the provisions of this article by filing in the office of the county clerk in the county in which its principal place of worship is located, a certificate, signed by the trustees in office at the time of such reincorporation whereby the majority of them setting forth that they desire to reincorporate under the provisions of this article, the corporate name by which such a church shall be known, the county, town, city or village where its principal place of worship is located and the names of the bishop and two or more persons appointed by the bishop from among the priests and deacons of such church, who shall constitute the initial board of trustees of said church. Immediately upon the filing of such certificate all the right, title, equity and interest of such a church in any estate, real or personal, together with all franchise and charter rights, shall be vested in the body corporate so created under this article and the original incorporation of such a church be null and void.

History: Add, L 1990, ch 912, § 1, eff Aug 29, 1990.

§ 454. Government of Incorporated Coptic Orthodox Churches

The bishop of the Coptic Orthodox Diocese in which the place of worship of an incorporated Coptic Orthodox Church is located and his successors in office shall, by virtue of his office, be a trustee of such a church. Two or more persons selected by the bishop from among the priests and deacons of such a church

in the manner provided from time to time by rules and regulations of the Coptic Orthodox Church adopted by the Synodical Committee for the Coptic Churches in Immigration shall also be trustees of such incorporated church, and the bishop and other such persons shall together constitute the board of trustees thereof. The bishop and other persons signing the certificate of incorporation shall be the trustees of such a church for the first year or until their successors are selected according to the rules, statutes, regulations and usages of the Coptic Orthodox Church adopted by the Synodical Committee for the Coptic Churches in Immigration. The trustees of every Coptic Orthodox Church shall have the custody and control of all temporalities and property, real and personal, belonging to such a church and of the revenues therefrom and shall administer the same in accordance with the rules, statutes, regulations and usages of the Coptic Orthodox Church of Alexandria adopted by Synodical Committee for the Coptic Churches in Immigration, provided, however, that no act or proceeding of the trustees of any such incorporated church shall be valid without the approval of the bishop of said diocese in which the place of worship of such a church is located, or in case of his absence or inability to act, without the approval of the vicar of such diocese.

History: Add, L 1990, ch 912, § 1, eff Aug 29, 1990.

§ 455. Disposition of property

Whenever a Coptic Orthodox parish shall hereafter be duly divided by the Coptic Orthodox bishop of the diocese in which said parish is located into two parishes within such diocese, then the Coptic Orthodox bishop or his successor shall have the right and power, of himself independently of any action or consent on the part of the trustees of the original Coptic Orthodox Church corporation to transfer assets, with or without valuable consideration, from the original Coptic Orthodox corporation to the new or second Coptic Orthodox Church corporation. Said transfer shall be made by said bishop or his successor after having complied with the requirements of this chapter in the same manner as the trustees of any religious corporation are compelled to do before making a transfer of church property.

History: Add, L 1990, ch 912, § 1, eff Aug 29, 1990.

ARTICLE 22
ORGANIZATIONS OF THE HINDU FAITH

§ 460. Application

1. This article applies to any unincorporated church affiliated with the Hindu faith, and to any heretofore incorporated church or body, so affiliated, which desires to reincorporate pursuant to this article. Independent churches may incorporate or reincorporate under this article in the manner provided in sections four hundred sixty-one and four hundred sixty-seven of this article, and all the provisions of this article shall apply to such churches as the context requires.

2. Nothing hereinafter provided shall prevent or prohibit any heretofore incorporated church or body, affiliated with the Hindu faith from maintaining and continuing the relationship which such church or body enjoyed at the time of the effective date of this article should such church or body determine not to reincorporate pursuant to this article.

History: L 2015, ch 468, § 2, eff Nov 20, 2015.

§ 461. Application for incorporation

Any unincorporated church or any heretofore incorporated church wishing to incorporate under this article shall execute, acknowledge and file a certificate of incorporation as hereinafter provided.

History: L 2015, ch 468, § 2, eff Nov 20, 2015.

§ 462. Qualification of voters

The following parties and no others shall be qualified voters for all purposes under this article: all persons eighteen years of age or over who are members in good and regular standing of the church or body by admission into membership therewith, in accordance with the standards for membership in the local church as determined by the local church itself.

History: L 2015, ch 468, § 2, eff Nov 20, 2015.

§ 463. Notice of meeting for incorporation

Notice of a meeting for the purpose of incorporating an unincorporated church shall be given as follows:

1. The notice shall be in writing and shall state, in substance, that a meeting of such unincorporated church will be held at its usual place of worship at a specified day and hour for the purpose of incorporating such church and electing three or more trustees, but not to exceed fifteen.

2. The notice must be signed by at least six qualified voters. A copy of such notice shall be publicly read at each of the two consecutive main worship services, of such unincorporated church preceding the meeting to incorporate, by the minister of such church, or if none, by the church member who has been designated by the membership or other authorized body of the church to conduct the worship service that day (the "officiating minister"); and at least fifteen days before the meeting for incorporation, a copy of such notice shall be posted at the place of worship.

History: L 2015, ch 468, § 2, eff Nov 20, 2015.

§ 464. Meeting for incorporation

1. At the meeting for incorporation held in pursuance of such notice, only qualified voters shall be eligible to vote.

2. The presence of one-third of the qualified voters or six qualified voters, whichever number is higher, shall be necessary to constitute a quorum of such meeting. The action of the meeting upon any matter or question shall be decided by a majority of the qualified voters present.

3. The minister of the church, or if none, the officiating minister, shall act as presiding officer of the meeting to incorporate. The presiding officer shall call the meeting to order and shall be the judge of the qualification of voters.

4. Such meeting shall decide by ballot whether the church shall be incorporated, the name of the proposed corporation, the names of the initial trustees, and the date, not more than fifteen months thereafter, on which the first annual election or affirmation of the trustees thereof after such meeting shall be held. The trustees shall hold office until their successors are elected or affirmed.

5. At the meeting for incorporation, a constitution and by-laws shall be adopted setting forth a form of church governance that is consistent with section four hundred sixty-five of this article.

History: L 2015, ch 468, § 2, eff Nov 20, 2015.

§ 465. Church governance

1. A church incorporated under this section shall provide in its certificate of incorporation or by-laws for trustees to be elected or appointed at large, or by virtue of their office. There shall be a minimum of three trustees. To the extent practicable, terms of office shall be for three years and staggered. Terms may be consecutive.

2. Provision shall also be made in its certificate of incorporation or by-laws for officers of the corporation to be elected or appointed at large or by virtue of their office. The president and secretary shall not be the same person. To the extent practicable, terms of office shall be for three years and staggered. Terms may be consecutive.

3. Provision shall also be made in its certificate of incorporation or by-laws for spiritual oversight of the church by an eldership board or a senior pandit, swami, guru or some combination of the above. Terms of office may be definite or indefinite as the by-laws may specify.

4. Provision shall also be made in its certificate of incorporation or by-laws for periodic affirmation of appointive positions by a designated body or board.

History: L 2015, ch 468, § 2, eff Nov 20, 2015.

§ 466. Certificate of incorporation

1. If at the meeting for incorporation it shall be decided that such unincorporated church shall become

incorporated, the presiding officer of the meeting and two others shall execute and acknowledge a certificate of incorporation, in which shall be stated the name or title by which such body shall be known in the law; the purpose of its organization; the names and addresses of the initial trustees, the county, town or city in which its principal place of worship is or is intended to be located; and a statement that the church is in affiliation with the Hindu faith.

2. On filing such certificate in the office of the county clerk of the county in which the principal office or place of worship of the corporation is or is intended to be located, such church shall be a corporation by the name stated in the certificate of incorporation.

History: L 2015, ch 468, § 2, eff Nov 20, 2015.

§ 467. Reincorporation of present incorporated churches

1. Any church heretofore incorporated may, subject to restrictions and limitations of existing laws, reincorporate under the provisions of this article, by filing in the county clerk's office in the county in which its principal place of worship is located, a certificate, signed and acknowledged by all the trustees of said church in office at the time of such reincorporation, setting forth that the said church by a majority vote of the members present at a duly called meeting of the membership, as determined by the by-laws of the existing corporation, desires to reincorporate under the provisions of this article. Such certificate shall set forth those items specified in section four hundred sixty-six of this article.

2. The reincorporated corporation shall be deemed a continuation of the previously organized corporation, but thereafter it shall have only such rights and powers and be subject only to such obligations as any corporation created under this article, provided, however, that all property rights and liabilities of the previously organized corporation shall be vested in and assumed by the reincorporated corporation. The corporate by-laws and officers of the reincorporated corporation shall be the same as those of its predecessor until changed pursuant to the said by-laws, provided they conform to the provisions of section four hundred sixty-five of this article.

History: L 2015, ch 468, § 2, eff Nov 20, 2015.

§ 468. Time, place and notice of corporate meetings

1. The by-laws shall make provisions for an annual corporate meeting and for giving appropriate notice to each voting member of the date and place of each such meeting.

2. Notices of any special meeting shall state the purpose or purposes for which the meeting is called and no business shall be transacted at such special meeting except that contained in such notice.

History: L 2015, ch 468, § 2, eff Nov 20, 2015.

§ 469. Corporate meetings

1. Each church shall determine the requirements for a quorum in their by-laws that shall not exceed fifty percent of the members.

2. The action of the meeting upon any matter or question shall be decided in a manner provided by the by-laws.

3. The presiding officer of any meeting shall be the senior pandit, swami or guru of the church or if none, as shall be set forth in the by-laws of the church.

History: L 2015, ch 468, § 2, eff Nov 20, 2015.

ARTICLE 23
ORGANIZATIONS OF THE SIKH FAITH

§ 470. Application

1. This article applies to any unincorporated church affiliated with the Sikh faith, and to any heretofore incorporated church or body, so affiliated, which desires to reincorporate pursuant to this article. Independent churches may incorporate or reincorporate under this article in the manner provided in sections four hundred seventy-one and four hundred seventy-seven of this article, and all the provisions of this article shall apply to such churches as the context requires.

2. Nothing hereinafter provided shall prevent or prohibit any heretofore incorporated church or body, affiliated with the Sikh faith from maintaining and continuing the relationship which such church or body enjoyed at the time of the effective date of this article should such church or body determine not to reincorporate pursuant to this article.

History: L 2015, ch 468, § 3, eff Nov 20, 2015.

§ 471. Application for incorporation

Any unincorporated church or any heretofore incorporated church wishing to incorporate under this article shall execute, acknowledge and file a certificate of incorporation as hereinafter provided.

History: L 2015, ch 468, § 3, eff Nov 20, 2015.

§ 472. Qualification of voters

The following parties and no others shall be qualified voters for all purposes under this article: all persons eighteen years of age or over who are members in good and regular standing of the church or body by admission into membership therewith, in accordance with the standards for membership in the local church as determined by the local church itself.

History: L 2015, ch 468, § 3, eff Nov 20, 2015.

§ 473. Notice of meeting for incorporation

Notice of a meeting for the purpose of incorporating an unincorporated church shall be given as follows:

1. The notice shall be in writing and shall state, in substance, that a meeting of such unincorporated church will be held at its usual place of worship at a specified day and hour for the purpose of incorporating such church and electing three or more trustees, but not to exceed fifteen.

2. The notice must be signed by at least six qualified voters. A copy of such notice shall be publicly read at each of the two consecutive main worship services, of such unincorporated church preceding the meeting to incorporate, by the minister of such church, or if none, by the church member who has been designated by the membership or other authorized body of the church to conduct the worship service that day (the "officiating minister"); and at least fifteen days before the meeting for incorporation, a copy of such notice shall be posted at the place of worship.

History: L 2015, ch 468, § 3, eff Nov 20, 2015.

§ 474. Meeting for incorporation

1. At the meeting for incorporation held in pursuance of such notice, only qualified voters shall be eligible to vote.

2. The presence of one-third of the qualified voters or six qualified voters, whichever number is higher, shall be necessary to constitute a quorum of such meeting. The action of the meeting upon any matter or question shall be decided by a majority of the qualified voters present.

3. The minister of the church, or if none, the officiating minister, shall act as presiding officer of the meeting to incorporate. The presiding officer shall call the meeting to order and shall be the judge of the qualification of voters.

4. Such meeting shall decide by ballot whether the church shall be incorporated, the name of the proposed corporation, the names of the initial trustees, and the date, not more than fifteen months thereafter, on which the first annual election or affirmation of the trustees thereof after such meeting shall be held. The trustees shall hold office until their successors are elected or affirmed.

5. At the meeting for incorporation, a constitution and by-laws shall be adopted setting forth a form of church governance that is consistent with section four hundred seventy-five of this article.

History: L 2015, ch 468, § 3, eff Nov 20, 2015.

§ 475. Church governance

1. A church incorporated under this section shall provide in its certificate of incorporation or by-laws for trustees to be elected or appointed at large, or by virtue of their office. There shall be a minimum of three trustees. To the extent practicable, terms of office shall be for three years and staggered. Terms may be consecutive.

2. Provision shall also be made in its certificate of incorporation or by-laws for officers of the corporation to be elected or appointed at large or by virtue of their office. The president and secretary shall not be the same person. To the extent practicable, terms of office shall be for three years and staggered. Terms may be consecutive.

3. Provision shall also be made in its certificate of incorporation or by-laws for spiritual oversight of the church by an eldership board or a senior granthi or guru or some combination of the above. Terms of office may be definite or indefinite as the by-laws may specify.

4. Provision shall also be made in its certificate of incorporation or by-laws for periodic affirmation of appointive positions by a designated body or board.

History: L 2015, ch 468, § 3, eff Nov 20, 2015.

§ 476. Certificate of incorporation

1. If at the meeting for incorporation it shall be decided that such unincorporated church shall become incorporated, the presiding officer of the meeting and two others shall execute and acknowledge a certificate of incorporation, in which shall be stated the name or title by which such body shall be known in the law; the purpose of its organization; the names and addresses of the initial trustees, the county, town or city in which its principal place of worship is or is intended to be located; and a statement that the church is in affiliation with the Sikh faith.

2. On filing such certificate in the office of the county clerk of the county in which the principal office or place of worship of the corporation is or is intended to be located, such church shall be a corporation by the name stated in the certificate of incorporation.

History: L 2015, ch 468, § 3, eff Nov 20, 2015.

§ 477. Reincorporation of present incorporated churches

1. Any church heretofore incorporated may, subject to restrictions and limitations of existing laws, reincorporate under the provisions of this article, by filing in the county clerk's office in the county in which its principal place of worship is located, a certificate, signed and acknowledged by all the trustees of said church in office at the time of such reincorporation, setting forth that the said church by a majority vote of the members present at a duly called meeting of the membership, as determined by the by-laws of the existing corporation, desires to reincorporate under the provisions of this article. Such certificate shall set forth those items specified in section four hundred seventy-six of this article.

2. The reincorporated corporation shall be deemed a continuation of the previously organized corporation, but thereafter it shall have only such rights and powers and be subject only to such obligations as any corporation created under this article, provided, however, that all property rights and liabilities of the previously organized corporation shall be vested in and

assumed by the reincorporated corporation. The corporate by-laws and officers of the reincorporated corporation shall be the same as those of its predecessor until changed pursuant to the said by-laws, provided they conform to the provisions of section four hundred seventy-five of this article.

History: L 2015, ch 468, § 3, eff Nov 20, 2015.

§ 478. Time, place and notice of corporate meetings

1. The by-laws shall make provision for an annual corporate meeting and for giving appropriate notice to each voting member of the date and place of each such meeting.

2. Notices of any special meeting shall state the purpose or purposes for which the meeting is called and no business shall be transacted at such special meeting except that contained in such notice.

History: L 2015, ch 468, § 3, eff Nov 20, 2015.

§ 479. Corporate meetings

1. Each church shall determine the requirements for a quorum in their by-laws that shall not exceed fifty percent of the members.

2. The action of the meeting upon any matter or question shall be decided in a manner provided by the by-laws.

3. The presiding officer of any meeting shall be the senior granthi or guru of the church or if none, as shall be set forth in the by-laws of the church.

History: L 2015, ch 468, § 3, eff Nov 20, 2015.

ARTICLE 24
ORGANIZATIONS OF THE ISLAMIC FAITH

§ 480. Application

1. This article applies to any unincorporated church affiliated with the Islamic faith, and to any heretofore incorporated church or body, so affiliated, which desires to reincorporate pursuant to this article. Independent churches may incorporate or reincorporate under this article in the manner provided in sections four hundred eighty-one and four hundred eighty-seven of this article, and all the provisions of this article shall apply to such churches as the context requires.

2. Nothing hereinafter provided shall prevent or prohibit any heretofore incorporated church or body, affiliated with the Islamic faith from maintaining and continuing the relationship which such church or body

enjoyed at the time of the effective date of this article should such church or body determine not to reincorporate pursuant to this article.

History: L 2015, ch 468, § 4, eff Nov 20, 2015.

§ 481. Application for incorporation

Any unincorporated church or any heretofore incorporated church wishing to incorporate under this article shall execute, acknowledge and file a certificate of incorporation as hereinafter provided.

History: L 2015, ch 468, § 4, eff Nov 20, 2015.

§ 482. Qualification of voters

The following parties and no others shall be qualified voters for all purposes under this article: all persons eighteen years of age or over who are members in good and regular standing of the church or body by admission into membership therewith, in accordance with the standards for membership in the local church as determined by the local church itself.

History: L 2015, ch 468, § 4, eff Nov 20, 2015.

§ 483. Notice of meeting for incorporation

Notice of a meeting for the purpose of incorporating an unincorporated church shall be given as follows:

1. The notice shall be in writing and shall state, in substance, that a meeting of such unincorporated church will be held at its usual place of worship at a specified day and hour for the purpose of incorporating such church and electing three or more trustees, but not to exceed fifteen.

2. The notice must be signed by at least six qualified voters. A copy of such notice shall be publicly read at each of the two consecutive main worship services, of such unincorporated church preceding the meeting to incorporate, by the minister of such church, or if none, by the church member who has been designated by the membership or other authorized body of the church to conduct the worship service that day (the "officiating minister"); and at least fifteen days before the meeting for incorporation, a copy of such notice shall be posted at the place of worship.

History: L 2015, ch 468, § 4, eff Nov 20, 2015.

§ 484. Meeting for incorporation

1. At the meeting for incorporation held in pursuance of such notice, only qualified voters shall be eligible to vote.

2. The presence of one-third of the qualified voters or six qualified voters, whichever number is higher, shall be necessary to constitute a quorum of such meeting. The action of the meeting upon any matter or question shall be decided by a majority of the qualified voters present.

3. The minister of the church, or if none, the officiating minister, shall act as presiding officer of the meeting to incorporate. The presiding officer shall call the meeting to order and shall be the judge of the qualification of voters.

4. Such meeting shall decide by ballot whether the church shall be incorporated, the name of the proposed corporation, the names of the initial trustees, and the date, not more than fifteen months thereafter, on which the first annual election or affirmation of the trustees thereof after such meeting shall be held. The trustees shall hold office until their successors are elected or affirmed.

5. At the meeting for incorporation, a constitution and by-laws shall be adopted setting forth a form of church governance that is consistent with section four hundred eighty-five of this article.

History: L 2015, ch 468, § 4, eff Nov 20, 2015.

§ 485. Church governance

1. A church incorporated under this section shall provide in its certificate of incorporation or by-laws for trustees to be elected or appointed at large, or by virtue of their office. There shall be a minimum of three trustees. To the extent practicable, terms of office shall be for three years and staggered. Terms may be consecutive.

2. Provision shall also be made in its certificate of incorporation or by-laws for officers of the corporation to be elected or appointed at large or by virtue of their office. The president and secretary shall not be the same person. To the extent practicable, terms of office shall be for three years and staggered. Terms may be consecutive.

3. Provision shall also be made in its certificate of incorporation or by-laws for spiritual oversight of the church by an eldership board or a senior imam, moulvi, maulana or some combination of the above. Terms of office may be definite or indefinite as the by-laws may specify.

4. Provision shall also be made in its certificate of incorporation or by-laws for periodic affirmation of appointive positions by a designated body or board.

History: L 2015, ch 468, § 4, eff Nov 20, 2015.

§ 486. Certificate of incorporation

1. If at the meeting for incorporation it shall be decided that such unincorporated church shall become incorporated, the presiding officer of the meeting and two others shall execute and acknowledge a certificate of incorporation, in which shall be stated the name or title by which such body shall be known in the law; the purpose of its organization; the names and addresses of the initial trustees, the county, town or city in which its principal place of worship is or is intended to be located; and a statement that the church is in affiliation with the Islamic faith.

2. On filing such certificate in the office of the county clerk of the county in which the principal office or place of worship of the corporation is or is intended to be located, such church shall be a corporation by the name stated in the certificate of incorporation.

History: L 2015, ch 468, § 4, eff Nov 20, 2015.

§ 487. Reincorporation of present incorporated churches

1. Any church heretofore incorporated may, subject to restrictions and limitations of existing laws, reincorporate under the provisions of this article, by filing in the county clerk's office in the county in which its principal place of worship is located, a certificate, signed and acknowledged by all the trustees of said church in office at the time of such reincorporation, setting forth that the said church by a majority vote of the members present at a duly called meeting of the membership, as determined by the by-laws of the existing corporation, desires to reincorporate under the provisions of this article. Such certificate shall set forth those items specified in section four hundred eighty-six of this article.

2. The reincorporated corporation shall be deemed a continuation of the previously organized corporation, but thereafter it shall have only such rights and powers and be subject only to such obligations as any corporation created under this article, provided, however, that all property rights and liabilities of the previously organized corporation shall be vested in and assumed by the reincorporated corporation. The corporate by-laws and officers of the reincorporated corporation shall be the same as those of its predecessor until changed pursuant to the said by-laws, provided they conform to the provisions of section four hundred eighty-five of this article.

History: L 2015, ch 468, § 4, eff Nov 20, 2015.

§ 488. Time, place and notice of corporate meetings

1. The by-laws shall make provision for an annual corporate meeting and for giving appropriate notice to each voting member of the date and place of each such meeting.

2. Notices of any special meeting shall state the purpose or purposes for which the meeting is called and no business shall be transacted at such special meeting except that contained in such notice.

History: L 2015, ch 468, § 4, eff Nov 20, 2015.

§ 489. Corporate meetings

1. Each church shall determine the requirements for a quorum in their by-laws that shall not exceed fifty percent of the members.

2. The action of the meeting upon any matter or question shall be decided in a manner provided by the by-laws.

3. The presiding officer of any meeting shall be the senior imam, moulvi or maulana of the church or if none, as shall be set forth in the by-laws of the church.

History: L 2015, ch 468, § 4, eff Nov 20, 2015.

TRANSPORTATION CORPORATIONS LAW

ARTICLE 1
SHORT TITLE; CLASSIFICATION; INCORPORATION; APPLICATION

§ 1.   Short title

This chapter shall be known as the "Transportation Corporations Law."

History: Add, L 1909, ch 219; amd, L 1926, ch 762, § 1, eff Oct 1, 1926, with substance transferred from former § 1.

§ 2.   Classification of transportation corporations

A transportation corporation shall be either,

1. A gas corporation, an electric corporation or a gas and electric corporation.

2. A telegraph corporation, a telephone corporation or a telegraph and telephone corporation.

3. A water–works corporation.

4. [Repealed]

5. A ferry corporation.

6. A pipe line corporation.

7. A freight terminal corporation.

8. A district steam corporation.

9. Sewage–works corporation.

History: Add, L 1909, ch 219; amd, L 1926, ch 762, § 1, eff Oct 1, 1926, with substance of former § 2 transferred to § 70.

Sub 9, add, L 1960, ch 1067; amd, L 1970, ch 828, § 1, eff Oct 1, 1970.

Sub 4, repealed, L 1983, ch 635, § 3, eff Jan 1, 1984.

CASE ANNOTATIONS

Where authority to furnish the electric power in a village has been vested in a "municipal commission" duly created by statute, the village is not a "transportation corporation" or "electric corporation"

under subd. 1 of this section. Buell v Herkimer (1935) 244 App Div 599, 280 NYS 253.

Company incorporated to construct, operate and maintain a community antenna system is a transportation corporation within the meaning of subsection 2 of this section and § 25. Harper v Kingston (1959) 17 Misc 2d 627, 188 NYS2d 577.

Pipeline cannot cross city streets without consent of city. Colonial Pipeline Co. v State Board of Equalization & Assessment (1975) 81 Misc 2d 696, 366 NYS2d 949, affd (1976, 2d Dept) 51 App Div 2d 793, 380 NYS2d 64, app gr (1976) 39 NY2d 710 and affd (1977) 41 NY2d 1057, 396 NYS2d 184, 364 NE2d 848.

Section 66 does not apply to the bankruptcy trustee of the New York State Railways inasmuch as it is not a transportation corporation as defined in this section. Tilton v Utica (1946, Sup) 60 NYS2d 249.

This law refers only to the formation of domestic corporations, and where a foreign corporation sought to secure an easement over private property for the construction of a pipeline it was not required to comply with the provisions of this law. Tennessee Gas Transmission Co. v Schmidt (1951, Sup) 108 NYS2d 435.

§ 3.   Incorporation

(a) A transportation corporation may be formed under this chapter, in accordance with the procedure for the formation of corporations set forth in article four of the business corporation law, by delivering to the department of state for filing a certificate of incorporation entitled "Certificate of incorporation of _____ (name of corporation) pursuant to section three of the transportation corporations law".

(b) In addition to the statements prescribed by section four hundred two of the business corporation law, a certificate of incorporation of a transportation corporation shall designate the particular kind of transportation corporation to be formed, and shall state:

1. If a gas corporation, an electric corporation, or a gas and electric corporation, the county or counties in which its operations are to be carried on;

2. If a telegraph corporation, a telephone corporation, or a telegraph and telephone corporation, the territory in which its operations are to be carried on;

3. If a water–works corporation, the cities, towns and villages to be supplied with water, and that the consent of the authorities of such cities, towns and villages required by this chapter has been obtained, and that such consent has been annexed thereto;

4. [Repealed]

5. If a ferry corporation, the places from and to which the ferry is to run;

6. If a pipe line corporation, the places from and to which the pipe line is to be maintained, as nearly as practicable, and the county or counties through which or in which it is to be maintained and operated;

7. If a freight terminal corporation, the limits of the locality in which its operations are to be carried on;

8. If a district steam corporation, the cities, towns and villages to be supplied with steam and that the consent of the authorities of such cities, towns and villages required by this chapter has been obtained, and that such consent has been annexed thereto.

History: Add, L 1909, ch 219; amd, L 1926, ch 762, § 1, L 1935, ch 979, L 1946, ch 598, § 1, L 1964, ch 734, § 2, eff June 1, 1964.

Sub (b), par 4, repealed, L 1983, ch 635, § 3, eff Jan 1, 1984.

§ 4. Applicability of business corporation law to transportation corporations

(a) The business corporation law applies to a corporation heretofore or hereafter formed under this chapter, or under any other statute or special act of this state, or under laws other than the statutes of this state, which has as its purpose or among its purposes a purpose for which a corporation may be formed under this chapter, except that in case of a conflict between the business corporation law and this chapter the provisions of this chapter shall govern. If there is in this chapter a provision relating to a matter embraced in the business corporation law and not in conflict therewith, both provisions shall apply. Any corporation to which the business corporation law is made applicable by this section shall be treated as a "corporation", "domestic corporation", or "foreign corporation", as such terms are used in the business corporation law, except that the purposes for which any such corporation may be formed under section three of this chapter shall not thereby be extended.

(b) For the purpose of this section and elsewhere in this chapter, the effective date of the business corporation law as to corporations to which the business corporation law is made applicable by this section shall be June first, nineteen hundred sixty–four.

History: Add, L 1964, ch 734, § 4, eff June 1, 1964.

Former § 4, add, L 1909, ch 219; amd, L 1926, ch 762; amd, L 1955, ch 633, § 8; repealed, L 1964, ch 734, § 3, eff June 1, 1964.

CASE ANNOTATIONS

Telephone utility's use of its poles was not limited to a use for telephone purposes; utility had statutory right to enter into contractual arrangements with others for use of space on its poles. New York Tel. Co. v North Hempstead (1975) 86 Misc 2d 487, 385 NYS2d 436, affd (1976, 2d Dept) 52 App Div 2d 934, 385 NYS2d 505, mod on other grounds (1977) 41 NY2d 691, 395 NYS2d 143, 363 NE2d 694.

§ 5. Application

A corporation heretofore or hereafter incorporated under a general law for a purpose or purposes for which a corporation may be formed under this chapter shall in respect to such purpose or purposes have all the powers and privileges conferred, and be subject to all the duties, liabilities and limitations imposed, on a corporation organized for such purpose or purposes under this chapter. Any corporation heretofore incorporated under a general law for any one or more of the purposes specified in this chapter, may exercise the powers now possessed by it to carry on any business in which it now may lawfully engage. A corporation heretofore incorporated under or by special law for such purpose or purposes shall in respect to such purpose or purposes have all the powers and privileges conferred, and be subject to the duties, liabilities and limitations imposed by this chapter, in so far as such duties, liabilities and limitations are not inconsistent with such special law.

History: Add, L 1909, ch 219; amd, L 1926, ch 762, § 1, L 1958, ch 223, § 2, eff March 18, 1958.

CASE ANNOTATIONS

Transportation Corporation Law § 5 implies that a multi–purpose company may be formed. Iroquois Gas Corp. v Jurek (1968, 4th Dept) 30 App Div 2d 83, 290 NYS2d 140.

Where the provisions of the Public Authorities Law were inconsistent with the provisions of the Transportation Corporation Law with regard to the procedures for alteration of existing bus routes, the relevant sections of the Transportation Corporation Law were inapplicable. County of Rensselaer v Capital Dist. Transp. Authority (1973, 3d Dept) 42 App Div 2d 445, 349 NYS2d 20.

Amendments by L 1926, c 762, to the Transp. Corp. Law, this section of which specifically excludes from its provisions any corporation theretofore incorporated, did not intend to interfere with standing charters at the time the statute went into effect, so that whether or not a corporation submits itself to the supervision of the authorities created by the Transp. Corp. Law, its power to do business cannot be affected, and its right to recover under its contracts must be sustained. Supervision Co. v Mogelewsky (1931) 139 Misc 256, 248, 248 NYS 243.

A domestic gas corporation organized under the Business Corporations Law for the purpose of purchasing, transporting, and selling natural gas at wholesale has all the powers and privileges and is subject to all the duties, liabilities, and limitations imposed by the Transportation Corporations Law. Home Gas Co. v Eckerson (1950) 197 Misc 793, 94 NYS2d 221.

§ 6. Merger of subsidiary corporations

(a) Any domestic transportation corporation or any foreign corporation authorized to do in this state any business which may be done in this state by a domestic transportation corporation, owning at least ninety–five percent of the outstanding shares of each class of any domestic corporation or corporations authorized to engage in business similar or incidental to the business which the possessor corporation is authorized to engage in, and any domestic transportation corporation owning at least ninety–five percent of the outstanding shares of each class of any foreign corporation authorized to do in this state any business which may be done in this state by a domestic transportation corporation and also authorized to engage in business similar or incidental to the business which the possessor corporation is authorized to engage in, may merge such corporation or corporations into itself without the authorization of the shareholders of any such corporation, in accordance with the procedure and with the effect set forth in article nine of the business corporation law for the merger of subsidiary corporations.

(b) Any omnibus corporation may be merged under this section with any railroad corporation, provided such railroad corporation shall have substituted stages, buses or motor vehicles for cars or trains upon tracks on any portion of its route in accordance with section one hundred twenty–one of the transportation law.

History: Add, L 1964, ch 734, § 5, eff June 1, 1964.

Former § 6, add, L 1909, ch 219; omitted, L 1926, ch 762, eff Oct 1, 1926, with substance transferred to § 72.

Sub (b), amd, L 1970, ch 267, § 44, eff March 1, 1971.

ARTICLE 2
GAS AND ELECTRIC CORPORATIONS

§ 10. Definitions

A gas corporation is a corporation organized to manufacture, to produce or otherwise acquire and to supply for public use artificial or natural gas or a mixture of both gases for light, heat or power and for lighting the streets and public and private buildings of cities, villages and towns in this state. An electric corporation is a corporation organized to manufacture, to produce or otherwise acquire, and to supply for public use electricity for light, heat or power, and for lighting streets, avenues, public parks and places and public and private buildings of cities, villages and towns within this state. A gas and electric corporation is a corporation organized for purposes of both a gas corporation and an electric corporation.

History: Add, L 1909, ch 219; amd, L 1926, ch 762, eff Oct 1, 1926, with substance transferred from § 60.

CASE ANNOTATIONS

Fact that utility was chartered as "gas corporation" under CLS Trans Corp § 10 rather than as "pipeline corporation" under CLS Trans Corp § 80 did not obligate it to transport and sell only its own natural gas, so there was no conflict with requirements of CLS Pub Ser § 66–d that utility also transport nonowned gas through its pipelines; legislature can redefine powers of corporations by statutory amendment to promote public interest, and utility was not being compelled to offer service greater or different than that authorized by its original charter. Rochester Gas & Electric Corp. v Public Service Com. (1988) 71 NY2d 313, 525 NYS2d 809, 520 NE2d 528.

Where authority to furnish electric power in village has been vested in a "municipal commission" duly created by statute, the village is not a "transportation corporation" or "electric corporation" under this section. Buell v Herkimer (1935) 244 App Div 599, 280 NYS 253.

A complaint to recover for electric current furnished landlord pursuant to the terms of lease by which the landlord agreed to use no other electric current must be dismissed, for contract is void as against public policy where the plaintiff, a domestic business corporation, was not organized under Art. 2 and is not subject to

regulations provided by Pub. Ser. Law. 8284 Corp. v Garey (1930) 137 Misc 197, 242 NYS 413.

See also Supervision Co. v Mogelewsky (1931) 139 Misc 256, 248 NYS 243.

A foreign business corporation engaged in the transportation of natural gas by pipe line from Pennsylvania to New York, where it is sold to a single purchaser, a public utility, is not a "gas corporation" within the meaning of this section. Penn–York Natural Gas Corp. v Maltbie (1937) 164 Misc 569, 299 NYS 1004.

§ 11. Powers

Every such corporation shall have the following powers:

1. A gas corporation and a gas and electric corporation shall have power to manufacture gas, and to acquire natural or artificial gas and to mix the gases and to sell and furnish gas for light, heat or power; and to lay conductors for gas in the streets, highways and public places, in each city, village and town in the county or counties named in its certificate of incorporation, with the consent of the municipal authorities of such city, village or town, and under such reasonable regulations as they may prescribe.

2. Every corporation having authority under any general or special law or under any charter or franchise, to lay down, erect or maintain pipes, conduits, ducts or other fixtures in, over or under the streets, highways and public places of any municipality for the purpose of furnishing or distributing natural gas, may acquire and supply for public use artificial gas.

Where any gas corporation is serving natural gas under permits or franchises permitting the laying or maintaining of mains or pipes and conveying natural gas, and the supply of natural gas has become inadequate or insufficient to give reasonable service to consumers in the municipalities served by it, such gas corporation may supply artificial gas or a mixture of natural and artificial gases under such permits or franchises.

3. An electric corporation and a gas and electric corporation shall have power to generate, acquire and supply electricity for heat or power in cities, towns and villages within this state, and to light the streets, highways and public places thereof, and the public and private buildings therein; and to make, sell or lease all machines, instruments, apparatus and other equipments therefor, and for transmitting and distributing electricity, to lay, erect and construct suitable wires or other conductors, with the necessary poles, pipes or other fixtures in, on, over and under the streets, avenues, public parks and places in such cities, towns or villages, with the consent of the municipal authorities thereof, and in such manner and under such reasonable regulations, as they may prescribe.

3–a. An electric corporation and a gas corporation shall have power and authority to acquire such real estate as may be necessary for its corporate purposes and the right of way through any property in the manner prescribed by the eminent domain procedure law.

3–b. The construction, use and maintenance by an electric corporation of transmission, distribution and service lines and wires in, over or under any street, highway or public place and the construction, use and maintenance by a gas corporation of transmission, distribution and service pipes, conduits, ducts or other fixtures in, over or under any trees, highway or public place, as may be necessary for its corporate purposes, are hereby declared to be public uses and purposes.

Where any person or corporation other than the state, a political subdivision thereof, or a municipality is the owner of any right, title or interest in or to any street, highway or public place, or in or to the land on which the street, highway or public place is located, an electric corporation or a gas corporation is hereby authorized and empowered to acquire the right to construct, use and maintain such lines or wires and such pipes, conduits, ducts or other fixtures, in, over or under such street, highway or public place, from such owner or owners, by petition in the manner prescribed by section four hundred two of the eminent domain procedure law to the supreme court in the county in which such street, highway or public place is situated. The corporation shall file with the court a certificate of the public service commission certifying that the right sought to be acquired is necessary and in the public interest and such certificate shall be conclusive evidence as to the matters lawfully certified therein.

After a hearing on such petition and any answer thereto, if the court shall find that such right to construct, use and maintain is necessary for the corporate purposes of the corporation, it shall enter its judgment adjudging that such right is necessary for the public use and that the corporation is entitled to construct, use and maintain its lines or wires or pipes, conduits, ducts or other fixtures in, over or under such street, highway or public place and adjudging pursuant to the eminent domain procedure law the compensation to be made by the corporation to the owner or owners.

4. Any two or more domestic gas corporations, electric corporations, gas and electric corporations, and any other domestic corporation formed for the purpose of engaging in any business in which domestic gas corporations, electric corporations or gas and electric corporations may engage, may merge or consolidate in accordance with the procedure and with the effect set forth in article nine of the business corporation law.

5. A corporation mentioned in this article or incorporated under or by any general or special law of this state for the purpose of supplying for public use electricity for light, heat or power in cities, towns or villages in this state, upon filing a certificate of amendment therefor, to which is annexed the consent required by section one hundred and eleven of this chapter, shall have all the rights, privileges and powers and be subject to all the restrictions of district steam corporations.

6. The term "municipal authorities" as used in subdivisions one and three of this section, shall be deemed to be the local legislative body of a city, the board of trustees of a village and the town board of a town. All consents in writing for the doing of acts mentioned in such subdivisions given before April fourteenth, nineteen hundred and twenty–two, in writing by the highway commissioners or town superintendent of highways or the town board of any town to any corporation organized under the provisions of this article shall be deemed to be the consents of the municipal authorities required by this section.

7. Subdivisions three and three–a of this section shall not apply to any merchant transmission company which:

(a) commences and ends in the state of New York;

(b) through its employees, agents, representatives, or assigns, has represented in testimony that the construction of such power transmission lines will increase electric rates in any part of the state; and

(c) which applied for and did not receive an early designation as a national interest electric transmission corridor under an act of congress commonly known as the Energy Policy Act of 2005.

History: Add, L 1909, ch 219; amd, L 1926, ch 762, § 1, eff Oct 1, 1926, with substance transferred from former § 61; L 1937, ch 816; L 1947, ch 622, § 1, eff April 5, 1947,2; L 1964, ch 734, § 6, eff June 1, 1964,7, eff June 1, 1964; L 1977, ch 840, § 91, eff July 1, 1978; L 2006, ch 741, § 1, eff Oct 3, 2006.

CASE ANNOTATIONS

1. Generally
2. Fixtures and installation of equipment, etc.
3. Municipal regulation, generally
4. Zoning
5. Corporate management

1. Generally

Under former § 61, the provision relating to the condemnation of land was inapplicable to cities. Oneonta Light & Power Co. v Schwarzenbach (1914) 164 App Div 548, 150 NYS 76, affd (1916) 219 NY 588, 114 NE 1075.

In a proceeding to review a determination and findings of a public utility condemning easements so as to permit it to operate and maintain electrical facilities in corridors within two rights of way owned by a railroad company, notwithstanding that the utility's broad powers of eminent domain under Trans Corp Law § 11(3–b) do not extend to the property of the State, a political subdivision thereof or a municipality, a public benefit corporation is neither identical with the State nor one of its political subdivisions and accordingly its property is not exempt from a taking by an electric or gas corporation, the power of acquisition granted by § 11(3–b) extends to property already devoted to a public use, and the utility successfully fashioned its taking so that the proposed condemnation comes within an exception to the prior public use doctrine. Long Island R. R. Co. v Long Island Lighting Co. (1984, 2d Dept) 103 App Div 2d 156, 479 NYS2d 355, affd (1985) 64 NY2d 1088, 489 NYS2d 881, 479 NE2d 226.

Electric utility company's condemnation of real property to permit construction of new operations center was not ultra vires since property was needed to carry out company's public function of servicing electrical power needs of surrounding communities as authorized by CLS Trans Corp § 11. 1521 Square, Inc. v Consolidated

Edison Co. (1986, 2d Dept) 125 App Div 2d 459, 509 NYS2d 577, later proceeding (1988, 2d Dept) 143 App Div 2d 1012, 533 NYS2d 591, resettlement den (1989, App Div, 2d Dept) 538 NYS2d 491, later proceeding (1989, 2d Dept) 147 App Div 2d 561, 538 NYS2d 490, app dismd, in part, app den, in part (1989) 74 NY2d 733, 544 NYS2d 817, 543 NE2d 82.

Public use was sufficiently demonstrated to support electric utility company's condemnation of real property where proposed operation center would accommodate construction, engineering, meter bureau and emergency service personnel, and would feature garage designed to maintain 130 vehicles, including overhead line and bucket trucks, splicing vans, service installation and emergency service vehicles. Neptune Associates, Inc. v Consolidated Edison Co. (1986, 2d Dept) 125 App Div 2d 473, 509 NYS2d 574, later proceeding (1988, 2d Dept) 143 App Div 2d 1012, 533 NYS2d 591, resettlement den (1989, App Div, 2d Dept) 538 NYS2d 491, later proceeding (1989, 2d Dept) 147 App Div 2d 561, 538 NYS2d 490, app dismd, in part, app den, in part (1989) 74 NY2d 733, 544 NYS2d 817, 543 NE2d 82.

Where electric utility company's existing operations center was inadequate both in size and accessibility, and lease on current facility would expire within 2 years, company's condemnation of real property for construction of new operations center was not ultra vires, since new center was necessary for continued performance of public duty to provide safe and efficient transmission of electric power, and thus acquisition was authorized under CLS Trans Corp § 11. Neptune Associates, Inc. v Consolidated Edison Co. (1986, 2d Dept) 125 App Div 2d 473, 509 NYS2d 574, later proceeding (1988, 2d Dept) 143 App Div 2d 1012, 533 NYS2d 591, resettlement den (1989, App Div, 2d Dept) 538 NYS2d 491, later proceeding (1989, 2d Dept) 147 App Div 2d 561, 538 NYS2d 490, app dismd, in part, app den, in part (1989) 74 NY2d 733, 544 NYS2d 817, 543 NE2d 82.

Fact that alternative sites were available and adequate to meet electric utility company's needs for construction of new operations center was not sufficient to invalidate company's condemnation of subject premises, especially where company evaluated size, location, zoning restrictions, roadway accessibility, and construction costs of over 40 available sites and chose petitioner's property as most appropriate. Neptune Associates, Inc. v Consolidated Edison Co. (1986, 2d Dept) 125 App Div 2d 473, 509 NYS2d 574, later proceeding (1988, 2d Dept) 143 App Div 2d 1012, 533 NYS2d 591, resettlement den (1989, App Div, 2d Dept) 538 NYS2d 491, later proceeding (1989, 2d Dept) 147 App Div 2d 561, 538 NYS2d 490, app dismd, in part, app den, in part (1989) 74 NY2d 733, 544 NYS2d 817, 543 NE2d 82.

Subd. 3 of this section was held to authorize an electric company to sell electric refrigerators subject to the supervision of the Public Service Commission for the avoidance of discriminatory or preferential rates, but on review it was held that under the Public Service Law the electric company might engage in such sales without filing schedules of prices and terms provided no undue preference or disadvantage was given to customers. In re City Ice & Fuel Co. (1940) 173 Misc 534, 18 NYS2d 588, app dismd (1940) 260 App Div 537, 23 NYS2d 376, app den (1941) 261 App Div 847, 25 NYS2d 1011.

2. Fixtures and installation of equipment, etc.

A transformer of electric current weighing upwards of five tons and occupying a space sixteen feet, eleven inches long by four feet, six inches wide and eight feet deep is not a conductor or other fixture within the meaning of subd. 3. Brooklyn Edison Co. v Davidson (1935) 269 NY 48, 198 NE 627.

A public utility company's franchise empowered it to lay conductors for gas in streets. Public Service Commission ordered company to install gas pressure regulating station in street. Held: whether such regulator is embraced within franchise should not be decided on conflicting affidavits of experts as to its nature, and manner, necessity and feasibility of its proposed installation in public streets, which, on the record, are question of fact. Brooklyn Union Gas Co. v Cashmore (1958) 4 NY2d 727, 171 NYS2d 115, 148 NE2d 322, on remand (1958) 21 Misc 2d 126, 194 NYS2d 298, affd (1959, 2d Dept) 9 App Div 2d 905, 195 NYS2d 604, app den (1960, 2d Dept) 10 App Div 2d 577, 196 NYS2d 606 and app den (1960) 7 NY2d 711.

In an action to recover damages for injuries sustained in tripping against the side of a manhole cover, in the light of the nature of the cover, its slight projection above the level of the surrounding dirt, and the availability of an adjacent paved area of sidewalk, there was no proof of negligence, the provisions of the Administrative Code requiring all covers to be flush with the sidewalk being inapplicable. Kaupferstein v Brooklyn Edison Co. (1943) 266 App Div 879, 43 NYS2d 23, affd (1944) 292 NY 561, 54 NE2d 686.

Poles of an electric company carrying electric power lines are obstructions incidental to the exercise of a statutory right and are not necessarily public nuisances. However, they must be so located as to avoid unreasonable and unnecessary dangers to travelers upon the highway. Sweet v State (1949) 195 Misc 494, 89 NYS2d 506.

The expenses of removing and relocating electric poles situated within the bounds of a county road because of reconstruction of such road is that of the company and not the county superintendent of highways. 1956 Ops St Compt File #8149.

Where a municipality accepts a dedication of streets subject to an easement granted to a utility, which has previously installed equipment, such as mains, pipes and wires, in, on or under those streets, that equipment does not become tangible property of a special franchise by virtue of such acceptance. 8 Op Counsel SBEA No. 61 (1985, Nov 21).

3. Municipal regulation, generally

As former §§ 60 and 61 empowered a gas company to run its mains through the cities, villages, and towns named in its charter, a village which had granted such company the right to lay mains in its public streets could not prevent it from laying other mains to supply the adjoining municipalities named in its charter. Northern Westchester Lighting Co. v President & Trustees of Ossining (1913) 154 App Div 789, 139 NYS 373, affd (1915) 214 NY 635, 108 NE 1102.

This section authorizes a corporation duly organized for the purpose of supplying gas for light to lay conductors through streets of a city with the consent of municipal authorities thereof and under such reasonable regulations as they may prescribe. New York v Woodhaven Gaslight Co. (1917) 181 App Div 188, 168 NYS 429.

A lighting company which has applied to the Board of Trustees of a village for a permit to erect and maintain poles and lines for the transmission of electricity in highways in the village is entitled, upon furnishing complete data with respect to its proposal, to a determination by the Board which, if not one of approval, should include affirmative, reasonable, regulatory proposals rather than merely a flat rejection of the application. Long Island Lighting Co. v Simonson (1947) 272 App Div 943, 72 NYS2d 52.

Even though the ordinance of a village does not expressly so provide, it is implicit that the village clerk is not empowered to issue a permit to a lighting company to erect and maintain poles and lines for the transmission of electricity in highways in the village without the approval of the Board of Trustees. The matter of regulation should be conducted directly between the lighting company and the Board. Long Island Lighting Co. v Simonson (1947) 272 App Div 943, 72 NYS2d 52.

Under subd. 3 of this section and Village Law, § 89, subd. 39, a village has the right to impose, as a condition for the erection of an electrical transmission line in the highways, that the line be placed underground. Long Island Lighting Co. v Shields (1948) 274 App Div 803, 79 NYS2d 657, app dismd (1948) 298 NY 696, 82 NE2d 589 and affd (1949) 299 NY 562, 85 NE2d 791.

A public utility corporation has a vested right to maintain its subsurface facilities as approved by the city. De Wald Constr. Corp. v Consolidated Edison Co. (1968) 58 Misc 2d 89, 294 NYS2d 571.

A town may make reasonable regulations for granting easements to electric and gas corporations over property owned by the town, and such an easement may be granted only with the town's consent, as the present law does not permit condemnation if the town refuses. 1961 Ops Atty Gen July 10.

4. Zoning

The right of a lighting company, by virtue of statutory authority and of franchises granted to it or its predecessor by a town, to erect, subject to regulation, a gas–manufacturing plant in the town, cannot be nullified by a town zoning ordinance enacted subsequent to the granting of such franchises. Long Island Lighting Co. v Griffin (1948) 297 NY 897, 79 NE2d 738.

Village zoning regulations cannot prohibit the erection and maintenance of power lines authorized by subd. Long Island Lighting Co. v Old Brookville (1948) 298 NY 569, 81 NE2d 104.

A zoning ordinance cannot nullify the right to erect a plant based on the authority of this section and a franchise granted by the town. Long Island Lighting Co. v Griffin (1947) 272 App Div 551, 74 NYS2d 348, affd (1948) 297 NY 897, 79 NE2d 738.

Action of village zoning board of appeals in denying electric company application for variance from zoning ordinance to permit construction of a tower for a natural–draft, closed–cycle, cooling system was error since the action contravened federal and state law; variance should issue with proper village authorities permitted limited regulation of local and incidental conditions with respect to proposed facilities in accordance with zoning ordinance, so long as such regulation was reasonable and not inconsistent with construction of proposed facility. Consolidated Edison Co. v Hoffman (1976, 2d Dept) 54 App Div 2d 761, 387 NYS2d 884, app dismd (1977) 41 NY2d 839, 393 NYS2d 402, 361 NE2d 1050 and app dismd (1977) 41 NY2d 899 and app gr (1977) 42 NY2d 801 and affd (1978) 43 NY2d 598, 403 NYS2d 193, 374 NE2d 105, 11 Envt Rep Cas 1346, 8 ELR 20250.

As a condition precedent to an application for the condemnation of real property, a power company is required to comply with a town zoning ordinance. New York State Electric & Gas Corp. v Statler (1953) 204 Misc 7, 122 NYS2d 190.

Where an electric power company had an absolute mandate by state law to furnish adequate electric service and sought to erect a high–tension electric transmission line, a village had no authority by a zoning ordinance to interfere with that right and abrogate state law and policy. Consolidated Edison Co. v Briarcliff Manor (1955) 208 Misc 295, 144 NYS2d 379.

5. Corporate management

A determination of the Public Service Commission disapproving a restricted stock option plan for key personnel of a gas corporation was beyond the administrative function of the Commission because it invaded the field of management. But the Public Service Commission's order was nonetheless confirmed where the proposed stock issue for the plan was not one within the purposes specified by § 69 of the Public Service Law. Brooklyn Union Gas Co. v Public Service Com. (1959, 3d Dept) 8 App Div 2d 210, 187 NYS2d 207, affd (1960) 8 NY2d 815, 202 NYS2d 322, 168 NE2d 390.

The businesses and activities of a gas and electric corporation and a district steam corporation are similar and incidental within the meaning of § 85 of the Stock Corporation Law so as to authorize a merger thereof under that section. 1952 Ops Atty Gen Nov 7.

§ 11–a.   [Repealed]

History: Add, L 1970, ch 386; repealed, L 1981, ch 713, § 1, eff Oct 19, 1981.

§ 12.   Gas and electricity must be supplied on application

Except in the case of an application for residential utility service pursuant to article two of the public service law, upon written application of the owner or occupant of any building within one hundred feet of any main of a gas corporation or gas and electric corporation, or a line of an electric corporation or gas and electric corporation, appropriate to the service requested, and payment by him of all money due from him to the corporation, it shall supply gas or electricity as may be required for lighting such building, notwithstanding there be rent or compensation in arrears for gas or electricity supplied, or for meter, wire, pipe or fittings furnished, to a former occupant thereof, unless such owner or occupant shall have undertaken or agreed with the former occupant to pay or to exonerate him from the payment of such arrears, and shall refuse or neglect to pay the same; and if for the space of ten days after such application, and the deposit of a reasonable sum as provided in the next section, if required, the corporation shall refuse or neglect to supply gas or electric light as required, such corporation shall forfeit and pay to the applicant the sum of ten dollars, and the further sum of five dollars for every day thereafter during which such refusal or neglect shall continue; provided that no such corporation shall be required to lay service pipes or wires for the purpose of supplying gas or electric light to any applicant where the ground in which such pipe or wire is required to be laid shall be frozen, or shall otherwise present serious obstacles to laying the same; nor unless the applicant, if required, shall deposit in advance with the corporation a sum of money sufficient to pay the cost of his proportion of the pipe, conduit, duct or wire required to be installed, and the expense of the installation of such portion.

History: Add, L 1909, ch 219; amd, L 1926, ch 762, § 1, with substance transferred from § 62, L 1965, ch 189, L 1981, ch 713, § 1, L 1981, ch 895, § 3, eff Sept 30, 1981, and applicable to those utility bills upon which full payment has not been received on or after such effective date.

CASE ANNOTATIONS

1. Generally
2. Construction and applicability of section
3. Extent of service required
4. Discontinuance or refusal of service
5. Tampering by customer
6. Action for penalty

1. Generally

A public utility applied to a town zoning board of appeals for a variance permitting it to use property in a residence use district as an electric distribution substation. The Appellate Division properly held that the board had no power to grant such an application because (1) the utility admittedly could not show facts warranting a variance because of practical difficulties of unnecessary hardship, and (2) acquisition of the plot in the public interest was not a substitute for the statutory prerequisite to a variance. Long Island Lighting Co. v East Rockaway (1953) 304 NY 932, 110 NE2d 743.

The Public Service Commission has the power to prohibit the submetering of electricity. Campo Corp. v Feinberg (1952) 279 App Div 302, 110 NYS2d 250, affd (1952) 303 NY 995, 106 NE2d 70.

Each day's default is complete in itself, and the consequences thereof neither detract from nor add to the cause of the action. Reiser v Edison Electric Illuminating Co. (1912) 76 Misc 563, 137 NYS 145.

This section requires that all applications for gas or electric service be made by the owner or occupant of the premises to be served, and, in the absence of written application by the owner of the premises, he cannot be held liable for service furnished to an occupant other than himself. Brewer v Brooklyn Union Gas Co. (1962) 33 Misc 2d 1015, 228 NYS2d 177.

2. Construction and applicability of section

A foreign corporation does not come under this section. People ex rel. Pennsylvania Gas Co. v Public Service Com. (1921) 196 App Div 514, 189 NYS 478.

This section has no application to a contract for the extension of pipelines. Hence, where a contract provided that a city could recover $ 1,000 liquidated damages against a public utility for its failure to extend pipelines within the fixed time, this was recoverable, since it was not a penalty and its effect was not limited by this section or the Pub. Ser. Law. North Hempstead v Public Service Corp. (1922) 200 App Div 44, 192 NYS 518, affd (1923) 235 NY 607, 139 NE 754.

A village in which the electric power is furnished by a "municipal commission" is not an electric transportation corporation within this section, notwithstanding the municipal commission is obligated to defend for and in the name of the village all actions relating to the generation and distribution of electric energy by the commission. Buell v Herkimer (1935) 244 App Div 599, 280 NYS 253.

A recipient of Supplemental Security Income benefits is not within the statutory definition of persons receiving public assistance within the meaning of the Transportation Corporations Law which proscribed discontinuance of utility service for nonpayment of bills. Thus, a 78–year old recipient of Supplemental Security Income benefits was not entitled to benefits provided for in the Transportation Corporations Law. In addition, since the record showed that the petitioner had received two emergency fuel for heating grants within the 12–month period preceding his application, he was not eligible for an additional grant under Soc Serv Law § 303. Termini v Hackett (1981, 4th Dept) 80 App Div 2d 730, 437 NYS2d 156.

This statute is penal and must be strictly construed. McMullin v New York Power & Light Corp. (1935) 157 Misc 515, 284 NYS 869, affd (1936) 249 App Div 695, 291 NYS 523.

3. Extent of service required

A tenant who signed a blank order, leaving the blanks unfilled with the exception of her residence, and who delivered the order to an employee of the company and was thereupon furnished with gas for two days made a sufficient written application to the company to bring her within this section. Shelley v Westchester Lighting Co. (1910) 139 App Div 690, 124 NYS 484, affd (1912) 204 NY 641, 97 NE 1116.

The duty of an electric company furnishing current for general purposes does not rest alone on this section or Pub. Ser. Law, § 65, which refer only to furnishing electricity for lighting purposes, but on its common–law obligation as a public service corporation to serve impartially every member of the community. People ex rel. Perceval v Public Service Com. (1914) 163 App Div 705, 148 NYS 583.

Where a gas company, at the request of the owner of a building, installed a particular type of gas meter, it performed its statutory duty under this section, and since no particular kind of meter is prescribed by the statute, the company is not required, at the request of a tenant, to change a prepayment meter theretofore installed by it for a black meter without the payment of the reasonable costs of change. Public Service Com. v Northern Union Gas Co. (1915) 168 App Div 731, 154 NYS 649, affd (1916) 217 NY 607, 111 NE 1098.

This section does not require an electric corporation to supply a particular kind of current, i.e., nonstandard "DC" current, upon a firm or non–temporary basis. Meerow Press, Inc. v Consolidated Edison Co. (1950) 277 App Div 839, 97 NYS2d 862, affd (1951) 302 NY 554, 96 NE2d 443.

The right to service is dependent upon the provisions of this section. McCormick v Westchester Lighting Co. (1931) 141 Misc 261, 252 NYS 454.

The making of a contract between the plaintiff and the defendant is precedent to the obligation of the defendant to furnish electric service. Silver's Lunch Stores, Inc. v United Electric Light & Power Co. (1932) 142 Misc 744, 255 NYS 515, mod on other grounds (1933) 146 Misc 554, 261 NYS 714.

No duty has ever been imposed by law or statute upon a public utility corporation to select for one of its customers electric service that will be most favorable and suitable for that customer. Silver's Lunch Stores, Inc. v United Electric Light & Power Co. (1932) 142 Misc 744, 255 NYS 515, mod on other grounds (1933) 146 Misc 554, 261 NYS 714.

A public utility corporation is under a statutory duty to the public to supply current from which it cannot escape except under certain defined circumstances. Esposito v Consolidated Edison Co. (1947, Mun Ct) 68 NYS2d 868.

This section does not prescribe any particular type or characteristics of electricity which a utility customer is entitled to demand and an electric utility obligated to furnish. The expressions "appropriate to the service requested" and "electricity as may be required for lighting such building" cannot reasonably be interpreted to mean "direct current" or "alternating current" or current of any specific phases, wires, volts, etc. Meerow Press, Inc. v Consolidated Edison Co. (1950, Sup) 95 NYS2d 55.

Except for this section there is no duty or obligation on the part of a gas company to furnish service to any applicant. The right conferred by this section on a consumer of gas is not such a right as may form the basis of a claim for confiscation or discrimination. United States Light & Heat Corp. v Niagara Falls Gas & Electric Light Co. (1931, CA2 NY) 47 F2d 567, cert den (1931) 283 US 864, 75 L Ed 1469, 51 S Ct 656.

4. Discontinuance or refusal of service

Sections 12 and 15 authorize an electric power corporation to discontinue and refuse electric service, though the indebtedness of the customer arose out of service provided at some other location. Whether or not petitioner, who was refused service, was actually indebted for electricity furnished to a store was a question of fact which could not be resolved upon application for a preemptory order of mandamus. Sulkin v Brooklyn Edison Co. (1932) 145 Misc 484, 261 NYS 245, affd (1932) 237 App Div 850, 261 NYS 929.

Where a lighting company seeks to cut off an existing supply of a consumer, the burden is on the corporation to justify its act. Manley v Consolidated Edison Co. (1946) 187 Misc 366, 63 NYS2d 353. See also Levine v Brooklyn Union Gas Co. (1911) 146 AD 464, 131 NYS 255.

Electric utility could not terminate services to customer where, despite previous unpaid bills, department of social services had guaranteed payment of future bills and of four months of such arrearages. Consolidated Edison Co. v McClain (1976) 87 Misc 2d 766, 386 NYS2d 770.

Where no application for public utility service was refused to public assistance recipient, where recipient was on public assistance during full period during which arrears in payment of utility bills accrued, and where accrued arrears were primarily incurred in a different dwelling than present dwelling of applicant, provisions of amendment to the Transportation Corporation Law stating that existence of preexisting debt incurred while applicant was not on public assistance could not serve as a bar to application for service and that four months of arrears would be paid by public welfare official charged with such duty would not be applicable to recipient protesting utility's intent to terminate her service unless arrears for both accounts were paid in full. Rivera v Berger (1976) 89 Misc 2d 586, 390 NYS2d 537.

A landlord's allegations that defendant public utility had terminated electric service to plaintiff's property in the middle of winter after plaintiff's tenant, the utility's customer, had ordered a final meter reading and shutoff of electrical service, causing the pipes to freeze and damage to occur, properly stated a cause of action in negligence against the utility where, though there can generally be no recovery against a utility for its negligence in furnishing service absent a contractual relationship between the injured party and the utility, the utility conceded that its past practice had been to continue service when a tenant customer moved even in the absence of a request for such service by the landlord, so that the utility could permissibly discontinue such practice only with due care, and where a provision in the utility's tariff that purported to limit its tort liability to instances of gross negligence was rendered ineffective by an administrative rule that prohibited the use of such disclaimers. Lanni v Rochester Gas & Electric Corp. (1983, City Ct) 120 Misc 2d 644, 466 NYS2d 248.

The extension of a creditors' receivership to include a mortgage foreclosure receivership constituted a change of the persons supplied or occupants of property under this section and § 15 so as to preclude a power company from discontinuing electric service on the refusal of the receiver for the creditors to pay a balance owing for electric current previously furnished. Kane v Roxy Theatres Corp. (1933, CA2 NY) 63 F2d 754, cert den (1933) 289 US 751, 77 L Ed 1496, 53 S Ct 695.

5. Tampering by customer

A public utility may discontinue the supply of electricity without notice where a consumer has misappropriated current by tampering with the meter. Morris v Consolidated Edison Co. (1943) 265 App Div 743, 40 NYS2d 825.

Where it appeared that plaintiff was the sole lessee of the premises and that access to the meters therein could be had solely by means of a key in the exclusive possession and control of plaintiff's representatives, the evidence established that plaintiff breached his contract to safeguard the meters from interference and tampering, and hence the statutory obligation to furnish service, as prescribed by this section, terminated. Hoberg v New York Edison Co. (1932) 144 Misc 726, 258 NYS 701.

Where defendant electric company by unilateral action determined that plaintiffs had tampered with its meter, fixed the amount which it claimed to be due from plaintiffs, and discontinued the electric service when plaintiffs, denying that they had tampered with the meter, refused to pay the sum, plaintiffs are entitled to a trial of the issues, and defendants will be compelled to supply electric service pending the trial of this action on condition that plaintiffs pay into court the amount in dispute, since the defendant should not be permitted to determine for itself, in advance of the trial, the merits of the action and arbitrarily to discontinue service. Manley v Consolidated Edison Co. (1946) 187 Misc 366, 63 NYS2d 353.

The refusal by a consumer who had tampered with the meter to pay the amount due for unmetered gas consumed warranted the gas company in refusing to restore the service. Rocha v Consolidated Edison Co. (1940, Sup) 22 NYS2d 157.

Where the evidence established that petitioner had not only tampered with gas meter but also had used unmetered gas of substantial amount and value, statutory obligation to supply service, which § 12 imposes on gas corporation, ceased and terminated. Rocha v Consolidated Edison Co. (1940, Sup) 22 NYS2d 157.

Where the evidence established that a customer had tampered with a meter, resulting in the use of unmetered gas of a substantial amount in value, the statutory obligation to supply service ceased. Where the obstruction of the meter destroyed the only accurate means of determining the exact amount of the consumer's gas consumption, proof, based on the utility company's experience in the gas business, showing the approximate amount of such consumption during the period that the meter was not registering and its value, is sufficient. Rocha v Consolidated Edison Co. (1940, Sup) 22 NYS2d 157.

For mere nonpayment of its lawful charges, an electric company may discontinue its service only after the statutory notice required by § 15 is given, but where there has been meter tampering, service may be discontinued without such notice. Esposito v Consolidated Edison Co. (1947, Mun Ct) 68 NYS2d 868.

In an action against a utility company to recover money paid under duress or mistake, the defense that the plaintiff interfered with the utility company's meter and equipment resulting in his deriving the sole benefit of unmetered current for which the defendant made a proper charge was an affirmative defense. Esposito v Consolidated Edison Co. (1947, Mun Ct) 68 NYS2d 868.

6. Action for penalty

Where defendant electric company contracted to supply plaintiff with current for light and power subject to the condition that plaintiff's equipment be approved by duly constituted authorities and, in addition to the certificates presented, demanded a certificate from a New York Board of Fire Underwriters which is not a government agency, such demand was not proper, and plaintiff is entitled to the statutory penalty for the refusal of a public utility to respond to a lawful demand for service. Tismer v New York Edison Co. (1920) 228 NY 156, 126 NE 729, reh den (1920) 228 NY 585, 127 NE 923.

A person may recover the statutory penalty when, after application and against protest, the gas was shut off solely because a prior tenant failed to pay for his gas. Shelley v Westchester Lighting Co. (1910) 139 App Div 690, 124 NYS 484, affd (1912) 204 NY 641, 97 NE 1116.

The penalty imposed by this section on a gas company applies not only to the refusal to begin a supply of gas but also when the existing supply has been cut off. Levine v Brooklyn Union Gas Co. (1911) 146 App Div 464, 131 NYS 255.

Where it is conceded that a customer tendered a two-dollar bill in payment of a current gas account of one dollar and sixty cents and that defendant refused to accept it unless certain alleged arrears, which had in fact been paid some time before, were also discharged, and, upon plaintiff's refusal to do so, turned off gas, it is not necessary for customer to keep her tender good or to pay the money into court in order to hold company for penalty of this section. Levine v Brooklyn Union Gas Co. (1911) 146 App Div 464, 131 NYS 255.

In an action under this section to recover the penalty therein provided, the defense that plaintiff owed defendant money for service rendered at another location and that defendant was justified in refusing to continue service at the new location until old bill was paid is good under this section and § 15. Clark v Utica Gas & Electric Co. (1928) 224 App Div 448, 231 NYS 308.

Under this section plaintiff was required to make application for the restoration of service as a prerequisite to bringing action. McMullin v New York Power & Light Corp. (1936) 249 App Div 695, 291 NYS 523.

A judgment directing a company to restore service to the plaintiff is not res judicata in an action to recover a penalty for failure to supply electricity under this section. Gordohn v Yonkers Electric Light & Power Co. (1949) 275 App Div 837, 86 NYS2d 329, amd on other grounds (1949) 275 App Div 852, 89 NYS2d 900.

In action arising from alleged economic damages suffered by 2 plaintiff commercial tenants as result of defendant electric company's inability to upgrade their electrical power service until 3 months after date agreed on with other plaintiffs who were customers of electric company, tenants failed to raise triable issues of fact on theory that they were direct, contractual customers of electric company where they never submitted written application for electrical power service, as required by CLS Trans Corp § 12. Tri–Tone Litho v Consolidated Edison Co. (1996, 1st Dept) 230 App Div 2d 625, 645 NYS2d 810.

The liability of defendant being penal, it must be strictly construed; it does not arise until defendant's neglect or refusal to comply with the statute has continued for ten days, and recovery by plaintiff should be limited to the amount which accrued prior to the com-

mencement of the action. Reiser v Edison Electric Illuminating Co. (1912) 76 Misc 563, 137 NYS 145.

In an action under this section to recover the penalty for failure of electric light company to supply current for lighting purposes, it is essential to a recovery that plaintiff prove he made application in writing to the company to furnish electric current to his premises. Reiser v Edison Electric Illuminating Co. (1912) 76 Misc 563, 137 NYS 145.

Where plaintiff purchased the stock, fixtures, and good will of a business from one who was then indebted to defendant for electric current provided in the place of business and, after payment of the customary deposit, was supplied with current for about ten days when it was shut off because of the indebtedness of the former owner and plaintiff, upon the advice of counsel, paid such indebtedness under protest, receiving therefor a receipted bill made out to the former owner, his complaint to recover back the money upon the theory that it was paid under duress will be dismissed, since the bill was paid voluntarily and with full knowledge that it was a just claim and since plaintiff did not avail himself of the right to sue for the penalties prescribed in this section. Becker v Brooklyn Edison Co. (1923) 121 Misc 96, 200 NYS 319.

An action for the violation of this section will be dismissed where the evidence is insufficient to warrant a finding that plaintiff made a written application in the first instance, and no written application was made after service was discontinued. McMullin v New York Power & Light Corp. (1935) 157 Misc 515, 284 NYS 869, affd (1936) 249 App Div 695, 291 NYS 523.

An action to enforce a penalty under this section will be dismissed where plaintiff's application for service was not made in good faith but merely as a subterfuge to secure service for a relative who was then in default in the payment of his bills. McMullin v New York Power & Light Corp. (1935) 157 Misc 515, 284 NYS 869, affd (1936) 249 App Div 695, 291 NYS 523.

This section has created a cause of action to recover a penalty which is independent of the common–law cause of action for breach of contract, and recovery in one will not bar recovery in the other. J. & K. Cohen Furniture Co. v Consolidated Edison Co. (1936) 160 Misc 941, 290 NYS 928.

Adjudication in plaintiff's favor in an action against a utility company for damages and the return of plaintiff's deposit for cutting off the supply of gas on plaintiff's premises establishes the essential premise, in an action to recover the statutory per diem penalty under this section, that the supply of gas was wrongfully withheld. J. & K. Cohen Furniture Co. v Consolidated Edison Co. (1936) 160 Misc 941, 290 NYS 928.

§ 13. [Repealed]

History: Add, L 1974, ch 1081, § 5; amd, L 1975, ch 198, § 12, L 1976, ch 125, § 2; repealed, L 1981, ch 713, § 1, eff Oct 19, 1981, L 1981, ch 895, § 4, eff Sept 30, 1981, and applicable to those utility bills upon which full payment has not been received on or after such effective date.

Former § 13, add, L 1909, ch 219; amd, L 1926, ch 762, § 1, with substance transferred from § 63, L 1933, ch 808, L 1935, ch 658, L 1936, ch 672, § 1, L 1940, ch 707, L 1944, ch 428; repealed, L 1970, ch 269, § 2, eff July 1, 1970, with substance transferred to Pub Serv Law § 120.

§§ 13–a–13–f. [Repealed]

History: § 13–a, add, L 1935, ch 658, § 2; amd, L 1936, ch 672, § 2, L 1940, ch 707, § 2; repealed, L 1943, ch 697, eff June 1, 1944, with substance transferred to Aband Prop L § 400, sub 1, par (a).

Former § 13–a, add, L 1934, ch 284; repealed, L 1935, ch 658, § 2, eff May 2, 1935, with substance transferred to Aband Prop L § 401.

§ 13–b, add, L 1935, ch 658, § 3; amd, L 1936, ch 672, § 3; repealed, L 1943, ch 697, eff June 1, 1944, with substance transferred to Aband Prop L § 40.

Former § 13–b, add, L 1934, ch 643; repealed, L 1935, ch 658, § 3.

§ 13–c, add, L 1935, ch 658, § 4; amd, L 1937, ch 776, L 1940, ch 707, § 3; repealed, L 1943, ch 697, eff June 1, 1944, with substance transferred to Aband Prop L § 403.

§ 13–d, add, L 1935, ch 658, § 4; amd, L 1940, ch 710, § 2; repealed, L 1943, ch 697, eff June 1, 1944.

§ 13–e, add, L 1935, ch 658, § 4; amd, L 1938, ch 454; repealed, L 1940, ch 710, § 3, L 1943, ch 697, eff June 1, 1944.

§ 13–f, add, L 1935, ch 658, § 4; repealed, L 1944, ch 428, § 2, eff June 1, 1944.

§ 14.　[Repealed]

History: Add, L, 1909, ch 219; amd, L 1926, ch 762, with substance transferred from § 64, L 1941, ch 469; repealed, L 1981, ch 713, § 1, eff Oct 19, 1981.

§ 15.　Refusal or neglect to pay rent

If any person supplied with gas or electric light by any such corporation, except residential customers supplied pursuant to article two of the public service law shall neglect or refuse to pay the rent or remuneration due for the same or for the wires, pipes or fittings let by the corporation, for supplying or using such gas or electric light or for ascertaining the quantity consumed or used as required by his contract with the corporation, or shall refuse or neglect, after being required so to do, to make the deposit required, such corporation may discontinue the supply of gas or electric light to the premises of such person; and the officers, agents or workmen of such corporation may enter into or upon such premises between the hours of eight o'clock in the forenoon and six o'clock in the afternoon, and separate and carry away any meter, pipe, fittings, wires or other property of such corporation, and may disconnect any meter, pipe, fittings, wires or other works whether the property of the corporation or not, from the mains, pipes or wires of the corporation. But the supply of gas or electric light shall not be discontinued for non–payment of bills rendered for service until and after a five–day written notice has been served upon such person either by delivering the same to such person personally or by mailing the same in post–paid wrapper addressed to such person at premises where service is rendered.

History: Add, L 1926, ch 762, with substance transferred from § 65; amd, L 1935, ch 481, L 1937, ch 545; L 1967, ch 495, L 1981, ch 713, § 11, L 1981, ch 895, § 5, eff Sept 30, 1981 (see 1981 note below).

Sub 1, formerly entire section, so designated sub 1, L 1967, ch 495; so designated entire section, L 1981, ch 713, § 11, L 1981, ch 895, § 5, eff Sept 30, 1981 (see 1981 note below).

Sub 2, add, L 1967, ch 495; deleted, L 1981, ch 713, § 11, L 1981, ch 895, § 5, eff Sept 30, 1981 (see 1981 note below).

CASE ANNOTATIONS

1. Generally
2. Extent of power to discontinue service
3. Trespass by utility company
4. Notice requirement
5. Tampering by customer
6. Burden of proof

1. Generally

This section and § 12 authorize an electric power corporation to discontinue and refuse electric service, though the indebtedness of the customer arose out of service provided at some other location. Sulkin v Brooklyn Edison Co. (1932) 145 Misc 484, 261 NYS 245, affd (1932) 237 App Div 850, 261 NYS 929.

Threat of putting customer out of business or subjecting him to serious penalty is coercion by utility and payment of gas and electricity bill made under protest in such circumstances may be recovered. Monroe v Niagara Mohawk Power Corp. (1976) 88 Misc 2d 876, 388 NYS2d 1003.

Where threat to discontinue gas and electric service to one's home is made by official of utility company, threat is equal to deed and one who is faced with that dilemma cannot be blamed for making payment under protest to avoid cutoff of service. Monroe v Niagara Mohawk Power Corp. (1976) 88 Misc 2d 876, 388 NYS2d 1003.

Where funds required to be advanced to public assistance recipient by local welfare agency upon her inability to pay public utility's bill were in category of an emergency assistance grant under section of Social Services Law providing for emergency assistance to needy families, section of state regulations relating to "advance allowance" for payment of utility bills with recoupment provisions was not applicable and, thus, county commissioner of social services would be required to pay to public utility the full amount of arrears owed by recipient for services rendered to her by public utility and, in order to avoid future shutoffs, commissioner should continue to make payment to utility for future services through voucher payment technique. Rivera v Berger (1976) 89 Misc 2d 586, 390 NYS2d 537.

2. Extent of power to discontinue service

Where the defendant defaulted in paying his gas and electric bill both at his business address and at his residence, which resulted in the business account being transferred to the residence account upon which the defendant agreed to make installment payments; after the defendant's further default, the plaintiff had a right to discontinue service and an injunction against such discontinuance was contrary to law. Dworman v Consolidated Edison Co. (1966, 1st Dept) 26 App Div 2d 535, 271 NYS2d 363.

Where a property owner fails to pay an amount due for electric service, the utility has the right to discontinue service to him and there is nothing in the statute limiting this right to any particular building or premises. Hayes v Niagara Mohawk Power Corp. (1970, 4th Dept) 35 App Div 2d 1072, 316 NYS2d 520, affd (1972) 30 NY2d 579, 330 NYS2d 795, 281 NE2d 843, reh den (1972) 30 NY2d 790.

The cutoff of electric service to plaintiff's drive–in restaurant for nonpayment of bills on January 19, 1966, after final notice as to the imminence of the cutoff on December 20, 1965, requiring payment of the unpaid bills by January 4, 1966 was proper, and did not constitute any violation of Public Service Law § 65. Brothers Drive–In, Inc. v Consolidated Edison Co. (1968) 56 Misc 2d 86, 288 NYS2d 106.

Electric utility could not terminate services to customer where, despite previous unpaid bills, department of social services had guaranteed payment of future bills and of four months of such arrearages. Consolidated Edison Co. v McClain (1976) 87 Misc 2d 766, 386 NYS2d 770.

If amendment to the Transportation Corporation Law limiting right of utility to terminate service for nonpayment of bills for such services rendered to person receiving public assistance was to be construed to require the continuation of service by the facility on the sole premise of prospective payment, limitation of utility to full remedy for unpaid arrears of civil judgment whose collectability would be extremely dubious, if not nil, would be, a deprivation of utility's property without due process, and the plain consequence of such a theory would be the passing along of the burden of such unpaid bills to other users of services of utility as uncollectable debts and would cause such other users, in effect, to pay for services which they had not and would not receive. Rivera v Berger (1976) 89 Misc 2d 586, 390 NYS2d 537.

Since language of statute permitting public utility to discontinue supply of gas or electricity for refusal to pay rent is discretionary in nature, such statute does not relieve utility of its common–law obligation to exercise ordinary care when a decision to discontinue is made. Pompeii Estates, Inc. v Consolidated Edison Co. (1977) 91 Misc 2d 233, 397 NYS2d 577.

Where public utility had in its files a letter written by builder concerning electrical service to be supplied to new home constructed by builder, reasonably prudent person examining such letter would realize that builder was not occupying such home, and utility was negligent in discontinuing electrical service to such home in the middle of winter after mailing disconnection notice to address of new home and without attempting to contact builder at builder's address. Pompeii Estates, Inc. v Consolidated Edison Co. (1977) 91 Misc 2d 233, 397 NYS2d 577.

Where Department of Social Services agreed to authorize payment for all of home relief recipients' future utility bills either by direct payment or voucher payment but refused to pay past payments due, recipients would be entitled to preliminary injunction mandating restoration of gas and electric service to their premises during pendency of action for permanent injunction mandating continuation of such service and for judgment declaring that utility company's refusal to supply utilities contravened the Transportation Corporations Law. Harrell v Consolidated Edison Co. (1977) 91 Misc 2d 714, 398 NYS2d 522.

Obvious purpose of section of Transportation Corporations Law providing it shall be unlawful for any gas or electric corporation to discontinue supply of gas or electricity to persons receiving public assistance for nonpayment of bills rendered for services if payment is to be paid directly by Department of Social Welfare was to assure a continuation of services to a person receiving public assistance whose account was not current but whose current service would be paid for directly by the Department of Social Services. Harrell v Consolidated Edison Co. (1977) 91 Misc 2d 714, 398 NYS2d 522.

Utility can properly discontinue service to a recipient of public assistance for nonpayment of bills for arrears, notwithstanding that local department of social services promises to directly pay all future utility bills. Fahey v Niagara Mohawk Power Corp. (1977) 91 Misc 2d 866, 398 NYS2d 810.

The extention of a creditors' receivership to include a mortgage foreclosure receivership constituted a change of the persons supplied or occupants of property under this section and § 12 so as to preclude a power company from discontinuing electric service on the refusal of the receiver for the creditors to pay a balance owing for electric current previously furnished. Kane v Roxy Theatres Corp. (1933, CA2 NY) 63 F2d 754, cert den (1933) 289 US 751, 77 L Ed 1496, 53 S Ct 695.

3. Trespass by utility company

Whether the entry of a gas company under this section was trespass depends on whether there was a neglect or refusal to pay the amount due for the gas supply. Dobbs v Northern Union Gas Co. (1912) 78 Misc 136, 137 NYS 785.

Where an agent of defendant gas company insisted upon entering plaintiff's premises and disconnecting the gas supply after plaintiff's wife had told him that the gas bill had been paid instead of verifying her statement by telephoning the company, defendant was liable in trespass for damages. Dobbs v Northern Union Gas Co. (1912) 78 Misc 136, 137 NYS 785.

Where utility discontinued gas and electric service to the plaintiffs' home, obtained an order of replevin for the meters, but such replevin order was set aside, a forcible entry by the utility thereafter, in order to remove the meters, was an abuse and constituted the utility a trespasser ab initio. Velardi v Consolidated Edison Co. (1970) 63 Misc 2d 623, 313 NYS2d 194.

4. Notice requirement

The provisions of the statute make it clear that the requirements as to notice of discontinuance of service are applicable only to persons having contracts for service with the corporation and no prior notice was required to be given to a tenant, where the power company discontinued service because of the nonpayment of charges by the landlord. Hayes v Niagara Mohawk Power Corp. (1970, 4th Dept) 35 App Div 2d 1072, 316 NYS2d 520, affd (1972) 30 NY2d 579, 330 NYS2d 795, 281 NE2d 843, reh den (1972) 30 NY2d 790.

Tenant who rented apartment for which electric service was paid by landlord was not entitled to written notice that electricity would be shut off for nonpayment of electric bills on other property owned by landlord. Hayes v Niagara Mohawk Power Corp. (1970, 4th Dept) 35 App Div 2d 1072, 316 NYS2d 520, affd (1972) 30 NY2d 579, 330 NYS2d 795, 281 NE2d 843, reh den (1972) 30 NY2d 790.

An injunction would issue to prevent discontinuance by defendant gas company to plaintiff property owner of gas service for nonpayment of bills where notice of intention to discontinue service was not given as required by this section prior to cutting off service and the gas company was attempting to require the owner of an apartment building to pay for service rendered to an occupant but not upon the owner's application. Brewer v Brooklyn Union Gas Co. (1962) 33 Misc 2d 1015, 228 NYS2d 177.

Under this section, as amended, it is very clear that a gas company cannot cut off service for failure to pay bills without giving a five–day written notice to the person who has requested the service and is liable for payment of the bills. Brewer v Brooklyn Union Gas Co. (1962) 33 Misc 2d 1015, 228 NYS2d 177.

Where gas furnished by corporation falling within the Transportation Corporations Law is sole source of heat of second floor apartment whose occupant is tenant of person occupying first floor of same building as store, if such corporation discontinues supply of gas to such apartment under terms of above statute, it is under duty to notify landlord occupying first floor, since he is obviously subject to damage that might result from freezing of water pipes on floor above. But where damage to landlord's property on first floor results from freezing and bursting of such pipes, question whether failure of such corporation to so notify landlord is proximate cause of such damage is matter for trial rather than for summary judgment. Cramer v Niagara Mohawk Power Corp. (1965) 45 Misc 2d 670, 257 NYS2d 380.

Assuming that the continuation of utility services rises to the status of a property right within the due process clause of the Constitution, a utility customer is accorded adequate due process under the provisions of Transportation Corporations Law § 15 if customer is given notice for termination and an opportunity to present to the utility company any evidence he may have, if he claims that his bill has been paid, and the determination of whether a utility bill has been paid does not involve such intricate questions of fact as to require the establishment of an independent quasi–judicial tribunal. Turner v Rochester Gas & Electric Corp. (1973) 74 Misc 2d 745, 345 NYS2d 421.

Utility company's proposed order for seizure of gas and electricity meters did not comply with due process requirement where letter to user advising that application and order had been filed did not include statement of the amount due or other specifics of claim or statement that demand for payment had been duly made, where no provision was made for service of the order, the affidavit or summons and complaint, there was no averment of facts sufficient to justify a breaking and entering, and order did not contain a particular description of meters to be seized or the place to be searched. Consolidated Edison Co. v Powell (1974) 77 Misc 2d 475, 354 NYS2d 311.

In action brought against public utility to recover damages arising out of the alleged wrongful termination of electricity at unoccupied house, evidence of utility's office practice of mailing disconnection notices established that utility complied with statutory requirement of mailing plaintiff such notice, notwithstanding fact that plaintiff never received such notice. Pompeii Estates, Inc. v Consolidated Edison Co. (1977) 91 Misc 2d 233, 397 NYS2d 577.

Although a public utility company was initially justified in disconnecting a consumer's gas service when a gas leak on the premises created a reasonable suspicion of an illegal bypass and the utility was denied access to the basement of the premises until the following day, since the utility company has an inherent right to disconnect service without prior notice when conditions indicate that life or property may be endangered, the utility company was not justified, after an inspection failed to establish the existence of a bypass, in continuing to withhold service for nonpayment of the amount the utility deemed owing for unmetered gas, inasmuch as the utility failed to give the consumer the five–day pretermination notice required under Trans Corp Law § 15 and otherwise failed to follow administrative procedures for the restoration of service while the dispute as to the amount due was being resolved; since the limitation of liability in the utility company's tariff to gross negligence is not applicable to the intentional termination of service, the consumer is entitled to damages for the loss of its subtenant due to the lack of heat and for the loss of contracts causally connected to the unheated premises, regardless of whether the contracts were enforceable under the statute of frauds or whether the consumer would have been in violation of the certificate of occupancy had it performed the contracts, but the utility company's misconduct in failing to restore the consumer's service would not warrant an award of punitive damages since such conduct does not rise to the level of malicious or wanton and reckless conduct or conduct resulting from a deliberate policy against the general public. Brooklyn Union Gas Co. v MacGregor's Custom Coach, Inc. (1983, Civ Ct) 122 Misc 2d 287, 471 NYS2d 470, mod on other grounds (1986, Sup App T) 133 Misc 2d 582, 509 NYS2d 446.

For mere nonpayment of its lawful charges, an electric company may discontinue its service only after the statutory notice required by this section is given, but where there has been meter tampering, service may be discontinued without such notice. Esposito v Consolidated Edison Co. (1947, Mun Ct) 68 NYS2d 868.

5. Tampering by customer

It was no defense to an action to recover for failure to comply with the provision in this section as to written notice that the electrical equipment in plaintiff's house had been so tampered with that the current used was not recorded. Fisher v Long Island Lighting Co. (1939) 280 NY 63, 19 NE2d 682.

A public utility may discontinue the supply of electricity without notice where a consumer has misappropriated the current by tampering with the meter. Morris v Consolidated Edison Co. (1943) 265 App Div 743, 40 NYS2d 825.

Statutory requirement of pretermination notice to customers who have not paid their bills, but not to customers who are alleged to have tampered with their meters, does not constitute state deprivation of the latter group of persons of equal protection of the laws since the distinction is rationally based on the fact that to require five–day notice to tamperers would in effect afford a period of grace to persons believed to be committing a misdemeanor and permit the continued existence of possibly dangerous conditions during that period. Taylor v Consolidated Edison Co. (1977, CA2 NY) 552 F2d 39, cert den (1977) 434 US 845, 54 L Ed 2d 111, 98 S Ct 147.

6. Burden of proof

Where the defense, in an action against an electric company for a penalty under § 12 for cutting off plaintiff's electric supply, was that plaintiff refused to pay a just claim for prior service at another location, defendant had the burden of justifying its act by alleging and proving the indebtedness and plaintiff's refusal to pay. Clark v Utica Gas & Electric Co. (1928) 224 App Div 448, 231 NYS 308.

Burden of proof to establish that payment of gas and electric bill was made under such coercion and duress as to allow its recovery is on customer. Monroe v Niagara Mohawk Power Corp. (1976) 88 Misc 2d 876, 388 NYS2d 1003.

To establish a prima facie case in an action to recover money paid a utility company under protest, plaintiff must prove that gas or electric current had been supplied to him as an owner or occupant, that he had duly paid all the charges for which he was billed after meter reading or measurement by the company, and that the company thereafter discontinued the service until he paid an additional sum of money for alleged unmetered current consumed and that he made such payment under protest to obtain a restoration of the service. Esposito v Consolidated Edison Co. (1947, Mun Ct) 68 NYS2d 868.

§ 16. No rent for meters to be charged

No gas corporation, electric corporation or gas and electric corporation directly or indirectly shall charge or collect rent on its gas meters, and any person, or corporation violating this provision shall be liable to a penalty of fifty dollars for each offense, to be sued for and recovered in the corporate name of the city, town or village where the violation occurs, in any court having jurisdiction, and when collected to be paid into the treasury of such city, town or village and to constitute a part of the contingent or general fund thereof.

History: Add, L 1926, ch 762, eff Oct 1, 1926, with substance transferred from § 66.

CASE ANNOTATIONS

A service charge reasonably computed and moderate in amount does not constitute "rent on a gas meter" within the meaning of this section. Rochester v Rochester Gas & Electric Corp. (1922) 233 NY 39, 134 NE 828.

Where, in an action to restrain defendant gas company from making a "service charge" on the ground that it constituted a violation of this section, it appeared that the Public Service Commission had authorized the charge after deciding that it did not constitute rental in violation of the statute, an injunction pendente lite was properly denied, since a decision of the Commission cannot be attacked collaterally unless its order was without the scope of its jurisdiction. North Hempstead v Public Service Corp. (1921) 199 App Div 189, 191 NYS 394.

This section will not allow a landlord or submetering company to increase the cost of electricity over that charged by the electric company on the ground that it is an assessment for meter service. Owners & Tenants Electric Co. v Tractenberg (1936) 158 Misc 677, 286 NYS 570.

§ 17. Construction over Indian reservation

A gas corporation, an electric corporation or a gas and electric corporation may contract with the chiefs of any nation of Indians over whose lands it may be necessary to construct its gas or electric lines for the right to construct such lines upon such lands, but no such contract shall vest in the corporation the fee of such lands nor the right to occupy the same for any purpose other than for the construction, operation and maintenance of such lines, nor shall such contract be valid or effectual until the same has been ratified by the county court of the county in which the lands are situated and approved by the public service commission pursuant to section sixty–eight of the public service commission law [public service law].[1]

History: Add, L 1926, ch 762, eff Oct 1, 1926, with substance transferred from § 67.

[1] The bracketed words have been inserted by the Publisher.

ARTICLE 3
TELEGRAPH AND TELEPHONE CORPORATIONS

§ 25. Definitions

A telegraph corporation is a corporation organized to construct, own, use and maintain a line or lines of electric telegraph wholly within or partly without this state, or to acquire and own any interest in any such line or lines, or any grants therefor or for any or all of such purposes. A telephone corporation is a corporation organized to construct, own, use and maintain a line or lines of electric telephone wholly within or partly without the state, or to acquire and own any interest in any such line or lines, or any grants therefor or for any or all of such purposes. A telegraph and telephone corporation is a corporation organized for both such telegraph and telephone purposes.

History: Add, L 1913, ch 495; amd, L 1926, ch 762, § 1, eff Oct 1, 1926, with substance transferred from § 100.

CASE ANNOTATIONS

A company incorporated for the purpose of doing a general telegraph and electric protective business by means of electrical alarms transmitted to central offices where watchmen are stationed to reply to the signals is a telegraph company. Holmes Electric Protective Co. v Williams (1920) 228 NY 407, 127 NE 315.

"Cable casting" has been defined as the distribution on a community antenna television system of television programs by means of high antenna or microwave transmission amplified and distributed by coaxial cable to the premises of its subscribers; it provides basically the same public service as noncable television and is so imbued with a public interest that it classifies as a public utility. Hoffman v Capitol Cablevision Systems, Inc. (1975) 82 Misc 2d 986, 372 NYS2d 482, affd (1976, 3d Dept) 52 App Div 2d 313, 383 NYS2d 674.

Easement which granted to power company and telephone company and "their respective successors and assigns the right, privilege and authority to construct, maintain, operate, repair and replace lines ... and appurtenances for the distribution of electricity and messages upon, under, along and across" plaintiffs' property authorized the companies to assign the right to a television cable company despite contention that the television facilities imposed an additional burden on plaintiffs which required payment of reasonable compensation to them. Hoffman v Capitol Cablevision Systems, Inc. (1975) 82 Misc 2d 986, 372 NYS2d 482, affd (1976, 3d Dept) 52 App Div 2d 313, 383 NYS2d 674.

Telephone utility's use of its poles was not limited to a use for telephone purposes; utility had statutory right to enter into contractual arrangements with others for use of space on its poles. New York Tel. Co. v North Hempstead (1975) 86 Misc 2d 487, 385 NYS2d 436, affd (1976, 2d Dept) 52 App Div 2d 934, 385 NYS2d 505, mod on other grounds (1977) 41 NY2d 691, 395 NYS2d 143, 363 NE2d 694.

A corporation engaged in the business of receiving, relaying and distributing television and radio broadcasts by means of wires is a telegraph and telephone corporation and should be formed pursuant to the Transportation Corporations Law. 1952 Ops Atty Gen July 21.

§ 26. Extension of lines

A telegraph corporation, a telephone corporation or a telegraph and telephone corporation heretofore or hereafter incorporated under or by any general or special law may construct, own, use and maintain any line of electric telegraph or telephone, whether or not the line and the territory in which it be located was described in its original certificate of incorporation, and whether wholly within or wholly or partly without the state, and may join with any other corporation in constructing, leasing, owning, using and maintaining such line, or hold or own any interest therein, or become lessees thereof, upon delivering to the department of state for filing a certificate of amendment. If the lines or territory are to be extended the certificate shall describe the territory in which the operations of the corporation are to be carried on.

History: Add, L 1915, ch 667, § 2; amd, L 1926, ch 762, § 1, with substance transferred from § 101, and substance of former § 26 transferred to §§ 66 and 67, L 1964, ch 734, § 8, eff June 1, 1964.

§ 27. Construction of lines

Any such corporation may erect, construct and maintain the necessary fixtures for its lines upon,

over or under any of the public roads, streets and highways; and through, across or under any of the waters within the limits of this state, and may erect, construct and maintain its necessary stations, plants, equipment or lines upon, through or over any other land, subject to the right of the owners thereof to full compensation for the same. If any such corporation can not agree with such owner or owners upon the compensation to be paid therefor, such compensation shall be ascertained in the manner provided in the eminent domain procedure law. Any such corporation is authorized, from time to time, to construct and lay lines of electrical conductors under ground in any city, village or town within the limits of this state, subject to all the provisions of law in reference to such companies not inconsistent with this section; provided that such corporation shall, before laying any such line in any city, village or town of this state, first obtain from the common council of cities, or other body having like jurisdiction therein, the trustees of villages, or the town superintendents of towns, permission to use the streets within such city, village or town for the purposes herein set forth. Nothing in this section shall limit, alter, or affect the provisions or powers relating or granted to telegraph corporations heretofore created by special act of the legislature of this state, except in so far as to confer on any such corporation the right to lay electrical conductors under ground.

History: Add, L 1926, ch 762, § 1, with substance transferred from § 102; amd, L 1977, ch 840, § 92, eff July 1, 1978 (see 1977 note below).

CASE ANNOTATIONS

1. In general
2. Constitutional matters
3. Relationship to other statutes and ordinances; federal matters
4. Application to particular entities
5. Nature of property right established
6. Obligations of construction and maintenance; nuisance
7. — Relocation
8. Procedural requirements

1. In general

Although defendant had no legal right to maintain 29 telegraph poles on plaintiff's farm, defendant could obtain such right by recourse to this section. Antonopulos v Postal Tel. Cable Co. (1941) 261 App Div 564, 26 NYS2d 403, affd (1942) 287 NY 712, 39 NE2d 931.

Unless town gave fair compensation, it lacked power to acquire an interest in telephone utility's special franchise to erect and maintain poles in public highways; town's use of such poles for street lighting equipment could not be justified as a valid exercise of town's police power. New York Tel. Co. v North Hempstead (1975) 86 Misc 2d 487, 385 NYS2d 436, affd (1976, 2d Dept) 52 App Div 2d 934, 385 NYS2d 505, mod on other grounds (1977) 41 NY2d 691, 395 NYS2d 143, 363 NE2d 694.

2. Constitutional matters

Since the franchise granted to a telephone company by Transportation Corporation Law § 27 is subject to the limitations imposed by the police power of the state and the State Department of Transportation is required to act in compliance with federal highway standards, the constitutionality of which statutes is not questioned, the refusal by the Department of Transportation to permit a telephone company to install cables under a controlled-access highway did not deny or impair any rights guaranteed to the telephone company by either the Constitution of the United States or of the state of New

York. New York Tel. Co. v Commissioner of New York State Dep't of Transp. (1970) 62 Misc 2d 6, 307 NYS2d 945.

3. Relationship to other statutes and ordinances; federal matters

An ordinance authorizing an antenna corporation to use city streets did not grant a franchise, but rather it granted the permission required by this section, before the corporation could use the city streets. Therefore, the provisions of subdivision 2, para. b of § 23 of the General City Law requiring public auction and public notice did not apply. Harper v Kingston (1959) 17 Misc 2d 627, 188 NYS2d 577.

In plaintiff city's declaratory judgment action brought only under N.Y. Transp. Corp. Law § 27 and City of Rome, N.Y., Charter § 33, seeking to compel defendant telephone company to negotiate a new franchise agreement, § 253 of the Telecommunications Act of 1996, 47 U.S.C.S. § 253, asserted only as a defense by the telephone company, did not confer federal jurisdiction to justify removal under 28 U.S.C.S. § 1441(c); the city's complaint did not comprehend a federal cause of action. City of Rome v Verizon Communs., Inc. (2004, CA2 NY) 362 F3d 168.

Town's franchise requirement for telecommunications companies seeking to provide service within the township were consistent with the town's right to approve or deny permission pursuant to N.Y. Trans. Corp. Law § 27; thus, to the extent that the local law was permissible under federal law, it was consistent with state law as well. Accordingly, the court denied the telecommunication's companies' motion for summary judgment and granted the town's motion for summary judgment with respect to this claim. TC Sys. v Town of Colonie (2003, ND NY) 263 F Supp 2d 471.

4. Application to particular entities

A corporation organized after the passage of former § 102, or its successor, cannot extend its lines within N.Y. city or lay additional lines without the consent of the municipal authorities. In re New York Independent Tel. Co. (1909) 133 App Div 635, 118 NYS 290, affd (1910) 200 NY 527, 93 NE 1126.

5. Nature of property right established

Telephone company's right to erect poles under section of the Transportation Corporations Law is a license or a privilege and not the grant of an interest in or appurtenant to real property. New York Tel. Co. v North Hempstead, 41 N.Y.2d 691, 395 N.Y.S.2d 143, 363 N.E.2d 694, 1977 N.Y. LEXIS 2018 (N.Y. 1977), abrogated, Corsello v Verizon N.Y., Inc., 18 N.Y.3d 777, 944 N.Y.S.2d 732, 967 N.E.2d 1177, 2012 N.Y. LEXIS 583 (N.Y. 2012).

Where defendant's franchise to maintain its conduits beneath the surface of a public street was dependent upon the continued existence of the street in question as a public highway and where, in the interest of the general public, the street was formally closed, that right was extinguished. Holden v New York Tel. Co. (1969, 2d Dept) 31 App Div 2d 812, 298 NYS2d 256.

Under Transportation Corporation Law § 27, a telephone company acquired a mere privilege or permit to use a portion of a public highway for a special purpose, subject to the public interest. New York Tel. Co. v Commissioner of New York State Dep't of Transp. (1970) 62 Misc 2d 6, 307 NYS2d 945.

Transportation Corporation Law, § 27 does not contemplate a condemnation of subsurface rights for the purpose of installation under private property. Buholtz v Rochester Tel. Corp. (1971) 65 Misc 2d 1071, 319 NYS2d 202, mod on other grounds (1973, 4th Dept) 40 App Div 2d 283, 339 NYS2d 775, app dismd (1974) 33 NY2d 939, 353 NYS2d 728, 309 NE2d 129.

Telephone utility's use of its poles was not limited to a use for telephone purposes; utility had statutory right to enter into contractual arrangements with others for use of space on its poles. New York Tel. Co. v North Hempstead (1975) 86 Misc 2d 487, 385 NYS2d 436, affd (1976, 2d Dept) 52 App Div 2d 934, 385 NYS2d 505, mod on other grounds (1977) 41 NY2d 691, 395 NYS2d 143, 363 NE2d 694.

Contrary to contention that attachment of lighting equipment to telephone utility's poles by town and its lighting district constituted an authorized de facto condemnation of an interest in real property because utility's special franchise to erect and maintain poles in public highways was an interest in real property, such franchise was not an interest in real property. New York Tel. Co. v North Hempstead (1975) 86 Misc 2d 487, 385 NYS2d 436, affd (1976, 2d Dept) 52 App Div 2d 934, 385 NYS2d 505, mod on other grounds (1977) 41 NY2d 691, 395 NYS2d 143, 363 NE2d 694.

Privileges secured hereunder constitute property rights which may not be withdrawn, impaired, or violated without compensation. 1912 Ops Atty Gen 61.

Where a municipality accepts a dedication of streets subject to an easement granted to a utility, which has previously installed equipment, such as mains, pipes and wires, in, on or under those streets, that equipment does not become tangible property of a special franchise by virtue of such acceptance. 8 Op Counsel SBEA No. 61 (1985, Nov 21).

6. Obligations of construction and maintenance; nuisance

Where a telephone company erects poles on a public highway under authority of this section, it must place them so that they will not interfere with or make dangerous the use of the highway by the public. Bailey v Bell Tel. Co. (1911) 147 App Div 224, 131 NYS 1000.

Since this section authorizes the placing of poles in streets, they are not an absolute nuisance as a matter of law. Permission to locate poles within the highway creates the implied condition that they must be so located as to avoid unreasonable and unnecessary danger to travelers upon such highway, and ordinarily that question is for the jury. Wagner v Amsterdam (1939) 256 App Div 144, 9 NYS2d 750.

Although a telephone company has the right to maintain its wires across a public highway, it cannot obstruct the reasonable use of the highway for moving a building 29 feet high by a person who has obtained the requisite permit therefor. New York Tel. Co. v Dittman (1916) 96 Misc 60, 159 NYS 625.

7. — Relocation

The plaintiff telephone company was not entitled to reimbursement from the defendant city for the expense of relocating in another street the company's telephone lines and other facilities which had lain in the public street, where the relocation was made necessary by the city's closing part of the street and using it as part of the site for a "middle income housing project" by conveying the site to a limited dividend corporation for development. New York Tel. Co. v Binghamton (1966) 18 NY2d 152, 272 NYS2d 359, 219 NE2d 184.

Where plans for the improvement of a highway are such as to require the relocation of the poles and wires of telephone or telegraph companies, it is incumbent upon the companies to relocate them at their own expense. 1913 Ops Atty Gen 176.

The expense of removing and relocating electric poles situated within the bounds of a county road because of reconstruction of such road is that of the company and not the county superintendent of highways. 1956 Ops St Compt File #8149.

8. Procedural requirements

Where there was no express reservation to limited use of telephone pole for municipal purposes in original grant to telephone company of right to erect and maintain poles in public streets and highways of town, and where grant of such right came from state and not from town, assent of town was in no wise required to authorize telephone company to erect its poles and, thus, there was no grant from the town to which a reservation in its favor could have been attached. New York Tel. Co. v North Hempstead, 41 N.Y.2d 691, 395 N.Y.S.2d 143, 363 N.E.2d 694, 1977 N.Y. LEXIS 2018 (N.Y. 1977), abrogated, Corsello v Verizon N.Y., Inc., 18 N.Y.3d 777, 944 N.Y.S.2d 732, 967 N.E.2d 1177, 2012 N.Y. LEXIS 583 (N.Y. 2012).

Village may grant telephone company permission to install lines in village streets without public hearing. 1967 Ops Atty Gen May 23.

A cable television company desiring to establish cable television facilities within the right–of–way of a public highway established by prescription or user must be franchised by the municipality in which such facilities will be provided and must also obtain the consent of the owner of the underlying fee to the roadbed. If such owner's consent cannot be obtained, the cable company is authorized to acquire the necessary land by eminent domain. Ops Atty Gen 83–66.

§ 28. Transmission of dispatches

Every such corporation shall receive dispatches from and for other telegraph or telephone lines or corporations, and from and for any person, and on payment of the usual charges for transmitting dispatches as established by the rules and regulations of such corporation, transmit the same with impartiality and good faith and in the order in which they are received, and if it neglects or refuses so to do, it shall pay one hundred dollars for every such refusal or neglect to the person sending or desiring to send any such dispatch and entitled to have it so transmitted,

Transportation Corporations Law

but arrangements may be made with the proprietors or publishers or [of] newspapers for the transmission for publication of intelligence of general and public interest out of its regular order.

History: Add, L 1926, ch 762, § 1, eff Oct 1, 1926, with substance transferred from § 103.

CASE ANNOTATIONS

The word "impartiality," as used in this section, requires impartiality of credit as well as impartiality in service, and, where financial standing of proposed customer is unquestioned, the refusal of credit customarily extended to others is arbitrary discrimination and a violation of statutory mandate of equality. People ex rel. Western Union Tel. Co. v Public Service Com. (1920) 230 NY 95, 129 NE 220, 12 ALR 960, remittitur den (1921) 230 NY 657, 130 NE 933.

Under this section a telegraph company presenting itself as a customer to another telegraph company is as much a part of the general public as any other customer and entitled to the same rights and privileges. People ex rel. Western Union Tel. Co. v Public Service Com. (1920) 230 NY 95, 129 NE 220, 12 ALR 960, remittitur den (1921) 230 NY 657, 130 NE 933.

In an action to recover for the death of plaintiff's intestate, alleged to have been caused by the failure of defendant to furnish telephone service so that a physician could not be promptly called, the defense that the liability of defendant was limited by schedule of rates filed with Commission was improperly stricken out. Emery v Rochester Tel. Corp. (1936) 271 NY 306, 3 NE2d 434.

The object of this section is punishment, not damages, and it should not be extended by implication to cover an act not within its obvious meaning. Saltzburg v Utica Home Tel. Co. (1913) 159 App Div 51, 144 NYS 309.

Action may not be brought to recover the penalty under this section on the ground that the telephone company removed a subscriber's telephone after his refusal to pay an unjustified claim for past services. Saltzburg v Utica Home Tel. Co. (1913) 159 App Div 51, 144 NYS 309.

Where plaintiff physician, who had contracted with defendant's predecessor for the special rate then given to physicians, was notified by defendant, after it acquired the rights of the original company, that the special rate was abolished but refused to pay the higher rate, and after due notice defendant discontinued service to him, he was not entitled to recover the penalty prescribed by this section. Kevand v New York Tel. Co. (1913) 159 App Div 628, 145 NYS 414, affd (1917) 222 NY 595, 118 NE 1064.

The penalty prescribed in this section has no reference to the unjustified act of a telephone company in suspending telephone service to a subscriber on the ground that he had failed to pay monthly telephone charges which had in fact been paid, since the relation of a subscriber to the telephone company is contractual, and his remedy is an action for breach of contract. Rose v New York Tel. Co. (1915) 167 App Div 691, 152 NYS 827.

A telegraph company sending messages to addresses both within and without the state is subject to both state and federal laws respecting discrimination in the transmission of messages. Klein v Western Union Tel. Co. (1939) 257 App Div 336, 13 NYS2d 441.

A telegraph company, in accepting, transmitting, and delivering messages is ordinarily entitled to a qualified privilege which rebuts any presumption of malice from the fact that a message is libelous per se as between the sender and the party mentioned therein, and, in order to justify a recovery, the party libeled must furnish evidence of actual or express malice or bad faith on the part of the carrier. Klein v Western Union Tel. Co. (1939) 257 App Div 336, 13 NYS2d 441.

A motion to set aside a verdict for plaintiff and for a new trial was granted in an action against defendant telegraph company for having received, transmitted, and delivered to nine separate addressees a telegram concerning plaintiff which, as between the sender and plaintiff, was concededly libelous per se, where it appeared that some of the addressees were within the state and others were without so that defendant was subject to both the Federal and State laws; that there was nothing to show that the statements were not true or that, as between the sender and the addressees, the telegram was not a privileged communication; that the verdict of the jury, so far as it found that defendant did not act in good faith, was contrary to the weight of the evidence; that the defendant, through one of its supervisors, had communicated with the sender of the telegram; and that the trial judge erred in his charge to the jury as to nominal damages and privilege. Klein v Western Union Tel. Co. (1939) 257 App Div 336, 13 NYS2d 441.

The telephone company is bound to furnish service to all who pay its proper charges and obey its reasonable regulations. Figari v New York Tel. Co. (1969, 2d Dept) 32 App Div 2d 434, 303 NYS2d 245.

This section is to be strictly construed; to be entitled to recover the penalty prescribed, plaintiff must bring his case plainly within the statute. Meyers v Western Union Tel. Co. (1913) 82 Misc 266, 143 NYS 574.

Where, owing to a mistake in the transmission of a prepaid telegram from Pittsburgh, Penn., through defendant's Buffalo, N. Y., office, it was received at the Dunkirk, N.Y., office as addressed to 707 Park Avenue instead of 709 Park Avenue, and there was no evidence of partiality, bad faith, or neglect on the part of defendant to perform its statutory duty, judgment in favor of plaintiff in an action to recover the penalty under this section will be reversed. Meyers v Western Union Tel. Co. (1913) 82 Misc 266, 143 NYS 574.

§ 29. Transfer of property to other corporations

Any such corporation may lease, sell or convey its property, rights, privileges and franchises, or any interest therein, or any part thereof to any telegraph, telephone or telegraph and telephone corporation organized under or created by the laws of this or any other state, and may acquire by purchase, lease or conveyance the property rights, privileges and franchises, or any interest therein or part thereof of any such corporation, and may make payments therefor in its own stock, money or property, or receive payment therefor in the stock, money or property of the corporation to which the same may be so sold, leased or conveyed.

History: Add, L 1926, ch 762, § 1, with substance transferred from § 104; amd, L 1964, ch 734, § 9, eff June 1, 1964.

CASE ANNOTATIONS

Where the property of a telephone company has been sold in compliance with this section, a stockholder who did not consent to such sale is not entitled to have appraisers appointed for the purpose of ascertaining the value of her stock under Stock Corp. Law, former § 17 [now § 21]. Where there is a conflict between that section and this one, the latter must prevail. In re Bronson (1917) 177 App Div 374, 164 NYS 179, affd (1917) 221 NY 661, 117 NE 1062.

The consent of stockholders to the sale of the property of a telephone company, in order to be binding, must be given at a stockholders' meeting. Ambler v Smith (1932) 237 App Div 226, 262 NYS 208.

§ 30. Special police officers of corporation operating signal systems

The police department or board of police of any city may, in addition to the police force now authorized by law, appoint a number of persons, not exceeding two hundred, who may be designated by any corporation operating a system of signaling by telegraph to a central office for police assistance, to act as special patrol officer in connection with such telegraph system. And the persons so appointed shall, in and about such service, have all the powers possessed by the members of the regular force, except as they may be limited by and subject to the supervision and control of the police department or board of police of such city. No person shall be appointed such special police officer who does not possess the qualifications required by such police department or board of police for such special service; and persons so appointed shall be subject, in case of emergency, to do duty as part of the regular police force of the city. The police department or board of police shall have power to revoke any such appointment at any time, and every person appointed shall wear a badge and uniform, to be furnished by such corporation and approved by the police department or board of police; such uniform shall be designated at the time of the first appointment and shall be the permanent uniform to be worn by such special police, and the pay of such special patrol officer and all expenses connected with their service shall be wholly paid by such corporation, and no expense or liability shall at any time be incurred or paid by the police department or board of police of any city, for or by reason of the services of such persons so appointed.

History: Add, L, 1909, ch 219; amd, L 1926, ch 762, § 1, eff Oct 1, 1926, with substance transferred from § 105; L 2018, ch 476, § 243, eff Dec 28, 2018.

Blackline Showing Effect of 2018 Amendments. — § 30. Special policemen police officers of corporation operating signal systems. The police department or board of police of any city may, in addition to the police force now authorized by law, appoint a number of persons, not exceeding two hundred, who may be designated by any corporation operating a system of signaling by telegraph to a central office for police assistance, to act as special patrolmen patrol officer in connection with such telegraph system. And the persons so appointed shall, in and about such service, have all the powers possessed by the members of the regular force, except as they may be limited by and subject to the supervision and control of the police department or board of police of such city. No person shall be appointed such special policeman police officer who does not possess the qualifications required by such police department or board of police for such special service; and persons so appointed shall be subject, in case of emergency, to do duty as part of the regular police force of the city. The police department or board of police shall have power to revoke any such appointment at any time, and every person appointed shall wear a badge and uniform, to be furnished by such corporation and approved by the police department or board of police; such uniform shall be designated at the time of the first appointment and shall be the permanent uniform to be worn by such special police, and the pay of such special patrolmen patrol officer and all expenses connected with their service shall be wholly paid by such corporation, and no expense or liability shall at any time be incurred or paid by the police department or board of police of any city, for or by reason of the services of such persons so appointed.

§ 30–a. Merger or consolidation of telephone corporations

Any two or more domestic telephone corporations may merge or consolidate with each other, in accordance with the procedure and with the effect set forth in article nine of the business corporation law.

History: Add, L 1950, ch 479; amd, L 1964, ch 734, § 11, eff June 1, 1964.

Section heading, amd, L 1964, ch 734, § 11, eff June 1, 1964.

§ 30–b. Merger or consolidation of telegraph corporations

Any two or more domestic telegraph corporations may merge or consolidate with each other, in accordance with the procedure and with the effect set forth in article nine of the business corporation law.

History: Add, L 1968, ch 960, eff June 22, 1968.

§ 31. Application of article

The provisions of this article shall apply to corporations owning, leasing, maintaining or operating or organized for the purpose of owning, leasing, maintaining or operating, a radio or wireless plant, equipment or system as a part of, or in conjunction with, a station or stations engaged in or designed to engage in public commercial intercourse by wireless telegraphy or telephony, and also corporations for the generation and distribution of music electrically; and such corporations shall possess the powers and be subject to all the duties granted to or imposed upon telegraph or telephone corporations thereby except that such corporations organized solely for the generation and distribution of music electrically shall not have or exercise the right of condemnation.

History: Add, L, 1909, ch 219; amd, L 1926, ch 762, § 1, eff Oct 1, 1926, with substance transferred from § 106.

CASE ANNOTATIONS

A corporation whose purpose is to engage in a mobile wireless message business is properly formed under this section. 1947 Ops Atty Gen Nov 21.

ARTICLE 4
WATER–WORKS CORPORATIONS

§ 40. Definition

A water–works corporation is a corporation organized to supply water by mains or pipes to any of the cities, towns or villages in this state, and the inhabitants thereof.

History: Add, L, 1909, ch 219; amd, L 1926, ch 762, § 1, eff Oct 1, 1926, with substance transferred from § 80 and substance of former § 40 transferred to § 80.

CASE ANNOTATIONS

The provisions of the Public Service Law and the Transportation Corporations Law with respect of rates and charges did not apply to a realty corporation which installed pipelines for the temporary supply of water to its purchasers. Malone v Custom Manor, Inc. (1956) 4 Misc 2d 976, 158 NYS2d 241.

§ 41. Municipal consent to incorporation

No certificate of incorporation of a waterworks corporation shall be filed unless there be annexed thereto a consent to the formation of the corporation, signed and acknowledged by the local authorities of each municipality named in such certificate. Such authorities shall be: in a city, a majority of the members of the board or body having charge of the water supply, or if there be no such board or body, a majority of the members of the local legislative body; in a village, a majority of the members of the board of trustees; in a town outside of a village, the town superintendent of highways and a majority of the members of the town board. Such consent to the formation of the corporation shall not be granted by said local authorities until ten days prior notice in writing of the application for such consent and until an engineering plan for proposed water system specifying location and size and type of wells, pumps, distribution mains and other facilities of the water supply and/or distribution system is furnished by the water works corporation to the local authorities and to the county water authority, and to the county water district if there be such authority or district where the proposed corporation seeks to operate; and until said authority or district has reported in writing to the municipality named in the certificate of incorporation its recommendations as to whether or not such consent should be granted, setting forth the reasons for such recommendation and a finding as to whether the proposed water supply and/or distribution system is reasonably comparable to standards of a county–wide water system and suitable for eventual integration with such county–wide water system. Said report shall be filed with such municipality on or before the tenth day after the giving of the notice aforesaid.

History: Add, L, 1909, ch 219; amd, L 1926, ch 762, § 1, with substance of former § 41 transferred to § 82, L 1960, ch 262, L 1969, ch 782, eff July 1, 1969.

CASE ANNOTATIONS

No provision of law exists requiring applicants for municipal consent for incorporation of water works corporations to be property owners. 1955 Ops Atty Gen Mar 24 (informal).

A water works corporation would not acquire an exclusive franchise to supply water to a municipality as a result of obtaining the consent required by § 41 of the Transportation Corporations Law from a municipal corporation. 1958 Ops St Compt File #1007.

When organizers make an application to a municipality for consent for incorporation of a water works corporation, the application need not be forwarded to a county water agency which is part of the county department of public works. However, the agency's aid may be requested by the municipality in determining whether or not consent should be granted. 1968 Ops St Compt File #680.

A town, as a condition to giving consent to the incorporation of a water–works corporation to serve a proposed condominium complex, may require the execution of an agreement by the condominium developer and the promoters of the water–works corporation which will provide safeguards with respect to the continued functioning of the water supply system. 1979 Op St Compt File #884.

§ 42.   Duty to supply water; contracts with municipalities

Such corporation shall supply each city, town or village through which the conduits or mains of such corporation may pass, or wherein such corporation may have organized, and the inhabitants thereof, with pure and wholesome water, at reasonable rates. The board of trustees of any incorporated village and the water commissioners or other board or officials performing the duties of water commissioners and having charge of the water supply of any city, shall have the power to contract in the name and behalf of the municipal corporation for the term of one year or more for the delivery by such corporation to the village or city of water, through hydrants or otherwise, for the extinguishment of fires and for sanitary and other public purposes. The amount agreed to be paid shall be annually raised as a part of the expenses of such village or city, and shall be assessed, levied and collected in the same manner as other expenses, and when collected shall be kept as a separate fund, and paid according to the terms and conditions of such contract. No such contract shall be made for a longer period than ten years nor for an annual amount exceeding in the aggregate two and one–half mills for every dollar of the taxable property of such village or city, except (a) upon the petition of a majority of the taxable inhabitants of any such village or city, or of the portion thereof to be supplied, or (b) upon a proposition to authorize the same submitted to a vote of the electors of the village or city, in the manner provided by the village law or city charter, and approved by a majority of the voters entitled to vote and voting thereon at an annual election or a special election duly called. Such contract shall be for a term not exceeding twenty years.

History: Add, L, 1909, ch 219; amd, L 1926, ch 762, § 1, eff Oct 1, 1926, with substance transferred from § 81 and substance of former § 42 transferred to § 83.

CASE ANNOTATIONS

1. Generally
2. Extent of obligation to supply water
3. Contracts for services
4. Rates

1. Generally

A water company is under duty to supply water to inhabitants and to municipality itself. It may impose a rule limiting wasteful use of water or bind a customer by any other reasonable regulation. Pond v New Rochelle Water Co. (1911) 143 App Div 69, 127 NYS 582, affd (1912) 206 NY 719, 100 NE 1132.

Statute of limitations barred plaintiffs' action against individual members of board of water supply, alleging violation of CLS Trans Corp § 42 (which deals with duty of water works corporation to supply water); timely service of summons and complaint in prior related action against water board did not toll statute in instant action on ground that defendants were "united in interest" within meaning of CLS CPLR § 203(b) since board members were not named as party defendants in prior action, and plaintiffs failed to show that their failure to join individual board members at outset was not due to inexcusable neglect. Fraccola v Utica Bd. of Water Supply (1988, 4th Dept) 142 App Div 2d 936, 531 NYS2d 154.

A Town Board may establish a water supply district without a petition of the taxpayers. 1921 Ops Atty Gen 340.

Expenses of contract between city and water–works corporation for provision of water to fire hydrants must be assessed through real property taxation. 1993 Ops Atty Gen I 93–16.

A water works corporation would not acquire an exclusive franchise to supply water to a municipality as a result of obtaining the consent required by § 41 of the Transportation Corporations Law from a municipal corporation. 1958 Ops St Compt File #1007.

2. Extent of obligation to supply water

A corporation organized for the purpose of supplying water to the authorities and inhabitants of the former town of Jamaica, now incorporated in N. Y. City, is required by statute to supply said authorities and inhabitants with pure and wholesome water at reasonable rates and, by virtue of the charter of greater New York, the Commissioner of Water Supply, Gas and Electricity, in his power to exercise superintendence, regulation, and control in respect of the supply of water by such company, may direct it to install new mains and hydrants at its own expense. New York v Jamaica Water Supply Co. (1917) 181 App Div 49, 167 NYS 763, affd (1919) 226 NY 572, 123 NE 859.

A peremptory mandamus order directing a water company operating on a town to extend its mains and instal fire hydrants in a water supply district established by the Town Board will be affirmed where it appears that the Town Board requested such extension of service and that the statutory limit of expenditure by the town will not be exceeded because of such extension. The duty and power of determining the need of extension of service is ministerial, not judicial, and the court has no power to determine the reasonableness of the requirements of the Board. Mamaroneck v New York Interurban Water Co. (1922) 203 App Div 122, 196 NYS 438, affd (1923) 235 NY 563, 139 NE 735.

Application by a village should be granted for a peremptory mandamus order to compel defendant water company to extend its water system in the village in and along the entire length of the street which was accepted by the village since the granting of the franchise to the water company. Massena v St. Lawrence Water Co. (1926) 126 Misc 524, 214 NYS 113.

3. Contracts for services

A property owner who has suffered fire loss has no cause of action against the water works company for breach of its statutory duty to furnish an adequate supply of water, since the breach of duty is to the city. Neither is an action maintainable for breach of contract in the absence of evidence of an intention that the company was to be answerable to the inhabitants, nor for a common law tort in the absence of malice. H. R. Moch Co. v Rensselaer Water Co. (1928) 247 NY 160, 159 NE 896, 62 ALR 1199.

Notwithstanding the charter of Greater New York provides that it shall be unlawful for the Commissioner of Water Supply to make contracts with water companies for water to be used for public purposes without the assent of the Board of Estimate and Apportionment and the written approval of certain municipal officers and that no contract for a public water supply may be made save in accordance with the requirements of the charter, where the city takes water from the mains of a water supply company which, by virtue of this section, is under a statutory duty to furnish water for public use in a district where the city has no other water supply available, it is liable for the reasonable value of the water used. Staten Island Water Supply Co. v New York (1911) 144 App Div 318, 128 NYS 1028.

The power of an incorporated village to contract for a water supply is in its Board of Trustees and Board of Water Commissioners, if such Board exists. Villa Park Ass'n v North Hempstead (1914) 162 App Div 45, 146 NYS 1047.

After a village has been incorporated within boundaries of a town, the Town Board has no authority to enter into contract with water company to furnish water for fire purposes to village within its boundaries, nor can it assess property in the village for its portion of the cost. Villa Park Ass'n v North Hempstead (1914) 162 App Div 45, 146 NYS 1047.

A contract between a water corporation and a city providing for reimbursement by the city for changes made by the water works corporation and expressly limited to ten years was not extended so as to constitute a continuing legal obligation on the city by the fact that for a time after its expiration the practical dealings of the parties with respect to reimbursement continued in accordance with the contract. New York Interurban Water Co. v Mt. Vernon (1918) 185 App Div 305, 173 NYS 38.

Where a contract between a village and a water company requiring the company to establish a waterworks and to supply a number of street hydrants had expired, and no fire protection was actually afforded by the company thereafter, it could not recover hydrant rentals on quantum meruit on the ground that because it did not seal its hydrants they were ready for use if fire had made such use necessary. Commonwealth Water Co. v Castleton (1920) 192 App Div 697, 183 NYS 753.

Nothing in this section precludes a city from agreeing to pay the cost of relocation of mains of a water company, supplying it with water, in connection with street grade changes. New Rochelle Water Co. v New Rochelle (1962) 34 Misc 2d 952, 227 NYS2d 741, mod on other grounds (1963, 2d Dept) 18 App Div 2d 922, 238 NYS2d 169.

4. Rates

In the absence of a schedule of rates fixed by a board or body so authorized by delegated authority, a water corporation has the power itself to promulgate reasonable rates, and such rates are prima facie reasonable. Silberberg v Citizens' Water Supply Co. (1921) 116 Misc 595, 190 NYS 349.

The reasonableness of the rates charged is a question of fact which may be judicially determined in an appropriate action. Follett v Waterworks Co. of Seneca Falls (1924) 123 Misc 825, 206 NYS 464.

Municipalities and the individuals resident therein, consumers of water supplied by a water company, may maintain an action to enjoin water company from charging unreasonable rates fixed in its schedule of increased water rates. Mamaroneck v New York Interurban Water Co. (1926) 126 Misc 382, 212 NYS 639.

§ 43. Powers

Every such corporation shall have the following additional powers:

1. To lay and maintain its pipes and hydrants for delivering and distributing water in any street, highway or public place of any city, town or village in which it has obtained the consent required by section forty–one of this article.

2. To lay its water pipes in any streets or avenues or public places of an adjoining city, town or village; provided that such right in an adjoining city or village having a population of more than twelve thousand inhabitants shall be subject to the permission of the local authorities thereof and upon such conditions as they may prescribe.

3. To cause examinations and surveys to be made to determine the proper location of its waterworks, and for such purpose by its officers, agents or servants to enter upon any lands or waters, subject to liability for all damages done.

4. To enter into appropriate agreements with the secretary of agriculture of the United States department of agriculture to operate without profit for the term specified therein for the purpose of qualifying to receive federal assistance pursuant to the consolidated farmers home administration act of nineteen hundred sixty–one and any federal laws amendatory and supplementary thereto. Any such agreement to operate without profit shall be subject to the approval of a majority of the stockholders entitled to vote threat at any regular or special stockholders' meeting. Any stockholder so entitled to vote who does not vote for or consent in writing to the taking of this action, shall, subject to and by complying with the provisions of section six hundred twenty–three of the business corporation law, have the right to receive payment of the fair value of his stock and the other rights and benefits provided by such section.

History: Add, L, 1909, ch 219; amd, L 1926, ch 762, § 1, eff Oct 1, 1926, with substance transferred from § 82 and substance of former § 43 transferred to § 84.

Sub 4, add, L 1966, ch 481, § 1, eff May 31, 1966.

CASE ANNOTATIONS

The right to maintain and operate a water system in the streets does not come from permission of village but direct from Legislature under this section. Waterloo Water Co. v Waterloo (1922) 200 App Div 718, 193 NYS 360.

The amendment to sub. 2 of this section providing that the permission of the adjoining town or city through which a water company desires to lay pipes must be obtained, is not applicable where work was commenced prior to the amendment. New York v Citizens' Water Supply Co. (1923) 204 App Div 783, 198 NYS 816, affd (1924) 237 NY 587, 143 NE 753.

§ 44.   Survey and map

Before taking or using any land, for its corporate purposes such corporation shall cause a survey and map to be made of the lands intended to be taken designating the land of the several owners or occupants thereof, which map shall be signed by the president and its secretary, and filed in the office of the county clerk of the county in which such lands are situated.

History: Add, L, 1909, ch 219; amd, L 1926, ch 762, § 1, eff Oct 1, 1926, with substance transferred from § 83 and substance of former § 44 transferred to § 85.

CASE ANNOTATIONS

The failure of petitioner to file the map required by this section was a jurisdictional defect as this section is mandatory. Old Homestead Water Co. v Treyz (1922) 202 App Div 98, 195 NYS 723, affd (1922) 234 NY 612, 138 NE 467.

A public service corporation supplying electricity which failed to file a map pursuant to this section cannot institute condemnation proceedings under its special act of incorporation and this section, but, having title to the major part of water–flow at site where it plans to develop additional power, it may maintain its action under Conser. Law, § 624, subd. 3, where Public Service Commission has granted an order pursuant to said statute declaring the contemplated acquisition necessary. In re Niagara, Lockport & Ontario Power Co. (1925) 125 Misc 269, 210 NYS 748.

§ 45.   Condemnation of real property

Any such corporation shall have the right to acquire real estate, or any interest therein, necessary for the purposes of its incorporation, and the right to lay, relay, repair and maintain conduits and water pipes with connections and fixtures, in, through or over the lands of others, the right to intercept and divert the flow of waters from the lands of riparian owners, and from persons owning or interested in any waters, and the right to prevent the flow of drainage of noxious or impure matters from the lands of others into its reservoirs or sources of supply. If any such corporation, which has made a contract with any city, town or village or with any of the inhabitants thereof for the supply of pure and wholesome water as authorized by section forty–two, shall be unable to agree upon the terms of purchase of any such property or rights, it may acquire the same by condemnation. But no such corporation shall have power to take or use water from any of the canals of this state, or any canal reservoirs as feeders, or any streams which have been taken by the state for the purpose of supplying the canals with water.

History: Add, L, 1909, ch 219; amd, L 1926, ch 762, § 1, eff Oct 1, 1926, with substance transferred from § 84 and substance of former § 45 transferred to § 86.

§ 46.   Corporations may contract with other cities, towns or villages; certificate of extension; effect of merger

When any such corporation has entered into a contract with the authorities of any city, town or village not mentioned in its certificate of incorporation, but situated in the same county as the city, towns or villages mentioned therein or in an adjoining county, to supply it with pure and wholesome water, it may file a certificate which shall be entitled and endorsed "certificate of extension of territory of_____pursuant to section forty–six of the transportation corporations law" (the blank space being filled in with the name of the corporation) and which shall state:

1. The name of the corporation, and, if it has been changed, the name under which it was originally incorporated.

2. The name of such other city, town or village to be so supplied with water.

Such certificate shall be signed and acknowledged by the president or a vice–president and the secretary or an assistant secretary of the corporation, who shall make and annex an affidavit that they have been authorized to execute and file the same by the vote of a majority of the directors of the corporation.

Such certificate shall be filed in each public office in which the certificate of incorporation is filed. Any corporation which has heretofore filed or shall file such certificate as aforesaid may thereupon supply any such city, town or village with water in the same manner and with the same rights and subject to the same requirements as if it had been named in the original certificate of incorporation, and as if such certificate of incorporation had had annexed thereto a consent to the formation of the corporation, signed and acknowledged by the local authorities of such municipal corporation, as defined in section forty–one of this chapter.

The right of merger of waterworks corporations shall not be limited to corporations operating in the same or adjoining counties, and if a waterworks corporation be merged pursuant to law with another waterworks corporation operating in the state, any municipal corporation or political subdivision of the state, and any public officer, board or body, authorized by statute to contract with such a merged corporation, shall have power and authority to contract and deal with the possessor corporation in the same manner and with the same effect as with such merged corporation.

History: Add, L, 1909, ch 219; amd, L 1926, ch 762, § 1, with substance transferred from § 85 and substance of former § 46 transferred to § 87, L 1929, ch 148, § 1, eff March 16, 1929.

CASE ANNOTATIONS

This section applies only to those contracts which place a water company in the same legal situation it holds in the territory of its original incorporation. People ex rel. Urban Water Supply Co. v

Connolly (1914) 164 App Div 163, 149 NYS 693, affd (1915) 213 NY 706, 108 NE 1105.

Woodbury, N.Y., Local Law No. 6, which prohibited the removal of groundwater for use outside of the village, except by intermunicipal agreement with the Village Board of Trustees, was preempted by the New York Transportation Corporations Law since the procedure for obtaining a certificate of extension did not require a water-works corporation to obtain the consent or permission of the municipality where it was originally incorporated, which comported with the policy in favor of the extension of water resources to less-advantageously situated municipalities. Woodbury Hgts. Estates Water Co., Inc. v Village of Woodbury (2013, 2d Dept) 111 App Div 3d 699, 975 NYS2d 101.

Water works corporation's challenge to Woodall, N.Y., Local Law No. 6, which prohibited the removal of groundwater for use outside of the village, except by intermunicipal agreement with the Village Board of Trustees, was ripe for adjudication since the corporation had obtained the written consent of a neighboring town to provide a proposed housing subdivision in the town with water and had filed a certificate of extension authorizing it to supply the town with water; the corporation's injury by virtue of Local Law No. 6 was present, rather than hypothetical, contingent or remote. Woodbury Hgts. Estates Water Co., Inc. v Village of Woodbury (2013, 2d Dept) 111 App Div 3d 699, 975 NYS2d 101.

§ 47. Merger or consolidation of waterworks corporations

Any two or more domestic waterworks corporations may merge or consolidate with each other, in accordance with the procedure and with the effect set forth in article nine of the business corporation law.

History: Add, L 1939, ch 447; amd, L 1964, ch 734, § 13, eff June 1, 1964.

Former § 47, add, L 1909, ch 219; omitted, L 1926, ch 762, with substance transferred to § 88.

Section heading, amd, L 1964, ch 734, § 13, eff June 1, 1964.

ARTICLE 5
[REPEALED]

§§ 60-69–d. [Repealed]

History: § 60, add, L 1909, ch 219; amd, L 1926, ch 762, with substance transferred from § 20 and substance of former § 60 transferred to § 10, L 1947, ch 784, § 6, L 1955, ch 633, § 9, L 1958, ch 223, § 1, L 1964, ch 734, § 14, L 1970, ch 267, § 45; repealed, L 1983, ch 635, § 3, eff Jan 1, 1984.

§ 60–a, add, L 1955, ch 633, § 7; repealed, L 1959, ch 169, § 2, eff March 24, 1959.

§ 61, add, L 1909, ch 219; amd, L 1926, ch 762, with substance transferred from § 21 and substance of former § 61 transferred to § 11, L 1955, ch 633, § 10; repealed, L 1983, ch 635, § 3, eff Jan 1, 1984.

§ 62, add, L 1909, ch 219; amd, L 1926, ch 762, with substance transferred from § 22 and substance of former § 62 transferred to § 12, L 1955, ch 633, § 11; repealed, L 1983, ch 635, § 3, eff Jan 1, 1984.

§ 63, add, L 1909, ch 219; amd, L 1926, ch 762, with substance transferred from § 23 and substance of former § 63 transferred to § 13, L 1954, ch 736, § 1, L 1970, ch 267, § 46; repealed, L 1983, ch 635, § 3, eff Jan 1, 1984.

§ 64, add, L 1909, ch 219; amd, L 1926, ch 762, with substance transferred from § 24 and substance of former § 64 transferred to § 14, L 1970, ch 267, § 47; repealed, L 1983, ch 635, § 3, eff Jan 1, 1984.

§ 65, add, L 1909, ch 219; amd, L 1926, ch 762, with substance transferred from § 25 and substance of former § 65 transferred to § 15, L 1970, ch 267, § 48; repealed, L 1983, ch 635, § 3, eff Jan 1, 1984.

§ 66, add, L 1909, ch 219; amd, L 1926, ch 762, with substance transferred from § 26 and substance of former § 66 transferred to § 16, L 1950, ch 755, § 3, L 1953, ch 449, § 1, L 1955, ch 633, § 12, L 1970, ch 267, § 49, L 1970, ch 801, § 1, L 1971, ch 1059, § 1, L 1972, ch 194, L 1974, ch 870, § 4; repealed, L 1983, ch 635, § 3, eff Jan 1, 1984.

§ 67, add, L 1922, ch 271; amd, L 1926, ch 762, with substance transferred from § 26 and substance of former § 67 transferred to § 17, L 1950, ch 755, § 4, L 1953, ch 449, § 2, L 1955, ch 633, § 13, L 1970, ch 267, § 50, L 1970, ch 801, § 2, L 1971, ch 1059, § 3, L 1972, ch 194, § 2, L 1974, ch 870, § 4; repealed, L 1983, ch 635, § 3, eff Jan 1, 1984.

§ 68, add, L 1928, ch 717, § 1; repealed, L 1983, ch 635, § 3, eff Jan 1, 1984.

§ 69, add, L 1926, ch 762; amd, L 1950, ch 755, § 5, L 1970, ch 801, § 3, L 1971, ch 1059, § 3, L 1974, ch 870, § 5; repealed, L 1983, ch 635, § 3, eff Jan 1, 1984.

§ 69–a, add, L 1928, ch 717, § 1; repealed, L 1983, ch 635, § 3, eff Jan 1, 1984.

§ 69–b, add, L 1928, ch 717, § 1; repealed, L 1983, ch 635, § 3, eff Jan 1, 1984.

§ 69–c, add, L 1928, ch 717, § 1; amd, L 1945, ch 855, § 74, L 1970, ch 267, § 51; repealed, L 1983, ch 635, § 3, eff Jan 1, 1984.

§ 69–d, add, L 1928, ch 717, § 1; amd, L 1970, ch 267, § 52; repealed, L 1983, ch 635, § 3, eff Jan 1, 1984.

ARTICLE 6
FERRY CORPORATIONS

§ 70. Definition

A ferry corporation is a corporation organized to operate a ferry, wholly within or partly without this state.

History: Add, L 1926, ch 762, § 1, eff Oct 1, 1926, with substance transferred from § 2.

CASE ANNOTATIONS

No burden is placed on interstate commerce by a statute which provides that a ferry corporation is a corporation organized to operate a ferry wholly within or partly without this State. Mascony Transport & Ferry Service, Inc. v Mitchell (1978) 94 Misc 2d 618, 405 NYS2d 380.

§ 71. Powers

Any such corporation shall have power to take by grant or by assignment a franchise or right to establish and operate a ferry or ferries, as specified in the certificate of incorporation, subject to the rights of any person, or municipal or other corporation.

In any case when an application is made to the local governing body of a county without the city of New York for a grant such local governing body is authorized to make such grant if a public necessity therefor is shown. Whenever it is shown to such local governing body upon an application for a grant that the tangible property of a ferry corporation, employed or to be employed in the exercise of a ferry franchise or right, is of the value of at least ten thousand dollars, such local governing body may grant such franchise or right for a period not exceeding fifteen years.

A ferry corporation, now enjoying a grant from a county court or such local governing body for a shorter period, shall be entitled to an extension thereof for a period not exceeding fifteen years from the time of granting such extension, on application and due proof to the local governing body of a county that its tangible property, employed in the exercise of such ferry franchise or right, is of the value of at least ten thousand dollars.

History: Add, L 1926, ch 762, with substance transferred from § 4; amd, L 1979, ch 123, § 3, eff May 22, 1979.

CASE ANNOTATIONS

By this section the State Legislature has delegated the granting of the privilege of establishing and operating a ferry to the county court. Ocean Beach Ferry Corp. v Ocean Beach (1948) 298 NY 30, 80 NE2d 137 (criticized as stated in Moriarty v Planning Bd. of Sloatsburg (1986, 2d Dept) 119 App Div 2d 188, 506 NYS2d 184).

Fact that water taxis and ferry serving village of Ocean Beach, Fire Island, are not prosecuted under ordinance governing landing of excursion boats and that, in a few instances, boats termed "excursion boats" were permitted to dock in the village without being prosecuted did not establish that ordinance was discriminatorily enforced against defendant, who was prosecuted for docking excursion boat in the village since there is a clear distinction between water taxis and excursion boats and ferry boat service was operated by village pursuant to franchise and other incidents involved docking for official or semiofficial purposes. People v Frederico (1976) 88 Misc 2d 32, 387 NYS2d 521, affd (1977) 91 Misc 2d 131, 397 NYS2d 515.

No burden is placed on interstate commerce by a statute which provides that a ferry corporation is a corporation organized to operate a ferry wholly within or partly without this State. Mascony Transport & Ferry Service, Inc. v Mitchell (1978) 94 Misc 2d 618, 405 NYS2d 380.

No burden is placed on interstate commerce by a statute which provides that any ferry corporation shall have the power to take by grant or by assignment a franchise or right to establish and operate a ferry or ferries. Mascony Transport & Ferry Service, Inc. v Mitchell (1978) 94 Misc 2d 618, 405 NYS2d 380.

A town board in which there is a public dock district does not possess the authority to require a ferry which uses the docking facilities therein to impose an additional fee on each passenger in order that such fee might be applied by the town toward reduction of assessments against real property in the public dock district. 1950 Ops St Compt File #4554.

§ 72. Posting schedule of rates

A corporation operating a ferry in this state, or between this state and any other state, shall post in a conspicuous and accessible place in each of its ferry houses, in plain view of the passengers, a schedule plainly printed in the English language, of its rates.

History: Add, L 1926, ch 762, § 1, eff Oct 1, 1926, with substance transferred from § 6.

ARTICLE 7
PIPE LINE CORPORATIONS

§ 80. Definition

A pipe line corporation is a corporation organized to construct and operate for public use, wholly within or partly without this state, except in the city of New York, lines of pipe for conveying or transporting therein petroleum, gas, liquids or any products or property, or, except in such city, to maintain and operate for public use for [which][1] such purposes lines of pipe already constructed.

History: Add, L, 1909, ch 219; amd, L 1926, ch 762, § 1, eff Oct 1, 1926, with substance transferred from § 40 and substance of former § 80 transferred to § 40.

[1] Brackets have been inserted around this word by the Publisher as it is superfluous.

CASE ANNOTATIONS

Although a pipeline company cannot exercise powers of condemnation except in connection with a public use (and the mere fact that it was incorporated under the Transportation Corporations Law does not per se render it a public service corporation), it is not required to prove that a contemplated pipeline will serve a public use before it can be permitted to enter upon lands of others to make an exploratory survey of a proposed right-of-way for the line. Northville Dock Pipe Line Corp. v Fanning (1968) 21 NY2d 616, 289 NYS2d 963, 237 NE2d 220, remittitur amd (1968) 22 NY2d 704, 291 NYS2d 812, 238 NE2d 920, remittitur amd (1968) 22 NY2d 828 and reh den (1968) 22 NY2d 827, stay den (1968) 22 NY2d 828, motion den (1968) 22 NY2d 742, 292 NYS2d 121, 239 NE2d 214.

Fact that utility was chartered as "gas corporation" under CLS Trans Corp § 10 rather than as "pipeline corporation" under CLS Trans Corp § 80 did not obligate it to transport and sell only its own natural gas, so there was no conflict with requirements of CLS Pub

Ser § 66–d that utility also transport nonowned gas through its pipelines; legislature can redefine powers of corporations by statutory amendment to promote public interest, and utility was not being compelled to offer service greater or different than that authorized by its original charter. Rochester Gas & Electric Corp. v Public Service Com. (1988) 71 NY2d 313, 525 NYS2d 809, 520 NE2d 528.

§ 81. Additional powers

Every such corporation shall have power:

1. To make such examinations and surveys as it may deem necessary for the selection of the most advantageous route, and for such purpose by its officers, agents or servants to enter upon the lands or waters of any person, subject to liability for all damage done thereto.

2. To lay out its route not exceeding fifty feet in width, but at the termini of such route and at all receiving and discharging points and at all places where machinery may properly be set up for the operation of such pipe line to take such additional land as may be necessary.

3. To convey through pipes any property, substance or product capable of transportation therein by means of any force, power or mechanical agency, and to erect and maintain all necessary and convenient buildings, stations, fixtures and machinery for the purposes of its incorporation.

4. To regulate the time and manner in which property shall be conveyed through its pipe lines, and the compensation to be paid, but such compensation shall not be at a rate in excess of twenty–five cents per one hundred miles for the transportation of forty–two gallons of any product conveyed through lines of one hundred miles in length or over, which shall be reckoned and adjusted upon the quantity or number of gallons delivered by such corporation.

History: Add, L, 1909, ch 219; amd, L 1926, ch 762, § 1, eff Oct 1, 1926, with substance transferred from § 49 and substance of former § 81 transferred to § 42.

Sub 2, amd, L 1949, ch 335, § 1, eff March 29, 1949.

CASE ANNOTATIONS

Although a pipeline company cannot exercise powers of condemnation except in connection with a public use (and the mere fact that it was incorporated under the Transportation Corporations Law does not per se render it a public service corporation), it is not required to prove that a contemplated pipeline will serve a public use before it can be permitted to enter upon lands of others to make an exploratory survey of a proposed right–of–way for the line. Northville Dock Pipe Line Corp. v Fanning (1968) 21 NY2d 616, 289 NYS2d 963, 237 NE2d 220, remittitur amd (1968) 22 NY2d 704, 291 NYS2d 812, 238 NE2d 920, remittitur amd (1968) 22 NY2d 828 and reh den (1968) 22 NY2d 827, stay den (1968) 22 NY2d 828, motion den (1968) 22 NY2d 742, 292 NYS2d 121, 239 NE2d 214.

In action for injunctive relief against owner's interference with pipeline company's survey for proposed pipeline, it is not necessary to show that the proposed pipeline will be employed for "public use" as a prerequisite to making a survey to ascertain "the most advantageous route," but, before granting injunction, Special Term should determine what measures must be taken and what security should be required to protect respondent from any damages which might result from the survey. Northville Dock Pipe Line Corp. v Fanning (1968) 21 NY2d 616, 289 NYS2d 963, 237 NE2d 220, remittitur amd (1968) 22 NY2d 704, 291 NYS2d 812, 238 NE2d 920, remittitur amd (1968) 22

NY2d 828 and reh den (1968) 22 NY2d 827, stay den (1968) 22 NY2d 828, motion den (1968) 22 NY2d 742, 292 NYS2d 121, 239 NE2d 214.

Court properly required city industrial development agency, as potential condemnor of property, to file $ 500,000 bond in favor of property owners to cover damages which might occur during its inspection of property; nothing in CLS EDPL § 404 prohibits requirement of such bond. Sun Co. v City of Syracuse Indus. Dev. Agency (1993, 4th Dept) 197 App Div 2d 912, 602 NYS2d 456, subsequent app (1995, 4th Dept) 209 App Div 2d 34, app dismd (1995) 86 NY2d 776, 631 NYS2d 603, 655 NE2d 700 and related proceeding (1996, 4th Dept) 224 App Div 2d 15, 646 NYS2d 741, related proceeding (1996, 4th Dept) 224 App Div 2d 30, 646 NYS2d 486, app dismd without op (1996) 89 NY2d 860, 653 NYS2d 281, 675 NE2d 1234 and app den (1997) 89 NY2d 811, 657 NYS2d 404, 679 NE2d 643 and app dismd without op (1996) 89 NY2d 860, 653 NYS2d 281, 675 NE2d 1234 and app den (1997) 89 NY2d 811, 657 NYS2d 403, 679 NE2d 642.

§ 81–a. Misconduct of officers and agents of pipe–line corporations

Any officer, agent or manager of a pipe–line corporation who:

1. Neglects or refuses to transport any product delivered for transportation, or to accept and allow a delivery thereof in the order of application, according to the general rules of the corporation, as provided by law; or,

2. Charges, accepts or agrees to accept for such receipt, transportation and delivery, a sum different from the amount fixed by such regulations; or,

3. Allows or pays, or agrees to allow or pay, or suffers to be allowed or paid or repaid, any draw–back, rebate or allowance, so that any person shall, by any advice, have or procure any transportation of products over such pipe–line at a less rate or charge than is fixed in such regulations,

is guilty of a misdemeanor, punishable by a fine not exceeding one thousand dollars, or by imprisonment not exceeding six months, or by both.

History: Add, L 1965, ch 1031, § 191, eff Sept 1, 1967, with substance derived from Penal Law § 669.

§ 82. Location of route

Before commencing the construction of its pipe line in any county, and before commencing any proceeding for the condemnation of real property, such a corporation shall plainly mark the route adopted and located by it by stakes consecutively numbered and placed not more than twenty rods apart, and shall make a map and survey of the route so located indicating thereon the points where such route crosses each parcel of land not theretofore acquired, and shall cause such map and survey to be certified by its president and engineer, and filed in the office of the clerk of each county into or through which such route passes. Such corporation shall give written notice of the filing of such map and survey to the owner or occupant of every such parcel of land, if he is known or can be ascertained, stating that such route passes over or across his lands, as indicated thereon by such line of stakes. Within fifteen days after the service of such notice, any such owner or occupant feeling aggrieved by such location may give ten days' written notice to the corporation, by service thereof upon its president, engineer, or any director, and like notice to the owner or occupant of any lands to be affected by the alteration of route to be proposed, of the time and place of an application to a special term of the supreme court in the judicial district in which the lands are situated for the appointment of commissioners to relocate such route. If the court shall determine that sufficient cause exists therefor, it shall appoint three disinterested persons as commissioners to examine the route located and the proposed alteration thereof, and direct the mode of proceeding. The commissioners shall report to the court the facts and their opinion as to the proposed alteration, and what, if any, alteration should be made in such route, and the court shall thereupon make an order finally determining the location of such route upon the lands embraced therein, and fixing and adjusting the costs, fees, and charges of the commissioners, and the costs and expenses of the proceedings, and directing by which party the same shall be paid. Payment thereof may be enforced by proceedings as for a contempt. Such corporation shall not begin to construct or lay its line of pipe, or commence proceedings for the condemnation of real property, in any county, until after the expiration of fifteen days from the service of the notice herein required, nor until all applications for a relocation of its route in such county, if any are made, have been finally determined.

History: Add, L, 1909, ch 219; amd, L 1926, ch 762, § 1, eff Oct 1, 1926, with substance transferred from § 41 and substance of former § 82 transferred to § 43.

CASE ANNOTATIONS

This law refers only to the formation of domestic corporations, and where a foreign corporation sought to secure an easement over private property for the construction of a pipeline it was not required to comply with provisions of this law. Tennessee Gas Transmission Co. v Schmidt (1951, Sup) 108 NYS2d 435.

§ 83. Condemnation of real property

In case such corporation is unable to agree for the purchase of any real property required for the purposes of its incorporation, and its route in the county in which such real property is situated has been finally located, it shall have the right to acquire title thereto by condemnation, but such corporation shall not locate its route or construct any line of pipe through or under any building, dooryard, lawn, garden or orchard, except by the consent of the owner thereof in writing duly acknowledged, nor through any cemetery or burial ground, nor within one hundred feet of any building except where such line is authorized by public officers to be laid across or upon any public highway. No such corporation shall lay or construct its line of pipe through or under a street in any city, unless it shall first obtain the consent of a majority of the owners of property abutting on that portion of the street in which its pipe line is to be laid. Such pipe line shall be laid with reasonable care and prudence.

History: Add, L, 1909, ch 219; amd, L 1926, ch 762, § 1, eff Oct 1, 1926, with substance transferred from § 42 and substance of former § 83 transferred to § 44.

CASE ANNOTATIONS

Although a pipeline company cannot exercise powers of condemnation except in connection with a public use (and the mere fact that it was incorporated under the Transportation Corporations Law does not per se render it a public service corporation), it is not required to prove that a contemplated pipeline will serve a public use before it can be permitted to enter upon lands of others to make an exploratory survey of a proposed right-of-way for the line. Northville Dock Pipe Line Corp. v Fanning (1968) 21 NY2d 616, 289 NYS2d 963, 237 NE2d 220, remittitur amd (1968) 22 NY2d 704, 291 NYS2d 812, 238 NE2d 920, remittitur amd (1968) 22 NY2d 828 and reh den (1968) 22 NY2d 827, stay den (1968) 22 NY2d 828, motion den (1968) 22 NY2d 742, 292 NYS2d 121, 239 NE2d 214.

The language of this section goes beyond fire protection and imposes a nondelegable duty to see that the line is laid with reasonable care and prudence. Denton v Buffalo Pipe Line Corp. (1939, Sup) 39 NYS2d 83, affd (1939) 258 App Div 844, 15 NYS2d 632.

The duty of a pipe line company which voluntarily built a bridge over an excavation on plaintiffs' premises pursuant to a written easement for the purpose of laying a pipeline did not end with the construction of a proper bridge but extended to the use of reasonable care to prevent a dangerous condition resulting from its removal. Whether the lapse of six hours and fifteen minutes after the planking was torn up was sufficient so that in the exercise of reasonable care the company should have discovered and remedied the condition was a question for the jury. Denton v Buffalo Pipe Line Corp. (1939, Sup) 39 NYS2d 83, affd (1939) 258 App Div 844, 15 NYS2d 632.

This law refers only to the formation of domestic corporations, and where a foreign corporation sought to secure an easement over private property for the construction of a pipeline it was not required to comply with provisions of this law. Tennessee Gas Transmission Co. v Schmidt (1951, Sup) 108 NYS2d 435.

§ 84. Railroad and highway crossings

Whenever it shall be necessary for any line of pipe of any such corporation to cross any railroad or highway, such line of pipe shall be laid under such railroad or highway, with the least injury practicable, and unless such right to cross shall be acquired by agreement, compensation shall be made to the railroad corporation, or in case of highways, to the public, in the manner prescribed in the eminent domain procedure law, but no exclusive right, title or use shall be so acquired against a railroad corporation, nor against the public in a highway. No such corporation shall take or use any lands, fixtures or structures of any railroad corporation, or acquire pursuant to the provisions of the eminent domain procedure law, any right or title to the lands of any such corporation, except for the purpose of a direct crossing.

History: Add, L, 1909, ch 219; amd, L 1926, ch 762, § 1, with substance transferred from § 43 and substance of former § 84 transferred to § 45, L 1977, ch 840, § 93, eff July 1, 1978.

§ 85. Construction across and along canals, rivers and creeks

No pipe line shall be constructed upon or across any of the canals of this state, except by the consent of and in the manner and upon the terms prescribed by the, commissioner of transportation, unless constructed upon a fixed bridge across such canal, and with the consent of the person for whose benefit such bridge is constructed and maintained, or upon such a bridge over the canal, at the crossing of a public highway or street, with the consent of the public officers having the supervision thereof, or of the municipal authorities of any village or city within whose limits such bridge may be, nor shall the pipes of any such corporation be laid through or along the banks of any of the canals of this state, nor through or under any of its rivers or creeks, unless such pipes shall be encased, so as to prevent leakage, in such manner as shall be approved by the commissioner of transportation.

History: Add, L, 1909, ch 219; amd, L 1926, ch 762, § 1, with substance transferred from § 44 and substance of former § 85 transferred to § 46, L 1968, ch 420, § 317, eff May 31, 1968.

§ 86. Consent of local authorities

No pipe lines shall be constructed across or along any public highway without the consent of the public officer or body having supervision thereof, upon such terms as may be agreed upon with him or it, and also in the case of any public highway in any city or village except as provided in section eighty–seven of this chapter, provided that if the highway be one under the sole supervision of a city or village or some official thereof then the authorization of the municipal authorities as required by section eighty–seven shall be sufficient without any other consent made necessary by this section. If such consent, except one required under section eighty–seven, or the consent of the municipal authorities required by the preceding section cannot be obtained, application may be made to the supreme court in the judicial district in which such highway or bridge is situated for an order permitting the corporation to construct its line across or along such highway, or upon such bridge. The application shall be by duly verified petition and notice which shall be served upon the public officer or body having supervision of the highway, or the municipal authorities of the village or city where such bridge is located in a case of consent required by the preceding section, and the court upon the hearing of the application may grant an order permitting the line to be constructed in such manner and upon such terms as it may direct.

History: Add, L 1926, ch 762, § 1, with substance transferred from § 45; amd, L 1938, ch 635, eff April 9, 1938.

§ 87. Construction through villages and cities

No pipe line shall be constructed into or through any incorporated village or city in this state, unless authorized by a resolution prescribing the route, manner of construction and terms upon which granted, adopted at a regular meeting of the board of trustees of the village or the legislative body of the city by a two–thirds vote thereof, but such resolution shall not affect any private right. No pavement shall be removed in any city under the provisions of this article, except as directed by the legislative body, nor until the corporation seeking to remove the same shall give a bond in such sum as the legislative body may require for relaying of any pavements removed. In case any pavement shall have been removed and not properly relaid, the city may sue such corporation, for the cost of relaying such pavement.

History: Add, L 1926, ch 762, § 1, eff Oct 1, 1926, with substance transferred from § 46.

§ 88. Over Indian reservations

Such corporations may contract with the chiefs of any nation of Indians over whose lands it may be necessary to construct its pipe line for the right to construct the same upon such lands, but no such contract shall vest in the corporation the fee of such lands, nor the right to occupy the same for any purpose other than for the construction, operation and maintenance of such pipe line, nor shall such contract be valid or effectual until the same has been ratified by the county court of the county in which the lands are situated.

History: Add, L 1926, ch 762, § 1, eff Oct 1, 1926, with substance transferred from § 47.

§ 89. Over state lands

The commissioner of general services shall have power to grant to any pipe line corporation any lands belonging to the people of this state which may be required for the purposes of its incorporation on such terms as may be agreed, or such corporation may acquire title thereto by condemnation, except that no pipe line corporation may condemn any canal lands abandoned pursuant to the provisions of article four of the public lands law, constituting chapter fifty of the laws of nineteen hundred nine, as amended, until after they have been sold and conveyed in the manner provided by the public lands law. If any lands owned by any county, city or town be required by such corporation for such purposes, the county, city or town officers having charge of such lands may grant them to the corporation upon terms and compensation agreed upon.

History: Add, L 1926, ch 762, § 1, with substance transferred from § 48; amd, L 1962, ch 60, § 26, eff Feb 27, 1962.

§ 90. Use of line to be public; storage; liable as common carrier; rates and charges

Every such corporation shall be a common carrier and its pipe lines subject to public use. All persons desiring to transport products shall have the right on equal terms to transportation in the order of application, on complying with the reasonable regulations and charges of such corporation. No application for transportation shall be valid beyond the quantity of products that the applicant shall then own and have ready for delivery. Every such corporation shall provide suitable and necessary receptacles for receiving all such products, and for storage at the place of delivery, until the same can reasonably be moved by the consignee. The time for delivery to the consignee shall be fixed by general regulation of the corporation, and shall be not less than two days after the same shall be ready for delivery and notice to such consignee. All rates and charges, for or connected with the transportation of any products, shall be uniform and be fixed by such corporation by general regulations, which shall be written or printed and posted and at all times open to public examination.

History: Add, L 1926, ch 762, eff Oct 1, 1926, with substance transferred from § 50.

§ 91. Receipts for property; cancellation of vouchers; delivery of property

No receipt, certificate or order of any kind shall be issued, made or accepted by any such corporation for any commodity unless the commodity represented thereby is actually in possession of the corporation. No commodity received for transportation by such corporation shall be delivered to any person without the presentation and surrender of all receipts, certificates or orders issued or accepted for the same. Whenever any such corporation shall have parted with the possession of any commodity and received therefor any receipt, certificate or order, such receipt, certificate or order, shall not be used again, but shall be mutilated and canceled, and such canceled receipt, certificate or order shall be preserved by such corporation and a record of the same kept by the secretary.

History: Add, L 1926, ch 762, § 1, eff Oct 1, 1926, with substance transferred from § 51.

§ 92. Semi–annual statements

Every such corporation shall make a semi–annual statement showing the quantity of all commodities on hand on the first day of the period for which the statement is made; the quantity received and delivered during such period, and the quantity on hand on the last day of such period, and the quantity represented by outstanding certificates, receipts or orders, and the credit balances on the books of the corporation. Such statement shall be made on or before the tenth day of the month succeeding the period for which the statement is made and verified by the oaths of the president and secretary, and shall be filed within three days thereafter in the office of the county clerk in the county in which the office of the corporation is located, and a true copy thereof shall be posted in a conspicuous place in its office for at least thirty days thereafter.

History: Add, L 1926, ch 762, § 1, with substance transferred from § 52; amd, L 1939, ch 214, § 1, eff April 5, 1939.

§ 93. Fences; farm crossings and use of line not inclosed

It shall not be necessary for any such corporation to fence the lands acquired for its corporate purposes. But, if not inclosed by a substantial fence, the owner of the adjoining lands from whom such lands were obtained, his heirs or assigns, may occupy and use such lands in any manner not injurious to the interests of the corporation and shall not be liable therefor, or for any trespass upon any such lands, except for wilful or negligent injury to the pipes, fixtures, machinery or personal property of the corporation. If the corporation shall keep such lands inclosed it shall construct and provide all suitable and necessary crossings with gates for the use and convenience of any owners of lands adjoining the portion of its lands so inclosed, and no claim shall be made by it against any owner of adjoining lands to make or contribute to the making or maintaining of any division fence between such adjoining lands and its lands. If it shall neglect to keep and maintain substantial fences along its lands the owners of adjoining lands may construct and maintain all farm or division fences, and all line fences crossed by such pipe line, in the same manner as though it had not acquired such lands for such pipe line, and it shall be liable for all injuries to such fences caused or done by any of its officers or agents, or any persons acting in their or its behalf, or by any laborer in its or their employ or in the employ of any of its contractors.

History: Add, L 1926, ch 762, § 1, eff Oct 1, 1926, with substance transferred from § 53.

ARTICLE 8
FREIGHT TERMINAL CORPORATIONS

§ 100. Definition
§ 101. Limitation of powers
§ 102. Rates; discrimination; liability
§ 103. Supervision
§ 104. Corporate acts subject to approval of commissioner of transportation
§ 105. Merger or consolidation of freight terminal corporations and other corporations formed for the purpose of engaging in business in which a freight terminal corporation may engage
§ 106. Condemnation; approval of commissioner of transportation
§ 107. Use of streets; municipal consent
§ 108. Regulation
§ 109. Inconsistent acts

§ 100. Definition

A freight terminal corporation is a corporation organized to supply, maintain and operate freight terminal facilities — including docks, wharves, bulkheads, basins, tugs, floats, lighters and other shipping, and wharfage and lighterage for the receipt, delivery, storage or handling of freight; terminal warehousing, terminal ways, terminal stations and stores; and terminal factory and show room facilities, including power, heat, light and machinery.

History: Add, L, 1909, ch 219; amd, L 1926, ch 762, § 1, eff Oct 1, 1926, with substance transferred from § 154 and substance of former § 100 transferred to § 25.

§ 101. Limitation of powers

Nothing in this article shall be so construed as to permit any such corporation to engage in manufacture or production, except for its own use, of power, heat, light, supplies and equipment or to carry on the business of generating, selling or distributing electricity for light, heat or power, nor shall the right, operation and use of such privileges be extended beyond the streets or marginal streets bounding or occupied by the property owned or operated by such corporation. No railroad corporation, and no corporation or joint–stock association engaged in carrying on an express business, shall either directly or indirectly, or through the medium of a holding company or otherwise, purchase, acquire or hold, any stock, bond or evidence of indebtedness issued by any such corporation.

History: Add, L, 1909, ch 219; amd, L 1926, ch 762, eff Oct 1, 1926, with substance transferred from § 154 and substance of former § 101 transferred to § 26.

§ 102. Rates; discrimination; liability.

Except as to terminal warehouses, show rooms and factories, such a corporation shall be a common carrier. Subject to regulation by the commissioner of transportation, such a corporation may make regulations and fix rates for each class of its business. Such corporation shall impartially serve all requiring its service within the locality described in its certificate of incorporation up to the maximum capacity of its plant and equipment. No receipt, certificate or order shall be made, issued or accepted by any such corporation for any commodity not actually in its possession.

History: Add, L, 1909, ch 219; amd, L 1926, ch 762, § 1, with substance transferred from § 155 and substance of former § 102 transferred to § 27, L 1970, ch 267, § 53, eff March 1, 1971.

§ 103. Supervision

Every such corporation shall be subject to supervision, control and regulation by the commissioner of transportation to the same extent as railroads and street railroads so far as the provisions of the transportation law are applicable.

History: Add, L, 1909, ch 219; amd, L 1926, ch 762, § 1, with substance transferred from § 156 and substance of former § 103 transferred to § 28, L 1970, ch 267, § 54, eff March 1, 1971.

§ 104. Corporate acts subject to approval of commissioner of transportation

It shall be necessary for such a corporation to secure the approval of the commissioner of transportation as a condition to the following corporate acts: The issuance of stock; the issuance of bonds, notes or other evidences of indebtedness, payable more than twelve months after the date of issuance; the mortgaging of property, privileges or franchises to secure its obligations; the increase or decrease of its capital or capital stock; the change of number of its shares; the purchase or acquisition of stocks, bonds or other evidences of indebtedness of any other corporation, domestic or foreign.

Such order of approval shall state that in the opinion of the commissioner the use of the capital to be obtained by the issue of such stock, bonds, notes, or evidences of indebtedness is reasonably required for the purposes of the corporation, and shall specify the amount of each issue thereof to which his approval is given.

History: Add, L, 1909, ch 219; amd, L 1926, ch 762, § 1, with substance of former § 104 transferred to § 29, L 1970, ch 267, § 55, eff March 1, 1971.

Section heading, amd, L 1970, ch 267, § 55, eff March 1, 1971.

§ 105. Merger or consolidation of freight terminal corporations and other corporations formed for the purpose of engaging in business in which a freight terminal corporation may engage

Any two or more domestic freight terminal corporations may merge or consolidate with each other, and any such corporation may merge or consolidate with any other domestic corporation formed for the purpose of engaging in any business in which a domestic freight terminal corporation may engage, in accordance with the procedure and with the effect set forth in article nine of the business corporation law.

History: Add, L, 1909, ch 219; amd, L 1926, ch 762, § 1, with substance of former § 105 transferred to § 30, L 1964, ch 734, § 16, eff June 1, 1964.

Section heading, amd, L 1964, ch 734, § 16, eff June 1, 1964.

§ 106. Condemnation; approval of commissioner of transportation

Every such freight terminal corporation shall have power to acquire by condemnation such real property, except that of a public service corporation, including the right of way through any property, as may be necessary for its corporate purposes. Such acquisition is hereby declared to be for a public use. No real property shall be condemned by any such corporation unless the commissioner of transportation shall first approve of such condemnation and issue a certificate that the property to be condemned is required for freight terminal accommodations needed by the public.

Property devoted to public use for streets, ferries, terminals or otherwise, whether operated by the public authorities or not, shall not be condemned except by permission of and subject to such conditions as may be imposed by the local authority in control thereof, in addition to the approval of the commissioner of transportation.

Nothing herein shall prevent the condemnation by the state or a municipal corporation of the property of a freight terminal corporation, whether or not such freight terminal corporation itself has therefore acquired such property by condemnation.

History: Add, L, 1909, ch 219; amd, L 1926, ch 762, § 1, with substance of former § 106 transferred to § 31, L 1970, ch 267, § 56, eff March 1, 1971.

Section heading, amd, L 1970, ch 267, § 56, eff March 1, 1971.

§ 107. Use of streets; municipal consent

Every such freight terminal corporation may acquire, use and enjoy the privilege to cross or otherwise use the streets adjacent to any terminal way or terminal station with the consent and on such terms as may be imposed by the local authority in control thereof, and subject to the approval of the commissioner of transportation. If such approval be granted, the commissioner of transportation shall issue a certificate (1) that such privilege is needed for public use; (2) that the exercise of such privilege will leave the street in the main available for ordinary street uses; and (3) that the exercise of such privilege will enhance and improve the service afforded by such street to the public. Such privilege shall be revocable by the city on such notice, not exceeding one year, as may be specified therein; but such revocation shall not be effective unless the commissioner of transportation approve of the same and certify that such privilege is no longer needed for public use or that the exercise of such privilege has failed to enhance or improve the service afforded by such street to the public.

History: Add, L 1926, ch 762, § 1; amd, L 1970, ch 267, § 57, eff March 1, 1971.

CASE ANNOTATIONS

A contract between a corporation organized under § 5 of the Stock Corporation Law and the City of New York providing that the corporation should operate a foreign trade zone previously operated by the City was not invalid because the City had contracted for the operation of freight terminal facilities with a corporation organized under the Stock Corporation Law. American Dock Co. v New York (1940) 174 Misc 813, 21 NYS2d 943, affd (1941) 261 App Div 1063, 26 NYS2d 704, affd (1941) 286 NY 658, 36 NE2d 696.

§ 108. Regulation

In construction and operation of its plant and equipment and in the transaction of its business, every such corporation shall be subject to all regulations as to construction, fire, health and safety imposed by law, ordinance or local authority.

History: Add, L 1926, ch 762, § 1, eff Oct 1, 1926, with substance transferred from § 158.

§ 109. Inconsistent acts

The provisions of any act and parts of acts, including the charter of Greater New York and the charter of any other city of the state, which are inconsistent with this article, and insofar only as they are inconsistent with this article, shall have no application to the rights, powers and obligations conferred or created by and under authority of this article or to any proceedings thereunder.

Nothing in this article shall be construed to prevent the organization of a corporation under the provisions of article four of the business corporation law for the purpose of owning, controlling or operating warehouses, docks, wharves or water craft, but no corporation formed for any such purpose under the provisions of the business corporation law shall have the right or power to acquire real property by condemnation.

History: Add, L 1926, ch 762, § 1, with substance transferred from § 159; amd, L 1964, ch 734, § 17, eff June 1, 1964.

ARTICLE 9
DISTRICT STEAM CORPORATIONS

§ 110. Definition
§ 111. Municipal consent to use streets
§ 112. Service to be furnished upon application
§ 113. Examination of meters by agent
§ 114. Entry by agent to cut off steam

§ 110. Definition

A district steam corporation is a corporation organized to supply steam to consumers from a central station or stations through pipes laid wholly or partly in the public streets.

History: Add, L 1926, ch 762, § 1, eff Oct 1, 1926, with substance transferred from Bus Corp Law § 12.

§ 111. Municipal consent to use streets

A district steam corporation shall have power to lay and maintain suitable pipes and conduits or other fixtures in and under the streets, parks and public places of the cities, villages or towns mentioned in its certificate of incorporation upon obtaining the written consent of the local authorities thereof and upon such reasonable regulations as they may prescribe. Such local authorities shall be: in a city, a majority of the members of the local legislative body; in a village, a majority of the members of the board of trustees; in a town, outside of a village, the town superintendent of highways and a majority of the members of the town board.

History: Add, L 1926, ch 762, § 1, eff Oct 1, 1926.

§ 112. Service to be furnished upon application

A district steam corporation, upon the application in writing of the owner or occupant of any building or premises, within one hundred feet of any street main laid down by any such corporation, and payment by him of all money due from him to it such corporation shall supply steam as may be required for heating such building or premises, notwithstanding there may be rent or compensation in arrears for steam supplied, or for meter, pipe or fittings furnished to a former occupant thereof, unless such owner or occupant shall have undertaken or agreed with the former occupant to pay or to exonerate him from the payment of such arrears, and shall refuse or neglect to pay the same. If, for the space of twenty days after such application, and the deposit, if required, of a reasonable sum to cover the cost of connection and two months' steam supply, the corporation shall refuse or neglect to supply steam as required, it shall forfeit to such applicant the sum of ten dollars and the further sum of five dollars for every day thereafter during which such refusal or neglect shall continue. No such corporation shall be required to lay a service pipe for the purpose of supplying steam to any applicant when the ground in which such pipe is required to be laid is frozen, or otherwise presents serious obstacles to laying the same, nor unless the applicant, if required, shall deposit in advance with the corporation a sum of money sufficient to pay for two months' steam supply and the cost of the necessary connections and of the erection of a meter and such other special apparatus as are required for use in connection with such steam supply, and provide the space and right of way necessary for the erection, maintenance and use of such connections and apparatus, and signify his assent in writing to the reasonable regulations of the corporation with reference to the supply of steam to consumers. For the purposes of this section, a district steam corporation shall not include a nonprofit cooperative corporation organized under the cooperative corporations law to make or produce and distribute steam solely for the use of its members.

History: Add, L 1926, ch 762, § 1, with substance transferred from Bus Corp Law § 12; amd, L 1985, ch 745, § 3, eff Aug 1, 1985.

§ 113. Examination of meters by agent

Any such corporation may make an agreement with any of its customers, by which any of its officers or agents shall be authorized at all reasonable times to enter any dwelling, store, building, room or place, supplied with steam by such corporation and occupied by such customer, for the purpose of inspecting and examining the meters, devices, pipes, fittings and appliances for supplying or regulating the supply of steam, and for ascertaining the quantity of steam consumed, or the quantity of water resulting from the condensation of steam consumed. Every such agreement shall further provide that such officer or agent shall exhibit his written authority if requested by the occupant of such dwelling, store, building, room or place. Any person who shall directly or indirectly prevent or hinder such officer or agent from entering such dwelling, store, building, room or place, or from making such inspection or examination, in violation

of such agreement, shall forfeit to the corporation the sum of twenty–five dollars for each offense.

History: Add, L 1926, ch 762, § 1, eff Oct 1, 1926, with substance transferred from Bus Corp Law § 13.

§ 114. Entry by agent to cut off steam

If any person, corporation or association supplied with steam by any such corporation, shall neglect or refuse to pay the rent or remuneration for such steam, or for the meter, device, pipes, fittings or appliances, furnished by such corporation it may thereupon prevent the steam from entering the premises of such person, persons, corporation or association. If a person is liable to a forfeiture, or to fine or imprisonment, for a wrong or offense committed against the corporation, its agents, or property for which such forfeiture, fine or penalty is imposed by law, such corporation may also prevent the steam from entering the premises of the person so liable, or if such person be an officer or agent of any corporation or association, prevent the steam from entering the premises of such corporation or association. In all cases in which such corporation is authorized to prevent the steam from entering any premises, it may, by its officers, agents or workmen, enter into or on such premises between the hours of eight o'clock in the forenoon and six o'clock in the afternoon and cut off, disconnect, separate and carry away any meter, device, pipe, fitting or other property of the corporation; and may cut off, disconnect and separate any meter, device, pipe or fitting, whether the property of the corporation or not, from the mains or pipes of such corporation.

History: Add, L 1926, ch 762, § 1, eff Oct 1, 1926, with substance transferred from Bus Corp Law § 14.

ARTICLE 10
SEWAGE–WORKS CORPORATIONS

§ 115. Definitions

As used in this article, the term:

1. "Sewage–works corporation" means a corporation heretofore or hereafter organized to provide a sewer system as hereinafter defined for the disposal of sewage, through an established system of pipe lines, treatment plants and other means of disposal, and which erects, operates, maintains and performs other necessary acts incidental thereto, disposal systems for sewer areas formed within towns or villages and other municipal areas of the state.

2. "Sewer system" means all sewer pipes and other appurtenances which are used or useful in whole or in part in connection with the collection, treatment or disposal of sewage, and other waste, including sewage pumping stations and sewage treatment and disposal plants and sites.

3. "Local governing body" means the legislative body of a city, town or village authorized by law to establish a sewer district or otherwise to provide sewage–works facilities in such city, town or village wherein is located the area to be served by the sewage–works corporation.

4. "Sewer district" means a county sewer district established pursuant to article five–A of the county law or a town sewer district established pursuant to article twelve or article twelve–A of the town law.

History: Add, L 1960, ch 1067, § 2; amd, L 1970, ch 828, § 3, eff Oct 1, 1970.

Sub 1, amd, L 1961, ch 60, § 1, eff July 1, 1961.

Sub 2, amd, L 1971, ch 1173, eff July 6, 1971.

Sub 4, add, L 1970, ch 828, § 3, eff Oct 1, 1970.

CASE ANNOTATIONS

Planned development homeowners were entitled to summary judgment declaring that defendant company owned and had statutory duty to maintain grinder pumps that pulverized and pumped waste from houses into developments' sewer systems where expert evidence established that pumps were indispensable component of centralized sewage systems, there was undisputed evidence that defendant or its predecessor had maintained and replaced pumps for 24 years, and there was evidence that subdivision developers and others had consistently represented to homeowners that defendant owned pumps. Huff v C. K. Sanitary Sys., Inc. (1999, 3d Dept) 260 App Div 2d 892, 688 NYS2d 801.

In action by public utility not subject to jurisdiction of Public Service Commission for judgment declaring that amended rate proposal which it had submitted to town was fair and reasonable and for judgment placing that rate proposed in effect, question of fact existed as to whether interim rate proposed by utility was reasonable one, precluding granting temporary mandatory injunction to effectuate that interim rate. Suffolk Sanitary Corp. v Town Bd. of Brookhaven (1975) 84 Misc 2d 373, 375 NYS2d 740.

The providing of sewer services constitutes the rendering of a regulated public utility service. A municipality may own and operate a public utility supplying sewer services to its residents and may acquire easements and rights of way for sewer purposes over school property by grant, without a referendum, from boards of education of school districts. 1975 Ops Atty Gen Oct 31 (informal).

Sewage–works corporation organized under Transportation Corporation Law may not reorganize as limited liability company. 1998 Ops Atty Gen I 98–47.

§ 116. Consent to incorporation

1. No certificate of incorporation of a sewage-works corporation shall be filed unless there be annexed thereto a certificate or certificates duly executed in behalf of the local governing bodies of the city, town or village, as the case may be, in which any part of a sewer system provided by such corporation is situate and, in the county of Suffolk, an additional certificate duly executed in behalf of the county sewer agency, consenting to the formation of the corporation for the area described in such certificate.

2. Upon receipt of a request for consent to incorporation, the local governing body shall grant or deny such request within sixty days thereafter or within sixty days after notice to it of the approval of maps and specifications of the proposed system filed with the department of health having jurisdiction pursuant to section one hundred seventeen of this article, whichever is later.

History: Add, L 1960, ch 1067, § 2; amd, L 1966, ch 290, § 1, eff June 1, 1966.

Section heading amd, L 1970, ch 828, § 4, eff Oct 1, 1970.

Sub 1, formerly entire section, so designated sub 1 and amd, L 1970, ch 828, § 4, eff Oct 1, 1970.

Sub 2, add, L 1970, ch 828, § 4, eff Oct 1, 1970.

CASE ANNOTATIONS

Developer's argument in a corporation's breach of contract case that the agreement with respect to sewer connection fees was not enforceable because the corporation was not an authorized sewage-works corporation under the Transportation Corporations Law was meritless; it was undisputed that the corporation's initial formation and authorization was proper and the record reflected the town's multiple consents to the corporation's requests to both extend its operating agreement with the town and to expand its service territory. While the corporation and/or the town may have subsequently failed to comply with the Transportation Corporations Law in other respects, there was no basis to conclude that the corporation's operation was deemed unauthorized by reason of such failures, and thus, the developers' counterclaim requesting a declaration that the corporation was not a valid sewage-works corporation was properly dismissed. Heritage Springs Sewer Works v Boghosian (2009, App Div, 3d Dept) 875 NYS2d 635.

After the State Board of Health has approved the transportation system to be employed by a corporation organized under this article, under this section the Town Board may exercise its discretion to give or withhold approval of the certificate of incorporation. 1960 Ops Atty Gen Dec 1.

Unless the Town Board consents to amendment of the certificate of incorporation of a sewage–works corporation formed under the Transportation Corporations Law, such corporation may not extend the territory it serves beyond the area described in its certificate. Such corporation may charge for services in accordance with a schedule of rates agreed to between the corporation and the local governing body, but in no event should its rates be unreasonable nor should it grant any of its customers an unreasonable preference. In the event a local governing body exercises its option to purchase a sewage–works corporation, only depreciation on an agreed schedule may be deducted from the purchase price. 1977 Op Atty Gen Feb 22.

Sewage–works corporation organized under Transportation Corporation Law may not reorganize as limited liability company. 1998 Ops Atty Gen I 98–47.

§ 117. Approval by department of health

A local governing body shall not consent to the establishment of a sewage–works corporation in any municipality unless there shall first be filed with the department of health, or city, county, or part–county department of health having jurisdiction, maps and specifications of the proposed system, and such department shall have given its approval thereof.

History: Add, L 1960, ch 1067, § 2; amd, L 1970, ch 828, § 5, eff Oct 1, 1970.

Section heading, amd, L 1970, ch 828, § 5, eff Oct 1, 1970.

§ 118. Inspection; cost certification

1. The local governing body, except in the county of Suffolk, the county sewer agency shall utilize any licensed professional engineer in its own personnel

staff, or retain a licensed professional engineer or engineering firm to cause the following to be undertaken and completed:

(a) Initial examinations of the plans and specifications and a report to the local governing body and in Suffolk county also to the county sewer agency on the feasibility and adequacy thereof including recommended modification and changes, if any;

(b) Inspections at reasonable intervals during and after the construction of the sewage-works systems and a report to the local governing body and in Suffolk county also to the county sewer agency on the progress thereof;

(c) A report to the local governing body and in Suffolk county also to the county sewer agency on the cost of construction of the sewage-works system and appurtenances thereto and acquisition of all lands and rights in land therefor, which, in turn, shall apprise the corporation of such cost report. As a part of his report, the licensed engineer or engineering firm shall have the right and duty to examine or have examined the books and records, including all underlying documentation, of the corporation as well as all reports submitted by the corporation to governmental agencies or authorities to ascertain and verify the costs of construction and acquisition. The services of a licensed certified public accountant or licensed public accountant may be utilized, where in the judgment of the engineer, they may be required to properly ascertain and verify the fiscal information to be included in the engineer's report.

(d) A report to the local governing body and in Suffolk county also to the county sewer agency that construction has been completed in accordance with the plans and specifications filed with and approved by the department of health having jurisdiction.

2. The cost of any such retained licensed professional engineering services shall be reimbursed to the local governing body or sewer agency by the corporation, in accordance with an agreement which shall be entered into between such local governing body or sewer agency and such corporation stating the cost of such services and the terms for payment thereof.

History: Add, L 1966, ch 290, § 2; amd, L 1969, ch 740, eff May 22, 1969; L 1970, ch 828, § 6, eff Oct 1, 1970; L 1971, ch 1171, eff July 6, 1971.

§ 119. Guaranties

1. The local governing body shall require the posting of a performance bond for the completion of the construction of the sewage-works system, and may require the posting of an additional bond or other guaranty for the payment of labor and material furnished in the course of such construction, and for the cost of retained engineering services to the local governing body or sewer agency.

2. The local governing body shall require a reasonable guaranty from the corporation that said corporation will continue to maintain and operate the system for a period of at least five years, in the form of a bond or other security acceptable to the local governing body in the amount of the estimated cost of the operation and maintenance of the sewage-works project, less the estimated revenues which are received from properties served, and to be utilized to defray such operation and maintenance costs, as reported by the licensed professional engineer or consulting engineering firm to the local governing body. The local governing body may, and on petition of the corporation shall, at any time review the adequacy of such bond or other security, to ascertain whether it should be modified on the basis of fiscal performance or other conditions.

3. (a) In addition to the guaranty, the stock of the corporation shall be placed in escrow and title thereto shall pass to the local governing body in the event of failure to complete the construction thereof, or in the event of abandonment or discontinuance of the maintenance and operation of the system by the corporation.

(b) In the county of Suffolk said stock placed in escrow may pass, with the consent of the local governing body and the board of supervisors to a county sewer agency in the event of failure to complete the construction of said sewer system, or in the event of abandonment or discontinuance of the maintenance and operation of said system by the corporation.

4. In the event of such abandonment or discontinuance of the maintenance and operation of the system, the local governing body shall have the right to continue the maintenance and operation of the system at the established rates, with the costs assessed against the users, and it may levy taxes, or sewer rents for such purposes in the same manner as if such facilities were owned by a city, town or village, as the case may be. The local governing body shall have such powers until such time as another corporation or agency may undertake to maintain and operate the sewer system, or until such time as it becomes a part of a municipal or sewer district system.

5. In Suffolk county in the event of an abandonment or discontinuance of the maintenance and operation of the sewer system, the county agency shall have the right to undertake to maintain and operate such sewer system, and it shall do so at the established rates, or such other rates as it may deem necessary, with the costs, including delinquent accounts, assessed against all of the users until such time as the sewer system is included in a sewer district which shall maintain and operate the sewer system.

History: Add, L 1960, ch 1067, § 2; amd, L 1961, ch 60, § 2, eff July 1, 1961; L 1965, ch 1069, § 3, eff July 21, 1965,4; L 1970, ch 828, § 7, eff Oct 1, 1970; L 1971, ch 1174, eff July 6, 1971.

CASE ANNOTATIONS

In an action by a town against a sewage disposal corporation that had provided services for a subdivision for over 10 years, the corporation would be allowed to discontinue operation since a reading of Trans Corp Law §§ 119 and 121, governing the duties and guarantees of a sewage–works corporation, indicated that the corporation had a duty to operate and maintain the system for five years and thereafter could abandon the facility and discontinue operation. Clifton Park v Rivercrest Sewerage Disposal Corp. (1981, 3d Dept) 81 App Div 2d 982, 440 NYS2d 85.

Plaintiff was entitled to a preliminary injunction enjoining a successor to a defunct sewage disposal corporation from disconnecting sewerage service and directing that service be maintained during the pendency of the action, even though the successor to the corporation contended that maintenance of the sewage service was economically unfeasible on the terms agreed to by the corporation, where irreparable harm would occur upon the termination of sewerage services, both to plaintiff and adjoining property owners, where defendant's continued maintenance of the service subsequent to the dissolution of the corporation, which had been a wholly owned subsidiary of defendant, was in accordance with a covenant of service contained in plaintiff's property deed and upon which he was entitled to rely, where plaintiff had no adequate remedy at law, and where defendant was not entitled to the benefits of the provision of Trans Corp Law § 119 relating to the abandonment of sewerage systems, in that defendant was not a sewage–works corporation. Paley v Copake Lake Dev. Corp. (1983, 3d Dept) 95 App Div 2d 903, 463 NYS2d 910.

The court has no power to compel defendant, a sewage works corporation (Transportation Corporations Law, art 10), to continue operation and maintenance of its sewage disposal system, as the defendant, after constructing the sewage facility without cost to the municipality and operating it for five years, may abandon the facility, discontinue its operation, and in such event, the local governing body becomes the sole stockholder of the facility and may continue the service until the system becomes part of a municipal or sewer district system. Clifton Park v Rivercrest Sewage Corp. (1978) 96 Misc 2d 122, 408 NYS2d 932.

Sewage–works corporation organized under Transportation Corporation Law may not reorganize as limited liability company. 1998 Ops Atty Gen I 98–47.

§ 120. Option

(a) The local governing body may, at the time of granting the consent to incorporation, require an option to purchase the system from the corporation or at any time shall have the right to purchase or acquire it by condemnation. The local governing body may exercise this option by serving written notice on the corporation, not less than ninety nor more than one hundred eighty days before the date of the taking.

(b) In Suffolk county and Saratoga county, the county sewer agency having the prior consent of the local governing body and the county legislature or a county district shall have an option to purchase the sewer system from the corporation by paying the cost thereof and for all additions and improvements as certified by the engineer as of the date of completion thereof pursuant to section one hundred eighteen, less depreciation on a schedule initially agreed upon but not to exceed thirty years, together with the cost of the land and other costs thereof as of the date of completion. The said county agency or county district may exercise its option by serving written notice on the corporation not less than ninety nor more than one hundred eighty days before the date of taking. The county agency or county district may, instead of making any cash payment agreed or required to be made to the corporation as compensation for such sewer system and land, elect to agree to pay the principal of and interest on outstanding bonds and mortgages issued by or on behalf of such corporation, having a principal amount not exceeding the amount

of such cash payment, as such principal and interest shall become due and payable. In the event the county agency does undertake to purchase, maintain and operate such sewer system, it shall do so at the rates established from time to time and agreed to between the county agency and the local governing body, with the costs, including delinquent accounts, assessed against the users until such time as the sewer system is included in a sewer district which shall maintain and operate the sewer system. Notwithstanding the foregoing provisions, in Suffolk county and Saratoga county a county district may elect to acquire the sewer system, including any and all plant sites and other real property pursuant to the provisions of the eminent domain procedure law and in such event the provisions of such law shall apply.

History: Add, L 1960, ch 1067, § 2, eff April 30, 1960; amd, L 1965, ch 1069, § 5; L 1969, ch 739; L 1970, ch 828, § 8, eff Oct 1, 1970, except that the provisions of sub (a) in effect immediately preceding Oct 1, 1970 shall continue in effect with respect to corporations consented to by the local governing body prior to Oct 1, 1970; L 1971, ch 1172, § 1; L 1977, ch 840, § 94; L 1983, ch 495, § 1, eff July 19, 1983.

CASE ANNOTATIONS

Unless the Town Board consents to amendment of the certificate of incorporation of a sewage–works corporation formed under the Transportation Corporations Law, such corporation may not extend the territory it serves beyond the area described in its certificate. Such corporation may charge for services in accordance with a schedule of rates agreed to between the corporation and the local governing body, but in no event should its rates be unreasonable nor should it grant any of its customers an unreasonable preference. In the event a local governing body exercises its option to purchase a sewage–works corporation, only depreciation on an agreed schedule may be deducted from the purchase price. 1977 Op Atty Gen Feb 22.

The purchase of a sewer treatment plant by a village from a corporation, organized under Article 10 of the Transportation Corporations Law is not subject to competitive bidding. 1960 Ops St Compt File #700.

Neither a town nor the Suffolk County sewer agency may purchase the stock of a sewerage disposal corporation in lieu of acquiring the assets thereof. 1968 Ops St Compt File #51.

§ 121. Duty to supply sewage–works facilities

A sewage–works corporation shall supply each city, town, village or other municipal area or district wherein such corporation operates, and the inhabitants therein, with facilities or make provision for the collection, treatment and disposal of sewage at fair, reasonable and adequate rates agreed to between the corporation and the local governing body or bodies, and, in addition, in the county of Suffolk, the county sewer agency, notwithstanding the provisions of any general, special or local law. Rates shall be reviewable at intervals of not more than five years or at any time by petition of the corporation or motion by the local governing body on written notice after a period of ninety days. The petition of a corporation shall be determined within ninety days of its filing, and in the event a determination is not rendered within such period of time, the petition shall be deemed approved. The local governing body of a city or village, or of a county or town on behalf of a sewer district or for a special sewer improvement shall have the power to contract with a sewage–works corporation for collection, treatment or disposal of sewage. No contract for such services shall be executed for a period greater than ten years.

History: Add, L 1960, ch 1067, § 2; amd, L 1966, ch 290, § 3, L 1970, ch 828, § 9, L 1981, ch 897, § 1, eff July 31, 1981.

Section heading, amd, L 1970, ch 828, § 9, eff Oct 1, 1970.

CASE ANNOTATIONS

1. In general
2. Environmental matters; SEQRA
3. Establishment of sewer rates and fees; increases
4. — Procedural matters, generally
5. — Timeliness; limitations and laches
6. — Evidence
7. Obligations of construction and maintenance
8. Discontinuance of operations

1. In general

Where passage of time created by town's own delay in considering public utility's application for rate increase resulted in submission of new empirical facts by utility, town could not assert that utility had not met mandate of Transportation Corporations Law that 90 days expire before review of any new proposal. Suffolk Sanitary Corp. v Town Bd. of Brookhaven (1975) 84 Misc 2d 373, 375 NYS2d 740.

Where a town had refused to allow a private sewage works corporation to collect sewage rates proposed by the town for the years 1979 through 1981, the corporation would be entitled to collect the preferred amount since, although the court had no rate–fixing power per se, it had the right and the duty "to prevent the confiscation of property without due process of law" and the refusal of the town to allow collection of the amount it considered fair and reasonable could bankrupt the corporation and defeat the purpose of the statute to promote private enterprise. Thus, the sewage works corporation would be entitled to collect a one–time assessment from its customers to pay tax arrears and avoid in rem foreclosure and provide operating revenue during the pendency of the action and, to the extent that the final rates established after trial were different, appropriate adjustments could be made in the customers' bills. Wild Oaks Utilities, Inc. v Green (1981, Sup) 112 Misc 2d 53, 445 NYS2d 941.

Summary judgment for a corporation in its claim that developers breached an agreement to provide sewage disposal services was error; N.Y. Transp. Corp. Law § 121 required a sewage-works corporation to provide sewer services at fair, reasonable, and adequate rates agreed to between the corporation and the local governing body, and, because there was no evidence that the town approved the connection fee, a determination of whether the provision of the agreement requiring the payment of such fees was enforceable and, accordingly, whether the developers were in material breach, depended on whether the fees were reasonable. This required, in turn, financial information which was in the corporation's exclusive control, and the developers therefore demonstrated the existence of a triable fact issue precluding summary judgment and should have been permitted to conduct appropriate discovery. Heritage Springs Sewer Works v Boghosian (2009, App Div, 3d Dept) 875 NYS2d 635.

Unless the Town Board consents to amendment of the certificate of incorporation of a sewage–works corporation formed under the Transportation Corporations Law, such corporation may not extend the territory it serves beyond the area described in its certificate. Such corporation may charge for services in accordance with a schedule of rates agreed to between the corporation and the local governing body, but in no event should its rates be unreasonable nor should it grant any of its customers an unreasonable preference. In the event a local governing body exercises its option to purchase a sewage–works corporation, only depreciation on an agreed schedule may be deducted from the purchase price. 1977 Op Atty Gen Feb 22.

A town may not conditionally create a sewer district, but may adopt a local law establishing requirements for town consent to the creation of a sewage–works corporation and the initial establishment of rates to be charged by that corporation. 1981 Op St Compt File #651.

2. Environmental matters; SEQRA

In an action by the state environmental conservation commissioner to restrain a sewage disposal corporation's violation of a prior consent order requiring the corporation to stop discharging effluent into a creek in excess of limitations, and requiring it to make certain repairs to its collection system, the corporation's violation of the consent order was properly restrained where the consent order was not subject to an alleged condition precedent that the corporation receive an increase in its rates from the village in order to obtain funds that were required to comply with the order, inasmuch as parol evidence of the alleged condition was properly excluded by the trial court absent any reference to the alleged condition precedent in the consent order, and in view of the fact that the order contained a provision for the corporation's application to the commissioner in order to seek relief or change with respect to the order. Flacke v Salem Hills Sewage Disposal Corp. (1982, 3d Dept) 91 App Div 2d 739, 457 NYS2d 992.

3. Establishment of sewer rates and fees; increases

In an action by a sewage disposal corporation seeking a judgment declaring that a rate approved by a village was not "fair, reasonable and adequate" within the meaning of Trans Corp Law § 121, the trial court erred in entering judgment in favor of the village where the evidence tended to establish that there was no basis for inferring that the sewage disposal corporation or its parent corporation had recouped the capital cost of a sewage treatment plant through the sale of homes in the village and, thus, insofar as the rate approved by the village excluded depreciation or return on investment on the basis of such an inference, the rate did not comply with the statutory requirement. Salem Hills Sewage Disposal Corp. v Voorheesville (1981, 3d Dept) 80 App Div 2d 479, 439 NYS2d 760.

In Article 78 proceeding, court would annual determination of town board which denied application for sewer rate increase by petitioner sewer works corporation which was wholly–owned subsidiary of developer of condominium complex, since town board erred in holding that capital assets still in name of developer could not be considered as part of petitioner's rate base, and by allowing its decision to be influenced by outrage of customers and unsubstantiated suggestion that sales material indicated that sewer rates would not rise significantly over time. Heritage Hills Sewage Works Corp. v Town Bd. of Somers (1993, 2d Dept) 189 App Div 2d 816, 592 NYS2d 439, related proceeding (1997, 2d Dept) 245 App Div 2d 450, 666 NYS2d 648.

In Article 78 proceeding by sewage works company to review town board's denial of company's application for sewer rate increase, board was collaterally estopped from arguing that company had recovered its capital costs through unit sales where that issue had been fully litigated with contrary result in prior rate proceeding involving same parties. Heritage Hills Sewage Works Corp. v Town Bd. (1997, 2d Dept) 245 App Div 2d 450, 666 NYS2d 648.

In Article 78 proceeding by sewage works company to review town board's denial of company's application for sewer rate increase, board substantially understated rate base, and thus minimum adequate rate to which company was entitled, where there was no rational basis for board's conclusion that company had received contributions in aid of construction from other developers in excess of contributions recognized by company in its application. Heritage Hills Sewage Works Corp. v Town Bd. (1997, 2d Dept) 245 App Div 2d 450, 666 NYS2d 648.

Although, in general, Supreme Court properly directed town to pay $ 360 tap–in fee to sewer company for each unit that had tapped into company's facilities, company was not entitled to recover tap–in fees incurred before May 8, 1990, where Appellate Division previously had decided that company was entitled to tap–in fees "for the six years prior to the commencement of this action," and action referred to in prior decision was commenced on May 8, 1996. Bennett Rd. Sewer Co. v Town Bd. (2000, 4th Dept) 273 App Div 2d 902, 709 NYS2d 768.

In action by public utility not subject to jurisdiction of Public Service Commission for judgment declaring that amended rate proposal which it had submitted to town was fair and reasonable and for judgment placing that rate proposal in effect, question of fact existed as to whether interim rate proposed by utility was reasonable one, precluding granting temporary mandatory injunction to effectuate that interim rate. Suffolk Sanitary Corp. v Town Bd. of Brookhaven (1975) 84 Misc 2d 373, 375 NYS2d 740.

Board's resolution setting sewer rates was proper because a letter was a sufficient request under N.Y. Transp. Corp. Law § 121 for the board to act, a formal hearing was not required, the board was not limited to information raised only at meetings, and it was reasonable to apply the sewer charges only to those units actually capable of currently using the system; considering the lack of increases for over 20 years, plus data showing that the corporation would be operating the sewer system at a loss even after the increase, the new rate was fair, reasonable, and adequate. Matter of Shellard v Town Bd. of Town of Queensbury (2010, 3d Dept) 70 App Div 3d 1288, 895 NYS2d 595.

4. — Procedural matters, generally

Because N.Y. Transportation Corporation Law § 121 provided that a town board could only rationally make any necessary determinations regarding rate-setting and revenue allocation with respect to new customers when, and if, they were actually acquired, it erred in prospectively allocating 80% of any future revenue that might be generated by the company's sale of excess sewage treatment capacity to its existing customers; accordingly, the trial court erred in denying the company's N.Y. C.P.L.R. art. 78 petition. Matter of Heritage Hills Sewage Works Corp. v Town Bd. of Town of Somers (2008, 2d Dept) 54 App Div 3d 673, 863 NYS2d 255.

Sewage works company was denied its right to impartial review of its application for sewer rate increase by town board where (1) board retained attorney who had prepared report and argued on behalf of chief opponent to increase at prior hearing, (2) that attorney then retained same rate consultant used in preparing earlier report, which had concluded that no increase was warranted, (3) board used rate year analysis even though Public Service Commission had used complete system analysis in reviewing rate increase by company's similarly situated sister water company, (4) board expanded its imputation of advances to include other investments made by company, and (5) board concluded that its calculations would afford company reasonable rate of return when, in fact, those calculations would not enable company to meet even interest payments on its debt. Heritage Hills Sewage Works Corp. v Town Bd. (1997, 2d Dept) 245 App Div 2d 450, 666 NYS2d 648.

In homeowners' action for preliminary injunction against sewage disposal company's imposition of de facto rate increase without complying with procedural formalities required by CLS Trans Corp § 121 and CLS Gen Mun § 452(5)(a), irreparable injury was probable where company announced that it would no longer continue to "gratuitously" maintain sewage grinder pumps, there would be serious risk of health hazards if single homeowner were unable to fix grinder pump, cost of repairing pump could exceed $ 1,000, and new pump might cost over $ 2,500. Huff v C.K. Sanitary Sys. (1998, 3d Dept) 246 App Div 2d 795, 667 NYS2d 766, later proceeding (1999, 3d Dept) 260 App Div 2d 892, 688 NYS2d 801.

In homeowners' action for preliminary injunction against sewage disposal company's imposition of de facto rate increase without complying with procedural formalities required by CLS Trans Corp § 121 and CLS Gen Mun § 452(5)(a), homeowners showed probability of success on merits where (1) company announced that it would no longer continue to "gratuitously" maintain sewage grinder pumps, (2) there was evidence that cost of maintaining entire sewer system, including repair and replacement of grinder pumps, had been borne by company and its predecessor through sewer rents collected from all homeowners connected to system, and (3) injunction sought would merely maintain what appeared to have been status quo for about 24 years. Huff v C.K. Sanitary Sys. (1998, 3d Dept) 246 App Div 2d 795, 667 NYS2d 766, later proceeding (1999, 3d Dept) 260 App Div 2d 892, 688 NYS2d 801.

Although town board made errors in denying sewer company's applications for rate increase, proper remedy was not to set new rate but to remit case to board for reconsideration of rate applications. Bennett Rd. Sewer Co. v Town Bd. (2000, 4th Dept) 273 App Div 2d 902, 709 NYS2d 768.

In the absence of a contractual agreement or local legislation so authorizing, a town may not charge back the cost of conducting an audit of a sewage works corporation to certify the reasonableness of a proposed rate increase by such corporation to that corporation. 1979 Op St Compt File #192.

The expenses incurred by a town board in setting rates to be charged by a sewage–works corporation to the residents of a sewer district within the town pursuant to section 121 of the Transportation Corporations Law are town expenses and may not be charged back to the district. 1981 Op St Compt File #803.

5. — Timeliness; limitations and laches

Four–month statute of limitations (CLS CPLR § 217) governed sewerage–works corporation's action against town for judgment declaring that it was entitled to rate increase, higher rates for industrial and commercial users, and application of same rates charged by town in sewer district to owners of unimproved property, as such claims could have been asserted in Article 78 proceeding and were plainly encompassed within grounds for mandamus to review

under CLS CPLR § 7803(3). Bennett Rd. Sewer Co. v Town Bd. (1998, 4th Dept) 243 App Div 2d 61, 672 NYS2d 587, later proceeding (2000, 4th Dept) 273 App Div 2d 902, 709 NYS2d 768.

Six–year limitations period under CLS CPLR § 213(2), rather than 4–month period under CLS CPLR § 217, governed action by plaintiff sewerage–works corporation for judgment declaring its right to tap–in fees which town was required to collect on its behalf for each unit that tapped into its sewer lines, as such claim involved obligation under plaintiff's agreement with town and was therefore action to enforce contract rather than one seeking relief under CLS CPL Art 78. Bennett Rd. Sewer Co. v Town Bd. (1998, 4th Dept) 243 App Div 2d 61, 672 NYS2d 587, later proceeding (2000, 4th Dept) 273 App Div 2d 902, 709 NYS2d 768.

Sewage disposal company was not entitled to dismissal, under CLS CPLR § 3211(a)(5), of homeowners' complaint, because statute of frauds defense did not apply, where homeowners' causes of action did not sound in contract but rather were based on company's attempts to impose de facto sewer rent increase without complying with procedural formalities required by CLS Trans Corp § 121 and CLS Gen Mun § 452(5)(a). Huff v C.K. Sanitary Sys. (1998, 3d Dept) 246 App Div 2d 795, 667 NYS2d 766, later proceeding (1999, 3d Dept) 260 App Div 2d 892, 688 NYS2d 801.

Customer was entitled to summary judgment on its petition seeking review of sewage rates because five years had passed since the last such review, and under N.Y. Transp. Corp. Law § 121, those rates were reviewable at intervals of not more than five years; the customer's petition was timely brought less than four months after date that such review should have been conducted. Matter of Home Depot U.S.A., Inc. v Town Bd. of the Town of Southeast (2010, App Div, 2d Dept) 895 NYS2d 142.

Trial court should have dismissed so much of a customer's consolidated proceeding as sought to compel a town board to consider the issues raised in the complaint because, although characterized as an N.Y. C.P.L.R. art. 78 proceeding in the nature of mandamus to compel, the portion of the proceeding seeking to have the sewage rates reviewed was properly accomplished by way of an N.Y. C.P.L.R. art. 78 proceeding in the nature of mandamus to review, and that claim was time barred; the customer failed to commence the proceedings within four months of the date when the determination setting the sewage rates became final and binding. Moreover, even if correctly characterized as a proceeding in the nature of mandamus to compel and therefore timely, the customer failed to demonstrate that it had a clear legal right under N.Y. Transp. Corp. Law § 121 to compel consideration of the issues raised. Matter of Home Depot U.S.A., Inc. v Town Bd. of the Town of Southeast (2010, App Div, 2d Dept) 895 NYS2d 142.

6. — Evidence

Town board arbitrarily denied rate increase to sewer company, even though company lost records of its actual construction costs for 4 of 7 sections of sewer system, where town did not deny that company built system, company submitted consulting civil engineer's expert testimony estimating construction costs, that testimony and numerous documents proved that current sewer rates were inadequate, and testimony of town's civil engineer that company could not recover costs of construction because it lost documents proving actual costs was irrational — as was board's reliance on it. Bennett Rd. Sewer Co. v Town Bd. (2000, 4th Dept) 273 App Div 2d 902, 709 NYS2d 768.

7. Obligations of construction and maintenance

Having correctly determined that sewer company owned grinder pumps that pulverized and pumped waste from houses into housing developments' sewer systems, Supreme Court properly declared that company had continuing obligation to repair, maintain or replace them pursuant to CLS Trans Corp Art 10, and properly enjoined company from charging additional fees for these services without town approval. Huff v C. K. Sanitary Sys., Inc. (1999, 3d Dept) 260 App Div 2d 892, 688 NYS2d 801.

8. Discontinuance of operations

In an action by a town against a sewage disposal corporation that had provided services for a subdivision for over 10 years, the corporation would be allowed to discontinue operation since a reading of Trans Corp Law §§ 119 and 121, governing the duties and guarantees of a sewage–works corporation, indicated that the corporation had a duty to operate and maintain the system for five years and thereafter could abandon the facility and discontinue operation. Clifton Park v Rivercrest Sewerage Disposal Corp. (1981, 3d Dept) 81 App Div 2d 982, 440 NYS2d 85.

§ 122. Powers

Every sewage-works corporation shall have the power:

1. To lay, maintain, repair and operate its pipes, conduits and sewers in any street, highway or public place of any city, town, village or other municipal area, in which it has obtained the consent required by section one hundred sixteen for the disposal, treatment and removal of sewage, and to operate and maintain and keep in repair its sewage disposal plants, and prescribe the manner in which sewer connections shall be made. No pipes, sewers or conduits shall be laid or repaired under any highway, road, street or avenue by such corporation, without the consent of the local governing body or its official in charge of highways or streets or if such highway be a state highway, or a highway constructed pursuant to section one hundred ninety-four or one hundred ninety-five or article six of the highway law, the consent of the state commissioner of transportation nor in any street, highway, road, avenue or public place in Suffolk county without the prior written consent of the county sewer agency or the county department of environmental control.

2. To cause examinations and surveys to be made for the purpose of determining the proper location of its disposal system, and, for such purpose by its officers, agents or servants, to enter upon any lands or waters, subject to liability for all damages done.

3. To enter into appropriate agreements with the secretary of agriculture of the United States department of agriculture to operate without profit for the term specified therein for the purpose of qualifying to receive federal assistance pursuant to the consolidated farmers home administration act of nineteen hundred sixty-one and any federal laws amendatory and supplementary thereto. Any such agreement to operate without profit shall be subject to the approval of a majority of the stockholders entitled to vote threat at any regular or special stockholders' meeting. Any stockholder so entitled to vote who does not vote for or consent in writing to the taking of this action, shall, subject to and by complying with the provisions of section six hundred twenty-three of the business corporation law, have the right to receive payment of the fair value of his stock and the other rights and benefits provided by such section.

History: Add, L 1960, ch 1067, § 2, eff April 30, 1960; amd, L 1961, ch 60, § 3; L 1966, ch 481, § 2, eff May 31, 1966; L 1968, ch 420, § 318; L 1970, ch 828, § 10, eff Oct 1, 1970; L 1971, ch 1178, eff July 6, 1971.

CASE ANNOTATIONS

Each sewage–works corporation must petition for sewer rate that is directly related to cost of operating and maintaining its own sewer system for its own users in its approved area of operation; there is no authority for municipal approval of combined sewer rate or increase for 2 sewage–works corporations, regardless of revenue needs or circumstances of either corporation. 1995 Ops Atty Gen I 95–49.

§ 123. Survey and map

Before taking or using any land, for its corporate purposes such corporation shall cause a survey and map to be made of the lands intended to be taken designating the land of the several owners or occupants thereof, which map shall be signed by the president and the secretary, and filed in the office of the clerk of the county in which such lands are situated.

History: Add, L 1960, ch 1067, § 2, eff April 30, 1960.

§ 124. Condemnation of real property

Any such corporation shall have the right to acquire real estate, or any interest therein, necessary for the purposes of its incorporation, and the right to lay, repair and maintain conduits and sewer pipes with connections and fixtures, and other necessary portions of the system, in, through or over the lands of others. If any such corporation, authorized by this article shall be unable to agree upon the terms of purchase of any such property or rights, it may acquire the same by condemnation. Notwithstanding the foregoing, in Suffolk county such corporation shall not have the right to condemn or use the land of others without first obtaining the prior written consent of the county sewer agency and the department of environmental control.

History: Add, L 1960, ch 1067, § 2; amd, L 1971, ch 1177, eff July 6, 1971.

CASE ANNOTATIONS

There is no authority for depriving a sewerage corporation of its right to acquire necessary property by condemnation, if unable to do so by purchase, after the corporation has been organized and complied with the other sections of this article. 1960 Ops Atty Gen Dec 1.

The providing of sewer services constitutes the rendering of a regulated public utility service. A municipality may own and operate a public utility supplying sewer services to its residents and may acquire easements and rights of way for sewer purposes over school property by grant, without a referendum, from boards of education of school districts. 1975 Ops Atty Gen Oct 31 (informal).

UNIFORM COMMERCIAL CODE

ARTICLE 1
GENERAL PROVISIONS

Editor's note. Article 1 of the Uniform Commercial Code is repealed and a new Article 1 is added. Some case annotations have been reassigned to the new sections.

PART 1
GENERAL PROVISIONS

§ 1-101.   Short Titles

(a) This act may be cited as the Uniform Commercial Code.

(b) This article may be cited as Uniform Commercial Code – General Provisions.

History: L 2014, ch 505, § 1, eff Dec 17, 2014.

CASE ANNOTATIONS

In an action to recover damages allegedly sustained as the result of the failure of the defendant trust company to perform its duty as collecting agent for the defendant in connection with shipments of grain, the plaintiff's motion for summary judgment was denied where the plaintiff, which knew that bills of lading were appropriated somehow without payment being received on the accompanying drafts, had an affirmative duty to notify the collecting agent of the alleged criminal activity immediately upon learning of it, rather than when financial losses were incurred, and where the plaintiff should not have been allowed to profit from the collecting agent's failure to comply with the stringent requirements of the UCC if it had actual knowledge of criminal activity and acquiesced therein as long as the asquiesence continued to be profitable. Joseph E. Seagram & Sons, Inc. v Bankers Trust Co. (1981, Sup) 110 Misc. 2d 525, 442 N.Y.S.2d 752

§ 1-102.   Scope of Article

This article applies to a transaction to the extent that it is governed by another article of this act.

History: L 2014, ch 505, § 1, eff Dec 17, 2014.

§ 1-103.   Construction of Uniform Commercial Code to Promote its Purposes and Policies; Applicability of Supplemental Principles of Law

(a) This act must be liberally construed and applied to promote its underlying purposes and policies, which are:

(1) to simplify, clarify, and modernize the law governing commercial transactions;

(2) to permit the continued expansion of commercial practices through custom, usage, and agreement of the parties; and

(3) to make uniform the law among the various jurisdictions.

(b) Unless displaced by the particular provisions of this act, the principles of law and equity, including the law merchant and the law relative to capacity to contract, principal and agent, estoppel, fraud, misrepresentation, duress, coercion, mistake, bankruptcy, and other validating or invalidating cause supplement its provisions.

History: L 2014, ch 505, § 1, eff Dec 17, 2014.

CASE ANNOTATIONS

Courts should not import comparative negligence principles into Uniform Commercial Code since code represents attempt to adjust risk of loss in commercial matters in fair and equitable manner not based on fault, but on allocating responsibility to party best able to prevent loss by exercise of care, with objective of promoting certainty and predictability in commercial transactions. Putnam Rolling Ladder Co. v Manufacturers Hanover Trust Co. (1989) 74 N.Y.2d 340, 547 N.Y.S.2d 611, 546 N.E.2d 904

Comparative negligence is not imported into Uniform Commercial Code. SOS Oil Corp. v Norstar Bank of Long Island (1990) 76 N.Y.2d 561, 561 N.Y.S.2d 887, 563 N.E.2d 258, 12 UCCRS2d 913

Equitable defense of mistaken payment did not relieve payor bank of liability for failing to timely dishonor check presented by payee who knew that check would be paid only if bank made mistake as (1) CLS UCC § 4-302, which displaces common-law principles of equity, provides limited defenses to untimely return or dishonor of items, and (2) permitting payor bank to avoid strict liability under § 4-302 by asserting mistaken payment would violate public policy by undermining predictability and finality of commercial paper transactions. Hanna v First Nat'l Bank (1995) 87 N.Y.2d 107, 637 N.Y.S.2d 953, 661 N.E.2d 683, 28 UCCRS2d 417

In action to recover damages for fraud, breach of contract, negligence and rescission, disclaimer and merger clauses in contracts for sale of property are ineffective to bar consideration of parol evidence of misrepresentation by seller unless clauses refer to particular subject matter as to which representations are alleged with sufficient specificity to put buyer on notice as to clauses' intended effect; accordingly, phrases "physical nature of premises" and "environmental matters" in contract cannot be said to fairly refer to presence of underground tanks containing possibly toxic chemicals. Hi Tor Industrial Park, Inc. v Chemical Bank (1985, 2d Dept) 114 A.D.2d 838, 494 N.Y.S.2d 751

Seller was entitled to summary judgment in action on account where buyer's only defense was that he was acting on behalf of

UCC

corporation but he did not allege that he disclosed agency relationship at time of contract. Rothschild Sunsystems, Inc. v Pawlus (1987, 3d Dept) 129 A.D.2d 933, 514 N.Y.S.2d 572, app den (1987) 70 N.Y.2d 610, 522 N.Y.S.2d 110, 516 N.E.2d 1223

In light of direct conflict between CLS UCC § 2-201 and more general statute of frauds in CLS Gen Oblig § 5-701, latter is no longer applicable to sale of goods, having been displaced by "particular provision" as provided by CLS UCC § 1-103. AP Propane, Inc. v Sperbeck (1990, 3d Dept) 157 A.D.2d 27, 555 N.Y.S.2d 211, 12 UCCRS2d 35, affd, ctfd ques ans (1991) 77 N.Y.2d 886, 568 N.Y.S.2d 908, 571 N.E.2d 78

An infant may not disaffirm a contract for necessaries (UCC § 1-103, successor provision to Pers Prop L § 83). Even here, the phrase "necessaries" does not possess a fixed interpretation, but must be measured against both the infant's standard of living and the ability and willingness of his guardian, if he has one, to supply the needed services or articles. Fisher v Cattani (1966) 53 Misc. 2d 221, 278 N.Y.S.2d 420

Pre-Code rule that one who receives before maturity note signed by maker for accommodation of another is not affected by mere fact that it was made without consideration, continues under Code. Franklin Nat'l Bank v Eurez Constr. Corp. (1969) 60 Misc. 2d 499, 301 N.Y.S.2d 845, 6 UCCRS 634

Where third person purchased money order for $286 from defendant bank, gave it to plaintiff to obtain release of automobile on which plaintiff had lien for towing and storage charges, immediately returned to defendant bank and ordered that payment be stopped on such money order, and was refunded purchase price thereof, bank in action by plaintiff was liable for face amount of such order, even though money orders are not specifically provided for in the Uniform Commercial Code. Under UCC § 1-103, court would apply law-merchant principle concerning money orders and enforce meaning given by merchants to such orders when issued by bank that person who purchases money order is authorized to bind bank's credit to limit stated in order, and in present case money order issued by defendant stated that it was "not valid over $1,000." Mirabile v Udoh (1977) 92 Misc. 2d 168, 399 N.Y.S.2d 869, 23 UCCRS 101(stating that phrase "not valid over $1,000" was concession by bank that purchaser of money order had authority to bind bank's credit to that amount)

In conversion under UCC § 3-419(1)(c) against depositary-collecting bank by payee of check that was mailed to payee by drawer, and was intercepted by third party who forged payee's endorsement, deposited check in account with defendant, and then withdrew all of check's proceeds from such account, court held (1) that since plaintiff agreed that defendant had acted in good faith and in accordance with reasonable commercial standards of banking business, and since defendant held no proceeds of check, defendant was insulated from direct liability to plaintiff by UCC § 3-419(3); and (2) that although defendant had agreed to facts that were sufficient to establish prima-facie contract claim against defendant in common-law action for money had and received, which action could be maintained under UCC § 1-103, good-faith defense allowed by UCC § 3-419(3) also applied to such common-law claim because UCC § 3-419(3) expressly provides that depositary-collecting bank is not liable in "conversion or otherwise" if bank satisfies statute's good-faith and reasonable-commercial-standards-of-dealing requirements. Moore v Richmond Hill Sav. Bank (1983, Civ Ct) 120 Misc. 2d 488, 466 N.Y.S.2d 131, later proceeding (1986, 2d Dept) 117 A.D.2d 27, 502 N.Y.S.2d 202, 1 UCCRS2d 135

Administrator was entitled to interest on the award of dividends in a wrongful registration suit brought under N.Y. U.C.C. Law § 8-404(b). Kirshtein v Americu Credit Union (2011, App Div, 4th Dept) 919 NYS2d 653, 74 UCCRS2d 164, subsequent app (2011, App Div, 4th Dept) 919 NYS2d 434.

Bankruptcy court rejected a creditor's administrative claim related to a contract dispute and the contract could not be rescinded due to an error after the goods were accepted and used, but unconscionability against the debtors required reformation. In re Owens Corning (2003, BC DC Del) 291 BR 329

In action by seller of steel slabs against buyer who had fully paid for all steel purchased, but had made many payments more than 15 days after receipt of steel shipments in violation of contract's express terms, for damages in form of interest at prevailing prime rates on buyer's late payments, under Pennsylvania common law, which was applicable under Pennsylvania UCC § 1-103, plaintiff seller, although entitled to recover interest on buyer's late payments, could do so only at statutorily fixed rate of six percent per year. Associated Metals &

Minerals Corp. v Sharon Steel Corp. (1983, SD NY) 590 F. Supp. 18, 39 UCCRS 892, affd without op (1983, CA2 NY) 742 F.2d 1431

In an ancillary proceeding conducted pursuant to 21 U.S.C.S. § 853(n) and Fed. R. Crim. P. 32.2(c) to determine whether diamond dealers, who alleged that they consigned diamonds to defendant, were the true owners of diamonds that were used in defendant's money laundering scheme, the Uniform Commercial Code was inapplicable because no third-party creditor rights were involved and N.Y. U.C.C. Law § 9-109 did not apply to the relationship between a consignor and a consignee; thus, in accordance with N.Y. U.C.C. Law § 1-103, the court used common law precepts to determined the parties rights. United States v Nektalov (2006, SD NY) 440 F Supp 2d 287, subsequent app (2006, CA2 NY) 2006 US App LEXIS 21701.

Article 8 of N.Y. U.C.C. Law did not displace substantive common law principles originally relied upon by the court, so on remand the result was same—as the corporation could not act on behalf of the individuals, no privity of contract existed between the individuals and the partnership—so the partnership's breach of oral contract to sell notes to partnership and breach of binding preliminary agreement claims failed. Highland Capital Mgmt., L.P. v Schneider (2008, SD NY) 533 F Supp 2d 345, motions ruled upon (2008, SD NY) 2008 US Dist LEXIS 7019.

§ 1-104.   Construction Against Implied Repeal

This act being a general act intended as a unified coverage of its subject matter, no part of it shall be deemed to be impliedly repealed by subsequent legislation if such construction can reasonably be avoided.

History: L 2014, ch 505, § 1, eff Dec 17, 2014.

§ 1-105.   Severability

If any provision or clause of this act or its application to any person or circumstance is held invalid, the invalidity does not affect other provisions or applications of this act which can be given effect without the invalid provision or application, and to this end the provisions of this act are severable.

History: L 2014, ch 505, § 1, eff Dec 17, 2014.

§ 1-106.   Use of Singular and Plural; Gender

In this act, unless the statutory context otherwise requires:

(1) words in the singular number include the plural, and those in the plural include the singular; and

(2) words of any gender also refer to any other gender.

History: L 2014, ch 505, § 1, eff Dec 17, 2014.

§ 1-107.   Section Captions

Section captions are part of this act. The subsection headings in article nine are not part of this act for purposes of construction.

History: L 2014, ch 505, § 1, eff Dec 17, 2014.

§ 1-108.   Relation to Electronic Signatures in Global and National Commerce Act

This article modifies, limits, and supersedes the federal Electronic Signatures in Global and National Commerce Act, 15 U.S.C. Section 7001 et seq., except that nothing in this article modifies, limits, or supersedes Section 7001(c) of that act or authorizes electronic delivery of any of the notices described in Section 7003(b) of that act.

History: L 2014, ch 505, § 1, eff Dec 17, 2014.

§ 1-109. [Repealed]

History: L 2014, ch 505, § 1, eff Dec 17, 2014.

PART 2
GENERAL DEFINITIONS AND PRINCIPLES OF INTERPRETATION

History: Add, L 1962, ch 553, eff Sept 27, 1964; amd, L 2014, ch 505, § 1, eff Dec 17, 2014.

§ 1-201.   General Definitions

(a) Unless the context otherwise requires, words or phrases defined in this section, or in the additional definitions contained in other articles of this act that apply to particular articles or parts thereof, have the meanings stated.

(b) Subject to definitions contained in other articles of this Act that apply to particular articles or parts thereof:

(1) "Action", in the sense of a judicial proceeding, includes recoupment, counterclaim, set-off, suit in equity, and any other proceeding in which rights are determined.

(2) "Aggrieved party" means a party entitled to pursue a remedy.

(3) "Agreement", as distinguished from "contract", means the bargain of the parties in fact, as found in their language or inferred from other circumstances, including course of performance, course of dealing, or usage of trade as provided in Section 1-303.

(4) "Bank" means a person engaged in the business of banking and includes a savings bank, savings and loan association, credit union, and trust company.

(5) "Bearer" means a person in control of a negotiable electronic document of title or a person in possession of a negotiable instrument, negotiable tangible document of title, or certificated security that is payable to bearer or indorsed in blank.

(6) "Bill of lading" means a document of title evidencing the receipt of goods for shipment issued by a person engaged in the business of directly or indirectly transporting or forwarding goods. The term does not include a warehouse receipt.

(7) "Branch" includes a separately incorporated foreign branch of a bank.

(8) "Burden of establishing" a fact means the burden of persuading the trier of fact that the existence of the fact is more probable than its nonexistence.

(9) "Buyer in ordinary course of business" means a person that buys goods in good faith, without knowledge that the sale violates the rights of another person in the goods, and in the ordinary course from a person, other than a pawnbroker, in the business of selling goods of that kind. A person buys goods in the ordinary course if the sale to the person comports with the usual or customary practices in the kind of business in which the seller is engaged or with the seller's own usual or customary practices. A person that sells oil, gas, or other minerals at the wellhead or minehead is a person in the business of selling goods of that kind. A buyer in ordinary course of business may buy for cash, by exchange of other property, or on secured or unsecured credit, and may acquire goods or documents of title under a preexisting contract for sale. Only a buyer that takes possession of the goods or has a right to recover the goods from the seller under article 2 may be a buyer in ordinary course of business. "Buyer in ordinary course of business" does not include a person that acquires goods in a transfer in bulk or as security for or in total or partial satisfaction of a money debt.

(10) "Conspicuous", with reference to a term, means so written, displayed, or presented that a reasonable person against which it is to operate ought to have noticed it. Whether a term is "conspicuous" or not is a decision for the court.

(11) "Consumer" means an individual who enters into a transaction primarily for personal, family, or household purposes.

(12) "Contract", as distinguished from "agreement", means the total legal obligation that results from the parties' agreement as determined by this act as supplemented by any other applicable laws.

(13) "Creditor" includes a general creditor, a secured creditor, a lien creditor, and any representative of creditors, including an assignee for the benefit of creditors, a trustee in bankruptcy, a receiver in equity, and an executor or administrator of an insolvent debtor's or assignor's estate.

(14) "Defendant" includes a person in the position of defendant in a counterclaim, cross-claim, or third-party claim.

(15) "Delivery", with respect to an electronic document of title means voluntary transfer of control and with respect to an instrument, a tangible document of title, or chattel paper, means voluntary transfer of possession.

(16) "Document of title" means a record (A) that in the regular course of business or financing is treated as adequately evidencing that the person in possession or control of the record is entitled to receive, control, hold, and dispose of the record and the goods the record covers and (B) that purports to be issued by or addressed to a bailee and to cover goods in the bailee's possession which are either identified or are fungible portions of an identified

mass. The term includes a bill of lading, transport document, dock warrant, dock receipt, warehouse receipt, and order for delivery of goods. An electronic document of title means a document of title evidenced by a record consisting of information stored in an electronic medium. A tangible document of title means a document of title evidenced by a record consisting of information that is inscribed on a tangible medium.

(17) "Fault" means a default, breach, or wrongful act or omission.

(18) "Fungible goods" means:

(A) goods of which any unit, by nature or usage of trade, is the equivalent of any other like unit; or

(B) goods that by agreement are treated as equivalent.

(19) "Genuine" means free of forgery or counterfeiting.

(20) "Good faith" means honesty in fact in the transaction or conduct concerned.

(21) "Holder" means:

(A) the person in possession of a negotiable instrument that is payable either to bearer or to an identified person that is the person in possession; or

(B) the person in possession of a negotiable tangible document of title if the goods are deliverable either to bearer or to the order of the person in possession; or

(C) the person in control of a negotiable electronic document of title.

(22) "Insolvency proceeding" includes an assignment for the benefit of creditors or other proceeding intended to liquidate or rehabilitate the estate of the person involved.

(23) "Insolvent" means:

(A) having generally ceased to pay debts in the ordinary course of business other than as a result of bona fide dispute;

(B) being unable to pay debts as they become due; or

(C) being insolvent within the meaning of federal bankruptcy law.

(24) "Money" means a medium of exchange currently authorized or adopted by a domestic or foreign government. The term includes a monetary unit of account established by an intergovernmental organization or by agreement between two or more countries.

(25) "Organization" means a person other than an individual.

(26) "Party", as distinguished from "third party", means a person that has engaged in a transaction or made an agreement subject to this act.

(27) "Person" means an individual, corporation, business trust, estate, trust, partnership, limited liability company, association, joint venture, government, governmental subdivision, agency, or instrumentality, public corporation, or any other legal or commercial entity.

(28) "Present value" means the amount as of a date certain of one or more sums payable in the future, discounted to the date certain by use of either an interest rate specified by the parties if that rate is not manifestly unreasonable at the time the transaction is entered into or, if an interest rate is not so specified, a commercially reasonable rate that takes into account the facts and circumstances at the time the transaction is entered into.

(29) "Purchase" means taking by sale, lease, discount, negotiation, mortgage, pledge, lien, security interest, issue or reissue, gift, or any other voluntary transaction creating an interest in property.

(30) "Purchaser" means a person that takes by purchase.

(31) "Record" means information that is inscribed on a tangible medium or that is stored in an electronic or other medium and is retrievable in perceivable form.

(32) "Remedy" means any remedial right to which an aggrieved party is entitled with or without resort to a tribunal.

(33) "Representative" means a person empowered to act for another, including an agent, an officer of a corporation or association, and a trustee, executor, or administrator of an estate.

(34) "Right" includes remedy.

(35) "Security interest" means an interest in personal property or fixtures which secures payment or performance of an obligation. "Security interest" includes any interest of a consignor and a buyer of accounts, chattel paper, a payment intangible, or a promissory note in a transaction that is subject to Article 9. "Security interest" does not include the special property interest of a buyer of goods on identification of those goods to a contract for sale under Section 2-401, but a buyer may also acquire a "security interest" by complying with article 9. Except as otherwise provided in Section 2-505, the right of a seller or lessor of goods under Article 2 or 2-A to retain or acquire possession of the goods is not a "security interest", but a seller or lessor may also acquire a "security interest" by complying with article 9. The retention or reservation of title by a seller of goods notwithstanding shipment or delivery to the buyer under section 2-401 is limited in effect to a reservation of a "security interest." Whether a transaction in the form of a lease creates a "security interest" is determined pursuant to section 1-203.

(36) "Send" in connection with a writing, record, or notice means:

(A) to deposit in the mail or deliver for transmission by any other usual means of communication with postage or cost of transmission provided for and properly addressed and, in the case of an instrument, to an address specified thereon or otherwise agreed, or if there be none to any address reasonable under the circumstances; or

(B) in any other way to cause to be received any record or notice within the time it would have arrived if properly sent.

(37) "Signed" includes using any symbol executed or adopted with present intention to adopt or accept a writing.

(38) "State" means a state of the United States, the District of Columbia, Puerto Rico, the United States Virgin Islands, or any territory or insular possession subject to the jurisdiction of the United States.

(39) "Surety" includes a guarantor or other secondary obligor.

(40) "Term" means a portion of an agreement that relates to a particular matter.

(41) "Unauthorized signature" means a signature made without actual, implied, or apparent authority. The term includes a forgery.

(42) "Warehouse receipt" means a document of title issued by a person engaged in the business of storing goods for hire.

(43) "Writing" includes printing, typewriting, or any other intentional reduction to tangible form. "Written" has a corresponding meaning.

History: L 2014, ch 505, § 1, eff Dec 17, 2014.

CASE ANNOTATIONS

1. Agreement
2. Bank
3. Buyer in ordinary course of business
4. Conspicuous
5. Contract
6. Creditor
7. Delivery
8. Document of title
9. Fungible
10. Good faith
11. Holder
12. Money
13. Notice
14. Notifying or giving notice
15. Notice received by organization
16. Party
17. Person
18. Presumption or presumed
19. Purchase
20. Representative
21. Security interests
22. Signature
23. Unauthorized signature or indorsement
24. Value
25. Warehouse receipt

1. Agreement

Under the Uniform Commercial Code, practical business people are not expected to govern their actions with reference to nice legal formalisms. Thus, when there is a basic agreement, however manifested and whether or not precise moment of such agreement can be determined, failure of parties to articulate agreement in precise legal language, with every difficulty and contingency considered and resolved, will not prevent formation of contract. However, if there is no basic agreement, the code will not imply one. And without an agreement, there can be no contract and without a contract, there can be no breach. This principle is explicitly recognized by UCC § 1-201(3) and (11), and UCC § 2-204(1) and (2). Kleinschmidt Div. of SCM Corp. v Futuronics Corp., 41 N.Y.2d 972,

395 N.Y.S.2d 151, 363 N.E.2d 701, 21 U.C.C. Rep. Serv. (CBC) 422, 1977 N.Y. LEXIS 2021 (N.Y. 1977).

Trial court erred in failing to grant a judgment in the amount of the deficiency to the lender since the borrowers', by their actions, orally agreed to an auction and the selection of an auctioneer; N.Y. U.C.C. Law § 30.30 did not require that the agreement be in writing. HSBC Bank USA v Econ. Steel, Inc., 298 A.D.2d 958, 747 N.Y.S.2d 661, 48 U.C.C. Rep. Serv. 2d (CBC) 1494, 2002 N.Y. App. Div. LEXIS 8979 (N.Y. App. Div. 4th Dep't 2002).

Trial court erred in granting a bank's motion for summary judgment in its action to foreclose a mortgage because the bank lacked standing inasmuch as it failed to demonstrate, prima facie, that it was a holder or assignee of the note prior to commencement of the action where the bank submitted the note with an allonge containing an endorsement, but the endorsement was not made in blank or payable to the bank. US Bank, N.A. v Zwisler, 147 A.D.3d 804, 2017 NY Slip Op 00682, 2017 NY Slip Op 682, 46 N.Y.S.3d 213, 91 U.C.C. Rep. Serv. 2d (CBC) 935, 2017 N.Y. App. Div. LEXIS 679 (N.Y. App. Div. 2d Dep't 2017).

Where depositor allegedly entered into oral agreement with bank concerning certain restrictions on his accounts and, pursuant to such agreement, sent letter to bank directing it not to pay any instruments drawn on his accounts unless instruments were on "printed checks of the bank", and where bank merely acknowledged "receipt" of customer's letter, such "receipt" could not be legally interpreted as general, unlimited lifetime "agreement," but at best was receipt of notice of stop payment and, in accord with UCC § 4-403(2) unless renewed in writing, was effective for only six months; stop payment order was not extended beyond statutory limitation by virtue of alleged "oral agreement" simultaneously made with written stop payment order. Dinerman v National Bank of North America, 89 Misc. 2d 164, 390 N.Y.S.2d 1002, 21 U.C.C. Rep. Serv. (CBC) 603, 1977 N.Y. Misc. LEXIS 1854 (N.Y. Sup. Ct. 1977).

Where a warranty, especially one expressly stated in a signed writing, is proved, the promisor should be allowed to disclaim "the bargain of the parties in fact as found in their language" (see UCC § 1-201(3)) only in an extraordinary case, such as one involving illegality or some other overriding consideration of public policy. Ainger v Michigan General Corp., 476 F. Supp. 1209, 1979 U.S. Dist. LEXIS 10155 (S.D.N.Y. 1979), aff'd, 632 F.2d 1025, 1980 U.S. App. LEXIS 13360 (2d Cir. N.Y. 1980) (construing NY UCC).

2. Bank

Life insurance company was "engaged in the business of banking" for purposes of CLS UCC § 4-406(4), even though it was not bank, where it performed same functions of bank in administering money market checking account which resembled ordinary checking account, in that company provided and retained customer's signature card, it issued checkbook, and it sent customer monthly statements. Woods v MONY Legacy Life Ins. Co., 84 N.Y.2d 280, 617 N.Y.S.2d 452, 641 N.E.2d 1070, 24 U.C.C. Rep. Serv. 2d (CBC) 1181, 1994 N.Y. LEXIS 3372 (N.Y. 1994).

3. Buyer in ordinary course of business

Auto wholesaler who purchases used autos from auto leasing or rental company does not qualify as "buyer in ordinary course of business." Hempstead Bank v Andy's Car Rental System, Inc., 35 A.D.2d 35, 312 N.Y.S.2d 317, 7 U.C.C. Rep. Serv. (CBC) 932, 1970 N.Y. App. Div. LEXIS 4129 (N.Y. App. Div. 2d Dep't 1970).

Where buyer of painting was not "buyer in ordinary course of business" under UCC § 1-201(9) because (1) person from whom buyer bought painting was not engaged in business of selling goods of that kind, and (2) buyer did not make purchase in good faith because he failed to make proper inquiry into ownership of painting, buyer could not successfully invoke, in suit by painting's owner to recover its possession or value, defense of statutory estoppel found in UCC § 2-403(2), which provides that entrusting possession of goods to one who deals in goods of that kind gives him power to transfer all rights of entruster to buyer in ordinary course of business. Porter v Wertz, 68 A.D.2d 141, 416 N.Y.S.2d 254, 26 U.C.C. Rep. Serv. (CBC) 876, 1979 N.Y. App. Div. LEXIS 10530 (N.Y. App. Div. 1st Dep't 1979), aff'd, 53 N.Y.2d 696, 439 N.Y.S.2d 105, 421 N.E.2d 500, 30 U.C.C. Rep. Serv. (CBC) 1582, 1981 N.Y. LEXIS 2344 (N.Y. 1981).

In action by receiver on note discounted by insolvent bank, where (1) defendant makers, on August 11, 1975, issued note, payable on May 14, 1976, to contractor-payee for services to be performed, (2) bank before its insolvency discounted note on December 12, 1975, (3) makers stopped payment on note on its maturity date (May 14, 1976)

UCC

and issued replacement note which was payable on August 12, 1976, (4) original note (note sued on) was not returned to makers at time of their issuance of replacement note, (5) on August 12, 1976, makers paid replacement note, even though original note still had not been returned to them, and (6) bank's receiver, after bank on May 14, 1976 had sent certificate and notice of protest to makers concerning original note, brought suit on such note in receiver's capacity as liquidator of bank's assets, court held (1) that under UCC § 3-201(1), receiver, as bank's transferee, had acquired bank's interest in note sued on, (2) that such note was unconditional on its face and did not refer to any other instrument, (3) that makers had known that note's payee intended to discount note to bank for value, (4) that when bank discounted note before its maturity, no breach of the underlying contract, and thus no defense to note, existed, (5) that fact that bank had had notice of possibility of breach of underlying contract did not mean that bank had taken note in bad faith within meaning of UCC § 1-201(9), (6) that evidence showed that bank was holder in due course under UCC § 3-302(1) and that bank's receiver had acquired such status under UCC § 3-201(1), and (7) that since makers' defenses, including defense of improvident payment of replacement note without return of original note (note sued on), could not be sustained because receiver was holder in due course, note sued on was required to be honored. Federal Deposit Ins. Corp. v Russo, 89 A.D.2d 575, 452 N.Y.S.2d 231, 34 U.C.C. Rep. Serv. (CBC) 599, 1982 N.Y. App. Div. LEXIS 17640 (N.Y. App. Div. 2d Dep't 1982), aff'd, 58 N.Y.2d 929, 460 N.Y.S.2d 532, 447 N.E.2d 81, 1983 N.Y. LEXIS 2892 (N.Y. 1983).

Buyers were entitled to summary judgment in lender's action for conversion, replevin, unjust enrichment, fraud, and civil conspiracy because they purchased the vehicles at issue in the ordinary course of business under N.Y. U.C.C. Law § 1-201(9), 9-320(a), and the lender failed to show a misrepresentation or a fiduciary relationship. Nissan Motor Acceptance Corp. v Scialpi, 94 A.D.3d 1067, 944 N.Y.S.2d 160, 2012 NY Slip Op 3153, 2012 N.Y. App. Div. LEXIS 3143 (N.Y. App. Div. 2d Dep't 2012).

A licensed automobile wrecker and junk dealer who purchased a two-year-old station wagon from a thief for $900 by placing $300 down, and who sold the vehicle for $1200 that same day, although he never obtained a bill of sale or registration certificate, was liable to the two owners, since the car had not been entrusted to a merchant who dealt in used cars and the defendant had not demonstrated that he was a "buyer in ordinary course of business" or that he was a "good faith purchaser for value". Atlas Auto Rental Corp. v Weisberg, 54 Misc. 2d 168, 281 N.Y.S.2d 400, 4 U.C.C. Rep. Serv. (CBC) 572, 1967 N.Y. Misc. LEXIS 1388 (N.Y. Civ. Ct. 1967), disapproved, Candela v Port Motors, 208 A.D.2d 486, 617 N.Y.S.2d 49, 25 U.C.C. Rep. Serv. 2d (CBC) 681, 1994 N.Y. App. Div. LEXIS 9380 (N.Y. App. Div. 2d Dep't 1994).

The fact that title has not yet been transferred as between the dealer and the consumer does not prevent the latter from being regarded as a buyer in the ordinary course of business, insofar as the secured creditor of the dealer is concerned, where the transaction between the dealer and the consumer is ordinary or typical in the trade. Chrysler Credit Corp. v Sharp, 56 Misc. 2d 261, 288 N.Y.S.2d 525, 5 U.C.C. Rep. Serv. (CBC) 226, 1968 N.Y. Misc. LEXIS 1867 (N.Y. Sup. Ct. 1968).

Where plaintiff bought truck from a merchant in the ordinary course of business, without knowledge of a security agreement entered into by the seller and later assigned to a bank, in repossessing the truck after the sale, bank was liable for conversion and damages. Makransky v Long Island Reo Truck Co., 58 Misc. 2d 338, 295 N.Y.S.2d 240, 5 U.C.C. Rep. Serv. (CBC) 1204, 1968 N.Y. Misc. LEXIS 1045 (N.Y. Sup. Ct. 1968).

Where automobile dealer sold two used cars to used car dealer but instructed him not to dispose of them until latter's check cleared the bank, which transaction constituted an entrustment, and second dealer violated instructions and conveyed the cars to a third dealer in a transaction wherein the value of the cars was applied in partial satisfaction of second dealer's pre-existing and running account, third dealer was not a buyer in the ordinary course of business within the code definition of the term which excludes a transaction by which payment is credited in total or partial satisfaction of a money debt and thus he did not take free of the instruction not to sell. Sherman v Roger Kresge, Inc., 67 Misc. 2d 178, 323 N.Y.S.2d 804, 9 U.C.C. Rep. Serv. (CBC) 858, 1971 N.Y. Misc. LEXIS 1389 (N.Y. County Ct. 1971), aff'd, 40 A.D.2d 766, 336 N.Y.S.2d 1015, 1972 N.Y. App. Div. LEXIS 6290 (N.Y. App. Div. 3d Dep't 1972).

A buyer in the ordinary course of business who takes free of a known and perfected security interest under UCC § 9-307(1) may be defined as one who purchases merchandise in the ordinary course of affairs from a merchant in the business of vending items of that nature within UCC § 1-201(9). Newton-Waltham Bank & Trust Co. v Bergen Motors, Inc., 68 Misc. 2d 228, 327 N.Y.S.2d 77, 9 U.C.C. Rep. Serv. (CBC) 1307, 1971 N.Y. Misc. LEXIS 1191 (N.Y. Civ. Ct. 1971), aff'd, 75 Misc. 2d 103, 347 N.Y.S.2d 568, 1972 N.Y. Misc. LEXIS 2184 (N.Y. App. Term 1972).

Where savings and loan association entered into floor-plan agreement with mobile-home dealer under which association would pay manufacturer for each home delivered to dealer, retain invoice and certificate of origin of each delivered unit, and dealer would execute demand note and security interest in delivered unit to association which it would hold until it received payment from dealer; where buyers of mobile home from dealer subsequently executed instalment contract reciting payment of specified down payment, delivery and acceptance of home, and granting by buyers of security interest therein; and where dealer assigned such contract to corporation that assigned it to defendant bank, and money paid for contract by defendant bank was transmitted to dealer who breached his obligation to savings and loan association and absconded, in action by subrogee of rights of savings and loan association against defendant bank to determine priority of security interests in such home, (1) buyers of home were good-faith purchasers in ordinary course of business under UCC § 1-201(9) who took home under UCC § 9-307(1) free of subrogee's security interest therein; (2) defendant bank's security interest in home therefore had priority over subrogee's security interest; and (3) subrogee's security interest attached to proceeds of sale in hands of absconding dealer. Integrity Ins. Co. v Marine Midland Bank-Western, 90 Misc. 2d 868, 396 N.Y.S.2d 319, 22 U.C.C. Rep. Serv. (CBC) 391, 1977 N.Y. Misc. LEXIS 2174 (N.Y. Sup. Ct. 1977).

When UCC §§ 1-201(9) and 9-307(1) are read together, the result, as noted in Official Comment 2, is that the buyer takes free if he merely knows that there is a security interest that covers the goods, but that he takes subject to such interest if he knows, in addition, that the sale was in violation of some term in the security agreement that was not waived by the words or conduct of the secured party. European-American Bank & Trust Co. v Sheriff of County of Nassau, 97 Misc. 2d 549, 411 N.Y.S.2d 851, 25 U.C.C. Rep. Serv. (CBC) 1137, 1978 N.Y. Misc. LEXIS 2834 (N.Y. Sup. Ct. 1978).

A buyer takes free of a security interest in goods created by a seller who is in the business of selling goods of that kind, even if the interest is perfected, if the buyer merely knows that there is a security interest which covers the goods, but takes subject to the interest if he knows, in addition, that the sale is in violation of some term in the security agreement not waived by the words or conduct of the secured party (Uniform Commercial Code, § 1-201, subd [9]; § 9-307, subd [1]), although it is not incumbent upon the buyer to make a search for any possible security interests; and, a buyer who takes free of a perfected security interest takes free of an unperfected one as well. European-American Bank & Trust Co. v Sheriff of County of Nassau, 97 Misc. 2d 549, 411 N.Y.S.2d 851, 25 U.C.C. Rep. Serv. (CBC) 1137, 1978 N.Y. Misc. LEXIS 2834 (N.Y. Sup. Ct. 1978).

Where (1) buyer purchased three boats under floor-plan arrangement whereby bank, as secured party, paid purchase price directly to seller and received from buyer security agreement and financing statement, and also a trust receipt for each boat, (2) financing statement was duly filed on April 24, 1978, thereby perfecting secured party's security interest in boats, (3) second bank claimed that boats were still property of seller and that second bank bank had previously perfected security interest in all of seller's property, including such boats, and (4) second bank also contended that sale of boats constituted bulk sale that was void as to second bank's rights, court held (1) that under definition of "bulk transfer" in UCC § 6-102(1) as a transfer, not in ordinary course of transferor's business, of major part of transferor's materials, merchandise, or other inventory, sale of boats in suit was not bulk transfer, (2) that such sale, instead of being an extraordinary sale, was only part of a continuing pattern of boat purchases that buyer had been making from seller for more than a year, (3) that such purchases involved deliveries that had been made on a regular basis, for a fair consideration, and without any intent to defraud creditors, (4) that under UCC § 1-201(9), buyer of boats was buyer in ordinary course of business, and (5) that since buyer had purchased boats without any knowledge of second bank's security interest therein, buyer under UCC § 9-307(1) took them free of such security interest. European-American Bank & Trust Co. v Sheriff of County of Nassau, 97 Misc. 2d 549, 411 N.Y.S.2d 851, 25 U.C.C. Rep. Serv. (CBC) 1137, 1978 N.Y. Misc. LEXIS 2834 (N.Y. Sup. Ct. 1978).

In conversion action by buyer of used boat from dealer against boat's former owner, where (1) defendant former owner delivered boat in suit to dealer as part payment for new boat that subsequently was not delivered to defendant on agreed delivery date, (2) dealer after receiving boat in suit from defendant sold it to plaintiff, and that (3) defendant thereafter retrieved boat and retained possession of it, court held (1) that plaintiff was buyer of boat in ordinary course of business within meaning of UCC § 1-201(9), which defines "buyer in ordinary course of business," and 2-403(2), which deals with effect of entrusting possession of goods to merchants who deals in goods of that kind, (2) that since defendant had entrusted boat to dealer, dealer under UCC § 2-403(2) had power to transfer to plaintiff all of defendant's rights to boat, and (3) that dealer's failure to transfer boat's registration certificate to plaintiff was not controlling because Vehicle and Traffic Law permitted boat's title to be transferred without deliver of registration certificate. Heiselman v Marcus, 128 Misc. 2d 94, 488 N.Y.S.2d 571, 41 U.C.C. Rep. Serv. (CBC) 395, 1985 N.Y. Misc. LEXIS 2885 (N.Y. Sup. Ct. 1985).

On application for order of seizure of boat (collateral), which was in possession of one defendant, prior to commencing action to recover boat's possession, original seller of boat, on buying it back from debtor, was not buyer in ordinary course of business under UCC § 1-201(9) because it knew that sale violated plaintiff's rights and that debtor was not in business of selling boats. Marine Midland Bank, N. A. v Smith Boys, Inc., 129 Misc. 2d 37, 492 N.Y.S.2d 355, 41 U.C.C. Rep. Serv. (CBC) 1843, 1985 N.Y. Misc. LEXIS 2692 (N.Y. Sup. Ct. 1985).

Under New Jersey law, which governed a dealer's agreement between a financing company and a New Jersey auto dealer, because the dealer was not licensed to sell motor vehicles in New Jersey, and, as a leasing company, it did not hold the subject cars as part of its sales inventory, when the dealer defaulted on a dealer's agreement with the financing company, the trial court properly found that the company was not a buyer in the ordinary course of business, as defined by N.Y. U.C.C. §§ 1-201(9) and 9-320(a); thus, the possessory interest sought by the company upon the dealer's default was subject to the security interests held by three creditors. Hann Fin. Serv. Corp. v Republic Auto Credit Group, LLC, 18 A.D.3d 434, 794 N.Y.S.2d 423, 57 U.C.C. Rep. Serv. 2d (CBC) 196, 2005 N.Y. App. Div. LEXIS 4784 (N.Y. App. Div. 2d Dep't 2005).

Furniture company's setting off debt owed it by drapery company against amount due on goods shipped to furniture company removed furniture company from buyer in ordinary course of business status, and consequently, bank's security interest in collateral continued pursuant to CLS UCC § 9-306(2). American Furniture Co. v Extebank, 676 F. Supp. 455, 5 U.C.C. Rep. Serv. 2d (CBC) 1511, 1987 U.S. Dist. LEXIS 12477 (E.D.N.Y. 1987).

4. Conspicuous

Exclusion of warranty of fitness, appearing in only print in paragraph form just before space for writing order, met Code "conspicuousness" requirement. Zicari v Joseph Harris Co., 33 A.D.2d 17, 304 N.Y.S.2d 918, 6 U.C.C. Rep. Serv. (CBC) 1246, 1969 N.Y. App. Div. LEXIS 2923 (N.Y. App. Div. 4th Dep't 1969), app. denied, 26 N.Y.2d 610, 309 N.Y.S.2d 1028, 1970 N.Y. LEXIS 1738 (N.Y. 1970).

Although lumber dealer's disclaimer of liability was printed in the smallest type appearing on his invoices, it could not be said to be inconspicuous when it appeared immediately following the conspicuous legend "NO CLAIMS ALLOWED UNLESS MADE IMMEDIATELY AFTER DELIVERY", and was preceded by the word "NOTE" in large capital letters. Velez v Craine & Clarke Lumber Corp., 41 A.D.2d 747, 341 N.Y.S.2d 248, 12 U.C.C. Rep. Serv. (CBC) 69, 1973 N.Y. App. Div. LEXIS 4988 (N.Y. App. Div. 2d Dep't 1973), rev'd, 33 N.Y.2d 117, 350 N.Y.S.2d 617, 305 N.E.2d 750, 13 U.C.C. Rep. Serv. (CBC) 793, 1973 N.Y. LEXIS 920 (N.Y. 1973).

Requirement of UCC § 2-316(2) and § 1-201(10) that language in warranty disclaimer be conspicuous was not satisfied where provisions of disclaimer were printed in type which was no larger than any other type on the entire page and actually was smaller than some of such other type. Nassau Suffolk White Trucks, Inc. v Twin County Transit Mix Corp., 62 A.D.2d 982, 403 N.Y.S.2d 322, 24 U.C.C. Rep. Serv. (CBC) 84, 1978 N.Y. App. Div. LEXIS 11018 (N.Y. App. Div. 2d Dep't 1978).

Where auto manufacturer's express written warranty, on which buyer relied, clearly stated (1) that it was given solely on behalf of dealer and no one else, and (2) that it excluded all other warranties, express or implied, including implied warranties of merchantability and fitness for particular purpose (see UCC §§ 2-314(1) and 2-315), court held (1) that manufacturer had made no express warranty on his own behalf (see UCC § 2-313(1)), (2) that under UCC § 1-201(10), conspicuousness of manufacturer's disclaimer was question for trial court, (3) that under UCC § 2-202, parol evidence could not be used to contradict unambiguous terms of written warranty sued on, and (4) that because buyer had sustained economic loss only and was not in privity with manufacturer, buyer could not recover from manufacturer on claim of breach of implied warranty. Arthur Jaffee Associates v Bilsco Auto Service, Inc., 89 A.D.2d 785, 453 N.Y.S.2d 501, 34 U.C.C. Rep. Serv. (CBC) 894, 1982 N.Y. App. Div. LEXIS 17898 (N.Y. App. Div. 4th Dep't 1982), aff'd, 58 N.Y.2d 993, 461 N.Y.S.2d 1007, 448 N.E.2d 792, 1983 N.Y. LEXIS 2944 (N.Y. 1983).

In lessor's action against lessee to recover unpaid rent due under lease of photocopying machine, implied warranty disclaimer in lease complied with both conspicuousness requirement of UCC § 2-316(2) and definition of "conspicuous" in UCC § 1-201(10), since such disclaimer appeared in only boldface print contained on first page of lease agreement under capitalized heading, "Terms and Conditions of Lease," and was not contained in boilerplate paragraphs set forth on back page of lease. Commercial Credit Corp v CYC Realty, Inc., 102 A.D.2d 970, 477 N.Y.S.2d 842, 39 U.C.C. Rep. Serv. (CBC) 108, 1984 N.Y. App. Div. LEXIS 19218 (N.Y. App. Div. 3d Dep't 1984).

In action by leasing company, as buyer of new automobile, and lessee of automobile from leasing company against manufacturer of automobile and dealer-seller for breach of express and implied warranties stemming from automobile's defective engine, which defendants did not successfully repair and which plaintiffs replaced with second-hand engine, under UCC § 1-201(10), question whether dealer's disclaimer was conspicuous was question of law for court. Carbo Industries, Inc. v Becker Chevrolet, Inc., 112 A.D.2d 336, 491 N.Y.S.2d 786, 41 U.C.C. Rep. Serv. (CBC) 1254, 1985 N.Y. App. Div. LEXIS 56477 (N.Y. App. Div. 2d Dep't 1985), dismissed, Carbo Indus. v Becker Chevrolet, Inc., 66 N.Y.2d 1035, 499 N.Y.S.2d 1030, 489 N.E.2d 1303, 1985 N.Y. LEXIS 18378 (N.Y. 1985).

Paint supplier was entitled to summary judgment dismissing bridge painting subcontractor's causes of action for breach of express and implied warranties of fitness for use for particular use where each invoice reflecting sale of paint and thinner by supplier to subcontractor contained conspicuous and thus effective disclaimer of all warranties, including that of fitness for particular purpose. Naftilos Painting, Inc. v Cianbro Corp., 275 A.D.2d 975, 713 N.Y.S.2d 626, 2000 N.Y. App. Div. LEXIS 9498 (N.Y. App. Div. 4th Dep't 2000).

Supreme court properly granted those branches of defendants' cross-motion for summary judgment dismissing the causes of action alleging breach of the implied warranty of fitness for a particular purpose, breach of the implied warranty of merchantability, and fraud in the inducement, and to recover consequential and incidental damages as defendants expressly and conspicuously disclaimed the implied warranties in the contract of sale; the recovery of consequential and incidental damages was barred by a limitation of liability provision in the contract of sale; and the alleged fraudulent misrepresentations were not collateral or extraneous to the contract of sale. Joka Indus., Inc. v Doosan Infracore Am. Corp., 153 A.D.3d 506, 59 N.Y.S.3d 470, 2017 N.Y. App. Div. LEXIS 5884 (N.Y. App. Div. 2d Dep't 2017).

Supreme court properly granted those branches of defendants' cross-motion for summary judgment dismissing the causes of action alleging breach of the implied warranty of fitness for a particular purpose, breach of the implied warranty of merchantability, and fraud in the inducement, and to recover consequential and incidental damages as defendants expressly and conspicuously disclaimed the implied warranties in the contract of sale; the recovery of consequential and incidental damages was barred by a limitation of liability provision in the contract of sale; and the alleged fraudulent misrepresentations were not collateral or extraneous to the contract of sale. Joka Indus., Inc. v Doosan Infracore Am. Corp., 2017 NY Slip Op 05941, 2017 NY Slip Op 5941, 2017 N.Y. App. Div. LEXIS 5884 (N.Y. App. Div. 2d Dep't 2017).

A disclaimer of warranties in type which was of the same size and style of print as a much larger paragraph and in the same size and style as the remainder of the contract was not "conspicuous". Hertz Commercial Leasing Corp. v Transportation Credit Clearing House,

UCC

59 Misc. 2d 226, 298 N.Y.S.2d 392, 6 U.C.C. Rep. Serv. (CBC) 132, 1969 N.Y. Misc. LEXIS 1785 (N.Y. Civ. Ct. 1969), rev'd, 64 Misc. 2d 910, 316 N.Y.S.2d 585, 1970 N.Y. Misc. LEXIS 2000 (N.Y. App. Term 1970).

Summary judgment was granted to seller for entire amount due in payment for certain air conditioning/heating units which allegedly did not comply with express warranties contained in advertising brochure, where front page of sales contract contained boldface disclaimer "Of Warranties, Express or Implied, of Merchantability or Fitness" not discussed by said contract, and where same page contained large bold print warning buyer to read contract. Pennsylvania Gas Co. v Secord Bros., Inc., 73 Misc. 2d 1031, 343 N.Y.S.2d 256, 1973 N.Y. Misc. LEXIS 2154 (N.Y. Sup. Ct. 1973), aff'd, 44 A.D.2d 906, 357 N.Y.S.2d 702, 1974 N.Y. App. Div. LEXIS 4899 (N.Y. App. Div. 4th Dep't 1974).

Printed portion of retail instalment contract purporting to exclude warranties specifically mentioned "merchantability," was of contrasting type and plainly visible, and was thus "conspicuous" within meaning of UCC, so that instrument contained valid exclusion of implied warranties of merchantability and of fitness. Pennsylvania Gas Co. v Secord Bros., Inc., 73 Misc. 2d 1031, 343 N.Y.S.2d 256, 1973 N.Y. Misc. LEXIS 2154 (N.Y. Sup. Ct. 1973), aff'd, 44 A.D.2d 906, 357 N.Y.S.2d 702, 1974 N.Y. App. Div. LEXIS 4899 (N.Y. App. Div. 4th Dep't 1974).

Where (1) first word of warranty disclaimer on label of containers of aluminum-to-plywood adhesive was "NON-WARRANTY" printed in capital letters, (2) such word was followed by disclaimer language in smaller, noncapitalized letters until beginning of last sentence, and (3) last sentence, printed in capital letters of same size as opening word "NON-WARRANTY," stated that "IF THE PURCHASER DOES NOT ACCEPT THE GOODS ON THESE TERMS, THEY ARE TO BE RETURNED AT ONCE, UNOPENED," such disclaimer under UCC § 1-201(10) was sufficiently conspicuous to have called buyer's attention to it. Basic Adhesives, Inc. v Robert Matzkin Co., 101 Misc. 2d 283, 420 N.Y.S.2d 983, 27 U.C.C. Rep. Serv. (CBC) 933, 1979 N.Y. Misc. LEXIS 2671 (N.Y. Civ. Ct. 1979).

The disclaimer of warranty on the label of a can of highly volatile wall tile adhesive, written in small print, in lower case except for the word "warranty", and without a border, is ineffective and does not constitute an affirmative defense to an action based on a fire in plaintiffs' home allegedly caused by the adhesive since such disclaimer is not so "conspicuous" that "a reasonable person against whom it is to operate ought to have noticed it" (Uniform Commercial Code, § 2-316, subd [2]; § 1-201, subd [10]); capital letters, large print, contrasting type or color and black borders are proper methods of making a message "conspicuous" in a form or label. Victor v Mammana, 101 Misc. 2d 954, 422 N.Y.S.2d 350, 27 U.C.C. Rep. Serv. (CBC) 1295, 1979 N.Y. Misc. LEXIS 2795 (N.Y. Sup. Ct. 1979).

The decision on whether a disclaimer of warranty is sufficiently "conspicuous" (Uniform Commercial Code, § 2-316, subd [2]) is to be made by the court (Uniform Commercial Code, § 1-201, subd [10]) and is not a question of fact for the jury at the time of trial and the court on a motion for summary judgment may, therefore, properly determine that the disclaimer of warranty on a can of highly volatile wall tile adhesive is an insufficient affirmative defense as a matter of law in an action based upon a fire in plaintiffs' home allegedly caused by the adhesive; in addition, even if the disclaimer is deemed "conspicuous", it is nonetheless an insufficient affirmative defense since a disclaimer is not effective against strangers to the contract who never saw it and defendant manufacturer failed to come forward with any evidence to rebut plaintiffs' assertions that they were unfamiliar with the can of adhesive left in their home and had never read the label. Victor v Mammana, 101 Misc. 2d 954, 422 N.Y.S.2d 350, 27 U.C.C. Rep. Serv. (CBC) 1295, 1979 N.Y. Misc. LEXIS 2795 (N.Y. Sup. Ct. 1979).

In action by lessee of gas station against oil company which alleged, inter alia, misrepresentation and breach of warranty concerning defective storage tanks and gasoline pumps supplied to plaintiff by defendant, UCC concepts of good faith and unconscionability would be applied by analogy to entire transaction even though loan of equipment was not sale under UCC §§ 2-102 and 2-105 where purchase of gasoline by plaintiff was consideration for equipment loaned; although disclaimers of warranties are not per se unconscionable under UCC § 2-316, disclaimer in equipment loan agreement of "all claims" would not be read to preclude action for misrepresentation that induced contract in first instance; disclaimer was not

enforceable in regard to warranties where it was located in body of form agreement and was indistinguishable from remainder of printing in contract and therefore was not "conspicuous" within meaning of UCC § 1-201(10); accordingly cause of action concerning misrepresentation and breach of warranty would not be dismissed. Laudisio v Amoco Oil Co., 108 Misc. 2d 245, 437 N.Y.S.2d 502, 31 U.C.C. Rep. Serv. (CBC) 436, 1981 N.Y. Misc. LEXIS 2188 (N.Y. Sup. Ct. 1981).

Defendant's disclaimers of merchantability, fitness, and other express and implied warranties satisfied, as matter of law, conspicuousness requirement of CLS UCC §§ 1-201(10) and 2-316(2) where relevant language was larger and contrasting in type. Farm Family Mut. Ins. Co. v Moore Business Forms, 164 Misc. 2d 656, 625 N.Y.S.2d 798, 1995 N.Y. Misc. LEXIS 161 (N.Y. Sup. Ct. 1995).

Trial court granted summary judgment to the finance company on its action against the company and guarantor for breach of a lease agreement and guaranty after the foreign company supplied the company with equipment, the company stopped making payments to the finance company after one payment under the lease agreement because the equipment broke down and could not be repaired, and the finance company sued the company and the guarantor; while the lease agreement's waiver of warranty provision was ineffective because it was not sufficiently conspicuous, commercial law expressly excluded the imputation of the implied warranties of merchantability and fitness for a particular purpose to finance leases, and the finance company was not responsible for the equipment's performance because the lease stated that the company and guarantor bought the machine "as is." Direct Capital Corp. v New ABI, Inc., 822 N.Y.S.2d 684, 2006 NY Slip Op 26408, 13 Misc. 3d 1151, 2006 N.Y. Misc. LEXIS 2839 (N.Y. Sup. Ct. 2006).

Buyer was entitled to summary judgment as to liability against a manufacturer on his claims of violations of the implied warranties of merchantability and fitness for a particular purpose because, inter alia, the parties' dealer agreement failed to effectively disclaim the implied warranty of merchantability since the purported disclaimer did not mention the term "merchantability" pursuant to N.Y. U.C.C. Law § 2-316(2), and the purported disclaimer was not conspicuous pursuant to N.Y. U.C.C. Law § 1-201(10); similarly, the agreement failed to effectively disclaim the implied warranty of fitness for a particular purpose since the purported disclaimer was not conspicuous pursuant to N.Y. U.C.C. Law § 2-316(2). Bimini Boat Sales, Inc. v Luhrs Corp., 69 A.D.3d 782, 892 N.Y.S.2d 548, 2010 NY Slip Op 462, 2010 N.Y. App. Div. LEXIS 444 (N.Y. App. Div. 2d Dep't 2010).

Seller of fabric was liable to buyer for breach of express warranties of merchantability and fitness for particular purpose, notwithstanding seller's invoice contained statement "No refunds after 5 days. Check goods before cutting," where buyer's purchase order stated that fabric was to be used for swimwear and that all "colors, prints and bonding processes must meet swimwear specifications," where buyer's order was based on sample supplied by seller and, although another fabric was substituted for sample fabric, such modification was initiated by seller, where seller's salesman assured buyer that substituted fabric would meet swimwear specifications, where fabric supplied and subsequently manufactured into swimsuits was defective and failed to meet minimum performance standards for colorfastness, and where buyer notified seller within 12 to 20 days after receipt of fabric that it had received substantial number of complaints with respect to colorfastness: (1) seller's invoice and shipment of goods did not constitute both acceptance and counteroffer under UCC § 2-207, binding buyer to terms of invoice, since language used did not clearly condition acceptance on additional terms nor were such terms conspicuous as defined by UCC § 1-201(10); (2) express warranties of merchantability and fitness for particular purpose were established under UCC § 2-313 based on buyer's order form, representations of seller's salesman and samples supplied by seller; (3) there was no showing that warranties of merchantability and fitness had been excluded or modified under UCC § 2-316; and (4) buyer, having given reasonable notice to seller under UCC § 2-607, was entitled to damages for credits issued to customers (including profits lost and costs of production for returns and allowances) plus cost of production of unsaleable swimsuits under UCC §§ 2-714 and 2-715, and to deduct such damages from purchase price under UCC § 2-717. Rite Fabrics, Inc. v Stafford—Higgins Co., 366 F. Supp. 1, 13 U.C.C. Rep. Serv. (CBC) 588, 1973 U.S. Dist. LEXIS 11787 (S.D.N.Y. 1973) (applying New York law).

5. Contract

Under the Uniform Commercial Code, practical business people are not expected to govern their actions with reference to nice legal formalisms. Thus, when there is a basic agreement, however manifested and whether or not precise moment of such agreement can be determined, failure of parties to articulate agreement in precise legal language, with every difficulty and contingency considered and resolved, will not prevent formation of contract. However, if there is no basic agreement, the code will not imply one. And without an agreement, there can be no contract and without a contract, there can be no breach. This principle is explicitly recognized by UCC § 1-201(3) and (11), and UCC § 2-204(1) and (2). Kleinschmidt Div. of SCM Corp. v Futuronics Corp., 41 N.Y.2d 972, 395 N.Y.S.2d 151, 363 N.E.2d 701, 21 U.C.C. Rep. Serv. (CBC) 422, 1977 N.Y. LEXIS 2021 (N.Y. 1977).

6. Creditor

Injunctive relief under CLS UCC § 8-317 would not be available to require debtors to transfer stock shares into New York so that they could be attached by New York sheriff where applicant for injunction did not yet have any money judgment and so was only mere claimant, not "creditor" under UCC, and where there was no indication that extra-state assets were going to be disposed of or that any award of money damages would be inadequate. Siy v McMicking, 134 Misc. 2d 164, 510 N.Y.S.2d 407, 1 U.C.C. Rep. Serv. 2d (CBC) 889, 1986 N.Y. Misc. LEXIS 3079 (N.Y. Sup. Ct. 1986).

Landlord was not protected "creditor" of tenant within meaning of Bulk Transfers Act at time of sale of tenant's assets, since tenant had not defaulted on any rent payment at time of sale, and thus no rent was due; definition of creditor under CLS UCC § 6-109 would not be construed to encompass claims that are not yet due, and are contingent. Sunrise Indus. Joint Venture v Ditric Optics, 873 F. Supp. 765, 26 U.C.C. Rep. Serv. 2d (CBC) 829, 1995 U.S. Dist. LEXIS 559 (E.D.N.Y. 1995).

7. Delivery

In an action to foreclose a mortgage, the trial court erred by granting plaintiff's motion for summary judgment because the plaintiff produced the mortgage, the unpaid note, and evidence of the appellant's default; however, the plaintiff failed to establish its standing because the note had been endorsed in blank and the affidavits of bank employees failed to establish physical delivery of the note to plaintiff prior to commencement of the action. U.S. Bank N.A. v Brody, 2017 N.Y. App. Div. LEXIS 8869 (N.Y. App. Div. 2d Dep't 2017).

Where holder of promissory notes delivers such notes to bank with instructions that bank sell interests therein and issue certificates of participation in notes, there has been constructive delivery of such notes with bank acting as agent of original holder and making constructive delivery to purchasers to extent of their interests in notes. Corporacion Venezolana de Fomento v Vintero Sales Corp., 452 F. Supp. 1108, 24 U.C.C. Rep. Serv. (CBC) 1199, 1978 U.S. Dist. LEXIS 18398 (S.D.N.Y. 1978).

Since UCC § 1-201(14) defines "delivery" as "voluntary transfer of possession" but does not specify whether it may be actual or constructive, court adopted former New York Negotiable Instruments Law, which defined "delivery" as "transfer of possession, actual or constructive, from one person to another," in light of general case-law agreement that because Uniform Commercial Code did not prescribe any new definition of the term, former definition of "delivery" should be deemed to continue. Corporacion Venezolana de Fomento v Vintero Sales Corp., 452 F. Supp. 1108, 24 U.C.C. Rep. Serv. (CBC) 1199, 1978 U.S. Dist. LEXIS 18398 (S.D.N.Y. 1978) (construing New York UCC; noting that constructive delivery may be accomplished through an agent).

8. Document of title

Court properly determined that "holding certificates" for platinum constitute negotiable "documents of title" within purview of CLS UCC § 7-403 since (1) evidence supported finding that commodities trading firms and banks accept holding certificates as collateral for loans, and consequently treat them as evidence that person in possession is entitled to receive commodities referred to therein, (2) platinum constitutes "goods" under CLS UCC Art 7 and thus issuer of certificate is "bailee" for purposes of Article 7, (3) identification of platinum by quantity and by grade meets identification requirement of CLS UCC § 1-201(15), and (4) fact that holding certificates stated "we are holding for the account or order of...," and promised to release platinum on surrender of certificate, rendered them negotiable. Bank

of New York v Amoco Oil Co., 35 F.3d 643, 24 U.C.C. Rep. Serv. 2d (CBC) 209, 1994 U.S. App. LEXIS 21123 (2d Cir. N.Y. 1994).

Bank, which accepted "holding certificates" for platinum as collateral for loan, was not deprived of holder in due course status for purposes of CLS UCC § 7-501 although it might have been aware that certificates arose out of lease agreement, since such knowledge did not constitute notice of defense against lease in absence of evidence that bank was aware of breach in underlying agreement. Bank of New York v Amoco Oil Co., 35 F.3d 643, 24 U.C.C. Rep. Serv. 2d (CBC) 209, 1994 U.S. App. LEXIS 21123 (2d Cir. N.Y. 1994).

A forged delivery order is neither a "document of title" nor a warehouse receipt under the provisions of this section because it cannot be said to have been issued in the regular course of business or financing, nor can it be treated as adequately evidencing that the person in possession of it is entitled to receive, hold, and dispose of the document and the good it covers. David Crystal, Inc. v Cunard S.S. Co., 223 F. Supp. 273, 1963 U.S. Dist. LEXIS 7867 (S.D.N.Y. 1963), aff'd, 339 F.2d 295, 1964 U.S. App. LEXIS 3630 (2d Cir. N.Y. 1964).

9. Fungible

Sugar in 100 pound bags fell within definition of fungible, UCC § 1-201(17); therefore, when delivery was tendered to warehousemen on behalf of buyer under UCC § 2-503(4), buyer acquired insurable interest in goods, title to goods, and at same time buyer bore risk of loss with respect to those goods, not withstanding warehousemen's failure to segregate sugar. Henry Heide, Inc. v Atlantic Mut. Ins. Co., 80 Misc. 2d 485, 363 N.Y.S.2d 515, 16 U.C.C. Rep. Serv. (CBC) 701, 1975 N.Y. Misc. LEXIS 2200 (N.Y. Sup. Ct. 1975).

10. Good faith

Bank did not act in bad faith when it took steps to safeguard checking account in which it held security interest as collateral for letter of credit issued to corporate account holder, even though bank acted before corporation's surety had presented draft to bank for payment, where bank had good reason to believe, at time of its actions, that corporation was insolvent and that bank would have to reimburse surety for corporation's anticipated inability to meet obligation for which surety issued bond. Gillman v Chase Manhattan Bank, N. A., 73 N.Y.2d 1, 537 N.Y.S.2d 787, 534 N.E.2d 824, 7 U.C.C. Rep. Serv. 2d (CBC) 945, 1988 N.Y. LEXIS 3537 (N.Y. 1988).

Bank did not violate implied standard of good faith inherent in every contract when it failed to warn corporate account holder of impending segregation of checking account once bank became insecure as to common law security interest it held in account, even though bank had shown continued confidence in corporation just prior to segregation by renewing letter of credit in exchange for which security interest was created; moreover, since there was no commercial bad faith in segregation, there could be no bad faith in bank's subsequent dishonor of checks drawn on segregated account. Gillman v Chase Manhattan Bank, N. A., 73 N.Y.2d 1, 537 N.Y.S.2d 787, 534 N.E.2d 824, 7 U.C.C. Rep. Serv. 2d (CBC) 945, 1988 N.Y. LEXIS 3537 (N.Y. 1988).

In an action by the owner of a valuable painting to recover the painting or its value, the defense of equitable estoppel, which provides that an owner may be estopped from setting up his own title and the lack of title in the vendor as against a bona fide purchaser for value where the owner has clothed the vendor with possession and other indicia of title, is not available to an art dealer who purchased the painting from a delicatessen employee who was not the owner and had no authority to dispose of it although he had obtained the painting from a person who rightfully had possession of it pursuant to an agreement with the true owner since the owner had consigned the painting for display only and conferred no other indicia of ownership; moreover, the owner's conduct did not in any way contribute to the deception practiced on the purchaser, and the purchaser was not a purchaser in good faith since he made no inquiry or investigation as to the true ownership of the painting. Porter v Wertz, 68 A.D.2d 141, 416 N.Y.S.2d 254, 26 U.C.C. Rep. Serv. (CBC) 876, 1979 N.Y. App. Div. LEXIS 10530 (N.Y. App. Div. 1st Dep't 1979), aff'd, 53 N.Y.2d 696, 439 N.Y.S.2d 105, 421 N.E.2d 500, 30 U.C.C. Rep. Serv. (CBC) 1582, 1981 N.Y. LEXIS 2344 (N.Y. 1981).

In an action by the owners of a valuable painting to recover the painting or its value, the defense of statutory estoppel (Uniform Commercial Code, § 2-403, subd [2], which provides that any entrusting of possession of goods to a merchant who deals in goods of that kind gives him power to transfer all rights of the entruster to a buyer in the ordinary course of business) is not available to an art dealer who purchased the painting from a delicatessen employee who

UCC

was not the owner of the painting and had no authority from the owner to dispose of it although he had obtained the painting from a person who rightfully had possession of it, since the art dealer was not a buyer in the ordinary course of business, defined as a person who in good faith and without knowledge that the sale to him is in violation of the ownership rights or security interest of a third party in the goods buys in ordinary course from a person in the business of selling goods of that kind (Uniform Commercial Code, § 1-201, subd [9]), inasmuch as the person from whom the dealer bought the painting was not an art dealer and never held himself out to be one and the dealer was not a person in good faith because he made no effort to verify whether the seller was the owner or authorized by the owner to sell the painting. Porter v Wertz, 68 A.D.2d 141, 416 N.Y.S.2d 254, 26 U.C.C. Rep. Serv. (CBC) 876, 1979 N.Y. App. Div. LEXIS 10530 (N.Y. App. Div. 1st Dep't 1979), aff'd, 53 N.Y.2d 696, 439 N.Y.S.2d 105, 421 N.E.2d 500, 30 U.C.C. Rep. Serv. (CBC) 1582, 1981 N.Y. LEXIS 2344 (N.Y. 1981).

Bank that paid checks on forged endorsements was not entitled to summary judgment dismissing payee's common-law contract causes of action where bank made no showing that it acted in good faith and in accordance with reasonable commercial standards under CLS UCC §§ 1-201(19) and 3-419. Lawyers' Fund for Client Protection v Gateway State Bank, 273 A.D.2d 565, 709 N.Y.S.2d 243, 2000 N.Y. App. Div. LEXIS 6686 (N.Y. App. Div. 3d Dep't 2000).

Payee on checks paid by defendant bank on forged endorsements was not entitled to summary judgment on its common-law contract causes of action, even though it produced evidence that on at least 50 prior occasions attorney/forger eliminated words "escrow account" from face of checks drawn on his escrow account, that on 4 occasions there were small overdrafts on that account, and that on numerous occasions there were checks drawn on escrow account to cover overdrafts in attorney's business account, where that evidence (1) was not germane to issue of whether bank acted in good faith and in accordance with reasonable commercial standards in accepting checks for deposit and (2) did not evoke duty of inquiry regarding payee's indorsement on deposited checks. Lawyers' Fund for Client Protection v Gateway State Bank, 273 A.D.2d 565, 709 N.Y.S.2d 243, 2000 N.Y. App. Div. LEXIS 6686 (N.Y. App. Div. 3d Dep't 2000).

Trial court improperly granted summary judgment dismissal of a physician's complaint, pursuant to N.Y. C.P.L.R. 3212, against a bank in his action alleging conversion and negligence, seeking to recover funds which were embezzled by use of fraudulent checks by the physician's former office manager and another, because whether the bank followed reasonably commercial standards in handling the checks was a question of fact; it was noted that the bank initially met its burden of showing proof of the affirmative defense under N.Y. U.C.C. Law § 3-419(3) and also, the physician had failed to show that the employees did not act with honesty in fact, as required by N.Y. U.C.C. Law § 1-201(19), but thereafter, the physician offered sufficient proof to combat the affirmative defense and render the issue ripe for the jury. Jones v Cmty. Bank of Sullivan County, 306 A.D.2d 679, 762 N.Y.S.2d 133, 51 U.C.C. Rep. Serv. 2d (CBC) 744, 2003 N.Y. App. Div. LEXIS 6664 (N.Y. App. Div. 3d Dep't 2003).

Receipt of a creditor's notice of a secured loan, together with a warning that making payments to the debtor instead of to the creditor would have constituted a violation of the security interest, deprived a transferee of the right to claim status as a buyer in the ordinary course of business; the transferee's subsequent acceptance of deliveries from the debtor, and payments to the debtor for those deliveries could not have been made in good faith. SK Global Am., Inc. v John Roberts, Inc., 6 A.D.3d 179, 778 N.Y.S.2d 5, 53 U.C.C. Rep. Serv. 2d (CBC) 401, 2004 N.Y. App. Div. LEXIS 3715 (N.Y. App. Div. 1st Dep't 2004).

A buyer who acquires property from one who has a voidable title must show that he was a "good faith purchaser for value", which requires "honesty in fact and the observance of reasonable commercial standards of fair dealing". Atlas Auto Rental Corp. v Weisberg, 54 Misc. 2d 168, 281 N.Y.S.2d 400, 4 U.C.C. Rep. Serv. (CBC) 572, 1967 N.Y. Misc. LEXIS 1388 (N.Y. Civ. Ct. 1967), disapproved, Candela v Port Motors, 208 A.D.2d 486, 617 N.Y.S.2d 49, 25 U.C.C. Rep. Serv. 2d (CBC) 681, 1994 N.Y. App. Div. LEXIS 9380 (N.Y. App. Div. 2d Dep't 1994).

To succinct Code definition of "good faith" as "honesty in fact", drafters of Code in Official Comment added that phrase "means at least what is here stated"; held, in short, "good faith" as used in Code stands for "honesty" and perhaps more. Star Credit Corp. v Molina,

59 Misc. 2d 290, 298 N.Y.S.2d 570, 6 U.C.C. Rep. Serv. (CBC) 70, 1969 N.Y. Misc. LEXIS 1705 (N.Y. Civ. Ct. 1969).

When the UCC intends to apply a concept of "good faith" beyond its definition in UCC § 1-201, subd 19 as "honesty in fact", a broader definition is provided, e.g. UCC § 2-103, subd 1(b), which adds the words "observance of reasonable commercial standards of fair dealing in the trade" to the definition of "good faith" as between merchants. Advanced Alloys, Inc. v Sergeant Steel Corp., 72 Misc. 2d 614, 340 N.Y.S.2d 266, 11 U.C.C. Rep. Serv. (CBC) 1230, N.Y. Misc. LEXIS 2273 (N.Y. Civ. Ct.), rev'd, 79 Misc. 2d 149, 360 N.Y.S.2d 142, 12 U.C.C. Rep. Serv. (CBC) 1173, 1973 N.Y. Misc. LEXIS 1264 (N.Y. App. Term 1973).

The phrase "in good faith", as used in UCC § 4-404 refers to the general definition of good faith contained in UCC § 1-201, subd, 19. Advanced Alloys, Inc. v Sergeant Steel Corp., 72 Misc. 2d 614, 340 N.Y.S.2d 266, 11 U.C.C. Rep. Serv. (CBC) 1230, N.Y. Misc. LEXIS 2273 (N.Y. Civ. Ct.), rev'd, 79 Misc. 2d 149, 360 N.Y.S.2d 142, 12 U.C.C. Rep. Serv. (CBC) 1173, 1973 N.Y. Misc. LEXIS 1264 (N.Y. App. Term 1973).

Drawee bank's payment of 14-month-old check without making inquiry of drawer was in good faith under UCC § 1-201, subd 19 and thus permissible under UCC § 4-404 where good faith of drawee bank was not disputed. Advanced Alloys, Inc. v Sergeant Steel Corp., 72 Misc. 2d 614, 340 N.Y.S.2d 266, 11 U.C.C. Rep. Serv. (CBC) 1230, N.Y. Misc. LEXIS 2273 (N.Y. Civ. Ct.), rev'd, 79 Misc. 2d 149, 360 N.Y.S.2d 142, 12 U.C.C. Rep. Serv. (CBC) 1173, 1973 N.Y. Misc. LEXIS 1264 (N.Y. App. Term 1973).

Neither a factor to whom general contractor improperly assigned receivables that should have been used to pay a subcontractor nor the subcontractor that asserted improper diversion on the part of the general contractor showed entitlement to summary judgment on the issue of whether the factor was protected as a bona fide purchaser for value, because further factual development was needed on the issue of good faith; the court used a definition of good faith drawn from New York common law and from the general definitions in the Uniform Commercial Code. LeChase Data/Telecom Servs., LLC v Goebert, 766 N.Y.S.2d 796, 2 Misc. 3d 195, 2003 N.Y. Misc. LEXIS 1344 (N.Y. Sup. Ct. 2003), aff'd in part, modified, 12 A.D.3d 1093, 785 N.Y.S.2d 222, 2004 N.Y. App. Div. LEXIS 13829 (N.Y. App. Div. 4th Dep't 2004).

Where guarantor of promissory note attempts to assert defense of fraud in inducement, rights of purchasers of limited interest in note cannot be defeated on ground that they breached duty to inquire and thus failed to act in good faith because circumstances of which holders had knowledge did not rise to level indicating that failure to inquire revealed deliberate desire to evade knowledge. Corporacion Venezolana de Fomento v Vintero Sales Corp., 452 F. Supp. 1108, 24 U.C.C. Rep. Serv. (CBC) 1199, 1978 U.S. Dist. LEXIS 18398 (S.D.N.Y. 1978).

The Uniform Commercial Code, in defining "good faith" as "honesty in fact in the conduct or transaction concerned" (UCC § 1-201(19), adopted a subjective standard for the good-faith test in UCC Article 3, which standard was generally applicable under the former Negotiable Instruments Law. Corporacion Venezolana de Fomento v Vintero Sales Corp., 452 F. Supp. 1108, 24 U.C.C. Rep. Serv. (CBC) 1199, 1978 U.S. Dist. LEXIS 18398 (S.D.N.Y. 1978) (construing New York UCC).

Where there was no reason for brokerage firm to suspect that delivery agent had any interest in securities delivered for principals' accounts, brokerage firm acted honestly in fact and therefore met good faith requirement of UCC § 1-201, subd 19, in crediting shares to principals' accounts rather than making payment to agent. Colonial Secur., Inc. v Merrill Lynch, Pierce, Fenner & Smith, Inc., 461 F. Supp. 1159, 1978 U.S. Dist. LEXIS 13844 (S.D.N.Y. 1978).

In determining status as holder in due course, bad faith represents more than failure to observe reasonable commercial standards; circumstances of which holder is aware must be such that failure to inquire signals desire to evade knowledge because of belief or fear that inquiry would reveal defense. Scarsdale Nat'l Bank & Trust Co. v Toronto-Dominion Bank, 533 F. Supp. 378, 33 U.C.C. Rep. Serv. (CBC) 996, 1982 U.S. Dist. LEXIS 10984 (S.D.N.Y. 1982).

Good faith is defined as honesty in fact in conduct of transaction concerned; since test is subjective, summary judgment is generally inappropriate when outstanding issues or questions involve intent or motive. French American Banking Corp. v Flota Mercante Grancolombiana, S.A., 609 F. Supp. 1352, 1985 U.S. Dist. LEXIS 20327 (S.D.N.Y. 1985).

In action by assignee-holder of note, which was secured by stock in foreign corporation that was purchased with note's proceeds, against husband-maker and wife-guarantor of note to obtain payment of unpaid interest and part of unpaid principal due, (1) defense that plaintiff did not act in good faith and commercially reasonable manner within meaning of UCC §§ 1-201(19), 1-203, and 2-103(1)(b) could not be sustained because of defendants' failure to show how plaintiff's acts constituted bad faith sufficient to relieve defendants from their obligation to pay; (2) plaintiff had not elected to retain collateral for note—which consisted of shares of stock in foreign corporation that had depreciated in value because they had been expropriated by government of country in which corporation was located—because plaintiff did not give written notice of such alleged election to defendants, as required by UCC § 9-505(2); (3) plaintiff did not discharge defendants from their obligation by oral waiver because plaintiff's alleged oral statements, even if proved, were insufficient under UCC § 3-605(1)(b), which requires renunciation of debt without consideration to be in writing signed and delivered to party to be discharged; (4) plaintiff's delay in making demand presentment, and giving notice of dishonor did not, under UCC § 3-511(2)(a), discharge defendants from their obligation because defendants had expressly waived such defenses by clause in note sued on; (5) defense of impairment of collateral (stock) for note under UCC § 3-606(1)(b) was not available to defendant husband because he was note's maker; (6) such defense also was not available to defendant wife, even if she were note's guarantor, because foreign government, rather than plaintiff, had impaired value of collateral (stock) by expropriation; and (7) defense that wife's liability as surety was discharged by certain modifications of her contractual obligations that were made without her consent (see UCC § 3-606(1)(a)) ignored fact that wife, in loan agreement signed by her, had expressly waived right to be notified of making of such modifications. Bank of Boston International v Arguello Tefel, 644 F. Supp. 1423, 3 U.C.C. Rep. Serv. 2d (CBC) 1069, 1986 U.S. Dist. LEXIS 20038 (E.D.N.Y. 1986) (applying NY UCC).

Seller could not have succeeded on its breach of contract claim even if the buyer had waived its right to timely delivery of an aircraft because the seller failed to prove that it had satisfied the conditions precedent to the buyer's obligation to purchase and the seller failed to prove that the buyer acted in bad faith when it rejected the aircraft because (1) the parties agreed that the buyer could have rejected the aircraft if the seller failed to satisfy the delivery conditions in any way, no matter how insignificant; (2) the deviations were not minor because two unapproved auxiliary center fuel tanks affected the aircraft's airworthiness; and (3) the seller contracted away any right it otherwise might have had to cure its failure to perform by March 31, 2004. Austrian Airlines Oesterreichische Luftverkehrs AG v UT Fin. Corp., 567 F. Supp. 2d 579, 2008 U.S. Dist. LEXIS 55072 (S.D.N.Y. 2008), aff'd, 336 Fed. Appx. 39, 2009 U.S. App. LEXIS 14565 (2d Cir. N.Y. 2009).

11. Holder

Where creditor bank, on date loan was due and after being informed by debtor that debtor would default, set off credit balances in debtor's accounts against amount of debt; where remittance check of debtor's customer, pursuant to prior agreement between debtor and bank, was taken by bank from debtor's post-office lockbox and indorsed and deposited in debtor's account; where after depositing such check, bank then exercised alleged right of setoff against it; and where customer then issued stop-payment order on check and bank sued customer for payment thereof, alleging that it had acquired holder-in-due-course status as to such check and that its right to receive payment was not affected by debtor's alleged failure to discharge contractual obligations to customer, (1) bank acted prematurely in setting off deposits in debtor's accounts on date loan was due; (2) although such premature setoff arguably became operative on following day, it did not determine issue as to whether bank was entitled to payment on check; (3) bank was mere holder of check under UCC § 1-201(20) and not holder in due course under UCC § 3-302(1), since it did not give value for check under UCC § 3-303(b) and UCC § 4-208(1); (4) failure to give value stemmed from fact that bank, after customer issued stop-payment order on check, reversed its provisional credit of check to debtor's account and thus reinstated that part of debtor's obligation against which such credit was set off; and (5) since bank did not give value for check and thus was not holder in due course, it could not recover on check. Marine Midland Bank-New York v Graybar Electric Co., 41 N.Y.2d 703, 395

N.Y.S.2d 403, 363 N.E.2d 1139, 21 U.C.C. Rep. Serv. (CBC) 1094, 1977 N.Y. LEXIS 2026 (N.Y. 1977).

In action by attorney of payee of four cashier's checks issued by defendant bank in exchange for four other checks on which stop-payment orders were subsequently issued, court, on affirming trial court's denial of summary-judgment motions of plaintiff and defendant, held (1) that plaintiff, who was at least holder under UCC § 1-201(20), had right under UCC § 3-301 to bring suit on cashier's checks; and (2) that if plaintiff was not holder in due course, defendant could assert defenses listed in UCC § 3-306(b) and (c), despite its acceptance of cashier's checks. Gates v Manufacturers Hanover Trust Company/Capital Region, 98 A.D.2d 829, 470 N.Y.S.2d 492, 37 U.C.C. Rep. Serv. (CBC) 1192, 1983 N.Y. App. Div. LEXIS 21156 (N.Y. App. Div. 3d Dep't 1983), overruled in part, Golden v Citibank, N.A., 23 N.Y.3d 935, 988 N.Y.S.2d 121, 2014 NY Slip Op 3192, 11 N.E.3d 194, 2014 N.Y. LEXIS 947 (N.Y. 2014).

Bank was not entitled to summary judgment in its action on promissory notes made payable to savings association, even though bank claimed that savings association merged into bank and that notes automatically became bank's property by operation of 12 CFR § 546.3, where bank did not submit copy of merger agreement or any other official document, nor did it submit affidavit by anyone with personal knowledge of facts attesting to merger. Home Sav. of America, F.A. v Lacher, 159 A.D.2d 235, 552 N.Y.S.2d 214, 1990 N.Y. App. Div. LEXIS 2281 (N.Y. App. Div. 1st Dep't 1990).

In action on promissory note which provided for repayment in 14 installments, court properly denied plaintiff's motion for summary judgment in lieu of complaint, without prejudice to renewal, where questions of fact were presented as to whether plaintiff (as assignee of note) was holder in due course of note, in that copy of note submitted by plaintiff bore on its back endorsement by plaintiff to nonparty institution, indicating that plaintiff had negotiated instrument after receiving it, and no longer had possession of it. American Inv. Bank N. A. v Dobbin, 209 A.D.2d 780, 617 N.Y.S.2d 999, 1994 N.Y. App. Div. LEXIS 10872 (N.Y. App. Div. 3d Dep't 1994).

Bank failed to establish that it had standing to recover on a promissory note because, while the bank appended a copy of the note to the complaint, the bank's submission of two different copies of the note with different endorsements in support of its motion for summary judgment failed to eliminate a triable issue of fact as to whether the bank was in possession of the original note at the time the action was commenced. Deutsche Bank Natl. Trust Co. v Webster, 142 A.D.3d 636, 2016 NY Slip Op 05846, 2016 NY Slip Op 05846, 2016 NY Slip Op 5846, 2016 NY Slip Op 5846, 37 N.Y.S.3d 283, 2016 N.Y. App. Div. LEXIS 5723 (N.Y. App. Div. 2d Dep't 2016)

Bank established that it had standing to prosecute a foreclosure action because the bank was in physical possession of the note, which was indorsed in blank and attached to the complaint, at the time the action was commenced; the bank was entitled to summary judgment because the bank submitted the mortgage, the note, and the affidavit of its vice president, attesting to the homeowner's default in the repayment of her mortgage loan obligation. JPMorgan Chase Bank, N.A. v Weinberger, 142 A.D.3d 643, 2016 NY Slip Op 05850, 2016 NY Slip Op 05850, 2016 NY Slip Op 5850, 2016 NY Slip Op 5850, 37 N.Y.S.3d 286, 2016 N.Y. App. Div. LEXIS 5730 (N.Y. App. Div. 2d Dep't 2016)

Assignee lacked standing in a foreclosure action because the assignee subsequently assigned both the note and mortgage to his then-bankruptcy attorney in March 2008 as partial payment for legal services, there was no evidence that the note was reassigned to the assignee prior to the commencement of the action in June 2010, and there was no evidence that the assignee was the holder of the original note at the time that he commenced the action. McCormack v Maloney, 160 A.D.3d 1098, 75 N.Y.S.3d 294, 2018 N.Y. App. Div. LEXIS 2384 (N.Y. App. Div. 3d Dep't 2018).

Assignee of a reverse mortgage lacked standing to pursue foreclosure action because it was not a holder in due course of the cash account agreement underlying the mortgage where, inter alia, the agreement was not a negotiable instrument and contained provisions that went well beyond definitions of negotiable instruments in the UCC. OneWest Bank, N.A. v FMCDH Realty, Inc., 165 A.D.3d 128, 83 N.Y.S.3d 612, 2018 N.Y. App. Div. LEXIS 6066 (N.Y. App. Div. 2d Dep't 2018).

Supreme court erred in ruling in favor of an assignee because triable issues of fact exist as to whether it was the holder of a note at the time the action was commenced; there was a triable issue of fact

UCC

as to whether the note was properly endorsed in blank by an allonge so firmly affixed thereto as to become a part thereof when it came into the possession of a bank, which later endorsed the note to the assignee. Bayview Loan Servicing, LLC, 166 A.D.3d 843, 2018 N.Y. App. Div. LEXIS 7992 (N.Y. App. Div. 2d Dep't 2018).

In an action to foreclose a mortgage, the supreme court properly granted plaintiff's motion for summary judgment because it made a prima facie showing of entitlement to judgment as a matter of law by producing the mortgage, the unpaid note, and evidence of default; plaintiff demonstrated that it was the holder of the note at the time the action, because a copy of the note, including an allonge containing an endorsement in blank, was among the various exhibits attached to the complaint. Bank of Am., N.A. v Tobin, 2019 N.Y. App. Div. LEXIS 96 (N.Y. App. Div. 2d Dep't 2019).

As a holder within the meaning of UCC § 1-201 subd 20, an escrow agent established a prima facie case on maker's dishonored check under UCC 3-307, subd 2, and it was no defense either that escrow agent could not himself sue on the check, or that the principal had failed to perform under the escrow agreement, where maker had prevented principal's performance, and where escrow agent, who had acknowledged the receipt of cash, could sue on check as trustee for principal, or as promisee of third party beneficiary contract under CPLR § 1004. Helman v Dixon, 71 Misc. 2d 1057, 338 N.Y.S.2d 139, 1972 N.Y. Misc. LEXIS 1377 (N.Y. Civ. Ct. 1972).

An escrow agent to whom a house buyer delivered a check to secure principal's performance of repairs to new house under escrow agreement was a "holder" under UCC § 1-201 subd 20 and entitled to sue on subsequently dishonored check under CPLR 1004 not only as the promisee of a third party beneficiary contract, but also as trustee for principal. Helman v Dixon, 71 Misc. 2d 1057, 338 N.Y.S.2d 139, 1972 N.Y. Misc. LEXIS 1377 (N.Y. Civ. Ct. 1972).

The Uniform Commercial Code, under UCC § 8-105(1), treats investment securities as negotiable instruments. The code also, in UCC § 1-201(20), defines a "holder" as one who is "in possession" of an investment security that is drawn, issued, or indorsed to him or to his order, or to bearer or in blank. Under the code's definition of a holder, therefore, possession is a significant factor, and the possessor of an instrument is a "holder" without regard to the legality or propriety of his possession. Stewart Becker, Ltd. v Horowitz, 94 Misc. 2d 766, 405 N.Y.S.2d 571, 1978 N.Y. Misc. LEXIS 2360 (N.Y. Sup. Ct. 1978).

The assignee of a collateral interest in the proceeds of promissory notes, who is in possession of the notes, which, however, were never indorsed over to its order, is not a holder of the notes and, therefore, has no status to effect an acceleration of payment under a clause therein authorizing such an acceleration at the option of the holder of the notes. Lipkowitz & Plaut v Affrunti, 95 Misc. 2d 849, 407 N.Y.S.2d 1010, 25 U.C.C. Rep. Serv. (CBC) 276, 1978 N.Y. Misc. LEXIS 2612 (N.Y. Sup. Ct. 1978).

Where (1) debtor sold corporate stock on July 25, 1974 to defendants for $180,000, and defendants executed promissory notes under pledge agreement securing payment of stock's purchase price and delivered them to escrowee, which also received the purchased stock, (2) debtor on March 19, 1975, with knowledge and consent of defendants and escrowee, assigned notes to creditor as collateral to secure payment of prior $60,000 debt, indorsed them to creditor's order, and delivered them to creditor which retained possession of them until August 24, 1976, a date following date on which debtor had fully debt due creditor, (3) on November 5, 1975, when defendants still owed debtor $135,000 on notes and notes were still in creditor's possession as collateral for payment of $28,000 balance then owed by debtor to creditor, debtor entered into agreement with plaintiff law firm and its client under which payments on prior debt owed by debtor to such client were extended, prospective lawsuit was settled, sums thus due to client were collateralized by assignment of debtor's interest in stock-payment notes, and notes themselves and pledge agreement securing them were also assigned to plaintiff on behalf of its client, subject to prior collater assignment in favor of debtor's first creditor, (4) first creditor on August 24, 1976 acknowledged to escrowee that debtor had fully discharged debt due it, delivered stock-payment notes in suit to plaintiff law firm, but never indorsed notes to plaintiff's order, (5) on August 25, 1976, plaintiff, defendants (purchasers of debtor's stock), debtor, and escrowee executed written acknowledgements of debtor's assignment of notes and pledge agreement to plaintiff, and plaintiff requested that it be paid next installment on notes, which was due on October 1, 1976, (5) on April 5, 1976, IRS assessed delinquent income-tax liability against debtor and filed notice of tax lien on August 4, 1976, (6) on October 1, 1976, escrowee paid installment payment due on notes to IRS, and (7) on October 5, 1976, plaintiff after due notice declared default on notes (because of failure to receive October 1, 1976 installment payment thereon) and under acceleration clause in notes demanded full payment thereof, court held (1) that plaintiff, as nominee for its client, acquired valid collateral assignment of proceeds of notes to extent that proceeds were not required to satisfy first creditor's prior security interest therein, (2) that under UCC § 3-202(3), debtor's indorsement and negotiation of notes to first creditor merely created partial assignment of notes' proceeds and did not divest debtor of ultimate right to all proceeds not required to satisfy debt owed to first creditor, (3) that debtor's remaining interest in notes' proceeds was the interest that debtor had assigned plaintiff as collateral on November 5, 1975, and that such assignment, under UCC § 9-204(1), gave plaintiff valid security interest in debtor's residuary interest in notes' proceeds, (4) that plaintiff's security interest in notes' proceeds was not perfected until August 24, 1976, when it became perfected under UCC § 9-305 by possession of notes following first creditor's delivery thereof to plaintiff, (5) that IRS tax lien was not superior to plaintiff's perfected security interest in notes, since neither plaintiff nor its client had received any notice of such lien until September 20, 1976, and (6) that neither plaintiff nor its client could accelerate unpaid balance due on notes, since plaintiff, as nominee for its client, was merely holder of security interest in notes and was not "holder" of notes within meaning of UCC § 1-201(20) because of first creditor's failure to indorse them to plaintiff's order. Lipkowitz & Plaut v Affrunti, 95 Misc. 2d 849, 407 N.Y.S.2d 1010, 25 U.C.C. Rep. Serv. (CBC) 276, 1978 N.Y. Misc. LEXIS 2612 (N.Y. Sup. Ct. 1978) (holding that plaintiff was entitled to receive, on behalf of its client, all installment payments due on notes, commencing with installment due on October 1, 1976).

Surety's guaranty of payment on promissory note and security interest in underlying investment did not make it holder in due course where surety was not in possession of note before acquiring it from prior holder in due course. National Union Fire Ins. Co. v Woodhead, 917 F.2d 752, 12 U.C.C. Rep. Serv. 2d (CBC) 1076, 1990 U.S. App. LEXIS 19202 (2d Cir. N.Y. 1990).

Acceptor of travelers checks with forged countersignatures did not qualify as holder where it was not shown that forger had countersigned in acceptor's presence under circumstances that would not put acceptor on notice of forgery. Xanthopoulos v Thomas Cook, Inc., 629 F. Supp. 164, 42 U.C.C. Rep. Serv. (CBC) 883, 1985 U.S. Dist. LEXIS 13541 (S.D.N.Y. 1985).

12. Money

For purposes of construing CLS Ins § 1110(a), current meaning of "money" must control; CLS UCC § 1-201(24) defines money as "a medium of exchange authorized or adopted by a domestic or foreign government as part of its currency" and, in modern operations, money does not only include cash but also drafts and checks. Insurance Department, Opinions of General Counsel, Opinion Number 03-10-17.

13. Notice

Subsequent creditor had actual knowledge under UCC §§ 9-401(2) and 1-201(25) of contents of improperly filed financing statement, and thus financing was effective against subsequent creditor, where subsequent creditor was aware at time that debtor came to it for loan that, except for about $13,000, all of debtor's $160,000 net worth was pledged for two prior bank loans and that pledge covered debtor's equipment. Enark Industries, Inc. v Bush, 86 Misc. 2d 985, 383 N.Y.S.2d 796, 19 U.C.C. Rep. Serv. (CBC) 685, 1976 N.Y. Misc. LEXIS 2557 (N.Y. App. Term 1976).

Neither a factor to whom general contractor improperly assigned receivables that should have been used to pay a subcontractor nor the subcontractor that asserted improper diversion on the part of the general contractor showed entitlement to summary judgment on the issue of whether the factor was protected as a bona fide purchaser for value, because further factual development was needed on the issue of lack of notice; the court used a definition of notice drawn from New York common law and from the general definitions in the Uniform Commercial Code. LeChase Data/Telecom Servs., LLC v Goebert, 766 N.Y.S.2d 796, 2 Misc. 3d 195, 2003 N.Y. Misc. LEXIS 1344 (N.Y. Sup. Ct. 2003), aff'd in part, modified, 12 A.D.3d 1093, 785 N.Y.S.2d 222, 2004 N.Y. App. Div. LEXIS 13829 (N.Y. App. Div. 4th Dep't 2004).

Funding company entered into a contractual relationship with network designer, and at the outset had a copy of its business plan and a right to copies of its business records; it had procedures in place to check with the network services provider to make sure that each individual invoice was payable before agreeing to purchase and advance funds against it; those kinds of considerations supported looking to N.Y. U.C.C. Law art. 1 rather than N.Y. U.C.C. Law arts. 3 and 4 for the standard of notice applicable to a factor seeking shelter as a good-faith purchaser. Further, N.Y. U.C.C. Law art. 9 does not define notice, N.Y. U.C.C. Law § 9-102(a), or refer to the definition of notice in N.Y. U.C.C. Law arts. 3 and 4, N.Y. U.C.C. Law § 9-102(b); therefore, N.Y. U.C.C. Law art. 1's general definitions and principles of construction and interpretation were most appropriately applicable, N.Y. U.C.C. Law § 9-102(c). Le Chase Data/Telecom Servs., LLC v Goebert, 6 N.Y.3d 281, 811 N.Y.S.2d 317, 2006 NY Slip Op 1247, 844 N.E.2d 771, 2006 N.Y. LEXIS 198 (N.Y. 2006).

Funding company's files contained a list of the network service provider's construction managers and their telephone numbers, and there were various e-mails and notes that referred to approval of the network designer's invoices by the provider's construction managers; that was because the funding company regularly contacted the provider's construction managers, and knew that the provider would not pay an invoice from the designer until a construction manager signaled satisfactory completion of the work billed. The funding company's knowledge that the provider's construction managers reviewed the designer's invoices for approval lead to the inference that the funding company should have known that a contractor's invoices were for construction work; thus, there was no triable issue of fact regarding notice under N.Y. U.C.C. Law § 1-201(25), the funding company was not entitled to protection of the exception in N.Y. Lien Law § 72(1) for a good-faith purchaser, and the contractor's motion for summary judgment was granted. Le Chase Data/Telecom Servs., LLC v Goebert, 6 N.Y.3d 281, 811 N.Y.S.2d 317, 2006 NY Slip Op 1247, 844 N.E.2d 771, 2006 N.Y. LEXIS 198 (N.Y. 2006).

Buyer took reasonable steps to notify seller as to defects in sweatshirts where buyer's and seller's representatives held meetings after first shipment was made to discuss sweatshirts, and seller's representatives thereafter deliberately failed to respond to communications from buyer after second shipment. Texpor Traders, Inc. v Trust Co. Bank, 720 F. Supp. 1100, 10 U.C.C. Rep. Serv. 2d (CBC) 1227, 1989 U.S. Dist. LEXIS 10753 (S.D.N.Y. 1989).

Buyer's rejection of allegedly defective merchandise is not rendered ineffective because seller receives no written notice of defects, because, UCC § 1-201 does not require written notice, furthermore, what constitutes reasonable notice depends on circumstances of each case Texpor Traders, Inc. v Trust Co. Bank, 720 F. Supp. 1100, 10 U.C.C. Rep. Serv. 2d (CBC) 1227, 1989 U.S. Dist. LEXIS 10753 (S.D.N.Y. 1989).

14. Notifying or giving notice

Where debtor, who had twice defaulted on agreement to purchase both stock in penthouse apartment and proprietary lease for apartment by first being evicted from apartment—which eviction constituted "Event of Default" under creditor's security agreement— and by not making final payment on note's due date, sought to have creditor's public sale of stock and lease declared void on grounds of lack of adequate notice of such sale and sale's commercial unreasonableness, court held (1) that notice of sale, which had been sent to both debtor's last known residential address in New York and his Texas bank, satisfied requirements of UCC §§ 9-504(3) and 1-201(26) and (38), since creditor was only required to take reasonable steps necessary to notify debtor, and debtor's actual receipt of such notice was not necessary; (2) that when debtor defaulted for second time by not making final payment on note, there was no debt left to accelerate and under UCC § 3-122(1)(a), cause of action on note accrued on day after its maturity without any demand for payment being necessary to charge debtor; (3) that creditor had right under UCC § 9-504(3) to sell collateral; and (4) that since issue of fact was presented as to whether collateral had been sold for commercially reasonable price, case would be remanded for trial of that issue. Dougherty v 425 Dev. Associates, 93 A.D.2d 438, 462 N.Y.S.2d 851, 36 U.C.C. Rep. Serv. (CBC) 354, 1983 N.Y. App. Div. LEXIS 17496 (N.Y. App. Div. 1st Dep't 1983).

Where letter of credit issued to insurance company contained no specific requirement that notice of intention not to renew it be addressed to particular person, delivery of notice to company's mailroom, addressed only to surname of contact person named in company's address on letter of credit, was sufficient under CLS UCC § 1-201(26), although 5 persons employed by company had same surname. National Union Fire Ins. Co. v Manufacturers Hanover Trust Co., 194 A.D.2d 327, 598 N.Y.S.2d 228, 21 U.C.C. Rep. Serv. 2d (CBC) 1, 1993 N.Y. App. Div. LEXIS 5522 (N.Y. App. Div. 1st Dep't 1993).

Depositor's failure to provide bank with written notice of forged checks within 14 days after bank statements were mailed, as required under deposit agreement, was not excused on ground that notification provision was ambiguous and that 14-day period should have been measured from actual receipt rather than mailing, since (1) plain language of agreement stated that written notice must be given within 14 days of "delivery or mailing," so that either method alone was sufficient to trigger running of notice period, and (2) although measuring 14 days from time of receipt would seem more fair time limit, proving (rather than presuming) receipt would be impracticable and would require needlessly expensive and cumbersome device of certified mail for all bank correspondence. Parent Teacher Ass'n, Public School 72 v Manufacturers Hanover Trust Co., 138 Misc. 2d 289, 524 N.Y.S.2d 336, 5 U.C.C. Rep. Serv. 2d (CBC) 679, 1988 N.Y. Misc. LEXIS 22 (N.Y. Civ. Ct. 1988).

Neither depositor (unincorporated association) nor its treasurer could claim nonreceipt or lack of knowledge to excuse their failure to notify bank of forged checks within 14-day contractual time period on ground that treasurer's husband had allegedly intercepted mailed bank statements to conceal forgery, since depositor must be deemed to have known that which its treasurer knew or should have known— that she was not in possession of statements at time when she should have been or that blank checks were missing. Parent Teacher Ass'n, Public School 72 v Manufacturers Hanover Trust Co., 138 Misc. 2d 289, 524 N.Y.S.2d 336, 5 U.C.C. Rep. Serv. 2d (CBC) 679, 1988 N.Y. Misc. LEXIS 22 (N.Y. Civ. Ct. 1988).

Buyer took reasonable steps to notify seller of defects in merchandise where buyer's representatives and seller's representatives met after first shipment to discuss merchandise and seller's representatives deliberately failed to respond to communications from buyer after second shipment. Texpor Traders, Inc. v Trust Co. Bank, 720 F. Supp. 1100, 10 U.C.C. Rep. Serv. 2d (CBC) 1227, 1989 U.S. Dist. LEXIS 10753 (S.D.N.Y. 1989).

In a case governed by the New York Uniform Commercial Code in which (1) it was undisputed that a buyer rejected the generators by a date certain, (2) whether the rejection was seasonable was a question for the jury, and (3) the buyer identified specific facts in the record showing that it communicated to the sellers that the generators were unsatisfactory or otherwise nonconforming almost immediately after the generators arrived in Iraq, the sellers' motion for summary judgment on the basis that the buyer accepted the generators by failing to reject them effectively was denied. GE Packaged Power, Inc. v Readiness Mgmt. Support, L.C., 510 F. Supp. 2d 1124, 2007 U.S. Dist. LEXIS 2645 (N.D. Ga. 2007).

15. Notice received by organization

Section 1-201 distinguishes between "giving" and "receiving" notice; notice requirement is satisfied even though notice is not actually received, as long as reasonable steps were taken to notify other party. Texpor Traders, Inc. v Trust Co. Bank, 720 F. Supp. 1100, 10 U.C.C. Rep. Serv. 2d (CBC) 1227, 1989 U.S. Dist. LEXIS 10753 (S.D.N.Y. 1989).

Notice received for particular transaction is effective from time it is brought to attention of individual conducting such transaction, or from time it would have been brought to such person's attention had he or organization exercised due diligence. Texpor Traders, Inc. v Trust Co. Bank, 720 F. Supp. 1100, 10 U.C.C. Rep. Serv. 2d (CBC) 1227, 1989 U.S. Dist. LEXIS 10753 (S.D.N.Y. 1989).

16. Party

Bank was not "party" to contract for sale of goods within meaning of CLS UCC § 2-609, and thus was not entitled to notice of buyer's demand on supplier for adequate assurance of due performance of contract for sale of oil products, where bank merely provided financing for supplier in transaction. BAII Banking Corp. v UPG, Inc., 985 F.2d 685, 20 U.C.C. Rep. Serv. 2d (CBC) 155, 1993 U.S. App. LEXIS 2705 (2d Cir. N.Y. 1993).

17. Person

The notation "Food for Love Acc't" does not indicate the name of a "person" as defined in UCC § 1-201, but signifies an account and suggests a direction to the drawee rather than a notice to the payee alerting it to any representational capacity in which the signature was executed. Star Dairy, Inc. v Roberts, 37 A.D.2d 1038, 326

N.Y.S.2d 85, 9 U.C.C. Rep. Serv. (CBC) 1374, 1971 N.Y. App. Div. LEXIS 2941 (N.Y. App. Div. 3d Dep't 1971).

18. Presumption or presumed

Blanket denials failed to overcome presumption of receipt of goods supported by receipted freight bill, check for freight charges, letter of notification, and actual delivery of merchandise. Eazor Express, Inc. v Lanza, 60 Misc. 2d 686, 303 N.Y.S.2d 571, 6 U.C.C. Rep. Serv. (CBC) 1088, 1969 N.Y. Misc. LEXIS 1288 (N.Y. County Ct. 1969).

The effect of the definition of "presumption" in UCC § 1-201(31) is to create a rebuttable presumption. The adversary has the burden of coming forward with evidence to overcome the presumption, and when such evidence is produced, the presumption disappears. Freeman Check Cashing, Inc. v State, 97 Misc. 2d 819, 412 N.Y.S.2d 963, 26 U.C.C. Rep. Serv. (CBC) 1186, 1979 N.Y. Misc. LEXIS 2006 (N.Y. Ct. Cl. 1979).

19. Purchase

Third party's argument that it paid value by making a down payment and paying installments under on a lease agreement was rejected, and N.Y. U.C.C. Law § 1-201(44) was inapplicable; the third party had not accepted delivery before it learned of the owner's security interest, and the down payment was to be refunded when the full contract price was paid. Snow Machs., Inc. v S. Slope Dev. Corp., 300 A.D.2d 906, 754 N.Y.S.2d 383, 50 U.C.C. Rep. Serv. 2d (CBC) 613, 2002 N.Y. App. Div. LEXIS 12412 (N.Y. App. Div. 3d Dep't 2002).

Defendant lender to buyer of debtor's property, who later liquidated the property, fell within the definition of "purchaser" in UCC § 1-201(32), and the lender's "purchase," as defined by UCC § 1-201(33), of the debtor's assets were subject to the same infirmities as the buyer's purchase for failure to comply with UCC art. 6. Comm. of Unsecured Creditors of Interstate Cigar Co. v Interstate Distrib., Inc. (In re Interstate Cigar Co.), 285 B.R. 789, 49 U.C.C. Rep. Serv. 2d (CBC) 267, 2002 Bankr. LEXIS 1362 (Bankr. E.D.N.Y. 2002), aff'd, app. denied, 42 Bankr. Ct. Dec. (LRP) 69, 2003 U.S. Dist. LEXIS 21845 (E.D.N.Y. 2003).

The term "purchaser of a limited interest" in UCC § 3-302(4) does not refer only to holders of security interest in negotiable property, but comprehends those who become purchasers of such property by any of the means specified in UCC § 1-201(32). Corporacion Venezolana de Fomento v Vintero Sales Corp., 452 F. Supp. 1108, 24 U.C.C. Rep. Serv. (CBC) 1199, 1978 U.S. Dist. LEXIS 18398 (S.D.N.Y. 1978) (construing New York UCC).

20. Representative

Individual who worked in seller's office constituted seller's "representative" for purposes of receiving notification of defects in shipments of goods, notwithstanding that he was not acting as seller's agent, where he was intimately involved in all discussions relating to goods and seller's president admittedly spoke with him virtually daily. Texpor Traders, Inc. v Trust Co. Bank, 720 F. Supp. 1100, 10 U.C.C. Rep. Serv. 2d (CBC) 1227, 1989 U.S. Dist. LEXIS 10753 (S.D.N.Y. 1989).

21. Security interests

Assignee of business' future "receivables" under factoring agreement had security interest in proceeds due under promissory note which business had received for sale of substantial share of business assets to third party, even though agreement provided that all receivables which were described in schedules prepared by business "will be bona fide existing obligations created by the sale and actual delivery of goods or the rendition of services to customers in the ordinary course of business," since agreement assigned all of business' receivables, including "all obligations of every kind at any time owing to" business. Berkowitz v Chavo Int'l, Inc., 74 N.Y.2d 144, 544 N.Y.S.2d 569, 542 N.E.2d 1086, 9 U.C.C. Rep. Serv. 2d (CBC) 4, 1989 N.Y. LEXIS 887 (N.Y. 1989).

Whether lease of mobile home, which contained option to purchase home for (a) additional $4,800 on January 1, 1975, (b) additional $3,600 on January 1, 1976, (c) additional $2,200 on January 1, 1977, or (d) additional $600 on January 1, 1978, was true lease or agreement for security interest could not be resolved, as declared by UCC § 1-201(37), solely by fact that lease included option to purchase. Instead, under UCC § 1-201(37), such lease would be agreement for security interest only if lessee had option to become owner of home for no additional consideration or for a nominal consideration. Van Alphen v Robinson, 71 A.D.2d 1039, 420 N.Y.S.2d 44, 1979 N.Y. App. Div. LEXIS 13401 (N.Y. App. Div. 3d Dep't 1979).

Where lease of dump trailer was not intended to create security interest in trailer, provisions of UCC Art 9 were inapplicable under UCC §§ 1-201(37) and 9-102(1)(a). Mileasing Co. v Hogan, 87 A.D.2d 961, 451 N.Y.S.2d 211, 1982 N.Y. App. Div. LEXIS 16492 (N.Y. App. Div. 3d Dep't 1982).

In action to determine priority of competing security interests in after-acquired restaurant equipment, where (1) plaintiff leased restaurant premises, together with furniture, fixtures, equipment, and improvements then located on premises, to two tenants, (2) lease provided that title to inventoried equipment listed in attached "schedule A" was to remain in plaintiff and that on expiration of lease, title to all additions, improvements, alterations, and replacements made during lease term was to vest in plaintiff, and (3) tenants thereafter purchased equipment from defendant and gave defendant purchase-money security interest in such equipment, court held (1) that although language in lease indicated that plaintiff lessor intended to reserve title to all after-acquired property on leased premises, such language was not sufficient to create security interest in such property under UCC § 1-201(37), (2) that fact that tenants were obligated by lease to leave all after-acquired equipment on leased premises was also insufficient to show intention to give plaintiff security interest in such equipment, and (3) that record, considered in its entirety, showed that lease did not create security interest in after-acquired equipment purchased by tenants from defendant. Mayflower Restaurant Corp. v Bejera Corp., 88 A.D.2d 716, 451 N.Y.S.2d 286, 33 U.C.C. Rep. Serv. (CBC) 1484, 1982 N.Y. App. Div. LEXIS 16956 (N.Y. App. Div. 3d Dep't 1982), app. dismissed, 57 N.Y.2d 604, 1982 N.Y. LEXIS 7135 (N.Y. 1982), app. dismissed, 57 N.Y.2d 774, 1982 N.Y. LEXIS 4347 (N.Y. 1982).

Whether lease is intended to create security interest depends on facts of each case rather than on form of agreement. All Good Leasing Corp. v Bimco Industries, Inc., 143 A.D.2d 788, 533 N.Y.S.2d 336, 1988 N.Y. App. Div. LEXIS 10209 (N.Y. App. Div. 2d Dep't 1988).

Equipment lease was security agreement that created security interest, not "a finance lease as that term is defined in UCC Art 2A," where it provided for "down payment" of $2,084.62 and 11 monthly payments of $525.21 plus tax, and plaintiff had option to purchase equipment for one dollar upon fulfillment of its lease obligation; thus, defendants' interest in equipment terminated upon completion of plaintiff's payment obligations, CLS Gen Oblig § 5-901 was inapplicable, and plaintiff had no cause of action under that statute. Citipostal, Inc. v Unistar Leasing, 283 A.D.2d 916, 724 N.Y.S.2d 555, 44 U.C.C. Rep. Serv. 2d (CBC) 691, 2001 N.Y. App. Div. LEXIS 4526 (N.Y. App. Div. 4th Dep't 2001).

Lease which provided defendant with option to renew for trifling yearly rental, which for all practical purposes amounted to making defendant owner of machine at end of lease for nominal consideration until total obsolescence, was intended for security within meaning of UCC § 1-210(37). Leasco Data Processing Equipment Corp. v Starline Overseas Corp., 74 Misc. 2d 898, 346 N.Y.S.2d 288, 12 U.C.C. Rep. Serv. (CBC) 1214, 1973 N.Y. Misc. LEXIS 1764 (N.Y. App. Term 1973), aff'd, 45 A.D.2d 992, 360 N.Y.S.2d 199, 1974 N.Y. App. Div. LEXIS 7628 (N.Y. App. Div. 1st Dep't 1974).

When the holder of promissory notes assigned his interest therein as collateral to secure payment of a prior indebtedness, a sum less than the aggregate amount of the notes, and indorsed and delivered them to that creditor, he did not irrevocably divest himself of the ultimate right to all of the proceeds of the notes, but retained ownership of those proceeds not required to satisfy that indebtedness, and, therefore, the negotiation of all of the notes operated only as a partial assignment of the proceeds of the notes; the interest retained by him was capable of being transferred and, when it was transferred by another collateral assignment, the transferee acquired a valid security interest as to his residuary interest in the notes, which security interest was perfected by a subsequent delivery of the notes to it. Lipkowitz & Plaut v Affrunti, 95 Misc. 2d 849, 407 N.Y.S.2d 1010, 25 U.C.C. Rep. Serv. (CBC) 276, 1978 N.Y. Misc. LEXIS 2612 (N.Y. Sup. Ct. 1978).

Leasing agreement between plaintiff lesssor and lessee of 2 hydraulic lifts constituted security interest where, although lease contained "no-purchase option" clause, purchase option agreement was executed along with lease which provided net purchase price of greater of 10 percent or $751, or then fair market value of equipment, and where (1) lessee was required to maintain all insurance coverage, (2) lessor was not in business of leasing such equipment but merely purchased equipment desired by lessee, (3) total rental payments under lease exceeded equipment's purchase price, (4) lease provided for repossession of equipment by lessor upon lessee's default and for liability of lessee for any resulting deficiency, and (5) lessor required guarantee executed by third party. Guardsman Lease Plan, Inc. v Gibraltar Transmission Corp., 129 Misc. 2d 887, 494 N.Y.S.2d 59, 42 U.C.C. Rep. Serv. (CBC) 943, 1985 N.Y. Misc. LEXIS 2721 (N.Y. Sup. Ct. 1985).

Transaction purporting to be lease of car would be construed as sale, with lease agreement serving to create security interest for benefit of lessor, where (1) agreement created pecuniary interest in lessee by virtue of her obligation to purchase car at end of lease or be liable for any deficiency resulting from lessor's resale of car (or, conversely, entitling lessee to equal share of any surplus from resale of car), together with fact that rental payments apparently represented retail price of car, and (2) other factors evinced attempt by lessor to protect its interest in car as collateral, including facts that lessee made "downpayment," was required to maintain full insurance coverage and pay all taxes, license and registration costs, and lessee covenanted to indemnify lessor from all claims, suits, or damages. Credit Car Leasing Corp. v De Cresenzo, 138 Misc. 2d 726, 525 N.Y.S.2d 492, 6 U.C.C. Rep. Serv. 2d (CBC) 1012, 1988 N.Y. Misc. LEXIS 160 (N.Y. Civ. Ct. 1988).

Creditor was not entitled to "lease" payments under 11 U.S.C.S. § 365(d)(10) on energy-saving equipment that was provided to a debtor under a Master Energy Services Agreement (MESA) where the MESA was a secured financing agreement and not a true lease; although the MESA was not a disguised security agreement under the bright-line test of N.Y. U.C.C. Law § 1-201(37), the economic realities of the underlying transaction indicated that it was a disguised security agreement. Duke Energy Royal, LLC v Pillowtex Corp. (In re Pillowtex, Inc.), 349 F.3d 711, 42 Bankr. Ct. Dec. (LRP) 45, 52 U.C.C. Rep. Serv. 2d (CBC) 18, 2003 U.S. App. LEXIS 23245 (3d Cir. Del. 2003).

Certain agreements for equipment between a Chapter 11 debtor and a purported lessor were not finance leases as they purported to be, but were rather disguised secured transactions under N.Y. U.C.C. Law § 1-201(37)(a) because (1) the agreements did not permit the debtor to terminate its payment obligations under the lease prior to the expiration of the lease term, (2) the remaining economic life of the equipment extended much further than the four-year lease term provided in the agreements, (3) the debtor possessed no option to renew the agreements at all, and (4) the purchase option price was so low that the debtor would certainly exercise it and would, in all probable circumstances, leave no meaningful reversion for the lessor. In re ECCO Drilling Co., Ltd., 390 B.R. 221, 50 Bankr. Ct. Dec. (LRP) 85, 2008 Bankr. LEXIS 2001 (Bankr. E.D. Tex. 2008).

Lease arrangement, under which owner sold equipment to a company whose only business was financing and not equipment maintenance, and company advanced funds to former owner's creditors, leased equipment to former owner with an option to buy, recorded an Article 9 UCC financing statement, and assigned the agreement to a bank, constituted a secured loan arrangement. National Equipment Rental, Ltd. v Hendrix, 565 F.2d 255, 1977 U.S. App. LEXIS 10778 (2d Cir. N.Y. 1977).

Seller of fuel oil could not claim to retain security interest in oil which it had delivered to broker for conveyance to buyer, and thus, as between seller and broker, seller could not bring action against third party buyer for misappropriation of oil, where no explicit agreement designating seller as security holder in oil was required as required by CLS UCC Art 9. In re Crysen/Montenay Energy Co., 902 F.2d 1098, 20 Bankr. Ct. Dec. (LRP) 807, 11 U.C.C. Rep. Serv. 2d (CBC) 881, 1990 U.S. App. LEXIS 7787 (2d Cir. N.Y. 1990).

Equipment lease transactions were security agreements under UCC § 1-201(37), and leasing corporation was "financing agency" and not seller of equipment under UCC § 2-104(2), where persons desirous of purchasing equipment or machinery applied to corporation for purchase money loan, corporation made commitments to advance money necessary for payment to manufacturer, plus sales tax, equipment was shipped by manufacturer directly to purchaser and invoice was sent to corporation, purchaser and corporation thereupon entered into security agreements in form of equipment leases with options to purchase at nominal extra charge, UCC financing statements were thereupon executed and delivered to purchaser and filed by corporation, corporation did not select or inspect any equipment, corporation did not maintain warehouse for storage of equipment or machinery, corporation did not carry leased property as assets on books or take any depreciation deductions, and corporation never took possession of any of leased equipment at end

of leased term. In re Sherwood Diversified Services, Inc., 382 F. Supp. 1359, 15 U.C.C. Rep. Serv. (CBC) 701, 1974 U.S. Dist. LEXIS 6442 (S.D.N.Y. 1974) (applying New York law).

Under UCC § 1-201(37), leasing agreements which provided for rental of computer equipment for specified monthly rental for first five years and for higher monthly rental for remainder of lease period, and which also gave lessee option to purchase such equipment for 2.7 per cent of equipment's total rental value, or 4 per cent of price lessor paid for equipment, were leases intended as security for payment by lessee of purchase price of equipment and thus were governed by UCC Article 9. National Equipment Rental, Ltd. v Priority Electronics Corp., 435 F. Supp. 236, 22 U.C.C. Rep. Serv. (CBC) 280, 1977 U.S. Dist. LEXIS 14719 (E.D.N.Y. 1977) (applying New York law, and noting that fact that total rentals under one lease exceeded cost of leased equipment by approximately 46 per cent, and that total rentals under other lease exceeded cost of leased equipment by approximately 30 per cent, also indicated that both leases were intended as security only and were not true leases).

Where (1) lessee leased heavy mining equipment from lessor under four separate leases, (2) leases did not contain purchase option at end of lease term, but stated that title to equipment remained in lessor and that lessee granted security interest in equipment to lessor, (3) one lease provided that in event of default, repossession, and sale of equipment, net sale proceeds, "less 15 percent of the total rent," would be credited to amount owed by lessee, (4) three leases provided that in event of default, repossession and sale, net proceeds of sale, "less 20 percent of the actual cost" of the equipment would be credited to amount owed by lessee, (5) equipment covered by one lease was repossessed and later destroyed by fire, (6) equipment covered by other three leases was repossessed and sold for less than total amount owed by lessee under such leases, and (7) lessor sued for deficiency judgment, court held (1) that assuming that parties' transactions came within scope of UCC §§ 1-201(37) and 9-102(2), dealing with leases intended as security and security interest created by conditional sales, lessor was entitled to judgment on most of its claims against lessee, (2) that equipment had been sold in commercially reasonable manner required by UCC § 9-504(3), (3) that fact that lessor was highest bidder on equipment sold at one sale did not make sale commercially unreasonable under UCC § 9-504(3), (4) that late charges imposed by leases were not unconscionable within meaning of UCC § 2-302(1), and (5) that provision in one lease for deduction of "15 percent of the total rent" from amount of sale proceeds to be credited to amount owed by lessee, and provision in other two leases for deduction of 20 percent of initial cost of equipment from amount of sale proceeds to be credited to amount owed by lessee, raised questions concerning unconscionability of such deductions. Leasing Service Corp. v Carbonex, Inc., 512 F. Supp. 253, 31 U.C.C. Rep. Serv. (CBC) 1789, 1981 U.S. Dist. LEXIS 9622 (S.D.N.Y. 1981) (applying NY UCC).

In action on equipment leases by creditor against debtor after latter's default, leases were intended as security under UCC §§ 1-201(37) and 9-102 where defendant had options to purchase for nominal percentages of total rent under leases (4.3 percent, 4 percent, and .75 percent respectively) and where leases provided for acceleration, repossession, and sale by plaintiff if defendant defaulted; provision in leases which allowed plaintiff to deduct 15 percent of total rent or 20 percent of initial price from sale proceeds as liquidated damages was unreasonable and impermissible variation of UCC § 9-504; liquidated damages could not be based on plaintiff's right to retain equipment where UCC § 9-505(2) provides that debt is satisfied if secured party elects to retain collateral and where this provision may not be waived by consent of parties; attorneys fees were not allowed under UCC § 9-504(1)(a) where request submitted was unreasonably high and where plaintiff failed to submit information upon which reasonable award could be calculated. Leasing Service Corp. v Carbonex, Inc., 522 F. Supp. 79, 31 U.C.C. Rep. Serv. (CBC) 1800, 1981 U.S. Dist. LEXIS 13175 (S.D.N.Y. 1981).

22. Signature

Employee's typewritten and handwritten initials on documents contained in benefit file where employee designations of retirement plan beneficiary were contained, did not constitute signature of employee under provisions of UCC §§ 1-201(39) and 3-401(2). Mohawk Airlines, Inc. v Peach, 61 A.D.2d 346, 402 N.Y.S.2d 496, 1978 N.Y. App. Div. LEXIS 9744 (N.Y. App. Div. 4th Dep't 1978), app. denied, 44 N.Y.2d 645, 1978 N.Y. LEXIS 4367 (N.Y. 1978), app.

UCC

denied, 44 N.Y.2d 838, 406 N.Y.S.2d 758, 378 N.E.2d 121, 1978 N.Y. LEXIS 2034 (N.Y. 1978).

Notation "verbally authorized by your depositor" on pre-authorized draft or "telecheck" can constitute signature under Uniform Commercial Code, but constitutes forged signature when unauthorized. Interbank of N.Y. v Fleet Bank, 189 Misc. 2d 20, 730 N.Y.S.2d 208, 45 U.C.C. Rep. Serv. 2d (CBC) 167, 2001 N.Y. Misc. LEXIS 270 (N.Y. Civ. Ct. 2001).

23. Unauthorized signature or indorsement

Where (1) plaintiff depositor was forced by criminals to withdrawl $1,000 from her savings account with defendant bank, and (2) bank's teller did not detect deliberate falsification by plaintiff of her age when furnishing biographical data required to make such withdrawl, court held (1) that signature made by plaintiff under duress was "unauthorized" under UCC §§ 1-201(43) and 3-404(1), and was unenforceable, under UCC § 3-305(2)(b), even as against holder in due course, and (2) that bank's failure to follow its own procedure for verifying plaintiff's age, which plaintiff had falsified in order to draw teller's attention to plaintiff's difficulty, demonstrated lack of good faith, under UCC § 3-404(1), in relying on plaintiff's unauthorized signature and rendered bank liable to plaintiff for full amount of her loss. Reynolds v Dime Sav. Bank, 121 Misc. 2d 463, 467 N.Y.S.2d 971, 1983 N.Y. Misc. LEXIS 3940 (N.Y. Civ. Ct. 1983).

Absence of signature of surety's authorized representative on check drawn by conservator on conservatee's account caused check to have "unauthorized signature" within meaning of CLS UCC §§ 1-201(43), 3-406, and 4-406 where conservator and surety had entered into joint control agreement with defendant bank requiring checks drawn on account to be signed by conservator and countersigned by surety. Fireman's Fund Ins. Co. v National Westminster Bank, 144 Misc. 2d 468, 543 N.Y.S.2d 604, 7 U.C.C. Rep. Serv. 2d (CBC) 1157, 1988 N.Y. Misc. LEXIS 852 (N.Y. Sup. Ct. 1988).

In action by Lawyers' Fund for Client Protection, as assignee and subrogee of infant whose attorney converted proceeds of 2 life insurance checks made payable to infant's guardian, by endorsing them in guardian's name without her knowledge and then depositing them into his escrow account at defendant bank, court dismissed bank's affirmative defense that it acted in accordance with reasonable commercial standards when it accepted checks for deposit, as attorney did not have actual or apparent authority to execute checks or other documents on behalf of trust, and fact that 2 sizeable instruments payable to noncustomer for whom no signature card was available were brought to bank by customer for deposit into his own account should have put bank on inquiry notice. Lawyers' Fund v Gateway State Bank, 181 Misc. 2d 660, 692 N.Y.S.2d 583, 1999 N.Y. Misc. LEXIS 250 (N.Y. Sup. Ct. 1999), modified in part and rev'd in part, 273 A.D.2d 565, 709 N.Y.S.2d 243, 2000 N.Y. App. Div. LEXIS 6686 (N.Y. App. Div. 3d Dep't 2000).

Depository/collecting bank was entitled to summary judgment dismissing action in which drawee/payor bank sought to recover on 4 pre-authorized drafts, or "telechecks," paid out from account of its customer, where customer executed affidavit of forgery with respect to each draft stating that he never authorized drafts to be issued, and there was no evidence presented that depository/collecting bank had knowledge that drafts were unauthorized. Interbank of N.Y. v Fleet Bank, 189 Misc. 2d 20, 730 N.Y.S.2d 208, 45 U.C.C. Rep. Serv. 2d (CBC) 167, 2001 N.Y. Misc. LEXIS 270 (N.Y. Civ. Ct. 2001).

24. Value

Definition of value is satisfied only where purchaser of goods gives seller credit on debt owed by seller to purchaser for purchase of goods. Kivort Steel, Inc. v Liberty Leather Corp., 110 A.D.2d 950, 487 N.Y.S.2d 877, 1985 N.Y. App. Div. LEXIS 48848 (N.Y. App. Div. 3d Dep't 1985).

Definition of "value" under UCC § 1-201(44)(b) is satisfied only if buyer of goods gives seller credit on pre-existing debt owed by seller to buyer. Kivort Steel, Inc. v Liberty Leather Corp., 110 A.D.2d 950, 487 N.Y.S.2d 877, 1985 N.Y. App. Div. LEXIS 48848 (N.Y. App. Div. 3d Dep't 1985).

Definition of value is satisfied only where purchaser of goods gives seller credit on debt owed by seller to purchaser for purchase of goods. Kivort Steel, Inc. v Liberty Leather Corp., 110 A.D.2d 950, 487 N.Y.S.2d 877, 1985 N.Y. App. Div. LEXIS 48848 (N.Y. App. Div. 3d Dep't 1985).

Brokerage firm was bona-fide purchaser of securities where it (1) acquired them for value within meaning of UCC §§ 8-302 and 1-201(44)(b) by receiving them for account of customer and in partial

satisfaction of preexisting claim, (2) acted honestly in fact in the transaction, thereby complying with good-faith requirement of UCC §§ 8-302 and 1-201(19), and (3) did not have notice of any adverse claim to securities. Colonial Secur., Inc. v Merrill Lynch, Pierce, Fenner & Smith, Inc., 461 F. Supp. 1159, 1978 U.S. Dist. LEXIS 13844 (S.D.N.Y. 1978) (applying NY UCC).

Brokerage firm which received stock for account of customer and promptly credited sales price to customer's account acquired stock in partial satisfaction of pre-existing claim (UCC § 1-201, subd 44(b)), and thus for value within meaning of UCC § 8-302. Colonial Secur., Inc. v Merrill Lynch, Pierce, Fenner & Smith, Inc., 461 F. Supp. 1159, 1978 U.S. Dist. LEXIS 13844 (S.D.N.Y. 1978).

25. Warehouse receipt

Warehouse receipt is document of title. Lofton v Mooney, 452 S.W.2d 617, 7 U.C.C. Rep. Serv. (CBC) 824, 1970 Ky. LEXIS 370 (Ky. 1970).

A forged delivery order is neither a "document of title" nor a warehouse receipt under the provisions of this section because it cannot be said to have been issued in the regular course of business or financing, nor can it be treated as adequately evidencing that the person in possession of it is entitled to receive, hold, and dispose of the document and the good it covers. David Crystal, Inc. v Cunard S.S. Co., 223 F. Supp. 273, 1963 U.S. Dist. LEXIS 7867 (S.D.N.Y. 1963), aff'd, 339 F.2d 295, 1964 U.S. App. LEXIS 3630 (2d Cir. N.Y. 1964).

§ 1-202.   Notice; Knowledge

(a) Subject to subsection (f), a person has "notice" of a fact if the person:

(1) has actual knowledge of it;

(2) has received a notice or notification of it; or

(3) from all the facts and circumstances known to the person at the time in question, has reason to know that it exists.

(b) "Knowledge" means actual knowledge. "Knows" has a corresponding meaning.

(c) "Discover", "learn", or words of similar import refer to knowledge rather than to reason to know.

(d) A person "notifies" or "gives" a notice or notification to another person by taking such steps as may be reasonably required to inform the other person in ordinary course, whether or not the other person actually comes to know of it.

(e) Subject to subsection (f), a person "receives" a notice or notification when:

(1) it comes to that person's attention; or

(2) it is duly delivered in a form reasonable under the circumstances at the place of business through which the contract was made or at another location held out by that person as the place for receipt of such communications.

(f) Notice, knowledge, or a notice or notification received by an organization is effective for a particular transaction from the time it is brought to the attention of the individual conducting that transaction and, in any event, from the time it would have been brought to the individual's attention if the organization had exercised due diligence. An organization exercises due diligence if it maintains reasonable routines for communicating significant information to the person conducting the transaction and there is reasonable compliance with the routines. Due diligence does not require an individual acting for the organization to communicate information unless the communication is part of the individual's regular duties or the individual has reason to know of the transaction and that the transaction would be materially affected by the information.

History: L 2014, ch 505, § 1, eff Dec 17, 2014.

§ 1-203. Lease Distinguished From Security Interest

(a) Whether a transaction in the form of a lease creates a lease or security interest is determined by the facts of each case.

(b) A transaction in the form of a lease creates a security interest if the consideration that the lessee is to pay the lessor for the right to possession and use of the goods is an obligation for the term of the lease and is not subject to termination by the lessee, and:

(1) the original term of the lease is equal to or greater than the remaining economic life of the goods;

(2) the lessee is bound to renew the lease for the remaining economic life of the goods or is bound to become the owner of the goods;

(3) the lessee has an option to renew the lease for the remaining economic life of the goods for no additional consideration or for nominal additional consideration upon compliance with the lease agreement; or

(4) the lessee has an option to become the owner of the goods for no additional consideration or for nominal additional consideration upon compliance with the lease agreement.

(c) A transaction in the form of a lease does not create a security interest merely because:

(1) the present value of the consideration the lessee is obligated to pay the lessor for the right to possession and use of the goods is substantially equal to or is greater than the fair market value of the goods at the time the lease is entered into;

(2) the lessee assumes risk of loss of the goods;

(3) the lessee agrees to pay, with respect to the goods, taxes, insurance, filing, recording, or registration fees, or service or maintenance costs;

(4) the lessee has an option to renew the lease or to become the owner of the goods;

(5) the lessee has an option to renew the lease for a fixed rent that is equal to or greater than the reasonably predictable fair market rent for the use of the goods for the term of the renewal at the time the option is to be performed; or

(6) the lessee has an option to become the owner of the goods for a fixed price that is equal to or greater than the reasonably predictable fair market value of the goods at the time the option is to be performed.

(d) Additional consideration is nominal if it is less than the lessee's reasonably predictable cost of performing under the lease agreement if the option is not exercised. Additional consideration is not nominal if:

(1) when the option to renew the lease is granted to the lessee, the rent is stated to be the fair market rent for the use of the goods for the term of the renewal determined at the time the option is to be performed; or

(2) when the option to become the owner of the goods is granted to the lessee, the price is stated to be the fair market value of the goods determined at the time the option is to be performed.

(e) The "remaining economic life of the goods" and "reasonably predictable" fair market rent, fair market value, or cost of performing under the lease agreement must be determined with reference to the facts and circumstances at the time the transaction is entered into.

History: L 2014, ch 505, § 1, eff Dec 17, 2014.

§ 1-204. Value

Except as otherwise provided in articles 3, 4, and 5, a person gives value for rights if the person acquires them:

(a) in return for a binding commitment to extend credit or for the extension of immediately available credit, whether or not drawn upon and whether or not a charge-back is provided for in the event of difficulties in collection;

(b) as security for, or in total or partial satisfaction of, a preexisting claim;

(c) by accepting delivery under a preexisting contract for purchase; or

(d) in return for any consideration sufficient to support a simple contract.

History: L 2014, ch 505, § 1, eff Dec 17, 2014.

§ 1-205. Reasonable Time; Seasonableness

(a) Whether a time for taking an action required by this act is reasonable depends on the nature, purpose, and circumstances of the action.

(b) An action is taken seasonably if it is taken at or within the time agreed or, if no time is agreed, at or within a reasonable time.

History: L 2014, ch 505, § 1, eff Dec 17, 2014.

CASE ANNOTATIONS

UNDER FORMER § 1-204

1. In general
2. Question of law or fact
3. Express time provision
4. Particular acts; in general
5. – Inspection
6. – Rejection or revocation
7. Particular circumstances; disability of party

1. In general

Although depository-collecting bank, under UCC § 4-213(4)(a), could not prevent customer from drawing against check deposited in his account after reasonable time had elapsed from bank's receipt of provisional settlement for check, bank and customer were free under UCC § 1-204(1) to agree on their own definition of "reasonable time," so long as time fixed was not manifestly unreasonable. Rapp v Dime Sav. Bank (1979) 48 N.Y.2d 658, 421 N.Y.S.2d 347, 396 N.E.2d 740, 27 UCCRS 501

Reasonable time for taking any action is dependent on the nature, purpose and circumstances of the action. White Devon Farm v Stahl (1976) 88 Misc. 2d 961, 389 N.Y.S.2d 724, 20 UCCRS 291

UCC

2. Question of law or fact

CLS UCC § 2-714 would permit purchaser of allegedly defective aluminum tubing to sue for breach of warranty for nonconforming goods, even if transaction constituted sale by sample, provided that reasonable notice of defect had been given; whether notice is given within reasonable time depends on circumstances of transaction under CLS UCC § 1-204, and court would not rule on such question as matter of law where disputed factual issues existed. Arkwin Industries, Inc. v Hadco Aluminum & Metal Corp. (1986, 2d Dept) 123 A.D.2d 806, 507 N.Y.S.2d 423

Where facts are not substantially in dispute, question of what is a reasonable time to inspect and reject goods that fail to conform to contract specifications is a matter to be resolved by the court. White Devon Farm v Stahl (1976) 88 Misc. 2d 961, 389 N.Y.S.2d 724, 20 UCCRS 291

3. Express time provision

Where a sales contract expressly creates an unlimited express warranty of merchantability which in a separate clause purports to indirectly modify the warranty without expressly mentioning the word merchantability, the language creating the unlimited express warranty must prevail over the time limitation insofar as the latter modifies the warranty, and the express warranty of merchantability includes latent shading defects and defendants may claim for such defects not reasonably discoverable within the time limits established by the contract if plaintiff was notified of these defects within a reasonable time after they were or should have been discovered. Wilson Trading Corp. v David Ferguson, Ltd. (1968) 23 N.Y.2d 398, 297 N.Y.S.2d 108, 244 N.E.2d 685

There was no merit to plaintiff's claim, based on CLS UCC § 1-204, that software's "Y2K" noncompliance was latent defect that could not be discovered during unreasonably short 90-day warranty period. Against Gravity Apparel, Inc. v Quarterdeck Corp. (1999, 1st Dept) 267 A.D.2d 44, 699 N.Y.S.2d 368, CCH Prod Liab Rep ¶ 15718

4. Particular acts; in general

Where default occurred in payment of an automobile retail installment contract in August of 1965 but the security holder did not make demand upon the dealer for performance of its repurchase agreement until October of 1966, and it was the custom and usage that the lending institution is required to repossess and return the vehicle for repurchase within a reasonable time after default and that 90 days is regarded as a reasonable time, the security holder could not enforce the repurchase agreement which contained no provision inconsistent with the custom and usage. Valley Nat'l Bank v Babylon Chrysler-Plymouth, Inc. (1967) 53 Misc. 2d 1029, 280 N.Y.S.2d 786, 4 UCCRS 385, affd (1967, 2d Dept) 28 A.D.2d 1092, 284 N.Y.S.2d 849, 4 UCCRS 732

In action to recover price of two used forklift trucks that plaintiff traded in to defendant dealer on acquiring new forklift truck from dealer, where (1) at time trade-in was allegedly made, plaintiff and dealer's salesmen signed "quotation" that reflected terms of parties' transaction and specified trade-in allowance of $6,300 for plaintiff's trucks, (2) quotation also stated that it was not binding unless signed by dealer's officer, and (3) three months after quotation was signed, dealer picked up plaintiff's trucks, made extensive repairs thereon, and offered to purchase them from plaintiff for $1,800 each because of their defective condition, court held (1) that parties intended to make trade-in and to allow plaintiff $6,300 for its trucks, (2) that absence of dealer's signature on parties' "quotation" would prevent enforcement of trade-in agreement under statute of frauds in UCC § 2-201(1), unless such agreement came within exception to statute of frauds, (3) that dealer's repair of trucks was inconsistent with plaintiff's ownership within meaning of UCC § 2-606(1)(c) and constituted acceptance of trucks, so as to bring trade-in agreement within exception to statute of frauds contained in UCC § 2-201(3)(c), dealing with effect of buyer's acceptance of goods under otherwise unenforceable sale contract, (4) that buyer's three-month delay in picking up trucks was unreasonable under UCC § 1-204(2) and prevented it from successfully claiming that trucks' value had depreciated to $1,800 each, and (5) that as a result, plaintiff was entitled to recover original "quotation" price of $6,300 for both trucks. Bora Machine & Die Works, Inc. v Clark Lift, Inc. (1981, Civ Ct) 108 Misc. 2d 591, 437 N.Y.S.2d 1011

5. – Inspection

There is no inflexible rule that the time to inspect goods to determine their conformance with contract specifications must coincide with passage of title. White Devon Farm v Stahl (1976) 88 Misc. 2d 961, 389 N.Y.S.2d 724, 20 UCCRS 291

6. – Rejection or revocation

Mere fact that because of seller's action the passing of title to stud horse was accelerated by some six months did not affect timing of obligation to inspect horse to determine its fitness for breeding purposes or decision to accept or reject the horse since, pursuant to agreement, it was only in the two-month period prior to stated date for passing of title and after end of racing season that seller was to have horse tested to determine his fitness for breeding purposes, actual inspection took place during such time and horse sustained no serious bodily injury during last months of racing; inspection and rejection in month before title would have passed absent acceleration was timely. White Devon Farm v Stahl (1976) 88 Misc. 2d 961, 389 N.Y.S.2d 724, 20 UCCRS 291

Taking into the nature, purpose, and circumstances, pursuant to N.Y. U.C.C. Law § 1-204(2), of the rejection, the rejection under N.Y. U.C.C. Law § 2-602(1) of the safes purchased by the buyer from the seller was timely under N.Y. U.C.C. Law § 1-204(1) after the buyer discovered that the safes did not meet the attack resistance specifications provided in the contract; the buyer acted reasonably in having the safe tested and in obtaining the testing protocols before rejecting the safes. New York City Off-Track Betting Corp. v Safe Factory Outlet, Inc. (2006, App Div, 1st Dept) 809 NYS2d 70

Where goods are effectively rejected for breach of warranty, the burden of proving they conform presumably remains on the seller, whereas upon acceptance the buyer has the burden to establish any breach. Miron v Yonkers Raceway, Inc. (1968, CA2 NY) 400 F.2d 112, 5 UCCRS 673

Buyer of precision parts timely revoked its acceptance, where (1) after buyer sought reasonable assurances in February 1981, it did not receive answer until September and seller's September response indicated that further assurances were forthcoming, (2) it was not until November that buyer learned that seller had no experience with precision parts operating under relevant conditions and that it was unlikely that parts could satisfy contract specifications, (3) any delay in revoking acceptance occurred because buyer reasonably relied on seller's assurances that parts would work, (4) buyer revoked its acceptance within reasonable time after learning that seller had been less than candid with its assurances, and (5) seller has not shown that it was prejudiced by alleged delay. Creusot-Loire International, Inc. v Coppus Engineering Corp. (1983, SD NY) 585 F. Supp. 45, 39 UCCRS 186

Buyer's rejection of allegedly defective merchandise is not rendered ineffective because seller receives no written notice of defects, because, UCC § 1-201 does not require written notice, furthermore, what constitutes reasonable notice depends on circumstances of each case Texpor Traders, Inc. v Trust Co. Bank (1989, SD NY) 720 F. Supp. 1100, 10 UCCRS2d 1227

7. Particular circumstances; disability of party

"Reasonable time" for buyer of polystyrene plastic to give notice of defective product (CLS UCC §§ 1-204, 2-607) could involve substantial period of time since (1) buyer was broker of plastic products and did not use plastic itself, but sold plastic product to third party "end-users," and (2) in most instances, defects would be discovered only when end-user actually molded plastic material, revealing defects such as black spots or brittleness. First Sec. Mortg. Co. v Goldmark Plastics Compounds (1994, ED NY) 862 F. Supp. 918, 25 UCCRS2d 66

§ 1-206. Presumptions

Whenever this act creates a "presumption" with respect to a fact, or provides that a fact is "presumed," the trier of fact must find the existence of the fact unless and until evidence is introduced that supports a finding of its nonexistence.

History: L 2014, ch 505, § 1, eff Dec 17, 2014.

§ 1-207. Statute of Frauds for Kinds of Personal Property Not Otherwise Covered

(a) Except in the cases described in subsection (b) of this section a contract for the sale of personal property is not enforceable by way of action or defense beyond five thousand dollars in amount or value of remedy unless there is some writing which indicates that a contract for sale has been made between the parties at a defined or stated price, reasonably identifies the subject matter, and is signed by the party against whom enforcement is sought or by his authorized agent.

(b) Subsection (a) of this section does not apply to contracts for the sale of goods (Section 2-201) nor of securities (Section 8-113) nor to security agreements (Section 9-203).

(c) Subsection (a) of this section does not apply to a qualified financial contract as that term is defined in paragraph two of subdivision b of section 5-701 of the general obligations law if either (1) there is, as provided in paragraph three of subdivision b of section 5-701 of such law, sufficient evidence to indicate that a contract has been made or (2) the parties thereto, by means of a prior or subsequent written contract, have agreed to be bound by the terms of such qualified financial contract from the time they reach agreement (by telephone, by exchange of electronic messages, or otherwise) on those terms.

History: L 2014, ch 505, § 1, eff Dec 17, 2014.

CASE ANNOTATIONS

1. In general

Trial court properly awarded judgment to the lenders plus statutory interest because the borrower failed to establish that the cashing of her check allegedly as payment in full constituted an accord and satisfaction where the note provided that the borrower would pay both principal and interest on the loan and the lender's indorsement of the back of the check with the words "without prejudice and under protest" constituted an explicit reservation of rights, thereby precluding an accord and satisfaction. Huimin Sun v Cai, 146 A.D.3d 760, 2017 NY Slip Op 00155, 2017 NY Slip Op 155, 45 N.Y.S.3d 155, 2017 N.Y. App. Div. LEXIS 155 (N.Y. App. Div. 2d Dep't 2017).

In an action by the receiver of a bank to recover a deficiency resulting from a default on a promissory note and security agreement, the agreement whereby a purchaser of sewing machines contracted with the bank for the sale of chattel paper was an enforceable contract under UCC § 1-206 where, although it contained a blank space in an "excess" transaction provision, the contract set forth an identified subject matter, indicated the parties and specified the price, and was signed by the party against whom enforcement was sought; Article 9 did not apply to the transaction since, strictly speaking, the sale of chattel paper is not a pure security transaction in that the paper is simply the property sold for value received. Federal Deposit Ins. Corp. v Herald Square Fabrics Corp., 81 A.D.2d 168, 439 N.Y.S.2d 944, 32 U.C.C. Rep. Serv. (CBC) 558, 1981 N.Y. App. Div. LEXIS 10509 (N.Y. App. Div. 2d Dep't 1981).

This section is not applicable to a "call option" since it does not involve the sale of a "security", but such a transaction is governed by UCC § 1-206. Cohn, Ivers & Co. v Gross, 56 Misc. 2d 491, 289 N.Y.S.2d 301, 5 U.C.C. Rep. Serv. (CBC) 390, 1968 N.Y. Misc. LEXIS 1562 (N.Y. App. Term 1968).

Oral agreement for sale of plaintiff's interest in dental practice, sale of his equipment, and interest in lease and dental business, including leaving his patients, patient lists and supplies, was unenforceable under CLS Gen Oblig § 5-701 since parties agreed that balance of purchase price would not be paid until 3 years after making agreement, even though plaintiff had fully performed his obligations; however, since transaction constituted sale of business, which is included in definition of personal property under CLS UCC § 9-106, contract was enforceable up to $5,000 under CLS UCC § 1-206. Beldengreen v Ashinsky, 139 Misc. 2d 766, 528 N.Y.S.2d 744, 6 U.C.C. Rep. Serv. (CBC) 1053, 1987 N.Y. Misc. LEXIS 2828 (N.Y. Civ. Ct. 1987).

Breach of contract claims that were unenforceable under CLS UCC § 1-206 beyond $5,000 because there was no writing were

nevertheless enforceable up to $5,000; however, under elementary res judicata principles, plaintiff's contract claims would merge in his $5,000 judgment, and he would be barred from recovering balance. Grappo v Alitalia Linee Aeree Italiane, 56 F.3d 427, 26 U.C.C. Rep. Serv. 2d (CBC) 657, 1995 U.S. App. LEXIS 13498 (2d Cir. N.Y. 1995).

Plaintiff's contract to sell customized version of his copyrighted training program was one for sale of "personal property" under CLS UCC § 1-206, not principally one for services, in that plaintiff's efforts to tailor program to purchaser's needs were plainly secondary to contract. Grappo v Alitalia Linee Aeree Italiane, 56 F.3d 427, 26 U.C.C. Rep. Serv. 2d (CBC) 657, 1995 U.S. App. LEXIS 13498 (2d Cir. N.Y. 1995).

Plaintiff's contract to sell customized version of his copyrighted training program, including training manuals and materials, was one for sale of personal property under CLS UCC § 1-206, not one for sale of "goods" under CLS UCC § 2-201, in that sale of non-exclusive license for copyrighted material was core of contract, and manuals would have been useless absent legal right to use them. Grappo v Alitalia Linee Aeree Italiane, 56 F.3d 427, 26 U.C.C. Rep. Serv. 2d (CBC) 657, 1995 U.S. App. LEXIS 13498 (2d Cir. N.Y. 1995).

Even though several letters or other writings could be resorted to for the agreed upon terms, these writings had to be connected either expressly or by the internal evidence of subject-matter and occasion. Oswald v Allen, 417 F.2d 43, 1969 U.S. App. LEXIS 10422 (2d Cir. N.Y. 1969).

In action for alleged breach of agreement to include clothing "contractor" in contemplated sale of corporation which supplied designs and materials and promoted sale of garments tailored by contractor, only writing contained no "defined or stated price," and so Code § 1-206 would make any contract unenforceable beyond $5,000. Olympic Junior, Inc. v David Crystal, Inc., 463 F.2d 1141, 10 U.C.C. Rep. Serv. (CBC) 1138, 1972 U.S. App. LEXIS 8832 (3d Cir. N.J. 1972) (construing both New York and New Jersey Codes).

Defendant was entitled to summary judgment in action for breach of alleged oral contract for plaintiff's purchase of corporate assets where plaintiff's evidence as to existence of oral agreement consisted only of letter signed by defendant's president, and of various unsigned internal memoranda of defendant connected to letter by parol evidence; materials could not be read together to satisfy statute of frauds (CLS UCC § 1-206) since letter's reference to "our verbal agreement" required speculation not only as to whether phrase referred to ground rules of negotiations or to ultimate agreement, but also as to specific nature of transaction. Horn & Hardart Co. v Pillsbury Co., 888 F.2d 8, 10 U.C.C. Rep. Serv. 2d (CBC) 60, 1989 U.S. App. LEXIS 15905 (2d Cir. N.Y. 1989).

Statute of frauds under UCC § 1-206 did not bar recovery by distributors against distiller upon oral agreement by distiller to relocate distributors with a new distributorship. Lee v Joseph E. Seagram & Sons, Inc., 413 F. Supp. 693, 19 U.C.C. Rep. Serv. (CBC) 1043, 1976 U.S. Dist. LEXIS 15412 (S.D.N.Y. 1976), aff'd, 552 F.2d 447, 1977 U.S. App. LEXIS 14306 (2d Cir. N.Y. 1977) (applying New York law).

Copyright sales are not excluded from purview of CLS UCC § 1-206, which applies to "general intangibles" as defined in Article 9 of UCC and to transactions excluded from Article 9 by § 9-104. Mellencamp v Riva Music, Ltd., 698 F. Supp. 1154, 1988 U.S. Dist. LEXIS 12420 (S.D.N.Y. 1988).

Series of signed and unsigned writings may not be read together so as to satisfy statute of frauds, where single signed writing failed to establish contractual relationship. Horn & Hardart Co. v Pillsbury Co., 703 F. Supp. 1062, 8 U.C.C. Rep. Serv. 2d (CBC) 354, 1989 U.S. Dist. LEXIS 398 (S.D.N.Y. 1989), aff'd, 888 F.2d 8, 10 U.C.C. Rep. Serv. 2d (CBC) 60, 1989 U.S. App. LEXIS 15905 (2d Cir. N.Y. 1989).

UNDER FORMER § 1-206

In an action by the receiver of a bank to recover a deficiency resulting from a default on a promissory note and security agreement, the agreement whereby a purchaser of sewing machines contracted with the bank for the sale of chattel paper was an enforceable contract under UCC § 1-206 where, although it contained a blank space in an "excess" transaction provision, the contract set forth an identified subject matter, indicated the parties and specified the price, and was signed by the party against whom enforcement was sought; Article 9 did not apply to the transaction since, strictly speaking, the sale of chattel paper is not a pure security transaction in that the paper is simply the property sold for value received. Federal Deposit Ins.

Corp. v Herald Square Fabrics Corp. (1981, 2d Dept) 81 A.D.2d 168, 439 N.Y.S.2d 944, 32 UCCRS 558

This section is not applicable to a "call option" since it does not involve the sale of a "security", but such a transaction is governed by UCC § 1-206. Cohn, Ivers & Co. v Gross (1968) 56 Misc. 2d 491, 289 N.Y.S.2d 301, 5 UCCRS 390

Oral agreement for sale of plaintiff's interest in dental practice, sale of his equipment, and interest in lease and dental business, including leaving his patients, patient lists and supplies, was unenforceable under CLS Gen Oblig § 5-701 since parties agreed that balance of purchase price would not be paid until 3 years after making agreement, even though plaintiff had fully performed his obligations; however, since transaction constituted sale of business, which is included in definition of personal property under CLS UCC § 9-106, contract was enforceable up to $5,000 under CLS UCC § 1-206. Beldengreen v Ashinsky (1987, Civ Ct) 139 Misc. 2d 766, 528 N.Y.S.2d 744, 6 UCCRS2d 1053

Breach of contract claims that were unenforceable under CLS UCC § 1-206 beyond $5,000 because there was no writing were nevertheless enforceable up to $5,000; however, under elementary res judicata principles, plaintiff's contract claims would merge in his $5,000 judgment, and he would be barred from recovering balance. Grappo v Alitalia Linee Aeree Italiane (1995, CA2 NY) 56 F.3d 427, 26 UCCRS2d 657, 62 ALR5th 805 (criticized in PKFinans Int'l Corp. v IBJ Schroder Leasing Corp. (1996, SD NY) 1996 US Dist LEXIS 9155) and judgment entered (1997, SD NY) 975 F. Supp. 297

Plaintiff's contract to sell customized version of his copyrighted training program was one for sale of "personal property" under CLS UCC § 1-206, not principally one for services, in that plaintiff's efforts to tailor program to purchaser's needs were plainly secondary to contract. Grappo v Alitalia Linee Aeree Italiane (1995, CA2 NY) 56 F.3d 427, 26 UCCRS2d 657, 62 ALR5th 805 (criticized in PKFinans Int'l Corp. v IBJ Schroder Leasing Corp. (1996, SD NY) 1996 US Dist LEXIS 9155) and judgment entered (1997, SD NY) 975 F. Supp. 297

Plaintiff's contract to sell customized version of his copyrighted training program, including training manuals and materials, was one for sale of personal property under CLS UCC § 1-206, not one for sale of "goods" under CLS UCC § 2-201, in that sale of non-exclusive license for copyrighted material was core of contract, and manuals would have been useless absent legal right to use them. Grappo v Alitalia Linee Aeree Italiane (1995, CA2 NY) 56 F.3d 427, 26 UCCRS2d 657, 62 ALR5th 805 (criticized in PKFinans Int'l Corp. v IBJ Schroder Leasing Corp. (1996, SD NY) 1996 US Dist LEXIS 9155) and judgment entered (1997, SD NY) 975 F. Supp. 297

Even though several letters or other writings could be resorted to for the agreed upon terms, these writings had to be connected either expressly or by the internal evidence of subject-matter and occasion. Oswald v Allen (1969, CA2 NY) 417 F.2d 43

In action for alleged breach of agreement to include clothing "contractor" in contemplated sale of corporation which supplied designs and materials and promoted sale of garments tailored by contractor, only writing contained no "defined or stated price," and so Code § 1-206 would make any contract unenforceable beyond $5,000. Olympic Junior, Inc. v David Crystal, Inc. (1972, CA3 NJ) 463 F.2d 1141 (construing both New York and New Jersey Codes)

Defendant was entitled to summary judgment in action for breach of alleged oral contract for plaintiff's purchase of corporate assets where plaintiff's evidence as to existence of oral agreement consisted only of letter signed by defendant's president, and of various unsigned internal memoranda of defendant connected to letter by parol evidence; materials could not be read together to satisfy statute of frauds (CLS UCC § 1-206) since letter's reference to "our verbal agreement" required speculation not only as to whether phrase referred to ground rules of negotiations or to ultimate agreement, but also as to specific nature of transaction. Horn & Hardart Co. v Pillsbury Co. (1989, CA2 NY) 888 F.2d 8, 10 UCCRS2d 60

Statute of frauds under UCC § 1-206 did not bar recovery by distributors against distiller upon oral agreement by distiller to relocate distributors with a new distributorship. Lee v Joseph E. Seagram & Sons, Inc. (1976, SD NY) 413 F. Supp. 693, 19 UCCRS 1043, affd (1977, CA2 NY) 552 F.2d 447, appeal after remand (1979, CA2 NY) 592 F.2d 39, 26 FR Serv 2d 1086 (applying New York law)

Copyright sales are not excluded from purview of CLS UCC § 1-206, which applies to "general intangibles" as defined in Article 9 of UCC and to transactions excluded from Article 9 by § 9-104. Mellencamp v Riva Music, Ltd. (1988, SD NY) 698 F. Supp. 1154

Series of signed and unsigned writings may not be read together so as to satisfy statute of frauds, where single signed writing failed to establish contractual relationship. Horn & Hardart Co. v Pillsbury Co. (1989, SD NY) 703 F. Supp. 1062, 8 UCCRS2d 354, affd (1989, CA2 NY) 888 F.2d 8, 10 UCCRS2d 60

§ 1-208. [Repealed]

History: L 2014, ch 505, § 1, eff Dec 17, 2014.

§ 1-209. [Repealed]

History: L 2014, ch 505, § 1, eff Dec 17, 2014.

PART 3
TERRITORIAL APPLICABILITY AND GENERAL RULES

§ 1-301. Territorial Applicability; Parties' Power to Choose Applicable Law

(a) Except as otherwise provided in this section, when a transaction bears a reasonable relation to this state and also to another state or nation, the parties may agree that the law either of this state or of such other state or nation shall govern their rights and duties so long as none of the parties to the transaction is a consumer and a resident of New York. Where a consumer is a resident of the state of New York, New York state law shall apply.

(b) In the absence of an agreement effective under subsection (a), and except as provided in subsection (c), this act applies to transactions bearing an appropriate relation to this state.

(c) If one of the following provisions of this act specifies the applicable law, that provision governs and a contrary agreement is effective only to the extent permitted by the law so specified:

(1) Section 2-402;

(2) Sections 2-A-105 and 2-A-106;

(3) Section 4-102;

(4) Section 4-A-507;

(5) Section 5-116;

(6) Section 8-110; and

(7) Sections 9-301 through 9-307.

History: L 2014, ch 505, § 1, eff Dec 17, 2014.

CASE ANNOTATIONS

UNDER FORMER § 1-105

1. In general
2. Choice of applicable law by agreement
3. – Reasonable relation

4. Choice of applicable law in absence of agreement

1. In general

In action by buyer of computer system for damages for system's failure to function properly, court held (1) that parties' designation under UCC § 1-105(1) of Massachusetts law to govern any claims of breach of their sales contract was immaterial, since such claims were governed by limitation period contained in UCC § 2-725(1), which was adopted by both New York and Massachusetts; (2) that contract in suit was not one for performance of services, as alleged by the buyer, but was one for purchase of goods within meaning of UCC § 2-106(1); (3) that action for breach of contract was not timely commenced by buyer, since breach occurred in January, 1971, and buyer did not commence suit until August 14, 1975, which was more than four years after cause of action accrued; (4) that action for fraud in the inducement was timely commenced, since the applicable statute of limitations under New Yorklaw for such action is either six years from commission of the fraud, or two years from discovery; (5) that UCC § 2-725(2), which deals with warranty that explicitly extends to future performance and provides that discovery of breach must await such performance, did not apply, since warranty under UCC § 2-725(2) must expressly refer to the future and implied warranty alleged by buyer, by its very nature, did not do so; and (6) that seller's attempts to repair computer system did not toll running of statute of limitations prescribed by UCC § 2-725(1). Triangle Underwriters, Inc. v Honeywell, Inc. (1979, CA2 NY) 604 F.2d 737, 26 UCCRS 1162, appeal after remand (1981, CA2 NY) 651 F.2d 132 (applying Massachusetts and New York UCC)

In action by buyer of computer system for damages for system's failure to function properly, court held (1) that parties' designation under UCC § 1-105(1) of Massachusetts law to govern their sales contract was immaterial, since buyer's breach-of-contract claims were governed by limitation period contained in UCC § 2-725(1), which had been adopted by both New York and Massachusetts; (2) that contract in suit was not one for performance of services, as alleged by buyer, but was one for purchase of goods within meaning of UCC § 2-106(1); (3) that action was not timely commenced by buyer, since breach had occurred in January, 1971 and buyer did not commence suit until August 14, 1975, which was more than four years after cause of action accrued; (4) that UCC § 2-725(2), which deals with warranty that explicitly extends to future performance and provides that discovery of breach must await such performance, did not apply, since warranty under UCC § 2-725(2) must expressly refer to the future and implied warranty alleged by buyer, by its very nature, did not do so; and (5) that seller's attempts to repair computer system did not toll running of statute of limitations prescribed by UCC § 2-725(1). Triangle Underwriters, Inc. v Honeywell, Inc. (1978, ED NY) 457 F. Supp. 765, 24 UCCRS 1088, affd in part and revd in part on other grounds (1979, CA2 NY) 604 F.2d 737, 26 UCCRS 1162, appeal after remand (1981, CA2 NY) 651 F.2d 132 (applying Massachusetts and New York UCC)

2. Choice of applicable law by agreement

Court would apply New York contract law in case involving closely-held family corporation where plaintiff was New York resident, company was New York corporation, New York was forum state, and, most importantly, agreement between parties specified that it was governed by New York law. Terwilliger v Terwilliger (2000, CA2 NY) 206 F.3d 240

Determination of whether the debtor had a pre-petition interest in creditor consignor's Botticelli painting sufficient for the bankruptcy trustee to prevail in his capacity as a hypothetical lien creditor under 11 U.S.C.S. § 544(a), was properly determined by the bankruptcy court, and the contractual choice of law provision was not enforced, where the creditor's argument did not address the limitation set forth in N.Y. U.C.C. § 1-105(2). In re Salander O'Reilly Galleries (2011, BC SD NY) 453 BR 106, related proceeding (2011, Sup) 32 Misc 3d 1223A.

It is established principle under UCC § 1-105, that parties to contract may consent, in absence of strong countervailing public policy of state, to law to be applied with respect to contract. Nederlandse Draadindustrie NDI B.V. v Grand Pre-Stressed Corp. (1979, ED NY) 466 F. Supp. 846, 26 UCCRS 406, affd without op (1979, CA2 NY) 614 F.2d 1289

In action by seller of steel slabs against buyer-who had fully paid for all steel purchased, but had made many payments more than 15 days after receipt of steel shipments in violation of contract's express terms-for damages in form of interest at prevailing prime rates on buyer's late payments, court held (1) that provision in parties' contract that contract would be governed by Pennsylvania law would be honored by New York courts under New York UCC § 1-105(1) because transaction bore reasonable relation to Pennsylvania; (2) that as a result, case was governed by Pennsylvania law. Associated Metals & Minerals Corp. v Sharon Steel Corp. (1983, SD NY) 590 F. Supp. 18, 39 UCCRS 892, affd without op (1983, CA2 NY) 742 F.2d 1431

3. – Reasonable relation

In a diversity action, concerning among other issues, "transactions in goods" within the scope of the U.C.C.'s article on sales, which were purchased by plaintiff, a New York corporation, from defendant, an Ohio corporation, the court, pursuant to the conflict of law rules of New York, the forum state, held that since New York was "appropriately related" to the transaction herein involved and Ohio was "reasonably related" to the "transaction," Ohio law governed insofar as the parties had agreed to let the law of Ohio govern the validity, interpretation and performance of the contract. County Asphalt, Inc. v Lewis Welding & Engineering Corp. (1971, CA2 NY) 444 F.2d 372, 15 FR Serv 2d 194, 9 UCCRS 206, cert den (1971) 404 US 939, 30 L Ed 2d 252, 92 S Ct 272

Reasonable relationship test was met where whiskey distributorship contracts between English exporters and New York importers, provided that they were to be governed by English law and where contracts were executed in United Kingdom, exporters were incorporated in United Kingdom, performance exporters occurred in United Kingdom, and payment was made and title to goods passed in United Kingdom. Fleischmann Distilling Corp. v Distillers Co. (1975, SD NY) 395 F Supp 221, 1975 CCH Trade Cases P 60337, 17 UCCRS 678 (applying New York law).

Reasonable relationship test was met where whiskey distributorship contracts between English exporters and New York importers, provided that they were to be governed by English law and where contracts were executed in United Kingdom, exporters were incorporated in United Kingdom, performance exporters occurred in United Kingdom, and payment was made and title to goods passed in United Kingdom. Fleischmann Distilling Corp. v Distillers Co. (1975, SD NY) 395 F. Supp. 221, 1975 CCH Trade Cases P 60337, 17 UCCRS 678 (applying New York law)

In action by English pipe manufacturer against American corporations for breach of contract for sale and distribution of plaintiff's pipes in United States, applicable law was that of England where contract contained explicit choice-of-law clause specifying that contract would be covered by English law; defendants' purchase in England of plaintiff's pipes provided "reasonable relation" between transaction and England, thus validating clause under UCC § 1-105(1). L. Orlik, Ltd. v Helme Products, Inc. (1977, SD NY) 427 F. Supp. 771 (applying New York law)

In action by seller of steel slabs against buyer who had fully paid for all steel purchased, but had made many payments more than 15 days after receipt of steel shipments in violation of contract's express terms for damages in form of interest at prevailing prime rates on buyer's late payments, provision in parties' contract that contract would be governed by Pennsylvania law would be honored by New York courts under New York UCC § 1-105(1) because transaction bears reasonable relation to Pennsylvania. Associated Metals & Minerals Corp. v Sharon Steel Corp. (1983, SD NY) 590 F. Supp. 18, 39 UCCRS 892, affd without op (1983, CA2 NY) 742 F.2d 1431

New York courts will honor choice of law provision in sales contracts so long as transaction bears "reasonable relationship" to state whose law is chosen; court turns to Pennsylvania law where purchase orders contain choice of law provision stating that they are to be governed by Pennsylvania law and where purchase orders indicate that items are to be delivered FOB in Pennsylvania. Associated Metals & Minerals Corp. v Sharon Steel Corp. (1983, SD NY) 590 F. Supp. 18, 39 UCCRS 892, affd without op (1983, CA2 NY) 742 F.2d 1431

4. Choice of applicable law in absence of agreement

Where evidence in bank's action on notes, which had been executed by diamond buyers in favor of seller and then negotiated by seller to bank, showed that bank, at time notes were negotiated to it, might have known that parties to underlying diamond transactions involved could have rescinded such agreements at any time without incurring liability, and that exercise of such right would have rendered notes executed under agreements void, court held (1) that sufficient relationship existed between underlying diamond transactions and state of New York to justify application of New York law under UCC

UCC

§ 1-105(1); and (2) that since triable issues of fact were raised as to whether bank was holder in due course of notes sued on within meaning of notice provisions of UCC §§ 3-302(1)(c) and 3-304(1)(b) and (4)(b), bank's motion for summary judgment on notes would be denied. Israel Discount Bank, Ltd. v Rosen (1983) 59 N.Y.2d 428, 465 N.Y.S.2d 885, 452 N.E.2d 1213, 36 UCCRS 574

Law of Massachusetts should apply to UCC claims arising from yacht repair problems, where yacht owner is resident of New York, but repairs were performed-and warranties allegedly breached-in Massachusetts by corporations residing there and elsewhere, because New York UCC only applies to transactions "bearing appropriate relation to" New York under CLS UCC § 1-105. Hadar v Concordia Yacht Builders (1995, SD NY) 886 F. Supp. 1082, CCH Prod Liab Rep P 14239, dismd (1997, SD NY) 1997 US Dist LEXIS 11182

In federal diversity action involving sale of goods, court would apply Massachusetts law to breach of warranty claims against builder, manufacturers and distributors of allegedly defective goods, although buyer resided in New York, where all defendants were residents of other states, and materials were purchased in other states and delivered to and used in Massachusetts (where warranties were allegedly breached); transaction lacked "appropriate relation" to New York for purposes of CLS UCC § 1-105. Hadar v Concordia Yacht Builders (1995, SD NY) 886 F. Supp. 1082, CCH Prod Liab Rep ¶ 14239, dismd (1997, SD NY) 1997 US Dist LEXIS 11182

§ 1-302. Variation by Agreement

(a) Except as otherwise provided in subsection (b) or elsewhere in this act, the effect of provisions of this act may be varied by agreement.

(b) The obligations of good faith, diligence, reasonableness, and care prescribed by this act may not be disclaimed by agreement. The parties, by agreement, may determine the standards by which the performance of those obligations is to be measured if those standards are not manifestly unreasonable. Whenever this act requires an action to be taken within a reasonable time, a time that is not manifestly unreasonable may be fixed by agreement.

(c) The presence in certain provisions of this act of the phrase "unless otherwise agreed", or words of similar import, does not imply that the effect of other provisions may not be varied by agreement under this section.

History: L 2014, ch 505, § 1, eff Dec 17, 2014.

CASE ANNOTATIONS

UNDER FORMER § 1-102

1. In general
2. Nature and purpose
3. Construction
4. – Policy of uniformity
5. Effect of agreements

1. In general

In action by insurer as subrogee of subcontractor for indemnification of claims settled by insurer, which claims arose out of fire in municipal filtration plant which started when spark from welding torch landed on defective plastic equipment supplied by defendant company to subcontractor for installation in plant, defense contention that policy of UCC § 1-102(2)(b) to permit continued expansion of commercial practices through custom, usage, and agreement of parties demonstrated legislative intent to allow "commercial-industrial specialists," such as subcontractor and defendant in present case, to regulate relationships among themselves and determine liability for defective products by agreement, had no merit because party injured by defective product was remote user thereof. Potsdam Welding & Machine Co. v Neptune Microfloc, Inc. (1977, 3d Dept) 57 A.D.2d 993, 394 N.Y.S.2d 744

CLS UCC § 1-102 imposes good faith standard unless otherwise agreed upon standard is set forth in contract. Gerard v Almouli (1984, CA2 NY) 746 F.2d 936, 39 UCCRS 1224

In action by receiver of failed bank predicated on promissory notes and guaranties, borrower's and guarantor's waiver of impairment of collateral defense under CLS UCC § 3-606 (resulting from their waiver of all recourse) was not "trumped" by CLS UCC § 1-102(3), which provides that obligations of good faith, diligence, reasonableness and care may not be disclaimed by agreement; general rule could not be invoked to satisfy specific requirement of § 3-606 that aggrieved party must have preserved its right of recourse. FDIC v Wrapwell Corp. (1996, SD NY) 922 F. Supp. 913

2. Nature and purpose

The purpose of this act, to be liberally construed, is specified as the stipulation, clarification and modernization of the law governing commercial transactions to permit the continued expansion of commercial practices through custom, usage and agreement of the parties; and the statute mandates a liberal administration to the end that an aggrieved party may be put in as good a position as if the other party had fully performed without consequential, special, or penal damages unless specifically provided for. Chrysler Credit Corp. v Sharp (1968) 56 Misc. 2d 261, 288 N.Y.S.2d 525, 5 UCCRS 226

Holding that "price" as set out in N.Y. U.C.C. Law § 9-103 includes negative equity (as does the new York Motor Vehicle Retail Installment Sales Act's definition of "cash sale price") serves the underlying purposes and policies of the Uniform Commercial Code because such a reading permits the continued expansion of commercial practices through custom, usage, and agreement of the parties. N.Y. U.C.C. Law § 1-102(2)(b). In re Petrocci (2007, BC ND NY) 370 BR 489, 63 UCCRS2d 705 (criticized in In re Pajot (2007, BC ED Va) 371 BR 139, 63 UCCRS2d 465) and (criticized in In re Blakeslee (2007, BC MD Fla) 377 BR 724) and (criticized in In re Westfall (2007, BC ND Ohio) 376 BR 210) and (criticized in In re Conyers (2007, BC MD NC) 2007 Bankr LEXIS 3773) and (criticized in In re Tuck (2007, BC MD Ala) 2007 Bankr LEXIS 4226) and (criticized in In re Johnson (2007, BC DC Or) 2007 Bankr LEXIS 4245).

3. Construction

Where repurchase agreement executed by automobile dealer failed to establish the time for performance, evidence of custom and usage showing that bank must repossess and return car for purchase within 90 days after default was admissible to establish what was a reasonable time, and bank's undue delay in repossession and demand precluded it from recovering from automobile dealer the amount due from the buyer under the contract less the amount received at the execution sale. Valley Nat'l Bank v Babylon Chrysler-Plymouth, Inc. (1967) 53 Misc. 2d 1029, 280 N.Y.S.2d 786, 4 UCCRS 385, affd (1967, 2d Dept) 28 A.D.2d 1092, 284 N.Y.S.2d 849, 4 UCCRS 732

A court should not seek to restrict the Code by interpretations which preserve former inconsistent rules or law. Chrysler Credit Corp. v Sharp (1968) 56 Misc. 2d 261, 288 N.Y.S.2d 525, 5 UCCRS 226

Due to supremacy clause of federal constitution, state Uniform Commercial Code statutes cannot be considered in isolation but instead must be read together with applicable federal statutes and regulations. Greater Buffalo Press, Inc. v Federal Reserve Bank (1989, CA2 NY) 866 F.2d 38, 7 UCCRS2d 956, cert den (1989) 490 US 1107, 104 L Ed 2d 1022, 109 S Ct 3159, later proceeding (1990, WD NY) 129 FRD 462, affd without op (1990, CA2 NY) 923 F.2d 843, cert den (1991) 500 US 942, 114 L Ed 2d 480, 111 S Ct 2238

4. – Policy of uniformity

Uniformity in the construction and application of the Code among the several states has been mandated by the Legislature, and therefore sister state interpretations are more than persuasive authority. Hertz Commercial Leasing Corp. v Transportation Credit Clearing House (1969) 59 Misc. 2d 226, 298 N.Y.S.2d 392, 6 UCCRS 132, revd on other grounds (1970) 64 Misc. 2d 910, 316 N.Y.S.2d 585

In Franklin Nat'l Bank v Eurez Constr. Corp. (1969) 60 Misc. 2d 499, 301 N.Y.S.2d 845, 6 UCCRS 634, directive of Code that it be liberally construed to promote its purposes and policies, one of which is "to make uniform the law among the various jurisdictions", was utilized by court in relying on cases from other jurisdictions holding that one who is not holder in due course but takes accommodation paper for value before it is due may enforce it against the accommodation maker, and that want of consideration is no defense to accommodation maker. Franklin Nat'l Bank v Eurez Constr. Corp. (1969) 60 Misc. 2d 499, 301 N.Y.S.2d 845, 6 UCCRS 634

5. Effect of agreements

In action by Federal Deposit Insurance Corporation (FDIC), as successor in interest to loan note given by debtor to insolvent bank, against guarantor of debtor's note who had given bank, as additional security for debtor's note, guarantor's half interest in mortgage note and mortgage on certain real estate, court held (1) that FDIC under UCC § 3-201(1) held insolvent bank's interest in debtor's note and that such interest included guarantor's half interest in mortgage note and realty mortgage; (2) that under UCC § 9-102(3), Uniform Commercial Code applies to pledge of realty paper as collateral, except in cases where mortgagee's creditor is attempting to enforce mortgagee's rights under mortgage; (3) that effect of judicial sale of realty represented by guarantor's interest in mortgage note and mortgage was to dispose of such note and mortgage as collateral that secured loan note given by debtor to insolvent bank; (4) that such disposition of collateral was required by UCC § 9-504(3) to be commercially reasonable; (5) that since such collateral disposition had not received judicial approval within meaning of UCC § 9-507(2), it could not conclusively be deemed to be commercially reasonable; (6) that because of material difference between realty's foreclosure-sale price and its alleged value, hearing on sale's commercial reasonableness was warranted; and (7) that FDIC's duty to sell such realty without undue delay could not be disclaimed by agreement under UCC § 1-102(3). Federal Deposit Ins. Corp. v Forte (1983, 2d Dept) 94 A.D.2d 59, 463 N.Y.S.2d 844, 37 UCCRS 354, appeal after remand (1988, 2d Dept) 144 A.D.2d 627, 535 N.Y.S.2d 75

In action by agent of federal Small Business Administration (SBA) against guarantors of debtor's loan to recover deficiency remaining after sale of debtor's collateral, guarantor under UCC § 1-102(3) may legally waive all rights and defenses, including defense of lack of commercial reasonableness (UCC § 9-504(3)) in sale of debtor's collateral, by terms of unconditional guaranty, provided that secured party was not guilty of bad faith in transaction. First City Div. of Chase Lincoln First Bank, N.A. v Vitale (1987, 3d Dept) 123 A.D.2d 207, 510 N.Y.S.2d 766, 2 UCCRS2d 1736 (criticized in Bank of China v Chan (1991, CA2 NY) 937 F.2d 780, 15 UCCRS2d 162) and (criticized in General Elec. Capital Corp. v Anfang (1995, N.Y. Sup) 27 UCCRS2d 284)

Chattel mortgages did not violate CLS UCC § 1-102(3), prohibiting debtor from waiving requirement of commercial reasonableness in disposition of collateral, where they contained provisions concerning prior notice to debtors of public sale of collateral, prior newspaper advertisement of sale, and mandatory terms of purchase, which were not "manifestly unreasonable." Orix Credit Alliance v East End Dev. Corp. (1999, 2d Dept) 260 A.D.2d 454, 688 N.Y.S.2d 191, 39 UCCRS2d 596

Bank was entitled to summary judgment dismissing action brought by depositor for wrongful payment of forged checks where (1) depositor failed to give written notice of irregularities to bank within 14 days after delivery of bank statements as required by deposit agreement, which was valid condition precedent to suit since it did not disclaim bank's liability nor absolve bank of its duty to use good faith and ordinary care, and (2) it was undisputed that bank statements were promptly delivered to home of depositor's agent; it was irrelevant whether bank was negligent or breached parties' agreement where depositor failed to comply with condition precedent which is element of depositor's cause of action. Parent Teacher Asso., Public School 72 v Manufacturers Hanover Trust Co. (1988, Civ Ct) 138 Misc. 2d 289, 524 N.Y.S.2d 336, 5 UCCRS2d 679

In action against bank which arranged for sale through its brokerage service of stock held as loan security, seeking consequential damages for failure to effect sale in time to afford lender favorable capital gains treatment, exculpatory clause in brokerage agreement absolving bank from liability for consequential damages would be held ineffective as disclaimer of liability under CLS UCC § 1-102(3), since secured creditor cannot avail itself of new contract disclaimer rights alien to original relationship between parties. Huther v Marine Midland Bank, N. A. (1989, City Ct) 143 Misc. 2d 697, 541 N.Y.S.2d 902

Under a Securities Investor Protection Act of 1970 liquidation, where the creditor had posted cash collateral with the debtor broker-dealer in exchange for loaned securities, the debtor's commingled cash was not subject to a constructive trust and all of the debtor's cash was property of the estate and the creditor's security interest could be avoided by the trustee, because, while the debtor was required to use reasonable care in preserving that collateral under N.Y. U.C.C. Law § 9-207(a) (2002), under N.Y. U.C.C. Law § 1-102, the parties had, by agreement, not unreasonably, provided that the debtor was not required to segregate the cash, and under N.Y. U.C.C. Law § 9-625, the creditor's only remedy was a claim for damages. Ferris, Baker, Watts, Inc. v Stephenson (In re MJK Clearing) (2002, BC DC Minn) 286 BR 109, 49 UCCRS2d 11

Parties' agreement, that Venezuelan account holder must notify bank of any irregularities in account statement within 30 days of mailing of statement, was not manifestly unreasonable due to known unreliability of Venezuelan mail delivery system, and thus such agreement effectively varied default standard of CLS UCC § 4-406(4) for determining whether customer's examination of its bank statement is reasonably prompt. Fundacion Museo de Arte Contemporaneo de Caracas-Sofia Imber v CBI-TDB Union Bancaire Privee (1998, SD NY) 996 F. Supp. 277, 36 UCCRS2d 766, affd (1998, CA2 NY) 160 F.3d 146, 37 UCCRS2d 123

§ 1-303.   Course of Performance, Course of Dealing, and Usage of Trade

(a) A "course of performance" is a sequence of conduct between the parties to a particular transaction that exists if:

(1) the agreement of the parties with respect to the transaction involves repeated occasions for performance by a party; and

(2) the other party, with knowledge of the nature of the performance and opportunity for objection to it, accepts the performance or acquiesces to it without objection.

(b) A "course of dealing" is a sequence of conduct concerning previous transactions between the parties to a particular transaction that is fairly to be regarded as establishing a common basis of understanding for interpreting their expressions and other conduct.

(c) A "usage of trade" is any practice or method of dealing having such regularity of observance in a place, vocation, or trade as to justify an expectation that it will be observed with respect to the transaction in question. The existence and scope of such a usage must be proved as facts. If it is established that such a usage is embodied in a trade code or similar record, the interpretation of the record is a question of law.

(d) A course of performance or course of dealing between the parties or usage of trade in the vocation or trade in which they are engaged or of which they are or should be aware is relevant in ascertaining the meaning of the parties' agreement, may give particular meaning to specific terms of the agreement, and may supplement or qualify the terms of the agreement. A usage of trade applicable in the place in which part of the performance under the agreement is to occur may be so utilized as to that part of the performance.

(e) Except as otherwise provided in subsection (f), the express terms of an agreement and any applicable course of performance, course of dealing, or usage of trade must be construed whenever reasonable as consistent with each other. If such a construction is unreasonable:

(1) express terms prevail over course of performance, course of dealing, and usage of trade;

(2) course of performance prevails over course of dealing and usage of trade; and

UCC

(3) course of dealing prevails over usage of trade.

(f) Subject to Section 2-209, a course of performance is relevant to show a waiver or modification of any term inconsistent with the course of performance.

(g) Evidence of a relevant usage of trade offered by one party is not admissible unless that party has given the other party notice that the court finds sufficient to prevent unfair surprise to the other party.

History: L 2014, ch 505, § 1, eff Dec 17, 2014.

CASE ANNOTATIONS

UNDER FORMER § 1-205

1. In general
2. Course of dealing
3. Usage of trade
4. – Negotiable instruments
5. – Risk of loss
6. Modification or waiver; express agreement
7. – Implied warranties
8. Evidence and burden of proof
9. – Presumptions

1. In general

In action for seller's breach of contract to sell investment securities that buyer had contracted to resell to third person, which breach caused buyer to make "cover" purchase of other securities to effect such resale, court held (1) that although UCC Art 8 contains no provision for buyer's remedies against seller for breach of contract to purchase securities, and although UCC § 2-105(1) expressly excludes investment securities from definition of "goods" for purposes of UCC Art 2, nevertheless, as indicated by Official Comment 1 to UCC § 2-105, buyer's remedies in Art 2 for breach of contract also apply by analogy to investment security transactions; (2) that under UCC § 2-712(2), buyer was entitled to recover as damages difference between cost of cover and contract price of securities in suit, plus incidental and consequential damages; and (3) that benefits that had accrued to buyer as result of its trading of its interest in securities in suit before seller's breach were not relevant to buyer's measure of damages for such breach. G. A. Thompson & Co. v Wendell J. Miller Mortg. Co. (1978, SD NY) 457 F. Supp. 996, 24 UCCRS 1285 (applying New York UCC)

2. Course of dealing

Summary judgment was properly granted to a seller in a commercial contract dispute because, while the seller established the contract price of the cranberry concentrate and that the concentrate was delivered to the buyer, the buyer did not raise an issue of fact whether a prior course of dealing or usage of trade altered the contract price under N.Y. U.C.C. Law § 1-205 because the affidavits of the buyer's president did not explain or supplement the unambiguous contract price but, rather, they impermissibly contradicted it under N.Y. U.C.C. Law § 2-202(a). Cliffstar Corp. v Cape Cod Biolab Corp. (2007, 4th Dept) 37 App Div 3d 1073, 829 NYS2d 779

Where the parties had a 12-year course of dealings, (as defined by N.Y. U.C.C. § 1-205), a customs broker's limitation on liability in a invoice was binding and enforceable absent gross negligence; therefore, the importer was entitled to amend its complaint, pursuant to N.Y. C.P.L.R. § 3025, to include a cause of action for gross negligence. United B Int'l Corp. v UTI United States, Inc. (2004, Sup) 5 Misc 3d 1013A, 798 N.Y.S.2d 714, 55 UCCRS2d 203

The term "course of dealing" refers to previous conduct between the parties indicating a common basis for interpreting expressions used by them, and proof of such conduct is limited to objective facts as distinguished from oral statements of agreements. Eskimo Pie Corp. v Whitelawn Dairies, Inc. (1968, SD NY) 284 F. Supp. 987, 5 UCCRS 702

Under UCC § 1-205(3), which provides that any usage of trade in vocation or trade in which parties are engaged, or any usage of trade of which parties are or should be aware, supplements terms of parties' agreement, statutory use of disjunctive "or" precluded seller of coal from asserting lack of knowledge that arbitration was customary in coal trade where seller did not deny that it was engaged

in such trade. Marion Coal Co. v Marc Rich & Co. International, Ltd. (1982, SD NY) 539 F. Supp. 903, 34 UCCRS 12 (applying N.Y. UCC)

Contrary to an assignee's claims, a corporation's Vendor Standards Manual and various purchase orders could have been explained or supplemented by course of dealing, usage of trade, or course of performance, all of which was admissible and relevant to the interpretation of the contracts in the corporation's motion for summary judgment. Feinberg v Federated Dept. Stores, Inc. (2007, Sup) 15 Misc 3d 299, 832 NYS2d 760, later proceeding (2007, NY App Div, 1st Dept) 2007 NY App Div LEXIS 4407

3. Usage of trade

Defendant, which agreed to supply plaintiff's tire needs for its fleet of trucks and other heavy equipment for one year, at price "not to exceed $60,000," with payments to be made "on a three month dating term," was not entitled to summary judgment in action to recover sums plaintiff expended, over and above contract price, to obtain tires from other sources for period covered by agreement where fact issue existed as to whether "three month dating term" required each invoice to be paid in 3 equal installments over 3 months following its receipt, until total of $60,000 had been paid, or whether contract required only equal monthly payments of $5,000, which could be deferred for up to 3 months; moreover, fact questions existed as to whether, at any time prior to plaintiff's delinquency, defendant's inability to supply needed tires substantially impaired value of whole contract, thereby entitling plaintiff to cancel, refuse further payment, and obtain damages, and if so, whether contract was effectively reinstated by plaintiff's attempt, in its cancellation letter, to exercise option to extend contract for additional year (apparently to increase damages available for defendant's purported breach). Cranesville Block Co. v Goodyear Tire & Rubber Co. (1994, 3d Dept) 208 A.D.2d 1157, 617 N.Y.S.2d 951

Where default occurred in payment of an automobile retail installment contract in August of 1965 but the security holder did not make demand upon the dealer for performance of its repurchase agreement until October of 1966, and it was the custom and usage that the lending institution is required to repossess and return the vehicle for repurchase within a reasonable time after default and that 90 days is regarded as a reasonable time, the security holder could not enforce the repurchase agreement which contained no provision inconsistent with the custom and usage. Valley Nat'l Bank v Babylon Chrysler-Plymouth, Inc. (1967) 53 Misc. 2d 1029, 280 N.Y.S.2d 786, 4 UCCRS 385, affd (1967, 2d Dept) 28 A.D.2d 1092, 284 N.Y.S.2d 849, 4 UCCRS 732

In action under federal Perishable Agricultural Commodities Act by seller of cabbage against buyer for balance of contract price, in which action buyer filed counterclaim alleging that seller had breached contract by failing to deliver all cabbage sold thereunder, court held (1) that evidence showed that after parties signed contract, price of cabbage increased dramatically; (2) that after such price increase, buyer inspected field where cabbage was growing and found that it was not growing in sufficient quantity or to large size desired by buyer; (3) that buyer's statement to seller at such inspection that buyer would be satisfied if "he got 400 tons out of the field," together with seller's failure to indicate that size of cabbage was factor that limited amount of cabbage sold under parties' contract, resulted in contract modification under which cabbage sold was not limited to large cabbage for which buyer had originally expressed preference; (4) that seller failed to demonstrate that "slaw cabbage" was term regularly used in trade within meaning of UCC § 1-205(2) to mean "large cabbage" or "12 cabbage heads or less per 50-pound bag"; and (5) that seller, who unsuccessfully contended that under UCC § 1-205(5) all of the evidence of trade usage in Georgia should have been considered because growing and bagging of cabbage had occurred in Georgia, failed to realize that relevant aspect of performing interstate contract in suit was delivery of cabbage from Georgia to New York. Williams v Curtin (1986, App DC) 257 US App DC 131, 807 F.2d 1046, 2 UCCRS2d 1169 (applying Ga and N.Y. UCC)

The term "usage of trade" refers to evidence of generalized industry practice or similar recognized custom, as distinguished from particular conversations or correspondence between the parties with respect to the terms of the agreement. Eskimo Pie Corp. v Whitelawn Dairies, Inc. (1968, SD NY) 284 F. Supp. 987, 5 UCCRS 702

In action by consignee of goods against carrier for misdelivery of goods to "notify party" (which subsequently went out of business), plaintiff was entitled to partial summary judgment on issue of liability where express terms of airway bill named plaintiff as person entitled to delivery so that under UCC § 1-205(4) trade usage that "notify party" was deemed consignee's agent for purposes of delivery was inapplicable; defendant's contention that delivery of goods to "notify party" was proper since it was true owner under letter of credit and other documents was irrelevant where defendant admittedly relied upon no document other than airway bill in its decision to deliver goods to "notify party" and where, in any event, issue of ownership did not affect defendant's contractual duty to deliver goods to consignee; plaintiff did not ratify misdelivery by demanding payment from "notify party" and then instituting suit against it. Kologel Co. v Down in the Village, Inc. (1982, SD NY) 539 F. Supp. 727, 34 UCCRS 12

Under UCC § 1-205(3), which provides that any usage of trade in vocation or trade in which parties are engaged, or any usage of trade of which parties are or should be aware, supplements terms of parties' agreement, statutory use of disjunctive "or" precluded seller of coal from asserting lack of knowledge that arbitration was customary in coal trade where seller did not deny that it was engaged in such trade. Marion Coal Co. v Marc Rich & Co. International, Ltd. (1982, SD NY) 539 F. Supp. 903, 34 UCCRS 12 (applying N.Y. UCC)

Applicable usage of trade in place where any part of performance is to occur shall be used in interpreting agreement as to that part of performance; thus, in action by soft drink bottler for preliminary injunction to restrain franchiser from terminating franchise agreement permitting plaintiff to distribute cola products where franchisor alleges that soft drink bottler will not exercise best efforts on behalf of franchisor's product when it begins to concurrently distribute competing cola product, contract clause providing for best efforts is interpreted to mean exclusive efforts, especially pattern of practice and usage by soft drink industry for distributors to distribute only one cola. Joyce Beverages of New York, Inc. v Royal Crown Cola Co. (1983, SD NY) 555 F. Supp. 271, 1982-83 CCH Trade Cases ¶ 65165

4. – Negotiable instruments

A check payable to "A/B" is a direction to pay in the alternative and a single valid indorsement by either A or B is sufficient. In an action against a bank which had cashed such a check, the plaintiff failed to present evidence establishing a course of dealing or usage of trade calling for two valid indorsements, where the plaintiff merely submitted affidavits of an attorney who stated his legal opinion as to the effect of a virgule, and submitted an affidavit recounting an instance in which employees of the bank had interpreted the symbol between two payees as requiring two indorsements. L. B. Smith, Inc. v Bankers Trust Co. (1981, 4th Dept) 80 A.D.2d 496, 439 N.Y.S.2d 543, 31 UCCRS 596, affd (1982) 55 N.Y.2d 942, 449 N.Y.S.2d 192, 434 N.E.2d 261

5. – Risk of loss

In action against ship owner for damages sustained as result of ship collision, where (1) plaintiff chartered ship to transport asphalt commercially, (2) ship was rammed by another ship and deemed to have been totally destroyed, since cost of repairing it would have been twice its fair-market value, (3) charter did not allocate risk of loss between parties, but merely required defendant owner to make maintenance repairs on ship and absolved owner from liability for damages caused by collision, and (4) plaintiff alleged that defendant had breached its charter duty to repair ship and sought damages for lost profits anticipated under full performance of charter, court held (1) that plaintiff could not recover under maritime doctrine of impossibility of performance, which focuses on whether loss was foreseeable, since parties could reasonably have foreseen that plaintiff would lose business and profits as result of ship collision, (2) that plaintiff also could not recover under doctrine of commercial impracticability set forth in UCC § 2-615(a), since trial court's finding that ship could be repaired only at unreasonable cost was not clearly erroneous, (3) that fact that defendant owner had received insurance proceeds that greatly exceeded ship's fair-market value did not prevent defendant from relying on defense of commercial impracticability, since application of such defense depends on reasonableness of expense in issue (here, cost of repairing totally demolished ship) and not on defendant's ability to pay commercially unreasonable expense, and (4) that risk of loss to ship was not allocated under UCC § 1-205(3) by custom in shipping industry. Asphalt International, Inc. v Enterprise Shipping Corp., S.A. (1981, CA2 NY) 667 F.2d 261, 33 UCCRS 570 (apparently applying UCC as rule of federal common law)

In action by diamond wholesaler against retailer to recover price of goods shipped under "all-risk" memorandum, custom and usage of industry established liability of consignee for full memorandum price of merchandise stolen while in his possession. Lipschutz v Gordon Jewelry Corp. (1974, SD Tex) 373 F. Supp. 375 (applying New York law)

6. Modification or waiver; express agreement

When custom and usage are inconsistent with the express terms of an agreement, the agreement terms control. Valley Nat'l Bank v Babylon Chrysler-Plymouth, Inc. (1967) 53 Misc. 2d 1029, 280 N.Y.S.2d 786, 4 UCCRS 385, affd (1967, 2d Dept) 28 A.D.2d 1092, 284 N.Y.S.2d 849, 4 UCCRS 732

In action by consignee of goods against carrier for misdelivery of goods to "notify party" (which subsequently went out of business), plaintiff was entitled to partial summary judgment on issue of liability where express terms of airway bill named plaintiff as person entitled to delivery so that under UCC § 1-205(4) trade usage that "notify party" was deemed consignee's agent for purposes of delivery was inapplicable; defendant's contention that delivery of goods to "notify party" was proper since it was true owner under letter of credit and other documents was irrelevant where defendant admittedly relied upon no document other than airway bill in its decision to deliver goods to "notify party" and where, in any event, issue of ownership did not affect defendant's contractual duty to deliver goods to consignee; plaintiff did not ratify misdelivery by demanding payment from "notify party" and then instituting suit against it. Kologel Co. v Down in the Village, Inc. (1982, SD NY) 539 F. Supp. 727, 34 UCCRS 12

7. – Implied warranties

Where buyer asserted unawareness of usage of trade as to exclusion of implied warranty of merchantability as to seeds, there was question of fact as to exclusion of warranty, precluding summary judgment for seller, even though written warranty exclusion was ineffective. Zicari v Joseph Harris Co. (1969, 4th Dept) 33 A.D.2d 17, 304 N.Y.S.2d 918, 6 UCCRS 1246, app den (1970) 26 N.Y.2d 610

An implied warranty may be excluded or modified by a course of dealing (Uniform Commercial Code, § 2-316, subd [3], par [c]; § 1-205, subd [1]); however, there is no exclusion where proof of such a course of dealing between plaintiff and third-party defendant is inconclusive and where the third-party defendant asserting the exclusion had notice and aided in the completion of a written agreement which contained an assignment of plaintiff's rights for breach of warranty against the third-party defendant. United States Leasing Corp. v Comerald Associates, Inc. (1979) 101 Misc. 2d 773, 421 N.Y.S.2d 1003, 27 UCCRS 1282

8. Evidence and burden of proof

Where trade usage must be resorted to for interpretation of contract, such trade usage would have to be demonstrated by something more than oral argument. Cable-Wiedemer, Inc. v A. Friederich & Sons Co. (1972) 71 Misc. 2d 443, 336 N.Y.S.2d 139

Exchange of drafts and the food manufacturing facility owner's and baby food manufacturer's failure to agree to the terms of the co-pack agreement did not constitute a sequence of previous conduct fairly to be regarded as establishing a common basis of understanding under N.Y. U.C.C. § 1-205(a). Promotion in Motion, Inc. v Beech-Nut Nutrition Corp. (2013, CA3 NJ) 2013 US App LEXIS 20622 (UNPUBLISHED).

9. – Presumptions

Trade usages sanctioned by passage of time are presumed to be within knowledge of parties regularly engaged in business, in present case shipment and carriage of goods by sea, and all contracts are presumed made with reference to trade usages and practice. Du Pont de Nemours International S.A. v S.S. Mormacvega (1972, SD NY) 367 F. Supp. 793, affd (1974, CA2 NY) 493 F.2d 97 (applying New York law)

§ 1-304. Obligation of Good Faith

Every contract or duty within this act imposes an obligation of good faith in its performance and enforcement.

History: L 2014, ch 505, § 1, eff Dec 17, 2014.

CASE ANNOTATIONS

UNDER FORMER § 1-203

1. In general
2. Applicability to particular parties
3. Commercial paper
4. Letters of credit

5. Sales

6. Secured transactions

7. Other commercial transactions

1. In general

Car rental agency was entitled to dismissal of customer's cause of action alleging breach of duty under CLS UCC § 1-203 to act in good faith regarding rental agreement since acting in bad faith, while factor which disqualifies party from benefiting from his acts, is not factor which imposes liability; Uniform Commercial Code does not permit recovery of money damages for not acting in good faith where no other basis for recovery is present. Super Glue Corp. v Avis Rent A Car System, Inc. (1987, 2d Dept) 132 A.D.2d 604, 517 N.Y.S.2d 764, 4 UCCRS2d 385, appeal after remand (1990, 2d Dept) 159 A.D.2d 68, 557 N.Y.S.2d 959, app den (1991) 77 N.Y.2d 801, 566 N.Y.S.2d 586, 567 N.E.2d 980

Party's actions may implicate implied covenant of good faith contained within Uniform Commercial Code when it acts so directly to impair value of contract for another party that it may be assumed that such actions are inconsistent with intent of parties; action presumed contrary to parties' intention must directly violate obligation that falls within their reasonable expectations, meaning implied promise must be so much part of contract as to be essential to effectuate contract's purpose. Bank of China v Chan (1991, CA2 NY) 937 F.2d 780, 15 UCCRS2d 162, later proceeding (1992, SD NY) 1992 US Dist LEXIS 15592

2. Applicability to particular parties

Allegations of bank's bad faith in handling letters of credit on behalf of corporation, and in causing corporation's demise, if proved, would be complete defense to guaranty signed by individual guarantor of corporation's debt. Bank of China v Chan (1991, CA2 NY) 937 F.2d 780, 15 UCCRS2d 162, later proceeding (1992, SD NY) 1992 US Dist LEXIS 15592

Words "or duty" were added to section to make it clear that third parties as well as parties to a contract have an obligation of good faith. In re Davidoff (1972, SD NY) 351 F. Supp. 440, 11 UCCRS 609

3. Commercial paper

Bank's business loan agreement containing provision whereby borrower waived rights to jury trial and to interpose setoffs and counterclaims would not be enforced to bar counterclaims based on fraud or violation of bank's fiduciary duty of good faith to its customer, since bank could not shield itself from its own tortious conduct. European American Bank v Mr. Wemmick, Ltd. (1990, 2d Dept) 160 A.D.2d 905, 554 N.Y.S.2d 628

Summary judgment was properly granted to plaintiff bank as holder in due course where defendant did not prove that bank took instruments in question with actual notice of defense of fraud or in bad faith. Banco Di Roma v Merchants Bank (1998, 1st Dept) 251 A.D.2d 139, 674 N.Y.S.2d 317, app den 92 N.Y.2d 808, 678 N.Y.S.2d 594, 700 N.E.2d 1230

Bank suing on instruments as holder in due course was entitled to summary judgment dismissing counterclaim for commercial bad faith where defendant did not produce evidence that bank participated in nonparty client's allegedly fraudulent scheme. Banco Di Roma v Merchants Bank (1998, 1st Dept) 251 A.D.2d 139, 674 N.Y.S.2d 317, app den 92 N.Y.2d 808, 678 N.Y.S.2d 594, 700 N.E.2d 1230

Summary judgment would be granted to bank in its action against payee who cashed check at bank branch with knowledge that payment had been stopped on instrument since CLS UCC § 1-203 imposes obligation to exercise good faith in performance of contract or duty; moreover, CLS UCC § 3-417(2) creates warranty of good title and rightfulness of transfer on part of transferee of instrument. Poughkeepsie Sav. Bank, FSB v Wagner (1990, Sup) 146 Misc. 2d 737, 552 N.Y.S.2d 545, 11 UCCRS2d 901

4. Letters of credit

Individual guarantor of corporation's debt raised genuine issue of material fact as to bank's good faith in handling letters of credit between corporation and foreign customers where (1) bank and corporation necessarily contemplated that bank would draw down master letters of credit when proper collection documents were presented, it would promptly remit all payments to corporation, it would handle collection documents with reasonable care, and it would take no action that would deliberately destroy corporation's commercial viability and its ability to pay its loans, and (2) documentary evidence was produced to show that bank had failed to perform such actions. Bank of China v Chan (1991, CA2 NY) 937 F.2d 780, 15

UCCRS2d 162, later proceeding (1992, SD NY) 1992 US Dist LEXIS 15592

5. Sales

"Outputs" contract under which bakery agreed to sell all breadcrumbs produced by it to promisee did not carry with it implication that bakery was obligated to manufacture breadcrumbs for full term of contract; rather, good faith termination of production of breadcrumbs was permissible under contract. Thus, summary judgment could not be entered in favor of either party to suit for breach of contract where unresolved issues of fact remained as to whether bakery acted in good faith in ceasing production of crumbs because of alleged economic unfeasibility. Feld v Henry S. Levy & Sons, Inc. (1975) 37 N.Y.2d 466, 373 N.Y.S.2d 102, 335 N.E.2d 320, 17 UCCRS 365

Court erred in finding that defendant breached implied covenant of good faith and fair dealing by failing to mitigate when faced with plaintiff's anticipatory breach, such as by seeking other customers for oil and suing plaintiff for difference in price; further, although defendant was entitled to respond to breach by terminating further performance, it was not required to do so, but could also continue to partially perform, subject only to standard of reasonableness, and then sue for partial breach (CLS UCC § 2-311(3)). Clark Oil Trading Co. v J. Aron & Co. (1998, 1st Dept) 256 A.D.2d 196, 683 N.Y.S.2d 12, 38 UCCRS2d 414, app dismd 93 N.Y.2d 953, 694 N.Y.S.2d 343, 716 N.E.2d 178

Modification of contract between merchant and consumer for sale of new car, under which consumer was obligated to pay higher price than that specified in original contract in order to obtain delivery and possession of car, was bad-faith modification under UCC §§ 2-209(1) and (2) and 2-103(1)(b) which gave consumer right to recover damages under UCC §§ 2-714(1), 2-607(2), and 1-203 after first giving seller notice of breach required by UCC § 2-607(3)(a). Palmer v Safe Auto Sales, Inc. (1982, Civ Ct) 114 Misc. 2d 964, 452 N.Y.S.2d 995

Buyer's determination that potatoes did not meet proper color standard was made in good faith, as required by CLS UCC § 1-203, where manner of visual testing utilized by buyer was reasonable and customary; buyer was not required to use photo-electric "Agtron" machine where contract did not specify manner of testing. Hubbard v UTZ Quality Foods (1995, WD NY) 903 F. Supp. 444, 28 UCCRS2d 562

Beverage company was entitled to summary judgment in an aluminum supplier's action alleging breach of the good faith duty under N.Y. U.C.C. § 1-203 in relation to the parties' aluminum supply contract; the evidence would not allow a jury to find that the beverage company breached its contractual duty to meet and discuss a new pricing mechanism in good faith after the aluminum supplier decided that the aluminum market had changed structurally. Novelis Corp. v Anheuser-Busch, Inc. (2008, ND Ohio) 559 F Supp 2d 877.

Seller could not have succeeded on its breach of contract claim even if the buyer had waived its right to timely delivery of an aircraft because the seller failed to prove that it had satisfied the conditions precedent to the buyer's obligation to purchase and the seller failed to prove that the buyer acted in bad faith when it rejected the aircraft because (1) the parties agreed that the buyer could have rejected the aircraft if the seller failed to satisfy the delivery conditions in any way, no matter how insignificant; (2) the deviations were not minor because two unapproved auxiliary center fuel tanks affected the aircraft's airworthiness; and (3) the seller contracted away any right it otherwise might have had to cure its failure to perform by March 31, 2004. Austrian Airlines Oesterreichische Luftverkehrs AG v UT Fin. Corp. (2008, SD NY) 567 F Supp 2d 579.

6. Secured transactions

Bank did not act in bad faith when it took steps to safeguard checking account in which it held security interest as collateral for letter of credit issued to corporate account holder, even though bank acted before corporation's surety had presented draft to bank for payment, where bank had good reason to believe, at time of its actions, that corporation was insolvent and that bank would have to reimburse surety for corporation's anticipated inability to meet obligation for which surety issued bond. Gillman v Chase Manhattan Bank, N. A. (1988) 73 N.Y.2d 1, 537 N.Y.S.2d 787, 534 N.E.2d 824, 7 UCCRS2d 945, 15 ALR5th 1039

Bank did not violate implied standard of good faith inherent in every contract when it failed to warn corporate account holder of impending segregation of checking account once bank became insecure as to common law security interest it held in account, even though bank had shown continued confidence in corporation just prior to segregation by renewing letter of credit in exchange for which security interest was created; moreover, since there was no commercial bad faith in segregation, there could be no bad faith in bank's subsequent dishonor of checks drawn on segregated account. Gillman v Chase Manhattan Bank, N. A. (1988) 73 N.Y.2d 1, 537 N.Y.S.2d 787, 534 N.E.2d 824, 7 UCCRS2d 945, 15 ALR5th 1039

Neither CLS UCC § 9-402(7) nor CLS UCC § 1-203 required secured party to refile properly and accurately filed financing statement on subsequent event of name change by debtor 6 weeks after acquiring secured party's assets; also, statute did not require special notation financing statement, even if known by secured party, where there was no finding of bad faith or wrongful intent attributable to secured party, and all that existed was mere possibility of and contractual authorization for name change, which occurred 6 weeks after acquisition of assets and with other key intervening developments and transactions. Fleet Factors Corp. v Bandolene Indus. Corp. (1995) 86 N.Y.2d 519, 634 N.Y.S.2d 425, 658 N.E.2d 202, 27 UCCRS2d 1105 appeal after remand (1971, CA8 Ark) 438 F.2d 254, 14 FR Serv 2d 1321

7. Other commercial transactions

Defendant bank was not entitled to summary judgment dismissing cause of action which alleged that manner in which it terminated line of credit agreement with plaintiff corporation and exercised its rights of set-off against corporate and personal bank accounts amounted to breach of duty of good faith and fair dealing implied in all contracts, where plaintiffs alleged that bank's actions were undertaken despite fact that no monetary default had occurred at time when bank could not have reasonably deemed itself to be insecure; although bank's actions were permitted by express terms of contract, which gave bank right to terminate line of credit at any time and without prior notice, bank's actions made it impossible for corporation to comply with demands. Advanced Safety Sys., Inc. v Manufacturers & Traders Trust Co. (1992, 4th Dept) 188 A.D.2d 1009, 592 N.Y.S.2d 159, related proceeding (1992, 4th Dept) 188 A.D.2d 1012, 592 N.Y.S.2d 295

Judgment, after nonjury trial, in favor of plaintiff in breach of contract action would be reversed where trial court properly determined that plaintiff, publishing sales representative, was "egregiously deceitful" in its representation of defendants, publishers with whom it had contracted, and thereby disregarded its obligation to act in good faith (CLS UCC § 1-203); such finding warranted dismissal of complaint since breach of obligation to act in good faith is disqualifying factor. Sussman Sales Co. v Kaufman (2000, 2d Dept) 269 A.D.2d 440, 702 N.Y.S.2d 918

In action for breach of unique contracts for sale of copper scrap which had been designed by defendant buyer to obtain copper from dealers who at time were reluctant to sell because of depressed copper prices, and which provided, inter alia, that price was to be mutually agreed upon between buyer and seller whenever seller wished to price contract and material was to be priced during Commodities Exchange trading hours (i.e. seller was entitled to hold price open until market advanced to point which would provide it with profit on scrap previously delivered), plaintiff seller was entitled to damages under UCC § 2-709 which would be based on mean Commodities Exchange price for copper during three month period prior to pricing date requested by plaintiff (less allowance for scrap discount) under either UCC § 2-305(3), as reasonable price fixed by injured party, or UCC § 2-305(1)(c), as price fixed in terms of agreed market; general obligation of good faith under UCC § 1-203 did not require plaintiff to invest in copper futures immediately upon being notified of defendant's breach in order to mitigate damages and protect its or defendant's exposure where plaintiff, scrap dealer, had little or no familiarity with Commodities Exchange dealings or hedging, unlike defendant which was fully acquainted with complexities of metals futures markets. Pepper's Steel & Alloys, Inc. v Lissner Minerals & Metals, Inc. (1979, SD NY) 494 F. Supp. 487

Intermediary bank did not owe duty of good faith and fair dealing to transferor bank in transferring funds from transferor's immediate transferee bank to another bank pursuant to "money back guarantee" provision of CLS UCC § 4-A-402, as there was no contract between transferor and intermediary bank. Grain Traders v Citibank, N.A. (1997, SD NY) 960 F. Supp. 784, 33 UCCRS2d 220, affd (1998, CA2 NY) 160 F.3d 97, 36 UCCRS2d 1141

§ 1-305. Remedies to be Liberally Administered

(a) The remedies provided by this act must be liberally administered to the end that the aggrieved party may be put in as good a position as if the other party had fully performed but neither consequential or special damages nor penal damages may be had except as specifically provided in this act or by other rule of law.

(b) Any right or obligation declared by this act is enforceable by action unless the provision declaring it specifies a different and limited effect.

History: L 2014, ch 505, § 1, eff Dec 17, 2014.

CASE ANNOTATIONS

UNDER FORMER § 1-106

Attorneys' fees incurred in action to recover loss of profits and incidental damages upon buyer's repudiation of contract are not in nature of protective expenses contemplated by Code. Neri v Retail Marine Corp. (1972) 30 N.Y.2d 393, 334 N.Y.S.2d 165, 285 N.E.2d 311, 10 UCCRS 950

Courts should not import comparative negligence principles into Uniform Commercial Code since code represents attempt to adjust risk of loss in commercial matters in fair and equitable manner not based on fault, but on allocating responsibility to party best able to prevent loss by exercise of care, with objective of promoting certainty and predictability in commercial transactions. Putnam Rolling Ladder Co. v Manufacturers Hanover Trust Co. (1989) 74 N.Y.2d 340, 547 N.Y.S.2d 611, 546 N.E.2d 904

In action by payee against drawee bank, rule of absolute liability stated in CLS UCC § 3-419(2) does not preclude setoff where payee has received all or part of proceeds of converted instrument. Mouradian v Astoria Fed. S&L (1997) 91 N.Y.2d 124, 667 N.Y.S.2d 340, 689 N.E.2d 1385, 34 UCCRS2d 267

Fees charged by defendant bank for returning customers' checks for insufficient funds, and for returning checks deposited by customers into their accounts which were subsequently dishonored by drawee bank for insufficient funds in drawer's account, were not "grossly excessive" so as to constitute impermissible penalties under UCC § 1-106(1), but were simply fixed charges for specified services to be rendered that were agreed to by customers when they opened their accounts with defendant. Jacobs v Citibank, N.A. (1983, 1st Dept) 92 A.D.2d 786, 459 N.Y.S.2d 781, affd (1984) 61 N.Y.2d 869, 474 N.Y.S.2d 464, 462 N.E.2d 1182, 37 UCCRS 1648

The purpose of this act, to be liberally construed, is specified as the stipulation, clarification and modernization of the law governing commercial transactions to permit the continued expansion of commercial practices through custom, usage and agreement of the parties; and the statute mandates a liberal administration to the end that an aggrieved party may be put in as good a position as if the other party had fully performed without consequential, special, or penal damages unless specifically provided for. Chrysler Credit Corp. v Sharp (1968) 56 Misc. 2d 261, 288 N.Y.S.2d 525, 5 UCCRS 226

In suit by owners of stock certificate against issuer and two brokerage firms for conversion of certificate by improperly transferring and surrendering it to issuer under purported signatures of owners which were (1) unauthorized and (2) guaranteed by defendant brokers, issuer was entitled to amend cross-claim against brokers to assert claim under UCC § 8-312(3), based on brokers' signature guarantees, for indemnification for legal fees and expenses in defending action, since UCC § 8-312(3)-which provides that guarantor "is liable" for any loss resulting from breach of warranties created by his signature guarantee-is required by UCC § 1-106(1) to be liberally construed and under such construction, "is liable" takes on meaning of "indemnification." O'Neal v General Electric Co. O'Neal v General Electric Co. (1983, Sup) 122 Misc. 2d 430, 470 N.Y.S.2d 67

Plaintiff was entitled to cash refund from store where she purchased defective coat, despite store's posted policy prohibiting cash refunds and allowing for store exchanges only, since (1) coat was covered by implied warranty of merchantability under CLS UCC § 2-314, (2) remedies under Uniform Commercial Code are to be liberally administered in order for aggrieved party to be put in as good position as if other party had fully performed (CLS UCC § 1-106), and (3) to give plaintiff store credit would not place her in her original position. Boys v Burlington Coat Factory (1988, City Ct) 138 Misc. 2d 626, 524 N.Y.S.2d 351, 6 UCCRS2d 367

Trial court's award of damages to an administrator in a wrongful registration suit brought under N.Y. U.C.C. Law § 8-404(b) was not improper because the corporation was unable to issue shares of stock to the administrator inasmuch as the corporation had been acquired by an investment group as the result of a merger transaction. Kirshtein v Americu Credit Union (2011, App Div, 4th Dept) 919 NYS2d 653, 74 UCCRS2d 164, subsequent app (2011, App Div, 4th Dept) 919 NYS2d 434.

In suit by depositary bank against drawee bank for wrongful dishonor of certified check for $60,000, where (1) drawee bank on June 8, 1981 stopped payment on check following telephone message from drawer that check had been lost, (2) on July 16, 1981, payees of check deposited it in passbook account with plaintiff, (3) check was received by drawee bank on July 22, 1981 and was returned unpaid on following day because of drawer's stop-payment order, (4) check was forwarded by Federal Reserve bank to plaintiff's correspondent bank, which returned check to plaintiff on November 3, 1981, after check's payees had withdrawn all funds from their passbook account with plaintiff, (5) on November 15, 1983, District Court ruled that plaintiff was entitled to payment of check, and (6) remaining issues in case involved consequential and punitive damages sought by plaintiff, court held (1) that under UCC § 1-106(1), consequential and punitive damages cannot be awarded unless they are specifically authorized by Uniform Commercial Code or some other rule of law, (2) that since plaintiff depositary bank was not customer, within meaning of UCC § 4-104(1)(e), of defendant drawee bank, plaintiff was not entitled to consequential damages under UCC § 4-402 for check's wrongful dishonor, (3) that plaintiff was entitled to try to prove consequential damages under "bad-faith" provision of UCC § 4-103(5), which deals with bank's liability for failure to exercise ordinary care in handling item, and (4) that plaintiff was not entitled to punitive damages under New York law. Casco Bank & Trust Co. v Bank of New York (1984, DC Me) 584 F. Supp. 763 (applying N.Y. UCC)

UCC § 1-106 prohibits punitive damages except as specifically provided, and punitive damages are not available for mere breach of contract absent evidence that conduct constituting breach was so malicious or morally culpable that it constitutes tort in and of itself. Computerized Radiological Services, Inc. v Syntex Corp. (1984, ED NY) 595 F. Supp. 1495, 40 UCCRS 49, affd in part and revd in part on other grounds (1986, CA2 NY) 786 F.2d 72, 42 UCCRS 1656

§ 1-306.   Waiver or Renunciation of Claim or Right After Breach

A claim or right arising out of an alleged breach may be discharged in whole or in part without consideration by agreement of the aggrieved party in an authenticated record.

History: L 2014, ch 505, § 1, eff Dec 17, 2014.

§ 1-307.   Prima Facie evidence by Third-party Documents

A document in due form purporting to be a bill of lading, policy or certificate of insurance, official weigher's or inspector's certificate, consular invoice, or any other document authorized or required by the contract to be issued by a third party is prima facie evidence of its own authenticity and genuineness and of the facts stated in the document by the third party.

History: L 2014, ch 505, § 1, eff Dec 17, 2014.

CASE ANNOTATIONS

UNDER FORMER § 1-202

In action by seller of restaurant linens against buyer for breach of contract, judgment for seller was reversed and remanded on ground that freight bills received from common carrier were inadmissible;

UCC § 1-202 could not be used as exception to hearsay rule where freight bills were not authorized or required by contract sued upon. Standard Textile Co. v National Equipment Rental, Ltd. (1981, 2d Dept) 80 A.D.2d 911, 437 N.Y.S.2d 398

CLS UCC § 1-202 establishes presumption of authenticity of bills of lading, but court must ultimately decide issue when accuracy or authenticity of document is questioned, and therefore, presumption cannot estop carrier from denying validity of document. Societe Generale v Federal Ins. Co. (1988, CA2 NY) 856 F.2d 461, 6 UCCRS2d 1236

Provision of CLS UCC § 1-202 that certain documents may be prima facie evidence of their own authenticity did not estop company, under whose name forged bills of lading had been issued, from denying validity of documents; statute merely establishes presumption of authenticity in absence of contrary evidence, and court must ultimately decide issue when authenticity is questioned. Societe Generale v Federal Ins. Co. (1988, CA2 NY) 856 F.2d 461, 6 UCCRS2d 1236

§ 1-308.   Performance or Acceptance Under Reservation of Rights

A party that with explicit reservation of rights performs or promises performance or assents to performance in a manner demanded or offered by the other party does not thereby prejudice the rights reserved. Such words as "without prejudice," "under protest," or the like are sufficient.

History: L 2014, ch 505, § 1, eff Dec 17, 2014.

CASE ANNOTATIONS

UNDER FORMER § 1-207

1. In general
2. Particular notations reserving rights
3. Particular notations inadequate to reserve rights

1. In general

Under UCC § 1-207, creditor may preserve right to balance of disputed claim by explicit reservation in his indorsement of check tendered by debtor as full payment, and thereby preclude accord and satisfaction; § 1-207 authorizes payee to indorse under protest and accept amount of check without entering accord and satisfaction or otherwise foresaking his claim to any additional sum allegedly due him. Horn Waterproofing Corp. v Bushwick Iron & Steel Co. (1985) 66 N.Y.2d 321, 497 N.Y.S.2d 310, 488 N.E.2d 56, 41 UCCRS 1591

Payment of contract debt by check or other commercial paper and its acceptance by creditor fall within reach of UCC § 1-207; consequently, debtor's tender of full payment check is Article 3 transactions which is governed by § 1-207, regardless of nature of contract underlying parties' commercial relationship. Horn Waterproofing Corp. v Bushwick Iron & Steel Co. (1985) 66 N.Y.2d 321, 497 N.Y.S.2d 310, 488 N.E.2d 56, 41 UCCRS 1591

Under UCC § 1-207, buyers of stock, by continuing to perform under contract, did not waive right to complain of sellers' retention of dividends where, although buyers made no explicit reservation of right to dividends, buyers' actions clearly indicated that they were not waiving any rights accruing to them. Deering Milliken, Inc. v Clark Estates, Inc. (1977, 1st Dept) 57 A.D.2d 773, 394 N.Y.S.2d 436, affd (1978) 43 N.Y.2d 545, 402 N.Y.S.2d 987, 373 N.E.2d 1212

UCC § 1-207 permits a party to accept, as long as he explicitly reserves his rights, whatever he can get by way of payment, performance, or other means without losing his right to sue for the balance of the payment. Ayer v Sky Club, Inc. (1979, 1st Dept) 70 A.D.2d 863, 418 N.Y.S.2d 57, 27 UCCRS 881, app dismd (1979) 48 N.Y.2d 705, 422 N.Y.S.2d 68, 397 N.E.2d 758

In action to recover under life insurance policy, beneficiary properly reserved her right to commence action, notwithstanding her negotiation of check from insurance company for premium paid for policy plus interest, where beneficiary's attorney acknowledged receipt of check and informed insurance company that beneficiary reserved right to commence action despite her negotiation of check; contrary result was not required by fact that beneficiary did not write reservation of rights on check itself. Masi v Equitable Variable Life

Ins. Co. (1991, 2d Dept) 178 A.D.2d 515, 577 N.Y.S.2d 146, 16 UCCRS2d 961

Defendant was entitled to dismissal of action on ground of accord and satisfaction where plaintiffs claimed that defendants owed them $125,000, plaintiffs accepted and deposited defendants' check for $30,000 explicitly tendered in full settlement of all claims, deposit was without any restrictive endorsement or other contemporaneous or prior reservation of rights, and nearly one week later plaintiffs purported to reserve their rights by letter. Sarbin v Southwest Media Corp. (1992, 1st Dept) 179 A.D.2d 567, 578 N.Y.S.2d 571, 17 UCCRS2d 10

Plaintiff's acceptance of check, without affixing words "without prejudice" or "under protest," did not constitute accord and satisfaction as matter of law where check itself bore no legend that it was intended to constitute payment in full. JRDM Corp. v U.W. Marx, Inc. (1998, 3d Dept) 252 A.D.2d 854, 675 N.Y.S.2d 691

In action by real estate agency seeking balance of $8,200 broker's commission, sellers were not entitled to dismissal under CLS UCC § 1-207 on grounds that they had tendered check for $6,000 and marked it with legend "in full accord and satisfaction for any real estate commission claimed" by agency, and that agency had accepted and cashed check without immediate protest so that no rights were reserved under § 1-207, since sellers never disputed amount owed before check was sent to agency and § 1-207 was not implicated absent pending dispute as to delivery, acceptance, or payment; accord and satisfaction pursuant to § 1-207 pertains only to procedure where one party is claiming as of right something which other feels is unwarranted. Century 21 Kaaterskill Realty v Grasso (1986, 3d Dept) 124 A.D.2d 316, 508 N.Y.S.2d 99, 2 UCCRS2d 1177

Trial court properly awarded judgment to the lenders plus statutory interest because the borrower failed to establish that the cashing of her check allegedly as payment in full constituted an accord and satisfaction where the note provided that the borrower would pay both principal and interest on the loan and the lender's indorsement of the back of the check with the words "without prejudice and under protest" constituted an explicit reservation of rights, thereby precluding an accord and satisfaction. Huimin Sun v Cai, 146 A.D.3d 760, 45 N.Y.S.3d 155 (N.Y. App. Div. 2d Dep't 2017).

Accord and satisfaction is obtainable under UCC § 1-207 only in cases where one party claims as of right something that other party disputes because he feels it is not warranted. Thus, in case where (1) corporate real-estate broker demanded payment of $8,200 commission from defendant; (2) defendant sent broker check for $6,000 "in full accord and satisfaction" of broker's claim; and (3) broker endorsed check, deposited it in its bank account, and sued defendant for $2,200, UCC § 1-207 was not applicable to case because defendant had never disputed amount owed before sending check to broker. Century 21 Kaaterskill Realty v Grasso (1986, 3d Dept) 124 A.D.2d 316, 508 N.Y.S.2d 99, 2 UCCRS2d 1177

Where (1) general contractor involved in payment dispute with steel supplier sent supplier check for certain sum as final payment of amount due and thereafter, in further effort to resolve dispute, sent supplier second check for slightly higher amount also as final payment of account, and (2) supplier, after first certifying both checks and holding them for several months, returned first check to general contractor, deposited second check with indorsement "without prejudice and under protest," and thereafter advised general contractor that it was still asserting its claim for entire amount allegedly due, court held (1) that UCC § 1-207 was inapplicable because supplier had made no reservation of its rights at time it had second check certified, and (2) that trial court correctly concluded as a result that an accord and satisfaction had occurred as to amount in dispute on date second check was certified. Lange-Finn Constr. Co. v Albany Steel & Iron Supply Co. (1978) 94 Misc. 2d 15, 403 N.Y.S.2d 1012, 24 UCCRS 11

Plaintiff's unequivocal, explicit and unambiguous reservation of rights on the back of a final payment check tendered in a commercial transaction, as well as in a letter to defendants immediately after the check was deposited, is more than adequate to satisfy the intent of section 1-207 of the Uniform Commercial Code, which permits a party to a code-covered transaction to preserve rights explicitly reserved and to accept whatever payment or performance he can obtain, a change in the common-law rule. Accordingly, accord and satisfaction was not effected by the deposit of said check and plaintiff's motion to strike the affirmative defense of accord and satisfaction raised by defendants was granted. Kroulee Corp. v A.

Klein & Co. (1980) 103 Misc. 2d 441, 426 N.Y.S.2d 206, 28 UCCRS 969

Claimant possessing tort cause of action for property damage could not, pursuant to CLS UCC § 1-207, preserve his right to balance allegedly owed by explicit reservation in his endorsement of negotiable instrument (check) tendered by defendant in full settlement of all claims, since (1) no debtor-creditor relationship arose from alleged tort, (2) there was no outstanding underlying obligation based on contract debt between parties, and none was created after tort since issues of negligence, duty, proximate cause and damages were unresolved, (3) there was no admission of liability by defendant or his insurer so as to create underlying obligation, (4) if claimant lost his tort claim, he would be obligated to return funds previously accepted, and (5) applying § 1-207 would discourage insurance companies from attempting to settle such cases; under circumstances, claimant's acceptance and deposit of check constituted accord and satisfaction as matter of law. Clarke v Yvans (1988, Civ Ct) 140 Misc. 2d 129, 530 N.Y.S.2d 465

2. Particular notations reserving rights

Where debtor presented "full payment" check for $500 in satisfaction of debt in amount of $1,080, and where creditor indorsed check below its notation, "Under Protest", thereby indicating its intent to preserve all rights to $580 balance, such explicit reservation of rights falls squarely within UCC § 1-207, and was effective means of precluding accord and satisfaction or any other prejudice to rights thus reserved. Horn Waterproofing Corp. v Bushwick Iron & Steel Co. (1985) 66 N.Y.2d 321, 497 N.Y.S.2d 310, 488 N.E.2d 56, 41 UCCRS 1591

The seller of certain specially manufactured goods adequately preserved its rights in accordance with UCC § 1-207, thus precluding an accord and satisfaction, where the seller, prior to negotiating the buyer's check and underneath the buyer's notation on the reverse side that "indorsement of this check constitutes payment in full," added its own notation that notwithstanding the buyer's notation, the seller "accepts this payment without prejudice and with full reservation of its rights to assert a claim" for the balance due on the contract. Braun v C.E.P.C. Distribs. (1980, 1st Dept) 77 A.D.2d 358, 433 N.Y.S.2d 447, 30 UCCRS 8, app den (1981) 52 N.Y.2d 704

In breach of contract action, seller preserved its rights under UCC § 1-207 so as to preclude accord and satisfaction which would have discharged buyer from further liability where, on receiving check from buyer which stated that indorsement of check constituted payment in full of all claims, seller indorsed and negotiated check but added notation that notwithstanding the foregoing it was accepting part payment without prejudice and with full reservation of rights to assert additional specified claims. Braun v C.E.P.C. Distribs. (1980, 1st Dept) 77 A.D.2d 358, 433 N.Y.S.2d 447, 30 UCCRS 8, app den (1981) 52 N.Y.2d 704

Creditor's endorsement on debtor's check which included words "without prejudice. Under protest. With reservation of all rights" was explicit reservation within meaning of CLS UCC § 1-207 which provides that creditor may preserve rights to balance of disputed claim by explicit reservation in its endorsement of check as full payment, thereby precluding accord and satisfaction. Pandick, Inc. v Sandusky Plastics, Inc. (1990, 1st Dept) 160 A.D.2d 236, 553 N.Y.S.2d 349, 11 UCCRS2d 759

Plaintiffs' acceptance of defendants' check did not constitute accord and satisfaction where plaintiff reserved its right to pursue remainder of its claim by writing on back of check that "(t)his check is deposited under protest, without prejudice and with preservation of all rights of the payee against the drawer of the check"; CLS UCC § 1-207 applied even though plaintiff's claim was for services rather than goods, since defendants paid by check. Metropolitan Knitwear v Trans World Fashions (1996, 1st Dept) 233 A.D.2d 241, 649 N.Y.S.2d 702, 31 UCCRS2d 671

Statement written on back of check by payee before cashing check, which included words "Cashed Under Protest" in two separate places, constituted express and unambiguous reservation under UCC § 1-207 of payee's right to demand balance alleged to be due from drawer. Aguiar v Harper & Row Publishers, Inc. (1982, Civ Ct) 114 Misc. 2d 828, 452 N.Y.S.2d 519, 34 UCCRS 6

Receipt and acceptance of check for unliquidated damages to plaintiff's automobile-which defendants intended to be full payment for such damages, but which plaintiff under UCC § 1-207 accepted as partial payment only by writing "without prejudice" on check to indicate claim for additional sum-did not constitute common-law accord and satisfaction of defendants' obligation in view of plaintiff's

UCC

explicit reservation of rights under UCC § 1-207. Cohen v Ricci (1983, City Ct) 120 Misc. 2d 712, 466 N.Y.S.2d 121

Conditional endorsement of negotiable instrument by payee preserves right of payee to seek amount in excess of accepted amount regardless of nature of underlying transaction; accordingly, conditional endorsement of check offered in satisfaction of claim for property damage with words "partial payment" does not constitute accord and satisfaction so as to bar payee from further recovery. McCreedy v Lopera (1985, Dist Ct) 130 Misc. 2d 292, 498 N.Y.S.2d 666

Claimant's acceptance of "full-payment" check offered as settlement of tort action, but with "No" written on back following printed legend stating that check represented payment for all damages, did not constitute accord and satisfaction barring further claims since CLS UCC § 1-207 changed common law rule and permits reservation of rights whenever negotiable instrument is used to make payment on existing debt, regardless of nature of underlying obligation between parties, and allows good-faith creditor to deposit "full-payment" check provided he indicates his intent to preserve all rights through use of words such as "without prejudice" or "under protest." DeVerna v Kinney Systems, Inc. (1989, Civ Ct) 142 Misc. 2d 271, 536 N.Y.S.2d 944, 7 UCCRS2d 1371, affd (1990, Sup App T) 146 Misc. 2d 276, 556 N.Y.S.2d 190

Employee who was injured in an automobile accident and sought payment under the underinsured motorist provision of his employer's insurance policy preserved his right to seek interest on an arbitrator's award by endorsing a check he received from a company that insured his employer "under protest," and the trial court confirmed the arbitrator's award and awarded interest on the amount the arbitrator awarded. Church Mut. Ins. Co. v Kleingardner (2003, Sup) 774 N.Y.S.2d 265

Where (1) utility by check refunded full amount of overcharge for electricity supplied to customer, but refused customer's demand for interest on such overcharge, and (2) customer negotiated refund check with indorsement that stated "negotiation of this check is not to be construed as waiver of... (customer's claim for interest payments)," court held (1) that UCC § 1-207-which provides that party who, with explicit reservation of rights, performs or assents to performance in manner demanded or offered by other party does not thereby prejudice rights reserved-is broad enough to allow one who claims right to interest to accept payment of principal under protest without waiving right to interest, (2) that as a result, defendant utility could not avoid customer's claim for accrued interest at statutory rate of six percent per year, and (3) that recovery of interest claimed to be due more than six years before action was commenced was barred by applicable statute of limitations. United States v Consolidated Edison Co. (1984, SD NY) 590 F. Supp. 266, 40 UCCRS 759 (applying N.Y. UCC)

3. Particular notations inadequate to reserve rights

In an action for specific performance of a contract to sell real estate, the trial court erred in denying seller's motion for summary judgment on the basis of accord and satisfaction where seller notified plaintiff that they considered him to be in breach of contract when plaintiff was unable to close by the requested date, where seller's attorney then sent plaintiff's attorney a check in the amount of plaintiff's down payment together with a letter which unequivocally stated that acceptance of the payment would act as a cancellation of the contract and release all existing obligations, where plaintiff subsequently received another check for the amount of interest earned on the down payment, where plaintiff deposited each of the checks with the following indorsement "without prejudice to and reserving any and all rights accruing to and vested in payee by reason of breach of contract...," and where before plaintiff deposited the checks, the seller sold the property in question to a third party; the negotiation of the checks constituted an accord and satisfaction under the common law and the words "without prejudice" were of no lawful effect. Gimby v Frost (1981, 2d Dept) 84 A.D.2d 806, 444 N.Y.S.2d 143, 33 UCCRS 805, app dismd (1982) 56 N.Y.2d 593

In an action to recover the balance due under a construction contract, recovery was barred by an accord and satisfaction created when plaintiff cashed defendant's check for a lesser amount than plaintiff claimed was due inasmuch as the check was accompanied by a covering letter from defendant conditioning it on its being "final payment to satisfy all charges" and clearly indicating that liquidated delay damages had been deducted from the contract price, despite the fact that plaintiff indorsed the check "Payment in Protest." William

Manfredi Constr. William Manfredi Constr. Corp. v Green Fan Co. (1982, 2d Dept) 87 A.D.2d 611, 448 N.Y.S.2d 43, 33 UCCRS 806

Although the acceptance of a check tendered as final payment in full for a disputed amount with an indorsement stating that the negotiation of the check is "without prejudice" or "under protest" does not result in an accord and satisfaction (Uniform Commercial Code, § 1-207), defendant's failure to expressly reserve its rights at the time it caused plaintiff's check tendered as a final payment for materials supplied by defendant on a construction project to be certified resulted in an accord and satisfaction. Where a check is tendered as payment in full for a disputed amount and the payee causes the check to be certified, an accord and satisfaction results since certification is equivalent to acceptance by the payee. Defendant only advised plaintiff that it was still asserting its claim for the entire balance after it caused plaintiff's check to be certified. Had defendant merely negotiated the check while reserving its rights, no accord and satisfaction would have occurred. Lange-Finn Constr. Co. v Albany Steel & Iron Supply Co. (1978) 94 Misc. 2d 15, 403 N.Y.S.2d 1012, 24 UCCRS 11

Creditor's scratching out of words "complete and final payment" entered by debtor over endorsement blocks on check, followed by creditor's endorsement and deposit of check for collection, did not constitute "explicit reservation of rights" which would preserve creditor's right to balance of disputed claim under CLS UCC § 1-207. Sullivan v Conant Valley Assoc., Ltd. (1990, Sup) 148 Misc. 2d 483, 560 N.Y.S.2d 617

§ 1-309. Option to Accelerate at Will

A term providing that one party or that party's successor in interest may accelerate payment or performance or require collateral or additional collateral "at will" or when the party "deems itself insecure," or words of similar import, means that the party has power to do so only if that party in good faith believes that the prospect of payment or performance is impaired. The burden of establishing lack of good faith is on the party against which the power has been exercised.

History: L 2014, ch 505, § 1, eff Dec 17, 2014.

CASE ANNOTATIONS

UNDER FORMER § 1-208

Plaintiff bank is entitled to liquidate municipal bonds held as collateral for loans made to defendant securities dealer since plaintiff had adequate cause to "deem itself insecure", a condition constituting default under the parties' security agreement, where defendant had engaged in wash sales to postpone the effect of losses occasioned by the declining bond market. Bankers Trust Co. v J. V. Dowler & Co. (1979) 47 N.Y.2d 128, 417 N.Y.S.2d 47, 390 N.E.2d 766, 26 UCCRS 549

Court erred in determining that note executed in November 1987 was demand note, notwithstanding "X" in box beside printed language stating that loan was payable "ON DEMAND, IF THE LENDER DEMANDS PAYMENT," since there was typewritten clause added to text of note stating that "notwithstanding the maturity date (of December 1, 2001), the bank may demand the entire amount of unpaid principal and accumulated interest be paid at any time after December 1, 1991"; typewritten clause controlled over printed language that came after box checked. Mundaca Inv. Corp. v Rivizzigno (1998, 4th Dept) 247 A.D.2d 904, 36 UCCRS2d 763

Under UCC § 1-208, conditional vendor of automobile was justified in exercising its "insecurity clause" and accelerating payment of balance due under conditional sales contract where conditional purchaser was charged with illegally transporting controlled substances in violation of state law, thereby subjecting vehicle to possible forfeiture proceedings by state and federal governments. Blaine v G.M.A.C. (1975) 82 Misc. 2d 653, 370 N.Y.S.2d 323, 17 UCCRS 641

N.Y. U.C.C. Law § 1-208 did not apply to the cross-default clause of a swap agreement, as the cross-default clause was not an acceleration clause, nor did it authorize additional collateral, nor was it "at will." Citibank, N.A. v United Subcontractors, Inc. (2008, SD NY) 581 F Supp 2d 640.

§ 1-310. Subordinated Obligations

An obligation may be issued as subordinated to performance of another obligation of the person obligated, or a creditor may subordinate its right to performance of an obligation by agreement with either the person obligated or another creditor of the person obligated. Subordination does not create a security interest as against either the common debtor or a subordinated creditor.

History: L 2014, ch 505, § 1, eff Dec 17, 2014.

CASE ANNOTATIONS

UNDER FORMER § 1-209

New York recognizes judicially created equitable doctrine known as "Rule of Explicitness," whereby parties may use subordination agreements to consent to payment of post-petition interest to senior creditors from funds that would otherwise go to junior creditors, but only if such subordination agreements contain specific language alerting junior creditors of enhanced risk and burden of allowing payment of senior creditor's post-petition interest demand. Southeast Banking Corp v First Trust of N.Y., N.A. (1999) 93 N.Y.2d 178, 688 N.Y.S.2d 484, 710 N.E.2d 1083, 34 BCD 326

ARTICLE 8
INVESTMENT SECURITIES

History: Add, L 1997, ch 566, § 5, eff Oct 10, 1997; amd, L 1997, ch 566, § 1a, eff Oct 10, 1997.

Former Art 8, add, L 1962, ch 553; repealed, L 1997, ch 566, § 5, eff Oct 10, 1997.

CASE ANNOTATIONS

UNDER FORMER ARTICLE 8

1. Under former § 8-102

Plaintiffs could not be either holders in due course or bona fide purchasers where they bought bearer bonds from third party with notice of adverse claims. Goldstein v Engel (1997, 1st Dept) 240 A.D.2d 280, 659 N.Y.S.2d 16, 35 UCCRS2d 970

Certificates of participation in eight promissory notes were not "investment securities" within meaning of UCC Article 8 where such certificates were not issued in "bearer" or "registered form" under UCC § 8-102(1)(c) and (d), and (2) none of such certificates was "one of a class or series or by its terms... divisible into a class or series of instruments" within meaning of UCC § 8-102(1)(a)(iii). Corporacion Venezolana de Fomento v Vintero Sales Corp. (1978, SD NY) 452 F. Supp. 1108, 24 UCCRS 1199, remanded without op (1979, CA2 NY) 607 F.2d 994 and remanded without op (1979, CA2 NY) 607 F.2d 994 (applying New York UCC; holding that banks to which such certificates were issued were holders of the underlying promissory notes, rather than owners of investment securities, and that their rights were therefore governed by UCC Article 3)

2. – Stock certificatees as security

Article 8 was intended to include all shares of stock and not merely those dealt with by security brokers. Previti v Rubenstein (1966, N.Y. Sup) 3 UCCRS 882

In determining whether certain stock rights were securities within the meaning of the Securities Exchange Act of 1934, the proposed final draft of 1950 of UCC § 8-102, which defined "security", was quoted by the court in Silverman v Landa (1962, CA2 NY) 306 F.2d 422

3. – Stock of closely-held corporation

Stock certificates of corporation which had fewer than four stockholders and whose only substantial asset was structure housing two professional offices, were "securities" within meaning of UCC § 8-102(1)(a); thus, alleged oral agreement among stockholders of corporation which, in effect, conferred upon each of them first refusal rights if any other stockholder wished to sell his stock, was unenforceable under UCC § 8-319. Pantel v Becker (1977) 89 Misc. 2d 239, 391 N.Y.S.2d 325, 21 UCCRS 274

4. – Other "securities"

Bearer bonds satisfy all three elements of CLS UCC § 8-102, and thus constitute "securities" as defined in that section. Vigilant Ins. Co. of Am. v Housing Auth. (1995) 87 N.Y.2d 36, 637 N.Y.S.2d 342, 660 N.E.2d 1121, 27 UCCRS2d 1285

Plaintiffs' claim that they were holders in due course of bearer bonds was without merit because those bonds, as certificated securities, were governed exclusively by CLS UCC Art 8, even though they might qualify as commercial paper under CLS UCC Art 3. Goldstein v Engel (1997, 1st Dept) 240 A.D.2d 280, 659 N.Y.S.2d 16, 35 UCCRS2d 970

UCC

A "call" is not a "security" within the definition of UCC § 8-102, thus, UCC § 8-319 is inapplicable to a call option. Cohn, Ivers & Co. v Gross (1968) 56 Misc. 2d 491, 289 N.Y.S.2d 301, 5 UCCRS 390

In suit by trustee in bankruptcy against bank which had allegedly received voidable preferences in violation of Bankruptcy Act, bankrupt's settlement of suit concerning reduction in value of collateral for loan was not voidable preference where collateral consisted of debenture in which defendant had perfected its security interest by possession; debenture was "security" within meaning of UCC § 8-102 where, inter alia, subordinated debentures of brokerage houses were recognized medium for investment; debenture was "instrument" under UCC § 9-105 where it was "security" under UCC § 8-102; security interest in debenture was perfected by possession, under UCC § 9-305, where it was "instrument" under UCC § 9-105; security interest attached immediately in collateral despite alleged ambiguity in security agreement to effect that it was to attach only in event of default, where construction of security agreement revealed intent to attach immediately and where, under UCC § 9-204, any attempt to postpone attachment must be explictly stated; filing, under UCC § 9-201, security agreement superceded previous subordination agreement and controlled rights and obligations among the parties. Allegaert v Chemical Bank (1980, CA2 NY) 657 F.2d 495, 6 BCD 1247

5. Under former § 8-103

Cooperative corporation's lien (for obligations other than maintenance) on unsold shares retained by sponsor, which had been pledged to lender to secure loan, was enforceable and had priority, even though security agreement provided that sponsor gave lender first and prior security interest "in and to all of [sponsor's] right, title and interest" in shares, and shares had been foreclosed upon and sold at auction by lender, where lien was stated both in bylaws of corporation and by endorsement on shares; shares of stock in corporation constituted "securities" within meaning of CLS UCC Art 8, and legend on shares gave sufficient notice under CLS UCC §§ 8-103 and 8-204 of corporation's lien and right to restrict transfer of shares based on provisions of bylaws and proprietary lease. ALH Properties Ten v 306-100th St. Owners Corp. (1993, 1st Dept) 191 A.D.2d 1, 600 N.Y.S.2d 443, 22 UCCRS2d 870, later proceeding (1993, N.Y. A.D., 1st Dept) 1993 N.Y. A.D. LEXIS 8889, app dismd without op (1994) 82 N.Y.2d 920, 610 N.Y.S.2d 154, 632 N.E.2d 464 and app gr (1995) 85 N.Y.2d 806, 627 N.Y.S.2d 322, 650 N.E.2d 1324 and mod, affd (1995) 86 N.Y.2d 643, 635 N.Y.S.2d 161, 658 N.E.2d 1034, 28 UCCRS2d 358

Legend on shares of stock of cooperative corporation, which stated generally that rights of "any holder" of shares were subject to provisions of corporation's bylaws, specifically set out that corporation could refuse to transfer shares until any indebtedness of shareholder to corporation was paid, and further stated that corporation had first lien on shares pursuant to bylaws and proprietary lease, gave sufficient notice under CLS UCC §§ 8 -103 and 8-204 of corporation's first lien and right to refuse transfer of shares based on provisions of both bylaws and proprietary lease. ALH Properties Ten v 306-100th St. Owners Corp. (1993, 1st Dept) 191 A.D.2d 1, 600 N.Y.S.2d 443, 22 UCCRS2d 870, later proceeding (1993, N.Y. A.D., 1st Dept) 1993 N.Y. A.D. LEXIS 8889, app dismd without op (1994) 82 N.Y.2d 920, 610 N.Y.S.2d 154, 632 N.E.2d 464 and app gr (1995) 85 N.Y.2d 806, 627 N.Y.S.2d 322, 650 N.E.2d 1324 and mod, affd (1995) 86 N.Y.2d 643, 635 N.Y.S.2d 161, 658 N.E.2d 1034, 28 UCCRS2d 358

6. Under former § 8-104

Petitioners were entitled to summary judgment for recission of stock purchase agreement under CLS UCC § 8-104 where it was undisputed that corporation was authorized by its certificate of incorporation to issue maximum of 200 shares of stock, and that petitioners were issued in excess of 550 shares of corporation's stock. Marino v Island Express Advertising, Inc. (1991, 2d Dept) 172 A.D.2d 525, 567 N.Y.S.2d 868, 15 UCCRS2d 1296

7. Under former § 8-105

The Uniform Commercial Code, under UCC § 8-105(1), treats investment securities as negotiable instruments. The code also, in UCC § 1-201(20), defines a "holder" as one who is "in possession" of an investment security that is drawn, issued, or indorsed to him or to his order, or to bearer or in blank. Under the code's definition of a holder, therefore, possession is a significant factor, and the possessor of an instrument is a "holder" without regard to the legality or propriety of his possession. Stewart Becker, Ltd. v Horowitz (1978) 94 Misc. 2d 766, 405 N.Y.S.2d 571

8. Under former § 8-107

"Adverse market conditions" or "market outs" in firm commitment underwriting agreement does not encompass decline in price of stock of company whose securities are to be underwritten; damages for breach of firm commitment underwriting agreement were properly awarded in amount of contract price pursuant to CLS UCC § 8-107, as 1982 amendment to § 8-107(2) was merely technical one and was not intended to effect any substantive change in New York's law of contract remedies. Walk-In Medical Centers, Inc. v Breuer Capital Corp. (1987, CA2 NY) 818 F.2d 260, 3 UCCRS2d 1885, later proceeding (1991, DC Colo) 778 F. Supp. 1116 and (criticized in Nycal Corp. v Inoco PLC (1997, SD NY) 988 F. Supp. 296)

In an action to recover damages for breach of a tender offer to purchase securities subsequently sold to another, the seller could recover the tender price for the securities, but the proper measure of damages was the difference between the resale price and the contract price, assuming that the resale is made in good faith and in a "commercially reasonable" manner. Bache & Co. v International Controls Corp. (1972, SD NY) 339 F. Supp. 341, 10 UCCRS 248, affd (1972, CA2 NY) 469 F.2d 696, 11 UCCRS 936

Under peculiar New York provision, the seller is relieved of any duty to mitigate damages by resale in the market prior to suing for the purchase price of tendered or delivered securities; there is not even the need for evidence that there is no available market or that efforts at resale would be unduly burdensome; the seller of securities is given the alternative of holding the rejected securities and recovering the purchase price. Bache & Co. v International Controls Corp. (1972, SD NY) 339 F. Supp. 341, 10 UCCRS 248, affd (1972, CA2 NY) 469 F.2d 696, 11 UCCRS 936 (applying New York law)

Where defendant unjustifiably terminates firm commitment underwriting agreement under "market out" claus, constituting breach of agreement, plaintiff is entitled to recover agreed price of securities under CLS UCC § 8-107(2). Walk-In Medical Centers, Inc. v Breuer Capital Corp. (1986, SD NY) 651 F. Supp. 1009, affd (1987, CA2 NY) 818 F.2d 260, 3 UCCRS2d 1885, later proceeding (1991, DC Colo) 778 F. Supp. 1116 and (criticized in Nycal Corp. v Inoco PLC (1997, SD NY) 988 F. Supp. 296)

9. Under former § 8-202

Payment under junior debentures need not be made where title to securities recited that it was "Convertible Subordinated Debenture" with further specific caveat of subordination to senior indebtedness, as set forth in indenture, and where senior debentures were in default. Kurtz v American Export Industries, Inc. (1975, 1st Dept) 49 A.D.2d 557, 370 N.Y.S.2d 599, affd (1976) 39 N.Y.2d 738, 384 N.Y.S.2d 774, 349 N.E.2d 874 and motion to dismiss app den (1976) 39 N.Y.2d 739, 384 N.Y.S.2d 774, 349 N.E.2d 875

10. Under former § 8-204

Court properly granted summary judgment to plaintiff brokerage house in action to recover for losses allegedly incurred in connection with sale of stock which was rejected for clearance by securities clearing house to which stock had been sent for re-registration by defendant (issuing corporation's transfer agent), where stock, which had initially been issued to issuing corporation's director and officer pursuant to "private placement" exemption authorized by Securities Act of 1933, bore no markings on certificates to alert subsequent transferees that they were unregistered and had been distributed in private placement; under CLS UCC § 8-204, restriction on transfer of security imposed by issuer, even though lawful, is ineffective against any person without actual knowledge thereof unless security is certificated and restriction is noted conspicuously thereon. Dean Witter Reynolds, Inc. v Selectronics, Inc. (1993, 1st Dept) 188 A.D.2d 117, CCH Fed Secur L Rep P 97757, 19 UCCRS2d 1156

Pledgee of stock is among persons protected generally by CLS UCC § 8-204 against restriction on transfer not conspicuously noted on security. Dean Witter Reynolds, Inc. v Selectronics, Inc. (1993, 1st Dept) 188 A.D.2d 117, CCH Fed Secur L Rep P 97757, 19 UCCRS2d 1156

Cooperative corporation's lien (for obligations other than maintenance) on unsold shares retained by sponsor, which had been pledged to lender to secure loan, was enforceable and had priority, even though security agreement provided that sponsor gave lender first and prior security interest "in and to all of [sponsor's] right, title and interest" in shares, and shares had been foreclosed upon and sold at auction by lender, where lien was stated both in bylaws of corporation and by endorsement on shares; shares of stock in corporation constituted "securities" within meaning of CLS UCC Art 8, and legend on shares gave sufficient notice under CLS UCC §§ 8-103 and

8-204 of corporation's lien and right to restrict transfer of shares based on provisions of bylaws and proprietary lease. ALH Properties Ten v 306-100th St. Owners Corp. (1993, 1st Dept) 191 A.D.2d 1, 600 N.Y.S.2d 443, 22 UCCRS2d 870, later proceeding (1993, N.Y. A.D., 1st Dept) 1993 N.Y. A.D. LEXIS 8889, app dismd without op (1994) 82 N.Y.2d 920, 610 N.Y.S.2d 154, 632 N.E.2d 464 and app gr (1995) 85 N.Y.2d 806, 627 N.Y.S.2d 322, 650 N.E.2d 1324 and mod, affd (1995) 86 N.Y.2d 643, 635 N.Y.S.2d 161, 658 N.E.2d 1034, 28 UCCRS2d 358

Legend on shares of stock of cooperative corporation, which stated generally that rights of "any holder" of shares were subject to provisions of corporation's bylaws, specifically set out that corporation could refuse to transfer shares until any indebtedness of shareholder to corporation was paid, and further stated that corporation had first lien on shares pursuant to bylaws and proprietary lease, gave sufficient notice under CLS UCC §§ 8 -103 and 8-204 of corporation's first lien and right to refuse transfer of shares based on provisions of both bylaws and proprietary lease. ALH Properties Ten v 306-100th St. Owners Corp. (1993, 1st Dept) 191 A.D.2d 1, 600 N.Y.S.2d 443, 22 UCCRS2d 870, later proceeding (1993, N.Y. A.D., 1st Dept) 1993 N.Y. A.D. LEXIS 8889, app dismd without op (1994) 82 N.Y.2d 920, 610 N.Y.S.2d 154, 632 N.E.2d 464 and app gr (1995) 85 N.Y.2d 806, 627 N.Y.S.2d 322, 650 N.E.2d 1324 and mod, affd (1995) 86 N.Y.2d 643, 635 N.Y.S.2d 161, 658 N.E.2d 1034, 28 UCCRS2d 358

A restriction contained in a certificate of incorporation requiring that the shares of stock, before being sold to anyone, be first offered for sale proportionally to the other holders of shares of stock in the corporation, is a valid and reasonable restriction binding the stockholders (Uniform Commercial Code, § 8-204) and therefore takes precedence and controls over the provisions in testator's will directing the executor to offer 25 percent of his shares for sale to a nonstockholder. A provision according the corporation a right or first option to purchase the stock is valid and enforceable provided the restraint on alienation of stock effectuates a lawful purpose and is in accord with public policy. In re Estate of Hatfield (1978) 93 Misc. 2d 472, 403 N.Y.S.2d 172, 24 UCCRS 210

A transferee is not bound by an unknown restriction which does not appear on the stock certificate. First Nat'l City Bank v Donbar Development Corp. (1968, N.Y. Sup App T) 4 UCCRS 1070

Fact that warrants to purchase stock failed to mention that warrants and underlying stock were subject to S.E.C. restriction on transfer, or that corporate issuer of warrants had no obligation to provide holders of warrants with unrestricted common stock, raised ambiguity as to terms of warrant contract that could not be resolved without reference to extrinsic evidence given general assumption that securities are free of adverse claims; thus, issuer was not entitled to summary judgment on holders' breach of contract claim, and matter would be remanded for receipt of extrinsic proof. Brass v American Film Technologies, Inc. (1993, CA2 NY) 987 F.2d 142, 19 UCCRS2d 1148

Corporate issuer of stock had no opportunity to legend its stock certificates, and thus had no responsibility under CLS UCC § 8-204 to notify investor who was holding warrants to purchase stock that S.E.C. had imposed transfer restrictions on warrants and underlying stock, where investor and his associates never exercised their stock purchase rights under warrants and never received any stock certificates. Brass v American Film Technologies, Inc. (1993, CA2 NY) 987 F.2d 142, 19 UCCRS2d 1148

Corporate issuer of warrants to purchase stock was not required, under CLS UCC § 8-204, to note on warrant certificate that S.E.C. rule imposed transfer restrictions on warrants and underlying stock since § 8-204 does not require that disclosure of transfer restrictions which must appear on face of one security must also appear on face of another security which purchaser might acquire; rather, statute applies only to restricted security actually acquired by purchaser. Brass v American Film Technologies, Inc. (1993, CA2 NY) 987 F.2d 142, 19 UCCRS2d 1148

Failure of corporate issuer of stock to disclose mandated restrictions of S.E.C. regarding transfer of warrants and underlying stock did not, as matter of law, subject issuer to suit for conversion where issuer had no obligation under CLS UCC § 8-204 to legend either warrants or stock certificates with such restriction. Brass v American Film Technologies, Inc. (1993, CA2 NY) 987 F.2d 142, 19 UCCRS2d 1148

Issuer of stock is not required by CLS UCC § 8-204 to include notice regarding limitations on transfer, where buyer purchased warrants that had originally been part of a private placement and

were not freely transferable, which buyer found out only when he sought to obtain original warrant document; consequently, buyer has no right to possess warrants covering unrestricted securities and suit for conversion against seller is insufficient as a matter of law. Brass v American Film Technologies, Inc. (1991, SD NY) 780 F. Supp. 1001, CCH Fed Secur L Rep ¶ 96531, reaffirmed, on reconsideration, complaint dismd (1992, SD NY) 1992 US Dist LEXIS 2375, remanded (1993, CA2 NY) 987 F.2d 142, 19 UCCRS2d 1148

11. Under former § 8-207

Since under UCC § 8-207, issuer of stock is permitted to treat registered owner as person exclusively entitled to vote, to receive notifications and otherwise to exercise all the rights and powers of an owner until the stock or other certificate is duly presented for registration of transfer, the transfer of record ownership of stock not only is necessary to effectuate or render complete the transfer of title to the stock but actually passes the "legal title" to the stock, making a stock transfer tax payable. Monarch Life Ins. Co. v State Tax Com. (1972, 3d Dept) 39 A.D.2d 31, 331 N.Y.S.2d 71, app gr (1972) 31 N.Y.2d 642 and affd (1973) 32 N.Y.2d 850, 346 N.Y.S.2d 272, 299 N.E.2d 684

12. Under former § 8-301

The Uniform Commercial Code furnishes useful analogies in determining the liability of a stock broker for the conversion of shares through selling stolen shares on the order of a thief. Hartford Acci. & Indem. Co. v Walston & Co. (1967) 21 N.Y.2d 219, 287 N.Y.S.2d 58, 234 N.E.2d 230, 5 UCCRS 205, reh gr (1968) 21 N.Y.2d 1041 and adhered to (1968) 22 N.Y.2d 672, 291 N.Y.S.2d 366, 238 N.E.2d 754

13. – "Bona fide purchaser"

Under UCC § 8-301(2), a bona-fide purchaser of securities acquires the rights possessed by his transferor and the securities themselves free of any adverse claim. *ERROR*Colonial Secur., Inc. v Merrill Lynch, Pierce, Fenner & Smith, Inc. (1978, SD NY) 461 F. Supp. 1159 (applying New York law)

14. – Not bona fide purchaser

Security interest of clearing broker in underwriter's warrant that entitled its holder to purchase certain securities was subject to equitable claims of shareholders of defunct securities dealer to whom warrant was issued (and who subsequently transferred warrant to clearing broker as security for loan before going out of business) where (1) prior to clearing broker's perfection of its security interest, dealer had promised to transfer portions of warrant to shareholders, and (2) clearing broker did not qualify as bona fide purchaser because it had actual notice of such adverse claims of shareholders at time of perfection. Pentech Int'l, Inc. v Wall Street Clearing Co. (1993, CA2 NY) 983 F.2d 441, 19 UCCRS2d 853

In action by liquidators of Bahamian bank against New York bank for either damages for conversion of Florida bank stock owned by Bahamian bank or imposition of constructive trust on such stock or its proceeds, where plaintiffs alleged (1) that officers of Bahamian bank had converted stock in suit to their own use, (2) that stock was later purchased by defendant New York bank as pledgee in purchase-money loan transaction, (3) that New York bank had had both actual and constructive notice of Bahamian bank's claim to stock at time New York bank purchased it, and (4) that in any case, New York bank had purchased stock under circumstances that showed bad faith, district court held (1) that Bahamian bank was beneficial owner of stock at time its officers appropriated it for their own use, (2) that conduct of officers of Bahamian bank constituted conversion under either New York law or law of Bahamas, (3) that officers of Florida bank, who had purchased stock in suit from officers of Bahamian bank and transferred it to defendant New York bank, had had notice of Bahamian bank's adverse claim to such stock and were not bona-fide purchasers under UCC § 8-302, (4) that defendant New York bank, which as pledgee was purchaser of such stock, was not bona-fide purchaser because its actions in taking stock in disregard of suspicious circumstances amounted to bad faith under New York UCC § 8-304(3) (not part of Official UCC), (5) that since New York bank was not bona-fide purchaser of such stock, it acquired under UCC § 8-301(1) only rights that its transferors and their transferors had possessed in stock and thus was liable to plaintiff liquidators of Bahamian bank for return of stock or appropriate damages therefor, (6) that although UCC § 8-301(1) provides that on delivery of security, purchaser acquires rights therein that his transferor had, such statute does not provide that purchaser assumes transferor's obligations or liabilities, (7) that therefore, even if transferors of stock to New York bank had been converters themselves, it did not follow under UCC § 8-301(1) that by accepting pledge of such stock from its

UCC

transferors, New York bank also became converter, so as to be liable in damages for conversion, (8) that constructive trust theory of damages was more appropriate remedy, (9) that constructive trust should be imposed on stock's proceeds in favor of plaintiff liquidators of Bahamian bank, and (10) that in lieu of imposition of constructive trust on stock's proceeds, plaintiffs were entitled to damages equal to value of such proceeds. Garner v First Nat'l City Bank (1979, SD NY) 465 F. Supp. 372(applying Fla and N.Y. UCC)

15. – "Holder in due course"

A holder in due course of a negotiable instrument acquires good title even though the paper was stolen and transferred by a thief. Hartford Acci. & Indem. Co. v Walston & Co. (1967) 21 N.Y.2d 219, 287 N.Y.S.2d 58, 234 N.E.2d 230, 5 UCCRS 205, reh gr (1968) 21 N.Y.2d 1041 and adhered to (1968) 22 N.Y.2d 672, 291 N.Y.S.2d 366, 238 N.E.2d 754

16. – Rights acquired by purchaser

Bank, who was pledgee of stock acquired by pledgors from corporate official converting same from corporation, acquires only right of its pledgor-transferor under UCC § 8-301 and does not have rights as bona fide purchaser under UCC § 8-303 since it had notice of adverse claim under UCC § 8-304 in that it willfully disregarded suspicious circumstances surrounding transfers of such stock. Garner v First Nat'l City Bank (1979, SD NY) 465 F. Supp. 372

17. – Liability for conversion

Stockbroker who purchased stolen treasury notes from bank which sold notes on behalf of bank's customer, was purchaser in good faith under UCC §§ 8-301 and 8-304 and, thus, was not liable for conversion of notes, notwithstanding transmittal slips from bank to broker stated that transactions were for account of named person, where broker bought notes without knowledge of any suspicious circumstances from bank with whom it had been dealing over the years. United States Fidelity & Guaranty Co. v Royal Nat'l Bank (1976, CA2 NY) 545 F.2d 1330, 20 UCCRS 726(applying New York law)

While bank-pledgee of stock has no greater rights in investment security than its pledgor-transferor had, UCC § 8-301 does not provide that purchaser assume obligations or liabilities of transferor and therefore, bank did not become converter upon acceptance of pledge and is not liable on basis of conversion measure of damages. Garner v First Nat'l City Bank (1979, SD NY) 465 F. Supp. 372

18. – Practice and procedure

Broker attempting to take advantage of bona fide purchaser protection of UCC § 8-301 must demonstrate compliance with "know your customer" rule (NYSE Rule 405). Cumis Ins. Soc., Inc. v E. F. Hutton & Co. (1978, SD NY) 457 F. Supp. 1380, CCH Fed Secur L Rep P 96576

19. Under former § 8-302

"Adverse claim" within meaning of CLS UCC § 8-302(1) is not limited to adverse ownership interest but may include any transfer with knowledge of violation of agreement. Fallon v Wall St. Clearing Co. (1992, 1st Dept) 182 A.D.2d 245, 586 N.Y.S.2d 953, 18 UCCRS2d 565, 21 UCCRS2d 79

The Code replaces the Uniform Stock Transfer Act in defining what constitutes value for the purpose of the transfer of shares of stock. Fried v Margolis (1961, CA2 NY) 296 F.2d 670, revd on other grounds (1963) 372 US 633, 10 L Ed 2d 33, 83 S Ct 969, reh den (1963) 373 US 928, 10 L Ed 2d 427, 83 S Ct 1522

20. – "Bona fide purchaser"

In action to recover value of stock which plaintiff alleged was subject of gift agreement between himself and prior owner, summary judgment is proper in favor of individual defendants who purchased stock for value, in good faith, and without notice of adverse claim so as to be bona fide purchasers; however, summary judgment will be denied against corporate defendant who allegedly had imputed knowledge of plaintiff's claim when it took delivery of stock in that its agent, attorney and director of corporation, had knowledge of prior owner's obligation to plaintiff. Center v Hampton Affiliates, Inc. (1985) 66 N.Y.2d 782, 497 N.Y.S.2d 898, 488 N.E.2d 828, 42 UCCRS 287

In action by alleged donee of stock to recover its value, where defendant purchased stock from decedent without actual and constructive knowledge of plaintiff's claim, defendant (1) was bona-fide purchaser for value and in good-faith within meaning of UCC § 8-302(1), (2) acquired stock under UCC § 8-302(3) free of plaintiff's adverse claim, and (3) was not liable to plaintiff for stock's value as matter of law. Benjamin Center v Hampton Affiliates, Inc. (1984, 2d Dept) 106 A.D.2d 422, 482 N.Y.S.2d 514, mod (1985) 66 N.Y.2d 782, 497 N.Y.S.2d 898, 488 N.E.2d 828, 42 UCCRS 287

Where (1) municipal bond dealer, prior to filing against it of involuntary petition in bankruptcy, (a) sold certain bonds to customer, (b) sent customer's nominee confirmation tickets concerning such sale, and (c) sent properly completed confirmation and delivery tickets concerning sale to defendant municipal-bond clearing facility in order to effectuate delivery of bonds to dealer's customer, and where (2) defendant clearing facility physically allocated specific bond certificates corresponding to dealer's instructions and recorded explicitly identifying information on bonds' delivery forms (including certificate numbers and name of dealer's customer), activities of dealer and defendant clearing facility constituted sufficient identification, "by book entry or otherwise," of bonds sold to customer under UCC § 8-313(1)(c), and dealer, by virtue of its contractual relationship with clearing facility, was not required by UCC § 8-313(1)(c) to have actual physical possession of certificates. Matthysse v Securities Processing Services, Inc. (1977, SD NY) 444 F. Supp. 1009, 23 UCCRS 435 (applying New York law; holding that possession of customer's bonds by clearing facility was sufficient to satisfy broker's possession requirement under UCC § 8-313(1)(c), and that under UCC § 8-302, customer was bona-fide purchaser of bonds who took them free of clearing facility's adverse claim thereto) (disapproved as stated in In re Bevill, Bresler & Schulman Asset Management Corp. (1986, DC NJ) 67 BR 557, CCH Fed Secur L Rep P 92966)

Brokerage firm was bona-fide purchaser of securities where it (1) acquired them for value within meaning of UCC §§ 8-302 and 1-201(44)(b) by receiving them for account of customer and in partial satisfaction of preexisting claim, (2) acted honestly in fact in the transaction, thereby complying with good-faith requirement of UCC §§ 8-302 and 1-201(19), and (3) did not have notice of any adverse claim to securities. *ERROR*Colonial Secur., Inc. v Merrill Lynch, Pierce, Fenner & Smith, Inc. (1978, SD NY) 461 F. Supp. 1159 (applying New York law)

21. – – Value given

Brokerage firm which received stock for account of customer and promptly credited sales price to customer's account acquired stock in partial satisfaction of pre-existing claim (UCC § 1-201, subd 44(b)), and thus for value within meaning of UCC § 8-302. Colonial Secur., Inc. v Merrill Lynch, Pierce, Fenner & Smith, Inc. (1978, SD NY) 461 F. Supp. 1159

22. – – Not bona fide purchaser

Commercial factor, who took possession of bearer bond as security for noninterest-bearing loan, which had no certain date for repayment and was made to individual with whom lender had had no prior personal transactions, was not a bona fide purchaser for value as against true owner of bond, which had been stolen. Brown v Rosetti (1971) 66 Misc. 2d 239, 319 N.Y.S.2d 1001, 8 UCCRS 730

Security interest of clearing broker in underwriter's warrant that entitled its holder to purchase certain securities was subject to equitable claims of shareholders of defunct securities dealer to whom warrant was issued (and who subsequently transferred warrant to clearing broker as security for loan before going out of business) where (1) prior to clearing broker's perfection of its security interest, dealer had promised to transfer portions of warrant to shareholders, and (2) clearing broker did not qualify as bona fide purchaser because it had actual notice of such adverse claims of shareholders at time of perfection. Pentech Int'l, Inc. v Wall Street Clearing Co. (1993, CA2 NY) 983 F.2d 441, 19 UCCRS2d 853

In action by liquidators of Bahamian bank against New York bank for either damages for conversion of Florida bank stock owned by Bahamian bank or imposition of constructive trust on such stock or its proceeds, where plaintiffs alleged (1) that officers of Bahamian bank had converted stock in suit to their own use, (2) that stock was later purchased by defendant New York bank as pledgee in purchase-money loan transaction, (3) that New York bank had had both actual and constructive notice of Bahamian bank's claim to stock at time New York bank purchased it, and (4) that in any case, New York bank had purchased stock under circumstances that showed bad faith, district court held (1) that Bahamian bank was beneficial owner of stock at time its officers appropriated it for their own use, (2) that conduct of officers of Bahamian bank constituted conversion under either New York law or law of Bahamas, (3) that officers of Florida bank, who had purchased stock in suit from officers of Bahamian bank and transferred it to defendant New York bank, had had notice of Bahamian bank's adverse claim to such stock and were not bona-fide purchasers under UCC § 8-302, (4) that defendant New York bank, which as pledgee was purchaser of such stock, was not bona-fide purchaser because its actions in taking stock in disregard of suspicious circumstances amounted to bad faith under New York UCC § 8-304(3) (not part of Official UCC), (5) that since New York bank was not bona-fide purchaser of such stock, it acquired under UCC § 8-301(1) only rights that its transferors and their transferors had possessed in stock and thus was liable to plaintiff liquidators of Bahamian bank for return of stock or appropriate damages therefor, (6) that although UCC § 8-301(1) provides that on delivery of security, purchaser acquires rights therein that his transferor had, such statute does not provide that purchaser assumes transferor's obligations or liabilities, (7) that therefore, even if transferors of stock to New York bank had been converters themselves, it did not follow under UCC § 8-301(1) that by accepting pledge of such stock from its transferors, New York bank also became converter, so as to be liable in damages for conversion, (8) that constructive trust theory of damages was more appropriate remedy, (9) that constructive trust should be imposed on stock's proceeds in favor of plaintiff liquidators of Bahamian bank, and (10) that in lieu of imposition of constructive trust on stock's proceeds, plaintiffs were entitled to damages equal to value of such proceeds. Garner v First Nat'l City Bank (1979, SD NY) 465 F. Supp. 372(applying Fla and N.Y. UCC)

23. – – Notice of invalidity

In action to recover value of stock which plaintiff alleged was subject of gift agreement between himself and prior owner, summary judgment is proper in favor of individual defendants who purchased stock for value, in good faith, and without notice of adverse claim so as to be bona fide purchasers; however, summary judgment will be denied against corporate defendant who allegedly had imputed knowledge of plaintiff's claim when it took delivery of stock in that its agent, attorney and director of corporation, had knowledge of prior owner's obligation to plaintiff. Center v Hampton Affiliates, Inc. (1985) 66 N.Y.2d 782, 497 N.Y.S.2d 898, 488 N.E.2d 828, 42 UCCRS 287

24. Under former § 8-303

Bank, who was pledgee of stock acquired by pledgors from corporate official converting same from corporation, acquires only right of its pledgor-transferor under UCC § 8-301 and does not have rights as bona fide purchaser under UCC § 8-303 since it had notice of adverse claim under UCC § 8-304 in that it willfully disregarded suspicious circumstances surrounding transfers of such stock. Garner v First Nat'l City Bank (1979, SD NY) 465 F. Supp. 372

25. Under former § 8-304

A selling broker is recognized as a "purchaser" under this section. Hartford Acci. & Indem. Co. v Walston & Co. (1967) 21 N.Y.2d 219, 287 N.Y.S.2d 58, 234 N.E.2d 230, 5 UCCRS 205, reh gr (1968) 21 N.Y.2d 1041 and adhered to (1968) 22 N.Y.2d 672, 291 N.Y.S.2d 366, 238 N.E.2d 754

Bank was not entitled to protection of CLS Gen Bus § 359-s since, in receiving securities as pledges, bank did not act as "third person" but was party to transfer; by receiving securities as pledges, it became purchaser of stock. Maloney v Stone (1993, 4th Dept) 195 A.D.2d 1065, 601 N.Y.S.2d 731, 23 UCCRS2d 226, related proceeding (1993, 4th Dept) 195 A.D.2d 1068, 601 N.Y.S.2d 883

Failure of bank to investigate borrower or his right to negotiate stolen bearer bonds that bank accepted as collateral for loan did not constitute bad faith precluding bank from enjoying status of bona fide purchaser. Gutekunst v Continental Ins. Co. (1973, CA2 NY) 486 F.2d 194, 13 UCCRS 522 (applying New York law)

Stockbroker who purchased stolen treasury notes from bank which sold notes on behalf of bank's customer, was purchaser in good faith under UCC §§ 8-301 and 8-304 and, thus, was not liable for conversion of notes, notwithstanding transmittal slips from bank to broker stated that transactions were for account of named person, where broker bought notes without knowledge of any suspicious circumstances from bank with whom it had been dealing over the years. United States Fidelity & Guaranty Co. v Royal Nat'l Bank (1976, CA2 NY) 545 F.2d 1330, 20 UCCRS 726(applying New York law)

In action to determine priority of two competing claims to proceeds of sale of Government National Mortgage Association (GNMA) certificate, where (1) first claimant gave certificate to brokerage firm as security for first claimant's purchase from such firm of one million dollars' worth of GNMA securities, (2) in order to perfect its security interest in certificate, brokerage firm had first claimant transfer certificate from Texas bank to New York trust company, (3) at time of transfer, certificate was registered in first claimant's name, (4) also at such time, trust company was brokerage firm's clearing agent and lender with which brokerage firm maintained general collateral agreement to secure its indebtedness to trust company in security-

dealing transactions and to which it had granted security interest in, and powers of secured party over, all of its securities in trust company's possession, (5) after delivery of certificate to trust company, brokerage firm had first claimant execute federal detached-assignment form to make certificate negotiable, (6) in executing such form, first claimant deleted provision therein which permitted reregistration of certificate in brokerage firm's name, (7) thereafter, trust company, despite first claimant's deletion in detached-assignment form of provision permitting reregistration of certificate, had certificate reregistered to order of brokerage firm and placed resulting new certificate in brokerage firm's general dealer account, with result (a) that it became part of trust company's collateral for brokerage firm's indebtedness to it, and (b) payments of principal and interest were thereafter made to brokerage firm, rather than to first claimant, and (8) after brokerage firm became bankrupt, first claimant instituted suit to recover proceeds of certificate's sale by bankruptcy court, court held (1) that principal issue was whether trust company, as second claimant of certificate's proceeds, could sustain such claim on its alleged status as bona-fide purchaser of certificate, (2) that because operative transactions involved had occurred in New York and certificate was in New York when trust company's alleged security interest therein was perfected, trust company's status as bona-fide purchaser was governed, under UCC § 9-103(1)(b), by New York version of UCC Article 8, (3) that under New York UCC § 8-301(1), trust company would acquire, on delivery of certificate to it, only transferor's rights therein, (4) that under New York UCC § 8-301(2), if trust company were bona fide purchaser as defined in New York UCC § 8-302, it would acquire certificate free of any adverse claims thereto, (5) that deletion in federal detached-assignment form of provision permitting reregistration of certificate did not put trust company on notice of first claimant's adverse claim under New York UCC § 8-304(1)(a), since certificate could have been transferred without reregistration, (6) that trust company also was not put on notice of adverse claim under New York UCC § 8-304(1)(b), since that subsection applies only to securities in bearer form, (7) that fact that trust company knew that certificate was to be used to secure brokerage firm's obligation to trust company, standing alone, did not show that trust company, within meaning of New York UCC § 8-304(2), had been aware of nature of relationship between first claimant and brokerage firm, (8) that under New York UCC § 8-304(3)-which is not part of Official Uniform Commercial Code-purchaser of security, in order to have notice of adverse claim thereto, must have actual knowledge of such claim or actual knowledge of such facts that his taking such security amounts to bad faith, (9) that under circumstances of present case, trust company's disregard of suspicious circumstances, of which it had actual knowledge, caused its taking of certificate to be in bad faith under New York UCC § 8-304(3), and (10) that trust company's suspicions should have been aroused when (a) it requested brokerage firm to have first claimant execute federal detached-assignment form permitting reregistration of certificate in brokerage firm's name, and (b) it noticed deletion in such form of provision permitting reregistration. In re Legel Braswell Government Sec. Corp. (1983, CA11 Fla) 695 F.2d 506, 35 UCCRS 595 (applying New York law)

Purchasers of corporate stock acquire only rights of converters they purchased from under UCC § 8-304 where purchasers had notice of adverse claim upon reading newspaper article after which they arranged and attended press conference with converters. Garner v First Nat'l City Bank (1979, SD NY) 465 F. Supp. 372

Bank, who was pledgee of stock acquired by pledgors from corporate official converting same from corporation, acquires only right of its pledgor-transferor under UCC § 8-301 and does not have rights as bona fide purchaser under UCC § 8-303 since it had notice of adverse claim under UCC § 8-304 in that it willfully disregarded suspicious circumstances surrounding transfers of such stock. Garner v First Nat'l City Bank (1979, SD NY) 465 F. Supp. 372

In action by liquidators of Bahamian bank against New York bank for either damages for conversion of Florida bank stock owned by Bahamian bank or imposition of constructive trust on such stock or its proceeds, where plaintiffs alleged (1) that officers of Bahamian bank had converted stock in suit to their own use, (2) that stock was later purchased by defendant New York bank as pledgee in purchase-money loan transaction, (3) that New York bank had had both actual and constructive notice of Bahamian bank's claim to stock at time New York bank purchased it, and (4) that in any case, New York bank had purchased stock under circumstances that showed bad faith, district court held (1) that Bahamian bank was beneficial owner

UCC

of stock at time its officers appropriated it for their own use, (2) that conduct of officers of Bahamian bank constituted conversion under either New York law or law of Bahamas, (3) that officers of Florida bank, who had purchased stock in suit from officers of Bahamian bank and transferred it to defendant New York bank, had had notice of Bahamian bank's adverse claim to such stock and were not bonafide purchasers under UCC § 8-302, (4) that defendant New York bank, which as pledgee was purchaser of such stock, was not bonafide purchaser because its actions in taking stock in disregard of suspicious circumstances amounted to bad faith under New York UCC § 8-304(3) (not part of Official UCC), (5) that since New York bank was not bona-fide purchaser of such stock, it acquired under UCC § 8-301(1) only rights that its transferors and their transferors had possessed in stock and thus was liable to plaintiff liquidators of Bahamian bank for return of stock or appropriate damages therefor, (6) that although UCC § 8-301(1) provides that on delivery of security, purchaser acquires rights therein that his transferor had, such statute does not provide that purchaser assumes transferor's obligations or liabilities, (7) that therefore, even if transferors of stock to New York bank had been converters themselves, it did not follow under UCC § 8-301(1) that by accepting pledge of such stock from its transferors, New York bank also became converter, so as to be liable in damages for conversion, (8) that constructive trust theory of damages was more appropriate remedy, (9) that constructive trust should be imposed on stock's proceeds in favor of plaintiff liquidators of Bahamian bank, and (10) that in lieu of imposition of constructive trust on stock's proceeds, plaintiffs were entitled to damages equal to value of such proceeds. Garner v First Nat'l City Bank (1979, SD NY) 465 F. Supp. 372(applying Fla and N.Y. UCC)

Unsuccessful bidder in coporate merger contest which purchased $425,000 shares of target corporation's treasury stock for value, in good faith, and without notice of any adverse claim thereto was bona fide purchaser under UCC §§ 8-301 and 8-304 (see also UCC § 8-302) and, on tendering stock to successful bidder, was entitled to payment therefor. Buffalo Forge Co. v Ogden Corp. (1983, WD NY) 555 F. Supp. 892, CCH Fed Secur L Rep P 99079, affd (1983, CA2 NY) 717 F.2d 757, CCH Fed Secur L Rep P 99501, cert den (1983) 464 US 1018, 78 L Ed 2d 724, 104 S Ct 550, later proceeding (1984, WD NY) 595 F. Supp. 593 (applying New York law)

26. Under former § 8-309

When a stockbroker is sued by the true owner of shares for conversion when the broker received the shares from a thief and paid the proceeds of the sale to the thief or his confederate, it is no defense that the owner of the shares may have been negligent in handling them. Hartford Acci. & Indem. Co. v Walston & Co. (1967) 21 N.Y.2d 219, 287 N.Y.S.2d 58, 234 N.E.2d 230, 5 UCCRS 205, reh gr (1968) 21 N.Y.2d 1041 and adhered to (1968) 22 N.Y.2d 672, 291 N.Y.S.2d 366, 238 N.E.2d 754

In action for specific performance of oral agreement to divide stock ownership of closed corporation, complaint should not have been dismissed where shares of stock in closed corporation were "securities" within meaning of UCC § 8-309, statute of frauds concerning securities and where that statute should have been read in conformity with UCC §§ 2-106, 2-201 and 2-304 which provide that price can be payable in money or otherwise; therefore under UCC § 8-319, services could constitute consideration sufficient to support contract. Gross v Vogel (1981, 2d Dept) 81 A.D.2d 576, 437 N.Y.S.2d 431, 31 UCCRS 224

Held that under above statute title to unindorsed securities may be transferred by delivery. In re Ruszkowski's Estate (1965) 45 Misc. 2d 380, 256 N.Y.S.2d 983

A stock certificate properly endorsed and delivered as an absolute gift to the donee is "transferred," even though transfer was not made on books of issuing corporation prior to donor's death. In re Ruszkowski's Estate (1965) 45 Misc. 2d 380, 256 N.Y.S.2d 983

Although a transfer of stock requires delivery under UCC § 8-309, title may pass by constructive delivery. Thus, if the parties so intend, title to stock passes to the buyer by delivery to an escrow agent for ultimate delivery to the buyer on payment of the purchase price or part thereof. Stewart Becker, Ltd. v Horowitz (1978) 94 Misc. 2d 766, 405 N.Y.S.2d 571

27. Under former § 8-311

Bank was not entitled to protection of CLS Gen Bus § 359-s since, in receiving securities as pledges, bank did not act as "third person" but was party to transfer; by receiving securities as pledges, it became purchaser of stock. Maloney v Stone (1993, 4th Dept) 195

A.D.2d 1065, 601 N.Y.S.2d 731, 23 UCCRS2d 226, related proceeding (1993, 4th Dept) 195 A.D.2d 1068, 601 N.Y.S.2d 883

Stock certificates' true owner whose forged signature was guaranteed by stock brokerage firm was not one of those encompassed within protective language of signature guarantee provision of UCC. Lowes v Merrill Lynch, Pierce, Fenner & Smith, Inc. (1973) 74 Misc. 2d 875, 344 N.Y.S.2d 55, 12 UCCRS 1198

Under Code provision stating that delivery occurs when person acquires possession of securities, "possession" cannot pass where shares allegedly possessed are not even in existence. Kaufman v Diversified Industries, Inc. (1972, CA2 NY) 460 F.2d 1331, cert den (1972) 409 US 1038, 34 L Ed 2d 487, 93 S Ct 517 and on remand (1973, SD NY) 356 F. Supp. 827 (applying New York law)

28. Under former § 8-312

In action against company that issued stock to plaintiff's husband during his lifetime and company that guaranteed husband's signature on certificates transferring stock to his girlfriend after his death, court properly granted summary judgment to defendants, dismissing plaintiff's claim that signature guarantee and reliance thereon were improper and deprived her of ownership of stock after her husband's death, since plaintiff failed to show that she was "person taking or dealing with the security in reliance on the guarantee" within purview of CLS UCC § 8-312 or that she suffered any loss resulting from breach of warranties under statute, where stock certificates admittedly had been transferred back to her by her husband's girlfriend, and value of stock had appreciated significantly during time she was deprived of its ownership and control. Conroy v Ford Motor Co. (1989, 3d Dept) 147 A.D.2d 885, 538 N.Y.S.2d 110, 8 UCCRS2d 160

In suit by owners of stock certificate against issuer and two brokerage firms for conversion of certificate by improperly transferring and surrendering it to issuer under purported signatures of owners which were (1) unauthorized and (2) guaranteed by defendant brokers, issuer was entitled to amend cross-claim against brokers to assert claim under UCC § 8-312(3), based on brokers' signature guarantees, for indemnification for legal fees and expenses in defending action, since UCC § 8-312(3)-which provides that guarantor "is liable" for any loss resulting from breach of warranties created by his signature guarantee-is required by UCC § 1-106(1) to be liberally construed and under such construction, "is liable" takes on meaning of "indemnification." O'Neal v General Electric Co. (1983, Sup) 122 Misc. 2d 430, 470 N.Y.S.2d 67

Plaintiff's complaint did not allege knowledge or connivance on part of defendants in alleged scheme to defraud; in sections of complaint alleging conspiracy to defraud, plaintiff does not name these defendants; held, plaintiff fails to state claim within asserted knowledge exception to UCC § 8-312(3) rule that guarantee of signature on securities document inures only to those "taking or dealing with the security in reliance on the guarantee." Wood v Wood (1970, SD NY) 312 F. Supp. 762, 7 UCCRS 1348 (applying New York law)

29. Under former § 8-313

Where decedent's transfer of stock to his son was registerd on corporation's books and stock certificate was issued only in son's name, although decedent retained possession of certificate until his death, court held (1) that symbolic delivery of certificate to son had occurred because of stock's transfer of record on corporation's books, and (2) that similar delivery of gift of stock occurs under UCC §§ 8-313 and 8-320. In re Estate of Carroll (1984, 2d Dept) 100 A.D.2d 337, 474 N.Y.S.2d 340, app withdrawn (1984) 63 N.Y.2d 702

Under statute defining "possession", the meaning of the term would be strained by a holding that possession of certain shares of stock passed where the shares allegedly possessed are not even in existence. Kaufman v Diversified Industries, Inc. (1972, CA2 NY) 460 F.2d 1331, cert den (1972) 409 US 1038, 34 L Ed 2d 487, 93 S Ct 517 and on remand (1973, SD NY) 356 F. Supp. 827

Bonds were delivered to purchaser under UCC § 8-313(1)(c) and Official Comment 1, even though purchaser did not take possession thereof, where (1) broker sent confirmation of purchase to purchaser; (2) broker's clearing house, acting under broker's instructions, placed certificate representing bonds in envelope addressed to purchaser, thereby identifying bonds as purchaser's property; and (3) possession of bonds by broker's clearing house satisfied statutory requirement that bonds be "in broker's possession." Louisiana State School Lunch Employees Retirement System v Legel, Braswell Government Sec. Corp. (1983, CA11 Fla) 699 F.2d 512, CCH Bankr L Rptr P 69087, 35 UCCRS 737 (applying New York law)

Book entry regulations of Treasury Department (31 CFR § 306.118) do not displace state law as to provide exclusive method of "delivery" of securities; pre-requisites for "delivery" under subsection (c) are that broker send security's purchaser confirmation of sale, that securities are in broker's possession and that securities are identified as belonging to purchaser; in order to satisfy "possession" requirement, broker need not have actual possession when securities are held by broker's clearing agent. Wichita Federal Sav. & Loan Asso. v Comark (1985, SD NY) 610 F. Supp. 406, 40 UCCRS 612

Municipality may not accept pledge of proportionate interest in single pool of obligations as security for its investments or deposits; however, pursuant to Joint investment agreement, municipalities may make joint investments and have obligations pledged to the credit of a single participant if joint investment agreement contains provisions stating that participant holding collateral will reimburse other participants if investment should fail. 1985 Op St Compt No. 85-47

30. – Delivery to third person

Where decedent's transfer of stock to his son was registerd on corporation's books and stock certificate was issued only in son's name, although decedent retained possession of certificate until his death, court held (1) that symbolic delivery of certificate to son had occurred because of stock's transfer of record on corporation's books, and (2) that similar delivery of gift of stock occurs under UCC §§ 8-313 and 8-320. In re Estate of Carroll (1984, 2d Dept) 100 A.D.2d 337, 474 N.Y.S.2d 340, app withdrawn (1984) 63 N.Y.2d 702

31. – Effect of delivery

A determination by the Surrogate that decedent had given 43 shares of stock to his son by valid inter vivos gift would be affirmed, notwithstanding some evidence leading to a contrary result, where the evidence established that each year decedent signed a transfer of a specific number of shares to be transferred on the back of the certificates he held and that, in every instance, both decedent and the donee each separately signed the new certificates, all of which were left with an accountant for safekeeping, so that the requisite elements of a valid inter vivos gift were established. In re Estate of Cristo (1982, 3d Dept) 86 A.D.2d 700, 446 N.Y.S.2d 555

Plaintiff was not shareholder of defendant corporation where (1) corporation loaned money to plaintiff's uncle in 1963, (2) in 1983, uncle delivered his certificate for stock in corporation to plaintiff, indorsed in blank, (3) plaintiff delivered certificate to president of corporation, and (4) president and plaintiff's uncle agreed that return of stock to corporation was in exchange for release of uncle's debt; although plaintiff maintained that corporation knew that he possessed stock, there was nothing indicating that corporation was on notice that plaintiff sought to stake claim to stock. Lapidus v Hiltzik (1990, 2d Dept) 160 A.D.2d 682, 553 N.Y.S.2d 458

Where (1) municipal bond dealer, prior to filing against it of involuntary petition in bankruptcy, (a) sold certain bonds to customer, (b) sent customer's nominee confirmation tickets concerning such sale, and (c) sent properly completed confirmation and delivery tickets concerning sale to defendant municipal-bond clearing facility in order to effectuate delivery of bonds to dealer's customer, and where (2) defendant clearing facility physically allocated specific bond certificates corresponding to dealer's instructions and recorded explicitly identifying information on bonds' delivery forms (including certificate numbers and name of dealer's customer), activities of dealer and defendant clearing facility constituted sufficient identification, "by book entry or otherwise," of bonds sold to customer under UCC § 8-313(1)(c), and dealer, by virtue of its contractual relationship with clearing facility, was not required by UCC § 8-313(1)(c) to have actual physical possession of certificates. Matthysse v Securities Processing Services, Inc. (1977, SD NY) 444 F. Supp. 1009, 23 UCCRS 435 (applying New York law; holding that possession of customer's bonds by clearing facility was sufficient to satisfy broker's possession requirement under UCC § 8-313(1)(c), and that under UCC § 8-302, customer was bona-fide purchaser of bonds who took them free of clearing facility's adverse claim thereto)(disapproved as stated in In re Bevill, Bresler & Schulman Asset Management Corp. (1986, DC NJ) 67 BR 557, CCH Fed Secur L Rep P 92966)

32. – Purchase by broker

UCC § 8-313 continues to recognize rule that when a broker purchases stock on behalf of a customer, title to that stock immediately vests in the purchaser. Tangorra v Hagan Investing Corp. (1971, 4th Dept) 38 A.D.2d 671, 327 N.Y.S.2d 131, CCH Fed Secur L Rep P 93373

33. Under former § 8-315

Reclamation as provided by UCC § 8-315 is limited to self-same security wrongfully diverted; thus, corporation had no possible right to reclaim 2000 shares of telephone company stock where shares in question were not those which corporation had originally loaned to third party so that he could make capital contribution to securities brokerage firm, which shares were sold on open market, but were, instead, 2000 shares of telephone company stock which third party had converted from securities brokerage firm. Peerless Mills, Inc. v American Tel. & Tel. Co. (1975, CA2 NY) 527 F.2d 445, 18 UCCRS 195 (applying New York law)

UCC § 8-315 provides that if owner may assert ineffectiveness of unauthorized endorsement against purchaser, then owner may reclaim or obtain possession on security or new certificated security; in addition, owner may recover damages against purchaser provided that latter is not bona fide purchaser who takes delivery of certificated security for value, in good faith, and without notice of any claim that transfer is wrongful. Land of Lincoln Sav. & Loan v Parr Sec. Corp. (1985, SD NY) 610 F. Supp. 265

34. Under former § 8-317

Injunctive relief under CLS UCC § 8-317 would not be available to require debtors to transfer stock shares into New York so that they could be attached by New York sheriff where applicant for injunction did not yet have any money judgment and so was only mere claimant, not "creditor" under UCC, and where there was no indication that extra-state assets were going to be disposed of or that any award of money damages would be inadequate. Siy v McMicking (1986, Sup) 134 Misc. 2d 164, 510 N.Y.S.2d 407, 1 UCCRS2d 889

In action by Philippine citizens for fraud in connection with stock investment in realty development in Spain, in which action one codefendant counterclaimed for $6,500,000 allegedly due on promissory notes issued by plaintiffs to pay for stock investment in suit, court held (1) that plaintiff held extensive assets in various securities outside United States; and (2) that counterclaiming defendant could not successfully base request for preliminary mandatory injunction against plaintiffs, which would direct them to transfer securities owned by them outside jurisdiction of New York state to New York state for attachment by sheriff, on UCC § 8-317(6) because (a) UCC § 8-317(6) does not change or eliminate well-established requirements for injunctive relief under New York law, and (b) New York requirements for injunctive relief include likelihood of ultimate success, irreparable injury, no adequate remedy at law, and balancing of equities, which requirements preclude issuance of injunction at creditor's mere request to compel assets outside jurisdiction of New York court to be brought within court's jurisdiction for attachment. Siy v McMicking (1986, Sup) 134 Misc. 2d 164, 510 N.Y.S.2d 407, 1 UCCRS2d 889

A levy by attachment against shares of stock is proper where directed against a bank holding the shares as custodian for the trustee of a voting trust to which the shares had been transferred, even though the voting trust agreement had been terminated by the time of the attachment. Proteus Food & Industries, Inc. v Nippon Reizo Kabushiki Kaisha (1968, N.Y. Sup) 4 UCCRS 961

The intent of the statute, providing that no levy upon an outstanding security is valid until it is actually seized by the officer, was not to determine what levy would suffice to entitle a sheriff to poundage or to enforce a money judgment against a judgment debtor but was rather enacted to protect bona fide purchasers for value of property subject to a judgment creditor's lien by invalidating a levy as to such parties unless the sheriff has taken actual possession. Knapp v McFarland (1972, CA2 NY) 462 F.2d 935, 18 ALR Fed 555

Code § 8-317 providing that no levy upon outstanding security shall be valid until it is actually seized by officer was not enacted for purpose of determining what levy would suffice to entitle sheriff to poundage or to enforce money judgment against judgment debtor, but was intended to define rights of third parties claiming interest in attached personal property. Knapp v McFarland (1972, CA2 NY) 462 F.2d 935, 18 ALR Fed 555 (applying New York law)

35. Under former § 8-318

It would seem that a rule of the New York Stock Exchange requiring the broker to use due diligence to learn the essential facts relative to its customers formulates what are "reasonable commercial standards." Hartford Acci. & Indem. Co. v Walston & Co. (1967) 21 N.Y.2d 219, 287 N.Y.S.2d 58, 234 N.E.2d 230, 5 UCCRS 205, reh gr (1968) 21 N.Y.2d 1041 and adhered to (1968) 22 N.Y.2d 672, 291 N.Y.S.2d 366, 238 N.E.2d 754

UCC

The Uniform Commercial Code, which apparently modifies the law in this state somewhat in favor of the selling broker, provides that the test of good faith of selling broker includes "observance of regional commercial standards if he be in the business of buying, selling, or otherwise dealing with securities". Hartford Acci. & Indem. Co. v Walston & Co. (1967) 21 N.Y.S.2d 219, 287 N.Y.S.2d 58, 234 N.E.2d 230, 5 UCCRS 205, reh gr (1968) 21 N.Y.2d 1041 and adhered to (1968) 22 N.Y.2d 672, 291 N.Y.S.2d 366, 238 N.E.2d 754

Where record, in action against bank for conversion of United States treasury notes that had been stolen from plaintiff and deposited with defendant by one of its customers, did not conclusively show that bank was in business of buying, selling, or otherwise dealing with securities, so as to be subject under UCC § 8-318 to reasonable commercial standards of such business, summary judgment against bank would be reversed because whether its conduct had conformed to reasonable commercial standards of securities business presented issue of fact that was inappropriate for resolution on motion for summary judgment. Insurance Co. of North America v Manufacturers Hanover Trust Co. (1984, 1st Dept) 106 A.D.2d 285, 483 N.Y.S.2d 3

In conversion action against bank which sold stolen treasury notes on behalf of its customer, bank acted in good faith and observed reasonable commercial standards pursuant to UCC § 8-318 in selling notes where, inter alia, bank had prior dealings with customer, nothing was suspect about customer's credentials, withdrawal by customer of large amount of cash from checking account which paid no interest was reasonable, transactions were in progress for more than one month without bank receiving any report that notes were missing or stolen, inquiries by bank addressed to appropriate federal agencies did not reveal that any of the notes were stolen or missing, customer did not disappear when funds were placed in suspense account, customer made personal daily visits to bank, and customer retained counsel to press his claim. United States Fidelity & Guaranty Co. v Royal Nat'l Bank (1976, CA2 NY) 545 F.2d 1330, 20 UCCRS 726(applying New York law)

36. Under former § 8-319

In action by investor against an individual who was president, chairman, and major stockholder of corporation, for specific performance and breach of contract for transfer of stock, summary judgment was properly refused even if writing was insufficient under statute of frauds, UCC § 8-319(a) where services (recruitment of other investors) and cash investments constituted payment under UCC § 8-319(b) and where issue of whether plaintiff's conduct was inequivocably referable to oral contract remained to be resolved. Palmerton v Envirogas, Inc. (1981, 4th Dept) 80 A.D.2d 996, 437 N.Y.S.2d 483, 31 UCCRS 226

In action for specific performance of oral agreement to divide stock ownership of closed corporation, complaint should not have been dismissed where shares of stock in closed corporation were "securities" within meaning of UCC § 8-309, statute of frauds concerning securities and where that statute should have been read in conformity with UCC §§ 2-106, 2-201 and 2-304 which provide that price can be payable in money or otherwise; therefore under UCC § 8-319, services could constitute consideration sufficient to support contract. Gross v Vogel (1981, 2d Dept) 81 A.D.2d 576, 437 N.Y.S.2d 431, 31 UCCRS 224

37. – Scope; "sale of securities"

The contract for the sale of a security comes within the statute of frauds. Mortimer B. Burnside & Co. v Havener Sec. Corp. (1966, 1st Dept) 25 A.D.2d 373, 269 N.Y.S.2d 724, 3 UCCRS 496

Plaintiff's purchase of stock from a named individual at the request of defendant would serve as consideration for defendant's agreement to transfer common stock purchase warrants to the plaintiff; and the transaction between plaintiff and defendant constituted a "sale" within the meaning of the Uniform Commercial Code, which to be enforceable must be in writing. Mortimer B. Burnside & Co. v Havener Sec. Corp. (1966, 1st Dept) 25 A.D.2d 373, 269 N.Y.S.2d 724, 3 UCCRS 496

An employment contract exchanging services for shares of stock constitutes the sale of a security within the meaning of UCC § 8-319, which requires such agreements to be in writing. Gross v Vogel (1981, 2d Dept) 81 A.D.2d 576, 437 N.Y.S.2d 431, 31 UCCRS 224

Action to enforce alleged oral subscription agreements, and to compel issuance of shares of stock in 2 corporations, was not barred by statute of frauds where plaintiffs argued that they had fully paid for their shares, and triable issues of fact existed as to whether sums paid by them unequivocally referred to purchase of shares; mere fact

that plaintiffs were never formally issued stock certificates did not preclude finding that they had rights of shareholders. Serdaroglu v Serdaroglu (1994, 2d Dept) 209 A.D.2d 600, 621 N.Y.S.2d 806

A "call" is not a "security" within the definition of UCC § 8-102; thus, UCC § 8-319 is inapplicable to a call option. Cohn, Ivers & Co. v Gross (1968) 56 Misc. 2d 491, 289 N.Y.S.2d 301, 5 UCCRS 390

Stock certificates of corporation which had fewer than four stockholders and whose only substantial asset was structure housing two professional offices, were "securities" within meaning of UCC § 8-102(1)(a); thus, alleged oral agreement among stockholders of corporation which, in effect, conferred upon each of them first refusal rights if any other stockholder wished to sell his stock, was unenforceable under UCC § 8-319. Pantel v Becker (1977) 89 Misc. 2d 239, 391 N.Y.S.2d 325, 21 UCCRS 274

UCC Sec 8-319 does not apply as a defense to an action brought to impress a constructive trust because of the breach of a confidential relationship. Macaluso v Lord (1967, N.Y. Sup) 4 UCCRS 45

38. – – Agency relationship

Temporary bankrupt corporation president's admission as to validity of oral contract made during deposition is not binding on stock sellers within meaning of New York statute of frauds governing sale of securities, since evidence established that he was not acting as agent of stock sellers at time alleged oral contract to sell stock. United Acquisition Corp. v Banque Paribas (1985, SD NY) 631 F. Supp. 797

39. – – Employment contracts

Employment contract involving transfer of title to shares of stock for price is "sale of securities"; held, not enforceable unless there is signed writing stating price and quantity of described securities. Bingham v Wells, Rich, Greene, Inc. (1970, 1st Dept) 34 A.D.2d 924, 311 N.Y.S.2d 508, 7 UCCRS 1051

40. – Necessity of writing

In action by employee against employer for breach of oral contract to transfer stock, employer's motion to dismiss employee's cause of action on ground that it was barred by writing requirement of statute of frauds in UCC § 8-319(a) should have been granted, since employer's concession, for purposes of its motion to dismiss that facts asserted in employee's complaint were true was not, as employee contended, affirmative admission sufficient under UCC § 8-319(d) to escape writing requirement of UCC § 8-319(a), but was only employer's recognition of procedural context in which its motion to dismiss arose. Boylan v G. L. Morrow Co. (1984) 63 N.Y.2d 616, 479 N.Y.S.2d 499, 468 N.E.2d 681

Transaction that contemplated transfer of all stock in corporation, if it constituted contract for sale of securities within meaning of UCC § 8-319(a), might not require formally executed contract if there existed writing, signed by party against whom enforcement of such contract was sought, which was sufficient to indicate that contract had been made for sale of stated quantity of described securities at stated price. APS Food Systems, Inc. v Ward Foods, Inc. (1979, 1st Dept) 70 A.D.2d 483, 421 N.Y.S.2d 223, 27 UCCRS 1381

Action to recover damages for breach of contract is barred by Statute of Frauds set forth in UCC 8-319(a), as alleged oral agreement involved exchange of plaintiff's services for defendant's shares of stock, and plaintiff's alleged performance does not fall under "payment" exception of UCC 8-319(b) to writing requirement since alleged performance was clearly not "unequivocally referable" to alleged oral agreement. Newman v Crazy Eddie, Inc. (1986, 2d Dept) 119 A.D.2d 738, 501 N.Y.S.2d 398, 1 UCCRS2d 1617

Restaurant employee's oral contract to purchase interest in restaurant was unenforceable as incapable of being performed within one year of its making where employee, under agreement, was not to be entitled to purchase interest, if at all, until completion of renovations and one full year of operations. LaJaunie v DaGrossa (1990, 1st Dept) 159 A.D.2d 349, 552 N.Y.S.2d 628

Action for accounting with regard to purported oral agreement between plaintiffs (as preparers of bid proposal for newsstands at railroad stations) and individual defendants (owner-operators of such newsstands), in which plaintiffs sought 50 percent of shares of stock in corporate defendant, was barred by statute of frauds set forth in CLS UCC 8-319, where plaintiffs submitted no writing to evidence alleged agreement. Himani v Mojawalla (1996, 2d Dept) 232 A.D.2d 455, 649 N.Y.S.2d 157, 33 UCCRS2d 889

Defendants were entitled to dismissal of cause of action for breach of agreement to tender shares of newly merged company where there were no written memoranda memorializing that agreement, which thus violated CLS UCC § 8-319, and plaintiffs' assertions were belied by language of plaintiff's resignation from company, which stated that he was not owed any "money, compensation or stock" in connection with merged companies. Allen v Bergleitner (1998, 3d Dept) 255 A.D.2d 668, 679 N.Y.S.2d 458

District court in tax fraud case correctly refused to give defendant's proposed instruction that clearing broker, as principal, could ratify acts of second broker, as agent, either by sending back securities order confirmations to agent, by failing to object to transactions after principal received confirmations from agent, or by any other conduct, such as recording transactions as if they were done, indicating intention to be bound by transactions, since (1) under CLS UCC § 8-319(A), acts of agent in contracting for purchase of securities would not be valid absent writing, and (2) agent's acts that are not valid unless performed pursuant to writing can only be ratified in writing. United States v Manko (1992, CA2 NY) 979 F.2d 900, cert den (1993) 509 US 903, 125 L Ed 2d 687, 113 S Ct 2993, post-conviction relief den (1995, SD NY) 1995 US Dist LEXIS 11953, vacated, remanded (1996, CA2 NY) 87 F.3d 50, 44 Fed Rules Evid Serv 929, 78 AFTR 2d 5135 and subsequent civil proceeding (1995, SD NY) 897 F. Supp. 1507, RICO Bus Disp Guide (CCH) P 8888, motion gr, in part sub nom United States v Manko (1997, SD NY) 1997 US Dist LEXIS 2578, post-conviction relief den, certif gr (1998, SD NY) 1998 US Dist LEXIS 10521, motion gr (1998, SD NY) 1998 US Dist LEXIS 18289 and related proceeding (1993, ED NY) 840 F. Supp. 198, RICO Bus Disp Guide (CCH) P 8642

Oral assurances by corporation that it would repurchase common stock held by plaintiffs on their resignation or retirement from corporation was unenforceable under statute of frauds governing contracts for sale of securities set forth in UCC § 8-319(a). Fischer v C. J. Lawrence & Co. (1979, SD NY) 481 F. Supp. 357 (apparently applying New York law)

41. – – Modification of written contract

The doctrine is well-established in New York that even where a contract provides that there shall be no waiver or amendment not evidenced by a writing, the prohibition of oral waiver may itself be waived and estoppel to assert the statute of frauds may be founded upon an oral agreement made after the execution of the principal agreement. Neonex International, Ltd. v Norris Grain Co. (1972, SD NY) 338 F. Supp. 845

42. – Sufficiency of writing

Alleged contract for sale of securities was not enforceable under UCC § 8-319(a) where it consisted of letter in which plaintiff agreed to sell back securities previously acquired from defendant at a future time and for a certain price and defendant, instead of being required to do anything at all under the alleged contract, was merely granted right to request return of such securities at specified price on one day's notice. Chase Manhattan Bank, N. A. v Mehlman (1977, 1st Dept) 59 A.D.2d 694, 398 N.Y.S.2d 686, affd (1978) 46 N.Y.2d 802, 413 N.Y.S.2d 922, 386 N.E.2d 833

A contract for the sale of securities, within the purview of section 8-319 of the Uniform Commercial Code, does not require a formally executed contract if there exists some writing signed by the party against whom enforcement is sought which is sufficient to indicate that a contract has been made for the sale of a stated quantity of described securities at a defined or stated price. APS Food Systems, Inc. v Ward Foods, Inc. (1979, 1st Dept) 70 A.D.2d 483, 421 N.Y.S.2d 223, 27 UCCRS 1381

Alleged oral shareholders' agreement violated securities statute of frauds in CLS UCC § 8-319 where underlying letter agreement did not give plaintiffs enforceable rights as claimed, because it failed to state quantity and price of shares to which plaintiffs claimed to be entitled. Baytree Assocs. v Forster (1997, 1st Dept) 240 A.D.2d 305, 659 N.Y.S.2d 19, 35 UCCRS2d 992, app den (1997) 90 N.Y.2d 810, 665 N.Y.S.2d 401, 688 N.E.2d 257

In action for, inter alia, breach of contract to transfer equity interest in defendant corporation in exchange for extinguishment of corporation's debt to plaintiffs, writing relied on by plaintiffs did not satisfy CLS UCC § 8-319(a) where that writing expressly contemplated execution of formal stock purchase and shareholder agreements, it lacked mechanism for ascertaining manner of governance and other material terms customarily included in such formal agreements, and thus it amounted to unenforceable agreement to agree. Steinberg v DiGeronimo (1998, 1st Dept) 255 A.D.2d 204, 680 N.Y.S.2d 93

In action by Netherlands corporation and individual who owned controlling interest in its parent company against multinational conglomerate, arising from plaintiffs' unsuccessful effort to purchase defendant's European photocopier business, enforceable contract existed under UCC § 2-204 where both parties had agreed upon essential terms and intended to be bound by final drafts, where none of terms that remained open were such, taken separately or together, as to prevent agreement from taking effect, where indefiniteness of purchase price was insignificant in light of formula provided for its determination, and where alleged need for approval by defendant's board of directors was without significance given involvement of board in agreements that had been reached; requirement of statute of frauds, UCC §§ 1-206, 2-201, and 8-319, was satisfied by final drafts, telexes to general managers of copier subsidiaries, and other letters and documents where memorandum required by statute of frauds need not be incorporated in single document that may be derived from several documents, and where signed and unsigned writings may be read together provided they refer to same matter or transaction; moreover, under UCC §§ 1-203, 2-305, defendant had duty to give effect to agreement which had been made and breached duty of good faith negotiation and performance by "bailing out" of what it came to see as a bad deal; however, plaintiffs could not recover for anticipatory breach of contract where they failed to demonstrate that they possessed ability to perform contract and come up with cash at closing since plaintiffs did not tender certified check for amount as calculated, and informal bank commitment letter did not establish their ability to close; accordingly, plaintiffs were not entitled to full expectation damages but were entitled to profits earned by business from date defendant obligated itself to run business for purchaser's account to date defendant repudiated agreement. Reprosystem, B. V. v SCM Corp. (1981, SD NY) 522 F. Supp. 1257, CCH Fed Secur L Rep P 98207 (disapproved by Golden v Garafalo (1982, CA2 NY) 678 F.2d 1139, CCH Fed Secur L Rep P 98656) and supp op (1982, SD NY) 565 F. Supp. 4, affd in part and revd in part (1984, CA2 NY) 727 F.2d 257, CCH Fed Secur L Rep P 99667, cert den (1984) 469 US 828, 83 L Ed 2d 54, 105 S Ct 110, later proceeding (1986, SD NY) 630 F. Supp. 1099

43. – – Tape recordings

Oral agreement between two shareholders of close corporation for sale of corporate stock was unenforceable under statute-of-frauds provisions of General Obligation Law and UCC § 8-319(a) because tape recording that set forth terms of such agreement did not constitute "writing" that would render agreement enforceable. Roos v Aloi (1985, Sup) 127 Misc. 2d 864, 487 N.Y.S.2d 637, 41 UCCRS 971

44. – Signature

Alleged oral agreement for option to purchase stock was unenforceable against alleged offeror not only because such agreement failed to comply with requirements that contract for sale of securities be in writing and be signed by person against whom it is sought to be enforced (UCC § 8-319), but also because plaintiff failed to meet burden of proving that defendant's board of directors had ever considered the option, as required by Business Corporation Law § 505(a). Scarpinato v National Patent Development Corp. (1973) 75 Misc. 2d 94, 347 N.Y.S.2d 623

Writing which indicated that share of security firm shareholder in certain underwriter's warrant issued to firm was 1.0 percent rather than 0.5 percent did not satisfy statute of frauds where both firm and its principal shareholder/officer were parties to contract with shareholder, and principal shareholder/officer signed only on line for his signature as agent for firm, not on line as officer. Pentech Int'l, Inc. v Wall Street Clearing Co. (1993, CA2 NY) 983 F.2d 441, 19 UCCRS2d 853

45. – Part performance

In action for specific performance of oral contract for sale of securities, court held that triable issue of fact existed as to whether plaintiff's payment to defendant of $11,000 constituted part performance that was clearly referable to alleged oral agreement and sufficient to remove it from statute of frauds in UCC § 8-319(b); and that if alleged oral agreement were established, plaintiff's recovery under UCC § 8-319(b) would be limited to extent of payment actually made by him. Ballan v Waterman (1984, 2d Dept) 103 A.D.2d 789, 477 N.Y.S.2d 432, app dismd (1985) 64 N.Y.2d 773, 485 N.Y.S.2d 990, 475 N.E.2d 457 and app dismd without op (1985) 64 N.Y.2d 604

Cause of action alleging oral stock purchase agreement was properly dismissed as barred by statute of frauds where there were no issues of fact warranting possible application of doctrines of promissory estoppel and partial performance; assuming that plaintiff was promised equity interest in exchange for his services on defendant's behalf, he suffered no unconscionable injury as evidenced by substantial weekly compensation he received, nor were his services "unequivocally referable" to alleged promise, as evidenced by his admission that no money had ever been applied toward purchase of equity interest. Coleman v CMI Transp. (1995, 1st Dept) 222 A.D.2d 285, 635 N.Y.S.2d 212, 30 UCCRS2d 1188

Plaintiffs' preparation of bid proposal for newsstands at railroad stations did not "unequivocally refer" to alleged oral agreement so as to excuse absence of writing under performance exception to statute of frauds, and thus defendants (owner-operators of such newsstands) were entitled to summary judgment in plaintiffs' action for accounting in which plaintiffs sought 50 percent of shares of stock in corporate defendant; while alleged oral agreement might "give significance" to plaintiffs' actions, actions were not "unintelligible or at least extraordinary" or explainable only with reference to oral agreement. Himani v Mojawalla (1996, 2d Dept) 232 A.D.2d 455, 649 N.Y.S.2d 157, 33 UCCRS2d 889

Delivery of 12,500 shares of stock to defendants in December, 1960, in exchange for $45,000 could not be said to have been unequivocally referable to contract alleged by plaintiff in his original complaint to have been made in February, 1961, whereby defendants allegedly obtained from plaintiff 12,500 shares of sports arena stock for which they agreed to pay $180,000 six years later, such that there was part performance of alleged contract sufficient to remove it from operation of UCC § 8-319. Konigsberg v Security Nat'l Bank (1975, SD NY) 66 FRD 439 (applying New York law)

46. – Confirmation in writing; letters

Doctor departing professional corporations is entitled only to $55,300 in full satisfaction of all claims made against corporations, despite his reliance on statutes of fraud at CLS Gen Oblig Law § 5-701(a)(1) and UCC § 8-319(a), where doctor endorsed and deposited February 1988 check, in conjunction with explicit letter and payment schedule outlining agreement discussed at prior meeting, as well as subsequent checks issued in accordance with outlined schedule, because signed checks and correspondence including letter-when pieced together-satisfy statutes of fraud. Lande v Radiology Specialists of Kingston P.C. (1992, SD NY) 806 F. Supp. 1084, 20 UCCRS2d 585

47. – – Objection within reasonable time

Since selling broker's confirmation can meet statute of frauds requirement if purchaser does not send written objections within 10 days after receipt under UCC § 8-319(c), time of delivery of confirmation is logical time for delivery of prospectus as required by Section 5(b)(1) of Securities Act of 1933. Byrnes v Faulkner, Dawkins & Sullivan (1977, CA2 NY) 550 F.2d 1303

48. – Judicial admissions

Because of Code provision that agreement within statute of frauds could still be enforced if party against whom enforcement is sought were to admit in his pleading, testimony or otherwise in court that agreement had been made, defendant on ground of statute of frauds before answer is served. Weiss v Wolin (1969) 60 Misc. 2d 750, 303 N.Y.S.2d 940, 6 UCCRS 1097

Document prepared by officer of defunct securities dealer, as well as officer's deposition identifying document and admitting contractual basis for dealer's obligation to its shareholders who claimed portions of underwriter's warrant that entitled its holder to purchase certain securities, constituted admission for purposes of CLS UCC § 8-319(d) in interpleader action brought by issuer of warrant, and thus shareholders established their right to warrant superior to claim of dealer's creditor (which had perfected security interest in warrant) even though majority of shareholders could not produce written shareholder agreement signed by dealer. Pentech Int'l, Inc. v Wall Street Clearing Co. (1993, CA2 NY) 983 F.2d 441, 19 UCCRS2d 853

49. – Practice and procedure

In action by employee against employer for breach of oral contract to transfer stock, employer's motion to dismiss employee's cause of action on ground that it was barred by writing requirement of statute of frauds in UCC § 8-319(a) should have been granted, since employer's concession, for purposes of its motion to dismiss that facts asserted in employee's complaint were true was not, as employee contended, affirmative admission sufficient under UCC § 8-319(d) to escape writing requirement of UCC § 8-319(a), but was only employer's recognition of procedural context in which its motion to dismiss arose. Boylan v G. L. Morrow Co. (1984) 63 N.Y.2d 616, 479 N.Y.S.2d 499, 468 N.E.2d 681

In action alleging that defendants fraudulently induced plaintiff to settle claims arising under 1982 partnership agreement, which involved mortgage lending venture, for substantially less than value of his partnership interest, defendants' motion to dismiss complaint on ground that plaintiff's underlying claims were totally valueless and unenforceable under UCC § 8-319 (which requires contracts for

sale of securities to be in writing) should have been denied as premature, where assertions in plaintiff's surreply papers suggested certain factual grounds that might defeat statute of frauds defense. Held v Kaufman (1998) 91 N.Y.2d 425, 671 N.Y.S.2d 429, 694 N.E.2d 430, subsequent app (1999, 2d Dept) 261 A.D.2d 509, 690 N.Y.S.2d 612

In an action to enforce an alleged option to purchase stock at a prescribed price, defendant's motion to dismiss the complaint was denied where defendant had failed to plead to the complaint and failed to deny the option agreement. It was held that summary judgment would not be granted where an issue was found to exist because facts which were wholly within the knowledge of the moving parties might be disclosed by cross-examination or pretrial examination. Weiss v Wolin (1969) 60 Misc. 2d 750, 303 N.Y.S.2d 940, 6 UCCRS 1097

50. Under former § 8-320

Where decedent's transfer of stock to his son was registerd on corporation's books and stock certificate was issued only in son's name, although decedent retained possession of certificate until his death, court held (1) that symbolic delivery of certificate to son had occurred because of stock's transfer of record on corporation's books, and (2) that similar delivery of gift of stock occurs under UCC §§ 8-313 and 8-320. In re Estate of Carroll (1984, 2d Dept) 100 A.D.2d 337, 474 N.Y.S.2d 340, app withdrawn (1984) 63 N.Y.2d 702

51. Under former § 8-404

Reasonable notice was given by 94-year-old lady to issuer of stock that stock had been stolen, so that issuer was obligated under UCC § 8-405(1) to issue new stock certificate to replace that which had been stolen; under applicable law, lady could not take cash in lieu of issuance of her shares of stock under UCC § 8-404. Weller v American Tel. & Tel. Co. (1972, Del Ch Ct) 290 A2d 842, 10 UCCRS 1221 (applying New York law)

In action against stock transfer agent for erroneously reissuing, in SEC Rule 144 sale transaction, plaintiff's stock in street name of plaintiff's broker rather than plaintiff's name, where (1) plaintiff, who wished to sell 6,571 shares of unregistered common stock in specified corporation, approached his broker to arrange for such sale pursuant to SEC Rule 144 and signed a "Form 144" and an "assignment separate from certificate," (2) broker without plaintiff's knowledge imprinted its own name in unfilled space for name of assignee of such assignment, (3) broker then mailed plaintiff's stock certificates and "assignment separate from certificate" to defendant transfer agent, together with cover letter requesting that agent reissue new, unlegended certificates in plaintiff's name, (4) transfer agent thereupon reissued single, unlegended certificate in name of plaintiff's broker instead of plaintiff, (5) broker subsequently became bankrupt, and (6) plaintiff failed to recover 1,344 of such shares because of their being commingled with other securities of broker that were held in its street name, court held that under UCC § 8-406(1)(b), providing that liability of stock transfer agent is same as that of issuer, and UCC § 8-404(1)(b), providing that issuer is not liable to owner who suffers loss as result of registration of transfer of security if issuer was under no duty to inquire into "adverse claims," defendant transfer agent was not liable for negligence or breach of fiduciary obligation to plaintiff because broker's cover letter to defendant, requesting reissuance of the stock in plaintiff's name, was not an "adverse claim" by the plaintiff or notice of an adverse claim to such stock, and the transfer transaction posed no apparent threat to plaintiff's ownership interest therein. Cohen v Bankers Trust Co. (1978, SD NY) 445 F. Supp. 794, CCH Fed Secur L Rep P 96300, 23 UCCRS 459 (applying Delaware and New York law; also holding that fact that stock was being freed for sale under SEC Rule 144 did not alter defendant's obligations to plaintiff)

52. Under former § 8-405

Where corporations wrongfully transferred stock upon forged signatures of the plaintiff trustee, in November of 1962, and notice of the illegal transfers reached the plaintiff trustee in July of 1963, § 8-405 of the Uniform Commercial Code would not be applied prospectively to bar the plaintiff trustee's cause of actions against the corporations by estopping her from asserting the ineffectiveness of the forged indorsement. Scovenna v American Tel. & Tel. Co. (1967) 54 Misc. 2d 74, 281 N.Y.S.2d 854, 4 UCCRS 329

Reasonable notice was given by 94-year-old lady to issuer of stock that stock had been stolen, so that issuer was obligated under UCC § 8-405(1) to issue new stock certificate to replace that which had been stolen; under applicable law, lady could not elect to take cash in lieu of issuance of her shares of stock under UCC § 8-404. Weller v

American Tel. & Tel. Co. (1972, Del Ch Ct) 290 A2d 842, 10 UCCRS 1221 (applying New York law)

53. Under former § 8-406

In action against stock transfer agent for erroneously reissuing, in SEC Rule 144 sale transaction, plaintiff's stock in street name of plaintiff's broker rather than plaintiff's name, where (1) plaintiff, who wished to sell 6,571 shares of unregistered common stock in specified corporation, approached his broker to arrange for such sale pursuant to SEC Rule 144 and signed a "form 144" and an "assignment separate from certificate," (2) broker without plaintiff's knowledge imprinted its own name in unfilled space for name of assignee of such assignment, (3) broker then mailed plaintiff's stock certificates and "assignment separate from certificate" to defendant transfer agent, together with cover letter requesting that agent reissue new, unlegended certificates in plaintiff's name, (4) transfer agent thereupon reissued single, unlegended certificate in name of plaintiff's broker instead of plaintiff, (5) broker subsequently became bankrupt, and (6) plaintiff failed to recover 1,344 of such shares because of their being commingled with other securities of broker that were held in its street name, court held that under UCC § 8-406(1)(b), providing that liability of stock transfer agent is same as that of issuer, and UCC § 8-404(1)(b), providing that issuer is not liable to owner who suffers loss as result of registration of transfer of security if issuer was under no duty to inquire into "adverse claims," defendant transfer agent was not liable for negligence or breach of fiduciary obligation to plaintiff because broker's cover letter to defendant, requesting reissuance of the stock in plaintiff's name, was not an "adverse claim" by the plaintiff or notice of an adverse claim to such stock, and the transfer transaction posed no apparent threat to plaintiff's ownership interest therein. Cohen v Bankers Trust Co. (1978, SD NY) 445 F. Supp. 794, CCH Fed Secur L Rep P 96300, 23 UCCRS 459 (applying Delaware and New York law; also holding that fact that stock was being freed for sale under SEC Rule 144 did not alter defendant's obligations to plaintiff)

PART 1
SHORT TITLE AND GENERAL MATTERS

History: Add, L 1997, ch 566, § 5, eff Oct 10, 1997.

Former Part 1, add, L 1962, ch 553; repealed, L 1997, ch 566, § 5, eff Oct 10, 1997.

§ 8-101.   Short Title

This Article may be cited as Uniform Commercial Code-Investment Securities.

History: Add, L 1997, ch 566, § 5, eff Oct 10, 1997.

Former § 8-101, add, L 1962, ch 553; repealed, L 1997, ch 566, § 5, eff Oct 10, 1997.

§ 8-102.   Definitions

(a) In this Article:

(1) "Adverse claim" means a claim that a claimant has a property interest in a financial asset and that it is a violation of the rights of the claimant for another person to hold, transfer, or deal with the financial asset.

(2) "Bearer form", as applied to a certificated security, means a form in which the security is payable to the bearer of the security certificate according to its terms but not by reason of an indorsement.

(3) "Broker" means a person defined as a broker or dealer under the federal securities laws, but without excluding a bank acting in that capacity.

(4) "Certificated security" means a security that is represented by a certificate.

(5) "Clearing corporation" means:

(i) a person that is registered as a "clearing agency" pursuant to 15 United States Code § 78-c(a)(23), as from time to time amended;

(ii) a federal reserve bank; or

(iii) any other person that provides clearance or settlement services with respect to financial assets that would require it to register as a clearing agency under the federal securities laws but for an exclusion or exemption from the registration requirement, if its activities as a clearing corporation, including promulgation of rules, are subject to regulation by a federal or state governmental authority.

(6) "Communicate" means to:

(i) send a signed writing; or

(ii) transmit information by any mechanism agreed upon by the persons transmitting and receiving the information.

(7) "Entitlement holder" means a person identified in the records of a securities intermediary as the person having a security entitlement against the securities intermediary. If a person acquires a security entitlement by virtue of Section 8-501(b)(2) or (3), that person is the entitlement holder.

(8) "Entitlement order" means a notification communicated to a securities intermediary directing transfer or redemption of a financial asset to which the entitlement holder has a security entitlement.

(9) "Financial asset", except as otherwise provided in Section 8-103, means:

(i) a security;

(ii) an obligation of a person or a share, participation, or other interest in a person or in property or an enterprise of a person, which is, or is of a type, dealt in or traded on financial markets, or which is recognized in any area in which it is issued or dealt in as a medium for investment; or

(iii) any property that is held by a securities intermediary for another person in a securities account if the securities intermediary has expressly agreed with the other person that the property is to be treated as a financial asset under this Article. As context requires, the term means either the interest itself or the means by which a person's claim to it is evidenced, including a certificated or uncertificated security, a security certificate, or a security entitlement.

(10) "Good faith", for purposes of the obligation of good faith in the performance or enforcement of contracts or duties within this Article, means honesty in fact and the observance of reasonable commercial standards of fair dealing.

(11) "Indorsement" means a signature that alone or accompanied by other words is made on a security certificate in registered form or on a separate document for the purpose of assigning, transferring, or redeeming the security or granting a power to assign, transfer, or redeem it.

(12) "Instruction" means a notification communicated to the issuer of an uncertificated security which directs that the transfer of the security be registered or that the security be redeemed.

(13) "Registered form", as applied to a certificated security, means a form in which:

(i) the security certificate specifies a person entitled to the security; and

(ii) a transfer of the security may be registered upon books maintained for that purpose by or on behalf of the issuer, or the security certificate so states.

(14) "Securities intermediary" means:

(i) a clearing corporation; or

(ii) a person, including a bank or broker, that in the ordinary course of its business maintains securities accounts for others and is acting in that capacity.

(15) "Security", except as otherwise provided in Section 8-103, means an obligation of an issuer or a share, participation, or other interest in an issuer or in property or an enterprise of an issuer:

(i) which is represented by a security certificate in bearer or registered form, or the transfer of which may be registered upon books maintained for that purpose by or on behalf of the issuer;

(ii) which is one of a class or series or by its terms is divisible into a class or series of shares, participations, interests, or obligations; and

(iii) which:

(A) is, or is of a type, dealt in or traded on securities exchanges or securities markets; or

(B) is a medium for investment and by its terms expressly provides that it is a security governed by this Article.

(16) "Security certificate" means a certificate representing a security.

(17) "Security entitlement" means the rights and property interest of an entitlement holder with respect to a financial asset specified in Part 5.

(18) "Uncertificated security" means a security that is not represented by a certificate.

(b) Other definitions applying to this Article and the sections in which they appear are:

"Appropriate person".	Section 8-107.
"Control".	Section 8-106.
"Delivery".	Section 8-301.
"Investment company security".	Section 8-103.
"Issuer".	Section 8-201.
"Overissue".	Section 8-210.
"Protected purchaser".	Section 8-303.
"Securities account".	Section 8-501.

(c) In addition, Article 1 contains general definitions and principles of construction and interpretation applicable throughout this Article.

(d) The characterization of a person, business, or transaction for purposes of this Article does not determine the characterization of the person, business, or transaction for purposes of any other law, regulation, or rule.

(e) The following definitions in Article 9 apply to this article:

Cooperative interest	Section 9-102(a)(27-b)
Cooperative organization	Section 9-102(a)(27-c)
Cooperative record	Section 9-102(a)(27-e)

History: Add, L 1997, ch 566, § 5, eff Oct 10, 1997.

Former § 8-102, add, L 1962, ch 553; amd, L 1963, ch 1003, § 17, L 1972, ch 416, L 1982, ch 18, § 1, L 1982, ch 928, § 3, L 1992, ch 450, § 1; repealed, L 1997, ch 566, § 5, eff Oct 10, 1997.

Sub (e), add, L 2001, ch 84, § 22, eff July 1, 2001.

CASE ANNOTATIONS

Securities intermediary obtained control over the depositor's security pursuant to N.Y. U.C.C. Law § 8-106(b), as the security was delivered by the depositor with the appropriate stock power and corporate resolution, and under N.Y. U.C.C. Law § 8-102(11), the depositor indorsed the security be delivering an irrevocable stock power wherein the depositor signed, assigned, and transferred the shares to the intermediary's clearing agent; the intermediary was not required by N.Y. U.C.C. Law § 8-303 to show that its control of the stock certificate was current. Dabbah Secs. Corp. v Croesus Capital Corp. (2002, A.D., 1st Dept) 747 N.Y.S.2d 82

Although defendant was granted a security interest in debtor's shares of a company, he never perfected his interest in the uncertificated shares by filing a UCC financing statement with the New York Department of State or by control over the investment property. As defendant only had an unperfected lien on debtor's shares, a Chapter 7 trustee, armed with the status of a hypothetical lien creditor, took debtor's 50 percent ownership in the company free of defendant's unperfected lien. Thaler v GJ & JF Realty Holdings, Inc. (In re Jaghab), 584 B.R. 472, 95 U.C.C. Rep. Serv. 2d (CBC) 826, 2018 Bankr. LEXIS 1151 (Bankr. E.D.N.Y. 2018).

§ 8-103. Rules for Determining Whether Certain Obligations and Interests are Securities or Financial Assets

(a) A share or similar equity interest issued by a corporation, business trust, joint stock company, or similar entity is a security.

(b) An "investment company security" is a security. "Investment company security" means a share or similar equity interest issued by an entity that is registered as an investment company under the federal investment company laws, an interest in a unit investment trust that is so registered, or a face-amount certificate issued by a face-amount certificate company that is so registered. Investment company security does not include an insurance policy or endowment policy or annuity contract issued by an insurance company.

(c) An interest in a partnership or limited liability company is not a security unless it is dealt in or traded on securities exchanges or in securities markets, its terms expressly provide that it is a security governed by this Article, or it is an investment company security. However, an interest in a partnership or limited liability company is a financial asset if it is held in a securities account.

(d) A writing that is a security certificate is governed by this Article and not by Article 3, even though it also meets the requirements of that Article. However, a negotiable instrument governed by Article 3 is a financial asset if it is held in a securities account.

(e) An option or similar obligation issued by a clearing corporation to its participants is not a security, but is a financial asset.

(f) A commodity contract, as defined in Section 9-102(a)(15), is not a security or a financial asset.

(g) A document of title is not a financial asset unless Section 8-102(a)(9)(iii) applies.

(h) An obligation, share, participation, or interest does not satisfy Section 8-102(a)(13)(ii) or 8-102(a)(15)(i) merely because the issuer or a person acting on its behalf:

(1) maintains records of the owner thereof for a purpose other than registration of transfer; or

(2) could, but does not, maintain books for the purpose of registra-tion of transfer.

History: Add, L 1997, ch 566, § 5, eff Oct 10, 1997; amd, L 2001, ch 84, § 23, eff July 1, 2001; L 2014, ch 505, § 24, eff Dec 17, 2014.

§ 8-104. Acquisition of Security or Financial Asset or Interest Therein

(a) A person acquires a security or an interest therein, under this Article, if:

(1) the person is a purchaser to whom a security is delivered pursuant to Section 8-301; or

(2) the person acquires a security entitlement to the security pursuant to Section 8-501.

(b) A person acquires a financial asset, other than a security, or an interest therein, under this Article, if the person acquires a security entitlement to the financial asset.

(c) A person who acquires a security entitlement to a security or other financial asset has the rights specified in Part 5, but is a purchaser of any security, security entitlement, or other financial asset held by

the securities intermediary only to the extent provided in Section 8-503.

(d) Unless the context shows that a different meaning is intended, a person who is required by other law, regulation, rule, or agreement to transfer, deliver, present, surrender, exchange, or otherwise put in the possession of another person a security or financial asset satisfies that requirement by causing the other person to acquire an interest in the security or financial asset pursuant to subsection (a) or (b).

History: Add, L 1997, ch 566, § 5, eff Oct 10, 1997.

Former § 8-104, add, L 1962, ch 553; amd, L 1982, ch 928, § 4; repealed, L 1997, ch 566, § 5, eff Oct 10, 1997.

§ 8-105. Notice of Adverse Claim

(a) A person has notice of an adverse claim if:

(1) the person knows of the adverse claim;

(2) the person is aware of facts sufficient to indicate that there is a significant probability that the adverse claim exists and deliberately avoids information that would establish the existence of the adverse claim; or

(3) the person has a duty, imposed by statute or regulation, to investigate whether an adverse claim exists, and the investigation so required would establish the existence of the adverse claim.

(b) Having knowledge that a financial asset or interest therein is or has been transferred by a representative imposes no duty of inquiry into the rightfulness of a transaction and is not notice of an adverse claim. However, a person who knows that a representative has transferred a financial asset or interest therein in a transaction that is, or whose proceeds are being used, for the individual benefit of the representative or otherwise in breach of duty has notice of an adverse claim.

(c) An act or event that creates a right to immediate performance of the principal obligation represented by a security certificate or sets a date on or after which the certificate is to be presented or surrendered for redemption or exchange does not itself constitute notice of an adverse claim except in the case of a transfer more than:

(1) one year after a date set for presentment or surrender for redemption or exchange; or

(2) six months after a date set for payment of money against presentation or surrender of the certificate, if money was available for payment on that date.

(d) A purchaser of a certificated security has notice of an adverse claim if the security certificate:

(1) whether in bearer or registered form, has been indorsed "for collection" or "for surrender" or for some other purpose not involving transfer; or

(2) is in bearer form and has on it an unambiguous statement that it is the property of a person other than the transferor, but the mere writing of a name on the certificate is not such a statement.

UCC

(e) Except as provided in section 9-516(e), filing of a financing statement under Article 9 is not notice of an adverse claim to a financial asset.

History: Add, L 1997, ch 566, § 5, eff Oct 10, 1997.

Former § 8-105, add, L 1982, ch 928, § 5; repealed, L 1997, ch 566, § 5, eff Oct 10, 1997.

Another § 8-105, add, L 1962, ch 553; amd, L 1964, ch 476, § 1; repealed, L 1982, ch 928, § 5, eff Dec 21, 1982.

Sub (e), amd, L 2001, ch 84, § 24, eff July 1, 2001.

CASE ANNOTATIONS

Order denying a turnover petition relating to accounts which were collateral for a line of credit was proper because the bank did not have notice of adverse claims pursuant to N.Y. U.C.C. Law § 8-105(a)(2); when the bank agreed to the line of credit, the funds had been on deposit for about 10 months, and no subpoena had been issued with respect to a limited liability company. The evidence in the record also supported the conclusion of the trial court that any notice to the corporation of an adverse claim could not have been imputed to the bank with respect to the collateral in issue as the clients of the corporation were not also clients of the bank. Matter of Scher Law Firm, LLP v DB Partners I, LLC (2012, App Div, 2d Dept) 948 NYS2d 335

Correspondence relating to the confiscation of certain shares in a corporation's margin account at a bank was insufficient to demonstrate that the bank had actual knowledge of third-party ownership of shares in the margin account; notice of third-party ownership was not sufficient to constitute notice of an adverse claim because there also had to be notice that a security was transferred in violation of the claimant's property interest-a condition that was absent. SEC v Credit Bancorp, Ltd. (2003, SD NY) 279 F. Supp. 2d 247, motion gr (2003, SD NY) 2003 US Dist LEXIS 20024

While two letters, together, were sufficient to raise suspicions that an adverse claim existed as to certain shares in a corporation's margin account at a bank, there was no evidence that the relevant bank officials, including the broker who opened the corporation's account, saw one of the letters or that the bank acted deliberately to preclude or inhibit the transmission of that letter to the broker. Although it was more likely than not that the broker received both of the letters, no evidence was provided for this speculation. SEC v Credit Bancorp, Ltd. (2003, SD NY) 279 F. Supp. 2d 247, motion gr (2003, SD NY) 2003 US Dist LEXIS 20024

While a letter was sufficient to raise suspicions that an adverse claim existed as to certain shares in a corporation's margin account at a bank, there was no evidence that the relevant bank officials, including the broker who opened the corporation's account, saw the letter or that the bank acted deliberately to preclude or inhibit transmission of that letter to the broker. SEC v Credit Bancorp, Ltd. (2003, SD NY) 279 F. Supp. 2d 247, motion gr (2003, SD NY) 2003 US Dist LEXIS 20024

Broker, who opened a corporation's margin account at a bank, and therefore the bank, were on notice of an adverse claim by a third-party corporation to the third-party corporation's shares in the corporation's margin account from the time that the broker failed to seek confirmation of oral assurances by an official of the corporation that there was nothing to worry about regarding the third-party corporation's shares; by not undertaking sufficient inquiries, the broker put the bank on notice of an adverse claim to all securities after the official and the broker spoke. Because the loans extended by the bank to the corporation after it was on notice of an adverse claim were rendered unsecured by that notice, the bank's request for leave to sell certain shares was denied, except to the extent that the shares were sold to cover loans extended before the bank was put on notice of an adverse claim. SEC v Credit Bancorp, Ltd. (2003, SD NY) 279 F. Supp. 2d 247, motion gr (2003, SD NY) 2003 US Dist LEXIS 20024

While receipt by a bank official responsible for a corporation's margin account of the credit facility agreements which the corporation had been using to defraud investors would have amounted to extremely strong evidence of an adverse claim to the securities in the margin account, no one responsible for the corporation's margin account ever saw the credit facility agreements; therefore, receipt of the credit facility agreements by the bank did not contribute to putting the bank on notice of an adverse claim. SEC v Credit Bancorp, Ltd. (2003, SD NY) 279 F. Supp. 2d 247, motion gr (2003, SD NY) 2003 US Dist LEXIS 20024

§ 8-106.   Control

(a) A purchaser has "control" of a certificated security in bearer form if the certificated security is delivered to the purchaser.

(b) A purchaser has "control" of a certificated security in registered form if the certificated security is delivered to the purchaser, and:

(1) the certificate is indorsed to the purchaser or in blank by an effective indorsement; or

(2) the certificate is registered in the name of the purchaser, upon original issue or registration of transfer by the issuer.

(c) A purchaser has "control" of an uncertificated security if:

(1) the uncertificated security is delivered to the purchaser; or

(2) the issuer has agreed that it will comply with instructions originated by the purchaser without further consent by the registered owner.

(d) A purchaser has "control" of a security entitlement if:

(1) the purchaser becomes the entitlement holder;

(2) the securities intermediary has agreed that it will comply with entitlement orders originated by the purchaser without further consent by the entitlement holder; or

(3) another person has control of the security entitlement on behalf of the purchaser or, having previously acquired control of the security entitlement, acknowledges that it has control on behalf of the purchaser.

(e) If an interest in a security entitlement is granted by the entitlement holder to the entitlement holder's own securitie intermediary, the securities intermediary has control.

(f) A purchaser who has satisfied the requirements of subsection (c) or (d) has control even if the registered owner in the case of subsection (c) or the entitlement holder in the case of subsection (d) retains the right to make substitutions for the uncertificated security or security entitlement, to originate instructions or entitlement orders to the issuer or securities intermediary, or otherwise to deal with the uncertificated security or security entitlement.

(g) An issuer or a securities intermediary may not enter into an agreement of the kind described in subsection (c)(2) or (d)(2) without the consent of the registered owner or entitlement holder, but an issuer or a securities intermediary is not required to enter into such an agreement even though the registered owner or entitlement holder so directs. An issuer or securities intermediary that has entered into such an agreement is not required to confirm the existence of the agreement to another party unless requested to do so by the registered owner or entitlement holder.

(h) Under subsection (c)(2) or (d)(2), authentication of a record does not impose upon the issuer or securities intermediary any duty not expressly agreed to by the issuer or securities intermediary in the record.

(i) A purchaser has "control" under subsection (c)(2) or (d)(2) even if any duty of the issuer or the securities intermediary to comply with instructions or entitlement orders originated by the purchaser is subject to any condition or conditions (other than further consent by the registered owner or the entitlement holder).

History: Add, L 1997, ch 566, § 5, eff Oct 10, 1997; amd, L 1962, ch 553; L 1982, ch 928, § 5, eff Dec 21, 1982; L 2001, ch 84, §§ 25, 26, eff July 1, 2001; L 2014, ch 505, § 25, eff Dec 17, 2014.

CASE ANNOTATIONS

Securities intermediary was a protected purchaser under N.Y. U.C.C. Law § 8-303, where the intermediary gave value to the depositor by receiving the certificate and crediting the depositor with ownership of the shares in accordance with N.Y. U.C.C. Law § 8-116, the intermediary had no notice of the restrictions on the certificate imposed by an agreement between the depositor and a third party, and the intermediary had obtained control over the security pursuant to N.Y. U.C.C. Law § 8-106(b). Dabbah Secs. Corp. v Croesus Capital Corp. (2002, A.D., 1st Dept) 747 N.Y.S.2d 82

Securities intermediary obtained control over the depositor's security pursuant to N.Y. U.C.C. Law § 8-106(b), as the security was delivered by the depositor with the appropriate stock power and corporate resolution, and under N.Y. U.C.C. Law § 8-102(11), the depositor indorsed the security be delivering an irrevocable stock power wherein the depositor signed, assigned, and transferred the shares to the intermediary's clearing agent; the intermediary was not required by N.Y. U.C.C. Law § 8-303 to show that its control of the stock certificate was current. Dabbah Secs. Corp. v Croesus Capital Corp. (2002, A.D., 1st Dept) 747 N.Y.S.2d 82

§ 8-107. Whether Indorsement, Instruction, or Entitlement Order is Effective

(a) "Appropriate person" means:

(1) with respect to an indorsement, the person specified by a security certificate or by an effective special indorsement to be entitled to the security;

(2) with respect to an instruction, the registered owner of an uncertificated security;

(3) with respect to an entitlement order, the entitlement holder;

(4) if the person designated in paragraph (1), (2), or (3) is deceased, the designated person's successor taking under other law or the designated person's personal representative acting for the estate of the decedent; or

(5) if the person designated in paragraph (1), (2), or (3) lacks capacity, the designated person's guardian, conservator, or other similar representative who has power under other law to transfer the security or financial asset.

(b) An indorsement, instruction, or entitlement order is effective if:

(1) it is made by the appropriate person;

(2) it is made by a person who has power under the law of agency to transfer the security or financial asset on behalf of the appropriate person, including, in the case of an instruction or entitlement order, a person who has control under Section 8-106(c)(2) or (d)(2); or

(3) the appropriate person has ratified it or is otherwise precluded from asserting its ineffectiveness.

(c) An indorsement, instruction, or entitlement order made by a representative is effective even if:

(1) the representative has failed to comply with a controlling instrument or with the law of the State having jurisdiction of the representative relationship, including any law requiring the representative to obtain court approval of the transaction; or

(2) the representative's action in making the indorsement, instruction, or entitlement order or using the proceeds of the transaction is otherwise a breach of duty.

(d) If a security is registered in the name of or specially indorsed to a person described as a representative, or if a securities account is maintained in the name of a person described as a representative, an indorsement, instruction, or entitlement order made by the person is effective even though the person is no longer serving in the described capacity.

(e) Effectiveness of an indorsement, instruction, or entitlement order is determined as of the date the indorsement, instruction, or entitlement order is made, and an indorsement, instruction, or entitlement order does not become ineffective by reason of any later change of circumstances.

History: Add, L 1997, ch 566, § 5, eff Oct 10, 1997.

Former § 8-107, add, L 1962, ch 553; amd, L 1964, ch 476, § 5, L 1982, ch 928, § 6; repealed, L 1997, ch 566, § 5, eff Oct 10, 1997.

CASE ANNOTATIONS

Because a decedent's last will and testament did not give an indorser authority to transfer certain stock certificates, the indorser was clearly not an appropriate person to request a medallion signature guaranty from a bank under N.Y. U.C.C. Law § 8-107; thus, the bank was entitled to summary judgment in its action to recoup funds paid in settlement under N.Y. U.C.C. Law § 8-306(h). Victory State Bank v Vidringstad (2009, Sup) 24 Misc 3d 878, 241 NYLJ 67, 885 NYS2d 161.

Because the term "capacity" in N.Y. U.C.C. Law § 8-107(a)(5) referred both to legal and mental capacity, the issue of whether a decedent lacked mental capacity at the time the decedent endorsed the transfer of certain shares of stock was an issue to be decided by a trier of fact; accordingly, the trial court properly denied the motions for summary judgment filed by a guarantor and the issuers. Kirshtein v Americu Credit Union (2009, App Div, 4th Dept) 882 NYS2d 610.

If a person lacks mental capacity, but has not been adjudicated an incompetent person, and does not have a designated guardian, conservator, or other similar representative, then the person nevertheless is not an appropriate person to make an indorsement and the indorsement is therefore not effective. Kirshtein v Americu Credit Union (2009, App Div, 4th Dept) 882 NYS2d 610.

§ 8-108. Warranties in Direct Holding

(a) A person who transfers a certificated security to a purchaser for value warrants to the purchaser,

UCC

and an indorser, if the transfer is by indorsement, warrants to any subsequent purchaser, that:

(1) the certificate is genuine and has not been materially altered;

(2) the transferor or indorser does not know of any fact that might impair the validity of the security;

(3) there is no adverse claim to the security;

(4) the transfer does not violate any restriction on transfer;

(5) if the transfer is by indorsement, the indorsement is made by an appropriate person, or if the indorsement is by an agent, the agent has actual authority to act on behalf of the appropriate person; and

(6) the transfer is otherwise effective and rightful.

(b) A person who originates an instruction for registration of transfer of an uncertificated security to a purchaser for value warrants to the purchaser that:

(1) the instruction is made by an appropriate person, or if the instruction is by an agent, the agent has actual authority to act on behalf of the appropriate person;

(2) the security is valid;

(3) there is no adverse claim to the security; and

(4) at the time the instruction is presented to the issuer:

(i) the purchaser will be entitled to the registration of transfer;

(ii) the transfer will be registered by the issuer free from all liens, security interests, restrictions, and claims other than those specified in the instruction;

(iii) the transfer will not violate any restriction on transfer; and

(iv) the requested transfer will otherwise be effective and rightful.

(c) A person who transfers an uncertificated security to a purchaser for value and does not originate an instruction in connection with the transfer warrants that:

(1) the uncertificated security is valid;

(2) there is no adverse claim to the security;

(3) the transfer does not violate any restriction on transfer; and

(4) the transfer is otherwise effective and rightful.

(d) A person who indorses a security certificate warrants to the issuer that:

(1) there is no adverse claim to the security; and

(2) the indorsement is effective.

(e) A person who originates an instruction for registration of transfer of an uncertificated security warrants to the issuer that:

(1) the instruction is effective; and

(2) at the time the instruction is presented to the issuer the purchaser will be entitled to the registration of transfer.

(f) A person who presents a certificated security for registration of transfer or for payment or exchange warrants to the issuer that the person is entitled to the registration, payment, or exchange, but a purchaser for value and without notice of adverse claims to whom transfer is registered warrants only that the person has no knowledge of any unauthorized signature in a necessary indorsement.

(g) If a person acts as agent of another in delivering a certificated security to a purchaser, the identity of the principal was known to the person to whom the certificate was delivered, and the certificate delivered by the agent was received by the agent from the principal or received by the agent from another person at the direction of the principal, the person delivering the security certificate warrants only that the delivering person has authority to act for the principal and does not know of any adverse claim to the certificated security.

(h) A secured party who redelivers a security certificate received, or after payment and on order of the debtor delivers the security certificate to another person, makes only the warranties of an agent under subsection (g).

(i) Except as otherwise provided in subsection (g), a broker acting for a customer makes to the issuer and a purchaser the warranties provided in subsections (a) through (f). A broker that delivers a security certificate to its customer, or causes its customer to be registered as the owner of an uncertificated security, makes to the customer the warranties provided in subsection (a) or (b), and has the rights and privileges of a purchaser under this section. The warranties of and in favor of the broker acting as an agent are in addition to applicable warranties given by and in favor of the customer.

History: Add, L 1997, ch 566, § 5, eff Oct 10, 1997.

Former § 8-108, add, L 1982, ch 928, § 7; repealed, L 1997, ch 566, § 5, eff Oct 10, 1997.

§ 8-109. Warranties in Indirect Holding

(a) A person who originates an entitlement order to a securities intermediary warrants to the securities intermediary that:

(1) the entitlement order is made by an appropriate person, or if the entitlement order is by an agent, the agent has actual authority to act on behalf of the appropriate person; and

(2) there is no adverse claim to the security entitlement.

(b) A person who delivers a security certificate to a securities intermediary for credit to a securities account or originates an instruction with respect to an uncertificated security directing that the uncertificated security be credited to a securities account makes to the securities intermediary the warranties specified in Section 8-108(a) or (b).

(c) If a securities intermediary delivers a security certificate to its entitlement holder or causes its entitlement holder to be registered as the owner of an uncertificated security, the securities intermediary makes to the entitlement holder the warranties specified in Section 8-108(a) or (b).

History: Add, L 1997, ch 566, § 5, eff Oct 10, 1997.

§ 8-110.   Applicability; Choice of Law

(a) The local law of the issuer's jurisdiction, as specified in subsection (d), governs:

(1) the validity of a security;

(2) the rights and duties of the issuer with respect to registration of transfer;

(3) the effectiveness of registration of transfer by the issuer;

(4) whether the issuer owes any duties to an adverse claimant to a security; and

(5) whether an adverse claim can be asserted against a person to whom transfer of a certificated or uncertificated security is registered or a person who obtains control of an uncertificated security.

(b) The local law of the securities intermediary's jurisdiction, as specified in subsection (e), governs:

(1) acquisition of a security entitlement from the securities intermediary;

(2) the rights and duties of the securities intermediary and entitlement holder arising out of a security entitlement;

(3) whether the securities intermediary owes any duties to an adverse claimant to a security entitlement; and

(4) whether an adverse claim can be asserted against a person who acquires a security entitlement from the securities intermediary or a person who purchases a security entitlement or interest therein from an entitlement holder.

(c) Except with respect to cooperative interests, the local law of the jurisdiction in which a security certificate is located at the time of delivery governs whether an adverse claim can be asserted against a person to whom the security certificate is delivered.

(d) "Issuer's jurisdiction" means the jurisdiction under which the issuer of the security is organized or, if permitted by the law of that jurisdiction, the law of another jurisdiction specified by the issuer. An issuer organized under the law of this State may specify the law of another jurisdiction as the law governing the matters specified in subsection (a)(2) through (5).

(e) The following rules determine a "securities intermediary's jurisdiction" for purposes of this section:

(1) If an agreement between the securities intermediary and its entitlement holder governing the securities account expressly provides that a particular jurisdiction is the securities intermediary's jurisdiction for purposes of this part, this article, or this act, that jurisdiction is the securities intermediary's jurisdiction.

(2) If paragraph (1) does not apply and an agreement between the securities intermediary and its entitlement holder governing the securities account expressly provides that the agreement is governed by the law of a particular jurisdiction, that jurisdiction is the securities intermediary's jurisdiction.

(3) If neither paragraph (1) nor paragraph (2) apply and an agreement between the securities intermediary and its entitlement holder governing the securities account expressly provides that the securities account is maintained at an office in a particular jurisdiction, that jurisdiction is the securities intermediary's jurisdiction.

(4) If none of the preceding paragraphs apply, the securities intermediary's jurisdiction is the jurisdiction in which the office identified in an account statement as the office serving the entitlement holder's account is located.

(5) If none of the preceding paragraphs apply, the securities intermediary's jurisdiction is the jurisdiction in which the chief executive office of the securities intermediary is located.

(f) A securities intermediary's jurisdiction is not determined by the physical location of certificates representing financial assets, or by the jurisdiction in which is organized the issuer of the financial asset with respect to which an entitlement holder has a security entitlement, or by the location of facilities for data processing or other record keeping concerning the account.

History: Add, L 1997, ch 566, § 5, eff Oct 10, 1997.

Sub (c), amd, L 2001, ch 84, § 27, eff July 1, 2001.

Sub (e), amd, L 2001, ch 84, § 28, eff July 1, 2001.

Sub (e), par (1), amd, L 2001, ch 84, § 28, eff July 1, 2001.

Sub (e), par (2), add, L 2001, ch 84, § 28, eff July 1, 2001.

Former sub (e), par (2), redesignated sub (e), par (3), L 2001, ch 84, § 28, eff July 1, 2001.

Sub (e), par (3), formerly sub (e), par (2), so designated sub (e), par (3) and amd, L 2001, ch 84, § 28, eff July 1, 2001.

Former sub (e), par (3), redesignated sub (e), par (4), L 2001, ch 84, § 28, eff July 1, 2001.

Sub (e), par (4), formerly sub (e), par (3), so designated sub (e), par (4) and amd, L 2001, ch 84, § 28, eff July 1, 2001.

Former sub (e), par (4), redesignated sub (e), par (5), L 2001, ch 84, § 28, eff July 1, 2001.

Sub (e), par (5), formerly sub (e), par (4), so designated sub (e), par (5) and amd, L 2001, ch 84, § 28, eff July 1, 2001.

§ 8-111.   Clearing Corporation Rules

A rule adopted by a clearing corporation governing rights and obligations among the clearing corporation and its participants in the clearing corporation is effective even if the rule conflicts with this article and affects another party who does not consent to the rule.

History: Add, L 1997, ch 566, § 5, eff Oct 10, 1997

§ 8-112. Creditor's Legal Process

(a) The interest of a debtor in a certificated security may be reached by a creditor only by actual seizure of the security certificate by the officer making the attachment or levy, except as otherwise provided in subsection (d). However, a certificated security for which the certificate has been surrendered to the issuer may be reached by a creditor by legal process upon the issuer.

(b) The interest of a debtor in an uncertificated security may be reached by a creditor only by legal process upon the issuer at its chief executive office in the United States, except as otherwise provided in subsection (d).

(c) The interest of a debtor in a security entitlement may be reached by a creditor only by legal process upon the securities intermediary with whom the debtor's securities account is maintained, except as otherwise provided in subsection (d).

(d) The interest of a debtor in a certificated security for which the certificate is in the possession of a secured party, or in an uncertificated security registered in the name of a secured party, or a security entitlement maintained in the name of a secured party, may be reached by a creditor by legal process upon the secured party.

(e) A creditor whose debtor is the owner of a certificated security, uncertificated security, or security entitlement is entitled to aid from a court of competent jurisdiction, by injunction or otherwise, in reaching the certificated security, uncertificated security, or security entitlement or in satisfying the claim by means allowed at law or in equity in regard to property that cannot readily be reached by other legal process.

History: Add, L 1997, ch 566, § 5, eff Oct 10, 1997.

§ 8-113. Statute of Frauds Generally Inapplicable

(a) Except as provided in subsection (b), a contract or modification of a contract for the sale or purchase of a security is enforceable whether or not there is a writing signed or record authenticated by a party against whom enforcement is sought, even if the contract or modification is not capable of performance within one year of its making.

(b) A contract or modification of a contract for the sale or purchase of a cooperative interest is void unless the contract or some note or memorandum thereof, expressing the consideration, is in writing, subscribed by the party to be charged, or by his lawful agency thereunto authorized by writing.

History: Add, L 1997, ch 566, § 5, eff Oct 10, 1997.

Sub (b), add, L 2001, ch 84, § 29, eff July 1, 2001.

Former sub (b), repealed, L 2001, ch 84, § 29, eff July 1, 2001.

CASE ANNOTATIONS

Defendants were entitled to summary judgment in action for breach of oral employment agreement on ground that plaintiff's claim was barred by statute of frauds applicable to sale of securities (CLS UCC § 8-601) in effect at time of alleged agreement where (1) plaintiff's deposition testimony showed that, at most, during pre-employment negotiations, individual defendants orally promised to give plaintiff "a piece of" defendant corporation, without mentioning any percentages, and (2) unsigned confirmatory e-mail allegedly sent by one individual defendant months later made only equivocal reference to.5 percent claimed by plaintiff, and did not satisfy subscription requirement of CLS UCC former § 8-319. Page v Muze, Inc. (2000, 2d Dept) 270 A.D.2d 401, 705 N.Y.S.2d 383

N.Y. Gen. Oblig. Law § 5-701 did not bar plaintiff venture capital investors' breach of contract claim against defendants, a start-up company and its founders, as the investment agreement provided that the investors had the right to purchase the founders' shares in three tranches over 18 months, and could be considered a "sale of securities" under N.Y. U.C.C. Law § 8-113; the investors would be allowed to present evidence that the transaction was a sale of securities and thus the court denied defendants' motion to dismiss. Spencer Trask Software & Info. Servs. LLC v RPost Int'l Ltd. (2003, SD NY) 383 F. Supp. 2d 428, motion gr (2003, SD NY) 2003 US Dist LEXIS 3954

Statutory revisions to N.Y. U.C.C. § 8-113 were designed to bring the law into step with prevailing mechanics of discrete securities transfers and was not intended to apply to certain financial transactions at issue in the case to negate the statute of frauds requirements set forth in N.Y. Gen. Oblig. Law § 5-701. Tradewinds Fin. Corp. v Repco Secs., Inc. (2004, A.D., 1st Dept) 773 N.Y.S.2d 395

§ 8-114. Evidentiary Rules Concerning Certificated Securities

The following rules apply in an action on a certificated security against the issuer:

(1) Unless specifically denied in the pleadings, each signature on a security certificate or in a necessary indorsement is admitted.

(2) If the effectiveness of a signature is put in issue, the burden of establishing effectiveness is on the party claiming under the signature, but the signature is presumed to be genuine or authorized.

(3) If signatures on a security certificate are admitted or established, production of the certificate entitles a holder to recover on it unless the defendant establishes a defense or a defect going to the validity of the security.

(4) If it is shown that a defense or defect exists, the plaintiff has the burden of establishing that the plaintiff or some person under whom the plaintiff claims is a person against whom the defense or defect cannot be asserted.

History: Add, L 1997, ch 566, § 5, eff Oct 10, 1997.

§ 8-115. Securities Intermediary and Others Not Liable to Adverse Claimant

A securities intermediary that has transferred a financial asset pursuant to an effective entitlement order, or a broker or other agent or bailee that has dealt with a financial asset at the direction of its customer or principal, is not liable to a person having an adverse claim to the financial asset, unless the securities intermediary, or broker or other agent or bailee:

(1) took the action after it had been served with an injunction, restraining order, or other legal process enjoining it from doing so, issued by a court of competent jurisdiction, and had a reasonable opportunity to act on the injunction, restraining order, or other legal process; or

(2) acted in collusion with the wrongdoer in violating the rights of the adverse claimant; or

(3) in the case of a security certificate that has been stolen, acted with notice of the adverse claim.

History: Add, L 1997, ch 566, § 5, eff Oct 10, 1997.

CASE ANNOTATIONS

It was undisputed that the investment company was acting as a securities intermediary for seven insurance companies and that none of the three enumerated exceptions in N.Y. U.C.C. Law 8-115 applied; but having found that the insurance companies were customers as to the brokerage accounts used to funnel funds as a party of a third party's fraud scheme, it was clear that the insurance companies were not persons having an adverse claim against the investment company, as the provision did not protect the investment company against claims by its own customers alleging that the investment company had failed to discharge its duty to ensure that transactions were authorized. Chaney v Dreyfus Serv. Corp. (2010, CA5 Miss) 595 F3d 219.

§ 8-116. Securities Intermediary as Purchaser for Value

A securities intermediary that receives a financial asset and establishes a security entitlement to the financial asset in favor of an entitlement holder is a purchaser for value of the financial asset. A securities intermediary that acquires a security entitlement to a financial asset from another securities intermediary acquires the security entitlement for value if the securities intermediary acquiring the security entitlement establishes a security entitlement to the financial asset in favor of an entitlement holder.

History: Add, L 1997, ch 566, § 5, eff Oct 10, 1997.

CASE ANNOTATIONS

Securities intermediary was a protected purchaser under N.Y. U.C.C. Law § 8-303, where the intermediary gave value to the depositor by receiving the certificate and crediting the depositor with ownership of the shares in accordance with N.Y. U.C.C. Law § 8-116, the intermediary had no notice of the restrictions on the certificate imposed by an agreement between the depositor and a third party, and the intermediary had obtained control over the security pursuant to N.Y. U.C.C. Law § 8-106(b). Dabbah Secs. Corp. v Croesus Capital Corp. (2002, A.D., 1st Dept) 747 N.Y.S.2d 82

PART 2
ISSUE AND ISSUER

History: Add, L 1997, ch 566, § 5, eff Oct 10, 1997.

Former Part 2, add, L 1962, ch 553; repealed, L 1997, ch 566, § 5, eff Oct 10, 1997.

§ 8-201. Issuer

(a) With respect to an obligation on or a defense to a security, an "issuer" includes a person that:

(1) places or authorizes the placing of its name on a security certificate, other than as authenticating trustee, registrar, transfer agent, or the like, to evidence a share, participation, or other interest in its property or in an enterprise, or to evidence its duty to perform an obligation represented by the certificate;

(2) creates a share, participation, or other interest in its property or in an enterprise, or undertakes an obligation, that is an uncertificated security;

(3) directly or indirectly creates a fractional interest in its rights or property, if the fractional interest is represented by a security certificate; or

(4) becomes responsible for, or in place of, another person described as an issuer in this section.

(b) With respect to an obligation on or defense to a security, a guarantor is an issuer to the extent of its guaranty, whether or not its obligation is noted on a security certificate.

(c) With respect to a registration of a transfer, issuer means a person on whose behalf transfer books are maintained.

History: Add, L 1997, ch 566, § 5, eff Oct 10, 1997.

Former § 8-201, add, L 1962, ch 553; amd, L 1963, ch 1003, § 18, L 1982, ch 928, § 8; repealed, L 1997, ch 566, § 5, eff Oct 10, 1997.

§ 8-202. Issuer's Responsibility and Defenses; Notice of Defect or Defense

(a) Even against a purchaser for value and without notice, the terms of a certificated security include terms stated on the certificate and terms made part of the security by reference on the certificate to another instrument, indenture, or document or to a constitution, statute, ordinance, rule, regulation, order, or the like, to the extent the terms referred to do not conflict with terms stated on the certificate. A reference under this subsection does not of itself charge a purchaser for value with notice of a defect going to the validity of the security, even if the certificate expressly states that a person accepting it admits notice. The terms of an uncertificated security include those stated in any instrument, indenture, or document or in a constitution, statute, ordinance, rule, regulation, order, or the like, pursuant to which the security is issued.

(b) The following rules apply if an issuer asserts that a security is not valid:

(1) A security other than one issued by a government or governmental subdivision, agency, or in-

UCC

strumentality, even though issued with a defect going to its validity, is valid in the hands of a purchaser for value and without notice of the particular defect unless the defect involves a violation of a constitutional provision. In that case, the security is valid in the hands of a purchaser for value and without notice of the defect, other than one who takes by original issue.

(2) Paragraph (1) applies to an issuer that is a government or governmental subdivision, agency, or instrumentality only if there has been substantial compliance with the legal requirements governing the issue or the issuer has received a substantial consideration for the issue as a whole or for the particular security and a stated purpose of the issue is one for which the issuer has power to borrow money or issue the security.

(c) Except as otherwise provided in Section 8-205, lack of genuineness of a certificated security is a complete defense, even against a purchaser for value and without notice.

(d) All other defenses of the issuer of a security, including nondelivery and conditional delivery of a security, are ineffective against a purchaser for value who has taken the security without notice of the particular defense.

(e) This section does not affect the right of a party to cancel a contract for a security "when, as and if issued" or "when distributed" in the event of a material change in the character of the security that is the subject of the contract or in the plan or arrangement pursuant to which the security is to be issued or distributed.

(f) If a security is held by a securities intermediary against whom an entitlement holder has a security entitlement with respect to the security, the issuer may not assert any defense that the issuer could not assert if the entitlement holder held the security directly.

History: Add, L 1997, ch 566, § 5, eff Oct 10, 1997.

Former § 8-202, add, L 1962, ch 553; amd, L 1964, ch 476, § 6, L 1982, ch 928, § 9; repealed, L 1997, ch 566, § 5, eff Oct 10, 1997.

§ 8-203.   Staleness as Notice of Defect or Defense

After an act or event, other than a call that has been revoked, creating a right to immediate performance of the principal obligation represented by a certificated security or setting a date on or after which the security is to be presented or surrendered for redemption or exchange, a purchaser is charged with notice of any defect in its issue or defense of the issuer, if the act or event:

(1) requires the payment of money, the delivery of a certificated security, the registration of transfer of an uncertificated security, or any of them on presentation or surrender of the security certificate, the money or security is available on the date set for

payment or exchange, and the purchaser takes the security more than one year after that date; or

(2) is not covered by subsection (1) and the purchaser takes the security more than two years after the date set for surrender or presentation or the date on which performance became due.

History: Add, L 1997, ch 566, § 5, eff Oct 10, 1997.

Former § 8-203, add, L 1962, ch 553; amd, L 1982, ch 928, § 9; repealed, L 1997, ch 566, § 5, eff Oct 10, 1997.

§ 8-204.   Effect of Issuer's Restriction on Transfer

A restriction on transfer of a security imposed by the issuer, even if otherwise lawful, is ineffective against a person without knowledge of the restriction unless:

(1) the security is certificated and the restriction is noted conspicuously on the security certificate; or

(2) the security is uncertificated and the registered owner has been notified of the restriction; or

(3) the restriction is on the transfer of a cooperative interest and the restriction is set forth in the cooperative record.

History: Add, L 1997, ch 566, § 5, eff Oct 10, 1997.

Former § 8-204, add, L 1962, ch 553; amd, L 1982, ch 928, § 10; repealed, L 1997, ch 566, § 5.

Amd, L 2001, ch 84, § 30, eff July 1, 2001.

Sub (2), amd, L 2001, ch 84, § 30, eff July 1, 2001.

Sub (3), add, L 2001, ch 84, § 30, eff July 1, 2001.

§ 8-205.   Effect of Unauthorized Signature on Security Certificate

An unauthorized signature placed on a security certificate before or in the course of issue is ineffective, but the signature is effective in favor of a purchaser for value of the certificated security if the purchaser is without notice of the lack of authority and the signing has been done by:

(1) an authenticating trustee, registrar, transfer agent, or other person entrusted by the issuer with the signing of the security certificate or of similar security certificates, or the immediate preparation for signing of any of them; or

(2) an employee of the issuer, or of any of the persons listed in subsection (1), entrusted with responsible handling of the security certificate.

History: Add, L 1997, ch 566, § 5, eff Oct 10, 1997.

Former § 8-205, add, L 1962, ch 553; amd, L 1982, ch 928, § 10; repealed, L 1997, ch 566, § 5, eff Oct 10, 1997.

§ 8-206.   Completion or Alteration of Security Certificate

(a) If a security certificate contains the signatures necessary to its issue or transfer but is incomplete in any other respect:

(1) any person may complete it by filling in the blanks as authorized; and

(2) even if the blanks are incorrectly filled in, the security certificate as completed is enforceable by a purchaser who took it for value and without notice of the incorrectness.

(b) A complete security certificate that has been improperly altered, even if fraudulently, remains enforceable, but only according to its original terms.

History: Add, L 1997, ch 566, § 5, eff Oct 10, 1997.

Former § 8-206, add, L 1962, ch 553; amd, L 1982, ch 928, § 10; repealed, L 1997, ch 566, § 5, eff Oct 10, 1997.

§ 8-207.   Rights and Duties of Issuer with respect to Registered Owners

(a) Before due presentment for registration of transfer of a certificated security in registered form or of an instruction requesting registration of transfer of an uncertificated security, the issuer or indenture trustee may treat the registered owner as the person exclusively entitled to vote, receive notifications, and otherwise exercise all the rights and powers of an owner.

(b) This Article does not affect the liability of the registered owner of a security for a call, assessment, or the like.

History: Add, L 1997, ch 566, § 5, eff Oct 10, 1997.

Former § 8-207, add, L 1962, ch 553; amd, L 1982, ch 928, § 10; repealed, L 1997, ch 566, § 5, eff Oct 10, 1997.

§ 8-208.   Effect of Signature of Authenticating Trustee, Registrar, or Transfer Agent

(a) A person signing a security certificate as authenticating trustee, registrar, transfer agent, or the like, warrants to a purchaser for value of the certificated security, if the purchaser is without notice of a particular defect, that:

(1) the certificate is genuine;

(2) the person's own participation in the issue of the security is within the person's capacity and within the scope of the authority received by the person from the issuer; and

(3) the person has reasonable grounds to believe that the certificated security is in the form and within the amount the issuer is authorized to issue.

(b) Unless otherwise agreed, a person signing under subsection (a) does not assume responsibility for the validity of the security in other respects.

History: Add, L 1997, ch 566, § 5, eff Oct 10, 1997.

Former § 8-208, add, L 1962, ch 553; amd, L 1963, ch 1003, § 19, L 1982, ch 928, § 10; repealed, L 1997, ch 566, § 5.

§ 8-209.   Issuer's Lien

A lien in favor of an issuer upon a certificated security is valid against a purchaser only if the right of the issuer to the lien is noted conspicuously on the security certificate or, in a case of a cooperative interest, is set forth in the cooperative record.

History: Add, L 1997, ch 566, § 5, eff Oct 10, 1997.

Amd, L 2001, ch 84, § 31, eff July 1, 2001.

CASE ANNOTATIONS

Cooperative corporation was entitled to partial summary judgment on issue of liability for shareholder's maintenance obligations, brought against bank that had lent shareholder money used to buy shares in cooperative corporation, even though bank had secured loan by perfecting security interest in those shares, where (1) shares of cooperative corporation are "securities" governed by CLS UCC Art 8, (2) CLS UCC § 8-209 provides that "[a] lien in favor of an issuer upon a certificated security is valid against a purchaser only if the right of the issuer of the lien is noted conspicuously on the security certificate, (3) legend on stock certificates stated that corporation "shall" at all times have "first lien" on shares of stock for any unpaid maintenance charges, and (4) thus, corporation had lien, enforceable against bank, on subject shares for any unpaid maintenance charges. Berkowners, Inc. v Dime Sav. Bank of N.Y., FSB. (2001, 2d Dept) 286 A.D.2d 695, 730 N.Y.S.2d 339

§ 8-210.   Overissue

(a) In this section, "overissue" means the issue of securities in excess of the amount the issuer has corporate power to issue, but an overissue does not occur if appropriate action has cured the overissue.

(b) Except as otherwise provided in subsections (c) and (d), the provisions of this Article which validate a security or compel its issue or reissue do not apply to the extent that validation, issue, or reissue would result in overissue.

(c) If an identical security not constituting an overissue is reasonably available for purchase, a person entitled to issue or validation may compel the issuer to purchase the security and deliver it if certificated or register its transfer if uncertificated, against surrender of any security certificate the person holds.

(d) If a security is not reasonably available for purchase, a person entitled to issue or validation may recover from the issuer the price the person or the last purchaser for value paid for it with interest from the date of the person's demand.

History: Add, L 1997, ch 566, § 5, eff Oct 10, 1997.

CASE ANNOTATIONS

Trial court's award of damages to an administrator in a wrongful registration suit brought under N.Y. U.C.C. Law § 8-404(b) was not improper because the corporation was unable to issue shares of stock to the administrator inasmuch as the corporation had been acquired by an investment group as the result of a merger transaction. Kirshtein v Americu Credit Union (2011, App Div, 4th Dept) 919 NYS2d 653, 74 UCCRS2d 164, subsequent app (2011, App Div, 4th Dept) 919 NYS2d 434.

PART 3
TRANSFER OF CERTIFICATED AND UNCERTIFICATED SECURITIES

UCC

History: Add, L 1997, ch 566, § 5, eff Oct 10, 1997.

Former Part 3, add, L 1962, ch 553; repealed, L 1997, ch 566, § 5, eff Oct 10, 1997.

§ 8-301.   Delivery

(a) Delivery of a certificated security to a purchaser occurs when:

(1) the purchaser acquires possession of the security certificate;

(2) another person, other than a securities intermediary, either acquires possession of the security certificate on behalf of the purchaser or, having previously acquired possession of the certificate, acknowledges that it holds for the purchaser; or

(3) a securities intermediary acting on behalf of the purchaser acquires possession of the security certificate, only if the certificate is in registered form and is (i) registered in the name of the purchaser, (ii) payable to the order of the purchaser, or (iii) specially indorsed to the purchaser by an effective indorsement and has not been indorsed to the securities intermediary or in blank.

(b) Delivery of an uncertificated security to a purchaser occurs when:

(1) the issuer registers the purchaser as the registered owner, upon original issue or registration of transfer; or

(2) another person, other than a securities intermediary, either becomes the registered owner of the uncertificated security on behalf of the purchaser or, having previously become the registered owner, acknowledges that it holds for the purchaser.

History: Add, L 1997, ch 566, § 5, eff Oct 10, 1997.

Former § 8-301, add, L 1962, ch 553; amd, L 1964, ch 476, § 7, L 1982, ch 928, § 11; repealed, L 1997, ch 566, § 5, eff Oct 10, 1997.

Sub (a), par (3), amd, L 2001, ch 84, § 32, eff July 1, 2001.

Article 8 of N.Y. U.C.C. Law did not displace substantive common law principles originally relied upon by the court, so on remand the result was same—as the corporation could not act on behalf of the individuals, no privity of contract existed between the individuals and the partnership—so the partnership's breach of oral contract to sell notes to partnership and breach of binding preliminary agreement

claims failed. Highland Capital Mgmt., L.P. v Schneider (2008, SD NY) 533 F Supp 2d 345, motions ruled upon (2008, SD NY) 2008 US Dist LEXIS 7019.

§ 8-302.   Rights of Purchaser

(a) Except as otherwise provided in subsections (b) and (c), a purchaser of a certificated or uncertificated security acquires all rights in the security that the transferor had or had power to transfer.

(b) A purchaser of a limited interest acquires rights only to the extent of the interest purchased.

(c) A purchaser of a certificated security who as a previous holder had notice of an adverse claim does not improve its position by taking from a protected purchaser.

History: Add, L 1997, ch 566, § 5, eff Oct 10, 1997.

Former § 8-302, add, L 1962, ch 553; amd, L 1963, ch 1003, § 20, L 1982, ch 928, § 12; repealed, L 1997, ch 566, § 5, eff Oct 10, 1997.

Sub (a), amd, L 2001, ch 84, § 33, eff July 1, 2001.

Buyer's good faith in purchasing certain securities was not properly measured against its compliance with reasonable commercial standards; rather the facts actually known to the broker's agent were so egregiously suspicious that his lack of investigation amounted to bad faith. MCC Proceeds, Inc. v Advest, Inc. (2002, 1st Dept) 293 A.D.2d 331, 743 N.Y.S.2d 1, CCH Blue Sky L Rep P 74267

Securities and Exchange Commission failed to show reasonable likelihood in prevailing on merits in suit against brokerage firm regarding alleged insider trading, even though firm's client was known inside trader, where firm had been directed to execute immediate transaction, and SEC did not suggest how firm could have swiftly and definitely assured itself that no insider information had been used; New York law requires dishonesty and not mere suspicion under CLS UCC § 8-302, and thus firm qualified as bona fide purchaser. SEC v Lehman Bros. (1998, CA1 Mass) 157 F.3d 2, CCH Fed Secur L Rep ¶ 90291, 36 UCCRS2d 852, sanctions allowed (DC Mass) 52 F. Supp. 2d 205

There was no conflict between federal and state law in insider trading case where brokerage firm (whose client was charged with insider trading) relied on Securities Exchange Act of 1934 § 29(b) (15 USCS § 78cc(b)) in which put option contracts are made unenforceable by buyer against seller where acquired through buyer's violation of "this chapter," and New York UCC provision relied on by Securities and Exchange Commission (CLS UCC § 8-302) merely gave SEC independent ground under New York law for saying that firm has no valid security interest (security interest that firm itself assumed it needed in order to prevail over SEC). SEC v Lehman Bros. (1998, CA1 Mass) 157 F.3d 2, CCH Fed Secur L Rep ¶ 90291, 36 UCCRS2d 852, sanctions allowed (DC Mass) 52 F. Supp. 2d 205

In plaintiff buyer's declaratory judgment action that argued the buyer was not liable under a merger agreement in which it was to purchase defendant seller's stock, intervenor shareholder's claim against the buyer for breach of contract was not automatically transferred under N.Y. Gen. Oblig. Law §§ 13-101, -107, or N.Y. U.C.C. Law § 8-302(a), when the shareholder later sold his stock, but, because issues involved controlling questions of New York law of first impression, and the case was exceptional where early appellate review would materially advance the case, the issues of whether the shareholders were intended third-party beneficiaries, and if so, whether shareholders' claims for damages for breach of contract against the buyer were automatically transferred to any subsequent purchasers of the seller's shares, were certified for interlocutory appeal under 28 U.S.C.S. § 1292(b). Consol. Edison, Inc. v Northeast Utils. (2004, SD NY) 318 F. Supp. 2d 181

Where defendants argued that the right to bring a claim for breach of the warrant agreement was not a right "in the security" and thus was not automatically transferred to the warrant purchasers when they purchased the warrants after the date of the breach, Consolidated Edison, Inc. v. Northeast Utilities, 318 F. Supp. 2d 181

(S.D.N.Y. 2004), which interpreted N.Y. U.C.C. Law § 8-302, a provision identical to Tex. Bus. & Com. Code Ann. § 8.302 (2004), undermined defendants' position. In Consolidated Edison, the court concluded that "rights in the security" included rights "vis-a-vis the issuer and vis-a-vis other potential holders," and that the rights against the issuer included contract rights, and further noted that a holder's rights in the security thus included the rights against the issuer under the contract embodied in the security as supplemented by federal and state law. R.A. Mackie & Co., L.P. v PetroCorp Inc. (2004, SD NY) 329 F. Supp. 2d 477

§ 8-303. Protected Purchaser

(a) "Protected purchaser" means a purchaser of a certificated or uncertificated security, or of an interest therein, who:

(1) gives value;

(2) does not have notice of any adverse claim to the security; and

(3) obtains control of the certificated or uncertificated security.

(b) In addition to acquiring the rights of a purchaser, a protected purchaser also acquires its interest in the security free of any adverse claim.

History: Add, L 1997, ch 566, § 5, eff Oct 10, 1997.

Former § 8-303, add, L 1962, ch 553; repealed, L 1997, ch 566, § 5, eff Oct 10, 1997.

CASE ANNOTATIONS

Securities intermediary was a protected purchaser under N.Y. U.C.C. Law § 8-303, where the intermediary gave value to the depositor by receiving the certificate and crediting the depositor with ownership of the shares in accordance with N.Y. U.C.C. Law § 8-116, the intermediary had no notice of the restrictions on the certificate imposed by an agreement between the depositor and a third party, and the intermediary had obtained control over the security pursuant to N.Y. U.C.C. Law § 8-106(b). Dabbah Secs. Corp v Croesus Capital Corp. (2002, A.D., 1st Dept) 747 N.Y.S.2d 82

Securities intermediary obtained control over the depositor's security pursuant to N.Y. U.C.C. Law § 8-106(b), as the security was delivered by the depositor with the appropriate stock power and corporate resolution, and under N.Y. U.C.C. Law § 8-102(11), the depositor indorsed the security by delivering an irrevocable stock power wherein the depositor signed, assigned, and transferred the shares to the intermediary's clearing agent; the intermediary was not required by N.Y. U.C.C. Law § 8-303 to show that its control of the stock certificate was current. Dabbah Secs. Corp. v Croesus Capital Corp. (2002, A.D., 1st Dept) 747 N.Y.S.2d 82

§ 8-304. Indorsement

(a) An indorsement may be in blank or special. An indorsement in blank includes an indorsement to bearer. A special indorsement specifies to whom a security is to be transferred or who has power to transfer it. A holder may convert a blank indorsement to a special indorsement.

(b) An indorsement purporting to be only of part of a security certificate representing units intended by the issuer to be separately transferable is effective to the extent of the indorsement.

(c) An indorsement, whether special or in blank, does not constitute a transfer until delivery of the certificate on which it appears or, if the indorsement is on a separate document, until delivery of both the document and the certificate.

(d) If a security certificate in registered form has been delivered to a purchaser without a necessary indorsement, the purchaser may become a protected purchaser only when the indorsement is supplied. However, against a transferor, a transfer is complete upon delivery and the purchaser has a specifically enforceable right to have any necessary indorsement supplied.

(e) An indorsement of a security certificate in bearer form may give notice of an adverse claim to the certificate, but it does not otherwise affect a right to registration that the holder possesses.

(f) Unless otherwise agreed, a person making an indorsement assumes only the obligations provided in Section 8-108 and not an obligation that the security will be honored by the issuer.

History: Add, L 1997, ch 566, § 5, eff Oct 10, 1997.

Former § 8-304, add, L 1962, ch 553; amd, L 1964, ch 476, § 8, L 1982, ch 928, § 13; repealed, L 1997, ch 566, § 5, eff Oct 10, 1997.

§ 8-305. Instruction

(a) If an instruction has been originated by an appropriate person but is incomplete in any other respect, any person may complete it as authorized and the issuer may rely on it as completed, even though it has been completed incorrectly.

(b) Unless otherwise agreed, a person initiating an instruction assumes only the obligations imposed by Section 8-108 and not an obligation that the security will be honored by the issuer.

History: Add, L 1997, ch 566, § 5, eff Oct 10, 1997.

Former § 8-305, add, L 1962, ch 553; amd, L 1982, ch 928, § 14; repealed, L 1997, ch 566, § 5, eff Oct 10, 1997.

§ 8-306. Effect of Guaranteeing Signature, Indorsement, or Instruction

(a) A person who guarantees a signature of an indorser of a security certificate warrants that at the time of signing:

(1) the signature was genuine;

(2) the signer was an appropriate person to indorse, or if the signature is by an agent, the agent had actual authority to act on behalf of the appropriate person; and

(3) the signer had legal capacity to sign.

(b) A person who guarantees a signature of the originator of an instruction warrants that at the time of signing:

(1) the signature was genuine;

(2) the signer was an appropriate person to originate the instruction, or if the signature is by an agent, the agent had actual authority to act on behalf of the appropriate person, if the person specified in the instruction as the registered owner was, in fact, the registered owner, as to which fact the signature guarantor does not make a warranty; and

(3) the signer had legal capacity to sign.

UCC

(c) A person who specially guarantees the signature of an originator of an instruction makes the warranties of a signature guarantor under subsection (b) and also warrants that at the time the instruction is presented to the issuer:

(1) the person specified in the instruction as the registered owner of the uncertificated security will be the registered owner; and

(2) the transfer of the uncertificated security requested in the instruction will be registered by the issuer free from all liens, security interests, restrictions, and claims other than those specified in the instruction.

(d) A guarantor under subsections (a) and (b) or a special guarantor under subsection (c) does not otherwise warrant the rightfulness of the transfer.

(e) A person who guarantees an indorsement of a security certificate makes the warranties of a signature guarantor under subsection (a) and also warrants the rightfulness of the transfer in all respects.

(f) A person who guarantees an instruction requesting the transfer of an uncertificated security makes the warranties of a special signature guarantor under subsection (c) and also warrants the rightfulness of the transfer in all respects.

(g) An issuer may not require a special guaranty of signature, a guaranty of indorsement, or a guaranty of instruction as a condition to registration of transfer.

(h) The warranties under this section are made to a person taking or dealing with the security in reliance on the guaranty, and the guarantor is liable to the person for loss resulting from their breach. An indorser or originator of an instruction whose signature, indorsement, or instruction has been guaranteed is liable to a guarantor for any loss suffered by the guarantor as a result of breach of the warranties of the guarantor.

History: Add, L 1997, ch 566, § 5, eff Oct 10, 1997.

Former § 8-306, add, L 1962, ch 553; amd, L 1963, ch 1003, § 21, L 1982, ch 928, § 15; repealed, L 1997, ch 566, § 5, eff Oct 10, 1997.

CASE ANNOTATIONS

Because a decedent's last will and testament did not give an indorser authority to transfer certain stock certificates, the indorser was clearly not an appropriate person to request a medallion signature guaranty from a bank under N.Y. U.C.C. Law § 8-107; thus, the bank was entitled to summary judgment in its action to recoup funds paid in settlement under N.Y. U.C.C. Law § 8-306(h). Victory State Bank v Vidringstad (2009, Sup) 24 Misc 3d 878, 241 NYLJ 67, 885 NYS2d 161.

§ 8-307.   Purchaser's Right to Requisites for Registration of Transfer

Unless otherwise agreed, the transferor of a security on due demand shall supply the purchaser with proof of authority to transfer or with any other requisite necessary to obtain registration of the transfer of the security, but if the transfer is not for value, a transferor need not comply unless the pur-

chaser pays the necessary expenses. If the transferor fails within a reasonable time to comply with the demand, the purchaser may reject or rescind the transfer.

History: Add, L 1997, ch 566, § 5, eff Oct 10, 1997.

Former § 8-307, add, L 1962, ch 553; amd, L 1982, ch 928, § 16; repealed, L 1997, ch 566, § 5, eff Oct 10, 1997.

§ 8-308.   [Repealed]

History: Add, L 1982, ch 928, § 17, eff Dec 21, 1982; repealed, L 1997, ch 566, § 5, eff Oct 10, 1997.

Former § 8-308, add, L 1962, ch 553; amd, L 1963, ch 1003, § 22; repealed, L 1982, ch 928, § 17, eff Dec 21, 1982.

§ 8-309.   [Repealed]

History: Add, L 1962, ch 553; amd, L 1982, ch 928, § 18, eff Dec 21, 1982; repealed, L 1997, ch 566, § 5, eff Oct 10, 1997.

§ 8-310.   [Repealed]

History: Add, L 1962, ch 553; amd, L 1982, ch 928, § 18; repealed, L 1997, ch 566, § 5, eff Oct 10, 1997.

§ 8-311.   [Repealed]

History: Add, L 1962, ch 553; amd, L 1982, ch 928, § 18; repealed, L 1997, ch 566, § 5, eff Oct 10, 1997.

§ 8-312.   [Repealed]

History: Add, L 1962, ch 553; amd, L 1982, ch 928, § 18; repealed, L 1997, ch 566, § 5, eff Oct 10, 1997.

§ 8-313.   [Repealed]

History: Add, L 1962, ch 553; amd, L 1963, ch 1003, §§ 23, 24, L 1964, ch 476, §§ 9, 10, 1964, L 1982, ch 928, § 19, L 1988, ch 708, § 1; repealed, L 1997, ch 566, § 5, eff Oct 10, 1997.

§ 8-314.   [Repealed]

History: Add, L 1962, ch 553; amd, L 1982, ch 928, § 20; repealed, L 1997, ch 566, § 5, eff Oct 10, 1997.

§ 8-315.   [Repealed]

History: Add, L 1962, ch 553; amd, L 1982, ch 928, § 20; repealed, L 1997, ch 566, § 5, eff Oct 10, 1997.

§ 8-316.   [Repealed]

History: Add, L 1962, ch 553; amd, L 1982, ch 928, § 20; repealed, L 1997, ch 566, § 5, eff Oct 10, 1997.

§ 8-317.   [Repealed]

History: Add, L 1962, ch 553, eff Sept 27, 1964; amd, L 1982, ch 928, § 20, eff Dec 21, 1982; repealed, L 1997, ch 566, § 5, eff Oct 10, 1997.

§ 8-318.   [Repealed]

History: Add, L 1962, ch 553; amd, L 1982, ch 928, § 20; repealed, L 1997, ch 566, § 5, eff Oct 10, 1997.

§ 8-319.   [Repealed]

History: Add, L 1962, ch 553; amd, L 1982, ch 928, § 20; repealed, L 1997, ch 566, § 5, eff Oct 10, 1997.

§ 8-320.   [Repealed]

History: Add, L 1962, ch 553; amd, L 1982, ch 928, § 20, L 1992, ch 450, § 2; repealed, L 1997, ch 566, § 5, eff Oct 10, 1997.

§ 8-321.   [Repealed]

History: Add, L 1982, ch 928, § 21; repealed, L 1997, ch 566, § 5, eff Oct 10, 1997.

PART 4
REGISTRATION

History: Add, L 1997, ch 566, § 5, eff Oct 10, 1997.

Former Part 4, add, L 1962, ch 553; repealed, L 1997, ch 566, § 5, eff Oct 10, 1997.

§ 8-401.   Duty of Issuer to Register Transfer

(a) If a certificated security in registered form is presented to an issuer with a request to register transfer or an instruction is presented to an issuer with a request to register transfer of an uncertificated security, the issuer shall register the transfer as requested if:

(1) under the terms of the security the person seeking registration of transfer is eligible to have the security registered in its name;

(2) the indorsement or instruction is made by the appropriate person or by an agent who has actual authority to act on behalf of the appropriate person;

(3) reasonable assurance is given that the indorsement or instruction is genuine and authorized (Section 8-402);

(4) any applicable law relating to the collection of taxes has been complied with;

(5) the transfer does not violate any restriction on transfer imposed by the issuer in accordance with Section 8-204;

(6) a demand that the issuer not register transfer has not become effective under Section 8-403, or the issuer has complied with Section 8-403(b) but no legal process or indemnity bond is obtained as provided in Section 8-403(d); and

(7) the transfer is in fact rightful or is to a protected purchaser.

(b) If an issuer is under a duty to register a transfer of a security, the issuer is liable to a person presenting a certificated security or an instruction for registration or to the person's principal for loss resulting from unreasonable delay in registration or failure or refusal to register the transfer.

History: Add, L 1997, ch 566, § 5, eff Oct 10, 1997.

Former § 8-401, add, L 1962, ch 5534; amd, L 1982, ch 928, § 22; repealed, L 1997, ch 566, § 5, eff Oct 10, 1997.

§ 8-402.   Assurance that Indorsement or Instruction is Effective

(a) An issuer may require the following assurance that each necessary indorsement or each instruction is genuine and authorized:

(1) in all cases, a guaranty of the signature of the person making an indorsement or originating an instruction including, in the case of an instruction, reasonable assurance of identity;

(2) if the indorsement is made or the instruction is originated by an agent, appropriate assurance of actual authority to sign;

(3) if the indorsement is made or the instruction is originated by a fiduciary pursuant to Section 8-107(a)(4) or (a)(5), appropriate evidence of appointment or incumbency;

(4) if there is more than one fiduciary, reasonable assurance that all who are required to sign have done so; and

(5) if the indorsement is made or the instruction is originated by a person not covered by another provision of this subsection, assurance appropriate to the case corresponding as nearly as may be to the provisions of this subsection.

(b) An issuer may elect to require reasonable assurance beyond that specified in this section.

(c) In this section:

(1) "Guaranty of the signature" means a guaranty signed by or on behalf of a person reasonably believed by the issuer to be responsible. An issuer may adopt standards with respect to responsibility if they are not manifestly unreasonable.

(2) "Appropriate evidence of appointment or incumbency" means:

(i) in the case of a fiduciary appointed or qualified by a court, a certificate issued by or under the direction or supervision of the court or an officer thereof and dated within 6 months before the date of presentation for transfer; or

(ii) in any other case, a copy of a document showing the appointment or a certificate issued by or on behalf of a person reasonably believed by an issuer to be responsible or, in the absence of that document or

UCC

certificate, other evidence the issuer reasonably considers appropriate.

History: Add, L 1997, ch 566, § 5, eff Oct 10, 1997.

Former § 8-402, add, L 1962, ch 553; amd, L 1981, ch 294, § 1, L 1982, ch 928, § 23; repealed, L 1997, ch 566, § 5, eff Oct 10, 1997.

§ 8-403. Demand that Issuer Not Register Transfer

(a) A person who is an appropriate person to make an indorsement or originate an instruction may demand that the issuer not register transfer of a security by communicating to the issuer a notification that identifies the registered owner and the issue of which the security is a part and provides an address for communications directed to the person making the demand. The demand is effective only if it is received by the issuer at a time and in a manner affording the issuer reasonable opportunity to act on it.

(b) If a certificated security in registered form is presented to an issuer with a request to register transfer or an instruction is presented to an issuer with a request to register transfer of an uncertificated security after a demand that the issuer not register transfer has become effective, the issuer shall promptly communicate, to the person who initiated the demand at the address provided in the demand and to the person who presented the security for registration of transfer or initiated the instruction requesting registration of transfer, a notification stating that:

(1) the certificated security has been presented for registration of transfer or the instruction for registration of transfer of the uncertificated security has been received;

(2) a demand that the issuer not register transfer had previously been received; and

(3) the issuer will withhold registration of transfer for a period of time stated in the notification in order to provide the person who initiated the demand an opportunity to obtain legal process or an indemnity bond.

(c) The period described in subsection (b)(3) may not exceed 30 days after the date of communication of the notification. A shorter period may be specified by the issuer if it is not manifestly unreasonable.

(d) An issuer is not liable to a person who initiated a demand that the issuer not register transfer for any loss the person suffers as a result of registration of a transfer pursuant to an effective indorsement or instruction if the person who initiated the demand does not, within the time stated in the issuer's communication, either:

(1) obtain an appropriate restraining order, injunction, or other process from a court of competent jurisdiction enjoining the issuer from registering the transfer; or

(2) file with the issuer an indemnity bond, sufficient in the issuer's judgment to protect the issuer and any transfer agent, registrar, or other agent of the issuer involved from any loss it or they may suffer by refusing to register the transfer.

(e) This section does not relieve an issuer from liability for registering transfer pursuant to an indorsement or instruction that was not effective.

History: Add, L 1997, ch 566, § 5, eff Oct 10, 1997.

Former § 8-403, add, L 1962, ch 553; amd, L 1982, ch 928, § 24; repealed, L 1997, ch 566, § 5, eff Oct 10, 1997.

§ 8-404. Wrongful Registration

(a) Except as otherwise provided in Section 8-406, an issuer is liable for wrongful registration of transfer if the issuer has registered a transfer of a security to a person not entitled to it, and the transfer was registered:

(1) pursuant to an ineffective indorsement or instruction;

(2) after a demand that the issuer not register transfer became effective under Section 8-403(a) and the issuer did not comply with Section 8-403(b);

(3) after the issuer had been served with an injunction, restraining order, or other legal process enjoining it from registering the transfer, issued by a court of competent jurisdiction, and the issuer had a reasonable opportunity to act on the injunction, restraining order, or other legal process; or

(4) by an issuer acting in collusion with the wrongdoer.

(b) An issuer that is liable for wrongful registration of transfer under subsection (a) on demand shall provide the person entitled to the security with a like certificated or uncertificated security, and any payments or distributions that the person did not receive as a result of the wrongful registration. If an overissue would result, the issuer's liability to provide the person with a like security is governed by Section 8-210.

(c) Except as otherwise provided in subsection (a) or in a law relating to the collection of taxes, an issuer is not liable to an owner or other person suffering loss as a result of the registration of a transfer of a security if registration was made pursuant to an effective indorsement or instruction.

History: Add, L 1997, ch 566, § 5, eff Oct 10, 1997.

Former § 8-404, add, L 1962, ch 553; amd, L 1982, ch 928, § 24; repealed, L 1997, ch 566, § 5, eff Oct 10, 1997.

CASE ANNOTATIONS

Trial court's award of damages to an administrator in a wrongful registration suit brought under N.Y. U.C.C. Law § 8-404(b) was not improper because the corporation was unable to issue shares of stock to the administrator inasmuch as the corporation had been acquired by an investment group as the result of a merger transaction. Kirshtein v Americu Credit Union (2011, App Div, 4th Dept) 919 NYS2d 653, 74 UCCRS2d 164, subsequent app (2011, App Div, 4th Dept) 919 NYS2d 434.

Instruction on the presumption of continuance was proper in a wrongful registration suit pursuant to N.Y. U.C.C. Law § 8-404 because there was no requirement that there be an adjudication of incompetency to warrant the instruction; rather, mere evidence of incompetency was sufficient, and evidence was presented that the transferee of the corporations' stock was incompetent. Kirshtein v Americu Credit Union (2011, App Div, 4th Dept) 919 NYS2d 653, 74 UCCRS2d 164, subsequent app (2011, App Div, 4th Dept) 919 NYS2d 434.

Administrator was entitled to interest on the award of dividends in a wrongful registration suit brought under N.Y. U.C.C. Law § 8-404(b). Kirshtein v Americu Credit Union (2011, App Div, 4th Dept) 919 NYS2d 653, 74 UCCRS2d 164, subsequent app (2011, App Div, 4th Dept) 919 NYS2d 434.

§ 8-405. Replacement of Lost, Destroyed, or Wrongfully taken Security Certificate

(a) If an owner of a certificated security, whether in registered or bearer form, claims that the certificate has been lost, destroyed, or wrongfully taken, the issuer shall issue a new certificate if the owner:

(1) so requests before the issuer has notice that the certificate has been acquired by a protected purchaser;

(2) files with the issuer a sufficient indemnity bond; and

(3) satisfies other reasonable requirements imposed by the issuer.

(b) If, after the issue of a new security certificate, a protected purchaser of the original certificate presents it for registration of transfer, the issuer shall register the transfer unless an overissue would result. In that case, the issuer's liability is governed by Section 8-210. In addition to any rights on the indemnity bond, an issuer may recover the new certificate from a person to whom it was issued or any person taking under that person, except a protected purchaser.

History: Add, L 1997, ch 566, § 5, eff Oct 10, 1997.

Former § 8-405, add, L 1962, ch 553; amd, L 1982, ch 928, § 24; repealed, L 1997, ch 566, § 5, eff Oct 10, 1997.

§ 8-406. Obligation to Notify Issuer of Lost, Destroyed, or Wrongfully taken Security Certificate

If a security certificate has been lost, apparently destroyed, or wrongfully taken, and the owner fails to notify the issuer of that fact within a reasonable time after the owner has notice of it and the issuer registers a transfer of the security before receiving notification, the owner may not assert against the issuer a claim for registering the transfer under Section 8-404 or a claim to a new security certificate under Section 8-405.

History: Add, L 1997, ch 566, § 5, eff Oct 10, 1997.

Former § 8-406, add, L 1962, ch 553; amd, L 1982, ch 928, § 24; repealed, L 1997, ch 566, § 5, eff Oct 10, 1997.

§ 8-407. Authenticating Trustee, Transfer Agent, and Registrar

A person acting as authenticating trustee, transfer agent, registrar, or other agent for an issuer in the registration of a transfer of its securities, in the issue of new security certificates or uncertificated securities, or in the cancellation of surrendered security certificates has the same obligation to the holder or owner of a certificated or uncertificated security with regard to the particular functions performed as the issuer has in regard to those functions.

History: Add, L 1997, ch 566, § 5, eff Oct 10, 1997.

Former § 8-407, add, L 1982, ch 928, § 25; repealed, L 1997, ch 566, § 5, eff Oct 10, 1997.

§ 8-408. [Repealed]

History: Add, L 1982, ch 928, § 25; repealed, L 1997, ch 566, § 5, eff Oct 10, 1997.

PART 5
SECURITY ENTITLEMENTS

History: Add, L 1997, ch 566, § 5, eff Oct 10, 1997.

§ 8-501. Securities Account; Acquisition of Security Entitlement from Securities Intermediary

(a) "Securities account" means an account to which a financial asset is or may be credited in accordance with an agreement under which the person maintaining the account undertakes to treat the person for whom the account is maintained as entitled to exercise the rights that comprise the financial asset.

(b) Except as otherwise provided in subsections (d) and (e), a person acquires a security entitlement if a securities intermediary:

UCC

(1) indicates by book entry that a financial asset has been credited to the person's securities account;

(2) receives a financial asset from the person or acquires a financial asset for the person and, in either case, accepts it for credit to the person's securities account; or

(3) becomes obligated under other law, regulation, or rule to credit a financial asset to the person's securities account.

(c) If a condition of subsection (b) has been met, a person has a security entitlement even though the securities intermediary does not itself hold the financial asset.

(d) If a securities intermediary holds a financial asset for another person, and the financial asset is registered in the name of, payable to the order of, or specially indorsed to the other person, and has not been indorsed to the securities intermediary or in blank, the other person is treated as holding the financial asset directly rather than as having a security entitlement with respect to the financial asset.

(e) Issuance of a security is not establishment of a security entitlement.

History: Add, L 1997, ch 566, § 5, eff Oct 10, 1997.

§ 8-502. Assertion of Adverse Claim against Entitlement Holder

An action based on an adverse claim to a financial asset, whether framed in conversion, replevin, constructive trust, equitable lien, or other theory, may not be asserted against a person who acquires a security entitlement under Section 8-501 for value and without notice of the adverse claim.

History: Add, L 1997, ch 566, § 5, eff Oct 10, 1997.

§ 8-503. Property Interest of Entitlement Holder in Financial Asset held by Securities Intermediary

(a) To the extent necessary for a securities intermediary to satisfy all security entitlements with respect to a particular financial asset, all interests in that financial asset held by the securities intermediary are held by the securities intermediary for the entitlement holders, are not property of the securities intermediary, and are not subject to claims of creditors of the securities intermediary, except as otherwise provided in Section 8-511.

(b) An entitlement holder's property interest with respect to a particular financial asset under subsection (a) is a pro rata property interest in all interests in that financial asset held by the securities intermediary, without regard to the time the entitlement holder acquired the security entitlement or the time the securities intermediary acquired the interest in that financial asset.

(c) An entitlement holder's property interest with respect to a particular financial asset under subsection (a) may be enforced against the securities inter-

mediary only by exercise of the entitlement holder's rights under Sections 8-505 through 8-508.

(d) An entitlement holder's property interest with respect to a particular financial asset under subsection (a) may be enforced against a purchaser of the financial asset or interest therein only if:

(1) insolvency proceedings have been initiated by or against the securities intermediary;

(2) the securities intermediary does not have sufficient interests in the financial asset to satisfy the security entitlements of all of its entitlement holders to that financial asset;

(3) the securities intermediary violated its obligations under Section 8-504 by transferring the financial asset or interest therein to the purchaser; and

(4) the purchaser is not protected under subsection (e). The trustee or other liquidator, acting on behalf of all entitlement holders having security entitlements with respect to a particular financial asset, may recover the financial asset, or interest therein, from the purchaser. If the trustee or other liquidator elects not to pursue that right, an entitlement holder whose security entitlement remains unsatisfied has the right to recover its interest in the financial asset from the purchaser.

(e) An action based on the entitlement holder's property interest with respect to a particular financial asset under subsection (a), whether framed in conversion, replevin, constructive trust, equitable lien, or other theory, may not be asserted against any purchaser of a financial asset or interest therein who gives value, obtains control, and does not act in collusion with the securities intermediary in violating the securities intermediary's obligations under Section 8-504.

History: Add, L 1997, ch 566, § 5, eff Oct 10, 1997.

CASE ANNOTATIONS

By alleging that defendant bank holding company issued loan to plaintiff shareholder's broker supported by demand promissory note securing loan with securities held in broker's account, and then sold plaintiff's shares and retained proceeds when broker defaulted, plaintiff sufficiently stated claim under CLS UCC § 8-503 to set aside defendant's security interest in shares and recover damages based on defendant's sale of shares and retention of proceeds. Nathan W. Drage, P.C. v First Concord Secs., Ltd. (2000, Sup) 184 Misc. 2d 92, 707 N.Y.S.2d 782, 41 UCCRS2d 673

§ 8-504. Duty of Securities Intermediary to Maintain Financial Asset

(a) A securities intermediary shall promptly obtain and thereafter maintain a financial asset in a quantity corresponding to the aggregate of all security entitlements it has established in favor of its entitlement holders with respect to that financial asset. The securities intermediary may maintain those financial assets directly or through one or more other securities intermediaries.

(b) Except to the extent otherwise agreed by its entitlement holder, a securities intermediary may not grant any security interests in a financial asset it is obligated to maintain pursuant to subsection (a).

(c) A securities intermediary satisfies the duty in subsection (a) if:

(1) the securities intermediary acts with respect to the duty as agreed upon by the entitlement holder and the securities intermediary; or

(2) in the absence of agreement, the securities intermediary exercises due care in accordance with reasonable commercial standards to obtain and maintain the financial asset.

(d) This section does not apply to a clearing corporation that is itself the obligor of an option or similar obligation to which its entitlement holders have security entitlements.

History: Add, L 1997, ch 566, § 5, eff Oct 10, 1997.

CASE ANNOTATIONS

Defendant bank holding company, having issued loan to plaintiff shareholder's broker which was supported by demand promissory note securing loan with securities held in broker's account, had perfected security interest in plaintiff's stock shares, even though plaintiff's broker violated CLS UCC § 8-504(b) by pledging shares as collateral without plaintiff's permission, since defendant obtained "control" of shares held by defendant pursuant to promissory note and pledged by plaintiff's broker. Nathan W. Drage, P.C. v First Concord Secs., Ltd. (2000, Sup) 184 Misc. 2d 92, 707 N.Y.S.2d 782, 41 UCCRS2d 673

§ 8-505. Duty of Securities Intermediary with respect to Payments and Distributions

(a) A securities intermediary shall take action to obtain a payment or distribution made by the issuer of a financial asset. A securities intermediary satisfies the duty if:

(1) the securities intermediary acts with respect to the duty as agreed upon by the entitlement holder and the securities intermediary; or

(2) in the absence of agreement, the securities intermediary exercises due care in accordance with reasonable commercial standards to attempt to obtain the payment or distribution.

(b) A securities intermediary is obligated to its entitlement holder for a payment or distribution made by the issuer of a financial asset if the payment or distribution is received by the securities intermediary.

History: Add, L 1997, ch 566, § 5, eff Oct 10, 1997.

§ 8-506. Duty of Securities Intermediary to Exercise Rights as directed by Entitlement Holder

A securities intermediary shall exercise rights with respect to a financial asset if directed to do so by an entitlement holder. A securities intermediary satisfies the duty if:

(1) the securities intermediary acts with respect to the duty as agreed upon by the entitlement holder and the securities intermediary; or

(2) in the absence of agreement, the securities intermediary either places the entitlement holder in a position to exercise the rights directly or exercises due care in accordance with reasonable commercial standards to follow the direction of the entitlement holder.

History: Add, L 1997, ch 566, § 5, eff Oct 10, 1997.

§ 8-507. Duty of Securities Intermediary to comply with Entitlement Order

(a) A securities intermediary shall comply with an entitlement order if the entitlement order is originated by the appropriate person, the securities intermediary has had reasonable opportunity to assure itself that the entitlement order is genuine and authorized, and the securities intermediary has had reasonable opportunity to comply with the entitlement order. A securities intermediary satisfies the duty if:

(1) the securities intermediary acts with respect to the duty as agreed upon by the entitlement holder and the securities intermediary; or

(2) in the absence of agreement, the securities intermediary exercises due care in accordance with reasonable commercial standards to comply with the entitlement order.

(b) If a securities intermediary transfers a financial asset pursuant to an ineffective entitlement order, the securities intermediary shall reestablish a security entitlement in favor of the person entitled to it, and pay or credit any payments or distributions that the person did not receive as a result of the wrongful transfer. If the securities intermediary does not reestablish a security entitlement, the securities intermediary is liable to the entitlement holder for damages.

History: Add, L 1997, ch 566, § 5, eff Oct 10, 1997.

§ 8-508. Duty of Securities Intermediary to change Entitlement Holder's Position to Other Form of Security Holding

A securities intermediary shall act at the direction of an entitlement holder to change a security entitlement into another available form of holding for which the entitlement holder is eligible, or to cause the financial asset to be transferred to a securities account of the entitlement holder with another securities intermediary. A securities intermediary satisfies the duty if:

(1) the securities intermediary acts as agreed upon by the entitlement holder and the securities intermediary; or

(2) in the absence of agreement, the securities intermediary exercises due care in accordance with reasonable commercial standards to follow the direction of the entitlement holder.

History: Add, L 1997, ch 566, § 5, eff Oct 10, 1997.

UCC

§ 8-509. Specification of Duties of Securities Intermediary by Other Statute or Regulation; Manner of Performance of Duties of Securities Intermediary and Exercise of Rights of Entitlement Holder

(a) If the substance of a duty imposed upon a securities intermediary by Sections 8-504 through 8-508 is the subject of other statute, regulation, or rule, compliance with that statute, regulation, or rule satisfies the duty.

(b) To the extent that specific standards for the performance of the duties of a securities intermediary or the exercise of the rights of an entitlement holder are not specified by other statute, regulation, or rule or by agreement between the securities intermediary and entitlement holder, the securities intermediary shall perform its duties and the entitlement holder shall exercise its rights in a commercially reasonable manner.

(c) The obligation of a securities intermediary to perform the duties imposed by Sections 8-504 through 8-508 is subject to:

(1) rights of the securities intermediary arising out of a security interest under a security agreement with the entitlement holder or otherwise; and

(2) rights of the securities intermediary under other law, regulation, rule, or agreement to withhold performance of its duties as a result of unfulfilled obligations of the entitlement holder to the securities intermediary.

(d) Sections 8-504 through 8-508 do not require a securities intermediary to take any action that is prohibited by other statute, regulation, or rule.

History: Add, L 1997, ch 566, § 5, eff Oct 10, 1997.

CASE ANNOTATIONS

Article 8 of N.Y. U.C.C. Law did not displace substantive common law principles originally relied upon by the court, so on remand the result was same—as the corporation could not act on behalf of the individuals, no privity of contract existed between the individuals and the partnership—so the partnership's breach of oral contract to sell notes to partnership and breach of binding preliminary agreement claims failed. Highland Capital Mgmt., L.P. v Schneider (2008, SD NY) 533 F Supp 2d 345, motions ruled upon (2008, SD NY) 2008 US Dist LEXIS 7019.

§ 8-510. Rights of Purchaser of Security Entitlement from Entitlement Holder

(a) In a case not covered by the priority rules in Article 9 or the rules stated in subsection (c), an action based on an adverse claim to a financial asset or security entitlement, whether framed in conversion, replevin, constructive trust, equitable lien, or other theory, may not be asserted against a person who purchases a security entitlement, or an interest therein, from an entitlement holder if the purchaser gives value, does not have notice of the adverse claim, and obtains control.

(b) If an adverse claim could not have been asserted against an entitlement holder under Section 8-502, the adverse claim cannot be asserted against a person who purchases a security entitlement, or an interest therein, from the entitlement holder.

(c) In a case not covered by the priority rules in Article 9, a purchaser for value of a security entitlement, or an interest therein, who obtains control has priority over a purchaser of a security entitlement, or an interest therein, who does not obtain control. Except as otherwise provided in subsection (d), purchasers who have control rank according to priority in time of:

(1) the purchaser's becoming the person for whom the securities account, in which the security entitlement is carried, is maintained, if the purchaser obtained control under Section 8-106(d)(1);

(2) the securities intermediary's agreement to comply with the purchaser's entitlement orders with respect to security entitlements carried or to be carried in the securities account in which the security entitlement is carried, if the purchaser obtained control under Section 8-106(d)(2); or (3) if the purchaser obtained control through another person under Section 8-106(d)(3), the time on which priority would be based under this subsection if the other person were the secured party.

(d) A securities intermediary as purchaser has priority over a conflicting purchaser who has control unless otherwise agreed by the securities intermediary.

History: Add, L 1997, ch 566, § 5, eff Oct 10, 1997.

Sub (a), amd, L 2001, ch 84, § 34, eff July 1, 2001.

Sub (c), add, L 2001, ch 84, § 35, eff July 1, 2001.

Former sub (c), repealed, L 2001, ch 84, § 35, eff July 1, 2001.

Sub (d), add, L 2001, ch 84, § 35, eff July 1, 2001.

CASE ANNOTATIONS

Because a motion by a receiver for, among other things, an order transferring certain securities from a corporation's accounts to the receiver was an action based on an adverse claim to a financial asset or security entitlement, N.Y. U.C.C. Law § 8-510(a) applied; the receiver sought to retrieve, for the benefit of all of the customers of a corporation, all assets of certain accounts belonging to the corporation that were not subject to valid liens. SEC v Credit Bancorp, Ltd. (2003, SD NY) 279 F. Supp. 2d 247, motion gr (2003, SD NY) 2003 US Dist LEXIS 20024

§ 8-511. Priority Among Security Interests and Entitlement Holders

(a) Except as otherwise provided in subsections (b) and (c), if a securities intermediary does not have sufficient interests in a particular financial asset to satisfy both its obligations to entitlement holders who have security entitlements to that financial asset and its obligation to a creditor of the securities intermediary who has a security interest in that financial asset, the claims of entitlement holders, other than the creditor, have priority over the claim of the creditor.

(b) A claim of a creditor of a securities intermediary who has a security interest in a financial asset held by a securities intermediary has priority over claims of the securities intermediary's entitlement holders who have security entitlements with respect to that financial asset if the creditor has control over the financial asset.

(c) If a clearing corporation does not have sufficient financial assets to satisfy both its obligations to entitlement holders who have security entitlements with respect to a financial asset and its obligation to a creditor of the clearing corporation who has a security interest in that financial asset, the claim of the creditor has priority over the claims of entitlement holders.

History: Add, L 1997, ch 566, § 5, eff Oct 10, 1997.

CASE ANNOTATIONS

Defendant bank holding company, having issued loan to plaintiff shareholder's broker which was supported by demand promissory note securing loan with securities held in broker's account, had perfected security interest in plaintiff's stock shares, even though plaintiff's broker violated CLS UCC § 8-504(b) by pledging shares as collateral without plaintiff's permission, since defendant obtained "control" of shares held by defendant pursuant to promissory note and pledged by plaintiff's broker. Nathan W. Drage, P.C. v First Concord Secs., Ltd. (2000, Sup) 184 Misc. 2d 92, 707 N.Y.S.2d 782, 41 UCCRS2d 673

PART 6
TRANSITION PROVISIONS FOR REVISED ARTICLE 8 AND FOR THE CONFORMING AMENDMENTS TO ARTICLES 1, 5, 9 AND 13

History: Add, L 1997, ch 566, § 5, eff Oct 10, 1997.

§ 8-601.   Savings Clause; Effect on Prior Perfected Security Interest

(a) As used in this Part, the term "this Act" means that chapter of the laws of 1997 which repealed former Article 8 of this code, added this article to this code, and made conforming amendments to provisions of other articles of this code.

(b) This Act does not affect an action or proceeding commenced before this Act takes effect. An oral contract or a modification of contract entered into before the date this Act takes effect does not become enforceable by reason of operation of Section 8-113.

(c) If a security interest in a security is perfected at the date this Act takes effect, and the action by which the security interest was perfected would suffice to perfect a security interest under this Act, no further action is required to continue perfection. If a security interest in a security is perfected at the date this Act takes effect but the action by which the security interest was perfected would not suffice to perfect a security interest under this Act, the security interest remains perfected for a period of 12 months after the effective date of this Act and continues perfected thereafter if appropriate action to perfect under this Act is taken within that period. If a security interest is perfected at the date this Act takes

effect and the security interest can be perfected by filing under this Act, a financing statement signed by the secured party instead of by the debtor may be filed within that period to continue perfection or thereafter to perfect.

History: Add, L 1997, ch 566, § 5, eff Oct 10, 1997.

§ 8-602.   Cross-References to former Article 8; Meaning or Interpretation

(a) Any reference made in law to a bond or other security or instrument to be issued hereafter under the authority of such law as being a negotiable instrument or security under former Article 8 of this code shall be deemed to mean and refer to such bond or other security or instrument issued on or after the effective date of this Act as being one to be governed by the provisions of this new Article 8.

(b) The provisions of subsection (a) shall not be deemed to impair in any manner the obligations of any bond or other security or instrument previously issued and in existence on the effective date of this Act and the same shall continue to be governed by its covenants. The provisions of this Act shall apply to such previously issued and existing bond or other security or instrument only to the extent that the provisions of this Act can be harmonized with the provisions of covenants existing on the effective date of this Act to which such bond or other security or instrument is subject on such date, without impairing its obligations.

History: Add, L 1997, ch 566, § 5, eff Oct 10, 1997.

ARTICLE 9
SECURED TRANSACTIONS

History: Add, L 2001, ch 84, § 36, eff July 1, 2001.

Former Article 9. add, L 1962, ch 553, eff Sept 27, 1964.

Former Article 9, repealed, L 2001, ch 36, § 36, eff July 1, 2001.

PART 1
GENERAL PROVISIONS

Subpart 1
Short Title, Definitions, and General Concepts

UCC

§ 9-107. Control of Letter-of-credit Right
§ 9-108. Sufficiency of Description

Subpart 2
Applicability of Article

§ 9-109. Scope
§ 9-110. Security Interests Arising Under Article 2 or 2-A

History: Add, L 2001, ch 84, § 36, eff July 1, 2001.

Former Part 1, add, L 1962, ch 553, eff Sept 27, 1964.

Former Part 1, repealed, L 2001, ch 84, § 36, eff July 1, 2001.

———

Subpart 1
Short Title, Definitions, and General Concepts

History: Add, L 2001, ch 84, § 36, eff July 1, 2001.

§ 9-101. Short Title

This article may be cited as Uniform Commercial Code-Secured Transactions.

History: Add, L 2001, ch 84, § 36, eff July 1, 2001.

Former § 9-101, add, L 1962, ch 553, eff Sept 27, 1964; repealed, L 2001, ch 84, § 36, eff July 1, 2001.

CASE ANNOTATIONS

UNDER FORMER § 9-101

In a suit brought by a shareholder against a housing corporation and other shareholders (collectively referred to as the housing corporation), there was no justification for the shareholder's filing of a financing statement against a garden unit apartment for which the shareholder alleged that funds were expended as no security agreement was ever entered into between the parties, the shareholder had no common law lien that was enforceable, and there was no authenticated record whereby the housing corporation authorized the filing. Since the filing of the UCC-1 financing statement was baseless, the shareholder was directed to terminate the same and pay the housing corporation statutory damages in the amount of $500. McDaniel v 162 Columbia Hgts. Hous. Corps. (2008, Sup) 21 Misc 3d 244, 863 NYS2d 346.

Where financing statements filed with secretary of state alone and not filed locally did not protect security interest, lien creditor had priority over holder of security interests. Package Machinery Co. v Cosden Oil & Chemical Co. (1976, 2d Dept) 51 A.D.2d 771, 380 N.Y.S.2d 248, 18 UCCRS 1316

Vessel owner's maritime lien on subfreights which was never perfected was not subject to Article 9 of the New York Uniform Commercial Code, and thus owner had priority over trustee without need to file or perfect under that article. In re Sterling Navigation Co. (1983, SD NY) 31 BR 619, 36 UCCRS 1368

Seller of fuel oil could not claim to retain security interest in oil which it had delivered to broker for conveyance to buyer, and thus, as between seller and broker, seller could not bring action against third party buyer for misappropriation of oil, where no explicit agreement designating seller as security holder in oil was executed as required by CLS UCC Art 9. In re Crysen/Montenay Energy Co. (1990, CA2 NY) 902 F.2d 1098, 20 BCD 807, 22 CBC2d 1385, CCH Bankr L Rptr ¶ 73394, 11 UCCRS2d 881

§ 9-102. Definitions And Index of Definitions

(a) Article 9 definitions. In this article:

(1) "Accession" means goods that are physically united with other goods in such a manner that the identity of the original goods is not lost.

(2) "Account", except as used in "account for", means a right to payment of a monetary obligation, whether or not earned by performance, (i) for proper-ty that has been or is to be sold, leased, licensed, assigned, or otherwise disposed of, (ii) for services rendered or to be rendered, (iii) for a policy of insurance issued or to be issued, (iv) for a secondary obligation incurred or to be incurred, (v) for energy provided or to be provided, (vi) for the use or hire of a vessel under a charter or other contract, (vii) arising out of the use of a credit or charge card or information contained on or for use with the card, or (viii) as winnings in a lottery or other game of chance operated or sponsored by a state, governmental unit of a State, or person licensed or authorized to operate the game by a State or governmental unit of a State. The term includes health-care-insurance receivables. The term does not include (i) rights to payment evidenced by chattel paper or an instrument, (ii) commercial tort claims, (iii) deposit accounts, (iv) investment property, (v) letter-of-credit rights or letters of credit, or (vi) rights to payment for money or funds advanced or sold, other than rights arising out of the use of a credit or charge card or information contained on or for use with the card.

(3) "Account debtor" means a person obligated on an account, chattel paper, or general intangible. The term does not include persons obligated to pay a negotiable instrument, even if the instrument constitutes part of chattel paper.

(4) "Accounting", except as used in "accounting for", means a record:

(A) authenticated by a secured party;

(B) indicating the aggregate unpaid secured obligations as of a date not more than 35 days earlier or 35 days later than the date of the record; and

(C) identifying the components of the obligations in reasonable detail.

(5) "Agricultural lien" means an interest in farm products:

(A) which secures payment or performance of an obligation for:

(i) goods or services furnished in connection with a debtor's farming operation; or

(ii) rent on real property leased by a debtor in connection with its farming operation; and

(B) which is created by statute in favor of a person that:

(i) in the ordinary course of its business furnished goods or services to a debtor in connection with a debtor's farming operation; or

(ii) leased real property to a debtor in connection with the debtor's farming operation; and

(C) whose effectiveness does not depend on the person's possession of the personal property.

(6) "As-extracted collateral" means:

(A) oil, gas, or other minerals that are subject to a security interest that:

(i) is created by a debtor having an interest in the minerals before extraction; and

(ii) attaches to the minerals as extracted; or

(B) accounts arising out of the sale at the well-head or mine head of oil, gas, or other minerals in which the debtor had an interest before extraction.

(7) "Authenticate" means:

(A) to sign; or

(B) with present intent to adopt or accept a record, to attach to or logically associate with the record an electronic sound, symbol, or process.

(8) "Bank" means an organization that is engaged in the business of banking. The term includes savings banks, savings and loan associations, credit unions, and trust companies.

(9) "Cash proceeds" means proceeds that are money, checks, deposit accounts, or the like.

(10) "Certificate of title" means a certificate of title with respect to which a statute provides for the security interest in question to be indicated on the certificate as a condition or result of the security interest's obtaining priority over the rights of a lien creditor with respect to the collateral. Such term includes another record maintained as an alternative to a certificate of title by the governmental unit that issues certificates of title if a statute permits the security interest in question to be indicated on the record as a condition or result of the security interest's obtaining priority over the rights of a lien creditor with respect to the collateral.

(11) "Chattel paper" means a record or records that evidence both a monetary obligation and a security interest in specific goods, a security interest in specific goods and software used in the goods, a security interest in specific goods and license of software used in the goods, a lease of specific goods, or a lease of specific goods and license of software used in the goods. In this paragraph, "monetary obligation" means a monetary obligation secured by the goods or owed under a lease of the goods and includes a monetary obligation with respect to software used in the goods. The term does not include (i) charters or other contracts involving the use or hire of a vessel or (ii) records that evidence a right to payment arising out of the use of a credit or charge card or information contained on or for use with the card. If a transaction is evidenced by records that include an instrument or series of instruments, the group of records taken together constitutes chattel paper.

(11-a) "Check" means (i) a draft, other than a documentary draft, payable on demand and drawn on a bank or (ii) a cashier's check or a teller's check. An instrument may be a check even though it is described on its face by another term, such as "money order". An instrument that (i) meets all of the requirements stated in Article 3 of this chapter to be a negotiable instrument other than stating that it is payable to order or bearer and (ii) otherwise qualifies as a check is a negotiable instrument and a check.

(12) "Collateral" means the property subject to a security interest or agricultural lien. The term includes:

(A) proceeds to which a security interest attaches;

(B) accounts, chattel paper, payment intangibles, and promissory notes that have been sold; and

(C) goods that are the subject of a consignment.

(13) "Commercial tort claim" means a claim arising in tort with respect to which:

(A) the claimant is an organization; or

(B) the claimant is an individual and the claim:

(i) arose in the course of the claimant's business or profession; and

(ii) does not include damages arising out of personal injury to or the death of an individual.

(14) "Commodity account" means an account maintained by a commodity intermediary in which a commodity contract is carried for a commodity customer.

(15) "Commodity contract" means a commodity future contract, an option on a commodity futures contract, a commodity option, or another contract if the contract or option is:

(A) traded on or subject to the rules of a board of trade that has been designated as a contract market for such a contract pursuant to federal commodities laws; or

(B) traded on a foreign commodity board of trade, exchange, or market, and is carried on the books of a commodity intermediary for a commodity customer.

(16) "Commodity customer" means a person for which a commodity intermediary carries a commodity contract on its books.

(17) "Commodity intermediary" means a person that:

(A) is registered as a futures commission merchant under federal commodities law; or

(B) in the ordinary course of its business provides clearance or settlement services for a board of trade that has been designated as a contract market pursuant to federal commodities law.

(18) "Communicate" means:

(A) to send a written or other tangible record;

(B) to transmit a record by any means agreed upon by the persons sending and receiving the record; or

(C) in the case of transmission of a record to or by a filing office, to transmit a record by any means prescribed by filing-office rule.

(19) "Consignee" means a merchant to which goods are delivered in a consignment.

(20) "Consignment" means a transaction, regardless of its form, in which a person delivers goods to a merchant for the purpose of sale and:

(A) the merchant:

(i) deals in goods of that kind under a name other than the name of the person making delivery;

(ii) is not an auctioneer; and

(iii) is not generally known by its creditors to be substantially engaged in selling the goods of others;

UCC

(B) with respect to each delivery, the aggregate value of the goods is $1,000 or more at the time of delivery;

(C) the goods are not consumer goods immediately before delivery; and

(D) the transaction does not create a security interest that secures an obligation.

(21) "Consignor" means a person that delivers goods to a consignee in a consignment.

(22) "Consumer debtor" means a debtor in a consumer transaction.

(23) "Consumer goods" means goods that are used or bought for use primarily for personal, family, or household purposes.

(24) "Consumer-goods transaction" means a consumer transaction in which:

(A) an individual incurs an obligation primarily for personal, family, or household purposes; and

(B) a security interest in consumer goods secures the obligation.

(25) "Consumer obligor" means an obligor who is an individual and who incurred the obligation as part of a transaction entered into primarily for personal, family, or household purposes.

(26) "Consumer transaction" means a transaction in which (i) an individual incurs an obligation primarily for personal, family, or household purposes, (ii) a security interest secures the obligation, and (iii) the collateral is held or acquired primarily for personal, family, or household purposes. The term includes consumer-goods transactions.

(27) "Continuation statement" means an amendment of a financing statement which:

(A) identifies, by its file number, the initial financing statement to which it relates; and

(B) indicates that it is a continuation statement for, or that it is filed to continue the effectiveness of, the identified financing statement.

(27-a) "Cooperative addendum" means a record that satisfies Section 9-502(e).

(27-b) "Cooperative interest" means an ownership interest in a cooperative organization, which interest, when created, is coupled with possessory rights of a proprietary nature in identified physical space belonging to the cooperative organization. A subsequent termination of the possessory rights shall not cause an ownership interest to cease being a cooperative interest.

(27-c) "Cooperative organization" means an organization which has as its principal asset an interest in real property in this state and in which organization all ownership interests are cooperative interests.

(27-d) "Cooperative organization security interest" means a security interest which is in a cooperative interest, is in favor of the cooperative organization, is created by the cooperative record, and secures only obligations incident to ownership of that cooperative interest.

(27-e) "Cooperative record" means those records which, as a whole, evidence cooperative interests and define the mutual rights and obligations of the owners of the cooperative interests and the cooperative organization.

(27-f) "Cooperative unit" means the physical space associated with a cooperative interest.

(28) "Debtor" means:

(A) a person having an interest, other than a security interest or other lien, in the collateral, whether or not the person is an obligor;

(B) a seller of accounts, chattel paper, payment intangibles, or promissory notes; or

(C) a consignee.

(29) "Deposit account" means a demand, time, savings, passbook, or similar account maintained with a bank. The term does not include investment property or accounts evidenced by an instrument.

(30) "Document" means a document of title or a receipt of the type described in Section 7-201(b).

(31) "Electronic chattel paper" means chattel paper evidenced by a record or records consisting of information stored in an electronic medium.

(32) "Encumbrance" means a right, other than an ownership interest, in real property. The term includes mortgages and other liens on real property.

(33) "Equipment" means goods other than inventory, farm products, or consumer goods.

(34) "Farm products" means goods, other than standing timber, with respect to which the debtor is engaged in a farming operation and which are:

(A) crops grown, growing, or to be grown, including:

(i) crops produced on trees, vines, and bushes; and

(ii) aquatic goods produced in aquacultural operations;

(B) livestock, born or unborn, including aquatic goods produced in aquacultural operations;

(C) supplies used or produced in a farming operation; or

(D) products of crops or livestock in their unmanufactured states.

(35) "Farming operation" means raising, cultivating, propagating, fattening, grazing, or any other farming, livestock, or aquacultural operation.

(36) "File number" means the number assigned to an initial financing statement pursuant to Section 9-519(a).

(37) "Filing office" means an office designated in Section 9-501 as the place to file a financing statement.

(38) "Filing-office rule" means a rule adopted pursuant to Section 9-526.

(39) "Financing statement" means a record or records composed of an initial financing statement

and any filed record relating to the initial financing statement.

(40) "Fixture filing" means the filing of a financing statement covering goods that are or are to become fixtures and satisfying Section 9-502(a) and (b). The term includes the filing of a financing statement covering goods of a transmitting utility which are or are to become fixtures.

(41) "Fixtures" means goods that have become so related to particular real property that an interest in them arises under real property law.

(42) "General intangible" means any personal property, including things in action, other than accounts, chattel paper, commercial tort claims, deposit accounts, documents, goods, instruments, investment property, letter-of-credit rights, letters of credit, money, and oil, gas, or other minerals before extraction. The term includes payment intangibles and software.

(43) "Good faith" means honesty in fact and the observance of reasonable commercial standards of fair dealing.

(44) "Goods" means all things that are movable when a security interest attaches. The term includes (i) fixtures, (ii) standing timber that is to be cut and removed under a conveyance or contract for sale, (iii) the unborn young of animals, (iv) crops grown, growing, or to be grown, even if the crops are produced on trees, vines, or bushes, and (v) manufactured homes. The term also includes a computer program embedded in goods and any supporting information provided in connection with a transaction relating to the program if (i) the program is associated with the goods in such a manner that it customarily is considered part of the goods, or (ii) by becoming the owner of the goods, a person acquires a right to use the program in connection with the goods. The term does not include a computer program embedded in goods that consists solely of the medium in which the program is embedded. The term also does not include accounts, chattel paper, commercial tort claims, deposit accounts, documents, general intangibles, instruments, investment property, letter-of-credit rights, letters of credit, money, or oil, gas, or other minerals before extraction.

(45) "Governmental unit" means a subdivision, agency, department, county, parish, municipality, or other unit of the government of the United States, a state, or a foreign country. The term includes an organization having a separate corporate existence if the organization is eligible to issue debt on which interest is exempt from income taxation under the laws of the United States.

(46) "Health-care-insurance receivable" means an interest in or claim under a policy of insurance which is a right to payment of a monetary obligation for health-care goods or services provided or to be provided.

(47) "Instrument" means a negotiable instrument or any other writing that evidences a right to the payment of a monetary obligation, is not itself a security agreement or lease, and is of a type that in ordinary course of business is transferred by delivery with any necessary indorsement or assignment. The term does not include (i) investment property, (ii) letters of credit, or (iii) writings that evidence a right to payment arising out of the use of a credit or charge card or information contained on or for use with the card.

(48) "Inventory" means goods, other than farm products, which:

(A) are leased by a person as lessor;

(B) are held by a person for sale or lease or to be furnished under a contract of service;

(C) are furnished by a person under a contract of service; or

(D) consist of raw materials, work in process, or materials used or consumed in a business.

(49) "Investment property" means a security, whether certificated or uncertificated, security entitlement, securities account, commodity contract, or commodity account.

(50) "Jurisdiction of organization", with respect to a registered organization, means the jurisdiction under whose law the organization is formed or organized.

(51) "Letter-of-credit right" means a right to payment or performance under a letter of credit, whether or not the beneficiary has demanded or is at the time entitled to demand payment or performance. The term does not include the right of a beneficiary to demand payment or performance under a letter of credit.

(52) "Lien creditor" means:

(A) a creditor that has acquired a lien on the property involved by attachment, levy, or the like;

(B) an assignee for benefit of creditors from the time of assignment;

(C) a trustee in bankruptcy from the date of the filing of the petition; or

(D) a receiver in equity from the time of appointment.

(53) "Manufactured home" means a structure, transportable in one or more sections, which, in the traveling mode, is eight body feet or more in width or 40 body feet or more in length, or, when erected on site, is 320 or more square feet, and which is built on a permanent chassis and designed to be used as a dwelling with or without a permanent foundation when connected to the required utilities, and includes the plumbing, heating, air-conditioning, and electrical systems contained therein. The term includes any structure that meets all of the requirements of this paragraph except the size requirements and with respect to which the manufacturer voluntarily files a certification required by the United States Secretary of Housing and Urban Development and complies

UCC

with the standards established under Title 42 of the United States Code.

(54) "Manufactured-home transaction" means a secured transaction:

(A) that creates a purchase-money security interest in a manufactured home, other than a manufactured home held as inventory; or

(B) in which a manufactured home, other than a manufactured home held as inventory, is the primary collateral.

(55) "Mortgage" means a consensual interest in real property, including fixtures, which secures payment or performance of an obligation.

(56) "New debtor" means a person that becomes bound as debtor under Section 9-203(d) by a security agreement previously entered into by another person.

(57) "New value" means (i) money, (ii) money's worth in property, services, or new credit, or (iii) release by a transferee of an interest in property previously transferred to the transferee. The term does not include an obligation substituted for another obligation.

(58) "Noncash proceeds" means proceeds other than cash proceeds.

(59) "Obligor" means a person that, with respect to an obligation secured by a security interest in or an agricultural lien on the collateral, (i) owes payment or other performance of the obligation, (ii) has provided property other than the collateral to secure payment or other performance of the obligation, or (iii) is otherwise accountable in whole or in part for payment or other performance of the obligation. The term does not include issuers or nominated persons under a letter of credit.

(60) "Original debtor", except as used in Section 9-310(c), means a person that, as debtor, entered into a security agreement to which a new debtor has become bound under Section 9-203(d).

(60-a) "Payment assurance device" means any device installed in a vehicle that can be used to remotely disable the vehicle.

(61) "Payment intangible" means a general intangible under which the account debtor's principal obligation is a monetary obligation.

(62) "Person related to", with respect to an individual, means:

(A) the spouse of the individual;

(B) a brother, brother-in-law, sister, or sister-in-law of the individual;

(C) an ancestor or lineal descendant of the individual or the individual's spouse; or

(D) any other relative, by blood or marriage, of the individual or the individual's spouse who shares the same home with the individual.

(63) "Person related to", with respect to an organization, means:

(A) a person directly or indirectly controlling, controlled by, or under common control with the organization;

(B) an officer or director of, or a person performing similar functions with respect to, the organization;

(C) an officer or director of, or a person performing similar functions with respect to, a person described in subparagraph (A);

(D) the spouse of an individual described in subparagraph (A), (B), or (C); or

(E) an individual who is related by blood or marriage to an individual described in subparagraph (A), (B), (C), or (D) and shares the same home with the individual.

(64) "Proceeds", except as used in Section 9-609(b), means the following property:

(A) Whatever is acquired upon the sale, lease, license, exchange, or other disposition of collateral;

(B) whatever is collected on, or distributed on account of, collateral;

(C) rights arising out of collateral;

(D) to the extent of the value of collateral, claims arising out of the loss, nonconformity, or interference with the use of, defects or infringement of rights in, or damage to, the collateral; or

(E) to the extent of the value of collateral and to the extent payable to the debtor or the secured party, insurance payable by reason of the loss or nonconformity of, defects or infringement of rights in, or damage to, the collateral.

(65) "Promissory note" means an instrument that evidences a promise to pay a monetary obligation, does not evidence an order to pay, and does not contain an acknowledgment by a bank that the bank has received for deposit a sum of money or funds.

(66) "Proposal" means a record authenticated by a secured party which includes the terms on which the secured party is willing to accept collateral in full or partial satisfaction of the obligation it secures pursuant to Sections 9-620, 9-621, and 9-622.

(66-a) "Prove" with respect to a fact means to meet the burden of establishing the fact (Section 1-201(8)).

(67) "Public-finance transaction" means a secured transaction in connection with which:

(A) debt securities are issued;

(B) all or a portion of the securities issued have an initial stated maturity of at least 20 years; and

(C) the debtor, obligor, secured party, account debtor or other person obligated on collateral, assignor or assignee of a secured obligation, or assignor or assignee of a security interest is a state or a governmental unit of a state.

(68) "Public organic record" means a record that is available to the public for inspection and is:

(A) a record consisting of the record initially filed with or issued by a state or the United States to form or organize an organization and any record filed with or issued by the state or the United States which amends or restates the initial record;

(B) an organic record of a business trust consisting of the record initially filed with a state and any record filed with the state which amends or restates the initial record, if a statute of the state governing business trusts requires that the record be filed with the state; or

(C) a record consisting of legislation enacted by the legislature of a state or the Congress of the United States which forms or organizes an organization, any record amending the legislation, and any record filed with or issued by the state or the United States which amends or restates the name of the organization.

(69) "Pursuant to commitment", with respect to an advance made or other value given by a secured party, means pursuant to the secured party's obligation, whether or not a subsequent event of default or other event not within the secured party's control has relieved or may relieve the secured party from its obligation.

(70) "Record", except as used in "for record", "of record", "record or legal title", and "record owner", means information that is inscribed on a tangible medium or which is stored in an electronic or other medium and is retrievable in perceivable form.

(71) "Registered organization" means an organization formed or organized solely under the law of a single state or the United States by the filing of a public organic record with, the issuance of a public organic record by, or the enactment of legislation by the state or the United States. The term includes a business trust that is formed or organized under the law of a single state if a statute of the state governing business trusts requires that the business trust's organic record be filed with the state.

(72) "Secondary obligor" means an obligor to the extent that:

(A) the obligor's obligation is secondary; or

(B) the obligor has a right of recourse with respect to an obligation secured by collateral against the debtor, another obligor, or property of either.

(73) "Secured party" means:

(A) a person in whose favor a security interest is created or provided for under a security agreement, whether or not any obligation to be secured is outstanding;

(B) a person that holds an agricultural lien;

(C) a consignor;

(D) a person to which accounts, chattel paper, payment intangibles, or promissory notes have been sold;

(E) a trustee, indenture trustee, agent, collateral agent, or other representative in whose favor a security interest or agricultural lien is created or provided for; or

(F) a person that holds a security interest arising under Section 2-401, 2-505, 2-711(3), 2-A-508(5), 4-210, or 5-118.

(74) "Security agreement" means an agreement that creates or provides for a security interest. A cooperative record that provides that the owner of a cooperative interest has an obligation to pay amounts to the cooperative organization incident to ownership of that cooperative interest and which states that the cooperative organization has a direct remedy against that cooperative interest if such amounts are not paid is a security agreement creating a cooperative organization security interest.

(75) "Send", in connection with a record or notification, means:

(A) to deposit in the mail, deliver for transmission, or transmit by any other usual means of communication, with postage or cost of transmission provided for, addressed to any address reasonable under the circumstances; or

(B) to cause the record or notification to be received within the time that it would have been received if properly sent under subparagraph (A).

(76) "Software" means a computer program and any supporting information provided in connection with a transaction relating to the program. The term does not include a computer program that is included in the definition of goods.

(77) "State" means a state of the United States, the District of Columbia, Puerto Rico, the United States Virgin Islands, or any territory or insular possession subject to the jurisdiction of the United States.

(78) "Supporting obligation" means a letter-of-credit right or secondary obligation that supports the payment or performance of an account, chattel paper, a document, a general intangible, an instrument, or investment property.

(79) "Tangible chattel paper" means chattel paper evidenced by a record or records consisting of information that is inscribed on a tangible medium.

(80) "Termination statement" means an amendment of a financing statement which:

(A) identifies, by its file number, the initial financing statement to which it relates; and

(B) indicates either that it is a termination statement or that the identified financing statement is no longer effective.

(81) "Transmitting utility" means a person primarily engaged in the business of:

(A) operating a railroad, subway, street railway, or trolley bus;

(B) transmitting communications electrically, electromagnetically, or by light;

(C) transmitting goods by pipeline or sewer; or

UCC

(D) transmitting or producing and transmitting electricity, steam, gas, or water.

(b) Definitions in other articles. The following definitions in other articles apply to this article:

"Applicant"	Section 5-102.
"Beneficiary"	Section 5-102.
"Broker"	Section 8-102.
"Certificated security"	Section 8-102.
"Clearing corporation"	Section 8-102.
"Contract for sale"	Section 2-106.
"Control" (with respect to a document of title	Section 7-106.
"Customer"	Section 4-104.
"Entitlement holder"	Section 8-102.
"Financial asset"	Section 8-102.
"Holder in due course"	Section 3-302.
"Issuer" (with respect to a letter of credit or letter-of-credit right)	Section 5-102.
"Issuer" (with respect to a security)	Section 8-201.
"Issuer" (with respect to document of title)	Section 7-102.
"Lease"	Section 2-A-103.
"Lease agreement"	Section 2-A-103.
"Lease contract"	Section 2-A-103.
"Leasehold interest"	Section 2-A-103.
"Lessee"	Section 2-A-103.
"Lessee in ordinary course of business"	Section 2-A-103.
"Lessor"	Section 2-A-103.
"Lessor's residual interest"	Section 2-A-103.
"Letter of credit"	Section 5-102.
"Merchant"	Section 2-104.
"Negotiable instrument"	Section 3-104.
"Nominated person"	Section 5-102.
"Note"	Section 3-104.
"Proceeds of a letter of credit"	Section 5-114.
"Prove"	Section 4-A-105.
"Sale"	Section 2-106.
"Securities account"	Section 8-501.
"Securities intermediary"	Section 8-102.
"Security"	Section 8-102.
"Security certificate"	Section 8-102.
"Security entitlement"	Section 8-102.
"Uncertificated security"	Section 8-102.

(c) Article 1 definitions and principles. Article 1 contains general definitions and principles of con-

struction and interpretation applicable throughout this article.

History: Add, L 2001, ch 84, § 36, eff July 1, 2001; amd, L 2014, ch 505, § 26, eff Dec 17, 2014; L 2018, ch 312, § 1, eff Oct 2, 2018.

Blackline Showing Effect of 2018 Amendments. — (a) Article 9 definitions. In this article:

(1) "Accession" means goods that are physically united with other goods in such a manner that the identity of the original goods is not lost.

(2) "Account", except as used in "account for", means a right to payment of a monetary obligation, whether or not earned by performance, (i) for property that has been or is to be sold, leased, licensed, assigned, or otherwise disposed of, (ii) for services rendered or to be rendered, (iii) for a policy of insurance issued or to be issued, (iv) for a secondary obligation incurred or to be incurred, (v) for energy provided or to be provided, (vi) for the use or hire of a vessel under a charter or other contract, (vii) arising out of the use of a credit or charge card or information contained on or for use with the card, or (viii) as winnings in a lottery or other game of chance operated or sponsored by a state, governmental unit of a State, or person licensed or authorized to operate the game by a State or governmental unit of a State. The term includes health-care-insurance receivables. The term does not include (i) rights to payment evidenced by chattel paper or an instrument, (ii) commercial tort claims, (iii) deposit accounts, (iv) investment property, (v) letter-of-credit rights or letters of credit, or (vi) rights to payment for money or funds advanced or sold, other than rights arising out of the use of a credit or charge card or information contained on or for use with the card.

(3) "Account debtor" means a person obligated on an account, chattel paper, or general intangible. The term does not include persons obligated to pay a negotiable instrument, even if the instrument constitutes part of chattel paper.

(4) "Accounting", except as used in "accounting for", means a record:

(A) authenticated by a secured party;

(B) indicating the aggregate unpaid secured obligations as of a date not more than 35 days earlier or 35 days later than the date of the record; and

(C) identifying the components of the obligations in reasonable detail.

(5) "Agricultural lien" means an interest in farm products:

(A) which secures payment or performance of an obligation for:

(i) goods or services furnished in connection with a debtor's farming operation; or

(ii) rent on real property leased by a debtor in connection with its farming operation; and

(B) which is created by statute in favor of a person that:

(i) in the ordinary course of its business furnished goods or services to a debtor in connection with a debtor's farming operation; or

(ii) leased real property to a debtor in connection with the debtor's farming operation; and

(C) whose effectiveness does not depend on the person's possession of the personal property.

(6) "As-extracted collateral" means:

(A) oil, gas, or other minerals that are subject to a security interest that:

(i) is created by a debtor having an interest in the minerals before extraction; and

(ii) attaches to the minerals as extracted; or

(B) accounts arising out of the sale at the wellhead or mine head of oil, gas, or other minerals in which the debtor had an interest before extraction.

(7) "Authenticate" means:

(A) to sign; or

(B) with present intent to adopt or accept a record, to attach to or logically associate with the record an electronic sound, symbol, or process.

(8) "Bank" means an organization that is engaged in the business of banking. The term includes savings banks, savings and loan associations, credit unions, and trust companies.

(9) "Cash proceeds" means proceeds that are money, checks, deposit accounts, or the like.

(10) "Certificate of title" means a certificate of title with respect to which a statute provides for the security interest in question to be

indicated on the certificate as a condition or result of the security interest's obtaining priority over the rights of a lien creditor with respect to the collateral. Such term includes another record maintained as an alternative to a certificate of title by the governmental unit that issues certificates of title if a statute permits the security interest in question to be indicated on the record as a condition or result of the security interest's obtaining priority over the rights of a lien creditor with respect to the collateral.

(11) "Chattel paper" means a record or records that evidence both a monetary obligation and a security interest in specific goods, a security interest in specific goods and software used in the goods, a security interest in specific goods and license of software used in the goods, a lease of specific goods, or a lease of specific goods and license of software used in the goods. In this paragraph, "monetary obligation" means a monetary obligation secured by the goods or owed under a lease of the goods and includes a monetary obligation with respect to software used in the goods. The term does not include (i) charters or other contracts involving the use or hire of a vessel or (ii) records that evidence a right to payment arising out of the use of a credit or charge card or information contained on or for use with the card. If a transaction is evidenced by records that include an instrument or series of instruments, the group of records taken together constitutes chattel paper.

(11-a) "Check" means (i) a draft, other than a documentary draft, payable on demand and drawn on a bank or (ii) a cashier's check or a teller's check. An instrument may be a check even though it is described on its face by another term, such as "money order". An instrument that (i) meets all of the requirements stated in Article 3 of this chapter to be a negotiable instrument other than stating that it is payable to order or bearer and (ii) otherwise qualifies as a check is a negotiable instrument and a check.

(12) "Collateral" means the property subject to a security interest or agricultural lien. The term includes:

(A) proceeds to which a security interest attaches;

(B) accounts, chattel paper, payment intangibles, and promissory notes that have been sold; and

(C) goods that are the subject of a consignment.

(13) "Commercial tort claim" means a claim arising in tort with respect to which:

(A) the claimant is an organization; or

(B) the claimant is an individual and the claim:

(i) arose in the course of the claimant's business or profession; and

(ii) does not include damages arising out of personal injury to or the death of an individual.

(14) "Commodity account" means an account maintained by a commodity intermediary in which a commodity contract is carried for a commodity customer.

(15) "Commodity contract" means a commodity future contract, an option on a commodity futures contract, a commodity option, or another contract if the contract or option is:

(A) traded on or subject to the rules of a board of trade that has been designated as a contract market for such a contract pursuant to federal commodities laws; or

(B) traded on a foreign commodity board of trade, exchange, or market, and is carried on the books of a commodity intermediary for a commodity customer.

(16) "Commodity customer" means a person for which a commodity intermediary carries a commodity contract on its books.

(17) "Commodity intermediary" means a person that:

(A) is registered as a futures commission merchant under federal commodities law; or

(B) in the ordinary course of its business provides clearance or settlement services for a board of trade that has been designated as a contract market pursuant to federal commodities law.

(18) "Communicate" means:

(A) to send a written or other tangible record;

(B) to transmit a record by any means agreed upon by the persons sending and receiving the record; or

(C) in the case of transmission of a record to or by a filing office, to transmit a record by any means prescribed by filing-office rule.

(19) "Consignee" means a merchant to which goods are delivered in a consignment.

(20) "Consignment" means a transaction, regardless of its form, in which a person delivers goods to a merchant for the purpose of sale and:

(A) the merchant:

(i) deals in goods of that kind under a name other than the name of the person making delivery;

(ii) is not an auctioneer; and

(iii) is not generally known by its creditors to be substantially engaged in selling the goods of others;

(B) with respect to each delivery, the aggregate value of the goods is $1,000 or more at the time of delivery;

(C) the goods are not consumer goods immediately before delivery; and

(D) the transaction does not create a security interest that secures an obligation.

(21) "Consignor" means a person that delivers goods to a consignee in a consignment.

(22) "Consumer debtor" means a debtor in a consumer transaction.

(23) "Consumer goods" means goods that are used or bought for use primarily for personal, family, or household purposes.

(24) "Consumer-goods transaction" means a consumer transaction in which:

(A) an individual incurs an obligation primarily for personal, family, or household purposes; and

(B) a security interest in consumer goods secures the obligation.

(25) "Consumer obligor" means an obligor who is an individual and who incurred the obligation as part of a transaction entered into primarily for personal, family, or household purposes.

(26) "Consumer transaction" means a transaction in which (i) an individual incurs an obligation primarily for personal, family, or household purposes, (ii) a security interest secures the obligation, and (iii) the collateral is held or acquired primarily for personal, family, or household purposes. The term includes consumer-goods transactions.

(27) "Continuation statement" means an amendment of a financing statement which:

(A) identifies, by its file number, the initial financing statement to which it relates; and

(B) indicates that it is a continuation statement for, or that it is filed to continue the effectiveness of, the identified financing statement.

(27-a) "Cooperative addendum" means a record that satisfies Section 9-502(e).

(27-b) "Cooperative interest" means an ownership interest in a cooperative organization, which interest, when created, is coupled with possessory rights of a proprietary nature in identified physical space belonging to the cooperative organization. A subsequent termination of the possessory rights shall not cause an ownership interest to cease being a cooperative interest.

(27-c) "Cooperative organization" means an organization which has as its principal asset an interest in real property in this state and in which organization all ownership interests are cooperative interests.

(27-d) "Cooperative organization security interest" means a security interest which is in a cooperative interest, is in favor of the cooperative organization, is created by the cooperative record, and secures only obligations incident to ownership of that cooperative interest.

(27-e) "Cooperative record" means those records which, as a whole, evidence cooperative interests and define the mutual rights and obligations of the owners of the cooperative interests and the cooperative organization.

(27-f) "Cooperative unit" means the physical space associated with a cooperative interest.

(28) "Debtor" means:

(A) a person having an interest, other than a security interest or other lien, in the collateral, whether or not the person is an obligor;

(B) a seller of accounts, chattel paper, payment intangibles, or promissory notes; or

(C) a consignee.

(29) "Deposit account" means a demand, time, savings, passbook, or similar account maintained with a bank. The term does not include investment property or accounts evidenced by an instrument.

(30) "Document" means a document of title or a receipt of the type described in Section 7-201(b).

(31) "Electronic chattel paper" means chattel paper evidenced by a record or records consisting of information stored in an electronic medium.

(32) "Encumbrance" means a right, other than an ownership interest, in real property. The term includes mortgages and other liens on real property.

UCC

(33) "Equipment" means goods other than inventory, farm products, or consumer goods.

(34) "Farm products" means goods, other than standing timber, with respect to which the debtor is engaged in a farming operation and which are:

(A) crops grown, growing, or to be grown, including:

(i) crops produced on trees, vines, and bushes; and

(ii) aquatic goods produced in aquacultural operations;

(B) livestock, born or unborn, including aquatic goods produced in aquacultural operations;

(C) supplies used or produced in a farming operation; or

(D) products of crops or livestock in their unmanufactured states.

(35) "Farming operation" means raising, cultivating, propagating, fattening, grazing, or any other farming, livestock, or aquacultural operation.

(36) "File number" means the number assigned to an initial financing statement pursuant to Section 9-519(a).

(37) "Filing office" means an office designated in Section 9-501 as the place to file a financing statement.

(38) "Filing-office rule" means a rule adopted pursuant to Section 9-526.

(39) "Financing statement" means a record or records composed of an initial financing statement and any filed record relating to the initial financing statement.

(40) "Fixture filing" means the filing of a financing statement covering goods that are or are to become fixtures and satisfying Section 9-502(a) and (b). The term includes the filing of a financing statement covering goods of a transmitting utility which are or are to become fixtures.

(41) "Fixtures" means goods that have become so related to particular real property that an interest in them arises under real property law.

(42) "General intangible" means any personal property, including things in action, other than accounts, chattel paper, commercial tort claims, deposit accounts, documents, goods, instruments, investment property, letter-of-credit rights, letters of credit, money, and oil, gas, or other minerals before extraction. The term includes payment intangibles and software.

(43) "Good faith" means honesty in fact and the observance of reasonable commercial standards of fair dealing.

(44) "Goods" means all things that are movable when a security interest attaches. The term includes (i) fixtures, (ii) standing timber that is to be cut and removed under a conveyance or contract for sale, (iii) the unborn young of animals, (iv) crops grown, growing, or to be grown, even if the crops are produced on trees, vines, or bushes, and (v) manufactured homes. The term also includes a computer program embedded in goods and any supporting information provided in connection with a transaction relating to the program if (i) the program is associated with the goods in such a manner that it customarily is considered part of the goods, or (ii) by becoming the owner of the goods, a person acquires a right to use the program in connection with the goods. The term does not include a computer program embedded in goods that consists solely of the medium in which the program is embedded. The term also does not include accounts, chattel paper, commercial tort claims, deposit accounts, documents, general intangibles, instruments, investment property, letter-of-credit rights, letters of credit, money, or oil, gas, or other minerals before extraction.

(45) "Governmental unit" means a subdivision, agency, department, county, parish, municipality, or other unit of the government of the United States, a state, or a foreign country. The term includes an organization having a separate corporate existence if the organization is eligible to issue debt on which interest is exempt from income taxation under the laws of the United States.

(46) "Health-care-insurance receivable" means an interest in or claim under a policy of insurance which is a right to payment of a monetary obligation for health-care goods or services provided or to be provided.

(47) "Instrument" means a negotiable instrument or any other writing that evidences a right to the payment of a monetary obligation, is not itself a security agreement or lease, and is of a type that in ordinary course of business is transferred by delivery with any necessary indorsement or assignment. The term does not include (i) investment property, (ii) letters of credit, or (iii) writings that evidence a right to payment arising out of the use of a credit or charge card or information contained on or for use with the card.

(48) "Inventory" means goods, other than farm products, which:

(A) are leased by a person as lessor;

(B) are held by a person for sale or lease or to be furnished under a contract of service;

(C) are furnished by a person under a contract of service; or

(D) consist of raw materials, work in process, or materials used or consumed in a business.

(49) "Investment property" means a security, whether certificated or uncertificated, security entitlement, securities account, commodity contract, or commodity account.

(50) "Jurisdiction of organization", with respect to a registered organization, means the jurisdiction under whose law the organization is formed or organized.

(51) "Letter-of-credit right" means a right to payment or performance under a letter of credit, whether or not the beneficiary has demanded or is at the time entitled to demand payment or performance. The term does not include the right of a beneficiary to demand payment or performance under a letter of credit.

(52) "Lien creditor" means:

(A) a creditor that has acquired a lien on the property involved by attachment, levy, or the like;

(B) an assignee for benefit of creditors from the time of assignment;

(C) a trustee in bankruptcy from the date of the filing of the petition; or

(D) a receiver in equity from the time of appointment.

(53) "Manufactured home" means a structure, transportable in one or more sections, which, in the traveling mode, is eight body feet or more in width or 40 body feet or more in length, or, when erected on site, is 320 or more square feet, and which is built on a permanent chassis and designed to be used as a dwelling with or without a permanent foundation when connected to the required utilities, and includes the plumbing, heating, air-conditioning, and electrical systems contained therein. The term includes any structure that meets all of the requirements of this paragraph except the size requirements and with respect to which the manufacturer voluntarily files a certification required by the United States Secretary of Housing and Urban Development and complies with the standards established under Title 42 of the United States Code.

(54) "Manufactured-home transaction" means a secured transaction:

(A) that creates a purchase-money security interest in a manufactured home, other than a manufactured home held as inventory; or

(B) in which a manufactured home, other than a manufactured home held as inventory, is the primary collateral.

(55) "Mortgage" means a consensual interest in real property, including fixtures, which secures payment or performance of an obligation.

(56) "New debtor" means a person that becomes bound as debtor under Section 9-203(d) by a security agreement previously entered into by another person.

(57) "New value" means (i) money, (ii) money's worth in property, services, or new credit, or (iii) release by a transferee of an interest in property previously transferred to the transferee. The term does not include an obligation substituted for another obligation.

(58) "Noncash proceeds" means proceeds other than cash proceeds.

(59) "Obligor" means a person that, with respect to an obligation secured by a security interest in or an agricultural lien on the collateral, (i) owes payment or other performance of the obligation, (ii) has provided property other than the collateral to secure payment or other performance of the obligation, or (iii) is otherwise accountable in whole or in part for payment or other performance of the obligation. The term does not include issuers or nominated persons under a letter of credit.

(60) "Original debtor", except as used in Section 9-310(c), means a person that, as debtor, entered into a security agreement to which a new debtor has become bound under Section 9-203(d).

(60-a) "Payment assurance device" means any device installed in a vehicle that can be used to remotely disable the vehicle.

(61) "Payment intangible" means a general intangible under which the account debtor's principal obligation is a monetary obligation.

(62) "Person related to", with respect to an individual, means:

(A) the spouse of the individual;

(B) a brother, brother-in-law, sister, or sister-in-law of the individual;

(C) an ancestor or lineal descendant of the individual or the individual's spouse; or

(D) any other relative, by blood or marriage, of the individual or the individual's spouse who shares the same home with the individual.

(63) "Person related to", with respect to an organization, means:

(A) a person directly or indirectly controlling, controlled by, or under common control with the organization;

(B) an officer or director of, or a person performing similar functions with respect to, the organization;

(C) an officer or director of, or a person performing similar functions with respect to, a person described in subparagraph (A);

(D) the spouse of an individual described in subparagraph (A), (B), or (C); or

(E) an individual who is related by blood or marriage to an individual described in subparagraph (A), (B), (C), or (D) and shares the same home with the individual.

(64) "Proceeds", except as used in Section 9-609(b), means the following property:

(A) Whatever is acquired upon the sale, lease, license, exchange, or other disposition of collateral;

(B) whatever is collected on, or distributed on account of, collateral;

(C) rights arising out of collateral;

(D) to the extent of the value of collateral, claims arising out of the loss, nonconformity, or interference with the use of, defects or infringement of rights in, or damage to, the collateral; or

(E) to the extent of the value of collateral and to the extent payable to the debtor or the secured party, insurance payable by reason of the loss or nonconformity of, defects or infringement of rights in, or damage to, the collateral.

(65) "Promissory note" means an instrument that evidences a promise to pay a monetary obligation, does not evidence an order to pay, and does not contain an acknowledgment by a bank that the bank has received for deposit a sum of money or funds.

(66) "Proposal" means a record authenticated by a secured party which includes the terms on which the secured party is willing to accept collateral in full or partial satisfaction of the obligation it secures pursuant to Sections 9-620, 9-621, and 9-622.

(66-a) "Prove" with respect to a fact means to meet the burden of establishing the fact (Section 1-201(8)).

(67) "Public-finance transaction" means a secured transaction in connection with which:

(A) debt securities are issued;

(B) all or a portion of the securities issued have an initial stated maturity of at least 20 years; and

(C) the debtor, obligor, secured party, account debtor or other person obligated on collateral, assignor or assignee of a secured obligation, or assignor or assignee of a security interest is a state or a governmental unit of a state.

(68) "Public organic record" means a record that is available to the public for inspection and is:

(A) a record consisting of the record initially filed with or issued by a state or the United States to form or organize an organization and any record filed with or issued by the state or the United States which amends or restates the initial record;

(B) an organic record of a business trust consisting of the record initially filed with a state and any record filed with the state which amends or restates the initial record, if a statute of the state governing business trusts requires that the record be filed with the state; or

(C) a record consisting of legislation enacted by the legislature of a state or the Congress of the United States which forms or organizes an organization, any record amending the legislation, and any record filed with or issued by the state or the United States which amends or restates the name of the organization.

(69) "Pursuant to commitment", with respect to an advance made or other value given by a secured party, means pursuant to the secured party's obligation, whether or not a subsequent event of default or other event not within the secured party's control has relieved or may relieve the secured party from its obligation.

(70) "Record", except as used in "for record", "of record", "record or legal title", and "record owner", means information that is inscribed on a tangible medium or which is stored in an electronic or other medium and is retrievable in perceivable form.

(71) "Registered organization" means an organization formed or organized solely under the law of a single state or the United States by the filing of a public organic record with, the issuance of a public organic record by, or the enactment of legislation by the state or the

United States. The term includes a business trust that is formed or organized under the law of a single state if a statute of the state governing business trusts requires that the business trust's organic record be filed with the state.

(72) "Secondary obligor" means an obligor to the extent that:

(A) the obligor's obligation is secondary; or

(B) the obligor has a right of recourse with respect to an obligation secured by collateral against the debtor, another obligor, or property of either.

(73) "Secured party" means:

(A) a person in whose favor a security interest is created or provided for under a security agreement, whether or not any obligation to be secured is outstanding;

(B) a person that holds an agricultural lien;

(C) a consignor;

(D) a person to which accounts, chattel paper, payment intangibles, or promissory notes have been sold;

(E) a trustee, indenture trustee, agent, collateral agent, or other representative in whose favor a security interest or agricultural lien is created or provided for; or

(F) a person that holds a security interest arising under Section 2-401, 2-505, 2-711(3), 2-A-508(5), 4-210, or 5-118.

(74) "Security agreement" means an agreement that creates or provides for a security interest. A cooperative record that provides that the owner of a cooperative interest has an obligation to pay amounts to the cooperative organization incident to ownership of that cooperative interest and which states that the cooperative organization has a direct remedy against that cooperative interest if such amounts are not paid is a security agreement creating a cooperative organization security interest.

(75) "Send", in connection with a record or notification, means:

(A) to deposit in the mail, deliver for transmission, or transmit by any other usual means of communication, with postage or cost of transmission provided for, addressed to any address reasonable under the circumstances; or

(B) to cause the record or notification to be received within the time that it would have been received if properly sent under subparagraph (A).

(76) "Software" means a computer program and any supporting information provided in connection with a transaction relating to the program. The term does not include a computer program that is included in the definition of goods.

(77) "State" means a state of the United States, the District of Columbia, Puerto Rico, the United States Virgin Islands, or any territory or insular possession subject to the jurisdiction of the United States.

(78) "Supporting obligation" means a letter-of-credit right or secondary obligation that supports the payment or performance of an account, chattel paper, a document, a general intangible, an instrument, or investment property.

(79) "Tangible chattel paper" means chattel paper evidenced by a record or records consisting of information that is inscribed on a tangible medium.

(80) "Termination statement" means an amendment of a financing statement which:

(A) identifies, by its file number, the initial financing statement to which it relates; and

(B) indicates either that it is a termination statement or that the identified financing statement is no longer effective.

(81) "Transmitting utility" means a person primarily engaged in the business of:

(A) operating a railroad, subway, street railway, or trolley bus;

(B) transmitting communications electrically, electromagnetically, or by light;

(C) transmitting goods by pipeline or sewer; or

(D) transmitting or producing and transmitting electricity, steam, gas, or water.

(b) Definitions in other articles. The following definitions in other articles apply to this article:

"Applicant"	Section 5-102.
"Beneficiary"	Section 5-102.
"Broker"	Section 8-102.
"Certificated security"	Section 8-102.
"Clearing corporation"	Section 8-102.
"Contract for sale"	Section 2-106.
"Control" (with respect to a document of title	Section 7-106.

UCC

"Customer"	Section 4-104.
"Entitlement holder"	Section 8-102.
"Financial asset"	Section 8-102.
"Holder in due course"	Section 3-302.
"Issuer" (with respect to a letter of credit or letter-of-credit right)	Section 5-102.
"Issuer" (with respect to a security)	Section 8-201.
"Issuer" (with respect to document of title)	Section 7-102.
"Lease"	Section 2-A-103.
"Lease agreement"	Section 2-A-103.
"Lease contract"	Section 2-A-103.
"Leasehold interest"	Section 2-A-103.
"Lessee"	Section 2-A-103.
"Lessee in ordinary course of business"	Section 2-A-103.
"Lessor"	Section 2-A-103.
"Lessor's residual interest"	Section 2-A-103.
"Letter of credit"	Section 5-102.
"Merchant"	Section 2-104.
"Negotiable instrument"	Section 3-104.
"Nominated person"	Section 5-102.
"Note"	Section 3-104.
"Proceeds of a letter of credit"	Section 5-114.
"Prove"	Section 4-A-105.
"Sale"	Section 2-106.
"Securities account"	Section 8-501.
"Securities intermediary"	Section 8-102.
"Security"	Section 8-102.
"Security certificate"	Section 8-102.
"Security entitlement"	Section 8-102.
"Uncertificated security"	Section 8-102.

(c) Article 1 definitions and principles. Article 1 contains general definitions and principles of construction and interpretation applicable throughout this article.

CASE ANNOTATIONS

1. Good faith purchaser
2. Consignment
3. Authentication requirement
4. Secured creditor
5. Purchase money security interest
6. Bad faith
7. Valid security agreement
8. Unperfected security interest
9. Under former § 9-106
10. Under former § 9-109
11. Under former § 9-105
12. – "Chattel paper"
13. – "Collateral"
14. – "Debtor"
15. – –Guarantor of obligation as debtor
16. – "Goods"
17. – "Instrument"
18. – "Security agreement"; financing statement as security agreement
19. – –Promissory note as security agreement
20. –"Secured party"
21. Under former § 9-112

1. Good faith purchaser
Funding company entered into a contractual relationship with network designer, and at the outset had a copy of its business plan and a right to copies of its business records; it had procedures in place to check with the network services provider to make sure that each individual invoice was payable before agreeing to purchase and advance funds against it; those kinds of considerations supported looking to N.Y. U.C.C. Law art. 1 rather than N.Y. U.C.C. Law arts. 3 and 4 for the standard of notice applicable to a factor seeking shelter as a good-faith purchaser. Further, N.Y. U.C.C. Law art. 9 does not define notice, N.Y. U.C.C. Law § 9-102(a), or refer to the definition of notice in N.Y. U.C.C. Law arts. 3 and 4, N.Y. U.C.C. Law § 9-102(b);

therefore, N.Y. U.C.C. Law art. 1's general definitions and principles of construction and interpretation were most appropriately applicable, N.Y. U.C.C. Law § 9-102(c). Le Chase Data/Telecom Servs., LLC v Goebert, 6 N.Y.3d 281, 811 N.Y.S.2d 317, 844 N.E.2d 771, 2006 N.Y. LEXIS 198 (N.Y. 2006).

Trial court properly granted summary judgment to a lender on a buyer's action for tortious interference with its contract with a borrower because, while the court erred in concluding that the buyer was not a debtor, the lender was entitled to repossess the equipment from the buyer inasmuch as the borrower's sale of the equipment to the buyer conclusively established an event of default occurred before the lender repossessed the equipment, and the lender was not liable for the acts of the repossessor as to the buyer's claims for tortious interference with contract and tortious interference with prospective business relations claims based on the manner of repossession and disposition of the equipment. Matter of Abele Tractor & Equip. Co., Inc. v Schaeffer, 2018 N.Y. App. Div. LEXIS 8694 (N.Y. App. Div. 3d Dep't 2018).

2. Consignment
In order for a transaction to fit under N.Y. U.C.C. Law § 9-102(a)(20), each of the attributes of a consignment as defined in § 9-102(a)(20) must be satisfied; the burden of proof with respect to each attribute falls on the party claiming to be protected by § 9-102(a)(20). Where a consignee filed for Chapter 7 bankruptcy relief, consignors were unable to prove that their transactions fit under § 9-102(a)(20) because they could not prove that the consignee was not an auctioneer and that the consignee was not generally known by its creditors to be substantially engaged in selling the goods of others. In re Morgansen's Ltd., 302 B.R. 784, 2003 Bankr. LEXIS 1726 (Bankr. E.D.N.Y. 2003), aff'd in part, 2005 U.S. Dist. LEXIS 43600 (E.D.N.Y. Sept. 27, 2005).

It was undisputed that during the term of the contract debtor held itself out to be a merchant only of certain jewelry. Since debtor dealt only in those certain goods and did not sell any other jewelry, it did not deal in goods under "a name other than the name of the person making delivery;" the arrangement accordingly was not be a consignment for purposes of application of U.C.C. art. 9. In re G.S. Distrib., 331 B.R. 552, 2005 Bankr. LEXIS 2006 (Bankr. S.D.N.Y. 2005).

Where dispute centered on who had superior rights to work of art that had been displayed in debtor's gallery, trustee was not entitled to summary judgment on claim it had superior right as assignee of creditor bank's perfected lien because trustee did not meet his burden to prove that definition of "consignment" under New York's Uniform Commercial Code had been met by transaction at issue. Jacobs v Kraken Inv. Ltd. (In re Salander-O'Reilly Galleries, LLC), 506 B.R. 600, 2014 Bankr. LEXIS 1101 (Bankr. S.D.N.Y. 2014), rev'd, 2014 U.S. Dist. LEXIS 181203 (S.D.N.Y. Nov. 25, 2014).

3. Authentication requirement
Because N.Y. U.C.C. Law § 9-203 did not require that a security agreement be signed by both parties to be enforceable, the fact that only the debtors signed both the promissory note and the contract of sale was enough to satisfy the authentication requirement of N.Y. U.C.C. Law § 9-102(a)(7). Ultimore, Inc. v Bucala (In re Bucala), 464 B.R. 626, 2012 Bankr. LEXIS 414 (Bankr. S.D.N.Y. 2012).

4. Secured creditor
Where debtors signed a note that included a paragraph under which the debtors agreed that a lien "may" be filed against the title of the collateral, the note clearly demonstrated the debtors' intent to grant the creditor a security interest because the note was replete with references to the creditor's status as a secured creditor. Ultimore, Inc. v Bucala (In re Bucala), 464 B.R. 626, 2012 Bankr. LEXIS 414 (Bankr. S.D.N.Y. 2012).

5. Purchase money security interest
In connection with the financed sale of a manufactured home, the seller held a purchase-money security interest in the home pursuant to N.Y. U.C.C. Law § 9-102(a)(54)(A) and § 9-103(b)(1), and the failure to perfect that interest did not result in a loss of its secured status. Ultimore, Inc. v Bucala (In re Bucala), 464 B.R. 626, 2012 Bankr. LEXIS 414 (Bankr. S.D.N.Y. 2012).

6. Bad faith
Defendants speculated that the corporation exercised its discretion to appraise and sell the pledged property in bad faith; however, they failed to create an issue of fact as to the alleged bad faith or the reasonableness of a potential auction sale of the collateral. Christie's Inc. v Davis, 247 F. Supp. 2d 414, 2002 U.S. Dist. LEXIS 23067 (S.D.N.Y. 2002).

7. Valid security agreement

Despite discrepancies in dates, an investment company asserted a valid security agreement under N.Y. U.C.C. § 9-102(73) with respect to a cooperative apartment based on its claim that a debtor borrowed money from it for expenses relating to the apartment, and the debtor also executed a demand promissory note for these funds as well as a confession of judgment in favor of the investment company. Micalden Invs. S.A. v Rostropovich, 535 F. Supp. 2d 433, 2008 U.S. Dist. LEXIS 16510 (S.D.N.Y. 2008).

8. Unperfected security interest

Court denied the bank's claims to the extent it sought treatment as a secured creditor or recission because under the plain terms of the bank's agreement with the debt fund, the bank did not take any collateral assignment, perfected or unperfected, of the interest in the participation agreement, and it was relevant that the bank's security interest was in the loan documents, and not in the participation agreement, because only the participation interest could possibly be construed as a "payment intangible"; a "payment intangible" was a general intangible under which the account debtor's primary obligation was a monetary obligation, U.C.C. § 9-102(a)(61), and a "general intangible" explicitly excluded instruments, such as the loan documents, which included a mortgage and a mortgage note, from its definition. U.C.C. § 9-102(a)(42). Under the UCC, the assignment of a payment intangible was automatically perfected, U.C.C. § 9-309(2), while under U.C.C. §§ 9-313(a); 9-312(a), a security interest in an instrument was perfected either by filing, or when the holder of the interest took actual or constructive possession of the instrument, and after the bank sold its participation interest a record was never authenticated acknowledging that it held the loan documents for the bank's benefit as would have been required by UCC § 9-313(c); as the bank had neither actual or constructive possession of the loan documents, its security interest in the loan documents was unperfected. SEC v Byers, 671 F. Supp. 2d 531, 2009 U.S. Dist. LEXIS 112494 (S.D.N.Y. 2009).

Although defendant was granted a security interest in debtor's shares of a company, he never perfected his interest in the uncertificated shares by filing a UCC financing statement with the New York Department of State or by control over the investment property. As defendant only had an unperfected lien on debtor's shares, a Chapter 7 trustee, armed with the status of a hypothetical lien creditor, took debtor's 50 percent ownership in the company free of defendant's unperfected lien. Thaler v GJ & JF Realty Holdings, Inc. (In re Jaghab), 584 B.R. 472, 2018 Bankr. LEXIS 1151 (Bankr. E.D.N.Y. 2018).

9. Under former § 9-106

Uniform Commercial Code § 9-318 and § 9-106 are apparently limited to instances of assignments of executory contracts. Gramatan Co. v D'Amico, 50 Misc. 2d 233, 269 N.Y.S.2d 871, 1966 N.Y. Misc. LEXIS 1933 (N.Y. Sup. Ct. 1966).

In suit by trustee in bankruptcy to recover commissions retained pursuant to agreement by former employee of bankrupt as repayment for monies that had been advanced, employer's right to retain commissions subsequently accruing was in effect right to refrain from paying commissions twice and was neither "contract right" subject to UCC §§ 1-201(37) or 9-106, nor "security interest" requiring perfection under UCC § 9-302. In re Sherman, 627 F.2d 594, 1980 U.S. App. LEXIS 15972 (2d Cir. N.Y. 1980).

Although UCC § 9-106 appears to include choses in action, assignability of choses in action is not unlimited; first, holder of security interest in chose in action has only qualified interest commensurate with debt or liabilities secured, and second, one can only assign chose in action that is sufficiently choate, such as claim that has already accrued, claim that is fully matured, or portion of expected recovery in pending lawsuit; assignment of truly future claim or interest does not work present transfer of property. Capital Nat'l Bank v McDonald's Corp., 625 F. Supp. 874, 1986 U.S. Dist. LEXIS 30710 (S.D.N.Y. 1986).

10. Under former § 9-109

A mobile home is a motor vehicle within the meaning of UCC § 9-302 which requires that a financing statement be filed to perfect a security interest therein. Recchio v Manufacturers & Traders Trust Co., 35 A.D.2d 769, 316 N.Y.S.2d 915, 1970 N.Y. App. Div. LEXIS 3635 (N.Y. App. Div. 4th Dep't 1970).

In junior mortgagee's action for damages for defendant's alleged impairment of plaintiff's security, where defendant under security agreement with dealer in modular homes had security interest in all of dealer's present or future inventory and also first mortgage on 2.39

acres of land acquired by dealer for use as sales lot, on which dealer installed two modular homes; where plaintiff held second mortgage on dealer's 2.39 acres as security for loan on which dealer defaulted; and where defendant after dealer's default quickly removed modular homes from dealer's lot pursuant to written authorization from officer of dealer's company, (1) homes placed by dealer on sales lot, although installed on concrete foundations and connected to utilities, were inventory and not real property or fixtures under UCC § 9-109(4), since they were goods intended for immediate or ultimate sale; (2) defendant held perfected purchase-money security interest in dealer's inventory under UCC § 9-401(1)(c) and UCC § 9-402(1), which under UCC § 9-312(3) took priority over plaintiff's junior-mortgage interest; and (3) defendant on dealer's default had right to take possession of homes on dealer's lot, since they were inventory collateral. Rakosi v General Electric Credit Corp., 59 A.D.2d 553, 397 N.Y.S.2d 416, 1977 N.Y. App. Div. LEXIS 13344 (N.Y. App. Div. 2d Dep't 1977).

The perfected security interest of a retail finance corporation who purchased a credit agreement signed by a "buyer in the ordinary course of business" from an automobile dealer had priority over the perfected interests of a bank which furnished floor plan financing to finance the dealer's acquisition and holding of motor vehicles for use and resale in the course of the dealer's business. Chrysler Credit Corp. v Sharp, 56 Misc. 2d 261, 288 N.Y.S.2d 525, 1968 N.Y. Misc. LEXIS 1867 (N.Y. Sup. Ct. 1968).

Automobiles financed under a floor plan arrangement and held by an automobile dealer are inventory held for sale to the public. Chrysler Credit Corp. v Sharp, 56 Misc. 2d 261, 288 N.Y.S.2d 525, 1968 N.Y. Misc. LEXIS 1867 (N.Y. Sup. Ct. 1968).

The Civil Court of the City of New York, which has no general equity jurisdiction (CCA, § 202), lacks subject matter jurisdiction over a creditor's action to hold defendant, as transferee, liable for the debt of a third party because of defendant's failure to comply with the Bulk Sales Act, which act is designed to prevent commercial fraud by declaring "ineffective" the sale or transfer of a debtor's bulk inventory if there is a failure to notify the creditors of such sale or transfer (Uniform Commercial Code, § 6-105), since, in order to obtain relief under the act, defrauded or unnotified general creditors must sue in equity to set aside the transfer or seek such other equitable remedies as the circumstances indicate and an action at law for a money judgment against the transferee for violations of the act cannot be maintained except in the exceptional case where the facts indicate tortious conduct or breach of contract; even if there were jurisdiction, the action would still be dismissed since the debtor was in the business of selling jewelry and diamonds and the sale to defendant of its office furniture and equipment, customers' lists, jewelry catalogues and a telephone listing was, therefore, not a bulk transfer of its inventory (Uniform Commercial Code, § 6-102), inventory being defined as goods held for sale. H. L. C. Imports Corp. v M & L Siegel, Inc., 98 Misc. 2d 179, 413 N.Y.S.2d 605, 1979 N.Y. Misc. LEXIS 2061 (N.Y. Civ. Ct. 1979).

In action by bank for conversion of boat which was purchased in New Jersey and subject to security interest perfected in New Jersey, against dealer that took possession of boat from debtor in New York as trade-in on new boat, bank was entitled to summary judgment even though no financing statement had been filed in New York within time provided in CLS UCC § 9-103, since boat was "consumer good" under CLS UCC § 9-109 and thus bank had "purchase money security interest" under CLS UCC § 9-107 which was perfected without need for further action under CLS UCC Art 9; provisions of § 9-103 which speak of expiration of period of perfection of security interest (when collateral is brought into New York while subject to security interest perfected under law of state from which it was removed) did not apply. Howell State Bank v Jericho Boats, Inc., 141 Misc. 2d 314, 533 N.Y.S.2d 363, 1988 N.Y. Misc. LEXIS 531 (N.Y. Sup. Ct. 1988).

Classifications contained in UCC § 9-109 are intended primarily for the purpose of determining which set of filing requirements is proper. In re Laminated Veneers Co., 471 F.2d 1124, 1973 U.S. App. LEXIS 12164 (2d Cir. N.Y. 1973).

Description of collateral contained in security agreement must be reasonably specific; and term "equipment" in omnibus clause of security agreement did not include two automobiles owned by debtor corporation. In re Laminated Veneers Co., 471 F.2d 1124, 1973 U.S. App. LEXIS 12164 (2d Cir. N.Y. 1973).

Sale of aircraft by airline was not a sale in ordinary course of business of airline, even though it is general practice in aviation industry for airlines to sell older aircraft in order to purchase newer

UCC

aircraft, as aircraft is capital equipment which is not subject to sale in ordinary course of business. Aircraft Trading & Services, Inc. v Braniff, Inc., 819 F.2d 1227, 1987 U.S. App. LEXIS 6730 (2d Cir. N.Y.), cert. denied, 484 U.S. 856, 108 S. Ct. 163, 98 L. Ed. 2d 118, 1987 U.S. LEXIS 4055 (U.S. 1987).

11. Under former § 9-105
12. – "Chattel paper"

Promissory note and purchase agreement executed by purchaser of business' assets did not qualify as "chattel paper," even though note evidenced monetary obligation running to business, where agreement created no security interest in goods sold thereunder, and instead note was offered in even exchange for sale of assets in which business retained no residual interest. Berkowitz v Chavo Int'l, Inc., 74 N.Y.2d 144, 544 N.Y.S.2d 569, 542 N.E.2d 1086, 1989 N.Y. LEXIS 887 (N.Y. 1989).

13. – "Collateral"

A security interest continued on behalf of a bank in the proceeds of a dishonored check, and the bank was entitled to deduct sums traceable as proceeds of the check from the accounts of depositors. Schwab v Walden Sav. Bank, 109 Misc. 2d 929, 441 N.Y.S.2d 195, 1981 N.Y. Misc. LEXIS 2495 (N.Y. Sup. Ct. 1981).

Diamonds held by bank in safe-deposit box as security for debt owed by customer were "collateral," although term "collateral" was not explicitly referred to in agreement creating debt, since diamonds were placed in safe-deposit box on bank premises, not in customer's safe deposit boxes, box was not to be opened except in presence of both customer and bank officer, and box was red-flagged to indicate that bank had interest in contents. European American Bank v Fulton, 139 Misc. 2d 747, 528 N.Y.S.2d 477, 1988 N.Y. Misc. LEXIS 261 (N.Y. Sup. Ct. 1988).

Defendant's mobile home remained personal property where it never became so permanently affixed to real property that it would despoil underlying land simply by its attempted removal, and thus bank was entitled to repossess mobile home as collateral for repayment of amount financed after defendants defaulted in repayment of their retail installment contract with bank and bank was notified that property on which mobile home was located was to be sold at tax sale. OnBank & Trust Co. v Hannold, 177 Misc. 2d 482, 676 N.Y.S.2d 412, 1998 N.Y. Misc. LEXIS 271 (N.Y. Sup. Ct. 1998), rev'd, 258 A.D.2d 720, 684 N.Y.S.2d 677, 1999 N.Y. App. Div. LEXIS 942 (N.Y. App. Div. 3d Dep't 1999).

Judgment holder, who sought possession of two patents owned by a debtor was entitled to obtained the same because the security agreement sufficiently set forth the term "general intangibles" and patents were included in such a term. The security agreement did not have to specifically identify the patents. Rice v Miller, 864 N.Y.S.2d 255, 21 Misc. 3d 573, 2008 N.Y. Misc. LEXIS 5502 (N.Y. Sup. Ct. 2008).

Consignment is defined, pursuant to N.Y. U.C.C. § 9-102(20), as a transaction, regardless of its form, in which a person delivers goods to a merchant for the purpose of sale; in an action where gem dealers consigned certain jewelry to a stylist who in turn attempted to pawn the jewels, the dealers motion to compel the return of the jewels by the police was granted. Gerald Modell Inc. v Morgenthau, 196 Misc. 2d 354, 764 N.Y.S.2d 779, 2003 N.Y. Misc. LEXIS 624 (N.Y. Sup. Ct. 2003).

14. – "Debtor"

In action to recover possession of motor home that plaintiff secured party had sold to debtor under retail installment contract and security agreement, where (1) plaintiff, although authorized to file financing statement, did not do so before assigning installment contract and security agreement to bank, (2) after contract and security agreement had been assigned to bank, debtor transferred title to home to third-party purchaser, (3) such purchaser resold home to another third party who, in turn, resold it to defendant, (4) after first third-party purchaser had purchased home, bank filed financing statement that listed only original buyer of home as "debtor," and (5) on original buyer's default in making payments, bank reassigned installment contract and security agreement to plaintiff, which sought to replevy home from last third-party purchaser, court held (1) that even though bank was aware that title to home had been transferred to first third-party purchaser, bank nevertheless, on filing its financing statement, listed only original buyer as "debtor" on such statement, (2) that financing statement, as a result, failed under UCC §§ 9-402(1) and 9-105(1)(d) to identify "debtor" properly in situation where owner of collateral and obligor on financing agreement were not the same person, (3) that plaintiff's security interest

was therefore not perfected, and (4) that since defendant third-party purchaser had purchased home out of ordinary course of business and without knowledge of plaintiff's unperfected security interest therein, defendant's ownership of home was free of such security interest under UCC § 9-301(1)(c). White Star Distributors, Inc. v Kennedy, 66 A.D.2d 1011, 411 N.Y.S.2d 751, 1978 N.Y. App. Div. LEXIS 14381 (N.Y. App. Div. 4th Dep't 1978).

Guarantor is "debtor" under CLS UCC § 9-105(1)(d) and thus may not waive defense that secured creditor failed to conduct liquidation sale in commercially reasonable manner. Marine Midland Bank, N. A. v Kristin Int'l, Ltd., 141 A.D.2d 259, 534 N.Y.S.2d 612, 1988 N.Y. App. Div. LEXIS 14437 (N.Y. App. Div. 4th Dep't 1988).

Where (1) dealer-assignor of car-purchase contract assigned to plaintiff agreed to repurchase contract if car purchaser should assert any claim or defense against plaintiff, (2) after plaintiff's repossession of car from, and institution of suit for deficiency judgment against, purchaser, purchaser asserted defenses against plaintiff, and (3) on dealer-assignor's refusal to repurchase contract, plaintiff assignee sued dealer-assignor for deficiency following car's sale, court held (1) that dealer-assignor was "debtor" under UCC § 9-105(1)(d) who was entitled under UCC § 9-504(3) to notice of car's sale, and (2) that plaintiff's failure to give such notice to dealer-assignor constituted absolute bar to plaintiff's recovery of deficiency judgment from it. Long Island Bank v Knight, 122 Misc. 2d 878, 473 N.Y.S.2d 901, 1983 N.Y. Misc. LEXIS 4158 (N.Y. App. Term 1983).

15. – –Guarantor of obligation as debtor

Under UCC § 9-402(1), a financing statement must include the name and address of the debtor. In this connection, however, the term "debtor" is defined by UCC § 9-105(1)(d) to include both the owner of the collateral and the obligor on the financing agreement if the owner and the obligor are not the same person. White Star Distributors, Inc. v Kennedy, 66 A.D.2d 1011, 411 N.Y.S.2d 751, 1978 N.Y. App. Div. LEXIS 14381 (N.Y. App. Div. 4th Dep't 1978).

Guarantor is "debtor" within meaning of UCC § 9-105(1)(d) and § 9-504(3), and thus is entitled to notice of disposition of collateral. Chase Manhattan Bank, N. A. v Natarelli, 93 Misc. 2d 78, 401 N.Y.S.2d 404, 1977 N.Y. Misc. LEXIS 2645 (N.Y. Sup. Ct. 1977).

A guarantor of payment of a secured party is entitled to the same notice of sale of the collateral as the debtor is entitled to (Uniform Commercial Code, § 9-504, subd [3]) since a gurantor is a "debtor" within the meaning of section 9-105 (subd [1], par [d]) of the Uniform Commercial Code which does not require the "debtor" to be the owner or have rights in the collateral. The debtor is only required to be an "obligor in any provision dealing with the obligation". It is imperative for the guarantor to receive notice of the dispositional sale in order to protect his right to reduce his potential liability at the sale. Requiring the secured party to give notice to the guarantor of the disposition of the collateral will not cause the creditor to suffer any prejudice or impose an undue burden. Chase Manhattan Bank, N. A. v Natarelli, 93 Misc. 2d 78, 401 N.Y.S.2d 404, 1977 N.Y. Misc. LEXIS 2645 (N.Y. Sup. Ct. 1977).

16. – "Goods"

In action for repossession of prefabricated diner assembled on property owned by another, brought after purchaser defaulted in payments due under security agreement, seller was not entitled to summary judgment foreclosing on its security interest under UCC Art 9, since question of fact existed as to whether diner was "movable" so as to constitute "goods" under CLS UCC § 9-105. J.K.S.P. Restaurant, Inc. v County of Nassau, 127 A.D.2d 121, 513 N.Y.S.2d 716, 1987 N.Y. App. Div. LEXIS 41351 (N.Y. App. Div. 2d Dep't 1987).

17. – "Instrument"

Promissory note executed by purchaser of business' assets qualified as "instrument" under CLS UCC § 9-105 where it constituted writing evidencing monetary obligation of purchaser running to business, it was not itself security agreement, and, notwithstanding payment restrictions attaching to note rendering it nonnegotiable, both note and agreement to which it was made subject were freely assignable. Berkowitz v Chavo Int'l, Inc., 74 N.Y.2d 144, 544 N.Y.S.2d 569, 542 N.E.2d 1086, 1989 N.Y. LEXIS 887 (N.Y. 1989).

Note was instrument within meaning of CLS UCC Art 9 and was within possessory requirement of CLS UCC § 9-304[1], notwithstanding argument that note was neither negotiable nor writing which evidenced right to payment of money of type which is in ordinary course of business transferred by delivery with any necessary indorsement or assignment within meaning of CLS UCC § 9-105[1][i]; while note was concededly nonnegotiable, nothing in note or contract to which it was subject restricted their assignability and there was no reason note could not be assigned along with contract. Berkowitz v Chavo International, Inc., 144 A.D.2d 263, 533 N.Y.S.2d 865, 1988 N.Y. App. Div. LEXIS 10959 (N.Y. App. Div. 1st Dep't 1988), app. dismissed, 73 N.Y.2d 974, 540 N.Y.S.2d 1007, 538 N.E.2d 359, 1989 N.Y. LEXIS 4994 (N.Y. 1989), aff'd, 74 N.Y.2d 144, 544 N.Y.S.2d 569, 542 N.E.2d 1086, 1989 N.Y. LEXIS 887 (N.Y. 1989).

In suit by trustee in bankruptcy against bank which had allegedly received voidable preferences in violation of Bankruptcy Act, bankrupt's settlement of suit concerning reduction in value of collateral for loan was not voidable preference where collateral consisted of debenture in which defendant had perfected its security interest by possession; debenture was "security" within meaning of UCC § 8-102 where, inter alia, subordinated debentures of brokerage houses were recognized medium for investment; debenture was "instrument" under UCC § 9-105 where it was "security" under UCC § 8-102; security interest in debenture was perfected by possession, under UCC § 9-305, where it was "instrument" under UCC § 9-105; security interest attached immediately in collateral despite alleged ambiguity in security agreement to effect that it was to attach only in event of default, where construction of security agreement revealed intent to attach immediately and where, under UCC § 9-204, any attempt to postpone attachment must be explicitly stated; filing, under UCC § 9-201, security agreement superceded previous subordination agreement and controlled rights and obligations among the parties. Allegaert v Chemical Bank, 657 F.2d 495, 1980 U.S. App. LEXIS 14761 (2d Cir. N.Y. 1980).

18. – "Security agreement"; financing statement as security agreement

The absence of a checkmark on a financing statement to show the debtor had authorized filing without her signature did not impair the creditor's security interest, where the statement was otherwise sufficient. Beneficial Finance Co. v Kurland Cadillac-Oldsmobile, Inc., 32 A.D.2d 643, 300 N.Y.S.2d 884, 1969 N.Y. App. Div. LEXIS 4018 (N.Y. App. Div. 2d Dep't 1969).

UCC-1 financing statement created security interest in manufactured home since it was signed by defendant, it named parties, it described plaintiff as secured party, and circumstances under which it was signed—at closing on sale of real property wherein plaintiff received note and purchase-money mortgage—evinced intent to create security interest in manufactured home. Lashua v La Duke, 272 A.D.2d 750, 707 N.Y.S.2d 542, 2000 N.Y. App. Div. LEXIS 5693 (N.Y. App. Div. 3d Dep't 2000).

Equipment lease was security agreement that created security interest, not "a finance lease as that term is defined in UCC Art 2A," where it provided for "down payment" of $2,084.62 and 11 monthly payments of $525.21 plus tax, and plaintiff had option to purchase equipment for one dollar upon fulfillment of its lease obligation; thus, defendants' interest in equipment terminated upon completion of plaintiff's payment obligations, CLS Gen Oblig § 5-901 was inapplicable, and plaintiff had no cause of action under that statute. Citipostal, Inc. v Unistar Leasing, 283 A.D.2d 916, 724 N.Y.S.2d 555, 2001 N.Y. App. Div. LEXIS 4526 (N.Y. App. Div. 4th Dep't 2001).

19. – –Promissory note as security agreement

Assignee of business' future "receivables" under factoring agreement had security interest in proceeds due under promissory note which business had received for sale of substantial share of business assets to third party, even though agreement provided that all receivables which were described in schedules prepared by business "will be bona fide existing obligations created by the sale and actual delivery of goods or the rendition of services to customers in the ordinary course of business," since agreement assigned all of business' receivables, including "all obligations of every kind at any time owing to" business. Berkowitz v Chavo Int'l, Inc., 74 N.Y.2d 144, 544 N.Y.S.2d 569, 542 N.E.2d 1086, 1989 N.Y. LEXIS 887 (N.Y. 1989).

Lender had enforceable security interest in equipment purchased by debtor with proceeds of loan, although preprinted standard form "security agreement" was not executed; promissory note signed by debtor met requirements of valid security agreement where it was signed by debtor, named parties, contained description of collateral, and specifically stated that it was to "secure the transfer" of collateral. Trinity Constr., Inc. v John R. Mott, Inc., 145 A.D.2d 720, 534 N.Y.S.2d 838, 1988 N.Y. App. Div. LEXIS 12330 (N.Y. App. Div. 3d Dep't 1988).

20. – "Secured party"

Where securities were pledged to broker who in turn pledged securities to bank for a loan, bank was a vendor of money in whose favor there existed a security interest and, therefore, was a "secured party" under the duty of exercising reasonable care for the preservation and protection of the collateral held by it. Grace v Sterling, Grace & Co., 30 A.D.2d 61, 289 N.Y.S.2d 632, 1968 N.Y. App. Div. LEXIS 4109 (N.Y. App. Div. 1st Dep't 1968).

CLS UCC § 9-105(1)(m) does not require that lender or secured party be licensed by state. Sloves Assocs. v Boudouris, 156 Misc. 2d 165, 592 N.Y.S.2d 236, 1992 N.Y. Misc. LEXIS 562 (N.Y. Civ. Ct. 1992).

In a suit brought by a shareholder against a housing corporation and other shareholders (collectively referred to as the housing corporation), there was no justification for the shareholder's filing of a financing statement against a garden unit apartment for which the shareholder alleged that funds were expended as no security agreement was ever entered into between the parties, the shareholder had no common law lien that was enforceable, and there was no authenticated record whereby the housing corporation authorized the filing. Since the filing of the UCC-1 financing statement was baseless, the shareholder was directed to terminate the same and pay the housing corporation statutory damages in the amount of $500. McDaniel v 162 Columbia Hgts. Hous. Corp., 863 N.Y.S.2d 346, 21 Misc. 3d 244, 2008 N.Y. Misc. LEXIS 4707 (N.Y. Sup. Ct. 2008).

21. Under former § 9-112

In dispute arising from stipulation granting plaintiff divorce from defendant and providing, inter alia, that she would hold, as collateral for defendant's assignment of certain rights encumbered by lien, assignment of his interest in certain medical partnership, no basis existed to award defendant any surplus from liquidation of plaintiff's collateral interest in medical partnership where (1) defendant had transferred his interest in that partnership to his partner's spouse for good and valuable consideration, subject to plaintiff's security interest, and (2) while plaintiff may have obtained windfall when she relinquished her security interest in exchange for $200,000, she was not unjustly enriched at defendant's expense. Strong v Strong, 277 A.D.2d 533, 715 N.Y.S.2d 499, 2000 N.Y. App. Div. LEXIS 11139 (N.Y. App. Div. 3d Dep't 2000).

The mere fact that the collateral was owned by the president of a corporation does not establish that a bank lending money to the corporation did not have a security interest in the property, because there may be a security interest in collateral not owned by the debtor. Recchio v Manufacturers & Traders Trust Co., 55 Misc. 2d 788, 286 N.Y.S.2d 390, 1968 N.Y. Misc. LEXIS 1833 (N.Y. Sup. Ct. 1968), rev'd, 35 A.D.2d 769, 316 N.Y.S.2d 915, 1970 N.Y. App. Div. LEXIS 3635 (N.Y. App. Div. 4th Dep't 1970).

§ 9-103. Purchase-money Security Interest; Application of Payments; Burden of Establishing

(a) Definitions. In this section:

(1) "purchase-money collateral" means goods or software that secures a purchase-money obligation incurred with respect to that collateral; and

(2) "purchase-money obligation" means an obligation of an obligor incurred as all or part of the price of the collateral or for value given to enable the debtor to acquire rights in or the use of the collateral if the value is in fact so used.

(b) Purchase-money security interest in goods. A security interest in goods is a purchase-money security interest:

(1) to the extent that the goods are purchase-money collateral with respect to that security interest;

(2) if the security interest is in inventory that is or was purchase-money collateral, also to the extent that the security interest secures a purchase-money obligation incurred with respect to other inventory in

which the secured party holds or held a purchase-money security interest; and

(3) also to the extent that the security interest secures a purchase-money obligation incurred with respect to software in which the secured party holds or held a purchase-money security interest.

(c) Purchase-money security interest in software. A security interest in software is a purchase-money security interest to the extent that the security interest also secures a purchase-money obligation incurred with respect to goods in which the secured party holds or held a purchase-money security interest if:

(1) the debtor acquired its interest in the software in an integrated transaction in which it acquired an interest in the goods; and

(2) the debtor acquired its interest in the software for the principal purpose of using the software in the goods.

(d) Consignor's inventory purchase-money security interest. The security interest of a consignor in goods that are the subject of a consignment is a purchase-money security interest in inventory.

(e) Application of payment in non-consumer-goods transaction. In a transaction other than a consumer-goods transaction, if the extent to which a security interest is a purchase-money security interest depends on the application of a payment to a particular obligation, the payment must be applied:

(1) in accordance with any reasonable method of application to which the parties agree;

(2) in the absence of the parties' agreement to a reasonable method, in accordance with any intention of the obligor manifested at or before the time of payment; or

(3) in the absence of an agreement to a reasonable method and a timely manifestation of the obligor's intention, in the following order:

(A) to obligations that are not secured; and

(B) if more than one obligation is secured, to obligations secured by purchase-money security interests in the order in which those obligations were incurred.

(f) No loss of status of purchase-money security interest in non-consumer-goods transaction. In a transaction other than a consumer-goods transaction, a purchase-money security interest does not lose its status as such, even if:

(1) the purchase-money collateral also secures an obligation that is not a purchase-money obligation;

(2) collateral that is not purchase-money collateral also secures the purchase-money obligation; or

(3) the purchase-money obligation has been renewed, refinanced, consolidated, or restructured.

(g) Burden of proof in non-consumer-goods transaction. In a transaction other than a consumer-goods transaction, a secured party claiming a purchase-money security interest has the burden of establishing the extent to which the security interest is a purchase-money security interest.

(h) Non-consumer-goods transactions; no inference. The limitation of the rules in subsections (e), (f), and (g) to transactions other than consumer-goods transactions is intended to leave to the court the determination of the proper rules in consumer-goods transactions. The court may not infer from that limitation the nature of the proper rule in consumer-goods transactions and may continue to apply established approaches.

History: Add, L 2001, ch 84, § 36; eff July 1, 2001.

Former § 9-103, add, L 1977, ch 866, § 7; amd, L 1982, ch 928, §§ 26, 27, L 1997, ch 566, § 6, eff Oct 10, 1997.

Former § 9-103, amd, L 2000, ch 471, § 5, eff Nov 1, 2000; repealed, L 2001, ch 84, § 36, eff July 1, 2001.

Prior § 9-103, add, L 1962, ch 553; amd, L 1963, ch 1003, §§ 25-27; repealed, L 1977, ch 866, § 7, eff July 2, 1978.

CASE ANNOTATIONS

N.Y. U.C.C. Law § 9-103 and any statute so directly governing the formation of security interests in personal and real property as New York's Motor Vehicle Retail Installment Sales Act (MVRISA) does can surely be deemed to have met the New York Court of Appeals' definition of statutes which relate to the same or to cognate subjects and are in pari materia and to be construed together; no intent to the contrary was clearly expressed by the New York state legislature in the MVRISA. Therefore, the two statutes are in pari materia, and the term "price," as used in N.Y. U.C.C. Law § 9-103, must be given the meaning set forth in MVRISA's definition of cash sales price, which includes negative equity. In re Petrocci (2007, BC ND NY) 370 BR 489, 63 UCCRS2d 705 (criticized in In re Pajot (2007, BC ED Va) 371 BR 139, 63 UCCRS2d 465) and (criticized in In re Blakeslee (2007, BC MD Fla) 377 BR 724) and (criticized in In re Westfall (2007, BC ND Ohio) 376 BR 210) and (criticized in In re Conyers (2007, BC MD NC) 2007 Bankr LEXIS 3773) and (criticized in In re Tuck (2007, BC MD Ala) 2007 Bankr LEXIS 4226) and (criticized in In re Johnson (2007, BC DC Or) 2007 Bankr LEXIS 4245).

Holding that "price" as set out in N.Y. U.C.C. Law § 9-103 includes negative equity (as does the new York Motor Vehicle Retail Installment Sales Act's definition of "cash sale price") serves the underlying purposes and policies of the Uniform Commercial Code because such a reading permits the continued expansion of commercial practices through custom, usage and agreement of the parties, N.Y. U.C.C. Law § 1-102(2)(b). In re Petrocci (2007, BC ND NY) 370 BR 489, 63 UCCRS2d 705 (criticized in In re Pajot (2007, BC ED Va) 371 BR 139, 63 UCCRS2d 465) and (criticized in In re Blakeslee (2007, BC MD Fla) 377 BR 724) and (criticized in In re Westfall (2007, BC ND Ohio) 376 BR 210) and (criticized in In re Conyers (2007, BC MD NC) 2007 Bankr LEXIS 3773) and (criticized in In re Tuck (2007, BC MD Ala) 2007 Bankr LEXIS 4226) and (criticized in In re Johnson (2007, BC DC Or) 2007 Bankr LEXIS 4245).

In connection with the financed sale of a manufactured home, the seller held a purchase-money security interest in the home pursuant to N.Y. U.C.C. Law § 9-102(a)(54)(A) and § 9-103(b)(1), and the failure to perfect that interest did not result in a loss of its secured status. Ultimore, Inc. v Bucala (In re Bucala) (2012, BC SD NY) 464 BR 626, 76 UCCRS2d 691.

U.S. Court of Appeals for the Second Circuit asked the New York Court of Appeals to determine if the portion of an automobile retail installment sale attributable to a trade-in vehicle's negative equity was part of the purchase-money obligation arising from the purchase of a new car, so it could resolve the issue of how negative equity would be treated under 11 U.S.C.S. § 1325(a) (hanging paragraph referencing paragraph 5). The Second Circuit looked at New York statutes and case law and found that New York law did not clearly answer the question whether an automobile retail installment sale attributable to a trade-in vehicle's negative equity was part of a debtor's purchase-money obligation arising from the purchase of a new car under N.Y. U.C.C. Law § 9-103 and other provisions of New York law. Reiber v GMAC, LLC (In re Peaslee) (2008, CA2 NY) 547 F3d 177, CCH Bankr L Rptr P 81341, 66 UCCRS2d 1052 (criticized in Nuvell Credit Co. v Callicott (In re Callicott) (2008, ED Mo) 396 BR 506, CCH Bankr L Rptr P 81363) and ques certified (2008, NY) 2008 NY Slip Op 9008, 2008 NY LEXIS 3385.

Because a buyer's debt to a lender was incurred at the time of a trade-in, under the same retail installment contract and for the same purpose of purchasing a newer vehicle, the buyer's financing of the negative equity of a trade-in vehicle was inextricably linked to the financing of a newer vehicle; accordingly, it satisfied the "close nexus" requirements of N.Y. U.C.C. Law § 9-103(a)(1), (2). Matter of Peaslee (2009) 13 NY3d 75, 885 NYS2d 1, 913 NE2d 387.

Under New York law, negative equity is considered a purchase-money obligation and therefore included in a purchase money security interest. Reiber v GMAC, LLC (In re Peaslee) (2009, CA2 NY) 585 F3d 53, CCH Bankr L Rptr P 81598.

Because negative equity was considered a purchase-money obligation and therefore included in a purchase money security interest under New York law, and the other conditions for avoiding cramdown under the hanging paragraph of 11 U.S.C.S. § 1325 were not contested by the parties, debtor-appellants' entire claims, including those portions attributable to the payoff of negative equity on their trade-in vehicles, had to be treated as secured claims; as a result, creditor-appellees were immune from cramdown and bifurcation of their full security interest in debtor-appellants' cars, including that portion deriving from the negative trade-in value of their prior cars. Reiber v GMAC, LLC (In re Peaslee) (2009, CA2 NY) 585 F3d 53, CCH Bankr L Rptr P 81598.

Where a court determined on remand that it was bound by Peaslee, a Second Circuit opinion, to conclude that a creditor's claim was secured by a purchase money security interest (PMSI) for purposes of the hanging paragraph in 11 U.S.C.S. § 1325(a) and thus, could not be bifurcated under 11 U.S.C.S. § 506, the court denied the debtors' motion for reconsideration and vacatur, as they failed to establish any grounds. With respect to their request for clarification, the court noted that the provisions of the Uniform Commercial Code (UCC) at issue in Peaslee, UCC § 9-103(a)(1)-(2) and Official Comment 3, were substantively identical in New York and Vermont, and that the ultimate focus of the decision was on the bankruptcy law question of whether the negative equity portion of a trade-in vehicle was part of a PMSI arising from the sale of the vehicle, and thus protected from cramdown by the "hanging paragraph" of 11 U.S.C.S. § 1325, which the Second Circuit answered in the affirmative. In re Munzberg (2011, BC DC Vt) 2011 Bankr LEXIS 260 (UNPUBLISHED).

UNDER FORMER § 9-107

Seller (which shipped printing press with unpaid balance owing to assignee of contract of sale after receiving payments toward purchase price financed by funds provided by bank in January 1989) had superior purchase-money security interest (PMSI) in printing press and its proceeds from inception of its contract with assignor in December 1988 where (1) seller expressly retained PMSI in both its contract with assignor and in subsequent purchase order, by which assignee obtained title, and (2) seller's security interest "attached" at time contract between it and assignor was entered into and partial payment of purchase price was made; further, since collateral was goods, seller perfected its security interest both by possession and by filing financing statement before it relinquished possession. Heidelberg E., Inc v Weber Lithography (1995, 2d Dept) 213 A.D.2d 127, 631 N.Y.S.2d 370, 27 UCCRS2d 1081

Auto dealer's antecedent purchase of inventory and finance company's subsequent reimbursement of purchase price were sufficiently "closely allied" such that finance company acquired purchase-money interest under CLS UCC § 9-107, where dealer clearly would not have been able to purchase expensive vehicles without finance company's backing, and purchase and loan transactions were only days apart. GE Capital Commer. Auto. Fin. v Spartan Motors, Ltd. (1998, 2d Dept) 246 A.D.2d 41, 675 N.Y.S.2d 626, 36 UCCRS2d 19, app gr (1998) 92 N.Y.2d 816, 683 N.Y.S.2d 759, 706 N.E.2d 747 and app dismd (1999) 93 N.Y.2d 870, 689 N.Y.S.2d 17, 711 N.E.2d 202

Where plaintiff purchased a mobile home and thereafter made an agreement with a woman whereby she took possession, assumed the monthly payments, and agreed that upon completion of the monthly payments ownership of the home would be transferred to her, plaintiff's interest in the mobile home was a purchase money security interest since it was "taken or retained by the seller of the collateral to secure all or part of its price." Recchio v Manufacturers & Traders Trust Co. (1968) 55 Misc. 2d 788, 286 N.Y.S.2d 390, 4 UCCRS 1133, revd on other grounds (1970, 4th Dept) 35 A.D.2d 769, 316 N.Y.S.2d 915

In action by bank for conversion of boat which was purchased in New Jersey and subject to security interest perfected in New Jersey, against dealer that took possession of boat from debtor in New York as trade-in on new boat, bank was entitled to summary judgment even though no financing statement had been filed in New York within time provided in CLS UCC § 9- 103, since boat was "consumer good" under CLS UCC § 9-109 and thus bank had "purchase money security interest" under CLS UCC § 9-107 which was perfected without need for further action under CLS UCC Art 9; provisions of § 9-103 which speak of expiration of period of perfection of security interest (when collateral is brought into New York while subject to security interest perfected under law of state from which it was removed) did not apply. Howell State Bank v Jericho Boats, Inc. (1988, Sup) 141 Misc. 2d 314, 533 N.Y.S.2d 363, 7 UCCRS2d 1215

§ 9-104. Control of Deposit Account

(a) Requirements for control. A secured party has control of a deposit account if:

(1) the secured party is the bank with which the deposit account is maintained;

(2) the debtor, secured party, and bank have agreed in an authenticated record that the bank will comply with instructions originated by the secured party directing disposition of the funds in the deposit account without further consent by the debtor;

(3) the secured party becomes the bank's customer with respect to the deposit account;

(4) the name on the deposit account is the name of the secured party or indicates that the secured party has a security interest in the deposit account; or

(5) another person has control of the deposit account on behalf of the secured party or, having previously acquired control of the deposit account, acknowledges that it has control on behalf of the secured party.

(b) Debtor's right to direct disposition. A secured party that has satisfied subsection (a) has control, even if the debtor retains the right to direct the disposition of funds from the deposit account.

(c) No implied duties of bank. The authentication of a record by the bank under subsection (a)(2) does not impose upon the bank any duty not expressly agreed to by the bank in the record. The naming of the deposit account in the name of the secured party or with an indication that the secured party has a security interest in the deposit account under subsection (a)(4) does not impose upon the bank any duty not expressly agreed to by the bank.

(d) Conditions not relevant. A secured party has control under subsection (a)(2) even if any duty of the bank to comply with instructions originated by the secured party directing disposition of the funds in the deposit account is subject to any condition or conditions (other than further consent by the debtor).

(e) No inferences. The procedures and requirements of subsection (a)(4) available to obtain control shall not be used in interpreting the sufficiency of a secured party's compliance with the procedures and requirements of subsection (a)(1), (a)(2) or (a)(3) to obtain control. The provisions of subsection (a)(4) shall create no inference regarding the requirements for compliance with subsection (a)(1), (a)(2) or (a)(3).

History: Add, L 2001, ch 84, § 36, eff July 1, 2001.

Former § 9-104, add, L 1962, ch 553; amd, L 1963, ch 1003, § 28, eff Sept 27, 1964; L 1977, ch 866, § 8, eff July 2, 1978, L 1979, ch 593, § 1, eff July 10, 1979, L 1988, ch 333, § 1, eff Oct 1, 1988.

Former § 9-104, amd, L 2000, ch 471, § 6, eff Nov 1, 2000; repealed, L 2001, ch 84, § 36, eff July 1, 2001.

Amd, L 2014, ch 505, § 27, eff Dec 17, 2014.

CASE ANNOTATIONS

Federal law would preempt any purported application of Uniform Commercial Code to margin transactions in view of pervasive federal regulating scheme that explicitly permits brokers to commingle customer funds and implicitly permits them to retain earnings on collateral posted for short sales; established practices of short sales and margin and UCC have peacefully co-existed for years, without any perception that UCC governed, much less outlawed, them. Levitin v Painewebber, Inc. (1998, CA2 NY) 159 F.3d 698, CCH Fed Secur L Rep ¶ 90286, 44 UCCRS2d 859, cert den 525 US 1144, 143 L Ed 2d 47, 119 S Ct 1039

§ 9-105.   Control of Electronic Chattel Paper

A secured party has control of electronic chattel paper if the record or records comprising the chattel paper are created, stored, and assigned in such a manner that:

(1) a single authoritative copy of the record or records exists which is unique, identifiable and, except as otherwise provided in paragraphs (4), (5), and (6), unalterable;

(2) the authoritative copy identifies the secured party as the assignee of the record or records;

(3) the authoritative copy is communicated to and maintained by the secured party or its designated custodian;

(4) copies or revisions that add or change an identified assignee of the authoritative copy can be made only with the participation of the secured party;

(5) each copy of the authoritative copy and any copy of a copy is readily identifiable as a copy that is not the authoritative copy; and

(6) any revision of the authoritative copy is readily identifiable as an authorized or unauthorized revision.

History: Add, L 2001, ch 84, § 36, eff July 1, 2001.

Former § 9-105, add, L 1962, ch 553; amd, L 1966, ch 416, L 1963, ch 1003, § 30 L 1977, ch 866, § 9, eff July 2, 1978, L 1982, ch 928, § 28, L 1997, ch 566, § 7, eff Oct 10, 1997.

Former § 9-105, amd, L 2000, ch 471, § 7, eff Nov 1, 2000; repealed, L 2001, ch 84, § 36, eff July 1, 2001.

§ 9-106.   Control of Investment Property

(a) Control under Section 8-106. A person has control of a certificated security, uncertificated security, or security entitlement as provided in Section 8-106.

(b) Control of commodity contract. A secured party has control of a commodity contract if:

(1) the secured party is the commodity intermediary with which the commodity contract is carried; or

(2) the commodity customer, secured party, and commodity intermediary have agreed that the commodity intermediary will apply any value distributed on account of the commodity contract as directed by the secured party without further consent by the commodity customer.

(c) Effect of control of securities account or commodity account. A secured party having control of all security entitlements or commodity contracts carried in a securities account or commodity account has control over the securities account or commodity account.

History: Add, L 2001, ch 84, § 36, eff July 1, 2001.

Former § 9-106, add, L 1962, ch 553; amd, L 1966, ch 416, § 3, L 1977, ch 866, § 10, L 1997, ch 566, § 8, eff Oct 10, 1997.

Former § 9-106, amd, L 2000, ch 471, § 8, eff Nov 1, 2000; repealed, L 2001, ch 84, § 36, eff July 1, 2001.

CASE ANNOTATIONS

1. Possession of patents
2. Adequate control of security entitlement
3. Security agreement requirements
4. Form IT-260
5. Indemnification language

1. Possession of patents

Judgment holder, who sought possession of two patents owned by a debtor was entitled to obtained the same because the security agreement sufficiently set forth the term "general intangibles" and patents were included in such a term. The security agreement did not have to specifically identify the patents. Rice v Miller, 864 N.Y.S.2d 255, 21 Misc. 3d 573, 66 U.C.C. Rep. Serv. 2d (CBC) 904, 2008 N.Y. Misc. LEXIS 5502 (N.Y. Sup. Ct. 2008).

2. Adequate control of security entitlement

Although defendant was granted a security interest in debtor's shares of a company, he never perfected his interest in the uncertificated shares by filing a UCC financing statement with the New York Department of State or by control over the investment property. As defendant only had an unperfected lien on debtor's shares, a Chapter 7 trustee, armed with the status of a hypothetical lien creditor, took debtor's 50 percent ownership in the company free of defendant's unperfected lien. Thaler v GJ & JF Realty Holdings, Inc. (In re Jaghab), 584 B.R. 472, 95 U.C.C. Rep. Serv. 2d (CBC) 826, 2018 Bankr. LEXIS 1151 (Bankr. E.D.N.Y. 2018).

Certificate of deposit (CD) and money market account held in street name by brokerage firm did not meet requirements of acceptable security under CLS Tax § 639(d) and 20 NYCRR § 154.11 where letter prepared by foreign financial institution and submitted by individual taxpayer stated that on notice from Department of Taxation and Finance on its letterhead indicating event of default, institution would liquidate account and forward proceeds to department; such letter in and of itself did not provide adequate control of security entitlement under CLS UCC §§ 8-106 and 9-106. NY Guidances Comm T & F NYT-G-06(1)I, 2006 N.Y. Tax LEXIS 257.

3. Security agreement requirements

In order for collateral offered by taxpayer to be considered acceptable security for purposes of CLS Tax § 639(d), taxpayer must submit security agreement in form of document that he has signed agreeing that Department of Taxation and Finance, as secured party, can initiate entitlement orders; such agreement must include (1) pledge of securities, (2) representation that no other party has been granted security interest in accounts, that no other party will be granted security interest in accounts, and that taxpayer is sole owner of accounts, (3) statement of taxpayer's and department's rights and remedies in event of default by taxpayer, and (4) statement that New York law will govern in event of litigation over provisions of security agreement or entitlement order. NY Guidances Comm T & F NYT-G-06(1)I, 2006 N.Y. Tax LEXIS 257.

4. Form IT-260

Signed Form IT-260 (New York State and City of New York Surety Bond Form Change of Resident Status - Special Accruals) was not applicable to certificate of deposit (CD) and money market account held in street name by brokerage firm because form only relates to securities that may be physically delivered to Department of Taxation and Finance; form does not relate to book-entry security and does not constitute agreement to entitlement order as required for acceptable security under CLS Tax § 639(d) and 20 NYCRR § 154.11. NY Guidances Comm T & F NYT-G-06(1)I, 2006 N.Y. Tax LEXIS 257.

5. Indemnification language

Indemnification language contained in letter to Department of Taxation and Finance by foreign financial institution on behalf of taxpayer was not acceptable for purposes of CLS Tax § 639(d) where letter called on department to agree to indemnify and hold harmless institution, its officers, directors, employees, agents, affiliates, representatives, and each of their heirs, successors, and assigns from and against any liability that might arise by institution acting on instructions of letter. NY Guidances Comm T & F NYT-G-06(1)I, 2006 N.Y. Tax LEXIS 257.

§ 9-107. Control of Letter-of-credit Right

A secured party has control of a letter-of-credit right to the extent of any right to payment or performance by the issuer or any nominated person if the issuer or nominated person has consented to an assignment of proceeds of the letter of credit under Section 5-114(c) or otherwise applicable law or practice.

History: Add, L 2001, ch 84, § 36, eff July 1, 2001.

Former § 9-107, add, L 1962, ch 553, eff Sept 27, 1964; repealed, L 2001, ch 84, § 36, eff July 1, 2001.

CASE ANNOTATIONS

Court properly determined that plaintiff's purchase-money security interest, filed in November 1994, had priority over defendant's perfected nonpossessory purchase-money security interest resulting from debtor's sale of collateral in December 1995, notwithstanding defendant's assertion that plaintiff's security interest was not purchase-money security interest because plaintiff failed to perfect her security interest within 20 days from debtor's receipt of collateral, since failure to perfect purchase-money security interest within 20 days from date of delivery of collateral does not result in loss of its "purchase money" status. Lashua v La Duke (2000, 3d Dept) 272 A.D.2d 750, 707 N.Y.S.2d 542, 41 UCCRS2d 930

§ 9-108. Sufficiency of Description

(a) Sufficiency of description. Except as otherwise provided in subsections (c), (d), and (e), a description of personal or real property is sufficient, whether or not it is specific, if it reasonably identifies what is described.

(b) Examples of reasonable identification. Except as otherwise provided in Section 9-502 and subsection (d), a description of collateral reasonably identifies the collateral if it identifies the collateral by:

(1) specific listing;

(2) category;

(3) except as otherwise provided in subsection (e), a type of collateral defined in this chapter;

(4) quantity;

(5) computational or allocational formula or procedure; or

(6) except as otherwise provided in subsection (c), any other method, if the identity of the collateral is objectively determinable.

(c) Supergeneric description not sufficient. A description of collateral as "all the debtor's assets" or "all the debtor's personal property" or using words of similar import does not reasonably identify the collateral.

(d) Investment property. Except as otherwise provided in subsection (e), a description of a security entitlement, securities account, or commodity account is sufficient if it describes:

(1) the collateral by those terms or as investment property; or

(2) the underlying financial asset or commodity contract.

(e) When description by type insufficient. A description only by type of collateral defined in this chapter is an insufficient description of:

(1) a commercial tort claim;

(2) in a consumer transaction, consumer goods, a security entitlement, a securities account, or a commodity account; or

(3) a cooperative interest.

History: Add, L 2001, ch 84, § 36, eff July 1, 2001.

Former § 9-108, add, L 1962, ch 553, eff Sept 27, 1964; repealed, L 2001, ch 84, § 36, eff July 1, 2001.

CASE ANNOTATIONS

UNDER FORMER § 9-108

District court properly determined that plaintiff had information sufficient to timely object were he so inclined, as the district court correctly used the objective standard in N.Y. U.C.C. Law § 9-108, and concluded that the account statements reasonably identified the payment orders underlying the wire transfers at issue; each of the monthly statements provided the dollar amount of the transfer, the date of the transfer, the total dollar amount transferred out of the account for that month, the account's total value at the end of that month, and the total dollar amount transferred out of the account for the year-to-date, and defendant assigned a unique identification number to every wire transfer listed on the statements. Youxin Ma v Merrill Lynch, Pierce, Fenner & Smith, Inc. (2010, CA2 NY) 597 F3d 84.

In connection with the financed sale of a manufactured home, the description of the collateral satisfied N.Y. U.C.C. Law § 9-108(a) because, despite the fact that the description of the collateral in the contract of sale and the promissory note were not identical, when the documents were read together, it was obvious that the two documents described the same collateral. Ultimore, Inc. v Bucala (In re Bucala) (2012, BC SD NY) 464 BR 626, 76 UCCRS2d 691.

N.Y. U.C.C. Law § 9-207 requires that the secured party be in "possession or control" of the collateral and thus a bank had no duty to a guarantor, under either the loan documents or the guarantee, the latter of which contained a broad and all encompassing consent to the bank's release of security, to collect more of the proceeds realized at the sale of the borrow's property than it did; the bank was properly granted summary judgment against the guarantor on the issue of liability, but the trial court erred in tracking the provision of the guarantee which, upon the borrower's default and the bank's unsatisfied demand for payment, gave the bank a lien against all of the guarantor's property "of every description," and accordingly, the attachment was limited to the personal property identified in a financial statement provided to the bank for the purposes of the loan extended to the borrower. Bank Leumi USA v Agati (2004, A.D., 1st Dept) 774 N.Y.S.2d 499

UCC

The title of a conditional vendor to removable fixtures installed upon realty is superior to the lien of a prior mortgage containing the standard "after-acquired" property clause, but a conditional vendor is bound to refrain from wilfully impairing the security of a real estate mortgagee and if, without the consent of the mortgagee, he removes equipment subject to the mortgage, he should be required to account to the mortgagee for its fair value, and if the equipment which was replaced without the mortgagee's consent was serviceable and of some value, the priorities may appropriately be reversed to the extent of the impairment of the mortgagee's security. Blancob Constr. Corp. v 246 Beaumont Equity, Inc. (1965, 1st Dept) 23 A.D.2d 413, 261 N.Y.S.2d 227, 2 UCCRS 995

Assignee of all receivables "now or hereafter" owned is assignee of accounts receivable and as such, under UCC § 9-204, has continuing security interest in present *and future* (court's emphasis) inventory of his debtor, and his lien prevails over a subsequent judgment creditor who levied prior to the secured party taking possession of the collateral. O'Hara & Shaver, Inc. v Empire Bituminous Products, Inc. (1971) 67 Misc. 2d 47, 323 N.Y.S.2d 190, 9 UCCRS 764

UNDER FORMER § 9-110

Order directing seizure of tractors and trailers which were listed as collateral in security agreement and which had been sold by debtor to defendants could not stand where there was factual question as to whether, under UCC § 9-306(2), creditor, by reason of its prior dealings with debtor, had authorized it to sell chattels free of any liens by asserting its right to receive "proceeds" if chattels were sold; order directing seizure of trailer not specifically mentioned in security agreement was improper under UCC §§ 9-110 and 9-203(1)(b) where general language in after-acquired property clause of security agreement was insufficient to cover vehicles other than those specifically listed, unless they were given and accepted in replacement of specified vehicles. Long Island Trust Co. v Porta Aluminum Corp. (1974, 2d Dept) 44 A.D.2d 118, 354 N.Y.S.2d 134, 14 UCCRS 833

Misdescription of collateral resulted in failure to perfect security interest in apartment; although security agreement and financing statement correctly described "stock" as certain number of shares of certain residential cooperative, those documents misdescribed "apartment" to which such shares were allocated as being located in different building. Fastag v Chemical Bank (1997, 1st Dept) 242 A.D.2d 445, 662 N.Y.S.2d 466, 35 UCCRS2d 1337

Defendant finance company, which acquired purchase-money security interest in 2 vehicles by its postpurchase advance of funds to auto dealer, had priority over "dragnet" lien previously acquired by plaintiff in connection with "floor plan" financing of dealer's inventory, notwithstanding plaintiff's claim that it lacked notice of inventory covered by defendant's security interest because dealer and defendant had diverged in practice from literal language of their contract which appeared to contemplate prepurchase advance of funds, where written identification of defendant's collateral was "reasonably specific" and plaintiff could not show how it relied to its detriment on when and how defendant discharged its individual financing obligations to dealer. GE Capital Commer. Auto. Fin. v Spartan Motors, Ltd. (1998, 2d Dept) 246 A.D.2d 41, 675 N.Y.S.2d 626, 36 UCCRS2d 19, app gr (1998) 92 N.Y.2d 816, 683 N.Y.S.2d 759, 706 N.E.2d 747 and app dismd (1999) 93 N.Y.2d 870, 689 N.Y.S.2d 17, 711 N.E.2d 202

On application for order of seizure of boat (collateral), which was in possession of one defendant, prior to commencing action to recover boat's possession, under UCC §§ 9-402(1) and 9-110, boat was adequately described in plaintiff's financing statement, even though statement did not include boat's serial number. Marine Midland Bank, N. A. v Smith Boys, Inc. (1985, Sup) 129 Misc. 2d 37, 492 N.Y.S.2d 355, 41 UCCRS 1843

Description of collateral contained in security agreement must be reasonably specific; and term "equipment" in omnibus clause of security agreement did not include two automobiles owned by debtor corporation. In re Laminated Veneers Co. (1973, CA2 NY) 471 F.2d 1124, 11 UCCRS 911 (applying New York law)

Unlike a financing statement which is designed merely to put creditors on notice that further inquiry is prudent, a security agreement embodies the intentions of the parties and is the primary source to which a creditor's or potential creditor's inquiry is directed and must be reasonably specific; thus term "equipment" in omnibus clause of security agreement did not include automobiles owned by bankrupt corporation. In re Laminated Veneers Co. (1973, CA2 NY) 471 F.2d 1124, 11 UCCRS 911

Description of triplex apartment contained in letter of credit was adequate to meet CLS UCC § 9-203 requirement that collateral be reasonably identified where letter stated that collateral consisted of 9,000 square-foot property owned by defendant located at specific address, that property was worth $6 million free and clear of any mortgage, and that it was not another property worth $1.8 million located at same address that was already held by plaintiff as collateral; fact that some additional research was needed for plaintiff to obtain precise apartment numbers of apartment did not require different result. Cantrade Private Bank Lausanne v Torresy (1995, SD NY) 876 F. Supp. 564, 26 UCCRS2d 971, judgment entered (1995, SD NY) 1995 US Dist LEXIS 8090, judgment entered sub nom CBG Banking Corp. Geneva v Torresy (1996, SD NY) 1996 US Dist LEXIS 12494

Subpart 2
Applicability of Article

History: Add, L 2001, ch 84, § 36, eff July 1, 2001.

### § 9-109.	Scope

(a) General scope of article. Except as otherwise provided in subsections (c) and (d), this article applies to:

(1) a transaction, regardless of its form, that creates a security interest in personal property or fixtures by contract;

(2) an agricultural lien;

(3) a sale of accounts, chattel paper, payment intangibles, or promissory notes;

(4) a consignment;

(5) a security interest arising under Section 2-401, 2-505, 2-711(3), or 2-A-508(5), as provided in Section 9-110;

(6) a security interest arising under Section 4-210 or 5-118; and

(7) a security interest in a cooperative interest.

(b) Security interest in secured obligation. The application of this article to a security interest in a secured obligation is not affected by the fact that the obligation is itself secured by a transaction or interest to which this article does not apply.

(c) Extent to which article does not apply. This article does not apply to the extent that:

(1) a statute, regulation, or treaty of the United States preempts this article;

(2) another statute of this State expressly governs the creation, perfection, priority, or enforcement of a security interest created by this state or a governmental unit of this state;

(3) a statute of another state, a foreign country, or a governmental unit of another state or a foreign country, other than a statute generally applicable to security interests, expressly governs creation, perfection, priority, or enforcement of a security interest created by the state, country, or governmental unit; or

(4) the rights of a transferee beneficiary or nominated person under a letter of credit are independent and superior under Section 5-114.

(d) Inapplicability of article. This article does not apply to:

(1) a landlord's lien, other than an agricultural lien, or a security interest in a cooperative interest;

(2) a lien, other than an agricultural lien, given by statute or other rule of law for services or materials, but Section 9-333 applies with respect to priority of the lien;

(3) an assignment of a claim for wages, salary, or other compensation of an employee;

(4) a sale of accounts, chattel paper, payment intangibles, or promissory notes as part of a sale of the business out of which they arose;

(5) an assignment of accounts, chattel paper, payment intangibles, or promissory notes which is for the purpose of collection only;

(6) an assignment of a right to payment under a contract to an assignee that is also obligated to perform under the contract;

(7) an assignment of a single account, payment intangible, or promissory note to an assignee in full or partial satisfaction of a preexisting indebtedness;

(8) a transfer of an interest in or an assignment of a claim under a policy of insurance or contract for an annuity including a variable annuity other than an assignment by or to a health-care provider of a health-care-insurance receivable and any subsequent assignment of the right to payment, but Sections 9-315 and 9-322 apply with respect to proceeds and priorities in proceeds;

(9) an assignment of a right represented by a judgment, other than a judgment taken on a right to payment that was collateral;

(10) a right of recoupment or set-off, but:

(A) Section 9-340 applies with respect to the effectiveness of rights of recoupment or set-off against deposit accounts; and

(B) Section 9-404 applies with respect to defenses or claims of an account debtor;

(11) the creation or transfer of an interest in or lien on real property, including a lease or rents thereunder, except to the extent that provision is made for:

(A) liens on real property in Section 9-203 and 9-308;

(B) fixtures in Section 9-334;

(C) fixture filings in Sections 9-501, 9-502, 9-512, 9-516, and 9-519;

(D) security agreements covering personal and real property in Section 9-604; and

(E) security interests in cooperative interests;

(12) an assignment of a claim arising in tort, other than a commercial tort claim, but Sections 9-315 and 9-322 apply with respect to proceeds and priorities in proceeds; or

(13) an assignment of a deposit account in a consumer transaction, but Sections 9-315 and 9-322 apply with respect to proceeds and priorities in proceeds.

History: Add, L 2001, ch 84, § 36, eff July 1, 2001.

Former § 9-109, add, L 1962, ch 553, eff Sept 27, 1964; repealed, L 2001, ch 84, § 36, eff July 1, 2001.

CASE ANNOTATIONS
UNDER FORMER § 9-102
1. Generally
2. Exclusions
3. – Real estate transactions
4. Transactions in property or Fixtures
5. – Motor vehicles
6. – Chattel paper or accounts
7. Assignments
8. Consignments
9. Leases creating security interests
10. – Not creating security interests
11. Purchase money security interests
12. Remedies; foreclosure and sale
UNDER FORMER § 9-104

UNDER FORMER § 9-102
1. Generally
A security interest is an interest in property which secures payment for the performance of an obligation. Under Article 9 the UCC does not adopt a title or lien theory of security interests and rights and obligations and remedies are not determined by the location of the title, but rather on function, compliance with statutory requirements, and the nature of the transaction. Chrysler Credit Corp. v Sharp (1968) 56 Misc. 2d 261, 288 N.Y.S.2d 525, 5 UCCRS 226

2. Exclusions
Where debtor was engaged in the business of originating residential mortgage loans and the debtor purchased subordinated notes from the brokerage which agreed to finance the note purchases under the parties' pre-existing master repurchase agreement (MRA), Uniform Commercial Code Article 9 did not apply because the MRA clearly provided for a purchase and sale of securities and not a security interest in the securities. Am. Home Mortg. Inv. Corp. v Lehman Bros. Inc. (In re Am. Home Mortg. Holdings, Inc.) (2008, BC DC Del) 388 BR 69, 50 BCD 17.

Pursuant to industry standard master repurchase agreements explicitly stating that parties "intend that all Transactions hereunder be sales and purchases and not loans," agreements were purchase and sale agreements, rather than secured loans, and, thus, CLS UCC § 9-102 did not apply to require broker-dealers to exercise their right to liquidate in good-faith and commercially reasonable manner. Granite Partners, L.P. v Bear, Stearns & Co. (1998, SD NY) 17 F. Supp. 2d 275, 1998-2 CCH Trade Cases ¶ 72301, 41 FR Serv 3d 1345, 36 UCCRS2d 1238, motion gr (1999, SD NY) 184 FRD 49, 42 FR Serv 3d 806, complaint dismd, in part (1999, SD NY) 58 F. Supp. 2d 228, 1999-2 CCH Trade Cases P 72604

3. – Real estate transactions
In action by Federal Deposit Insurance Corporation (FDIC), as successor in interest to loan note given by debtor to insolvent bank, against guarantor of debtor's note who had given bank, as additional security for debtor's note, guarantor's half interest in mortgage note and mortgage on certain real estate, court held (1) that FDIC under UCC § 3-201(1) held insolvent bank's interest in debtor's note and that such interest included guarantor's half interest in mortgage note and realty mortgage; (2) that under UCC § 9-102(3), Uniform Commercial Code applies to pledge of realty paper as collateral, except in cases where mortgagee's creditor is attempting to enforce mortgagee's rights under mortgage; (3) that effect of judicial sale of realty represented by guarantor's interest in mortgage note and mortgage was to dispose of such note and mortgage as collateral that secured loan note given by debtor to insolvent bank; (4) that such disposition of collateral was required by UCC § 9-504(3) to be commercially reasonable; (5) that since such collateral disposition had

UCC

not received judicial approval within meaning of UCC § 9-507(2), it could not conclusively be deemed to be commercially reasonable; (6) that because of material difference between realty's foreclosure-sale price and its alleged value, hearing on sale's commercial reasonableness was warranted; and (7) that FDIC's duty to sell such realty without undue delay could not be disclaimed by agreement under UCC § 1-102(3). Federal Deposit Ins. Corp. v Forte (1983, 2d Dept) 94 A.D.2d 59, 463 N.Y.S.2d 844, 37 UCCRS 354, appeal after remand (1988, 2d Dept) 144 A.D.2d 627, 535 N.Y.S.2d 75

4. Transactions in property or Fixtures

In action for repossession of prefabricated diner assembled on property owned by another, brought after purchaser defaulted in payments due under security agreement, seller was not entitled to summary judgment foreclosing on its security interest under UCC Art 9, since question of fact existed as to whether diner was "movable" so as to constitute "goods" under CLS UCC § 9-105. J.K.S.P. Restaurant, Inc. v County of Nassau (1987, 2d Dept) 127 A.D.2d 121, 513 N.Y.S.2d 716, 3 UCCRS2d 825

5. – Motor vehicles

Automobile "lease agreement" was, in fact, secured transaction within meaning of Article 9 of Uniform Commercial Code where agreement was of indefinite duration and, at its inception, passed all risks and indicia of ownership of vehicle to purported lessee, in that lessee not only insured against any loss to leasing company of its capitalized cost, but after 26 months, was entitled to any surplus funds if and when car was sold, and where at end of 56 months, car would, at option of leasee, pass to her at no cost, since monthly installment payments would have equaled capitalized cost of vehicle. Right of debtor to receive notice of intended disposition of collateral after default may not be limited under UCC § 9-501(1), (3)(b), and inasmuch as leasing company failed to comply with notice provision of UCC § 9-504(3) before selling repossessed vehicle, it was precluded from recovering deficiency judgment and could only recover sums owed to it prior to repossession as well as repossession charges. clsAvis Rent A Car System, Inc. v Franklin (1975) 82 Misc. 2d 66, 366 N.Y.S.2d 83, 16 UCCRS 895 (disapproved by Security Trust Co. v Thomas (1977, 4th Dept) 59 A.D.2d 242, 399 N.Y.S.2d 511, 22 UCCRS 1305)

6. – Chattel paper or accounts

Under Article 9, all forms of secured transactions, such as conditional sales and chattel mortgages, are treated in the same manner. Miller v Bonafied Ready Mix Corp. (1967, N.Y. Sup) 4 UCCRS 881

7. Assignments

Under revised N.Y. U.C.C. Law § 9-109, a description of collateral in a security agreement needed to include a more specific description other than "all tort claims." to meet the requirements for attachment. Christine Falls of New York, Inc. v Algonquin Power Corp. (In re Franklin Indus. Complex, Inc.) (2007, BC ND NY) 377 BR 32

In action to determine priority of right to collateral (note secured by deed of trust) that corporate debtor had assigned three times to secure its obligations, where (1) California bank in 1972 made loan of $300,000 to corporate debtor and loans of $170,000 to each of three individuals associated with corporate debtor, (2) such loans were secured by 1972 deed of trust on California property owned by corporate debtor, (3) in 1974, corporate debtor formed joint venture with plaintiff to develop certain California real estate owned by corporate debtor, which included property subject to 1972 deed of trust given to secure California bank's loans to corporate debtor and three individuals associated with debtor, (4) pursuant to joint-venture agreement with plaintiff, corporate debtor sold property to be developed for note secured by deed of trust to such property, and such note and deed constituted collateral sued for, (5) in May, 1974, corporate debtor assigned collateral in suit to California bank, which had loaned corporate debtor $300,000, to secure principal of $240,000, and bank took possession of collateral and retained it during corporate debtor's subsequent assignments thereof, (6) in January, 1975, corporate debtor made second assignment of collateral in suit, which incorporated its first assignment, by assigning collateral (a) first to California bank to secure corporate debtor's obligation of $280,000, and (b) then to first Chicago bank to secure debtor's obligation of over one million dollars, (7) thereafter, corporate debtor repaid its $280,000 debt to California bank with funds from $275,000 loan obtained from second Chicago bank, but did not repay debt to first Chicago bank, (8) in March, 1976, corporate debtor assigned collateral in suit to both California bank and second Chicago bank to secure loans made by California bank to three individuals associated with corporate debtor, (9) in May, 1976, Federal Deposit Insurance

Corporation (FDIC), as liquidator of California bank which had been corporate debtor's creditor and had become insolvent, obtained California bank's rights to collateral in suit and took possession of it, (10) in 1978, first Chicago bank also became insolvent, and FDIC obtained such bank's rights to collateral in suit and sold them to plaintiff in June, 1979, on corporate debtor's default on underlying debt to first Chicago bank, and (11) plaintiff brought suit for possession of collateral when FDIC, as liquidator of California bank, refused to surrender it, district court awarded summary judgment and granted ownership of a collateral interest in the note and deed to first Chicago bank. On appeal, summary judgment was reversed and the matter remanded as the record raised a material issue of fact as to the bank's knowledge, or participation in relevant events and, therefore, its status as a good faith purchaser. Landmark Land Company v Sprague, (1982) 701 F.2d 1065

8. Consignments

Where the consignee of ladies' accessories entered an agreement with a manufacturer of ladies' gloves, whereby the manufacturer would deliver gloves on consignment directly to stores with title to the gloves remaining in the manufacturer and the consignee receiving a commission for having arranged the retail sales, and the goods were never delivered to the consignee's place of business; the assignee of creditors of the consignee had no right to merchandise remaining in possession of the manufacturer previously consigned nor to any proceeds received by the manufacturer from the sale of merchandise previously consigned. In re Mincow Bag Co. (1968, 1st Dept) 29 A.D.2d 400, 288 N.Y.S.2d 364, 5 UCCRS 60, affd (1969) 24 N.Y.2d 776, 300 N.Y.S.2d 115, 248 N.E.2d 26, 6 UCCRS 112

A true consignment of merchandise intended for sale in which there is no obligation to pay for the goods unless they are sold is not subject to this Article except as provided in § 2-326. In re benefit of Mincow Bag Co. (1967) 53 Misc. 2d 599, 279 N.Y.S.2d 306, 4 UCCRS 197, affd (1968, 1st Dept) 29 A.D.2d 400, 288 N.Y.S.2d 364, 5 UCCRS 60, affd (1969) 24 N.Y.2d 776, 300 N.Y.S.2d 115, 248 N.E.2d 26, 6 UCCRS 112

In an ancillary proceeding conducted pursuant to 21 U.S.C.S. § 853(n) and Fed. R. Crim. P. 32.2(c) to determine whether diamond dealers, who alleged that they consigned diamonds to defendant, were the true owners of diamonds that were used in defendant's money laundering scheme, the Uniform Commercial Code was inapplicable because no third-party creditor rights were involved and N.Y. U.C.C. Law § 9-109 did not apply to the relationship between a consignor and a consignee; thus, in accordance with N.Y. U.C.C. Law § 1-103, the court used common law precepts to determined the parties rights. United States v Nektalov (2006, SD NY) 440 F Supp 2d 287, subsequent app (2006, CA2 NY) 2006 US App LEXIS 21701.

9. Leases creating security interests

Contract which required plaintiff to purchase sophisticated billing machine and lease it to defendant for 5 years and 4 months at fixed monthly rental, with option to defendant of renewing lease at its expiration for yearly rental in same amount at monthly rental during term, was "title retention contract and lease intended as a security" to which Article 9, rather than Article 2, of UCC applied. Leasco Data Processing Equipment Corp. v Starline Overseas Corp. (1973) 74 Misc. 2d 898, 346 N.Y.S.2d 288, 12 UCCRS 1214, affd (1974, 1st Dept) 45 A.D.2d 992, 360 N.Y.S.2d 199, app dismd (1974) 35 N.Y.2d 645 and app dismd (1974) 35 N.Y.2d 963, 365 N.Y.S.2d 179, 324 N.E.2d 557

Automobile "lease agreement" was, in fact, secured transaction within meaning of Article 9 of Uniform Commercial Code where agreement was of indefinite duration and, at its inception, passed all risks and indicia of ownership of vehicle to purported lessee, in that lessee not only insured against any loss to leasing company of its capitalized cost, but after 26 months, was entitled to any surplus funds if and when car was sold, and where at end of 56 months, car would, at option of leasee, pass to her at no cost, since monthly installment payments would have equaled capitalized cost of vehicle. Right of debtor to receive notice of intended disposition of collateral after default may not be limited under UCC § 9-501(1), (3)(b), and inasmuch as leasing company failed to comply with notice provision of UCC § 9-504(3) before selling repossessed vehicle, it was precluded from recovering deficiency judgment and could only recover sums owed to it prior to repossession as well as repossession charges. Avis Rent A Car System, Inc. v Franklin (1975) 82 Misc. 2d 66, 366 N.Y.S.2d 83, 16 UCCRS 895 (disapproved by Security Trust Co. v Thomas (1977, 4th Dept) 59 A.D.2d 242, 399 N.Y.S.2d 511, 22 UCCRS 1305)

Where (1) lessee leased heavy mining equipment from lessor under four separate leases, (2) leases did not contain purchase option at end of lease term, but stated that title to equipment remained in lessor and that lessee granted security interest in equipment to lessor, (3) one lease provided that in event of default, repossession, and sale of equipment, net sale proceeds, "less 15 percent of the total rent," would be credited to amount owed by lessee, (4) three leases provided that in event of default, repossession and sale, net proceeds of sale, "less 20 percent of the actual cost" of the equipment would be credited to amount owed by lessee, (5) equipment covered by one lease was repossessed and later destroyed by fire, (6) equipment covered by other three leases was repossessed and sold for less than total amount owed by lessee under such leases, and (7) lessor sued for deficiency judgment, court held (1) that assuming that parties' transactions came within scope of UCC §§ 1-201(37) and 9-102(2), dealing with leases intended as security and security interest created by conditional sales, lessor was entitled to judgment on most of its claims against lessee, (2) that equipment had been sold in commercially reasonable manner required by UCC § 9-504(3), (3) that fact that lessor was highest bidder on equipment sold at one sale did not make sale commercially unreasonable under UCC § 9-504(3), (4) that late charges imposed by leases were not unconscionable within meaning of UCC § 2-302(1), and (5) that provision in one lease for deduction of "15 percent of the total rent" from amount of sale proceeds to be credited to amount owed by lessee, and provision in other two leases for deduction of 20 percent of initial cost of equipment from amount of sale proceeds to be credited to amount owed by lessee, raised questions concerning unconscionability of such deductions. Leasing Service Corp. v Carbonex, Inc. (1981, SD NY) 512 F. Supp. 253, 31 UCCRS 1789 (applying New York law)

In action on equipment leases by creditor against debtor after latter's default, leases were intended as security under UCC §§ 1-201(37) and 9-102 where defendant had options to purchase for nominal percentages of total rent under leases (4.3 percent, 4 percent, and .75 percent respectively) and where leases provided for acceleration, repossession, and sale by plaintiff if defendant defaulted; provision in leases which allowed plaintiff to deduct 15 percent of total rent or 20 percent of initial price from sale proceeds as liquidated damages was unreasonable and impermissible variation of UCC § 9-504; liquidated damages could not be based on plaintiff's right to retain equipment where UCC § 9-505(2) provides that debt is satisfied if secured party elects to retain collateral and where this provision may not be waived by consent of parties; attorneys fees were not allowed under UCC § 9-504(1)(a) where request submitted was unreasonably high and where plaintiff failed to submit information upon which reasonable award could be calculated. Leasing Service Corp. v Carbonex, Inc. (1981, SD NY) 522 F. Supp. 79, 31 UCCRS 1800

10. – Not creating security interests

Where lease of dump trailer was not intended to create security interest in trailer, provisions of UCC Art 9 were inapplicable under UCC §§ 1-201(37) and 9-102(1)(a). Mileasing Co. v Hogan (1982, 3d Dept) 87 A.D.2d 961, 451 N.Y.S.2d 211

Where lease of dump trailer was not intended to create security interest in trailer, provisions of UCC Art 9 were inapplicable under UCC §§ 1-201(37) and 9-102(1)(a). Mileasing Co. v Hogan (1982, 3d Dept) 87 A.D.2d 961, 451 N.Y.S.2d 211

In action to determine priority of competing security interests in after-acquired restaurant equipment, where (1) plaintiff leased restaurant premises, together with furniture, fixtures, equipment, and improvements then located on premises, to two tenants, (2) lease provided that title to inventoried equipment listed in attached "schedule A" was to remain in plaintiff and that on expiration of lease, title to all additions, improvements, alterations, and replacements made during lease term was to vest in plaintiff, and (3) tenants thereafter purchased equipment from defendant and gave defendant purchase-money security interest in such equipment, court held (1) that although language in lease indicated that plaintiff lessor intended to reserve title to all after-acquired property on leased premises, such language was not sufficient to create security interest in such property under UCC § 1-201(37), (2) that fact that tenants were obligated by lease to leave all after-acquired equipment on leased premises was also insufficient to show intention to give plaintiff security interest in such equipment, and (3) that record, considered in its entirety, showed that lease did not create security interest in after-acquired equipment purchased by tenants from defendant. Mayflower Restaurant Corp. v Bejera Corp. (1982, 3d

Dept) 88 A.D.2d 716, 451 N.Y.S.2d 286, 33 UCCRS 1484, app dismd (1982) 57 N.Y.2d 604 and app dismd (1982) 57 N.Y.2d 774

11. Purchase money security interests

Finance company's purchase money security interest in defendant's inventory was not circumscribed by precise language of parties' written security agreement, which appeared to contemplate only one method of inventory financing (i.e., advance of funds prior to purchase transaction) where, in fact, it was not unusual for parties to pursue same end by finance company's posttransaction reimbursement to defendant for inventory purchases. GE Capital Commer. Auto. Fin. v Spartan Motors, Ltd. (1998, 2d Dept) 246 A.D.2d 41, 675 N.Y.S.2d 626, 36 UCCRS2d 19, app gr (1998) 92 N.Y.2d 816, 683 N.Y.S.2d 759, 706 N.E.2d 747 and app dismd (1999) 93 N.Y.2d 870, 689 N.Y.S.2d 17, 711 N.E.2d 202

12. Remedies; foreclosure and sale

Mortgage pledgee may institute action to foreclose on real property under Real Property Actions and Proceedings Law without first proceeding to foreclose its security interests under CLS UCC Art 9, provided that pledgor is joined as party, either as plaintiff or defendant. Bank of Tokyo Trust Co. v Urban Food Malls (1996, 1st Dept) 229 A.D.2d 14, 650 N.Y.S.2d 654, 31 UCCRS2d 1132

UNDER FORMER § 9-104

Secured lending bank could not recover proceeds of auto insurance policy upon destruction of collateral by fire where bank was not named as loss payee, and where, prior to 1977 revision of UCC, insurance claims were excluded under UCC § 9-104(g). First Nat'l Bank v Merchant's Mut. Ins. Co. (1980) 49 N.Y.2d 725, 426 N.Y.S.2d 267, 402 N.E.2d 1168, 28 UCCRS 1181

Insurance payments made because of casualty loss of collateral are "proceeds" pursuant to provision of UCC § 9-306(1), effective July, 1978, which includes "insurance payable by reason of loss or damage to collateral..... except to extent it is payable to a person other than a party to the security agreement"; where automobile accident occurred in 1975, the above language of UCC § 9-306(1) is not relevant, and UCC § 9-104(g) which states that UCC Art 9 does not apply to a transfer of an interest or claim in or under any insurance policy is applicable. First Nat'l Bank v Merchant's Mut. Ins. Co. (1980) 49 N.Y.2d 725, 426 N.Y.S.2d 267, 402 N.E.2d 1168, 28 UCCRS 1181

In action by bank to foreclose mortgage given as security for loan, fact that note did not contain description of property in compliance with UCC § 9-203 did not bar foreclosure where collateral was real estate and therefore governed by UCC § 9-104(j) which exempts security interests solely in land from coverage under Code and where even if Code had been applicable, mortgage itself, not note, would have constituted security agreement and mortgage contained adequate description of property. State Bank of Albany v Fioravanti (1980) 51 N.Y.2d 638, 435 N.Y.S.2d 947, 417 N.E.2d 60, 30 UCCRS 731

CLS UCC Art 9 is inapplicable to transfer of interest in bank deposit. Gillman v Chase Manhattan Bank, N. A. (1988) 73 N.Y.2d 1, 537 N.Y.S.2d 787, 534 N.E.2d 824, 7 UCCRS2d 945, 15 ALR5th 1039

Corporation's transfer of its "general intangibles" to bank as collateral for certain loans did not confer on bank security interest in corporation's tort claims. J. A. R. Constr. Co. v Dorskind (1996, 2d Dept) 233 A.D.2d 423, 650 N.Y.S.2d 268

Transaction between local housing authority and United States whereby housing authority pursuant to its statutory powers granted to United States security interest prior to everyone else in world, including judgment creditor, was excluded from operative provisions of Uniform Commercial Code under § 9-104. Union Nat'l Bank v First Merrick Constr. Corp. (1975) 81 Misc. 2d 658, 367 N.Y.S.2d 434

Assignment of a real estate mortgage, which secures a promissory note that is included in such assignment, as collateral for a bank loan is not a secured transaction under UCC Art 9 because it is specifically excluded by UCC § 9-104(j). Rucker v State Exchange Bank (1978, Fla App D1) 355 So 2d 171, 23 UCCRS 1020 (criticized in In re Staff Mortg. & Inv. Corp. (1980, CA9 Cal) 625 F.2d 281, 6 BCD 1385, 29 UCCRS 639) and (criticized in Landmark Land Co. v Sprague (1981, SD NY) 529 F. Supp. 971, 33 UCCRS 53)

Filing was not necessary to perfect assignment of judgment under UCC since § 9-104(h) specifically excludes right represented by judgment from Article 9 of UCC. Law Research Service, Inc. v Martin Lutz Appellate Printers, Inc. (1974, CA2 NY) 498 F.2d 836, 14 UCCRS 1027 (applying New York law)

Under security agreement granting creditor security interest in inventory and equipment and further providing that debtor would

UCC

maintain insurance policy on collateral with creditor as payee, and providing that security interest was to continue in proceeds from inventory, creditor had valid security interest in proceeds of fire insurance policy upon destruction of inventory under UCC § 9-306(1), where party's clear intention was to give secured party benefit of insurance proceeds; UCC § 9-104(g), providing that Article Nine does not apply "to a transfer of an interest or claim in or under any policy of insurance" is applicable only in situations where parties to security agreement attempt to create direct security interest in insurance policy by making policy itself immediate collateral securing transaction, and not to situations where security agreement creates both direct security interest in inventory and/or equipment and requires debtor to provide his creditor with further protection by insuring collateral. PPG Industries, Inc. v Hartford Fire Ins. Co. (1976, CA2 NY) 531 F.2d 58, 76-1 USTC P 9257, 18 UCCRS 569, 37 AFTR 2d 946 (applying New York law)

In action to determine priority of right to collateral (note secured by deed of trust) that corporate debtor had assigned three times to secure its obligations, where (1) California bank in 1972 made loan of $300,000 to corporate debtor and loans of $170,000 to each of three individuals associated with corporate debtor, (2) such loans were secured by 1972 deed of trust on California property owned by corporate debtor, (3) in 1974, corporate debtor formed joint venture with plaintiff to develop certain California real estate owned by corporate debtor, which included property subject to 1972 deed of trust given to secure California bank's loans to corporate debtor and three individuals associated with debtor, (4) pursuant to joint-venture agreement with plaintiff, corporate debtor sold property to be developed for note secured by deed of trust to such property, and such note and deed constituted collateral sued for, (5) in May, 1974, corporate debtor assigned collateral in suit to California bank, which had loaned corporate debtor $300,000, to secure principal of $240,000, and bank took possession of collateral and retained it during corporate debtor's subsequent assignments thereof, (6) in January, 1975, corporate debtor made second assignment of collateral in suit, which incorporated its first assignment, by assigning collateral (a) first to California bank to secure corporate debtor's obligation of $280,000, and (b) then to first Chicago bank to secure debtor's obligation of over one million dollars, (7) thereafter, corporate debtor repaid its $280,000 debt to California bank with funds from $275,000 loan obtained from second Chicago bank, but did not repay debt to first Chicago bank, (8) in March, 1976, corporate debtor assigned collateral in suit to both California bank and second Chicago bank to secure loans made by California bank to three individuals associated with corporate debtor, (9) in May, 1976, Federal Deposit Insurance Corporation (FDIC), as liquidator of California bank which had been corporate debtor's creditor and had become insolvent, obtained California bank's rights to collateral in suit and took possession of it, (10) in 1978, first Chicago bank also became insolvent, and FDIC obtained such bank's rights to collateral in suit and sold them to plaintiff in June, 1979, on corporate debtor's default on underlying debt to first Chicago bank, and (11) plaintiff brought suit for possession of collateral when FDIC, as liquidator of California bank, refused to surrender it, district court awarded summary judgment and granted ownership of a collateral interest in the note and deed to first Chicago bank. On appeal, summary judgment was reversed and the matter remanded as the record raised a material issue of fact as to the bank's knowledge, or participation in relevant events and, therefore, its status as a good faith purchaser. Landmark Land Company v Sprague, (1982) 701 F.2d 1065

CLS UCC § 9-104(i) does no more than exempt holders of setoff rights from filing requirements of CLS UCC Art 9, and does not remove commercial transactions or conflicts from operation of Uniform Commercial Code whenever priority of set-off is involved. MNC Commercial Corp. v Joseph T. Ryerson & Son, Inc. (1989, CA2 NY) 882 F.2d 615, CCH Bankr L Rptr ¶ 73031, 9 UCCRS2d 9

Subsequently arising setoff cannot take priority over perfected security interest in receivables under CLS UCC Art 9 based on "first in time, first in right" rule of CLS UCC § 9-312. MNC Commercial Corp. v Joseph T. Ryerson & Son, Inc. (1989, CA2 NY) 882 F.2d 615, CCH Bankr L Rptr ¶ 73031, 9 UCCRS2d 9

In action between bank which held prior federally recorded security interest in airplane and bailee which held possessory lien for storage charges, under UCC §§ 9-104(c) and 9-310, possessory lien had priority over bank's interest. Industrial Nat'l Bank v Butler Aviation International, Inc. (1974, ED NY) 370 F. Supp. 1012 (applying New York law)

Transaction between export-import company and sales corporation whereby export-import company undertook to perform contract between sales corporation and buyer of shoes to import and deliver shoes to buyer, was assignment of contract rights by sales corporation to export-import company within meaning of UCC § 9-104(f) and, thus, was not secured transaction with scope of Article 9. American East India Corp. v Ideal Shoe Co. (1975, ED Pa) 400 F. Supp. 141, 17 UCCRS 527, affd without op (1978, CA3 Pa) 568 F.2d 768 (applying New York law) and (superseded by statute as stated in Bank Brussels Lambert v Credit Lyonnais (Suisse) (2000, SD NY) 2000 US Dist LEXIS 1438)

§ 9-110.   Security Interests Arising Under Article 2 or 2-A

A security interest arising under Section 2-401, 2-505, 2-711(3), or 2-A-508(5) is subject to this article. However, until the debtor obtains possession of the goods:

(1) the security interest is enforceable, even if Section 9-203(b)(3) has not been satisfied;

(2) filing is not required to perfect the security interest;

(3) the rights of the secured party after default by the debtor are governed by Article 2 or 2-A; and

(4) the security interest has priority over a conflicting security interest created by the debtor.

History: Add, L 2001, ch 84, § 36, eff July 1, 2001.

Former § 9-110, add, L 1962, ch 553; amd, L 1964, ch 476, § 11, eff Sept 27, 1964; repealed, L 2001, ch 84, § 36, eff July 1, 2001.

CASE ANNOTATIONS

UNDER FORMER § 9-113

Seller (which shipped printing press with unpaid balance owing to assignee of contract of sale after receiving payments toward purchase price financed by funds provided by bank in January 1989) had superior purchase-money security interest (PMSI) in printing press and its proceeds from inception of its contract with assignor in December 1988 where (1) seller expressly retained PMSI in both its contract with assignor and in subsequent purchase order, by which assignee obtained title, and (2) seller's security interest "attached" at time contract between it and assignor was entered into and partial payment of purchase price was made; further, since collateral was goods, seller perfected its security interest both by possession and by filing financing statement before it relinquished possession. Heidelberg E., Inc v Weber Lithography (1995, 2d Dept) 213 A.D.2d 127, 631 N.Y.S.2d 370, 27 UCCRS2d 1081

§ 9-111.   [Repealed]

History: Former § 9-111, add, L 1962, ch 553, eff Sept 27, 1964; repealed, L 2001, ch 84, § 36, eff July 1, 2001.

§ 9-112.   [Repealed]

History: Add, L 1962, ch 553, eff Sept 27, 1964; repealed, L 2001, ch 84, § 36, eff July 1, 2001.

CASE ANNOTATIONS

UNDER FORMER § 9-112

In dispute arising from stipulation granting plaintiff divorce from defendant and providing, inter alia, that she would hold, as collateral for defendant's assignment of certain rights encumbered by lien, assignment of his interest in certain medical partnership, no basis existed to award defendant any surplus from liquidation of plaintiff's collateral interest in medical partnership where (1) defendant had transferred his interest in that partnership to his partner's spouse for good and valuable consideration, subject to plaintiff's security interest, and (2) while plaintiff may have obtained windfall when she relinquished her security interest in exchange for $200,000, she was not unjustly enriched at defendant's expense. Strong v Strong (2000, 3d Dept) 277 A.D.2d 533, 715 N.Y.S.2d 499, 42 UCCRS2d 1204

The mere fact that the collateral was owned by the president of a corporation does not establish that a bank lending money to the corporation did not have a security interest in the property, because there may be a security interest in collateral not owned by the debtor. Recchio v Manufacturers & Traders Trust Co. (1968) 55 Misc. 2d 788, 286 N.Y.S.2d 390, 4 UCCRS 1133, revd on other grounds (1970, 4th Dept) 35 A.D.2d 769, 316 N.Y.S.2d 915

§ 9-113. [Repealed]

History: Add, L 1962, ch 553; amd, L 1994, ch 114, § 4, eff June 30, 1995; repealed, L 2001, ch 84, § 36, eff July 1, 2001.

§ 9-114. [Repealed]

History: Add, L 1977, ch 866, § 11, eff July 2, 1978; repealed, L 2001, ch 84, § 36, eff July 1, 2001.

§ 9-115. [Repealed]

History: Add, L 1997, ch 566, § 9, eff Oct 10, 1997; repealed, L 2001, ch 84, § 36, eff July 1, 2001.

§ 9-116. [Repealed]

History: Add, L 1997, ch 566, § 9, eff Oct 10, 1997; repealed, L 2001, ch 84, § 36, eff July 1, 2001.

PART 2
EFFECTIVENESS OF SECURITY AGREEMENT; ATTACHMENT OF SECURITY INTEREST; RIGHTS OF PARTIES TO SECURITY AGREEMENT

Subpart 1
Effectiveness and Attachment

Subpart 2
Rights and Duties

History: Add, L 2001, ch 84, § 36, eff July 1, 2001.

Former Part 2, add, L 1962, ch 553, eff Sept 27, 1964; repealed, L 2001, ch 84, § 36, eff July 1, 2001.

Subpart 1
Effectiveness And Attachment

History: Add, L 2001, ch 84, § 36, eff July 1, 2001.

§ 9-201. General Effectiveness of Security Agreement

(a) General effectiveness. Except as otherwise provided in this chapter, a security agreement is effective according to its terms between the parties, against purchasers of the collateral, and against creditors.

(b) Applicable consumer laws and other law. A transaction subject to this article is subject to:

(1) any applicable rule of law which establishes a different rule for consumers;

(2) any other statute or regulation of this state which regulates the rates, charges, agreements and practices for loans, credit sales or other extensions of credit;

(3) any consumer protection statute or regulation of this state.

(c) Other applicable law controls. In case of conflict between this article and a rule of law, statute, or regulation described in subsection (b), the rule of law, statute, or regulation controls. Failure to comply with a statute or regulation described in subsection (b) has only the effect the statute or regulation specifies.

(d) Further deference to other applicable law. This article does not:

(1) validate any rate, charge, agreement, or practice that violates a rule of law, statute, or regulation described in subsection (b); or

(2) extend the application of the rule of law, statute, or regulation to a transaction not otherwise subject to it.

History: Add, L 2001, ch 84, § 36, eff July 1, 2001.

Former § 9-201, add, L 1962, ch 553, eff Sept 27, 1964; repealed, L 2001, ch 84, § 36, eff July 1, 2001.

CASE ANNOTATIONS

UNDER FORMER § 9-201

In connection with the financed sale of a manufactured home, the fact that the creditor did not file a motor vehicle lien or any other perfection document had no effect on the granting of a security interest under N.Y. U.C.C. Law § 9-201(a) because, even an unperfected secured creditor, had greater rights in its collateral than any other creditor, unless the UCC provided otherwise. Ultimore, Inc. v Bucala (In re Bucala) (2012, BC SD NY) 464 BR 626, 76 UCCRS2d 691.

Provision in two security agreements, executed to secure payment of two notes evidencing loans made by bank to debtor, that collateral secured all existing and subsequently incurred indebtedness of debtor to bank was valid and effective under UCC § 9-201 and § 9-204(5) to continue bank's lien on collateral, even after debtor paid the two notes, where debtor had incurred other indebtedness to bank which remained unpaid. National Bank of Northern New York v Shaad (1977, 4th Dept) 60 A.D.2d 774, 400 N.Y.S.2d 965, 23 UCCRS 775

In action to recover deficiency judgments for payments due under 17 motor vehicle leases, lessor was not entitled to summary judgment since there was triable issue of fact as to whether leases were secured transactions under CLS UCC Art 9 where (1) defendant presented evidence that leases were intended to finance purchase of vehicles and therefore were secured transactions rather than true leases, (2) leases assigned various indicia of ownership of vehicles to defendant, such as duty to pay registration, taxes and insurance, and (3) leases provided that, on default, amount due would be accelerated, vehicles would be sold, and defendant would be liable for any deficiency. All

UCC

Good Leasing Corp. v Bimco Industries, Inc. (1988, 2d Dept) 143 A.D.2d 788, 533 N.Y.S.2d 336

Insurance company which, as part of claim settlement, obtained title to car covered by security interest, was liable to secured party for unpaid balance under UCC § 9-201, even though car was total loss and had no value; insurance company was not buyer of automobiles in ordinary course of business under UCC § 9-307. General Motors Acceptance Corp. v Allstate Ins. Co. (1974) 77 Misc. 2d 849, 355 N.Y.S.2d 78, 14 UCCRS 1229

In suit by trustee in bankruptcy against bank which had allegedly received voidable preferences in violation of Bankruptcy Act, bankrupt's settlement of suit concerning reduction in value of collateral for loan was not voidable preference where collateral consisted of debenture in which defendant had perfected its security interest by possession; debenture was "security" within meaning of UCC § 8-102 where, inter alia, subordinated debentures of brokerage houses were recognized medium for investment; debenture was "instrument" under UCC § 9-105 where it was "security" under UCC § 8-102; security interest in debenture was perfected by possession, under UCC § 9-305, where it was "instrument" under UCC § 9-105; security interest attached immediately in collateral despite alleged ambiguity in security agreement to effect that it was to attach only in event of default, where construction of security agreement revealed intent to attach immediately and where, under UCC § 9-204, any attempt to postpone attachment must be explictly stated; filing, under UCC § 9-201, security agreement superceded previous subordination agreement and controlled rights and obligations among the parties. Allegaert v Chemical Bank (1980, CA2 NY) 657 F.2d 495, 6 BCD 1247

Under UCC, parties to security agreement were free to decide who should have right to possession of collateral. American Honda Motor Co. v United States (1973, SD NY) 363 F. Supp. 988, 32 AFTR 2d 5886 (applying New York law)

In a bondholder's suit for a declaratory judgment that it was entitled to certain bond proceeds, an insurer's argument that the bondholder's security interests were not perfected failed because under N.Y. U.C.C. § 9-201(a), the bondholder, as a secured creditor, had greater rights in the collateral — here, the bond proceeds — than other creditors. Wachovia Bank Nat'l Ass'n v Encap Golf Holdings, LLC (2010, SD NY) 690 F Supp 2d 311.

§ 9-202.   Title to Collateral Immaterial

Except as otherwise provided with respect to consignments or sales of accounts, chattel paper, payment intangibles, or promissory notes, the provisions of this article with regard to rights and obligations apply whether title to collateral is in the secured party or the debtor.

History: Add, L 2001, ch 84, § 36, eff July 1, 2001.

Former § 9-202, add, L 1962, ch 553, eff Sept 27, 1964; repealed, L 2001, ch 84, § 36, eff July 1, 2001.

CASE ANNOTATIONS

UNDER FORMER § 9-202

Plaintiff could claim that his rights under CLS UCC §§ 9-504 and 9-505 were violated, even though, pursuant to agreements between parties, plaintiff did not secure title to stock purchased by him. Berton v Tabat Marine (1996, 2d Dept) 232 A.D.2d 441, 648 N.Y.S.2d 347

In order to meet the needs of the modern credit world, the Code ignores the question of the location of title. Chrysler Credit Corp. v Sharp (1968) 56 Misc. 2d 261, 288 N.Y.S.2d 525, 5 UCCRS 226

Since the UCC has abolished the technical distinctions between the various security devices, the federal bankruptcy courts should no longer feel compelled to engage in the purely theoretical exercise of locating "title;" nor should considerations of where "title lies" influence the courts in the exercise of their equitable discretion in ruling upon a security holder's petition for reclamation of collateral. In re Yale Express System, Inc. (1966, CA2 NY) 370 F.2d 433, 3 UCCRS 1007, appeal after remand (1967, CA2 NY) 384 F.2d 990, 4 UCCRS 783 (superseded by statute as stated in In re Timbers of

Inwood Forest Associates, Ltd. (1986, CA5 Tex) 793 F.2d 1380, 14 BCD 1029, 15 CBC2d 509, CCH Bankr L Rptr P 71238)

§ 9-203.   Attachment and Enforceability of Security Interest; Proceeds; Supporting Obligations; Formal Requisites

(a) Attachment. A security interest attaches to collateral when it becomes enforceable against the debtor with respect to the collateral, unless an agreement expressly postpones the time of attachment.

(b) Enforceability. Except as otherwise provided in subsections (c) through (i), a security interest is enforceable against the debtor and third parties with respect to the collateral only if:

(1) value has been given;

(2) the debtor has rights in the collateral or the power to transfer rights in the collateral to a secured party; and

(3) one of the following conditions is met:

(A) the debtor has authenticated a security agreement that provides a description of the collateral and, if the security interest covers timber to be cut, a description of the land concerned;

(B) the collateral is not a certificated security and is in the possession of the secured party under Section 9-313 pursuant to the debtor's security agreement;

(C) the collateral is a certificated security in registered form and the security certificate has been delivered to the secured party under Section 8-301 pursuant to the debtor's security agreement; or

(D) the collateral is deposit accounts, electronic chattel paper, investment property, letter-of-credit rights, or electronic documents, and the secured party has control under Section 7-106, 9-104, 9-105, 9-106, or 9-107 pursuant to the debtor's security agreement.

(c) Other UCC provisions. Subsection (b) is subject to Section 4-210 on the security interest of a collecting bank, Section 5-118 on the security interest of a letter-of-credit issuer or nominated person, Section 9-110 on a security interest arising under Article 2 or 2-A, and Section 9-206 on security interests in investment property.

(d) When a person becomes bound by another person's security agreement. A person becomes bound as debtor by a security agreement entered into by another person if, by operation of law other than this article or by contract:

(1) the security agreement becomes effective to create a security interest in the person's property; or

(2) the person becomes generally obligated for the obligations of the other person, including the obligation secured under the security agreement, and acquires or succeeds to all or substantially all of the assets of the other person.

(e) Effect of new debtor becoming bound. If a new debtor becomes bound as debtor by a security agreement entered into by another person:

(1) the agreement satisfies subsection (b)(3) with respect to existing or after-acquired property of the new debtor to the extent the property is described in the agreement; and

(2) another agreement is not necessary to make a security interest in the property enforceable.

(f) Proceeds and supporting obligations. The attachment of a security interest in collateral gives the secured party the rights to proceeds provided by Section 9-315 and is also attachment of a security interest in a supporting obligation for the collateral.

(g) Lien securing right to payment. The attachment of a security interest in a right to payment or performance secured by a security interest or other lien on personal or real property is also attachment of a security interest in the security interest, mortgage, or other lien.

(h) Security entitlement carried in securities account. The attachment of a security interest in a securities account is also attachment of a security interest in the security entitlements carried in the securities account.

(i) Commodity contracts carried in commodity account. The attachment of a security interest in a commodity account is also attachment of a security interest in the commodity contracts carried in the commodity account.

History: Add, L 2001, ch 84, § 36, eff July 1, 2001.

Former § 9-203, add, L 1962, ch 553, eff Sept 27, 1964; amd, L 1977, ch 866, § 12, L 1982, ch 928, § 29, L 1983, ch 321, § 4, L 1997, ch 566, § 10, eff Oct 10, 1997.

Former § 9-203, repealed, L 2001, ch 84, § 36, eff July 1, 2001.

Amd, L 2014, ch 505, § 28, eff Dec 17, 2014.

CASE ANNOTATIONS

UNDER FORMER § 9-203
I. Generally
1. In general
2. Construction
II. Enforceability
3. In general
4. Attachment
5. Description of collateral
6. – Description by reference
7. – General descriptions
8. – Miscellaneous
9. Particular documents or acts creating security interest
10. – Letters or course of conduct
11. – Oral agreements
12. Perfection
13. Priority
14. Proceeds
15. Writing requirement
16. – Formal requirements
17. – – Signature

Security interest may be enforceable even in the absence of perfection under N.Y. U.C.C. Law § 9-203[a]; a third party, who knew of the owner's interest prior to closing with the purchaser of snow machines, had a responsibility to ensure that the owner's interest no longer existed at the time of closing. Snow Machs., Inc. v S. Slope Dev. Corp. (2002, A.D., 3d Dept) 754 N.Y.S.2d 383

Music distributor's summary judgment motion was granted on its claim for foreclosure of its security interest set forth in a distribution agreement between the distributor and a music production company, where it was undisputed that the company granted the distributor a security interest in certain company property and that the company had the rights to that property. EMI Music Mktg. v Avatar Records, Inc. (2004, SD NY) 317 F. Supp. 2d 412

UNDER FORMER § 9-203

I. Generally
1. In general

Debtor's proposed compromise with a tenant-creditor did not constitute the unauthorized use of a secured creditor's cash collateral because under New York's Uniform Commercial Code, the creditor's security interest in rents attached only when debtor had rights in the collateral or power to transfer rights in collateral. In the context of this case, involving rights of a landlord-debtor and tenant-creditor, a claim for recoupment by the tenant-creditor was superior to even the bankruptcy estate's interest in prospective rents, and the secured creditor's interest only encumbered debtor's property interest in rents received by debtor. In re Tara Retail Grp., Inc., 2018 Bankr. LEXIS 655 (Bankr. N.D. W. Va. Feb. 14, 2018).

In an action by the receiver of a bank to recover a deficiency resulting from a default on a promissory note and security agreement, the agreement whereby a purchaser of sewing machines contracted with the bank for the sale of chattel paper was an enforceable contract under UCC § 1-206 where, although it contained a blank space in an "excess" transaction provision, the contract set forth an identified subject matter, indicated the parties and specified the price, and was signed by the party against whom enforcement was sought; Article 9 did not apply to the transaction since, strictly speaking, the sale of chattel paper is not a pure security transaction in that the paper is simply the property sold for value received. Federal Deposit Ins. Corp. v Herald Square Fabrics Corp. (1981, 2d Dept) 81 A.D.2d 168, 439 N.Y.S.2d 944, 32 UCCRS 558

Court would dismiss Article 78 petition to review commissioner's determination sustaining additional sales and use tax assessment against taxpayer who contended that transfer of equipment to it from closely related corporation was not bulk sale but rather was in settlement of valid security interest, since collateral was never in possession of secured party, and taxpayer failed to show that executed written security agreement had ever existed; statute of frauds barred parol evidence of security agreement, particularly as transaction was not at arm's length. Talco Contractors v New York State Tax Comm'n (1988, 3d Dept) 140 A.D.2d 834, 528 N.Y.S.2d 219

Security agreement can be found through collective examination of various documents none of which, standing alone, could satisfy requirements for security agreement found in UCC § 9-203. In re Coffee Cupboard, Inc. (1983, BC ED NY) 33 BR 668, 37 UCCRS 1360

For security interest to be valid and enforceable against both debtor and third parties, three requirements must be met: debtor must sign description of collateral, security interest must attach, and security interest must be perfected. Allegaert v Chemical Bank (1980, CA2 NY) 657 F.2d 495, 6 BCD 1247

Allegation that corporation impermissibly failed to remit profits from investment of security deposits, or to apply profits to reduce secured obligation, stated cause of action under CLS Gen Oblig § 7-101, but not under CLS UCC § 9-203. Steinmetz v Toyota Motor Credit Corp. (1997, ED NY) 963 F. Supp. 1294, 35 UCCRS2d 660

2. Construction

A perfected security interest obtained by compliance with and pursuant to UCC § 9-302(1)(d) and § 303 is not invalid against the debtor or third parties by reason of noncompliance with UCC § 9-203. Recchio v Manufacturers & Traders Trust Co. (1968) 55 Misc. 2d 788, 286 N.Y.S.2d 390, 4 UCCRS 1133, revd on other grounds (1970, 4th Dept) 35 A.D.2d 769, 316 N.Y.S.2d 915

II. Enforceability
3. In general

Defendant, which had acquired security interest in vehicle, was not owner thereof so as to be liable for its negligent use merely because defendant took actions consistent with its rights as lienholder under CLS UCC Art 9 when vehicle lessor defaulted on its obligations; thus, defendant was properly granted summary judgment in action for injuries sustained while plaintiff was passenger in vehicle. Kelly v Fleet Bank (2000, 2d Dept) 271 A.D.2d 654, 706 N.Y.S.2d 190, app den 96 N.Y.2d 702, 722 N.Y.S.2d 794, 745 N.E.2d 1016

Cooperative's claim for arrears in payment of maintenance charges, standing alone and in absence of proof of security agreement, did not give rise to enforceable right under CLS UCC Art 9 to take possession and dispose of tenants' shares in cooperative apartment to satisfy maintenance claim. Saada v Master Apts., Inc. (1991, Sup) 152 Misc. 2d 861, 579 N.Y.S.2d 536, 18 UCCRS2d 298

4. Attachment

Seller (which shipped printing press with unpaid balance owing to assignee of contract of sale after receiving payments toward purchase price financed by funds provided by bank in January 1989) had superior purchase-money security interest (PMSI) in printing press and its proceeds from inception of its contract with assignor in December 1988 where (1) seller expressly retained PMSI in both its contract with assignor and in subsequent purchase order, by which assignee obtained title, and (2) seller's security interest "attached" at time contract between it and assignor was entered into and partial payment of purchase price was made; further, since collateral was goods, seller perfected its security interest both by possession and by filing financing statement before it relinquished possession. Heidelberg E., Inc v Weber Lithography (1995, 2d Dept) 213 A.D.2d 127, 631 N.Y.S.2d 370, 27 UCCRS2d 1081

Exacting qualification of postponing attachment must be strictly construed, and only unequivocal showing of explicit agreement can effect postponement; agreement to postpone attachment which is merely inferred from words or conduct is not explicit agreement within meaning of UCC. Allegaert v Chemical Bank (1980, CA2 NY) 657 F.2d 495, 6 BCD 1247

5. Description of collateral

Unlike a financing statement which is designed merely to put creditors on notice that further inquiry is prudent, a security agreement embodies the intentions of the parties and is the primary source to which a creditor's or potential creditor's inquiry is directed and must be reasonably specific; thus term "equipment" in omnibus clause of security agreement did not include automobiles owned by bankrupt corporation. In re Laminated Veneers Co. (1973, CA2 NY) 471 F.2d 1124, 11 UCCRS 911

Description of collateral contained in security agreement must be reasonably specific. In re Laminated Veneers Co. (1973, CA2 NY) 471 F.2d 1124, 11 UCCRS 911 (applying New York law)

6. – Description by reference

Where there was security agreement complete on its face and containing no reference to financing statement, maturity date appearing only on financing statement would not be read into security agreement, security agreement was enforceable according to its terms as between parties, and secured party's claim was therefore superior to that of assignee as successor in interest to debtor assignor when secured party took possession of merchandise. In re Marta Cooperative, Inc. (1973) 74 Misc. 2d 612, 344 N.Y.S.2d 676, 12 UCCRS 955

7. – General descriptions

Description of collateral contained in security agreement must be reasonably specific; and term "equipment" in omnibus clause of security agreement did not include two automobiles owned by debtor corporation. In re Laminated Veneers Co. (1973, CA2 NY) 471 F.2d 1124, 11 UCCRS 911 (applying New York law)

8. – Miscellaneous

In action by bank to foreclose mortgage given as security for loan, fact that note did not contain description of property in compliance with UCC § 9-203 did not bar foreclosure where collateral was real estate and therefore governed by UCC § 9-104(j) which exempts security interests solely in land from coverage under Code and where even if Code had been applicable, mortgage itself, not note, would have constituted security agreement and mortgage contained adequate description of property. State Bank of Albany v Fioravanti (1980) 51 N.Y.2d 638, 435 N.Y.S.2d 947, 417 N.E.2d 60, 30 UCCRS 731

Order directing seizure of tractors and trailers which were listed as collateral in security agreement and which had been sold by debtor to defendants could not stand where there was factual question as to whether, under UCC § 9-306(2), creditor, by reason of its prior dealings with debtor, had authorized it to sell chattels free of any liens by asserting its right to receive "proceeds" if chattels were sold; order directing seizure of trailer not specifically mentioned in security agreement was improper under UCC §§ 9-110 and 9-203(1)(b) where general language in after-acquired property clause of security agreement was insufficient to cover vehicles other than those specifically listed, unless they were given and accepted in replacement of specified vehicles. Long Island Trust Co. v Porta Aluminum

Corp. (1974, 2d Dept) 44 A.D.2d 118, 354 N.Y.S.2d 134, 14 UCCRS 833

Description of triplex apartment contained in letter of credit was adequate to meet CLS UCC § 9-203 requirement that collateral be reasonably identified where letter stated that collateral consisted of 9,000 square-foot property owned by defendant located at specific address, that property was worth $6 million free and clear of any mortgage, and that it was not another property worth $1.8 million located at same address that was already held by plaintiff as collateral; fact that some additional research was needed for plaintiff to obtain precise apartment numbers of apartment did not require different result. Cantrade Private Bank Lausanne v Torresy (1995, SD NY) 876 F. Supp. 564, 26 UCCRS2d 971, judgment entered (1995, SD NY) 1995 US Dist LEXIS 8090, judgment entered sub nom CBG Banking Corp. Geneva v Torresy (1996, SD NY) 1996 US Dist LEXIS 12494

9. Particular documents or acts creating security interest

In action to determine priority of right to collateral (note secured by deed of trust) that corporate debtor had assigned three times to secure its obligations, where (1) California bank in 1972 made loan of $300,000 to corporate debtor and loans of $170,000 to each of three individuals associated with corporate debtor, (2) such loans were secured by 1972 deed of trust on California property owned by corporate debtor, (3) in 1974, corporate debtor formed joint venture with plaintiff to develop certain California real estate owned by corporate debtor, which included property subject to 1972 deed of trust given to secure California bank's loans to corporate debtor and three individuals associated with debtor, (4) pursuant to joint-venture agreement with plaintiff, corporate debtor sold property to be developed for note secured by deed of trust to such property, and such note and deed constituted collateral sued for, (5) in May, 1974, corporate debtor assigned collateral in suit to California bank, which had loaned corporate debtor $300,000, to secure principal of $240,000, and bank took possession of collateral and retained it during corporate debtor's subsequent assignments thereof, (6) in January, 1975, corporate debtor made second assignment of collateral in suit, which incorporated its first assignment, by assigning collateral (a) first to California bank to secure corporate debtor's obligation of $280,000, and (b) then to first Chicago bank to secure debtor's obligation of over one million dollars, (7) thereafter, corporate debtor repaid its $280,000 debt to California bank with funds from $275,000 loan obtained from second Chicago bank, but did not repay debt to first Chicago bank, (8) in March, 1976, corporate debtor assigned collateral in suit to both California bank and second Chicago bank to secure loans made by California bank to three individuals associated with corporate debtor, (9) in May, 1976, Federal Deposit Insurance Corporation (FDIC), as liquidator of California bank which had been corporate debtor's creditor and had become insolvent, obtained California bank's rights to collateral in suit and took possession of it, (10) in 1978, first Chicago bank also became insolvent, and FDIC obtained such bank's rights to collateral in suit and sold them to plaintiff in June, 1979, on corporate debtor's default on underlying debt to first Chicago bank, and (11) plaintiff brought suit for possession of collateral when FDIC, as liquidator of California bank, refused to surrender it, district court awarded summary judgment and granted ownership of a collateral interest in the note and deed to first Chicago bank. On appeal, summary judgment was reversed and the matter remanded as the record raised a material issue of fact as to the bank's knowledge, or participation in relevant events and, therefore, its status as a good faith purchaser. Landmark Land Company v Sprague, (1982) 701 F.2d 1065

Despite discrepancies in dates, an investment company asserted a valid security agreement, which was enforceable under N.Y. U.C.C. § 9-203, with respect to a cooperative apartment based on its claim that a debtor borrowed money from it for expenses relating to the apartment, and the debtor also executed a demand promissory note for these funds as well as a confession of judgment in favor of the investment company. Micalden Invs. S.A. v Rostropovich (2008, SD NY) 535 F Supp 2d 433.

10. – Letters or course of conduct

Letter allegedly establishing assignment of foreign exchange contract rights to bank did not measure up to security agreement under UCC since it failed to contain "description of the collateral" as required by § 9-203(1)(a). Moreover, bank failed to file financing statement, as required by §§ 9-302(1) and 9-303 and, thus, failed to obtain valid and perfected assignment of contract rights. Purported assignment was not exempt from filing under UCC § 9-302(10)(e) since, at time assignee allegedly assigned contract worth $1,000,000, assignee's total "outstanding accounts or contract rights" were $4,439,300; thus, assignment transferred just under 20 percent of assignee's accounts, including assigned contract right, which constituted "significant part" of assignee's outstanding accounts, especially in view of high absolute value of transaction at issue. Miller v Wells Fargo Bank International Corp. (1975, SD NY) 406 F. Supp. 452, 18 UCCRS 489, affd (1976, CA2 NY) 540 F.2d 548 (applying New York law)

Parties plainly contemplated "conditional assignment" as security for debtor's obligation to pay union trust funds, and it was valid, even though document purporting to constitute assignment of accounts receivable admittedly does not contain description of collateral, where letter agreement, read together with UCC-1 financing statement, is sufficient to constitute security agreement and conditional assignment, because parties created enforceable security interest under CLS UCC § 9-203. King v Tuxedo Enters. (1997, ED NY) 975 F. Supp. 448, 35 UCCRS2d 1372

11. – Oral agreements

The fact that the security agreement in goods resold by the buyer to a third person is oral does not affect its validity as against other creditors under UCC § 9-302(1)(d) and § 9-303. Recchio v Manufacturers & Traders Trust Co. (1968) 55 Misc. 2d 788, 286 N.Y.S.2d 390, 4 UCCRS 1133, revd on other grounds (1970, 4th Dept) 35 A.D.2d 769, 316 N.Y.S.2d 915

12. Perfection

An attorney's charging lien created by Jud Law § 475 did not take precedence over a bank's security interest in the underlying money judgment since, notwithstanding that the attorney's lien attached at the commencement of the underlying litigation, the bank's security interest vested pursuant to UCC § 9-203, which was perfected without the necessity of filing a financing statement and prior to the commencement of the litigation. Effective Communications West, Inc. v Board of Cooperative Educational Services etc. (1981, 4th Dept) 84 A.D.2d 941, 446 N.Y.S.2d 684, 33 UCCRS 736

Claim of bank that loaned money to seller of coffee to proceeds of contract for sale of coffee to buyer is granted summarily, where bank produced security agreement signed by seller describing collateral accounts receivable and indicating that bank gave value to seller and that seller had rights in collateral, and where bank gave notice of its security interest in account to account debtor, because bank met criteria in CLS UCC ' 9-203(1) for creation, attachment, and perfection of security interest in seller's account, and because bank's security interest attached prior to security agreement between coffee trading company and its lender. Continental Coffee Prods. Co. v Banque Lavoro S.A. (1994, SD NY) 852 F. Supp. 1235, 25 UCCRS2d 542

13. Priority

Court would order debtors to return property to secured creditor on basis of security agreement between parties, notwithstanding debtors' contention that nonparty held superior security interest in same property; mere existence of potentially senior lien constituted no defense under CLS UCC § 9-312, and priority dispute would be proper subject of dispute only between secured parties. Midlantic Commercial Leasing Corp. v D.B.A. Knits, Inc. (1990, 1st Dept) 167 A.D.2d 117, 561 N.Y.S.2d 436

Defendant finance company, which acquired purchase-money security interest in 2 vehicles by its postpurchase advance of funds to auto dealer, had priority over "dragnet" lien previously acquired by plaintiff in connection with "floor plan" financing of dealer's inventory, notwithstanding plaintiff's claim that it lacked notice of inventory covered by defendant's security interest because dealer and defendant had diverged in practice from literal language of their contract which appeared to contemplate prepurchase advance of funds, where written identification of defendant's collateral was "reasonably specific" and plaintiff could not show how it relied to its detriment on when and how defendant discharged its individual financing obligations to dealer. GE Capital Commer. Auto. Fin. v Spartan Motors, Ltd. (1998, 2d Dept) 246 A.D.2d 41, 675 N.Y.S.2d 626, 36 UCCRS2d 19, app gr (1998) 92 N.Y.2d 816, 683 N.Y.S.2d 759, 706 N.E.2d 747 and app dismd (1999) 93 N.Y.2d 870, 689 N.Y.S.2d 17, 711 N.E.2d 202

The perfected security interest of a retail finance corporation who purchased a credit agreement signed by a "buyer in the ordinary course of business" from an automobile dealer had priority over the perfected interests of a bank which furnished floor plan financing to finance the dealer's acquisition and holding of motor vehicles for use

and resale in the course of the dealer's business. Chrysler Credit Corp. v Sharp (1968) 56 Misc. 2d 261, 288 N.Y.S.2d 525, 5 UCCRS 226

14. Proceeds

Where secured creditor alleged that it was entitled to, as proceeds of its security interest in an automobile owned by debtor, a portion of money received by debtor in settlement of a state court lawsuit for personal injury to himself and property damage to automobile, where action was settled for $25,000 in state court pursuant to New York State Insurance Law, and where nowhere in such settlement was there any indication as to what portion was allocated for personal injuries or property damages for pain and suffering, inasmuch as there was damage to vehicle, some portion of money received in settlement of state court action constituted proceeds of damaged vehicle as defined by § 9-306(1) of New York Uniform Commercial Code; creditor was entitled to security interest in that portion of proceeds that represented damage to automobile. In re Territo (1983, BC ED NY) 32 BR 377, 11 BCD 20, 36 UCCRS 1762, later proceeding (1984, BC ED NY) 36 BR 667, CCH Bankr L Rptr ¶ 69759

Because a creditor may perfect a lien in the private economic value of a license granted by the Federal Communications Commission (FCC) to the extent that such lien does not violate the FCC's public right to regulate license transfers, noteholders had a valid lien on the economic value of the debtor's license to use an S-Band spectrum, and nothing in N.Y. U.C.C. § 9-203 or 11 U.S.C.S. § 552 invalidated this lien. Sprint Nextel Corp. v U.S. Bank Nat'l Ass'n (In re Terrestar Networks, Inc.) (2011, BC SD NY) 457 BR 254.

15. Writing requirement

In absence of written security agreement signed by debtor, as required by UCC § 9-203(1)(a), creditor's action to recover possession of racehorse from debtor under security agreement allegedly executed by parties was barred, since UCC § 9-203(1)(a), as noted in Official Comment 5 to that section, functions as a "statute of frauds." Oksner v Murphy (1982, 2d Dept) 89 A.D.2d 995, 454 N.Y.S.2d 323, 34 UCCRS 996

Tax Commissioner properly found that transfer of certain equipment to taxpayer was bulk sale subject to sales and use tax under CLS Tax § 1141, rather than settlement of valid security interest, since taxpayer was unable to produce executed written security agreement, and failed to prove content of missing security agreement by parol evidence where UCC-1 financing statements and other documents offered as evidence contained incongruous descriptions of collateral and testimony adduced at hearing did not clarify specific terms of agreement. Talco Contractors v New York State Tax Comm'n (1988, 3d Dept) 140 A.D.2d 834, 528 N.Y.S.2d 219

16. – Formal requirements

UCC-1 financing statement created security interest in manufactured home since it was signed by defendant, it named parties, it described collateral, it described plaintiff as secured party, and circumstances under which it was signed-at closing on sale of real property wherein plaintiff received note and purchase-money mortgage-evinced intent to create security interest in manufactured home. Lashua v La Duke (2000, 3d Dept) 272 A.D.2d 750, 707 N.Y.S.2d 542, 41 UCCRS2d 930

In an action for conversion by seizure and sale of property covered by security agreement allegedly void presented triable issues of fact as to the validity of the agreement, precluding summary judgment, where agreement was undated, did not specify the amount of the debt, or the terms of repayment and was signed by an individual in his own name and not in his capacity as an officer of the debtor corporation but the agreement did name the debtor corporation in the body thereof, listed the collateral covered by it, and the individual signing it was in fact the president of the debtor authorized to sign. Cherno v Bank of Babylon (1968) 57 Misc. 2d 801, 293 N.Y.S.2d 577

17. – – Signature

Security agreement which named the debtor corporation in the body thereof, listed the collateral covered by it, and the individual signing it was in fact the president of the debtor authorized to sign by resolution on file with the bank, and was signed on a line preceded by the word "by" with corporate seal affixed, raised issues as to the validity of the security agreement sufficient to defeat a motion for summary judgment although the agreement was undated, did not specify the amount of the debt, nor the terms of repayment and was signed by the individual in his own name and not in his capacity as an officer of the debtor corporation. Cherno v Bank of Babylon (1968) 57 Misc. 2d 801, 293 N.Y.S.2d 577

UCC

Because N.Y. U.C.C. Law § 9-203 did not require that a security agreement be signed by both parties to be enforceable, the fact that only the debtors signed both the promissory note and the contract of sale was enough to satisfy the authentication requirement of N.Y. U.C.C. Law § 9-102(a)(7). Ultimore, Inc. v Bucala (In re Bucala) (2012, BC SD NY) 464 BR 626, 76 UCCRS2d 691.

§ 9-204. After-acquired Property; Future Advances

(a) After-acquired collateral. Except as otherwise provided in subsection (b), a security agreement may create or provide for a security interest in after-acquired collateral.

(b) When after-acquired property clause not effective. A security interest does not attach under a term constituting an after-acquired property clause to:

(1) consumer goods, other than an accession when given as additional security, unless the debtor acquires rights in them within 10 days after the secured party gives value; or

(2) a commercial tort claim.

(c) Future advances and other value. A security agreement may provide that collateral secures, or that accounts, chattel paper, payment intangibles, or promissory notes are sold in connection with, future advances or other value, whether or not the advances or value are given pursuant to commitment.

History: Add, L 2001, ch 84, § 36, eff July 1, 2001.

Former § 9-204, Add, L 1962, ch 553; amd, L 1977, ch 866, § 13, eff July 2, 1978; repealed, L 2001, ch 84, § 36, eff July 1, 2001.

CASE ANNOTATIONS

UNDER FORMER § 9-204
I. Generally
1. Creation of security interest
2. "Rights in collateral"
3. – Documents of title
4. – What constitutes; creation
5. – Particular applications
II. After-Acquired Property
6. Conditional sale as affecting
7. Language creating coverage
8. Priority
9. Truth-In-Lending Act
10. – Violation of 10-day rule
11. – Not violative of 10-day rule
III. Future Advances
12. In general
13. Language creating coverage
IV. Particular Collateral
14. Inventory
15. – Particular applications

UNDER FORMER § 9-204

I. Generally
1. Creation of security interest
Where (1) debtor sold corporate stock on July 25, 1974 to defendants for $180,000, and defendants executed promissory notes under pledge agreement securing payment of stock's purchase price and delivered notes to escrowee, which also received the purchased stock, (2) debtor on March 19, 1975, with knowledge and consent of defendants and escrowee, assigned notes to creditor as collateral to secure payment of prior $60,000 debt, indorsed them to creditor's order, and delivered them to creditor which retained possession of them until August 24, 1976, a date following date on which debtor had fully discharged debt due creditor, (3) on November 5, 1975, when defendants still owed debtor $135,000 on notes and notes were still in creditor's possession as collateral for payment of $28,000 balance

then owed by debtor to creditor, debtor entered into agreement with plaintiff law firm and its client under which payments on prior debt owed by debtor to such client were extended, prospective lawsuit was settled, sums thus owe to client were collateralized by assignment of debtor's interest in stock-payment notes, and notes themselves and pledge agreement securing them were also assigned to plaintiff on behalf of its client, subject to prior collateral assignment in favor of debtor's first creditor, (4) first creditor on August 24, 1976 acknowledged to escrowee that debtor had fully discharged debt due it, delivered stock-payment notes in suit to plaintiff law firm, but never indorsed notes to plaintiff's order, (5) on August 25, 1976, plaintiff, defendants (purchasers of debtor's stock), debtor, and escrowee executed written acknowledgements of debtor's assignment of notes and pledge agreement to plaintiff, and plaintiff requested that it be paid next installment on notes, which was due on October 1, 1976, (5) on April 5, 1976, IRS assessed delinquent income-tax liability against debtor and filed notice of tax lien on August 4, 1976, (6) on October 1, 1976, escrowee paid installment payment due on notes to IRS, and (7) on October 5, 1976, plaintiff after due notice declared default on notes (because of failure to receive October 1, 1976 installment payment thereon) and under acceleration clause in notes demanded full payment thereof, court held (1) that plaintiff, as nominee for its client, acquired valid collateral assignment of proceeds of notes to extent that proceeds were not required to satisfy first creditor's prior security interest therein, (2) that under UCC § 3-202(3), debtor's indorsement and negotiation of notes to first creditor merely created partial assignment of notes' proceeds and did not divest debtor of ultimate right to all proceeds not required to satisfy debt owed to first creditor, (3) that debtor's remaining interest in notes' proceeds was the interest that debtor had assigned to plaintiff as collateral on November 5, 1975, and that such assignment, under UCC § 9-204(1), gave plaintiff valid security interest in debtor's residuary interest in notes' proceeds, (4) that plaintiff's security interest in notes' proceeds was not perfected until August 24, 1976, when it became perfected under UCC § 9-305 by possession of notes following first creditor's delivery thereof to plaintiff, (5) that IRS tax lien was not superior to plaintiff's perfected security interest in notes, since neither plaintiff nor its client had received any notice of such lien until September 20, 1976, and (6) that neither plaintiff not its client could accelerate unpaid balance due on notes, since plaintiff, as nominee for its client, was merely holder of security interest in notes and was not "holder" of notes within meaning of UCC § 1-201(20) because of first creditor's failure to indorse them to plaintiff's order. Lipkowitz & Plaut v Affrunti (1978) 95 Misc. 2d 849, 407 N.Y.S.2d 1010, 25 UCCRS 276 (holding that plaintiff was entitled to receive, on behalf of its client, all installment payments due on notes, commencing with installment due on October 1, 1976)

In suit by trustee in bankruptcy against bank which had allegedly received voidable preferences in violation of Bankruptcy Act, bankrupt's settlement of suit concerning reduction in value of collateral for loan was not voidable preference where collateral consisted of debenture in which defendant had perfected its security interest by possession; debenture was "security" within meaning of UCC § 8-102 where, inter alia, subordinated debentures of brokerage houses were recognized medium for investment; debenture was "instrument" under UCC § 9-105 where it was "security" under UCC § 8-102; security interest in debenture was perfected by possession, under UCC § 9-305, where it was "instrument" under UCC § 9-105; security interest attached immediately in collateral despite alleged ambiguity in security agreement to effect that it was to attach only in event of default, where construction of security agreement revealed intent to attach immediately and where, under UCC § 9-204, any attempt to postpone attachment must be explicitly stated; filing, under UCC § 9-201, security agreement superceded previous subordination agreement and controlled rights and obligations among the parties. Allegaert v Chemical Bank (1980, CA2 NY) 657 F.2d 495, 6 BCD 1247

2. "Rights in collateral"
Notwithstanding any agreement between debtor and creditor, if debtor has no rights in collateral, no security interest in that collateral comes into existence. In re Emergency Beacon Corp. (1981, CA2 NY) 665 F.2d 36, 32 UCCRS 788, later proceeding (1981, CA2 NY) 666 F.2d 754, 8 BCD 605, CCH Bankr L Rptr P 68522, 32 FR Serv 2d 1431, later proceeding (1983, BC SD NY) 27 BR 757, later proceeding (1984, BC SD NY) 40 BR 113, later proceeding (1984, BC SD NY) 43 BR 672, later proceeding (1985, SD NY) 48 BR 341, 41 UCCRS 1544, later proceeding (1985, SD NY) 48 BR 356, 13 BCD 204, later proceeding (1985, BC SD NY) 52 BR 828, later proceeding

(1986, BC SD NY) 58 BR 399 and affd (1987, SD NY) 71 BR 117, CCH Bankr L Rptr P 71717 and affd in part and revd in part (1985, SD NY) 52 BR 979, affd (1986, CA2 NY) 790 F.2d 285, CCH Bankr L Rptr P 71154, 4 FR Serv 3d 1194

3. – Documents of title

UCC's phrase "documents of title" does not refer to vehicle certificates of title; it does not appear that vehicle certificate of title carries with it certitude invisioned by UCC's term "document of title" since it cannot be treated as "adequately evidencing" ownership of vehicle. In re Emergency Beacon Corp. (1981, CA2 NY) 665 F.2d 36, 32 UCCRS 788, later proceeding (1981, CA2 NY) 666 F.2d 754, 8 BCD 605, CCH Bankr L Rptr P 68522, 32 FR Serv 2d 1431, later proceeding (1983, BC SD NY) 27 BR 757, later proceeding (1984, BC SD NY) 40 BR 113, later proceeding (1984, BC SD NY) 43 BR 672, later proceeding (1985, SD NY) 48 BR 341, 41 UCCRS 1544, later proceeding (1985, SD NY) 48 BR 356, 13 BCD 204, later proceeding (1985, BC SD NY) 52 BR 828, later proceeding (1986, BC SD NY) 58 BR 399 and affd (1987, SD NY) 71 BR 117, CCH Bankr L Rptr P 71717 and affd in part and revd in part (1985, SD NY) 666 F.2d 979, affd (1986, CA2 NY) 790 F.2d 285, CCH Bankr L Rptr P 71154, 4 FR Serv 3d 1194

4. – What constitutes; creation

Even where creditor and debtor agreed to postpone time of attaching of creditor's security interest in debtor's collateral until event of default should occur, creditor under UCC § 9-204(1) had security interest in collateral where construction of security agreement revealed intent to attach immediately and where, under UCC § 9-204, any attempt to postpone attachment must be explicitly stated; filing, under UCC § 9-201, security agreement superceded previous subordination agreement and controlled rights and obligations among the parties. Allegaert v Chemical Bank (1980, CA2 NY) 657 F.2d 495, 6 BCD 1247

5. – Particular applications

When the holder of promissory notes assigned his interest therein as collateral to secure payment of a prior indebtedness, a sum less than the aggregate amount of the notes, and indorsed and delivered them to that creditor, he did not irrevocably divest himself of the ultimate right to all of the proceeds of the notes, but retained ownership of those proceeds not required to satisfy that indebtedness, and, therefore, the negotiation of all of the notes operated only as a partial assignment of the proceeds of the notes; the interest retained by him was capable of being transferred and, when it was transferred by another collateral assignment, the transferee acquired a valid security interest as to his residuary interest in the notes, which security interest was perfected by a subsequent delivery of the notes to it. Lipkowitz & Plaut v Affrunti (1978) 95 Misc. 2d 849, 407 N.Y.S.2d 1010, 25 UCCRS 276

II. After-Acquired Property

6. Conditional sale as affecting

The title of a conditional vendor to removable fixtures installed upon realty is superior to the lien of a prior mortgage containing the standard "after-acquired" property clause, but a conditional vendor is bound to refrain from wilfully impairing the security of a real estate mortgagee and if, without the consent of the mortgagee, he removes equipment subject to the mortgage, he should be required to account to the mortgagee for its fair value, and if the equipment which was replaced without the mortgagee's consent was serviceable and of some value, the priorities may appropriately be reversed to the extent of the impairment of the mortgagee's security. Blancob Constr. Corp. v 246 Beaumont Equity, Inc. (1965, 1st Dept) 23 A.D.2d 413, 261 N.Y.S.2d 227, 2 UCCRS 995

7. Language creating coverage

Possibly, between the parties to the security agreement, the ambiguous provision to the effect that it creates a security for "any and all liabilities... now existing or hereafter arising" might be found, on parol testimony, to mean that it does apply to subsequent deliveries, but so to find under UCC § 9-204(3) where third-party claimants to the fund were involved would be to stretch its language beyond what is reasonable and beyond what is just. Rusch Factors, Inc. v Passport Fashion, Ltd. (1971) 67 Misc. 2d 3, 322 N.Y.S.2d 765, 9 UCCRS 507, affd (1971, 1st Dept) 38 A.D.2d 690, 327 N.Y.S.2d 536, app den (1972) 30 N.Y.2d 482

Assignee of all receivables "now or hereafter" owned is assignee of accounts receivable and as such, under UCC § 9-204, has continuing security interest in present and future (court's emphasis) inventory of his debtor, and his lien prevails over a subsequent judgment creditor who levied prior to the secured party taking possession of the collateral. O'Hara & Shaver, Inc. v Empire Bituminous Products, Inc. (1971) 67 Misc. 2d 47, 323 N.Y.S.2d 190, 9 UCCRS 764

"Dragnet" clause of chattel mortgage agreement encompassed contemporaneously made real estate bond and mortgage and therefore also covered the debt arising from the default on foreclosure of the real estate mortgage. In re Riss Tanning Corp. (1972, CA2 NY) 468 F.2d 1211, 11 UCCRS 601

"Dragnet" clause of chattel mortgage agreement stating that equipment was security for note "as well as for payment of any other obligation or liability due or to become due whether now existing or hereafter arising" encompassed contemporaneously made real estate bond and mortgage and therefore also covered debt arising from default on foreclosure of that mortgage. In re Riss Tanning Corp. (1972, CA2 NY) 468 F.2d 1211, 11 UCCRS 601 (applying New York law)

8. Priority

Where a security agreement has already been executed, a security interest in subsequent accounts receivable attaches as soon as the accounts become due, and prevails over a judgment lien thereafter obtained. Space-Tronics, Inc. v International Business Machines Corp. (1966, N.Y. Sup) 3 UCCRS 902

9. Truth-In-Lending Act

In an action by a lender to recover the balance due on a loan following the debtors' default, a counterclaim by the debtors based on a violation of the Truth in Lending Act (US Code, tit 15, § 1601 *et seq.*)in that the disclosure statement described the security interest as covering the debtors' automobile as well as all "household consumer goods of every kind now owned or hereafter acquired" by the debtors, was not time barred since although subdivision (e) of section 1640 of title 15 of the United States Code provides that such an action against a lender is to be commenced within one year from the date of the occurrence of the violation and the action was commenced more than three years after the loan was made, the counterclaim arose out of the transaction sued upon and is not untimely. Public Loan Co. v Hyde (1979) 47 N.Y.2d 182, 417 N.Y.S.2d 238, 390 N.E.2d 1162, 26 UCCRS 781

10. – Violation of 10-day rule

A disclosure statement made by a lender which describes the security interest as covering all "household consumer goods of every kind now owned or hereafter acquired" is in direct conflict with subdivision (2) of section 9-204 of the Uniform Commercial Code, which limits the security interest a creditor may take in consumer goods to those acquired within 10 days after the creditor gives value, and is also in violation of Regulation Z (12 CFR 226.8 [b] [5]), which was adopted pursuant to the provisions of the Truth in Lending Act (US Code, tit 15, § 1601 *et seq.*)and requires a clear identification of the property to which the security interest relates; accordingly, inasmuch as the security interest was not properly and clearly set forth because it was unlawfully overstated and overbroad, the lender is liable to the debtor in an amount of twice the finance charge imposed, pursuant to subdivision (a) of section 1640 of title 15 of the United States Code. Public Loan Co. v Hyde (1979) 47 N.Y.2d 182, 417 N.Y.S.2d 238, 390 N.E.2d 1162, 26 UCCRS 781

Provision in disclosure statement that lender had security interest in all of debtor's "household consumer goods of every kind now owned or hereafter acquired" violated UCC § 9-204(2), which limits creditor's security interest in consumer goods to goods acquired within 10 days after creditor gave value. Public Loan Co. v Hyde (1979) 47 N.Y.2d 182, 417 N.Y.S.2d 238, 390 N.E.2d 1162, 26 UCCRS 781

A failure on the part of a lender to disclose that the scope of its security interest in after-acquired consumer goods is limited to those acquired within 10 days after the lender gives value (Uniform Commercial Code, § 9-204, subd [2]) constitutes an affirmative misstatement of the scope of the lender's security interest, is violative of the Federal Truth in Lending Act (US Code, tit 15, § 1639) and a regulation promulgated thereunder, and renders the lender liable to the debtors for the statutory penalty of twice the finance charge (US Code, tit 15, § 1640); however, while section 353 of the New York Banking Law incorporates that Federal act and regulation to the extent of requiring the disclosure of all items required to be disclosed thereby, the improper disclosure statement here is not so blatant or substantial a violation of that section as to justify imposition of the drastic sanctions provided for in section 358 of the Banking Law, pursuant to which one who violates section 353 thereof is guilty of a misdemeanor and the underlying debt is totally invalidated. Public Loan Co. v Hyde (1978, 3d Dept) 63 A.D.2d 193, 406 N.Y.S.2d 907,

UCC

app gr (1978) 45 N.Y.2d 711 and affd (1979) 47 N.Y.2d 182, 417 N.Y.S.2d 238, 390 N.E.2d 1162, 26 UCCRS 781

In action by borrower under federal Truth-in-Lending Act (15 USCS § 1601 et seq.), defendant creditor's disclosure statement and security agreement violated both Truth-in-Lending Act and UCC § 9-204(4)(b), dealing with attachment of security interest under after-acquired property clause to consumer goods given as additional security where debtor acquires rights in such goods within ten days after secured party gives value, since creditor's security agreement claimed interest beyond scope permitted by UCC § 9-204(4)(b) by failing to allow for ten-day limitation that statute provided for. Conrad v Beneficial Finance Co. (1977) 91 Misc. 2d 643, 398, 398 N.Y.S.2d 499, 22 UCCRS 1221

Creditor's failure to disclose 10 day limitation on security interests and after acquired consumer goods violates Truth in Lending Act (15 USCS § 1639). McKimmie v AVCO Financial Services Co. (1981, WD NY) 504 F. Supp. 1286, 31 UCCRS 700

11. – Not violative of 10-day rule

The failure of plaintiff finance company to state in its combined promissory note and disclosure statement that under State law the security interest covering defendants' after-acquired household consumer goods was limited to those goods acquired by defendants within 10 days after the loans were made (Uniform Commercial Code, § 9-204, subd [4], par [b]) did not violate the disclosure requirements of the Federal Truth in Lending Act (US Code, title 15, § 1639, subd [a], par [8]) and the regulations thereunder which only require that the fact that after-acquired property will be subject to a security interest "be clearly set forth in conjunction with the description or identification of the type of security interest held, retained or acquired" (12 CFR 226.8 [b] [5]). The note and disclosure statement did reveal that a security interest was sought in after-acquired household goods. The omission to specify the limitation of the security interest in defendants' consumer goods to those acquired within 10 days is not significant enough to justify the total forfeiture of the principal and interest of the loans which would result under sections 353 and 358 of the Banking Law for a failure to properly disclose under the Federal act. A note and disclosure statement need not incorporate all portions of the State law in order not to run afoul of the Federal Truth in Lending Act which only requires a description of the security interest to be retained and clear identification of the property to which it relates. The Federal act gives the consumer the right to know the terms on which a lender will extend him credit, but does not give the consumer the right to know all the creditor's rights and duties under State law. Interlakes Financial Corp. v Payne (1978) 92 Misc. 2d 770, 401 N.Y.S.2d 713

III. Future Advances

12. In general

Under UCC § 9-204(3), obligations covered by a security agreement may include future advances or other value, whether or not given pursuant to commitment. State Bank of Albany v Fioravanti (1979, 3d Dept) 70 A.D.2d 1011, 418 N.Y.S.2d 202, affd (1980) 51 N.Y.2d 638, 435 N.Y.S.2d 947, 417 N.E.2d 60, 30 UCCRS 731 (holding that mortgages for future advances are valid)

13. Language creating coverage

Provision in two security agreements, executed to secure payment of two notes evidencing loans made by bank to debtor, that collateral secured all existing and subsequently incurred indebtedness of debtor to bank was valid and effective under UCC § 9-201 and § 9-204(5) to continue bank's lien on collateral, even after debtor paid the two notes, where debtor had incurred other indebtedness to bank which remained unpaid. National Bank of Northern New York v Shaad (1977, 4th Dept) 60 A.D.2d 774, 400 N.Y.S.2d 965, 23 UCCRS 775

IV. Particular Collateral

14. Inventory

Where the validity of a security agreement which secures both present and future advances and covers both existing and after-acquired inventory is not controverted, the security interest attached to such inventory. William Iselin & Co. v Burgess & Leigh Ltd. (1967) 52 Misc. 2d 821, 276 N.Y.S.2d 659, 3 UCCRS 1168

15. – Particular applications

State and city tax stamps affixed to cigarette packs were not "accessions" under CLS UCC § 9-314, and thus wholesale distributor of cigarettes did not possess type of rights in tax stamps which could be subject to security interest by third party, since tax stamps have no intrinsic commercial value and distributor was, at most, agent for state and city for purposes of collecting cigarette tax; accordingly, secured lender's motion for summary judgment declaring it owner of

escrow account containing proceeds of sale of tax stamps would be denied. Lincoln First Commercial Corp. v New York State Tax Com. (1987, Sup) 136 Misc. 2d 478, 518 N.Y.S.2d 904

§ 9-205. Use or Disposition of Collateral Permissible

(a) When security interest not invalid or fraudulent. A security interest is not invalid or fraudulent against creditors solely because:

(1) the debtor has the right or ability to:

(A) use, commingle, or dispose of all or part of the collateral, including returned or repossessed goods;

(B) collect, compromise, enforce, or otherwise deal with collateral;

(C) accept the return of collateral or make repossessions; or

(D) use, commingle, or dispose of proceeds; or

(2) the secured party fails to require the debtor to account for proceeds or replace collateral.

(b) Requirements of possession not relaxed. This section does not relax the requirements of possession if attachment, perfection, or enforcement of a security interest depends upon possession of the collateral by the secured party.

History: Add, L 2001, ch 84, § 36, eff July 1, 2001.

Former § 9-205, add, L 1962, ch 553; amd, L 1977, ch 866, § 14, eff July 2, 1978; repealed, L 2001, ch 84, § 36, eff July 1, 2001.

CASE ANNOTATIONS

UNDER FORMER § 9-205

The perfected security interest of a retail finance corporation who purchased a credit agreement signed by a "buyer in the ordinary course of business" from an automobile dealer had priority over the perfected interests of a bank which furnished floor plan financing to finance the dealer's acquisition and holding of motor vehicles for use and resale in the course of the dealer's business. Chrysler Credit Corp. v Sharp (1968) 56 Misc. 2d 261, 288 N.Y.S.2d 525, 5 UCCRS 226

Under UCC, parties to security agreement were free to decide who should have right to possession of collateral. American Honda Motor Co. v United States (1973, SD NY) 363 F. Supp. 988, 32 AFTR 2d 5886 (applying New York law)

§ 9-206. Security Interest Arising in Purchase or Delivery of Financial Asset

(a) Security interest when person buys through securities intermediary. A security interest in favor of a securities intermediary attaches to a person's security entitlement if:

(1) the person buys a financial asset through the securities intermediary in a transaction in which the person is obligated to pay the purchase price to the securities intermediary at the time of the purchase; and

(2) the securities intermediary credits the financial asset to the buyer's securities account before the buyer pays the securities intermediary.

(b) Security interest secures obligation to pay for financial asset. The security interest described in subsection (a) secures the person's obligation to pay for the financial asset.

(c) Security interest in payment against delivery transaction. A security interest in favor of a person that delivers a certificated security or other financial asset represented by a writing attaches to the security or other financial asset if:

(1) the security or other financial asset:

(A) in the ordinary course of business is transferred by delivery with any necessary indorsement or assignment; and

(B) is delivered under an agreement between persons in the business of dealing with such securities or financial assets; and

(2) the agreement calls for delivery against payment.

(d) Security interest secures obligation to pay for delivery. The security interest described in subsection (c) secures the obligation to make payment for the delivery.

History: Add, L 2001, ch 84, § 36, eff July 1, 2001.

Former § 9-206, add, L 1962, ch 553, eff Sept 27, 1964; amd, L 1963, ch 1003, § 31, eff Sept 27, 1964; repealed, L 2001, ch 84, § 36, eff July 1, 2001.

CASE ANNOTATIONS

UNDER FORMER § 9-206
1. Waiver
2. – Defenses waived and not waived
3. – – Failure of consideration; nonperformance
4. – – Fraud in the inducement
5. Enforceability of waiver
6. – Good faith
7. – Relation of assignee to seller
8. – Particular applications

UNDER FORMER § 9-206

1. Waiver
Clause in lease of photocopier equipment which provided, pursuant to UCC § 9-206(1), that lessee would not assert against assignee any defenses or counterclaims that he might have against lessor, was not void as being contrary to public policy. Bankers Trust Co. v Litton Systems, Inc. (1979, CA2 NY) 599 F.2d 488, 26 UCCRS 513 (applying New York law)

Under UCC § 9-206(1), written agreement by buyer of dump trucks that it would not assert against assignee of sale contract any claims, defenses, or offsets that it might have against seller, which agreement was clear as to both its terms and meaning and was supported by consideration, was enforceable by assignee against buyer. Credit Alliance Corp. v David O. Crump Sand & Fill Co. (1979, SD NY) 470 F. Supp. 489, 27 UCCRS 291 (applying New York law)

2. – Defenses waived and not waived
In suit by assignee of equipment lease, after repossession-sale of leased equipment following lessee's default in payment of rentals, for deficiency judgment against lessee, lessee had expressly waived, within meaning of UCC § 9-206(1), fraud defense that lessee had against lessor-assignor, and such waiver was valid under UCC § 9-206(1) because plaintiff assignee had taken lease assignment for value, in good faith, and without notice of any defense to lessee's enforcement, and thus was holder in due course. Leasing Service Corp. v River City Constr., Inc. (1984, CA11 Ala) 743 F.2d 871, 39 UCCRS 1054 (applying Ala and N.Y. UCC)

3. – – Failure of consideration; nonperformance
Assignee who does not take assignment "in good faith" is not entitled to protection of "cut-off" provisions of Code § 9-206, so that whatever claims and defenses consumer has with respect to instalment contracts may be asserted against assignee thereof; held, where seller had delivered only freezer and not frozen food called for by contract, assignee was not entitled to maintain action for payments due but could repossess freezer. Star Credit Corp. v Molina (1969) 59 Misc. 2d 290, 298 N.Y.S.2d 570, 6 UCCRS 70

4. – – Fraud in the inducement
Where (1) certain estoppel documents were substantial equivalent of agreement by lessee of machines that it would not assert against an assignee any claim or defense that it might have against the lessor, and (2) where such agreement by lessee was enforceable under UCC § 9-206(1) by assignee who took assignment for value, in good faith, and without notice of a claim or defense thereto, court would hold that in addition to certain defenses, which on an earlier appeal had been held to be barred by estoppel documents in suit, lessee also could not assert against an assignee defense of original lessor's fraud in the inducement where record failed to raise triable issue that assignee had had knowledge or notice of such fraud. B. V. D. Co. v Marine Midland Bank-New York (1977, 1st Dept) 60 A.D.2d 544, 400 N.Y.S.2d 63, 23 UCCRS 792

In action by successor in interest to assignee of lease of telephone equipment to recover accrued rent installments, where (1) lease contained clause that in event of its assignment, defendant lessee would not assert against assignee any claims or defenses that he might have against lessor, and (2) defendant alleged, as defense to action, that he had been fraudulently induced to enter into the lease, court held that such defense could not be asserted against plaintiff because it did not come within exception in UCC § 9-206(1) that defenses assertable against holder in due course of negotiable instrument can also be asserted against an assignee, regardless of any agreement to the contrary, since (1) only fraud in the factum can be asserted against a holder in due course, and (2) defendant had merely alleged fraud in the inducement. Federal Deposit Ins. Corp. v Kassel (1979, 2d Dept) 72 A.D.2d 787, 421 N.Y.S.2d 609, 27 UCCRS 1426

With respect to provision in UCC § 9-206(1) that agreement by buyer or lessee, that he will not assert against assignee any claim or defense that he may have against seller or lessor is enforceable by assignee who had taken assignment for value, in good faith, and without notice of any claim or defense, except as to defenses of type that can be asserted against holder in due course of negotiable instrument under UCC Article 3 (see UCC § 3-305(2)), fraud in the inducement is not defense of type that can be asserted against holder in due course under Article 3. Chase Manhattan Bank, N. A. v Finger Lakes Motors, Inc. (1979) 102 Misc. 2d 48, 423 N.Y.S.2d 128, 28 UCCRS 220

Fraud in the inducement is an insufficient defense to a waiver of defenses provision in an assignment clause (Uniform Commercial Code, § 9-206, subd [1]) since fraudulent inducement is not a defense "of a type which may be asserted against a holder in due course", in that fraud in the inducement renders an obligation voidable, but not void, and is also not an available misrepresentation defense (Uniform Commercial Code, § 3-305, subd [2], pars [b], [c]); however, plaintiff bank, the assignee of an equipment lease and guarantee executed by defendants as part of a franchise agreement with the assignor, a muffler franchisor, is not entitled to summary judgment to recover the balance due and owing under the lease and remains vulnerable to defendants' claim of fraud in the inducement at this juncture since it failed to submit any proof sufficient to meet its burden of establishing that it took the assignment in good faith and without notice of any claims or defenses; defendants' allegations that the assignor entered into the lease and franchise agreements with the express purpose of fleecing the defendants and that plaintiff had notice of the assignor's fraudulent conduct raise a triable issue of fact as to notice sufficient to defeat plaintiff's motion for summary judgment. Chase Manhattan Bank, N. A. v Finger Lakes Motors, Inc. (1979) 102 Misc. 2d 48, 423 N.Y.S.2d 128, 28 UCCRS 220

5. Enforceability of waiver
If assignee of lease concerning computers and computer equipment took assignment for value, in good faith and without notice of concurrent agreement that lease, would not be effective if certain acceptable and satisfactory equipment were not delivered, assignee could recover on lease notwithstanding lessor's alleged failure to deliver equipment where lease provided that lessee would not assert against assignee any defenses, counterclaims or offsets which it might have against lessor. National Bank of North America v De Luxe Poster Co. (1976, 2d Dept) 51 A.D.2d 582, 378 N.Y.S.2d 462, 18 UCCRS 802

CLS UCC § 9-206 sanctions enforcement of clause in equipment lease in which lessee acknowledges assignment of lease to assignee and agrees to make payments due under lease notwithstanding any

UCC

defenses it may have against lessor where assignee takes assignment for value without notice of any defenses. Manufacturers & Traders Trust Co. v Murdevski (1987, 4th Dept) 126 A.D.2d 952, 511 N.Y.S.2d 723

The waiver by the lessee of vending machines of any claims that it may have against the lessor is valid. Fairfield Lease Corp. v Colonial Aluminum Sales, Inc. (1966, N.Y. Sup) 3 UCCRS 858

6. – Good faith

Stating that "good faith" as used in UCC § 9-206 means more than "honesty in fact", the Civil Court of New York City held that where an assignee sought to bar a consumer from asserting claims and defenses to the underlying obligations and evidence disclosed the assignee had taken the contracts at a discount of 22 percent from face value within 24 hours of their execution and before the seller could possibly have made a credit investigation of the buyer, the assignee had not taken the contract "in good faith" and was not entitled to protection of "cut-off" provisions of § 9206. Star Credit Corp. v Molina (1969) 59 Misc. 2d 290, 298 N.Y.S.2d 570, 6 UCCRS 70

7. – Relation of assignee to seller

A buyer who executes a conditional sales contract containing covenant not to assert against an assignee any defense, counterclaim or offset on account of breach of warranty or otherwise is bound by its agreement and the fact that the assignee is a subsidiary of the assignor seller is not sufficient to cast doubt upon assignee's status as a bona fide purchaser for value. B. W. Acceptance Corp. v Richmond (1965) 46 Misc. 2d 447, 259 N.Y.S.2d 965, 2 UCCRS 627

8. – Particular applications

Assignee of agreement for lease of telephone equipment was entitled to summary judgment in its action against lessee for payments due under lease, despite lessee's defense that equipment was defective and that lessor had failed to comply with terms of separate maintenance agreement, where lessee admitted that he did not make such payments, lease contained clause that lessee acknowledged assignment of lease to assignee and agreed to make payments due notwithstanding any defenses it might have against lessor, and lessee did not controvert assignee's statement in moving papers that it had no knowledge of such defenses at time that it took assignment and advanced funds to lessor. Manufacturers & Traders Trust Co. v Murdevski (1987, 4th Dept) 126 A.D.2d 952, 511 N.Y.S.2d 723

Defendant equipment lessee raised triable issues of fact as to whether plaintiff, as assignee of lessor, took lease in good faith and without notice of lessee's claims that equipment was defective, which, if resolved in lessee's favor, would render assignee subject to lessee's claims and defenses, despite lease provision that lessee would not assert any claims or defenses against assignee, where (1) assignee did not explain why it did not send lessee notice of assignment until almost one year after purported assignment, 6 months after lessee ceased making lease payments, and one month after assignor sent notice of default and threatened to accelerate payments as provided in lease, (2) both notice of default and notice of assignment were signed by same person, and (3) assignor and assignee shared same business address, suite, and attorneys. Norwest Fin. Leasing, Inc. v Parish of St. Augustine (1998, 1st Dept) 251 A.D.2d 125, 674 N.Y.S.2d 312

In action for lessee's conceded default in payment under computer lease, assignee of lease was entitled to summary judgment despite lessee's claim that lessor breached various warranties under lease and that lease was void due to lessor's fraudulent inducement, since lessee had agreed not to assert defenses against lessor's assignee, and such agreement was binding under CLS UCC § 9-206; lessee's allegation that assignee of lease, as financing agent for lessor, knew or should have known that leased equipment was defective and that lessor would be subject to defenses in action to enforce lease, was insufficient to raise triable issue as to assignee's bad faith or notice of lessee's defenses. Norstar Bank of Upstate New York v Corrigan (1987, Sup) 136 Misc. 2d 920, 519 N.Y.S.2d 447, 4 UCCRS2d 1621

Assignee of seller's purchase money security interest was entitled to enforce provision of sales agreement whereby purchaser agreed to waive all defenses and counterclaims against seller's assignee, provided that assignment was made for value, in good faith, and without notice of claims and defenses (CLS UCC § 9-206), since seller did not retain purchase money security interest in goods. Siemens Credit Corp. v Marvik Colour, Inc. (1994, SD NY) 859 F. Supp. 686, 24 UCCRS2d 705

Subpart 2
Rights And Duties

History: Add, L 2001, ch 84, § 36, eff July 1, 2001.

§ 9-207. Rights and Duties of Secured Party Having Possession or Control of Collateral

(a) Duty of care when secured party in possession. Except as otherwise provided in subsection (d), a secured party shall use reasonable care in the custody and preservation of collateral in the secured party's possession. In the case of chattel paper or an instrument, reasonable care includes taking necessary steps to preserve rights against prior parties unless otherwise agreed.

(b) Expenses, risks, duties, and rights when secured party in possession. Except as otherwise provided in subsection (d), if a secured party has possession of collateral:

(1) reasonable expenses, including the cost of insurance and payment of taxes or other charges, incurred in the custody, preservation, use, or operation of the collateral are chargeable to the debtor and are secured by the collateral;

(2) the risk of accidental loss or damage is on the debtor to the extent of a deficiency in any effective insurance coverage;

(3) the secured party shall keep the collateral identifiable, but fungible collateral may be commingled; and

(4) the secured party may use or operate the collateral:

(A) for the purpose of preserving the collateral or its value;

(B) as permitted by an order of a court having competent jurisdiction; or

(C) except in the case of consumer goods, in the manner and to the extent agreed by the debtor.

(c) Duties and rights when secured party in possession or control. Except as otherwise provided in subsection (d), a secured party having possession of collateral or control of collateral under Section 7-106, 9-104, 9-105, 9-106, or 9-107:

(1) may hold as additional security any proceeds, except money or funds, received from the collateral;

(2) shall apply money or funds received from the collateral to reduce the secured obligation, unless remitted to the debtor; and

(3) may create a security interest in the collateral.

(d) Buyer of certain rights to payment. If the secured party is a buyer of accounts, chattel paper, payment intangibles, or promissory notes or a consignor:

(1) subsection (a) does not apply unless the secured party is entitled under an agreement:

(A) to charge back uncollected collateral; or

(B) otherwise to full or limited recourse against the debtor or a secondary obligor based on the non-payment or other default of an account debtor or other obligor on the collateral; and

(2) subsections (b) and (c) do not apply.

History: Add, L 2001, ch 84, § 36, eff July 1, 2001.

Former § 9-207, add, L 1962, ch 553, eff Sept 27, 1964; repealed, L 2001, ch 84, § 86, eff July 1, 2001.

Amd, L 2014, ch 505, § 29, eff Dec 17, 2014.

CASE ANNOTATIONS

UNDER FORMER § 9-207

1. In general; duty of care
2. Disclaimer of duty
3. Duty to preserve value
4. – Duty of government as to Treasury bills
5. Duty to record security interest
6. Proof of negligence or bad faith

N.Y. U.C.C. Law § 9-207 requires that the secured party be in "possession or control" of the collateral; although a sale was part of a plan worked out between a borrower and a bank to reduce the former's debts to the latter, including debts for which a guarantor was liable, the bank had no duty to the guarantor, under either the loan documents or the guarantee, the latter of which contained a broad and all encompassing consent to the bank's release of security, to collect more of the proceeds realized at the sale than it did, and the bank was properly granted summary judgment against the guarantor on the issue of liability. Bank Leumi USA v Agati (2004, A.D., 1st Dept) 774 N.Y.S.2d 499

Under a Securities Investor Protection Act of 1970 liquidation, where the creditor had posted cash collateral with the debtor broker-dealer in exchange for loaned securities, the debtor's commingled cash was not subject to a constructive trust and all of the debtor's cash was property of the estate and the creditor's security interest could be avoided by the trustee, because, while the debtor was required to use reasonable care in preserving that collateral under N.Y. U.C.C. Law § 9-207(a) (2002), under N.Y. U.C.C. Law § 1-102, the parties had, by agreement, not unreasonably, provided that the debtor was not required to segregate the cash, and under N.Y. U.C.C. Law § 9-625, the creditor's only remedy was a claim for damages. Ferris, Baker, Watts, Inc. v Stephenson (In re MJK Clearing) (2002, BC DC Minn) 286 BR 109, 49 UCCRS2d 11

UNDER FORMER § 9-207

1. In general; duty of care

Mere fact that collateral is stolen while in possession of secured party does not establish secured party's liability to debtor where debtor fails to establish that precautions taken by secured party to safeguard property were not reasonable. Bud-Lee Ski Centers, Inc. v State (1986, 2d Dept) 116 A.D.2d 715, 497 N.Y.S.2d 768, 42 UCCRS 1789

Bank which loaned money to corporation and took physical possession of corporation's assets on default by corporation was not bound to honor exclusive supply contract between corporation and subsidiary in absence of contract requiring such action, notwithstanding facts that bank and plaintiff had entered into intercreditor agreement which provided plaintiff with superior security interest in subsidiary, and subsidiary's only asset with value was exclusive supply agreement. Spielman v Acme Nat'l Sales Co. (1991, 3d Dept) 169 A.D.2d 218, 572 N.Y.S.2d 400

Bank which loaned money to corporation and took physical possession of corporation's assets on default by corporation was not assignee of corporation so as to be bound by exclusive supply agreement between corporation and subsidiary since nothing in agreement between bank and corporation manifested intent to "assign" present or future interest in corporation's assets to bank.

Spielman v Acme Nat'l Sales Co. (1991, 3d Dept) 169 A.D.2d 218, 572 N.Y.S.2d 400

Bank which loaned money to corporation and took physical possession of corporation's assets on default by corporation was not successor of corporation so as to be bound by exclusive supply agreement between corporation and subsidiary since bank's possession and control of corporation's assets, undertaken by bank on corporation's default pursuant to security agreement, amounted to substantive change in ownership, rather than one of mere form. Spielman v Acme Nat'l Sales Co. (1991, 3d Dept) 169 A.D.2d 218, 572 N.Y.S.2d 400

Bank was entitled to retain, as security for corporate loan, collateral from plaintiff's personal loan after personal loan had been paid in full, and bank was also entitled to summary judgment dismissing causes of action alleging breach of contract in refusing to return collateral where (1) corporate loan was personally guaranteed by plaintiff, (2) at time personal loan was paid off and plaintiff requested return of security, corporate loan was in default and seriously undersecured, (3) plaintiff was president and minority shareholder of corporation involved, (4) promissory notes signed with respect to both loans provided that plaintiff assigned to bank security interest in any other property of plaintiff in possession or control of bank, and (5) personal guarantee provided that all property of plaintiff would be held by bank subject to lien and security interest in its favor as security for liabilities of plaintiff to bank. Reich v Bowery Sav. Bank (1992, 2d Dept) 183 A.D.2d 884, 583 N.Y.S.2d 978, app den (1992) 80 N.Y.2d 758, 589 N.Y.S.2d 308, 602 N.E.2d 1124

Bank which arranged for sale through its brokerage service of stock held as loan security, in order to enable lender to realize favorable capital gains treatment available only upon sale of stock by December 31, 1986, would be held liable for consequential damages resulting from failure to sell stock until January 7, 1987, having breached CLS UCC § 9-207 duty to use reasonable care in custody and preservation of collateral in its possession. Huther v Marine Midland Bank, N. A. (1989, City Ct) 143 Misc. 2d 697, 541 N.Y.S.2d 902

Federal law would preempt any purported application of Uniform Commercial Code to margin transactions in view of pervasive federal regulating scheme that explicitly permits brokers to commingle customer funds and implicitly permits them to retain earnings on collateral posted for short sales; established practices of short sales and margin and UCC have peacefully co-existed for years, without any perception that UCC governed, much less outlawed, them. Levitin v Painewebber, Inc. (1998, CA2 NY) 159 F.3d 698, CCH Fed Secur L Rep ¶ 90286, 44 UCCRS2d 859, cert den 525 US 1144, 143 L Ed 2d 47, 119 S Ct 1039

Under UCC § 3-606(1)(b), providing that party to instrument is discharged if holder, without such party's consent, unjustifiably impairs collateral for instrument and UCC § 9-207(1), which defines impairment of collateral, party to loan transaction-other than the party actually pledging collateral that was subsequently unjustifiably impaired-is discharged only if he was entitled to look to collateral for reimbursement of any payment made to creditor. Thus, Iranian debtors who executed notes and loan agreement, and Iranian corporation which guaranteed debtors' obligations to creditor, were not discharged under UCC §§ 3-606(1)(b) and 9-207(1) from their direct and secondary obligations under such notes, loan agreement, and to guaranty agreement, even assuming that collateral given was unjustifiably impaired, where they were not entitled to look to collateral for reimbursement of payments made to creditor. American Express International Banking Corp. v Sabet (1980, SD NY) 512 F. Supp. 463 (ovrld in part on other grounds as stated in FDIC v Wrapwell Corp. (1996, SD NY) 922 F. Supp. 913)(applying New York law)

In action by holder in due course to recover on three secured promissory notes which (1) had been validly executed by maker and assigned to plaintiff prior to maker's death as evidence of plaintiff's assumption of maker's total liability to certain third parties, and (2) had matured after maker's death, court held on plaintiff's motion for partial summary judgment under F R Civ P 56, (1) that case was especially suited for application of Rule 56 in order to eliminate defendant executors' unworthy defenses, which were employed solely for dilatory purposes, (2) that no absolute defenses to promissory note (see, for example, UCC §§ 3-305(2) (defenses against holder in due course), and 3-407 (material alteration of instrument)) applied to notes in suit, (3) that since evidence showed that plaintiff had not foreclosed on notes' collateral and that defendants were still dealing with collateral as owners, defendants could not successfully claim that notes sued on had been discharged by plaintiff's acceptance of such collateral, (4) that creditor under UCC § 9-207 can retain and protect collateral received as security for debt until such debt is satisfied, and (5) that retention of collateral by creditor under UCC § 9-207 cannot be equated with election by creditor under UCC § 9-505(2) to satisfy debt only with collateral in absence of written notice from creditor, which is required by UCC § 9-505(2), that creditor has made such election. Hanam, B.V. v Kittay (1984, SD NY) 589 F. Supp. 1042 (applying New York law)

2. Disclaimer of duty

Even if there was valid agreement exempting secured party's assignee from use of reasonable care in preservation of collateral, where assignee did not respond to assignor's letter indicating that assignor was relying on assignee to record judgment note, assignee was estopped from raising exemption; held, exemption or exculpation clause was not effective as against duty of care imposed by UCC § 9-207(1). Congress Financial Corp. v Sterling-Coin Op Machinery Corp. (1972, CA3 Pa) 456 F.2d 451, 10 UCCRS 199 (applying New York law)

3. Duty to preserve value

A sub-pledge of negotiable securities is under the duty to exercise reasonable care for the preservation and protection of their value. Grace v Sterling, Grace & Co. (1968, 1st Dept) 30 A.D.2d 61, 289 N.Y.S.2d 632, 5 UCCRS 297

Under both the common law and UCC § 9-207(1), the creditor is under a special duty to the surety to exercise reasonable care in protecting and preserving the collateral. Executive Bank of Ft. Lauderdale v Tighe (1978, 2d Dept) 66 A.D.2d 70, 411 N.Y.S.2d 939, 25 UCCRS 786, appeal after remand (1980, 2d Dept) 75 A.D.2d 574, 426 N.Y.S.2d 585, 29 UCCRS 367, appeal after remand (1981) 54 N.Y.2d 330, 445 N.Y.S.2d 425, 429 N.E.2d 1054, 32 UCCRS 894

Bank, which held plaintiff's stock shares as collateral, did not fail to exercise reasonable care in their custody and preservation, even though bank had assigned corporate note and all collateral to Federal Deposit Insurance Corporation (FDIC) and stock was worthless by time FDIC settled with plaintiff, where stock did not decline in value until it had been in FDIC's possession for 8 months, and there was no evidence that plaintiff ever requested that bank sell stock before it lost its value. Reich v Bowery Sav. Bank (1992, 2d Dept) 183 A.D.2d 882, 583 N.Y.S.2d 980, 19 UCCRS2d 611, app den (1992) 80 N.Y.2d 758, 589 N.Y.S.2d 308, 602 N.E.2d 1124

Bank owed duty to preserve value of corporation's accounts receivable by drawing down master letters of credit issued to both corporation and its customer when shipping documents were properly presented where bank acted (1) as banker to both parties in issuing letters of credit, and (2) as creditor, following corporation's default, with possession of collateral (letters of credit that allowed collection of accounts receivable); duty existed regardless of whether bank's allegedly commercially unreasonable acts took place before or after date of default. Bank of China v Chan (1991, CA2 NY) 937 F.2d 780, 15 UCCRS2d 162, later proceeding (1992, SD NY) 1992 US Dist LEXIS 15592

Individual guarantor of corporate debt raised genuine issue of fact as to commercial reasonableness of bank's handling of corporation's accounts receivable where guarantor supported with documentary evidence his allegations that bank dishonored letters of credit and temporarily lost both shipping documents and payments of corporation's foreign customers, and bank simply alleged, without proof, that all dishonored letters of credit involved discrepancies between terms of letters and shipping documents which corporation presented. Bank of China v Chan (1991, CA2 NY) 937 F.2d 780, 15 UCCRS2d 162, later proceeding (1992, SD NY) 1992 US Dist LEXIS 15592

UCC § 9-207(2)(c) did not create property right in motorists that was enforceable through Takings Clause to have interest on advance toll payments made as part of computerized toll payment system returned to motorist, since motorists did not incur debt when they prepaid tolls. Rosenfeld v Port Auth. (2000, ED NY) 108 F. Supp. 2d 156, 42 UCCRS2d 269

4. – Duty of government as to Treasury bills

Where debtor sold vehicles that were subject to security interest to third party, secured party was entitled, on default, to enforce its right of possession against third party; failure of third party to surrender property immediately upon default and demand prevented secured party from using collateral under UCC § 9-207(4) or reselling or leasing it under UCC § 504(1), and third party was liable to secured party for loss of use of property as element of damages. Long Island Trust Co. v Porta Aluminum, Inc. (1975, 2d Dept) 49 A.D.2d 579, 370

N.Y.S.2d 166, 17 UCCRS 619, appeal after remand (1978, 2d Dept) 63 A.D.2d 670, 404 N.Y.S.2d 682, 24 UCCRS 252

5. Duty to record security interest

In action by lessor of 2 hydraulic lifts to recover upon guarantee by third party of obligation of lessee who defaulted in making payments under lease and transferred lifts to its former landlord, where lease constituted security interest, lessor's failure to file financing statement did not impair collateral to detriment of third party and thus, third party's obligation on its guarantee was not discharged to any extent; since landlord was legal owner of hydraulic lifts, and by whatever means lessee's former landlord took possession of property from lessee, it remained that landlord took possession of property that did not belong to lessee. Guardsman Lease Plan, Inc. v Gibraltar Transmission Corp. (1985, Sup) 129 Misc. 2d 887, 494 N.Y.S.2d 59, 42 UCCRS 943

6. Proof of negligence or bad faith

Secured party is not negligent when it permits removal of repossessed collateral by secured and judgment creditors of debtor where judgment creditor has secured court order directing that secured party turn over property and where, with respect to secured creditor, party in possession of collateral has ascertained legitimacy of creditor's claim and obtained receipt for each item of property taken. Bud-Lee Ski Centers, Inc. v State (1986, 2d Dept) 116 A.D.2d 715, 497 N.Y.S.2d 768, 42 UCCRS 1789

§ 9-208. Additional Duties of Secured Party Having Control of Collateral

(a) Applicability of section. This section applies to cases in which there is no outstanding secured obligation and the secured party is not committed to make advances, incur obligations, or otherwise give value.

(b) Duties of secured party after receiving demand from debtor. Within 10 days after receiving an authenticated demand by the debtor:

(1) a secured party having control of a deposit account under Section 9-104(a)(2) shall send to the bank with which the deposit account is maintained an authenticated statement that releases the bank from any further obligation to comply with instructions originated by the secured party;

(2) a secured party having control of a deposit account under Section 9-104(a)(3) shall:

(A) pay the debtor the balance on deposit in the deposit account; or

(B) transfer the balance on deposit into a deposit account in the debtor's name;

(3) a secured party, other than a buyer, having control of electronic chattel paper under Section 9-105 shall:

(A) communicate the authoritative copy of the electronic chattel paper to the debtor or its designated custodian;

(B) if the debtor designates a custodian that is the designated custodian with which the authoritative copy of the electronic chattel paper is maintained for the secured party, communicate to the custodian an authenticated record releasing the designated custodian from any further obligation to comply with instructions originated by the secured party and instructing the custodian to comply with instructions originated by the debtor; and

(C) take appropriate action to enable the debtor or its designated custodian to make copies of or revisions to the authoritative copy which add or change an identified assignee of the authoritative copy without the consent of the secured party;

(4) a secured party having control of investment property under Section 8-106(d)(2) or 9-106(b) shall send to the securities intermediary or commodity intermediary with which the security entitlement or commodity contract is maintained an authenticated record that releases the securities intermediary or commodity intermediary from any further obligation to comply with entitlement orders or directions originated by the secured party;

(5) a secured party having control of a letter-of-credit right under Section 9-107 shall send to each person having an unfulfilled obligation to pay or deliver proceeds of the letter-of-credit to the secured party an authenticated release from any further obligation to pay or deliver proceeds of the letter-of-credit to the secured party; and

(6) a secured party having control of an electronic document shall:

(A) give control of the electronic document to the debtor or its designated custodian;

(B) if the debtor designates a custodian that is the designated custodian with which the authoritative copy of the electronic document is maintained for the secured party, communicate to the custodian an authenticated record releasing the designated custodian from any further obligation to comply with instructions originated by the secured party and instructing the custodian to comply with instructions originated by the debtor; and

(C) take appropriate action to enable the debtor or its designated custodian to make copies of or revisions to the authoritative copy which add or change an identified assignee of the authoritative copy without the consent of the secured party.

History: Add, L 2001, ch 84, § 36, eff July 1, 2001.

Former § 9-208, add, L 1962, ch 553, eff Sept 27, 1964; repealed, L 2001, ch 84, § 36, eff July 1, 2001.

Amd, L 2014, ch 505, § 30, eff Dec 17, 2014.

§ 9-209. Duties of Secured Party If Account Debtor Has Been Notified of Assignment

(a) Applicability of section. Except as otherwise provided in subsection (c), this section applies if:

(1) there is no outstanding secured obligation; and

(2) the secured party is not committed to make advances, incur obligations, or otherwise give value.

(b) Duties of secured party after receiving demand from debtor. Within 10 days after receiving an authenticated demand by the debtor, a secured party shall send to an account debtor that has received notification of an assignment to the secured party as assignee under Section 9-406(a) an authenticated record that releases the account debtor from any further obligation to the secured party.

(c) Inapplicability to sales. This section does not apply to an assignment constituting the sale of an account, chattel paper, or payment intangible.

History: Add, L 2001, ch 84, § 36, eff July 1, 2001.

§ 9-210. Request for Accounting; Request Regarding List of Collateral or Statement of Account

(a) Definitions in this section:

(1) "Request" means a record of a type described in paragraph (2), (3), or (4).

(2) "Request for an accounting" means a record authenticated by a debtor requesting that the recipient provide an accounting of the unpaid obligations secured by collateral and reasonably identifying the transaction or relationship that is the subject of the request.

(3) "Request regarding a list of collateral" means a record authenticated by a debtor requesting that the recipient approve or correct a list of what the debtor believes to be the collateral securing an obligation and reasonably identifying the transaction or relationship that is the subject of the request.

(4) "Request regarding a statement of account" means a record authenticated by a debtor requesting that the recipient approve or correct a statement indicating what the debtor believes to be the aggregate amount of unpaid obligations secured by collateral as of a specified date and reasonably identifying the transaction or relationship that is the subject of the request.

(b) Duty to respond to requests. Subject to subsections (c), (d), (e), and (f), a secured party, other than a buyer of accounts, chattel paper, payment intangibles, or promissory notes or a consignor, shall comply with a request within 14 days after receipt:

(1) in the case of a request for an accounting, by authenticating and sending to the debtor an accounting; and

(2) in the case of a request regarding a list of collateral or a request regarding a statement of account, by authenticating and sending to the debtor an approval or correction.

(c) Request regarding list of collateral; statement concerning type of collateral. A secured party that claims a security interest in all of a particular type of collateral owned by the debtor may comply with a request regarding a list of collateral by sending to the debtor an authenticated record including a statement to that effect within 14 days after receipt.

(d) Request regarding list of collateral; no interest claimed. A person that receives a request regarding a list of collateral, claims no interest in the collateral when it receives the request, and claimed an interest in the collateral at an earlier time shall comply with the request within 14 days after receipt by sending to the debtor an authenticated record:

(1) disclaiming any interest in the collateral; and

UCC

(2) if known to the recipient, providing the name and mailing address of any assignee of or successor to the recipient's interest in the collateral.

(e) Request for accounting or regarding statement of account; no interest in obligation claimed. A person that receives a request for an accounting or a request regarding a statement of account, claims no interest in the obligations when it receives the request, and claimed an interest in the obligations at an earlier time shall comply with the request within 14 days after receipt by sending to the debtor an authenticated record:

(1) disclaiming any interest in the obligations; and

(2) if known to the recipient, providing the name and mailing address of any assignee of or successor to the recipient's interest in the obligations.

(f) Charges for responses. A debtor is entitled without charge to one response to a request under this section during any six-month period. The secured party may require payment of a charge not exceeding $25 for each additional response.

History: Add, L 2001, ch 84, § 36, eff July 1, 2001.

PART 3
PERFECTION AND PRIORITY

History: Add, L 2001, ch 84, § 36, eff July 1, 2001.

Former Part 3, add, L 1962, ch 553, eff Sept 27, 1964; repealed, L 2001, ch 84, § 36, eff July 1, 2001.

Subpart 1
Law Governing Perfection And Priority

History: Add, L 2001, ch 84, § 36, eff July 1, 2001.

§ 9-301. Law Governing Perfection and Priority of Security Interests

Except as otherwise provided in Sections 9-303 through 9-306, the following rules determine the law governing perfection, the effect of perfection or nonperfection, and the priority of a security interest in collateral:

(a) Except as otherwise provided in this section, while a debtor is located in a jurisdiction, the local law of that jurisdiction governs perfection, the effect of perfection or nonperfection, and the priority of a security interest in collateral.

(b) While collateral is located in a jurisdiction, the local law of that jurisdiction governs perfection, the effect of perfection or nonperfection, and the priority of a possessory security interest in that collateral.

(c) Except as otherwise provided in subsection (d), while tangible negotiable documents, goods, instruments, money, or angible chattel paper is located in a jurisdiction, the local law of that jurisdiction governs:

(1) perfection of a security interest in the goods by filing a fixture filing;

(2) perfection of a security interest in timber to be cut; and

(3) the effect of perfection or nonperfection and the priority of a nonpossessory security interest in the collateral.

(d) The local law of the jurisdiction in which the wellhead or minehead is located governs perfection, the effect of perfection or nonperfection, and the priority of a security interest in as-extracted collateral.

(e) When collateral is a cooperative interest, the law of this state governs perfection, the effect of perfection or nonperfection, and the priority of the security interest in such collateral.

History: Add, L 2001, ch 84, § 36, eff July 1, 2001.

Former § 9-301, add, L 1962, ch 553; amd, L 1977, ch 866, § 15, eff July 2, 1978; amd, L 1977, ch 866, § 15, eff July 2, 1978, L 1985, ch 717, § 1, eff Aug 31, 1985, and applicable to collateral received by a debtor on or after August 31, 1985, L 1997, ch 566, § 11, eff Oct 10, 1997.

Former § 9-301, repealed, L 2001, ch 84, § 36, eff July 1, 2001.

Amd, L 2014, ch 505, § 31, eff Dec 17, 2014.

CASE ANNOTATIONS

Where a debtor, which was a New York corporation, received an unexpected refund from a Canadian supplier, under former N.Y. U.C.C. Law § 9-103(3)(b), the status of a creditor's security interest in the refund, which was a general intangible, was governed by the law of New York. In re Iroquois Energy Mgmt., LLC (2002, BC WD NY) 284 BR 28

Under N.Y. U.C.C. §§ 9-301(a) and -307(e) and 13 Pa. Cons. Stat. §§ 9301 and 9307(e), whether an insurance company had perfected a security interest in the assets of a judgment creditor was governed by New York law, as the judgment creditor was organized as a New York corporation and was therefore "located" in New York. Sentry Select Ins. Co. v LBL Skysystems (U.S.A.), Inc. (2007, ED Pa) 486 F Supp 2d 496, stay den (2007, ED Pa) 2007 US Dist LEXIS 46654.

UNDER FORMER § 9-103

Creditors, whose perfected security interest in painting under Swiss law was lost when it was removed from Switzerland to New York warehouse, were not entitled to 4-month grace period of CLS UCC § 9-103(1)(d)(i) to reperfect security interest in New York by reason of Switzerland's Private International Law Statute, which provides that acquisition and loss of rights in moveable goods are governed by law of country of location at time of event giving rise to acquisition or loss, since (1) New York law provides that in determining grace period reference is made to law of jurisdiction from which collateral was removed, and (2) even if New York substantive law applied, § 9-103(1)(d)(i) provides only for extension of perfected security interest, and creditors had lost their perfected security interest. Fortune Finans AB v Andersson (1993, 1st Dept) 192 A.D.2d 124, 600 N.Y.S.2d 460, 21 UCCRS2d 352

Creditors, who had perfected security interest in painting under Swiss law prior to its removal to warehouse in New York, were not entitled to modification of orders of attachment to exclude painting from their scope on theory that they reperfected security interest in New York within 4 months after painting's arrival there, but after orders of attachment were issued and painting was levied on, where warehouse was unaware of creditors' security interest under Swiss law; under CLS UCC § 9-103(1)(d)(i), creditor is required to reperfect security interest in collateral which is subject to security interest perfected under law of another jurisdiction from which it was removed on sooner of either 4 months or expiration of perfection under law of other jurisdiction, and because under Swiss law creditors' security interest expired on transfer of painting to New York warehouse without notice of their interest, they could not avail themselves of statute's 4-month grace period for reperfection. Fortune Finans AB v Andersson (1993, 1st Dept) 192 A.D.2d 124, 600 N.Y.S.2d 460, 21 UCCRS2d 352

Transaction between contractor and surety for completion of public improvement project following contractor's default was not intended to have effect as security. Aetna Casualty & Surety Co. v Perrotta (1970) 62 Misc. 2d 252, 308 N.Y.S.2d 613, 7 UCCRS 358

Where New Jersey was chief place of business of debtor which had entered into security agreement as to traxcavator, a heavy construction machine, rights of parties were governed by New Jersey law. Foley Machinery Co. v John T. Brady Co. (1970) 62 Misc. 2d 777, 310 N.Y.S.2d 49, 7 UCCRS 872

Truck was not sold in ordinary course of business; buyer had no knowledge of Florida source of origin of truck; buyer inquired of seller and checked proper county offices in New York and found that no liens had been filed against truck; Florida bank held chattel mortgage on truck; bank had permitted seller, who had acquired title in Florida, to register title in New York; both New York and Florida are title states; seller had failed to use proceeds of sale to pay off lien; held, lien of bank was subordinated to buyer's purchase interest. Seely v First Bank & Trust (1970) 64 Misc. 2d 845, 315 N.Y.S.2d 374, 8 UCCRS 559

One who takes title to incoming auto subject to security interest of assignee of conditional vendor during four months from time auto entered jurisdiction cannot prevail over assignee under UCC § 9-103(3). Newton-Waltham Bank & Trust Co. v Bergen Motors, Inc. (1971) 68 Misc. 2d 228, 327 N.Y.S.2d 77, affd (1972) 75 Misc. 2d 103, 347 N.Y.S.2d 568

Lien created in Massachusetts enjoyed superiority in New York for period of 4 months from date auto arrived in New York without any further measures being undertaken by conditional vendor's assignee, who sought to recover from New York purchaser, to localize such foreign security interest. Newton-Waltham Bank & Trust Co. v Bergen Motors, Inc. (1971) 68 Misc. 2d 228, 327 N.Y.S.2d 77, affd (1972) 75 Misc. 2d 103, 347 N.Y.S.2d 568

Where (1) defendant purchased automobile at execution sale with full knowledge of plaintiff's perfected security interest therein and had it stored in codefendant's garage in effort to keep vehicle from plaintiff, and (2) plaintiff did not consent or request such storage of vehicle, court held (1) that plaintiff's security interest was superior, under UCC § 9-103(2)(a) & (4), to codefendant garageman's lien for storage charges, (2) that lien issue was not controlled by UCC § 9-310, as alleged by garageman, and (3) that defendant, after buying vehicle at execution sale with knowledge of plaintiff's security interest therein, was legally obligated to resolve favorably plaintiff's secured interest before she could do anything with vehicle. O'Connor v B. J. Auto Make Ready Corp. (1979) 101 Misc. 2d 665, 421 N.Y.S.2d 758, mod (1982, Sup App T) 115 Misc. 2d 575, 455 N.Y.S.2d 164, 35 UCCRS 725

In action by tax-sale purchaser of truck for conversion of truck by bank which had perfected security interest therein, where (1) debtor bought truck on August 23, 1979 under installment-sale-and-security-agreement contract that gave bank security interest in truck, (2) on September 11, 1979, debtor was issued New Jersey certificate of title to truck that contained notation of bank's lien, (3) debtor registered truck in New York on September 19, 1979, but never obtained New York certificate of title, (4) truck was sold to plaintiff by Internal Revenue Service (IRS) on December 17, 1980, for debtor's nonpayment of delinquent taxes, and IRS certificate of sale gave plaintiff all of debtor's interest in truck, (5) on December 22, 1980, bank notified plaintiff by letter of its lien on truck and requested plaintiff to pay balance owed on truck's purchase, (6) on December 23,

1980, plaintiff was issued New York certificate of title to truck that contained no notation of bank's lien, and (7) bank repossessed truck on February 3, 1981, court held (1) that since bank had perfected its security interest in truck in New Jersey, bank's security interest, under UCC § 9-103(2)(b), continued indefinitely in New York without any need for bank to reperfect it until truck was "registered" in another jurisdiction, (2) that term "registration," as used in UCC § 9-103(2)(b), means issuance of "certificate of title" and not mere "nontitle registration" under vehicle-and-traffic statute that permits vehicle to be operated on registering state's highways, (3) that when debtor registered truck in New York on September 19, 1979 under New York vehicle-and-traffic law, bank did not lose its status as creditor with perfected security interest in truck because such registration did not require notation of bank's security interest, (4) that because plaintiff had had ample notice of bank's lien on truck when plaintiff bought it at IRS tax sale and because plaintiff had also made title-and-lien search on truck, plaintiff was aware of bank's prior lien and of fact that truck was not then covered by New York certificate of title, and (5) that as a result, plaintiff's subsequent "clean" New York certificate of title, which was issued on December 23, 1980 without any notation thereon of bank's lien, was ineffective to prevent bank from lawfully repossessing truck. Brewton Trading Corp. v Midland Bank & Trust Co. (1982, Sup) 115 Misc. 2d 475, 454 N.Y.S.2d 510, 34 UCCRS 980

In action by bank for conversion of boat which was purchased in New Jersey and subject to security interest perfected in New Jersey, against dealer that took possession of boat from debtor in New York as trade-in on new boat, bank was entitled to summary judgment even though no financing statement had been filed in New York within time provided in CLS UCC § 9- 103, since boat was "consumer good" under CLS UCC § 9-109 and thus bank had "purchase money security interest" under CLS UCC § 9-107 which was perfected without need for further action under CLS UCC Art 9; provisions of § 9-103 which speak of expiration of period of perfection of security interest (when collateral is brought into New York while subject to security interest perfected under law of state from which it was removed) did not apply. Howell State Bank v Jericho Boats, Inc. (1988, Sup) 141 Misc. 2d 314, 533 N.Y.S.2d 363, 7 UCCRS2d 1215

In action to determine priority of right to collateral (note secured by deed of trust) that corporate debtor had assigned three times to secure its obligations, where (1) California bank in 1972 made loan of $300,000 to corporate debtor and loans of $170,000 to each of three individuals associated with corporate debtor, (2) such loans were secured by 1972 deed of trust on California property owned by corporate debtor, (3) in 1974, corporate debtor formed joint venture with plaintiff to develop certain California real estate owned by corporate debtor, which included property subject to 1972 deed of trust given to secure California bank's loans to corporate debtor and three individuals associated with debtor, (4) pursuant to joint-venture agreement with plaintiff, corporate debtor sold property to be developed for note secured by deed of trust to such property, and such note and deed constituted collateral sued for, (5) in May, 1974, corporate debtor assigned collateral in suit to California bank, which had loaned corporate debtor $300,000, to secure principal of $240,000, and bank took possession of collateral and retained it during corporate debtor's subsequent assignments thereof, (6) in January, 1975, corporate debtor made second assignment of collateral in suit, which incorporated its first assignment, by assigning collateral (a) first to California bank to secure corporate debtor's obligation of $280,000, and (b) then to first Chicago bank to secure debtor's obligation of over one million dollars, (7) thereafter, corporate debtor repaid its $280,000 debt to California bank with funds from $275,000 loan obtained from second Chicago bank, but did not repay debt to first Chicago bank, (8) in March, 1976, corporate debtor assigned collateral in suit to both California bank and second Chicago bank to secure loans made by California bank to three individuals associated with corporate debtor, (9) in May, 1976, Federal Deposit Insurance Corporation (FDIC), as liquidator of California bank which had been corporate debtor's creditor and had become insolvent, obtained California bank's rights to collateral in suit and took possession of it, (10) in 1978, first Chicago bank also became insolvent, and FDIC obtained such bank's rights to collateral in suit and sold them to plaintiff in June, 1979, on corporate debtor's default on underlying debt to first Chicago bank, and (11) plaintiff brought suit for possession of collateral when FDIC, as liquidator of California bank, refused

to surrender it, district court awarded summary judgment and granted ownership of a collateral interest in the note and deed to first Chicago bank. On appeal, summary judgment was reversed and the matter remanded as the record raised a material issue of fact as to the bank's knowledge, or participation in relevant events and, therefore, its status as a good faith purchaser. Landmark Land Company v Sprague, (1982) 701 F.2d 1065

In bankruptcy proceeding involving priority of right to debtor's boat as between bankruptcy trustee and secured party who had loaned debtor money to buy boat, where (1) seller transferred title to debtor by executing form on back of boat's certificate of title, but did not give certificate to debtor, (2) secured party's security interest was not noted on boat's certificate of title, and no new certificate was applied for, and (3) secured party filed financing statements only in New York and not in Florida where debtor kept boat, court held (1) that since boat was covered by Florida certificate of title at time of sale, Florida law, under UCC § 9-103(2)(b), governed perfection of secured party's security interest, (2) that boat's certificate of title was not required to be issued to debtor, and that such certificate was invalid under Florida law 15 days after boat's transfer to debtor, (3) that debtor's failure to obtain new Florida certificate of title did not convert boat into "mobile goods" within meaning of UCC § 9-103(3), (4) that secured party's filing of financing statements in New York, where debtor resided, was insufficient under UCC § 9-302(3)(c) to perfect security interest in boat because it was subject to Florida certificate-of-title statute, and (5) that as a result, boat belonged to bankruptcy trustee as lien creditor under bankruptcy code. Payment Plans, Inc. v Strell (1983, CA2 NY) 717 F.2d 25, 36 UCCRS 1337 (applying New York law)

Where a house trailer was purchased in Virginia and the certificate of title issued by that state showed a bank's conditional sales contract as a lien thereon, it was unnecessary for the security holder to perfect its lien in New York within four months after the trailer was moved there, for subsection (4), rather than subsection (3) was controlling. In re White (1967, ND NY) 266 F. Supp. 863, 4 UCCRS 421

Where bankrupt, using money borrowed from New York bank, purchased second hand truck in Ohio and acquired clean certificate of title in Ohio, bank's security interest not being noted on title certificate as required by Ohio law, bankrupt registered vehicle in Ohio using title certificate, although bank knew nothing of Ohio registration and title certificate nor of bankrupt's intention to register vehicle there, and although truck was garaged principally in New York, in accordance with UCC § 9-103(4) law of Ohio determined existence of perfected security interest prior to bank's lawful repossession of truck in state of New York and bank, therefore, did not obtain perfected security interest in New York by filing financing statement in New York. In re Osborn (1975, ND NY) 389 F. Supp. 1137, 16 UCCRS 827 (applying New York law)

In action by ultimate assignee of collateral following refusal by prior assignee to relinquish possession of collateral, California law governs issue relating to perfection of security interest since collateral was in California in possession of bank at all times during which parties to action could claim that their purported security interest became perfected. Landmark Land Co. v Sprague (1981, SD NY) 529 F. Supp. 971, 33 UCCRS 53, revd (1983, CA2 NY) 701 F.2d 1065

§ 9-302.   Law Governing Perfection and Priority of Agricultural Liens

While farm products are located in a jurisdiction, the local law of that jurisdiction governs perfection, the effect of perfection or nonperfection, and the priority of an agricultural lien on the farm products.

History: Add, L 2001, ch 84, § 36, eff July 1, 2001.

Former § 9-302, add, L 1962, ch 553; amd, L 1963, ch 1003, § 32, L 1964, ch 476, § 12, L 1966, ch 416, L 1977, ch 866, § 16, eff July 2, 1978, L 1982, ch 928, § 30, L 1997, ch 566, § 12, eff Oct 10, 1997.

Former § 9-302, repealed, L 2001, ch 84, § 36, eff July 1, 2001.

§ 9-303. Law Governing Perfection and Priority of Security Interests in Goods Covered by a Certificate of Title

(a) Applicability of section. This section applies to goods covered by a certificate of title, even if there is no other relationship between the jurisdiction under whose certificate of title the goods are covered and the goods or the debtor.

(b) When goods covered by certificate of title. Goods become covered by a certificate of title when a valid application for the certificate of title and the applicable fee are delivered to the appropriate authority. Goods cease to be covered by a certificate of title at the earlier of the time the certificate of title ceases to be effective under the law of the issuing jurisdiction or the time the goods become covered subsequently by a certificate of title issued by another jurisdiction.

(c) Applicable law. The local law of the jurisdiction under whose certificate of title the goods are covered governs perfection, the effect of perfection or nonperfection, and the priority of a security interest in goods covered by a certificate of title from the time the goods become covered by the certificate of title until the goods cease to be covered by the certificate of title.

History: Add, L 2001, ch 84, § 36, eff July 1, 2001.

Former § 9-303, add, L 1962, ch 553, eff Sept 27, 1964; amd, L 1963, ch 1003, § 33, L 1997, ch 566, § 13, eff Oct 10, 1997.

Former § 9-303, repealed, L 2001, ch 84, § 36, eff July 1, 2001.

§ 9-304. Law Governing Perfection and Priority of Security Interests in Deposit Accounts

(a) Law of bank's jurisdiction governs. The local law of a bank's jurisdiction governs perfection, the effect of perfection or nonperfection, and the priority of a security interest in a deposit account maintained with that bank.

(b) Bank's jurisdiction. The following rules determine a bank's jurisdiction for purposes of this part:

(1) If an agreement between the bank and its customer governing the deposit account expressly provides that a particular jurisdiction is the bank's jurisdiction for purposes of this part, this article, or this chapter, that jurisdiction is the bank's jurisdiction.

(2) If paragraph (1) does not apply and an agreement between the bank and its customer governing the deposit account expressly provides that the agreement is governed by the law of a particular jurisdiction, that jurisdiction is the bank's jurisdiction.

(3) If neither paragraph (1) nor paragraph (2) applies and an agreement between the bank and its customer governing the deposit account expressly provides that the deposit account is maintained at an office in a particular jurisdiction, that jurisdiction is the bank's jurisdiction.

(4) If none of the preceding paragraphs apply, the bank's jurisdiction is the jurisdiction in which the office identified in an account statement as the office serving the customer's account is located.

(5) If none of the preceding paragraphs apply, the bank's jurisdiction is the jurisdiction in which the chief executive office of the bank is located.

History: Add, L 2001, ch 84, § 36, eff July 1, 2001.

Former § 9-304, add, L 1962, ch 553; amd, L 1977, ch 866, § 17, eff July 2, 1978, L 1982, ch 928, § 31, L 1988, ch 333, §§ 2, 3, L 1997, ch 566, § 14, eff Oct 10, 1997.

Former § 9-304, amd, L 2000, ch 471, § 9, eff Nov 1, 2000; repealed, L 2001, ch 84, § 36, eff July 1, 2001.

Amd, L 2014, ch 505, § 32, eff Dec 17, 2014.

CASE ANNOTATIONS

Where a mortgage banker perpetrated a fraud by issuing to a warehouse lender and a correspondent lender duplicate original notes and mortgages for the same loans, a successor to the correspondent lender had a priority interest in the loans because the correspondent lender was the first to perfect its security interest under N.Y. U.C.C. Law § 9-304(1) by taking possession of the notes. Although the warehouse lender was the first to record mortgage assignments, the warehouse lender did not have a priority interest because the mortgages followed the notes. Provident Bank v Cmty. Home Mortg. Corp. (2007, ED NY) 498 F Supp 2d 558, 63 UCCRS2d 155

§ 9-305. Law Governing Perfection and Priority of Security Interests in Investment Property

(a) Governing law: general rules. Except as otherwise provided in subsections (c) and (d), the following rules apply:

(1) While a security certificate is located in a jurisdiction, the local law of that jurisdiction governs perfection, the effect of perfection or nonperfection, and the priority of a security interest in the certificated security represented thereby.

(2) The local law of the issuer's jurisdiction as specified in Section 8-110(d) governs perfection, the effect of perfection or nonperfection, and the priority of a security interest in an uncertificated security.

(3) The local law of the securities intermediary's jurisdiction as specified in Section 8-110(e) governs perfection, the effect of perfection or nonperfection, and the priority of a security interest in a security entitlement or securities account.

(4) The local law of the commodity intermediary's jurisdiction governs perfection, the effect of perfection or nonperfection, and the priority of a security interest in a commodity contract or commodity account.

(b) Commodity intermediary's jurisdiction. The following rules determine a commodity intermediary's jurisdiction for purposes of this part:

(1) If an agreement between the commodity intermediary and commodity customer governing the commodity account expressly provides that a particular jurisdiction is the commodity intermediary's

jurisdiction for purposes of this part, this article, or this chapter, that jurisdiction is the commodity intermediary's jurisdiction.

(2) If paragraph (1) does not apply and an agreement between the commodity intermediary and commodity customer governing the commodity account expressly provides that the agreement is governed by the law of a particular jurisdiction, that jurisdiction is the commodity intermediary's jurisdiction.

(3) If neither paragraph (1) nor paragraph (2) applies and an agreement between the commodity intermediary and commodity customer governing the commodity account expressly provides that the commodity account is maintained at an office in a particular jurisdiction, that jurisdiction is the commodity intermediary's jurisdiction.

(4) If none of the preceding paragraphs apply, the commodity intermediary's jurisdiction is the jurisdiction in which the office identified in an account statement as the office serving the commodity customer's account is located.

(5) If none of the preceding paragraphs apply, the commodity intermediary's jurisdiction is the jurisdiction in which the chief executive office of the commodity intermediary is located.

(c) When perfection governed by law of jurisdiction where debtor located. The local law of the jurisdiction in which the debtor is located governs:

(1) perfection of a security interest in investment property by filing;

(2) automatic perfection of a security interest in investment property created by a broker or securities intermediary; and

(3) automatic perfection of a security interest in a commodity contract or commodity account created by a commodity intermediary.

(d) Cooperative interests. Subsections (a) through (c) do not apply to cooperative interests.

History: Add, L 2001, ch 84, § 36, eff July 1, 2001.

Former § 9-305, add, L 1962, ch 553; amd, L 1977, ch 866, § 18, L 1982, ch 928, § 32, L 1997, ch 566, § 15, eff Oct 10, 1997.

Former § 9-305, amd, L 2000, ch 471, § 10, eff Nov 1, 2000; repealed, L 2001, ch 84, § 36, eff July 1, 2001.

CASE ANNOTATIONS

Where a mortgage banker perpetrated a fraud by issuing to a warehouse lender and a correspondent lender duplicate original notes and mortgages for the same loans, a successor to the correspondent lender had a priority interest in the loans because the correspondent lender was the first to perfect its security interest under N.Y. U.C.C. Law § 9-304(1) by taking possession of the notes. Although the warehouse lender was the first to record mortgage assignments, the warehouse lender did not have a priority interest because the mortgages followed the notes. Provident Bank v Cmty. Home Mortg. Corp. (2007, ED NY) 498 F Supp 2d 558, 63 UCCRS2d 155

§ 9-306.   Law Governing Perfection and Priority of Security Interests in Letter-of-credit Rights

(a) Governing law: issuer's or nominated person's jurisdiction. Subject to subsection (c), the local law of the issuer's jurisdiction or a nominated person's jurisdiction governs perfection, the effect of perfection or nonperfection, and the priority of a security interest in a letter-of-credit right if the issuer's jurisdiction or nominated person's jurisdiction is a state.

(b) Issuer's or nominated person's jurisdiction. For purposes of this part, an issuer's jurisdiction or nominated person's jurisdiction is the jurisdiction whose law governs the liability of the issuer or nominated person with respect to the letter-of-credit right as provided in Section 5-116.

(c) When section not applicable. This section does not apply to a security interest that is perfected only under Section 9-308(d).

History: Add, L 2001, ch 84, § 36, eff July 1, 2001.

Former § 9-306, add, L 1962, ch 553; amd, L 1977, ch 866, § 19, eff July 2, 1978, L 1997, ch 566, § 16, eff Oct 10, 1997.

Former § 9-306, repealed, L 2001, ch 84, § 36, eff July 1, 2001.

CASE ANNOTATIONS

UNDER FORMER § 9-305
1. In general
2. Instruments
3. Money
4. Documents
5. Chattel paper
6. Possession by bailee or agent
7. Effect on third parties

UNDER FORMER § 9-305

1. In general

Under the statute, the actions of one seeking to repossess certain personal property from a defaulting vendee were insufficient to perfect the vendor's security interest. L. B. Smith, Inc. v Foley (1972, WD NY) 341 F. Supp. 810, 72-1 USTC P 9230, 11 UCCRS 41, 29 AFTR 2d 567

Under UCC, parties to security agreement were free to decide who should have right to possession of collateral. American Honda Motor Co. v United States (1973, SD NY) 363 F. Supp. 988, 32 AFTR 2d 5886 (applying New York law)

2. Instruments

Where a security interest in the proceeds of promissory notes was perfected before the holder of that interest received notice of the existence of a previously filed Internal Revenue Service lien, the holder's right to the proceeds of the notes is not affected by the lien. Lipkowitz & Plaut v Affrunti (1978) 95 Misc. 2d 849, 407 N.Y.S.2d 1010, 25 UCCRS 276

In suit by trustee in bankruptcy against bank which had allegedly received voidable preferences in violation of Bankruptcy Act, bankrupt's settlement of suit concerning reduction in value of collateral for loan was not voidable preference where collateral consisted of debenture in which defendant had perfected its security interest by possession; debenture was "security" within meaning of UCC § 8-102 where, inter alia, subordinated debentures of brokerage houses were recognized medium for investment; debenture was "instrument" under UCC § 9-105 where it was "security" under UCC § 8-102; security interest in debenture was perfected by possession, under UCC § 9-305, where it was "instrument" under UCC § 9-105; security interest attached immediately in collateral despite alleged ambiguity in security agreement to effect that it was to attach only in event of default, where construction of security agreement revealed intent to attach immediately and where, under UCC § 9-204, any attempt to postpone attachment must be explictly stated; filing, under UCC § 9-201, security agreement superceded previous subordination agreement and controlled rights and obligations among the parties. Allegaert v Chemical Bank (1980, CA2 NY) 657 F.2d 495, 6 BCD 1247

3. Money

Bank's segregation of corporate account did not constitute preferential transfer under CLS Dr & Cr § 15 where bank had required for issuance of irrevocable letter of credit to corporation's surety, and which created perfected security interest in account balance in bank's favor due to rule (under CLS UCC § 9-305) that bank's possession of that collateral served to perfect the interest. Gillman v Chase Manhattan Bank, N. A. (1987, 2d Dept) 135 A.D.2d 488, 521 N.Y.S.2d 729, app gr (1988) 72 N.Y.2d 803, 532 N.Y.S.2d 369, 528 N.E.2d 521 and affd (1988) 73 N.Y.2d 1, 537 N.Y.S.2d 787, 534 N.E.2d 824, 7 UCCRS2d 945, 15 ALR5th 1039

Assignee of rights of designated recipients of escrowed funds of bankrupt corporation under reorganization plan confirmed by Bankruptcy Court had priority to bankruptcy distributions, over claims of bank as judgment creditor of assignors, where assignment was made in 1989, assignee took possession of last note in 1990, and bank's claims did not arise until 1996. Norstar Bank, N.A. v Davis (1997, 4th Dept) 238 A.D.2d 892, 661 N.Y.S.2d 106

Dispute over priority to escrowed funds of bankrupt corporation under reorganization plan was not affected by either (1) "Consent Modification Agreement" by which designated recipient of funds conveyed its ownership interest in bankrupt corporation, or (2) Bankruptcy Court's confirmation of reorganization plan extinguishing recipient's stock rights in bankrupt corporation, where assignee's interest in bankruptcy distributions was not traceable to recipient's interest as stockholder in bankrupt corporation. Norstar Bank, N.A. v Davis (1997, 4th Dept) 238 A.D.2d 892, 661 N.Y.S.2d 106

Assignee of rights of designated recipients of escrowed funds of bankrupt corporation under reorganization plan confirmed by Bankruptcy Court was not collaterally estopped from asserting its claim of priority to bankruptcy distributions where bankruptcy proceeding concerned claims of creditors of bankrupt corporation, priority suit concerned claims of creditors of those creditors, there was thus no identity of issue, and there was no inconsistency between assignee's present claim and its position taken in bankruptcy proceeding. Norstar Bank, N.A. v Davis (1997, 4th Dept) 238 A.D.2d 892, 661 N.Y.S.2d 106

4. Documents

Service of order of attachment, which was later vacated, upon garnishee in possession of stock certificates was insufficient to perfect assignee's security interest in stock and to place garnishee and assignor's creditor on notice that assignee had secured interest in shares, whereas garnishee and assignor's creditor, by possession, did properly perfect their security interests under UCC § 9-305. Friedman v Fein (1974, 2d Dept) 46 A.D.2d 886, 361 N.Y.S.2d 397

5. Chattel paper

Under UCC § 9-305, possessory security interest in ordinary chattel paper requires no filing for perfection. State Tax Com. v Shor (1977) 43 N.Y.2d 151, 400 N.Y.S.2d 805, 371 N.E.2d 523

Where (1) debtor sold corporate stock on July 25, 1974 to defendants for $180,000, and defendants executed promissory notes under pledge agreement securing payment of stock's purchase price and delivered notes to escrowee, which also received the purchased stock, (2) debtor on March 19, 1975, with knowledge and consent of defendants and escrowee, assigned notes to creditor as collateral to secure payment of prior $60,000 debt, indorsed them to creditor's order, and delivered them to creditor which retained possession of them until August 24, 1976, a date following that on which debtor had fully debt due creditor, (3) on November 5, 1975, when defendants still owed debtor $135,000 on notes and notes were still in creditor's possession as collateral for payment of $28,000 balance then owed by debtor to creditor, debtor entered into agreement with plaintiff law firm and its client under which payments on prior debt owed by debtor to such client were extended, prospective lawsuit was settled, sums thus due to client were collateralized by assignment of debtor's interest in stock-payment notes, and notes themselves and pledge agreement securing them were also assigned to plaintiff on behalf of its client, subject to prior collateral assignment in favor of debtor's first creditor, (4) first creditor on August 24, 1976 acknowledged to escrowee that debtor had fully discharged debt due it,

delivered stock-payment notes in suit to plaintiff law firm, but never indorsed notes to plaintiff's order, (5) on August 25, 1976, plaintiff, defendants (purchasers of debtor's stock), debtor, and escrowee executed written acknowledgements of debtor's assignment of notes and pledge agreement to plaintiff, and plaintiff requested that it be paid next installment on notes, which was due on October 1, 1976, (5) on April 5, 1976, IRS assessed delinquent income-tax liability against debtor and filed notice of tax lien on August 4, 1976, (6) on October 1, 1976, escrowee paid installment payment due on notes to IRS, and (7) on October 5, 1976, plaintiff after due notice declared default on notes (because of failure to receive October 1, 1976 installment payment thereon) and under acceleration clause in notes demanded full payment thereof, court held (1) that plaintiff, as nominee for its client, acquired valid collateral assignment of proceeds of notes to extent that proceeds were not required to satisfy first creditor's prior security interest therein, (2) that under UCC § 3-202(3), debtor's indorsement and negotiation of notes to first creditor merely created partial assignment of notes' proceeds and did not divest debtor of ultimate right to all proceeds not required to satisfy debt owed to first creditor, (3) that debtor's remaining interest in notes' proceeds was the interest that debtor had assigned to plaintiff as collateral on November 5, 1975, and that such assignment, under UCC § 9-204(1), gave plaintiff valid security interest in debtor's residuary interest in notes' proceeds, (4) that plaintiff's security interest in notes' proceeds was not perfected until August 24, 1976, when it became perfected under UCC § 9-305 by possession of notes following first creditor's delivery thereof to plaintiff, (5) that IRS tax lien was not superior to plaintiff's perfected security interest in notes, since neither plaintiff nor its client had received any notice of such lien until September 20, 1976, and (6) that neither plaintiff not its client could accelerate unpaid balance due on notes, since plaintiff, as nominee for its client, was merely holder of security interest in notes and was not "holder" of notes within meaning of UCC § 1-201(20) because of first creditor's failure to indorse them to plaintiff's order. Lipkowitz & Plaut v Affrunti (1978) 95 Misc. 2d 849, 407 N.Y.S.2d 1010, 25 UCCRS 276 (holding that plaintiff was entitled to receive, on behalf of its client, all installment payments due on notes, commencing with installment due on October 1, 1976)

6. Possession by bailee or agent

Seller (which shipped printing press with unpaid balance owing to assignee of contract of sale after receiving payments toward purchase price financed by funds provided by bank in January 1989) had superior purchase-money security interest (PMSI) in printing press and its proceeds from inception of its contract with assignor in December 1988 where (1) seller expressly retained PMSI in both its contract with assignor and in subsequent purchase order, by which assignee obtained title, and (2) seller's security interest "attached" at time contract between it and assignor was entered into and partial payment of purchase price was made; further, since collateral was goods, seller perfected its security interest both by possession and by filing financing statement before it relinquished possession. Heidelberg E., Inc v Weber Lithography (1995, 2d Dept) 213 A.D.2d 127, 631 N.Y.S.2d 370, 27 UCCRS2d 1081

In action to determine priority of right to collateral (note secured by deed of trust) that corporate debtor had assigned three times to secure its obligations, where (1) California bank in 1972 made loan of $300,000 to corporate debtor and loans of $170,000 to each of three individuals associated with corporate debtor, (2) such loans were secured by 1972 deed of trust on California property owned by corporate debtor, (3) in 1974, corporate debtor formed joint venture with plaintiff to develop certain California real estate owned by corporate debtor, which included property subject to 1972 deed of trust given to secure California bank's loans to corporate debtor and three individuals associated with debtor, (4) pursuant to joint-venture agreement with plaintiff, corporate debtor sold property to be developed for note secured by deed of trust to such property, and such note and deed constituted collateral sued for, (5) in May, 1974, corporate debtor assigned collateral in suit to California bank, which had loaned corporate debtor $300,000, to secure principal of $240,000, and bank took possession of collateral and retained it during corporate debtor's subsequent assignments thereof, (6) in January, 1975, corporate debtor made second assignment of collateral in suit, which incorporated its first assignment, by assigning collateral (a) first to California bank to secure corporate debtor's obligation of $280,000, and (b) then to first Chicago bank to secure debtor's obligation of over one million dollars, (7) thereafter, corporate debtor repaid its $280,000 debt to California bank with funds from $275,000 loan obtained from second Chicago bank, but did not repay debt to first Chicago bank, (8) in March, 1976, corporate debtor assigned collateral in suit to both California bank and second Chicago bank to secure loans made by California bank to three individuals associated with corporate debtor, (9) in May, 1976, Federal Deposit Insurance Corporation (FDIC), as liquidator of California bank which had been corporate debtor's creditor and had become insolvent, obtained California bank's rights to collateral in suit and took possession of it, (10) in 1978, first Chicago bank also became insolvent, and FDIC obtained such bank's rights to collateral in suit and sold them to plaintiff in June, 1979, on corporate debtor's default on underlying debt to first Chicago bank, and (11) plaintiff brought suit for possession of collateral when FDIC, as liquidator of California bank, refused to surrender it, district court awarded summary judgment and granted ownership of a collateral interest in the note and deed to first Chicago bank. On appeal, summary judgment was reversed and the matter remanded as the record raised a material issue of fact as to the bank's knowledge, or participation in relevant events and, therefore, its status as a good faith purchaser. Landmark Land Company v Sprague, (1982) 701 F.2d 1065

7. Effect on third parties

Sale of unfinished textile fabrics by converter (i.e., one who finishes textiles into dyed and patterned fabrics) to another converter was in ordinary course of first converter's business within meaning of UCC § 9-307(1), even though predominant business purpose of converters was converting of unfinished textiles into finished fabrics, and thus second converter took fabric free from manufacturer's security interest in textiles, although manufacturer's security interest was perfected by possession of goods under UCC § 9-305, where it was shown that converters often purchased unfinished textiles in excess of their requirements, selling such excess through brokers to other converters, and that converters buy such goods if price is satisfactory or particular goods are not available from manufacturers, both of which conditions were satisfied in present case. Tanbro Fabrics Corp. v Deering Milliken, Inc. (1976) 39 N.Y.2d 632, 385 N.Y.S.2d 260, 350 N.E.2d 590, 19 UCCRS 385

§ 9-307.   Location of Debtor

(a) "Place of business." In this section, "place of business" means a place where a debtor conducts its affairs.

(b) Debtor's location: general rules. Except as otherwise provided in this section, the following rules determine a debtor's location:

(1) A debtor who is an individual is located at the individual's principal residence.

(2) A debtor that is an organization and has only one place of business is located at its place of business.

(3) A debtor that is an organization and has more than one place of business is located at its chief executive office.

(c) Limitation of applicability of subsection (b). Subsection (b) applies only if a debtor's residence, place of business, or chief executive office, as applicable, is located in a jurisdiction whose law generally requires information concerning the existence of a nonpossessory security interest to be made generally available in a filing, recording, or registration system as a condition or result of the security interest's obtaining priority over the rights of a lien creditor with respect to the collateral. If subsection (b) does not apply, the debtor is located in the District of Columbia.

(d) Continuation of location: cessation of existence, etc. A person that ceases to exist, have a residence, or have a place of business continues to be located in the jurisdiction specified by subsections (b) and (c).

(e) Location of registered organization organized under state law. A registered organization that is organized under the law of a state is located in that state.

(f) Location of registered organization organized under federal law; bank branches and agencies. Except as otherwise provided in subsection (i), a registered organization that is organized under the law of the United States and a branch or agency of a bank that is not organized under the law of the United States or a state are located:

(1) in the state that the law of the United States designates, if the law designates a state of location;

(2) in the state that the registered organization, branch, or agency designates, if the law of the United States authorizes the registered organization, branch, or agency to designate its state of location, including by designating its main office, home office, or other comparable office; or

(3) in the District of Columbia, if neither paragraph (1) nor paragraph (2) applies.

(g) Continuation of location: change in status of registered organization. A registered organization continues to be located in the jurisdiction specified by subsection (e) or (f) notwithstanding:

(1) the suspension, revocation, forfeiture, or lapse of the registered organization's status as such in its jurisdiction of organization; or

(2) the dissolution, winding up, or cancellation of the existence of the registered organization.

(h) Location of United States. The United States is located in the District of Columbia.

(i) Location of foreign bank branch or agency if licensed in only one state. A branch or agency of a bank that is not organized under the law of the United States or a state is located in the state in which the branch or agency is licensed, if all branches and agencies of the bank are licensed in only one state.

(j) Location of foreign air carrier. A foreign air carrier under the Federal Aviation Act of 1958, as amended, is located at the designated office of the agent upon which service of process may be made on behalf of the carrier.

(k) Section applies only to this part. This section applies only for purposes of this part.

History: Add, L 2001, ch 84, § 36, eff July 1, 2001.

Former § 9-307, add, L 1962, ch 553; amd, L 1977, ch 866, § 20, eff July 2, 1978.

Former § 9-307, repealed, L 2001, ch 84, § 36, eff July 1, 2001.

Amd, L 2014, ch 505, § 33, eff Dec 17, 2014.

CASE ANNOTATIONS

Under N.Y. U.C.C. §§ 9-301(a) and -307(e) and 13 Pa. Cons. Stat. §§ 9301 and 9307(e), whether an insurance company had perfected a security interest in the assets of a judgment creditor was governed by

New York law, as the judgment creditor was organized as a New York corporation and was therefore "located" in New York. Sentry Select Ins. Co. v LBL Skysystems (U.S.A.), Inc. (2007, ED Pa) 486 F Supp 2d 496, stay den (2007, ED Pa) 2007 US Dist LEXIS 46654.

Subpart 2
Perfection

History: Add, L 2001, ch 84, § 36, eff July 1, 2001.

§ 9-308. When Security Interest or Agricultural Lien Is Perfected; Continuity of Perfection

(a) Perfection of security interest. Except as otherwise provided in this section and Section 9-309, a security interest is perfected if it has attached and all of the applicable requirements for perfection in Sections 9-310 through 9-316 have been satisfied. A security interest is perfected when it attaches if the applicable requirements are satisfied before the security interest attaches.

(b) Perfection of agricultural lien. An agricultural lien is perfected if it has become effective and all of the applicable requirements for perfection in Section 9-310 have been satisfied. An agricultural lien is perfected when it becomes effective if the applicable requirements are satisfied before the agricultural lien becomes effective.

(c) Continuous perfection; perfection by different methods. A security interest or agricultural lien is perfected continuously if it is originally perfected by one method under this article and is later perfected by another method under this article, without an intermediate period when it was unperfected.

(d) Supporting obligation. Perfection of a security interest in collateral also perfects a security interest in a supporting obligation for the collateral.

(e) Lien securing right to payment. Perfection of a security interest in a right to payment or performance also perfects a security interest in a security interest, mortgage, or other lien on personal or real property securing the right.

(f) Security entitlement carried in securities account. Perfection of a security interest in a securities account also perfects a security interest in the security entitlements carried in the securities account.

(g) Commodity contract carried in commodity account. Perfection of a security interest in a commodity account also perfects a security interest in the commodity contracts carried in the commodity account.

(h) Cooperative organization security interest. A cooperative organization security interest becomes perfected when the cooperative interest first comes into existence and remains perfected so long as the cooperative interest exists.

History: Add, L 2001, ch 84, § 36, eff July 1, 2001.

Former § 9-308, add, L 1962, ch 553; amd, L 1963, ch 1003, § 34, L 1977, ch 866, § 21, eff July 2, 1978.

Former § 9-308, repealed, L 2001, ch 84, § 36, eff July 1, 2001.

CASE ANNOTATIONS

UNDER FORMER § 9-303

The title of a conditional vendor to removable fixtures installed upon realty is superior to the lien of a prior mortgage containing the standard "after-acquired property" clause, but a conditional vendor is bound to refrain from wilfully impairing the security of a real estate mortgagee and if, without the consent of the mortgagee, he removes equipment subject to the mortgage, he should be required to account to the mortgagee for its fair value, and if the equipment which was replaced without the mortgagee's consent was serviceable and of some value, the priorities must appropriately be reversed to the extent of the impairment of the mortgagee's security. Blancob Constr. Corp. v 246 Beaumont Equity, Inc. (1965, 1st Dept) 23 A.D.2d 413, 261 N.Y.S.2d 227, 2 UCCRS 995

A perfected security interest obtained by compliance with and pursuant to UCC § 9-302(1)(d) and § 303 is not invalid against the debtor or third parties by reason of noncompliance with UCC § 9203. Recchio v Manufacturers & Traders Trust Co. (1968) 55 Misc. 2d 788, 286 N.Y.S.2d 390, 4 UCCRS 1133, revd on other grounds (1970, 4th Dept) 35 A.D.2d 769, 316 N.Y.S.2d 915

Where New York debtor assigned accounts receivable to New York creditor under terms of security agreement and secured creditor complied with all steps required by UCC to perfect its security interest in such accounts, New York creditor's perfected security interest attached as soon as accounts came into existence and took priority over interest of Colorado creditor, as lien creditor under writ of attachment, with respect to accounts owed debtor by Colorado account debtors. Barocas v Bohemia Import Co. (1974) 33 Colo App 263, 518 P2d 850, 14 UCCRS 191 (applying New York law)

Where seller of mobile homes assigned instalment contracts thereon to bank which filed financing statement within 10 days, bank was entitled to repossess on default in making payments. Citizens Nat'l Bank v Osetek (1973, SD NY) 353 F. Supp. 958, 12 UCCRS 378

Letter allegedly establishing assignment of foreign exchange contract rights to bank did not measure up to security agreement under UCC since it failed to contain "description of the collateral" as required by § 9-203(1)(a). Moreover, bank failed to file financing statement, as required by §§ 9-302(1) and 9-303 and, thus, failed to obtain valid and perfected assignment of contract rights. Purported assignment was not exempt from filing under UCC § 9-302(1)(e) since, at time assignee allegedly assigned contract worth $1,000,000, assignee's total "outstanding accounts or contract rights" were $4,439,300; thus, assignment transferred just under 20 percent of assignee's accounts, including assigned contract right, which constituted "significant part" of assignee's outstanding accounts, especially in view of high absolute value of transaction at issue. Miller v Wells Fargo Bank International Corp. (1975, SD NY) 406 F. Supp. 452, 18 UCCRS 489, affd (1976, CA2 NY) 540 F.2d 548 (applying New York law)

§ 9-309. Security Interest Perfected upon Attachment

The following security interests are perfected when they attach:

(1) a purchase-money security interest in consumer goods, except as otherwise provided in Section 9-311(b) with respect to consumer goods that are subject to a statute or treaty described in Section 9-311(a);

(2) an assignment of accounts or payment intangibles which does not by itself or in conjunction with other assignments to the same assignee transfer a significant part of the assignor's outstanding accounts or payment intangibles;

(3) a sale of a payment intangible;

(4) a sale of a promissory note;

UCC

(5) a security interest created by the assignment of a health-care-insurance receivable to the provider of the health-care goods or services;

(6) a security interest arising under Section 2-401, 2-505, 2-711(3), or 2-A-508(5), until the debtor obtains possession of the collateral;

(7) a security interest of a collecting bank arising under Section 4-210;

(8) a security interest of an issuer or nominated person arising under Section 5-118;

(9) a security interest arising in the delivery of a financial asset under Section 9-206(c);

(10) a security interest in investment property created by a broker or securities intermediary;

(11) a security interest in a commodity contract or a commodity account created by a commodity intermediary;

(12) an assignment for the benefit of all creditors of the transferor and subsequent transfers by the assignee thereunder;

(13) a security interest created by an assignment of a beneficial interest in a decedent's estate; and

(14) a sale by an individual of an account that is a right to payment of winnings in a lottery or other game of chance.

History: Add, L 2001, ch 84, § 36, eff July 1, 2001.

Former § 9-309, add, L 1962, ch 553; amd, L 1982, ch 928, § 33, L 1997, ch 566, § 17, eff Oct 10, 1997.

Former § 9-309, repealed, L 2001, ch 84, § 36, eff July 1, 2001.

Amd, L 2014, ch 505, § 34, eff Dec 17, 2014.

CASE ANNOTATIONS

Bathtub was not "ordinary" building material, and creditor retained its security interest in the tub pursuant to N.Y. U.C.C. Law § 9-334(a), where the tub was purchased at a specialty store, incorporated luxury features and other items, such that it was something more than a container to hold water, and the total cost of the items was cost $4,266. Because this collateral was a consumer good, the lien became immediately perfected under N.Y. U.C.C. Law § 9-309(1), without need for filing a financing statement. In re Ryan (2007, BC WD NY) 360 BR 50.

§ 9-310. When Filing Required to Perfect Security Interest or Agricultural Lien; Security Interests and Agricultural Liens to Which Filing Provisions Do Not Apply

(a) General rule: perfection by filing. Except as otherwise provided in subsection (b) and Section 9-312(b), a financing statement must be filed to perfect all security interests and agricultural liens.

(b) Exceptions: filing not necessary. Except as provided in subsection (d), the filing of a financing statement is not necessary to perfect a security interest:

(1) that is perfected under Section 9-308(d), (e), (f), or (g);

(2) that is perfected under Section 9-309 when it attaches;

(3) in property subject to a statute, regulation, or treaty described in Section 9-311(a);

(4) in goods in possession of a bailee which is perfected under Section 9-312(d)(1) or (2);

(5) in certificated securities, documents, goods, or instruments which is perfected without filing, control, or possession under Section 9-312(e), (f), or (g);

(6) in collateral in the secured party's possession under Section 9-313;

(7) in a certificated security which is perfected by delivery of the security certificate to the secured party under Section 9-313;

(8) in deposit accounts, electronic chattel paper, electronic documents, investment property, or letter-of-credit rights which is perfected by control under Section 9-314;

(9) in proceeds which is perfected under Section 9-315;

(10) that is perfected under Section 9-316; or

(11) that is a cooperative organization security interest.

(c) Assignment of perfected security interest. If a secured party assigns a perfected security interest or agricultural lien, a filing under this article is not required to continue the perfected status of the security interest against creditors of and transferees from the original debtor.

(d) Special rule for cooperative interests. Except for a cooperative organization security interest, a security interest in a cooperative interest may be perfected only by filing a financing statement.

History: Add, L 2001, ch 84, § 36, eff July 1, 2001.

Former § 9-310, add, L 1962, ch 553, eff Sept 27, 1964; repealed, L 2001, ch 84, § 36, eff July 1, 2001.

Amd, L 2014, ch 505, § 35, eff Dec 17, 2014.

CASE ANNOTATIONS

In an interpleader action, an insurance company that had properly perfected a security interest in a judgment creditor's assets under N.Y. U.C.C. Law § 9-310(a) by filing a financing statement that met the requirements of N.Y. U.C.C. Law § 9-502(a) was found to be entitled to the proceeds of an award obtained by the judgment creditor in a breach of contract suit; the insurance company's claim took priority under N.Y. U.C.C. Law § 9-322(a) over that of a claimant that had obtained a default judgment against the judgment creditor in a separate suit. Sentry Select Ins. Co. v LBL Skysystems (U.S.A.), Inc. (2007, ED Pa) 486 F Supp 2d 496, stay den (2007, ED Pa) 2007 US Dist LEXIS 46654.

UNDER FORMER § 9-302

A mobile home is a motor vehicle within the meaning of this section which requires that a financing statement must be filed to perfect a security interest therein. Recchio v Manufacturers & Traders Trust Co. (1970, 4th Dept) 35 A.D.2d 769, 316 N.Y.S.2d 915

Under UCC § 9-302(1)(d), a valid financing statement, properly filed, perfects a security interest in a motor vehicle. Until that time, under UCC § 9-301(1)(c), a buyer not in the ordinary course of business, to the extent that he gives value and receives delivery of the collateral without knowledge of the unperfected security interest, takes free of such interest. White Star Distributors, Inc. v

Kennedy (1978, 4th Dept) 66 A.D.2d 1011, 411 N.Y.S.2d 751, 25 UCCRS 1446

Plaintiff was entitled to summary judgment in legal malpractice action alleging failure to perfect security interest because of failure to file security agreement under CLS UCC § 9-302(1) where (1) plaintiff engaged defendant attorney to secure debt owed by customer, (2) security agreement contained typed clause dictating how existing debt would be repaid, followed by printed clause declaring that collateral also secured future debts, and (3) debtors became insolvent after paying off original debt, but with outstanding balance from later purchases; typed clause did not supersede printed clause since typed clause was not inconsistent with, or preclusive of, collateral's use to secure future advances. S & D Petroleum Co. v Tamsett (1988, 3d Dept) 144 A.D.2d 849, 534 N.Y.S.2d 800

Corporate client was entitled to summary judgment in legal malpractice action where (1) it was uncontroverted that its attorney filed financing statement for it in county clerk's office, but failed to file it with Department of State, and attorney assured client that its security interest was "okay" and that its lien would follow property, and (2) debtor who acquired property from client filed bankruptcy and, because of failure to perfect security interest, subsequent creditor repossessed property. Deb-Jo Constr. v Westphal (1994, 4th Dept) 210 A.D.2d 951, 620 N.Y.S.2d 678

Failure of attorney to file financing statement in manner required by law to perfect his client's security interest constitutes negligence or malpractice as matter of law. Deb-Jo Constr. v Westphal (1994, 4th Dept) 210 A.D.2d 951, 620 N.Y.S.2d 678

Seller (which shipped printing press with unpaid balance owing to assignee of contract of sale after receiving payments toward purchase price financed by funds provided by bank in January 1989) had superior purchase-money security interest (PMSI) in printing press and its proceeds from inception of its contract with assignor in December 1988 where (1) seller expressly retained PMSI in both its contract with assignor and in subsequent purchase order, by which assignee obtained title, and (2) seller's security interest "attached" at time contract between it and assignor was entered into and partial payment of purchase price was made; further, since collateral was goods, seller perfected its security interest both by possession and by filing financing statement before it relinquished possession. Heidelberg E., Inc v Weber Lithography (1995, 2d Dept) 213 A.D.2d 127, 631 N.Y.S.2d 370, 27 UCCRS2d 1081

Where petitioner's security interest was perfected by proper filing, it thereupon took priority over all unfiled and unperfected interests, including the rights of judgment creditors who thereafter issued execution, since under Rule 5202(a) CPLR such creditors are perfected only by the issuance of execution; and, upon default in payments due on the indebtedness secured by the interest, petitioner became entitled to immediate possession of the collateral under the provisions of § 9-503. William Iselin & Co. v Burgess & Leigh Ltd. (1967) 52 Misc. 2d 821, 276 N.Y.S.2d 659, 3 UCCRS 1168

A house trailer is a motor vehicle within the meaning of the Uniform Commercial Code provision requiring filing with respect to motor vehicles which are to be licensed or registered in this state, and therefore mortgagee who perfected his security interest by filing the same was entitled to possession of a trailer as opposed to the owner of a retail instalment contract whose filing had expired prior to the mortgagee's perfecting of his security interest. Albany Discount Corp. v Mohawk Nat'l Bank (1967) 54 Misc. 2d 238, 282 N.Y.S.2d 401, 4 UCCRS 669, mod on other grounds (1968, 3d Dept) 30 A.D.2d 623, 290 N.Y.S.2d 576, on reh (1968, 3d Dept) 30 A.D.2d 919, 292 N.Y.S.2d 300, app gr (1969) 23 N.Y.2d 647 and affd (1971) 28 N.Y.2d 222, 321 N.Y.S.2d 94, 269 N.E.2d 809, 8 UCCRS 1310

As the security interest of the seller in consumer goods comes into being and is perfected concomitantly with the delivery of the goods to the buyer, the seller's interest has priority over a security interest thereafter created by the buyer in favor of a third person. Recchio v Manufacturers & Traders Trust Co. (1968) 55 Misc. 2d 788, 286 N.Y.S.2d 390, 4 UCCRS 1133, revd on other grounds (1970, 4th Dept) 35 A.D.2d 769, 316 N.Y.S.2d 915

In action by bank for conversion of boat which was purchased in New Jersey and subject to security interest perfected in New Jersey, against dealer that took possession of boat from debtor in New York as trade-in on new boat, bank was entitled to summary judgment even though no financing statement had been filed in New York within time provided in CLS UCC § 9- 103, since boat was "consumer good" under CLS UCC § 9-109 and thus bank had "purchase money security interest" under CLS UCC § 9-107 which

was perfected without need for further action under CLS UCC Art 9; provisions of § 9-103 which speak of expiration of period of perfection of security interest (when collateral is brought into New York while subject to security interest perfected under law of state from which it was removed) did not apply. Howell State Bank v Jericho Boats, Inc. (1988, Sup) 141 Misc. 2d 314, 533 N.Y.S.2d 363, 7 UCCRS2d 1215

The bankruptcy judge erred in treating appellant life insurance issuer's right to retain commissions as a "security interest" requiring perfection under UCC § 9-302 since appellant's right to refrain from paying $22,494.40 in commissions a second time, commissions which were earned before the bankruptcy petition was filed, hardly falls within the scope of the definitions for "security interest". In re Sherman (1980, CA2 NY) 627 F.2d 594, 6 BCD 872, 23 CBC 65, CCH Bankr L Rptr P 67497, 29 UCCRS 262

In bankruptcy proceeding involving priority of right to debtor's boat as between bankruptcy trustee and secured party who had loaned debtor money to buy boat, where (1) seller transferred title to debtor by executing form on back of boat's certificate of title, but did not give certificate to debtor, (2) secured party's security interest was not noted on boat's certificate of title, and no new certificate was applied for, and (3) secured party filed financing statements only in New York and not in Florida where debtor kept boat, court held (1) that since boat was covered by Florida certificate of title at time of sale, Florida law, under UCC § 9-103(2)(b), governed perfection of secured party's security interest, (2) that boat's certificate of title was not required to be issued to debtor, and that such certificate was invalid under Florida law 15 days after boat's transfer to debtor, (3) that debtor's failure to obtain new Florida certificate of title did not convert boat into "mobile goods" within meaning of UCC § 9-103(3), (4) that secured party's filing of financing statements in New York, where debtor resided, was insufficient under UCC § 9-302(3)(c) to perfect security interest in boat because it was subject to Florida certificate-of-title statute, and (5) that as a result, boat belonged to bankruptcy trustee as lien creditor under bankruptcy code. Payment Plans, Inc. v Strell (1983, CA2 NY) 717 F.2d 25, 36 UCCRS 1337 (applying New York law)

Letter allegedly establishing assignment of foreign exchange contract rights to bank did not measure up to security agreement under UCC since it failed to contain "description of the collateral" as required by § 9-203(1)(a). Moreover, bank failed to file financing statement, as required by §§ 9-302(1) and 9-303 and, thus, failed to obtain valid and perfected assignment of contract rights. Purported assignment was not exempt from filing under UCC § 9-302(1)(e) since, at time assignee allegedly assigned contract worth $1,000,000, assignee's total "outstanding accounts or contract rights" were $4,439,000; thus, assignment transferred just under 20 percent of assignee's accounts, including assigned contract right, which constituted "significant part" of assignee's outstanding accounts, especially in view of high absolute value of transaction at issue. Miller v Wells Fargo Bank International Corp. (1975, SD NY) 406 F. Supp. 452, 18 UCCRS 489, affd (1976, CA2 NY) 540 F.2d 548 (applying New York law)

§ 9-311. Perfection of Security Interests in Property Subject to Certain Statutes, Regulations, and Treaties

(a) Security interest subject to other law. Except as otherwise provided in subsection (d), the filing of a financing statement is not necessary or effective to perfect a security interest in property subject to:

(1) a statute, regulation, or treaty of the United States whose requirements for a security interest's obtaining priority over the rights of a lien creditor with respect to the property preempt Section 9-310(a);

(2) a certificate-of-title statute of this state or regulations promulgated thereunder, to the extent such statute or regulations provide for a security interest to be indicated on the certificate as a condition or result of perfection; or

UCC

(3) a statute of another jurisdiction which provides for a security interest to be indicated on a certificate of title as a condition or result of the security interest's obtaining priority over the rights of a lien creditor with respect to the property.

(b) Compliance with other law. Compliance with the requirements of a statute, regulation, or treaty described in subsection (a) for obtaining priority over the rights of a lien creditor is equivalent to the filing of a financing statement under this article. Except as otherwise provided in subsection (d) and Sections 9-313 and 9-316(d) and (e) for goods covered by a certificate of title, a security interest in property subject to a statute, regulation, or treaty described in subsection (a) may be perfected only by compliance with those requirements, and a security interest so perfected remains perfected notwithstanding a change in the use or transfer of possession of the collateral.

(c) Duration and renewal of perfection. Except as otherwise provided in subsection (d) and Section 9-316(d) and (e), duration and renewal of perfection of a security interest perfected by compliance with the requirements prescribed by a statute, regulation, or treaty described in subsection (a) are governed by the statute, regulation, or treaty. In other respects, the security interest is subject to this article.

(d) Inapplicability to certain inventory. During any period in which collateral subject to a statute specified in subsection (a)(2) is inventory held for sale or lease by a person or leased by that person as lessor and that person is in the business of selling goods of that kind, this section does not apply to a security interest in that collateral created by that person.

History: Add, L 2001, ch 84, § 36, eff July 1, 2001.

Former § 9-311, add, L 1962, ch 553, eff Sept 27, 1964; repealed, L 2001, ch 84, § 36, eff July 1, 2001.

Amd, L 2014, ch 505, § 36, eff Dec 17, 2014.

§ 9-312. Perfection of Security Interests in Chattel Paper, Deposit Accounts, Documents, Goods Covered by Documents, Instruments, Investment Property, Letter-of-credit Rights, and Money; Perfection by Permissive Filing; Temporary Perfection Without Filing or Transfer of Possession

(a) Perfection by filing permitted. A security interest in chattel paper, negotiable documents, instruments, or investment property may be perfected by filing.

(b) Control or possession of certain collateral. Except as otherwise provided in Section 9-315(c) and (d) for proceeds:

(1) a security interest in a deposit account may be perfected only by control under Section 9-314;

(2) and except as otherwise provided in Section 9-308(d), a security interest in a letter-of-credit right may be perfected only by control under Section 9-314; and

(3) a security interest in money may be perfected only by the secured party's taking possession under Section 9-313.

(c) Goods covered by negotiable document. While goods are in the possession of a bailee that has issued a negotiable document covering the goods:

(1) a security interest in the goods may be perfected by perfecting a security interest in the document; and

(2) a security interest perfected in the document has priority over any security interest that becomes perfected in the goods by another method during that time.

(d) Goods covered by nonnegotiable document. While goods are in the possession of a bailee that has issued a non-negotiable document covering the goods, a security interest in the goods may be perfected by:

(1) issuance of a document in the name of the secured party;

(2) the bailee's receipt of notification of the secured party's interest; or

(3) filing as to the goods.

(e) Temporary perfection: new value. A security interest in certificated securities, negotiable documents, or instruments is perfected without filing or the taking of possession or control for a period of 20 days from the time it attaches to the extent that it arises for new value given under an authenticated security agreement.

(f) Temporary perfection: goods or documents made available to debtor. A perfected security interest in a negotiable document or goods in possession of a bailee, other than one that has issued a negotiable document for the goods, remains perfected for 20 days without filing if the secured party makes available to the debtor the goods or documents representing the goods for the purpose of:

(1) ultimate sale or exchange; or

(2) loading, unloading, storing, shipping, transshipping, manufacturing, processing, or otherwise dealing with them in a manner preliminary to their sale or exchange.

(g) Temporary perfection: delivery of security certificate or instrument to debtor. A perfected security interest in a certificated security or instrument remains perfected for 20 days without filing if the secured party delivers the security certificate or instrument to the debtor for the purpose of:

(1) ultimate sale or exchange; or

(2) presentation, collection, enforcement, renewal, or registration of transfer.

(h) Expiration of temporary perfection. After the 20-day period specified in subsection (e), (f), or (g) expires, perfection depends upon compliance with this article.

(i) Cooperative interests. Subsections (a) through (h) do not apply to cooperative interests.

History: Add, L 2001, ch 84, § 36, eff July 1, 2001.

Former § 9-312, add, L 1962, ch 553; amd, L 1977, ch 866, § 22, eff July 2, 1978, L 1982, ch 928, § 34, L 1985, ch 717, § 2, eff Aug 31, 1985, and applicable to collateral received by a debtor on or after August 31, 1985, L 1997, ch 566, § 18, eff Oct 10, 1997.

Former § 9-312, repealed, L 2001, ch 84, § 36, eff July 1, 2001.

Amd, L 2014, ch 505, § 37, eff Dec 17, 2014.

CASE ANNOTATIONS

1. **Secured interest priority**
2. **Payment intangible**
3. **Under former § 9-304**

1. Secured interest priority

Bank had control over the New York account at issue pursuant to N.Y. U.C.C. Law § 9-104 by virtue of its maintenance of the New York account. Because the bank perfected its interest in the New York account pursuant to N.Y. U.C.C. Law § 9-312(b)(1) at least as early as February 20, 2007, its interest was superior to respondent's July 21, 2008 judgment lien and respondent's petition for a turn-over order as to the New York account was denied. Joseph Stephens & Co. v Cikanek, 588 F. Supp. 2d 870, 67 U.C.C. Rep. Serv. 2d (CBC) 384, 2008 U.S. Dist. LEXIS 98900 (N.D. Ill. 2008).

Although defendant was granted a security interest in debtor's shares of a company, he never perfected his interest in the uncertificated shares by filing a UCC financing statement with the New York Department of State or by control over the investment property. As defendant only had an unperfected lien on debtor's shares, a Chapter 7 trustee, armed with the status of a hypothetical lien creditor, took debtor's 50 percent ownership in the company free of defendant's unperfected lien. Thaler v GJ & JF Realty Holdings, Inc. (In re Jaghab), 584 B.R. 472, 95 U.C.C. Rep. Serv. 2d (CBC) 826, 2018 Bankr. LEXIS 1151 (Bankr. E.D.N.Y. 2018).

2. Payment intangible

Court denied the bank's claims to the extent it sought treatment as a secured creditor or recission because under the plain terms of the bank's agreement with the debt fund, the bank did not take any collateral assignment, perfected or unperfected, of the interest in the participation agreement, and it was relevant that the bank's security interest was in the loan documents, and not in the participation agreement, because only the participation interest could possibly be construed as a "payment intangible"; a "payment intangible" was a general intangible under which the account debtor's primary obligation was a monetary obligation. U.C.C. § 9-102(a)(61), and a "general intangible" explicitly excluded instruments, such as the loan documents, which included a mortgage and a mortgage note, from its definition. U.C.C. § 9-102(a)(42). Under the UCC, the assignment of a payment intangible was automatically perfected, U.C.C. § 9-309(2), while under U.C.C. §§ 9-313(a); 9-312(a), a security interest in an instrument was perfected either by filing, or when the holder of the interest took actual or constructive possession of the instrument, and after the bank sold its participation interest a record was never authenticated acknowledging that it held the loan documents for the bank's benefit as would have been required by UCC § 9-313(c); as the bank had neither actual or constructive possession of the loan documents, its security interest in the loan documents was unperfected. SEC v Byers, 671 F. Supp. 2d 531, 71 U.C.C. Rep. Serv. 2d (CBC) 364, 2009 U.S. Dist. LEXIS 112494 (S.D.N.Y. 2009).

3. Under former § 9-304

Judgment creditor had prior right to proceeds due under promissory note held by judgment debtor, even though third party had entered into factoring agreement with debtor prior to judgment which had given third party security interest in all debtor's "receivables," including proceeds of note, where note did not constitute chattel paper and third party failed to take possession of note in order to perfect whatever security interest it might have had by virtue of agreement with debtor. Berkowitz v Chavo Int'l., Inc., 74 N.Y.2d 144,

544 N.Y.S.2d 569, 542 N.E.2d 1086, 9 U.C.C. Rep. Serv. 2d (CBC) 4, 1989 N.Y. LEXIS 887 (N.Y. 1989).

In action between judgment creditor and secured party over who had priority to obligation denominated as promissory note but concededly nonnegotiable, judgment creditor's lien had priority since secured party did not have actual possession of note at time it was levied upon by sheriff and thus failed to perfect its security interest therein as required by CLS UCC § 9-304[1]. Berkowitz v Chavo International, Inc., 144 A.D.2d 263, 533 N.Y.S.2d 865, 1988 N.Y. App. Div. LEXIS 10959 (N.Y. App. Div. 1st Dep't 1988), app. dismissed, 73 N.Y.2d 974, 540 N.Y.S.2d 1007, 538 N.E.2d 359, 1989 N.Y. LEXIS 4994 (N.Y. 1989), aff'd, 74 N.Y.2d 144, 544 N.Y.S.2d 569, 542 N.E.2d 1086, 9 U.C.C. Rep. Serv. 2d (CBC) 4, 1989 N.Y. LEXIS 887 (N.Y. 1989).

Subject to certain exceptions, security interest in instrument can be perfected only by secured party's taking possession of instrument as required by CLS UCC § 9-304[1]. Berkowitz v Chavo International, Inc., 144 A.D.2d 263, 533 N.Y.S.2d 865, 1988 N.Y. App. Div. LEXIS 10959 (N.Y. App. Div. 1st Dep't 1988), app. dismissed, 73 N.Y.2d 974, 540 N.Y.S.2d 1007, 538 N.E.2d 359, 1989 N.Y. LEXIS 4994 (N.Y. 1989), aff'd, 74 N.Y.2d 144, 544 N.Y.S.2d 569, 542 N.E.2d 1086, 9 U.C.C. Rep. Serv. 2d (CBC) 4, 1989 N.Y. LEXIS 887 (N.Y. 1989).

Note was instrument within meaning of CLS UCC Art 9 and was within possessory requirement of CLS UCC § 9-304[1], notwithstanding argument that note was neither negotiable nor writing which evidenced right to payment of money of type which is in ordinary course of business transferred by delivery with any necessary indorsement or assignment within meaning of CLS UCC § 9-105[1][i]; while note was concededly nonnegotiable, nothing in note or contract to which it was subject restricted their assignability and there was no reason note could not be assigned along with contract. Berkowitz v Chavo International, Inc., 144 A.D.2d 263, 533 N.Y.S.2d 865, 1988 N.Y. App. Div. LEXIS 10959 (N.Y. App. Div. 1st Dep't 1988), app. dismissed, 73 N.Y.2d 974, 540 N.Y.S.2d 1007, 538 N.E.2d 359, 1989 N.Y. LEXIS 4994 (N.Y. 1989), aff'd, 74 N.Y.2d 144, 544 N.Y.S.2d 569, 542 N.E.2d 1086, 9 U.C.C. Rep. Serv. 2d (CBC) 4, 1989 N.Y. LEXIS 887 (N.Y. 1989).

Defendant's security interest in cooperative apartment was not perfected by filing of UCC financing statements prior to effective date of CLS UCC § 9-304(7), which permitted perfection of such security interest only by filing, and thus could not defeat plaintiff's rights as bona fide purchaser in physical possession of stock certificate and proprietary lease attributable to apartment. Morgan v Gordon & Co., 210 A.D.2d 30, 618 N.Y.S.2d 817, 1994 N.Y. App. Div. LEXIS 12381 (N.Y. App. Div. 1st Dep't 1994), app. denied, 85 N.Y.2d 807, 628 N.Y.S.2d 50, 651 N.E.2d 918, 1995 N.Y. LEXIS 1165 (N.Y. 1995).

In action to determine priority of right to collateral (note secured by deed of trust) that corporate debtor had assigned three times to secure its obligations, where (1) California bank in 1972 made loan of $300,000 to corporate debtor and loans of $170,000 to each of three individuals associated with corporate debtor, (2) such loans were secured by 1972 deed of trust on California property owned by corporate debtor, (3) in 1974, corporate debtor formed joint venture with plaintiff to develop certain California real estate owned by corporate debtor, which included property subject to 1972 deed of trust given to secure California bank's loans to corporate debtor and three individuals associated with debtor, (4) pursuant to joint-venture agreement with plaintiff, corporate debtor sold property to be developed for note secured by deed of trust to such property, and such note and deed constituted collateral sued for, (5) in May, 1974, corporate debtor assigned collateral in suit to California bank, which had loaned corporate debtor $300,000, to secure principal of $240,000, and bank took possession of collateral and retained it during corporate debtor's subsequent assignments thereof, (6) in January, 1975, corporate debtor made second assignment of collateral in suit, which incorporated its first assignment, by assigning collateral (a) first to California bank to secure corporate debtor's obligation of $280,000, and (b) then to first Chicago bank to secure debtor's obligation of over one million dollars, (7) thereafter, corporate debtor repaid its $280,000 debt to California bank with funds from $275,000 loan obtained from second Chicago bank, but did not repay debt to first Chicago bank, (8) in March, 1976, corporate debtor assigned collateral in suit to both California bank and second Chicago bank to secure loans made by California bank to three individuals associated

UCC

with corporate debtor, (9) in May, 1976, Federal Deposit Insurance Corporation (FDIC), as liquidator of California bank which had been corporate debtor's creditor and had become insolvent, obtained California bank's rights to collateral in suit and took possession of it, (10) in 1978, first Chicago bank also became insolvent, and FDIC obtained such bank's rights to collateral in suit and sold them to plaintiff in June, 1979, on corporate debtor's default on underlying debt to first Chicago bank, and (11) plaintiff brought suit for possession of collateral when FDIC, as liquidator of California bank, refused to surrender it, district court awarded summary judgment and granted ownership of a collateral interest in the note and deed to first Chicago bank. On appeal, summary judgment was reversed and the matter remanded as the record raised a material issue of fact as to the bank's knowledge, or participation in relevant events and, therefore, its status as a good faith purchaser. Landmark Land Co. v Sprague, 701 F.2d 1065, 1983 U.S. App. LEXIS 30033 (2d Cir. N.Y. 1983).

§ 9-313.   When Possession by or Delivery to Secured Party Perfects Security Interest Without Filing

(a) Perfection by possession or delivery. Except as otherwise provided in subsection (b), a secured party may perfect a security interest in tangible negotiable documents, goods, instruments, money, or tangible chattel paper by taking possession of the collateral. A secured party may perfect a security interest in certificated securities by taking delivery of the certificated securities under Section 8-301.

(b) Goods covered by certificate of title. With respect to goods covered by a certificate of title issued by this state, a secured party may perfect a security interest in the goods by taking possession of the goods only in the circumstances described in Section 9-316(d).

(c) Collateral in possession of person other than debtor. With respect to collateral other than certificated securities and goods covered by a document, a secured party takes possession of collateral in the possession of a person other than the debtor, the secured party, or a lessee of the collateral from the debtor in the ordinary course of the debtor's business, when:

(1) the person in possession authenticates a record acknowledging that it holds possession of the collateral for the secured party's benefit; or

(2) the person takes possession of the collateral after having authenticated a record acknowledging that it will hold possession of collateral for the secured party's benefit.

(d) Time of perfection by possession; continuation of perfection. If perfection of a security interest depends upon possession of the collateral by a secured party, perfection occurs no earlier than the time the secured party takes possession and continues only while the secured party retains possession.

(e) Time of perfection by delivery; continuation of perfection. A security interest in a certificated security in registered form is perfected by delivery when delivery of the certificated security occurs under Section 8-301 and remains perfected by delivery until the debtor obtains possession of the security certificate.

(f) Acknowledgment not required. A person in possession of collateral is not required to acknowledge that it holds possession for a secured party's benefit.

(g) Effectiveness of acknowledgment; no duties or confirmation. If a person acknowledges that it holds possession for the secured party's benefit:

(1) the acknowledgment is effective under subsection (c) or Section 8-301(a), even if the acknowledgment violates the rights of a debtor; and

(2) unless the person otherwise agrees or law other than this article otherwise provides, the person does not owe any duty to the secured party and is not required to confirm the acknowledgment to another person.

(h) Secured party's delivery to person other than debtor. A secured party having possession of collateral does not relinquish possession by delivering the collateral to a person other than the debtor or a lessee of the collateral from the debtor in the ordinary course of the debtor's business if the person was instructed before the delivery or is instructed contemporaneously with the delivery:

(1) to hold possession of the collateral for the secured party's benefit; or

(2) to redeliver the collateral to the secured party.

(i) Effect of delivery under subsection (h); no duties or confirmation. A secured party does not relinquish possession, even if a delivery under subsection (h) violates the rights of a debtor. A person to which collateral is delivered under subsection (h) does not owe any duty to the secured party and is not required to confirm the delivery to another person unless the person otherwise agrees or law other than this article otherwise provides.

(j) Cooperative interests. Subsections (a) through (i) do not apply to cooperative interests.

History: Add, L 2001, ch 84, § 36, eff July 1, 2001.

Former § 9-313, add, L 1962, ch 553; amd, L 1977, ch 866, § 23, eff July 2, 1978.

Former § 9-313, repealed, L 2001, ch 84, § 36, eff July 1, 2001.

Amd, L 2014, ch 505, § 38, eff Dec 17, 2014.

CASE ANNOTATIONS

1. **Holder in due course without notice**
2. **Authentication**
3. **Lien limitation**
4. **Payment intangible**
5. **Agency**
6. **Under former § 9-305**
7. **–In general**
8. **–Instruments**
9. **–Money**
10. **–Documents**
11. **–Chattel paper**
12. **–Possession by bailee or agent**
13. **–Effect on third parties**
7. **Particular applications**

1. **Holder in due course without notice**
Defendant assignees, who provided warehouse loans to the debtor to finance mortgage originations and who were assigned the mortgages and notes by the debtor, had perfected security interests in the

notes due to possession under UCC § 9-304(1), and because the assignees were holders in due course without notice of the plaintiff disbursing agents claims under UCC § 9-318, the assignees defeated the claims of the disbursing agent which were based on the debtor's dishonored checks. Broward Title Co. v Jacobs (In re AppOnline.com, Inc.), 285 B.R. 805, 49 U.C.C. Rep. Serv. 2d (CBC) 531, 2002 Bankr. LEXIS 1382 (Bankr. E.D.N.Y. 2002), aff'd, app. dismissed, 321 B.R. 614, 2003 U.S. Dist. LEXIS 26258 (E.D.N.Y. 2003).

2. Authentication

By signing a check for proceeds from a sale of cattle, and making the check payable jointly to both a debtor and a creditor, an agent for an auctioneer authenticated a record acknowledging possession of collateral for the benefit of a creditor, so as to effect perfection under N.Y. U.C.C. Law § 9-313(c)(1). Thus, the creditor's lien in the cattle was perfected upon the issuance of the check, and since the check was issued outside the preference period in 11 U.S.C.S. § 547(b)(4), there was no preferential transfer. Heyer v Conesus Milk Producers Coop. Ass'n (In re Clayson), 341 B.R. 137, 46 Bankr. Ct. Dec. (LRP) 85, 59 U.C.C. Rep. Serv. 2d (CBC) 341, 2006 Bankr. LEXIS 555 (Bankr. W.D.N.Y. 2006).

3. Lien limitation

Carrier had general lien that was not perfected as against bank's prior purchase money security interest on all of debtor's property, beyond freight charges for current goods, because carrier's lien was limited to cargo which was in carrier's possession. In re World Imps., Ltd. v OEC Group N.Y., 498 B.R. 58, 2013 Bankr. LEXIS 3329 (Bankr. E.D. Pa. 2013), aff'd, 526 B.R. 127, 2015 U.S. Dist. LEXIS 7675 (E.D. Pa. 2015).

4. Payment intangible

Court denied the bank's claims to the extent it sought treatment as a secured creditor or recission because under the plain terms of the bank's agreement with the debt fund, the bank did not take any collateral assignment, perfected or unperfected, of the interest in the participation agreement, and it was relevant that the bank's security interest was in the loan documents, and not in the participation agreement, because only the participation interest could possibly be construed as a "payment intangible"; a "payment intangible" was a general intangible under which the account debtor's primary obligation was a monetary obligation. U.C.C. § 9-102(a)(61), and a "general intangible" explicitly excluded instruments, such as the loan documents, which included a mortgage and a mortgage note, from its definition. U.C.C. § 9-102(a)(42). Under the UCC, the assignment of a payment intangible was automatically perfected, U.C.C. § 9-309(2), while under U.C.C. §§ 9-313(a); 9-312(a), a security interest in an instrument was perfected either by filing, or when the holder of the interest took actual or constructive possession of the instrument, and after the bank sold its participation interest a record was never authenticated acknowledging that it held the loan documents for the bank's benefit as would have been required by UCC § 9-313(c); as the bank had neither actual or constructive possession of the loan documents, its security interest in the loan documents was unperfected. SEC v Byers, 671 F. Supp. 2d 531, 71 U.C.C. Rep. Serv. 2d (CBC) 364, 2009 U.S. Dist. LEXIS 112494 (S.D.N.Y. 2009).

5. Agency

In an action in which plaintiff lender alleged that defendant seller failed to deliver bills of lading that served as security for loans that plaintiff made to a borrower, the alleged pledge of the bills of lading was not perfected under N.Y. U.C.C. Law § 9-313(c) because there was no allegation that defendant, while holding the bills of lading, was plaintiff's agent or was acting on plaintiff's behalf. Ancile Inv. Co. v Archer Daniels Midland Co., 784 F. Supp. 2d 296, 74 U.C.C. Rep. Serv. 2d (CBC) 91, 2011 U.S. Dist. LEXIS 23443 (S.D.N.Y. 2011).

6. Under former § 9-305

7. –In general

Under the statute, the actions of one seeking to repossess certain personal property from a defaulting vendee were insufficient to perfect the vendor's security interest. L. B. Smith, Inc. v Foley, 72-1 U.S. Tax Cas. (CCH) ¶230, 341 F. Supp. 810, 11 U.C.C. Rep. Serv. (CBC) 41, 1972 U.S. Dist. LEXIS 15489 (W.D.N.Y. 1972).

Under UCC, parties to security agreement were free to decide who should have right to possession of collateral. American Honda Motor Co. v United States, 363 F. Supp. 988, 1973 U.S. Dist. LEXIS 11940 (S.D.N.Y. 1973).

8. –Instruments

Where a security interest in the proceeds of promissory notes was perfected before the holder of that interest received notice of the existence of a previously filed Internal Revenue Service lien, the holder's right to the proceeds of the notes is not affected by the lien. Lipkowitz & Plaut v Affrunti, 95 Misc. 2d 849, 407 N.Y.S.2d 1010, 25 U.C.C. Rep. Serv. (CBC) 276, 1978 N.Y. Misc. LEXIS 2612 (N.Y. Sup. Ct. 1978).

In suit by trustee in bankruptcy against bank which had allegedly received voidable preferences in violation of Bankruptcy Act, bankrupt's settlement of suit concerning reduction in value of collateral for loan was not voidable preference where collateral consisted of debenture in which defendant had perfected its security interest by possession; debenture was "security" within meaning of UCC § 8-102 where, inter alia, subordinated debentures of brokerage houses were recognized medium for investment; debenture was "instrument" under UCC § 9-105 where it was "security" under UCC § 8-102; security interest in debenture was perfected by possession, under UCC § 9-305, where it was "instrument" under UCC § 9-105; security interest attached immediately in collateral despite alleged ambiguity in security agreement to effect that it was to attach only in event of default, where construction of security agreement revealed intent to attach immediately and where, under UCC § 9-204, any attempt to postpone attachment must be explicitly stated; filing, under UCC § 9-201, security agreement superceded previous subordination agreement and controlled rights and obligations among the parties. Allegaert v Chemical Bank, 657 F.2d 495, 6 Bankr. Ct. Dec. (LRP) 1247, 29 U.C.C. Rep. Serv. (CBC) 993, 1980 U.S. App. LEXIS 14761 (2d Cir. N.Y. 1980).

9. –Money

Bank's segregation of corporate account did not constitute preferential transfer under CLS Dr & Cr § 15 where bank had valid security agreement with corporation which bank had required for issuance of irrevocable letter of credit to corporation's surety, and which created perfected security interest in account balance in bank's favor due to rule (under CLS UCC § 9-305) that bank's possession of that collateral served to perfect the interest. Gillman v Chase Manhattan Bank, N.A., 135 A.D.2d 488, 521 N.Y.S.2d 729, 1987 N.Y. App. Div. LEXIS 52451 (N.Y. App. Div. 2d Dep't 1987), aff'd, 73 N.Y.2d 1, 537 N.Y.S.2d 787, 534 N.E.2d 824, 7 U.C.C. Rep. Serv. 2d (CBC) 945, 1988 N.Y. LEXIS 3537 (N.Y. 1988).

Assignee of rights of designated recipients of escrowed funds of bankrupt corporation under reorganization plan confirmed by Bankruptcy Court had priority to bankruptcy distributions, over claims of bank as judgment creditor of assignors, where assignment was made in 1989, assignee took possession of last note in 1990, and bank's claims did not arise until 1996. Norstar Bank, N.A. v Davis, 238 A.D.2d 892, 661 N.Y.S.2d 106, 1997 N.Y. App. Div. LEXIS 4682 (N.Y. App. Div. 4th Dep't 1997).

Dispute over priority to escrowed funds of bankrupt corporation under reorganization plan was not affected by either (1) "Consent Modification Agreement" by which designated recipient of funds conveyed its ownership interest in bankrupt corporation, or (2) Bankruptcy Court's confirmation of reorganization plan extinguishing recipient's stock rights in bankrupt corporation, where assignee's interest in bankruptcy distributions was not traceable to recipient's interest as stockholder in bankrupt corporation. Norstar Bank, N.A. v Davis, 238 A.D.2d 892, 661 N.Y.S.2d 106, 1997 N.Y. App. Div. LEXIS 4682 (N.Y. App. Div. 4th Dep't 1997).

Assignee of rights of designated recipients of escrowed funds of bankrupt corporation under reorganization plan confirmed by Bankruptcy Court was not collaterally estopped from asserting its claim of priority to bankruptcy distributions where bankruptcy proceeding concerned claims of creditors of bankrupt corporation, priority suit concerned claims of creditors of those creditors, there was thus no identity of issue, and there was no inconsistency between assignee's present claim and its position taken in bankruptcy proceeding. Norstar Bank, N.A. v Davis, 238 A.D.2d 892, 661 N.Y.S.2d 106, 1997 N.Y. App. Div. LEXIS 4682 (N.Y. App. Div. 4th Dep't 1997).

10. –Documents

Service of order of attachment, which was later vacated, upon garnishee in possession of stock certificates was insufficient to perfect assignee's security interest in stock and to place garnishee and assignor's creditor on notice that assignee had secured interest in shares, whereas garnishee and assignor's creditor, by possession, did properly perfect their security interests under UCC § 9-305. Friedman v Fein, 46 A.D.2d 886, 361 N.Y.S.2d 397, 1974 N.Y. App. Div. LEXIS 3513 (N.Y. App. Div. 2d Dep't 1974).

11. –Chattel paper

Under UCC § 9-305, possessory security interest in ordinary chattel paper requires no filing for perfection. State Tax Com. v Shor, 43 N.Y.2d 151, 400 N.Y.S.2d 805, 371 N.E.2d 523, 1977 N.Y. LEXIS 2447 (N.Y. 1977).

Where (1) debtor sold corporate stock on July 25, 1974 to defendants for $180,000, and defendants executed promissory notes under pledge agreement securing payment of stock's purchase price and delivered notes to escrowee, which also received the purchased stock, (2) debtor on March 19, 1975, with knowledge and consent of defendants and escrowee, assigned notes to creditor as collateral to secure payment of prior $60,000 debt, indorsed them to creditor's order, and delivered them to creditor which retained possession of them until August 24, 1976, a date following date on which debtor had fully debt due creditor, (3) on November 5, 1975, when defendants still owed debtor $135,000 on notes and notes were still in creditor's possession as collateral for payment of $28,000 balance then owed by debtor to creditor, debtor entered into agreement with plaintiff law firm and its client under which payments on prior debt owed by debtor to such client were extended, prospective lawsuit was settled, sums thus due to client were collateralized by assignment of debtor's interest in stock-payment notes, and notes themselves and pledge agreement securing them were also assigned to plaintiff on behalf of its client, subject to prior collateral assignment in favor of debtor's first creditor, (4) first creditor on August 24, 1976 acknowledged to escrowee that debtor had fully discharged debt due it, delivered stock-payment notes in suit to plaintiff law firm, but never indorsed notes to plaintiff's order, (5) on August 25, 1976, plaintiff, defendants (purchasers of debtor's stock), debtor, and escrowee executed written acknowledgements of debtor's assignment of notes and pledge agreement to plaintiff, and plaintiff requested that it be paid next installment on notes, which was due on October 1, 1976, (5) on April 5, 1976, IRS assessed delinquent income-tax liability against debtor and filed notice of tax lien on August 4, 1976, (6) on October 1, 1976, escrowee paid installment payment due on notes to IRS, and (7) on October 5, 1976, plaintiff after due notice declared default on notes (because of failure to receive October 1, 1976 installment payment thereon) and under acceleration clause in notes demanded full payment thereof, court held (1) that plaintiff, as nominee for its client, acquired valid collateral assignment of proceeds of notes to extent that proceeds were not required to satisfy first creditor's prior security interest therein, (2) that under UCC § 3-202(3), debtor's indorsement and negotiation of notes to first creditor merely created partial assignment of notes' proceeds and did not divest debtor of ultimate right to all proceeds not required to satisfy debt owed to first creditor, (3) that debtor's remaining interest in notes' proceeds was the interest that debtor had assigned to plaintiff as collateral on November 5, 1975, and that such assignment, under UCC § 9-204(1), gave plaintiff valid security interest in debtor's residuary interest in notes' proceeds, (4) that plaintiff's security interest in notes' proceeds was not perfected until August 24, 1976, when it became perfected under UCC § 9-305 by possession of notes following first creditor's delivery thereof to plaintiff, (5) that IRS tax lien was not superior to plaintiff's perfected security interest in notes, since neither plaintiff nor its client had received any notice of such lien until September 20, 1976, and (6) that neither plaintiff not its client could accelerate unpaid balance due on notes, since plaintiff, as nominee for its client, was merely holder of security interest in notes and was not "holder" of notes within meaning of UCC § 1-201(20) because of first creditor's failure to indorse them to plaintiff's order. Lipkowitz & Plaut v Affrunti, 95 Misc. 2d 849, 407 N.Y.S.2d 1010, 25 U.C.C. Rep. Serv. (CBC) 276, 1978 N.Y. Misc. LEXIS 2612 (N.Y. Sup. Ct. 1978) (holding that plaintiff was entitled to receive, on behalf of its client, all installment payments due on notes, commencing with installment due on October 1, 1976).

12. –Possession by bailee or agent

Seller (which shipped printing press with unpaid balance owing to assignee of contract of sale after receiving payments toward purchase price financed by funds provided by bank in January 1989) had superior purchase-money security interest (PMSI) in printing press and its proceeds from inception of its contract with assignor in December 1988 where (1) seller expressly retained PMSI in both its contract with assignor and in subsequent purchase order, by which assignee obtained title, and (2) seller's security interest "attached" at time contract between it and assignor was entered into and partial payment of purchase price was made; further, since collateral was goods, seller perfected its security interest both by possession and by

filing financing statement before it relinquished possession. Heidelberg E., Inc v Weber Lithography, 213 A.D.2d 127, 631 N.Y.S.2d 370, 27 U.C.C. Rep. Serv. 2d (CBC) 1081, 1995 N.Y. App. Div. LEXIS 9236 (N.Y. App. Div. 2d Dep't 1995).

In action to determine priority of right to collateral (note secured by deed of trust) that corporate debtor had assigned three times to secure its obligations, where (1) California bank in 1972 made loan of $300,000 to corporate debtor and loans of $170,000 to each of three individuals associated with corporate debtor, (2) such loans were secured by 1972 deed of trust on California property owned by corporate debtor, (3) in 1974, corporate debtor formed joint venture with plaintiff to develop certain California real estate owned by corporate debtor, which included property subject to 1972 deed of trust given to secure California bank's loans to corporate debtor and three individuals associated with debtor, (4) pursuant to joint-venture agreement with plaintiff, corporate debtor sold property to be developed for note secured by deed of trust to such property, and such note and deed constituted collateral sued for, (5) in May, 1974, corporate debtor assigned collateral in suit to California bank, which had loaned corporate debtor $300,000, to secure principal of $240,000, and bank took possession of collateral and retained it during corporate debtor's subsequent assignments thereof, (6) in January, 1975, corporate debtor made second assignment of collateral in suit, which incorporated its first assignment, by assigning collateral (a) first to California bank to secure corporate debtor's obligation of $280,000, and (b) then to first Chicago bank to secure debtor's obligation of over one million dollars, (7) thereafter, corporate debtor repaid its $280,000 debt to California bank with funds from $275,000 loan obtained from second Chicago bank, but did not repay debt to first Chicago bank, (8) in March, 1976, corporate debtor assigned collateral in suit to both California bank and second Chicago bank to secure loans made by California bank to three individuals associated with corporate debtor, (9) in May, 1976, Federal Deposit Insurance Corporation (FDIC), as liquidator of California bank which had been corporate debtor's creditor and had become insolvent, obtained California bank's rights to collateral in suit and took possession of it, (10) in 1978, first Chicago bank also became insolvent, and FDIC obtained such bank's rights to collateral in suit and sold them to plaintiff in June, 1979, on corporate debtor's default on underlying debt to first Chicago bank, and (11) plaintiff brought suit for possession of collateral when FDIC, as liquidator of California bank, refused to surrender it, district court awarded summary judgment and granted ownership of a collateral interest in the note and deed to first Chicago bank. On appeal, summary judgment was reversed and the matter remanded as the record raised a material issue of fact as to the bank's knowledge, or participation in relevant events and, therefore, its status as a good faith purchaser. Landmark Land Co. v Sprague, 701 F.2d 1065, 1983 U.S. App. LEXIS 30033 (2d Cir. N.Y. 1983).

13. –Effect on third parties

Sale of unfinished textile fabrics by converter (i.e., one who finishes textiles into dyed and patterned fabrics) to another converter was in ordinary course of first converter's business within meaning of UCC § 9-307(1), even though predominant business purpose of converters was converting of unfinished textiles into finished fabrics, and thus second converter took fabric free from manufacturer's security interest in textiles, although manufacturer's security interest was perfected by possession of goods under UCC § 9-305, where it was shown that converters often purchased unfinished textiles in excess of their requirements, selling such excess through brokers to other converters, and that converters buy such goods if price is satisfactory or particular goods are not available from manufacturers, both of which conditions were satisfied in present case. Tanbro Fabrics Corp. v Deering Milliken, Inc., 39 N.Y.2d 632, 385 N.Y.S.2d 260, 350 N.E.2d 590, 19 U.C.C. Rep. Serv. (CBC) 385, 1976 N.Y. LEXIS 2721 (N.Y. 1976).

7. Particular applications

Trial court erred in granting a receiver's motion to, among other things, permit a sale of mortgaged property and mandating the lender's discharge of the mortgage because the receiver's deposit of the money into the escrow account of the lender's attorney—contingent upon the occurrence of the trial court's determination of the long-pending summary judgment motions—was not tantamount to possession of the collateral by the lender, the Uniform Commercial Code did not authorize the trial court to substitute the lender's collateral, and the receiver did not have the same power as a bankruptcy trustee to dispose of real property free and clear of all liens and mortgages. Krupnick v Windy Ridge Corp., 147 A.D.3d 1247, 2017 NY Slip Op 01419, 2017 NY Slip Op 1419, 48 N.Y.S.3d 536, 2017 N.Y. App. Div. LEXIS 1391 (N.Y. App. Div. 3d Dep't 2017).

§ 9-314. Perfection by Control

(a) Perfection by control. A security interest in investment property, deposit accounts, letter-of-credit rights, electronic chattel paper, or electronic documents may be perfected by control of the collateral under Section 7-106, 9-104, 9-105, 9-106, or 9-107.

(b) Specified collateral: time of perfection by control; continuation of perfection. A security interest in deposit accounts, electronic chattel paper, letter-of-credit rights, or electronic documents is perfected by control under Section 7-106, 9-104, 9-105, or 9-107 when the secured party obtains control and remains perfected by control only while the secured party retains control.

(c) Investment property: time of perfection by control; continuation of perfection. A security interest in investment property is perfected by control under Section 9-106 from the time the secured party obtains control and remains perfected by control until:

(1) the secured party does not have control; and

(2) one of the following occurs:

(A) if the collateral is a certificated security, the debtor has or acquires possession of the security certificate;

(B) if the collateral is an uncertificated security, the issuer has registered or registers the debtor as the registered owner; or

(C) if the collateral is a security entitlement, the debtor is or becomes the entitlement holder.

(d) Cooperative interests. Subsections (a) through (c) do not apply to cooperative interests.

History: Add, L 2001, ch 84, § 36, eff July 1, 2001.

Former § 9-314, add, L 1962, ch 553, eff Sept 27, 1964; repealed, L 2001, ch 84, § 36, eff July 1, 2001.

Amd, L 2014, ch 505, § 39, eff Dec 17, 2014.

§ 9-315. Secured Party's Rights on Disposition of Collateral and in Proceeds

(a) Disposition of collateral: continuation of security interest or agricultural lien; proceeds. Except as otherwise provided in this article and in Section 2-403(2):

(1) a security interest or agricultural lien continues in collateral notwithstanding sale, lease, license, exchange, or other disposition thereof unless the secured party authorized the disposition free of the security interest or agricultural lien; and

(2) a security interest attaches to any identifiable proceeds of collateral.

(b) When commingled proceeds identifiable. Proceeds that are commingled with other property are identifiable proceeds:

(1) if the proceeds are goods, to the extent provided by Section 9-336; and

(2) if the proceeds are not goods, to the extent that the secured party identifies the proceeds by a method of tracing, including application of equitable principles, that is permitted under law other than this article with respect to commingled property of the type involved.

(c) Perfection of security interest in proceeds. A security interest in proceeds is a perfected security interest if the security interest in the original collateral was perfected.

(d) Continuation of perfection. A perfected security interest in proceeds becomes unperfected on the 21st day after the security interest attaches to the proceeds unless:

(1) the following conditions are satisfied:

(A) a filed financing statement covers the original collateral;

(B) the proceeds are collateral in which a security interest may be perfected by filing in the office in which the financing statement has been filed; and

(C) the proceeds are not acquired with cash proceeds;

(2) the proceeds are identifiable cash proceeds; or

(3) the security interest in the proceeds is perfected other than under subsection (c) when the security interest attaches to the proceeds or within 20 days thereafter.

(e) When perfected security interest in proceeds becomes unperfected. If a filed financing statement covers the original collateral, a security interest in proceeds which remains perfected under subsection (d)(1) becomes unperfected at the later of:

(1) when the effectiveness of the filed financing statement lapses under Section 9-515 or is terminated under Section 9-513; or

(2) the 21st day after the security interest attaches to the proceeds.

History: Add, L 2001, ch 84, § 36, eff July 1, 2001.

Add, L 1962, ch 553, eff Sept 27, 1964; repealed, L 2001, ch 84, § 36, eff July 1, 2001.

CASE ANNOTATIONS

UNDER FORMER § 9-306
I. In General; "Proceeds"
1. Generally; excluded transactions
2. Insurance as proceeds
3. – Not proceeds
II. Security Interest as Continuing
4. In general
5. "Sale, exchange, or other disposition"
6. Transfer not in ordinary course
7. Unauthorized disposition; waiver
8. Authorized disposition; waiver
9. Identifiable proceeds
III. Insolvency Proceedings
10. In general
IV. Rights as to Returned or Repossessed Goods
11. In general

In a suit brought by a shareholder against a housing corporation and other shareholders (collectively referred to as the housing corporation), there was no justification for the shareholder's filing of a financing statement against a garden unit apartment for which the shareholder alleged that funds were expended as no security agreement was ever entered into between the parties, the shareholder had no common law lien that was enforceable, and there was no authenticated record whereby the housing corporation authorized the filing. Since the filing of the UCC-1 financing statement was baseless, the shareholder was directed to terminate the same and pay the housing corporation statutory damages in the amount of $500. McDaniel v 162 Columbia Hgts. Hous. Corps. (2008, Sup) 21 Misc 3d 244, 863 NYS2d 346.

Under a Securities Investor Protection Act of 1970 liquidation, where the creditor had posted cash collateral with the debtor broker-dealer in exchange for loaned securities, the debtor's commingled cash was not subject to a constructive trust and all of the debtor's cash was property of the estate and the creditor's security interest could be avoided by the trustee, because, while under N.Y. U.C.C. § 9-315(a)(2), (b)(2), (c), a security interest could attach to commingled proceeds, the creditor was unable to trace its cash. Ferris, Baker, Watts, Inc. v Stephenson (In re MJK Clearing) (2002, BC DC Minn) 286 BR 109, 49 UCCRS2d 11

UNDER FORMER § 9-306

I. In General; "Proceeds"

1. Generally; excluded transactions

Insurance payments made because of casualty loss of collateral are "proceeds" pursuant to provision of UCC § 9-306(1) added effective July, 1978, which includes "insurance payable to a person other than a party to the security agreement"; where automobile accident occurred in 1975, language of UCC § 9-306(1) is not relevant and UCC § 9-104(g), which states that UCC Art 9 does not apply to a transfer of an interest or claim in or under any insurance policy is applicable. First Nat'l Bank v Merchant's Mut. Ins. Co. (1980) 49 N.Y.2d 725, 426 N.Y.S.2d 267, 402 N.E.2d 1168, 28 UCCRS 1181

While a security interest continues under UCC § 9-306(2) in any identifiable proceeds of the collateral, the term "identifiable proceeds" may not be extended to include a "cause of action." Bank of New York v Margiotta (1979) 99 Misc. 2d 423, 416 N.Y.S.2d 493, 26 UCCRS 1032

2. Insurance as proceeds

Insurance payments made because of casualty loss of collateral are "proceeds" pursuant to provision of UCC § 9-306(1) added effective July, 1978, which includes "insurance payable to a person other than a party to the security agreement"; where automobile accident occurred in 1975, language of UCC § 9-306(1) is not relevant and UCC § 9-104(g), which states that UCC Art 9 does not apply to a transfer of an interest or claim in or under any insurance policy is applicable. First Nat'l Bank v Merchant's Mut. Ins. Co. (1980) 49 N.Y.2d 725, 426 N.Y.S.2d 267, 402 N.E.2d 1168, 28 UCCRS 1181

Insurance carrier, by paying fire loss proceeds to policyholder, was not thereby rendered liable in conversion to policyholder's landlords who had filed UCC-1 financing statements covering destroyed collateral, where insurance contract was between policyholder and carrier only; there is no need to subject insurance claims process to vagaries surrounding adequacy of UCC-1 filings inasmuch as secured party always has conventional option of having itself named in insurance contract as loss payee or additional insured. Badillo v Tower Ins. Co. (1999) 92 N.Y.2d 790, 686 N.Y.S.2d 363, 709 N.E.2d 104, 38 UCCRS2d 991

In action by lending bank to recover damages resulting from impairment of its security interest after debtor's law firm released insurance proceeds covering loss of secured property to debtor instead of to bank, law firm was not entitled to summary judgment based on alleged lack of notice of bank's claims where, in addition to constructive notice provided by UCC-1 filings, bank had consistently asserted its rights in insurance proceeds from time of debtor's loss of secured collateral. Bank of India v Weg & Myers, P.C. (1999, 1st Dept) 257 A.D.2d 183, 691 N.Y.S.2d 439, 38 UCCRS2d 996

Although assignment of Medicaid accounts receivable is invalid as against Department of Social Services, Medicaid provider can grant security interest in such receivables which is valid as against third parties, and such security interest attaches once Department approves provider's claim and authorizes payment (CLS UCC § 9-306(1) and (2)). In re Estate of Angiulli (1990, Sur) 148 Misc. 2d 796, 561 N.Y.S.2d 626, 14 UCCRS2d 1197, affd (1991, 4th Dept) 178 A.D.2d 948, 580 N.Y.S.2d 889

Where secured creditor alleged that it was entitled to, as proceeds of its security interest in an automobile owned by debtor, a portion of money received by debtor in settlement of a state court lawsuit for personal injury to himself and property damage to automobile, where action was settled for $25,000 in state court pursuant to New York State Insurance Law, and where nowhere in such settlement was there any indication as to what portion was allocated for personal injuries or property damages for pain and suffering, inasmuch as there was damage to vehicle, some portion of money received in settlement of state court action constituted proceeds of damaged vehicle as defined by § 9-306(1) of New York Uniform Commercial Code; creditor was entitled to security interest in that portion of proceeds that represented damage to automobile. In re Territo (1983, BC ED NY) 32 BR 377, 11 BCD 20, 36 UCCRS 1762, later proceeding (1984, BC ED NY) 36 BR 667, CCH Bankr L Rptr ¶ 69759

Under security agreement granting creditor security interest in inventory and equipment and further providing that debtor would maintain insurance policy on collateral with creditor as payee, and providing that security interest was to continue in proceeds from inventory, creditor had valid security interest in proceeds of fire insurance policy upon destruction of inventory under UCC § 9-306(1), where party's clear intention was to give secured party benefit of insurance proceeds; UCC § 9-104(g), providing that Article Nine does not apply "to a transfer of an interest or claim in or under any policy of insurance" is applicable only in situations where parties to security agreement attempt to create direct security interest in insurance policy by making policy itself immediate collateral securing transaction, and not to situations where security agreement creates both direct security interest in inventory and/or equipment and requires debtor to provide his creditor with further protection by insuring collateral. PPG Industries, Inc. v Hartford Fire Ins. Co. (1976, CA2 NY) 531 F.2d 58, 76-1 USTC P 9257, 18 UCCRS 569, 37 AFTR 2d 946 (applying New York law)

Prior to New York's adoption of 1972 amendments to Article 9, insurance payments were not "proceeds" under New York UCC § 9-306(1) because (1) such funds were excluded from Article 9 coverage by New York UCC § 9-104(g), which provides that Article 9 does not apply to transfer of interest or claim in, or under, any insurance policy; and (2) 1977 amendment of New York UCC § 9-306(1), which included insurance payments within definition of "proceeds," did not apply retroactively to funds paid before July 2, 1978. Sanchez v United States (1982, CA2 NY) 696 F.2d 213, 83-1 USTC P 9126, 35 UCCRS 244, 51 AFTR 2d 399 (applying New York law)

In view of policy considerations behind Article 9, as well as policy of 26 USCS § 6323 to give preference to security interests as defined by that provision, creditor had security interest in proceeds of insurance which took precedence over government's tax lien where creditor had security interest in debtor's inventory and where parties intended proceeds of insurance on that collateral to be further security for loan. PPG Industries, Inc. v Hartford Fire Ins. Co. (1974, SD NY) 384 F. Supp. 91, 74-2 USTC P 9823, 15 UCCRS 928, 35 AFTR 2d 331, affd (1976, CA2 NY) 531 F.2d 58, 76-1 USTC P 9257, 18 UCCRS 569, 37 AFTR 2d 946 (applying New York law)

Proceeds from fire insurance policy covering secured collateral constituted "proceeds" within meaning of UCC § 9-306(1), and hence were subject to secured party's security interest, where security agreements required debtor to procure insurance on collateral in favor of secured party, "proceeds" box in both security agreements was checked, rider to second security agreement assigned all sums payable under such insurance to secured party as further security for its loan, and rider was attached to insurance policy making loss payable to secured party "as interests may appear." Firemen's Fund American Ins. Co. v Ken-Lori Knits, Inc. (1975, ED NY) 399 F. Supp. 286, 16 UCCRS 1407 (apparently applying New York law)

3. – Not proceeds

Insurance covering auto destroyed by fire in 1975 was not "proceeds" within the meaning of UCC § 9-306 as such statute read prior to amendment effective July 2, 1978. First Nat'l Bank v Merchant's Mut. Ins. Co. (1980) 49 N.Y.2d 725, 426 N.Y.S.2d 267, 402 N.E.2d 1168, 28 UCCRS 1181

Where (1) first buyer of dry cleaning and laundry equipment violated security agreement with seller by not procuring insurance on equipment, (2) first buyer later sold equipment to another buyer, who procured insurance on it before it was destroyed by fire, and (3) insurer refused to pay insurance proceeds to secured creditor of first buyer, court held that secured creditor had no right to such proceeds under UCC § 9-306(1) because (1) purpose of UCC § 9-306(1) is to declare secured party's right to proceeds, including insurance proceeds, that are received by debtor on debtor's disposal of collateral, and (2) in present case, insurance proceeds were not received by secured party's debtor (first buyer). McGraw-Edison Credit Corp. v Allstate Ins. Co. (1978, 2d Dept) 62 A.D.2d 872, 406 N.Y.S.2d 337, 24 UCCRS 767

A secured creditor has no statutory right to recover insurance proceeds directly from the insurer of the debtor's buyer; section 9-306 of the Uniform Commercial Code was enacted to state a secured party's right to proceeds received by the debtor on disposition of the collateral, and, effective July 2, 1978 (L 1977, ch 866), it was specifically amended to provide that "Insurance payable by reason of loss or damage to the collateral is proceeds, except to the extent that it is payable to a person other than a party to the security agreement", thus making it clear that a secured creditor has a statutory right to share in insurance proceeds payable to the debtor, but not in insurance proceeds payable to a third party. McGraw-Edison Credit Corp. v Allstate Ins. Co. (1978, 2d Dept) 62 A.D.2d 872, 406 N.Y.S.2d 337, 24 UCCRS 767

II. Security Interest as Continuing

4. In general

Court erred in granting buyer's motion for summary judgment dismissing action to enforce security interest in excavator where fact question existed as to whether security interest was created by seller. John Deere Indus. Equip. Co. v Daman Cable Specialists (1996, 4th Dept) 233 A.D.2d 907, 649 N.Y.S.2d 262

Under the Uniform Commercial Code, title to goods passes at delivery, with only the reservation of a security interest by the seller permitted (Uniform Commercial Code, § 2-401, subd [1]); rules on chattel mortgages and conditional sales are now governed by article 9 of the code, and are considered as a single security device and, while under section 9-306 a security interest continues in any identifiable proceeds of collateral covered by the security agreement and a third party may be liable in conversion for paying those proceeds without satisfying the secured party's interest, there is no justification for extending the statute to include a cause of action within the meaning of identifiable proceeds. Accordingly, in a negligence action by plaintiff bank against defendant driver of a borrowed car in which the bank had a security interest, which car was destroyed in an accident, allegedly because of defendant's negligence, defendant was granted summary judgment since plaintiff failed to state a cause of action. Bank of New York v Margiotta (1979) 99 Misc. 2d 423, 416 N.Y.S.2d 493, 26 UCCRS 1032

Properly perfected security interest of creditor of deceased Medicaid provider continued in proceeds of Medicaid and non-Medicaid receivables after administrator of decedent's insolvent estate received payment from Department of Social Services; thus, such proceeds never became part of estate, administrator acted improperly in using proceeds to pay funeral and administration expenses, and summary judgment would accordingly be granted to creditor sustaining objections to fiduciary's account. In re Estate of Angiulli (1990, Sur) 148 Misc. 2d 796, 561 N.Y.S.2d 626, 14 UCCRS2d 1197, affd (1991, 4th Dept) 178 A.D.2d 948, 580 N.Y.S.2d 889

5. "Sale, exchange, or other disposition"

Plaintiff, which took assignment of security agreement from seller of motor boat and inboard motor and properly filed financing statement covering such "consumer goods" in county of original debtor's residence, had greater priority as to collateral than defendants, which purchased boat and motor without knowledge of plaintiff's security interest after series of sales, made without plaintiff's knowledge, including trade in of collateral by original debtor to original seller as part of purchase of new boat, and seller's resale of collateral to another purchaser, since no exceptions to general rule that security interest continues in collateral despite its sale (UCC 9-306(2)) were applicable. Marine Midland Bank, N. A. v Smith Boys, Inc. (1985, Sup) 129 Misc. 2d 37, 492 N.Y.S.2d 355, 41 UCCRS 1843

6. Transfer not in ordinary course

Subsequent purchasers of aircraft containing engine subject to unperfected chattel mortgage and who were not buyers in ordinary course of business took aircraft and engine not free of chattel mortgage, but took property with priority over chattel mortgage holder's subordinate claim, however, subsequent purchaser who took with notice of perfected chattel mortgage purchased aircraft and engine subject to chattel mortgage which had been perfected. Aircraft Trading & Services, Inc. v Braniff, Inc. (1987, CA2 NY) 819 F.2d 1227, 3 UCCRS2d 1297, cert den (1987) 484 US 856, 98 L Ed 2d 118, 108 S Ct 163

7. Unauthorized disposition; waiver

In action to enforce security interest in livestock, seeking damages for defendant's conversion of certain cows purchased by him from debtor, plaintiff was entitled to judgment notwithstanding verdict where (1) plaintiff had perfected security interest in debtors' cattle and defendant's purchase of cows was subject thereto, (2) defendant did not take free of plaintiff's security interest because check of record and diligent inquiry would have revealed that sale was inconsistent with express "no sale" restriction of security agreement, and because defendant was purchaser of farm products from one engaged in farming operations, (3) despite proof that plaintiff may have known of a few prior sales of "cull" cows, there was no proof that it acquiesced in sale of valuable animals such as those purchased by defendant, and (4) there was no testimony that debtors sold cows or that defendant purchased them in good-faith reliance on plaintiff's failure to object to prior sales. Lake Ontario Production Credit Asso. v Partnership of Grove (1988, 4th Dept) 138 A.D.2d 930, 526 N.Y.S.2d 985, 6 UCCRS2d 1597, later proceeding (1988, 4th Dept) 138 A.D.2d 932, 526 N.Y.S.2d 1023, app den (1988) 72 N.Y.2d 806, 532 N.Y.S.2d 847, 529 N.E.2d 177

In action seeking to trace proceeds from unauthorized sale of secured goods into hands of debtors' law firm, court properly granted judgment as matter of law to firm, which received proceeds in ordinary course of debtors' business and in exchange for legal services rendered, since CLS UCC § 9-306, with certain exceptions, allows secured party to trace proceeds from unauthorized sale of collateral only insofar as they remain in debtor's hands. Lake Ontario Production Credit Asso. v Partnership of Grove (1988, 4th Dept) 138 A.D.2d 930, 526 N.Y.S.2d 985, 6 UCCRS2d 1597, later proceeding (1988, 4th Dept) 138 A.D.2d 932, 526 N.Y.S.2d 1023, app den (1988) 72 N.Y.2d 806, 532 N.Y.S.2d 847, 529 N.E.2d 177

Lending bank was entitled to partial summary judgment on its conversion cause of action against debtor's law firm, which released insurance proceeds covering loss of secured property to debtor instead of bank, because once law firm had notice of outstanding right of possession to proceeds by secured creditor it became stakeholder as to those proceeds notwithstanding its additional role as debtor's attorney. Bank of India v Weg & Myers, P.C. (1999, 1st Dept) 257 A.D.2d 183, 691 N.Y.S.2d 439, 38 UCCRS2d 996

When furniture company resold goods it obtained from debtor, it converted collateral that was subject to creditor's security interest, and furniture company is thus liable for conversion of goods. American Furniture Co. v Extebank (1987, ED NY) 676 F. Supp. 455, 5 UCCRS2d 1511

8. Authorized disposition; waiver

Order directing seizure of tractors and trailers which were listed as collateral in security agreement and which had been sold by debtor to defendants could not stand where there was factual question as to whether, under UCC § 9-306(2), creditor, by reason of its prior dealings with debtor, had authorized it to sell chattels free of any liens by asserting its right to receive "proceeds" if chattels were sold. Long Island Trust Co. v Porta Aluminum Corp. (1974, 2d Dept) 44 A.D.2d 118, 354 N.Y.S.2d 134, 14 UCCRS 833

9. Identifiable proceeds

Corporate officers of debtor were not personally liable for conversion of proceeds from sale of inventory in which creditor had perfected security interest under UCC § 9-306(3)(a) where security agreement, rather than requiring creditor to segregate specific proceeds of each sale from debtor's general funds, merely required debtor to pay "amounts due." Independence Discount Corp. v Bressner (1975, 2d Dept) 47 A.D.2d 756, 365 N.Y.S.2d 44

Where security agreement providing that creditor would have security interest in inventory of retailer and in proceeds of sale of each item of inventory did not impose duty upon retailer to pay over to creditor specific proceeds of sale of each item covered by agreement, but merely provided that upon sale or other disposition of any item of inventory, retailer was obligated to immediately pay amounts due to creditor, there was no specific fund from which payment had to be made, and thus corporate officer's commingling of proceeds of sales with other funds was not conversion of proceeds. Independence Discount Corp. v Bressner (1975, 2d Dept) 47 A.D.2d 756, 365 N.Y.S.2d 44

Automobile credit company, seeking to recover from state money paid by dealer in satisfaction of sales tax liability, failed to state cause of action in alleging that such money constituted proceeds of sales of vehicles by dealer, and that pursuant to duly filed security agreement, credit company had perfected security interest in vehicles and in proceeds of sales, since money paid to state did not constitute "identifiable cash proceeds" which remained subject to credit company's prior perfected and superior security interest under CLS UCC § 9-306(3)(b); dealer incurred sales tax liability in ordinary course of its business (CLS Tax § 1132(a)), and there were no allegations to demonstrate that payments were fraudulent conveyances or that state acted in collusion with dealer to defraud credit company. Ford Motor Credit Co. v State (1996, 3d Dept) 219 A.D.2d 202, 641 N.Y.S.2d 742, 30 UCCRS2d 368, app den (1996) 88 N.Y.2d 813, 651 N.Y.S.2d 15, 673 N.E.2d 1242

Lending bank was entitled to summary judgment on its claim that debtor's law firm, by releasing insurance proceeds following loss of secured property to debtor instead of to bank, impaired its security interest and violated equitable lien which arose by virtue of debtor's express covenant in loan agreement to secure all proceeds of assets as collateral for debt. Bank of India v Weg & Myers, P.C. (1999, 1st Dept) 257 A.D.2d 183, 691 N.Y.S.2d 439, 38 UCCRS2d 996

Under the Uniform Commercial Code, title to goods passes at delivery, with only the reservation of a security interest by the seller permitted (Uniform Commercial Code, § 2-401, subd [1]); rules on chattel mortgages and conditional sales are now governed by article 9 of the code, and are considered as a single security device and, while under section 9-306 a security interest continues in any identifiable proceeds of collateral covered by the security agreement and a third party may be liable in conversion for paying those proceeds without satisfying the secured party's interest, there is no justification for extending the statute to include a cause of action within the meaning of identifiable proceeds. Accordingly, in a negligence action by plaintiff bank against defendant driver of a borrowed car in which the bank had a security interest, which car was destroyed in an accident, allegedly because of defendant's negligence, defendant was granted summary judgment since plaintiff failed to state a cause of action. Bank of New York v Margiotta (1979) 99 Misc. 2d 423, 416 N.Y.S.2d 493, 26 UCCRS 1032

Financing agent that loaned automobile dealer funds for purchase of inventory and had continuing security interest in proceeds from sale of inventory, although such proceeds were commingled with other funds in general account maintained by dealer in defendant bank, since (1) proceeds under CLS UCC § 9-306 are "identifiable" despite commingling when they can be traced under principles of trust accounting, (2) there was no compelling reason to reject "lowest intermediate balance" method of tracing whereby it was assumed that debtor spent proceeds in which there was security interest last, and (3) fact that financing agent was aware of, and permitted, commingling did not waive its right to proceeds; thus, financing agent would be granted summary judgment on its claim for priority as secured creditor, and bank's claim for setoff would be denied. General Motors Acceptance Corp. v Norstar Bank, N.A. (1988, Sup) 141 Misc. 2d 349, 532 N.Y.S.2d 685, 7 UCCRS2d 566

Creditor has valid security interest in that portion of personal injury settlement which represents settlement for damages suffered by secured vehicle in automobile accident, where installment contract which gave rise to perfected security interest in automobile provides that creditor shall have security interest in vehicle and any money or goods received for that vehicle. In re Territo (1983, BC ED NY) 32 BR 377, 11 BCD 20, 36 UCCRS 1762, later proceeding (1984, BC ED NY) 36 BR 667, CCH Bankr L Rptr P 69759

Where secured party had perfected security interest in all of debtor's present and future accounts and contract rights, including proceeds therefrom, where debtor obtained purchase orders for shoes from buyer and assigned purchase orders to export-import company, and where export-import company performed purchase orders and delivered shoes to buyer, account generated by export-import company's performance of debtor-buyer contract did not constitute "proceeds" of that contract within meaning of UCC § 9-306. American East India Corp. v Ideal Shoe Co. (1975, ED Pa) 400 F. Supp. 141, 17 UCCRS 527, affd without op (1978, CA3 Pa) 568 F.2d 768 and (superseded by statute as stated in Bank Brussels Lambert v Credit Lyonnais (Suisse) (2000, SD NY) 2000 US Dist LEXIS 1438)(applying New York law)

III. Insolvency Proceedings
10. In general

Where (1) plaintiff factor made cash advances to debtor, debtor as security assigned accounts receivable to plaintiff, and plaintiff perfected security interest in such accounts, and (2) debtor breached

factoring agreement (a) by assigning fictitious accounts to plaintiff, and (b) by not notifying legitimate account debtors to make payments to plaintiff, with result that debtor wrongfully received such payments, court held that since debtor had acted in illegal manner and plaintiff had right to identifiable proceeds of collateral under UCC § 9-306(4)(a) and (b), plaintiff was entitled to equitable relief in form of injunction and accounting despite its remedy at law for damages. Crocker Commercial Services, Inc. v Davan Enterprises, Inc. (1982, 1st Dept) 88 A.D.2d 877, 451 N.Y.S.2d 781, 34 UCCRS 328

Under a Securities Investor Protection Act of 1970 liquidation, where the creditor had posted cash collateral with the debtor broker-dealer in exchange for loaned securities, the debtor's commingled cash was not subject to a constructive trust and all of the debtor's cash was property of the estate and the creditor's security interest could be avoided by the trustee, because, while under N.Y. U.C.C. § 9-315(a)(2), (b)(2), (c), a security interest could attach to commingled proceeds, the creditor was unable to trace its cash. Ferris, Baker, Watts, Inc. v Stephenson (In re MJK Clearing) (2002, BC DC Minn) 286 BR 109, 49 UCCRS2d 11

IV. Rights as to Returned or Repossessed Goods
11. In general

In action against bank to recover possession of car that bank, which held perfected security interest in car, had repossessed and sold at public sale, court held (1) that plaintiff, who had had no knowledge of bank's security interest, could acquire under UCC § 9-306(2) no greater right to car than that possessed by marshal who had seized car and sold it at public auction; (2) that marshal's right to car was subject to bank's security interest; (3) that although bank had right under UCC §§ 9-306(2) and 9-503 to repossess car, notice of sale sent by bank to plaintiff was defective under UCC § 9-504(3) because it did not inform plaintiff of time and place of car's sale, and also gave only one day's notice of such sale; and (4) that since plaintiff was entitled to proper notification of sale, he could recover from bank, under UCC § 9-507(1), any loss caused by bank's failure to give proper notification. Fitzpatrick v Bank of N.Y. (1983, Sup App T) 124 Misc. 2d 732, 480 N.Y.S.2d 157, on remand (1984, Civ Ct) 125 Misc. 2d 1069, 480 N.Y.S.2d 864

§ 9-316.   Effect of Change in Governing Law

(a) General rule: effect on perfection of change in governing law. A security interest perfected pursuant to the law of the jurisdiction designated in Section 9-301(a) or 9-305(c) remains perfected until the earliest of:

(1) the time perfection would have ceased under the law of that jurisdiction;

(2) the expiration of four months after a change of the debtor's location to another jurisdiction; or

(3) the expiration of one year after a transfer of collateral to a person that thereby becomes a debtor and is located in another jurisdiction.

(b) Security interest perfected or unperfected under law of new jurisdiction. If a security interest described in subsection (a) becomes perfected under the law of the other jurisdiction before the earliest time or event described in that subsection, it remains perfected thereafter. If the security interest does not become perfected under the law of the other jurisdiction before the earliest time or event, it becomes unperfected and is deemed never to have been perfected as against a purchaser of the collateral for value.

(c) Possessory security interest in collateral moved to new jurisdiction. A possessory security interest in collateral, other than goods covered by a certificate of title and as-extracted collateral consisting of goods, remains continuously perfected if:

(1) the collateral is located in one jurisdiction and subject to a security interest perfected under the law of that jurisdiction;

(2) thereafter the collateral is brought into another jurisdiction; and

(3) upon entry into the other jurisdiction, the security interest is perfected under the law of the other jurisdiction.

(d) Goods covered by certificate of title from this state. Except as otherwise provided in subsection (e), a security interest in goods covered by a certificate of title which is perfected by any method under the law of another jurisdiction when the goods become covered by a certificate of title from this state remains perfected until the security interest would have become unperfected under the law of the other jurisdiction had the goods not become so covered.

(e) When subsection (d) security interest becomes unperfected against purchasers. A security interest described in subsection (d) becomes unperfected as against a purchaser of the goods for value and is deemed never to have been perfected as against a purchaser of the goods for value if the applicable requirements for perfection under Section 9-311(b) or 9-313 are not satisfied before the earlier of:

(1) the time the security interest would have become unperfected under the law of the other jurisdiction had the goods not become covered by a certificate of title from this state; or

(2) the expiration of four months after the goods had become so covered.

(f) Change in jurisdiction of bank, issuer, nominated person, securities intermediary, or commodity intermediary. A security interest in deposit accounts, letter-of-credit rights, or investment property which is perfected under the law of the bank's jurisdiction, the issuer's jurisdiction, a nominated person's jurisdiction, the securities intermediary's jurisdiction, or the commodity intermediary's jurisdiction, as applicable, remains perfected until the earlier of:

(1) the time the security interest would have become unperfected under the law of that jurisdiction; or

(2) the expiration of four months after a change of the applicable jurisdiction to another jurisdiction.

(g) Subsection (f) security interest perfected or unperfected under law of new jurisdiction. If a security interest described in subsection (f) becomes perfected under the law of the other jurisdiction before the earlier of the time or the end of the period described in that subsection, it remains perfected thereafter. If the security interest does not become perfected under the law of the other jurisdiction before the earlier of that time or the end of that period, it becomes unperfected and is deemed never to have been perfected as against a purchaser of the collateral for value.

(h) Effect on filed financing statement of change in governing law. The following rules apply to collateral to which a security interest attaches within four months after the debtor changes its location to another jurisdiction:

(1) A financing statement filed before the change pursuant to the law of the jurisdiction designated in Section 9-301(a) or 9-305(c) is effective to perfect a security interest in the collateral if the financing statement would have been effective to perfect a security interest in the collateral had the debtor not changed its location.

(2) If a security interest perfected by a financing statement that is effective under paragraph (1) becomes perfected under the law of the other jurisdiction before the earlier of the time the financing statement would have become ineffective under the law of the jurisdiction designated in Section 9-301(a) or 9-305(c) or the expiration of the four-month period, it remains perfected thereafter. If the security interest does not become perfected under the law of the other jurisdiction before the earlier time or event, it becomes unperfected and is deemed never to have been perfected as against a purchaser of the collateral for value.

(i) Effect of change in governing law on financing statement filed against original debtor. If a financing statement naming an original debtor is filed pursuant to the law of the jurisdiction designated in Section 9-301(a) or 9-305(c) and the new debtor is located in another jurisdiction, the following rules apply:

(1) The financing statement is effective to perfect a security interest in collateral in which the new debtor has or acquires rights before or within four months after the new debtor becomes bound under Section 9-203(d), if the financing statement would have been effective to perfect a security interest in the collateral had the collateral been acquired by the original debtor.

(2) A security interest that is perfected by the financing statement and which becomes perfected under the law of the other jurisdiction before the earlier of the expiration of the four month period or the time the financing statement would have become ineffective under the law of the jurisdiction designated in Section 9-301(a) or 9-305(c) remains perfected thereafter. A security interest that is perfected by the financing statement but which does not become perfected under the law of the other jurisdiction before the earlier time or event becomes unperfected and is deemed never to have been perfected as against a purchaser of the collateral for value.

History: Add, L 2001, ch 84, § 36, eff July 1, 2001.

Former § 9-316, add, L 1962, ch 553, eff Sept 27, 1964; repealed, L 2001, ch 84, § 36, eff July 1, 2001.

Amd, L 2014, ch 505, § 40, eff Dec 17, 2014.

_____

Subpart 3
Priority

History: Added, L 2001, ch 84, § 36, eff July 1, 2001.

§ 9-317. Interests That Take Priority over or Take Free of Security Interest or Agricultural Lien

(a) Conflicting security interests and rights of lien creditors. A security interest or agricultural lien is subordinate to the rights of:

(1) a person entitled to priority under Section 9-322; and

(2) except as otherwise provided in subsection (e), a person that becomes a lien creditor before the earlier of the time:

(A) the security interest or agricultural lien is perfected; or

(B) one of the conditions specified in Section 9-203(b)(3) is met and a financing statement covering the collateral is filed.

(b) Buyers that receive delivery. Except as otherwise provided in subsection (e), a buyer, other than a secured party, of tangible chattel paper, tangible documents, goods, instruments, or a certificated security takes free of a security interest or agricultural lien if the buyer gives value and receives delivery of the collateral without knowledge of the security interest or agricultural lien and before it is perfected.

(c) Lessees that receive delivery. Except as otherwise provided in subsection (e), a lessee of goods takes free of a security interest or agricultural lien if the lessee gives value and receives delivery of the collateral without knowledge of the security interest or agricultural lien and before it is perfected.

(d) Licensees and buyers of certain collateral. A licensee of a general intangible or a buyer, other than a secured party, of accounts, electronic chattel paper, electronic documents, general intangibles, or investment property other than a certificated security takes free of a security interest if the licensee or buyer gives value without knowledge of the security interest and before it is perfected.

(e) Purchase-money security interest. Except as otherwise provided in Sections 9-320 and 9-321, if a person files a financing statement with respect to a purchase-money security interest before or within 20 days after the debtor receives delivery of the collateral, the security interest takes priority over the rights of a buyer, lessee, or lien creditor which arise between the time the security interest attaches and the time of filing. The preceding sentence does not apply to cooperative interests.

History: Add, L 2001, ch 84, § 36, eff July 1, 2001.

Former § 9-317, add, L 1962, ch 553, eff Sept 27, 1964; repealed, L 2001, ch 84, § 36, eff July 1, 2001.

Amd, L 2014, ch 505, § 41, eff Dec 17, 2014.

CASE ANNOTATIONS

Pursuant to N.Y. U.C.C. Law § 9-317(b), one who purchases property in which another holds a security interest takes title free and clear of that interest, if the buyer gives value and receives delivery of the collateral without knowledge of the security interest before it is perfected. Snow Machs., Inc. v S. Slope Dev. Corp. (2002, A.D., 3d Dept) 754 N.Y.S.2d 383

UNDER FORMER § 9-301

I. Generally
1. In general

In action to recover possession of motor home that plaintiff secured party had sold to debtor under retail installment contract and security agreement, where (1) plaintiff, although authorized to file financing statement, did not do so before assigning installment contract and security agreement to bank, (2) after contract and security agreement had been assigned to bank, debtor transferred title to home to third-party purchaser, (3) such purchaser resold home to another third party who, in turn, resold it to defendant, (4) after first third-party purchaser had purchased home, bank filed financing statement that listed only original buyer of home as "debtor," and (5) on original buyer's default in making payments, bank reassigned installment contract and security agreement to plaintiff, which sought to replevy home from last third-party purchaser, court held (1) that even though bank was aware that title to home had been transferred to first third-party purchaser, bank nevertheless, on filing its financing statement, listed only original buyer as "debtor" on such statement, (2) that financing statement, as a result, failed under UCC §§ 9-402(1) and 9-105(1)(d) to identify "debtor" properly in situation where owner of collateral and obligor on financing agreement were not the same person, (3) that plaintiff's security interest was therefore not perfected, and (4) that since defendant third-party purchaser had purchased home out of ordinary course of business and without knowledge of plaintiff's unperfected security interest therein, defendant's ownership of home was free of such security interest under UCC § 9-301(1)(c). White Star Distributors, Inc. v Kennedy (1978, 4th Dept) 66 A.D.2d 1011, 411 N.Y.S.2d 751, 25 UCCRS 1446

Under UCC § 9-302(1)(d), a valid financing statement, properly filed, perfects a security interest in a motor vehicle. Until that time, under UCC § 9-301(1)(c), a buyer not in the ordinary course of business, to the extent that he gives value and receives delivery of the collateral without knowledge of the unperfected security interest, takes free of such interest. White Star Distributors, Inc. v Kennedy (1978, 4th Dept) 66 A.D.2d 1011, 411 N.Y.S.2d 751, 25 UCCRS 1446

2. Application

In special proceeding to determine rights to fund in connection with public improvement contract, under UCC § 9-301, surety who had posted payment bonds was not subject to filing requirements of code in regard to payments assigned to it by contractor under agreement of indemnity after contractor's default. Orciouli v August Bohl Contracting Co. (1981, 3d Dept) 80 A.D.2d 13, 437 N.Y.S.2d 792, 32 UCCRS 318

Issues arising between an assignee for the benefit of creditors and the owner of machinery allegedly leased to the debtor are not controlled by the Uniform Commercial Code, where the lease agreement had been signed prior to the effective date of the Code. In re General Assignment for benefit of Creditors of Merkel, Inc. (1965) 46 Misc. 2d 270, 259 N.Y.S.2d 514, 2 UCCRS 742

3. Knowledge of security interest as affecting priority

Misspelling of names on UCC-1 financing statement rendered plaintiff's security interest in debtor's crops unperfected where debtor "Peter Dragan, doing business as Dragan Grain Farms" was listed on statement as "Dragon Grain Farms and Peter Dragon, individually," but plaintiff's unperfected rights were superior to those of buyer who purchased crops with actual knowledge of plaintiff's security interest; thus, affidavit of plaintiff's treasurer, asserting that she wrote and phoned purchaser objecting to its purchase of crops, raised fact issue as to purchaser's actual knowledge of plaintiff's security interest. Reisdorf Bros., Inc. v Clinton Corn Processing Co. (1987, 4th Dept) 130 A.D.2d 951, 516 N.Y.S.2d 375, 3 UCCRS2d 1956

The fact that the corporation to which plaintiff bank made loans secured by a restaurant equipment security agreement had not yet filed its certificate of incorporation at the time the security agreement was entered into and the first advance made, does not constitute an affirmative defense to plaintiff's action to recover on its security interest from defendants, the purchasers of the restaurant equipment at a mortgage foreclosure sale, since the doctrine of de facto corporation is applicable, it being necessary in order to establish the existence of a de facto corporation that there is a law under which the corporation might be organized, an attempt to organize the corporation and an exercise of corporate powers thereunder; in any event, the corporation subsequently adopted the security agreement by accepting loans from plaintiff after the date the certificate of incoporation was filed; since it was the corporate entity which entered into the contract with plaintiff and not the corporation's president, individually, it was proper to list the corporation as the debtor on the financing statement, which sufficiently described the restaurant equipment covered by the security agreement (Uniform Commercial Code, § 9-402); accordingly, in the event that defendants are unable to prove that the equipment was owned by the corporation's president, individually, the restaurant equipment they purchased is subject to plaintiff's valid perfected security interest even assuming that they purchased the equipment for value and without knowledge of plaintiff's interest. Bankers Trust Co. v Zecher (1980) 103 Misc. 2d 777, 426 N.Y.S.2d 960, 29 UCCRS 323

Subsequent purchasers of aircraft, engine of which was subject to unperfected chattel mortgage, where purchase was made without knowledge of existence of chattel mortgage and before chattel mortgage was perfected, had superior rights to aircraft and its engine over holder of security. Aircraft Trading & Services, Inc. v Braniff, Inc. (1987, CA2 NY) 819 F.2d 1227, 3 UCCRS2d 1297, cert den (1987) 484 US 856, 98 L Ed 2d 118, 108 S Ct 163

4. – Knowledge immaterial

In dispute between assignee for benefit of creditors and bank claiming security interest in proceeds from sale of collateral, bank held superior interest under UCC § 9-301(3) where, under New York version of UCC § 9-402, change of name of debtor firm did not affect perfection of filing made under former name, regardless of whether bank had knowledge of change of name. In re Pasco Sales Co. (1974) 77 Misc. 2d 724, 354 N.Y.S.2d 402, 14 UCCRS 1059

II. Receivers In Equity and Assignees For Benefit of Creditor

5. Assignee over unperfected security interest

Assignee of rights of designated recipients of escrowed funds of bankrupt corporation under reorganization plan confirmed by Bankruptcy Court had priority to bankruptcy distributions, over claims of bank as judgment creditor of assignors, where assignment was made in 1989, assignee took possession of last note in 1990, and bank's claims did not arise until 1996. Norstar Bank, N.A. v Davis (1997, 4th Dept) 238 A.D.2d 892, 661 N.Y.S.2d 106

Dispute over priority to escrowed funds of bankrupt corporation under reorganization plan was not affected by either (1) "Consent Modification Agreement" by which designated recipient of funds conveyed its ownership interest in bankrupt corporation, or (2) Bankruptcy Court's confirmation of reorganization plan extinguishing recipient's stock rights in bankrupt corporation, where assignee's interest in bankruptcy distributions was not traceable to recipient's interest as stockholder in bankrupt corporation. Norstar Bank, N.A. v Davis (1997, 4th Dept) 238 A.D.2d 892, 661 N.Y.S.2d 106

Assignee of rights of designated recipients of escrowed funds of bankrupt corporation under reorganization plan confirmed by Bankruptcy Court was not collaterally estopped from asserting its claim of priority to bankruptcy distributions where bankruptcy proceeding concerned claims of creditors of bankrupt corporation, priority suit concerned claims of creditors of those creditors, there was thus no identity of issue, and there was no inconsistency between assignee's present claim and its position taken in bankruptcy proceeding. Norstar Bank, N.A. v Davis (1997, 4th Dept) 238 A.D.2d 892, 661 N.Y.S.2d 106

Under the terms of the above statute an unrecorded conditional sale is an unperfected security interest which is subordinate to the rights of an assignee for the benefit of creditors. In re General Assignment for Ben. of Creditors of Merkel, Inc. (1965) 45 Misc. 2d 753, 258 N.Y.S.2d 118, 2 UCCRS 489, revd on other grounds (1966, 2d Dept) 25 A.D.2d 764, 269 N.Y.S.2d 190, 3 UCCRS 459

6. Miscellaneous

A lease that reveals that it possesses none of the vital characteristics, such as a right or obligation on the part of the lessee to acquire title, which transmuted it from a lease into a conditional bill of sale, enables the lessor to recover the leased property from the lessee's assignee for benefit of creditors. In re General Assignment for benefit of Creditors of Merkel, Inc. (1965) 46 Misc. 2d 270, 259 N.Y.S.2d 514, 2 UCCRS 742

III. Lien Creditors

7. In general

Ten-day filing requirement for "super-perfection" under § 9-301(2) applies only to lien creditors and trustees in bankruptcy, not purchasers, and then only with respect to liens which precede actual filing date. Marine Midland Bank, N. A. v Smith Boys, Inc. (1985, Sup) 129 Misc. 2d 37, 492 N.Y.S.2d 355, 41 UCCRS 1843

8. Lien creditor over unperfected security interest

Under the statute, a person, who becomes a lien creditor of the conditional vendee without knowledge of the conditional vendor's security interest and prior to the perfection of that security interest, would take priority over the conditional vendor with respect to interest in the subject property. L. B. Smith, Inc. v Foley (1972, WD NY) 341 F. Supp. 810, 72-1 USTC P 9230, 11 UCCRS 41, 29 AFTR 2d 567

Under UCC § 9-301(4), even a lien creditor would take subject to valid security interest obtained by surety of two construction companies in contract rights of such companies where (1) surety, instead of allowing its debtors to default, agreed to advance more than two million dollars in order to enable debtors to complete their bonded construction projects, and (2) such advance was made "pursuant to a commitment entered into without knowledge of the lien." John G. Lambros Co. v Aetna Casualty & Surety Co. (1979, SD NY) 468 F. Supp. 624, 27 UCCRS 266 (applying New York law)

9. – Lease intended as security interest

An instrument designated a machinery lease contract providing for semi-annual rental payments over a 5-year term and for an option to purchase at the end of the term for a sum less than 10 percent of the aggregate rental, is a security interest and not a lease, and if not recorded, is an unperfected interest as against a lien creditor without knowledge of the instrument. In re General Assignment for Ben. of Creditors of Merkel, Inc. (1965) 45 Misc. 2d 753, 258 N.Y.S.2d 118, 2 UCCRS 489, revd on other grounds (1966, 2d Dept) 25 A.D.2d 764, 269 N.Y.S.2d 190, 3 UCCRS 459

10. Place of filing

Where financing statements filed with secretary of state alone and not filed locally did not protect security interest, lien creditor had priority over holder of security interests. Package Machinery Co. v Cosden Oil & Chemical Co. (1976, 2d Dept) 51 A.D.2d 771, 380 N.Y.S.2d 248, 18 UCCRS 1316

11. Judgment lien creditor over unperfected security interest

Judgment creditor had prior right to proceeds due under promissory note held by judgment debtor, even though third party had

UCC

entered into factoring agreement with debtor prior to judgment which had given third party security interest in all debtor's "receivables," including proceeds of note, where note did not constitute chattel paper and third party failed to take possession of note in order to perfect whatever security interest it might have had by virtue of agreement with debtor. Berkowitz v Chavo Int'l, Inc. (1989) 74 N.Y.2d 144, 544 N.Y.S.2d 569, 542 N.E.2d 1086, 9 UCCRS2d 4, reconsideration den (1989) 74 N.Y.2d 893, 547 N.Y.S.2d 850, 547 N.E.2d 105

IV. Secured Interests

12. In general

Under UCC § 9-302(1)(d), a valid financing statement, properly filed, perfects a security interest in a motor vehicle. Until that time, under UCC § 9-301(1)(c), a buyer not in the ordinary course of business, to the extent that he gives value and receives delivery of the collateral without knowledge of the unperfected security interest, takes free of such interest. White Star Distributors, Inc. v Kennedy (1978, 4th Dept) 66 A.D.2d 1011, 411 N.Y.S.2d 751, 25 UCCRS 1446

In action to recover possession of motor home that plaintiff secured party had sold to debtor under retail installment contract and security agreement, where (1) plaintiff, although authorized to file financing statement, did not do so before assigning installment contract and security agreement to bank, (2) after contract and security agreement had been assigned to bank, debtor transferred title to home to third-party purchaser, (3) such purchaser resold home to another third party who, in turn, resold it to defendant, (4) after first third-party purchaser had purchased home, bank filed financing statement that listed only original buyer of home as "debtor," and (5) on original buyer's default in making payments, bank reassigned installment contract and security agreement to plaintiff, which sought to replevy home from last third-party purchaser, court held (1) that even though bank was aware that title to home had been transferred to first third-party purchaser, bank nevertheless, on filing its financing statement, listed only original buyer as "debtor" on such statement, (2) that financing statement, as a result, failed under UCC §§ 9-402(1) and 9-105(1)(d) to identify "debtor" properly in situation where owner of collateral and obligor on financing agreement were not the same person, (3) that plaintiff's security interest was therefore not perfected, and (4) that since defendant third-party purchaser had purchased home out of ordinary course of business and without knowledge of plaintiff's unperfected security interest therein, defendant's ownership of home was free of such security interest under UCC § 9-301(1)(c). White Star Distributors, Inc. v Kennedy (1978, 4th Dept) 66 A.D.2d 1011, 411 N.Y.S.2d 751, 25 UCCRS 1446

The rights of a holder of a perfected security interest are superior to this of a lien creditor, and are also superior to those of a third party purchaser at a sheriff's sale. General Motors Acceptance Corp. v Stotsky (1969) 60 Misc. 2d 451, 303 N.Y.S.2d 463, 6 UCCRS 844

Fact that assignee of security agreement did not file financing statement within 10 days after collateral came into possession of initial debtor was irrelevant with respect to purchaser of consumer goods who acquired collateral after date of filing. Marine Midland Bank, N. A. v Smith Boys, Inc. (1985, Sup) 129 Misc. 2d 37, 492 N.Y.S.2d 355, 41 UCCRS 1843

Where a defendant took possession of the property pursuant to the lease agreement, and not the contract of sale, the defendant was a lessee, not a buyer, and N.Y. U.C.C. Law § 9-317(b) was inapplicable; although N.Y. U.C.C. Law § 1-201(14) provides that "delivery" refers to a voluntary transfer of possession, to benefit under N.Y. U.C.C. Law § 9-317(b), the transfer of possession must be clearly referable to the ultimate purchase and not to a grant of temporary possession under a lease agreement. Snow Machs., Inc. v S. Slope Dev. Corp. (2002, A.D., 3d Dept) 754 N.Y.S.2d 383

13. Perfected security interest over lien creditor

Where secured party's security interest in collateral was perfected at time of assignment and account debtor's assignee had notice of assignment, secured party's rights were protected by continuation statement unilaterally filed by secured party within time limits prescribed by Code, so that secured party's claim to collateral was superior to that of assignee as lien creditor. In re Marta Cooperative, Inc. (1973) 74 Misc. 2d 612, 344 N.Y.S.2d 676, 12 UCCRS 955

14. – Assignments

Where New York debtor assigned accounts receivable to New York creditor under terms of security agreement and secured creditor complied with all steps required by UCC to perfect its security

interest in such accounts, New York creditor's perfected security interest attached as soon as accounts came into existence and took priority over interest of Colorado creditor, as lien creditor under writ of attachment, with respect to accounts owed debtor by Colorado account debtors. Barocas v Bohemia Import Co. (1974) 33 Colo App 263, 518 P2d 850, 14 UCCRS 191 (applying New York law)

15. Perfected security interest over unperfected

Finance company which takes possession of debtor's stock certificate and proprietary lease prior to time federal tax lien is filed has perfected security interest and interest in proceeds of sale of debtor's stock in co-operative apartment corporation superior to federal tax lien since under Uniform Commercial Code § 9-301 shares in co-operative apartment are personal property for purposes of Uniform Commercial Code. Superior Financial Corp. v Haskell (1983, SD NY) 556 F. Supp. 199, 83-1 USTC P 9211, 35 UCCRS 996, 51 AFTR 2d 950

16. Perfected security interest over judgment creditor

Where petitioner's security interest was perfected by proper filing, it thereupon took priority over all unfiled and unperfected interests, including the rights of judgment creditors who thereafter issued execution, since under Rule 5202(a) CPLR such creditors are perfected only by the issuance of execution; and, upon default in payments due on the indebtedness secured by the interest, petitioner became entitled to immediate possession of the collateral under the provisions of § 9-503. William Iselin & Co. v Burgess & Leigh Ltd. (1967) 52 Misc. 2d 821, 276 N.Y.S.2d 659, 3 UCCRS 1168

Once purchase money security agreement is entered into and financing statement evidencing that agreement is filed in accordance with requirements of Code, then secured party acting in good faith acquires rights which are superior to subsequent judgment creditors and third party purchasers. General Motors Acceptance Corp. v Stotsky (1969) 60 Misc. 2d 451, 303 N.Y.S.2d 463, 6 UCCRS 844

Since security interests perfected by proper filing take priority over all unfiled and unperfected interests (Uniform Commercial Code, § 9-301) and liens of judgment creditors are perfected only by the issuance of an execution pursuant to CPLR 5202 (subd [a]), the lien of plaintiff judgment creditor levied upon against defendant debtor corporation's bank accounts in June, 1977 was subsequent and subordinate to the security interest filed and perfected in October, 1975 by defendant's bank under an accounts receivable agreement by which defendant assigned its accounts receivable to the bank as security for indebtedness and upon defendant's default the bank was entitled under such agreement and section 151 of the Debtor and Creditor Law to apply the funds in defendant's cash collateral, general and payroll accounts to defendant's debt without regard to plaintiff's levy against them. Cibro Petroleum Products, Inc. v Fowler Finishing Co. (1977) 92 Misc. 2d 450, 400 N.Y.S.2d 322, 23 UCCRS 517

Security interest of bank in debtor's cash collateral account, which was perfected by proper filing on October 20, 1975, had priority under UCC § 9-301(1)(b) over lien of creditor who obtained judgment against debtor and had execution issue on judgment on June 2, 1977 against debtor's cash collateral account with bank, since under state law, lien of judgment creditor could not be perfected until issuance of execution on judgment. Cibro Petroleum Products, Inc. v Fowler Finishing Co. (1977) 92 Misc. 2d 450, 400 N.Y.S.2d 322, 23 UCCRS 517 (vacating execution levy made by judgment creditor on cash collateral account in suit)

17. Unperfected security interests as between parties

In action involving priority of rights in debtor's collateral (corn), where plaintiff made operating advances to debtor doing business as "Dragon Grain Farms" in exchange for security interest in debtor's 1981 corn crop, and plaintiff's filed financing statement listed debtor as "Dragon Grain Farms and Peter Dragon, individually," on reversing trial court's grant of summary judgment for defendant buyers, (1) misspelling of debtor's own name and also his d/b/a name was so seriously misleading, within meaning of UCC § 9-402(1) and (8), as to render plaintiff's security interest in debtor's corn crop unperfected; (2) although plaintiff's security interest was unperfected, plaintiff's rights would still be superior under UCC § 9-301(1)(c) to rights of buyer who purchased debtor's corn with actual knowledge of plaintiff's security interest therein; and (3) evidence in record of defendant buyers' actual knowledge of plaintiff's security interest was sufficient to preclude grant of summary judgment in their favor. Reisdorf Bros., Inc. v Clinton Corn Processing Co. (1987, 4th Dept) 130 A.D.2d 951, 516 N.Y.S.2d 375, 3 UCCRS2d 1956

V. Tax Liens

18. In general

United States was within "lien creditor" definition of UCC § 9-301 where it had filed its tax lien and had what was in effect a judgment at the time it made its tax assessment. L. B. Smith, Inc. v Foley (1972, WD NY) 341 F. Supp. 810, 72-1 USTC P 9230, 11 UCCRS 41, 29 AFTR 2d 567

19. Tax lien creditors versus perfected security interest; place of filing

Since possessory security interest in cooperative-apartment stock is similar to possessory security interest in ordinary chattel paper, which under UCC § 9-305 requires no filing for perfection, creditor's security interest in apartment stock-which was perfected under UCC § 9-305 when creditor acquired possession of stock certificate from debtor in 1975-took priority, under federal income-tax law (26 USCS § 6323(h)(1)) and UCC § 9-301(3)(b), over federal income-tax lien on debtor's property which did not become effective against holder of valid security interest until filing of notice of such tax lien in 1977. Superior Financial Corp. v Haskell (1983, SD NY) 556 F. Supp. 199, 83-1 USTC P 9211, 35 UCCRS 996, 51 AFTR 2d 950 (applying New York law)

VI. Trustee in Bankruptcy

20. In general

Ten-day filing requirement for "super-perfection" under § 9-301(2) applies only to lien creditors and trustees in bankruptcy, not purchasers, and then only with respect to liens which precede actual filing date. Marine Midland Bank, N. A. v Smith Boys, Inc. (1985, Sup) 129 Misc. 2d 37, 492 N.Y.S.2d 355, 41 UCCRS 1843

On application for order of seizure of boat (collateral), which was in possession of one defendant, prior to commencing action to recover boat's possession, plaintiff's failure to file within 10 days after debtor took possession of boat was not relevant, since "super-perfection" filing requirement of UCC § 9-301(2) applies only to lien creditors and trustees in bankruptcy with respect to liens that preceded actual filing date. Marine Midland Bank, N. A. v Smith Boys, Inc. (1985, Sup) 129 Misc. 2d 37, 492 N.Y.S.2d 355, 41 UCCRS 1843

§ 9-318. No Interest Retained in Right to Payment That Is Sold; Rights and Title of Seller of Account or Chattel Paper with Respect to Creditors and Purchasers

(a) Seller retains no interest. A debtor that has sold an account, chattel paper, payment intangible, or promissory note does not retain a legal or equitable interest in the collateral sold.

(b) Deemed rights of debtor if buyer's security interest unperfected. For purposes of determining the rights of creditors of, and purchasers for value of an account or chattel paper from, a debtor that has sold an account or chattel paper, while the buyer's security interest is unperfected, the debtor is deemed to have rights and title to the account or chattel paper identical to those the debtor sold.

History: Add, L 2001, ch 84, § 36, eff July 1, 2001.

Add, L 1962, ch 553; amd, L 1977, ch 866, § 24, eff July 2, 1978; repealed, L 2001, ch 84, § 36, eff July 1, 2001.

CASE ANNOTATIONS

When part of the collateral pledged in a security agreement was a promissory note containing an arbitration agreement, the lender who executed the security agreement was an assignee of its borrower's interests under the promissory note and was subject to the arbitration clause. Sea Spray Holdings, Ltd. v Pali Fin. Group, Inc. (2003, SD NY) 269 F. Supp. 2d 356, costs/fees proceeding, application gr, in part (2003, SD NY) 2003 US Dist LEXIS 13980

§ 9-319. Rights and Title of Consignee with Respect to Creditors and Purchasers

(a) Consignee has consignor's rights. Except as otherwise provided in subsection (b), for purposes of determining the rights of creditors of, and purchasers for value of goods from, a consignee, while the goods are in the possession of the consignee, the consignee is deemed to have rights and title to the goods identical to those the consignor had or had power to transfer.

(b) Applicability of other law. For purposes of determining the rights of a creditor of a consignee, law other than this article determines the rights and title of a consignee while goods are in the consignee's possession if, under this part, a perfected security interest held by the consignor would have priority over the rights of the creditor.

History: Add, L 2001, ch 84, § 36, eff July 1, 2001.

CASE ANNOTATIONS

Where dispute centered on who had superior rights to work of art that had been displayed in debtor's gallery, trustee was not entitled to summary judgment on claim it had superior right as assignee of creditor bank's perfected lien because trustee did not meet his burden to prove that definition of "consignment" under New York's Uniform Commercial Code had been met by transaction at issue. Jacobs v Kraken Inv. Ltd. (In re Salander-O'Reilly Galleries, LLC) (2014, BC SD NY) 506 BR 600, 59 BCD 82

§ 9-320. Buyer of Goods

(a) Buyer in ordinary course of business. Except as otherwise provided in subsection (e), a buyer in ordinary course of business, other than a person buying farm products from a person engaged in farming operations, takes free of a security interest created by the buyer's seller, even if the security interest is perfected and the buyer knows of its existence.

(b) Buyer of consumer goods. Except as otherwise provided in subsection (e), a buyer of goods from a person who used or bought the goods for use primarily for personal, family, or household purposes takes free of a security interest, even if perfected, if the buyer buys:

(1) without knowledge of the security interest;

(2) for value;

(3) primarily for the buyer's personal, family, or household purposes; and

(4) before the filing of a financing statement covering the goods.

(c) Effectiveness of filing for subsection (b). To the extent that it affects the priority of a security interest over a buyer of goods under subsection (b), the period of effectiveness of a filing made in the jurisdiction in which the seller is located is governed by Section 9-316(a) and (b).

(d) Buyer in ordinary course of business at wellhead or minehead. A buyer in ordinary course of business buying oil, gas, or other minerals at the wellhead or minehead or after extraction takes free of an interest arising out of an encumbrance.

(e) **Possessory security interest not affected.** Subsections (a) and (b) do not affect a security interest in goods in the possession of the secured party under Section 9-313.

History: Add, L 2001, ch 84, § 36, eff July 1, 2001.

CASE ANNOTATIONS

UNDER FORMER § 9-307
1. Who "creates" security interest
2. Type of collateral
3. Buyers in ordinary course
4. – Persons protected
5. – Knowledge of security interest
6. – Knowledge of violation
7. – Security interests as to which buyer takes free
8. – Security interests as to which buyer takes subject
9. – Conversion action or the like
10. Buyers of consumer goods
11. Buyers not in ordinary course; future advances

Receipt of a creditor's notice of a secured loan, together with a warning that making payments to the debtor instead of to the creditor would have constituted a violation of the security interest, deprived a transferee of the right to claim status as a buyer in the ordinary course of business; the transferee's subsequent acceptance of deliveries from the debtor, and payments to the debtor for those deliveries, could not have been made in good faith. SK Global Am., Inc. v John Roberts, Inc. (2004, A.D., 1st Dept) 778 N.Y.S.2d 5

Under New Jersey law, which governed a dealer's agreement between a financing company and a New Jersey auto dealer, because the dealer was not licensed to sell motor vehicles in New Jersey, and, as a leasing company, it did not hold the subject cars as part of its sales inventory, when the dealer defaulted on a dealer's agreement with the financing company, the trial court properly found that the company was not a buyer in the ordinary course of business, as defined by N.Y. U.C.C. §§ 1-201(9) and 9-320(a); thus, the possessory interest sought by the company upon the dealer's default was subject to the security interests held by three creditors. Hann Fin. Serv. Corp. v Republic Auto Credit Group, LLC (2005, A.D., 2d Dept) 794 N.Y.S.2d 423

UNDER FORMER § 9-307

1. Who "creates" security interest
Court erred in granting buyer's motion for summary judgment dismissing action to enforce security interest in excavator where fact question existed as to whether security interest was created by buyer. John Deere Indus. Equip. Co. v Daman Cable Specialists (1996, 4th Dept) 233 A.D.2d 907, 649 N.Y.S.2d 262

Security interest is "created" only by party granting interest. Marine Midland Bank, N. A. v Smith Boys, Inc. (1985, Sup) 129 Misc. 2d 37, 492 N.Y.S.2d 355, 41 UCCRS 1843

2. Type of collateral
A buyer takes free of a security interest in goods created by a seller who is in the business of selling goods of that kind, even if the interest is perfected, if the buyer merely knows that there is a security interest which covers the goods, but takes subject to the interest if he knows, in addition, that the sale is in violation of some term in the security agreement not waived by the words or conduct of the secured party (Uniform Commercial Code, § 1-201, subd [9]; § 9-307, subd [1]), although it is not incumbent upon the buyer to make a search for any possible security interests; and, a buyer who takes free of a perfected security interest takes free of an unperfected one as well. European-American Bank & Trust Co. v Sheriff of County of Nassau (1978) 97 Misc. 2d 549, 411 N.Y.S.2d 851, 25 UCCRS 1137

3. Buyers in ordinary course
Buyers were entitled to summary judgment in lender's action for conversion, replevin, unjust enrichment, fraud, and civil conspiracy because they purchased the vehicles at issue in the ordinary course of business under N.Y. U.C.C. Law § 1-201(9), 9-320(a), and the lender failed to show a misrepresentation or a fiduciary relationship. Nissan Motor Acceptance Corp. v Scialpi (2012, 2d Dept) 94 App Div 3d 1067.

The finance company to which the seller has assigned the sales contract made with a buyer in ordinary course prevails over the lender financing the seller. Chrysler Credit Corp. v Sharp (1968) 56 Misc. 2d 261, 288 N.Y.S.2d 525, 5 UCCRS 226

Insurance company which, as part of claim settlement, obtained title to car covered by security interest, was liable to secured party for unpaid balance under UCC § 9-201, even though car was total loss and had no value; insurance company was not buyer of automobiles in ordinary course of business under UCC § 9-307. General Motors Acceptance Corp. v Allstate Ins. Co. (1974) 77 Misc. 2d 849, 355 N.Y.S.2d 78, 14 UCCRS 1229

Where (1) plaintiff purchased used car from dealer, (2) such car, prior to plaintiff's purchase, was subject of security agreement that defendant secured party had perfected by filing of financing statement, and (3) original purchaser of car sold it to third person, who in turn resold it to dealer from whom plaintiff purchased it, court held (1) that although plaintiff was buyer in ordinary course of business under UCC § 9-307(1), he was not protected in his purchase because security interest in car had been created by original purchaser of car, instead of plaintiff's seller, and (2) that plaintiff was also not protected under UCC § 9-307(2), since secured party had filed financing statement covering car before plaintiff purchased it. Lindsley v Financial Collection Agencies, Inc. (1978) 97 Misc. 2d 263, 410 N.Y.S.2d 1002, 25 UCCRS 889

When UCC §§ 1-201(9) and 9-307(1) are read together, the result, as noted in Official Comment 2, is that the buyer takes free if he merely knows that there is a security interest that covers the goods, but that he takes subject to such interest if he knows, in addition, that the sale was in violation of some term in the security agreement that was not waived by the words or conduct of the secured party. European-American Bank & Trust Co. v Sheriff of County of Nassau (1978) 97 Misc. 2d 549, 411 N.Y.S.2d 851, 25 UCCRS 1137

4. – Persons protected
Sale of unfinished textile fabrics by converter (i.e., one who finishes textiles into dyed and patterned fabrics) to another converter was in ordinary course of first converter's business within meaning of UCC § 9-307(1), even though predominant business purpose of converters was converting unfinished textiles into finished fabrics, and thus second converter took fabric free from manufacturer's security interest in textiles, although manufacturer's security interest was perfected by possession of goods under UCC § 9-305, where it was shown that converters often purchased unfinished textiles in excess of their requirements, selling such excess through brokers to other converters, and that converters buy such goods if price is satisfactory or particular goods are not available from manufacturers, both of which conditions were satisfied in present case. Tanbro Fabrics Corp. v Deering Milliken, Inc. (1976) 39 N.Y.2d 632, 385 N.Y.S.2d 260, 350 N.E.2d 590, 19 UCCRS 385

5. – Knowledge of security interest
Where plaintiff bought truck from a merchant in the ordinary course of business, without knowledge of a security agreement entered into by the seller and later assigned to a bank, in repossessing the truck after the sale, bank was liable for conversion and damages. Makransky v Long Island Reo Truck Co. (1968) 58 Misc. 2d 338, 295 N.Y.S.2d 240, 5 UCCRS 1204

A buyer takes free of a security interest in goods created by a seller who is in the business of selling goods of that kind, even if the interest is perfected, if the buyer merely knows that there is a security interest which covers the goods, but takes subject to the interest if he knows, in addition, that the sale is in violation of some term in the security agreement not waived by the words or conduct of the secured party (Uniform Commercial Code, § 1-201, subd [9]; § 9-307, subd [1]), although it is not incumbent upon the buyer to make a search for any possible security interests; and, a buyer who takes free of a perfected security interest takes free of an unperfected one as well. European-American Bank & Trust Co. v Sheriff of County of Nassau (1978) 97 Misc. 2d 549, 411 N.Y.S.2d 851, 25 UCCRS 1137

Where (1) buyer purchased three boats under floor-plan arrangement whereby bank, as secured party, paid purchase price directly to seller and received from buyer security agreement and financing statement, and also a trust receipt for each boat, (2) financing statement was duly filed on April 24, 1978, thereby perfecting secured party's security interest in boats, (3) second bank claimed that boats were still property of seller and that second bank bank had previously perfected security interest in all of seller's property, including such boats, and (4) second bank also contended that sale of boats constituted bulk sale that was void as to second bank's rights, court held (1) that under definition of "bulk transfer" in UCC § 6-102(1) as a transfer, not in ordinary course of transferor's business, of major part of transferor's materials, merchandise, or other inventory, sale of boats in suit was not bulk transfer, (2) that such sale, instead of being an extraordinary sale, was only part of a continuing pattern of boat purchases that buyer had been making from seller for more than a year, (3) that such purchases involved deliveries that had been made on a regular basis, for a fair consideration, and without any intent to defraud creditors, (4) that under UCC § 1-201(9), buyer of boats was buyer in ordinary course of business, and (5) that since buyer had purchased boats without any knowledge of second bank's security interest therein, buyer under UCC § 9-307(1) took them free of such security interest. European-American Bank & Trust Co. v Sheriff of County of Nassau (1978) 97 Misc. 2d 549, 411 N.Y.S.2d 851, 25 UCCRS 1137

6. – Knowledge of violation

A buyer takes free of a security interest in goods created by a seller who is in the business of selling goods of that kind, even if the interest is perfected, if the buyer merely knows that there is a security interest which covers the goods, but takes subject to the interest if he knows, in addition, that the sale is in violation of some term in the security agreement not waived by the words or conduct of the secured party (Uniform Commercial Code, § 1-201, subd [9]; § 9-307, subd [1]), although it is not incumbent upon the buyer to make a search for any possible security interests; and, a buyer who takes free of a perfected security interest takes free of an unperfected one as well. European-American Bank & Trust Co. v Sheriff of County of Nassau (1978) 97 Misc. 2d 549, 411 N.Y.S.2d 851, 25 UCCRS 1137

7. – Security interests as to which buyer takes free

Where savings and loan association, entered into floor-plan agreement with mobile-home dealer under which association would pay manufacturer for each home delivered to dealer, retain invoice and certificate of origin of each delivered unit, and dealer would execute demand note and security interest in delivered unit to association which it would hold until it received payment from dealer; where buyers of mobile home from dealer subsequently executed instalment contract reciting payment of specified down payment, delivery and acceptance of home, and granting by buyers of security interest therein; and where dealer assigned such contract to corporation that assigned it to defendant bank, and money paid for contract by defendant bank was transmitted to dealer who breached his obligation to savings and loan association and absconded, in action by subrogee of rights of savings and loan association against defendant bank to determine priority of security interests in such home, (1) buyers of home were good-faith purchasers in ordinary course of business under UCC § 1-201(9) who took home under UCC § 9-307(1) free of subrogee's security interest therein; (2) defendant bank's security interest in home therefore had priority over subrogee's security interest; and (3) subrogee's security interest attached to proceeds of sale in hands of absconding dealer. Integrity Ins. Co. v Marine Midland Bank-Western (1977) 90 Misc. 2d 868, 396 N.Y.S.2d 319, 22 UCCRS 391

A buyer takes free of a security interest in goods created by a seller who is in the business of selling goods of that kind, even if the interest is perfected, if the buyer merely knows that there is a security interest which covers the goods, but takes subject to the interest if he knows, in addition, that the sale is in violation of some term in the security agreement not waived by the words or conduct of the secured party (Uniform Commercial Code, § 1-201, subd [9]; § 9-307, subd [1]), although it is not incumbent upon the buyer to make a search for any possible security interests; and, a buyer who takes free of a perfected security interest takes free of an unperfected one as well. European-American Bank & Trust Co. v Sheriff of County of Nassau (1978) 97 Misc. 2d 549, 411 N.Y.S.2d 851, 25 UCCRS 1137

On application for order of seizure of boat (collateral), which was in possession of one defendant, prior to commencing action to recover boat's possession, although person to whom original seller resold boat was buyer in ordinary course of business, he did not take free of plaintiff's security interest under UCC § 9-307(1), since such interest had been created by debtor (original buyer of boat), rather than by original seller, and as a result, plaintiff assignee had priority of right to boat. Marine Midland Bank, N. A. v Smith Boys, Inc. (1985, Sup) 129 Misc. 2d 37, 492 N.Y.S.2d 355, 41 UCCRS 1843

8. – Security interests as to which buyer takes subject

Plaintiff, who purchased a used automobile from a car dealer which was subject to an outstanding security instrument lien created by an earlier owner, is not entitled to protection from the prior perfected security interest afforded to consumers under subdivision (1) of section 9-307 of the Uniform Commercial Code which provides that a "buyer in ordinary course of business... takes free of a security interest created by his seller", since the security interest in question was not created by plaintiff's seller, but was instead created by an earlier owner. Plaintiff is not entitled to any additional protection from the existing security interest since a finance statement covering the automobile had been filed. (Uniform Commercial Code, § 9-307, subd [2].) Accordingly, plaintiff's purchase from the car dealer is subject to the perfected security interest. Lindsley v Financial Collection Agencies, Inc. (1978) 97 Misc. 2d 263, 410 N.Y.S.2d 1002, 25 UCCRS 889

Where (1) plaintiff purchased used car from dealer, (2) such car, prior to plaintiff's purchase, was subject of security agreement that defendant secured party had perfected by filing of financing statement, and (3) original purchaser of car sold it to third person, who in turn resold it to dealer from whom plaintiff purchased it, court held (1) that although plaintiff was buyer in ordinary course of business under UCC § 9-307(1), he was not protected in his purchase because security interest in car had been created by original purchaser of car, instead of plaintiff's seller, and (2) that plaintiff was also not protected under UCC § 9-307(2), since secured party had filed financing statement covering car before plaintiff purchased it. Lindsley v Financial Collection Agencies, Inc. (1978) 97 Misc. 2d 263, 410 N.Y.S.2d 1002, 25 UCCRS 889

A buyer takes free of a security interest in goods created by a seller who is in the business of selling goods of that kind, even if the interest is perfected, if the buyer merely knows that there is a security interest which covers the goods, but takes subject to the interest if he knows, in addition, that the sale is in violation of some term in the security agreement not waived by the words or conduct of the secured party (Uniform Commercial Code, § 1-201, subd [9]; § 9-307, subd [1]), although it is not incumbent upon the buyer to make a search for any possible security interests; and, a buyer who takes free of a perfected security interest takes free of an unperfected one as well. European-American Bank & Trust Co. v Sheriff of County of Nassau (1978) 97 Misc. 2d 549, 411 N.Y.S.2d 851, 25 UCCRS 1137

9. – Conversion action or the like

Where plaintiff bought truck from a merchant in the ordinary course of business, without knowledge of a security agreement entered into by the seller and later assigned to a bank, in repossessing the truck after the sale, bank was liable for conversion and damages. Makransky v Long Island Reo Truck Co. (1968) 58 Misc. 2d 338, 295 N.Y.S.2d 240, 5 UCCRS 1204

10. Buyers of consumer goods

The fact that title has not yet been transferred as between the dealer and the consumer does not prevent the latter from being regarded as a buyer in the ordinary course of business, insofar as the secured creditor of the dealer is concerned, where the transaction between the dealer and the consumer is ordinary or typical in the trade. Chrysler Credit Corp. v Sharp (1968) 56 Misc. 2d 261, 288 N.Y.S.2d 525, 5 UCCRS 226

Where the buyer of an automobile cannot make the cash down payment but trades in her automobile and makes a specific promise as to when she will pay the cash she is to be deemed in ordinary course. Chrysler Credit Corp. v Sharp (1968) 56 Misc. 2d 261, 288 N.Y.S.2d 525, 5 UCCRS 226

Where plaintiff bought truck from a merchant in the ordinary course of business, without knowledge of a security agreement entered into by the seller and later assigned to a bank, in repossessing the truck after the sale, bank was liable for conversion and damages. Makransky v Long Island Reo Truck Co. (1968) 58 Misc. 2d 338, 295 N.Y.S.2d 240, 5 UCCRS 1204

11. Buyers not in ordinary course; future advances

Auto wholesaler purchased autos in which bank held security interest from auto leasing and rental company; held, this was not purchase from person engaged in business of selling cars and wholesaler was not entitled to "buyer in ordinary course of business" status. Hempstead Bank v Andy's Car Rental System, Inc. (1970, 2d Dept) 35 A.D.2d 35, 312 N.Y.S.2d 317, 7 UCCRS 932

One who buys an auto from a seller who is not engaged in the selling of autos as a systematic economic enterprise cannot qualify as a "buyer in the ordinary course of business" within UCC § 9-307. Newton-Waltham Bank & Trust Co. v Bergen Motors, Inc. (1971) 68 Misc. 2d 228, 327 N.Y.S.2d 77, affd (1972) 75 Misc. 2d 103, 347 N.Y.S.2d 568

UCC

Subsequent purchasers of aircraft, engine of which was subject to unperfected chattel mortgage, where purchase was made without knowledge of existence of chattel mortgage and before chattel mortgage was perfected, had superior rights to aircraft and its engine over holder of security. Aircraft Trading & Services, Inc. v Braniff, Inc. (1987, CA2 NY) 819 F.2d 1227, 3 UCCRS2d 1297, cert den (1987) 484 US 856, 98 L Ed 2d 118, 108 S Ct 163

State law determines priority as between holder of unperfected lien on airplane engine and subsequent purchasers of airplane, even though federal law requires that all interests in aircraft or aircraft parts be recorded with FAA. Aircraft Trading & Services, Inc. v Braniff, Inc. (1987, CA2 NY) 819 F.2d 1227, 3 UCCRS2d 1297, cert den (1987) 484 US 856, 98 L Ed 2d 118, 108 S Ct 163

§ 9-321. Licensee of General Intangible and Lessee of Goods In Ordinary Course of Business

(a) "Licensee in ordinary course of business." In this section, "licensee in ordinary course of business" means a person that becomes a licensee of a general intangible in good faith, without knowledge that the license violates the rights of another person in the general intangible, and in the ordinary course from a person in the business of licensing general intangibles of that kind. A person becomes a licensee in the ordinary course if the license to the person comports with the usual or customary practices in the kind of business in which the licensor is engaged or with the licensor's own usual or customary practices.

(b) Rights of licensee in ordinary course of business. A licensee in ordinary course of business takes its rights under a nonexclusive license free of a security interest in the general intangible created by the licensor, even if the security interest is perfected and the licensee knows of its existence.

(c) Rights of lessee in ordinary course of business. A lessee in ordinary course of business takes its leasehold interest free of a security interest in the goods created by the lessor, even if the security interest is perfected and the lessee knows of its existence.

History: Add, L 2001, ch 84, § 36, eff July 1, 2001.

§ 9-322. Priorities among Conflicting Security Interests in And Agricultural Liens on Same Collateral

(a) General priority rules. Except as otherwise provided in this section, priority among conflicting security interests and agricultural liens in the same collateral is determined according to the following rules:

(1) Conflicting perfected security interests and agricultural liens rank according to priority in time of filing or perfection. Priority dates from the earlier of the time a filing covering the collateral is first made or the security interest or agricultural lien is first perfected, if there is no period thereafter when there is neither filing nor perfection.

(2) A perfected security interest or agricultural lien has priority over a conflicting unperfected security interest or agricultural lien.

(3) The first security interest or agricultural lien to attach or become effective has priority if conflicting

security interests and agricultural liens are unperfected.

(b) Time of perfection: proceeds and supporting obligations. For the purposes of subsection (a)(1):

(1) the time of filing or perfection as to a security interest in collateral is also the time of filing or perfection as to a security interest in proceeds; and

(2) the time of filing or perfection as to a security interest in collateral supported by a supporting obligation is also the time of filing or perfection as to a security interest in the supporting obligation.

(c) Special priority rules: proceeds and supporting obligations. Except as otherwise provided in subsection (f), a security interest in collateral which qualifies for priority over a conflicting security interest under Section 9-327, 9-328, 9-329, 9-330, or 9-331 also has priority over a conflicting security interest in:

(1) any supporting obligation for the collateral; and

(2) proceeds of the collateral if:

(A) the security interest in proceeds is perfected;

(B) the proceeds are cash proceeds or of the same type as the collateral; and

(C) in the case of proceeds that are proceeds of proceeds, all intervening proceeds are cash proceeds, proceeds of the same type as the collateral, or an account relating to the collateral.

(d) First-to-file priority rule for certain collateral. Subject to subsection (e) and except as otherwise provided in subsection (f), if a security interest in chattel paper, deposit accounts, negotiable documents, instruments, investment property, or letter-of-credit rights is perfected by a method other than filing, conflicting perfected security interests in proceeds of the collateral rank according to priority in time of filing.

(e) Applicability of subsection (d). Subsection (d) applies only if the proceeds of the collateral are not cash proceeds, chattel paper, negotiable documents, instruments, investment property, or letter-of-credit rights.

(f) Limitations on subsections (a) through (e). Subsections (a) through (e) are subject to:

(1) subsection (g) and the other provisions of this part;

(2) Section 4-210 with respect to a security interest of a collecting bank;

(3) Section 5-118 with respect to a security interest of an issuer or nominated person; and

(4) Section 9-110 with respect to a security interest arising under Article 2 or 2-A.

(g) Priority under agricultural lien statute. A perfected agricultural lien on collateral has priority over a conflicting security interest in or agricultural lien on the same collateral if the statute creating the agricultural lien so provides.

(h) Special priority rules: cooperative interests.

(1) With respect to all amounts secured, a cooperative organization security interest has priority over all other security interests in a cooperative interest.

(2) As to security interests in cooperative interests other than cooperative organization security interests, Section 9-323(h) provides special rules for future advances.

History: Add, L 2001, ch 84, § 36, eff July 1, 2001.

CASE ANNOTATIONS

1. In general
2. Under former § 9-312
3. –General rules of priority
4. – –Perfected interest; order of filing
5. – –Unperfected interests
6. –Inventory secured purchase money security interests
7. –Non-inventory secured purchase money security interests

1. In general

In an interpleader action, an insurance company that had properly perfected a security interest in a judgment creditor's assets under N.Y. U.C.C. Law § 9-310(a) by filing a financing statement that met the requirements of N.Y. U.C.C. Law § 9-502(a) was found to be entitled to the proceeds of an award obtained by the judgment creditor in a breach of contract suit; the insurance company's claim took priority under N.Y. U.C.C. Law § 9-322(a) over that of a claimant that had obtained a default judgment against the judgment creditor in a separate suit. Sentry Select Ins. Co. v LBL Skysystems (U.S.A.), Inc., 486 F. Supp. 2d 496, 2007 U.S. Dist. LEXIS 37520 (E.D. Pa. 2007), aff'd, 281 Fed. Appx. 93, 2008 U.S. App. LEXIS 11996 (3d Cir. Pa. 2008).

2. Under former § 9-312
3. –General rules of priority

Court would order debtors to return property to secured creditor on basis of security agreement between parties, notwithstanding debtors' contention that nonparty held superior security interest in same property; mere existence of potentially senior lien constituted no defense under CLS UCC § 9-312, and priority dispute would be proper subject of dispute only between secured parties. Midlantic Commercial Leasing Corp. v D.B.A. Knits, Inc., 167 A.D.2d 117, 561 N.Y.S.2d 436, 1990 N.Y. App. Div. LEXIS 13036 (N.Y. App. Div. 1st Dep't 1990).

4. – –Perfected interest; order of filing

Where (1) secured party's loan to debtor was secured by interest in debtor's accounts receivable, (2) after loan was made, debtor sold goods to third party, who was obligated to pay debtor specified sum therefore, (3) debtor owed money to still another third party and entered into arrangement with both third parties whereby money owing to debtor from first third party would be set off against money that debtor owed to second third party, and (4) secured party sought to pierce such arrangement and reach receivables owed to debtor by first third party, court held that in absence of proof that arrangement between debtor and such third parties predated secured transaction between plaintiff and debtor, plaintiff's perfected security interest prevailed under UCC § 9-312 over the presumably subsequent and unperfected security interest of second third party. Bank Leumi Trust Co. v Collins Sales Service, Inc., 65 A.D.2d 735, 410 N.Y.S.2d 617, 1978 N.Y. App. Div. LEXIS 13539 (N.Y. App. Div. 1st Dep't 1978), aff'd, 47 N.Y.2d 888, 419 N.Y.S.2d 474, 393 N.E.2d 468, 27 U.C.C. Rep. Serv. (CBC) 582, 1979 N.Y. LEXIS 2158 (N.Y. 1979).

Court properly determined that plaintiff's purchase-money security interest, filed in November 1994, had priority over defendant's perfected nonpossessory purchase-money security interest resulting from debtor's sale of collateral in December 1995, notwithstanding defendant's assertion that plaintiff's security interest was not purchase-money security interest because plaintiff failed to perfect her security interest within 20 days from debtor's receipt of collateral, since failure to perfect purchase-money security interest within 20 days from date of delivery of collateral does not result in loss of its "purchase money" status. Lashua v La Duke, 272 A.D.2d 750, 707 N.Y.S.2d 542, 41 U.C.C. Rep. Serv. 2d (CBC) 930, 2000 N.Y. App. Div. LEXIS 5693 (N.Y. App. Div. 3d Dep't 2000).

A house trailer is a motor vehicle within the meaning of the Uniform Commercial Code provision requiring filing with respect to motor vehicles which are to be licensed or registered in this state, and therefore mortgagee who perfected his security interest by filing the same was entitled to possession of a trailer as opposed to the owner of a retail instalment contract whose filing had expired prior to the mortgagee's perfecting of his security interest. Albany Discount Corp. v Mohawk Nat'l Bank, 54 Misc. 2d 238, 282 N.Y.S.2d 401, 4 U.C.C. Rep. Serv. (CBC) 669, 1967 N.Y. Misc. LEXIS 1353 (N.Y. Sup. Ct. 1967), modified, 30 A.D.2d 623, 290 N.Y.S.2d 576, 1968 N.Y. App. Div. LEXIS 3877 (N.Y. App. Div. 3d Dep't 1968), aff'd, 30 A.D.2d 919, 292 N.Y.S.2d 300, 1968 N.Y. App. Div. LEXIS 3313 (N.Y. App. Div. 3d Dep't 1968).

In an action seeking monetary damages from defendant for merchandise sold and delivered by plaintiff, who had a validly executed, filed and perfected security agreement for a quantity of the merchandise sold, plaintiff's request for a replevin of the disputed inventory for purposes of sale as provided for in the Uniform Commercial Code was granted, although the intervenor bank had a perfected security interest in defendant's inventory which was superior to that of plaintiff's security interest; a creditor may not unilaterally prevent seizure of a debtor's assets solely as an incident of the status of preferred party, and whether as judgment creditor or secured party plaintiff has the right to replevy the collateral held by defendant, who is in default of payment of its obligations to plaintiff, although the intervenor's lien will have priority over plaintiff's with regard to proceeds of any sale of the repossessed collateral. Roemer & Zeller, Inc. v Ace Transmission Center, Inc., 114 Misc. 2d 415, 454 N.Y.S.2d 377, 1982 N.Y. Misc. LEXIS 3490 (N.Y. Sup. Ct. 1982).

In action to determine priority of right to collateral (note secured by deed of trust) that corporate debtor had assigned three times to secure its obligations, where (1) California bank in 1972 made loan of $300,000 to corporate debtor and loans of $170,000 to each of three individuals associated with corporate debtor, (2) such loans were secured by 1972 deed of trust on California property owned by corporate debtor, (3) in 1974, corporate debtor formed joint venture with plaintiff to develop certain California real estate owned by corporate debtor, which included property subject to 1972 deed of trust given to secure California bank's loans to corporate debtor and three individuals associated with debtor, (4) pursuant to joint-venture agreement with plaintiff, corporate debtor sold property to be developed for note secured by deed of trust to such property, and such note and deed constituted collateral sued for, (5) in May, 1974, corporate debtor assigned collateral in suit to California bank, which had loaned corporate debtor $300,000, to secure principal of $240,000, and bank took possession of collateral and retained it during corporate debtor's subsequent assignments thereof, (6) in January, 1975, corporate debtor made second assignment of collateral in suit, which incorporated its first assignment, by assigning collateral (a) first to California bank to secure debtor's obligation of $280,000, and (b) then to first Chicago bank to secure debtor's obligation of over one million dollars, (7) thereafter, corporate debtor repaid its $280,000 debt to California bank with funds from $275,000 loan obtained from second Chicago bank, but did not repay debt to first Chicago bank, (8) in March, 1976, corporate debtor assigned collateral in suit to both California bank and second Chicago bank to secure loans made by California bank to three individuals associated with corporate debtor, (9) in May, 1976, Federal Deposit Insurance Corporation (FDIC), as liquidator of California bank which had been corporate debtor's creditor and had become insolvent, obtained California bank's rights to collateral in suit and took possession of it, (10) in 1978, first Chicago bank also became insolvent, and FDIC obtained such bank's rights to collateral in suit and sold them to plaintiff in June, 1979, on corporate debtor's default on underlying debt to first Chicago bank, and (11) plaintiff brought suit for possession of collateral when FDIC, as liquidator of California bank, refused to surrender it, district court awarded summary judgment and granted ownership of a collateral interest in the note and deed to first Chicago bank. On appeal, summary judgment was reversed and the matter remanded as the record raised a material issue of fact as to the bank's knowledge, or participation in relevant events and, therefore, its status as a good faith purchaser. Landmark Land Co. v Sprague, 701 F.2d 1065, 1983 U.S. App. LEXIS 30033 (2d Cir. N.Y. 1983).

Subsequently arising setoff cannot take priority over perfected security interest in receivables under CLS UCC Art 9 based on "first in time, first in right" rule of CLS UCC § 9-312. MNC Commercial

Corp. v Joseph T. Ryerson & Son, Inc., 882 F.2d 615, 9 U.C.C. Rep. Serv. 2d (CBC) 9, 1989 U.S. App. LEXIS 10136 (2d Cir. N.Y. 1989).

Lender had perfected security interest senior to consigner's interest in inventory sold to debtors prior to date consigner filed its financing statement because lender had filed first financing statement and it did not have actual knowledge of consignment interest when it executed the loan with debtors. TSA Stores, Inc. v M J Soffe, LLC (In re TSAWD Holdings, Inc.), 2018 Bankr. LEXIS 3681 (Bankr. D. Del. Nov. 26, 2018).

5. – –Unperfected interests

Where (1) secured party's loan to debtor was secured by interest in debtor's accounts receivable, (2) after loan was made, debtor sold goods to third party, who was obligated to pay debtor specified sum therefore, (3) debtor owed money to still another third party and entered into arrangement with both third parties whereby money owing to debtor from first third party would be set off against money that debtor owed to second third party, and (4) secured party sought to pierce such arrangement and reach receivables owed to debtor by first third party, court held that in absence of proof that arrangement between debtor and such third parties predated secured transaction between plaintiff and debtor, plaintiff's perfected security interest prevailed under UCC § 9-312 over the presumably subsequent and unperfected security interest of second third party. Bank Leumi Trust Co. v Collins Sales Service, Inc., 65 A.D.2d 735, 410 N.Y.S.2d 617, 1978 N.Y. App. Div. LEXIS 13539 (N.Y. App. Div. 1st Dep't 1978), aff'd, 47 N.Y.2d 888, 419 N.Y.S.2d 474, 393 N.E.2d 468, 27 U.C.C. Rep. Serv. (CBC) 582, 1979 N.Y. LEXIS 2158 (N.Y. 1979).

In absence of a writing in form of filed financing statement to protect plaintiff's interest in mobile home and in absence of his possession of mobile home, which he had given to woman under oral agreement that she would assume monthly payments and that ownership of home would be transferred to her when all payments were made, plaintiff in replevin action had no enforceable security interest, and defendant, which had obtained chattel mortgage security agreement from woman to secure payment of demand note, had valid security interest and was entitled to possession of mobile home upon default on note. Recchio v Manufacturers & Traders Trust Co., 55 Misc. 2d 788, 286 N.Y.S.2d 390, 4 U.C.C. Rep. Serv. (CBC) 1133, 1968 N.Y. Misc. LEXIS 1833 (N.Y. Sup. Ct. 1968), rev'd, 35 A.D.2d 769, 316 N.Y.S.2d 915, 8 U.C.C. Rep. Serv. (CBC) 565, 1970 N.Y. App. Div. LEXIS 3635 (N.Y. App. Div. 4th Dep't 1970).

6. –Inventory secured purchase money security interests

In junior mortgagee's action for damages for defendant's alleged impairment of plaintiff's security, where defendant under security agreement with dealer in modular homes had security interest in all of dealer's present or future inventory and also first mortgage on 2.39 acres of land acquired by dealer for use as sales lot, on which dealer installed two modular homes; where plaintiff held second mortgage on dealer's 2.39 acres as security for loan on which dealer defaulted; and where defendant after dealer's default quickly removed modular homes from dealer's lot pursuant to written authorization from officer of dealer's company, (1) homes placed by dealer on sales lot, although installed on concrete foundations and connected to utilities, were inventory and not real property or fixtures under UCC § 9-109(4), since they were goods intended for immediate or ultimate sale; (2) defendant held perfected purchase-money security interest in dealer's inventory under UCC § 9-401(1)(c) and UCC § 9-402(1), which under UCC § 9-312(3) took priority over plaintiff's junior-mortgage interest; and (3) defendant on dealer's default had right to take possession of homes on dealer's lot, since they were inventory collateral. Rakosi v General Electric Credit Corp., 59 A.D.2d 553, 397 N.Y.S.2d 416, 22 U.C.C. Rep. Serv. (CBC) 204, 1977 N.Y. App. Div. LEXIS 13344 (N.Y. App. Div. 2d Dep't 1977).

7. –Non-inventory secured purchase money security interests

Guarantor was not liable to seller of beer distributorship for buyer's failure to pay purchase price after it filed Chapter 11 bankruptcy petition where seller failed to perfect its purchase money security interest within 20 days under CLS UCC § 9-312(4). Port Distrib. Corp. v Pflaumer, 70 F.3d 8, 28 U.C.C. Rep. Serv. 2d (CBC) 248, 1995 U.S. App. LEXIS 32055 (2d Cir. N.Y. 1995).

§ 9-323. Future Advances

(a) When priority based on time of advance. Except as otherwise provided in subsection (c), for purposes of determining the priority of a perfected security interest under Section 9-322(a)(1), perfection of the security interest dates from the time an advance is made to the extent that the security interest secures an advance that:

(1) is made while the security interest is perfected only:

(A) under Section 9-309 when it attaches; or

(B) temporarily under Section 9-312(e), (f), or (g); and

(2) is not made pursuant to a commitment entered into before or while the security interest is perfected by a method other than under Section 9-309 or 9-312(e), (f), or (g).

(b) Lien creditor. Except as otherwise provided in subsections (c) and (h), a security interest is subordinate to the rights of a person that becomes a lien creditor to the extent that the security interest secures an advance made more than 45 days after the person becomes a lien creditor unless the advance is made:

(1) without knowledge of the lien; or

(2) pursuant to a commitment entered into without knowledge of the lien.

(c) Buyer of receivables. Subsections (a) and (b) do not apply to a security interest held by a secured party that is a buyer of accounts, chattel paper, payment intangibles, or promissory notes or a consignor.

(d) Buyer of goods. Except as otherwise provided in subsection (e), a buyer of goods other than a buyer in ordinary course of business takes free of a security interest to the extent that it secures advances made after the earlier of:

(1) the time the secured party acquires knowledge of the buyer's purchase; or

(2) 45 days after the purchase.

(e) Advances made pursuant to commitment: priority of buyer of goods. Subsection (d) does not apply if the advance is made pursuant to a commitment entered into without knowledge of the buyer's purchase and before the expiration of the 45 day period.

(f) Lessee of goods. Except as otherwise provided in subsection (g), a lessee of goods, other than a lessee in ordinary course of business, takes the leasehold interest free of a security interest to the extent that it secures advances made after the earlier of:

(1) the time the secured party acquires knowledge of the lease; or

(2) 45 days after the lease contract becomes enforceable.

(g) Advances made pursuant to commitment: priority of lessee of goods. Subsection (f) does not apply if the advance is made pursuant to a commitment entered into without knowledge of the lease and before the expiration of the 45 day period.

(h) Priority with respect to cooperative interests. The following rules apply for purposes of determining under Section 9-322(a)(1) the priority of a perfected security interest in a cooperative interest:

(1) Perfection of the security interest with respect to a future advance dates from the time of the filing under Section 9-310(d) if all of the following are true:

(A) The security agreement states the maximum amount to be advanced pursuant to commitment;

(B) The future advance is made pursuant to that commitment;

(C) The future advance plus the outstanding sum of any prior advances is not more than the stated maximum amount; and

(D) The filed financing statement includes a cooperative addendum disclosing that the security agreement contains a commitment to make future advances.

(2) Except as provided in paragraph (1), perfection of the security interest with respect to a future advance dates from the time the advance is made.

(3) For purposes of paragraph (1), no amendment of a security agreement shall adversely affect the priority of any other security interest in the same cooperative interest that was perfected prior to the amendment.

(4) This subsection applies only to advances made subsequent to an initial advance.

History: Add, L 2001, ch 84, § 36, eff July 1, 2001.

§ 9-324. Priority of Purchase-money Security Interests

(a) General rule: purchase-money priority. Except as otherwise provided in subsection (g), a perfected purchase-money security interest in goods other than inventory or livestock has priority over a conflicting security interest in the same goods, and, except as otherwise provided in Section 9-327, a perfected security interest in its identifiable proceeds also has priority, if the purchase-money security interest is perfected when the debtor receives possession of the collateral or within 20 days thereafter.

(b) Inventory purchase-money priority. Subject to subsection (c) and except as otherwise provided in subsection (g), a perfected purchase-money security interest in inventory has priority over a conflicting security interest in the same inventory, has priority over a conflicting security interest in chattel paper or an instrument constituting proceeds of the inventory and in proceeds of the chattel paper, if so provided in Section 9-330, and, except as otherwise provided in Section 9-327, also has priority in identifiable cash proceeds of the inventory to the extent the identifiable cash proceeds are received on or before the delivery of the inventory to a buyer, if:

(1) the purchase-money security interest is perfected when the debtor receives possession of the inventory;

(2) the purchase-money secured party sends an authenticated notification to the holder of the conflicting security interest;

(3) the holder of the conflicting security interest receives the notification within five years before the debtor receives possession of the inventory; and

(4) the notification states that the person sending the notification has or expects to acquire a purchase-money security interest in inventory of the debtor and describes the inventory.

(c) Holders of conflicting inventory security interests to be notified. Subsections (b)(2) through (4) apply only if the holder of the conflicting security interest had filed a financing statement covering the same types of inventory:

(1) if the purchase-money security interest is perfected by filing, before the date of the filing; or

(2) if the purchase-money security interest is temporarily perfected without filing or possession under Section 9-312(f), before the beginning of the 20-day period thereunder.

(d) Livestock purchase-money priority. Subject to subsection (e) and except as otherwise provided in subsection (g), a perfected purchase-money security interest in livestock that are farm products has priority over a conflicting security interest in the same livestock, and, except as otherwise provided in Section 9-327, a perfected security interest in their identifiable proceeds and identifiable products in their unmanufactured states also has priority, if:

(1) the purchase-money security interest is perfected when the debtor receives possession of the livestock;

(2) the purchase-money secured party sends an authenticated notification to the holder of the conflicting security interest;

(3) the holder of the conflicting security interest receives the notification within six months before the debtor receives possession of the livestock; and

(4) the notification states that the person sending the notification has or expects to acquire a purchase-money security interest in livestock of the debtor and describes the livestock.

(e) Holders of conflicting livestock security interests to be notified. Subsections (d)(2) through (4) apply only if the holder of the conflicting security interest had filed a financing statement covering the same types of livestock:

(1) if the purchase-money security interest is perfected by filing, before the date of the filing; or

(2) if the purchase-money security interest is temporarily perfected without filing or possession under Section 9-312(f), before the beginning of the 20-day period thereunder.

(f) Software purchase-money priority. Except as otherwise provided in subsection (g), a perfected purchase-money security interest in software has priority over a conflicting security interest in the same collateral, and, except as otherwise provided in Section 9-327, a perfected security interest in its identifiable proceeds also has priority, to the extent that the purchase-money security interest in the goods in which the software was acquired for use has priority in the goods and proceeds of the goods under this section.

(g) Conflicting purchase-money security interests. If more than one security interest qualifies for priority in the same collateral under subsection (a), (b), (d), or (f):

(1) a security interest securing an obligation incurred as all or part of the price of the collateral has priority over a security interest securing an obligation incurred for value given to enable the debtor to acquire rights in or the use of collateral; and

(2) in all other cases, Section 9-322(a) applies to the qualifying security interests.

History: Add, L 2001, ch 84, § 36, eff July 1, 2001.

§ 9-325. Priority of Security Interests in Transferred Collateral

(a) Subordination of security interest in transferred collateral. Except as otherwise provided in subsection (b), a security interest created by a debtor is subordinate to a security interest in the same collateral created by another person if:

(1) the debtor acquired the collateral subject to the security interest created by the other person;

(2) the security interest created by the other person was perfected when the debtor acquired the collateral; and

(3) there is no period thereafter when the security interest is unperfected.

(b) Limitation of subsection (a) subordination. Subsection (a) subordinates a security interest only if the security interest:

(1) otherwise would have priority solely under Section 9-322(a) or 9-324; or

(2) arose solely under Section 2-711(3) or 2-A-508(5).

History: Add, L 2001, ch 84, § 36, eff July 1, 2001.

§ 9-326. Priority of Security Interests Created by New Debtor

(a) Subordination of security interest created by new debtor. Subject to subsection (b), a security interest that is created by a new debtor in collateral in which the new debtor has or acquires rights and is perfected solely by a filed financing statement that would be ineffective to perfect the security interest but for the application of Section 9-316(i)(1) or 9-508 is subordinate to a security interest in the same collateral which is perfected other than by such a filed financing statement.

(b) Priority under other provisions; multiple original debtors. The other provisions of this part determine the priority among conflicting security interests in the same collateral perfected by filed financing statements described in subsection (a). However, if the security agreements to which a new debtor became bound as debtor were not entered into by the same original debtor, the conflicting security interests rank according to priority in time of the new debtor's having become bound.

History: Add, L 2001, ch 84, § 36, eff July 1, 2001; amd, L 2014, ch 505, § 42, eff Dec 17, 2014.

§ 9-327. Priority of Security Interests in Deposit Account

The following rules govern priority among conflicting security interests in the same deposit account:

(a) A security interest held by a secured party having control of the deposit account under Section 9-104 has priority over a conflicting security interest held by a secured party that does not have control.

(b) Except as otherwise provided in subsections (c) and (d), security interests perfected by control under Section 9-314 rank according to priority in time of obtaining control.

(c) Except as otherwise provided in subsection (d), a security interest held by the bank with which the deposit account is maintained has priority over a conflicting security interest held by another secured party.

(d) A security interest perfected by control under Section 9-104(a)(3) has priority over a security interest held by the bank with which the deposit account is maintained.

History: Add, L 2001, ch 84, § 36, eff July 1, 2001.

§ 9-328. Priority of Security Interests in Investment Property

The following rules govern priority among conflicting security interests in the same investment property:

(a) A security interest held by a secured party having control of investment property under Section 9-106 has priority over a security interest held by a secured party that does not have control of the investment property.

(b) Except as otherwise provided in paragraphs (c) and (d), conflicting security interests held by secured parties each of which has control under Section 9-106 rank according to priority in time of:

(1) if the collateral is a security, obtaining control;

(2) if the collateral is a security entitlement carried in a securities account and:

(A) if the secured party obtained control under Section 8-106 (d) (1), the secured party's becoming the person for which the securities account is maintained;

(B) if the secured party obtained control under Section 8-106 (d) (2), the securities intermediary's agreement to comply with the secured party's entitlement orders with respect to security entitlements carried or to be carried in the securities account; or

(C) if the secured party obtained control through another person under Section 8-106 (d) (3), the time on which priority would be based under this paragraph if the other person were the secured party; or

(3) if the collateral is a commodity contract carried with a commodity intermediary, the satisfaction of the requirement for control specified in Section 9-106 (b) (2) with respect to commodity contracts carried or to be carried with the commodity intermediary.

(c) A security interest held by a securities intermediary in a security entitlement or a securities account maintained with the securities intermediary has priority over a conflicting security interest held by another secured party.

(d) A security interest held by a commodity intermediary in a commodity contract or a commodity account maintained with the commodity intermediary has priority over a conflicting security interest held by another secured party.

(e) A security interest in a certificated security in registered form which is perfected by taking delivery under Section 9-313 (a) and not by control under Section 9-314 has priority over a conflicting security interest perfected by a method other than control.

(f) Conflicting security interests created by a broker, securities intermediary, or commodity intermediary which are perfected without control under Section 9-106 rank equally.

(g) In all other cases, priority among conflicting security interests in investment property is governed by Sections 9-322 and 9-323.

(h) Subsections (a) through (g) do not apply to cooperative interests.

History: Add, L 2001, ch 84, § 36, eff July 1, 2001.

§ 9-329. Priority of Security Interests in Letter-of-credit Right

The following rules govern priority among conflicting security interests in the same letter-of-credit right:

(a) A security interest held by a secured party having control of the letter-of-credit right under Section 9-107 has priority to the extent of its control over a conflicting security interest held by a secured party that does not have control.

(b) Security interests perfected by control under Section 9-314 rank according to priority in time of obtaining control.

History: Add, L 2001, ch 84, § 36, eff July 1, 2001.

§ 9-330. Priority of Purchaser of Chattel Paper or Instrument

(a) Purchaser's priority: security interest claimed merely as proceeds. A purchaser of chattel paper has priority over a security interest in the chattel paper which is claimed merely as proceeds of inventory subject to a security interest if:

(1) in good faith and in the ordinary course of the purchaser's business, the purchaser gives new value and takes possession of the chattel paper or obtains control of the chattel paper under Section 9-105; and

(2) the chattel paper does not indicate that it has been assigned to an identified assignee other than the purchaser.

(b) Purchaser's priority: other security interests. A purchaser of chattel paper has priority over a security interest in the chattel paper which is claimed other than merely as proceeds of inventory subject to a security interest if the purchaser gives new value and takes possession of the chattel paper or obtains control of the chattel paper under Section 9-105 in good faith, in the ordinary course of the purchaser's business, and without knowledge that the purchase violates the rights of the secured party.

(c) Chattel paper purchaser's priority in proceeds. Except as otherwise provided in Section 9-327, a purchaser having priority in chattel paper under subsection (a) or (b) also has priority in proceeds of the chattel paper to the extent that:

(1) Section 9-322 provides for priority in the proceeds; or

(2) the proceeds consist of the specific goods covered by the chattel paper or cash proceeds of the specific goods, even if the purchaser's security interest in the proceeds is unperfected.

(d) Instrument purchaser's priority. Except as otherwise provided in Section 9-331(a), a purchaser of an instrument has priority over a security interest in the instrument perfected by a method other than possession if the purchaser gives value and takes possession of the instrument in good faith and without knowledge that the purchase violates the rights of the secured party.

(e) Holder of purchase-money security interest gives new value. For purposes of subsections (a) and (b), the holder of a purchase-money security interest in inventory gives new value for chattel paper constituting proceeds of the inventory.

(f) Indication of assignment gives knowledge. For purposes of subsections (b) and (d), if chattel paper or an instrument indicates that it has been assigned to an identified secured party other than the purchaser, a purchaser of the chattel paper or instrument has knowledge that the purchase violates the rights of the secured party.

History: Add, L 2001, ch 84, § 36, eff July 1, 2001.

§ 9-331. Priority of Rights of Purchasers of Instruments, Documents, and Securities under Other Articles; Priority of Interests in Financial Assets and Security Entitlements under Article 8

(a) Rights under Articles 3, 7, and 8 not limited. This article does not limit the rights of a holder in due course of a negotiable instrument, a holder to which a negotiable document of title has been duly negotiated, or a protected purchaser of a security. These holders or purchasers take priority over an earlier security interest, even if perfected, to the extent provided in Articles 3, 7, and 8.

(b) Protection under Article 8. This article does not limit the rights of or impose liability on a person to the extent that the person is protected against the assertion of a claim under Article 8.

(c) Filing not notice. Filing under this article does not constitute notice of a claim or defense to the holders, or purchasers, or persons described in subsections (a) and (b).

(d) Section not applicable to cooperative interests. Subsections (a), (b), and (c) do not apply to cooperative interests.

History: Add, L 2001, ch 84, § 36, eff July 1, 2001.

CASE ANNOTATIONS
UNDER FORMER § 9-309

A purchaser who has paid a factor for the seller (which factor has a security interest in the invoice) has no claim against the factor for the seller's default; he can look to the seller only. Nor can a claim against a factor be based on payment due to a mistake if the alleged mistake is that the buyer believed the seller would perform or had performed. Crompton-Richmond Co. v Raylon Fabrics, Inc. (1969, 1st Dept) 33 A.D.2d 741, 305 N.Y.S.2d 850

§ 9-332. Transfer of Money; Transfer of Funds from Deposit Account

(a) Transferee of money. A transferee of money takes the money free of a security interest unless the transferee acts in collusion with the debtor in violating the rights of the secured party.

(b) Transferee of funds from deposit account. A transferee of funds from a deposit account takes the funds free of a security interest in the deposit account unless the transferee acts in collusion with the debtor in violating the rights of the secured party.

History: Add, L 2001, ch 84, § 36, eff July 1, 2001.

§ 9-333. Priority of Certain Liens Arising by Operation of Law

(a) "Possessory lien." In this section, "possessory lien" means an interest, other than a security interest or an agricultural lien:

(1) which secures payment or performance of an obligation for services or materials furnished with respect to goods by a person in the ordinary course of the person's business;

(2) which is created by statute or rule of law in favor of the person; and

(3) whose effectiveness depends on the person's possession of the goods.

(b) Priority of possessory lien. A possessory lien on goods has priority over a security interest in the goods unless the lien is created by a statute that expressly provides otherwise.

History: Add, L 2001, ch 84, § 36, eff July 1, 2001.

CASE ANNOTATIONS
UNDER FORMER § 9-310

Carrier had general lien that was not perfected as against bank's prior purchase money security interest on all of debtor's property, beyond freight charges for current goods, because carrier's lien was limited to cargo which was in carrier's possession. In re World Imps., Ltd. v OEC Group N.Y., 498 B.R. 58, 2013 Bankr. LEXIS 3329

(Bankr. E.D. Pa. 2013), aff'd, 526 B.R. 127, 2015 U.S. Dist. LEXIS 7675 (E.D. Pa. 2015).

Carrier had general lien that was not perfected as against bank's prior purchase money security interest on all of debtor's property, beyond freight charges for current goods, because carrier's lien was limited to cargo which was in carrier's possession. In re World Imps., Ltd. v OEC Group N.Y. (2013, BC ED Pa) 498 BR 58.

Although assignee of claims of medical assistance supplier could not enforce assignment against county department of social services, assignment was enforceable as to all others, and, by filing its security interest in claims prior in time to State's tax warrant, assignee's claim took priority over State's claim for withholding taxes. IMFC Professional Services, Inc. v State (1977, 4th Dept) 59 A.D.2d 1047, 399 N.Y.S.2d 804

Although assignee of claims of medical assistance supplier could not enforce assignment against county department of social services, assignment was enforceable as to all others, and, by filing its security interest in claims prior in time to State's tax warrant, assignee's claim took priority over State's claim for withholding taxes. IMFC Professional Services, Inc. v State (1977, 4th Dept) 59 A.D.2d 1047, 399 N.Y.S.2d 804

Assignee of retail installment contract involving automobile purchased in New Jersey was not entitled to order of seizure under CLS CPLR § 7102, even though assignee had perfected security interest in vehicle in New Jersey and owner had defaulted in his payments, where assignee was aware of owner's New York residence but failed to perfect its security interest in New York under CLS Veh & Tr § 2118, and thus lien sale in New York (which was properly held after owner left vehicle with garageman and failed to pay bill for repair and storage) terminated assignee's New Jersey security interest. General Motors Acceptance Corp. v Farkos (1987, 2d Dept) 133 A.D.2d 738, 520 N.Y.S.2d 27

In action to recover possession of automobile after sale to lienholder, assignee of retail installment contract covering vehicle was not entitled to assert owner's statutory defenses to notice of lien for repair and storage which garageman gave to vehicle's owner after owner failed to claim vehicle or pay bill, since assignee held perfected security interest in vehicle only in another state and defenses were personal to owner. General Motors Acceptance Corp. v Farkos (1987, 2d Dept) 133 A.D.2d 738, 520 N.Y.S.2d 27

Under this section and section 184 of the Lien Law artisan's lien for automobile repair had priority over automobile purchase lien arising out of installment sales contract which was in default. Schleimer v Arrowhead Garage, Inc. (1965) 46 Misc. 2d 607, 260 N.Y.S.2d 271, 2 UCCRS 753, affd (1966) 49 Misc. 2d 775, 267 N.Y.S.2d 995

Plaintiff's prior perfected security interest in an automobile which was purchased by defendant at a public aution subject to the security interest and then stored by defendant at codefendant's garage, is superior to the subsequent bailee's lien for garage storage charges; section 9-310 of the Uniform Commercial Code, which provides that the lien of an individual in possession of goods for which he furnished some service or materials in the course of his business takes priority over a perfected security interest in such goods, is inapplicable since plaintiff neither requested nor consented to the storage of the vehicle (Lien Law, § 184) and cannot incur any liability for the storage charges by reason of defendant's having stored the vehicle at a garage; since the lien for storage charges was incurred at the specific request of defendant, who had full knowledge that the sale of the vehicle was subject to plaintiff's security interest, she appears to be the party liable for the storage charges. O'Connor v B. J. Auto Make Ready Corp. (1979) 101 Misc. 2d 665, 421 N.Y.S.2d 758, mod (1982, Sup App T) 115 Misc. 2d 575, 455 N.Y.S.2d 164, 35 UCCRS 725

Under UCC § 9-310, storage-lien of garage on automobile subject to security interest had priority over such security interest, and garage could detain vehicle until its lien charges were paid. O'Connor v B.J. Auto Make Ready Corp. (1982, Sup App T) 115 Misc. 2d 575, 455 N.Y.S.2d 164, 35 UCCRS 725

Reading CLS Lien § 184 in conjunction with CLS UCC § 9-310, lien under former statute has priority over perfected security interest unless lienholder allows property out of his possession subsequent to 30 days from accrual of lien. ITT Commercial Fin. Corp. v Kallmeyer & Sons Truck Tire Serv., Inc. (1993, Sup) 156 Misc. 2d 505, 593 N.Y.S.2d 951

In action between bank which held prior federally recorded security interest in airplane and bailee which held possessory lien for storage charges, under UCC §§ 9-104(c) and 9-310, possessory lien had priority over bank's interest. Industrial Nat'l Bank v Butler Aviation International, Inc. (1974, ED NY) 370 F. Supp. 1012

§ 9-334. Priority of Security Interests in Fixtures and Crops

(a) Security interest in fixtures under this article. A security interest under this article may be created in goods that are fixtures or may continue in goods that become fixtures. A security interest does not exist under this article in ordinary building materials incorporated into an improvement on land.

(b) Security interest in fixtures under real property law. This article does not prevent creation of an encumbrance upon fixtures under real property law.

(c) General rule: subordination of security interest in fixtures. In cases not governed by subsections (d) through (h), a security interest in fixtures is subordinate to a conflicting interest of an encumbrancer or owner of the related real property other than the debtor.

(d) Fixtures purchase-money priority. Except as otherwise provided in subsection (h), a perfected security interest in fixtures has priority over a conflicting interest of an encumbrancer or owner of the real property if the debtor has an interest of record in or is in possession of the real property and:

(1) the security interest is a purchase-money security interest;

(2) the interest of the encumbrancer or owner arises before the goods become fixtures; and

(3) the security interest is perfected by a fixture filing before the goods become fixtures or within 20 days thereafter.

(e) Priority of security interest in fixtures over interests in real property. A perfected security interest in fixtures has priority over a conflicting interest of an encumbrancer or owner of the real property if:

(1) the debtor has an interest of record in the real property or is in possession of the real property and the security interest:

(A) is perfected by a fixture filing before the interest of the encumbrancer or owner is of record; and

(B) has priority over any conflicting interest of a predecessor in title of the encumbrancer or owner;

(2) before the goods become fixtures, the security interest is perfected by any method permitted by this article and the fixtures are readily removable:

(A) factory or office machines;

(B) equipment that is not primarily used or leased for use in the operation of the real property; or

(C) replacements of domestic appliances that are consumer goods;

(3) the conflicting interest is a lien on the real property obtained by legal or equitable proceedings after the security interest was perfected by any method permitted by this article; or

(4) the security interest is:

(A) created in a manufactured home in a manufactured-home transaction; and

(B) perfected pursuant to a statute described in Section 9-311(a)(2).

(f) Priority based on consent, disclaimer, or right to remove. A security interest in fixtures, whether or not perfected, has priority over a conflicting interest of an encumbrancer or owner of the real property if:

(1) the encumbrancer or owner has, in an authenticated record, consented to the security interest or disclaimed an interest in the goods as fixtures; or

(2) the debtor has a right to remove the goods as against the encumbrancer or owner.

(g) Continuation of paragraph (f)(2) priority. The priority of the security interest under paragraph (f)(2) continues for a reasonable time if the debtor's right to remove the goods as against the encumbrancer or owner terminates.

(h) Priority of construction mortgage. A mortgage is a construction mortgage to the extent that it secures an obligation incurred for the construction of an improvement on land, including the acquisition cost of the land, if a recorded record of the mortgage so indicates. Except as otherwise provided in subsections (e) and (f), a security interest in fixtures is subordinate to a construction mortgage if a record of the mortgage is recorded before the goods become fixtures and the goods become fixtures before the completion of the construction. A mortgage has this priority to the same extent as a construction mortgage to the extent that it is given to refinance a construction mortgage.

(i) Priority of security interest in crops. A perfected security interest in crops growing on real property has priority over a conflicting interest of an encumbrancer or owner of the real property if the debtor has an interest of record in or is in possession of the real property.

(j) Subsection (i) prevails. Subsection (i) prevails over any inconsistent provisions with this article or any other chapter of law.

History: Add, L 2001, ch 84, § 36, eff July 1, 2001.

CASE ANNOTATIONS

Bathtub was not "ordinary" building material, and creditor retained its security interest in the tub pursuant to N.Y. U.C.C. Law § 9-334(a), where the tub was purchased at a specialty store, incorporated luxury features and other items, such that it was something more than a container to hold water, and the total cost of the items was cost $4,266. Because this collateral was a consumer good, the lien became immediately perfected under N.Y. U.C.C. Law § 9-309(1), without need for filing a financing statement. In re Ryan (2007, BC WD NY) 360 BR 50.

§ 9-335. Accessions

(a) Creation of security interest in accession. A security interest may be created in an accession and continues in collateral that becomes an accession.

(b) Perfection of security interest. If a security interest is perfected when the collateral becomes an accession, the security interest remains perfected in the collateral.

(c) Priority of security interest. Except as otherwise provided in subsection (d), the other provisions of this part determine the priority of a security interest in an accession.

(d) Compliance with certificate-of-title statute. A security interest in an accession is subordinate to a security interest in the whole which is perfected by compliance with the requirements of a certificate-of-title statute under Section 9-311 (b).

(e) Removal of accession after default. After default, subject to Part 6, a secured party may remove an accession from other goods if the security interest in the accession has priority over the claims of every person having an interest in the whole.

(f) Reimbursement following removal. A secured party that removes an accession from other goods under subsection (e) shall promptly reimburse any holder of a security interest or other lien on, or owner of, the whole or of the other goods, other than the debtor, for the cost of repair of any physical injury to the whole or the other goods. The secured party need not reimburse the holder or owner for any diminution in value of the whole or the other goods caused by the absence of the accession removed or by any necessity for replacing it. A person entitled to reimbursement may refuse permission to remove until the secured party gives adequate assurance for the performance of the obligation to reimburse.

History: Add, L 2001, ch 84, § 36, eff July 1, 2001.

CASE ANNOTATIONS

UNDER FORMER § 9-314

A purchaser who has paid a factor for the seller (which factor has a security interest in the invoice) has no claim against the factor for the seller's default; he can look to the seller only. Nor can a claim against a factor be based on payment due to a mistake if the alleged mistake is that the buyer believed the seller would perform or had performed. Crompton-Richmond Co. v Raylon Fabrics, Inc. (1969, 1st Dept) 33 A.D.2d 741, 305 N.Y.S.2d 850

§ 9-336.   Commingled Goods

(a) "Commingled goods." In this section, "commingled goods" means goods that are physically united with other goods in such a manner that their identity is lost in a product or mass.

(b) No security interest in commingled goods as such. A security interest does not exist in commingled goods as such. However, a security interest may attach to a product or mass that results when goods become commingled goods.

(c) Attachment of security interest to product or mass. If collateral becomes commingled goods, a security interest attaches to the product or mass.

(d) Perfection of security interest. If a security interest in collateral is perfected before the collateral becomes commingled goods, the security interest that attaches to the product or mass under subsection (c) is perfected.

(e) Priority of security interest [.] * Except as otherwise provided in subsection (f), the other provisions of this part determine the priority of a security interest that attaches to the product or mass under subsection (c).

* The bracketed punctuation has been inserted by the Publisher.

(f) Conflicting security interests in product or mass [.] * If more than one security interest attaches to the product or mass under subsection (c), the following rules determine priority:

(1) A security interest that is perfected under subsection (d) has priority over a security interest that is unperfected at the time the collateral becomes commingled goods.

(2) If more than one security interest is perfected under subsection (d), the security interests rank equally in proportion to the value of the collateral at the time it became commingled goods.

* The bracketed punctuation has been inserted by the Publisher.

History: Add, L 2001, ch 84, § 36, eff July 1, 2001.

§ 9-337.   Priority of Security Interests in Goods Covered by Certificate of Title

If, while a security interest in goods is perfected by any method under the law of another jurisdiction, this state issues a certificate of title that does not show that the goods are subject to the security interest or contain a statement that they may be subject to security interests not shown on the certificate:

(a) a buyer of the goods, other than a person in the business of selling goods of that kind, takes free of the security interest if the buyer gives value and receives delivery of the goods after issuance of the certificate and without knowledge of the security interest; and

(b) the security interest is subordinate to a conflicting security interest in the goods that attaches, and is perfected under Section 9-311 (b), after issuance of the certificate and without the conflicting secured party's knowledge of the security interest.

History: Add, L 2001, ch 84, § 36, eff July 1, 2001.

§ 9-338.   Priority of Security Interest or Agricultural Lien Perfected by Filed Financing Statement Providing Certain Incorrect Information

If a security interest or agricultural lien is perfected by a filed financing statement providing information described in Section 9-516(b)(5) which is incorrect at the time the financing statement is filed:

(1) the security interest or agricultural lien is subordinate to a conflicting perfected security interest in the collateral to the extent that the holder of the conflicting security interest gives value in reasonable reliance upon the incorrect information; and

(2) a purchaser, other than a secured party, of the collateral takes free of the security interest or agricultural lien to the extent that, in reasonable reliance upon the incorrect information, the purchaser gives value and, in the case of tangible chattel paper,

tangible documents, goods, instruments, or a security certificate, receives delivery of the collateral.

History: Add, L 2001, ch 84, § 36, eff July 1, 2001; amd, L 2014, ch 505, § 43, eff Dec 17, 2014.

§ 9-339. Priority Subject to Subordination

This article does not preclude subordination by agreement by a person entitled to priority.

History: Add, L 2001, ch 84, § 36, eff July 1, 2001.

Subpart 4
Rights Of Bank

History: Add, L 2001, ch 84, § 36, eff July 1, 2001.

§ 9-340. Effectiveness of Right of Recoupment or Set-off Against Deposit Account

(a) Exercise of recoupment or set-off. Except as otherwise provided in subsection (c), a bank with which a deposit account is maintained may exercise any right of recoupment or set-off against a secured party that holds a security interest in the deposit account.

(b) Recoupment or set-off not affected by security interest. Except as otherwise provided in subsection (c), the application of this article to a security interest in a deposit account does not affect a right of recoupment or set-off of the secured party as to a deposit account maintained with the secured party.

(c) When set-off ineffective. The exercise by a bank of a set-off against a deposit account is ineffective against a secured party that holds a security interest in the deposit account which is perfected by control under Section 9-104(a)(3), if the set-off is based on a claim against the debtor.

History: Add, L 2001, ch 84, § 36, eff July 1, 2001.

§ 9-341. Bank's Rights and Duties with Respect to Deposit Account

Except as otherwise provided in Section 9-340 (c), and unless the bank otherwise agrees in an authenticated record, a bank's rights and duties with respect to a deposit account maintained with the bank are not terminated, suspended, or modified by:

(a) the creation, attachment, or perfection of a security interest in the deposit account;

(b) the bank's knowledge of the security interest; or

(c) the bank's receipt of instructions from the secured party.

History: Add, L 2001, ch 84, § 36, eff July 1, 2001.

§ 9-342. Bank's Right to Refuse to Enter into or Disclose Existence of Control Agreement

This article does not require a bank to enter into an agreement of the kind described in Section 9-104(a)(2), even if its customer so requests or directs. A bank that has entered into such an agreement is not required to confirm the existence of the agreement to another person unless requested to do so by its customer.

History: Add, L 2001, ch 84, § 36, eff July 1, 2001.

PART 4
RIGHTS OF THIRD PARTIES

History: Add, L 2001, ch 84, § 36, eff July 1, 2001.

Former Part 4, add, L 1962, ch 553, eff Sept 27, 1964; repealed, L 2001, ch 84, § 36, eff July 1, 2001.

§ 9-401. Alienability of Debtor's Rights

(a) Other law governs alienability; exceptions. Except as otherwise provided in subsection (b) and Sections 9-406, 9-407, 9-408, and 9-409, whether a debtor's rights in collateral may be voluntarily or involuntarily transferred is governed by law other than this article.

(b) Agreement does not prevent transfer. An agreement between the debtor and secured party which prohibits a transfer of the debtor's rights in collateral or makes the transfer a default does not prevent the transfer from taking effect.

History: Add, L 2001, ch 84, § 36, eff July 1, 2001.

Former § 9-401, add, L 1962, ch 553; amd, L 1963, ch 1003, §§ 3, 35-37, L 1964, ch 476, § 13, L 1967, ch 680, § 105, L 1977, ch 866, § 25, eff July 2, 1978, L 1988, ch 333, § 4, eff Oct 1, 1988.

Former § 9-401, repealed, L 2001, ch 84, § 36, eff July 1, 2001.

CASE ANNOTATIONS

UNDER FORMER § 9-311

When the holder of promissory notes assigned his interest therein as collateral to secure payment of a prior indebtedness, a sum less than the aggregate amount of the notes, and indorsed and delivered them to that creditor, he did not irrevocably divest himself of the ultimate right to all of the proceeds of the notes, but retained ownership of those proceeds not required to satisfy that indebtedness, and, therefore, the negotiation of all of the notes operated only as a partial assignment of the proceeds of the notes; the interest retained by him was capable of being transferred and, when it was transferred by another collateral assignment, the transferee acquired a valid security interest as to his residuary interest in the notes, which security interest was perfected by a subsequent delivery of the notes to it. Lipkowitz & Plaut v Affrunti (1978) 95 Misc. 2d 849, 407 N.Y.S.2d 1010, 25 UCCRS 276

Where the debtor makes a prohibited assignment of the collateral he is bound by his act as against the transferee and cannot avoid the transfer on the ground that it was contrary to the security agreement. Miller v Bonafied Ready Mix Corp. (1967, N.Y. Sup) 4 UCCRS 881

Where New York debtor assigned accounts receivable to New York creditor under terms of security agreement and secured creditor complied with all steps required by UCC to perfect its security interest in such accounts, New York creditor's perfected security interest attached as soon as accounts came into existence and took priority over interest of Colorado creditor, as lien creditor under writ of attachment, with respect to accounts owed debtor by Colorado account debtors. Barocas v Bohemia Import Co. (1974) 33 Colo App 263, 518 P2d 850, 14 UCCRS 191 (applying New York law)

§ 9-402. Secured Party Not Obligated on Contract of Debtor or in Tort

The existence of a security interest, agricultural lien, or authority given to a debtor to dispose of or use collateral, without more, does not subject a secured party to liability in contract or tort for the debtor's acts or omissions.

History: Add, L 2001, ch 84, § 36, eff July 1, 2001.

Former § 9-402, add, L 1962, ch 553; amd, L 1963, ch 1003, §§ 38-41, L 1964, ch 476, §§ 14, 15, L 1970, ch 899, § 1, L 1977, ch 866, § 26, eff July 2, 1978.

Former § 9-402, repealed, L 2001, ch 84, § 36, eff July 1, 2001.

CASE ANNOTATIONS

UNDER FORMER § 9-317

Bank which loaned money to corporation and took physical possession of corporation's assets on default by corporation was not assignee of corporation so as to be bound by exclusive supply agreement between corporation and subsidiary since nothing in agreement between bank and corporation manifested intent to "assign" present or future interest in corporation's assets to bank. Spielman v Acme Nat'l Sales Co. (1991, 3d Dept) 169 A.D.2d 218, 572 N.Y.S.2d 400

Bank which loaned money to corporation and took physical possession of corporation's assets on default by corporation was not successor of corporation so as to be bound by exclusive supply agreement between corporation and subsidiary since bank's possession and control of corporation's assets, undertaken by bank on corporation's default pursuant to security agreement, amounted to substantive change in ownership, rather than one of mere form. Spielman v Acme Nat'l Sales Co. (1991, 3d Dept) 169 A.D.2d 218, 572 N.Y.S.2d 400

Bank which loaned money to corporation and took physical possession of corporation's assets on default by corporation was not bound to honor exclusive supply contract between corporation and subsidiary in absence of contract requiring such action, notwithstanding facts that bank and plaintiff had entered into intercreditor agreement which provided plaintiff with superior security interest in subsidiary, and subsidiary's only asset with value was exclusive supply agreement. Spielman v Acme Nat'l Sales Co. (1991, 3d Dept) 169 A.D.2d 218, 572 N.Y.S.2d 400

Credit corporation, which was assignee of "lease" of crane containing provision that title to crane would pass to lessee upon completion of payment schedule, was assignee of security interest and, under UCC § 9-317, was not liable in contract or tort for acts or omissions of lessor or lessee. Brandes v Pettibone Corp. (1974) 79 Misc. 2d 651, 360 N.Y.S.2d 814, 16 UCCRS 205

§ 9-403. Agreement Not to Assert Defenses Against Assignee

(a) "Value." In this section, "value" has the meaning provided in Section 3-303. In this section the meaning of "obligor" is not limited to the meaning given it in Section 9-102(a)(59). In this section the term "person entitled to enforce the instrument" means (i) the holder of the instrument, (ii) a nonholder in possession of the instrument who has the rights of a holder, or (iii) a person not in possession of the instrument who is entitled to enforce the instrument pursuant to Article 3 of this chapter. A person may be a person entitled to enforce the instrument even though the person is not the owner of the instrument or is in wrongful possession of the instrument.

(b) Agreement not to assert claim or defense. Except as otherwise provided in this section, an agreement between an account debtor and an assignor not to assert against an assignee any claim or defense that the account debtor may have against the assignor is enforceable by an assignee that takes an assignment:

(1) for value;

(2) in good faith;

(3) without notice of a claim of a property or possessory right to the property assigned; and

(4) without notice of:

(A) a defense of the obligor based on (i) infancy of the obligor to the extent it is a defense to a simple contract, (ii) duress, lack of legal capacity, or illegality of the transaction which, under other law, nullifies the obligation of the obligor, (iii) fraud that induced the obligor to sign the instrument with neither knowledge nor reasonable opportunity to learn of its character or its essential terms, or (iv) discharge of the obligor in solving proceedings;

(B) a defense of the obligor stated anywhere in Article 3 of this chapter or a defense of the obligor that would be available if the person entitled to enforce the instrument were enforcing a right to payment under a simple contract; and

(C) a claim in recoupment of the obligor against the assignor if the claim arose from the transaction that gave rise to the assigned obligation, but the claim of the obligor may be asserted against an assignee only to reduce the amount owing on the assigned obligation at the time the action is brought.

(c) When subsection (b) not applicable. An assignee takes subject to the defenses listed in paragraph (b)(4)(A), but is not subject to defenses of the obligor stated in paragraph (b)(4)(B) or claims in recoupment stated in paragraph (b)(4)(C) against a person other than the enforcing assignee.

(d) Omission of required statement in consumer transaction. In a consumer transaction, if a record evidences the account debtor's obligation, law other than this article requires that the record include a statement to the effect that the rights of an assignee are subject to claims or defenses that the account debtor could assert against the original obligee, and the record does not include such a statement:

(1) the record has the same effect as if the record included such a statement; and

(2) the account debtor may assert against an assignee those claims and defenses that would have been available if the record included such a statement.

(e) Rule for individual under other law. This section is subject to law other than this article which establishes a different rule for an account debtor who is an individual and who incurred the obligation primarily for personal, family, or household purposes.

(f) Other law not displaced. Except as otherwise provided in subsection (d), this section does not displace law other than this article which gives effect to an agreement by an account debtor not to assert a claim or defense against an assignee.

History: Add, L 2001, ch 84, § 36, eff July 1, 2001.

Former § 9-403, add, L 1962, ch 553; amd, L 1963, ch 1003, § 42, L 1964, ch 476, §§ 16, 17, L 1965, ch 743, § 1, L 1967, ch 689, § 1, L 1970, ch 899, § 2, L 1977, ch 866, § 27, L 1982, ch 692, § 1, L 1986, ch 453, § 4, L 1988, ch 333, § 5, L 1990, ch 561, §§ 8, 9, L 1991, ch 648, § 9, L 1996, ch 309, § 247, eff July 13, 1996.

Former § 9-403, repealed, L 2001, ch 84, § 36, eff July 1, 2001.

CASE ANNOTATIONS

Attorneys who represented plaintiffs in connection with sale of their business, and filed financing statement to perfect their security interest in purchasers' property, were not entitled to summary judgment dismissing action alleging that they committed malpractice by allowing security interest to lapse, as triable issues existed as to whether "continuous representation" rule applied so as to impose duty on them to file CLS UCC § 9-403 continuation statement, where record showed that, after closing of sale of plaintiffs' business, they advised plaintiffs in regard to purchaser's default on its debt, and represented plaintiffs in purchaser's bankruptcy proceedings. Berman v Cullen & Dykman (2000, 2d Dept) 276 A.D.2d 515, 713 N.Y.S.2d 762

Malpractice claim based on law firm's failure to file CLS UCC § 9-403 continuation statement accrued when original financing statement lapsed. Berman v Cullen & Dykman (2000, 2d Dept) 276 A.D.2d 515, 713 N.Y.S.2d 762

In a breach of contract action brought by a bank against a mortgage company, the federal district court was correct in holding an equipment lease contract, and particularly a "hell or high water" clause contained therein, valid under New York law; the bank purchased the lease assignment in good faith and for value. Wells Fargo Bank, N.A. v BrooksAmerica Mortg. Corp. (2005, CA2 NY) 419 F.3d 107, 57 UCCRS2d 980

Where a landlord assigned a lease to a mortgagee, N.Y. U.C.C. Law § 9-403(c) did not prohibit a tenant from asserting constructive eviction as a defense to the mortgagee's claims arising from the lease agreement because the defense of constructive eviction was similar to the defenses of fraud and duress in that it went to the very existence of the agreement rather than a failure to perform in accordance with the terms of the agreement. ReliaStar Life Ins. Co. v Home Depot U.S.A., Inc. (2009, CA2 NY) 570 F3d 513.

Government's motion for summary judgment was granted because the Uniform Commercial Code (UCC) liens filed pursuant to N.Y. U.C.C. Law § 9-403 by the inmate against a federal judge and prosecutor were entirely without merit because the inmate could not possess a common law copyright in his name because the concept of common law copyright was preempted by the Copyright Act of 1976, 17 U.S.C.S. § 301(a), and a name was not a proper subject for copyright. United States v Ramirez (2003, SD NY) 291 F. Supp. 2d 266

§ 9-404. Rights Acquired by Assignee; Claims and Defenses Against Assignee

(a) Assignee's rights subject to terms, claims, and defenses; exceptions. Unless an account debtor has made an enforceable agreement not to assert defenses or claims, and subject to subsections (b) through (e), the rights of an assignee are subject to:

(1) all terms of the agreement between the account debtor and assignor and any defense or claim in recoupment arising from the transaction that gave rise to the contract; and

(2) any other defense or claim of the account debtor against the assignor which accrues before the account debtor receives a notification of the assignment authenticated by the assignor or the assignee.

(b) Account debtor's claim reduces amount owed to assignee. Subject to subsection (c) and except as otherwise provided in subsection (d), the claim of an account debtor against an assignor may be asserted against an assignee under subsection (a) only to reduce the amount the account debtor owes.

(c) Rule for individual under other law. This section is subject to law other than this article which establishes a different rule for an account debtor who is an individual and who incurred the obligation primarily for personal, family, or household purposes.

(d) Omission of required statement in consumer transaction. In a consumer transaction, if a record evidences the account debtor's obligation, law other than this article requires that the record include a statement to the effect that the account debtor's recovery against an assignee with respect to claims and defenses against the assignor may not exceed amounts paid by the account debtor under the record, and the record does not include such a statement, the extent to which a claim of an account debtor against the assignor may be asserted against an assignee is determined as if the record included such a statement.

(e) Inapplicability to health-care-insurance receivable. This section does not apply to an assignment of a health-care-insurance receivable.

History: Add, L 2001, ch 84, § 36, eff July 1, 2001.

Former § 9-404, add, L 1977, ch 866, § 28, eff July 2, 1978, L 1982, ch 692, § 2, L 1986, ch 453, § 5, L 1990, ch 561, § 10, eff Jan 1, 1991, L 1996, ch 309, § 248, eff July 13, 1996.

Former § 9-404, repealed, L 2001, ch 84, § 36, eff July 1, 2001.

Prior § 9-404, add, L 1962, ch 553; amd, L 1964, ch 476, § 18, L 1965, ch 959, § 1; repealed, L 1977, ch 866, § 28, eff July 2, 1978.

CASE ANNOTATIONS

In General
UNDER FORMER § 9-318
I. Generally
1. In general

II. Defenses Against Assignee
2. In general
3. Waiver
4. Contract terms, claims, and defenses
5. Defenses accruing prior to notice
III. Modification or Substitution
6. In general
IV. Notice of Assignment
7. In general
8. Service and proof of notice
9. Sufficiency of notice

In General.

Staffing company's breach of a staffing agreement in failing to pay contractors provided a consulting company with a defense under N.Y. U.C.C. Law § 9-404(a)(1) to a financing company's claim to receivables owed by the consulting company to the staffing company, and its payments to those contractors gave rise to a claim in recoupment under § 9-404, because, inter alia, the staffing company's breach of the staffing agreement was material. Riviera Fin. of Tex., Inc. v Capgemini US, LLC (2013, CA2 NY) 2013 US App LEXIS 3202 (UNPUBLISHED).

UNDER FORMER § 9-318

I. Generally
1. In general

Vehicle purchaser was properly held liable to assignee where it made payment to defunct car dealership despite receiving notice of dealer's assignment of right to receive payment to plaintiff since (1) CLS UCC § 9-318(3) requires account debtor to make payment consistent with any assignment of which it has notice, even absent agreement to do so, (2) dealer expressly appointed plaintiff "as its attorney...to...receive...payment of the accounts hereby assigned," and (3) assignment was supported by plaintiff's extension of credit to dealer. General Motors Acceptance Corp. v Scio Volunteer Fire Dep't (1993, 4th Dept) 191 A.D.2d 981, 595 N.Y.S.2d 145

Uniform Commercial Code § 9-318 and § 9-106 are apparently limited to instances of assignments of executory contracts. Gramatan Co. v D'Amico (1966) 50 Misc. 2d 233, 269 N.Y.S.2d 871, 3 UCCRS 544

Assignee cannot be liable to an account debtor for the assignor's breach because the U.C.C. distinguishes finance assignments from general assignments. And, under N.Y. U.C.C. Law § 9-404(b) and the antecedent case law codified therein, an account debtor could not pursue affirmative relief against a financing assignee for the assignor's breach. Riviera Fin. of Tex., Inc. v Capgemini U.S., LLC (2012, SD NY) 855 F Supp 2d 179.

II. Defenses Against Assignee
2. In general

UCC § 9-318(1)(a), by its terms, subjects the rights of the assignee only to those claims or defenses that the account debtor has against the assignor. Bank Leumi Trust Co. v Collins Sales Service, Inc. (1979) 47 N.Y.2d 888, 419 N.Y.S.2d 474, 393 N.E.2d 468, 27 UCCRS 582

In action by assignee of account against account debtor in which debtor sought to offset judgment obtained by third party against debtor for sum that was identical to debt owed by plaintiff's assignor to such third party, court held (1) that evidence showed clearly that truck delivered to account debtor by assignor was encumbered-in violation of provisions of UCC § 2-312(1)(a) and (b) concerning warranty of good title to conveyed goods and freedom of goods from security interest or other lien-by debt owed by assignor to third party; (2) that as result of third party's obtaining judgment on such debt in suit against account debtor, debtor under UCC § 9-318(1)(a) had right to offset judgment against claim that assignor might make against debtor under their contract; and (3) that such defense should also be available to account debtor under UCC § 9-318(1)(a) in present action by assignee on same claim. Marine Midland Bank, N.A. v Murray Walter, Inc. (1984, 4th Dept) 101 A.D.2d 691, 475 N.Y.S.2d 679, 38 UCCRS 673, 39 UCCRS 691

In action by assignee on equipment lease, which lessor-assignor and lessee-account debtor had agreed was subject to Uniform Commercial Code remedies in event of default, lessee-account debtor could assert against assignee any claim concerning defects in leased equipment that it could have asserted against lessor-assignor, since UCC § 9-318(1) provides that in absence of contrary agreement, rights of assignee are subject to any defenses or claims arising out of

contract between account debtor and assignor. General Electric Credit Corp. v Xerox Corp. (1985, 4th Dept) 112 A.D.2d 30, 490 N.Y.S.2d 407

Assignees of promissory note acquired no greater rights than those of assignor and took subject to all defenses and counterclaims existing against assignors, including any defenses and counterclaims that accrued before debtor received notification of assignment. Caprara v Charles Court Assocs. (1995, 3d Dept) 216 A.D.2d 722, 627 N.Y.S.2d 836

3. Waiver

In action by plaintiff-assignee to recover payments due from defendant account debtor on invoices issued by assignor over 8-month period, neither party was entitled to summary judgment where triable issue of fact existed as to defendant's claim that plaintiff waived direct payment requirement under assignment by permitting defendant to remit payments directly to assignor during period in question. Abrams & Co. v ITS Equip. & Leasing Corp. (1995, 2d Dept) 216 A.D.2d 503, 628 N.Y.S.2d 784

4. Contract terms, claims, and defenses

In action by assignee of account against account debtor in which debtor sought to offset judgment obtained by third party against debtor for sum that was identical to debt owed by plaintiff's assignor to such third party, court held (1) that evidence showed clearly that truck delivered to account debtor by assignor was encumbered-in violation of provisions of UCC § 2-312(1)(a) and (b) concerning warranty of good title to conveyed goods and freedom of goods from security interest or other lien-by debt owed by assignor to third party; (2) that as result of third party's obtaining judgment on such debt in suit against account debtor, debtor under UCC § 9-318(1)(a) had right to offset judgment against claim that assignor might make against debtor under their contract; and (3) that such defense should also be available to account debtor under UCC § 9-318(1)(a) in present action by assignee on same claim. Marine Midland Bank, N.A. v Murray Walter, Inc. (1984, 4th Dept) 101 A.D.2d 691, 475 N.Y.S.2d 679, 38 UCCRS 673, 39 UCCRS 691

Where account debtor's unrelated breach-of-contract claim against assignor of debtor's account arose after debtor had received notice of account's assignment, debtor under UCC § 9-318(1)(b) could not use such claim as defense to assignee's right to receive proceeds of account assigned. Rosenthal & Rosenthal, Inc. v John Kunstadt, Inc., 106 A.D.2d 277, 482 N.Y.S.2d 287 (Div. 1st Dep't 1984), app. dismissed, 64 N.Y.2d 1129 (1985), overruled in part, DS-Concept Trade Invest LLC v Wear First Sportswear, Inc., 128 A.D.3d 585, 10 N.Y.S.3d 60 (Div. 1st Dep't 2015).

In action by assignee of proceeds of letter of credit against advising and paying bank that asserted right of setoff against such proceeds after acknowledging their assignment, where foreign bank issued irrevocable letter of credit in favor of foreign beneficiary who was purchaser of goods sold by United States seller, beneficiary assigned proceeds of letter to seller as payment for goods, and defendant United States bank, "advising and paying bank" with respect to letter of credit, acknowledged assignment, but claimed right of setoff against them on ground that beneficiary-assignor owed bank amount of setoff in prior, unrelated letter-of-credit transaction, court held that under UCC § 9-318(1), rights of assignee in absence of contrary agreement are subject to account debtor's defenses or claims under contract with assignor, and to account debtor's defenses or claims with respect to assignor that accrued before account debtor received notice of assignment of his account; that foreign bank that issued letter of credit was party obligated on such account, or "account debtor," under § 9-318(1); that defendant bank, in its capacity as "advising bank" under § 5-103(1)(e), did not under § 5-107(1) have any obligation to honor drafts drawn against letter of credit and thus was not "account debtor" so as to have right of setoff against letter's proceeds prior to notification of assignment of such proceeds; that defendant's "paying-bank" designation did not transform it into "account debtor" with right of setoff against letter's proceeds as against plaintiff assignee; and that after its acceptance of assignment by foreign beneficiary of proceeds of letter of credit in suit to plaintiff seller, defendant could not treat such proceeds as belonging to foreign beneficiary and assert right of setoff. Bamberger Polymers International Corp. v Citibank, N. A. (1983, Sup) 124 Misc. 2d 653, 477 N.Y.S.2d 931, 37 UCCRS 1263

When car dealer leases vehicle to consumer via retail installment contract later assigned to finance company, finance company in collecting payments due under contract is subject to any defenses consumer has against dealer which can be asserted as offset against recovery on contract, such as counterclaims for negligent repairs to and defects in vehicle, since it would be inconsistent with covenant of fair dealing implied in all contracts to clearly prohibit agreement not to assert defenses against assignee of retail installment contract for sale of automobile, as in CLS Pers P § 302(9), and at same time permit such practice with respect to contract to lease vehicle. Ford Motor Credit Co. v Sofia (1990, Civ Ct) 147 Misc. 2d 651, 559 N.Y.S.2d 109, mod on other grounds (1992, Sup App T) 151 Misc. 2d 567, 581 N.Y.S.2d 520

Defendant assignees, who provided warehouse loans to the debtor to finance mortgage originations and who were assigned the mortgages and notes by the debtor, had perfected security interests in the notes due to possession under UCC § 9-304(1), and because the assignees were holders in due course without notice of the plaintiff disbursing agents claims under UCC § 9-318, the assignees defeated the claims of the disbursing agent which were based on the debtor's dishonored checks. Broward Title Co. v Jacobs (In re AppOnline.com, Inc.) (2002, BC ED NY) 285 BR 805

Creditor's security interest in payments due to hardcover publisher from paperback publisher was subject to author's third-party interest in preexisting agreement between publishers, so that creditor could claim none of 2/3 share of amount due to hardcover publisher which had vested in author on execution of agreement, since, under CLS UCC § 9-318, rights of assignee (creditor) were subject to contract between account debtor (paperback publisher) and assignor (hardcover publisher) and any claim arising therefrom, and hardcover publisher did not own and could not validly assign author's share to creditor without author's consent. Septembertide Pub., B.V. v Stein & Day, Inc. (1989, CA2 NY) 884 F.2d 675, 9 UCCRS2d 817

5. Defenses accruing prior to notice

In action by assignee of account, where account debtor raised defense based on assignor's alleged breach of contract out of which assigned debt arose and counterclaim predicated on apparently unrelated, unpaid loan, notice of assignment would only have relevance to counterclaim and not to defense, because only claims arising independently of contract between account debtor and assignor which accrue after notification are cut off thereby. Gateway Nat'l Bank v Saxe, Bacon & Bolan (1972, 1st Dept) 40 A.D.2d 653, 336 N.Y.S.2d 668, 11 UCCRS 668

In action by assignee of transportation company for balance due under contract with State Park Commission, state, as "account debtor," was entitled to assert claim against transportation company for uncollected withholding taxes which became due before state had notice of assignment. Central State Bank v State (1973) 73 Misc. 2d 128, 341 N.Y.S.2d 322, 12 UCCRS 373

III. Modification or Substitution

6. In general

Provision in plumbing subcontract which prohibited subcontractor's assignment, without written consent of general contractor (account debtor) for which plumbing services were to be performed, of any proceeds from, or interest in such contract, was legally ineffective under express terms of UCC § 9-318(4). Aetna Casualty & Surety Co. v Bedford-Stuyvesant Restoration Constr. Corp. (1982, 1st Dept) 90 A.D.2d 474, 455 N.Y.S.2d 265, 34 UCCRS 1425

Assignees of promissory note were not entitled to summary judgment in action to recover on note where pre-assignment letter from assignors to debtors created issue of fact regarding alleged modification of note, assignees failed to offer evidence of date when debtors had been notified of assignment, and assignees conceded that debtors had valid claim against assignors at time of assignment, although they disputed amount. Caprara v Charles Court Assocs. (1995, 3d Dept) 216 A.D.2d 722, 627 N.Y.S.2d 836

Bank was not entitled, under CLS UCC § 9-318(2), to notification of buyer's demand on supplier for adequate assurance of due performance of contract for sale of oil products where bank merely provided financing for supplier in transaction and was not supplier's assignee; statute addresses cases in which obligor and assignor agree to changes in contract which adversely affect rights of assignee. BAII Banking Corp. v UPG, Inc. (1993, CA2 NY) 985 F.2d 685, 20 UCCRS2d 155, 37 ALR5th 807

IV. Notice of Assignment

7. In general

As general rule, notice is necessary in order to charge debtor with duty of payment to assignee. Caprara v Charles Court Assocs. (1995, 3d Dept) 216 A.D.2d 722, 627 N.Y.S.2d 836

8. Service and proof of notice

Where creditor with perfected security interest in debtor's accounts and contract rights brought action against state to recover money held by state on account for debtor in payment for certain survey and design work performed for state by debtor, and where state claimed right to set off unpaid withholding taxes and unemployment insurance contributions owed by debtor to state: (1) Under UCC § 9-318, state was account debtor and, thus, secured creditor was subject to any defense or claim that state had against debtor before state received notification of assignment of account; (2) Secured party's filing of financing statement with department of state did not constitute actual notice to state of such assignment and, thus, state's right to assert claims for unpaid taxes and unemployment insurance was not cut off until secured party made demand on state controller for money due to debtor. Chase Manhattan Bank (N. A.) v State (1975, 3d Dept) 48 A.D.2d 11, 367 N.Y.S.2d 580, 17 UCCRS 250, affd (1976) 40 N.Y.2d 590, 388 N.Y.S.2d 896, 357 N.E.2d 366, 20 UCCRS 577, remittitur amd (1977) 42 N.Y.2d 1016

Evidence supported finding of notification of assignment within UCC § 9-318(3) where invoices were mailed in envelopes with return address and were not returned and where check used to pay invoice bore invoice number notation in lower left corner. Taubenhaus v Jung Factors, Inc. (1972, Tex Civ App Houston (14th Dist)) 478 SW2d 149

9. Sufficiency of notice

Assignee of account was entitled to summary judgment in action against debtor where assignor's invoices were stamped with notice which stated "Payable to [assignee]. Remittance is to be made only to them...," thus apprising debtor that account had been assigned to assignee; moreover, for purposes of deciding whether issue of fact existed concerning account debtor's knowledge of assignment, it was persuasive that debtor had paid assignee on 3 separate occasions on receiving identically stamped invoices from 2 different assignors. Capital Factors, Inc. v Caldor, Inc. (1992, 1st Dept) 182 A.D.2d 532, 582 N.Y.S.2d 1012, 18 UCCRS2d 315

Defendant equipment lessee raised triable issues of fact as to whether plaintiff, as assignee of lessor, took lease in good faith and without notice of lessee's claims that equipment was defective, which, if resolved in lessee's favor, would render assignee subject to lessee's claims and defenses, despite lease provision that lessee would not assert any claims or defenses against assignee, where (1) assignee did not explain why it did not send lessee notice of assignment until almost one year after purported assignment, 6 months after lessee ceased making lease payments, and one month after assignor sent notice of default and threatened to accelerate payments as provided in lease, (2) both notice of default and notice of assignment were signed by same person, and (3) assignor and assignee shared same business address, suite, and attorneys. Norwest Fin. Leasing, Inc. v Parish of St. Augustine (1998, 1st Dept) 251 A.D.2d 125, 674 N.Y.S.2d 312

Bank, as assignee of security interest in security-agreement debtor's accounts receivable owed by account debtor under 1981 oil-purchase-and-resale contract-which contract contained broad arbitration provision that bank wished to avoid-(1) was subject to such arbitration provision under UCC § 9-318(1)(a), since (a) it was part of oil-purchase-and-resale contract in suit, and (b) account debtor had not waived any claims allowed it under UCC § 9-318(1); and (2) bank also could not avoid arbitration of account debtor's subsequent 1982 claim against security-agreement debtor on ground that account debtor had had notice of bank's assignment with meaning of UCC § 9-318(1)(b)-which prohibits account debtor from asserting against assignor any claims or defenses that arise after account debtor has received notice of assignment-since bank's notification to account debtor did not reasonably identify rights assigned, as required by UCC § 9-318(3). Banque de Paris et des Pays-Bas v Amoco Oil Co. (1983, SD NY) 573 F. Supp. 1464 (applying UCC as rule of federal law)

§ 9-405. Modification of Assigned Contract

(a) Effect of modification on assignee. A modification of or substitution for an assigned contract is effective against an assignee if made in good faith. The assignee acquires corresponding rights under the modified or substituted contract. The assignment may provide that the modification or substitution is a breach of contract by the assignor. This subsection is subject to subsections (b) through (d).

(b) Applicability of subsection (a). Subsection (a) applies to the extent that:

(1) the right to payment or a part thereof under an assigned contract has not been fully earned by performance; or

(2) the right to payment or a part thereof has been fully earned by performance and the account debtor has not received notification of the assignment under Section 9-406(a).

(c) Rule for individual under other law. This section is subject to law other than this article which establishes a different rule for an account debtor who is an individual and who incurred the obligation primarily for personal, family, or household purposes.

(d) Inapplicability to health-care-insurance receivable. This section does not apply to an assignment of a health-care-insurance receivable.

History: Add, L 2001, ch 84, § 36, eff July 1, 2001.

Former § 9-405, add, L 1962, ch 553; amd, L 1965, ch 743, § 2, L 1967, ch 689, § 2, L 1977, ch 866, § 29; L 1982, ch 692, § 3, L 1986, ch 453, § 6, L 1990, ch 561, § 11, L 1996, ch 309, § 249, eff July 13, 1996.

Former § 9-405, repealed, L 2001, ch 84, § 36, eff July 1, 2001.

§ 9-406. Discharge of Account Debtor; Notification of Assignment; Identification and Proof of Assignment; Restrictions on Assignment of Accounts, Chattel Paper, Payment Intangibles, and Promissory Notes Ineffective

(a) Discharge of account debtor; effect of notification. Subject to subsections (b) through (h), an account debtor on an account, chattel paper, or a payment intangible may discharge its obligation by paying the assignor until, but not after, the account debtor receives a notification, authenticated by the assignor or the assignee, that the amount due or to become due has been assigned and that payment is to be made to the assignee. After receipt of the notification, the account debtor may discharge its obligation by paying the assignee and may not discharge the obligation by paying the assignor.

(b) When notification ineffective. Subject to subsection (g), notification is ineffective under subsection (a):

(1) if it does not reasonably identify the rights assigned;

(2) to the extent that an agreement between an account debtor and a seller of a payment intangible limits the account debtor's duty to pay a person other than the seller and the limitation is effective under law other than this article; or

(3) at the option of an account debtor, if the notification notifies the account debtor to make less than the full amount of any installment or other periodic payment to the assignee, even if:

(A) only a portion of the account, chattel paper, or payment intangible has been assigned to that assignee;

(B) a portion has been assigned to another assignee; or

(C) the account debtor knows that the assignment to that assignee is limited.

(c) Proof of assignment. Subject to subsection (g), if requested by the account debtor, an assignee shall seasonably furnish reasonable proof that the assignment has been made. Unless the assignee complies, the account debtor may discharge its obligation by paying the assignor, even if the account debtor has received a notification under subsection (a).

(d) Term restricting assignment generally ineffective. Except as otherwise provided in subsection (e) and Sections 2-A-303 and 9-407, and subject to subsection (g), a term in an agreement between an account debtor and an assignor or in a promissory note is ineffective to the extent that it:

(1) prohibits, restricts, or requires the consent of the account debtor or person obligated on the promissory note to the assignment or transfer of, or the creation, attachment, perfection, or enforcement of a security interest in, the account, chattel paper, payment intangible, or promissory note; or

(2) provides that the assignment or transfer or the creation, attachment, perfection, or enforcement of the security interest may give rise to a default, breach, right of recoupment, claim, defense, termination, right of termination, or remedy under the account, chattel paper, payment intangible, or promissory note.

(e) Inapplicability of subsection (d) to certain sales. Subsection (d) does not apply to the sale of a payment intangible or promissory note.

(f) Subsection (b)(3) not waivable. Subject to subsection (g), an account debtor may not waive or vary its option under subsection (b)(3).

(g) Rule for individual under other law. This section is subject to a rule of law, statute, rule or regulation other than this article which establishes a different rule for an account debtor who is an individual and who incurred the obligation primarily for personal, family, or household purposes.

(h) Inapplicability. This section does not apply to:

(1) an assignment of a health care insurance receivable to the extent such assignment conflicts with other law or the parties have otherwise agreed in writing that such receivable is non-assignable,

(2) a claim or right to receive compensation for injuries or sickness as described in 26 U.S.C. § 104(a)(1) and (2), as amended from time to time, or

(3) a claim or right to receive benefits under a special needs trust as described in 42 U.S.C. § 1396p (d)(4), as amended from time to time.

History: Add, L 2001, ch 84, § 36, eff July 1, 2001.

Former § 9-406, Add, L 1962, ch 553; amd, L 1965, ch 743, § 3, L 1967, ch 689, § 3, L 1977, ch 866, § 30, L 1982, ch 692, § 4, L 1986, ch 453, § 7, L 1990, ch 561, § 12, L 1996, ch 309, § 250, eff July 13, 1996.

Former § 9-406, repealed, L 2001, ch 84, § 36, eff July 1, 2001.

CASE ANNOTATIONS

Trial court erred in granting a bank's motion to dismiss, pursuant to N.Y. C.P.L.R. 3211(a)(1), an action by a purchaser to recover on three invoices owed by the bank; a blanket notice of payment redirection letter was sufficient to inform the bank of the sale of the invoices to the purchaser pursuant to N.Y. U.C.C. Law § 9-406(c), as the letter reasonably identified the rights to be assigned and notified the bank to direct payment to the purchaser's address. Hamilton Group (Del.), Inc. v Fed. Home Loan Bank (2003, A.D., 4th Dept) 767 N.Y.S.2d 332

Trial court properly denied account debtors' motion to dismiss a factor's action to collect on accounts receivable, because the factor presented evidence including testimony by the factor's comptroller and receipts from a carrier which raised clear factual issues as to whether the factor mailed notice of the assignment of the accounts to the debtors as required by N.Y. U.C.C. Las § 9-406, and the debtors' claims that they did not receive the notice did not afford a basis for dismissal. IIG Capital LLC v Archipelago, L.L.C. (2007, 1st Dept) 36 App Div 3d 401, 829 NYS2d 10

Professional service corporations' motion for partial summary judgment was granted as to insurers' defense of lack of standing in insurers' action for a declaratory judgment that the corporations were ineligible for no fault reimbursement because the corporations were entitled to a declaration that they were not ineligible for no fault reimbursement by reason of having assigned the claims pursuant to an accounts receivable financing agreement; a no fault insurer who pays the health care provider is not exposed to the risk of double-paying a factored claim. AIU Ins. Co. v Deajess Med. Imaging, P.C. (2009, Sup) 241 NYLJ 42, 882 NYS2d 812.

Creditor did not violate the discharge injunction by attempting to enforce its security interest against a bankruptcy debtor's disability benefits under an employee benefit plan, since the creditor had a valid lien in the benefits which survived discharge, and former N.Y. U.C.C. Law § 9-318(4) (now codified at N.Y. U.C.C. Law § 9-406(d)(1)) rendered unenforceable a spendthrift clause in the plan. In re Johnson (2010, BC ED Mich) 439 BR 416.

Former N.Y. U.C.C. Law § 9-318(4) (now codified at N.Y. U.C.C. Law § 9-406(d)(1)) was not preempted by the Employee Retirement Income Security Act (ERISA) under 29 U.S.C.S. § 1144(a) to permit the application of an anti-assignment clause in an employee benefit plan, since § 9-318(4) was a generally applicable statute which did not specifically refer to ERISA plans or single out such plans for special treatment. In re Johnson (2010, BC ED Mich) 439 BR 416.

§ 9-407. Restrictions on Creation or Enforcement of Security Interest in Leasehold Interest or in Lessor's Residual Interest

(a) Term restricting assignment generally ineffective. Except as otherwise provided in subsection (b), a term in a lease agreement is ineffective to the extent that it:

(1) prohibits, restricts, or requires the consent of a party to the lease to the assignment or transfer of, or the creation, attachment, perfection, or enforcement of a security interest in, an interest of a party under the lease contract or in the lessor's residual interest in the goods; or

(2) provides that the assignment or transfer or the creation, attachment, perfection, or enforcement of the security interest may give rise to a default,

breach, right of recoupment, claim, defense, termination, right of termination, or remedy under the lease.

(b) Effectiveness of certain terms. Except as otherwise provided in Section 2-A-303(7), a term described in subsection (a)(2) is effective to the extent that there is:

(1) a transfer by the lessee of the lessee's right of possession or use of the goods in violation of the term; or

(2) a delegation of a material performance of either party to the lease contract in violation of the term.

(c) Security interest not material impairment. The creation, attachment, perfection, or enforcement of a security interest in the lessor's interest under the lease contract or the lessor's residual interest in the goods is not a transfer that materially impairs the lessee's prospect of obtaining return performance or materially changes the duty of or materially increases the burden or risk imposed on the lessee within the purview of Section 2-A-303(4) unless, and then only to the extent that, enforcement actually results in a delegation of material performance of the lessor.

History: Add, L 2001, ch 84, § 36, eff July 1, 2001.

Former § 9-407, add, L 1962, ch 553, eff Sept 27, 1964; amd, L 1963, ch 1003, § 43, L 1964, ch 476, § 19, L 1966, ch 608, § 6, L 1982, ch 692, § 6, L 1986, ch 453, § 8, L 1990, ch 561, § 13, L 1996, ch 309, § 251, eff July 13, 1996.

Former § 9-407, repealed, L 2001, ch 84, § 36, eff July 1, 2001.

§ 9-408. Restrictions on Assignment of Promissory Notes, Health-care-insurance Receivables, and Certain General Intangibles Ineffective

(a) Term restricting assignment generally ineffective. Except as otherwise provided in subsection (b), a term in a promissory note or in an agreement between an account debtor and a debtor which relates to a health-care-insurance receivable or a general intangible, including a contract, permit, license, or franchise, and which term prohibits, restricts, or requires the consent of the person obligated on the promissory note or the account debtor to, the assignment or transfer of, or creation, attachment, or perfection of a security interest in, the promissory note, health-care-insurance receivable, or general intangible, is ineffective to the extent that the term:

(1) would impair the creation, attachment, or perfection of a security interest; or

(2) provides that the assignment or transfer or the creation, attachment, or perfection of the security interest may give rise to a default, breach, right of recoupment, claim, defense, termination, right of termination, or remedy under the promissory note, health-care-insurance receivable, or general intangible.

(b) Applicability of subsection (a) to sales of certain rights to payment. Subsection (a) applies to a security interest in a payment intangible or promissory note only if the security interest arises out of a sale of the payment intangible or promissory note.

(c) Limitation on ineffectiveness under subsection (a). To the extent that a term in a promissory note or in an agreement between an account debtor and a debtor which relates to a health-care-insurance receivable or general intangible would be effective under law other than this article but is ineffective under subsection (a), the creation, attachment, or perfection of a security interest in the promissory note, health-care-insurance receivable, or general intangible:

(1) is not enforceable against the person obligated on the promissory note or the account debtor;

(2) does not impose a duty or obligation on the person obligated on the promissory note or the account debtor;

(3) does not require the person obligated on the promissory note or the account debtor to recognize the security interest, pay or render performance to the secured party, or accept payment or performance from the secured party;

(4) does not entitle the secured party to use or assign the debtor's rights under the promissory note, health-care-insurance receivable, or general intangible, including any related information or materials furnished to the debtor in the transaction giving rise to the promissory note, health-care-insurance receivable, or general intangible;

(5) does not entitle the secured party to use, assign, possess, or have access to any trade secrets or confidential information of the person obligated on the promissory note or the account debtor; and

(6) does not entitle the secured party to enforce the security interest in the promissory note, health-care-insurance receivable, or general intangible.

(d) Inapplicability. This section does not apply to:

(1) a claim or right to receive compensation for injuries or sickness as described in 26 U.S.C. § 104(a)(1) and (2), as amended from time to time, or

(2) a claim or right to receive benefits under a special needs trust as described in 42 U.S.C. § 1396p (d)(4), as amended from time to time.

History: Add, L 2001, ch 84, § 36, eff July 1, 2001.

Former § 9-408, add, L 1977, ch 866, § 31, eff July 2, 1978; repealed, L 2001, ch 84, § 36, eff July 1, 2001.

Prior § 9-408, add, L 1962, ch 553; amd, L 1965, ch 959, § 2; renumbered § 9-409, L 1977, ch 866, § 31, eff July 2, 1978.

§ 9-409.   Restrictions on Assignment of Letter-of-credit Rights Ineffective

(a) Term or law restricting assignment generally ineffective. A term in a letter-of-credit or a rule of law, statute, regulation, custom, or practice applicable to the letter of credit which prohibits, restricts, or requires the consent of an applicant, issuer, or nominated person to a beneficiary's assignment of or creation of a security interest in a letter-of-credit right is ineffective to the extent that the term or rule of law, statute, regulation, custom, or practice:

(1) would impair the creation, attachment, or perfection of a security interest in the letter-of-credit right; or

(2) provides that the assignment or the creation, attachment, or perfection of the security interest may give rise to a default, breach, right of recoupment, claim, defense, termination, right of termination, or remedy under the letter-of-credit right.

(b) Limitation on ineffectiveness under subsection (a). To the extent that a term in a letter-of-credit is ineffective under subsection (a) but would be effective under law other than this article or a custom or practice applicable to the letter-of-credit, to the transfer of a right to draw or otherwise demand performance under the letter-of-credit, or to the assignment of a right to proceeds of the letter-of-credit, the creation, attachment, or perfection of a security interest in the letter-of-credit right:

(1) is not enforceable against the applicant, issuer, nominated person, or transferee beneficiary;

(2) imposes no duties or obligations on the applicant, issuer, nominated person, or transferee beneficiary; and

(3) does not require the applicant, issuer, nominated person, or transferee beneficiary to recognize the security interest, pay or render performance to the secured party, or accept payment or other performance from the secured party.

History: Add, L 2001, ch 84, § 36, eff July 1, 2001.

Former § 9-409, added as § 9-408, L 1962, ch 553; amd, L 1965, ch 959, § 2; renumbered § 9-409, L 1977, ch 866, § 31, eff July 2, 1978.

Former § 9-409, repealed, L 2001, ch 84, § 36, eff July 1, 2001.

Former § 9-409, add, L 1964, ch 476, § 20; renumbered § 9-410, L 1977, ch 866, § 31, eff July 2, 1978.

§ 9-410.   [Repealed]

History: Added as § 9-409, L 1964, ch 476, § 20; renumbered § 9-410, L 1977, ch 866, § 31, eff July 2, 1978.

Repealed, L 2001, ch 84, § 36, eff July 1, 2001.

PART 5
FILING

Subpart 1
Filing Office; Contents and Effectiveness of Financing Statement

§ 9-501.   Filing Office

History: Add, L 2001, ch 84, § 36, eff July 1, 2001.

Former Part 5, add, L 1962, ch 553, eff Sept 27, 1964; repealed, L 2001, ch 84, § 36, eff Juy 1, 2001.

Subpart 1
Filing Office; Contents And Effectiveness Of Financing Statement

History: Add, L 2001, ch 84, § 36, eff July 1, 2001.

§ 9-501.   Filing Office

(a) Filing offices. Except as otherwise provided in subsection (b), if the law of this state governs perfection of a security interest or agricultural lien, the office in which to file a financing statement to perfect the security interest or agricultural lien is:

(1) the office designated for the filing or recording of a record of a mortgage on the related real property, if:

(A) the collateral is as-extracted collateral or timber to be cut; or

(B) the financing statement is filed as a fixture filing and the collateral is goods that are or are to become fixtures; or

(C) the collateral is a cooperative interest; or

(2) the office of the secretary of state, in all other cases, including a case in which the collateral is goods that are or are to become fixtures and the financing statement is not filed as a fixture filing.

(b) Filing office for transmitting utilities. The office in which to file a financing statement to perfect a security interest in collateral, including fixtures, of a transmitting utility is the office of the secretary of state. The financing statement also constitutes a fixture filing as to the collateral indicated in the financing statement which is or is to become fixtures.

(c) The term "filing officer" or "recording officer" means the county clerk of the county, except in the counties of Bronx, Kings, New York, and Queens where it means the city register in the county; and the term "filing officer" includes the secretary of state where a filing is made in the department of state.

History: Add, L 2001, ch 84, § 36, eff July 1, 2001.

Former § 9-501, add, L 1962, ch 553; amd, L 1977, ch 866, § 32, eff July 2, 1978.

Former § 9-501, repealed, L 2001, ch 84, § 36, eff July 1, 2001.

CASE ANNOTATIONS

UNDER FORMER § 9-401
I. Generally
1. In general
2. Necessity of filing
II. Place of Filing
3. Residence of debtor; farm goods, etc.
4. Secretary of State
III. Mistake as to Place of Filing
5. In general
6. Good faith
7. Actual knowledge of financing statement
8. – Trustee in bankruptcy or the like
IV. Change in Circumstances Controlling Filing
9. Motor vehicles

UNDER FORMER § 9-401

I. Generally
1. In general
A financing statement, pursuant to the relevant sections of UCC Article 9, is a notice only, intended to make the general public aware of a prior interest in collateral so that proper inquiry can be made; the security agreement is the contract, and it determines the collateral involved. Allis-Chalmers Credit Corp. v Bank of Utica (1981, Sup) 110 Misc. 2d 283, 441 N.Y.S.2d 852

2. Necessity of filing
Corporate client was entitled to summary judgment in legal malpractice action where (1) it was uncontroverted that its attorney filed financing statement for it in county clerk's office, but failed to file it with Department of State, and attorney assured client that its security interest was "okay" and that its lien would follow property, and (2) debtor who acquired property from client filed bankruptcy and, because of failure to perfect security interest, subsequent creditor repossessed property. Deb-Jo Constr. v Westphal (1994, 4th Dept) 210 A.D.2d 951, 620 N.Y.S.2d 678

Failure of attorney to file financing statement in manner required by law to perfect his client's security interest constitutes negligence or malpractice as matter of law. Deb-Jo Constr. v Westphal (1994, 4th Dept) 210 A.D.2d 951, 620 N.Y.S.2d 678

II. Place of Filing
3. Residence of debtor; farm goods, etc.
Lender was entitled to summary judgment in lieu of complaint in its action to recover amount of defendant's guaranty of borrower's promissory note, which was secured in part by art collection, where (1) parties were entitled to set by agreement standards by which to measure fulfillment of lender's duty to dispose of art collateral in commercially reasonable may, so long as such standards were not manifestly unreasonable, (2) option agreement's valuation of collection, based in part on 1993 professional appraisal, was not manifestly unreasonable on its face and was not controverted by any competent evidence, (3) fact that art works were not acquired by lender until at least 2 years after execution of option agreement did

not negate reasonableness of agreed valuation, because both debtor and creditor were protected against later fluctuations in value, (4) borrower, which executed bills of sale transferring art collateral to lender, necessarily had notice of such transactions, and (5) option agreement did not require separate notice to borrower of exercise of lender's option. Leonia Bank PLC v Kouri (2001, 1st Dept) 286 A.D.2d 654, 730 N.Y.S.2d 501, 45 UCCRS2d 253

On application for order of seizure of boat (collateral), which was in possession of one defendant, prior to commencing action to recover boat's possession, plaintiff bank, to which security agreement entered into by debtor (original purchaser of boat) was assigned by original seller, had properly filed financing statement covering boat (consumer goods) in county of debtor's residence, as required by UCC § 9-401(1)(a), and under UCC § 9-401(3), no refiling was required when boat was moved to another county. Marine Midland Bank, N. A. v Smith Boys, Inc. (1985, Sup) 129 Misc. 2d 37, 492 N.Y.S.2d 355, 41 UCCRS 1843

4. Secretary of State

Where financing statements filed with secretary of state alone and not filed locally did not protect security interest, lien creditor had priority over holder of security interests. Package Machinery Co. v Cosden Oil & Chemical Co. (1976, 2d Dept) 51 A.D.2d 771, 380 N.Y.S.2d 248, 18 UCCRS 1316

In junior mortgagee's action for damages for defendant's alleged impairment of plaintiff's security, where defendant under security agreement with dealer in modular homes had security interest in all of dealer's present or future inventory and also first mortgage on 2.39 acres of land acquired by dealer for use as sales lot, on which dealer installed two modular homes; where plaintiff held second mortgage on dealer's 2.39 acres as security for loan on which dealer defaulted; and where defendant after dealer's default quickly removed modular homes from dealer's lot pursuant to written authorization from officer of dealer's company, (1) homes placed by dealer on sales lot, although installed on concrete foundations and connected to utilities, were inventory and not real property or fixtures under UCC § 9-109(4), since they were goods intended for immediate or ultimate sale; (2) defendant held perfected purchase-money security interest in dealer's inventory under UCC § 9-401(1)(c) and UCC § 9-402(1), which under UCC § 9-312(3) took priority over plaintiff's junior-mortgage interest; and (3) defendant on dealer's default had right to take possession of homes on dealer's lot, since they were inventory collateral. Rakosi v General Electric Credit Corp. (1977, 2d Dept) 59 A.D.2d 553, 397 N.Y.S.2d 416, 22 UCCRS 204

Failure of assignee of present and future accounts receivable to file financing statement with secretary of state voided lien as against assignor's creditors, including assignee for benefit of creditors; filing only in city register's office in county in which assignor had its place of business was not enough to properly perfect security interest under UCC § 9-401(1)(c). In re National New York Packing & Shipping Co. (1975) 82 Misc. 2d 1010, 372 N.Y.S.2d 274, 16 UCCRS 214

Test to be used to determine whether debtor has "place of business" in more than one county for purposes of filing financing statement and perfecting security interest under UCC § 9-401(1)(c) is the "notoriety" test. Enark Industries, Inc. v Bush (1976) 86 Misc. 2d 985, 383 N.Y.S.2d 796, 19 UCCRS 685

In order for location to qualify as place of business for purposes of UCC § 9-401(1)(c), debtor must actually conduct business at that location; actual business operations alone are insufficient to render location "place of business," and operations at location must be sufficiently notorious so that class of probable, potential creditors are aware of place of business. In re Alithochrome Corp. (1983, BC SD NY) 31 BR 352, 36 UCCRS 1784, vacated (1983, BC SD NY) 34 BR 354

In action between trustee in bankruptcy of contract knitting firm and creditors seeking to reclaim machinery, filing with secretary of state was sufficient to perfect security interest under UCC § 9-401(1)(c) as to those creditors whose security interests were created while debtor had place of business in more than one county in state; relative secrecy of one place of business was not fatal where its presence was known to those in trade. In re Mimshell Fabrics, Ltd. (1974, CA2 NY) 491 F.2d 21, 14 UCCRS 227

If central and local filing are both required, a local filing is not sufficient to cure the defect of failing to file in a central office. Filing in such a manner is not a mere irregularity and cannot be overlooked. In re Dumont-Airplane & Marine Instruments, Inc. (1962, SD NY) 203 F. Supp. 511, 1 UCCRS 579

Although bank, which filed financing statement in county clerk's office, failed to perfect its security interest by dual filing with Department of State as required by New York UCC, if subsequent creditor had all knowledge which it would have had if its officer had visited county clerk's office and read financing statement, under New York law it had actual notice of contents of financing statement. In re Davidoff (1972, SD NY) 351 F. Supp. 440, 11 UCCRS 609

III. Mistake as to Place of Filing

5. In general

If central and local filing are both required, a local filing is not sufficient to cure the defect of failing to file in a central office. Filing in such a manner is not a mere irregularity and cannot be overlooked. In re Dumont-Airplane & Marine Instruments, Inc. (1962, SD NY) 203 F. Supp. 511, 1 UCCRS 579

6. Good faith

Term "good faith" error, pursuant to CLS UCC § 9-401(2), is intended to apply to filing defects in general, not only to creditor's uncertainty with respect to location of filing. P.T. Bank Cent. Asia v Chinese Am. Bank (1997, 1st Dept) 229 A.D.2d 224, 654 N.Y.S.2d 117, 31 UCCRS2d 611

Foreclosure judgment did not extinguish mortgagee's security interest in real estate tax refund, as tax refund constituted "mortgaged property" as expressly defined in subject mortgages and thus, when received, it was subject to mortgagee's security interest and was available to satisfy its deficiency judgment against mortgagor. Board of Managers, Horizon Condo. v Glick Dev. Affiliates (2000, 1st Dept) 276 A.D.2d 386, 714 N.Y.S.2d 68, 43 UCCRS2d 752, app den 97 N.Y.2d 605, 737 N.Y.S.2d 53, 762 N.E.2d 931

In action to determine priority between municipal real estate tax lien on mobile home affixed to realty and purchase-money security interest of bank in such home, which interest, although improperly perfected, had attached under UCC § 9-204(1) before home was affixed to realty, court held (1) that since municipality was deemed to have had knowledge of bank's security interest and its good faith, but improper filing, bank's security interest in home was effectively perfected under UCC § 9-401(2) as of March 18, 1975; and (2) that although municipality was allegedly in position of subsequent purchaser for value of interest in realty to which home was attached within meaning of UCC § 9-313(4)(a), bank's perfected security interest in home had priority over municipality's real estate tax lien under UCC § 9-313(4) because (a) municipality was deemed to have had knowledge of bank's security interest, and (b) municipality's tax lien came into existence on April 16, 1975 after bank's security interest had been perfected. Commercial v Block 136, Lot 2, Now Lot 13 (1981) 179 NJ Super 307, 431 A2d 862, 34 UCCRS 760

7. Actual knowledge of financing statement

Irrespective of lapse of first filing, second filing in full compliance with requirements of CLS UCC Art 9 remains effective against creditor with actual knowledge of contents of financing statement. P.T. Bank Cent. Asia v Chinese Am. Bank (1997, 1st Dept) 229 A.D.2d 224, 654 N.Y.S.2d 117, 31 UCCRS2d 611

Subsequent creditor had actual knowledge under UCC §§ 9-401(2) and 1-201(25) of contents of improperly filed financing statement, and thus financing was effective against subsequent creditor, where subsequent creditor was aware at time that debtor came to it for loan that, except for about $13,000, all of debtor's $160,000 net worth was pledged for two prior bank loans and that pledge covered debtor's equipment. Enark Industries, Inc. v Bush (1976) 86 Misc. 2d 985, 383 N.Y.S.2d 796, 19 UCCRS 685

Where it appeared that party claiming security interest had all the knowledge which it would have had if it had visited the clerk's office and read the financing statement, it had actual notice under New York law despite fact that there was a defect in the filing of the statement. In re Davidoff (1972, SD NY) 351 F. Supp. 440, 11 UCCRS 609

8. – Trustee in bankruptcy or the like

An assignee for benefit of creditors stands in the position of a lien creditor by operation of law at the time of the assignment and is not charged with knowledge of the existence of an alleged prior security interest which has not been perfected because it was filed in a wrong office. In re Worldwide Handbag Co. (1967, N.Y. Sup) 4 UCCRS 608

IV. Change in Circumstances Controlling Filing

9. Motor vehicles

Initial filing of financing statement covering motor boat and inboard motor continued to be effective even though location of collateral changed. Marine Midland Bank, N. A. v Smith Boys, Inc. (1985, Sup) 129 Misc. 2d 37, 492 N.Y.S.2d 355, 41 UCCRS 1843

Where (1) debtors, at time security interest attached to mobile home purchased from creditor, were actually living in Fulton County, New York, (2) debtors, before August 6, 1973, moved to Herkimer County, New York, where home had been delivered and installed on its site, (3) on August 6, 1973, bank which was secured creditor's assignee filed financing statement in Fulton County, (4) debtors filed petition in bankruptcy, and (5) bank reassigned its interest in security agreement to plaintiff which repossessed home, plaintiff had secured-creditor status as against debtor's general creditors because (1) under UCC § 9-401(1)(a), proper place for filing financing statement covering consumer goods was county of debtor's actual residence at time security interest attached, and (2) after plaintiff's security interest had been perfected by filing in proper place, under UCC § 9-401(3), it remained effective, regardless of number of times or places debtors or collateral might thereafter move. In re Knapp (1978, CA2 NY) 575 F.2d 341, 23 UCCRS 1354 (applying New York law, and rejecting contention of bankruptcy trustee that county of debtors' residence at time financing statement was filed should control plaintiff's status as secured creditor)

§ 9-502. Contents of Financing Statement; Record of Mortgage as Financing Statement; Time of Filing Financing Statement; Contents of Cooperative Addendum

(a) Sufficiency of financing statement. Subject to subsection (b), a financing statement is sufficient only if it:

(1) provides the name of the debtor;

(2) provides the name of the secured party or a representative of the secured party;

(3) indicates the collateral covered by the financing statement; and

(4) in the case of a cooperative interest, indicates the number or other designation and the street address of the cooperative unit.

(b) Real-property-related financing statements. Except as otherwise provided in Section 9-501(b), to be sufficient, a financing statement that covers as-extracted collateral or timber to be cut, or which is filed as a fixture filing and covers goods that are or are to become fixtures, or, unless a cooperative addendum is filed, which covers a cooperative interest, must satisfy subsection (a) and also:

(1) indicate that it covers this type of collateral;

(2) indicate that it is to be filed in the real property records;

(3) provide a description of the real property to which the collateral is related, including the location of the real estate by reference to a book and page number in a deed or mortgage index maintained in the county clerk's office in the county where the property is situate or by street and number and town or city, or, if the real estate is in the city of New York, by county, except that if the real estate is in the city of New York or counties of Nassau or Onondaga, where the block system of recording or registering and indexing conveyances is in use, the statement must also specify the block and lot number in which the real estate is situated; and

(4) if the debtor does not have an interest of record in the real property, provide the name of a record owner.

(c) Record of mortgage as financing statement. A record of a mortgage is effective, from the date of recording, as a financing statement filed as a fixture filing or as a financing statement covering as-extracted collateral or timber to be cut only if:

(1) the record indicates the goods or accounts that it covers;

(2) the goods are or are to become fixtures related to the real property described in the record or the collateral is related to the real property described in the record and is as-extracted collateral or timber to be cut;

(3) the record satisfies the requirements for a financing statement in this section, but:

(A) the record need not indicate that it is to be filed in the real property records; and

(B) the record sufficiently provides the name of a debtor who is an individual if it provides the individual name of the debtor or the surname and first personal name of the debtor, even if the debtor is an individual to whom Section 9-503(a)(4) applies; and

(4) the record is duly recorded.

(d) Filing before security agreement or attachment. A financing statement may be filed before a security agreement is made or a security interest otherwise attaches.

(e) Contents of cooperative addendum. A cooperative addendum is sufficient only if it satisfies subsection (a) and also:

(1) if not filed simultaneously with the initial financing statement, identifies, by its file number, the initial financing statement to which the addendum relates;

(2) indicates the street address of the cooperative unit;

(3) indicates the county in which the cooperative unit is located;

(4) indicates the city, town, or village in which the cooperative unit is located;

(5) indicates the real property tax designation associated with the real property in which the cooperative unit is located as assigned by the local real property tax assessing authority; and

(6) indicates the name of the cooperative organization.

History: Add, L 2001, ch 84, § 36, eff July 1, 2001.

Former § 9-502, add, L 1962, ch 553; amd, L 1977, ch 866, § 33, eff July 2, 1978.

Former § 9-502, repealed, L 2001, ch 84, § 36, eff July 1, 2001.

Amd, L 2014, ch 505, § 44, eff Dec 17, 2014.

CASE ANNOTATIONS

UNDER FORMER § 9-402
1. In general; scope
2. Purpose
3. Sufficiency of financing statement, generally
4. Misspelling of debtor's name
5. Misstatement of debtor's corporate or trade name

UCC

6. Use of debtor's trade name only

7. Misidentification of secured party

8. Failure to identify owner of collateral

9. Effect of debtor's change of name or corporate structure

10. Signatures; particular applications

11. Addresses of parties, generally

12. Knowledge of security agreement

13. Description; particular applications

14. – After-acquired property

15. – Accuracy of description of single item of collateral

16. – General terms of description

17. – – "Equipment"

18. – Inventory

19. Minor errors

20. Security agreement as financing statement

21. Amendment or continuation of security agreement

22. Assignment of security interest of priority

In an interpleader action, an insurance company that had properly perfected a security interest in a judgment creditor's assets under N.Y. U.C.C. Law § 9-310(a) by filing a financing statement that met the requirements of N.Y. U.C.C. Law § 9-502(a) was found to be entitled to the proceeds of an award obtained by the judgment creditor in a breach of contract suit; the insurance company's claim took priority under N.Y. U.C.C. Law § 9-322(a) over that of a claimant that had obtained a default judgment against the judgment creditor in a separate suit. Sentry Select Ins. Co. v LBL Skysystems (U.S.A.), Inc. (2007, ED Pa) 486 F Supp 2d 496, stay den (2007, ED Pa) 2007 US Dist LEXIS 46654.

UNDER FORMER § 9-402

1. In general; scope

Sections 65 and 70 of the New York Personal Property Law which provide the effect and method of filing conditional sales contracts have now been superseded by §§ 9-402 and 9-403(1) of the UCC. In re Mutual Board & Packaging Corp. (1965, CA2 NY) 342 F.2d 294, 2 UCCRS 451

2. Purpose

The purpose of filing is to put the public generally on notice of the prior interest in collateral so that inquiry can be made. Bank of Utica v Smith Richfield Springs, Inc. (1968) 58 Misc. 2d 113, 294 N.Y.S.2d 797, 5 UCCRS 1197

The purpose of the statute is to avoid the real estate type of closing where all parties go to the clerk's office, check the records, execute the financing statement and file it secure in the knowledge that the creditor has first priority. The statute was designed to allow a creditor to pre-empt first rights against the borrower. Bank of Utica v Smith Richfield Springs, Inc. (1968) 58 Misc. 2d 113, 294 N.Y.S.2d 797, 5 UCCRS 1197

Uniform Commercial Code § 9-402 adopts a system of "notice filing" which merely indicates that the secured party may have a security interest in the collateral described, the purpose of the filed statement being to give sufficient information necessary to put a searcher on inquiry, and the secured party has the duty to make sure of proper filing and indexing. John Deere Co. v William C. Pahl Constr. Co. (1969) 59 Misc. 2d 872, 300 N.Y.S.2d 701, 6 UCCRS 840, affd (1970, 4th Dept) 34 A.D.2d 85, 310 N.Y.S.2d 945, 7 UCCRS 795

A financing statement, pursuant to the relevant sections of UCC Article 9, is a notice only, intended to make the general public aware of a prior interest in collateral so that proper inquiry can be made; the security agreement is the contract, and it determines the collateral involved. Allis-Chalmers Credit Corp. v Bank of Utica (1981, Sup) 110 Misc. 2d 283, 441 N.Y.S.2d 852

3. Sufficiency of financing statement, generally

In action to recover possession of motor home that plaintiff secured party had sold to debtor under retail installment contract and security agreement, where (1) plaintiff, although authorized to file financing statement, did not do so before assigning installment contract and security agreement to bank, (2) after contract and security agreement had been assigned to bank, debtor transferred title to home to third-party purchaser, (3) such purchaser resold home to another third party who, in turn, resold it to defendant, (4) after first third-party purchaser had purchased home, bank filed financing statement that listed only original buyer of home as "debtor," and (5) on original buyer's default in making payments, bank reassigned installment contract and security agreement to plaintiff, which sought to replevy home from last third-party purchaser, court held (1) that even though bank was aware that title to home had been

transferred to first third-party purchaser, bank nevertheless, on filing its financing statement, listed only original buyer as "debtor" on such statement, (2) that financing statement, as a result, failed under UCC §§ 9-402(1) and 9-105(1)(d) to identify "debtor" properly in situation where owner of collateral and obligor on financing agreement were not the same person, (3) that plaintiff's security interest was therefore not perfected, and (4) that since defendant third-party purchaser had purchased home out of ordinary course of business and without knowledge of plaintiff's unperfected security interest therein, defendant's ownership of home was free of such security interest under UCC § 9-301(1)(c). White Star Distributors, Inc. v Kennedy (1978, 4th Dept) 66 A.D.2d 1011, 411 N.Y.S.2d 751, 25 UCCRS 1446

Under UCC § 9-402(1), a financing statement must include the name and address of the debtor. In this connection, however, the term "debtor" is defined by UCC § 9-105(1)(d) to include both the owner of the collateral and the obligor on the financing agreement if the owner and the obligor are not the same person. White Star Distributors, Inc. v Kennedy (1978, 4th Dept) 66 A.D.2d 1011, 411 N.Y.S.2d 751, 25 UCCRS 1446

Financing statement under name of "Gail Keaton" was insufficient to give minimum information necessary to put person searching financing statements on inquiry where person was searching for "Charlene Gail Keaton;" thus, financing statement filed by seller of mobile home was defective and seller's interest was subordinate to interest of mobile home park which levied against mobile home for rent due. First Manufactured Housing Credit Corp. v Clarkson Mobile Home Park, Inc. (1989, 3d Dept) 148 A.D.2d 901, 539 N.Y.S.2d 529, 8 UCCRS2d 1259, app den (1989) 74 N.Y.2d 611, 546 N.Y.S.2d 555, 545 N.E.2d 869

Defendant finance company, which acquired purchase-money security interest in 2 vehicles by its postpurchase advance of funds to auto dealer, had priority over "dragnet" lien previously acquired by plaintiff in connection with "floor plan" financing of dealer's inventory, notwithstanding plaintiff's claim that it lacked notice of inventory covered by defendant's security interest because dealer and defendant had diverged in practice from literal language of their contract which appeared to contemplate prepurchase advance of funds, where written identification of defendant's collateral was "reasonably specific" and plaintiff could not show how it relied to its detriment on when and how defendant discharged its individual financing obligations to dealer. GE Capital Commer. Auto. Fin. v Spartan Motors, Ltd. (1998, 2d Dept) 246 A.D.2d 41, 675 N.Y.S.2d 626, 36 UCCRS2d 19, app gr (1998) 92 N.Y.2d 816, 683 N.Y.S.2d 759, 706 N.E.2d 747 and app dismd (1999) 93 N.Y.2d 870, 689 N.Y.S.2d 17, 711 N.E.2d 202

Junior secured noteholders (JSNs) were entitled to lien on released and reaquired collateral because JSNs' interest in reaquired mortgage loans was perfected under New York law due to filing of financing statements that were sufficient to engage interested parties in further inquiry. Official Comm. of Unsercured Creditors v UMB Bank, N.A. (In re Capital) (2013, BC SD NY) 501 BR 549.

4. Misspelling of debtor's name

Misspelling of names on UCC-1 financing statement rendered plaintiff's security interest in debtor's crops unperfected where debtor "Peter Dragan, doing business as Dragan Grain Farms" was listed on statement as "Dragon Grain Farms and Peter Dragon, individually," but plaintiff's unperfected rights were superior to those of buyer who purchased crops with actual knowledge of plaintiff's security interest; thus, affidavit of plaintiff's treasurer, asserting that she wrote and phoned purchaser objecting to its purchase of crops, raised fact issue as to purchaser's actual knowledge of plaintiff's security interest. Reisdorf Bros., Inc. v Clinton Corn Processing Co. (1987, 4th Dept) 130 A.D.2d 951, 516 N.Y.S.2d 375, 3 UCCRS2d 1956

Financing statement filed under name of "Charline Gail Keaton" would give minimum information necessary to put person searching financing statements on inquiry where person was searching for "Charlene Gail Keaton," notwithstanding minor deviation in spelling. First Manufactured Housing Credit Corp. v Clarkson Mobile Home Park, Inc. (1989, 3d Dept) 148 A.D.2d 901, 539 N.Y.S.2d 529, 8 UCCRS2d 1259, app den (1989) 74 N.Y.2d 611, 546 N.Y.S.2d 555, 545 N.E.2d 869

Misspelling of corporate debtor's name-"Ranelli" instead of "Ranalli"-on filed financing statement was seriously misleading and amounted to no filing at all, so that security interest was ineffective as to person in possession. John Deere Co. v William C. Pahl Constr. Co. (1969) 59 Misc. 2d 872, 300 N.Y.S.2d 701, 6 UCCRS 840, affd (1970, 4th Dept) 34 A.D.2d 85, 310 N.Y.S.2d 945, 7 UCCRS 795

5. Misstatement of debtor's corporate or trade name

Plaintiff creditor's financing statement substantially complied with filing requirements of CLS UCC § 9-402 in naming of debtor, and thus gave sufficient notice of plaintiff's security interest to defendant creditor, where statement listed debtor's name as "Kohn's Supermarket d/b/a Best K Foods, Inc." whereas debtor's name of incorporation was "The Kohn's Supermarket, Inc."; moreover, defendant had actual notice that debtor was conducting business as "Kohn's Supermarket" where it had taken over debtor's premises and had complete access to debtor's business records, and where signs at debtor's place of business read "Kohn's Supermarket." TMMB Funding Corp. v Associated Food Stores, Inc. (1988, 2d Dept) 136 A.D.2d 540, 523 N.Y.S.2d 161, 5 UCCRS2d 1527

Financing statement describing debtor as "Nara Dist. Inc." when in fact correct name of debtor was "Nara Non Food Distributing Inc." was sufficient as putting any interested person fairly on notice that there might be an outstanding lien against the Nara intended. In re Nara Non Food Distributing, Inc. (1970) 66 Misc. 2d 779, 322 N.Y.S.2d 194, 9 UCCRS 747, affd (1971, 2d Dept) 36 A.D.2d 796, 320 N.Y.S.2d 1014

6. Use of debtor's trade name only

Filing of financing statement only under business name was not adequate notice of lien against bankrupt individual where goods were purchased in individual rather than business name. In re Leichter (1972, CA2 NY) 471 F.2d 785, 11 UCCRS 673 (superseded by statute as stated in In re Bennett Funding Group (1996, BC ND NY) 203 BR 30, 32 UCCRS2d 331)

7. Misidentification of secured party

The fact that the corporation to which plaintiff bank made loans secured by a restaurant equipment security agreement had not yet filed its certificate of incorporation at the time the security agreement was entered into and the first advance made, does not constitute an affirmative defense to plaintiff's action to recover on its security interest from defendants, the purchasers of the restaurant equipment at a mortgage foreclosure sale, since the doctrine of *de facto* corporation is applicable, it being necessary in order to establish the existence of a *de facto* corporation that there is a law under which the corporation might be organized, an attempt to organize the corporation and an exercise of corporate powers thereunder; in any event, the corporation subsequently adopted the security agreement by accepting loans from plaintiff after the date the certificate of incoporation was filed; since it was the corporate entity which entered into the contract with plaintiff and not the corporation's president, individually, it was proper to list the corporation as the debtor on the financing statement, which sufficiently described the restaurant equipment covered by the security agreement (Uniform Commercial Code, § 9-402); accordingly, in the event that defendants are unable to prove that the equipment was owned by the corporation's president, individually, the restaurant equipment they purchased is subject to plaintiff's valid perfected security interest even assuming that they purchased the equipment for value and without knowledge of plaintiff's interest. Bankers Trust Co. v Zecher (1980) 103 Misc. 2d 777, 426 N.Y.S.2d 960, 29 UCCRS 323

Where chapter 7 trustee sought to exercise his avoidance powers under 11 U.S.C.S. §§ 544(a)(1) and 547(b), creditor's recording of a U.C.C.-1 financing statement identifying in general certain specific cows as the collateral complied with N.Y. U.C.C. Law § 9-502, and gave notice of the creditor's valid claim to the cows. Collins v Angell (In re Baker) (2012, BC ND NY) 465 BR 359.

8. Failure to identify owner of collateral

In action to recover possession of motor home that plaintiff secured party had sold to debtor under retail installment contract and security agreement, where (1) plaintiff, although authorized to file financing statement, did not do so before assigning installment contract and security agreement to bank, (2) after contract and security agreement had been assigned to bank, debtor transferred title to home to third-party purchaser, (3) such purchaser resold home to another third party who, in turn, resold it to defendant, (4) after first third-party purchaser had purchased home, bank filed financing statement that listed only original buyer of home as "debtor," and (5) on original buyer's default in making payments, bank reassigned installment contract and security agreement to plaintiff, which sought to replevy home from last third-party purchaser, court held (1) that even though bank was aware that title to home had been transferred to first third-party purchaser, bank nevertheless, on filing its financing statement, listed only original buyer as "debtor" on such

statement, (2) that financing statement, as a result, failed under UCC §§ 9-402(1) and 9-105(1)(d) to identify "debtor" properly in situation where owner of collateral and obligor on financing agreement were not the same person, (3) that plaintiff's security interest was therefore not perfected, and (4) that since defendant third-party purchaser had purchased home out of ordinary course of business and without knowledge of plaintiff's unperfected security interest therein, defendant's ownership of home was free of such security interest under UCC § 9-301(1)(c). White Star Distributors, Inc. v Kennedy (1978, 4th Dept) 66 A.D.2d 1011, 411 N.Y.S.2d 751, 25 UCCRS 1446

Under UCC § 9-402(1), a financing statement must include the name and address of the debtor. In this connection, however, the term "debtor" is defined by UCC § 9-105(1)(d) to include both the owner of the collateral and the obligor on the financing agreement if the owner and the obligor are not the same person. White Star Distributors, Inc. v Kennedy (1978, 4th Dept) 66 A.D.2d 1011, 411 N.Y.S.2d 751, 25 UCCRS 1446

9. Effect of debtor's change of name or corporate structure

Neither CLS UCC § 9-402(7) nor CLS UCC § 1-203 required secured party to refile properly and accurately filed financing statement on subsequent event of name change by debtor 6 weeks after acquiring secured party's assets; also, statute did not require special notation financing statement, even if known by secured party, where there was no finding of bad faith or wrongful intent attributable to secured party, and all that existed was mere possibility of and contractual authorization for name change, which occurred 6 weeks after acquisition of assets and with other key intervening developments and transactions. Fleet Factors Corp. v Bandolene Indus. Corp. (1995) 86 N.Y.2d 519, 634 N.Y.S.2d 425, 658 N.E.2d 202, 27 UCCRS2d 1105

In dispute between assignee for benefit of creditors and bank claiming security interest in proceeds from sale of collateral, bank held superior interest under UCC § 9-301(3) where, under New York version of UCC § 9-402, change of name of debtor firm did not affect perfection of filing made under former name, regardless of whether bank had knowledge of change of name. In re Pasco Sales Co. (1974) 77 Misc. 2d 724, 354 N.Y.S.2d 402, 14 UCCRS 1059

10. Signatures; particular applications

The absence of a checkmark on a financing statement to show the debtor had authorized filing without her signature did not impair the creditor's security interest, where the statement was otherwise sufficient. Beneficial Finance Co. v Kurland Cadillac-Oldsmobile, Inc. (1969, 2d Dept) 32 A.D.2d 643, 300 N.Y.S.2d 884, 6 UCCRS 539

Financing statement was not "signed by the debtor" as required by UCC § 9-402(1), where debtor was "P. S. C. Products Corporation" and where statement was signed by officer of debtor corporation under legend which identified debtor as "Pacific Supply Co., division of P. S. C. Products Corp." In re Pasco Sales Co. (1976, 2d Dept) 52 A.D.2d 138, 383 N.Y.S.2d 42, 19 UCCRS 959 (superseded by statute as stated in In re Bennett Funding Group (1996, BC ND NY) 203 BR 30, 32 UCCRS2d 331)

In an action for conversion by seizure and sale of property covered by security agreement allegedly void presented triable issues of fact as to the validity of the agreement, precluding summary judgment, where agreement was undated, did not specify the amount of the debt, or the terms of repayment and was signed by an individual in his own name and not in his capacity as an officer or the debtor corporation but the agreement did name the debtor corporation in the body thereof, listed the collateral covered by it, and the individual signing it was in fact the president of the debtor authorized to sign. Cherno v Bank of Babylon (1968) 57 Misc. 2d 801, 293 N.Y.S.2d 577

Under New York Code § 9-402(2)(c) (subsection not contained in "official" or "uniform" version of Code) financing statement, indicating that filing without debtor's signature was authorized, was properly treated as proof that security agreement did in fact authorize such filing. Bank of North America v Bank of Nutley (1967) 94 NJ Super 220, 227 A2d 535, 4 UCCRS 56 (applying New York law)

11. Addresses of parties, generally

Under UCC § 9-402(1), a financing statement must include the name and address of the debtor. In this connection, however, the term "debtor" is defined by UCC § 9-105(1)(d) to include both the owner of the collateral and the obligor on the financing agreement if the owner and the obligor are not the same person. White Star Distributors, Inc. v Kennedy (1978, 4th Dept) 66 A.D.2d 1011, 411 N.Y.S.2d 751, 25 UCCRS 1446

UCC

12. Knowledge of security agreement

A financing statement is sufficient if it indicates the types or describes the items of collateral. Bank of Utica v Smith Richfield Springs, Inc. (1968) 58 Misc. 2d 113, 294 N.Y.S.2d 797, 5 UCCRS 1197

13. Description; particular applications

UCC-1 financing statement created security interest in manufactured home since it was signed by defendant, it named parties, it described collateral, it described plaintiff as secured party, and circumstances under which it was signed-at closing on sale of real property wherein plaintiff received note and purchase-money mortgage-evinced intent to create security interest in manufactured home. Lashua v La Duke (2000, 3d Dept) 272 A.D.2d 750, 707 N.Y.S.2d 542, 41 UCCRS2d 930

Description of collateral was sufficient without boat's serial number. Marine Midland Bank, N. A. v Smith Boys, Inc. (1985, Sup) 129 Misc. 2d 37, 492 N.Y.S.2d 355, 41 UCCRS 1843

On application for order of seizure of boat (collateral), which was in possession of one defendant, prior to commencing action to recover boat's possession, under UCC §§ 9-402(1) and 9-110, boat was adequately described in plaintiff's financing statement, even though statement did not include boat's serial number. Marine Midland Bank, N. A. v Smith Boys, Inc. (1985, Sup) 129 Misc. 2d 37, 492 N.Y.S.2d 355, 41 UCCRS 1843

14. – After-acquired property

Financing statement covering "motor vehicles" is sufficiently specific under Code § 9-402(1) to perfect security interest of bank loaning money on chattel mortgage for three named automobiles; adding words "after acquired", while advisable, is not necessary where debtor is retail auto agency obviously buying and selling autos. Bank of Utica v Smith Richfield Springs, Inc. (1968) 58 Misc. 2d 113, 294 N.Y.S.2d 797, 5 UCCRS 1197

15. – Accuracy of description of single item of collateral

Plaintiff who sold farm tool to defendant and filed UCC 1 financing statement containing incorrect serial number was not entitled to order under CLS CPLR § 7102 permitting sheriff to seize tool from defendant since it failed to demonstrate probability of success on merits; CLS UCC § 9-402 does not require exactitude in describing collateral, but by listing tool's serial number in effort to be more exact, plaintiff ran risk of subjecting its security interest to attack if it did so incorrectly. John Deere Co. v Richards (1987, Sup) 136 Misc. 2d 923, 519 N.Y.S.2d 450, 4 UCCRS2d 1252

16. – General terms of description

A filed financing statement covering "motor vehicles" is sufficiently specific under UCC § 9-402 to perfect the security interest of a bank loaning on a chattel mortgage for three named automobiles as opposed to an interest of the seller of the automobiles to receive payment for those cars because of a worthless check. Bank of Utica v Smith Richfield Springs, Inc. (1968) 58 Misc. 2d 113, 294 N.Y.S.2d 797, 5 UCCRS 1197

17. – – "Equipment"

Unlike a financing statement which is designed merely to put creditors on notice that further inquiry is prudent, a security agreement embodies the intentions of the parties and is the primary source to which a creditor's or potential creditor's inquiry is directed and must be reasonably specific; thus term "equipment" in omnibus clause of security agreement did not include automobiles owned by bankrupt corporation. In re Laminated Veneers Co. (1973, CA2 NY) 471 F.2d 1124, 11 UCCRS 911

18. – Inventory

In junior mortgagee's action for damages for defendant's alleged impairment of plaintiff's security, where defendant under security agreement with dealer in modular homes had security interest in all of dealer's present or future inventory and also first mortgage on 2.39 acres of land acquired by dealer for use as sales lot, on which dealer installed two modular homes; where plaintiff held second mortgage on dealer's 2.39 acres as security for loan on which dealer defaulted; and where defendant after dealer's default quickly removed modular homes from dealer's lot pursuant to written authorization from officer of dealer's company, (1) homes placed by dealer on sales lot, although installed on concrete foundations and connected to utilities, were inventory and not real property or fixtures under UCC § 9-109 (4), since they were goods intended for immediate or ultimate sale; (2) defendant had perfected purchase-money security interest in dealer's inventory under UCC § 9-401(1)(c) and UCC § 9-402(1), which under UCC § 9-312(3) took priority over plaintiff's junior-mortgage interest; and (3) defendant on dealer's default had right to take possession of homes on dealer's lot, since they were inventory collateral. Rakosi v

General Electric Credit Corp. (1977, 2d Dept) 59 A.D.2d 553, 397 N.Y.S.2d 416, 22 UCCRS 204

19. Minor errors

Failure of finance company to check box opposite provision that debtor had signed security agreement authorizing finance company to file statement was minor error which could not seriously mislead one who searched file; held, financing statement was effective. Beneficial Finance Co. v Kurland Cadillac-Oldsmobile, Inc. (1969, 2d Dept) 32 A.D.2d 643, 300 N.Y.S.2d 884, 6 UCCRS 539

20. Security agreement as financing statement

A conditional sales contract in proper form and timely filed with correct recording office has been filed in compliance with this section even though recorder erroneously returned instrument for an acknowledgment. In re Mutual Board & Packaging Corp. (1965, CA2 NY) 342 F.2d 294, 2 UCCRS 451

21. Amendment or continuation of security agreement

In dispute between assignee for benefit of creditors and bank claiming security interest in proceeds from sale of collateral, bank held superior interest under UCC § 9-301(3) where, under New York version of UCC § 9-402, change of name of debtor firm did not affect perfection of filing made under former name, regardless of whether bank had knowledge of change of name. In re Pasco Sales Co. (1974) 77 Misc. 2d 724, 354 N.Y.S.2d 402, 14 UCCRS 1059

22. Assignment of security interest of priority

Plaintiff's security interest in all present and future Medicaid and Medicare accounts receivable of ambulance company, which plaintiff perfected on May 11, 1972 by filing financing statement in accordance with UCC § 9-402, had priority over state tax warrant for sum owed by ambulance company for employee income-withholding taxes, which warrant was filed on October 8, 1975 and under which state tax department had levied on Medicaid payments owed to ambulance company by county department of social services. In such case, priority of plaintiff's security-interest lien was not affected by state statute providing that assignment of claim of supplier of medical assistance was invalid as against any social services district since such statute, although prohibiting enforcement of plaintiff's assignment against any social services district, did not prohibit enforcement of such assignment as against any other person. IMFC Professional Services, Inc. v State (1977, 4th Dept) 59 A.D.2d 1047, 399 N.Y.S.2d 804

Where 1966 loan was secured by assignment of contract right, where financing statement filed in 1966 was in compliance with UCC § 9-402(1) and where secured party made subsequent loans to debtor in 1967 and 1968, even if 1966 and 1967 notes did not contain future advance clauses, secured party maintained position of perfected secured creditor with respect to 1968 loan which was also secured by assignment of contract rights covered by 1966 note and financing statement. In re Estate of Gruder (1977) 89 Misc. 2d 477, 392 N.Y.S.2d 203, 21 UCCRS 287

§ 9-503.   Name of Debtor and Secured Party

(a) Sufficiency of debtor's name. A financing statement sufficiently provides the name of the debtor:

(1) except as otherwise provided in paragraph (3), if the debtor is a registered organization or the collateral is held in a trust that is a registered organization, only if the financing statement provides the name that is stated to be the registered organization's name on the public organic record most recently filed with or issued or enacted by the registered organization's jurisdiction of organization which purports to state, amend, or restate the registered organization's name;

(2) subject to subsection (f), if the collateral is being administered by the personal representative of a decedent, only if the financing statement provides, as the name of the debtor, the name of the decedent and, in a separate part of the financing statement, indicates that the collateral is being administered by a personal representative;

(3) if the collateral is held in a trust that is not a registered organization, only if the financing statement:

(A) provides, as the name of the debtor:

(i) if the organic record of the trust specifies a name for the trust, the name specified; or

(ii) if the organic record of the trust does not specify a name for the trust, the name of the settlor or testator; and

(B) in a separate part of the financing statement:

(i) if the name is provided in accordance with subparagraph (A)(i), indicates that the collateral is held in a trust; or

(ii) if the name is provided in accordance with subparagraph (A)(ii), provides additional information sufficient to distinguish the trust from other trusts having one or more of the same settlors or the same testator and indicates that the collateral is held in a trust, unless the additional information so indicates;

(4) subject to subsection (g), if the debtor is an individual to whom this State has issued a driver's license or non-driver photo identification card that has not expired, only if the financing statement provides the name of the individual which is indicated on the driver's license or non-driver photo identification card;

(5) if the debtor is an individual to whom paragraph (4) does not apply, only if the financing statement provides the individual name of the debtor or the surname and first personal name of the debtor; and

(6) in other cases:

(A) if the debtor has a name, only if the financing statement provides the organizational name of the debtor; and

(B) if the debtor does not have a name, only if it provides the names of the partners, members, associates, or other persons comprising the debtor, in a manner that each name provided would be sufficient if the person named were the debtor.

(b) Additional debtor-related information. A financing statement that provides the name of the debtor in accordance with subsection (a) is not rendered ineffective by the absence of:

(1) a trade name or other name of the debtor; or

(2) unless required under subsection (a)(6)(B), names of partners, members, associates, or other persons comprising the debtor.

(c) Debtor's trade name insufficient. A financing statement that provides only the debtor's trade name does not sufficiently provide the name of the debtor.

(d) Representative capacity. Failure to indicate the representative capacity of a secured party or representative of a secured party does not affect the sufficiency of a financing statement.

(e) Multiple debtors and secured parties. A financing statement may provide the name of more than one debtor and the name of more than one secured party.

(f) Name of decedent. The name of the decedent indicated on the order appointing the personal representative of the decedent issued by the court having jurisdiction over the collateral is sufficient as the "name of the decedent" under subsection (a)(2).

(g) Multiple driver's licenses. If this State has issued to an individual more than one driver's license or non-driver photo identification card of a kind described in subsection (a)(4), the one that was issued most recently is the one to which subsection (a)(4) refers.

(h) Definition. In this section, the "name of the settlor or testator" means:

(1) if the settlor is a registered organization, the name that is stated to be the settlor's name on the public organic record most recently filed with or issued or enacted by the settlor's jurisdiction of organization which purports to state, amend, or restate the settlor's name; or

(2) in other cases, the name of the settlor or testator indicated in the trust's organic record.

History: Add, L 2001, ch 84, § 36, eff July 1, 2001.

Former § 9-503, add, L 1962, ch 553, eff Sept 27, 1964; repealed, L 2001, ch 84, § 36, eff July 1, 2001.

Amd, L 2014, ch 505, § 45, eff Dec 17, 2014.

CASE ANNOTATIONS

Court properly determined that a debtor's action against a creditor for personal injuries that he sustained during an altercation with a repossessor was subject to the three-year statute of limitations in N.Y. C.P.L.R. 214(2). Because an employer of an independent contractor was not generally liable for an injury caused to a third party by the acts or omissions of the independent contractor or its employees, and because N.Y. U.C.C. Law § 9-503 imposed a nondelegable duty on the creditor to keep the peace in the course of a repossession, the statute created a new liability for a wrong that no other statute of limitations prescribed. GMAC v Vucich (2005, A.D., 3d Dept) 787 N.Y.S.2d 745

Because there was a question of fact as to whether an employee of a company hired by a lender to repossess a vehicle from the borrowers acted in self-defense, the trial court properly denied the borrowers' motion for partial summary judgment on their cause of action for breach of the peace during a repossession under former N.Y. U.C.C. Law § 9-503. General Motors Acceptance Corp. v Vucich (2006, App Div, 3d Dept) 818 NYS2d 327.

§ 9-504.   Indication of Collateral

A financing statement sufficiently indicates the collateral that it covers if the financing statement provides:

(1) a description of the collateral pursuant to Section 9-108; or

(2) an indication that the financing statement covers all assets or all personal property.

History: Add, L 2001, ch 84, § 36, eff July 1, 2001.

Former § 9-504, add, L 1962, ch 553, eff Sept 27, 1964, amd, L 1977, ch 866, § 34, eff July 2, 1978.

Former § 9-504, repealed, L 2001, ch 84, § 36, eff July 1, 2001.

In action on promissory note issued in connection with sale of boat, neither party was entitled to summary judgment where there were triable issues of fact as to whether private sale of boat by bank to plaintiff took place in "commercially reasonable" manner under CLS UCC § 9-504(3) regarding adequacy of price and notice provided to defendant of sale. Drucker v Alfieri (2000, 2d Dept) 273 A.D.2d 436, 711 N.Y.S.2d 747

In action on promissory note issued in connection with sale of boat, neither party was entitled to summary judgment where there were triable issues of fact as to whether private sale of boat by bank to plaintiff took place in "commercially reasonable" manner under CLS UCC § 9-504(3) regarding adequacy of price and notice provided to defendant of sale. Drucker v Alfieri (2000, 2d Dept) 273 A.D.2d 436, 711 N.Y.S.2d 747

§ 9-505. Filing and Compliance with Other Statutes and Treaties for Consignments, Leases, Other Bailments, and Other Transactions

(a) Use of terms other than "debtor" and "secured party." A consignor, lessor, or other bailor of goods, a licensor, or a buyer of a payment intangible or promissory note may file a financing statement, or may comply with a statute or treaty described in Section 9-311(a), using the terms "consignor", "consignee", "lessor", "lessee", "bailor", "bailee", "licensor", "licensee", "owner", "registered owner", "buyer", "seller", or words of similar import, instead of the terms "secured party" and "debtor".

(b) Effect of financing statement under subsection (a). This part applies to the filing of a financing statement under subsection (a) and, as appropriate, to compliance that is equivalent to filing a financing statement under Section 9-311(b), but the filing or compliance is not of itself a factor in determining whether the collateral secures an obligation. If it is determined for another reason that the collateral secures an obligation, a security interest held by the consignor, lessor, bailor, licensor, owner, or buyer which attaches to the collateral is perfected by the filing or compliance.

History: Add, L 2001, ch 84, § 36, eff July 1, 2001.

Former § 9-505, add, L 1962, ch 553; amd, L 1963, ch 1003, § 44, L 1977, ch 866, § 35, eff July 2, 1978.

Former § 9-505, repealed, L 2001, ch 84, § 36, eff July 1, 2001.

§ 9-506. Effect of Errors or Omissions

(a) Minor errors and omissions. A financing statement substantially satisfying the requirements of this part is effective, even if it has minor errors or omissions, unless the errors or omissions make the financing statement seriously misleading.

(b) Financing statement seriously misleading. Except as otherwise provided in subsection (c), a financing statement that fails sufficiently to provide the name of the debtor in accordance with Section 9-503(a) is seriously misleading.

(c) Financing statement not seriously misleading. If a search of the records of the filing office under the debtor's correct name, using the filing office's stand-

ard search logic, if any, would disclose a financing statement that fails sufficiently to provide the name of the debtor in accordance with Section 9-503(a), the name provided does not make the financing statement seriously misleading.

(d) "Debtor's correct name." For purposes of Section 9-508(b), the "debtor's correct name" in subsection (c) means the correct name of the new debtor.

History: Add, L 2001, ch 84, § 36, eff July 1, 2001.

Former § 9-506, add, L 1962, ch 553, eff Sept 27, 1964; repealed, L 2001, ch 84, § 36, eff July 1, 2001.

There was a clear and material mismatch between the collateral descriptions contained in the Pledge and the "UCC-1" financing statement; the descriptions were irreconcilable and made the UCC-1 seriously misleading and ineffective under New York law. Any reasonable person viewing the Pledge would conclude that debtor had granted the purported creditor a lien on its membership interest in another entity, which is intangible personal property; by contrast, a reasonable person viewing the UCC-1 would conclude that debtor had granted the purported creditor a security interest in identifiable condominium units in Manhattan. In re 11 East 36th, LLC, 2015 Bankr. LEXIS 277 (Bankr. S.D.N.Y. 2015), aff'd, 2016 U.S. Dist. LEXIS 36548 (S.D.N.Y. Mar. 21, 2016).

UCC-1 Financing Statements filed by creditor, having neither used the approved additional party form, nor having contained any direction to look beyond first page of the UCC-1 for additional debtor information, were seriously misleading with respect to two additional debtors and therefore ineffective to perfect a security interest in its assets. Official Comm. of Unsecured Creditors v Regions Bank (In re Camtech Precision Mfg.) (2011, BC SD Fla) 443 BR 190, judgment entered (2011, BC SD Fla) 73 UCCRS2d 369.

§ 9-507. Effect of Certain Events on Effectiveness of Financing Statement

(a) Disposition. A filed financing statement remains effective with respect to collateral that is sold, exchanged, leased, licensed, or otherwise disposed of and in which a security interest or agricultural lien continues, even if the secured party knows of or consents to the disposition.

(b) Information becoming seriously misleading. Except as otherwise provided in subsection (c) and Section 9-508, a financing statement is not rendered ineffective if, after the financing statement is filed, the information provided in the financing statement becomes seriously misleading under Section 9-506.

(c) Change in debtor's name. If the name that a filed financing statement provides for a debtor becomes insufficient as the name of the debtor under Section 9-503(a) so that the financing statement becomes seriously misleading under Section 9-506:

(1) the financing statement is effective to perfect a security interest in collateral acquired by the debtor before, or within four months after, the filed financing statement becomes seriously misleading; and

(2) the financing statement is not effective to perfect a security interest in collateral acquired by the debtor more than four months after the filed financing statement becomes seriously misleading, unless an amendment to the financing statement which renders the financing statement not seriously mis-

leading is filed within four months after the financing statement became seriously misleading.

History: Add, L 2001, ch 84, § 36, eff July 1, 2001.

Add, L 1962, ch 553, eff Sept 27, 1964; repealed, L 2001, ch 84, § 36, eff July 1, 2001.

Amd, L 2014, ch 505, § 46, eff Dec 17, 2014.

§ 9-508. Effectiveness of Financing Statement If New Debtor Becomes Bound by Security Agreement

(a) Financing statement naming original debtor. Except as otherwise provided in this section, a filed financing statement naming an original debtor is effective to perfect a security interest in collateral in which a new debtor has or acquires rights to the extent that the financing statement would have been effective had the original debtor acquired rights in the collateral.

(b) Financing statement becoming seriously misleading. If the difference between the name of the original debtor and that of the new debtor causes a filed financing statement that is effective under subsection (a) to be seriously misleading under Section 9-506:

(1) the financing statement is effective to perfect a security interest in collateral acquired by the new debtor before, and within four months after, the new debtor becomes bound under Section 9-203(d); and

(2) the financing statement is not effective to perfect a security interest in collateral acquired by the new debtor more than four months after the new debtor becomes bound under Section 9-203(d) unless an initial financing statement providing the name of the new debtor is filed before the expiration of that time.

(c) When section not applicable. This section does not apply to collateral as to which a filed financing statement remains effective against the new debtor under Section 9-507(a).

History: Add, L 2001, ch 84, § 36, eff July 1, 2001.

§ 9-509. Persons Entitled to File a Record

(a) Person entitled to file record. A person may file an initial financing statement, amendment that adds collateral covered by a financing statement, or amendment that adds a debtor to a financing statement only if:

(1) the debtor authorizes the filing in an authenticated record or pursuant to subsection (b) or (c); or

(2) the person holds an agricultural lien that has become effective at the time of filing and the financing statement covers only collateral in which the person holds an agricultural lien.

(b) Security agreement as authorization. By authenticating or becoming bound as debtor by a security agreement, a debtor or new debtor authorizes the filing of an initial financing statement, and an amendment, covering:

(1) the collateral described in the security agreement; and

(2) property that becomes collateral under Section 9-315(a)(2), whether or not the security agreement expressly covers proceeds.

(c) Acquisition of collateral as authorization. By acquiring collateral in which a security interest or agricultural lien continues under Section 9-315(a)(1), a debtor authorizes the filing of an initial financing statement, and an amendment, covering the collateral and property that becomes collateral under Section 9-315(a)(2).

(d) Person entitled to file certain amendments. A person may file an amendment other than an amendment that adds collateral covered by a financing statement or an amendment that adds a debtor to a financing statement only if:

(1) the secured party of record authorizes the filing; or

(2) the amendment is a termination statement for a financing statement as to which the secured party of record has failed to file or send a termination statement as required by Section 9-513(a) or (c), the debtor authorizes the filing, and the termination statement indicates that the debtor authorized it to be filed.

(e) Multiple secured parties of record. If there is more than one secured party of record for a financing statement, each secured party of record may authorize the filing of an amendment under subsection (d).

History: Add, L 2001, ch 84, § 36, eff July 1, 2001.

CASE ANNOTATIONS

In a suit brought by a shareholder against a housing corporation and other shareholders (collectively referred to as the housing corporation), there was no justification for the shareholder's filing of a financing statement against a garden unit apartment for which the shareholder alleged that funds were expended as no security agreement was ever entered into between the parties, the shareholder had no common law lien that was enforceable, and there was no authenticated record whereby the housing corporation authorized the filing. Since the filing of the UCC-1 financing statement was baseless, the shareholder was directed to terminate the same and pay the housing corporation statutory damages in the amount of $500. McDaniel v 162 Columbia Hgts. Hous. Corps. (2008, Sup) 21 Misc 3d 244, 863 NYS2d 346.

Creditor had a valid security interest in a bankruptcy debtor's assets pursuant to a financing statement, even though the financing statement was filed before the debtor and creditor executed security agreements, since the unauthorized filing of the otherwise sufficient financing statement became authorized, and the financing statement became effective, upon the debtor's post-filing authorization or ratification of the filing by executing the security agreements. Official Comm. of Unsecured Creditors of Adoni Grp., Inc. v Capital Business Credit, LLC (In re Adoni Grp., Inc.), 530 B.R. 592, 60 Bankr. Ct. Dec. (LRP) 262, 2015 Bankr. LEXIS 1865 (Bankr. S.D.N.Y. 2015).

§ 9-510. Effectiveness of Filed Record

(a) Filed record effective if authorized. A filed record is effective only to the extent that it was filed by a person that may file it under Section 9-509.

(b) Authorization by one secured party of record. A record authorized by one secured party of record does not affect the financing statement with respect to another secured party of record.

UCC

(c) Continuation statement not timely filed. A continuation statement that is not filed within the six-month period prescribed by Section 9-515(d) is ineffective.

History: Add, L 2001, ch 84, § 36, eff July 1, 2001.

CASE ANNOTATIONS

In a suit brought by a shareholder against a housing corporation and other shareholders (collectively referred to as the housing corporation), there was no justification for the shareholder's filing of a financing statement against a garden unit apartment for which the shareholder alleged that funds were expended as no security agreement was ever entered into between the parties, the shareholder had no common law lien that was enforceable, and there was no authenticated record whereby the housing corporation authorized the filing. Since the filing of the UCC-1 financing statement was baseless, the shareholder was directed to terminate the same and pay the housing corporation statutory damages in the amount of $500. McDaniel v 162 Columbia Hgts. Hous. Corps. (2008, Sup) 21 Misc 3d 244, 863 NYS2d 346.

Creditor had a valid security interest in a bankruptcy debtor's assets pursuant to a financing statement, even though the financing statement was filed before the debtor and creditor executed security agreements, since the unauthorized filing of the otherwise sufficient financing statement became authorized, and the financing statement became effective, upon the debtor's post-filing authorization or ratification of the filing by executing the security agreements. Official Comm. of Unsecured Creditors of Adoni Grp., Inc. v Capital Business Credit, LLC (In re Adoni Grp., Inc.), 530 B.R. 592, 60 Bankr. Ct. Dec. (LRP) 262, 2015 Bankr. LEXIS 1865 (Bankr. S.D.N.Y. 2015).

§ 9-511.   Secured Party of Record

(a) Secured party of record. A secured party of record with respect to a financing statement is a person whose name is provided as the name of the secured party or a representative of the secured party in an initial financing statement that has been filed. If an initial financing statement is filed under Section 9-514(a), the assignee named in the initial financing statement is the secured party of record with respect to the financing statement.

(b) Amendment naming secured party of record. If an amendment of a financing statement which provides the name of a person as a secured party or a representative of a secured party is filed, the person named in the amendment is a secured party of record. If an amendment is filed under Section 9-514(b), the assignee named in the amendment is a secured party of record.

(c) Amendment deleting secured party of record. A person remains a secured party of record until the filing of an amendment of the financing statement which deletes the person.

History: Add, L 2001, ch 84, § 36, eff July 1, 2001.

§ 9-512.   Amendment of Financing Statement

(a) Amendment of information in financing statement. Subject to Section 9-509, a person may add or delete collateral covered by, continue or terminate the effectiveness of, or, subject to subsection (e), otherwise amend the information provided in, a financing statement by filing an amendment that:

(1) identifies, by its file number, the initial financing statement to which the amendment relates; and

(2) if the amendment relates to an initial financing statement filed in a filing office described in Section 9-501(a)(1), provides the date and time that the initial financing statement was filed and the information specified in Section 9-502(b).

(b) Period of effectiveness not affected. Except as otherwise provided in Section 9-515, the filing of an amendment does not extend the period of effectiveness of the financing statement.

(c) Effectiveness of amendment adding collateral. A financing statement that is amended by an amendment that adds collateral is effective as to the added collateral only from the date of the filing of the amendment.

(d) Effectiveness of amendment adding debtor. A financing statement that is amended by an amendment that adds a debtor is effective as to the added debtor only from the date of the filing of the amendment.

(e) Certain amendments ineffective. An amendment is ineffective to the extent it:

(1) purports to delete all debtors and fails to provide the name of a debtor to be covered by the financing statement; or

(2) purports to delete all secured parties of record and fails to provide the name of a new secured party of record.

History: Add, L 2001, ch 84, § 36, eff July 1, 2001.

§ 9-513.   Termination Statement

(a) Consumer goods. A secured party shall cause the secured party of record for a financing statement to file a termination statement for the financing statement if the financing statement covers consumer goods and:

(1) there is no obligation secured by the collateral covered by the financing statement and no commitment to make an advance, incur an obligation, or otherwise give value; or

(2) the debtor did not authorize the filing of the initial financing statement.

(b) Time for compliance with subsection (a). To comply with subsection (a), a secured party shall cause the secured party of record to file the termination statement:

(1) within one month after there is no obligation secured by the collateral covered by the financing statement and no commitment to make an advance, incur an obligation, or otherwise give value; or

(2) if earlier, within 20 days after the secured party receives an authenticated demand from a debtor.

(c) Other collateral. In cases not governed by subsection (a), within 20 days after a secured party receives an authenticated demand from a debtor, the secured party shall cause the secured party of record for a financing statement to send to the debtor a termination statement for the financing statement or file the termination statement in the filing office if:

(1) except in the case of a financing statement covering accounts or chattel paper that has been sold or goods that are the subject of a consignment, there is no obligation secured by the collateral covered by the financing statement and no commitment to make an advance, incur an obligation, or otherwise give value;

(2) the financing statement covers accounts or chattel paper that has been sold but as to which the account debtor or other person obligated has discharged its obligation;

(3) the financing statement covers goods that were the subject of a consignment to the debtor but are not in the debtor's possession; or

(4) the debtor did not authorize the filing of the initial financing statement.

(d) Effect of filing termination statement. Except as otherwise provided in Section 9-510, upon the filing of a termination statement with the filing office, the financing statement to which the termination statement relates ceases to be effective. Except as otherwise provided in Section 9-510, for purposes of Section 9-519(g), 9-522(a), and 9-523(c), the filing with the filing office of a termination statement relating to a financing statement that indicates that the debtor is a transmitting utility also causes the effectiveness of the financing statement to lapse.

(e) Cooperative Interests.

(1) "Cooperative Interest Settlement" means the time and place at which an owner of a cooperative interest transfers the cooperative interest, or refinances or pays off the debt secured by the cooperative interest.

(2) Upon an authenticated demand with sufficient notice by a debtor, the secured party shall deliver to a cooperative interest settlement a termination statement or partial release and any component of the cooperative record of which it took possession, which shall be released to the debtor upon payment of the debt secured by the cooperative interest and the discharge of any obligation of the secured party to make further advances. Unless the secured party has agreed otherwise or the cooperative interest settlement takes place at the offices of the secured party, the secured party or its agent shall be entitled to a reasonable fee for attendance at the cooperative interest settlement.

(3) Upon payment of the debt secured by a cooperative interest other than at a cooperative interest settlement and the discharge of any obligation of the secured party to make further advances, the secured party shall arrange for a termination statement or partial release to be filed within one month of receipt of the payment or discharge of the obligation to make further advances, whichever is later, and shall send to the debtor any component of the cooperative record of which it took possession.

History: Add, L 2001, ch 84, § 36, eff July 1, 2001.

Court properly denied debtor's application to compel lender to accept early payment of secured loan without future interest charges and to file termination statement under CLS UCC § 9-404 since (1) security agreement is subject to general rule that, under contract to pay money with interest, creditor cannot be forced to accept payment in advance, (2) debtor failed to set forth any reason to permit prepayment without penalty, and (3) statutes that permit party to prepay debts without penalty did not apply. Trinity Constr., Inc. v John R. Mott, Inc. (1988, 3d Dept) 145 A.D.2d 720, 534 N.Y.S.2d 838, 8 UCCRS2d 831

Where the debtor under a chattel mortgage had paid off the entire obligation, but the holder of the paper refused to send a statement that he no longer claimed a security interest under the document, the debtor was not restricted to the rights afforded to her by the Uniform Commercial Code and could properly pursue the remedy given her by § 414(2) of the Personal Property Law which permitted her to recover the amount equal to the credit service charge imposed by the transaction. Tyler v Eastern Discount Corp. (1968) 55 Misc. 2d 1002, 286 N.Y.S.2d 948, 5 UCCRS 273

Where the debtor under a chattel mortgage had paid off the entire obligation, but the holder of the paper refused to send a statement that he no longer claimed a security interest under the document, the debtor was not restricted to the rights afforded to her by the Uniform Commercial Code and could properly pursue the remedy given her by § 414(2) of the Personal Property Law which permitted her to recover the amount equal to the credit service charge imposed by the transaction. Tyler v Eastern Discount Corp. (1968) 55 Misc. 2d 1002, 286 N.Y.S.2d 948, 5 UCCRS 273

§ 9-514. Assignment of Powers of Secured Party of Record

(a) Assignment reflected on initial financing statement. Except as otherwise provided in subsection (c), an initial financing statement may reflect an assignment of all of the secured party's power to authorize an amendment to the financing statement by providing the name and mailing address of the assignee as the name and address of the secured party.

(b) Assignment of filed financing statement. Except as otherwise provided in subsection (c), a secured party of record may assign of record all or part of its power to authorize an amendment to a financing statement by filing in the filing office an amendment of the financing statement which:

(1) identifies, by its file number, the initial financing statement to which it relates;

(2) provides the name of the assignor; and

(3) provides the name and mailing address of the assignee.

(c) Assignment of record of mortgage. An assignment of record of a security interest in a fixture covered by a record of a mortgage which is effective as a financing statement filed as a fixture filing under Section 9-502(c) may be made only by an assignment of record of the mortgage in the manner provided by law of this state other than this chapter.

History: Add, L 2001, ch 84, § 36, eff July 1, 2001.

UCC

§ 9-515. Duration and Effectiveness of Financing Statement; Effect of Lapsed Financing Statement

(a) Five-year effectiveness. Except as otherwise provided in subsections (b), (e), (f), (g), and (h), a filed financing statement is effective for a period of five years after the date of filing.

(b) Public-financed or manufactured-home transaction. Except as otherwise provided in subsections (e), (f), (g), and (h), an initial financing statement filed in connection with a public-financed transaction or manufactured-home transaction is effective for a period of 30 years after the date of filing if it indicates that it is filed in connection with a public-financed transaction or manufactured-home transaction.

(c) Lapse and continuation of financing statement. The effectiveness of a filed financing statement lapses on the expiration of the period of its effectiveness unless before the lapse a continuation statement is filed pursuant to subsection (d). Upon lapse, a financing statement ceases to be effective and any security interest or agricultural lien that was perfected by the financing statement becomes unperfected, unless the security interest is perfected otherwise. If the security interest or agricultural lien becomes unperfected upon lapse, it is deemed never to have been perfected as against a purchaser of the collateral for value.

(d) When continuation statement may be filed. A continuation statement may be filed only within six months before the expiration of the five-year period specified in subsection (a) or the thirty-year period specified in subsection (b) or the fifty-year period specified in subsection (h), whichever is applicable.

(e) Effect of filing continuation statement. Except as otherwise provided in Section 9-510, upon timely filing of a continuation statement, the effectiveness of the initial financing statement continues for a period of five years commencing on the day on which the financing statement would have become ineffective in the absence of the filing. Upon the expiration of the five-year period, the financing statement lapses in the same manner as provided in subsection (c) unless, before the lapse, another continuation statement is filed pursuant to subsection (d). Succeeding continuation statements may be filed in the same manner to continue the effectiveness of the initial financing statement.

(f) Transmitting utility financing statement. If a debtor is a transmitting utility and a filed initial financing statement so indicates, the financing statement is effective until a termination statement is filed.

(g) Record of mortgage as financing statement. A record of a mortgage that is effective as a financing statement filed as a fixture filing under Section 9-502(c) remains effective as a financing statement filed as a fixture filing until the mortgage is released or satisfied of record or its effectiveness otherwise terminates as to the real property.

(h) Cooperative interest transaction. An initial financing statement covering a cooperative interest is effective for a period of 50 years after the date of the filing of the initial financing statement if a cooperative addendum is filed simultaneously with the initial financing statement or is filed before the financing statement lapses.

History: Add, L 2001, ch 84, § 36, eff July 1, 2001; amd, L 2014, ch 505, § 47, eff Dec 17, 2014.

CASE ANNOTATIONS

UNDER FORMER § 9-404

Under evidence that the debtor had signed a security agreement authorizing the filing of a financing statement without her signature, that the motor vehicle was covered by the security agreement, and that the debtor had signed and delivered a promissory note to plaintiff, the fact that finance company failed to check the box opposite the provision that the debtor had signed a security agreement authorizing plaintiff to file the financing statement was a minor error which could not seriously mislead one who searched the file. Beneficial Finance Co. v Kurland Cadillac-Oldsmobile, Inc. (1969, 2d Dept) 32 A.D.2d 643, 300 N.Y.S.2d 884, 6 UCCRS 539

Bank was entitled to summary judgment on issue of liability in action against attorney and abstract company for failure to file financing statement with Secretary of State, causing bank to lose its secured position on loan, despite fact that copy of financing statement and check for filing costs were mailed to Secretary of State on day following closing, since no return receipt was ever received, check for filing fees was never returned or negotiated, and no completed copy of financing statement was returned; mere mailing of financial statement did not constitute "presentation" to filing officer under CLS UCC § 9-403, as financing statement must be received by filing officer before it is presented, and evidence of receipt is required. Peoples Nat'l Bank v Weiner (1987, 2d Dept) 129 A.D.2d 782, 514 N.Y.S.2d 772, 3 UCCRS2d 1615

Irrespective of lapse of first filing, second filing in full compliance with requirements of CLS UCC Art 9 remains effective against creditor with actual knowledge of contents of financing statement. P.T. Bank Cent. Asia v Chinese Am. Bank (1997, 1st Dept) 229 A.D.2d 224, 654 N.Y.S.2d 117, 31 UCCRS2d 611

Court erred in denying landlords' motion for summary judgment to recover proceeds of fire insurance policy which tenant's insurer paid to tenant where insurer did not object to landlords' submission of uncertified documents in support of their motion, UCC-1 financing statements submitted by landlords completely defeated insurer's claim of lack of notice, insurer did not argue that tenant fraudulently induced it to issue policy, or that tenant breached any of policy conditions before loss occurred, and tenant's only misrepresentation concerned proper recipient of proceeds after valid claim was submitted. Badillo v Tower Ins. Co. (1997, 1st Dept) 243 A.D.2d 413, 663 N.Y.S.2d 207, 36 UCCRS2d 234, app gr (1998) 92 N.Y.2d 803, 677 N.Y.S.2d 73, 699 N.E.2d 433 and revd, summary judgment den (1999) 92 N.Y.2d 790, 686 N.Y.S.2d 363, 709 N.E.2d 104, 38 UCCRS2d 991

In estate administration proceeding, where (1) deceased, on purchase of pharmacy, gave seller promissory note secured by security agreement that was duly filed in county clerk's office on December 1, 1971 and with secretary of state of New York on December 2, 1971, (2) filed instruments reflected maturity date of November 15, 1981, (3) decedent left unpaid balance on promissory note given seller, and (4) seller did not renew his security interest by filing continuation statement, as provided by UCC § 9-403(2), on or before December 2, 1976 (which was expiration of 5-year period specified by UCC § 9-403(2)), court held that seller forfeited his preferred standing and became mere general creditor of deceased. In re Estate of Sweeney (1978) 95 Misc. 2d 22, 406 N.Y.S.2d 255, 24 UCCRS 797

A creditor of a decedent, who had duly filed a security agreement but failed to renew his security interests by failing to file renewal certificates, as required by section 9-403 of the Uniform Commercial Code, which provides that the effectiveness of a filing statement lapses on the expiration of a five-year period unless a continuation statement is filed prior to the lapse, thereby forfeited his secured and preferred standing and became a general creditor with respect to the assets of decedent's estate. In re Estate of Sweeney (1978) 95 Misc. 2d 22, 406 N.Y.S.2d 255, 24 UCCRS 797

Guarantor of payment under lease/purchase agreement covering sound and lighting equipment for theater was not discharged from obligation on ground that secured party, after principal's default and sale of some of equipment, impaired collateral under CLS UCC § 3-606(1)(b) by not filing fixtures financing statement under CLS UCC § 9-403(7) as to equipment left in theater, since such equipment did not become trade fixtures under CLS UCC § 9-313(1)(a), but remained personal property covered by secured party's dual filing under CLS UCC § 9-401(1)(c). Norstar Leasing Services, Inc. v Colonie Coliseum Enterprises, Inc. (1989, Sup) 145 Misc. 2d 388, 546 N.Y.S.2d 942, 11 UCCRS2d 328

Sections 65 and 70 of the New York Personal Property Law which provide the effect and method of filing conditional sales contracts have now been superseded by §§ 9-402 and 9-403(1) of the UCC. In re Mutual Board & Packaging Corp. (1965, CA2 NY) 342 F.2d 294, 2 UCCRS 451

A conditional sales contract in proper form and timely filed with correct recording office has been filed in compliance with this section even though recorder erroneously returned instrument for an acknowledgment. In re Mutual Board & Packaging Corp. (1965, CA2 NY) 342 F.2d 294, 2 UCCRS 451

Date stamp and filing number on financing statement were prima facie evidence of filing with city register's office on that date, notwithstanding evidence that on later date financing statement temporarily could not be found; debtor's contention that secured party had duty to insure proper filing and indexing was without merit. In re May Lee Industries, Inc. (1974, SD NY) 380 F. Supp. 1, 15 UCCRS 528, affd (1974, CA2 NY) 501 F.2d 1407, 15 UCCRS 532(applying New York law)

Judgment creditor's presentation of financing statement, with tender of proper fee, was legal equivalent of filing and perfected creditor's security interest, despite fact that financing statement was returned to creditor unfiled, where no defect in financing statement appeared on its face, and where financing statement was accepted without alteration when presented for second time. Chemical Bank v Barron (1987, SD NY) 663 F. Supp. 367, 3 UCCRS2d 1966

§ 9-516. What Constitutes Filing; Effectiveness of Filing

(a) What constitutes filing. Except as otherwise provided in subsection (b), communication of a record to a filing office and tender of the filing fee or acceptance of the record by the filing office constitutes filing.

(b) Refusal to accept record; filing does not occur. Filing does not occur with respect to a record that a filing office refuses to accept because:

(1) the record is not communicated by a method or medium of communication authorized by the filing office;

(2) an amount equal to or greater than the applicable filing fee is not tendered;

(3) the filing office is unable to index the record because:

(A) in the case of an initial financing statement, the record does not provide a name for the debtor;

(B) in the case of an amendment or correction statement, the record:

(i) does not identify the initial financing statement as required by Section 9-512 or 9-518, as applicable; or

(ii) identifies an initial financing statement whose effectiveness has lapsed under Section 9-515;

(C) in the case of an initial financing statement that provides the name of a debtor identified as an individual or an amendment that provides a name of a debtor identified as an individual which was not previously provided in the financing statement to which the record relates, the record does not identify the debtor's last name; or

(D) in the case of a record filed in the filing office described in Section 9-501 (a) (1), the record does not provide a sufficient description of the real property to which it relates;

(4) in the case of an initial financing statement or an amendment that adds a secured party of record, the record does not provide a name and mailing address for the secured party of record;

(5) in the case of an initial financing statement or an amendment that provides a name of a debtor which was not previously provided in the financing statement to which the amendment relates, the record does not:

(A) provide a mailing address for the debtor; or

(B) indicate whether the debtor is an individual or an organization;

(C) if the financing statement indicates that the debtor is an organization, provide:

(i) a type of organization for the debtor, or

(ii) a jurisdiction of organization for the debtor; or

(6) in the case of an assignment reflected in an initial financing statement under Section 9-514(a) or an amendment filed under Section 9-514(b), the record does not provide a name and mailing address for the assignee; or

(7) in the case of a continuation statement, the record is not filed within the six-month period prescribed by Section 9-515(d).

(c) Rules applicable to subsection (b). For purposes of subsection (b):

(1) a record does not provide information if the filing office is unable to read or decipher the information; and

(2) a record that does not indicate that it is an amendment or identify an initial financing statement to which it relates, as required by Section 9-512, 9-514, or 9-518, is an initial financing statement.

(d) Refusal to accept record; record effective as filed record. A record that is communicated to the filing office with tender of the filing fee, but which the filing office refuses to accept for a reason other than one set forth in subsection (b), is effective as a filed record except as against a purchaser of the collateral which gives value in reasonable reliance upon the absence of the record from the files.

(e) Special rule for cooperative interests; record effective as notice. A filing that includes a cooperative addendum covering a cooperative interest constitutes notice of the existence of the security interest in the cooperative interest as of the date of the filing of the cooperative addendum, except as against a purchaser of the collateral which gives value in reasonable reliance upon the absence of the record from the files.

UCC

History: Add, L 2001, ch 84, § 36, eff July 1, 2001.

§ 9-517.   Effect of Indexing Errors

The failure of the filing office to index a record correctly does not affect the effectiveness of the filed record.

History: Add, L 2001, ch 84, § 36, eff July 1, 2001.

CASE ANNOTATIONS

Florida Secured Transaction Registry did not make an indexing error in filing a creditor's UCC-1 Financing Statements because the creditor's UCCs were seriously misleading as to two additional debtors. Official Comm. of Unsecured Creditors v Regions Bank (In re Camtech Precision Mfg.) (2011, BC SD Fla) 443 BR 190, judgment entered (2011, BC SD Fla) 73 UCCRS2d 369.

§ 9-518.   Claim Concerning Inaccurate or Wrongfully Filed Record

(a) Correction statement. A person may file in the filing office a correction statement with respect to a record indexed there under the person's name if the person believes that the record is inaccurate or was wrongfully filed.

(b) Sufficiency of correction statement. A correction statement must:

(1) identify the record to which it relates by:

(A) the file number assigned to the initial financing statement to which the record relates; and

(B) if the correction statement relates to a record filed in a filing office described in Section 9-501(a)(1), the date and time that the initial financing statement was filed and the information specified in Section 9-502(b);

(2) indicate that it is a correction statement; and

(3) provide the basis for the person's belief that the record is inaccurate and indicate the manner in which the person believes the record should be amended to cure any inaccuracy or provide the basis for the person's belief that the record was wrongfully filed.

(c) Record not affected by correction statement. The filing of a correction statement does not affect the effectiveness of an initial financing statement or other filed record.

(d) Special proceeding to redact or expunge a falsely filed or amended financing statement.

(1) Provided he or she is an employee of the state or a political subdivision thereof, a person identified as a debtor in a financing statement filed pursuant to this subpart may bring a special proceeding against the named filer of such statement or any amendment thereof to invalidate the filing or amendment thereof where such statement was falsely filed or amended; except that an attorney who is not an employee of the state or a political subdivision thereof may also bring a special proceeding hereunder where he or she represents or has represented the respondent therein in a criminal court. Such special proceeding shall be governed by article four of the civil practice law and rules, and shall be commenced in the supreme court of Albany county, the county of the petitioner's residence or a county within the judicial district in which any property covered by the financing statement is located. No fee pursuant to article eighty of the civil practice law and rules shall be collected in such special proceeding.

(2) The petition in a special proceeding hereunder shall plead that:

(A) the financing statement filed or amended by the respondent pursuant to section 9-509 was falsely filed or amended to retaliate for: (i) the performance of the petitioner's official duties in his or her capacity as an employee of the state or a political subdivision thereof, or (ii) in the case of a special proceeding brought by an attorney who is not an employee of the state or a political subdivision thereof, to retaliate for the performance of the petitioner's duties in his or her capacity as an attorney for the respondent in a criminal court; and

(B) such financing statement does not relate to an interest in a consumer-goods transaction, a commercial transaction, or any other actual transaction between the petitioner and the respondent; and

(C) the collateral covered in such financing statement is the property of the petitioner; and

(D) prompt redaction or invalidation of the financing statement is necessary to avert or mitigate prejudice to the petitioner.

(3) If the court makes a written finding that the allegations in paragraph two of this subsection are established, the court shall order the expungement of such statement or its redaction in the public records in the office in which the financing statement is filed, as appropriate, and may grant any additional relief authorized by section 9-625. In such case, the court shall cause a copy of its order to be filed with the secretary of state or other appropriate filing office pursuant to this chapter. Upon a finding that the respondent has engaged in a repeated pattern of false filings as found under this subsection, the court also may enjoin the respondent from filing or amending any further financing statement pursuant to this article without leave of the court. If the respondent is incarcerated at the time the court issues an order containing such an injunction, the court shall cause the head of the correctional facility in which the respondent is incarcerated to receive a copy of such determination. The head of such a facility shall cause a copy of such order to be provided to the respondent. In any instances of the issuance of such an injunction where the respondent has defaulted, the court shall direct service of such injunction upon the respondent.

History: Add, L 2001, ch 84, § 36, eff July 1, 2001; amd, L 2013, ch 490, § 4, eff Nov 1, 2013.

CASE ANNOTATIONS

In a suit brought by a shareholder against a housing corporation and other shareholders (collectively referred to as the housing corporation), there was no justification for the shareholder's filing of a financing statement against a garden unit apartment for which the shareholder alleged that funds were expended as no security agreement was ever entered into between the parties, the shareholder had no common law lien that was enforceable, and there was no authenticated record whereby the housing corporation authorized the filing. Since the filing of the UCC-1 financing statement was baseless, the shareholder was directed to terminate the same and pay the housing corporation statutory damages in the amount of $500. McDaniel v 162 Columbia Hgts. Hous. Corps. (2008, Sup) 21 Misc 3d 244, 863 NYS2d 346.

Subpart 2
Duties And Operation Of Filing Office
History: Add, L 2001, ch 84, § 36, eff July 1, 2001.

§ 9-519. Numbering, Maintaining, and Indexing Records; Communicating Information Provided in Records

(a) Filing office duties. For each record filed in a filing office, the filing office shall:

(1) assign a unique number to the filed record;

(2) create a record that bears the number assigned to the filed record and the date and time of filing;

(3) maintain the filed record for public inspection; and

(4) index the filed record in accordance with subsections (c), (d), and (e).

(b) File number. A file number must include a digit that:

(1) is mathematically derived from or related to the other digits of the file number; and

(2) aids the filing office in determining whether a number communicated as the file number includes a single-digit or transpositional error.

(c) Indexing: general. Except as otherwise provided in subsections (d) and (e), the filing office shall:

(1) index an initial financing statement according to the name of the debtor and index all filed records relating to the initial financing statement in a manner that associates with one another an initial financing statement and all filed records relating to the initial financing statement; and

(2) index a record that provides a name of a debtor which was not previously provided in the financing statement to which the record relates also according to the name that was not previously provided.

(d) Indexing: real-property-related financing statement. If a financing statement is filed as a fixture filing or covers as-extracted collateral, or timber to be cut, or a cooperative interest, the filing office shall index it:

(1) under the names of the debtor and of each owner of record shown on the financing statement as if they were the mortgagors under a mortgage of the real property described; and

(2) to the extent that the law of this state provides for indexing of records of mortgages under the name of the mortgagee, under the name of the secured party as if the secured party were the mortgagee thereunder, and;

(3) if the real estate is in the City of New York or in Nassau, Onondaga, or any other county where the block system of recording or registering and indexing conveyances is in use, according to the block in which the real estate is situated; the filing officer may index such statements according to the names of the record owners of the real estate in a single consolidated index installed and maintained by him pursuant to section five hundred twenty-nine of the county law.

(e) Indexing: real-property-related assignment. If a financing statement is filed as a fixture filing or covers as-extracted collateral, timber to be cut or a cooperative interest, the filing office shall index an assignment filed under Section 9-514(a) or an amendment filed under Section 9-514(b):

(1) under the name of the assignor as grantor; and

(2) to the extent that the law of this state provides for indexing a record of the assignment of a mortgage under the name of the assignee, under the name of the assignee; and

(3) if the real estate is in the City of New York or in Nassau, Onondaga, or any other county where the block system of recording or registering and indexing conveyances is in use, according to the block in which the real estate is situated; the filing officer may index such assignments according to the names of the record owners of the real estate in a single consolidated index installed and maintained by him pursuant to section five hundred twenty-nine of the county law.

(f) Retrieval and association capability. The filing office shall maintain a capability:

(1) to retrieve a record by the name of the debtor and:

(A) if the filing office is described in Section 9-501(a)(1), by the file number assigned to the initial financing statement to which the record relates and the date and time that the record was filed or recorded; or

(B) if the filing office is described in Section 9-501(a)(2), by the file number assigned to the initial financing statement to which the record relates; and

(2) to associate and retrieve with one another an initial financing statement and each filed record relating to the initial financing statement; and

(3) if the real estate is in the City of New York or in Nassau, Onondaga, or any other county where the block system of recording or registering and indexing conveyances is in use, to retrieve a record according to the block in which the real estate is situated.

(g) Removal of debtor's name. The filing office may not remove a debtor's name from the index until one year after the effectiveness of a financing statement naming the debtor lapses under Section 9-515 with respect to all secured parties of record.

(h) Timeliness of filing office performance. The filing office shall perform the acts required by subsections (a) through (e) at the time and in the manner prescribed by filing-office rule, but not later than two

UCC

business days after the filing office receives the record in question.

(i) Inapplicability to real-property-related filing office. Subsections (b) and (h) do not apply to a filing office described in Section 9-501(a)(1).

History: Add, L 2001, ch 84, § 36, eff July 1, 2001.

§ 9-520.   Acceptance and Refusal to Accept Record

(a) Mandatory refusal to accept record. A filing office shall refuse to accept a record for filing for a reason set forth in Section 9-516(b) and may refuse to accept a record for filing only for a reason set forth in Section 9-516(b).

(b) Communication concerning refusal. If a filing office refuses to accept a record for filing, it shall communicate to the person that presented the record the fact of and reason for the refusal and the date and time the record would have been filed had the filing office accepted it. The communication must be made at the time and in the manner prescribed by filing-office rule but, in the case of a filing office described in Section 9-501(a)(2), in no event more than two business days after the filing office receives the record.

(c) When filed financing statement effective. A filed financing statement satisfying Section 9-502(a) and (b) is effective, even if the filing office is required to refuse to accept it for filing under subsection (a). However, Section 9-338 applies to a filed financing statement providing information described in Section 9-516(b)(5) which is incorrect at the time the financing statement is filed.

History: Add, L 2001, ch 84, § 36, eff July 1, 2001.

§ 9-521.   Uniform Form of Written Financing Statement; Amendment; and Cooperative Addendum

(a) Initial financing statement form. A filing office that accepts written records may not refuse to accept a written initial financing statement in the form promulgated by the department of state except for a reason as set forth in Section 9-516(b).

(b) Amendment form. A filing office that accepts written records may not refuse to accept a written financing statement amendment in the form promulgated by the department of state except for a reason as set forth in Section 9-516 (b).

(c) Cooperative addendum form. A filing office that accepts written records may not refuse to accept a written cooperative addendum in the form promulgated by the department of state except for a reason as set forth in Section 9-516 (b).

History: Add, L 2001, ch 84, § 36, eff July 1, 2001.

§ 9-522.   Maintenance and Destruction of Records

(a) Post-lapse maintenance and retrieval of information. The filing office shall maintain a record of the information provided in a filed financing statement for at least one year after the effectiveness of the financing statement has lapsed under Section 9-515 with respect to all secured parties of record. The record must be retrievable by using the name of the debtor and:

(1) if the record was filed in the filing office described in Section 9-501(a)(1), by using:

(A) the file number assigned to the initial financing statement to which the record relates and the date and time that the record was filed; and

(B) in the case of collateral which is a cooperative interest, the real property tax designation associated with the real property in which the cooperative unit is located as assigned by the local real property tax assessing authority; or

(2) if the record was filed in the filing office described in Section 9-501(a)(2), by using the file number assigned to the initial financing statement to which the record relates.

(b) Destruction of written records. Except to the extent that a statute governing disposition of public records provides otherwise, the filing office immediately may destroy any written record evidencing a financing statement. However, if the filing office destroys a written record, it shall maintain another record of the financing statement which complies with subsection (a).

History: Add, L 2001, ch 84, § 36, eff July 1, 2001.

§ 9-523.   Information from Filing Office; Sale or License of Records

(a) Acknowledgment of filing written record. If a person that files a written record requests an acknowledgment of the filing, the filing office shall send to the person an image of the record showing the number assigned to the record pursuant to Section 9-519(a)(1) and the date and time of the filing of the record. However, if the person furnishes a copy of the record to the filing office, the filing office may instead:

(1) note upon the copy the number assigned to the record pursuant to Section 9-519 (a) (1) and the date and time of the filing of the record; and

(2) send the copy to the person.

(b) Acknowledgment of filing other record. If a person files a record other than a written record, the filing office shall communicate to the person an acknowledgment that provides:

(1) the information in the record;

(2) the number assigned to the record pursuant to Section 9-519(a)(1); and

(3) the date and time of the filing of the record.

(c) Communication of requested information. The filing office shall communicate or otherwise make available in a record the following information to any person that requests it:

(1) whether there is on file on a date and time specified by the filing office, but not a date earlier

than three business days before the filing office receives the request, any financing statement that:

(A) designates a particular debtor or, if the request so states, designates a particular debtor at the address specified in the request;

(B) has not lapsed under Section 9-515 with respect to all secured parties of record; and

(C) if the request so states, has lapsed under Section 9-515 and a record of which is maintained by the filing office under Section 9-522(a);

(D) is filed in the filing office described in Section 9-501(a)(1), if the request indicates the real property tax designation associated with the real property as assigned by the local real property tax assessing authority.

(2) the date and time of filing of each financing statement,

(3) the information provided in each financing statement,

(4) whether there is on file any notice of federal tax lien, or a certificate or notice affecting such lien, on the date and time specified in such record naming a particular debtor; and

(5) the date and time of filing of each such notice or certificate of or affecting a federal tax lien.

(d) Medium for communicating information. In complying with its duty under subsection (c), the filing office may communicate information in any medium. However, if requested, the filing office shall communicate information by issuing its written certificate.

(e) Timeliness of filing office performance. The filing office, except by a filing office described in Section 9-501 (a) (1), shall perform the acts required by subsections (a) through (d) at the time and in the manner prescribed by filing-office rule, but not later than two business days after the filing office receives the request.

(f) Public availability of records. At least weekly, the secretary of state shall offer to sell or license to the public on a nonexclusive basis, in bulk, copies of all records filed in it under this part, in every medium from time to time available to the filing office.

History: Add, L 2001, ch 84, § 36, eff July 1, 2001.

CASE ANNOTATIONS

UNDER FORMER § 9-407

Article 9 of Uniform Commercial Code, § 9-407, requiring issuance of certificate showing whether financing statement is on file naming particular debtor, manifests intent to protect certain class of people, and Secretary of State's error in issuing such certificate is therefore actionable. Hudleasco, Inc. v State (1977) 90 Misc. 2d 1057, 396 N.Y.S.2d 1002, 22 UCCRS 545, affd (1978, 3d Dept) 63 A.D.2d 1042, 405 N.Y.S.2d 784

Language of New York version of UCC § 9-407, pertaining to obtaining information from filing officer, is mandatory and not discretionary. Thus, filing officer's erroneous certification to inquirer that there was no record on file of any financing statement pertaining to debtor was not discretionary act, but was actionable error committed in performance of ministerial duty. Hudleasco, Inc. v State (1977)

90 Misc. 2d 1057, 396 N.Y.S.2d 1002, 22 UCCRS 545, affd (1978, 3d Dept) 63 A.D.2d 1042, 405 N.Y.S.2d 784

In negligence action by creditor against state for failure of state officer to issue accurate certificate of information on request made under UCC § 9-407(2), where (1) plaintiff sought certified listing of all filed financing statements that named plaintiff's debtor-namely, "All-Glass Boat Sales, Inc. d/b/a Marlin Marine"-as debtor on such statements, (2) state officer sent plaintiff certified listing of all secured debts of another debtor named "American Felt and Filter Company," (3) one creditor of "American Felt and Filter Company" notified plaintiff that it was not creditor of plaintiff's debtor, (4) despite such notice, plaintiff did not attempt to obtain correct information from state officer concerning filed financing statements of other creditors that named plaintiff's debtor as debtor in such statements, and (5) on subsequent default of plaintiff's debtor, plaintiff sustained loss because another creditor had valid priority to collateral put up by plaintiff's debtor, court held (1) that although state officer had been negligent in issuing inaccurate certificate of information to plaintiff, state's liability for such negligence was not absolute, (2) that plaintiff's reliance on such certificate was unreasonable because certificate was clearly unresponsive to plaintiff's request, and (3) that plaintiff's unreasonable reliance on certificate was substantial cause of its loss, thus preventing plaintiff from being entitled to any damages for such loss. ITT Diversified Credit Corp. v State (1982, Ct Cl) 115 Misc. 2d 716, 454 N.Y.S.2d 530, 34 UCCRS 1442

§ 9-524.   Delay by Filing Office

Delay by the filing office beyond a time limit prescribed by this part is excused if:

(a) the delay is caused by interruption of communication or computer facilities, war, emergency conditions, failure of equipment, or other circumstances beyond control of the filing office; and

(b) the filing office exercises reasonable diligence under the circumstances.

History: Add, L 2001, ch 84, § 36, eff July 1, 2001.

§ 9-525.   Fees

Fees for filing and services under this chapter shall be determined in accordance with section ninety-six-a of the executive law.

History: Add, L 2001, ch 84, § 36, eff July 1, 2001.

§ 9-526.   Filing-office Rules

(a) Adoption of filing-office rules. The secretary of state shall adopt and publish rules to implement this article. The filing-office rules must be consistent with this article.

(b) Harmonization of rules. To keep the filing-office rules and practices of the filing office in harmony with the rules and practices of filing offices in other jurisdictions that enact substantially this part, and to keep the technology used by the filing office compatible with the technology used by filing offices in other jurisdictions that enact substantially this part, the secretary of state, so far as is consistent with the purposes, policies, and provisions of this article, in adopting, amending, and repealing filing-office rules, shall:

(1) consult with filing offices in other jurisdictions that enact substantially this part; and

(2) consult the most recent version of the Model Rules promulgated by the International Association

UCC

of Corporate Administrators or any successor organization; and

(3) take into consideration the rules and practices of, and the technology used by, filing offices in other jurisdictions that enact substantially this part.

History: Add, L 2001, ch 84, § 36, eff July 1, 2001.

§ 9-527. Duty to Report

The secretary of state shall report to the governor, the temporary president of the senate and the speaker of the assembly on the first day of July, two thousand two, on the first day of July, two thousand three and biennially on the first day of July thereafter, on the operation of the filing office. In addition to a statement on the operation of the filing office, the report shall contain a statement of the extent to which:

(a) the filing office rules are not in harmony with the rules of the filing offices in other jurisdictions that enact substantially this part and the reasons for such variation; and

(b) the filing office rules are not in harmony with the most recent version of the Model Rules promulgated by the International Association of Corporate Administrators, or any successor organization, and the reasons for these variations.

History: Add, L 2001, ch 84, § 36, eff July 1, 2001.

PART 6
DEFAULT

History: Add, L 2001, ch 84, § 36, eff July 1, 2001.

Subpart 1
Default And Enforcement Of Security Interest
History: Add, L 2001, ch 84, § 36, eff July 1, 2001.

§ 9-601. Rights after Default; Judicial Enforcement; Consignor or Buyer of Accounts, Chattel Paper, Payment Intangibles, or Promissory Notes

(a) Rights of secured party after default. After default, a secured party has the rights provided in this part and, except as otherwise provided in Section 9-602, those provided by agreement of the parties. A secured party:

(1) may reduce a claim to judgment, foreclose, or otherwise enforce the claim, security interest, or agricultural lien by any available judicial procedure; and

(2) if the collateral is documents, may proceed either as to the documents or as to the goods they cover.

(b) Rights and duties of secured party in possession or control. A secured party in possession of collateral or control of collateral under Section 7-106, 9-104, 9-105, 9-106, or 9-107 has the rights and duties provided in Section 9-207.

(c) Rights cumulative; simultaneous exercise. The rights under subsections (a) and (b) are cumulative and may be exercised simultaneously.

(d) Rights of debtor and obligor. Except as otherwise provided in subsection (g) and Section 9-605, after default, a debtor and an obligor have the rights provided in this part and by agreement of the parties.

(e) Lien of levy after judgment. If a secured party has reduced its claim to judgment, the lien of any levy that may be made upon the collateral by virtue of an execution based upon the judgment relates back to the earliest of:

(1) the date of perfection of the security interest or agricultural lien in the collateral;

(2) the date of filing a financing statement covering the collateral; or

(3) any date specified in a statute under which the agricultural lien was created.

(f) Execution sale. A sale pursuant to an execution is a foreclosure of the security interest or agricultural lien by judicial procedure within the meaning of this section. A secured party may purchase at the sale and thereafter hold the collateral free of any other requirements of this article.

(g) Consignor or buyer of certain rights to payment. Except as otherwise provided in Section 9-607(c), this part imposes no duties upon a secured party that is a consignor or is a buyer of accounts, chattel paper, payment intangibles, or promissory notes.

History: Add, L 2001, ch 84, § 36, eff July 1, 2001; amd, L 2014, ch 505, § 48, eff Dec 17, 2014.

CASE ANNOTATIONS

Note unambiguously provided that the corporation had the rights of a secured party under the New York Uniform Commercial Code to foreclose on an amount of the pledged property with an aggregate value of twice the outstanding debt. Christie's Inc. v Davis (2002, SD NY) 247 F. Supp. 2d 414, 49 UCCRS2d 684

§ 9-602. Waiver and Variance of Rights and Duties

Except as otherwise provided in Section 9-624, to the extent that they give rights to a debtor or obligor and impose duties on a secured party, the debtor or obligor may not waive or vary the rules stated in the following listed sections:

(a) Section 9-207 (b) (4) (C), which deals with use and operation of the collateral by the secured party;

(b) Section 9-210, which deals with requests for an accounting and requests concerning a list of collateral and statement of account;

(c) Section 9-607 (c), which deals with collection and enforcement of collateral;

(d) Sections 9-608 (a) and 9-615 (c) to the extent that they deal with application or payment of non-cash proceeds of collection, enforcement, or disposition;

(e) Sections 9-608 (a) and 9-615 (d) to the extent that they require accounting for or payment of surplus proceeds of collateral;

(f) Section 9-609 to the extent that it imposes upon a secured party that takes possession of collateral without judicial process the duty to do so without breach of the peace;

(g) Sections 9-610 (b), 9-611, 9-613, and 9-614, which deal with disposition of collateral;

(h) Section 9-615 (f), which deals with calculation of a deficiency or surplus when a disposition is made to the secured party, a person related to the secured party, or a secondary obligor;

(i) Section 9-616, which deals with explanation of the calculation of a surplus or deficiency;

(j) Sections 9-620, 9-621, and 9-622, which deal with acceptance of collateral in satisfaction of obligation;

(k) Section 9-623, which deals with redemption of collateral;

(l) Section 9-624, which deals with permissible waivers; and

(m) Sections 9-625 and 9-626, which deal with the secured party's liability for failure to comply with this article.

History: Add, L 2001, ch 84, § 36, eff July 1, 2001.

§ 9-603. Agreement on Standards Concerning Rights and Duties

(a) Agreed standards. The parties may determine by agreement the standards measuring the fulfillment of the rights of a debtor or obligor and the duties of a secured party under a rule stated in Section 9-602 if the standards are not manifestly unreasonable.

(b) Agreed standards inapplicable to breach of peace. Subsection (a) does not apply to the duty under Section 9-609 to refrain from breaching the peace.

History: Add, L 2001, ch 84, § 36, eff July 1, 2001.

CASE ANNOTATIONS

Foreclosure sale of drilling rigs, conducted in accordance with credit agreements, was commercially reasonable even though it attracted few prospective buyers and resulted in bid below market value; price was not so inadequate as to shock conscience, and debtors could not complain about adequacy of preparation for sale because they prevented creditor from taking possession of collateral prior to sale. Adobe Trucking, Inc. v PNC Bank (In re Adobe Trucking, Inc.) (2014, CA5 Tex) 2014 US App LEXIS 314 (UNPUBLISHED).

§ 9-604. Procedure If Security Agreement Covers Real Property, Fixtures, or Cooperative Interests

(a) Enforcement: personal and real property. If a security agreement covers both personal and real property, a secured party may proceed:

(1) under this part as to the personal property without prejudicing any rights with respect to the real property; or

(2) as to both the personal property and the real property in accordance with the rights with respect to the real property, in which case the other provisions of this part do not apply.

(b) Enforcement: fixtures. Subject to subsection (c), if a security agreement covers goods that are or become fixtures, a secured party may proceed:

(1) under this part; or

(2) in accordance with the rights with respect to real property, in which case the other provisions of this part do not apply.

(c) Removal of fixtures. Subject to the other provisions of this part, if a secured party holding a security interest in fixtures has priority over all owners and encumbrancers of the real property, the secured party, after default, may remove the collateral from the real property.

(d) Injury caused by removal. A secured party that removes collateral shall promptly reimburse any encumbrancer or owner of the real property, other than the debtor, for the cost of repair of any physical injury caused by the removal. The secured party need not reimburse the encumbrancer or owner for any diminution in value of the real property caused by the absence of the goods removed or by any necessity of replacing them. A person entitled to reimbursement may refuse permission to remove until the secured party gives adequate assurance for the performance of the obligation to reimburse.

(e) Enforcement: cooperative interests. A security interest in a cooperative interest may be enforced only as provided in Section 9-601(a).

History: Add, L 2001, ch 84, § 36, eff July 1, 2001.

§ 9-605. Unknown Debtor or Secondary Obligor

A secured party does not owe a duty based on its status as secured party:

(a) to a person that is a debtor or obligor, unless the secured party knows:

(1) that the person is a debtor or obligor;

(2) the identity of the person; and

(3) how to communicate with the person; or

(b) to a secured party or lienholder that has filed a financing statement against a person, unless the secured party knows:

(1) that the person is a debtor; and

(2) the identity of the person.

History: Add, L 2001, ch 84, § 36, eff July 1, 2001.

§ 9-606. Time of Default for Agricultural Lien

For purposes of this part, a default occurs in connection with an agricultural lien at the time the secured party becomes entitled to enforce the lien in accordance with the statute under which it was created.

History: Add, L 2001, ch 84, § 36, eff July 1, 2001.

§ 9-607. Collection and Enforcement by Secured Party

(a) Collection and enforcement generally. If so agreed, and in any event after default, a secured party:

(1) may notify an account debtor or other person obligated on collateral to make payment or otherwise render performance to or for the benefit of the secured party;

(2) may take any proceeds to which the secured party is entitled under Section 9-315;

(3) may enforce the obligations of an account debtor or other person obligated on collateral and exercise the rights of the debtor with respect to the obligation of the account debtor or other person obligated on collateral to make payment or otherwise render performance to the debtor, and with respect to any property that secures the obligations of the account debtor or other person obligated on the collateral;

(4) if it holds a security interest in a deposit account perfected by control under Section 9-104 (a) (1), may apply the balance of the deposit account to the obligation secured by the deposit account; and

(5) if it holds a security interest in a deposit account perfected by control under Section 9-104 (a) (2) or (3), may instruct the bank to pay the balance of the deposit account to or for the benefit of the secured party.

(b) Nonjudicial enforcement of mortgage. If necessary to enable a secured party to exercise under subsection (a) (3) the right of a debtor to enforce a mortgage nonjudicially, the secured party may record in the office in which a record of the mortgage is recorded:

(1) a copy of the security agreement that creates or provides for a security interest in the obligation secured by the mortgage; and

(2) the secured party's sworn affidavit in recordable form stating that:

(A) a default has occurred with respect to the obligation secured by the mortgage; and

(B) the secured party is entitled to enforce the mortgage nonjudicially.

(c) Commercially reasonable collection and enforcement. A secured party shall proceed in a commercially reasonable manner if the secured party:

(1) undertakes to collect from or enforce an obligation of an account debtor or other person obligated on collateral; and

(2) is entitled to charge back uncollected collateral or otherwise to full or limited recourse against the debtor or a secondary obligor.

(d) Expenses of collection and enforcement. A secured party may deduct from the collections made pursuant to subsection (c) reasonable expenses of collection and enforcement, including reasonable attorney's fees and legal expenses incurred by the secured party.

(e) Duties to secured party not affected. This section does not determine whether an account debtor, bank, or other person obligated on collateral owes a duty to a secured party.

History: Add, L 2001, ch 84, § 36, eff July 1, 2001; amd, L 2014, ch 505, § 49, eff Dec 17, 2014.

CASE ANNOTATIONS

1. In general

Order was entered granting plaintiffs' (P) motion to deposit funds into the court registry and to dismiss and discharge P as: (1) P filed an interpleader action as to the monies debtor (D) claimed under a settlement agreement with P and defendant claimed under a security agreement with D; (2) P were disinterested stakeholders and filed their motion in good faith; and (3) defendant had notified P that it was owed the disputed monies pursuant to a security agreement with D governed by New York law. Shuffle Tech Int'l, LLC v Poydras-Talrick Holdings, LLC (In re DigiDeal Corp.), 2017 Bankr. LEXIS 4287 (Bankr. E.D. Wash. Dec. 14, 2017).

§ 9-608. Application of Proceeds of Collection or Enforcement; Liability for Deficiency and Right to Surplus

(a) Application of proceeds, surplus, and deficiency if obligation secured. If a security interest or agricultural lien secures payment or performance of an obligation, the following rules apply:

(1) A secured party shall apply or pay over for application the cash proceeds of collection or enforcement under Section 9-607 in the following order to:

(A) the reasonable expenses of collection and enforcement and, to the extent provided for by agreement and not prohibited by law, reasonable attorney's fees and legal expenses incurred by the secured party;

(B) the satisfaction of obligations secured by the security interest or agricultural lien under which the collection or enforcement is made; and

(C) the satisfaction of obligations secured by any subordinate security interest in or other lien on the collateral subject to the security interest or agricultural lien under which the collection or enforcement is made if the secured party receives an authenticated demand for proceeds before distribution of the proceeds is completed.

(2) If requested by a secured party, a holder of a subordinate security interest or other lien shall furnish reasonable proof of the interest or lien within a reasonable time. Unless the holder complies, the secured party need not comply with the holder's demand under paragraph (1)(C).

(3) A secured party need not apply or pay over for application noncash proceeds of collection and enforcement under Section 9-607 unless the failure to do so would be commercially unreasonable. A secured party that applies or pays over for application noncash proceeds shall do so in a commercially reasonable manner.

(4) A secured party shall account to and pay a debtor for any surplus, and the obligor is liable for any deficiency.

(b) No surplus or deficiency in sales of certain rights to payment. If the underlying transaction is a sale of accounts, chattel paper, payment intangibles, or promissory notes, the debtor is not entitled to any surplus, and the obligor is not liable for any deficiency.

History: Add, L 2001, ch 84, § 36, eff July 1, 2001.

§ 9-609. Secured Party's Right to Take Possession after Default

(a) Possession; rendering equipment unusable; disposition on debtor's premises. After default, a secured party:

(1) may take possession of the collateral; and

(2) without removal, may render equipment unusable and dispose of collateral on a debtor's premises under Section 9-610.

(b) Judicial and nonjudicial process. A secured party may proceed under subsection (a):

(1) pursuant to judicial process; or

(2) without judicial process, if it proceeds without breach of the peace.

(c) Assembly of collateral. If so agreed, and in any event after default, a secured party may require the debtor to assemble the collateral and make it available to the secured party at a place to be designated by the secured party which is reasonably convenient to both parties.

History: Add, L 2001, ch 84, § 36, eff July 1, 2001.

CASE ANNOTATIONS

1. **Simultaneous pursuit of multiple remedies**
2. **Commercially reasonable conduct**
3. **Right to repossession**

1. Simultaneous pursuit of multiple remedies

In a breach of contract case involving a corporate aircraft in which the creditor moved for summary judgment against the personal guarantors after a default, there were no genuine issues of material fact as to whether the creditor acted in a commercially reasonable manner by instituting the present action before selling the aircraft. Not only were the creditor's rights under the New York Uniform Commercial Code cumulative, they could be exercised simultaneously; additionally, the terms of the security agreement and the personal guarantees permitted the creditor to take possession of the aircraft upon default and concurrently pursue other remedies against the guarantors. Ctr. Capital Corp. v JR Lear 60-099, LLC, 674 F. Supp. 2d 569, 2009 U.S. Dist. LEXIS 117315 (D. Del. 2009).

2. Commercially reasonable conduct

Plaintiffs raised a triable issue of fact as to the commercial reasonableness of the individual's conduct regarding the preservation of the collateral securing the promissory note, as the individual, as the secured party, was obligated to exercise reasonable care in the custody and preservation of collateral in his possession; the individual's ownership and control of the corporation made his enforcement of his immediate right to possession of his collateral a simple matter. Nugent v Hubbard, 130 A.D.3d 893, 15 N.Y.S.3d 71, 2015 N.Y. App. Div. LEXIS 6094 (N.Y. App. Div. 2d Dep't 2015).

3. Right to repossession

Trial court properly granted summary judgment to a lender on a buyer's action for tortious interference with its contract with a borrower because, while the court erred in concluding that the buyer was not a debtor, the lender was entitled to repossess the equipment from the buyer inasmuch as the borrower's sale of the equipment to the buyer conclusively established an event of default occurred before the lender repossessed the equipment, and the lender was not liable for the acts of the repossessor as to the buyer's claims for tortious interference with contract and tortious interference with prospective business relations claims based on the manner of repossession and disposition of the equipment. Matter of Abele Tractor & Equip. Co., Inc. v Schaeffer, 2018 N.Y. App. Div. LEXIS 8694 (N.Y. App. Div. 3d Dep't 2018).

§ 9-610. Disposition of Collateral after Default

(a) Disposition after default. After default, a secured party may sell, lease, license, or otherwise dispose of any or all of the collateral in its present condition or following any commercially reasonable preparation or processing.

(b) Commercially reasonable disposition. Every aspect of a disposition of collateral, including the method, manner, time, place, and other terms, must be commercially reasonable. If commercially reasonable, a secured party may dispose of collateral by public or private proceedings, by one or more contracts, as a unit or in parcels, and at any time and place and on any terms.

(c) Purchase by secured party. A secured party may purchase collateral:

(1) at a public disposition; or

(2) at a private disposition only if the collateral is of a kind that is customarily sold on a recognized market or the subject of widely distributed standard price quotations.

UCC

(d) **Warranties on disposition.** A contract for sale, lease, license, or other disposition includes the warranties relating to title, possession, quiet enjoyment, and the like which by operation of law accompany a voluntary disposition of property of the kind subject to the contract.

(e) **Disclaimer of warranties.** A secured party may disclaim or modify warranties under subsection (d):

(1) in a manner that would be effective to disclaim or modify the warranties in a voluntary disposition of property of the kind subject to the contract of disposition; or

(2) by communicating to the purchaser a record evidencing the contract for disposition and including an express disclaimer or modification of the warranties.

(f) **Record sufficient to disclaim warranties.** A record is sufficient to disclaim warranties under subsection (e) if it indicates "There is no warranty relating to title, possession, quiet enjoyment, or the like in this disposition" or uses words of similar import.

History: Add, L 2001, ch 84, § 36, eff July 1, 2001.

CASE ANNOTATIONS

In dispute arising from stipulation granting plaintiff divorce from defendant and providing, inter alia, that she would hold, as collateral for defendant's assignment of certain rights encumbered by lien, assignment of his interest in certain medical partnership, no basis existed to award defendant any surplus from liquidation of plaintiff's collateral interest in medical partnership where (1) defendant had transferred his interest in that partnership to his partner's spouse for good and valuable consideration, subject to plaintiff's security interest, and (2) while plaintiff may have obtained windfall when she relinquished her security interest in exchange for $200,000, she was not unjustly enriched at defendant's expense. Strong v Strong (2000, 3d Dept) 277 A.D.2d 533, 715 N.Y.S.2d 499, 42 UCCRS2d 1204

Limited liability company (LLC) member's causes of action seeking surplus under N.Y. U.C.C. Law §§ 9-610 and 9-616 should have been dismissed because the lender was not obliged to sell the collateral (the member's interest in the LLC) after the member defaulted on the loan. Barbarito v Zahavi (2013, 1st Dept) 107 App Div 3d 416, 968 NYS2d 422.

Foreclosure sale was valid because, despite the defects in the notice of sale that the mortgagee mailed to the mortgagor, the notices were addressed to the wrong cooperative apartment number and to the wrong zip code, the record indicated that the mortgagor's doorman signed for both certified letters; furthermore, N.Y. U.C.C. § 9-504(3) (current version at N.Y. U.C.C. § 9-610(b)) did not require actual notice of sale, only that the mortgagee took reasonable steps to provide the notification, which the mortgagee did in this case. DeRosa v JP Morgan Chase (2004, A.D., 1st Dept) 774 N.Y.S.2d 120

Creditor had a right to exploit and rehabilitate collateral by retaining a manager for that purpose, because N.Y. U.C.C. Law § 9-610(a) authorized the creditor, as a secured lender, to sell, lease, license, or otherwise dispose of any or all of the collateral in its present condition or following any commercially reasonable preparation or processing. Nothing in the law precluded a creditor's retention of an interim manager to effect a commercially reasonable rehabilitation of the collateral. Prudential Secs. Credit Corp., LLC v TeeVee Toons, Inc. (2005, 1st Dept) 16 A.D. 3d 192, 791 N.Y.S.2d 95

Even though a guarantor waived the defense of impairment of collateral when co-signing for a friend's truck loan, once the friend had defaulted, and the lender, after releasing its lien, had allowed the friend to bring payments current and resume possession, but had not notified the guarantor of the new arrangement, when the lender sued the guarantor after a second default, the guarantor raised a triable issue of fact as to the commercial reasonableness of the lender's actions and the defense of waiver was not available in a post-default

context. ESL Fed. Credit Union v Bovee (2005, Sup) 9 Misc 3d 256, 801 NYS2d 482, 56 UCCRS2d 517.

Summary judgment was erroneously granted to a cooperative buyer in its action, seeking specific performance of the closing of title, as the sale pursuant to a private auction under N.Y. U.C.C. Law § 9-610(b) did not conflict with the terms of the cooperative's governing documents, which prohibited transfer to the buyer; the buyer was not an individual, as required by the governing documents. LI Equity Network, LLC v Village in the Woods Owners Corp. (2010, App Div, 2d Dept) 910 NYS2d 97.

Because a creditor had been in possession of the debtors' collateral for over two years, the commercial reasonableness of its delay in disposing the collateral under N.Y. U.C.C. Law § 9-610(a), (b) could not be disposed of on a motion to dismiss. Tee Vee Toons Inc. v Prudential Secs. Credits Corp. LLC (2005, Sup) 234 NYLJ 58, costs/fees proceeding (2006, 1st Dept) 35 App Div 3d 308, 825 NYS2d 366, subsequent app (2006, 1st Dept) 35 App Div 3d 309, 827 NYS2d 49.

In a suit between creditors, where plaintiff, who made letters of credit available to a certain women's clothing company, although it did not file any evidence of this debt, alleged two fraudulent conveyances by defendant, which had factoring agreements with the company, which were filed, and which entered into a new factoring agreement with a new company created by the primary owner of the old company, whereby the old company's obligations to it were satisfied, defendant did not have a duty as a secured creditor to dispose of the old company's assets under N.Y. U.C.C. Law § 9-610(a) (2000) because the factoring agreement provided that defendant "might," but it was not required, to take possession of the company's assets in the event of a default. Chemtex, LLC v St. Anthony Enters. (2007, SD NY) 490 F Supp 2d 536.

In a breach of contract case involving a corporate aircraft in which the creditor moved for summary judgment against the personal guarantors after a default, no genuine issue of material fact existed with regard to the commercial reasonableness of the creditor's preservation of and/or attempts to dispose of the aircraft. The mere fact that the creditor possessed the aircraft for six months prior to filing the present summary judgment motion, and that the guarantors contended that the creditor may not have kept up with the aircraft's contractual maintenance program did not raise issues of material fact sufficient to warrant denial of summary judgment. Ctr. Capital Corp. v JR Lear 60-099, LLC (2009, DC Del) 674 F Supp 2d 569.

Limited liability company (LLC) member's causes of action seeking surplus under N.Y. U.C.C. Law §§ 9-610 and 9-616 should have been dismissed because the lender was not obliged to sell the collateral (the member's interest in the LLC) after the member defaulted on the loan. Barbarito v Zahavi (2013, 1st Dept) 107 App Div 3d 416, 968 NYS2d 422.

Foreclosure sale of drilling rigs, conducted in accordance with credit agreements, was commercially reasonable even though it attracted few prospective buyers and resulted in bid below market value; price was not so inadequate as to shock conscience, and debtors could not complain about adequacy of preparation for sale because they prevented creditor from taking possession of collateral prior to sale. Adobe Trucking, Inc. v PNC Bank (In re Adobe Trucking, Inc.) (2014, CA5 Tex) 2014 US App LEXIS 314 (UNPUBLISHED).

§ 9-611. Notification Before Disposition of Collateral

(a) "Notification date." In this section, "notification date" means the earlier of the date on which:

(1) a secured party sends to the debtor and any secondary obligor an authenticated notification of disposition; or

(2) the debtor and any secondary obligor waive the right to notification.

(b) **Notification of disposition required.** Except as otherwise provided in subsection (d), a secured party that disposes of collateral under Section 9-610 shall send to the persons specified in subsection (c) a reasonable authenticated notification of disposition.

(c) Persons to be notified. To comply with subsection (b), the secured party shall send an authenticated notification of disposition to:

(1) the debtor;

(2) any secondary obligor; and

(3) if the collateral is other than consumer goods:

(A) any other person from which the secured party has received, before the notification date, an authenticated notification of a claim of an interest in the collateral;

(B) any other secured party or lienholder that, 10 days before the notification date, held a security interest in or other lien on the collateral perfected by the filing of a financing statement that:

(i) identified the collateral;

(ii) was indexed under the debtor's name as of that date; and

(iii) was filed in the office in which to file a financing statement against the debtor covering the collateral as of that date; and

(C) any other secured party that, 10 days before the notification date, held a security interest in the collateral perfected by compliance with a statute, regulation, or treaty described in Section 9-311(a).

(d) Subsection (b) inapplicable: perishable collateral; recognized market. Subsection (b) does not apply if the collateral is perishable or threatens to decline speedily in value or is of a type customarily sold on a recognized market.

(e) Compliance with subsection (c) (3) (B). A secured party complies with the requirement for notification prescribed by subsection (c) (3) (B) if:

(1) not later than twenty days or earlier than thirty days before the notification date, the secured party requests, in a commercially reasonable manner, information concerning financing statements indexed under the debtor's name in the office indicated in subsection (c) (3) (B); and

(2) before the notification date, the secured party:

(A) did not receive a response to the request for information; or

(B) received a response to the request for information and sent an authenticated notification of disposition to each secured party or other lienholder named in that response whose financing statement covered the collateral.

(f) Additional pre-disposition notice for cooperative interests.

(1) In addition to such other notification as may be required pursuant to subsection (b) of this section and section 9-613 of this article, a secured party whose collateral consists of a residential cooperative interest used by the debtor and whose security interest in such collateral secures an obligation incurred in connection with financing or refinancing of the acquisition of such cooperative interest and who proposes to dispose of such collateral after a default with respect to such obligation, shall send to the debtor, not less than ninety days prior to the date of the disposition of the cooperative interest, an additional pre-disposition notice as provided herein.

(2) The notice required by this subsection shall be in bold, fourteen-point type and shall be printed on colored paper that is other than the color of the notice required by subsection (b) of this section, and the title of the notice shall be in bold, twenty-point type. The notice shall be on its own page.

(3) The notice required by this subsection shall appear as follows:

Help for Homeowners at Risk of Foreclosure

New York State Law requires that we send you this information about the foreclosure process. Please read it carefully.

Notice

You are in danger of losing your home. You are in default of your obligations under the loan secured by your rights to your cooperative apartment. It is important that you take action, if you wish to avoid losing your home.

Sources of Information and Assistance

The State encourages you to become informed about your options, by seeking assistance from an attorney, a legal aid office, or a government agency or non-profit organization that provides counseling with respect to home foreclosures.

To locate a housing counselor near you, you may call the toll-free helpline maintained by the New York State Banking Department at [----------] [---------] (enter number) or visit the Department's website at [----------] [----------] (enter web address).

One of these persons or organizations may be able to help you, including trying to work with your lender to modify the loan to make it more affordable.

Foreclosure rescue scams

Be careful of people who approach you with offers to "save" your home. There are individuals who watch for notices of foreclosure actions or collateral sales in order to unfairly profit from a homeowner's distress. You should be extremely careful about any such promises and any suggestions that you pay them a fee or sign any papers that transfer rights of any kind to your cooperative apartment. State law requires anyone offering such services for profit to enter into a contract which fully describes the services they will perform and fees they will charge, and which prohibits them from taking any money from you until they have completed all such promised services.

(4) The banking department shall prescribe the telephone number and web address to be included in the notice.

(5) The banking department shall post on its website or otherwise make readily available the name

and contact information of government agencies or non-profit organizations that may be contacted for information about the foreclosure process, including maintaining a toll-free helpline to disseminate the information required by this subsection.

History: Add, L 2001, ch 84, § 36, eff July 1, 2001.

Sub (f), add, L 2009, ch 507, § 2, eff Jan 14, 2010.

CASE ANNOTATIONS

Notices provided were not adequate to provide notice to the owner or to a third-party bidder that the sale encompassed, in addition to the aircraft, damages against debtor airline for breach of the lease. In particular, (i) while the acceleration notice requested that the owner trustee deliver instruments of title to obtain title to the "collateral," it also made it clear that the intended foreclosure sale referred only to the aircraft, (ii) there was no indication in the record that the owner trustee ever delivered instruments specifically conveying title to the lease, and (iii) the foreclosure notices also did not indicate to the owner trustee, to the beneficiary of the owner trust, or to a prospective purchaser that the lease or any proceeds thereunder were being sold. In re Northwest Airlines Corp. (2008, BC SD NY) 383 BR 575.

In a suit between creditors, where plaintiff, who made letters of credit available to a certain women's clothing company, although it did not file any evidence of this debt, alleged two fraudulent conveyances by defendant, which had factoring agreements with the company, which were filed, and which entered into a new factoring agreement with a new company created by the primary owner of the old company, whereby the old company's obligations to it were satisfied, even assuming defendant had a duty as a secured creditor to dispose of the old company's assets under N.Y. U.C.C. Law § 9-610(a) (2000), plaintiff would not have received any of the proceeds from such a sale because it was an unsecured creditor and thus, it was not entitled to notice of the sale of the assets under N.Y. U.C.C. Law § 9-611(c) (2000). Chemtex, LLC v St. Anthony Enters. (2007, SD NY) 490 F Supp 2d 536

§ 9-612.   Timeliness of Notification Before Disposition of Collateral

(a) Reasonable time is question of fact. Except as otherwise provided in subsection (b), whether a notification is sent within a reasonable time is a question of fact.

(b) 10-day period sufficient in non-consumer transaction. In a transaction other than a consumer transaction, a notification of disposition sent after default and 10 days or more before the earliest time of disposition set forth in the notification is sent within a reasonable time before the disposition.

History: Add, L 2001, ch 84, § 36, eff July 1, 2001.

§ 9-613.   Contents and Form of Notification Before Disposition Of Collateral: General

Except in a consumer-goods transaction, the following rules apply:

(a) The contents of a notification of disposition are sufficient if the notification:

(1) describes the debtor and the secured party;

(2) describes the collateral that is the subject of the intended disposition;

(3) states the method of intended disposition;

(4) states that the debtor is entitled to an accounting of the unpaid indebtedness and states the charge, if any, for an accounting; and

(5) states the time and place of a public disposition or the time after which any other disposition is to be made.

(b) Whether the contents of a notification that lacks any of the information specified in subsection (a) are nevertheless sufficient is a question of fact.

(c) The contents of a notification providing substantially the information specified in subsection (a) are sufficient, even if the notification includes:

(1) information not specified by subsection (a); or

(2) minor errors that are not seriously misleading.

(d) A particular phrasing of the notification is not required.

(e) The following form of notification and the form appearing in Section 9-614(c), when completed, each provides sufficient information:

NOTIFICATION   OF   DISPOSITION   OF COLLATERAL

To: (Name of debtor, obligor, or other person to which the notification is sent)

From: (Name, address, and telephone number of secured party)

Name of Debtor(s): (Include only if debtor(s) are not an addressee) (For a public disposition:)

We will sell (or lease or license, as applicable) the (describe collateral) (to the highest qualified bidder) in public as follows:

Day and Date:_____

Time: _____

Place: _____

(For a private disposition:)

We will sell (or lease or license, as applicable) the (describe collateral) privately sometime after (day and date).

You are entitled to an accounting of the unpaid indebtedness secured by the property that we intend to sell (or lease or license, as applicable) (for a charge of $). You may request an accounting by calling us at (telephone number).

History: Add, L 2001, ch 84, § 36, eff July 1, 2001.

§ 9-614.   Contents and Form of Notification Before Disposition of Collateral: Consumer-goods Transaction

In a consumer-goods transaction, the following rules apply:

(a) A notification of disposition must provide the following information:

(1) the information specified in Section 9-613(a);

(2) a description of any liability for a deficiency of the person to which the notification is sent;

(3) a telephone number from which the amount that must be paid to the secured party to redeem the collateral under Section 9-623 is available; and

(4) a telephone number or mailing address from which additional information concerning the disposition and the obligation secured is available.

(b) A particular phrasing of the notification is not required.

(c) The following form of notification, when completed, provides sufficient information:

(Name and address of secured party)

(Date)

NOTICE OF OUR PLAN TO SELL PROPERTY

(Name and address of any obligor who is also a debtor)

Subject: (Identification of Transaction)

We have your (describe collateral), because you broke promises in our agreement.

(For a public disposition:)

We will sell (describe collateral) at public sale. A sale could include a lease or license. The sale will be held as follows:

Date: _____
Time: _____
Place: _____

You may attend the sale and bring bidders if you want.

(For a private disposition:)

We will sell (describe collateral) at private sale sometime after (date). A sale could include a lease or license.

The money that we get from the sale (after paying our costs) will reduce the amount you owe. If we get less money than you owe, you (will or will not, as applicable) still owe us the difference. If we get more money than you owe, you will get the extra money, unless we must pay it to someone else.

You can get the property back at any time before we sell it by paying us the full amount you owe (not just the past due payments), including our expenses. To learn the exact amount you must pay, call us at (telephone number). If you want us to explain to you in writing how we have figured the amount that you owe us, you may call us at (telephone number) (or write us at (secured party's address)) and request a written explanation. (We will charge you $ for the explanation if we sent you another written explanation of the amount you owe us within the last six months.)

If you need more information about the sale call us at (telephone number) (or write us at (secured party's address).

We are sending this notice to the following other people who have an interest in (describe collateral) or who owe money under your agreement:

(Names of all other debtors and obligors, if any)

(d) A notification in the form of subsection (c) is sufficient, even if additional information appears at the end of the form.

(e) A notification in the form of subsection (c) is sufficient, even if it includes errors in information not required by subsection (a), unless the error is misleading with respect to rights arising under this article.

(f) If a notification under this section is not in the form of subsection (c), law other than this article determines the effect of including information not required by subsection (a).

History: Add, L 2001, ch 84, § 36, eff July 1, 2001.

§ 9-615. Application of Proceeds of Disposition; Liability For Deficiency and Right to Surplus

(a) Application of proceeds. A secured party shall apply or pay over for application the cash proceeds of disposition under Section 9-610 in the following order to:

(1) the reasonable expenses of retaking, holding, preparing for disposition, processing, and disposing, and, to the extent provided for by agreement and not prohibited by law, reasonable attorney's fees and legal expenses incurred by the secured party;

(1-a) in the case of a cooperative organization security interest, the holder thereof in the amount secured thereby;

(2) the satisfaction of obligations secured by the security interest or agricultural lien under which the disposition is made;

(3) the satisfaction of obligations secured by any subordinate security interest in or other subordinate lien on the collateral if:

(A) the secured party receives from the holder of the subordinate security interest or other lien an authenticated demand for proceeds before distribution of the proceeds is completed; and

(B) in a case in which a consignor has an interest in the collateral, the subordinate security interest or other lien is senior to the interest of the consignor; and

(4) a secured party that is a consignor of the collateral if the secured party receives from the consignor an authenticated demand for proceeds before distribution of the proceeds is completed.

(b) Proof of subordinate interest. If requested by a secured party, a holder of a subordinate security interest or other lien shall furnish reasonable proof of the interest or lien within a reasonable time. Unless the holder does so, the secured party need not comply with the holder's demand under subsection (a) (3).

(c) Application of noncash proceeds. A secured party need not apply or pay over for application noncash proceeds of disposition under Section 9-610 unless the failure to do so would be commercially unreasonable. A secured party that applies or pays over for application noncash proceeds shall do so in a commercially reasonable manner.

(d) Surplus or deficiency if obligation secured. If the security interest under which a disposition is made secures payment or performance of an obligation, after making the payments and applications required by subsection (a) and permitted by subsection (c):

(1) unless subsection (a)(4) requires the secured party to apply or pay over cash proceeds to a consignor, the secured party shall account to and pay a debtor for any surplus; and

(2) the obligor is liable for any deficiency.

(e) No surplus or deficiency in sales of certain rights to payment. If the underlying transaction is a sale of accounts, chattel paper, payment intangibles, or promissory notes:

(1) the debtor is not entitled to any surplus; and

(2) the obligor is not liable for any deficiency.

(f) Calculation of surplus or deficiency in disposition to person related to secured party. The surplus or deficiency following a disposition is calculated based on the amount of proceeds that would have been realized in a disposition complying with this part to a transferee other than the secured party, a person related to the secured party, or a secondary obligor if:

(1) the transferee in the disposition is the secured party, a person related to the secured party, or a secondary obligor; and

(2) the amount of proceeds of the disposition is significantly below the range of proceeds that a complying disposition to a person other than the secured party, a person related to the secured party, or a secondary obligor would have brought.

(g) Cash proceeds received by junior secured party. A secured party that receives cash proceeds of a disposition in good faith and without knowledge that the receipt violates the rights of the holder of a security interest or other lien that is not subordinate to the security interest or agricultural lien under which the disposition is made:

(1) takes the cash proceeds free of the security interest or other lien;

(2) is not obligated to apply the proceeds of the disposition to the satisfaction of obligations secured by the security interest or other lien; and

(3) is not obligated to account to or pay the holder of the security interest or other lien for any surplus.

History: Add, L 2001, ch 84, § 36, eff July 1, 2001.

CASE ANNOTATIONS

Debtor could not avoid a bank's deficiency claim by reason of the voluntary surrender of the collateral prior to the petition for Chapter 13 bankruptcy relief because the claim was not subject to the treatment that 11 U.S.C.S. §§ 1322(b)(2) and 1325(a)(5) would have applied to secured claims. Pursuant to N.Y. U.C.C. Law § 9-615(d) (2002), the debtor became liable for the deficiency after the application of the sale proceeds; thus, when the debtor filed his bankruptcy petition, the bank no longer enjoyed the status of a secured creditor under 11 U.S.C.S. § 506(a), and the bank was entitled to assert its deficiency as an unsecured claim. In re Krotje (2007, BC WD NY) 370 BR 515

§ 9-616. Explanation of Calculation of Surplus or Deficiency

(a) Definitions. In this section:

(1) "Explanation" means a writing that:

(A) states the amount of the surplus or deficiency;

(B) provides an explanation in accordance with subsection (c) of how the secured party calculated the surplus or deficiency;

(C) states, if applicable, that future debits, credits, charges, including additional credit service charges or interest, rebates, and expenses may affect the amount of the surplus or deficiency; and

(D) provides a telephone number or mailing address from which additional information concerning the transaction is available.

(2) "Request" means a record:

(A) authenticated by a debtor or consumer obligor;

(B) requesting that the recipient provide an explanation; and

(C) sent after disposition of the collateral under Section 9-610.

(b) Explanation of calculation. In a consumer-goods transaction in which the debtor is entitled to a surplus or a consumer obligor is liable for a deficiency under Section 9-615, the secured party shall:

(1) send an explanation to the debtor or consumer obligor, as applicable, after the disposition and:

(A) before or when the secured party accounts to the debtor and pays any surplus or first makes written demand on the consumer obligor after the disposition for payment of the deficiency; and

(B) within fourteen days after receipt of a request; or

(2) in the case of a consumer obligor who is liable for a deficiency, within fourteen days after receipt of a request, send to the consumer obligor a record waiving the secured party's right to a deficiency.

(c) Required information. To comply with subsection (a)(1)(B), a writing must provide the following information in the following order:

(1) the aggregate amount of obligations secured by the security interest under which the disposition was made, and, if the amount reflects a rebate of unearned interest or credit service charge, an indication of that fact, calculated as of a specified date:

(A) if the secured party takes or receives possession of the collateral after default, not more than thirty-five days before the secured party takes or receives possession; or

(B) if the secured party takes or receives possession of the collateral before default or does not take possession of the collateral, not more than thirty-five days before the disposition;

(2) the amount of proceeds of the disposition;

(3) the aggregate amount of the obligations after deducting the amount of proceeds;

(4) the amount, in the aggregate or by type, and types of expenses, including expenses of retaking, holding, preparing for disposition, processing, and

disposing of the collateral, and attorney's fees secured by the collateral which are known to the secured party and relate to the current disposition;

(5) the amount, in the aggregate or by type, and types of credits, including rebates of interest or credit service charges, to which the obligor is known to be entitled and which are not reflected in the amount in paragraph (1); and

(6) the amount of the surplus or deficiency.

(d) Substantial compliance. A particular phrasing of the explanation is not required. An explanation complying substantially with the requirements of subsection (a) is sufficient, even if it includes minor errors that are not seriously misleading.

(e) Charges for responses. A debtor or consumer obligor is entitled without charge to one response to a request under this section during any six-month period in which the secured party did not send to the debtor or consumer obligor an explanation pursuant to subsection (b)(1). The secured party may require payment of a charge not exceeding 25 dollars for each additional response.

History: Add, L 2001, ch 84, § 36, eff July 1, 2001.

CASE ANNOTATIONS

Limited liability company (LLC) member's causes of action seeking surplus under N.Y. U.C.C. Law §§ 9-610 and 9-616 should have been dismissed because the lender was not obliged to sell the collateral (the member's interest in the LLC) after the member defaulted on the loan. Barbarito v Zahavi (2013, 1st Dept) 107 App Div 3d 416, 968 NYS2d 422.

§ 9-617. Rights of Transferee of Collateral

(a) Effects of disposition. A secured party's disposition of collateral after default:

(1) transfers to a transferee for value all of the debtor's rights in the collateral;

(2) discharges the security interest under which the disposition is made; and

(3) discharges any subordinate security interest or other subordinate lien other than liens created under any law of this state that are not to be discharged.

(b) Rights of good-faith transferee. A transferee that acts in good faith takes free of the rights and interests described in subsection (a), even if the secured party fails to comply with this article or the requirements of any judicial proceeding.

(c) Rights of other transferee. If a transferee does not take free of the rights and interests described in subsection (a), the transferee takes the collateral subject to:

(1) the debtor's rights in the collateral;

(2) the security interest or agricultural lien under which the disposition is made; and

(3) any other security interest or other lien.

History: Add, L 2001, ch 84, § 36, eff July 1, 2001.

§ 9-618. Rights and Duties of Certain Secondary Obligors

(a) Rights and duties of secondary obligor. A secondary obligor acquires the rights and becomes obligated to perform the duties of the secured party after the secondary obligor:

(1) receives an assignment of a secured obligation from the secured party;

(2) receives a transfer of collateral from the secured party and agrees to accept the rights and assume the duties of the secured party; or

(3) is subrogated to the rights of a secured party with respect to collateral.

(b) Effect of assignment, transfer, or subrogation. An assignment, transfer, or subrogation described in subsection (a):

(1) is not a disposition of collateral under Section 9-610; and

(2) relieves the secured party of further duties under this article.

History: Add, L 2001, ch 84, § 36, eff July 1, 2001.

§ 9-619. Transfer of Record or Legal Title

(a) "Transfer statement." In this section, "transfer statement" means a record authenticated by a secured party stating:

(1) that the debtor has defaulted in connection with an obligation secured by specified collateral;

(2) that the secured party has exercised its post-default remedies with respect to the collateral;

(3) that, by reason of the exercise, a transferee has acquired the rights of the debtor in the collateral; and

(4) the name and mailing address of the secured party, debtor, and transferee.

(b) Effect of transfer statement. A transfer statement entitles the transferee to the transfer of record of all rights of the debtor in the collateral specified in the statement in any official filing, recording, registration, or certificate-of-title system covering the collateral. If a transfer statement is presented with the applicable fee and request form to the official or office responsible for maintaining the system, the official or office shall:

(1) accept the transfer statement;

(2) promptly amend its records to reflect the transfer; and

(3) if applicable, issue a new appropriate certificate of title in the name of the transferee.

(c) Transfer not a disposition; no relief of secured party's duties. A transfer of the record or legal title to collateral to a secured party under subsection (b) or otherwise is not of itself a disposition of collateral under this article and does not of itself relieve the secured party of its duties under this article.

History: Add, L 2001, ch 84, § 36, eff July 1, 2001.

UCC

§ 9-620. Acceptance of Collateral in Full or Partial Satisfaction of Obligation; Compulsory Disposition of Collateral

(a) Conditions to acceptance in satisfaction. Except as otherwise provided in subsections (g) and (h), a secured party may accept collateral in full or partial satisfaction of the obligation it secures only if:

(1) the debtor consents to the acceptance under subsection (c);

(2) the secured party does not receive, within the time set forth in subsection (d), a notification of objection to the proposal authenticated by:

(A) a person to which the secured party was required to send a proposal under Section 9-621; or

(B) any other person, other than the debtor, holding an interest in the collateral subordinate to the security interest that is the subject of the proposal;

(3) if the collateral is consumer goods, the collateral is not in the possession of the debtor when the debtor consents to the acceptance; and

(4) subsection (e) does not require the secured party to dispose of the collateral or the debtor waives the requirement pursuant to Section 9-624.

(b) Purported acceptance ineffective. A purported or apparent acceptance of collateral under this section is ineffective unless:

(1) the secured party consents to the acceptance in an authenticated record or sends a proposal to the debtor; and

(2) the conditions of subsection (a) are met.

(c) Debtor's consent. For purposes of this section:

(1) a debtor consents to an acceptance of collateral in partial satisfaction of the obligation it secures only if the debtor agrees to the terms of the acceptance in a record authenticated after default; and

(2) a debtor consents to an acceptance of collateral in full satisfaction of the obligation it secures only if the debtor agrees to the terms of the acceptance in a record authenticated after default or the secured party:

(A) sends to the debtor after default a proposal that is unconditional or subject only to a condition that collateral not in the possession of the secured party be preserved or maintained;

(B) in the proposal, proposes to accept collateral in full satisfaction of the obligation it secures; and

(C) does not receive a notification of objection authenticated by the debtor within twenty days after the proposal is sent.

(d) Effectiveness of notification. To be effective under subsection (a)(2), a notification of objection must be received by the secured party:

(1) in the case of a person to which the proposal was sent pursuant to Section 9-621, within 20 days after notification was sent to that person; and

(2) in other cases:

(A) within 20 days after the last notification was sent pursuant to Section 9-621; or

(B) if a notification was not sent, before the debtor consents to the acceptance under subsection (c).

(e) Mandatory disposition of consumer goods. A secured party that has taken possession of collateral shall dispose of the collateral pursuant to Section 9-610 within the time specified in subsection (f) if:

(1) sixty percent of the cash price has been paid in the case of a purchase-money security interest in consumer goods; or

(2) sixty percent of the principal amount of the obligation secured has been paid in the case of a non-purchase-money security interest in consumer goods.

(f) Compliance with mandatory disposition requirement. To comply with subsection (e), the secured party shall dispose of the collateral:

(1) within 90 days after taking possession; or

(2) within any longer period to which the debtor and all secondary obligors have agreed in an agreement to that effect entered into and authenticated after default.

(g) No partial satisfaction in consumer transaction. In a consumer transaction, a secured party may not accept collateral in partial satisfaction of the obligation it secures.

(h) Special provisions for cooperative interests. A secured party whose collateral consists of a residential cooperative interest used by the debtor and whose security interest in such collateral secures an obligation incurred in connection with financing or refinancing of the acquisition of such cooperative interest and who chooses to accept that cooperative interest in full satisfaction of the debtor's obligation may do so.

(1) If the secured party sends a proposal to take the cooperative interest in full satisfaction of the debtor's obligation, the proposal shall be accompanied by a notice in the form and manner prescribed in subsection (f) of section 9-611 of this subpart, unless the secured party has previously sent the debtor such notice. A debtor consents to an acceptance of a cooperative interest in full satisfaction of the obligation it secures only if the debtor agrees to the terms of the proposal in a record authenticated after default.

(2) A debtor may propose to the secured party that it take the cooperative interest in full satisfaction of the obligation it secures. The proposal shall be ineffective unless the secured party consents to the proposal in an authenticated record.

History: Add, L 2001, ch 84, § 36, eff July 1, 2001.

Sub (a), opening par, amd, L 2009, ch 507, § 3, eff Jan 14, 2010.

Sub (h), add, L 2009, ch 507, § 3, eff Jan 14, 2010.

CASE ANNOTATIONS

Creditor's strict foreclosure against a bankruptcy debtor's assets was valid since the debtor's default occurred when the debtor initially failed to pay a note to the creditor, rather than when the debtor also failed to pay under a subsequent forbearance agreement, and the debtor expressly consented to strict foreclosure in the forbearance agreement as required by N.Y. U.C.C. Law § 9-620(c); the debtor was not contractually obligated to redeem or sell the assets under the forbearance agreement, and the debtor's failure to do so was not a default and did not give rise to liability. In re CBGB Holdings, LLC (2010, BC SD NY) 439 BR 551, 53 BCD 226.

Where a debtor alleged, in support of its argument that a transfer at issue in a state court action against it did not fall within an exclusion in its directors and officers liability policies, that the state court plaintiffs' allegations concerning a restructuring transaction could be interpreted as a discharge of debt via a strict foreclosure on excess cash flow certificates by note holders under N.Y. U.C.C. Law §§ 9-620 and 9-622, its argument failed. Those allegations were inconsistent with such a transaction because none of the required elements under N.Y. U.C.C. Law § 9-620 were alleged by the state court plaintiffs, and there was no allegation that any of the procedural requirements of N.Y. U.C.C. Law §§ 9-620 or 9-621 were followed with respect to the restructuring transaction. Welch v United States (2010, CA7 Ill) 604 F3d 408.

Defendants' motions to dismiss plaintiff's claim for declaratory relief under Article 9 of the New York Uniform Commercial Code was denied because plaintiff had pled facts suggesting that it was the rightful owner of the patents and that all three defendants had asserted ownership of the patents; there was a controversy involving ownership of the patents that would be resolved by the declaratory relief that plaintiff requested. digiGAN, Inc. v iValidate, Inc. (2004, SD NY) 71 USPQ2d 1455, 52 UCCRS2d 1022, magistrate's recommendation (2004, SD NY) 2004 US Dist LEXIS 8705 (UNPUBLISHED).

§ 9-621. Notification of Proposal to Accept Collateral

(a) Persons to which proposal to be sent. A secured party that desires to accept collateral in full or partial satisfaction of the obligation it secures shall send its proposal to:

(1) any person from which the secured party has received, before the debtor consented to the acceptance, an authenticated notification of a claim of an interest in the collateral;

(2) any other secured party or lienholder that, 10 days before the debtor consented to the acceptance, held a security interest in or other lien on the collateral perfected by the filing of a financing statement that:

(A) identified the collateral;

(B) was indexed under the debtor's name as of that date; and

(C) was filed in the office or offices in which to file a financing statement against the debtor covering the collateral as of that date; and

(3) any other secured party that, 10 days before the debtor consented to the acceptance, held a security interest in the collateral perfected by compliance with a statute, regulation, or treaty described in Section 9-311(a).

(b) Proposal to be sent to secondary obligor in partial satisfaction. A secured party that desires to accept collateral in partial satisfaction of the obligation it secures shall send its proposal to any secondary obligor in addition to the persons described in subsection (a).

History: Add, L 2001, ch 84, § 36, eff July 1, 2001.

CASE ANNOTATIONS

Where a debtor alleged, in support of its argument that a transfer at issue in a state court action against it did not fall within an

exclusion in its directors and officers liability policies, that the state court plaintiffs' allegations concerning a restructuring transaction could be interpreted as a discharge of debt via a strict foreclosure on excess cash flow certificates by note holders under N.Y. U.C.C. Law §§ 9-620 and 9-622, its argument failed. Those allegations were inconsistent with such a transaction because none of the required elements under N.Y. U.C.C. Law § 9-620 were alleged by the state court plaintiffs, and there was no allegation that any of the procedural requirements of N.Y. U.C.C. Law §§ 9-620 or 9-621 were followed with respect to the restructuring transaction. Welch v United States (2010, CA7 Ill) 604 F3d 408.

Defendants' motions to dismiss plaintiff's claim for declaratory relief under Article 9 of the New York Uniform Commercial Code was denied because plaintiff had pled facts suggesting that it was the rightful owner of the patents and that all three defendants had asserted ownership of the patents; there was a controversy involving ownership of the patents that would be resolved by the declaratory relief that plaintiff requested. digiGAN, Inc. v iValidate, Inc. (2004, SD NY) 71 USPQ2d 1455, 52 UCCRS2d 1022, magistrate's recommendation (2004, SD NY) 2004 US Dist LEXIS 8705 (UNPUBLISHED).

§ 9-622. Effect of Acceptance of Collateral

(a) Effect of acceptance. A secured party's acceptance of collateral in full or partial satisfaction of the obligation it secures:

(1) discharges the obligation to the extent consented to by the debtor;

(2) transfers to the secured party all of a debtor's rights in the collateral;

(3) discharges the security interest or agricultural lien that is the subject of the debtor's consent and any subordinate security interest or other subordinate lien; and

(4) terminates any other subordinate interest.

(b) Discharge of subordinate interest notwithstanding noncompliance. A subordinate interest is discharged or terminated under subsection (a), even if the secured party fails to comply with this article.

History: Add, L 2001, ch 84, § 36, eff July 1, 2001.

CASE ANNOTATIONS

Where a debtor alleged, in support of its argument that a transfer at issue in a state court action against it did not fall within an exclusion in its directors and officers liability policies, that the state court plaintiffs' allegations concerning a restructuring transaction could be interpreted as a discharge of debt via a strict foreclosure on excess cash flow certificates by note holders under N.Y. U.C.C. Law §§ 9-620 and 9-622, its argument failed. Those allegations were inconsistent with such a transaction because none of the required elements under N.Y. U.C.C. Law § 9-620 were alleged by the state court plaintiffs, and there was no allegation that any of the procedural requirements of N.Y. U.C.C. Law §§ 9-620 or 9-621 were followed with respect to the restructuring transaction. Welch v United States (2010, CA7 Ill) 604 F3d 408.

§ 9-623. Right to Redeem Collateral

(a) Persons that may redeem. A debtor, any secondary obligor, or any other secured party or lienholder may redeem collateral.

(b) Requirements for redemption. To redeem collateral, a person shall tender:

(1) fulfillment of all obligations secured by the collateral; and

(2) the reasonable expenses and attorney's fees described in Section 9-615(a)(1).

UCC

(c) When redemption may occur. A redemption may occur at any time before a secured party:

(1) has collected collateral under Section 9-607;

(2) has disposed of collateral or entered into a contract for its disposition under Section 9-610; or

(3) has accepted collateral in full or partial satisfaction of the obligation it secures under Section 9-622.

History: Add, L 2001, ch 84, § 36, eff July 1, 2001.

CASE ANNOTATIONS

Credit union that repossessed debtors' vehicle four days before the debtors declared Chapter 7 bankruptcy violated the stay that was imposed pursuant to 11 U.S.C.S. § 362 when it refused to return the vehicle to the debtors until they paid $ 817 in arrears they owed, provided proof of insurance, and signed a reaffirmation agreement, and the court ordered the credit union to pay costs the debtors incurred to rent a replacement vehicle, the debtors' attorney's fees, and the amount in arrears it collected from the debtors, and also ordered the credit union to pay the debtors' actual damages a second time as punitive damages. The debtors had the right to redeem the vehicle under N.Y. U.C.C. Law § 9-623(a), the vehicle was part of their bankruptcy estate under 11 U.S.C.S. § 541, and the credit union had an obligation under 11 U.S.C.S. § 542(a) to return the vehicle after it learned that the debtors declared bankruptcy. In re Velichko (2012, BC SD NY) 473 BR 64

Because plaintiff debtor had an equitable interest under N.Y. U.C.C. Law § 9-623 to redeem a repossessed vehicle before defendant secured creditor's sale, under 11 U.S.C.S. §§ 362, 363, 541, 542, the secured creditor had to first return the vehicle upon the debtor's Chapter 13 filing, and only then could it seek adequate protection, thus, retaining the vehicle was a willful violation of the automatic stay for which it was liable for damages, costs, and attorney's fees under § 362(k)(1). Weber v SEFCU (In re Weber) (2013, CA2) 719 F3d 72 (criticized in Stephens v Guaranteed Auto, Inc. (In re Stephens) (2013, BC ND Ga) 2013 Bankr LEXIS 2730).

§ 9-624. Waiver

(a) Waiver of disposition notification. A debtor or secondary obligor may waive the right to notification of disposition of collateral under Section 9-611 only by an agreement to that effect entered into and authenticated after default.

(b) Waiver of mandatory disposition. A debtor may waive the right to require disposition of collateral under Section 9-620 (e) only by an agreement to that effect entered into and authenticated after default.

(c) Waiver of redemption right. Except in a consumer-goods transaction, a debtor or secondary obligor may waive the right to redeem collateral under Section 9-623 only by an agreement to that effect entered into and authenticated after default.

History: Add, L 2001, ch 84, § 36, eff July 1, 2001.

Subpart 2
Noncompliance With Article
History: Add, L 2001, ch 84, § 36, eff July 1, 2001.

§ 9-625. Remedies for Secured Party's Failure to Comply with Article

(a) Judicial orders concerning noncompliance. If it is established that a secured party is not proceeding in accordance with this article, a court may order or restrain collection, enforcement, or disposition of collateral on appropriate terms and conditions.

(b) Damages for noncompliance. Subject to subsections (c), (d), and (f), a person is liable for damages in the amount of any loss caused by a failure to comply with this article. Loss caused by a failure to comply may include loss resulting from the debtor's inability to obtain, or increased costs of, alternative financing.

(c) Persons entitled to recover damages; statutory damages if collateral is consumer goods. Except as otherwise provided in Section 9-628:

(1) a person that, at the time of the failure, was a debtor, was an obligor, or held a security interest in or other lien on the collateral may recover damages under subsection (b) for its loss; and

(2) if the collateral is consumer goods, a person that was a debtor or a secondary obligor at the time a secured party failed to comply with this part may recover for that failure in any event an amount not less than the credit service charge plus 10 percent of the principal amount of the obligation or the time-price differential plus 10 percent of the cash price.

(d) Recovery when deficiency eliminated or reduced. A debtor whose deficiency is eliminated under Section 9-626 may recover damages for the loss of any surplus. However, a debtor or secondary obligor whose deficiency is eliminated or reduced under Section 9-626 may not otherwise recover under subsection (b) for noncompliance with the provisions of this part relating to collection, enforcement, disposition, or acceptance.

(e) Statutory damages: noncompliance with specified provisions. In addition to any damages recoverable under subsection (b), the debtor, consumer obligor, or person named as a debtor in a filed record, as applicable, may recover five hundred dollars in each case from a person that:

(1) fails to comply with Section 9-208;

(2) fails to comply with Section 9-209;

(3) files a record that the person is not entitled to file under Section 9-509 (a);

(4) fails to cause the secured party of record to file or send a termination statement as required by Section 9-513 (a), (c), or (e);

(5) fails to comply with Section 9-616 (b) (1) and whose failure is part of a pattern, or consistent with a practice, of noncompliance; or

(6) fails to comply with Section 9-616 (b) (2).

(f) Statutory damages: noncompliance with Section 9-210. A debtor or consumer obligor may recover damages under subsection (b) and, in addition, five hundred dollars in each case from a person that, without reasonable cause, fails to comply with a request under Section 9-210. A recipient of a request under Section 9-210 which never claimed an interest in the collateral or obligations that are the subject of a request under that section has a reasonable excuse for failure to comply with the request within the meaning of this subsection.

(g) Limitation of security interest: noncompliance with Section 9-210. If a secured party fails to comply with a request regarding a list of collateral or a statement of account under Section 9-210, the secured party may claim a security interest only as shown in the list or statement included in the request as against a person that is reasonably misled by the failure.

History: Add, L 2001, ch 84, § 36, eff July 1, 2001; amd, L 2014, ch 505, § 50, eff Dec 17, 2014.

CASE ANNOTATIONS

In a suit brought by a shareholder against a housing corporation and other shareholders (collectively referred to as the housing corporation), there was no justification for the shareholder's filing of a financing statement against a garden unit apartment for which the shareholder alleged that funds were expended as no security agreement was ever entered into between the parties, the shareholder had no common law lien that was enforceable, and there was no authenticated record whereby the housing corporation authorized the filing. Since the filing of the UCC-1 financing statement was baseless, the shareholder was directed to terminate the same and pay the housing corporation statutory damages in the amount of $500. McDaniel v 162 Columbia Hgts. Hous. Corps. (2008, Sup) 21 Misc 3d 244, 863 NYS2d 346.

Under a Securities Investor Protection Act of 1970 liquidation, where the creditor had posted cash collateral with the debtor broker-dealer in exchange for loaned securities, the debtor's commingled cash was not subject to a constructive trust and all of the debtor's cash was property of the estate and the creditor's security interest could be avoided by the trustee, because, while the debtor was required to use reasonable care in preserving that collateral under N.Y. U.C.C. Law § 9-207(a) (2002), under N.Y. U.C.C. Law § 1-102, the parties had, by agreement, not unreasonably, provided that the debtor was not required to segregate the cash, and under N.Y. U.C.C. Law § 9-625, the creditor's only remedy was a claim for damages. Ferris, Baker, Watts, Inc. v Stephenson (In re MJK Clearing) (2002, BC DC Minn) 286 BR 109, 49 UCCRS2d 11

§ 9-626. Action in Which Deficiency or Surplus is in Issue

(a) Applicable rules if amount of deficiency or surplus is in issue. In an action arising from a transaction, other than a consumer transaction, in which the amount of a deficiency or surplus is in issue, the following rules apply:

(1) A secured party need not prove compliance with the provisions of this part relating to collection, enforcement, disposition, or acceptance unless the debtor or a secondary obligor places the secured party's compliance in issue.

(2) If the secured party's compliance is placed in issue, the secured party has the burden of establishing that the collection, enforcement, disposition, or acceptance was conducted in accordance with this part.

(3) Except as otherwise provided in Section 9-628, if a secured party fails to prove that the collection, enforcement, disposition, or acceptance was conducted in accordance with the provisions of this part relating to collection, enforcement, disposition, or acceptance, the liability of a debtor or a secondary obligor for a deficiency is limited to an amount by which the sum of the secured obligation, expenses, and attorney's fees exceeds the greater of:

(A) the proceeds of the collection, enforcement, disposition, or acceptance; or

(B) the amount of proceeds that would have been realized had the non-complying secured party proceeded in accordance with the provisions of this part relating to collection, enforcement, disposition, or acceptance.

(4) For purposes of paragraph (3)(B), the amount of proceeds that would have been realized is equal to the sum of the secured obligation, expenses, and attorney's fees unless the secured party proves that the amount is less than that sum.

(5) If a deficiency or surplus is calculated under Section 9-615(f), the debtor or obligor has the burden of establish- ing that the amount of proceeds of the disposition is signif icantly below the range of prices that a complying disposition to a person other than the secured party, a person related to the secured party, or a secondary obligor would have brought.

(b) Non-consumer transactions; no inference. The limitation of the rules in subsection (a) to transactions other than consumer transactions is intended to leave to the court the determination of the proper rules in consumer transactions. The court may not infer from that limitation the nature of the proper rule in consumer transactions and may continue to apply established approaches.

History: Add, L 2001, ch 84, § 36, eff July 1, 2001.

§ 9-627. Determination of Whether Conduct Was Commercially Reasonable

(a) Greater amount obtainable under other circumstances; no preclusion of commercial reasonableness. The fact that a greater amount could have been obtained by a collection, enforcement, disposition, or acceptance at a different time or in a different method from that selected by the secured party is not of itself sufficient to preclude the secured party from establishing that the collection, enforcement, disposition, or acceptance was made in a commercially reasonable manner.

(b) Dispositions that are commercially reasonable. A disposition of collateral is made in a commercially reasonable manner if the disposition is made:

(1) in the usual manner on any recognized market;

(2) at the price current in any recognized market at the time of the disposition; or

(3) otherwise in conformity with reasonable commercial practices among dealers in the type of property that was the subject of the disposition.

(c) Approval by court or on behalf of creditors. A collection, enforcement, disposition, or acceptance is commercially reasonable if it has been approved:

(1) in a judicial proceeding;

(2) by a bona fide creditors' committee;

(3) by a representative of creditors; or

UCC

(4) by an assignee for the benefit of creditors.

(d) Approval under subsection (c) not necessary; absence of approval has no effect. Approval under subsection (c) need not be obtained, and lack of approval does not mean that the collection, enforcement, disposition, or acceptance is not commercially reasonable.

History: Add, L 2001, ch 84, § 36, eff July 1, 2001.

CASE ANNOTATIONS

1. Commercially reasonable

Borrower was not entitled to injunctive relief on the ground that a nonjudicial sale of the shares of stock issued in connection with her cooperative apartment and proprietary lease to her apartment for the current market value would not be commercially reasonable because disposition of the borrower's collateral would be commercially reasonable if made at the price current in any recognized market. Matter of Chase v Wells Fargo Bank, N.A., 135 A.D.3d 751, 24 N.Y.S.3d 673 (2d Dep't 2016).

Foreclosure sale was valid because the sale was conducted in a commercially reasonable manner, despite the mortgagor's protestations, without any support, that the sale price was only 45 percent of the market value of the property. DeRosa v JP Morgan Chase (2004, A.D., 1st Dept) 774 N.Y.S.2d 120

§ 9-628. Nonliability and Limitation on Liability of Secured Party; Liability of Secondary Obligor

(a) Limitation of liability of secured party for noncompliance with article. Unless a secured party knows that a person is a debtor or obligor, knows the identity of the person, and knows how to communicate with the person:

(1) the secured party is not liable to the person, or to a secured party or lienholder that has filed a financing statement against the person, for failure to comply with this article; and

(2) the secured party's failure to comply with this article does not affect the liability of the person for a deficiency.

(b) Limitation of liability based on status as secured party. A secured party is not liable because of its status as secured party:

(1) to a person that is a debtor or obligor, unless the secured party knows:

(A) that the person is a debtor or obligor;

(B) the identity of the person; and

(C) how to communicate with the person; or

(2) to a secured party or lienholder that has filed a financing statement against a person, unless the secured party knows:

(A) that the person is a debtor; and

(B) the identity of the person.

(c) Limitation of liability if reasonable belief that transaction not a consumer-goods transaction or consumer transaction. A secured party is not liable to any person, and a person's liability for a deficiency is not affected, because of any act or omission arising out of the secured party's reasonable belief that a transaction is not a consumer-goods transaction or a consumer transaction or that goods are not consumer goods, if the secured party's belief is based on its reasonable reliance on:

(1) a debtor's representation concerning the purpose for which collateral was to be used, acquired, or held; or

(2) an obligor's representation concerning the purpose for which a secured obligation was incurred.

(d) Limitation of liability for statutory damages. A secured party is not liable to any person under Section 9-625 (c) (2) for its failure to comply with Section 9-616.

(e) Limitation of multiple liability for statutory damages. A secured party is not liable under Section 9-625 (c) (2) more than once with respect to any one secured obligation.

History: Add, L 2001, ch 84, § 36, eff July 1, 2001.

PART 7
TRANSITION

History: Add, L 2001, ch 84, § 36, eff July 1, 2001.

§ 9-700. Definitions

The following words and terms when used in this part 7 shall have the following meanings:

"Former Article 9." The provisions of article 9 of the Uniform Commercial Code of this state as in effect before the effective date of Revised Article 9.

"Revised Article 9." The provisions of article 9 of the Uniform Commercial Code of this state, as amended by the chapter of the laws of 2001 which added these words and as they may be further amended.

History: Add, L 2001, ch 84, § 36, eff July 1, 2001.

§ 9-701. Effective Date

Revised Article 9 takes effect on July 1, 2001.

History: Add, L 2001, ch 84, § 36, eff July 1, 2001.

CASE ANNOTATIONS

N.Y. U.C.C. Law § 9-702(c) provided that Revised Article 9 did not affect an action, case, or proceeding commenced before Revised Article 9 took effect, and Revised Article 9 became effective on July 1, 2001 under N.Y. U.C.C. Law § 9-701, thus, since the seller's adversary proceeding against the debtor asserting a right to stop goods in transit under N.Y. U.C.C. Law §§ 2-702, 2-705 and its challenge to the debtor's secured creditor's interest was commenced on March 30, 2001, Old Article 9 applied. Cargill Inc. v Trico Steel Co. (In re Trico Steel Co.) (2002, BC DC Del) 282 BR 318

§ 9-702. Savings Clause

(a) Pre-effective-date transactions or liens. Except as otherwise provided in this part, Revised Article 9 applies to a transaction or lien within its scope, even if the transaction or lien was entered into or created before Revised Article 9 takes effect.

(b) Continuing validity. Except as otherwise provided in subsection (c) and Sections 9-703 through 9-709:

(1) transactions and liens that were not governed by Former Article 9, were validly entered into or created before Revised Article 9 takes effect, and would be subject to Revised Article 9 if they had been entered into or created after Revised Article 9 takes effect, and the rights, duties, and interests flowing from those transactions and liens remain valid after Revised Article 9 takes effect; and

(2) the transactions and liens may be terminated, completed, consummated, and enforced as required or permitted by Revised Article 9 or by the law that otherwise would apply if Revised Article 9 had not taken effect.

(c) Pre-effective-date proceedings. Revised Article 9 does not affect an action, case, or proceeding commenced before Revised Article 9 takes effect.

History: Add, L 2001, ch 84, § 36, eff July 1, 2001.

CASE ANNOTATIONS

N.Y. U.C.C. Law § 9-702(c) provided that Revised Article 9 did not affect an action, case, or proceeding commenced before Revised Article 9 took effect, and Revised Article 9 became effective on July 1, 2001 under N.Y. U.C.C. Law § 9-701, thus, since the seller's adversary proceeding against the debtor asserting a right to stop goods in transit under N.Y. U.C.C. Law §§ 2-702, 2-705 and its challenge to the debtor's secured creditor's interest was commenced on March 30, 2001, Old Article 9 applied. Cargill Inc. v Trico Steel Co. (In re Trico Steel Co.) (2002, BC DC Del) 282 BR 318

Revised Article 9 of the New York Uniform Commercial Code did not apply to transactions that occurred before the effective date of the revisions unless the parties had affirmatively opted to have the revised provisions apply to their transaction that was memorialized by agreements that were executed before the revised code provisions were put into effect. Christine Falls of New York, Inc. v Algonquin Power Corp. (In re Franklin Indus. Complex, Inc.) (2007, BC ND NY) 377 BR 32

Where the pre-2001 version of the New York Uniform Commercial Code did not govern a purported assignment of a malpractice claim, pursuant to N.Y. U.C.C. Law § 9-702(b)(2), the assignment of the tort claim remained valid under revised Article 9 and could be enforced pursuant to the common law of New York. Algonquin Power Income Fund v Christine Falls of N.Y., Inc. (2013, CA2 NY) 2013 US App LEXIS 2038 (UNPUBLISHED).

§ 9-703. Security Interest Perfected Before Effective Date

(a) Continuing priority over lien creditor: perfection requirements satisfied. A security interest that is enforceable immediately before Revised Article 9 takes effect and would have priority over the rights of a person that becomes a lien creditor at that time is a perfected security interest under Revised Article 9 if, when Revised Article 9 takes effect, the applicable requirements for enforceability and perfection under Revised Article 9 are satisfied without further action.

(b) Continuing priority over lien creditor: perfection requirements not satisfied. Except as otherwise provided in Section 9-705 and subsection (c), if, immediately before this article takes effect, a security interest is enforceable and would have priority over the rights of a person that becomes a lien creditor at that time, but the applicable requirements for enforceability or perfection under this article are not satisfied when this article takes effect, the security interest:

(1) is a perfected security interest for one year after this article takes effect;

(2) remains enforceable thereafter only if the security interest becomes enforceable under Section 9-203 before the year expires; and

(3) remains perfected thereafter only if the applicable requirements for perfection under this article are satisfied before the year expires.

(c) Special rule for cooperative interests: perfection requirements not satisfied. If, immediately before Revised Article 9 takes effect, a security interest in a cooperative interest is enforceable and would have priority over the rights of a person that becomes a lien creditor at that time, but the applicable requirements for perfection under Revised Article 9 are not satisfied when Revised Article 9 takes effect, the security interest:

(1) is a perfected security interest for 5 years after Revised Article 9 takes effect; and

(2) remains perfected thereafter only if the applicable requirements for perfection under Revised Article 9 are satisfied before the 5 years expire.

History: Add, L 2001, ch 84, § 36, eff July 1, 2001.

§ 9-704. Security Interest Unperfected Before Effective Date

A security interest that is enforceable immediately before Revised Article 9 takes effect but which would be subordinate to the rights of a person that becomes a lien creditor at that time:

(a) remains an enforceable security interest for one year after Revised Article 9 takes effect;

(b) remains enforceable thereafter if the security interest becomes enforceable under Section 9-203 when Revised Article 9 takes effect or within one year thereafter; and

(c) becomes perfected:

(1) without further action, when Revised Article 9 takes effect if the applicable requirements for perfection under Revised Article 9 are satisfied before or at that time; or

(2) when the applicable requirements for perfection are satisfied if the requirements are satisfied after that time.

History: Add, L 2001, ch 84, § 36, eff July 1, 2001.

§ 9-705. Effectiveness of Action Taken Before Effective Date

(a) Pre-effective-date action; one-year perfection period unless reperfected. If action, other than the filing of a financing statement, is taken before Revised Article 9 takes effect and the action would have resulted in priority of a security interest over the rights of a person that becomes a lien creditor had the security interest become enforceable before Revised Article 9 takes effect, the action is effective to perfect a security interest that attaches under Revised Article 9 within one year after Revised Article 9 takes effect. An attached security interest becomes unperfected one year after Revised Article 9 takes effect unless the security interest becomes a perfected security interest under Revised Article 9 before the expiration of that period.

(b) Pre-effective-date filing. The filing of a financing statement before Revised Article 9 takes effect is effective to perfect a security interest to the extent the filing would satisfy the applicable requirements for perfection under Revised Article 9.

(c) Pre-effective-date filing in jurisdiction formerly governing perfection. Revised Article 9 does not render ineffective an effective financing statement that, before Revised Article 9 takes effect, is filed and satisfies the applicable requirements for perfection under the law of the jurisdiction governing perfection as provided in Former Section 9-103. However, except as otherwise provided in subsections (d) and (e) and Section 9-706, the financing statement ceases to be effective at the earlier of:

(1) the time the financing statement would have ceased to be effective under the law of the jurisdiction in which it is filed; or

(2) June thirtieth, 2006.

(d) Continuation statement. The filing of a continuation statement after Revised Article 9 takes effect does not continue the effectiveness of the financing statement filed before Revised Article 9 takes effect. However, upon the timely filing of a continuation statement after Revised Article 9 takes effect and in accordance with the law of the jurisdiction governing perfection as provided in Part 3, the effectiveness of a financing statement filed in the same office in that jurisdiction before Revised Article 9 takes effect continues for the period provided by the law of that jurisdiction.

(e) Application of subsection (c) (2) to transmitting utility financing statement. Subsection (c) (2) applies to a financing statement that, before Revised Article 9 takes effect, is filed against a transmitting utility and satisfies the applicable requirements for perfection under the law of the jurisdiction governing perfection as provided in Former Section 9-103 only to the extent that Part 3 provides that the law of a jurisdiction other than the jurisdiction in which the financing statement is filed governs perfection of a security interest in collateral covered by the financing statement.

(f) Application of Part 5. A financing statement that includes a financing statement filed before Revised Article 9 takes effect and a continuation statement filed after Revised Article 9 takes effect is effective only to the extent that it satisfies the requirements of Part 5 for an initial financing statement.

History: Add, L 2001, ch 84, § 36, eff July 1, 2001.

§ 9-706. When Initial Financing Statement Suffices to Continue Effectiveness of Financing Statement

(a) Initial financing statement in lieu of continuation statement. The filing of an initial financing statement in the office specified in Section 9-501 continues the effectiveness of a financing statement filed before Revised Article 9 takes effect if:

(1) the filing of an initial financing statement in that office would be effective to perfect a security interest under Revised Article 9;

(2) the pre-effective-date financing statement was filed in an office in another state or another office in this state; and

(3) the initial financing statement satisfies subsection (c).

(b) Period of continued effectiveness. The filing of an initial financing statement under subsection (a) continues the effectiveness of the pre-effective-date financing statement:

(1) if the initial financing statement is filed before Revised Article 9 takes effect, for the period provided in Former Section 9-403 with respect to a financing statement; and

(2) if the initial financing statement is filed after Revised Article 9 takes effect, for the period provided in Section 9-515 with respect to an initial financing statement.

(c) Requirements for initial financing statement under subsection (a). To be effective for purposes of subsection (a), an initial financing statement must:

(1) satisfy the requirements of Part 5 for an initial financing statement;

(2) identify the pre-effective-date financing statement by indicating the office in which the financing statement was filed and providing the dates of filing and file numbers, if any, of the financing statement and of the most recent continuation statement filed with respect to the financing statement; and

(3) indicate that the pre-effective-date financing statement remains effective.

History: Add, L 2001, ch 84, § 36, eff July 1, 2001.

§ 9-707. Amendment of Pre-effective-date Financing Statement

(a) "Pre-effective-date financing statement". In this section, "pre-effective-date financing statement" means a financing statement filed before Revised Article 9 takes effect.

(b) Applicable law. After Revised Article 9 takes effect, a person may add or delete collateral covered by, continue or terminate the effectiveness of, or otherwise amend the information provided in, a pre-effective-date financing statement only in accordance with the law of the jurisdiction governing perfection as provided in Part 3. However, the effectiveness of a pre-effective-date financing statement also may be terminated in accordance with the law of the jurisdiction in which the financing statement is filed.

(c) Method of amending: general rule. Except as otherwise provided in subsection (d), if the law of this state governs perfection of a security interest, the information in a pre-effective-date financing statement may be amended after Revised Article 9 takes effect only if:

(1) the pre-effective-date financing statement and an amendment are filed in the office specified in Section 9-501;

(2) an amendment is filed in the office specified in Section 9-501 concurrently with, or after the filing in that office of, an initial financing statement that satisfies Section 9-706 (c); or

(3) an initial financing statement that provides the information as amended and satisfies Section 9-706 (c) is filed in the office specified in Section 9-501.

(d) Method of amending: continuation. If the law of this state governs perfection of a security interest, the effectiveness of a pre-effective-date financing statement may be continued only under Section 9-705 (d) and (f) or 9-706.

(e) Method of amending: additional termination rule. Whether or not the law of this state governs perfection of a security interest, the effectiveness of a pre-effective-date financing statement filed in this state may be terminated after Revised Article 9 takes effect by filing a termination statement in the office in which the pre-effective-date financing statement is filed, unless an initial financing statement that satisfies Section 9-706 (c) has been filed in the office specified by the law of the jurisdiction governing perfection as provided in Part 3 as the office in which to file a financing statement.

History: Add, L 2001, ch 84, § 36, eff July 1, 2001.

§ 9-708. Persons Entitled to File Initial Financing Statement Or Continuation Statement

A person may file an initial financing statement or a continuation statement under this part if:

(a) the secured party of record authorizes the filing; and

(b) the filing is necessary under this part:

(1) to continue the effectiveness of a financing statement filed before Revised Article 9 takes effect; or

(2) to perfect or continue the perfection of a security interest.

History: Add, L 2001, ch 84, § 36, eff July 1, 2001.

§ 9-709. Priority

(a) Law governing priority. Revised Article 9 determines the priority of conflicting claims to collateral. However, if the relative priorities of the claims were established before Revised Article 9 takes effect, Former Article 9 determines priority.

(b) Priority if security interest becomes enforceable under Section 9-203. For purposes of Section 9-322(a), the priority of a security interest that becomes enforceable under Section 9-203 of Revised Article 9 dates from the time Revised Article 9 takes effect if the security interest is perfected under Revised Article 9 by the filing of a financing statement before Revised Article 9 takes effect which would not have been effective to perfect the security interest under Former Article 9. This subsection does not apply to conflicting security interests each of which is perfected by the filing of such a financing statement.

History: Add, L 2001, ch 84, § 36, eff July 1, 2001.

§ 9-710. Transitional Provision for Maintaining and Searching Local-Filing Office Records

(a) In this Section:

(1) "Local-filing office" means a filing office, other than the department of state, that is designated as the proper place to file a financing statement under Section 9-401 of Former Article 9. The term applies only with respect to a record that covers a type of collateral as to which the filing office is designated in that section as the proper place to file.

(2) "Former-Article-9 records" means:

(A) financing statements and other records that have been filed in a local-filing office before the effective date of this Article, and that are, or upon processing and indexing will be, reflected in the index maintained, as of the effective date of this Article, by the local-filing office for financing statements and other records filed in the local-filing office before the effective date of this Article, and

(B) the index as of the day before the effective date of this Article.

The term does not include records presented to a local-filing office for filing after the effective date of this Article, whether or not the records relate to financing statements filed in the local-filing office before the effective date of this Article.

(3) "Cooperative interest", "mortgage", "as-extracted collateral", "fixture filing", "goods" and "fixtures" have the meanings set forth in this Article.

(b) A local-filing office must not accept for filing a record presented on or after the effective date of this Article, whether or not the record relates to a financing statement filed in the local-filing office before the effective date of this Article.

(c) Until at least seven years after the effective date of this Article, each local-filing office shall maintain all former-Article-9 records in accordance with Former Article 9. A former-Article-9 record that is not reflected on the index maintained on the day before the effective date of this Article by the local-filing office must be processed and indexed as soon as

UCC

practicable but in any event no later than thirty days after the effective date of this Article.

(d) Until at least seven years after the effective date of this Article, each local-filing office shall respond to requests for information with respect to former-Article-9 records relating to a debtor and issue certificates, in accordance with Former Article 9. The fees charged for responding to requests for information relating to a debtor and issuing certificates with respect to former-Article-9 records shall be the fees in effect under Former Article 9 on the day before the effective date of this Article, unless a different fee is later determined in accordance with section ninety-six-a of the executive law.

(e) Subsequent to seven years after the effective date of this Article, each local-filing office may re

move and destroy, in accordance with any then applicable record retention law of this state, all former-Article-9 records, including the related index.

(f) This section shall not apply, with respect to financing statements and other records, to a filing office in which mortgages or records of mortgages on real property are required to be filed or recorded, if:

(1) the collateral is timber to be cut or as-extracted collateral; or

(2) the record is or relates to a financing statement filed as a fixture filing and the collateral is goods that are or are to become fixtures; or

(3) the collateral is a cooperative interest.

History: Add, L 2001, ch 84, § 36, eff July 1, 2001.

INDEX
Abbreviation Guide

———

The following abbreviations appear throughout the index:

VOLUME ONE

VOLUME TWO

Index

BANKS AND BANKING—Cont'd

Industrial banks.
Cemetery corporation deposit of permanent maintenance fund in bank by, N-PCL V1 §1401

Names.
Bank holding company, corporate venue, BCL V1 §302

Religious organization.
Power of trustee to transfer property in trust to bank or trust company, ReligCorp V1 §5

Safe deposit boxes.
Power of attorney as to, GenOblig V2 §5-1502D

Savings not to be used in corporate name, BCL V1 §301

Savings banks.
Cemetery corporation, deposit of permanent maintenance fund by, N-PCL V1 §1401

Securities.
Exemption of securities which are legal investments for savings banks, GenBus V2 §359-f

Secured transactions.
Definition of bank, UCC V1 §9-102
Security interests in deposit accounts.
Control agreements.
Rights of banks with respect to agreements, UCC V1 §9-342
Perfection and priority, UCC V1 §9-304
Rules of priority, UCC V1 §9-327
Rights and duties of banks, UCC V1 §9-341
Set-off or recoupment, UCC V1 §9-340
Transfer of funds from deposit account, UCC V1 §9-332

Securities.
Abandoned property, AbandProp V2 §500, 501
Dealer in securities defined, GenBus V2 §359-e
Exemption of securities from regulation, GenBus V2 §359-f

State comptroller.
Report and delivery of abandoned accounts and securities, AbandProp V2 §501, 502

Stockholders.
Directors.
Stockholder rights plans, BCL V1 §717

Superintendent of banks.
Securities issued by corporation under supervision of superintendent of banks as exempt from regulation, GenBus V2 §359-f

Superintendent of financial services.
Limited partnership, approval of name, Partn V1 §121-102

BAPTIST CHURCHES, ReligCorp V1 §130 to 140

Certificate of incorporation, ReligCorp V1 §132

Change or modification.
Date of annual corporate meetings, changing of, ReligCorp V1 §135
Number of trustees, changing of, ReligCorp V1 §136

Control of trustees, by corporate meetings, ReligCorp V1 §139

Corporate meetings, ReligCorp V1 §133 to 136, 138

Incorporation of, ReligCorp V1 §130 to 132

Meetings.
Corporate, ReligCorp V1 §133
Incorporation, ReligCorp V1 §130, 131
Trustees, ReligCorp V1 §137

Membership corporations, transfers of property to incorporated churches by, ReligCorp V1 §140

Notice.
Corporate meetings, ReligCorp V1 §133
Meeting for incorporation, ReligCorp V1 §130
Meetings of trustees, ReligCorp V1 §137

Organization and conduct of corporate meetings, ReligCorp V1 §134

Pastoral relation and form of worship sections, inapplicable, ReligCorp V1 §27

Qualification of voters, ReligCorp V1 §131, 134

Quorum.
At meeting for incorporation, ReligCorp V1 §131
At meeting of trustees, ReligCorp V1 §137

Transfers of property, by or to, ReligCorp V1 §140

Trustees.
Generally, ReligCorp V1 §131, 132, 134 to 139
Vacancies among trustees, ReligCorp V1 §138

Worship, trustees not to change nature or order of, ReligCorp V1 §139

BAR ASSOCIATIONS.

Name of, N-PCL V1 §301

BATTLE GROUNDS.

Historical societies, as holding property, N-PCL V1 §1408

BENEFIT CORPORATIONS, BCL V1 §1701 to 1709

Applicability of provisions, BCL V1 §1701

Certificates, specific language required, BCL V1 §1709

Definitions, BCL V1 §1702

Directors and officers.
Standard of conduct, BCL V1 §1707

Election by existing corporation to become benefit corporation, BCL V1 §1704

Formation, BCL V1 §1703

Purposes of corporation.
General or specific public benefits, BCL V1 §1706

Reports.
Annual benefit report, BCL V1 §1708

Termination of status as, BCL V1 §1705

BENEVOLENT ORDERS.

Injunctions, benevolent, humane, or charitable corporation, injunction against use of name of, GenBus V2 §135

Not-for-profit corporation.
Applicability of not-for-profit corporation law, N-PCL V1 §103
Name of corporation, N-PCL V1 §301

Securities regulation, exemption of securities issued by benevolent corporation, GenBus V2 §359-f

State department, filing fees, Exec V2 §96

BIBLES.

Incorporation, congregations for purpose of, ReligCorp V1 §50, 50-aa, 51-a

BLANKS.

Nonprofit corporations, counting blank votes in number of votes cast, N-PCL V1 §613

BLIND PERSONS.

Corporations, term blind not to be used in corporate name, BCL V1 §301

Legislature, education and support of blind persons, provision for, NY Const V2 Art VII §8

Limited partnership, handicapped not to be used in name of, Partn V1 §121-102

BLUE SKY LAW, GenBus V2 §352 to 359-h. (See SECURITIES REGULATION)

BOILERS AND BOILER ROOMS.

Corporations, purpose clause in certificate of incorporation, BCL V1 §112, 201

BONA FIDE PURCHASERS.

Partnership, effect of excess authority on transfer to good faith purchaser, Partn V1 §21

BOND ISSUES.

Binding share exchanges, effect on contracts in connection with convertible securities provisions, indentures, etc., BCL V1 §913

Broker-dealers and salesmen, filing fees, GenBus V2 §359-e

Freight terminal corporations, issuance of bonds, notes, or other evidences of indebtedness, TransCorp V1 §104

Industrial bonds or securities.
Abandoned property, industrial revenue bond, AbandProp V2 §500

Land banks, N-PCL V1 §1611

Power of attorney.
Business operating transactions, GenOblig V2 §5-1502E
Generally, GenOblig V2 §5-1502C

Publication.
Fictitious transactions in securities, GenBus V2 §339

Public corporations, obligations issued by, NY Const V2 Art X §5 to 8

BONDS, SURETY.

Limited partnership. (See LIMITED PARTNERSHIP)

Partnership. (See PARTNERSHIP)

Power of attorney.
Business operating transactions, GenOblig V2 §5-1502E
Claims and litigations, GenOblig V2 §5-1502H
Forms, GenOblig V2 §5-1502C

BONUSES.

Cemetery corporations, payment of bonus for purchase of land, N-PCL V1 §1401

BOOKS AND PAPERS.

Definitions, UCC V1 §9-105

Securities regulation.
Designation of person to receive service of subpoena duces tecum, GenBus V2 §352-a, 352-b
Destruction of obsolete evidence seized under subpoena duces tecum, GenBus V2 §359-h
Generally, GenBus V2 §352
Immunity of witness, GenBus V2 §359
Pre-trial examination, GenBus V2 §354 to 357
Receiver taking possession of, GenBus V2 §353-a
Refusal to produce, as prima facie proof of fraudulent practice, GenBus V2 §353

BREAST CANCER.

Research.
Gift for breast cancer research and education, Tax V2 §209-D

BRIDGES AND TUNNELS.

Private or local bill, building of bridges, bill providing for, NY Const V2 Art III §17

Transportation corporations, construction of pipeline across canals, TransCorp V1 §85

BROKERS.

Association of brokers, approval of certificate of incorporation for, N-PCL V1 §404

Power of attorney, contract with broker under, GenOblig V2 §5-1502C

BROOKLYN SOCIETY FOR PREVENTION OF CRUELTY TO CHILDREN, N-PCL V1 §1403

BUILDING AND CONSTRUCTION CONTRACTS AND WORK.

Corporations, purpose clause in certificate of incorporation, BCL V1 §201

Soldiers' monuments, erection of, N-PCL V1 §1405

Index

Index

Index

Index

Index

Index

Index

Index

Index

Index

SECURITIES REGULATION—Cont'd

Witnesses and subpoenas.
Designation of person to receive service of subpoena, GenBus V2 §352-a, 352-b
Fraud cases, GenBus V2 §354
Generally, GenBus V2 §352
Immunity of witness, GenBus V2 §359
Refusal to be sworn or examined as prima facie proof of fraudulent practice, GenBus V2 §353

SECURITY TAKEOVER DISCLOSURE ACT, BCL V1 §1600 to 1613

Administration, BCL V1 §1608
Attorneys' fees, private right of action, BCL V1 §1613
Banks and bank holding companies, exclusions, BCL V1 §1610
Bid for takeover of corporation, prohibition of, BCL V1 §1605
Enforcement, BCL V1 §1606
Exemptions and exclusions, BCL V1 §1612
Financial disclosure, requirement of, BCL V1 §1602
Fraudulent, deceptive, or manipulative practices, BCL V1 §1609, 1611, 1612
Hearings and investigations, BCL V1 §1604, 1612
Immunity from prosecution, BCL V1 §1607, 1609
Notice and service of process and papers, BCL V1 §1608, 1610
Penalties and violations, BCL V1 §1607
Prohibition of takeover bid, BCL V1 §1605
Prosecution, BCL V1 §1607, 1609
Public hearing, BCL V1 §1604, 1612
Public utilities, exclusions, BCL V1 §1610
Registration statement, contents of, BCL V1 §1603
Regulations, BCL V1 §1601
Saving clause of statute, BCL V1 §1613
Savings and loan holding companies, exclusions, BCL V1 §1610
Secretary of state, designation as agent for service, BCL V1 §1610
Target company, defined for purpose of bids, BCL V1 §1601
Violations and penalties, BCL V1 §1607

SEPARATE MAINTENANCE.

Jurisdiction over nonresidents, CPLR V2 §302

SEPSIS.

Infection control guidelines, Educ V2 §6505-b

SETOFF.

Secured transactions.
Banks.
Security interests in deposit accounts, UCC V1 §9-340

SETTLEMENTS.

Structured settlements.
Secured transactions.
Third parties.
Assignments.
Restrictions on assignments, UCC V1 §9-406

SEVENTH DAY BAPTIST CHURCHES.

Property of extinct churches, ReligCorp V1 §17-a

SEVERANCE PAY.

Business corporations, wages for which stockholders liable, BCL V1 §630

SEWERS AND SEWAGE.

Acquisition of property for.
Generally, TransCorp V1 §124
Approval or consent.
Department of health, approval by, TransCorp V1 §117

Incorporation, consent to, TransCorp V1 §116
Sewage disposal systems, TransCorp V1 §115 to 124
Approval by state department of health, TransCorp V1 §117
Bond, TransCorp V1 §119
Certificate of costs, TransCorp V1 §118
Classification, TransCorp V1 §2
Condemnation of property, TransCorp V1 §124
Duty to supply facilities, TransCorp V1 §121
Employment of engineer, TransCorp V1 §118
Federal assistance, authority and procedure for obtaining, TransCorp V1 §122
Guarantees, TransCorp V1 §119
Inspection, TransCorp V1 §118
Municipal consent to incorporation, TransCorp V1 §116
Option of local governing body to purchase system, TransCorp V1 §120
Powers of, TransCorp V1 §122
Rates for services, petition for review of rates, time limits as to, TransCorp V1 §121
Saratoga county, generally, TransCorp V1 §120
Survey and map, TransCorp V1 §123
Sewer and sewage districts.
Definition of terms, TransCorp V1 §115
Service of summons, CPLR V2 §311
Transportation.
Definition of terms, TransCorp V1 §115
Saratoga county, sewer systems, TransCorp V1 §120

SEX OFFENSES.

Firefighters.
Criminal background check for sex offenders, N-PCL V1 §1402

SHAKER ACT.

Generally, ReligCorp V1 §202

SHARES.

Corporations, BCL V1 §501 to 630
Partnership. (See PARTNERSHIP)

SHIPMENTS AND SHIPPERS.

Franchise tax on transportation companies, determination and computation of tax, Tax V2 §184

SHIPS AND SHIPPING.

Ferries, TransCorp V1 §70 to 72

SHORT MERGER ACT.

Corporations, BCL V1 §901 to 913

SHORT SALES.

Power of attorney-in-fact as to, GenOblig V2 §5-1502C

SHORT STATUTES OF LIMITATIONS, CPLR V2 §217

SICKNESS OR ILLNESS.

Legislature, protection against hazards of sickness, power to provide for, NY Const V2 Art VII §8
Nonprofit corporations, quorum necessary for filling of vacancies, director's illness affecting, N-PCL V1 §705

SIGNATURE.

Limited partnership. (See LIMITED PARTNERSHIP)
Power of attorney, GenOblig V2 §5-1502E

SIGNS AND SIGNALS.

Telegraph and telephone corporations, signal systems operated by special policemen of, TransCorp V1 §30

SIKH FAITH, ORGANIZATIONS OF, ReligCorp V1 §470 to 479

Applicability of provisions, ReligCorp V1 §470
Application for incorporation, ReligCorp V1 §471
Certificate of incorporation, ReligCorp V1 §476
Governance of church, ReligCorp V1 §475
Meetings.
Annual corporate meeting, ReligCorp V1 §478
Conduct of meeting for incorporation, ReligCorp V1 §474
Notice of meeting for incorporation, ReligCorp V1 §473
Presiding officer, ReligCorp V1 §479
Quorum, ReligCorp V1 §479
Qualification of voters, ReligCorp V1 §472
Reincorporation of existing incorporated churches, ReligCorp V1 §477

SIMILAR BUSINESS.

Incorporation certificate, purpose clause in, BCL V1 §201

SINGLE PERSONS.

Nonprofit corporations, shelter for unmarried mothers, N-PCL V1 §404

SIX YEAR LIMITATION PERIODS, CPLR V2 §213

SMALL BUSINESS INVESTMENT COMPANIES.

Name, exception as to restriction on use of term investment in corporate name, BCL V1 §302

SMALL CLAIMS.

Appearance.
Generally, CPLR V2 §321

SOCIAL SERVICES.

Adult care facilities.
Title or regulation, exceeding requirements of, N-PCL V1 §404
Blind persons.
Corporate name, approval by state department of social services of use of terms blind in, BCL V1 §301
Business corporations, power of corporations to make donations for public welfare, BCL V1 §202
Business license waiver for practice of certain professional services, Educ V2 §6503-a
Children or minors.
Cities, power to provide welfare services to children, NY Const V2 Art VIII §1
Counties, power to provide welfare services to children, NY Const V2 Art VIII §1
Inmates, care and education provided by counties, NY Const V2 Art VIII §1
Town, care and education of inmates provided by.
Generally, NY Const V2 Art VIII §1
Municipalities' power to provide for care and education of inmates, NY Const V2 Art VIII §1
Religious corporations, acquisition of property for homes, ReligCorp V1 §225-n, 279
Cities.
Children, power to provide welfare services for, NY Const V2 Art VIII §1
Contributions, wages for which stockholders liable, contributions by employer as, BCL V1 §630
Corporations.
State department of social services, approval of use of terms blind or handicapped in corporate name, BCL V1 §301

Index

Index

Index

Index

We are the unwavering partner for

90%

of the Fortune 500®

We serve

180,000⁺

corporate customers

We provide solutions to

3,000⁺

financial market customers

We support over

10,000

law firms, including the most prominent in the U.S.

CSC

CSC® is the world's leading provider of business, legal, tax, and digital brand services to companies around the globe. We are the business behind business. We are the trusted partner for 90% of the Fortune 500®, more than half of the Best Global Brands (Interbrand®), nearly 10,000 law firms, and more than 3,000 financial organizations. We are committed to reducing risk and cost for our clients by providing a suite of services designed to streamline workflows, compliance, monitoring, and reporting solutions.

REPRESENTATION SERVICES

For more than a century, successful companies have relied on CSC to support all of their corporate filing, formation, and transaction needs. Whether your company manages one or thousands of entities, we have the tools and expertise to keep them on track.

- **Formations:**
  Whether forming a corporation or limited liability structure, our compliance experts will guide your company through the process and get your entities started.
- **Articles of amendment:**
  CSC can prepare and file all the certificates required to amend any entity's formation documents.
- **Dissolutions or withdrawals:**
  CSC will complete and file the appropriate state forms in instances where your company must dissolve or withdraw a business entity.
- **Mergers:**
  From the due diligence phase to post-closing, CSC provides a complete solution for merger transactions.
- **Certificates of Good Standing:**
  CSC can order Certificates of Good Standing for entities from the secretary of state in all 50 states and the District of Columbia, providing evidence that your company has satisfied annual report, franchise tax, and other obligations.

UNIFORM COMMERCIAL CODE

CSC has provided Uniform Commercial Code (UCC) services for nearly six decades. Today we serve thousands of financial institutions, including many of the world's largest lenders—from commercial banks, capital finance companies, and large leasing enterprises, to legal firms that specialize in secured transactions.

CSC processes millions of UCC searches and filings annually, and monitors millions more for expiration or continuation. Our solutions are scalable to your needs. CSC currently delivers custom interfaces to more than 120 major financial institutions and leasing companies. We'll do the same for you. We provide rapid, integrated services with standard or proprietary loan applications. Our vast correspondent network enables CSC to provide timely fulfillment of search and filing orders at the federal, state, and local levels throughout the U.S.

*For more information, call **800.927.9800** or visit us at **cscglobal.com.***

DELAWARE TRUST

Delaware Trust provides a full suite of corporate trust and agency, independent director, private equity networking, and special purpose entity services to corporations, law firms, financial institutions, institutional investors, and private equity firms. A wholly owned subsidiary of CSC, Delaware Trust is not affiliated with any bank, lender, or other third party.

INDEPENDENT DIRECTOR SERVICES

CSC offers a full suite of independent director services to address a variety of needs. Think of us as a boutique provider of customizable services, with an expert team ready to assist you from pre-closing through completion of your deal. Our experienced staff has provided directors for more than 20,000 transactions, including:

- Independent directors for bankruptcy remote and other special purpose entities formed in conjunction with real estate finance and securitization transactions.
- Independent directors for distressed companies in both pre-bankruptcy and restructuring situations. Our directors are well versed in the intricacies of distressed situations and director fiduciary duties as they relate to companies that are insolvent or are entering the zone of insolvency.
- Directors for special purpose entities formed for tax and risk management strategies, project finance transactions, and trademarks and intellectual property protection.
- Springing member services (also known as special member services) for limited liability companies.

DIGITAL BRAND SERVICES

The digital world changes fast. CSC will help you navigate it. We help businesses around the world effectively manage, promote, and secure their valuable brand assets against the threats of the online world.

Leading companies around the world choose CSC as their trusted partner to gain control of their digital assets, maximize their online potential, and increase online security against brand risks.

Consolidate and Secure—CSC centralizes your digital assets and keeps them secure and fully operational, 24/7

Monitor and Enforce—Our tailored and evolving solutions help prevent revenue loss and brand abuse by identifying and eliminating digital infringements and counterfeiting

Optimize and Promote—We optimize your assets to seize control of growth opportunities, regain lost web traffic, and maximize the return on investment of your digital portfolio

CSC's Digital Brand Services helps more than half the 100 Best Global Brands® and a growing share of Global 2000® corporations. Our expertise and global reach—with offices throughout North America, Europe, Australia, and Asia—give our customers peace of mind that no matter how fast the digital world changes, we're here to keep their intellectual property secure. We are the business behind business℠.

For complete details on our suite of law firm products and services, visit cscglobal.com or contact a customer service representative at 800.927.9800.

CSC

The CSC® Library of Publications offers you a wide array of valuable resources. Whether you're looking for important jurisdictional updates or forming a limited liability company, these books offer you the information you need most—in a format that is compact, concise, and convenient.

THE CSC BUSINESS ENTITY JURISDICTIONAL LIBRARY

You'll appreciate the valuable resources offered by the CSC Jurisdiction Library. Each book offers the state's key business statutes, including: corporation, LLC, LLP, LP and nonprofit laws. The books also include annotations, amendments, and the statutes' legislative history. Softbound for portability, updated annually—no filing required.

Delaware Laws Governing Business Entities (Spring and Fall Editions)

Volume 1 (annotated statutes and rules) features a corporate fees and taxes payable chapter, the full text of the Chancery Court Rules, and Articles 1, 8, and 9 of the Uniform Commercial Code, plus the Delaware General Corporation Law, Limited Liability Act, and more. This title also includes Blackline Notes showing the effect of the most recent amendments, and a complete analysis of amendments.

Volume 2 (annotations from all state and federal courts) contains annotations of cases decided under Delaware business entity law in all state and federal courts; case annotations are organized by statute, section-by-section, then by state and federal court.

Business Entity Jurisdiction Books from CSC
Select the jurisdiction you need.

- **California** Laws Governing Business Entities
- **Colorado** Laws Governing Business Entities
- **Connecticut & Rhode Island** Laws Governing Business Entities
- **Delaware** Laws Governing Business Entities Volumes 1 & 2 (Spring and Fall)
- **Georgia** Laws Governing Business Entities
- **Florida** Laws Governing Business Entities
- **Illinois** Laws Governing Business Entities
- **Maryland & District of Columbia Laws** Governing Business Entities

- **Massachusetts** Laws Governing Business Entities
- **Nevada** Laws Governing Business Entities
- **New Jersey** Laws Governing Business Entities
- **New York** Laws Governing Business Entities Volumes 1 & 2 (Spring and Fall)
- **North Carolina** Laws Governing Business Entities
- **Pennsylvania** Laws Governing Business Entities
- **Texas** Laws Governing Business Entities
- **Utah** Laws Governing Business Entities
- **Virginia** Laws Governing Business Entities
- **Washington** Laws Governing Business Entities

*For more information, call **800.927.9800** or visit us at **cscglobal.com**.*

CORPORATE GOVERNANCE AND COMPLIANCE PUBLICATIONS

The Directors' Handbook
(with interactive CD-ROM)

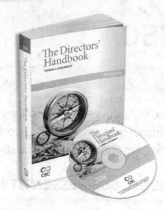

- One of today's leading guides to corporate governance
- A well-written, easy-to-understand resource for directors, officers, attorneys, corporate secretaries, and others involved in board activities
- The book tackles key issues faced by today's directors in the aftermath of the Sarbanes-Oxley Act and privatized enforcement processes
- Valuable insight and information give directors clear guidance on how to best manage complex corporate situations

Qualifying to Do Business in Another State: The CSC® 50-State Guide to Qualification

- Helps readers determine whether their business activities trigger qualification requirements
- Lists those activities that do not trigger qualification requirements
- Offers clear insight on whether certain Internet activities trigger qualification requirements
- Provides annotated qualification statutes for 50 states
- Includes CD-ROM with editable PDF Qualification Forms
- Includes the following quick-reference charts:
  – What Constitutes Business for Qualification Purposes;
  – The Consequences of Not Qualifying

Symonds & O'Toole on Delaware Limited Liability Companies, Second Edition

- Access statutory changes, practice recommendations, and up-to-date forms
- Tap into expert information on drafting LLC agreements
- Gain practical insight into case law interpreting the statute
- Consult comprehensive legislative history
- Coverage includes: LLC Formation and Organization; Drafting the LLC Agreement; Financing the LLC; Members and Managers; Ownership, Voting and LLC Interests; Indemnification and Other Liability Protections; Fiduciary Duties; Series LLCs; Creditors' Rights, Protections and Remedies; Mergers, Conversions and Other Fundamental Transactions; Dissolution, Winding Up and Termination of the LLC

2018 UPDATES NOW AVAILABLE

Egan on Entities: Corporations, Partnerships and Limited Liability Companies in Texas

This treatise combines scholarly analysis and practical guidance on business entity law in a manner that will aid legal practitioners, company executives, and students in understanding business entities in Texas, whether formed in Texas or Delaware, and in addressing related complexities that inevitably arise in navigating the critical decisions that must be made with respect to such entities.

*For more information, call **800.927.9800** or visit us at **cscglobal.com**.*